THE SHORTER OXFORD ENGLISH DICTIONARY

THE SHORTER OXFORD ENGLISH DICTIONARY

ON HISTORICAL PRINCIPLES

PREPARED BY

WILLIAM LITTLE

H. W. FOWLER AND JESSIE COULSON

REVISED AND EDITED BY

C. T. ONIONS

THIRD EDITION

COMPLETELY RESET

WITH ETYMOLOGIES REVISED BY

G. W. S. FRIEDRICHSEN

AND WITH REVISED ADDENDA

VOLUME I

A–MARKWORTHY

CLARENDON PRESS · OXFORD

Oxford University Press, Walton Street, Oxford OX2 6DP
Oxford New York Toronto
Delhi Bombay Calcutta Madras Karachi
Kuala Lumpur Singapore Hong Kong Tokyo
Nairobi Dar es Salaam Cape Town
Melbourne Auckland
and associated companies in
Beirut Berlin Ibadan Nicosia

Oxford is a trade mark of Oxford University Press

Published in the United States
by Oxford University Press, New York

Plain Edition ISBN 0 19 861126 9
Thumb Index Edition ISBN 0 19 861127 7

First Published February 1933
Reprinted with Corrections March 1933, April 1933
Reprinted 1934. Second Edition 1936. Reprinted 1939
Third Edition 1944. Reprinted with Corrections 1947
Reprinted 1950, 1952, 1955
With Corrections and Revised Addenda 1956
Reprinted with Corrections 1959, 1962, 1964, 1965, 1967, 1968, 1970, 1972
Reset with Revised Etymologies and Addenda 1973, 1974
1975 (With Corrections), 1977, 1978, 1980, 1983, 1984, 1985, 1986

Printed in Great Britain
at the University Printing House, Oxford
by David Stanford
Printer to the University

PUBLISHERS' NOTE

THIS reset version of the *Shorter Oxford*, prepared by members of the O.E.D. Department in Oxford, as well as presenting this famous Dictionary in a fresh and elegant type-face, incorporates two new features. The etymologies of all words in the body of the Dictionary have been revised by Dr. G. W. S. Friedrichsen, former colleague of the late Dr. C. T. Onions; this major undertaking represents more than eight years' work by Dr. Friedrichsen. The second main feature is the inclusion of a fresh set of Addenda, drawn chiefly from the material assembled for the new Supplement to the *O.E.D.* (the first volume of which was published in the autumn of 1972), and presenting notable accessions to the English language in the period since the *O.E.D.* appeared. The entries in the main text of the Dictionary remain essentially as they were, pending the completion of the Supplement to the *O.E.D.* towards the end of the present decade.

The publishers wish to acknowledge the contributions of the following: Dr. G. W. S. Friedrichsen, working in Washington far from his friends and colleagues in Oxford; Mr. N. S. Doniach for his assistance with the etymologies of Arabic and Hebrew words; those responsible for the proof-reading of the main text of the reset version (a task occupying five years in all), notably Mrs. Jessie Coulson, who has been associated with the *S.O.E.D.* in one way or another since the late 1920s, Mrs. J. E. A. Field, Miss G. A. Rathbone, Mrs. A. Wallace-Hadrill, and Mrs. J. M. Wilson; and the other members of the O.E.D. Department who were responsible for the preparation of the Addenda (see note at the head of the Addenda).

August 1972

PREFACE TO THE FIRST EDITION

THIS Dictionary is an abridgement officially authorized by the Delegates of the Oxford University Press of *A New English Dictionary on Historical Principles*, later known as *The Oxford English Dictionary*. The need for such an abridged form of the great work was envisaged at the outset. The publication of this work is, in fact, a fulfilment of one of the provisions of the agreement entered into in the year 1879 between the Philological Society and the Oxford University Press. The relevant clause of the Indenture runs as follows:

> The Delegates may (if and whenever they think fit) prepare and publish any Dictionaries compiled or abridged from the principal Dictionary, and in such form as they may think fit, and may deal with the same in all respects at their discretion.

It was not until 1902 that the project of an abridgement was initiated. It was clear that the editors and staff engaged on the principal work had their hands too full to undertake it. A scholar from outside was found for the task in the late Mr. William Little, Fellow of Corpus Christi College, Oxford, who was asked to submit specimens in 1902, and with him negotiations were officially entered into on 24 April 1903. The work was carried on steadily by him until his death in January 1922. By this time he had prepared entirely without assistance the manuscript for the letters A to T and V, and had passed for printing about one-third of the whole dictionary.

Upon his death the materials left by him were placed in my hands for revision and completion. The gaps in the manuscript 'copy' were filled by Mr. H. W. Fowler, who abridged U and X, Y, Z, and by Mrs. E. A. Coulson, who was responsible for W. In the earlier stages of my editorship I was assisted by two experienced members of the Oxford Dictionary staff, Mr. F. J. Sweatman, M.A. Oxon., and Mr. J. W. Birt. Since 1924, when these assistants could no longer be spared for the work, the following ladies have successively taken part: Mrs. J. W. Alden (Miss A. M. Savage), M.A. Oxon., and three graduates in English of the University of Leeds, Mrs. E. A. Coulson (Miss J. Senior), Miss M. Dawn, and Miss S. M. Mills. The services rendered by all these helpers and their share in bringing the work to a successful conclusion are here gratefully acknowledged.

The aim of this Dictionary is to present in miniature all the features of the principal work. It is designed to embrace not only the literary and colloquial English of the present day together with such technical and scientific terms as are most frequently met with or are likely to be the subject of inquiry, but also a considerable proportion of obsolete, archaic, and dialectal words and uses. The Oxford Dictionary was compiled and edited from materials amounting to over five million quotations, derived from English works of literature and records of all kinds, and resulted in 15,000 large quarto pages, in which nearly half a million words are recorded with more than one and a half million illustrative quotations. This abridgement, *The Shorter Oxford English Dictionary*, presents, therefore, a quintessence of those vast materials. The method reflects exactly that of the principal work. It is historical in its representation of the chronological sequence in the development of meaning. It gives the etymologies of words in such a form as to exhibit every significant stage of their history from their place of origin. The meanings are illustrated by quotations either exactly dated or assigned to their authors; the range of the texts used in these illustrations is shown in the list of Authors and Books Cited which is printed on pp. xv–xxii. Idiomatic phrases are treated with a fullness that is unusual if not unparalleled in dictionaries of similar compass. Like the original work, this abridgement is not intended to provide a direct commentary on the peculiar vocabulary of any one author, but an attempt has been made to record the special words and meanings and even the oddities of important writers. Many provincialisms also that have some currency in standard literature or are of signal importance historically are treated here, though it may be with extreme brevity. It has been possible in many places to supplement the word-content of the original dictionary and its chronological evidence from the collections gathered by many hands during the last fifty years with a view to a grand supplement or an extensive revision of that work. It has been the aim of the compilers to keep a due proportion between the various interests, and not to exaggerate the etymological side at the expense of the semantic, and, though it has been impossible to preserve entirely the readability of the principal work, the definitions have much of their original fullness, so that the ample and leisurely character of the parent work is in a measure retained.

It is hoped that both the student and the general reader will find in this work what they may reasonably expect to find in a historical dictionary of English compressed within 2,500 quarto pages, which covers not only the history of the general English vocabulary from the days of King Alfred down to the present time, but includes also a large number of obsolete, archaic, provincial, and foreign words and phrases, and a multitude of terms of art and science. In short, it is hoped that it may be found acceptable as a lexical companion to English literature. For those who possess the great Oxford Dictionary the 'Shorter' will serve as a key to its treasures, for those who do not it will form the only possible substitute.

C. T. ONIONS

Oxford
December, 1932

INTRODUCTION

THE following sections contain an exposition of the contents and method of this Dictionary, with directions for its use.

§ 1. The GENERAL ORDER AND ARRANGEMENT of an article is as follows (all possible features, which are of necessity not present in all or even the majority of words, being taken into account). (i) The catchword in heavy type, preceded where necessary by a diacritic mark of the status of the word († obsolete, ‖ alien), is followed by (ii) the pronunciation in phonetic transcript (§ 3), where this is not sufficiently indicated by stress-marks in the catchword itself, or unless the word is obsolete (the pronunciation being then omitted), and (iii) the notation of the part of speech (except where the word is a substantive and there is no word of another part of speech spelt in the same way). Next comes (iv) the indication of the modern currency of the word, unless already noted by a symbol, e.g. whether it is now literary, colloquial, slang, or surviving only in archaic, historical, dialectal, or other limited use. Then follows, where appropriate, (v) a statement of variant spellings or inflexional forms in heavy type with their pronunciations, if these have some special importance. The next item, which is a feature of all articles, is the indication of (vi) the earliest appearance of the word, which is shown either by the symbols OE., ME., late ME. (§ 4), or by a precise date. This is succeeded by (vii) the etymology enclosed within square brackets (§ 5); (viii) the specification of the word as belonging to some art or science (*Mus.*, *Bot.*, etc., for which see pp. xxiii–xxv) if it is entirely so restricted; (ix) the meanings, numbered or lettered, with specification of their status and with the date of their first appearance, or, if they are obsolete, an indication of their last known occurrence (§ 6). After each group of senses there is normally (x) a block of quotations with dates or indications of authorship, numbered according to the senses which they exemplify (§ 6). (xi) Groups of idiomatic phrases or attributive uses and combinations conclude the article, unless there are (xii) derivatives of minor importance, which are appended with an introductory 'Hence' or 'So' (§ 7).

§ 2. The VOCABULARY of this Dictionary is designed to include all words in regular literary and colloquial use, together with a selection of those which belong to the terminology of the arts and sciences and those which are current only in archaic or dialectal use, as well as of words now obsolete but of importance during some period of our literature.

The individual words of the vocabulary may be classified in various ways. In this work a broad distinction is made between *natives* and *denizens* (naturalized foreigners) on the one hand, and *aliens* (non-naturalized foreigners) on the other. *Natives* are words of Old English origin, *denizens* are borrowings from foreign languages which have acquired full English citizenship, *aliens* are words that retain their foreign appearance and to some extent their foreign sound. This last group is distinguished by the prefixing of ‖ to the catchword.

Words are also classifiable according to the sphere of their currency and usage. Where they do not belong to the language *common* to literature and everyday speech the circumstances of their use call for some characterization. Hence the necessity for such labels as, on the one hand, *obsolete* (marked by †), *literary*, *colloquial*, *slang*, *dialectal*, *local*, *archaic*, *vulgar*, and on the other, *Art*, *Natural History*, *Mathematics*, and so on. The composition of a vocabulary under these aspects may be usefully pictured in such a diagram as that devised by Sir James Murray, which is here reproduced with some modifications from Vol. I, p. xxvii, of the *Oxford English Dictionary*:

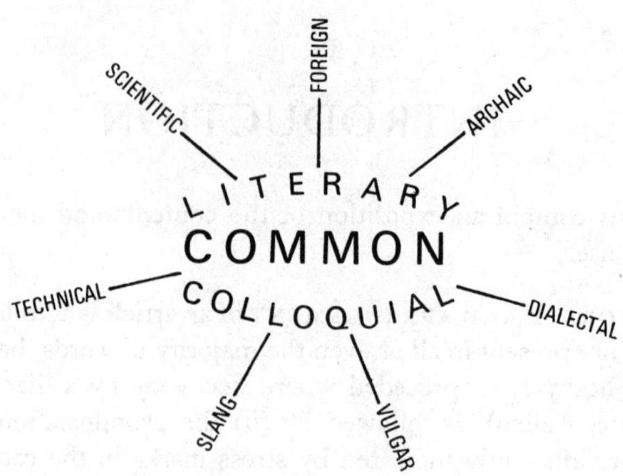

The centre is occupied by 'common' words, in which literary and colloquial usage meet. 'Scientific', 'foreign', and 'archaic' words are the specially learned outposts of the literary language; 'technical' and 'dialectal' words blend with the common language both in speech and in literature. 'Slang' touches the technical terminology of trades and occupations, as in 'nautical slang', 'University slang'; 'slang', 'vulgar' speech, and 'dialect' form a group of lower or less dignified status; 'dialectal' and 'archaic' words are allied in so far as they are outcrops of older strata of the language. In addition to and interpenetrating the common vocabulary with all its ramifications and outliers, there is a vast number of proper names, which either themselves acquire connotative value or give rise to derivatives which take their place among the ordinary words of the language.

Words created for one special occasion are here called *nonce-words*.

Where it has been found necessary to recognize variants of form having equal or nearly equal claims to be considered standard, a double, occasionally a triple, catchword indicates the diversity of usage, priority of place corresponding to priority of usage. Besides variants current in Britain, certain conventional spellings (as *honor*) of the United States have been recorded.

Exigencies of space have determined the arrangement of many compound words in groups under their first element, which usually appear in other dictionaries as 'main words'. Other linguistic elements that cannot be classed as words, viz. prefixes and suffixes, and the letters of the alphabet, are entered in their alphabetical places and receive the same historical treatment as words.

Entries of variant spellings referred to their standard form have been limited to those which are not easily recognizable, alternatives such as those between *y* and *i*, *s* and *z*, *c* and *s*, *k* and *c* being generally ignored. The word to which cross-reference is made is printed in SMALL CAPITALS.

§ 3. The PRONUNCIATION is noted within round brackets by means of a phonetic alphabet, the application of which is shown in the Key to the Pronunciation printed on p. xxix. The additional consonant-signs employed in the phonetic system are þ, ð, ʃ, ʒ, ŋ, and ɹ. The symbol ɹ (reversed r) represents the letter r used finally or before a consonant, where no r-sound is normally heard in the educated speech of southern England, although the preceding vowel may be lengthened, or followed by a voice-glide, or both. When, however, a word ending with the letter r is closely followed by another beginning with a vowel, an r-sound is usually inserted by many speakers in the pronunciation, as in *far and near* (fā̆r ǣnd nīᵊɹ).

Each simple sound is indicated regularly by the same single symbol. Short quantity in vowels is left unmarked, long quantity is denoted by the macron ¯; the mark generally employed to indicate short quantity ˘ is here used to denote *obscuration of quality*. The main or primary stress is indicated by a turned period · after the vowel of the stressed syllable. Subordinate or secondary stress, where it falls otherwise than in the normal place (i.e. on the second syllable from the main stress), is marked : as in *cry:stalliza·tion, boo·kse:ller*. In obsolete words and in some current words, especially compounds of obvious formation or derivatives or cognates of a word that is entered with full pronunciation, the stress only is marked without further notation. Varieties in the pronunciation of a word are recorded as fully as possible, priority of position in the record being given to the variety which according to the available evidence has the more extensive currency.

In the system as a whole variation is extensively recognized, and allowance is made for local or class divergence from the standard range, but not, as a rule, for dialectal, colonial, or American varieties. Thus, the divergent pronunciations of the vowels of such words as *fast*, *bath*, and *cough*, *lost*, *soft* are shown, special symbols, (ɑ) and (ǫ̇) respectively, being used to indicate that such local or individual varieties exist. Again, discrimination has been made between the vowels of *fir* (fə̄ɹ) and *fur* (fɒ̄ɹ), where south-of-England speakers make no distinction. Similarly, a difference is noted between the (ǫ) of *scotch* and the (ọ) of *watch*, the (ǭ) of *for* and the (ọ̄) of *war*, and the northerly pronunciation (ō^{ə}) of vowels of words like *fort*, *port*, *mourn* is recognized, where the southerly has (ǭ), which is, on the other hand, the general sound in *form*, *short*, and *morn*. Use is made of small 'superior' letters, ^{i} and ^{u}, to express the final elements of those diphthongs which are fully developed only with certain classes of speakers, e.g. in *fate* (fē^{i}t), *note* (nō^{u}t), as distinguished from the generally received diphthongs of *eye* (əi), *boy* (boi), *bow* (bɑu), *few* (fiū̆). Similar recognition is given to the variation between *ū̆*, ū, and ^{i}*ū̆*, ^{i}ū which is illustrated by the pronunciation of *lieu*, *lure*, *illuminant*. A 'superior' turned e (^{ə}) is used for the vowel-element developed between ī, ē, ō, ū, ɑu, etc. and r, as in *pier* (pī^{ə}ɹ), *pare* (pē^{ə}ɹ), *pour* (pō^{ə}ɹ), *poor* (pū^{ə}ɹ), *weary* (wī^{ə}·ri), *scour* (skɑu^{ə}ɹ); the modern southern development of (ū^{ə}ɹ) to (ō^{ə}ɹ), e.g. (ʃū^{ə}ɹ), (ʃō^{ə}ɹ), is not admitted, nor the monophthongal pronunciation in words like *door*, i.e. (dǭɹ) as opposed to (dō^{ə}ɹ).

In general, 'superior' letters indicate elements that are present or absent according to individual or other usage, and are therefore used in such cases as *promptitude* (prǫ·m^{p}titiū̆d), *standstill* (stæ·n^{d}stil).

An outstanding feature of the phonetic system is the recognition of the primary or ideal value of the many vowels that undergo obscuration or reduction in unstressed positions, but which may at any time revert to their full quality, as in rhetorical utterance, in singing, and in any cases of deliberate or affected precision. Examples are: *accept* (æ̆kse·pt), *confer* (kǫ̆nfə̄·ɹ), *judgement* (dʒɒ·dʒmĕnt), *dislocate* (di·slŏke^{i}t)—contrast *action* (æ·kʃən), *mental* (me·ntăl), *local* (lō^{u}·kăl); here the unstressed obscured vowel is in normal speech the 'mid-mixed' vowel (ə) of the second syllable of *ever* (e·vəɹ), towards which the majority of obscured vowels tend; *mistress* (mi·strės), *billet* (bi·lėt), *useless* (yū̆·slės), where (ė) represents a 'raised' variant of (e) which approaches (i); *beauteous* (biū̆·tĭəs), where (ĭ) represents a reduced form of the short vowel of *Hebe* (hī·bi). In words like *fracture*, *measure*, the historical or ideal pronunciations are (fræ·ktiŭɹ), (me·ʒ^{i}ŭɹ), from which may be deduced the common colloquial forms (fræ·ktʃəɹ), (me·ʒəɹ). The following equations show the general equivalents in ordinary speech, and in the majority of other phonetic systems, of the different types of obscured vowels:

æ̆ ă ĕ ĭ ŏ ǫ̆ ŭ } = ə
ɒ̆ ĕ ŏ ǫ̆ ŭ }
ė *ĭ* = i.

§ 4. CHRONOLOGY. Every independent word and meaning is attested by an indication of the period, or the first date, of its occurrence. If the record begins before the middle of the twelfth century (*c* 1150), it is regarded as falling within the Old English period and is marked OE.; if within that date and the middle of the fourteenth century (*c* 1150–*c* 1350) it is marked ME., the later ME. period (*c* 1350–1450) being specified as late ME. After that period, and in exceptional instances even somewhat before 1450, dating by the year is used.

The earliest known meaning of a word has no date attached, since it has already been indicated at the beginning of the article; but for each succeeding sense a date is given at the end of the definition. The latest limit of an obsolete word or sense is shown by means of the year preceded by a dash, as –1759.

§ 5. The ETYMOLOGY is given within square brackets. The etymologies of all words have been revised, and for the most part rewritten, ultimately on the basis of the material presented in the *Oxford Dictionary of English Etymology* (1966), which embodies recent research on the etymologies of English and of the other languages concerned. In many cases matter from the *Oxford English Dictionary* which had been omitted in the earlier editions of *S.O.E.D.* has been restored.

What is usually called the 'etymology' of a word ought to provide an account of its immediate provenance, whether by traditional descent or as a loan-word from another language, or by its formation in English by the composition of two words, or the combination of a word or stem with a prefixal or suffixal element.

The forms from which the English word is derived, whether by descent or by adoption from another language, may be further traced to their ultimate source, so far as this is known, as may be thought expedient or necessary.

The symbol :– means 'normal development from', 'regular phonetic descendant of'; the symbol – means 'adoption of', 'adopted from'; e.g. *civility* – (O)Fr. *civilité*. The formula 'ad.', = derived by adaptation, i.e. with adjustment to English speech habits, has been abandoned, the abbreviations 'a.' (= adopted) and 'ad.' (= adapted) now being merged into one sign –, so that *serous* (hitherto 'ad. F. *séreux*') now appears as '– Fr. *séreux*'.

The stricter attention given to the immediate derivation and the domestic history of words has resulted in the abandonment of many references to Latin (or Greek) words or elements. Thus, for instance, OSCULANT (1826) is explained as [f. OSCULATE (in sense 3, *Nat. Hist.*) + -ANT.] and not [ad. L. *osculantem*, f. *osculari* to kiss.]; INCUBATOR (1854) is [f. INCUBATE *v.* + -OR 2.], not from L. *incubator* 'one who lies in any place; oppressor, unlawful possessor'; POTENTIOMETER (1881) is from POTENTIAL *sb.*, not from L. *potentia*.

Many words ascribed to Latin are actually variants of English words resulting from the replacement of a prefix or suffix by a different one; thus INFIX (1881) is after PREFIX, SUFFIX, whilst MUSCULAR (1681) is a variant of the earlier † MUSCULOUS by suffix-substitution, not derived from a non-existent 'mod.L. **muscularis*'. The free use of postulated but unrecorded Latin and Greek words has been abandoned, as in the case of CANONICITY, which is f. CANONIC + -ITY, not 'f. L. type **canonicitas*'.

Words of Germanic (Gmc.) descent are referred to their OE. (sometimes ON.) form with all known relevant collaterals in other Gmc. languages (together with their later forms) in the order Old Frisian, Old Saxon, Old High German, Old Norse, Gothic. Late adoptions from a Gmc. language, as from ON. or from MLG. and/or MDu. are supported by the corresponding correlative forms. The siglum LDu. (Low Dutch) is used conventionally, as in *O.D.E.E.*, to include both (Middle) Low German and (Middle) Dutch, especially when the word in one or other of those dialects is not recorded, but may be presumed to have existed, and the English could be derived from either or both. Indo-European (IE.) forms are given occasionally, as may be expedient.

Words of Romanic provenance are referred to their proximate origin, usually French or Old French, the earlier history of which, when known, is indicated. The siglum (O)Fr., adopted from *O.D.E.E.*, is used for mod. Fr. forms that go back to OFr.; thus 'OFr. *evangile*, mod. *évangile*', is compendiously written '(O)Fr. *évangile*', with the accent to indicate the modern spelling. OFr. in this work includes the language of the fourteenth century.

Latin words are distinguished conventionally as L. (or cl.L.) down to A.D. *c* 200, late L. from *c* 200 to *c* 600, med.L. from *c* 600 to *c* 1500, and mod.L. from *c* 1500 on. Popular Latin (pop.L.), also termed Vulgar Latin (vulg.L., VL.) is the Latin spoken by the mass of the people, as distinct from the more formal written Latin, e.g. *bellus, caballus, ossum, testa* (*capum*), as against *pulcher, equus, os, caput.*

The designation Chr.L. is proper to the earlier adoptives from, or after, the Greek, exemplified by *Angelus, apostolus, baptisma, -um, baptizare, diaconus, episcopus, evangelium, martyr, presbyter, Trinitas*; eccl.L. is applicable to later (theological, etc.) terms used by patristic and later writers; e.g. *anathema, catholicus, essentia, essentialis, pascha, paschalis, persona, substantia,* etc.; but the distinction is not consistently maintained; words in the latter group may be described as late L., or med.L.

§ 6. MEANINGS, DEFINITIONS, QUOTATIONS, AUTHORITIES. The meanings are arranged with as strict a regard as possible for their appearance in order of time. They are liable to all the qualifications to which words themselves are liable; thus they may be marked † (obsolete), *arch., dial., U.S., nonce-use,* and so forth, or as pertaining to some branch of science or art. In a word of long and intricate history, the meanings are usually divided into groups having roman numeral headings, within which the meanings have an independent numeration in arabic figures. For the method of dating see § 4.

Two devices are used in order to specify the application of definitions. (i) The object of a transitive verb is placed in its grammatical position in a definition, within round brackets. Such parts of a definition as are not universally applicable, as well as qualifications of its extent, are similarly treated. (ii) Additions, as of prepositions or adverbs, or an infinitive, *in italic type* indicate that the italicized words do or may enter into the construction accompanying or dependent upon the word when used in the sense defined. Examples are: *Tend*.. To watch over and wait upon (the sick or helpless); *Beat*.. To drive (a person) by blows *away, off, from, into,* etc.; *Force*.. To compel or constrain (a person, oneself, etc.) *to do* a thing; *Layman*.. an 'outsider' or non-expert (esp. in relation to law or medicine); *Chit*.. a (very young) child.

When the form of the catchword is used anywhere in the course of an article, it may be abbreviated for economy of space by means of the initial letter followed by a full stop.

The chief sources of the illustrative quotations, which are placed under number- or letter-headings according to the sections to which they apply, are catalogued in the list of Authors and Books Cited, printed below, pp. xv–xxii. Authors' names are printed in small capitals (e.g. SCOTT); for certain common abbreviations of these see pp. xxiii–xxv. Occasionally, an example of a current usage is supplied from a casual source; this is marked *mod.* (= a modern example). It has been found necessary in respect of some words or meanings whose history has been treated at considerable length in the original Dictionary, and with more detail than could be presented here, merely to refer by means of the abbreviation N.E.D. (or O.E.D.) to the fuller statement there given. Modern dictionaries in general are referred to as Dicts.

§ 7. PHRASES, COMBINATIONS, and MINOR DERIVATIVES commonly form a block or blocks at the end of the article, phrases in italic or in thick type, obvious (undefined) combinations in italics. Specialized verbal phrases with adverbs or prepositions are displayed in thick type, as are also special combinations, i.e. those compound words of which the meaning cannot at once be inferred from their elements, as well as derivatives the status of which does not warrant their insertion as 'main words' of the vocabulary in their alphabetical sequence.

PROPRIETARY NAMES

THIS Dictionary includes some words which are or are asserted to be proprietary names or trade marks. Their inclusion does not imply that they have acquired for legal purposes a non-proprietary or general significance nor any other judgement concerning their legal status. In cases where the editorial staff have established in the records of the Patent Offices of the United Kingdom and of the United States that a word is registered as a proprietary name or trade mark this is indicated, but no judgement concerning the legal status of such words is made or implied thereby.

AUTHORS AND BOOKS CITED

Abernethy, John, 1764–1831
Academy, The (1869–99)
Adams, George, 1750–95
Adams, Thomas, fl. 1612–53
Addison, Joseph, 1672–1719
Ainsworth, William Harrison, 1805–82
Aird, Thomas, 1802–76
Akenside, Mark, 1721–70
Alcott, Louisa M., 1832–88
Alford, Henry, 1810–71
Alison, Sir Archibald, 1792–1867
Allardyce, Alexander, 1846–96
Allbutt, Thomas C., ed. *A System of Medicine*, 1896–9
Allen, Grant, 1848–99
Allingham, William, 1824–89
Andrewes, Lancelot, 1555–1626
Anglo-Saxon Chronicle, The (Thorpe, 1861; Earle and Plummer, 1892, 1899)
Anson, George, 1697–1762
Arber, Edward, ed. *An English Garner* (1877–96)
Arbuthnot, John, 1667–1735
Argyll, 8th Duke of 1823–1900
Arnold, Matthew, 1822–88
Arnold, Thomas, 1795–1842
Arnolde, Richard, d. 1521?
Ascham, Roger, 1515–68
Ashmole, Elias, 1617–92
Athenæum, The (1828–1901)
Atterbury, Francis, 1662–1732
Auckland, William Eden, 1st Baron 1744–1814
Austen, Jane, 1775–1817
Austin, Sarah, 1793–1867
Ayliffe, John, 1676–1732
Aytoun, William E., 1813–65

Bacon, Francis, Ld. 1561–1626
Bacon, Nathaniel, 1593–1660
Badham, Charles D., 1806–57
Bagehot, Walter, 1826–77
Bailey, Nathan, *An Universal Etymological English Dictionary* (1721, etc.)
Baillie, Robert, 1599–1662
Bain, Alexander, 1810–77
Baker, Sir Richard, 1568–1645
Baker, Sir Samuel W., 1821–93
Baldwin, William, fl. 1547
Bale, John, 1495–1563
Balfour, John H., 1808–84
Bancroft, Abp. Richard, 1544–1610
Barbour, John, 1316?–95
Barckley, Sir Richard, *Discourse of the Felicitie of Man* (1598)
Barclay, James, fl. 1774
Baret, John, d. 1580?
Barham, Richard H., 1788–1845
Baring-Gould, Sabine, 1834–1924
Barlow, Joel, 1754–1812
Barlow, Peter, 1776–1862
Barlow, Bp. William, d. 1613
Barnes, Robert, 1495–1540
Barnes, William, 1801–86
Barrère and Leland, *Dictionary of Slang*, etc. (1888–90)
Barrie, Sir James M., 1860–1937
Barrow, Isaac, 1630–77
Bartlett, John R., *Dictionary of Americanisms* (1848, etc., 1876)
Baxter, Richard, 1615–91
Bayne(s), Paul, d. 1617
Beaconsfield, Earl of: see Disraeli
Beale, Francis, fl. 1656
Beattie, James, 1735–1803
Beaumont, Francis, and Fletcher, John, 1584–1616 and 1579–1625
Beckford, Peter, 1740–1811
Beckford, William, 1759–1844
Becon, Thomas, 1512–67
Bedell, Bp. William, 1571–1642
Bedwell, William, d. 1632
Beeton, Mrs. Isabella M., *Book of Household Management* (1861)
Behn, Mrs. Aphra, 1640–89
Bell, A. M., *The Principles of Speech* (1863)
Bell, William, *Dictionary of the Law of Scotland* (1838)
Ben Israel, Manasseh, 1604–57
Benlowes, Edward, 1603?–76
Bentham, Jeremy, 1748–1832
Bentley, Richard, 1662–1742
Bentley, Robert, *Manual of Botany* (1861)
Berkeley, Bp. George, 1685–1753
Berkeley, Hon. George C. G. F., 1800–81
Berkeley, Miles J., 1803–89
Berners, John Bourchier, Baron 1467–1533
Berry, Miss Mary, 1763–1802
Besant, Mrs. Annie, 1847–1933
Besant, Sir Walter, 1836–1901
Best, Thomas, *A Concise Treatise on the Art of Angling* (1787)
Beveridge, William, 1637–1705
Bewick, Thomas, 1753–1828
Bible; Wyclif's, 1382, 1388; Coverdale, 1535; Great or Cranmer's, 1539; Geneva, 1560; Bishops', 1568; Douay, 1609–10; Authorized, 1611; Revised N.T., 1881; O.T., 1884; Apocrypha, 1894. The version quoted is that of 1611, unless otherwise noted. (See p. xxvii for abbreviations of titles.) See also *New Testament.*
Billingsley, Sir Henry, d. 1608
Bingham, Joseph, 1668–1723
Birch, Thomas, 1705–66
Birrell, Augustine, 1850–1933
Black, Charles C., fl. 1870
Black, William, 1841–98
Blackie, John Stuart, 1809–95
Blackmore, Richard D., 1825–1900
Blackstone, Sir William, 1723–80
Blades, William, 1824–90
Blair, Robert, 1593–1666
Blair, Robert, 1699–1746
Blake, William, 1757–1827
Blith, Walter, fl. 1649
Bloomfield, Robert, 1766–1823
Blount, Thomas, 1618–79
Blundevil, Thomas, fl. 1560
Blunt, John H., 1823–84
Bokenham, Osbern, 1393–1447?
'Boldrewood, Rolf' (T. A. Browne), 1826–1915
Bolingbroke, H. St. John, Viscount 1678–1751
Bolton, Robert, 1572–1631
Bonnycastle, John, 1750?–1821
Book of Common Prayer, The (1549, 1552, 1559, 1662)
Boorde (or Borde), Andrew, 1490?–1549
Booth, David, 1766–1846
Borrow, George, 1803–81
Boswell, James, 1740–95
Bosworth, Joseph, and Toller, T. N., *An Anglo-Saxon Dictionary* (1882–98); *Suppl.* (1908–21)
Botoner, William, 1415–1482?
Bouvier, John, *Law Dictionary of the U.S.A.* (1843–56)
Bowen, Charles S. C., Baron 1835–94
Boyle, Hon. Robert, 1627–91
Braddon, Mary E., 1837–1915
Bradley, Henry, 1845–1923
Bradley, Richard, d. 1732
Bradshaw, Henry, d. 1513
Bramhall, Abp. J., 1594–1663
Brand, John, 1744–1806
Brassey, Annie, Lady 1839–87
Brathwaite, Richard, 1588?–1673
Brent, Sir Nathaniel, 1573?–1652
Brereton, Sir William, 1604–61
Breton, Nicholas, 1545?–1626?
Brevint, Daniel, 1616–95
Brewster, Sir David, 1781–1868
Bridges, Robert, 1844–1930
Bright, John, 1811–89
Brinsley, John, fl. 1663
British Association for the Advancement of Science, Reports of the (1831–)
Brodie, Sir Benjamin C., 1783–1862
Brome, Richard, d. 1652?
Brontë, Charlotte, 1816–55
Brontë, Emily J., 1818–48
Broome, William, 1689–1745
Brougham, Henry Peter, Lord 1778–1868
Broughton, Rhoda, 1840–1920
Brown, John, 1810–82
Brown, Thomas, 1663–1704
Brown, Thomas, *Modern Farriery* (1847)
Browne, Sir Thomas, 1605–82
Browne, William, 1591–1643?
Browning, Mrs Elizabeth Barrett, 1806–61
Browning, Robert, 1812–89
Bryant, Thomas, *Practice of Surgery* (1872)
Bryant, William Cullen, 1794–1878
Bryce, James, 1838–1922
Buchan, William, 1729–1805
Buchanan, Robert, 1813–66
Buck, Albert H., ed. *Handbook of the Medical Sciences* (1885–90)
Buckland, Francis T., 1826–80
Buckland, William, 1784–1856
Buckle, Henry T., 1821–62
Buckle, John S., *Manufacturer's Compendium* (1864)
Budgell, Eustace, 1686–1737
Bull, Bp. George, 1634–1710
Buller, Sir Francis, 1746–1800
Bulwer, John, fl. 1654
Bulwer-Lytton: see Lytton
Bunsen, Frances, Baroness 1791–1876
Bunyan, John, 1628–88
Burgon, John W., 1813–88
Burke, Edmund, 1729–97
Burnaby, Andrew, 1734?–1812
Burnet, Bp. Gilbert, 1643–1715
Burnet, Thomas, 1635?–1715
Burnett, James, Lord Monboddo, 1714–99
Burney, Frances: see D'Arblay

Burney, William, ed. *Falconer's Dictionary of the Marine* (1815)
Burns, Robert, 1759–96
Burrow, Edward J., 1785–1861
Burton, Henry, 1578–1648
Burton, Richard F., 1821–90
Burton, Robert, 1577–1640
Bury, Lady Charlotte S. M., 1775–1861
Butler, Alban, 1711–73
Butler, Bp. Joseph, 1692–1752
Butler, Samuel, *Hudibras* (1663–4, –78)
Byron George Gordon, 6th Baron 1788–1824

Cable, George W., 1844–1925
Caine, Sir T. H. Hall, 1853–1931
Cairns, John, 1818–92
Calhoun, John C., d. 1850
Calthorpe, Sir Henry, 1586–1637
Camden, William, 1551–1623
Cameron, Lucy L., 1781–1858
Campbell, Thomas, 1777–1844
Campion, Thomas, d. 1619
Canning, George, 1770–1827
Cant, Andrew, 1590?–1663
Capgrave, John, 1393–1464
Carew, Richard, 1555–1620
Carew, Thomas, 1595?–1639?
Carey, Henry, d. 1743
Carlyle, Jane B. Welsh, 1801–66
Carlyle, Thomas, 1795–1881
Carpenter, William B., 1813–85
'Carroll, Lewis' (C. L. Dodgson), 1832–98
Carte, Thomas, 1686–1754
Cartwright, William, 1611–43
Cary, Henry F., 1772–1844
Casaubon, Meric, 1599–1671
Cassell's Encyclopædic Dictionary (1879–88)
Cassell's Supplementary Volume (1902)
Catholic Dictionary, A (1884, 1897)
Catholicon Anglicum (*c* 1483)
Caulfeild, J. M., *Seamanship Notes* (1886)
'Cavendish' (H. Jones), 1831–99
Cavendish, George, 1500–61?
Caxton, William, 1422?–91
Cayley, Arthur, 1821–95
Cecil, Robert, Earl of Salisbury, 1563?–1612
Centlivre, Susanna, 1667?–1723
Century Dictionary, The (1889–91)
—— *Supplement* (1909)
Challoner, Bp. Richard, 1691–1781
Chalmers, Alexander, 1759–1834
Chaloner, Edward, *Six Sermons* (1625)
Chaloner, Sir Thomas, 1521–65
Chambers, Ephraim, *Cyclopædia; or, an universal dictionary of arts and sciences* (1728, etc.)
Chambers, Sir E. K., 1866–1954
Chambers, Robert, 1802–71
Chambers's Cyclopædia of English Literature (1844)
Chambers's Encyclopædia (1860–68)
Chapman, George, 1559?–1634
Chapone, Hester, 1727–1801
Charles I, 1600–49
Charles II, 1630–85
Chatham, William Pitt, Earl of 1708–78
Chatterton, Thomas, 1752–70
Chatto, William A., 1799–1864
Chaucer, Geoffrey, 1340?–1400
Chesterfield, P. D. Stanhope, 4th Earl 1694–1773
Chesterton, Gilbert K., 1874–1936
Cheyne, George, 1671–1743
Child, Francis J., ed. *English and Scottish Ballads* (1857, 1882–98)
Chillingworth, William, 1602–44
Chitty, Sir J. W., 1828–99

Churchill, Charles, 1731–64
Churchill, John, *Voyages and Travels* (1704)
Cibber, Colley, 1671–1757
Clare, John, 1793–1864
Clarendon, Edward Hyde, 1st Earl of 1609–74
Clarke, Hyde, *New and Comprehensive Dictionary of the English Language* (1855)
Clarke, Mary Cowden, 1809–98
Cleveland, John, 1613–58
Clissold, F., *The Ascent of Mont Blanc* (1823)
Clough, Arthur H., 1819–61
Cobbett, William, 1763–1835
Cobden, Richard, 1804–65
Cockburn, Henry Thomas, Lord 1779–1854
Cockburn, John, 1652–1729
Cockeram, Henry, *The English Dictionarie* (1623)
Cocks, Richard, *Diary in Japan* (1615–22)
Cogan, Henry, fl. 1650
Coke, Sir Edward, 1552–1634
Coke, Roger, fl. 1696
Colebrooke, Henry T., 1765–1837
Coleridge, Hartley, 1796–1849
Coleridge, Samuel T., 1772–1834
Colet, John, 1467?–1519
Collier, Jeremy, 1650–1726
Collins, Mortimer, 1827–76
Collins, William, 1721–59
Collins, William Wilkie, 1824–89
Colman, George (the elder), 1732–94
Colman, George (the younger), 1762–1836
Colvil, Samuel, *Whiggs Supplication* (1681)
Combe, William, 1741–1823
Conder, Eustace, *The Basis of Faith* (1877)
Conder, Josiah, 1789–1855
Congreve, William, 1670–1729
Conway, Moncure D., 1832–1907
Conybeare, Bp. John, 1692–1755
Cook, Captain James, 1728–79
Cook, Moses, *The Manner of Raising .. Forrest Trees* (1676)
Cooper, James Fenimore, 1789–1851
Cooper, Samuel, 1780–1848
Copland, Robert, fl. 1530
Corbet, John, 1620–80
'Cornwall, Barry': see Procter, Bryan W.
Cornwalleys, Henry, fl. 1693
Cornwallis, Sir William, d. 1631?
Cory, William J., 1823–92
Coryate, Thomas, 1577?–1617
Cotgrave, John, fl. 1655
Cotgrave, Randle, *Dictionarie of the French and English Tongues* (1611, 1632)
Cotton, Charles, 1630–87
Cotton, John, 1584–1652
Coues, Elliott, *Birds of the Northwest* (1873)
Coverdale, Miles, 1488–1568
Cowley, Abraham, 1618–67
Cowper, William, 1731–1800
Cox, Homersham, *The Institutions of the English Government* (1863)
Crabb, George, 1778–1851
Crabbe, George, 1754–1832
Craig, John, *A New Universal .. Dictionary of the English Language* (1849)
Craik, Mrs. Dinah M., 1826–87
Cranmer, Thomas, 1489–1556
Crashaw, Richard, 1613?–49
Crockett, Samuel R., 1860–1914
Croker, John W., 1780–1857
Cromwell, Oliver, 1599–1658
Cromwell, Thomas, Earl of Essex, 1485?–1540
Crookes, William, *Dyeing and Calico-printing* (1874)

Crowe, William, 1745–1829
Crowne, John, d. 1703?
Crozier, A. A., *Dictionary of Botanical Terms* (1892)
Cruise, William, d. 1824
Crump, Arthur, *On Banking, Currency, and the Exchanges* (1866)
Cudworth, Ralph, 1617–88
Culpepper, Nicholas, 1616–54
Cursor Mundi (XIV–XV)
Curzon, Hon. Robert, 1810–73
Cussans, John E., 1837–99

Dale, Robert W., 1829–95
Dallas, Alexander J., *Reports of Cases .. Adjudged in the Courts of Pennsylvania* (1790–1807)
Dampier, William, 1652–1715
Dana, James Dwight, *A System of Mineralogy* (1837 etc.)
Dana, Richard H., 1787–1879
Dana, Richard H., Jr., 1815–82
Daniel, George, 1616–57
Daniel, Samuel, 1562–1619
Danneley, John F., 1786–1834?
D'Arblay, Madame (Frances Burney), 1752–1840
Darwin, Charles R., 1809–82
Darwin, Erasmus, 1731–1802
Dasent, Sir George W., 1817–96
Daubeny, Charles G. B., 1795–1867
Davenant, Sir William, 1606–68
Davies, Sir John, 1569–1626
Davies, John (of Hereford), 1565?–1618
Davies, John (of Kidwelly), 1627?–93
Davies, Myles, 1662–1715?
Davy, Sir Humphry, 1778–1829
Day, John, fl. 1606
Dee, John, 1527–1608
De Foe, Daniel, 1661?–1731
Dekker, Thomas, 1570?–1641?
Delany, Mrs. Mary, 1700–88
De Lolme, John L., 1740?–1807
Deloney, Thomas, 1543?–1607?
De Morgan, Augustus, 1806–71
Denham, Sir John, 1615–69
Denham, Michael A., d. 1859
Dennis, John, 1657–1734
De Quincey, Thomas, 1785–1859
Derham, William, 1657–1735
Dering, Sir Edward, 1598–1644
De Vere, Sir Aubrey, 1788–1846
De Vere, Aubrey Thomas, 1814–1902
De Vere, M. Schele, *Americanisms* (1872)
D'Ewes, Sir Simonds, 1602–50
Dibdin, Charles, 1745–1814
Dibdin, Thomas Frognall, 1776–1847
Dicey, Edward, 1832–1911
Dickens, Charles, 1812–70
Digby, Sir Kenelm, 1603–65
Digges, Sir Dudley, 1583–1639
Digges, Thomas, d. 1595
Disraeli, Benjamin, Earl of Beaconsfield 1804–81
D'Israeli, Isaac, 1766–1848
Dixon, William Hepworth, 1821–79
Dobson, H. Austin, 1840–1921
Dodsley, Robert, 1703–64
Dodwell, Henry, 1641–1711
Donne, John, 1573–1631
Doran, John, 1807–78
Douglas, Bp. Gavin, 1474?–1522
Douglas, Sir Howard, 1776–1861
Douland, or Dowland, John, 1563?–1626?
Dowden, Edward, 1843–1913
Doyle, Sir A. Conan, 1859–1930
Drayton, Michael, 1563–1631
Drummond, Henry, 1851–97

Drummond, William (of Hawthornden), 1585–1649
Dryden, John, 1631–1700
Du Cange, Sieur Charles Dufresne, *Glossarium Mediæ et Infimæ Latinitatis* (ed. 1883–7)
Duff, M. E. Grant, 1829–1906
Dufton, William, *Nature and Treatment of Deafness* (1844)
Dugdale, Sir William, 1605–86
Dunbar, William, 1465?–1530?
Duncan, Archibald, *Life of Lord Nelson* (1806)
D'Urfey, Thomas, 1653–1723
Dyer, John, 1700?–58

Earle, John, 1824–1903
Eden, Richard, 1521?–76
Edgeworth, Maria, 1767–1849
Egan, Pierce, 1772–1849
Eikon Basilike (1648)
'Eliot, George' (Mary Ann Evans), 1819–80
Elizabeth, Queen, 1533–1603
Ellis, William, d. 1758
Ellwood, Thomas, 1639–1713
Elphinstone, Mountstuart, 1779–1859
Elyot, Sir Thomas, 1499?–1546
Emanuel, Henry, *Diamonds and Precious Stones* (1865)
Emerson, Peter H., b. 1856
Emerson, Ralph W., 1803–82
Encyclopædia Britannica (ed. 9) 1875–89; (ed. 10) 1902–3; (ed. 11) 1910–11; (ed. 12) 1922; (ed. 13) 1926
Encyclopædia Metropolitana (1818–45)
English Review, The (1905–6)
Erskine, John, 1695–1768
Essex, Arthur Capel, Earl of 1631–83
Etherege, Sir George, 1635?–91
Evelyn, John, 1620–1706

Faber, Frederick W., 1814–63
Faber, George S., 1773–1854
Fabyan, Robert, d. 1513
Fairbairn, Andrew M., 1838–1912
Fairfax, Nathaniel, 1637–90
Fairfax, Thomas, 3rd Baron 1612–71
Fairholt, Frederick W., 1814–66
'Fairless, Michael' (Margaret F. Barber), 1869–1901
Falconer, William, 1732–69
Family Dictionary (1725)
Faraday, Michael, 1791–1867
Farmer, J. S., and Henley, W. E., *Slang and its Analogues* (1890–1904)
Farquhar, George, 1678–1707
Farrar, Frederic W., 1831–1903
Fawcett, Henry, 1833–84
Fawkes, Francis, 1720–77
Featley, Daniel, 1582–1645
Feltham, Owen, 1602?–68
Fenn, George Manville, 1831–1909
Fennell: see *Stanford Dictionary*
Fergusson, Robert, 1750–74
Fergusson, William, 1808–77
Ferrier, James F., 1808–64
Ferrier, Susan E., 1782–1854
Ferris, Richard, fl. 1590
Fessenden, Thomas G., 1771–1837
Fiddes, Richard, 1671–1725
Field, Nathaniel, 1587–1633
Fielding, Henry, 1707–54
Fielding, Sarah, 1710–68
Fisher, Bp. John, 1459–1535
Fisher, Samuel, 1605–65
Fiske, John, 1842–1901
FitzGerald, Edward, 1809–83
Flavel, John, 1630?–91

Flecknoe, Richard, d. 1678?
Fleetwood, Bp. William, 1656–1723
Fleming, Abraham, 1552?–1607
Fleming, David Hay, 1849–1931
Fleming, Robert, 1630–94
Fletcher, Giles (the elder), 1549?–1611
Fletcher, Giles (the younger), 1588?–1623
Fletcher, John, 1579–1625
Fletcher, Phineas, 1582–1650
Florio, John, 1553?–1625
Flower and the Leaf, The (*a* 1500)
Floyer, Sir John, 1649–1734
Folkingham, William, fl. 1610–20
Fonblanque, Albany, 1793–1872
Foote, Samuel, 1720–77
Forbes, Edward, 1815–54
Ford, John, fl. 1639
Ford, Richard, 1796–1858
Fordyce, James, 1720–96
Forrest, Thomas, 1729?–1802?
Forrest, Sir William, fl. 1581
Forster, John, 1812–76
Fortescue, Sir John, 1394?–1476?
Fortnightly Review, The (1865–1912)
Foster, William, ed. *English Factories in India* [1618–69]
Four Centuries of English Letters [15th–18th c.] (ed. W. B. Scoones 1880)
Fowler, Thomas, 1832–1904
Foxe, John, 1516–87
Francis, Francis, 1822–86
Franklin, Benjamin, 1706–90
Freeman, Edward A., 1823–92
French, John, 1616?–57
Frith, John, 1503–33
Froude, James Anthony, 1818–94
Fulbecke, William, 1560–1603?
Fulke, William, 1538–89
Fuller, Thomas, 1608–61
Fullerton, Lady Georgiana C., 1812–85
Funk and Wagnalls' Standard Dictionary of the English Language (1893–5, etc.)

Gage, John, 1786–1842
Gage, Thomas, d. 1656
Gale, Thomas, 1507–87
Galsworthy, John, 1867–1933
Galt, John, 1779–1839
Garrard, William, *The Art of Warre* (*a* 1587)
Garrick, David, 1717–79
Gascoigne, George, 1525?–77
Gaskell, Mrs. Elizabeth Cleghorn, 1810–65
Gataker, Thomas, 1574–1654
Gauden, Bp. John, 1605–62
Gaule, John, fl. 1660
Gay, John, 1685–1732
Gayton, Edmund, 1608–66
Gee, George E., *The practical gold-worker* (1877)
Geikie, Sir Archibald, 1835–1924
Geikie, James, 1839–1915
Gerard, or Gerarde, John, 1545–1612
Gesta Romanorum, The (*c* 1440)
Gibbon, Edward, 1737–94
Gibbs, Henry Hucks, 1st Baron Aldenham 1819–1907
Gibson, William, fl. 1720
Gifford, William, 1756–1826
Gilbert, Sir Geoffrey, 1674–1726.
Gilbert, William Schwenk, 1836–1911
Gilchrist, James, *The Etymologic Interpreter* (1824)
Gladstone, William Ewart, 1809–98
Glanvill, Joseph, 1636–80
Glapthorne, Henry, fl. 1639
Glasse, Mrs. Hannah, fl. 1747
Gleig, George R., 1796–1888
Glouc.: see Robert of Gloucester

Glover, Richard, 1712–85
Goddard, Thomas, *Plato's Demon* (1684)
Godefroy, Frédéric, *Dictionnaire de l'ancienne langue française* (1881–92)
Godstow Nunnery, The English register of (*c* 1450)
Godwin, Mrs. Mary Wollstonecraft: see Wollstonecraft
Godwin, William, 1756–1836
Golding, Arthur, 1536?–1605?
Goldsmith, Oliver, 1728–74
Gooch, Benjamin, fl. 1775
Good, John Mason, 1764–1827
Goode, George Brown, 1851–96
Goodwin, Thomas, 1600–80
Googe, Barnaby, 1540–94
Gordon, Adam Lindsay, 1833–70
Gordon, Charles George, 1833–85
Gore, Bp. Charles, 1853–1932
Gosse, Sir Edmund W., 1849–1928
Gosse, Philip Henry, 1810–88
Gosson, Stephen, 1554–1624
Gouge, William, 1578–1653
Goulburn, Edward Meyrick, 1818–97
Gould, George M., *A New Medical Dictionary* (1890)
Gould, John, 1804–81
Gower, John, 1325?–1408
Grafton, Richard, d. 1572?
Grahame, Kenneth, 1859–1932
Grant, David, 1823–86
Grant, James, 1802–79
Gray, Asa, 1810–88
Gray, Thomas, 1716–71
Green, John Richard, 1837–83
Green, Thomas Hill, 1836–82
Greene, Robert, 1560?–92
Gregory, William, 1803–58
Gresley, William S., *A Glossary of Terms used in Coalmining* (1883)
Greville, Charles C. F., 1794–1865
Greville, Fulke, 1st Baron Brooke 1554–1628
Grew, Nehemiah, 1641–1712
Griffiths, Frederick Augustus, d. 1869
Grimalde, Nicholas, 1519–62
Grindal, Abp. Edmund, 1519?–83
Grose, Francis, 1731?–91
Grote, George, 1794–1871
Grove, Sir George, 1820–1900
Grove, Sir William, 1811–96
Guest, Edwin, 1800–80
Guillim, John, 1565–1621
Gunter, Archibald C., 1847–1907
Gurnall, William, 1617–79
Gurwood, John, 1790–1845
Guthry, Bp. Henry, 1600?–76
Gwilt, Joseph, *An Encyclopædia of Architecture* (1842, 1859)

Habington, William, 1605–54
Hacket, Bp. John, 1592–1670
Hadley, James, *Essays philological and critical* (*a* 1872)
Haggard, Sir H. Rider, 1856–1925
Hakewill, George, 1578–1649
Hakewill, William, 1574–1655
Hakluyt, Richard, 1552?–1616
Hale, Sir Matthew, 1609–76
Hales, John, 1584–1656
Haliburton, Thomas Chandler, 1796–1865
Hall, Edward, *c* 1489–1547
Hall, Fitzedward, 1825–1901
Hall, Granville S., 1846–1924
Hall, Bp. Joseph, 1574–1656
Hallam, Henry, 1777–1859
Halliwell (afterwards Halliwell-Phillipps), James O., 1820–89
Hamerton, Philip Gilbert, 1834–94

Hamilton, James, 1814–67
Hamilton, Abp. John, 1511?–71
Hamilton, Richard W., 1794–1848
Hamilton, Sir William, 1788–1856
Hammond, Henry, 1605–60
Hampole, Richard Rolle of, 1290?–1349
Hanmer, Meredith, 1543–1604
Hanmer, Sir Thomas, 1677–1746
Hardy, Thomas, 1840–1928
Hare, Augustus J. C., 1834–1903
Hare, Julius C., 1795–1855
Harewood, Harry, *A Dictionary of Sports* (1835)
Harington, Sir John, 1561–1612
Harlan, George C., *Eyesight* (1879)
Harpsfield, Nicholas, 1519?–75
Harraden, Beatrice, 1864–1936
Harrington, James, 1611–77
Harris, Chapin A., *A Dictionary of Dental Science* (1849)
Harris, James, 1709–80
Harris, John, 1667?–1719
Harris, Moses, fl. 1766–85
Harris, Robert, 1581–1658
Harrison, Sarah, *The Housekeeper's Pocket-book* (1739)
Harsnett, Samuel, 1561–1631
Harte, F. Bret, 1839–1902
Hartley, David, 1705–57
Hartlib, Samuel, d. 1670?
Harvey, Christopher, 1597–1663
Harvey, Gabriel, 1545?–1630
Hatton, Joseph, 1841–1907
Hatzfeld, Adolphe and Darmesteter, Arsène, *Dictionnaire général de la langue française* (1895–1900)
Havelok, Lay of (*a* 1300)
Haward, Nicholas, fl. 1569
Hawes, Stephen, d. 1523?
Hawker, Robert S., 1803–75
Hawkins, Sir John, 1532–95
Hawkins, Sir John, 1719–89
Hawkins, Sir Richard, *c* 1560–1622
Hawthorne, Julian, 1846–1934
Hawthorne, Nathaniel, 1804–64
Hayward, Sir John, 1564?–1627
Haywood, Mrs., *The Whole Art of Cookery, etc.* (1771)
Hazlitt, William, 1778–1830
Hazlitt, William C., 1834–1913
Head, Richard, 1637?–86?
Healey, John, d. 1610
Hearn, William E., 1826–88
Hearne, Thomas, 1678–1735
Heber, Bp. Reginald, 1783–1826
Helps, Sir Arthur, 1813–75
Hemans, Felicia D., 1793–1835
Henfrey, Arthur, 1819–59
Henley, William E., 1849–1903
Henry, Matthew, 1662–1714
Henslow, John S., 1796–1861
Herbert, George, 1593–1633
Herbert, Sir Thomas, 1606–82
Herrick, Robert, 1591–1674
Herschel, Sir John F. W., 1792–1871
Hervey, James, 1714–58
Hewlett, Joseph T. J., 1800–47
Hexham, Henry, 1585?–1650?
Heylin, Peter, 1600–62
Heywood, John, 1497?–1580?
Heywood, Thomas, d. 1650?
Hickeringill, Edmund, 1631–1708
Hieron, Samuel, 1576?–1617
Higden's Polychronicon, 1432–50; see also Trevisa
Higgins, John, fl. 1570–1602
Hiles, John, *A Complete Dictionary of Musical Terms* (1871)

Hill, John, 1716?–75
Hill, Thomas, fl. 1590
Hill, Thomas, d. 1653
Hitchcock, Robert, fl. 1580–91
Hobbes, Thomas, 1588–1679
Hoblyn, Richard D., 1803–86
Hoby, Sir Edward, 1560–1617
Hoccleve, Thomas, 1370?–1450?
Hogarth, George, 1783–1870
Hogg, James, 1770–1835
Holbrook, M. L., *Hygiene of the Brain and Nerves* (1878)
Holcroft, Thomas, 1745–1809
Holinshed, Raphael, d. 1580?
Holland, Josiah G., 1819–81
Holland, Philemon, 1552–1637
Holme, Randle, 1627–99
Holmes, Edward, 1797–1859
Holmes, Oliver Wendell, 1809–94
Holtzapffel, Chas. and J. J., *Turning and Mechanical Manipulation* (1843–50)
Holwell, William, 1726–98
Holyday, Barten, 1593–1661
Holyoake, Francis, 1567–1653
Home, Sir Everard, 1756–1832
Hone, William, 1780–1842
Hood, Thomas, 1799–1845
Hook, Theodore E., 1788–1841
Hook, Walter F., 1798–1875
Hooker, Sir Joseph D., 1817–1911
Hooker, Richard, 1554?–1600
Hooker, Sir William J., 1785–1865
Hooper, Bp. John, d. 1555
Hooper, Robert, 1773–1835
Hope, Alexander J. Beresford, 1820–87
Horne, Bp. George, 1730–92
Hotten, John C., *A Dictionary of Modern Slang* (1859, etc.)
House of Commons, Journals of the (1547–)
House of Lords, Journals of the (1509–)
Housman, Alfred E., 1859–1936
Houston, Edwin J., *A Dictionary of Electrical Words* (1889)
Howell, James, 1594?–1666
Howells, William D., 1837–1920
Howitt, Mary, 1799–1888
Howitt, William, 1792–1879
Howson, Bp. John, 1557?–1632
Hoyle, Edmond, 1672–1769
Hughes, Thomas, 1822–96
Huloet, Richard, fl. 1552
Hume, David, 1711–76
Hunt, J. H. Leigh, 1784–1859
Hunt, William Holman, 1827–1910
Hunter, James, *Dictionary of Farriery* (1796)
Hussey, Robert, 1801–56
Hutchinson, Horace G., 1859–1932
Hutchinson, Lucy, fl. 1665
Hutchinson, Thomas, 1711–80
Hutton, Charles, 1737–1823
Huxley, Thomas H., 1825–95
Hyne, C. J. Cutcliffe W., 1866–1944

Imison, John, d. 1788
Index Kewensis (1893–5); *Suppl.* (1901–26)
Ingelow, Jean, 1820–97
Ingoldsby Legends by R. H. Barham
Innes, Cosmo, 1798–1874
Instructions and regulations for the formations and movements of the cavalry (1796)
Irving, Edward, 1792–1834
Irving, Washington, 1783–1859

Jackson, Benjamin D., 1846–1927
Jackson, Thomas, 1579–1640
Jacob, Giles, *A New Law Dictionary* (1729)
James VI, King of Scotland, afterwards James I of England, 1566–1625

James, Charles, *A New and Enlarged Military Dictionary* (1802)
James, George P. R., 1799–1860
James, Henry, 1843–1916
Jameson, Mrs. Anna B., 1794–1860
Jameson, Robert, 1774–1854
Jamieson, John, 1759–1838
Jefferies, Richard, 1848–87
Jefferson, Thomas, 1743–1826
Jellicoe, John Rushworth, 1st Earl 1859–1935
Jephson, Robert, 1736–1803
Jerrold, Douglas W., 1803–57
Jesse, E.: see Knapp, J. L.
Jevons, William Stanley, 1835–82
Jewel, John, 1522–71
Johnson, Samuel, 1709–84 (*A Dictionary of the English Language*, 1755, 1773)
Jones, John, fl. 1579
Jones, Thomas Rymer, 1810–80
Jones, Sir William, 1746–94
Jonson, Ben, 1573?–1637
Jortin, John, 1698–1770
Jowett, Benjamin, 1817–93
'Junius' Letters (1769–72)

Kames, Henry Home, Lord 1696–1782
Kane, Elisha K., 1820–57
Keatinge, Maurice B., *Travels through France and Spain* (1816)
Keats, John, 1795–1821
Keble, John, 1792–1866
Keightley, Thomas, 1789–1872
Kemble, Frances A., 1809–93
Kemble, John M., 1807–57
Ken, Bp. Thomas, 1637–1711
Kent, James, *Commentaries on American Law* (1826–30)
Ker, William P., 1855–1923
Kersey, John, fl. 1720
Key, Thomas H., 1799–1875
King, William, 1663–1712
Kinglake, Alexander W., 1809–91
Kingsley, Charles, 1819–75
Kingsley, Henry, 1830–76
Kingsmill or Kingesmyll, Andrew, 1538–69
Kipling, Rudyard, 1865–1936
Kirby, William, 1759–1850
Kirwan, Richard, 1733–1812
Klein, Edward E., 1844–1925
Knapp, John L., 1767–1845
Knight, Charles, 1791–1873
Knight, Edward H., *Dictionary of Mechanics* (1874–7); *Suppl.* (1884)
Knolles, Richard, 1550?–1610
Knox, John, 1505–72
Knox, Robert, 1791–1862
Knox, Vicesimus, 1752–1821
Kyd, Thomas, 1557?–95?

Lamb, Charles, 1775–1834
Lamb, Mary Ann, 1764–1847
Lambarde, William, 1536–1601
Landor, Walter S., 1775–1864
Lane, Edward W., 1801–76
Lang, Andrew, 1844–1912
Langhorne, John, 1735–79
Langland, William, 1330?–1400?
Lankester, Sir E. Ray, 1847–1929
Lardner, Dionysius, 1793–1859
Latham, John, 1740–1837
Latham, Robert G., 1812–88
Latimer, Hugh, 1485?–1555
Laud, Abp. William, 1573–1645
Law, William, 1686–1761
Laȝamon's *Brut* (XIII)
Lee, Frederick G., d. 1902
Lee, Nathaniel, 1653?–92

'Lee, Vernon' (Violet Paget), 1856–1935
Leland, John, 1506?–52
L'Estrange, Sir Roger, 1616–1704
Lever, Charles J., 1806–72
Lewes, George H., 1817–78
Lewins, William, *Her Majesty's Mail* (1864)
Lewis, Charlton T., and Short, Charles, *A Latin Dictionary* (1879)
Lewis, John, 1675–1747
Liddell, Henry G., and Scott, Robert, *A Greek–English Lexicon* (ed. 8, 1897)
Lindley, John, 1799–1865
Lingard, John, 1771–1851
Linnæus (Carl von Linné), 1707–78
Linton, Mrs. E. Lynn, 1822–98
Lithgow, William, 1582–1645?
Littleton's, Sir T., Tenures (1538)
Littré, Émile, *Dictionnaire de la langue française* (1863–77)
Livingstone, David, 1813–73
Locke, John, 1632–1704
Lockhart, John G., 1794–1854
Lockyer, J. Norman, 1836–1920
Lodge, Thomas, 1558?–1625
Longfellow, Henry Wadsworth, 1807–82
Lotze's, R. H., Logic, B. Bosanquet, tr. (1884)
Loudon, John C., 1783–1843
Lovelace, Richard, 1618–58
Lovell, Archibald, fl. 1679–87
Lover, Samuel, 1797–1868
Lowell, James Russell, 1819–91
Lower, Sir William, 1600?–62
Lowth, Bp. Robert, 1710–87
Lubbock, Sir John, 1834–1913
Ludlow, John M., 1821–1911
Lupton, Thomas, fl. 1583
'Lyall, Edna' (Ada E. Bayly), 1857–1903
Lydekker, Richard, 1849–1915
Lydgate, John, 1370?–1451?
Lyell, Sir Charles, 1797–1875
Lyly, John, 1554?–1606
Lyndesay, Sir David, 1490–1555
Lyte, Henry, tr. *Dodoens' Niewe Herball* (1578)
Lyttelton, George, 1st Baron 1709–73
Lytton, Edward G. E. L. Bulwer-Lytton, 1st Baron 1803–73

Mabbe, James, 1572–1642?
Macaulay, Thomas Babington, Lord 1800–59
McCarthy, Justin, 1830–1912
McCosh, James, 1811–94
McCulloch, John R., 1789–1864
Macdonald, George, 1824–1905
McDonogh, Felix, fl. 1820–26
McDougall, William, 1871–1938
Macfarren, Sir George A., 1813–87
Macgillivray, William, 1796–1852
Mackenzie, Sir George, 1636–91
Mackenzie, Sir Morell, 1837–92
Mackenzie, Murdoch, d. 1797
Mackintosh, Sir James, 1765–1832.
Maclaren, Walter S. B., 1853–1912
Macpherson, James, 1736–96
Mahaffy, John P., 1839–1919
Maine, Sir Henry J. S., 1822–88
Maitland, Samuel R., 1792–1866
Mallock, William H., 1849–1923
Malone, Edmund, 1741–1812
Malory, Sir Thomas, fl. 1470
Malthus, Thomas R., 1766–1834
Malynes, Gerard de, fl. 1586–1641
Mandeville, Bernard, 1670?–1733
Manley, Thomas, 1628–90
Manning, Cdl. Henry E., 1808–92
Mansel, Henry L., 1820–71
Manson, George J., *The Sporting Dictionary* (1895)
Manton, Thomas, 1620–77
Manwood, John, d. 1610
Marbeck, John, d. 1585?
Markham, Gervase, 1568?–1637
Marlowe, Christopher, 1564–93
Marryat, Frederick, 1792–1848
Marshall, Alfred, 1842–1924
Marshall, John, 1818–91
Marshall, William H., 1745–1818
Marston, John, 1575?–1634
Martin, Sir Theodore, 1816–1909
Martineau, Harriet, 1802–76
Martineau, James, 1805–1900
Marvell, Andrew, 1621–78
Masefield, John, 1878–1967
Maskelyne, Mervin H. N. S., 1823–1911
Mason, Charlotte M. S., 1842–1923
Mason, George, 1735–1806
Mason, Jas., *The Principles of Chess* (1894)
Mason, John, fl. 1750
Massinger, Philip, 1583–1640
Masson, David, 1822–1907
Mather, Cotton, 1663–1728
Maudsley, Henry, 1835–1918
Maunder, Samuel, 1785–1849
Maundeville, Sir John, *Travels* (*c* 1400)
Maundrell, Henry, 1665–1701
Maurice, Frederick Denison, 1805–72
Maury, Matthew F., 1806–73
Max-Müller, Friedrich, 1823–1900
Maxwell, William Hamilton, 1792–1850
May, Thomas, 1595–1650
May, Sir Thomas Erskine, 1815–86
Mayhew, A. L., and Skeat, W. W., *A concise dictionary of Middle English* (1888)
Mayhew, Henry, *London Labour and the London Poor* (1851–61)
Mayne, Jasper, 1604–72
Mayne, Robert G., *An Expository Lexicon of the Terms .. of Medical and General Science* (1853–60)
Medwin, Thomas, 1788–1869
Melmoth, William, 1710–99
Melville, George J. Whyte, 1821–78
Melville, Herman, 1819–91
Mendes da Costa, Emanuel, 1717–91
Meredith, George, 1828–1909
Merivale, Charles, 1808–93
Meynell, Wilfrid, 1877–1948
Miall, Louis C., 1842–1921
Middleton, Thomas, 1570?–1627
Miege, Guy, 1644–1718?
Mill, James, 1773–1836
Mill, John Stuart, 1806–73
Miller, Hugh, 1802–56
Milman, Henry Hart, 1791–1868
Milton, John, 1608–74 (*Paradise Lost* (*P.L.*) 1667, *Paradise Regained* (*P.R.*) 1671, *Samson Agonistes* (*S.A.*) 1671)
Minsheu, John, fl. 1617
Mirror for Magistrates, A (1559, etc.)
Mitchell, Donald G., 1822–1908
Mitford, Miss Mary R., 1787–1855
Mivart, St. George J., 1827–1900
Moir, David M., 1798–1851
Mollett, John W., *An Illustrated Dictionary of Words used in Art and Archæology* (1883)
Monboddo, James Burnett, Lord 1714–99
Monmouth, Henry Carey, 2nd Earl 1596–1661
Monro, Alexander, 1697–1767
Montagu, Elizabeth, 1720–1800
Montagu, George, 1751–1815
Montagu, Lady Mary Wortley, 1689–1762
Montagu, Bp. Richard, 1577–1641
Moore, Sir Jonas, 1617–79
Moore, Thomas, 1779–1852
More, Hannah, 1745–1833
More, Henry, 1614–87
More, Sir Thomas, 1478–1535
Morgan, Conwy Lloyd, 1852–1936
Morgan (formerly Owenson), Sydney, Lady 1783?–1859
Morier, James J., 1780?–1849
Morley, John, 1838–1923
Morley and Muir: see Watts, Henry
Morris, John, 1810–86
Morris, Sir Lewis, 1833–1907
Morris, William, 1834–96
Morse, Jedidiah, 1761–1826
Mortimer, Thomas, 1730–1810
Morton, John C., 1821–88
Moryson, Fynes, 1566–1630
'Mostyn, Sydney': see Russell, W. C.
Motherwell, William, 1797–1835
Motley, John Lothrop, 1814–77
Motteux, Peter A., 1660–1718
Moxon, Joseph, 1627–1700
Mozley, James Bowling, 1813–78
Müller, Friedrich Max-: see Max-Müller, F.
Mulcaster, Richard, 1530?–1611
Munday, Anthony, 1553–1633
Munro, Neil, *The Lost Pibroch* (1896)
Murchison, Sir Roderick Impey, 1792–1871
Murphy, Arthur, 1727–1805
Murray, David Christie, 1847–1907
Murray, Sir James A. H., 1837–1915
Murray, Lindley, 1745–1826
Musgrave, George Musgrave, 1798–1883
Mynshul, Geffray, 1594?–1668

N. & Q. = *Notes and Queries*
Napier, Robina, ed. *Johnsoniana* (1884)
Napier, Sir William F. P., 1785–1860
Nares, Edward, 1762–1841
Nares, Robert, 1753–1829
Nashe, Thomas, 1567–1601
National Review, The (1883–1950)
Naunton, Sir Robert, 1563–1635
Naval accounts and inventories of the reign of Henry VII (1485–97)
Neal, Daniel, 1678–1743
Neale, John M., 1818–66
Nelson, Horatio Nelson, 1st Viscount 1758–1805
Nesse, Christopher, 1621–1705
Nevile, Thomas, fl. 1769
New Testament (versions). Tindale, 1526, 1534; Geneva, 1557; Rheims, 1582. See also *Bible*
Newman, Edward, 1801–76
Newman, Cdl. John Henry, 1801–90
Newton, Sir Isaac, 1642–1727
Nichol, John P., 1804–59
Nichols, John, 1745–1826
Nicholson, Henry A., 1844–99
Nicholson, Peter, 1765–1844
Nicholson, William, 1753–1815
Nicol, Alexander, fl. 1739–66
Nicolas, Sir Nicholas H., 1799–1848
Nicolson, Abp. William, 1655–1727
Nightingale, Florence, 1820–1910
Noad, Henry M., 1815–77
Norris, John (of Bemerton), 1657–1711
Norris, William E., 1847–1925
North, Roger, 1653–1734
North, Sir Thomas, 1535?–1601?
Norton, Caroline E. S., 1808–77
Norton, Thomas, 1532–84
Notes and Queries (1850–)
Noyes, Alfred, 1880–1958
Nugent, Thomas, 1700?–72

Occleve, Thomas: see Hoccleve, T.
Ogilby, John, 1600–76
Ogilvie, John, 1797–1867
Ogilvie-Grant, William, R., 1863–1924
Old English Chronicle: see *Anglo-Saxon*
Oldham, John, 1653–83
Oldys, William, 1696–1761
Oliphant, Laurence, 1829–88
Oliphant, Margaret O. W., 1828–97
Olmsted, Frederick L., 1822–1903
Opie, John, 1761–1807
Orm(in), *Ormulum* (*c* 1200)
Orrery, John Boyle, 5th Earl of Cork and 1707–62
Osborn, Hon. Mrs. Sarah, *Political and Social Letters* (1721–71)
Osborne, Dorothy (Lady Temple), 1627–95
Osborne, Francis, 1593–1659
Otway, Thomas, 1652–85
'Ouida' (Mlle L. de La Ramée), 1839–1908
Ouseley, Sir Frederick A. G., 1825–89
Overbury, Sir Thomas, 1581–1613
Owen, John, 1616–83
Owen, Richard, 1804–92
Oxford University Calendar (1810–)

Page, David, 1814–79
Paget, Francis E., 1806–82
Paley, William, 1743–1805
Palgrave, Sir Francis, 1788–1861
Palgrave, Francis T., 1824–97
Palgrave, William G., 1826–88
Palsgrave, John, d. 1554
Parker, John Henry, 1806–84
Parker, Abp. Matthew, 1504–75
Parkman, Francis, 1823–93
Parnell, Thomas, 1679–1718
Parr, Bartholomew, 1750–1810
Parr, Samuel, 1747–1825
Parry, Sir William E., 1790–1855
Paston Letters, The (1422–1509)
Pater, Walter H., 1839–94
Patmore, Coventry K. D., 1823–96
Patrick, Bp. Simon, 1626–1707
Pattison, Mark, 1813–84
Payn, James, 1830–98
Paynell, Thomas, fl. 1528–68
Peabody, Andrew P., 1811–93
Peacock, Thomas Love, 1785–1866
Peake, James, *Rudiments of Naval Architecture* (1849)
Pearce, Bp. Zachary, 1690–1774
Pearson, George, 1751–1828
Pecock, Reginald, 1395?–1460?
Peele, George, 1558?–1597?
Pegge, Samuel, 1704–96
Pembroke, Mary Herbert, Countess of 1555?–1621
Penn, William, 1644–1718
Pennant, Thomas, 1726–98
Pepys, Samuel, 1633–1703
Percy, Thomas, 1729–1811; ed. *Reliques of Ancient English Poetry* (1765)
Perkins, Charles C., 1823–86
Pettie, George, 1548–89
Petty, Sir William, 1623–87
Phillips, Edward, *The New World of Words* (1658, 1662, 1678, 1696, 1706)
Phillips, Henry, fl. 1865–81
Phillips, John, 1800–74
Phillips, William, 1775–1828
Phillpotts, Eden, 1862–1960
Piers Plowman: see Langland, W.
Pindar, Peter: see Wolcot, John
Pinkerton, John, 1758–1826
Piozzi, Hester Lynch (Mrs. Thrale), 1741–1821

Planché, James R., *A Cyclopædia of Costume* (1876–9)
Plat, or Platt, Sir Hugh, 1552–1611?
Playfair, John, 1748–1819
Plot, Robert, 1640–96
Pocock, Nicholas, 1814–97
Pococke, Bp. Richard, 1704–65
Poe, Edgar A., 1809–49
Pollock, Sir Frederick, 1845–1937
Pomfret, John, 1667–1702
Pope, Alexander, 1688–1744
Porson, Richard, 1759–1808
Porter, George R., 1792–1852
Potter, Christopher, 1591–1646
Potter, Humphry T., *A New Dictionary of Cant* (*a* 1790)
Powel, David, 1552?–98
Powell, John J., 1755?–1801
Prescott, William H., 1796–1859
Preston, Richard Graham, Visct. 1648–95
Price, Bonamy, 1807–88
Prichard, James C., 1786–1848
Prideaux, Humphrey, 1648–1724
Priestley, Joseph, 1733–1804
Pringle, Sir John, 1707–82
Prior, Matthew, 1664–1721
Prior, Richard C. A., *On the popular names of British Plants* (1863)
Procter, Bryan W. ('Barry Cornwall'), 1787–1874
Proctor, Richard A., 1837–88
Promptorium Parvulorum (*c* 1440, etc.)
Prynne, William, 1600–69
Pugin, Augustus W. N., 1812–52
Punch, or the London Charivari (1840–)
Purcell, John, 1674?–1730
Purchas, Samuel, 1575?–1626
Pusey, Edward B., 1800–82
Puttenham, George, d. 1590

'Q' (Sir Arthur T. Quiller-Couch), 1863–1944
Quain, Sir Richard, 1816–98
Quarles, Francis, 1592–1644
Quarterly Review, The (1809–1967)
Quincey, Thomas De: see De Quincey
Quincy, John, d. 1722

Radcliffe, Mrs. Ann, 1764–1823
Raffald, Mrs. Elizabeth, 1733–81
Ralegh, Sir Walter, 1552?–1618
Ramsay, Allan, 1686–1758
Ramsay, Sir Andrew C., 1814–91
Randolph, Thomas, 1605–35
Rankine, William J. M., 1820–72
Raphson, Joseph, *A Mathematical Dictionary* (1702)
Rawlinson, George, 1812–1902
Ray, John, 1627–1705
Raymond, Rossiter W., *Glossary of mining and metallurgical terms* (1881)
Reade, Charles, 1814–84
Recorde, Robert, 1510?–58
Rees, Abraham, 1743–1825
Reid, Thomas, 1710–96
Reynolds, Bp. Edward, 1599–1676
Reynolds, Sir Joshua, 1723–92
Rhys, Sir John, 1840–1915
Rich, Barnaby, 1540?–1617
Richardson, George Fleming, 1796?–1848
Richardson, Samuel, 1689–1761
Rickman, Thomas, 1776–1841
Ridley, Bp. Nicholas, 1500?–55
Risdon, Tristram, 1580?–1640
'Rita' (Eliza M. J. von Booth, Mrs. W. D. Humphreys) d. 1938
Ritchie, Anne Isabella, Lady d. 1918
Ritson, Joseph, 1752–1803
Rivers, Anthony Wydeville, Earl 1442?–83

Robert of Gloucester's *Chronicle* (1297)
Robertson, Frederick W., 1816–53
Robertson, William, 1721–93
Roby, Henry J., 1830–1915
Rochester, John Wilmot, 2nd Earl 1647–80
Rogers, James E. Thorold, 1823–90
Rogers, Samuel, 1763–1855
Rogers, Thomas, d. 1616
Rogers, Woodes, d. 1732
Roland, George, *A treatise on the theory and practice of the Art of Fencing* (1823)
Rolland, John, fl. 1560
Rolle, Richard, of Hampole: see Hampole
Rolleston, George, 1829–81
Rolt, Richard, 1725?–70
Romaunt of the Rose, The (lines 1–1705, Chaucer *a* 1366; lines 1706– anon. *c* 1400)
Roper, William, 1496–1578
Roscoe, Sir Henry E., 1833–1915
Roscommon, Wentworth Dillon, 4th Earl of 1633?–85
Rose, John B., fl. 1866
Ross, Sir James Clark, 1800–62
Rossetti, Christina G., 1830–94
Rossetti, Dante Gabriel, 1828–82
Rossiter, William, fl. 1871
Row, William, *Supplement to R. Blair's Autobiography* (1676)
Rowe, Nicholas, 1674–1718
Rowlands, Samuel, 1570?–1630?
Rowley, William, 1585?–1642?
Rudimentary Treatise on Navigation, A (1850) by J. Greenwood
Ruskin, John, 1819–1900
Russell, Rachel, Lady 1636–1723
Russell, William Clark, 1844–1911

Saintsbury, George E. B., 1845–1933
Sala, George A. H., 1828–96
Sale, George, 1697?–1736
Salkeld, John, 1576–1660
Salmon, George, 1819–1904
Salmon, William, 1644–1713
Sandahl, B., *Middle English Sea Terms* (1951, 1958)
Sanderson, Bp. Robert, 1587–1663
Sandys, Abp. Edwin, 1516?–88
Sandys, George, 1578–1644
Sandys, William, 1792–1874
Savage, Richard, d. 1743
Sayce, Archibald H., 1846–1933
Schaff, Philip, 1819–93
Sclater, William, 1575–1626
Scoresby, William, 1789–1857
Scots Magazine, The (1739–1817)
Scott, Sir G. Gilbert, 1811–78
Scott, George Gilbert, *English Church Architecture* (1881)
Scott, Michael, 1789–1835
Scott, Sir Walter, 1771–1832
Scribner's Magazine (1887–1939)
Scriven, John, *A practical treatise on Copyhold Tenure* (1816)
Scrivener, Frederick H. A., 1813–91
Scrivener, S. C., *Our Fields and Cities* (1890)
Sedley, Sir Charles, 1639?–1701
Seebohm, Henry, 1832–95
Seeley, Sir John R., 1834–95
Selborne, Roundell Palmer, 1st Earl 1812–95
Selden, John, 1584–1654
Sewel, William, 1654–1720
Shadwell, Thomas, 1642?–92
Shaftesbury, Anthony Ashley Cooper, 3rd Earl of 1671–1713
Shakespeare, William, 1564–1616 (see p. xxvii for abbreviations of titles)
Shand, Alexander I., d. 1907
Sharp, William, 1855–1905

Sharpe, Richard Bowdler, 1847–1909
Sharpe, Samuel, 1799–1881
Sharrock, Robert, 1630–84
Shaw, George Bernard, 1856–1950
Shaw, Vero K., *The Illustrated Book of the Dog* (1879–81)
Sheffield, John, Duke of Buckingham 1648–1721
Shelley, Mrs. Mary Wollstonecraft, 1797–1851
Shelley, Percy Bysshe, 1792–1822
Shelton, Thomas, fl. 1612–20
Shelvocke, George, fl. 1690–1728
Shenstone, William, 1714–63
Sheridan, Richard Brinsley, 1751–1816
Sheridan, Thomas, 1719–88
Sherlock, Bp. Thomas, 1678–1761
Sherwood, Mrs. Mary Martha, 1775–1851
Shipley, Orby, 1832–1916
Shirley, James, 1596–1666
Shorthouse, Joseph H., 1834–1903
Sidney, Sir Philip, 1554–86
Simmonds, Peter L., *A Dictionary of Trade Products* (1858, 1892)
Simpson, Sir James Y., 1811–70
Sims, George R., 1847–1922
Singleton, Robert C., 1810–81
Skeat, Walter W., 1835–1912
Skelton, John, 1460?–1529
Skene, William F., 1809–92
Sloane, Thomas O'Conor, *The Standard Electrical Dictionary* (1893)
Smart, Christopher, 1722–71
Smeaton, John, 1724–92
Smiles, Samuel, 1812–1904
Smith, Adam, 1723–90
Smith, Albert R., 1816–60
Smith, Bosworth, 1839–1908
Smith, Charlotte, 1749–1806
Smith, Capt. George, *Universal Military Dictionary* (1779)
Smith, Goldwin, 1823–1910
Smith, Horatio ('Horace'), 1779–1849
Smith, James, 1775–1839
Smith, Capt. John, 1580–1631
Smith, Sydney, 1771–1845
Smith, Walter C., *Kildrostan* (1884)
Smith, Sir William, 1813–93
Smollett, Tobias G., 1721–71
Smyth, R. Brough, 1830–89
Smyth, William H., *The Sailor's Word-book* (1867)
Somerville, Alexander, 1811–85
Somerville, Mrs. Mary, 1780–1872
Somerville, William, 1675–1742
South, Robert, 1634–1716
Southey, Robert, 1774–1843
Soyer, Alexis B., 1809–58
Spectator, The (J. Addison, R. Steele, etc.), 1711–14
Speed, John, 1532?–1629
Spelman, Sir Henry, 1564?–1641
Spelman, Sir John, 1594–1643
Spence, Ferrand, fl. 1686
Spencer, Herbert, 1820–1903
Spenser, Edmund, 1552?–99 (*The Faerie Queene* (*F.Q.*) 1590, 1596)
Spurgeon, Charles H., 1834–92
Stainer, Sir John, 1840–1901
Stanford Dictionary of Anglicised Words and Phrases, The, ed. C. A. M. Fennell (1892)
Stanhope, George, 1660–1728
Stanhope, Lady Hester L., 1776–1839
Stanhope, Philip H., 5th Earl 1805–75
Stanley, Arthur Penrhyn, 1815–81
Stanley, Sir Henry Morton, 1841–1904
Stanley, Thomas, 1625–78
Stark, John, *Elements of Natural History* (1828)

Starkey, George, d. 1665
Starkey, Thomas, 1499?–1538
Steele, Sir Richard, 1672–1729
Stephen, Sir James, 1789–1859
Stephen, Sir James Fitzjames, 1829–94
Stephen, Sir Leslie, 1832–1904
Sterne, Laurence, 1713–68
Sternhold, Thomas, d. 1549
Stevenson, Robert Louis, 1850–94
Stewart, Balfour, 1828–87
Stewart, Dugald, 1753–1828
Stillingfleet, Benjamin, 1702–71
Stillingfleet, Bp. Edward, 1635–99
Stirling, Sir William Alexander, Earl of 1567?–1640
Stirling, James H., 1820–1909
Stocqueler, Joachim H., 1800–85
Stoddart, Thomas T., 1810–80
Stonehouse, William B., *The History and Topography of the Isle of Axholme* (1839)
Stow, John, 1525?–1605
Stowe, Mrs. Harriet Elizabeth Beecher, 1812–96
Strafford, Thomas Wentworth, Earl of 1593–1641
Stratmann, F. H., *Dictionary of the Old English Language* (1878; ed. H. Bradley, 1891)
Strutt, Joseph, 1749–1802
Strype, John, 1643–1737
Stubbs, Bp. William, 1825–1901
Sturmy, Samuel, *The Mariners Magazine* (1683)
Suckling, Sir John, 1609–42
Sullivan, James, 1744–1808
Surflet, Richard, fl. 1600
Surrey, Henry Howard, Earl of, 1517?–47
Surtees, Robert S., 1803–64
Sutcliffe, Halliwell, 1870–1932
Swainson, William, 1789–1855
Swan, Annie S. (Mrs. Burnett Smith), 1860–1943
Sweet, Henry, 1845–1912
Swift, Jonathan, 1667–1745
Swinburne, Algernon Charles, 1837–1909
Swinburne, Henry, 1560?–1623
Sydenham Society Lexicon of Medicine and Allied Sciences (1879–99)
Sylvester, Josuah, 1563–1618
Symonds, John Addington, 1840–93

Tate, Nahum, 1652–1715
— — and Brady, Nicholas, *A new version of the Psalms of David* (1696)
Tatler, The (R. Steele, etc.), 1709–11
Taverner, John, *Certaine Experiments concerning Fish and Fruite* (1600)
Taverner, Richard, 1505?–75
Taylor, Ann, 1782–1866, and Jane, 1783–1824
Taylor, Bayard, 1825–78
Taylor, Sir Henry, 1800–86
Taylor, Isaac, 1787–1865
Taylor, Jeremy, 1613–67
Taylor, John (Water poet), 1580–1653
Taylor, Thomas, 1576–1633
Temple, Sir William, 1628–99
Ten Brink's Early English Literature, tr. (1883)
Tennyson, Alfred, Lord 1809–92
Termes de la Ley, Les (1624)
Thackeray, Anne Isabella: see Ritchie, A. I.
Thackeray, William Makepeace, 1811–63
Theobald, Lewis, 1688–1744
Thirlwall, Bp. Connop, 1797–1875
Thomas, Joseph, 1811–91
Thompson, Francis J., d. 1907
Thompson, Silvanus P., 1851–1916
Thomson, James, 1700–48

Thomson, Thomas, 1773–1852
Thomson, Abp. William, 1819–90
Thomson, Sir William, 1st Baron Kelvin, 1824–1907
— — and Tait, P. G., *Treatise on Natural Philosophy* (1867)
Thoreau, Henry D., 1817–62
Thoresby, Ralph, 1658–1725
Thynne, Francis, 1545?–1608
Ticknor, George, 1791–1871
Tillotson, Abp. John, 1630–94
Times, The (1788–)
Timme, Thomas, d. 1620
Tindal, Matthew, 1657–1733
Tindale, William, d. 1536
Todd, Henry J., 1763–1845
Todhunter, Isaac, 1820–84
Tomlins, Sir Thomas E., Jacob's *Law Dictionary* (1797)
Tomson, Laurence, 1539–1608
Tonstall, or Tunstall, Bp. C., 1474–1559
Tooke, John H., 1736–1812
Topsell, Edward, d. 1638?
Tourneur, Cyril (1575?–1626)
Tout, Thomas F., *History of England* (1890)
Traill, Henry Duff, 1842–1900
Trapp, John, 1601–69
Treasury of Botany, The (1866)
Trench, Abp. Richard C., 1807–86
Trevelyan, Sir George O., 1838–1928
Trevisa, John de, 1326–1412
Trimmer, Joseph, *Practical geology and mineralogy* (1841)
Tristram, Henry B., 1822–1906
Trollope, Anthony, 1815–82
Trollope, Thomas A., 1810–92
Tryon, Thomas, 1634–1703
Tucker, Abraham, 1705–74
Tucker, Josiah, 1712–99
Tupper, Martin F., 1810–89
Turberville, George, 1540?–1610?
Turner, George J., ed. *Select Pleas of the Forest* (1901)
Turner, Sharon, 1768–1847
Turner, William, *A new Herball* (1551); *the seconde parte* (1562)
Turton, William, 1762–1835
Tusser, Thomas, 1524?–80
Tutchin, John, 1661?–1707
'Twain, Mark' (S. L. Clemens), 1835–1910
Twining, Thomas, 1735–1804
Tylor, Edward B., 1832–1917
Tyndale, William: see Tindale, W.
Tyndall, John, 1820–93
Tyrrell, James, 1642–1718
Tyrwhitt, Thomas, 1730–86
'Tytler, Sarah' (Henrietta Keddie), 1827–1914

Udall, John, 1560?–92
Udall, Nicolas, 1505–56
Underwood, Michael, 1736–1820
Ure, Andrew, 1778–1857
Urquhart, Sir Thomas, 1611–60
Ussher, James, 1581–1656

Vanbrugh, Sir John, 1664–1726
Vansittart, Henry, 1732–70
Vaughan, Henry, 1622–95
Vaughan, Thomas, 1622–66
Vaux, James Hardy, *Vocabulary of the Flash Language* (1812)
Venables, Edmund, 1819–95
Venner, Tobias, 1577–1660
Vere, Sir Francis, 1560–1609
Victoria, Queen, 1819–1901
Vigfusson, Gudbrand, *An Icelandic–English Dictionary* (1874)

Villiers, George, 2nd Duke of Buckingham 1628–87
Vince, Samuel, 1749–1821
Vines, Sydney H., 1849–1934
Voyle, George E., and Stevenson, G. de Saint-Clair, *A Military Dictionary* (1876)

Walker, Francis A., 1840–97
Walker, John, 1732–1807
Walker, Obadiah, 1616–99
Wall, Edward J., *A Dictionary of Photography* (1889)
Wallace, Alfred R., 1823–1913
Waller, Edmund, 1606–87
Wallis, John, 1616–1703
Wallis, Thomas, *The Farrier's and Horseman's Complete Dictionary* (1764)
Walpole, Horace, 1717–97
Walton, Izaak, 1593–1683
Warburton, Rowland E. Egerton, 1804–91
Warburton, Bp. William, 1698–1779
Ward, Edward, 1667–1731
Ward, Mrs. Humphry, 1851–1920
Ward, Lester F., 1841–1913
Ward, Nathaniel, 1578–1652
Ward, Bp. Samuel, 1577–1640
Ward, William, 1769–1823
Warner, Charles Dudley, 1829–1900
Warner, Susan, 1819–85
Warner, William, 1558?–1609
Warton, Joseph, 1722–1800
Warton, Thomas, 1728–90
Washington, George, 1732–99
Waterhouse, George R., 1810–88
Waterland, Daniel, 1683–1740
Watson, Joseph Y., *British Mining* (1843)
Watson, Bp. Richard, 1737–1816
Watts, Henry, *A Dictionary of Chemistry* (1859, etc.; 1872–82; ed. Morley and Muir, 1888–94)
Watts, Isaac, 1674–1748
Waugh, Edwin, 1817–90
Weale, John, 1791–1862
Webster, John, 1580?–1625?
Webster, Noah, *A Dictionary of the English Language* (1828, etc.; 1864)
Webster's International Dictionary (1890, etc.)
— *New International Dictionary* (1911, etc.)
Weever, John, 1576–1632
Wellington, Arthur Wellesley, 1st Duke of 1769–1852
Wells, Herbert G., 1866–1946
Wesley, Charles, 1707–88
Wesley, John, 1703–91
West, Alfred S., 1846–1932
West, Gilbert, 1703–56
Westminster Gazette, The (1893–1927)
Westwood, John O., 1805–93
Weyman, Stanley J., 1855–1928
Wharton, Henry, 1664–95
Wharton, John J. S., *A Law Lexicon* (1848; ed. 5, 1872)
Whately, Abp. Richard, 1787–1863
Whewell, William, 1794–1866
Whistler, James M., 1834–1903
Whiston, William, 1667–1752
Whitaker's Almanac (1868–)
White, Gilbert, 1720–93
White, Henry Kirke, 1785–1806
White, Stewart E., 1873–1946
Whitgift, Abp. John, 1530?–1604
Whitman, Walt, 1819–92
Whitney, William D., 1827–94
Whyte-Melville, G. J.: see Melville
Wilkes, John, 1727–97
Wilkins, Bp. John, 1614–72
Williams, Roger, 1604?–83
Willis, Nathaniel P., 1806–67
Wilson, Alexander, 1766–1813
Wilson, Sir Daniel, 1816–92
Wilson, Horace H., 1786–1860
Wilson, John, 1627?–96
Wilson, John, 1785–1854
Windham, William, 1750–1810
Wiseman, Cdl. Nicholas P. S., 1802–65
Wither, George, 1588–1667
Withering, William, 1741–99
Wolcot, John (Peter Pindar), 1738–1819
Wollaston, William, 1660–1724
Wollstonecraft (afterwards Godwin), Mary, 1759–97
Wolseley, Garnet J. W., Viscount 1833–1913
Wood, Anthony, 1632–95
Wood, Mrs. Henry, 1814–87
Wood, James, 1760–1839
Wood, John G., 1827–89
Woodbury, Walter E., *The Encyclopædia of Photography* (1892)
Woodhead, Abraham, 1609–78
Woodward, John, 1665–1728
Woolsey, Theodore D., 1801–89
Worcester, Joseph E., 1784–1865
Wordsworth, William, 1770–1850
Worlidge, John, fl. 1669–98
Wotton, Sir Henry, 1568–1639
Wotton, William, 1666–1727
Wright, Thomas, 1810–77
Wyatt, Sir Thomas, 1503?–1542
Wycherley, William, 1640?–1716
Wyclif, John, d. 1384

Yarranton, Andrew, 1616–84?
Yarrell, William, 1784–1856
Yates, Edmund H., 1831–94
Yeats, William B., 1865–1939
Yellow Book, The (1894–97)
Yonge, Charlotte M., 1823–1901
Youatt, William, 1776–1847
Young, Arthur, 1741–1820
Young, Edward, 1683–1765
Young, Thomas, 1773–1829
Yule, Sir Henry, 1820–89

Zangwill, Israel, 1864–1926
Zouch, Thomas, 1737–1815

LIST OF ABBREVIATIONS, SIGNS, ETC.

In this list the abbreviations are printed in the type that is normally used for them, but there are variations for special cases.

a	*ante*, 'before', 'not later than'
a.	adjective
abbrev.	abbreviated, abbreviation (of)
abl.	ablative
Abp.	Archbishop
absol.	in absolute use, absolutely
abstr.	abstract
acc., accus.	accusative
act.	active
adj.	adjective, adjectival
adv.	adverb
advb.	adverbial, -ly
Æol.	Æolic
Aero., *Aeronaut.*	in Aeronautics
AFr.	Anglo-French
Afr.	African
agent-n.	agent-noun
Agric.	in Agriculture
AL.	Anglo-Latin
Alb.	Albanian
Alch.	in Alchemy
Alg.	in Algebra
allus.	allusively
alt.	altered, alteration (of)
alt. f.	altered form of
Amer.	American
Amer. Hist.	in American History
Amer. Ind.	American Indian
anal.	analogy
Anat.	in Anatomy
Anc. Hist., etc.	in Ancient History, etc.
Anglo-Ind.	Anglo-Indian
Anglo-Ir.	Anglo-Irish
Anthrop.	in Anthropology
aphet.	aphetic, aphetized
Apocr.	Apocrypha
app., appar.	apparently
appos.	appositive, -ly
Arab.	Arabic
Aram.	Aramaic
arch.	archaic
Arch., *Archit.*	in Architecture
Archæol.	in Archæology
Arith.	in Arithmetic
Arm.	Armenian
assim.	assimilated, -ation
assoc.	associated, -ation
Astr., *Astron.*	in Astronomy
Astrol.	in Astrology
astrol.	astrological
attrib.	attributive, -ly
attrib. and *Comb.*	in attributive uses and combinations
augm.	augmentative
Austral.	Australian
Av.	Avestic
A.V.	Authorized Version
Bacteriol.	in Bacteriology
Beaum. & Fl.	Beaumont & Fletcher
bef.	before
betw.	between
bibl.	biblical
Biochem.	in Biochemistry
Biol.	in Biology
Biol. Chem.	in Biological Chemistry
B. Jons.	Ben Jonson
Bot.	in Botany
Bot. L.	in Botanical Latin
Bp.	Bishop
Br.	Branch
Braz.	Brazilian
Brit. N. Amer.	British North America
Bulg.	Bulgarian
Byz.	Byzantine
c	*circa*, 'about'
c.	century
Camb.	Cambridge
cap.	capital letter
Cat., Catal.	Catalan
catachr.	catachrestic, -ally
cc.	centuries
Cdl.	Cardinal
Celt.	Celtic
Cent. Dict.	Century Dictionary
CEur.	Common European
Cf., cf.	*confer*, 'compare'
CGmc.	Common Germanic
Chem.	in Chemistry
Chesterf.	Chesterfield
Ch. Hist.	in Church History
Chin.	Chinese
Chor.	Chorus
Chr. L.	Christian Latin
Chron., *Chronol.*	in Chronology
CIE.	Common Indo-European
Cinemat., *Cinematogr.*	in Cinematography
cl.	clause
Class. Antiq.	in Classical Antiquities
cl. Gr., L.	classical Greek, Latin
cogn., cogn. w.	cognate with
collect.	collective, -ly
colloq.	colloquial, -ism, -ly
Com.	Common
comb.	combining
Comb.	in combination
Comm.	in Commercial usage
Comm. Law	in Commercial Law
comp.	compound
comp., compar.	comparative
Comp. Anat.	in Comparative Anatomy
compl.	complement
Conch., *Conchol.*	in Conchology
concr.	concrete, -ly
conj.	conjunction, conjunctive
conjug.	conjugation
conn.	connected
cons.	consonant
const., const. w.	construed with
constr.	construction
contemp.	contemporary
contempt.	in contemptuous use
contr.	contracted, contraction
Corn.	Cornish
correl.	correlative
corresp.	corresponding
corrupt.	corruption
Cotgr.	Cotgrave
CRom.	Common Romanic
Crim.Goth.	Crimean Gothic
Cryst., *Crystall.*	in Crystallography
CSlav.	Common Slavonic
Cursor M.	*Cursor Mundi*
d.	died
Da.	Danish
dat.	dative
D'chess	Duchess of
def.	definition
def. art.	definite article
dem., demons.	demonstrative
deriv.	derivation, derivative, -s
derog.	derogatory
dial.	dialect, dialectal, -ly
Dict.	Dictionary
Dicts.	in Dictionaries
dim.	diminutive
dissim.	dissimilated, -ation
dist.	distinguished
distrib.	distributive
Dor.	Doric
Drumm. of Hawth.	Drummond of Hawthornden
Du.	Dutch
dub.	dubious
Eccl.	in Ecclesiastical usage
eccl. Gr.	ecclesiastical Greek
Eccl. Hist.	in Ecclesiastical History
eccl. L.	ecclesiastical Latin
Econ.	in Economics
ed.	edited by, edition (of)
E.D.D.	*The English Dialect Dictionary*, ed. J. Wright
EE.	Early English
EFris.	East Frisian
e.g.	*exempli gratia*, 'for example'
Egyptol.	in Egyptology
EInd.	East Indian
E. Ind.	in the East Indies
Electr.	in Electricity
Electr. Engin.	in Electrical Engineering
ellipt.	elliptical, -ly
Embryol.	in Embryology
e.midl.	east midland
emph.	emphatic
Eng.	English
Eng. Hist.	in English History
Engin.	in Engineering
Ent., *Entomol.*	in Entomology
Epil.	Epilogue
equiv., equivs.	equivalent, -s
erron.	erroneous, -ly
esp.	especially
etc.	et cetera
Eth.	Ethiopian
Ethnol.	in Ethnology
etym.	etymology
etymol.	etymological
euphem.	euphemistic, -ally
ex.	example
exc.	except
exclam.	exclamation
f.	form of, formation (on), formed (on), from

F.	French
fam.	familiar, -ly
fem.	feminine
ff.	forms, forms of
fig.	in figurative use
Finn.	Finnish
fl.	*floruit*, 'flourished'
Flem.	Flemish
Fo.	(First) Folio edition of Shakespeare's plays
foll.	following, following word or article
Fortif.	in Fortification
Fr.	French
Frank.	Frankish
freq.	frequent, -ly
frequent.	frequentative
Fr. Hist.	in French History
Fris.	Frisian
fut.	future
G.	German
Gael.	Gaelic
Gallo-Rom.	Gallo-Roman
Gaul.	Gaulish
Gen.	General
gen.	general, -ly
gen., genit.	genitive
Geog.	in Geography
Geol.	in Geology
Geom.	in Geometry
Gmc.	Germanic
GOLDSM.	Goldsmith
Goth.	Gothic
Gr.	Greek
Gram.	in Grammar
gram.	grammar
Gr. Antiq.	in Greek Antiquities
Gr. Ch.	in the Greek Church
Gr. Hist.	in Greek History
Gr.-L.	Græco-Latin
Heb.	Hebrew
Her.	in Heraldry
Herb.	among herbalists
HG.	High German
Hind.	Hindustani
Hist.	in historical use
hist.	historical
Hort.	in Horticulture
Hydraul. Engin.	in Hydraulic Engineering
hyperbol.	hyperbolically
ib., ibid.	*ibidem*, 'in the same book or passage'
Icel.	Icelandic
Ichth., Ichthyol.	in Ichthyology
id.	*idem*, 'the same'
i.e.	*id est*, 'that is'
IE.	Indo-European
imit.	imitative
immed.	immediate, -ly
imper.	imperative
impers.	impersonal
impf.	imperfect
improp.	improper, -ly
incl.	including
incorr.	incorrect
ind., indic.	indicative
indef., indef. art.	indefinite, indefinite article
Indo-Eur.	Indo-European
Indo-Gmc.	Indo-Germanic
inf., infin.	infinitive
infl.	inflected, influenced
instr.	instrumental
int., interj.	interjection
interrog.	interrogative, -ly
intr.	intransitive, -ly
Ir.	Irish
Irel.	Ireland
iron.	ironical, -ly
irreg.	irregular, -ly
It.	Italian
J., (J.)	Johnson's *Dictionary*
Jam.	Jamieson's *Scottish Dictionary*
Jap.	Japanese
Jav.	Javanese
joc.	jocular, -ly
Jurisp.	in Jurisprudence
L.	Latin
lang., langs.	language, -s
LANGL.	Langland
Lat.	Latin
Law-L.	Law-Latin
Ld.	Lord
LDu.	Low Dutch
Lett.	Lettish
LG.	Low German
Linn.	Linnæus
lit.	literal, -ly
lit. and *fig.*	in literal and figurative use
Lith.	Lithuanian
Liturg.	in liturgical use
LONGF.	Longfellow
LXX	Septuagint
LYDG.	Lydgate
m.	masculine
Magn.	in Magnetism
Manuf.	in .. Manufacture
masc.	masculine
Math.	in Mathematics
MAUNDEV.	Maundeville
M.Bret.	Middle Breton
MDu.	Middle Dutch
(M)Du.	Middle and modern Dutch
ME.	Middle English
Mech.	in Mechanics
M.E.D.	*Middle English Dictionary*
Med.	in Medicine
med.L.	mediæval Latin
Metall.	in Metallurgy
Metaph.	in Metaphysics
metath.	metathetic
Meteorol.	in meteorology
Mex.	Mexican
MHG.	Middle High German
midl.	midland
Mil., Milit.	in military usage
MILT.	Milton
Min.	in Mineralogy
MIr.	Middle Irish
MLG.	Middle Low German
(M)LG.	Middle and modern Low German
Mme.	Madame
mod.	modern
mod.L.	modern Latin
MSc.	Middle Scottish
MSw.	Middle Swedish
Mus.	in Music
MWelsh	Middle Welsh
Myth., Mythol.	in Mythology
n.	neuter, northern, noun
NAfr.	North-African
NAmer.	North American
Nat. Hist.	in Natural History
Nat. Phil., Nat. Philos.	in Natural Philosophy
Nat. Sci.	in Natural Science
Naut.	in Nautical language
n. dial.	in northern dialects
N.E.D.	*A New English Dictionary on Historical Principles*
NEFr.	North-eastern French
neg.	negative
n. Eng.	northern English
neut.	neuter
NFris.	North Frisian
N.O.	Natural Order
nom.	nominative
nonce-wd.	nonce-word
north.	northern, in northern dialects
Northumb.	Northumbrian
Norw.	Norwegian
N.S.W.	New South Wales
N.T.	New Testament
num. adj.	numeral adjective
Numism.	in Numismatics
N.W., n.w.	north-west, -western
N.Z.	New Zealand
obj.	object
obl.	oblique
OBret.	Old Breton
OBrit.	Old British
Obs., obs.	obsolete
obsc.	obscure, -ly
Obsol.	obsolescent
Obstet. Surg.	in Obstetrical Surgery
occ., occas.	occasional, -ly
OCelt.	Old Celtic
OCorn.	Old Cornish
OE.	Old English (= Anglo-Saxon)
O.E.D.	Oxford English Dictionary
OFr.	Old French
(O)Fr.	Old and modern French
OFris.	Old Frisian
OGael.	Old Gaelic
OHG.	Old High German
OIcel.	Old Icelandic
OIr.	Old Irish
OL.	Old Latin
OLFrank., OLG.	Old Low Frankish, German
OLith.	Old Lithuanian
ON.	Old Norse
ONFr.	Old Northern French
ONorth.	Old Northumbrian
OPers.	Old Persian
opp.	opposed (to)
OPruss.	Old Prussian
Org. Chem., Organ. Chem.	in Organic Chemistry
orig.	original, -ly
Ork.	Orkney
Ornith.	in Ornithology
Orthogr.	in Orthography
OS.	Old Saxon
OScand.	Old Scandinavian
OSl., OSlav.	Old Slavonic
OSp.	Old Spanish
OSw.	Old Swedish
O.T.	Old Testament
OW.	Old Welsh
Oxf.	Oxford
Palæogr.	in Palæography
Palæont.	in Palæontology
PALSGR.	Palsgrave
pa. pple.	passive or past participle
parasynth.	parasynthetic
pass.	passive, -ly
pa. t.	past tense
Path., Pathol.	in Pathology
perh.	perhaps

pers.	person, -al
Pers.	Persian
Peruv.	Peruvian
Petrog.	in Petrography
pf.	perfect
Pg.	Portuguese
Pharm.	in Pharmacy
Pharm. Chem.	in Pharmaceutical Chemistry
Phil.	in Philosophy
Philol.	in Philology
Philos.	in Philosophy
Phœn.	Phœnician
phonet.	phonetic, -ally
Photogr.	in Photography
phr.	phrase, -s
Phren.	in Phrenology
Phys.	in Physiology
Phys. Chem.	in Physical Chemistry
Physiog.	in Physiography
Physiol.	in Physiology
Physiol. Chem.	in Physiological Chemistry
pl., pl.	plural
poet.	poetical
Pol.	Polish
Pol. Econ.	in Political Economy
Polit.	in Politics
pop.	popular, -ly
pop.L.	popular Latin
poss.	possessive, possible, possibly
post-Aug.	post-Augustan Latin
post-cl.	post-classical Latin
ppl.	participial
pple.	participle
Pr.	Provençal
pr.	present
prec.	preceding word or article
pred.	predicate
predic.	predicative, -ly
Pref.	Preface
pref.	prefix
pre-hist.	prehistoric
prep.	preposition
pres.	present
pret.	preterite
prim.	primitive
priv.	privative
prob.	probably
Promp. Parv.	*Promptorium Parvulorum*
pron.	pronominal, pronounced
pron.	pronoun
pronunc.	pronunciation
prop.	proper, -ly
Pros.	in Prosody
Prov.	Provençal
Prov., prov.	proverb
provb.	proverbial, -ly
Psych., *Psychol.*	in Psychology
Qo., Qos	Quarto edition, -s
quot., quots.	quotation(s)
q.v.	*quod vide*, 'which see'
R. C. Ch.	in the Roman Catholic Church
rec.	recent
redupl.	reduplicated, -ation(s)
ref.	reference
refash.	refashioned, -ing
refl.	reflexive
reg.	regular
rel.	relative
rel.	related (to)
repl.	replaced, -ing
repr.	representative (of), represented, representing, representation(s)
Rhet.	in Rhetoric
rhet.	rhetorical, -ly
Rom.	Roman, Romance, Romanic
Rom. Antiq.	in Roman Antiquities
Rom. Hist.	in Roman History
Rum.	Rumanian
Russ.	Russian
R.V.	Revised Version
S., s.	South, southern
S. Afr.	South African
S. Amer.	South American
sb.	substantive
Sc.	Scotch, Scots, Scottish
sc., scil.	*scilicet*, 'understand' or 'supply'
Scand.	Scandinavian
Sc. Hist.	in Scottish History
schol. L.	scholastic Latin
Scotl.	Scotland
Sculpt.	in Sculpture
s. dial.	in southern dialects
Seismol.	in Seismology
Sem.	Semitic
Serb.	Serbian
SHAFTESB.	Shaftesbury
SHAKS.	Shakespeare
Shetl.	Shetland
sing.	singular
Sinh.	Sinhalese
Skr.	Sanskrit
sl.	slang
Slav.	Slavonic
Sp.	Spanish
sp.	spelling
spec.	specific, -ally
sp. gr.	specific gravity
Sport.	in Sporting use
Stock Exch.	on the Stock Exchange
str.	strong
subj.	subject, subjunctive
subord. cl.	subordinate clause
subseq.	subsequent, -ly
subst.	substantival, -ly
suff.	suffix
superl.	superlative
Surg.	in Surgery
s.v.	*sub voce*, 'under the word'
S.W., s.w.	South West, south-western
s.w. dial.	in south-western dialect(s)
Sw., Swed.	Swedish
Syd. Soc. Lex.	*The New Sydenham Society's Lexicon*
syll.	syllable(s)
synon.	synonymous
Syr.	Syriac
t.	tense
techn.	in technical use
Telegr.	in Telegraphy
Teut.	Teutonic
Theatr.	in theatrical language
Theol.	in Theology
Tokh.	Tokharian
tr.	translation of
trans.	transitive, -ly
transf.	transferred
transf. and *fig.*	in transferred and figurative use
Trig.	in Trigonometry
Turk.	Turkish
Typog.	in Typography
Tyrol.	Tyrolese
Ukr.	Ukrainian
ult.	ultimate, -ly
unc.	uncertain
unexpl.	unexplained
Univ.	University
unkn.	unknown
U.S.	in the English of the U.S.A.
U.S.(A.)	(the) United States (of America)
usu.	usually
v.	verb
var. (in 'stress var.')	variable
var., vars.	variant, -s (of)
vb.	verb
vbl.	verbal
vbl. sb.	verbal substantive
viz.	*videlicet*, 'namely'
voc.	vocative
Vulg.	the Vulgate
vulg.	vulgar, -ly
W.	Welsh, West
w.	with
west.	western
WFr.	West French
WFris.	West Frisian
WGmc.	West Germanic
WIE.	western Indo-European
W. Ind., *W. Indies*	in the West Indies
wk.	weak
wk. vb.	weak verb
w. midl.	w. midland, w. midland dialect(s)
WORDS.	Wordsworth
WS.	West Saxon
WYCL.	Wyclif
Zool.	in Zoology

SIGNS AND OTHER CONVENTIONS

Before a word or sense

† = obsolete

‖ = not naturalized, alien

¶ = catachrestic or erroneous use

In the etymologies

:– = regular or normal phonetic descendant of

* indicates a word or form not actually found but of which the existence is inferred

The printing of a word in SMALL CAPITALS indicates that further information will be found under the word so referred to.

Roman numbers in small capitals indicate the date by centuries; thus XIV = (in the) fourteenth century.

– before a date indicates that the date so marked is that of the latest recorded use of the word or sense.

In quotations, . . indicates that a word or words have been omitted.

ABBREVIATIONS OF TITLES OF BOOKS OF THE BIBLE

Gen/esis
Exod/us
Lev/iticus
Num/bers
Deut/eronomy
Josh/ua
Judg/es
Ruth
1 Sam/uel
2 Sam/uel
1 K(in)gs
2 K(in)gs
1 Chr/on/icles
2 Chr/on/icles
Ezra
Neh/emiah
Esther
Job
Ps/alms
Prov/erbs
Eccl/es/iastes
S(ong) of S/olomon; Cant/icles
Isa/iah
Jer/emiah
Lam/entations
Ezek/iel
Dan/iel
Hos/ea
Joel
Amos
Obad/iah
Jonah
Mic/ah
Nahum
Hab/akkuk
Zeph/aniah
Hag/gai
Zech/ariah
Mal/achi
1 Esd/ras
2 Esd/ras
Tobit
Judith
Rest of Esther
Wisd/om of Solomon
Eccl(esiastic)us
Baruch
S(ong) of (the) III Ch/ildren
Sus/anna
Bel & (the) Dr/agon
Pr(ayer) of Man/asseh
1 Macc/abees
2 Macc/abees

(St.) Matt/hew
(St.) Mark
(St.) Luke
(St.) John
Acts
Rom/ans
1 Cor/inthians
2 Cor/inthians
Gal/atians
Eph/esians
Phil/ippians
Col/ossians
1 Thess/alonians
2 Thess/alonians
1 Tim/othy
2 Tim/othy
Tit/us
Philem/on
Heb/rews
Ja(me)s
1 Pet/er
2 Pet/er
1 John
2 John
3 John
Jude
Rev/elation

ABBREVIATIONS OF TITLES OF SHAKESPEARE'S WORKS

All's Well	All's Well that Ends Well
Ant. & Cl.	Antony and Cleopatra
A.Y.L.	As You Like It
Com. Err.	The Comedy of Errors
Compl.	A Lover's Complaint
Cor(iol).	Coriolanus
Cymb.	Cymbeline
Ham(l).	Hamlet, Prince of Denmark
1 Hen. IV	The First Part of King Henry IV
2 Hen. IV	The Second Part of King Henry IV
Hen. V	The Life of King Henry V
1 Hen. VI	The First Part of King Henry VI
2 Hen. VI	The Second Part of King Henry VI
3 Hen. VI	The Third Part of King Henry VI
Hen. VIII	The Famous History of the Life of King Henry VIII
(K.) John	The Life and Death of King John
Jul. C(æs).	Julius Cæsar
Lear	King Lear
L.L.L.	Love's Labour's Lost
Lucr.	The Rape of Lucrece
Macb.	Macbeth
Meas. for M.	Measure for Measure
Merch. V.	The Merchant of Venice
Merry W.	The Merry Wives of Windsor
Mids. N. (D.)	A Midsummer-Night's Dream
Much Ado	Much Ado about Nothing
Oth.	Othello, the Moor of Venice
Per.	Pericles, Prince of Tyre
Phœnix	The Phœnix and the Turtle
Pilgr.	The Passionate Pilgrim
Rich. II	The Tragedy of King Richard II
Rich. III	The Tragedy of King Richard III
Rom. & Jul.	Romeo and Juliet
Sonn.	Sonnets
Tam. Shr.	The Taming of the Shrew
Temp.	The Tempest
Timon	Timon of Athens
Tit. A.	Titus Andronicus
Tr. & Cr.	Troilus and Cressida
Twel. N.	Twelfth-Night; or, What You Will
Two Gent.	The Two Gentlemen of Verona
Ven. & Ad.	Venus and Adonis
Wint. T.	The Winter's Tale

KEY TO THE PRONUNCIATION

For a description of the phonetic system employed in this dictionary, see the Introduction, §3, pp. x and xi. The pronunciations given are those in use in the educated speech of southern England (the so-called 'Received Standard'), and the keywords given are to be understood as pronounced in such speech.

I. VOWELS

The symbol ¯ placed over a vowel-letter denotes length.

ORDINARY	LONG	OBSCURE
a as in Fr. *à la* mode (a la mod)	ā as in *a*lms (āmz), b*a*r (bāɹ)	ă as in *a*mœb*a* (ămī·bă)
‖ai ... *ay*ah (ai·ă), s*ai*ga (sai·gă)		
‖au ... G. fr*au* (frau)		
æ ... m*a*n (mæn)		ǣ ... *a*ccept (ǣkse·pt), mani*a*c (mē^{i}·nıǣk)
ɑ ... p*a*ss (pɑs), ch*a*nt (tʃɑnt)*		
ɑu ... l*ou*d (lɑud), n*ow* (nɑu)		
ʋ ... c*u*t (kʋt), s*o*n (sʋn)	ʋ̄ ... c*u*rl (kʋ̄ɹl), f*u*r (fʋ̄ɹ)	ʋ̆ ... dat*u*m (dē^{i}·tʋ̆m)
e ... y*e*t (yet), t*e*n (ten)	ē^{ə} ... th*e*re (ðē^{ə}ɹ), p*ea*r, p*a*re (pē^{ə}ɹ)	ĕ ... mom*e*nt (mō^{u}·mĕnt), sev*e*ral (se·vĕrăl)
		ė ... add*e*d (æ·dėd), *e*state (ėstē^{i}·t)
‖*e* ... Fr. attach*é* (ataʃe)	ē^{i} ... r*ei*n, r*ai*n (rē^{i}n), th*ey* (ðē^{i})	ĕ ... separ*a*te *adj.* (se·părĕt)
‖ę ... Fr. ch*e*f (ʃęf)	‖ę̄ ... Fr. f*ai*re (fę̄r)	
	ə̄ ... f*i*r (fə̄ɹ), f*e*rn (fə̄ɹn), *ea*rth (ə̄ɹþ)	ə ... *the general obscure vowel, used in the notation of* -*e*r (əɹ), -ous (əs), -*s*ion (ʒən, ʃən), -*t*ion (ʃən)
əi ... *I, eye* (əi), b*i*nd (bəind)		
‖ə ... Fr. coup de grace (kudəgrās)		
i ... s*i*t (sit), m*y*st*i*c (mi·stik)	ī^{ə} ... b*ie*r (bī^{ə}ɹ), cl*ea*r (klī^{ə}ɹ)	ĭ ... van*i*ty (væ·nĭti)
i ... Psych*e* (səi·*ki*), r*e*act (r*i*,æ·kt)	ī ... th*ie*f (þīf), s*ee* (sī)	ĭ ... r*e*main (rĭmē^{i}·n), b*e*lieve (bĭlī·v)
o ... ach*o*r (ē^{i}·koɹ) m*o*rality (moræ·lĭti)	ō^{ə} ... b*oa*r, b*o*re (bō^{ə}ɹ), gl*o*ry (glō^{ə}·ri)	ŏ ... the*o*ry (þī·ŏri)
oi ... *oi*l (oil), b*oy* (boi)		
o ... her*o* (hī^{ə}·ro), z*oo*logy (zo,ǫ·lŏdʒi)	‖ō ... Fr. ch*o*se (ʃōz)	ŏ ... vi*o*let (vəi·ŏlėt), par*o*dy (pæ·rŏdi)
	ō^{u} ... s*o*, s*ow*, s*ew* (sō^{u}), s*ou*l (sō^{u}l)	
ǫ ... wh*a*t (hwǫt), w*a*tch (wǫtʃ)	ǭ ... f*ou*ght (fǭt), w*a*lk (wǭk), w*a*rt (wǭɹt)	ǫ̆ ... *au*thority (ǫ̆þǫ·rĭti)
ǫ, ǫ̀ ... g*o*t (gǫt), s*o*ft (sǫ̀ft)*	ǭ ... sh*o*rt (ʃǭɹt), th*o*rn (þǭɹn)	ǫ̆ ... c*o*nnect (kǫ̆ne·kt), amaz*o*n (æ·măzǫ̆n)
‖ö ... Fr. j*eu*ne (ʒön), G. K*ö*ln (köln)	‖ȫ ... Fr. c*œu*r (kȫr)	
‖ö ... Fr. p*eu* (pö)	‖ȫ ... G. G*oe*the (gȫtĕ), Fr. j*eû*ne (ʒȫn)	
u ... f*u*ll (ful), b*oo*k (buk)	ū^{ə} ... p*oo*r (pū^{ə}ɹ), m*oo*rish (mū^{ə}·riʃ)	ŭ ... thankf*u*l (þæ·ŋkfŭl)
iu ... d*u*ration (diurē^{i}·ʃən)	iū, ^{i}ū pure (piū^{ə}ɹ), l*u*re (l^{i}ū^{ə}ɹ)	iŭ, ^{i}ŭ verd*u*re (və̄·ɹdiŭɹ), meas*u*re (me·ʒ^{i}ŭɹ)
u ... *u*nt*o* (ʋ·nt*u*), fr*u*gality (fr*u*gæ·lĭti)	ū ... t*wo* m*oo*ns (tū mūnz)	ŭ ... altog*e*ther (ǭltŭge·ðəɹ)
iu ... Matth*ew* (mæ·þiu), virt*ue* (və̄·ɹtiu)	iū, ^{i}ū f*ew* (fiū), l*u*te (l^{i}ūt)	iŭ ... circ*u*lar (sə̄·ɹkiŭlăɹ)
‖ü ... G. M*ü*ller (mü·lĕr)		
‖ü ... Fr. j*u*ste (ʒüst), d*u*ne (dün)	‖ǖ ... G. gr*ü*n (grǖn), Fr. p*u*r (dǖr)	

The incidence of main stress is shown by a raised point (·) after the vowel-symbol, and a secondary stress by a raised double point (:).

II. CONSONANTS

b, d, f, k, l, m, n, p, t, v, z *have their usual English values*

		(FOREIGN)
g as in *g*ó (gō^{u})	þ as in *th*in (þin), ba*th* (bɑþ)	ṅ *marks nasalization of the preceding vowel,* as in Fr. env*i*ron (aṅvīroṅ)
h ... *h*o! (hō^{u})	ð ... *th*en (ðen), ba*th*e (bē^{i}ð)	n^{v} ... Sp. se*ñ*or (sen^{v}ō·r)
r ... *r*un (rʋn), te*rr*ier (te·riəɹ)	ʃ ... *sh*op (ʃǫp), di*sh* (diʃ)	χ ... G. a*ch* (aχ), Sc. lo*ch* (lǫχ)
ɹ ... he*r* (hə̄ɹ), fa*r*ther (fā·ɹðəɹ)*	tʃ ... *ch*op (tʃǫp), di*tch* (ditʃ)	χ^{y} .... G. i*ch* (iχ^{y}) Sc. li*ch*t (liχ^{y}t)
s ... *s*ee (sī), *s*ucce*ss* (sʋ̆kse·s)	ʒ ... vi*s*ion (vi·ʒən), *j*eu (ʒö)	γ .... G. sa*g*en (zā·γĕn)
w ... *w*en (wen)	dʒ ... *j*u*dg*e (dʒʋdʒ)	γ^{y} ... G. le*g*en (lē·γ^{y}ĕn), re*g*nen (rē·γ^{y}nĕn)
hw ... *wh*en (hwen)	ŋ ... si*ng*i*ng* (si·ŋiŋ), i*n*k (iŋk)	
y ... *y*es (yes)	ŋg ... fi*ng*er (fi·ŋgəɹ)	

* The symbols a and ǫ̀ are used to indicate respectively the local or individual variants æ, ā (e.g. in *castle*) and ǫ, ǭ (e.g. in *salt*). For ɹ, see Introduction, § 3, p. x.

Small 'superior' letters are used (*a*) to express the glide element of the diphthongs ə̄^{ə}, ī^{ə}, ō^{ə}, ū^{ə}, *e*^{i}, ē^{i}, ō^{u}, and of the triphthongs ɑu^{ə}, əi^{ə}, iū^{ə}; (*b*) to denote an element that may or may not be present in a local or an individual pronunciation, as (l^{i}ūt) *lute*, (win^{d}mil) *windmill*; (*c*) to indicate the palatal or labial modification of certain consonants (see third column of Consonants above).

A break , is used to indicate syllabic division when necessary to avoid ambiguity.

' indicates that a following l, m, or n is syllabic, as in (ē^{i}·b'l) *able*, (rū·mătiz'm) *rheumatism*, (ī·t'n) *eaten*.

A (ē^{i}), the first letter of the Roman and English Alphabet (Gr. *Alpha*, Heb. *Aleph*); repr. orig. in Eng., as in L., the 'low-back-wide' vowel, formed with the widest opening of jaws, pharynx, and lips. Pl. *aes*, A's, *As*.

For its principal sounds see KEY TO THE PRONUNCIATION.

II. Besides serial order, *A* or *a* signifies *spec.* **1.** *Mus.* The 6th note of the diatonic scale of C major, or the first of the relative minor scale of C. Also, the scale of a composition with A as its key-note. **2.** *Naut.* See A 1 below. **3.** In *Logic*: a universal affirmative. **4.** In *Law, reasoning*, etc.: any one thing or person. **5.** In *Algebra*: *a, b, c*, etc., stand for known quantities, *x, y, z* for unknown.

III. *Abbreviations.* A., a., *a.* = **1.** *anno*, as A.D. *anno domini*, in the year of our Lord; A.M. *anno mundi*, in the year of the world; A.U.C. *anno urbis conditæ*, in the year of the founding of the City (Rome). **2.** *ante*, as a.m. *ante meridiem*, before noon; a. or *a* 1600. **3.** *adjective*; *active* (verb). **4.** *artium*, as A.B. (= B.A.) *artium baccalaureus*, A.M. (= M.A.) *artium magister*, Bachelor, and Master, of Arts. **5.** *alto.* **6.** *accepted* (of bills). **7.** *Associate*, as A.L.S. Associate of the Linnean Society. **8.** R.A. Royal Artillery, Academy, or Academician; F.B.A. Fellow of the British Academy; F.S.A. Fellow of the Society of Antiquaries. **9.** A.B. able-bodied seaman. **10.** *ā* or *āā* in Med. ANA, q.v. **11.** A.C. or a.c., alternating current.

IV. *Phrases.* **1. A per se**, A by itself, *esp.* as a word; hence *fig.* (also † **Apersie,** † **Apersey,** † **A per C**) the first, best, or unique person or thing; = mod. *A* 1. **2.** A 1. Used of ships in first-class condition, as to hull (A), and stores (1). (Lloyd's Register.) Hence *colloq.* *A* 1, U.S. *A No.* 1 = prime, first-class, e.g. An A number one cook MRS. STOWE.

† **A,** *adj.*[1] definite numeral. *Obs.* or *dial.* [OE. *ān*, one, later *ā* bef. a cons., became in the south *on* (*oon, one*), *o* (*oo*) and finally *one*; *an* and *a* becoming the 'indef. article'. See next wd. In the north *an(e* and *a* had both senses.] See AN(E, O *a.*, and ONE.

A (toneless ă, ə; emph. ē^{i}), *adj.*[2], called 'indefinite article'. Bef. a vowel-sound **an** (ăn, emph. æn). A weakening of OE. *ān*, 'one', which, *c* 1150, became proclitic and toneless, ăn, ă; see prec. wd. *An* is freq. bef. a cons. to 1300, bef. sounded *h* till after 1700. Now *an* is used bef. a vowel-sound or *h* mute; *a* bef. a cons., sounded *h*, and *eu-*, *u-* pronounced *iu, iū*, as *a host, a eunuch, a unit.* But in *unaccented* syllables, many writers retain *an* bef. sounded *h*, some bef. *eu, u*, as *an historian, an university.* About the 15th cent. *a* or *an* was commonly joined with its sb. as *aman, anadder, anewt.* Hence, by mistaken division, words like ADDER, NEWT. *A* is strictly *adjective*, and requires a sb. Meanings:—**1.** One, some, any ME. **2.** *A* with numeral adjectives = some, a matter of, about OE. **3.** A certain, a particular ME. **4.** The same 1551. **5.** In each, to or for each. This was orig. the prep. *a*, OE. *an, on*, defining time, as in twice *a* day; afterwards identified with the 'indef. art.', and extended from time to space, measure, weight, number. See A *prep.*[1]

1. A tree, a wish, an ice, a pouring rain (*mod.*) A Daniel SHAKS. A Poland TENNYSON. Also, following the adj. preceded by *how, so, as, too*, and in *many a, such a, what a!* Ho, such a one! *Ruth* 4:1. Behold, how great a matter a little fire kindleth *James* 3:5. What manner a man = *cujusmodi homo?* As fine a child as you shall see (*mod.*). Appar. bef. pl. nouns (*of* omitted): A dozen (of) men. A certayne noble knightis .. she kept LD. BERNERS. Poore a thousand crownes *A.Y.L.* I. i. 2. More than a dozen times TYNDALL. **2.** A ii hundred speres LD. BERNERS. And a many merry men with him *A.Y.L.* I. i. 121. *Obs.* except in *a few, a great many, a good many*, and in dial. **3.** Phr. *Once on a time.* **4.** These foyles have all a length *Haml.* v. ii. 277. *Mod.* Fowls of a feather. Two at a time. **5.** A peny a daye TINDALE *Matt.* 20:2. Twentie poundes a bowe 1584. Four pieces of eight a man DE FOE. A penny a mile, sixpence a pound (*mod.*).

A, also **a'** (ǭ), *adj.*[3] [From ALL; *l* lost as in *alms, talk*; *a'* is the current sp. in modern literary Scotch.] = ALL.

† **A** (ă), *pron. Obs.* or *dial.* [for HA = HE, HEO, HI, *he* (*Haml.* III. iii. 74), *she* (*it*), *they*, when stressless, chiefly in S. and W.] ME.

† **A,** *v.* for **ha, ha'**, worn down f. HAVE (cf. Fr. *a* = L. *habet*). Frequent in 13–17th c.; since, chiefly *colloq.* or *dial.* (TENNYSON *Northern Farmer*), and usu. spelt *ha, ha'*.

† **A,** *adv.* Also **aa, o, oo.** [OE. *ā, āwa*, replaced in 13th c. by Norse *aʒ, ai, ei, ay, aye.* See AYE and O.] Ever, always.

A (ă), *prep.*[1], also **o.** [Worn down proclitic f. OE. prep. *an, on.* Now repl. by *on, in*, etc., exc. in phr. like *go a begging*, etc., and in compounds like *abed, alive, asleep*, etc.] **1.** Superposition: on; as *a bed*, etc. ME. **2.** Motion: on, upon, on to; as *a field*, etc. ME. **3.** Juxtaposition: on, at; as in *a right* (or *left*) *half* ME. † **4.** Position or situation: in; as *a Rome* –1660. **5.** Direction or position: towards; as *a back*, etc. ME. **6.** Partition: in, into; as *a pieces* ME. † **7.** Position in a series: at, in; as *a first*, etc. ME. **8.** Time: in, on, by; as *a night* OE. With OE. genitives *a nights, nowadays.* Esp. with advbs. of repetition: *once a day* (OE. *on dæġe*). See A *adj.*[2] 5, and cf. Fr. *deux francs par jour.* † **9.** Manner: in, with, etc.; as *a this wise*, *a purpose* = on purpose –1695. † **10.** Capacity: in any one's name, esp. *a God's name* –1702. **11.** State: in; as *a live*, etc. ME. **12.** Process: in course of; as in *whilst these things were a doing* STOW. ME. In mod.Eng. *were doing, were being done.* **13.** Action; **a.** with *be*: engaged in; as in *They had ben a fyghtyng* LD. BERNERS. Mod., *been fighting.* **b.** with vb. of motion: as in *to go a begging*, etc. ME.

† **A** (ă, ə), *prep.*[2] ME. [Worn down from *of*, and once used for it in *men a war, time a day*, etc.] **1.** Of, *esp.* in *a clock* = of the clock. **2.** After *manner, kind, sort*, etc., *of* in its reduced form was identified with the 'indef. art.'; thus, What manner of man? *cujusmodi homo?* became 'what manner a man?'

1. Cloth a gold *Much Ado* III. iv. 19. It's sixe a clock B. JONS. **2.** No maner a person LD. BERNERS.

† **A,** *conj.* ME. [Occurs before a consonant for *an*; see AN, AN', *conj.*] **1.** = And. **2.** = *And, an'*, if.

† **A,** *interj.* ME. [var. of O, AH.] **1.** O! exclam. of surprise, admiration. **2.** Ah! of grief. **3.** Before proper names as a war-cry, as *A Warwick!* **4.** As in *merrily hent the Stile-a* SHAKS., for metre; now burlesque. Cf. O! as in 'My Nannie, O'.

A, a- (ă, ə) *particle* or *prefix*, reduced form (now s.w. dial.) of I-[1], Y-, the prefix of pa. pples. late ME.

An' we have all a-left the spot W. BARNES.

A-, *prefix.* **1.** OE. **a-**, orig. *ar-* away, on, up, out, as in *a-rise.* Sometimes confused with OFr. *a-* :– L. *ad-, ac-, af-*, etc., as in *a(c)-curse*, etc. **2.** ME. **a-** :– OE. *an, on*, in, on, engaged in, at, as in *asleep*, etc. See A *prep.*[1] **3.** ME. **a-** :– OE. *of* prep. off, from, of, as in *akin*, etc. See A *prep.*[2] **4.** ME. **a-** :– OE. *and-*, against, opposite, as in *a-long.* **5.** ME. **a-** for AT, as in *ado*, early N. Eng. *at do* = inf. *to do.* **6. a-** for *i-, y-* :– *ʒe-*; see A *particle.* **7.** ME. **a-** = Fr. pref. *a-* :– L. *ad-* to, at, expressing addition, increase, change *into.* In 15th c., as in Fr., most words from OFr. with (and some without) this prefix were treated as if formed directly from L. Cf. *a(d)dress, a(f)fect, a(c)curse* = OE. *a-* + *curse.* **8.** ME. **a-** = Fr. *a-* :– L. *ab* off, away, from, as in *a-soil.* **9.** ME. **a-** = AFr. *a*, OFr. *e-, es-* :– L. *ex-* out, utterly, as in *abash.* **10.** ME. **a-** :– AFr. *an-*, OFr. *en-*, as in *abushment*, etc. **11.** *a-*, as used by Spenser and others, is often due to vague form-association only. **12. a-,** f. L. *a* = *ad*, to, reduced to *a-* bef. *sc-, sp-, st-*, as in *a-scend*, etc. See AD-. **13. a-,** f. L. *a* = *ab* from, off, away; only bef. *v*, as in *avert*; see AB-. **14. a-,** f. Gr. ἀ- used bef. a cons. for ἀν = *without, not, -less* as in *adamant, apetalous*, etc. In *agnostic*, etc., *a-* = *un-, non-*, and is used also with techn. words from L., as *a-sexual.*

-a, *suffix.* **1.** OE. **-a** (:– Gmc., *-on*), nom. ending, as in *ox-a* = ME. *ox-e*, mod.E. *ox.* A com. ending of OE. names and titles, as *Bæda.* **2.** Gr. and L. **-a,** nom. ending of fem. nouns (*esp.* Nat. Hist. terms, and names of women), often adopted unchanged, as *idea, soda, Diana*, etc. **3.** Mod. Rom. **-a,** ending of fem. nouns, names of women, and occ. a sex-suffix, as *stanza*; *Eva*; *donn-a*, etc. **4.** Gr. and L. **-a,** pl. ending of neut. nouns, occ. adopted unchanged, as *data, Mammalia*, etc.

‖ **Aal** (āl). 1875. [Hind.] A species of *Morinda*, whose roots yield a red dye. Also, the dye.

‖ **Aam** (ām, ǭm). 1526. [Du. *aam*, = G. *ahm, ohm*, – (ult.) Gr. ἄμη bucket.] A Du. and Ger. liquid measure, varying from 37 to 41 gallons; a cask.

‖ **Aard-vark** (ā·ɹdvāɹk). 1833. [S. Afr. Du., f. *aarde* earth + *vark* pig.] An insectivorous quadruped (*Orycteropus capensis*), one of the Edentata, intermediate between Armadillos and Ant-eaters.

‖ **Aard-wolf** (ā·ɹdwulf). 1833. [S. Afr. Du., f. *aarde* earth + *wolf* wolf.] A S. Afr. carnivorous quadruped (*Proteles lalandii*), intermediate between the dogs, hyenas, and civets.

Aaronic, -al (e^{ə}rǫ·nik, -ăl), *a.* 1874. [f. the prop. name; see -IC, -ICAL.] Pertaining to Aaron, Levitical, high-priestly.

Aaron's-beard (ē^{ə}·rənzbī^{ə}·ɹd). 1549. [*Ps.* 133:2.] *Herb.* A name, *esp.* of the Great St. John's wort (*Hypericum calycinum*), and locally of other plants.

Aaron's rod. 1834. **1.** [*Num.* 17:8.] *Herb.* A name of plants, *esp.* the Great Mullein or Hag-taper (*Verbascum thapsus*), and the Golden Rod (*Solidago virgaurea*). **2.** [*Exod.* 7:9.] *Arch.* A rod with a serpent twined about it, used as an ornament.

‖ **Ab** (æb). 1833. [Heb.] The 5th month of the Heb. sacred year, the 11th of the civil year. The 12th month of the Syrian year, = August.

Ab-, *pref.* repr. L. *ab*, 'off, away, from'. In rec. formations, e.g. *ab-oral*, *ab-* = 'position away from'.

Aba (æ·bă). 1876. A new altazimuth instrument, designed by M. d'Abbadie [and named after him] for determining latitude, etc., without the sextant.

‖ **Abaca** (æ·băkă), **-ka.** The native name of the palm (*Musa textilis*) which furnishes Manilla Hemp; also, its fibre.

Abacinate (ăbæ·sine^{i}t), *v. rare.* [– *abacinat-*, pa. ppl. stem of med.L. *abacinare*, f. *ab* AB- + *bacinus* BASIN; see -ATE[3].] To blind by placing hot irons or metal plates before the eyes. Hence **Abacina·tion.**

‖ **Abaci·scus.** [L., – Gr. ἀβακίσκος, dim. of ἄβαξ ABACUS.] *Arch.* **1.** A tile or square in a mosaic pavement. † **2.** = ABACUS.

Abacist (æ·băsist). ME. [– med.L. *abacista*, f. L. *abacus*; see -IST.] One who uses an abacus in casting accounts; a calculator.

† **Aback.** *rare.* [– Fr. *abaque* – L. *abacus.*] A square tablet or compartment.

Aback (ăbæ·k), *adv.* [OE. *on* (A *prep.*[1] 5, A- *pref.* 2) + *bæc* BACK *sb.*[1] Now chiefly *Naut.*] **1.** Backwards. Also *fig.* **2.** In the rear, behind OE. Also *fig.* **3.** *Naut.* Of sails: Laid back against the mast, with the wind in front 1697. Also of the ship. Hence **To be taken aback,** to be caught in front suddenly, through a shift of wind, and driven astern; *fig.* to be disconcerted by a sudden check.

2. When tyme is, to holde thyself abacke SKELTON.

† **Abackward,** *adv.* ME. [f. ABACK *adv.* + -WARD.] Early f. BACKWARD. Chaucer.

Abactinal (æ:bˌæktəi·năl), *a.* 1857. [f. AB- + ACTINAL.] *Zool.* Remote from the actinal area. See ACTINAL.

† **Aba·ctor.** 1659. [– L., f. *abigere, -act-* drive away; see -OR 2 a.] A stealer of cattle by herds.

‖ **Aba·culus.** [L., dim. of *abacus* (foll.); see -ULE.] *Arch.* = ABACISCUS.

Abacus (æ·băkŏs). Pl. **-ci.** ME. [– L. *abacus*, f. Gr. ἄβαξ slab, orig. drawing-board covered with dust – Heb. *'ābāq* dust.] † **1.** A board strewn with sand, for drawing figures, etc. **2.** A calculating frame, *esp.* one with sliding balls on wires 1686. **3.** The upper member of the capital of a column, supporting the architrave 1563. † **4.** = ABACK *sb.* **5.** *Gr. & Rom. Antiq.* A sideboard 1853.

† **Abada.** *a* 1599. [– Pg. *abada*, perh. Malay.] The rhinoceros. PURCHAS.

Abaddon (ăbæ·dən). ME. [– Heb. *'abaddôn* destruction (*Prov.* 15:11).] In *Rev.* 9:11 = Gr. Ἀπολλύων destroyer, 'the angel of the bottomless pit'. Hence the pit itself MILT. *P.R.* iv. 624.

Abaft (ăbɑ·ft). ME. [A *prep.*[1] 5 + *bi* BY + *æftan*; see BAFT and AFT.] **A.** *adv.* † **1.** Backwards ME. **2.** Back ME. Usu. *Naut.* **B.** *prep.* Behind.

A. 2. Her works were rotten a. ANSON. **B.** Just a. the beam MAURY.

† **Abai·sance.** ME. [– OFr. *abaissance*, f. *abaissier* ABASE; see -ANCE.] A low bow –1721.

Abai·ser. 1849. Burnt black or ivory black; used to lower the tones of colours in painting.

† **Abalienate** (æbˌēi·liĕneit), *v.* 1554. [– *abalienat-*, pa. ppl. stem of L. *abalienare*, f. *ab* AB- + *alienare* estrange; see ALIEN, -ATE[3].] **1.** *Rom. Law.* To make that another's which was ours. **2.** To remove; estrange –1652. **3.** To cause aberration of (mind) –1652. Hence **Aba:liena·tion.**

Abalone (æbălōu·ni). *U.S.* 1883. [– Mexican Sp. *abulón*.] An edible mollusc, the sea-ear.

† **Aba·nd,** *v.* 1559. [Contr. f. ABANDON.] **1.** To forsake SPENSER. **2.** To banish –1559.

† **Abando·n, -ou·n,** *adv.* ME. [– OFr. *à bandon*; see BANDON *sb.*] Under one's control; at one's discretion.

Abandon (ăbæ·ndən), *v.* ME. [– OFr. *abandoner*, f. *à bandon*; see prec. and cf. Fr. *mettre à bandon*.] † **1.** To reduce under control, subdue –1533. **2.** To give up to the control of another, surrender *to* another ME.; esp. *refl.* to surrender oneself 1564. **3.** *trans.* To relinquish a claim to underwriters (also *absol.*) 1755. **4.** To cease to hold, use, or practise; to give up, renounce ME.; to desert, leave without help 1490. † **5.** *refl.* To let oneself loose, rush headlong –1530. † **6.** To put to the ban, banish –1660.

2. To a. a place to the enemy HUME. *refl.* Abandon'd to her sorrow *Twel. N.* I. iv. 19. **3.** To a. a Ship to the Insurers 1755. **4.** Abandoning . . of images 1577. To a. the Dutch war BURKE. MILT. *Sams.* 118. To a. one's own flesh and blood DE FOE, the helm of justice BURKE. **6.** Abandoned from thy bed *Tam. Shr.* Ind. ii. 112. Hence **Aba·ndoner.**

† **Abando·n, -ou·n(e,** *sb.*[1] ME. [– OFr. *abandon*; see ABANDON *adv.*] = BANDON. *At, in abandoun*: recklessly.

Abandon (abæ·ndən), *sb.*[2] ? *Obs.* 1755. [f. ABANDON *v.*; cf. Fr. *abandon* in same senses.] The act of abandoning; *spec.* of insured property.

‖ **Abandon** (ăba·ndoṅ), *sb.*[3] 1850. [mod.Fr. See ABANDONMENT.] *lit.* Surrender to natural impulses; hence, freedom from constraint or convention.

Abandoned (abæ·ndənd), *ppl. a.* ME. [f. ABANDON *v.* + -ED[1].] **1.** Forsaken, cast off 1477. **2.** Self-given up *to* ME. Now always to evil. Hence (without *to*): Profligate 1692.

1. A poor, a. woman 1704. A. finery LEVER. **2.** A. to sorrow SHAKS., to despair DE FOE, to vice SCOTT. A. youth PRIOR, writings STEELE. Hence **Aba·ndonedly** *adv.* profligately; also unconventionally (f. ABANDON *sb.*[3]).

Aba:ndonee·. 1848. [f. ABANDON *v.* + -EE[1].] One to whom anything is formally abandoned; *spec.* an underwriter.

Abandonment (abæ·ndənmĕnt). 1611. [– (O)Fr. *abandonnement*, f. *abandonner*; see ABANDON *v.*, -MENT.] **1.** The action of abandoning or the condition of being abandoned 1611. **2.** *Comm. Law.* Abandoning an interest or claim; *esp.* in *Marine Insurance* 1809. **3.** Self-abandonment 1860. **4.** = ABANDON *sb.*[3]

1. A. of pretences BURKE, of reason BYRON. **3.** True A. .. the nearest way to God VAUGHAN. **4.** A manner frank even to a. DISRAELI.

‖ **Abandum.** [med.L. *abandum*, etc., – OFr. *abandon* ABANDON *sb.*[1]] *Law.* 'Anything sequestered, proscribed, or abandoned' TOMLINS.

† **A·banet, a·bnet.** 1707. [Heb. *'abnēṭ* belt (*Lev.* 8:13).] A girdle of fine linen, worn esp. by Jewish priests.

† **Abanni·tion.** 1656. [f. med.L. *abannire*.] Banishment.

Abarticulation (æ:bărti:kiulēi·ʃən). 1751. [– mod.L. *abarticulatio* = Gr. ἀπάρθρωσις (Galen); see AB-, ARTICULATION.] *Anat.* Articulation allowing free motion in the joint.

Abase (ăbēi·s), *v.* ME. [– OFr. *abaissier*, f. *à* AD- + *baissier* :– Rom. **bassiare*, f. late L. *bassus* short of stature. Infl. by BASE *a.*] **1.** To lower (physically). *arch.* 1477. **2.** To lower in rank, office, etc.; humiliate; degrade ME. † **3.** To lower in price or value, debase (coin) –1736.

1. To a. one's eyes SHAKS. **2.** He dyd a. hym selfe TONSTALL. To a. the proud 1762. **3.** The peece of ix pence was abaced to sixpence 1569. Hence **Aba·sedly** *adv.* **Aba·ser.**

Abased (ăbēi·st), *ppl. a.* 1611. [f. ABASE *v.* + -ED[1].] **1.** In the senses of the vb. **2.** *Her.* = Fr. *abaissé*: Turned downwards, as wings on a shield. Also said of a charge, when lowered; opp. to *enhanced*. 1741.

Abasement (ăbēi·smĕnt). 1561. [f. as prec., or – Fr. *abaissement*; see -MENT.] The action of abasing or condition of being abased.

Abash (ăbæ·ʃ), *v.* ME. [– AFr. *abaïss-* (see A- *prefix* 9) = OFr. *esbaïss-*, stem of *e(s)baïr*, mod. *ébahir*; f. *es-* EX-[1] + *baïr* astound, f. *ba!* int., or OFr. *baer* (mod. *bayer*) yawn.] **1.** To destroy the self-possession of, to disconcert with sudden shame, consciousness of error, presumption, etc. ME. † **2.** *intr.* To stand confused, etc. –1585.

1. The lyon with his crye abassheth all other bestes 1496. To a. the gainsayer 1863. **2.** The herte of man sholde not abasshe CAXTON. Hence **Aba·shed** *ppl. a.* put to confusion. **Aba·shedly** *adv.* **Aba·shless** *a.* unabashed BROWNING. **Aba·shment,** confusion from shame, etc.

Aba·sk, *adv.* 1866. [A *prep.*[1] 11 + BASK *v.*] Basking.

†‖ **Abassi, -s.** 1753. [f. Shah *Abas* II.] A silver coin of Persia, worth about twelvepence.

† **Aba·stard,** *v.* 1610. [– OFr. *abastardir* (mod. *abâtardir*), f. *à* AD- (see A- *prefix* 7) + *bastard*; cf. med.L. *abastardare* declare illegitimate.] To render bastard; to debase –1651. var. † **Aba·stardize, -ise.**

Abate (ăbēi·t), *v.*[1] ME. [– OFr. *abatre* :– Rom. **abbatt(u)ere*, f. *ad* AD- + L. *batt(u)ere* beat. See A- *prefix* 7.] **1.** *trans.* To beat down, destroy. *Obs.* exc. in *Law*. Hence, to put an end to; as (*Law*) to *abate* a nuisance, an action, a writ ME. **2.** *intr.* (through *refl.*) To become null and void 1602. † **3.** To bring down physically, socially, or mentally. Also *intr.* Also with *of*: To curtail of. –1651. **4.** To bring down in size, amount, value, force ME. Also *intr.* **5.** To lower in force or intensity ME. Also *intr.* **6.** To strike off a part, deduct ME. **7.** *fig.* To bar or except 1588. **8.** With *of*: To deduct something from. *arch.* 1644. † **9.** *Falconry.* To beat with the wings; *usu.* BATE –1575.

1. Ye gates of Bruges. . were abated FABYAN. **2.** Commissions shall not a. by the death of his majesty DE FOE. **3.** Abatid and defouled in helle CHAUCER. *Lear* II. iv. 161. **4.** To a. (= blunt) the edge of envy BACON, the edge of a sword HEYWOOD. The waters were abated *Gen.* 8:3. To a. a party SCOTT. *intr.* The legacies must a. proportionately 1768. **5.** Nor (was) his naturall force abated *Deut.* 34:7. **6.** To a. something of his morning price 1866. A. me two shillings a week FRANKLIN. **7.** Abating his brutality, etc. JOHNSON. **8.** The guide abating of his pace SCOTT.

Aba·te, *v.*[2] 1528. [– AFr. *abatre*, earlier *enbatre* (see A- *pref.* 10), in phr. *se enbatre* or *abatre en*. Confused with prec.] *Law. refl.* To thrust oneself tortiously into a tenement between the death of the owner and the accession of the legal heir. Usu. *intr.*

† **Aba·te,** *sb.* ME. [f. ABATE *v.*[1]; cf. Fr. *abat*.] Depression, diminution; subtraction.

Abatement[1] (ăbēi·tmĕnt). 1513. [– OFr. *abatement*, f. *abatre* ABATE *v.*[1]; see -MENT.] **1.** The action of abating; the being abated (see quots.). **2.** The result of abating; decrease, deduction, drawback 1624. *lit.* and *fig.*, and *techn.* in *Comm.* **3.** *Her.* A mark of depreciation 1610.

1. A. of writs PERKINS, of nuisances BLACKSTONE. *Plea in a.*, a defendant's plea, showing cause against being impleaded or sued. Much a. of my hopes CROMWELL. A. of a storm 1794, of the energies 1878. **2.** An A. to his Riches BACON. An a. out of the purchase money 1858.

Aba·tement[2]. ME. [– AFr. *abatement*, f. *abatre* ABATE *v.*[2]; see -MENT.] The action of abating; tortious entry.

Aba·ter[1]. 1732. [f. ABATE *v.*[1] + -ER[1].] He who or that which abates.

Aba·ter[2]. 1660. [f. ABATE *v*[1] + -ER[4].] A plea in abatement.

Abatis (æ·bătis), **Abattis.** 1766. [– Fr. *abatis*, OFr. *abateïs*, f. *abatre* fell, ABATE *v.*[1], + *-eïs* :– Rom. **-aticium*; cf. -ISE[2], -ICE.] *Mil.* A defence formed by placing felled trees lengthwise one over the other with their branches towards the enemy's line. Hence **A·batised** *ppl. a.*

‖ **Abatjour** (abaʒū·r). [Fr.] A skylight.

Abator[1] (ăbēi·təɹ, -tǫ:ɹ). 1592. [– late AFr. *abator, -tour*, f. *abatre*; see ABATE *v.*[1], -OR 2.] **1.** One who abates a nuisance, etc. **2.** = ABATER[1]. 1592.

Aba·tor[2]. 1531. [– late AFr. *abator, -tour*, f. *abatre* = *enbatre*; see ABATE *v.*[2], -OR 2.] One who abates; see ABATE *v.*[2]

‖ **Abattoir** (abatwā·r). 1840. [Fr., f. *abattre* fell (see ABATE *v.*[1]) + *-oir* -ORY[1].] A public slaughter-house for cattle.

Abature (æ·bătiŭr). 1575. [– (O)Fr. *abature*, f. *abatre*; see ABATE *v.*[1], -URE.] The traces of a stag in the underwood.

† **Aba·ve,** *v.* ME. [– OFr. *abaubir* disconcert (mod. *ébaubir*), repr. L. *ad* + *balbum* stammering.] To put or be put to confusion. var. **Abaw(e.**

Aba·xial, *a.* 1857. [f. AB- + AXIAL.] *Bot.* = ABAXILE.

Abaxile (æbˌæ·ksəil), *a.* 1854. [f. AB- + AXILE.] Off the axis; eccentric.

† **Abay** (ăbēi·). ME. [– OFr. *abai* (mod. *aboi* in phr. *être, mettre aux abois*); see BAY *sb.*[4]] **1.** Barking; esp. when closing round the prey. The dogs then *stand at a.*, and the prey *is at a.* (mod. *at bay*). Hence **2.** To be in extremities –1670.

2. Like a wild Beast at abbay MILT.

Abb (æb). OE. [f. A- *pref.* 1 + WEB; cf. OE. *āwef, ōwef*, whence WOOF.] The woof or weft in a web. Also *attrib.*

‖ **Abba** (æ·bă). ME. [eccl.L., – N.T. Gr. – Aramaic (Syriac) *'abbā*.] Father. **1.** An invocation, 'Abba, father' (*Mark* 14:36). **2.** A title given to bishops and patriarchs in Syriac and Coptic churches.

Abbacy (æ·băsi). ME. [– eccl.L. *abbacia*, var. of *-tia*, f. *abbat-* ABBOT; see -ACY.] The office, or term of office, of an abbot.

‖ **Abbate** (abbā·te). [It., :– eccl.L. *abbatem* ABBOT.] An Italian abbot; = Fr. *abbé*.

† **A·bbatess, A·bbotess.** [OE. *abbadisse*, etc. – eccl.L. *abbadissa, -tissa*; see ABBESS.] = ABBESS.

Abbatial (ăbēi·ʃ'ăl), *a.* 1642. [– med.L. *abbatialis* or Fr. *abbatial*; see ABBOT, -IAL.] Of or pertaining to an abbacy, abbot, or abbess. var. † **Abba·tical.**

† **A·bbatie.** ME. [– eccl.L. *abbatia*; see ABBACY.] = ABBACY.

‖ **Abbé** (abe). 1780. [Fr., :– eccl.L. *abbas, abbat-* ABBOT.] The Fr. equivalent of Eng. *abbot*, but in France extended to everyone who wears an ecclesiastical dress (Littré) Cf. ABBATE.

Abbess (æ·bės). [– (O)Fr. *abbesse* :– eccl. L. *abbadissa, -tissa*, f. *abbat-* ABBOT; see -ESS[1].] The female superior of a nunnery.

Abbey (æ·bi). [– OFr. *ab(b)eïe* (mod. *abbaye*) :– med.L. *abbatia*; see ABBACY, -Y[3].] **1.** A society of *monks* governed by an *abbot*, or of *nuns* under an *abbess*. Hence—**a.** the office of an abbot. **b.** the corporation. **c.** the buildings. **2.** The Abbey Church, as *Westminster A.* 1557. Also, as in *Battle A.*, of residences which were once abbeys. **3.** Scotl.: The precincts of the A. of Holyrood, as a sanctuary for debtors 1709.

Abbot (æ·bət). [OE. *abbud, -od, -ot*, – eccl.L. *abbas, abbat-* – Gr. ἀββᾶς – Syriac *'abbā* ABBA.] The head or superior of an abbey OE. After the Reformation, occ. applied to the layman to whom the revenues were impropriated.

Anselm a. of S. Ædmund *O.E. Chron.* The lay a. of Marney DISRAELI. *Abbat of the people*, a Genoese magistrate. †*A. of Misrule*, †*A. of Unreason*, applied ironically to the leader in mediæval revels. Hence **A·bbotcy, A·bbotship** = ABBACY.

† **A·bbotric.** OE. [f. ABBOT + OE. *rīce* kingdom.] An abbacy –1711.

Abbreviate (ăbrī·vi,ět), *ppl. a.* late ME. [f. late L. *abbreviatus*, pa. pple. of *abbreviare*, f. *ab* or *ad* (see AB-, AD-) + *breviare*, f. *brevis* BRIEF *adj.*; see -ATE[2].] **A.** *adj.* † **a.** = ABBREVIATED. **b.** *Nat. Hist.* Relatively short. † **B.** *sb.* An abridgement –1716. † **Abbre·viately** *adv.*

Abbreviate (ăbrī·vi,eⁱt), *v.* late ME. [f. *abbreviat-*, pa. ppl. stem of late L. *abbreviare*; see prec., -ATE[3], and cf. ABRIDGE.] † **1.** *trans.* To shorten by omitting details –1672; to epitomize –1648; in *Math.*, to reduce to lower terms– 1796; † *intr.* to speak or write briefly –1622. **2.** *trans.* To shorten by cutting off a part (see quots.).

1. It is one thing to a. by contracting, another by cutting off BACON. **2.** Of time, etc.: To a. one's life BURTON, Devotions FULLER, the long way MILT. So of vowels, etc.: To make short. Of words or symbols: To contract (*the common mod. use*); Exancester abbreviated to. . Exeter DE FOE. Hence **Abbre·viated** *ppl. a.* = ABBREVIATE *ppl. a.*

Abbreviation (ăbrīvi,ēⁱ·ʃən). 1460. [– Fr. *abbréviation* or late L. *abbreviatio*, f. as prec.; see -ION.] **1.** The act of abbreviating 1530. **2.** The result of abbreviating 1460; an abridgement; *esp.* of a word or symbol 1727.

2. Smiffle is. . an a. for Smithfield THACKERAY.

Abbreviator (ăbrī·vi,eⁱtəɹ). 1532. [– med.L. (Isidor), f. as prec.; see -OR 2.] **1.** One who abbreviates 1615. **2.** An officer who draws up the pope's briefs 1532. † **3.** A school of physicians so named –1605.

Abbre·viature. 1614. [f. as prec. + -URE; cf. obs. Fr. *abréviature*.] † **1.** Abbreviation –1673; an abbreviated condition –1650. **2.** An abridgement 1650; a contraction 1630.

2. To write by abbreviatures SIR T. BROWNE.

A B C (ēⁱ:bī:sī·), *sb.* ME. **1.** The alphabet. [So in OFr.] †**2.** An alphabetical acrostic –1597. **3.** A spelling-book, or primer ME.; hence *fig.* the first elements (of a subject). Also *attrib.* as in **ABC-** or **abcee-book.**

2. Chaucer's A B C, called *La Prière de Nostre Dame* 1597. **3.** The A B C of religion FARRAR.

‖ **Abdest** (ā·bdest). [Pers. *āb-dast*, f. *āb* water + *dast* hand.] The Moslem rite of washing the hands before prayer.

Abdicate (æ·bdikeⁱt), *v.* 1541. [f. *abdicat-*, pa. ppl. stem of L. *abdicare* renounce, f. *ab* AB- + *dicare* proclaim; see -ATE[3].] **1.** *trans.* To disown; *esp.* to disinherit children (= L. *abdicare filium*) 1541. † **2.** To depose *from* 1621; esp. *refl.* to divest oneself of an office (L. *abdicare se magistratu*) –1689. † **3.** To discard –1689. **4.** To give up (a right, office, etc.) either formally or by default 1633. **5.** *absol.* (by ellipsis). To renounce sovereignty, etc. 1704.

1. To a. or disinherit children MILT. **2.** King James. . had by demise abdicated himself EVELYN. **3.** To a. idolatry BP. HALL. **4.** To a. thrones DE FOE, authority PRESCOTT, a power RUSKIN. Hence **A·bdicable** *a.* **A·bdicant** *adj.* abdicating; *sb.* one who abdicates. **A·bdica:tive** *a.* causing or implying abdication. **A·bdica:tor.**

A·bdicated, *ppl. a.* 1688. [f. prec. + -ED[1].] **1.** Formerly renounced (of a possession, right, etc.). **2.** Deposed (see ABDICATE 2), self-deposed 1691.

Abdication (æbdikēⁱ·ʃən). 1552. [– L. *abdicatio*; see ABDICATE *v.*, -ION.] **1.** The action of formally disowning. Now only techn. in Rom. Law. † **2.** Deposition 1660. **3.** Resignation (formal or virtual); *esp.* of sovereignty, etc. 1618. **4.** *Comm. Law.* Surrender of ownership to underwriters 1755.

3. A. of all power and authority BURKE. The A. of Licinius GIBBON.

A·bditory. 1658. [– med.L. *abditorium*, f. *abdit-*, pa. ppl. stem of L. *abdere* hide + *-orium* -ORY[1].] A concealed repository.

Abdomen (æ̆bdōᵘ·mĕn, æ·bdŏmen). 1541. [– L. *abdomen*, of unkn. origin.] † **1.** *orig.* Fat round the belly –1692. **2.** *Anat.* The belly; the lower cavity of the body from the diaphragm downwards, sometimes including the pelvic cavity; often in *Nat. Hist.* the outer surface of the belly 1615. **3.** *Zool.* In some *Arthropoda* (insects, spiders, etc.), the posterior division of the body 1788.

Abdominal (æ̆bdǫ·minăl). 1746. [– mod.L. *abdominalis*, f. *abdomin-*, stem of *abdomen* (prec.) + *-alis* -AL[1].] **A.** *adj.* **1.** *Anat.* and *Zool.* Of or pertaining to the abdomen. **2.** *Zool.* Epithet of an order of fishes; see **B. B.** *sb.* An abdominal fish; in *pl.* **Abdominals,** ‖ **Abdominales,** an order of soft-finned osseous fishes, having the ventral fins under the abdomen and behind the pectorals.

‖ **Abdominalia** (æ̆bdǫ:minēⁱ·liă). [mod.L., n. pl. of *abdominalis* (prec.); see -IA[2].] *Zool.* An order of the Cirripedes, having three abdominal segments bearing three pairs of cirri.

Abdominoscopy (æ̆bdǫ:minǫ·skǒpi). 1851. [f. L. *abdomen, -min-* + Gr. -σκοπία viewing; cf. -SCOPE.] Examining the abdomen for disease by percussion, inspection, measurement, etc.

Abdo·minous, *a.* 1651. [f. as prec. + -OUS.] Big-bellied.

Abdu·ce, *v. arch.* 1537. [– L. *abducere*, f. *ab* AB- + *ducere* lead.] = ABDUCT.

If we a. the eye into either corner SIR T. BROWNE.

Abducent (æ̆bdiū·sĕnt), *ppl. a.* 1713. [– *abducent-*, pr. ppl. stem of L. *abducere*; see prec., -ENT.] Drawing away or out. Chiefly *Anat.*, as *abducent* muscles, nerves. Opp. to *adducent.*

Abduct (æ̆bdɒ·kt), *v.* 1834. [– *abduct-*, pa. ppl. stem of L. *abducere* (prec.).] **1.** To lead or take away illegally; to kidnap. **2.** To draw away (a limb, etc.) from its natural position 1836.

Abduction (æ̆bdɒ·kʃən). 1626. [– late L. *abductio*, f. as prec.; see -ION. Cf. Fr. *abduction.*] **1.** A leading away. **2.** *spec.* Carrying off or leading away illegally a wife, child, voter, etc. 1768. **3.** *Phys.* Withdrawing a limb, etc., outward from the medial line 1666. **4.** *Surg.* The separation of contiguous parts after a transverse fracture 1753. **5.** *Logic.* A syllogism, with the major premiss certain, the minor only probable; apagoge 1696.

Abductor (æ̆bdɒ·ktəɹ). 1615. [mod.L., f. as prec.; see -OR 2.] **1.** *Anat.* A muscle which draws any part of the body from its normal position, or from the median line. Also *attrib.* **2.** One who abducts 1847.

A-be. *Sc.* [Prob. = *at be*, north. inf. = to be.] In *let a be*: let alone SCOTT.

Abeam (ăbī·m), *adv.* 1836. [f. A *prep.*[1] 5 + BEAM *sb.*] *Naut.* In a line at right angles to the ship's length, opposite to its centre; abreast. Const. *of.*

Abear (ăbēᵊ·ɹ), *v.* [OE. *aberan*, f. A- *pref.* 1 + *beran* BEAR *v.*[1]] † **1.** To bear, carry OE. **2.** To endure, with *cannot. dial.* or *vulgar.* OE. † **3.** *refl.* To demean oneself 1596.

2. She couldn't a. the men DICKENS. **3.** Thus did the knight himselfe a. SPENSER. Hence † **Abea·r** *sb.* **Abea·rance.** † **Abea·ring** *vbl. sb.* behaviour.

Abecedarian (ēⁱ:bīsīdēᵊ·riăn); also **ABCD-arian; abcedarian.** 1603. [f. late L. *abecedarius* (see foll.); see -ARIAN.] **A.** *adj.* **1.** Pertaining to the alphabet; arranged alphabetically, as *A. psalms*, e.g. the 119th 1665. **2.** Pertaining to one learning the alphabet 1651. **B.** *sb.* A teacher or learner of A B C or rudiments 1603.

Abecedary (ēⁱ:bīsī·dări), *a.* and *sb.*[1] 1580. [– late L. *abecedarius*, f. *a, b, c, d*; see -ARY[1].] = ABECEDARIAN.

†**Abece·dary,** *sb.*[2] ME. [– med.L. *abecedarium*, subst. use of n. adj. (sc. *manuale* manual); see prec., -ARY[1].] An ABC-book; a primer –1660.

Abed (ăbe·d), *adv.* OE. [f. A *prep.*[1] = OE. *on* + BED *sb.*] In bed (*arch.*); laid up 1660.

The King's a bed *Macb.* II. i. 12. A. with gout 1873. **To bring a-bed**: to deliver of a child. Usu. *pass.* Also *fig.*

† **Abe·de,** *v.* OE. [f. *ā-* away, back + *bēodan* announce.] To announce.

Abedge, abeie, etc., obs. ff. ABYE *v.*

Abei·gh, *adv. Sc.* 1707. [perh. f. A *prep.*[1] 4 + ON. *beigr, beygr* fear.] At a shy distance, aloof.

Abele (ăbī·l, ēⁱ·bĕl). 1681. [– Du. *abeel* – OFr. *abel, aubel* :– med.L *albellus*, dim. of *albus* white (cf. ALBUM).] The white poplar (*Populus alba*).

Plantations . . of abeles SWIFT.

Abe·lian, A·belite, Abelo·nian. 1751. [f. *Abel*, second son of Adam and Eve (*Gen.* 4).] *Eccl. Hist.* One of a sect of heretics in Africa, said by Augustine of Hippo to have lived in continence after marriage, like 'righteous Abel'.

Abelmosk (ēⁱ·b'lmǫsk). [(ult.) – Arab. *ḥabbu-l-misk* musk-mallow.] A genus of plants of the order *Malvaceæ*.

Aberdevine (æ·bəɹdĕvəi:n). 1735. [Of unkn. origin.] A bird, the Siskin (*Carduelis spinus*), closely related to the goldfinch.

Abernethy (æ·bəɹnī:þi). 1837. [f. name of John *Abernethy*, surgeon (1764–1831).] A hard biscuit flavoured with caraway-seeds.

† **Abe·rr,** *v.* 1536. [– L. *aberrare*, f. *ab* AB- + *errare* wander, ERR.] To go astray –1658. Also *fig.*

Aberrance (ăbe·răns). 1665. [f. foll.; see -ANCE.] The action of straying; vagary. So **Abe·rrancy,** the quality or condition of being aberrant 1646.

Aberrant (ăbe·rănt), *a.* 1830. [– *aberrant-*, pres. ppl. stem of L. *aberrare* ABERR; see -ANT.] **1.** Straying from the right path. *lit.* and *fig.* 1848. **2.** Deviating from the normal type: *esp.* in *Nat. Hist.* 1830.

Aberrate (æ·bĕreⁱt), *v. rare.* 1765. [– *aberrat-*, pa. ppl. stem of L. *aberrare* ABERR; see -ATE[3].] To diverge from the straight path; to produce aberration, as in optics.

Aberration (æbĕrēⁱ·ʃən). 1594. [– L. *aberratio*, f. as prec.; see -ION.] **1.** The action of wandering away. *lit.* and *fig.* 1615. **2.** A wandering of the intellect 1823. **3.** Deviation from the normal type 1846. **4.** *Optics.* The non-convergence of rays of light to one focus 1753. **5.** *Astron.* An apparent displacement of a heavenly body, occasioned by the joint effect of the earth's motion and the non-instantaneous transmission of light; called also *aberration of light* 1856.

1. A comet with long aberrations CARLYLE. *fig.* The aberrations of my life BP. HALL. **2.** Shades of mental a. SCOTT. **3.** Aberrations of structure and of function BUCKLE. **4.** *Spherical a.*, that due to the failure of a spherical mirror to cause all the rays to meet in one point. *Chromatic a.*, that due to the different refrangibilities of the coloured constituents of white light. **5.** *Diurnal a.*, that due to the motion of the earth on its axis. *Annual a.*, that due to motion in its orbit. *Planetary a.*, that due to the motion of the planet while its light is passing to the earth. Hence **Aberra·tional** *a.* eccentric.

† **Aberu·ncate,** *v.* [f. *aberuncare*, in 17th c. erron. f. L. *averruncare*, by confusion w. L. *eruncare* (f. *e* EX- + *runcare* to weed); see AVERRUNCATE.] To extirpate. **Aberunca·tor,** erron. f. AVERRUNCATOR, an instrument for lopping trees.

Abet (ăbe·t), *v.* ME. [– OFr. *abeter*, f. *a* AD- + *beter* hound on, cogn. w. BAIT *v.*[1]] † **1.** To urge on –1587. **2.** *esp.* in a bad sense: To incite, instigate (†*to*, or *in*) 1590. † **3.** To maintain, uphold –1725. **4.** *esp.* in a bad sense: To encourage, countenance 1779.

2. He will a. them in their damnable courses 1593. **3.** To a. their opinions SIR T. BROWNE, the cause of truth WOLLASTON. **4.** To a. vice and vanity JOHNSON, an invasion FREEMAN. Hence **Abe·tter**; see ABETTOR. **Abe·tting** *vbl. sb.*

† **Abet,** *sb.* ME. [– OFr. *abet*; see prec.] **1.** Fraud –1460. **2.** Encouragement (of an offence) SPENSER.

Abetment (ăbe·tmĕnt). ME. [– AFr. *abetement*; see ABET *v.*, -MENT.] **1.** The action or fact of abetting (*usu.* an offence). †**2.** Deception –1586. †**3.** A bet –1615. var. **Abe·ttal.**

Abettor (ăbe·təɹ, -oɹ). Also **Abetter,** exc. in *Law.* 1514. [– AFr. *abettour*, f. *abeter*; see ABET *v.*, -OR 2.] **1.** *Law* and *gen.* One who abets an offence 1514. **2.** *gen.* A supporter, adherent 1580. Now only in a bad sense.

Abevacuation (æ:bĭvæ:kiu,ēi·ʃən). 1851. [f. AB- + EVACUATION; cf. ABARTICULATION.] *Med.* An incomplete evacuation. Also evacuation by the passage of matter from one organ into another.

Abeyance (ăbēi·ăns). 1528. [– AFr. *abeiance*, OFr. *abeance*, f. *abeer* aspire after, f. *a-* AD- + *beer*, *baer* gape (mod. *bayer*, *béer*) :– med.L. *batare* gape; cf. BAY *sb.*³ and see -ANCE.] **1.** *Law.* Expectation or contemplation of law; the position of being without an owner 1528. **2.** A state of suspension; dormant condition 1660.

1. In a., that is to say alonely in the remembrance..and consideration of the lawe *Littleton's Tenures.* **2.** His honour is in a. BURKE. Hence **Abey·ancy,** a state of abeyance. **Abey·ant** *a.* dormant.

Abhominable, abhomination, etc., the spelling of ABOMINABLE, etc., in OFr. and in Eng. to 17th c., as if f. *ab homine* 'inhuman, beastly'. So † **Abhominal** *a.* –1659.

Abhor (æbhǭ·ɹ), *v.* 1449. [– L. *abhorrēre*, f. *ab* AB- + *horrēre* stand aghast. Partly from Fr. *abhorrer.*] **1.** *trans.* To shrink from with horror. *lit.* and *fig.* 1449. †**2.** To cause horror or disgust (usu. *impers.*) –1604. †**3.** *intr.* To shrink with horror *from* –1656. †**4.** To differ entirely *from* –1671.

1. *fig.* To a. all manner of meate *Ps.* 107:18. Which..ye abhorre to doe MILTON. **2.** It do's abhorre me *Oth.* IV. ii. 162. **3.** The Italians abhorring from being sea men 1617. Hence **Abho·rred** *ppl. a.* detested; horrified *Haml.* V. i. 206. **Abho·rring** *vbl. sb.* = ABHORRENCE 1, 3; †*ppl. a.* repulsive.

Abhorrence (æbhǫ·rĕns). 1660. [f. ABHORRENT; see -ENCE.] **1.** The action of abhorring 1660. **2.** An expression of abhorrence; in *Eng. Hist.*, applied to certain addresses presented to Charles II. 1678. **3.** That which excites abhorrence 1752.

1. Out of a just Abhorrence of such a..Council, etc. *Address to Chas. II* 1680. (Hence sense 2.) **3.** Politics are my a. COWPER.

†**Abho·rrency.** 1605. [f. as prec.; see -ENCY.] **1.** The quality of being abhorrent –1709. **2.** = ABHORRENCE 3.

Abhorrent (æbhǫ·rĕnt), *ppl. a.* 1619. [– *abhorrent-*, pr. ppl. stem of L. *abhorrēre* ABHOR; see -ENT.] **1.** Abhorring; having abhorrence *of* 1749. **2.** Opposed *to* 1619; repugnant, inconsistent 1720. **3.** Abhorred 1833.

1. A. of excess 1869. **2.** The persons most a. from blood and treason BURKE. Similars are not a. from similars 1822. Not a. to nature KEMBLE. **3.** Pride, a. as it is J. TAYLOR. Hence **Abho·rrently** *adv.*

Abhorrer (æbhǭ·rəɹ). 1611. [f. ABHOR *v.* + -ER¹.] **1.** One who abhors. **2.** *Eng. Hist.* One who signed an address of ABHORRENCE 1680.

‖ **Abib** (ēi·bib). [– Heb. *ābīb* spike of corn.] A Jewish month, 1st of the eccl. year, 7th of the civil year, called later Nisan.

Abidance (ăbəi·dăns). 1647. [f. next + -ANCE.] **1.** Abiding, dwelling. var. **Abi·dal.** **2.** With *by*: Conformity to 1875.

1. A. in the holy hill FULLER. **2.** A. by rules HELPS.

Abide (ăbəi·d), *v. str.* Pa. t. **abode,** also **abided.** Pa. pple. **abode, abided, abidden.** [OE. *ābīdan*, f. A- *pref.* 1 + *bīdan* BIDE; cogn. w. Goth. *usbeidan.*]

I. *intr.* **1.** To wait, stay, remain OE. **2.** To reside ME. **3.** To continue to be ME. **4.** To abide *by*: to remain with, true to 1509. **5.** To stand firm 1398.

1. A. you here with the asse *Gen.* 22:5. Tho' much is taken, much abides TENNYSON. Their guilt..abides upon you LAW. **2.** Neither abode in any house *Luke* 8:27. **3.** The town abode frenche LD. BERNERS. **4.** To a. by authority 'JUNIUS', measures EDGEWORTH, rules TYNDALL. **5.** But thou Lorde..abydest COVERDALE.

II. *trans.* **1.** To wait for, await the issue of, endure ME. **2.** To await defiantly, to face ME. **3.** To await submissively ME. **4.** To put up with (now only in neg. and interrog. sentences) 1526.

1. Abit his tyme JAMES I. A. my removal SCOTT. The fiery lake which abideth him E. IRVING. **2.** To a. the brunt of the service CROMWELL, battle SCOTT. **3.** To abyde the lawe CAXTON. To a. thy Kingly doome *Rich. II*, V. vi. 23. **4.** I cannot a. physic 1585, the country H. MARTINEAU.

¶Occas. confused with ABYE = pay for, as in *Jul. Cæs.* III. ii. 119. Hence **Abi·ding** *vbl. sb.* the action or state of one who abides; † an abode; hence **abiding-place,** place of abode; *ppl. a.* lasting, and in comb. **law-abiding,** adhering to the law. **Abi·dingly** *adv.*

Abider (ăbəi·dəɹ). 1543. [f. prec. + -ER¹.] One who abides (see ABIDE *v.* I. 1, 2; II. 2).

Abietene (æ·bi,ĕtīn). 1875. [f. L. *abies, abiet-* fir + -ENE.] A hydrocarbon distilled from the resin or balsam of the nut-pine (*Pinus sabiniana*).

Abietic (æbi,e·tik), *a.* 1864. [f. as prec. + -IC.] *Chem.* Of or pertaining to fir. *Abietic acid*, a monobasic acid, $C_{20}H_{30}O_2$, the essential constituent of resin.

Abietin(e (æ·bi,ĕtin). [f. as prec. + -IN¹, -INE⁵.] *Chem.* A neutral resin extracted from Strasburg turpentine or Canada balsam, products of *Abies* or fir. Hence **Abieti·nic** *a.*, as *abietinic acid*, a bibasic resinous acid, $C_{44}H_{64}O_5$, obtained from species of fir.

Abietite (æ·bi,ĕtəit). [f. as prec. + -ITE¹ 4.] *Chem.* A sugar, $C_6H_8O_3$, obtained from the needles of the silver-fir, analogous to mannite.

Abigail (æ·bigeil). 1666. [f. the name of the 'waiting gentlewoman' in *The Scornful Lady* (Beaum. & Fl.); also see 1 *Sam.* 25.] A lady's-maid. Hence **A·bigailship.**

An antiquated A., dressed in her lady's cast clothes SMOLLETT.

† **Abiliment,** obs. f. HABILIMENT.

Ability (ăbi·lĭti). ME. [– OFr. *ablete* :– L. *habilitas, -tat-*, f. *habilis*; see ABLE, -ITY.] †**1.** Fitness –1678. **2.** Capacity in an agent. **3.** Bodily or mental power 1549. **4.** Pecuniary power. *arch.* 1502. **5.** A power of the mind, a faculty. Usu. *pl.* 1587.

2. Abilite to lerne sciences CHAUCER. Habilitie to annoy HOOKER. Of a. in law to take liverie of seisin 1528. **3.** A. to lift a great stone 1576. Inferior to Condorcet in point of a. BUCKLE. **4.** Out of my leane and low a. Ile lend you something *Twel. N.* III. iv. 378. **5.** His abilities were useful rather than splendid GIBBON.

† **Abi·me,** earliest f. ABYSM –1616.

Abiogenesis (æ:bio,dʒe·nĕsis). 1870. [f. Gr. ἄβιος (f. ἀ A- *pref.* 14 + βίος life) + γένεσις GENESIS.] *Biol.* The production of living by not-living matter; 'spontaneous generation'. (Introduced by Prof. Huxley in *Brit. Assoc. Rep.* lxxvi.) Hence **A:biogene·tic** *a.* **A:biogene·tically** *adv.* **A:bio·genist,** one who believes in a. **A:bio·genous** *a.* produced by spontaneous generation. **A:bio·geny** = ABIOGENESIS.

Abiological (æ:biŏlǫ·dʒikăl), *a.* [f. Gr. ἀ- A- *pref.* 14 + BIOLOGICAL.] Pertaining to the study of inanimate things.

Abirritate (æb,i·riteit), *v.* [f. L. *ab* AB- *pref.* + IRRITATE *v.*¹] *Med.* To diminish irritation. Hence **Abi·rritant** *a.* and *sb.* a soothing agent. **Abi:rrita·tion** *Med.*, a depressed condition (opp. to irritation) of the tissues. **Abi·rritative** *a.*

Abit, obs. 3rd sing. of ABIDE *v.*

Abject (æ·bdʒĕkt), *ppl. a.* ME. [– L. *abjectus*, pa. pple. of *abicere* reject, f. *ab* AB- + *jacere* throw. Orig. *abje·ct*, pple. and adj. Later, repl. by *abjected* as pple., *a·bject* remaining as adj. and sb.] †**1.** *pple.* Cast off, rejected –1614. **2.** *adj.* Cast down, brought low in condition, low-lying 1520. **3.** Low in regard, mean-spirited, despicable 1548. As *sb.* 1534.

2. A. fortune MILT. The a. heirs of an illustrious name MACAULAY. **3.** Seruile, a. drudges 2 *Hen. VI*, IV. i. 105. An a. liar MACAULAY. *sb.* Servants and abjects flout me G. HERBERT. Hence **A·bjectly** *adv.* **A·bjectness.**

† **Abje·ct,** *v.* 1475. [f. prec. Cf. *content* vb. from adj.] **1.** To cast off, *lit.* and *fig.* –1650; to cast down, degrade –1640. Hence † **Abje·cted** *ppl. a.*, † **Abje·ctedness.**

Abjection (æbdʒe·kʃən). ME. [– (O)Fr., or L. *abjectio*; see ABJECT *ppl. a.*, -ION.] †**1.** The action of casting down –1653. **2.** The condition of one cast down, degradation, low estate ME. †**3.** The action of casting off; rejection –1655. †**4.** That which is cast off; refuse. Usu. *fig.* –1534.

2. A. of mind or seruilitie HOOKER. The a. and uncivilisedness of Glasgow M. ARNOLD. **3.** A. from God 1607. **4.** These dregges and a. of all menn 1534.

Abjudge (æbdʒʊ·dʒ), *v. rare.* 1855. [f. L. *ab* AB- + JUDGE, repr. L. *abjudicare* (see foll.).] To take away by judicial decision. Opp. to *adjudge.*

Abjudicate (æbdʒiū·dikeit), *v. Obs.* 1602. [– *abjudicat-*, pa. ppl. stem of L. *abjudicare*, f. *ab* AB- + *judicare* to JUDGE; see -ATE³.] **1.** To pass judgement against, reject as illegal. **2.** = ABJUDGE. Hence **Abju:dica·tion.**

† **A·bjugate,** *v.* [– *abjugat-*, pa. ppl. stem of L. *abjugare*, f. *ab* AB- + *jugum* yoke; see -ATE³.] To unyoke.

† **Abju·nct,** *ppl. a.* 1610. [– *abjunct-*, pa. ppl. stem of L. *abjungere* detach, f. *ab* AB- + *jungere* join; see -ATE².] Disjoined. Hence **Abju·nctive** *a. rare.*

Abjuration (æ:bdʒiurēi·ʃən). 1514. [– (O)Fr., or late L. *abjuratio*; see next and -ATION.] **1.** Renunciation on oath; forswearing (*esp.* of heresies). Also *fig.* **2.** Official repudiation on oath of any principle 1650.

1. A. of his blasphemous heresies FULLER. *fig.* An a. of friendship 1842. **2.** A. of doctrines of the Church of Rome 1726. Hence *Oath of Abjuration*, i.e. disclaiming allegiance to the Pretender or any one claiming through him. *Abjuration of the realm, a town*, etc.: an oath taken to leave it for ever.

Abjure (æbdʒiūᵊ·ɹ), *v.* 1480. [– L. *abjurare* deny on oath, f. *ab* AB- + *jurare* swear.] **1.** To renounce on oath; to recant 1501. *trans.* and *absol.* †**2.** To cause to recant –1542. **3.** To disclaim solemnly; to reject upon oath 1597. Also *absol.*

1. This..Magicke I heere a. *Temp.* V. i. 51. **2.** All such must be burned, or ellis ab-Iuryd THYNNE. **3.** To a. pleasures MILT., the badges of Popery MACAULAY, the Pretender 1863. *To a. the realm*, etc.: to swear to leave it for ever. Hence **Abju·rement, Abju·rer.**

‖ **Abkari** (ăbkā·ri), also **abcaree.** 1797. [– Pers. *āb-kārī*, water (liquor)-business.] The manufacture or sale of spirits; hence, in Anglo-Ind., the excise duty on such manufacture, etc.

† **Abla·ctate,** *v. rare.* [– *ablactat-*, pa. ppl. stem of late L. *ablactare* wean, f. *ab* AB- + *lactare* suckle; see -ATE³.] To wean from the breast.

Ablactation (æblæktēi·ʃən). 1656. [– late L. *ablactatio*; see prec. and -ATION.] **1.** The weaning of the young from the mother. **2.** *Hort.* 'Grafting by approach', inarching 1676.

† **Abla·queate,** *v. rare.* ME. [– *ablaqueat-*, pa. ppl. stem of L. *ablaqueare* disentangle, f. *ab* AB- + *laqueare* (f. *laqueus* noose); see -ATE³. To loosen or remove the soil round roots. Hence † **Ablaquea·tion.**

Ablaste·mic, *a.* 1881. [f. Gr. ἀ- A- *pref.* 14 + βλάστημος growth + -IC.] Non-germinal.

† **Abla·te,** *v. rare.* 1542. [– *ablat-*, pa. ppl. stem of L. *auferre* take away; see -ATE³.] To take away.

Ablation (æblēi·ʃən). 1577. [– Fr., or late L. *ablatio*; see prec. and -TION.] **1.** The action of taking away. †**2.** *Med.* Subsidence of acute symptoms 1671. **3.** *Surg.* Surgical removal of any part of the body 1846. **4.** *Geol.* Surface waste of rocks or glaciers 1860.

1. Ablations of goods HAKLUYT. **2.** The a. of the disease 1671. **3.** A. of the nipple, the mamma MILLER. **4.** The a. of the ice TYNDALL.

Ablatitious (æblăti·ʃəs), *a.* 1833. [f. L. *ablat-* (see ABLATE) + -ITIOUS; cf. ADDITITIOUS.] Tending to take away, diminishing. *A. force* (*Astr.*), that which diminishes the gravitation of a satellite towards its planet.

Ablative (æ·blătiv), *a.* and *sb.* ME. [– (O)Fr. *ablatif, -ive* or L. *ablativus*; see ABLATE, -IVE.] **1.** *Gram.* Name of a case found in L. and other Aryan languages, but not in Gr., and expressing primarily *direction from* a place, or *time*. In L. it expressed also the *source, cause, instrument* and *agent, manner*, and sometimes *place* and *time* of an action or event. Often used as *sb.* [sc. *case.*] † **2.** = prec. –1713.

1. We learn from a fragment of Cæsar's work, *De Analogia*, that he was the inventor of the term a. in Latin MAX-MÜLLER. *A. absolute*, in L. Grammar, an a. case of a noun with a participle in concord, expressing the time, occasion, etc. of a fact stated, as *sole oriente, tenebræ aufugiunt.* **2.** A. directions . . to vnteach error BP. HALL.

‖ **Ablaut** (a·blaut). 1871. [mod.G., f. *ab* off + *laut* sound.] *Philol.* Vowel permutation, as in *sing, sang, song, sung*, uninfluenced by a succeeding vowel (contrast *Umlaut*).

Ablaze (ăblē^{i}·z), *adv.* and *a.*, prop. **a blaze**; earlier **on blaze.** ME. [f. A *prep.*[1] + BLAZE.] In a blaze. Also *fig.* In brilliant colours 1851. In the glow of excitement 1840.

Set a. by lightning TYNDALL. *fig.* A. with gorse and broom W. BLACK. A. with anger 1879.

Able (ē^{i}·b'l), *a.* ME. [– OFr. *(h)able* :– L. *habilis* (f. *habēre* have), 'easy to be handled', hence 'fit'. In Eng. the silent *h* was dropped, though *habile*, refash. after Fr. or L., still exists; see -IL, -ILE.]

I. *pass.* † **1.** Complaisant ME.; manageable –1710. † **2.** Suitable –1717. † **3.** Liable (*to*). *Obs.* exc. *dial.* ME.

1. The Hands are the most habil members of the Body 1710. **2.** To the next a. Tree with him BROME.

II. *act.* **1.** Having the qualifications for, and means of, doing anything; having sufficient *power* ME. *spec.* Legally qualified 1708. † **2.** Strong, materially or physically, vigorous –1690; wealthy –1665. **3.** Having mental power 1577.

1. Abeler þen þow To alle manere gode *c* 1450. A. to take care of myself TYNDALL. *spec.* Admission . . in Law is when . . the Bishop allows a clerk to be a. 1708. **2.** Of a. bodie *All's Well* IV. v. 86. A very a. citizen in Gracious Street PEPYS. **3.** A. pastours 1587, men *Ex.* 18:21, heads DRYDEN. An abler general 1792. *Comb.* **a.-bodied** *a.* having a body free from disability and fit for service; hence **-bodiedness.** Hence † **A·bleness.**

† **Able,** *v.* ME. [f. ABLE *a.*; cf. (O)Fr. *habiller*, used in all the senses of the Eng. vb.] **1.** *trans.* To fit; make ready. (Const. *to, into, unto.*) –1583. **2.** To attire 1450. **3.** = ENABLE. –1693. **4.** To make strong; to empower legally –1631; hence, to vouch for –1605.

3. If God shall me a. EVELYN. **4.** I'll a, 'em *Lear* IV. vi. 172. Hence **A·bling** *vbl.sb.*

-able, – Fr. *-able* :– L. *-abilis*, adjectival suffix, the form taken by the suffix *-bili-* (see -BLE) when added to vbs. in *-are*, Fr. *-er*; extended in Fr. to verbs of all conjugations, and also (as occas. in post-classical L., e.g. *amicabilis* AMIABLE, AMICABLE, f. *amicus*) to nouns, as in *charitable, equitable, peaceable.* Orig. found in English only in words from Fr. or L., as *separable* (– Fr. *séparable* or L. *separabilis*), but subsequently used to form many adjs. by analogy directly from the stem of Engl. vbs. in *-ate*, as *appreciable* from *appreciate, educable* from *educate, extricable* from *extricate.* Later, prob. by confusion with the unrelated adj. ABLE, freely used to form adjs. from vbs. of all types (*bearable, reliable*), sbs. (*clubbable, saleable*) and verbal phrases (*get-at-able*). In new formations now always passive in sense but earlier freq. active, as in *comfortable, suitable.*

Ablegate (æ·blĭge^{i}t), *sb.* [– mod.Fr. *ablégat* (XVIII) or L. *ablegatus*; see next.] A papal envoy, who brings to a newly appointed cardinal his insignia of office.

† **A·blegate,** *v. rare.* 1657. [– *ablegat-*, pa. ppl. stem of L. *ablegare* dismiss, f. *ab* AB- + *legare* send on a charge or mission; see -ATE[3].] To send abroad or to a distance –1665. Hence † **Ablega·tion.**

† **Able·nd,** *v.* OE. [f. A- *pref.* 1 + *blendan*, to blind.] To blind (temporarily). Also *fig.* –ME.

† **Ablepsy.** *rare.* 1652. [– late L. *ablepsia*, f. Gr. ἀβλεψία, f. ἀ A- *pref.* 14 + βλέπειν see; see -Y[3].] Blindness. *lit.* and *fig.*

† **Ablesse.** Coined by CHAPMAN, after *noblesse*, etc.

Ablet (æ·blėt), also **ablen.** [– (O)Fr. *ablette*, dim. of *able*, = med.L. *abula*, f. L. *albula*, sb. use of fem. of *albulus* whitish, f. *albus* white.] A fish, the Bleak, *Leuciscus alburnus.*

Ablings, -ins (ē^{i}·blinz), *adv. north.* 1597. [f. ABLE *a.* + -LING[2].] Possibly.

Abloom (ăblū·m), *adv.* 1855. [f. A *prep.*[1] 11 + BLOOM *sb.*[1]] In or into bloom.

† **Ablow·,** *v.* OE. [f. A- *pref.* 1 + *blāwan* BLOW *v.*[1]] **1.** To blow upon or into. *lit.* and *fig.* –ME. **2.** *intr.* and *trans.* To puff up. *lit.* and *fig.* –ME.

† **Ablu·de,** *v. rare.* 1612. [– L. *abludere* differ from, f. *ab* AB- + *ludere* play.] To differ (*from*) –1655.

Abluent (æ·bluěnt). 1751. [– *abluent-*, pres. ppl. stem of L. *abluere* wash off, f. *ab* AB- + *luere* wash; see -ENT.] *Med.* **A.** *adj.* Washing away (impurities). **B.** *sb.* An abstergent.

Ablush (ăblʊ·ʃ), *adv.* and *a.* 1852. [f. A *prep.*[1] + BLUSH *sb.*] Blushing.

† **Ablu·ted,** *ppl. a.* 1650. [f. L. *ablut-* (next) + -ED[1].] Washed away.

Ablution (æblⁱū·ʃən). ME. [– (O)Fr., or late L. *ablutio*, f. *ablut-*, *abluere* wash off, f. *ab* AB- + *luere* wash; see -TION.] **1.** The act of washing clean: *spec.* † **a.** Of substances, in Alchemy and Chem. –1754. **b.** Of the body: as a religious rite 1533; generally 1748. **c.** Of chalice and paten after, and, in R.C. Ch., of the priest's hands before, during, and after, the celebration. **2.** The water, etc., used in ablution; *spec.* the wine and water used to rinse the chalice and wash the priest's hands after the communion 1718. † **b.** A lotion 1671.

1. b. Ablutions, in the East, . . a part of religious worship 1856. The scanty ablutions of the morning 1859. **2.** Cast the ablutions in the main POPE. Hence **Ablu·tionary** *a.*

Ably (ē^{i}·bli), *adv.* ME. [f. ABLE *a.*; see -LY[2].] In an able manner.

-ably, compd. suffix, f. ABLE + -LY[2], supplying advbs. to adjs. in *-able.*

Abnegate (æ·bnĭge^{i}t), *v.* 1657. [– *abnegat-*, pa. ppl. stem of L. *abnegare* refuse, f. *ab* AB- + *negare* deny; see -ATE[3].] **1.** To deny oneself (anything), to renounce (a right, etc.) 1657. **2.** To abjure, as a tenet 1755.

1. To a. the personal enjoyment of life MILL. **2.** To a. the very possibility of Heroism CARLYLE. Hence **A·bnega:tive** *a.* **A·bnega:tor.**

Abnegation (æ:bnĭgē^{i}·ʃən). 1554. [– (O)Fr. or late L. *abnegatio*; see prec., -ATION.] **1.** Denial; rejection (of a doctrine, etc.) 1554. **2.** Self-denial; renunciation 1639; self-abnegation 1657. (*Self* now often expressed.)

1. A. of Christe KNOX, of the responsibility of choice 1875. **2.** A. of the world MRS. JAMESON, of authority MOTLEY. The Pretences of Romanists to A., to a Self-denying Life PENN.

Abnormal (æbnǫ·ɹmăl), *a.* 1835. [orig. ANORMAL, refash. after L. *abnormis* (see ABNORMOUS).] Deviating from the type; contrary to rule or system; unusual 1835.

The wing of a bat is an a. structure DARWIN. A. compassion 1878. Hence **Abnorma·lity,** the quality or state of being a.; an a. feature or act. **Abno·rmally** *adv.*

Abnormity (æbnǫ·ɹmĭti). 1731. [– late L. *abnormitas*, f. *abnormis*; see next., -ITY.] The quality of being abnormal; a monstrosity 1859. Usu. depreciatory.

An a. . . like a calf born with two heads MRS. WHITNEY.

Abnormous (æbnǫ·ɹməs), *a.* 1742. [f. L. *abnormis* irregular (f. *ab* AB- + *norma* rule) + -OUS.] 'Irregular, misshapen.' J.

A character of an a. cast 1771.

Aboard (ăbō^{ə}·ɹd), *adv.* and *prep.* 1494. [f. A *prep.*[1] + BOARD, and Fr. *à bord*, the Fr. *bord* (= 1. plank; 2. ship; 3. edge) giving the uses, and ME. *shippes borde*, etc., the derivation.]

A. *adv.* **1.** On board; on or on to or into a ship, etc. 1509. **2.** Alongside (*hard, close*) 1494. ¶ *Catachr.* ? = abroad, adrift SPENSER.

1. Remember whom thou hast aboord *Temp.* I. i. 21. Aboord, aboord for shame *Haml.* I. iii. 56. **2.** To keep the coast a. COOK. *Phrases*: **To lay** (a ship) **aboard**: to place one's own alongside of (it) 1593. **To fall aboard**: to fall foul of (a ship). Also *fig.* with *with* or *of*: to quarrel 1604. **To bring aboard**: to bring to land. **To come to aboard** (Fr. *venir, arriver à bord*): to land. **To haul the tacks aboard**: 'to bring their weather clues down to the chess-tree', to set the courses.

B. *prep.* [*of* omitted.] In senses A. 1, 2. ¶ *Catachr.*? = across the breadth of SPENSER. Is he a. the fleet? SOUTHEY. He came a. my ship DE FOE. Haul a. the shore FULLER.

Aboard, obs. f. ABORD *v.* and *sb.*

Abode (ăbō^{u}·d), *sb.*[1] [ME. *abād, abōd*, vbl. sb. of ABIDE.] † **1.** The action of waiting –1596. † **2.** A temporary stay –1749. **3.** Habitual residence 1576. **4.** A place of habitation; house or home 1614.

1. *Without a.*, at once. Your patience for my long a. *Merch. V.* II. vi. 21. **3.** The Countrey where you make a. SHAKS. **4.** Paradise, Adam's a. MILT. Abodes of . . pain 1767.

† **Abode,** *sb.*[2] 1600. [f. ABEDE *v.*, on the analogy of BODE *sb.*[2]] An omen.

† **Abode,** *v.* 1593. [f. prec., on the analogy of BODE *v.*] To presage, BODE, FOREBODE. Shaks.

Abode, past tense of ABIDE.

† **Abodement**[1]. [f. ABODE *v.* + -MENT; an early instance of a native vb. with this suffix.] An omen. SHAKS.

† **Abodement**[2]. [irreg. f. ABODE *sb.*[1] + -MENT, perh. infl. by prec.] Abiding –1616.

† **Aboding,** *vbl. sb.* and *ppl. a.* [f. ABODE *v.* + -ING[1], [2].] Boding.

Abolish (ăbǫ·liʃ), *v.* 1490. [– Fr. *aboliss-*, *abolir*, f. L. *abolēre* destroy, f. *ab* AB- + *olēre* grow; see -ISH[2].] To put an end to; to annul; to demolish or destroy. Now only of institutions, customs, and practices. Formerly *from, out of.*

To a. idoles *Isa.* 2:18, the Bastille CARLYLE, pestilence KINGSLEY. Hence **Abo·lishable** *a.* **Abo·lisher. Abo·lishment** = ABOLITION.

Abolition (æbŏli·ʃən). 1529. [– Fr., or L. *abolitio*, f. *abolit-*, pa. ppl. stem of *abolēre*; see prec., -ION.] **1.** The act of abolishing; the being abolished; destruction 1529. *spec.* The abolition of the slave-trade; called familiarly 'abolition' 1788. Hence *attrib.* † **2.** A putting out of memory; an amnesty –1809.

1. The a. of eternal guilt JER. TAYLOR. *spec.* To promote the a. in France 1808. The A. party W. PHILLIPS, movement KEMBLE. Hence **Aboli·tionary** *a.* destructive. **Aboli·tionism,** opposition to negro slavery. **Aboli·tionist,** one who aims at a., *esp.* of negro slavery. **Aboli·tionize** *v.* to teach abolitionism. In U.S.

‖ **Abolla** (ăbǫ·lă). [L., – Gr. ἀμβολά = ἀναβολή mantle, lit. something thrown back, f. ἀνά ANA- + βολή, f. βάλλειν throw.] A woollen cloak worn by the soldiers and lower classes of ancient Rome.

‖ **Aboma** (ăbō^{u}·mă). [Pg., of Afr. origin. (Congo).] A large S. American serpent, *Epicratis cenchria.*

‖ **Abomasum, -us** (æbo,mē^{i}·sŏm, -ŏs). 1706. [mod.L., f. *ab* AB- + OMASUM.] The fourth, and true digestive, stomach of ruminants.

Abominable (ăbǫ·minăb'l), *a.* ME. [– (O)Fr., – L. *abominabilis*, f. *abominari* to deprecate as an ill omen, f. *ab* AB- + *omen* OMEN *sb.*; see -ABLE. In med.L., OFr., and Eng. (XIV–XVII) commonly spelt *abhom-*, as if from *ab* + *homin-*, *homo* man, quasi 'inhuman'.] **1.** Exciting disgust; offensive; odious. **2.** *colloq.* Very unpleasant 1860. Also as *adv.*

1. Abhominable and beastly touches *Meas. for M.* III. ii. 25. A. practices BURKE. **2.** The road was a. TYNDALL. As an intensive: 'A bomynable (= terrible) syght of monks' J. BERNERS. Hence **Abo·minableness,** the quality of being a. **Abo·minably** *adv.* loathsomely; *colloq.* very badly.

Abominate (ăbǫ·mine^{i}t), *v.* 1644. [– *abominat-*, pa. ppl. stem of L. *abominari*; see prec., -ATE[3].] **1.** To feel extreme disgust towards; to abhor. **2.** *colloq.* To dislike strongly 1880.

1. The Egyptians . . abominated flesh-eaters 1728. **2.** Steele . . abominated operas 1880. Hence **Abo·minate, Abo·minated** *ppl. adjs.* **Abo·minator.**

Abomination (ăbǫ:minē^{i}·ʃən). ME. [– (O)Fr., – L. *abominatio*, f. as prec.; see -ION.] **1.** The feeling of disgust and hatred; loathing. † **2.** A state exciting disgust; pollution –1480. **3.** A degrading vice ME. **4.** An object that excites disgust and hatred (followed by *unto, to*); *esp.* an idol ME.

1. To have in abominacion MORE. **3.** Antony, most large in his abhominations *Ant. & Cl.* III. vi. 94. An a. is committed in Israel *Mal.* 2:11. **4.** Lying lips are an a. to the Lord *Prov.* 12:22.

† **Abo·mine,** *v.* [– (O)Fr. *abominer* – L. *abominari* ABOMINATE *v.*] = ABOMINATE *v.*

Aboo·n, *adv.* and *prep.* Sc. and n. form of ABOVE. Also *poet.*

Aboral (æbōᵊ·răl), *a.* 1857. [f. AB- + ORAL *a.*] *Zool.* Pertaining to the part away from the mouth.

Abord (ăbōᵊ·ɹd), *v. arch.* 1509. [– (O)Fr. *aborder*; see ABOARD *adv.* Cf. ACCOST *v.*] † **1.** To approach; to land on –1691. **2.** To accost. *arch.* 1611.

† **Abo·rd,** *sb.* 1611. [– Fr., f. *aborder*; see prec.] Approach, or way of approach.

Aboriginal (æbŏri·dʒinăl). 1667. [irreg. f. next + -AL¹.] **A.** *adj.* **1.** First or earliest known; primitive; indigenous. *spec.* Earlier than (European) colonists. 1788. **2.** Pertaining to aborigines, or to native races 1851.

1. A. forests LYELL, Iberians FORD. The English are not a. STUBBS. **2.** The a. fleets of ancient Caledonia D. WILSON.

B. *sb.* An original inhabitant, opp. to colonist 1767. *fig.* Of words 1858.

The thoughtless a. DARWIN. Hence **Abori·ginalism,** the due recognition of native races. **A:bori:gina·lity,** the quality of being a. **A:bori·ginally** *adv.* from the earliest known times.

Aborigines (æbori·dʒiniz, -iz). 1547. [L. *aborigines*, usu. explained as f. *ab origine* from the beginning, but this is not certain. At first pl. only; for sing. ABORIGINAL and *aborigine* (æ:bŏri·dʒini) have been used.] **1.** The inhabitants of a country (orig. of Italy and of Greece) *ab origine*. Also *fig.* **2.** *spec.* The natives, as opp. to colonists 1789. **3.** Used of animals and plants 1677.

1. Meere A.; that is, Homelings and not forren brought in HOLLAND. **3.** An invasion of one plant over the a. DARWIN. Hence (from *sing.*) **A:bori·ginary,** an aboriginal inhabitant.

† **Abo·rsement.** 1540. var. f. *abortment* (see ABORT *v.*).

† **Abo·rsive,** *a.* 1639. [f. *abors-*, late L. var. of *abort-*, pa. ppl. stem of L. *aboriri* to miscarry + -IVE.] Abortive from the first FULLER.

Abort (ăbǭ·ɹt), *v.* 1580. [– *abort-*, pa. ppl. stem of L. *aboriri* to miscarry, f. *ab* AB- + *oriri* come into being.] **1.** To miscarry. *trans.* and *intr.* Also *fig.* 1614. **2.** *Biol.* To become sterile; to be checked in normal development, so as to remain rudimentary or to shrink away 1862. Hence **Abo·rted** *ppl. a.* born before its time; *Biol.* checked in development. **Abo:rtifa·cient** *a.* causing premature delivery; as *sb.* [sc. *drug*]. **Abǫ·rting** *vbl. sb.* a miscarrying; *ppl. a.* producing abortions. † **Abo·rtment,** abortion.

† **Abo·rt.** 1603. [– L. *abortus*; see prec.] A miscarriage (*lit.* and *fig.*) 1621; the offspring of a miscarriage 1603.

Abortion (ăbǭ·ɹʃən). 1547. [– L. *abortio*, f. *aboriri*; see ABORT *v.*, -TION.] **1.** Giving untimely birth to offspring; the procuring of premature delivery so as to destroy offspring. Also *fig.* 1710. **2.** *Biol.* Arrest of development of any organ (see ABORT *v.* 2) 1842. **3.** The imperfect offspring of a miscarriage; hence used *fig.* of the result of any action 1640. Hence **Abo·rtional** *a.* **Abo·rtionist,** one who procures abortion.

Abortive (ăbǭ·ɹtiv). ME. [– (O)Fr. *abortif, -ive* – L. *abortivus*, f. *abort-*, pa. ppl. stem of *aboriri* ABORT *v.*; see -IVE.]

A. *adj.* † **1.** Pertaining to abortion; born prematurely –1664; causing abortion –1753; miscarrying –1662. **2.** Coming to nought 1593. **3.** *Biol.* Arrested in development (see ABORT *v.* 2) 1794.

1. A. be it [the child] *Rich. III*, I. ii. 21. *A. parchment*: that derived from a still-born animal. Also as *sb.* in same sense. Plunged in that a. gulf MILT. *P.L.* II. 441. **2.** A. pride 2 *Hen. VI*, IV. i. 60. An a. attempt SCOTT. **3.** Thorns . . are a. branches 1834.

B. *sb.* [The adj. used *absol.*] † **1.** An a. progeny –1760. † **2.** An a. delivery –1587. † **3.** An imperfect result of an action –1706. † **4.** An a. drug –1647.

3. My conjecture (although it is an a.) HOLLAND. Hence **Abo·rtively** *adv.* **Abo·rtiveness.**

† **Abo·rtive,** *v.* 1615. [f. prec. Cf. NEGATIVE *v.*] To cause abortion –1699; *intr.* to miscarry –1692.

† **Abote,** *ppl. a.* ? = *abeaten* or *abated. Chaucer's Dreme.*

Abought, obs. pa. t. and pple. of ABYE.

Abound (ăbau·nd), *v.*¹ ME. [– OFr. *abunder, abonder* – L. *abundare* overflow, f. *ab*, AB- + *undare* flow, f. *unda* wave. In XIV–XVI spelt *hab-* by association w. L. *habēre* have.] **1.** To overflow; to be plentiful ME. † **2.** To be rich, to have to overflowing –1765. **3.** To abound, be wealthy *in* ME.; teem *with* ME. † **4.** To go at large, expatiate ME. † **5.** To pour forth –1631.

1. To make al grace abounde in you WYCLIF. Rheumaticke diseases doe a. *Mid. N.* II. i. 105. **2.** But I have all and a. *Phil.* 4: 18. **3.** I abounde in joye WYCLIF. To a. in Teares *Wint. T.* II. i. 120. A faithfull man shall a. with blessings *Prov.* 28: 20. **4.** To let others **abound in their own sense** (= follow their own opinion) BURKE. Hence **Abou·nder,** one who abounds. **Abou·nding** *vbl. sb.* abundance; *ppl. a.* full-flowing, plentiful, † affluent.

† **Abou·nd,** *v.*² ME. [f. A- *pref.* 11, or A *particle* = I-¹, Y-, + BOUND *v.*¹] To limit –1627.

About (ăbau·t), *adv.* and *prep.* [OE. *onbūtan*, f. *on* in, on (see A *prep.*¹) + *būtan* outside of; see BUT *prep.*] **A.** (without obj.) *adv.* **I.** Position. **1.** Around the outside; on or towards every side; all round OE. **2.** On any side; near ME. **3.** Nearly, all but — of quantity OE.; of quality 1614.

1. Hannibal byseged hem all aboute TREVISA. *Temp.* V. i. 180. So *cast, look about.* **2.** He hangs a. doing nothing (*mod.*). **3.** A girl of a. seven 1802. A. right DICKENS, finished (*mod.*).

II. Motion. **1.** Round, in revolution OE.; in succession ME. **2.** Half round or less 1535. **3.** In circumference 1598. **4.** In a circuitous course, up and down OE.; hence, on the move, astir; prevailing (as a disease) ME.; with inf. or vbl. sb., on the point of.

1. **To come a.**: to revolve (as time); to come to pass. **To bring a.**: to cause to revolve; bring to pass. To twist a man's neck a. STERNE. Turn and turn v. MAYHEW. **2.** *Turn, face a. To the right a.*: in the opposite direction. *The wrong way a.*: by the wrong end or side. So *The other way a. To bring one a.* (or round), i.e. from illness, etc. *Naut.* To *make, put, go, a.*, to *go a. ship*, on the opposite tack. **3.** In the waste two yards a. *Merry Wives* I. ii. 44. The sure way (though most a.) BACON. **4.** He ledde him a. *Deut.* 32:10. To move furniture a. (*mod.*). A., my Braine *Haml.* II. ii. 617. Small-pox is a. (*mod.*). *To go a. to do*: to endeavour. A. to storm 1665. A. concluding SMEATON.

B. (with obj.) *prep.* **I.** Position. **1.** On the outside of; on or towards every side of; all round OE. **2.** Somewhere near, in or near ME; hence, in attendance on ME.; at hand 1567. **3.** Connection: Attached to as an attribute or circumstance 1603; near so as to meddle with, concerned with ME.; touching, concerning ME. **4.** Of time, and quantity: Near, close to OE.

1. My crown a. my brows TENNYSON. To lay a. one HIERON. **2.** The meadows a. Oxford (*mod.*). Have this (herb) a. you MILT. *Comus* 647. **3.** *A. his business*: away, i.e. to attend to his own affairs. What are you a.? (*mod.*). Much Adoe a. Nothing 1599. Indifferent a. what happens HUME. **4.** Aboute prime CHAUCER, a. midnight SHAKS. A. my stature SHAKS.

II. Motion. **1.** Round (opp. to across, over, or into). *arch.* OE. **2.** To and fro in 1534; hence, frequenting 1593.

1. To beat *a. the bush.* See BUSH. To get a. the Cape DAMPIER. **2.** Cowslips dotted a. the field (*mod.*). A 'blood' or dandy a. town THACKERAY.

Comb.: **a.-sledge,** the largest hammer used by smiths; **-ward, -s** *adv.* trying, being a. to.

† **Abouts, aboutes,** *adv.* and *prep.* ME. [prob. north., with *-es* for *-en.*] A genitival form of ABOUT, still found in HEREABOUTS, etc.

Above (ăbʋ·v). OE. [f. A *prep.*¹ repr. OE. *on*, as in ABOUT, + OE. *bufan*, f. *be* BY *prep.* and *adv.* + *ufan* above. North. and orig. advb.] **A.** (without obj.) *adv.* **1.** Overhead, vertically up, on high OE; in heaven ME. **2.** On the outside; covering all. ? *Obs.* ME. **3.** Higher (in various senses; see quots.). **4.** In addition 1596.

1. The clouds a. *Prov.* 8:28. A wooden stair leading a. DICKENS. Every perfect gift is from aboue *James* 1:17. **3.** Higher in place ME., position or order OE.: A. were the snowy peaks (*mod.*). *A.-written, -said,* etc. † *fig.* Thou shalt be a. and . . not . . beneath *Deut.* 28:13. Higher in rank, etc. ME.: A higher court, etc. Also *ellipt.* The a. will show (*mod.*). **4.** Stand indebted **over and above** *Merch. V.* IV. i. 413.

B. (with obj.) *prep.* **1.** Over; vertically up from; on the top of OE. **2.** Relatively over, covering. ? *Obs.* ME. **3.** Higher than (in various senses; see quots.). **4.** In addition to 1581.

1. The sky that hangs a. our heads SHAKS. **3.** Higher up than OE.; beyond the level or reach of ME.; and *fig.* superior to (the influence of): A. the 45th degree of N. latitude MORSE; *Above ground*: out of the grave, alive; A. the din (*mod.*); A. the anxieties of human love WORDSW. *fig.* Higher in rank or position than ME.: Abune my station SCOTT. Higher in degree or quality: *a. all*, beyond all; *a. measure*, beyond what is meet. Higher in number, quantity, etc.; Not a. once *Haml.* II. ii. 455. A. a hundred were present (*mod.*). **4.** He earns a large sum **over and above** his salary (*mod.*).

C. Elliptically (quasi-*a.* and *sb.*). **1.** By *ellipsis* of a pple. *above* stands attributively, as 'the above explanation'; or *above* may be used absol., as 'the above will show', etc. 1779. † **2.** With a possessive case, *at, to mine,* etc., *above*: something above what I am –1484.

Above-board (ăbʋ·v,bōᵊɹd), *adv.* (and *a.*) 1616. Openly, without concealment. *lit.* and *fig.* Orig. a gambling term.

Abovesaid (ăbʋ·v,se:d), *ppl. a. arch.* ME. Mentioned higher up; aforesaid. So **above-bounden, -cited, -found, -given, -mentioned, -named, -written.**

† **Abow,** *v.* OE. [OE. *ābūgan*, f. A- *pref.* 1 + *būgan* BOW *v.*¹] To bend or make to bend; *fig.* to do homage, submit.

Abracadabra (æ:brăkădæ·bră). 1696. [L., first found in Q. Serenus Sammonicus (II), ult. – Gr. *ΑΒΡΑϹΑΔΑΒΡΑ*, in which *C* (i.e. *S*) was read as *C* (i.e. *K*); rel. to ABRAXAS.] A cabalistic word, written in various arrangements, and used as a charm, to cure agues, etc. A spell; a mysterious word without meaning; gibberish.

The new a. of science, 'organic evolution' 1879.

Abrade (ăbrēⁱ·d), *v.* 1677. [– L. *abradere* scrape off, f. *ab* AB- + *radere* scrape; cf. ABRASE.] **1.** To rub or wear off (a part *from*). **2.** To rub away. *lit.* and *fig.* 1748.

2. To a. the popularity . . of a government 1804. To a. the stomach KANE, rocks LYELL. Hence **Abra·der.**

† **Abraham, Abram,** *a.* 1599. Corrupt ff. AUBURN. *Coriol.* II. iii. 21.

Abraham-man, Abram-man. 1561. [Possibly in allusion to the parable of the beggar Lazarus in *Luke* 16.] One of a class of pretended lunatics who wandered over England seeking alms, after the dissolution of the religious houses. Hence **To sham Abram**: to feign sickness.

† **Abrai·d,** *v*¹. [OE. *abreġdan*, f. A- *pref.* 1 + BRAID *v.*¹] **1.** To wrench out (a sword) –ME. **2.** To start –1600; to startle –1596. **3.** To shout out; *trans.* and *intr.* Also *refl.* To exert oneself; to frequent LYDGATE.

† **Abrai·d,** *v.*² late ME. [f. A- *pref.* 1 + BRAID *v.*² Cf. EMBRAID *v.*¹, UPBRAID.] To upbraid –1599.

Abra·nchial, *a.* 1861. [f. Gr. ἀ- A- *pref.* 14 + βράγχια gills + -AL¹.] = ABRANCHIATE. So **Abra·nchian** *a.* and *sb.*

Abranchiate (ăbræ·ŋkiĕt), *a.* 1855. [f. as prec. + -ATE².] *Zool.* Having no gills.

† **Abra·se,** *ppl. a.* 1600. [– L. *abrasus*; see next.] Rubbed smooth –1688.

Abra·se, *v.* 1593. [– *abras-*, pa. ppl. stem of L. *abradere*; see ABRADE.] To rub off or away; abrade. Hence † **Abra·sing** *vbl. sb.* **Abra·sive** *a.* having the property of abrading.

Abrasion (ăbrēⁱ·ʒən). 1656. [– L. *abrasio*, f. *abras-*; see prec. and -ION.] **1.** Rubbing off or away. *lit.* and *fig.* 1656. **2.** The result of rubbing off; † débris; an abraded place 1740. **3.** *Med.* Wearing away the mucus which covers the membranes by corrosive medicines. Cf. Fr. *abrasion*. 1751.

1. A. of coins CRUMP, of the skin H. M. STANLEY. **2.** A bed-sore . . a simple a. BRYANT.

‖ **Abraum Salts** (a·b,raum sǫlts). 1753. [– G. *abraumsalze* f. *abraum* waste product + *salze* salts.] Mixed salts found at Stassfurt in Prussia, and also in the Isle of Wight, now used for producing chloride of potassium.

‖**Abraxas.** [late L., rel. to ABRACADABRA.] A cabalistic word sometimes inscribed on gems as a charm.

Abray, false f. ABRAID *v.* SPENSER.

Abrazite (æ·brăzeit). 1847. [f. Gr. ἀ- A- *pref.* 14 + βράζειν to boil + -ITE¹ 2 b.] *Min.* = GISMONDITE.

Abrazi·tic, *a.* [f. prec. + -IC.] *Min.* Not effervescing when melted before the blow-pipe.

Abreast (ăbre·st), *adv.* 1450. [f. A *prep.*[1] + BREAST.] **1.** With breasts, or fronts, in a line; side by side (in advancing) 1599. **2.** *Naut.* With the ships equally distant, and parallel 1697. **3.** *Naut.* On a parallel with the beam.

1. A breach that 16 men might enter a. 1675. *A. of*, parallel to, or alongside of something stationary. *lit.* and *fig.* A. of Millbank MARRYAT, of truth LOWELL. *A. with*, keeping up with 1655; often *fig.*

† **Abrenou·nce,** *v.* 1537. [– OFr. *abrenoncier* – late L. *abrenuntiare* f. *ab* AB- + *renuntiare* RENOUNCE *v.*] To repudiate; to contradict –1656.

Many a. [theyr parentes] . . and cast them of LATIMER. var. † **A:brenu·nciate** *v.*

A:brenuncia·tion. *arch.* 1641. [– OFr. *abrenonciation* or late L. *abrenuntiatio*; see prec., RENUNCIATION.] Renunciation; retractation.

† **Abre·ption.** 1681. [– late L. *abreptio*, f. *abrept-*, pa. ppl. stem of *abripere* snatch away.] Snatching away; separation.

‖ **Abreuvoir** (abrövwa·r). [Fr., f. *abreuver* cause to drink.] In masonry, an interstice to be filled up with mortar or cement.

Abricock, -coct, -cot, obs. ff. APRICOT.

Abridge (ăbri·dʒ), *v.* ME. [– OFr. *abregier*, *abreger* :– late L. *ab-*, *adbreviare* f. *ab* off or *ad* to + *breviare* shorten, f. *brevis* short; see BRIEF *a.*] Always *trans.* **1.** To shorten in duration. **2.** To make shorter in words, while retaining the sense; to epitomize ME.; esp. (*Law*) to shorten a count or declaration 1691. **3.** To cut short, curtail; *esp.* rights, privileges, etc. **4.** With a person :—Constr. *of*, also *from*, *in*. To stint, curtail in, debar from. ME.

1. God sal abrege his days HAMPOLE. To a. a visit SMOLLETT, labour HT. MARTINEAU. **2.** Efnard . . abridged the French Psalter 1611. **3.** To a. a train FULLER, the naturall Liberty of man HOBBES. **4.** Abridged in his freedom SOUTH. Hence **Abri·dgeable, -gable** *a.* capable of, or liable to, abridgement. **Abri·dgedly** *adv.* **Abri·dger.**

Abridgement, -gment (ăbri·dʒmĕnt). [– (O)Fr. *abrégement*; see prec. and -MENT.] **1.** The act of abridging; *fig.* a means of whiling away the time; the being abridged 1797. **2.** An epitome or compendium of a larger work 1523, or of a subject 1609. **3.** *Law.* Omission of parts of a plaint or demand 1641.

1. Abridgements of liberty MACAULAY. What a. (? = means of shortening) haue you for this euening *Mids. N.* v. i. 39. **2.** A mere meagre a. FREEMAN. To be Master of the Sea, is an a. of Monarchy BACON. An a. of all that was pleasant in man GOLDSM. *Retal.* 94.

Abroach (ăbrōᵘ·tʃ), *adv.* ME. [– Anglo-Fr. *abroche*, f. OFr. *abrochier*; see next, A- *pref.* 1.] **1.** Broached, pierced. Also *fig.* **2.** In a state to be diffused; astir 1528.

1. A butt of strong beer a. SMOLLETT. **2.** Who set this auncient quarrell new a.? *Rom. & Jul.* I. i. 111. Phr. **To set abroach**: to pierce and leave running; to set a-foot.

† **Abroa·ch,** *v.* ME. [– OFr. *abrochier*, *abrocher*, f. *a-* AD- + *brochier* to prick, pierce; see BROACH *v.*[1]] To pierce (a cask, etc.). Also *fig.* –1530.

Abroad (ăbrǭ·d). ME. [f. A *prep.*[1] + BROAD *sb.*]

A. *adv.* **1.** Widely, over a broad surface; widely scattered; widely apart, wide spread; hence, *Naut.* = *spread.* **2.** At large; *fig.* current 1500. **3.** Out of one's house ME., or home country 1450. **4.** Wide of the mark; 'out' 1838.

1. The love of God is shed a. in our hearts *Rom.* 5:5. Sands [blown] like Sibels leaues a. *Tit. A.* IV. i. 106. With Dutch colours a. 1667. **2.** Ther's villanie a. *L.L.L.* I. i. 190. **3.** Dining a. with a friend BORROW. The badger ventures a. at dusk (*mod.*). Imported *from abroad* MACAULAY. So, I must a. (*ellipt.* for *go a.*). **4.** Only a little a. DICKENS.

B. *prep.* [With place expressed.] *arch.* Throughout 1523. Also as *adj.*

A. the world BAXTER.

Abrogate (æ·brŏgĕt), *a.* and *pple. arch.* 1460. [– L. *abrogatus*, pa. pple. of *abrogare* repeal, f. *ab* AB- + *rogare* propose a law; see -ATE[2].] Repealed.

Abrogate (æ·brŏgeⁱt), *v.* 1526. [– *abrogat-*, pa. ppl. stem of L. *abrogare*; see prec., -ATE[3].] **1.** To repeal (a law, etc.). **2.** To do away with 1588.

1. To a. a Law by the Sword MILT. To a. the pope's power FULLER. **2.** Please you to a. scurilitie *L.L.L.* IV. ii. 55. Hence **A·brogable** *a.* **A·brogative** *a.* having the quality of abrogating. **A·brogator.**

Abrogation (æbrŏgēⁱ·ʃən). 1535. [– Fr. *abrogation* or L. *abrogatio* repeal of a law, f. as prec. + -ION.] The act of abrogating. (Not now used of persons or concrete things.)

The A. of King James by the people S. JOHNSON. A. of a right 1866.

Abroo·d, *adv.* ME. [A *prep.*[1] + BROOD *sb.*] On its brood or eggs. Also *fig.*

† **Abroo·k,** *v.* [f. A *pref.* 11 + BROOK *v.*] To brook. 2 *Hen. VI*, II. iv. 10.

Abrupt (ăbrɒ·pt), *a.* and *sb.* 1583. [– L. *abruptus* broken off, steep, pa. pple. of *abrumpere* break off, f. *ab* AB- + *rumpere* break.] † **1.** Broken away (from restraint). **2.** Broken off. ? *Obs.* 1607. **3.** Characterized by sudden interruption or change 1591. **4.** Precipitous 1618. **5. a.** *Bot.* Truncated. **b.** *Geol.* Suddenly cropping out. **6.** As *sb.* An a. place; an abyss. (Only in MILT. *P.L.* II. 409.)

3. Your a. departure 1 *Hen. VI*, II. iii. 30. The a. style . . hath many breaches B. JONS. **4.** A. ravines STANLEY. Hence **Abru·ptness** (in senses 2, 3, 4).

† **Abru·pt,** *v.* 1643. [– *abrupt-*, pa. ppl. stem of L. *abrumpere*; see prec.] To break off, sever. Sir T. BROWNE. Hence **Abru·pted** *ppl. a.* **Abru·ptedly** *adv.*

Abruption (ăbrɒ·pʃən). 1606. [– L. *abruptio*, f. as prec.; see -ION.] **1.** A breaking off, an interruption. *arch.* **2.** A sudden breaking away (of portions of a mass) 1657.

1. Sudden a. of all intercourse MILMAN. **2.** Removal . . by a. BRYANT.

Abruptly (ăbrɒ·ptli), *adv.* 1590. [f. ABRUPT *a.* + -LY[2].] **1.** In an abrupt manner; see ABRUPT *a.* 2, 3, 4. **2.** *Bot.* As in *abruptly pinnate*, pinnate without an intermediate leaflet at the end.

Abs-, *pref.*, repr. L. *abs-*, the form of AB- off, away, from, used bef. c-, q-, t-.

Abscess (æ·bsĕs). 1543. [– L. *abscessus* a going away, abscess (Celsus), f. *abscess-*, pa. ppl. stem of *abscedere*, f. *abs* ABS- + *cedere* go; see CEDE *v.*] A collection of pus or purulent matter formed by a morbid process in a cavity of the body. Hence **A·bscessed** *ppl. a.*

† **Absce·ssion.** 1599. [– L. *abscessio* a going away, f. as prec.; see -ION.] **1.** Departure; cessation of a pain, etc. –1659. **2.** = ABSCESS. 1610.

Abscind (ăbsi·nd), *v. arch.* 1657. [– L. *abscindere* cut off, f. *ab* AB- + *scindere* cut asunder.] To cut off. *lit.* and *fig.*

Absciss(e (æ·bsis). Pl. **-es**; oftener as L. **abscissa** (ăbsi·sa), pl. **– æ**; also **-as.** 1698. [– mod.L. *abscissa* (sc. *linea*), subst. use of fem. pa. pple. of *abscindere*; see prec.] *Geom.* A line or distance cut off; *spec.* the portion of a given line intercepted between a fixed point within it, and an ordinate drawn to it from a given point without it.

Abscission (ăbsi·ʒən). 1612. [– L. *abscissio*, f. *abscindere* ABSCIND *v.*; see -ION.] A cutting off (*lit.* and *fig.*); † the state of being cut off –1649. var. **Absci·sion.**

Abscond (ăbskǫ·nd), *v.* 1565. [– L. *abscondere* hide or stow away, f. *abs* ABS- + *condere* put together, stow. Cf. OFr. *abscondre.*] † **1.** *trans.* To hide away. *Obs.* or *arch.* 1612. Also *refl.* **2.** *intr.* (refl. pron. omitted.) To hide oneself; to go away hurriedly and secretly 1565.

1. The Alps a. their heads POMFRET. **2.** Some few absconded CARLYLE. Hence **Absco·ndedly** *adv.* **Absco·ndence.** **Absco·nder,** a runaway from justice.

Absee, obs. f. A B C.

Absence (æ·bsĕns). ME. [– (O)Fr. – L. *absentia*, f. *absent-* ABSENT; see -ENCE.] **1.** The state of being absent or away; also the time of duration of such state. **b.** *poet.* An absent form or face. **2.** Absence (*of mind*): inattention; abstraction 1710. **3.** At Eton College, roll-call 1856.

1. Not when I was present only, but now moche more in myne a. TINDALE *Phil.* 2:12. A. has plac'd her in a fairer light YOUNG. A. of the sonne ME. **2.** Disquietude, a. of mind is on every face CARLYLE. var. † **A·bsency.**

Absent (æ·bsĕnt). ME. [– (O)Fr. *absent*, – L. *absent-*, pa. ppl. stem of *absens*, functioning as pres. pple. of *abesse* be away, f. *ab* AB- + *esse* be; see -ENT.] **A.** *adj.* **1.** Away, not present; wanting, not existing 1718. **2.** Absent-minded, paying no attention to present objects, etc. 1710. † **B.** *sb.* [sc. *person*] –1699.

A. 1. An a. friend 1716. Crevasses . . are . . totally a. TYNDALL. **2.** I became a. and thoughtful SMOLLETT. Hence **A·bsently** *adv.* with absence of mind. **A·bsentness,** absent-mindedness.

Comb.: **a.-minded** *a.* = ABSENT 2; **-mindedly** *adv.* = ABSENTLY; **-mindedness** = ABSENCE 2.

Abse·nt, *v.* ME. [– (O)Fr. *absenter* or late L. *absentare* keep away, be away, f. as prec.] **1.** *trans.* To keep away 1530. Also *refl.* † **2.** *intr.* To stay away –1709. † **3.** *trans.* (*from* omitted). To leave 1695.

1. A. thee from felicitie awhile *Haml.* v. ii. 358. **3.** To a. the kingdom 1695. Hence **Abse·nted** *ppl. a.* **Abse·nter,** one who absents himself. **Abse·nting** *vbl. sb.* being or going away. † **Abse·ntment,** staying away.

Absenta·tion. 1800. [f. ABSENT *v.* + -ATION, after PRESENTATION.] Absenting oneself.

Absentee (æbsĕntī·). 1537. [f. ABSENT *v.* + -EE[1].] One who is absent on any occasion. *spec.* A landlord, etc., who lives away from his country or home. Also *attrib.*

Occasional absentees for business, health, or diversion SWIFT. A. proprietors HALLAM. In 157 benefices the incumbent was an a. HT. MARTINEAU. Hence **Absentee·ism** 1829, **Absentee·ship,** the practice or condition of being an a.

Absey, -sie, obs. f. A B C.

Absinth(e (æ·bsinþ, Fr. absæ̃nt). 1612. [– Fr. *absinthe* – L. *absinthium* – Gr. ἀψίνθιον wormwood.] **1.** The plant *Absinthium* or wormwood. **2.** Essence of wormwood; also *fig.* 1865. **3.** A liqueur originally distilled from wine and wormwood 1854. Hence **Absi·nthial** *a.* pertaining to wormwood; bitter. **Absi·nthian** *a.* **Absi·nthiate** *v.* to impregnate with wormwood. **Absi·nthic** *a.* belonging to a., as *absinthic acid.* **Absi·nthine** *a.* having the nature of a.; bitter. **A·bsinthism,** a disease like alcoholism, arising from a.

Absinthin (ăbsi·nþin). 1853. [f. L. *absinthium* (see prec.) + -IN[1].] *Chem.* The bitter principle of wormwood, *Artemisia absinthium.*

Absinthium (ăbsi·nþiŏm). ME. [L., see ABSINTH(E.] *Bot.* The wormwood, *Artemisia absinthium* of Linnæus, a bitter and aromatic plant.

Absinthole (ăbsi·nþoᵘl). 1879. [f. ABSINTH(E + *-ole*; see -OL 3.] *Chem.* $C_{10}H_{16}O$. A liquid camphor obtained from the oil of wormwood.

Absis, obs. f. APSIS.

† **Absi·st,** *v.* 1614. [– L. *absistere* withdraw, f. *ab* AB- + *sistere* stand.] To desist.

† **Absoil, -soyle,** *v.* 1450. [– OFr. *absoillir*, etc., refash. from *asoillir* ASSOIL *v.* after L. *absolvere.*] = ASSOIL; to absolve.

† **Absolent, -solete,** erron. ff. due to a confusion between ABSOLUTE, 'completed', and OBSOLETE.

Absolute (æ·bsŏliut), *a.* ME. [– L. *absolutus* freed, completed, pa. pple. of L. *absolvere* ABSOLVE; partly infl. by OFr. *absolut* (earlier *asolu*, mod. *absolu*). The senses are mostly Latin.] Orig. a *pple.*; then *adj.* Formerly compared *absoluter*, *-est.*

I. † **1.** *pple.* Detached, disengaged *from* ME. † **2.** Untrammelled, absorbed *in* –1483; essential ME.

II. 1. Absolute in quality or degree; perfect ME. **2.** Complete, entire 1574. **3.** Pure, mere 1563.

1. A. counsils 1550. Masters of the a. art of language RUSKIN. **2.** An a. *Johannes fac totum* GREENE. An A. Impossibility CUDWORTH. **3.** *A. Alcohol*, perfectly free from water.

III. 1. Absolute in position or relation; independent 1533. Hence, **2.** Arbitrary, despotic 1612. **3.** *Gram.* Detached from the usual syntactic construction, as in *ablative absolute* 1527. **4.** Real, actual; opp. to *relative* and *comparative* 1666.

1. God's a. power TINDALE. A. owners 1576. **2.** A. Monarchy is Tyranny; but a. Democracy is Tyranny and Anarchy both LD. BOLINGBROKE. **4.** A. misery, but happiness only comparative JOHNSON.

IV. Free from condition or mental limitation. † **1.** Positive –1676. **2.** Unqualified, unconditional (*esp.* in *Logic*) 1625. **3.** *Metaph.* Existing without relation to any other being; self-existent (*mod.*). **4.** *Metaph.* Capable of being known or conceived out of relation; unconditioned (*mod.*). **5.** *Metaph.* Considered apart from its being subjective or objective 1809.

1. I am a. 'Twas very Cloten *Cymb.* IV. ii. 106. **2.** My thoughts were sincere and a. CHARLES I. An a. proposition BOWEN. **3.** By the A. is meant that which exists in and by itself, having no necessary relation to any other being MANSEL. **4.** Whatever can be known (or conceived) out of relation . . is the known A. 1856.

¶ In the metaphysical uses the word tends to become substantival: *the Absolute*, i.e. that which is absolute.

Absolutely (æ·bsŏliutli), *adv.* 1489. [f. prec. + -LY².] In an ABSOLUTE manner, or degree; without condition, or limitation.

Absoluteness (æ·bsŏliutnĕs). 1570. [f. as prec. + -NESS.] The quality of being ABSOLUTE, in various senses. (See ABSOLUTE *a.*) Also catachr. for *Obsoleteness.*

Absolution (æbsŏliū·ʃən). ME. [–(O)Fr., – L. *absolutio*, f. *absolut-*, pa. ppl. stem of *absolvere* ABSOLVE *v.*; see -ION.] **1.** An absolving, or formal setting free (*from* guilt, sentence, or obligation); remission (*of* sin or penance). **2.** *spec.* Remission of sins declared by eccl. authority. (*The earliest use.*) ME. Also, the formula of remission 1520. **3.** Forgiveness of offences generally ME. † **4.** *Rom. Law.* A legal acquittal 1600. †**5.** Delivery (of words) –1637.

1. A bull of a. from oaths . . taken STUBBS. **2.** Without Confession to a Priest no a. 1638. The A., . . to be pronounced by the Priest alone, standing *Comm. Prayer* (Rubric). **3.** A. after the fact FREEMAN. **5.** The composition [of some language] full, the a. plenteous B. JONS.

Absolutism (æ·bsŏliutiz'm). 1753. [f. ABSOLUTE *a.* + -ISM, after Fr. *-isme.*] The practice of, or adherence to, the absolute. **1.** *Theol.* The dogma of God's acting absolutely as to salvation; the doctrine of predestination 1753. **2.** *Polit.* The practice of absolute government; despotism 1830.

Absolutist (æ·bsŏliutist), *sb.* and *a.* 1830. [f. as prec. + -IST, after Fr. *-iste.*] **1.** *Polit.* A partisan of absolutism in government 1830. **2.** *Metaph.* One who maintains the absolute identity of subject and object 1856. **3.** *adj.* Despotic 1837.

Absolutory (ăbsǫ·liutəri), *a.* 1640. [– L. *absolutorius* serving for acquittal; see ABSOLUTE *a.* and -ORY².] Absolving.

Absolve (ăbsǫ·lv, ăbz-), *v.* 1535. [– L. *absolvere* free, acquit, f. *ab* AB- + *solvere* to loose. Replacing ASSOIL.] **1.** To set or pronounce free (*from* guilt, etc.; *from the consequences of* crime or sin) 1538. **2.** *spec.* To give absolution to; also with *of* or *for* 1535. **3.** To remit (a sin or crime) 1592. **4.** To pronounce not guilty; *esp.* in Rom. Law 1628. **5.** To set free (*from*, † *of* obligations) 1649. † **6.** To clear up, resolve –1667. † **7.** To clear off (a task, etc.) –1801.

1. Absolved from any notorious crime CLARENDON. **2.** To make confession, and to be absolu'd *Rom. & Jul.* III. v. 233. I dare not a. him of robbing a priest KINGSLEY. **3.** The Pope for pay absolueth euery thing 1592. **4.** Absolves the just, and dooms the guilty POPE. **5.** To a. himselfe of those ties MILT. Hence **Abso·lvable** *a.* † **Absolvatory**, erron. f. ABSOLUTORY, q.v. **Abso·lved** *ppl. a.* set free, † solved. **Abso·lver,** one who pronounces absolution, or acquits. **Abso·lving** *vbl. sb.* acquitting, † solving.

Absolvent (ăbsǫ·lvĕnt, ăbz-). 1651. [–*absolvent-*, pres. ppl. stem of L. *absolvere*; see prec. and -ENT.] *ppl. a.* Acquitting 1837. As *sb.* One who absolves 1651.

Absonant (æ·bsŏnănt), *a.* 1564. [f. as foll. + -ANT; cf. *consonant, dissonant.*] Discordant, harsh. Also *fig.* Const. *to, from.*

†**Absonous** (æ·bsŏnəs), *a.* 1622. [f. L. *absonus* out of tune (f. *ab* AB- + *sonus* sound) + -OUS.] *lit.* Out of tune; *fig.* incongruous. Const. *to.*

Absorb (ăbsǭ·ɹb), *v.* Pa. pple. **absorbed,** formerly **absorpt.** 1490. [– (O)Fr. *absorber* or L. *absorbēre* swallow up, f. *ab* AB- + *sorbēre* suck in.] **I.** † **1.** To swallow up; as water, etc.; also *fig.* –1800. **2.** Hence, To incorporate 1553. **3.** To engross the attention or faculties 1830.

1. To be absorpt . . in a lake of fire T. BURNET. **2.** *To be absorbed*, to be swallowed up, so as no longer to exist apart. Into the English nation his own followers were gradually absorbed FREEMAN. **3.** To get absorbed in a book KANE.

II. 1. To suck or drink in 1626. **2.** To take up by chemical or molecular action 1707.

1. The clay refuses to a. the water HUXLEY. **2.** It is possible to a. hydrogen in certain metals ROSCOE. Hence **Absorbabi·lity,** the quality of being absorbable. **Abso·rbable** *a.* capable of being absorbed. **Abso·rbed** *ppl. a.* swallowed up; *fig.* engrossed. **Abso·rbedly** *adv.* with engrossed attention. **Abso·rbedness,** engrossed attention. **Abso·rber,** one who, or that which, absorbs. **Abso·rbing** *ppl. a.* swallowing, imbibing; incorporating; *fig.* engrossing. **Abso·rbingly** *adv.*

Absorbency (ăbsǭ·ɹbĕnsi). 1762. [f. as next; see -ENCE, -ENCY.] † **1.** The action of absorbing. **2.** The quality of being absorbent 1859.

Absorbent (ăbsǭ·ɹbĕnt). 1718. [– *absorbent-*, pres. ppl. stem of L. *absorbēre* ABSORB; see -ENT.] **A.** *adj.* Absorbing; absorptive.

B. *sb.* **1.** An absorbing substance, *esp.* chalk, magnesia, etc., in *Med.*, which absorb the acidity of the stomach. Also *fig.* **2.** *Physiol.* (in *pl.*) The vessels (e.g. the lacteals in animals, the extremities of the roots in plants) through which the process of absorption is carried on 1753.

1. *fig.* The country gentlemen, the absorbents of every prejudice LD. COCKBURN.

† **Absorbi·tion.** [– late L. *absorbitio* a swallowing up (Augustine), f. L. *sorbitio* a drink, broth, f. *sorbēre* suck in; see ABSORB, -ITION.] = ABSORPTION. SIR T. BROWNE.

Absorpt (ăbsǭ·ɹpt), *ppl. a. arch.* 1528. [– *absorpt-*, pa. ppl. stem of L. *absorbēre* ABSORB.] = later ABSORBED.

A. in yellow care 1736.

Absorption (ăbsǭ·ɹpʃən). 1597. [– L. *absorptio*, f. *absorpt-*; see prec., -ION.] **I.** † **1.** The swallowing up of bodies –1753. **2.** The swallowing up by inclusion in or assimilation to something else, *esp.* (*Med.* and *Path.*) of tissues or deposits 1741. **3.** Engrossment of the faculties 1855.

1. The a. or burial 1597. **2.** The a. of dialects by the Latin 1860, of peasant-holdings SEELEY. **3.** The a. of the English mind in the war DICKENS.

II. 1. The sucking in of fluid, light, etc. 1744. Also *attrib.* **2.** *Physiol.* The imbibing of fluids by the vessels and tissues of the body, *esp.* by the lacteals of the intestine 1753.

1. A. of radiant heat TYNDALL. **2.** The functions of digestion and a. CARPENTER.

Absorptive (ăbsǭ·ɹptiv), *a.* 1664. [f. as prec. + -IVE.] Having the quality of absorbing. *fig.* Engrossing. Hence **Abso·rptiveness. A:bsorpti·vity.**

Absquatulate (æbskwǫ·tiulēⁱt), *v.* 1830. [A joc. U.S. formation with reminiscence of *abscond, squattle* decamp, *perambulate.*] *intr.* To depart hurriedly or secretly, decamp, abscond.

Abstain (ăbstēⁱ·n), *v.* ME. [– AFr. *astener*, = (O)Fr. *abstenir*, :– L. *abstinēre* to withhold, f. *abs* ABS- + *tenēre* hold. The form *abstain* is – the tonic stem of OFr. *abstenir.*] † **1.** *refl.* To keep *oneself* (*of, from*) –1535. **2.** *intr.* To refrain (*from*) ME.; *esp.* from wine, etc. 1534. † **3.** *trans.* To keep back –1658.

1. To absteyne them selues from Idols COVERDALE. **2.** Many . . nolens volens . . do asteine [from meate] BOORDE. **3.** To a. men from marying MILT. Hence **Abstai·ning** *vbl. sb.* = ABSTINENCE; *ppl. a.* practising abstinence.

Abstainer (ăbstēⁱ·nəɹ). 1535. [f. prec.] One who abstains; *esp.* one who abstains from alcoholic drinks; in older writers a Nazarite.

Abstemious (ăbstī·miəs), *a.* 1610. [f. L. *abstemius*, f. *abs* ABS- + base of *temetum* intoxicating drink; see -OUS.] **1.** Dispensing with wine and rich food; temperate; sparing 1624. **2.** Abstinent (from other things). *rare.* 1610.

1. An absteinous life HEYWOOD. Mother and father were a. CARLYLE. The meal of the Saracens was a. SCOTT. **2.** Be more a., Or else good night your vow *Temp.* IV. i. 53. Hence **Abste·mious-ly** *adv.*, **-ness.**

Abstention (ăbste·nʃən). 1521. [– Fr., or late L. *abstentio*, f. *abstent-*, pa. ppl. stem of L. *abstinēre* ABSTAIN; see -ION.] † **1.** The act of restraining –1653. **2.** The act or state of refraining 1624. Hence **Abste·ntionist,** a partisan of a. **Abste·ntious** *a.* self-restraining.

Absterge (ăbstə̄·ɹdʒ), *v.* 1541. [–(O)Fr. *absterger* or L. *abstergēre* wipe away, f. *abs* ABS- + *tergēre* wipe.] To wipe away; to cleanse; *fig.* to purge.

Thynges yᵗ absterge or wasshe moderatly R. COPLAND. Hence **Abste·rgent** *a.* cleansing; *sb.* [sc. *substance*]. **Abste·rsion,** the act or process of cleansing or purging. **Abste·rsive** *a.* having the quality of cleansing or purging; *sb.* [sc. *agent*]. **Abste·rsiveness. Abste·rsory** *a.* abstersive.

† **Abste·rse,** *v.* 1646. [– *absters-*, pa. ppl. stem of L. *abstergēre*; see prec.] = ABSTERGE.

Abstinence (æ·bstinĕns). ME. [–(O)Fr., – L. *abstinentia*, f. as ABSTINENT; see -ENCE.] **1.** The action or practice of abstaining (*from*) ME. *spec.* Abstaining from hostilities, an armistice ME. **2.** *absol.* Continence (the oldest sense); fasting; abstaining from alcoholic beverages, total abstinence ME.

1. Jewish a. from certaine kinds of meates HOOKER. The truce or a. BURTON. **2.** Agayns glotonye the remedie is a. CHAUCER. A. ingenders maladies *L.L.L.* IV. iii. 259.

Abstinency (æ·bstinĕnsi). 1576. [f. as prec.; see -ENCY.] The quality of being abstinent; fasting; a fast. (Never used with *from.*)

Abstinent (æ·bstinĕnt). ME. [–(O)Fr. *abstinent* – *abstinent-*, pres. ppl. stem of L. *abstinēre* ABSTAIN; see -ENT.] **A.** *adj.* Refraining; *esp.* from indulgence of appetite. **B.** *sb.* One who abstains, a faster. In *Eccl. Hist.* the *Abstinents* were a sect who appeared in the 3rd c. Hence **A·bstinently** *adv.*

Abstract (æ·bstrækt). ME. [– obs. Fr. *abstract* or L. *abstractus*, pa. pple. of *abstrahere*, f. *abs* ABS- + *trahere* draw.]

A. *pple.* and *adj.* † **1.** Derived –1496. † **2.** = ABSTRACTED 1. Const. *from.* –1765. **3.** = ABSTRACTED 2. *arch.* 1509. **4.** Separated from matter, practice, or particulars; ideal; abstruse. Opp. to *concrete.* 1557. **5.** *absol.* 'The abstract'; the ideal 1615. Hence **A·bstract-ly** *adv.*, **-ness.**

2. The more a. from the body . . the more fit [etc.] J. MORRIS. **3.** Steady step and a. air 1860. A. numbers 1557, names HOBBES, substances CUDWORTH, ideas COLERIDGE, science HERSCHELL, reasoning 1870. **5.** Justice in the a., is nothing 1628.

B. *sb.* **1.** One thing concentrating in itself the virtues of several; a compendium 1561; *spec.* a summary or epitome 1528. Also *attrib.* **2.** An abstract term 1530.

1. A man who is the a. of all faults, That all men follow *Ant. & Cl.* I. iv. 9. An a. of all that was said BURNET. **Abstract of title** (*Law*): an epitome of the evidences of ownership. **2.** Substantives . . suche as the Logicians call abstractes 1530.

Abstract (ăbstræ·kt), *v.* 1542. [partly – prec., partly – *abstract-*, pa. ppl. stem of L. *abstrahere* (see prec.).] **1.** *trans.* To withdraw, take away; *euphem.* to take away secretly, etc.; to purloin 1542. Also *absol.* † *Chem.* To extract –1725. **2.** *trans.* To draw off; disengage *from* 1557. *absol.* To divert. **3.** *refl.* To withdraw oneself, to retire *from. lit.* and *fig.* 1671. **4.** To separate in mental conception; to consider apart from the concrete 1612. † **5.** To derive. Cf. ABSTRACT *a.* 1. 1610. **6.** To epitomize 1678.

1. The brande abstracted and abjected BOORDE. Property abstracted by the Arabs 1852. **2.** To a. the mixed people each from other SELDEN. To soothe and to a. LAMB. **3.** To a. oneself from one's own interest STEELE. *Abstracting from*, withdrawing in thought from (*Obs.* or *arch.*). Abstracting from his crimes JENISON. **4.** We must . . a. the notions of time, of space, and of matter GIBBON. **6.** This system I . . abstracted GIBBON. Hence **Abstra·cter.**

Abstracted (ăbstræ·kted), *ppl. a.* 1615. [f. prec.] **1.** Drawn off; separate, apart *from* 1660. **2.** Withdrawn from the contemplation of present objects; absent in mind 1643. † **3.** Separated from the concrete, ideal; abstruse (replaced by ABSTRACT *a.* 4) –1823.

1. The Evil one a. stood From his own evil MILT. **2.** An a. thinker 1731, mood SCOTT. **3.** A. ideas of virtue JOHNSON. Hence **Abstra·ctedly** *adv.* **Abstra·ctedness,** † abstractness; † disinterestedness; absence (of mind); ideality.

Abstraction (æbstræ·kʃən). 1549. [–(O)Fr., or late L. *abstractio*; see ABSTRACT and -ION.] **1.** The act of abstracting (see ABSTRACT *v.* 1). **2.** *Chem.* The drawing off, or exhaling away, a menstruum from the subject it had been put to dissolve; distillation; cohobation 1753. **3.** The act of separating in thought 1647. **4.** The result of abstracting; a mere idea; something visionary 1644. **5.** Seclusion from things of sense 1649. **6.** Absence of mind 1790.

1. Justice must have . . a. from all affections R. COKE. A wrongful a. of wealth from [etc.] MILL. **3.** A. is thus . . a negation to one or more objects, in consequence of its [the mind's] concentration on another SIR W. HAMILTON. **4.** Death is a mighty a., like Night HAZLITT. **6.** Wrapped up in grave a. BOSWELL. Hence **Abstra·ctionist,** one who deals with abstractions. † **A:bstracti·tious** *a.* resulting from a.

Abstractive (æbstræ·ktiv). 1490. [–med.L. *abstractivus*, f. as prec.; see -IVE.] **A.** *adj.* Of abstracting tendency or character (see ABSTRACT *v.* 1, 4, 6). **B.** *sb.* Anything abstractive; *spec.* an abstract 1611. Hence **Abstra·ctively** *adv.* in the abstract; separately. **Abstra·ctiveness.**

† **Abstru·de,** *v.* 1627. [– L. *abstrudere*; see next.] To thrust away.

Abstruse (æbstrū·s), *a.* 1599. [–Fr. *abstrus, -use*, or L. *abstrusus*, pa. pple. of *abstrudere* conceal, f. *abs* ABS- + *trudere* thrust.] † **1.** Hidden, secret –1762. **2.** Remote from apprehension; recondite 1599.

1. Hidden in the most a. dungeons SHELTON. **2.** The abstruser parts of a discourse SWIFT. Hence **Abstru·sely** *adv.* **Abstru·seness. Abstru·sity,** (*arch.*) abstruseness; anything abstruse.

† **Absu·me,** *v.* 1596. [– L. *absumere* take away, f. *ab* AB- + *sumere* take.] To waste away –1756. Hence † **Absu·mption,** the process of wasting away –1661.

Absurd (æbsɒ̄·ɹd). 1557. [– Fr. *absurde* or L. *absurdus* incongruous, f. *ab* AB- (as in *absonus* ABSONOUS) + a base perh. identical with that of *susurrus* murmur.] **A.** *adj.* † **1.** *Mus.* Inharmonious 1617. **2.** Out of harmony with reason or propriety; in mod. use, plainly opposed to reason, and *hence* ridiculous, silly 1557. † **B.** *sb.* [sc. *thing*] –1635. Now ABSURDITY.

2. A fault, To reason most a. *Haml.* I. ii. 103. Froward and A. men for Businesse BACON. Don't be a. 1874. Hence **Absu·rdly** *adv.* **Absu·rdness.**

Absurdity (æbsɒ̄·ɹdīti). 1528. [–Fr. *absurdité* or L. *absurditas*; see ABSURD, -ITY.] † **1.** *Mus.* Lack of harmony 1674. **2.** The state or quality of being ABSURD (sense 2); folly 1528. **3.** Anything absurd, e.g. a statement, action, or custom 1528.

2. The a. of delaying reformation JOHNSON. A piece of prolix a. CARLYLE. **3.** An a. in Philosophy SIR T. BROWNE. Anachronisms or absurdities MCCARTHY.

Absurdum (æbsɒ̄·ɹdɒ̆m). [L., subst. use of n. sing. of *absurdus* ABSURD.] An absurd or illogical conclusion or condition. See REDUCTIO AD ABSURDUM.

Abthain, -thane (æ·bþēⁱn). 1535. [– med.L. *abthania* for Gael. *abdhaine* abbacy.] **1.** Erron. use: a 'Superior Thane'. **2.** An abbacy (*Sc.*). Hence **A·bthainry, -thanrie,** an abbacy; the territory and jurisdiction of an abbot. **A·bthanage,** the jurisdiction of the supposed ABTHANE.

Abumbral (æ:bˌɒ·mbrăl), *a.* *Zool.* Short for next.

Abumbrellar (æ:bˌɒmbre·lăɹ), *a.* [f. L. *ab* AB- + UMBRELLA, the disk of *Acalepha*, + -AR¹.] In sea-blubbers: Pertaining to that surface of the *velum* which is turned away from the 'umbrella'; opp. to *adumbrellar.*

‖**Abuna** (ăbū·nă). 1635. [Eth.; = 'our father'.] The Patriarch of the Abyssinian Ch.

Abundance (ăbɒ·ndăns). ME. [– OFr. (*h*)*abundance* (mod. *abondance*), – L. *abundantia*, f. *abundant-*, pres. ppl. stem of *abundare* ABOUND; see -ANCE.] **1.** Overflowing state or condition; superfluity; hence, *loosely*, plentifulness ME. **2.** A large quantity, or (less correctly) number ME. **3.** Affluence ME.

1. The . . aboundance of his love 1535. **2.** A. of good things DE FOE. A. who want a morsel of bread FIELDING. Also † with nouns: Wine a. HOBBES; and † adjs.: A. better SWIFT. **3.** The a. of the rich will not suffer him to sleep *Ecclus* 5:12. var. † **Abu·ndancy.**

Abundant (ăbɒ·ndănt), *a.* ME. [– L. *abundant-*; see prec. and -ANT.] **1.** Overflowing, more than enough; plentiful; (orig. of fluids) *c* 1450. **2.** Possessing in superfluity; wealthy (*in*, † *of*) ME. Also quasi-*adv.*

1. Where synne is haboundant charity waxeth colde 1509. **2.** In labours moare aboundant TINDALE. Hence **Abu·ndantly** *adv.*

Abune, obs. north. form of ABOVE.

Aburst (ăbɒ̄·ɹst), *adv.* ME. [f. A *prep.*¹ 11 + BURST *sb.*] † **1.** In a burst (of rage, etc.). **2.** Bursting (*mod.*).

Abuse (ăbiū·z), *v.* ME. [–(O)Fr. *abuser*, Rom. **abusare*, f. *abus-*; see next.] † **1.** *Sc.* To disuse –1471. **2.** To misuse; to take a bad advantage of 1413. † **3.** To misrepresent; to adulterate. *refl.* To make false pretensions. –1749. † **4.** To misuse any one's confidence; to impose upon him –1776. *refl.* and *pass.* To be deceived –1743. **5.** To ill-use 1556. **6.** To violate. *arch.* 1553. **7.** To wrong with words; to malign 1604.

2. The liberty of the press may be abused JUNIUS. To a. an opportunity SCOTT, authority FREEMAN. **3.** Abused by translators 1702. He hath been grossly abused to you FIELDING. **4.** 'The serpent me abusit' LYNDESAY. **5.** To a. one's wife and family (*mod.*). **7.** Of life as honest As you that thus a. me *Oth.* v. i. 123. Hence **Abu·sed** *ppl. a.* worn out; misused; deceived. **Abu·sedly** *adv.* **Abusee·**, correl. to ABUSER¹. † **Abu·sement,** a misleading. **Abu·ser¹**, one who abuses (in senses 2, 4, 6, 7).

Abuse (ăbiū·s), *sb.* 1486. [–(O)Fr. *abus* or L. *abusus*, – *abus-*, pa. ppl. stem of L. *abuti* use up, misuse, f. *ab* AB- + *uti* use. Replacing ABUSION.] † **1.** The process of using up –1539. **2.** Improper use, perversion 1538; in *Rhet.* catachresis 1589. **3.** An improper usage, a corrupt practice 1486. † **4.** Imposture, deceit –1653. † **5.** Ill-usage –1682. **6.** Violation, defilement (now only in *self-a.*) 1580. **7.** Injurious speech 1559.

2. A. of language MILL, of terms BROUGHAM, of the eyes HARLAN. **3.** The abuses of the courte CAXTON. The hoary head of inveterate a. BURKE. **4.** Or is it some a.? *Haml.* IV. vii. 51. **5.** The a. of Falstaffe *Merry W.* v. iii. 8. **7.** Treasonable abuses *Meas. for M.* v. i. 347. After exchanging a good deal of a. MACAULAY. Hence † **Abu·seful** *a.* abounding in abuse. **Abu·sefully** *adv.* abusively.

Ab-usefulness. *rare.* Used by Ruskin for, Capability of improper use.

† **Abu·ser²**. 1646. [f. ABUSE *v.* + -ER⁴, after *waiver*, etc.] Illegal or wrongful use –1734.

† **Abu·sh(e, abu·sse, abu·sche,** *v.* ME. [Reduced form of AMBUSH *v.*; see A- *pref.* 10.] To ambush –1350. Hence † **Abu·shment,** ambush.

† **Abu·sion.** ME. [– OFr., – L. *abusio*; see ABUSE *sb.*, -ION.] **1.** Misuse, perversion –1558; *esp.* of the truth –1640; in *Rhet.* catachresis –1636. **2.** Violation of law, or right, or propriety –1718. **3.** Injurious language –1587.

Abusive (ăbiū·siv), *a.* 1583. [–(O)Fr. *abusif, -ive* or late L. *abusivus*; see ABUSE *sb.*, -IVE.] Characterized by abuse: hence **1.** Misapplied; in *Rhet.* catachrestic 1583. **2.** Full of abuses (*arch.*) 1589. † **3.** Deceitful –1667. † **4.** Given to ill-using –1669. **5.** Scurrilous 1621.

1. The a. acception . . of the English word 'priest' FULKE. **2.** The a. enormities of . . our times NASHE. **3.** Th' a. Shews of sense S. DANIEL. An a. treaty BACON. **5.** An a. satire HOWELL. Hence **Abu·sively** *adv.* incorrectly; with foul language. **Abu·siveness.**

Abut (ăbɒ·t), *v.* ME. [(1) – AL. *abuttare*, f. *a-* AD- + *butta* BUTT *sb.*⁶; (2) –(O)Fr. *abouter*, †*abuter*, f. *a* AD- + *bouter* BUTT *v.*¹] **1.** To end at, border *on* 1463. Also *trans.* (*on* omitted). **2.** To end *on*, or *against*; to lean *upon* at one end 1578. Also *trans.* (*on* omitted). **3.** To cause to end *against* 1802.

1. [Selborne parish] abuts on twelve parishes WHITE. Abutting Southwark Park 1882. **2.** The Chapter House abutted on the south aisle MILMAN. Hence **Abu·tter,** one who or that which abuts; *spec.* an owner of contiguous property. **Abu·tting** *ppl. a.* projecting towards; touching.

Abutilon (ăbiū·tilǫn). 1731. [mod.L., – Arab. *abū tīlūn* Indian mallow.] *Bot.* A genus of plants (N. O. *Malvaceæ*).

Abutment (ăbɒ·tmĕnt). 1644. [f. ABUT *v.* + -MENT; cf. (O)Fr. *aboutement* meeting or joining end to end.] **1.** The meeting end to end; the place of junction. **2.** The action of abutting 1870. **3.** *Arch.* The solid part of a pier, wall, etc., which supports the thrust or lateral pressure of an arch 1793. **4.** That upon which anything abuts or leans 1734.

1. At the abutments of four stately ways EVELYN. **3.** The abutments of a bridge mean the walls adjoining the land 1823. **4.** The whole scheme and a. of the . . project NORTH.

Abuttal (ăbɒ·tăl). 1630. [f. ABUT *v.* (in sense 1) + -AL¹.] Abutment; *pl.* the parts in which land abuts on neighbouring lands. Hence † **Abu·ttalling** *vbl. sb.* the declaration of abuttals.

Aby, abye (ăbəi·), *v.* *arch.* ME. [OE. *ābyćgan* redeem (= Goth. *usbugjan*); see A- *pref.* 1, BUY *v.*] † **1.** To buy –1503. **2.** To pay the penalty for, usu. with *sore, dearly*, etc. *arch.* ME. **3.** To pay; suffer. *arch.* ME. † **4.** *absol.* To pay the penalty, to atone –1596. † **5.** *absol.* To endure, remain; = ABIDE –1596.

1. Thus dere abought is Love CHAUCER. **2.** They shall a. it! SCOTT. **3.** Thou wouldst a. A heavy fate MORRIS. **5.** Nought that wanteth rest can long a. SPENSER.

Abysm (ăbi·z'm). ME. [– OFr. *abi(s)me* (mod. *abîme*), – med.L. *abysmus*, alt. of *abyssus* ABYSS by assimilation to Gr. *-ισμός* -ISM.] **1. a.** The great deep, supposed to be, *spec.*: **b.** a subterraneous reservoir of waters ME.; **c.** hell, the infernal regions 1509. **2.** Any deep immeasurable space or cavity. *lit.* and *fig.* Also *attrib.* 1495.

1. b. Ocean's bed Over the a. COLERIDGE. **c.** Into th' Abisme of hell *Ant. & Cl.* III. xiii. 147. **2.** The Abysme of Time *Temp.* I. ii. 50. Hence **Aby·smal** *a.* of, pertaining to, or resembling an abyss. *lit.* and *fig.* **Aby·smally** *adv.* unfathomably.

Abyss (ăbi·s). ME. [– late L. *abyssus* – Gr. *ἄβυσσος* bottomless, f. *ἀ-* A- *pref.* 14 + *βυσσός*, var. of *βυθός* depth.] **1.** The great deep, the primal chaos; the bowels of the earth; the infernal pit; see ABYSM. **2.** A bottomless gulf; any unfathomable cavity or void space 1639. Also *fig.* **3.** *Her.* The centre of an escutcheon 1753.

1. The depe bottomlesse abisse of the yerth 1534. **2.** The awful a. which separates us from the stars HERSCHEL. *fig.* An abyssus of goodness BACON. Abysses of disgrace BURKE.

Aby·ss, *v.* [f. prec.] To engulf. LOWELL.

Aby·ssal, *a.* 1691. [– late L. *abyssalis*, f. *abyssus* ABYSS; see -AL.¹ Cf. Fr. *abyssal.*] Unfathomable. *Abyssal Zone*, the belt of water below 300 fathoms.

‖ **Abyssus** (ăbi·sɒ̆s). [L.] Earlier f. ABYSS.

† **Ac,** *conj.* [OE. *ac.*] But –1535.

Ac-, *pref.*, assim. form of L. *ad-*, bef. *c-* (*k-*) and *qu-*. Occ., but erron., for *a-* = OFr. *an-*, *en-* :– *in-*, or *es-* :– *ex-*, as in EE. *acumbre*, OFr. *encombrer*, and also for *a-* = OE. *a-* or *on-*, as in *a(c)curse*, etc. Only *a-* is pronounced.

-ac, *suffix*, also **-aque, -ak(e, -ack,** repr. Gr. *ακός, -ακή, -ακόν* = adj. suffix *-κός*, of or belonging to, w. sb. in *-ια, -ιος, -ιον*, as *καρδιακ-ός cardiac*, etc. Hence L. *cardiacus*, etc., whence Fr. words in *-aque*. Eng. words, e.g. *ammoniac, maniac*, etc., are adopted partly from Fr., partly from Gr. or L.; see also -ACAL.

Acacia¹ (ăkēⁱ·ʃiă). 1543. [– L., – Gr. *ἀκακία*, prob. f. base of *ἀκή* point, in ref. to its thorns.] **1.** *Bot.* A genus of leguminous shrubs or trees, of the *Mimosa* tribe, yielding Gum Acacia, Gum Arabic, Catechu, etc. **2.** *pop.* The North-American Locust-tree or False-Acacia (*Robinia pseud-acacia*) 1664. **3.** *Med.* The inspissated juice of the unripe fruit of species of *Acacia* and *Mimosa* 1601.

† **Aca·cia²**. Something like a roll or bag, seen on medals in the hands of consuls or emperors since Anastasius. Chambers *Cycl.* 1751.

Acacine (æ·kăsin). [f. ACACIA¹ + -INE⁵.] Pure gum arabic.

Academe (ækădī·m). *poet.* 1588. [– L. *Academia*; in Milton – *Academus*; see Hor. *Ep.* II. ii. 45.] = ACADEMY 1, 3.

Our Court shall be a little Achademe *L.L.L.* I. i. 13. The olive grove of A. MILT. Hence **Acade·mial** *a.* academic. † **Acade·mian,** a disciple of Plato; an academician.

Academic (ækăde·mik). 1586. [–(O)Fr. *académique* or L. *academicus*; see ACADEMY, -IC.] **A.** *adj.* **1.** Of the school or philosophy of Plato; sceptical 1610. **2.** Of or belonging to an academy; collegiate, scholarly 1588. **3.** Of or belonging to a learned society; belonging to an Academician 1879. **4.** Not leading to a decision; unpractical (*mod.*).

1. A very a. faith HUME. **2.** An academicke life BP. HALL. Rusticity and a. seclusion CARLYLE. **4.** A purely a. discussion (*mod.*).

B. *sb.* [The adj. used *absol.*] **1.** A Platonist 1586. **2.** A member of a college or university 1587; *pl.* academical robes 1823. **3.** = ACADEMICIAN. *rare.* 1751. **4.** pl. *Academics*, the *Academica* of Cicero.

1. The schools Of academics old and new MILT. **2.** The uniform habit of the academics, the square cap and gown GIBBON. Hence **Acade·micism,** a tenet of the A. philosophy.

Academical (ækăde·mikăl). 1587. [f. prec. + -AL[1]; see -ICAL.] **A.** *adj.* = ACADEMIC *a.* 1, 2, 3, 4. **B.** *sb. pl.* Academical robes 1823. Hence **Acade·mically** *adv.* platonically; sceptically; in relation to an academy.

Academician (ăkæ:dĕmi·ʃăn). 1749. [–Fr. *académicien*; see ACADEMIC and -ICIAN.] **1.** A member of an academy, or society for promoting arts and sciences; orig. used of the Fr. Academies, and the Eng. Royal Academy 1755. **2.** = ACADEMIC *sb.* 2. *rare.* 1749.

Academy (ăkæ·dĕmi). 1474. [–Fr. *académie* or L. *academia* – Gr. ἀκαδημία, ἀκαδήμεια, f. Ἀκάδημος name of a man; see -Y[3].] The name of a garden near Athens where Plato taught 1474. **2.** The school or system of Plato 1677. **3.** An institution for the study of the arts and sciences, e.g. a university; *pop.* a school claiming to rank between a college and an ordinary school (a sense discredited in Eng.) 1549; † *fig.* the arts taught in an academy, or a treatise on them –1754. **4.** Hence, a place of training, *esp.* in a special art, etc., as a Riding A., the Royal Military A., etc. 1570. **5.** A Society for the promotion of literature, art, or science, as the French A., the Royal A., called in Eng. 'the Academy' 1691. **6.** *Artists' slang.* Short for *A.-figure.* Also *attrib.*

3. The oldest A. in Scotland is that of Perth GRANT. *fig.* That living a. of love-lore my Lady Vane H. WALPOLE. **4.** *A.* is particularly . . a riding-school 1751. *Comb.* **a.-figure,** a drawing, half-life-size, in crayon or pencil, from the nude. Hence † **Aca·demism,** the Academic doctrine. † **Aca·demist,** a Platonist; a sceptic; an ACADEMICIAN (sense 1); a pupil in a riding-school. **Aca·demize** *v.* (*rare*) to form into an a.

Acadialite (ăkē[i]·diăləit). [f. as foll. + -LITE.] *Min.* A reddish chabazite.

Acadian (ăkē[i]·dian), *a.* and *sb.* 1790. [f. *Acadia*, latinized f. *Acadie*, French name of Nova Scotia; see -IAN.] Of or native to Nova Scotia.

Acajou (a·kaʒu). 1725. [Fr.; see CASHEW.] **1.** The Cashew or Cashew-nut. **2.** A medicine yielded by the mahogany tree (Fr. *acajou*) 1879.

-acal, comp. suffix = -AC (q.v.), often used subst., + -AL[1], repr. L. *-alis, -ale, of the nature of* or *connected with* the *attribute* in *-ac.*

† **Acale, ak-,** *ppl. a.* [ME. *acale*, prob. f. OE. *ofcalen*, pa. pple. of *ofcalan*, f. *of* (see A- *pref.* 3) + *calan* be cold.] Cold –1393.

‖ **Acalepha** (ækălī·fa), *sb. pl.* 1846. [mod.L. sb. pl. (prop. adj. sc. *animalia*), – Gr. ἀκαλήφη nettle; see -A *suffix* 4. Also *Acalephæ* fem. pl.; see -Æ *pl. suffix.*] *Zool.* A class of radiate marine animals, including the Jellyfishes and Medusas, possessing the power of stinging. Occ. called sea-nettles. (Sing. *Acaleph, Acalephan.*) Hence **Acale·phan** *a.* and *sb.* **Acale·phoid** *a.*

Aca·lycine, *a.* 1858. [– mod.L. *acalycinus*, f. Gr. ἀ- A- *pref.* 14 + κάλυξ, -υκ- CALYX, + -INE[1].] *Bot.* Having no calyx. var. **Acaly·cinous.**

Acaly·culate, *a.* [f. A- *pref.* 14 + L. *calyculus*, dim. of *calyx* CALYX; see -ATE.[2]] *Bot.* Having no calyculus or accessory calyx.

Acanth (ăkæ·nþ). 1662. [– Fr. *acanthe* – L. *acanthus* ACANTHUS.] = ACANTHUS.

Acanthite (ăkæ·nþəit). [f. Gr. ἄκανθα thorn + -ITE[1] 2b.] *Min.* An iron-black sulphide of silver, found at Freiberg, etc.

Acantho-, ad. Gr. ἀκανθο-, combining form of ἄκανθα, with sense of 'thorn, thorny'.

acantho-ce·phalous [Gr. κεφαλή] *a. Bot.* spiny-headed; **-cladous** [Gr. κλάδος] *a. Bot.* with spiny branches; **-logical** *a. Zool.* pertaining to the study of spines; **-phorous** [Gr. -φόρος] *a. Bot.* spine-bearing; **-pterous** [Gr. πτερόν.] *a.* spiny-winged; spiny-finned = **-pterygious**; ‖ **-ptery·gii** [Gr. πτερύγιον] *sb. pl. Zool.* an order of Fishes, a group of the Osseous sub-division, having spiny rays in the dorsal fins; hence **-ptery·gian** *a.* and *sb.* [sc. *fish*], **-ptery·gious** *a.*

Acanthus (akæ·nþŏs). 1616. [L., – Gr. ἄκανθος bear's-foot (as in Corinthian capitals) f. ἄκανθα thorn, f. ἀκή sharp point.] **1.** *Bot.* A genus of herbaceous plants (monopetalous exogens, N. O. *Acanthaceæ*). *pop.* Chiefly *A. spinosus*, Bear's Breech or Brank-Ursine 1616. **2.** *Arch.* A conventionalized leaf of *A. spinosus*, used in Corinthian and Composite capitals 1751.

1. Beares-breech, called of the Latines A. 1616. Hence **Acantha·ceous** *a.* of the type of the A., epithet of N. O. *Acanthaceæ.* **Aca·nthine** *a.* pertaining to the A.

Aca·psular, *a.* 1879. [f. A- *pref.* 14 + L. *capsula* CAPSULE + -AR[1].] *Bot.* Having no capsule.

Aca·rdiac, *a.* 1879. [f. Gr. ἀκάρδιος, f. ἀ- A- *pref.* 14 + καρδία heart, + -AC.] *Physiol.* Without a heart.

‖ **Acariasis** (ækărəi·ăsis). 1828. [f. Gr. ἄκαρι mite + -ASIS.] *Path.* A skin-disease, caused by *Acari.*

‖ **Acaridæ** (ăkæ·ridī), *sb. pl.* 1847. [mod.L., f. ACARUS + *-idæ*; see -ID[3].] *Zool.* A family of Arachnida, comprising mites and ticks. (Sing. *Acaridan.*) Hence **Aca·ridan** *a.* and *sb.*

Acarpellous (ækaɹpe·ləs), *a.* 1879. [f. Gr. ἀ- A- *pref.* 14 + mod.L. *carpellus* CARPEL + -OUS.] *Bot.* Having no carpels.

Acar·pous, *a.* [f. Gr. ἀ- A- *pref.* 14 + καρπός fruit + -OUS.] *Bot.* Unfruitful.

‖ **Acarus** (æ·kărŏs). Pl. **acari.** 1658. [mod. L., f. Gr. ἀκαρί mite.] *Zool.* A genus of Arachnida, embracing the cheese-mite, etc.; a mite. Hence **A·caricide,** a preparation for killing *Acari.* **A·carine** *a.* **A·caroid** *a.*

† **Acast,** *v.* ME. [f. A- *pref.* 1 + CAST *v.*] To cast away.

Acatalectic (ăkætăle·ktik), *a.* 1589. [– late L. *acatalecticus*, f. Gr. ἀκατάληκτος + *-īcus* -IC, or f. *a-* A- *pref.* 14 + Gr. καταληκτικός CATALECTIC *a.*] *Pros.* Not catalectic; complete in its syllables: also as *sb.* [sc. *verse*].

Acatalepsy (akæ·tălepsi). 1605. [– schol.L. *acatalepsis*, – Gr. ἀκαταληψία incomprehensibility, f. ἀ- A- *pref.* 14 + κατά thoroughly + λῆψις a seizing.] Incomprehensibility (of the object):—a Sceptic term; correl. of Agnosticism.

Acatale·ptic, *a. rare.* 1731. [– schol. L. *acatalepticus* (Fr. *acataleptique*), f. Gr. ἀκατάληπτος incomprehensible + *-icus* -IC, perh. after Gr. καταληπτικός conveying direct apprehension; see prec.] Relating to acatalepsy; incomprehensible.

† **Acate.** ME. [– AFr. *acat* ((O)Fr. *achat*) purchase, f. *acater* (OFr. *achater*, mod. *acheter*) buy :– Rom. **accaptare*, f. *ad* AC- + L. *captare* catch, f. *capt- capere* take. See CATE.] **1.** Purchasing. CHAUCER. **2.** *pl.* or *collect. sing.* Things purchased; dainties –1692. (Aphet. to CATES *c* 1460.)

Bread, wine, acates B. JONS.

† **Aca·ter, -tour.** ME. [:– AFr. *acatour* (OFr. *achatour*, mod. *acheteur*) buyer, f. *acater* buy + *-our* -OR 2; see prec. and CATER *sb.*[1]] A purveyor –1637. Hence † **Aca·tery,** provisions purchased; also, the store-room for them –1751.

Acaudate (ăkǭ·de[i]t), *a.* 1879. [f. A- *pref.* 14 + CAUDATE.] Tailless. var. **Acaudal.**

Acaulescent (æ·kǫle·sĕnt), *a.* 1854. [f. A-*pref.* 14 + CAULESCENT.] *Bot.* Apparently stemless. vars. **Acau·line, Acaulo·se, Acaulous** [all f. mod.L. *acaulis*, Fr. *acaule*].

Accadian (ăkē[i]·dian). [f. *Accad, Akkad*, an ancient city mentioned in *Gen.* 10:10 along with Babel, Erech and Calneh, in the land of Shinar; see -IAN.] A pre-Assyrian language preserved in cuneiform inscriptions.

Accede (ækṡī·d). ME. [– L. *accedere* approach, f. *ad* AC- + *cedere* go; see CEDE *v.* and cf. (O)Fr. *accéder.*] **1.** To come forward, approach –1677. **2.** To arrive at, or enter upon an office, etc. Const. *to.* 1756. **3.** To give one's adhesion; to assent *to* († *unto*) ME.

1. A property, acceding, or seceding, changes its subject. F. HALL. **2.** To a. to the purple BURTON, to a post 1879. **3.** To a. to a confederacy THIRLWALL. Hence **Acce·dence,** the action of acceding. **Acce·der.** *rare.*

‖ **Accelerando** (ækselĕræ·ndo[u]). [It.; cf. foll.] *Mus.* A direction: With gradual increase of speed.

† **Acce·lerate,** *ppl. a.* 1527. [– *accelerat-*, pa. ppl. stem of L. *accelerare*, f. *ad* AC- + *celer* swift; see -ATE[2].] Quickened.

Accelerate (ække·lĕre[i]t), *v.* 1530. [f. prec. or as prec.; see -ATE[3].] **1.** To quicken a motion or a thing in motion 1601. **2.** To hasten the occurrence of 1530; hence, to antedate 1855. **3.** *intr.* To become swifter 1646.

1. Every step accelerates the rapidity of the descent JUNIUS. A. your crucible 1631. **2.** The commons accelerated the grant STUBBS. Invention . . accelerated the baptism of Constantine MILMAN. Hence **Acce·lerated** *ppl. a. Accelerated motion*: motion continually increased in velocity. **Acce·leratedly** *adv.* **Acce·lerating** *vbl. sb.* and *ppl. a. Accelerating force*: a force that produces continually increased motion. **Acce·lerative, Acce·leratory** *adjs.* pertaining or tending to acceleration.

Acceleration (ækselĕrē[i]·ʃən). 1531. [–(O)Fr., or L. *acceleratio*, f. as prec.; see -ION.] **1.** The action of accelerating, or the being accelerated; increased speed 1534. **2.** The extent to which anything is accelerated; in *Nat. Phil.* the rate of increase per unit of time 1656.

1. A. of plants COWLEY. With what a. I advance towards death JOHNSON. **2.** *Uniform*, or *constant a.*: the unvarying amount per second added to the rate at which a body is moving, e.g. under the influence of gravity. *Astr.* and *Physics.* A. of the *fixed stars*; the time (3′ 55·9″) which the stars gain upon the sun in passing the meridian each day. Of the *planets*, the increased velocity of their advance from aphelion to perihelion. Of the *moon*, an increase (about 11″ per century) in the speed of the moon's mean motion. Of the *tides*, the amount by which high or low water occurs at any place before the calculated time.

Accelerator (ækse·lĕre[i]təɹ). 1611. [f. ACCELERATE *v.* + -OR 2.] **1.** He who or that which accelerates; *spec.* certain nerves and muscles that accelerate organic functions; also, a light mailcart used by postmen. **b.** An apparatus to regulate the speed of the engine in a motor-vehicle, esp. for increasing speed 1900.

† **Acce·nd,** *v.* ME. [– L. *accendere* kindle, f. *ad* AC- + **candere*, rel. to *candēre* shine.] To kindle, set on fire. *lit.* and *fig.* –1720.

† **Acce·nsed,** *ppl. a.* 1573. [f. *accensus*, pa. pple. of L. *accendere* (prec.) + -ED[1].] Kindled, set on fire –1760.

Acce·nsion. *arch.* 1646. [– late L. *accensio*; f. as prec. + -ION.] Kindling or being kindled.

Accent (æ·ksĕnt), *sb.* 1538. [–(O)Fr., or L. *accentus* (f. *ad* AC- + *cantus* song, CHANT), rendering προσῳδία PROSODY.] **1.** A prominence given to one syllable in a word, or in a phrase 1581.

Accent in Gr. (προσῳδία) and L. meant orig. variety of musical pitch in pronouncing the syllables of a word; later, stress only. The grammatical varieties of accent in Eng. are all varieties of stress.

2. a. The marks, (´) *acutus*, (`) *gravis*, (^) *circumflexus*, indicating the nature and position of a spoken accent in a word. **b.** Marks (mostly ´`^), distinguishing the qualities of sound indicated by a letter, called diacritical accents, and in Eng. ` to show that *-ed* is pronounced 1596. **c.** Marks placed over and under Heb. consonants, as signs of tone and of interpunctuation; hence *fig.* the minutest particular (of the Mosaic law) 1610. **3.** The mode of utterance peculiar to an individual, locality, or nation 1600. **4.** The way in which anything is said 1538. **5.** *poet.* A significant tone or sound; a word; *pl.* speech 1595. **6.** *Pros.* The stress laid at intervals on certain syllables of a verse, the succession constituting the rhythm 1588. **7.** *Mus. Anciently*: the marks placed over words to show the notes, turns, or phrases to which they were to be sung. *Now*: stress recurring at intervals generally fixed, but variable by syncopation and cross accentuation 1609. **8.** *fig.* Distinctive stress; a distinguishing mark, character or tone 1639.

1. Though we doe not obserue quantitie, yet we obserue the a. very precisely SIDNEY. 2. b. *Accento*: an a. or point ouer anie letter to giue it a due sound FLORIO. c. Every pricke and a. of the law HOLLAND. 3. A slight a., a strong provincial a., an Irish, American, etc. a. (*mod.*). 4. With like timerous a. *Oth.* I. i. 75. Mild was his a. DRYDEN. In broken accents SWIFT. 5. That any a. breaking from thy tongue Should scape . . mine eare *K. John* v. vi. 95. In State[s] vnborne, and Accents yet vnknowne *Jul. C* III. i. 113. 6. You finde not the apostrophas, and so misse the a. *L. L. L.* IV. ii. 124. 8. These are the . . accents of honour in the German service FULLER. That which gave a. to Abraham's faith GURNAL. Hence **A·ccentless** *a.*

Accent (ǣkse·nt), *v.* 1530. [– Fr. *accenter*, f. *accent* (prec.).] **1.** To pronounce with accent or stress; to emphasize. **2.** To mark with a (written) accent. **3.** To pronounce, intone 1639. **4.** *fig.* To mark emphatically; to heighten 1655.

1. I can nat a. aryght in . . latyn PALSGR. 3. Sounds, accented by a thousand voices SCOTT. 4. Piers, accented at the cardinal points by [etc.] 1877.

Accentor (ǣkse·ntəɹ). [med.L. (Isidor) one who sings with another, f. *ad* AC- + CANTOR.] **1.** *Mus.* One who sings the leading part. **2.** A genus of birds, including the hedge-sparrow. *U.S.* The water-thrush.

Accentual (ǣkse·ntiu,ăl, *a.* 1610. [f. L. *accentus* ACCENT *sb.* + -AL[1].] Of or belonging to accent.

A. iambics, verses with alternate strong and weak instead of long and short syllables. Hence **Acce:ntua·lity** (*rare*), the quality of being a.; in *pl.* a. particulars. **Acce·ntually** *adv.*

Accentuate (ǣkse·ntiu,eⁱt), *v.* 1731. [f. med.L. *accentuare* (as prec.); see -ATE[3]; cf. Fr. *accentuer*.] **1.** To pronounce or mark with an accent. **2.** *fig.* To mark strongly, emphasize.

1. The French never a. their words or their feelings HARE. 2. To a. antagonism LECKY.

Accentuation (ǣkse:ntiu,ēⁱ·ʃən). 1818. [f. prec., see -ION; cf. med.L. *accentuatio*, Fr. *accentuation*.] **1.** The marking of accent in speech 1827. **2.** The notation of accents in writing 1846. **3.** Mode of pronunciation 1818. **4.** *fig.* Emphasizing 1875.

† **Acce·pt**, *ppl. a.* MF. [– L. *acceptus*, pa. pple. of *accipere*; see next.] = ACCEPTED. –1599.

Accept (ǣkse·pt), *v.* Pa. pple. †*accept*, *accepted*. ME. [– (O)Fr. *accepter* or L. *acceptare*, f. *accept-*, pa. ppl. stem of *accipere*, f. *ad* Ac- + *capere* take.] To take or receive what is offered. Hence, **1.** To take or receive with consenting mind; to receive with favour 1380. **2.** To receive as adequate; hence, to admit 1530. **3.** To take upon oneself as a responsibility 1524. (In senses 1–3 often with *of*.) **4.** *Comm.* To accept a bill or draft: to agree or promise to pay when due 1665. Also *absol.*

1. To a. (as a prospective husband) *Merch. V.* I. ii. 102. His ring I doe a. *Ibid.* IV. ii. 9. **To accept the person** or **face of**: To favour (*esp.* on corrupt grounds). **To accept persons**: To show favouritism. [A Hebraism, in N. T. Gr. προσωποληπτεῖν, Vulg. *acceptare personam*.] 2. A fact which we may a. FREEMAN. To a. an apology (*mod.*). **To accept service of a writ**: to agree to consider it as validly served. 3. To a. the siege of Calais WOLSEY, a post M. PATTISON. Hence **Acce·pted** *ppl. a.* well-received; † acceptable. **Acce·ptedly** *adv.* **Acce·pter**, one who accepts; see sense 1, quots. **Acce·ptive** *a.* fit for acceptance; † ready to accept. **Acce·ptor** = ACCEPTER; he who accepts a bill of exchange.

Acceptability (ǣkseptăbi·lĭti). 1660. [– late L. *acceptabilitas*, f. as next. + *-itas* -ITY. In later use f. next. + -ITY.] = ACCEPTABLENESS.

Acceptable (ǣkse·ptăb'l, æ·kseptăb'l), *a.* ME. [–(O)Fr. – late L. *acceptabilis*; see ACCEPT *v.*, -ABLE.] Orig., and still poet., *a·cceptable*. Worthy or likely to be accepted; pleasing, welcome.

What a. thynge shal I offre vnto the Lorde COVERDALE *Mic.* 6: 6. Hence **Acce·ptableness. Acce·ptably** *adv.*

Acceptance (ǣkse·ptăns). 1574. [– OFr.; see ACCEPT *v.*, -ANCE.] **1.** The act or fact of accepting, as a pleasure, a satisfaction of claim, or duty 1596; *esp.* favourable reception (of persons) 1596; belief 1669. **2.** The state of being accepted 1649. **3.** = ACCEPTATION 3. 1716. **4.** Acceptableness 1593. **5.** *Comm.* (see ACCEPT *v.* 4.) The formal engagement to pay when due; the bill itself when 'accepted'. **6.** *Law.* An agreeing to the act of another by some act which binds the person in law 1574.

1. A. of the Crown FREEMAN. The vocalist . . sang with marked a. (*mod.*). The assertion finds a. in every rank FARADAY. *Acceptance of persons*: partiality. See ACCEPT 1, quots. 2. Holiness . . a Condition of Final A. WESLEY. 3. The proper a. of the word 1857. 4. The Canon ! . . A man of such a. BROWNING. 5. To get acceptances into circulation 1865.

Acce·ptancy. 1856. [f. prec., see -ANCY.] Willingness to receive. MRS. BROWNING.

Acce·ptant. 1596. [– (O)Fr. *acceptant*, pres. pple. of *accepter*; see ACCEPT *v.*, -ANT.] **A.** *adj.* Willingly receiving. Const. *of*. †**B.** *sb.* One who ACCEPTS; *spec.* the acceptor of a bill 1596.

Acceptation (æ:kseptēⁱ·ʃən). ME. [– (O)Fr., – late L. *acceptatio*; see ACCEPT *v.*, -ION.] † **1.** *gen.* = ACCEPTANCE 1. –1692. **2.** = ACCEPTANCE 2. *arch.* 1594. **3.** The sense in which a word, etc. is accepted 1614. † **4.** = ACCEPTANCE 5. 1622.

3. The different acceptations of the word Knowledge LOCKE.

Acce:ptila·tion. 1562. [– L. *acceptilatio*, = *accepti latio* a formal discharging from debt.] *Rom. Law.* The remission of a debt by an acquittance without payment. *fig.* Free remission.

† **Acception** (ǣkse·pʃən). ME. [– L. *acceptio*; see ACCEPT *v.*, -ION. Partly – (O)Fr. *acception*.] **1.** The act of accepting –1662. **2.** *A. of persons* or *faces*. [A Hebraism, in Gr. προσωποληψία, L. *acceptio personæ*.] Corrupt acceptance or favouritism –1677. See ACCEPT 1. quots. **3.** = ACCEPTATION 3 –1711.

1. Acception or takyng of money CAXTON. 3. This A. of the term 1711.

Access (æ·ksės, ǣkse·s). ME. [– (O)Fr. *accès* or L. *accessus* approach, f. *access-* pa. ppl. stem of *accedere* ACCEDE. *A·ccess* is now usual.] **1.** Approaching or being approached in various senses (see quots.) ME. **2.** A way or means of approach. *lit.* and *fig.* 1605. **3.** A coming as an addition (replaced by ACCESSION) 1576. **4.** A (sudden) coming on of illness, anger, etc., a fit ME.; † *spec.* an ague fit –1751. Also *fig.* (mod., after Fr. *accès*).

1. = † Entrance: At our a. to the pope's presence GARDINER. = Admittance: He importunes accesse to you *A.Y.L.* I. i. 98. = Accessibility: Lord Chesterfield's easiness of a. BOSWELL. Opp. to *recess*: The Sunnes a. and departure HEALEY. The a. and recess of Parliament MAY. = ACCESSION: Our a. to the Crowne CHARLES I. 2. The Accesses of the Island MILT. Every a. to the conscience DALE. 3. I from . . thy looks receive A. in every virtue MILT. An a. of tone 1881. 4. The A. of Fevers HARTLEY. An a. of tone 1881. 4. The A. of Fevers HARTLEY. An a. of paralysis TICKNOR. *fig.* An a. of jealousy SOUTHEY. ¶ Frequently written for EXCESS. Cf. sense 3. Hence † **Acce·ssive** *a.* pressing in; accessible. †**Acce·ssively** *adv.* pressingly. **Acce·ssless,** inaccessible.

Accessary (æ·ksĕsări, ǣkse·sări). 1480. [– med.L. *accessarius* (*minister secundarius ecclesiæ*, Du Cange), f. as prec. + *-arius* -ARY[1]. The sb. is etymologically *accessary*, the adj. *accessory*, but in use no distinction is practicable. A·ccessary is the hist. pronunc.] **A.** *sb.* **1.** One who gives his accession (formerly *access*) to an act or undertaking. In *Law*: One who aids or abets in an offence, either before or after the fact. **2.** Anything contributory or subordinate 1534.

1. There are no accessaries in Treason FINCH. 2. The attention . . is distracted by the accessaries MRS. JAMESON.

B. *adj.* **1.** Of persons: Acceding *to*. In *Law*: Participant, privy 1594. † **2.** Of things: Subordinate, adventitious; (repl. by ACCESSORY) –1691.

1. Both houses of Parliament were . . made a. to the legal murders of this reign HALLAM. Hence **Acce·ssarily** *adv.* consentingly. **Acce·ssariness,** privity.

Accessible (ǣkse·sib'l), *a.* 1610. [– (O)Fr., or late L. *accessibilis*; see ACCESS, -IBLE.] **1.** Capable of being used as an access (*to*). **2.** Capable of being entered or reached; get-at-able 1642; *fig.* open to the influence of (const. *to*) 1818.

1. With one ascent A. from earth MILT. 2. Bold, a. coasts HOWELL. Evidence not a. to contemporaries MAY. *fig.* A. to bribery 1881. Hence **Acce:ssibi·lity.**

Accession (ǣkse·ʃən). 1588. [– (O)Fr., or L. *accessio*; see ACCESS, -ION.] The action of going to, and its result. Hence, **1.** Approach, admittance: = ACCESS 1. 1652. † **2.** Advance, arrival –1656. **3.** Coming to a dignity, etc., *esp.* the throne 1769. **4.** A coming to as an addition in various senses (see quots.) 1588; *esp.* (*Law*) Addition to property by natural growth or artificial improvement, which the owner acquires by Accession 1768. † **5.** A coming on of disease, etc. = ACCESS 4. –1827.

1. A. of air SIR H. DAVY, of solar light KANE. 4. = Joining: The a. of piety to patience T. ADAMS. = Assent: A. to an affair SIR J. MELVIL. *Deed of A.*, in Sc. Law, a deed by which creditors bind themselves to concur in a trust executed by their debtor for the general behoof. = Addition: A. of strength WELLESLEY. A. to a library HALLAM. 5. Accessions of folly SOUTHEY. Hence **Acce·ssional** *a.* additional.

‖ **Acce·ssit.** Short for PROXIME ACCESSIT.

Accessory (æ·ksėsəri, ǣkse·səri). 1549. [– med.L. *accessorius*, *-orium*, f. as ACCESS + *-orius* -ORY. Partly through (O)Fr. *accessoire*. See ACCESSARY.] **A.** *adj.* **1.** Of things: Coming as an accession; additional 1618. **2.** = ACCESSARY *a.* 1.

B. *sb.* **1.** An accessory thing; an adjunct 1549. **2.** = ACCESSARY *sb.* 1.

1. All pleasures else I accessories call HOLLAND. 2. Accessories to his bold riot MILT. Hence **Accessorial** *a.* supplementary. **Accessorily** *adv.* additionally. **Accessoriness,** secondary character.

‖ **Acciaccatura** (attʃa:kkătū·ră). 1876. [It.] *Mus.* A. 'grace', consisting of a small note performed quickly before an essential note of a melody; a 'crush-note'.

† **A·ccidence**[1]. ME. [– OFr., – L. *accidentia* sb. fem. what happens, chance; see ACCIDENT, -ENCE, -ENCY.] Hap; fortuitous circumstance –1811. Hence **Accide·ntial,** *a.* non-essential.

Accidence[2] (æ·ksidĕns). 1509. [– L. *accidentia* (tr. Gr. παρεπόμενα accompanying things), n.pl. of *accidens* ACCIDENT, taken as fem. sing.; see -ENCE.] **1.** That part of Grammar which treats of the Accidents or inflexions of words. **2.** Hence, The rudiments of any subject 1562.

1. Aske him some questions in his A. *Merry W.* IV. i. 16. 2. The Accedence of Armorie 1562.

Accident (æ·ksidĕnt). ME. [– (O)Fr., f. *accident-*, pres. ppl. stem of L. *accidens* (in late L. use, accident or chance), f. *accidere* happen, f. *ad* Ac- + *cadere* fall; see -ENT.] **I.** Anything that happens. **1.** † An event; *esp.* an unforeseen contingency; a disaster ME. **2.** Chance, fortune. (By a. = L. *per accidens.*) 1490. † **3.** *Med.* An unfavourable symptom –1671. † **4.** A casual appearance or effect –1765. **5.** An irregularity in the landscape 1870.

1. Of mouing Accidents by Flood and Field *Oth.* I. iii. 135. *The chapter of accidents*: the unforeseen course of events. A railway a., insurance against accidents (*mod.*). 2. By a. or design FREEMAN. 4. Non a. for noon adversité Was seyn in hir CHAUCER. 5. Taking advantage of every a. of the ground 1878.

II. That which is present by chance, and so non-essential. **1.** *Logic.* An attribute which is not part of the essence ME. **2.** Hence, any non-essential accompaniment. **3.** *Her.* A note or mark that may be retained or omitted in a coat of arms 1610. † **4.** *Gram. pl.* (L. *accidentia.*) The changes, such as gender, number, case, etc., to which words are subject –1612. Now ACCIDENCE.

1. When the breed is conuerted into the . . body of our lord the accidentes abyden|. . whytnesse, roundenesse and sauoure CAXTON. 2. The brilliant accidents of birth, beauty [etc.] DISRAELI. Hence † **Accide·ntary** *a.* fortuitous; non-essential. † **Accide·ntarily** *adv.* **A·ccidented** *ppl. a.* characterized by accidents. (Cf. Fr. *accidenté.*)

† **A·ccident,** *a.* 1509. [– L. *accident-*, *accidens* (see prec.) befalling, accidental.] Accidental. Hence †**A·ccidently** *adv.* by chance: non-essentially.

Accidental (æksĭde·ntăl). ME. [– late L. *accidentalis*; see ACCIDENT, -AL[1]; cf. Fr. *accidentel* (XVI).] **A.** *adj.* **1.** Happening by, or pertaining to, chance; casual, fortuitous 1506. **2.** *Logic.* Pertaining to accidents; non-essential 1553. **3.** Incidental, subsidiary 1386.

1. The jury . . find only a. death (*mod.*). Thy sinn's not accidentall, but a Trade *Meas. for M.*

III. i. 149. **2.** The propositions in which accidents were predicated of it [the subject] were called a. MILL. **3.** A. benefits JOHNSON. *Accidental* sharps, flats, naturals (*Mus.*); so called only when they occur bef. particular notes, and not in the *signature* of the keys. *Accidental* colours (in *Optics*): complementary colours, due to subjective sensation. *Accidental* lights (in *Painting*): 'secondary lights; effects of light other than ordinary daylight', FAIRHOLT.

B. *sb.* **a.** A casual property, see A 2. **b.** *Mus.* A sharp, flat, or natural, occurring not at the commencement, but before a particular note; see A 3 (quots.). **c.** *Painting. pl.* Those unusual effects produced by artificial light, proceeding from a fire, candle, etc. Hence **Accide·ntalism,** in *Painting*, the effect produced by a. lights; *Med.* a system which treats disease as an a. modification of health. **A·ccidenta·lity** = ACCIDENTALNESS. **Accide·ntally** *adv.* by chance; † non-essentially. **Accide·ntalness,** the quality or fact of being a.

† **Accidie.** ME. [– AFr. *accidie* = OFr. *accide*, – med. L. *accīdia*, alt. of late L. *acēdia* – Gr. ἀκηδία listlessness. Cf. ACEDY.] Sloth, torpor.

The synne of Accidie CHAUCER.

Accipenser, see ACIPENSER.

† **Acci·pient,** *ppl. a.* [– *accipient-*, pres. ppl. stem of L. *accipere*; see ACCEPT *v.*, -ENT.] 'One who receives.' (Dicts.)

‖ **Accipiter** (æ̆ksi·pitəɹ). 1874. [L.] **1.** *Zool.* A bird of prey, one of the *Accipitres*, or *Raptores*. **2.** *Surg.* A bandage for the nose, resembling a hawk's claw. Hence **Acci·pitral** *a.* rapacious; keen-sighted. **Acci·pitrine** *a.* hawk-like.

Accise, earlier form of EXCISE; see ASSIZE.

‖ **Acci·smus.** 1753. [mod.L., – Gr. ἀκκισμός, f. ἀκκίζεσθαι affect indifference.] *Rhet.* A feigned refusal of something desired.

† **Acci·te,** *v.* 1506. [– *accit-*, pa. ppl. stem of L. *accire* summon, f. *ad* AC- + *ciēre* call; see CITE *v.*] **1.** To summon –1674. **2.** To quote –1631. **3.** To excite –1637.

1. Stanislaus . . whom . . valour accited . . into the Tauric fields MILT. **3.** To a. So ravenous . . an Appetite B. JONS.

Acclaim (ăklēⁱ·m), *v.* ME. [In branch II – L. *acclamare* to applaud, f. *ad* AC- + *clamare* to shout, w.sp. assim. to CLAIM *v.*; in branch I from med.L. sense to claim.] † **I.** To lay claim to –1717.

II. 1. To applaud 1633; to name with applause as 1749. **2.** *intr.* To shout applause 1652. **3.** *trans.* To shout; *spec.* to utter an ACCLAMATION 1690.

1. To a. speeches 1881. The . . high Gods . . Acclaimed her victress SWINBURNE. **3.** Acclaiming, 'Glory be to Thee, O Lord' 1690. Hence **Acclai·m,** a shout of applause. *poet.* **Acclai·mable** *a.* **Acclai·mer. Accla·matory** *a.*

Acclamation (æklămēⁱ·ʃən). 1541. [– L. *acclamatio*; see prec., -ATION.] **1.** The action of acclaiming. † **a.** Calling to. **b.** Loud or eager approval, or shouting 1585. **2.** An exclamation: † **a.** of dislike; † **b.** of approval. Hence **c.** Approbation however expressed 1541. † **3.** *Rhet.* A brief isolated sentence in a discourse, emphasizing what precedes it –1675.

1. To sing with a. unto the Lord ABP. SANDYS. **b.** The general a. of all the powers JOHNSON. [A Bill] passed *by a.* FROUDE. **2.** That sad a., Blessed are the wombs which bare not 1673. The acclamations of the soldiers proclaimed him Emperor GIBBON. **3.** Plain a. of Amen MILT.

Acclimata·tion. 1859. [– Fr., f. *acclimater*; see next, -ATION.] = ACCLIMATIZATION.

Acclimate (ăkləi·mĕt), *v.* 1792. [– Fr. *acclimater*, f. *à* to, AC- + *climat* CLIMATE *sb.*] = ACCLIMATIZE, now more common. *lit.* and *fig.* Hence **Accli·matable** *a.* **Accli·matement** (*rare*).

Acclimation (æklimēⁱ·ʃən). 1853. [f. prec. + -ION, on analogy of *narrate, narration*; see -ATE³, -ATION.] = ACCLIMATIZATION.

Acclimatization (ăkləi:mătəizēⁱ·ʃən). 1830. [f. next + -ATION.] **1.** The process of habituating, or being habituated, to a new climate. Also *attrib.* **2.** A thing which has been acclimatized.

1. A. gardens J. BULLER. **2.** The turkey . . one of our best acclimatisations OWEN.

Acclimatize (ăkləi·matəiz), *v.* 1836. [f. Fr. *acclimater* ACCLIMATE + -IZE.] To habituate, or become habituated, to a new or unusual climate. *lit.* and *fig.*

Acclimatized to unfamiliar ecclesiastical surroundings M. DAVIES. Hence **Accli·mati:zer. Accli·matizing** *vbl. sb.* = ACCLIMATIZATION.

Acclivity (ăkli·vĭti). 1614. [– L. *acclivitas*, f. *acclivis*, *-us* sloping upward, f. *ad* AC- + *clivus* slope; see -ITY.] An ascending slope. Hence **Accli·vitous** *a.*

Accli·vous, *a.* 1731. [f. L. *acclivus* (see prec.) + -OUS.] Sloping upward.

Accloy (ăkloi·), *v. arch.* [ME. *acloy* – OFr. *encloyer* (mod. *enclouer*) :– med.L. *inclavare* drive in a nail, f. *in* in + *clavare* to nail, f. L. *clavus* nail. Later aphet. to CLOY. For ME. *a-* – OFr. *en-*, see A- *pref.* 10; for the sp. *accloy*, cf. A- *pref.* 7.] **1.** To prick with a nail, shoeing a horse; to lame. *lit.* and *fig.* **2.** To stop up an aperture as with a nail, etc.; to obstruct, clog, choke 1430. **3.** To overfill ME.; to nauseate 1519; to weary 1530.

2. The laws by which the flesh Accloys the spirit BROWNING. **3.** Accloyed with bribes PAYNELL, examples JEWEL. Hence **Acclo·ying** *vbl. sb.* overloading.

Accoast, *v.*; **accoasting,** *vbl. sb.* The older ff. of ACCOST, ACCOSTING, in the sense of *coast, border upon.*

† **Accoi·l,** *v.* [– OFr. *acoillir* (mod. *accueillir*) :– med.L. *accolligere* to associate, f. *ad* AC- + L. *colligere* gather. See COIL *v.*¹, ³.] To collect. (Only in Spenser.) **Accoi·l,** *sb. rare.* [– OFr. *acoil* (mod. *accueil*).] Reception.

Accolade (ækolēⁱ·d, akola·d). 1623. [– Fr., – Pr. *acolada*, f. Rom. **accollare* embrace about the neck, f. L. *ad* + *collum* neck; see next, -ADE.] **1.** *prop.* An embrace; the technical name of the salutation, consisting at different times of an embrace, a kiss, or a blow on the shoulders with the flat of a sword, marking the bestowal of knighthood. **2.** *Mus.* A vertical line or brace, used to couple two or more staves 1882.

1. Could [the Pope] receive [the Czar] with . . an insincere a. WISEMAN. Hence **Accola·ded** *ppl. a.* knighted.

† **Acco·ll,** *v.* [ME. *acole* – OFr. *acoler* :– Rom. **accollare* (see prec.); sp. assim. to later Fr. *accoller* (mod. *accoler*).] To embrace –1557.

Accolled, *ppl. a.* 1723. [f. ACCOLL. Fr. *accolé* is more used.] *Her.* **1.** Collared, gorged. **2.** Intertwined. **3.** Conjoined, united, jugate, as two shields, two lozenges, or two busts on a coin. var. **A·ccollated.**

† **Acco·mmodate,** *ppl. a.* 1525. [– L. *accommodatus*, pa. pple. of *accommodare*; see next, -ATE².] Suited; suitable, fit.

Accommodate (ăkǫ·modēⁱt), *v.* 1531. [– *accommodat-*, pa. ppl. stem of L. *accommodare*, f. *ad* AC- + *commodus* fitting; see -ATE³.] **1.** To ascribe fittingly (a thing *to* a person) –1676; to adjust (one thing or person *to* another); † *intr.* to adapt oneself *to* –1677; to show the correspondence of one thing to another; to make consistent (const. *to*, † *unto*, † *with*) 1603. **2.** To adjust, reconcile (things or persons); to bring to agreement 1597; *intr.* to come to terms 1648. † **3.** To fit (a thing for use); to repair (Fr. *raccommoder*) –1812; to facilitate –1703. **4.** To fit or furnish a person *with* 1597; to oblige 1663; *esp.* with lodgings, etc. 1715.

1. To a. the eye to different distances BREWSTER. The intention of Poets, unto which they a. their verses HOLLAND. **2.** To a. a quarrel 1677, opinions MACAULAY. I hope we shall a. with the Danes 1801. **3.** Well accommodated for our lodgment HENRY. To a. a cure MASSINGER. **4.** A Souldier is better accommodated, then with a wife 2 *Hen. IV*, III. ii. 72. To a. with cash for a cheque (*mod.*). The honour of accommodating [the Queen] at his house 1772. Hence **Acco·mmodable** *a.* suitable. † **Acco·mmodately** *adv.* † **Acco·mmodateness. Acco·mmodating** *vbl. sb.* the action of the vb.; *ppl. a.* suiting; hence, *adj.* affording accommodation; pliant, conciliatory; pliable, open to corruption. **Acco·mmodatingly** *adv.* **Acco·mmodator,** he who, or that which, accommodates.

Accommodation (ăkǫ:mōdēⁱ·ʃən). 1604. [– (O)Fr., or L. *accommodatio*, f. *accommodare*; see prec., -ION.] **1.** The action of accommodating, or the being accommodated; adaptation, adjustment 1644. **2.** Adaptation of a word, expression, or system to something different from its original purpose 1724. **3.** Self-adaptation; obligingness 1768. **4.** An arrangement of a dispute; a settlement, compromise 1645. **5.** The supplying with what is requisite. **6.** Anything which supplies a want, or affords aid or refreshment; *esp.* lodgings and entertainment at an inn, etc. 1604. **7.** Pecuniary aid in an emergency; a loan 1824.

1. The a. of the eye to the vision of external objects BREWSTER. **2.** The adaptation or a. of a prophecy TRENCH. **3.** His object in these accommodations was [etc.] HALLAM. **4.** An a. between the belligerents PRESCOTT. **5.** The a. of life JOHNSON. **6.** Progress . . is from necessaries to accommodations REYNOLDS. A. for our sick men CROMWELL. The Hummums . . has good accommodations PORTER. **7.** An a. of £100 from Ballantine LOCKHART.

Phrases. *Accommodation Bill*, a bill not representing an actual commercial transaction, but for the purpose of raising money on credit. *Accommodation land*: land, generally in the neighbourhood of a town or fair, having a special rental value owing to its being required by some one, to whom it is let temporarily, for the purposes of his business or property; e.g. land let to a butcher, to fatten his stock for killing, or the like. *Accommodation price*: the price, always in excess of the mere agricultural rental value, paid for such land.

Accommodative (ăkǫ·mōdēⁱtiv), *a.* 1841. [f. ACCOMMODATE *v.* + -IVE.] Tending to accommodate. Hence **Acco·mmoda:tiveness.**

† **Acco·mpanable, -iable,** *a.* 1548. [– OFr. *acompagnable*, f. *acompagner* ACCOMPANY + *-able* -ABLE; cf. COMPANABLE.] Companionable.

Accompaniment (ăkɒ·mpănimĕnt). 1744. [– (O)Fr. *accompagnement*, f. as prec.; see -MENT.] **1.** Anything that accompanies; something attending or added, by way of ornament, for symmetry, or the like 1756. **2.** *Mus.* The subsidiary part or parts, instrumental or vocal, added for the sake of effect to a musical composition; *esp.* the instrumental part which sustains the voice 1744. **3.** *Her.* The belt, mantlings, etc., applied about the shield, by way of ornament.

Accompany (ăkɒ·mpăni), *v.* 1460. [– (O)Fr. *accompagner*, f. *a-* A- 7 + *compaign* COMPANION *sb.*¹; later assim. to COMPANY.] **1.** † To add or conjoin *to* –1587; to send (or give) *with* the addition of 1629; † *refl.* to unite oneself *with* –1650. † **2.** *intr.* (refl. pron. omitted.) To keep company *with*; *euphem.* to cohabit with –1760; *absol.* to combine –1577. **3.** *trans.* (*with* omitted.) † To keep company with; *euphem.* to cohabit with –1660; to convoy, escort, attend *c.* 1460; used *fig.* of things personified 1477. **4.** To go with as an attribute or attendant phenomenon 1731. **5.** *Mus.* To a. (singing, a piece, the singer): To join a singer or player by singing or playing an accompaniment.

1. With fresh souldiours to them accompanied FOXE. To a. the word with a blow (*mod.*). **3.** Shee . . bid her . . accompanie her solitarie father SIDNEY. The ladies accompanied the gentlemen in hunting parties STRUTT. Accompanied by his wife FREEMAN. *Déjeuner*, accompanied by half a bottle of Bordeaux HAMERTON. **4.** The ejections of scoriæ were accompanied by bellowings PHILLIPS.

¶ *Accompanied* now takes *by* with personal or active agents, *with* only when the agency is secondary. Hence **Acco·mpanier.** LAMB. **Acco·mpanist, -yist. Acco·mpanying** *vbl. sb.* going, or acting with; or giving as an accompaniment, *esp.* in *Music*; *ppl. a.* attending; attached, appended.

† **Acco·mplement.** 1587. [f. AC- + COMPLEMENT (in obs. sense II. 1, 2); cf. † *accomplement* (XVII) = COMPLIMENT *sb.* & *v.*] Anything that completes or perfects; see ACCOMPLISHMENT.

Accomplice (ăkǫ·mplis). 1485. [alt. of COMPLICE, prob. by association w. *accompany*.] An associate in crime or guilt. Const. *of*; also *with* the criminal, *in* the crime. Also *playfully* (*rare*).

An a. of [Catiline's] Crime DRYDEN. Our . . Generall, And . . his accomplices SHAKS. Hence **Acco·mpliceship** (*rare*), **Accompli·city** (*rare*), the state of being an a.

Accomplish (ăkǫ·mpliʃ), *v.* ME. [– OFr. *acompliss-*, extended stem of *acomplir* (mod. *acc-*), – (w. change of suffix) Rom. **accomplēre* f. *ad*, AC- + L. *complēre* fill, complete;

see COMPLISH, -ISH[2]. The hist. pronunc. is ăkɒ·mpliʃ. **1.** *trans.* To perform, carry out. † *intr.* –1509. **2.** To complete (a work 1477, time 1574, a distance 1855). **3.** To equip completely 1588. **4.** To perfect in mental acquirements; to finish off 1475.

1. The desire accomplished is sweet to the soule *Prov.* 13:19. **2.** To a. seuentie yeeres *Dan.* 9:2, half a league or more PRESCOTT. **3.** The Armourers accomplishing the Knights *Hen. V*, IV. Chor. 12. **4.** Thou art a Gentleman: .. well-accomplish'd *Two Gent.* IV. iii. 13. Hence **Acco·mplishable** *a.* practicable. **Acco·mplisher.**

Accomplished (ăkǫ·mpliʃt), *ppl. a.* 1475. [f. prec.] **1.** Fulfilled, completed 1577. **2.** Perfect; *esp.* in acquirements, etc. 1475. †**3.** Fully versed *in*.

1. Not yet eight years a. HOLINSHED. A. service SOUTHEY. **2.** An a. courtier *Cymb.* I. v. 103. A. speaking is an art BLACKIE.

Accomplishment (ăkǫ·mpliʃmĕnt). 1460. [f. ACCOMPLISH + -MENT. after Fr. *accomplissement.*] **1.** The action of accomplishing, or the being accomplished; completion. **2.** The act of perfecting, or the being perfected; perfection 1561. **3.** An achievement or attainment 1599. **4.** Anything that completely equips, as accoutrement; in mod. use, an ornamental attainment or acquirement; occas. a superficial acquirement.

1. The A. of the Duke of York's marriage with the princess of Modena JOHNSON. **2.** The finishing stroke and very A. of Virtue SHAFTESBURY. **3.** A harmony—the a. of correct and vigilant judgement MRS. RADCLIFFE. **4.** The external Accomplishments of Kingly prosperity MILT. To fold and seal a letter adroitly is not the lowest of accomplishments DE QUINCEY.

Accompt, *v.* and *sb.*, arch. f. ACCOUNT.

Accomptant, arch. f. ACCOUNTANT. **Accompter,** obs. f. *Accounter* (ACCOUNT *v.*).

Accord (ăkǭ·ɹd), *v.* OE. [– OFr. *acorder* (mod. *acc-*):– Rom. * *accordare* f. L. *ad* AC-, after *concordare* CONCORD *v.*] *lit.* To bring heart to heart. **1.** † *trans.* To cause to agree, to reconcile (persons) –1702; † *refl.* and *pass.* to reconcile oneself *with* –1786; to compose (quarrels or differences) ME.; † to attune *to* –1663. **2.** *intr.* (refl. pron. suppressed). To come to an agreement (see quots.) ME.; † to agree *to*, to assent or consent *to* –1674; of things: To be in harmony *with* ME.; † *impers.* to be suitable or proper (L. *convenit*) –1556. **3.** *trans.* (prep. omitted). † To agree upon –1676; to agree to grant; hence, in 19th c., to grant *to*, to award.

1. We wolde gladly acorde you and hym LD. BERNERS. Musyque accordeth alle thinges CAXTON. To a. a difference LONGF. **2.** Two dogges and one bone Maye never a. in one 1500. We may ..a. *with* the Emperour HOLCROFT. To a. *in* common sentiments HALE. To. a. *of* the time to begin H. SMITH. So *upon*. †With *subord. cl.*: I acord wel *that it ys so* CHAUCER. You, to his love must a. *A.Y.L.* V. iv. 139. His principles and practice do not a. well together (*mod.*). Do that thyng quhilk accords 1556. **3.** All business being thus accorded 1676. The glimpses of eternity To saints accorded WORDSW. Hence **Acco·rdable** *a.* accordant; reconcilable. **Acco·rdancy,** agreement. **Acco·rded** *ppl. a.* reconciled; granted. **Acco·rder,** one who agrees, or bestows. **Acco·rdment,** reconcilement.

Accord (ăkǭ·ɹd). ME. [– OFr. *acord* (mod. *acc-*), f. *acorder* (prec.)] **1.** Reconciliation; concurrence of opinion, will, or action; consent ME. **2.** A formal act of reconciliation; a treaty ME. **3.** *Law.* An extrajudicial arrangement 1625. **4.** Harmonious correspondence, e.g. of colours and tints; *esp.* of sounds: Agreement in pitch and tone; harmony ME. †**5.** Assent to a proposal; permission –1602.

1. True A. is an Union of .. the Will and Affections R. JONES. Family a. COWPER. A. of hands and back and forward steps WORDSW. *To be of, at a.* with: to a gree with. *With* (†*of*) *one a.*: with unanimity. **2.** The pees and the acord y made..CAXTON. A general a. with Holland MOTLEY. **4.** The ayres and accords of the Harpe BACON. **5.** This gentle and unforced a. of Hamlet *Haml.* I. ii. 123. *Of* († *by*, † *on*) *one's own a.*: of one's own motion.

† **Acco·rd,** *adv.* or *a.* ME. [shortened f. pa. pple. *accorded.*] In accord. CHAUCER.

Accordance (ăkǭ·ɹdăns). ME. [– OFr. *acordance*, f. *acorder* ACCORD *v.*; see -ANCE.] The state of being in accord, or the act of agreeing or granting; harmony; conformity.

The accordaunce Of .. songe *Rom. Rose* 498. The degree of a. PHILLIPS. *In a. with* (rarely *to*): in conformity to.

Accordant (ăkǭ·ɹdănt), *a.* ME. [– OFr., pres. pple. of *acorder* ACCORD *v.*] **1.** Conformable *to, with.* **2.** *absol.* † Concurring in mind, agreeable –1599; agreeing in action or motion; *esp.* of sounds: harmonious 1764. †**3.** Appropriate, fitting –1574.

A. with reason FABYAN, with the pride of London MISS YONGE. **2.** If hee found her a. *Much Ado* I. i. 14. A. strings R. LLOYD, action KINGLAKE. **3.** With warrantie a. *Littleton's Ten.* Hence **Acco·rdantly** *adv.*

According (ăkǭ·ɹdiŋ), *ppl. a.* and *adv.* ME. [f. ACCORD *v.* + -ING[2].] *ppl. adj.* †**1.** Corresponding *to* –1532. **2.** *absol.* Agreeing in nature or action; consentient 1450. †**3.** Appropriate, fitting –1674. **4.** *adv.* † *absol.* = ACCORDINGLY 4.

2. This a. voice of national wisdom BURKE. The a. hearts of men TENNYSON. **4.** Thou [hast] a stubborne soule..And squar'st thy life a. *Meas. for M.* v. i. 487. *Phr.* According *as*: exactly or just as. According *to*: in a manner consistent with; †suitably to.

Accordingly (ăkǭ·ɹdiŋli), *adv.* ME. [f. prec. + LY[2].] †**1.** Harmoniously –1514. †**2.** Becomingly, suitably –1634. †**3.** In the order specified; respectively –1603. **4.** In accordance with the premises; correspondingly 1599; in natural sequence 1688.

4. When you have seene more .. proceed a. *Much Ado* III. ii. 125. *Phr.* † Accordingly *to*: conformably to. Accordingly *as*: just as.

Accordion (ăkǭ·ɹdiən). 1842. [– G. *akkordion*, f. It. *accordare* tune (an instrument) + *-ion*, as in *orchestrion.*] A portable musical hand-instrument, consisting of a small pair of bellows and a range of keys, which on being pressed admit wind to metal reeds. Also as *adj.*, folding like an a. Hence **Acco·rdionist.**

Accost (ăkǫ·st), *v.* 1578. [– Fr. *accoster* – It. *accostare*:– Rom. * *accostare*, f. L. *ad* AC- + *costa* rib side. Formerly often spelt *accoast*, after *coast.*] †**1.** *intr.* To lie alongside –1611; *trans.* to border on –1662; to go alongside of, to COAST –1603. †**2.** *refl.* To accost oneself *with*, keep beside (rare); *intr.* to draw near *to* –1635. **3.** *trans.* To approach for any purpose; to face; to make up to. *arch.* 1599. **4.** To address 1612. **5.** To solicit in the street for an improper purpose 1887.

1. *trans.* If his land accosteth the sea FULLER. **3.** A. is front her, boord her, woe her, assail her *Tw. Night* I. iii. 52. **4.** [They] thus .. a. him soon MILT. Hence **Acco·st** *sb.* salutation. **Acco·stable** *a.* ready to accost; approachable. **Acco·sted** *ppl. a. Her.* placed side by side. **Acco·sting** *vbl. sb.* †a coming alongside: advance (towards intercourse). †**Acco·stment,** the action of accosting.

‖ **Accouche** (ăku·ʃ, ăkau·tʃ), *v.* 1867. [– Fr. *accoucher*; see A- *pref.* 7, COUCH *v.*] To act as midwife.

‖ **Accouchement** (akuʃmaǹ, ăku·ʃmĕnt, ăkau·tʃmĕnt) 1809. [Fr., f. *accoucher*; see prec., -MENT.] Delivery in child-bed.

‖ **Accoucheur** (akuʃö·r). 1759. [Fr., f. as prec. + *-eur* -OR 2.] A man midwife; also formerly = next.

‖ **Accoucheuse** (akuʃö·z, -ə̄·z). 1867. [Fr. fem. of prec.] A midwife.

† **Accounsel,** *v.* ME. [– OFr. *aconseillier*, f. *a* A- *pref.* 7 + *conseillier* COUNSEL *v.*] To COUNSEL –1649.

Account (ăkau·nt), *v.* [ME. *acunte, acounte* – OFr. *acunter, aconter*, f. *à*- A- *pref.* 7 + *conter* COUNT *v.* Formerly also *a(c)compt*: see next.] †**1.** To count, count up –1582; *absol.* –1776; to calculate, reckon –1788; to reckon in –1826. Also with *to*, † *on*, † *that*. **2.** *intr.* To render or receive an account ME.; *trans.* to render account of 1614; to render an account for trust moneys; to explain; to answer for (see quots.) 1679. **3.** *trans.* To estimate, value, hold (a thing to be so and so). Also with *inf.* or *subord. cl.* So, to account *of*; to think *much*, etc. of a thing. ME. †**4.** To narrate. *trans.* and *intr.* ME.

1. He [a grocer] must be able to .. a. A. SMITH. The Hejerà .. is accounted from the year of the flight of Mahomet .. from Mecca 1788. All sorts of graces accounted *to* you D. JERROLD. **2.** Ramnarain was ready to a. fairly JAS. MILL. All receipts should be accounted to a finance committee M. PATTISON. At once accounting for his deep arrears DRYDEN. To a. for the greater cold TYNDALL. The terrier accounted for one, the keeper for another THACKERAY. **3.** [I] therein doe a. my selfe well paid *Merch. V.* IV. i. 417. Wee are accounted *as* sheepe *Rom.* 8:36. They are nothing to be accounted of I. TAYLOR. Hence **Accou·nted** *ppl. a.* reckoned. † **Accou·nter,** one who accounts or narrates. **Accou·nting** (*vbl. sb.* †computing; also *attrib.*; with *for*: answering for, explaining; *ppl. a.* †counting; that keeps accounts (*arch.*). **Accou·ntment,** the work of accounting, responsibility.

Account (ăkau·nt), *sb.* [ME. *acunt, acount* – AFr. *acunt*, OFr. *acont*, later *a(c)compt*, f. *acunter*; see prec. The former var. *accompt*, like the French, is assim. to L. *computum.*] **1.** Counting, reckoning, calculation ME. **2.** A statement of moneys received and paid, with calculation of the balance; also one of the heads under which accounts are kept in a ledger ME.; the preparing a statement of money transactions 1646. **3.** A reckoning in one's favour; advantage 1611. **4.** A statement of the administration of money in trust 1513; hence, a statement as to responsibilities generally; answering for conduct, e.g. on the Last Day ME.; †also in same sense pl. was used as sing. **a.** of money –1762; **b.** of responsibility or conduct –1564. **5.** *Law.* A writ or action against a bailiff, receiver, etc., who refuses to render account 1622. **6.** Estimation, consideration, importance ME. **7.** A relation, report or description 1614.

1. Quick at accounts (*mod.*). *To cast accounts*, to make calculations. *Money of a*, denominations of money used in reckoning only. **2.** At many times I brought in my accompts *Timon* II. ii. 142. *To open or close an a. with one. To render* or *send in an a.*: to give a statement of money due. *A. current*: a running account. *Joint a.*: one entered into by two parties not otherwise in partnership. *To keep accounts* (pl.). *To balance or square accounts*: to pay or receive the balance shown. *Cash A., Suspense A.*, etc. *For the a.* (*Stock Exchange*): not for cash, but for settlement on the next settling-day. *In a. with*: in relations requiring the keeping of an a. *with*. *To place* or *pass to a.*: to debit or credit a person's a. *with*. *For a. of*: to be accounted to for. *On a.*: as an interim payment on a. of something in process. *On one's a.*: in his behalf and at his expense. *On one's own a. On a. of*: because of; † concerning. Commissioners of public a. HALLAM. **3.** Wherein they expected *to find their own a.* SWIFT. A kind which cannot *be turned to any a.* HT. MARTINEAU. **4.** The ordinary cannot demand accompt for them PERKINS. Claudio shall render me a deere a. *Much Ado* IV. i. 338. He has gone to his a. MARRYAT. *To give a. of*: to account for. *To give a good a. of*: to be successful with. Accompts to be made to the King LAMBARDE. We shall render an accompts for [their] lives BECON. **5.** A. does not lie against an infant TOMLINS. **6.** A Scholler .. of good accompt B. JONS. *To make a. of*, to esteem. *To take* (*into*) *a.* (*of*): to notice. *To leave out of a. To lay one's a. with* (*on, for*): to reckon upon. (*Orig. Sc.*) **7.** An accompt of my poore voyage CAMPION. He trusted nobody's a. of it DICKENS. Hence † **Accou·ntless** *a.* beyond count; irresponsible.

attrib. and *Comb.* **A.-book,** one prepared for the keeping of accounts. **A. day,** day of reckoning. **A. Sales,** a detailed account of the sale of a parcel of goods.

† **Accou·nt,** *pa. pple.* 1548. Short f. ACCOUNTED.

Accountable (ăkau·ntăb'l), *a.* 1583. [– AFr. *accountable*; see ACCOUNT *v.*, -ABLE; cf. OFr. *acomptable.*] **1.** Liable to be called to account; responsible (*to, for*) 1583; also simply 1642. †**2.** To be counted on –1709. †**3.** To be computed –1589; attributable *to* –1681. **4.** Explicable. (Cf. *unaccountable.*) 1665. Also with *for* 1745.

1. I am a. to no man STEELE. A. to the volunteer for the residue of the sum WELLINGTON. **4.** A very a. obstinacy GEO. ELIOT. Hence **Accoun:tabi·lity, Accou·ntableness,** responsibility (*to, for*). **Accou·ntably** *adv.*

Accountant (ăkau·ntănt). 1453. [– Law Fr., use of pres. pple. of OFr. *aconter*; see ACCOUNT *v.*, -ANT.] † **A.** *adj.* Giving or liable to give an account –1649.

B. *sb.* **1.** One accountable or responsible. In *Law*, the defendant in action of Account 1453. **2.** One who counts; a calculator 1646. **3.** One who professionally makes up accounts; an officer in a public office who has charge of the accounts 1539. †**4.** A narrator –1655.

1. Any crown debtor or a. to the crown WILLIAMS. It is no plea by an a. that he was robbed TOMLINS. **2.** He is an excellent A. STEELE. **3.** *A.-General*, the superintending accountant in various public offices. Skilful accountants JEVONS. Hence **Accou·ntancy,** the art or practice of an a. **Accou·ntantship,** the office of an a.

† **Accou·ple,** *v.* 1486. [– OFr. *acopler* (mod. *accoupler*) to join in a couple :– Rom. **accopulare* f. *ad* AC- + L. *copulare*; see COUPLE *v.* Sp. refash. as in Fr.] To couple –1635.

Accou·plement. 1483. [– Fr.] † **1.** The action of coupling; marriage union –1594. **2.** In *Carpentry.* A tie or brace. † **Accou·pling,** *vbl. sb.* 1525. [f. ACCOUPLE.] Coupling; *esp.* union in marriage.

† **Accou·rage,** *v.* [– OFr. *aco(u)ragier*, var. of *encoragier* ENCOURAGE *v.*, f. *a* (cf. A- *pref.* 7) + *coragier* f. *corage* COURAGE *sb.*] To encourage. SPENSER.

† **Accou·rt,** *v.* [f. COURT *v.*; see A- *pref.* 11.] To court. SPENSER.

Accoutre (ăkū·təɹ), *v.* 1606. [–(O)Fr. *accoutrer*, earlier *acoustrer* orig. to equip gen. (later, with clothing), f. *a-* A- *pref.* 7 + *cousture* (mod. *couture*) sewing :– Rom. **consutura*, f. L. *consut-*, pa. ppl. stem of *consuere* sew together; see CON-, SEW *v.*[1]] To equip, array.

Aptly accoustred, and armed Cap-a-pe DEKKER. He accoutred me with other necessaries SWIFT. Hence **Accou·tred** *ppl. a.* (The only part of the vb. much used.)

Accoutrement (ăkū·təɹmĕnt). 1549. [– Fr. *accoutrement*, †*accoustrement*; see prec., -MENT.] **1.** Apparel, outfit, equipment. (Usu. *pl.*) *Milit.* Equipments other than arms and dress. **2.** The process of accoutring or being accoutred 1598.

Point deuice in your accoustrements *A.Y.L.* III. ii. 402. The war-contractor and the a.-maker 1858.

† **Accoy,** *v.* ME. [– OFr. *acoier*, f. *a* (A- *pref.* 7) + *coi* quiet; see COY *a.* & *vb.*] To quiet; *hence*, to soothe, to silence, or daunt –1647.

With kind words accoyd SPENSER.

† **Accrea·se,** *v.* ME. [– OFr. *acreiss-*, tonic stem of *acreistre* (mod. *accroître*) :– L. *accrescere* increase f. *ad* AC- + *crescere* grow. Superseded by INCREASE.] To increase. *trans* and *intr.* Hence **Accrea·se** *sb.* increase.

Accredit (ăkre·dit), *v.* 1620. [– Fr. *accréditer* (earlier *acr-*), f. *a-* A- *pref.* 7 + *crédit* CREDIT, after phr. *mettre à crédit*, lit. 'put to credit'.] **1.** To put into credit, to set forth as credible; to vouch for 1620. **2.** To furnish with credentials; to authorize as an envoy. Const. *to, at.* 1794.

1. His censure will (to use the new..phrase) a. his praises COWPER. *Phr.* To a. *one with something*: to vouch for it as his. Mr. Bright.. was accredited with having said [etc.] 1880. **2.** Accredited at St. Petersburg KINGLAKE. var. † **Accre·ditate** *v.*, whence **Accredita·tion,** the action of accrediting, or being accredited. **Accre·dited** *ppl. a.* furnished with credentials; authoritatively sanctioned.

Accrementitial (æ:krĭmĕnti·ʃăl), *a.* 1879. [– Fr. *accrémentitiel*, f. *accrémentition*; see next, and cf. -IAL.] *Biol.* Pertaining to accrementition.

Accrementition (æ:krimĕnti·ʃən). 1879. [– Fr. *accrémentition*, f. med.L. *accrementum* increase + *-ition* -ITION.] *Biol.* Organic growth, by development of blastema, or by fission of cells; = ACCRETION.

Accresce (ăkre·s), *v.* 1634. [– L. *accrescere*, f. *ad* AC- + *crescere* grow; cf. ACCREASE.] **1.** To accrue (in Rom. Law). † **2.** *trans.* To add to 1652. Hence **Accre·scence,** continuous growth; an accretion. **Accre·scency,** an accretion. **Accre·scent** *a.* growing continuously; *Bot.* growing larger after flowering.

Accrete (ăkrī·t), *v.* 1784. [– *accret-* pa.ppl. stem of L. *accrescere*; see prec.] **1.** *intr.* To grow together by adhesion; to grow *to* 1869. **2.** *trans.* To cause to grow or unite *to* 1871.

Accre·te, *ppl. a.* 1824. [– L. *accretus*, pa. pple. of *accrescere* ACCRESCE *v.*] **1.** Formed by accretion; factitious. **2.** *Bot.* Grown together; said of parts normally separate 1847.

Accretion (ăkrī·ʃən). 1615. [– L. *accretio*; see prec., -ION.] **1.** Continued growth. **2.** The growing together of particles, or of parts normally separate 1655; anything so formed 1873. **3.** The process of growth by external addition 1626. **4.** The adhesion of external matter or things so as to cause increase 1713; that which so adheres, an extraneous addition 1653. **5.** *Law.* **a.** = ACCESSION. 1830. **b.** The increase of an inheritance or legacy by the addition of the share of a failing co-heir or co-legatee 1880.

1. The tendency of all power is to a. HELPS. **2.** The drop, gathered by a. of minute particles, may be snow, ice, or water PHILLIPS. The Bible—an a. of casual writings H. ROGERS. **3.** Inanimate Bodies.. have an A., but no Alimentation BACON. **4.** The a. after *K* pure, of the palatal semi-vowel *y* DOUSE. The accretions of age MERIVALE.

Accre·tive, *a.* 1665. [f. L. *accret-* (see ACCRETE *v.*) + -IVE.] Belonging to accretion.

† **Accriminate,** *a.* 1655. [rare var. of INCRIMINATE by substitution of AC- *pref.* for IN[2]-.] To accuse of crime. Hence † **Accrimina·tion,** accusation of crime.

Accroach (ăkrōᵘ·tʃ), *v.* ME. [– OFr. *acrocher* (mod. *acc-*) hook in, draw in with a hook, f. *a-* A- *pref.* 7 + *croc* hook; see CROOK, CROUCH.] *prop.* To draw with a hook; hence, **1.** To draw to oneself, acquire ME. **2.** With *to oneself*: To usurp what is not one's own 1520. **3.** *intr.* To encroach 1530.

2. They had attempted to a. to themselves royal power STUBBS. Hence **Accroa·ching** *vbl. sb.* the act of drawing to oneself; usurping sovereign power. **Accroa·chment.**

Accrual (ăkrū·ăl). [f. ACCRUE *v.* + -AL[1].] = ACCRETION 5 b. *attrib.*, as *a. basis.*

† **Accrue** (ăkrū·), *sb.* 1577. [subst. use of AFr. *acru*, pa. pple. of *acreistre* ACCREASE; so mod. Fr. *accrue* sb., increase.] Accession, reinforcement. (Cf. CREW.)

Accrue (ăkrū·), *v.* 1470. [f. prec.] **1.** To fall (*to* any one) as a natural growth or increment; to come as an accession or advantage. Const. *unto, to.* **2.** To arise or spring (*from, by,* †*of*) as a natural growth or result. Used *esp.* of interest 1589. † **3.** To grow, grow up 1604. † **4.** *trans.* To collect 1594.

1. Lands left to the shore.. accrew wholly to the King 1622. **2.** Interest begins to a. from the moment [etc.] MCCULLOCH. Hence **Accrue·d** *ppl. a.* accumulated by growth; *Her.* full grown. **Accrue·ment,** the action of accruing as a natural accession, or as *interest*; that which accrues or has accrued. **Accru·er** (*Law*), the action of accruing; = ACCRETION 5 b. **Accru·ing** *vbl. sb.* natural growth; *ppl. a.* arising in due course.

Accubation (æ:kiubēⁱ·ʃən). 1646. [– L. *accubatio*, MS. var. of *accubitio*, f. *accubare* lie near to, f. *ad* AC- + *cubare* lie; see -ATION.] † **1.** The ancient posture of reclining at table –1656. **2.** *Med.* = ACCOUCHEMENT. 1879.

Accumbent (ăkʌ·mbĕnt). 1656. [– *accumbent-*, pres. ppl. stem of L. *accumbere* lay oneself down, esp. at table, f. *ad* AC- + *-cumbere*, rel. to *cubare* lie; see -ENT.] **A.** *ppl. a.* **1.** Reclining at table 1727. **2.** *Bot.* Lying against anything; opp. to *incumbent.* Applied to the cotyledons of an embryo when their edges lie against the folded radicle. **B.** *sb.* One who reclines, or is, at table 1656.

† **Accu·mber,** *v.* [ME. *acombre, acumbre*, for earlier *en-*; see A- *pref.* 10, AC-, ENCUMBER.] To encumber, oppress, crush.

Acoombred with the cloaked hatred of Cain *Homilies.* Hence † **Accu·mbrance,** the act of encumbering. † **Accu·mbrous** *a.* cumbrous. CHAUCER.

Accumulate (ăkiū·miulĕt), *ppl. a.* 1533. [– L. *accumulatus*, pa. pple. of *accumulare*, f. *ad* AC- + *cumulus* heap; see -ATE[2].] Heaped up by additions. As pple. replaced by ACCUMULATED.

Accumulate (ăkiū·miŭleⁱt), *v.* [f. as prec.; see -ATE[3].] **1.** *trans.* To heap up in a mass, to pile up; to collect. *fig.* 1529. *absol.* 1858. Occas. *lit.* (*after Lat.*) 1809. **2.** To take (*degrees*) by ACCUMULATION; also *absol.* 1691. **3.** *intr.* (from refl.) To go on increasing 1759.

1. To a. piles of wealth *Hen. VIII*, III. ii. 107, an immense debt BURKE, authorities 1798. To a. beyond our wants 1858. **3.** Where wealth accumulates GOLDSMITH.

Accumulation (ăkiūmiŭlēⁱ·ʃən). 1490. [– L. *accumulatio*, f. as prec.; see -ATION and cf. (O)Fr. *accumulation.*] **1.** The action of accumulating. *lit.* and *fig.* 1606. **2.** The process of growing into a heap; *spec.* the growth of money by the addition of interest to principal 1490. **3.** The combination of several acts or exercises into one; *spec.* the taking of higher and lower degrees together, or at a shorter interval than is usual 1753. **4.** An accumulated mass; a pile 1490.

1. Quicke a. of renowne *Ant. & Cl.* III. i. 19. The instinct of a. HAMERTON. **2.** The a. of ruins and rubbish from above STANLEY. **3.** To say the divine offices by a. 1865. **4.** An a. of knowledge JOHNSON, of capital CARLYLE, of snow HUXLEY.

Accumulative (ăkiū·miŭlĕtiv), *a.* 1651. [f. ACCUMULATE *v.* + -IVE.] **1.** Arising from accumulation; cumulative. **2.** Tending to increase in amount 1857. **3.** Given to accumulate 1817. Hence **Accu·mulatively** *adv.* **Accu·mulativeness.**

Accumulator (ăkiū·miŭleⁱtəɹ). 1691. [f. ACCUMULATE *v.*; see -OR 2.] **1.** One who amasses 1748. **2.** One who takes degrees by ACCUMULATION 1691. **3.** Anything that accumulates, *spec.* An apparatus for accumulating electricity. 1877.

† **Accur(re,** *v.* 1555. [– L. *accurrere* to run to, f. *ad* AC- + *currere* run; cf. Fr. *accourir.*] To run to; to meet –1651. ¶ Often for OCCUR.

Accuracy (æ·kiŭrĕsi). 1662. [f. next; see -ACY.] The state of being ACCURATE; precision, correctness.

Experiments that require a greater a. R. WALLER. A. of singing HUXLEY.

Accurate (æ·kiŭrĕt), *a.* 1612. [– L. *accuratus* performed with care, f. *accurare* apply care to, f. *ad* AC- + *curare* care for, f. *cura* care; see CURE.] † **1.** Executed with care –1738. **2.** Of things and persons: Exact, correct, as the result of care 1612. **3.** Of things: Conforming to a standard, or to truth; precise, correct 1651.

1. Acurat diaries BURTON. A. attempts 1738. **2.** An a. knowledge of mineralogy SULLIVAN. An a. and learned printer DIBDIN. **3.** An a. term BURKE, solution (*mod.*). Hence **A·ccurately** *adv.* with careful exactness; without error or defect. **A·ccurateness.** (Properly of a person.)

Accurse (ăkɔ̄·ɹs), *v. arch. Pa. pple.* **accursed, accurst.** ME. [f. A- *pref.* 1 + OE. *cursian* to curse, f. *curs* CURSE *sb.*; for the sp. *acc-* see A- *pref.* 7.] To pronounce or imprecate a curse upon; to devote to perdition, or misery.

She had purchased a curse of the pope, to a curse all yᵉ said barons FABYAN. Accursed Above all cattle MILT. Hence **Accu·rsed, accu·rst** *ppl. a.* lying under a curse; worthy of, or bringing with it, a curse; also *absol.* **Accu·rsedly** *adv. arch.* **Accu·rsedness.** *arch.* † **Accu·rsing** *vbl. sb.* the act of pronouncing a curse; excommunication.

† **Accurtation.** 1583. [– med.L. *accurtatio* f. *accurtare* shorten f. L. *curtare*, f. *curtus* short; cf. CURT.] Shortening –1594.

Accusant (ăkiū·zănt). 1611. [– obs. Fr., pres. pple. of *accuser* ACCUSE; see -ANT.] One who accuses.

Accusation (ækiuzēⁱ·ʃən). ME. [–(O)Fr. *accusation* – L. *accusatio*, f. *accusat-* pa. ppl. stem of *accusare*; see ACCUSE *v.*, -ATION.] **1.** The act of accusing, or the being accused. **2.** The charge, or the declaration containing it; an indictment ME.

1. Be thou constant in the a. *Much Ado* II. ii. 55. Under the a. of his country BURKE. **2.** To this a. I will not plead 1862.

Accusative (ăkiū·zătiv), *a.* ME. [–(O)Fr. *accusatif, -ive* or L. *accusativus* (sc. *casus* case), f. pa. ppl. stem of *accusare* (see ACCUSE *v.*, -IVE). L. (*casus*) *accusativus* renders Gr. (πτῶσις) αἰτιατική (case) of accusing.] *Gram.* In inflected languages the name of the case expressing primarily destination; hence, the case expressing the object of transitive verbs, i.e. the destination of the verbal action; applied, in uninflected languages, to the *relation* in which the object stands. Usu. sb. (*case* being omitted). † **2.** (From ACCUSE *v.*) Accusatory ME.

1. The fourte case is accusatif case *Gesta Rom.* (1879) 417. **2.** A very a. age SIR E. DERING. Hence **Accu:sati·val** *a.* **Accu·satively** *adv.* in an a. manner; relating to the a. case.

† **Accusator, -our.** ME. [– *accusat-*, pa. ppl. stem of L. *accusare*; see ACCUSE *v.*, -OR 2.] An accuser.

Accusatorial (ăkiū:zătōᵊ·riăl), *a.* 1823. [f. L. *accusatorius* + -AL[1]; cf. -ORIAL.] Of or pertaining to an accuser.

A. procedure, that in which the.. prosecutor is.. a different person from the judge BENTHAM. Hence **Accu·satorially** *adv.* by means of a formal accuser.

Accusatory (ăkiū·zatəri), *a.* 1601. [– L. *accusatorius*; see prec. and -ORY[2].] Of the nature of an accusation.

Accuse (ăkiū·z), *v.* [ME. *acuse* – OFr. *ac(c)user*, (mod. *acc-*):– L. *accusare* to call to account, f. *ad* AC- + *causa* CAUSE.] **1.** To charge with a fault; to blame; also with *as*, †*for*, or *subord. cl.* 1513. **2.** To accuse *of* (†*for*, †*in*, †*upon*): To charge with the crime of ME.; also *absol.* (obj. omitted), and *intr.* **3.** To betray, disclose, and *fig.* to indicate, or make known (*rare*) ME.

1. He had accused him to the king BURNET. Such frugal virtue malice may a. DRYDEN. Accused as accessary to the crime (*mod.*). **2.** Atreus accused himself of murdre LYDGATE. Who is he that accuseth (*mod.*). They accusen falsely agaynste Chryste WYCLIF. **3.** The distribution of the scene accuses an absence of motive or thought 1864. Hence **Accu·sable** *a.* liable to be accused; liable to the charge *of*. **Accu·sably** *adv.* **Accu·sal**, the act of accusing. †**Accu·se**, accusation 2 *Hen. VI*, III. i. 160. **Accu·sed** *ppl. a.* charged with a crime or fault. (Usu. *the accused*: the prisoner at the bar.) †**Accu·sement**, the action of accusing. **Accu·sing** *vbl. sb.* the action of accusing; *ppl. a.* blaming; reproachful. **Accu·singly** *adv.*

Accuser (ăkiū·zəɹ). ME. [f. prec.] One who accuses or blames; *esp.* one who prosecutes in a court of justice.

Satan.., The tempter ere the a. of mankind MILT.

†**Accusor, -our.** ME. [– AFr. *ac(c)usour* (mod. Fr. *accuseur*) = OFr. *acusor*, *-eor*,:– L. *accusator* ACCUSATOR; repl. by prec.] Early ff. ACCUSER.

Accustom (ăkɒ·stəm), *v.* [late ME. *acustum(e* – AFr. *acustumer*, OFr. *acostumer* (mod. *accoutumer*), f. *a-* A- *pref.* 7 + *costume* CUSTOM *sb.*] †**1.** *trans.* To make customary or familiar; to practise habitually. Freq. in pass., *to be accustomed*. –1768. †**2.** *intr.* To become familiar, to consort or cohabit with –1670. **3.** *trans.* To habituate (*to*, †*in*, †*into*, †*for*, †*with*, or *to do*) 1478. Also *refl.* and †*intr.*

1. Such..thanks As..friends a. on the shore MARLOWE. **2.** With the best man we a. openly MILTON. **3.** The ear..is accustomed to stillness RUSKIN. *refl.* With servants, never a. yourself to ..passionate language CHATHAM. *intr.* Those.. who..a. to wash their heads EVELYN. Hence †**Accu·stom** *sb.* habit. †**Accu·stomable** *a.* usually practising or practised. **Accu·stomably** *adv.* customarily. †**Accu·stomance,** customary use or practice. †**Accu·stomarily** *adv.* usually. **Accu·stomary** *a. arch.* usual. †**Accu·stomate** *ppl. a.* accustomed. **Accu·stoming** *vbl. sb.* †making oneself familiar with, consorting; habituating.

Accustomed (ăkɒ·stəmd), *ppl. a.* 1483. [f. ACCUSTOM *v.*] **1.** Made customary; habitual. †**2.** Frequented by customers –1772.

1. Th' a. sight of death *A.Y.L.* III. v. 4. **2.** A well a. shop SMOLLETT. Hence **Accu·stomedly** *adv.* **Accu·stomedness,** the quality or fact of being a.

Ace (ēˈs). [ME. *as*, *aas* – (O)Fr. *as*:– L. *as* unity, unit.] **1.** *One* at dice, or the side of the die marked with one pip, and counting as one; afterwards extended to cards, dominoes, etc. *Ambs ace*, both aces; *deuce ace* (OFr.) two aces at one throw (now taken as *deuce* + *ace* = 2 and 1; so *trey ace*, *syce ace*, etc.). **b.** A point at rackets, lawn tennis, etc. **2.** *fig.* Bad luck, loss (= the lowest throw); the perfection (= the best card) ME. **b.** An aviator who has brought down three enemy machines, a crack aviator 1917. **3.** *fig.* A single point, a jot, particle, or atom 1528.

1. *Cymb.* II. iii. 3. **2.** The a. and wale o' honest men BURNS. **3. To bate an ace:** to make the slightest abatement. Bating him that a., he was a truly great man R. NORTH. **Within an ace of:** on the very point of. I was within an a. of being talked to death T. BROWN. Hence **Ace** *v.* to score an ace against (an opponent) cf. 1b above.

-acea, L. suffix, pl. neut. of *-aceus* = belonging to, etc.; see -ACEOUS. Used (in neut. pl. sc. *animalia*) to form names of classes or orders of animals, as *Crustacea*, etc.

-aceæ, L. suffix, pl. fem. of *-aceus*, as above. Used (in fem. pl. sc. *plantæ*) to form names of orders or families of plants, as *Rosaceæ*, etc.

-acean, f. L. *-aceus* + -AN. As an adj. = *-aceus*; as a sb. = sing. to collect. pls. in *-acea*.

Acediamine (æːsidəi·ăməin). 1877. [f. ACE(TIC + DIAMINE.] *Chem.* An amine of composition $C_2N_2H_6$.

†**Acedy.** 1623. [Later f. ACCIDIE – late L. *acēdia*.] Torpor.

Aceldama (ăke·l-, ăse·ldămă). ME. [Gr. Ἀκελδαμά – Aram. *ḥaḳēl dᵉmâ* field of blood.] The name of the field near Jerusalem bought with the blood-money received by Judas Iscariot. Hence *fig.* A field of bloodshed.

fig. What an A. Sicily has been BURKE.

Acenaphthene (æːsinæ·fþīn). 1877. [f. ACE(TIC + NAPHTHENE.] *Chem.* A compound substance of the Naphthalene group, $C_{12}H_{10}$.

Acenaphthylene (æːsinæ·fþilīn). 1877. [f. ACE(TIC + NAPHTHA + -YL + -ENE.] *Chem.* A compound substance of the Naphthalene group, $C_{12}H_8$, having two atoms of H less than Acenaphthene.

Ace·ntric, *a.* 1852. [f. A- *pref.* 14 + CENTRIC, after *eccentric*.] Without a centre.

-aceous (ēˈ·ʃəs), *suffix*, f. L. *-ace-us*, *-a*, *-um* of the nature of + -OUS; cf. -EOUS. Used in Nat. Hist. to supply adjs., resembling L. words in *-aceus*, to nouns in *-acea*, *-aceæ*; also in other words, as *cretaceous*, etc.

†**Acephal.** 1549. [– Fr. *acéphale* or late L. *acephalus*; see ACEPHALI.] **A.** *adj.* = ACEPHALOUS. **B.** *sb.* [sc. *animal*] = ACEPHALAN. 1607.

‖ **Acephala** (ăse·fălă), *sb. pl.* 1847. [late L., – Gr. ἀκέφαλα adj. neut. pl. = headless (sc. *animalia*); see -A *suffix* 4.] One of the two great divisions of molluscs. *Sing.* ACEPHALAN, or ACEPHAL.

Acephalan (ăse·fălăn). 1856. [f. prec. + -AN 1.] **A.** *adj.* Of or pertaining to the ACEPHALA. **B.** *sb.* [sc. *animal*.]

‖ **Acephali** (ăse·făləi), *sb. pl.* 1600. [med. L. (Isidor) pl. of *acephalus* without a chief – Gr. ἀκέφαλος headless, without a chief, f. ἀ- A- *pref.* 14 + κεφαλή head.] **1.** *Nat. Hist.* (Imaginary) men or animals without heads. **2.** *Eccl. Hist.* A name of various Christian bodies, which owned either no leader, no earthly head, or no bishop 1625. †**3.** *Eng. Hist.* Certain Levellers of the time of K. Henry I 1721. Hence †**Acepha·lian** *a.* and *sb.* †**Ace·phalist** (*rare*); also **Ace·phalite.**

Acephalocyst (ăse·fălo,sist). 1836. [– mod.L. *acephalocystis*; see prec., CYST.] A headless bladder-worm; a name for the hydatids. They are now known to be the *larvæ* of one of the tapeworms (*Tæniadæ*), which enlarges into a globular cyst, with the head inverted and so invisible. Hence **Ace:phalocy·stic** *a.*

Acephalous (ăse·făləs), *a.* 1731. [f. as ACEPHALI + -OUS.] **1.** Headless. **2.** Having or owning no leader or chief 1751. **3.** *Zool.* Having no part of the body specially organized as a head, e.g. *A. Molluscs* = ACEPHALA 1741. **4.** *Bot.* With the natural head aborted or cut off 1880. **5.** Lacking the beginning, as an imperfect manuscript or verse 1753.

1. An a. pedigree GROTE. **2.** An a. body politic was inconceivable SIR F. PALGRAVE. **5.** An a. structure of sentence DE QUINCEY.

Acerate (æ·serēˈt). 1847. [f. L. *acer* maple + -ATE⁴.] *Chem.* A salt of aceric acid.

Acerb (ăsɜ·ɹb), *a.* 1657. [– L. *acerbus* harsh to the taste; cf. Fr. *acerbe*.] Sour and bitter, as unripe fruit; also *fig.*

Acerbate (æ·səɹbeˈt), *v.* 1731. [– *acerbat-*, pa. ppl. stem of *acerbare*, f. *acerbus*; see prec., -ATE³.] To sour or embitter; usu. *fig.* Hence **Ace·rbate** *ppl. a.* embittered.

Acerbic (ăsɜ·ɹbik), *a.* 1865. [f. L. *acerbus*.] Sour or harsh.

Acerbity (ăsɜ·ɹbĭti). 1572. [– Fr. *acerbité* or L. *acerbitas*; see ACERB *a.*, -ITY.] **1.** Sourness of taste, with astringency 1611. **2.** *fig.* Of men, their words, etc.: Sharpness and bitterness, keen harshness 1572.

2. A. of pain BARROW. The a. of political warfare DISRAELI.

Aceric (ăse·rik), *a.* 1847. [f. L. *acer* maple + -IC 1.] Pertaining to the maple, as *aceric acid*, which is found in its sap.

Acerose (æːsĕrōᵘ·s), *a.* 1721. [– L. *acerosus*, f. *acus*, *acer-* chaff; see -OSE¹. In sense 2 erron. referred to *acus* needle, or *acer* sharp.] **1.** Like, or mixed with chaff (Dicts.). **2.** *Bot.* Needle-shaped and rigid, as pine-leaves 1785. var. **A·cerous.**

Acervate (ăsɜ·ɹvĕt), *ppl. a.* 1848. [– *acervatus*, pa. pple. of *acervare* heap up, f. *acervus* heap; see -ATE².] Heaped, growing in heaps or clusters. Hence **Ace·rvately** *adv.* **Acerva·tion,** accumulation. **Ace·rvative** *a.* tending to heaping up. **Ace·rvuline** *a.* of the form of little heaps.

Acescence (ăse·sĕns). 1765. [– Fr.; see ACESCENT, -ENCE.] The act of turning sour; acetous fermentation.

Acescency (ăse·sĕnsi). 1756. [f. next; see -ENCY.] The quality or state of turning sour; incipient or slight sourness.

Acescent (ăse·sĕnt). 1731. [– Fr., or *acescent-*, pres. ppl. stem of L. *acescere* to become sour; see -ENT.] **A.** *adj.* Turning sour; or tending to turn acid; slightly sour, turned. *lit.* and *fig.* **B.** *sb.* [sc. *substance*.]

Acet-. *Chem.* In comb. = ACETIC, ACETYL bef. a vowel, as in *acet-amide*, etc.; cf. ACETO-.

Acetable (æ·sĭtăb'l). 1551. [– L. *acetabulum* (next), the form now used.] **1.** An ancient fluid measure; a saucerful; = half a gill. **2.** = ACETABULUM 2 b. 1684.

‖ **Acetabulum** (æsĭtæ·biŭlŏm). ME. [L., f. *acetum* vinegar + *-abulum* dim. of *-abrum* = a holder.] **1.** *Rom. Antiq.* A cup for holding vinegar at table; hence a measure, half a gill. **2.** *Animal Physiol.* A cup-shaped cavity or organ: as, **a.** A sucker of the cuttle-fish or other cephalopod 1661. **b.** The socket of the thigh-bone 1709; *Hence*, **c.** The socket of any joint in insects 1828. **d.** A placental lobe, in ruminants. **3.** *Bot.* The receptacle of certain fungi. Hence **Aceta·bular** *a.* cup-like; sucker-shaped. **Aceta:buli·ferous** *a.* bearing acetabula. **Aceta·buliform** *a.* saucer-shaped.

Acetal (æ·sĭtæl). 1869. [f. ACET(IC + AL(COHOL.] *Chem.* A colourless liquid found in preparing spirit of wine, the *diethylate of ethylidene or ethidene* $CH_3–CH(OC_2H_5)_2$.

Acetaldehyde (æːsĭtæ·ldĭhəid). 1877. [contr. for *acetic aldehyde*.] *Chem.* Common or ethyl aldehyde.

Acetamide (æ·sĭtăməiːd, ăse·tăməid). 1873. [f. as next + AMIDE.] *Chem.* The primary AMIDE in which the replacing acid radical is ACETYL; $C_2H_3O.NH_2$; a white crystalline solid, nearly neutral.

Acetanilide (æːsĭtæ·niləid). 1864. [f. ACET(YL) + ANILIDE.] *Chem.* A compound of aniline and acetyl, $C_6H_5.NH.C_2H_3O$. Erron. *acetaniline*.

†**A·cetars, a·cetaries,** *sb. pl.* 1612. [– L. *acetaria* (sc. *olera*) salad herbs, subst. use of n. pl. of **acetaris*, f. *acetum* vinegar; see -ARY².] Salad plants –1775. Hence **Aceta·rious** *a.* used in salads, as cress, etc.

Acetary (æ·sĭtări). 1674. [– med.L. *acetarium* (Du Cange) vinegar container (for L. ACETABULUM), f. *acetum* vinegar; see -ARY¹.] An acid pulpy substance in the pear, etc., enclosed in a mass of calculous particles towards the base of the fruit.

Acetate (æ·sĭteˈt). 1827. [f. ACET(IC + -ATE⁴; cf. Fr. *acétate*.] *Chem.* A salt formed by combining acetic acid with a base; as *A. of lead*.

A·cetated, *ppl. a.* 1791. [irreg. f. prec. + -ED¹.] Treated with acetic acid.

Aceta·tion. 1863. [irreg. f. L. *acetum* vinegar + -ATION.] = ACETIFICATION.

Acetic (ăsĭ·tik, ăse·tik), *a.* 1808. [– Fr. *acétique*, f. L *acetum* vinegar + *-ique* -IC.] Of the nature of or pertaining to vinegar.

Phr. **Acetic acid:** The special acid of which vinegar is a diluted or crude form, produced by fermentation. Chemically, the monatomic monobasic acid of the ethyl or dicarbon series $C_2H_4O_2$. *Anhydrous acetic acid*, a synonym of *acetic anhydride*. *Acetic series*: The series of compound bodies containing the radical ACETYL C_2H_3O; as *A. ether*, *A. oxide* or *anhydride*.

Acetify (ăse·tifəi), *v.* 1864. [f. L. *acetum* vinegar + -FY.] To subject to, or undergo, acetous fermentation. Hence **Ace:tifica·tion,** the action of converting into vinegar. **Ace·tifier,** an apparatus for producing vinegar.

Acetimeter (æːsĭti·mĭtəɹ). 1875. [– Fr. *acétimètre*, f. L. *acetum* vinegar + *-mètre* -METER.] An instrument for measuring the strength of vinegar, or other acids. Hence **A:cetime·trical** *a.* var. **Aceto·meter.**

A:ceti·metry. 1875. [– Fr. *acétimétrie*, f. as prec. + *-ie* -Y[3]; see -METRY.] The determination of the strength or sourness of vinegar or acetic acid, or the proportion of it in any substance.

Acetin (æ·sĭtin). 1874. [f. ACET- + -IN[1].] Acetic glycerine; class name of a series consisting of glycerine, in which one, two, or all the three hydrogen atoms are replaced by acetyl C_2H_3O, thus forming *mono-*, *di-*, or *tri-acetin*.

† **A·cetite,** earlier f. ACETATE.

A·cetize, *v.* [f. L. *acetum* vinegar + -IZE.] = ACETIFY.

Aceto-. *Chem.* In comb. = ACETIC, ACETYL bef. a cons. (cf. ACET-), as in *aceto-chloride*, etc.

Acetone (æ·sĭtōᵘn). 1858. [f. ACET(IC + -ONE.] *Chem.* A colourless limpid liquid related to acetic acid, but containing less oxygen; pyro-acetic spirit. It is the acetic ketone, and is called also *Dimethyl ketone*. Hence ‖ **A:cetonæ·mia,** *Med.* a morbid state, marked by the presence of a. in the blood. **A·cetonami:ne,** *Chem.* a compound amine, obtained by heating a. with ammonia. **A·cetonate,** *Chem.* a salt of acetonic acid. **Aceto·nic** *a.* derived from a. **A:cetoni·tril,** *Chem.* an alcoholic cyanide or hydrocyanic ether; the *nitril* of the acetic series, called also *Ethenyl nitril* and *Methyl cyanide*.

Acetose (æ:sĭtōᵘ·s), *a.* 1533. [– late L. *acetosus* sour, f. L. *acetum* vinegar; see -OSE[1]; cf. OFr. *acetos*, Fr. *acéteux*.] Tasting like vinegar; sour. Hence **Aceto·sity,** the quality of being a. var. † **Aceto·sous** *a.*

† **A:ceto·se, -ouse.** 1547. [– OFr. *acetose*, med.L. *acetosa*, subst. use of fem. of late L. *acetosus*; see prec.] The herb Sorrel or Sorrel Dock (*Rumex acetosa*).

Acetous (æ·sĭtəs), *a.* 1778. [– late L. *acetosus*; see ACETOSE *a.*, -OUS.] Of, pertaining to, or having the qualities of vinegar; sour. Also *fig.*

fig. Till all France were grown a., virulent CARLYLE. *Acetous fermentation*: The chemical reaction by which sugar or alcohol is changed into vinegar. † *Acetous acid*: A name given to vinegar in the erroneous belief that it contained less oxygen than Acetic acid.

Acetyl (æ·sĭtil). 1864. [f. ACET(IC + -YL.] *Chem.* A monatomic radical C_2H_3O, the basis of the acetic series. Also *attrib.* and in *Comb.* Hence **Acety·lic** *a.*

Acetylene (ăse·tilīn). 1864. [f. ACETYL + -ENE.] *Chem.* A gaseous hydrocarbon, C_2H_2, used as an illuminant. Also *a. gas, lamp.*

‖ **Ach** (ăχ), *int.* [G. and Celtic.] Ah!

Achænocarp (ăkī·nokāɹp). 1880. [f. Gr. ἀ- A- *pref.* 14 + χαίνειν gape + καρπός fruit; see ACHENE.] A fruit which is an achene.

† **Acha·fe,** *v.* ME. [– AFr. *achaufer* – OFr. *eschaufer* (see A- *pref.* 9), f. *es-* EX- + *chaufer* warm: see CHAFE, ESCHAUFE.] To heat; *fig.* to heat with passion –1490.

† **Acha·pe,** *v.* [ME. *achape* – OFr. *achaper*, var. of *eschaper* (mod. *échapper*); see ESCAPE.] A by-form of ESCAPE.

† **Achaque.** [Sp.] Ailment. HOWELL.

‖ **Achar** (ătʃā·ɹ). *Anglo-Ind.* [Pers. *āchār*.] Pickles.

† **Acha·rne,** *v. rare.* ME. [–(O)Fr. *acharner*, f. *a-* AD- + *charn* flesh:– L. *caro, carn-*.] To thirst for blood. Hence ‖ **Acha·rnement,** bloodthirsty fury.

Achate (æ·kăt), *sb.*[1] *arch.* ME. [– OFr. *acate, achate* – L. *achates*; see AGATE.] An agate.

† **Acha·te,** *sb.*[2] ME. [–(O)Fr. *achat* f. *achater*; see next and cf. ACATE.] **1.** Purchase –1691. **2.** *pl.* Things purchased; CATES –1644.

† **Acha·te,** *v. rare.* 1601. [– OFr. *achater*, (also mod.) *acheter* to purchase:– Rom. * *accaptare* f. *ad* AC- + L. *captare* seize.] To purchase.

† **Acha·tour.** ME. [– AFr. *achatour*, earlier *acatour*, f. *achater* (see prec.) + *-our* -OUR; cf. ACATER.] A purchaser of provisions, *esp.* for the royal household; a purveyor –1751.

Ache, ake (ēᶦk), *v.* OE. [orig. a strong vb. like *take, shake*. Historically the vb. is *ake*, the sb. *ache*, as in *bake, batch*, etc. Both are written *ache*, but pronounced *ake*, since Johnson's erron. derivation from Gr. ἄχος; see next wd.] **1.** To be in pain; *esp.* in continuous or prolonged pain; to throb with pain. † **2.** *trans.* To make to ache –1566.

1. Lat our hedes nevere ake CHAUCER. Thy sorrow aches in me MRS. BROWNING. Hence **A·chage** (after *breakage*) *Joc.* Aching state. **A·cher,** he who, or that which, aches. **A·chingly** *adv.*

Ache (ēᶦk), *sb.*[1] [OE. *æće* is a deriv. of vb. *ac-an* to ACHE, orig. with *c* (k) palatalized to *ch* (tʃ), as in *make, match*, etc. Till 1700 the sb. was *atche* (ătʃ, ētʃ), pl. *atches* (ătʃès, ētʃès); see prec.] A pain; *esp.* a continuous or abiding pain, physical or mental.

[Ile] Fill all thy bones with Aches, make thee rore *Temp.* I. ii. 370. *Much Ado* III. iv. 56. Hence **A·cheless** *a.* without ache.

† **Ache** (ēᶦtʃ), *sb.*[2] ME. [– (O)Fr. *ache*:– L. *apium* parsley – Gr. ἄπιον.] An umbelliferous plant; prop. Smallage (i.e. *Small-Ache*); also *parsley*.

Ache (ēᶦtʃ), *sb.*[3] Name of the letter H, q.v.

† **Achea·t, achete,** *v.* ME. [– ME. *achete* sb. – AFr. var. of OFr. *eschete* ESCHEAT; see A- *pref.* 9.] To escheat; to do one out of.

† **Ache·ck,** *v.* [f. A *particle* + CHECK *v.*[1]] To check. CHAUCER.

† **Achee·r,** *v.* [var. of contemp. ENCHEER; see A- *pref.* 10, EN-[1].] To cheer –1660.

Acheilary (ăkəi·lări), *a.* 1868. [f. Gr. ἀ- A- *pref.* 14 + χεῖλος lip + -ARY[1].] *Bot.* Wanting the lip of the corolla. Better *achilary.*

Achei·lous, *a.* 1879. [f. as prec. + -OUS.] *Bot.* Without a lip. Better *achilous*.

Achene (ăkī·n), also **achæne.** 1845. [– mod.L. *achænium*, irreg. f. Gr. ἀ- A- *pref.* 14 + χαίνειν to gape. See ACHÆNOCARP.] *Bot.* A monospermal seed-vessel which does not open, with a separate pericarp; any small brittle seed-like fruit; a 'naked seed'. Hence **Ache·nial** *a.*

‖ **Acheron** (æ·kĕrọn). 1590. [L., – Gr. Ἀχέρων.] A fabled river of the Lower World; hence, the infernal regions. Hence **Achero·ntic, -al** *a.* of or belonging to Acheron, infernal; gloomy; waiting to cross Acheron, moribund.

† **Ache·soun.** ME. [– OFr. *acheson, achaison*:–L. *occasio* OCCASION; refash. ENCHESOUN, ENCHEASON; aphet. to CHESOUN; see A- *pref.* 10.] Occasion, purpose.

Achieve (ătʃī·v), *v.* ME. [– (O)Fr. *achever* come or bring to an end, f. OFr. phr. *a chief* to (a) head, to an end, repr. L. *ad* and Rom. **capum*, for L. *caput*; see AD-, CHIEF.] **1.** To finish, to carry out successfully, to bring to an end. *absol.* 1607. † **2.** *intr.* To come to an end; result, turn out –1534. **3.** Of an end: To attain, to reach successfully. † **4.** *intr.* To attain successfully *to* –1587.

1. He that nought nassayeth, nought nacheveth CHAUCER. Bid them atchieue me, and then sell my bones *Hen. V*, IV. iii. 91. *absol.* He does atcheeue as soone As draw his sword *Coriol.* IV. vii. 23. **3.** Some atchieue greatnesse *Twel. N.* v. i. 378. To a. its [the policy's] necessary ends 1882. Hence **Achie·vable** *a.* † **Achie·vance,** achievement. **Achie·ver.**

Achievement (ătʃī·vmĕnt). 1475. [f. prec. or – (O)Fr. *achèvement*; see –MENT.] **1.** The action of achieving. **2.** Anything achieved; a feat, a victory 1593. **3.** *Her.* An escutcheon or ensign armorial, granted in memory of some achievement 1548. (In this sense corrupted to **hatchment.**)

1. Within the bounds of possible a. SOUTHEY. **2.** The achievements of genius BREWSTER. **3.** The Hachementes wer borne onely by Capitaynes 1548.

Achi·ll, *adv.* 1870. [f. A *prep.*[1] + CHILL *sb.*] In a state of chill.

Achillean (æ:kilī·ăn), *a.* 1637. [f. *Achilles* + -AN.] Resembling Achilles; invulnerable, invincible.

† **Achillize,** *v.* 1672. [f. as prec. + -IZE.] To play Achilles with.

Achilous. [Better form of ACHEILOUS.] *Bot.* Without lips.

Achi·me, *adv.* 1860. [f. A *prep.*[1] + CHIME *sb.*[1]] Chiming.

‖ **Achio·te, acho·te.** 1796. [Sp. *achiote* – native Amer. *achiotl*.] The seeds of the Arnotto (*Bixa orellana*); the red colouring matter they yield.

Achirite (æ·kirəit). [f. *Achir* Mahméd + -ITE[1] 2b.] = DIOPTASE.

Achlamydate (ăklæ·midĕt), *a.* 1877. [f. Gr. ἀ- A- *pref.* 14 + χλαμυδ-, χλαμύς cloak + -ATE[2].] *Zool.* Of Molluscs: Having no mantle.

Achlamydeous (æklămi·diəs), *a.* 1830. [f. as prec. + -EOUS.] *Bot.* Having no envelope; without apparent calyx and corolla.

† **Acho·ke,** *v.* ME. [f. A- *pref.* 1 + CHOKE *v.*] To choke.

Acholous (æ·kŏləs). [f. Gr. ἀ- A- *pref.* 14 + χολή bile + -OUS.] Lacking bile.

‖ **Achor** (ēᶦ·koɹ). 1585. [L., – Gr. ἀχώρ scald, scurf.] *Med.* A scaly eruption in the hair scalp, constituting scald-head.

Achroite (æ·kro,əit). [f. Gr. ἄχροος colourless + -ITE[1] 2b: see ACHROOUS.] *Min.* Colourless tourmaline from Elba.

Achromatic (æ:kromæ·tik), *a.* 1766. [– Fr. *achromatique*, f. Gr. ἀχρώματος + *-ique* -IC; see A- *pref.* 14, CHROMATIC.] **1.** *Optics.* Free from colour; not showing colour from decomposition in transmitting light. Also *sb.* [sc. *lens*]. **2.** *Biol.* Of tissue: Uncoloured 1882.

1. The human eye is not a. TYNDALL. *sb.* An a. of four inches aperture 1878. Hence **A:chroma·tically** *adv.* so as to produce freedom from colour. **Achro:mati·city, Achro·matism,** the state or quality of being a. **Achromati·stous** *a.* (*rare*) achromatic. **Achro:matiza·tion,** the action or process of rendering a. **Achro·matize** *v.* to render a. **Achro·mato:psy,** *Med.* colour-blindness. † **Achro·mic** *a.* [improp. formed] = ACHROMATIC. **Achro·mous** *a.* (*rare*) colourless.

Achronical, -ly, incorr. ff. ACRONYCAL, -LY.

Achronism (æ·krŏniz'm). *nonce-wd.* [f. Gr. ἄχρονος (f. ἀ- A- *pref.* 14 + χρόνος time), + -ISM.] The state of timelessness. 1877. ¶ Occ. for ANACHRONISM, as if *an achronism.*

Achroö-, combining form of ACHROOUS, as in *achroödextrin*, colourless dextrin, etc.

Achroous (æ·kroəs), *a.* 1879. [f. Gr. ἄχροος (f. ἀ- A- *pref.* 14 + χρόα, χροιά colour) + -OUS.] Colourless; achromatic.

Achylous (ăkəi·ləs), *a.* 1879. [f. Gr. ἄχυλος + -OUS; see A- *pref.* 14, CHYLE.] *Phys.* Without chyle.

Achy·mous, *a.* 1879. [f. Gr. ἄχυμος + -OUS; see A- *pref.* 14, CHYME.] *Phys.* Without chyme.

‖ **Acicula** (ăsi·kiŭlă). Pl. **aciculæ.** 1875. [late L., dim. of *acus* needle.] *Nat. Hist.* A slender needle-like body, such as the spines or prickles of some animals and plants, or some crystals. var. **A·cicle.** Hence **Aci·cular** *a.* needle-like. **Aci·cularly** *adv.* **Aci·culate** *a.* furnished with aciculæ; marked as with needle-scratches; *improp.* = ACICULAR. **Aci·culated** *ppl. a.* marked or striated with fine lines, as if by a needle. **Aci·culiform** *a.* needle-shaped. **Aci·culine** *a.* = ACICULAR. **Aci·culite** (*Min.*) = AIKINITE, or Acicular Bismuth.

Acid (æ·sid). 1626. [– Fr. *acide* or L. *acidus*, f. *acēre* to be sour.] **A.** *adj.* **1.** Sour, tart, sharp to the taste; tasting like vinegar. Also *fig.* **2.** *Chem.* Having the essential properties of an acid 1727. **3.** *Min.* = ACIDIC 2. 1874.

1. [Sorrel] is a cold and a. herb BACON. *fig.* In his a. manner BOSWELL. Rather an a. expression of countenance DISRAELI. *A. drop*: a sweet made of sugar flavoured with tartaric acid 1836. **2.** *A. salt*, a salt that retains part of the replaceable hydrogen of a dibasic acid.

B. *sb.* A sour substance; *spec.* in *Chem.* a substance belonging to a class of compounds of hydrogen with another element or elements (oxygen being generally the third element), the commonest of which are sour, and have the property of neutralizing alkalis, and of changing vegetable blues to red 1696. **A. test**: testing for gold with aquafortis; *fig.* a crucial test 1893.

Of Acids, Vitriol is the chiefest, Sea-salt next to that E. PHILLIPS.

Acidic (ăsi·dik), *a.* 1877. [f. prec. + -IC.] *Min.* Applied to the element in a mineral compound which forms an oxygen or other salt with a basic element, e.g. the silicon in silicate of lime 1880. **2.** Abounding in an acidic element, usu. silicon 1877.

Acidify (ăsi·difəi), *v.* 1797. [f. as prec. + -FY; cf. Fr. *acidifier*.] **1.** To make acid or sour.

Chem. To convert into an ACID. Also *fig.* **2.** *intr.* (*refl.*) To become acid.

1. *fig.* His thin existence all acidified into rage CARLYLE. Hence **Aci·difi:able** *a.* **Aci·difiant** *a.* acidifying. **Acidi·fic** *a.* (*Min.*) applied to the oxygen, sulphur, etc., in a mineral which is an oxygen, sulphur, etc., salt of any basic element. **Aci:difica·tion,** the act or process of acidifying. **Aci·difier,** anything that acidifies. **Aci·difying** *ppl. a.* forming an acid.

Acidimeter (æ:sidi·mĭtəɹ). 1839. [f. ACID + -METER; cf. Fr. *acidimètre.*] An instrument for measuring the strength of acids. Hence **A:cidime·trical** *a.* **A:cidi·metry,** the process of measuring the strength of acids.

Acidity (ăsi·dĭti). 1620. [– Fr. *acidité* or late L. *aciditas*; see ACID, -ITY.] The quality or state of being acid.

Acidosis (æsidōᵘ·sis). 1905. [f. ACID + -OSIS.] *Path.* An acid condition of the blood such as occurs in diabetes.

Acidulate (ăsi·diŭleⁱt), *v.* 1732. [f. L. *acidulus* sourish (see ACID, -ULOUS) + -ATE³.] To make somewhat acid or sour; to flavour with an acid. Also *fig.*

fig. [No] compliment not acidulated with scorn MACAULAY.

Acidulous (ăsi·diŭləs), *a.* 1769. [f. as prec. + -OUS.] Sub-acid. Also *fig.* Sour-tempered. *fig.* Gloomy and a. CARLYLE. var. **Aci·dulent.**

† **Acier.** Also **asser.** [OFr. *acer, acier* :– low L. *aciarium* (sc. *ferrum*), f. *acies* edging or pointing iron.] Steel (prop. Fr.).

Acierage (æ·siĕrėdʒ). [– Fr. *aciérage*, f. *acier* steel + *-age* -AGE.] The process of plating with steel.

‖ **Acies.** *Obs.* 1646. [L. *acies* edge, keenness, sharpness.] Keen attention or aim of eye, ear, etc.

A·ciform, *a.* [f. L. *acus* needle + -FORM.] Needle-shaped.

‖ **Acinaces** (ăsi·năsīz, ăki·năkīz). [L., for Gr. ἀκινάκης, orig. Pers.] *Anc. Hist.* A short sword or scimitar. Hence **A:cina·ciform, aci·naciform** *a.* scimitar-shaped, as in *Bot.* of leaves, etc.

Acinetic (æsine·tik), *a.* 1879. [f. Gr. ἀκίνητος motionless + -IC; cf. KINETIC.] *Med.* Preventing motion. var. **Acine·sic** (improp. formation).

Acinetiform (æsinī·tifǫɹm), *a.* 1877. [f. mod.L. *acineta* (f. Gr. ἀκίνητος motionless) + -FORM.] Having the form of *Acinetæ*, a genus of infusoria with suckers which are not in constant motion like the cilia or flagella of other infusoria.

‖ **Acinus** (æ·sinŏs). Pl. **acini.** 1731. [L. *acinus*, a berry growing in a cluster; also a kernel.] † **1.** A berry which grows in clusters, as grapes, etc.; the cluster. **2.** *Bot.* One of the small fleshy berries or drupes which make up such fruits as the blackberry; the compound fruit itself 1830. **3.** The stones or seeds of grapes or berries 1731. **4.** *Anat.* A racemose gland; a blind end of a duct of a secreting gland, which has several lobes 1751. Hence **A:cina·ceous** *a.* consisting of acini, formed like a blackberry or raspberry. **Aci·niform, a·ciniform** *a.* clustered, or full of small kernels, like grapes. **A:cino·se** *a.* consisting of *acini*; resembling, or composed of, a cluster of small berries. **A·cinous** *a.* = ACINOSE.

-acious (-ēⁱʃəs), *suffix*, forming adjs. meaning 'given to, inclined to, abounding in'; f. L. *-aci-* (nom. *-ax*), adj. ending added chiefly to vb. stems (Fr. *-ace*) + -OUS; as in *vivacious*, etc.

‖ **Acipenser** (æsipe·nsəɹ). 1853. [L.] *Zool.* The sturgeon.

-acitate (-æ·siteⁱt), *suffix* = *-aci-* (see -ACIOUS) + *-t-* (see -TY) + -ATE, forming vbs. on adjs. in *-aci-ous*, or sbs. in *-aci-ty*, as *capacitate* to endow with capacity.

-acity (-æ·sĭti), *suffix*, – Fr. *-acité* – L. *-acitat-*, f. *-aci-* (see -ACIOUS) + *-tat-* (see -TY), as *voracity*, the quality of being voracious.

† **Acker.** ME. [Of uncertain origin; prob. a variant of EAGRE, the 'bore' on tidal rivers, called by Lyly *agar*.] †**1.**? Flood tide; bore –1552. **2.** A ripple, or furrow on the water; a 'cat's-paw' 1808.

Acker, obs. f. ACRE.

† **Ackno·w, aknow,** *v.* [OE., f. *on* in, on + *cnāwan* to know (by the senses), to recognize; the prefix afterwards reduced, as usual, to *o-*, *a-* (see A- *pref.* 2), and at length corruptly written *ac-* in imitation of *ac-* before *c-*, *k-*, *q-* in words adopted from L.] **1.** To recognize –1430; to acknowledge, confess –1561. **2.** In pa. pple. Informed *of* –1490. **3.** To be acknown: To be (self-) recognized in relation to anything; hence, to avow (*to* a person) –1639.

3. Be not aknowne on't; I have vse for it *Oth.* III. iii. 319.

Acknowledge (ăknǫ·lėdʒ), *v.* 1481. [Either from obs. *acknowledge* sb. (XVI), like the earlier KNOWLEDGE *v.*, f. KNOWLEDGE *sb.*; or f. KNOWLEDGE *v.*, like ACKNOW *v.* on KNOW. By XVI the earlier verbs *knowledge* and *a(c)know* (exc. in pa. pple.) were obs., and *acknowledge* took their place.] **1.** To own the knowledge of; to confess; to admit as true 1553. **2.** To recognize or confess (a person or thing to be something); or, *simply*, to own the claims of 1481. **3.** To own as genuine, or valid in law; to avow or assent to, in legal form. **4.** To own as an obligation; hence, to acknowledge (the receipt of) a letter 1667.

1. He loued .. your daughter, and meant to a. it this night *Much Ado* I. ii. 13. **2.** The kingdomes that a. Christ 1 *Hen. IV*, III. ii. 111. Agents too vile to be acknowledged MACAULAY. **3.** To a. a release PINKERTON. **4.** But they his gifts acknowledg'd none MILT. Hence **Acknow·ledgeable** *a.* recognizable. **Acknow·ledged** *ppl. a.* recognized; admitted as true, valid, or authoritative. **Acknow·ledgedly** *adv.* **Acknow·ledger.** †**Acknow·ledging** *ppl. a.* expressing esteem or gratitude. (Fr. *reconnaissant.*)

Acknowledgement (ăknǫ·lėdʒmĕnt). Also **acknowledgment.** 1594. [f. prec. + -MENT.] **1.** The act of acknowledging; confession, admission, avowal. †**2.** Recognition –1616. **3.** The act of recognizing the position or claims of 1611. **4.** A declaration or avowal of an act or document so as to give it legal validity 1651. **5.** The owning, or due recognition, of a gift or benefit received, or of a message 1612; hence, something given or done in return for a favour or message.

1. With this a., That God fought for us *Hen. V*, IV. viii. 124. **3.** All such places as owe a. to the Dutch JAS. MILL. **4.** A. of indebtedness (*mod.*). A virtual a. of the contract (*mod.*). **5.** I am, with all a., etc. W. GOULD. A. of help (*mod.*). A small a. of my gratitude (*mod.*). *Comb.* **a.-money,** a sum paid at the death of a landlord, in a. of the new one.

Acla·stic, *a. rare.* 1879. [f. Gr. ἄκλαστος unbroken, f. κλάζειν to break + -IC.] *Nat. Phil.* Not refracting.

Aclinic (ăkli·nik), *a.* 1850. [f. Gr. ἀκλινής unbending, f. ἀ- A- *pref.* 14 + κλίνειν to bend + -IC. Cf. Fr. *aclinique.*] Without inclination. Said of the magnetic equator, or *aclinic line*, where the magnetic needle lies horizontal.

A-clock, early f. **o'clock**; see A *prep.*² and CLOCK.

Acme (æ·kmi). 1570. [– Gr. ἀκμή. First spelt as Eng. by Venner in 1620.] The highest point or pitch; the culmination or perfection; *esp.* †a. the period of full growth –1844; **b.** the crisis of a disease (*arch.*) 1630.

The mark and ἀκμή of our language B. JONS. In Achilles, courtesy reaches to its acmè GLADSTONE. **a.** One that can instruct your youth, And keepe your Acme in the state of truth B. JONS. **b.** The a. of a disease 1752, of frenzy CARLYLE.

Acne (æ·kni). 1835. [– mod.L. *acne*, deduced from a misreading, ἀκνάς for ἀκμάς, acc. pl. of Gr. ἀκμή eruption on the face. See prec.] *Path.* Tubercular tumours, chiefly in the face.

Acnode (æ·knōᵘd). 1873. [f. L. *acus* needle + NODE.] *Geom.* An isolated point belonging to a locus or curve: = *conjugate point* (CONJUGATE *a.* 6). Hence **Acno·dal** *a.* of or pertaining to acnodes.

† **A-coast,** *adv.* 1599. [f. A *prep.*¹ + COAST; see ACOST.] **1.** At one side, by the coast. **2.** Ashore.

Acock (akǫ·k), *adv.* 1846. [f. A *prep.*¹ + COCK *sb.*⁴] In cocked fashion; defiantly.

A-cock-bill, *adv.* 1708. [In XVIII, *a cock-bell*, f. A *prep.*¹ + *cock-bell* (later *-bill*); see COCK-BILL.] *Naut.* Having the bills cocked or pointing upwards. Said of the anchor when it hangs from the cathead ready for dropping; also of the yards when placed at an angle with the deck.

A-cock-horse, *phr.* [f. A *prep.*¹ + COCK-HORSE.] See COCK-HORSE.

Acold (ăkōᵘ·ld), *a. arch.* ME. [prob. orig. *a-cōlod, a-cōled*, pa. pple.; see ACOOL *v.*] Chilled, cold.

Tom's a-cold *K. Lear* III. iv. 59. The owl for all his feathers was a-cold KEATS.

† **Aco·ld,** *v.* [OE. *acaldian* (= OHG. *irkalten*, MHG., G. *erkalten*), f. A- *pref.* 1 + *caldian*, *ćealdian* become cold; cf. ACALE *ppl. a.*, ACOOL *v.*] To become or make cold –1440.

Aco·logy. *rare.* 1847. [f. Gr. ἄκος cure, remedy + -λογία -LOGY; cf. Fr. *acologie.*] *Med.* The doctrine of therapeutic agents.

Acolyctine (ækoli·ktəin). [f. *Aco(nitum lyc(octonum* + *-tine* after ACONITINE.] *Chem.* An organic base obtained from *Aconitum lycoctonum*; aconine.

Acolyte (æ·kŏləit). [– OFr. *acolyt* (mod. *-yte*), or eccl. L. *acolytus, -itus, -ithus* – Gr. ἀκόλουθος following, follower (whence *acolutus* in Cyprian, Augustine, Gregory). See COLET.] **1.** *Eccl.* One belonging to the highest of the minor orders (also, a layman) whose duties are concerned with attendance at the altar and carrying candles ME. **2.** An attendant; a devoted follower 1829.

1. The Acholite, which we call Benet or Cholet .. 1555. **2.** The acolytes of chivalry SCOTT. Hence **A·colyteship.** vars. † **Acolouthite, Acolythist.**

† **A-co·mpass,** *adv.* [– OFr. *a compas*, f. *a* to + *compas* circle.] In a circle. CHAUCER.

Acondylous (ăkǫ·ndiləs), *a.* 1853. [f. Gr. ἀ- A- *pref.* 14 + κόνδυλος joint + -OUS.] *Nat. Hist.* Not jointed.

Acone·lline. 1876. [dim. f. ACONINE; see -EL².] *Chem.* An organic base obtained from the root of the aconite. var. **Aconella.**

Aconic (ăkǫ·nik), *a.* 1877. [irreg. contr. f. ACONITIC; cf. next.] *Chem.* In *Aconic Acid*: A non-saturated monobasic acid, $C_5H_4O_4$. Also used in comb. as *citraconic*, etc.

Aconine (æ·kŏnəin). [irreg. contr. f. ACONITINE; cf. prec.] *Chem.* An alkaloid found in the root of aconite.

Aconite (æ·kŏnəit). 1578. [– Fr. *aconit* or L. *aconitum* – Gr. ἀκόνιτον.] **1.** *Bot.* A poisonous plant of the order *Ranunculaceæ*; *esp.* Monk's-hood or Wolf's-bane (*Aconitum napellus*). **2.** An extract from *Aconitum napellus* used in pharmacy. *poet.* Deadly poison. 1597.

1. One [sorte] is..Aconit that baneth or killeth Panthers. The other..Woolfs LYTE. **2.** *Aconite* ..styled 'The Homœopathic Lancet' H. BUCK. Wine is A. to men COWLEY. **Winter Aconite:** *Eranthis hyemalis.* Hence **Aconi·tal** *a. rare.* **Aco·nitate,** *Chem.* a salt of Aconitic acid. **Aconi·tic** *a.*, *Chem.* in *Aconitic acid*, a basic triatomic acid $(C_6H_3O_3)'''(OH)_3$ existing in monkshood, etc.

Aconitine (ăkǫ·nitəin). 1847. [f. ACONITE + -INE⁵; cf. Fr. *aconitine.*] *Chem.* The essential principle of aconite, a poisonous vegetable alkaloid, with a bitter taste. var. **Aconi·tia.**

† **Acoo·l,** *v.* [OE. *acōlian*, f. A- *pref.* 1 + *cōlian* be or become cold; cf. ACALE *ppl. a.*, ACOLD *v.*] To wax cold; *trans.* to cool.

† **Aco·p,** *adv. rare.* [A *prep.*¹ + COP *sb.*²] On the top; on high. B. JONS.

Acopic (ăkǫ·pik), *a.* and *sb.* [f. Gr. ἄκοπος (f. ἀ- A- *pref.* 14 + κόπος weariness) + -IC.] *Med.* Removing fatigue.

Acorn (ēⁱ·kǫɹn). [OE. *æcern* acorn, also mast of trees, = MLG. *ackeren* (Du. *aker*) acorn, MHG. *ackeran, eckern* oak or beech mast, ON. *akarn* acorn, Goth. *akran* fruit, produce (rendering Gr. καρπός); rel. to OE. *æcer* ACRE, thus orig. meaning produce of uncultivated land. In Eng., LDu. and ON. restricted to the fruit of the oak, and since XV–XVI assoc. w. *oak* and *corn*, as in *ake-, oke-corn*, and the mod. sp. *acorn.*] † **1.** Fruit generally, or mast of trees –ME. **2.** The fruit or seed of the oak-tree; an oval nut growing in a *cupule* OE. **3.** *Naut.* A conical piece of wood fixed on the point of the spindle, above the vane, on the mast-head.

1. To slaken .. hunger with acornes of okes CHAUCER. **2.** His fill of pesen and oke cornes Bp. FISHER. Bearing mast or okehornes HULOET. Brused acrons [quasi – Gr. ἄκρον top] PLAT. *Comb.* **Sea-a.** = ACORN-SHELL; **a.-barnacle** = ACORN-SHELL. Hence **A·corned** *a.* furnished with or (*Her.*) bearing acorns; fed or filled with acorns.

Acorn-shell. 1764. A multivalve Cirriped (*Balanus*), allied to the Barnacles.

‖ **Acorus** (æ·kǒrɒs). 1714. [L., = Gr. ἄκορος (Dioscorides).] A genus of plants (N. O. *Orontiaceæ*), including the Sweet Flag or Galingale (*A. calamus*).

Acosmism (ăkǫ·zmiz'm). 1847. [f. Gr. ἀ- A- *pref.* 14 + κόσμος world + -ISM.] Denial of the existence of the universe, or of a universe as distinct from God.
The a. of Spinoza and the atheism of Comte J. MARTINEAU. Hence **Aco·smist,** one who professes a.

† **Aco·st,** *adv.* ME. [– OFr. *a coste*, f. *a* to, at + *coste* side :– L. *costa* rib, later side. Afterwards treated as if f. Eng. A- *prep.*[1] + COAST in the restricted sense of 'shore'.] **1.** On or by the side. **2.** Ashore.

Acotyledon (ăkǫ:tilī·dən). 1819. [f. mod.L. pl. *acotyledones*, perh. through Fr. *acotylédone*; see A- *pref.* 14, COTYLEDON.] *Bot.* A plant which has no distinct cotyledons, or seed-lobes; as a fern, fungus, etc. Hence **Acotyle·donous** *a.*

‖ **Acouchi** (ăku·ʃi). 1866. [Native name in Guiana.] *Bot. Acouchi* resin, or balsam: the balsam of *Icica heterophylla*.

Acou·chy. 1831. [– Fr. *acouchi, agouchi*; see AGOUTI.] *Zool.* A small rodent allied to the guinea-pig and agouti; the Surinam Rabbit.

Acoumeter (akau·mītəɹ). 1847. [irreg. f. Gr. ἀκούειν to hear + -METER.] An instrument for measuring the power of the sense of hearing. Hence **Acou·metry.**

† **Acou·nter,** *v.* [ME. var. of ENCOUNTER; see A- *pref.* 10.] To encounter. Hence † **Acou·nter, -tre** *sb.* an encounter.

† **Acou·p(e,** *v.* ME. [– OFr. *acolper, acouper* to accuse, f. *a* A- *pref.* 7 + *coulper* blame :– L. *culpare*, f. *culpa* fault; or f. OFr. *enculper* etc. :– L. *inculpare* INCULPATE, with ME *a-* for *en-*: see A- *pref.* 10.] To accuse.

Acoustic (ăkau·stik, ăkū·-), *a.* 1605. [– Gr. ἀκουστικός pertaining to hearing, f. ἀκούειν to hear; see -IC. Cf. Fr. *acoustique* (XVIII).] **1.** Pertaining to the sense of hearing, used in hearing; adapted to aid hearing; pertaining to the science of audible sounds. **2.** as *sb.* A medicine or appliance which aids hearing. In *pl.*: see ACOUSTICS.
1. Acoustique Art BACON. An a. instrument 1743. *A.* or *speaking* tubes 1822. A. nerves 1878, telegraphy 1879. Hence **Acou·stical** *a.* of or pertaining to acoustics; promoting hearing. **Acou·stically** *adv.* in relation to the hearing of sounds. **A:cousti·cian,** one versed in acoustics.

Acoustico-, comb. f. ACOUSTIC.

Acoustics (ăkau·stiks, ăkū·-), *sb. pl.* 1683. [See ACOUSTIC, -ICS.] **1.** The science of the phenomena of hearing. **2.** The acoustic properties of a building 1898.

Acquaint (ăkwēⁱ·nt). *arch.* ME. [– OFr. *acoint* familiar, friendly :– Rom. **accognitus*, pa. pple. of L. *accognoscere*; see next. Cf. QUAINT *a.*] **A.** *ppl. a.* = ACQUAINTED (*with*). **B.** *sb.* An acquaintance. CHAUCER.

Acquaint (ăkwēⁱ·nt), *v.* [ME. *aqueynte, acointe* – OFr. *acointier* to make known, also refl. (mod. Fr. *s'accointer*) :– med.L. *accognitare* to make known, f. pa. ppl. stem of L. *accognoscere* to know, recognize, f. *ad* AC- + *cognoscere* to know.] To make known. † **1.** *refl.* To make oneself known, become known (*to*) –1483; hence *intr.* to become acquainted, or familiar –1774. **2.** *refl.* To make oneself to have, to give, or gain for, oneself acquaintance *with* any one. Now only in *pass.* ME. **3.** *refl.* and *trans.* To give (oneself or any one) experimental knowledge of (a thing) 1567; † *trans.* to familiarize (const. *with*, or *inf. phr.*) –1658. **4.** *trans.* To inform, make cognizant or aware (*with, that,* † *of*) 1559; *ellipt* to inform 1590; † to tell or make known –1678.
1. *intr.* Though the Choiseuls will not a. with you WALPOLE. **2.** A. now thy selfe with him *Job* 22: 21. We're acquainted now SOUTHEY. **3.** Acquainting mine heart with wisedome *Eccles.* 2: 3. A. yourself with your new duties (*mod.*). *trans.* A. them to pronounce some examples BRINSLEY. **4.** It were a peece of honestie to a. the King withall *Wint. T.* IV. iv. 696. *ellipt.* He begged her to a. him immediately FIELDING. Hence † **Acquai·ntable** *a.* easy to be acquainted with.

Acquaintance (ăkwēⁱ·ntăns). ME. [– OFr. *acointance* f. *acointier*; see prec., -ANCE. For the sp. w. *ac-* cf. ACKNOWLEDGE *v.*] **1.** Knowledge of a person or thing which is more than mere recognition, and less than intimacy. **2.** The state of being acquainted (const. *with*, † *of*, or *obj. gen.* as 'her', 'our' a.) 1300. **3.** A person or persons with whom one is acquainted. (Orig. *collect.*, now usu. *sing.*, with pl. *acquaintances.*) ME.
1. An a. with [books] such as only . . study could give BRYCE. † *To take a. of* = *mod.* **to make the a. of,** to form an a. with. **2.** I shall desire you of more a. *Mids. N.* III. i. 185. Let's . . drink unto Our better a. BYRON. **3.** He was his a. and familyar MORE. A crowd of acquaintances GIBBON. Hence **Acquai·ntanceship** = ACQUAINTANCE 2. **Acquai·ntancy** = prec. † **Acquai·ntant** = ACQUAINTANCE 3.

Acquainted (ăkwēⁱ·ntĕd), *ppl. a.* ME. [f. ACQUAINT *v.* + ED[1].] **1.** Familiar, through being known 1314. **2.** Having mutual knowledge. Const. *with.* ME. **3.** Having personal or experimental knowledge. Const. *with, of.* 1480. † **4.** Accustomed. Const. *with, to.* –1683.
1. As things a. and familiar to us 2 *Hen. IV*, V. ii. 139. The a. sword SOUTHEY. Upon a. ground LAMB. **2.** I pray you be better a. *Cymb.* I. iv. 132. **3.** A. with griefe *Isa.* 53: 3, with English politics GEO. ELIOT. **4.** A. only with a very moderate fortune CLARENDON. Hence **Acquai·ntedness,** the state or degree of acquaintance.

Acquest (ăkwe·st). 1613. [– Fr. (XVI) † *acquest* (OFr. *aquest*, mod. *acquêt*; med.L. (XIII) *acquestum*) :– Rom. * *acquæsitum*, subst. use of n. pa. pple. of * *acquærere* ACQUIRE.] **1.** A thing acquired 1622. *spec.* (*Law.*) Property gained otherwise than by inheritance. † **2.** = ACQUIST 1. –1787.
1. New Acquests are more Burthen, then Strength BACON. Acquests in the Study and Practice of the Law 1671. **2.** In the a. of Independence J. BARLOW.

Acquiesce (ækwi,e·s), *v.* 1620. [– L. *acquiescere* remain at rest, assent to, f. *ad* AC- + *quiescere* to rest; see QUIET. Cf. Fr. *acquiescer.*] † **1.** *intr.* To remain at rest; to rest satisfied *in*, *under* –1788. **2.** To agree tacitly to, concur *in*, † *to*, † *with* 1651. † **3.** *trans.* To bring to rest, appease –1659.
1. We were not made to a. in life and health BURKE. **2.** We . . a. [in the word of the Church] HOBBES. To a. in the propriety of . . COWPER, the necessity of . . SCOTT. var. † **Acquie·scate** *v.* Hence **Acquie·scing** *vbl. sb.* tacitly agreeing; *ppl. a.* silently compliant. **Acquie·scingly** *adv.*

Acquiescence (ækwi,e·sĕns). 1631. [f. prec. + -ENCE; cf. Fr. *acquiescence.*] **1.** The action or condition of acquiescing (sense 1). **2.** Silent or passive assent to, or compliance with, measures or proposals. Also with *in*, † *with*, † *to*.
1. A life of worldly a. J. MARTINEAU. **2.** The Chief Justice smiled a. DARWIN. A. in the charges levied ROGERS. vars. † **Acquie·scement, Acquie·scency.**

Acquiescent (ækwi,e·sĕnt). 1753. [– *acquiescent-*, pres. ppl. stem of L. *acquiescere* ACQUIESCE *v.*; see -ENT.] **A.** *adj.* Acquiescing; disposed to acquiesce. **B.** *sb.* One who acquiesces 1810. Hence **Acquie·scently** *adv.*

† **Acqui·et,** *v.* 1548. [– med.L. *acquietare* put at rest, f. *ad* AC- + late L. *quietare* (Priscian) to quiet.] To set at rest, quiet –1613.

Acquire (ăkwəiᵊ·ɹ), *v.* [ME. *acquere* – OFr. *aquerre* :– Rom. **acquærere*, for L. *acquirere* f. *ad* AC- + *quærere* seek. Superseded *c* 1600 by the latinized form *acquire*; cf. mod. Fr. *acquérir.*] **1.** To gain, or get as one's own (by one's own exertions or qualities) 1435. **2.** To receive, to come into possession of 1613.
1. What w'acquire by Pains and Art BUTLER. **2.** The Idler acquires weight by lying still JOHNSON. Hence **Acqui·rable** *a.* **Acquirabi·lity. Acqui·red** *ppl. a.* gained, opp. to *innate* or *inherited.* **Acqui·rer. Acqui·ring** *vbl. sb.* the action of gaining; the thing gained. † **Acqui·ry,** the process of acquiring.

Acquirement (ăkwəiᵊ·ɹmĕnt). 1630. [f. prec. + -MENT.] **1.** The action of acquiring 1712. **2.** That which is acquired; an attainment. Opp. to a (material) *acquisition*, or a natural *gift*. 1630. Also *collect.* 1868.
1. Rules for the A. of a Taste ADDISON. The a. of knowledge MRS. SHELLEY. **2.** His acquirements were . . considerable LD. BROUGHAM. A man of ability and a. SEELEY.

† **A·cquisite,** *a.* 1532. [– L. *acquisitus*, pa. pple. of *acquirere* ACQUIRE *v.*] Acquired. Also as pa. pple. of ACQUIRE.

Acquisition (ækwizi·ʃən). ME. [– L. *acquisitio*, f. *acquisit-*, pa. ppl. stem of *acquirere* ACQUIRE *v.*; see -ITION.] **1.** The action of acquiring; see ACQUIRE *v.* **2.** A thing acquired or gained 1477.
1. The a. of Wealth HOBBES. **2.** The English acquisitions in Guinea 1686.

Acquisitive (ăkwi·zĭtiv), *a.* 1637. [f. as ACQUISITE + -IVE, partly through Fr. *acquisitif, -ive* – late L. *acquisitivus.*] † **1.** Belonging to one by acquisition –1642. **2.** Able, or given, to make acquisitions 1846.
2. A. Louis Fourteenths CARLYLE. The Perceptive or A. Faculty BOWEN. Hence **Acquisiti·tious** *a.* ?*Obs.* Acquired, not *native* or *innate.* **Acqui·sitively** *adv.*

Acquisitiveness (ăkwi·zĭtivnĕs). 1826. [f. prec. + -NESS.] The quality of being acquisitive; desire of possession. (A faculty to which phrenologists allot a special 'organ'.)

Acquist (ăkwi·st). 1613. [var. of ACQUEST, after L. *acquisitum* (see ACQUISITE *a.*), med.L. *acquistum*, It. *acquisto*. Commonly used for the action, while *acquest* is more common for the result.] **1.** The action of acquiring, acquisition. † **2.** = ACQUEST 1. –1677.

Acquit (ăkwi·t), *v.* [ME. *acwite, aquite* – OFr. *acuiter, a(c)quiter* – med.L. *acquitare* to acquit, pay a debt, f. *ad* AC- + *quitare* QUIT *v.* As in *quit*, the vowel was long (*aquite*) to XVI, and even XVII. Cf. REQUITE *v.*] To quiet a claim; hence, to satisfy the creditor; to clear the debtor.

I. 1. To discharge a claim, debt, or liability ME. † **2.** To perform the duties of (an office) 1530. **3.** To requite (a benefit or injury). *arch.* ME. † **4.** To atone for (an offence) –1600.
1. To . . acquite Your . . promise QUARLES. To a. an obligation 'JUNIUS'. **3.** Make us that we a. not evil for evil 1535.

II. To pay off; to repay, be quits with –1599.

III. † **1.** To set free, release, by paying or cancelling a debt –1630. **2.** To set free, release *of* or *from* a duty, obligation, or burden 1463. **3.** To clear from a charge, to declare not guilty *of* ME. † **4.** *refl.* To deliver, rid, oneself *of* –1753. **5.** To discharge oneself (*of* duty or responsibility). Hence, *simply*, To discharge one's duties, perform one's part. late ME.
1. Twelf pens to me, and I the wil acquite CHAUCER. **3.** Three others were acquitted after . . trial MCCARTHY. **5.** He . . acquitted himself like a man 1878. Hence **Acqui·t** *ppl. a. arch.* = *acquitted.* † **Acqui·t** *sb.* the act of acquitting. **Acqui·tment** (? *Obs.*), the action of acquitting; release. **Acqui·tted** *ppl. a.* exonerated. **Acqui·tter.**

Acquittal (ăkwi·tăl). ME. [f. prec. + -AL[1].] † **1.** Payment, or retribution; amends –1749. **2.** = ACQUITTANCE 2. *Obs.* exc. in *Law.* 1463. **3.** A setting free by verdict, sentence, or other legal process 1535. **4.** Discharge (of duty) 1656.

Acquittance (ăkwi·tăns), *sb.* ME. [– OFr. *aquitance*, f. *aquiter* + *-ance* -ANCE.] **1.** The action of clearing off debt, or other obligation ME. **2.** Hence (the result): Release, discharge ME. **3.** A writing in evidence of discharge; a release, a receipt ME. Also *attrib.* † **4.** Release (from danger or trouble) –1631. **5.** = ACQUITTAL 3. **6.** = ACQUITTAL 4. *rare.*
1. This may be an a. of favours upon the turf JUNIUS. **3.** You can produce acquittances For such a summe *L. L. L.* II. i. 161. Hence **Acqui·ttance** *v.* to discharge. *Rich. III*, III. vii. 233.

Acraldehyde (æ:kræ·ldĭhəid). 1869. [f. L. *acer, acr-* ACRID + ALDEHYDE.] *Chem.* One of the polymeric modifications of ALDEHYDE.

‖ **Acrania** (ăkrēⁱ·niă). 1849. [mod.L., f. Gr. ἀ- A- *pref.* 14 + κρανίον skull + -IA[1].] Absence of the skull. Hence **Acra·nial** *a.*

† **A·crasy.** 1596. [– Gr., confusing ἀκρασία ill-temperature (f. ἄκρατος unmixed, untempered, intemperate), with ἀκρασία want of self-command (f. ἀκρατής powerless, incontinent).] Irregularity, disorder, intemperance. Personified in Spenser.
Guyon . . Doth . . Acrasy defeat SPENSER *F.Q.* II. xii. *motto.*

† **Acra·ze,** *v.* 1549. [A- *pref.* 11 + CRAZE *v.*] To weaken, impair. Hence † **Acra·zed** *ppl. a.* impaired in body, or mind.

Acre (ē^i·kəɹ). *Pl.* **acres.** [OE. *æcer* = OFris. *ekker*, OS. *akkar* (Du. *akker*), OHG. *ackar* (G. *acker*), ON. *akr*, Goth. *akrs* – Gmc. **akraz* :– IE. **agros*, repr. also by L. *ager*, Gr. ἀγρός, Skr. *ájras* field.] **1.** A piece of tilled or arable land, a field OE. *Obs.* exc. in *God's Acre* [from mod. Ger.] a churchyard, and prop. names, as *Long Acre*. Used *rhet.* in *pl.* for *lands*, etc. **2.** A measure of land, orig. as much as a yoke of oxen could plough in a day; later limited by statute to a piece 40 poles long by 4 broad (= 4840 sq. yds.), or its equivalent.

1. Nabot.. had an Aker of a Vine yerd CAXTON. *Broad acres*, extensive lands. **2.** Now would I give a thousand furlongs of sea for an a. of barren ground *Temp.* I. i. 70. Their estates were bound to the last a. BURKE. Also *loosely*: Acres of despatches CARLYLE. † An **a. length,** 40 poles or a furlong (*i.e.* furrow-length); † an **a. breadth,** 4 poles or 22 yards.

¶ **Acre** or **Acre-fight** (from L. *acram* (for *pugnam*) *committere*, where *acram* is a bad tr. of OE. *camp* combat, confused with L. *campus*, and so with *acre*) exists only in Cowel and mod. Dicts.

Hence **A·creable** *a.* per acre. **A·creage,** extent of acres; acres collectively; also *attrib.* **A·cred** *a.* possessing landed estates.

Acrid (æ·krid), *a.* 1712. [irreg. f. L. *acer*, *acr-* sharp, pungent + -ID[1], prob. after *acid*.] **1.** Bitter and hot to the taste; pungent, stinging, corrosive to the eyes, skin, etc. **2.** Bitterly irritating to the feelings. (Stronger than *acrimonious*.) 1781.

1. Corroded by some a. humour REID. [Sweat] turning a. MRS. BROWNING. **2.** Tacitus grows more a. .. to the last MERIVALE. Hence **Acri·dity,** the quality of being a.; irritant bitterness of speech or temper. **A·cridly** *adv.* **A·cridness,** acridity. var. † **A·crious** *a.*

Acridine (æ·kridəin). 1877. [f. ACRID + -INE[5].] *Chem.* A crystalline substance, $C_{12}H_9N$, of the diphenyl group, extracted from coal-tar oil.

Acrimonious (æ:krimōᵘ·niəs), *a.* 1612. [f. next + -OUS.] **1.** = ACRID 1. *arch.* **2.** Bitter and irritating in disposition or manner 1775.

1. An a. kinde of salt SIR T. BROWNE. **2.** An a. contest SCOTT, expression MACAULAY. Hence **A:crimo·niously** *adv.* **A:crimo·niousness.**

Acrimony (æ·krimǝni). 1542. [– Fr. *acrimonie* or L. *acrimonia* pungency, f. *acer*, *acr-*; see ACRID, -MONY.] **1.** The quality of being ACRID 1. *arch.* **2.** Irritating bitterness of temper 1618.

2. Cleon attacked him with great a. LANGHORNE. A. of expression WELLINGTON.

† **A·crisy.** 1721. [– Gr. ἀκρισία want of judgement, f. ἀ- A- *pref.* 14 + κρίσις judgement.] **1.** A matter left undecided; also, want of judgement. **2.** An undecided state or condition of a disease. var. † **Acrisia.**

‖ **Acrita** (æ·krită), *sb. pl.* 1835. [mod.L. (sc. *animalia*) – Gr. ἄκριτα, n. pl. of ἄκριτος undistinguishable; see -A 4.] *Zool.* A division of the animal kingdom lacking a distinct nervous system. Hence **A·critan** *a.* and *sb.* (as sing. of prec.). **A·crite** *a.* acritan.

Acritical (ăkri·tikăl), *a.* 1864. [f. A- *pref.* 14 + CRITICAL *a.*] *Med.* Not having or indicating a crisis.

Acritochromacy (æ:krito,krōᵘ·măsi). 1879. [f. Gr. ἄκριτος undistinguishing + χρῶμα, χρωματ- colour; see -ACY.] Colour-blindness, achromatopsy.

† **A·critude.** [– L. *acritudo* sharpness, f. *acer*, *acr-* sharp; see -TUDE.] = ACRIDITY. –1753.

† **A·crity.** 1619. [– L. *acritas* sharpness, f. *acer*, *acr-* sharp; see -ITY.] Sharpness.

Acro-. Gr. ἀκρο- comb. f. ἄκρος *a.* terminal, topmost; *sb.* a tip, peak, summit.

acro-ca·rpous [Gr. καρπός] *a.*, terminal-fruited; **-cepha·lic** [Gr. κεφαλή] *a.*, having a lofty skull, better *-cephalous*; **-ce·phaly,** loftiness of skull; **-chord** [see next], a snake of the genus *Achrocordus*, family *Hydridæ*, having a fusiform body covered with tricuspid scales; **-cho·rdon** [Gr. χορδή], a hard elongated wart; a hanging wart; **-dont** [Gr. ὀδόντ-] *sb.* and *a.*, having teeth firmly soldered to the ridge of the jaw-bones, as lizards; **-gen** [Gr. -γενης], a plant having a stem with the growing point at its extremity, opp. to *Thallogens*; hence, **-ge·nic, -genous** *adjs.*; **-graphy** [Gr. -γραφία], the art of making blocks in relief, as a substitute for wood-engraving; **-lith** [Gr. λίθος], a statue with the head and extremities of stone, the trunk usu. of wood; hence, **-lithan, -li·thic** *adjs.*; **-lo·gic** [Gr. λόγος] *a.*, pertaining to, or founded on, initials; **-petal** [L. *petere*] *a.*, tending towards the summit or apex; said of the order in which the parts of a plant arise; hence, **-petally** *adv.*; **-spire** [Gr. σπεῖρα], the first leaf that appears when corn sprouts, forming a developed plumule; also as *vb.*; hence, **-spired** *ppl. a.*; **-spiring** *vbl. sb.*; **-spore** [Gr. σπόρος; see SPORE], a spore produced at the apex of a hypha or cellular filament in certain fungi, a basidiospore; hence, **-sporous** *a.*

‖ **A:croa·ma.** Pl. **a:croa·mata.** 1580. [Gr. ἀκρόαμα anything heard, f. ἀκροᾶσθαι hear.] **1.** A rhetorical declamation (as opp. to an argument) 1852. **2.** *Anc. Phil.* Oral teaching heard only by the initiated; *esoteric* as opp. to *exoteric* doctrines. Hence **A:croama·tic** *adj.* orally communicated; esoteric, secret; *sb. pl.* [ellipt. after Gr. τὰ ἀκροαματικά] Aristotle's lectures to the initiated on the esoteric parts of his philosophy. Also † **Acroama·tical** *a.*

‖ **Acroasis** (æ:kroē^i·sis). Pl. **acroases.** 1655. [L. *acroasis* – Gr. ἀκρόασις something listened to, f. as prec.] *Anc. Hist.* A discourse listened to. Hence, **A:croa·tic** *a.* and *sb.*

Acrobat (æ·krŏbæt). 1825. [– Fr. *acrobate* – Gr. ἀκροβάτης, f. ἀκρόβατος walking on tiptoe, f. ἄκρος ACRO- + -βατος, f. base of βαίνειν to walk.] A rope-dancer; a gymnast; a tumbler. *lit.* and *fig.* **A:croba·tic** *a.* **A:croba·tically** *adv.* **A:croba·tics** *sb. pl.* **A·crobatism.**

Acro·ck. 1615. [Fr. *à croc.*] With a prop or support.

Acrolein (ăkrōᵘ·li,in). 1869. [f. L. *acer*, *acr-* sharp, pungent + *olēre* smell + -IN[1].] *Chem.* A colourless acrid liquid (C_3H_4O), of pungent irritating odour, formed in the destructive distillation of glycerin. It is the aldehyde of allyl.

‖ **Acromion** (ăkrōᵘ·miən). 1615. [– Fr., or its source Gr. ἀκρώμιον, f. ἄκρος point + ὦμος shoulder.] *Phys.* The outer extremity of the shoulder-blade. Also *attrib.* as *a. process.* Hence **Acro·mial** *a.*

Acronarcotic (æ:kro,naɹkǫ·tik), *a.* 1882. [irreg. f. L. *acer*, *acr-* pungent + NARCOTIC *a.*] Having both acrid and narcotic qualities.

Acronych (ăkrǫ·nik), *a.* [– Gr. ἀκρόνυχος at nightfall, f. ἄκρος ACRO- + νύξ night.] = next.

Acro·nychal, -ycal, *a.* 1594. [f. prec. + -AL[1]; also erron. spelt *-ical*, as if f. χρόνος time.] Happening in the evening or at nightfall, vespertine, as the a. rising or setting of a star. (*Not* 'rising in the evening *and* setting at sunrise'.) Opp. to *cosmical*. Hence **Acro·nychally** *adv.* var. **A:crony·ctous.**

Acroo·k, *adv.* 1480. [A *prep.*[1] + CROOK *sb.*] In a bend; crookedly.

Acrophony (ækrǫ·fŏni). 1880. [f. Gr. ἀκρο- ACRO- + -φωνία voice, sound.] The sound of the initial; the use of the picture-symbol or hieroglyph of an object to represent phonetically the initial syllable or sound of the name of the object; *e.g.* of the symbol of an *ox*, '*aleph*', to represent *a*. Hence **A:crophone·tic** *a.* pertaining to a.

Acropolis (ăkrǫ·pŏlis). 1662. [– Gr. ἀκρόπολις, f. ἄκρος topmost + πόλις city.] The elevated part, or the citadel, of a Greek city; *esp.* that of Athens. Also *fig.*

[The] A. of Man's body, the Head HY. MORE.

Across (ăkrǫ·s), aphet. **cross.** [ME. *a croiz*, *o cros*, *a cros*, whence *acros*, *acrosse* (XV), with occas. vars. *in*, *on crosse* (XV, XVI) – OFr. *a croix*, *en croix*; later assim. to native formations in A- *pref.*[1]]

A. *adv.* **1.** In the form of a cross, crosswise, crossing 1480. **2.** Crossing the length-line, transversely; through 1523. **3.** On the other side (as the result of crossing) 1816. † **4.** Not straight; obliquely, amiss –1687.

1. A warrior frowns in stone, his legs a. 1771. **2.** H'as broke my head a-crosse *Twel. N.* v. i. 178. To swim a. the Channel (*mod.*). **3.** We shall soon be a. (*mod.*). **4.** The squint-eyed pharisees looke a-crosse at all the actions of Christ BP. HALL.

B. *prep.* [The adv. with obj. expressed.] **1.** Direction: At right angles, or any angle, with 1626. **2.** Motion: From side to side of, not lengthwise; through, over 1591. **3.** Position: On the other side of, beyond 1750.

1. A. the theatre 1697. [An] arch..a. the river J. WILSON. Her bow a. her shoulder flung COLLINS. *To come across*: to come upon incidentally. **2.** When my..Falcon made her flight acrosse Thy Fathers ground *Wint. T.* IV. iv. 15. *Across the country*: straight through between two points without regard to paths. To sweep a. one's memory G. O. TREVELYAN. **3.** 'The king a. the water!' *Jacobite Toast.*

Acrostic (ăkrǫ·stik). 1587. [– Fr. *acrostiche* or Gr. ἀκροστιχίς, f. ἀκρο- ACRO- + στίχος line of verse. The etymol. sp. *acrostich* has been superseded through association w. -IC.] A short poem, etc., in which the initial, the last, or the middle letters of the lines, or all of them, taken in order, spell a word, phrase, or sentence, and thus form a *single*, a *double*, or a *triple* acrostic. See also TELESTICH. **2.** An ABECEDARIAN poem 1753. † **3.** The beginning or end of a verse –1753. Hence **Acro·stic** *a.*[1] pertaining to acrostics (in senses 1, 2). **Acro·stichally, -cally** *adv.* **Acrosti·chic** *a.* **Acro·sticism,** acrostic arrangement or character.

Acro·stic, *a.*[2] 1602. [A factitious formation from ACROSS *adv.*, or obs. *acrossed* crosswise.] Folded across; erratic, zigzag.

Acrostichoid (ăkrǫ·stikoid), *a.* 1882. [f. *acrostich* ACROSTIC + -OID.] An epithet of a genus of ferns, N.O. *Polypodiaceæ*, due to the peculiar distribution of the sori.

Acroteleutic (æ:kro,tĕliū·tik). 1753. [f. Gr. ἀκροτελεύτιον fag-end, hence burden or chorus (f. ἀκρο- ACRO- + τελευτή end) + -IC.] *Eccl.* The end of a verse or psalm, or something added thereto to be sung by the people.

Acroter (ăkrōᵘ·təɹ). 1678. [– Fr. *acrotère* – L. *acroteria* (pl., in Vitruvius) – Gr. ἀκρωτήρια (pl.) f. ἄκρος extreme, endmost, highest.] **1.** *Arch.* In *pl.* **acroteria** or **acroters,** prop. 'The pedestals, often without bases, placed on the centre and sides of pediments for the reception of figures.' Gwilt. Also, incorr., the statues. 1706. † **2.** 'The pinnacles or other ornaments standing in ranges on the horizontal coping or parapets of a building.' Gwilt. –1759. † **3.** *Med.* The extremities of the body, the hands, feet, and head –1753. vars. **A:crote·rium, A:crote·rion.** Hence **A:crote·rial** *a.*

Acrotic (ăkrǫ·tik), *a.* 1853. [irreg. f. Gr. ἀκρότης extreme + -IC.] *Path.* Pertaining to the outside.

Acrotism (æ·krŏtiz'm). 1853. [f. Gr. ἀ- A- *pref.* 14 + κρότος sound of striking + -ISM.] *Med.* Lack of pulsation.

Acrotomous (ăkrǫ·tŏməs), *a.* [f. Gr. ἀκρότομος having the top cut off + -OUS.] *Min.* Having a cleavage parallel with the base.

† **A-cry,** *adv.* 1593. [A *prep.*[1] + CRY *v.*] In a cry, crying.

Acryl (æ·kril). [f. ACR(OLEIN + -YL.] *Chem.* The hypothetical radical of the allyl series, C_3H_3O. Hence **A·crylate,** a salt of acrylic acid. **Acrylic** *a.* of or containing a. *Acrylic acid*, $C_2H_3O.OH$, formed by the oxidation of acrolein.

Act (ækt), *sb.* ME. [Mainly – L. *actus* doing, playing a part, dramatic action, act of a piece, *actum* public transaction, (pl.) records, register, f. *act-* (see next): partly through Fr. *acte* – L.] **1.** A thing done; a deed ME.; a deed implying a state 1751. † **2.** Fact or reality; opp. to intention, possibility, etc. –1677. † **3.** ? Active principle –1730. **4.** The process of doing; action, operation. (L. *actus.*) *arch.* 1494. **5.** A thing transacted in council, etc.; hence, a decree. (L. *actum*, pl. *acta.*) 1458. **6.** A record of transactions or decrees; an instrument in writing. (L. *actum*, pl. *acta.*) 1535. **7.** A 'performance' of part of a play; *hence*, One of the main divisions of a drama, completing a definite part of the action. Also *fig.* (L. *actus.*) 1613. **8.** In the Universities, a thesis publicly maintained by a candidate for a degree. Also *attrib.* 1641. † **9.** An *auto da fé*, or act of faith; a burning of heretics –1709.

1. The worthie Actes of the ancient Brytaines

POWEL. An a. of bankruptcy BLACKSTONE. The a. of a madman (*mod.*). **2.** If I in a., consent, or sinne of thought Be guiltie *John* IV. iii. 135. **3.** God is a pure A. BEVERIDGE. **4.** Wise in Conceit, in A. a very sot DRAYTON. *Act of God*: action of uncontrollable natural forces in causing an accident. *In act*: in the very doing; on the point of. (L. *in actu.*) Taken in adultery, in the very a. *John* 8: 4. **5.** By new a. of Parliament 3 *Hen. VI*, II. ii. 91. A. of Attainder 1839. **6.** Credit..shall be given to the public acts, records, etc. of every other state *Constit. U.S.* iv. § 1. *Acts* (*of the Apostles*). **7.** Away then: our A.'s ended FLETCHER. The..first a. of our great drama FREEMAN. **8.** Attendance to keep Acts GATAKER. attrib. *A. Sunday, A. Sermon, Act* (i.e. Trinity) *Term*. Hence **A·ctless** *a.* inactive.

Act (ækt), *v.* 1594. [– *act-*, pa. ppl. stem of L. *agere* drive, carry on, do. Prob. infl. by ACT *sb.*] † **1.** *trans.* To put in motion; actuate, animate –1748; to bring (a thing or process) into action –1791. **2.** To carry out in action. *arch.* 1610. **3.** To carry out in mimic action; to perform (a play); *fig.* in a bad sense: To simulate 1594. **4.** *intr.* (obj. suppressed). To perform on the stage 1598. **5.** To perform on the stage of existence; to do, as opp. to *think, speak*, etc.; to comport or demean oneself 1684. Also with *for, as, on, upon, up to*. **6.** Of things: To put forth energy, produce effects, exert influence, fulfil functions 1751. Also with *on*.

1. Thy senses flue that acte thy life WARNER. Self-love..acts the soul POPE. **2.** To a. her.. abhord commands *Temp.* I. ii. 273. Acting the law we live by TENNYSON. **3.** Acting her passions on our stately stage DRAYTON. Sunderland acted calumniated virtue to perfection MACAULAY. *To act a part*, or *the part of*: You have still an honourable part to a. 'JUNIUS'. *To act* (*any one*), *lit.* and *fig.*: He that acteth another is said to beare his Person, and a. in his name HOBBES. Acting the lover SWIFT. **4.** Say who acts best? J. MARSTON. **5.** Acting..from..disinterested motives SIR R. PEEL. In overcoming the hostility of the West, William acted as he always did a. FREEMAN. Acting as Chaplain MACAULAY. I a. for my brother (*mod.*). To a. *on* a maxim (*mod.*). Your lordship acts up to your tenets LANDOR. **6.** When several causes a. at once JEVONS. The brake refused to a. (*mod.*). Hence **A·ctable** *a.* capable of being acted (on the stage), or carried out in practice. **A·cted** *ppl. a.* carried out in action; performed (*esp.* dramatically); feigned.

Actinal (æ̆ktəi·năl, æ·ktinăl), *a.* 1857. [f. Gr. ἀκτίς, ἀκτιν- ray + -AL¹.] *Zool.* Pertaining to that part of a radiate animal which contains the so-called mouth, etc.

Acting (æ·ktiŋ), *vbl. sb.* 1601. [f. ACT *v.* + -ING¹.] **1.** Execution. **2.** The performance of deeds; in *pl.* doings, practices, etc. 1603. **3.** The performing of plays, etc.; simulation 1664. **4.** The putting forth of energy, activity, etc. 1647.

1. Betweene the a. of a dreadfull thing, And the first motion *Jul. C.* II. i. 63. **2.** The great actings which are now on foot SCOTT. *Comb.* **a.-order,** *spec.* an order to act in a vacant office, pending an appointment by the ultimate authority.

A·cting, *ppl. a.* 1597. [f. as prec. + -ING².] **1.** Performing (dramatically). **2.** Putting forth activity. **3.** Performing temporary or special duties, as *Acting-Captain, -Manager*, etc. 1797.

‖ **Actinia** (æ̆kti·niă). Pl. **actiniæ, actinias.** 1748. [mod.L., f. Gr. ἀκτίς, ἀκτιν- ray + -IA².] *Zool. prop.* A genus of the family *Actiniadæ*; *pop.*, any animal of the family; a Sea-Anemone.

Actiniform (æ̆kti·nifǭɹm), *a.* 1843. [f. as prec. + -FORM.] Of a radiated form, like a sea-anemone. var. **A·ctinoid** *a.*

Actinism (æ·ktiniz'm). 1844. [f. as prec. + -ISM. Cf. Fr. *actinisme*.] † **1.** The radiation of heat or light, or that branch of Philosophy which treats of it. **2.** That property in light-rays which produces chemical changes, as in photography. Hence **Acti·nic** *a.*

Actinium (æ̆kti·niŏm). 1881. [f. as prec. + -IUM.] *Chem.* **1.** A supposed chemical element, so called because light affects its salts. **2.** A radio-active element. Symbol Ac. 1904.

Actino-, a. Gr. ἀκτινο- comb. f. of ἀκτίς (gen. ἀκτῖνος), a ray, a beam.

actino-che·mistry, that branch which treats of the chemical energies in solar rays; **-graph** [Gr. γράφος], an instrument for recording the variations in the power of the solar rays; **-lite** [Gr. λίθος], a bright green variety of Hornblende, occurring usu. in fasciculated crystals; var., † **a·ctinote**; hence, **-li·tic** *a.*; **-mere** [Gr. μέρος], a portion of the surface of a radiated animal cut off by any two meridional lines reaching from pole to pole; **-meter** [Gr. μέτρον], an instrument for measuring the intensity of the sun's heating rays; hence, **-me·tric(al** *a.*; **-metry** [Gr. -μετρια], the measurement of the radiation of heat from surfaces; **-mo·rphous** [Gr. μορφή] *a.*, of radiated shape; **-phone** [Gr. -φωνος], an apparatus for the production of sound by actinic rays; hence, **-pho·nic** *a.*; **-phorous** [Gr. -φορος] *a.*, bearing radiating spines; **-stome** [Gr. στόμα], the mouth of a radiated animal; **-zo·a** [Gr. ζῷα] *sb. pl.* a class of radiated animals, partly *Cœlenterata*, partly *Zoophytes*, containing the sea-anemones and coral polypes; hence, **-zo·al** *a.*

Action (æ·kʃən). ME. [– (O)Fr. *action* – L. *actio*, f. *act-* pa. ppl. stem of *agere* ACT *v.*; see -ION.]

I. *Generally.* **1.** The process or condition of acting or doing, the exertion of energy or influence; working, agency, operation ME. **2.** A thing done, a deed; in *pl.* conduct. Viewed as occupying time in doing, as distinguished from ACT. 1600. **3.** The thing represented as done in a drama, poem, etc. 1712. † **4.** *pl.* The acts or records of a court, etc. –1635. **5.** Gesture, esp. in oratory; gesture and attitude in *Sculpt.* and *Painting*; trained movements of the body, etc., in animals 1579. **6.** The way in which an instrument acts; also, the mechanism by which this is effected 1845.

1. A Womans thought runs before her a. *A.Y.L.* IV. i. 141. The word a. is properly applied to those exertions which are consequent on volition D. STEWART. *Quantity of a.* in *Physics*: the momentum of a body multiplied into the time. The accioun or werkynges of Penitence CHAUCER. 1842 Chemical a. 1842. Schemes were put in a. against her life HALLAM. *A. of a verb, verbal a.*: the action expressed by a verb. Submit the whole to the a. of a slow fire SOYER. **2.** When our Actions do not, Our feares do make vs Traitors *Macb.* IV. ii. 3. The Actions of men [are] the best Interpretors of their thoughts LOCKE. **3.** The a. of Paradise Lost ADDISON, of the Iliad 1751. **5.** Sute the A. to the Word, the Word to the A. *Haml.* III. ii. 19. The roan has good knee-a. (*mod.*). **6.** The a. of the air-pump 1845. The grand pianoforte with the new a. DICKENS.

II. *Specifically.* **1.** The taking of legal process to establish a claim or obtain remedy; legal process; the right to raise such process ME. **2.** A legal process or suit 1483. **3.** Active operation against an enemy, fighting 1604; a fight 1599. † **4.** Acting of plays; a play –1710; **5.** A devotional exercise 1825. † **6.** A share in a joint-stock company (Fr.) 1641.

1. *To take a.*: to institute legal proceedings; hence, *gen.* to take steps. *Property in a.*, i.e. not in possession, but recoverable by legal process. (Earliest Eng. sense.) If one calls a merchant bankrupt, a. lies TOMLINS. He took prompt a. to defend his rights (*mod.*). Mr. Fang, haue you entred the A.? SHAKS. **3** Cleared ship for A. 1805. A general a. WELLINGTON. **5.** The a. of Thanksgiving 1855. **6.** African actions fell to £30 EVELYN. Hence **A·ction** *v.* to institute a legal action against. **A·ctionable** *a.* affording grounds for an a. at law. **A·ctionably** *adv.* **A·ctional** *a.* of or pertaining to a. or actions. † **A·ctionary,** a shareholder in a joint-stock company. **A·ctioner,** an artisan who makes the ACTION (sense 6) of an instrument. **A·ctionist** (*a*) = ACTIONARY (*obs.*); (*b*) one who lays stress on (oratorical) a. **A·ctionless** *a.* void of a., inert. † **A·ctious** *a.* energetic.

† **A·ctivate,** *v.* 1626. [f. ACTIVE *a.* + -ATE³.] To move to activity. Cf. ACTUATE.

Active (æ·ktiv), *a.* ME. [– L. *activus*, f. *act-* (see ACT *v.*) + *-ivus* -IVE; partly through (O)Fr. *actif, -ive.*] *gen.* Characterized by action. Hence **1.** Practical, *esp.* with *life*, opp. to *contemplative, speculative, theoretical* ME. **2.** Originating or communicating action; spontaneous; opp. to *passive* ME. Also *absol.*, sc. *qualities, forces*. **3.** *Gram.* **a.** *prop.* An epithet of Voice in verbs used transitively; opp. to *Passive, Reflexive*, or *Middle*. That form of the vb. in which the logical subject of the action is made the grammatical subject of the assertion, as shown by inflections, position, etc. **b.** *Less correctly*, said of verbs themselves, either (1) by opposing *action* in Active verbs to *passion* in Passive verbs, and to the action or state which is neutral in Neuter verbs, or (2) by opposing *action* in *Active* (*Transitive* or *Intransitive*) verbs to *existence* or *state* in *Neuter* verbs. **4.** Working, effective; opp. to *quiescent* or *extinct* 1640. **5.** Abounding in action; energetic; diligent, brisk 1597. **6.** On the credit side of the balance-sheet; opp. to *passive*. (Fr.)

1. Actyf lyf or contemplatyf LANGL. My speculative and a. instruments *Oth.* I. iii. 271. **2.** The treasons of Eadwine were often passive rather than a. FREEMAN. **4.** A. benevolence BOSWELL, volcanos LYELL, poison LIVINGSTONE, service FREEMAN. **5.** The most a. fellow in Europe SHAKS. A. to pursue POPE. Less a. than he was COWPER. A. demand FAWCETT, markets (*mod.*). Hence **A·ctively** *adv.* † practically; spontaneously; *Gram.* in the manner of an active vb.; energetically, briskly. **A·ctiveness** = ACTIVITY 2.

Activity (æ̆kti·vĭti). 1530. [– Fr. *activité* or late L. *activitas*, f. as prec.; see -ITY.] **1.** The state of being active; the exertion of energy, action 1549. **2.** Energy, diligence, liveliness 1530. † **3.** Physical exercise, athletics –1710. **4.** Anything active, e.g. a force or operation 1646.

1. The Supreme Being (who is Activity itself) 1664. **2.** The a. of France BURKE, of a volcano 1869, in the iron market (*mod.*). **4.** Activities without purpose LAMB.

Acton (æ·ktən). ME. [– OFr. *auqueton, hocqueton* (mod. *hoqueton*), prob. – Prov. *alcoton* – Arab. *alḳuṭun* cotton; see AL- *pref.*², COTTON.] A stuffed jerkin, worn under the mail; later, a jacket of leather, plated with mail.

Cranstoun's lance..Through shield..and a. past SCOTT. var. **Haqueton.**

Actor (æ·ktəɹ). ME. [– L., f. *act-* (see ACT *v.*) + *-or* -OR 2. Cf. (O)Fr. *acteur* (XIII).] † **1.** An overseer, or factor (tr. L. *actor*). † **2.** He who conducts an action; a plaintiff; an advocate; a public prosecutor. *Obs.* exc. in *Rom. Law*. 1413. **3.** One who acts, or takes part in any action; a doer 1603. **4.** A stage-player 1581.

3. Condemn the fault, and not the a. of it *Meas. for M.* II. ii. 37. **4.** *Rich. II*, v. ii. 24. Pitt was essentially an a. J. R. GREEN. *Comb.* **a.-manager,** a manager who is also an a. Hence **A·ctorship,** the quality of a (dramatic) actor.

Actress (æ·ktrės). Also **actrice.** 1589. [f. prec. + -ESS¹.] † **1.** A female ACTOR (sense 3); replaced by ACTOR –1712. **2.** A female player on the stage 1700.

Actual (æ·ktiuăl), *a.* [ME. *actuel* – (O)Fr. *actuel* – late L. *actualis* active, practical, f. *actus* ACT *sb.*; see -AL¹. The sp. *-al* assim. to the L.] † **1.** = ACTIVE 1. –1647. **2.** Existing in act or fact; real. Also *absol.* in *pl.* = actualities. **3.** Existing or acting at the time; present, current 1642.

1. Walking, and other actuall performances *Macb.* v. i. 13. **2.** Their own actuall miseries HOBBES. Not in a. rebellion 'JUNIUS'. The a. proceeds JAS. MILL. **3.** Their a. lord BROWNING. The a. position of affairs (*mod.*). Hence **A·ctualness,** = ACTUALITY.

Actualism (æ·ktiuăliz'm). 1860. [f. prec. + -ISM.] The doctrine that all existence is active, not inert or dead.

Actuality (æ:ktiu,æ·lĭti). ME. [– OFr. *actualité* entity (mod.Fr. *actualité* is a neologism) or med.L. *actualitas*, f. *actualis* ACTUAL *a.* + *-itas* -ITY.] † **1.** Capacity of action –1677. **2.** The state of being ACTUAL (sense 2); reality 1675; *pl.* actual conditions or circumstances 1665. **3.** Realism in description 1850.

2. To sacrifice a truth of a. to a truth of feeling RUSKIN. *pl.* The actualities of the case M. DAVIES. **3.** [Her] characters..have a flavour of a. W. E. HENLEY. var. **A·ctualness.**

Actualize (æ·ktiuăləiz), *v.* 1810. [f. ACTUAL *a.* + -IZE; cf. Fr. *actualiser*.] **1.** To make ACTUAL; to realize in action. **2.** To represent realistically 1881.

1. When these possibilities are actualized DE QUINCEY. Hence **A:ctualiza·tion.**

Actually (æ·ktiuăli), *adv.* 1470. [f. ACTUAL *a.* + -LY²; cf. late L. *actualiter* practically; in sense 3 after Fr. *actuellement*.] † **1.** With deeds, actively –1660; energetically –1485. **2.** In act or fact; really 1587. **3.** As a present fact, at present 1663. **4.** As a matter of fact; indeed; even 1762.

2. The rates of interest a. paid in business

JEVONS. 3. The party a. in power (*mod.*). 4. I a. found the door standing open (*mod.*).

Actuary (æ·ktiuări). 1553. [– L. *actuarius* keeper of accounts, f. *actus* ACT *sb.*; see -ARY[1].] **1.** A registrar or notary, who keeps record of the acts of a court 1553. **2.** An official in an insurance office who compiles tables of mortality, estimates rates of premium, etc.; or one whose profession it is to solve monetary problems depending on Interest and Probability, in connection with life, fire, or other accidents, etc. Hence **Actua·rial, Actua·rian** *adjs.* of or pertaining to actuaries or their profession.

Actuate (æ·ktiu,e^{i}t), *v.* 1596. [– *actuat-*, pa. ppl. stem of med.L. *actuare*, f. *actus* ACT *sb.*; see -ATE[3].] † **1.** To reduce to action 1596; to render active, to excite –1751. **2.** To inspire (a thing) with active properties. *arch.* 1642. Also *absol.* **3.** To move to mechanical action. Also *fig.* 1645. **4.** To act upon the will, as motives do 1741. † **5.** *intr.* To act –1657.

2. The soul is a spirit that actuates the natural body HY. MORE. 3. To a. or put in motion the system of wheels or pinions G. ADAMS. 4. Every liberal motive that can a. an Authour BOSWELL. Hence † **A·ctuate** *ppl. a.* = ACTUATED. **A·ctuated** *ppl. a.* rendered actual, or active. **A·ctuating** *vbl. sb.* carrying out in practice; animating; *ppl. a.* moving, inspiring.

Actuation (æ·ktiu,ē^{i}·ʃən). 1630. [– med.L. *actuatio* efficacity, f. as prec.; see -ION. In mod. use f. prec.] A communication of motion, a bringing into action; impulse, movement.

The best designs are spoiled by faulty a. 1879.

† **A:ctuo·se**, *a. rare.* 1677. [– L. *actuosus* full of activity, f. *actus*; see ACT *sb.*, -OSE[1]; cf. OFr. *actueus.*] Very active. Hence † **Actuo·sity.**

† **A·cture.** *rare.* 1593. [f. as ACT *v.* + -URE.] Action.

Actu·rience. 1880. [f. as prec.; see -URIENT, -ENCE.] Desire to act.

Acuate (æ·kiuĕt), *ppl. a.* 1471. [– *acuat-*, pa. ppl. stem of med.L. *acuare*, var. of L. *acuere* sharpen, make pointed; see -ATE[2].] Sharp-pointed. Hence † **A·cuate** *v.* to sharpen. *lit.* and *fig.* **A:cua·tion** (*rare*), sharpening; var. † **Acui·tion.**

Acuity (ăkiū·ĭti). 1543. [– Fr. *acuité* or med.L. *acuitas*, f. *acuere* sharpen; see ACUTE *a.*, -ITY. Cf. OFr. *aiguëté.*] Sharpness; as of a needle, an acid, wit.

Aculeate (ăkiū·liĕt), *a.* 1605. [– L. *aculeatus* furnished with a sting or prickle, f. *aculeus*, dim. of *acus* needle; see -ATE[2].] **1.** *Zool.* Having a sting 1661. **2.** *Bot.* Set with prickles 1870. **3.** *fig.* Pointed, stinging 1605.

3. Words may be a. BACON. Hence **Acu·leated** *ppl. a.* In *Nat. Hist.* Pointed; armed with prickles; also *fig.* **Acu:lea·tion,** pointedness.

Aculeiform (ăkiū·li,ifǫɹm), *a. Bot.* 1857. [f. L. ACULEUS + -FORM.] Like a prickle.

Aculeolate (ăkiū·liolĕt), *a. Bot.* 1858. [f. L. *aculeolus*, dim. of *aculeus* (see next) + -ATE[2].] Set with small prickles.

‖ **Aculeus** (ăkiū·liŏs). Pl. **aculei.** 1828. [L.] **1.** *Zool.* The sting of an insect, etc. **2.** *Bot.* A prickle; as in the rose 1878. Hence † **Acu·leous** *a.* aculeate. *rare.*

† **Acumble**, *v.* ME. [Of unkn. origin.] To benumb.

Acumen (ăkiū·mĕn). 1531. [– L. *acumen* point, acuteness, f. *acuere* sharpen; see ACUTE *a.*] **1.** Sharpness of wit; penetration of perception; keenness of discrimination. **2.** *Bot.* A tapering point 1794.

1. The jest or *a.* [of epigrams] CASAUBON. Metaphysical a. REID.

Acuminate (ăkiū·minĕt), *ppl. a.* 1605. [– L. *acuminatus* pointed, f. *acumen*, *-min-* (prec.); see -ATE[2].] **1.** Pointed, tapering to a point, *esp.* in *Nat. Hist.* 1646. Also quasi-*sb.* † **2.** Having acumen. *rare.* 1645.

Acuminate (ăkiū·mine^{i}t), *v.* 1611. [f. as prec. + -ATE[3], or f. late L. *acuminare.*] **1.** *trans.* To sharpen; to give poignancy or keenness to. † **2.** *intr.* To rise or taper to a point.

1. Tones. .to a. even despair COWPER. 2. Hierarchies acuminating. .in a cone of Prelaty MILT. Hence **Acu·minated** *ppl. a.* pointed (*lit.* and *fig.*); made keen in discernment or attention. **Acu·minating** *ppl. a.* rising or tapering to a point. **Acu:mina·tion,** the giving point to (*lit.* and *fig.*); a tapering point; direction to a point. **Acu:mino·se** *a.* terminating in a flat narrow end. **Acu·minous** *a.* marked by acumen; acute.

Acupressure (æ:kiupre·ʃ^{i}ŭɹ, -ʃəɹ). 1859. [f. L. *acu* with a needle + PRESSURE.] Prof. Simpson's method of arresting hæmorrhage from wounded arteries by the pressure of a needle passed across their mouths or tubes.

Acupunctuate (æ:kiupɒ·ŋktiu,e^{i}t), *v.* 1865. [f. as prec. + PUNCTUATE.] To prick with a needle; also *fig.*

Acupuncture (æ:kiupɒ·ŋktiŭɹ, -tʃəɹ), *sb.* 1684. [f. as prec. + PUNCTURE.] Pricking with a needle; a prick so made. *spec.* The insertion of needles into living tissues for remedial purposes. Hence **A:cupu·ncture** *v.* = ACUPUNCTUATE. **A:cupu:nctura·tion,** the practice or process of a.; var. **A:cupu:nctua·tion.**

Acustom, -ance, obs. ff. ACCUSTOM, -ANCE.

Acute (ăkiū·t), *a.* 1570. [– L. *acutus*, pa. pple. of *acuere* sharpen, f. *acus* needle.] **1.** Sharp at the end, coming to a point. **2.** Of diseases: Coming sharply to a crisis, not *chronic*. Also *fig.* 1667. **3.** Acting keenly on the senses (see quots.) 1609. **4.** Of the senses or nervous system: Sensitive or responsive to impressions, finely-strung 1762. **5.** Of the intellect: Discerning, penetrating, sharp-witted, shrewd, clever 1588. Aphet., *esp.* in U.S., to *cute*. Also quasi-*sb.* (sc. *accent.*)

1. An *a. angle* is that which is lesse than a right angle *Euclid*. Leaves may be a. 1842. 3. Of pain, pleasure, etc.: Intense. The pleasure is not. .a., or of great intensity BAIN. Of sounds: Shrill, high. The most a. [stave] is called the soprano OUSELEY. *A. accent*; see ACCENT 1, 2. 4. Her feelings were very a. MISS AUSTEN. 5. A most a. Iuuenal *L.L.L.* III. i. 67. An a. logician REID, observer DAVY. A cute thing (U.S.). *sb.* Marked with acutes 1824. *Comb.* **a.-angled,** having an a. angle. Hence † **Acutangular** *a.* † **Acu·te** *v.* to sharpen; to mark, etc., with an a. accent. **Acu·tely** *adv.* **Acu·tish** *a.* somewhat a.

Acuteness (ăkiū·tnės). 1646. [f. prec. + -NESS.] The quality of being ACUTE (in senses 1, 2, 3, 4); said of material things, of disease, of pain, etc., of sounds, of the senses or feelings, of the mental faculties.

Acuti-, a combining form of L. *acutus* sharp, in Eng. words formed on or after mod. L.; as **acutifoliate** *a.* sharp-leaved.

Acuto-, comb. advb. form of ACUTE, as in **acuto-nodose**, *acutely* nodose, or in **acuto-grave**, *acute* + grave.

-acy, *suffix* of sbs. [A branch of -CY.] Forming sbs. of quality, state, or condition. **1.** as = L. *-acia*, on adjs. in *-aci-*, as 'fallacy'; **2.** as = L. *-at-i-a* (med.L. *-acia*), on nouns in *-at-* (nom. *-as*), as 'abbacy'; **3.** as = med. L. *-atia*, on nouns in *-atus*, as 'advocacy'; **4.** repr. Gr. sbs. of state in *-άτεια*, as 'piracy', and in *-cracy* Gr. sbs. in *-κρατία*, as 'aristocracy'.

Ad. Colloq. abbrev. of ADVERTISEMENT.

‖ **Ad,** L. prep. = 'to' in **ad hoc,** for this or the particular purpose; also *attrib.*; **ad nauseam,** to a sickening extent; **ad referendum,** subject to reference; **ad rem,** to the point or purpose. Also AD EUNDEM, etc.

Ad-, *pref.* **1.** repr. L. *ad* prep. 'to', with sense of motion to, change into, addition, or intensification. Assimilated bef. *c, f, g, l, n, p, q, r, s, t*, and prob. bef. *b*, as in *ab-* for *ad-breviare*; reduced to *a-* bef. *sc, sp, st*. In the 15th c. words borrowed from OFr., etc. were refash. after L., and all words since formed follow L. spelling. *Ad-* 'at', opp. to *ab-* 'away from', as in *ad-oral, ab-oral*, is recent.

2. At the same time *ad-* was substituted for *a-* where *a-* was really L. *ab*, OFr. *en (an), es*, OE. *a (ar), on, æt*, etc.; as in *a(d)vance, a(d)debted, a(c)curse, a(l)lay, a(d)miral*, etc.

-ad, *suffix* of sbs. **1.** repr. Gr. *-άδ-α* (nom. *-άς*) forming **a.** Collective numerals, as *monad*, etc. **b.** Fem. patronymics (var. *-id*), as *Dryad*, pl. *Dryades*, etc. Hence used **c.** in names of Poems, as *Iliad* the lay (*ᾠδή*) of Ilium, *Dunciad*, etc.; and **d.** to form family names of plants, as *liliad*, etc. **2.** – Fr. *-ade*, in *salad*, etc.; see -ADE.

II. suffix forming advs. and adjs. in the sense of 'towards' (the part denoted by the main element of the word), as DEXTRAD, DORSAD, LATERAD, VENTRAD, etc.

Adactylous (ădæ·ktiləs), *a.* 1858. [f. Gr. *ἀ-* A- *pref.* 14 + *δάκτυλος* finger + -OUS.] Without fingers, toes, or claws.

† **Adad** (ădæ·d), *int.* [var. of EGAD.] Exclam. of asseveration or emphasis –1763.

Adage (æ·dėdʒ). 1548. [– Fr., – L. *adagium* f. *ad* AD- + **agjo* (whence *aio*) I say.] A traditional maxim; a proverb.

The a. . .That Beggers mounted, runne their Horse to death 3 *Hen. VI*, I. iv. 126. Also *Macb.* I. vii. 45. Hence **Ada·gial** *a.* of the nature of an a.

‖ **Adagio** (ădā·dʒ^{i}o). 1746. [It.] *Mus.* **A.** *adv.* A direction: Slowly. **B.** *adj.* Of movement: Slow. **C.** *sb.* A piece of music in a. time. Also *fig.*

† **A·dagy,** 17th c. var. of ADAGE.

Adam (æ·dăm). 1569. [Heb. *'ādām* man.] **1.** The Biblical name of the first man, the father of the human race; hence, *fig.* the unregenerate condition or character. **2.** = ADAM'S ALE.

1. Whipt th'offending Adam out of him *Hen. V*, I. i. 29. *Comb.* **Adam's ale,** water (*joc.*); **-apple,** a variety of Lime (*Citrus limetta*), of Orange or Shaddock; the projection in the neck formed by the thyroid cartilage (supposed to have been caused by a piece of the apple that stuck in Adam's throat); **-flannel,** the Great Mullein (*Verbascum thapsus*); **-needle,** occ. name of the Shepherd's Needle (*Scandix pecten-veneris*); **-wine,** Sc. = ADAM'S ALE. Hence **Ada·mic, -al** *a.* like Adam; free, naked, fallen. **Ada·mically** *adv.*

Adamant (æ·dămănt). OE. [– OFr. *adamaunt, ade-* – L. *adamant-*, nom. *adamas* – Gr. *ἀδαμαντ-*, nom. *ἀδάμας*, orig. adj. = invincible, f. *ἀ-* A- *pref.* 14 + *δαμᾶν* tame. The sense 'magnet, loadstone' arose from association of med.L. *adamas* w. L. *adamare* have a strong liking for (f. *amare* love). See DIAMOND.] An alleged rock or mineral, of contradictory and fabulous properties. Now a poet. or rhet. name for impregnable hardness. **1.** Not identified OE. Also *fig.* † **2.** The diamond 1393–1794. † **3.** The loadstone or magnet 1366–1656. Also *fig.* and *attrib.*

1. The dore was al of A. eterne CHAUCER. Gates of burning a. MILT. *fig.* The sharp a. of Fate CARLYLE. 2. A., precyowse stone *c* 1440. The a. . .will not be fil'd But by itself 1598. 3. As true to thee as steel to a. 1614. The grace of God's spirit, like the true loadstone or a. BP. HALL. *fig.* A great A. of acquaintance BACON. *Mids.N.D.* II. i. 195. *attrib.* An a. heart 1677. A. walls B. TAYLOR. Hence † **Adama·ntive** *a.* (?misprint for *adamantine*).

† **Adamante·an,** *a.* [f. L. *adamanteus* (as prec.) + -AN.] Of adamant. MILT.

Adamantine (ædămæ·ntin), *a.* ME. [– L. *adamantinus* – Gr. *ἀδαμάντινος* f. *ἀδάμας*; see ADAMANT, -INE[2].] **1.** Made of, or like, adamant; unbreakable, impenetrable, impregnable. † **2.** Like the loadstone; magnetic –1655.

1. A state a. . .that is invincible HOLLAND. A. laws HY. MORE, rock MILT., fortitude MACAULAY, purity of a woman RUSKIN. **A. spar,** old name of CORUNDUM.

Adama·ntoid. [f. Gr. *ἀδαμαντ-*, stem of *ἀδάμας* ADAMANT + -OID.] A form of crystal in the diamond, bounded by 48 equal triangles. DANA.

Adambulacral (æ:d,æmbiulē^{i}·krăl), *a.* 1872. [f. AD- + AMBULACRUM + -AL[1].] *Zool.* Next to the ambulacra, in echinoderms.

Adamite (æ·dămait). 1628. [f. ADAM + -ITE[1] 1.] **A.** *sb.* **1.** A descendant of Adam, a human being; also, a name for the section of the human race derived from Adam 1635. **2.** An imitator of Adam, an unclothed man; the name of certain sects, ancient and modern 1628. Hence † **Adami·tic** *a.* **A·damitism.** **B.** *adj.* Descended from Adam; human.

A·damite, *sb.*[2] 1837. [f. M. *Adam*, of Paris, + -ITE[1] 2b.] *Min.* A zinc olivenite.

A·damsite. 1837. *Min.* = MUSCOVITE.

A-da·nce, *adv.* 1869. [A *prep.*[1] 11.] Dancing.

A-da·ngle, *adv.* 1855. [A *prep.*[1] 11.] Dangling.

‖ **Adansonia** (ădănsō^{u}·niă). 1852. [f. *Adanson*, French naturalist, + -IA[1].] *Bot.* A genus (N.O. *Bombaceæ*) consisting of two species of gigantic trees, the Baobab, Monkey-bread, or Ethiopian Sour Gourd of W. and Central

Africa, and the Cream of Tartar Tree, or Sour Gourd of N. Australia.

Adapt (ădæ·pt), *v.* 1611. [– (O)Fr. *adapter* – L. *adaptare*, f. *ad* AD- + *aptare*, f. *aptus* fit, suitable; see APT *a.*] **1.** To fit, to make suitable (*to, for*). **2.** To alter so as to fit for a new use 1774.

1. The structure of the outer ear is adapted to collect and concentrate the vibrations BAIN. **2.** A Comedy adapted from the French 1849. Hence † **Ada·pt** *ppl. a.* suited; fit. **Ada·pted** *ppl. a.* fitted, fit (*to, for*); altered so as to fit. **Ada·ptedness,** the quality of being adapted. **Ada·ption** = ADAPTATION. **Ada·ptive** *a.* characterized by, or given to, adaption. **Ada·ptively** *adv.* so as to suit special conditions. **Ada·ptiveness,** the quality of being adaptive. var. † **Ada·ptate** *v.* CUDWORTH.

Adaptable (ădæ·ptăb'l), *a.* 1800. [f. prec. + -ABLE.] Capable of being adapted. Hence **Adaptabi·lity** (*to, for*). **Ada·ptableness.**

Adaptation (ædæptēi·ʃən). 1610. [– Fr., – med.L. *adaptatio*; see ADAPT *v.*, -ION.] **1.** The action or process of adapting (*to*). **2.** The process of modifying so as to suit new conditions 1790. **3.** The condition of being adapted; anything adapted.

2. Powers of self-a. KINGSLEY. **3.** The a. of immortality to our true wants J. MARTINEAU. This play is an a. from the French (*mod.*). Hence **Adapta·tional** *a.*

Ada·ptative, *a.* 1857. [f. ADAPT *v.* + -ATIVE.] = ADAPTIVE. Hence **Ada·ptativeness.**

Adapter, rarely **-or** (ădæ·ptəɹ). 1801. [f. ADAPT *v.*] **1.** One who ADAPTS (in senses 1, 2). **2.** A connecting part; in *Chem.* a tube joining two pieces of apparatus.

Ada·ptitude. 1842. [f. ADAPT, after APTITUDE.] Adaptedness.

‖ **Adar** (ēi·dăɹ). ME. [Heb. *'adār.*] The twelfth month of the Heb. eccl. year, the sixth of the civil year.

† **Adarticula·tion.** 1753. [f. AD- + ARTICULATION; cf. ABARTICULATION.] *Anat.* A loose jointing of two bones; = ARTHRODIA.

‖ **Adatis, -ais, addatys** (æ·dătis). 1687. Indian muslin.

† **Adau·nt,** *v.* ME. [– OFr. *adanter*, var. of *adonter* (later *addomter*) f. *a* AD- + *danter* DAUNT *v.*] To subdue –1597.

† **Ada·w,** *v.*[1] ME. [f. A- *pref.* 1 + DAW *v.*[1]; cf. MHG. *ertagen.*] To awake or awaken –1530.

Til that he be adawed verrayly CHAUCER.

† **Adaw·,** *v.*[2] 1557. [Probably obs. ADAWE *adv.* in some such phrase as 'they did him *adawe*', *i.e.* out of life, to death, was mistaken for a verb infinitive, *quasi* 'to quell, crush, put down', and this later fancied to be a compound of *awe*, after *ad-apt*, etc.; see AD- 2.] To subdue, daunt –1654.

Adawed with some dreadfull spright SPENSER.

† **Adaw·e,** *adv.* ME. [for *o dawe* = *of dawe*, *of daȝe* :– OE. *of dagum* from life (lit., from days).] Out of life. Usu. with vbs. *bring, do*: To kill –1513.

Adawn (ădǭ·n), *adv.* [A *prep.*[1] 11.] Dawning.

Aday, a-day (ădēi·), *adv.* ME. [A *prep.*[1] 8.] † **1.** By day. **2.** Daily 1500.

2. A peny a daye TINDALE.

Adays, a-days, *adv. phr.* ME. [A *prep.*[1] 8 + *day's*, gen. sing. of *day*. In OE. the gen. *dæȝes* was used advb., = by day; subsequently the gen. was strengthened by the prep. *a* = in, on.] † **1.** By day –1765. **2. Now-a-days:** At the present day ME.

1. Pining a daies..waking a nights BURTON. **2.** Reason and loue keepe little company together now-adayes *Mids.N.D.* III. i. 148.

Add (æd), *v.* ME. [– L. *addere*, f. *ad* AD- + *dare* give, put.] **1.** To join or unite (a thing *to* another), so as to increase the number, quantity, or importance; to give by way of increased possession. **2.** (obj. unexpressed.) To make an addition *to*; to augment 1591. **3.** To say or write in addition; to go on to say, etc., ME. **4.** To unite into one sum; often with *together*. *absol.* To perform the process of addition. So to *add up*; to *add in*, to include in a sum. 1509.

1. Lat vs..adden reuerence to suffisaunce and to power CHAUCER. To a. 3 to 5 HUTTON. All these things shall be added unto you *Matt.* 6:33. **2.** It adds to our labour (*mod.*). **3.** But let me a., Sir Robert's mighty dull POPE. **4.** To a. together the ideas of two days, or two years LOCKE. Hence **A·ddable** *a.* capable of being added, or added to. **A·ddible** *a.* capable of being added; whence **Addibi·lity.**

‖ **Addax** (æ·dăks). 1693. [L., – an African wd.; see Plin. *H. N.* xi. 37.] A boviform antelope, allied to the Nyl-ghau and Gnu, inhabiting N. Africa. (*Oryx nasomaculata.*)

† **Addee·m,** *v.* [A- *pref.* 11.] To adjudge. SPENSER.

‖ **Addendum** (ăde·ndŏm). Pl. **addenda** (ade·ndă). 1794. [L., gerundive of *addere* ADD *v.*] A thing to be added.

Adder[1] (æ·dəɹ). 1580. [f. ADD + -ER[1].] He who adds.

Adder[2] (æ·dəɹ). [OE. *nǣd(d)re*, corresp. to OS. *nādra* (MDu. *nadre*, Du. *adder*), OHG. *nātara* (G. *natter*), and (with different vowel-grade) ON. *naðr*, *naðra*, Goth. *nadrs*. The initial *n* was lost in ME. (XIV–XV) through the erroneous division of *a naddre* as *an addre*, as in *apron, auger, eyas, ouch, umpire.*] † **1.** A serpent. *fig.* The old serpent, the devil. –1513. **b.** A dragon, or flying serpent ME. **2.** A viper. *spec.* The Common Viper (*Pelias berus*). OE. **b.** By extension, Applied to the *asp, basilisk, cockatrice*, etc. In mod. Zoology to species of *Clotho*, etc., as the Puff Adder and Horned Adder of Africa, Death Adder of N. Australia, etc. ME. **3. Flying Adder,** *Adder-fly*: the Dragon-fly. **4. Sea Adder,** *Syngnathus acus.*

1. Eue, seide he, ðat neddre bold ME. Grete addren comen flynge ME. **2.** It is the bright day that brings forth the A. *Jul. Cæs.* II. i. 14. Stung with adders and Scorpions MILT. **b.** They are like the deafe adder [*marg.* or aspe] *Ps.* 58: 4.

Comb.: **a.-bead,** a prehistoric, perh. Druidic, amulet; **-bolt,** a dragon-fly; **-deaf** *a.*, see 2 b, quot.; **-footed** *a.*, dragon-footed; **-pike,** the sting-fish (*Trachinus vipera*); **-stone** = -BEAD; † **adder's fry,** brood of vipers; **-meat,** the Greater Stitchwort; **-mouth** (U. S.), plants of the genus *Microstylis*; **-spear** = ADDER'S-TONGUE.

A·dder's-grass. 1551. *Herb.* **1.** The Early Spring Orchis (*O. mascula*). **2.** = next.

A·dder's-tongue. 1578. *Herb.* A genus of ferns (*Ophioglossum*); also Wake Robin, Lily of the Valley, etc.

Adderwort (æ·dəɹwŏɹt). OE. Bistort.

Addice, early f. ADZE.

Addict (æ·dikt), *sb.* 1909. [f. next.] One who is addicted to the habitual and excessive use of a drug or the like.

† **Addict,** *ppl. a.* 1529. [– L. *addictus* assigned by decree, made over, pa. pple. of *addicere*, f. *ad* AD- + *dicere* appoint, allot. Now repl. by ADDICTED.] **1.** Formally made over or bound *to* –1583. **2.** Self-addicted, devoted *to* –1790.

Addict (ădi·kt), *v.* 1560. [f. next.] **1.** *Rom. Law.* To deliver over formally by judicial sentence *to*; *fig.* to make over, give up 1586. Also † *refl.* **2.** To devote or apply habitually to a practice 1577. Also *refl.* and *pass.*

1. *fig.* The..day he addicts..to study 1670. **2.** He can [not] a. his mind to..profitable business TOPSELL. *refl.* To a. themselves to Sack SHAKS., to vice PRIESTLEY.

Addicted (ădi·ktėd), *ppl. a.* 1534. [orig. f. ADDICT *ppl. a.* + -ED[1], the verb being inferred later.] **1.** *Rom. Law.* Delivered over judicially; devoted. † **2.** Attached by one's own act (*to* a person, etc.) –1709. **3.** Self-addicted *to*, prone 1561. † **4.** *without const.* Devoted –1652.

1. We be virgins, and a. to virginitie GREENE. **2.** A. to Marius his master 1642. **3.** A. to a melancholy *Twelfth N.* II. v. 222, to wine or strong drinke T. TAYLOR, stealing 1865. **4.** Your Honors most a., T. B. 1594. Hence **Addi·ctedness.**

Addiction (ădi·kʃən). 1604. [– L. *addictio*, f. *addict-*, pa. ppl. stem of *addicere*; see ADDICT *ppl. a.*, -ION. In the later senses from ADDICT *v.*] **1.** *Rom. Law.* A formal giving over by sentence of court; hence, a dedication to a master 1625. **2.** The state of being (self-) addicted *to* 1641. † **3.** The way in which one is addicted; bent, inclination –1675.

2. A. to tobacco JOHNSON, to bad habits MILL. **3.** *Oth.* II. ii. 6.

Additament (æ·ditămĕnt). 1460. [– OFr. *additement*, or L. *additamentum*, f. *addit-*, pa. ppl. stem of *addere* ADD; see -MENT.] Anything added or appended.

Pretty additaments..to that main structure LAMB.

Addition (ădi·ʃən), *sb.* ME. [– (O)Fr., or L. *additio*, f. *addit-*; see prec., -ION.] **1.** The action or process of adding (see ADD *v.*) ME. **2.** That which is added; an appendix, accession, etc. ME. **3.** *spec.* † **a.** Something added to a man's name, to distinguish him; 'style' of address –1726. † **b.** *Her.* Something added to a coat of arms, as a mark of honour; opp. to *abatement* –1753. † **c.** *Mus.* A dot placed on the right side of a note, to lengthen it by one half –1753.

1. Without a. or diminishing *Com. Err.* II. ii. 130. **2.** Ireland..and other Additions to the Crown PETTY. **3. a.** How do you Lieutenant? The worser, that you giue me the a. *Oth.* IV. i. 105. **b.** *Tr. & Cr.* IV. v. 141. Hence † **Addi·tion** *v.* to surname or style. † **Addi·tionary** *a.* additional.

Additional (ădi·ʃənăl). 1639. [f. prec. + -AL[1].] **A.** *adj.* Existing in addition; added 1646. **B.** *sb.* Something added; an addition; an 'extra' 1639. Hence **Addi·tionally** *adv.*

Addititious (æditi·ʃəs), *a.* 1748. [f. late L. *additicius* additional (Tertullian), f. *addit-* (see ADDITAMENT) + *-icius* (see -ITIOUS[1]).] Due to, or of the nature of, an addition. *A. force* (*Astr.*), that which increases the gravitation of a satellite towards its planet.

Additive (æ·ditiv), *a.* 1699. [– late L. *additivus*, f. *addit-* (see ADDITAMENT) + *-ivus* -IVE. Cf. Fr. *additif, -ive.*] Disposed to addition; to be added. Hence **A·dditively** *adv.* var. † **A·dditory.**

Addle (æ·d'l). [OE. *adela*, cogn. w. MLG. *adele*, MDu. *adel*, (Du. *aal*, G. *adel*), OSw. *adel* in *ko-adel* cow's urine.] **A.** *sb.* **1.** Stinking urine or liquid filth; mire OE. **2.** The dry lees of wine. (Dicts.)

B. *adj.* **1.** As in **Addle egg** (tr. med.L. *ovum urinæ*, which is a perversion of L. *ovum urinum*, repr. Gr. οὔριον ᾠόν wind-egg.). Rotten or putrid; producing no chicken ME. **2.** *fig.* Empty, idle; muddled, unsound *a* 1593.

1. No more then I esteeme an a. egge *Tr. & Cr.* I. ii. 145. *Rom. & Jul.* III. i. 25. **2.** A. head LYLY, epistle 1800. His brains grow a. DRYDEN.

Comb.: **a.-brain, -head, -pate,** one whose brain is addled, a stupid bungler; **-brained, -headed, -pated** *adjs.*; **-headedness,** fatuity. Hence **A·ddleness,** putrefaction.

Addle (æ·d'l), *v.*[1] 1712. [Inferred from earlier *addled*, ADDLE *adj.* + -ED[1].] **1.** To make addle; to confuse; to make abortive. **2.** *intr.* To grow addle. *lit.* and *fig.* 1812. So **A·ddled** *ppl. a.* **A·ddlement,** the process of addling or being addled. **A·ddling** *vbl. sb.*[1] decomposition of an egg; muddling of the wits.

† **Addle** (æd'l), *v.*[2] ME. [– ON. *ǫðla*, refl. *ǫðlask* to acquire (for oneself) property, f. *óðal* property. See ODAL.] To earn. Also *absol.* Of crops: To yield 1580. Hence † **A·ddling** *vbl. sb.*[2] earning.

† **Addoo·m,** *v.* [A- *pref.* 11.] To adjudge. SPENSER.

Addorsed (ădǭ·ɹst), *ppl. a.* 1572. [f. L. *ad* + *dorsum*; cf. Fr. *adossé.*] *Her.* Turned back to back, as two animals on a shield.

Address (ădre·s), *v.* ME. [– (O)Fr. *adresser* :– Rom. **addrictiare*, f. *ad* AD- + **drictus*, for L. *directus* straight, direct (see DIRECT *v.*).] **I.** To make straight or right, in various senses, now obs.; see quots.

† To put 'to rights', to set in order. [He] dyuers great batelles addressed LD. BERNERS. A Parlament being call'd, to addres many things MILT. We will that you..a. several Schedules Q. ELIZABETH. *intr.* Let vs addresse to tend on Hector's heeles SHAKS. † To make right or ready in attire; to clothe; to don. Addressed her selfe in Mans apparell JEWEL. To a. a frock of heavy mail BROWNING.

II. To direct. † **1.** To aim (*Obs.* exc. in *Golf*, 'to a. the ball') ME.; to send, refer, introduce *to* 1475; † *refl.* to betake oneself –1683. **2.** To send as a written message *to*; to dedicate 1636. **3.** To direct spoken words, a prepared speech, etc., *to* 1490; *refl.* to a. *oneself* in speech *to* 1665; † *intr.* to a. *to*; and *techn.* to present an address, and to 'pay addresses', to court –1765; *trans.* (*to* omitted) to speak directly to 1718.

1. Towards Eve addressed his way MILT. I addressed him to Lord Mordaunt EVELYN. Ship to be addressed to Charterers 1882. **2.** To a. a letter to the public 'JUNIUS'. *To a. a letter*: *techn.* to 'direct' it. Letters are..sometimes addressed 'London' only *P.O. Guide.* **3.** To a. (*to* a person) prayers CAXTON, vows DRYDEN, discourse MACAULAY. Addressed the House of Peers MACAULAY. A. the Chair! (*mod.*).

III. † *trans.* To direct (to an object) –1591; *refl.* to apply oneself to 1393; † *intr.* (refl. pron. omitted) to set about –1725.

Hence **Addre·ssee,** the person to whom a document is addressed. **Addre·sser,** one who addresses; one who signs or delivers an address, or directs a message to any one. † **Addre·ssion,** the direction of one's course CHAPMAN. **Addre·ssor,** one who signs an address, or one who addresses a formal document.

Address (ădre·s), *sb.* 1539. [partly f. prec., partly – (O)Fr. *adresse.*] † **1.** The action of making ready or the being ready –1788; an appliance –1598; dress –1660. **2.** General preparedness; skill, dexterity, adroitness 1598. **3.** The action of directing or dispatching 1882. † **4.** The action of sending, or dedicating, a writing –1705. **5.** The direction or superscription of a letter 1712. **6.** † The act of addressing oneself to any one –1704; *esp.* dutiful or courteous approach, courtship. Now in *pl.* 1539. **7.** Bearing in conversation 1674. **8.** A formal speech of congratulation, thanks, etc.; *esp.* in reply to the Royal Speech at the opening of Parliament; a set discourse (less oratorical than a *speech*, less systematic than a *sermon*) 1751.

2. His ready a.: for no man ever resolved quicker or spoke clearer BACON. The a. of an accomplished intriguer MERIVALE. **5.** This letter is to your a. (*mod.*). **6.** Our addresses to Heaven 1704. To make sham addresses to the older lady FIELDING. **7.** His a...was abrupt, unceremonious CARLYLE. **8.** Lord Liverpool moved the A. 1870. Short and stirring addresses (*mod.*).

Addressed (ădre·st), *ppl. a.*; also **addrest.** ME. [f. ADDRESS *v.* + -ED[1].] † **1.** Erected –1595. † **2.** Well-ordered –1597. † **3.** Prepared; dressed as food –1633. **4.** Arrayed. *arch.* ME. **5.** Directed, sent 1598. **6.** Directed as a letter. Hence † **Addre·ssedness.**

Adduce (ădiū·s), *v.* 1616. [– L. *adducere*, f. *ad* AD- + *ducere* lead, bring.] To bring forward for consideration; to cite.

To a. authorities BRENT, arguments W. ROBERTSON, reasons BOWEN. Hence **Addu·ceable, -ible** *a.* **Addu·ced** *ppl. a.* **Addu·cer.**

Adducent (ădiū·sĕnt), *a.* 1694. [– *adducent-*, pr. ppl. stem of L. *adducere* (prec.); see -ENT.] *Phys.* Drawing towards a given point; as *adducent* muscles = ADDUCTORS. Opp. to *abducent.*

Adduct (ădɒ·kt), *v.* 1836. [– *adduct-*, pa. ppl. stem of L. *adducere* (as prec.).] *Phys.* To draw towards a common centre or median line.

Adduction (ădɒ·kʃən). 1656. [– Fr., or late L. *adductio*, f. as prec.; see -ION.] **1.** The action of adducting; see prec. **2.** The action of adducing; see ADDUCE. 1764.

Adductive (ădɒ·ktiv), *a.* 1638. [f. as ADDUCT *v.* + -IVE. Cf. med.L. *adductivus* (XIV).] Bringing to something else; *spec.* of the change wrought in transubstantiation.

Adductor (ædɒ·ktəɹ). 1746. [mod.L. use of L. *adductor* bringer-to, f. as prec.; see -OR 2. Cf. Fr. *adducteur.*] *Phys.* A muscle which draws any limb, or part of the body, towards the trunk or main axis, or which folds extended parts of the body. Also *attrib.*

† **Addu·lce,** *v.* 1475. [In XV, *adoulce* – OFr. *ad(d)oulcir* (mod. *adoucir*), f. *ad-* AD- + *dou(l)x* sweet, :– L. *dulcis*; cf. late L. *(ad)-dulcare* sweeten.] To sweeten; to soothe.

-ade, *suff.* of sbs. **1.** – Fr. *-ade*, – Pr. *-āda*, fem. of pa. pple. as sb., meaning **a.** an action done, as in *blockade*; **b.** the body concerned, as in *ambuscade*; **c.** the product, as in *arcade*. The native Fr. form is *-ée*, as in *entrée*. **2.** – Fr. *-ade*, – Gr. -αδ-α (nom. -ας), as in *decade* (usu. *decad*). **3.** – Sp. or Pg. *-ado*, It. *-ato*, masc. of 1, as in *brocade*, the product, and in *renegade*, the person affected.

A-dead (ăde·d), *adv.* [A- *pref.* 11.] Dead.

Adeem (ădī·m), *v.* 1845. [– L. *adimere* take away, f. *ad* AD- + *emere* take, assim. to REDEEM.] To take away, *spec.* in *Rom. Law*, to revoke a legacy.

A-deep (ădī·p), *adv.* [A *prep.*[1]] Deeply. MRS. BROWNING.

‖ **Adelantado** (ā:delantā·do). 1599. [Sp.] A Sp. grandee; a lord-lieutenant or governor. B. JONS.

‖ **Adelaster** (ædilæ·stəɹ). 1866. [f. Gr. ἄδηλος not manifest + ἀστήρ, ἀστερ- star.] *Bot.* A provisional name for a plant of which the flowers and therefore its genus are unknown.

Adeling. See ATHELING.

Adelopod(e (ădī·lŏpǫd). 1847. [f. Gr. ἄδηλος not seen + πούς, ποδ- foot.] *Zool.* An animal whose feet are hidden.

‖ **-adelphia** (ăde·lfiă), *terminal element.* 1858. [– Gr. -αδελφία (in comb.) brotherhood, f. ἀδελφός brother.] *Bot.* Collection of stamens into a bundle; as in the class-names *Monadelphia*, etc.

Adelphic (ăde·lfik), *a.* 1847. [– Gr. ἀδελφικός brotherly; see prec., -IC.] *Bot.* Having the stamens united into a parcel or parcels.

Adelpholite (ăde·lfŏləit). 1868. [f. Gr. ἀδελφός brother; see -LITE.] *Min.* A Columbate of iron and manganese. DANA.

Adelphous (ăde·lfəs), *a.* 1855. [f. Gr. ἀδελφός + -OUS; cf. ADELPHIC.] *Bot.* Having the stamens grouped or united; usu. in comp. as *monadelphous*, etc.

† **Ade·mpt,** *ppl. a.* ME. [– L. *ademptus*, pa. pple. of *adimere* take away; see ADEEM *v.*] Taken away –1561.

Ademption (ăde·mʃən). 1590. [– L. *ademptio*, f. *adempt-*; see prec., -ION.] A taking away; in *Law*, revocation of a grant or bequest.

‖ **A·den.** *Obs.* Pl. **adenes.** [– Gr. ἀδήν, ἀδένα gland; perh. through late L. *aden* (Oribasius).] A gland –1775.

Aden-, adeni-, adeno-, comb. forms of prec.

‖ **adenalgia** (ædenæ·ldʒiă) [mod.L. *-algia*], pain, a painful swelling, in a gland; **adeniform** (ăde·nifǫɹm, æ·dėni-) [L. *-formis*] *a.*, gland-like; **a·denocele** [Gr. κήλη], an adenoid tumour; **adeno·graphy** [Gr. -γραφία], description of the glandular system; **a·denoid, -al** [Gr. -ειδης] *a.*, gland-like; **a·denoids** *sb. pl.*, an overgrowth of the glandular tissue on the back of the upper part of the throat, called also *adenoid vegetations*; **adeno·logy** [Gr. -λογία], the part of Physiology which treats of the glands; hence **a:denolo·gical** *a.*; **adeno·pathy** [Gr. -παθία], disease of the glandular system; **adeno·phorous** [Gr. -φορος], *a.*, bearing or producing glands; **a:denophy·llous** [Gr. φύλλον] *a.*, glandular-leaved; **adeno·tomy** [Gr. -τομία], dissection of or incision into a gland.

Adenose (æ:dĕnōᵘ·s), *a.* 1853. [f. ADEN + -OSE[1]; so late L. *adenosus* (Oribasius).] Glandular. var. **A·denous.**

‖ **Adephaga** (ăde·făgă), *sb. pl.* 1842. [mod. – Gr. ἀδηφάγα (sc. ζῷα), sb. use of n. pl. of ἀδηφάγος gluttonous, f. Ionic ἄδην to one's fill + -φαγος eating; see -PHAGY.] A family of Beetles, also called *Carnivora.*

‖ **Adeps** (æ·deps). 1657. [L., = soft fat, grease.] Animal fat, lard.

Adept (ăde·pt). 1685. [– L. *adeptus* having attained, pa. pple. of *adipisci* attain, acquire.] **A.** *adj.* Completely versed (*in*); well-skilled 1691.

B. *sb.* [In med.L. *adeptus* used subst. = One who *has attained* the great secret of Alchemy. In Eng. the L. form *adeptus* was at first used.] Hence, One who is skilled in all the secrets of anything 1685.

Queens became adepts in Des Cartes' philosophy REID. Hence † **Ade·ptical** *a.* alchemical. † **Ade·ptist,** a skilled alchemist. **Ade·ptness,** the quality of being a. **Ade·ptship,** the condition or rank of an a.

† **Ade·ption.** 1548. [– L. *adeptio* an attaining, f. as prec., see -ION. Cf. OFr. *adepcion.*] Attainment.

Adequacy (æ·dĭkwĕsi). 1808. [f. next, see -ACY.] The state or quality of being ADEQUATE.

Adequate (æ·dĭkwĕt), *a.* 1617. [– L. *adæquatus*, pa. pple. of *adæquare* equalize, f. *ad* AD- + *æquus* equal; see -ATE[2]. Cf. (O)Fr. *adéquat.*] Const. *to*, † *with.* † **1.** Equal in magnitude or extent –1750. **2.** Commensurate in fitness; sufficient, suitable 1617. **3.** *Logic.* Fully representing 1690.

1. Not a. to the expectations JOHNSON. **2.** Is language a. to describe it? 1860. A. to the disease JAS. MILL. **3.** A. ideas LOCKE. An a. definition MILL. Hence **A·dequately** *adv.* **A·dequateness.** **Adequa·tion,** the action of equalizing, or fact of equalling; an equivalent.

† **A·dequate,** *v.* 1599. [– as prec.; see -ATE[3].] To make or be equal or sufficient.

A·dequative, *a.* 1823. [irreg. f. ADEQUATE *a.* + -IVE.] = ADEQUATE 2. Scott.

Adesmy (ăde·smi). 1879. [f. Gr. ἄδεσμος unbound (f. ἀ- A- *pref.* 14 + δεσμός bond) + -Y[3].] *Bot.* Defective coherence or adherence between vegetable organs.

Adessenarian (æde:sĭnēᵊ·riăn). 1751. [f. mod.L. *adessenarii*; f. L. *adesse* be present (f. *ad-* AD- + *esse* be) + *-arius*; see -ARIAN.] *Eccl. Hist.* One who held the real presence of Christ's body in the Eucharist, but not by transubstantiation.

‖ **Ad eundem** (*i,ɒ·*ndem), of admission *to the same* degree in another university.

Adevism (æ·dīviz'm). 1878. [f. Gr. ἀ- A- *pref.* 14 + Skr. *dēva* god + -ISM.] A denial of the legendary deities, as distinguished from *atheism.* MAX-MÜLLER.

Adfe·cted, *ppl. a.* 1695. [Specialized var. of AFFECTED.] Compounded. *Math.* Of equations: Containing different powers of an unknown quantity.

Adfiliate, -ation, obs. vars. AFFILIATE, -ATION.

Adflu·xion. 1829. var. of AFFLUXION.

Adglu·tinate, *a.* = AGGLUTINATE.

Adhere (ædhīᵊ·ɹ), *v.* 1597. [– (O)Fr. *adhérer* or L. *adhærēre*, f. *ad* AD- + *hærēre* stick.] **1.** To stick fast, to cleave, *to* a substance, as by grasping or being glued 1651. Also *fig.* **2.** To cleave *to* a person or party; to be a follower 1597. **3.** To cleave *to*, continue to maintain, an opinion, practice, etc. 1656. † **4.** *without const.* To 'hang together'; to agree –1605. **5.** *Bot.* To be adnate 1857.

1. These mouldings nearly a. to the stone RUSKIN. *fig.* Flattery adheres to power GIBBON. **2.** Meane men must adheare BACON. To a. to the King's enemies 1690, to the Church of Rome MACAULAY. **3.** To a. to a plan B. TAYLOR, a decision (*mod.*). **4.** Nor time nor place did then a. *Macb.* I. vii. 52. Hence **Adhe·rer** (? *Obs.*), one who adheres (*to* an act, etc.). **Adhe·ring** *vbl. sb.* the act or process of sticking, etc.; *ppl. a.* clinging, etc.

Adherence (ædhīᵊ·rĕns). 1612. [f. ADHERE *v.*; see -ANCE, -ENCE. Cf. late & med.L. *adhærentia.*] **1.** The action of adhering (see ADHERE 1, 2, 3, 5). † **2.** An instance of adhering; adherent matter or circumstance –1667.

Adhe·rency. *arch.* 1582. [f. as prec.; see -ANCY, -ENCY.] **1.** The quality or state of being adherent 1647. † **2.** That which is adherent; adhering matter, etc. –1681. † **3.** An adhering party; a following –1662.

1. By virtue of its a...in the flesh JER. TAYLOR.

Adhe·rent. ME. [– (O)Fr. *adhérent* – L. *adhærent-*, pres. ppl. stem of *adhærēre* ADHERE *v.*; see -ENT.] **A.** *adj.* **1.** Sticking fast *to*, attached materially 1615. **2.** *fig.* Attached as a circumstance 1588. † **3.** Attached as a partisan or follower (*to*) –1602. **4.** *Bot.* Adnate 1830.

1. Vpon a rocke, and a. G. SANDYS. **3.** To be a. to the King's enemies FULBECKE.

B. *sb.* **1.** A partisan, follower, supporter (*of*) *c* 1460. † **2.** That which adheres –1645.

1. Luther and his adherentes MORE. Hence **Adhe·rently** *adv.*

Adhesion (ædhī·ʒən). 1624. [– Fr. *adhésion* or L. & med.L. *adhæsio*, f. *adhæs-*, pa. ppl. stem of L. *adhærēre* ADHERE.] **1.** The action of sticking *to*, by attraction, viscosity of surface, or grasping. An instance of such action. *Path.* Unnatural union of surfaces due to inflammation. 1645. Also *fig.* **2.** Attaching oneself, or remaining attached, to a person, party, or tenet 1624. **3.** *Psych.* Intimate and involuntary association of ideas and action 1855. **4.** *Bot.* Coalescence of normally *unlike* parts; opp. to *cohesion* 1857. **5.** Anything which adheres; an appendage, etc. *rare.* 1743.

1. The a. of the Finger to the Tube BOYLE. **2.** A. unto authority SIR T. BROWNE, to Rome HUSSEY, to an accustomed policy KINGLAKE. *To give in one's a.*: to join as a supporter. **5.** Casting off all noxious adhesions CARLYLE.

Adhesive (ædhī·siv), *a.* 1670. [f. as prec. + -IVE.] **1.** Sticky 1775. **2.** Prepared so as to adhere, as in *adhesive label* 1854. **3.** *fig.* Apt or tending to adhere, cling to, or persevere in 1670.

1. A plaster, moderately a. GOOCH. 3. A. to the track J. THOMSON. Hence **Adhe·sively** *adv. rare.*

Adhesiveness (ædhī·sivnės). 1815. [f. prec. + -NESS.] **1.** The quality of being ADHESIVE. *lit.* and *fig.* 1839. **2.** *Phren.* The faculty of forming and maintaining attachments to persons. *Psych.* The tendency to association of ideas. 1815.

† **Adhi·bit,** *ppl. a.* 1528. [– L. *adhibitus*, pa. ppl. of *adhibēre* bring to, employ in, f. *ad* AD- + *habēre* have, hold.] **1.** Brought in *to* 1543. **2.** Brought into application –1671.

Adhibit (ădhi·bit), *v.* 1528. [f. prec. or as prec.] **1.** To take or let in, admit. **2.** To affix 1567. **3.** To apply, use; *esp.* as a remedy 1654.

1. The witnesses adhibited 1880. 2. We a. our seals BOSWELL. 3. Let this bolus be adhibited 1725. Hence **Adhibi·tion,** the action of adhibiting.

‖ **Ad hominem** (æ:d hǫ·minem). 1748. [L. *ad* to, *hominem*, acc. of *homo* man.] Of arguments, etc.: Directed to the preferences or principles of the individual, not to abstract truth.

† **Adho·rt** *v.*, † **Adhorta·tion,** † **Adho·rtatory,** *a.* [vars. of EXHORT, etc., – L. *adhortari*, f. *ad-* AD- + *hortari* encourage.] = EXHORT, etc.

Adiabatic (æ:diăbæ·tik), *a.* 1877. [f. Gr. ἀδιάβατος not to be passed through (f. ἀ- A- *pref.* 14 + βατός passable) + -IC; cf. Fr. *adiabatique.*] *Physics.* Impassable (*sc.* to heat); pertaining to a condition where no heat enters or leaves a system. Hence **Adiaba·tically** *adv.*

Adiactinic (æ:diæ̆kti·nik), *a.* 1880. [A- *pref.* 14 + DIACTINIC.] *Chem.* Opaque to the actinic rays.

‖ **Adiantum** (ædi,æ·ntǒm). 1706. [L., – Gr. ἀδίαντον maidenhair, sb. use of n. adj. 'unwetted' (sc. φυτόν plant), f. ἀ- A- *prep.* 14 + διαίνειν to wet.] *Bot.* **1.** A genus of ferns, of which True Maidenhair (*A. capillus-veneris*) is a rare native of Britain. **2.** *Herb.* and *pop.* The Black Maidenhair (*Asplenium a.-nigrum*).

Adiaphorism (ædi,æ·fǒriz'm). 1866. [f. as next; see -ISM.] Theological indifference; latitudinarianism.

Adiaphorist (ædi,æ·fǒrist). 1564. [– mod.L. *adiaphorista*, f. Gr. ἀδιάφορος indifferent; see -IST.] **A.** *sb.* **1.** An indifferentist in theology 1645. **2.** *Eccl. Hist.* One of the moderate Lutherans, who held some things, condemned by Luther, to be indifferent 1564. var. **Adia·phorite. B.** *adj.* Theologically indifferent (*mod.*). Hence **Adiaphori·stic** *a.*, relating to adiaphorism or the *adiaphora.*

‖ **Adiaphoron** (ædi,æ·fǒron), *a.* and *sb. arch.* Pl. **adiaphora.** 1553. [Gr., neut. of ἀδιάφορος; see prec.] A thing indifferent in the eyes of the Church.

Adiaphorous (ædi,æ·fǒrəs), *a.* 1635. [f. as prec. + -OUS. Cf. mod.L. *adiaphorus* (Bacon).] **1.** Indifferent, non-essential; neutral. var. † **Adia·phoral.** † **2.** *Chem.* Neutral; neither alkaline nor acid –1691. **3.** *Med.* Doing neither harm nor good (*mod.*).

† **Adia·phory.** [– Gr. ἀδιαφορία indifference; see prec., -Y³.] Indifferentism.

‖ **Adiapneustia** (æ:diăpniū·stiă). 1706. [Gr., f. ἀ- A- *pref.* 14 + διά through + πνευστ-, f. πνέειν breathe; see -Y³.] *Med.* Defective or impeded perspiration.

Adiathermic (æ:diăþɔ̄·ɹmik), *a.* 1867. [f. Gr. ἀ- A- *pref.* 14 + DIATHERMIC.] *Physics.* Impervious to heat.

Adicity (ædi·sĭti). 1882. [f. AD- 1, after ATOMICITY.] *Chem.* Combining capacity of an element.

Adieu (ădiū·). [Late ME. *adew(e)* – AFr. *adeu*, (O)Fr. *adieu*, f. *à* to + *dieu* God :– L *deus*; sp. refash. after Fr.] **A.** *int.* Good-bye! farewell! (*arch.*) *fig.* = Away! an end to. **B.** *adv.* † *To go adieu*: to go away –1575. *To bid or say adieu* (*to*): to take leave of. late ME. Hence **C.** *sb.* A leave-taking; a parting word; a farewell; esp. *to make or take adieu.* late ME.

A. *fig.* Adew my song ASHMOLE. A. to all ideas of nobility HUME. C. Too cold an a. SHAKS. His adieus were not long MISS AUSTEN.

† **Adi·ght,** *v.* [ME., f. A- *pref.* 1 + *dihten* compose, set in order; see DIGHT *v.*] To put in order; equip, dress –1581.

‖ **Ad infinitum** (æ:d infināi·tǒm). 1678. [L. *ad* to, *infinitum* infinity.] Without end, for ever.

Adinole (æ·dinō͞ul). 1837. [Origin unkn.] *Min.* A variety of ALBITE.

‖ **Ad interim** (æ:d i·ntĕrim). 1787. [L. *ad* to, for, *interim* adv. meanwhile, used subst.] *adv.* Meanwhile. *adj.* Temporary 1818.

† **Adinve·ntion.** ME. [– late L. *adinventio* invention, f. *adinvent-*, pa. ppl. stem of late L. *adinvenire* find out; see INVENT *v.*, -ION. Cf. OFr. *adinvention.*] An invented addition –1630.

Adipe·scent, *a.* 1847. [f. L. *adeps, adip-* fat + -ESCENT.] Becoming fatty.

Adipic (ădi·pik), *a.* 1877. [f. as prec. + -IC 1 b.] *Chem.* In *Adipic acid*, $C_6H_{10}O_4$, a dibasic, diatomic acid, obtained by the action of nitric acid on fats.

Adipocere (æ·dipo,sīəɹ). 1803. [– Fr. *adipocire* (XVIII), f. L. *adeps, adip-* fat + Fr. *cire* wax :– L. *cera.*] A greyish white fatty substance, chiefly *Margarate of Ammonia*, generated in dead bodies buried in moist places or submerged in water. Hence **Adipo·cerate** *v.* to convert into a. **Adipo·cera·tion,** the process of changing into a. **Adipoce·riform** *a.* **Adipo·cerous** *a.*

Adipose (æ:dipōus). 1743. [– mod.L. *adiposus* f. L. *adeps, adip-* fat; see -OSE¹. Cf. Fr. *adipeux.*] **A.** *adj.* Of or pertaining to adeps, or animal fat; fatty. *Adipose tissue*: the vesicular structure which contains the fat. **B.** *sb.* [sc. *substance.*] The animal fat 1865. Hence **A:dipo·seness,** the state of being fat. **Adipo·sity,** fatness; or tendency to fatness. var. (less techn.) **A·dipous.**

Adipsous (adi·psəs), *a.* 1879. [f. Gr. ἄδιψος not thirsty (f. ἀ- A- *pref.* 14 + δίψα thirst) + -OUS.] *Med.* Allaying thirst.

A·dipsy (æ·dipsi). [f. as prec. + -Y³.] Absence of thirst.

Adit (æ·dit). 1602. [– L. *aditus*, f. *adit-*, pa. ppl. stem of *adire* approach, f. *ad* AD- + *ire* go.] **1.** An approach; *spec.* a horizontal opening by which a mine is entered or drained. **2.** Access, entrance 1847.

1. Soughs or adits to drain them RAY. 2. A. to the executive HELPS.

Adjacency (ădʒē¹·sĕnsi). 1646. [– L. *adjacentia* (n. pl., in sense 2), f. as next; in mod. use f. next; see -ENCE, -ENCY.] **1.** The quality or state of being adjacent 1805. var. † **Adja·cence** –1652. **2.** That which lies near. *pl.* Adjacent places, environs. 1646.

1. The a. of some great . . river DE QUINCEY. 2. The Palais Royal and adjacencies CARLYLE.

Adjacent (ădʒē¹·sĕnt). ME. [– *adjacent-*, pres. ppl. stem of L. *adjacēre* lie near, f. *ad* AD- + *jacēre* lie down; see -ENT.] **A.** *adj.* Lying near *to*; adjoining; bordering. (Not necessarily *touching.*)

Adjacent angles: the angles which one straight line makes with another on which it stands. Parts . . a. to London DE FOE. Hence **Adja·cently** *adv.*

B. † *sb.* That which lies near; a neighbour –1725.

† **Adject.** ME. [– L. *adjectus*, pa. pple. of *adicere* lay to, f. *ad* AD- + *jacere* lay, throw.] **A.** *ppl. a.* (adje·ct). Joined –1612. **B.** *sb.* (a·dject). An addition –1677.

Adject (ădʒe·kt), *v.* ME. [– L. *adjectare* put to, add, frequent. of *adicere*; see prec.] To add or join.

They adjected this Condition 1733.

Adjection (ădʒe·kʃən). ME. [– L. *adjectio* addition, f. *adject-*; see ADJECT *ppl. a.*, -ION.] **1.** The action of adding or joining. † **2.** That which is added –1704.

1. Without a. Of your assistance B. JONS.

Adjectitious (ædʒekti·ʃəs), *a.* 1652. [f. late L. *adjectitius* additional (f. as prec.) + -OUS; see -ITIOUS¹.] Additional.

Adjectival (ædʒektəi·văl), *a.* 1797. [f. next + -AL¹; a mod. substitute for ADJECTIVE *a.* in sense 1.] Of or belonging to the adjective.

Adjective (æ·dʒektiv). ME. [–(O)Fr. *adjectif, -ive* – late L. *adjectivus, -iva*, f. *adject-* (see ADJECT *ppl. a.*) + *-ivus* -IVE. First in *noun adjective*, rendering late L. *nomen adjectivum* (Priscian), tr. Gr. ὄνομα ἐπίθετον.] **A.** *adj.* **1.** *Gram.* Forming an adjunct to a noun substantive; dependent on a sb. as an attribute. **2.** Hence, *gen.* Dependent 1622. **3.** Of *Law*: Relating to procedure; opp. to *substantive* 1808.

1. Scotland is like a noun a. that cannot stand without a substantive ME. 2. The women were treated . . as a. beings GROTE.

B. *sb.* [The adj. used *absol.*] **1.** A 'Noun Adjective', a word added to the name of a thing, and signifying an attribute of the thing 1509. **2.** Hence, *gen.* That which cannot stand alone; a dependent; an accessory 1639.

2. Those Northern Adjectives, not able to subsist without England 1658.

Hence **A·djective** *v.* to make adjectival. **A·djectived** *ppl. a.* made a.; used as an a. **A·djectively** *adv.* **A·djectiving** *vbl. sb.* the making adjectival.

Adjoin (ădʒoi·n), *v.* [ME. *ajoine* – OFr. *ajoin-, ajoign-*, stem of *ajoindre* (mod. *adjoindre*) :– L. *adjungere*, f. *ad* AD- + *jungere* join.] **1.** † To join on, unite, *to* or *unto* –1659; *fig.* to join on as an adjunct or supplement (*arch.*) ME. Also *refl.* and *intr.* † **2.** *intr.* To be or lie close, contiguous (*to, on, with*) –1794. **3.** *trans.* (*to* omitted.) To be contiguous to or in contact with 1745.

¶ Used erron. for ENJOIN. [See A- *pref.* 10.]

1. Mortiz'd and adjoined *Haml.* III. iii. 20. 3. The head of the tomb adjoins the west wall 1870. Hence **Adjoi·ned** *ppl. a.* † joined, united; appended or subjoined. † **Adjoi·nedly** *adv.* unitedly. **Adjoi·ning** *ppl. a.* lying next; *fig.* pertaining; connected.

† **Adjoi·nant.** 1494. [– OFr. *ajoinant*, pr. pple. of *ajoindre*; see prec., -ANT.] **A.** *ppl. a.* Adjoining –1602. **B.** *sb.* One living close by 1548.

† **Adjoint,** *sb.*¹ 1597. [– Fr. *adjoint*, pa. pple. of *adjoindre* associate, after late L. *adjunctus* ally, in med.L. ally, colleague ('*socius, collega*', Du Cange), pa. pple. of L. *adjungere* join to; see ADJOIN, ADJUNCT.] A helper; an adjunct –1700.

‖ **Adjoint** (adʒoań, æ·dʒoint), *sb.*² [Fr.; see prec.] A French civil officer who assists the maire; a sub-professor in a French college.

Adjourn (ădʒɔ̄·ɹn), *v.* ME. [– OFr. *ajorner* (mod. *ajourner*) f. phr. *à jorn* (*nomé*) to an (appointed) day, i.e. *à* AD-, *jorn* :– late L. *diurnum* day (whence Fr. *jour*), n. of L. *diurnus* daily; cf. DIURNAL, JOURNAL.] † **1.** *trans.* To appoint (one) a day for his appearance; to cite, or summon for, or remand to, a stated day –1660. **2.** To defer or put off ME. **3.** To adjourn (a meeting): To put off or defer proceedings to another day 1494. **4.** *intr.* (and † *refl.*) Of persons: To suspend proceedings and disperse for a time, or *sine die.* Also, to separate in order to meet elsewhere; hence *colloq.* to go in a body to another place. 1641.

2. Fro place to place to adiourne it 1559. This day a. your cares POPE. 3. To a. Parlyament FABYAN, a Court SHAKS., the Senate 1741. 4. The House . . then adjournd themselves MARVELL. From the Church the people adjourned to the hippodrome GIBBON. They thence adjourned to eat ice at a pastry-cook's JANE AUSTEN. Hence † **Adjou·rnal,** adjournment. **Adjou·rned** *ppl. a.* † cited; postponed. **Adjou·rning** *vbl. sb.* adjournment. **Adjou·rnment,** the act of adjourning; the state of being adjourned.

† **Adjou·st,** *v.* ME. [– OFr. *ajoster, ajuster*, later *adjouster* (mod. *ajouter* add), place beside :– Rom. **adjuxtare* f. L. *ad* AD- + *juxta* close to. See ADJUST *v.*] **1.** To put a thing (to one); to suggest –1521. **2.** To put one thing to another; to add –1530.

Adjudge (ădʒɒ·dʒ), *v.* [ME. *aiuge* – OFr. *ajuger* (mod. *adjuger*) :– L. *adjudicare* to grant or award; see next.] **1.** *trans.* To decide judicially ME. **2.** To pronounce or decree by judicial sentence 1563. † **3.** To determine in one's own judgement, judge –1729. **4.** To condemn ME. **5.** To award, grant, or impose judicially (*to* or *unto*) 1494.

1. And so was it adjudged in the Court of Common Pleas COKE. 2. The grant was adjudged void FULLER. 3. Divers adjudged that he was a scrivener's sone HAWARD. 4. Adjudging my family to beggary BURKE. Charles was adjudged to die P. BAYNE. 5. Hard to a. the garland SELDEN. Hence **Adju·dged** *ppl. a.* (senses 1, † 2, 4, 5). **Adju·dger,** an awarder. **Adju·dging** *vbl. sb.* (senses 1, 4, 5). **Adju·dg(e)ment,** the act of adjudging.

Adjudicate (ădʒ¹ū·dikeⁱt), *v.* 1700. [– *adjudicat-*, pa. ppl. stem of L. *adjudicare*, f. *ad* AD- + *judicare* (f. *judex, judic-* judge); see -ATE³.] † **1.** *trans.* To award judicially –1731. **2.** *trans.* To try and determine judicially 1775. **3.** *intr.* To act as a judge, or court of judgement 1840.

2. Adjudicated a bankrupt 1870. **3.** He ought not to a. as to his own fees 1857. Hence **Adju·dicative** *a.* having the character of adjudicating. **Adju·dicator,** one who settles a question, or awards a prize. **Adju·dica·ture,** the process of adjudicating.

Adjudication (ădʒ¹ū:dikēⁱ·ʃən). 1691. [– Fr., or late L. *adjudicatio*, f. *adjudicat-*; see prec., -ION.] **1.** The act of adjudicating; see ADJUDICATE 1, 2. **2.** A judicial sentence or award 1782. **3.** *Law.* A decree in bankruptcy 1869. **4.** *Sc. Law.* An attachment of heritable estate as security, etc.

1. An a. in his favour PENNANT. The a. of the medal SMILES. **2.** Any a. in favour of natural rights BURKE.

† **A·djument.** 1607. [– L. *adjumentum*, contr. f. *adjuvamentum*, f. *adjuvare* assist; see ADJUVANT, -MENT.] Help; a helper –1663.

Adjunct (æ·dʒɒŋkt). 1588. [– *adjunct-*, pa. ppl. stem of L. *adjungere* join to, f. *ad* AD- + *jungere* join.] **A.** *adj.* Joined or added; subordinate 1595.

Every humour hath his a. pleasure SHAKS. *Sonn.* xci.

B. *sb.* (Cf. Fr. *adjoint.*) **1.** Something joined to another, but subordinate, as auxiliary, or dependent upon it 1588. **2.** A person joined to another in some office or service 1639. **3.** A personal addition or enhancement 1610; a qualifying addition to a word or name 1608. **4.** *Gram.* Any word or words expanding the subject, predicate, etc., of a sentence 1589. **5.** *Logic.* Anything added to the essence; a non-essential attribute 1588.

1. Learning is but an a. to our selfe *L.L.L.* IV. iii. 314. The charters with their adjuncts STUBBS. **2.** Colleagues, or rather Adjuncts, in the duties of the Office 1877. **3.** The Adjuncts of a strong and subtil Capacity NAUNTON. Geographical adjuncts 'West', 'East', etc. FREEMAN. **5.** To differ more in adjuncts . . than in innate quality I. TAYLOR. Hence **Adju·nctive** *a.* having the quality of contributing (*to*) or forming an a. **Adju·nctively** *adv.* as an a.

Adjunction (ădʒɒ·ŋkʃən). 1603. [– L. *adjunctio*, f. *adjunct-*; see prec., -ION.] **1.** The act of joining on or adding 1618. **2.** That which is joined on, etc. ? *Obs.* 1603.

Adjuration (æ:dʒ¹urēⁱ·ʃən). ME. [– Fr., or L. *adjuratio* f. *adjurat-*, pa. ppl. stem of *adjurare*; see ADJURE *v.*, -ION.] The action of adjuring (see ADJURE 2); an earnest appeal 1611; *spec.* in exorcism ME.

An a. as vain as it was earnest FROUDE. Come, draw thy circle, speak thine a. B. TAYLOR.

Adjuratory (ădʒ¹ūᵊ·rătəri), *a.* 1815. [– late L. *adjuratorius*, f. *adjurator*, agent-noun of L. *adjurare*; see prec., -OR 2, -ORY².] Containing a solemn charge or appeal.

Adjure (ădʒ¹ūᵊɹ), *v.* ME. [– L. *adjurare* swear to, (later) put to an oath, conjure, f. *ad* AD- + *jurare* swear (f. *jus, jur-* oath).] † **1.** To put (one) to his oath; to bind under the penalty of a curse –1643. **2.** To charge or entreat solemnly, as if under oath, or under the penalty of a curse 1483.

1. Thy father adjured the people, saying: Cursed be the man that [etc.] 1 *Sam.* 14:28. **2.** His friends adjured him to take more care of [his] life MACAULAY. Hence **Adju·rement,** a solemn entreaty. **Adju·rer, -or,** one who adjures. **Adju·ring** *ppl. a.* charging upon oath; exorcising.

Adjust (ădʒɒ·st), *v.* 1611. [– Fr. (XVI) *adjuster* (mod. *ajuster*), refash., after *juste* JUST *a.*, from OFr. *ajoster* (mod. *ajouter* add); see ADJOUST *v.*] **1.** To arrange, compose, harmonize (differences, discrepancies, accounts) 1611. † **2.** *ellipt. intr.* To a. (*sc.* differences, or oneself): To come to terms –1733. **3.** To arrange suitably (*to, by, with*) something else 1664. **4.** To arrange suitably in relation to its parts; to regulate, systematize 1667; *esp.* of clothes, armour, etc. 1735.

1. To a. Accounts COWLEY, the preliminaries of a Treaty STEELE, a difficulty DE FOE, pretensions H. WALPOLE, the books JAS. MILL. **3.** To a. the event to the prediction ADDISON, means to end BURKE, the marvellous with the probable *a* 1746. **4.** The scientifically adjusted court precedency of France BURTON. See them . . a. their clothes POPE. Hence **Adju·stable** *a.* † **Adju·stage.** *rare.* = ADJUSTMENT. Also = ADJUTAGE. **Adju·sting** *vbl. sb.* the process of arranging or disposing suitably.

Adjuster (ădʒɒ·stəɹ). 1756. [f. prec. + -ER¹.] One who adjusts; *spec.* in *average adjuster*: One who professionally assesses and apportions claims arising out of loss, etc., at sea.

Adjustment (ădʒɒ·stmĕnt). 1644. [– OFr. *adjustement* (mod. *aj-*), f. *adjuster*; see ADJUST *v.*, -MENT.] **1.** The process of adjusting. **2.** The state of being adjusted; settlement 1689. **3.** An arrangement whereby things are adjusted 1736. **4.** *Comm.* The settlement among various parties of their several claims, liabilities, or payments; as the *a. of the policy*, or *of general average* in Marine Insurance 1670.

1. The a. of the whole SIR J. REYNOLDS, of the eye TYNDALL, of the Calendar 1881. **2.** A mode of bringing [questions] to an amicable a. WELLINGTON. **3.** Wheels and verniers, and delicate adjustments TYNDALL.

Adjutage, ajutage (ădʒ¹ū·tĕdʒ, æ·dʒ¹ūtĕdʒ). 1707. [– Fr. *ajutage, ajoutage*, f. *ajouter*; see ADJOUST *v.*, ADJUST *v.*, -AGE.] *lit.* An adjustment; hence in *Hydraulics*, The efflux-tube of an artificial fountain.

Adjutancy (æ·dʒ¹ŭtănsi). 1791. [f. next; see -ANCY.] **1.** The office or rank of an adjutant 1820. **2.** *fig.* Official order. BURKE.

Adjutant (æ·dʒ¹ŭtănt). 1600. [– *adjutant-*, pr. ppl. stem of L. *adjutare*, frequent. of *adjuvare*, f. *ad* AD- + *juvare* help; see -ANT.] **A.** *adj.* Helping.

B. *sb.* **1.** An assistant or helper. Now *rare.* 1622. **2.** *Mil.* An officer who assists the superior officers in the details of military duty 1600. **3.** *Ornith.* A gigantic species of stork (*Ciconia argala*) native to India; so called from its gait. (Called also **a.-bird, -crane, -stork.**) 1798.

1. The Hands [and other] . . adjutants of man's wit BULWER. **2.** He would sit in his pavilion, and manage all by adjutants BACON.

A:djutant-ge·neral. [See GENERAL *a.* 9.] **1.** *Mil.* An officer who assists the general of an army 1645. **2.** Among the Jesuits, a superintendent of a province or country, acting under the supervision of the General of the Order 1753.

A·djutator. 1647. [Identical in form w. late L. *adjutator* (Oribasius) = L. *adjutor*, f. *adjut-*, pa. ppl. stem of *adjutare* help; see ADJUTANT, -OR 2 b.] *lit.* A helper. Orig. a corruption of AGITATOR, q.v.

† **Adju·te,** *v.* 1524. [– Fr. (XVI) *adjouter* (now *ajouter*) add; see ADJOUST *v.*, ADJUTAGE.] To add –1633.

† **Adju·tor**¹. 1531. [– L. *adjutor* helper, f. *adjut-*; see ADJUTATOR, -OR 2 b.] A helper –1652. Occ. = ADJUTANT *sb.* 2.

† **Adju·tor**². 1541. [irreg. – OFr. *ajutoire* help, arm, later *adjutoire* (now obs.), – L. *adjutorium* help (in med.L. also helper) – *adjut-* (see prec.) + *-orium* -ORY¹. See next.] Properly the *humerus*; also the *ulna*.

† **A·djutory.** 1541. [– L. *adjutorium* help, in med.L. also helper, f. *adjutor*; see prec.] **A.** *adj.* Helping. *spec.* in *Phys.* of certain bones of the arm –1706. **B.** *sb.* **1.** A helper 1552. **2.** *Phys.* = ADJUTOR² 1541. **3.** Help –1678.

Adjuvant (æ·dʒ¹uvănt). 1609. [– Fr., or L. *adjuvant-*, pres. ppl. stem of *adjuvare*, f. *ad* AD- + *juvare* to help; see -ANT.] *adj.* Aiding 1614. *sb.* [The adj. used *absol.*] A help, or helper 1609. *spec.* in *Med.* A substance added to a prescription to assist the action of the base.

† **A·djuvate,** *v.* 1599. [– *adjuvat-*, pa. ppl. stem of L. *adjuvare*; see prec., -ATE³.] To aid –1708.

Adlegation (æ:dlĭgēⁱ·ʃən). 1753. [mod. use of L. *adlegatio* (usu. *allegatio*; see ALLEGATION), f. *ad* in addition + *legare* depute.] The right claimed by the states of the old German Empire of associating their delegates with those of the Emperor in treaties, etc. relating to the common concerns of the empire. Distinguished from *legation*.

‖ **Ad libitum** (æ:d li·bitŏm). 1705. [L. *ad* to, *libitum* pleasure.] At one's pleasure; as much as one likes. In *Music* opp. to *obbligato*. Abbrev. **ad lib.**

Admarginate (ædmā·ɹdʒineⁱt), *v.* 1834. [app. f. AD- + MARGINATE *v.*] To add in the margin.

Admaxillary (ædmæ·ksilări), *a.* 1881. [f. AD- + MAXILLARY.] Connected with the jaw.

Admeasure (ædme·ʒ¹ŭɹ, -ʒəɹ), *v.* [ME. *amesure* – OFr. *amesurer* :– med.L. *admensurare* (in Eng. senses), f. *ad* AD- + late L. *mensurare*; see MEASURE *v.*] † **1.** To assign a measure or limit to –1627. † **2.** To apply a measure to –1697. **3.** To measure out to; to apportion 1641.

3. To a. and apportion [the common] TOMLINS. Hence **Admea·surer.**

Admeasurement (ædme·ʒ¹ŭɹmĕnt, -ʒər-). 1598. [– OFr. *amesurement*; see prec., -MENT.] **1.** The process of applying a measure in order to ascertain dimensions 1626. **2.** Size, dimensions 1790. **3.** The ascertainment and apportionment of just shares, e.g. in an inheritance or common 1598.

1. A. by acre BACON. **2.** Accurate admeasurements in feet and cubits MAURICE. **3.** By writ of a. of pasture BLACKSTONE. var. **Adme:nsura·tion.**

† **Admerveyle, -ayle,** *v.* 1474. [– late OFr. *admerveillier*, refash., through erron. assoc. w. L. *ad*, from OFr. *amerveillier*, var. of *esmerveillier* (mod. *ém-*), f. *es-* :– L. *ex* + *merveillier* MARVEL *v.* See AMARVEL *v.*] To marvel, marvel at –1506.

Adminicle (ædmi·nik'l). Also **-cule.** 1556. [– L. *adminiculum* prop, support, f. *ad* AD- and dim. *-culum* -CULE.] **1.** Anything that aids or supports. **2.** *Law.* Supporting or corroboratory evidence. *Sc. Law.* Any writing tending to prove the existence and tenor of a lost deed. 1706. **3.** *Archæol.* In *pl.* Ornaments which surround the figure on coins, etc. 1751.

1. Fasting and sackcloth . . as adminicles . . to . . prayer 1597. **2.** Only as adminicles of testimony SCOTT. Hence **A:dmini·cular** *a.* var. † **Admini·culary** *a.* and *sb.*

Adminiculate (æ:dmini·kiŭleⁱt), *v.* [– *adminiculat-*, pa. ppl. stem of L. *adminiculare*, f. *adminiculum*; see prec., -ATE³.] *Sc. Law.* To support by corroboratory evidence. Hence **Adminicula·tion.**

‖ **Adminiculum** (æ:dmini·kiŭlŏm). Pl. **-a.** [L. see ADMINICLE.] *Entom.* In *pl.* The short spines or teeth on the abdomen of certain pupæ or grubs. KIRBY.

Administer (ædmi·nistəɹ), *v.* [ME. *amynistre* – OFr. *aministrer, amenestrer* – L. *administrare*, f. *ad* AD- + *ministrare* (see MINISTER); later refash. after latinized (O)Fr. *ad-*.] **1.** *trans.* To manage as a steward, to carry on. Also *absol.* ME. **2.** *Law.* To manage and dispose of the estate of a deceased person, either under a will or under *Letters of Administration* c 1430; also *absol.* 1602. **3.** *trans.* To execute or dispense 1495; to tender (an oath *to*) 1593. **4.** To apply, as medicine, etc. 1541. **5.** Hence *fig.* To dispense, give (anything beneficial; also (*joc.*) a *rebuke*, a *blow*, etc.) *to* 1489; *intr.* to minister *to* 1712.

1. To a. the gouernement LYDG., the secular affairs of a church HOBBES, a charity 1756, Athens GROTE, the finances of a college M. PATTISON. **3.** To admynystre Ryght and Justyce FISHER. To a. the sacraments ABP. SANDYS, the Lord's Supper WESLEY, extreme unction PRESCOTT. † *To be administered*: to receive the sacrament. The Oath that we a. *Rich. II*, I. iii. 182. **5.** To a. posset to the Gossips THACKERAY. Hence **Admi:niste·rial** *a.* pertaining to the administration or government. **Admi·nistrable** *a.* † **Admi·nistrer,** one who administers; fem. † **Admi·nistress.** var. **Admi·nistrate** *v.* (a sacrament, oath, medicine); hence † **Admi·nistrate** *ppl. a.* administered.

† **Admi·nister,** *sb.* [– L., = attendant, f. *ad* AD- + *minister* servant; see MINISTER *sb.*] A minister or administrator –1677.

Administrant (ædmi·nistrănt), *a.* 1602. [– Fr., pr. pple. of *administrer*; see ADMINISTER *v.*, -ANT.] Executive. As *sb.* An acting officer.

Administration (ædmi:nistrēⁱ·ʃən). ME. [– (O)Fr., or – L. *administratio*, f. *administrat-*, pa. ppl. stem of *administrare*; see ADMINISTER *v.*, -ION.] † **1.** The action of administering; service, attendance –1791; execution *of* –1611. **2.** Management ME.; *ellipt.* the management of public affairs, government 1681; the executive part of the legislature, the ministry

1731. **3.** *Law.* The management and disposal of the estate of a deceased person by an executor or administrator. *spec.* Authority to administer, conferred by *Letters of Administration.* 1538. **4.** The action of administering something to others (see ADMINISTER *v.* 3, 4) ME.

1. [While] the Physician continues his a. HALE. The a. of an office BARCKLEY. **2.** The a. of a few fields..of a great country RUSKIN. Every measure of your grace's a. JUNIUS. A succession of weak administrations MACAULAY. **4.** The a. of the sacrament ME., of war HALE, of an antidote WOOD. Hence **Administra·tional** *a.*

Administrative (ædmi·nistrēⁱ:tiv), *a.* 1731. [– Fr. *administratif, -ive* or L. *administrativus,* f. as prec.; see -IVE.] **1.** Pertaining to management; executive. **2.** *absol.* An administrative body 1876. Hence **Admi·nistra:tively** *adv.*

Administrator (ædmi·nistrēⁱ:təɹ, æ:dministrēⁱ·toɹ). 1514. [– L., f. as prec.; see -OR 2. Cf. Fr. *administrateur.*] **1.** One who administers (see ADMINISTER 1) 1533; *absol.* one who has the faculty of organizing 1855. **2.** One who executes or dispenses; one who applies, proffers, or gives (see ADMINISTER 3, 4, 5) 1563. **3.** *Law.* **a.** One appointed trustee, steward, etc., during a minority or legal incapacity 1599. **b.** One appointed to administer an estate in default of an executor; an executor dative 1514.

1. The a. of Holstein 1705. The first of living administrators MACAULAY. **2.** Administrators of Sacraments 1563, of justice 1865. Hence **Admi·nistratorship.**

Admi·nistratrix. Pl. **-trixes** (triksėz), **-trices** (trisīz). 1626. [f. prec.; see -TRIX. Cf. Fr. *administratrice.*] A female administrator; *spec.* a woman appointed to administer an intestate estate. Also **-tress** (*rare*).

Admirable (æ·dmirăb'l), *a.* 1596. [–(O)Fr., – L. *admirabilis*; see ADMIRE *v.*, -ABLE.] †**1.** To be wondered at –1794. Hence, **2.** Exciting pleased surprise, or wonder united with approbation. In mod. usage the idea of *wonder* is lost. 1598. Also as *adv.* SHAKS.

1. Oh 'tis braue warres. Most a. *All's Well* II. i. 26. **2.** A gentleman..of a. discourse *Merry W.* II. ii. 234. His wife takes a. care of him DICKENS. Hence **A·dmirableness. A·dmirably** *adv.* †wonderfully; excellently.

Admiral (æ·dmirăl), *sb.* [ME. *amyrayl, admira(i)l* – (O)Fr. *amiral,* †*admira(i)l* – (through med.L. *a(d)miralis, -allus*) Arab. *'amir* military commander, with termination of unc. origin; see AMEER, EMIR. The forms in *ad-*, which arose from the treatment of *am-* as = Fr. *am-* :– L. *adm-*, were associated with med.L. *admirabilis,* etc.] †**1.** An emir or prince under the Sultan; any Saracen Commander –1561. **2.** The commander-in-chief of a navy 1460. **3.** A naval officer of the highest rank; a flag-officer *c* 1425. **4.** The privileged commander of a fishing or merchant fleet 1708. **5.** *Admiral-ship* (cf. Fr. *le vaisseau amiral*): The ship which carries the admiral; the Flagship. **6.** Two species of butterfly; the *Red Admiral* (*Vanessa atalanta*), and the *White Admiral* (*Limenitis sibylla*). **7.** *Conch.* = *Admiral-shell*: a shell of the genus *Conus.*

1. Sone of the admyralle of babylone CAXTON. **2.** Erle of Kente made Admyral of Englond CAXTON. *Lord High Admiral*: the full title of an officer or magistrate who had formerly the administrative duties now discharged by five *Lords Commissioners of the Admiralty,* and the judicial functions now vested in the *High Court of Admiralty.* **3.** One Giles..a petty A. of four Ships MILT. *A. of the Fleet,* an officer ranking with a field-marshal; *A., Vice-A.,* and *Rear-A.,* officers ranking with a general, lieutenant-general, and major-general respectively. *Admirals of the Red, White,* or *Blue*: so called from the colours hoisted by them. Hence *A. of the Blue,* (*joc.*) a *tapster* (from his blue apron): The A. of the Blue, crys, Coming Sir! 1731. **5.** The mast Of some great Ammiral [It. *ammiraglia*] MILT. *Comb.* **a.-in-chief,** or **-in-general,** the supreme naval commander. Hence **A·dmiralling** *vbl. sb.* (cf. *a-colonelling,* HUDIBRAS). **A·dmiralship,** the position of an a.; ability to perform the duties of an a.

† **A·dmiral,** *a.* [var. of ADMIRABLE, through *admirabilis,* a med.L. form of ADMIRAL *sb.*] Admirable –1650.

Admiralty (æ·dmirălti). ME. [– OFr. *admiral(i)té* (mod. *amirauté*); see ADMIRAL *sb.*, -TY¹. Cf. AL. *admiralitas.*] **1.** The office or jurisdiction of an admiral ME. †**2.** The navy –1626. **3.** The naval branch of the Executive; now in England the *Lords Commissioners of the A.* 1459. **4.** The maritime branch of the administration of justice 1589. **5.** With *the*: The building where the Lords of the Admiralty transact business 1617. **6.** The command of the seas, pre-eminence on the sea. 1893.

1. His Badge or Token of the Amiraltye LELAND. **3.** The admiralties of the allied powers MACAULAY. **4.** *Court of A.*: the tribunal for the trial of maritime causes, formerly presided over by the Lord High Admiral, but now transferred to the Probate, Divorce, and Admiralty Division of the High Court of Justice. This judge of the A., Judge Jenkins PEPYS.

† **Admi·rance.** [– OFr., f. *admirer* ADMIRE *v.*; see -ANCE.] Admiration. SPENSER.

Admiration (æ:dmirēⁱ·ʃən). 1490. [– (O)Fr., or L. *admiratio,* f. *admirat-*, pa. ppl. stem of *admirari*; see next, -ION.] **1.** The action of wondering or marvelling. *arch.* 1506. **2.** Wonder mingled with reverence, esteem, approbation; gratified contemplation 1589. † **3.** Admirableness –1642. **4.** An object of admiration; a marvel 1490. **5.** *Note of admiration*: the mark (!).

1. A. is the daughter of ignorance FULLER. **2.** The test of true a. is pleasure MOZLEY. **3.** Admir'd Miranda! Indeede the top of a. *Temp.* III. i. 38. **4.** Bring in the a. SHAKS. The prince..is the a. of the whole court 1716. **5.** To skip over all sentences where he spied a note of a. at the end SWIFT.

Admire (ădməiᵊ·ɹ), *v.* 1590. [– Fr. *admirer* (OFr. *amirer*) or L. *admirari* wonder at, f. *ad* AD- + *mirari* wonder.] **1.** *intr.* To feel or express surprise or astonishment. *arch.* **2.** *trans.* To view with wonder or surprise; to marvel at. *arch.* 1590. Hence **3.** To gaze on with ADMIRATION (sense 2) 1594. †**4.** To astonish –1650.

1. Admiring at the miracle FULLER. We may..a. that so beastly a drunkard lived so long FULLER. **2.** Examples rather to be admired then imitated FULLER. **3.** To a. the knowledge and promptness of [a] guide TYNDALL. Hence **A·dmira:tive** *a. rare,* characterized by admiration. **A·dmiratively** *adv.* † **Admi·re** *sb.* admiration. **Admi·red** *ppl. a.* regarded with admiration; astonished. **Admi·redly** *adv.* in an admired manner; surprisingly. **Admi·ring** *vbl. sb.* viewing with ADMIRATION (sense 2); *ppl. a.* full of admiration; †causing admiration. **Admi·ringly** *adv.* with admiration.

Admirer (ădməiᵊ·rəɹ). 1605. [f. ADMIRE *v.* + -ER.¹] **1.** One who admires (see ADMIRE *v.* 2, 3). **2.** A lover 1704.

Admissible (ădmi·sĭb'l), *a.* 1611. [– Fr., or med.L. *admissibilis*; see next, -IBLE.] **1.** Allowable, as an idea or project 1611, or (*Law*) as judicial proof 1849. **2.** Worthy of being admitted to an office or relation, or to the use of a place 1775.

1. An a. supposition HALE. Parol evidence..is a. 1849. **2.** A. to the English markets MᶜCULLOCH. Hence **Admi:ssibi·lity. Admi·ssibleness.**

Admission (ădmi·ʃən). 1494. [– L. *admissio,* f. *admiss-*, pa. ppl. stem of *admittere*; see ADMIT *v.*, -ION.] **1.** The action of admitting to a place and its privileges, a society, or class of things. Also, the fact of being admitted, access. 1622. **2.** Institution or acceptance into an office or position 1494. **3.** The admitting (*of* anything) as proper, valid, or true 1538. **4.** *Law,* and *gen.* A concession, an acknowledgement 1808.

1. The a. of poor suitors without fee BACON. The free a. of the light of Heaven RUSKIN. **2.** This formal a. of St. Matthias into the number of the Apostles BEVERIDGE. **3.** The a. of supernatural truths SULLIVAN. **4.** His wife's a. that she had agreed to pay [etc.] 1808.

Admissive (ădmi·siv), *a.* 1778. [f. as prec. + -IVE.] Characterized by admitting; tending to admit. var. **Admi·ssory** *a.*

Admit (ădmi·t), *v.* ME. [– L. *admittere,* f. *ad* AD- + *mittere* send.] **I.** As a voluntary agent. **1.** To allow to enter, let in, receive; *spec.* in *Law,* into the possession of a copyhold estate. **2.** *fig.* To consent to, permit ME.; to acknowledge, as lawful, etc. 1538; to concede, as true, etc. 1532. Also with *of* 1649.

1. Obsolete words are admitted JOHNSON. To a. air TYNDALL. Admitted a Commoner 1713, to benefices BP. BURNET. Mirth, a. me of thy crew MILT. **2.** She will a. no kinde of suite *Twel. N.* I. ii. 45. To a. a prayer SHENSTONE, delay JAS. MILL. To a. a title SHAKS. *John* II. i. 200, a claim to tribute WELLESLEY. To a. the outline of a story FREEMAN.

II. As an involuntary agent. **1.** *trans.* To be the channel of admission to; to afford entrance 1703. **2.** To have room for 1661. **3.** To lie open to, be compatible with. *arch.* 1538. Also with *of* 1718.

1. This order admits the whole party (*mod.*). **2.** The passage admits two abreast (*mod.*). **3.** My loue admits no qualifying crosse *Tr. & Cr.* IV. iv. 9. [His] conduct admitted..of no apology MAR. EDGEWORTH. Hence **Admi·ttable** *a.* orig. = ADMISSIBLE, now lit.: Capable of being admitted to a place or as a fact; var. **Admittible. Admi·ttedly** *adv.* by general admission. **Admi·tter,** one who admits (senses I. 1, 2). † **Admi·ttie** (*rare*), admittance. B. JONS. **Admi·tting** *vbl. sb.* willing or official reception; mental assent; acknowledgement.

Admittance (ădmi·tăns). 1589. [f. prec. + -ANCE.] **1.** The action of admitting (see ADMIT I. 1); permission to enter; the fact of being admitted 1593. †**2.** Admissibility –1598. †**3.** Admitting as valid, true, etc. –1622.

1. 'Tis Gold which buyes a. *Cymb.* II. iii. 73. A. to office in the Church HOOKER, into favor 1743. A. is the last stage..of copyhold assurances BLACKSTONE. **2.** A gentleman..of great a. *Merry W.* II. ii 235. **3.** A. of a tenet 1635.

Admix (ădmi·ks), *v. rare.* 1533. [f. AD- + MIX *v.*, perh. after L. *admiscēre* mix with, or through the taking of ADMIXT *ppl. a.* as an Eng. pa. pple. *admix-t.*] To mingle with something else. *trans.* and *intr.*

Admixt (ădmi·kst), *ppl. a.* ME. [– L. *admixtus,* pa. pple. of *admiscēre* mix with, f. *ad* AD- + *miscēre* mix; see prec.] Mingled with.

Admixtion (ădmi·kstiən). ME. [– L. *admixtio,* f. *admixt-*, pa. ppl. stem of *admiscēre*; see ADMIXT *ppl. a.*, -ION.] The mingling of one thing with another.

Admixture (ădmi·kstiŭɹ). 1605. [f. AD- + MIXTURE, replacing ADMIXTION. Cf. MIXTION, MIXTURE.] **1.** The action of mingling as an ingredient; the fact of being so mingled 1605. **2.** That which is mixed with anything; an alloy 1665.

Admonish (ădmǫ·niʃ), *v.* [ME. *amoneste* – OFr. *amonester* – Rom. **admonestare,* unexplained deriv. of L. *admonēre,* f. *ad* AD- + *monēre* advise. The final *t,* esp. in pa. t. and pa. ppl. forms, was taken as an inflexion, and the final syll. *-es* (etc.) then assim. to -ISH²; the initial syll. was latinized to *ad-*.] **1.** *gen.* To put in mind of duties; to counsel, to warn ME. †**2.** To inculcate ME. **3.** To put in mind, charge, exhort, *to do* ME. **4.** To put in mind, warn (*of, against, for, that,* etc.) 1541. **5.** To put in mind, inform (*of, that,* etc.) 1574.

1. A. him as a brother 2 *Thess.* 3:15. **3.** Admonyst your people to do well their deuoyre LD. BERNERS. **4.** He would admonest..him of his lacke in diligence ELYOT. **5.** He shall be admonished of the King's pleasure BRAMHALL. Hence **Admo·nisher,** a monitor. **Admo·nishingly** *adv.*

Admonishment (ădmǫ·niʃmĕnt). ME. [– OFr. *a(d)monestement*; see prec., -MENT.] The action of admonishing, or being admonished; an ADMONITION (sense 2).

Admonition (æ:dmŏni·ʃən). ME. [– OFr. *amonition* (mod. *ad-*) – L *admonitio,* f. *admonit-*, pa. ppl. stem of *admonēre*; see ADMONISH *v.*, -ION.] **1.** The action of admonishing; authoritative counsel; warning, reproof. **2.** An act of admonishing; a statement of counsel or (ecclesiastical) censure 1526.

1. These things..are written for our a. 1 *Cor.* 10:11. A. or reproof JOHNSON. **2.** A. is the lowest of Ecclesiasticall censures FULLER. Hence †**Admoni·tioner,** a monitor; *spec.* in *pl.* The Puritans who in 1571 presented an a. to Parliament, condemning the ceremonies of the Church of England. var. **Admo·nitor,** fem. **Admo·nitrix**; hence **Admo:nito·rial** *a.* (*rare*) = ADMONITORY.

Admonitory (ădmǫ·nitəri), *a.* 1594. [– med.L. *admonitorius,* f. *admonit-* (see prec., -ORY²); in mod. use f. prec.] Of or pertaining to an admonitor; giving admonition.

An a. glance SCOTT. A raised a. finger DICKENS.

Admortization, var. of AMORTIZATION.

† **Admo·ve,** *v.* ME. [– L. *admovēre* move to or towards, f. *ad* AD- + *movēre* move.] **1.** To move to or towards –1646. **2.** To ad-

vance 1839. Hence **Admo·tive** *a.* characterized by motion towards.

†**Adna·scent,** *a.* 1664. [– *adnascent-*, pr. ppl. stem of L. *adnasci* grow to, upon (for *adg-*, commonly *ag-*), f. *ad* Ag- + *nasci* be born.] Growing or produced upon something else. Hence **Adna·scence,** adhesion of parts to each other by the whole surface.

Adnate (æ·dnēⁱt), *a.* 1661. [– L. *adnatus*, pa. pple. of *adnasci*; see prec., -ATE².] †**1.** Acquired –1677. **2.** *Phys.* and *Bot.* Attached congenitally by the whole surface; grown to congenitally 1661.

Adnation (ædnēⁱ·ʃən). 1842. [f. prec.; see -ATION.] Growth to; *esp.* in *Bot.* of different whorls of the inflorescence to each other.

Adnominal (ædnǫ·minăl), *a.* 1845. [f. L. *adnomen, -min-*, var. of *agnomen*, + -AL¹. See next.] Of or belonging to an adnoun; attached to a noun.

The adjective in [its attributive use] is a. 1860.

Adnoun (æ·dnaun). 1753. [mod. f. L. *ad* to + NOUN, on the model of *adverb*. Also in mod.Fr. *adnom*, and mod.L. *adnomen*; the cl. L. *agnomen* had a different sense.] An adjective; *spec.* an adj. used substantively.

† **Adnu·mber,** *v.* [f. L. *ad* to + NUMBER *v.*, after L. *adnumerare* count or reckon to; cf. ADMIX *v.*] To count in –1561.

Ado (ădū·), *sb.*, prop. *v. inf.* = **at do.** [ME. *a do* (see A- *pref.* 5), f. adoption of ON. *at* w. infin. (in Eng. *to*) + Do; cf. the corresp. Eng. phr. *to do* (Do *v.* IV. 2); see AT *prep.* VI.] **1.** *pres. inf.* To do; *esp.* in *to have ado.* (Cf. Fr. *avoir affaire*, orig. *avoir à faire.*) **2.** In doing; astir 1577. Hence, through *much ado*, etc., by taking the adverbs as adjs. qualifying *ado*: **3.** *sb.* (pl. rare, *adoes, ados*). Doing, fuss ME. **4.** Labour, trouble 1485.

1. I will nowt have a. ther with *Paston Lett.* **2.** An eager bustling, that rather keeps a. than does anything 1628. **3.** *Without more ado* FREEMAN. **4.** Quaking bogs, which we shall have our own ados to make..habitable CARLYLE.

† **Ado,** *pa. pple.* 1554. [For earlier *ido, ydo, ydon*; see A *particle.*] Done. *Dead for ado*: dead and done with. *Once for ado*: once for all. –1642.

-ado, *suffix* of sbs. **1.** – Sp. or Pg. *-ado* masc. of pa. pple., as *desperado* :– L. *desperatus*. **2.** Refash. of sbs. in *-ade* – Fr. *-ade* fem. (= Sp. *-ada*, It. *-ata*), perh. on the erron. analogy of *renegade* = *renegado*.

‖ **Adobe** (ădōᵘ·bi, ădōᵘ·b). 1834. [Sp., through U.S. from Mexico.] An unburnt brick dried in the sun. Also *attrib.*

† **Ado·d,** *int.* 1708. [For *Ah God!* Cf. *adad*, etc.] –1762.

Adolescence (ædole·sěns). ME. [– (O)Fr., – L. *adolescentia*; see ADOLESCENT, -ENCE.] The process or condition of growing up; the growing age; youth; the period between childhood and maturity, extending from 14 to 25 in males, from 12 to 21 in females. Also *fig.*

fig. [A Disease] of National A. CARLYLE.

Adolescency (ædole·sěnsi). ME. [– L. *adolescentia*, f. as next + *-ia* -Y³; see -ENCY.] The quality or state of being adolescent; *youthfulness*, as opp. to *youth.*

Adolescent (ædole·sěnt). 1482. [– (O)Fr. *adolescent* – *adolescent-*, pres. ppl. stem of L. *adolescere*, f. *ad* AD- + *alescere* grow up; see -ESCENT.] **A.** *sb.* A person in the age of adolescence. **B.** *adj.* Growing from childhood to maturity 1785.

B. I see Near manhood in thy a. limbs B. TAYLOR.

† **Adon.** [– Fr. *Adon* (XVI) or late L. *Adon* – Gr.; see ADONIS.] Adonis; a fop. SHAKS.

‖ **Adonai** (ădōᵘ·nāi, ædonēⁱ·əi). 1483. [Heb.] A name of the Supreme Being; in O.T. 'Lord'; substituted by the Jews, in reading, for *Jahveh*, the 'ineffable name'.

Adonic (ădǫ·nik). 1678. [– Fr. *adonique* – med.L. *adonicus*; cf. late Gr. ἀδώνιος, L. *adonium*, Fr. *adonien.*] **A.** *adj.* Of or relating to Adonis; in *Pros.* used of a metre, consisting of a dactyl and a spondee (– ◡ ◡ | – –). **B.** *sb.* [sc. *verse* or *line.*] 1753. var. **Ado·nian.**

Adonis (ădōᵘ·nis). 1597. [L., – Gr. Ἄδωνις, Ἄδων, – Phœn. *adōni* my lord, *adōn* lord.] **1.** In Gr. Mythology, a youth beloved by Venus for his beauty: hence, a beau 1765. †**2.** A kind of wig –1775. **3.** A genus of plants, N.O. *Ranunculaceæ*, including Pheasant's Eye 1597. **4.** A butterfly (*Polyommatus Adonis*).

2. A fine flowing a. or white periwig 1775. Hence **Adone·an** *a.* **A·donize** *v.* to dandify. *trans.* and *intr.*

† **Ado·nist.** 1751. [f. ADONAI + -IST.] In *pl.*: A Hebrew sect, differing from the Jehovists, *esp.* as to whether the word Adonai is always read for the word Jehovah.

† **A-doors,** prop. **a doors, a door.** 1526. A phonetic reduction of both *of doors* (A *prep.*², A- *pref.* 3), and *at doors* (A- *pref.* 5).

Cf. Driven out of doores with it *Com. Err.* IV. iv. 36. As you went in at doors MARLOWE.

† **Ado·perate,** *v.* [– *adoperat-*, pa. ppl. stem of med.L. *adoperare* use, employ, see *ad* AD- and OPERATE *v.*] To bring into operation –1681. Hence **Ado:pera·tion.**

Adopt (ădǫ·pt), *v.* 1548. [– (O)Fr. *adopter* or L. *adoptare* choose for oneself, f. *ad* AD- + *optare* choose.] **1.** To take voluntarily into any relationship 1548; *esp.* that of a son 1604. **2.** To take up from another, and use as one's own 1607; *spec.* in *Philol.* To take a foreign word into use without changing its form (*mod.*). **3.** To take (a course, etc.) as a matter of choice 1769. † **4.** *causal.* To affiliate, attach, to any one. [L. *se alicui adoptare.*] POPE. † **5.** To christen or rechristen –1601.

1. To a. as heyre HALL, as sonne in law BARCKLEY, as favourites JOHNSON. Rather to a. a Child, than get it *Oth.* I. iii. 191. **2.** To a. a policy SHAKS., systems CHESTERFIELD, Egyptian habits FROUDE. **3.** He adopted one posture H. MARTINEAU. The resolutions were adopted 1875. **4.** Adopted to a foreign land POPE. Hence **Ado:ptabi·lity,** capability of being adopted; *concr.* an adoptable thing. **Ado·ptable** *a.* **Ado·ptedly** *adv.* **Ado·ptive** *a.* due to adoption; having the habit of adopting. **Ado·ptively** *adv.* by way of adoption.

† **Ado·ptant.** 1671. [– Fr. – *adoptant-*, pres. ppl. stem of L. *adoptare*; see prec., -ANT.] One who adopts.

Adopter (ădǫ·ptəɹ). 1572. [f. ADOPT *v.*] **1.** One who adopts, *esp.* an adoptive father. **2.** One who adopts an opinion, etc. (see ADOPT *v.* 2, 3) 1829. **3.** *Chem.* = ADAPTER 2.

Adoption (ădǫ·pʃən). ME. [– (O)Fr., or L. *adoptio*, f. *adopt-*, pa. ppl. stem of *adoptare*; see ADOPT *v.*, -ION.] **1.** The action of adopting or fact of being adopted (see ADOPT *v.* 1) ME. **2.** Taking up and treating as one's own 1598; *spec.* in *Philol.* taking a foreign word into use without changing its form; a word so taken; also used *passively* 1755.

1. The friends thou hast, and their a. tride *Haml.* I. iii. 62. A. into immortal palaces LAMB. **2.** The country of his own a. SEELEY. Which [words] depend for their a. on the suffrage of futurity JOHNSON. Hence **Ado·ptional** *a.* † **Ado·ptious** *a.* of or connected with a. SHAKS.

Adoptionist (ădǫ·pʃənist). 1847. [f. ADOPTION + -IST, after med.L. *adoptiani.*] *Eccl. Hist.* One of a sect who maintained that Jesus Christ is the son of God by adoption only. Also used *attrib.*

‖ **Ador.** ME. [L.] Sacrificial grain, spelt.

Adorable (ădōᵊ·răb'l), *a.* 1611. [– Fr., or L. *adorabilis*, f. *adorare* ADORE, *v.*; see -ABLE.] **1.** Worthy of divine worship. **2.** By exaggeration, said of anything to which one is passionately attached or for which one has a great regard 1710.

1. The a. wisdom of God BURKE. **2.** A. places SHAFTESBURY. Hence **Adorabi·lity. Ado·rableness. Ado·rably** *a.*

Adoral (ædōᵊ·răl), *a.* 1882. [f. AD- + ORAL *a.* Cf. ABORAL *a.*] Situated at the mouth. Hence **A:do·rally** *adv.*

Adoration (ædŏrēⁱ·ʃən). 1543. [– (O)Fr., or L. *adoratio*, f. *adorat-*, pa. ppl. stem of *adorare*; see next, -ATION.] **1.** The act of worshipping, or paying divine honours. **2.** *fig.* The exhibition of profound regard and love 1601. **3.** *techn.* A method of electing a pope by a low reverence before the same candidate from two-thirds of the voters present 1599.

1. A. is..the prostration of the Soul 1866. **2.** How does he loue me? With adorations *Twel. N.* I. v. 274.

Adore (ădōᵊ·ɹ), *v.* [ME. *aoure* – OFr. *aourer* :– L. *adorare* to address, salute, (eccl.) worship, f. *ad* AD- + *orare* (see ORATE *v.*). Refash. after L. and (O)Fr. *adorer* (XV).] **1.** *trans.* To make an act of the mind and will in acknowledgement of the infinite perfection of (God); to make an outward reverence expressing such an act, e.g. a bow, genuflexion, etc. **b.** To venerate with relative or representative honours 1582. **c.** To elect (a pope) by ADORATION 1670. **d.** *absol.* or *intr.* 1582. **2.** To regard with the utmost reverence and affection 1594. ¶ Confused with ADORN.

1. To preye and adoure god Almyghty CAXTON. The host, which he publicly adored SMOLLETT. **2.** My soul adores judiciall schollership MARSTON. ¶ The hore Congealed litle drops, which doe the morne adore SPENSER. Hence † **Ado·rative** *a.* pertaining to adoration. † **Ado·rement,** *rare.* **Ado·rer,** a worshipper; *fig.* a lover. **Ado·ringly** *adv.*

Adorn (ădǭ·ɹn), *v.* [ME. *aourne* – OFr. *ao(u)rner* :– L. *adornare*, f. *ad* AD- + *ornare* furnish, deck. Refash. after L., and (O)Fr. *adorner.*] **1.** To be an ornament to; to beautify, add lustre to ME.; also *fig.* ME.; and hence, of persons 1534. **2.** To furnish with ornaments; to deck or embellish (*with*) ME. Also *fig.* † **3.** To deck out speciously, dress up –1622. ¶ By confusion with ME. *adoren*: To adore 1470.

1. A Garland to adorne Her Tresses MILT. *fig.* The piety which adorns his character 1888. A new Cibber shall the stage a. POPE. **2.** Aourned as a king CAXTON. As a bride adorneth herselfe with her jewels *Isa.* 61:10. The..vertues with which he has adorned his mind BURKE. Hence † **Adorn** *sb.* adornment. † **Adorna·tion,** the act of adorning, ornament. **Ado·rned** *ppl. a.* furnished with ornaments, or with qualities that give distinction. **Ado·rner. Ado·rningly** *adv.*

† **Ado·rn,** *a. rare.* [f. It. *adorno*, short f. *adornato* :– L. *adornatus*; see ADORN *v.*] Adorned.

Made so a. for thy delight the more MILT.

† **Adorna·tion.** 1597. [– OFr., or med.L. *adornatio*, f. L. *adornat-*, pa. ppl. stem of *adornare*; see ADORN *v.*, -ATION.] The act of adorning; ornament.

Adornment (ădǭ·ɹnměnt). 1480. [In XV *aournement* – OFr. *aournement*, later *a-do(u)rnement*, to which Eng. was conformed; see ADORN *v.*, -MENT.] **1.** The action of adorning. **2.** That which adorns; an ornament. With *pl.* 1489.

Adosculation (ædǫ:skiulēⁱ·ʃən). 1674. [f. AD- + OSCULATION.] Impregnation by mere contact, without intromission.

‖ **Adossée** (adose, ado·si), *ppl. a.* [pa. pple. of (O)Fr. *adosser* turn the back to, f. *à* to + *dos* back. Cf. ADDORSED *ppl. a.*] *Her.* = ADDORSED.

Adown (ădau·n). *arch.* [OE. *adūn(e)*, reduced f. *ofdūne*, f. *of* (see A- *pref.* 3) + dat. of *dūn* hill; early aphet. to DOWN *adv.*, see DOWN *sb.*¹] **A.** *adv.* **1.** To a lower place; downward, down OE. *fig.* ME. † **2.** In a lower place; *esp.* on earth OE.

1. His..collar hung a. SCOTT. **2.** In this erthe adoun CHAUCER.

B. *prep.* (with obj.) Downwards upon or along ME. Also *fig.*

Adoune the staire CHAUCER. A. the sky PHILLIPS, the Pyrenees BYRON. *fig.* A. life's latter days M. ARNOLD. Hence † **Adownright** = DOWNRIGHT. † **Adow·nward** *adv.* = DOWNWARD; *prep.* = ADOWN *prep.*

Adp-, obs. f. APP-.

Adpress (ædpre·s), *v.* 1872. [– *adpress-*, pa. ppl. stem of *adprimere* press to, f. *ad* AD- + *premere* (see PRESS *v.*¹).] To press close to. Hence **Adpre·ssed** *ppl. a.* pressed close to, as hairs on stems.

‖ **Adpromissor** (æ:dpromi·səɹ, -oɹ). [late L., = one who is security, f. L. *adpromittere*, f. *ad* AD- + *promittere*; see PROMISE *v.*] *Rom. Law.* One who gives bail or security.

Adq-, obs. f. ACQ-.

Adra·d, *ppl. a. arch.* ME. [prob. weakened form of *of-drad*, pa. pple. of *of-drede* frighten, terrify.] Frightened.

I was the less a. Of what might come MORRIS.

Adradial (ædrēⁱ·diăl), *a.* 1880. [f. AD- + RADIAL.] *Zool.* Situated near or beside a ray. **b.** *sb.* An adradial organ.

† **Adrea·d,** *v.* OE. [A- *pref.* 4.] To dread.

† **Adrea·med,** *pple.* 1556. [prob. f. A *particle* + DREAM *sb.* or *v.*] *To be a.*, to dream.

Adrenal (æd,rī·năl), *a.* and *sb.* 1875. [f. AD- 1 + RENAL *a.*] *Anat.* = SUPRARENAL.

Hence **Adrenalin** (-re·nălin), a crystalline substance extracted from the adrenal glands, used as a hæmostatic.

† **Adre·nch,** *v.* ME. only. [f. A- *pref.* 1 + DRENCH, OE. *drencan.*] To give to drink; *trans.* to submerge, drown; *refl.* to drown (oneself); *intr.* to 'go down', as a ship. *lit.* and *fig.*

Adrift (ădri·ft), *adv.* 1624. [f. A *prep.*[1] + DRIFT. Cf. *afloat.*] Drifting, at the mercy of wind and tide. *fig.* 1690.

With all his..trees a. MILT. *fig.* The mind..a. YOUNG.

† **Adrip,** *adv.* 1867. [A *prep.*[1] + DRIP.] Dripping.

Adrogate (æ·drogeʲt), *v.* Also **arrogate.** 1649. [Specialized form of ARROGATE *v.*] *Rom. Law.* To adopt a person who was at the time his own master or *sui juris.* Hence **A·drogated** *ppl. a.* adopted when *sui juris.* **A:droga·tion.** Also **arrogation. A·droga:tor,** he who adrogates. Also **arrogator.**

Adroit (ădroi·t), *a.* 1652. [– (O)Fr. *adroit,* f. adv. phr. *à droit* according to right, i.e. *à* to + *droit* :– Rom. **drictum,* see ADDRESS *v.*] Possessing address or readiness of resource, either bodily or mental; dexterous, active, clever.

A. cavalry EVELYN, wrestlers 1825, intriguers MOTLEY. Hence **Adroi·tly** *adv.* **Adroi·tness,** the quality of being a.; skill and readiness, either bodily or mental.

† **Adro·p.** 1471. *Alch.* Lead; the philosopher's stone. B. JONS.

Adrostral (ædrǫ·străl), *a.* 1878. [f. AD- 1 + ROSTRAL *a.*] *Zool.* Pertaining to or at the beak or snout.

Adry·, *adv.* 1599. [f. A- *pref.* 11 + DRY *a.*, after *athirst,* etc.] In a dry condition; thirsty.

Ads, var. of ODS, 'minced' form of *God's.*

Adscititious (æ:dsiti·ʃəs), *a.*; also **asc-.** 1620. [f. *adscit-*, pa. ppl. stem of L. *adsciscere* admit, adopt, f. *ad* AD- + *sciscere,* inceptive of *scire* know, + -ITIOUS[1], after *adventitious.*] Assumed, adopted from without; supplemental; additional.

A. habits EVELYN. Initial vowels..not radical, but a. MÜLLER. Hence **A:dsciti·tiously** *adv.*

Adscript (æ·dskript). 1822. [– L. *adscriptus*; see ASCRIPT *ppl. a.* Cf. Fr. *adscrit.*] **A.** *adj.* **1.** Written after, opp. to *subscript.* **2.** For med.L. *adscriptus* (*glebæ*), attached (to the soil), and hence transferred with it. Said of feudal serfs. **B.** *sb.* = *adj.* **2** used subst. var. **Adscri·pted** *ppl. a.* Hence **Adscripti·tious** *a.* bound by adscription.

Adscription (ǣdskri·pʃən). 1660. [– L. *adscriptio*; see ASCRIPTION.] **1.** = ASCRIPTION 1857. † **2.** *spec.* Circumscribing or inscribing geometrical figures –1660. **3.** Attachment as an ADSCRIPT 1872.

Adsignify (ǣdsi·gnifəi), *v. rare.* 1798. [– L. *adsignificare* show, denote, f. *ad* AD- + *significare*; see SIGNIFY *v.*] To signify an action with an addition of time, as in tenses. Hence **Adsi:gnifica·tion.**

Adsorption (ædsǭ·ɹpʃən). 1882. [f. L. *ad* AD- + AB)SORPTION.] Condensation of gases on surfaces of solids.

† **Adspira·tion.** = ASPIRATION.

Adstipulate (ǣdsti·piŭleʲt), *v.* [– *adstipulat-*, pa. ppl. stem of L. *adstipulari* stipulate with, f. *ad* AD- + *stipulari* bargain; cf. ASTIPULATE.] *Rom. Law.* To act as second stipulant or receiving party to a bargain. Hence **Adsti:pula·tion,** the addition of, or acting as, a second stipulant. **Adsti·pula:-tor,** a second stipulant who stipulates in the same terms as the first.

Adstrict, -ion, -ory, obs. vars. of ASTRICT, -ION, -ORY.

Adstringe, -ent, obs. vars. of ASTRINGE, -ENT.

‖ **Adula·ria,** 1798. [f. Fr. *adulaire adj.* (f. *Adula,* name for eastern Lepontine Alps, Switzerland) + -IA[1].] A variety of Orthoclase.

Adulate (æ·diŭleʲt), *v.* 1777. [– *adulat-*, pa. ppl. stem of L. *adulari* fawn upon; see -ATE[3].] To flatter basely or slavishly. Hence **A·dula:tor.**

Adulation (æ:diŭleʲ·ʃən). ME. [– (O)Fr., or L. *adulatio,* f. *adulat-*; see prec., -ION.] Servile flattery or homage; exaggerated and hypocritical praise.

Flatery and adulacioun CHAUCER. Titles blowne from a. *Hen. V,* IV. i. 271.

Adulatory (æ·diŭlătəri), *a.* 1611. [– L. *adulatorius,* f. as prec.; see -ORY[2]. Cf. Fr. *adulatoire.*] Of or belonging to an adulator; servilely or fulsomely flattering.

A. addresses BURKE. A style rather too a. HALLAM.

Adullamite (ădɒ·lămait). ME. [f. *Adullam,* name of a Canaanite city, + -ITE[1] 1.] **1.** *prop.* An inhabitant of Adullam; see *Gen.* 38:12. **2.** A frequenter of the cave of Adullam. *fig.* A name founded on the application by John Bright of 1 *Sam.* 22:1, 2, to certain members of the British House of Commons who in 1866 seceded from the Liberal party on the question of Parliamentary Reform.

2. The little third party were at once christened the Adullamites MCCARTHY.

Adult (ădɒ·lt), æ·dɒlt), *a.* 1531. [– L. *adultus,* pa. pple. of *adolescere*; see ADOLESCENT; cf. Fr. *adulte.*] Grown up, having reached the age of maturity. *fig.* Full-grown 1670. As *sb.* [sc. *person*] 1658.

Adult Baptism: the baptism of adults only; opp. to *Infant Baptism.* Hence † **Adu·lted** *ppl. a.* grown to maturity. *rare.* **Adu·lthood. Adu·ltness.**

† **Adu·lter.** [ME. *avouter* – OFr. *avoutre, aoutre* :– L. *adulter*; in XV–XVI partly assim. to L. as *advou(l)ter* (cf. later OFr. *advoultre*), in XVI–XVII completely as *adulter.*] An adulterer.

† **Adu·lter,** *v.* [ME. *avoutre* – OFr. *avoutrer, aoutrer* :– L. *adulterare* debauch, corrupt, f. *adulter* (prec.); in XV partly, XVI completely, assim. to L.; cf. prec.] **1.** To commit adultery –1775. **2.** *fig.* = ADULTERATE –1651.

Adulterant (ădɒ·ltĕrănt). 1755. [– *adulterant-*, pres. ppl. stem of L. *adulterare* (see prec.); perh. inferred f. ADULTERATE *v.*; see -ANT.] **A.** *sb.* That which adulterates. **B.** *adj.* Adulterating 1881.

Adulterate (ădɒ·ltĕrĕt), *ppl. a.* 1590. [– *adulterat-*, pa. ppl. stem of L. *adulterare*; see ADULTER *v.*, -ATE[2].] **1.** Stained by adultery, either in origin or conduct; adulterous. **2.** Spurious; base in origin or by intermixture 1592.

1. Possest with an a. blot *Com. Err.* II. ii. 142. Th' a. Hastings *Rich. III,* IV. iii. 69. **2.** Th' a. Beauty of a falsed Cheek DANIELL. To discern between true and a. Justice HOBBES. A. copper SWIFT.

Adulterate (ădɒ·ltĕreʲt), *v.* 1531. [f. as prec.; see -ATE[3]. Superseded ADULTER *v.*] † **1.** *intr.* = mod. *To commit adultery* –1698. † **2.** *trans.* To debauch –1678. **3.** To render counterfeit, corrupt, debase, *esp.* by base admixture 1531.

1. She adulterates hourely with thine Vnckle Iohn SHAKS. *John* III. i. 56. **2.** To murder Uriah and a. his wife MILT. **3.** To a. coin with a more base metal ELYOT, scripture with false gloses MORE, our tongue with strange words ADDISON. Hence **Adulterated** *ppl. a.* = ADULTERATE *a.* 1, 2. **Adu·lterately** *adv.* **Adu·lterateness. Adu·lterator,** † an adulterer; one who debases, etc., by spurious admixture.

Adulterer (ădɒ·ltĕrəɹ). [ME. *avouterer,* f. *avoutre* (ADULTER *v.*) + -ER[1]. Partly, then completely, assim. to L. *adulter*; replacing ADULTER *sb.* in XVII.] **1.** One who commits adultery ME. Of a woman *c* 1550. † **2.** = ADULTERATOR –1650.

Adulteress (ădɒ·ltĕrĕs, -trĕs). [ME. *avoutresse* – OFr. (f. *avoutre* ADULTER *sb.* + *-esse* -ESS[1]), later assim. to L. Formally the fem. of ADULTER, not of prec.] A woman who commits adultery.

Adulterine (ădɒ·ltĕrəin), *a.* 1542. [– L. *adulterinus,* f. *adulter* adulterer; see ADULTER *sb.*, -INE[1]. Cf. Fr. *adultérin.*] **1.** Born of adultery 1751. **2.** Of or relating to adultery (*mod.*). **3.** *fig.* Due to adulteration; spurious 1542. **4.** Illegal, unlicensed; *esp.* in *Eng. Hist.* Adulterine castles, guilds 1640.

Adulterize (ădɒ·ltĕrəiz), *v. arch.* 1611. [f. ADULTER *sb.* + -IZE.] To commit adultery. Hence **Adu·lterism.** *rare.*

Adulterous (ădɒ·ltĕrəs), *a.* 1470. [f. ADULTER *sb.* + -OUS, on anal. of words in *-ous* from Fr. or L.] **1.** Pertaining to or characterized by adultery. † **2.** = ADULTERINE 1. –1607. **3.** Pertaining to or characterized by adulteration. *arch.* 1567.

1. A. Anthony SHAKS. An a. union 1884. **3.** An a. mixture SMOLLETT. Hence **Adu·lterously** *adv.*

Adultery (ădɒ·ltĕri). [ME. *avoutrie,* etc., – OFr. *avout(e)rie,* etc., f. *avoutre* adulterer, see ADULTER sb., -Y[3]. From XV assim. to L. *adulter(ium).*] **1. a.** Violation of the marriage bed; sexual relation of a married person with one who is not his or her lawful spouse, whether unmarried (*single adultery*) or married to another (*double adultery*). In moral theology sometimes extended to irregular sexual intercourse gen.; in biblical use, idol-worship, idolatry (cf. *fornication*); *Eccl.* enjoyment by one of a benefice during the lifetime of the lawful incumbent or the translation of a bishop. † **2.** Adulteration –1673.

1. Of [Dame Katryne Swynford] in double Avoutry gottyn 1485. Whosoeuer loketh on a woman to lust after her, hath committed aduoutrie with her already in his hart *Matt.* 5:28 (Geneva). A. was long unknown at Sparta THIRLWALL. **b.** Shee..committed a. with stones and with stockes *Jer.* 3:9. **2.** Th' adulteries of Art B. JONS.

Adumbrate (æ·dɒ̆mbrēʲt), *v.* 1581. [– *adumbrat-*, pa. ppl. stem of L. *adumbrare,* f. *ad* AD- + *umbrare* to shadow, f. *umbra*; see -ATE[3].] † **1.** To shade (and so complete) a sketch 1599. **2.** To represent the shadow of; to outline; to sketch 1641. **3.** *fig.* To represent by 'shadow' or emblem; to typify; hence, to foreshadow 1581. **4.** To overshadow, darken 1670.

2. Adumbrated and obscurely indicated 1692. **3.** Noah is adumbrated to us..in Prometheus GALE. **4.** Good qualities..adumbrated by..defects 1670. Hence **Adu·mbral** *a.* shady; *Zool.* = ADUMBRELLAR. **Adu·mbrative** *a.* having the attribute of adumbrating. **Adu·mbratively** *adv.*

Adumbration (ædɒmbrēʲ·ʃən). 1531. [– L. *adumbratio,* f. as prec.; see -ION.] † **1.** Shading in painting –1531. **2.** Representation in outline; *concr.* a sketch; a shadowy figure; a faint description 1552. **3.** Symbolic representation 1622. **4.** *Her.* An outline figure 1610. **5.** Overshadowing; obscuration 1653.

2. Far-off hints and adumbrations LOWELL. The Prime Minister's a. of measures 1882. **3.** An Emblem or A. of our passage through life HARTLEY.

Adumbrellar (æ:dɪɒmbre·lăɹ), *a.* 1881. [f. AD- + UMBRELLA + -AR[1].] *Zool.* Pertaining to the upper surface of the *velum,* which is turned towards the 'umbrella' or disc, in sea-blubbers; opp. to *abumbrellar.*

Adunation (ædiunēʲ·ʃən). 1555. [– eccl. L. *adunatio,* f. *adunat-*, pa. ppl. stem of *adunare* unite to, f. *ad* AD- + *unare* make one, f. *unus* one; see -ION. Cf. OFr. *adunation.*] Union into one.

Adunc (ădɒ·nk), *a.* 1626. [– L. *aduncus* bent, f. *ad* AD- + *uncus* hook.] Hooked. Hence † **Adu·ncity,** hookedness. **Adu·ncous** *a.* hooked, incurved.

Adu·ncate, *v.* 1823. [– *aduncat-*, pa. ppl. stem of late L. *aduncare* to curve, bend, f. prec.; see -ATE[3].] To curve inward. (Only in pa. pple.)

† **Adu·re,** *v.* ME. [– L. *adurere* set fire to, f. *ad* AD- + *urere* burn.] To burn completely; to scorch, parch –1626. Hence † **Adu·rent** *ppl. a.* BACON.

A-du·sk, *adv.* 1856. [A *prep.*[1] 11 + DUSK.] In dusk, dark. MRS. BROWNING.

Adust (ădɒ·st), *ppl. a.* ME. [– Fr. *aduste* or L. *adustus,* pa. pple. of *adurere*; see ADURE *v.*] **1.** Scorched; burnt up; parched. Also *fig.* 1550. **2.** Brown, as if scorched; sunburnt 1596. **3.** *Med.* Characterized by dryness of the body, heat, thirst, burnt colour of the blood and little serum in it, etc. *Obs.* exc. in gen. sense, atrabilious, sallow, gloomy, etc. ME.

1. The Lybian air a. MILT. A. wine 1684. An a. taste 1755. **2.** Here [in Spain] everything is a. and tawny FORD. **3.** Choller a., and melancholie 1576. Hence † **Adu·st** *v.* to burn; to dry up with heat. Also *fig.* **Adu·sted** *ppl. a.* = ADUST *a.* † **Adu·stive** *a.* fiery.

Adu·st, *adv.* and *a.* 1863. [A *prep.*[1] 11 + DUST.] In a dusty condition.

† **Adustion.** 1533. [– (O)Fr., or L. *adustio* burning, f. *adust-*, pa. ppl. stem of *adurere*; see ADUST ppl. a., -ION.] **1.** The action of making ADUST –1725. **2.** The state of being ADUST (senses 1, 3) –1725.

‖ **Ad valorem** (æ:d vălōᵊ·rem). 1711. [L.] 'In proportion to the value'; a phrase applied to a mode of levying customs duties upon goods when these are taxed at rates proportioned to their estimated value.

Silk goods [pay] an *ad valorem* duty of 30 per cent. 1825.

Advance (ădvɑ·ns), *v.* [ME. *avaunce* – (O)Fr. *avancer*, :– Rom. **abantiare*, f. late L. *abante* before (whence Fr. *avant*), f. L. *ab* off, away + *ante* before. The sp. *adv-*, as in OFr., arose from association with *av-* originating in *adv-*, as in *aventure*, ADVENTURE.] **I.** To move forward *in place*. **1.** To move, put, or push forward (*lit.* and *fig.*) 1509; *intr.* and *fig.* to go forward, make progress in life, etc. 1513. **2.** Of a process or thing in course: To forward, help on ME.; *refl.* and *intr.* to progress towards completion 1644. **3.** To put forward for notice, present 1509.

1. Brauely a. your. .shields HEYWOOD. They had. .advanced about a mile DE FOE. *fig.* To a. in knowledge LOCKE, in life JOHNSON, commercially CRUMP. **2.** To a. hostile preparations WELLESLEY, one's views KANE. As the work advances (*mod.*). **3.** To a. arguments BENTLEY, a claim SOUTHEY.

II. To move forward *in time*. **1.** To make earlier 1481. **2.** To pay before due; and hence, to pay or lend on security of future reimbursement 1679.

1. The . benefits my death advances you TOURNEUR. **2.** I will a. him £50 on your note-of-hand (*mod.*).

III. To move upward. **1.** To raise or lift up. *lit.* and *fig. arch.* 1475. **2.** To raise or promote in rank, etc., to put in a better position ME. **3.** *Law.* To provide for children, *esp.* in anticipation of the provisions of a will, etc. ME. †**4.** *fig.* To extol; to boast –1660. **5.** To raise in † amount, rate, or price 1691. *intr.* 1882. †**6.** To be over and above. (Cf. It. *avanzare*.) –1601.

1. The fringed Curtains of thine eyes aduance *Temp.* I. ii. 408. Advancing high The. .floating Pageantry WORDSW. **2.** To a. preests and clerks by prebends [etc.] 1461. To a. his family FREEMAN. **4.** Praise and a. [the Lord] for ever FRITH. **5.** The Bank has advanced the rate of discount to 5% 1882. Rupee paper has fractionally advanced 1884. Hence †**Adva·nceable** *a.* **Adva·ncingly** *adv.*

Advance (ădvɑ·ns), *sb.* 1496. [– prec.; partly after Fr. *avance*.] **I.** A going forward, onward, or upward. **1.** Forward motion; also *ellipt.* the order to move forward *a* 1674; *fig.* progress 1668; a step forward 1860. **2.** A personal approach, an overture 1678. **3.** A rise in amount, value, or price 1677.

1. The enemy's a. CLARENDON. The A. will be sounded 1868. These are the days of a. TENNYSON. A very great a. DICKENS. **2.** To make advances towards a reconciliation MACAULAY. **3.** An a. in the. .rate of discount CRUMP.

II. A putting forward. †**1.** = ADVANCEMENT –1696. †**2.** The putting forward of statements; an allegation –1699. **3.** Payment in anticipation, or on security; hence, a loan 1681.

3. A weeks wages a. SWIFT. Life assurances. .as security for advances CRUMP.

III. A being forward. The state of being before, to the front, or above 1668.

Much in a. of the rates of goods CHILD. Hutton was in a. of the speculation of his time HUXLEY. *In advance*: **a.** Of place, Ahead; **b.** Of time, Beforehand; **c.** In the position of having advanced money on account.

Comb., etc.: **a.-guard,** a guard before or in front of the main body of an army; **-proofs, -sheets,** parts of a work supplied previously to publication.

Advanced (ădvɑ·nst), *ppl. a.* 1460. [f. ADVANCE *v.* + -ED[1].] **1.** Moved forward, standing to the front 1795. **2.** *fig.* Far on in life, time, etc. 1534. †**3.** Promoted –1681. †**4.** Raised (physically) –1673. **5.** Raised (in amount) 1782.

1. A. guard, post, works (*Mil.*). **2.** A. period of life DIGBY, beliefs SIR T. BROWNE, truths of mathematics MILL, political opinions (*mod.*).

Advancement (ădvɑ·nsmĕnt). ME. [– (O)Fr. *avancement*; see ADVANCE *v.*, -MENT.] **1.** Promotion, preferment. **2.** *Law.* The promotion of children in life, *esp.* by advancing money, etc. (see ADVANCE *v.* III. 3); the money so advanced ME. †**3.** Vaunting –1646. **4.** Furtherance of a thing in process; improvement 1551. †**5.** A going forward (*lit.* and *fig.*); see ADVANCE *v.* –1825. **6.** Advancing or forward condition 1793. †**7.** Payment in advance –1649.

1. What a. may I hope from thee *Haml.* III. ii. 62. The Advancements of every Person according to his Merit MILT. **4.** The Proficience and A. of Learning BACON. **6.** Water-melons in good a. HAWTHORNE.

Advancer (ădvɑ·nsəɹ). 1496. [f. ADVANCE *v.* + -ER[1].] **1.** One who advances, see the vb. †**2.** *Rhet.* Amplification, auxesis, or climax. PUTTENHAM. **3.** A second branch of a buck's horn 1496.

Advantage (ădvɑ·ntĕdʒ). [ME. *avantage* – (O)Fr. *avantage*, f. *avant* before; see ADVANCE *v.*, -AGE. Aphet. to VANTAGE.] **I.** Superior position. **1.** The position, state, or circumstance of being *in advance*, or having the better of another in any respect; superiority, *esp.* in contest or debate ME. **2.** In *Tennis*, the next point after DEUCE, a temporary superiority, not the game. Also *attrib.* 1641. †**3.** = VANTAGE-GROUND –1663. †**4.** A time of vantage, a chance –1667. **5.** A favouring circumstance; opp. to *disadvantage* 1483.

1. The A. or Height of all the dry Land RAY. The Gauls maintained their a. GIBBON. To have, gain, get, give *a. of, over,* † *on*: superiority over. I have seen the hungry ocean gain A. on the kingdom of the shore SHAKS. To have *the a. of*: to have a personal knowledge which is not reciprocal. **2.** It is but an a. to the dozen, it is no winning cast MILT. **4.** Make use of time, let not a. slip SHAKS. **5.** Ile use the a. of my power *Rich. II*, III. iii. 42. *To take, make one's a. of* a thing: to use any favourable condition it offers. To take an ill a. of his absence *Merry Wiv.* III. iii. 116. *To take at a.*: when the position favours the taker. *To play upon a.*: to cheat. To turn rook and play upon a. SEDLEY.

II. The result of a superior position. **1.** Benefit; increased well-being ME. †**2.** Pecuniary profit, interest –1665. †**3.** Overplus, excess –1642.

1. Nailed, For our a., on the bitter Crosse SHAKS. *To a.*: Favourably. True Wit is Nature to a. dress'd POPE. **2.** To lend or borrow upon a. *Merch. V.* I. iii. 71. **3.** As many to th'vantage *Oth.* IV. iii. 84.

Hence **Advanta·geous** *a.* of advantage; †overreaching, *rare.* **Advanta·geous-ly** *adv.*, **-ness.**

Advantage (ădvɑ·ntĕdʒ), *v.* 1496. [– prec., or (O)Fr. *avantager*.] **1.** To give an advantage to 1598. **2.** To further the progress of 1586. †**3.** To add to the amount or value of –1673. **4.** To benefit, profit 1526. † *absol.* –1668. † *refl.* –1693. †**5.** To gain –1557.

1. Advantaged in their payes 1598. How dress advantages Women RICHARDSON. **2.** To a. a cause WASHINGTON, agriculture BRIGHT. **4.** To a. a statue by the addition of colour RUSKIN. What shall it avauntage a man TINDALE. They will. .*a. themselves of* the wind. Hence †**Adva·ntageable** *a.* tending to a.

Advehent (æ·dvĭhĕnt), *a.* 1836. [– *advehent-*, pres. ppl. stem of L. *advehere* carry, convey (to), f. *ad* AD- + *vehere* carry.] Afferent.

Advene (ădvī·n), *v.* 1606. [– (O)Fr. *advenir*, or L. *advenire* arrive at, f. *ad* AD- + *venire* come.] To accede or come (*to*); to be superadded. *trans.* To reach 1839.

†**Adve·nient,** *a.* 1594. [– *advenient-*, pres. ppl. stem of L. *advenire*; see prec., -ENT.] Superadded; adventitious.

Advent (æ·dvĕnt). OE. [– OFr. *advent*, refash. after L. of *auvent* (mod. *avent*) – L. *adventus* arrival, f. *advent-*, pa. ppl. stem of *advenire*; see ADVENE *v.*, -ENT.] **1.** *Eccl.* The season including the four Sundays immediately preceding the festival of the Nativity OE. **2.** The Coming of Christ as Saviour of the world. Hence his Second Coming as Judge, and the Coming of the Holy Spirit. ME. **3.** Any important arrival; any arrival 1742.

3. The a. of the Normans STRUTT. Expecting still his a. home TENNYSON. Hence **A·dventist,** one who holds millenarian views 1876. Also SECOND A.

‖ **Adventi·tia,** *sb. pl.* 1876. [L., n. pl. of *adventicius* adj.; see next.] *Phys.* Membranous structure, covering but not belonging to an organ.

Adventitious (ædvĕnti·ʃəs), *a.* 1603. [f. L. *adventicius* coming from abroad, strange, (f. *advent-*, see ADVENT) + -OUS; see -ITIOUS[1].] **1.** Of the nature of an addition from without; supervenient, accidental, casual. **2.** *Law.* Falling to a man by mere fortune, or from a stranger; not *profectitious* 1651. **3.** *Nat. Hist.* esp. *Bot.* Appearing casually or in unusual places 1676.

1. An a., no mother-language HOWELL. An a. population GROTE. **3.** A. streaks, in leaves GREW, in buds GRAY, in roots OLIVER. var. †**Adventi·tial** *a.* Hence **Adventi·tiously** *adv.* **Adventi·tiousness.**

†**Adve·ntive,** *a.* 1605. [f. L. *advent-* (see ADVENE *v.*) + -IVE, after ADVENTITIOUS.] = ADVENTITIOUS. As *sb.* An immigrant. BACON.

†**Adve·ntry.** [Formed by B. JONSON on *adventer*, a XVI–XVII form of ADVENTURE *v.*; cf. *entry* f. *enter*.] An adventure.

Adventure (ădve·ntiŭɹ, -tʃəɹ). [ME. *aventure* – (O)Fr. *aventure* :– Rom. **adventura*, sb. use (sc. *res* thing) of fut. pple. of *advenire*; see ADVENT, -URE. The form *adv-* is due to XV–XVI refash. of Fr., after L. The contr. form *aunter* (XIII–XVI) was due to initial stress. Aphet. to VENTURE.] †**1.** That which happens without design; chance, hap, luck ME. †**2.** A chance occurrence. Also in *Law.* –1727. †**3.** A trial of one's chance; a venture, or experiment –1790. **4.** Chance of danger or loss; risk, jeopardy ME. **5.** A hazardous enterprise or performance ME.; hence, a novel or exciting incident 1570. **6.** A pecuniary venture, a speculation 1625. **7.** Adventurous activity, enterprise ME.

1. To leave to the a. of uncertain pity HOOKER. †**Per,** †**by,** †**of a.**: by chance. †**An,** †**on,** †**in,** †**upon,** †**for a.**: In case, lest, for fear. **2.** *Aventure* is a mischance, causing the death of a man, without felony BLOUNT. **3.** *To give the a.*: to try the venture. *To stand in a.*: To hang in doubt. To try the faire a. of tomorrow SHAKS. *John* V. v. 22. †**At a., -s**: At hazard, recklessly. To draw a bow *at aventure* (not *at a venture*) 1 *Kings* 22:34. †**At all a., -s**: At random; at any risk. A mind floating at all adventures LOCKE. **4.** For my sake *to put* thy life *in a.* 1598. So in *Mar. Insur.* **5.** To walk alone in London seemed of itself an a. C. BRONTË. **6.** My East India a. EVELYN. **7.** A yearning after a. 1825. The spirit of a. BURTON. Hence **Adve·nturesome** *a.* given to running risks. **Adve·nturesomeness.**

Adventure (ădve·ntiŭɹ, -tʃəɹ), *v.* [– (O)Fr. *aventurer* f. *aventure*; see prec.] **1.** *trans.* To take the chance of; to venture upon ME. **2.** To risk the loss of; to imperil ME. Also *refl.* **3.** *intr.* To risk oneself, to venture (*in, into, on, upon*); to dare to undertake; also *fig.* ME. †**4.** *intr.* To come by chance, befall. Usu. *impers.* ME.

1. I'll a. chiding FORD. **2.** We had adventured our lives and liberties GODDARD. To a. themselves abroad POTTER. **3.** To a. uppon the exploit SHAKS., on a shore unknown BYRON, to be sent to th' Towre SHAKS. Hence **Adve·ntured** *ppl. a.* risked; gained at a risk. **Adve·nturing** *vbl. sb.* risking; trial; *ppl. a.* venturesome.

Adventurer (ădve·ntiŭrəɹ). 1474. [– Fr. *aventurier*, † *adv-*, f. *aventure* ADVENTURE *sb.*; see -ER[2].] †**1.** A gamester 1474. **2.** One who seeks adventures (see ADVENTURE *sb.* 5) 1667; *esp.* a soldier of fortune; also, a volunteer 1548. **3.** One who undertakes or shares in commercial adventures; a speculator; a *Merchant Adventurer* 1609. **4.** One who lives by his wits 1663.

2. Military adventurers ready to flock to any standard THIRLWALL. **3.** *Adventurers* (Eng.), shareholders in a mining enterprise RAYMOND. **4.** Needy adventurers were generally found in waiting GOLDSM.

Adventuress (ădve·ntiŭrĕs). 1754. [f. prec.; see -ESS[1].] A woman who lives by her wits.

Adventurous (ădve·ntiŭrəs), *a.* ME. [– OFr. *aventuros, -ous, -eus* f. *aventure*; see ADVENTURE *sb.*, -OUS.] †**1.** Fortuitous ME. only. †**2.** Full of risk; perilous –1637. **3.** Prone to incur risk, rash ME. **4.** Enterprising (without *rashness*) ME.

2. To pass through this a. glade MILT. **3.** A. Eve MILT. A. hypotheses WHITNEY. **4.** An a. people BURKE. Hence **Adve·nturous-ly** *adv.*, **-ness.**

Adverb (æ·dvɜ̄ɹb). 1530. [– Fr. *adverbe* or L. *adverbium*, f. *ad* AD- + *verbum* word, VERB; lit. rendering of Gr. ἐπίρρημα something additional (ἐπί) to the predication (ῥῆμα).] *Gram.* One of the Parts of Speech; a word used to express the attribute of an attribute; one that qualifies an adj., vb., or other advb. Also *attrib.*

Adverbial (ădvɜ̄·ɹbiăl), *a.* 1591. [– late L. *adverbialis* or Fr. *adverbial*; see prec., -AL[1].]

Of or pertaining to or of the nature of an adverb 1611; given to the use of adverbs. *rare.* 1710. As *sb.* 1591. Hence **Adve:rbia·lity,** the quality of being a. **Adve·rbialize** *v.* to make an adverb of. **Adve·rbially** *adv.* **Adve:rbia·tion,** a phraseological adverb. EARLE.

† **Adve·rsant,** *ppl. a.* ME. [– *adversant-*, pres. ppl. stem of L. *adversari* oppose oneself to, f. *adversus*; see ADVERSE *a.*, -ANT. Cf. late L. *adversans* opposing, contrary.] Opposing; adverse (*to*) –1630.

‖ **Adversaria** (ædvəɹsēᵊ·riă), *sb. pl.* 1610. [L., subst. use of n. pl. (sc. *scripta* writings) of *adversarius* lying before one (see next), in mercantile use, collection of items as they occur, waste-book, day-book.] A commonplace book; = MISCELLANEA; also, commentaries or notes on a text, etc.

Adversary (æ·dvəɹsări). ME. [– OFr. *adversarie* (mod. *-aire*) – L. *adversarius* opposed, opponent, f. *adversus* against; see ADVERSE *a.*, -ARY[1].] In Shaks. *a·dversary*, in MILT. also *adve·rsary*. **A.** *sb.* **1.** One who or that which takes up a position, or acts, as an antagonist; an enemy. *spec.* The Devil. **2.** *pl.* = ADVERSARIA, commentaries.

1. His ancient Knot of dangerous Adversaries *Rich. III*, III. i. 182. Or shall the A. thus obtain His end MILT.

B. *adj.* Opposed. *arch.* ME. In *Law.* An a. suit: one in which an opposing party appears.

The a. Champion BOLTON. Hence **Adversa·rious** *a.* hostile. SOUTHEY.

Adversative (ădvɜ̄·ɹsătiv), *a.* 1533. [– Fr. *adversatif, -ive* or late L. *adversativus* (Priscian), f. *adversat-*, pa. ppl. stem of L. *adversari* (f. *adversus*; see next), + -IVE.] **1.** Expressive of opposition, contrariety, or antithesis. †**2.** Of adverse nature –1603. As *sb.* 1556. Hence **Adve·rsatively** *adv.*

Adverse (æ·dvɜ̄rs), *a.* ME. [– OFr. *advers*, refash. after L. of *avers* :– L. *adversus* standing opposite, hostile, pa. pple. of *advertere* turn towards, f. *ad* AD- + *vertere* turn.] **1.** Acting in opposition to, actively hostile. **2.** Opposing any one's interests; hence, unfavourable, injurious, calamitous. Const. *to.* ME. **3.** Opposite in position 1623.

1. Aduerse Foreyners SHAKS. A. winds DIGBY, power MILT., gales CRABBE, critics HELPS. *Adverse possession* (Law): possession of land by a person not the owner during a certain time without acknowledgement of the right of the real owner. **2.** In prosperous days They swarm, but in a. withdraw their heads MILT. A. to the cause of slavery BRIGHT. **3.** The a. hills BLACKIE. Hence †**Adve·rse** *v.* to oppose. **A·dversely** *adv.* **A·dverseness.**

Adversifoli-ate, -ous (ădvɜ̄ɹsifōᵘ·liĕt, -əs), *a.* [f. L. *adversus* opposite + *folium* leaf + -ATE[2], -OUS.] *Bot.* Having leaves placed opposite to each other on the stem.

† **Adve·rsion.** 1647. [– L. *adversio*, f. *advers-*, pa. ppl. stem of L. *advertere*; see ADVERT *v.*, -ION.] Attention.

Adversity (ădvɜ̄·ɹsĭti). ME. [– (O)Fr. *adversité*, refash. after L. of *aversité* – L. *adversitas* opposition (Pliny), misfortune (Cassiodorus), f. *adversus*; see ADVERSE *a.*, -ITY.] †**1.** Opposition, contrariety –ME. **2.** The condition of adverse fortune; distress, trial, or affliction; an adverse circumstance; a calamity, etc. ME. †**3.** Perversity –1606.

2. A. findeth few friends HOLINSHED. *A.Y.L.* II. i. 12. **3.** Well said, a. (= perverse one) *Tr. & Cr.* v. i. 14.

Advert (ădvɜ̄·ɹt), *v.* [Late ME. *averte, adverte* – (O)Fr. *avertir*, XIV–XVI also †*advertir* (now only) admonish, warn, f. Rom. **advertire*, for L. *advertere* turn towards, direct (*animum* the attention) to (cf. ANIMADVERT *v.*), f. *ad* AD- + *vertere* turn.] †**1.** To turn towards (*lit.* or *fig.*). *rare.* Only in ME. **2.** *intr.* = ADVERTISE 1. *arch.* ME. **3.** *esp.* To refer *to* in speech or writing 1777. †**4.** *trans.* = ADVERTISE 2. –1692. †**5.** To give warning of –1513. ¶ Erron. for AVERT.

2. To a. to the means of strengthening..the Nizam WELLINGTON. **3.** I shall now a. to some other matters PRIESTLEY. Hence **Adve·rtent** *ppl. a.* attentive. ?*Obs.*

Advertence (ădvɜ̄·ɹtĕns). ME. [– (O)Fr. *advertence*, also † *avertence*, f. *avertir, adv-*, (see ADVERT *v.*) + *-ence* -ENCE; cf. med.L. *advertentia* attention, notice.] The action of adverting or attending; occ. = ADVERTENCY.

Advertency (ădvɜ̄·ɹtĕnsi). 1646. [f. prec.; see -ENCY.] The quality or habit of being advertent or attentive.

Advertise (æ·dvəɹtaiz, *Sc.* ædvərtəi·z), *v.* [late ME. *avertise, adv-*, – *a(d)vertiss-*, lengthened stem of (O)Fr. *avertir*, also OFr. *advertir*; see ADVERT *v.*] †**1.** *intr.* To take note, consider –1526. †**2.** *trans.* To take note of, attend to, observe –1606. **3.** *trans.* To call the attention of (another); to notify, admonish, or formally warn 1490. **4.** Hence (pers. obj. omitted), To give notice of, make generally known 1588; *esp.* to make publicly known, by announcement *in* a journal, by circular, etc. 1750. **5.** †To give warning or information (*of*) –1765; *esp.* by public notice in a journal, by placard, etc. 1772.

3. To consider thereof and a. me timely MARVELL. Advertised by me of his design SMOLLETT. **4.** Twenty things that are not to be advertised, you know M. EDGEWORTH. To a. a reward H. WALPOLE, a sale of slaves BURKE. Phr. *To a. for*: to ask for by public notice. Hence **Adve:rtisee·**, one advertised for, or aimed at by advertising. **A:dverti·ser,** one who advertises (senses 4, 5); a journal publishing advertisements. **Ad:verti·sing** *vbl. sb.* † warning, information; a bringing into notice, *esp.* by advertisement; *ppl. a.* † adverting, attentive; issuing advertisements.

Advertisement (ădvɜ̄·ɹtizmĕnt). 1460. [Earlier *avertisement* – Fr. *avertissement*, f. *avertiss-*; see prec., -MENT.] †**1.** Attention, heed –1651. †**2.** Admonition, instruction –1715. †**3.** Information, notification –1716. **4.** A notification, a notice. *arch.* 1460. **5.** A public announcement by the town-crier, in print, etc.; *spec.* a paid announcement in a newspaper 1582.

2. The advertisements came to him from..many hands BURNET. **4.** An a. to the reader DIBDIN. **5.** My griefs cry lowder than a. *Much Ado* v. i. 32. An a. of the particulars in the common newspapers DE FOE.

Advice (ădvəi·s). [ME. *avis* – (O)Fr. *avis* :– Rom. **advisum*, f. L. *ad* AD- + *visum* (as in *mihi visum est* for cl. L. *mihi videtur*), n. pa. pple. of *vidēre* see (*vidēri* seem); refash. (XV) after L. *ad*, through Fr. *advis* (XIV–XVI), introduced by Caxton.] †**1.** The way in which a matter is looked at; opinion, judgement –1651. †**2.** Prudence, wisdom –1523. †**3.** Weighing of opinions; consultation –1654. **4.** Opinion given or offered as to action; used *spec.* in *Med.* and *Law.* ME. †**5.** The result of consultation; determination, plan –1704. †**6.** An act; a *senatus consultum.* *rare.* –1661. **7.** Information given, notice; news; in *pl.* Communications from a distance. *spec.* in *Comm.* Formal notice from a party concerned. 1490. **8.** = ADVICE-BOAT.

3. *To take a.*: to deliberate. Consider of it, take aduise *Judg.* 19:30. **4.** *Macb.* IV. ii. 68. Ill of fever, and come only for a. PEPYS. **5.** Changing aduice on the sudden SAVILE. **7.** A mail from Holland, which brought me several Advices STEELE. To give a banker a. of bills becoming due CRUMP.

Comb. **a.-yacht, -boat,** one employed to bring intelligence; a dispatch-boat; see ADVISO.

Hence † **Advi·ceful** *a.* considerate; full of counsel.

Advisable (ădvəi·zăb'l), *a.* 1647. [f. next + -ABLE.] **1.** Open to advice 1661. **2.** Proper to be advised; expedient 1647.

1. An a. and teachable temper WESLEY. **2.** A course Now not a. COWPER. Hence **Advi:sabi·lity,** advisableness. **Advi·sableness,** readiness to be advised; expediency. **Advi·sably** *adv.*

Advise (ădvəi·z), *v.* [ME. *avise* – (O)Fr. *aviser* :– Rom. **advisare* f. L. *ad* AD- + *visare*, for L. *visere*, frequent. of *vidēre* to see; refash. (XV) after L. *ad-* and Fr. (XV–XVI) *adviser.*] †**1.** To look at, consider; also, to watch for –1603. †**2.** To look at *mentally*; to consider –1677; *spec.* in *Sc. Law*, to consider together ('take into *avizandum*') 1609. †**3.** To purpose –1586. †**4.** *refl.* To bethink oneself (Fr. *s'aviser*), reflect –1656; †*intr.* to ponder, deliberate –1671. Hence **5.** To consider in company, to hold a consultation 1513. **6.** To offer counsel; to give advice 1375. **7.** *trans.* To give counsel to, to counsel, caution ME. **8.** To give (formal) notice, to inform, apprise 1591; *Comm.* to announce (an event, transaction).

4. Aduise you what you say *Twel. N.* IV. ii. 102. *intr.* A. Forthwith how thou oughtst to receive him MILT. **5.** He must *a. with* his Council MISS YONGE. **7.** Well use that trick no more I would a. you MARLOWE. He advised distrust SOUTHEY. **8.** The States are advised that [etc.] STEELE. *Comm.* Have these drafts been advised? Hence **Advi·ser,** one who advises (senses 7, 8); † a dispatch-boat, an A(D)VISO. **Advi·sership,** the office of an adviser. † **Advi·sive** *a.* advising. **Advi·sory** *a.* having the attribute of advising.

Advised (ădvəi·zd), *ppl. a.* ME. [f. ADVISE *v.* + -ED[1]. Cf. ADVISY.] †**1.** *pple.* Having considered (*of*) –1633; hence *adj.* Deliberate, wary –1702. **2.** Considered, deliberate; hence judicious ME. **3.** Of persons: † determined –1483; counselled 1596; apprised 1599.

1. Are you a-uis'd o' that *Merry Wiv.* I. iii. 106. A Prince ought to be slow and a. 1702. With the *well-a.* is wisdome *Prov.* 13:10. **2.** The more a. the deed is, the lesse a. it is FULLER. **3.** The a. measures RUSKIN. *Hen. V*, II. Cho. 12. Hence **Advi·sedly** *adv.* (esp. in sense 2). **Advi·sedness,** the quality of being advised.

Advisement (ădvəi·zmĕnt). ME. [– OFr. *a(d)visement*, f. *aviser* ADVISE *v.*; cf. med.L. *a(d)visamentum.*] †**1.** The process of advising (see ADVISE 1, 2, 5). **2.** = ADVICE 4, 5.

† **Advi·so.** Pl. **-oes.** 1591. [– Sp. *aviso* (whence the rather later AVISO), with sp. assim. to L. *ad-*, as in *advice*, etc.; see AVISO.] **1.** Intelligence. = ADVICE 7. **2.** *pompously*, A suggestion 1591. **3.** A dispatch- or advice-boat; var. of AVISO. 1624.

2. The honest advisoes of faith SIR T. BROWNE.

† **Advisy, advisee,** *ppl. a.* [ME. *avise(e)*, *a(d)visy* – (O)Fr. *avisé*, pa. pple. of *aviser* ADVISE *v.* See ADVISED *ppl. a.*] Well-advised; circumspect –1513.

Advocacy (æ·dvŏkĕsi). ME. [– OFr. *avocacie, ad-*, – med.L. *advocatia* (see ADVOCATION), f. *advocat-*, see ADVOCATE *sb.*, -CY.] **1.** The function of an advocate; pleading for or supporting. **2.** = ADVOWSON, ADVOCATION 5. 1876.

Advocate (æ·dvŏkĕt), *sb.* ME. [– (O)Fr. *avocat* – L. *advocatus* legal witness or counsellor, (later) advocate, sb. use of pa. pple. of *advocare* to call in as witness or counsellor, f. *ad* AD- + *vocare* to call; see -ATE[1]. Assim. XV to L. form *ad-*, after Fr. (XIV–XVI).] **1.** One who pleads the cause of any one in a court of justice; counsel. (The techn. title where Roman law is retained; also in many special tribunals.) **2.** *fig.* and *gen.* One who pleads, intercedes, or speaks for another ME.; used *spec.* of Christ as the intercessor for sinners ME. **3.** One who argues on behalf of a proposal or tenet. Const. *of.* 1735. †**4.** An ADVOWEE ME.

Faculty of Advocates: the collective bar in Scotland. *Lord Advocate*, the Scotch Attorney-General. *Judge-Advocate*, an officer who conducts the prosecution before a court-martial, the supreme officer being the *Judge-Advocate-General*. *Devil's Advocate* (*advocatus diaboli*), one who pleads against the admission of a candidate for canonization.

1. Of advocates or (as we..call them) counsel, there are two species, barristers and sergeants BLACKSTONE. **2.** We have an Advocate with the Father 1 *John* 2:1. **3.** Advocates for folly dead and gone POPE, of the system of caste MÜLLER. Hence **A·dvocateship** (in senses 1, 2, 3).

A·dvocate, *v.*[1] 1555. [– *advocat-*, pa. ppl. stem of L. *advocare*; see prec., -ATE[3].] †**1.** To call (*to* oneself). **2.** *Sc. Law.* To ADVOKE 1609.

Advocate (æ·dvŏkeᶦt), *v.*[2] 1641. [f. ADVOCATE *sb.*] †**1.** *intr.* To act as advocate *for.* *arch.* †**2.** *trans.* To defend (by action) –1666. **3.** To argue in favour of; to recommend publicly 1767.

3. The only [sensible] thing that has been advocated BURKE. To a. publication MERIVALE, a view TYNDALL. Hence **A·dvocating** *vbl. sb.* (in sense 3).

Advocation (ædvokēᶦ·ʃən). 1474. [– OFr. *a(d)vocacion* – L. *advocatio* (see ADVOWSON), f. *advocat-*; see ADVOCATE *sb.*, -ION. Cf. ADVOKE *v.*] **I.** n. of action f. L. *advocare*. †**1.** A convocation –1474. **2.** *Sc. Law.* The calling of an action before itself by a superior court. (See ADVOKE.) 1528. †**3.** The act of calling to one's aid –1753.

II. n. of office f. L. *advocatus*. †**1.** The function of an ADVOCATE 1, 2; advocacy –1767.

†2. = ADVOCATE 4; protection of a church; = ADVOWSON –1661.

1. Alas..My A. is not now in tune *Oth.* III. iv. 123.

Advocator (æ·dvǒkeⁱtəɹ). 1482. [– late L. = consoler, advocate, f. *advocat-*; see ADVOCATE *sb.*, -OR 2.] †1. A patron (saint); also = ADVOCATE 1, 2. 2. = ADVOCATE 3.

Advocatory (æ·dvǒkeⁱ:təri), *a.* 1864. [f. ADVOCATE *v.*² + -ORY².] Pertaining to the advocate.

† **A·dvocatress.** 1641. [f. ADVOCATOR + -ESS¹; see -TRESS. Prob. refash. from earlier *advocatrice.*] † -trix.

† **Advo·ke,** *v.* 1533. [– obs. Fr. *advoquer*, earlier *avoquer*; see AVOKE.] To summon; *esp.* to summon a cause to a higher tribunal –1655.

Advoteresse, obs. f. ADULTERESS. **Advoulter, advouter, -er, -ess, -ous, -y,** obs. ff. ADULTER, -ER, -ESS, -OUS, -Y.

Advowee (ǣdvau:ī·). 1691. [– AFr. *avowé*, *advowé* patron (mod.Fr. *avoué* solicitor) :– L. *advocatus*; see ADVOCATE *sb.*, -EE¹.] 1. = AVOWÉ, q.v. 2. The advocate, protector, or patron of an eccl. office. Subsequently, One who holds the advowson.

† **Advow·ry,** var. of AVOWRY.

† **Advow·sance, -ante, -sement.** [Corrupt formations on *advowson* or *advowsen* (= *advowsing*) from an imaginary *advowse.*]

Advowson (ǣdvau·zən, -z'n), *sb.* ME. [– AFr. *a(d)voweson*, *a(d)voeson*, OFr. *avoeson* :– L. *advocatio*, *-ōn-*, f. *advocat-*; see ADVOCATE *sb.*, -ION. Cf. ADVOCACY, ADVOCATION. Refash. after L. Aphet. *voweson.*] The 'patronage' of an eccl. house or office; the right of presentation to a benefice or living. (*orig.* The obligation to be its *advocate*; see ADVOWEE.)

The traffic in advowsons has never been..prevented 1865. var. † **Advow·sonage.**

Advoyer, obs. f. AVOYER.

Adward, obs. var. of AWARD *sb.* (Spenser).

† **Adwe·sch,** *v.* OE. [f. A- *pref.* 1 + *dwǣscan* to extinguish.] To quench.

‖ **Adynamia** (ædinē·mia). 1830. [mod.L., – Gr. ἀδυναμία f. ἀ- A- *pref.* 14 + δύναμις power. Cf. Fr. *adynamie.*] *Med.* Lack of vital power, as in some fevers. var. **Adynamy.**

Adynamic (ædinæ·mik), *a.* 1829. [f. prec. + -IC; cf. Fr. *adynamique.*] 1. *Med.* Of or pertaining to adynamia; asthenic. 2. *Nat. Phil.* Characterized by the absence of force 1879.

Adytum (æ·ditǒm). Pl. **adyta.** 1673. [– L. *adytum* – Gr. ἄδυτον, sb. use of n. sing. of ἄδυτος impenetrable, f. ἀ- A- *pref.* 14 + -δυτος vbl. adj. f. δύειν enter.] The innermost part of a temple; the secret shrine whence oracles were delivered; hence *fig.* A private chamber, a sanctum.

Adze, adz (ædz). [OE. *adesa*, ME. *adese*, later *adys*, *addis*, *add(e)s*; *adze* from XVIII. Of unkn. origin.] A tool, like an axe with the blade set at right angles to the handle and curving inwards towards it; used for chipping or slicing away the surface of wood. Hence **Adze** *v.* to dress with an a.

† **Adzoo·ks.** [See ADS.] –1841.

Æ, also ae, orig. a short vowel midway between *a* and *e* = *a* in *man*, replaced by *e* or *ee* in 13th c., and reintroduced for L. *æ*, Gr. *αι* in 16th c. Here retained only (1) in EE. words that became obs. bef. changing to *e*, as *ǣ* river (OE. *eá*); (2) in words directly adopted or formed from L. and Gr. which became obs. bef. changing to *e*; or which indicate ancient things, as *ægis*, or are techn. as *ætiology*. Classical scholars incline to pronounce æ long (ī) in all positions.

† **Æ,** *sb.*¹ [OE. *ēa*, *ē*, *ǣ* = OFris. *ā*, *ē*, OS., OHG. *aha*, ON. *á*, Goth. *ahwa*, cogn. w. L. *aqua.*] A river. Cf. EA. –1205.

† **Æ,** *sb.*² [OE. *ǣ*, *ǣw*, cogn. w. OFris. *ēwa*, *ēwe*, OS. *ēo*, *ēu*, OHG. *ēwa.*] Law; hence legal custom, rite, marriage –1200. *Comb.* **æubreche,** adultery.

Ae (ē), Sc. form of north. ME. *a*, OE. *ān*, one; see A *adj.*¹

Æ-, *pref.* Stress form of OE. *a-* (see A- *pref.* 1) used with sbs. and adjs. Out, off, onward, away; hence priv. = *un-*, *-less.*

-æ (-ī), *pl. suffix* of L. nouns of 1st decl. in *-a*, and romanized form of Gr. *-αι* pl. of nouns. In all words completely popularized it yields to -s, as *arenas*, etc.

Æcern, æcirn, obs. ff. ACORN.

‖ **Æcidium** (isi·diǒm). Pl. **-a.** 1867. [mod. L., dim. of Gr. ἀικία injury. *Bot.* The cup-shaped fruit borne on the mycelium of certain parasitic fungi.

Ædicule (e·dikiul). 1832. [– L. *ædicula*, dim. of *ædes* dwelling; see -CULE. Cf. Fr. *édicule.*] A small house or room; a niche.

Ædile (ī·dəil). 1580. [– L. *ædilis*, sb. use of adj. 'having to do with buildings', f. *ædes*, *ædis* building; see -ILE.] *Rom. Antiq.* A magistrate in Rome, who had charge of public buildings, shows, police, etc.; hence, a municipal officer. As *adj.* 1880. Hence **Æ·dileship, Ædi·lity,** the office, or term of office, of an ædile. **Æ:dili·tian** *a.* pertaining to an ædile.

Ægemony, obs. var. of HEGEMONY.

‖ **Æger** (ī·dʒəɹ), *a.* 1861. [L.] The L. word for 'sick', used at the Eng. Universities in excusing absence on account of illness; hence, a note alleging sickness.

‖ **Ægilops** (e·dʒilǫps). 1601. [L., = Gr. αἰγίλωψ, f. αἴγιλος herb eaten by goats (f. αἴξ, αἰγός goat) + ὤψ eye.] 1. *Med.* An ulcer or fistula in the inner angle of the eye. †2. *Herb.* The wild-oat or other corn-weed grass –1753. 3. *Bot.* A genus of South European grasses 1872. 4. A species of Oak (*Quercus ægilops*) 1706.

Ægirite (e·dʒirəit, ī·-). 1837. [f. *Ægir*, Scand. god of the sea + -ITE¹ 2 b.] *Min.* An ore of the Amphibole group of Bisilicates.

‖ **Ægis** (ī·dʒis). 1704. [L. – Gr. αἰγίς, shield of Zeus.] A shield, or defensive armour; *esp.* that of Jupiter or Minerva. Also *fig.* A protection 1793. *attrib.* 1793.

fig. The æ. of the laws THIRLWALL.

Ægophony (igǫ·fǒni). 1853. [f. Gr. αἴξ, αἰγ- goat + -φωνία -PHONY.] *Path.* A tremulous resonance of the voice, like the bleating of a kid, heard in pleurisy.

† **Æ·gritude.** 1532. [– L. *ægritudo* f. *æger* sick; see -TUDE.] Sickness –1647.

‖ **Ægrotat** (ī·grotæt, īgrōᵘ·tæt). 1794. [3rd pers. sing. pres. indic. of L. *ægrotare* be sick, f. *æger* sick.] In Eng. Univ. use, a certificate of illness; also, a place awarded in an examination list to one who has such a certificate.

Aeipathy (eˌəi·păþi). 1853. [f. Gr. ἀεί ever + -πάθεια feeling; see -PATHY.] *Med.* An inveterate disease.

Æneid (inīˌid, ī·niˌid). 1490. [– *Æneid-*, stem of L. *Æneis* (*-idis*, *-idos*) the epic, f. *Æneas*; see -ID². Cf. Fr. *Énéide.*] An epic poem by Virgil, with Æneas as hero; also, one of the twelve books of this poem.

Aeneous (eˌī·niˌəs), *a.* 1815. [f. L. *a(h)eneus* brazen (f. æs bronze) + -OUS.] Brassy; brass-coloured.

Ænigma, -tic, etc.; see ENIGMA, -TIC, etc.

Æni·gmatite. *Min.* [f. Gr. αἴνιγμα, -ματ- enigma + -ITE¹ 2 b.] A variety of AMPHIBOLE.

Æolian (iˌōᵘ·liăn), *a.* 1789. [f. L *Æolius* f. *Æolis*, *Æolia*, or *Æolus* + -AN; see -IAN. Cf. Fr. *éolien.*] 1. Of Æolis or Æolia, in Asia Minor; Æolic. 2. Of Æolus, god of the winds; hence of, produced by, or borne on the wind; aerial.

1. *Æolian mode* (*Mus.*): 'the ninth of the church modes.' GROVE. 2. *Æ. harp*: a stringed instrument producing musical sounds under a current of air.

Æolic (iˌǫ·lik), *a.* 1674. [– L. *Æolicus* – Gr. Αἰολικός; see prec., -IC.] = ÆOLIAN 1.

Æolic digamma: the sixth letter of the early Greek Alphabet, surviving in the Æolic dialect. *Æ. mode*; see ÆOLIAN 1.

Æolipyle, -pile (ī·ǒlipəil, iˌǫ·lipəil). Also **eo-** 1611. [– Fr. *éolipyle* (XVI) – L. *Æoli pylæ* (= Gr. πύλαι) the doorway of Æolus; see *Vitruvius* i. 6.] A pneumatic instrument, illustrating the force with which vapour generated by heat in a closed vessel rushes out by a narrow aperture. First described by Hero of Alexandria.

Æolist (ī·ǒlist). [– L. *Æolus* god of winds + -IST.] A pretender to inspiration SWIFT. Hence **Æoli·stic** *a.* long-winded.

Æolo-, combining form of *Æolus*, the impersonation of wind, as in *æolodicon*, *æolodion*, etc., names of musical wind-instruments.

Æolotropy (ī:ǒlǫ·trǒpi). 1881. [f. Gr. αἰόλος changeful + -τροπία turning.] Change of physical qualities on change of position, opp. to *isotropy*; anisotropy. Hence **Æolotro·pic** *a.* not isotropic.

Æon, eon (ī·ǭn). 1647. [– eccl.L. *æon* – Gr. αἰών age.] An age, or the whole duration, of the world, or of the universe; an immeasurable period of time; eternity. 2. The personification of an age. In *Platonic philosophy*, A power existing from eternity 1647.

1. Æons of æons CARLYLE. 2. The Valentinian thirty Gods and Æons CUDWORTH. Hence **Æonial, Æonian** *adjs.* everlasting.

Æquoreal (īkwōᵊ·riăl), *a.* 1838. [f. L. *æquoreus* (f. *æquor* sea) + -AL¹.] Oceanic.

Ærarian (īrēᵊ·riăn), *a.* 1850. [f. L *ærarius* fiscal, *ærarium* treasury (f. *æs*, *ær-* bronze) + -AN; see -IAN.] Connected with the treasury; fiscal. As *sb.* [sc. *citizen.*] A Roman citizen, unenfranchised, who paid only a poll-tax (*æra pendebat*).

Aerate (ē·əreⁱt), *v.* 1794. [f. L. *aer* air + -ATE³, after Fr. *aérer.*] 1. To expose to the mechanical action of air, to supply with air 1856. 2. To expose to the chemical action of air; to oxygenate (the blood) by respiration 1794. 3. To charge with carbonic acid gas. Hence **Aerated** *ppl. a.* (in all senses).

Aeration (ē:ərēⁱ·ʃən). 1578. [f. as prec. + -ATION.] †1. Exposure to the open air. 2. Supplying with fresh air; airing 1835. 3. Exposure to the chemical action of the air (see AERATE 2) 1836. 4. The charging with carbonic acid or oxygen.

Aerator (ē·əreⁱtəɹ). 1861. [f. AERATE *v.* + -OR 2.] That which supplies or charges with air.

Aerial (ēᵊ·riăl, ēˌīᵊ·riăl), *a.* and *sb.* 1604. [f. L. *aerius* – Gr. ἀέριος (f. ἀήρ air) + -AL¹.] 1. Composed of air; aeriform, gaseous 1664. 2. Thin as air, ethereal; unsubstantial; ideal, imaginary 1610. 3. Light as air, airy 1606. 4. Of, pertaining to, or produced in the air; atmospheric 1604. 5. Existing, moving, or growing in the air; *spec.* with ref. to locomotion in the air 1620. 6. Placed at any airy height, elevated. Also *fig.* 1620. B. *sb.* An a. wire 1902.

2. A. bodies HOBBES, beings SCOTT, architecture (= building castles in the air) DICKENS, distinctions MILMAN. 4. Th'Eriall blew *Oth.* II. i. 39. *A. perspective* is the expression of space by any means whatever RUSKIN. 5. A. Spirits or devils BURTON, travellers DICKENS, roots for climbing GRAY. Towns a. on the waving tree POPE. 6. **A. railway,** a track consisting of overhead wires, etc., supporting carriages, usu. driven by electricity. **A. wire,** a wire supported in the air for radiating or receiving the waves of wireless telegraphy. Hence **Ae·rially** *adv.*

Aerie, aery, eyrie, eyry (ēᵊ·ri, īᵊ·ri). 1581. [– med.L. *airea*, *eyria*, *aeria*, *-ea*, prob. f. (O)Fr. *aire* lair, (earlier also) nature, origin, kind, = Pr. *agre* family, race, stock :– L. *agrum* piece of ground, in Rom. native country, lair.] 1. The nest of any bird of prey, *esp.* of an eagle; also of ravens, etc., which build high in the air; used *fig.* of a high-perched human dwelling or retreat. 2. The brood in the nest; *fig.* a noble stock of children 1594.

1. And like an Eagle o're his ayerie towers SHAKS. *John* V. ii. 149. 2. fig. *Haml.* II. ii. 354.

Aeriferous (ē:əri·fĕrəs), *a.* 1687. [f. L. *aer* air + -FEROUS.] Bearing or conveying air.

Aeriform (ē·ərifǭɹm), *a.* 1620. [f. L. *aer* air + -FORM.] Of the form of air, gaseous 1620; *fig.* unsubstantial 1821.

Aerify (ē·ərifəi), *v. rare.* [f. L. *aer* air + -FY.] 1. *trans.* To make aeriform. 2. = AERATE 1847. Hence **A:erifa·ction,** the action of aerifying. **A:erifica·tion,** the act of becoming air; aerifaction.

Aero- (ēᵊ·rǒ, ē·ərǒ), repr. Gr. ἀερο-, comb. f. ἀήρ AIR.

Aerobatics (-bæ·tiks) [after *acrobatics*], evolutions performed with an aeroplane, esp. for display; so **-batic** *a.* **Aerodyna·mics** [DYNAMICS], (*a*) the branch of pneumatics which treats of air and other gases in motion, and of their mechanical effects; (*b*) the art of moving through the air by some mechanism; the use of flying machines, aviation; so **-dyna·mic** *a.* **Ae·rogram,** (*a*) a message sent 'through the air', i.e. by wireless telegraphy; (*b*) a telegram conveyed partly by aeroplane. **Aero·graphy** [Gr. *-γραφία*], description of the atmosphere. **Aerohy·drous** *a.* used of minerals which contain water in their cavities. **Aero·logy** [Gr. *-λογία*], the part of science which treats of the atmosphere. **Ae·romancy** [Gr. *μαντεία*], divination by air, including augury; later, weather-forecasting. **Aero·meter** [Gr. *μέτρον*], an instrument for measuring the weight or density of air and gases; so **-me·tric** *a.* **Aero·-metry** [Gr. *-μετρία*], the science of pneumatics. **Ae·rophyte** [Gr. *φυτόν*], a plant growing wholly in the air, as epiphytal orchids, etc.; *pl.* **-phyta,** esp. lichens. **Ae·roscepsy** [Gr. *σκέψις*], **-o·scopy** [Gr. *-σκοπία*], the observation of the air; = AEROMANCY. **Aerosi·derite** [Gr. *σιδηρίτης*], a meteorite consisting of iron ore. **Ae:roside·rolite** [Gr. *σίδηρος* + *λίθος*], a meteorite intermediate between stone and iron. **Ae·rosphere** [Gr. *σφαῖρα*], the body of air that surrounds the earth. **b.** In various names of aeroplanes or flying machines or their parts, as *aero-biplane, -car, -engine, -surface.*

Aerobe (*ē*·ərōᵘb). *Biol.* 1879. [–(with assim. to *microbe*) Fr. *aérobie* (Pasteur), f. G. *ἀήρ* air + *βίος* life.] A microbe living on free oxygen derived from air.

Aerodrome (ēᵊ·rŏ-, *ē*·ərŏdrōᵘm). 1891. [f. AERO- + Gr. *δρόμος* course.] † **1.** An aeroplane –1896. **2.** A course for the use of flying machines; a tract of level ground from which aeroplanes or airships can start 1902.

Aerolite (*ē*·arŏləit). 1815. [alt. f. AEROLITH; see -LITE.] A mass which has fallen to the earth through the atmosphere; a meteorite. In later usage, a mass of stone, not of meteoric iron. Hence **Aeroli·tic** *a.*

Aerolith (*ē*·ərŏlip). 1819. [f. AERO + -LITH; cf. Fr. *aérolithe.*] = prec.

Aeronaut (ēᵊ·rŏnǫt, *ē*·ərŏnǫt). 1784. [– Fr. *aéronaute*, f. Gr. *ἀήρ* air + *ναύτης* sailor, f. *ναῦς* ship. (The first balloon ascent was made in 1783.)] One who sails through the air; a balloonist. *fig.* A gossamer spider 1845. Hence **Ae:ronau·tic, -al** *a.* **Ae·ronautism,** ballooning.

Aeronautics (-nǭ·tiks). 1753. [– mod.L. *aeronautica*, f. as prec.; see -ICS. Cf. Fr. *aéronautique.*] The science, art, or practice of aerial navigation.

Aeroplane (ēᵊ·rŏ-, *ē*·ərŏplēⁱn). 1866. [In sense 1, f. AERO- + PLANE *sb.*³; in sense 2 – Fr. *aéroplane*, f. Gr. *ἀερο-*, *ἀήρ* AIR *sb.* + *-πλανος* wandering.] † **1.** A plane for aerostatic experiment; the plane of a flying machine –1905. **2.** A heavier-than-air flying machine having one or more such planes (*monoplane, biplane, triplane*) and driven by a motor. Also *attrib.* 1884.

Aerostat (ēᵊ·rŏstæt, *ē*·ərŏstæt). 1784. [– Fr. *aerostat*, f. Gr. *ἀερο-* AERO- + *στατός* standing.] **1.** Early name for a balloon or machine capable of supporting weight in the air. **2.** An aeronaut 1870.

Aerostatic (ēᵊ:rŏstæ·tik, *ē*:ərŏ-), *a.* 1785. [– Fr. *aérostatique*, f. as prec.; see -IC.] **1.** Pertaining to the balancing or weighing of air; pneumatic 1791. **2.** Aeronautic 1785. var. **Ae:rosta·tical** *a.*

Aerostatics (ēᵊ:rŏstæ·tiks), *sb. pl.* 1753. [f. prec., after *hydrostatics*; see -ICS.] The branch of pneumatics which treats of the equilibrium and pressure of air and gases, and of bodies sustained in them; hence including AERONAUTICS.

Aerostation (*ē*:ərŏstēⁱ·ʃən). 1785. [– Fr. *aérostation*, improp. f. *aérostat*, as if = L. *-atus.*] † **1.** Aerostatics –1792. **2.** The art of raising and guiding balloons, etc., in the air; aerial navigation 1785.

‖ **Æruginous** (irū·dʒinəs), *a.* 1605. [– L. *æruginosus*, f. *ærugo, -gin-* verdigris, f. *æs, ær-* bronze; see -OUS.] Of the nature or colour of verdigris, or copper-rust.

‖ **Ærugo** (irū·go). 1753. [L.; see prec.] The rust of copper, or brass, verdigris; the rust of any metal.

Aery (*ē*·əri, ēᵊ·ri), *a. poet.* 1586. [– L. *aerius*, f. *aer* AIR; the suffix has been associated with -Y¹.] Aerial; hence ethereal, incorporeal.

A. tongues that syllable men's names MILT. *Comb.* **a.-light.**

Aery, var. of AERIE.

Æschynite (*ī*·skinəit). [f. Gr. *αἰσχύνη* disgrace + -ITE¹ 2 b.] *Min.* A blackish mineral of the tantalite group found in Russia.

Æsculapius (īskiulēⁱ·piŏs). Also **Esc-.** 1714. [L.] The Roman god of medicine; *fig.* a physician. Hence **Æscula·pian** *a.* belonging to Æ.; medicinal.

Æsculetin (īskiulī·tin). 1877. [f. as next, with dim. infix *-et-*; see -ET; cf. ACON(ELL)INE f. ACONINE.] *Chem.* A bitter crystalline substance ($C_9H_6O_4$) found in æsculin.

Æsculin (*ī*·skiŭlin). 1877. [f. L. *æsculus* winter or Italian oak, in mod. Bot. the horse-chestnut, + IN¹.] *Chem.* A glucoside contained in the bark of the horse-chestnut, etc.; $C_{21}H_{24}O_{13}$.

Æsthesics (īsþī·siks, e-). 1879. [f. Gr. *αἴσθησις* perception (on the rare anal. of *φυσικός* f. *φύσις*, the regular *æsthetics* being preoccupied + -ICS.] An abstract science of feeling. G. H. LEWES.

‖ **Æsthesis** (īsþī·sis). 1851. [Gr.; see prec.] The perception of the external world by the senses. Hence **Æsthe:sioge·nic** *a.* producing sensation. **Æsthesio·meter,** an instrument for measuring the tactile sensibility of patients.

Æsthesodic (īsþĭsǫ·dik), *a.* 1878. [f. Gr. *αἴσθησις* perception + *ὁδός* path, way + -IC. Cf. Fr. *esthésodique.*] *Phys.* Of nerves: Providing a path for sensory impulses.

Æsthete (*ī*·spīt, e·spīt). 1881. [f. next, after *athlete, athletic*, but cf. Gr. *αἰσθητής* one who perceives.] One who professes a superior appreciation of what is beautiful, and endeavours to carry out his ideas in practice.

Æsthetic (īsþe·tik, e-). 1798. [– Gr. *αἰσθητικός*, f. *αἰσθητά*, things perceptible by the senses (f. *αἰσθέσθαι* perceive), as opposed to *νοητά* things thinkable or immaterial. Misapplied in G. by Baumgarten to 'criticism of taste', and so used in Eng. since 1830.] **A.** *adj.* † **1.** Received by the senses –1798. **2.** Of or pertaining to the appreciation or criticism of the beautiful 1831. **3.** Having or showing refined taste; in accordance with good taste 1871.

2. A wash of quite fluid Æ. tea CARLYLE. **3.** He must have æ. wall-paper and a dado 1888.

B. *sb.* usu. pl. **æsthetics,** as collect. sing. † **1.** The science of the conditions of sensuous perception –1803. **2.** The philosophy of taste, or of the perception of the beautiful 1833.

2. Two professors of the science [of art] and æsthetic M. PATTISON. Hence **Æsthe·tical** *a.* of or relating to æsthetics. **Æsthe·tically** *adv.* **Æstheti·cian,** one devoted to æsthetics. **Æsthe·ticism,** the quality of being æsthetic; æsthetic doctrine; susceptibility to æsthetic influences. **Æsthe·ticist,** a professor of æstheticism. **Æsthe·ticize** *v.* to render æsthetic.

Æ:stho-physio·logy. 1855. [irreg. f. Gr. *αἰσθ-* perceive + PHYSIOLOGY.] The scientific study of the organs of sensation.

Æstival, estival (*ī*·stivăl, *ī*stəi·văl, also e-), *a.* ME. [– (O)Fr. *estival* – L. *æstivalis*, f. *æstivus* of summer, f. *æstus* heat; see -IVE, -AL.¹] **1.** Of or belonging to summer, or the summer solstice. **2.** Appearing or produced in summer.

2. Vernal, æ., and autumnal garlands SIR T. BROWNE.

Æstivate (*ī*·stiveⁱt, e-), *v.* Also **e-.** 1626. [– *æstivat-*, pa. ppl. stem of L. *æstivare* reside during the summer, f. *æstivus*; see prec., -ATE³. Cf. Fr. *estiver.*] To spend the summer; *esp.* (Zool.) in a state of torpor. Cf. *hibernate.*

Æstivation, e- (īstivēⁱ·ʃən, e-). 1625. [f. as prec.; see -ION.] † **1.** The spending of summer; summer retreat –1755. **2.** *Zool.* Summer-torpor; opp. to *hibernation.* Also *fig.* 1845. **3.** *Bot.* Internal arrangement of a flower-bud, before expansion; præfloration 1830.

† **Æ·stive,** *a.* Also **e-.** [– L. *æstivus* pertaining to summer, or heat; see ÆSTIVAL.] = ÆSTIVAL 1.

† **Æ·stuary.** 1706. [– L. *æstuarium* (prop. adj. = tidal); see ESTUARY, -ARY¹.] **1.** = ESTUARY. **2.** A vapour-bath.

† **Æ·stuate,** *v.* 1620. [– *æstuat-*, pa. ppl. stem of L. *æstuare* be hot, f. *æstus* heat; see -ATE³.]. To boil, to heave. Hence †**Æ·stuation** feverish disturbance, ebullition. †**Æstuous** *a.* heaving. † **Æ·sture** (an irregular form), boiling. CHAPMAN.

Aetheogam (e,ī·þīogæm). 1845. [f. Gr. *ἀήθης* unusual + *γάμος* marriage; see -GAM.] *Bot.* A cryptogam. Hence **Aetheo·gamous** *a.* =CRYPTOGAMOUS.

Æther, -ial, etc., occas. vars. ETHER, -EAL, etc.

† **Æthiops mineral.** [– L. *æthiops* – Gr. *Αἰθίοψ* Ethiopian; see ETHIOPS.] *Chem.* Quicksilver and sulphur ground together to a dark powder –1755.

Æ·thogen. [f. Gr. *αἶθος* fire + -GEN.] *Chem.* Boric nitride, which gives a phosphorescent light under the blowpipe. (Dicts.)

Æthrioscope (*ī*·þriŏskōᵘp). 1832. [f. Gr. *αἰθρία* open sky + *-σκοπός, -σκοπίον* observer; see -SCOPE.] An instrument for indicating the variations of solar radiation.

Ætiology (īti,ǫ·lŏdʒi, e·ti-). 1555. [– late L. *ætiologia* (Isidore) – Gr. *αἰτιολογία*, f. *αἰτία* cause + *-λογία* -LOGY.] **1.** The assignment of a cause; also, the wherefore of a command, etc. **2.** The science or philosophy of causation; the part of any special science which deals with causes 1660; *spec.* that part of medical science which investigates the causes of disease 1684.

1. The æ. of the drinking customs 1884.

†‖ **Aeti·tes.** [– L. *aetites* – Gr. *ἀετίτης* of the eagle, f. *ἀετός* eagle.] The eagle-stone; a hollow nodule of argillaceous oxide of iron, having a loose nucleus, fabled to be found in the eagle's nest.

† **Ævite·rnal,** *a.* [f. L. *æviternus* (see ETERNAL) + -AL¹.] Endless, eternal –1660. † **Ævite·rnity,** eternity.

†‖ **Æ·vum.** [L., = an age.] = ÆON. –1660.

Af-, *pref.* **1.** = L. *ad-* bef. *f-*, OFr. *a-*, refash. later with *ff*, after L. **2.** Occas. for *a-* (not = L. *af-*), as in *af(f)ray.*

Afar (ăfā·ɹ), *adv.* ME. [f. A- 2, 3 (= ON, OF) + FAR *adv.*] **1.** From far. With *see*, etc.; used of the thing seen. Now usu. with *from.* **2.** Far, at or to a distance. (In prose with *off.*)

1. To strike. .thy foeman from a farre 1611. **2.** In Stronds a-farre remote SHAKS. Abraham. .saw the place afarre off *Gen.* 22:4.

† **Afea·r,** *v.* OE. [f. A- *pref.* 1 + *fǣran* frighten; cf. AFEARD.] To frighten –1596.

† **Afea·r, afe·re, afei·r.** ME. [A *prep.*¹ 11 + FEAR *sb.*] **A.** *adv.* In fear. **B.** *conj.* Lest. (*Sc.*)

Afeard, -ed (ăfīᵊ·ɹd), *ppl. a.* ME. [f. AFEAR *v.* + -ED¹; superseded in gen. use by AFRAID.] Frightened.

Afer (*ī*·fəɹ). [L. = African.] The south-west wind. MILT.

Affability (æfăbi·līti). 1483. [– (O)Fr. *affabilité* – L. *affabilitas*; see next, -ITY.] The quality of being AFFABLE; courteousness.

A. .is where a man speaketh courteysly with a sweet speech or countenance ELYOT. His usual politeness and a. THACKERAY.

Affable (æ·făb'l), *a.* 1540. [– (O)Fr. *affable* – L. *affabilis* easy to be spoken to, f. *affari* to address, f. *ad* + *fari* to speak; see -ABLE.] Easy of conversation or address; civil and courteous, esp. with inferiors, etc.; kindly and polite.

Raphaël, The a. archangel MILT. *P.L.* vii. 42. Gentle his look, and a. his mien 1723. Hence **A·ffableness. A·ffably** *adv.*

Affabrous (æ·făbrəs), *a. rare.* [f. L. *affaber* made with art (f. *ad* AF- + *faber* skilful) + -OUS.] Workmanlike.

Affair (ăfēᵊ·ɹ). ME. [– AFr. *afere*, OFr. *afaire* (mod. *affaire*), f. phr. *à faire* to do; cf. ADO.] **1.** What one has to do, or has to do with; business; *more vaguely*, a concern 1611. **2.** *esp.* (in *pl.*) Ordinary pursuits of life 1484; commercial or professional business 1519; public business 1605. **3.** *sing.* Used vaguely of any proceeding which it is not desired to be precise about 1702. **4.** Loosely of material things, as a prop to an epithet 1802. † **5.** Performance –1596. † **6.** Fortune, rank. CAXTON. Cf. OFr. *de haute afaire.*

1. What is your affaire in Elsenour? *Haml.* I. ii. 174. An a. of a few days (*mod.*). **2.** The affairs of mankind 1869. Men of affairs, trained to business SMILES. That in the Field; this in Affairs of State DRYDEN. **3.** In our Dialect. .a lady is said to have an a. BERKELEY. An a. of honour (a duel) 1753. The a. was fiercely disputed SCOTT. **4.** His wife was no grand a. MAR. EDGEWORTH. The Plata is, in truth, a poor a. DARWIN.

† **Affa·mish,** *v.* 1568. [– Fr. *affamer*, OFr. *afamer*, see A- *prefix* 7, FAMISH *v.*] To starve.

trans. and *intr.* Hence † **Affa·mished** *ppl. a.* **Affa·mishment.**

Affatuate (ăfæ·tiuĕt), *a.* [f. INFATUATE *ppl. a.* by substitution of prefix AF-.] Infatuated. So **Affa·tuated** *ppl. a.*

† **Affe·ct,** *sb.* ME. [– L. *affectus*, n. of completed action, f. *afficere*; see AFFECT *v.*[2] Cf. OFr. *affect.*] **1.** Mental disposition (*esp.* opp. to *chere*, outward appearance, or to *effect*) –1626; desire, passion (opp. to *reason*) –1619. **2.** Natural tendency –1606; *esp.* kind disposition towards –1633. **3.** Bodily disposition, *esp.* disease, affection –1679.

1. The affects and Passions of the Heart and Spirits BACON *Sylva* § 97. **2.** For euery man with his affects is borne *L.L.L.* I. i. 152. **3.** Of great vse for the affects of the lungs 1616.

† **Affe·ct,** *ppl. a.* ME. [– L. *affectus*, pa. pple. of *afficere*; see AFFECT *v.*[2] Hence AFFECTED II.] = AFFECTED II –1538.

Affect (ăfe·kt), *v.*[1] 1483. [– Fr. *affecter* or L. *affectare* aim at, profess to have, f. *affect-*, pa. ppl. stem of *afficere*; see next.] † **1.** To aim at, seek –1794. **2.** To like, love. *arch.* 1550; *esp.* To like to use, frequent 1589; † *absol.* –1645; of animals and plants: To haunt 1616. **3.** To assume ostentatiously 1605; with *inf.*: To profess 1720. **4.** To assume falsely; to pretend 1661; with *inf.* 1603.

1. Have I affected wealth or honour 2 *Hen. VI*, IV. vii. 104. To a. the skies POPE, to be made equall vnto *Ecclus.* 13: 11. **2.** She did a. me *Twel. N.* II. v. 28. Making Peace or Warre, As thou affects *Ant. & Cl.* I. iii. 71. To a. new fashions 1586, the back benches 1862. **3.** To a. a saucy roughnes *Lear* II. ii. 102, a stern demeanour GIBBON. **4.** He had ever affected a haughty indifference DISRAELI. To a. to be surprised 1879. Hence **Affe·cter, -or,** † a lover; an ostentatious user (*of* anything). var. † **Affectate** *v.*

Affect (ăfe·kt), *v.*[2] 1606. [– Fr. *affecter* or *affect-*, pa. ppl. stem of L. *afficere* act upon, influence, f. *ad* AF- + *facere* do.] **1.** To attack as a disease. † **2.** *Law.* To attaint *with* a crime –1726. **3.** To have an effect on the feelings 1662 (cf. AFFECTED III), or on things 1631. **4.** To allot specially *to* 1611.

1. The inward gangrene affected their vitals DE FOE. **2.** To a. with Fraud 1726. **3.** To a. the amount of the dividends 1840. **4.** Affected to his special service THACKERAY. Hence **Affe·ctible** *a. rare.* **Affe:ctibi·lity.**

† **Affecta·te(d,** *ppl. a.* [– L. *affectatus*, pa. pple. of *affectare*, AFFECT *v.*[1]; see -ATE[2], -ED[1].] = AFFECTED I, 2, 3.

Affectation (æfektē[i]·ʃən). 1548. [– Fr. *affectation* or L. *affectatio*, f. pa. ppl. stem of *affectare*; see AFFECT *v.*[1], -ATION.] † **1.** An aiming at –1711; liking for –1795. Const. *of.* **2.** An ostentatious fondness for, or display of 1548. **3.** Artificiality of manner 1593. **4.** Pretence 1581.

1. The A. of being Gay STEELE. A. of the manners. .of France GIBBON. **2.** A. of eloquence 1548, of Latin 1861. **3.** The essence of a. is that it be assumed CARLYLE. Mere a. 1873. Hence **Affecta·tionist.** var. **Affe·ctedness.**

Affected (ăfe·ktėd), *ppl. a.* Really *three* words.

I. Pa. pple. of AFFECT *v.*[1] 1588. † **1.** Aimed at –1649; loved –1705. **2.** Assumed artificially 1594; pretended 1663. **3.** Full of AFFECTATION (sense 3) 1588.

1. A work assigned rather than by me chosen or a. MILT. **2.** I have not used any a. style MILT. Real or a. levity 1879. **3.** Too spruce, too a., too odde *L.L.L.* v. i. 15.

II. adj. f. AFFECT *ppl. a.* + -ED[1]. 1535. **1.** Disposed, inclined 1587. † **2.** *esp.* *Well-* or *ill*-disposed (*to*) –1690. Cf. *disaffected.* † **3.** Of the body –1615.

1. How stands the country a. towards you BUNYAN.

III. Pa. pple. of AFFECT *v.*[2] 1579. **1.** Attacked by a disease. Const. *with* or *absol.* 1619. **2.** Mentally influenced (*by*), *esp.* by sorrow, or *absol.* 1626. **3.** Of things: Influenced, acted upon (*by* or *absol.*) 1748. **4.** Specially allotted (see AFFECT *v.*[2] 4).

1. The a. part of a city 1806. **2.** Deeply a. by his own reproaches GIBBON. **3.** Finances. .materially a. 1783. **4.** Horses a. . .to military purposes 1871.

Affe·ctedly, *adv.* 1596. [f. AFFECTED I + -LY[2]; cf. OFr. *affecteement.*] † **1.** Purposely –1738; affectionately –1611. **2.** Artificially 1617. **3.** Hypocritically 1656.

2. A. vaine SIR T. BROWNE. The person a. described as Lupus is really. .Wulfstan. FREEMAN. **3.** An a. sympathising voice, like an undertaker's F. NIGHTINGALE.

Affe·cting, *ppl. a.* 1598. [f. AFFECT *v.*[1] 1 and 4 and *v.*[2]] † **1.** Loving –1619. † **2.** Using AFFECTATION (sense 3) –1611. **3.** [f. AFFECT *v.*[2]] † Impressive –1779; thrilling, touching 1720.

2. A drawling-affecting rogue SHAKS. **3.** An a. farewell. Hence **Affe·ctingly** *adv.*

Affection (ăfe·kʃən), *sb.* ME. [– (O)Fr. *affection*, – L. *affectio* (favourable) disposition or inclination, f. *affect-*, pa. ppl. stem of *afficere*; see AFFECT *v.*[2], -ION.] **I.** The action of affecting; the being affected 1660.

1. The a. of our bodily organs from without MILL.

II. 1. An emotion of the mind ME.; † *esp.* passion, lust, as opp. to reason –1736. **2.** † Mental tendency –1756; *esp.* disposition, inclination towards ME.; good disposition towards, love ME. *Esp.* in *pl.*

1. God gave them up to vile affections *Rom.* i. 26. **2.** How do you know he loues her? *John.* I heard him swear his a. *M. Ado* II. i. 175. This yong Maides affections *Oth.* I. iii. 112.

III. A state of the body; *esp.* disease 1541. It was an a. of the heart 1853.

IV. In *Metaph. esp.* in *pl.* [= L. *affectus.*] A property or attribute of a thing 1567.

Thought is. .an a. of perishable matter 1860.

† **V.** = AFFECTATION –1776.

Three-pil'd Hyperboles, spruce a. *L.L.L.* v. i. 407. Hence **Affe·ctional** *a.* having affections (*mod.*). † **Affe·ctionally** *adv.* earnestly. † **Affe·ctioned** *ppl. a.* = AFFECTIONATE. † **Affe·ctious** *a.* loving.

Affe·ction, *v.* 1584. [– (O)Fr. *affectionner*, f. *affection* (prec.).] To love.

Can you a. the 'o-man *Merry W.* I. i. 234.

Affectionate (ăfe·kʃənĕt), *a.* 1494. [– med. L. *affectionatus* devoted, or its deriv., Fr. *affectionné*; see AFFECTION *sb.*, -ATE.[2]] † **1.** Disposed mentally –1657. † **2.** Biased –1611. † **3.** Passionate –1726. † **4.** Eager –1750. † **5.** Well-affected *to* –1761. **6.** Loving 1586; of things: Tender 1586.

4. I am. .zealous and a. to recede as little from antiquity BACON. Their labours, however zealous or a. JOHNSON. **5.** A. to the French government HUME. **6.** Your most loving and a. brother JAMES VI. Your. .a. Seruant Gonerill *Lear* IV. vi. 276. An a. farewell (*mod.*). Hence † **Affe·ctionate** *v.* = AFFECTION *v.* Also *refl.* † **Affe·ctionated** *ppl. a.* = AFFECTIONATE 1, 2, 5, 6. **Affe·ctionateness,** the quality of being a.

Affectionately (ăfe·kʃənĕtli), *adv.* 1588. [f. prec. + -LY[2]; cf. Fr. *affectionnément.*] † **1.** Zealously –1723. **2.** Lovingly 1606.

Affective (ăfe·ktiv), *a.* 1549. [– Fr. *affectif*, *-ive* – late L. *affectivus*; see AFFECT *v.*[2], -IVE.] † **1.** *rare.* = AFFECTING. **2.** Pertaining to the emotions, opp. to *intellectual* (see AFFECT *sb.*) 1623. Hence **Affe·ctively** *adv.*

† **Affe·ctual,** *a.* 1483. [– OFr. *affectuel* – med.L. *affectualis* with affection; f. *affectus* AFFECT *sb.* + *-alis* -AL.[1]] **1.** Earnest –1581. **2.** = AFFECTIVE 2. 1655. Hence † **Affe·ctually** *adv.*

† **Affe·ctuous,** *a.* 1460. [– OFr. *affectueus* – late L. *affectuosus*, f. as prec.; see -OUS, -UOUS.] **1.** Eager –1656; loving –1575. **2.** = AFFECTING 2. 1674. Hence † **Affe·ctuously** *adv.*

† **Affee·ble,** *v.* 1480. [– OFr. *afebler* grow weak, f. *à* AD- + *febler*; see FEEBLE.] To enfeeble –1599.

Affee·r, *v.* 1467. [– OFr. *afeurer*, AFr. *aferer* – med.L. *afforare* fix the price, f. *ad* AF- + L. *forum* market. **1.** To assess an amercement. **2.** *fig.* To confirm –1605. *Macb.* IV. iii. 34. Hence † **Affee·rance. Affee·rment. Affee·ror.**

† **Affei·r,** *v.* *n. dial.* ME. [– OFr. *aferir* belong, pertain.] To fall by right. = EFFEIR. Hence † **Affei·ring** *ppl. a.* † **Afferant** *ppl. a.* and *sb.*

Afferent (æ·fĕrĕnt), *a.* 1839. [– *afferent-*, pres. ppl. stem of L. *afferre* bring to, f. *ad* AF- + *ferre* bring. Cf. Fr. *afférent.*] *Phys.* Conducting inwards, as *afferent nerves.* Opp. to *efferent.*

‖ **Affettuoso** (affettu,ō·so), *a.* 1796. [It.] *Mus.* A direction: With feeling.

Affiance (ăfəi·ăns). ME. [– OFr. *afiance*, f. *afier* to trust; see AFFY *v.*, -ANCE.] **1.** Trust *in*, *on* 1330. † **2.** Confidence, assurance –1753. **3.** Plighting of faith; *esp.* of troth on agreement of marriage –1809. † **4.** Affinity –1601.

1. My Lancelot, thou in whom I have. .a. TENNYSON. **3.** After a. and troth plight between them.

Affi·ance, *v.* 1523. [– OFr. *afiancer*, f. *afiance*; see prec.] To promise; *esp.* in marriage. Usu. in pass., with *to.* Hence **Affi·anced** *ppl. a.*

Affi·ant. 1807. [– Fr. *affiant*; see AFFY *v.*, -ANT.] *U.S.* One who makes an affidavit.

† **Affich(e,** *v.* ME. [Fr., f. *afficher* to fix, AFFIX *v.*] To affix.

Affidavit (æfidē[i]·vit). 1622. [3rd. pers. sing. perf. of med.L. *affidare* declare on oath; see AFFY *v.*] *Law.* A written statement, *sworn* by deponent, *taken* by the judge; in pop. usage *made* or *taken* by deponent. *Slang.* On my *davy.*

Affi·ed, *ppl. a.* *arch.* 1500. [f. AFFY *v.* + -ED[1].] = AFFIANCED. Also *fig.*

† **Affi·le,** *v.* ME. [– (O)Fr. *afiler* sharpen:– Rom. **affilare* f. *ad* AF- + L. *filum* thread, later, cutting edge.] To sharpen –1520.

Affiliable (ăfi·liăb'l), *a.* 1862. [f. AFFILI(ATE) *v.* + -ABLE.] Capable of being affiliated on or causally traced to. Const. *on, upon.*

Affiliate (ăfi·li,e[i]t), *v.* 1761. [– *affiliat-*, pa. ppl. stem of med.L. *affiliare*, f. *ad* AF- + *filius* son, prob. after Fr. *affilier*; see -ATE[3].] **1.** To adopt as a branch, or a member of a society 1761; *intr.* (for *refl.*) to connect oneself *with* 1860. Const. *to, with.* **2.** *Law.* To fix the paternity of an illegitimate child; hence, to ascribe a child *to* its father 1834. Also *fig.*

1. The party. .that affiliates with the Republicans 1860. **2.** To a. a child on a person as the. .putative Father thereof 1834. Hence **Affi·liated** *ppl. a.* Usu. *fig.*

Affiliate (afi·liĕt), *a.* 1868. [f. as prec.; see -ATE[1], [2].] Affiliated. As *sb.* An associate 1879.

Affiliation (ăfili,ē[i]·ʃən). 1751. [– Fr. *affiliation* – med.L. *affiliatio*, f. *affiliat-*, pa. ppl. stem of *affiliare*; see AFFILIATE *v.*, -ION.] **1.** Adoption of a son 1751. **2.** Adoption, by a society, of branches 1799. **3.** Fixing the paternity of a child. *fig.* The fathering of a thing upon any one; also, the assignment of anything to its origin 1830.

Affi·nal, *a.* 1609. [f. L. *affinis* bordering on, related, + -AL[1]; cf. *celestial, terrestrial* f. L. *celestis, terrestris.*] Related by marriage; from the same stock.

Affi·ne. 1509. [– L. *affinis* related, see AFFINITY; cf. OFr. *afin*, mod. *affin*, which may partly be the source.] **A.** *sb.* A relation by marriage; a connection. **B.** *adj.* Closely related 1650.

Affi·ned, *ppl. a.* 1597. [f. prec. or as prec. + -ED[1], perh. after OFr. *afiné.*] **1.** Related. **2.** Bound by any tie (*arch.*) 1604.

2. A. to loue the Moore *Oth.* I. i. 39.

Affi·nitive, *a.* 1651. [f. next + -IVE, after *infinity, -ive.*] Connected by affinity.

Affinity (ăfi·niti). ME. [– OFr. *afinité* (mod. *aff-*) – L. *affinitas*, f. *affinis* bordering on, related, f. *ad* AF- + *finis* border; see -ITY.] **1.** Relationship by marriage, opp. to *consanguinity*; *collect.* relations by marriage. In *R.C.Ch.*: The spiritual relationship between sponsors and their godchild. **2.** Kinship generally; *collect.* kindred ME. **3.** *Philol.* Structural resemblance in languages suggestive of a common stock 1599. **4.** *Nat. Hist.* Structural resemblance in animals, plants, or minerals, suggestive of a common stock or type 1794. **5.** *fig.* Causal relationship or connection; family likeness 1533. † **6.** Vicinity –1770. **7.** † Relationship by inclination; companionship –1611; hence *fig.* Any natural friendliness or attraction 1616. **8.** *esp.* Chemical attraction; the tendency of certain elements or their compounds to unite and form new compounds 1753. **9.** A spiritual attraction believed to exist between persons; also, the subjects of the affinity 1868.

1. Related by a. to the royal house 1849. The bar of spiritual a. FREEMAN. **2.** The a. and brotherhood of mankind 1794. **5.** The spiritual a. between Luther and Bunyan 1861. **7.** Now Jehosaphat. .joyned a. with Ahab 2 *Chron.* 18: 1. With this hath. .the Spaw water great a. 1652.

Affirm (ăfə·ɹm), *v.* [ME. *afferme* – OFr. *afermer* (mod. *affirmer*):– L. *affirmare*, f. *ad* AF- + *firmus* FIRM *a.* In XVI the sp. was assim. to L., as in Fr.] †**1.** To make firm –1534. **2.** *Law.* To confirm, ratify 1386. †**3.** To confirm or maintain (a statement) –1670; hence, to state positively ME.; to make a solemn AFFIRMATION (sense 5) ME. **4.** *Logic* and *Gram.* To make a statement in the affirmative (as opp. to the *negative*) 1581.

2. To a. a sentence CHAUCER, a judgement COKE. **3.** If my Lord affirm'd that black was white POPE. Permitted by law to a. instead of swearing 1863. **4.** For Grammer sayes..two negatiues affirme SIDNEY. Hence **Affi·rmable** *a.* †affirmative; capable of being affirmed. **Affi·rmably** *adv.* **Affi·rmant** *a.* affirming; *sb.* on who affirms; var **Affirmer. Affi·rmatory** *a.* assertive.

Affirmance (ăfɔ̄·ɹmăns). 1494. [– OFr. *af(f)ermance*, f. *afermer*; see prec., -ANCE.] **1.** A confirming 1531; in *Law*, ratification 1528. **2.** A (strong) declaration 1494.

1. The a. of the decree 1808. **2.** Till a. breeds a doubt COWPER.

Affirmation (æfəɹmē̆ⁱ·ʃən). 1533. [– Fr., or L. *affirmatio*, f. *affirmat-*, pa. ppl. stem of *affirmare*; see AFFIRM *v.*, -ION.] **1.** Confirmation; in *Law*, ratification. **2.** The action of declaring true; *esp.* affirmative (opp. to negative) assertion 1611. **3.** *Logic.* An affirmative judgement or proposition 1656. **4.** That which is asserted; a statement 1593. **5.** *Law.* A solemn declaration, having the value and penalties of an oath, by persons who conscientiously decline taking an oath 1695.

2. Vpon warrant of bloody a. *Cymb.* I. iv. 63. A single nod implies an a. DARWIN. **4.** Paul's a., who saith..1593.

Affirmative (ăfɔ̄·ɹmătiv). ME. [– (O)Fr. *affirmatif, -ive* – late L. *affirmativus*, f. as prec.; see -IVE.] **A.** *adj.* †**1.** Corroborative –1674; positive –1734. **2.** *Logic.* Expressing the agreement of the two terms of a proposition 1570. **3.** Hence, Asserting that the fact is so; answering 'yes'. Opp. to *negative.* 1628. †**4.** *Math.* Positive or real, opp. to *negative* –1789.

1. Be not confident and a. in an uncertain matter JER. TAYLOR. **3.** An a. answer H. SPENCER.

B. *sb.* [sc. *mode, proposition, statement.*] **1.** The affirmative mode in a proposition ME. **2.** An affirmative word or proposition, opp. to a *negative* 1588. †**3.** An assertion –1660.

1. They all *.answered in the a.* DE FOE. **2.** If your foure negatiues make your two affirmatiues *Twel. N.* v. i. 24. **3.** That a. which sayes the Loadstone is poison SIR T. BROWNE. Hence **Affi·rmatively** *adv.* in an a. manner.

†**Affi·rmly, Affe·rmely,** *adv.* [f. after OFr. *aferméement*, f. *afermé*, pa. pple. of *afermer*, with -LY² repr. Fr. *-ment*; see AFFIRM *v.*] Firmly –1525.

Affix (ăf·iks), *v.* 1533. [– (O)Fr. *affixer* or med.L. *affixare*, f. *ad* AF- + *fixare* FIX. First in Sc. pa. pple. *affix(i)t*; cf. MIX.] **1.** To fix or fasten (*to, on, upon*) 1533. †**2.** *intr.* To cling or be attached *to* –1695. **3.** To attach, add, as a seal, a signature, a postscript, etc., *to* 1658. Also *fig.* 1665. †**4.** *trans.* To fix upon –1725.

1. Affixed to a vessel 1734, *fig.* to one's studies FULLER. **3.** To a. a price DIBDIN, notes 1878. *fig.* To a. ridicule to people 1734, blame 1805, salaries to a profession HUME. Hence **Affi·xed** *ppl. a.* attached; †fixed upon. **Affi·xer.**

Affix (æ·fiks), *sb.* 1612. [subst. use of L. *affixus* fastened to, pa. pple. of *affigere*, f. *ad* AF- + *figere*; see FIX *v.*] That which is attached or added 1642; *esp.* in *Gram.* An addition to a root, stem, or word; a prefix; a suffix 1612.

Affixture (ăfi·kstiŭɹ). 1793. [f. AFFIX *v.*, after FIXTURE.] The action of affixing; the being affixed; attachment. vars. **Affixa·tion,** †**Affi·xion.**

Afflate (ăflē̆ⁱ·t), *v. rare.* 1599. [– L. *afflat-*; see foll., -ATE³.] To blow or breathe upon. Hence **Affla·ted** *ppl. a.* inspired. **Affla·tion.** inspiration.

Afflatus (ăflē̆ⁱ·tŏs). 1665. [– L. *afflatus*, f. *afflat-*, pa. ppl. stem of *afflare* blow upon, f. *ad* AF- + *flare* blow.] †**1.** Hissing. [L. *afflatus serpentis.*] **2.** The inspiration of supernatural knowledge; an overmastering impulse, poetic or other 1665. **3.** *Med.* A form of erysipelas, which comes on suddenly.

2. A migratory a. LIVINGSTONE.

†**Affli·ct,** *ppl. a.* ME. [– OFr. *aflit*:– L. *afflictus*, pa. pple. of *affligere*; see next.] Afflicted –1583.

Afflict (ăfli·kt), *v.* ME. [– L. *afflictare* or *afflict-*, pa. ppl. stem of *affligere* dash against, distress, f. *ad* AF- + *fligere* strike; partly through prec. Cf. OFr. *afflicter.*] †**1.** To cast down –1667; *intr.* to become downcast ME. **2.** *trans.* To trouble grievously; *refl.* to grieve 1535.

1. Reassembling our afflicted Powers MILT. **2.** It is their virtues that a...him JUNIUS. Hence †**Affli·ct** *sb.* = AFFLICTION. **Affli·cter. Affli·ctingly** *adv.*

Affliction (ăfli·kʃən). ME. [– (O)Fr. *affliction* – L. *afflictio*, f. *afflict-*(prec.); see -ION.] †**1.** The action of inflicting grievous pain. *spec.* in religion, Self-discipline, mortification –1628. **2.** The state of being afflicted ME. **3.** That which afflicts; a calamity, pain, etc. 1598.

1. Feede him with bread of a., and with water of a. 2 *Chron.* 18:26. **2.** I have seen the affliccioun of my puple WYCLIF *Ex.* iii. 7. A. of spirit *Haml.* III. ii. 324. **3.** Every former a. had its charm MISS AUSTEN. Hence **Affli·ctionless** *a.*

Afflictive (ăfli·ktiv), *a.* 1611. [–(O)Fr. *afflictif, -ive,* – med.L. *afflictivus*, f. as prec.; see -IVE.] Tending to afflict; painful; trying. Const. *to.* Hence **Affli·ctively** *adv.*

†**Afflue·**, *v.* [– (O)Fr. *affluer*, f. L. *affluere* flow towards, f. *ad* AF- + *fluere* flow.] To flow towards; to flock –1521.

Affluence (æ·flⁱuĕns). ME. [– (O)Fr. *affluence* or L. *affluentia*, f. *affluent-*; see next, -ENCE.] **1.** A flowing towards; a concourse 1600. **2.** A plentiful flow; profusion 1447; *ellipt.* wealth 1603.

1. Great a. of company CARLYLE. **2.** A. in rethoryk 1447, of teeres CAXTON, of all things 1633, of snows LONGF. They lived in..a. STEELE. var. †**A·ffluency** (in senses 2, 3).

Affluent (æ·flⁱuĕnt), *a.* ME. [– (O)Fr. *affluent* – L. *affluent-*, pres. ppl. stem of *affluere*; see AFFLUE *v.*, -ENT.] †**1.** Flowing toward a place –1759. **2.** Flowing freely or abundantly 1816. *fig.* Of the gifts of fortune, etc.: Plenteous 1413. **3.** Hence, Wealthy. Also *fig.* Const. *in*; *of* rare. 1769. **4.** *sb.* [The adj. used *absol.*] A tributary stream 1833.

1. A. blood HARVEY. **2.** An a. mane SOUTHEY, fountain 1863, fortune GOLDSM. **3.** An a. retreat 'JUNIUS'. A. in expressions [etc.] 1855. **4.** The.. Missouri, with its a., the Mississippi 1833. Hence **A·ffluently** *adv.*

Afflux (æ·flɒks). 1611. [– med.L. *affluxus*, f. *afflux-*, pa. ppl. stem of *affluere*; see AFFLUE *v.* Cf. Fr. *afflux.*] **1.** A flowing towards a point; *esp.* in *Med.* of humours. **2.** An accession 1661.

1. The a. of the sea 1635, of matter [to the lungs] 1661, of air 1794, of purchasers 1872. **2.** An increased a. of blood 1859. var. **Afflu·xion.**

†**A·ffodill.** ME. [– med.L. *affodilus*, var. of L. *asphodilus*; see ASPHODEL.] **1.** Asphodel, or King's Spear (*Asphodelus*) –1615. **2.** = DAFFODIL –1611.

Afforce (ăfō̆ᵊ·ɹs), *v.* [ME. *af(f)orce* – OFr. *aforcier* in the same senses, f. *à* + *force* FORCE *sb.*¹] †**1.** To apply force ME.: ravish ME.; attempt –1528. †**2.** To add force to, reinforce ME. **3.** *Eng. Hist.* To strengthen by adding new members.

3. It was the practice to a. the jury HALLAM. Hence **Affo·rcement,** †**Afforciament,** a strengthening (sense 3); † a fort.

Afford (ăfō̆ᵊ·ɹd), *v.* [Late OE. *ġeforþian* advance, promote, accomplish, f. *ġe-* Y- + *forþian* to further, f. *forþ* FORTH. For ME. *a-* see A- *pref.* 6; change of *th* to *d* as in *burden, murder.*] †**1.** To further; to accomplish –ME. **2.** To manage (*to do*); with *can*: To have the means, be able 1449; to spare, to bear the expense of 1833. **3.** Without *can*: To give of what one has 1596. Of things: To be capable of yielding 1581; to yield naturally 1600.

2. To a. that their sons may be good for nothing SWIFT. He could a. to suffer WORDSW. To a. Another Rib MILT., beer 1833. **3.** Welcome what he doth a. G. HERBERT. The world affords no law to make thee rich *Rom. & Jul.* v. i. 73. To a. an instance 1782. Olives..a. most oil when..ripe RAY. Hence **Affo·rdable** *a.* that can be afforded, spared, or yielded. **Affo·rder.**

Afforest (ăfǫ·rĕst), *v.* 1502. [– med.L. *afforestare* (Charter of Forests, 1217), f. *ad* AF- + *foresta* FOREST *sb.*] To convert into forest. Hence **Affo:resta·tion,** the action of the vb. or its result.

Affranchise (ăfræ·ntʃiz, -ʃəiz), *v.* 1475. [– OFr. *afranchiss-*, lengthened stem of *afranchir* (mod. *aff-*), f. *à* :– L. *ad*, AF- + *franc* free. Cf. ENFRANCHISE *v.*] To free from servitude, or from a vow, etc. Hence **Affra·nchisement.**

†**Affra·p,** *v.* [f. A- *pref.* 11 + FRAP *v.*] To strike. SPENSER.

Affray (ăfrē̆ⁱ·), *v.* ME. [– AFr. *afrayer*, OFr. *effreer, esfreer* (mod. *effrayer*) :– Rom. **exfridare*, f. L. *ex* EX-¹ + Rom. **fridus* – Gmc. **friþuz* peace (whence OE. *friþ* FRITH *sb.*¹). See AFRAID.] **1.** To disturb or startle (*arch.*) ME. **2.** To frighten; *esp.* in pass. (*arch.*) ME. **3.** To frighten away (*arch.*) ME.

1. The kettle-drum And..clarionet a. his ears KEATS. **2.** He was affrayde 1315. **3.** To afray us from the euil 1610. Hence **Affray·ed** *ppl. a.* alarmed KEATS. **Affray·er.**

Affray (ăfrē̆ⁱ·), *sb.* ME. [– AFr. *affrai* = OFr. *effrei, esfrei* (mod. *effroi*), f. the vb.] †**1.** An attack, or assault –1583. †**2.** Alarm; terror –1596. **3.** † A disturbance –1810; *esp.* a breach of the peace, caused by fighting or riot in a public place 1482.

3. The tumult and a. SCOTT. An A. is a common wrong BLOUNT

Affreight (ăfreⁱ·t), *v. rare.* 1847. [– Fr. *affréter*, f. *à* :– L. *ad* AF- + *fréter*, f. *fret*; see FREIGHT, to which sp. was assim.] To hire a ship to carry cargo. Hence **Affrei·ghter. Affrei·ghtment,** the hiring of a ship to carry cargo.

†**Affre·t,** *sb.* [Origin unkn.] Furious onset SPENSER.

Affricate (æ·frikĕt). *Phonetics.* 1880. [– L. *affricatus*, pa. pple. of *affricare* rub on or against, f. *ad* AF- + *fricare* rub.] A combination of a stop with a following fricative, as G. *pf.* Also **Affri·cative, A·ffricated** *a.*

†**Affrie·nded,** *pa. pple.* [f. A- *pref.* 11 + FRIEND *sb.* + -ED.] Made friends. SPENSER.

†**Affri·ght,** *ppl. a.* [OE. *āfyrhted*, pa. pple. of **āfyrhtan*, see A- *pref.* 1, FRIGHT *v.* Cf. next.] = next.

Affright (ăfrəi·t), *v. arch.* 1589. [f. A- *pref.* 11 + FRIGHT *v.*] To frighten, to terrify. Now *poet.* for FRIGHTEN.

The Scar-Crow that affrights our children so 1 *Hen. VI*, I. iv. 43. Hence **Affri·ght** *sb.* the action of causing terror; *concr.* a cause of terror; the state of terror; whence **Affri·ghtful** *a.*, **-ly** *adv.* **Affri·ghten** *v.* var. of AFFRIGHT *v.* **Affri·ghter. Affri·ghtment,** †the action of frightening; the fact or state of being frightened. All *arch.*

Affrighted (ăfrəi·tĕd), *ppl. a.* 1604. [f. prec. + -ED¹.] Struck with sudden fear; alarmed.

Th'a. Globe *Oth.* v. ii. 100. Hence **Affri·ghtedly** *adv.*

Affront (ăfrɒ·nt), *v.* [– OFr. *afronter* strike in the face :– Rom. **affrontare*, f. L. phr. *ad frontem* to the face; see AF-, FRONT *sb.*] **1.** To insult to the face or openly. **2.** To put to the blush; to cause to feel ashamed ME. **3.** To face in defiance; confront 1563. **4.** † To meet of purpose, accost –1633; to face in position (*arch.*) 1600. †**5.** To set face to face –1606.

1. Not to honor vs, but to a. vs 1577. To a. the Divine Goodness GLANVILLE. **2.** Lord Sandwich affronted his Grace of Grafton extremely H. WALPOLE. **3.** Who, him affronting soone, to fight was readie prest SPENSER. To a. death 1856, great risk KINGLAKE. **4.** To a., as 'twere by accident *Haml.* III. i. 31. What affronts our gaze BROWNING. Hence **Affro·nted** *ppl. a.* injured in one's feelings; †brazen-faced. **Affro·ntedly** *adv.* shamelessly. †**Affro·ntedness. Affro·ntee,** one who receives an affront. **Affro·nter,** † a deceiver; one who affronts. **Affro·nting** *vbl. sb.* insulting; facing; *ppl. a.* openly offensive. **Affro·ntingly** *adv.* **Affro·ntingness,** insulting manner. **Affro·ntive** *a.* of affronting character or tendency.

Affront (ăfrɒ·nt), *sb.* 1598. [f. prec.; cf. Fr. *affront.*] **1.** An open insult; a word or act of intentional disrespect. **2.** Felt indignity 1662. †**3.** An encounter or meeting (see AFFRONT *v.* 3, 4) –1678; a position of hostility –1648.

1. Phr. *To offer an affront to, put an a. on.* **2.** Candidates are..not very susceptible of affronts COWPER.

‖ **Affrontee** (afronte, ăfrɒ·ntī), *a.* 1751. [– Fr. *affronté*, pa. pple. of *affronter* AFFRONT *v.*; see -EE[1].] *Her.* **1.** Front to front. **2.** Looking frontwise 1766.

Affu·se, *v. rare.* 1683. [– *affus-*, pa. ppl. stem of L. *affundere* pour upon, f. *ad* AF- + *fundere* pour.] To pour upon. Hence **Affu·sed** *ppl. a.*

Affusion (ăfiū·ʒən). 1615. [– Fr. *affusion* or late L. *affusio*, f. *affus-*; see prec., -ION.] A pouring on or into; e.g. of water upon the body, as (*Med.*) in fevers, or in one method of baptism. Also *fig.*

† **Affy·**, *v.* [– OFr. *afier*:– med.L. *affidare* bind oneself in loyalty, f. L. *ad* AF- + *fidare* trust.] **1.** To trust. *trans.*, *refl.*, and *intr.* Const. *to*, *on*, *in*. –1642. **2.** To affirm on one's faith –1617. **3.** To make fast by solemn promise; to espouse –1627; to affiance –1705. Also *fig.*

1. I do affie In thy vprightnesse *Tit. A.* I. i. 47. **3.** The Prince affyes [Philippa] at the last DRAYTON. I would not a. my daughter to you ROWE. Hence † **Affy·** *sb.* trust.

† **A·fgod.** [OE., f. *af*, *æf* off, away + GOD, corresp. to ON. *afguð*, OHG. *abgot*; cf. Goth. *afguþs* impious.] A false god.

Afield (ăfī·ld), *adv.* OE. [A *prep.*[1] 1 + FIELD *sb.*] **1.** On or in the field, *esp.* of labour or battle. **2.** To or into the field; *hence*, to battle ME; away from home; also *fig.* ME.

1. Æneas is a. *Tr. & Cr.* v. iii. 67. **2.** They a. Their cattle drive HOBBES.

Afire (ăfəi^ə·ɹ), *adv.* and *a.* ME. [A *prep.*[1] 11 + FIRE *sb.*] On or in fire; burning. Also *fig.*

Aflame (ăflē^i·m), *adv.* and *a.* 1555. [A *prep.*[1] 11 + FLAME *sb.*] In or into flame; in a glow. Also *fig.* 1798.

fig. All a. with curiosity W. W. COLLINS.

Afla·t, *adv.* ME. [A *prep.*[1] + FLAT *sb.*[2]] In a flat position.

Aflau·nt, *adv.* 1568. [A *prep.*[1] 11 + FLAUNT *sb.*] In a flaunting state.

A-fli·cker, *adv.* [A *prep.*[1] 11 + FLICKER *sb.*[1]] In a flickering state. BROWNING.

Afloat (ăflō^u·t), *adv.* and *a.* [OE. *on flot(e)*, *a flote* on the sea (A *prep.*[1], FLOAT *sb.*); in ME. partly after ON. *á flot(i)* and OFr. *en flot*; from XVI prob. a new formation.] **1.** In a floating condition, opp. to *aground*; at sea, opp. to *in dock*, *ashore* OE.; buoyed up in the air 1825. **2.** In a state of overflow or submersion 1591. **3.** *fig.* Unembarrassed; having one's head above water 1538. **4.** Started 1559; in full swing 1604. **5.** In currency 1586; *esp.* in *Comm.* of negotiable instruments (*mod.*). **6.** Adrift 1714.

1. He commanded the force a. WELLINGTON. The quantity of wheat a. 1879. **2.** The main deck was a. MARRYAT. **5.** Various rumours were a. BRIGHT. To keep bills a. 1888.

Aflow·er, *adv.* and *a.* 1876. [A *prep.*[1] 11 + FLOWER *sb.*] Flowering.

Aflu·tter, *adv.* 1830. [A *prep.*[1] 11 + FLUTTER *sb.*] In a flutter.

Afoa·m, *adv.* 1849. [A *prep.*[1] 11 + FOAM *sb.*] In a state of foam.

Afoot (ăfu·t), *adv.* ME. [A *prep.*[1] + FOOT *sb.*; orig. in pl. *a* (*on*) *foten* = *on feet*, partly after ON. *á fótum.*] **1.** On foot, *i.e.* on one's own feet. **2.** Astir, on the move 1530; hence, in active existence or operation 1601.

1. He was mounted and I a. DICKENS. **2.** Mischeefe thou art a. *Jul. C.* III. ii. 265. *Comb.* **afoot-back** (after *a-horse-back*). GREENE.

Afore (ăfō^ə·ɹ). *dial.* and *Naut.* [OE. *onforan* (ME. *on-*, *aforen*), f. *on* prep. + *foran* adv. = before, in front, prop. dat. of *for*, used as adj. or sb.; cf. BEFORE, TOFORE. Later ME. *afore* is f. ON *prep.* + FORE *adv.* and *prep.*] **A.** *adv.* **1.** Of place: In front; in or into the forepart. **2.** Of time: Before ME. **B.** *prep.* **1.** Of place: Before OE. **2.** Of rank, etc.: In precedence of ME. **C.** *conj.* [*ellipt.*] Sooner than ME. Still used in comb. in **aforesaid** 1418.

Aforehand (ăfō^ə·ɹhænd), *adv. arch.* ME. [f. AFORE *prep.* + HAND *sb.*, after earlier *beforehand*, which survives.] In anticipation. † As *adj.* Prepared, provided for the future –1748.

Aforethought (ăfō^ə·ɹþǭt). 1581. [f. AFORE *adv.* + *thought*. App. tr. of Old Law-Fr. *prepense*; see PREPENSED *ppl. a.*] **A.** *ppl. a.* Thought before; premeditated. **B.** *sb. rare.* Premeditation 1851.

A. With malice a. COKE.

Aforetime (ăfō^ə·ɹtəim), *adv.* 1535. [f. AFORE *prep.* + TIME *sb.*, after earlier *beforetime.*] Before in time, formerly. Rarely *attrib.* as adj. or *absol.* as sb. Var. † **-times.**

† **Afo·reward,** *adv.* ME. [f. AFORE + -WARD.] First in rank; in front –1380.

‖ **A fortiori** (ē^i fō^əɹʃiō^ə·rəi). [L. (sc. *argumento*).] With stronger reason.

Afraid (ăfrē^i·d), *ppl. a.* [ME. *af(f)raied*, *-ayed*, pa. pple. of AFFRAY, superseding AFEARD. For the sp. *-aid* (XVI) cf. STAID.] As *pple.* Alarmed, frightened; hence as *adj.*, In a state of fear, moved by fear. (As adj. it never stands bef. a noun.) Const. *of*; *inf.*; *lest*, *that* (with subj.); *of* with gerund = *lest* with subj.

Back they recoild affraid MILT. A. of truth KINGSLEY. Willing to wound, and yet a. to strike POPE. I am a. that it is too true 1888. A. of being known as the author 1855.

Afreet, -it, -ite (æ·frīt). 1802. [Arab. *'ifrīt* 'a powerful demon', in the Koran 27:39.] A demon of Moslem mythology.

†‖ **Afre·sca,** *adv.* [It. *affresco.*] In fresco. EVELYN.

Afre·sh, *adv.* 1509. [A- *pref.* 3 + FRESH.] Anew, freshly.

Dead Henries wounds Open their congeal'd mouthes and bleed a. *Rich. III*, I. ii. 56.

African (æ·frikăn), *a.* and *sb.* 1564. [– L. *Africanus*, f. *Africa* + *-anus* -AN.] Belonging to or characteristic of, a native or inhabitant of, Africa. Hence **A·fricanism** 1641, **A·fricanize** *v.* 1853.

Africander (æ·frikændəɹ). 1834. [– S. Afr. Du. *Afrikaander*, f. next, after *Hollander* Dutchman.]. A white (esp. Dutch) native of S. Africa.

Afrikaans (æfrikā·ns). 1908. [S. Afr. Du., = Du. *Afrikaansch* African.] = TAAL.

†**Afro·nt,** *adv.* ME. [A *prep.*[1] 5 + FRONT *sb.*, corresp. to Fr. *de front.*] Face to face –1601; in front –1621; in a front, abreast –1621. Also as *prep.* –1622.

These foure came all a. and..thrust at me SHAKS.

Aft (ɑft), *adv.* 1628. [prob. alt. of earlier *abaft*, *baft*, after LG., Du. *achter* abaft, AFTER; no historical connection w. OE. *æftan* behind.] **1.** *Naut.* In or near the stern; towards the stern. † **2.** Of time: Earlier –1676.

1. *Fore and a.*: from stem to stern, lengthwise 1618.

After (ɑ·ftəɹ), *adv.* [OE. *æfter*, corresp. to OFris. *efter*, OS., OHG. *aftar*, ON. *aptr*, Goth. *aftra*; prob. compar. deriv. (see -THER) of Gmc. **af-*, cogn. w. Gr. ἀπό OF (I.E. **ap-*) or ὀπίσω behind (IE. **op-*).] **A.** *adv.* Behind in place or order OE.; later in time, next following OE.

Jill came tumbling a. *Nurs. Rhyme.* That happened in the week a. 1888.

B. *prep.* **1.** Moving in the rear of, behind OE.: with vbs., adjs., and sbs. of action: In pursuit of, in search of OE. **2.** Following in time, in succession to OE.; after the interval of OE.; subsequent to and later than OE.; subsequent to and in consequences of OE.; subsequent to and notwithstanding 1603. **3.** Next to in order or importance ME. **4.** According to, in harmony with OE.; in imitation of, like ME.; in a manner proportionate to (*arch.*) OE.; at (the rate of) 1530.

1. A. them, nay, before them if we can 2 *Hen. VI*, v. iii. 27. To *be after*: trying to get or do, or get into the company of. To *look*, *see after* (a thing gone, going, etc.): to attend to. To *call*, etc., *after*: to seek to get, etc., by calling. To enquire a. one's health SHERIDAN. Greedy a. power MACAULAY. **2.** A. me cometh a man that is preferred before me *John* 1: 30. Time a. time (*mod.*). A. two years' absence (*mod.*). Long a. dark 1832. I'll work a. hours DICKENS. A. his behaviour to his parents what could you expect? (*mod.*). The Roman occupation was, *after all*, very superficial FREEMAN. **3.** Codrus a. Phoebus sings the best DRYDEN. **4.** A. our lawe he ought to dye *John* 19: 7. A. his oracle Dr. Johnson GIBBON. And Corin called it a. his name cornewayle CAXTON. So to *draw*, *model*, *compose a.* Giue them a. the worke of their handes *Ps.* 28: 4. A. the Rate of 12*s.* per Gallon 1702.

C. *conj.* **1.** Of time: with *that* (*arch.*); or *simply* ME. † **2.** Of manner: According as; const. *that* or *as* –1587; or *simply* –1634.

1. A. I am rysen ageyne TINDALE *Matt.* 26: 32 [WYCLIF A. that I schal rise aȝen].

After (ɑ·ftəɹ), *a.* [OE. *æfter(r)a*, f. prec. (cf. OHG. *aftaro*); later the adv. in attrib. use; see next.] Of time. † **1.** The second (of two) –ME. **2.** Next OE.; later, *esp.* in *Comb.* 1594. **3.** Of place: Nearer the rear, further aft. Chiefly *Naut.* ME. Hence † **A·fterness,** the quality of being after.

After- *in comb.* is used in many relations, in some of which the use of the hyphen indicates no more than that the grammatical relation is not that of preposition and object.

a.-band, a later band or bond after a release; **-blow** = AFTERCLAP; **-born** *ppl. a.*, born after the father's death or last will; younger; † **-brain,** the posterior lobe, the cerebellum; **-cabin;** † **-cast,** a second throw (at dice), an experimental result; **-damp,** the choke-damp left in a mine after an explosion; **-eatage** = AFTERGRASS; † **-eye,** to look after; **-growth,** an AFTERMATH; growth afterwards; **-knowledge,** knowledge after the event; **-leech,** the hinder edge (of a sail); **-liver,** survivor; **-nose,** *Entom.*, a triangular piece below the antennæ and above the nasus; **-reckoning;** **-roll,** the roll of the waves after a storm; also *fig.*; **-sails,** all those on the after-masts, and on the stays between the main and mizen masts; **-shine** = AFTERGLOW; **-sum,** the purchase money paid after the deposit; **-taste,** a taste which comes after swallowing anything; also *fig.*; **-winter,** a renewal of winter; **-wise,** wise after the event; **-world,** future generation; **-wrist,** the metacarpus; **-yards,** *Naut.* the yards in the main and mizen masts.

Afterbirth (ɑ·ftəɹbə̄ɹþ). 1587. [Also †*afterburden*, perh. directly – G. *afterbürde* (Luther, *Deut.* 28: 57), also *aftergeburt*; cf. Icel. *eftirburðr*, OSw. *efterbörd*, Da. *efterbyrd.*] **1.** The secundine or placenta, which is expelled from the womb after the infant. Also *fig.* **2.** *Rom. Law.* Birth after a father's death or last will 1875. **3.** Late-born children 1871. Also † **A·fter-bu:rthen, -den** (in sense 1).

Afterclap (ɑ·ftəɹklæp). ME. An unexpected stroke after the recipient has ceased to be on his guard; a surprise happening after an affair is supposed to be at an end.

Fear of afterclaps H. MELVILLE.

† **A·fterco:mer.** ME. A successor; *pl.* posterity –1705.

After-course (ɑ·ftəɹkō^ə·ɹs). 1580. † **1.** A later course at dinner. **2.** Subsequent course. (Prop. two wds.) 1859.

Aftercrop (ɑ·ftəɹkrǫp). 1562. A second crop in one season. Hence **A·ftercrop** *v.*

† **A·fterdeal.** 1481. [Cf. G. *nachteil.*] A disadvantage –1634.

After-dinner (ɑ:ftəɹ-di·nəɹ). 1576. † **1.** *sb.* The time after dinner; the afternoon –1618. **2.** *attrib.* Occurring after dinner; *esp.* before leaving the table 1730.

1. Upon an a. RALEIGH. **2.** An a. anecdote 1826.

After-game (ɑ·ftəɹgē^i·m). 1631. A second game played to improve on the result of the first; *hence*, a new plan to meet a miscarriage.

Afterglow (ɑ·ftəɹglō^u). 1873. A glow that remains after the disappearance of any light, *esp.* that in the western sky after sunset; also *fig.*

After-grass (ɑ·ftəɹgrɑs). 1681. The grass which grows after the first crop or after harvest.

After-guard (ɑ·ftəɹgāɹd). 1826. *Naut.* The men who are stationed on the quarter-deck and poop, to work the after-sails.

† **A·fterhand,** *adv.* ME. [orig. *after the hand.*] Afterwards –1658.

After-image (ɑ·ftər,i:mėdʒ). 1879. The impression of a vivid sensation, retained after the external cause is withdrawn.

Afterings (ɑ·ftəriŋz), *sb. pl.* 1796. [f. AFTER *adv.* + -ING[1]; cf. *innings.*] The milk drawn last from a cow. Still *dial.*

A·fter-life. **1.** A future life 1615. **2.** The later period of one's life 1817.

Aftermath (ɑ·ftərmaþ). Also **-mowth.** 1523. [f. AFTER- + MATH. Cf. LATTERMATH.] Second or later mowing; the crop of grass which springs up after the mowing in early summer. Also *attrib.* and *fig.*

fig. The a. of the great rebellion COLERIDGE.

Aftermost (ɑ·ftəɹməst, -mo^ust), *a. superl.* [In sense 1, OE. *æftemest* (corresp. to Goth. *aftumists* last); in sense 2, independent f. AFTER + -MOST.] † **1.** Hindmost; last in time –ME. **2.** *Naut.* Furthest aft 1773.

Afternoon (ɑːftəɹnū·n). ME. [Cf. L. *post meridiem*.] The time from mid-day to evening. Also *fig.* and *attrib.*
fig. In the a. of her best dayes *Rich. III*, III. vii. 186. *attrib.* A. tea 1879.

After-pain (ɑ·ftəɹpēⁱːn). 1556. A pain which follows later; *esp.* (in *pl.*) the pains that follow child-birth. Also *fig.*

A·fterpiece. 1806. **1.** A farce or short piece after the play. Also *fig.* **2.** *Naut.* The heel of a rudder.

† **A·fterspring.** 1583. **1.** Posterity –1587. **2.** A second spring –1670. Also *fig.*

A:fter-su·pper. 1590. The time between supper and bed-time. *Obs.* exc. *attrib.*

Afterthought (ɑ·ftəɹþǭt). 1661. **1.** A subsequent thought. **2.** Reflection after the act; hence, a later explanation or evasion 1684.

Afterward (ɑ·ftəɹwəɹd), *adv.* [Late OE. *æfterwearde* (see AFTER-, -WARD).] † **1.** Behind –ME.; *Naut.* afterward –1618. **2.** Subsequently ME. † **3.** Of order: next –1581.

A·fterwards, *adv.* ME. [f. prec. + *-es, -s*; see -WARDS.] At a later time.
In the a. metropolitan city NEWMAN.

After-wit (ɑ·ftəɹwiːt). *arch.* 1509. † **1.** Later knowledge –1680. **2.** † Second thought –1607; *esp.* wisdom after the event 1579.
2. A. is everybody's wit 1736. Hence **A·fter-wi:tted** *a.* wise when too late.

A·fterwo:rt. 1725. The second run of beer.

A·ftward, *adv.* [f. AFT *adv.* + -WARD.] Towards the stern.

Ag-, *pref.* = L. *ad-* bef. *g*, OFr. *a-*, refash. later after L., exc. in *agree*. Occ. for *a-* not = L. *ad-*.

‖ **Aga, agha** (ăgā·, æ·gă). 1600. [– Turk. *ağa* master, lord.] A chief officer, military or civil, in the Ottoman empire; also, a title of distinction.

† **Aga·d,** *int.* = EGAD, q.v.

Agadic (ăgæ·dik), *a.* 1878. [f. *Agada*, latinized form of HAGGADA, + -IC.] Of or pertaining to the Haggada, legendary (Rabbinic).

Again (ăge·n, ăgēⁱ·n). [WS. *ongēan, ongēn*, later *agēn*, Anglian *ongægn, ongegn*, ME. *aȝen, ayen* and *aȝain, aȝein*; corresp. to OS. *angegin*, OHG. *ingagan, ingegin(i)* (G. *entgegen*, opposite), ON. *í gegn* against. A Gmc. phr. f. ON or IN + **ȝaȝan-*, **ȝaȝin-* direct, straight. ME. forms in *aȝ-, ay-* were superseded XVI by *ag-* from Scand.] **A.** *adv.* † **1.** Back –1480. **2.** In return, in reply (*arch.*) ME. **3.** Back into a former position OE.; anew, once more ME. **4.** Once repeated 1593. **5.** Anywhere besides (*arch.*) 1555. **6.** On the other hand; besides 1533.
1. Turn a. Whittington (*arch.*). *To and a.*: to and fro. **2.** I maruell why I answer'd not againe *A.Y.L.* III. v. 132. To *ring, echo*, etc., *a.*; to *creak, crack, ache, shine, gleam*, etc., *a.* **3.** Here we are a. (*mod.*). Not look upon his like a. *Haml.* I. ii. 188. **Now and again**: now and then. Also † *ever and a.* **4.** Lent shall bee as long againe as it is 2 *Hen. VI*, IV. iii. 7. **5.** There is not, in the world a. 1626. **6.** But now a., see what succeeds RICHARDSON.
†**B.** *prep.* = AGAINST I. 1, II. 1, 2, III. 2, 3, IV, V. † **C.** *conj.* Against the time that –1632.

† **Agai·n-** [the *adv.*], was formerly used in many combs., all now obs. In meaning it answered to L. *re-*, esp. in the senses of opposition, reciprocal action, and repetition.
† **a.-buy** *v.*, to redeem; hence † **-buyer**; †**-come** *v.*, to encounter; †**-rise** *v.*, to rebel; †**-say** *v.*, to say nay; to speak against; to reverse; hence †**-say** *sb.*, objection, †**-sayer**; **-stand** *v.*, to resist; hence †**-stander**; †**-turn** *v.*, to return.

Against (ăge·nst, ăgēⁱ·nst). [ME. *aȝaines*, etc., f. *aȝein*, etc. + *-es*, n. gen. sing. ending used advb.; see AGAIN. For parasitic *-t* cf. *amidst, amongst*.] **A.** *prep.* **I.** Of position. **1.** Facing, in full view of (now usu. *over against*) ME.; † with (L. *apud*) –1520; *fig.* in regard to ME. **2.** Near, adjoining. Still *dial.* 1531.
1. Sat backwards over a. me 1741. 'Gainst the fire SHAKS. Ageynste the Lorde ys mercy 1520. Their rights as a. each other (*mod.*).

II. Of motion. † **1.** Towards –1634. **2.** Toward and into contact with ME; hence, supported by 1591; having as background 1805.
2. To kyke aȝens the pricke WYCLIF. *To run a.*: to meet accidentally. Leane thine aged back a. mine Arme 1 *Hen. VI*, II. v. 43.

III. Of motion or action in opposition to. **1.** Counter to ME. **2.** Not in conformity with ME. **3.** Towards with hostile intent (*arch.*) ME.; in active opposition to OE.; in resistance to OE.
1. To swimme a. the Tyde 3 *Hen. VI*, I. iv. 20. *A. the hair* (Fr. *à contrepoil*), *a. the grain*: opposed to the natural bent. **2.** A. my general notions BURKE. **3.** His hand will be a. euery man *Gen.* 16:12. So *to fight, speak, act a., a declaration, law, protest a.*, and the like. My lectures a. pride GOLDSM. So *to be a., to run, play*, etc., *a.* Proof a. their enmitie *Rom. & Jul.* II. ii. 73. Caution a. pickpockets (*mod.*).

IV. Of mutual opposition or relation. In exchange for ME.; in the opposite scale 1531.
To set off a.: to enter on the *opposite* side to a previous entry.

V. Of time. † Drawing towards –1634; *esp.* in preparation for ME.
A sermon to write a. the Assizes WESLEY.
B. *conj.* By the time that, before (*arch.*) ME.
A. father comes home DICKENS.
C. *adv. rare.* = AGAIN *adv.*

† **Agai·nward,** *adv.* ME. [f. AGAIN *adv.* + WARD; cf. *backward, outward*.] Back again –1634; in reply –1520; once more –1541; *vice versa* –1579; on the other hand –1534.

Agalactous (ægălæ·ktəs), *a.* 1879. [f. Gr. ἀγάλακτος (f. ἀ- A- *pref.* 14 + γαλακτ- milk) + -OUS; cf. Fr. *agalacte*.] *Med.* Having no milk to suckle with.

Agalaxy (æ·gălæksi). 1731. [– Gr. ἀγαλαξία for -τία; see prec., -Y³.] *Med.* A failure of milk in a mother after childbirth. var. ‖ **Agala·ctia.**

† **Aga·lloch.** 1633. [– late L. *agallochum*, – Gr. ἀγάλλοχον.] The fragrant resinous heartwood of *Aquilaria*; also called *agila-, aloes-, eagle-wood*. Lindley.

Agalmatolite (ægælmæ·tŏləit). 1832. [f. Gr. ἄγαλμα, -ματ- statue, image + -LITE.] *Min. prop.* The 'Figurestone' or Pagodite; also other soft minerals, which are easily carved.

Agama (æ·gămă). 1817. [Carib.] *Zool.* A genus of lizards; *pop.* one British West Indian species. Hence **Aga·mian** *a.* and *sb.* name of a sub-family of the iguanians (including the genus *A.*). **A·gamoid** *a.* resembling an agama.

† **A-ga·me,** *adv.* [f. A *prep.*¹ 9 + GAME *sb.*] In sport. CHAUCER.

Agami (æ·gămī) 1833. [– Fr. *agami* (Barrère 1741), native name in Guiana.] The Trumpeter, a bird allied to the Crane.

Agamic (agæ·mik), *a.* 1850. [f. Gr. ἄγαμος unmarried + -IC; cf. AGAMOUS *a.*] *Biol.* Characterized by the absence of sexual action; † *Bot.* = CRYPTOGAMIC. Hence **Aga·mically** *adv.*

† **A·gamist.** [f. late L. *agamus* – Gr. ἄγαμος (prec.) + -IST.] A professed celibate –1656.

Agamogenesis (æːgămoˌdʒe·nėsis). 1864. [f. Gr. ἄγαμος (see prec.) + γένεσις generation.] *Biol.* Generation without sexual union (as by simple division, or by buds); asexual reproduction. Hence **A:gamogene·tic** *a.* relating to a.; generating or generated without sexual union. **A:gamogene·tically** *adv.*

Agamous (æ·gaməs), *a.* 1847. [f. Gr. ἄγαμος unmarried (f. ἀ- A- *pref.* 14 + γάμος marriage) + -OUS.] *Biol.* Asexual.

Agamy (æ·gămi). 1796. [– Gr. ἀγαμία celibacy; see -Y³.] Absence or non-recognition of the marriage relation.

Aganglionic (ăgæːŋgliˌǫ·nik), *a.* 1836. [f. A- *pref.* 14.] *Phys.* Without ganglia.

‖ **Aganippe.** 1630. A fountain on Mount Helicon sacred to the Muses; *fig.* poetic power or method.

Agape (ăgēⁱ·p), *adv.* 1667. [f. A- *pref.* 11 + GAPE *sb.*] On the gape; *fig.* in wondering expectation.
A rabbit mouth that is ever a. TENNYSON.

‖ **Agape** (æ·găpi). Pl. **agapæ.** 1696. [Gr. ἀγάπη brotherly love.] A 'love-feast' held by the early Christians in connection with the Lord's Supper.

A·gaphite. 1837. [Named after *Agaphi*, a naturalist; see -ITE¹ 2 b.] A kind of turquoise.

Agar-agar (ēⁱ·garˌēⁱ·gaɹ). 1820. [Malay.] An E. Indian seaweed from which a gelatinous substance is extracted for use in soup and for a culture medium. Also **a·gar.**

Agaric (æ·gărik, ăgæ·rik). 1533. [– L. *agaricum* (Pliny) – Gr. ἀγαρικόν tree fungus. Cf. Fr. *agaric* (XV).] **1.** *Herb.* and *Pharm.* One of various species of *Polyporus*, esp. *P. officinalis*, the 'Female Agarick', a cathartic, and *P. igniarius*, the 'Male Agarick', used as tinder, etc. *arch.* **2.** *Bot.* A mushroom; *prop.* one of the genus *Agaricus* 1777. **3.** = *A.-mineral.*
2. And agarics and fungi SHELLEY. A foulflesh'd a. TENNYSON. *Comb.* **a.-mineral,** a light, spongy variety of carbonate of lime, called also Rock-milk, allied to stalactites.

Aga·sp, *adv.* 1800. [A *prep.*¹ 11 + GASP *sb.*] Gasping.

† **Aga·st, agha·st,** *v.* [ME. *agast*, short form of pa. pple. of † *agaste* frighten; see GAST *v.* The sp. with *gh-* (XVIII) is due to assoc. w. GHASTLY *a.*] Now only in pa. pple. *agast*, erron. AGHAST.] To frighten; to take fright –1596. Hence † **Aga·sted** *ppl. a.*

Agastric (ăgæ·strik), *a.* 1836. [f. Gr. ἀ- A- *pref.* 14 + γαστήρ, -τρ- belly + -IC.] *Zool.* Having no distinct alimentary canal.

Agate (æ·gět), *sb.* 1570. [– (O)Fr. *agate*, also †*agathe* – L. *achates* – Gr. ἀχάτης. See ACHATE *sb.*¹] **1.** A precious stone; one of the semi-pellucid variegated chalcedonies, having the colours arranged in stripes or bands, or blended in clouds, and classed accordingly, as *moss a., ribbon a.*, etc. † **2.** *fig.* A diminutive person, from the small figures cut in agates for seals –1599. **3.** An instrument used by gold-wire-drawers for burnishing 1751. **4.** *Typog.* The U.S. name of the type called in Eng. *ruby* 1871.
2. If low, an agot very vildlie cut *M. Ado* III. i. 65. Also 2 *Hen. IV*, I. ii. 19. *Comb.* **a.-shell,** one of the tropical genus *Achatina*. Hence **A·gated** *ppl. a.* marked like an a. **Agati·ferous** *a.* producing, or rich in, agates. **Aga·tiform** *a.* a.-like; var. **A·gatine.** **A·gatized** *ppl. a.* converted into a. **A·gaty** *a.* of the nature of a.

Agate (ăgēⁱ·t), *adv.* 1554. [A *prep.*¹ 11 + GATE *sb.*²] On the way; a-going.

Agathism (æ·găþiz'm). *rare.* 1830. [f. Gr. ἀγαθός good + -ISM.] The doctrine that all things tend towards good; opp. to *optimism*. Hence **A·gathist.**

A:gatho-, comb. f. Gr. ἀγαθός good.
a.-demon [Gr. δαίμων], a good genius; whence **-demonic** *a.*; **-ka:kolo·gical** *a.* composed of good and evil (*nonce-wd.*).

‖ **Agave** (ăgēⁱ·vi). 1830. [– L. *Agave* – Gr, Ἀγαύη, prop. fem. of ἀγαυός illustrious.] *Bot.* A genus of plants (N.O. *Amaryllidaceæ*), including the American Aloe.

Agaze (ăgēⁱ·z), *adv.* 1430. [f. A *prep.*¹ 11 + GAZE *v.*] Gazing.

† **Aga·zed, -sed,** *ppl. a.* ME. [perh var. of *agast* AGHAST, affected by prec.] Affrighted –1600.

Age (ēⁱdʒ), *sb.* ME. [– OFr. *age*, earlier *aëge, eäge* (mod. *âge*):– Gallo-Rom. **ætaticum*, f. L. *ætas, ætat-*, f. *ævum* age of time; see ÆON.] **I.** A period of existence. **1.** The time that anything has lived or existed ME. **2.** The whole or ordinary duration of life 1535. **3.** Such duration as ordinarily brings maturity ME.; any length of life which qualifies for anything ME. **4.** A naturally distinct period or stage of life; *esp.* old age ME.; hence, the effects of age: Senility, maturity 1460.
1. Of the a. of twelue yeeres *Mark* 5:42. *The Moon's age*: the time since the occurrence of the new moon. Of what a. is the day? MASSINGER. **2.** The a. of man has greatly diminished 1853. **3.** *Full age*, in Eng. Law, 21 years; *age of discretion*, 14 years. To come of a. (*mod.*). No limitation of a. (*mod.*). **4.** One man in his time playes many parts, His Acts being seuen ages *A.Y.L.* II. vii. 143. A. with his stealing steps *Haml.* V. i. 79. When the a. is in, the wit is out *Much Ado* III. v. 37. This wine lacks a. 1888.

II. A period of time. **1.** The generation to which any one belongs ME. **2.** A generation 1535. **3.** A long but indefinite period ME.; often *loosely* in exaggeration 1590; also, a century. (Cf. Fr. *siècle*.) 1594. **4.** *Hist.* A great period of human history marked by certain characters, real or mythical ME. **5.** *Geol.* A great period or stage of the physical history of the Earth; an æon 1855.

1. The follies of the a. POPE. 3. Thro' the ages one increasing purpose runs TENNYSON. It is an a. since we met 1813. 4. The Golden, the Patriarchal, the Bronze A., the A. of the Reformation, the Middle Ages, the Prehistoric A. 5. The Ice A. or Glacial Epoch KINGSLEY. Hence **Age** *v.* to grow, or make, old. **A·geing, a·ging** *ppl. a.* **A·geless** *a.* without old a. or limits of duration. **A·ge-long** *a.* long as an a. † **A·gemate,** a coeval.

-age, *suffix* of abstr. nouns, formed from names of things, or persons, or vbs. of action, as *language, baronage, wreckage,* etc. [OFr. *-age* (whence med.L. *-agium*):– late L. *-aticum,* neut. of adjs. in *-aticus.*] That which belongs or is functionally related to.

Aged (ēⁱ·dʒĕd; sense 3 ēⁱdʒd), *ppl.a.* 1440. [f. the vb. + -ED¹, after Fr. *âgé.*] **1.** Old. Also *fig.* **2.** Belonging to old age 1588. **3.** Of or at the age of. 1637.

1. An a. man FREEMAN. Ag'd in vertue 1611. 2. A. wrinkles, cramps SHAKS. Hence **A·gedly** *adv.* ? *Obs.* **A·gedness,** the quality of being old, or of a stated age.

Agelast (æ·dʒĭlæst). 1877. [– Gr. ἀγέλαστος not laughing, f. ἀ- A- *pref.* 14 + γελαστός laughable, f. γελᾶν to laugh.] One who does not laugh.

Agen, *poet.* = southern pronunc. of AGAIN.

Agency (ēⁱ·dʒĕnsi). 1658. [– med.L. *agentia*; see AGENT, -CY.] **1.** The faculty of an agent, or of acting; action 1658; intermediation 1674. **2.** Action personified 1784. **3.** *Comm.* The office or function of an agent or factor 1745. **4.** An establishment where business is done for another 1861.

1. The moral a. of the Supreme Being 1762. The A. of the Romish Factors with the King of Spain 1674. 2. An invisible a. arrested his progress BECKFORD. 3. The contract of a. 1875. 4. Reuter's A. 1882.

† **Age·nd,** now **agendum.** Pl. † **agends, agenda.** 1629. [– L. *agendum,* sb. use of n. gerundive of *agere* (see AGENT). Only the pl. *agenda* is in ordinary use.] **1.** *pl.* Things to be done; opp. to matters of belief 1753. † **2.** *Eccl.* Matters of ritual –1775. **3.** The items of business to be done at a meeting 1882.

Agenesis (ădʒe·nĕsis). 1853. [f. Gr. ἀ- A- *pref.* 14 + γένεσις birth.] *Phys.* Imperfect development of the body or any part of it. var. **Agenesia.** Hence **Agene·sic** *a.*

Agennesis (ædʒĕnī·sis). 1847. [f. Gk. ἀ- A- *pref.* 14 + γέννησις engendering.] Male sterility. var. **Agennesia.**

Agent (ēⁱ·dʒĕnt). 1579. [– *agent-,* pres. ppl. stem of L. *agere* act, do.] **A.** *adj.* Acting; opp. to *patient* (*arch.*) 1620.

B. *sb.* **1.** One who or that which acts; opp. to the *patient,* or the *instrument* 1600. **2.** The efficient cause 1656; hence, any natural force, or substance, which produces phenomena, as *electricity, actinism, chloroform,* etc. 1756. **3.** One who does the *actual work,* as opp. to the employer; a deputy, steward, emissary, etc. 1593. **4.** Of things: The material cause or instrument 1579.

3. **A.-general** *spec.* the representative, under a high commissioner for the Dominion, of each of the States of Australia and of certain Provinces of Canada. 4. *Two Gent.* I. iii. 46. 5. Comb. *a. -noun,* etc. Hence † **A·gent** *v.* to act as a. in. **A·gentess.** WALPOLE. **Agential** (eⁱdʒe·nʃăl) *a.* of or pertaining to an a., or agency. **A·gentship** = AGENCY 3.

Ager, obs. f. EAGER *sb.,* tide, bore.

‖ **Agera·sia.** 1706. [Gr. ἀγηρασία eternal youth, f. ἀ- A- *pref.* 14 + γῆρας old age; see -Y³.] The quality of not growing old.

Ageratum (ădʒe·rătŏm, *pop.* ædʒərēⁱ·tŏm). 1567. [mod. L. – L. *ageraton* – Gr. ἀγήρατον, prop. n. of ἀγήρατος not growing old, f. ἀ- A- *pref.* 14 + γῆρας, -ατ- old age.] † **1.** *Herb.* An 'everlasting' flower, known to the ancients. **2.** *Bot.* A genus of plants (N.O. *Compositæ,* Div. *Eupatoriæ*) 1866.

† **Age·t,** *v.* OE. [f. A- *pref.* 1 + GET *v.*] To seize –1490.

† **Age·te(n, aȝe·te(n,** *v.* OE. [f. A- *pref.* 1 + OE. *ġēotan* pour, corresp. to OS. *agiotan,* OHG. *argiozan,* Goth. *usgiutan.*] To pour out, shed –ME.

‖ **Ageu·stia.** 1853. [Gr. ἀγευστία, f. ἄγευστος not tasting; see -Y³.] *Med.* Loss of the sense of taste.

† **Aggela·tion.** *rare.* 1681. [– med.L. *aggelatio* (*ag-* in Du. Cange) frost, freezing, f. L. *ad* AG- + *gelatio,* f. *gelare* freeze. See -ATION.] A freezing to.

† **Agge·nerate,** *v.* 1660. [– *aggenerat-,* pa. ppl. stem of late L. *aggenerare,* beget in addition, f. L. *ad* AG- + *generare*; see -ATE³.] To beget as an addition. Hence † **Aggenera·tion.**

‖ **Agger** (æ·dʒəɹ). ME. [L.] A mound; *esp.* in *Rom. Antiq.* the rampart of a camp.

Aggerate (æ·dʒĕreⁱt), *v. rare.* 1553. [– *aggerat-,* pa. ppl. stem of L. *aggerare* to heap up, f. *agger* heap; see -ATE³.] To heap up. *lit.* and *fig.*

Aggeration (ædʒĕrēⁱ·ʃən). 1692. [– L. *aggeratio,* f. *aggerat-*; see prec., -ION.] A heaping up; in *Archæol.* the supposed raising of a mound, as an inclined plane for the erection of standing stones, etc., as at Stonehenge.

† **Agge·st,** *v.* 1655. [– *aggest-,* pa. ppl. stem of L. *aggerere* carry to, heap up, f. *ad* AG- + *gerere* carry.] To heap up. Hence † **Agge·stion,** accumulation.

Agglomerate (ăglǫ·mĕreⁱt), *v.* 1684. [– *agglomerat-,* pa. ppl. stem of L. *agglomerare* add or join to, f. *ad* AG- + *glomerare* wind into a ball, f. *glomus* clew, ball; see -ATE³. Cf. Fr. *agglomérer.*] † **1.** To wind or roll into a ball. **2.** To gather together in a rounded mass; to heap together mechanically 1684. **3.** *intr.* To collect in a mass. *lit.* and *fig.* 1730.

2. Working men..agglomerated..in great towns 1878. 3. The hard agglomerating salts THOMSON. Hence **Agglo·merated** *ppl. a.* gathered into a ball; heaped loosely together. **Agglo·merating** *ppl. a.* uniting into a hard mass. **Agglo·merative** *a.*

Agglomerate (ăglǫ·mĕrĕt). 1828. [f. as prec.; see -ATE¹, ².] **A.** *adj.* Gathered into a ball or cluster, or (*Bot.*) a rounded head of flowers.

B. *sb.* **1.** A collection of things rudely thrown together 1831. **2.** *Geol.* A mass of volcanic or eruptive fragments, united by heat; opp. to a *conglomerate* 1830.

Agglutinant (ăglⁱū·tinănt). 1684. [– *agglutinant-,* pres. ppl. stem of L. *agglutinare*; see next, -ANT¹. Perh. partly through Fr. *agglutinant.*] **A.** *adj.* Gluing; uniting closely.

B. *sb.* **1.** Any sticky substance which causes bodies to adhere together 1752. † **2.** *Med.* A medicine supposed to adhere to and supply the waste of tissue –1751.

Agglutinate (ăglⁱū·tinĕt), *ppl. a.* 1541. [– L. *agglutinatus,* pa. pple. of *agglutinare* fasten to with glue, f. *gluten* glue; see -ATE². Cf. Fr. *agglutiné.*] **1.** United as with glue; glued together. **2.** *Philol.* Consisting of root words combined by AGGLUTINATION (sense 2) 1850.

Agglutinate (ăglⁱū·tineⁱt), *v.* 1586. [– *agglutinat-,* pa. ppl. stem of L. *agglutinare*; see prec., -ATE.³ Cf. Fr. *agglutiner.*] **1.** To unite as with glue; to cement. **2.** *Phys.* To cause to adhere 1620. **3.** To compound simple words 1830. **4.** *trans.* and *intr.* To turn into glue 1869. Hence **Agglu·tinated** *ppl. a.* cemented together. **Agglu·tinating** *ppl. a.* gluing together; *Philol.* (see AGGLUTINATION 2).

Agglutination (ăglⁱū:tinēⁱ·ʃən). 1541. [– Fr. *agglutination* or f. prec.; see -ATION.] **1.** The action of agglutinating; the state of being agglutinated. **2.** *Philol.* The combining of simple or root words into compounds, without material change of form or loss of meaning 1830. **3.** That which is agglutinated; a mass or group 1615.

Agglutinative (ăglⁱū·tineⁱ:tiv, -ĕtiv), *a.* 1634. [– Fr. *agglutinatif, -ive* or f. as prec.; see -IVE.] **1.** Of or pertaining to agglutination; adhesive, cementing 1734. † **2.** *Med.* = AGGLUTINANT *sb.* 2. 1634. **3.** *Philol.* Characterized by agglutination 1652.

Un-tru-th-ful-ly preserve[s] an a. character 1875.

Ag(g)ra·ce, *v. arch.* [f. A- *pref.* 11 + GRACE *v.*] † **1.** To favour. SPENSER. **2.** To grace 1825. Hence † **Aggra·ce** *sb.* favour.

Aggrandize (æ·grăndaiz), *v.* 1634. [f. *agrandiss-,* lengthened stem (see -ISH²) of (O)Fr. *agrandir,* prob. – It. *aggrandire,* f. *ag* AG- + *grandire* – L. *grandire,* f. *grandis* GRAND; assim. to vbs. in -IZE.] **1.** To increase, magnify, or intensify; to increase the power, rank, or wealth of. Also *refl.* 1682. **2.** To make to appear greater; to exaggerate 1687; to exalt 1753. † **3.** *intr.* To become greater –1704.

1. To a. tortures 1634, distress 1748, the Russian Empire 1780, power RUSKIN. 2. To a. the man, and to lower the babies RICHARDSON. Hence **A·ggrandizable** *a.* **A·ggrandizer.**

Aggrandizement (ăgræ·ndizmĕnt). Also **-isement.** 1656. [– Fr. *agrandissement*; see prec., -MENT.] **1.** The action of aggrandizing; the state of being aggrandized. **2.** *lit.* Increase in size 1830. var. † **Aggrandiza·tion.**

† **Aggra·te,** *v.* 1591. [– It. † *aggratare* (Florio, mod. *aggradare*), f. *ag-* AG- + *grato* pleasing; cf. AGREE *v.*] **1.** To gratify. SPENSER. **2.** To thank –1633.

† **A·ggravable,** *a.* 1664. [f. L. *aggravare* (see next) + -BLE, after *separable,* etc.] Tending to aggravation. –1733.

† **A·ggravate,** *ppl. a.* 1471. [– L. *aggravatus,* pa. pple. of *aggravare* make heavier, f. *ad* AG- + *gravare,* f. *gravis* heavy; see -ATE².] **1.** Burdened. *lit.* and *fig.* –1510. **2.** *Eccl.* Under censure –1481. **3.** Made more serious, heightened –1733.

Aggravate (æ·grăveⁱt), *v.* 1530. [– *aggravat-,* pa. ppl. stem of L. *aggravare*; see prec., -ATE³; prob. through (O)Fr. *aggraver.*] † **1.** To put weight upon; to load, *esp.* with a 'gravamen' or charge –1678. **2.** † To add weight to –1698; *esp.* to make worse (things evil, offences, etc.) 1596. **3.** To exasperate; *fam.* to arouse the evil feelings of 1611. **4.** To add weight unduly; to exaggerate (cf. 2) 1555.

2. To introduce new mischiefs or to a...the old BURKE. Falsehood will..a. your guilt FIELDING. 3. Threats only served to a. people THACKERAY. 4. I have not..aggravated your sense or words MARVELL. Hence **A·ggrava:tingly** *adv.* **A·ggrava:tive** *a.* and *sb. rare,* tending to a. **A·ggrava:tor.**

Aggravation (ægrăvēⁱ·ʃən). 1481. [– Fr. *aggravation* – med.L. *aggravatio,* f. *aggravat-*; see prec., -ION.] † **1.** Oppression 1481. † **2.** Accusation –1675. **3.** *Eccl.* An ecclesiastical censure 1611. **4.** An increasing, or being increased, in gravity or seriousness 1615. † **5.** Exaggeration –1743. **6.** *fam.* The action of irritating. **7.** An extrinsic circumstance which increases the guilt or misery of a calamity or crime 1552.

5. Rhetorical aggravations BENTLEY. 7. An a. of their sin..that they commit it after Baptism BAXTER.

Aggregate (æ·grigĕt, -eⁱt), *ppl. a.* and *sb.* ME. [– L. *aggregatus,* pa. pple. of *aggregare* bring or add to a flock, f. *ad* AG- + *gregare,* f. *grex* flock; see -ATE².]

A. *ppl. a.* **1.** Collected into one; formed by the collection of many units into one, collective 1659. **2.** *spec.* **a.** *Law.* Composed of many individuals united into one association 1625; **b.** *Zool.* Consisting of distinct animals united into one organism 1835; **c.** *Bot.* Consisting of florets united within a common involucre; occ. of fruit, etc.: Collected into one mass 1693; **d.** *Geol.* Composed of distinct minerals, combined into one rock 1795; † **e.** *Gram.* Collective –1756. **3.** quasi-*sb.* [sc. *state,* etc.] 1777.

1. The a. amount of labour expended..is called the cost of production ROGERS. 2. a. Each chapter is a *corporation aggregate* 1862. 3. Man *in the aggregate* 1777.

B. *sb.* **1.** Sum total 1656; an assemblage of units 1650. **2.** *spec.* **a.** *Physics.* A mass of homogeneous particles, opp. to a *compound* 1692; **b.** *Geol.* A mass of minerals formed into one rock 1830; **c.** *Build.* Material added to lime to make concrete 1881.

1. A Multitude considered as one a. HOBBES. Hence **A·ggregately** *adv.* collectively.

Aggregate (æ·grigeⁱt), *v.* 1509. [– *aggregat-,* pa. ppl. stem of L. *aggregare*; see prec., -ATE³.] **1.** To gather together into one whole; to mass. Also *refl.* and *intr.* 1855. **2.** To unite *to* (occ. *with*) an association, etc.; to add as a member 1651. **3.** *ellipt.* [from sb.] To amount in the aggregate to (*colloq.*) 1865.

1. *intr.* We see the polar snows aggregating 1870. 2. That great..apostle, who..was aggregated to the other twelve TRENCH. Hence **A·ggregated,** orig. **A·ggregate** *ppl. a.* collected; collective; *Zool.* = AGGREGATE *a.* 2 b; † *Bot.* = AGGREGATE *a.* 2 c. **A·ggregator,** an adherent; a compiler.

Aggregation (ægrĭgē^{i}·ʃən). 1547. [f. prec. + -ION, or – Fr. †*aggrégation* (mod. *ag-*).] **1.** The action of aggregating; or of adding one particle *to* an amount; the state of being aggregated (see AGGREGATE *v.* 1, 2) 1564. **2.** *concr.* A whole, a mass, formed by aggregating items 1547.
1. Learning is..the a. of many mens sentences and acts 1564. His a. to the society of free-masons 1796. Their individuall imperfections.. are.. enlarged by their a. SIR T. BROWNE. **2.** The Church..an a. of Believers 1638.

Aggregative (æ·grĭge^{i}:tiv), *a.* 1644. [– Fr. *agrégatif, -ive*, f. as prec.; see -IVE.] **1.** Relating or tending to aggregation; collective. **2.** Gregarious 1837.
1. Fancy, or the a. and associative power COLERIDGE. **2.** His a. nature CARLYLE.

Aggregato- (ægrĭgē^{i}:to), combining form, = AGGREGATELY-.

† **Aggre·ge, -e·dge,** *v.* ME. [– OFr. *agregier* :– Gallo-Rom. **aggreviare*, f. *ad* AG- + Rom. **grevis* for L. *gravis* heavy. See AGGRIEVE *v.*] **1.** To make, or be, heavy, or dull –1393. **2.** To make, become, or cause to appear, graver –1696. **3.** To charge –1600.

† **Aggre·ss,** *sb.* 1678. [– late L. *aggressus* attack; see next.] Attack –1698.

Aggress (ăgre·s), *v.* 1575. [– Fr. †*aggresser* (OFr. *agresser*) – *aggress-*, pa. ppl. stem of L. *aggredi* attack, f. *ad* AG- + *gradi* walk, step.] † **1.** To approach. **2.** *intr.* To make an attack *on*; to begin the quarrel 1714; *trans.* to attack 1775.
2. The moral law says—Do not a. H. SPENCER. Hence **Aggre·ssing** *vbl. sb.* and *ppl. a.* commencing the attack.

Aggression (ăgre·ʃən). 1611. [– Fr. *agression* or L. *aggressio* attack, f. *aggress-*; see prec., -ION.] **1.** An unprovoked attack; the first attack in a quarrel; an assault. **2.** The practice of making such attacks 1704.
1. An a. upon their..liberties SCOTT. **2.** A war of a. 1799.

Aggressive (ăgre·siv), *a.* 1824. [f. as prec. + -IVE; cf. Fr. *agressif, -ive.*] **1.** Marked by aggression; offensive; also quasi- *sb.* [sc. *course*] 1845. **2.** Disposed to attack others 1840.
1. A. pleasantry SYD. SMITH. Hence **Aggre·ssively** *adv.* **Aggre·ssiveness.**

Aggressor (ăgre·səɹ). 1678. [– late L. *aggressor* attacker, f. as prec.; see -OR 2. Cf. Fr. *agresseur.*] He who makes an aggression; he who makes the first attack in or begins a quarrel.

Aggrie·vance (ăgrī·văns). ME. [– OFr. *agrevance*, f. *agrever* (see prec.); sp. assim. to next.] † **1.** That which burdens or oppresses –1664. **2.** Oppression 1587. † **3.** Aggravation –1506.

Aggrieve (ăgrī·v), *v.* [ME. *agreve* – OFr. *agrever* make heavier :– Gallo-Rom. **aggrevare*, f. *ad* AG- + **grevare* GRIEVE *v.* Cf. AGGREGE. Mod. sp. assim. to GRIEVE *v.*] **1.** To bear heavily upon; to grieve, oppress. ? *Obs.* exc. in *pass.* † **2.** *intr.* To grieve –1559. † **3.** To make more grave or serious –1590.
1. Both were alike aggrieved MACAULAY. Hence **Aggrie·ved** *ppl. a.* † hurt in spirit, now *grieved*; injuriously affected, having a grievance; † hurt; † aggravated. **Aggrie·vedness. Aggrie·vement,** the action of aggrieving.

Aggroup (ăgrū·p), *v.* 1695. [– Fr. *agrouper* – It. *aggroppare*, f. *groppo* GROUP.] To GROUP. *trans.* and *intr.* Hence **Aggrou·ped** *ppl. a.* **Aggrou·pment.**

‖ **Aggry, -ri.** 1819. [Origin unkn.] A name for the glass beads, resembling the adder bead of the Britons, found buried in Africa.

Agha, var. AGA.

Aghast (ăgɑ·st), *ppl. a.* ME. [Variant sp. (first in Sc., XV) of obs. *agast*; see AGAST, AGHAST *v.*] Affrighted; *esp.* in mod. use, Seized with the physical signs of terror, or amazement. Const. *at*, † *of*, *with.* ¶ *catachrestic.* Ghastly.
With..eyes agast MILT. A. with terror PRESCOTT. Hence **Agha·stness.**

† **A·gible,** *a.* 1613. [– OFr. *agible* (morally) licit – med.L. *agibilis* feasible, f. *agere* do; see -IBLE.] Practicable. Also used *subst.*

Agile (æ·dʒil, -əil), *a.* 1577. [– (O)Fr. *agile* – L. *agilis*, f. *agere* do; see -ILE.] **1.** Having the faculty of quick motion; nimble, ready. † **2.** Easily moved –1694.
1. His a. arme *Rom. & Jul.* III. i. 171. A robust and a. frame 1844. Hence **A·gilely** *adv.*

Agility (ădʒi·lĭti). ME. [– (O)Fr. *agilité* – L. *agilitas, -tat-*; see prec., -ITY.] The quality of being agile; readiness, nimbleness, activity, dexterity in motion.
The a. of their wit BACON, of youth COWPER.

Agio (æ·dʒio, ē^{i}·dʒi$_{i}$o). 1682. [– It. *aggio.*] **1.** The percentage charged for changing paper-money into cash, or an inferior for a more valuable currency; the excess value of one currency over another. **2.** *loosely,* Money-changing 1817.
2 Chabot, disfrocked Capuchin, skilful in a. CARLYLE.

Agiotage (æ·dʒiotėdʒ). 1829. [– Fr. *agiotage*, f. *agioter* speculate, f. *agio* – It. *aggio* (prec.); see -AGE.] Exchange business; *loosely,* speculation in stocks and shares.
Vanity and a. are to a Parisian the oxygen and hydrogen of life LANDOR.

Agist (ădʒi·st), *v.* ME. [– OFr. *agister* (mod. *agîter*), f. *a* AD- + *gister* to lodge :– Rom. **jacitare*, frequent. of *jacēre* lie.] **1.** To take in cattle to remain and feed, at a certain rate; *orig.* to admit for a stated time into a forest. **2.** *intr.* To remain and feed 1598. **3.** To charge (lands, etc.) with a rate 1691.
3. To a. lands to keep out the sea 1691. Hence **Agi·sted** *ppl. a.* taken in to feed; of pasture, etc.: Eaten by cattle taken in at a certain rate. **Agi·sting** *vbl. sb.* and *ppl. a.* taking in to pasture; feeding on hired pasture.

Agistment (ădʒi·stmĕnt). ME. [– OFr. *agistement*; see prec., -MENT.] **1.** The action of agisting. **2.** The herbage of a forest, or the right to it 1598. **3.** The rate or profit made upon agisting 1577. **4.** Any rate charged upon pasture lands; esp. *agistment tithe*, paid to the vicar or rector by the occupier 1527. vars. † **Agi·stage,** † **Agista·tion.**

Agistor, -er (ădʒi·stəɹ). ME. [– AFr. *agistour*, f. *agister*; see AGIST *v.*, -OUR.] One who agists. *spec.* An officer of the royal forests, who took charge of cattle agisted, and accounted for the proceeds. var. † **Agista·tor.**

† **A·gitable,** *a.* 1548. [– Fr., or L. *agitabilis*; see AGITATE *v.*, -BLE.] Capable of being agitated –1661.

† **A·gitant.** 1670. [– Fr. *agitant*, pres. pple. of *agiter* stir up; see next, -ANT.] One who stirs in, or plans, a course of action –1698.

Agitate (æ·dʒite^{i}t), *v.* 1586. [– *agitat-*, pa. ppl. stem of L. *agitare* move to and fro, frequent. of *agere* drive; see -ATE³.] † **1.** To actuate; = ACT *v.* 1. –1748. **2.** To move to and fro, shake 1599; *fig.* to perturb 1586. **3.** To perturb, excite, or stir up by appeals, etc. 1822. † **4.** To act as an agent –1654. **5.** To revolve in the mind; to contrive busily (*arch.*) 1648. **6.** To discuss, or push forward 1643. **7.** *absol.* To keep up an agitation (*for*) 1828.
1. Who..agitates the whole THOMSON. **2.** To a. a fan SCOTT, the souls of one's hearers HOR. SMITH. **3.** Each consul agitates the people in favour of his own views 1855. **4.** Viceroyes.. to a. his State-affaires WOOD. **5.** To a. desperate designs 1649. **6.** Before a repeal was..agitated BURKE. **7.** If you..expect success, *agitate, agitate, agitate* 1828. Hence **A·gitated** *ppl. a.* (in senses † 1, 2, 6). **A·gita:tedly** *adv.* **A·gitating** *vbl. sb.* the action of the vb.; *ppl. a.* acting as 'Agitators' (see AGITATOR 1); exciting. † **A·gitative** *a.* tending to a.

Agitation (ædʒitē^{i}·ʃən). 1569. [– Fr. *agitation* or L. *agitatio*, f. *agitat-*; see prec., -ION.] **1.** The action of agitating, or state of being agitated (see AGITATE *v.* † 1, 2, 3) 1573. **2.** Mental tossing to and fro; consideration 1569. † **3.** Busy scheming –1626. † **4.** *Eng. Hist.* The action of the 'Agitators' of 1647. **5.** The keeping of an object before public attention by appeals, etc.; public excitement 1828.
1. Motion or a. of the body 1711. The a. of the sea MAURY. America has been kept in continual a. In strange agitations and surprises DE FOE. **2.** The business in a. FULLER. **5.** The antislavery a. 1863. Hence **Agita·tional** *a.*

‖ **Agitato** (adʒitā·to), *a.* [It.] *Mus.* A direction: With agitation.

Agitator (æ·dʒite^{i}təɹ). 1647. [– L. *agitator*; see AGITATE *v.*, -OR 2.] † **1.** *Eng. Hist.* An agent (see AGITATE 4); a name for the delegates of the private soldiers of the Parliamentary Army 1647–9; in which use it varied with ADJUTATOR, a corruption infl. by *Adjutant*, and *Adjutor*. **2.** One who keeps up a political agitation 1780. **3.** An apparatus for shaking 1871.
1. Those elective tribunes called Agitators HALLAM. **2.** The great a. Daniel O'Connell 1853. Hence **A:gitato·rial** *a.*

Aglare (ăglē^{ə}·ɹ), *adv.* 1872. [A *prep.*¹ 11.] In a glare.

Agleam (ăglī·m), *adv.* 1870. [A *prep.*¹ 11.] Gleaming.

Aglet, ai- (æ·glĕt, ē^{i}-). ME. [– (O)Fr. *aiguillette*, dim. of *aiguille* needle :– late L. *acucula* pine-needle, dim. of *acus* needle.] **1.** The metal tag (or *point*) of a lace 1440. **2.** Hence, any metallic tag, pendent, or spangle worn as an ornament on the dress 1514; *esp.* an *aiguillette* 1843. **3.** Round white stay-laces 1882. **4.** *Herb.* A catkin of hazel, etc. 1578.
2. Golden aygulets, that glistred bright SPENSER *F. Q.* II. iii. 26. **4.** [The willow] glints his steely aglets in the sun LOWELL.
Comb. **a.-babie,** ? a doll decked with aglets *Tam. Shr.* I. ii. 80.

A-glimmer (ăgli·məɹ), *adv.* 1860. [A *prep.*¹ 11.] In or into a glimmering state.

Aglitter (ăgli·təɹ), *adv.* 1865. [A *prep.*¹ 11.] In a glitter.

Aglossal (ăglǫ·săl), *a.* 1870. [f. Gr. ἄγλωσσος (f. ἀ- A- *pref.* 14 + γλῶσσα tongue) + -AL¹.] *Zool.* Tongueless.

Aglow (ăglō^{u}·), *adv.* 1817. [A *prep.*¹ 11.] In a glow of warmth, colour, or excitement.
The Fletshorn was all a. TYNDALL. A. with delight W. BLACK.

Aglutition (æglĭuti·ʃən). 1847. [f. A- *pref.* 14 + DEGLUTITION by substitution of prefix.] *Path.* Inability to swallow.

† **Agly·, -ey·,** *adv. Sc.* [A *prep.*¹ 11 + GLEY.] Asquint, askew. BURNS.

Agminate (æ·gminė^{i}t), *a.* 1859. [– L. *agmen, -min-* troop + -ATE².] Grouped. var. **A·gminated.**

Agnail (æ·gnē^{i}l). [OE. *angnægl*, corresp. to OFris. *ongneil*, OHG. *ungnagel* (G. dial. *anneglen, einnegeln*), f. **ang-* compressed, tight, painful + *nægl* NAIL *sb.* in the sense of 'hard excrescence in the flesh'.] † **1.** A corn on the toe or foot –1783. **2.** A painful swelling about the toe- or finger-nail 1578. **3.** A 'hang-nail' 1847.

Agname (æ·gnē^{i}m). 1834. [f. AG- + NAME *sb.*, after L. AGNOMEN.] A name in addition to the name and surname; a 'to-name', a sobriquet.

Agnate (æ·gne^{i}t), *sb.* (*a.*) 1534. [– L. *agnatus*, f. *ad* AG- + *(*g*)*natus* born; cf. ADNATE *a.*] **1.** A descendant by male links from the same male ancestor. **2.** A descendant from a common male ancestor 1868. **3.** *adj.* Related by the father's side 1860; *fig.* akin 1782. Hence **Agna·tic** *a.* related on the father's side. **Agna·tically** *adv.* **Agna·tion,** descent from a common male ancestor through male links only; descent from a common male ancestor, opp. to *cognation*; kinship by descent.

Agnathous (æ·gnăþəs), *a.* 1879. [f. Gr. ἀ- A- *pref.* 14 + γνάθος jaw + -OUS.] *Phys.* Having no jaws.

Agnification (æ:gnifikē^{i}·ʃən). *rare.* 1863. [f. L. *agnus* lamb + -FICATION.] The representing (of persons) as lambs or sheep.

† **Agni·tion.** 1569. [– L. *agnitio*, f. *agnit-*, pa. ppl. stem of *agnoscere* acknowledge, f. *ad* AG- + *gnoscere* KNOW *v.*] Recognition, acknowledgement –1678.

Agnize (ægnəi·z), *v. arch.* 1535. [f. L. *agnoscere* (see prec.), after *cognize, recognize*; see -IZE.] **1.** To recognize (*arch.*) 1611; † to own *for, as*, etc. –1737. **2.** To recognize the existence of, confess (*arch.*) 1543.
2. I do a. A Naturall..Alacartie, I finde in hardnesse *Oth.* I. iii. 232.

Agnoiology (ægnoi$_{i}$ǫ·lŏdʒi). 1856. [f. Gr. ἄγνοια ignorance + -LOGY.] *Philos.* The philosophy of ignorance.

Agnoites, -etes (æ·gno$_{i}$əits, -īts). 1586. [– med.L. *agnoetæ* – Gr. ἀγνοηταί, f. ἀγνοεῖν be ignorant.] *Eccles.* A sect who held that Christ was ignorant of some things. Hence **A·gnoetism.**

‖ **Agnomen** (ægnō^{u}·men). 1753. [L., f. *ad* AG- + *(*g*)*nomen* name.] *Rom. Antiq.* A second cognomen or fourth name, occas. assumed by the Romans, as Publius Cornelius Scipio *Africanus*; *loosely*, a 'to-name'.

His a. of Bean, or white SCOTT. Hence **Agno·minal** *a. rare.* ? *Obs.* **Agno·minate** *v. rare*, to nickname. ? *Obs.*

Agnomination (ægnǫ:mineⁱ·ʃən). Also **adn-, ann-.** 1588. [In sense 2, – L. *agnominatio* paronomasia; in sense 1, f. †*agnominate* v., or late and med.L. *agnominare* give a surname to, f. AGNOMEN; see -TION.] **1.** The giving of an agnomen; the agnomen. *rare.* 1775. **2.** *Rhet.* Paronomasia 1588; alliteration 1595.

Agnostic (ægnǫ·stik), *sb.* and *a.* 1870. [f. A- *pref.* 14 + GNOSTIC.] One who holds that the existence of anything beyond material phenomena, e.g. of a First Cause, or of noumena, cannot be known; *adj.* pertaining to agnostics or agnosticism.

The word was suggested by Thomas Henry Huxley (1825–95): it has been taken to refer to the Unknown God (Ἀγνώστῳ Θεῷ) of Acts 17: 23.

Hence **Agno·stically** *adv.* **Agno·sticism,** the doctrine of agnostics.

‖ **A·gnus.** late ME. = AGNUS DEI.

‖ **Agnus Castus** (æ·gnǒs kæ·stǒs). ME. [L., – Gr. ἄγνος, the name of the tree, confused with ἁγνός, whence *castus.*] A tree (*Vitex agnus-castus*), called also Chaste-tree and Abraham's Balm.

‖ **Agnus Dei** (æ·gnǒs dī·əi, a·gnus dē·ī). ME. [L., 'Lamb of God'.] In *R.C. Ch.* **a.** A part of the mass beginning with the words *Agnus Dei*; also the music set to it. **b.** A figure of a lamb bearing a cross or flag 1629. **c.** A cake of wax stamped with such a figure and blessed by the Pope 1583.

† **Ago·**, *v.* OE. [f. A- *pref.* 1 + GO *v.*] To go forth –ME.; to go away –1674. Of time: To pass –1550.

Ago, agone (ăgōᵘ·, ăgǫ·n). ME. [pa. pple. of prec., used as adj. with noun of time.] **A.** *ppl. a.* Gone by; past. (Now *follows* its noun.) **B.** *adv.* in *Long ago*: in time long gone, long since 1366.

A. It was ago fif year ME. Drunke..an hour agone *Twel. N.* v. i. 204. **B.** So yore agoo CHAUCER. Dead and gone long ago 1833.

Agog (ăgǫ·g), *adv.* 1542. [prob. (w. substitution of A *prep.*[1]) repr. late OFr. *en gogues*, i.e. *en* in + pl. of *gogue* merriment, pleasantry, of unkn. origin.] In eager expectation; on the move, astir. Const. *inf.*, *on, upon, for, with, about.*

To sette on gogge 1575. A. on mischief TRAPP.

Agoing; see A *prep.*[1] 13 and GO *v.*

‖ **Agon** (æ·gōᵘn). Pl. (usu.) *agones* (ăgōᵘ·niz). 1660. [Gr. ἀγών contest.] *Gr. Antiq.* A public celebration of games, a contest for the prize at the games; also *fig.*

† **A·gonal, -el.** 1610. [perh. – med.L. **agonale* (= *liber agonalis*), ult. f. Chr. L. *agon* – Chr. Gr. ἀγών martyrdom.] A martyrology –1695.

Agone (ăgǫ·n), *ppl. a. arch.* and *poet.* = AGO.

Agonic (ăgǫ·nik), *a.* 1863. [f. Gr. ἄγωνος, ἀγώνιος (f. ἀ- A- *pref.* 14 + γωνία angle) + -IC.] Having or making no angle.

Agonic line: the irregular line passing through the two magnetic poles of the earth along which the magnetic needle points directly north or south; the line of no magnetic variation.

Agonistic (ægǒni·stik), *a.* 1648. [– late L. *agonisticus* – Gr. ἀγωνιστικός pertaining to a contestant (ἀγωνιστής); see AGON, -IST, -ISTIC.] Pertaining to the ancient Greek athletic contests; *hence*, athletic. **2.** *Rhet.* Polemic, combative 1660. **3.** Strained, aiming at effect 1843.

2. [Dr. Parr] consumed his power in a. displays DE QUINCEY. **3.** A. posture-makers CARLYLE. var. **Agoni·stical** *a.* (senses 1, 2); whence **Agoni·stically** *adv.* Hence **Agoni·stics** [pl. of adj. used *subst.*], the science of athletic combats.

Agonize (æ·gǒnəiz), *v.* 1583. [– Fr. *agoniser* or late L. *agonizare* (after Gr. ἀγωνίζεσθαι).] **1.** To torture 1583; *intr.* to suffer or writhe with agony, to be in the throes of death 1664. **2.** *intr.* To contend in the arena; to wrestle. Usu. *fig.* 1711. **3.** *fig.* To make convulsive efforts for effect 1865.

1. Where dying victims a. in pain FALCONER. **3.** To a. after originality 1865. Hence **A·gonized** *ppl. a.* subjected to or expressing agony. **A·goni:zedly** *adv.* **A·gonizer.** **A·gonizing** *vbl. sb.* the action of the vb.; *ppl. a.* torturing; suffering or writhing with agony; in the throes of death. **A·goni:zingly** *adv.*

Agonothet(e (ăgōᵘ·nǒþīt, -þet). 1626. [– Gr. ἀγωνοθέτης f. ἀγών contest + θέτης disposer.] A director of the public games of Greece. Hence **Ago:nothe·tic** *a.*

Agony (æ·gǒni). ME. [–(O)Fr. *agonie* or late L. *agonia* – Gr. ἀγωνία contest, mental struggle, f. ἀγών contest; see -Y[3].] **1.** Anguish of mind, sore distress, a paroxysm of grief ME.; hence, a paroxysm of pleasure 1725. **2.** *spec.* The mental anguish of Christ in Gethsemane ME. **3.** The throes or pangs of death. (Now rare *simply.*) 1549. **4.** Extreme bodily suffering with throes or writhing 1607. **5.** A struggle or contest 1677.

1. The *agony column*: the column in a newspaper containing distressful advertisements for missing relatives, etc. An a. of confusion and despair 'JUNIUS'. Agonies of delight POPE. **2.** As cried Christ ere his a. TENNYSON. **3.** Mirth cannot moue a soule in agonie *L.L.L.* v. ii. 867. **5.** The crisis, or essential a. of the Battle CARLYLE.

† **A-good,** *adv.* 1536. [f. A *prep.*[1] 11 + GOOD *a.*] Heartily –1671.

I made her weep a. *Two Gent.* IV. iv. 170.

‖ **Agora** (æ·gorǎ). 1820. [Gr. ἀγορά place of assembly, market-place.] *Gr. Antiq.* An assembly; hence, the place of assembly, *esp.* the market-place.

A:gorapho·bia. 1873. [mod.L., f. Gr. ἀγορά (prec.) + -PHOBIA.] *Path.* Morbid dislike of public places.

† **A-go·re-blood.** 1580. [A *prep.*[1]: see GORE *sb.*[1]] In or with clotted blood –1609.

Agouti, -ty (ăgū·ti). Also **aguti.** 1731. [– Fr. *agouti* or Sp. *aguti* – Tupi *aguti.*] A genus of rodents of the Guinea-pig family.

Agrace, obs. var. of AGGRACE *v.*

Agraffe (ăgræ·f). 1707. [– Fr. *agrafe*, f. *agrafer* to hook.] A hook, which fastens to a ring, used as a clasp.

‖ **Agraphia** (ăgræ·fiă). 1871. [mod.L., f. Gr. ἀ- A- *pref.* 14 + -γραφία writing; see -GRAPHY. Cf. Fr. *agraphie.*] *Med.* Inability to write (a form of brain-disease). Hence **Agra·phic** *a.* characterized by a.

Agrarian (ăgrēᵊ·riăn). 1618. [– L. *agrarius* (f. *ager, agr-* land) + -AN; see -ARY[1], -ARIAN.] **A.** *adj.* **1.** *Rom. Hist.* Relating to the land: epithet of a law (*Lex agraria*) for the division of conquered lands. **2.** Hence, Connected with landed property 17..; or with cultivated land, or its cultivation 1792. **3.** *Bot.* Growing wild in the fields 1843.

2. *Agrarian outrage*, one originating in discord between landlords and tenants. An a. war 1833. [Member] of the a. society 1792.

B. *sb.* **1.** An agrarian law 1656. **2.** One in favour of a redistribution of the land 1818.

2. An A. of three hours standing SOUTHEY.

Agrarianism (ăgrēᵊ·riăniz'm). 1808. [f. prec. + -ISM.] **1.** The principle of an equal division of lands. **2.** Political agitation or dissension arising from dissatisfaction with the existing tenure of the land 1861.

Agrarianize (ăgrēᵊ·riănəiz), *v.* 1846. [f. as prec. + -IZE.] **1.** To apportion land by an agrarian law. (Mod. Dicts.) **2.** To imbue with agrarianism 1883.

† **A·gre,** *v.* [– OFr. *agrier, aigrier* (cf. mod. Fr. *aigrir*) to torment, f. *aigre* sour; see EAGER *a.*] To vex. CAXTON.

† **Agrea·t,** *adv.* 1502. [A *prep.*[1] + GREAT *a.* Cf. Fr. *en gros.*] In gross; by the lot –1632.

† **Agree·**, *adv.* ME. only. [–(O)Fr. *à gré*, f. *à* to + *gré* liking; see GREE *sb.*[2]] Kindly, in good part. Phr. *To take a.*

Agree (ăgrī·), *v.* ME. [– (O)Fr. *agréer* :– Rom. * *aggratare*, f. L. *ad* AG- + *gratus* pleasing, agreeable; cf. GREE sb.[2]] † **1.** To please –1475; to accept favourably (Fr. *prendre à gré*) –1642. † **2.** To reconcile, arrange, conciliate (persons or things) –1785. Still of *accounts*, etc. To concert –1718. **3.** *refl.* and *intr.* To accede, consent *to*, grant. Const. *inf., to, absol.*, with *cl.* ME. **4.** *intr.* (? for *refl.*) To come into accord or harmony; *esp.* to come to terms about the price, etc., to contract. ? *Obs.* Const. *with.* 1489. Also *on, as to*, † *of, inf.*, or with *cl.* 1523. **5.** To be in harmony; to have no causes of variance. (Simply, or *together*; *with.*) 1548. To concur *with* a person *in, as to, that, with* an opinion 1494. **6.** Of things: to accord (*simply*, or *with*) 1494; to be consistent, correspond † *to, with* 1526. **7.** *Gram.* To be in concord; to take the same gender, number, case, or person 1530. **8.** † To be suitable *to* –1671; to do well *with* († of a person) –1697, (of food, climate, etc.) 1661.

1. The principles to be agreed by all BACON. **2.** To a. the balance, the items of an account (*mod.*), Whan..this..trewse was agreed LD. BERNERS. POPE *Il.* iv. 186. **3.** To a. to make a trial TYNDALL, to any couenants SHAKS., that to be law which [etc.] 1658, that a thing is so (*mod.*). **4.** Did a. for a cabinet to give my wife PEPYS. To a. on terms of reconciliation FREEMAN. To a. to differ 1810, that the matter should stand over (*mod.*). **5.** Two of a trade can ne'er a. GAY. One point in which they all a. 'JUNIUS'. **6.** At last..our jarring notes a. *Tam. Shr.* v. ii. 1. The beginning agreeth with the ende BARET. **8.** She wondered whether the climate would a. with her THACKERAY. Hence † **Agree·** *sb.* agreement. **Agree·r,** an adherent. **Agree·ing** *vbl. sb.* a coming into or being in harmony; *ppl. a.* † conformable *to*; concurring: † suiting; † = AGREEINGLY. **Agree·ingly** *adv.* in an agreeing manner. **Agree·ingness,** the quality of agreeing.

Agreeability (ăgrī:ăbi·lĭti). ME. [In ME., – OFr. *agreableté*, f. *agreable*; re-formed XVIII on AGREEABLE *a.*; see -ITY, -ILITY.] The quality of being agreeable, *esp.* in disposition.

All..a. (surely I may make words when at a loss) MISS BURNEY.

Agreeable (ăgrī·ăb'l), *a.*; also **agreable.** ME. [– (O)Fr. *agréable*, f. *agréer*; see AGREE *v.*, -ABLE.] **1.** To one's liking; pleasant. **2.** Having a liking (*to*); pleased, contented (*to do*). Now *colloq.* 1467. † **3.** Agreeing together –1601. **4.** † Suitable, fitting –1692; † consistent (*with*) –1783; conformable (*unto, to*) ME. **5.** *adv.* = AGREEABLY 1549. † **6.** *sb.* [sc. *person.*] *pl.* [sc. *things.*] Cf. *An incapable*; *eatables.* –1822.

1. An a. man—he who agrees with us DISRAELI. A. to my likynge CHAUCER. **2.** If Ann's a., I say ditto THACKERAY. **4.** Very a. with your general kindness BOSWELL. A. to all experience BAIN. **5.** The Earl entered, a. to the Prince's summons SCOTT. Hence **Agree·ableness,** the quality of being a., pleasingness. **Agree·ably** *adv.* in a way which is pleasing, suitable *to*, or in conformity *with*; † correspondingly; † similarly; † fittingly.

Agreed (ăgrī·d), *ppl. a.* ME. [f. the vb.] † **1.** Contented; made pleasing. ME. only. **2.** Brought into harmony; united in feeling or sentiment ME. **3.** At one in opinion 1613. **4.** Settled by common consent. Now *agreed on.* 1596. **5.** As a rejoinder: Consented to. = 'I agree to the proposal'. 1794.

2. Can two walke together except they be a. *Amos* 3: 3. **3.** Are you all a., Lords? SHAKS. **4.** It stands a. by all voices SHAKS. Your dowry 'greed on *Tam. Shr.* II. i. 272.

Agreement (ăgrī·mĕnt). ME. [– OFr. *agreement* agreement, favour (mod. *agrément*) f. *agreer*; see AGREE *v.*, -MENT.]

† **1.** The action of pleasing –1494; consenting –1483; setting at one, atoning –1577. **2.** A coming into accord; a mutual understanding; a covenant, or treaty 1400. **3.** *Law.* A contract duly executed and legally binding 1536. **4.** Accordance in sentiment, action, etc.; absence of dissension 1528; mutual conformity of things, affinity ME. **5.** *Gram.* Concord; see AGREE *v.* 7. **6.** Usu. *pl.* Agreeable qualities, etc. = Fr. *les agrémens.* 1692.

2. Were not of the a. with the King LD. BERNERS. **4.** You loued better..discorde then agremente 1548. What a. hath the Temple of God with idoles? 2 *Cor.* 6: 16. **6.** The charms and Agreements natural to women DRYDEN. var. † **Agree·-ance.**

† **Agre·st,** *a.* ME. [–(O)Fr. *agreste* – L. *agrestis* rustic, f. *ager, agr-* field.] Belonging to the country, wild; rustic, rude –1775. As *sb.* A rustic –1480. Hence † **Agre·sted** *ppl. a.* countrified.

Agrestial (ăgre·stiăl), *a.* 1607. [f. L. *agrestis* + -AL[1]; see prec.] Inhabiting the fields or open country; wild, uncouth; *spec.* in *Bot.* growing wild in cultivated land. vars. **Agre·stian** *a.* (and *sb.*) **Agre·stic** *a.*

Agricole (æ·grikōᵘl). 1656. [–(O)Fr. *agricole* – L. *agricola*, f. *ager, agr-* field + *-cola* inhabitant, cultivator.] A husbandman. vars. † **Agri·colist,** † **A·gricu:ltor.** Hence **Agri·colous** *a.*

Agriculture (æ·grikɒ:ltiŭr, -tʃəɹ). 1603. [– Fr. *agriculture* or L. *agricultura* tillage of the land; see prec., CULTURE.] The science and art of cultivating the soil; including the gathering in of the crops and the rearing of live stock; farming (in the widest sense). *spec.* Tillage (*rare*) 1862.

spec. Not fields for a., but pastures for cattle STANLEY. Hence **Agricu·ltural** *a.* of or pertaining to a. **Agricu·lturalist,** one engaged in a.; var. **Agricu·lturer** (*pop.*).

Agriculturist (ægrikɒ·ltiŭrist). 1760. [f. prec. + -IST.] At first, A student of the science of agriculture; later, A farmer.

The theoretical a., and the practical farmer 1814.

† **Agrie·f,** *adv.* ME. [A *prep.*[1] 13.] In grief. *To take a.*: to take it ill; opp. of *to take a-gree, in gree.*

Agrimony (æ·grimə̆ni). [ME. *egremoine* – (O)Fr. *aigremoine*; later *agrimony* – L. *agrimonia,* misreading for L. *argemonia* (Pliny, Celsus) – Gr. ἀργεμώνη.] **1.** A genus of plants (N.O. *Rosaceæ*); esp. *A. eupatoria.* **2.** A name of other plants; as Hemp A., *Eupatoria cannabina*; Water A., *Bidens*; Wild A., *Potentilla anserina* 1578.

Agrin (ăgri·n), *adv.* 1847. [A *prep.*[1] 13.] Grinning.

Agriologist (ægri,ǫ·lŏdʒist). 1882. [f. Gr. ἄγριος savage + -LOGY + -IST.] One versed in the history and customs of savages.

† **A·griot.** 1611. [– OFr. *agriote* (mod. *griotte*).] A sour kind of cherry.

† **Agri·se,** *v.* [OE. *āgrīsan,* ME. *agrise*; see A- *pref.* 1; cf. *grisly.*] **1.** To quake –1598; to abhor –1468; also *impers.* –1596; to horrify, or be horrified –1647.

‖ **Agrodolce** (a:grodo·ltʃe), *a.* [It., *agro* sour, *dolce* sweet] = AIGRE-DOUX.

‖ **A·grom.** 1753. [– Gujarati *agrūn.*] An Indian term for a rough and cracked condition of the tongue.

Agronomic (ægronǫ·mik), *a.* 1817. [– Fr. *agronomique,* f. *agronome* agriculturist + *-ique* -IC; cl. Gr. ἀγρονόμος meant overseer of country districts.] Of or pertaining to agronomy. vars. **Agrono·mial, Agrono·mical** *adjs.* Hence **Agrono·mics** [the adj. as sb. pl. or coll. sing.], the science of agronomy. **Agro·nomist, A·gronome** (*rare*), a student of agronomics.

Agronomy (ăgrǫ·nŏmi). 1814. [– Fr. *agronomie,* f. as prec. + *-ie* -Y[3]; see -NOMY.] The management of land, rural economy.

† **Agro·pe,** *v.* ME. only. [f. A- *pref.* 1.] To grope out, search.

‖ **Agrostis** (ăgrǫ·stis). 1753. [– late L. *agrostis* couch-grass – Gr. ἄγρωστις dog's-tooth grass, f. ἀγρός field.] *Bot.* A genus of grasses known as *Bent.*

Agrostography (ægrǫ̆stǫ·grăfi). 1753. [f. prec. + -GRAPHY.] Description of grasses. Hence **Agro:stogra·phic, -al** *a.*

Agrostology (ægrǫ̆stǫ·lŏdʒi). 1847. [f. as prec. + -LOGY.] That part of botany which treats of grasses. Hence **Agro:stolo·gic, -al** *a.* **Agrosto·logist,** one skilled in a.

†**Agro·te,** *v.* ME. only. [perh f. A- *pref.* 1 + *grot* a particle.] To cram. (Cf. GROUT.)

Aground (ăgrau·nd), *adv.* ME. [A *prep.*[1] 1.] † **1.** On or to the earth –1562. **2.** On or to the strand or shallow bottom of any water; opp. to *afloat* 1500. Also *fig.*

2. We run ourselves a. *Temp.* I. i. 4. Fast a. SOUTHEY.

‖ **Agrypnia** (ăgri·pniă). 1684. [late L. – Gr. ἀγρυπνία.] *Med.* Sleeplessness.

Agrypnode (ăgri·pnōᵘd), *a.* 1879. [– Gr. ἀγρυπνώδης making sleepless; see prec.] *Med.* Sleep-preventing.

Agrypnotic (ægripnǫ·tik), (*a.*) *sb.* 1879. [– Fr. *agrypnotique,* f. as prec., after *hypnotique* HYPNOTIC.] *Med.* Anything which produces wakefulness.

Ague (ēⁱ·giu). ME. [–(O)Fr. *ague*:– med. L. *acuta,* sb. use (sc. *febris* fever) of fem. of L. *acutus* ACUTE *a.*] † **1.** An acute fever –1611. **2.** *esp.* A malarial fever, with paroxysms, consisting of a cold, a hot, and a sweating stage. (At first *esp.* of the hot stage, now *esp.* of the cold.) ME. **3.** *fig.* Any fit of shaking or shivering 1589.

1. Brennyng Aguwes LANGL. **2.** That same A. that hath made you leane *Jul. Cæs.* II. ii. 113. **3.** This vain a. of the mind SCOTT. *Comb.* **a.-cake,** an enlargement of the spleen caused by a.; **-drop,** a solution of potassic arseniate, used for a.; **-grass,** *Aletris farinosa*; **-shake** *v.* to shake as with a.; **-shell,** the Hawk's-Bill; **-spell,** a charm against a.; † **-tree,** the Sassafras. Hence **A·gue** *v.* to affect as with a. (*rare*). **A·gued** *ppl. a.* affected as with a. **A·guey** *a.* = AGUISH.

† **Agui·lt.** [OE. *āgyltan,* f. A- *pref.* 1 + *gyltan*; see GUILT *v.*] To sin –1450; to wrong –1420; to declare guilty –1530.

† **Agui·se,** *sb.* 1483. [f. GUISE; the pref. either for *on* (cf. A *prep.*[1]), or opp. to *dis-* in *disguise*; cf. *ac(c)ord, discord.*] **1.** Dress, array –1647. **2.** as *v.* To array –1598. Hence † **Agui·sed** *ppl. a.* arrayed.

Aguish (ēⁱ·giu,iʃ), *a.* 1616. [f. AGUE + -ISH[1].] **1.** Of the character of, or tending to produce, ague 1627. **2.** Subject to ague 1616. **3.** *fig.* Like an ague; shivering; intermittent 1633.

1. A low a. fever 1856. A rich a. flat 1850. **3.** Panics..of the a. or intermittent type 1865. Hence **A·guishly** *adv.* **A·guishness.**

Agu·sh, *adv.* 1858. [A *prep.*[1] 11.] Gushing.

Agynary (æ·dʒinări), *a.* 1879. [– Fr. *agynaire,* f. Gr. ἀ- A- *pref.* 14 + γυνή woman; see -ARY[1].] *Bot.* Without female organs, as some double flowers. var. **Agyna·rious.**

Agynic (ădʒi·nik), *a.* 1879. [– Fr. *agynique,* f. as prec. + *-ique* -IC.] *Bot.* Having the stamens non-adherent to the ovary.

† **Agynous,** *a.* 1847. [f. A- *pref.* 14 + Gr. γυνή woman + -OUS.] *Bot.* Without female organs.

Agyrate (ădʒəiᵊ·reⁱt), *a.* 1847. [f. A- *pref.* 14 + GYRATE *a.*] *Bot.* Not disposed in whorls or circles.

Ah (ā), *int.* ME. [Earliest form *a* – OFr. *a* (later and mod. *ah*); cf. It., Sp. *ah,* L. *ā, āh,* Gr. ἆ, ἀᾶ, etc.] An exclam. expressing **a.** sorrow, regret, a vain wish; **b.** surprise, admiration 1826; **c.** entreaty, appeal, remonstrance ME.; **d.** dislike, contempt, mockery ME.; **e.** opposition (*mod.*).

a. They shall not lament for him, saying Ah my brother *Jer.* 22: 18. So *Ah me!* (north. *eh me!*) **c.** Ah, Clifford, murther not this innocent child 3 *Hen. VI,* I. iii. 8. **d.** Ah thou that destroyest the Temple *Mark* 15: 29.

Aha (ăhā·, ăhā·), *int.* ME. [AH + HA.] An exclam. of † surprise, satisfaction, mockery or irony.

Aha, var. HA-HA, *sb.*, a sunk fence.

† **A hall,** *phr.* 1592. [*A* as in A *interj.* 3; cf. *a-hey, ahoy.*] = 'Make room (for a dance)' –1808.

Ahead (ăhe·d), *adv.* 1628. [A *prep.*[1] 5.] Orig. *Naut.* Now used *fig.* in all senses. **1.** At the head, in advance (of a moving company). **2.** In the direct line of one's motion 1725. **3.** Pointing forward 1596; forward 1762. **4.** Forward or onward rapidly; headlong; also *fig.* unrestrainedly 1643.

1. The..Dolphin gets a. DRYDEN. **2.** They saw it..right a. DE FOE. **3.** To fire directly a., or astern 1873. **4.** Galloping straight a. BROWNING. *Phr.* **go-a-head** *a.*; **ahead of:** away in front of.

Aheap (ăhī·p), *adv.* 1827. [A *prep.*[1] 11.] All of a heap.

A-hei·ght. *arch.* 1605. [A *prep.*[1] 5.] Aloft. Looke vp a height *Lear* IV. vi. 58.

Ahem (ăhe·m), *int.* 1763. [Lengthened f. *hem!*] An exclam. to attract attention, or gain time.

A-hey (ăhēⁱ·), *int.* 1705. [*A* = A *interj.* 3; cf. A HALL, AHOY.] Hey! ho!

† **A-high** (ăhəi·), *adv.* ME. [A *prep.*[1] 5.] On high –1823; aloud –1489.

† **A-high-lone,** *adv. phr.* 1597. Prob. emphatic for *alone,* i.e. all-one, divided as *a-lone*; see HIGH *adv.* 2 –1664.

Ahi·nd, ahi·nt, *adv.* and *prep. dial.* 1768. [f. A- *pref.* 2 + HIND; cf. *afore* = *before.*] Behind.

† **A-ho·ld,** *adv.* [A *prep.*[1] 13.] Close to the wind, so as to hold or keep to it. *Temp.* I. i. 52.

A-ho·rseback. *adv. arch.* 1490. [A *prep.*[1] 1.] On horseback.

Ahoy·, *int.* 1751. [A *int.* + HOY; cf. A HALL, A-HEY.] *Naut.* A call used in hailing.

Ahull (ăhɒ·l), *adv.* 1582. [A *prep.*[1]] *Naut.* With sails furled, and the helm lashed alee; said of ships in a storm.

Ahungered (ăhɒ·ŋgəɹd), *ppl. a. arch.* ME. [prob. repr. a var. of ME. *ofhungred,* OE. *ofhyngrod,* pa.pple. of *ofhyngran,* f. *of-* (see A- *pref.* 3) + *hyngran* HUNGER *v.*; cf. ANHUNGERED, ENHUNGERED, ATHIRST.] = AN-HUNGERED. Also † **Ahu·ngry** *a.*

A-hu·nt, *adv.* 1875. [A *prep.*[1] 11.] On the hunt.

Ai (ā·i). 1693. [– Braz. word repr. the animal's cry; prob. through Fr. *aï* (†*hay,* † *haiit*).] *Zool.* A kind of Sloth (*Bradypus tridactylus*).

Aiblins, var. of ABLINGS.

Aid (ēⁱd), *v.* 1483. [– OFr. *aïdier* (mod. *aider*) :– L. *adjutare,* frequent. of *adjuvare,* f. *ad* AD- + *juvare* help, assist.] **1.** To give support to; to help, assist, succour. **2.** *absol.* and with *inf.* 1601.

1. Aide..with victuals, weapons, money, or ships 1 *Macc.* 8: 26. **2.** Heaven ayding *All's Well* IV. iv. 12. Hence **Ai·dable** *a.* capable of † aiding, or being aided. **Ai·dance,** aid. **Ai·ded** *ppl. a,* assisted. **Ai·der,** one who, or that which, aids.

Aid (ēⁱd), *sb.* 1460. [– OFr. *aïde* (mod. *aide*):– Rom. **adjuta,* sb. use of fem. pa. pple. of *adjuvare*; see prec.] **1.** Help, succour, relief 1475. **2.** *Eng. Law.* Help in defending an action, legally claimed from some one who has a joint interest in the defence 1625. **3.** Anything helpful; *esp.* in *pl.* aids and appliances 1597. **4.** *Eng. Hist.* A pecuniary grant in aid to the king; *later,* an exchequer loan 1460. **5.** A pecuniary contribution by a vassal to his lord 1590. **6.** *Fr. Hist.* (*pl.*) Customs-dues 1714. **7.** An assistant; *pl.* auxiliaries. (Cf. Fr. *aide,* and Eng. *help.*) 1569.

1. Dispatch Those Centuries to our a. *Coriol.* I. vii. 3. **2.** *To pray in aid*: to claim a. *Aid-prayer*: the appeal for aid. **3.** Exercise..an a. to Physick 1711. **5.** Aids, 'Pur faire fitz chiualer & pur file marier' H. SWINBURNE. **6.** *Court of Aids*: the Court that supervised the customs-dues. Hence **Ai·dful** *a.* full of aid, helpful. **Ai·dless** *a.* † useless; unassisted.

Aidant (ēⁱ·dănt), *a.* 1475. [– OFr. *aiant, aidant,* pres. pple. of *aider* AID *v.*; see -ANT.] Assisting 1483. As *sb. rare.* A helper 1475.

Aide, short for AIDE-DE-CAMP.

‖ **Aide-de-camp** (ed-də-kaṅ, ēⁱ·d-də-kǫ:ŋ). Pl. **aides-de-camp.** 1670. [Fr., lit. 'camp adjutant'.] *Mil.* An officer who assists a general in the field, by conveying his orders, procuring him intelligence, etc.

† **Ai·el.** Also **ayle, ayel,** etc. ME. [– OFr. *aïel,* (also mod.) *aïeul* :– Rom. **aviolus,* dim. of L. *avus* grandfather.] A grandfather –1502.

Writ of Aile, Ayle, Ayel, Ael (Law): one which lay where a stranger had dispossessed the heir of lands of which his grandfather died seised.

Aiger, obs. f. EAGER *sb.* tidal bore.

Aiglet, obs. f. AGLET.

Aiglette, obs. f. EAGLET.

Aigre, obs. f. EAGER *a.* sour.

‖ **Aigre-doux, -ce,** *a.* 1523. [Fr.] Mixed of sweet and sour.

Aigrette (ēⁱ·grėt). 1645. [Fr.; see EGRET.] **1.** The Lesser White Heron; see EGRET 1845. **2.** A tuft of feathers, like an Egret's; a spray of gems, etc., worn on the head 1645. **3.** In *Science* applied to the pappus of the Dandelion, etc.; the tufts on the heads of insects, etc.; rays of light from behind the moon in solar eclipses 1816.

†‖ **Aigue-marine.** 1765. [Fr., f. OFr. *aigue* (:– L. *aqua* water) + *marin, -e* of the sea; see AQUAMARINE.] AQUAMARINE.

Aiguille (ēⁱ·gwīl, -wil). 1816. [– Fr. *aiguille* needle; cf. AGLET.] A slender, sharply pointed peak; *esp.* those of the Alps. Hence **Ai:guille·sque** *a.* shaped like an a.

Aiguillette (ēⁱ:gwile·t). 1816. [– Fr. *aiguillette*; see AGLET.] = AGLET. Hence **Ai:guille·tted** *a.*

Aik, aiken, obs. north. f. OAK, OAKEN.

Aikinite (ēⁱ·kinəit). 1837. [f. A. *Aikin* + -ITE[1] 2 b.] *Min.* A sulpharsenite ore, crystallizing in the orthorhombic system.

Ail (ēⁱl), *v.* [OE. *eġlan, eġlian,* f. *eġle* troublesome, rel. to Goth. *agls* disgraceful, *aglo* oppression, *usagljan* oppress.] † **1.** *trans.* To afflict (*rare*) ME. **2.** *impers.* To trouble, affect unusually. (Now only in *interrog., rel.,* and *indef.* sentences.) OE. † **3.** To hinder –1563. **4.** *intr.* To be ill ME.; or † in trouble –1817.

2. What ayleth the people that they wepe? COVERDALE. **4.** And when he ails..he is..peevish RICHARDSON. Hence **Ai·ling** *vbl. sb.* = AILMENT; *ppl. a.* ill, suffering. **Ai·lment,** the fact of ailing; disorder.

Ail (ēⁱl), *sb.*[1] ME. [In mod. use f. AIL *v.*] Trouble; ailment.

† **Ail,** *sb.*[2] [OE. *eġl*, cogn. w. G. dial. *egel*, *agel*.] The awn of barley, etc. –1787.

‖ **Ailanto, ailantus** (e^{i}læ·nto, -tǒs). 1845. [f. *Aylanto*, Tree of the gods, the Amboyna name; whence mod.L. *Ailantus*, corrupted in Eng. to *Ailanthus*, after Gr. ἄνθος.] *Bot.* An East Indian tree (N.O. *Simarubaceæ*), grown in S. Europe for shade, and for its leaves, the favourite food of a species of silkworm. Erron. called 'Japan Varnish'. Hence **Aila·ntery,** a grove of a. trees. **Aila·nthic** *a. Chem.* of or belonging to the A., as *ailanthic acid*. **Aila·ntine,** improp. **aila·nthine** *a.* of or belonging to the A., or the A. silkworm; *sb.* silk from the A. silkworm (*Bombyx cynthia*).

Ailette (e^{i}le·t). 1440. [– Fr. *ailette*, dim. of *aile* wing :– L. *ala*.] A steel plate worn by men-at-arms on their shoulders, whence the mod. epaulette.

Aim (ē^{i}m), *v.* [ME. *ame*, later *aime*, partly – OFr. *amer*, dial. var. of *esmer* :– L. *æstimare* (see ESTIMATE *v.*); partly – OFr. *ae(s)mer* :– Rom. **adæstimare*.] † **1.** To esteem; to reckon; to guess –1602; to plan –1604. **2.** *intr.* To calculate or direct one's course, to attain; *fig.* to endeavour earnestly. Const. *at*; *dat. inf.*; occas. *for*, perh. after *make for*. ME. **3.** *intr.* To calculate the direction of anything about to be launched (at an object), as a missile, a blow, etc.; *fig.* to try to hit, or obtain. Const. *at*. ME. **4.** *trans.* To direct (a missile, or blow); *esp.* to direct with the eye, or point a gun, etc. (*at*); *fig.* to direct any proceeding against 1573. **5.** *absol.* To take aim; to form designs 1588.

2. A. for the Steeple *Guide Eng.Lakes*. **3.** A. at his breast POPE. **4.** Mrs. Bull aimed a knife at John ARBUTHNOT. **5.** I aime a Mile beyond the Moone *Tit. A.* IV. iii. 65. Hence **Aimed** *ppl. a.* † estimated; directed at a mark, etc. **Ai·mer.**

Aim (ē^{i}m), *sb.* [f. prec.] † **1.** Conjecture –1625; course, direction –1679. **2.** The act of aiming ME. Also *fig.* **3.** A mark or butt (*Obs.* in lit. sense) –1632; *fig.* an object, purpose 1625.

1. Aimes and ghesses JEWEL. **2.** A certaine aime he tooke At a faire Vestall *Mids. N.* II. i. 157. † **To give aim:** to guide by informing of the result of a preceding shot. † **To cry aim:** to encourage archers by crying out '*Aim!*' Free from..selfish A. WESLEY. **3.** The aym of Punishment is not a revenge, but terrour HOBBES. Hence **Ai·mful** *a.* full of purpose; whence **Ai·mfully** *adv.* **Ai·mless** *a.* purposeless; whence **Ai·mlessly** *adv.*, **Ai·mlessness.**

Ain't (ē^{i}nt). 1778. Later variant of AN'T, now illiterate or dial.

Air (ē^{ə}ɹ). ME. [In branch I – (O)Fr. *air* – L. *aer* – Gr. ἀήρ; in branch II – Fr. *air* (XVI), prob. repr. OFr. *aire* place, site, disposition :– L. *ager*, *agr-*, infl. by L. *area* AREA (see AERIE); branch III repr. It. *aria* (see ARIA).] I. Atmospheric air. **1.** The gaseous substance which envelops the earth, and is breathed by all land animals; one of the four elements of the ancients, now known to be a mechanical mixture of oxygen and nitrogen, carbonic acid gas, and traces of other substances as contaminations ME. Also *fig.* † **2.** Any aeriform body, as a *gas*, a *vapour* –1819. **3.** The whole body of air *surrounding*, or (pop.) *above* the earth ME. Also *fig.* **4.** A special state of the atmosphere, as *night air*, etc. 1479; *esp.* fresh air ME.; miasma ME.; † effluvium, odour ME. **5.** Air in motion; a breeze, current, or draught 1535. † **6.** Breath; *fig.* popular applause –1821. † **7.** Hence, inspiration, whispers –1660. **8.** *fig.* (Cf. 3 and 5.) Public exposure, publicity 1601.

1. As transparent, as colourless, as invisible as the a. we breathe HUXLEY. **3.** A bird of the aire shall carry the voyce *Eccles.* 10:20. An open air meeting (*mod.*). **In the air:** 1. *a.* In men's minds everywhere abroad; *b.* in an uncertain state. 2. *Mil.* Protruded into the open country, with its flank unprotected. 3. *To build (castles) in the air*: to form unsubstantial projects. **4.** The cold winter a. 1649; one's native a. POPE; change of a. 1860. Abroad to take the a. MASSINGER. Foul a. and gas fumes 1861. Hunting conies by the a. 1607. **5.** Bring with thee ayres from Heaven or blasts from Hell *Haml.* I. iv. 41. In the a. of the door 1888. **8.** *To take air*: to 'get wind'. Least the deuice take ayre *Twel. N.* III. iv. 144.

II. Manner, appearance. **1.** Outward appearance, look, style 1596. **2.** Of a person: Mien, gesture, manner (*arch.*) 1599; † mood –1728. **3.** An affected appearance 1660. † **4.** Stylishness –1816.

1. Seest thou not the ayre of the Court in these enfoldings? *Wint. T.* IV. iv. 755. With the a. of a secret POPE, of a paradox HUME. **2.** Her a., if not her words BYRON. With a decisive a. BUTLER. **3.** Taking the a. of a supercilious mentor GEO. ELIOT. To give oneself airs FIELDING.

III. In music [= musical *mode*]. **1.** Connected succession of musical sounds; song-like music, melody 1590. **2.** *concr.* A piece of music to be sung or played as a 'solo', with or without a distinct harmonized accompaniment; a melody 1604; † a sprightly tune or song –1789. **3.** The predominant part of a harmonized composition, in part-music usu. the soprano part 1819. † **4.** A part-song 1597.

1. Any ayre of musicke *Merch. V.* v. i. 76.

Comb.: **a.-ball,** a ball inflated with a., a toy; **-bath,** an arrangement for drying chemical substances; **-bed,** one with a mattress inflated with a.; **-bladder,** (1) a sac filled with a. in an animal or plant; also, a vesicle in glass, etc.; (2) the swimming-bladder of fishes; **-bone,** a bone for the reception of a., as in birds; **-box,** (1) the air-chamber of a fire-engine or life-boat; (2) a square wooden tube used in mining to convey a. into the face of a single drift; **-brake,** one worked by condensed a.; **-brick,** one perforated for ventilation; **-canal, -casing,** the casing enclosing the base of a steamer chimney, to keep heat off the deck; **-castle,** a visionary project; **-cavity,** an intercellular space in water-plants; **-cell,** any small cavity filled with a.; *esp.* (in *pl.*) small cells in the lungs of animals, forming the extremities of the ramifications of the bronchial tubes; air-cavities in plants; **-chamber,** (1) any cavity filled with a. in an animal or plant; (2) in a pump, etc., a receptacle containing a., which, when compressed, maintains a constant pressure upon the water; an air-vessel; whence **-chambered** *a.*; **-cock,** a stop-cock to let a. out or in; **-cushion,** one inflated with a.; **-drain,** a covered channel round a foundation to prevent damp; **-duct,** a passage for a., *esp.* to the air-bladder of fishes; **-engine,** one actuated by heated a.; **-fountain,** one actuated by compressed a.; **-grating,** one for the entrance of a. under floors, etc.; **-gun,** one projecting balls, etc., by compressed a.; **-hammer,** one moved by compressed a.; **-head, -ing,** a smaller passage in a mine, driven parallel with the gate-road, to carry a. for ventilation; **-holder,** an air-tight vessel or receiver; **-hole,** one to admit a.; *spec.* a breathing-place in the ice, in rapid rivers; the cavities in a metal casting, produced by a.; **-jacket,** one with air-tight lining, to give buoyancy in water, when inflated; **-line,** (*a*) a bee-line; (*b*) a line of aircraft; **-monger,** a visionary projector; **-pillow** (see **-cushion**); **-pipe,** one of the bronchial tubes; a ventilating pipe; **-plant,** an epiphyte, which has roots unconnected with the ground; **-poise,** an instrument for weighing a.; **-port**[1], a port-hole in a ship for ventilation; **-pump,** a machine for exhausting the a. out of a vessel by the strokes of a piston; **-root,** the root of an epiphyte, which hangs in a.; **-sac** (= **-cell**); **-scuttle** (= **-port**[1]); **-shaft,** a straight passage, *usu.* vertical, for admitting a. into a mine or tunnel; **-stone,** an aerolite; **-stove,** one which heats a. passing between its surface and its casing; **-thermometer,** one measuring temperature by the expansion of a column of a.; **-threads,** those of the gossamer spider seen floating in the a.; **-tight** *a.*, impermeable to a. 1760; whence **-tightly** *adv.*; **-trap,** one for preventing the escape of foul a. from sewers, etc.

b. In comb. relating to flying machines or aviation, as *a.-base*, *-fleet*, *-line*, *-liner*, *-mail*, *-pilot*, *-sickness*; **a. force,** that part of the forces of a country (in Great Britain, Royal Air Force, abbrev. R.A.F.) which consists of officers and men with the necessary flying machines; so **a.-commodore, -marshal; -port**[2] [PORT *sb.*[1]], a place containing an aerodrome at which flying machines start on or land from their voyages; so **-station; a. raid,** a raiding attack by aircraft upon an enemy; **-worthy** *a.*, in fit condition to travel through the air.

Hence **Ai·rless** *a.* void of air; stuffy; still.

Air (ē^{ə}ɹ), *v.* 1530. [f. prec.] **1.** *trans.* To expose to the open air; to ventilate. **2.** To expose to heat, dry or warm at the fire 1610. **3.** *refl.* To expose oneself to the fresh air 1611. Also *intr.* (*arch.*) 1633. **4.** *fig.* To wear openly; and hence, to show off 1611. Also *refl.* and *intr.* 1670.

1. To a. doublet and cloak SCOTT, a room 1861. **2.** Air'd at the fire 1759. **3.** To a. myself in my native fields LAMB. **4.** I begge..leaue to ayre this jewel *Cymb.* II. iv. 98. Airing a snowy hand TENNYSON. Hence **Aired** (ē^{ə}ɹd) *pple.* and *a.* ventilated, or dried by heat; in *comb.* having an air (said of breath, manner, mien, tune). **Ai·rer,** one who or that which airs; *spec.* a frame for airing clothes. **Ai·ring** *vbl. sb.* the action of AIR *v.* 1, 2; a walk, ride, or drive to take the air; exercising horses in the open air.

Air (ē^{ə}ɹ), *Sc.* *ēr*), *adv.* [Sc. form of ERE.] † Formerly; early.

Air day or late day SCOTT.

Air(e, Sc. f. EYRE, a circuit court.

† **Air-balloo·n.** 1753. [f. AIR *sb.* + BALLOON; cf. G. *luftballon*, Fr. *ballon aérostatique*.] = BALLOON.

Aircraft (ē^{ə}·ɹ,kraft). 1907. [CRAFT 8.] Flying machines collectively.

† **Aire,** *sb.*[1] 1581. [– OFr. *aire* :– L. *ara* altar.] An altar –1652.

† **Aire,** *sb.*[2] ME. [See AERIE.] Early f. AERIE –1706. Hence † **Aire** *v.* to build an aerie.

Airedale (ē^{ə}·ɹdē^{i}l). A district in the W. Riding of Yorkshire; *A. terrier*, a breed of large rough-haired dogs.

Airily (ē^{ə}·rili), *adv.* 1766. [f. AIRY *a.* + -LY[2].] In an airy manner; thinly, lightly; with light hearts, gaily; jauntily. So **Ai·riness.**

Airman (ē^{ə}·ɹmæ̆n). 1910. [f. AIR + MAN *sb.*, after *seaman*.] The pilot of an aeroplane or airship. So **Ai·rwoman.** So **Ai·rmanship** [after *seamanship*] 1864.

Airplane (ē^{ə}·ɹplē^{i}n). 1907. [alt. of AEROPLANE, after AIR *sb.*] = AEROPLANE 2.

Airship (ē^{ə}·ɹʃip). 1888. [f. AIR *sb.* + SHIP *sb.*[1], after G. *luftschiff*.] A dirigible motor-driven balloon, usu. cigar-shaped.

Airt (ē^{ə}·ɹt, *Sc.* ērt), *sb.* 1470. [– Gael. *aird*, *ard* (= OIr. *aird*, Ir. *ard*) height, top, quarter of the compass.] A quarter of the compass; a direction. Hence **Airt** *v.* to guide.

Ai·r-ve:ssel. 1676. [f. AIR *sb.* + VESSEL; cf. Fr. *vaisseau aérien*.] **1.** *Nat. Hist.* Any vessel used for containing air; *esp.* the tracheæ of insects, and the spiral vessels in plants. **2.** *Hydraul.* = AIR-CHAMBER. 1819.

Airway (ē^{ə}·ɹwe^{i}). 1859. [f. AIR *sb.* + WAY *sb.*] **1.** A passage for air, esp. one for ventilation in a mine. **2.** The route of a service of aeroplanes or airships 1908.

Airy (ē^{ə}·ri), *a.* ME. [f. AIR *sb.* + -Y[1].] **I.** Of the atmosphere. **1.** † Atmospheric, aerial –1677; performed in the air 1624; placed high in the air, lofty; hence, heavenly (*poet.*) 1590. **2.** Exposed to the air; breezy 1596.

1. The a. voyage 1878. The aery Mountain DENHAM. A. brows MARLOWE. **2.** A more a. mode of life JOHNSON.

II. Of the substance. **1.** Composed of air, air-like, immaterial ME.; light or buoyant as air 1598; elastic 1642; sprightly 1644; delicate in imagination 1779. **2.** Unsubstantial as air; unreal 1590; superficial, flippant 1598; visionary 1667. † **3.** Assuming airs –1606; of a good air –1699.

1. Thin a. shapes ADDISON. From her a. tread SCOTT. A. Songs and Galiards 1674. The fancy of Spenser; and..the a. dream that hovers over it HAZLITT. **2.** A. nothings *Mids. N.* v. i. 16. An ayrie, and meere borrow'd thing B. JONS. An a. metaphysician BURKE.

Airy, obs. and dial. f. AREA.

Aisle (əil). [ME. *ele* – OFr. *ele* (mod. *aile*) :– L. *ala* wing; in Eng., through confusion with *ile*, *isle* island, spelt *ile* (XV–XVIII), *isle* (XVI–XVIII) and finally (after Fr. *aile*) *aisle* (XVIII–).] **1.** A wing or lateral division of a church; the part on either side of the nave, usu. divided from it by a row of pillars. Also *fig.* † **2.** *Cross aisle*: a transept –1772. **3.** Also, **a.** Any division of a church 1762; **b.** (quasi ALLEY) A passage in a church between the rows of pews or seats 1731.

1. Long iles extend POPE. A double isle RAY. As he treads the solemn aile 1782. *fig.* Aisles of the forest 1854, of the pine B. TAYLOR. **3. b.** '*Aisle* [..to be written *aile*.] The walks in a church or wings of a quire' JOHNSON. Hence **Aisled** *adj.* furnished with aisles; *pple.* placed in an a. **Ai·sleless** *a.* unfurnished with aisles.

Ait[1] (ē^{i}t). [OE. *iġġaþ*, *iġ(e)oþ*, *iġ(e)þ*, ME. *yȝet*, *eit*, later *ait*, *eyot*. Ult. f. *ieġ* ISLAND + dim. suffix *-aþ*. Final *t* perh. due to AFr. influence.] An islet or small isle; *esp.* one in a river.

Ait[2], **aitt,** Sc. and north. = OAT.

Aitch (the letter); see ACHE *sb.*[3] and H.

Aitch-bone (ē^{i}·tʃbō^{u}:n). ME. [orig. *nache-*, *nage-bone* – OFr. *nache*, *nage*, pl. *naches* :– late L. *naticas*, acc. pl. of *naticæ*, f. L. *natis* buttock. For loss of *n-* cf. ADDER.] The bone of the rump, or the cut of beef lying over it.

Aith, obs. or dial. f. OATH.

Aitiology, obs. var. of ÆTIOLOGY.

Ajar (ădʒā·ɹ), *adv.*[1] ME. [f. A *prep.*[1] 11 + *char* CHARE *sb.*[1]] On the turn, slightly opened, as a door. Erron. *at jar.*

The dim lattice is a. SCOTT.

Ajar, *adv.*[2] 1553. [f. A *prep.*[1] 11 + JAR *sb.*; reduction of earlier *at (a) jar.*] In a jarring state, out of harmony.

A. with the world HAWTHORNE.

Ajee (ădʒī·), *adv. Sc.* and *dial.* Also **agee.** 1733. [f. A *prep.*[1] 11 + JEE *sb.*] Aside; (of a gate) ajar. Also *fig.*

Ajog (ădʒǫ·g), *adv.* 1879. [A *prep.*[1] 11.] On the jog.

Ajoint (ădʒoi·nt), *adv.* 1840. [f. A *prep.*[1] 11 + JOINT *sb.*] **a.** On a joint or pivot. **b.** Jointed, supple.

Ake, earlier and better f. ACHE *v.*

† **Akehorne,** obs. var. of ACORN.

Aker, obs. f. ACRE; var. of ACKER, tidal bore.

Aketon, -toun, obs. vars. of ACTON, HAQUETON.

Akimbo (ăki·mbo[u]), *adv.* [Late ME. *in kenebowe*, later (by assimilation to A *prep.*[1]), *a* or *on kenbow, a kembo, akimbo*, prob. – ON. phr. **i keng boginn* 'bent in a curve' (cf. *kengboginn* crooked); see BOW *v.*[1]] The hand resting on the hips, and the elbow turned outwards.

With his arm a. 1727. Both arms a. BROWNING.

Akin (ăki·n). 1558. [f. A *prep.*[2] + KIN.] **A.** *adv.* **1.** Of kin, by way of blood relationship. **2.** Of things: Of nature or character, in character 1633. See also KIN 3 b.

2. To love, Fear's neare akinne P. FLETCHER.

B. *adj.* (Only as pred. or compl.) **1.** Of the same kin; related by blood 1586. **2.** Of things: Allied in character, etc. 1603.

1. A. to the royal family 1839 **2.** The sensation was a. to giddiness TYNDALL. Hence † **Aki·nd** *a.* FULLER.

‖ **Akinesia** (ækinī·siă). 1878. [– Gr. ἀκινησία quiescence f. ἀ- A- *pref.* 14 + κίνησις motion.] *Phys.* Paralysis of the motor nerves. Also **Akinesis.** Hence **Akine·sic** *a.*

Akmite (æ·kməit). 1837. [f. Gr. ἀκμή point + -ITE[1] 2 b.] *Min.* A bisilicate of the Amphibole group.

Aknee (ănī·), *adv.* ME. [OE. *on cneowe*; see A *prep.*[1], KNEE.] On one's knee or knees.

Aknow, obs. f. ACKNOW *v.*

Akre, obs. or dial. var. of ACORN, due to taking *akern* as pl.

Al, obs. f. ALL, retained in comp. in *albeit, almighty*, etc.

Al-, *pref.*[1] = L. *ad-* bef. *l*, OFr. *a-*, refash. later after L. as *al-*. Occas. for *a-* (not = L. *al-*), as in *a(l)lay.*

Al-, *pref.*[2], the Arab. article, as in *alcohol*, etc.

-al, *suffix*[1], of adjs. and sbs. **1.** *adj.* repr. L. *-alis* = 'of the kind of, pertaining to'. In Eng. *-al* is suffixed to any L. sb., as in *bas-al*, etc.; to Gr. sbs., as in *baptismal*, etc.; to L. adjs. in *-eus, -ius, -uus, -rnus, -is*, and Gr. adjs. in *-κός, -οειδής*, as *comical, spheroidal.* **2.** *sb.* Adjs. in *-al-* used subst. in L. have been adopted in Eng.; and OFr. *-aille, -ail, -al*, f. L. *-alia* (neut. pl.) became an Eng. formative of nouns of action, as in AFr. *arrivaille* arrival.

-al, *suffix*[2] (= *al*cohol or *al*dehyde), as in *chloral, ethal, ural, veronal.*

‖ **A la** (a·la). 1646. [Fr. *à la* (sc. *mode*).] After the (specified) manner, method, or style, as *à la française*; hence *à la Reine* (= *à la mode de la Reine*), etc.

‖ **Ala** (ē[i]·lă). Pl. **alæ** (ē[i]·lī). 1755. [L. *ala* wing, arm-pit, side apartment.] **1.** Any wing-like process; *esp.* (*Phys.*) a lateral cartilage of the nose; (*Bot.*) † an axil; a side petal of a papilionaceous corolla 1794. **2.** *Arch.* A side apartment of a Roman house. Cf. AISLE. 1832.

† **Alaba·ndine.** ME. [– med.L. *alabandina* (sc. *gemma*), f. *Alabanda* in Caria. See ALMANDINE.] **1.** = ALMANDINE –1656. **2.** = next.

Alabandite (ælăbæ·ndəit). [f. as prec. + -ITE[1] 2 b.] *Min.* A native iron-black submetallic sulphide of manganese, called also *manganblende.* DANA.

Alabarch (æ·lăbāɹk). 1727. [– dissim. f. L. *arabarches* (Juvenal) – Gr. ἀραβάρχης, also ἀλαβάρχης.] Title of the chief magistrate of the Jews at Alexandria under the Ptolemies.

Alabaster (æ·lăbɑ:stəɹ, æ:lăbɑ·stəɹ). ME. [– OFr. *alabastre* (mod. *albâtre*) – L. *alabaster, -trum* – Gr. ἀλάβαστος, -τρος, prob. of foreign origin.] **1.** A term for *sulphate* of lime or gypsum, occurring white, yellow, red, or clouded (*Modern* or *Gypseous A.*); also for the varieties of stalagmitic *carbonate* of lime used by the ancients (*Oriental* or *Calcareous A.*). **2.** A box for unguents, made of alabaster ME. † **3.** A liquid measure = half the sextary. **4.** *adj.* (*sb.* as *attrib.*) Of or like alabaster 1526.

1. Like his Grandsire cut in Alablaster *Merch. V.* I. i. 84. **4.** An a. boxe of precious oyntment TINDALE. Babes'..a. innocent arms SHAKS. vars. **Alabla·ster** (16–17th c.), ‖ **Alabastri·tes.** Hence **Alaba·strine** *a.* of or like a.

‖ **Alaba·strum.** 1706. [L., = pointed form of rose-bud (Pliny), transf. use of *alabaster* (prec.) casket for perfumes.] *Bot.* A flower-bud.

Alablaster, obs. f. ALABASTER and ARBLASTER.

‖ **A la carte** (ælakā·ɹt, Fr. alakart). 1826. [Fr. = by the card.] Said of meals ordered by separate items: opp. to TABLE D'HOTE.

Alack (ălæ·k), *int.* 1480. [f. A *int.* + LACK *sb.*[2], after ALAS.] An exclam. of pity or shame; hence of regret or surprise. *arch., poet.*, or *dial.*

A.! our friend is gone TENNYSON. **Alack the day! alack-a-day:** shame to, woe worth, the day! Aphet. *lack-a-day*, of surprise only.

† **Ala·ck,** *adv. rare.* 1528. [A *prep.*[1] 11 + LACK *sb.*[1]] Lacking –1587.

† **Ala·crious,** *a.* 1602. [f. L. *alacris*, var. of *alacer* (see foll.) + -OUS; cf. *hilarious.*] Lively. Hence † **Ala·criously** *adv.* † **Ala·criousness.** var. **Ala·critous** (*rare*).

Alacrity (ălæ·kriti). 1510. [– L. *alacritas*, f. *alacer, alacr-* brisk; see -ITY.] Cheerful readiness, promptitude, liveliness, sprightliness.

That meruelouse alacritee languished MORE. A. of spirit *Rich. III*, V. iii. 73, [of] Visage STEELE. Grateful a. SCOTT.

‖ **Alala·.** 1675. [Dor. Gr. ἀλαλά loud shout, war-cry.] A Greek battle-cry. HOBBES.

Ala·lia. 1878. [Gr. ἀλαλία f. ἀ- A- *pref.* 14 + λαλία talking, speech.] *Med.* Loss of speech.

Alalite (æ·lăləit). [f. *Ala*, in Tyrol, + -LITE.] A Malacolite or Diopside. DANA.

‖ **Alameda** (alămē·dă). 1843. [Sp.] A public walk, shaded with trees.

† **Alami·re.** 1528. [f. *a, la, mi, re*, names of musical notes.] *Mus.* The lowest tone but one in Aretine's scale –1760.

Alamoda·lity. 1753. [– mod.L. *alamodalitas*, f. foll.; see -ALITY.] The quality of being *à la mode.*

A.—a good and pregnant word SOUTHEY.

Alamode, ‖ **à la mode** (æ·lămō[u]d, Fr. alamo·d). 1649. [Fr. *à la mode* according to the manner or fashion; cf. MODE.] **1.** *phr.* In the fashion. **2.** as *adj.* Fashionable 1650. † **3.** *subst.* A fashion or mood –1683. **4.** A thin light glossy black silk 1676.

2. *A. silk*; see 4. *A. beef*: scraps of beef boiled down into a stew. **4.** The alamodes of Lyons MACAULAY.

Alamort, ‖ **à la mort** (ælămǭ·ɹt, Fr. alamō·r). 1592. [– Fr. *à la mort* to (the) death; see AMORT.] **1.** *adv.* To the death. **2.** *adj.* Sick to death; dispirited.

2. What sweeting all-mort? *Tam. Shr.* IV. iii. 36.

† **Alan.** ME. [– OFr. *alan, alant*, = med.L. *alanus.*] A wolf-hound. CHAUCER.

Aland (ălæ·nd), *adv.* ME. [A *prep.*[1]] † In the country –1568; ashore (*arch.*); to the land ME.

Alanine (æ·lănəin). 1863. [f. AL(DEHYDE) + -INE[5], the *-an-* inserted for euphony.] **1.** The 'acid' monamide $C_3H_7NO_2$, derived from lactic acid by replacement of the alcoholic hydroxyl by NH_2. **2.** (in pl.) A name for the group of acid amides, derived from the lactic series.

Ala·ntin. 1847. [f. G. *alant* elecampane + -IN[1].] *Chem.* = INULIN.

Alar (ē[i]·laɹ), *a.* 1839. [– L. *alaris* f. *ala* wing; see -AR[1].] **1.** Of or belonging to wings 1847; wing-shaped 1839. **2.** *Bot.* and *Phys.* Axillary 1858.

† **Ala·rge,** *v.* ME. [– OFr. *alargier, -ir* f. *à* :– L. *ad* + *large* LARGE *a.*] To increase –1560. Also *intr.* (OFr. *s'alargir.*)

Alarm (ălā·ɹm), *sb.* Also **alarum** (now pronounced ălē[ə]·ɹəm, ălæ·rəm). ME. [– (O)Fr. *alarme* – It. *allarme*, = *all' arme* 'to arms!'] **I.** As a phrase. † **1.** *int.* An exclam. = 'To arms' –1600. † **2.** quasi-sb. The call to arms, by crying *alarme!* or otherwise. With *cry, sound*, etc. –1594.

1. Crying al'arme, help HOLLAND. **2.** Strike alarum, drummes SHAKS.

II. As *sb.* with *pl.* **1.** A call to arms 1548; news of approaching hostility 1812. **2.** A sound to warn of danger, or to arouse; *esp.* a sudden peal rung out by a tocsin, or a chime by a clock 1592. Also *fig.* **3.** The mechanism which sounds the a.; also *fig.* Usu. *alarum.* 1586. **4.** A warning of danger of any kind 1591. **5.** *Fencing.* A step or stamp made on the ground with the advancing foot 1579. **6.** A din (*arch.*) 1523. † **7.** A sudden attack; a surprise –1681. **8.** A state of excitement caused by danger apprehended 1587.

1. The..scouts Bring swift alarums in SOUTHEY. **2.** *fig.* An alarum against Usurers LODGE. **4.** Your ..benevolence *took the alarm* 'JUNIUS'. So *to give the a.* **6.** This alarum in the elements KEATS. **8.** A blanket in th' Alarum of feare caught vp *Haml.* II. ii. 532.

Comb.: **alar(u)m-bell,** one rung as a signal of danger; also *fig.*; **alar(u)m-clock, -watch,** one which rings loudly at any pre-appointed hour; **alar(u)m-gauge,** an appliance to give warning of a dangerous pressure of steam or deficiency of water in a boiler; **a.-gun, -cannon,** one fired to give a.; **-post,** a post appointed for each regiment to march to in case of an a.; **-word,** a watchword. Hence **Ala·rmism,** the profession or practice of the alarmist. **Ala·rmist,** a panic-monger.

Alarm (ălā·ɹm), *v.* 1590. [f. prec.] † **1.** To call to arms –1718; to rouse to action –1768. **2.** To arouse to a sense of danger, to put on the alert 1651. **3.** To keep in excitement 1661. **4.** To excite with sudden fear or apprehension of danger 1653.

2. For the purpose of alarming the guards MACAULAY. **4.** I am alarmed at the aspect of affairs 1888. Hence **Ala·rmable** *a.* liable to be alarmed. **Ala·rmed** *ppl. a.* aroused, on the watch; disturbed. **Ala·rmedly** *adv.* **Ala·rming** *ppl. a.* disturbing with apprehension of danger. **Ala·rmingly** *adv.*

Alarum, var. of ALARM, now only poet., or in senses of sb. II, 2, 3.

Alary (ē[i]·lări), *a.* 1658. [– L. *alarius* (also *alaris*) f. *ala* wing.] Of or pertaining to wings or *alæ.*

Alas (ăla·s), *int.* ME. [– OFr. *a las(se), helas* (mod. *hélas*) = 'ah! weary (that I am)!' = *a* AH + *las(se)* :– L. *lassus* weary.] An exclam. of unhappiness, sorrow, pity, etc.

Alas the heauy day *Oth.* IV. ii. 42.

‖ **Alastor** (ăla·stǫɹ). *rare.* 1810. [Gr. ἀλάστωρ avenging deity, f. ἀ- A- *pref.* 14 + λαστ-, f. λαθεῖν forget.] A relentless spirit; a Nemesis.

Alate (ălē[i]·t), *adv. arch.* ME. [A *prep.*[2]] Of late.

Alate (ē[i]·le[i]t), *a.* 1668. [– L. *alatus* winged f. *ala* wing; see -ATE[2].] Having wings or wing-like appendages. var. **A·lated** *a.*

Alatern(us (ælătə·ɹnǒs). 1607. [– L. *alaternus*; cf. Fr. *alaterne.*] *Bot.* An evergreen shrub (*Rhamnus alaternus*) of the genus *Rhamnaceæ* or Buckthorns.

Alation (e[i]lē[i]·ʃən). [f. L. *ala* wing + -ATION, after *foliation*; cf. Fr. *alation.*] A winged condition; the mode in which the wings of insects are disposed.

Alaunt, var. of ALAN.

† **Alay·,** *v.* 1508. [Origin unkn.] Term of art: To carve (a pheasant).

Alb (ælb). [OE. *albe* – eccl. L. *alba*, subst. use of L. *albus* white.] A tunic of white cloth, reaching to the feet, and enveloping the person; worn by priests in religious ceremonies, and occ. by consecrated kings.

[Sigismund] was buryed in his regall a. 1606.

Albacore (æ·lbăkǭ[ə]ɹ). 1579. [– Pg. *albacor, -ora*, f. Arab. *al* AL-[2] + *bakr* young camel or *bakūr* premature, precocious.] A fish; prop. a large species of Tunny (*Thynnus*), found in the Atlantic; also loosely, of other species. var. **Albicore** (Fr.).

Alban (æ·lbăn). 1863. [f. L. *albus* white + -AN.] A white crystalline resinous substance extracted from gutta-percha on treatment with alcohol, etc.

Albata (ælbēⁱ·tă). 1848. [– L. *albata*, fem. of *albatus* clothed in white, f. *albus* white; cf. -ATE².] A white metallic composition; German silver.

† **Alba·tion.** 1612. [– med.L. *albatio*, f. late L. *albare* make white, f. *albus* white. See -ATION.] **1.** *Alchem.* = ALBIFICATION. **2.** Dusting; ? orig. with a white powder 1612.

Albatross (æ·lbătrǫs). 1681. [app. alt., by assoc. w. L. *albus* white, of † *alcatras* pelican, gannet, sea-mew, frigate-bird – Sp., Pg. *alcatraz*, var. of Pg. *alcatruz*, orig. bucket, corresp. to Sp. *alcaduz*, *arcaduz* – Arab. *alḳādūs* the pitcher, f. *al* AL-² + *ḳādūs* – Gr. κάδος jar. See ALCATRAS.] † **1.** The Frigate-bird, = ALCATRAS 2. –1753. **2.** A family of birds allied to the Petrels (Order *Tubinares*), inhabiting the Pacific and Southern Oceans. The great Albatross, *Diomedea exulans*, is the largest of sea-birds.

Albe. 1697. [Anglicized form of ALBUM.] *Rom. Antiq.* A register.

†**Albe·**, *conj.* late ME. [= *all be*, contr. of *all be it* ALBEIT.] Also **al be, allbe, all be.** = ALBEIT. –1825.

Albedo (ælbī·do). 1859. [– eccl. L. *albedo* whiteness f. L. *albus* white.] Whiteness; *spec.* in *Astr.* The proportion of the solar light incident upon an element of the surface of a planet, which is again reflected from it.

Albeit (ǫlbī·it), *conj.* ME. [prop. a phrase *all be it (that)* = *all though it be (that)*; see ALL *adv.*] **1.** Admitting (*that*) 1460. **2.** Although ME. **3.** In *contr. cl.*: even if 1795.

2. All bee it he coulde not saye naye MORE. 3. A certain (a. uncertain) morrow THACKERAY.

Albert (æ·lbəɹt). 1883. [In full *Albert chain*, named after Prince Albert (d. 1861), Consort of Queen Victoria.] A kind of watch-chain.

Albertite (æ·lbəɹtəit). 1875. [f. *Albert* (county), New Brunswick + -ITE¹ 2 b.] *Min.* A jet-black bituminous mineral found in New Brunswick.

A·lbert-type. 1875. [f. name of inventor.] A method of printing in ink from photographic plates; also, the picture so printed.

Albescent (ælbe·sěnt), *a.* 1831. [– *albescent-*, pres. ppl. stem of L. *albescere* grow white, f. *albus* white; see -ESCENT.] Growing or passing into white.

Albespyne, -ine (æ·lbėspəin). ME. [– OFr. *albespine* (mod. *aubépine*) :– L. *alba spina.*] Whitethorn, hawthorn. *arch.*

†**Albeston(e.** ME. [early var. of ASBESTOS, – OFr. *a(l)beston* – med.L. *albeston*, alt. f. L. *asbestos* – Gr. ἄσβεστος; see ASBESTOS.] = ASBESTOS –1567.

A·lbicant, *ppl. a.* 1879. [– *albicant-*, pres. ppl. stem of L. *albicare* make or become white, f. *albus* white; see -ANT.] Growing white.

Albication (ælbikēⁱ·ʃən), 1879. [– *albicat*pa. ppl. stem of L. *albicare*: see prec., -ATION.] The process of growing white; *esp.* the development of light patches, bands, etc. in the foliage of plants.

Albicore, var. of ALBACORE.

† **Albifica·tion.** ME. [– (O)Fr. *albification* – med.L. *albificatio*, f. *albificare*, f. *albus* white; see -FICATION.] *Alchem.* The process or art of making white –1592.

Albiflo·rous, *a.* 1879. [f. L. *albus* + *flor-* + -OUS.] *Bot.* White-flowered.

Albin(e (æ·lbin). 1817. [f. L. *albus* white + -INE⁵.] *Min.* An opaque white apophyllite found in Bohemia.

Albines (æ·lbinz), *sb. pl.* 1879. [f. L. *albus* white + -INE¹.] *Phys.* Small colourless bodies found with aleuron grains.

Albino (ælbī·no, ælbəi·no). Pl. **-os.** 1777. [– Sp., Pg. *albino*, f. *albo* white + *-ino* (-INE¹); orig. applied by the Portuguese to white African Negroes.] **1.** A human being having a congenital deficiency of colouring pigment in the skin, hair, and eyes, so that the former are white, and the eyes pink. **2.** Applied also to animals, as white mice, etc., and to plants lacking chlorophyll 1859. Hence **A·lbiness,** a female a. **A·lbinism, Albi·noism,** the condition of being an a.

Albite (æ·lbəit). 1843. [f. L. *albus* white + -ITE¹ 2 b.] *Min.* White or soda feldspar. Hence **Albi·tic** *a.* of the nature of, or containing, a.

A·lbolith. 1875. [f. L. *albus* white + Gr. λίθος stone; see -LITH.] A white cement made from magnesia and silica.

‖ **Albora·k.** *Obs.* 1635. [Arab. *al-burāḳ.*] A white mule; *esp.* the winged steed said to have carried Mohammed up to heaven.

‖ **Albugo** (ælbiū·go). ME. [L., f. *albus* white.] A disease of the eye, in which a white opaque spot forms on the transparent cornea. Hence **Albugi·nean** *a.* of or like the white fibrous tissue of the eye. **Albugi·neous** *a.* = ALBUGINEAN; albuminous. †**Albu·ginousness.**

‖ **Album**¹ (æ·lbŏm). Pl. **albums.** 1651. [– L. *album* a blank tablet; orig. used as L.] **1.** *Rom. Antiq.* A tablet on which the prætor's edicts and other public matters were recorded for public information 1753. **2.** A blank book in which to insert autographs, verses, drawings, stamps, etc. 1651. **3.** A Visitors' Book 1775. Hence **Albumean** *a.* relating to albums; **Albumess,** a female keeper of an a. (*Nonce-wds.*) LAMB.

†‖ **A·lbum**². 1527. [med.L. *album* (sc. *malum* disease), subst. use of n. sing. of *albus* white.] **1.** *Path.* Leucorrhea. **2.** Rent paid in white money or silver –1775.

Albumen (ælbiū·men). 1599. [– L. *albumen*, *-min-*, f. *albus* white.] **1.** The white of an egg. **2.** The substance which exists nearly pure in the white of an egg, and is a constituent of animal solids and fluids, and of the tuberous roots and seeds of plants; see ALBUMIN 1800. **3.** *Bot.* The substance which surrounds the embryo in many seeds; the endosperm or perisperm 1677. Hence **Albu·menize** *v.* to cover, coat, or impregnate, with a. **Albu·menizer,** one who albumenizes.

Albumin (ælbiū·min). 1869. [– Fr. *albumine* (XVIII), f. L. *albumin-*; see prec.] A class of ALBUMINOIDS, comprising those soluble in water (= ALBUMEN 2), in dilute acids, and in alkalis (*acid* or *alkali albumins*). Hence **Albu·minate,** a combination of a. with certain bases, in which the a. acts as a very feeble acid. **Albu·minated** *ppl. a.* albuminized. **Albu:mini·ferous** *a.* producing a. **Albu:mini·meter,** a polarizing apparatus for measuring the a. in a liquid. **Albu·minin,** the substance of the cells enclosing the white of birds' eggs. **Albu:mini·parous** *a.* producing a. **Albu·minize** *v.* (*Biol.*) to convert into a.; whence **Albu:miniza·tion,** reconversion of a tissue into a. ‖ **Albu:mino·sis,** *Path.* a condition of the blood in which there is an excess of a.

Albumino- (ælbiū·mino), comb. f. ALBUMEN. **1.** *adv.* Albuminously, as in **a.-fibrous. 2.** *adj.* Albuminous, as in **a.-chloride.**

Albuminoid (ælbiū·minoid), *a.* 1859. [see ALBUMEN, -OID.] Like albumen. As *sb.* (in *pl.*) = *Albuminoid Principles*: Organic compounds which form the chief part of the tissues of animals and plants, = PROTEIDS. 1873. Hence **Albu:minoi·dal** *a.*

Albuminose (ælbiū:minōᵘ·s), *a.* 1847. [f. as ALBUMEN + -OSE¹.] = ALBUMINOUS 1859. As *sb.* A crystalloid substance derived from albumen by the action of pepsin in weak acid solutions 1847.

Albuminous (ælbiū·minəs), *a.* 1791. [f. as prec. + -OUS.] **1.** Of the nature or character of albumen or albumin. **2.** *Bot.* Containing albumen in the seed; see ALBUMEN 3. **3.** *fig.* Insipid 1865. Hence **Albu·minousness.**

‖ **Albuminuria** (ælbiū:miniūᵊ·riă). 1854. [f. L. *albumin-* (see ALBUMEN) + Gr. οὖρον urine + -IA¹.] *Path.* The escape of albumen in the urine.

Alburn (æ·lbŏɹn). 1753. **1.** = ALBURNUM. **2.** A fish; the Bleak (in L. *alburnus*).

Alburnum (ælbŏ·ɹnŏm). 1664. [L. *alburnum* (Pliny) sap-wood, f. *albus* white.] The sap-wood in exogenous trees. Hence **Albu·rnous** *a.* of, or of the nature of, a.

Alcade, var. of ALCALDE; and erron. f. ALCAYDE.

Alcahest, var. of ALKAHEST.

Alcaic (ælkē·ik). Also **alch-.** 1630. [– late L. *alcaicus* – Gr. ἀλκαϊκός, f. Ἀλκαῖος Alcæus; see -IC.] *adj.* Of or pertaining to Alcæus, a lyric poet of Mytilene (*c* 600 B.C.), or his metre 1637. *sb.* in *pl.* Alcaic strophes.

Alcaid, var. of ALCAYDE.

‖ **Alcalde** (alka·lde). 1615. [– Sp. *alcalde*, – Arab. *al-ḳāḍī* the judge; see AL-², CADI. Cf. Fr. *alcade.*] A sheriff or justice, in Spain and Portugal.

Alcali, etc. obs. var. of ALKALI, etc.

‖ **Alca·nna, -na.** 1625. [– Sp. *alcana*, *alcaña* (med.L. *alcanna* XIII) – Arab. *al-ḥinnā'*; see HENNA and cf. ALKANET, ORCANET.] *Bot.* Egyptian Privet (*Lawsonia inermis*, N.O. *Lythraceæ*), or its leaves, etc., used by Orientals to dye parts of the body reddish orange; henna.

Alcargen, alcarsin; see ALK-.

‖ **Alcarraza** (ælkără·ză, Sp. alkără·þă). 1818. [Sp., – Arab. *al-karrāz* the pitcher; see AL-².] A porous earthenware vessel used for cooling water by evaporation.

† **A·lcatras, -ace, -ash.** 1564. [– Sp., Pg. *alcatraz*, var. of Pg. *alcatruz* bucket of a 'noria', or water-raising wheel for irrigation; see ALBATROSS. App. orig. applied to the pelican, which was supposed to draw up water in its beak.] ‖ **1.** Sp. and Pg. name of the Pelican; applied also to sea-mews, etc. † **2.** Eng. name for the Frigate Bird, *Tachypetes aquilus* –1692. † **3.** ? A kind of albatross, prob. *Diomedea fuliginosa* –1775.

‖ **Alcavala** (alkăvā·lă). 1776. [Sp. *alcabala*, Pg. *alcavala* – Arab. *al-ḳabāla* the tax, duty. See AL-², GABELLE.] A tax of ten per cent. upon sales. ADAM SMITH.

‖ **Alcayde** (ælkēⁱ·d, Sp. alkai·de). 1502. [– Sp. *alcaide* – Arab. *al-ḳā'id* the leader, f. *al* AL-² + *ḳā'id*, pr. pple. of *ḳāda* lead.] The governor of a fortress; the warden of a prison; (in Spain, Portugal, Barbary, etc.). Occ. confused with ALCALDE.

‖ **Alcazar** (alkā·þar). 1615. [– Sp. *alcazar* – Arab. *al-ḳaṣr* the castle – L. *castrum* fortified camp; see AL-².] A palace, fortress.

† **Alce.** 1541. [L. *alce*, also *alx*, pl. *alces* (Cæsar); cf. Gr. ἄλκη (Pausanias). See ELK¹.] An elk –1753.

Alchemic, -al (ælke·mik, -ăl), *a.*; also **alchym-.** 1815. [f. ALCHEMY + -IC, after CHEMIC, -AL¹; cf. Fr. *alchimique.*] Of or belonging to alchemy. Also *fig.* Hence **Alche·mically** *adv.*

Alchemist (æ·lkĭmist). 1514. [– OFr. *alkemiste* (mod. *alchimiste*) or med.L. *alchemista* (XIII), f. *alchemia*; see ALCHEMY, -IST.] One who studies or practises alchemy.

You are an Alcumist, make Gold of that *Timon* v. i. 117. var. † **A·lchemister.** Hence **Alchemi·stic, -al** *a.* † **A·lchemistry,** alchemy.

Alchemize (æ·lkĭməiz), *v.* 1603. [f. prec. after *baptist*, *baptize*; see -IZE.] To change, as by alchemy.

Till the sunshine, striking this [i.e. the hair], A. its dulness MRS. BROWNING.

Alchemy (æ·lkĭmi). [ME. *alkamy(e*, *alkemye* – OFr. *alkemie*, *alkamie* (mod. *alchimie*) – med.L. *alchimia*, *-chemia* – Arab. *alkīmīā*, f. *al* AL-² + *kīmīā* – Gr. χημία, χημεία art of transmuting metals (Suidas). The common variant *alchymy* (XVI–XVIII) arose by assoc. w. Gr. χυμεία infusion, f. χεῖν to pour. Cf. CHEMISTRY.] **1.** The chemistry of the Middle Ages and 16th c.; limited to the pursuit of the transmutation of baser metals into gold, and the search for the alkahest and the panacea. Also *fig.* † **2.** A composition, mainly of brass, imitating gold; 'alchemy gold'; also, a trumpet made of this –1812. Also *fig.*

1. It has been [said] that A. was the mother of Chemistry WHEWELL. *fig.* Guilding pale streames with heauenly alcumy SHAKS. *Sonn.* xxxiii. 2. Cherubim Put to their mouths the sounding alchymie MILT. *P.L.* ii. 516. Hence † **A·lchemy** *v.* [f. the *sb.* 2] to plate, or to alloy. Cf. to *tin*, *lacquer*, etc.

Alchim-; see ALCHEM-.

† **Alchitran, alkitran.** ME. [– OFr. *alketran*, *alquitran* – Sp. *alquitran* – Arab. *al-qaṭrān*, *-kiṭrān* the resin of fir-trees.] The resin or pitch of fir-trees; extended to **a.** oil of

cedar and juniper; **b.** mineral pitch, bitumen, etc. –1658.

Alchym-: see ALCHEM-.

Alcoate, -hate, short f. ALCOHOLATE (see ALCOHOL).

Alcohol (æ·lkŏhǫl). 1543. [– Fr. (now *alcool*) or med.L. *alcohol* – Arab. *alkuḥl* collyrium, f. *al* AL-² + *kuḥl* KOHL¹.] † **1.** *orig.* The fine metallic powder used in the East to stain the eyelids, etc.: powdered antimony; also, occas., powdered galena –1819. † **2.** Any impalpable powder, produced by trituration, or esp. by sublimation –1812. † **3.** By extension to fluids: An essence or 'spirit', obtained by distillation –1794. *fig.* Quintessence 1830. **4.** Pure spirit of wine; or (pop.) any liquor containing it 1753. **5.** *Organ. Chem.* A class of compounds, of the same type as spirit of wine, composed of carbon, hydrogen, and oxygen, some of which are liquid and others solid 1850.

1. *Alcohól*: a drug called Antimonium MINSHEU. **2.** *Alcohol martis*: reduced iron. The *alcohol of Sulphur* SIR H. DAVY. **3.** *Alcohol of wine*: essence or spirit of wine. *fig.* The a. of egotism COLERIDGE. **4.** *Absolute or anhydrous alcohol*: a. entirely free from water. Pure spirits, called a. VINCE. **5.** *Common* (vinous or vinic) *Alcohol*, the best known, is a *primary, monatomic, dicarbon* or *ethyl* alcohol, $C_2H_5.OH$. Others are Methyl alcohol ($CH_3.OH$), Propyl ($C_3H_7.OH$), Butyl ($C_4H_9.OH$), Amyl ($C_5H_{11}.OH$), etc., the number being unlimited. Hence **A·lcohola:te,** a. crystalline compound in which a. acts as water of crystallization. **Alcoho·lature,** an alcoholic tincture made from fresh plants.

Alcoholic (ælkohǫ·lik), *a.* 1790. [f. prec. + -IC.] **1.** Of or belonging to alcohol. **2.** Preserved in alcohol 1852. **3.** Using alcohol 1856. As *sb. pl.* = alcoholic liquors.

1. A. strength 1836. **2.** An a. specimen DANA. **3.** A. thermometers 1856. Hence **Alcoho·lically** *adv.* **Alcoholi·city,** a. quality.

Alcoholism (æ·lkŏhǫli:z'm). 1852. [– mod.L. *alcoholismus* (Magnus Huss, 1852), f. as prec.; see -ISM.] The action of alcohol upon the human system; diseased condition produced by it.

Alcoholize (æ·lkŏhǫləi:z), *v.* 1686. [– Fr. *alcooliser*, f. as prec.; see -IZE.] † **1.** To sublimate –1686. † **2.** To rectify –1799. **3.** To saturate with, or subject to the influence of, alcohol 1862. Hence **A:lcoholiza·tion. A·lcoholi:zing** *vbl. sb.* converting into or saturating with alcohol.

Alcoholometer (æ:lkŏhǫlǫ·mĭtəɹ). 1859. [f. ALCOHOL + -METER; cf. Fr. *alcoolomètre.*] An instrument for measuring the proportion of absolute alcohol in a liquor. vars. **Alcoho·lmeter, Alcoo·meter.** Hence **Alcoholome·tric, -al** *a.* Also **Alcoometrical,** of or pertaining to alcoholometry.

Alcoholometry (æ:lkŏhǫlǫ·mĕtri). 1863. [f. as prec. + -METRY; cf. Fr. *alcoolométrie.*] The process of testing the proportion of absolute alcohol in a liquor. var. **Alcoo·metry.**

†‖ **Alco·nde.** 1486. [Sp., f. Arab. *al* AL-² + Sp. *conde* COUNT *sb.*²] A (Spanish) Count.

A:lcoothio·nic, *a.* [f. ALCOHOL + Gr. θεῖον sulphur + -IC.] = ŒNOTHIONIC.

Alcoran (ælkorā·n, æ·lkorăn, -æn). *arch.* ME. [– (O)Fr. *alcoran* – Arab. *al-kur'ān*; see AL-², KORAN¹.] The sacred book of the Mohammedans; the Koran (now the usual form).

As the Turkes doe, bidde men belieue in Machometes alchoran MORE. Hence **Alcoran** *v.* to make into a Koran. † **Alcora·nal, Alcora·nic,** † **Alcora·nish** *adjs.* of or belonging to the Koran. **Alcora·nist,** one who adheres to the letter of the Koran.

‖ **Alcorno·co, -que.** 1832. [Sp., Pg. *alcornoque* cork-oak, ult. (through Arab.) f. L. *quercus* oak.] The cork-oak, the bark of which (*Spanish A. bark*) is used in tanning. Also *American A.*, yielding a bark formerly used in medicine.

Alcove (æ̆lkōᵘv, æ·lkōᵘv). 1623. [– Fr. *alcôve* – Sp. *alcoba* – Arab. *al-kubba*, f. *al* AL-² + *kubba* vault, vaulted chamber.] **1.** A vaulted recess; a recess in a chamber for a bed; a recess or niche in a wall 1786. **2.** A recess in a garden, orig. in the garden-wall or hedge; any bower or summerhouse 1706.

2. The alcoves of box and yew COLERIDGE. Hence **Alco·ved** *ppl. a.* vaulted, arched.

Alcyon, var. of HALCYON.

Alcyon (æ·lsiǫn). *Zool.* = ALCYONIUM.

Alcyonarian (æ:lsiǫnē³·riăn), *a.* 1878. [f. mod.L. *Alcyonaria*, f. next + -AN.] Belonging to the *Alcyonaria*, a sub-order of Actinoid Zoophytes; see ALCYONIUM. As *sb.* A zoophyte of that group.

‖ **Alcyonium** (ælsi,ōᵘ·niŏm). 1752. [mod.L., = Gr. ἀλκυόνειον (-ιον Dioscorides) Bastard-sponge, so called from its resemblance to the nest of the ἀλκυών, HALCYON.] *Zool.* A genus of zoophytes, giving its name to the sub-order *Alcyonaria*, forming firm fleshy masses, and including 'Dead Man's Fingers', or 'Cow's Paps'. Hence **Alcyo·nic** *a.* **A·lcyonite,** a fossil zoophyte related to *Alcyonium.* **A·lcyonoid** *a.* allied to A.; also used *subst.*

† **Ald,** *a.* Now *dial.* [OE. *ald*, surviving dial. for standard OLD; see AULD, ELD *a.*, OLD.] See OLD.

† **Ald,** *sb.* ME. [var. of ELD *sb.* infl. by the adj. *ald* (prec.).] Age; an age; old age –1551.

† **Alday,** *adv.* ME. [= ALL DAY.] Every day; *hence,* Always –1483.

‖ **Alde·a, -dee.** *Obs.* 1698. [Sp. *aldea*, Pg. *aldeia* (cf. Fr. *aldée*) village – Arab *al-ḍay'a*, f. *al* AL-² + *ḍay'a* farm, village.] A Pg. village or villa –1780.

Aldehyde (æ·ldĭhəid). 1850. [f. *al. dehyd.*, abbrev. of *alcohol dehydrogenatum* dehydrogenated alcohol.] **1.** A colourless volatile fluid of suffocating smell, obtained by the oxidation of Alcohol. **2.** A class of compounds of the same type, each derived from its alcohol by removal of two atoms of hydrogen. (Called also *Aldides.*) 1863.

2. Thus Methyl Alcohol CH_4O, Methyl Aldehyde CH_2O. Hence **A·ldehydate,** a salt in which a. acts as a monobasic acid. **Aldehy·dic** *a.*

Alder (ǭ·ldəɹ), *sb.*¹ [OE. *alor, aler*, rel. to MLG. *aller*, MDu. *else*, OHG. *elira, erila* (G. *erle*), ON. *ǫlr*, conn. w. L. *alnus*. Forms with glide-*d* appear XIV.] A tree (*Alnus glutinosa*) related to the Birch, and common in wet places OE. **2.** Extended to other shrubs or trees, as **Black Alder, A. Buckthorn** (Europ.), *Rhamnus frangula*; Black A. (N. Amer.), *Prinos verticillatus*; White A. (N. Amer.), *Clethra alnifolia*; (S. Afr.), *Platylophus trifoliatus*; Red A. (S. Afr.), *Cunonia capensis*.

Comb. **a.-carr,** a piece of wet ground where alders grow.

† **A·lder,** *sb.*² [OE. *aldor, ealdor* chief, prince f. *ald, eald* old (see ALD *a.*) + *-or* suffix forming sbs. Cf. ELDER *sb.*²] **1.** Parent, ancestor. OE. only. **2.** Chief, prince, lord –ME. (In OE. tr. L. *senior, princeps, magistratus*, etc.) Hence † **A·lderdom,** lordship.

† **Alder-,** later var. of ME. *aller-, alre*, OE. *alra*, gen. pl. of ALL (q.v., D 2), as in *alderbest* (Chaucer), *alderliefest* (Chaucer, Shakespeare).

† **A·lderling.** 1655. [prob. f. ALDER *sb.*¹ + -LING.¹] A species of trout; cf. dial. *allertrout.*

Alderman (ǭ·ldəɹmæn). [OE. *aldormann*, f. *aldor* ALDER *sb.*² + MAN *sb.*] † **1.** A noble or man of high rank; the governor of a district. **2.** = ALDER *sb.*² 2. † **3.** The chief officer or warden of a guild 1130. **4.** A municipal officer ranking next to the mayor (as still in U.S.A.), formerly (and still in the city of London) representing a ward; now, in England and Wales generally, a co-opted member of a borough or county council.

1 a. Brightnothus, aldermanne, erle, or duke of northumberlande THYNNE. **b.** 'Senators' or Aldermen BOLTON. **3.** What an Alderman's pace he comes GAULE. An A. of Cripplegate COWPER. Hence **A·ldermanate,** the dignity of a.; the body of aldermen. **A·ldermancy,** the office of a. **Alderma·nic,** † **-al** *a.* of, pertaining to, or like, an a. † **Alderma·nikin,** *a.* a little a. **Alderma·nity,** (joc.) the quality of an a.; the body of aldermen. **A·ldermanlike** *a.* and *adv.* **A·ldermanly** *a.* **A·ldermanship,** the office, position, or quality of an a. **A·ldermane:ss,** † **A·lderwo:man,** † **A·ldress,** the wife of an a.

Aldermanry (ǭ·ldəɹmænri). ME. [f. prec. + -RY.] A district of a borough having its own alderman, a ward; also, the dignity of an alderman.

Aldern (ǭ·ldəɹn), *a.* OE. [f. ALDER *sb.*¹ + -EN⁴.] Of alder. As *sb.* = ALDER *sb.*¹ ME.

Aldide (æ·ldəid). *Chem.* [f. ALD(EHYDE) + -IDE.] See ALDEHYDE 2.

Aldine (ǭ·ldəin), *a.* 1802. [– mod.L. *Aldinus*, f. *Aldus*, latinized f. *Aldo*; see -INE¹.] Printed or produced by Aldus Manutius, a Venetian printer in the 16th c.; the title of a modern series of books; also of certain styles of display types.

Aldol (æ·ldǫl). 1874. [f. ALD(EHYDE + ALCOH)OL.] A clear viscid neutral liquid, $CH_3.CH(OH).CH_2.CHO$, polymerous with acetyl aldehyde.

Ale (ē¹l). [OE. *alu* (*ealu*), gen., dat. *alop*, gen. pl. *ealeþa* = OS. *alo-*, OHG. *al-*, ON. *ǫl* :– Gmc **aluþ-* (*t*-stem).] **1.** A beverage made from an infusion of malt by fermentation, flavoured with hops, or other bitters. † **2.** In **'the ale'** (phr.), **a.** The ale drinking; **b.** The public supply, and hence the alehouse –1617. **3.** A festival at which much ale was drunk. (Cf. *a tea.*) See also BRIDAL. OE.

Ale and *beer* were orig. synonymous; but now 'beer' is the generic name for all malt liquors, 'ale' being the name for the lighter coloured kinds.

1. Item, she brewes good Ale *Two Gent.* III. i. 304. **Buttered ale**: sugar, cinnamon, butter, and beer brewed without hops. PEPYS. **2.** † **At the ale,** To goe *to the Ale* with a Christian *Two Gent.* II. v. 61. *In his Ales*: under the influence of a. *Hen. V*, IV. vii. 47. **3.** There were *leet-, scot-, church-, clerk-, bed-*, and *bride-ales* SKEAT.

Comb.: **a.-barrel,** 36 (formerly 32) gallons; **-bench,** one before or in an ale-house; **-bush,** a tavern sign; **-draper,** an ale-house keeper; hence **-drapery; -fat** = *a.-vat*; **-firkin,** 9 (formerly 8) gallons; **-grains,** refuse malt left after brewing; **-house,** a house where a. is retailed; also *attrib.*; **-kilderkin,** a half-barrel of a.; † **-knight,** a votary of the ale-house; **-pole,** one set up as the sign of an ale-house; **-score, -shot,** a reckoning for a. consumed; † **silver,** a tax paid by ale-sellers within the City of London; † **-stake** = *a.-pole*; a tippler; **-tap,** prop. the tap whence ale is drawn, hence the room or place where it is kept; **-taster** = ALE-CONNER; † **-toast,** a toast in a., *fig.* a roisterer; **-vat,** one in which a. is brewed; **-wort,** the fermenting infusion of malt; **-yeast,** yeast produced in brewing ale.

Aleatory (ē¹·li,ătəri), *a.* 1693. [– L. *aleatorius*, f. *aleator* dicer, f. *alea* die, dice; see -ORY².] Dependent on the throw of a die; *hence*, dependent on uncertain contingencies, as an *aleatory contract.*

† **A·leberry.** ME. [f. ALE- + OE. *briw*, pottage, brewis; erron. assoc. w. berry, as in *bread-berry.*] Ale boiled with spice, sugar, and sops of bread –1630.

‖ **A·lec.** 1520. [L. *al(l)ec* fish sauce, garum.] A herring; a pickle made of small herrings. Hence **A·lecize** *v.* to dress with a. sauce.

Aleconner (ē¹·lkǫ:nəɹ). ME. [f. ALE + CONNER¹.] An inspector of ale. Still a titular office in some boroughs.

Alecost (ē¹·lkǫst). 1589. [f. ALE- + COST, – L. *costum*, – Gr. κόστος a plant used as spice.] = COSTMARY, q.v.

Alectryomachy (ăle:ktri,ǫ·măki). [f. Gr. ἀλεκτρυών cock + -μαχία -MACHY.] Cock-fighting. A Dict. wd. var. **Ale:ctoro·machy.**

Alectryomancy (ăle·ktri,omæ:nsi). 1684. [f. as prec.; see -MANCY.] Divination by means of a cock with grains of corn. var. **Ale·ctoro:mancy.**

‖ **Alectryon** (ăle·ktri,ǫn). [Gr. ἀλεκτρυών.] A cock. LONGF.

Alee (ălī·), *adv.* ME. [f. A *prep.*¹ + LEE *sb.*¹, partly after ON. *á hlé*; cf. ALOFT.] *Naut.* On or toward the lee or sheltered side of a ship; away from the wind.

The helm was *put alee* JAMES.

Ale·ft, *adv.* ME. [A *prep.*¹ 3.] On or to the left.

Alegar (æ·lĭgăɹ, ē¹·lĭgăɹ). 1542. [f. ALE + *-egar*, (see EAGER *a.*) of *vinegar*; cf. BEEREGAR.] Sour ale; malt vinegar.

A. is to ale what vinegar is to wine 1881.

† **Ale·ger,** *a.* [– Fr. *allègre* – It. *allegro* – L. *alacer, alacr-* brisk.] Cheerful. BACON.

Ale-hoof (ē¹·lhūf). ME. [prob. alt. of *hayhove*, f. *hay* hedge (OE. *heġe*) + *hove* ground-ivy, (OE. *hōfe*), perh. in allusion to its alleged use instead of hops in brewing.] The herb ground-ivy (*Nepeta glechoma*). Also *hay-, hey-, horse-hove.*

Alei·ptic, *a. rare.* 1660. [– Gr. ἀλειπτικός f. ἀλείπτης gymnastic trainer; see -IC.] Belonging to gymnastic training.

Alembic (ăle·mbik). ME. [– OFr. *alembic* (mod. *alambic*) – med.L. *alembicus* – Arab.

al-'inbīk, f. *al* AL-² + *'inbīk* still – Gr. ἄμβιξ, ἀμβικ- cup, beaker, cap of a still, alembic. Cf. LIMBECK.] An apparatus formerly used in distilling, consisting of a *cucurbit* or gourd-shaped vessel, and the *cap* or *alembic* proper, the beak of which conveyed the products to a *receiver*. Also *fig.*
fig. The hot spirit drawn out of the a. of hell which in France is now so furiously boiling BURKE. Hence † **Ale·mbic, Ale·mbicate** *vbs.* to distil as in an a.

Alembroth (ăle·mbrǫþ). 1471. [Origin unkn.] *Alchem.* An old name for the double chloride of mercury and ammonium, once believed to be an alkahest.

† **Ale·ngth.** ME. [A *prep.*¹ 5.] **A.** *adv.* Lengthwise –1601. **B.** *prep.* Lengthwise to –1540.

† **Alepine, alapeen.** 1739. [– Fr. *alépine* (XVII) – Arab. *ḥalabī* from Aleppo.] A mixed stuff of wool and silk, or mohair and cotton.

‖ **Alerce** (ăle·rþe). 1845. [Sp. *alerce* larch – Arab.] An American tree allied to the larch.

Alerion (ălīᵊ·riən). 1605. [– Fr. *alérion* = med.L. *alerio*, of unkn. origin.] *Her.* An eagle without beak or feet.

Alert (ălə̄·ɹt). 1598. [– Fr. *alerte*, earlier *allerte*, *à l'airte* – It. *all' erta* on the look-out, f. *alla* at the + *erta* look-out (tower). Cf. ALARM *sb.*] **A.** *adv.* On the look-out; hence *adj.* (in the pred.) Watchful, wide-awake. *Mil.* 1598. *gen.* 1735. **B.** *adj.* Quick in attention and motion, lively, active 1712. **C.** *sb.* [mod.Fr. *alerte*, a military call. Cf. *alarm.*] **1.** The call to 'look out' for an attack; hence, a sudden attack 1803. **2. On the alert:** on the watch (replacing *alert* adv. = *all' erta*).
B. An a., joyous, and lively old soul SCOTT. C. **1.** No man ever saw me drunk when an a. was expected SCOTT. **2.** For ever on the a. 1882. Hence **Ale·rtly** *adv.* **Ale·rtness.**

Alethiology (ălī:þi,ǫ·lŏdʒi). *rare.* 1837. [f. G. ἀλήθεια truth + -LOGY.] The part of logic treating of truth.

Ale·tte. *arch.* 1816. [Fr. *alette*, dim. of *aile* wing :– L. *ala.*] A small wing; a pilaster or buttress.

Aleuromancy (ăliūᵊ·romæ:nsi). *rare.* 1656. [– Fr. *aleuromancie*, f. Gr. ἄλευρον flour; see -MANCY.] Divination by means of meal or flour.

Aleurometer (æliurǫ·mītəɹ). 1844. [f. Gr. ἄλευρον flour; see -METER.] An instrument for measuring the quantity of gluten in flour.

Aleuron(e (ăliūᵊ·rən, -ōᵘn). 1869. [f. Gr. ἄλευρον flour + -ONE b.] An albuminoid or proteinous substance found in granules in seeds, etc. Hence **Aleuro·nic** *a.* of or pertaining to a.

Alevin (æ·lĕvin). 1868. [–(O)Fr. *alevin*, also OFr. *alevain* :– Rom. **allevamen*, f. L. *allevare* set up, raise up, f. *ad* AL-¹ + *levare* raise.] Young fish, fry.

† **Alew·.** *rare.* = HALLOO. SPENSER.

A·le-wife¹. ME. [f. ALE- + WIFE in sense of *woman.*] A woman that keeps an ale-house.
Marrian Hacket the fat A. of Wincot SHAKS.

Ale-wife² (ēⁱ·lwəif). Pl. **-wives.** 1867. [Origin unkn.] An American fish (*Clupea serrata*) allied to the herring.

† **Alexa·nder,** *sb.* 1500. Alexandrian work; a species of striped silk.

† **Alexa·nder,** *v. nonce-wd.* To praise as an Alexander. DRYDEN.

Alexanders (ælĕgza·ndəɹz). [OE. – med.L. *alexandrum*; ME. *alisaundre* – OFr. *allis-sa(u)ndre*, *-derie* – med.L. *alexandrum* = *Petro-selinum alexandrinum*, also *P. macedonicum.*] An umbelliferous plant (*Smyrnium olusatrum*), called also Horse-parsley, formerly used for salads.

Alexander's Foot. 1597. A composite plant (*Anacyclus pyrethrum*), also called Pellitory of Spain, allied to camomile.

Alexandrine (ælĕgza·ndrin), *a.* and *sb.*¹ 1589. [– Fr. *alexandrin* (XV), f. *Alexandre*, title of an OFr. romance (XII–XIII) concerning Alexander the Great, in which the metre is used; see -INE¹.] **A.** *adj.* Applied to a line of six feet, the Fr. heroic verse, used in Eng. to vary the heroic verse of five feet. **B.** *sb.* An A. line or verse 1667.
A needless A. ends the song That like a wounded snake, drags its slow length along POPE.

Alexandrine, *a.* and *sb.*². 1500. [– Fr. *alexandrin* – L. *alexandrinus*, f. *Alexandria.*] Of or belonging to Alexandria; *esp.* a kind of embroidery.

Alexandrite (ælĕgza·ndrəit). 1837. [named after *Alexander* I, Czar of Russia; see -ITE¹ 2 b.] *Min.* A variety of chrysoberyl found in the Ural mountains.

Ale:xipha·rmic, *a.* 1671. [Modified f. ALEXIPHARMAC, Gr. ἀλεξιφάρμακον; see -IC.] Having the quality or nature of an antidote against poison. As *sb.* An antidote or counter-poison 1683. vars. † **Ale:xipha·rmac,** ‖ **Ale:xipharmacon.** Hence † **Ale:xipha·rmical** *a.*, var. † **Ale:xipha·rmacal.**

Ale:xipyre·tic, *a.* 1753 [f. Gr. ἀλεξι- warding off + πυρετός fever + -IC.] Helpful against fever. Also as *sb.*

Ale:xite·ric, *a.* 1694. [f. med.L. *alexiterium* alexitery (– Gr. ἀλεξιτήριον safeguard) + -IC.] *prop.* Able to ward off contagion; but *used as* = ALEXIPHARMIC 1706. As *sb.* A preservative against contagion or poison 1694. vars. † **Ale:xite·rial** *a.*, † **Ale:xite·rical** *a.*, † **Ale·xitery** *a.* and *sb.*

‖ **Alezan** (aləzaṅ·). 1848. [Fr. *alezan* – Sp. *alazan* – Arab.] A sorrel horse.

Alfa·lfa. 1845. [– Sp. *alfalfa*, formerly *alfalfez* – Arab. *al-fasfasa* a green fodder.] A variety of Lucerne.

‖ **Alfaqui** (alfăkī·). 1615. [Sp. *alfaqui*, – Arab. *al-fakīh*, f. *al* AL-² + *fakīh* one skilled in divine things.] A Moslem priest.

† **Alfe·res.** 1591. [– OSp., Pg. *alféres* (mod. Sp. *alférez*) ensign – Arab. *al-fāris* the horse-man, knight, cavalier.] An ensign, a standard-bearer.

† **Alfet.** OE. [– med.L. *alfetum* – OE. *ālfæt*, f. *āl* burning + *fæt* VAT.] The cauldron used in the ordeal of scalding water –ME.

† **A·lfin, a·lphin.** ME. [– OFr. *alfin, aufin* – Sp., Pg. *alfil* – Arab. *al-fīl*, f. *al* AL-² + *fīl* elephant.] Former name of the *bishop* in chess –1801.

† **Alfo·rge, -rja.** 1611. [Pg. *alforge*, Sp. *alforja* – Arab.] **1.** A wallet, a saddle-bag –1779. **2.** The cheek pouch of a baboon –1748.

‖ **Alfresco** (alfre·sko), *adv.* 1753. [It. *al fresco* in the open (air), on fresh (plaster).] † **1.** = FRESCO –1764. **2.** In the open air; also *attrib.* open-air 1753.
2. Here a. SMOLLETT. An a. emporium 1881.

‖ **Alga** (æ·lgă). Pl. **algæ** (æ·ldʒī). 1551. [L.] A sea-weed; in *pl.* A division of cryptogamic plants, including sea-weeds, kindred fresh-water plants, and some aerial species. var. **Alg** (*rare*). Cf. Fr. *algue.*

Algæology, -ist, bad ff. ALGOLOGY, -IST.

Algal (æ·lgăl), *a.* 1846. [f. L. ALGA + -AL¹.] Of the nature of an alga. As *sb.* An ally of the *algæ.* 1848.

†**Algara·d.** 1649. [– Fr. *algarade* – Sp. *algarada* – Arab. *al-ġāra*, f. *al* AL-² + *ġāra* raid.] A raid.

† **Algarde.** ME. only. [f. name of place.] A Spanish wine formerly in repute. DRUMM. OF HAWTH.

† **Algarot, -oth.** 1706. [– Fr. *algaroth*, f. Victor *Algarotti*, a physician of Verona.] *Chem.* An emetic, a compound of trichloride and trioxide of antimony.

‖ **Algarro·ba.** 1845. [Sp. – Arab. *al-ḵar-rūba* CAROB.] **1.** The CAROB tree and bean. **2.** A S. Amer. mimosa with pods of like flavour.

Algate, -s, *adv.* Now *dial.* ME. [lit. *alle gate* = every way; see GATE *sb.*² The *-s* is analogical.] † **1.** Always –1587. † **2.** Any how –1580. † **3.** At any rate –1600. † **4.** All the way, altogether –1625. † **5.** After all –1614. **6.** Everywhere. *n. dial.* Cf. *any gate*, etc.

Algazel, early f. GAZELLE.

Algebra (æ·ldʒībră). 1541. [– It., Sp., med.L. *algebra* – Arab. *al-jabr* f. *al* AL-² + *jabr* reunion of broken parts, f. *jabara* set broken bones, reunite. The full Arabic term for algebraic computation was *'ilm al-jabr wa'l- mukābala* the science of restoration to normal and equating like with like.] † **1.** The surgical treatment of fractures –1623. **2.** The part of mathematics which investigates the relations and properties of numbers by means of general symbols; a calculus of symbols combining according to defined laws 1551. A textbook of algebra (*mod.*).
2. Tell what hour o' th' day The clock does strike by A. BUTLER *Hud.* I. i. 126. Hence **Algebra·ic** *a.* of or pertaining to or occurring in a. (possessive gen.). **Algebra·ical** *a.* of or relating to a. (objective gen.). **Algebra·ically** *adv.* by algebraic processes. † **A·lgebraism, -rism,** an expression in a.; algebraic symbolism. **A·lgebra:ist, -rist,** one versed in a.; var. † **Algebri·cian. A·lgebraize, -rize,** to reduce to terms of or solve by a.

Algedo·nic, *a.* 1894. [f. Gr. ἄλγος pain + ἡδονή pleasure + -IC.] Concerned with pleasure and pain.

Algefacient (æ:ldʒifēⁱ·ʃiənt), *a.* 1879. [f. L. *algēre* be cold + -FACIENT.] *Med.* Cooling.

A·lgerite. [Named (1849) after Fr. *Alger*; see -ITE¹ 2 b.] *Min.* A kind of Wernerite.

Alge·tic, *a.* 1879. [irreg. f. Gr. ἀλγεῖν feel pain + -IC, after *emetic*, etc.] Causing or relating to pain.

Algid (æ·ldʒid), *a.* 1626. [– L. *algidus*, f. *algēre* be cold; see -ID¹.] Cold, chilly; *esp.* of one stage of an ague.
The a. breath of the desert wind BURTON. Hence **Algi·dity,** chilliness; *esp.* that due to collapse.

Algist (æ·ldʒist). 1869. [f. ALGA + -IST.] One who studies algæ.

Algodonite (ælgǫ·dŏnəit). [Named (1857) from *Algodones*, near Coquimbo; see -ITE¹ 2 b.] *Min.* A native arsenite of copper, Cu_6As, whitish and lustrous.

Algoid (æ·lgoid), *a.* 1874. [f. ALGA + -OID.] Like an alga.

Algology (ælgǫ·lŏdʒi). 1849. [f. ALGA + -LOGY. Cf. Fr. *algologie.*] The part of Botany which relates to algæ. Hence **Algolo·gical** *a.* **Algo·logist,** a student of a.

Algor (æ·lgŏɹ). ME. [– L. *algor* cold.] Cold, chilliness; *esp.* in the onset of fever.

Algorism (æ·lgŏriz'm). ME. [– OFr. *augori(s)me, algorisme* – med.L. *algorismus* f. (with assim. to *-ismus* -ISM) Arabicized Pers. *al- Ḵuwārizmī* the man of Ḵuwārizm (ancient name of Khiva), surname of the Arab mathematician 'Abū Ja'far Muhammad ibn Mūsa (IX), through the European translation of whose work on algebra the Arabic numerals became generally known. Cf. the use of *Euclid* for plane geometry.] The Arabic, or decimal system of numeration; *hence*, arithmetic. Also *attrib.*
Corruptlye written..Augrim for algorisme, as the Arabians sounde it RECORDE. Hence **Algori·smic** *a.* arithmetical.

Algorithm. [refash. (XVII) of ALGORISM through association w. Gr. ἀριθμός number, perh. through Fr. *algorithme* (XVII), which superseded OFr. *algorisme.*] ALGORISM.

Algous (æ·lgəs), *a.* 1742. [– L. *algosus* f. ALGA; see -OUS.] Of, pertaining to, or full of sea-weeds.

‖ **Alguazil** (ælgwăzi·l, Sp. algwăþi·l). 1598. [Early Sp. *alguazil* (mod. *-cil*) – Arab. *al-wazīr* f. *al* AL-² + *wazīr* (senior) minister of state, VIZIER.] Orig. the same word as *vizier*; at first a *justice*, later a *warrant-officer*, or *serjeant.*
The gripe of the vile alguazils of Impey MACAULAY.

Algum (æ·lgɒm). 1578. [Heb. *'algūm.*] A Biblical tree, called also (1 *Kings* 10:11) ALMUG; prob. sandal-wood.
Algume trees 2 *Chron.* 2:8.

‖ **Alhagi** (ælhă·dʒi). 1769. [mod.L. (Rauwolf 1537) – Arab. *al-kāj*, used by Avicenna.] *Bot.* A genus of leguminous plants, some of which yield a kind of manna.

Alhambra (ælhæ·mbră). [– Sp. – Arab. *al-ḥamrā'* the red, f. *al* AL-² + fem. of *aḥmar*, named after Muhammad ibn al-Aḥmar, who built it in 1273.] The palace of the Moorish kings at Granada. Hence **Alhambre·sque** *a.* like the A. in style.

‖ **Alha·ndal.** *Obs.* 1683. [Arab. *al-ḥanḏal.*] *Pharm.* The purgative extract of the Colocynth (*Citrullus colocynthis*).

Alhenna: see ALCANNA, HENNA.

Alias (ēⁱ·liăs, æ·-). 1535. [– L. *alias* at another time, otherwise.] **A.** *adv.* Otherwise (called or named). Now *italicized.*
Violent testie magistrates (alias Fooles) *Cor.* II. i. 48.

B. *sb.* (with *pl.* **aliases.**) **1.** Another name; an assumed name 1605. †**2.** *Law.* A second writ, containing the words *Sicut alias præcepimus*, issued after a first had failed –1809.

1. An *Aliàs* or double name CAMDEN. 2. A second [writ]..called an *alias* BLACKSTONE.

Alibi (æ·libəi), *adv.* 1727. [– L. *alibi*, contr. f. *aliubi*, f. *alius* other + *ibi* there, *ubi* where.] Elsewhere –1777. As *sb.* The plea of having been *elsewhere* at the time of any alleged act 1774.

To prove that..he was a. ERSKINE. *sb.* An a. was set up MACAULAY.

Alible (æ·lib'l), *a.* 1656. [f. L. *alibilis*, f. *alere* nourish; see -BLE.] Nutritive, nourishing. Hence **Alibi·lity,** nutritive quality.

Alicant (ælikæ·nt). 1500. A Spanish wine made at Alicante.

Butter'd beer, coloured with Alligant 1625. Cf. *Merry W.* II. ii. 69.

Alidad(**e** (ælidæ·d, æ·lidēd). ME. [orig. *allidatha, alhidada* – med.L. – Arab. *al-'idāda* revolving radius of a graduated circle, f. *'aḍud* upper arm, radius; in mod. form – Fr. *alidade*.] The index (Chaucer's *Rule*) of an astrolabe, quadrant, or other graduated instrument, carrying the sights or telescope, and showing the degrees cut off on the arc of the instrument.

Alien (ē·liĕn). ME. [– OFr. *alien* :– L. *alienus* belonging to another person or place, f. *alius* other.] **A.** *adj.* **1.** *gen.* Belonging to another person, place, or family; *esp.* to a foreign nation or allegiance. **2.** Foreign in nature, character, or origin 1673. **3.** Far removed from, inconsistent with ME.; repugnant, or opposed *to* 1720; *fig.* unkindly (*rare*) 1849.

1. Ruth..in tears amid the a. corn KEATS. A. domination MACAULAY. **Alien Priory:** one owing obedience to a mother-abbey in a foreign country. 2. A. pleasures BURKE. 3. His looks A. from Heaven MILT.

B. *sb.* [the adj. used absol.] **1.** A stranger, a foreigner ME. Also *fig.* **2.** *esp.* A resident foreign in origin and not naturalized 1330. **3.** One excluded *from* (citizenship, privileges, etc.) 1549. **4.** *Bot.* A plant orig. introduced from other countries 1847.

1. An a. in a strange land *Ex.* 18:3. *fig.* An a. from my mother's heart DICKENS. 3. Aliens from God's mercies J. H. NEWMAN.

Comb.: **a.-friend, (-amy), -enemy,** one owing allegiance to a country which is in alliance or at war with the country in which he resides; **aliens duty,** the special duty formerly paid by aliens on mercantile transactions; **-looking,** of foreign appearance.

Alien (ē·liĕn), *v.* ME. [– (O)Fr. *aliéner* :– L. *alienare* estrange or make another's, f. *alienus*; see prec.] = ALIENATE, the later form. **1.** To convert into an alien. Usu. *fig.* To estrange. **2.** To transfer the property or ownership of anything. [Often written *aliene* (ē·lyīn).] ME. †**3.** *refl.* and *intr.* To turn away, go off –1541.

1. Alien'd from their duty CLARENDON. 2. To a. the crown RALEIGH, land 1658. Hence **A·liened** *ppl. a.* = ALIENATED. **A:lienee·**, one to whom property is transferred. **A·liening** *vbl. sb* = ALIENATING. **A·lienor,** one who transfers property to another.

Alienable (ē·liĕnăb'l), *a.* 1611. [f. prec. + -ABLE; cf. Fr. *aliénable*.] Capable of being alienated. Hence **Alienabi·lity.**

Alienage (ē·liĕnėdʒ). 1809. [f. ALIEN *sb.* + -AGE.] The state or legal standing of an alien.

† **A·lienate,** *ppl. a.* and *sb.* ME. [– L. *alienatus*, pa. pple. of *alienare*; see ALIEN *v.*, -ATE[2].] **1.** Estranged –1814. **2.** Foreign in nature –1660. **3.** *Bot.* = ALIENATED. As *sb.* An alien –1566.

Alienate (ē·liĕneˈt), *v.* 1513. [– *alienat-*, pa. ppl. stem of L. *alienare*; see ALIEN *v.*, -ATE[3].] **1.** = ALIEN *v.* 1. 1548. **2.** = ALIEN *v.* 2. **3.** *fig.* To turn away, transfer 1621. †**4.** To alter –1587.

1. To a. colonies from the mother country BURKE. 2. To A. the Crown DRYDEN. 3. To a. capital from its natural channels 1832. 4. To a. one's purpose FOXE. Hence **A·lienated** *ppl. a.* estranged; transferred to another owner; † altered. **A·lienating** *vbl. sb.* and *ppl. a.* **A·lienator.**

Alienation (ē:liĕnē·ʃən). ME. [–(O)Fr. *alienation* or L. *alienatio*, f. *alienat-* (see prec.) + *-io* -ION.] **1.** The action of estranging, or state of estrangement. **2.** The action of transferring ownership to another ME.; diversion of anything to a different purpose 1828. **3.** The state of being alienated (sense 2) 1818. **4.** Loss or derangement of mental faculties; insanity. (So in L.) 1482. †**5.** Alteration 1615.

1. The a. of the people from..the sanctuary A. P. STANLEY. 2. The a. of Lands to the Church BRAMHALL. 4. A state of mental a. 1862.

Aliene, var. of ALIEN *v.* and obs. f. ALIEN *sb.* and *a.*

Alienigenate (ē:liĕni·dʒĕneˈt), *a.* 1855. [f. L. *alienigenus* (f. *alienus* ALIEN *a.* + *-genus* born) + -ATE[2] 2.] Alien-born.

Alienism (ē·liĕniz'm). 1816. [f. ALIEN *sb.* + -ISM.] **1.** The position of being an alien. **2.** The study and treatment of mental diseases 1881.

A·lienist. 1864. [– Fr. *aliéniste*; see ALIENATION 4, -IST.] One who treats mental diseases.

† **A·liet.** [ME. *aliete* – med.L. *alietus* – Gr. ἁλιάετος sea-eagle, prob. osprey.] The osprey or sea-eagle (Wyclif); *Her.* a merlin or sparrow-hawk.

† **Ali·fe,** *adv* [prob. f. *lief* dear, but confused w. *life*, quasi 'as one's life'.] In *To love a.*: to love dearly –1693.

A·liform, *a.* 1836. [– mod.L. *aliformis*, f. L. *ala* wing; see -FORM. Cf. Fr. *aliforme*.] Wing-shaped.

Alight (ăləi·t), *v.*[1] [OE. *alīhtan*, f. A- *pref.* 1 + *līhtan*; see LIGHT *v.*[1]] **1.** To spring; to dismount *from*, † *of*, to descend *out of* OE.; † to mount –1509. **2.** To land; to dismount or descend for a time; to stop ME. †**3.** To go or come down –1483. **4.** To descend and settle (opp. to *falling*); to land on a spot by floating, flying, etc. ME. **5.** To fall (*on* or *upon*) as a blow, etc. (*arch.*) ME. **6.** To chance upon (*rare*) 1858.

1. To a. from a hors 1475, out of a Coach CLARENDON. 2. A-lighted at your gate *Merch. V.* II. ix. 87. To a. at an inn 1824, at a station 1872. 4. I alit upon my feet POE. 6. To a. on a collection of MSS. FROUDE. Hence † **Ali·ght** *ppl. a.* alighted, arrived.

† **Ali·ght,** *v.*[2] late ME. [perh. f. A- *pref.* 1 + LIGHT *v.*[1] or LIGHT *a.*[2]; but cf. OE. *ġelīhtan*, which may have been the source.] To lighten; to relieve –1483. var. †**Ali·ghten.**

† **Ali·ght,** *v.*[3] OE. [repr. OE. *onlīhtan* (A- *pref.* 2, LIGHT *v.*[2]) and *alīhtan* (A- *pref.* 1), both 'shine upon, light up' unless *alīhtan* (once) is only a later form of *onlīhtan*.] To light up; to light (a fire, etc.) –1634. var. †**Ali·ghten.**

Ali·ght, *a.* ME. [prob. evolved from phr. †*on* (also *of, in*) *a light fire* (XVI–XVIII) ablaze, where *light* (= LIGHT *a.*[2]) appears to be pa. pple. of LIGHT *v.*[2]] **1.** Lighted; on fire. Also *fig.* **2.** Lighted up 1842. Also *fig.*

1. A Beacon..to be kept a. 1743. 2. [A] Chapel scarcely a. THACKERAY.

Align, aline (ăləi·n), *v.* 1693. [–(O)Fr. *aligner*, f. phr. *à ligne* into line; see LINE *sb.*[2] Earliest sp. *aline*; later after Fr.] **1.** To range or place in a line; to bring into line. **2.** *intr.* To fall into line 1877. **3.** To bring two or more points into a straight line, e.g. the sights of a rifle and the mark 1860.

Alignment (ăləi·nmĕnt). 1790. [–(O)Fr. *alignement*, f. *aligner*; see prec., -MENT.] **1.** Arrangement in a line or lines; used *spec.* of soldiers 1808; *concr.* a line of things arranged, a military 'line'. **2.** The drawing of a straight line so that it shall pass through a particular point 1869. **3.** Bringing into line; straightening 1879.

1. The alignments or stone avenues of Kermario 1881. The alignement of a battalion, of a camp, JAMES.

Alike (ăləi·k), *a.* [OE. *ġelīc*, = OFris. *gelīk*, OS. *gelīc*, OHG. *gilīh*, ON. *glíkr*, Goth. *galeiks* :– Gmc *ʒalīkaz, f. *ʒa- Y- + *līkam form, body (see LYCHGATE, LIKE). ME. *ilich*(*e, ilik*(*e* was prob. reinforced or superseded in certain areas by ON. *álíkr*, corresp. to OE. *anlīc, on-*, OHG *analīh*, Goth. *analeiks*.] Like one another, similar or identical in form or character. (Usu. predicatively; and of things in pl.)

Male, twins, both a. *Com. Err.* I. i. 56. Hence † **Ali·kewise.**

Ali·ke, *adv.* [OE. *ġelīċe* (ME. *ilyche, aliche, olike, ilike*), f. *ġelīċ* with adv. ending *-e*, corresp. to OHG. *gilīhho*, Goth. *galeiko*. Partly from ON. *álíka*, corresp. to OE. *anlīċe*, OHG. *analīhho*, Goth. *analeiko* (cf. prec.).] In the same or like manner, equally, similarly.

Nature..kind a. to all GOLDSM.

Aliment (æ·limĕnt). 1477. [– Fr. *aliment* or L. *alimentum*, f. *alere* nourish.] That which nourishes or feeds; nutriment; *fig.* that which sustains or supports 1631. **2.** *Sc. Law* and *gen.* = ALIMONY 1640.

1. A., medicine, and poison BACON. 2. Some pension or a. from the Court CARLYLE. Hence **Alime·ntal** *a.* of or pertaining to a.; nutritive, **Alime·ntally** *adv.*

A·liment, *v.* 1490. [–(O)Fr. *alimenter* – late L. *alimentare*, f. L. *alimentum* (prec.).] **1.** † To nourish; *fig.* to support 1663. **2.** *Sc. Law* and *gen.* To provide maintenance for 1629. Hence **A·limenter,** one who or that which affords aliment. **A·limenting** *vbl. sb.* maintenance.

Alimentary (ælime·ntări), *a.* 1615. [– L. *alimentarius*, f. as prec.; see -ARY[1].] **1.** Of the nature of ALIMENT; nutritious. **2.** Concerned with the function of nutrition 1620. **3.** Connected with maintenance 1751.

Alimentary Canal: the whole passage through the body by which food is received, digested, etc. Hence † **Alime·ntariness,** the quality of being a.

Alimentation (æ:limĕntē·ʃən). 1590. [– Fr. *alimentation* or med.L. *alimentatio*, f. *alimentat-*, pa. ppl. stem of *alimentare* ALIMENT *v.*; see -ION.] **1.** The action of affording aliment 1656. **2.** Process of being nourished 1605. **3.** Maintenance 1590.

2. Plants..have an Accretion, but no A. BACON.

Alimentative (ælime·ntĕtiv), *a. rare.* 1881. [f. ALIMENT *v.* + -ATIVE; cf. next.] Connected with the supply of aliment. Hence **Alime·ntativeness,** better form of next.

Alime·ntiveness. 1825. [f. ALIMENT *v.* + -IVE + -NESS, after Fr. *alimentativité*.] The instinct which impels an animal to seek food, to which phrenologists assign an 'organ'.

Alimony (æ·limăni). 1655. [– L. *alimonia*, f. *alere*; see -MONY.] **1.** Nourishment; maintenance 1656. Also *fig.* **2.** *esp.* The allowance made to a woman, out of her husband's estate, for her maintenance, on separation from him for certain causes 1655.

Aline, -ment, vars. of ALIGN, -MENT.

Aliped (æ·liped), *a.* 1847. [– L. *alipes -ped-*, f. *ala* wing + *pes* foot.] Wing-footed, as the bat. As *sb.* A cheiropterous animal. (Dicts.)

Aliquant (æ·likwănt), *a.* 1695. [– Fr. *aliquante* – fem. (*-a*) of L. *aliquantus* somewhat, f. *alius* some or other + *quantus* how great.] *Math.* In *aliquant part*: Contained in another, but not dividing it evenly; opp. to *aliquot*. Thus 3 is an a. part of 7.

Aliquot (æ·likwǫt), *a.* 1570. [– Fr. *aliquote*, med.L. *aliquota* fem. (AL. *partes aliquotæ* XIII), f. L. *aliquot* some, several, f. *alius* one of two + *quot* how many.] *Math.* In *aliquot part*: Contained in another, and dividing it without a remainder. Thus 2 is an a. part of 6. As *sb.* An aliquot part 1610.

‖ **Alisma** (ăli·zmă). 1736. [L. – Gr. ἄλισμα water-plantain.] *Bot.* A genus of aquatic endogenous plants, the type of N.O. *Alismaceæ*; esp. *A. plantago*. Hence **Alisma·ceous** *a.* of or belonging to the Alismads. **Ali·smad,** a plant of the order *Alismaceæ*. **Ali·smal** *a.* of or pertaining to alisma. **Ali·smoid** *a.* a.-like.

A·lisonite. 1837. [Named after R. E. *Alison* of Chili; see -ITE[1] 2 b.] A kind of COVELLITE.

Alispheno- (ælisfī·no), comb. f. of next.

Alisphenoid (ælisfī·noid), *a.* 1846. [f. L. *ala* wing + SPHENOID *a.*] *Phys.* Forming the wing of the sphenoid bone at the base of the skull, or pertaining to this part. As *sb.* An a. bone 1849. Hence **A:lisphenoi·dal** *a.* pertaining to the wings of the sphenoid bone.

† **Ali·te** = *a lite*, a little; see LITE.

Alitrunk (æ·litrɒŋk). 1816. [f. L. *ala* wing + *truncus* trunk.] The segment of the thorax to which an insect's wings are attached.

-ality, *comp. suffix* of sbs. = -AL + -ITY, the quality of being.

† **Ali·ve,** *v.* OE. [f. A- *pref.* 1 + LIVE *v.*] To live.

Alive (ăləi·v), *adv.* [OE. phr. *on life* ME. *on live, olive, alive*; see A *prep.*[1] 11, LIFE.]

1. In life; living. 2. (Emphatic, intensive, or expletive.) *colloq.* ME. 3. *fig.* Unextinguished, unabated, unforgotten 1602. 4. In a sentient condition; sensitive, awake, fully conscious 1732. 5. In an active condition; vivacious, brisk, quick in action 1748. 6. In a state of commotion, stirring or swarming *with* 1808.

1. Let me on-lif go 1500. A. or dead *Merch. V.* II. ii. 75. 2. Any man alive = any man in the world. Man Alive! 1845. Sakes alive! (U.S.) 1860. 3. To keep discontent a. MACAULAY. 4. A. to the impression of shame BENTHAM. 5. *To look alive*: to make haste. 6. The river .. a. with wherries MACAULAY.

† **Ali·ves,** *adv.* ME. [= prec. with gen. *lives* for dat. *live*; cf. LIVES.]

Ali·zarate. 1875. [f. next + -ATE[1] 1 c.] *Chem.* A salt of alizaric acid.

‖ **Alizari** (ăliză·ri). 1850. [Fr. and Sp. *alizari*, f. Arab. *al-ʿiṣara* juice pressed out, f. *ʿaṣara* press (grapes or olives).] *Comm.* The Madder of the Levant. Hence **Aliza·ric** *a.*; *esp.* in *alizaric acid* = phthalic acid.

Alizarin (ăli·zărin). 1835. [– Fr. *alizarine*; see prec., -IN[1].] *Chem.* The red colouring matter of the madder root ($C_{14}H_8O_4$).

Alkahest (æ·lkăhest). Also **alc-, alch-.** 1641. [prob. invented by Paracelsus, after Arab.] *Alchemy.* The 'universal solvent'. *fig.* An intellectual a., melting the universe into an idea 1866. Hence **Alcahe·stic, -al** *a.* all-dissolving.

Alkalamide (æ·lkălămaid). 1863. [f. ALKALI + AMIDE.] *Chem.* A compound ammonia in which two or more atoms of hydrogen are replaced by *acid-* and *base-*radicles.

Alkalescent (ælkăle·sĕnt), *a.* 1732. [f. ALKALI + -ESCENT; cf. Fr. *alcalescent*, which may be the source.] Becoming or tending to become alkaline. As *sb.* [sc. *substance.*] 1750. Hence **Alkale·scence,** the process of becoming, or tendency to become, alkaline; slight alkaline character; var. **Alkale·scency.**

Alkali (æ·lkăli). Pl. **alkalis,** occ. **-ies.** [Late ME. *alcaly* – med.L. *alkali* – Arab. *al-ḳalī* calcined ashes of Salsoia and Salicornia, f. *ḳala* fry, roast; see AL-[2], KALI.] 1. *orig.* A saline substance obtained by lixiviating the calcined ashes of marine plants; soda-ash. 2. *Bot.* The plant Saltwort (*Salsola kali*) 1578. 3. Any substance having the characteristics of soda 1612. 4. *Comm.* Any form of alkaline substance, as common soda, caustic soda, caustic potash, etc., used in commerce or the arts 1822. 5. *Chem.* A series of BASES, analogous to and including soda, potash, and ammonia, highly soluble in water, producing corrosive solutions, which neutralize strong acids, and turning vegetable yellows to brown, reds to blue, and purples to green 1813.

Comb.: **a.-metal** = ALKALINE metal; **-waste,** a by-product, sulphide of calcium. Hence † **Alka·lic** *a.* = ALKALINE. **A·lkalify** *v.* to make into or become an a., or alkaline; hence **A·lkalifi·able** *a.* † **Alkaligen,** a name for nitrogen. **Alkali·genous** *a.* generating a., or alkaline qualities. † **Alkali·meter,** an instrument for measuring the amount of a. in a solution. **Alkalime·tric, -al** *a.* **Alkali·metry,** the measurement of the strength of alkalis.

Alkaline (æ·lkălain), *a.* 1677. [f. prec. + -INE[1]; cf. Fr. *alcalin* (1700).] Of or pertaining to or of the nature of alkalis. Also used *fig.* and *subst.* 2. **Alkaline metals:** those whose hydroxides are alkalis, *viz.* potassium, sodium, cæsium, lithium, and the hypothetical ammonium. **Alkaline earths:** the oxides of calcium, strontium, and barium. Hence **Alkali·nity,** the quality of being a. **A·lkalinize,** to make a. var. † **Alka·lious.**

† **Alka·lizate,** *ppl. a.* 1622. [– mod.L. *alkalizatus*; see ALKALI, -IZE, -ATE[2].] Alkalized, alkaline –1753. Hence † **Alka·lizateness** = ALKALINITY. **Alkaliza·tion,** the action of alkalizing.

Alkalize (æ·lkălaiz), *v.* 1749. [f. ALKALI + -IZE; cf. Fr. *alcaliser.*] To render alkaline.

Alkaloid (æ·lkăloid). 1831. [– G. *alkaloid*; see ALKALI, -OID. Cf. Fr. *alcaloïde.*] *Chem.* A body resembling an alkali in properties. Applied *gen.* to all nitrogenous basic substances, or to all nitrogenous organic bases; *spec.* to the *Vegetable alkalis*, very bitter in taste, and acting powerfully on the animal system. Also *attrib.* Hence **Alkaloi·dal** *a.* of the nature of an a.

Alkanet (æ·lkănet). ME. [– Sp. *alcaneta*, f. *alcana* (med.L. *alchanna*), corresp. to OFr. *alchanne, arcanne* – Arab. *al-ḥinnā'*: see AL-[2], HENNA, and cf. ALCANNA, ORCANET.] 1. A dye-material yielding a fine red colour (see 2). 2. The plant whose root yields the dye, *Anchusa* or *Alkanna tinctoria*, N.O. *Boraginaceæ*, Orchanet, Dyer's or Sp. Bugloss, Bugloss of Languedoc 1567. 3. Applied also to: **a.** Common (Eng.) A. (*Anchusa officinalis*); **b.** Evergreen A. (*A. sempervirens*); **c.** Bastard A. (*Lithospermum arvense*); **d.** Alkanet (Amer.), (*L. canescens*).

Alkanna: see ALCANNA.

Alkargen (ælkā·ɹdʒĕn). 1877. [f. ALKAR(SIN) + (OXY)GEN.] = CACODYLIC ACID.

Alkarsin (ælkā·ɹsin). 1850. [f. ALK(ALI) + ARS(ENIC) + -IN[1].] *Chem.* A poisonous, spontaneously inflammable, liquid, smelling of garlic, supposed to be a mixture of cacodyl and its oxidation products; called also *Cadet's fuming liquor.*

†‖ **Alkeda·vy.** 1631. [– (perh. indirectly) Arab. *al-ḳāḍawī* of the CADI or ALCALDE.] The palace of a cadi. HEYWOOD.

‖ **Alkekengi** (ælkĭke·ndʒi). ME. [– med.L. – Arab. *al-kākanj*, f. *al* AL-[2] + Pers. *kākanj* kind of medicinal resin, (also) nightshade.] *Bot.* A plant (*Physalis alkekengi* Linn.) N.O. *Solanaceæ*, called also Winter-Cherry from its scarlet berries.

† **Alkermes** (ælkɔ̄·ɹmīz). 1605. [– Fr. *alkermès*, – (ult.) Arab.; see AL-[2], KERMES.] 1. The Kermes, or Scarlet Grain insect (the female of *Coccus ilicis*) –1718. 2. A confection of which the Kermes, formerly supposed to be a berry, was an ingredient –1753.

† **A·lkin,** *a.* ME. [Genitive phr., sing. or pl., *alles cynnes, alra cynna*, placed bef. the sb.; hence treated as adj., and ult. shortened to *alkin(s)*.] Of every kind; every kind of –1552.

All (ǭl). [OE. *all, (eall)* = OFris. *al, ol*, OS., OHG. *al*, ON. *allr*, Goth. *alls*, prob.:– Gmc. **alnaz*, ppl. formation on **al-*, as in OS., OHG. *alung* completely, and **ala-* of Goth. *alaniuwi* quite new, *alamannam* all mankind.] **A.** *adj.* 1. with *sb. sing.* The whole amount, extent, substance, or compass of; the whole OE.; all that is possible 1594. 2. With *sb. pl.* The entire number of, without exception. (Bef. the sb., etc., exc. poet.) OE. 3. = Every. L. *omnis*. *Obs.* exc. with *kind*, and *manner* –1570. 4. = Any whatever (in exclusive sentences and clauses) ME. Also *absol.* 5. As antecedent to relative: all *that*, all *those* OE. 6. Followed by *of*: in *sing.* The whole; in *pl.* Every individual 1800. 7. as *pl.* = All men OE. 8. as *sing.* = Everything OE.

1. All flesh is as grass 1 *Pet.* 1:24. I in all haste was sent SHAKS. All this while SHAKS. I see it all now (mod.). 2. Th' abstracts of all faults That all men follow *Ant. & Cl.* I. iv. 9. So *all those, all mine*, etc., *all we* now *we all*, or *all of us*. 3. Alle manere of marchaundises MAUNDEV. All kind of drollery 1888. 4. Things without all remedie *Macb.* III. ii. 11. *Beyond all question, doubt*, etc. *To deny, disclaim, etc., all intention.* 5. All what thou commandst MILT. 6. *All of it*, etc. 7. O God, and fadir of alle WYCLIF. 8. All is not lost MILT. So in **all but:** everything short of; *hence* almost. **And all:** and all the rest, *et cetera*; *hence* as well. **And all that:** and all the rest of it. **All in all:** all things in all respects. **When all comes (goes) to all:** when everything is summed up. **At all:** in every or any way (now only in neg., interrog., or hypothet. sentences or clauses). **For all:** notwithstanding. **In all:** all together; *also*, in whole. **Of all:** formerly *ellipt.* = most of all. **With all:** see WITHAL. **All and some:** distributed to each part of the whole; also, in *sing.* the sum total. So *one and all, all and sundry*, etc.

B. *sb.* 1. Everything that we have, or that concerns or pertains to us 1627. Also in *pl.* 2. Whole being, entirety, totality 1674. 3. Whole system of things, the Universe 1598.

1. Our All is at stake ADDISON. To pack up one's alls FIELDING. 2. An all of rotten Formulas CARLYLE. 3. The wide circle of the All CARLYLE.

C. *adv.* 1. *All* adj.; separated from its sb., appeared to refer to the predicate, hence, to qualify it, as *adv.*: Wholly, completely, altogether, quite OE. 2. Even, just (*arch.*) 1579. 3. All through, wholly, without admixture 1705.

1. It [the City] is all full of lies *Nahum* 3:1. It succeeded all other wise ELYOT. So † **all thing** *Macb.* III. i. 14. 2. All in the Downs the fleet was moored GAY. 3. Paces all 1705.

Special constructions. 1. **All one.** Also **all a.** Quite the same. 2. Pleonastic in † **All-whole:** entire. So † **All-wholly,** † **-utterly.** 3. Emphatic in *All so, too* = Quite. 4. With adv. *the*: just so much. All the better *A.Y.L.* I. ii. 102. 5. With advbs. of place: In all directions, in every part; as **All along, All over, All round,** etc. † 6. *All* emphasised the particle combined with a vb.; *esp. to-* = as under (L. *dis*), as in *all to-broken*, quite broken in pieces; and, as **allto, alto** = wholly, was applied to other vbs., as in *all-to dirtied* LATIMER, *all-to-be-fooled* BUNYAN.

D. Obsolete uses of early inflected forms.

† 1. The gen. sing. **alles:** altogether, at all –1320. † 2. The gen. pl. **alra, alre, aller, alder, alther,** 'of all' –1600; esp. *absol.* bef. a superlative: Mine Alder liefest Soueraigne 2 *Hen. VI*, I. i. 28. Occ. written *all there.* Also, as in *our, your, their aller* = mod. *of us all*, etc.

E. All- in *comb.*

1. *adj.* with sb. **four(s** (sc. *extremities*). The *-s* is recent. **To be (stand) on all fours:** to be even with; **-hail,** *int., sb.*, and *v.* a salutation: *lit.* (I wish you) all health! **-might,** omnipotence; † **-night,** a service of food, fuel, or light for the whole night; **-power** = *a.-might.* 2. *adj.* with adv. ALGATE; ALWAYS; **-where** (*arch.*) everywhere; **-whither,** in every direction (*rare*). 3. *subst.* (*genit.*) with sb. = 'of all'. **-father,** *orig.* Odin; Jupiter; God. 4. *subst.* (*obj.*) with vb. inf. **-hold,** that which holds all. 5. *advb.* with sb. **-bone,** the Greater Stitchwort (*Stellaria holostea* L.); **-heart,** the elm-tree; **-rail; -slavery; -talk; -wool.** 6. *advb.* with adj. = 'wholly, infinitely'. **-holy; -mighty; -witty;** and since 1600 with any adj. of quality, esp. *poet.*; with forms in *-ent*, and *-ive*; and with pr. pple., often as obj. of the vbl. action. 7. *advb.* with *pa. pple.* = completely; occ. = by all; freq. in SHAKS.

‖ **Alla Breve** (a:lla brē·ve). 1806. [It., = according to the BREVE.] *Mus. Orig.* With a breve or four minims to every bar; *now*, in quick common time, counted with two minims in the bar.

‖ **A·lla Cape·lla.** 1847. [It., = according to (the manner of) the chapel.] *Mus.* = prec.

Allagite (æ·lădʒait). [f. Gr. ἀλλαγή change + -ITE[1] 2 b.] *Min.* A carbonated variation of RHODONITE, dull-green or reddish-brown in colour.

Allagostemonous (æ:lăgo,stī·mənəs), *a.* 1880. [f. Gr. ἀλλαγή change + στήμων thread + -OUS.] *Bot.* With stamens inserted alternately on the torus and on the petals.

Allah (æ·lă). 1702. [– Arab. *'allāh*, for *al-'ilāh*, i.e. *al* AL-[2], *ilāh* god = Aram. *ʿlāh*, Heb. *ʿlōah*,; see ELOHIM.] The Moslem name of the Deity.

Allamotti, -monti, -moth, dial. names for the Stormy Petrel.

Allan, var. of ALAN; and AULIN.

Allanite (æ·lănait). 1843. [Named after T. *Allan*; see -ITE[1] 2 b.] *Min.* A brownish-black mineral, akin to Epidote, a cerium-epidote.

Allantoid (ălæ·ntoid). 1633. [– Gr. ἀλλαντοειδής (Galen), f. ἀλλᾶς, ἀλλᾶντ- sausage + -ειδής -OID; cf. Fr. *allantoïde.*] *Phys.* **A.** *adj.* Of or pertaining to the allantois. **B.** *sb.* = ALLANTOIS 1667.

Allantoidian (ælæ̆ntoi·diăn). 1861. [– Fr. *allantoïdien*; see prec., -IAN.] *Zool.* **A.** *adj.* Having the fœtus furnished with an allantois. **B.** *sb.* [sc. *animal.*]

Allantoin (ălæ·nto,in). 1845. [f. ALLANTOIS + -IN[1]; cf. Fr. *allantoïne.*] *Chem.* A crystalline substance, $C_4N_4H_6O_3$, the nitrogenous constituent of the allantoic fluid.

Allantois (ălæ·nto,is). 1646. [mod.L., spurious form evolved from *allantoides* – Gr. ἀλλαντοειδής ALLANTOID.] *Phys.* The fœtal membrane (named from its form in a calf) found only in mammals, birds, and reptiles, which lies under the chorion, and forms a means of communication between the fœtal and maternal blood. Hence **Allanto·ic** *a.*

Allanturic (ælæ̆ntiūᵊ·rik), *a.* 1863. [f. ALLANTOIN + URIC *a.*] Obtained from allantoin or from uric acid.

† **Alla·trate,** *v.* 1583. [– *allatrat-*, pa. ppl. stem of *allatrare* bark at, f. *ad* AL-[1] + *latrare* bark.] To bark out. *rare.*

Allay (ălē[i]·), *v.*[1] OE. [f. A- *pref.* 1 + LAY *v.*; OE. *alecgan* (= OHG. *irleggen* (G. *erlegen*), Goth. *uslagjan*), ME. *alegge*, superseded by *aleie*, *alay* (see LAY *v.*). Later (XVI) sp. *all-* after words derived f. L. *adl-*, *all-*. The sense-development has been infl. by formal association w. ALLAY *v.*[2,3], ALLEGE *v.*[2]]

† **1.** To lay down, set aside; *hence*, to annul –ME.; to quell –ME.; to overthrow (a principle, etc.) –1659. **3.** To put down or repress; to assuage, 'lay' a storm 1488. **3.** To quell or put down; to appease ME. † **4.** *intr.* To subside, cease; to become mild –1723. **5.** (see ALLEGE *v.*[1]) To subdue; to abate, alleviate ME. **6.** (see ALLAY *v.*[2]) To temper or abate 1514; to mitigate 1603.

2. Alay (the wild waters) *Temp.* I. ii. 2. **3.** To a. wrath 1600, distrusts 1623, panic 1880. **5.** To a. Thir appetite MILT. *P.L.* x. 566, grief BEATTIE. **6.** To a. or dim the whiteness of paper FLORIO. To a. a crime PRYNNE. Hence [f. ALLAY *v.*[1] (*v.*[2])] **Allayed** *ppl. a.* † alloyed; tempered; modified; laid (cf. *inlaid*). **Allay·er,** he who or that which allays. **Allay·ing** *vbl. sb.* † cessation; dilution; mitigation; † alloying; *ppl. a.* diluting, tempering. † **Allay·ment,** admixture with a modifying element *Cymb.* I. v. 22.

† **Allay·,** *v.*[2] ME. [– ONFr. *aleyer, alayer* (mod. *aloyer*), var. of OFr. *alier* ALLY *v.* :– L. *alligare* bind up, f. *ad* AL-[1] + *ligare* bind. Replaced by ALLOY *v.*] To mix (metals); *esp.* with a baser metal. Also *fig.* –1796.

fig. Debased and allayed with superstitious intents FULLER.

† **Allay·,** *v.*[3] ME. [– OFr. *aleier, alaier* declare on oath :– L. *allegare* produce in evidence, f. *ad* AL-[1] + *legare* depute, send. Replaced by ALLEGE *v.*[2]] To cite, allege –1470.

† **Allay·,** *sb.*[1] ME. [– ONFr. *aley, alai* (mod. *aloi*) f. *aleier, alayer, aloyer*; see ALLAY *v.*[2] Replaced by ALLOY *sb.*] **1.** = ALLOY. *lit.* and *fig.* **2.** *fig.* Alien element –1774. **3.** *fig.* Composition. Cf. Fr. *de bon aloi.* –1690. **4.** (f. ALLAY *v.*[1]) Dilution –1632; abatement –1758; repression –1726.

† **Allay·,** *sb.*[2] 1486. [– AFr. *alais* = OFr. *eslais* (see A- *pref.* 9) dash forward, leap, f. *eslaissier* let out, let off. Cf. RELAY *sb.*] The act of laying on the hounds –1630.

† **Alle·ct,** *v.* 1528. [– L. *allectare* allure, entice, frequent. of *allicere*, f. *ad* AL-[1] + *lacere* entice.] To entice –1552. Hence †**Alle·ction,** enticement. †**Alle·ctive** *a.* enticing; *sb.* that which can entice.

† **A·llegate,** *v.* 1529. [– *allegat-*, pa. ppl. stem of L. *allegare* produce in evidence; see ALLAY *v.*[3]] = ALLEGE *v.*[2] –1639.

Allegation (ælĭgē[i]·ʃən). 1483. [– (O)Fr. *allégation* or L. *allegatio*, f. *allegat-*; see prec., -ION.] **1.** The action of alleging or making a charge before a tribunal; that which is charged. † **2.** An excuse –1622. **3.** An assertion 1532; *esp.* a mere assertion 1635. † **4.** Quotation; the matter quoted –1673.

1. To sweare False allegations 2 *Hen. VI*, III. i. 181. **3.** I thought their allegations but reasonable STEELE. His wild a. BOSWELL.

† **Alle·ge,** *v.*[1] ME. [– OFr. *aleger, allegier* (mod. *alléger*) :– late L. *alleviare* lighten, cl. L. *allevare* (f. *ad* AL-[1] + *levare* raise), infl. by *levis* light. See ALLEVIATE *v.*] = ALLAY *v.*[1] 5. –1530. Hence † **Alle·geance**[1], alleviation; var. † **Alle·gement**[1], **ale-**.

Allege (ăle·dʒ), *v.*[2] ME. [– AFr. *alegier* = OFr. *esligier* (see A- *pref.* 9) :– Rom. **exlitigare* clear at law, f. L. *ex* EX- + *lis, lit-* lawsuit; used in the senses of L. *allegare*, replacing ALLAY *v.*[3]] **1.** To declare on oath before a tribunal; hence, to plead. *Obs.* exc. *fig.* **2.** To cite, quote *for* or *against* (*arch.*) ME. **3.** Hence *gen.* To plead as an excuse; to adduce as reason ME. **4.** To advance, as being able to prove; *hence*, to assert without proof ME.

1. The Prosecutor alleged That [etc.] STEELE. **2.** They alleage Moses . . for tithes MILT. **3.** To a. excuses to the contrary 1598. **4.** Where much is alleged, something must be true GIBBON. Hence **Alle·geable** *a.* † **Alle·geance**[2], the action of alleging; allegation. **Alle·ged** *ppl. a.* adduced as legal ground, or as a reason; quoted; asserted as provable; asserted but not proved. **Alle·gedly** *adv.* † **Alle·gement**[2], allegation. **Alle·ger.**

Allegiance (ălī·dʒăns, ălī·dʒ[i]ăns). ME. [– AFr. **aligeance* (AL. *alligantia*), f. OFr. *ligeance* (AL. *ligantia*), f. *lige* LIEGE; see -ANCE. The prefix *al-* was perh. due to association w. *alligantia* ALLIANCE.] † **1.** The relation of a liege lord ME. only. **2.** The relation or duties of a liegeman to his lord; the tie of a subject to his sovereign or government ME. **3.** *fig.* The recognition of the claims which any one has to our respect and duty 1732.

2. Subjects may be freed from their Allegeance HOBBES. **3.** A. to a lady SCOTT, to natural science HERSCHELL. var. **Alle·giancy.** Hence **Alle·giant** *a.* loyal.

Allegoric, -al (ælĭgǫ·rik, -ăl), *a.* ME. [– late L. *allegoricus* – Gr. ἀλληγορικός; see ALLEGORY, -IC. Cf. Fr. *allégorique* (XVI).] Of or pertaining to allegory; of the nature of an allegory; constituting or containing an allegory.

What kingdom, Real or allegorick, I discern not MILT. *P.R.* iv. 389. Its chimeras, its harpies, its allegorical figures BURKE. Hence **Allego·rically** *adv.* **Allego·ricalness.** (Dicts.)

Allegorist (æ·lĭgŏrist). 1684. [– Fr. *allégoriste* – Gr. ἀλληγοριστής; see ALLEGORY, -IST.] One who writes allegories, or writes or expounds allegorically.

Bunyan . . the first of allegorists MACAULAY.

Allegorize (æ·lĭgŏrəiz), *v.* 1581. [– Fr. *allégoriser* or late L. *allegorizare* (Jerome), f. L. *allegoria* ALLEGORY; see -IZE.] **1.** To make or treat as allegorical 1596. **2.** *intr.* To expound allegorically; to construct or utter allegories 1581.

1. To a. *away* the History of the Crucifixion 1667. To a. Christ *out of* His Divinity PENN. **A·llegorizer. A:llegoriza·tion.**

Allegory (æ·lĭgŏri). ME. [– (O)Fr. *allégorie* – L. *allegoria* – Gr. ἀλληγορία speaking otherwise, f. ἄλλος other + -ἀγορία speaking.] **1.** Description of a subject under the guise of some other subject of aptly suggestive resemblance. **2.** An instance of such description; an extended metaphor 1534. **3.** An allegorical representation; an emblem 1639.

‖ **Allegresse** (alegre·s, ælĭgre·s), 1652. [Fr.] Gaiety, gladsomeness.

‖ **Allegretto** (allegre·tto), *a.* 1879. [It., dim. of ALLEGRO.] *Mus.* Somewhat brisk.

‖ **Allegro** (It. allē·gro). 1632. [It.] **A.** *adj.* Lively, gay MILT. **B.** *adv.* and *adj. Mus.* Brisk, lively 1721. **C.** *sb.* [sc. *movement*] 1777.

Alleleu (ælĭl[i]ū·). An outcry. CARLYLE.

Allelomorph (ælī·lomǭɹf). 1902. [f. Gr. ἀλλήλ- one another + μορφή form.] *Biol.* Each of a pair of mutually exclusive characters, one or the other of which is exhibited without intermixture in descendants of a cross between parental forms respectively possessing them. Hence **Alle:lomo·rphic** *a.*

Alleluia (ælĭl[i]ū·iă), *int.* and *sb.*[1] ME. [– eccl.L. *alleluia* – Gr. ἀλληλουϊα, the LXX repr. of Heb. HALLELUJAH *int.* and *sb*[1].] = HALLELUJAH. Hence **Allelu:ia·tic** *a.*

Allelu·ia, *sb.*[2] 1543. [Origin unkn.] The woodsorrel.

‖ **Allemande** (aləmāñ·d, -ma·nd, æ·lĕmænd æ·lmænd). 1685. [– Fr. (sc. *danse*) *allemande* German (dance); see ALMAIN.] **1.** A name of various German dances 1775. **2.** A piece of music forming one of the movements of the Suite 1685.

Allemontite (ælĕmǫ·ntəit). 1837. [f. *Allemont*, in Dauphiné, + -ITE[1] 2 b.] A native alloy of arsenic and antimony.

Allenarly (ăle·năɹli). *north.* and *Sc.* ME. [f. ALL *adv.* + ANERLY.] **1.** *adv.* Only, solely. **2.** *adj.* Only, sole 1533.

Allene, = ALLYLENE.

† **Alle·niate,** *v. rare.* [f. L. *ad* AL-[1] + *lēnis* soft, gentle + -ATE[3], after *alleviate.*] To soften –1642.

Allerion, var. of ALERION.

† **Alle·ve,** *v.* 1546. [– OFr. *alevier* relieve, alleviate – late L. *alleviare*; see ALLEGE *v.*[1]] To relieve. Hence † **Alle·vement.**

† **Alle·viate,** *ppl. a.* 1471. [– *alleviatus*, pa. pple. of late L. *alleviare*; see foll.] Alleviated –1671.

Alleviate (ălī·vi,ē[i]t), *v.* 1528. [– *alleviat-*, pa. ppl. stem of late L. *alleviare*; see ALLEGE *v.*[1], -ATE[3].] † **1.** To make lighter –1666. **2.** To relieve, mitigate 1528. † **3.** To extenuate –1777.

2. To a. sorrows BP. HALL, sufferings 1871. **3.** To a. a crime BLACKSTONE. Hence **Alle·viative** *a.* of an alleviating tendency. Also *sb.* **Alle·viator,** he who, or that which, alleviates. **Alle·viatory** *a.* having the attribute of relieving.

Alleviation (ălī:vi,ē[i]·ʃən). 1625. [– OFr. *alleviation* or med.L. *alleviatio*, f. as prec.; see -ION.] The action of lightening weight, gravity, severity, or pain; relief, mitigation.

It [is] an a. of misery not to suffer alone JOHNSON.

Alley (æ·li). ME. [– OFr. *alee* (mod. *allée*) walking, passage, f. *aller* walk, go :– L. *ambulare* walk; cf. AMBLE *v.*] † **1.** A passage in or into a house –1525. Also *fig.* **2.** *esp.* A walk or passage in a garden, park, etc., bordered with trees or bushes; an avenue ME. **3.** A passage between buildings; hence, a lane; in *U.S.* a *Mews* 1510. **4.** A long narrow enclosure for playing at bowls, skittles, etc. ME. Also *fig.* **5.** A passage between the rows of pews or seats in a church 1464. In the south superseded by AISLE. **6.** The space between two compositors' stands, etc. in a printing-office 1871. **7.** A free space between two lines of any kind 1756.

2. A thick pleached a. in my orchard *Much Ado* I. ii. 10. Every a. green . . of this wild wood MILT. *Comus* 311. **3.** *Blind Alley*: one that is closed at the end; a *cul de sac*. *The Alley, esp.* Change Alley, London, scene of the gambling in South Sea stocks. Hence **A·lleyed** *ppl. a.* laid out as an a., or with alleys.

Alley, var. of ALLY, a kind of marble.

All-fired (ǭ·l-fəi[ə]·ɹd), *a. slang.* 1837. [euphem. for *hell-fired.*] Infernal. (Chiefly in U.S.). Hence **A·ll-fi:redly** *adv.*

All-flower-water. 1839. [Origin unkn.] Cow's urine; as a remedy.

All Fools' Day. 1712. [With joc. ref. to *All Saints, All Souls.*] The 1st of April; pop. appropriated to practising upon people's credulity.

All fours (ǭ·l fō[ə]·ɹz). 1707. [i.e. *all four points.*] **1.** A game of cards, played by two; called after the *four* points, *high, low, Jack,* and *the game*, which make 'all-fours'. **2.** A game at dominoes, in which only four or its multiples count. See also ALL E. 1.

Allgood (ǭ·lgud), *sb.* 1578. [ALL E 6.] The herb (*Chenopodium bonus-henricus*), also called English Mercury, and Good King Henry.

All-hallow, -s (ǭ:lhæ·lo[u]z). [OE. *ealra hālgena dæġ* day of all saints, ME. *alle halewene day*, later *al halow*. With *-s* from XV. See HALLOW *sb.*[1] HALLOWE'EN, HALLOWMAS.] **1.** All saints (collectively). **2.** = All hallows' day, Nov. 1, or All-hallowmas (*arch.*) 1503.

Phrases *All hallows' day*: All Saints' day. *All-hallow Eve, Mass, tide*, the eve, feast, season, of All Saints; cf. HALLOW-E'EN. † *All-hallown Summer*: = *Indian Summer*, or *St. Martin's Summer*. 1 *Hen. IV*, I. ii. 178.

Alliable (ăləi·ăb'l), *a. rare.* 1795. [– Fr. *alliable*, f. *allier*; see ALLY *v.*, -ABLE.] Able to enter into alliance or union.

Alliaceous (æli,ē[i]·ʃəs), *a.* 1792. [– mod.L. *alliaceus*, f. L. *allium* garlic; see -ACEOUS.] **a.** Of or pertaining to *Allium*. **b.** Smelling or tasting like garlic and onions.

† **A·lliage.** ME. [– Fr. *alliage*, f. as next; see -AGE.] Alliance –1546.

Alliance (ăləi·ăns), *sb.* ME. [– OFr. *aliance* (mod. *alliance*) f. *alier*; see ALLY *v.*, -ANCE.] The state of union or combination; uniting or combining. **1.** Union by marriage, affinity; consanguinity. **2.** Combination for a common object; *esp.* between sovereign states ME. **3.** Community in nature or qualities; affinity 1677. † **4.** *collect.* People united by kinship or friendship (? for *Alliants*) –1655; also, a kinsman, relation, or ally –1654. **5.** *Bot.* A group of Natural Orders. LINDLEY. ¶ By confusion, for ALLEGIANCE 1581.

1. So streighte a bonde of alyaunce or consanguinitie COVERDALE. **2.** The Holy Alliance SEELEY. **4.** Therefore let our A. be combined *Jul. C.* IV. i. 43. Hence **Alli·ance** *v. rare*, to ally or ally oneself. **Alli·ancer,** one who joins or belongs to an a. *rare.*

† **Alli·ant,** *a.* 1551. [– OFr. *aliant* sb., ally, Fr. *alliant* pres. pple., f. as prec.; see -ANT.] In league; akin. As *sb.* An ally –1656.

Allice, allis (æ·lis). 1620. [irreg. – (O)Fr. *alose* :– late L. *alausa* (Ausonius) small fish in the Moselle.] A fish, usu. called the **allice-shad** (*Alosa communis*).

Allicholly, joc. = MELANCHOLY. SHAKS.

† **Alli·cit,** *v.* 1725. [irreg. f. *allicere*, after ELICIT *v.*] To entice, attract. Hence (through Fr.) †**Alli·ciate** *v.* to allure. **Alli·cient** *ppl. a.* attracting; *sb.* that which attracts. †**Alli·ciency,** the quality of being attractive.

Allied (ăləi·d), *ppl. a.* ME. [f. ALLY *v.*] **1.** United, joined; *esp.* by kindred or affinity, or by league or treaty. **2.** *fig.* Connected in nature, or qualities; akin 1603.

1. A Lady..alide vnto the Duke *Two Gent.* IV. i. 49. **2.** Great wits are sure to madness near a. DRYDEN.

Alligate (æ·ligeɪt), *v.* ? *Obs.* 1626. [– *alligat-*, pa. ppl. stem of L. *alligare* bind to, f. *ad* AL-¹ + *ligare* bind; see -ATE³.] † **1.** To tie or unite –1677. **2.** To perform the operation of ALLIGATION 1671.

Alligation (æligē¹·ʃən). 1542. [– L. *alligatio*, f. as prec.; see -ION.] **1.** The action of attaching; the state of being attached 1555. **2.** The 'Rule of Mixtures'; the arithmetical method of solving questions concerning the mixing of articles of different qualities or values 1542.

Alligator (æ·ligeitəɹ). 1568. [– Sp. *el lagarto* the lizard (repr. **lacarto* for L. *lacerta* LIZARD), which was applied spec. to the large saurians of the New World.] **1.** A genus of Saurians of the crocodile family, also called Caymans, belonging to America; pop. all large American Saurians, some of which are true crocodiles. **2.** Anything operating by jaws, as (*Mining*) **a.** A rock-breaker. **b.** A 'Squeezer' for the puddle-ball.

1. In his..shop a tortoyrs hung, An Allegater stuft [*1st Qo.* Aligarta.] *Rom. & Jul.* v. i. 43 (*1st Fo.*).

Comb.: **a. apple,** the fruit of a W. Indian tree, *Anona palustris*; **a. pear,** the fruit of a W. Indian tree, *Persea gratissima* or *Laurus persea*; **a. tortoise,** a large marsh tortoise (*Chelydra serpentina*, fam. *Emydidæ*), called also the Snapping Turtle, found in Carolina; **a. wood,** the timber of a W. Indian tree, *Guarea swartzii*.

Allineate (ăli·niˌeɪt), *v. rare.* 1864. [mod. f. L. *ad* AL-¹ + *linea* line + -ATE³, after DELINEATE *v.*] = ALIGN.

Allineation, alin- (ălini,ē¹·ʃən). 1837. [f. as prec. + -ATION, after DELINEATION.] **1.** = ALIGNMENT 1. 1860. **2.** = ALIGNMENT 3. **3.** The position of two or more bodies in a straight line with a given point 1882.

Allision (ăli·ʒən). ? *Obs.* 1631. [– late L. *allisio*, f. *allis-*, pa. ppl. stem of *allido* dash against, f. *ad* AL-¹ + *lædo* strike violently; see -ION.] The action of dashing against.

Alli·teral, *a. rare.* 1850. [f. ALLITER(ATE), after *literal.*] Marked by alliteration.

Alliterate (ăli·tĕreɪt), *v.* 1816. [f. next; see -ATE³.] **1.** *intr.* Of words: To begin alliteratively, to constitute ALLITERATION. **2.** To compose alliteratively 1826. Hence **Alli·terate** *ppl. a.* alliterated. **Alli·terated** *ppl. a.* composed with or marked by alliteration. **Alli·terating** *ppl. a.* producing alliteration. **Alli·terative** *a.* pertaining to or marked by alliteration. **Alli·teratively** *adv.* **Alli·terativeness. Alli·tera:tor,** one who uses alliteration.

Alliteration (ăli:tĕrē¹·ʃən). 1656. [– mod.L. *alliteratio* (XV), f. L. *ad* AL-¹ + *littera* LETTER + *-atio* -ATION.] **1.** *gen.* The commencing of two or more words in close connection with the same letter or sound. **2.** The commencement of certain accented syllables in a verse with the same consonant or consonantal group, or with different vowel sounds, as in OE. and Teut. versification 1774.

1. Apt Alliteration's artful aid CHURCHILL. Taxation no Tyranny..was..nothing but a jingling a. MACAULAY. **2.** Cf. In *a*bit as an ermite · vnholy of werkes, Ich *w*ente forth in þe *w*orlde · *w*onders to hure *Piers Ploughman.* Hence **Alli:tera·tional** *a.* abounding in a.

Allitu·ric, *a.* [f. ALL(OXAN) + *-it-* (meaningless) + URIC.] *Chem.* In *Alliturie acid*, a product of the disintegration of alloxantin.

‖ **Allium** (æ·liŏm). 1807. [L., = garlic.] *Bot.* A genus of Liliaceous plants comprising garlic, onion, leek, chive, shallot, etc.

Allness (ǭ·lnės). 1652. [f. ALL + -NESS.] Universality.

† **Allobro·gical,** *a.* 1640. [f. L. *allobrogicus* of the Allobroges + -AL¹, perh. allusively: cf. Fr. *allobroge* (XVI) loutish fellow.] A term applied in 17th c. to Presbyterians and Calvinists, in allusion to the fact that Geneva was anciently a town of the Allobroges.

Allocate (æ·lŏkeɪt), *v.* 1640. [– *allocat-*, pa. ppl. stem of med.L. *allocare*, f. L. *ad* AL-¹ + *locare* place, LOCATE; see -ATE³.] **1.** To set apart for a special purpose or person; to apportion, assign. **2.** To attach locally 1842. **3.** To fix the locality of 1881.

2. Lasswade, to which..we a. ourselves DE QUINCEY.

† **A·llocate,** *sb.* 1709. [– med.L. *allocatum* allowance, subst. use of n.sing. of pa. pple. of *allocare*; see prec., -ATE¹.] A grant.

Allocation (ælokē¹·ʃən). 1535. [– med.L. *allocatio* allowance, f. as prec.; see -ION; in later use – Fr. *allocation* (XVII) or f. ALLOCATE *v.*] **1.** The action of apportioning or assigning to a special person or purpose 1833; † a portion of revenue, etc. so assigned –1658. **2.** Allowing an item in an account; also, the item so allowed 1658. **3.** Disposition, arrangement 1656. **4.** Localization 1855.

1. The a. of powers under the Constitution 1876. **4.** The a. of the..albuminous electric pulp in a special cavity OWEN.

‖ **Alloca·tur.** [med.L., 'it is allowed'.] *Law.* A certificate duly given at the end of an action, allowing costs.

Allochro·ic, *a.* 1879. [f. Gr. ἀλλόχροος changed in colour + -IC.] Changeable in colour.

Allochroite (ăelǫ·kroˌəit). 1837. [f. as prec. + -ITE¹ 2 b.] *Min.* An iron-garnet, a sub-variety of Andradite, found in Norway, etc. DANA.

Allochromatic (æ:loˌkromæ·tik), *a.* 1879. [f. Gr. ἄλλος different + χρῶμα, -ματ- colour + -IC.] Of or pertaining to change of colour.

Allochroous (ăelǫ·kroˌəs), *a.* 1811. [f. as ALLOCHROIC + -OUS.] Changing colour.

Alloclase (æ·loklēⁱs). 1875. [– G. *alloklas* (1866), f. Gr. ἄλλος different + κλάσις fracture.] *Min.* = next.

Alloclasite (ăelǫ·klăsəit). 1868. [f. as prec. + -ITE¹ 2 b.] A mineral containing sulphur, arsenic, bismuth, and cobalt, with traces of iron, etc.

Allocution (ælokiū·ʃən). 1615. [– L. *allocutio*, f. *allocut-*, pa. ppl. stem of *alloqui* address, f. *ad* AL-¹ + *loqui* speak.] **1.** *Rom. Antiq.* An address by a general to his soldiers; hence, in *R.C.Ch.*, by the Pope to his clergy, or to the Church 1689. **2.** *gen.* The action of addressing; hortatory address 1615.

1. The text of the a. WISEMAN. **2.** This vigorous a. to..his Hareem THACKERAY.

Allod, alod (æ·lǫd). 1689. [Anglicized f. med.L. *allodium.* Cf. Fr. † *alode* (COTGR.).] = ALLODIUM.

† **Allo·dge.** ME. [– OFr. *alogier*, f. *a* :– L. *ad* + *logier* (mod. *loger*) LODGE *v.*; cf. med.L. *allogiare*, It. *alloggiare.*] To lodge. Hence † **Allo·dgement.**

Allodial, al- (ălōᵘ·diăl), *a.* 1656. [– med.L. *al(l)odialis*, f. *allodium* + -AL¹; cf. Fr. *allodial* (XVII).] **1.** Of or pertaining to an allodium; or to the *a.* (opp. to the *feudal*) *system* 1747. **2.** Owning an allodium 1857. As *sb.* Allodial lands 1769; an allodial holder 1778.

2. The a. holder who held his land of no other man FREEMAN. Hence **Al(l)o·dialism,** the a. system. **Al(l)o·dialist,** an a. proprietor; var. **al(l)o·diary. Al(l)o:dia·lity,** the quality of holding or being held in free ownership. **Al(l)o·dially** *adv.*

Allo:difica·tion. 1875. [f. next + -FICATION.] *Law.* The conversion of land into allodium.

Allodium, al- (ălōᵘ·diŏm). 1628. [– med.L. *allodium* (Domesday Book), f. Frankish **allōd-* (whence Fr. *alleu*) 'entire property' (in latinized forms *alodis, alaudes*), f. *all* ALL + *ōd* (OHG. *ōt*, OE. *ēad*, ON. *auðr*) estate, property, wealth.] An estate held, not of a superior, but in absolute ownership; opp. to *feudum* or *feud*.

For in the law of England we have not properly a. COKE.

‖ **Allœo·stropha,** *a.* or *sb. pl* [– Gr. ἀλλοιόστροφα adj. pl. neut., consisting of irregular strophes, f. ἀλλοῖος different + στροφή strophe.] Verse consisting of irregular strophes. MILT. *Sams.* Pref.

Allœotic, -al (æliˌǫ·tik, -ăl) *a.* [– Gr. ἀλλοιωτικός alterative, f. ἀλλοιοῦν alter.] *Med.* Alterative.

Allogamy (ăelǫ·gămi). 1879. [f. Gr. ἄλλος different + -γαμία marriage.] *Bot.* Cross-fertilization.

Allogeneous (ælodʒī·niˌəs), *a. rare.* [f. Gr. ἀλλογενής of another race (f. ἄλλος other + γένος kind) + -OUS.] Diverse in kind. Hence **A:llogene·ity.**

Allograph (æ·lǫ́grɑf). [f. Gr. ἄλλος other + -GRAPH, as opp. to *autograph.*] A writing or signature made by one person for another.

Allomerism (ăelǫ·mĕriz'm). [f. Gr. ἄλλος. other + μέρος part + -ISM.] *Chem.* Variation in chemical constitution without change of crystalline form.

Allomerous (ælǫ·mĕrəs), *a.* [f. as prec. + -OUS.] Characterized by allomerism.

Allomorphite (ælomǭ·ɹfəit). [f. Gr. ἄλλος different + μορφή shape + -ITE¹ 2 b.] *Min.* A mineral, allied to barytes or barite, having the form and cleavage of ANHYDRITE.

† **Allo·nge,** *sb.*¹ [– Fr. *allonge* lengthening, drawing out, f. *allonger*, f. *long* LONG *a.*¹] **1.** A lunge. (Dicts.) **2.** A long rein. J.

‖ **Allonge** (alǭṅ·ʒ), *sb.*² 1862. [Re-adoption of prec.] A slip of paper annexed to a bill of exchange, etc. to give room for more endorsements.

Allonym (æ·lŏnim). 1867. [– Fr. *allonyme*, f. Gr. ἄλλος other + -ώνυμος named, f. ὄνομα name.] **a.** The name of some one else assumed by the author of a work. **b.** A work bearing such a name. Hence **Allo·nymous** *a.*

† **Alloo·,** *v.* 1708. [For HALLOO.] To urge on with cries.

A:llopalla·dium. 1837. [f. Gr. ἄλλος + PALLADIUM.] *Min.* Native palladium crystallizing under the hexagonal system.

Allopath (æ·lŏpæþ). 1830. [– Fr. *allopathe*, back-formation from *allopathie* ALLOPATHY.] A practitioner of allopathy.

Allopathic (ælopæ·þik), *a.* 1830. [– Fr. *allopathique*; see next, -IC.] Of or pertaining to allopathy. var. **A:llopathe·tic.** Hence **Allopa·thically** *adv.*; var. **A:llopathe·tic-ally.**

Allopathy (ăelǫ·păþi). 1842. [– G. *allopathie* (Hahnemann), f. Gr. ἄλλος other + παθεία -PATHY.] 'The curing of a diseased action by the inducing of another of a different kind, yet not necessarily diseased.' Opp. to HOMŒOPATHY.

Allo·phanate. [f. next + -ATE⁴.] *Chem.* A salt of allophanic acid.

Allophane (æ·lofēⁱn). 1843. [– Gr. ἀλλοφανής appearing otherwise, f. ἄλλος other + φαίνειν show, appear.] *Min.* A hydrated silicate of alumina, usu. sky-blue, losing its colour under the blowpipe; whence the name.

Allopha·nic, *a.* [f. prec. + -IC.] Of or pertaining to anything which changes colour or appearance; as *A. acid* $C_2H_4N_2O_3$.

Allophite (æ·lofəit). 1880. [f. Gr. ἄλλος different + OPHITE¹; cf. G. *allophit* (1873), of parallel formation.] *Min.* A hydrous silicate of the Margarophyllite section, inferior in hardness to serpentine.

Allophyle (æ·lofil). *rare.* 1577. [– eccl.L. *allophylus* – Gr. ἀλλόφυλος alien, f. ἄλλος other + φυλή tribe.] An alien; a Philistine. As *adj.* = ALLOPHYLIAN.

Allophylian (ælofi·liăn), *a.* and *sb.* 1844. [f. as prec. + -IAN.] Of a race or stock which is not Aryan or Semitic; used esp. of Asiatic and European languages; occas. = Turanian.

Allophytoid (æloˑfitoid). 1858. [f. Gr. ἄλλος different + *phytoid* (f. φυτόν plant + -OID).] *Bot.* A separated vegetable bud differing from the parent plant.

Alloquial (ălōᵘ·kwiăl), *a. rare.* 1840. [f. L. *alloquium* address (f. *alloqui*; see ALLOCUTION) + -AL [1], after *colloquial*.] Of, or pertaining to, the action of addressing others; contrasted with *colloquial*. Hence **Allo·quiali:sm,** a phrase or manner of address.

Allot (ălǫ·t), *v.* 1547. [– OFr. *aloter* (mod. *allotir*), f. *a* :– L. *ad* AL-[1] + *lot* LOT *sb.*] **1.** To distribute by lot, or in such way that the recipients have no choice; to assign shares authoritatively; to apportion 1574. **2.** To assign as a lot or portion *to*; to appoint (without distribution) 1547; hence, to appropriate to a special person or purpose 1574. † **3.** To appoint, destine (a person *to do*) –1677. **4.** U.S. *colloq.* To reckon (*upon*) 1816.

2. The..end that was allotted him SURREY. Ten years I will a. to the attainment of knowledge JOHNSON. 4. And I a. we must economise 1840. Hence **Allo·ttable** *a.* **Allo·ttee,** one to whom an allotment is made. **Allo·tter,** one who allots. † **Allo·ttery,** allotted share *A.Y.L.* I. i. 77.

Allotheism (æ·loˌþīːiz'm). 1660. [f. Gr. ἄλλος other + θεός god + -ISM.] The worship of strange gods.

Allotment (ălǫ·tmĕnt). 1574. [f. prec. + -MENT; cf. Fr. † *allotement*.] **1.** The action of allotting. **2.** Lot in life, destiny 1674. **3.** A share or portion, *esp.* of land, allotted to a special person or purpose 1629. † **4.** *Comm.* The division of a ship's cargo into equal portions, to be distributed among purchasers by lot –1751.

2. The stinted allotments of earthly life CARLYLE. *Comb.* **a. system,** the division of land into small plots to be held for cultivation by the poorer classes at a small rent.

Allotrophic (ælotrǫ·fik), *a.* 1879. [f. Gr. ἄλλος different + -τροφος nourishing (f. τρέφειν nourish) + IC.] *Med.* Variable as to nutritive properties, without any change in physical or chemical characters.

Allotropic, -al (ælotrǫ·pik, -ăl), *a.* 1849. [f. Gr. ἀλλότροπος (see ALLOTROPY) + -IC + AL[1].] Of or pertaining to ALLOTROPY. Hence **Allotro·pically** *adv.* **Allo:tropi·city** (*rare*). So **A·llotrope,** an allotropic form.

Allotropism (ælǫ·trŏpiz'm). 1851. [f. as prec. + -ISM.] Allotropy as a principle or process.

Allotropize (ælǫ·trŏpəiz), *v. rare.* [f. as prec. + -IZE.] To change allotropically.

Allotropy (ælǫ·trŏpi). [– Gr ἀλλότροπος of another form, f. ἄλλος different + τρόπος manner; see -Y[3].] The variation of physical properties without change of substance, first noticed by Berzelius in charcoal and the diamond.

† **A:ll ou·t,** *adv.* ME. **1.** Completely, quite –1638; esp. in *to drink a.*, to empty a bumper; cf. CAROUSE. **B.** *sb.* A bumper –1611.

A:ll o·ver, *adv.* 1577. **1.** Over the whole extent, in every part, e.g. of the body. **2.** Finished; done for (*mod.*). **3.** *adj.* (from 1) *colloq.* Indisposed all over the body 1851.

2. *It is all over with* = L. *actum est de.* Hence (from 3) **A·ll-o·verishness,** general indisposition. *colloq.*

Allow (ălau·), *v.* ME. [– OFr. *alouer* (later *allouer*), 1. praise :– L. *allaudare* extol, f. *ad* AL-[1] + *laudare* praise; 2. bestow, assign :– med.L. *allocare*, f. *ad* AL[1]- + *locare* place, stow, ALLOCATE. Many uses blend 1 and 2.] **I.** Fr. *alouer* :– L. *allaudare*. **1.** *trans.* † To praise, commend –1783; to approve of, sanction (*arch.*) ME.; *intr.* with *upon*, *of* 1543; to accept as satisfactory (*arch.*) ME.; † *intr.* with *of* –1748. **2.** To accept as true or valid, to admit 1548; *intr.* with *of* 1528; with *subord. cl.* to concede 1643; with *compl.* to admit a thing *to be* 1593; to conclude, opine, or state as an opinion formed (*Eng.* and *Amer. dial.*) 1580. **3.** *trans.* To concede, permit (an action, etc.) 1558; with *inf.* 1637; *refl.* to permit oneself to indulge *in*, † *to* 1605; *intr.* to admit *of* 1732.

1. Upon reasonable cause to be allowed by a justice of the peace BLACKSTONE. 2. It will be allowed us that marriage is a human society MILT. Allowed for law 1798. I 'lowed I'd make him sorry fur it *Scrib. Mag.* 3. Where many sorts of worship be allowed HOBBES. His..madness Allows itself to anything *Lear* III. vii. 107.

II. Fr. *allouer* :– L. *allocare*. **1.** † To assign as a right or due –1596; to give, or let any one have, as his share, or as what he needs ME.; † to portion, endow –1712. **2.** † To place to one's credit, count to one –1667; hence, † to deduct from the debit, to abate –1530; *gen.* to add or deduct (so much) on account of something not formally appearing 1663.

1. The Law allowes it, And the Court awards it *Merch. V.* IV. i. 303. A. him but his plaything of a pen POPE. 2. To a. an hour for time lost in changing trains 1888. Hence **Allow·er,** one who allows (senses I. 1, 2, 3). **Allow·ment,** sanction, approval.

Allowable (ălau·ăb'l), *a.* ME. [– OFr. *alouable* (mod. *allouable*), f. *alouer*; see prec., -ABLE.] † Laudable –1702; acceptable 1552; admissible, probable 1682; permissible, legitimate 1568.

Prayer for the dead is not..a. COVERDALE. Hence **Allow·ableness. Allow·ably** *adv.*

Allowance (ălau·ăns), *sb.* ME. [– OFr. *alouance*, f. *alouer*; see ALLOW *v.*, -ANCE.] The action of allowing; a thing allowed. **1.** † Praise –1633; approbation, sanction, voluntary acceptance (*arch.*) 1552; †acknowledgement –1756; permission, sufferance 1628. **2.** The action of placing to one's credit, admitting in an account, or allotting on account of expenses 1574; † a sum allowed in account, a consideration –1574. **3.** A limited portion or sum, *esp.* of money, or food 1440. **4.** Rebate, deduction, discount 1530. **5.** *fig.* The taking into account of mitigating or extenuating circumstances 1676. † **6.** A balance –1552.

1. The a. of slavery in the South FREEMAN. 2. Illiberalite of Parents in a. towards their Children BACON. 3. They consider this A. [Pin-money] as a kind of Alimoney ADDISON. The short A., the Bread and Water of a Prison 1711. A scant a. of star-light MILT. *Comus* 308. 4. *To make allowance*: to add or deduct, in order to provide for incidental circumstances. An a. for the waste of the Timber 1663. 5. To make Allowances for Conduct STEELE.

Allowance (ălau·ăns), *v.* 1839. [f. the sb. Cf. *portion*, etc.] **1.** To put upon an allowance; to limit in the amount allowed. **2.** To supply in limited quantities 1840.

Allowed (ălau·d), *ppl. a.* ME. [f. ALLOW.] † **1.** Praised, accepted as satisfactory –1728. **2.** Licensed 1589; acknowledged 1749; allotted 1440; remitted 1674.

2. An a. printer 1589, fool *Twel. N.* I. v. 101. The a. and established models of good breeding CHESTERF. Hence **Allow·edly** *adv.*

Alloxan (ælǫ·ksăn). 1853. [f. ALL(ANTOIN) + OXA(LIC) + -AN I. 2.] *Chem.* An organic compound $C_4H_2N_2O_4$, one of the oxidation products of uric acid. Hence **Allo·xanate,** a salt of alloxanic acid. **Alloxa·nic** *a.*

Alloxantin (ælǫksæ·ntin). 1853. [f. prec. + -IN[1], with euphonic *-t-*.] *Chem.* An organic compound $C_8H_4N_4O_7$.

Alloy (ăloi·), *sb.* 1598. [– (O)Fr. *aloi* mixture, f. *aloier*, earlier *aleier* :– L. *alligare* bind up, f. *ad* AL-[1] + *ligare* bind. Repl. ALLAY *sb.*[1]] **1.** Fineness, standard, of gold or silver 1604; † agio of exchange –1672. **2.** A baser metal mixed with a nobler, *esp.* in gold and silver coinage 1719. **3.** The condition of mixture 1827. **4.** An amalgam; *formerly*, a compound containing a baser metal 1656. † **5.** *fig.* Intrinsic quality –1674. **6.** *fig.* Admixture of that which lowers in character or value; alien element 1625.

4. **Native alloy:** one of osmium and iridium occurring with native platinum. 6. A base a. of moral cowardice C. BRONTË.

Alloy (ăloi·), *v.* 1661. [– Fr. *aloyer*, f. *aloi* (prec.). Repl. ALLAY *v.*] **1.** To mix with a baser metal, so as to reduce in standard 1691. **2.** To mix metals 1822; *intr.* (*refl.*) to enter into combination with another metal 1839. **3.** *fig.* To debase by admixture 1703. **4.** *fig.* To temper, moderate 1661.

Hence **Alloy·age,** the art or process of alloying metals.

Allozooid (æːlozōᵘ·oid). 1858. [f. Gr. ἄλλος different + ζῷον living being + -OID.] *Biol.* A separated animal bud differing in nature from the parent.

All-red, *a.* 1895. Used to indicate a telegraph-line, a trading route, etc., lying throughout in territory of the British Empire. (From the practice of colouring British and Imperial territory red in our maps.)

A:ll(-)rou·nd. 1805. **A.** *adv.* Everywhere around; affecting equally all the parts or every one in a circle or company 1871. **B.** *prep.* Around all the parts of 1805. **C.** *adj.* Including everything or every one in a given circle.

C. *An all-round man:* one who has ability in all departments. Hence **A:ll-rou·nder,** he who or that which is all round; an all-round man.

All saints. 1580. The saints in heaven collectively. The festival, called also **All Saints' Day** (Nov. 1). Also = ALL-HALLOW *tide*.

Allseed (ǭ·lsīd). A name for various many-seeded plants. **a.** The genus *Polycarpon*. **b.** A species of Goosefoot (*Chenopodium polyspermum*). **c.** *Radiola millegrana*. **d.** The Knot-grass (*Polygonum aviculare*).

All souls. The souls of all the pious dead. The festival on which the Ch. of Rome makes supplications on their behalf, called also **All Souls' Day** (Nov. 2). **All Souls' Eve,** the evening of Nov. 1.

Allspice (ǭ·lspəis). 1621. [f. ALL + SPICE, as combining the flavour of cinnamon, nutmeg, and cloves.] **1.** An aromatic spice, Jamaica Pepper or Pimenta, the dried berry of *Eugenia pimenta* or Allspice Tree (N.O. *Myrtaceæ*) of the West Indies. **2.** A name of other aromatic shrubs: **A. Tree** or **Carolina A.,** *Calycanthus floridus*; **Japan A.,** *Chimonanthus fragrans*; **Wild A.,** *Lindera benzoin*. Hence **A·llspi:cy** *a. nonce-wd.*, hot.

Allthing. *Obs.* or *dial.* Everything.

Allude (ăl'ū·d), *v.* 1535. [– L. *alludere* play or dally with, touch lightly upon, f. *ad* AL-[1] + *ludere* engage in play.] † **1.** To mock –1577; to play upon words, to refer by play of words –1607; to refer by play of fancy (*trans.* and *intr.*) –1665. **2.** *intr.* To have or make an indirect or passing reference to (not = *refer*) 1533. † **3.** *trans.* To refer a thing *to*, as a thing to its author –1634. † **4.** To hint, suggest –1677.

2. Quotations which a. to the Perjuries of the Fair STEELE. He often alluded to his poverty 1837.

‖ **Allumette** (alüme·t). 1848. [Fr., f. *allumer* set light to.] A match for lighting.

† **Allu·mine,** *v.* 1581. [– Fr. † *alluminer* (OFr. *aluminer*) set light to, illumine – Rom. **alluminare* for cl. L. *illuminare* ILLUMINE *v.*] To illuminate.

† **Allu·minor.** 1483. [– AFr. *alluminour*; see prec., -OUR.] An illuminator, a limner –1607.

† **Allu·rance.** 1580. [f. next + -ANCE.] Enticement. † **Allu·rant** *ppl. a.* enticing.

Allure (ăl'ūᵊ·ɹ), *v.* ME. [– OFr. *alurer*, f. *a* :– L. *ad* AL-[1] + *luere* LURE *sb.*[1]] **1.** To attract or tempt by something flattering or advantageous; to entice; to win over. **2.** To fascinate, charm 1612; †to attract, elicit –1794.

1. He..Allur'd to brighter worlds and led the way GOLDSM. Allured by hopes of relief JOHNSON. 2. The..Sun..Allur'd his eye MILT. *P. L.* III. 5. 73. Hence **Allu·rer,** he who, or that which, allures. **Allu·ring** *vbl. sb.* the action of attracting with the prospect of advantage; † fascination; *ppl. a.* tempting, seductive, attractive, fascinating. **Allu·ring-ly** *adv.*, **-ness** (*rare*).

† **Allu·re,** *sb.*[1] 1548. [f. prec.] = ALLUREMENT –1758.

‖ **Allure** (alür), *sb.*[2] 1882. [Fr., f. *aller* go; see -URE.] Gait, mien, air.

Allurement (ăl'uᵊ·ɹmĕnt). 1548. [f. ALLURE *v.* + -MENT.] **1.** The action of alluring; enticement 1561. **2.** Fascination, charm 1579. **3.** That which allures; a lure, bait 1548.

1. Though Adam by his wife's a. fell MILT. *P.R.* II. 131. 3. Allurements to enlist in the army 1825.

Allusion (ăl'ū·ʒən). 1548. [– Fr. *allusion* or late L. *allusio*, f. *allus-*, pa. ppl. stem of *alludere* ALLUDE *v.*] † **1.** Illusion –1618. † **2.** A word-play –1731. † **3.** A symbolical reference –1781. **4.** A covert or implied reference 1612.

Allusive (ăl'ū·siv), *a.* 1605. [f. as prec. + -IVE.] † **1.** Punning –1656. **2.** Symbolical (*arch.*) 1605. **3.** Containing allusion 1607.

1. *Her. Allusive Arms*, called also *canting* or *punning* arms: those in which the charges play upon

the bearer's name or title, as the martlets (OFr. *arondel*) borne by the Earls of Arundel. Hence **Allu·sive-ly** *adv.*, **-ness.** var. † **Allu·sory.**

† **All-utterly,** *adv.* ME. Wholly; absolutely –1651.

Alluvial (ălˡū·viăl), *a.* 1802. [f. ALLUVIUM + -AL¹; cf. Fr. *alluvial.*] Of, pertaining to, or consisting of alluvium. var. **Allu·vian** (*rare*).

Alluvion (ălˡū·viən). 1536. [– Fr. *alluvion* – L. *alluvio*, f. *ad* AL-¹ + *-luvio* washing, f. *luere* wash.] **1.** The wash of water against the shore or a river-bank. **2.** An inundation; a flood 1550. **3.** The matter deposited by a flood 1731; *esp.* ALLUVIUM 1779. **4.** *Law.* The imperceptible action of flowing water in forming new land 1751.

3. Spreading..a...over its meadows 1841.

Alluvium (ălˡū·viŏm). Pl. **-ia, -iums.** 1665. [– L., n. of *alluvius* washed against, f. *ad* AL-¹ + *luv-* of *luere* (cf. prec.).] Deposits of earth, sand, etc., left by water flowing over land that is not permanently submerged; *esp.* those left in river valleys and deltas. Also *fig.*

† **A:ll-who·le.** ME. [Cf. Fr. *tout entier.*] *adj.* Entire –1588. *adv.* Entirely –1601. Hence † **A:ll-who·lly** *adv.*

A·llwo:rk. 1830. Work, *esp.* domestic, of all kinds. *Maid of all-work*: a general servant.

Ally (ăləi·), *v.* ME. [– OFr. *alier*, analogical alt. of *aleier*; see ALLOY *sb.*, ALLAY *v.*², ALLIGATE *v.*] **1.** *trans.* To unite for a special object; now chiefly of marriage, association of sovereign states, and union of nature or spirit. Const. *to*, *with*. **2.** *intr.* To enter into alliance (*arch.*) ME. † **3.** *trans.* To mix. (Cf. *allay*, *alloy*.) –1500.

1. In..mariage alied to the emperour ME. He allied himself closely to Castlemaine MACAULAY. **2.** No foreign power will a. with us 1825.

Ally (æ·ləi, ăləi·), *sb.*¹ ME. [In the sense of 'kindred, kinship' – OFr. *alié*, subst. use of pa. pple. of *alier* (prec.); in the sense of 'allied person or people', f. the vb. For the loss of final *-é* cf. ASSIGN *sb.*², COSTIVE *a.*] † **I.** *abstr.* Kinship –1592; alliance –1587. † **II.** *collect.* Kindred –1460. **III.** *individual.* † **1.** A relative –1654. **2.** *fig.* Anything akin to another by structure, properties, etc. 1697. **3.** One united with another by treaty or league; now usu. of sovereigns or states 1598. **4.** *fig.* Anything auxiliary to another 1853.

1. This Gentleman the Princes neere Alie *Rom. & Jul.* III. i. 114. **2.** The alkaline metals and their allies 1888. **3.** Ammon, the ancient a. of Israel A. P. STANLEY. **4.** Tractarianism..the..a. of Rome 1853.

Ally, alley, alay (æ·li), *sb.*² 1720. [abbrev. of *alabaster*; cf. *Willy*, etc.] A marble of real alabaster.

Allyl (æ·lil). 1854. [f. L. *allium* garlic + -YL.] *Chem.* A monovalent hydro-carbon radical, C_3H_5. Also *attrib.*, as in *allyl alcohol* C_3H_5OH, *allyl sulphide* $(C_3H_5)_2S$, etc. Hence **A·llylami:ne,** the ammonia of the a. series $C_3H_5NH_2$, also called Acrylamine. **A·llylate,** a salt of a., as *sodium allylate* C_3H_5ONa. **A·llylene,** a divalent hydro-carbon radical, C_3H_4, isomeric with acetylene. Also called *propine*. **Ally·lic** *a.* **A·llylin,** a viscid liquid, a by-product in the preparation of allyl alcohol.

Alma, almah (æ·lmă). Also **alme(h.** 1814. [– Arab. *'ālima* adj. fem. learned (in music and dancing), f. *'alama* know.] An Egyptian dancing-girl.

Almacantar (ælmăkæ·ntəɹ). ME. [– med.L. *almucantarath* or Fr. (XVI) *almicantarat, almucantara* – Arab. *almuḳanṭarāt* pl., sun-dial, f. *ḳanṭara* bridge, arch; see AL-².] *pl.* Circles of the sphere parallel to the horizon; parallels of altitude. **2.** The name of an instrument for the determination of time and latitude 1880.

Comb. **a.-staff,** an instrument formerly used to take observations of the sun at its rising and setting, in order to correct the compass.

Almadia (ælmădī·ă). 1681. [– Arab. *al-ma'dīya* ferry-boat.] A river-boat. **1.** An Indian boat, 80 ft. long, and very swift. **2.** An African canoe, made of bark or of a hollowed trunk 1753.

Almagest (æ·lmădʒest). ME. [– OFr. *almageste*, ult. – Arab. *al-majisṭī* (see AL-²), – Gr. μεγίστη greatest (sc. σύνταξις composition).] The great astronomical treatise of Ptolemy; also, other great textbooks of astrology and alchemy.

‖ **Alma·gra.** 1703. [Sp. – Arab. *al-maǧar, al-muǧra* red ochre.] A deep red ochre, the *sil atticum* of the ancients, found in Spain.

† **A·lmain.** Also **-ayn, -an(e.** ME. [– OFr. *aleman* (mod. *allemand*) – med.L. *alamannus* – OHG *aleman.*] **A.** *adj.* German –1665. **B.** *sb.* **1.** A German –1698. **2.** A kind of dance, or dance-music; = ALLEMANDE (*arch.*) 1549.

† **A·lmaine, -any.** ME. [– OFr. *alemaigne* – late L. *allemania* the country of the *Alemanni.*]

A:lmain-ri·vets. 1530. Light armour, made flexible by overlapping plates sliding on rivets. First used in Germany.

‖ **A:lma Ma·ter.** 1715. [L., = bounteous mother.] A title given by the Romans, *esp.* to Ceres and Cybele, and transferred in Eng. to Universities and schools, regarded as 'fostering mothers' to their *alumni*.

Almanac (ǭ·lmănæ̆k). ME. [– med.L. *almanac(h* (Roger Bacon, 1267) – late Gr. ἀλμενιχιακά (Eusebius); ult. origin unkn.] An annual table, or book of tables, containing a calendar of months and days, with astronomical data and calculations, ecclesiastical and other anniversaries, etc., and, in former days, astrological and astrometeorological forecasts.

Looke in the A., finde out the Moone-shine *Mids. N.* III. i. 54. Falshood and Lying..like Almanackes of the last yeare, are now gon out DEKKER. You would reduce all history to..an a. BOSWELL.

Almandine (æ·lmăndin, æ·lmăndəi:n). 1658. [– Fr. † *almandine*, alt. of † *alabandine* – med.L. *alabandina* (sc. *gemma* gem), f. *Alabanda* city of Caria. See ALABANDINE.] An alumina iron garnet of a violet or amethystine tint.

Turkis and agate and almondine TENNYSON.

Almandite (æ·lmăndəit). [f. as prec. + -ITE¹ 2 b.] Dana's name for almandine as a mineral, a variety of garnet.

† **A·lma:nner.** Comb. f. *all manner* used *attrib.* ME. [orig. a genitive = 'of every sort'; see MANNER and ALL.] –1526.

Alme(h; see ALMA.

‖ **Almendro·n.** 1852. [Sp., augm. of *almendra* almond.] The Brazil-nut tree (*Bertholletia excelsa*).

Almery, obs. f. AMBRY.

Almes(se, obs. f. ALMS.

†**Almi:ght,** *a.* OE. [f. ALL + *might*, prob. pa. pple. of MAY *v.*¹ in the primary sense of 'to have power.'] = ALMIGHTY. Usu. *poet.* –1546. † **Almi·ghtful,** *a.* ME. only. [f. ALL *adv.* + MIGHTFUL.] All-powerful; var. † **Almi·ghtiful.** † **Almi·ghtin,** *sb.* and *a.* ME. only. [var. of ALMIGHTY.] Used in apposition to *God*; also alone.

Almighty (ǭlməi·ti), *a.* OE. [f. ALL *adv.* + MIGHTY *a.*; OE. *ælmihtiǵ*, corresp. to OFris. *elmachtich*, OS. *alomahtig*, OHG. *alamahtīc*, ON. *almáttigr.*] All-powerful, omnipotent. **1.** *attrib.* With *God*, etc. OE.; absol. *The Almighty* OE. Occas. in superl. 1598. **2.** *gen.* All-powerful ME. ¶ *slang.* Mighty, great; exceedingly 1824.

1. I am the almightie God, walke before me *Gen.* 17:1. Doth the Almightie peruert iustice? *Job* 8:3. **2.** Almighty Sampson CHAUCER. The a. dollar (a phr. due to) W. IRVING. 'Almighty' nonsense (to speak *transatlanticè*) DE QUINCEY. vars. † **Almi·ght,** † **Almi·ghtend.** Hence **Almi·ghtily** *adv.* **Almi·ghtiness.**

Almirah, -myra (ælməi·ră). 1878. [– Urdu *almari* – Pg. *almario* :– L. *armarium*; see AMBRY.] Anglo-Ind. for a cupboard, press, chest of drawers, etc.

† **A·lmistry.** [perh. *joc.* for *all-mystery.*] B. JONS.

† **Almner,** var. of ALMONER.

Almoign, almoin (æ̆lmoi·n). ME. [As *almon(e* – OFr. *almone* (mod. *aumône*), see ALMS; *almoin* is late AFr., perh. due to confusion w. *alimonium*, the senses of the two words partially overlapping.] † **1.** Alms; alms-chest ME. **2.** Tenure by divine service, or by performing some religious duty. **Frank almoin** or *free alms* (L. *libera eleemosyna*); the tenure of lands, etc., bestowed upon God, that is, given to a religious corporation for pure and perpetual alms, free from any temporal service; perpetual tenure by free gift of charity.

† **A·lmonage.** 1655. [– OFr. *almosnage* almsgiving, f. *almosner* give alms; see ALMS, -AGE.] In **Frank almonage** = *frank almoin*; see ALMOIGN. –1667.

Almond (ā·mənd). ME. [– OFr. *alemande, a(l)mande* (mod. *amande*), for **almandle* – med.L. *amandula* – Gr. ἀμυγδάλη; *al-* app. due to association w. Rom. words in AL-².] **1.** The kernel of a drupe, the produce of the almond tree, of which there are two kinds, the sweet and the bitter. **2.** The tree, *Amygdalus Communis* (N.O. *Rosaceæ*) 1697. **3.** Anything made with almonds, or like almonds in shape, or almond blossom in colour; *esp.* the tonsils, called *almonds of the throat, jaws,* or *ears* (*arch.*) 1578. Also a pigeon, the Almond Tumbler 1867.

2. Mark well the flowering Almonds in the Wood DRYDEN. **3.** Balls, or rather almonds, of purple marble RUSKIN. Cream colour..and a. 1879.

Comb.: **a.-butter,** a preparation of cream, whites of eggs, and blanched almonds; **-kernel** (= ALMOND 1, 3); **-milk,** a preparation of sweet blanched almonds and water; **-oil,** the expressed oil of bitter almonds, or benzoic aldehyde; **a. tree,** the tree that bears almonds, also *fig.* grey hair; **a. tumbler** (see ALMOND 3); **a. willow,** *Salix amygdalina*; **-worts,** the plants of N.O. *Drupaceæ*. Hence **A·lmondy** *a.* having, or suggesting, almonds.

A:lmond-fu·rnace. 1674. [Corruption of *Allemand*, i.e. German, *furnace*.] A furnace used to separate metals from dross, and to reduce slag of litharge to lead.

Almoner¹ (ā·mənəɹ, æ·lmənəɹ). [– AFr. *aumoner*, OFr. *-ier*, earlier *au-*, *a(u)lmosnier* (mod. *aumônier*) :– Rom. **almosinarius*, for med.L. *eleēmosynarius* ELEEMOSYNARY used subst.; see -ER², ALMS.] A distributor of alms on behalf of a person or a community, e.g. a sovereign, a religious house (*Hereditary High A.* and *Lord High A.* are officers of the royal household of Great Britain). **b.** A hospital official who has duties concerning patients' payments and their general welfare 1892. † **2.** An alms-giver ME.

1. Judas..Was iesu crist aumoner ME. *fig.* The sun is the a. of the Almighty HERSCHEL. **2.** An amner to the poore that helpless cry 1591.

† **A·lmoner**². ME. [– AFr. *aumener*, (O)Fr. *aumonière* (med.L. *almonaria*) :– Rom. **eleemosinaria* (sc. *bursa, arca*); see prec.] An alms-purse; a bag –1460. var. **Alner.**

A·lmonership. 1847. [f. ALMONER¹ + -SHIP.] The office of an almoner.

Almonry (æ·lmŏnri). 1480. [orig. – OFr. *au(l)mosnerie* (mod. *aumônerie*), f. *aulmosnier* (XII) ALMONER¹; subseq. f. ALMONER¹; see -ERY², -RY.] **1.** A place where alms were distributed. † **2.** = ALMONER² 1536. Cf. AMBRY.

† **Almose.** 1483. [var. of ALMS.] = ALMS 1, 2. Also as sing. –1587.

Almost (ǭ·lmoᵘst, -məst, when emph. ǭ·lmōᵘ·st), *adv.* Aphet. **'most.** OE. [f. ALL + MOST *adv.* = *mostly*; OE. *ælmǣst* for the most part, ME. *almest(e*; *almost* from XIV.] † **1.** *adj.* or *adv.* Mostly all; for the most part –1658. **2.** *adv.* Very nearly, all but ME.

1. The women..do that work a. 1658. **2.** With *vb.* or *attrib.*: A. thou perswadest mee to be a Christian *Acts* 26:28. Almost was never hang'd 1639. With *sb.*: You are a. come to part a. a fray *Much Ado* V. i. 113. *Almost no* = scarcely any; *Almost never* = scarcely ever, etc. † To intensify an interrog. (L. *quis fere*): Whom a. can we see who opens his arms to his enemies? SOUTH.

† **Almous.** ME. Sc. **awmous.** [– ON. *almusa, ǫlmusa*; see ALMS.] = ALMS 1, 2. *sing.* and *pl.*

Alms (āmz). [OE. *ælmysse, -messe*, corresp. to OFris. *ielmisse*, OS. *alamosna*, OHG. *alamuosa(n)*, ON. *almusa, ǫlmusa* :– Gmc. **alemos(i)na* – pop.L., Rom. **alimosina*, alt., prob. through L. *alimonia* ALIMONY, of Christian L. *eleēmosyna* (Tertullian) – Gr. ἐλεημοσύνη compassionateness, f. ἐλεήμων compassionate, f. ἔλεος mercy.] **1.** Charitable relief of the poor; charity; *esp.* as a religious duty. Const. with *do, make, work*; later, with *give*, etc. **a.** *collect.* without pl. OE. **b.** as *sing.* A charitable donation ME. **c.** as *pl.* Things given in charity 1557. † **2.** *fig.* A good deed, a service to God, a charity. Often *ironic.* –1623. **3.** *Law.* Tenure by a., see ALMOIGN; **free alms** = *frank almoign.* **Reasonable alms**: a part of an intestate estate allotted to the poor.

1. a. Hir hond mynistre of fredom and almesse CHAUCER. **b.** To ask an a. ADDISON. **c.** For a. are but the vehicles of prayer DRYDEN. **2.** If he be hungry it is a. to feed him SANDERSON.

Comb.: **a.-basket**, that containing the public a. *L.L.L.* v. i. 41; **-deed** = ALMS 2; † **-drink**, the remains of liquor, reserved for alms-people; **-fee**, Peter's pence or Rome-scot; **-folk**, persons supported by a.; † almsgivers; **-gift**, almsgiving, also = ALMOIGN; **-land**, land held in frank almoign. **A·lmsgi:ving.** 1690. The giving of alms. So **-gi:ver** 1630.

A·lms-house. ME. A house founded by private charity, *esp.* for the aged poor. *Formerly*, The house belonging to a monastery, where alms and hospitality were dispensed.

A·lmsman. OE. **1.** One supported by alms; a bedesman. Also *fig.* **2.** An almsgiver (*arch.*) 1483.

1. My gay Apparrell, for an Almes-mans Gowne SHAKS.

Almucantar, -urie, obs. ff. ALMACANTAR.

Almuce, early f. AMICE.

Almug (æ·lmɒg). 1611. [Heb.] An erron., but in Eng. more usual, sp. of ALGUM.

† **Almury.** [– (ult.) Arab. *almurī*, f. *al* AL-[2] + *murī* indicator.] The 'denticle' or pointer on the astrolabe. CHAUCER.

† **Almu·ten.** 1625. [Corrupt f. OFr. *almutaz* – Arab. *al-mu'tazz*, f. *al* AL-[2] + *mu'taz* prevailing.] *Astrol.* The ruling planet in the horoscope –1721.

Alnage (ǭ·lnedʒ). 1477. [– OFr. *alnage* (mod. *aunage*) f. *aulner* (mod. *auner*) measure by the ell, f. *alne, au(l)ne* ELL[1]; see -AGE.] **1.** Measurement by the ell. *spec.* Official measurement and inspection of woollen cloth. **2.** The fee for such measurement 1622.

Alnager (ǭ·lnedʒəɹ). ME. [– OFr. *alnegeor*, f. *alnage* (prec.); see -OR 2.] A sworn officer to examine and attest the measurement and quality of woollen goods. vars. † **A·lner, Aulner.**

† **Alna·th.** ME. [– Arab. *al-naṭḥ*, f. *naṭaḥa* butt, aim at with the horns.] *Astrol.* The first star in the horns of Aries. CHAUCER.

Alod, -ial, -iality, etc., vars. of ALLOD, etc.

Aloe (æ·lo). [OE. *al(e)we* – L. *aloē* – Gr. ἀλόη plant and drug; (also) agalloch; in late ME. reinforced by OFr. *aloes* (mod. *aloès*) or its source, *aloēs*, gen. sing. of L. *aloē*, as in LIGN-ALOES; whence the frequent use of the word in pl. form.] † **1.** *pl.* The fragrant resin or wood of the AGALLOCH. See LIGN-ALOES. –1741. **2.** A genus of plants (N.O. *Liliaceæ*, sect. *Aloinæ*) with bitter juice ME. **3.** (Usu. *pl.*) A nauseous bitter purgative, procured from the inspissated juice of the plants ME. *fig.* Bitter experiences 1526. **4.** *pop.* A name of other plants resembling the a., *esp.* the AGAVE or American Aloe 1682.

1. Thy garments are like myrre, Aloes and Cassia *Ps.* 44: 8. **3.** *fig.* The bitter aloes of the law 1617. Hence **A·loed** *ppl. a.* mixed with, or as with, or planted with, aloes.

† **Aloe·dary.** 1753. [– mod.L. *aloedarium*, – Gr. ἀλοηδάριον, f. ἀλόη ALOE.] **1.** *Med.* A purgative, chiefly aloes. **2.** *Bot.* A treatise on the Aloe 1753.

Aloetic (ælo,e·tik). 1706. [f. ALOE + -IC, after *diuretic*.] **A.** *ad.* **1.** *Med.* Like, or containing aloes. **2.** *Chem. Aloetic Acid*: a yellow amorphous powder, $2C_7H_2N_2O_5.H_2O$, formed by the action of nitric acid on aloes 1855. **B.** *sb.* [sc. *medicine*] 1706.

Aloft (ălǫ·ft), *adv.* ME. [– ON. *á lopt* (of motion), *á lopti* (of position), i.e. *á* in, on, to (see A *prep.*[1]), *lopt* air, sky (cogn. w. OE. *lyft*, OHG. *luft*, Goth. *luftus*; cf. LOFT, LIFT). Cf. ALEE.] † **1.** Up, as a star –1577; *fig.* ruling –1601. **2.** In heaven (*arch.*) ME.; high above the earth, on high ME.; † on the top –1718. Also *fig.* **3.** Of direction: Into the air, up, on high; also *fig.* ME. **4.** *Naut.* On or to a higher part of the ship ME. † **5.** *prep.* On the top of; above –1613.

2. A..cherub that sits up a. DIBDIN. Fame sits a. POPE. **3.** Blow her a. DE FOE. **4.** Our sayles are a loft BARCLAY. **5.** I breathe again A. the flood SHAKS.

Alogian (ălōᵘ·dʒiăn). 1675. [– med.L. *alogiani*, f. Gr. ἀλόγιοι (f. ἀ- A- *pref.* 14 + λόγος, translated '*Word*' in John 1:1); see -AN.] One of a sect who denied the divinity of the 'Logos'.

Alogotrophy (ælǒgǫ·trǒfi). 1753. [– mod.L. *alogotrophia*, f. Gr. ἄλογος unreasonable + τροφή nourishment; see -Y[3].] *Med.* Excessive nutrition, e.g. of the bones, resulting in deformity.

† **A·logy.** 1646. [– L. *alogia* – Gr. ἀλογία unreasonableness, f. ἄλογος unreasonable; see -Y[3].] Absurdity. SIR T. BROWNE.

Aloid (æ·lo,id), *a.* 1853. [irreg. f. ALOE + -OID.] Resembling aloes.

Aloin (æ·lo,in). 1841. [f. ALOE + -IN[1].] *Chem.* The bitter purgative principle in aloes, $C_{17}H_{18}O_7$, which forms in crystals.

Alomancy, var. of HALOMANCY.

Alone (ălōᵘ·n), *a.* and *adv.* [ME. *al ane, al one*, i.e. OE. *all* entirely (ALL), *āna* by oneself (f. *ān* ONE). Aphet. to LONE.] **1.** *lit.* Quite by oneself, unaccompanied; *fig.* alone of its kind, unique 1535; alone in action or feeling ME. **2.** *attrib.* Sole, unique (*rare*) 1547. **3.** Taken or acting by itself (*esp.* after, or separated from, the sb.) ME. **4.** Also of a number, in all prec. senses: By themselves ME. **5.** With no one else in the same case; exclusively. (Bef., after, or separated from the sb.) ME. **6.** *adv.* With vb., adj., phr., or cl.: Only, merely, exclusively ME.

1. Never less a. than when..a. HOWELL. A. on a wide sea COLERIDGE. A. in an opinion (*mod.*). So *me al-one* (or *al me one*; see ONE), *mine alone, my lone* (now *dial.*). To **let** or **leave alone**: to leave to their own efforts, abstain from interfering. Let me a. for swearing *Twel. N.* III. iv. 201. **2.** The a. God 1564. **3.** A man lyueth not in breed aloon WYCLIF *Matt.* 4: 4. **4.** They two allone ME. **5.** By him a. and onely UDALL. 'Tis not a. my Inky Cloake *Haml.* I. ii. 77. Hence † **Alo·nely** *a.* and *adv.* only, sole, solitary; solely, solitarily. **Alo·neness.**

Along (ălǫ·ŋ), *a.*[1] *arch.* and *dial.* [OE. *ġelang* depending, belonging, = OS. *gilang* ready, OHG. *gilang* neighbouring, :– WGmc. *ʒi- + *laŋg LONG; see A, *particle*, and A- *pref.* 6.] In *Along of* (earlier *on*, in OE. *æt*): Pertaining, owing to; on account of. (Common in London and south. dial.)

And long of her it was That [etc.] *Cymb.* V. v. 271. A. of him and you DICKENS.

Along (ălǫ·ŋ), (*a.*[2]), *adv.* and *prep.* [OE. *andlang* through the length of, = OS. *and-, antlang*, f. WGmc. *and- opposite + *lang- extended, LONG. Cf. ENDLONG.] † **A.** *adj.* (only in OE.) Extending lengthwise, livelong. Merged in *all long*: as *all night long.*

B. *prep.* Orig. adj. with *gen.* Cf. *ahead of*, etc. Through the whole length of, from end to end of, whether *within*, or *by the side of* (often with *all*) OE.; following the line of, opp. to *across* OE.; parallel to the length of ME.

The..Tempest raves a. the plain THOMSON. Stealing..a. the coast JOHNSON.

C. *adv.* [The prep. with obj. omitted.] **1.** In a line with the length; lengthwise. Now only with *by* and as in next. ME. **2.** With vbs. of motion: Onward in the line of motion. Also *fig.* (see quots.) ME. **3.** *ellipt.* (*with* omitted, but its force retained.) In company, with (some one) 1590. **4.** Lengthwise; at full length. Often with *all.* ME. † **5.** In full. (? = Fr. *au long.*) –1588. † **6.** Afar. (? = Fr. *au loin.*) –1580.

1. A. by the king's high way *Numb.* 20: 17. **2.** *To get along*: to get on. *Get along!*: be off! *Along with*: on the way. or in company *with*; together *with*; in conjunction *with.* Then I must lug you a. with me, Says the saucy Arethusa DIBDIN. **3.** The Knave..took a. his rusty Hanger 1682. *All along*: throughout. All a...a burden FREEMAN. **4.** Vnder yond..Trees lay thee all a. *Rom. & Jul.* V. iii. 3. *Comb.* **a.-ships**, lengthwise to the ship.

Alongshore (ălǫ·ŋʃǭᵊ·ɹ), *adv.* 1779. [f. ALONG *prep.* + SHORE. Aphet. LONG-SHORE.] Along *by*, or *on*, the shore.

Alongside (ălǫ·ŋsəi·d), *adv.* 1707. [ALONG *prep.* + SIDE *sb.*[1]] **A.** *adv.* Along or parallel to the side *of*; with *of*: side by side with; also *fig.* 1781. **B.** *prep.* [*of* omitted.] Side by side with 1793.

A. *fig.* A. of him stood his maternal uncle FREEMAN.

Alo·ngst. ME. [orig. *alonges*, advb. gen. in *-es*; for the parasitic *-t* cf. *against, amidst, amongst.*] **A.** *prep.* † Through the length of, opp. to *across*, etc. –1630; by the side of 1580. † **B.** *adv.* Onwards by the side of –1599; opp. to *athwart* –1737; together *with* –1817; as far as (a place indicated) –1650. *Comb.* **a.-ships** = *along-ships*; see ALONG *adv.*

Aloof (ălū·f), *adv.* 1532. [Early forms *a luf, aloufe, on luffe*, i.e. *a* A *prep.*[1], LUFF *sb.*, prob. after Du. *te loef.*] † **1.** *phr. Naut.* The order to keep the ship's head to the wind; now LUFF –1678. Also *fig.* **2.** *adv. Naut.* Away to the windward 1532. **3.** Hence *gen.* At a distance (*from*), apart; *esp.* with *hold, keep*, etc. 1540; from a distance 1547; also *fig.* **4.** As *compl.* or *pred.*: At a distance 1607. As † *prep.* [= aloof from.] (*rare*) –1667.

3. No frende draweth nere, I syt alowfe 1540. Purple cliffs, a. descried TENNYSON. *fig.* **To stand, keep, hold aloof** (*from*): to take no part in, show no sympathy with. **4.** To keepe [dangers] aloofe BACON. *prep.* The great Luminarie Alooff the vulgar Constellations thick MILT. *P.L.* III. 577. Hence **Aloo·fness**, the state of being a. (*lit.* and *fig.*).

‖ **Alope·cia.** ME. [– L. *alopecia* – Gr. ἀλωπεκία fox-mange, also baldness in man, f. ἀλώπηξ, ἀλωπεκ- fox; see -Y[3].] *Med.* Baldness. Hence **Alo·pecist**, one who treats baldness.

Alorcinic (æ:lǫɹsi·nik), *a.* 1875. [f. AL(OE + ORCIN + -IC.] *Chem.* In *Alorcinic Acid*, $C_9H_{10}O_3$, produced by melting potash upon aloes.

Alose (ălōᵘ·s), *sb.* 1591. [– Fr. *alose* :– late L. *alausa* (Ausonius).] A fish (*Alosa communis*), commonly called ALLICE, or *Allice-shad.*

† **Alo·se,** *v.* [– OFr. *aloser*, f. *a* :– L. *ad* AL-[1] + (O)Fr. *los* (now arch.) :– L. *laus*, or pl. *laudes* used as sing.] To praise; also *refl.*; to report (in a bad sense). Only in ME.

‖ **Alouatte** (ælu,æ·t). 1778. [– Fr. *alouate*; origin unkn.] The Howling Monkey, *Mycetes seniculus*, of S. America.

Aloud (ălau·d), *adv.* ME. [A *prep.*[1] + LOUD *a.*; cf. A-HIGH *adv.*, ALOW *adv.*[1]] In a loud voice; with great noise; loudly; also *fig.* (*colloq.*).

He wepte alowde *Gen.* 45: 2.

† **Alou·t,** *v.* OE. [In form = OE. *ālūtan* lurk, in sense *alūtan* to stoop. The *a-* is A- *pref.* 1.] To stoop; to fall over –1480; *esp.* to bow in worship *to* –1500.

Alow (ălōᵘ·), *adv.*[1] ME. [f. A *prep.*[1] 9 + LOW *a.* Cf. *aloud, afar.*] Opp. to *aloft.* Below; downwards. Also *fig. Naut.* In or into the lower part of a vessel 1509.

Toss'd..aloft and then a. DRYDEN.

Alow (ălōu·, ălɒu·), *adv.*[2] *n. dial.* ME. [f. A *prep.*[1] 11 + LOW *sb.*[2]] Ablaze.

† **Alow·,** *v.*; also **all-.** 1530. [f. A- *pref.* 1 + LOW *v.*[1]] To lower. *lit.* and *fig.* –1576.

Alp[1] (ælp). 1551. [In pl. – Fr. *Alpes* – L *Alpes* – Gr. Ἄλπεις, variously explained as (i) 'white' (snow-capped), and (ii) 'high'.] **1.** *pl.* The mountain range which separates France and Italy, etc. *sing.* A single peak. (In Switzerland the pasture-land on the mountain side.) **2.** Any high, *esp.* snow-capped, mountain 1598. Also *fig.*

2. O're many a Frozen, many a Fierie A. MILT. *P.L.* II. 620. *fig.* This adamantine a. of wedlock. MILT.

Alp[2] (ælp). ME. [Origin unkn.] A bullfinch.

† **Alp**[3]. [ME. var. of obs. *elp*, short f. OE. *elpend* elephant.] Elephant.

‖ **Alp**[4]. 1836. [G. *alp* nightmare, demon.] A demon.

Alpaca (ǣlpæ·kă). 1792. [– Sp. *alpaca* (also *paco*) – Quechua *alpako* (also *pako, pakollama*), f. *pako* reddish-brown.] **1.** A Peruvian quadruped, a species of llama, having long fine woolly hair 1811. Also *attrib.* **2.** = alpaca wool 1792; also, the fabric made of it. Often *attrib.* 1838.

Alpenstock (æ·lpěnstǫk). 1829. [G., f. *Alpen* Alps + *stock* stick.] A long staff, pointed with iron, used in climbing, *esp.* in the Alps.

† **Alpe·stral.** *rare.* 1664. [prob. f. It. *alpestre* (whence Fr. *alpestre*) Alpine, mountainous – med.L. *alpestris*; see -AL[1].] **A.** *adj.* Alpine. **B.** *sb.* An alpine species –1675.

Alpe·strian. 1861. [f. It. or Fr. (as prec.) + -IAN.] An Alpine climber.

Alpha (æ·lfă). ME. [– L. – Gr. ἄλφα – Heb. *'eleph* pl., cattle, the first letter of the Heb. alphabet, formed from the hieroglyph of an ox's head.] **1.** Name of the letter A, α, in the Gr. alphabet 1626; hence, the beginning, *esp.* in **Alpha and Omega,** used of God. **2.** The first in numerical sequence. *esp.* **a.** *Astr.* The chief star in a constellation. **b.** *Chem.* The first of a series of isomerous modifications of a compound 1863. **c.** *Alpha rays* or *α-rays,* the first of three types of rays emitted by radioactive substances, consisting of positively-charged particles. Also *alpha* (or *α*) *particles.* 1904.

1. I am alpha and oo, the bigynnyng and endyng, seith the Lord God WYCLIF *Rev.* 1:8. **2.** Alpha and Beta Capricorni 1869. A. naphthol 1880.

Alphabet (æ·lfăbet), *sb.* 1513. [– late L. *alphabetum* (Tertullian), f. Gr. ἄλφα + βῆτα, the first two Greek letters as a name for all; cf. ABC.] **1.** *orig.* The set of letters used in writing the Gr. language; hence, any set of characters repr. the simple sounds in a language, or in speech. Also *attrib.* **2.** *fig.* The key to any study; the first rudiments 1588. † **3.** An index –1825; a series –1727.

2. I (of these) will wrest an A., And..learne to know thy meaning *Tit. A.* III. ii. 44. Hence **A·lphabet** *v.* (esp. in U.S.) = ALPHABETIZE 2. **A:lphabeta·rian,** one learning his a., a beginner; one who studies alphabets. † **A·lphabeta:ry** *a.* rudimentary; *sb.* = ALPHABETARIAN.

Alphabetic, -al (æ·lfăbe·tik, -ăl), *a.* 1642. [f. prec. + -IC; cf. Fr. *alphabétique.*] **1.** Arranged in the order of the alphabet. **2.** Of, pertaining to, or by means of an alphabet 1736. † **3.** *fig.* Literal, strict. *rare.*

3. An alphabetical servility MILT. Hence **Alphabe·tically** *adv.*

Alphabetics (ælfăbe·tiks). 1865. [f. as prec.; see -IC 2.] The science of the expression of spoken sounds by letters.

Alphabetism (æ·lfăbĕti:z'm). 1867. [f. ALPHABET + -ISM.] **1.** Symbolization of spoken sounds by means of an alphabet 1879. **2.** The use of certain letters of the alphabet as a signature, etc.

Alphabetize (æ·lfăbĕtəiz), *v.* 1867. [f. as prec. + -IZE.] **1.** To express by alphabetic letters; to reduce to writing. **2.** To arrange alphabetically 1880.

Alphenic (ælfe·nik). 1657. [– Fr. *alphenic* – Sp. *alfeñique* sugar paste – Arab. *al-fānīd* f. *al* AL-[2] + Pers. *pānīd* refined sugar.] *Pharm.* White barley sugar.

† **Alphitomancy.** 1652. [– Fr. *alphitomantie,* f. Gr. ἀλφιτόμαντις diviner by barley meal (f. ἄλφιτον barley groats); see -MANCY.] Divination by barley-meal –1721.

A:lphitomo·rphous, *a.* 1879. [f. Gr. ἄλφιτον barley groats + μορφή form + -OUS.] Like barley-meal in form; said of certain microscopic fungi.

Alphonsin (æ̆lfǫ·nsin). 1751. [f. *Alphonsus* Ferrier, of Naples.] *Surg.* An instrument with three elastic branches, for extracting bullets from the body.

Alphonsine (æ̆lfǫ·nsin), *a.* 1678. Of Alphonso the Wise, King of Castile; applied to astronomical tables invented by him, etc.

‖ **Alphos** (æ·lfǫs). 1706. [– Gr. ἀλφός a dull-white leprosy, whence L. *alphus* (Celsius).] *Path.* Non-contagious leprosy.

† **Alpieu·.** 1693. [– Fr. *alpiou* – It. *al più,* lit. for the more, for most.] In the game of basset, a mark put on a card to indicate that the player doubles his stake after winning –1768.

Alpine (æ·lpəin), *a.* 1607. [– L. *alpinus*; see ALP, -INE[1].] Of or pertaining to the Alps; lofty.

A. plants 1759, snows HOOK. An a. height GROTE.

Alpinist (æ·lpinist). 1881. [– Fr. *alpiniste*; see ALPINE, -IST.] An alpine climber.

Alpist (æ·lpist). ? *Obs.* Also **alpia.** 1597. [– Fr. *alpiste* – It. *alpista*; see ALP, -IST.] Birdseed, *esp.* the seed of the Canary Grass (*Phalaris canariensis*).

‖ **Alquifou** (ælkifū·). 1819. [– Fr. *alquifoux* – Sp. *alquifol* – Arab. *al-kuḥl* ALCOHOL.] A lead ore, resembling antimony when broken, used by potters to make a green glaze.

Already (ǭlre·di), *adv.* ME. [ALL *adv.* + READY.] † **1.** *adj.* (*compl.*) Fully prepared –1509. **2.** *adv.* Beforehand; previously to some specified time; by this time, thus early.

2. It hath beene a. of olde time *Eccles.* 1: 10. ¶ Sense 1 can still be traced in: The three Scotch regiments were a. in England MACAULAY.

Alright, frequent sp. of *all right* 1893.

† **Als.** Chiefly *north.* ME. An intermediate form between *alse* = *alswa* ALSO and AS, and used like them.

Alsatia (æ̆lsē[i]·ʃ[i]ă). 1688. [– med.L. *Alsatia, Alsacia,* whence Fr. *Alsace,* latinized f. G. *Elsass,* lit. 'foreign settlement'.] **1.** The province of Alsace, a debatable ground between France and Germany, whence: **2.** Cant name for the precinct of White Friars in London, once a sanctuary for debtors and criminals; hence, an asylum for criminals. Hence **Alsatian** *a.* of or belonging to A.; *sb.* an inhabitant of A.; a debtor or criminal in sanctuary. *A.* (*wolf-dog*): see WOLF-DOG 3.

‖ **Al segno** (al se·nyo). [It., = to the sign or mark.] *Mus.* A direction: Go back to the sign 𝄋 and repeat.

Alsike (æ·lsik). 1852. [f. *Alsike* in Sweden.] A species of clover, *Trifolium hybridum.*

Alsinaceous (ælsinē[i]·ʃəs), *a.* 1835. [f. L. *alsine* – Gr. ἀλσίνη wall pellitory + -ACEOUS.] *Bot.* Allied to, or like, chickweed.

Also (ǭ·lso[u]), *adv.* [OE. *alswā* (WS. *ealswā*), (= OFris. *alsa,* OHG. *alsō*), f. ALL + SO *adv.*; see AS *adv.*] **A.** Demonstrative. † **1.** Wholly or quite so; in this or that very manner –ME.; in like manner, likewise –1710. **2.** Further, too; replacing OE. *éac,* EKE. ME.

2. Not in Words onely, but in Woes a. 2 *Hen. IV,* II. iv. 459. Not only futile, but..a. injurious BUCKLE.

B. Correlative. *Obs.* replaced by As, So.

C. Relative and conjunctive. † As –1458; † with *subj.* As though ME.

† **Alsoo·n,** *adv.* ME. [= *als soon,* i.e. *as soon.*] **1.** As soon (*as*). Cf. F. *aussitôt que.* –1579. **2.** *absol.* At once. [Fr. *aussitôt.*] –ME.

Alstonite (ǭ·lstənəit). [f. *Alston* in Cumberland + -ITE[1] 2 b.] = BROMLITE.

† **Alt[1].** 1623. [– obs. Fr. *alte,* or modification of earlier ALTO *sb.*[1] after Fr.] In *To make alt*: a halt –1664.

Alt[2] (ælt). 1535. [– It. *alto* ALTO *sb.*[2]; cf. G. *alt* XVI.] *Mus.* High tone; *spec.* in *In alt*: in the octave above the treble stave beginning with G. Also *fig.*: In an exalted frame of mind.

Altaian (æ̆ltē·iăn), *a.* and *sb.* 1874. [– Fr. *altaïen,* f. *Altaï,* a mountain range in Central Asia; see -AN.] Belonging to the neighbourhood of the Altai Mountains. var. **Alta·ic** *a.*

Altaite (æ̆ltē·əit). [f. as prec. + -ITE[1] 2 b.] *Min.* A tellurid of silver, or of lead and silver.

‖ **Altaltissimo** (altalti·simo). 1855. [It.] The very highest summit. BROWNING.

Altar (ǭ·ltəɹ). [OE. *altar, alter,* corresp. to OFris. *altar(e),* OS., OHG., ON. *altari, alteri*; Gmc. – late L. *altar, -are, -arium,* for L. *altaria* n. pl. Forms repr. OFr. *auter* appear XIII; present form (XVI) adapted to Latin.] **1.** A raised structure, with a plane top, on which to place or sacrifice offerings to a deity; also *fig.* **2.** The raised structure consecrated to the celebration of the Eucharist ME.; the 'holy table' of the Eng. Prayer-book, which occupies the place of the altars removed after the Reformation 1549. **3.** *fig.* A place consecrated to devotional exercises, as in *Family altar* 1693. **4.** A metrical composition, written or printed in the form of an altar (*arch.*) 1680. **5.** The constellation *Ara* 1556.

1. The altare of burnt offrynges *Exod.* 38:1 *fig.* The sacred a. of peace BURKE. **2.** *High Altar,* the chief a. in a cathedral or church. It was not to be accounted an a. but the communion-table BRERETON. Receive this kingly sword brought now from the a. of God *Eng. Coron. Service* (where alone the word remains in authoritative use). *To lead a bride to the a.,* i.e. to the place where the marriage service in a church is concluded; whence 'hymeneal a.'

Comb.: **a.-bread,** that used in the Communion; **-cloth,** the linen cloth used at the Communion or the Mass; the silk frontal; **-fire,** the fire on an a.; *fig.* religious rite; **-front, -frontal, -facing,** a movable frame or hanging of silk, etc., placed in front of the a., the *antependium*; **-piece,** a painting or sculpture placed behind and over an a.; a reredos; **-plate,** the communion plate; **-pyx,** a pyx for holding the consecrated elements; **-rails,** those separating the sacrarium; **-screen,** the screen at the back of an a.; **-stone,** *esp.* the slab forming the top of an a.; the super-altar; **-table** = *a.-stone*; † **-thane,** a mass-priest; **-tomb,** a raised tomb resembling an a.; **-ways,** = *Altarwise.*

Hence **A·ltarage.** **1.** The revenue from oblations at an a. **2.** A fund to maintain an a. and a priest to say masses at it. **A·ltared** *ppl. a.* furnished with, or treated as, an a. **A·ltarist,** a vicar of a church; one who sees to what is necessary for the service of the altars. **A·ltarless** *a. poet.* **A·ltarlet,** a small a. **A·ltarwise** *adv.* after the manner, or in the position, of an a.

Altazimuth (ælt,æ·zimɒþ). 1860. [f. AL-T(ITUDE) + AZIMUTH.] An instrument for determining altitudes and azimuths.

Alter (ǭ·ltəɹ), *v.* ME. [– (O)Fr. *altérer* – late L. *alterare,* f. *alter* other.] **1.** To make otherwise or different in some respect, without changing the thing itself; to modify. **2.** *intr.* (for *refl.*) To become otherwise, to undergo some change 1590. † **3.** To affect mentally –1674. † **4.** *intr.* To administer alterative medicines –1684.

1. To a. a decree *Merch. V.* IV. i. 219, a design BURKE. **2.** The law of the Medes and Persians which altereth not *Dan.* 6:12. Hence **A·lterer,** he who or that which alters. **A·ltering** *vbl. sb.* alteration; *ppl. a.* making or becoming otherwise; † *Med.* = ALTERATIVE.

Alterable (ǭ·ltərăb'l), *a.* 1526. [– (O)Fr. *altérable* or med.L. *alterabilis*; see prec., -ABLE.] † **1.** Liable to alter or vary –1696. **2.** Capable of being altered 1574.

2. Laws..a. by Parliament 1744. Substances a. by fire PLAYFAIR. Hence **A:lterabi·lity** = ALTERABLENESS. **A·lterableness** *a.* the quality of being a. **A·lterably** *adv.*

Alterant (ǭ·ltərănt). 1626. [– Fr. *altérant*; see ALTER *v.*, -ANT.] **A.** *adj.* Producing alteration. **B.** *sb.* Anything which alters 1750; *spec.* † an alterative medicine –1753.

† **A·lterate,** *ppl. a.* ME. [– *alteratus,* pa. pple. of late L. *alterare*; see ALTER *v.*, -ATE[2].] = ALTERED –1531.

† **A·lterate,** *v.* 1475. [– *alterat-,* pa. ppl. stem of late L. *alterare*; see prec., -ATE[3].] var. of ALTER –1693.

Alteration (ǭltərē[i]·ʃən). 1482. [– (O)Fr. *altération* or late L. *alteratio*; see prec., -ION.] **1.** The action of altering. **2.** An altered condition 1532. † **3.** A distemper –1663. † **4.** *Mus.* Doubling the proper value of a note –1609.

1. He's full of a. *Lear* V. i. 3. **2.** Ere long I might perceave Strange a. in me MILT. *P.L.* IX. 599.

Alterative (ǭ·ltərĕtiv). ME. [– med.L. *alterativus,* f. as prec., see -IVE; cf. Fr. *altératif, -ive.*] **A.** *adj.* Tending to produce alteration; *esp.* of medicines which alter the processes of nutrition, and reduce them to healthy action 1605. **B.** *sb.* An alterative medicine or treatment ME.

Altercate (æ·ltəɹke[i]t, ǭ·l-). 1530. [– *altercat-,* pa. ppl. stem of L. *altercari, -are* to wrangle; see -ATE[3].] To dispute vehemently or angrily; to contend in words; to wrangle. Hence † **A·ltercative** *a.* scolding.

Altercation (æ·ltəɹkē[i]·ʃən, ǭ·l-). ME. [– (O)Fr. *altercation* – L. *altercatio,* f. as prec.; see -ION.] **1.** The action of altercating (see ALTERCATE); the conduct of a case by question and answer (L. *altercatio*) 1779. **2.** A vehement or angry dispute, a wrangle 1552.

‖ **Alter ego** (æ·ltər e·go). 1537. [L., = other or second self (Cicero).] A second self; an intimate.

Alterity (æ̆lte·rĭti, ǭl-). 1642. [– Fr. *altérité* or late L. *alteritas*; see ALTER *v.*, -ITY.] The being different; otherness.

Altern (æ̆ltə̄·ɹn, ǭl-; æ·ltəɹn, ǭ·l-), *a.* 1644. [– L. *alternus* every other; cf. Fr. *alterne.*] **1.** Alternate 1644. **2.** *Cryst.* Having upper and lower faces corresponding in form, but alternate with each other in the position of their sides and angles. **3.** quasi-*adv.* In turns 1677.

3. The greater to have rule by Day, The less by Night alterne MILT. *P.L.* VII. 348. *Altern base*: in oblique-angled triangles the difference or sum of the segments formed by a perpendicular falling from the vertex according as it cuts the base or base produced. Hence † **Alte·rnacy**, alternate condition. † **Alte·rnal** *a.* = ALTERNATE.

Alternant (ǣltə̄·ɹnănt, ǭl-), *ppl. a.* 1640. [– *alternant-*, pres. ppl. stem of L. *alternare*; see next, -ANT; cf. Fr. *alternant.*] Alternating; *Min.* consisting of alternating layers (*mod.*). As *sb.* [sc. *quantity*.] 1882.

Alternate (ǣltə̄·ɹnĕt, ǭl-). 1513. [– L. *alternatus*, pa. pple. of *alternare* do things by turns, f. *alternus*, f. *alter*; see ALTERN *a.*, ALTER *v.*, -ATE².] **A.** *adj.* **1.** Done or changed by turns, coming each after one of the other kind. **2.** Said of a series or whole made up of such alternate members 1650. **3.** Alternatively taken; — about; every second 1697. **4.** Alternately placed; occurring first on one side and then on the other of an axial line, *esp.* in *Bot.* of *leaves*, and in *Geom.* of *angles* 1570. **5.** Reciprocal 1716. † **6.** Inter-changed 1590. **7.** quasi-*adv.* By turns 1712.

1. A. day and night (*mod.*). A. smiles and frowns both insincere T. BROWN. **2.** Smooth a. verse CRABBE. **Alternate generation:** *Biol.* genealogical succession by a. processes, as first by budding, and next by sexual reproduction, and so on. **3.** He and I go on a. days, or *day about* (*mod.*). **Alternate proportion:** that obtained by comparing antecedent to antecedent and consequent to consequent 1660. **7.** Wane and wax a. like the moon POPE.

B. *sb.* [the adj. used *absol.*] **1.** That which alternates with something else; a vicissitude, an alternative 1718. **2.** (U.S.) A second, or substitute (*mod.*).

Alternate (æ·ltəɹneᶦt, ǭl-), *v.* 1599. [– *alternat-*, pa. ppl. stem of L. *alternare*; see prec., -ATE³.] **1.** *trans.* To arrange, do, perform, or cause to occur, in alternation 1599. **2.** *intr.* To succeed one another by turns, in time or space 1700. **3.** *intr.* To consist of alternations. Const. *between.* 1823. **4.** *intr.* To appear alternately *with* 1831.

1. Who..Hymns about the..Throne A. all night long MILT. *P.L.* v. 657. Hence **A·lterna:ting** *ppl. a.* (in senses 2, 3, 4); spec. *alternating current* (Electr.), a current which reverses its direction at regular intervals (abbrev. *A.C.* or *a.c.*). **A·lterna:tingly** *adv.*

Alternately (ǣltə̄·ɹnĕtli, ǭl-), *adv.* 1552. [f. ALTERNATE *a.* + -LY².] **1.** In alternate order; time about. **2.** By taking the alternate terms 1695. **3.** On each side in turn 1751.

Alternation (æltəɹnēᶦ·ʃən, ǭl-). 1611. [– Fr. *alternation* or L. *alternatio*; see ALTERNATE *v.*, -ION.] **1.** The action of two things succeeding each other by turns; alternate succession or occurrence. **2.** Taking the members of a series alternately 1695. **3.** Successive change in a scene or action 1633. **4.** The state of being in alternate order 1830. **5.** The doing of anything by two actors in turn; reading or singing antiphonally 1642. **6.** *erron.* Permutation 1751.

1. The a. of pleasure and pain GOLDSM. **Alternation of generations** = *alternate generation*; see ALTERNATE *a.* 2 (quots.).

Alternative (ǣltə̄·ɹnĕtiv, ǭl-). 1590. [– Fr. *alternatif*, *-ive* or med.L. *alternativus*, f. as prec.; see -IVE.] **A.** *adj.* **1.** Stating or offering either of two things 1590. **2.** Of two things: Such that one or the other may be chosen, the choice of either involving the rejection of the other. (Sometimes of more than two things.) 1861. Also (*ellipt.*) the other (of two) 1838. **3.** Disjunctive 1753. † **4.** Alternate –1716.

2. I accept the statements as a. statements FREEMAN. The a. supposition 1838. **3.** The a. conjunctions are either—or [etc.] BAIN.

B. *sb.* [the adj. used *absol.*] That which is alternative. **1.** A statement or offer of two things of which either may be agreed to, but not both; permission to choose between two things 1624. ¶ The only use in Johnson. **2.** *loosely*, Either of two courses open to choose between. Cf. 'no other alternative'. 1814. *esp.* The remaining course. Cf. 'no alternative' (also = no choice; see 1). 1760. **3.** Also, one of more than two courses which may be chosen 1848. † **4.** Alternation –1782.

1. The brief a. of Mahomet, death or the Koran 1853. **2.** But two alternatives,..Rome, and.. Atheism J. H. NEWMAN. There was no a. in my uncle Toby's wardrobe STERNE. **3.** [I prefer] the fourth and last of these alternatives GLADSTONE. Hence **Alte·rnatively** *adv.* in a way that offers a choice between two; † by turns. † **Alte·rnativeness**, the quality of being a., or alternate.

Alte:rni-, comb. form of L. *alternus* (see ALTERN); = ALTERNATE or ALTERNATELY, as in *alterni-foliate*.

Alternity (ǣltə̄·ɹnĭti, ǭl-). *rare.* 1646. [In sense 1 – OFr. *alternité* alternation or med.L. *alternitas*; in mod. use f. L. *alternus* (see ALTERN *a.*) + -ITY.] † **1.** Alternation. **2.** The counterchange of vowels, and correspondency of consonants, in certain Welsh rhymes 1856.

† **A·lternize**, *v.* [f. ALTERN *a.* + -IZE; cf. *modernize.*] To alternate. MME. D'ARBLAY.

‖ **Althæa** (ǣlþī·ă). 1669. [L. – Gr. ἀλθαία marsh mallow, f. ἀλθεῖν to heal.] *Bot.* A genus of plants (N.O. *Malvaceæ*), including the marsh mallow and the hollyhock; often extended to the genus *Hibiscus*.

‖ **Althing** (ǭ·lþiŋ). [Icel. *alþing*, ON. *alþingi* general assembly.] The general assembly of Iceland. Hence **Althingman**, a member of the A.

Althionic (ælþiˌǫ·nik), *a.* 1858. [f. AL(COHOL) + Gr. θεῖον sulphur + -IC; cf. *thionic* (THIO-).] *Chem.* In *Althionic Acid*, $C_2H_6SO_4$, produced by heating alcohol with an excess of sulphuric acid.

Although (ǭlðōᵘ·), *conj.* ME. [Now a var. of, but orig. two words and more emphatic than, THOUGH. See ALL, and THOUGH.] Even though, though..even; though; granting that, supposing that.

A. all shall be offended, yet will not I *Mark* 14:29 (R.V.)

Alti-, comb. form of L. *altus* high, and *alte* highly.

† **A·ltify**, *v.* ?*nonce-wd.* [f. ALTI- + -FY, after *magnify*.] To make high. FULLER.

Alti·loquence. 1731. [f. med.L. *altiloquus* pompous talker + -ENCE, after *grandi-*, *magniloquence*.] Pompous language.

Altimeter (ǣlti·mĭtəɹ). 1847. [f. ALTI- + -METER; cf. med.L. *altimeter* (Papias).] An instrument for taking altitudes geometrically. So **Alti·metry** 1696.

‖ **Alti·ncar.** 1753. [– (ult.) Arab. *altinkār*, cf. med.L., Sp. *atincar*; see TINCAL.] = TINCAL.

Altisonant (ǣlti·sōnănt), *a.* 1620. [f. L. *altisonus* high-sounding (f. *alti-* ALTI- + *sonare* to sound) + -ANT.] High-sounding, pompous, loud.

‖ **Altissimo** (ɑlti·ssimo). 1819. [It., superl. of *alto*.] *Mus.* In the phr. *In altissimo*: in the second octave above the treble stave, beginning with G.

† **Alti·tonant**, *a.* 1627. [– *altitonant-*, stem of L. *altitonans* (f. *alti-* ALTI- + *tonare* to thunder); see -ANT.] Thundering from on high –1656.

Altitude (æ·ltitiud). ME. [– L. *altitudo*, f. *altus* high; see -TUDE.] **1.** *gen.* Vertical extent or distance; the quality of being high or deep. **2.** *Geom.* The height of a triangle, etc., measured by a perpendicular to the base or base produced 1570. **3.** Height above a base (e.g. the ground, or sea-level); loftiness 1535. **4.** *Astr.* Height expressed by angular distance above the horizon ME. **5.** *sing.* A height; *pl.* high regions ME. **6.** *fig.* High degree of any quality; high rank, power, etc. ME. † **7.** *fig.* in *pl.* Lofty mood, airs, phrases, etc. –1782.

1. The a. which thou hast perpendicularly fell *Lear* IV. vi. 53. **3.** A toure..that in a. euened the stars 1583. **6.** Euen in the a. of popedome 1596. **7.** If we would see him in his altitudes NORTH. Hence **Altitu·dinal** *a.* relating to a. **A:ltitudina·rian** *a.* pertaining to the heights (of fancy, doctrine, etc.); *sb.* one given to lofty thoughts, etc.

† **A·lto**, *sb.*¹ 1591. [– Sp. *alto* in phr. *alto hacer*, adaptation of G. *halt machen* make a stop, halt; cf. ALT¹.] A halt –1622.

Alto (ɑ·lto), *sb.*² 1784. [– It. *alto* high (sc. *canto* song) :– L. *altus* high.] *Mus.* **A.** *sb.* **1.** The highest male voice, the counter-tenor; also, the musical part for it 1819. **2.** The female voice of similar range, or the musical part sung by it, more strictly the *contralto* 1881. **3.** One who has an alto voice 1784. **4.** = ALT². 1862. **5.** A tenor violin [It.] 1833. **B.** *attrib.* as *adj.* Belonging to the a. 1845. **Alto clef:** the C clef when placed on the third line of the stave. **Alto-ripieno:** a tenor part, used only occ. in a grand chorus.

‖ **Alto-** (ɑ·lto), It. = high-, used in comb. **1.** *Mus.*, as **a.-clarinet, -fagotto, -viola,** instruments like, but higher in pitch than, the clarinet, etc. **2.** *Sculpt.* (See ALTO-RELIEVO.)

Altogether (ǭltŭge·ðəɹ). ME. [comb. of ALL and TOGETHER. Orig. a strengthening of *all*, but now advb.] **A.** *adj.* A strengthened form of ALL *a.* † **1.** The whole together; the total –1611; (*pl.* now *all together*) –1663. **B.** *adv.* [cf. ALL *adv.*] **1.** Everything being included; in all respects; wholly, quite ME. **2.** Uninterruptedly 1700. **3. For altogether:** for all time to come, for good. Also without *for.* 1548. **C.** *sb.* A whole, a *tout ensemble* 1667.

B. 1. Thou wast a. born in sins *John* 9:34. **C.** American fingers impart a finish and an a. (this is ..better than..*tout-ensemble*) 1865. Hence **Altoge·therness**, unity of being (*rare*).

Alto-relievo (ɑ:lto rĭlī·vo). Pl. **-os.** 1717. [It. *alto-rilievo*, occas. so spelt in Eng.] High relief; sculpture, etc., in which the figures project more than half their thickness from the background. Hence *concr.* A sculpture, etc., in high relief.

Altruism (æ·ltruˌiz'm). 1853. [– Fr. *altruisme* (A. Comte, 1830), – It. *altrui* somebody else, what is another's (cf. Fr. *autrui*) :– Rom. **alteri huic* 'to this other'; see -ISM.] Regard for others, as a principle of action; opp. to egoism or selfishness.

The religion of humanity, whose great moral principle is a. 1877. Hence **A·ltruist**, one who professes a. **Altrui·stic** *a.* of or pertaining to a.; benevolent. **Altrui·stically** *adv.*

† **A·ltumal**, *a.* 1711. [f. L. *altum* the deep + -AL¹.] In *altumal cant*: maritime language –1753.

Aludel (æ·lᶦudel). 1559. [– Fr. *aludel* – Sp. – Arab. *al-'uṯāl* the apparatus; see AL-².] *Chem.* A pear-shaped pot of earthenware or glass, open at both ends, so that a series could be fitted one above another; used in sublimation.

Alum (æ·ləm). ME. [– OFr. *alum* (mod. *alun*) :– L. *alumen*, rel. to *aluta* tawed leather.] A whitish transparent mineral salt, crystallizing in octahedrons, very astringent; chemically a double sulphate of aluminium potassium. In *Mod. Chem.* (with *pl.*) extended to include *Potash, Soda, Ammonia, Silver alum*, etc.; also *Iron, Manganese, Chrome, Chrome-ammonia alums*, etc.; and in *Min.* various native minerals which are chemically either alums proper, or pseudo-alums.

While chalk and a. and plaster are sold to the poor for bread TENNYSON.

Comb.: **a. cake,** a massive and porous sulphate of alumina, mixed with silica, made from fine clay; **a.-rock, -schist, -shale, -slate,** thin-bedded rocks, found in various formations, which yield a.; **-root,** the astringent roots of various plants; **-stone** = ALUNITE. Hence **A·lum** *v.* to treat with a.

‖ **Alumbrado** (a:lumbrā·do). 1671. [Sp., = enlightened, pa. pple. of *alumbrar*.] One of the Sp. *Illuminati* or Perfectionists of the 16th c.; hence, any one claiming illumination.

Alumian (ălᶦū·miăn). [irreg. f. ALUM + -IAN.] *Min.* A white sulphate of aluminium.

Alumina (ălᶦū·mină). 1790. [f. L. *alumen*, *alumin-*, after names of other earths, as *soda*, *potassa*, *magnesia*; cf. Fr. *alumine.*] One of the earths; the only oxide (Al_2O_3) of Aluminium, the basis of alum, the chief constituent of all clays, and found crystallized as the sapphire. Hence **Alu·minate** *sb.* a compound of alumina with one of the stronger bases. **Alu·minate** *v.* to treat with alum.

Alumine (æ·lᶦuməin). 1791. [– Fr. *alumine* (prec.).] *Chem. arch.* = ALUMINA.

Aluminiferous (ălᶦū:mini·fĕrəs), *a.* 1849. [f. L. *alumen*, *alumin-* ALUM + -FEROUS.] Alum-bearing.

Aluminiform (ălᶦū·minifǭ:ɹm, æ:lᶦumi·ni-), *a.* 1864. [f. as prec. + -FORM.] Having the form of an alum.

Aluminio- (æ:lᶦumi·nio), comb. form of ALUMINIUM, as in *Aluminio-silicate*.

Aluminite (ălᶦū·minəit). 1868. [f. L. *alumen*, *alumin-* ALUM + -ITE¹ 2 b.] *Min.* An opaque whitish native hydrosulphate of alumina; WEBSTERITE.

Aluminium (æːlⁱumi·niŏm). 1812. [alt. f. of ALUMINUM in conformity w. names of other metals in -IUM.] A metal, white, sonorous, ductile, and malleable, very light, not readily oxidized or tarnished. In *Chem.* it has the symbol Al, is trivalent, has *alumina* as its oxide, and the *alums* as its chief salts.
Comb. Aluminium-bronze, an alloy of a. and copper. Hence **Alumi·nic** *a.*

Aluminize (ălⁱū·minəiz), *v. rare.* 1857. [f. L. *alumen, alumin-* ALUM + -IZE.] To treat with alum; to alum.

Alumino- (ălⁱū·mino), comb. form of ALUMINA, ALUMINUM, implying the union of these with another element.

Aluːmino·se, *a.* 1879. [– L. *aluminosus*; see -OSE¹.] = ALUMINOUS. Hence **Aluːmino·sity** (*rare*).

Aluminous (ălⁱū·minəs), *a.* 1541. [f. as prec. + -OUS; cf. Fr. *alumineux.*] Of the nature of or containing alum or alumina.
A. or clayey soils TRIMMER.

Alu·minum. [Modification by Davy (1812) of his earlier name *alumium*, subseq. altered to ALUMINIUM. *Aluminum* is usual in U.S.] = ALUMINIUM.

Alumish (æ·ləmiʃ), *a.* 1562. [f. ALUM + -ISH¹.] Somewhat like alum. var. † **Alu·minish.**

†**Alu·mium.** See ALUMINUM.

Alumniate (ălɒ·mniˌĕt). *rare.* 1879. [irreg. f. ALUMNUS + -ATE¹, after *noviciate.*] The period of pupilage.

‖ **Alumnus** (ălɒ·mnŭs). Pl. **-i.** 1645. [L., = nursling, pupil, f. *alere* nourish, bring up.] The nursling or pupil of any school, university, etc.

Aluni·ferous, *a.* 1879. [f. Fr. *alunifère* (f. *alun* ALUM + *-fère* = -FEROUS) + -OUS.] = ALUMINIFEROUS.

Alunite (æ·lⁱunəit). 1868. [– Fr. *alunite*, f. *alun* ALUM + *-ite* -ITE¹ 2 b.] *Min.* A mineral, also called Alum-stone and Aluminilite, consisting of common alum together with normal hydrate of aluminium.

Alunogen (ălⁱū·nŏdʒĕn). 1868. [– Fr. *alunogène*, f. *alun* ALUM + *-gène* -GEN.] *Min.* A hydrous sulphate of alumina, occurring as a feathery efflorescence; also called *Keramohalite, hair-salt*, and *feather-alum.*

† **A·lure.** ME. [– OFr. *aleüre, alure* (mod. *allure*), f. *aller* go + *-ure* -URE.] A place to walk in; *esp.* a passage behind the parapets of a castle, or round the roof of a church; a cloister –1851.

Alutaceous (ælⁱutē̆ⁱ·ʃəs), *a.* 1873. [f. late L. *alutacius*, (f. L. *aluta* soft leather) + -OUS; see -ACEOUS.] Of the quality or colour of tawed leather.

Alveary (æ·lviˌări). 1580. [– L. *alvearium, alveare*, f. *alveus* bee-hive; see -ARY¹.] **1.** A bee-hive; a title given to an early polyglot Dictionary. **2.** *Anat.* The hollow of the outer ear, where the wax is found 1719.

Alveated (æ·lviˌeⁱtĕd), *ppl. a.* 1623. [f. L. *alveatus* hollowed out (f. *alveus* deep cavity) + -ED¹; see -ATE².] Hollow like a hive, vaulted, or trenched.

Alveolar (ǣlvī·ŏlăɹ, æ·lviŏlăɹ), *a.* 1799. [f. ALVEOLUS + -AR¹; cf. Fr. *alvéolaire.*] **1.** Of or pertaining to the sockets of the teeth, or to that part of the upper jaw, the *alveolar arch*, in which the teeth are placed. **2.** Socket-shaped 1858. **3.** *sb.* The alveolar processes of the maxillary bone, in which the teeth are fixed 1874.
1. The English *t* and *d* are not strictly *dental*, they are *a.* 1880. var. **Alve·olary.** Hence **Aːlveola·riform** *a.* shaped like cells in a honey-comb.

Alveolo- (ǣlvī·ŏlo), comb. form of ALVEOLUS: Of or pertaining to the sockets of the teeth or the alveolar arch, as in **alveolo-condylean plane,** that bounded by the centre of the upper alveolar arch and the base of the occipital condyles.

‖ **Alveolus** (ǣlvī·ŏlŏs). Pl. **-i.** 1706. [L., dim. of *alveus* cavity.] A small cavity; *hence* **a.** the socket of a tooth; **b.** the cell of a honey-comb; **c.** the conical chamber of a Belemnite, or the conical body found in it. var. **A·lveole.** Hence **Alve·olate** *a.* honey-combed; pitted with small cavities. **Alve·oliform** *a.* celled like a honey-comb. **Alve·olite,** a fossil Zoophyte found in the chalk.

‖ **A·lveus.** 1695. [L., = deep cavity; channel or bed of a river.] The channel of a river; the trough of the sea.

Alvine (æ·lvəin), *a.* 1754. [– mod.L. *alvinus*, f. L. *alvus* belly; see -INE¹.] Pertaining to the abdomen or its contents.

Alway (ǭ·lweⁱ, *arch.* ǭ·lwē̆ⁱ·), *adv.* OE. [orig. two words, in the acc. of space = *all the way*, but soon transferred to time also. Now *arch.* and *poet.*; repl. in prose by ALWAYS.] **1.** Throughout all time. **2.** = ALWAYS 1. ME. **†3.** = ALWAYS 3. –1475.

Always (ǭ·lweⁱz, -wêz), *adv.* ME. [gen. case of *all way*, prob. distrib. 'at every time'. Cf. *sometimes* and *some time*. The distinction is now lost.] **1.** At all times; opp. to *sometimes*, etc. **2.** = ALWAY 1; through all time; opp. to *for a time* ME. **3.** Still, nevertheless, however; now, in any or every circumstance, anyway.
1. Man never is, but a. to be blest POPE *Ess. Man* I. 92. **2.** To be..Had in remembrance a. with delight MILT. *P.L.* III. 704.

Aly (ē̆ⁱ·li), *a.*; also **aley.** 1624. [f. ALE + -Y¹.] Of or like ale.

† **Aly·pum, -us.** 1611. [– L. *alypon* (Pliny) – Gr. ἄλυπον.] An unknown plant of anodyne properties –1621.

Alyssum (ăli·sŏm). 1551. [– L. *alysson* (Pliny) – Gr. ἄλυσσον.] *Bot.* **1.** A genus of Cruciferous plants, including *A. Saxatile* or Gold-dust. **2.** *pop.* **Sweet Alyssum** (or *A·lison*), (*Königa maritima*), A small cruciferous plant with white flowers.

Am (æm, əm, 'm, m), *v.*, 1st sing. pres. ind. of vb. BE. *Am, art, is, are*, are the only survivals in Eng. of the original substantive vb. (Skr. *as-*, Gr. ἐσ-, L. *es-*, Goth. *is-*, *i-*). See BE.

Amability (æmăbi·liti). 1604. [– Fr. *amabilité* or L. *amabilitas*, f. *amabilis* lovely, f. *amare* love; see -BLE.] Lovableness.

† **A·mable, -ile,** *a.* ME. [late ME – OFr. *amable* (mod. *aimable*) :– L. *amabilis* (see prec.); *amabile* (XVI) – L.] Lovely, lovable –1677.

Amacra·tic, *a.* [irreg. f. Gr. ἅμα together + κράτος strength + -IC.] Uniting actinic rays into one focus, as an *amacratic lens.*

‖ **Amadavat** (æːmădăvæ·t). Also **ava-.** 1777. [f. *Ahmadabad* (Gujerat, India) whence the birds were orig. brought.] An Indian song-bird (*Estrilda amandava*), brown in colour with white spots.

Amadelphous (æmăde·lfəs), *a.* 1879. [irreg. f. Gr. ἅμα together + ἀδελφός brother + -OUS.] Gregarious.

Amadou (æ·mădū). 1815. [– Fr. *amadou* – mod. Pr. *amadou* lit. 'lover', so called for its quick kindling.] Tinder, touchwood, punk (the sterile part of the fruit body of the fungus *Fomes fomentarius*).

‖ **Amah** (ā·mă). 1839. [Anglo-Ind. – Pg. *ama* nurse.] A wet-nurse.

Amain (ămē̆ⁱ·n), *adv.* 1540. [f. A *prep.*¹ + MAIN *sb.*¹; earlier † *with main.*] **1.** *lit.* In, or with, full force; vehemently, violently; in full force of numbers 1601. **2.** At full speed 1563; without delay 1600. **3.** Exceedingly. (Cf. L. *valde.*) 1587.
1. The blood gushed out a. HOOD. **2.** They fled a. 1587. Housewives left a. Their broken tasks 1821. **3.** They..thrive in wealth a. MILT. *P.R.* II. 429.

† **Amai·n(e,** *v.* 1553. [– (O)Fr. *amener* lower (sail), strike (colours), f. *a* AD- + *mener* **bring**; cf. A- *pref.* 7.] **1.** To lower (*esp.* the topsail) –1627; *fig.* to abate 1578. **2.** *intr.* To lower the topsail in sign of yielding; to yield 1593. **3.** To conduct. (Cf. Fr. *amenée.*) *rare.* 1553.

Amalgam (ămæ·lgăm), *sb.* 1471. [– Fr. *amalgame* or med.L. *amalgama*, prob. ult. f. Gr. μάλαγμα emollient.] **1.** *orig.* A soft mass formed *esp.* by combination with mercury; *hence now*, any mercurial alloy. **2.** By extension, An intimate mixture of any two or more substances 1626. **3.** *fig.* A complete combination of various elements. Also *attrib.* 1790. **4.** An alloy 1840.
1. Native amalgam, an a. of mercury with silver or gold, found in Columbia, etc. **2.** The Body of the Wood will [become] a kind of Amalgama BACON *Sylva* § 99. **3.** Custom is an a. of sense and folly HONE. **4.** Quackery—a necessary ..a. for truth CARLYLE. Hence †**Ama·lgamize** *v.* to soften, *esp.* with mercury.

Ama·lgam, *v. arch.* ME. [– med.L. *amalgamare*; see prec. Cf. Fr. *amalgamer.*] **† 1.** = AMALGAMATE 1, 2. **2.** *trans.* To coat with amalgam 1789. **3.** = AMALGAMATE 4. 1827. Hence **Ama·lgamable** *a.*

Amalgamate (ămæ·lgămĕt), *ppl. a.* 1642. [– med.L. *amalgamatus*, pa. pple. of *amalgamare*; see prec., -ATE².] **1.** Combined or alloyed 1642. **2.** Coalesced; *spec.* of languages 1849.

Amalgamate (ămæ·lgămeⁱt), *v.* 1660. [– *amalgamat-*, pa. ppl. stem of *amalgamare*; see AMALGAM *v.*, -ATE³.] **1.** To soften by combining with mercury; *hence*, to alloy with mercury. **2.** *intr.* To combine with mercury 1751. **3.** To mix so as to form a uniform compound 1821. **4.** *fig.* To combine (two elements, or one *with* another) in a homogeneous whole. *trans.* 1802. *intr.* 1797.
3. Wayland..amalgamated the drugs SCOTT. **4.** [The Romans] were ordained..to a. the materials of Christendom COLERIDGE. Two banks of issue had amalgamated CRUMP. Hence **Ama·lgamative** *a.* tending to or marked by amalgamation.

Amalgamation (ămæːlgamē̆ⁱ·ʃən). 1612. [f. AMALGAMATE *v.* + -ION (see -ATION), perh. through Fr. *amalgamation.*] **1.** The action of amalgamating (see AMALGAMATE *v.* 1). **2.** *fig.* The action of combining into one uniform whole 1775. **3.** The state of being united with mercury; hence, a mixture of metals generally 1753. **4.** *fig.* A homogeneous union 1828.
2. The a. of the Saxons and Normans DE LOLME. **3.** An a. of copper with tin 1874. **4.** A close a. between ecclesiastical and civil authority GLADSTONE.

Amalgamator (ămæ·lgămeⁱtəɹ). Occ. **-er.** 1838. [f. AMALGAMATE *v.* + -OR 2.] One who or that which amalgamates: *spec.* **a.** One who amalgamates public companies; **b.** The apparatus used for extracting silver from its ore by combining it with mercury.

Ama·lic, *a.* 1863. [f. Gr. ἀμαλός weak + -IC 1b.] *Chem.* In *Amalic Acid*: a product of the decomposition of caffeine by chlorine, having a feeble acid reaction.

Amandin(e (ămǣ·ndin). 1845. [– Fr. *amandine*, f. *amande* almond; see -IN¹, -INE⁵.] **a.** The albumen contained in sweet almonds. **b.** A kind of cold cream made from it.

Amanitine (æmănəi·təin). 1847. [f. Gr. ἀμανῖται a kind of fungus + -INE⁵.] The active narcotic principle of poisonous fungi.

Amanuensis (ămæːniuˌe·nsis). Pl. **-es** (iz). 1619. [– L. *amanuensis* (Suetonius) clerk, secretary, f. *a manu* in *servus a manu* slave at hand, + *-ensis* belonging to; see -ESE.] One who copies or writes from dictation.

‖ **Amaracus** (ămæ·răkŏs). ME. [– L. *amaracus* – Gr. ἀμάρακος marjoram.] An aromatic plant, the dittany of Crete (*Origanum dictamnus*).

Amarant(h (æ·mărænt, -ænþ). 1551. [– Fr. *amarante* or mod.L. *amaranthus*, alt. after names in *-anthus* (Gr. ἄνθος flower) of L. *amarantus* – Gr. ἀμάραντος, f. *ἀ-* A- *pref.* 14 + *μαραν-*, stem of μαραίνειν wither.] **1.** An imaginary flower that never fades. Also *attrib.* 1616. **2.** A genus of plants (*Amarantus*, N.O. *Amarantaceæ*) with coloured foliage, including Prince's Feather and Love-lies-bleeding 1551. **3.** A purple colour 1690.
1. Thir Crowns inwove with Amarant and Gold, Immortal Amarant MILT. *P.L.* III. 353. **2.** Sad Amaranthus, in whose purple gore Me seemes I see Amintas wretched fate SPENSER *F.Q.* III. vi. 45. **Globe Amaranth**: *Gomphrena globosa.* Hence **Aːmarant(h)a·ceous** *a.* of the nature of a. **Amara·nt(h)ad,** an ally of the genus A. **Amara·nt(h)oid** *a.* and *sb.* resembling, or an ally of, a.

Amarant(h)ine (æmăræ·ntin, -þin), *a.*; **amarantin** MILT. 1667. [f. prec. + -INE¹.] **1.** Of or pertaining to amarant(h). **2.** Fadeless, immortal 1781. **3.** Amarant(h-coloured 1874.
1. Amarantin Shade MILT. *P.L.* XI. 78. **2.** A. joys COWPER. **3.** A. glosses HARDY.

Amarine (ămēᵊ·rəin), *sb.* 1839. [f. L. *amarus* bitter + -INE⁵.] *Chem.* A bitter vegetable principle; *spec.* the alkaloid ($C_{21}H_{18}N_2$) formed by the action of ammonia on essence of bitter almonds, also called BENZOLINE.

† **Ama·ritude.** 1490. [– L. *amaritudo* bitterness, f. *amarus* bitter; see -TUDE.] Bitterness –1666.

† **Ama·rvel,** *v.* ME. [– OFr. *amerveillier,* earlier *es-* (see A- *pref.* 9), f. *es* :– L. *ex* + *merveillier* MARVEL *v.*] To strike with wonder; usu. in pass. –1530.

Amaryllid (æmări·lid) 1830. [– *Amaryllid-,* stem of L. *Amaryllis*; see next.] *Bot.* A plant of the same order as the genus *Amaryllis.* Hence **Amary:llida·ceous** *a.* of or pertaining to the *Amaryllidaceæ,* a Nat. Ord. including Amaryllis, Narcissus, and Snowdrop; var. **A:marylli·deous.**

‖ **Amaryllis** (æmări·lis). 1794. [mod.L. use of L. *Amaryllis* – Gr. Ἀμαρυλλίς, name of a country girl in Theocritus, Virgil, and Ovid.] *Bot.* A genus of bulbous plants, typical of the N.O. *Amaryllidaceæ*; applied also to allied genera.

Here and there, on sandy beaches A milky-bell'd a. blew TENNYSON.

Amass (ămæ·s), *v.* 1481. [– (O)Fr. *amasser* or med.L. *amassare* :– Rom. **admassare,* f. L. *ad* AD- + *massa* MASS *sb.*[2]] **1.** *gen.* To collect into a mass or masses, pile up 1594; *intr.* to assemble (*arch.*) 1572. **2.** *esp.* To accumulate as one's own. (The earliest, now the usual sense.) 1481.

1. To a. [things] into one 1644, balls 1694. **2.** To a. grete tresours CAXTON, stores of knowledge 1712, gold POPE, materials SMILES. Hence **Ama·ssable** *a. rare.* **Ama·sser,** one who amasses.

Amassment (ămæ·smĕnt). 1665. [– obs. Fr. *amassement*; see prec., -MENT.] The action or result of amassing.

That famous a. of troops KINGLAKE.

Ama·te, *v.*[1] *Obs.* or *arch.* ME. [– OFr. *amater* cast down, f. *a* AD- + *mater,* f. *mat* dejected; see MATE *a.*] To cast down.

A half-blown flow'ret which cold blasts a. KEATS.

† **Ama·te,** *v.*[2] 1596. [f. A- *pref.* 11 + MATE *v*[2].] To be a mate to; to equal –1642.

Amateur (æmătɔ̄·ɹ, æ·mătiuəɹ). 1784. [– Fr. *amateur* – It. *amatore* :– L. *amator* lover.] **1.** One who loves, is fond *of,* or has a taste for, anything. **2.** One who cultivates anything as a pastime; hence occas. = dabbler 1803. **3.** *attrib.* Done by amateurs 1848.

1. Amateurs of a superficial philosophy 1817. **2.** Not amateurs..but professional men DE QUINCEY. **3.** A. theatricals 1849. A. running records 1882. Hence **Amateu·rish** *a.* suggesting an a., having the faults of a. work. **Amateu·rishly** *adv.*, **-ness. A·mateurism,** the characteristic practice of an a. **A·mateurship,** the quality or character of an a.

Amative (æ·mătiv), *a.* 1636. [– med.L. *amativus,* f. *amat-* pa. ppl. stem of L. *amare* to love + *-ivus* -IVE; cf. -ATIVE.] Disposed to loving. Hence **A·mativeness** *Phren.* propensity to love, or sexual passions 1815.

Amatol (æ·mătǫl). 1918. A high explosive compounded of *am*monium nitrate and trinitro*tol*uene.

Amatorial (æmătōə·riăl), *a.* 1603. [f. as next + -AL[1].] **1.** Of or pertaining to a lover, or love-making. **2.** Epithet of the oblique muscles of the eye, which assist in *ogling* 1751.

Amatory (æ·mătəri). 1599. [– L. *amatorius,* f. *amator* lover, f. *amat-* pa. ppl. stem of *amare* to love; see -ORY[2].] **A.** *adj.* Of or pertaining to a lover, love-making, or sexual love. **B.** *sb.* A philtre 1635.

A. An a. poem 1772, poet 1840, sentiment THACKERAY. Hence † **Amato·rious** *a.*

‖ **Amaurosis** (æmǭrōu·sis). 1657. [mod.L. – Gr. ἀμαύρωσις, f. ἀμαυροῦν darken, f. ἀμαυρός dim.] *Med.* Partial or total loss of sight, from disease of the optic nerve, usu. without external change in the eye.

An A. or Gutta Serena 1704. Hence **Amauro·tic** *a.* affected with a.

† **Amay·,** *v.* ME. [– ONFr. *amaier* = OFr. *esmaier* (see A- *pref.* 9) :– Rom. **exmagare*; see DISMAY.] To dismay –1485.

Amaze (ămēi·z), *v.* [OE. *āmasian,* pa. pple. *āmasod,* whence ME. *amased,* f. A- *pref.* 1 + **mas-,* perh. as in Norw., Da. *mase* be busy or active. See MAZE *v.*] † **1.** To craze –1642; to perplex –1642; to fill with panic –1706. **2.** To overwhelm with wonder; to astound or greatly astonish 1592; *intr.* to be astounded (*arch.*) 1589; † *refl.* to bewilder oneself –1678.

2. Crystal eyne, Whose full perfection all the world amazes *Ven. & Ad.* 634. I amaze me MILT.

Amaze (ămēi·z), *sb.* Also *a maze.* ME. [f. prec.] † **1.** = AMAZEMENT † 1. **2.** Extreme wonder. (Chiefly poet.) 1579.

2. With pleasure and a., I stood transported ADDISON. Hence † **Ama·zeful** *a.* amazing; amazed.

Amazed (ămēi·zd), *ppl. a.* ME. [See AMAZE *v.*] In the senses of the vb.

I am a. at your passionate words *Mids.N.* III. ii. 220. Hence **Ama·zedly** *adv.* **Ama·zedness.**

Amazement (ămēi·zmĕnt). 1595. [f. AMAZE *v.* + -MENT.] *orig.* Loss of one's wits. † **1.** Mental stupefaction, frenzy –1746; bewilderment –1722; consternation –1756. **2.** Overwhelming wonder 1602.

1. Behold, destraction, frenzie, and a., Like witlesse Antickes, one another meete *Tr. & Cr.* V. iii. 85. This A. of the Magistrates DE FOE. Amazements and panick terrors MILT. **2.** Wonder and a. *Acts* 3:10.

† **Amazia** (ămēi·ziă). 1874. [mod.L., f. Gr. ἀ- (A- *pref.* 14) + μαζος breast + -IA[1].] *Med.* Non-development of the breasts in a female.

Amazing (ămēi·ziŋ). 1530. [f. AMAZE *v.* + -ING[1].] **1.** *vbl. sb.* The action of causing AMAZEMENT. † **2.** *ppl. a.* Causing AMAZEMENT –1781. **3.** Astounding, great beyond expectation 1704. **4.** quasi-*adv.* Wonderfully 1824.

2. Let thy blowes..Fall like a. thunder on the Caske Of thy amaz'd, pernicious enemy SHAKS. **3.** A. generosity 1704. An a. assertion BURKE. Hence **Ama·zingly** *adv.* (Now often hyperbol. in colloq. use for: Very.)

Amazon (æ·măzǫn). Pl. **-ons**; also 4–7 **-ones.** In 6–7 *amā·zon.* ME. [– L. *Amazon* – Gr. Ἀμαζών, -όνος, explained by the Greeks as meaning 'breastless' (as if f. ἀ- A- *pref.* 14 + μαζός breast), but prob. of foreign origin. Cf. (O)Fr. *amazone.*] **1.** *pl.* A race of female warriors alleged to exist in Scythia. **2.** Hence, A female warrior (*lit.* and *fig.*) 1578. **3.** *transf.* A strong, tall, or masculine woman 1758.

2. Belike she minds to play the A. 3 *Hen. VI,* IV. i. 106.

Comb.: **a.-ant,** a species of red ant, of which the neuters capture and enslave the young of other species; also, the neuters alone; **-stone,** a bright verdigris-green variety of orthoclase, worn as an amulet.

Amazonian (æmăzōu·niăn), *a.* 1594. [f. L. *amazonius* + -AN; see -IAN.] **1.** Of or pertaining to the Amazons; warlike, or masculine, as a woman 1594. **2.** Of the river Amazon, or its basin 1863. **3.** *sb.* An Amazon (fabulous) 1704.

Amazonite (æ·măzǫnəit). 1601. [f. AMAZON + -ITE[1] 1, 2 b.] † **1.** An Amazon –1630. **2.** *Min.* = AMAZON-STONE.

Ambage (æ·mbĕdʒ). Pl. **ambages** (æ·mbĕdʒĕz, *or as L.* æmbēi·dʒīz). ME. [– (O)Fr. *ambages* – L. *ambages* circuits, circumlocutions, f. *amb-* both ways + *agere* to drive (cf. AMBIGUOUS *a.*). Naturalized in XVI, but latterly treated as Latin.] **I.** Of language (from Fr.; pron. *a·mbages*; with *sing.*). **1.** Equivocation, deceitful ambiguities (*arch.*). † **2.** Obscure language –1713; circumlocutions –1678. † **3.** *Rhet.* (in *sing.*) Periphrasis 1589.

1. Ambages, and treacherous Counsels NORTH.

II. Of paths, ways. [From, or as L. *ambā·ges.*] **1.** Circuitous paths, windings (*arch.*) 1615; *fig.* indirect proceedings; delaying practices 1546. † **2.** Dark ways of action. (Cf. Livy I. 56.) –1797.

1. *fig.* He shall, by Ambages of diets, bathings, etc. prolong life BACON. Hence **Amba:gio·sity,** circuitousness (*rare*). **Amba·gious** *a.* full of ambages: **a.** circumlocutory; **b.** circuitous. **Amba·giously** *adv.* **Amba·giousness,** the quality of being ambagious (*rare*). † **Amba·gitory** *a.* ambagious. (Coined by SCOTT.)

Ambassade, em- (æ·m-, e·mbăsē·d). *Obs.* or *arch.* ME. [– Fr. *ambassade* (XV, superseding OFr. *ambassée* AMBASSY) – It. *ambasciata* – Pr. *ambaisada* embassy – **ambaisa* – Goth. *andbahti* office, service f. *andbahts* servant; see AMBASSADOR.] **1.** = AMBASSY 1. 1450. **2.** = AMBASSY 3. 1450. **3.** = AMBASSY 2. 1560.

Ambassador, em- (æm-, ĕmbæ·sădəɹ). ME. [ME. *ambass(i)atour, embassatour, -dour,* etc., – Fr. *ambassadeur* – It. *ambasciator,* ult. :– Rom. **ambactiator* (*-orem*), f. **ambactiare* go on a mission, f. med.L. *ambactia, ambaxia* (Salic and Burgundian Laws), f. Gmc. **ambaχtaz* (Goth. *andbahts* servant, OE. *ambeht* servant, messenger, OHG. *ambaht,* G. *amt*) – L. *ambactus* servant, vassal (Ennius, Cæsar), a Gaulish word, **ambactos.* The var. *embassador* was common in XVII–XVIII, and is still used in U.S.] **1.** An official messenger sent by or to a sovereign or public body; *esp.* a minister of high rank sent by one sovereign or state on a mission to another, an *A. Extraordinary.* **2.** (= *Ordinary* or *Resident A.,* formerly *A. Leger.*) A minister of the highest rank who permanently represents his sovereign or country at a foreign court, and has a right to a personal interview with the foreign sovereign or chief magistrate 1603. **3.** An appointed or official messenger (now only *fig.*) 1483. **4.** *A. Plenipotentiary*: one with full power to sign treaties, and act for his sovereign 1603.

2. Intends you for his swift A., Where you shall be an everlasting Leiger *Meas. for M.* III. i. 58. **3.** An Embassador of loue *Merch. V.* II. ix. 92. Hence **Amba:ssado·rial** *a.* of or pertaining to an a. **Amba·ssadorship,** the office, position, or function of an a.; var. † **Amba·ssadry.**

Ambassadress (æmbæ·sădrĕs). 1594. [f. prec.; see -ESS[1].] **1.** A female ambassador or messenger; var. **ambassadrix. 2.** The wife of an AMBASSADOR (*leger*) 2; var. † **amba·ssadrice.**

Ambassage, em- (æ·m-, e·mbăsĕdʒ). Also **imb-.** [An Eng. formation, app. on OFr. *ambasse* message, embassy + -AGE. The usual sp. is *embassage.* Cf. AMBASSY.] † **1.** = AMBASSY 1. –1640. **2.** = AMBASSY 2. 1548. **3.** = AMBASSY 3. 1605. See also EMBASSAGE.

† **Amba·ssiate.** ME. [– med.L. *ambassiata,* (XIV) for **ambactiata,* pa. ppl. stem of Rom. **ambactiare*; see AMBASSADOR, -ATE[1].] **1.** The business of an ambassador –1548. **2.** An embassy –1580. **3.** A single envoy –1535.

Ambassy, em- (æ·m-, e·mbăsi). 1588. [– OFr. *ambassée,* superseded by *ambassade*; see AMBASSADE, EMBASSY, -Y[5].] **1.** The mission, function, or office of an ambassador 1600. **2.** The message brought by an ambassador 1606. **3.** A body of men sent as ambassadors; an ambassador and his suite or surroundings 1732.

‖ **Ambe** (æ·mbi). 1711. [Gr. ἄμβη, Ion. for ἄμβων a projecting edge.] **1.** *Surg.* An apparatus for reducing dislocations of the shoulder. **2.** *Anat.* A superficial crest of a bone 1879.

Amber (æ·mbəɹ), *sb.*[1] ME. [– (O)Fr. *ambre* – Arab. *'anbar* (orig.) AMBERGRIS, (later) amber. Cf. late L. *ambar* a perfumed substance, med.L. *ambar* stercus piscis (Du Cange).] † **1.** *orig.* = AMBERGRIS (*greece of amber, gris, gray amber*). –1718. Also *attrib.* † **2. White Amber**: Spermaceti –1611. **3.** A yellowish fossil resin, used for ornaments, etc., which when rubbed becomes *electric* (f. ἤλεκτρον its Gr. name). † **4.** An amulet made of a. –1691. **5.** *fig.* Amber-coloured 1735. **6.** An alloy of four parts of gold with one of silver (L. *electrum,* Gr. ἤλεκτρον) ME. **7.** = LIQUIDAMBAR 1569. **8.** (*local*) St. John's-wort. **9.** *adj.* [cf. Fr. *ambré.*] Amber-coloured.

1. [Perfuming] the air with a., aloes-wood, etc. 1718. **3.** Thicke A., or Plum-Tree Gumme *Haml.* II. ii. 200. Like a fly in a. 1847. † *Spirit of amber*: succinic acid. **6.** Out of the midst thereof as the colour of a. [WYCLIF electre] *Ezek.* 1:4. **9.** Robed in flames and a. light MILT. *L'Alleg.* 61.

Comb.: **a. Fauna,** the animals whose remains are found in a.; **a. Flora,** the plants found in a.; **a.-forest,** the primeval forest the trees of which yielded a.; **-pear,** an AMBRETTE; **-seed,** the seeds of *Abelmoschus moschatus,* musk-seed, Ambrette, used as a perfume; **-tree,** a name of the genus *Anthospermum*; **-varnish,** copal varnish. Hence **A·mbering** *vbl. sb.* giving a scent of a. **A·mbery** *a.* of the nature or colour of a.

† **A·mber,** *sb.*[2] [OE. *amber, -or,* corresp. to OS. *ēmbar,* OHG. *ambar* (later *eimbar, einbar,* G. *eimer* bucket) – Rom. form with *-b-* repr. L. *amphora* – Gr. ἀμφορεύς vessel with two handles.] A dry measure of four bushels.

Amber, *sb.,*[3] obs. f. AMBRY.

Amber (æ·mbəɹ), *v. rare.* 1616. [f. the *sb.* Cf. Fr. *ambrer,* pa. pple. *ambré* ambered.] **1.** To perfume with ambergris 1616. **2.** To make amber-coloured 1809. **3.** To preserve in amber 1882.

Amber-days; see EMBER-DAYS.

Ambergris (æ·mbəɹgrīs). 1481. [– (O)Fr. *ambre gris* 'grey amber'. To this substance the name *amber* orig. belonged (cf. AMBER *sb.*[1]); after its extension to the resin, dist. in Fr. as *ambre jaune* 'yellow amber', ambergris received its distinctive designation of 'grey'. Various early spellings show assim. to *grease*.] A wax-like substance of ashy colour, found floating in tropical seas, and as a morbid secretion in the intestines of the sperm-whale. Used in perfumery, and formerly in cookery.
In pastry built, or from the spit, or boiled, Gris-amber-steam'd MILT. *P.R.* II. 341. Praise is like a.; a little whiff of it..is very agreeable POPE.

Ambidexter (æ:mbide·kstəɹ). 1532. [– late L. *ambidexter*, f. *ambi-* on both sides + L. *dexter* right-handed.] **A.** *adj.* **1.** *lit.* Right-handed on both sides, able to use both hands equally well 1646. **2.** Double-dealing 1613. **3.** Two-sided 1806.
1. Only man is a. SIR T. BROWNE. **2.** A. Lawyers 1705. **3.** An a. controversialist 1839.
B. *sb.* **1.** [sc. *man.*] Also *fig.* 1598. **2.** *Law.* One who takes money on both sides 1532. **3.** double-dealer 1555.
3. Ambidexters, or..such as can shift on both sides 1555. Hence **A:mbidexte·rity,** the power of using both hands alike; many-sided resourcefulness; double-dealing. **A:mbide·xtral** *a.* belonging to both sides.

Ambidext(e)rous (æ:mbide·kstrəs), *a.* 1646. [f. prec. + -OUS.] = AMBIDEXTER. Hence **A:mbide·xt(e)rously** *adv.* **A:mbide·xtrousness.**

Ambient (æ·mbiĕnt). 1596. [– Fr. *ambiant* or L. *ambient-*, pres. ppl. stem of *ambire* go round, f. *ambi-* on both sides + *ire* go; see -ENT.] **A.** *adj.* **†1.** Revolving –1620. **2.** Circling about (something). *rare.* 1655. **3.** Lying round, surrounding, encompassing 1596; *esp.* as a fluid; circumfused 1605. ¶ Misused for 'limpid', of the air.
1. A. years CHAPMAN. **2.** A. Winds, That course about the quarters of the globe DISRAELI. **3.** Opening to the a. light MILT. *P.L.* VI. 481.
B. *sb.* [The adj. used *absol.*] **†1.** A canvasser 1649. **2.** An encompassing circle or sphere 1624. **3.** *Astrol.* The ambient air or sky 1686.

Ambigenal (æ̆mbi·dʒĕnal), *a.* 1727. [f. med.L. *ambigenus* of two kinds, hybrid (f. L. *ambi-* both + *-genus* -born, -natured) + -AL[1]. See -GEN.] Of two kinds, hybrid. (Used to describe a kind of hyperbola.)

Ambigenous (æ̆mbi·dʒĕnəs), *a.* 1850. [f. as prec. + -OUS.] Of two kinds; *spec.* applied to a multifoliate calyx, externally leaf-like and internally petaloid.

† Ambigu. 1688. [– Fr.: prop. adj. = AMBIGUOUS.] A banquet at which a medley of dishes are set on together –1753.

Ambiguity (æmbigiū·iti). ME. [– (O)Fr. *ambiguité* or L. *ambiguitas*; see next, -ITY.] **† 1.** Subjectively: Hesitation, doubt –1590; *concr.* an uncertainty –1658. **2.** Objectively: Double or dubious meaning ME.; *concr.* an equivocal expression 1591.
2. To clear the..laws..from a. MACAULAY. Without ambages or ambiguities DRYDEN.

Ambiguous (æ̆mbi·giu,əs), *a.* 1528. [f. L. *ambiguus* shifting, doubtful, f. *ambigere* go round, f. *ambi-* both ways + *agere* drive; see -OUS, -UOUS.] **I.** Objectively. **1.** Doubtful; not clearly defined 1528. **2.** Open to more than one interpretation; equivocal. (The common use.) 1532. **3.** Of doubtful position or classification 1603.
1. A. shadows 1800, distances RUSKIN. **2.** Answers..dark, A., and with double sense deluding MILT. *P.R.* I. 435. **3.** Mungrell and a. shapes FLORIO.
II. Subjectively. **† 1.** Hesitating, doubtful –1649. **2.** Of doubtful issue 1612; hence, not to be trusted 1756. **3.** Of oracles, etc.: Using words of doubtful or double meaning 1566.
1. Doubtfull and a. in all thir doings MILT. **2.** A. paths 1850. **3.** Antinous..thus a. spoke POPE. Hence **Ambi·guously** *adv.* **Ambi·guousness.**

Ambilævous, -levous (æ:mbilī·vəs), *a. rare.* 1646. [f. L. *ambi-* on both sides + *lævus* left + -OUS, after *ambidextrous.*] Left-handed on both sides; clumsy.

Ambi·parous, *a.* 1879. [f. L. *ambi-* both + *-parus* producing; see -PAROUS.] *Bot.* Of a bud: Containing both flowers and leaves.

Ambit (æ·mbit). ME. [– L. *ambitus* circuit, compass, f. *ambire*; see AMBIENT.] **1.** A circuit, compass, or circumference 1597; *esp.* a space round a house, castle, etc., the liberties, verge. **2.** The limits of a district 1845; *fig.* the compass of actions, words, etc. 1691.
2. The a. of the manor DIGBY, of legislation 1882.

Ambition (æ̆mbi·ʃən), *sb.* ME. [– (O)Fr. *ambition* – L. *ambitio*, f. *ambit-*, pa. ppl. stem of *ambire*; see AMBIENT, -ION.] **1.** The eager or inordinate desire of honour or preferment. **† 2.** Ostentation; pride of state –1631. **3.** A strong desire *of*, (occ. *for*), *to be* or *do* anything creditable, etc. 1607; the object of such a desire 1602. **† 4.** Canvassing. (L. *ambitio.*) 1531.
1. Cromwel, I charge thee, fling away A., By that sinne fell the Angels SHAKS. **3.** The pitiful a. of possessing..more acres BURKE. Their a. is in heaven RUSKIN. **4.** I..used no a. to commend my deeds MILT. *Sams.* 246. Hence **Ambi·tionist,** one ruled by a. **Ambi·tionless** *a.*

Ambition (æ̆mbi·ʃən), *v.* 1628. [– Fr. *ambitionner*; cf. *raisonner.*] **† 1.** *trans.* To move to ambition. **2.** To desire strongly. (Const. *simple obj.*, *inf.*, or *cl.*) 1664.

Ambitious (æ̆mbi·ʃəs), *a.* ME. [– (O)Fr. *ambitieux* or L. *ambitiosus*, f. *ambit-*; see AMBITION *sb.*, -OUS.] **1.** Full of AMBITION (sense 1). **2.** Strongly desirous *of*, **†** *for*, *to be*, or *do* 1513. **3.** *fig.* As if aspiring; swelling, towering 1601. **4.** Of works of art, etc.: Aspiring or pretentious 1751. **† 5.** quasi-*sb.* [sc. *man.*] –1563.
1. With a. aim Against the Throne and Monarchy of God MILT. *P.L.* I. 41. **2.** I am a. for a motley coat *A.Y.L.* II. vii. 43. A. of long words 1855. **3.** I haue seene Th'a. Ocean swell *Jul. C.* I. iii. 7. **4.** An a. attempt ended in failure (*mod.*). Hence **Ambi·tious-ly** *adv.* in an a. manner; **-ness.**

Amble (æ·mb'l), *v.* ME. [– (O)Fr. *ambler*:– L. *ambulare* to walk.] **1.** *intr.* Of horses, etc.: To move by lifting the two feet on one side together, alternately with the two feet on the other; hence, to move at a smooth or easy pace. **2.** To ride at an easy pace ME. **3.** Hence, to walk, dance, etc., like an ambling horse, or *fig.* of any easy motion 1596.
1. I will tell you who time ambles withal *A.Y.L.* III. ii. 328. [The mare] ambles most 1690. **2.** To a. the circuit with the Judges WYCHERLEY. **3.** The skipping King, hee ambled vp and downe 1 *Hen. IV*, III. ii. 60. How fast your thoughts a. H. WALPOLE. Hence **A·mbler,** a horse, mule, etc., or person that ambles. **A·mbling** *vbl. sb.* motion in an amble; *ppl. a.* moving in an amble. **A·mblingly** *adv.*

Amble (æ·mb'l), *sb.* ME. [f. prec.; cf. Fr. *amble* (XVI).] **1.** The pace described in prec. (sense 1), and *loosely*, an easy pace. **2.** Of persons: A movement suggesting an amble 1607.
1. A fine easy a. B. JONS. The usual pace of [mules] is an a. JEPHSON. **2.** His Antick a. 1607.

Ambleocarpous (æ:mbli,o,kā·ɹpəs), *a.* 1847. [f. Gr. ἀμβλοῦσθαι miscarry + καρπός fruit + -OUS.] *Bot.* Having the seeds entirely, or largely, abortive.

‖ **Amblosis** (æ̆mblōᵘ·sis). 1706. [Gr. ἀμβλωσις abortion; see prec.] *Med.* Abortion. Hence **Amblo·tic** *a.* causing abortion; *sb.* [sc. *medicine.*]

Amblygon (æ·mbligǫn); also **ambligon.** 1570. [– Fr. *amblygone* or late L. *ambligonius* – Gr. ἀμβλυγώνιος obtuse-angled, f. ἀμβλύς blunt + γωνία angle.] **† A.** *adj.* Obtuse-angled –1796. **B.** *sb.* [sc. *figure*, esp. *triangle.*] 1570. Hence **Ambly·gonal** *a.* (*rare*); vars. **†Ambly·go·nial, †Ambly·gonous. Ambly·gonite** (*Min.*) a typical greenish white translucent mineral, occurring in obtuse-angled rhombic prisms, and consisting of alumina, lithia, potash, soda, iron, and fluoric acid.

‖ **Amblyopia** (æmbli,ōᵘ·piă). 1706. [– Gr. ἀμβλυωπία dimsightedness, f. ἀμβλυωπός, f. ἀμβλύς dull + ὤψ, ὠπ- eye; see -IA[1].] *Path.* Impaired vision, due to defective sensibility of the retina, etc.; the early stage of *amaurosis.* var. **A·mblyopy.** Hence **Amblyo·pic** *a.*

Ambo (æ·mbo). Pl. **ambos** (-oᵘz), also L. **ambones.** 1641. [– med.L. *ambo, ambon-*, – Gr. ἄμβων rim, ridge; in med.Gr. pulpit.] The pulpit or reading-desk in early Christian churches; an oblong enclosure with steps at both ends.

Ambodexter, etc., obs. f. AMBIDEXTER, etc.

Ambo·lic, *a.* 1879. Abortifacient.

Ambon (æ·mbǫn). 1725. [– Gr. ἄμβων (see AMBO), ridge or edge of a cup.] **† 1.** = AMBO –1794. **2.** *Anat.* The margin of the sockets of the large bones. (So in Galen.) 1811.

Amboyna (wood) (æ̆mboi·nă). 1866. [– *Amboyna*, island of the Moluccas.] The wood of the *Pterospermum indicum* (N.O. *Sterculiaceæ*).

Ambreate (æ·mbri,eⁱt). 1839. [f. next + -ATE[4].] *Chem.* A salt of Ambreic acid.

Ambreic (æ̆mbrī·ik), *a.* 1831. [f. AMBER + -IC.] *Chem.* Of or pertaining to ambrein or ambergris, as *Ambreic Acid.*

Ambrein (æ·mbri,in). 1832. [– Fr. *ambréine*, f. *ambre*; see AMBER, -IN[1].] *Chem.* A crystalline fatty substance, the main constituent of ambergris.

Ambrette (ambre·t). 1725. [– Fr. *ambrette*, f. *ambre* AMBER + *-ette* -ETTE.] **1.** A pear with an odour of musk. **2.** The seeds of *Hibiscus abelmoschus*, used in perfumery 1858.

Ambrite (æ·mbrəit). [– G. *ambrit* (1861), f. *amber, ambra* amber + *-it* = -ITE[1] 2b.] *Min.* A yellowish-grey, sub-transparent fossil resin found in New Zealand.

Ambrology (æ̆mbrǫ·lŏdʒi). 1879. [f. AMBER + -LOGY.] The natural history of amber.

Ambrose (æ·mbroᵘz). ME. [–(O)Fr. *ambroise* :– L. *ambrosia*, name of several plants; see next.] **1.** *Herb.* An English plant: the Wood Sage (*Teucrium scorodonia*); also *Chenopodium botrys.* **† 2.** = AMBROSIA 1. –1621.

Ambrosia (æ̆mbrōᵘ·ziă, -ʒiă) 1567. [– L. *ambrosia* – Gr. ἀμβροσία immortality, elixir of life, f. ἄμβροτος immortal.] **1.** *Gr. Myth.* The fabled food (1590), drink (1567), or unguent (1667), of the immortals. Also *fig.* **2.** *transf.* Water, oil, and fruits mixed as a libation; also a perfumed draught 1685. **3.** *fig.* Something divinely sweet to taste or smell 1731. **4.** Bee-bread 1609. **5.** *Herb.* A name of plants; see AMBROSE 1597. **6.** *Mod. Bot.* A genus (N.O. *Compositæ*) of weeds allied to Wormwood. *A. artemisifolia* is the Oak of Jerusalem.
1. Drinkes Nectar, eates diuine A. MARSTON. His dewie locks distill'd A. MILT. *P.L.* V. 57. **3.** The a. of her lips DE QUINCEY. Hence **† Ambro·siac** *a.* ambrosial. **† Ambro·siate** *a.* formed or furnished with a. var. **† A·mbrosie, -y.**

Ambro:sia·ceous, *a.* 1879. [f. prec. + -ACEOUS.] *Bot.* Akin to the genus *Ambrosia.*

Ambrosial (æ̆mbrōᵘ·ziăl, -ʒiăl), *a.* 1596. [f. L. *ambrosius* – Gr. ἀμβρόσιος pertaining to the immortals; see AMBROSIA, -AL[1].] **1.** Immortal, celestial; *orig.* belonging to or worthy of the gods 1596; *transf.* belonging to heaven 1637; *fig.* divinely fragrant; occas. divinely beautiful 1667. **2.** Of pollen or bee-bread (*rare*) 1816.
1. A. food POPE, locks 1866, oil 1870. A. fruits, fetched from the tree of life, And from the fount of life a. drink MILT. *P.R.* IV. 586. The broad a. aisles of lofty lime TENNYSON. Hence **Ambro·sially** *adv.* **Ambro·sian** *a.*[1] = AMBROSIAL.

Ambrosian (æmbrōᵘ·zian), *a.*[2] 1609. [– late L. *ambrosianus*, f. *Ambrosius*, Bishop of Milan (d. 397); see -AN.] **1.** Of, pertaining to, or instituted by St. Ambrose. **2.** Of the Ambrosian Library at Milan 1724.
1. *A. rite or office*: one used in the A. church of Milan. *A. chant*: a chant now merged in the Gregorian. **2.** The A. manuscript 1724.

Ambrosin (æ·mbrosin). 1753. [– med.L. *ambrosinus* (sc. *nummus*); see prec. and cf. -IN[2].] A coin bearing the figure of St. Ambrose on horseback.

Ambrosine (æ·mbrosin). 1872. [f. AMBER + ROSIN *sb.*; see -INE[5].] *Min.* A resinous mineral of eocene age, related to amber, found near Charleston, S.C.

Ambrotype (æ·mbrŏtəip). 1855. [origin unkn.] U.S. name for a photograph on glass, with lights given by the silver, and shades by a dark background showing through.

Ambry, aum- (ɑ·mbri). [Late ME. *almarie*, later *aumery*, *aumbry* (XVI) – OFr. *almarie*, var. of *armarie* (mod. *armoire*) – L. *armarium* closet, chest, f. *arma* utensils.] **1.** *gen.* A repository; a cupboard; a locker, a press; **†** *fig.* = treasury –1628. **2.** *spec.* A place for keeping victuals (*arch.* and *dial.*) ME.; a locker, or recess in the wall of a church, for sacramental vessels, etc. (*arch.*) ME.; † archives –1775. ¶ Corruptly for ALMONRY (*Almry* or *Ambry Close*, Westminster, was orig. *Almonry Close*).

Ambs-ace (æ:mz ēⁱ·s). ME. [– OFr. *ambes as* :– L. *ambo* both, *as* ACE.] *lit.* Double ace, the lowest throw at dice; hence *fig.* bad luck; worthlessness ME.; next to nothing 1679. ? *Obs.*

I had rather be in this choise, than throw Ames-ace for my life *All's Well*, II. iii. 85.

‖ **Ambulacrum** (æmbiuleⁱ·krŏm, -æ·krŏm). Pl. **-a.** 1837. [L., = walk, avenue, f. *ambulare* to walk.] An avenue or double row of pores for the protrusion of the tube-feet, as in an echinoderm. Hence **Ambula·cral** *a.* of or pertaining to the ambulacra of echinoderms. ‖**Ambulacra·ria, -aire,** a series of the perforated coronal pieces in an echinus. **Ambula·criform** *a.* having the shape of ambulacra.

Ambulance. 1819. [– Fr. *ambulance*, replacing *hôpital ambulant*, mobile (horse-drawn) field ambulance, f. *ambulant* – pres. ppl. stem of L. *ambulare* to walk; see next, -ANCE.] Not in gen. use bef. the Crimean war. **1.** A moving hospital, attending an army as it moves, so as to succour the wounded without delay. Often *attrib.* 1819. **2.** An ambulance waggon or cart for conveying the wounded off the field, etc. 1854.

1. *attrib.* A. waggons 1860, men 1864.

Ambulant (æ·mbiŭlănt), *a.* 1654. [– *ambulant-*, pres. ppl. stem of L. *ambulare* to walk; see -ANT. Cf. Fr. *ambulant.*] **1.** Walking, moving about. **2.** Shifting, unfixed (*rare*) 1810.

1. An a. 'Revolutionary Army' CARLYLE.

Ambulate (æ·mbiŭleⁱt), *v. rare.* 1623. [– *ambulat-*, pa. ppl. stem of L. *ambulare* to walk; see -ATE³.] To walk, move about. Hence **A·mbulative** *a.* always moving. ? *Obs.*

Ambulation (æmbiŭleⁱ·ʃən). 1541. [– L. *ambulatio* walking, f. *ambulat-*; see prec., -ION.] **1.** The action of walking, moving about 1574. † **2.** The spreading of a gangrene –1751.

Ambulator (æ·mbiŭleⁱtəɹ). 1652. [mod. use of L. *ambulator*, f. as prec.; see -OR 2.] **1.** One who walks about. **2.** An instrument for measuring distances on the road, also called *perambulator* 1859.

Ambulatory (æ·mbiŭlătəri), *a.* 1622. [– L. *ambulatorius* moveable, mobile, f. as prec.; see -ORY³.] **1.** Of or pertaining to a walker, or walking. **2.** Adapted for walking 1835. **3.** Unfixed in abode; movable 1622. **4.** *fig.* Shifting, temporary, mutable. (So in Fr.) 1631.

1. A. exercise 1622, life 1796. **3.** Many [schools] are a. 1845. **4.** A man's will is a., or alterable, untill death 1651. They..think virtue and vice a. MRS. PIOZZI. var. **A:mbulato·rial** (in senses 1, 2).

A·mbulatory, *sb.* 1623. [– med.L. *ambulatorium*, subst. use of *-orius*; see prec., -ORY¹.] A place (open or *esp.* covered) for walking in; an arcade, a cloister.

†**A·mbuling,** *ppl. a.* [f. Fr. *ambulant*, f. OFr. *ambuler*, – L. *ambulare* to walk; or f. L. *ambulans, -ant-* AMBULANT.] In *Ambuling Communion*, an observance of the Lord's Supper while moving about –1655.

Amburbial (æmbŭ·rbiăl), *a.* 1656. [– L. *amburbialis* pertaining to the *amburbium*, f. *ambi-* about + *urbs, urbi-* city; see -AL, -IAL.] *Rom. Antiq.* Connected with the city; *esp.* with the expiatory procession round Rome.

Ambury, var. of ANBURY.

Ambuscade (æ:mbŏskēⁱ·d), *sb.* 1582. [– Fr. *embuscade* – It. *imboscata* or Sp. *emboscada*, Pg. *embuscada*; see AMBUSH, -ADE, -ADO.] **1.** = AMBUSH 1 (and now more formal). **2.** = AMBUSH 2. 1674. **3.** *fig.* = AMBUSH 4. 1794.

2. The lurking a. 1814. **3.** The a. of a fallacy 1844.

Ambuscade (æmbŏskēⁱ·d), *v.* 1592. [f. the sb.] To lie, or conceal, in ambush. Hence **Ambusca·ded** *ppl. a.* placed in ambuscade; ambushed. **Ambusca·der,** one who lies in ambush.

Ambusca·do, *sb. arch.* Pl. **-os, †-oes, †-o's.** 1592. [refash. of AMBUSCADE after Sp.; see -ADO 2. Usual in 17th c.] **1.** = AMBUSCADE 1. † **2.** = AMBUSCADE 2. –1726. **3.** *fig.* 1640.

1. Of cutting Forraine throats, of Breaches, Ambuscados, Spanish Blades *Rom. & Jul.* I. iv. 84. Hence † **Ambusca·doed** *ppl. a.* ambuscaded.

Ambush (æ·mbuʃ), *sb.* 1489. [– OFr. *embusche*, f. *embuschier*; see next.] **1.** *strictly.* A military disposition consisting of troops concealed in a wood, etc., in order to surprise an enemy. (See AMBUSCADE 1.) † **2.** The force (*pl.* troops) so disposed –1653. **3.** Any persons (or person) lying in wait 1573. **4.** *fig.* 1592. ¶ Confused with AMBAGES 1602.

1. Then Ionathans men that lay in a. rose vp 1 *Macc.* 9:40. *To make, construct, lay an a.* **2.** The Ambushes rose, and put themselves [etc.] 1653. **3.** Once I did lay an a. for your life *Rich. II*, I. i. 137. **4.** The ambushes of envy JOHNSON.

Ambush (æ·mbuʃ), *v.* ME. [– OFr. *embuschier* :– Rom. **imboscare* 'to put in a wood', f. *in* IM-¹ + **boscus* wood; see BUSH *sb.*¹] **1.** To place in ambush, in order to surprise an enemy. *Obs.* or *arch.* **2.** *intr.* (refl. pron. omitted) To lie down in ambush; lie in wait 1626. **3.** *trans.* To waylay, attack from an ambush 1631.

2. The archest chin Mockery ever embush'd in M. ARNOLD. **3.** This party were ambushed..and defeated 1780. Hence **A·mbushed** *ppl. a.* placed or lying in ambush; also *fig.*

Ambushment (æ·mbuʃmĕnt, formerly embu·ʃ-). *arch.* ME. [– OFr. *ambuschement*, f. *ambuschier*; see AMBUSH *v.*, -MENT.] **1.** = AMBUSH 1. † **2.** = AMBUSH 2. ME. † **3.** A surprise party –1655. † **4.** *fig.* Devices to entrap –1641.

Ambu·stion. 1623. [– Fr. *ambustion* or L. *ambustio*, f. *ambust-* pa. ppl. stem of *amburere* burn around, f. *ambi-* on both sides + *urere* burn.] A burn, a scald. ? *Obs.*

Amebean, var. of AMŒBÆAN.

‖ **Ameer** (ămiᵊ·ɹ). Also **amír.** 1614. [– (through Pers. and Urdu) Arab. *'āmīr* commander. As a historical Saracen title commonly spelt EMIR; the sp. *Amír, Ameer* is used of mod. Indian and Afghan rulers.] † **1.** = EMIR –1679. **2.** The title of various Moslem rulers in Scinde and (*esp.*) in Afghanistan 1803. Hence **Amee·rship,** the position of an A.

† **A·mel,** *sb.* ME. [– AFr. *amail* = OFr. *esmail* (A- *pref.* 9), f. Gmc.: see ENAMEL *sb.*] Enamel. Also *attrib.* –1625. Hence † **A·mel** *v.* to enamel; **A·meled, a·melled** *ppl. a.*; † **A·meling** *vbl. sb.*

Amelanchier (æmĕlæ·nʃiəɹ). 1741. [– Savoy *amelancier* the medlar.] *Bot.* A genus of small trees, allied to the Medlar.

Amelcorn (æ·mĕlkŏɹn). 1578. [– Du., G. *amelkorn*, f. L. *amylum* (– Gr. ἄμυλον) starch + *korn* corn.] An inferior wheat, the Larger Spelt (*Triticum vulgare dicoccum*); French Rice.

† **A·m(e)let.** 1761. [– obs. Fr. *amelette*, now *omelette*; see OMELET.] = OMELET.

Ame·liorable, *a.* 1807. [f. next + -ABLE.] Capable of amelioration.

Ameliorate (ămī·liŏreⁱt), *v.* 1767. [alt. of earlier MELIORATE after Fr. *améliorer*, refash. after L. *melior* better of OFr. *ameillorer*, f. *meilleur* better.] **1.** To make better, improve. **2.** *intr.* To grow better 1789.

1. In every human being there is a wish to a. his own condition MACAULAY. Hence **Ame·liora:tive** *a.* tending to a. **Ame·liora:ter.**

Amelioration (ămī:liŏrēⁱ·ʃən). 1659. [– Fr. *amelioration* (XV); see prec., and cf. MELIORATION.] **1.** The action of making better; the being made better; improvement. **2.** *concr.* An improvement 1776.

1. In a course of a. BURKE. **2.** Buildings..and other ameliorations A. SMITH.

Amen (ēⁱ:me·n, *often* ā:me·n). OE. [– eccl.L. *amen* – Gr. ἀμήν – Heb. *'āmēn* certainty, truth, f. *'āman* strengthen, confirm; adopted in Greek by the LXX, whence in the N.T. and in early Christian use in Greek and Latin.] **A.** *int.* or *adv.* **1.** (from L.) = Finis. **2.** After a prayer or wish: Be it so really! ME. **3.** After a statement, confession of faith, etc.: It is so in truth OE. **4.** As retained in the Bible from Gr. or Heb.: Truly, verily ME.

2. But delyuere vs fro yuel. Amen *that is so be it* WYCLIF *Matt.* 6:13.

B. *sb.* **1.** The concluding word *Amen!* ME. **2.** An expression of assent or belief 1579. **3.** *transf.* Conclusion 1677. **4.** A title of Christ (*Rev.* 3:14); = The faithful one.

1. No better word to say, then A. 1597. **2.** False doctrine strangled by its own a. MRS. BROWNING. **3.** The A. of my life HALE.

Amen (ēⁱ:me·n), *v.* 1854. [f. the sb.] To say Amen to; to ratify solemnly, say the final word to.

Amenable (ămī·năb'l), *a.* 1596. [Earliest form (XVI–XVIII) *amesnable*, presumably – legal AFr. **ame(s)nable*, f. (O)Fr. *amener* bring to, f. *a* AD- + *mener* bring, lead :– (pop.) L. *minare* drive (animals), for L. *minari* threaten; see MENACE *sb.*, -ABLE.] **1.** Liable to answer (*to* a tribunal, etc., or *absol.*); responsible. **2.** Of things: Liable to the legal authority of 1768. **3.** *loosely*, Liable (*to* a charge, etc.) 1863. **4.** *fig.* Capable of being tested by. Const. *to.* 1845. **5.** Responsive *to*; tractable 1803.

1. Not amesnable to Law SPENSER. **3.** A. to an imputation 1876. **4.** A. to the touch, but invisible to the eye BUCKLE. **5.** [Not] a. to discipline WELLINGTON. Will..is a. to habit MILL. Hence **Ame:nabi·lity,** the quality of being a. (senses 1, 5). **Ame·nableness,** the quality or state of being a. **Ame·nably** *adv.*

† **Amena·ge,** *v. rare.* [– Fr. *aménager*, f. *a* AD- + *ménage*; see MÉNAGE.] To domesticate. SPENSER.

† **Amenance, -aunce,** 1591. [– OFr. *amenance*, f. *amener*; see AMENABLE *a.*, -ANCE.] Conduct, bearing –1739.

Amend (ăme·nd), *v.* ME. [–(O)Fr. *amender* :– Rom. **admendare*, alt. by prefix-substitution of L. *emendare* EMEND *v.* Aphet. MEND *v.*] **1.** To free from faults, correct, convert; to rectify (*arch.*); *esp.* to emendate 1483. *intr.* To reform oneself ME. **2.** To make alterations (in a bill before Parliament) (see AMENDMENT 2) 1777. **3.** To repair; to restore (*arch.*). Now usu. MEND. ME. † **4.** To heal (the sick); to cure (a disease) –1804; *intr.* to recover –1611. **5.** To improve. *trans.* ME. *intr.* (*rare*) 1530. † **6.** To better, surpass –1500. † **7.** To make amends for an offence. (Cf. MEND.) –1635.

1. If here One Sinner doth a. Strait there is Joy H. VAUGHAN. To a. his civil government BURKE. A *mandamus* may not be amended after return TOMLINS. **3.** Dame Gurton these breeches amended 1575. **4.** *intr.* Th' affliction of my mind amends *Temp.* V. i. 115. **5.** To punish you by the heeles, would a. the attention of your eares SHAKS. Hence **Ame·nd** *sb.*; see AMENDS. **Ame·ndable** *a.* capable of being amended. **Ame·ndableness. Ame·ndatory** *a.* of or pertaining to amendment; tending to amend (U.S.). **Ame·nder** (usu. with *of*), one who or that which amends.

‖ **Amende-honorable** (amañ·d onora·bl'). 1670. [Fr. (see AMENDS). Treated as Eng. in XVIII, now usu. as Fr. Occas. without *honorable*. Orig. a public and humiliating acknowledgement of crime, now *fig.*] Public apology and reparation to one who has been injured or offended in his honour. Cf. AMENDS 2.

Amendment (ăme·ndmĕnt). ME. [–(O)Fr. *amendement*; see AMEND *v.*, -MENT.] The action or result of amending. **1.** Removal of faults or errors, reformation; esp. (*Law*) in a writ or process 1607. **2.** The alteration of a bill before Parliament; hence *concr.* a proposed alteration (which if adopted may even defeat the measure) 1696. *In a Public Meeting*: A proposed alteration submitted as a resolution for adoption; occas., a counter-motion. † **3.** Repair –1682. **4.** Improvement ME.; *esp.* in health 1526. † **5.** Reparation ME. only.

1. I see a good a. of life in thee: from Praying, to Purse-taking 1 *Hen. IV*, I. ii. 114. A. of the law GOLDSM. **2.** A Bill..was agreed to with some amendments 1710. **4.** What hope is there of his maiesties a.? He hath abandon'd his Physitions, Madam *All's Well* I. i. 12.

Amends (ăme·ndz). ME. [– OFr. *amendes* pecuniary fine, penalties, pl. of *amende* reparation, f. *amender* AMEND. Used as a collect. sing. with sing. vb., *amend* being rare in Eng.] † **1.** A fine (= L. *pœnæ*) –1618. **2.** Reparation, compensation, satisfaction. *pl.* in form ME. † *sing.* –1668. † **3.** Improvement *esp.* in health –1709.

2. To make amends we have many..ballads COWPER. To make an honourable Amends ADDISON. To make amend in time MARVELL. **3.** But here I feel a. MILT. *Sams.* 9. Hence † **Ame·ndsful** *a. rare*, making compensation.

Amene (ămī·n), *a.* ME. [– OFr. *amene* (implied in *amenement* pleasantly) – L. *amœnus* pleasant; in later use from L.] Agreeable. var. †**Ame·nous.**

Amenity (ămī·nĭti, ăme·nĭti). ME. [– (O)Fr. *aménité* or L. *amœnitas*; see prec., -ITY.] **1.** The quality of being pleasant or agreeable. **2.** *pl.* † Pleasant places 1644; pleasant ways or manners 1841; the pleasurable features of an estate 1928.

1. The a. of the climate PRESCOTT, of Erasmus DIBDIN. **2.** The amænities of nature H. WALPOLE. Amenities of authors D'ISRAELI, of home life 1866.

‖**Amenorrhœa** (ăme:norī·ă). 1804. [mod.L. f. Gr ἀ- A- *pref.* 14 + μήν month + -ροια flowing.] *Med.* Absence or suppression of the menstrual discharge. Hence **Amenorrhœ·al** *a.*

Ament (ame·nt). 1791. [– L. AMENTUM.] *Bot.* = AMENTUM.

Amental (ăme·ntăl), *a.*[1] (and *sb.*) 1847. [f. as prec. + -AL[1].] *Bot.* Bearing catkins.

Ame·ntal, *a.*[2] *nonce-wd.* 1877. [f. A- *pref.* 14 + MENTAL *a.*[1]] Denying or dispensing with the existence of mind.

‖ **Amentum** (ăme·ntŏm). Pl. **-a.** 1770. [L., = thong or strap.] A catkin. Hence **Amenta·ceous** *a.* of the nature of, or bearing, catkins. **Amenti·ferous** *a.* bearing catkins. **Ame·ntiform** *a.* catkin-shaped.

† **Ame·nty.** 1623. [– L. *amentia* madness, f. *amens* mad, f. *a* away from + *mens ment-* mind; see -Y[3].] *Path.* Madness.

† **Amenuse,** *v.* ME. [– AFr. *amenuser* = OFr. *amenuisier* (mod. *amenuiser*), f. *a* AD- + *menuisier* make smaller :– Rom. **minutiare*, f. L. *minutia* smallness; see MINUTIA, AMINISH *v.*] *trans.* To make less –1554. *intr.* –1481.

Amerce (ămɜ̄·ɹs), *v.* [ME. *amercy* – AFr. *amercier*, orig. in *estre amercié*, be placed at the mercy of another (as to the amount of a fine), f. phr. *à merci* at (the) mercy.] **1.** To fine arbitrarily; *fig.* and *loosely*, to exact something from; to punish 1570. **2.** Also with the penalty expressed (see quots.) 1500.

1. To be amerced to the Crown 1863. To be amerced for sins unknown BYRON. **2.** To be amerc'd a Supper 1725. He would a. him in half his wages SCOTT. A. him with the loss of his Kingdom MILT. Amerced of heaven MILT. *P.L.* I. 604. Hence **Ame·rciable** *a.*; also † **ame·rceable,** liable to be amerced. **Ame·rcing** *vbl. sb.* mulcting. var. † **Ame·rciate.**

Amercement (ămɜ̄·ɹsmĕnt). [– AFr. *amerciment*, f. *amercier*; see prec., -MENT.] **1.** The infliction of a penalty or fine at the 'mercy' of the inflicter (orig. one lighter than the fixed fines) 1513. **2.** The fine itself ME. Also *fig.*

1. Liable to an a. from the Crown for raising a false accusation BLACKSTONE. **2.** Yt is necessary to..levie the sayd amerciments 1483.

Amerciament (ămɜ̄·ɹsiămĕnt). ME. [– med.L. *amerciamentum*, f. *amerciare*, latinization of AFr. *amercier* AMERCE.] = AMERCEMENT (in both senses).

Amerced, and by the A. affeered to 10*s.* 1714.

American (ăme·rikăn). 1578. [– mod.L. *Americanus*, f. *America* (1507).] **A.** *adj.* **1.** Belonging to the continent of America. **2.** † **a.** Belonging to the British colonies in North America –1775. **b.** Belonging to the United States.

2. b. *A. cloth*, an enamelled oilcloth used chiefly for covering tables, chairs, etc.

B. *sb.* **1.** An aborigine of the American continent; now called an 'American Indian' 1578. **2.** A native of America, *esp.* a citizen of the United States 1765.

1. Worse Than ignorant Americans MASSINGER. **2.** We Americans are terribly in earnest about making ourselves HOWELLS.

Americanism (ăme·rikăni:z'm). 1794. [f. prec. + -ISM.] **1.** Attachment to the United States 1808. **2.** Anything peculiar to the United States; *esp.* a word or phrase (the usual, and earliest, Eng. use) 1794.

1. The leaven of A. 1861. **2.** I hate this shallow A. which hopes to get rich by credit EMERSON.

Ame·ricanist. 1881. [f. as prec. + -IST.] One who makes a special study of subjects pertaining to America, as its ethnology, etc.

Americanize (ăme·rikănəi:z), *v.* 1816. [f. as prec. + -IZE.] **1.** *strictly*, To make American; *esp.* to naturalize as a citizen of the United States 1816. **2.** *loosely*, To make American in character. (A dyslogistic term of Eng. party politics.) 1830. **3.** *intr.* To become American in character, etc. 1875.

2. They say we must not..A. our institutions BRIGHT. Hence **Ame:ricaniza·tion,** the process of Americanizing. **Ame·ricanized** *ppl. a.* made American, or like the American.

Americo-, comb. form of America, as in **Americo-mania,** a craze for what is American.

Ames-ace, obs. f. AMBS-ACE.

Amess, obs. f. AMICE.

‖ **Ametabola** (æ:mĭtæ·bŏlă), *sb. pl.* 1870. [mod.L. adj. pl. neut. (sc. *insecta*) – Gr. ἀμετάβολα, f. ἀ- A- *pref.* 14 + μετάβολος changeable.] *Zool.* A sub-class of insects, e.g. Lice, etc., which do not undergo metamorphosis. Hence **Ame:tabo·lian** *a.* belonging to the *Ametabola*; *sb.* [sc. *insect.*] **Ame:tabo·lic, Ameta·bolous** *adjs.*, not undergoing metamorphosis.

Ame·tallous, *a.* 1879. [f. A- *pref.* 14 + METAL *sb.* + -OUS.] Non-metallic.

Amethyst (æ·mĭþist). [ME. *ametist* – OFr. *ametiste* (mod. *améthyste*) – L. *amethystus* – Gr. ἀμέθυστος, subst. use (sc. λίθος stone) of adj., f. ἀ- A- *pref.* 14 + *μέθυστος intoxicated; the stone was so named because it was supposed to prevent intoxication.] **1.** A precious stone of a clear purple or bluish violet colour, consisting of quartz coloured by manganese, or by a compound of iron and soda. Also *fig.* **2.** *Her.* The colour of the A., purple violet 1572. Also *attrib.* = AMETHYSTINE 2. 1601.

1. The amethist staieth drunkennesse LODGE. **Oriental Amethyst:** a rare violet variety of sapphire. *fig.* Towers of a. KEATS.

Amethystine (æmĭþi·stin), *a.* 1670. [– L. *amethystinus* – Gr. ἀμεθύστινος; see prec., -INE[1].] **1.** Of, or containing, amethyst. **2.** Amethyst-coloured; violet-purple 1671.

2. A. flowers 1671, wings DISRAELI, ether 1870.

‖ **Ametropia** (æmĭtrōᵘ·piă). 1875. [mod.L. f. Gr. ἀ- A- *pref.* 14 + μέτρον measure + ὤψ, ὠπ- eye + -ια -IA[1].] *Path.* Any abnormal condition of the refraction of the eye. Hence **Ametro·pic** *a.*

Ametrous (ămī·trəs), *a.* 1879. [f. Gr. ἀ- A- *pref.* 14 + μήτρα womb + -OUS.] *Path.* Having no uterus.

† **Ami, amy(e.** ME. only. [– (O)Fr. *ami, amie* :– L. *amicus, amica* friend.] A friend, a lover.

Amiability (ēⁱ:miăbi·lĭti). 1807. [f. next; see -ILITY.] **1.** The quality of being AMIABLE. **2.** Lovableness (better AMABILITY, q.v.) 1869.

Amiable (ēⁱ·miăb'l), *a.* ME. [–(O)Fr. *amiable* :– L. *amicabilis* friendly, f. *amicus* friend (see AMICABLE); later infl. in sense by Fr. *aimable* lovable, likeable.] **1.** (= L. *amicabilis.*) † Friendly; kind –1491; kindly disposed (? U.S.) 1875; of conduct, temper, mood, etc.: Friendly ME. † **2.** (= L. *amabilis.*) Lovable –1788; of things (*arch.*) ME. **3.** Having pleasing qualities of heart (a fusion of senses 1 and 2) 1749.

1. Lay an a. siege to the honesty of this Ford's wife *Merry W.* II. ii. 243. In no a. temper MACAULAY. †**Amiable numbers:** see AMICABLE. **2.** We are a. or odious in the Eyes of our great Judge ADDISON. This a. home of the dead M. ARNOLD. **3.** The a. temper of pity FIELDING. Hence **A·miableness,** (*a*) = AMABILITY; (*b*) = AMIABILITY. **A·miably** *adv.* † amicably; † lovably; good-temperedly.

Amiant(h (æ·mi,ænt, -ænþ). ME. [– Fr. *amiante* or L. *amiantus*; see next.] = next. Now *poet.*

‖**Amiant(h)us** (æmi,æ·ntŏs, -þŏs). 1668. [– L. *amiantus* – Gr. ἀμίαντος, f. ἀ- A- *pref.* 14 + μιαίνειν to defile. For the sp. *-th* cf. AMARANTH.] *Min.* **1.** A variety of asbestos, splitting into fibres, which have been woven into a fabric. **2.** A fibrous kind of greenish chrysolite 1862.

1. Here is amianthus, as fine and soft as any cotton thread RUSKIN. Hence **Amia·nt(h)iform** *a.* of the structure of a. **Amia·nt(h)ine** *a.* of the nature of a. **Amia·nt(h)inite,** a variety of actinolite. **Amia·nt(h)oid** *a.* a.-like; *sb.* [sc. *mineral*] = ASBESTOID; whence **Amiant(h)oi·dal** *a.* a.-like.

Amic (æ·mik), *a.* 1863. [f. AM(MONIA or AM(IDE + -IC.] *Chem.* Of or pertaining to ammonia, of the nature of an amide; *esp.* in *Amic acid*, an acid amide; e.g. *lactamic* acid.

Amicable (æ·mikăb'l), *a.* 1532. [– late L. *amicabilis*, f. L. *amicus* friend; see -ABLE, AMIABLE.] **1.** *gen.* Friendly. **2.** *esp.* Of arrangements: Done with mutual goodwill; harmonious 1609. † **3.** Kindly, genial –1691.

1. Each a. guest POPE. **2.** An a. settlement of all differences 1794. *Amicable suit*: a friendly action instituted by agreement between the parties, in order to secure a judicial decision on a point of law. **3. Amicable** (or *amiable*) **numbers:** numbers which are mutually equal to the whole sum of each other's aliquot parts, e.g. 284 and 220. Hence **A:micabi·lity,** the quality of being a.; *concr.* friendly relations. **A·micableness, A·micably** *adv.*

† **Amical,** *a.* 1652. [– L. *amicalis*; see prec., -AL[1].] Friendly –1691.

Amice[1] (æ·mis). [Late ME. *amis, ames(s)* – med.L. *amicia, amisia*, of obscure formation; superseding the var. † *amit* (XIV) – OFr. *amit* (mod. *amict*):– L. *amictus* outer garment, cloak (see AMIT(E). Formally not distinct from next.] † **1.** *gen.* A loose wrap ME. **2.** *Eccl.* An oblong or square piece of white linen, worn by clerics about the neck and shoulders, and originally also covering the head 1532. **3.** *Loosely* of other garments 1641.

2. As the Jewes dyd fyrst couer Chrystes face..so hath the Priest..an Amise put vpon his head BP. WATSON. var. † **Ami·ct.**

Amice[2] (æ·mis). [late ME. *amisse* – OFr. *aumusse* – med.L. *almucia, -ium*, of unkn. orig. Now often spelt *almuce* with assimilation to med.L. See prec.] **1.** A cap, a hood or hooded cape, later a badge, made of, or lined with, grey fur, worn by the clergy. † **2.** The fur of the marten or grey squirrel, used as in 1. –1598.

1. Morning fair..in a. gray MILT. *P.R.* IV. 427.

Amid (ămi·d). [OE. *on middum, on middan, on midre*, i.e. *on* (see A *prep.*[1]) with obl. case of MID in concord w. a sb.; ME. *amidde.*] † **A.** *adv.* In the midst –1581.

B. *prep.* **1.** In the middle *of.* Now only *poet.* OE. **2.** *more loosely*, Near the middle of, surrounded by (with *sing.* or *pl. sb.*). Chiefly *poet.* ME. **3.** *esp.* In relation to the circumstances of an action 1513.

2. And all a. them stood the Tree of Life MILT. **3.** A. the broil SCOTT, general shouts of dissent FREEMAN.

Amid-, comb. form of AMIDE, used instead of AMIDO- bef. vowels.

A·midated, *ppl. a.* 1878. [f. foll. + -ATE[3] + -ED[1].] *Chem.* Converted into an amide.

Amide (æ·məid, ăməi·d in comb.). 1850. [f. AM(MONIA) + -IDE.] *Chem.* † **1.** *orig.* A name given to derivatives of ammonia (NH_3) in which one atom of H was exchanged for a metal or organic radical, acid or basic, these being viewed as compounds of the *metal*, etc., with *amidogen* (NH_2). **2.** *Mod. Chem.* Generic name of the compound ammonias in which one or more atoms of hydrogen are replaced by an *acid* radical 1863. **3.** Extended to ALKALAMIDES. **4.** *Acid amide*: AMIC ACID, or ALANINE. Hence **Ami·dic** *a.* of or derived from an a.

Amidide (æ·midəid). 1854. [f. AMIDE + -IDE.] *Chem.* A simple compound of amidogen with another element or complex radical.

Amidin (æ·midin). 1833. [f. *amid-* the common Romanic form of L. *amylum* starch (as in Fr. *amidon*, etc.) + -IN[1].] *Chem.* **1.** The soluble matter in the granules of starch. **2.** Starch in solution 1839.

Amidmost (ămi·dmoᵘst, -əst). [mod. f. *amid* or *midmost.*] *adv.* In the very middle. *prep.* In the very centre of. MORRIS.

Amido- (ăməi·do), comb. form of AMIDE, used also in phrases as *amido compounds*, etc.

Amidogen (ăməi·dŏdʒen). 1850. [f. AMIDO- + -GEN.] *Chem.* The hypothetical radical (NH_2) of the primary amides and amines (equal to ammonia minus one of its hydrogen atoms).

Amidships (ămi·dʃips), *adv.* 1692. [alt., by association w. AMID, of MIDSHIPS.] In, *occas.* to or towards, the middle of a ship.

Amidst (ămi·dst). ME. [f. ME. *amidde* AMID + advb. gen. -S, with subseq. addition of parasitic -*t* as in *against, amongst.*] **A.** *adv.* In the middle.

B. *prep.* **1.** In or into the middle of (with *sing.* or *pl. sb.*) ME. **2.** Amongst, in the course of (with *sing.* or *pl. sb.*) ME.

1. The fruit of this fair tree a. The garden MILT. *P.L.* ix. 661. Lost, Amids the moving waters CHAPMAN. **2.** To smile a. adversity 1756. A. his ascetic follies 1849.

Amidulin (ami·diŭlin). 1879. [f. *amid-* as in AMIDIN, prob. after INULIN; see -IN¹. Cf. Fr. *amiduline.*] *Chem.* A soluble preparation of starch.

† **Ami·dward.** ME. [f. AMID + -WARD, after *downward*, etc.] *adv.* Towards or near the middle -1513. *prep.* Towards or near the middle of ME. only.

‖ **Amildar** (æ·mǝldāɹ). 1799. [Pers. and Urdu, f. Arab. *ʻamal* work + Pers. *dār* holding, holder.] A native factor in India; *esp.* a collector of revenue.

† **Ami·nded,** *pa. pple.* 1578. [f. A- *pref.* 6 + MINDED.] Minded -1640.

Amine (æ·mǝin, ămǝi·n in comb.). 1863. [f. AM(MONIA) + -INE.] *Chem.* Generic name of the *compound ammonias*, in which one or more atoms of hydrogen are replaced by alcohol or other base-radicals.

† **Ami·nish,** *v.* 1477. [Refash. of AMENUSE, after *diminish.*] To diminish -1530.

Amir, var. of AMEER.

Amiral, -el, -eld, obs. ff. ADMIRAL.

Amiss (ămi·s). [ME. *a mis, on mis*, prob. – ON. *á mis* so as to miss, or not to meet, i.e. *á* ON, *mis*, identical in form w. the prefix *mis-* MIS-¹, rel. to MISS *v.*] **A.** *adv.* Away from the mark. **1.** Erroneously, missing its object ME. **2.** Defectively, falling short of its object; faultily ME. **3.** *euphem.* Wrongly ME.

1. Our Archyers shet neuer arowe amys CAXTON. **2.** I cannot be lodged amisse in this house 1579. **3.** Apt to see wrong, and speak a. H. MARTINEAU.

Phrases. **1. To come** or **happen amiss:** to happen out of order or untowardly. **2. To do, deal,** or **act a.:** to err; *euphem.* to do wrong. **3. To take** (a thing) **a.:** *orig.* to miss its meaning (i.e. *(a)misstake*); *now*, to misinterpret its motive and take offence at it. So **To think a.**

B. quasi-*adj.* [Never *attrib.*] Out of order; deficient, faulty ME.; *esp.* negatively, *Not amiss*: not beside the mark 1513; not bad 1860.

What is amisse? You are, and doe not know't *Macb.* II. iii. 102. It is likewise not a. to hope JOHNSON.

C. † *sb.* [The *adv.* or *adj.* used subst.] An error or fault; hence *euphem.* an evil deed -1700. *Haml.* IV. v. 18.

Amissible (ămi·sĭb'l), *a.* 1672. [– eccl.L. *amissibilis*, f. *amiss-* pa. ppl. stem of *amittere* lose, AMIT.] Liable to be lost. Hence **Ami:ssibi·lity,** possibility of being lost or losing. So † **Ami·ssive** *a.* tending to or marked by loss.

Amissing (ămi·siŋ), *ppl. a.* 1634. [The phr. *amissing* (see A *prep.*¹ 12, 13); chiefly Sc.] = MISSING.

† **Ami·ssion.** 1623. [–(O)Fr. *amission* or L. *amissio*; see AMISSIBLE *a.*, -ION.] LOSS.

† **Ami·t,** *v.* 1525. [– L. *amittere* lose; see AMISSION.] To lose. Occ. with *of.* -1756.

† **Amit(e,** *sb.* ME. [– OFr. *amit* (now *amict*); see AMICE.] **1.** = AMICE¹ 1, 2. **2.** = AMICE². ME.

Amity (æ·mĭti). 1474. [–(O)Fr. *amitié* :– Rom. **amicitas, -at-* (= L. *amicitia*) f. *amicus* friend; see -ITY.] Friendship, friendliness; friendly relations, *esp.* of a public character between states or individuals.

Treaties of a. and commerce G. DUFF. Ancient amities DISRAELI.

‖ **Amma** (æ·mă). 1706. [mod.L. for Gr. ἅμμα anything tied or made to tie.] *Surg.* A band or truss.

Ammelide (æ·mĭlǝid). 1846. [f. AM(MONIA + MEL(AM + -IDE.] *Chem.* A white powder, $C_6N_9H_9O_3$, produced by concentrated sulphuric acid acting on melam; regarded as acid amide of cyanuric acid.

Ammeline (æ·mĭlǝin). 1846. [f. as prec. + -INE⁵.] *Chem.* A white powder, 2 CyH_2N. CyH.O, produced by boiling melam with dilute sulphuric acid, etc.; an amic base of cyanuric acid.

Ammeter (æ·mĭtǝɹ). 1882. [f. AM(PÈRE) + -METER.] An instrument for measuring electric current.

Ammi (æ·mi). 1551. [– L. *ammi* – Gr. ἄμμι. Cf. Fr. *ammi.*] *Bot.* Bishop-weed. var. †‖ **A·mmeos** (Gr. gen. taken as nom.).

Ammiral, -ant, obs. ff. ADMIRAL.

†‖ **Ammi·tes, am-.** 1750. [Gr. ἀμμίτης sandstone, f. ἄμμος sand.] *Min.* OOLITE.

Ammo-, comb. form of AMMONIUM, implying conjunction of that basyl with an element, as in *Ammopalladium.*

Ammodyte (æ·mŏdǝit). 1607. [– L. *ammodytes* – Gr. ἀμμοδύτης sand-burrower, f. δύειν to dive.] *Zool.* † **1.** A venomous snake of S. Europe, the Sand Natter -1774. **2.** The sand-eel, *Ammodytes* 1698.

Ammonia (ămō̆ᵘ·niă). 1799. [mod.L. (Bergman, 1782), so named as being obtained from *sal-ammoniac*; see next.] **1.** A colourless gas with pungent smell and strong alkaline reaction, NH_3, called also *Spirit of Hartshorn*, and *Volatile* or *Animal Alkali.* **2.** *pop.* *Ammonia*, or spec. *Liquid Ammonia*: a solution of a. in water 1850. **3.** *Chem.* Applied to a series of compounds in which one or more hydrogen atoms of NH_3 are replaced by an acid radical 1863.

Ammoniac (ămō̆ᵘ·niæ̆k). [ME. *armoniak, amm-* – OFr. *armoniac* (XIV) (cf. med.L. *armoniacum*), *ammoniac* (XV) – L. *ammoniacus, -um* – Gr. ἀμμωνιακός *-όν* of Ammon, used subst. for a salt and a gum obtained from a region in Libya near the temple of Jupiter Ammon.] **A.** *adj.* **1.** In *Sal Ammoniac*, i.e. Salt of Ammon, a hard white opaque crystalline salt, chemically called Ammonium Chloride, formerly *Muriate of Ammonia.* (Supposed to have been prepared from the dung of camels near the temple of Jupiter Ammon.) **2.** in *Gum Ammoniac*, i.e. gum of Ammon, a gum-resin, of peculiar smell and bitterish taste, the inspissated juice of an umbelliferous plant (*Dorema ammoniacum*) found wild from N. Africa to India. Used in medicine, and as a cement. 1627. **3.** Ammoniacal 1646.

B. *sb.* **1.** = Gum Ammoniac. Also **ammoniacum.** 1420. † **2.** = Ammonia. [mod.Fr. *ammoniaque.*] -1802.

Ammoniacal (æmŏnǝi·ăkăl), *a.* 1732. [f. prec. + -AL¹; cf. Fr. *ammoniacal*; see -ACAL.] Of, pertaining to, or of the nature of ammonia.

Ammoniaco- (æmŏnǝi·ăko), comb. form of AMMONIAC or AMMONIACAL; also = AMMONIA +, as in *a.-magnesian phosphate.*

Ammoni·acum; see AMMONIAC *sb.* 1.

† **Ammo·niate.** 1844. [f. AMMONIA + -ATE⁴.] *Chem.* A combination of ammonia and a metallic oxide. Hence **Ammo·niated** *ppl. a.* combined with ammonia.

Ammonic, -al (ămǫ·nik, -ăl), *a. rare.* 1869. [f. AMMONIUM + -IC, -ICAL.] Of or derived from ammonia or ammonium.

Ammonio- (ămō̆ᵘ·nio), comb. form of AMMONIUM, indicating the presence of that basyl or its salts in a compound.

Ammonite (æ·mŏnǝit). 1706. [– mod.L. *ammonites* (Bruguière), f. med.L. name *cornu Ammonis* 'horn of Ammon', given to these fossils from their resemblance to the involuted horn of Jupiter *Ammon* + -ITE¹ 2 a.] **1.** A fossil genus of Cephalopods, with whorled chambered shells; once thought to be coiled snakes petrified, and called *Snake-stones.* (SCOTT *Marmion* II. xiii.) † **2.** = AMMITES, i.e. oolite -1753. Hence **A:mmoniti·ferous** *a.*

Ammonium (ămō̆ᵘ·niŏm). 1808. [– mod.L. *ammonium* (Berzelius, 1803), f. AMMONIA + -IUM.] *Chem.* The radical, NH_4, supposed to exist in the salts of ammonia, which behaves in composition as a monatomic alkaline metal, replacing sodium and potassium. *attrib.* in **a. alum** (see ALUM); **a. amalgam,** an amalgam of a. and mercury.

† **Ammo·niuret.** 1839. [f. AMMONIA + -URET.] *Chem.* = AMMONIATE. Hence **Ammo·niuretted** *ppl. a.* combined with ammonia (or ammonium). ? *Obs.*

Ammo·philous, *a.* 1879. [f. Gr. ἄμμος sand + φίλος loving + -OUS; see -PHILOUS.] Sand-loving.

Ammunition (æmiuni·ʃǝn), *sb.* 1626. [– Fr. † *am(m)unition*, resulting from a wrong analysis of *la munition* the supplies (see MUNITION) as *l'amunition.*] **1.** Military stores or supplies; *orig.* of all kinds; *now*, powder, shot, shell; and, in extension, offensive missiles generally. Also *fig.* **2.** *attrib.* as *a.-boots, -bread*, etc., those supplied as equipment or rations.

Ammuni·tion, *v.* 1644. [f. the sb.] To supply with ammunition. Hence **Ammuni·tioned** *ppl. a.*

Amnemonic (æmnĭmǫ·nik), *a.* 1879. [f. Gr. ἀ- A- *pref.* 14 + μνημονικός of memory; see MNEMONICS.] *Path.* Marked by loss of memory.

‖ **Amnesia** (æmnī·siă). 1786. [mod.L. – Gr. ἀμνησία forgetfulness.] *Path.* Loss of memory. Hence **Amne·sic** *a.*

Amnestic (æ̆mne·stik), *a.* 1879. [f. Gr. ἀμνηστία forgetfulness + -IC.] *Med.* Causing loss of memory.

Amnesty (æ·mnĕsti), *sb.* 1580. [– Fr. † *amnestie* (mod. *amnistie*) or L. *amnestia* – Gr. ἀμνηστία oblivion.] **1.** Forgetfulness; an intentional overlooking 1592. **2.** An act of oblivion, a general overlooking or pardon of past offences, by the ruling authority 1580.

1. Reconcilement. .by an a., and passing over that which is past BACON. **2.** An act of a. and indulgence BURKE. Hence **A·mnesty** *v.* to give a. to: proclaim a.

Amnion (æ·mniǫn). 1667. [– mod.L. – Gr. ἀμνίον caul, dim. of ἀμνός lamb. Cf. Fr. *amnion.*] *Phys.* The innermost membrane enclosing the fœtus before birth. Also *attrib.*

Amnios (æ·mniǫs). 1657. [– Gr. (Galen) ἀμνειός or ἄμνιος (sc. χιτών, ὑμήν) caul; cf. Fr. *amnios* (XVI), AMNION.] **1.** *Phys.* = AMNION. **2.** *Bot.* The fluid produced within the sac which receives the embryo-rudiment 1816.

‖ **Amniota** (æmni,ō̆ᵘ·tă), *sb. pl.* 1879. [mod. L., formed anomalously after AMNIOTIC.] The vertebrates, including reptiles, birds, and mammals, which possess an amnion.

Amniotic (æmni,ǫ·tik), *a.* 1822. [irreg. f. AMNIOS + -OTIC (cf. *chaotic* f. *chaos*); cf. Fr. *amniotique.*] Of, pertaining to, or characterized by, an amnion; as *Phys.* the *a. liquid*, *Bot.* the *a. sac.* var. **A·mnic** (*rare*).

Amœba (ămī·bă). Pl. **-bæ, -bas.** 1841. [– mod.L. – Gr. ἀμοιβή change, alternation.] *Zool.* A microscopic animalcule (class *Protozoa*) having no constant form. Hence **Amœ·biform** *a.* amœba-like; proteiform. var. **Amœboid.**

Amœbæan (æmĭbī·ăn), *a.*; also **amebean.** 1658. [f. L. *amœbæus* alternate – Gr. ἀμοιβαῖος interchanging + -AN.] Alternately answering; responsive.

Amoibite (ămoi·bǝit). [– G. *amoibit* (von Kobell, 1844) f. Gr. ἀμοιβή change; see -ITE¹ 2 b.] *Min.* A variety of Gersdorffite.

† **Amoi·nder,** *v. rare.* 1601. [– OFr. *amoindrer* (mod. *amoindrir*) lessen, f. *a* AD- + *moindre* less.] To diminish -1631.

† **Amo·lish,** *v.* 1624. [– *amoliss-*, lengthened stem of obs. Fr. *amolir* – L. *amoliri* remove forcibly, f. *a* AB- + *moliri* construct; cf. *demolish.*] To remove forcibly -1640. Hence † **Amoli·tion,** displacement.

† **Amo·llish,** *v.* 1474. [– OFr. *amolir* (mod. *amollir*) soften, f. *a* AD + *molir* :– L. *mollire* soften.] To soften, appease -1483. Hence † **Amo·llishment.**

‖ **Amomum** (ămō̆ᵘ·mŏm). ME. [L., = an aromatic shrub, – Gr. ἄμωμον] *Bot.* A genus of aromatic plants (N.O. *Zingiberaceæ*), including the species which yield Cardamoms and Grains of Paradise. Hence **Amo·meous** *a.*

Among (ămɒ·ŋ). [OE. *onġemang, -mong*, i.e. *on* (A- *prep.*¹, *ġemang*, assemblage, crowd, mingling (see MENG *v.*, MINGLE *v.*); later *onmang, onmong*, whence *amang, among.*] **A.** *prep.* In the crowd of, *hence* associated with. **1.** Surrounded by (occ. = *in*) OE. **2.** In company or association with or beside; in the house, city, or country of. (= L. *apud*, Fr. *chez*, Ger. *bei.*) ME. **3.** In the number or class of ME.; *esp.* pre-eminent among ME. † **4.** During, in course of -1691. **5.** With or by (the members of a group) generally ME.

6. Divided between ME.; by the joint action of 1597; reciprocally between ME.

1. 'Mong Boyes, Groomes, and Lackeyes *Hen. VIII*, v. ii. 18. Amonge a basket ful of roses CHAUCER. 2. The Cananites dwelt a. them at Gaser COVERD. 3. Amonge all elementes water is prouffytablest TREVISA. He is a Saul a. the people 1884. 5. Vsed..emonge marchantes CAXTON. Popular a. the Irish SYD. SMITH. 6. What are they a. so many *John* 6:9. You haue a. you kill'd a sweet and innocent Ladie *Much Ado* v. i. 194. They quarrelled a. themselves ADDISON.

B. *adv.* [The prep. used *ellipt.*] † **1.** During this (period), at the same time –1598. † **2.** Betweenwhiles –1606. † **3.** Of place: Together, among *something else* –1624.

Amongst (ămɒ·ŋst), *prep.* [ME. *amonges* f. AMONG + advb. gen. -S; for the parasitic *-t* cf. AMIDST, AGAINST.] = AMONG in all senses exc. 4, but less usual in the primary local sense, and, when so used, generally implying dispersion, intermixture, or shifting position.

‖ **Amontillado** (amǫntilʸā·do). 1825. [Sp.; f. *Montilla*, a town in Spain + *-ado* -ATE².] Formerly, a specially dry sherry; now, sherry of a matured type. **b.** *attrib.* in fig. sense 1862.

Amoral (eⁱ,mǫ·răl), *a.* 1882. [A- *pref.* 14 + MORAL *a.*] Non-moral. Hence **-ism**, etc.

†**A·moret.** ME. [– OFr. *amoret, -ette* (mod. *amourette* AMOURETTE), dim. of *amor* :– L. *amor* love; see -ET, -ETTE.] **1.** An amorous girl; a paramour –1794. **2.** = AMORETTO –1598. **3.** A love-knot –1423. **4.** A love sonnet –1594. **5.** *pl.* Love-glances; dalliances –1651. Cf. AMOURETTE.

‖ **Amoretto** (æmore·to, It. amore·tto). 1596. [It., dim. of *amore* love; cf. prec.] † A lover; † a love-sonnet; † a love-trick; a cupid.

‖ **Amorino** (amorī·no). Pl. **-i.** [It., dim. of *amore.*] A cupid.

Amorist (æ·mŏrist). 1581. [f. L. *amor* or Fr. *amour* + -IST.] One who professes (usu. sexual) love.

Hence **Amori·stic** *a. rare.*

† **A-mo·rnings,** *adv.* ME. [A *prep.*¹ 8.] In the morning; every morning –1633.

†‖ **Amoro·sa.** 1634. [It.] A female lover; a wanton.

†‖ **Amoro·so.** 1616. [It.] A lover –1706.

Amorous (æ·mŏrəs), *a.* ME. [– OFr. *amorous* (mod. *amoureux*) – med.L. *amorosus* f. L. *amor* love; see -OUS.] **1.** Habitually inclined to love. Also *fig.* of things. **2.** In love, enamoured, fond. Also *fig.* of things. (Const. *absol.*; or with *on, of,* † *in.*) ME. **3.** Showing love or fondness (sexual or general) ME. **4.** Of or pertaining to (sexual) love ME. † **5.** *passively.* Lovable, lovely –1611.

2. Our..Musitian groweth a. *Tam. Shr.* III. i. 63. A. on Hero *Much Ado* II. i. 161. Amerous of that lady 1450. 3. His eyen gray and a. LD. BERNERS. 4. Fful is the place..Of songis amerous CHAUCER. 5. O mother of God moste..a. 1557. Hence **A·morously** *adv.* in the way of love. **A·morousness,** the quality of being a.; var. † **Amoro·sity.**

Amorpha (ămǭ·ɹfă). 1753. [f. Gr. ἄμορφος shapeless; see -A *suff.* 4.] *Bot.* A genus of N. American deciduous shrubs, with long spiked clusters of purple flowers.

Amorphism (ămǭ·ɹfiz'm). 1852. [f. as prec. + -ISM.] Want of regular form; *esp.* want of crystalline structure.

Amorpho- (ămǭ·ɹfo), comb. f. AMORPHOUS.

Amorphophyte (ămǭ·ɹfŏfəit). 1879. [f. AMORPHO- + -PHYTE.] *Bot.* A plant having flowers of irregular or anomalous form.

Amorphous (ămǭ·ɹfəs), *a.* 1731. [f. mod.L. *amorphus* – Gr. ἄμορφος (f. ἀ- A- *pref.* 14 + μορφή shape) + -OUS.] **1.** Having no determinate shape; unshapely; belonging to no type. **2.** *Min.* and *Chem.* Uncrystallized 1801. **3.** *Geol.* Without definite parts 1830. **4.** *Biol.* Without definite structure 1848. **5.** *fig.* Unorganized, ill-digested 1837.

1. An a. hat D'ISRAELI. 5. An a. Sansculottism taking form CARLYLE. var. **Amorpho·se** *a.* (*rare*). Hence **Amo·rphous·ly** *adv.*, **-ness.**

‖ **Amorphozoa** (ămǭ:ɹfo,zoᵘ·ă), *sb. pl.* 1857. [mod.L., f. AMORPHO- + Gr. ζῷα animals; see -A *suffix* 4.] *Zool.* Protozoa, e.g. sponges, which have no regular form. Hence **Amorphozo·ary,** a compound amorphozoic organism. **Amorphozo·ic** *a.*

Amo·rphy. 1704. [– Gr. ἀμορφία; see -Y³.] Shapelessness. (Used in jest by Swift.)

† **A-morrow,** *adv.* OE. [A *prep.*¹ 8.] In the morning; next morning –1480.

Amort (ămǭ·ɹt), *adv.* and *pred. a.* 1590. [orig. *all amort* – (w. assim. to ALL) Fr. *à la mort* to the death; cf. ALAMORT. The unqualified *amort* (XVII) has the appearance of being – Fr. *à mort.*] In the state or act of death; inanimate; *fig.* spiritless.

All a. [*obpressam*] for feare HOLLAND. Halfe a-mort 1619. Now a., alive now BROWNING.

Amortization, -isation (ămǭ:ɹtizēⁱ·ʃən). 1672. [f. next + -ATION; cf. med.L. *a(d)mortizatio.*] **1.** The act of alienating lands in mortmain, i.e. to a community having perpetual existence. **2.** The extinction of a debt, *esp.* by means of a sinking fund. *concr.* The money thus paid 1864. var. **Amo·rtizement, -ise-.**

Amortize, -ise (ămǭ·ɹtiz), *v.* ME. [– *amortiss-*, lengthened stem of (O)Fr. *amortir* :– Rom. **admortire*, f. *ad* AD- + *mors, mort-* death; the sp. -IZE is due to med.L. *amortizare.*] † **1.** *trans.* To deaden –1656; *intr.* to droop 1480. **2.** To alienate (lands) in mortmain, i.e. to a corporation ME. **3.** To extinguish a debt, etc., usu. by means of a sinking fund 1882.

2. To render inalienable or..a. the crown lands STUBBS. 3. To a. the Egyptian Debt 1882. Hence **Amo·rtizable, -isable** *a.* extinguishable. **Amo·rtized, -ised** *ppl. a.* † destroyed; held in, or as in, mortmain; held in commission.

Amotion (ămōᵘ·ʃən). *arch.* 1641: [– L. *amotio* removing; see AMOVE *v.*², MOTION *sb.*] **1.** The action of removing; ousting; *esp.* removal of a person from office. **2.** Deprivation of possession 1653.

Amount (ămau·nt), *v.* ME. [– OFr. *amunter, amo(u)nter* f. *amont* upward, i.e. *à mont* :– L. *ad montem* to the hill, upward; see MOUNT *sb.*¹ and cf. PARAMOUNT *a.*] † **1.** *intr.* To go up, mount –1631; to mount up –1706. **2.** To come up to (a number or quantity); † *trans.* with simple, or quasi-advb. obj. –1480; *intr.* with *to* 1546. † **3.** *intr.* To result –1650. **4.** † *trans.* To mean, signify –1460; *intr.* with *to*: To be tantamount *to* ME. † **5.** *causal.* To cause to rise, to raise –1655.

2. *intr.* Which doth a. to three odde Duckets more *Com. Err.* IV. i. 30. 4. *intr.* The proofs..do not a. to a demonstration ADDISON. Hence **Amou·nting** *ppl. a.* † resulting; with *to*: Equalling in sum or effect.

Amount (ămau·nt), *sb.* 1710. [f. the vb.] **1.** The sum total to which anything mounts up; *spec.* the sum of the principal and interest 1796. **2.** *fig.* The full value, effect, or significance 1732. **3.** A quantity or sum viewed as a total 1833.

1. The A. of the said Drawback 1710. 2. The whole a. of that enormous fame POPE. 3. The a. of resistance which William met with FREEMAN.

Amour (ămūᵊ·ɹ, Fr. amu·r). ME. [– (O)Fr. *amour* :– L. *amor* love, related to *amare* to love. The Fr. word was reintroduced in XVI, when the early anglicized *a·mour* had become obs. or was (temporarily) repl. by the L. *amor* (XVI–XVII). Cf. PARAMOUR.] † **1.** *gen.* Love, affection –1742; *pl.* the tender affections (L. *amores*, Fr. *amours*) –1727. **2.** A love-affair, love-making. (Now only joc. of honourable love-making.) 1567. **3.** *usually,* An intrigue 1626.

1. † *In amours* (with): in love (*with*). 3. Intrigue, that's an old phrase; ..a. sounds better DRYDEN.

Amourette (amure·t). 1865. [– Fr. *amourette*; see AMORET.] **1.** A petty amour. **2.** The Love-grass (*Briza media*) 1866.

‖ **Amour-propre** (amur,pro·pr'). 1818. [Fr., = self-respect.] Sensitive self-love; self-esteem.

† **Amo·ve,** *v.*¹ [ME. *amoeve, ameve* – *ameuv-*, tonic stem of OFr. *amover, amouvoir,* f. *a* AD- + *mover* MOVE *v.*; cf. med.L. *admovere, amm-*. App. infl. by OFr. *esmover* (mod. *émouvoir*), see EMOVE *v.*] **1.** To set in motion, excite –1590; *esp.* to move the feelings of (Fr. *émouvoir*) -1596. **2.** To arouse. SPENSER.

Amove (ămū·v), *v.*² 1494. [– OFr. *amover* or L. *amovēre*, f. *a* AB- + *movēre* move.] **1.** To remove from a position; to dismiss (a person) from an office. (Now only in *Law.*) † **2.** To remove (things immaterial) –1664. Hence **Amo·vable** *a.*, also **amovible,** removable. † **Amo·val,** removal.

Ampassy. *dial.* See AMPERSAND.

Ampelideous (æmpĭli·dĭəs), *a.* 1879. [f. mod.L. *ampelideæ*, f. Gr. ἄμπελος vine + -OUS.] *Bot.* Of the vine family.

Ampelite (æ·mpĭləit). 1751. [– L. *ampelitis* – Gr., in ἀμπελῖτις γῆ, an earth sprinkled on the vine.] *Min.* A bituminous earth; perh. cannel coal. Hence **Ampeli·tic** *a.*

Ampelography (æmpĭlǫ·grăfi). 1879. [– Fr. *ampélographie*, f. Gr. ἄμπελος vine; see -GRAPHY.] The scientific description of the vine.

A·mper. OE. A tumour; a blemish. (Cf. ANBURY.) Now *dial.*

Ampère (ãnpe·r, æmpēᵊ·ɹ). 1881. [f. A. M. *Ampère*, French physicist (d. 1876); adopted by the Congrès Électrique at Paris, 1881.] *Electr.* The unit of current; the current that one volt can send through one ohm.

Amperometer (æmpĕrǫ·mĭtəɹ). 1882. [f. prec. + -METER.] *Electr.* = AMMETER.

Ampersand (æmpəɹsæ·nd). 1837. Also **ampassy-, ampussy-, ampus-.** For the old way of naming the character & '*and* per se—*and*', i.e. '& by itself = and'. Found in all dial. glossaries.

Of all the types in a printer's hand Commend me to the A. *Punch* 17 Apr. 1869.

Amphi-, *prefix* – Gr. ἀμφι- both, of both kinds, on both sides, about, around. Used in derivatives, etc.

Amphiarthrosis (æ:mfi,aɹþrōᵘ·sis). 1836. [f. AMPHI- + ARTHROSIS.] *Anat.* A form of jointing combining diarthrosis and synarthrosis, in which the bones are united by an elastic cartilage, admitting of a certain amount of movement; as in the carpus, etc. Hence **A:mphiarthro·dial** *a.* characterized by a.

‖ **Amphibia** (æ̆mfi·biă), *sb. pl.* 1609. [mod. L. – Gr. ἀμφίβια (sc. ζῷα animals), subst. use of ἀμφίβιος (f. ἀμφι- + βίος life); see -A suffix 4, -IA².] **I.** *sing.* *-um, -on,* pl. *-a, -ums.* **1.** A being that is equally at home in water or on land. **2.** *fig.* A being of ambiguous or double position 1645.

2. Ask these a. what names they would have. What..papists? no..protestants? no 1645.

II. *pl.* only. *Zool.* † **a.** Reptiles (including mod. Amphibia). LINNÆUS. **b.** Mammals (including seals, etc.). CUVIER. **c.** Since Macleay, the fourth division of Vertebrata, intermediate between reptiles and fishes, whose young have gills like fishes, as frogs, newts, etc.

Hence **Amphi·bial** *a.* and *sb.* (*rare*) = AMPHIBIAN. **Amphi·bian** *a.* of double or doubtful nature; of or pertaining to the A.; *sb.* one of the A. **Amphi·biolite, -lith,** the fossil remains of an amphibian.

Amphibiology (æ̆mfi:bi,ǫ·lŏdʒi). 1840. [f. prec. + -LOGY.] A scientific treatise on the Amphibia; the part of zoology which treats of Amphibia. Hence **Amphi:biolo·gical** *a.*

Amphibious (æ̆mfi·biəs), *a.* 1643. [f. as prec. + -OUS.] **1.** Living both on land and in water 1654. **2.** Of, pertaining to, suited for, or connected with, both land and water 1646. **3.** Combining two lives, positions, classes, qualities, etc. 1643.

1. Th' a. Otter 1735. The a. tribe as willow, osier, etc. 1813. 2. A floating island, an a. spot WORDSW. 3. I have considered this a. Pope CARLYLE. Hence **Amphi·bious-ly** *adv.*, **-ness.** (Dicts.)

Amphibium, (L.) sing. form of AMPHIBIA.

Amphibole¹ (æ·mfibŏᵘl). 1606. [– Fr. – L. *amphibolum* – Gr. ἀμφίβολον, f. ἀμφί- AMPHI- + βάλλειν to throw.] † **1.** An ambiguity; = AMPHIBOLY –1668. **2.** Hornblende. So named by Haüy 1801, in allusion to the great variety in composition, etc., assumed by the genus. Dana includes under it Actinolite, Asbestos, Hornblende, Tremolite, etc. (The pronounc. æ̆mfi·bŏli is erron.) 1833. Hence **Amphibo·lic,** † **-al** *a.* equivocal; of, or of the nature of, the mineral amphibole; var. **Amphi·boline. Amphi·bolite, -yte,** = Hornblende-rock or Diabase.

‖ **Amphibole**² (æ̆mfi·bŏli). 1854. [Gr. ἀμφιβολή.] *Gr. Antiq.* A casting-net.

Amphibology (æ:mfibǫ·lŏdʒi). ME. [– (O)Fr. *amphibologie* – late L. *amphibologia*, for cl.L. *amphibolia* – Gr. ἀμφιβολία (-βολογία) ambiguity.] **1.** = AMPHIBOLY 1. **2.** = AMPHIBOLY 2. 1589. Hence **Amphi:bolo·gical** *a.*

ambiguous, *prop.* of a sentence or phrase; equivocating. **Amphibo·logism,** an amphibolous construction or phrase (*rare*).

Amphi:bolosty·lous, *a.* 1879. [f. Gr. ἀμφίβολος AMPHIBOLE[1] + στῦλος column + -OUS.] *Bot.* Having a non-apparent style.

Amphi·bolous, *a.* 1641. [f. late L. *amphibolus* – Gr. ἀμφίβολος ambiguous + -OUS; see AMPHIBOLE[1].] † **1.** Of double or doubtful character or sense –1660. **2.** *Path.* Spreading on both sides 1880.

Amphiboly (æ̆mfi·bŏli). 1588. [– L. *amphibolia*: see AMPHIBOLOGY. Cf. OFr. *amphibolie.*] **1.** Ambiguous discourse; a quibble. (AMPHIBOLOGY is earlier and more pop.) 1610. **2.** *Logic.* Ambiguity arising from uncertain construction, where the individual words are unequivocal. In pop. use confused with equivocation. 1588.

Amphibrach (æ·mfi͵bræk). Also **-us, -ys, -ee.** 1589. [– L. *amphibrachys* (later *-us*) – Gr. ἀμφίβραχυς, short at both ends.] *Gr. and L. Pros.* A foot consisting of a long between two short syllables, as *ămātă*. Occas. now with reference to accent, as *drama·tic.*

So Prior: 'As Chlŏē came īntŏ thĕ rōom t'ŏthĕr dāy' GRAY.

Amphi·bryous, *a.* 1866. [f. Gr. ἀμφι- AMPHI- + βρύειν to swell + -OUS.] *Bot.* Growing by additions all over the periphery.

Amphica·rpous, *a.* 1866. [f. Gr. ἀμφι- AMPHI- + καρπός fruit + -OUS.] *Bot.* Having fruit of two kinds, or at two times.

Amphichro·ic, *a.* 1876. [f. Gr. ἀμφι- AMPHI- + -χροος coloured + -IC.] Having a double action on test colours in chemistry.

Amphicœ·lous, *a.* 1869. [f. Gr. ἀμφι- AMPHI- + κοῖλος hollow + -OUS.] *Phys.* Concave on both sides, double concave, as vertebræ. So **Amphicœ·lian.**

† **A·mphicome.** [– Gr. ἀμφίκομος with hair all round, f. ἀμφι- AMPHI- + κόμη hair.] A kind of figured stone, round, but rugged, once used in divination (Chambers).

Amphictyonic (æmfi:kti͵ǫ·nik), *a.* 1753. [– Gr. ἀμφικτυονικός; see next, -IC.] Of the Amphictyons; also *transf.*

Amphictyons (æ̆mfi·kti͵ǫ̆nz), *sb. pl.* 1586. [– Gr. ἀμφικτύονες, orig. ἀμφικτίονες, they that dwelt round.] *Gr. Hist.* Deputies from the states of ancient Greece composing a council.

Amphictyony (æ̆mfi·kti͵ǫ̆ni). 1835. [– Gr. ἀμφικτυονία, -εία, f. prec.; see -Y[3].] *Gr. Hist.* A confederation of Amphictyons; a league of neighbouring states for the common interest.

† **Amphid(e** (æ·mfid). 1842. [f. Gr. ἀμφι- AMPHI- + -IDE.] *Chem.* An obs. name for salts viewed by Berzelius as compounds of two oxides, sulphides, selenides, or tellurides, as distinct from the *haloid* salts.

A·mphidisc. 1867. [f. Gr. ἀμφι- AMPHI- + δίσκος round plate.] *Zool.* Asteroid spicules, resembling two toothed wheels united by an axle, which form a layer surrounding the gemmules of sponges.

† **Amphidro·mic, -al,** *a.* 1658. [f. Gr. ἀμφιδρομία running round + -IC, -ICAL.] Pertaining to the Amphidromia (an Attic festival at the naming of a child, when friends carried it round the hearth, and then named it).

Amphigam (æ·mfi͵gæm). 1845. [– Fr. *amphigame* (De Candolle), f. Gr. ἀμφι- AMPHI- + γάμος marriage.] *Bot.* A name of plants having no distinct sexual organs, also called *Agamæ*. Hence **Amphi·gamous** *a.* of or pertaining to Amphigams.

‖ **Amphigastria** (æmfi͵gæ·striă), *sb. pl.* 1842. [mod.L., f. Gr. ἀμφι- AMPHI- + γαστήρ belly + -IA[2].] *Bot.* Scale-like leaves developed on the under side of some Liverworts.

Amphigean (æ̆mfi·dʒī·ăn), *a. rare.* 1864. [f. Gr. ἀμφι- AMPHI- + γῆ earth + -AN.] Extending all over the earth from the equator to both poles.

Amphigen[1] (æ·mfi͵dʒen). 1879. [– Fr. *amphigène*, f. Gr. ἀμφι- AMPHI- + -γενής; see -GEN 2.] *Bot.* = THALLOGEN.

† **A·mphigen**[2]. 1842. [f. as prec.; see -GEN 1.] *Chem.* An element, as oxygen, sulphur, selenium, tellurium, capable of forming, in combination with metals, both acids and bases (Berzelius).

Amphigene (æ·mfi͵dʒīn). 1803. [– Fr. *amphigène* (Haüy), f. as prec.] *Min.* = LEUCITE. (Rejected by Dana.) Hence **Amphi·genite, -yte,** a lava containing a., or leucite.

Amphigenous (æ̆mfi·dʒĕnəs), *a.* 1835. [f. AMPHIGEN[1, 2] + -OUS.] **1.** *Bot.* Growing all round a central point. **2.** *Chem.* Of the nature or class of an amphigen 1879.

Amphigony (æ̆mfi·gŏni). 1876. [f. Gr. ἀμφι- AMPHI- + γονία engendering.] Sexual reproduction. Hence **Amphigo·nic** *a.* pertaining to a.; bisexual. **Amphi·gonous** *a.* pertaining to both parents.

‖ **Amphigouri, -gory** (æ:mfigū̃ə·ri, æ·mfi͵gŏri). 1809. [Fr. (XVIII), app. a learned (jocular) formation f. Gr. ἀμφί round about + *allégorie* ALLEGORY.] A burlesque writing without sense, as a nonsense-verse.

Amphilogism (æ̆mfi·lŏdʒiz'm). *rare.* 1866. [f. Gr. ἀμφίλογος doubtful + -ISM.] A circumlocution.

† **Amphi·logy** [f. Gr. ἀμφιλογία dispute, f. ἀμφίλογος disputed, uncertain; see -LOGY.] Ambiguity. (Dicts.)

Amphimacer (æ̆mfi·măsəɹ). 1589. [– L. *amphimacrus* – Gr. ἀμφίμακρος long at both ends.] *Gr. and L. Pros.* A foot consisting of a short between two long syllables, as *cārĭtās*, or (mod.) *multitude*, etc.

‖ **Amphioxus** (æmfi͵ǫ·ksǫ̆s). 1836. [mod. L., f. Gr. ἀμφί- + ὀξύς tapering at both ends.] *Zool.* A genus (containing one species) of fishes called also the Lancelet, the lowest of the vertebrates.

We cannot regard A. as a fish *Athenæum*.

Amphipneust (æ·mfi͵pniūst). Pl. **-s,** or collect. **amphipneusta.** 1841. [f. Gr. ἀμφι- AMPHI- + -πνευστος breathing.] *Zool.* An Amphibian having both lungs and gills, as the Proteus and Siren.

Amphipod (æ·mfi͵pǫd). 1835. [f. next.] *sb.* One of the *Amphipoda*. *adj.* = AMPHIPODOUS. 1852.

‖ **Amphipoda** (æ·mfi·pŏdă), *sb. pl.* As sing. AMPHIPOD. 1837. [mod.L. (sc. *animalia*), f. Gr. ἀμφι- AMPHI- + πούς, ποδ- foot, footed; see -A *suffix* 4.] *Zool.* An order or sub-order of the sessile-eyed Crustacea, having feet of two kinds, as the common sand-hopper. Hence **Amphi·podan** *a.* of or pertaining to the A.; var. **Amphi·podous. Amphipo·diform** *a.*

Amphiprostyle (æ̆mfi·prŏstəil). 1706. [– L. *amphiprostylus* – Gr. ἀμφιπρόστυλος, f. ἀμφι- AMPHI- + πρόστυλος PROSTYLE.] *Arch.* A temple having a portico in the rear as well as the front, but without columns at the sides.

‖ **Amphisa·rca.** 1854. [mod.L. f. Gr. ἀμφι- AMPHI- + σάρξ, σαρκ- flesh; see -A suffix 2.] *Bot.* A hard-rinded berry, succulent within and woody without, as a calabash.

‖ **Amphisbæna** (æmfisbī·na). ME. [L. (Pliny) – Gr. ἀμφίσβαινα, f. ἀμφίς both ways + βαίνειν go, walk.] **1.** A fabled serpent, with a head at each end, and able to move in either direction: now a poet. conception. **2.** *Zool.* A worm-like genus of lizards, having head and tail scarcely distinguishable 1833.

1. Complicated monsters head and taile, Scorpion, and Asp, and A. dire MILT. *P.L.* x. 524. Hence **Amphisbæ·nian** *a.* **Amphisbæ·nic** *a.* of the nature of an a. **Amphisbæ·nous** *a.* walking equally in opposite directions.

Amphiscians (æ̆mfi·fiănz), *sb. pl.* 1622. [f. med.L. *Amphiscii* (also used) – Gr ἀμφίσκιοι (f. ἀμφι- AMPHI- + -σκιά shadow) + -AN.] Inhabitants of the torrid zone, whose shadows at one time fall northward, at another southward.

Amphistome (æ·mfi͵stōᵘm). 1880. [– mod.L. *amphistoma*, f. Gr. ἀμφι- AMPHI- + στόμα mouth.] *Zool.* A genus of worms, having suckers at both ends of the body. Hence **Amphi·stomoid** *a.* like or akin to the Amphistomes.

Amphistylic (æmfi͵stəi·lik), *a.* 1876. [f. Gr. ἀμφι- AMPHI- + στῦλος pillar + -IC.] Having piers supporting both upper and lower mandibular arches, as the skulls of certain sharks.

Amphitheatre, -ter (æ·mfi͵þĭ·ătəɹ). 1546. [– L. *amphitheatrum* – Gr. ἀμφιθέατρον; see AMPHI-, THEATRE. Cf. Fr. *amphithéatre.*] † **1.** *etymol.* A double theatre –1807. **2.** Hence, An oval or circular building, with seats rising behind and above each other, around an open space or arena 1546. **3.** A place of public contest, an arena 1640. **4.** A semicircular rising gallery in a theatre 1882. † **5.** *fig.* Surrounding scene –1711. **6.** *transf.* A level surrounded by rising slopes 1772. **7.** *Hort.* An arrangement of shrubs and trees resembling an a. 1753.

2. The students gathered in the a. to see a painful operation 1883. **4.** A. stalls DICKENS. Hence **A:mphithe·atred** *ppl. a.* formed into, or provided with, an a. **A:mphithea·tric, -al** *a.* of or pertaining to or resembling an a. **A:mphithea·trically** *adv.*

Amphithere (æ·mfi͵þīəɹ). 1859. [– mod.L. *amphitherium* (also in use), f. Gr. ἀμφι- AMPHI- + θηρίον beast.] *Palæont.* An extinct genus of small marsupials.

Amphi·tropal, *a.* 1847. [f. Gr. ἀμφι- AMPHI- + -τρόπος turning + -AL[1].] *Bot.* Of an embryo. So curved as to have both apex and radicle presented to the hilum. var. **Amphi·tropous.**

‖ **Amphitryon** (æ̆mfi·tri͵ǫ̆n). 1862. [f. Molière's *Amphitryon* III. v.] A host, a dinner-giver.

Amphodarch (æ·mfŏdăɹk). 1878. [– Gr. ἀμφοδάρχης, f. ἄμφοδον quarter of a town + -αρχης ruler.] *Gr. Ant.* One governing a quarter of a town.

‖ **Amphora** (æ·mfŏră). Pl. **-æ.** 1465. [L., – Gr. ἀμφορεύς.] **1.** *Cl. Antiq.* A two-handled vessel, for holding wine, oil, etc. **2.** A liquid measure, Greek, = about 9 gals.; or Roman (also called quadrantal), = 6 gals. 7 pts. **3.** *Bot.* The lower part of a pyxis 1821. var. † **Amphore** (in senses 1, 2). Hence **A·mphoral** *a.* of, pertaining to, or like an a.

Amphoric (æmfǫ·rik), *a.* 1839. [– mod.L. *amphoricus*, f. AMPHORA, see -IC; cf. Fr. *amphorique.*] **1.** = AMPHORAL (*rare*). **2.** *Med.* Like the sound produced by blowing or speaking into an amphora, etc., as in *a. cough*, etc. Hence **Amphori·city,** a. quality.

Amphoteric (æmfote·rik), *a. rare.* 1849. [f. Gr. ἀμφότερος, compar. of ἀμφώ both + -IC.] Both acid and alkaline.

Ample (æ·mp'l), *a.* 1481. [– (O)Fr. *ample* – L. *amplus.*] **1.** Extending far; broad, wide, spacious. (Now always *eulogistic.*) 1548. **2.** Roomy, capacious; copious 1596. **3.** Of things immaterial: Large in extent or amount 1481; *esp.* full, complete 1592; liberal, unstinted 1536. **4.** Of a writing, etc.: Copious 1592.

1. This a. third of our faire kingdome *Lear* I. i. 82. Ruling in large and a. Emperie SHAKS. **2.** That a. hous SPENSER *F.Q.* III. xi. 49. **3.** A more a. and large commission 1542. A. justice JUNIUS, provision 1834. 4. An ampler description 1670. Hence **A·mpleness** (*arch.*). **A·mply** *adv.* in an a. manner.

† **A·mple, amply,** *v.* ME. [– OFr. *amplier*, *ampleer* – L. *ampliare* extend, f. *amplus* AMPLE *a.*] = AMPLIFY –1533.

† **Ample·ct,** *v.* 1525. [– L. *amplecti*, med.L. *amplectare.*] To embrace –1657. var. † **Ample·x.**

Amplexation (æmplĕksē·ʃən). *rare.* 1615. [– late and med.L. *amplexatio*, f. *amplexat-*, pa. ppl. stem of L. *amplexare*, *-ari* embrace; see -ION.] † **1.** Embracing. **2.** *Surg.* A method of treating fracture of the clavicle.

Amplexicaudate (æ̆mple:ksi͵kǭ·deᶦt), *a.* 1879. [f. L. *amplexus* embrace + *cauda* tail + -ATE[2].] *Ent.* Having the tail enveloped in the interfemoral membrane.

Amplexicaul (æ̆mple·ksikǭl), *a.* 1760. [– mod.L. *amplexicaulis* (Linnæus), f. L. *amplexus* embrace + *caulis* stem.] *Bot.* Embracing the stem, said of sessile leaves. var. **Ample:xicau·line.**

Amplexifoliate (æ̆mple:ksi͵fōᵘli͵ᵉ̆t), *a.* 1879. [f. L. *amplexus* embrace + FOLIATE *a.*] *Bot.* Having leaves which clasp the stem.

† **A·mpliate,** *v.* 1513. [– *ampliat-*, pa. ppl. stem of L. *ampliare* widen, f. *amplus* AMPLE *a.*] To enlarge; to amplify –1686. Hence **A·mpliate,** † **A·mpliated** *ppl. adjs.* enlarged, amplified.

Ampliation (æmpli͵ēᶦ·ʃən). *arch.* 1509. [– (O)Fr. *ampliation* or L. *ampliatio*; see prec., -ION.] **1.** Enlarging; amplification. **2.** That which is added in enlarging; an enlargement or extension 1590. **3.** *Law.* Deferring of judgement for further consideration 1656.

Ampliative (æ·mpliĕtiv), *a.* 1842. [– Fr. *ampliatif* (med.L. *ampliativus* XIV), f. as prec. + -IVE.] *Logic.* Enlarging a simple conception by predicating of it something which is not directly implied in it.

Amplification (æ:mplifikēi·ʃən). 1546. [– (O)Fr. *amplification* or L. *amplificatio*; see AMPLIFY, -FICATION.] The action of amplifying. **1.** Enlargement. *concr.* That which is added. **2.** Augmentation in extent, importance, significance, etc. *concr.* An enlarged representation. 1569. *esp.* Extension of meaning 1551. **3.** *Rhet.* The extension of a simple statement by rhetorical devices; making the most of a thought, etc. 1553. **4.** Additions made; statement as amplified 1567.

2. *Amplification of the predicate* (in *Gram.*) = extension of the predicate. **3.** A. is the spinning-wheel of the *bathos*, which draws out and spreads it POPE. No a. at all, but a positiue and measured truth BACON.

A·mplifica:tory, *a. rare.* [f. AMPLIFICATION + -ORY[2].] Of the nature of enlargement.

Amplifier (æ·mplifəi,əɹ). 1546. [f. next.] One who or that which amplifies or enlarges. **b.** *spec.* An apparatus for increasing the strength of wireless signals; also, a loud speaker used for making a voice more audible.

Amplify (æ·mplifəi), *v.* ME. [– Fr. *amplifier* – L. *amplificare* enlarge f. *amplus* large; see -FY.] † **1.** To enlarge in space or capacity –1636; in volume or amount –1626. Also *intr.* (*refl.*) –1600. **2.** Of things immaterial: To extend in amount, importance, etc. 1549. **3.** To expand (a story, etc.) ME. **4.** *intr.* To enlarge, expatiate 1590. **5.** To magnify, exaggerate 1561.

1. To a. states 1636, sounds BACON. **2.** To a. one's jurisdiction 1767. **3.** Instead of saying.. Turnus died, he amplifies his death 1751. **4.** He would a. so much, he would often lose his way 1670.

Amplitude (æ·mplitiūd). 1549. [– Fr. *amplitude* or L. *amplitudo*, f. *amplus* AMPLE; see -TUDE.] The quality of being AMPLE. **1.** Extension in space; *chiefly* width, breadth 1599. **2.** Of things immaterial: Width, breadth, fullness; copiousness 1605. **3.** Wide (mental) range 1575. **4.** Excellence, splendour 1549. **5.** *Astr.* Angular distance at rising or setting from the eastern or western point of the horizon 1627. **6.** Extent of motion in space; *esp.* (in *Physics*), *A. of a vibration*: the distance a particle moves from side to side in one vibration 1837.

1. An a. of form and stature, answering to her mind LAMB. **2.** The a. of the divine charity 1850. **3.** As for the A. of his Lordship's mynde 1575. **4.** The state and a. of their Empire FULLER. **5.** *Magnetic Amplitude*: The a. reckoned from the eastern and western points as shown by the compass.

‖ **Ampu·lla.** Pl. **-æ.** ME. [L., two-handled big-bellied flask or pot, dim. of *ampora*, var. of AMPHORA.] **1.** *Rom. Antiq.* A small globular flask or bottle, with two handles. **2.** A vessel for holding consecrated oil, etc. 1598. **3.** *Biol.* Any vessel shaped like an ampulla; the dilated end of any canal, duct, etc., in an animal; the spongiole of a root 1821. var. † **A·mpul** (in senses 1, 2). Hence **Ampulla·ceous** *a.* like an a.; bottle-shaped, inflated. **A·mpullar, A·mpullary** *adjs.* of the form or character of an a. **A·mpullate** *a.* furnished with, or shaped like, an a.; bellied; var. **A·mpullated** *ppl. a.* **Ampu·lliform** *a.* flask-shaped, bulging.

Ampullosity (æmpǒlǫ·sĭti). *rare.* 1868. [– It. *ampullosità* f. med.L. *ampullosus* bombastic, f. AMPULLA; see -ITY, -OSITY.] Inflated inanity; bombast. BROWNING.

Ampus-and, ampussy; see AMPERSAND.

Amputate (æ·mpiuteit), *v.* 1638. [– *amputat-*, pa. ppl. stem of L. *amputare*, f. *am-* for *amb-* around, AMBI- + *putare* prune, lop; see -ATE[3].] **1.** *gen.* To lop off or prune. *Obs.* exc. as *fig.* **2.** *spec.* To cut off a limb, or any projecting part of the body. Also *absol.* 1639. Hence **A·mputated** *ppl. a.* cut off, as a limb, etc. **A·mputating** *vbl. sb.* amputation. **A·mputator,** one who amputates. *lit.* and *fig.*

Amputation (æmpiutēi·ʃən). 1611. [– Fr. *amputation* or L. *amputatio*, f. *amputat-*; see prec., -ION.] **1.** The operation of amputating (see AMPUTATE). Also *attrib.* **2.** *fig.* Excision, *e.g.* of sentences, etc.; pruning 1664.

2. 'Twas he..Made those that represent the nation Submit and suffer a. BUTLER *Hudibr.* II. I. 364.

‖ **Ampyx** (æ·mpiks). [Gr. ἄμπυξ.] *Gr. Antiq.* A broad metal band worn on the forehead of ladies of rank; also, the headband of horses.

‖ **Amrita** (ǣmrī·tă). Also **Amreeta.** 1810. [Skr. *amṛita* (= Gr. ἄμ(β)ροτος) immortal.] Immortal, ambrosial.

The A.-cup of immortality SOUTHEY.

† **A·msel, amzel.** 1705. [app. – G. *amsel* blackbird.] The Blackbird, or the Ring Ousel.

†‖ **Amtman** (a·mtmăn). 1587. [G.; cf. AMBASSADOR.] One in charge; a bailiff, steward, magistrate, etc.

Amuck (ămʊ·k), *a.* and *adv.*; also **amock, amok.** 1663. [– Malay *āmoq* fighting furiously, in homicidal frenzy.] **1.** Orig. *adj.* or *sb.* A frenzied Malay. **2.** To **run amuck:** to run viciously, frenzied for blood. (Here orig. *adj.*) 1672. **3.** *fig.* Wild, or wildly. (Usu. with *run.*) Const. *on, at, against,* (*with, of*). 1689. ¶ Erron. treated as *muck* sb.

3. Too discreet To run a muck, and tilt at all I meet POPE. ¶ Runs an Indian muck at all he meets DRYDEN.

Amulet (æ·miŭlėt). 1601. [– L. *amulētum* (Varro, Pliny), of unkn. origin. Cf. Fr. *amulette* (XVII).] **1.** Anything worn as a charm against evil, disease, witchcraft, etc. Also *fig.* 1621. † **2.** *Med.* A medicine whose virtue or mode of operation is occult –1753.

1. Amulets against agues SIR T. BROWNE. *fig.* He is our A., our Sun BURTON. Hence † **Amule·tic** *a.* of or pertaining to amulets; *sb.* [sc. *medicine.*]

Amuse (ămiū·z), *v.* 1480. [– (O)Fr. *amuser* entertain, † deceive, f. *à* AD- + *muser* stare stupidly; see MUSE *v.* Not in SHAKS.] † **1.** *intr.* To gaze in astonishment –1681; *trans.* to cause to muse or stare, to puzzle –1741. † **2.** To occupy the attention of. Const. *upon, with, about, to.* (esp. *refl.* and *pass.*) –1734. **3.** To divert the attention of; to beguile, mislead. (The usual sense in 17–18th c.) *arch.* 1480. **4.** To keep in expectation, in order to gain or waste time (*arch.*) 1639; † to keep up for a purpose –1693. **5.** To divert (one's) attention from serious business; *hence,* to divert; *esp.* to tickle the fancy of. Const. *with, by, in, at.* 1631. **6.** To beguile, while away 1771.

1. To..stupify, fluster, and a. the senses SWIFT. **2.** Amused and engrossed by the things of sense WATTS. **3.** Tools of the Devil, to cheat and a. the world DE FOE. Their Fleet was to a. ours whilst they cross from Leghorn NELSON. **4.** Amused with vain expectations 1777. **5.** To a. himself with trifles 1687. **6.** He did this to a. their concern 1771. Hence **Amu·sable** *a.* capable of being amused. **Amusee·**, the person amused. **Amu·ser. Amu·sing-ly** *adv.*, **-ness.**

Amusement (ămiū·zmĕnt). 1611. [– Fr. *amusement*; see prec., -MENT.] The action of amusing, or a thing done to amuse. † **1.** Musing –1712; bewilderment –1699. **2.** The action of amusing (sense 3). *arch.* 1692. † **3.** A diversion to gain or waste time –1710. **4.** The action of amusing or state of being amused (sense 5) 1698. **5.** *concr.* A pastime, play, game, etc. (Orig. *depreciatively.*) 1673.

1. Useless a. and dispute LOCKE. **4.** A. is the happiness of those that cannot think POPE. When men are rightly occupied, their a. grows out of their work RUSKIN. **5.** Plays and other amusements 1753.

† **Amusette** (æmiuze·t). 1761. [– Fr. *amusette* little amusement, plaything; see AMUSE *v.*, -ETTE.] A light field-cannon, invented by Marshal Saxe.

Amusive (ămiu·ziv), *a.* 1728. [f. AMUSE *v.* after *abusive*, etc.; see -IVE.] Such as to amuse. † **1.** Illusive –1760; recreative –1753. **2.** Interesting; *esp.* fitted to make one smile or laugh 1760. **3.** Tending to amusement 1781. Hence **Amu·sively** *adv.* **Amu·siveness.**

A-mu·tter, *adv.* 1856. [A *prep.*[1] 11.] Muttering. MRS. BROWNING.

Amyctic (ămi·ktik), *a.* 1853. [– late L. *amycticus* – Gr. ἀμυκτικός scratching.] *Med.* Excoriating, irritating, vellicating.

† **A·mydon, -oun.** ME. [– Fr. *amidon* starch – med.L. *amidum*; see AMYL[1].] Finest flour –1616.

Amyelencephalic (ămǝi:ĕlensĭfæ·lik), *a.* 1875. [f. Gr. ἀμύελος without marrow + ἐγκέφαλος brain + -IC.] *Phys.* Having the central nervous system wanting.

Amyelotrophy (ămǝi:ĕlǫ·trǒfi). 1879. [f. Gr. ἀ- A- *pref.* 14 + μυελός marrow + -τροφία nourishment; see -Y[3].] *Path.* Atrophy of the spinal cord.

Amyelous (ămǝi·ĕləs), *a.* [f. Gr. ἀμύελος without marrow + -OUS.] *Phys.* Wanting the spinal cord.

Amy·gdal. ? *Obs.* [In OE., ME., – L. *amygdala* (-*um*) – Gr. ἀμυγδάλη (-ον) almond; in XVI – Fr. *amygdale* tonsil.] † **1.** An almond –ME. **2.** *pl.* The tonsils; also, the almonds of the ear 1541. Hence **Amy:gdala·ceous** *a.* *Bot.* akin to the almond. **Amy·gdalate** *a.* made of almonds; † *sb.* = *almond-milk* (see ALMOND); *Chem.* a salt of Amygdalic acid. **Amygda·lic** *a.* *Chem.* of or pertaining to almonds. *Amygdalic Acid*, $C_{20}H_{26}O_{12}$, derived from amygdalin by boiling with an alkali. **Amygdali·neous** *a.* belonging to the almond tribe.

Amygdalin (ămi·gdălin). 1865. [f. as prec. + IN[1].] *Chem.* $C_{20}H_{27}NO_{11} + 3H_2O$; a GLUCOSIDE found crystalline in almonds, etc., and amorphous in cherry-laurel leaves, etc.

‖ **Amygdalitis** (-ǝi·tis). 1876. [f. as prec. + -ITIS.] *Med.* Inflammation of the tonsils.

Amygdaloid (ămi·gdăloid), *a.* 1791. [f. as prec. + -OID. Cf. Fr. *amygdaloïde.*] Almond-shaped; having almond-shaped nodules 1836. As *sb.* *Geol.* An igneous rock, usually trappean, containing almond-shaped nodules or geodes of agate, chalcedony, calc-spar, etc. Hence **Amygdaloi·dal** *a.*

Amygdule (ămi·gdiŭl). 1877. [f. L. *amygdala* almond + -ULE.] *Geol.* An agate pebble.

† **A·myl**[1]. 1572. [– L. *amylum* – Gr. ἄμυλον starch.] Starch; finest flour –1601. Cf. AMYDON.

Amyl[2] (æ·mil). 1850. [– L. *amylum* starch + -YL. Cf. Fr. *amyle.*] *Chem.* The monatomic alcohol radical of the pentacarbon series C_5H_{11}, also called *Pentyl* or *Quintyl*.

attrib. = amylic: as in **Amyl alcohol,** $CH.2CH_3.(C_2H_4)OH$, a burning acrid oily liquid, the chief constituent of Fusel oil; **Amyl hydride,** = *pentane*; **Ethyl-amyl-acetate,** the essence of jargonelle pears.

Hence **A·mylami:ne,** an amine in which one hydrogen atom of ammonia is replaced by amyl. **A·mylate,** a salt of the radical amyl, in which amyl replaces the oxygenated group in a metallic salt. **A·mylene,** the diatomic hydrocarbon, or olefine, of the pentacarbon series, C_5H_{10}, formed by the removal of one atom of water from amyl alcohol; it has anæsthetic properties. **Amy·lic** *a.* of or pertaining to amyl; = AMYL *attrib.*

Amylaceous (æmilēi·ʃəs), *a.* 1830. [f. as prec. + -ACEOUS. Cf. Fr. *amylacé.*] Of the character or nature of starch; starchy.

Amylo-, comb. form of AMYL[1, 2]. Hence: **amylo-ce:llulo·se** [L. *cellulosus*], a supposed constituent of starch granules, which is coloured copper-red by iodine; **-gen,** soluble starch; **-ly·tic** [Gr. -λυτικός] *a.*, converting starch into dextrine and sugar; **-meter** [Gr. μέτρον], an instrument for testing the amount of starch, in potatoes, etc.; **-sy·nthesis** [Gr. σύνθεσις], the formation of starch by assimilation.

Amyloid (æ·miloid). 1857. [f. L. *amylum* starch + -OID. Cf. Fr. *amyloïde.*] **A.** *adj.* Starch-like. **B.** *sb.* **1.** Any non-nitrogenous starchy food 1872. **2.** A starch-like substance forming the cell-walls in the cotyledons of various plants. **3.** An albuminoid developed in diseased degeneration of various animal organs. Also *attrib.* Hence **Amyloi·dal** *a.*

Amylose (æ:milōu·s). 1877. [f. as prec. + -OSE[2].] *Chem.* A subdivision of the *Carbohydrates*. The Amyloses are dextrin, starch, inulin, glycogen, cellulose, tunicin, and gum, all having the composition $C_6H_{10}O_5$, or a multiple thereof.

Amyosthenic (ămǝi,ǫsþe·nik). 1879. [f. Gr. ἀ- A- *pref.* 14 + μῦς, μυ- muscle + -σθένεια strength + -IC.] *Med.* A medicine which depresses muscular action.

Amyo·trophy. 1879. [f. Gr. ἀ- A- *pref.* 14 + μῦς, μυ- muscle; cf. ATROPHY.] *Path.* Atrophy of muscle. Hence **Amyotro·phic** *a.*

A·myous, *a.* 1879. [f. Gr. ἄμυος not showing muscle + -OUS.] *Path.* Wanting in muscle.

‖ **Amyris** (æ·miris). 1865. *Bot.* A genus of tropical trees and shrubs, yielding resinous products.

Amzel, var. of AMSEL.

† **An,** *adj.*[1] Earlier form of the numeral ONE; retained in the north. See ANE, A *adj.*[2], and ONE.

An (toneless ăn, ən; emph. æn), *adj.*[2], *indef. article.* The older and fuller form of *a*, now retained only bef. a vowel sound, by most writers bef. *h*, and by some bef. *eu*, *ū* (= *yū*), in unaccented syllables. For its history, and signification, see A *adj.*[2]

An, an' (ăn, ən, 'n), *conj.* [weakened from AND.] **1.** = AND, *conj. co-ordinate.* (L. *et.*) OE. Rare after 1500, exc. in dial. as *an'*, and in common pronunc. **2.** = AND, *conj. conditional.* = *if.* (L. *si.*) *arch*, and *dial.* Rare bef. 1600; exc. in *an't* (= *an it*), occurring only once in the 1st Folio of SHAKS. Mod. writers make *an'* for 'and', L. *et*, dial. or illiterate, but *an'* or *an* for 'and', L. *si*, arch. Dialectally both are *an'*; the intensified *and if*, *an if*, still exists in s.w. dial. as *nif*.

2. There, an't shall please you *L.L.L.* v. ii. 584. Nay then two treyes, an if you grow so nice *Ibid.* v. ii. 232.

† **An,** *prep.* The orig. form of ON, in Anglo-Saxon also absorbing *in*. After 11th c. *on* prep. occ. became *ăn* bef. vowels, as *an edge*, etc. (see A *prep.*[1]), but later again this became *on*, or *in*, exc. in go *an* (now *a*) hawking, twice *an* hour. See AN- *pref.* 1, and A *prep.*[1]

Each particular haire to stand an end *Haml.* I. v. 19. Set my pugging tooth an edge *Wint. T.* IV. iii. 7.

An-, *prefix.* **1.** OE. and ME. **an-** = AN *prep.* (see prec.). Cf. A- *pref.* **2.** *Obs.*, exc. as in *anon, anent;* etc. **2.** ME. **an-,** reduced f. OE. *and-*, against; see AND-. † **3.** ME. **an-** :– OE. *án* one. **4.** ME. **an-** = Anglo-Norm. *an-*, OFr. *en-* :– L. *in-* = in, into, as ANOINT (L. *inunctum*), etc. **5.** ME. **an-,** for earlier *a-* = OE. *a-* (A- *pref.* 1), or OFr. *a-* :– L. *ab-*, *ad-*, *ex-*, *ob-*, as *a(n)s-aumple*, refash. *example*, or changed to *ensample*. **6.** ME. **an-,** earlier *a-*, = OFr. *a-* :– L. *an-* = *ad-* 'to', bef. *n-*, as in *a(n)nounce*. See AD-. **7. an-,** repr. L. *an-* = *ad-* bef. *n-*, as in *annul*, etc. **8. an-,** repr. L. *an-* bef. certain cons., for *am-*, *amb-*, *ambi-* on both sides, about. **9. an-,** repr. Gr. ἀν- for ἀνά up, back, etc. (see ANA-) bef. a vowel; also in *anchor*[2], *anchoret*. **10. an-,** repr. Gr. ἀν-, not, without (bef. cons. ἀ-; see A- *pref.* 14); esp. in scientific words.

-an, *suffix.* **I.** Derivative. **1.** repr. L. *-anus*, *-ana*, *-anum*, of or belonging to. Orig. in ME. *-ain*, or (after *i*) *-en*, after OFr., but later refash. *-an.* *Esp.* added to proper names; 'belonging to a place', as *Oxonian*, etc.; 'following a founder', or 'a system', as *Lutheran, Anglican*, etc.; and (*Zool.*) 'belonging to a class or order', as *crustacean*, etc. Prop. these are all adjs., but many are used subst. as in L. In L. this termination was added to others, as *-ius*, in *ianus*, whence -IAN, which is in use merely a euphonic var. of *-an*; cf. *Corinthian, Roman*. **2.** in *Chem.* for *-ane*, as in *azotan* (obs.).

† **II.** Inflectional. † **1.** In OE. *pl.* ending = ME. *-en*, as *ox-en* :– OE. *ox-an*. Hence (dat. or loc. sing.) in advb. or prep. forms, as *beforan*. † **2.** In OE. pres. inf. ending, = ME. *-en*, *-e*, as OE. *writan*, ME. *write(n*; now *write*.

Ana (ēⁱ·nă, ā·nă). *suff.* and *sb.* 1727. [– L. *-ana* in neut. pl. of adjs. in *-anus* (see -AN *suffix* 1), as in (*Dicta*) *Virgiliana*. Used in Fr. as sb. sing. *un ana.*] **A.** *suffix.* Sayings of a person, literary trifles, gossip, etc., of a place; anecdotes of, notes about, or publications bearing upon 1741.

Shakespeariana 1863.

B. *sb.* **1.** *collect. sing.* (with *pl.*) A collection of the sayings or table talk of any one 1727. **2.** *collect. pl.* Clever sayings or anecdotes of any one; notes, etc., relating to a person or place; literary gossip ?1755.

1. Boswell's Life of Johnson..the *Ana* of all *Anas* SOUTHEY. **2.** Ere days that deal in ana TENNYSON.

‖ **Ana** (æ·nă), *adv.* Often written *ăă* or *ā*. 1500. [med.L. – Gr. ἀνά (see next) as advb.] In prescriptions: Throughout, of each, of every one alike: *hence* formerly, 'an equal quantity or number'.

Ana of each does the just Mixture make COWLEY.

Ana-, *pref.*, repr. Gr. ἀνά up, in place or time, back, again, anew, in words and derivatives from Gr.

Ana, var. of ANNA, Indian money.

Anabaptism (ænăbæ·ptiz'm). 1577. [– eccl.L. *anabaptismus* (Augustine) – Gr. ἀναβαπτισμός, f. ἀνά over again + βαπτισμός baptism. Cf. Fr. *anabaptisme* (XVI).] **1.** Rebaptism. (The orig. sense in L.) Also *transf.* 1645. **2.** The doctrine of the Anabaptists; also, occas. of modern Baptists (see next). 1577. So † **Anaba·ptistry.**

Anabaptist (ænăbæ·ptist). 1532. [– Fr. *anabaptiste* or mod.L. *anabaptista* (XVI), f. eccl.L. *anabaptismus* (Augustine); see prec.] **1.** *lit.* One who baptizes over again (whether *frequently*, or *once*). Hence **2.** *Ch. Hist.* Name of a sect which arose in Germany in 1521. **3.** Applied (invidiously) to the Baptists; and occas. (loosely) to other non-Anglicans 1586. Also *attrib.*

3. Baptists never called themselves *ana*baptists; as they did not admit that immersion..was *baptism* [without] an intelligent concurrence..on the part of the recipient 1883. *attrib.* An..a. preacher SWIFT. Hence **A:nabapti·stic, -al** *a.* connected with or attributed to Anabaptists; **-ly** *adv.*

Anabaptize (æ:năbæ̀ptəi·z), *v.* 1637. [– med.L. *anabaptizare* – Gr. ἀναβαπτίζειν baptize repeatedly or over again, f. ἀνά over again + βαπτίζειν baptize.] To re-baptize, re-christen: *hence*, to re-name.

Marvell..now anabaptized Dr. Turner as Mr. Smirke H. COLERIDGE.

‖ **Anabas** (æ·năbæs). 1845. [mod.L. (Cuvier) – Gr. ἀναβάς, pres. pple. of ἀναβαίνειν walk up.] A genus of acanthopterygian fishes, which sometimes leave the water, and even climb trees.

‖ **Anabasis** (ănæ·băsis). 1706. [Gr., = going up, f. ἀνά up + βάσις going.] **1.** A going up, a military advance; *esp.* that of Cyrus the younger into Asia, as narrated by Xenophon. † **2.** *Med.* The course of a disease to its climax 1706.

1. General Sherman's great a. 1864.

†‖ **Ana·bathrum.** 1623. [L., a. Gr. ἀνάβαθρον elevated seat.] A raised platform; a pulpit –1759.

Anabatic (ænăbæ·tik), *a.* 1811. [– Gr. ἀναβατικός pertaining to ἀναβάτης 'one who ascends', f. ἀναβαίνειν walk up; see -IC.] *Med.* Of or belonging to ANABASIS (sense 2); increasing (as a fever).

Anabiotic (æ:năbəi,ǫ·tik), *a.* 1879. [f. Gr. ἀναβίωσις return to life, on the anal. of words in -OSIS, -OTIC.] *Med.* Stimulant or tonic.

†‖ **Anabro·sis.** 1721. [Gr. ἀνάβρωσις eating up.] *Med.* Corrosion of the soft parts of the body. Hence † **Anabro·tic** *a.*

‖ **Anaca·mpsis.** 1879. [Gr. ἀνάκαμψις bending back, f. ἀνά back + κάμπτειν to bend.] Reflection; reaction. Hence **Anaca·mptic, -al,** *a.* causing or suffering reflection; chiefly of echoes. **Anaca·mptically** *adv.* by way of a. † **Anaca·mptics,** (*a*) = *Catoptrics* (see CATOPTRIC); (*b*) the branch of Acoustics, that relates to reflection of sound.

Anacard (æ·năkaɹd). 1541. [– med.L. *anacardus*, mod.L. *anacardium*, – Gr. ἀνακάρδιον, f. ἀνά like + καρδίον heart-shaped ornament. Cf. Fr. *anacarde*.] The nut of the Cashew (*Anacardium occidentale*); also, any plant of N.O. *Anacardiaceæ* (Lindley). Hence **Anaca·rdate.** *Chem.* See ANACARDIC. **Anaca:rdia·ceous** *a. Bot.* belonging to the *Anacardiaceæ*, as the Cashew, and the trees that produce mangoes, pistachios, etc.

Anacardic (ænăkā·ɹdik), *a.* 1863. [f. mod. L. *anacardium* (prec.) + -IC.] Of the Cashew-nut; as in *anacardic acid*, $C_{44}H_{64}O_7$, extracted from it by the action of ether. Its salts are **anacardates.**

Anacathartic (æ:nă,kăþā·ɹtik). 1696. [f. Gr. ἀνά upward + CATHARTIC.] *Med. adj.* Causing *anacatharsis*, i.e. vomiting or expectoration. *sb.* [sc. *drug*, etc.] Now written ANOCATHARTIC.

‖ **A:nacephalæo·sis.** *rare.* 1696. [late L. – Gr. ἀνακεφαλαίωσις; see next.] Recapitulation.

Anacephalize (ænăse·fāləiz), *v.* ? *Obs.* 1654. [f. Gr. ἀνακεφαλ(αιοῦν) recapitulate (f. ἀνά up, back + κεφαλή head) + -IZE.] To recapitulate.

‖ **Anacharis** (ănæ·kăris). 1848. [mod.L., f. Gr. ἀνά up + χάρις grace.] A N. American water-weed (*A. alsinastrum* or *Elodea canadensis*), which appeared unaccountably in Britain in 1842, and rapidly filled canals, ditches, and ponds, all over the country.

Anachoret(e, anachorite, var. ANCHORET.

Ana·chorism. *nonce-wd.* [f. Gr. ἀνά back + χωρίον country, place, to match *anachronism.*] Something foreign to the country. LOWELL.

Anachronic, -al (ænăkrǫ·nik, -ăl), *a.* 1807. [f. next, after pairs of words like *synchronic*, *synchronism*; see -IC. Cf. Fr. *anachronique*.] Erroneous in date or order; marked by anachronism. Hence **Anachro·nically** *adv.*

Anachronism (ănæ·krŏniz'm). 1646. [– Fr. *anachronisme* or Gr. ἀναχρονισμός, f. ἀναχρονίζεσθαι refer to a wrong time, f. ἀνά back + χρόνος time.] **1.** An error in computing time, or fixing dates; reference of an event, etc., to a wrong date. Used *etymologically* of a date which is too early (*prochronism*), but also of too late a date (*parachronism*). **2.** Anything done or existing out of date; *hence*, any former thing, which is, or would be, out of harmony with the present; a *practical a.* 1816.

2. A pilgrimage now seems an a. 1859. Hence **Ana·chronist,** one who commits an a. (DE QUINCEY.) **Ana:chroni·stic** *a.* of the nature of, or involving, a. **Ana·chronize** *v.* to transfer to a wrong time. (LOWELL.) **Ana·chronous** *a.* involving a.; **-ly** *adv.*

† **Anack.** 1615. [origin unkn.] Oatmeal bread –1750.

Anaclastic (ænăkla·stik), *a.* 1753. [f. Gr. ἀνάκλαστος reflected f. ἀνακλάειν bend back (ἀνά ANA- + κλάειν break) + -IC.] **1.** *Opt.* Pertaining to, or produced by, refraction 1796. **2.** Springing back with a crackling sound 1753. As *sb.* (*pl.*) [Cf. *acoustics*.] = Dioptrics 1696.

1. *Anaclastic curves*: certain apparent curves seen at the bottom of a vessel full of water, etc., caused by refraction. **2.** *Anaclastic glasses*: low phials, with very thin, slightly convex, bottoms, which become concave, and again convex, with a crackling noise, as the air in the phials is sucked out or returned.

Anaclete (æ·năklīt). *rare.* 1817. [– Gr. ἀνάκλητος called back (to service), f. ἀνακαλεῖν to recall.] The Recalled; a name given to Julian the Apostate.

Anacœnosis (æ:nă,sinōᵘ·sis). 1589. [med.L. (Isidor), = communication, – Gr. ἀνακοίνωσις, f. ἀνακοινοῦν communicate; see -OSIS.] *Rhet.* A figure, by which the speaker applies to his hearers or opponents for their opinion upon the point in debate.

‖ **Anacoluthia** (æ:năkolⁱū·þiă). 1856. [mod. L. – Gr. ἀνακολουθία want of sequence; see next, -IA[1].] A want of grammatical sequence; the passing to a new construction before the original one is completed.

‖ **Anacoluthon** (æ:năkolⁱū·þǫn). Pl. **-a** (**-ons**). 1706. [late L. – Gr. ἀνακόλουθον, n. sing. of adj. 'lacking sequence', f. ἀν- AN- *pref.* 10 + ἀκόλουθος following.] *Gram.* An instance of anacoluthia. Hence **A:nacolu·thic** *a.* of or pertaining to anacoluthia; lacking grammatical sequence; **-ally** *adv.*

Anaconda (ænăkǫ·ndă). Also **-o.** 1768. [Unexpl. alt. of *anacandaia* (Ray, 1693), for Sinh. *henakandayā* whip-snake, f. *hena* lightning + *kanda* stem.] Orig. A large Ceylonese snake (? *Python reticulatus*, or *P. molurus* Gray); *spec.* applied (erron.) to a large S. Amer. Boa (*Eunectes murinus* Gray), called in Brazil *sucuriuba*; *loosely*, any large snake which crushes its prey.

Anacreontic (ănæ:kri,ǫ·ntik), *a.* 1656. [– late L. *anacreonticus*, f. Gr. Ἀνακρέων, -οντ-; see -IC.] Of, or after the manner of, the Greek poet Anacreon. As *sb.* [sc. *poem.*] 1656. Hence **Ana:creo·ntically** *adv.*

Anacrotism (ănæ·krŏtiz'm). 1879. [f. Gr. ἀνά up + κρότος striking, clapping + IC.] *Phys.* A secondary oscillation or notch in the upward portion of the curve obtained in a sphygmographic tracing. Hence **Anacro·tic** *a.* (More fully *anadicrotic.*)

‖ **Anacru·sis.** 1833. [mod.L. – Gr. ἀνάκρουσις prelude, f. ἀνακρούειν, f. ἀνά up, ANA- + κρούειν strike.] *Pros.* A syllable at the beginning of a verse, before the just rhythm.

Anadem (æ·nădėm). *poet.* 1604. [– L. *anadema* – Gr. ἀνάδημα head-band. Cf. DIADEM.] A wreath for the head; a chaplet, a garland.

Anadems of flowers DRAYTON.

† **A·nadesm.** 1658. [– Gr. ἀνάδεσμα snood, ἀνάδεσμος snood, bandage for woman's breast. Cf. late L. *anadesmus* (surgical) bandage.] A bandage for wounds.

Anadicro·tic, fuller f. ANACROTIC.

‖ **Anadiplosis** (æ:nă,diplōu·sis). 1589. [Gr. ἀναδίπλωσις repetition, f. ἀναδιπλοῦν to double; see -OSIS.] *Rhet.* Reduplication; the beginning of a sentence, line, or clause with the concluding, or any prominent, word of the preceding.

As thus: Comforte it is for man to haue a wife, Wife chast, and wise..*Anadiplosis* PUTTENHAM.

Anadrom (æ·nădrǫm). 1859. [– Fr. *anadrome* – Gr. ἀνάδρομος running up (of fish entering a river).] An anadrŏmous fish.

Anadromous (ănæ·drŏməs), *a.* 1753. [f. Gr. ἀνάδρομος (see prec.) + -OUS.] **1.** *Zool.* Ascending rivers to spawn. **2.** *Bot.* Of ferns: Having their lowest secondary branches on the anterior side of the pinnæ 1881.

‖ **Anæmia** (ănī·miă). 1836. [mod.L. – Gr. ἀναιμία, f. ἀν- AN- *pref.* 10 + αἷμα blood; see -IA[1].] *Path.* Lack of blood, or of red corpuscles in the blood. Hence **Anæ·mial, Anæ·mic** *adjs.* bloodless; of or pertaining to a.

Anæmo·trophy. 1860. [f. Gr. ἀν- AN- *pref.* 10 + αἷμα blood + -τροφία nourishment.] *Path.* Deficient nourishment of the blood.

Anære·tic. 1879. [– Gr. ἀναιρετικός destructive.] *Med.* An agent which tends to destroy tissue.

Anaerophyte (ănē·əro,fəit). 1876. [f. Gr. ἀν- AN- *pref.* 10 + ἀήρ air + φυτόν plant; see -PHYTE.] *Bot.* A plant which does not need a direct supply of air.

‖ **Anæsthesia** (ænėsþī·siă, ænīs-). 1721. [mod.L. – Gr. ἀναισθησία f. ἀν- AN- *pref.* 10 + αἴσθησις sensation.] Loss of feeling or sensation; insensibility. Also *fig.* var. † **Anæsthe·sis.** Hence **Anæsthe·siant** *adj.* producing a.; *sb.* an anæsthetic. **Anæ:sthesi·meter,** an instrument for measuring the amount of an anæsthetic administered.

Anæsthetic (ænėsþe·tik, -þī·tik), *a.* 1847. [f. Gr. ἀναίσθητος insensible; see prec., -IC.] **1.** Insensible 1848. **2.** *fig.* Unfeeling (*rare*) 1860. **3.** Producing, or connected with the production of, insensibility 1847. **4.** *sb.* [sc. *agent.*] 1848.

1. An a. state SIMPSON. **2.** A cold a. temperament 1860. **3.** An a. agent, operation SIMPSON. Hence **Anæsthe·tically** *adv.* as, or in the way of, an a.; so as to produce anæsthesia.

Anæsthetize (ăne·spĭtəiz, ănī·-), *v.* 1848. [f. as prec. + -IZE.] To render insensible. Hence **Anæsthe·tist,** one who administers anæsthetics. **Anæ:sthetiza·tion,** the process of rendering insensible; subjection to anæsthetics.

‖ **Anagennesis** (ænă,dʒenī·sis). 1879. [– Gr. ἀναγέννησις regeneration.] A reproduction of structure.

Anaglyph (æ·năglif). 1651. [– Gr. ἀναγλυφή work in low relief, f. ἀνά ANA- + γλύφειν carve.] **1.** An ornament worked in low relief. **2.** A superimposed stereogram 1909. Hence **Anagly·phic** *a.*; *sb.* (*pl.*) = ANAGLYPTICS.

Anaglyptic (ænăgli·ptik), *a.* 1656. [– late L. *anaglypticus* – Gr. ἀναγλυπτικός; see prec., -IC.] Of or pertaining to ANAGLYPHS. As *sb.* (*pl.*) The art of carving in low relief, chasing, embossing, etc. 1662.

Anaglyptograph (ænăgli·ptŏgraf). 1876. [f. Gr., ἀνάγλυπτος embossed; see prec., – GRAPH.] A machine for producing representations in relief, of coins, medals, etc. Hence **Anaglypto·graphy,** the art of engraving such representations.

‖ **Anagnorisis** (ænăgnǫ·risis). 1800. [Gr. ἀναγνώρισις recognition.] Recognition; the *dénouement* in a drama.

Anagnost (æ·năgnǫst). ? *Obs.* 1601. [– L. *anagnostes* – Gr. ἀναγνώστης reader.] A reader, a prelector; the reader of the lessons in church.

‖ **Anagoge** (ænăgōu·dʒi). 1706. [eccl.L. – Gr. ἀναγωγή (religious or ecstatic) elevation, mystical sense, f. ἀνάγειν lift up, f. ἀν- ANA- + ἄγειν lead.] † **1.** Spiritual elevation, esp. to understand mysteries –1751. **2.** Mystical or spiritual interpretation 1849. Hence **Anago·gic** *adj.* of or pertaining to a.; mystical, spiritualized; *sb.* one skilled in explaining the Scriptures; *sb. pl.* anagogic studies, or practices. **Anago·gical** *a.* of words, etc.: mystical, spiritual, allegorical; *catachr.* of persons. **Anago·gically** *adv.* with a hidden spiritual sense.

A·nagogy. 1519. [Analogical var. of prec., perh. after Fr. *anagogie* (XVI).] ANAGOGE.

Anagram (æ·năgræm). 1589. [– Fr. *anagramme* or mod.L. *anagramma*, f. Gr. ἀνά ANA- + γράμμα letter.] **1.** A transposition of the letters of a word, name, or phrase, whereby a new one is formed. † **2.** *loosely* or *fig.* A transposition, a mutation –1678.

1. This *Gustavus* (whose a. is *Augustus*) was a great Captain HOWELL.

† **A·nagram,** *v. rare.* 1630. [f. the sb.] To ANAGRAMMATIZE. *trans.* and *intr.* –1751.

Anagrammatic, -al (æ:nă,grămæ·tik, -ăl), *a.* 1605. [f. mod.L. *anagrammat-*, *anagramma* (see ANAGRAM) + -IC, + -AL[1]. Cf. Fr. *anagrammatique.*] Of or pertaining to an anagram, performed or produced by transposition of letters. Hence **A:nagramma·tically** *adv.*

Anagrammatize (ænăgræ·mătəiz), *v.* 1591. [– mod.L. *anagrammatizare* – Gr. ἀναγραμματίζειν transpose the letters of a word; cf. Fr. *anagrammatiser* (XVI) and see -IZE.] To transpose so as to form an ANAGRAM.

Others..a. it from *Eva* into *væ*, because (they say) she was the cause of all our woe 1637. Hence **Anagra·mmatism,** the formation of anagrams; var. † **Anagra·psis. Anagra·mmatist,** a maker (or book) of anagrams; var. † **A·nagrammist** (*rare*).

† **A·nagraph.** [– Gr. ἀναγραφή record, f. ἀνά ANA- + γραφή writing.] An inventory. (Dicts.)

Anal (ē[i]·năl), *a.* 1769. [– mod.L. *analis*; see ANUS, -AL[1]; cf. Fr. *anal.*] **1.** Of or pertaining to the anus 1836. **2.** Situated near the anus 1769.

Analcite, -ime (ănæ·lsəit, -əim). [orig. *analcime* (cf. Fr. *analcime*, G. *analzim*), f. Gr. ἀν- AN- *pref.* 10 + ἄλκιμος stout, brave; Dana substituted *analcite*, f. as prec. + ἀλκή strength + -ITE[1] 2 b.] *Min.* One of the Zeolite section of Hydrous Silicates, occurring in trap rocks.

Analects (æ·nălekts), *sb. pl.* 1623. [– L. *analecta* – Gr. ἀνάλεκτα (n. pl.) things gathered up, f. ἀναλέγειν, f. ἀνά ANA- + λέγειν gather. Freq. in L. form.] † **1.** Crumbs; gleanings –1721. **2.** Literary gleanings. (Usu. as a title.) 1658.

1. No trencher-a. 1643. **2.** The Confucian A. 1861.

‖ **Analemma** (ænăle·mă). 1652. [L. (Vitruvius) – Gr. ἀνάλημμα sun-dial.] † **1.** *orig.* A sort of sundial. (? in Eng.) **2.** An orthographical projection of the sphere, made on the plane of the meridian; used in dialling, etc. 1652. **3.** A gnomon or astrolabe, having the projection on a plate of wood or brass, with a horizon or cursor fitted to it, formerly used in solving problems 1667. **4.** A scale of the sun's daily declination drawn from tropic to tropic on artificial terrestrial globes 1832.

A·nalepsy. ? *Obs.* ME. [– med.L. *anale(m)psia* – Gr. ἀνάληψία (later -μψ-) taking up or back. In mod. use direct – Gr.] *Med.* **1.** Epilepsy arising from stomachic disorder. **2.** The support given in the treatment of a fractured limb 1860.

Analeptic (ænăle·ptik), *a.* 1661. [– late L. *anale(m)pticus* – Gr. ἀναληπτικός restorative; see -IC. Cf. Fr. *analeptique* (XVI).] *Med.* Restorative, strengthening. As *sb.* [sc. *medicine* or *aliment.*] 1671. var. † **Anale·ptical.**

‖ **Analgesia** (ænăldʒī·siă). 1706. [mod.L. – Gr. ἀναλγησία, painlessness.] *Med.* Insensibility to pain; opp. to *anæsthesia*, total insensibility. Hence **Analge·sic** *a.* tending to remove pain; *sb.* [sc. *drug.*] (Better *analgetic.*)

Anallagmatic (æ:nælæ̆gmæ·tik), *a.* 1869. [f. Gr. ἀν- AN- *pref.* 10 + ἄλλαγμα, -ματ- change + -IC.] *Math.* Not changed in form by inversion, as the sphere.

† **Ana·logal,** *a.* 1631. [f. L. *analogus* + -AL[1]; see ANALOGOUS.] = ANALOGOUS. (Freq. in 17th c.)

Analogic (ænălǫ·dʒik), *a.* 1677. [– Fr. *analogique* or L. *analogicus* – Gr. ἀναλογικός; see ANALOGUE, -IC.] Of or belonging to, or † constituted by, analogy.

Analogical (ænălǫ·dʒikăl), *a.* 1570. [f. as prec. + -AL[1].] † **1.** *Math.* Proportional 1570. **2.** Of the nature of analogy 1609. **3.** Expressing an analogy, metonymic; as the *apple* of the eye 1623. † **4.** Figurative 1638. **5.** = ANALOGIC 1854. **6.** = ANALOGOUS (*arch.*) 1644.

2. A. or inductive reasoning PRICE. **3.** When a country which has sent out colonies is termed the mother country, the expression is a. MILL. Hence **Analo·gically** *adv.* **Analo·gicalness,** the quality of being a.; fitness for illustration. *rare.*

† **Ana·logism.** *rare.* 1656. [– Gr. ἀναλογισμός line of reasoning, proportionate calculation, f. ἀναλογίζεσθαι reckon up.] **1.** *Math.* The constitution of a proportion –1667. **2.** An argument from cause to effect; *a priori* reasoning 1656. **3.** *Med.* Diagnosis by analogy –1753.

Analogize (ănæ·lŏdʒəiz), *v.* 1655. [– Gr. ἀναλογίζεσθαι; see prec., -IZE; in later use f. ANALOGY; cf. obs. Fr. *analogiser.*] **1.** *intr.* To employ analogy; *orig.* to reason by proportion. **2.** *trans.* To figure 1743; to make, or show to be, analogous 1802. **3.** *intr.* (for *refl.*) To be in general harmony 1733.

3. Exceptions..a. with special providences in the mundane order F. HALL. Hence **Ana·logist,** one who seeks, or argues from, analogies. **Ana:logi·stic** *a.* of or pertaining to (linguistic) analogists. **Ana·logizing** *vbl. sb.* the perception of analogies, analogical reasoning.

‖ **Ana·logon.** Pl. **-a.** 1810. [irreg. subst. use of n. sing. of Gr. ἀνάλογος adj. proportionate, conformable.] = ANALOGUE.

Analogous (ănæ·lŏgəs), *a.* 1646. [f. L. *analogus* (Varro) – Gr. ἀνάλογος (see prec.) + -OUS.] **1.** Having analogy; similar in attributes, circumstances, relations, or uses; *esp.* in *Nat. Hist.* 1664. Const. *to.* **2.** = ANALOGICAL 3 (*rare*) 1671.

1. We are in a state of trial..a. or like to our moral and religious trial BUTLER. The bristles and quils in other Animals..are a. to the hairs in a man 1664. **2.** Nouns are either Univocal, Equivocal, or A. ABP. THOMSON. Hence **Ana·logous-ly** *adv.*, **-ness.**

Analogue (æ·nălǫg). 1826. [– Fr. *analogue* – Gr. ἀνάλογον ANALOGON.] **1.** An analogous word or thing 1837. **2.** *esp.* in *Nat. Hist.* **a.** A part of an animal or plant representative of a different part in another. Strictly said of organs of different origin. 1826. **b.** A species or tribe in one region, or at one period, which represents a different species or tribe elsewhere or at a different epoch 1830. **c.** A representative in a different class or group 1835.

1. 'Renard the Fox' has its a. among the Kafirs SAYCE. **2.** The fossil shells with their recent analogues LYELL. The fishes, marine analogues of flying creatures G. ALLEN.

Analogy (ănæ·lŏdʒi). 1536. [– Fr. *analogie* or L. *analogia* (Varro) – Gr. ἀναλογία equality of ratios, proportion (orig. math.), f. ἀνάλογος; see ANALOGON.] **1.** *Math.* Proportion; agreement of ratios 1557; hence, † due proportion –1774. **2.** Equivalency or likeness of relations. Const. *to, with, between.* 1550. **3.** *more vaguely,* Similarity 1605. † **4.** A simile or similitude –1651. **5.** = ANALOGUE 1646. **6.** *Logic.* **a.** Resemblance of relations or attributes as a ground of reasoning. **b.** Presumptive reasoning based on the assumption that if things have some similar attributes, their other attributes will be similar. 1602. **7.** *Language.* Similarity of formative or constructive processes. (*Form-association* is the term now used where the *forms* only of words are considered.) 1659. **8.** *Nat. Hist.* Resemblance of form or function without identity of essence 1814.

2. Which three parts active [experimental, philosophical, magical] have a correspondence and a. with the three parts speculative BACON. **3.** Places, Persons..which bear a Resemblance, or at least some remote A., with what we find represented

ADDISON. 5. The child is the a. of a people yet in childhood LYTTON. 6. A. is of weight..towards determining our Judgment BUTLER. A., however, is not proof, but illustration STUBBS.

† **A·nalyse,** *sb.* 1638. [– Fr. *analyse* – mod.L. *analysis* ANALYSIS.] = ANALYSIS –1730.

Analyse, -ze (æ·nălaiz), *v.* 1601. [perh. orig. f. as prec.; later infl. by Fr. *analyser* (XVIII) = *faire l'analyse*; see ANALYSIS.] *Prim. signification,* To take to pieces. To make an ANALYSIS of; to separate, distinguish, or ascertain the elements of anything complex, as a material collection, chemical compound, light, sound, a miscellaneous list, account, or statement, a sentence, phrase, word, conception, feeling, action, process, etc.

To a. the process of inference MILL, the sensations of pleasure and pain DARWIN, the nature of Jacobinism COLERIDGE, limestone SMEATON, samples of water 1888, a poem MOORE, lines into syllables JOHNSON, light BREWSTER. Hence **A·naly:sable, -zable** *a.* capable of being analysed. **A:nalysa·tion, -za·tion,** analysis. **A·nalysed, -zed** *ppl. a.* resolved or reduced to its elements.

Analyser, -zer (æ·nălaizər). 1627. [f. prec. + -ER¹.] **1.** He who or that which analyses. **2.** In the polariscope, the part which exhibits the fact that the light has been polarized 1863.

1. Bacon—the great a. of common sense 1869.

Analysis (ănæ·lisis). Pl. **analyses** (-īz). 1581. [– med.L. *analysis* – Gr. ἀνάλυσις, f. ἀναλύειν unloose, f. ἀνά up, back + λύειν to loose.] **1.** The resolution of anything complex into its simple elements, opp. to *synthesis*; the exact determination of its components. *Obs.* of things material. **2.** *concr.* A tabular statement, a synopsis or conspectus, of the results of the above process 1668. Specifically. **3.** *Chem.* The resolution of a chemical compound into its *proximate* or *ultimate* elements; the determination of its elements, or of the foreign substances which it may contain 1655. **4.** *Opt.* The resolution of light into its prismatic constituents 1831. **5.** *Literature.* The critical examination of any production, so as to exhibit its elements in simple form 1644. **6.** *Gram.* The ascertainment of the elements composing a sentence, or any part of it 1612. **7.** *Math. Ancient a.*: the proving of a proposition by resolving it into simpler propositions already proved or admitted. *Modern a.*: the resolving of problems by reducing them to equations. 1656. **8.** *Logic.* The tracing of things to their sources; the discovery of general principles underlying concrete phenomena 1680.

1. A. is not the business of the Poet. His office is to portray, not to dissect. MACAULAY. **2.** A. of.. In Memoriam 1862. **3.** *Qualitative analysis* determines *what* the elements of a chemical compound are, *quantitative* in what quantity each is present, by weight (*gravimetrical*) or by volume (*volumetrical*) O.E.D. **5.** Such, in brief a., was the memorable Declaration of Elizabeth MOTLEY. **6.** *Logical, Syntactic, or Sentence Analysis*: the resolution of the sentence into elements having definite relations to the whole sentence and to each other, as *subject* and *predicate* with their respective *enlargements*. **8.** A. finds out causes by their effects WATTS.

Analyst (æ·nălist). 1656. [– Fr. *analyste,* f. *analyser,* by assoc. w. pairs in *-iser, -iste* (-IZE, -IST).] One who makes an ANALYSIS, *esp.* in *Math.* 1656; and *Chem.* (the common use now) 1800.

Analytic (ænăli·tik), *a.* 1590. [– late L. *analyticus* – Gr. ἀναλυτικός, f. ἀναλύειν; see ANALAYSIS, -IC.] **A.** *adj.* **1.** Of, pertaining to, or in accordance with ANALYSIS; resolving compounds into their elements 1601. **2.** Addicted to analysis; analytical 1805.

B. *sb.* mostly *pl.* **analytics,** tr. L. *analytica,* – Gr. ἀναλυτικά, adj. pl. neut. used subst. as title of Aristotle's treatises on Logic. **1.** *gen.* The science and art of ANALYSIS 1641. **2.** *spec.* That part of Logic which treats of analysis 1590; †the application of Algebra to geometry –1751.

Analy·tical, *a.* 1525. [f. as prec. + -AL¹; see -ICAL.] **1.** Of or pertaining to analytics; employing the analytic method; *lang.* expressing the elements of a proposition or complex notion by distinct words, instead of combining several into one word, as *with a sword* for *gladio* 1873. **2.** = ANALYTIC *a.* 1. 1656. Hence **Analy·tically** *adv.*

‖ **Anamnesis** (ænæmnī·sis). 1657. [Gr. ἀνάμνησις remembrance.] The recalling of things past; reminiscence.

The doctrine of A., in Plato, according to which the soul had pre-existed in a purer state, and there gained its ideas 1876. Hence **Anamne·stic** *a.* recalling to mind; aiding the memory; †*sb.* [sc. *medicine* or *symptom.*]

Anamorphism (ænămǭ·ɹfiz'm). 1836. [f. Gr. ἀνά up + μορφή form + -ISM.] **1.** Distorted projection. **2.** Progression from a lower to a higher type 1852. Hence **Anamo·rphous** *a.* distorted (*rare*).

Anamorphose (ænămǭ·ɹfoᵘs, -ōs), *v. rare.* [f. next; cf. METAMORPHOSE.] To represent by ANAMORPHOSIS.

Anamorphosis (ænămǭ·ɹfŏsis). 1727. [– Gr. ἀναμόρφωσις transformation, f. ἀνά ANA- + μορφοῦν to change; see -OSIS.] **1.** A distorted projection or drawing of anything, which, when viewed from a particular point, or by reflection from a suitable mirror, appears regular and properly proportioned; a deformation. **2.** *Bot.* Abnormal transformation, due to degeneration or change in the habit of a plant 1830. **3.** = ANAMORPHISM 2. 1852.

Anan, obs. f. ANON.

Anan (ănæ·n), *int. Obs.* or *dial.* 1553. Same wd. as ANON *adv.* orig. in answer to a call, 'Presently,' and later = 'I beg your pardon! Sir? Eh?' See 1 *Hen. IV,* II. iv. 71.

Ananas (ănēⁱ·năs, -ā·năs). Also **anana.** 1613. [– Fr. *ananàs* or Sp. *ananás* – Guarani *anănā.*] **1.** The pineapple plant (*Ananassa sativa*) or fruit. **2.** An allied West Indian fruit (*Bromelia pinguin*).

Anandrious (ǣnæ·ndri,əs), *a.* 1879. [f. Gr. ἀνανδρία want of virility + -OUS. Cf. next.] *Med.* Without virility; impotent.

Anandrous (ǣnæ·ndrəs), *a.* 1847. [f. Gr. ἄνανδρος without males (f. ἀν- AN- *pref.* 10 + ἀνήρ, ἀνδρ- male) + -OUS.] *Bot.* Having no stamens, as the females of diœcious, or the female flowers of monœcious plants.

Ana·ntherous, *a.* 1866. [f. AN- *pref.* 10 + ANTHER + -OUS.] *Bot.* Destitute of anthers. var. **Ana·ntherate.**

Ana·nthous, *a.* 1866. [– Gr. ἀνανθής flowerless (f. ἀν- AN- *pref.* 10 + ἄνθος flower) + -OUS.] *Bot.* Flowerless.

Ana·nthropism. [f. Gr. ἀν- AN- *pref.* 10 + ἄνθρωπος human being + -ISM.] A lack of humanity. SEELEY.

Ananym (æ·nănim). *rare.* 1867. [Loosely f. Gr. ἀνά + ὄνυμα, ANONYM having another meaning.] The real name written backwards.

Anapæst (æ·năpest, -pīst). 1678. [– L. *anapæstus* – Gr. ἀνάπαιστος reversed, f. ἀνά ANA- + παίειν to strike.] *Pros.* **1.** A reversed dactyl, a metrical foot, consisting of two short syllables followed by a long one. **2.** A verse composed of, or containing, such feet 1846.

1. For your *anapestus*..ye haue..*mănĭfōld mōnĭlĕsse,* etc. PUTTENHAM.

Anapæstic (ænăpe·stik, -ī·stik), *a.* 1699. [– late L. – Gr.; see prec., -IC.] Composed of anapæsts. As *sb.* Verses containing anapæstic feet 1699.

sb. Where an a. is terminated by a trochee BENTLEY. Hence **Anapæ·stical** *a.* **Anapæ·stically** *adv.* in a. rhythm (*rare*).

Anapa·ganize, *v. rare.* [f. ANA- + PAGANIZE.] To make pagan again. SOUTHEY.

Anapeiratic (æ:năpairæ·tik), *a.* 1879. [irreg. f. Gr. ἀναπειρᾶσθαι.] *Path.* Resulting from the habitual use of certain muscles for a long time.

† **A-na·pes** 1575. In *Fustian a napes* = o Napes, of Naples –1627.

‖ **Anaphora** (ănæ·fŏră). 1589. [L. – Gr. ἀναφορά repetition, f. ἀνα- ANA- + φέρειν carry.] *Rhet.* The repetition of the same word or phrase in several successive clauses.

Anaphrodisiac (ǣn,æ:frodi·ziăk), *a.* 1823. [f. Gr. ἀν- AN- *pref.* 10 + ἀφροδισιακός venereal.] That diminishes sexual appetite. As *sb.* [sc. *drug.*] An antaphrodisiac 1865.

Anaphroditic (ǣn,æ:frodi·tik), *a.* 1879. [f. Gr. ἀναφρόδιτος without love + -IC.] *Biol.* Developed without concourse of sexes.

Anaphroditous (ǣn,æ:frodai·təs), *a.* 1879. [f. as prec. + -OUS.] Without sexual appetite.

Anaplasty (æ·năplasti). 1879. [– Fr. *anaplastie,* f. Gr. ἀνάπλαστος, ppl. adj. f. ἀναπλάσσειν form anew; see -Y³.] *Surg.* Reparation of external lesions by the use of adjacent healthy tissue. Hence **Anapla·stic** *a.* of or pertaining to a.

‖ **Anaplerosis** (æ:năplirōᵘ·sis). 1680. [Gr. ἀναπλήρωσις, f. ἀναπληροῦν fill up; see -OSIS.] The filling up of a deficiency. Hence **A:naplero·tic** *a.* tending to supply deficiencies of tissue; *sb.* (in *pl.*) an anaplerotic substance.

Anapnograph (ănæ·pnŏgraf). 1870. [f. Gr. ἀναπνοή respiration; see -GRAPH.] An instrument for registering the movements and amount of expiration and inspiration.

Anapno·ic, *a.* 1879. [f. as prec. + -IC.] Pertaining to respiration.

Anapnometer (ænăpnǫ·mĭtəɹ). 1860. [f. as prec. + -METER.] A spirometer.

Anapodeictic (ǣn,æ:podai·ktik), *a. rare.* [f. Gr. ἀν- AN- *pref.* 10 + ἀποδεικτικός demonstrable.] Undemonstrable.

Anapophysis (ænăpǫ·fisis). 1854. [f. Gr. ἀνά back + ἀπόφυσις offshoot.] *Phys.* A small bony process, projecting backward from the neural arch of the vertebræ. Hence **A:napophy·sial,** of or pertaining to an a.

Anaptotic (ænăptǫ·tik), *a.* 1850. [f. Gr. ἀνά again + ἄπτωτος indeclinable + -IC. Cf. APTOTIC.] Falling back from inflection, as *a. languages.*

Anarch (æ·năɹk). 1667. [– Gr. ἄναρχος without a chief, f. ἀν- AN- *pref.* 10; see -ARCH.] An author of anarchy; a leader of revolt. As *adj.* Without government; anarchical (*rare*) 1822.

The A. old MILT. *P.L.* II. 988. Lo! the great Anarch's ancient reign restor'd POPE. Hence **Ana·rchal** *a.* (*rare*) = ANARCH *a.*

Anarchic (ănā·ɹkik), *a.* 1790. [f. as prec. + -IC, after Gr. ἀρχικός; cf. Fr. *anarchique.*] Of or belonging to anarchy; lawless.

Anarchical (ănā·ɹkikăl), *a.* 1597. [f. as prec. + -ICAL.] **1.** = prec. **2.** Connected with, tending to, or involving anarchy 1649.

1. That..a. little commonwealth MOTLEY. **2.** A. doctrines 1797, efforts 1847. var. **Ana·rchial.** Hence **Ana·rchically** *adv.*

Anarchism (æ·năɹkiz'm). *rare.* 1642. [f. as prec. + -ISM; in more recent use dependent on Fr. *anarchisme.*] The principles or practice of anarchy, or anarchists.

Anarchist (æ·năɹkist). 1678. [f. as prec. + -IST; in more recent use dependent on Fr. *anarchiste* (XVIII).] One who admits of no ruling power; an advocate of anarchy; one who upsets settled order. quasi-*adj.* 1812.

Anarchize (æ·năɹkaiz), *v.* 1800. [f. as prec. + -IZE.] To reduce to anarchy; to destroy the settled order of.

Anarchy (æ·năɹki). 1539. [– med.L. *anarchia* – Gr. ἀναρχία, f. ἄναρχος without a chief, f. ἀν- AN- *pref.* 10 + ἀρχός leader. So Fr. *anarchie.*] **1.** Absence of government; a state of lawlessness due to the absence or inefficiency of the supreme power; political disorder. **2.** *transf.* Absence or non-recognition of authority in any sphere 1667; moral or intellectual disorder 1656.

1. This unleful lyberty or lycence of the multytude is called an Anarchie TAVERNER. A Polity without an Head..would..be..Anarchy HY. MORE. **2.** The waste Wide Anarchie of Chaos MILT. *P.L.* X. 283. An a. of thought,—a perpetuity of mental revolutions W. GROVE. Hence **Ana·rchial** *a.*

† **Ana·reta.** 1647. [incorr. f. *anæreta,* latinized f. Gr. ἀναιρέτης destroyer, murderer.] *Astrol.* The planet that destroys life –1819.

Anarthrous (ǣnā·ɹþrəs), *a.* 1808. [f. Gr. ἀν- AN- *pref.* 10 + ἄρθρον joint, definite article + -OUS.] **1.** Of Greek sbs.: Used without the article. **2.** *Phys.* Jointless; or apparently so 1879. Hence **Ana·rthrously** *adv.* without the (Gr.) article. **Ana·rthrousness.**

Anasarca (ænăsā·ɹkă). ME. [– med.L. *anasarc(h)a* – Gr. ἀνάσαρξ adj. (Galen) = ἀνὰ σάρκα (ἀνά ANA-, σάρξ flesh).] *Path.* A dropsical affection of the subcutaneous cellular tissue of a limb, etc. Also *transf.* and *fig.*

1807. Hence **Anasa·rcous** *a.* of the nature or showing signs of a.

Anasei·smic, *a.* 1881. [f. Gr. ἀνά up + σεισμός earthquake + -IC.] Of an earthquake shock: Moving vertically.

† **Anasta·ltic,** *a.* 1775. [– Gr. ἀνασταλτικός tending to check.] Styptic. As *sb.* Restringent medicines.

Anastatic (ænăstæ·tik), *a.* 1849. [f. Gr. ἀνάστατος, ppl. formation on ἀνιστάναι set up.] Of the nature of revival; *spec.* of a printing process, in which facsimiles are produced by a transfer process from zinc plates.

Anastomose (ănæ·stŏmōᵘz), *v.* 1697. [– Fr. *anastomoser* (XVIII), f. *anastomose* ANASTOMOSIS.] † *trans.* To connect by ANASTOMOSIS. *intr.* To inosculate. Said of blood-vessels, rivers, branches of trees, etc. Hence **Ana·stomosed** *ppl. a.* connected by anastomosis. **Ana·stomosing** *vbl. sb.* = ANASTOMOSIS; *ppl. a.* inosculating; var. **Anastomo·sant.**

‖ **Anastomosis** (anæ:stŏmōᵘ·sis). Pl. **-o·ses.** 1615. [mod.L. – Gr. ἀναστόμωσις, f. ἀναστομοῦν furnish with a mouth or outlet f. ἀνά ANA- + στόμα mouth; see -OSIS.] Intercommunication between two vessels, channels, or branches, by a connecting cross branch. Orig. of the cross connections between the arteries and veins, etc.; now of those of any branching system.

The African name..Tanganyika, signifying an a., or a meeting-place R. BURTON.

Anastomotic (ănæ·stŏmǫ·tik). 1657. [– Gr. ἀναστομωτικός proper for opening; see ANASTOMOSIS, -OTIC. In sense 2 f. directly on ANASTOMOSIS.] † **1.** (As in L.) Of medicines: Designed to open the mouths of vessels. (Occ. also, *anastomatic.*) –1721. **2.** Pertaining to or forming ANASTOMOSIS 1836.

‖ **Anastrophe** (anæ·strŏfi). 1577. [Gr. ἀναστροφή turning back, f. ἀνά back + στρέφειν turn. Cf. med.L. *anastrophe* (IX).] *Rhet.* Inversion or unusual order of words or clauses, as 'All Italy about I went'.

Anatase (æ·nătēⁱs). 1843. [– Fr. *anatase* – Gr. ἀνάτασις extension, f. ἀνά ANA- + τείνειν stretch.] *Min.* Haüy's name for OCTAHEDRITE.

† **A·nathem,** *sb.* 1555. [– Fr. *anathème* or eccl.L. *anathema* (next).] **1.** = ANATHEMA 1. *rare.* **2.** = ANATHEMA 2. –1648.

Anathema (ănæ·þĭmă). Pl. **anathemas;** also, in sense 3, **anathe·mata.** 1526. [– eccl.L. *anathema* excommunicated person, sentence of excommunication – Gr. ἀνάθεμα, orig. 'a thing devoted', later 'an accursed thing' (see *Rom.* 9:3), orig. var. of ἀνάθημα votive offering, f. ἀνατιθέναι set up.] **1.** Anything accursed, or consigned to damnation. Also quasi-*adj.* **2.** The formal act, or formula, of consigning to damnation; *spec.* the great curse of the Church, excommunicating a person; or denouncing a doctrine or practice as damnable 1590. Hence *gen.*, Any imprecation 1691. **3.** [= ἀνάθημα, better pron. ænăþī·mă.] A thing devoted to divine use 1581.

1. Paul wished to become a. himself, so he could thereby save his brethren A. TUCKER. **2.** The Pope ..has condemned the slave trade—but no.. heed is paid to his a. GLADSTONE. 'Confound the man!' was my mental a. LYTTON. Hence **A:nathema·tic** *a.* of the nature of, or pertaining to, an offering (*rare*). † **Ana:thema·tical** *a.* of the nature of an a.; *sb.* = ANATHEMA. † **Ana·thematism,** an ecclesiastical denunciation.

Anathema Maranatha (mærănēⁱ·þă). 1526. [Gr. ἀνάθεμα; Μαρὰν ἀθά = Aramaic *mᵉran ᵃthā* 'the Lord has come'. The pronunc. should be (măræ:n,ăthā).] Taken erron. as a portentously intensified *Anathema. Maran atha* forms a distinct sentence.

Let him be Anathema. Maranatha. *1 Cor.* 16:22.

Anathematize (ănæ·þĭmătəiz), *v.* 1566. [– (O)Fr. *anathématiser* – eccl.L. *anathematizare* – Gr. ἀναθεματίζειν, f. ἀνάθεμα, -ματ- ANATHEMA; see -IZE.] **1.** *trans.* To pronounce an anathema against (see ANATHEMA 2). **2.** *absol.* To curse 1837. var. **Ana·themize.** Hence **Ana:thematiza·tion,** the action of anathematizing; var. † **Ana:themiza·tion. Ana·themati:zer.**

Anatheme (æ·năþīm). 1654. [Anglicized f. ANATHEMA in sense 3.] An offering dedicated to God.

† **Anati·ferous,** *a. rare.* 1646. [f. mod.L. *anatiferus* (f. L. *anas, -at-* duck + *-ferus* producing) + -OUS; see -FEROUS.] Producing ducks or geese; *i.e.* producing barnacles, once supposed to grow on trees, and dropping off into water, to turn to Tree-geese (Pennant II. 238).

Anatocism (ănæ·tŏsiz'm). *arch.* 1656. [– L. *anatocismus* (Cicero) – Gr. ἀνατοκισμός compound interest, f. τόκος interest.] Compound interest.

Anatomic, -al (ænătǫ·mik, -ăl), *a.* 1586. [– Fr. *anatomique* or late L. *anatomicus*; see ANATOMY, -IC, -ICAL.] Of or pertaining to the study or practice of anatomy. **2.** Of anatomy; structural; also *transf.* 1627. Hence **Anato·mically** *adv.*

Anato·mico-, comb. form of ANATOMIC.

Ana·tomiless, *a. rare.* [f. ANATOMY + -LESS.] Devoid of anatomy. RUSKIN.

Anatomism (ănæ·tŏmiz'm). 1860. [– Fr. *anatomisme*, f. *anatomie* ANATOMY; see -ISM.] **1.** Analysis or display of anatomic structure 1870. **2.** The doctrine that the phenomena of life are explained by the anatomical structure of living organisms. (Cf. ANIMISM.) 1860.

Anatomist (ănæ·tŏmist). 1569. [– Fr. *anatomiste* or med.L. **anatomista*, f. *anatomizare*; see ANATOMY, -IST.] **1.** One skilled in (*esp.* human) anatomy 1594. Also *fig.*

Anatomize (ănæ·tŏməiz), *v.* 1541. [– Fr. *anatomiser* or med.L. *anatomizare*; see ANATOMY, -IZE.] **1.** To dissect; to cut up an animal or vegetable body in order to lay open the position, structure, and relations of its various parts. Also *absol.* 1870. **2.** *fig.* To lay open minutely; to analyze 1553

1. A. me into atomies 1596. **2.** To a. wit GREENE, a town or country HOWELL, the doctrine of free government BURKE. Hence **Ana:tomiza·tion,** dissection; † anatomic structure. **Ana·tomi:zer.**

Anatomy (ănæ·tŏmi). 1528. [–(O)Fr. *anatomie* – late L. *anatomia* – Gr. ἀνατομία, f. ἀνά up, ANA- + -τομία -TOMY.] **1.** The artificial separation of the parts of an organized body, in order to discover their position, structure, and economy; dissection 1541; † with *quick, live*: Vivisection –1668. † **2.** *concr.* A body, or part, anatomized; a subject for dissection –1751. **3.** A model of the body, as dissected 1727. **4.** *pop.* A skeleton 1594; a skeleton with the skin left, a mummy 1586; a living being reduced to skin and bone 1590; also *transf.* and *fig.* 1605. Cf. ATOMY. **5.** The bodily frame 1592. **6.** The science of the structure of organized bodies, divided into *Animal A.* or *Zootomy, Vegetable, Human,* and *Comparative* 1541; a treatise on the science 1528. **7.** Anatomical structure 1579. **8.** Detailed examination or analysis 1569. † **9.** Chemical analysis –1686.

2. They must ha' dissected, and made an Anatomie o' me B. JONS. **4.** Death..Thou fell A. SHAKS. *John* III. iv. 40. More like an a. than a living person SOUTHEY. One Pinch: a hungry leane-fac'd Villain, A meere Anatomie *Com. Err.* v. 238. **5.** In what vile part of this Anatomie Doth my name lodge *Rom. & Jul.* III. iii. 106. **8.** The Anatomy of Melancholy: what it is [etc.] BURTON (*title*). var. † **A·natome** (3 syll.).

Anatopism (ănæ·tŏpiz'm). *rare.* 1812. [f. Gr. ἀνά·ANA- + τόπος place + -ISM.] A putting of a thing out of its proper place.

Anatreptic (ænătre·ptik), *a.* 1655. [f. Gr. ἀνατρεπτικός overturning, f. ἀνά ANA- + τρέπειν turn; see -IC.] Overturning; a subdivision of Platonic Discourse.

Anatripso·logy. 1839. [f. Gr. ἀνάτριψις (see next) + -LOGY.] *Med.* The doctrine of the use of friction.

Anatri·ptic, *a.* 1879. [f. Gr. ἀνάτριπτος (f. ἀνατρίβειν rub up) + -IC.] *Med.* Belonging to, or characterized by, friction, as a medicine.

† **Anatron.** 1706. [– Sp. † *anatrón* – Arab. *an-naṭrūn*, i.e. *an* = AL-² + *naṭrūn* NATRON.] Native carbonate of soda; see NATRON.

Anatropous (ănæ·trŏpəs), *a.* 1847. [f. mod.L. *anatropus* (f. Gr. ἀνά + –τροπος, f. τρέπειν turn) + -OUS.] *Bot.* Having its nucleus inverted, opp. to *orthotropous*: said of the ovule of phanerogamous plants. var. **Ana·tropal.**

Anatta, anatto (ănæ·tă, *-o*). Also **annatto, annotto.** 1682. [– native name.] An orange-red dye, procured in Central America from the pulp surrounding the seeds of the *Bixa orellana*; used to colour cheese, etc.

† **Anau·nter.** Still *dial.* ME. [= AN *prep.* + *aunter*, early f. ADVENTURE.] In peril; lest.

Anaxagorean (ænæ̆ksæ:gŏrī·ăn), *a.* 1586. [f. L. *Anaxagoras* + -EAN.] Of or pertaining to Anaxagoras, a Greek philosopher who taught that matter was eternal, but was combined into bodies by a supreme intelligence. Also as *sb.*

Anaxa·gorize, *v.* [f. as prec. + -IZE.] To hold the principles of Anaxagoras. CUDWORTH.

Anaxima·ndrian, *a.* 1678. [f. *Anaximander* + -IAN.] Adhering to the tenets of Anaximander. Also as *sb.*

Anbury, amb- (æ·nbəri, æ·m-). 1598. [perh. f. *ang-* in OE. *angnæġl* AGNAIL, *angseta* carbuncle, pimple + BERRY *sb.*¹ in the sense of red mark or pustule.] **1.** A soft tumour or spongy wart on horses and oxen. **2.** A diseased affection of the roots of turnips, etc.; called also 'finger and toe' 1750.

-ance, *suffix*; – Fr. *-ance* :– L. *-antia, -ēntia, -entia.* Since 1500 various words orig. in *-ance* from Fr. have been altered back to *-ence* after L., and more recent words have taken *-ence* or *-ance* according to the L. vowel. Hence much inconsistency, as in *dependance, -dence, resistance, subsistence.* As a living formative *-ance* has occas. been added to native vbs., as *forbear-ance, ridd-ance,* etc.

Ancestor (æ·nsĕstəɹ). [ME. *auncetre, ancestre* – OFr. *ancestre* (mod. *ancêtre*):– L. *antecessor* predecessor, f. *antecēdere* precede, f. *ante* before + *cēdere* go (cf. CEDE *v.*). ME. *ancestre* is the antecedent of the present form through *ancestour*, by assim. to *-tour, -tor*; see -OR 2.] **1.** One from whom a person is descended, either by the father or mother; a forefather (usu. one more remote than a grandfather). Also of animals, and *fig.* **2.** *Biol.* An organized being of a lower type, whence others of a later type are inferred to have been developed 1863.

1. Tyme, that eldith our auncessours ME. When I am sleeping with my Ancestors 2 *Hen. IV,* IV. iv. 61. *fig.* Eldest Night and Chaos, ancestors of Nature MILT. *P.L.* II. 894. The institutions, the wisdom, of our ancestors BURKE. **2.** The a. of the African elephant RAMSAY. Hence **Ancesto·rial** *a.* = ANCESTRAL. **Ancesto·rially** *adv.* by inheritance from one's ancestors.

Ancestral (æ̆nse·străl), *a.* 1523. [Earlier *a(u)ncestrel* – OFr. *ancestrel*, mod. *ancestral*, to which the mod.Eng. sp. conforms; see ANCESTOR, -AL¹.] **1.** Of, belonging to, or inherited from ancestors 1579; *esp.* in *Law* 1523. **2.** *Biol.* Of, pertaining to, or constituting the original, or an earlier, type (see ANCESTOR 2) 1862. var. **Ance·strial** (*rare*).

Ancestress (æ·nsĕstrĕs). 1580. [f. ANCESTOR + -ESS¹.] A female ancestor.

Ancestry (æ·nsĕstri). ME. [Eng. modification (due to *ancestre*) of OFr. *ancesserie*; see ANCESTOR, -Y³, -RY.] **1.** The relation or condition of ancestors; progenitorship; *hence*, distinguished or ancient descent. **2.** *collect.* The line or body of ancestors. (Cf. *tenantry*, etc.) ME.

1. Som worthy blood of Auncetrye CHAUCER. A son, whose Death disgraced his a. DRYDEN. **2.** Our a., a gallant Christian race COWPER.

Anchithere (æ·ŋkiþīᵊɹ). 1879. [– mod.L. *anchitherium*, f. Gr. ἄγχι near + θηρίον wild beast.] *Palæont.* A fossil Eocene and Miocene animal having three toes on each foot; regarded as an ancestor of the horse.

Anchoic (æ̆ŋkōᵘ·ik), *a.* 1863. [f. Gr. ἄγχειν throttle, suffocate + -IC.] *Chem.* In *Anchoic acid*: a dibasic acid, $C_9H_{16}O_4$, emitting suffocating fumes.

Anchor (æ·ŋkəɹ), *sb.*¹ [OE. *ancor, -er, -ra* (= OFris., (M)LG., (M)Du. *anker*, late OHG. *anchar* (G. *anker*), ON. *akkeri*), – L. *ancora* – Gr. ἄγκυρα. In ME. reinforced by (O)Fr. *ancre*. The present sp. follows the erron. L. *anchora*.] **1.** An appliance for holding a ship, etc., fixed in a particular place, by mooring it to the bottom of the sea or river; a heavy iron, composed of a long shank, with a ring at one end for the cable, and at the other two arms or flukes, tending upwards, with barbs on each side. **2.** *fig.* That which gives stability or security ME. **3.** *transf.* Any contrivance or instrument which holds fast or gives security; also, an anchor-shaped appendage, as the spicules on Holothuroids 1855. **4.** *Arch.* An ornament shaped like an anchor or arrow-head; used with the egg ornament 1663.

The largest anchor is the SHEET-anchor; next are the BOWER-anchors; the smallest is the KEDGE-anchor.

1. The a. is foul, that is, the Cable has got about the Fluke 1692. Anchors of rusty fluke TENNYSON. **2.** Which hope we haue as an anker of the soule *Heb.* 6:19. Say Warwicke was our A.: what of that? 3 *Hen. VI*, v. iv. 13. This sheet-anchor of happiness, Religion CHATHAM.

Phrases (from sense 1). *lit. and fig.* **1. At (an, the,** *obs.*) **anchor,** in OE. *on ancre*: anchored. **2. To come to (an) anchor:** = ANCHOR *v.* 2, 4. **3. To cast anchor:** to drop the a.; *hence*, to take up a position. Also of the ship: *she* cast a. **4. To weigh anchor:** to take up the a., so as to sail away. **5. The anchor comes home:** *i.e.* is dragged from its hold. So, a ship *drags her a.* *To slip the a.*, to let it go by letting the cable slip.

Comb.: **a.-frost,** the clogging of a mill-wheel with ice below the water-surface; **-ice,** ground-ice; **-lining** = *bill-boards* (see BILL *sb.*²); **-plate,** a heavy piece of timber or metal, serving as a point of support (*e.g.* for the cables of a suspension-bridge); **-ring,** the great ring for attaching the cable; **-shackle,** an iron loop used instead of an a.-ring; **-stock,** a bar which crosses the top of an a., at right angles to the shank, and also to the plane of the arms; also as *v.*; **-tow,** the cable of an a.; **-watch,** a part of a crew kept on duty while the ship lies at a.

† **A·nchor,** *sb.*² [OE. *ancra, ancor, -er* – OIr. *anchara*, shortened f. eccl.L. *anachoreta* ANCHORET.] **1.** An ANCHORET –1604. **2.** An ANCHORESS –1466.

1. And anchors cheere [*i.e.* chair] in prison be my scope *Haml.* III. ii. 229 (2nd Qo.). **2.** *Ancren Riwle*, the 'Rule of Nuns' 1884.

Anchor (æ·ŋkəɹ), *v.* ME. [–(O)Fr. *ancrer*, = med.L. *anc(h)orare*.] **1.** To secure with an anchor; to place at, or bring to, anchor. **2.** *intr.* To cast or come to anchor. (Said of crew or ship.) 1578. **3.** *fig.* To fix as with an anchor 1594. **4.** *fig. refl.* and *intr.* To fix oneself, one's attention, etc. 1581.

3. Till that my Nayles were anchor'd in thine eyes *Rich. III*, IV. iv. 231. **4.** Whilst my Inuention . . anchors on Isabell *Meas. for M.* II. iv. 4.

Anchorage[1] (æ·ŋkərėdʒ). 1516. [f. ANCHOR *sb.*¹ + -AGE, after Fr. *ancrage*.] **1.** The action of anchoring; lying at anchor 1611. **2.** Conditions admitting of anchoring, *esp.* anchorage-ground 1706. **3.** *transf.* A position of support, a hold 1860. **4.** *fig.* A stay for the mind or feelings 1677. **5.** Anchorage-dues 1516. **6.** A ship's anchors 1588.

4. The Church a., . the new a. in the Bible FROUDE. **6.** The Barke . . Returnes . . From whence . . she weigh'd her A. *Tit. A.* I. i. 73.

A·nchorage[2]. 1593. [f. ANCHOR *sb.*² + -AGE; cf. *hermitage*.] The retreat of an anchoret.

Anchored (æ·ŋkəɹd), *ppl. a.* 1611. [f. the vb.] **1.** With the anchor dropt; held fast by the anchor; firmly fixed, at rest. **2.** Furnished with anchors; or, *esp.* in *Her.*, with anchor-like appendages 1611.

Anchoress, ancress (æ·ŋkŏrės, æ·ŋkrės). ME. [f. ANCHOR *sb.*² + -ESS¹.] A female anchoret.

Yef ho were ankeras or nonne 1450.

Anchoret, -ite (æ·ŋkŏrėt, -əit). 1460. [– med.L. *anc(h)orita*, eccl.L. *anchorēta* – eccl. Gr. ἀναχωρητής, f. ἀναχωρεῖν retire, retreat, f. ἀνά back, ANA- + χωρεῖν withdraw, f. χώρα, χῶρος place. Superseded ANCHOR *sb.*²] **1.** One who has withdrawn or secluded himself from the world, usu. for religious reasons; a recluse, a hermit. *masc.* and *fem.* Also *attrib.* 1847. **2.** *Ch. Hist.* The recluses of the East. (Often *anachoret.*) 1553. **3.** *fig.* Any one of secluded habits 1616.

1. The severity of an a. JOHNSON. **3.** Th'anachorit of love DRUMM. OF HAWTH. Hence **Anchore·tic, -al** *a.* of, pertaining to, or like an a. **A·nchore:tish, -i:tish** *a.* hermit-like. **A·nchoretism, -it-,** the practice of an a.

Anchoring (æ·ŋkəriŋ), *vbl. sb.* 1593. [f. ANCHOR *v.* + -ING¹.] **1.** The action or state of lying at anchor; anchorage. **2.** *transf.* Fixing securely 1767. **3.** *ppl. a.* Coming to or lying at anchor; holding firm 1605.

1. Good a., cleane ground R. HAWKINS. *Comb.*: **a.-ground, -place,** one suited for anchoring; **-room,** space for anchoring; **-stone,** one used instead of an anchor.

Anchorite, -itish, vars. of ANCHORET, -ISH.

A·nchoritess. *arch.* [f. ANCHORITE + -ESS¹.] = ANCHORESS. FULLER.

A·nchorless, *a. rare.* 1863. [f. ANCHOR *sb.*¹ + -LESS.] Without an anchor; *fig.* drifting.

Anchovy (æntʃōᵘ·vi, occ. æ·ntʃŏvi). 1596. [– Sp., Pg. *anchova, anchoa*; has been supposed to be :– Rom. **apiu(v)a* – Gr. ἀφύη some small fish, but G. *anchovi(s), anschovis* (– Du. *ansjovis*) has been referred to Basque *anchu.*] A small fish of the Herring family (*Engraulis encrasicholus*), found esp. in the Mediterranean, and pickled for exportation.

Item, Anchoues, and Sacke after supper ijs. vid. 1 *Hen. IV*, II. iv. 588. *Comb.*: **a.-pear,** a West Indian fruit, eaten like the mango; also the tree (*Grias cauliflora*) which bears it; **-toast.**

‖ **Anchusa** (æŋkiū·să). [– L. *anchusa* (Pliny) – Gr. ἄγχουσα, ἔγχ-.] A hairy-stemmed plant of the genus so named, which includes alkanet. Hence **Anchu·sic** *a.* in *A. acid* = **A·nchusin,** the colouring matter of alkanet, a dark-red amorphous powder 1863.

Anchylose, ank- (æ·ŋkilōᵘz), *v.* 1787. [Back-formation from ANCHYLOSIS, after *anastomosis, -ose*, etc.] **1.** To effect anchylosis in; *usu.* in *pass.* to be solidly united bone to bone. **2.** *intr.* To grow stiff. Of two bones: To grow together. 1833. Hence **A·nchylosed, ank-** *ppl. a.* grown together; stiffened; *fig.* cramped.

‖ **Anchylosis, ank-** (æŋkilōᵘ·sis). 1713. [– mod.L. – Gr. ἀγκύλωσις, f. ἀγκυλοῦν to crook, f. ἀγκύλος crooked; see -OSIS. *Ch, k* substituted for regular *c* to denote the *k*-sound (cf. Fr. *ankylose*).] The formation of a stiff joint by consolidation of the articulating surfaces; the coalescence of two bones originally distinct. Also *fig.* Hence **Anchylo·tic, ank-** *a.* of or pertaining to a.

† **A·nciency.** 1548. [alt. of ANCIENTY, as if f. ppl. adj. in -ENT, after *decent, decency*, etc.] The quality of being ancient –1759.

Ancient (ēⁱ·nʃĕnt), *a.* and *sb.*¹ [ME. *auncien, -ian* – AFr. *auncien*, (O)Fr. *ancien*, repr. Rom. **antianus*, **anteanus*, f. L. *ante* before, ANTE- + *-anus* -AN.] **A.** *adj.* Of date. **1.** Belonging to time past (*arch.*) 1490; † whilom, ex- –1718; *esp.* belonging to times *long* past, old ME. **2.** *spec.* Belonging to the period before the fall of the Western Roman Empire; opp. to *modern*, and *mediæval* 1605. ** Of duration. **3.** Of early origin, going far back 1475; hence, time-worn, hoary 1586. **4.** Of living beings: Old, of great age (*arch.*) ME.; having the wisdom, etc., of age, venerable (*arch.*) 1460; old-fashioned (*rare*) 1598; veteran, senior (now *old*) ME. **5.** *Law.* In *Ancient tenure, Tenure of ancient demesne*: that existing in those manors which belonged to the crown in the reigns of Edward the Confessor and William the Conqueror 1607.

1. Thy antient kindness BUNYAN. They mourned their a. leader lost POPE. (Cf. Fr. *ancien gouverneur.*) A. weapons of war 1777, civilisation 1836. **2.** The antient languages 1808. **A.** art 1846, literature 1875. **3.** O thou awncient Israel *Baruch* 4:5. Contending. . for a. rights 1855. These times are the a. times, when the world is a. BACON. This a. city, Memphis YOUNG. **4.** Farewell, auncient Lady *Rom. & Jul.* II. iv. 150. The precepts of a. experience JOHNSON. An a. ditty, long since mute KEATS. Respect to be had to graue and a. souldiers 1598.

B. *sb.* **1.** One who lived in ancient times. Usu. in *pl. The Ancients*: *esp.* the Greeks, Romans, etc. 1541; the classic authors 1615. **2.** *The Ancient of Days*; the Almighty. *Dan.* 7:9. **3.** An aged man (or animal); a patriarch 1502. † **4.** An ancestor (*rare*) –1649; a senior (usu. *his ancient*) –1659. **5.** An Elder (*arch.*) 1534. **6.** A senior member of the Inns of Court or of Chancery. 1563.

1. If Mr. Shakespear had not read the ancients HALES. The same . . Ancient [Plutarch] 1763. **4.** Reinolds was . . bred up in the same college . . with Jewel his a. and R. Hooker his contemporary FULLER.

Ancient (ēⁱ·nʃĕnt), *sb.*² *arch.* 1554. [corrupt. of ENSIGN by assoc. of such forms as *ensyne* w. *ancien*, ANCIENT *sb.*¹] **1.** An ensign, or standard: *pl.* insignia, colours. **2.** A standard-bearer, an 'ensign' (in full † **ancient-bearer**). 1596.

1. A red a., on the mizen-top DE FOE. **2.** Hee is call'd aunchient Pistoll *Hen. V*, III. vi. 20.

Anciently (ēⁱ·nʃĕntli), *adv.* 1502. [f. ANCIENT *a.* + -LY².] **1.** In ancient times; † formerly –1774. **2.** † Of long standing –1686; like something old HAWTHORNE.

Ancientness (ēⁱ·nʃĕntnės). 1537. [f. as prec. + -NESS.] The quality of being ANCIENT (now *antiquity*); † ancient condition –1657; † seniority –1628.

Ancientry (ēⁱ·nʃĕntri). *arch.* 1580. [f. ANCIENT *a.* + -RY; cf. *peasantry.*] **1.** The quality or estate of being ANCIENT. † **2.** Ancestry SPENSER; *collect.* elders –1611. **3.** Antiquity 1755; *pl.* or *collect.* antiquities 1866.

1. I allow my a. H. WALPOLE. **2.** The Auncientry of the Parish 1589. **3.** I love those tales of a. 1839.

† **A·nciently.** ME. [– AFr. *auncienté*, (O)Fr. *ancienneté*; see -TY¹.] **1.** Antiquity –1602; *concr.* the ancients 1556. **2.** Old standing –1623; agedness –1569; seniority –1775.

‖ **Ancile** (ænsəi·li). 1600. [L., pl. *ancilia.*] The sacred tutelary shield of Rome, said to have fallen from heaven.

Ancillary (æ·nsilări), *a.* 1667. [– L. *ancillaris*, f. *ancilla* handmaid, fem. dim. of *anculus* servant; see -ARY².] **1.** Subservient, subordinate (*to*). **2.** *lit.* (after L.) Of or pertaining to maid-servants (*rare* and *affected*) 1852.

1. Rather a. than essential H. TAYLOR. **2.** The a. beauty THACKERAY.

† **Ancille.** [ME. *ancelle* (also *ancille* – L.) – OFr. *ancele*, mod. *ancelle* :– L. *ancilla* handmaid.] A handmaid –1500. var. ‖ **Anci·lla.** [L.]

Ancipital (ænsi·pităl), *a. rare.* 1794. [f. L. *anceps, -cipit-* two-headed (f. *an* = *ambi* both + *caput, capit-* head) + AL¹; cf. BICEPS.] Having two sharp edges. vars. **Anci·pitate, Anci·pitous.**

Anci·stroid, *a.* 1879. [– Gr. ἀγκιστροειδής hook-shaped, f. ἄγκιστρον hook; see -OID.] Hook-shaped.

Ancle, var. of ANKLE.

† **A·ncoly.** 1561. [– Fr. *ancolie*, OFr. *anquelie, aquelee*, etc. :– med.L. *aquile(g)ia.*] Columbine –1578.

A·ncome. *Obs.* or *dial.* ME. [prob. var. of north.ME. *on-come* (XIV) visitation, access of disease.] A boil forming unexpectedly; also, later, a whitlow.

‖ **Ancon** (æ·ŋkǫn). Pl. **anco·nes.** 1706. [L. *ancon* – Gr. ἀγκών elbow.] **1.** *Phys.* The elbow. **2.** *Arch.* The corner or quoin of a wall, etc. 1706. Also, a truss or console supporting a cornice at the flank 1823.

Ancon sheep: A race with long bodies and short legs, the fore-legs crooked; bred from a single lamb so born in 1791. Hence **A·nconal** *a.* of or pertaining to the elbow; vars. **Anco·neal, Anco·neous. A·nconoid** *a.* elbow-like.

† **A·ncony.** 1674. [Origin unkn.] A form of bloom –1825.

Ancor, obs. form of ANCHOR.

†‖ **Ancora.** 1712. [It.] = Fr. ENCORE. Mr. Froth cried out *Ancora* ADDISON.

Ancoral (æ·ŋkŏrăl), *a. rare.* 1852. [– L. *ancoralis*, pertaining to an anchor; see ANCHOR *sb.*¹, -AL¹.] *Zool.* Of or pertaining to an anchor; anchor-like, as the feet of some parasitic crustacea.

-ancy, *suffix.* [– L. *-antia*, forming abstr. sbs. on ppl. adjs. in *-antem* (see -ANT).] Mod. Eng. var. of -ANCE, expressing *quality, state*, or *condition*, as opp. to *action* (Fr. *-ance*). Many words orig. in *-nce* have been refash. accordingly, as *constancy, infancy*, etc.

Ancyroid (ænsəi·roid), *a.* 1839. [– mod.L. *ancyroides* – Gr. ἀγκυροειδής; see ANCHOR *sb.*¹, -OID.] *Phys.* Anchor-shaped, as the coracoid process of the scapula; also, the middle cornu of the lateral ventricle of the brain.

And (ænd, ənd, *fam.* ən, 'n), *conj.*¹ formerly *prep.* [OE. *and, ond*, corresp. to OFris.

and(a), ande, end(a), en, OS. *ande, endi* (Du. *en*), OHG. *anti, enti* (G. *und*) and Skr. *átha* (:– **ntha*) thereupon, also. Connection w. OE. *and-* (as in *andswaru* ANSWER *sb.*), ON. *and-*, Goth. *anda-*, and Skr. *anti* over against, Gr. ἀντί against, L. *ante* before, and OE. *ende* END *sb.*, etc., is no longer gen. accepted. See also AN *conj.*] **†A.** *prep.* (with *dat.*) Before; besides. OE. only.

B. *conj. co-ordinate.* Side by side with, along with, in addition to. **I.** Connecting words. **1.** Simply connective OE. **2.** Expressing continuous repetition (of groups, or indefinite) OE. **3.** Emphatic. **a.** opp. to *or* (mod.); **b.** = and other (expressing a difference of quality) 1569. **4.** Connecting an adj. adverbially with another which follows, esp. *fam.* after *nice, fine* 1592. **†5.** Bef. both words: = Both — and —. (A Latinism.) –1520. **6.** When many notions, etc., are connected, *and* is now expressed only with the last, exc. rhetorically ME.

1. *One and twenty*; (cf. *twenty-one*). (*And* is used also to connect fractions to wholes, pence to shillings, etc., but not different denominations of weights and measures, nor in 'railway time'.) **And all:** see ALL. **2.** Yea, two and two, Newgate fashion 1 *Hen. IV*, III. iii. 104. Higher still and higher SHELLEY. **3. b.** Alack, there be roses and roses, John! BROWNING. (Cf. Molière's 'il y a fagots et fagots' 1666, as against 1569.) **4.** His slow and mouing finger *Oth.* IV. ii. 56. Nice and warm 1888.

II. Connecting co-ordinate clauses or sentences. **1.** Simply connective. **a.** additive OE. **b.** adversative OE. **2.** Introducing a consequence, actual or predicted OE. **3.** Introducing an amplificative clause OE. **4.** Connecting two vbs. in the sense of *to* with the inf., *esp.* after *go, come, send, try* 1671.

1. b. Hee said, I goe sir, and went not *Matt.* 21: 30. **2.** A pretty young woman, and I did kiss her PEPYS. This do, and thou shalt liue *Luke* 10: 28. **3.** Scrooge signed it: and Scrooge's name was good upon 'Change DICKENS. **4.** To try and teach the erring soul MILT. *P.R.* I. 224.

III. Introductory. **1.** Continuing the narration OE.; occ. = 'Yes! and' 1847. **2.** In expressing surprise at, or asking the truth of, what one has heard 1788. As quasi-*adv.* **3.** Also; even. (A Latinism.) ME. *Obs.* or *arch.*

1. You are now to obey me. And I will KINGSLEY. **2.** And are you really going? 1888. **3.** She brought to him her beauty and truth, But and broad earldoms three LOWELL.

C. *conj. conditional,* = If. [Prob. elliptical; cf. *so*; or conn. w. the introductory *and*. Others write *an*, as in *an't* = *and it* (*c* 1600). See AN *conj.*] **1.** If; also 'and if', 'an' if' ME. **2.** Concessive: Even if, although ME. **†3.** = as if –1606; whether, L. *an* (*illiterate* or *dial.*) –1602. ¶ Also used *subst.* 1638.

1. And you will not, sir, Ile take my heeles *Com. Err.* I. ii. 94. But and yf that evill servaunt shall say TINDALE *Matt.* 24: 48. **3.** I will roar you an 'twere any Nightingale *Mids. N.* I. ii. 86. *subst.* Absolutely, and without any ifs and ands CUDWORTH.

†And, *conj.*[2] *after comparatives.* 1463. [An erroneous literary expansion of northern dial. *'an, en* 'than', formally confused with *an'*, dial. and familiar form of prec.] = THAN *conj.*

A made a finer end..and it had beene any Christome child *Hen. V*, II. iii. 12.

†And-, *pref.* Against, in return, toward. In OE. it remained only in sbs. and adjs.; and now as *an-* in *answer*. When proclitic, as in vbs., it became *on-*, and later *a-* as in *along* (see A *pref.* 4).

-and, *suffix.* Ending of pr. pple. in northern dial., repr. OE. *-ende*, ME. and mod. *-ing*.

†Anda·batism. 1630. [f. L. *andabata* a Roman gladiator who fought mounted, in a helmet without eyeholes + -ISM.] The practice of a hoodwinked gladiator; contention in the dark DRUMM. OF HAWTH.

Andalusite (ændăl[i]ū·səit). 1837. [f. *Andalusia* + -ITE[1] 2 b.] *Min.* A hard silicate of alumina, in rhombic crystals of various colour, first found in Spain.

‖ **Andante** (anda·nte, ændæ·nti). 1742. [It., pr. pple. of *andare* go.] *Mus. adj.* Of movement: Moderately slow and distinct. Also as advb. *sb.* [sc. *movement* or *piece.*] 1784.

‖ **Andantino** (andantī·no). 1819. [It., dim. of prec.] *Mus. adj. orig.* Rather slower than andante; but freq.: With less of andante, *i.e.* rather quicker. *sb.* [sc. *movement* or *piece.*] 1845.

Andean (æ·ndi,ăn), *a.* 1839. [f. *Andes* + -AN, -EAN.] Of, pertaining to, or like the Andes.

Andesine (æ·ndīzin). 1862. [var. of foll.; see -INE[5].] *Min.* = next.

Andesite (æ·ndīzəit). 1850. [f. *Andes* + -ITE[1] 2 b.] *Min.* A silicate of alumina, lime, and soda, found in the Andes and elsewhere. Hence **Andesi·tic** *a.*

Andiron (æ·ndəi:əɹn). [ME. *aundyre, -yrne, -erne* – OFr. *andier* (mod. *landier* for *l'andier*) w. assim. of the second syll. to IRON *sb.*[1]] A horizontal bar, one of a pair, sustained on short feet, with an upright pillar, usually ornamental, in front, placed at each side of the hearth to support burning wood.

‖ **Andou·ille.** ? *Obs.* 1605. [(O)Fr. :– Rom. **anducla*, of unkn. origin.] A kind of sausage.

‖ **Andouille·t.** ? *Obs.* 1706. [Fr. *andouillette*, dim. of prec.; see -ETTE.] 'Minced Veal with Bacon..roll'd into a Paste.' Phillips.

Andrana·tomy. ? *Obs.* 1811. [f. Gr. ἀνήρ, ἀνδρ- man + ANATOMY.] The dissection of the human (*esp.* male) body.

A·ndrew. 1618. **†1.** A broad-sword, an Andrea Ferrara (*rare*). **†2.** A valet. CONGREVE. **3.** See MERRYANDREW.

Andro-, comb. form of Gr. ἀνήρ, ἀνδρ- a man, a male.

andro-diœ·cious [Gr. διά + οἰκία] *a.*, *Bot.* with flowers on one plant hermaphrodite, and on the other staminate only; **-dy·namous** [Gr. δύναμις] *a.*, *Bot.* having stamens and petals unusually developed; **-mo·rphous** [Gr. -μορφος] *a.*, having the form of a male; **-pe·tal** [+ PETAL], *Bot.* a petal produced from a stamen; **-pe·talar, -pe·talous** *adjs.*, *Bot.* made double by having the stamens changed into petals; **-phagous** [Gr. -φαγος] *a.*, man-eating, anthropophagous; **-phore** [Gr. φόρος (φερ-)], *Bot.* the column formed by the united filaments in monadelphous plants; *Zool.* the male gonophore of some *Physaphoridæ*; **-sphinx** [+ SPHINX], a sphinx whose human portion is male; **-spore** [Gr. σπόρος], *Bot.* the zoospore which in some *Algæ* produces the male reproductive organs; **-tomous** *a.*, *Bot.* having the filaments of the stamens divided into two parts; **† -tomy** = ANTHROPOTOMY.

‖ **Andrœ·cium.** 1839. [mod.L., f. ANDRO- + Gr. οἰκίον house.] *Bot.* The male organs of a flower collectively.

Androgyne (æ·ndrŏdʒin). 1552. [–(O)Fr. *androgyne* or L. *androgynus, -gyne* – Gr. ἀνδρόγυνος, -γύνη f. ἀνδρο- ANDRO- + γυνή woman.] **1.** A being of both sexes; a hermaphrodite. **†2.** An effeminate man; a eunuch (*rare*) –1742. **3.** *Bot.* An androgynous plant 1785. Hence **Andro·gynal** *a.* = ANDROGYNOUS. **Andro·gynally** *adv.* **Andro·gynary** *a.* having both stamens and pistils developed into petals, as the double narcissus. **Andro·gyny**, hermaphroditism.

Androgynism (ændrǫ·dʒiniz'm). 1869. [f. prec. + -ISM.] *Bot.* Change from the diœcious to the monœcious condition.

Androgynous (ændrǫ·dʒinəs), *a.* 1628. [f. as prec. + -OUS.] **1.** Uniting the (physical) characters of both sexes; hermaphrodite 1651. **†2.** Hence, effeminate 1628. **3.** *Astrol.* Of planets: Both hot and cold 1652. **4.** *Bot.* Bearing both stamens and pistils in the same flower, or on the same plant 1793.

1. Many of the rabbins are of opinion that Adam was created a. 1751.

Android (æ·ndroid). *rare.* 1727. [– mod.L. *androides* (also used), f. Gr. ἀνδρο- ANDRO- + -ειδης -OID. Cf. Fr. *androïde.*] An automaton resembling a human being. Hence **Andrōi·dal** *a.*

† A·ndrolepsy. *rare.* [– Gr. ἀνδρολημψία seizure of men; see -Y[3].] An Athenian custom whereby, if a citizen were killed abroad, and his death unatoned for, three subjects of the offending country were seized as reprisals.

Andromed(e (æ·ndrŏmėd). 1876. [– Gr. 'Ανδρομέδη, wife of Perseus.] *Astr.* A system of meteors radiating from a point in Andromeda.

Andromeda (ændrǫ·mĭdă). 1706. [L. – Gr. 'Ανδρομέδη, wife of Perseus.] **1.** A constellation of the northern hemisphere. **2.** *Bot.* A genus of shrubs (N.O. *Ericaceæ*), native to Britain and N. America 1794.

-androus, *Bot. suffix* of adjs., f. mod.L. *-andrus* (– Gr. -ανδρος adj. ending, f. ἀνήρ, ἀνδρ- man). = 'having..male organs or stamens', as *triandrous*, etc.

† Ane, *a.* [OE. *ān* ONE.] **1.** *ān-e*: repr. inflections of *ān* 'one'; and after the sb. = 'only'; see ONE –ME. **2.** In ME., n. dial., var. of *an* (*ane* = *ān*), as def., or indef. article, according to the stress. See AN *adj.*[1] **3.** In 16th c. literary *Sc.* = One, an, a. **4.** In mod. Sc. and n. dial., *absol.* = one; the adj. form being *a, ae.*

-ane, *suffix.* **1.** Occas. Eng. – L. *-anus*, esp. in words that have also a form in *-an*, as *humane*. **2.** *Chem.* Hofmann's formative of the names of the saturated hydrocarbons of comp. C_nH_{2n+2}, also called *paraffines*, as *Methane*, etc.

Anear (ănī[ə]·ɹ). 1608. [f. A *prep.*[1] 5 + NEAR *a.*, after *afar.*] *adv.* Well-nigh; near, opp. to *afar* 1798. *prep.* Near, near to 1732.

adv. The lady..well a-near Does fall SHAKS. Now..far, and now a-near SCOTT. *prep.* A. some river's bank 1879.

Anea·r, *v. arch.* 1534. [f. A- *pref.* 11 + NEAR *v.*] **† 1.** *intr.* To draw near *to* –1583; to be near 1583. **2.** *trans.* To approach 1586.

Aneath (ănī·þ, *Sc.* ăne·þ), *prep.* 1801. [alt. of *beneath* after *afore*/*before, aside*/*beside.*] Beneath.

Anecdotage (æ·nekdo[u]tėdʒ). 1823. [f. next + -AGE.] **1.** Anecdotes; anecdotic literature. **2.** *joc.* Garrulous old age [after *dotage*] 1835.

2. A man who has reached his a.—to use a pun.. conveyed from Wilkes M. COLLINS.

Anecdote (æ·nekdo[u]t). 1676. [– Fr. *anecdote* or mod.L. *anecdota* pl. – Gr. ἀνέκδοτα things unpublished, n.pl. of ἀνέκδοτος adj., f. ἀν- AN- *pref.* 10 + ἔκδοτος published, f. ἐκ out + διδόναι give.] **1.** *pl.* Secret, or hitherto unpublished narratives or details of history. **2.** The narrative of an interesting or striking incident or event. (*At first,* An item of gossip.) 1761. Also *collect.*

1. Anecdotes of Florence, or the secret history of the House of Medicis F. SPENCE (*title*). **2.** An after-dinner a. 1888. Hence **A·necdotal** *a.* **A·necdoted** *ppl. a.* made the subject of an a. (*rare*). **Anecdo·tic, -al** *a.* = *anecdotal*; addicted to anecdote. **Anecdo·tically** *adv.* **Anecdotist** (æ·nĕkdo[u]tist, ăne·kdŏtist), a relater of anecdotes.

Anelace (**anelate** in Blount), var. ANLACE.

Anele (ănī·l), *v. arch.* ME. [f. *an-*, OE. *on-* (AN- *pref.* 1) + ME. *elien*, f. OE. *ele* – L. *oleum* OIL. Cf. ANOIL *v.*] To anoint; *esp.* to give extreme unction to. Hence **Ane·led** *ppl. a.* **† Ane·ler. Ane·ling** *vbl. sb.*

Anelectric (ænĭle·ktrik), *a.* 1830. [f. AN- *pref.* 10 + ELECTRIC.] **† a.** Non-electric. **b.** Parting rapidly with electricity. As *sb.* **† a.** A body which does not become electric, when rubbed. **b.** A metal, etc., which being a good conductor parts rapidly with electricity. 1863.

Anele·ctrode. 1834. [f. Gr. ἀνά up + ELECTRODE; cf. ANODE.] The positive pole of a galvanic battery.

‖ **Anelectrotonus** (æ:nĭlektrǫ·tŏnŏs). 1873. [f. Gr. ἀν = ἀνά up + ἤλεκτρον amber (see ELECTRIC) + τόνος tension.] *Phys.* A state of depressed irritability produced in a nerve near the positive pole of an electric current which traverses it. Hence **Anele:ctroto·nic** *a.*

Anelytrous (ăne·litrəs), *a.* 1847. [f. Gr. ἀνέλυτρος (f. ἀν- AN- *pref.* 10 + ἔλυτρον covering) + -OUS.] *Ent.* Not having elytra or wing-cases.

Anemious (ănī·mi,əs), *a. rare.* 1879. [– Gr. ἀνέμιος windy + -OUS.] Windy, growing in windy places.

Anemo- (ăne·mŏ, ænĭmǫ·), comb. f. Gr. ἄνεμος wind.

anemo·cracy [Gr. κρατεία], *nonce-wd.*, a government by the wind; **-gram** [Gr. γράμμα], a prepared sheet marked by an anemograph; **-graph** [Gr. -γραφος], an instrument for recording on paper the direction and force of the wind; **-gra·phic** *a.*; **-graphy** [Gr. -γραφία], (*a*) description of, or a treatise on, the winds; (*b*) the art of recording the direction and force of the wind; **-logy** [+ -LOGY], the science of the winds; **-lo·gical** *a.*; **-philous** [Gr. φίλος], *a.*, wind-loving, wind-fertilized; **-scope** [Gr. -σκοπος], an instrument for showing the direction of the wind, or foretelling a change of weather.

Anemometer (ænĭmǫ·mĭtəɹ). 1727. [f. Gr. ἄνεμος wind + -METER.] **1.** An instrument for measuring the force of the wind. **2.** An apparatus for indicating the wind-pressure in an organ 1876. Hence **Ane:mome·tric, -al** *a.* **Ane:mome·trograph** = *anemograph*; see ANEMO-. **Anemo·metry,** the measurement of the force or velocity of the wind.

Anemone (ăne·məni, *Bot. L.* ænĭmōu·ni). 1551. [– L. *anemone* – Gr. ἀνεμώνη wind-flower, f. ἄνεμος wind.] **1.** *Bot.* A genus of plants (family *Ranunculaceæ*), of which one (*A. nemorosa*), the wind-flower, is common in Britain. Also *attrib.* **2.** *Zool.* **Sea Anemone:** pop. name of various Actinoid Zoophytes 1773.

1. Woods with anemonies in flower till May M. ARNOLD. Hence **Anemo·nic** *a. Chem.* derived from the a. **Ane·monin,** *Chem.* an acrid crystalline substance, obtained from the a. var. **Anemony.**

Anencephalous (ænĕnse·faləs), *a.* 1836. [f. Gr. ἀνεγκέφαλος (Galen) without brain (f. ἀν- AN- *pref.* 10 + ἐγκέφαλος brain) + -OUS; cf. Fr. *anencéphale.*] *Phys.* Brainless; wanting the brain. var. **Ane:ncepha·lic.** Hence **Anence·phaloid** *a.* partially, or tending to be, a.

An-e·nd. *arch.* ME. [See AN *prep.*, and END.] †**1.** At last. **2.** To the end; continuously (*arch.*) ME. **3.** On end (*arch.*) 1593.

2. † *Most an end*: almost uninterruptedly, mostly. **3.** Mine haire be fixt an end 2 *Hen. VI*, III. ii. 318.

Anent (ăne·nt), *prep.* [OE. phr. *on efen, efn,* or *emn* (ME. *onevent, anont, anentes,* (also mod. dial.) *anenst*; *anent* from XIV), i.e. ON, *efen* EVEN *a.* = OS. *an eban,* MHG. *eneben, nebent,* (also mod.) *neben.* The suffix *-es, -s* appears *c.* 1200.] **1.** † In a line with, beside (OE. only); † on a par with –ME.; in the company of, by (L. *apud,* Fr. *chez*). (Still *dial.*) **2.** Fronting, over against (*arch.* or *dial.*) ME. **3.** In respect or reference to, concerning. (*Sc.* and affected by Eng. writers.) ME. **4.** *adv.* (obj. understood). Opposite (*dial.*) 1520.

Ane·nterous, *a.* 1847. [f. Gr. ἀν- AN- *pref.* 10 + ἔντερα bowels + -OUS.] *Zool.* Having no intestine.

Ane:piplo·ic, *a.* 1879. [f. Gr. ἀν- AN- *pref.* 10 + ἐπίπλοον EPIPLOÖN + -IC.] *Phys.* Having no epiploon, or omentum.

† **A·nerly,** *adv. north.* ME. [f. ANE one; the *-er-* is unexplained, but cf. *formerly,* etc., and ALLENARLY.] Only; only just –1513.

Aneroid (æ·nĕroid), *a.* 1848. [– Fr. *anéroïde,* f. Gr. ἀ- A- *pref.* 14 + νηρός wet, damp + *-oïde* -OID (used arbitrarily).] Of a barometer, in which the pressure of the air is measured, not by the aid of a fluid, as mercury, but by its action on the elastic lid of a box exhausted of air. As *sb.* [Short for 'Aneroid barometer'.] 1849.

Anes, earlier f. ONCE. *Sc.*

‖ **Anesis** (æ·nĭsis). 1811. [Gr. ἄνεσις remission.] *Med.* The abatement of symptoms.

Anesthetic, var. of ANÆSTHETIC.

Anet (æ·net). ME. [– L. *anethum* – Gr. ἄνηθον, dial. form of ἄνισον dill, ANISE; later reinforced by Fr. *aneth, anet.*] The herb Dill (*Anethum graveolens*). *Comb.* **anetseed,** the seed of a. **A·nethated** *ppl. a.* prepared or mixed with dill.

Anethene (æ·nĭþīn). 1874. [f. L. *anethum* (prec.) + -ENE.] *Chem.* The most volatile part of the essential oil of dill, fennel, etc.; $C_{10}H_{16}$.

Anethol (æ·nĭþǫl). 1863. [f. as prec. + -OL.] *Chem.* An essential principle of the oils of anise, fennel, etc.; $C_{10}H_{12}O$.

Ane·tic, *a.* 1853. [– late L. *aneticus* abating – Gr. ἀνετικός relaxing; see ANESIS.] *Med.* Assuaging, soothing.

Aneuch, north. f. ENOUGH.

Aneurysm, -ism (æ·niuriz'm). 1656. [– Gr. ἀνεύρυσμα dilatation, f. ἀνευρύνειν widen out, f. ἀνά ANA- + εὐρύνειν widen, f. εὐρύς wide. The unetymological sp. with *i* is the commoner. Cf. Fr. *anévrisme.*] *Path.* A morbid dilatation of an artery, due to disease, or to a tumour caused by rupture, of the arterial coats. Hence **Aneury·smal, -i·smal** *a.* marked or affected by a.; var. † **Aneurysma·tic, -al.**

Anew (ăniū·), *adv.* [ME. *of newe, of the newe, o newe,* i.e. OF, A- *pref.* 3, NEW *a.*, prob. after OFr. *de neuf, de nouveau,* L. *de novo.*] **1.** Once more, afresh, as a new action. **2.** In a new way ME. †**3.** Newly, opp. to *of old* –1728; freshly –1582.

† **Anew·,** *v.* late ME. [perh. f. A- *pref.* 1 + NEW *v.*; cf. OHS. *irniuwōn* (G. *erneuen*) renew.] To renew –1690.

† **A·nfract.** *rare.* 1567. [– L. *anfractus* a bending.] A winding –1611.

Anfractuose (ænfræ:ktiu,ōu·s), *a. rare.* 1691. [– L. *anfractuosus*; see prec., -OSE¹; cf. Fr. *anfractueux.*] Winding, sinuous.

Anfractuosity (ænfræ:ktiu,ǫ·sĭti). 1596. [– Fr. *anfractuosité,* f. late L. *anfractuosus* winding, f. L. *anfractus* a bending; see -OSITY.] **1.** *lit.* Sinuosity; usu. *concr.* in *pl.* winding crevices, channels, etc.; *spec.* the sinuous depressions separating the convolutions of the brain 1687. **2.** *fig.* Involution, intricacy; *concr.* in *pl.* 1652.

2. The anfractuosities of the human mind JOHNSON. var. **Anfra·cture.**

Anfractuous (ænfræ·ktiu,əs), *a.* 1621. [f. L. *anfractus* a bending + -OUS; cf. Fr. *anfractueux.*] Sinuous; circuitous; spiral.

Angary (æ·ngări). 1880. [– Fr. *angarie* – It. *angaria* – late L. *angaria* forced service – Gr. ἀγγαρεία, f. ἄγγαρος courier.] The right of a belligerent to use and destroy neutral property.

Angel (ēi·ndʒĕl). ME. [– OFr. *angele* – Chr.L. *angelus* – Gr. ἄγγελος messenger. Superseded OE. *engel,* corresp. to OFris. *angel, engel,* OS. *engil,* OHG. *angil, engil* (Du., G. *engel*), ON *engill,* Goth. *aggilus* (perh. immed. – Gr.); one of the earliest Gmc. adoptions from L.] **1.** A ministering spirit or divine messenger; one of an order of spiritual beings superior to man in power and intelligence, who are the attendants and messengers of the Deity OE.; hence **b.** one of the fallen spirits, who rebelled against God OE.; **c.** a guardian or attendant spirit (*lit.* and *rhet.*) ME.; **d.** *fig.* a person who resembles an angel in attributes or actions 1592. **2.** Any messenger of God, as a prophet or preacher (a Hellenism) ME.; a pastor or minister of a Church ME.; *poet.* a messenger ME; *fig.* in *angel of death* 1574. **3.** *transf.* A conventional figure with wings 1536. **4.** An old Eng. gold coin, orig. called ANGEL-NOBLE, having as its device the archangel Michael and the dragon. Its value varied from 6*s.* 8*d.* to 10*s.* 1488. **5.** *attrib.* = ANGELIC 1611.

1. Thou hast maad hym a litil lesse than aungels WYCLIF *Ps.* 8:6. Angels are bright still, though the brightest fell *Macb.* IV. iii. 22. **b.** The deuill and his angels *Matt.* 25:41. **c.** There is no euill Angell but Loue *L.L.L.* I. i. 78. **d.** O, speake againe, bright Angell *Rom. & Jul.* II. ii. 26. **2.** To the aungel of the chirche of Smyrna, wrijte thou WYCLIF *Rev.* 2:8. The dear good a. of the spring, The nightingale B. JONS. **4.** His stripes washed off With oil of angels MASSINGER.

Comb.: † **a.-bed,** an open bed without bed-posts; **-cornice,** one decorated with figures of angels; **angels' eyes,** the plant, germander speedwell; **-fish,** one of the *Squalidæ* or Shark family, named from the wing-like expansion of its pectoral fins, the Monk-fish, Fiddle-fish, Shark-ray; † **-gold,** standard gold; **-like,** *adv.*; **-noble,** see ANGEL 4; † **-proof,** the gold standard of the a.; **-shot** (Fr. *ange*), a kind of chain-shot, made of the (2 or 4) segments of a bullet, attached by chains to a disk; † **-water** [for Angelica-water], a perfume, orig. consisting chiefly of Angelica, subseq. of ambergris, rose, myrtle, and orange-flower waters.

Hence **A·ngelhood,** the condition of an a.; a brotherhood of angels. † **Ange·lify** *v.* (*rare*), also **A·ngelize** *v.* (*arch.*), to make into or like an a. **Angelo·latry,** angel-worship. **Angelo·logy,** that part of theology which treats of angels; doctrine as to angels. **Angelo·phany,** the visible manifestation of angels.

A·ngelate. 1863. [f. ANGELIC *a.*² + -ATE⁴.] *Chem.* A salt of angelic acid.

Angelet (ēi·ndʒĕlĕt). 1481. [alt. of (O)Fr. *angelot,* substituting the more familiar -ET for -OT¹. See ANGELOT.] † **1.** A gold coin; a half-angel. **2.** A little angel; *fig.* a pretty child 1823.

Angelic (ændʒe·lik), *a.*¹ 1485. [– (O)Fr. *angélique* – late L. *angelicus* – Gr. ἀγγελικός; see ANGEL, -IC.] **1.** Of or pertaining to angels; of angel kind. **2.** Like an angel; *hence,* of superhuman intelligence, innocence, purity, sweetness, etc. 1510.

1. The angelyk visyon CAXTON. *Angelic Salutation,* the *Ave Maria* (Luke 1:28). Th' a. guards MILT. [Satan's] Wit and Angelick Faculties STEELE. **2.** Fair a. Eve MILT. *P.L.* v. 74. *Angelic doctor* (i.e. spiritual as an angel): Thomas Aquinas.

Ange·lic, *a.*² 1863. [f. next + -IC.] *Chem.* Of or derived from angelica; as in *Angelic acid* $C_5H_8O_2$, occurring in the root of *A. archangelica,* etc.

‖ **Angelica** (ændʒe·likă). 1578. [med.L., short for *herba angelica* 'angelic plant'.] **1.** An aromatic umbelliferous plant (*A. archangelica,* or *A. officinalis*), used in cookery and medicine; the genus, of which this plant is the type. Also *attrib.* 1641. **2.** Short for **a.** Angelica-water (cf. ANGEL-*water*). **b.** Candied angelica root 1653.

Ange·lical, *a.* 1509. [f. ANGELIC *a.*¹ + -AL¹; see -ICAL.] **1.** = ANGELIC 1 (*arch.*). **2.** = ANGELIC 2. 1577. **3.** Of or pertaining to a divine messenger or pastor. Cf. ANGEL 2. (*rare*) 1678. Hence **Ange·lically** *adv.* † **Ange·licalness** (*rare*).

Angelina (ændʒĕlī·nă). 1663. [f. ANGEL; see -INA².] *Bot.* A genus of *Leguminosæ,* native esp. to tropical America.

Angelot (æ·ndʒĕlǫt). *arch.* 1525. [– (O)Fr. *angelot,* dim. of OFr. *angele* ANGEL; see -OT¹. Cf. ANGELET.] † **1.** A Fr. gold coin struck by Louis XI, bearing the image of St. Michael and the dragon; also an Eng. piece coined at Paris by Henry VI. † **2.** A cheese, made in Normandy [and stamped with the coin. Littré.] –1719. **3.** A musical instrument 1678.

‖ **Angelus** (æ·ndʒĕlŏs). 1727. [L., '*Angelus domini nuntiavit Mariæ*'.] **1.** A devotional exercise commemorating the Incarnation, in which the Angelic Salutation is thrice repeated, said by Roman Catholics, at morning, noon, and sunset, at the sound of a bell. **2.** Short for *Angelus-bell* 1847.

2. Softly the A. sounded LONGF.

Anger (æ·ŋgəɹ), *sb.* ME. [– ON. *angr* grief, f. the base **aŋg-* narrow, repr. also by ON. *ǫngr,* Goth. *aggwus,* and OE. *enge,* OS., OHG. *engi* (Du., G. *eng*) narrow; rel. to L. *angere* (see ANGUISH *sb.*).] † **1.** That which pains or afflicts, or the feeling which it produces; trouble, vexation, sorrow –1475. **2.** The active feeling provoked against the agent; passion, rage; wrath, ire ME. **3.** Inflammatory state of any part of the body; physical pain. (Still *dial.*) ME.

1. Syknesses and angres LANGL. **2.** A., which is a desire of revenge; Hatred, which is inveterate a. BURTON. A. is the executive power of justice MANNING. **3.** Where the greatest a. and soreness still continued TEMPLE (J.). Hence **A·ngerless** *a.* **A·ngerly** *adv.* (*arch.*) † painfully; † furiously; = ANGRILY; also as adj.: angry.

Anger (æ·ŋgəɹ), *v.* ME. [– ON. *angra* grieve, vex, f. *angr* grief; see prec.] † **1.** To distress, vex, hurt –1440. **2.** Hence, to make angry, enrage ME.; *intr.* (refl. pron. omitted; *rare*) ME. † **3.** To irritate or inflame a sore –1760.

2. You have both pleased and angered me JOHNSON. **3.** Itch most hurts when anger'd to a sore POPE. Hence **A·ngered** *ppl. a.* provoked to wrath (*lit.* and *fig.*); inflamed; flushed as with rage.

† **A·ngild.** [OE., f. AN- *pref.* 1 + *gildan* to pay.] In OE. law, compensation for injury. (Erron. taken later as 'single payment'.)

‖ **Angina** (æ·ndʒĭnă, ændʒəi·nă, f. supposed L. *angīna*). 1590. [– L. *angina* quinsy – Gr. ἀγχόνη strangling, assim. to L. *angere* (see ANGUISH *sb.*).] *Path.* **1.** Quinsy. **2.** (In full *Angina pectoris.*) A dangerous disease, marked by sudden and severe pain in the lower part of the chest, with a feeling of suffocation; called also *breast-pang, heart-stroke,* and *spasm of the chest* 1772. Hence **A·nginous** *a.* (sense 2).

Angio-, a comb. form, repr. Gr. ἀγγεῖον a vessel. Occ. spelt *angeio-*; but Roman *ī* = Gr. ει. Exc. in ændʒi,ǫ· (stress on *o*), pronunc. should be ændʒəi·o, but æ·ndʒi,o is common.

angioca·rpian [Gr. καρπός], *Bot.* an angiocarpous plant; **-ca·rpous** *a.*, *Bot.* having the fruit in an envelope not constituting part of the calyx; **-graph** [Gr. -γραφος], a kind of sphygmograph; **-graphy** [Gr. -γραφία], a description (*a*) of vessels, instruments, etc., used by any nation, (*b*) of the blood-vessels; **-logy** [Gr. -λογία], the part of anatomy which treats of the blood-vessels; **-monospe·rmous** [+ MONOSPERMOUS] *a.*, *Bot.* bearing solitary seeds each in its own pod; **-scope** [Gr. -σκοπος], an instrument for examining the capillary vessels of animals and plants; **-sperm** [Gr. -σπερμος f. σπέρμα], *Bot.* a plant which has its seeds enclosed in a seed-vessel; opp. to *gymnosperms*; **-spe·rmal, -spe·rmatous, -spe·rmous** *adjs.*; **-sporous** [Gr. σπόρος] *a.*, *Bot.* having spores enclosed in a hollow receptacle, as the puff-ball, etc.; **-stomous** [Gr. -στομος, but cf. L. *angere* for sense] *a.*, *Conch.* having a narrow opening, as some univalve shells; **-te·nic** [Gr. τεν- stem of τείνειν] *a.*, *Med.* tending to stretch the blood-vessels: applied to inflammatory fevers; **-tomy** [Gr. -τομία], the anatomy of the blood-vessels.

† **A·ngiport.** *rare.* 1647. [– L. *angiportus* narrow lane, f. *angere* to compress + *portus* harbour.] A narrow entrance, or opening in a wall –1652.

Angle (æ·ng'l), *sb.*[1] *arch.* [OE. *angul* = OS., OHG. *angul* (G. *angel*), ON. *ǫngull.*] **1.** A fishing-hook; often also the line and rod. †**2.** *fig.* A person or thing that catches like a hook –1598. **3.** [f. the vb.] An act of angling 1874.

1. Giue me mine A., weele to th' Riuer *Ant. & Cl.* II. v. 10. **2.** A woman..is a very a., hir hert is a net *Ecclus.* 7:26. *Comb.* **a.-worm,** a worm for bait.

Angle (æ·ŋg'l), *sb.*[2] ME. [– (O)Fr. *angle* or L. *angulus* corner, dim. of **angus.*] **1.** The space included between two meeting lines or planes; hence in *Geom.* the degree of inclination of two lines to each other. **2.** The meeting-point of two lines not in the same direction. Also *fig.* 1605. **3.** A corner, viewed (*a*) as a retreat, (*b*) as a projection. Also *fig.* ME. **4.** An outlying spot, a nook. Also *fig.* (*arch.*) ME. **5.** A sharp projection; *hence*, an angular fragment. Also *fig.* 1684. **6.** *Astrol.* Any of the four 'houses', at the cardinal points of the compass ME.

The inclination of two lines in the same plane is a plane angle, formed either by straight lines (*rectilineal*), or curved (*curvilineal*); if on the surface of a sphere it is a *spherical* angle; the space included by more than two plane angles meeting at a point is a *solid* angle. From measurement by angle in physics, mechanics, etc., come such phrases as *angle of application, depression, deviation, elevation, incidence, inclination, position, reflection, refraction, repose, rest, traction, vision*; and *To take the angle.*

1. *At angles with*: so placed as to form an a. with, opp. to *parallel*. *On the angle*: obliquely. **3.** For truth will seek no angles 1655. No bonch nor a. PUTTENHAM. **4.** Whom I left..In an odde A. of the Isle *Temp.* I. ii. 223. **5.** The fractured angles of upturned ice KANE.

Comb.: **a.-bar,** the upright bar at the a. of a polygonal window; also = *a.-iron*; **-bead,** a vertical bead fixed to an exterior a., flush with the surface of the plaster; **-brace,** a piece of timber fixed to the adjacent sides of a quadrangular framing; **-iron,** an L-shaped piece of iron, used to secure or strengthen framework; **-meter,** an instrument for measuring angles, *esp.* a CLINOMETER; **-staff** = *a.-bead*; **-tie** = *a.-brace*; **-wise,** *adv.*

Angle (æ·ŋg'l), *sb.*[3] OE. [– L. *Anglus*, pl. *Angli*, in Tacitus *Anglii* – Gmc. **Aŋgli-* (whence OE. *Engle*; cf. ENGLISH) the people of *Angul* (mod. *Angeln*), a district of Schleswig so called from its shape, the same word as ANGLE *sb.*[1]] *pl.* A Low German tribe that settled in Britain, formed the kingdoms of Northumbria, Mercia, and East Anglia, and finally gave their name to the ENGLISH people.

Angle (æ·ŋg'l), *v.*[1] 1496. [f. ANGLE *sb.*[1]; cf. to *hook.*] **1.** To fish with a hook and bait. Const. *for*, † *to*. Also *trans.* (*rare.*) 1866. **2.** *fig.* To use artful or wily means to catch a person or thing; to 'fish'. Const. *for*. 1589. † Also *trans.* –1683.

1. It is but a sory lyfe and an yuell to stande anglynge all day to catche a few fysshes 1530. **2.** Shee..did a. for mee, madding my eagernesse with her restraint *All's Well* V. iii. 212. Shooes which.. angled their Charity, that pass'd along OLDHAM.

A·ngle, *v.*[2] 1575. [f. ANGLE *sb.*[2]] †**1.** *intr.* To run into a corner. **2.** *refl.* To move in angles 1876. Hence **A·ngled** *ppl. a.* † driven into, or stationed in, a corner; placed at angles; having an angle or angles; also **-angled** in comb.

Angleberry, anle-. 1600. [perh. var. of ANBURY, or *ang-berry.*] A fleshy excrescence resembling a strawberry, found growing on the feet of cattle, etc.

Angler (æ·ŋglə.ɪ). 1552. [f. ANGLE *v.*[1] + -ER[1].] **1.** One who angles (*lit.* and *fig.*). **2.** *Zool.* A British fish (*Lophius piscatorius* Linn.), so named from its preying on small fish, which it attracts by moving certain wormlike filaments attached to the head and mouth. Called also Sea Devil, Frog or Toad Fish, and Fishing Frog. 1766.

Anglesite (æ·ŋglĭsəit). 1837. [f. *Anglesea* (where first found) + -ITE[1] 2b.] *Min.* The native sulphate of lead, lead vitriol.

Anglian (æ·ŋgliăn), *a.* and *sb.* 1726. [f. L. *Angli* (see ANGLE *sb.*[3]) + -AN.] Of or pertaining to the Angles. *East Anglian*, of East Anglia or the East Angles. var. **A·nglic** *a.*

Anglican (æ·ŋglikăn), *a.* and *sb.* 1635. [– med.L. *Anglicanus* (*Anglicana Ecclesia*, Magna Carta), f. *Anglicus*, f. *Anglus* ANGLE *sb.*[3]; see -IC, -AN.] **1.** Of or belonging to the Church of England (esp. as reformed) and churches in communion therewith, and so dependent upon the see of Canterbury. **2.** English. *rare.* 1860. **B.** *sb.* An adherent of the Anglican Communion 1797.

1. A. orders GLADSTONE, doctrine and discipline MACAULAY. *A. chant*: a harmonized melody of two strains (consisting each of a reciting note and a cadence) to which the psalms and the canticles are commonly sung in the Anglican Communion. **B.** Whether Catholicks, Anglicans, or Calvinists BURKE. Hence **A·nglicanism.**

Anglicism (æ·ŋglisiz'm). 1642. [f. L. *Anglicus*; see prec., -ISM. Hence Fr. *anglicisme.*] **1.** Anglicized language; *hence*, an idiom specially English. †**2.** An English fashion 1787. **3.** English political principles or methods 1873.

1. Dr. B. has abundance of pure Anglicisms in his Latin BENTLEY.

Anglicize (æ·ŋglisəiz), *v.* 1748. [f. as prec. + -IZE.] To make English in form or character; to English. Also *intr.* (*rare*). Hence **A:nglicizaˑtion,** the making English.

Anglify (æ·ŋglifəi), *v.* 1751. [f. L. *Angli* (see ANGLE *sb.*[3]) + -FY.] = prec. (Rather out of use.) Hence **A·nglifica·tion.**

Angling (æ·ŋgliŋ), *vbl. sb.* 1496. [f. ANGLE *v.*[1] + -ING[1].] The action or art of fishing with a rod. Also *fig.* 1674.

Uncertain anglings for distinction CARLYLE.

A·nglish, *a. rare.* [f. ANGLE *sb.*[3] + -ISH[1].] Anglian. CARLYLE.

Anglo- (æ·nglo), comb. form of L. *Anglus* English. For history see ANGLO-SAXON. **1.** **a.** English, of England: as in ANGLO-CATHOLIC, -SAXON; **A.-Danish,** pertaining to the Danes in England; **-French,** the French retained and separately developed in England; **-Latin,** Anglicized Latin; *a.-Judaic, -Jewish, -Norman.* **b.** Of English race, origin, descent, as *Anglo-American*, etc. **2.** English *and*; English in connection with; as *Anglo-Russian*, etc.

Anglo-Caˑtholic. 1841. [ANGLO-.] **A.** *adj.* Catholic of the Anglican communion. **B.** *sb.* **1.** *Hist.* An Englishman who, without wishing to sever the English from the Catholic Church, was in favour of its national independence 1858. **2.** *Modern.* A member of the Church of England who maintains its 'catholic' character 1849. Hence **Anglo-Catholicism,** Catholicism of the Anglican type.

Anglo-Indian (æ:ŋglo,i·ndian), *a.* and *sb.* 1861. [ANGLO- 1b.] (A person) of British birth, now or formerly resident in India; also, of mixed European and Indian parentage, Eurasian.

A·ngloman, -e. *rare.* 1860. [– Fr. *anglomane*, f. *anglomanie* ANGLOMANIA.] Anglomaniac.

Anglomania (æŋglo,mēi·niă). Occas. **anglomany.** 1787. [f. ANGLO- + -MANIA, after Fr. *anglomanie.*] A mania for what is English. Hence **Angloma·niac** *sb.* (*rare*) a rabid partisan of what is English.

Anglophobe (æ·ŋglŏfōᵘb). 1866. [– Fr.; see ANGLO-, -PHOBE.] One afflicted with ANGLOPHOBIA.

Anglopho·bia. 1816. [f. ANGLO- + -PHOBIA.] Intense fear or hatred of England. **Anglopho·bic** *a.* (*rare*). **Anglopho·bist** (*rare*) = ANGLOPHOBE.

Anglo-Saxon (æ:ŋglo,sæ·ksən), *sb.* and *a.* [– mod.L. *Anglo-Saxones* pl., for med.L. *Angli Saxones* (Paulus Diaconus, VIII), designation of Continental origin for the 'English Saxons'; after OE. *Angulseaxe, -seaxan*, in hybrid form *Angulsaxones.*] **1.** English Saxon, Saxon of England; opp. *orig.* to the 'Old Saxons' of the continent. Hence, opp. also to the Angles. **A.** *sb.* (the only contemporary use) OE. **B.** *adj.* In O.E.D. and in this Dictionary, the language of England bef. 1100 is called OE.; *Anglo-Saxon* when used = the Saxon (as opp. to the Anglian) *dialects* of OE. **2.** Extended to the entire Old English people and language before the Norman Conquest. (This use dates from Camden. Subseq. the word was explained as = *Angle* + *Saxon*, a union of Angle and Saxon, whence ANGLO- 2, q.v.) **A.** *sb.* 1610. **B.** *adj.* (*absol.* The Old English language.) 1610. **3.** Used rhet. for *English* in its ethnological sense. **A.** *sb.* 1853. **B.** *adj.* 1840. Hence **Anglo-Saˑxondom,** the Anglo-Saxon domain; the Anglo-Saxons collectively; rhet. for Great Britain and the United States. **Anglo-Saˑxonism,** **a.** anything peculiar to the Anglo-Saxon race; *esp.* a word, phrase, or habit of speech belonging to the Old English; **b.** the sentiment of being Anglo-Saxon (sense 3) ethnologically; **a** belief in the Anglo-Saxon race.

Angola (ǽŋgōᵘ·lă). 1827. A corruption of ANGORA; the fabric made of Angora wool.

Angor (æ·ŋgǒɹ). ME. [– OFr. *angor* :– L. *angor* strangling, vexation, f. *angere* squeeze, strangle; see -OR 1, -OUR.] †**1.** Anguish –1711. **2.** *spec.* A feeling of anxiety and constriction in the precordial region; cf. *angina* 1666.

Angora (ǽŋgōᵊ·ră). 1819. [Modern form of ancient Ἄγκυρα Ancyra.] **1.** A town in Asia Minor, giving its name to a goat, and to its silk-like wool; also to a cat, etc. **2.** The fabric ANGOLA 1867.

Angostura; see ANGUSTURA.

Angry (æ·ŋgri), *a.* ME. [f. ANGER *sb.* + -Y[1]; cf. *hungry*. Compar. *-ier, -iest.*] †**1.** Full of trouble actively, troublesome –1667; affected by trouble, vexed –1485. **2.** Feeling or showing resentment against the agent or cause of trouble; enraged, wrathful. Const. *at, about* the occasion; *at, with* the person. ME. **3.** Moved or excited by anger 1509. **4.** Looking or acting as if in anger ME.; red (*rare*) 1632. **5.** Habitually under the influence of anger, choleric, passionate (*arch.*) ME. **6.** Inflamed, smarting 1579. **7.** Sharp, keen (*rare*) ME.

2. A. letters to his angrier mistress 1864. A. with you *Hen. V*, IV. i. 217, at him *Timon* III. iii. 13. **3.** The a. trade of war COTTON. **4.** Now.. Doth..warre bristle his a. crest SHAKS. *John* IV. iii. 149. An angrie countenance *Prov.* 25:23. A. masses of cloud TYNDALL. Sweet rose, whose hue angrie and brave [etc.] G. HERBERT. **5.** Honour, this busie, a. thing ROWE. **7.** I never ate with angrier appetite TENNYSON. Hence **A·ngrily** *adv.* **A·ngriness.**

Ångström (unit). 1897. [The name of A. J. *Ångström* (1814–1874), a Swedish physicist.] A hundred-millionth of a centimetre, used in expressing short wave-lengths (abbrev. Å.U., A.U.).

Anguiform (ǽ·ŋgwifǫɹm), *a.* 1800. [f. L. *anguis* snake + -FORM; cf. Fr. *anguiforme.*] Snake-shaped.

†**Anguille, anguelle.** 1500. [– Fr. *anguille* eel :– L. *anguilla*, dim. of *anguis* snake.] 'A sort of small worms cast up by sick hawks.' Hence **Angui·lliform** *a.* eel-shaped.

Anguillule (ǽŋgwi·liul). 1860. [f. L. *anguilla* eel + -ULE; cf. Fr. *anguillule.*] A small eel-shaped creature; *esp.* one of the *Anguillulidæ* or eels found in sour paste or vinegar.

Anguine (æ·ŋgwin), *a.* 1657. [– L. *anguinus*, f. *anguis* snake; see -INE[1].] Of or resembling a snake or serpent.

Anguineous (ǽŋgwi·nĭəs), *a. rare.* 1656. [f. as prec. + -OUS; see -EOUS.] Snake-like; as in Newton's *Anguineous Hyperbola.*

Anguish (æ·ŋgwiʃ), *sb.* ME. [– OFr. *anguisse* (mod. *angoisse*) :– L. *angustia* straitness, pl.

straits, distress, f. *angustus* narrow, tight, f. **angh-* in *angere* squeeze, strangle; see -ISH². Cf. ANGER *sb.*, ANGINA, ANGOR.] Formerly with *pl.* Excruciating or oppressive bodily or mental suffering; pain, or grief.

Anguysshes as of the child berere WYCLIF *Jer.* 4:31. One paine is lesned by anothers a. *Rom. & Jul.* I. ii. 47. I wil speake in the a. of my spirit *Job* 7:11.

Anguish (æ·ŋgwiʃ), *v.* ME. [– OFr. *anguissier* (mod. *angoisser*) – eccl.L. *angustiare* to distress; see prec.] To distress with severe pain or grief, excruciate. Also *intr.* (refl. pron. omitted). Hence **A·nguished** *ppl. a.* sorely distressed; expressing pain.

A·nguishous, *a. Obs.* or *dial.* ME. [– OFr. *anguissus, angoissos* (mod. *angoisseux*) :– med.L. *angustiosus*; see ANGUISH *sb.*, -OUS.] Tormenting –1554; distressed –ME.; anxious –1503.

Angular (æ·ŋgiŭlăɹ), *a.* 1597. [– L. *angularis*. f. *angulus* ANGLE *sb.*²; see -AR¹. Cf. Fr. *angulaire*.] **1.** Having an angle or angles, sharp-cornered 1598. **2.** Constituting, placed in or at, an angle 1597; measured by angle 1674. **3.** Having the joints and bones prominent. Of action: Jerky, abrupt, awkward. 1850. **4.** Stiff and formal; unaccommodating; cantankerous 1840.

1. A. handwriting 1863. 2. An a. aperture of 60° 1867. 3. The a. female in black bombazine O. W. HOLMES. Many bows and a deal of a. politeness HAWTHORNE. Hence **A·ngularly** *adv.* in or with angles; at (acute) angles; in an a. manner; see ANGULAR 3.

Angularity (æŋgiulæ·riti). 1642. [f. prec. + -ITY.] **1.** The quality or state of being ANGULAR. *concr.* in *pl.* Angular outlines, sharp corners 1853. **2.** Want of rounded outline. Of manner: Crankiness. 1848.

Angulate (æ·ŋgiŭlĕt), *a.* 1794. [– L. *angulatus*, f. *angulus* ANGLE *sb.*² + *-atus* -ATE².] Formed with corners; angled. Hence **A·ngulate** *v.* to make cornered. **A·ngulately** *adv.* with angles or corners. **Angula·tion,** a making angulate; angular formation or position.

Angulato- (æ:ŋgiŭleⁱto), comb. f. L. *angulatus* used advb. Angulately.

Angulo- (æ:ŋgiŭlo), comb. f. L. *angulus* (see ANGLE *sb.*²) used advb., as in *a.-dentate*, angularly toothed.

Angulo·meter. *rare.* 1859. [f. prec. + -METER.] An instrument for measuring external angles.

A:ngulo·se, *a. rare.* [See ANGULOUS *a.*, -OSE¹.] = ANGULOUS.

Anguloso- (æŋgiulōᵘ:so), comb. f. L. *angulosus*, used advb., as in *a.-gibbous*, gibbous with the curved sides almost forming angles.

Angulous (æ·ŋgiuləs), *a.* ? *Obs.* 1656. [– Fr. *anguleux* or L. *angulosus*; see ANGLE *sb.*², -OUS.] Having angles or corners; angular.

‖ **Anguria** (æŋgiūᵊ·riă). 1611. [mod.L. – Gr. ἀγγούριον water-melon. See -IA².] *Bot.* A plant of the gourd family; also its fruit.

† **Angu·st,** *a.* 1599. [– Fr. † *anguste* or L. *angustus* narrow, f. *angere* squeeze tight.] Strait, compressed –1661.

Angu·state, *a.* 1847. [– *angustat-*, pa. ppl. stem of L. *angustare* make narrow, f. *angustus*; see prec., -ATE².] Narrowed, as leaves at the base. Hence **Angusta·tion,** contraction.

Angusti- (æŋgʊ·sti), comb. f. L. *angustus* narrow; as in *angustifoliate, -ous* narrow-leaved; *angustirostrate*, with narrow beak.

†‖ **Angu·stia.** *rare.* [L. = 'narrowness'; in eccl. L. 'anguish'.] Straits. SIR T. BROWNE.

Angustu·ra, or **Angostura.** 1791. A town on the Orinoco, now Ciudad Bolivar. It gives its name to a bark, the produce of *Galipea* or *Cusparia febrifuga*, a febrifuge and tonic.

† **Anha·ng,** *v.* ME. only. [app. var. of *ahang* (OE. *ahōn*), through confusion of AN- *pref.* 1 and A- *pref.* 1.] To hang. *trans.* and *intr.*

Anharmonic (æ:nhaɹmǫ·nik), *a.* 1863. [– Fr. *anharmonique*, f. Gr. ἀν- AN- *pref.* 10 + *harmonique* HARMONIC.] *Math.* Not harmonic. Applied to the *section* of a line by four points A, B, C, D, when their mutual distances are such that $\frac{AB}{CB}$ is unequal to $\frac{AD}{CD}$; the ratio between these two quotients is called the *anharmonic ratio* of AC.

Anhelation (ænhĭlēⁱ·ʃən). *arch.* 1623. [– Fr. *anhélation* or L. *anhelatio* panting, f. *anhelare*; see next, -ATION.] **1.** A difficulty with breathing, panting; asthma. **2.** *fig.* Panting, aspiration (*after*) 1631.

† **Anhe·le,** *v.* ME. [– OFr. *aneler* (mod. *anhéler*): – L. *anhelare* pant, breathe with difficulty.] **1.** ? To blow, puff. ME. only. **2.** *fig.* To pant *for*, aspire *to* –1536.

† **Anhe·lous,** *a.* 1661. [f. L. *anhelus* panting + -OUS; see prec.] Short of breath, panting –1684.

Anhidrotic (ænhidrǫ·tik), *a.* 1880. [f. AN- *pref.* 10 + HIDROTIC.] *Med.* Tending to check perspiration. As *sb.* [sc. *medicine*.]

Anhistous (ænhi·stəs), *a.* 1880. [f. Gr. ἀν- AN- *pref.* 10 + ἱστόν web, tissue + -OUS; cf. Fr. *anhiste*.] *Biol.* Of tissue: Without recognizable structure.

Anhungered (ænhʊ·ŋgəɹd), *ppl. a. arch.* ME. [alt. of AHUNGERED by substitution of AN- *pref.* 5 for A- *pref.* 3.] **1.** Overcome with hunger, hungry. **2.** *fig.* Eagerly desirous 1848.

† **An-hu·ngry,** *a. rare.* 1607. [var. of *a-hungry*; see prec., AHUNGERED.] Hungry –1681.

Anhydride (ænhəi·drəid). 1863. [f. Gr. ἄνυδρος waterless (f. ἀν- AN- 10 + ὕδωρ, ὑδρ- water) + -IDE.] *Chem.* A compound formed by the union of oxygen with another element, without hydrogen, but which, on exposure to water, absorbs hydrogen and becomes an acid. Also called *anhydrous acids*, because produced by expelling the water from oxy-acids.

Anhydrite (ænhəi·drəit). 1831. [f. as prec. + -ITE¹ 2 b.] *Min.* Anhydrous gypsum or sulphate of lime.

Anhydro- (ænhəi:dro), combining form of next, as in *anhydro-borate*, etc.

Anhydrous (ænhəi·drəs), *a.* 1819. [f. as ANHYDRIDE + -OUS.] **1.** *Chem.* Having no water in its composition: said of *salts*, *crystals*, destitute of water of crystallization, etc. **2.** *transf.* Sapless, dried up 1872. var. **Anhy·dric.**

‖ **A·nicut, ann-.** 1784. [Anglo-Ind. – Tamil *aṇai-kaṭṭu* dam-building.] The dam constructed across a river to fill, and regulate the supply of, the irrigating channels.

Anidioma·tic, -al, *a. rare.* Landor's substitutes for *unidiomatic, -al.*

† **Anie·ntise, -ish,** *v.* ME. [– *anientiss-*, lengthened stem of OFr. *aniantir, -er*, (mod. *anéantir*), annihilate, f. *à* to + *neient, nient* (mod. *néant*) nothing, :– Gallo-Rom. *ne gente* (*gens, gent-* crowd, people).] **1.** To bring to naught, annul, destroy –1483. **2.** To bring low, reduce –1530. var. **Anie·nte.** Hence † **Anie·ntisement,** annihilation.

Anigh (ənəi·). 1773. [f. NIGH *adv.*, after ANEAR.] *adv.* Nigh 1868. *prep.* Near to 1773.

Anight (ănəi·t), *adv. arch.* [ME. *a niht*, OE. *on niht*, i.e. ON *prep.*, NIGHT *sb.*; see A *prep.*¹ 8.] By night, at night.

They mete neuer but a nyght ME.

Anights (ănəi·ts), *adv. arch.* 1440. [Fusion of *on niht*, and *nihtes* advb. gen.] = prec., though *-s* is occas. taken as pl.

Such [men] as sleepe a-nights *Jul. C.* I. ii. 193.

Anil (æ·nil). 1581. [– Fr. or Pg. *anil* – Arab. *an-nil*, i.e. *al* AL-² + Arab. and Pers. *nīl* – Skr. *nīlī* indigo, f. *nīla* dark blue.] **1.** The Indigo shrub 1712. **2.** The indigo dye 1581. **3.** Formative of names of aniline compounds and derivatives; as **anilamic** = PHENYLAMIC, **chloranil** $C_6Cl_4O_2$.

Anile (æ·nəil), *a.* 1652. [– L. *anilis*, f. *anus* old woman; see -ILE.] Of or like an old woman; weak-minded.

Anilic (ăni·lik), *a.* 1863. [f. ANIL + -IC.] **1.** Of or pertaining to anil; as in *Anilic* (or *Indigotic*) *Acid* 1868. **2. -anilic** in comb. = of aniline.

Anilide (æ·niləid). 1863. [f. ANIL + -IDE, = *Anil(ine am)ide*.] *Chem.* A species of alkalamide related to aniline as amides to amines: hence called *phenylamide*.

Aniline (æ·niləin). 1850. [– G. *anilin* (C. J. Fritzsche, 1841); see ANIL, -INE⁵.] *Chem.* A chemical base yielding many beautiful dyes; obtained orig. by distilling indigo with caustic potash, now from coal-tar, etc. It is a colourless, oily, aromatic, volatile liquid, $C_6H_5(NH_2)$, which may be viewed as ammonia in which one hydrogen atom is replaced by the compound radical phenyl C_6H_5, hence also called *Phenylamine*. Also *attrib.* 1864.

Anility (ăni·liti). 1623. [– L. *anilitas*, f. *anus* old woman; see -ITY.] The state of being an old woman; dotage. In fig. use stronger than *senility*.

† **A:nimadve·rsal.** [f. ANIMADVERT, after *reversal*.] The faculty of perceiving; consciousness. HY. MORE.

Animadversion (æ:nimădvə·ɹʃən). 1599. [– Fr. *animadversion* or L. *animadversio*; see ANIMADVERT *v.*] † **1.** The action or the faculty of noticing –1795; (with *pl.*) notice, monition, warning –1712. **2.** The action of taking judicial cognizance of offences, and of inflicting punishment; *concr.* with *pl.* a penal visitation (*arch.*) 1646. **3.** The utterance of criticism or reproof; *concr.* a criticism, *esp.* one implying censure 1599.

2. A power whose lightest measure of a. would be banishment ALISON. 3. [A temper] of a. and cavil M. PATTISON. 3. Some sharp animadversions HALLAM.

† **A:nimadve·rsive,** *a.* 1642. [See next, -IVE.] Percipient –1685.

Animadvert (æ:nimădvə̄·ɹt), *v.* 1637. [– L. *animadvertere*, i.e. *animum advertere* turn the mind to, f. *ad* AD-* + *vertere*, *vers-* turn.] † **1.** *trans.* To turn the mind to, observe –1679. **2.** *intr.* To take note, remark, bethink oneself. Const. *simply*, or with *that* (*arch.*). 1642. **3.** *intr.* To take judicial cognizance of; *hence*, to proceed by way of punishment or censure (*arch.*) 1671. **4.** To comment critically (*on*) 1665.

3. The law will a. hereon as an injury BLACKSTONE. 4. To a. on defects HALLAM. Hence **A:nimadve·rter,** also **-ve·rsor,** one who animadverts (*arch.*).

Animal (æ·nimăl). 1541. [As adj., – (O)Fr. *animal* or L. *animalis*, in med.L. bestial, f. *anima* vital breath, see -AL¹; as sb. ult. – L. *animal*, for *animale*, subst. use of n. adj.]

A. *sb.* **1.** A living being, endowed with sensation and voluntary motion, but in the lowest forms distinguishable from vegetable forms only by evident relationship to other animal forms 1602. **2.** One of the lower animals; a brute or beast, as distinguished from man. (Often limited *pop.* to quadrupeds, and *fam.* to those used by man.) 1600. **3.** A human being in whom the animal nature has the ascendancy. Cf. *creature*. 1588. **4.** *slang* var. for 'hog' in 'go the whole hog' 1838. † **5.** *ellipt.* in *pl.* Animal spirits –1647.

1. What a piece of work is a man!..the Parragon of Animals *Haml.* II. ii. 20. When an organism receives nutritive matter by a mouth..it is called an a. OWEN. 2. He..feasts the a. he dooms his feast POPE. We fastened our animals to trees round the camp-fire 1888. 3. He is onely an a., onely sensible in the duller parts *L.L.L.* IV. ii. 27.

B. *adj.* [See above. Like L. *animalis*, treated in med. Eng. occas. as a deriv. of *anima*, occas. of *animus*, but in mod. use connected with the sb. *animal* only.] † **1.** Connected with sensation, innervation, and will; opp. to *vital* and *natural*. Occas. = psychical. See ANIMAL SPIRITS. –1668. **2.** Of or pertaining to the functions of animals; opp. to *intellectual* and *spiritual* 1651. **3.** Carnal; opp. to *moral*, *spiritual* 1633. **4.** = sb. used *attrib.*; opp. to *vegetable* 1646.

1. Motions proceeding from sense..called a. motions HOBBES. 2. The A. Œconomy 1718. The mere a. courage of the soldier FREEMAN. 3. The a. nature..the a. appetites FROUDE.

Comb. and *phrases*: **a. charcoal,** that formed by charring a. substance; **a. electricity,** that developed in certain animals, as the torpedo and electric eel; **a. food; a. flower,** one of the actinozoa, as the sea-anemone; **a. heat,** the constant temperature maintained within the bodies of living animals; **a. kingdom,** the whole species of animals viewed scientifically, as one of the three great divisions of natural objects; **a. magnetism** = MESMERISM; **a. myth,** one founded upon the habits of animals; **a. painter, painting, piece; a. plant,** a zoophyte or polype, as coral; **a. world.**

Hence **Anima·lic** *a. rare.* † **A·nimalish** *a.* of the nature of an a. CUDWORTH.

Animalcula, *sb. pl.*; see ANIMALCULE.

Animalcular (ænimæ·lkiŭlăɹ), *a. rare.* 1753. [f. as next + -AR[1].] Of or pertaining to animalcules 1765, or †animalculism –1807. var. **Anima·lculine.**

Animalcule (ænimæ·lkiŭl). 1509. [– mod.L. *animalculum* (whence also Fr. *animalcule*), dim. of *animal*; see ANIMAL *sb.*, -CULE.] †**1.** A small or tiny animal, as a mouse, or any invertebrate –1831. **2.** A microscopic animal: *esp.* of the *Rotifera* and *Infusoria* 1677.

1. The basest of created animalcules, the Spider CARLYLE.

Animalculism (ænimæ·lkiŭliz'm). 1874. [f. as prec. + -ISM.] *Phys.* or *Path.* The theory that animalcules are (1) the germs of life, and (2) the cause of diseases, and thus explain phenomena. Hence **Anima·lculist,** an adherent of A.; one who makes a study of animalcules.

† **Animali·llio.** [f. ANIMAL, w. dim. ending as in It. *-iglio*, Sp. *-illo* (-ilʸo).] A tiny animal. HOWELL.

Animalism (æ·nimăliz'm). 1831. [f. ANIMAL + -ISM.] **1.** Animal activity; sensuality. **2.** The doctrine which views men as mere animals 1857. **3.** A merely sensual being (*rare*) 1868.

1. Healthy a. KINGSLEY. A face..without a vestige of a. 1868. 3. Girls, Hetairai,..Hired animalisms TENNYSON.

Animalist (æ·nimălist). 1837. [f. as prec. + -IST.] **1.** One who takes the 'animal' side of a discussion. **2.** An adherent of ANIMALISM 2; a sensualist 1851. **3.** = ANIMALCULIST 1874.

Animality (ænimæ·lĭti). 1615. [– Fr. *animalité*; see ANIMAL, -ITY.] **1.** The sum of the animal qualities and functions; vital power. **2.** The merely animal nature, as opp. to the moral and spiritual; animalhood 1646. **3.** Animal nature, life; opp. to *vegetable* or *inorganic* matter 1647. **4.** The animal series 1770.

2. Ignorance and a. 1868. A. and primitive barbarism 1878.

Animalize (æ·nimăləiz), *v.* 1741. [f. ANIMAL + -IZE, partly through Fr. *animaliser.*] †**1.** To represent in animal form. **2.** To convert into animal substance 1770. **3.** To reduce to animal nature; to sensualize 1806.

3. Has sensualized and animalized its character ARNOLD. Hence **A:nimaliza·tion,** the act of animalizing (senses 2, 3); ‖ distribution of animal existence, animal population. [Fr.]

Animally (æ·nimăli), *adv.* 1600. [f. as prec. + -LY[2].] †**1.** Psychically, in respect of the *anima*, animal soul –1678. **2.** Physically, opp. to *intellectually* 1866.

Animal spirits (formerly, **spirit**). [See ANIMAL *adj.* 1.] †**1.** *orig.* The supposed 'spirit' or principle of sensation and voluntary motion; answering to nerve fluid, nerve force, nervous action –1777. †**2.** Nerve, animal courage –1719. **3.** *coll. pl.* Nervous vivacity, healthy animalism 1739.

3. She had high animal spirits JANE AUSTEN.

† **A·nimant,** *a. rare.* 1677. [– *animant-*, pres. ppl. stem of L. *animare* quicken; see ANIMATE *ppl. a.* and *sb.*, -ANT.] Having life; animated 1678. As *sb.* [sc. *creature.*] 1677.

† **Anima·stic,** *a.* 1651. [– med.L. *animasticus* pertaining to the soul, f. L. *anima* breath, life. For the (hybrid) suffix, cf. ONOMASTIC *a.*] Spiritual, opp. to *material*; occ. = ANIMATE –1855. † As *sb.* Psychology. SIR W. HAMILTON.

Animate (æ·nimet), *ppl. a.* and *sb.* 1546. [– *animat-*, pa. ppl. stem of L. *animare* quicken, f. *anima* air, breath, life, soul; see -ATE[2].] **A.** *pple.* and *adj.* †**1.** *pple.* Animated, inspired –1640. **2.** *adj.* Endowed with life 1605. **3.** Lively 1801. **4.** Pertaining to animals 1828.

2. Phylosophers..have affirmed the..loadstone to be a. 1605.

B. † *sb.* A living thing –1669.

Animate (æ·nimeⁱt), *v.* 1538. [f. as prec.; see -ATE[3].] **1.** To give life to, quicken, vivify 1542. **2.** To give the appearance of life to (*arch.*) 1612. **3.** To impart vividness or interest to, enliven 1670. **4.** To fill with boldness; inspirit 1538; † *intr.* to become animated –1782. **5.** To inspire, incite 1583. **6.** To actuate, or put in motion 1646.

2. Poetry..which..animates matter JOHNSON. 3. To a. a play FLECKNOE, the song POPE. 4. The shouting animates their hearts DRYDEN. 5. Animated by religious zeal MARLOWE. 6. Motion ..which animates the bullet TYNDALL. Hence **A·nimatingly** *adv.* **A·nimative** *a.* having the faculty of animating. **A·nimator, -er,** he who or that which animates.

Animated (æ·nimeⁱtėd), *ppl. a.* 1532. [f. prec. + -ED[1].] **1.** Endowed with life 1534; *fig.* appearing alive 1711. **2.** Full of activity; spirited; vivacious 1585. **3.** Inspired, actuated, encouraged 1532. †**4.** Pertaining to animated beings 1753.

1. *Animated Nature*: that portion which is alive; the animal world. Heroes in a. marble frown POPE. 2. The discussion was a. PRESCOTT. 3. Our newly a. common enemies MILT. 4. A. pathology E. CHAMBERS. Hence **A·nimatedly** *adv.*

Animation (ænimēⁱ·ʃən). 1597. [– L. *animatio*, f. as prec.; see -ION.] **1.** The action of animating (see ANIMATE *v.*); quickening. **2.** The state of being alive, animateness (*arch.*) 1615. **3.** Vivacity, sprightliness 1790. †**4.** Inspiration –1664; *esp.* encouragement –1680.

1. The fourth act that goeth to make man, is called A. HOWELL. 2. Suspended a. 1837. 3. Johnson..talked with great a. BOSWELL. 4. A great a. of my..endeavours 1616.

‖ **Animé** (a·nime, æ·nimi), *sb.* 1577. [Fr., perh. = 'alive' with insects; or a native name.] A name for resins, *esp.* that obtained from a West Indian tree (*Hymenæa Courbaril*).

‖ **Animé** (a·nime), *a.* 1731. [Fr., = animated, excited, aroused.] *Her.* In action and showing a desire to fight; having the eyes, etc. of a different tincture from the animal itself.

Animine (æ·niməin). 1863. [f. ANIM(AL + -INE[5].] *Chem.* An organic base obtained from bone-oil, etc.

Animism (æ·nimiz'm). 1832. [f. L. *anima* + -ISM.] **1.** The doctrine of the *anima mundi* (Stahl 1720); the doctrine that the phenomena of animal life are produced by an immaterial *anima*, or soul, distinct from matter. **2.** The attribution of a living soul to inanimate objects and natural phenomena 1866. **3.** By extension: Spiritualism; the belief in the existence of soul or spirit apart from matter 1880.

2. Polytheism..takes very largely the form of a. 1877. Hence **A·nimist,** an adherent of a. **Animi·stic** *a.* of or belonging to a. or animists.

Animosity (ænimǫ·sĭti). ME. [–(O)Fr. *animosité* or late L. *animositas*, f. *animosus* spirited, f. *animus* spirit, mind; see -OSITY.] †**1.** Spiritedness, courage –1670. **2.** Excitement of feeling against any one; active enmity 1605.

1. Confirming his wavering hand unto the a. of that attempt SIR T. BROWNE. 2. The more affinity there is between theological parties, the greater commonly is their a. HUME.

† **A·nimous,** *a. rare.* 1620. [– Fr. *animeux*, – late L. *animosus*; see prec., -OUS.] Spirited; also, hot-tempered.

Animus (æ·nimɒs). No pl. 1831. [– L. *animus* spirit, mind.] Actuating feeling, bias, animating (usu. hostile) temper; *hence,* animosity.

Anion (æ·niǫn). 1834. [– Gr. ἀνιόν n. pres. pple. of ἀνιέναι go up.] *Electr.* Faraday's term for an ion carrying a negative charge of electricity by virtue of which it is attracted, on electrolysis, to the anode. Cf. CATION.

Anis-, *Chem.* comb. form of L. *anisum* anise, forming names of compounds derived from oil of anise, as **A·nisal,** short for *anisic aldehyde*, etc.

Anisanthous (æ:nəisæ·nþəs), *a.* 1880. [f. Gr. ἄνισος unequal + ἄνθος flower + -OUS.] *Bot.* Having perianths of different form.

Anisated (æ·niseⁱtėd), *ppl. a.* 1880. [f. ANISE + -ATE[3] + -ED[1], perh. after Fr. *anisé.*] Mixed or flavoured with aniseed.

Anise (æ·nis). ME. [–(O)Fr. *anis* :– L. *anisum* – Gr. ἄνισον. Cf. ANET.] **1.** An umbelliferous plant (*Pimpinella anisum*), a native of the Levant, anciently confused with the Dill (*Anethum graveolens*), prob. the anise of the Bible of 1611. **2.** *fig.* See *Matt.* 23:23. 1741.

Aniseed (æ·nisīd). [ME. *annes, aneys sede.*] **1.** The seed of the anise. Also *attrib.* 1698. **2.** = ANISETTE (*rare*) 1756.

‖ **Anisette** (ɑnize·t). 1837. [Fr., in full *anisette de Bordeaux*, f. *anis* ANISE + *-ette* -ETTE.] A liqueur flavoured with aniseed.

Anisic (æ̆ni·zik), *a.* 1863. [f. ANISE + -IC.] Of or derived from anise, as in *a. series, acid*, etc.

Aniso-, comb. form of Gr. ἄνισος unequal, a formative *esp.* of negatives of corresponding terms in Iso-.

a:niso·bryous [Gr. βρύειν] *a., Bot.* = *anisodynamous*; **-dacty·lic** [Gr. δάκτυλος] *a., Zool.* unequal-toed (said of those insessorial birds called *Anisodactyles*); **-dy·namous** [Gr. δύναμις] *a., Bot.* growing more strongly on one side of the axis than on the other; **-gynous** [Gr. γυνή] *a., Bot.* having the carpels not equal in number to the sepals; **-me·ric** [Gr. μέρος] *a., Chem.* not composed of the same proportions of the same elements; **-merous** *a.*, not having equal, or the same number of, parts, unsymmetrical; *esp.* in *Bot.* having unequal numbers of parts in different whorls; **-me·tric** [Gr. μέτρον] *a.*, of unequal measurement, consisting of unequal or nonsymmetrical parts; **-metro·pia** [Gr. μέτρον + ὤψ, ὦπα], *Path.* inequality in the refractive power of the two eyes; **-metro·pic** *a.*; **-pe·talous** [Gr. πέταλον] *a., Bot.* with unequal petals; **-phy·llous** [Gr. φύλλον] *a., Bot.* with unequal leaves; **-pterous** [Gr. πτερόν], *a.*, having unequal wings; *esp.* in *Bot.* of fruit, flowers, etc.; **-ste·monous** [Gr. στήμων] *a., Bot.* having the stamens unequal in number to the petals or sepals; **-sthe·nic** [Gr. σθένος], *a.*, of unequal strength; **-stomous** [Gr. στόμα] *a., Bot.* having unequal mouths, as in a calyx unequally divided; **-tropal, -tropous** *a.* = ANISOTROPIC; **-tropy** [Gr. -τροπία], the quality of being anisotropic, æolotropy.

Anisotropic (æ̆nəi:sotrǫ·pik), *a.* 1879. [f. ANISO- + Gr. τροπικός of turning.] Possessing the power both of right- and left-handed polarization; æolotropic.

Anker (æ·ŋkəɹ); also **ankor, anchor.** 1673. [– LG., Du. (whence G.) *anker* – med.L. *anceria, ancheria* of unkn. origin.] **1.** A liquid measure used in various parts. That of Rotterdam, once used in England, holds 10 old wine or 8½ imperial gallons. **2.** A cask or keg of the above capacity 1750.

Ankerite (æ·ŋkərəit). 1843. [f. Prof. *Anker* of Styria + -ITE[1] 2b.] *Min.* A mineral closely allied to Dolomite, with the magnesia largely replaced by iron, with or without magnesia.

Ankle, ancle (æ·ŋk'l). ME. [– ON. **ankul-* (OSw. *ankol*, OIcel. *ǫkkla*), corresp. to OFris. *ankel*, MLG. *enkel*, MDu. *ankel*, OHG. *anchal, enchil* (G. *enkel*); f. **aŋk-* :– IE. **aŋg-*, as in L. *angulus* ANGLE *sb.*[2]. Superseded OE. *ancléow*, ME. *anclow, anclee.*] The joint which connects the foot with the leg; the slender part between this and the calf.

His stockings..downe giued to his Anckle *Haml.* II. i. 80. Hence **A·nkled** *ppl. a.* furnished with ankles (*rare*).

Anklet (æ·ŋklėt). 1832. [f. prec. + -LET, after *bracelet.*] An ornament or fetter for the ankle.

Ankylose, -osis, vars. of ANCHYLOSE, -OSIS.

Anlace (æ·nlăs, -ĕs). *arch.* [ME. *aunlaz, anla(a)s*, of unkn. origin.] A short two-edged knife or dagger, broad at the hilt, and tapering to a point, formerly worn at the girdle. (Obs. bef. 1500. Used loosely by mod. poets.)

† **A·nlet.** 1557. [– OFr. *anelet*, dim. of *anel* :– L. *anellus*, dim. of *anulus*; cf. ANNULET.] A small ring –1660.

Anna (æ·nă). 1727. [– Hind. *ānā* (Panjabi *ānnā*).] An East Indian money of account; the 16th part of a rupee.

¶ In Anglo-Indian speech 'a 6-anna share' = $\frac{6}{16}$, '4 annas of dark blood' = a quadroon, etc.

Annabergite (ænăbə·ɹgəit). 1852. [f. *Annaberg*, in Saxony; see -ITE[1] 2 b.] *Min.* A hydrous arsenate of nickel, apple-green in colour, occurring in capillary crystals, or as an earthy mass.

A·nnal, *sb.* sing. form of ANNALS. Hence † **A·nnal** *v.* to compose annals, chronicle (*rare*). **A·nnalism,** annal-writing (*rare*). **A·nnalist,** a writer of annals; also *ellipt.*

and *transf.* **A·nnalistic** *a.* of or proper to the annalist or annals. † **A·nnalize** *v.* to chronicle.

Annals (æ·nălz), *sb. pl.* 1536. [– Fr. *annales* or L. *annales* masc. pl. (sc. *libri* books) of *annalis* yearly, f. *annus* year; see -AL[1].] **1.** A narrative of events written year by year 1563; *sing.* the record of a single year, or a single item, in a chronicle 1699; also *attrib.* **2.** Historical records generally 1581. **3.** Masses said for the space of a year 1536.

1. Annals..contain the mere jottings down of unconnected events STUBBS. The annal of that year BENTLEY. *attrib.* The annal Text MILT. **2.** The short and simple annals of the poor GRAY.

† **A·nnary.** [f. L. *annus* year + -ARY[1], after *diary*.] An annual record. FULLER.

Annates (æ·ne[i]ts, -ĕts). 1534. [– pl. of Fr. *annate* – med.L. *annata* year's space, work, or proceeds, f. *annus* year.] **1.** The first-fruits, or one year's revenue, paid to the Pope by bishops, etc., of the R.C. Church on their appointment to a see or benefice.

The annates of English benefices, transferred to the Crown at the Reformation, were given up in the reign of Queen Anne to form the fund known as Queen Anne's Bounty.

2. *Sc. Law.* A half-year's salary, in addition to the stipend, which is legally due to the executors of a deceased minister 1571.

Anneal (ănī·l), *v.* [OE. *onǣlan*, f. *on* (see AN *prep.*) + *ǣlan* kindle, burn, bake, f. *āl* fire, burning, = OS. *ēld*, ON. *eldr*.] † **1.** To set on fire, kindle (*lit.* and *fig.*) –ME. † **2.** To subject to the action of fire; to fire, bake, fuse, glaze –1668. **3.** To burn in colours upon glass, earthenware, or metal, to enamel by encaustic process (*arch.*) 1580. **4.** To toughen after fusion by exposure to continuous and slowly diminished heat, as glass, steel, etc. 1664. Also *fig.*

3. When thou dost a. in glasse thy storie G. HERBERT. **4.** *fig.* The mind to strengthen and a. SCOTT. Hence **Annea·ler,** he who or that which anneals (*rare*).

† **Anne·ct,** *v.* 1531. [– L. *annectere*, f. *ad* AN- *pref.* 7 + *nectere* tie, fasten. See ANNEX *v.*] = ANNEX –1737.

Annectent (ăne·ktĕnt), *a.* 1826. [f. as prec.; see -ENT.] Joining on, connecting.

Transitional or a. characters OWEN.

Annelid(e (æ·nĕlid). 1834. [– Fr. *annélide* or mod.L. *annelida*; see next.] *Zool. sb.* One of the *Annelida. adj.* Of or pertaining to the *Annelida* 1855. vars. **Anne·lidan** *a.* and *sb.*, **Anneli·dian** *a.*

‖ **Annelida** (ăne·lidă), *sb. pl.* 1834. [mod.L., n.pl., f. Fr. *annelé's* 'ringed animals' (Lamarck, 1801), ppl. a. f. *anneler*, f. OFr. *anel* (mod. *anneau*) ring; see ANLET.] *Zool.* A class of animals (*Articulata* Cuvier) comprising the Red-blooded worms with bodies composed of annular segments.

Anne·lidous. *rare.* 1845. [f. as prec. + -OUS.] Of the nature of an annelid.

Anneloid (æ·neloid). 1869. [f. as prec. + -OID.] *Zool.* An animal resembling the *Annelida*.

Annex (ăne·ks), *v.* ME. [– (O)Fr. *annexer*, f. *annex-*, pa. ppl. stem of L. *annectere*, f. *ad* AN- *pref.* 7 + *nectere* tie, bind.] **1.** To join (*to*) (*arch.*). **2.** To unite materially, as an accessory (*arch.*) 1605. **3.** To join as an addition to existing possessions 1509. **4.** To append 1450. **5.** To affix (a seal, or signature) (*arch.*) 1603. **6.** To attach as an attribute ME., condition 1588, or consequence 1538.

2. Ye a... Periwiges and counterfeite Haire PRYNNE. **3.** Julius Cæsar annexed Brittaine to the Romaine emperie 1534. **6.** It is annexed to the Soveraignty, to be Judge HOBBES. Salvation is not annexed to a right knowledge of geometry M. ARNOLD. Hence **Anne·xable** *a.* † **A·nnexary,** an adjunct. **Anne·xed** *ppl. a.*; also **annext. Anne·xer,** one who annexes (territory). **Anne·xment,** an adjunct (*rare*). *Haml.* III. iii. 21.

Annex(e (ăne·ks), *sb.* 1540. [– Fr. *annexe* – L. *annexum*, subst. use of pa. pple. of *annectere*; see prec.] † **1.** An adjunct, accessory –1686. **2.** *Sc. Law.* An appurtenance 1540. **3.** An appendix 1647. **4.** From mod.Fr. *annexe*: A supplementary building; a wing 1861.

3. The annex to the Anglo-Turkish convention of 1878 (*mod.*). **4.** Newnham and Girton, and..the Woman's Annex at Harvard 1883.

Annexation (ænĕksē[i]·ʃən). 1611. [– med.L. *annexatio*; see prec., -ION.] **1.** The action of annexing (see ANNEX *v.* 1, 3, 6) 1634. † **2.** The thing annexed 1611.

1. France..by the a. of Piedmont, had overstepped the Alps BRYCE. The a. of punishment to vicious acts 1833.

Annexa·tionist. 1845. [f. prec. + -IST.] One who advocates annexation (of territory). Also *attrib.* or *adj.* 1852.

Used in *U.S.* (1845) of the 'annexation' of Texas.

Annexion (ăne·kʃən). *arch.* 1600. [– late L. *annexio*; see ANNEX *v.*, -ION.] **1.** = ANNEXATION 1. 1611. † **2.** The thing annexed; an adjunct –1748.

2. With the annexions of fair gems enrich'd SHAKS. Hence **Anne·xionist** = ANNEXATIONIST.

† **Anni·hil,** *v.* 1490. [– (O)Fr. *annihiler* – late L. *annihilare* (Jerome), f. *ad* AD- + *nihil* nothing.] = ANNIHILATE –1595.

Annihilable (ănəi·hĭlăb'l), *a.* 1677. [f. prec. + -ABLE.] Capable of being annihilated.

Annihilate (ănəi·hĭlĕt), *ppl. a. arch.* ME. [– late L. *annihilatus*, pa. pple. of *annihilare*; see ANNIHIL *v.*, -ATE[2].] **1.** Reduced to nothing. † **2.** Made null and void –1587.

Annihilate (ănəi·hĭle[i]t), *v.* 1525. [f. as prec. + -ATE[3], superseding ANNIHIL *v.*] **1.** To reduce to nothing, blot out of existence 1586. **2.** To make null and void, cancel, abrogate 1525; to treat as non-existent (*arch.*) 1542. **3.** To extinguish virtually 1630. **4.** To destroy the collective or organized existence of anything 1808.

1. Ye Gods! a. but space and time, And make two lovers happy POPE. **2.** To a. arguments 1665, rights 'JUNIUS', law 1836, exploits SMOLLETT. **3.** Thou who with thy frown Annihilated senates BYRON. **4.** To a. an army WELLINGTON, the fleet of Napoleon 1879. Hence **Anni·hilated** *ppl. a.* utterly destroyed. **Anni·hilative** *a.* such as to a.; crushing. **Anni·hilator,** he who, or that which, utterly destroys.

Annihilation (ănəi:hĭlē[i]·ʃən). 1638. [– (O)Fr. *annihiliation* (XIV), f. *annihilat-* pa. ppl. stem of late L. *annihilare*; see ANNIHILATE *v.*, -ION.] **1.** The action of annihilating (see ANNIHILATE *v.* 1, 2, 4). **2.** The state of being annihilated 1677.

1. Suppose the a. of all matter PRIESTLEY. An a. of credit 1796, of an army 1796. **2.** Political a. 1851.

Annihilationism (ănəi:hĭlē[i]·ʃəniz'm). 1881. [f. prec. + -ISM.] *Theol.* The doctrine of the total annihilation of the wicked after death. Hence **Anni:hila·tionist.**

A·nnist. [-IST.] A partisan of Queen Anne. SWIFT.

Anniversarily (ænivɜ̄·ɹsărĭli), *adv.* 1631. [f. next + -LY[2].] By annual return.

Anniversary (ænivɜ̄·ɹsări). ME. [– L. *anniversarius* returning yearly, f. *annus* year + *versus* turning + *-arius* -ARY[1]; used subst. in med.L. *anniversaria* (sc. *dies* day), *-arium* (sc. *festum* feast); cf. (O)Fr. *anniversaire*; see -ARY[1], [2].] **A.** *adj.* **1.** Returning at the same date yearly; annual 1552; † *loosely*, repeated each year –1738. † **2.** Completed in a year –1704. **3.** [*attrib.* use of *sb.*] Of or pertaining to an anniversary 1654.

B. *sb.* [sc. *day, service*, etc.] **1.** The yearly return of any remarkable date, the day on which some interesting event is annually celebrated ME. **2.** The celebration which takes place on such a date; *orig.* a mass in memory of someone on the day of his death ME. † **3.** *R.C.Ch.* The commemorative service performed daily for a year after a person's death –1753.

‖ **Anno Domini** (æ·no dǫ·minəi). 1579. [L., = in the year of the Lord.] In the year of the Christian era; **b.** *jocular colloq.* as *sb.* Advanced or advancing age 1885.

Annominate (ănǫ·mine[i]t), *v. rare.* 1765. [var. of AGNOMINATE (see AGNOMEN), after med.L. and Fr. sp. *ann-*.] To call by some epithet or title.

Annomination (ănǫminē[i]·ʃən). 1753. [var. of AGNOMINATION, prob. – Fr. *annomination*, med.L. *annominatio*.] **1.** Paronomasia. † **2.** Alliteration 1775.

‖ **Annonce** (anõ̂s). *rare.* 1807. [Fr.] = ANNOUNCEMENT.

Annotate (æ·nŏte[i]t), *v.* 1733. [– *annotat-*, pa. ppl. stem of L. *annotare* put a note to, f. *ad-* AN- *pref.* 7 + *nota* mark, NOTE *sb.*[2]; see -ATE[3].] **1.** To add notes to (a work or author) 1755. **2.** *intr.* To add or make notes. Const. *on, upon.* 1733.

2. It was Coleridge's habit to a. with a pencil 1882. var. † **Anno·te.** Hence **A·nnotated** *ppl. a.* furnished with notes. **A·nnotative** *a.* of the nature of annotation.

Annotation (ænotē[i]·ʃən). 1460. [– Fr. *annotation* or L. *annotatio*, f. as prec.; see ION.] **1.** The action of annotating 1570. † **2.** Chronological reckoning –1669. **3.** *concr.* (usu. *pl.*) A note, by way of explanation or comment 1528.

3. The minute..with annotations in the margin 1528.

Annotator (æ·nŏte[i]təɹ). 1663. [f. as ANNOTATE *v.* + -OR 2; cf. Fr. *annotateur* (XVI), med. L. *annotator* in same sense.] One who annotates; a commentator. Hence **Anno·tatory** *a.* of or pertaining to an a., or his work.

† **A·nnotine.** *rare.* [– L. *annotinus* of last year, f. *annus* year.] *Bot.* A tree of which the fruit does not ripen in a single season; *e.g.* the fig. Hence **Anno·tinous** *a.* a year old.

Annotto, var. of ANATTA.

Announce (ănau·ns), *v.* 1483. [– Fr. *annoncer* :– L. *annuntiare*, f. *ad* AN- *pref.* 6 + *nuntiare*, f. *nuntius* messenger.] **1.** To deliver news; to make public or official intimation of; to proclaim 1485. **2.** *ellipt.* To intimate the approach or presence of 1761. **3.** To make manifest to the senses, or mind 1781.

1. Who..publish laws, a. Or life or death PRIOR. The angel..announced to them that he was rysen CAXTON. **2.** Dinner was announced 1802. **3.** His feeble efforts announced his degenerate spirit GIBBON. Hence **Annou·ncer** 1611; *spec.*, in broadcasting, a person who announces the subjects of a programme and the items of news (1922).

Announcement (ănau·nsmĕnt). 1798. [f. prec. + -MENT.] The action of announcing; public or official notification.

Annoy (ănoi·), *sb.* Aphet. to NOY. [ME. *anui, anoy* – OFr. *anui, anoi* (mod. *ennui*) :– Rom. **inodio*, from the L. phr. *mihi in odio est* it is hateful to me (cf. ODIUM).] **1.** A disturbed or ruffled feeling arising from impressions, etc., which one dislikes. Orig. = mod. Fr. *ennui*; now active discomfort. **2.** That which causes the feeling; annoyance ME.

1. His *ennui* amounted to a. 1812. *To work*, † *do, annoy*: to cause trouble, to molest. Hence † **Annoy·ous** *a.* disturbing; troubled. † **Annoy·ously** *adv.*

Annoy (ănoi·), *v.* Also aphet. to NOY. [ME. *anue, anoie* – OFr. *anuier, anoier* (mod. *ennuyer*); cf. late L. *inodiare* make loathsome, f. **inodio* (see prec.).] † **1.** *intr.* To be odious, or a cause of trouble (*to*, or *dat.*); *trans.* to trouble, bore (= Fr. *ennuyer*) –1534. **2.** *trans.* To affect so as to ruffle, trouble, vex. (Refers to the feeling, rather than the action; hence freq. in pass.) ME. † *intr.* (refl. pron. omitted.) –1555. **3.** To molest, injure; *esp.* in *Mil.* ME. *absol.* ME. † **4.** To derange affect injuriously –1721.

1. Ye all are anoyed and wery of all goodness LD. BERNERS. **2.** She will not be annoy'd with suters *Tam. Shr.* I. i. 189. **3.** The works on the hills would a. the town NELSON. When fears a. BLAKE. Hence **Annoy·er. Annoy·ing-ly** *adv.*, **-ness.**

Annoyance (ănoi·ăns). ME. [– OFr. *anoiance*, f. *anoier*; see prec., -ANCE.] **1.** The action of annoying; molestation. **2.** The state of feeling caused by what annoys; vexation 1502. **3.** Anything annoying, a nuisance 1502.

2. A. and trouble of mind MILT. **3.** *Jury of Annoyance*: one appointed to report upon public nuisances. Hence **Annoy·ancer,** he who, or that which, annoys. [Cf. *conveyancer*.]

Annual (æ·niuăl). late ME. [Earliest form *annuel* – (O)Fr. *annuel* – late L. *annualis*, for L. *annuus* and *annalis*, f. *annus* year; see -AL[1].] **A.** *adj.* Of, belonging to, or reckoned by, the year; yearly. **2.** Recurring once every year 1548. **3.** Repeated yearly and occupying the whole year 1635. **4.** Lasting for a year only. late ME.

1. Three thousand Crownes in Annuall fee *Haml.* II. ii. 73. Annual Register 1650. **2.** So stears the.. crane Her a. Voiage MILT. *P.L.* VII. 431. **3.** The a. course of the sun FROUDE. **4.** A. parliaments STUBBS, plants BACON. Hence **A·nnually** *adv.* yearly.

B. *sb.* 1. In *R.C. Ch.* A mass said either daily for a year after, or yearly on the anniversary of, a person's death; *also*, the payment for it. **2.** A yearly payment, tribute, allowance, etc. *Obs.* exc. in *Sc. Law*, where *annual* = quit-rent. 1622. **3.** Anything that lasts only for a year; *esp.* an annual plant (perpetuating itself by seed) 1710. **4.** A book published once a year; a year-book 1689.

3. Oaths are the children of fashion; they are.. almost annuals SWIFT. Like an a. in a garden, which must be raised anew every season DE FOE. Hence **A·nnualist,** a contributor to an a. **A·nnualize** *v.* to write for an a. SOUTHEY.

Annuary (æ·niuări). 1550. [– late L. *annuarius* annual, med.L. *annuarium* anniversary, f. *annus* year; see -ARY[1].] † *adj.* = ANNUAL *a.* –1651. *sb.* † **1.** A priest who says annual masses 1550. **2.** = ANNUAL *sb.* 4. 1856.

† **Annueller.** ME. [– OFr. *annueler*, in med.L. *annuellarius*; see ANNUAL, –ER[2] 2.] A priest who celebrates ANNUALS –1528.

A·nnuent, *a.* 1727. [– *annuent-*, pres. ppl. stem of L. *annuere* nod to; see -ENT.] Nodding; *spec.* of the muscles which nod the head.

† **Annui·sance.** ME. [– OFr. *anuisance*, f. *anuire*, f. *a* (A- *pref.* 7) + *nuire* to hurt; see NUISANCE.] Nuisance, injury –1751.

Annuitant (ăniu·itănt). 1720. [f. next, after *accountant*, etc.; see -ANT.] One who holds, or receives, an annuity. Also *fig.*

Annuity (ăniu·iti). ME. [– Fr. *annuité* – med.L. *annuitas*, f. *annuus* ANNUAL; see -ITY.] **1.** A yearly allowance, or income. **2.** *Law.* The grant of an annual sum for a term of years, for life, or in perpetuity, chargeable primarily upon the grantor's person, and his heirs if named; opp. to *rent-charge* ME. **3.** An investment of money, entitling the investor to receive a series of equal annual payments, made up of both principal and interest, except in the case of perpetual annuities; *also*, the annual sum thus paid 1693.

In *perpetual annuities* the payments cease only on repayment of the principal; in *deferred* or *reversionary annuities* they commence after some specified time or event.

Annul (ănɒ·l), *v.* ME. [– OFr. *anuller*, *adnuller* (mod. *annuler*):– late L. (Vulg.) *annullare*, f. *ad* AN- *pref.* 7 + *nullum* nothing, n. sing. of *nullus* none, NULL *a.*] **1.** To reduce to nothing, extinguish. **2.** To put an end to (an action, etc.); to abolish, cancel ME. **3.** To destroy the force of; to render void in law ME.

1. Light..to me is extinct, And all her various objects of delight Annulled MILT. *Sams.* 70. **2.** Intellect annuls Fate EMERSON. **3.** To a. a pardon SELDEN, a contract 1786, statutes MACAULAY. Hence **Annu·llable** *a.* (*rare*). † **A·nnullate** *v.* = ANNUL. † **Annulla·tion,** the act of annulling, or being annulled. **Annu·ller.**

Annular (æ·niŭlăɹ), *a.* 1571. [– Fr. *annulaire* or L. *annularis*, f. *annulus*; see ANNULUS, -AR[1].] **1.** Of or pertaining to a ring or rings; ring-like; ring-formed, ringed; *esp.* in *Phys.* of ringed or ring-like structures 1691. **2.** = ANNULARY 2. 1648.

1. An a. body like a Wasp 1664. **2.** His a. finger 1648.

Phrases. Annular space, that between an inner and an outer ring or cylinder. *A. ligament* (*Phys.*), a muscular band girding the wrist and ankle. *A. process* or *protuberance* (in the brain), the *Pons Varolii*, a ring-like process of the medulla oblongata. *A. Eclipse* of the sun (*Astr.*), when the dark body of the moon is seen projected upon the sun's disc, leaving a ring of light visible all round. *A. vault* (*Arch.*), a vaulted roof over an annular space between two concentric walls. Hence **Annula·rity,** a. quality or form. **A·nnularly** *adv.* after the manner or form of a ring or rings.

Annulary (æ·niulări), *a.* 1623. [– L. *annularius*, f. as prec.; see -ARY[1].] † **1.** = ANNULAR 1. –1691. **2.** Bearing the ring. (Said of the fourth finger of the left hand.) Also as *sb.* [sc. *finger.*] 1623.

‖ **Annulata** (æniulē·i·tă), *sb. pl.* 1847. [L., n. pl. (sc. *animalia*) of *annulatus*; see next.] = ANNELIDA (the commoner name); occ. = ANNULOSA; see ANNULATE 2.

Annulate (æ·niŭlĕt), *a.* 1830. [– L. *annulatus* furnished with a ring, f. ANNULUS; cf. ANNULAR *a.*, -ATE[2].] **1.** Furnished or marked with a ring or rings; *esp.* in *Bot.* **2.** = ANNULATED 3. 1852.

Annulated (æ·niŭleⁱted), *ppl. a.* 1668. [f. prec. + -ED[1].] **1.** That wears rings. **2.** Furnished with rings; marked with ring-like lines, ridges, or grooves; *Her.* having an annulet 1668. **3.** Composed of rings, or a series of ring-like segments united so as to form a tube 1748.

Annulation (æniulē·i·ʃən). 1829. [f. ANNULATE; see -ATION.] The formation of rings or ring-like divisions; *concr.* a ring.

Annulet (æ·niŭlĕt). 1572. [f. L. *annulus* ring + -ET; perh. refash. of earlier ANLET.] **1.** A little ring 1598. **2.** *Her.* A small circle worn as a charge 1572. **3.** *Arch.* A small fillet encircling a column 1727.

1. Crosslets, pendulets,..annulets, bracelets 1602.

Annulment (ănɒ·lmĕnt). 1491. [f. ANNUL + -MENT.] The act of reducing to nothing, or declaring void. var. † **Annu·llity** [perh. after *nullity*].

Annuloid (æ·niŭloid), *a.* 1855. [f. L. *annulus* + -OID.] Ring-like. In *Zool.* applied by Huxley to the *Annuloida*; see next.

‖ **Annuloida** (æniuloi·dă), *sb. pl.* 1851. [prop. *-oidea*, mod.L. n. pl. adj. (sc. *animalia*); see prec. and -A 4.] *Zool.* The Annuloid animals, a modification of the *Annulosa*, placed between them and the *Infusoria* (Huxley).

‖ **Annulosa** (æniulōᵘ·să), *sb. pl.* 1855. [mod. L. n. pl. adj. (sc. *animalia*); see next and -A 4.] *Zool.* The ANNULOSE animals, including the higher *Articulata*. Hence **Annulo·san,** one of the *Annulosa*.

Annulose (æniuloᵘ·s), *a.* 1826. [f. mod.L. *annulosus*; see ANNULUS and -OSE[1].] **1.** Ringed or ring-like. **2.** *Zool.* Having the body formed of a series of ring-like segments 1835.

Annulus (æ·niŭlɒ̆s). Pl. **-i.** 1563. [L., late form of *ānulus*, dim. of *ānus* ring; see ANUS.] **1.** A ring, or ring-like body. **2.** *Geom.* A ring, or solid formed by the revolution of a circle about a straight line exterior to its circumference as an axis, and in the plane of the said circle 1802. **3.** *Bot.* In ferns: The ring of cells round the sporangia. In mosses: The elastic external ring of epidermal cells with which the brim of the sporangium is furnished. In fungi: The portion of the veil which remains like a collar round the stalk. 1830. **4.** *Astr.* A ring of light, as in an annular eclipse 1871.

Annum [acc. of L. *annus*], year, in *per annum*; see PER.

† **Annu·merate,** *ppl. a.* ME. only. [– L. *annumeratus*, pa. pple. of *annumerare* add to, f. *ad* AN- *pref.* 7 + *numerare* to number.] Reckoned in. Hence † **Annu·merate** *v.* † **Annu:mera·tion.**

Annunciade (ănɒnsi,ēⁱ·d). 1706. [– Fr. *annonciade* – It. *annunziata*, f. *annunziare*; see ANNOUNCE *v.*, -ADE.] **a.** A military order, thus re-named in 1439, in honour of the Annunciation of the angel Gabriel; **b.** A female religious order founded by Queen Jane of France; a nun of that order.

¶ The Eng. forms of wds. derived from L. *annuntiare* follow the med. spelling *annunciare*.

† **Annu·nciate,** *ppl. a.* ME. [– *annunciatus*, med.L. sp. of L. *annuntiatus*, pa. pple. of *annuntiare*; see ANNOUNCE *v.*, -ATE[2].] Announced (*esp.* beforehand) –1509.

Annunciate, -tiate (ănɒ·nʃi,eⁱt), *v.* 1536. [f. as prec.; see -ATE[3].] **1.** To proclaim = ANNOUNCE 1. **2.** To proclaim as coming, ready, etc. 1652.

2. They who did a. unto the blessed Virgin the conception of the Saviour PEARSON. Hence † **Annu·nciable** *a.* (*rare*). **Annu·nciative** *a.* characterized by or proper to annunciation (*rare*).

Annunciation (ănɒ:nsi,ēⁱ·ʃən). ME. [– (O)Fr. *annonciation* – late L. *annuntiatio*, f. *annuntiare* ANNOUNCE; see -ATION.] **1.** The action of announcing; the matter so announced, announcement 1563. **2.** *esp.* The intimation of the incarnation, made by the angel Gabriel to the Virgin Mary ME. **3.** The church festival commemorating that event; Lady-day (March 25) ME.

2. No subject has been more frequently treated.. than that of the A. RUSKIN.

Annunciator (ănɒ·nʃi,eⁱtəɹ). 1753. [– late L. *annunciator*; see ANNUNCIATE *v.*, -OR 2.] He who, or that which, announces; *spec.* **a.** an officer of the Gr. Ch., who gave notice of holy days; **b.** an indicator, used in hotels, etc., to show where attendance is desired.

Ano- (ēⁱ·no), comb. f. L. *anus*, as in *ano-perinæal*, pertaining to anus and perinæum.

Ano- (æ:no), *pref.* – Gr. ἄνω adv. 'upward'.

Anocarpous (ænokā·ɹpəs), *a.* 1880. [f. ANO- *pref.* + καρπός fruit + -OUS.] *Bot.* Of ferns: Bearing fructification on the upper part of the frond.

Anocathartic (æ:no,kăþā·ɹtik), *a.* and *sb.* 1853. [f. ANO- *pref.* + CATHARTIC.] Emetic.

Anode (æ·nōᵘd). 1834. [– Gr. ἄνοδος way up, f. ἀνά up, ANA- + ὁδός way.] *Electr. strictly*: The path by which an electric current leaves the positive pole, and enters the electrolyte, on its way to the negative pole (Faraday). *loosely*: The positive pole. In both senses opp. to *cathode*.

Anodic (ænǫ·dik), *a.* 1853. [f. as prec. + -IC.] *Med.* Of nerve force: Proceeding upwards.

Anodon(t (æ·nŏdǫn, -ǫnt). 1847. [mod.L. *anodonta*, f. Gr. ἀν- AN- *pref.* 10 + ὀδούς, ὀδοντ- tooth; see -A 4.] *Zool.* A genus of bivalve molluscs, without teeth on the hinge of their shell; e.g. fresh-water mussels.

Anodyne (æ·nŏdəin). 1543. [– L. *anodynus* (Celsus) – Gr. ἀνώδυνος free from pain, f. ἀν- AN- *pref.* 10 + ὀδύνη pain. As *sb.* – late L. *anodynon*. Cf. Fr. *anodin*, *-ine*, perh. the immed. source.] **A.** *adj.* Having the power of assuaging pain; also *fig.* var. † **Ano·dynous. B.** *sb.* **1.** A medicine or drug which alleviates pain 1543. **2.** *fig.* Anything that soothes the feelings 1550.

2. Time..the only a. of sorrow BREWSTER.

Anoetic (æno,e·tik), *a. rare.* [– Gr. ἀνόητος inconceivable (f. ἀ- A- *pref.* 14 + νοητός perceivable) + -IC.] Unthinkable. FERRIER.

Anogenic (æno,dʒe·nik), *a.* 1878. [f. ANO- *pref.* + Gr. -γενης produced + -IC; see -GEN.] Developed up- or inwardly.

† **Anoi·l,** *v.* ME. [var. of ENOIL – OFr. *enuiler* (mod. *enhuiler*), perh. affected by ANELE.] To anoint with oil; *spec.* to administer extreme unction –1688.

† **Anoi·nt,** *ppl. a. etc.* ME. [– AFr. *anoint* (see AN- *pref.* 4), OFr. *enoint*, pa. pple. of *enoindre* :– L. *inungere*, f. *in* IN- *pref.*[2] + *ungere* anoint.] Anointed –1450.

Anoint (ănoi·nt), *v.* [ME. *anoynt(e)*, *enoynt(e)*, f. prec.] **1.** To smear or rub over with oil or unguent; to oil, grease, apply ointment to. **2.** *spec.* To apply or pour on oil, etc., as a religious ceremony, as at baptism or on consecration ME. † **3.** *fig.* To besmear with flattery –1483. **4.** To moisten or rub with any substance ME; hence, *ironically*: To beat soundly, to 'baste' 1500.

1. A. thine eyes with eye salue, that thou mayest see *Rev.* 3:18. Fragrant oils the stiffen'd limbs a. DRYDEN. **2.** All kynges of fraunce ben enoynted at Raynes CAXTON. **4.** Jesus made clay, and anointed mine eyes *John* 9:11. Hence **Anoi·nter,** one who anoints; *spec.* one of a 17th-c. sect, who anointed people before admitting them. † **Anoi·ntment,** the action of anointing; ointment.

Anointed (ănoi·nted), *ppl. a.* ME. [f. prec. + -ED[1].] **1.** Smeared or rubbed with oil, etc., *esp.* as a sacred rite; *fig.* consecrated (*rare*) 1597. **2.** *absol.* A consecrated one. *The Lord's Anointed*: Christ or the Messiah; also, a king by divine right. 1529.

Anointing (ănoi·ntiŋ). ME. [f. as prec. + -ING[1].] **1.** The action of oiling the body. **2.** *fig.* The application of oil on consecration to an office ME. † **3.** Ointment –1561. Also *attrib.*

Anoli, -is (ănōᵘ·li, -is). 1706. [Native name in the Antilles; cf. Fr. *anolis.*] *Zool.* A genus of lizards of the Iguana family, found in the West Indies.

† **Ano·mal,** *a.* 1569. [– (O)Fr. *anomal* – late L. *anomalus* – Gr. ἀνώμαλος uneven, f. ἀν- AN- *pref.* 10 + ὁμαλός even, f. ὁμός same.] Irregular, anomalous –1681. As *sb.* [sc. *thing.*] –1665.

Anomaliped (ănǫ·măliped), *a. rare.* 1847. [f. L. *anomalus* (see ANOMAL) + *ped-* (*pes*); cf. Fr. *anomalipède.*] Having an anomalous foot; having the middle toe united to the exterior by three phalanges, and to the interior by one only. As *sb.* [sc. *bird.*]

Anomalism (ănǫ·măliz'm). *rare.* 1668. [f. Gr. ἀνώμαλος (see ANOMAL) + -ISM.] Anomalousness; an example of irregularity.

Anomalist (ănǫ·mălist). *rare.* 1860. [f. as prec. + -IST.] One who held that language was conventional or arbitrary in its origin.

Anomalistic, -al (ănǫ:măli·stik, -ăl), *a.* 1727. [f. as prec. + -IC, + -AL.] **1.** Of or pertaining to an anomaly, or anomalist. **2.** *Astr.* Pertaining to the anomaly or angular distance of a planet from its perihelion.

2. *Anomalistic year*: the time occupied by the earth (or other planet) in passing from perihelion to perihelion, which is 365 d. 6 h. 13′ 49·3″. *Anomalistic month*: the time occupied by the moon in passing from perigee to perigee, etc.

Anomalo- (ănǫ·mălo), comb. form of Gr. ἀνώμαλος irregular; as in **Anomalogo·natous** [Gr. γονατ- (γόνυ)] *a.*, *Zool.* of or belonging to the *Anomalogonati*, an order of birds lacking the *rectus femoris* muscle.

Anomalous (ănǫ·măləs), *a.* 1646. [f. late L. *anomalus* (see ANOMAL) + -OUS.] **1.** With *to*: Unequal, unconformable, incongruous (*arch.*) **2.** *simply*: Unconformable to the common order; irregular; abnormal 1655.

2. A. Feavers 1667, structure DARWIN, Nouns 1706. Hence **Ano·malous-ly** *adv.*, **-ness.**

Anomaly (ănǫ·măli). 1571. [– L. *anomalia* (Varro) – Gr. ἀνωμαλία; see ANOMAL *a.*, -Y[3].] **1.** Unevenness, inequality, of condition, motion, etc. **2.** Irregularity, deviation from the common or natural order, exceptional condition or circumstance. *concr.* An anomalous thing or being. 1664. **3.** *Astr.* The angular distance of a planet, etc., from its last perihelion or perigee; so called because the first irregularities of planetary motion were discovered in the discrepancy between the actual and the computed distance 1669. **4.** *Mus.* A small deviation from a perfect interval, in tuning instruments with fixed notes 1830.

2. Time changes a. into system HALLAM. There is no greater a. in nature than a bird that cannot fly DARWIN. The anomalies or irregularities of the [English] tongue WATTS.

Anomo- (æ:nǫ̈mo, ănǫ:mŏ), comb. form of Gr. ἄνομος without law, f. ἀ + νόμος.

a.-bra·nchiate [Gr. βράγχια], *Zool. adj.* having gills of irregular structure; *sb.* [sc. *crustacean*]; **-ca·rpous** [Gr. καρπός] *a.*, *Bot.* bearing unusual fruit; **-dont** [Gr. ὀδοντ-] *a.* and *sb.*, *Zool.* having irregular or no teeth, applied to a genus of fossil reptiles; **-phy·llous** [Gr. φύλλον] *a.*, *Bot.* having leaves irregularly placed; **-rho·mboid** [Gr. ῥομβοειδής], *Cryst.* a name given to varieties of crystalline spars, which always fracture into irregular rhomboids; **-rhomboi·dal** *a.*

Anomœo·mery. *rare.* [f. Gr. ἀνομοιομερής.] The theory that the ultimate atoms of matter are dissimilar. CUDWORTH.

Anomouran, -muran (ænomūᵊ·răn), *a.* 1877. [f. *Anom(o)ura* (mod.L. f. Gr. ἄνομος + οὐρά) + -AN.] *Zool.* Of the *Anomoura* or stalk-eyed crustacea, which have no regular type in the abdomen or tail. As *sb.* One of the *Anomoura*. Hence **Anom(o)u·ral** *a.* having the character of the *Anomoura*. var. **Anomou·rous** *a.*

† A·nomy. 1591. [– Gr. ἀνομία lawlessness, f. ἄνομος lawless + -ία -Y[3].] Disregard of (divine) law; lawlessness –1755.

Anon (ănǫ·n). [OE. *on ān* into one, *on āne* in one, i.e. ON and acc. and dat. of *ān* ONE.] **† 1.** In one course, straight on, even –ME. **† 2.** *strictly*, Straightway, at once. (Occ. revived by mod. writers.) –1611. **3.** By misuse: Soon, in a little while 1526. **4.** Now or here again 1588. **5.** A response by a servant, etc.: 'Presently, coming', and later = 'Beg your pardon! Sir! Eh?' See ANAN.

1. *Anon to*: even to; = L. *usque ad.* **2.** He that heareth the word, & a. with ioy receiueth it *Matt.* 13:20. † *Anon so* or *as*: as soon as ever (Fr. *aussitot que*). † *Anon after, after anon*: directly after. **3.** † *Till anon*: until by and by. Thou do'st me yet but little hurt; thou wilt a. *Temp.* II. ii. 84. **4.** Now for this Cardinal, a. for another 1670. *Ever and anon*: every now and then *L.L.L.* v. ii. 102.

Anonaceous (ænonēⁱ·ʃəs), *a.* [See below and -ACEOUS.] Of or pertaining to the family *Anonaceæ*, typified by the genus *Anona* (custard-apple, alligator-apple, sour-sop, sweet-sop).

Anonad (ănōᵘ·năd). 1847. [f. as prec. + -AD 1.] *Bot.* A plant of the N.O. *Anonaceæ.*

Anonym (æ·nǫ̈nim). 1812. [subst. use of Gr. ἀνώνυμος; see next.] **1.** A person who remains nameless. **2.** A pseudonym 1866. Hence **† Ano·nymal** *a.* anonymous (*rare*). **Anony·mity,** the state of being anonymous. (Used of an author or writings.) 1829.

Anonymous (ănǫ·niməs), *a.* 1601. [f. late L. *anonymous* – Gr. ἀνώνυμος without name (f. ἀ- A- *pref.* 14 + ὄνομα name) + -OUS.] **1.** Nameless; of unknown name. Also *subst.* 1603. **2.** *transf.* Of unknown or unavowed authorship 1676. **3.** Illegitimate (*rare*) 1881.

1. A. correspondents STEELE, altars PALEY. **2.** An a. book EVELYN, pamphlet MORSE, attack BREWSTER. Hence **Ano·nymous-ly** *adv.*, **-ness. Ano:nymu·ncule** [after L. *homunculus*], a petty a. writer.

Anophyte (æ·nǫ̈fəit). 1850. [– mod.L. *anophytum*; see ANO- *pref.*, -PHYTE.] *Bot.* A name of the non-vascular acrogens, or mosses, etc.

Anoplothere (ænǫ·plǫ̈þīᵊr). 1815. [– Fr. *anoplothère*, f. Gr. ἄνοπλος unarmed, f. ἀν- AN- *pref.* 10 + ὅπλον weapon + θηρίον beast.] Also **anoplotherium.** *Palæont.* A Middle Eocene pachydermatous quadruped, having no apparent means of defence. Hence **Anoplothe·roid** *a.* like an a.; also used *subst.*

Anopluriform (ænoplⁱūᵊ·rifǫ̈ɹm), *a.* 1816. [f. Gr. ἄνοπλος unarmed (see prec.) + οὐρά tail + -FORM.] *Zool.* Of the form of the *Anoplura* (insects having no tail appendage); louse-like.

† A·nopsy. 1646. [– mod.L. *anopsia*, f. Gr. ἀν- AN- *pref.* 10 + ὄψις vision + -ία -Y[3].] Want of sight.

Anorexy (æ·nore:ksi). 1598. [– late and med.L. *anorexia* (also used) – Gr. ἀνορεξία want of appetite.] *Path.* Want of appetite. Hence **Anore·ctous** *a.* without appetite.

Anorgano·logy. 1876. [f. AN- *pref.* 10 + ORGANOLOGY.] The part of Natural Science relating to inorganic objects.

† Anormal (ănǫ·ɹmăl), *a.* 1835. [– Fr. *anormal*, var. of *anomal*. In Eng. taken as f. L. *a* + *norma*, referred to L. *abnormis*, and refash. later ABNORMAL.] = ABNORMAL.

† Ano·rn, *v.* [ME. *aourne* – OFr. *aörner*, *aöurner* :– L. *adornare*, with A- *pref.* 2 (*an-*) for A- *pref.* 7. Confused also with *anourn*, inf. of vb. ANOURE.] To deck, dress; = ADORN –1558. To worship. (See ANOURE.) WYCLIF. Hence **† Ano·rnament,** adornment.

Anorthic (ænǭ·ɹþik), *a.* 1864. [f. Gr. ἀν- AN- *pref.* 10 + ὀρθός straight + -IC.] *Cryst.* Irregular in crystallization; called also *triclinic*, etc.

Anorthite (ænǭ·ɹþəit). 1833. [f. as prec. + -ITE[1] 2 b.] *Min.* Lime-feldspar, a mineral occurring in small triclinic glassy crystals.

‖ **Anortho·pia.** 1849. [mod.L., f. Gr. ἀν- AN- *pref.* 10 + ὀρθός straight + -ωπία vision, f. ὤψ, ὠπ- eye; see -IA[1].] *Path.* Obliquity of vision.

Anorthoscope (ænǭ·ɹþoˌskoᵘp). 1842. [f. as prec.; see -SCOPE.] An optical toy for viewing distorted figures drawn on a rotating disc.

‖ **Ano·smia.** 1811. [mod.L., f. Gr. ἀν- AN- *pref.* 10 + ὀσμή smell; see -IA[1].] *Path.* Loss of the sense of smell.

Another (ănʊ·ðəɹ), *a.*, and *pron.* [ME. *an other* (in two words as late as XVI), i.e. AN *adj.*[1], OTHER *adj.*, *pron.* (*sb.*); superseded the simple *ōþer* of OE.] **1.** One more; orig. *a second* of two; subseq. *an additional.* (Pl. *other*: with sb. understood, *others.*) *fig.* A second in effect; a counterpart to 1577. **2.** A different; different in effect (const. *than, from* catachr.) ME. **3.** Contrasted with *one.* (Esp. in sense 2.) ME.

1. Clarence hath not a. day to liue *Rich. III*, I. i. 150. 'You are a.,' cries the sergeant FIELDING. *Such another*; another of the same sort. *fig.* Another Nelson 1888. **2.** Let a. man praise thee, and not thine owne mouth *Prov.* 27:2. Of persons (with *poss.* **another's**; *pl.* **others**): Arte thou he that shall come: or shall we loke for a.? TINDALE Another's knowledge BACON. He is nowe become a. man 1588. **3.** One man's meat is a. man's poison *Provb.* Of two things only (now *the other*): Let's go hand in hand, not one before a. *Com. Err.* V. i. 425. *One with another*: (*a*) all together; (*b*) taken on the average. *One another*: a compound reciprocal pron. with poss. *one another's* (now *each other's*). Said of two or more.

† Ano·ther-gates, *a.* 1594. [f. prec. + GATE *sb.*[2]; see OTHERGATES *adv.* and *adj.*] Of another sort –1693. var. **† Ano·ther-gaines.**

Ano·therguess, *a. arch.* 1625. [Reduction of *anothergets* for ANOTHER-GATES; *-guess* is misleading.] = prec.

I wish you anothergets wife than Socrates had HOWELL. var. **† Ano·therguise.**

Anotta, anotto, vars. of ANATTA.

† Anou·r, *sb.* ME. only. [ME. – AFr. *anour*, var. of OFr. (*h*)*onor*, (*h*)*onur* :– L. *honor*. See ANOURE *v.*, HONOUR *sb.*] Honour, worship.

Anou·ra. [mod.L., f. Gr. ἀν- AN- *pref.* 10 + οὐρά tail; see -A 4.] *Zool.* An order of tailless Amphibians; see ANOUROUS.

† Anou·re, *v.* ME. [repr. 1. AFr. *anourer* = OFr. *onourer, onurer* :– L. *honorare*; 2. OFr. *aörer* :– L. *adorare*. See ANORN, ADORE, HONOUR *v.*] To adore, worship, or honour. ¶ To deck (see ANORN). Hence **† Anou·rement** = ADORNMENT.

Anourous (ănūᵊ·rəs, ănau·-), *a.* 1838. [f. as ANOURA + -OUS.] *Zool.* Tailless, as the frog and toad, or (less correctly) the crab.

Anp-, freq. earlier spelling of AMP-.

‖ **Ansa** (æ·nsă). *Pl.* **ansæ.** Formerly **anse, -s.** 1665. [L. *ansa* handle (of a vessel).] A name applied to the apparent ends of Saturn's ring seen projecting like two handles beyond the disc.

Anserated (æ·nsĕreⁱtėd), *ppl. a.* 1678. *Her.* Of a cross: Having the extremities cleft and terminated in the heads of serpents, eagles, etc.

Anserine (æ·nsĕrəin), *a.* 1839. [– L. *anserinus*, f. *anser* goose; see -INE[1].] **1.** Of, pertaining to, or of the nature of, a goose. **2.** Stupid; as the goose is erron. supposed to be. So **A·nserous** *a.* 1826.

‖ **Anspessa·de.** 1751. [Fr.; see LANCEPESADE.] An officer in the foot below a corporal.

Answer (a·nsəɹ), *sb.* [OE. *andswaru*, corresp. to OFris. *ondser*, OS. *antswōr*, ON. *andsvar* :– Gmc **andswarō*, f. **and-* against, opposite + **swar-*, base of OE. *swerian* SWEAR. Orig. a solemn affirmation in rebutting a charge.] **1.** A reply made to a charge; a defence. *spec.* in *Law.* The counter-statement made in reply to a complainant's bill of charges ME. **2.** A reply to an objection; a reply in writing or debate, setting forth arguments opposed to those previously advanced 1534. **3.** A reply to a question. (The common use.) OE. **4.** A reply to an appeal, address, remark, letter, etc.; a response, rejoinder ME. **5.** The solution of a problem 1592. **6.** A practical reply; anything done in return. In *Fencing*, the return hit. 1535. **7.** *Mus.* A re-echoing or reproduction of sounds 1869.

1. To dampne a man with-oute answere CHAUCER. **2.** An a. to the Protest of the Free Church 1846. **3.** Grim andswaru *Beowulf.* I will bee a foole in question, hoping to bee the wiser by your a. *All's Well* II. ii. 42. **4.** I called my seruant, and he gaue me no answere *Job* 19:16. There must be a. to his doubt TENNYSON. **6.** The a. was..a volley of musketry DARWIN. Hence **A·nswerless** *a.* having no a., having no possible a. (*rare*).

Answer, *v.* [OE. *andswarian*, f. prec.; cf. OFris. *ondswera*, ON. *andsvara*.] **I.** To answer to a charge. **1.** *intr.* To speak in reply to a charge, defend oneself OE.; with *for*: To answer charges in regard to ME. **2.** *intr.* To speak or undertake responsibility *for* ME. To guarantee. Const. *for.* 1728. **3.** *trans.* To make a defence against; *hence*, to justify (*arch.*) 1552. **4.** To reply to, meet an objection or argument ME. **5.** To meet practically, atone for; esp. *intr.* Const. *for.* ME. **6.** To satisfy a pecuniary claim, pay; *hence*, to be sufficient for (a liability) 1581. **7.** To repay, recoup 1587. **8.** To fulfil (wishes, etc.) 1653; to suit 1714. **9.** *intr.* (*ellipt.*). To serve the purpose, succeed. Also: To turn out (well or ill). 1783.

1. To a. at the bar of public opinion (*mod.*). We that haue good wits, haue much to a. for *A.Y.L.*

v. i. 13. **2.** When Miss Browning 'answered for it' Miss Phoebe gave up doubting MRS. GASKELL. **3.** To a. the stealing of a cup MARLOWE. **4.** To a. an argument 1526, Forgeries 1635, a protest 1888, Locke (*mod.*). **5.** Grievouslie hath Cæsar answered for it *Jul. C.* III. ii. 85. **6.** His fortunes cannot a. his expense 1608. To a. a fine 1770. **8.** I shall..a. your hopes WALTON. **9.** It answered..as a speculation FROUDE.

II. To answer a question, etc. **1.** To speak or write in reply to a question, remark, etc.; *also*, To reply to an implied question OE. **2.** Coupled with *say*. (A Hellenism of the N.T.) *arch.* OE. **3.** *trans.* or *absol.* To solve a problem put as a question in an examination 1742. **4. To answer to a name:** to answer when addressed by the name; to have the name of 1599. **5.** To say or sing antiphonally 1611. **6.** To make a responsive sound, as an echo ME. **7.** To reply favourably. Cf. I. 8. 1593. **8.** To reply to a knock, bell, or other practical request or signal 1597.

1. To a. their question directly DE FOE. No man was able to a. him a word *Matt.* 22:46. **4.** I a. to that name *Much Ado* V. iv. 73. **6.** The woods shall a., and their echo ring POPE. **7.** Doubt not ye the Gods have answer'd TENNYSON.

III. To correspond. **1.** *trans.* To act in conformity with, to obey; *esp.* of a ship: *To answer the helm* 1610. **2.** *intr.* To act in sympathy with 1684; *trans.* to repeat 1599. **3.** To give back in kind 1576. **4.** *intr.* To correspond with (in any respect). Const. *to.* ME. †*trans.* To come up to –1789.

1. I come, to a. thy best pleasure *Temp.* I. ii. 190. **2.** Fire answers fire SHAKS. **3.** Able to answere feast with feast 1601. **4.** I wish she had answered her picture as well SHERIDAN.

Answerable (ɑ·nsərăb'l), *a.* 1548. [f. ANSWER *v.* and *sb.* + -ABLE.] **1.** Liable to be called to account; responsible. **2.** Such as responds to demands, etc.; suitable (*arch.*) 1571. **3.** Corresponding, accordant (*arch.*) 1580; proportional, commensurate (*to*) 1617; equivalent, adequate *to* (*arch.*) 1581. **4.** *pass.* Able to be answered (*rare*) 1697.

1. He was a. with his head, if [etc.] 1781. A. to the power which appointed him FREEMAN, for what we do NEWMAN. **2.** Her treatment..was not a. to her merits RICHARDSON. **3.** With a thickness a. to their height EVELYN. Revenue.. not a. to its necessary expenditure WELLINGTON. Hence **A·nswerableness,** correspondency (*arch.*); responsibility. **A·nswerably** *adv.* in an answerable manner (*absol.* or with *to*).

Answerer (ɑ·nsərəɹ). 1511. [f. ANSWER *v.* + -ER[1].] **1.** One who replies to a charge, argument, etc. 1533. **2.** One who replies to a question or appeal 1556. †**3.** One responsible –1539.

Ant (ænt). Pl. **ants.** [OE. *æmet(t)e* = MLG. *āmete, ēmete*, OHG. *ămeiza* (G. *ameise*):– WGmc **āmaitja, *aimaitja*, f. **ā-* off, away + **mait-* to cut, hew. The OE. forms gave two ME. types, (i) *am(e)te*, whence *ant* (the prevailing standard form) and (ii) *emete* (see EMMET).] **1.** A small social insect of the Hymenopterous order, celebrated for its industry; an emmet, a pismire. **2. White ant:** A destructive social insect of the Neuropterous order, also called Termite 1729.

Goe to the Ant [*Wycl.* ampte, amte, *Coverd.* Emmet], thou sluggard *Prov.* 6:6. *Comb.*: **a.-bear,** the great ant-eater, *Myrmecophaga jubata*; **-catcher** = ANT-THRUSH; **-eggs, ants' eggs,** the larvæ of ants (a favourite food of young pheasants); **-fly,** a winged ant; **-heap, -hill, -hillock,** the mound raised over an ant's nest; **-rice,** the grains of *Aristida oligantha*, harvested by ants; **-worm,** the larva of the ant.

Ant, obs. form of AUNT, and of AND.

An't (ānt), contraction of *are n't, are not* 1706; colloq. for *am not*; also illiterate or dial. for *is not, have* or *has not.* Cf. AIN'T.

† **An't** (ănt). Var. of *on't*, prop. 'on it', but freq. = *o't* 'of it'. 1589. See ON.

Ant-, *pref.*, short f. ANTI- 'against', bef. vowels, and *h-*.

-ant[1], *suffix*, – Fr. *-ant* :– L. *-entem, -āntem, -ēntem*, pres. pple. ending (see -ENT); sometimes – *-āntem* only. Fr. words in *-ant*, repr. some L. *-ānt*, some L. *-ent, -ēnt*, became after adoption in Eng. *-au·nt*, and again *-ant* with change of stress. Some have since been refash. with *-ent* after L., as *pendant, -ent*, etc. Hence, much inconsistency and uncertainty in the spelling.

-ant[2], a corruption of *-an*, due to confusion of *-an, -and, -ant*, as in *pheasan(t, truan(t, tyran(t*, etc.

‖ **Anta** (æ·ntă). Usu. in pl. **antæ.** 1751. [L. *antæ* (pl.). Cf. ANTES.] *Arch.* A square pilaster on either side of a door, or at the corner of a building.

Antacid (ænt,æ·sid), *a.* 1732. [f. ANT- + ACID.] Corrective of acidity, *esp.* in the stomach. As *sb.* A remedy for, or preventive of, acidity. var. **Antiacid.**

Antacrid (ænt,æ·krid), *a.* 1853. [f. ANT- + ACRID.] Corrective of acridity in the secretions.

Antæ; see ANTA.

Antagonism (ǣntæ·gŏniz'm). 1838. [prob. – Fr. *antagonisme*; see next, -ISM.] **1.** The mutual resistance of two opposing forces, physical or mental; active opposition to a force. Const. *between* two things; *to, against, with* a thing. **2.** An opposing force or principle 1840.

2. As if resulting from mighty and equal antagonisms DE QUINCEY. var. † **Anta·gony.** MILT.

Antagonist (ǣntæ·gŏnist). 1599. [– Fr. *antagoniste* or late L. *antagonista* (Jerome) – Gr. ἀνταγωνιστής, f. ἀνταγωνίζεσθαι struggle against. See ANT-, AGONIZE *v.*] **1.** One who contends with another in any contest; an opponent, an adversary; an impersonal agent acting in opposition 1711. **2.** *Phys.* A muscle which counteracts another 1706. **3.** Used *attrib.* as sb., or adj.: = ANTAGONISTIC 1671.

1. Satan..A. of Heaven's Almightie King MILT. *P.L.* x. 387. Marke what good vse our A. makes of this conclusion PRYNNE. Fire and air act as antagonists in boiling 1794.

Antagonistic, -al (ǣntæ:gŏni·stik, -ăl), *a.* 1632. [f. prec. + -IC, + -AL.] Of the nature of an ANTAGONIST 1, 2. Hence **Antagoni·stically** *adv.*

Antagonize (ǣntæ·gŏnəiz), *v.* 1634. [– Gr. ἀνταγωνίζεσθαι, f. ἀντ- ANT- + ἀγωνίζεσθαι struggle against, f. ἀγών contest, AGON.] † **1.** *trans.* To compete with, rival. **2.** To act in antagonism to, contend with, oppose actively 1742; in U.S. used of forces not of the same kind, e.g. a person may antagonize (i.e. oppose) a bill 1882. **3.** *Phys.* To counteract the action of; hence, to neutralize 1833. **4.** *intr.* To act in antagonism 1861. **5.** *trans.* To render antagonistic 1882. Hence **Anta·gonized** *ppl. a.* (sense 5). **Anta·gonizer,** *Phys.* (*rare*) = ANTAGONIST 2. **Anta·gonizing** *ppl. a.* acting in opposition; mutually opposing.

Antalgic (ǣnt,æ·ldʒik), *a.* 1753. [f. ANT- + Gr. ἄλγος pain + -IC.] *Med.* Tending to prevent or mitigate pain 1775. As *sb.* = ANODYNE.

Antalkali (ænt,æ·lkăli). 1834. [f. ANT- + ALKALI.] *Med.* Anything which counteracts the action of an alkali, *esp.* in the system. Hence **Anta·lkaline** *a.* and *sb.*

Antambulacral (æ:nt,æmbiulē·krăl, -æ·krăl), *a.* Also **anti-amb-.** 1870. [f. ANT- + AMBULACRAL.] *Zool.* Opposite to what is ambulacral, as the upper side of a star-fish.

‖ **Antana·clasis.** ? *Obs.* 1646. [– Gr. ἀντανάκλασις, f. ἀνακλᾶν reflect, bend back.] *Rhet.* **1.** Repeating a word in a different or even contrary sense 1657. **2.** 'A returning to the matter after a parenthesis' (J.) 1646.

1. 'That Abraham against hope believed in hope'..is an a. MANTON.

† **Antanago·ge.** 1589. [f. ANT- + Gr. ἀναγωγή.] *Rhet.* Retorting a charge when unable to answer it. (Now only in Dicts.)

Antaphrodisiac (æ:nt,æfrodi·ziæk), *a.* 1742. [f. ANT- + APHRODISIAC *a.*] Tending to counteract venereal desire. As *sb.* [sc. *medicine*, etc.] 1753.

Antaphroditic (æ:nt,æfrodi·tik), *a.* 1706. [f. ANT- + Gr. 'Αφροδίτη + -IC.] Of use against venereal disease 1755. *sb.* 1. [sc. *medicine.*] 1706. † **2.** = ANTAPHRODISIAC 1719.

Antapoplectic (æ:nt,æpople·ktik), *a.* 1697. [f. ANT- + APOPLECTIC.] *Med.* Tending to prevent or cure apoplexy. † *sb.* [sc. *medicine.*] 1753.

† **A·ntarchy.** *rare.* 1656. [– mod.L. *antarchia*, f. Gr. ἀντ- ANT- + -αρχία government, f. ἄρχειν to rule. See -Y[3].] Opposition to government.

Antarctic (ǣntā·ɹktik), *a.* [Late ME. *antartik* – OFr. *antartique* (mod. *-arctique*), or L. *antarcticus* – Gr. ἀνταρκτικός opposite to the north; later refash. after Gr. form.] **1.** Opposite to the arctic; pertaining to the south polar regions; southern. † **2.** *fig.* Contradictory, antipodean –1711. As *sb.* [The adj. used *ellipt.*] The south pole, or the regions adjacent ME.

1. *Antarctic Pole*, the South Pole of earth or heavens. *A. Circle*, the parallel of 66° 32′ South. A. flora 1881.

Antarthritic (ænt,ăɹþri·tik), *a.* 1706. [f. ANT- + ARTHRITIC.] *Med.* Tending to prevent or relieve gout 1775. *sb.* [sc. *medicine.*] 1706.

Antasthmatic (ænt,æsþmæ·tik), *a.* 1681. [f. ANT- + ASTHMATIC.] *Med.* Tending to prevent or relieve asthma. As *sb.* [sc. *medicine.*]

Antatrophic (ænt,ătrǫ·fik), *a.* 1811. [f. ANT- + ATROPHIC.] *Med.* Tending to counteract atrophy. Also as *sb.*

Ante, obs. f. ANT, AUNT. See also *ANTE.

Ante-, L. *prep.* and *adv.*, used in composition with vbs., vbl. sbs., other sbs., and adjs. derived from phrases, as *ante-mundane*, f. *antemund(um* + *-ane*.

A. *sbs.* (Main stress on *a·nte*: *a·ntechapel.*) **1.** Of position: usu. = A smaller introductory —; as **a.-portico; -stomach;** also **-bath,** an apartment opening into the bath; **-church** = ANTECHAPEL; **-nave,** the western part of a divided nave; **-number,** the preceding number. (Since 1600.) **2.** Of time or order: = A previous —, *or* A something previous to —; **-predicament; -taste;** also **-eternity,** the quality of having existed from all eternity; **-noon,** the forenoon. (Since 1600.)

B. *adjs.* (Main stress not on *ante*: *ante-nu·ptial, ante-wa·r*. Usu. of 19th c.) **1.** Of position: = Before, in front of —; **a.-cæcal,** before the *cæcum*; **-initial,** prefatory; **-pectoral,** in front of the breast. **2.** Of time or order: = Occurring or existing in the time before (a fact etc. implied or expressed); **a.** with adj. ending: **-baptismal; -Christian; -historic; -jentacular,** before breakfast; **-judiciary,** taking place before judgement; **-Mosaic; -Norman; -nuptial; -patriarchal,** existing before the patriarchs; **-posthumous,** posthumous (professedly), but written before; **-reformational. b.** with sb., forming attrib. phr.: *-communion, -reformation, -war*. In this sense *ante-* varies with *pre-*.

Ante-, freq. earlier spelling of ANTI-.

† **A:nte-a·cted,** *ppl. a. rare.* 1607. [f. L. *ante actus*, i.e. *ante* ANTE-, *actus* pa. pple. of *agere* to act.] Previously done or spent –1620.

Anteal (æ·ntiăl), *a. rare.* 1852. [f. L. *ante* before + -AL[1].] Pertaining to what is in front.

†‖ **Ante-a·mbulo.** 1609. [L., f. *ante* before + *ambulo* walker, f. *ambulare* to walk.] One whose business it is to walk in front, an usher.

A·nt-ea:ter. 1764. **1.** A group of the *Edentata* having long thread-like viscous tongues. They comprise the Ant-eaters proper (*Myrmecophaga* of S. America, the Scaly Ant-eaters (*Manis*), and the Aardvark (*Orycteropus*). **2.** The Aculeated, or Porcupine Ant-eater (*Echidna*), found in Australia 1868. **3.** A bird, the ANT-THRUSH 1827.

A:nteceda·neous, *a.* 1630. [app. var. of contemp. *precedaneous* (= XVII. L. *precedaneus*); see next, -ANEOUS.] Preliminary or previous.

Antecede (æntĭsī·d), *v. arch.* 1624. [– L. *antecedere*, f. *ante* ANTE- + *cedere* go, CEDE.] **1.** To go before, in time, place, or rank; to surpass. **2.** *intr.* To go or come before 1628.

Antecedence (æntĭsī·dĕns). 1535. [– Fr. *antécédence* (XVI) or L. *antecedentia*; see prec., -ENCE.] **1.** The action or fact of going before, priority 1651. † **2.** That which goes before, *spec.* an antecedent, a premiss 1535. **3.** *Astr.* A motion from east to west; retrograde motion 1669.

Antecedency (æntĭsī·dĕnsi). 1598. [f. L. *antecedentia*; see prec., -ENCY.] **1.** The quality or condition of being antecedent. † **2.** An antecedent state of things; in *pl.* = ANTECEDENT 5. –1748.

Antecedent (æntĭsī·dĕnt), *sb.* ME. [– as next; subst. use of the adj. as in French, and in Latin as a term of philosophy.] **1.** A thing or circumstance which goes before in time or order; often also implying causal relation with its *consequent* 1612. Hence **2.** *Logic.* (Opp. to *consequent.*) The statement upon which any consequence logically depends;

hence, the premisses of a syllogism (*obs.*); the first part of a conditional proposition ME. **3.** *Gram.* The substantive to which a following (*esp.* a relative) pronoun refers ME. **4.** *Math.* The first of two terms between which a ratio is expressed; the first and third in a series of four proportionals 1570. **5.** *pl.* The events of a person's past history; also used of institutions, etc. 1841. †**6.** *lit.* = ANTE-AMBULO –1632.

1. Circumstances..governed by a long chain of antecedents BUCKLE. **2.** You have shewn us the a., now let us have the *ergo* 1587. **5.** They will.. sift what the French call their antecedents 1841.

Antecedent (æntĭsī·dĕnt), *a.* 1543. [– (O)Fr. *antécédent* or *antecedent-*, pres ppl. stem of L. *antecedere*; see ANTECEDE *v.*, -ENT.] **1.** Preceding, in time or order. Also with *to*, † *unto*, and quasi-*advb.* **2.** *ellipt.* Previous to investigation; presumptive, *a priori* 1794.

1. A period a. to all contemporary..records 1878. **2.** The a. improbability of miracles. 1859. Hence **Antece·dently** *adv.* before in time or causality; *a priori*.

† **Antece·ll**, *v. rare.* 1635. [– L. *antecellere* be prominent.] To excel –1642.

Antecessor (æ:ntĭse·səɹ, æ·ntĭ-). ME. [In XV *-our* (see -OUR) – L. *antecessor* (in late and med.L. senses), f. *ante* before + *cess-*, pa. ppl. stem of *cedere* go; see ANCESTOR.] **1.** One who goes before (*esp.* in office); a predecessor; † an ancestor –1660. †**2.** A professor of civil law 1751. †**3.** *pl.* One of the advanced guard of an army 1753.

1. Our fathers and Antecessours of olde tyme LD. BERNERS.

Antechamber (æ·ntiˌtʃēⁱ·mbər). 1656. [XVII *antichamber* – Fr. *antichambre* – It. *anticamera*; see ANTE-, CHAMBER *sb.*] A room leading to the chief apartment, in which visitors wait; *orig.* the room admitting into the (royal) bed-chamber. Also *fig.* and *transf.*

Ante-chapel (æ·ntiˌtʃæpĕl). 1703. [f. ANTE + CHAPEL.] A University term for the outer part at the west end of a chapel.

Antedate (æ·ntĭdēⁱt), *sb.* 1580. [f. ANTE + DATE *sb.*] A date affixed or assigned, earlier than the actual date. †**2.** *fig.* Anticipation 1624.

Antedate (æ·ntĭdēⁱ:t), *v.* 1587. [f. prec. *sb.*; cf. *date.*] **1.** To affix or assign an earlier than the true date to. **2.** To carry back to an earlier time 1600. **3.** To accelerate 1640. **4.** To precede in date 1664. **5.** To anticipate 1611.

1. To a. a letter 1858, a vow 1631. **2.** By Reading a Man does as it were A. his Life J. COLLIER. **3.** A fright of his Mother..antedated his nativity FULLER. **5.** Antedating My Lord's command 1611.

Antediluvial (æ:ntĭdilⁱū·viăl), *a. rare.* 1823. [f. as next + -AL¹.] Older than the Flood. Hence **A:ntedilu·vially** *adv.*

Antediluvian (æ:ntĭdilⁱū·viăn), *a.* 1646. [f. ANTE- + L. *diluvium* DELUGE + -AN.] **1.** Existing before the Noachian deluge 1657. **2.** Referring to the period before the Flood 1646. **3.** Of the sort which obtained before the Flood 1698. **4.** Very antiquated. (Disparaging.) 1726. **5.** *sb.* [The adj. used *absol.*] One who lived before the Flood; *fig.* one who is very old 1684.

1. The a. language HARTLEY. **3.** An a. lease of life 1846. **4.** A sorry a. makeshift of a building LAMB.

† **A·ntefact.** *rare.* 1623. [– L. *ante factum*; see ANTE-, FACT.] A thing done before.

Confession was of antefacts, not post facts FULLER.

Antefix (æ·ntĭfiks). Usu. in *pl.* 1832. [– L. *antefixum*, pl. *-a* 'something fixed in front', f. *ante* ANTE- + subst. use of *fixus*; see FIX *v.*] Ornaments on the eaves and cornices of ancient buildings, to conceal the ends of the tiles; also ornamental heads, etc., making the spouts from the gutters. Hence **Ante·fi·xal** *a.*

A·nteflexed, *ppl. a. rare.* 1872. [f. ANTE- + *flex-*, pa. ppl. stem of L. *flectere* to bend + -ED¹.] Bent forward; *spec.* of the uterus. Hence **Anteflexion**, a bending forward; *spec.* of the uterus (*rare*).

‖ **Antefurca** (æntĭfɒ̄·ɹkă). 1826. [mod.L., f. L. *ante* in front + *furca* fork.] *Ent.* In cockroaches, an internal forked projection from the sternal wall of the anterior somite of the thorax.

† **Antela·tion.** *rare.* 1553. [– med.L. *antelatio* prerogative, f. *antelat-*, pa. ppl. stem of L. *anteferre* prefer.] Precedence –1623.

Antelope (æ·ntĭlōᵘp). ME. [– OFr. *antelop* (once, XIII (Brunetto Latini), also *antelu*), or med.L. *ant(h)alopus* – med. Gr. ἀνθόλοψ, of which the source and orig. meaning are unknown.] Any species of the deer-like ruminant genus *Antilope* (Pallas), characterized by cylindrical, annulated horns, and the possession of a lachrymal sinus, and grouped as *True* Antelopes, *Bush* A., *Capriform* A., and *Bovine* A. The name is now pop. associated with the first. Also *attrib.*

The Gr., L., and OFr. antelope was a creature haunting the banks of the Euphrates, very savage, hard to catch, and having long saw-like horns. This is the heraldic animal.

The a. and wolfe both fiers and fell SPENSER *F.Q.* I. vi. 26. To the group of true Antelopes also belongs the Gazelle CARPENTER.

Antelucan (æntĭlⁱū·kăn), *a.* 1654. [– L. *antelucanus* before dawn, f. *ante* ANTE- + *lux*, *luc-* light; see -AN.] Of or pertaining to the hours before dawn.

Antemeridian (æ:ntĭˌmĕri·diăn), *a. rare.* 1656. [– L. *antemeridianus* of the fore-noon, f. phr. *ante meridiem* before noon; see MERIDIAN *a.*] Of or belonging to the forenoon.

Antemetic (æntˌĭme·tik), *a.* 1706. [f. ANT- + EMETIC.] Tending to check vomiting. Also as *sb.* [sc. *medicine.*]

Antemundane (æntĭmɒ·ndēⁱn), *a.* 1731. [f. ANTE- + L. *mundus*, after *mundane.*] Existing or occurring before the creation of the world.

Antemu·ral. *? Obs.* 1774. [– eccl.L. *antemurale* (Jerome) protecting wall, f. *ante* ANTE- + *murus* wall.] A strong high wall with turrets, called also the barbican.

Antenatal (æntĭnēⁱ·tăl), *a.* 1817. [f. ANTE- + NATAL.] Happening or existing before birth.

‖ **Antenna** (ænte·nă). Pl. **-æ,** occas. **-as.** 1698. [– L. *antenna*, prop. *antemna* sail-yard, used in pl. as tr. of Aristotle's κεραῖοι 'horns' of insects.] **1.** *Zool.* A sensory organ, occurring in pairs on the heads of insects and crustacea; pop. called *horns* or *feelers.* **2.** *Bot.* Two long processes in the male flower of certain orchids, which when touched eject the pollinium from the flower 1862. **3.** A wireless aerial 1902.

1. The antennæ are organs of touch HUXLEY. Hence **Ante·nnal, Ante·nnary** *adjs.* of, relating to, or of the nature of antennæ. **Antenni·ferous** *a.* bearing antennæ. **Ante·nniform** *a.* of the form of antennæ.

Antennule (ænte·niūl). 1845. [dim. of ANTENNA; see -ULE.] *Zool.* A tiny organ of the nature of an antenna. Hence **Ante·nnular, -y** *a.* of the nature of small antennæ.

Ante-orbital (æntiǭ·ɹbităl), *a.* Also **ant-.** 1839. [f. ANTE- + ORBIT eyesocket + -AL¹.] *Phys.* Situated in front of the eyes.

Antepagment (æntĭpæ·gmĕnt). 1678. [– L. *antepagmentum* (also used, pl. *-a*), f. *ante* ANTE- + *pangere* fasten; see -MENT.] *Arch.* One of the jambs or moulded architraves of a door.

Antepa·schal, *a. rare.* 1660. [f. ANTE- + L. *pascha* passover + -AL¹.] Coming before the Passover, or before Easter.

A·ntepast. Also **anti-.** 1590. [f. ANTE- + L. *pastus* food; cf. REPAST *sb.*] † A whet taken before a meal; also, a foretaste.

An a. of the odium they were to incur H. WALPOLE.

‖ **Antependium** (æntĭpe·ndiŏm). Often **anti-.** 1696. [med.L., f. *ante* before + *pendĕre* hang.] A covering for the front of the altar, used in R.C. and some Anglican churches; occas. used for FRONTAL.

Antepenult (æ:ntĭˌpĭnɒ·lt), *a.* and *sb.* 1585. [abbrev. of next.] = ANTEPENULTIMATE.

‖ **Antepenultima** (æ:ntĭˌpĭnɒ·ltimă). 1581. [Late L. (*syllaba*) *antepænultima* last (syllable) but two, f. *ante* before + *pænultima*; see PENULTIMA.] *Pros.* The last syllable but two of a word.

Antepenultimate (-ɒ·ltimĕt), *a.* 1727. [f. ANTE- + PENULTIMATE.] The last but two. Orig. of syllables; but extended to order in place or time. 1730. Also as *sb.* 1727.

Antephialtic (æ:ntˌefiˌæ·ltik), *a.* 1853. [– mod.L. *antephialticus* (Hoffmann, *a* 1740), f. Gr. ἀντί against + ἐφιάλτης nightmare; see -IC.] *Med.* Good against the nightmare. Also as *sb.*

Antepileptic (æ:ntˌepile·ptik), *a.* 1656. [f. ANT- + EPILEPTIC.] *Med.* Good against epilepsy. Also as *sb.*

† **A·nteport.** *rare.* 1644. [– It. *antiporta*, f. *anti* = L. *ante* before + *porta* gate, door.] **1.** An outer gate or door. **2.** A hanging in front of a door –1669.

Anteposition (æntĭpozi·ʃən). *rare.* 1753. [n. of action deduced from earlier † *antepone* or its source, L. *anteponere* to place before; cf. *postpone, postposition.* See -ITION.] The placing of anything in front; *esp.* (*Gram.*) of a word which normally follows.

Antepra·ndial, *a.* 1847. [f. ANTE- + L. *prandium* dinner + -AL¹; cf. *postprandial.*] Before-dinner.

Anterior (æntīᵊ·riəɹ), *a.* 1611. [– Fr. *antérieur* or L. *anterior*, f. *ante* before, after *posterior*; see ANTE-, -IOR.] **1.** Of place: Fore, more to the front; opp. to *posterior.* **2.** Of time, etc.: Preceding, former, earlier 1794. Also with *to.* (Thus *anterior* is comparative in sense, but not in const.) 1728. Hence **Anterio·rity**, the quality of being a. **Ante·riorly** *adv.*

A·ntero-, Eng. comb. f. assumed L. **anterus*, positive of ANTERIOR; = Front, fore.

a.-frontal, pertaining to the front part of the forehead; **-parietal,** belonging to the front of the parietal or side plates of the skull; **-posterior,** front and back, forward and backward.

Ante-room (æ·ntĭˌrūm). 1762. [after Fr. *antichambre* or It. *anticamera*; see ANTECHAMBER.] A room before, or forming an entrance to, another.

Antes (æ·ntīz), *sb. pl.* 1789. [– Fr. *antes* (pl.) repr. L. *antæ*; see ANTA.] *Arch.* = ANTÆ.

A·ntescript. *rare.* 1831. [after *postscript.*] A note written in front or on the top of a letter, etc.; *also*, The whole letter before the postscript.

† **Antestature.** 1706. [– Fr. *antestature*, Sp. *antestatura*, f. L. *ante* before + *statura* a standing; see STATURE.] 'A small intrenchment, raised in haste, to dispute the rest of the ground, when the enemy has gained part.'

Ante-temple (æ·ntĭtemp'l). 1703. [– med. L. *antetemplum*, tr. Gr. πρόναος PRONAOS.] The portico of a church or of an ancient temple; occas. = *ante-nave* (see ANTE-).

† **A·ntethem(e.** 1494. [prob. – med.L. **antethema* theme leading up to (the main subject of a sermon); see ANTE-, THEME.] The text prefixed to a sermon as its theme or motto –1561.

Antetype (æ·ntĭtəip). 1612. [f. ANTE- + TYPE.] A preceding type; an earlier example.

Anteversion (æntĭvə·ɹʃən). 1853. [f. ANTE- + VERSION; cf. Fr. *antéversion.*] = ANTEFLEXION.

Antevert (æntĭvə̄·ɹt), *v.* 1649. [– L. *antevertere* anticipate, prevent, f. *ante* before + *vertere* turn.] †**1.** To avert beforehand –1677. **2.** To turn forward 1870. Hence **Anteve·rted** *ppl. a.* = ANTEFLEXED.

Anth-, Gr. ἀνθ, comb. form of ἀντί (see ANTI-) bef. an aspirate. Often in mod. scientific wds. *anti-*, as in *anthelix, anti-helix.*

Anthelion (ænþī·liŏn, ænt,h-). Pl. **-a.** 1670. [– Gr. ἀνθήλιον, neut. of ἀνθήλιος, earlier ἀντήλιος opposite to the sun, f. ἀντί ANTI- + ἥλιος sun.] A luminous ring or nimbus seen surrounding the shadow of the observer's head projected on a cloud or fogbank opposite the sun.

Anthelix; see ANTI-HELIX.

Anthelmintic (ænþĕlmi·ntik), *a.* 1684. [f. ANTH- + ἕλμινς, ἑλμινθ- worm + -IC.] *Med.* Of use against intestinal worms. Also as *sb.* 1706.

Anthem (æ·nþĕm), *sb.* [OE. *antefn, antifne* – late L. *anti·phona*, for *antiphō·na* ANTIPHON. The later forms indicate the foll. development of the pronunc.: *ante·ne, ante·m(ne), a·ntem, a·nthem* (XV, cf. OFr. *anthaine*; perh. infl. by *hymne* hymn); the sp. w. *th* finally affected the pronunc., as in *author.*] **1.** A composition, in prose or verse, sung antiphonally; an ANTIPHON. *Obs.* or *arch.* OE. **2.** A composition in unmeasured prose (usu. from the Scriptures or Liturgy) set to music for sacred use ME. **3.** *loosely* in poetry: Any song of praise or gladness. Also used of the Eng. National Anthem (techn. a *hymn*). 1591.

1. Continuing..untill an Anthymne was sung LESTRANGE. **2.** For my voice, I haue lost it with hallowing and singing of Anthemes SHAKS. **3.** Thy plaintive a. fades Past the near meadows KEATS.

Anthem (æ·nþĕm), *v.* 1628. [f. the sb.; cf. to *chant*, etc.] *trans.* To celebrate in an anthem.

Anthemy (æ·nþĭmi). *rare.* 1880. [f. Gr. ἀνθ-, ἄνθος flower. Also mod. L. *anthemia.*] *Bot.* A flower-cluster of any kind.

Anther (æ·nþəɹ). 1791. [– Fr. *anthère* or mod.L. *anthera,* in cl.L. medicine extracted from flowers, – Gr. ἀνθηρά, fem. of ἀνθηρός of flowers, f. ἄνθος flower.] *Bot.* That part of the stamen containing the pollen, which when mature is shed forth for the fertilization of the ovary.

Comb.: **a.-dust,** pollen; **-valve,** the opening by which the pollen is shed. Hence **A·ntheral** *a.* **Antheri·ferous** *a.* a.-bearing. **Anthe·riform** *a.* a.-shaped. **A·ntherless** *a.* without anthers. **Anthero·genous** *a.* produced or developed from anthers, as petals in a double rose. **A·ntheroid** *a.* anther-like in appearance or functions.

‖ **Antheridium** (ænþĕri·diŏm). 1854. [mod. L., f. *anthera* (prec.) + Gr. -ιδιον dim. suffix.] *Bot.* Oblong or globular sperm cells found in Cryptogams, answering to the anthers of flowering plants. Hence **Antheri·dial** *a.* pertaining to, or of the nature of, an a.

† **A·ntherine.** Also **anterne.** 1710. [perh. f. Gr. ἀνθηρός flowery; see -INE.] A kind of poplin –1739.

A:ntherozo·oid, -zo·id. 1854. [f. ANTHER + -o- + ZOOID.] *Bot.* One of the minute moving bodies in the antheridia of cryptogams. Hence **A:ntherozooi·dal, -zoi·dal** *a.*

‖ **Anthesis** (ǣnþī·sis). 1835. [Gr. ἄνθησις flowering, f. ἀνθεῖν to blossom.] Full bloom.

† **A·nthine,** *a.* 1656. [– L. *anthinus* – Gr. ἄνθινος of flowers.] Derived from or flavoured with flowers. As *sb.* (= L. *anthinum mel.*) Honey, oil, or wine flavoured with flowers.

Antho- (ǣnþōᵘ, -o, -ŏ, -ǫ), comb. form, f. Gr. ἄνθος flower.

antho·bian [Gr. βίος] *a., Ent.* an animal (*esp.* a beetle) living in or feeding on flowers. **-ca·rpous** [Gr. -καρπος] *a., Bot.* of or pertaining to the *Anthocarpi* (Lindley), fruits composed of flowers and fruit proper blended into a mass, as in the pine-apple; **-ce·phalous** [Gr. -κεφαλος] *a.,* having a flower-like head; **-cy·anin(e** [Gr. κύανος], also **-cyane, -kyan,** the blue colouring matter in plants; **-graphy** [Gr. -γραφία], *Bot.* the scientific description of flowers; **-lite** [Gr. λίθος], *Geol.* a name for certain fossil plants resembling flowers; *Min.* a variety of Amphibolite; ‖ **-lysis** [Gr. λύσις], *Bot.* a retrograde metamorphosis of a flower, in which parts normally combined are separated; **-ma·nia** [Gr. μανία], an extravagant passion for flowers; **-phore** [Gr. -φορος], *Bot.* the stalk which in some flowers raises the receptacle above the calyx; **-phorous** [see prec.] *a.,* flower-bearing; **-si·derite** [Gr. σιδηρίτης], *Min.* a hydrous silicate of iron occurring in feathery flowers; **-sperm** [Gr. σπέρμα], *Bot.* a little coloured concretion scattered in the tissue of certain Fucoids; **-taxy** [Gr. -ταξία], *Bot.* arrangement of flowers according to their inflorescence; **-xa·nthin(e** [Gr. ξανθός], now called *xanthophyll.*

A·nthoid, *a.* 1859. [f. Gr. ἄνθος flower + -OID.] Flower-like.

Anthology (ǣnþǫ·lŏdʒi). 1640. [– Fr. *anthologie* or med.L. *anthologia* (cf. L. *anthologica*) – Gr. ἀνθολογία, f. ἄνθος flower; see -LOGY.] **1.** A collection of the flowers of verse, i.e. small choice poems, *esp.* epigrams; orig. applied to the Gr. collections so called. **2.** Any other literary collection 1856. **3.** 'A collection of flowers' (J.) 1755. **4.** A hymnal [= Gr. ἀνθολόγιον] 1775. †**5.** A treatise on flowers. [Cf. *zoology*, etc.; also in Fr.] –1706.

1. Anthologies are sickly things 1851. Hence **Antholo·gical** *a.* † treating of flowers; of or relating to a literary a. **Antho·logist,** the compiler of an a.

Anthony (St.), the patron saint of swineherds, to whom one of each litter was usually vowed. Hence *pop.* **Anthony** = the smallest pig of a litter. **Anthony's** or **St. Anthony's fire,** a popular name of erysipelas (from the tradition that those who sought his intercession recovered from that distemper in 1089).

He will follow him like a St. Anthony's Pig FULLER.

Anthood (æ·nt,hud). 1879. [f. ANT + -HOOD.] Ant nature; ants collectively.

Anthophyllite (ænþofi·ləit, -ǫ·filəit). 1843. [f. mod.L. *anthophyllum* clove + -ITE[1] 2 b.] *Min.* A variety of hornblende, so called from its colour. Hence **Anthophylli·tic** *a.*

† **A·nthos.** 1585. [– Gr. ἄνθος flower.] Rosemary, 'the flower' *par excellence.*

‖ **Anthozoa** (ænþozōᵘ·ă), *sb. pl.* ? *Obs.* 1851. [mod.L., f. Gr. ἄνθος flower + ζῷα animals; see -A 4.] *Zool.* Another name for Actinozoa, including sea-anemones, coralline, polypes, etc. Hence **Anthozo·ic** *a.*

Anthozo·oid. 1877. [f. ANTHO- + ZOOID.] *Zool.* An individual animalcule of a compound Zoophyte.

Anthra-. *Chem.* Abbrev. of *Anthrac-,* stem of ANTHRACENE, forming compound names of Anthracene derivatives, as **anthraqui·none,** $C_{14}H_8O_2$, obtained by oxidation of anthracene, crystallizing in pale yellow needles. It is the source of artificial alizarin.

Anthracene (æ·nþrăsīn). 1863. [f. Gr. ἄνθραξ, -ακ- coal + -ENE.] *Chem.* A complex hydrocarbon, $C_{14}H_{10}$, obtained from coal-tar. It belongs to the Benzol group. Also *attrib.*, as in *Anthracene Red,* artificial alizarine. var. **Anthracin.**

Anthracic (ǣnþræ·sik), *a.* 1881. [f. as prec. + -IC.] Of or pertaining to anthrax. Hence **Anthra·ciform** *a.* having the form or appearance of anthrax: so **A·nthracoid** *a.*

Anthracite (æ·nþrăsəit). 1601. [– Gr. ἀνθρακῖτις kind of coal; see ANTHRAX, -ITE[1] 2 b.] † **1.** A stone described by Pliny, perh. hydrophane –1750. **2.** The non-bituminous variety of coal, called also Glance Coal, Blind Coal, and Stone Coal. Also *attrib.* 1812. Hence **Anthraci·ferous** *a.* yielding a. **Anthraci·tic** *a.* of, pertaining to, or resembling, a. **A·nthraciti:sm,** the anthracitic condition (of coal). **A·nthracitous** *a.* containing or characterized by a.

Anthracometer (æ:nþrăkǫ·mītəɹ). 1847. [f. Gr. ἄνθραξ, -ακ- coal (see ANTHRAX) + -METER.] An instrument for measuring the carbonic acid in a mixture. Hence **A:nthracome·tric** *a.*

Anthraconite (ǣnþræ·kŏnəit). 1843. [f. as prec. + Gr. -ωνη female descendant, derivative, + -ITE[1] 2 b.] *Min.* Von Moll's name for common black marble and the black bituminous limestones called swinestones or stinkstones.

Anthracothere (æ·nþrăko,þiᵊ:ɹ). 1833. [– mod.L. *anthracotherium,* f. as prec. + Gr. θηρίον beast.] A pachyderm quadruped whose remains occur in Tertiary lignites and coal.

Anthracoxen(e (æ·nþrăkǫksī:n). 1863. [f. as prec. + Gr. ξένος stranger.] *Min.* A brownish-black resin-like substance, occurring in amorphous masses which alternate with layers of coal, in the coal-beds of Bohemia.

Anthrax (æ·nþræks). ME. [– late L. *anthrax* carbuncle – Gr. ἄνθραξ coal, carbuncle.] **1.** A carbuncle, or malignant boil. **2.** 'Splenic fever' in sheep and cattle, caused by minute organisms introduced into the blood, which multiply rapidly. Also 'malignant pustule', caused in man by infection from animals so affected. 1876.

Anthropic, -al (ǣnþrǫ·pik, -ăl), *a. rare.* 1859. [– Gr. ἀνθρωπικός human, f. ἄνθρωπος human being; see -IC.] Of or belonging to a human being; human.

Anthropo-, repr. Gr. ἀνθρωπο-, stem and comb. form of ἄνθρωπος man.

Anthropocentric (ǣnþrōᵘ:po,se·ntrik), *a.* 1863. [f. prec. + CENTRIC = *-centred.*] Centring in man; regarding man as the central fact of the universe, to which all surrounding facts have reference.

Anthropogeny (ænþropǫ·dʒĕni). 1839. [f. as prec. + -GENY.] The investigation of the origin of man.

Anthropoglot (ǣnþrōᵘ·pǫglǫt). 1847. [– Gr. ἀνθρωπόγλωττος speaking man's language, f. as prec. + γλῶττα tongue.] An animal with a tongue like a man's, e.g. a parrot.

Anthropography (ænþropǫ·grăfi). 1570. [f. as prec. + -GRAPHY.] † **1.** A description of the structure of man –1839. **2.** The branch of anthropology which treats of the geographical distribution of the races of mankind, and their local variations; ethnography 1834.

Anthropoid (æ·nþrŏpoid, ǣnþrōᵘ·po,id), *a.* 1832. [– Gr. ἀνθρωποειδής of human form; see ANTHROPO-, -OID.] Of human form, man-like 1837. As *sb.* **a.** A being that is human in form only 1832. **b.** An anthropoid ape 1863. Hence **Anthropoi·dal** *a.*

Anthropolatry (ænþropǫ·lătri). *rare.* 1658. [f. ANTHROPO- + -LATRY.] Man-worship.

Anthropolite, -lith (ǣnþrōᵘ·pŏləit, -liþ). 1848. [f. ANTHROPO- + -LITE, -LITH.] A petrified man.

Anthropological (-lǫ·dʒikal), *a.* 1825. [f. as next + -ICAL.] Of, pertaining to, or connected with, anthropology; relating to the nature of man, or the natural history of mankind. So **Anthropolo·gic** (*rare*). Hence **Anthropolo·gically** *adv.*

Anthropologist (ænþropǫ·lŏdʒist). 1805. [f. next + -IST.] One who pursues the science of anthropology.

Anthropology (-ǫ·lŏdʒi). 1593. [See ANTHROPO-, -LOGY, and cf. mod.L. *anthropologia* (1595), Fr. *anthropologie* (XVI).] **1.** The science of man, or of mankind, in the widest sense. (The orig. Eng. meaning.) 1593. **b.** The science of the nature of man, embracing Human Physiology and Psychology. (The restricted sense current to *c* 1860.) 1706. **c.** The study of man as an animal 1861. † **2.** A speaking in terms of men; anthropomorphic language –1751.

Anthropomancy (ǣnþrōᵘ·pomæ:nsi). 1618. [f. ANTHROPO- + -MANCY.] Divination by the entrails of men.

Anthropometry (ænþropǫ·mĕtri). 1839. [f. ANTHROPO- + -METRY.] The measurement of the human body with a view to determine its average dimensions, etc., at different ages and in different races or classes. Hence **Anthro:pome·tric, -al** *a.* of, belonging to, or skilled in, a. **Anthro:pome·trically** *adv.* in regard to a.

Anthropomorphic, -al (ǣnþrōᵘ:pomǭ·ɹfik, -ăl), *a.* 1827. [f. as ANTHROPOMORPHOUS; see -IC, -ICAL.] Of the nature of anthropomorphism. **a.** Treating the Deity as having a human form and character. **b.** Attributing a human personality to anything impersonal or irrational 1858.

a. The a. language of the Pentateuch WESTCOTT. **b.** The a. abstractions which we call nations Black. Hence **Anthro:pomo·rphically** *adv.*

Anthropomorphism (-mǭ·ɹfiz'm). 1753. [f. as ANTHROPOMORPHOUS; see -ISM.] **1.** Ascription of a human form and attributes to the Deity, or of a human attribute or personality to anything impersonal or irrational. **2.** The use of terms applicable to men in speaking of God 1833.

1. The a. of the vulgar GIBBON. **2.** The strong a. of the Hebrew Scriptures COLERIDGE. Hence **Anthro:pomo·rphist,** one who uses a.

Anthropomorphite (-mǭ·ɹfəit). 1561. [– eccl.L. *anthropomorphitæ* (Augustine) – eccl. Gr. ἀνθρωπομορφῖται; see ANTHROPOMORPHOUS, -ITE[1] 1.] **1.** One ascribing (as an article of religious belief) a human form to God; *spec.* applied to **a.** A sect that arose in Egypt in the 4th c.; **b.** A party in the Western Church in the 10th c. **2.** *attrib.* or as *adj.* = ANTHROPOMORPHITIC 1662. Hence **Anthropomorphi·tic, -al** *a.* of or proper to anthropomorphites 1662.

Anthropomorphitism (-mǫ·ɹfitiz'm). 1664. [f. prec. + -ISM.] **a.** The doctrine of anthropomorphites. **b.** Anthropomorphism.

Anthropomorphize (-mǭ·ɹfəiz), *v.* 1845. [f. as ANTHROPOMORPHOUS; see -IZE.] *trans.* To render, or regard as, anthropomorphous. Also *absol.*

Anthropomorphology (-mǫɹfǫ·lŏdʒi). [f. as prec.; see -LOGY.] = ANTHROPOMORPHISM **2.** Hence **Anthropomorpholo·gically** *adv.*

Anthropomorphosis (-mǫɹfōᵘ·sis, -mǫ·ɹfōsis). 1863. [f. as prec.; see -OSIS.] Transformation into human shape.

Anthropomorphous (-mǫ·ɹfəs), *a.* 1753. [f. Gr. ἀνθρωπόμορφος of human form (f. ἄνθρωπος human being + μορφή form) + -OUS.] **1.** Having the form of a man. **2.** = ANTHROPOMORPHIC 1858. Hence **Anthropomo·rphously** *adv.* (*rare*).

Anthropono·mical, *a.* ? *Obs.* 1734. [f. ANTHROPO- + (ECO)NOMICAL.] Concerned with the laws which regulate human action.

Anthropopathy (-pǫ·păþi). 1647. [f. ANTHROPO- + -PATHY; cf. *anthropomorphite* (XVI), *-ist* (XVII), *-ism* (XVIII). Cf. mod.L. *anthropopathia* (Calvin).] Ascription of human feelings and passions (to the Deity, etc.).

Expressions which spoke of God by what is called a.—that is, as subject to wrath, repentance, and other human emotions FARRAR. var. **Anthropo·pathism.** Hence **Anthropopa·thic** *a.*, **-ally** *adv.*

‖ **Anthropophagi** (-pǫ·fădʒəi), *sb. pl.* 1552. [L., pl. of *anthropophagus* – Gr. ἀνθρωποφάγος man-eating; see ANTHROPO-, -PHAGOUS.] Man-eaters, cannibals. Rarely in sing. *anthropophagus.*

The Canibals that each others eate, The Anthropophague *Oth.* I. iii. 144. Hence **Anthro·popha·gic, -al** *a.* of, connected with, or relating to anthropophagy. † **Anthropophagi·nian.** *rare.* [app. after *Carthaginian.*] Used as sing. to *Anthropophagi Merry W.* IV. v. 9. **Anthropo·phagism,** cannibalism. **Anthropo·phagist, Anthropo·phagite,** a habitual cannibal. **Anthropo·phagistic** *a.*

Anthropo·phagous, *a.* 1831. [f. as prec. + -OUS.] Man-eating, cannibal. Hence **Anthropo·phagously** *adv.* (*rare*).

Anthropophagy (ænþropǫ·fădʒi). 1638. [– Gr. ἀνθρωποφαγία; see ANTHROPOPHAGI.] The eating of men, cannibalism.

Anthropopho·bia. *nonce-wd.* [f. ANTHROPO- + -PHOBIA.] Aversion to man.

Anthropophuism (ænþropǫ·fiu,iz'm). 1858. [f. Gr. ἀνθρωποφυής of man's nature (f. ἄνθρωπος human being + φυή nature) + -ISM.] The ascription of a human nature to the gods. Hence **Anthropophui·stic** *a.* ascribing a human nature to the gods; having such a nature ascribed.

Anthroposophist (ænþropǫ·sŏfist). [f. ANTHROPO- + SOPHIST.] One furnished with 'the wisdom of men'. (Cf. 1 *Cor.* 2:5, 13.) KINGSLEY.

Anthroposophy (-pǫ·sŏfi). 1742. [f. ANTHROPO- + Gr. σοφία wisdom; in more recent use contrasted w. *theosophy.*] The knowledge of the nature of man. *Also,* Human wisdom.

Anthropotomy (ænþropǫ·tŏmi). 1855. [f. ANTHROPO- + -TOMY.] Anatomy of the human body. Hence **Anthro:poto·mical** *a.* **Anthropo·tomist,** one who studies human anatomy.

Anthropu·rgic, *a. rare.* 1838. [f. Gr. ἀνθρωπουργός man-making (but taken, on anal. of θεουργός (see THEURGY), as = operating as man) + IC.] Wrought or acted upon by man.

Anthypnotic, anthysteric: see ANTI-HY-.

‖ **Anthypophora** (ænþipǫ·fŏră). Also **anti-hyp-.** 1589. [L. – Gr. ἀνθυποφορά, f. ἀντί against (ANTH-) + ὑποφορά allegation; cf. -A 2.] *Rhet.* Counter-inference or allegation. Hence **Anthypophore·tic** *a.*

Anti-, *prefix*¹; repr. Gr. ἀντι-, ἀντ-, ἀνθ- (see ANT-, ANTH-), 'opposite, against, in exchange, instead, representing, rivalling, simulating'; in Eng. used in compounds already formed in Gr., or others modelled on them. Also as a living formative, with sbs. expressed, or implied in adjs., and in the derivatives of these, after *antichrist, antichristian,* and *antipope,* the only examples in use bef. 1600. Shakespeare has no *anti-* combinations.

Combinations. **I.** Sbs. in which *anti-* attributively qualifies a sb. The main stress is on *a·nti* (a·nti,ki:ng). **1.** Formed on the type of ANTICHRIST; = 'Opposed, in opposition, opponent, rival', whence 'pretended, spurious, pseudo-': as *anti-bishop, -Cæsar, -Messiah,* etc. **b.** The opposite or reverse of; an opponent of: as *anti-hero, -Paul,* etc. **2.** With names of things: **a.** = Opposed, opposing, opposite, opposition-, counter-; as *anti-Bartholomew, -decalogue, -endowment, -parliament, -Rome,* etc. **b.** = The opposite, contrary, or reverse of; as ANTICLIMAX, *-poison,* etc. **II.** Adjs. and attrib. phrases, with sb. expressed, as *anti-zealot,* or implied in an adj., as *anti-national.* The stress is *not* on *anti-* (anti,-ca·tholic). **3.** Adjs., formed on the type of ANTICHRISTIAN = Opposed to Christ, Christians, or what is Christian: as *anti-national,* or (rarely) *anti-church-ian,* etc. Occ. *anti-* simply reverses the sense of the adj.: as *anti-grammatical, -warlike,* etc. **4.** Attrib. phrases, consisting of *anti-* governing a sb., where *anti-* may be considered as a preposition = *against.* Examples are: **anti-aircraft** (defence, gun 1914); **anti-court** party (perhaps the earliest *c* 1650); **Anti-combination** (laws), **Anti-Corn-Law** (league), **Anti-rent** (agitation), **Anti-slavery** (society), **Anti-state-church** (association), **Anti-vaccination** (league). **III.** Sbs. uniform with, or formed on the preceding adjs. and attrib. phrases. Stress not on *anti-* (anti-ca·lvinist). **5.** Combs. in which *anti-* is prefixed to a personal appellation: as *anti-Arminian, -Calvinist, -episcopist, -missionary.* **6.** Combs. chiefly in -IST, as *anti-alcoholist,* etc. **7.** Names **a.** of systems, as *anti-slavery,* etc.; **b.** of material agents or appliances, as **anti-ferment; anti-erysipelas,** a plant so named from its use; **anti-huff,** a substance used to adulterate cheese, etc. **8.** Abstract sbs., chiefly in *-ism,* as *anti-negroism,* etc.

Anti-, *pref.*² Var. of ANTE- 'before', being the form in It., OFr., and occ. in L., hence sometimes in Eng. words from these, as *antichamber,* etc.

Anti-acid, -aphrodisiac, -apoplectic, -arthritic, -asthmatic: see ANTACID, etc.

‖ **Antiæ** (æ·nti,ī), *sb. pl.* 1874. [L., for *antiæ comæ* forelocks, f. *antius* fore.] *Zool.* Forelocks.

‖ **Antiar** (æ·ntʃăɹ, æ·ntiăɹ). [– Jav. *antjar, antshar.*] The Upas tree of Java, *Antiaris toxicaria*; also, the poison obtained from it. Hence **A·ntiarin,** the poisonous principle of the Upas tree.

Anti-attrition (æ:nti,ătri·ʃən). 1833. [ANTI-¹ 7.] That which resists attrition. *spec.* Any compound applied to machinery to resist the effects of friction; as black lead mixed with grease, etc. Also *fig.*

‖ **Antibacchius** (æ:nti,băkəi·ŏs). 1589. [late L. – Gr. ἀντιβάκχειος; see BACCHIUS.] *Pros.* A reversed bacchius, a foot of two long and one short syllable. Hence **Antiba·cchic** *a.*

Antibi·lious, *a.* 1835. [ANTI-¹ 3.] Of use against biliousness.

Antibio·tic, *a. rare.* 1860. [f. ANTI-¹ 3 + Gr. βιωτικός fit for life.] Opposed to a belief in the presence or possibility of life.

† **Anti-Birmingham.** 1681. [ANTI- 5.] *Eng. Hist.* An anti-Whig, a Tory; a nickname given to the opponents of the Exclusion Bill in 1680; its supporters were nicknamed by Tories 'Birmingham (= counterfeit) Protestants'.

Antibody (æ·nti,bǫdi). 1901. [tr. G. *antikörper*: ANTI- 2a.] *Biol. Chem.* A body formed in the blood, etc., to attack a toxin, etc.

Antibrachial (æntì,bræ·kiăl), *a.* 1836. [f. ANTI *pref.*² + BRACHIUM + -AL¹.] *Anat.* Of or pertaining to the forearm.

Antiburgher (æ:ntibɒ̄·ɹgəɹ). 1766. [ANTI-¹ 5.] A section of the Secession Church in Scotland, which held it unscriptural to take the Burgess Oath: see BURGHER.

Antic (æ·ntik). 1529. [– It. *antico* ancient, ANTIQUE, used in Eng. as synon. with *grottesco* GROTESQUE.] **A.** *adj.* **1.** *Arch.* and *Decorative Art.* Grotesque, in composition or shape; bizarre 1548. **2.** Absurd from incongruity, grotesque, in gesture, shape, or attire 1590. † **3.** Grinning, like 'antics' in architecture –1697.

1. Whether *Grotesca* (as the Italians) or Antique worke (as wee call it) should be receiued WOTTON. **2.** An Anticke disposition *Haml.* I. v. 172. Antick shapes 1642. To be sung in an a. Cope MILT. **3.** Your mimick mouthes, your antick faces QUARLES.

B. *sb.* † **1.** *Arch.* and *Decorative Art.* A monstrous, fantastic, or incongruous representation of objects of the animal or the vegetable kingdom, as in tracery, or sculpture –1830. **2.** A grotesque gesture, posture, or trick; also *fig.* of behaviour. (Usu. in *pl.*) 1529. † **3.** A grotesque theatrical representation –1673. **4.** A performer who plays a grotesque part, a clown, mountebank, etc. 1564. Also *transf.* and *fig.*

1. Woven with antickes and wyld ymagery SPENSER. Gargils or Antiques HOLLAND. **3.** Some. show, or pageant, or anticke, or fire-worke *L.L.L.* v. i. 119. **4.** Jugglers and dancers, antics, mummers, mimics MILT. *Sams.* 1325. *Rich. II*, III. ii. 162.

Antic (æ·ntik), *v.* 1589. [f. prec.] † **1.** *trans.* To make antic or grotesque 1606. **2.** *intr.* To perform antics 1589.

Anticachectic (æ:nti,kăke·ktik), *a.* 1719. [f. ANTI¹- + CACHECTIC *a.*, after *anti-narcotic.*] *Med.* Used against cachexy. Also as *sb.*

† **Antica·mera.** 1625. [It.; see ANTECHAMBER.] An antechamber –1670.

Anticatarrhal (æ:nti,kătā·răl), *a.* 1753. [ANTI-¹ 3.] Of use against catarrh. Also as *sb.*

Antica·tholic, *a.* 1819. [ANTI-¹ 3.] Opposed to what is catholic. Also as *sb.*

Anticausotic (æ:nti,kǭsǫ·tik), *a.* 1753. [f. ANTI-¹ 3 + Gr. καῦσις burning + -OTIC.] *Med.* Of use against a burning fever. Also as *sb.*

Anticeremonial (æ:nti,serĭmōᵘ·niăl), *a.* 1655. [ANTI-¹ 3 or 4.] Opposed to ceremonies. var. † **Anticeremo·nian.**

† **Anti-chamber,** var. of ANTECHAMBER.

Antichlor(e (æ·nti,klōᵊɹ). 1869. [f. ANTI-¹ 7 + CHLOR(INE.] *Chem.* A substance used to remove the last traces of chlorine in bleaching.

Antichrist (æ·nti,krəist). [ME. *ante-, anticrist* (later assim. to L. and Gr.) – OFr, *antecrist* (mod. *antéchrist*) – eccl.L. *antichristus* – Gr. ἀντίχριστος (1 John 2:18), f. ἀντί ANTI-¹ + χριστός CHRIST.] **1.** An opponent of Christ. **2.** The title of a great personal opponent of Christ and His kingdom, expected to appear before the end of the world ME.

1. The first Antichrist, Simon Magus PUSEY. **2.** God shal make shorte the tyme of Antecryst FISHER. The question, whether the Pope be A. HOBBES.

Antichristian (ænti,kri·stiăn), *a.* 1531. [f. prec., after *Christian*; often treated as f. ANTI-¹ + CHRISTIAN, and in 17–18th c. hyphened.] **A.** *adj.* **1.** Of or pertaining to Antichrist 1532. **2.** Opposed to what is Christian or to Christianity. (Often *anti-christian.*) 1587.

1. Tindales antichristen heresyes MORE. **2.** Shelley's a. opinions 1870.

B. *sb.* † **1.** A follower of Antichrist –1753. **2.** An opponent of Christianity 1621.

2. Toland, the great oracle of the anti-christians SWIFT. Hence **Antichri·stianism,** the system of Antichrist; the quality of being opposed to Christianity; anything a.; var. † **Antichristia·nity.** † **Antichri·stianize** *v.* to oppose Christ. **Antichri·stianly** *adv.*

† **Anti·chronism.** 1612. [Improper use of Gr. ἀντιχρονισμός use of one tense for another, f. ἀντί ANTI-¹ + χρόνος time, tense + -ισμος -ISM.] Contradiction of true chronology; anachronism –1728.

‖ **Antichthon** (ænti·kþōᵘn), *pl.* † **-chthones** (-·kþōnīz). 1601. [Gr. ἀντίχθων, prop. adj. (sc. γῆ earth), f. ἀντί opposite to + χθών earth, ground.] **1.** A (supposed) second Earth on the opposite side of the sun 1655. † **2.** *pl.* The inhabitants of the opposite side of the earth –1684.

Anticipant (ænti·sipănt), *a.* 1626. [– *anticipant-*, pres. ppl. stem of L. *anticipare*; see ANTICIPATE *v.*, -ANT; cf. Fr. *anticipant.*] **1.** Operating in advance. **2.** Apprehending beforehand, expectant 1798. **3.** As *sb.* One who anticipates 1854.

2. Wakening guilt, a. of Hell SOUTHEY. **3.** O meek a. of that sure pain [etc.] M. ARNOLD.

† **Anticipate,** *ppl. a.* 1549. [– L. *anticipatus*, pa. pple. of *anticipare*; see next, -ATE².] Anticipated.

Anticipate (ænti·sipeᵉit), *v.* 1532. [– *anticipat-*, pa. ppl. stem of L. *anticipare* take beforehand, anticipate, f. *ante* ANTE- + *cip-*, var. of base of *capere* take; see -ATE³. Partly after Fr. *anticiper.*] † **1.** To seize beforehand –1783. **2.** To use or spend in advance 1674. **3.** To deal with (a thing) or perform (an action) before another; to forestall 1605; to be before (another) in acting 1682. **4.** To observe or practise or cause to happen, earlier than the due date 1534. **5.** † *intr.* To occur earlier –1646; *trans.* to precede (*rare*) 1855. **6.** To take into consideration

fore the due time; also *absol.* 1532. **7.** To realize beforehand (a certain future event) 1643; to look for (an uncertain event) as certain. Const. *simple obj.* or *subord. cl.* 1749.
2. To a. one's income 1883. **3.** To a. the vengeance of heaven GOLDSM. To be anticipated by one's predecessors 1877. **4.** To a. a payment 1751. **6.** He is to a. consequences and provide for the future 1796. **7.** My fears A. thy words SMOLLETT. Those, not in the secret, anticipated an acquittal 1839. Hence † **Anti·cipately** *adv.*

Anticipation (æntiːsipē̆ⁱ·ʃən). 1548. [– Fr. *anticipation* or L. *anticipatio*, f. *anticipat-*; see prec., -ION.] **1.** The action of anticipating (see ANTICIPATE 1, 2); the using of money before it is at one's disposal; the sum so used. **2.** Prior action that 'prevents', provides for, or precludes the action of another 1553. **3.** Assignment to too early a time; *hence*, observance in advance 1774. **4.** Occurrence in advance of the due time; *ellipt.* the amount of such earlier occurrence. *Obs.* in gen. sense. –1697. **b.** *Mus.* The introduction in advance of part of a chord which is to follow 1819. **5.** Intuitive preconception; *a priori* knowledge; presentiment 1549. † **6.** The formation of opinions before examining the evidence, prepossession, prejudice –1711. **7.** The action of realizing a thing before it occurs 1711. **8.** Expectation 1809.
1. Restrained from a. by the settlement LD. ST. LEONARDS. **2.** So shall my a. preuent your discovery *Haml.* II. ii. 304. **6.** Men give themselves up to the first anticipations of their mind LOCKE. **7.** And when the thoughts on evil pore, A. makes it more 1764. **8.** The a. of many readers COLERIDGE.

Anti·cipative, *a.* 1559. [f. ANTICIPATE *v.* + -IVE.] **1.** Having the faculty or habit of anticipating. **2.** Of the nature of anticipation 1664. Hence **Anti·cipatively** *adv.*

Anti·cipator. Also **-er.** 1598. [f. ANTICIPATE *v.* + -OR 2.] One who anticipates. Hence **Anti·cipatory** *a.* of or pertaining to an anticipator; of the nature of anticipation. **Anti·cipatorily** *adv.*

Anticivic (æntiˌsi·vik), *a. rare.* 1805. [– Fr. *anticivique*; see ANTI-¹ 3 and CIVIC.] Opposed to citizenship, *esp.* to the Fr. doctrine of citizenship of 1789.

Anticivism (æntiˌsi·viz'm). *rare.* [– Fr. *anticivisme*; see ANTI-¹ 8 + CIVISM.] Opposition to citizenship (as in prec.) CARLYLE.

A·nticize, *v. rare.* [f. ANTIC *sb.* + -IZE; cf. *criticize.*] To play antics. BROWNING.

Anticlastic (æntiˌklæ·stik), *a.* 1879. [f. Gr. ἀντί contrary + κλαστός 'bent' f. κλᾶν to break; cf. SYNCLASTIC.] Applied to a surface having two curvatures, transverse to each other, in opposite directions, as the surface of a saddle.

Anticlimax (æːntiˌklai·mæks). 1727. [ANTI-¹ 2.] **1.** *Rhet.* The opposite of climax; the addition of a particular which suddenly lowers the effect. **2.** A descent in contrast to a previous rise 1858.
1. *A.* . . 'Dalhoussy the great God of war, Lieutenant colonel to the Earl of Mar' POPE. **2.** [His] later years, were only an a. MCCARTHY.

Anticlinal (æntiˌklai·năl), *a.* 1833. [f. Gr. ἀντί against + κλίνειν to lean, slope + -AL¹.] **1.** *Geol.* Forming a ridge, in which strata lean against each other, and whence they dip in opposite directions. Opp. to *synclinal.* **2.** *Anat.* (A vertebra) having an upright spine, towards which the spines on both sides incline 1870. As *sb.* [sc. *fold, axis, crest*, or *line.*] 1849.

Anticline (æ·ntiˌklain). 1861. [f. as prec., after *incline.*] An anticlinal fold.

A·nticly, *adv. arch.* 1556. [f. ANTIC *a.* + -LY².] Grotesquely.
Go antiquely, and show outward hideousnesse *Much Ado* V. i. 96. So † **A·nticness,** oddity (*rare*).

Anticonvellent (æːntiˌkǫnve·lĕnt), *a.* 1876. [f. *anti-*¹ 3 + *convellent-*, pres. ppl. stem of L. *convellere* convulse.] *Med.* Of use against convulsions. Also as *sb.* So **A:nticonvu·lsive** *a.* and *sb.*

Anticor (æ·ntiˌkōᵊːɹ). 1607. [f. ANTI- + L. *cor* heart.] A swelling which breaks out in the breast of a horse, etc., over against the heart.

Anticorrosion (æntiˌkǫrōᵘ·ʒən). 1851. [ANTI-¹ 7.] A substance which prevents corrosion.

Anticous (æ̆ntai·kəs), *a.* 1870. [f. L. *anticus* front + -OUS, after POSTICOUS.] *Bot.* Fronting the axis of the whorl to which it belongs.

Anticyclone (æ·ntiˌsai·kloᵘn). 1877. [ANTI-¹ 2.] *Meteor.* The rotatory outward flow of air from an atmospheric area of high pressure; also, the whole system of high pressure and outward flow.

Anticyclonic (æːntiˌsaiklǫ·nik), *a. Meteor.* **1.** [f. ANTI-¹ 3 + CYCLONIC.] Opposed to cyclones or cyclonic theories 1860. **2.** [f. ANTICYCLONE.] Of or pertaining to an anticyclone 1871. Hence **Anticyclo·nically** *adv.* after the manner of an anticyclone.

Antidicoma·rianite. 1625. [– eccl.Gr. ἀντιδικομαριανῖται, f. ἀντίδικος adversary + Μαρία Mary; in med.L. *antidicomaritæ*; see -ITE¹ 1.] *pl.* Adversaries of Mary; Oriental Christians of the 4th c., who denied the perpetual virginity of the mother of Jesus. So **Antidicoma·rian** *a.* and *sb.*

† **Anti·dotary,** *a.* 1541. [– med.L. *antidotarius, -arium*, f. *antidotum*; see next, -ARY¹. Cf. Fr. *antidotaire.*] Of the nature of an antidote –1657. As *sb.* **1.** [sc. *application.*] 1583. **2.** A book describing antidotes; occas. = A dispensary –1727.

Antidote (æ·ntidoᵘt). 1543. [– Fr. *antidote* or L. *antidotum* – Gr. ἀντίδοτον, subst. use of n. of ἀντίδοτος, f. ἀντί ANTI-¹ + δο-, stem of διδόναι give.] A medicine given to counteract the action of poison, or an attack of disease. Const. *against, for, to.* Also *fig.*
Where are poysons, antidots are most G. HERBERT. His very mirth is an a. to all gaiety GOLDSM. Hence **A·ntidotal** *a.* of, pertaining to, or of the nature of an a. **Antido·tally** *adv.*; also † **Antido·tically.**

Antidote (æ·ntidoᵘt), *v.* 1630. [f. prec., after med.L. *antidotare*, Fr. *antidoter* (XVI).] † **1.** *trans.* To furnish with an antidote; fortify against poison. Also *fig.* –1703. **2.** To apply an antidote to, counteract. Also *fig.* 1661.

Antidromous (æ̆nti·drŏməs), *a.* 1878. [f. Gr. ἀντί against + -δρομος running + -OUS.] Running in an opposite direction round an axis. var. **Anti·dromal.**

Antidysenteric (æːntiˌdisĕnte·rik), *a.* 1853. [ANTI-¹ 3 + DYSENTERY + -IC.] *Med.* Of use against dysentery. Also as *sb.*

Antidysuric (æːntiˌdisiūᵊ·rik), *a.* [f. ANTI-¹ 3 + DYSURY + -IC.] *Med.* Of use against dysury.

Anti-emetic, -ephialtic, vars. of ANTEMETIC, etc.

Anti-ethnic (æntiˌe·þnik), *a.* 1861. [f. ANTI-¹ 3 + ETHNIC.] Against the Gentiles, or non-Jewish nations.

Antifebrile (æntiˌfe·bril, fī-), *a.* 1661. [ANTI-¹ 3.] *Med.* Of use against fever. As *sb.* [sc. *substance.*] 1661. var. **Antifebri·fic** (erron. *-febritick*).

Antifriction (æntiˌfri·kʃən). 1837. [ANTI-¹ 7.] That which prevents friction. Also *fig.*
Oil of flattery, the best patent a. known CARLYLE.

Antigalactic (æːntiˌgălæ·ktik), *a.* 1847. [f. ANTI-¹ 3 + Gr. γάλαξ, γάλακτ- milk + -IC.] Of use in preventing the secretion of milk. Also as *sb.*

Anti-Ga·llican, *a.* 1755. [f. ANTI-¹ 3 + GALLICAN.] Opposed to what is French 1765. *sb.* One opposed to the French 1755. var. **Anti-Ga·llic.** Hence **Anti-Ga·llicanism.**

Anti-god (æ·ntiˌgǫd). 1684. [ANTI-¹ 1.] He who or that which is opposed to God. *Hence* **b.** A rival deity; **c.** An evil demon.

Antigorite (æ̆nti·gŏrəit). 1862. [f. *Antigorio* in Piedmont + -ITE¹ 2b.] *Min.* A variety of serpentine.

Antigro·pelos. 1848. [Said to be made up from Gr. ἀντί against + ὑγρός wet + πηλός mud (which should give *anthygropē·los*).] Waterproof leggings.

Anti-guggler (æntigʋ·gləɹ). 1794. [f. ANTI-¹ 6 + *guggle* = GURGLE + -ER¹.] A siphon inserted into carboys, etc., in drawing off liquor, so as to admit the air without gurgling.

Antihelix, anthelix (æntiˌhī·liks, æ·nþīliks). 1721. [– Gr. ἀνθέλιξ inner curvature of the ear, f. ἀντί opposite + ἕλιξ outer curvature.] *Anat.* The curved elevation within the helix or outer rim of the ear.

Antihydropic (æːntiˌhəidrǫ·pik), *a.* 1742. [f. ANTI-¹ 3 + HYDROPIC.] *Med.* Of use against dropsy. Also as *sb.*

Antihypnotic (æːntiˌhipnǫ·tik), *a.* Also **anthypn-.** 1681. [f. ANTI-¹ 3 + HYPNOTIC.] *Med.* Tending to prevent sleep. Also as *sb.*

Antihysteric (æːntiˌhiste·rik), *a.* 1747. [f. ANTI-¹ 3 + HYSTERIA + -IC.] *Med.* Of use against hysteria. Also as *sb.*

Anti-icteric (æːntiˌikte·rik), *a.* 1853. [f. ANTI-¹ 3 + ICTERIC.] *Med.* Of use against jaundice. Also as *sb.*

Anti-Jacobin (æntiˌdʒæ·kŏbin), *a.* 1809. [ANTI-¹ 3.] Opposed to the party called Jacobins in France in 1789; hence, opposed to the French Revolution, and to those who sympathized with democratic principles, who were nicknamed *Jacobins* by Mr. Pitt's followers. As *sb.* One opposed to the Jacobins, etc.; also, name of a weekly paper started in 1797. Hence **Anti-Ja·cobinism.**

A:ntilibra·tion. *rare.* 1858. [f. ANTI-¹ 3 + LIBRATION.] Counterpoising.

Antilithic (æntiˌli·þik), *a.* 1853. [f. ANTI-¹ 3 + LITHIC *a.*¹] *Med.* Of use against stone in the bladder. Also as *sb.*

Antilogarithm (æntiˌlǫ·gărip'm). 1675. [ANTI-¹ 2.] *Math.* † **1.** The complement of the logarithm of a sine, tangent, or secant; or the difference between that and the logarithm of 90 degrees –1796. **2.** The number to which the logarithm belongs 1675. Hence **Antilogari·thmic** *a.*

Antilogy (æ̆nti·lŏdʒi). 1614. [– Fr. *antilogie* (= med.L. *antilogium*, later *-ia*) – Gr. ἀντιλογία contradiction, f. ἀντί against + -λογία -LOGY.] A contradiction in terms, or ideas.
Speculation ends in a series of insoluble antilogies SIR W. HAMILTON.

Antilopine (æ̆nti·lŏpəin), *a.* Also **ante-.** 1827. [f. mod.L. *antilopus*, generic name of the *antelope*, + -INE¹.] Of or pertaining to the antelope.

Antilyssic (æntiˌli·sik), *a.* [f. ANTI-¹ 3 + *lyssa* (– Gr. λύσσα rabies) + -IC.] *Med.* Of use against hydrophobia. Also as *sb.*

Antimacassar (æːntiˌmăkæ·səɹ). 1852. [f. ANTI-¹ 7 + MACASSAR.] A covering thrown over sofas, chairs, etc., to protect them from grease in the hair, etc., or as an ornament.

† **Antimagistra·tical,** *a.* 1645. [ANTI-¹ 3.] Opposed to the power or claims of civil magistrates –1669. var. † **Antimagi·strical** *a.* (*rare*).

Antima·son. [ANTI-¹ 5.] One professing opposition to freemasonry. (U.S. politics.) Hence **Antimaso·nic,** *a.* **Antima·sonry,** opposition to freemasonry.

Antimasque, -mask (æntiˌma·sk). 1613. [ANTI-¹ 2.] A grotesque interlude between the acts of a masque. (Occ. made *Anticmasque.*) Hence **A·ntima·squer, -ker,** a performer in an a.

Antimere (æ·ntimīᵊɹ). 1877. [f. Gr. ἀντί opposite + μέρος part.] *Biol.* Usu. pl. *antimeres*, or as L. *antimera*: Opposite divisions or halves. Hence **Antime·ric** *a.*

‖ **Antimetabole** (æːntiˌmĭtæ·bŏli). 1589. [late L. – Gr. ἀντιμεταβολή, f. ἀντί in opposite direction + μεταβολή turning about.] *Rhet.* Repetition of words or ideas in inverse order.

‖ **Antimetathesis** (æːntiˌmĭtæ·þĭsis). [Gr. ἀντιμετάθεσις counterchange, f. ἀντί against; see METATHESIS.] *Rhet.* Inversion of the members of an antithesis.

Antimeter (æ̆nti·mĭtəɹ). 1819. [f. Gr. ἀντί, expressing equivalence, + -METER.] An obsolete instrument, called also *Reflecting Sector*, for measuring small angles.

Antimona·rchical, *a.* 1625. [ANTI-¹ 3.] Opposed to monarchy. vars. † **Antimona·rchial, Antimona·rchic.** Hence **Antimonar·chically** *adv.*

Antimo·narchy. 1648. [ANTI-¹ 7.] Opposition to monarchy. Hence **Antimo·narchist.**

Antimonate (æ·ntimonēⁱːt, -mōᵘ·neⁱt). 1854. [f. ANTIMONY + -ATE⁴.] *Chem.* A salt of Antimonic acid.

Antimonial (æntimōᵘ·niăl), *a.* 1605. [– mod.L. *antimonialis*; see ANTIMONY, -AL¹.]

1. Of or pertaining to antimony. **2.** Containing antimony in combination 1771. **3.** *sb.* A medicine containing antimony 1727.

1. *Antimonial cups*: cups made of glass of antimony, to communicate emetic qualities to wine. **2.** *Antimonial wine*: sherry containing tartarated antimony. A. arsenic, copper, etc. (*mod.*).

Antimo·niate. 1801. [– mod.L. *antimoniatum*, f. med.L. *antimonium*; see ANTIMONY, -ATE⁴.] = ANTIMONATE. Hence **Antimo·niated** *ppl. a.* treated with antimony.

Antimonic (æntimǫ·nik), *a.* 1834. [f. ANTIMONY + -IC.] Of or pertaining to antimony. In *Chem.* applied to compounds in which antimony combines as a pentad; as *Antimonic acid* (prop. *A. oxide*), or *Antimony pentoxide* Sb_2O_5.

Antimonide (æ·ntimonəi:d, -mōᵘ·nəid). 1863. [f. as prec. + -IDE.] *Chem.* A compound of antimony with hydrogen, a metal, or an organic radical. Also called STIBIDE, and formerly ANTIMONIURET.

A:ntimonio·so-, comb. f. ANTIMONIOUS.

Antimonious (æntimōᵘ·niəs), *a.* 1833. [f. as prec. + -OUS.] Of the nature of, or containing, antimony. In *Chem.* applied to compounds in which antimony combines as a triad; as *Antimonious Chloride* $SbCl_3$, etc. var. **Antimo·nous.**

Antimonite (æ·ntimonəi:t, -mōᵘ·nəit). 1834. [f. as prec. + -ITE¹ 4 b.] **1.** *Chem.* A salt of antimonious acid. **† 2.** = STIBNITE.

Antimo·niuret. 1841. [f. as prec. + -URET.] *Chem.* See ANTIMONIDE. Hence **Antimo·niuretted** *ppl. a.* combined with antimony (in a gaseous state).

Antimony (æ·ntiməni). 1477. [– med.L. *antimonium* (Constantinus Africanus of Salerno, XI), of unkn. origin.] A brittle metallic elementary body, of bright bluish-white colour and flaky crystalline texture. Symbol Sb (*Stibium*). **a.** *Alchem.* and *Pharm.* Orig. applied to the native trisulphide (called also *grey antimony*, or *Stibnite*), the στίμμι, *stibium* of the ancients, and *al-kuḥl* of the Arabs (see ALCOHOL); the *antimonium, proteus, leo ruber*, etc., of the alchemists. **b.** *Chem.* The simple element. (Called earlier *Regulus of Antimony.*) 1788.

Combs., etc.: **Antimony blende** = Red A.; **A. bloom** = White A.; **A. glance** = Grey A. (see a); **A. ochre**, *Cervantite*; **A. vermilion**, a red pigment precipitated from an antimonial solution; **Butter of A.**, an old name of the trichloride, a translucent fatty mass; **Crocus of A.**, an impure sulphide of a. and sodium; **Glass of A.**, an oxysulphide fused; **Red A.** = *Kermesite*; **Saffron of A.** = Red A.; **Tartarated A.**, tartar emetic.

Antinational (ænti,næ·ʃənăl), *a.* [ANTI-¹ 3.] Opposed to one's own nation, or to a national party.

Antinephritic (æ:nti,nĭfri·tik), *a.* 1678. [ANTI-¹ 3.] *Med.* Of use against disease of the kidneys. Also as *sb.*

Antinomian (æntinōᵘ·miăn). 1645. [f. med.L. *Antinomi*, f. Gr. ἀντί against + νόμος law; see -IAN.] **A.** *adj.* Of or pertaining to the antinomians. **B.** *sb.* One who maintains that the moral law is not binding upon Christians, under the law of grace 1645. *spec.* One of a sect alleged to hold this opinion, which arose in Germany in 1535. var. **† Anti·nomist** *sb.* Hence **Antino·mianism, † Anti·nomism,** the doctrine or practice of antinomians. **† Antinomianize** *v.* to teach antinomianism.

Antinomy (ænti·nŏmi). 1592. [– L. *antinomia* – Gr. ἀντινομία conflict of laws, f. ἀντί against + νόμος law; cf. Fr. *antinomie*, -Y³.] **1.** A contradiction in a law, or between two equally binding laws. **† 2.** A contradictory law, statute, or principle; an authoritative contradiction –1656. **3.** A contradiction between conclusions which seem equally logical, reasonable, or necessary; a paradox; intellectual contradictoriness 1802.

1. The antinomies or contradictions of the Code and Pandects GIBBON. **2.** His own a., or counter-statute MILT. var. **A·ntinome** (*rare*), Hence **Antino·mic, -al** *a.* of, pertaining to, or characterized by a.

Anti-odontalgic (æ:nti,ōᵘdǫntæ·ldʒik), *a.* 1817. [ANTI-¹ 3.] *Med.* Of use against toothache. Also as *sb.*

Anti-orgastic (æ:nti,ǫɹgæ·stik), *a.* 1880. [ANTI-¹ 3.] *Med.* Allaying excitement, sedative.

Antiparallel (ænti,pæ·rălĕl). *rare.* 1660. [ANTI-¹ 2.] **† 1.** Parallel but opposed. **2.** *Geom. pl.* Two lines which make with two other lines angles equal each to each, but contrary ways, one being exterior and the other interior 1796.

Antiparalytic, -al (æ:nti,pærăli·tik, -ăl), *a.* 1755. [ANTI-¹ 3.] *Med.* Of use against paralysis. Also as *sb.*

Antiparliame·ntary, *a.* 1643. [ANTI-¹ 3.] **1.** Opposed to (the Long) Parliament or the parliamentary party. *Obs.* or *Hist.* vars. **† Antiparliame·ntal, Antiparliamenta·rian. 2.** Against parliamentary usage 1656.

† Antiparliamentee·r. 1643. [Cf. *pamphleteer.*] A writer or speaker against (the Long) Parliament.

Antipathetic, -al (ǣntipăþe·tik, -ăl), *a.* 1601. [f. as ANTIPATHY, after PATHETIC *a.*] Having an antipathy or constitutional aversion; opposed in nature or tendency (*to*). Hence **Antipathe·tically** *adv.* var. **† Anti·pathous.**

Antipathic (ænti,pæ·þik), *a.* 1830. [f. ANTIPATHY + -IC, after Fr. *antipathique.*] Of or belonging to antipathy; of contrary nature or character (*to*); *spec.* in *Med.* having or producing the contrary symptoms.

Antipathist (ǣnti·păþist). *rare.* 1817. [f. as prec. + -IST.] One possessed by an antipathy; a natural enemy.

Antipathize (ǣnti·păþəiz), *v.* ? *Obs. rare.* 1633. [f. as prec. + -IZE.] **1.** *intr.* To feel the opposite. **2.** *trans.* To render antipathetic 1667.

Antipathy (ǣnti·păþi). 1601. [– Fr. *antipathie* or L. *antipathia* – Gr. ἀντιπάθεια, f. ἀντιπαθής opposed in feeling, f. ἀντί ANTI-¹ + πάθος, παθε-; see PATHOS, -Y³.] **† 1.** Contrariety of feeling, disposition, or nature; natural incompatibility. Opp. to *sympathy.* –1692. **2.** Feeling against; constitutional or settled aversion 1606. **3.** *concr.* That which is † contrary in nature, or the object of antipathy 1622.

1. No contraries hold more a., Then I, and such a knaue *Lear* II. ii. 93. **2.** A Sect, whose chief Devotion lies In odd perverse Antipathies BUTLER.

Antipendium, var. of ANTE-; see ANTI-².

Antiperiodic (æ:nti,piəri,ǫ·dik), *a.* 1861. [ANTI-¹ 3.] *Med.* Destroying the periodicity of diseases that run a typical course.

Antiperistaltic (æ:nti,peristæ·ltik), *a.* 1706. [ANTI-¹ 3.] *Phys.* Contrary to peristaltic motion; acting upwards.

Antiperistasis (æ:nti,pĕri·stăsis). *arch.* 1598. [– Gr. ἀντιπερίστασις surrounding so as to compress, f. ἀντί against + περίστασις standing round; cf. Fr. *antiperistase* (XVI).] Opposition or contrast of circumstances; resistance or reaction roused against any action.

Having their penury doubled by the a. of others plenty FULLER. Hence **A:ntiperista·tic, -al** *a.* heightened by contrast, **-ally** *adv.* (*rare*).

Antipestilential (æ:nti,pestile·nʃăl), *a.* 1683. [ANTI-¹ 3.] *Med.* Of use against the plague, etc. Also as *sb.*

A. pills DE FOE.

Antipha·rmic, *a.* 1853. [f. ANTI-¹ 3 + Gr. φάρμακον poison + -IC.] *Med.* = ALEXIPHARMIC.

Antiphlogistian (æ:nti,flodʒi·stiăn), *a.* 1788. [f. ANTI-¹ 3 + *phlogistian* (see PHLOGISTON).] Opposed to the theory of phlogiston, or the existence of an element of pure fire. As *sb.* An opponent of this theory.

Antiphlogistic (æ:nti,flodʒi·stik), *a.* 1744. [f. ANTI-¹ 3 + PHLOGISTIC *a.*] **1.** = prec. adj. 1788. **2.** *Med.* Counteracting inflammation 1769; also *fig.* (*rare*) 1840. As *sb.* [sc. *medicinal agent.*] 1744.

2. *fig.* A cooling a. speech HOOD.

Antiphlogistin (æ:nti,flodʒi·stin). 1901. [f. ANTI-¹ 3 + PHLOGIST(ON) + -IN¹.] A proprietary preparation used as an anodyne, antiseptic, and antiphlogistic.

Antiphon (æ·ntifŏn). 1500. [– eccl.L. *antiphona* – Gr. (τά) ἀντίφωνα, n. pl. of ἀντίφωνος responsive, f. ἀντί ANTI-¹ + φωνή sound; see ANTHEM.] **1.** A versicle or sentence sung by one choir in response to another 1652. **2.** = ANTHEM 1. 1500. **3.** *techn.* A short piece of plain-song introduced before a psalm or canticle, the meaning of which it illustrates and enforces 1775. **4.** *transf.* A response, answer 1651.

Antiphonal (ǣnti·fŏnăl), *a.* 1691. [f. prec. + -AL¹; cf. OFr. *antiphonal.*] **1.** Of the nature of an antiphon; sung alternately 1719. **2.** Responsive in sound, or (*transf.*) other effect 1848. As *sb.* = ANTIPHONARY 1691.

1. A. singing was first brought into the church of Milan BINGHAM. Hence **Anti·phonally** *adv.* So **Antipho·nic** *a.* mutually responsive. **Antipho·nically** *adv.*

Antiphonary (ǣnti·fŏnări 1681. [– eccl.L. *antiphonarium* (see ANTIPHON, -ARY¹), whence, through OFr. *antiphonier*, the earlier *antiphoner.*] A book of antiphons. vars. **† Anti·phonar, Anti·phoner** (the earliest word).

Antiphony (ǣnti·fŏni). 1592. [f. ANTIPHON + -Y³, partly through OFr. *antiphonie.*] **1.** Opposition of sound; or harmony produced by it 1603. **2.** = ANTIPHON 1. 1592. **3.** Antiphonal singing. Also *fig.* 1753. **4.** *concr.* = ANTIPHON 2. 1868. **† 5.** = ANTIPHON 3. –1753. **6.** *transf.* A response or echo 1657.

3. Life answering life across the vast profound In full a. MRS. BROWNING. **6.** The eccho or a., which these..exclaimers hope..to draw..from their audience SHAFTESBURY.

‖ **Antiphrasis** (ǣnti·frăsis). 1533. [Late L. – Gr. ἀντίφρασις, f. ἀντιφράζειν express by the opposite.] *Rhet.* Use of words in a sense opposite to their proper meaning.

You are pastors, but it is by an a., *a minime pascendo* CROMWELL. Hence **Antiphra·stic** *a.*, **-ally** *adv.*

Antiphthisic (ænti,ti·zik), *a.* 1853. [ANTI-¹ 3.] *Med.* Tending to check phthisis. Also as *sb.*

Antiplastic (ænti,plæ·stik), *a.* [f. ANTI-¹ 3 + PLASTIC *a.*] *Med.* Unfavourable to the process of healing or granulation. Also used of medicines which impoverish the blood. *Syd. Soc. Lex.*

Antipleuritic (æ:nti,pluri·tik), *a.* 1712. [ANTI-¹ 3.] Of use against pleurisy. Also as *sb.*

Antipodagric, -al (æ:nti,podæ·grik, -ăl), *a.* 1712. [ANTI-¹ 3.] *Med.* Of use against gout. Also as *sb.*

Antipodal (ǣnti·pŏdăl), *a.* 1646. [f. ANTIPODES + -AL¹.] **1.** Of or pertaining to the ANTIPODES. **2.** *transf.* Directly opposite (*to*) 1664.

Antipodean (ǣnti:pŏdī·ăn), *a.* 1651. [irreg. f. ANTIPODES, perh. after *European.*] **1.** Of or pertaining to the opposite side of the world; *esp.* Australasian 1861. **2.** *joc.* Having everything upside down 1852. **3.** *fig.* Diametrically opposed (*to*) 1651. var. **† Antipo·dian** (better).

Antipodes (ǣnti·pŏdīz), *sb. pl.* ME. [– Fr. *antipodes* or late L. *antipodes* – Gr. ἀντίποδες pl. of ἀντίπους having the feet opposite, f. ἀντί opposite + πούς, ποδ- foot. Formerly trisyllabic, *a·ntipodes*, with sg. *antipode*; the four-syllable form shows reversion to L. and Gr.] **† 1.** Those who dwelt directly opposite to each other on the globe, as it were feet against feet –1837. **† 2.** *fig.* Those who in any way resemble the dwellers on the opposite side of the globe 1605. **3.** Places on the surface of the earth directly opposite to each other, or the place which is directly opposite to another (*esp.* to our own region) 1549. **4.** *transf.* The exact opposite of a person or thing. (With sing. *antipode.*) 1641. **† 5.** As adv. (sb. in apposition) in *To walk antipodes to*, etc. –1718.

2. He will neuer be one of the A., to tread opposite to the present world BACON. **3.** I will goe on the slightest arrand now to the Antypodes *Much Ado* II. i. 273. **4.** Fools..are a. unto the wise SIR T. BROWNE. *At antipodes*: in direct opposition. Hence **Anti·podist**, a believer in the antipodes (when the belief was heresy); as *adj.* = ANTIPODAL. **† Anti·podite**, an inhabitant of the antipodes.

Antipole (æ·nti,pōᵘ:l). 1822. [ANTI-¹ 2.] The opposite pole. *fig.* The direct opposite.

Antipope (æ·nti,pōᵘp). 1579. [orig. – Fr. *antipape* – med.L. *antipapa*, after *antichristus.*] A pope elected in opposition to one held to be canonically chosen; *spec.* of those who resided at Avignon during 'the great schism of the West'. (So called by adversaries.)

Antipruritic (æ:nti,pruri·tik), *a.* 1876. [f. ANTI-¹ 3 + L. *pruritis* + -IC.] *Med.* Tending to relieve itching.

Antipsoric (æntipsǫ·rik), *a.* 1853. [f. ANTI-[1] 3 + Gr. ψώρα itch + -IC.] *Med.* Of use against the itch. Also as *sb.*

‖ **Antipto·sis.** 1657. [Late L. – Gr. ἀντίπτωσις, f. ἀντί in exchange + πτῶσις case.] *Gram.* The use of one case for another.

Antipyic (æntiˌpəi·ik), *a.* 1853. [– Fr. *antipyique*, f. Gr. ἀντί ANTI-[1] + πύον pus; see -IC.] *Med.* Tending to prevent suppuration. Also as *sb.*

Antipyretic (æ:ntiˌpire·tik), *a.* 1681. [f. ANTI-[1] 3 + PYRETIC.] *Med.* Tending to prevent fever. Also as *sb.*

Antipyrotic (æ:ntiˌpirǫ·tik), *a.* 1839. [f. ANTI-[1] 3 + *pyrotic* (f. Gr. πυρωτικός burning) caustic.] *Med.* Of use against burns. As *sb.* Anything so used.

Antiquarian (æntiˌkwēᵊ·riăn), *a.* 1610. [f. as ANTIQUARY; see -ARIAN.] **1.** Of or connected with the study of antiquities 1771. **2.** Applied to a large size of drawing paper 1875. **3.** As *sb.* [The adj. used *absol.*] An antiquary 1610.

1. A. researches FREEMAN. Hence **Antiqua·rianism,** the profession, etc., of the a. **Antiqua·rianize** *v. colloq.* to play the a. **Antiqua·rianly** *adv.* (*rare*).

‖ **Antiqua·rium.** *rare.* 1881. [mod.L., neut. of L. *antiquarius*; see next, -ARIUM.] A repository of antiquities.

Antiquary (æ·ntiˌkwări). 1563. [– L. *antiquarius*, f. *antiquus*; see ANTIQUE, -ARY[1]. Cf. Fr. *antiquaire*.] **A.** *adj.* Of antiquity; ancient (*rare*) 1606.

Here's Nestor Instructed by the A. times *Tr. & Cr.* II. iii. 262.

B. *sb.* [sc. *man, thing.*] †**1.** A man of great age –1635. †**2.** An official custodian or recorder of antiquities. (A title bestowed by Hen. VIII upon Leland.) –1763. **3.** A professed student, or collector, of antiquities. (*Orig.* a student of early history, *now* opp. to *archæologist.*) 1586.

3. Antiquaries, who hold everything worth preserving, merely because it has been preserved 1762.

Antiquate (æ·ntiˌkwĕt), *ppl. a. arch.* 1537. [– L. *antiquatus*, pa. pple. of *antiquare* (f. *antiquus* ANTIQUE) restore (a thing) to its former condition; in eccl.L. make old; see -ATE[2].] = ANTIQUATED.

Antiquate (æ·ntiˌkweⁱt), *v.* 1596. [f. prec.; see -ATE[3].] **1.** To make old, or obsolete; to abolish as out of date. **2.** To give an antique colour or appearance to 1821.

1. He [the Pope] antiquates the precepts of Christ MARVELL. Hence **Antiqua·tion,** the action of making, or state of being, antiquated; abolition; the production of an appearance of age.

Antiquated (æ·ntiˌkweⁱtĕd), *ppl. a.* 1623. [f. prec.] **1.** Grown old, inveterate 1670. **2.** Obsolete 1623. **3.** So old as to be unworthy to survive; often 'old-world' 1692. **4.** Old-fashioned, as surviving from, or as imitating, earlier usage 1675. **5.** Of persons: Very old, superannuated. Also *fig.* 1678.

1. A. prejudices BURKE. **2.** Reviving a. laws 1695. **3.** Deride. .the a. folly BENTLEY. **4.** A. phraseology FREEMAN. **5.** [An] a. Sybil ADDISON.

Antique (ǣntī·k, æ·ntik). 1530. [– Fr. *antique* or L. *antiquus, anticus*, f. *ante* before + *-icus* (as in *posticus* f. *post*); orig. identical in form and pronunc. with ANTIC, but finally differentiated after 1700.] **A.** *adj.* **1.** Ancient, olden. (Now usu. rhet. = of the 'good old times'.) 1541. **2.** Having existed since olden times; aged, venerable (*arch.*) 1536. **3.** Old-fashioned; out of date. 1647. **4.** Of, belonging to, or after the manner of the ancients (of Greece and Rome) 1734; or of any ancient time, archaic 1753. **5.** *Bookbinding.* See ANTIQUE *v.* **6.** *Typogr.* Of a type in which all the lines are of uniform thickness 1871.

1. The anticke world SPENSER. The Senatours of th' antique Rome *Hen. V*, V. Prol. 26. **2.** In place of things of antick use BUTLER *Hud.* II. I. 792. Antique walls GIBBON. **4.** A group that's quite a., Half naked, loving, natural, and Greek BYRON.

B. *sb.* [The adj. used *ellipt.*; sc. *man, thing.*] †**1.** A man of ancient times; *pl.* the Ancients –1598. **2.** A relic of ancient art, or of the past 1530. **3.** *The antique*: ancient work in art, antique style 1751.

2. Pictures, medals, intaglios, and antiques of all kinds GOLDSM. **3.** Drawing from the a. 1859. Hence **Anti·quely** *adv.* †anciently; in an a. manner. **Anti·queness. Anti·quish** *a.* (*rare*).

Antique, occ. sp. of ANTIC in 16–17th c.

Antique (ǣntī·k), *v.* 1753. [f. the adj.] To bind (books) after an antique manner, by ornamenting the edges with ramifications, etc.

Antiquist (æ·ntikwist, ǣntī·kist). *rare.* 1784. [f. ANTIQUE + -IST.] †An antiquary; a collector or connoisseur of antiques.

Antiquitarian (æntiˌkwitēᵊ·riăn). 1641. [f. ANTIQUITY + -ARIAN; cf. *humanitarian*.] One attached to the practices or opinions of antiquity.

Antiquity (ǣnti·kwĭti). ME. [–(O)Fr. *antiquité* – L. *antiquitas*, f. *antiquus*; see ANTIQUE, -ITY.] **1.** The quality of being ancient; long standing 1450. †**2.** Old age (of human life); seniority –1677. **3.** Ancient character 1850. ****Elliptical senses. **4.** The time of antiquity; *esp.* the time of the ancient Greeks and Romans ME. **5.** The people (or writers, etc.) of ancient times collectively; the Ancients 1538. **6.** (Now *pl.* or *collect.*) Matters, customs, precedents, etc., of earlier times; ancient records 1557. **7.** (Now usu. *pl.*) Relics, or monuments of antiquity 1513. Also *attrib.*

2. Is not your voice broken?. .and euery part about you blasted with A. 2 *Hen. IV*, I. ii. 208. **3.** [An] air of a. MAX-MÜLLER. **4.** A is like fame, *caput inter nubila condit* BACON. **5.** That indigested heap, and frie of Authors, which they call A. MILT. **7.** Antiquities are history defaced, or some remnants of history which have escaped the shipwreck of time BACON.

Antirachitic (æ:ntiˌrăki·tik), *a.* 1853. [f. ANTI-[1] 3 + *rachitic* (see RACHITIS).] *Med.* Tending to cure spinal disease.

Antirrhinum (æntĭrəi·nŏm). Pl. **-s.** 1551. [– L. – Gr. ἀντίρρινον, f. ἀντί opposite + ῥίς, ῥιν- nose, from the resemblance of the flower to an animal's mouth.] *Bot.* A genus of Scrophulariaceous plants, also called Snapdragon.

A. or Calves-snout 1741.

Antisabbatarian (æ:ntiˌsæbătēᵊ·riăn), *a.* 1645. [ANTI-[1] 3, 5.] Opposed to the observance of the Sabbath by Christians. Also as *sb.*

‖ **Antiscii** (ǣnti·siˌəi, -i·ʃiˌəi), *sb. pl.* 1706. [Late L. – Gr. ἀντίσκιοι, pl. masc. of, ἀντίσκιος, throwing a shadow the opposite way, f. ἀντί opposite + σκιά shadow.] Those who live on the same meridian, but on opposite sides of the equator, so that their shadows fall at noon in opposite directions. Hence **Anti·scian** *a.* of or pertaining to the Antiscii; *sb.* (*pl.*) = ANTISCII.

Antiscion (ǣnti·ʃiǫn). 1658. [app. repr. Gr. ἀντίσκιον (sc. ζῴδιον sign of the zodiac); see prec.] *Astrol.* Applied to signs of the Zodiac equidistant on opposite sides from Cancer and Capricorn.

Antiscolic (æntiˌskǫ·lik), *a.* 1880. [irreg. f. ANTI- 3 + Gr. σκώληξ worm + -IC.] *Med.* = ANTHELMINTIC.

Antiscorbutic (æntiˌskǫɹbiu·tik), *a.* 1696. [ANTI-[1] 3.] Of use against scurvy. Also as *sb.*

Antiscriptural (æntiˌskri·ptiŭrăl), *a.* 1677. [ANTI-[1] 3.] Opposed to Holy Scripture.

Antiscrofulous (æntiˌskrǫ·fiŭləs), *a.* 1880. [ANTI-[1] 3.] *Med.* Of use against scrofula.

Antisepalous (æntiˌse·păləs), *a.* 1879. [f. Gr. ἀντί opposite + SEPAL + -OUS.] *Bot.* Placed opposite to the sepals.

‖ **Antisepsis** (æntiˌse·psis). 1875. [mod.L., f. ANTI-[1] 3 + SEPSIS.] *Med.* The principle of antiseptic surgical treatment.

Antiseptic (æntiˌse·ptik), *a.* 1751. [f. ANTI-[1] 3 + SEPTIC.] Counteracting putrefaction; *fig.* preventing moral decay 1820. Also as *sb.* (*lit.* and *fig.*).

A. bandages TYNDALL. *fig.* Not divine men, yet useful a. products of their generation CARLYLE. Hence **Antise·ptically** *adv.* **Antise·pticist,** one who believes in ANTISEPSIS.

Antisocial (æntiˌsōᵘ·ʃăl), *a.* 1797. [ANTI-[1] 3.] **1.** Opposed to society or companionship. **2.** Opposed to the principles on which society is constituted 1802.

Antispasmodic (æ:ntiˌspæzmǫ·dik), *a.* 1681. [ANTI-[1] 3.] Good against spasms. Also as *sb.*

Antispast (æ·ntiˌspæst). 1706. [– late L. *antispastus* – Gr. ἀντίσπαστος f. ἀντισπᾶν draw in the contrary direction.] *Pros.* A metrical foot composed of an iambus and a trochee, as Ἀλέξανδρος.

Antispastic (æntiˌspæ·stik), *a.* 1541. [– Gr. ἀντισπαστικός, see prec.; as med. term, late L. *antispasticus* (Oribasius).] **1.** *Med.* Tending to divert. **2.** *Pros.* Consisting of, or containing, antispasts 1811. **3.** As *sb.* *Med.* An a. agent 1719.

Antisplenetic (æ:ntiˌsplīne·tik), *a.* 1734. [ANTI-[1] 3.] *Med.* Good against disease of the spleen. Also as *sb.*

‖**Antistrophe** (ǣnti·strŏfi). 1605. [– late L. – Gr. ἀντιστροφή, f. ἀντιστρέφειν turn against; see STROPHE.] **1.** The returning movement, from left to right, in Greek choruses and dances, answering to the strophe; the lines of choral song recited during this movement; any choral response 1619. **2.** An inverse correspondence 1605. **3.** *Rhet.*, etc. **a.** Repetition of words in inverse order. **b.** The figure of retort, or turning an opponent's plea against him 1625.

2. An inverse correspondency with the Nile (north and south, therefore, as the a. of south and north) DE QUINCEY. Hence **Antistro·phic** *a.* of or pertaining to antistrophes; *sb.* (*pl.*) the lyrical part of Greek dramas. **Antistro·phically** *adv.* (*rare*). **Anti·strophize** *v.* (*rare*), to form an a.

‖ **Antistrophon** (ǣnti·strŏfǫn). 1611. [n. sing. of Gr. ἀντίστροφος turned in an opposite way, f. ἀντιστρέφειν; see prec.] *Rhet.* An argument that is retorted upon an opponent.

Antistruma·tic. 1676. [f. ANTI-[1] 3 + *strumatic* (f. STRUMA).] *Med. adj.* = next. *sb.* A remedy for scrofula.

Antistrumous (æntiˌstrū·məs), *a.* 1861. [f. ANTI-[1] + STRUMOUS *a.*] *Med.* Tending to cure scrofula.

Antisyphilitic (æ:ntiˌsifĭli·tik), *a.* 1830. [ANTI-[1] 3.] Of use against syphilis. Also as *sb.*

Antitetanic (æ:ntiˌtĭtæ·nik), *a.* 1875. [ANTI-[1] 3.] *Med.* Good against tetanus. Also as *sb.*

Antithalian (æntiˌþēⁱ·liăn), *a.* [f. ANTI-[1] 3 + *Thalia*, the Muse of Comedy + -AN.] Opposed to festivity. PEACOCK.

Antitheism (æntiˌþī·iz'm). 1833. [ANTI-[1] 8.] The doctrine of antitheists.

Antitheist (æntiˌþī·ist). 1860. [ANTI-[1] 5.] One opposed to belief in the existence of a God. Hence **A:ntithei·stic** *a.*

Antithesis (ǣnti·þĭsis). Pl. **antitheses.** 1529. [– late L. – Gr. ἀντίθεσις, f. ἀντιτιθέναι, f. ἀντί against + τιθέναι to set, place; cf. THESIS.] **1.** *Rhet.* An opposition or contrast of ideas, expressed by using in contiguous sentences or clauses, words which are strongly contrasted with each other; as '*thou* shalt *wax*, and *he* shall *dwindle*'. **2.** The second of two such opposed clauses; a counter-thesis 1533. **3.** By extension: Direct opposition (between two things); contrast. Const. *of, between*, †*with*. 1631. **4.** The opposite. Const. *of, to*. 1831.

1. All arm'd with points, antitheses, and puns POPE. **3.** The a. of natural and revealed religion KINGSLEY. **4.** The very a. to a great dramatist MACAULAY. Hence **Anti·thesize** *v.* to form antitheses or put into a. (*rare*). **Anti·thesizer** (*rare*).

Antithet (æ·ntiþet). 1580. [– L. *antitheton* – Gr. ἀντίθετον n. sing. of adj. ἀντίθετος placed in opposition; see prec.] †**1.** = ANTITHESIS 1. –1610. **2.** An antithetic statement 1605.

Antithetic (æntiþe·tik), *a.* 1610. [ult. – Gr. ἀντιθετικός; see prec., -IC.] That is of the nature of antithesis, *esp.* in *Rhet.*; directly opposite 1864. **2.** Consisting of two opposites 1842.

2. The dual or a. character of force involved in the term polarity W. GROVE. So **Antithe·tical** *a.* connected with, containing, or using antithesis; marked by direct opposition 1583. **Antithe·tically** *adv.*

Antitoxin (æntitǫ·ksin). 1892. [ANTI-[1] 2 b.] A substance having the property of counteracting a toxin.

Anti-trade (æ·ntiˌtrēⁱ:d), *attrib. phr.* and *sb.* 1853. [ANTI-[1] 2.] A wind that blows steadily in the opposite direction to the trade-wind.

‖ **Antitragus** (æ·ntiˌtrēⁱ:gŏs). 1842. [ANTI-[1] 2.] *Anat.* A protuberance of the outer ear, opposite to the tragus.

Antitrinitarian (æ:ntiˌtrinĭtēᵊ·riăn). 1641. [ANTI-[1] 3.] *adj.* Opposed to the doctrine of the Trinity 1665. *sb.* One who rejects that doctrine 1641. Hence **Antitrinita·rianism.**

Antitropal (ǣnti·trŏpăl), *a.* 1855. [f. Gr. ἀντί against + -τροπος turning + -AL¹. Cf. ATROPOUS *a.*] *Bot.* Of an embryo: Inverted, so as to have the radicle at the extremity of the seed, opposite to the hilum. So **Anti·tropous.**

Antitype (æ·nti,təip). 1635. [– late L. *antitypus* – Gr. ἀντίτυπος, prop. adj. corresponding as an impression to the die, f. ἀντί opposite to + τύπος stroke, stamp, die.] That which is represented by the type or symbol. Hence **A·ntitypal** *a.* (*rare*). **Antity·pical** *a.* of the nature of or pertaining to an a.

† **Anti·typous,** *a. rare.* 1678. [f. Gr. ἀντίτυπος force-resisting (see prec.) + -OUS.] Resisting force; material, solid.

Antitypy (ǣnti·tĭpi). *rare.* 1605. [– Gr. ἀντιτυπία resistance of a hard body, f. as prec. + -ία -Y³.] Resistance of matter to force of penetration, compression, or motion.

Antivariolous (æ:nti,vărəi·ŏləs), *a.* 1880. [ANTI-¹ 3.] *Med.* Good against small-pox.

Antivenereal (æ:nti,vĭnī³·riăl), *a.* 1676. [ANTI-¹ 3.] *Med.* Of use against venereal disease.

A:ntivermi·cular, *a.* 1717. [ANTI-¹ 3.] = ANTIPERISTALTIC.

Antizymic (ænti,zi·mik), *a.* 1804. [f. ANTI-¹ 3 + Gr. ζύμη leaven + -IC.] Opposing fermentation. *sb.* An a. substance.

Antizymotic (æ:nti,zimǫ·tik, -zəimǫ·tik). 1875. [f. ANTI-¹ 3 + ZYMOTIC *a.*] *adj.* = prec. *sb.* A substance that prevents fermentation.

Antler (æ·ntləɹ). [late ME. *auntelere* – AFr. var. of OFr. *antoillier* (mod. *andouiller*), of unkn. origin.] **1.** *orig.* The lowest (forward-directed) branch of the horn of a stag, etc.; later, any branch, the lowest being then the *brow-antler*, and the next *bes-antler*. **2.** Hence *pop.*: The branched horn of a stag, etc. 1829.

1. Huge stags with sixteen antlers MACAULAY. 2. A vaulted apartment garnished with stags' antlers SCOTT. Hence **A·ntlerless** *a.* without antlers.

Antlered (æ·ntləɹd), *ppl. a.* 1818. [f. prec + -ED².] **1.** Bearing antlers; adorned with stags' horns 1828. **2.** *transf.* 1870.

1. An a. stag BRYANT, hall SCOTT. 2. A. fern DISRAELI.

‖ **Antlia** (æ·ntli,ă). 1828. [L. *antlia* instrument for drawing up water – Gr. ἀντλία bilge water, ἀντλίον bucket.] *Ent.* The proboscis or haustellum of insects, with which they suck up juices. Hence **A·ntliate** *ppl. a.* furnished with an a.

A·nt-li:on. 1815. [tr. Gr. μυρμηκο-λέων in the LXX.] A neuropterous insect, or genus of insects (*Myrmeleon*), the larva of which lies in wait for and devours ants.

Anto·cular, *a. rare.* 1870. [– L. *ante* before + *ocularis* pertaining to the eye, f. *oculus* eye; see -AR¹.] Placed in front of the eye.

‖ **Antœci** (ænti·səi), *sb. pl.* 1622. [late L. – Gr. ἄντοικοι f. ἀντί opposite + -οικος dwelling.] The dwellers under the same meridian, on opposite sides of the equator, and equally distant from it. Hence **Antœ·cian** *a.* of or belonging to the opposite latitude; *sb.* (*pl.*) = ANTŒCI.

‖ **Antonomasia** (æ:ntǭnomē¹·ziă, ǣntǫ:no). 1589. [L. – Gr. ἀντονομασία use of an epithet, etc., for a proper name.] The substitution of an epithet, etc., or the name of an office or dignity, for a person's proper name, as *the Iron Duke* for Wellington. Also, conversely, the use of a proper name to express a general idea, as in calling a wise judge *a Daniel*. Hence **Antonoma·stically** *adv.* (*rare*).

Antonym (æ·ntŏnim). 1870. [– Fr. *antonyme*, f. Gr. ἀντί ANTI-¹, after *synonyme* SYNONYM.] A term which is the opposite of another, a counter-term.

Antorbital, var. ANTE-ORBITAL.

Antozone (ænt,ō^u·zō^un). 1862. [f. ANT- + OZONE.] *Chem.* A gaseous product, once supposed to be a permanently positive variety of oxygen, but now shown to be hydrogen dioxide H_2O_2. Hence **Anto·zonide.**

Anto·zonite. 1868. [f. prec. + -ITE¹ 2b.] *Min.* A dark violet-blue Fluorite.

Antral (æ·ntrăl), *a. rare.* 1880. [f. L. *antrum* cave + -AL¹.] Of the nature of, or pertaining to, a cavity.

Antre (æ·ntəɹ). 1604. [– Fr. *antre* :– L. ANTRUM.] *poet.* A cave, a cavern.

Antars vast, and Desarts idle *Oth.* I. iii. 140.

Antrorse (æntrǭ·ɹs), *a.* 1858. [– mod.L. *antrorsus*, f. L. **antero-* + *versus*, after *extrorsus*, etc.] Bent forward or upward.

Antroversion (æntrovō̆·ɹʃən). 1880. [f. *antro-* for ANTERO- + L. *versio* turning; see VERSION.] = ANTEVERSION.

Antrove·rt, *v. rare.* 1854. [f. as prec. + L. *vertere* to turn.] To turn or bend forward.

‖**Antrum** (æ·ntrŏm). Pl. **-a.** ME. [L. – Gr. ἄντρον cave.] A cavern; *spec.* in *Phys.* of cavities in the body.

‖ **Antrustion** (ǣntrɒ·stiən). 1848. [– Fr. *antrustion* or med.L. *antrustio* (in Salic Law, etc.) f. OFrank. **an-trōstjo*, = OHG. *trōst* help, protection.] A voluntary follower of Old Frankish princes at the period of the national migrations. Hence **Antru·stionship.**

A·ntsigne. 1576. Obs. f. ENSIGN, as if f. *ante* + *signum*.

A·nt-thru:sh. 1863. [ANT *sb.*] A bird of the Thrush family, which lives on ants, etc.

Anura, -ous, vars. of ANOURA, -OUS.

Anury (æ·niŭri). 1876. [– mod.L. *anuria*, – Gr. ἀν- AN- *pref.* 10 + οὖρον urine + -ία -Y³.] *Path.* Absence or lack of urine.

‖ **Anus** (ē¹·nŏs). 1658. [– L. *ānus*, orig. ring; cf. ANNULAR.] **1.** The posterior opening of the alimentary canal, through which the excrements are ejected. **2.** An opening at the base of a flower 1730.

Anvil (æ·nvil), *sb.* [OE. *anfilte* (earlier *onfilti*), *anfealt*, corresp. to MDu. *aenvilte*, OHG. *anafalz* (G. dial. *afilts, amfilt, anefilt*), to which are parallel MLG. *anebelte, -bolt*, MDu. *aen-, anebelt, -bilt* (Du. *aanbeeld, aambeeld*), and OHG. *anabōz* (G. *amboss*); all based on Gmc. **ana* ON + vbl. stem meaning 'beat' (cf. FELT *sb.*¹) and perh. all modelled on L. *incus* anvil, f. *in* IN-¹ + *cūd-*, stem of *cūdere* beat.] **1.** The block (usually of iron) on which the smith hammers and shapes his metal; also *fig.* **2.** *transf.* Anything like a smith's anvil in shape or use; esp. (*Phys.*) one of the bones of the ear, the incus 1687.

1. Bitwene þe anfelde and þe hamoure ME. Him that smote the anuill *Isa.* 41:7. *fig.* Hammering me vpon the anvild CAMDEN. *On* or *upon the anvil*: in preparation, in hand; He has now on the a. another scheme BURKE.

Comb.: **a.-proof,** the standard of hardness of an a.; **-rock,** a kind of Sandstone, so named from the form of two masses of it in Kentucky.

A·nvil, *v.* 1607. [f. the sb.] **1.** *trans.* To fashion on an anvil; usu. *fig.* **2.** *intr.* To work at an anvil 1882.

Anxiety (ǣŋzəi·ěti). 1525. [– Fr. *anxiété* or L. *anxietas*, f. *anxius* (next); see -ITY, -TY¹.] **1.** The quality or state of being ANXIOUS; solicitude, concern. **2.** Strained or solicitous desire (*for*, or *to effect*) 1769. **3.** *Path.* A condition of agitation and depression, with a sensation of tightness and distress in the præcordial region 1661.

1. There dyed he without grudge, without anxietie MORE. 2. A...for the general welfare 'JUNIUS'.

Anxious (æ·ŋkʃəs), *a.* 1623. [– L. *anxius*, f. *anx-* pa. ppl. stem of *angere* choke, oppress; see ANGUISH, -IOUS. Cf. Fr. *anxieux*.] **1.** Troubled in mind about some uncertain event; being in disturbing suspense; concerned, solicitous. Const. † *of, for, about* 1711. **2.** Fraught with trouble, distressing, worrying. (*Obs.* exc. as transf. use of 1.) 1667. **3.** Full of desire and endeavour (*to effect*) 1742.

1. A., and cast down 1636. A. for their own safety MACAULAY. 2. A. cares MILT. *P.L.* viii. 185. 3. A. to please BLAIR. Hence **A·nxious·ly** *adv.*, **-ness** (*rare*).

Any (e·ni), *a.* and *pron.* [OE. *ǣnig* = OFris. *ēnich*, OS. *ēnig*, MLG. *einich*, MDu. *ēnich* (Du. *eenig*), OHG. *einag* (G. *einig*), ON. *einigr*, Goth. *ainaha* :– Gmc. **ainazaz, -izaz*, f. **ain-* ONE + *-*iʒ-* -Y¹. Cf. L. *ūnicus* UNIQUE *a.* The ME. forms, *eny, ei*, were south., *any* midl., *ony* midl. and north. Fem. and pl. forms in *-e* also existed in ME. The living mod.Eng. word is *eny*.] *Primarily adj.* **1.** *gen.* In *sing.* = A — no matter which, or what. In *pl.* = Some — no matter which, of what kind, or how many. **a.** Used primarily in interrog., hypothet., and condit. forms of speech OE. **b.** With a preceding neg.: = None at all, of any kind, etc., not even one OE. **c.** In affirm. sentences: = (constructively) *Every* one of the sort named ME. **2.** Quantitative: = A quantity or number however great or small 1526. **3.** Qualitative: Of any kind or sort whatever; = earlier ANY-KYNS. Occas. *depreciatory*: Any, however imperfect 1866. **4.** *absol.*, esp. after a sb. already expressed, or bef. *of* ME. † **5.** Either (of *two*). Still dial., esp. north. –1585. **6.** *pronominally.* = Any one, anybody; in *pl.* any persons OE. **7.** *adverbially*, esp. with comp. adjs., as *any sooner*, etc.: In any degree, at all ME. **8. Any one. a.** as *adj.* (e:ni wɒ·n) Any single; **b.** *absol.* as in 'any one of them'; **c.** *pron.* (e·ni,wɒn) Any person. ME. **9.** In *comb.* with interrog. wds., which then become indefinite.

1. a. Who wil shew vs any good *Ps.* 4:6. b. Not to be done at any time BURKE. c. Any time these three hundred yeeres *Merry W.* I. i. 11. *At any rate, in any case*: whatever the circumstances may be. 2. Haue ye here eny meate *Luke* 24:41. 4. If there be any of him left, Ile bury it *Wint. T.* III. iii. 136. 5. Anie of them both THYNNE. 6. Please they any, That serue many 1562. 7. Any longer SHAKS. more 1680, farther STEELE, the worse 1875.

Anybody (e·ni,bǫdi, -bǒdi), *sb.* or *pron.* 1490. **1.** comb. of ANY and BODY in the sense of *person*: Any person. See ANY *a.* 1. Formerly two words. **2.** Qualitative. **a.** In interrog. or hypothet. expressions, *laudatory*: a person of some importance. **b.** In affirm. expressions, *depreciatory*: an ordinary person. 1826.

1. If he doe..finde any body in the house *Merry W.* I. iv. 4. 2. Everybody was there who is a. DISRAELI. Two or three anybodies J. BRIGHT.

Anyhow (e·ni,hau). 1740. [see ANY 9.] **1.** *adv.* In any way or manner whatever. **2.** *advb. conj.* In any case, at least 1825.

1. Done a., no profitable one CARLYLE. 2. Any how, it must be acknowledged [etc.] NEWMAN.

† **Any-kyn, -s.** ME. only. [orig. genitive phr. = 'of any kind', afterwards, with loss of *-s*, looking like an adj. = 'any kind of'.] Any kind or manner.

Anything (e·ni,þiŋ), *pron., sb., adv.* OE. **1.** *pron.* A comb. of ANY and THING, in the widest sense of the latter. See ANY *a.* Orig. always two words; now rarely exc. when stress is upon *thing*. **2.** *sb.* Thing of any kind 1596. **3.** *adv.* Any whit, in any measure OE.

1. If ye shall ask any thing in my name, I will do it *John* 14:14. 2. She is my house..my oxe, my asse, my a. *Tam. Shr.* III. ii. 234. 3. Yf my lady your wyf come ony thyng nyghe yowe CAXTON. Hence **A:nythinga·rian** [after *trinitarian*, etc.], one who professes no creed in particular. (A contemptuous term.)

Anyway (e·ni,we¹), *adv.* and *conj.* 1570. [Cf. ANYWAYS, and *always, alway*.] **1.** *adv.* In any way or manner, anyhow; in any measure. **2.** *advb. conj.* In any case 1859.

1. Anything that sauoureth any way of newnesse BIBLE *Transl.* Pref. 1.

Anyways (e·ni³we¹z). 1560. [ANY + -WAYS, as in ALWAYS.] = prec. 1, 2.

Anywhen (e·ni,hwe:n), *adv.* 1831. [see ANY 9.] At any time, ever. *Rare* in literature.

† **A·nywhence,** *adv. rare.* 1613. [see ANY 9.] From anywhere.

Anywhere (e·ni,hwē³·ɹ, -hwĕɹ). ME. [see ANY 9. Preceded by *owhere, aywhere* –1485.] In any place. Formerly two words.

Anywhither (e·ni,hwi:ðəɹ), *adv. arch.* 1611. [See ANY 9. Preceded by *owhither*.] To or towards any place.

Anywise (e·ni,wəiz), *adv.* OE. [for *in any wise* (also used); OE. *on ǣnige wīsan*.] In any manner, way, or case; at all.

Any law or usage to the contrary hereof in a. notwithstanding 1775.

Aonian (e,ō^u·niăn), *a.* 1607. [f. L. *Aonia* – Gr. Ἀονία + -AN.] Of or belonging to Aonia, a region of ancient Bœotia, containing the mountains Helicon and Cithaeron, sacred to the Muses or 'Aonian maids'.

Above th' Aonian mount MILT. *P.L.* 1. 15.

Aorist (ē·ŏrist), *a.* 1581. [– Gr. ἀόριστος undefined (sb. sc. χρόνος time, Dionysius Thrax), f. ἀ- A- *pref.* 14 + ὁριστός delimited, f. ὁρίζειν define (cf. HORIZON).] *Gram.* One of the past tenses of the Gr. verb, which denotes a simple past occurrence, with none of the limitations of the other past tenses. Hence **Aori·stic** *a.* undefined; of or pertaining to the aorist tense. **Aori·stically** *adv.*

Aorta (eɪǭ·ɹtă). 1594. [– Gr. ἀορτή, by Hippocrates used pl. for the branches of the wind-pipe, by Aristotle for the great artery, f. **aor-*, var. of **aer-* of ἀείρειν (:– **aerj-*) to raise; cf. ARTERY.] *Phys.* The great artery or trunk of the arterial system, from its origin in the left ventricle of the heart to its division into the two iliac arteries. Hence **Ao·rtal, Ao·rtic** *adjs.*

Ap-, *pref.*[1] = L. *ad-* bef. initial *p-*. In OFr. *ad-*, *ap-* became *a-*, and in this form the Fr. wds. were adopted in Eng., as *a-part, a-ply*, etc. Later the *p* was again doubled, after L. See AD- *pref.* 2, A- *pref.* 10.

Ap-, *pref.*[2] = Gr. ἀπ', short for ἀπό off.

Ap-, *pref.*[3] [Welsh *ap*, f. *map* son; cf. *Mac.*]

Apace (ăpēⁱ·s), *adv.* ME. [– OFr. *a pas* at (a considerable) pace, i.e. *a* (:– L. *ad* at), *pas* step, PACE *sb.*] *lit.* At a pace, *i.e.* at a good pace (orig. of the pace of men); *hence*, With speed; swiftly; †immediately –1723.

He commeth to hym apaas CHAUCER. Kings of armies did flee a. *Ps.* 68:12. Like water yᵗ runneth a pace 1535 Hoording wealth a. 1604. An ill weed growes a. 1611.

Apache (ăpæ·ʃ). 1902. [– Fr. *apache*, a use of the name of a war-like tribe of N. Amer. Indians. Cf. MOHOCK.] A type of robber and assassin frequenting Paris, etc.; *gen.* a ruffian.

‖ **Apagoge** (æpăgōᵘ·dʒi). 1727. [Gr. ἀπαγωγή leading away, f. ἀπάγειν lead off. A term of Aristotelian logic.] †**1.** *Logic.* = ABDUCTION. **2.** A demonstration which proves a thing by showing the impossibility or absurdity of denying it; a *reductio ad absurdum* 1753. †**3.** *Math.* The passage from one proposition, which has been demonstrated, to the proof of another 1753. Hence **Apago·gic, -al** *a.* of, pertaining to, or of the nature of a. **Apago·gically** *adv.*

Apaid (ăpēⁱ·d), *ppl. a. arch.* ME. [f. APAY *v.*] **1.** Satisfied, pleased. †**2.** Repaid –1748.

Apair, Apale, Apall; see APP-.

Apaise, apayse, obs. ff. APPEASE.

Apanage, app- (æ·pănėdʒ). 1602. [– (O)Fr. *apanage*, f. OFr. *apaner* dower (a daughter), – med.L. *appanare* provide with means of subsistence, f. L. *ad* AP- *pref.*[1] + *panis* bread; see -AGE.] **1.** The provision made for the maintenance of the younger children of kings, princes, etc.; orig. a province, jurisdiction, or office. **2.** *loosely*, A perquisite 1835. **3.** A dependent territory or property; a dependency 1807. **4.** *transf.* A specially appointed, or natural accompaniment, endowment, or attribute 1663.

2. The diplomatic service..the a. of the wealthy FREEMAN. **3.** Ireland..the..appanage of our empire SYD. SMITH. **4.** Had he thought it fit, That wealth should be the appenage of wit SWIFT. Hence **A·panaged** *ppl. a.* endowed with an a.

Apanthropy (æpˌæ·nþrŏpi). *rare.* 1753. [– Gr. ἀπανθρωπία dislike of men, f. ἀπό AP- *pref.*[2] + ἄνθρωπος human being + -ία -Y[3]. Cf. Fr. *apanthropie.*] A form of melancholy characterized by a dislike to society.

Apar-; see later APPAR-.

‖ **A·parithme·sis.** 1753. [Gr. ἀπαρίθμησις, f. ἀπαριθμεῖν to count off.] *Rhet.* A figure: Enumeration.

Apart (ăpā·ɹt), *adv.* ME. [– OFr. *apart* (mod. *à part*) :– L. *ā parte* at the side, i.e. *ā* A- *pref.* 8 + abl. of *pars* side, PART *sb.*] **1.** To one side, aside, to a place removed from the general body. **2.** Apart from each other; asunder ME. **3.** Separately in thought, or consideration 1577. **4.** Separately in action or function; individually ME. Also (with ellipsis of *standing*, etc.) = Separate. (Cf. Fr. *c'est un homme à part.*) 1786. **5.** *fig.* Aside, away from all employment, etc. (Fr. *mettre, laisser à part.*) (*arch.*) 1477. Also *absol.* as 'jesting apart' (Fr. *raillerie à part*) = Laid aside 1732. **6.** Away from common use for a special purpose 1604. Const. *from* (in all senses) 1617. *Rarely* prepositional (*from* omitted) 1615.

1. Get thee a-part and weepe *Jul. C.* III. i. 282. Judas being a. with the Elders 2 *Macc.* 13:13. **2.** The Spartans lived in villages a. 1728. **3.** Let us view each ingredient a. 1756. **4.** Power..exercised either collectively, or a. and severally SELDEN. A class a. MACAULAY. **5.** Lay a. all filthinesse *James* 1:21. **6.** Places *set apart* for the worship of God 1680. A. this city, in the harbour CHAPMAN. Hence **Apa·rt** *v.* to set aside. **Apa·rtness,** aloofness.

Apartment (ăpā·ɹtmĕnt). 1641. [– Fr. *appartement* – It. *appartamento*, f. *appartare* to separate, f. *a parte* APART; see -MENT.] **1.** A suite of rooms in a house or building allotted to the use of an individual or party (*arch.*). **2.** A single room in a house; with pl. *apartments* in sense 1. 1715. †**3.** Quarters –1719. †**4.** A compartment –1727.

1. My a. consisted of three elegant..rooms GIBBON. **2.** I stole..to the window of my a. SCOTT. **3.** My Appartment in the tree DE FOE *Crusoe* 54. Hence **Apa:rtme·ntal** *a.* (*rare*).

† **Apa·ss,** *v.* ME. [– OFr. *apasser*, f. *à* A- *pref.* 7 + *passer* to pass.] To pass on or by. Rarely *trans.*

Apathaton, corrupt f. *epitheton.* SHAKS.

Apathetic, -al (æpăþe·tik, -ăl), *a.* 1744. [f. APATHY, after PATHETIC, -ICAL; see -IC, -AL[1].] Of, or pertaining to, apathy; unemotional; indifferent. Hence **Apathe·tically** *adv.*

Apathist (æ·păþist). *rare.* 1640. [f. APATHY + -IST.] One addicted to apathy.

A·pathize, *v. rare.* [f. as prec. + -IZE.] To render insensible.

Apathy (æ·păþi). 1603. [– Fr. *apathie* – L. *apathia* – Gr. ἀπάθεια f. ἀπαθής without feeling, f. ἀ- A- *pref.* 14 + παθε- PATHOS; see -Y[3].] **1.** Freedom from, or insensibility to, suffering, passion, or feeling; passionless existence. **2.** Indolence of mind, indifference to what normally excites emotion or interest 1733. Also *transf.* (of the markets, etc.) 1881.

1. A. was considered by the Stoics as the highest condition of Humanity LEWES. **2.** A certain a., or sluggishness in his nature PRESCOTT.

Apatite (æ·pătəit). 1803. [– G. *apatit* (Werner 1786), f. Gr. ἀπάτη deceit; so named from its diverse and deceptive forms; see -ITE[1] 2 b.] *Min.* A native crystallized phosphate of lime, varying in colour from white to green, blue, violet, brown; transparent, translucent or opaque. Also *transf.*

Apay (ăpēⁱ), *v. arch.* ME. [– OFr. *apaier* :– Rom. **adpacare* f. L. *ad* A- *pref.* 7 + *pacare* please, satisfy, orig. to pacify, f. *pax, pac-* peace. See APPEASE *v.*, PAY *v.*[1]] **1.** To satisfy, content (*arch.*). †**2.** To repay –1631.

Ape (ēⁱp), *sb.* [OE. *apa* m., *ape* fem. = OS. *apo* (Du. *aap*), OHG. *affo* m., *affe* fem. (G. *affe*), ON. *api* :– Gmc **apan-*.] **1.** An animal of the monkey tribe (*Simiadæ*); the generic name before 'monkey', and still occas. so used, esp. with reference to their resemblance to, and mimicry of, men. **2.** *spec.* A member of the *Simiadæ*, having no tail nor cheek-pouches; as the gorilla, chimpanzee, orang-utan, and gibbons 1699. **3.** *fig.* One who plays the ape; an imitator, a mimic. Usu. contemptuous. ME. †**4.** *transf.* A fool –1741. †**5.** as *adj.* Foolish –1509.

1. Apes With foreheads villanous low *Temp.* IV. i. 249. **2.** An a., properly so called, is without a tail 1764. **3.** O sleepe, thou A. of death *Cymb.* II. ii. 31. **4.** *God's ape*: a natural born fool. The titled a., her husband RICHARDSON.

Phrases: *To play the ape*: to imitate (badly). † *To make any one his ape, to put an ape in his hood*: to befool or dupe him. CHAUCER. *To lead apes in hell*: the supposed consequence of dying an old maid. *To say an ape's paternoster*: to chatter with cold.

Comb., etc.: †**a.-bearer, -carrier,** a strolling buffoon, who carried a monkey about; † **-leader,** an old maid, see Phrases; **Sea Ape:** the fish *Squalus Vulpes*, Sea Fox, or Thresher. Hence **A·pedom** (*rare*). **A·pehood.**

Ape (ēⁱp), *v.* 1632. [f. the sb.] To imitate, *esp.* absurdly.

To a. the sprightliness of wit JOHNSON. Art.. doth a. nature 1663. Hence **Aped** *ppl. a.* counterfeit. **A·per** (*rare*).

A-peak (ăpī·k), *adv.* (*a.*) 1596. [orig. *a pike* – Fr. *à pic*, i.e. *à*, AT, *pic* PEAK *sb.*[2] (to which the second syll. was assimilated).] *Naut.* In a vertical position; vertical. Also *fig.*

A *ship* drawn directly over the anchor is *apeak*; the *anchor* is *apeak* when the cable has been sufficiently hove in to bring the ship over it. *Oars apeak*: held vertically.

Apel-: see later sp. APPEL-.

Apelles (ăpe·līz). 1630. A Gr. painter in the time of Alexander the Great; occas. (connotatively) = a master artist.

Apen-; see later sp. APPEN-.

Apepsy (ăpe·psi). 1678. [– mod.L. *apepsia* – Gr. ἀπεψία, f. ἀ- A- *pref.* 14 + πέπτειν to digest; see PEPTIC, -Y[3].] *Med.* Lack of digestive power.

Aper-; see later sp. APPER-.

‖ **Aperçu** (apersü·). 1882. [Fr.] A summary exposition, a conspectus.

Aperient (ăpīᵊ·riĕnt), *a.* 1626. [– *aperient-*, pres. ppl. stem of L. *aperire* to open; see -ENT.] *Med.* Opening the bowels; laxative. Also as *sb.*

‖ **Aperitif** (aperitif). 1894. [Fr. *apéritif*, used subst., – med.L. *aperitivus*, var. of late L. *apertivus* (*Cælius Aurelianus*), f. L. *apertus*, pa. pple. of *aperire* to open.] An alcoholic drink taken before a meal as an appetizer.

Aperitive (ăpe·rĭtiv), *a.* and *sb.* 1582. [var. of *apertive* (see APERT), after Fr. *apéritif, -ive*, older *apertif*, – late L. *apertivus*; see prec., -IVE.] = APERIENT *a.* and *sb.*

A per se, apersee; see A. (the letter).

Apert (ăpē·ɹt). *arch.* ME. [– OFr. *apert* – L. *apertus*, pa. pple. of *aperire* to open. Aphet. PERT *a.*] *adj.* Open, public ME.; †evident –1674; †expert –1483; †outspoken, insolent (cf. PERT) –1688. †*adv.* Openly, plainly, publicly –1556. Hence † **Ape·rtion,** the action of opening; an opening. **Ape·rtive,** *a.* †open; also = APERIENT. **Ape·rtness,** the quality of being open; †plainness of speech.

Ape·rtly, *adv.* ? *Obs.* ME. [f. prec. + -LY[2].] Openly; evidently; boldly.

Aperto·meter. 1880. [f. L. *apertus* open + -O- + -METER.] An appliance attached to a microscope for measuring the angular aperture of object-glasses.

Aperture (æ·pərtiŭɹ). 1649. [– L. *apertura*, f. *apert-*, pa. ppl. stem of *aperire* to open; see APERT, -URE.] †**1.** The process of opening –1708. **2.** An opening; a gap, cleft, chasm, or hole 1665. **3.** *Opt.* The space through which light passes in any optical instrument. Also *attrib.* 1664. **4.** *Geom.* The space included within two right lines which meet in a point and make an angle 1706.

Apery (ēⁱ·pəri). 1616. [f. APE *sb.* + -ERY 2.] **1.** The practice of an aper, aping 1616; a silly or apish action 1851. **2.** A collection or colony of apes 1862.

2. More apish than all the apes of all aperies KINGSLEY.

Apet-; see later sp. APPET-.

Apetaloid (ăpe·tăloid), *a.* 1870. [f. as next + -OID.] *Bot.* Of apetalous form.

Apetalous (ăpe·tăləs), *a.* 1706. [f. mod.L. *apetalus* (– Gr. ἀπέταλος leafless) + -OUS.] *Bot.* Without petals.

Apex (ēⁱ·pĕks). Pl. **apices** (ĕi·pisīz, æ·p-), **apexes.** 1603. [– L. *apex* peak, tip.] **1.** (*As in L.*; see quot.) *rare.* 1603. **2.** The tip, top, peak, or pointed end of anything, as of a mountain, spire, shell, leaf, etc.; the vertex of a triangle or cone 1610. Also *fig.* **3.** A horn on a Hebrew letter (= κεραία *Matt.* 5:18 in Vulg.); hence †*fig.* A tittle, a jot –1680.

1. A hat of..wool, whose top ended in a cone, and was thence called an a. B. JONSON. **2.** The a. of the dome 1848. *Apex* (U.S. *Min.*), the end or edge of a vein nearest the surface 1881. **3.** Every a. or tittle JACKSON. Hence **A·pexed** *ppl. a.* pointed.

Aph-, repr. Gr. ἀφ', var. of ἀπό 'off, away from', bef. an aspirated vowel.

Aphæresis (ăfīᵊ·rĭsis). Also **aphe-.** 1611. [– late L. – Gr. ἀφαίρεσις, f. ἀφαιρεῖν take away, f. ἀπό APO- + αἱρεῖν to take.] *Gram.* The taking away of a letter or syllable at the beginning of a word. Hence **Aphære·tic** *a.* (*rare*).

Apha·nesite. [irreg. f. Gr. ἀφανής unseen; cf. APHANITE.] *Min.* = CLINOCLASITE.

‖ **Aphaniptera** (æfăni·ptĕră), *sb. pl.* 1835. [mod.L., f. Gr. ἀφανής unseen + -πτερος winged.] *Zool.* A small order of insects, having only rudimentary scales for wings. Hence **Aphani·pterous** *a.*

Aphanite, -yte (æ·fănəit). 1862. [f. Gr. ἀφανής unseen + -ITE[1] 2 b.] *Min.* A compact dark-coloured hornblende rock, uniform in texture and showing no distinct grains (whence its name); also called *Corneine*. Hence **Aphani·tic** *a.*

Aphanozygous (æfănǫ·zigəs), *a.* 1871. [f. Gr. ἀφανής unseen + ζυγόν (for ζύγωμα cheek-bone) + -OUS.] *Anthrop.* Having the cheek-bones invisible from above.

‖ **Aphasia** (ăfē·ziă). 1867. [mod. L. – Gr. ἀφασία, f. ἄφατος speechless, f. ἀ- A- *pref.* 14 + φάναι speak; see -IA¹.] *Path.* Loss of the faculty of speech, as a result of cerebral affection.

Aphasic (ăfæ·zik), *a.* 1867. [f. prec. + -IC.] Suffering from aphasia. *sb.* One suffering from aphasia; var. **Apha·siac** (the better form).

Aphelion (ăfī·liŏn). Pl. **aphelia.** 1656. [Græcized form (Kepler) of mod.L. *aphelium*, f. Gr. ἀπό APO-, APH- + ἥλιος sun, after L. *apogæum* APOGEE.] *Astr.* That point of a planet's or comet's orbit at which it is furthest from the sun. Also *fig.*

Apheliotropic (ăfī:li,otrǫ·pik), *a.* 1880. [f. APH- + *heliotropic*; see HELIOTROPE.] Turning away from the sun; said of leaves, etc. Hence **Aphe:liotro·pically** *adv.* **Aphe:lio·-tropism,** the habit of bending away from the light.

‖ **Aphemia** (ăfī·miă). 1864. [mod.L. f. ἀ- A- pref. 14 + φήμη voice, speech + -ία -Y³.] *Path.* Loss of power of articulation; *spec.* a form of APHASIA, in which words are still understood and conceived. Hence **Aphe·mic** *a.* and *sb.*

Aphesis (æ·fĭsis). 1880. [– Gr. ἄφεσις letting go, f. ἀφιέναι, f. ἀπό APO- APH- + ἱέναι let go, send. Suggested by Sir J. A. H. Murray.] The gradual and unintentional loss of a short unaccented vowel at the beginning of a word; as in *squire* for *esquire*, etc. It is a special and frequent form of *Aphæresis*. Hence **Aphe·tic** *a.* pertaining to, or resulting from, a. **Aphe·tically** *adv.* by way of a. **A·phetism,** a word resulting from a., as *squire*, etc. **A·phetize** *v.* to shorten by aphesis.

‖ **A·pheta.** 1647. [med.L. – Gr. ἀφέτης, a starter in races.] *Astrol.* The giver of life in a nativity. Hence **Aphe·tic, -al** *a.* life-giving.

Aphidian (ăfi·diăn). 1855. [f. *aphid-*, stem of mod.L. APHIS, + -IAN.] *adj.* Of or pertaining to aphides. *sb.* One of the aphides.

Aphilanthropy (æfilæ·nþrŏpi). *? Obs.* 1753. [f. A- *pref.* 14 + PHILANTHROPY.] **1.** 'Want of love to mankind'. J. **2.** *Med.* A form of melancholy in which solitude is preferred; anthropophobia.

‖ **Aphis** (æ·fis). Pl. **aphides** (æ·fidīz). 1771. [– mod.L. *aphis*, first used by Linnæus, and based on ἄφις in Aldrovandi's 'De animalibus insectis' (1602). The Gr. ἄφις first appears (as = L. *cimex* bug) in 1523, and is prob. an error for κόρις bug, κορ having been mis-read as αφ.] A family of minute insects, also called *plant-lice*, which are very destructive. They are prodigiously prolific, multiplying by parthenogenesis; and are tended by ants for the honey-dew which they yield, whence occas. called *ant-cows*.

Comb. **a.-lion,** *Chrysopa perla*. Hence **Aphidiphagous, Aphidi·vorous** *adjs.*, feeding on aphides, like the lady-bird. **Aphido·logist,** a student of the *Aphides*.

Aphlogistic (æflodʒi·stik), *a.* 1831. [f. Gr. ἀφλόγιστος uninflammable + -IC.] Without flame.

Aphlogistic or *Flameless Lamp*: Sir H. Davy's lamp, in which a coil of platinum wire is kept in a state of flameless ignition by spirit.

Aphonic (ăfǫ·nik), *a. rare.* 1827. [f. Gr. ἄφωνος voiceless + -IC.] Having no vocal sound.

Aphony (æ·fŏni). 1684. [– mod.L. *aphonia* (oftener used) – Gr. ἀφωνία speechlessness.] Inability to produce vocal sound, or voice.

Aphorism (æ·fŏriz'm). 1528. [– Fr. *aphorisme* or late L. *aphorismus* – Gr. ἀφορισμός definition, f. ἀφορίζειν define, f. ἀπό APO-, APH- + ὁρίζειν set bounds to, f. ὅρος boundary.] **1.** A 'definition' or concise statement of a principle in any science. **2.** Any principle or precept expressed shortly and pithily; a maxim 1590.

1. Knowledge, while..in aphorisms and observations..is in growth BACON. **2.** Is not thy common talk found aphorisms MARLOWE. 'Tis an old Aphorisme *Oderunt omnes quem metuunt* HOWELL. Hence **A:phorisma·tic** *a.* [irreg. f. Gr. ἀφόρισμα.] aphorismic or aphoristic. † **A·phorismer,** a dealer in aphorisms (MILT.). **Aphori·smic** *a.* having the form of aphorisms. **A·phori:sming** *ppl. a.* dealing in aphorisms (*rare*).

Aphorist (æ·fŏrist). 1713. [f. APHORIZE; see -IST.] One who writes or utters aphorisms. Hence **Aphori·stic** *a.* of or pertaining to an aphorist; of the nature of an aphorism. **Aphori·stically** *adv.* pithily.

Aphorize (æ·fŏrəiz), *v. rare.* 1669. [f. APHORISM; see -IZE.] To write or speak in aphorisms; to make terse general reflections.

Aphrite (æ·frəit). 1868. [f. Gr. ἀφρός foam + -ITE¹ 2 b.; = *foam-stone*.] *Min.* A carbonate of lime or calcite.

Aphrizite (æ·frizəit). [f. Gr. ἀφρίζειν to foam + -ITE¹ 2 b.] *Min.* Black tourmaline from Krageröe in Norway.

Aphrodisiac (æfrodi·ziæc), *a.* 1719. [– Gr. ἀφροδισιακός, f. ἀφροδίσιος, f. Ἀφροδίτη goddess of love ('foam-born') f. ἀφρός foam.] Venereal; having a venereal tendency 1830. *sb.* A drug, etc., inducing venereal desire 1719. Also *fig.*

Aphrodisian (æfrodi·ziăn), *a.* 1860. [f. Gr. ἀφροδίσιος (see prec.) + -AN.] Belonging to Venus, devoted to sensual love.

‖ **Aphrodite** (æfrodəi·tī), *sb.*¹ 1658. [Gr. Ἀφροδίτη; see APHRODISIAC.] **1.** The Grecian Venus. **2.** *Zool.* A genus of marine worms with bristles of iridescent hues; also called *Sea-mouse* 1857.

Aphrodite (æ·frodəit), *sb.*² 1837. [f. prec., taken as 'foam-stone' from its ending -ITE; cf. APHRITE.] *Min.* A soft opaque milk-white mineral, consisting mostly of bisilicate of magnesium, allied to Sepiolite or meerschaum.

A·phronitre. *? Obs.* ME. [– L. *aphronitrum* – Gr. ἀφρόνιτρον, for ἀφρὸς νίτρου 'foam of nitre'.] Foam of nitre; saltpetre.

Aphrosi·derite. 1847. [f. Gr. ἀφρός foam + σίδηρος iron + -ITE¹ 2 b.] *Min.* A soft ferruginous dark olive-green mineral, a variety of Prochlorite.

‖ **Aphtha** (æ·fþă). 1657. [L. – Gr. ἄφθα, mostly in pl.; conn. w. ἅπτειν to set on fire.] *Path.* The infantile disease 'thrush', and, in the plural, the small white specks on the mouth and tongue which characterize it. Hence **A·phthous** *a.* of the nature of, or characterized by, a.

Aphthitalite (æfþi·tăləit). 1835. [f. Gr. ἄφθιτος undecaying + -LITE.] *Min.* A native sulphate of potash found upon lava; called also Vesuvian salt, Aphthalose, Arcanite, and Glaserite.

Aphthong (æ·fþǫŋ). 1847. [– Gr. ἄφθογγος voiceless, ἄφθογγον (sc. γράμμα) consonant.] A letter which is not sounded in the pronunciation of a word; a mute.

Aphthonite (æ·fþŏnəit). [f. Gr. ἄφθονος plentiful + -ITE¹ 2 b.] *Min.* A steel-grey ore, resembling, or identical with, tetrahedrite. Corruptly *Aftonite*.

Aphyllous (ăfi·ləs), *a.* 1830. [f. mod.L. *aphyllus* – Gr. ἄφυλλος (f. ἀ- A- *pref.* 14 + φύλλον leaf) + -OUS.] *Bot.* Naturally leafless.

Apiaceous (ē¹pi,ē¹·ʃəs), *a.* 1839. [f. mod.L. *Apiaceæ*, f. L. *apium* celery; see -ACEOUS.] *Bot.* Of the N.O. *Apiaceæ* or *Umbelliferæ*; umbelliferous.

Apian (ē¹·piăn), *a.* 1862. [– L. *apianus*, f. *apis* bee; see -AN.] Of or belonging to bees.

Apiary (ē¹·piări). 1654. [– L. *apiarium* bee-house, f. *apis* bee; see -ARY¹.] A place where bees are kept. Hence **Apia·rian** *a.* pertaining to bee-hives or bee-keeping; *sb.* = next (*rare*). **A·piarist,** one who keeps an a.

Apical (æ·pikăl, ē¹·pi-), *a.* 1828. [f. L. *apic-*, stem of *apex* APEX + -AL¹.] Of, belonging to, or at an apex, summit, or tip. Hence **A·pically** *adv.* **A·picifi:xed** *ppl. a.* fixed to the apex.

Apicilar, Apici·llary = APICULAR.

Api·cial, incorr. var. of APICAL.

Apician (ăpi·ʃăn), *a.* 1699. [f. *Apicius*, a Roman epicure + -AN.] Of or pertaining to epicures or to luxurious diet.

A pick a back, apickaback; see PICK-A-BACK.

Apicular (ăpi·kiŭlaɹ), *a. rare.* 1854. [f. mod.L APICULUS + -AR¹.] Of or belonging to a little apex.

Apiculate (ăpi·kiŭlĕt), *a.* 1830. [f. as prec. + -ATE².] Having a minute apex. So **Api·culated** *ppl. a.*

Apiculture (ē¹·pi,kɒ:ltiŭr, -tʃəɹ). 1864. [f. L. *apis* bee, after *agriculture*.] Bee-keeping or -rearing.

‖ **Apiculus** (ăpi·kiŭlŏs). 1863. [mod.L., dim. of *apex*, *apic-*; see APEX, -ULE.] A minute point or tip.

Apiece (ăpī·s), *adv.* ME. [orig. two words, A *adj.*², PIECE *sb.*] For each piece, thing, or (*colloq.*) person; each, for each, to each; severally, individually.

Six waterpottes of stone..contaynynge two or thre fyrkins a pece TINDALE *John* 2:6.

† **A-pie·ces,** *advb. phr.* 1560. [f. A *prep.*¹ 6.] In pieces, to pieces –1678. *fig.* –1663.

A-pi·nch, *advb. phr.* [A *prep.*¹ 11.] So as to pinch. MRS. BROWNING.

Apiocrinite (æpi,ǫ·krinəit). 1830. [f. Gr. ἄπιον pear + κρίνον lily + -ITE¹ 2 b, after *encrinite*.] *Palæont.* The pear-encrinite, a stalked echinoderm of the Oolite, so called from its shape.

Apiol (ē̆i·pi,ǫl). 1872. [f. L. *apium* parsley + -OL.] *Chem.* and *Med.* Parsley-camphor, obtained by distilling parsley seeds with water.

Apio·logist. *rare.* [f. L. *apis* + -LOGIST.] A scientific student of bees. EMERSON.

Apish (ē¹·piʃ), *a.* 1532. [f. APE *sb.* + -ISH¹.] **1.** Like an ape 1570. **2.** Ape-like in manner; befitting an ape; affected, silly, trifling 1532. **3.** Foolishly imitative 1579.

1. Two devilish apes, or a. devils RUSKIN. **2.** He bowed with a thousand a. congees SMOLLETT. **3.** We are but too a., apt to be led much by examples SANDERSON. Hence **A·pishly** *adv.* **A·pishness.**

A·pism. [f. APE.] The practice of aping. CARLYLE.

Apjohnite (æ·p,dʒǫnəit) 1847. [f. *Apjohn*, its first analyzer, + -ITE¹ 2 b.] *Min.* Manganese alum; a double sulphate of potash and manganese, occurring in fibrous or asbestiform masses, white, and lustrous.

† **Apla·ce,** *advb. phr.* ME. [f. A *prep.*¹ + *place*; cf. Fr. *en place*.] Into this place, in place –1637.

Aplacental (æplăse·ntăl), *a.* 1857. [f. A- *pref.* 14 + PLACENTAL.] *Zool.* Having no placenta.

Aplanatic (æplănæ·tik), *a.* 1794. [f. Gr. ἀπλάνητος free from error (f. ἀ- A- *pref.* 14 + πλανᾶν wander) + -IC.] Free from (spherical) aberration, as a compound lens. Hence **Apla·natism,** a state or condition.

Aplastic (ăplæ·stik), *a.* 1839. [f. A- *pref.* 14 + PLASTIC *a.*] Characterized by, or tending to, irregularity or absence of organic structure (techn. *aplasia*).

‖ **Aplomb** (a,plǫn·). 1828. [Fr., f. *à plomb* 'according to the plummet'.] **1.** The perpendicular; perpendicularity 1872. **2.** Confidence, self-possession 1828. Also *attrib.*

Aplotomy (ăplǫ·tŏmi). 1852. [f. Gr. ἁπλοῦς, ἁπλο- simple + -TOMY.] *Surg.* Simple incision.

‖ **Apnœa** (æpnī·ă). 1719. [mod.L. – Gr. ἄπνοια, f. ἄπνους breathless.] *Path.* Suspension or cessation of breathing.

Apo-, *pref.*; repr. Gr. ἀπό- off, from, away; quite. In mod. scientific words = 'detached', as *apo-carpous*.

Apocalypse (ăpǫ·kălips). ME. [– (O)Fr. *apocalypse* – eccl.L. *apocalypsis* – Gr. ἀποκάλυψις, f. ἀποκαλύπτειν uncover, f. ἀπό APO- + καλύπτειν cover.] **1.** The revelation of the future granted to St. John in the isle of Patmos; also the book of the New Testament containing it. **2.** Any revelation or disclosure ME.

1. He who saw Th' Apocalyps MILT. *P.L.* IV. 2. **2.** The A. of all State-arcana SWIFT.

Apocalypst (ăpǫ·kălipst). *rare.* 1829. [irreg. = *apocalypt*, or *apocalyptist*.] A revealer of the unknown.

Apocalypt (ăpǫ·kălipt). *rare.* 1834. [– Gr. *ἀποκαλύπτης, f. ἀποκαλύπτειν; see APOCALYPSE.] = APOCALYPTIST.

Apocalyptic (ăpǫ·kăli·ptik), *a.* (*sb.*) 1629. [– Fr. *apocalyptique* (Rabelais) – Gr. ἀποκαλυπτικός, f. ἀποκαλύπτειν; see APOCALYPSE -IC.]

1. Of or pertaining to the Apocalypse of St. John 1663. 2. Of the nature of a revelation 1683. † 3. Of persons: Dealing with the Apocalypse, or with prophetic revelations generally –1690. 4. *sb.* The writer of the Apocalypse, St. John the Divine; also = APOCALYPST 1629. Hence **Apo:caly·ptical** *a.* = APOCALYPTIC *a.* 3. **Apo:caly·ptically** *adv.* after the manner, or by means, of revelation or of the Apocalypse; (*joc.*) so as to reveal what should be concealed.

Apocalyptist (ăpǫ:kăli·ptist). *rare.* 1864. [f. Gr. ἀποκαλύπτειν (see prec.) + -IST.] The writer of the Apocalypse.

Apocarpous (æpokā·ɹpəs), *a.* 1830. [f. Gr. ἀπό APO- + καρπός fruit + -OUS.] *Bot.* Having the carpels distinct.

‖ **Apocatastasis** (æ:po,kătæ·stăsis). *rare.* 1678. [L. – Gr. ἀποκατάστασις re-establishment.] 1. Restoration, re-establishment. 2. *Path.* Return to a previous condition 1753. 3. *Astr.* Return to the same apparent position. (So in Gr.) 1822.

Apocathartic (æ:po,kaþā·ɹtik), *a.* 1859. [– Gr. ἀποκαθαρτικός; see APO-, CATHARTIC.] *Med.* Purging. Also as *sb.*

Apocopate (ăpǫ·kŏpeᶦt, -ĕt), *ppl. a.* 1850. [– mod.L. *apocopatus*, f. APOCOPE; see -ATE².] Cut short by apocope.

Apocopate (ăpǫ·kŏpeᶦt), *v.* 1851. [f. as prec.; see -ATE³.] To cut off (*esp.* the last letter or syllable of a word). Hence **Apo:copa·tion,** the action of apocopating; apocopated state.

‖ **Apocope** (ăpǫ·kŏpi). 1591. [– late L. – Gr. ἀποκοπή, f. ἀποκόπτειν to cut off, f. ἀπό APO- + κόπτειν to cut.] The cutting off or omission of the last letter or syllable of a word. Hence **Apoco·pic** *a.*

Apocrisiary (æpokri·ziări). Also **apo·crisary.** ME. [– med.L. *apocrisiarius* delegate, f. Gr. ἀπόκρισις answer; see -ARY¹.] A person appointed to give and receive answers; *spec.* a papal nuncio.

Apocrustic (æpokrʊ·stik), *a.* Also **apocroustic.** 1706. [– med.L. *apocrusticus* – Gr. ἀποκρουστικός, f. ἀποκρούειν beat off, repel; see -IC.] *Med.* Having power to repel, astringent. Also as *sb.*

Apocrypha (ăpǫ·krifă). ME. [neut. pl. (sc. *scripta* writings) of eccl.L. *apocryphus*, – Gr. ἀπόκρυφος hidden, f. ἀποκρύπτειν to hide; see APO-, CRYPT.] † **A.** *adj.* Of unknown authorship; spurious; uncanonical (see *sb.*); false –1690.

B. *sb.* 1. A writing of doubtful authorship or authenticity; *spec.* those books included in the Septuagint and Vulgate, which were not originally written in Hebrew and not counted genuine by the Jews, and which, at the Reformation, were excluded from the Sacred Canon by the Protestant party. Also *attrib.* 1539. 2. [As in Gr.] Hidden things (*rare*) 1839.

1. What's now apocrypha, my wit, In time to come may pass for holy writ POPE. var. † **Apocryph(e,** † **-crif(e.**

Apocryphal (ăpǫ·krifăl), *a.* 1590. [f. prec. + -AL¹.] 1. Of doubtful authenticity; spurious, false, mythical; *spec.* Of or belonging to the Jewish and early Christian uncanonical literature 1615. 2. Sham, counterfeit 1610.

1. If but one word be true. . In all th' a. romance BUTLER *Hud.* III. i. 492. 2. A whoreson, upstart a. captain B. JONSON. Hence **Apo·cryphalist,** one who supports the inclusion of the Apocrypha in the Bible (*rare*). **Apo·cryphally** *adv.* (*rare*). **Apo·cryphalness** (*rare*).

† **Apo·cryphate,** *a.* 1486. [f. as prec. + -ATE².] Of apocryphal origin; spurious –1655.

Apocynaceous (ăpǫ:sinēᶦ·ʃəs), *a.* 1883. [f. mod.L. *Apocynaceæ* (f. *Apocynon* dog's-bane – Gr. ἀπόκυνον, f. ἀπό APO- + κύων, κυν- dog) + -OUS; see -ACEOUS.] *Bot.* Of or belonging to the N.O. *Apocynaceæ*, or Dog-banes. var. **Apocy·neous.**

Apod(e (æ·pǫd, æ·poᵘd). 1601. [– Gr. ἄπους, ἀποδ- without feet, f. ἀπό APO- + πούς foot; cf. Fr. *apode.*] *Zool. adj.* Footless 1816. *sb.* (usu. *pl.* = mod.L. *Apodes, Apoda.*) Term applied to birds, fish, and reptiles, in which feet or ventral fins are either absent or only rudimentary. Hence **A·podal** *a.* lacking feet or ventral fins.

Apodeme (æ·pŏdīm). 1852. [– mod.L. *apodema* (also used), f. Gr. ἀπό APO- + δέμας body, frame.] *Zool.* One of the processes on the exoskeleton of the thorax of *Arthropods*, which serve as attachment for muscles, etc. Hence **Apo·demal** *a.* of or pertaining to an a.; var. **Apode·matal.**

Apodiabolosis (æ:po,dəiăbŏlōᵘ·sis). *rare.* 1827. [f. Gr. διάβολος, after *apotheosis.*] A making or treating as diabolical.

Apodictic, -deictic (æpodi·ktik, -dəi·ktik), *a.* 1652. [– L. *apodicticus* – Gr. ἀποδεικτικός, f. ἀποδεικνύναι demonstrate, f. ἀπό APO- + δεικνύναι show.] Of clear demonstration; established incontrovertibly. (By Kant applied to a judgement enouncing a necessary and hence *absolute* truth.) var. **Apodi·ctical, -dei·ctical** (*arch.*). Hence **Apodi·ctically, -dei·ctically** *adv.*

‖ **Apodio·xis.** ? *Obs.* 1657. [– Gr. ἀποδίωξις expulsion, f. ἀποδιώκειν drive away.] *Rhet.* A figure: Rejecting an argument or objection with indignation as absurd.

‖ **Apodixis, -deixis** (æpodi·ksis, -dei·ksis). ? *Obs.* 1623. [L. *apodixis* – Gr. ἀπόδειξις demonstration; see APODICTIC.] Demonstration, absolute proof.

‖ **Apodosis** (ăpǫ·dŏsis). 1638. [– late L. (Donatus) – Gr. ἀπόδοσις 'a giving back', f. ἀποδιδόναι, f. ἀπό APO- + διδόναι give.] The concluding clause of a sentence (opp. to *protasis*); now usu. the consequent clause in a conditional sentence, as 'If thine enemy hunger, *feed him*'.

Apodous (æ·podəs), *a.* 1816. [f. Gr. ἀποδ- (see APODE) + -OUS.] *Zool.* Footless, apod.

‖ **Apodyterium** (æpo,ditīᵊ·riŏm). 1695. [L. – Gr. ἀποδυτήριον, f. ἀποδύειν to strip.] A dressing-room; *orig.* one in which clothes were deposited by those preparing for the bath or *palæstra.*

Apogæic, -gaic (æpodʒī·ik, -gē·ik), *a.* 1839. [f. Gr. ἀπόγαιος (see APOGEE) + -IC.] = APOGEAN. So **Apoge·al** *a.*

Apogean (æpodʒī·ăn), *a.* 1644. [f. as prec. + -AN.] **a.** Proceeding off from the earth or land. **b.** Of or pertaining to apogee.

Apogee (æ·podʒī). 1594. [– Fr. *apogée* or mod.L. *apogæum, -eum* – Gr. ἀπόγαιον, -ειον, subst. use (sc. διάστημα distance) of neut. of adjs. ἀπόγαιος, -ειος far from the earth, f. ἀπό APO- + γαι- γει-, stems of γῆ (γαῖα) earth.] *Astr.* 1. The point in the orbit of the moon, etc., at which it is furthest from the earth; also, the greatest distance of the sun from the earth in *aphelion.* (A term of the Ptolemaic astronomy which viewed the earth as the centre of the universe.) † 2. The meridional altitude of the sun on the longest day –1646. 3. Hence *fig.* **a.** The most distant spot. **b.** The highest point, climax. 1600.

1. A., if the sun be supposed to revolve, Aphelion, if the earth WOODHOUSE. 3. The trade of the Netherlands. . had by no means reached its a. MOTLEY.

Apogeotropic (æ:po,dʒī,otrǫ·pik), *a.* 1880. [f. (by Darwin, 1880) Gr. ἀπό from + γῆ earth (see GEO-) + τροπικός turning.] *Bot.* Turning away from the ground. Hence **A:pogeotro·pically** *adv.*

Apogeotropism (æ:po,dʒi,ǫ·trŏ,piz'm). 1880. [f. as prec. + -ISM.] The tendency of leaves, etc., to turn away from the earth.

Apograph (æ·pogrɑf). 1601. [– Gr. ἀπόγραφον, f. ἀπογράφειν to copy.] An exact transcript.

Apoious (ăpoi·əs), *a. rare.* 1880. [f. Gr. ἄποιος without quality + -OUS.] Having no active qualities; neutral; *e.g.* water.

Apojove (æ·po,dʒōᵘv). 1867. [– Fr. *apojove* – mod.L. *apojovium*, f. Gr. ἀπό APO- + L. *jov-* (stem of *Jupiter*), after APOGEE.] *Astr.* The point in the orbit of a satellite of Jupiter at which it is furthest from the planet.

Apolar (ăpōᵘ·lăɹ), *a.* 1859. [f. A- *pref.* 14 + POLAR.] *Biol.* Having no poles or fibrous processes, as certain nerve-cells.

Apolaustic (æpolǭ·stik), *a.* 1871. [– Gr. ἀπολαυστικός, f. ἀπολαύειν enjoy; see -IC.] Given to enjoyment; self-indulgent.

The lordly, a., and haughty undergraduate 1880.

Apollinarian (ăpǫ:linēᵊ·riăn), *a.* 1586. [f. L. *Apollinaris* of Apollo (also proper name) + -AN; see -ARIAN.] 1. Sacred to or in honour of Apollo 1753; var. † **Apo·llinar.** 2. Of or pertaining to Apollinaris of Laodicea (4th c.), who held heretical opinions on the Incarnation 1659. As *sb.* An adherent of Apollinaris 1586; var. **Apollina·rist** (? *obs.*).

Apollonian (æpǫlōᵘ·niăn), *a.* 1663. [f. L. *Apollonius* – Gr. Ἀπολλώνιος of Apollo (also proper name) + -AN; see -IAN.] 1. Pertaining to or resembling Apollo, the sun-god of the Greeks and Romans, the patron of music and poetry; var. **Apollo·nic.** 2. Of Apollonius of Perga, a geometer and investigator of conic sections 1727.

Apollo·nicon. 1834. [f. as prec., after *harmonicon.*] A chamber-organ of great power, first exhibited in 1817.

‖ **Apollyon** (ăpǫ·liǫn). ME. [– L. (Vulg.) *Apollyon* – Gr. (N.T.) Ἀπολλύων (*Rev.* 9:11, tr. ABADDON), subst. use of pres. pple. of ἀπολλύναι, intensive of ὀλλύναι destroy.] The destroyer; a name given to the Devil. (See *Rev.* 9:3–11.) Hence **Apollyonist,** a subject of Apollyon.

† **Apo·loger.** 1621. [f. L. *apologus* (see APOLOGUE) + -ER¹ 4.] A fabulist –1653.

Apologetic (ăpǫ:lŏdʒe·tik). 1605. [– Fr. *apologétique* – late L. *apologeticus* – Gr. ἀπολογητικός fit for defence, f. ἀπολογεῖσθαι; see APOLOGY.] **A.** *adj.* 1. Of the nature of a defence; vindicatory 1649. 2. Regretfully acknowledging or excusing fault or failure 1855.

2. A subdued and a. tone MACAULAY.

B. *sb.* 1. A formal apology for a defence of a person, doctrine, course, etc. 1605. 2. *pl.* or *collect. sing.* The defensive method of argument; often *spec.* The argumentative defence of Christianity 1733.

2. The science of apologetics. . was unknown till the attacks of the adversaries of Christianity assumed a learned and scientific character 1834. Hence **Apo:loge·tical** *a.* = APOLOGETIC *a.*; **-ly** *adv.*

† **Apolo·gical,** *a.* 1607. [f. Gr. ἀπολογία, or ἀπόλογος + -ICAL.] Of the nature of an apology, or of an apologue –1665.

Apologist (ăpǫ·lŏdʒist). 1640. [– Fr. *apologiste*, f. Gr. ἀπολογίζεσθαι render an account, f. ἀπόλογος; see APOLOGUE.] One who apologizes for, or defends by argument; a literary champion.

Mr. Hume, the staunch a. . of all the Stuarts LD. BROUGHAM.

Apologize (ăpǫ·lŏdʒəiz), *v.* 1597. [– Gr. ἀπολογίζεσθαι render an account (see prec.); now assoc. w. APOLOGY.] 1. *intr.* To make or serve as an APOLOGY; to offer defensive arguments; to make excuses. Also in mod. usage: To acknowledge and express regret for a fault without defence. Const. *for.* † 2. *trans.* (*for* omitted.) (*rare*) 1733.

1. They had very little wine, which the governor apologised for DE FOE. 2. T' apologise his late offence SWIFT. Hence **Apo·logi:zer,** one who apologizes; earlier = APOLOGIST.

Apologue (æ·pŏlǫg). Also 6–7 **-logy.** 1552. [– Fr. *apologue* or L. *apologus* – Gr. ἀπόλογος story, account, f. ἀπό APO- + λόγος discourse; see -LOGY.] An allegorical story intended to convey a useful lesson. (*Esp.* a fable in which the actors or speakers are animals or inanimate things.)

To teach the people in apologies, bringing in how one beast talketh with another LATIMER.

Apology (ăpǫ·lŏdʒi), *sb.* 1533. [– Fr. *apologie* or late L. *apologia* – Gr. ἀπολογία speech in defence, f. ἀπολογεῖσθαι speak in ones own defence; see -LOGY.] 1. The pleading off from a charge or imputation; defence or vindication from accusation or aspersion. 2. Justification, explanation, or excuse 1588. 3. A frank acknowledgement, by way of reparation, of offence given, or an explanation that offence was not intended, with expression of regret for any given or taken 1594. 4. A poor substitute 1754.

1. Apologie of Syr Thomas More, Knyght; made by him, after he had geuen ouer the Office of Lord Chancellor of Englande MORE (*title*). An A. for the Bible BP. WATSON. 2. His *enter* and *exit* shall bee strangling a Snake; and I will haue an Apologie for that purpose *L.L.L.* V. i. 142. 3. In her face excuse Came Prologue, and Apologie to prompt MILT. *P.L.* IX. 854. 4. Gibbon. . had no nose at all, only an a. for one 1858. Hence † **Apo·logy** *v.* to apologize (*rare*).

A:pomeco·meter. 1869. [f. Gr. ἀπό APO- + μῆκος length; see -METER.] An instrument for measuring the distance of objects.

A:pomeco·metry. 1570. [f. as prec.; see -METRY.] The art or science of measuring the distances of objects.

Apomorphia (æpomǭ·ɹfiǎ). 1869. [f. Gr. ἀπό + MORPHIA.] *Chem.* A white crystalline powder, $C_{17}H_{17}NO_2$, obtained by heating morphia with an excess of hydrochloric acid: also **Apomorphine.** It is a prompt emetic.

‖ **Aponeurosis** (æ:po,niurōᵘ·sis). Pl. **-es.** 1676. [mod.L. – Gr. ἀπονεύρωσις (Galen), f. νεῦρον sinew; see -OSIS.] *Phys.* A white, shining, fibrous membrane, serving as the sheath of a muscle, or forming the connection of a muscle and a tendon. Hence **A:poneuro·graphy,** the description of aponeuroses. **A:poneuro·logy,** the science of aponeuroses. **A:poneuro·tic** *a.* **A:poneuro·tomy,** dissection of the aponeuroses.

A-poo·p, *adv.* 1809. [f. A *prep.*[1] 5 + POOP *sb.*] On the poop, astern.

Apopemptic (æpope·mptik). *rare.* 1753. [– Gr. ἀποπεμπτικός, f. ἀποπέμπειν send away; see -IC.] *adj.* Pertaining to dismissal; valedictory. *sb.* [sc. *hymn.*]

Apopetalous (æpope·tǎləs), *a.* 1875. [f. Gr. ἀπό APO- + πέταλον petal + -OUS.] *Bot.* Having the petals distinct or free.

‖ **Apophasis** (ǎpǫ·fǎsis). 1657. [Late L. *apophasis* – Gr. ἀπόφασις denial.] *Rhet.* A figure in which we feign to deny or pass over what we really say or advise.

† **A:pophlegma·tic, -al,** *a.* 1727. [– Gr. ἀποφλεγματικός promoting discharge of phlegm; see APO-, PHLEGM, -IC.] *Med.* Promoting the removal of phlegm. Also as *sb.* [sc. *agent.*] var. **Apophlegma·tizant** (prob. f. mod.L.).

† **Apophle·gmatism.** 1615. [– late L. *apophlegmatismus* – Gr. ἀποφλεγματισμός, f. ἀποφλεγματίζειν purge away phlegm; see APO-, PHLEGM, -ISM.] *Med.* **1.** The action of purging phlegm from the head. **2.** An apophlegmatic agent or treatment.

Apophthegm, apothegm (æ·pǒþėm). 1553. [– Fr. *apophthegme* or mod.L. *apophthegma* – Gr. ἀπόφθεγμα, f. ἀποφθέγγεσθαι speak one's opinion plainly, f. ἀπό APO- + φθέγγεσθαι speak.] A terse, pointed saying, embodying an important truth in few words; a pithy or sententious maxim.

Johnson suddenly uttered . . an a., at which many will start: 'Patriotism is the last refuge of a scoundrel' BOSWELL. Hence **A:pophthegma·tic, -al, apothegm-** *a.* of, pertaining to, or of the nature of, an a.; addicted to the use of apophthegms; sententious, pithy. **A:pophthegma·tically, apothegm-** *adv.* **Apophthe·gmatist, apothegm-,** a professed maker of apophthegms. **Apophthe·gmatize, apothegm-** *v.* to write or speak in apophthegms.

Apophyge (ǎpǫ·fidʒi). 1563. [– Gr. ἀποφυγή escape, in later use 'the curve with which the shaft escapes into the base or capital', f. ἀποφύγειν flee away. L. *apophygis* in Vitruvius is erron. f. the Greek.] *Arch.* The part of a column where it springs out of its base, or joins its capital, usually moulded into a concave sweep or cavetto.

Apophyllite (ǎpǫ·filəit, æpofi·ləit). 1810. [f. Gr. ἀπό off + φύλλον leaf + -ITE[1] 2 b.] *Min.* A zeolitic mineral, a hydrated silicate of lime and potash, with a trace of fluorine; occurring in glassy square prisms or octahedrons, or laminated masses, with a pearly lustre.

Apophyllous (æpofi·ləs), *a. rare.* 1875. [f. as prec. + -OUS.] *Bot.* Having the sepals free.

‖ **Apophysis** (ǎpǫ·fisis). Pl. **-es.** Also **apophyse.** 1611. [mod.L. – Gr. ἀπόφυσις offshoot, f. ἀπό off + φύσις growth.] **1.** *Phys.* A natural protuberance or process, arising from, and forming a continuous part of, a bone. **2.** *Bot.* A dilatation of the base of the theca or spore-case in some mosses 1794. Hence **Apo·physate** *a.* furnished with an a. (*rare*). **Apophy·sial** (less correctly **apophysal**) *a.* belonging to, or of the nature of, an a.; var. **Apo·physary.**

Apoplectic, -al (æpople·ktik, -ǎl), *a.* 1611. [– Fr. *apoplectique* or late L. *apoplecticus*, – Gr. ἀποπληκτικός (see APOPLEXY).] **1.** Of, pertaining to, or causing apoplexy. **2.** Suffering from, or showing signs of, apoplexy. Also *fig.* 1721. †**3.** = ANTAPOPLECTIC –1753. **4.** *sb.* One liable to, or suffering from, apoplexy 1670.

1. One of your stiff-starched a. cravats DICKENS. **2.** A short-necked a. sort of fellow JANE AUSTEN. **3.** A. balsam ADDISON. Hence **Apople·ctically** *adv.* **Apople·ctiform** *a.* having the form of apoplexy.

A·poplex. *arch.* 1533. [– late L. *apoplexis* (= *apoplexia*) – Gr. ἀπόπληξις, var. of ἀποπληξία APOPLEXY.] = APOPLEXY.

A·poplex, *v. arch.* 1602. [f. prec. sb.] To strike with apoplexy, benumb.

Sure, that sense Is apoplex'd *Haml.* III. iv. 73.

Apoplexy (æ·po,pleksi). ME. [– (O)Fr. *apoplexie* – late L. *apoplexia* – Gr. ἀποπληξία, f. ἀποπλήσσειν disable by a stroke, f. ἀπό APO- + πλήσσειν strike.] A malady, sudden in its attack, which arrests the powers of sense and motion; usually caused by an effusion of blood or serum in the brain, and preceded by giddiness, partial loss of muscular power, etc. Also *transf.* or *fig.* **2.** Occas. applied to the effusion of blood in other organs 1853.

1. This Apoplexie is (as I take it) a kind of Lethargie, a sleeping of the blood, a horson Tingling *2 Hen. IV*, I. ii. 126. The Apoplexie or falling euill in Hawkes MARKHAM. **2.** *A. cutaneous*, a sudden determination of blood to the skin MAYNE.

† **Apore·tic,** † **-al,** *a. rare.* 1605. [– Fr. *aporétique* – Gr. ἀπορητικός, f. ἀπορεῖν be at a loss, f. ἀ- A- *pref.* 14 + πόρος passage; see -IC, -ICAL.] Full of doubts and objections –1688.

‖ **Aporia** (ǎpōᵊ·riǎ, -ǫ·riǎ). 1589. [– late L. *aporia* – Gr. ἀπορία doubt, perplexity, f. ἄπορος impassable; see prec., -Y[3].] *Rhet.* A figure: Doubt.

Aporose (æ:porōᵘ·s), *a.* 1865. [– mod.L. *aporosus*, f. A- *pref.* 14 + med.L. *porosus*; see POROUS *a.*, -OSE[1].] Not porous; *spec.* of the corals of the sub-order *Aporosa.*

† **Aporrhœ·a.** 1646. [Late L. – Gr. ἀπόρροια effluence, emanation, f. ἀπορρεῖν flow off.] An emanation, effluvium –1681.

A-port (ǎpōᵊ·ɹt), *adv.* 1626. [f. A *prep.*[1] 5 + PORT *sb.*[5]] On or towards the port side of the ship, the left side when looking forward. *To put the helm a-port* (= 'to port the helm'): to move the rudder to the starboard side, making the ship turn to the right.

Apose·palous, *a.* 1875. [f. Gr. ἀπό APO- + SEPAL + -OUS.] *Bot.* Having free sepals.

‖ **Aposiopesis** (æ:po,səi,opī·sis). 1578. [L. (Quintilian) – Gr. ἀποσιώπησις, f. ἀποσιωπᾶν be silent.] *Rhet.* A figure, in which the speaker suddenly halts, as if unable or unwilling to proceed.

A., an excellent figure for the ignorant, as 'What shall I say?' when one has nothing to say POPE. Hence **A:posiope·tic** *a.*

Aposi·tic, *a.* 1853. [– Gr. ἀποσιτικός, f. ἀπόσιτος without appetite, f. ἀπό APO- + σῖτος food.] *Med.* Tending to diminish appetite; causing *apositia* or distaste for food.

Apostasy (ǎpǫ·stǎsi). Also **-acy.** ME. [– eccl.L. *apostasia* – late Gr. ἀποστασία, for ἀπόστασις defection; see -Y[3].] **1.** Abandonment or renunciation of one's religious faith or moral allegiance. **b.** *R.C.Ch.* The action of quitting a religious order or renouncing vows without legal dispensation 1532. **2.** The abandonment of principles or party generally 1579.

1. Raphael . . had forewarned Adam by dire example to beware Apostasie MILT. *P.L.* VII. 44. **2.** A. from every good principle 1773.

Apostate (ǎpǫ·stět). ME. [– (O)Fr. *apostate* or eccl.L. *apostata* – late Gr. ἀποστάτης runaway slave, apostate, f. ἀπο- APO- + στατ-, rel. to ἱστάναι to stand.] **A.** *sb.* **1.** One guilty of APOSTASY 1; a pervert. **b.** *R.C.Ch.* One who renounces a religious order without legal dispensation ME. **2.** A turncoat, a renegade ME.

1. High in the midst. . Th' A. in his Sun-bright Chariot sate MILT. *P.L.* vi. 100. **2.** Apostates, to their own Country, and Cause 1687.

B. *adj.* Guilty of APOSTASY; renegade, infidel; rebellious ME. **2.** Deserting principles or party; perverted 1671.

1. So spake th' Apostate Angel MILT. **2.** Those a. abilities of men STEELE. Hence † **Apo·state** *v.* = APOSTATIZE. **Aposta·tic** *a.* (*rare*) = APOSTATE *a.* 1. **Aposta·tical** *a.* of the nature of apostates or apostasy; † withdrawing, retrograde. **Apo·statism,** the practice of apostatizing.

Apostatize (ǎpǫ·stǎtəiz), *v.* 1552. [– med.L. *apostatizare*, earlier *apostatare*, f. *apostata* APOSTATE; see -IZE.] **1.** To be guilty of APOSTASY (*from, to*). **2.** To abandon a principle, desert a party 1648.

2. He apostatized from your cause CROMWELL.

† **A·postem(e, -tume, -thume.** ME. [– OFr. *aposteme, apostume* (XIII) – L. *apostema* (med.L. *apostuma*) – Gr. ἀπόστημα separation of purulent matter into an abscess, f. ἀποστα-, ἀποστῆναι (cf. *abs-cess*). Corruptions are, in OFr. *apostume* (as if f. L. *postumus*), changed later to *empostume*; hence Eng. *impostume*, IMPOSTHUME (cf. *posthumous*), in XVIII the only form. Accented *a·postem* by Johnson.] A gathering of purulent matter in any part of the body; an abscess. Also *fig.* Hence † **Apo·stemate, -umate** *a.* formed into an a.; festering; *sb.* = APOSTEM. † **Apo·stemate, -umate** *v. pass* to be affected with an a.; *intr.* to fester. † **Apo:stema·tion,** etc., the formation of an a.; = APOSTEM. **Aposte·matous** *a.* of the nature of an a.; characterized by abscesses.

‖ **A posteriori** (ēⁱ pǫste:ri,ōᵊ·rəi, ā poste:rīō·ri), *advb.* (and *adj.*) *phr.* 1710. [L., opp. to *a priori.*] A phrase used to characterize reasoning from effects to causes, from experience and not from axioms; empirical, inductive; inductively.

Knowledge *a posteriori* is a synonym for knowledge empirical or from experience SIR W. HAMILTON.

Aposthume, -ation, etc.; see APOSTEME.

Apostil, -ille (ǎpǫ·stil), *sb.* 1527. [– OFr. *apostille* (also *apostil* XV–XVI), f. *apostiller*, f. *postille* POSTIL.] A marginal note, comment, or annotation.

The world. . was to move upon protocols and apostilles MOTLEY. Hence **Apo·stil** *v.* to write marginal notes to (*rare*).

Apostle (ǎpǫ·s'l). [OE. *apostol* (whence ME. *apostel, -yl*) – eccl.L. *apostolus* – Gr. ἀπόστολος messenger, f. ἀποστέλλειν send forth. Reinforced or superseded by adoption of OFr. *apostle* (mod. *apôtre*).] † **1.** (As in Gr.) One sent, a messenger; applied in N.T. to Jesus Christ –1611. **2.** Any of the twelve witnesses whom Jesus Christ sent forth to preach his Gospel; also, later, Barnabas (*Acts* 13:2, 14:14), and Paul, the Apostle of the Gentiles OE. **3.** One who in any way imitates or resembles the Apostles ME.; *esp.* the missionary who first plants Christianity in any region ME.; the chief advocate of a new principle or system 1810. † **4.** The Acts and Epistles of the Apostles –1794. † **5.** A letter dimissory; *pl.* in *Rom. Law.* A short statement of the case, sent up by a lower to a higher court, when an appeal is made –1753.

1. Neither is an a. greater then he that sent him *Rhem.* John 13:16. **2.** The glorious company of the Apostles praise Thee *Te Deum.* **3.** The king's booted apostles 1659. Boniface has gained the title of the A. of Germany 1844. M. Comte is. . an a. of science 1870.

Comb., etc.: **a. skulls,** very long and narrow skulls; **a. spoons,** old-fashioned silver spoons, the handles of which end in figures of the Apostles. Hence **Apo·stlehood,** the office or position of an a. (*arch.*). So **Apo·stleship. Apo·stolize** *v.* (*rare*), *trans.* to proclaim (a message); *intr.* to act as or like an a.

† **Apostoi·le.** ME. only. [– OFr., AFr. *apostoile*, later Central Fr. *apostoile*:– late L. *apostolicus*, prop. adj.; see APOSTOLIC.] The pope.

Apostolate (ǎpǫ·stǒleⁱt). 1642. [– eccl.L. *apostolatus*; see APOSTLE, -ATE[1].] The office or position of an apostle; leadership in a propaganda.

I no otherwise assume the A. of England. . than I assume the A. of all Europe WESLEY.

Aposto·lian. [f. APOSTOLIC by substitution of suffix; see -IAN.] = APOSTOLIC *sb.*

Apostolic (æpǒstǫ·lik). 1477. [– Fr. *apostolique* or eccl.L. *apostolicus* – Gr. ἀποστολικός, f. ἀπόστολος; see APOSTLE, -IC.] **A.** *adj.* **1.** Pertaining to or contemporaneous with the Apostles 1549. **2.** Of the nature or character of the Apostles 1549. **3.** Of or pertaining to the pope as successor of St. Peter; papal 1477.

1. And a. statues climb To crush the imperial urn BYRON. **2.** A. charity COWPER, devotion to the service of the poor DE QUINCEY. **3.** Dependent on the A. See LINGARD. Hence **Aposto·licism,** profession of, or claim to, apostolicity. **Apo:stoli·city,** the quality of being a. in character or origin.

B. *sb.* A heretical sect, who imitated the Apostles, in wandering about without staves, shoes, money, or bags 1580.

Aposto·lical, *a.* (*sb.*) 1546. [– OFr. *apostolical* or med.L. *apostolicalis*; see prec., -AL[1], -ICAL.] **1.** Connected with or relating to the Apostles, or to what is apostolic 1577. **2.** Of the Apostolic See 1546. **3.** Formerly (and still occas.) = APOSTOLIC 1548. **4.** *sb.* One who maintains the doctrine of apostolical succession 1839.

1. *Apostolical succession* (*Eccl.*), an uninterrupted transmission of spiritual authority through a succession of bishops from the Apostles downwards. Hence **Aposto·lically** *adv.* **Aposto·licalness.** ? *Obs.*

Apostrophe[1] (ăpǫ·strŏfi). Also † **-phy.** 1533. [– L. *apostrophe* – Gr. ἀποστροφή turning away to one in particular, f. ἀποστρέφειν, f. ἀπό away + στρέφειν turn.] **1.** *Rhet.* A figure, in which a speaker or writer suddenly stops in his discourse, and turns to address pointedly some person or thing, either present or absent; an exclamatory address. (Not confined, as occas. stated, to a person *present* (Quintilian), and the *absent* or *dead.*) **2.** *Bot.* The aggregation of protoplasm and chlorophyll-grains on the cell-walls adjacent to other cells; opp. to *epistrophe* 1875.

1. The a. to light at the commencement of the third book [of *Paradise Lost*] COLERIDGE.

Apostrophe[2] (ăpǫ·strŏfi). Also † **-phus** 1588. [– Fr. *apostrophe* or late L. *apostrophus* – late Gr. ἀπόστροφος mark of elision, subst. use (sc. προσῳδία accent) of adj. 'turned away', f. ἀπό away + στροφ- (see prec.); prop. of three syllables, but erron. assim. to prec.] † **1.** The omission of one or more letters in a word –1642. **2.** The sign (') used to indicate the omission of a letter, as in *o'er*; and as a sign of the mod. Eng. genitive or possessive case, as in *boy's*, *men's*, *Moses'*, etc. 1588.

It orig. marked merely the omission of *e* in writing, as in folio's = *folioes* nom. pl., but was gradually disused exc. in, and extended to all, possessives.

You finde not the apostrophas [? apostrophus], and so misse the accent *L.L.L.* IV. ii. 123.

Apostrophic (æpo,strǫ·fik), *a.* 1795. [f. APOSTROPHE[1], [2] + -IC.] **1.** Of, pertaining to, or given to the use of, rhetorical apostrophe 1820; var. **Apo·strophal. 2.** Of or pertaining to the grammatical apostrophe 1795.

Apostrophize (ăpǫ·strŏfəiz), *v.* 1611. [f. as prec. + -IZE.] **1.** *Rhet.* To address in an apostrophe 1725. Also *absol.* **2.** To omit one or more letters of a word; to mark with the sign (') the omission of letters 1611. Hence **Apo·strophized** *ppl.* a. (in both senses).

Apostume, -ation, etc.; see APOSTEME, etc.

Apotactite (æpotæ·ktəit). 1727. [– med.L. *apotactitæ* (pl.) – late Gr. ἀποτακτῖται 'renouncers', f. ἀποτάσσεσθαι part from, bid adieu to (a person); cf. *Luke* 9:61.] One of an early Christian sect, who renounced all their possessions in imitation of the early church in Jerusalem.

† **Apotelesm** (ăpǫ·tĭlez'm). *rare.* 1636. [– Gr. ἀποτέλεσμα, f. ἀποτελεῖν bring to an end, f. ἀπό off + τελεῖν finish.] **1.** (as in Gr.) The result, the sum and substance. **2.** *Astrol.* The casting of a horoscope 1753. Hence **Apotelesma·tic** *a.* of or pertaining to the casting of horoscopes.

†**Apo·thec.** 1591. [– OFr. *apotheque* shop, – L. *apotheca* – Gr. ἀποθήκη storehouse.] A shop, or storehouse; *esp.* for drugs. Also *fig.* –1657.

Apothecary (ăpǫ·pĭkări). [ME. *apotecarie* – OFr. *apotecaire*, *-icaire* (mod. *apothicaire*), – late L. *apothecarius* storekeeper, f. *apotheca*; see prec., -ARY[1].] † **1.** *orig.* One who kept a store or shop of non-perishable commodities, spices, drugs, comfits, preserves, etc. **2.** *spec.* The earlier name for : One who prepared and sold drugs for medicinal purposes; now called a druggist or pharmaceutical chemist. The modern apothecary is a general medical practitioner, by licence of the Apothecaries Company; but in pop. usage the term is archaic. ME. † **3.** [cf. OFr. *apotecarie*, and late L. *apothecaria.*] Drugs collectively; a store of drugs; medical treatment by drugs –1621. **4.** *attrib.* 1562.

2. *Apothecaries' Weight*: that by which drugs are compounded. O, true Apothecary: Thy drugs are quicke *Rom. & Jul.* V. iii. 119. **4.** A. shops 1601.

‖**Apothecium** (æpopĭ·ʃiŏm). Pl. **-a.** 1830. [mod.L. – Gr. ἀποθήκη (see APOTHEC) + *-ium*, as in *basidium*, etc.] The shield or spore-case, containing the fructification in lichens.

Apothegm, -them, vars. of APOPHTHEGM.

Apothem (æ·pǒpĕm). [mod. f. Gr. ἀποτιθέναι to deposit, after θέμα, f. τιθέναι to place; see THEME, and cf. Fr. *apothème.*] **1.** *Math.* In a regular polygon : The perpendicular dropped from the centre upon one of the sides. Cf. *off-set.* **2.** The insoluble brown deposit which forms in vegetable extracts exposed to the air (Berzelius) 1859.

Apotheosis (æpopĭ·ŏsis, ăpǫ:pi,ŏ[u]·sis). 1605. [– eccl.L. *apotheosis* (Tertullian) – Gr. ἀποθέωσις, f. ἀποθεοῦν deify, f. θεός god.] **1.** The action of ranking, or fact of being ranked, among the gods; deification; divine status. **2.** The exaltation of any person, principle, practice, etc.; the canonization of saints; a deified ideal 1651. **3.** *loosely*, Ascension to glory, release from life; resurrection 1649.

1. That which the Grecians call *Apotheosis*. . was the supreme honour which a man could attribute unto man BACON. **2.** The a. of Milton 1739, of familiar abuses COLERIDGE. **3.** His Majesties Speech upon the Scaffold, and His Death or A. 1649.

Apotheosize (æpopĭ·ŏsəiz, ăpǫ·pi,osəi:z), *v.* 1760. [f. prec. + -IZE.] To elevate to, or as if to, the rank of a god; to exalt. var. **Apo·theose.**

‖ **Apothesis** (ăpǫ·pĭsis). 1811. [1. – Gr. ἀπόθεσις, lit. 'laying in store'; 2. Vitruvius's var. *apothesis* of his *apophygis*; see APOPHYGE.] **1.** (As in Gr.) The setting of a fractured or dislocated limb. **2.** *Arch.* = APOPHYGE.

Apotome (ăpǫ·tŏmi). Also **-tomy.** 1571. [– Gr. ἀποτομή cutting off, f. ἀποτέμνειν cut off; see -TOMY.] **1.** *Math.* The difference of two quantities, commensurable only in power (*i.e.* in their squares, etc.); as between $\sqrt{2}$ and 1, which is the difference between the diagonal and side of a square. **2.** *Mus.* A variety of semitone 1696.

Apo·tropous, *a.* 1880. [f. Gr. ἀπότροπος turned away (f. ἀποτρέπειν turn away) + -OUS.] *Bot.* Turned away.

Apozem (æ·pŏzĕm). *arch.* Also † **-zeme.** 1603. [– (O)Fr. *apozème* or late L. *apozema* – Gr. ἀπόζεμα decoction, f. ἀποζεῖν to boil.] *Med.* A decoction or infusion. Hence † **Apoze·mical** *a.*

† **Appai·r, apai·r,** *v.* [ME. *ampayr, apaire* – OFr. *empeir(i)er, amp-* (mod. *empirer*) :– Rom. **impejorare* for L. *pejorare* make worse, f. *pejor* worse. For the ME. pref. *a-* see A- *pref.* 10. The *-pp-* is erron., after words like *appear.*] **1.** *trans.* To IMPAIR –1643. **2.** *intr.* (refl. pron. omitted) To deteriorate –1581.

Appal, appall (ăpǭ·l), *v.* ME. [– OFr. *apal(l)ir* grow pale, be dismayed, also trans., make pale, f. *a-* AD- + *palir* (mod. *pâlir*) PALE *v.*[2]] † **1.** *intr.* To wax pale or dim ME. only; *fig.* to fail, decay –1596; to lose savour, etc., to become flat or stale (cf. PALL *v.*) –1568. † **2.** To lose heart, become dismayed 1450. † **3.** *trans.* To make pale –1583; *fig.* to cause to fade or fail, to impair –1616. † **4.** To quell (anger, pride, etc.) (*rare*) –1598. **5.** To cause the heart of (any one) to sink, to dismay 1532. Also *absol.*

5. A man. . that dare looke on that which might appall the Diuell *Macb.* III. iv. 59. *absol.* Thoughts that awe but not appal KEBLE. Hence † **Appa·l, appall** *sb.* the act of appalling; dismay (*rare*). **Appa·lled** *ppl. a.* † made pale or faint; made flat or stale (cf. PALLED); bereft of courage, etc., by sudden terror, dismayed; also *fig.* **Appa·llingly** *adv.* **Appa·lment,** consternation (*rare*).

† **Appale, apale** (ăpē[i]·l), *v.* 1500. [Doubtful whether (1) an adoption of obs. Fr. *appalir*, (2) an assimilation of APPAL *v.* to PALE *a.* or *v.*[2] or (3) an independent new formation on PALE *a.* or *v.*[2] See APPAL *v.*] **1.** *intr.* = APPAL *v.* 1. –1598. **2.** *trans.* = APPAL *v.* 3, 5. –1686.

2. Make mad the guilty and apale the free *Haml.* II. ii. 590. Hence † **Appa·lement,** the action of dismaying; dismay.

‖ **Appa·lto.** [It., f. *appaltare* let or farm out.] A monopoly. DISRAELI.

Appanage, var. of APANAGE.

Apparail, -ment, obs. f. APPAREL, etc.

† **Apparance.** *rare.* 1546. [– OFr. *aparance*, f. *aparer* prepare :– L. *apparare*; see APPARATUS.] Preparation –1594.

†**A·pparate.** *rare.* 1600. [See -ATE[1].] Anglicized f. APPARATUS.

† **Appara·tion.** 1533. [– L. *apparatio*, f. *apparare* prepare; see APPARATUS, -ION.] Preparation –1657.

Apparatus (æpărē[i]·tŏs). Pl. (*rare*) **-atus, -atuses.** 1628. [– L. *apparatus*, f. *apparare* make ready, f. *ad* AP- *pref.*[1] + *parare* PREPARE.] † **1.** The work of preparing; preparation –1722. **2.** The things collectively in which preparation consists, and by which its processes are maintained; equipments, material, machinery; material appendages or arrangements 1628. **3.** *esp.* The mechanical requisites for scientific experiments or investigations 1727; the organs by which natural processes are carried on 1718; materials for the critical study of a document 1727.

1. An a. and necessary introduction thereunto 1638. **2.** The gaudy a. of female vanity 1767. **3.** The whole a. of vision BUTLER.

Apparel (ăpæ·rĕl), *v. arch.* [ME. *aparaile* – OFr. *apareiller* (mod. *app-*) :– Rom. **adpariculare* make equal or fit, f. *ad* AP- *pref.*[1] + **pariculum* (Fr. *pareil* like), dim. of L. *par* equal.] Usually *trans.* or *refl.* † **1.** *trans.* To make ready or prepare (*for*) –1631. **2.** To furnish with things necessary ME.; † to equip for fighting –1672. **3.** To array with proper clothing; to attire. (The ordinary sense, but now *arch.*, and not in spoken use.) ME. Also *fig.* (*arch.*)

2. Ryal shippes. . ful wel arayd and enparelled and enarmed CAXTON. **3.** They which are gorgeously apparelled *Luke* 7:25. *fig.* When thou wert appareld in thy flesh TOURNEUR. Apparelled in celestial light WORDSW. Looke sweet, speake faire. . Apparell vice like vertues harbenger *Com. Err.* III. ii. 12. Hence **Appa·relment,** † preparation; *concr.* equipment, apparel (*rare*).

Apparel (ăpæ·rĕl), *sb.* ME. [– OFr. *apareil* (mod. *app-*), f. *apareiller*; see prec.] † **1.** The work of fitly preparing –1485; *concr.* materials requisites, apparatus –1725; furniture, appendages (as of a house, gun, etc.) –1535. **2.** The outfit of a ship (*arch.*) ME. **3.** Personal outfit or attire; clothing, raiment (*arch.*) ME. † **4.** Aspect –1526. **5.** † Ornament ME. only; *esp.* ornamental embroidery on certain eccles. vestments (*revived*) 1485.

1. Socrates sayde That women ben thapparayles to cacche men CAXTON. **2.** Tackle, A., Provisions, etc. 1882 (*Charter-party*). **3.** The Apparell oft proclaimes the man *Haml.* I. iii. 72. Style (the apparell of matter) 1610. **5.** The Albe. . should be made. . with apparells. . worked in silk PUGIN.

† **Appa·rence, -ance.** ME. [– OFr. *aparence, -a(u)nce*, f. *apareir* APPEAR; see -ENCE, -ANCE. Refash. as APPEARANCE, after APPEAR *v.*] **1.** = APPEARANCE (in all senses) –1686. **2.** The position of being heir apparent –1628.

Apparency (ăpē[ə]·rĕnsi, ăpæ·r-). *arch.* ME. [f. prec., or late L. *apparentia* (Tertullian); see APPEAR *v.*, -ENCY, -ANCY.] † **1.** Appearance –1684. **2.** The quality of being apparent; visibility; show of reason 1604. **3.** The position of being heir apparent 1741.

Apparent (ăpē[ə]·rĕnt, ăpæ·r-), *a.* ME. [– OFr. *aparant, -ent* (mod. *apparent*) – L. *apparent-*, pres. ppl. stem of *apparēre* APPEAR.] **1.** Meeting the eyes, showing itself; visible, plainly seen (*arch.*). † **2.** Conspicuous –1603. **3.** Manifest to the understanding; evident, obvious; palpable ME. † **4.** Likely so far as appearances go –1754. **5.** Seeming, as distinct from (though not necessarily opposed to) what really *is*. Contrasted with *real*. (The commonest sense now.) 1645. † **6.** *sb.* [by ellipsis.] An heir apparent. Also *fig.* –1646.

1. An Owl-eyed buzzard that. . sees not things apparent WITHER. **3.** The mind is repelled by useless and a. falsehood JOHNSON. In *Heir apparent*, etc.: Manifest, evident; applied to one who will undoubtedly inherit, if he survive the present possessor; opp. to heir *presumptive*. **4.** The three a. candidates are Fox, Pitt, and Murray H. WALPOLE. **5.** His real merit, and a. fidelity GIBBON. **6.** Next to thy selfe, and my young Rouer, he's Apparant to my heart *Wint. T.* I. ii. 178. Hence †**Appa·rent** *v.* to make a. (*rare*). **Appa·rentness** (*rare*).

Appa·rently, *adv.* ME. [f. prec. adj. + -LY².] †**1.** Evidently; visibly –1651. **2.** Evidently to the understanding; clearly 1553. **3.** Seemingly; contrasted with *really*. (See APPARENT 5.) 1566. **4.** So far as one can judge 1846.

1. The Prophets..who saw not God a. like unto Moyses HOBBES.

Apparition (æpări·ʃən). 1481. [– (O)Fr. *apparition* (in OFr. the Epiphany) or L. *apparitio* attendance, service, f. *apparit-*, pa. ppl. stem of *apparēre* appear at a summons, attend; see APPEAR *v.*, -ITION.] **1.** The action of appearing, or becoming visible 1525. **2.** *Astr.* The first appearance of a star, etc., after disappearance or occultation 1556. †**3.** The manifestation of Christ; the Epiphany; the season commemorating it –1703. **4.** *Astr.* Visibility, *esp.* of a star, planet, or comet 1601. †**5.** Semblance –1667; form or aspect –1660. **6.** That which appears; an appearance, *esp.* if remarkable or unexpected; a phenomenon 1481. **7.** *spec.* An immaterial appearance as of a real being; a spectre, phantom, ghost. (The sense now current.) 1601. Also *transf.* or *fig.* †**8.** An illusion, a sham –1679.

1. A sudden a. of the foul fiend SCOTT. The a. of a new public body in the state M. ARNOLD. **4.** The circle of *perpetual apparition*, between which and the elevated pole the stars never set HERSCHEL. **6.** The steamer was such a terrible a. to them LIVINGSTONE. **7.** I thinke it is the weakenesse of mine eyes That shapes this monstrous A. *Jul. C.* IV. iii. 277. Hence **Appari·tional** *a.* spectral, subjective.

Apparitor (ăpæ·ritəɹ). 1528. [– L. *apparitor* public servant, f. *apparit-*, pa. ppl. stem of *apparēre*; see -OR 2.] **1.** The servant or attendant of a civil or eccles. officer. **2.** *spec.* **a.** (*Rom. Antiq.*) A general name for the public servants of the Roman magistrates 1533. **b.** A beadle in a University, etc., who carries the mace 1727. **3.** *gen.* A herald, pursuivant, usher (*lit.* and *fig.*) 1561. **4.** One who appears (*rare*) 1843.

1. All the hell pestering rabble of Sommers and Apparitors MILT. **2. a.** Six hundred apparitors, who would be styled at present either secretaries, or clerks, or ushers, or messengers GIBBON.

†**Appa·ssionate,** *ppl. a.* 1580. [– It. *appassionato*.] Impassioned –1609. Hence †**Appa·ssionate** *v.* to impassion.

†**Appa·st.** 1580. [– obs. Fr. *appast* (mod. *appas, appât*) food, bait, f. *a* :– L. *ad* to + *past* :– L. *pastus* food; see REPAST.] Food, bait –1633.

‖**Appaumé** (apō·me), *ppl. a.* 1864. [Fr., f. *à* to + *paume* palm of the hand.] *Her.* With the hand open, so as to display the palm.

Appay, late-sp. of APAY *v.*

†**Appea·ch,** *v.* [ME. *apeche* (see A- *pref.* 10) – AFr. *enpecher*, OFr. *empechier* IMPEACH *v.*] **1.** To impede, delay 1460. **2.** To impeach –1650. **3.** To asperse (honour, character, etc.) –1700. **4.** To inform against (a crime, etc.) –1658. **5.** *intr.* To 'peach'. *All's Well* I. iii. 197. Hence †**Appea·cher,** one who impeaches; an informer. †**Appea·chment,** a criminal charge.

Appeal (ăpī·l), *v.* [ME. *apele* – OFr. *apeler* (mod. *appeler*) to call :– L. *appellare* accost, address, appeal to, impeach, f. *ad* AP- *pref.*¹ + *pell-* of *pellere* drive.] **I.** *trans.* To appeal a person. *Obs.* or *Hist.* **1.** To call (one) to answer before a tribunal; in *Law*: To accuse of a crime which the accuser undertakes to prove. *spec.* **a.** To impeach *of* treason. **b.** To turn 'approver', and accuse an accomplice of treason or felony. **c.** To accuse of a heinous crime, in respect of which the accuser demands reparation. *Obs.* exc. *Hist.* **2.** To challenge (*arch.*) ME. †**3.** To claim as judge (*rare*) ME. only; to call to witness (*rare*) –1649.

1. To appeale a man is as much as to accuse him COKE. **3.** To a. Cesar WYCLIF *Acts* 25:12, the testimony of God MILT.

II. *intr.* Const. *to*. **1.** To remove a case from an inferior to a higher court; also *fig.* ME. **2.** To call upon an authority for sanction or decision in one's favour ME.; also *fig.* ME. **3.** To call *to* a witness, etc., for corroboration ME. **4.** To make entreaty, or earnest request, *to* a person *for* a thing 1540. **5.** To address oneself *to* some principle, faculty, class, etc., in expectation of support 1794.

1. They appeale from custome to reason HOBBES. *fig.* To a. from Philip drunk to Philip sober. *Provb. phr. To appeal to the country* (sc. *from parliament*): to dissolve parliament after an adverse vote in the House of Commons, in order to take the sense of the constituencies on the question. **2.** *fig.* To a. to the sword MACAULAY. **3.** I a. to the judicious observers for the truth, etc. STEELE. **4.** I appell to your Highnes for mercy T. CROMWELL. **5.** He appealed to their sense of feudal honour FREEMAN. Pictures a. to the eye, arguments to the reason (*mod.*).

III. *trans.* To appeal a thing. To remove to a higher tribunal 1481.

To a. a case of taste to a court of final judicature LOWELL. Hence **Appea·lable** *a.* that can be appealed against, or *to*. **Appea·ler,** one who makes an appeal, or brings an accusation. **Appea·lingly** *adv.* imploringly. **Appea·lingness.**

Appeal (ăpī·l), *sb.* ME. [– OFr. *apel* (mod. *appel*), f. *apeler*; see prec.] **1.** A calling to account before a legal tribunal; in *Law*: A criminal accusation made by one who undertook under penalty to prove it. See APPEAL *v.* 1. *Obs.* exc. *Hist.* †**2.** A challenge –1700. **3.** The transference of a case from an inferior to a higher court; the application for such transference; the transferred case ME. *transf.* as *an appeal to the country* 1799. **4.** The call to an authority for vindication, or to a witness for corroboration. Cf. APPEAL *v.* 5, 6. 1626. **5.** A call for help, etc.; an entreaty 1859. **6.** Language addressed *to*, or likely to influence, some particular principle, faculty, class, etc. 1833.

1. Aumerle is guiltie of my true Appeale *Rich. II*, IV. i. 79. An a. of treason TOMLINS, of felony COX. **3.** *Court of Appeal*: a court for re-hearing cases previously tried in inferior courts. **4.** They saw no hope but in an a. to arms FREEMAN.

Appear (ăpiᵊ·ɹ), *v.* [ME. *apere* – *aper-*, tonic stem of OFr. *apareir*, (mod. *apparoir*) :– L. *apparēre*, f. *ad* AP- *pref.*¹ + *parēre* come into view.] **1.** To come forth into view, as from concealment, or from a distance; to become visible. **2.** To be in sight, be visible ME. **3.** To present oneself formally before a tribunal; *hence*, to act as counsel ME. **4.** To come before the public in any character or capacity; to come out 1607. **5.** To be plainly set forth in a document; to be declared; to occur 1531. **6.** To be plain, manifest ME; *impers.* ME. **7.** To be in one's opinion; to seem. Also *impers.* ME. **8.** To seem, as distinguished from *to be*; to be to the superficial observer 1599.

1. The Dutch begin to a. again near Gravesend MARVELL. Aperede an ongel of heuene in here slepe ME. **3.** Mr. —— appeared for the prosecution (*mod.*). **4.** To a. at St. James's Coffee House ADDISON, in print POPE. **5.** As more large apperyth in for-sayde autoryte 1531. **6.** It doth appeare, you are a worthy Judge *Merch. V.* IV. i. 236. **8.** That they may appeare vnto men to fast *Matt.* 6:16. Hence †**Appea·r** *sb.* appearance (*rare*). **Appea·rer** (senses 1, 3). **Appea·ringly** *adv.* seemingly.

Appearance (ăpiᵊ·răns). [ME. *aparaunce*, APPARENCE – OFr. *aparance*, *-ence* (mod. *apparence*) :– late L. *apparentia*, f. *apparent-*, pres. ppl. stem of L. *apparēre*; assim. in form to prec.] **1.** The action of appearing (see APPEAR 1). **2.** The action of appearing formally; *esp.* in a court to answer or prosecute a suit or charge; called *making* or *putting in* an appearance ME. **3.** The action of coming before the public, etc., in any character 1671; the coming out of a book 1882. **4.** Occurrence in a document 1868. **5.** Show, parade 1591. **6.** Appearing or seeming to be; semblance ME.; †likelihood –1793; †*subjectively*, perception –1627. **7.** Apparent form, look, aspect ME.; *pl.* the general 'look' of things 1677. **8.** *esp.* as opp. to *reality*: Outward look or show ME. **9.** *concr.* That which appears, or meets the view; *esp.* a natural phenomenon 1666; an apparition 1470.

1. The a. of the fleet was unlooked for FREEMAN. **2.** All men must put in a personal a. at the last Assize SPURGEON. **3.** The gravity of my behaviour at my very first a. in the world ADDISON. **5.** All who pretend to make an A. STEELE. **6.** *To all appearance*: so far as appears to any one. With the a. of safety SMEATON. **7.** Thou hast a grim apparence *Coriol.* IV. v. 66. *pl.* Appearances are all in your favour (*mod.*). **8.** To preserve an a. of consistency PALEY. *To save* or *keep up appearances*: to maintain artificially the outward signs. **9.** Natural appearances COWPER. Whose..sword Had three times slaine th' a. of the King 2 *Hen. IV*, I. ii. 128. var. †**Appea·rency.**

Appeasable (ăpī·zăb'l), *a.* 1549. [– OFr. *apaisable*; see APPEASE and -ABLE.] Capable of being appeased.

Appease (ăpī·z), *v.* [ME. *apese* – AFr. *apeser*, OFr. *apaisier* (mod. *apaiser*), f. *a* AD- + *pais* PEACE *sb.*] **1.** To bring to peace, settle (strife, etc.); †to calm (persons) –1774. Also *fig.* **2.** To pacify (anger, etc.); also *fig.*; to propitiate (him who is angry) ME. **3.** To assuage, allay, or relieve ME. **4.** To pacify, by satisfying demands (*lit.* and *fig.*) 1548. Also †*refl.* and †*intr.* in all senses.

1. To a. a mutiny BACON, a disordred city KNOLLES. **2.** To a. enmity by blandishments and bribes JOHNSON, the incensed Father MILT. *P.L.* v. 846. **3.** To a. anxiety 1828. **4.** To apease mennes bodyly thruste CAXTON. Bacchus appeased him [Vulcan] with wine NEWTON. Hence **Appea·ser,** one who or that which appeases. †**Appea·sive** *a.* tending to appease (*rare*).

Appeasement (ăpī·zmĕnt). ME. [– OFr. *apaisement*; see APPEASE, -MENT.] **1.** The action or process of appeasing. **2.** Pacification, satisfaction 1586. var. †**Appea·se** (*rare*).

Appellant (ăpe·lănt). 1480. [– (O)Fr. *appellant*, pres. pple. of *appeler* APPEAL.]

A. *adj.* **1.** *Law* and *gen.* Appealing: **a.** accusing, challenging; **b.** appealing to a higher tribunal; **c.** asking or crying for aid. 1593. **2.** *Law.* Appellate 1818.

B. *sb.* **1.** One who appeals another of treason, etc.; see APPEAL *v.* 1. *Obs.* exc. *Hist.* Hence, †A challenger –1671. **2.** One who APPEALS (senses II, 1, 2) 1611. **b.** *Ch. Hist.* in pl. The Jansenists and others who appealed to a general council against the 'Unigenitus' bull 1753. **3.** One who APPEALS (senses II. 3, 4) 1704.

1. Answer thy a... Who now defies thee thrice to single fight MILT. *Sams.* 1220. **3.** An humble..a. for the laurel SWIFT.

Appellate (ăpe·lĕt). 1726. [– L. *appellatus*, pa. pple. of *appellare* APPEAL; see -ATE².] *ppl. a.* Appealed to; taking cognizance of appeals 1768. †*sb.* One who is appealed against (*rare*) 1726.

Appellate (æ·pĕleⁱt), *v. rare.* 1765. [See prec., -ATE³.] To call, designate.

Appellation (æpĕlēⁱ·ʃən). ME. [– (O)Fr. *appellation* – L. *appellatio*, f. as prec. + *-io* -ION.] †**1.** (f. OFr. *apeler.*) = APPEAL *sb.* 3 (–1679); the action of appealing or calling on –1671. **2.** (f. Fr. *appeler*, or L. *appellare.*) Calling by a name, nomenclature 1581. **3.** A designation or name given to a person, thing, or class ME.

3. Stenny, an a. he always used of and towards the Duke CLARENDON. Hence **Appella·tional** *a.*

Appellative (ăpe·lătiv). 1520. [– late L. *appellativus*, f. as prec.; see -IVE and cf. Fr. *appellatif*.] **A.** *adj.* **1.** Designating a class; *common* as opp. to *proper*. †**2.** Of the nature of an APPELLATION (sense 3) –1654. **3.** Of or pertaining to the giving of names 1860.

B. *sb.* **1.** A common noun, or name applicable to each member of a class 1591. **2.** A designation, or descriptive name 1632.

2. Wily Will justified his a. SCOTT. Hence **Appe·llatively** *adv.* as a common noun.

†**Appe·llatory,** *a.* 1553. [– late L. *appellatorius*, f. as prec. + *-orius* -ORY².] Pertaining to an appellant or an appeal –1726.

Appellee (æpĕlī·, ăpe:lī·). 1531. [– Fr. *appelé*, pa. pple. of *appeler* APPEAL; see -EE¹.] *Law.* **1.** One who is appealed against. (See APPEAL *v.* I. 1, 2.) †**2.** The defendant in an appeal; now called the *respondent*. COTGR.

Appellor (ăpe·lǭ:ɹ, æ:pelǭ·ɹ). ME. [– AFr. *apelour*, = OFr. *apeleor* :– L. *appellator* appellant, f. *appellat-*, pa. ppl. stem of *appellare* APPEAL; see -OR 2.] One who accuses of crime, challenges, or informs against an accomplice.

Appenage, obs. f. APANAGE.

† **Appe·nd,** *v.*[1] ME. [– OFr. *apendre* depend on, belong to :– L. *appendere* (in cl. L. only trans.) for *appendĕre*, f. *ad* AP- *pref.*[1] + *pendĕre* hang (intr.). Not conn. in Eng. w. APPEND *v.*[2]] *intr.* To belong, pertain, or be proper *to* –1470. Hence **Appe·nding** *ppl. a.* = APPENDANT.

Append (ăpe·nd), *v.*[2] 1646. [– L. *appendere* hang to, f. *ad* AP- *pref.*[1] + *pendere* hang.] *trans.* **1.** To hang on, attach as a pendant 1646. **2.** To attach as an accessory 1779, or as an appendix 1843.

2. Some additional remarks..are appended MILL.

Appendage (ăpe·ndėdʒ). 1649. [f. prec. + -AGE.] **1.** That which is attached as if by being hung on; a subsidiary, but not an essential, adjunct 1713; *esp.* an addition to territory or property 1667; *Nat. Hist.* a subsidiary organ 1785. Also *transf.* of persons 1838.

1. Dwelling-houses and their appendages 1876. Antennæ and other appendages used for feeling 1874. The dance..being..merely an a. to the Song 1763. Hence **Appe·ndaged** *ppl. a.* having an a.

Appendance, -ence (ăpe·ndĕns). 1523. [– OFr. *apendance*, f. *apendre* APPEND *v.*[1]; see -ANCE.] †**1.** A dependent possession –1662. †**2.** An extraneous adjunct or concomitant –1677. **3.** *Law.* The fact of being appendant 1832.

† **Appe·ndancy, -ency.** 1615. [f. as prec.; see -ENCY, -ANCY.] **1.** The quality or state of being appendant 1641. **2.** = APPENDANCE 2. –1669.

Appendant, -ent (ăpe·ndĕnt). 1509. [– OFr. *apendant* (mod. *app-*), f. *apendre*; see APPEND *v.*[1],[2]. Orig. apprehended as f. APPEND *v.*[1], but subseq. infl. by APPEND *v.*[2]]

A. *adj.* Const. *to, on.* **1.** *Law.* Attached or belonging as an additional but subsidiary right 1523. **2.** Attached in a subordinate relation; adjunct 1577. **3.** Attendant, consequent 1509. **4.** *lit.* Hanging attached (*to*) 1576.

1. Those tenantes that haue commen appendaunt 1523. Liberties..a. to manors SELDEN. **3.** A pleasure embased with no a. sting SOUTH. **4.** The seal a. by a silken cord 1874.

B. *sb.* [the adj. used *absol.*] *arch.* **1.** *Law.* A lesser right or property attached by prescription to one more important 1525. **2.** An appendage; a dependency 1587; also *transf.* of persons 1641. **3.** A consequent quality, property, principle, etc. 1587. **4.** An appendix; a pendant 1570.

3. The numerous corollaries or appendents COLERIDGE.

Appe·ndical, *a.* 1850. [f. L. *appendix, -ic-* + -AL[1].] Of the nature of an appendix.

† **Appe·ndicate,** *v. rare.* 1677. [f. as prec. + -ATE[3].] To append. Hence † **Appe:ndica·tion,** addition by way of appendix (*rare*).

† **Appe·ndice,** *v. rare.* 1661. [f. *appendice* sb.; see APPENDIX.] To add as an appendix –1702. *intr.* To form an appendix. Hence **Appe·ndicing** *ppl. a.* appendant.

Appendicitis (ăpendisəi·tis). 1886. [f. L. *appendix, -ic-* + -ITIS.] *Med.* Inflammation of the vermiform appendix of the cæcum.

Appendicle (ăpe·ndik'l). 1611. [– L. *appendicula*, dim. of *appendix, -ic-*; see -CULE.] A small appendix or appendage. Hence **Appendi·cular** *a.* belonging to, or of the nature of, an a. **Appendi·culate** *a.* furnished with appendicles; forming an a.; var. **Appendi·culated** *ppl. a.*

Appendicularian (æpĕndi:kiŭlēᵊ·riăn), *a.* 1880. [f. mod.L. *Appendicularia* (see prec.) + -AN.] *Zool.* Pertaining to the *Appendicularia*, a family of minute ascidian molluscs, with long tail-appendages. Also as *sb.*

Appendix (ăpe·ndiks), *sb.* Pl. **-ices** (-isīz) and **-ixes.** 1542. [– L. *appendix, -ic-*, f. *appendere* APPEND *v.*[2] A sing. *appendice* after Fr. occurs XVII.] = APPENDAGE, but more restricted in use. **1.** A subsidiary extraneous adjunct; a dependency. *Obs.* exc. as in 2. 1592. † *transf.* of persons –1692. **2.** An addition subjoined to a document or book, having some contributory value, but not essential to completeness 1549. **3.** *Biol.* A small process developed from the surface of any organ 1615. †**4.** A subsidiary accompaniment; an accessory –1699.

1. Normandy, once an A. of the Crown of England HOWELL. My children..are but the Appendixes of me 1692. **2.** Towards the end whereof is an A. or Postscript 1638. **4.** Idleness is an a. to nobility BURTON.

Appendix (ăpe·ndiks), *v. rare.* 1755. [f. the sb.] To add as an appendix. Hence **Appe·ndixed** *ppl. a.*

Appennage, obs. f. APANAGE.

Appense (ăpe·ns), *a. rare.* 1829. [– L. *appensus*, pa. pple. of *appendere* APPEND *v.*[2]] *Bot.* Hung up, pendulous.

† **Appe·ntice.** *rare.* 1616. [– Fr. *appentis*, OFr. *apentis*, whence aphetic PENTICE; see PENTHOUSE, -ICE.] A lean-to building, a penthouse.

† **Apperceive,** *v.* [ME. *aperceive* – tonic stem of OFr. *aperceveir* (mod. *apercevoir*) :– Rom. **appercipēre* for **appercipĕre*, f. *ad-* AP- *pref.*[1] + *percipere* PERCEIVE.] To perceive, recognize, notice –1614.

Apperception (æpəɹse·pʃən). 1753. [– Fr. *aperception* – mod.L. *apperceptio* (Leibnitz); see AD-, AP-, PERCEPTION.] *Metaph.* **1.** The mind's perception of itself as a conscious agent; self-consciousness. **2.** Mental perception, recognition 1839.

1. A...by which we are conscious of our own existence, and conscious of our own perceptions REID.

† **Appe·ril.** *rare.* 1607. [f. A- *pref.* 11 + PERIL *sb.*] Peril –1632.

Faith, I will bail him, at mine own a. B. JONS.

Appertain (æpəɹtēⁱ·n), *v.* ME. [– OFr. *apartenir* (mod. *app-*) :– Rom. **appartenēre* for late L. *appertinēre*, f. *ad* AP- *pref.*[1] + *pertinēre* PERTAIN.] **1.** *intr.* To belong as parts to the whole, or as members to a family or class, and hence, to the head of the family; to be related, akin *to* 1450. **2.** To belong, or be suited, proper, or appropriate *to* ME. **3.** To pertain, relate ME. † *impers.* –1623. † *absol. As appertains*: as is proper –1611. †**4.** *trans.* (*to* omitted.) To belong to, befit –1601.

1. All the men that appertained unto Korah *Numb.* 16:32. **2.** Do all rites, That appertaine unto a buriall *Much Ado* IV. i. 210. Hence † **Appertai·nance,** var. of APPURTENANCE. † **Appertai·nment** (*rare*) *Tr. & Cr.* II. iii. 87. **Appertinance, -ence,** obs. ff. APPURTENANCE. **Appe·rtinent,** var. of APPURTENANT, esp. in the non-legal sense.

† **Appertise, -yse.** 1480. [– (O)Fr. *apertise*, f. *apert*; see APERT.] Evidence of skill, *esp.* in arms.

† **Appe·te,** *v.* ME. [– (O)Fr. *appéter* – L. *appetere* strive after, f. *ad-* AP- *pref.*[1] + *petere* seek.] To seek after, desire –1685.

Appetence (æ·pĭtĕns). 1610. [– Fr. *appétence* or L. *appetentia* longing after, f. *appetere*; see prec., -ENCE.] The action of seeking for; appetite, desire.

Appetency (æ·pĭtĕnsi). 1627. [– L. *appetentia*; see prec., -ENCY.] **1.** *strictly*, The state of longing for, desiring; appetite, passion. Also = APPETENCE. Const. *of, for, after.* 1631. **2.** Instinctive inclination or propensity 1802. **3.** Of things inanimate: Natural tendency, affinity 1627. **4.** *Metaph.* Suggested by Sir W. Hamilton as a term including both desire and volition 1836.

1. Brutish appetencies 1652. An a. after literary distinction MASSON.

Appetent (æ·pĭtĕnt). ME. [– *appetent-*, pa. ppl. stem of L. *appetere*; see APPETE *v.*, -ENT.] **1.** Longing, eagerly desirous. Const. *after, of.* **2.** *Metaph.* Connected with desire and volition 1837.

1. A. after glory and renown 1646.

Appetible (æ·pĭtib'l), *a.* 1471. [– L. *appetibilis* desirable, f. *appetere*; see APPETE *v.*, -IBLE.] *adj.* †**1.** Attractive. **2.** Worthy of being sought after; desirable 1622. † Also as *sb.* SOUTH.

2. The a. fruit 1847. Hence **A:ppetibi·lity.** ? *Obs.*

† **Appeti·sse,** *v.* [– Fr. *appetisser* (COTGR.), OFr. *apeticier* diminish, f. *a-* :– L. *ad* + *petit* small.] To make small. CAXTON.

Appetite (æ·pĭtəit), *sb.* [ME. *apetyte* – OFr. *apetit* (mod. *appétit*) – L. *appetitus*, f. *appetere* seek after, f. *ad-* AP- *pref.*[1] + *petere* seek.] Const. *for*; formerly *to, of,* and *inf.* **1.** Bent of the mind; desire, inclination, disposition. **2.** *vaguely,* Inclination, preference, liking, fancy (*arch.*) 1490. **3.** *esp.* The determinate desire to satisfy the natural necessities, or fulfil the natural functions, of the body; one of those instinctive cravings which secure the preservation of the individual and the race ME. **4.** *spec.* Craving for food, hunger. Also *fig.* ME. **5.** Capacity for, or feeling as regards, food; relish ME. †**6.** Of things: Natural tendency towards –1667. **7.** The object of desire (*arch.*) ME. **8.** A whet. (So in Fr.) 1693.

1. Obeying without reflection the a. of the moment GROTE. Such an a. for consolation SHERIDAN. **2.** *To* or *after one's appetite*: just as one pleases. **3.** The most violent Appetites in all Creatures are Lust and Hunger ADDISON. **4.** Now good digestion waite on A., And health on both *Macb.* III. iv. 38. **5.** I have seen a Man in Love.. lose his A. ADDISON. Hence † **A·ppetite** *v.* to have an a. for; to satisfy. **A·ppetited** *ppl. a.* furnished with an a.

Appetition (æpĭti·ʃən). 1603. [– L. *appetitio* strong desire after, f. *appetit-*, pa. ppl. stem of *appetere*; see APPETE *v.*, -ION.] The direction of desire towards an object or purpose; seeking after.

Appetitive (æ·pĭtəitiv, ăpe·tĭtiv), *a.* 1577. [– Fr. *appétitif, -ive* or med.L. *appetitivus*; see APPETITE, -IVE.] **1.** Characterized by appetite. **2.** Giving an appetite; attractive (*rare*) 1864.

Appetize (æ·pĭtəiz), *v. rare.* [Back-formation from *appetizing* – (O)Fr. *appétissant*, w. ending assim. to -IZE, -ING[2].] To give appetite, to cause relish for food. Hence **A·ppetized** *ppl. a.* furnished with an appetite. **A·ppetizement,** hunger (*rare*). **A·ppetizer,** a whet or stimulant to appetite. **A·ppetizing** *ppl. a.* exciting a desire, *esp.* for food; stimulating the appetite. **Appeti·zingly** *adv.*

Applaud (ăplǭ·d), *v.* 1536. [– L. *applaudere*, f. *ad* AP- *pref.*[1] + *plaudere* to clap, partly after Fr. *applaudir.*] **1.** *intr.* To clap the hands in expression of approbation; *hence,* to express approval loudly 1598. †**2.** To applaud *to*: To give approbation *to* –1685; to express agreement with –1635. **3.** *trans.* To express approval of audibly, or in any way 1591.

1. Caps, hands, and tongues, a. it to the clouds *Haml.* IV. v. 107. **3.** I would a. thee to the very Eccho, That should a. again *Macb.* V. iii. 54. O that our Fathers would a. our loues *Two Gent.* I. iii. 48. Hence † **Applau·d** *sb.* applause. **Applau·ded** *ppl. a.* loudly approved. **Applau·der.** **Applau·dingly** *adv.*

Applause (ăplǭ·z), *sb.* 1596. [– L. *applausus*, f. *applaus-*, pa. ppl. stem of *applaudere* (prec.).] **1.** Approbation loudly expressed 1596; marked approval or commendation 1601. †**2.** Agreement or assent. Cf. APPLAUD *v.* 2. *rare.* 1612. †**3.** The object of applause 1623.

1. Hearing a. and vniversall shout *Merch. V.* III. ii. 144. The Censures and Applauses of Men 1714. **3.** The applause! delight! the wonder of our stage B. JONS. Hence † **Applau·sible** *a.* worthy to be applauded (*rare*).

Applausive (ăplǭ·siv), *a.* 1605. [f. as prec. + -IVE; cf. med.L. *applausivus* favourable.] **1.** Loudly expressive of approbation 1609; approbative 1628. †**2.** Worthy of applause –1607. Hence **Applau·sively** *adv.*

Apple (æp'l). [OE. *æppel*, corresp. to OFris., OS., (M)Du. *appel*, OHG. *apful* (G. *apfel*), ON. *epli* (n.), Crim. Goth. *apel* :– Gmc. **aplu-*, rel. to **ab(a)la*, **ablu-*, repr. by IE. cogns.] **1.** The round firm fleshy fruit of a Rosaceous tree (*Pyrus malus*), found wild, as the Crab-apple, in Europe, etc., and cultivated in innumerable varieties all over the two Temperate Zones OE.; short for APPLE-TREE 1626. **2.** Any fruit, or similar vegetable production; esp. such as in some respect resemble the Apple OE.; *Bot.* any fruit of the structure of the Apple; a pome 1729. **3.** Hence forming part of many names of fruits; as † **Apple Punic,** the pomegranate; **Apple of Sodom,** or *Dead Sea Fruit*, of fair appearance externally, but turning, when grasped, into smoke and ashes; supposed by some to be the fruit of *Solanum sodomeum*, by others of *Calotropis procera*; *fig.* any hollow disappointing thing ME.; **Apple of Adam** = ADAM'S APPLE;

Apple of Love = LOVE-APPLE. **4.** The fruit of the 'forbidden tree' (Milton) OE. **5.** Anything like an apple in form or colour, as *Golden Apple*: the Orb in the British Regalia OE.

1. A goodly a. rotten at the heart *Merch. V.* I. iii. 102. There's small choise in rotten apples *Tam. Shr.* I. i. 139. **2.** The fruit or apples of Palm-trees TOPSELL. **5.** A round bal or hollow a. of glasse 1601.

Phrases: **Apple of discord:** the golden a. inscribed 'For the fairest', thrown by Eris, the personification of discord, into the assembly of the gods, and contended for by Juno, Minerva, and Venus; whence, any subject of dissension. **Apple of the eye:** the pupil, which was supposed to be a globular solid body. Used as a symbol of that which is most cherished.

Combs.: **a.-aphis,** the insect (*Lachnus lanigerus*) which produces **a.-blight,** a cottony substance found on trees; **-brandy,** a spirit distilled from cider; **-corer**; **-eating** *a., fig.* easily tempted; † **-fallow** *a.*, yellowish-red, bay; **-fly,** a small green fly found sometimes within an apple; † **-garth,** an orchard; † **-gray** *a.*, streaky in colour like an a.; **-jack,** U.S. name for *a.-brandy*; **-moth,** *Tortrix pomana*; **-shell, -snail,** a family of Gasteropods, so named from their shape; † **-squire,** a pimp; **-tree**; **-wife, -woman,** one who keeps a stall for the sale of apples; **-worm,** the maggot bred in apples; † **-yard** = *-garth*.

To upset the apple-cart: see UPSET *v.*

Apple (æp'l), *v. rare.* OE. [f. the sb.] **1.** To form or turn into apples; to bear apples. **2.** *intr.* To gather apples 1799.

A·pple-John. Also **John-Apple.** 1597. [f. St. John's Day, when it is ripe.] An apple said to keep two years, and to be ripe when much withered.

A dish of Apple-Iohns 2 *Hen. IV*, II. iv. 5.

Apple-pie. 1590. A pie made with apples; *transf.* the Willow-herb.

Apple-pie bed: a bed in which, as a practical joke, the sheets are so folded that a person cannot get his legs down. *Apple-pie order*: complete order. [Explained as '*Cap-a-pie-order*', but this phr. is not found.]

† **Appli·able,** *a.* 1499. [f. APPLY *v.* + -ABLE; earlier than APPLICABLE.] **1.** Ready to apply oneself *to*; docile, well-disposed –1699. Hence **2.** Capable of being APPLIED; having reference –1679. Hence † **Appli·ableness.** † **Appli·ably** *adv.*

Appliance (ăplǝi·ăns). 1561. [f. APPLY *v.* + -ANCE.] † **1.** Compliance; subservience –1603. **2.** The action of applying 1561. **3.** A thing applied as means to an end; apparatus 1597.

1. Too noble, to conserue a life In base appliances *Meas. for M.* III. i. 89. **2.** Acted-on. . by the a. of birch-rods CARLYLE. **3.** Aske God for Temp'rance; that's th' a. onely which your disease requires *Hen. VIII*, I. i. 124. Hence **Appli·ancy,** adaptability, pliancy (*rare*).

† **Appli·ant,** *a.* ME. [– OFr. *apliant*, pres. pple. of *aplier*; see APPLY *v.*, -ANT.] Pliant; diligent; pertinent *to* (*rare*).

Applicable (æ·plikăb'l), *a.* 1563. [– (O)Fr. *applicable* or med.L. *applicabilis*; see APPLY *v.*, -ABLE.] † **1.** = APPLIABLE 1. –1674. **2.** Capable of being applied; having reference. (See APPLY *v.*) 1660. **3.** Fit or suitable 1835. Hence **A·pplicableness** (*rare*), **Appli:cabi·lity.**

Applicant (æ·plikant), *a.* (*sb.*) 1485. [orig. – OFr. *aplicant* pleader; in mod. use based on APPLICATION; see -ANT.] † **1.** Pliant, docile (*rare*). **2.** Applying (*rare*). **3.** *sb.* One who applies or makes request 1485.

Applicate (æ·plikeⁱt, -ĕt). 1534. [– L. *applicatus*, pa. pple. of *applicare*; see APPLY *v.*, -ATE².] **A.** *adj.* † **1.** Closely adapted, suited; inclined towards 1652. **2.** Put to practical use; applied, concrete 1796.

2. A. number = concrete HUTTON.

B. *sb.* **1.** In Conic Sections: An ordinate 1706. **2.** An applied department; an application 1855.

2. Geometry and its applicates 1855.

† **A·pplicate,** *v.* 1531. [– *applicat-*, pa. ppl. stem of L. *applicare*; see APPLY *v.*, -ATE³.] By-form of APPLY.

Application (æplikēⁱ·ʃǝn). 1493. [– (O)Fr. *application* – L. *applicatio* joining or attaching (oneself) to – *applicat-*, pa. ppl. stem of *applicare*; see APPLY *v.*, -ION.] The action of applying; the thing applied. **1.** The action of putting a thing to another 1632; *esp.* in *Geom.* 1727. **2.** The putting on of a medicament; the remedy so applied 1601. **3.** The bringing of anything to bear practically upon another; *spec.* in *Theol.* of 'the redemption purchased by Christ' 1647. **4.** The putting of anything to a use or purpose; employment 1538. **5.** The bringing of a general or figurative statement to bear upon a particular case, or upon matters of practice; the moral of a fable 1493; the capacity of being thus used; relevancy 1842. **6.** The action of applying one's self closely *to* a task, diligence 1605; the object of such diligence 1734. † **7.** Obsequiousness 1605. **8.** *Astr.* The action of approaching. ? *Obs.* 1594. **9.** The action of making an † appeal, request, or petition *to* a person; the request so made 1647.

1. The place of a. of a force 1879. **2.** Application Of Medicines to th' Imagination BUTLER *Hud.* II. iii. 287. **3.** A sufficient a. of legal penalties MILL. **4.** The a. of the loadstone to navigation 1794. **5.** The a. of the Law to the present case HOBBES. A parable, related without any a. or moral BUTLER. This has no a. to present circumstances 1888. **6.** A. for ever so short a time kills me LAMB. **9.** Frequent applications to God in prayer BP. BURNET.

Applicative (æ·plikeⁱtiv, -ĕtiv), *a.* 1638. [f. L. *applicat-* (see prec.) + -IVE; cf. Fr. *applicatif*.] Characterized by being put into actual contact with anything 1680; practical 1638. Hence **A·pplicatively** *adv.* practically.

Applicator (æ·plikeⁱtǝɹ). *rare.* 1659. [f. as prec. + -OR 2.] He who (*obs.*) or that which applies.

Applicatory (æ·plikatǝ̆ɹi), *a.* 1540. [f. as prec. + -ORY¹,².] Having the property of applying to practical use; † applicable 1649; † making application or request –1673. † As *sb.* A means of applying to practical use –1667. Hence **A·pplicato:rily** *adv.* by way of application or request.

Applied (ăplǝi·d), *ppl. a.* 1500. [f. APPLY *v.* + -ED¹.] † **1.** Folded (*rare*). **2.** Put to practical use; practical, as opp. to *abstract* or *theoretical* 1656. Hence † **Appli·edly** *adv.* (*rare*).

Appli·er. 1565. [f. APPLY *v.* + -ER¹.] He who, or that which, applies.

† **Appli·que, -i·ke,** *v.* 1483. [– Fr. *appliquer*, OFr. *apliquier* – L. *applicare*; see APPLY *v.*] By-form of APPLY *v.*

‖ **Appliqué** (aplike), *sb.* 1841. [Fr., pa. pple. of *appliquer* (prec.) used as sb.] Work applied to or laid on another material; *spec.* a trimming cut out in outline and laid on another surface. Also in metal-work. Hence **Appliquéd.**

Applot (ăplǫ·t), *v.* 1647. [f. PLOT, app. after *lot, allot*.] To divide into plots or parts; to apportion. Hence **Applo·tment,** apportionment.

Apply (ăplǝi·), *v.* [ME. *aplie* – OFr. *aplier* :– L. *applicare*, f. *ad-* AP- *pref.*¹ + *plicare* to fold.] **I.** To put a thing into practical contact with another. **1.** *trans.* To bring into contact; to put close *to*; *esp.* in *Geom.* 1660. † **2.** *intr.* To come into, or be in, contact –1793. **3.** *trans.* To place (a plaster, etc.) in contact with the body; *hence*, to administer any remedy 1541; *fig.* to bring (a thing) to bear upon 1596. **4.** To appropriate *to* 1460; to put to use, dispose of 1502. **5.** To use (a word) in special reference *to* (a thing) 1628. **6.** To bring (a law, test, etc.) into contact with facts, to put into practical operation 1586. **7.** To refer (a general or figurative statement) *to* a particular instance ME. **8.** *intr.* To have a valid reference *to* 1790. † **9.** *trans.* To refer, ascribe –1709; to compare, liken –1661

1. He shal applie to hym hooli men WYCLIF *Numb.* 16:5. To a. light, heat, a foot-rule *to* (*mod.*). **3.** A. the iuyce to any wound 1579. To a. comfort to him who is not. . ready for it FULLER. **4.** To a. the Poll money to the use of the warre MARVELL. **6.** The Difficulty is how to a. this Rule SHERLOCK. **7.** I leave you to a. the remark FORDYCE. **8.** It will a. no less to our own case1866.

II. To bring oneself into close contact with a pursuit. **1.** To give or devote (any faculty) assiduously *to*, or *to do* 1450; also *refl.* and *intr.* † **2.** *trans.* To handle vigorously; to wield, practise. Replaced by PLY. –1667. † **3.** To keep at (a person) *with*. See PLY. –1594.

1. That we may applie oure hertes vnto wyssdome *Ps.* 89:12. Let your remembrance a. to Banquo *Macb.* III. ii. 30. **2.** The birds thir quire a. MILT.

III. To bend, conform, or adapt *to*. *trans.*, † *refl.*, and † *intr.* ME.

Wholy applyinge himselfe to the Kings humour 1533.

IV. To bend or direct *to*. (Cf. L. *applicare* (*navem*), and ACCOST, ADDRESS.) † **1.** To bring (a ship) to land; to direct or steer (her course, one's course, etc.) –1613; *intr.* to land; to steer, go –1819. † **2.** *trans.* To address or direct (words) to –1744. **3.** *intr.* with *to*. † **a.** To appeal to. **b.** To address oneself for information or aid. Also *refl.* 1642.

3. b. Exiles, who had come. . to a. for succour MACAULAY. Hence **Apply·ing** *vbl. sb.* application; plying. † **Apply·ment** = APPLICATION, APPLIANCE.

‖ **Appoggiatura** (appo:ddʒătū·ră). 1753. [It. Cf. Fr. APPUI.] *Mus.* A grace-note or passing tone prefixed as a support to an essential note of a melody. *transf.* A prop, a point of support.

Appoint (ăpoi·nt), *v.* [ME. *apoint(e* – OFr. *apointer*, f. *à point* to a point, into condition; see POINT *sb.*¹] **I.** To come, or bring matters, to a point. **1.** *intr.* (and *pass.*) † To arrange definitely –1660; to make an appointment (*arch.*) 1509; *trans.* to arrange (*arch.*) 1588; to make an appointment for a meeting with 1528. **2.** † *refl.* and *pass.* To make up one's mind –1586; *intr.* to resolve (*arch.*) 1440.

1. Apointed to be playd to Morowe night 1604. **2.** The Lord had appointed to defeate the good counsell of Ahithophel 2 *Sam.* 17:14.

II. To determine authoritatively. **1.** *trans.* To fix (a time, *later* a place) for any act ME.; to fix **a.** *that* it shall be, **b.** a thing 1538. † **2.** To grant authoritatively –1764. **3.** *Law.* To declare an appointment under a power. (See APPOINTMENT 5.) 1601. **4.** To ordain, devote, destine (a person or thing) *to* or *for* (*arch.*); *to do* or *suffer* (*arch.*) 1496. **5.** To ordain, set up, nominate 1460.

1. The time appointed for execution DE FOE. T' a. Who should attend on him *Hen. VIII*, I. i. 74. **4.** The Creator. . has appointed every thing to a certain Use BUDGELL. Appointed to be tried DE FOE. **5.** Who appointed you, then ?1888. To a. a Committee ADDISON.

III. (Cf. Fr. *en bon point*.) † To put in order, make ready –1615; *esp.* to equip completely, to furnish. *Obs.* exc. in pa. pple. 1490.

Lodgings. . well-appointed 1660. Thus appointed . . he was in readiness to depart SCOTT.

IV. After Fr. and L. † **1.** To point to or at, to point out –1556. † **2.** To arraign (*rare*) –1674.

2. A. not heavenly disposition, father MILT. *Sams.* 373. Hence **Appoi·ntable** *a* (? *Obs.*) capable of being, or proper to be, appointed. **Appoi:ntee,** one who is nominated to an office, or one in whose favour a power of APPOINTMENT is exercised. **Appoi·nter,** one who ordains, or nominates. (See also APPOINTOR.)

Appoi·nt, *sb.* 1555. [f. the vb. Cf. Fr. *appoint*.] † **1.** Agreement –1565. † **2.** Equipment 1592. **3.** *Comm.* Settlement *per appoint*: Exact and independent settlement, *i.e.* not by payments on account, etc.

Appointed (ăpoi·ntĕd), *ppl. a.* 1535. [f. as prec. + -ED¹.] **1.** Fixed beforehand 1585; fixed by authority 1535. **2.** With *well, ill,* etc.: Fitted out, equipped 1535.

‖ **Appointé** (apwăṅte), *a.* 1753. [Fr.] *Her.* Touching at the point or end.

Appointment (ăpoi·ntmĕnt). ME. [– OFr. *apointement*, f. *apointer*; see APPOINT *v.* -MENT.] † **1.** The action of agreeing; a pact, contract –1745; *spec.* the act of capitulating; terms of capitulation –1605. **2.** *spec.* An agreement for a meeting; engagement, assignation 1530. † **3.** Purpose –1606. **4.** The action of ordaining what is to be done; direction, ordinance 1440. **5.** *Law.* The act of declaring the destination of any specific property, in exercise of a power conferred for that purpose 1601. **6.** The action of nominating to, or placing in, an office; the office itself 1658. **7.** Equipment, outfit, furniture, or any article thereof. Now usu. *pl.* 1575. † **8.** An allowance paid, *esp.* to a public officer –1761.

2. For missing your meetings and appointments *Merry W.* III. i. 92. **3.** No certain purpose or a. MORE. **4.** According to a natural order or a. BUTLER. **5.** An a. . . to a charitable use BLACKSTONE. **6.** A poor baronet, hoping for an a. GEO. ELIOT. **7.** I have not one a. . . which I set so much store by, as I do by these jackboots STERNE. **8.** He had the appointments of an ambassador BURNET.

Appointor (ăpoi·ntǫ̆r). 1882. [f. APPOINT *v.* + -OR 2 d.] *Law.* The legal form of APPOINTER: The person who exercises a power of appointment.

† **Appo·rt,** *sb.* ME. [– OFr. *aport* action of bringing, f. *aporter* bring to.] **1.** Demeanour –1606. **2.** *pl.* Things brought; offerings; revenues –1530. So † **Appo·rt,** *v.* to bring; *intr.* to arrive *at.*

Apportion (ăpōᵊ·ɹʃən), *v.* 1574. [– (O)Fr. *apportionner* or med.L. *apportionare*; see AP- *pref.*¹, PORTION *v.*] **1.** To assign (*to*) as a proper portion; to allot 1587. **2.** To portion out, to share 1574. **3.** To proportion (*arch.*) 1615.

1. His guardians had apportioned to him an allowance DISRAELI. **2.** To a. the expenses of production between the two MILL. Hence **Appo·rtionable** *a.*

†**Appo·rtionate,** *v.* 1523. [– *apportionat-*, pa. ppl. stem of med.L. *apportionare*; see prec., -ATE³.] = APPORTION *v.*

Apportionment (ăpōᵊ·ɹʃənmĕnt). 1628. [f. APPORTION *v.* + -MENT; cf. med.L. *apportionamentum* in Eng. law.] **1.** The act of distributing or allotting in proper shares. **2.** The state or fact of being thus distributed 1681.

† **Appo·se,** *v.*¹ [ME. *apose, opose* – OFr. *aposer*, var. of *oposer* OPPOSE. Aphet. to POSE *v.*²] **1.** To confront with objections or hard questions; to examine –1615. *absol.* and *intr.* –1581. **2.** *spec.* To examine as to accounts, to audit –1738.

1. Thus beginneth the Master to a. his Scholar 1553. I would I might a. CAMPION. Hence † **Appo·sal,** a posing question; legal examination of accounts. † **Appo·ser,** an examiner; an Exchequer officer who audited the sheriffs' accounts (till 1833).

Appose (ăpōᵘ·z, emphatic æ:pōᵘ·z), *v.*² 1593. [Formed to represent L. *apponere*; see next and cf. POSE *v.*¹] **1.** To put one thing *to* another, as a seal to a document; to put (food) before. **2.** To place in apposition or juxtaposition 1800.

1. Atrides..food sufficient Appos'd before them, and the peers appos'd their hands to it CHAPMAN.

Apposite (æ·pŏzit), *a.* 1621. [– L. *appositus*, pa. pple. of *apponere* apply, f. *ad-* AP- *pref.*¹ + *ponere* to place; see POSITION *sb.*] **1.** Well put or applied; appropriate (*to*). † **2.** Of persons: Ready with apt remarks –1788.

1. Her language is not copious but apposit HABINGTON. Hence **A·pposite-ly** *adv.*, **-ness.**

Apposition¹ (æpozi·ʃən). 1659. [– OFr. *aposicion, apposition*, var. of *opposition*, in med. L. sense of *opponere*; see APPOSE *v.*¹] A public disputation by scholars; a formal examination by question and answer; still applied to the Speech Day at St. Paul's School, London.

Apposition² (æpozi·ʃən). ME. [– Fr. *apposition* or late L. *appositio*, f. *apposit-*, pa. ppl. stem of *apponere*; see APPOSITE *a.*, -ION.] **1.** The action of apposing (see APPOSE² 1); application 1541; † that which is apposed, an addition –1655. **2.** The placing of things in contact, or side by side 1660; the being so placed, juxtaposition, parallelism 1606. † **3.** *Rhet.* The addition of a parallel word, etc., by way of explanation or illustration of another –1638. **4.** *Gram.* The placing of a word beside, or in syntactic parallelism with, another; *spec.* the addition of one sb. to another, or to a noun clause, as an attribute or complement; the position of the sb. so placed 1440.

1. By the A. of a Publick Seal 1726. **2.** The cut surfaces and edges of the wounds are to be brought into a. T. BRYANT. **4.** In various forms of a., especially that of the word to the sentence JOWETT. Hence **Apposi·tional** *a.* of or belonging to a.; **-ly** *adv.*

Appositive (ăpǫ·zitiv), *a.* 1693. [– late L. *appositivus* subsidiary (Priscian), f. as prec.; see -IVE.] Of, pertaining to, or standing in apposition. Also as *sb.* Hence **Appo·sitively** *adv.* in a. construction.

Appraisal (ăprēⁱ·zăl). 1817. [f. next + -AL¹ 2.] The act of appraising; the setting of a price. Also *fig.*

Appraise (ăprēⁱ·z), *v.* 1535. [alt., by assimilation to PRAISE *v.*, of APPRIZE *v.*²] **1.** To fix a price for; *esp.* as an official valuer. **2.** *transf.* To estimate the amount, or worth of. Also *refl.* 1841.

1. All this morning at Pegg Kite's..appraising her goods that her mother has left PEPYS. **2.** Appraised his [the infant's] weight TENNYSON. Hence **Apprai·sable** *a.* **Apprai·singly** *adv.*

Appraisement (ăprēⁱ·zmĕnt). 1642. [f. prec. + -MENT.] **1.** The action of appraising; valuation by an official appraiser. **2.** Estimated value 1703. **3.** *transf.* Estimation of worth generally 1858.

Appraiser (ăprēⁱ·zəɹ). 1529. [f. as prec. + -ER¹.] One who appraises: *spec.* a licensed valuer. Also *transf.*

The appraisers sworn to appraise goods sold under distress for rent 1857.

† **A·pprecate,** *v. rare.* 1631. [– *apprecat-*, pa. ppl. stem of L. *apprecari* pray to, f. *ad-* AP- *pref.*¹ + *precari* pray.] To pray for, devoutly wish, *to* –1674. Hence † **Appreca·tion.** † **A·pprecatory** *a.* intercessory.

Appreciable (ăprī·ʃi,ăb'l), *a.* 1818. [– Fr. *appréciable*, f. *apprécier*; see APPRECIATE *v.*, -ABLE.] **1.** Capable of being appreciated, valued, or recognized by the mind. **2.** Perceptible, sensible 1820.

1. An a. interest 1818. Hence **Appre·ciably** *adv.*

Appreciate (ăprī·ʃi,eⁱt), *v.* 1655. [– *appreciat-*, pa. ppl. stem of late L. *appretiare* set a price on, f. *ad-* AP- *pref.*¹ + *pretium* PRICE *sb.*; see -ATE³ and cf. (O)Fr. *apprécier*. Not in Johnson.] **1.** *trans.* To form an estimate of worth, quality, or amount 1769. **2.** To estimate aright 1798; *esp.* to be sensitive to, or sensible of, any delicate impression or distinction 1833. **3.** To esteem adequately or highly 1655. **4.** To raise in value; opp. to *depreciate* 1779; *intr.* (esp. in U.S.) 1789.

1. The..want of candour..with which Priestley appretiated Hume 1817. **2.** A blind man is able to a. sound, touch, etc., but not colours F. HALL. **3.** To a. Homer GLADSTONE. **4.** Gold has been steadily appreciating in value 1882. Hence **Appre·ciated,** adequately valued; enhanced in exchangeable value. **Appre·ciatingly** *adv.*

Appreciation (ăprīʃi,ēⁱ·ʃən). Late ME. [– Fr. *appréciation* – late L. *appreciatio*, f. as prec.; see -ION. Found once *c* 1400; then not till XVII.] **1.** The action of setting a money value upon; appraisement (*rare*) 1799. **2.** The action of estimating; deliberate judgement 1604. **3.** Perception, *esp.* of delicate impressions or distinctions. late ME. **4.** Adequate or high estimation 1650. **5.** Rise in exchangeable value. See APPRECIATE 4. 1789.

2. A. of the condition of things 1880. **3.** A. of the intricacies of a country 1879. **4.** A. of scenery 1870. **5.** A considerable a. in the value of Gold 1883.

Appreciative (ăprī·ʃi,ĕtiv), *a.* 1850. [f. APPRECIATE *v.* + -IVE.] Showing APPRECIATION (senses 3, 4).

Kindly a. words 1850. Hence **Appre·ciative-ly** *adv.*, **-ness.**

Appreciator (ăprī·ʃi,eⁱtəɹ). 1842. [f. APPRECIATE *v.* + -OR 2.] One who values adequately or highly.

Appreciatory (ăprī·ʃi,ătəri), *a.* 1819. [f. as prec. + -ORY².] Of or befitting an appreciator; appreciative. Hence **Appre·ciatorily** *adv.*

Appredicate (ăpre·dikeⁱt). 1837. [– mod. L. *appraedicatum* (= Gr. προσκατηγορούμενον); see PREDICATE.] The copula, considered as not included in the predicate.

Apprehend (æprǐhe·nd), *v.* ME. [– Fr. *appréhender* or L. *apprehendere*, f. *ad-* AP- *pref.*¹ + *prehendere* seize.] **I.** Physical. **1.** To lay hold upon, seize (*lit.* and *fig.*) *arch.* 1572. **2.** To seize in name of law, arrest 1548. † **3.** To take possession of –1652; to embrace (an offer, etc.) –1633.

2. To fynde sum occasion..to attache and apprehende him UDALL.

II. Mental. † **1.** *gen.* To learn. Also *absol.* –1680. **2.** To become or be conscious by the senses of 1635; † to feel –1670. **3.** To lay hold of with the intellect; to see; to catch the meaning of; also *absol.* 1577. **4.** To understand (a thing *to be*); to take as; also *absol.* 1614. **5.** To anticipate (*mostly* things adverse) 1603. **6.** To anticipate with fear 1606.

1. Thereby they provoke many to a. virtue ELYOT. **2.** To a. a voice from heaven HOBBES. **3.** Each man..avails him of what worth He apprehends in you BROWNING. As soone..apprehended as read 1631. Cousin, you a. passing shrewdly *Much Ado* II. i. 84. **4.** They apprehended it a great courtesy done unto them FULLER. In general, I a., the later French critics have given the preference to Racine HALLAM. **5.** A man that apprehends death no more dreadfully, but as a drunken sleepe *Meas. for M.* IV. ii. 149. **6.** Which makes me much a. the end of those honest Worthies SIR T. BROWNE. Hence **Apprehe·nded** *ppl. a.* arrested; conceived; dreaded. **Apprehe·nder,** one who seizes, or arrests; one who feels, or understands. **Apprehe·ndingly** *adv.* by apprehending.

Apprehensible (æprǐhe·nsib'l), *a.* 1631. [– late L. *apprehensibilis*, f. *apprehens-*, pa. ppl. stem of L. *apprehendere* APPREHEND; cf. Fr. *appréhensible.*] Capable of being apprehended (see APPREHEND II. 5, 6). Const. *by, to.* Hence **Apprehe:nsibi·lity. Apprehe·nsibly** *adv.* (*rare*).

Apprehension (æprǐhe·nʃən). ME. [– Fr. *appréhension* or late L. *apprehensio*, f. as prec.; see -ION.] *gen.* The action of seizing upon, seizure. The mental senses are the earliest. **I.** Physical. **1.** The action of laying hold of; prehension (*rare*) 1646. **2.** *Law.* The action of taking manual possession 1832. **3.** Seizure or arrest in the name of justice or authority 1577.

1. [A lobster's claw is] a part of a. SIR T. BROWNE. **3.** A warrant for his a. was obtained 1881.

II. Mental. **1.** † *gen.* The action of learning –1641; sensible perception (*arch.*) 1590. † **2.** Sympathetic perception –1644. **3.** The action of grasping with the intellect; conception, intellection 1597. **4.** The apprehensive faculty; understanding 1570. **5.** The product, or the abiding result, of grasping mentally; a conception; a view, notion, or opinion 1579. **6.** Anticipation; *chiefly* of things adverse 1603. **7.** Dread 1648.

2. Dark night..The eare more quicke of a. makes *Mids. N.* III. ii. 178. **3.** The love and a. of duty BACON. **4.** Simple a. denotes..the soul's naked intellection of an object GLANVILL. O the quick a. of women DEKKER. **5.** Which, according to vulgar a., swept away his legs JOHNSON. **6.** The sence of death is most in a. *Meas. for M.* III. i. 78. **7.** I looked about with some a. 1709.

Apprehensive (æprǐhe·nsiv), *a.* ME. [– Fr. *appréhensif, -ive* or med.L. *apprehensivus*, f. as prec.; see -IVE.] † **1.** In the habit of seizing, ready to embrace (an opportunity, etc.) –1641. **2.** Pertaining to, or apt for, the laying hold of sensuous or mental impressions ME. **3.** Of faculties: Showing apprehension; intelligent 1621. **4.** Of persons, etc.: Perceptive; *hence,* quick to learn. Const. *of.* 1601. **5.** Having an apprehension or notion; conscious, sensible. Const. *of* or *subord. cl.* (*arch.*) 1611. **6.** Anticipative of something adverse. (The usual sense.) Const. *simply,* with *of,* or *subord. cl., from, for.* 1633. † **7.** Apprehensible 1692.

1. A. of occasions wherein [etc.] LD. STRAFFORD. **2.** My a. tenderest parts MILT. *Sams.* 623. **3.** A sense so a. and discriminant NEWMAN. **4.** More fond of Miracles, than a. of Truth MILT. **6.** Noah's niece, being a. of the deluge, set out for Ireland H. WALPOLE. He was a. an operation would be necessary 1802. Hence **Apprehe·nsively** *adv.* with anticipation, *esp.* of danger. **Apprehe·nsiveness,** fearfulness.

† **Appre·nd,** *v. rare.* 1567. [– Fr. *apprendre* learn or L. *apprendere*, contr. f. *apprehendere* APPREHEND.] To seize; to grasp mentally –1642.

Apprentice (ăpre·ntis), *sb.* [Late ME. *aprentys* – OFr. *aprentis* (mod. *apprenti*), nom. of *aprentif*, f. *aprendre* learn (see prec.) + *-tis, -tif* :– L. *-ivus*; see -IVE, -ICE 2. Aphet. PRENTICE.] **1.** A learner of a craft; one who is bound by legal agreement to serve an employer for a period of years, with a view to learn some handicraft, trade, etc., in which the employer is reciprocally bound to instruct him. **2.** A barrister-at-law of less than 16 years' standing. *Obs.* exc. *Hist.* ME. **3.** By extension: A beginner, a tyro 1489. **4.** *adj.* or *attrib.* ME.

2. Barristers (first stiled apprentices)..who answered to our bachelors BLACKSTONE. **3.** As yet they were apprentices to piracy FULLER.

Apprentice (ăpre·ntis), *v.* 1631. [f. the sb.] To bind as an apprentice; to indenture. Hence **Appre·nticement** (*rare*).

Apprenticeship (ăpre·ntisʃip). 1592. [f. APPRENTICE *sb.* + -SHIP; repl. *Apprenticehood.*]

1. The position of an apprentice (see APPRENTICE 1); service as an apprentice; also *transf.* or *fig.* 1592. 2. The period for which an apprentice is bound 1667. 3. *Hence*: A period of seven years 1780.

1. *Serving his apprenticeship* in the military art MACAULAY. [An] a. in Sanskrit grammar MAX-MÜLLER. 3. Three 'prenticeships have passed away..Since I was bound to life HOOD. vars. †**Appre·nticeage**, †**Appre·nticehood.**

Appress (ǣpre·s), *v.* 1791. [– *appress-*, pa. ppl. stem of L. *apprimere*, f. *ad-* AP- *pref.*[1] + *premere* press.] = ADPRESS.

† **Appre·st.** ME. [– OFr. *apreste* (mod. *apprêt*) preparation, f. *aprester* make ready, f. *a* :– L. *ad* + *prest* (mod. *prêt*) :– L. *præstus* ready. Cf. IMPREST *a.* and *sb.*[1]] Provision; *esp.* pecuniary provision, loan –1570.

Appre·ve, *v.*, pa. pple. **approven.** *Obs.* or *dial.* ME. [– OFr. *apreuv-*, tonic stem of *aprover*, whence APPROVE *v.*[1]. For the vocalism, cf. ME. *preve* prove, *meve* move.] = APPROVE *v.*[1].

Apprise (ăprəi·z), *v.*[1]; also **apprize.** 1694. [– *appris, -ise*, pa. pple. of Fr *apprendre* teach. (causative of the sense 'learn'); see APPREHEND *v.*]
1. To impart information to; acquaint. Hence in *pass.* To be aware 1712. 2. To notify, advise (*rare*) 1817.

1. The adjoining cell, as the reader is apprised, was occupied by Gurth SCOTT.

Apprize, -ise (ăprəi·z), *v.*[2] *arch.* ME. [– OFr. *aprisier*, f. *a* :– L. *ad* AP- *pref.*[1] + *pris* PRICE *sb.*] 1. *Sc. Law.* To put up for sale at a set price, appraise 1533. 2. To value, appreciate ME. Hence † **Appri·zement,** appraisement. **Appri·zer, -ser,** one who appraises; *Sc. Law*, a creditor for whose behoof an appraisal is made.

Appro. (æ·pro), abbrev. of *approbation* or *approval*, in *on a.*, said of goods sent for a customer's examination with a view to purchase.

Approach (ăpr$ō^u$·tʃ), *v.* [ME. *aproch(e* – OFr. *aproch(i)er* (mod. *approcher*) :– eccl. L. *appropiare*, f. *ad-* AP- *pref.*[1] + *propius* nearer, comp. of *prope* near.] 1. *intr.* To come nearer, or draw near, in space. Const. *simply*, or with *to*. *trans.* To come near to ME. Also *fig.* 2. *trans.* Of lines, etc.: To be so situated in space that the parts lie successively nearer to a given point or line 1598. 3. To come near to a person: *i.e.* into personal relations. *intr.* with *to* (*arch.*) ME. *trans.* ME. 4. *euphem.* Of sexual relations 1611. 5. Of time, etc.: To draw nigh ME. 6. To come near, be nearly equal. *intr.* with *to* ME. *trans.* 1698. 7. *Mil.* To make approaches to (see APPROACH *sb.* 6). 8. *causal.* To bring near locally; approximate (*arch.*) 1541. Also *fig.*

1. A., thou Beacon to this vnder Globe *Lear* II. ii. 170. Approch the Chamber *Macb.* II. iii. 76. 2. Here the boundary approaches, but does not quite reach the river (*mod.*). 3. I cannot a. her without Awe STEELE. 5. When now the Nuptial time Approaches DRYDEN. 6. He..thought even to have approached Homer TEMPLE. 7. Ground.. easy to A., and as..dangerous to Storm CLARENDON. 8. So saying he approached to the fire a three-footed stool SCOTT. Hence **Approa·cher. Approa·ching** *vbl. sb.* the action of drawing near; *spec.* in *Mil.* and *Hort.* = APPROACH *sb.* 6, 7; *ppl. a.* drawing or coming near (*lit. and fig.*). **Approa·chment,** †approach; affinity.

Approach (ăpr$ō^u$·tʃ), *sb.* 1489. [f. the vb.; cf. Fr. *approche.*] 1. The act of approaching (see APPROACH *v.* 1) 1555; † *spec.* nearer advance of an enemy –1652. 2. *pl.* Movements towards personal relations; advances 1642. 3. Access (*arch.*) 1563; an access 1633. 4. A drawing near in time or circumstance 1593. 5. A coming near in quality or character 1750. 6. *Mil.* Entrenchments, etc., by which the besiegers draw closer to the besieged; also *fig.* 1633. 7. *Hort.* The bringing of the branch of one tree close to that of another for grafting; called also ablactation or inarching 1658.

1. The a. of a Comet to the Earth WHISTON. 2. What Approaches, Smiles, Shrugs, Habits, are.. requirable from them 1654. 3. Honour hath in it ..the a. to kings 1626. The station and its approaches 1878. 4. Death's a. 2 *Hen. VI*, III. iii. 6. Signs of the a. of a reaction SEELEY. Hence **Approa·chless** *a. poet.* unapproachable.

Approachable (ăpr$ō^u$·tʃăb'l), *a.* 1571. [f. APPROACH *v.* + -ABLE; cf. Fr. *approchable.*] Capable of being approached; accessible (*lit.* and *fig.*) 1611.

This Truth..a. by most CARLYLE. Hence **Approa:chabi·lity. Approa·chableness.**

† **A·pprobate,** *ppl. a.* ME. [– L. *approbatus*, pa. pple. of *approbare*; see APPROVE *v.*[1], -ATE[2].] Approved formally, or authoritatively –1577.

Approbate (æ·prŏbe^{i}t), *v.* 1470. [– *approbat-*, pa. ppl. stem of L. *approbare* see APPROVE *v.*[1], -ATE[3].] 1. To approve expressly; to sanction authoritatively. Obs. in England, but in use in U.S., often as simply = *approve.* 2. *Sc. Law.* To approve as valid. Also *transf.* 1836.

1. *To approbate and reprobate*: to take advantage of the parts of a deed which favour one, and repudiate the rest. Hence **A·pprobated** *ppl. a.* = APPROVED. **A·pprobator** (*rare*), one who sanctions; an approver. ? *Obs.* **A·pproba:tory** *a.* of the nature of or tending to approbation or sanction. (Orig. in phr. *letter approbatory.*)

Approbation (æprobē^i·ʃən). ME. [– (O)Fr. *approbation* – L. *approbatio*, f. as prec.; see -ION.] † 1. The action of proving true; confirmation –1718. 2. The action of declaring good or true; sanction 1502. 3. Approval expressed or felt 1548. b. *On approbation*: see APPRO. † 4. Probation –1654.

1. Would I had put my Estate..on th' a. of what I haue spoke *Cymb.* I. iv. 134. 2. Received the royal a. 1839. 3. Nods of A. BUDGELL. 4. This day, my sister should the Cloyster enter, And there receiue her a. *Meas. for M.* I. ii. 183.

Approbative (æ·prŏbe^{i}tiv), *a. arch.* 1611. [– Fr. *approbatif, -ive* or med.L. *approbativus* approving, f. as prec.; see -IVE.] Expressing approbation or approval. Hence **A·pproba:tiveness,** the quality of being a.; in *Phrenol.* love of approbation.

† **Appro·mpt,** *v. rare.* [f. AP- *pref.*[1] + PROMPT *v.*] To make ready; stimulate. BACON.

Approof (ăprū·f). *arch.* ME. [– OFr. *aprove, apreuve* (whence XV *apref*) f. *aprouver*, tonic stem *apreuv-* (whence APPREVE *v.*); see APPROVE *v.*[1], PROOF *sb.*] 1. The act of proving; trial. 2. Sanction, approbation 1439.

1. A Souldier..and of verie valiant approofe *All's Well* II. v. 3. 2. *Meas. for M.* II. iv. 174.

Appropinquate (æpropi·ŋkwe^{i}t), *v. arch.* 1623. [– *appropinquat-*, pa. ppl. stem of L. *appropinquare* to approach, f. *propinquus* neighbouring, f. *prope* near; see -ATE[3].] To come near *to*. † *trans.* To bring near (*rare*) 1646. Hence **Ap:propin·qua·tion,** the action of coming or bringing near; approach. **Appropi·nquity,** nearness (*rare*). So † **Appropi·nque** *v.* BUTLER, *Hud.* I. iii. 590.

† **Appro·pre, appro·prie.** ME. [– OFr. *aproprier* (mod. *app-*) acquire – late L. *appropriare*; see APPROPRIATE *v.*] = APPROPRIATE 1, 2, 3, 5.

Appropriable (ăpr$ō^u$·pri,ăb'l), *a.* 1646. [f. prec. + -ABLE.] Capable of being appropriated.

† **Appro·priament.** 1633. [– med.L. *appropriamentum*, f. late L. *appropriare* APPROPRIATE; see -MENT and cf. OFr. *apropriement.*] A characteristic.

Appropriate (ăpr$ō^u$·pri,ĕt), *ppl. a.* 1525. [– late L. *appropriatus*, pa. pple. of *appropriare* make one's own, f. *ad-* AP- *pref.*[1] + *proprius* own, PROPER; see -ATE[2].] *pple.* or *adj.* 1. Annexed or attached (*to*), as a possession; appropriated. *spec.* in *Eccl.* Annexed as a benefice to a religious corporation 1599. † 2. Selfish 1627; individual 1796. 3. Attached as an attribute, quality or right; peculiar, own. Const. *absol.*, *to.* 1525. 4. Specially suitable, proper. Const. *to, for.* 1546. Also as † *sb.* [sc. *thing*, or *attribute.*] –1642.

3. Honour, a. to the Soveraign only HOBBES. 4. Prayers..a. for the great solemnity FREEMAN. Hence **Appro·priate-ly** *adv.*, **-ness.**

Appropriate (ăpr$ō^u$·pri,e^{i}t), *v.* 1528. [– prec., or *appropriat-*, pa. ppl. stem of late L. *appropriare*; see prec., -ATE[3]. Superseded (XVII) APROPRE, -IE.] 1. † To make over to any one as his own; to set apart –1723. Const. *to oneself*; = next. 1583. 2. *ellipt.* To take for one's own, or to oneself 1635. 3. *Eccl.* To annex (a benefice) to some religious corporation as its property 1528. 4. To assign to a special purpose. Const. *to, for.* 1605. 5. To assign or attribute specially or exclusively *to* (*arch.*) 1533. 6. To make, or select as, appropriate *to*; to suit (*arch.*) 1594.

1. The name 'priesthood'..was never appropriated by the apostles to themselves 1876. 4. After appropriating £18,424 for the payment of interest on debentures 1882. 5. The word presumption I a. to the internal feeling COLERIDGE. Hence **Appro·priated** *ppl. a.* (in senses 1, 4, 5, 6, repl. APPROPRIATE as pple.).

Appropriation (ăpr$ō^u$:pri,ē^i·ʃən). ME. [– (O)Fr. *appropriation* – late L. *appropriatio*, f. *appropriat-*; see prec., -ION.] 1. The making of a thing private property, *esp.* one's own; taking to one's own use; *concr.* the thing so appropriated. 2. *Eccl.* Transference to a religious corporation of the tithes and endowments intended for the maintenance of religious ordinances in a parish; *concr.* the benefice or tithes so appropriated ME. 3. Assignment of anything to a special purpose; *concr.* the thing (*esp.* money) so assigned –1690. † 4. Special attribution; a special attribute –1690.

1. The rapacious a. of the abbey lands M. PATTISON. 3. *Appropriation Bill*: a Bill in Parliament, allotting the revenue to the various purposes to which it is to be applied. 4. Hee makes it a great a. to his owne good parts, that he can shoo him [his horse] himselfe *Merch. V.* I. ii. 46.

Appropriative (ăpr$ō^u$·pri,ĕtiv), *a.* 1655. [f. APPROPRIATE *v.* + -IVE.] Of appropriating character or tendency. Hence **Appro·pria:tiveness.**

Appropriator (ăpr$ō^u$·pri,e^{i}tər). 1726. [– med.L. *appropriator* (sense 2), f. as prec.; see -OR 2.] 1. One who appropriates 1840. 2. The religious corporation that owns the fees and endowments of a benefice 1726; var. † **Approprietary** [– later *appropriétarius*] (*rare*).

Approvable (ăprū·văb'l), *a.* 1449. [f. APPROVE *v.*[1] + -ABLE.] Able to be approved; worthy of approval. Hence **Appro·vableness.**

Approval (ăprū·văl). 1690. [f. APPROVE *v.*[1] + -AL[1]. Rare bef. 1800; now usual.] The action of approving; sanctioning approbation.

Mankind had stamped its a. upon certain actions MILL *On approval*: see APPRO.

Approvance (ăprū·văns). *arch.* 1592. [– OFr. *aprovance*, f. *aprover*; see next, -ANCE.] = APPROOF, APPROVAL.

Approve (ăprū·v), *v.*[1] [ME. *aprove* – OFr. *aprover* (mod. *approuver*) :– L. *approbare* make good, assent to as good, f. *ad-* AP- *pref.*[1] + *probus* just, good. The tonic stem *apreuv-* of OFr. *aprover* gave APPREVE *v.*] I. [= Fr. *approuver.*] † 1. To make good; to prove, demonstrate –1677. † 2. To attest with some authority, to confirm –1781. 3. To demonstrate practically, display, make proof of. Also *refl.* 1551. 4. To confirm authoritatively. *Hence* techn. for confirming the sentence of a court-martial ME. 5. To pronounce to be good, commend ME. *intr.* Const. † *on, of,* 1658. 6. *trans.* To recommend oneself, one's qualities, etc., as worthy of approval; to commend *to* 1611.

1. One thing..which must approue thee honest *Cymb.* V. v. 245. 2. What damned error, but some sober brow Will..approue it with a text *Merch. V.* III. ii. 79. 3. Opportunities to a. his stoutness and worth EMERSON. 'Tis an old lesson; Time approves it true BYRON. He..approved himself a very vile person 1656. 5. I entirely a. that precaution WELLINGTON. Would his grandfather a. of what he had done KINGSLEY. 6. Without approving the heart to God CROMWELL.

II. [= Fr. *éprouver.*] † 1. To put to the proof; to try –1770. † 2. To find by experience –1651.

1. Nay, taske me to my word: approue me Lord 1 *Hen. IV*, IV. i. 9. Hence **Appro·vingly** *adv.*

Appro·ve, approw·, *v.*[2] 1483. [Lawyer's form (XVII) of *approue*, var. of *approwe* – OFr. *apprower, appro(u)er*, f. *à* AP- *pref.*[1] + *pro, prou* advantage, profit. See IMPROVE *v.*[2], PROUD *a.*] *Law.* To make profit to oneself of (*e.g.* land), by increasing the value or rent. *esp.* Said of a lord of a manor enclosing common land, as permitted by the Statute of Merton (20 Hen. III. c. iv.). Cf. IMPROVE.

Approved (ăprū·vd), *ppl. a.* ME. [f. APPROVE *v.*[1] + -ED[1].] 1. Proved by experience, tried; † convicted –1635. **2.** Pronounced good; sanctioned, esteemed 1667.

1. The old a. mode BURKE. To knit my soul to an approued wanton *Much Ado* IV. i. 45. **2.** *Approved-of*: regarded with commendation. Hence **Appro·ved-ly** *adv.*, **-ness** (*rare*).

Approvement[1] (ăprū·vmĕnt). 1615. [– OFr. *aprovement*, later *approuvement* (Cotgrave), f. *aprover*; see APPROVE *v.*[1], -MENT.] **1.** The proving guilty, or convicting, by becoming 'approver' 1768. **2.** † Approbation –1665; that which is approved 1673.

The doctrine of a. has been obsolete now for 150 years 1824.

Appro·vement[2], **approw·ment.** 1475. [– OFr. *aproement*, *aproue-*, *aprowe-* profit, f. *aproer* etc.; see APPROVE *v.*[2], -MENT.] **1.** The action of approving (see APPROVE *v.*[2]). Cf. IMPROVEMENT. † **2.** The profits themselves 1489.

Approver[1] (ăprū·vəɹ). ME. [f. APPROVE *v.*[1] + -ER[1]; cf. OFr. *aproveur*.] **1.** One who proves or offers to prove (another) guilty; *hence*, an informer. Now restricted to: One who confesses a felony and turns king's (queen's) or state's evidence. † **2.** One who tests –1691. **3.** One who confirms or commends 1548.

1. An A., while he is in that service, hath a Peny a day 1679.

† **Appro·ver**[2], **approw·er.** ME. [– AFr. *aprouour* f. *aprouer*; see APPROVE *v.*[2] In med.L. *apruator*, *approuator*. Ought to be written *apprower*. See -OUR, in later use apprehended as, and repl. by, -ER.[1]] One who looks after the profit of an employer; a steward or bailiff; an agent –1758.

Approximate (ăprǫ·ksimĕt), *a.* (*sb.*) 1646. [– *approximatus*, pa. pple. of late L. *approximare* (Tertullian) draw near to, f. *ad-* AP- *pref.*[1] + *proximus* very near, next; see -ATE[2].] **1.** Very near; nearly resembling. **2.** *Phys. Sc.* Set very close together 1839. **3.** *ellipt.* Reasonably or nearly correct 1816. **4.** *sb.* An approximate result or quantity (*rare*) 1784.

1. Three a. faunas DARWIN. **3.** A. uniformity 1853.

Approximate (ăprǫ·ksimeʲt), *v.* 1660. [f. prec., or – *approximat-* pa. ppl. stem of late L. *approximare*; see prec., -ATE[3].] **1.** *trans.* To bring close or near, to cause to approach (*to*). Rarely of physical motion. **2.** *intr.* To come near or close (*to*). Rarely of physical motion; commonly of conceptions to which ideas of space are transferred. 1789. **3.** *trans.* [the prep. omitted.] To come close to, approach closely 1789.

1. Shakespeare approximates the remote, and familiarizes the wonderful JOHNSON. **2.** The shores gradually a. 1835. **3.** Rentals approximating £4,000 per annum 1883. Hence **Appro·ximated** *ppl. a.* brought close; nearly reached; approximate. **Appro·ximately** *adv.* nearly; *ellipt.* with near approach to accuracy. **Appro·ximator.**

Approximation (ăprǫ:ksimēʲ·ʃən). 1646. [f. prec. + -ION; cf. late L., med.L. *approximatio*, Fr. *approximation* (XV).] **1.** The action of approximating (see APPROXIMATE *v.*); approach, proximity (*lit.* and *fig.*). † **b.** *spec.* in *Med.* Communication of a disease by contact –1753; † **c.** in *Hort.* = APPROACH *sb.* 7. 1765. **2.** A coming or getting near to identity in quantity, quality, or degree; an approach to a correct estimate or conception. *concr.* The result of such a process. 1660. **3.** *Math.* A process of solving problems, wherein a continual approach is made to the exact quantity 1695.

1. The world's decay and a. to its period 1664. An a. of feeling among those whom opinions have divided SOUTHEY.

Approximative (ăprǫ·ksimetiv), *a.* 1830. [f. APPROXIMATE *v.* + -IVE; cf. Fr. *approximatif*, *-ive*.] Of approximate character; nearly reaching accuracy. Hence **Appro·ximative-ly** *adv.*, **-ness.**

‖ **Appui** (apüi, ăpwī·), *sb.* 1573. [Fr.; see next. At one time naturalized.] † **1.** Support, stay, prop –1601. **2.** *Mil.* Defensive support. Also *fig.* 1809. **3.** *Horsemanship.* The reciprocal sense of the action of the bridle between the horse's mouth and the horseman's hand 1727.

2. *Point of appui*: Any fixed object or marker upon which a body of troops is directed to commence its formation into line.

Appui, appuy, *v.* 1656. [– Fr. *appuyer* lean or rest upon.] To prop or stay; *spec.* in *Mil.* to post (troops) near some point which affords support.

The enemy have their right appuied upon these mountains 1813.

Appulse (ăpʋ·ls). 1626. [– L. *appulsus* driving towards, f. *appuls-*, pa. ppl. stem of *appellere*, f. *ad-* AP- *pref.*[1] + *pellere* drive.] **1.** A driving toward or against. † *spec.* The running of a ship towards a point. Also *fig.* 1642. **2.** *Astr.* The arrival of a star or planet at the meridian or other point; the coming into conjunction of two heavenly bodies –1668.

1. The continual a. of fresh sap GREW.

† **Appu·nctuation.** *rare.* [– med.L. *appunctuatio* agreement, f. *appunctuat-*, pa. ppl. stem of *appunctuare* settle, define, f. *ad-* AP- *pref.*[1] + *punctum* point, after Fr. *appointer* adjust, etc. See APPOINT *v.*] The action of defining; determination.

Appurtenance (ăpʋ·ɹtĭnăns). [ME. *apurtena(u)nce* – AFr. *apurtenaunce*, OFr. *apart-*, *apertenance* :– Rom. **appertinentia*, f. late L. *appertinēre* APPERTAIN; see -ANCE.] **1.** *Law* and *gen.* A thing that belongs to another, belonging; a minor property, right, or privilege, belonging to another as principal, and passing with it; an appendage. **2.** A contributory adjunct, an accessary ME; *esp.* in *pl.* the mechanical accessories employed in any function or system; apparatus, gear. Also *fig.* ME. **3.** The fact or state of appertaining 1846.

2. The a. of Welcome is Fashion and Ceremony *Haml.* II. ii. 388. The Pope, with his appertinences the Prelats MILT. All the appurtenances of a great establishment 1840. Hence † **Appu·rtenanced** *ppl. a.* furnished with, as an a.

Appartenant (ăpʋ·ɹtĭnănt), *a.* (*sb.*) ME. [– OFr. *apartenant*, pres. pple. of *apartenir* APPERTAIN; see -ANT.] **1.** Belonging as a property or right (*to*); *spec.* in *Law*, constituting an APPURTENANCE (sense 1). **2.** Appertaining as if by right (*to*); appropriate to; pertinent ME. **3.** *sb.* A belonging 1483.

1. Villeins a. to the soil of the master HALLAM **2.** Euery thing, That to the feste was apertinent CHAUCER. **3.** All the appertinents Belonging to his Honour *Hen. V*, II. ii. 87.

Apricate (æ·prikeʲt), *v. rare.* 1697. [– *apricat-*, pa. ppl. stem of L. *apricare* bask in the sun, *apricus* exposed (to the sun); see -ATE[3].] **1.** *intr.* To bask in the sun. **2.** *trans.* To expose to sunlight 1851. Hence **Aprica·tion.**

Apricot (ēʲ·prikǫt). 1551. [Earliest forms *abrecock*, *apricock*, pl. *ab-*, *aprecox* – Pg. *albricoque* or Sp. *albaricoque* – Arab. *al-barḳūḳ*, i.e. *al* AL-[2], *barḳūḳ* – late Gr. πραικόκιον (Dioscorides), Byz. Gr. βερίκοκκον – L. *præcoquum*, *-cocum*, neut. (sc. *malum*) of var. of *præcox* early-ripe (see PRECOCIOUS *a.*). The later Eng. forms show assimilation to Fr. *abricot*, and subsequent alt. of *abr-* to *apr-*, perh. after L. *apricus* sunny.] **1.** A stone-fruit allied to the plum, of an orange colour, roundish-oval shape, and delicious flavour. **2.** The tree which bears this fruit (*Prunus armeniaca*) 1573. Also *attrib.*

1. Yond dangling Apricocks *Rich. II*, III. iv. 29.

April (ēʲ·pril). ME. [– L. *Aprilis* prop. adj. (sc. *mensis* month), whence (O)Fr. *avril*, adopted earlier in Eng. *averil* (XIII).] The fourth month of the year. *attrib.* 1579. Also *fig.* (in reference to April showers, etc.) and *attrib.*

Half-opening buds of A. TENNYSON. The vncertaine glory of an Aprill day *Two Gent.* I. iii. 85. *fig.* The Aprill's in her eyes, it is Loue's spring *Ant. & Cl.* III. ii. 43. And hopes and light regrets that come Make April of her tender eyes TENNYSON. *Comb.*: **a.-fool**, one who is sportively imposed upon, on the first of April, or *April-fool-day*; †**-gentleman**, a newly-married husband; **-gowk** (i.e. *cuckow*), north. for **-fool.**

‖ **A priori** (ēʲ pri,ōᵊ·rəi), *advb.* (and *adj.*) *phr.* 1710. [L.; cf. *a posteriori*.] **1.** A phrase used to characterize reasoning from causes to effects, from abstract notions to their consequences, from assumed axioms (and not from experience); deductive; deductively. **2.** Hence *loosely*, Previous to any special examination, presumptively 1834. **3.** *Metaph.* Prior to experience; innate in the mind 1841.

1. Nor can we *a priori* determine the value of any new instrument SMEATON. **2.** An *a priori* conjecture FARRAR. **3.** The term *a priori* is now.. employed [by the Kantian school] to characterise those elements of knowledge which..as native to, are potentially in, the mind antecedent to the act of experience SIR W. HAMILTON. Hence **Aprio·rity**, the quality of being innate in the mind; practice of *a priori* reasoning.

Aproctous (ăprǫ·ktəs), *a.* 1870. [f. Gr. ἀ- A- *pref.* 14 + πρωκτός anus + -OUS.] *Phys.* Having no anus.

Apron (ēʲ·prən, ēʲ·pəɹn), *sb.* ME. [Evolved by misdivision of *a napron* as *an apron* (cf. *adder*, *auger*, *umpire*); ME. *napron* – OFr. *naperon* (mod. *napperon*), f. *nape*, *nappe* table-cloth :– L. *mappa*, napkin (see MAP *sb.*). For Rom. initial *n.* repr. L. *m* cf. Fr. *natte* :– L. *matta*, Fr. *nèfle* :– L. *mespilus*. For misdivision of *a napron* see A *adj.*[2]] **1.** An article of dress, orig. of linen, worn in front of the body, to protect the clothes from dirt or injury, or simply as a covering. **2.** A similar garment worn officially by bishops, deans, Freemasons, etc. 1704. **3.** Anything like an apron in shape or function, *esp.* the leather covering for the legs in a gig, etc. 1875. **4.** Technical uses:

a. A platform placed at the bottom of a sluice or entrance to a dock, so as to intercept the fall of water. **b.** in *Gunnery*, A square piece of lead laid over the touch-hole. **c.** in *Ship-building*, A kind of false or inner stem, fayed on the aftside of the stem, to strengthen it. **d.** in *Plumbing*, A strip of lead which conducts the drip of a wall into the gutter. **e.** in *Mech.* The piece that holds the cutting tool in a planing machine. **f.** *Theatr.* The stage-area in front of the curtain.

5. *Apron of a roast goose or duck*: the skin covering the belly, which encloses the stuffing 1755.

1. A Napron of worsted 1569. Where is thy Leather A., and thy Rule *Jul. C.* I. i. 7. **2.** *Green apron*: a lay preacher (contemptuous).

Comb. etc.: **a.** †**-man**, a mechanic; †**-rogue** = *-man*; **-squire** = APPLE-SQUIRE. Hence **A·pronful**, the quantity that can be held in an a. **A·pronless** *a.*

Apron (ēʲ·prən), *v.* 1865. [f. the sb.] To cover with, or as with, an apron. Hence **A·proned** *ppl. a.* having an apron (usu. in *comb.*); formerly: Mechanic. † **Apronee·r,** one who wears an apron; a shopman or mechanic. (Used of the Parliamentary party during the Civil Wars.) †**A·proner,** one who wears an apron; a barman, waiter.

A·pron-string. 1542. The string with which an apron is tied on.

Apron-string hold or *tenure*: tenure in virtue of a wife, or during her life-time only. *Tied to the apron-strings of* (a mother, etc.): unduly controlled by.

‖ **Apropos** (apropō·). 1668. [Fr. *à propos*, i.e. *à* to *propos* plan, purpose.] Const. *to*, *of*. **A.** *adv.* **1.** To the purpose; opportunely. **2.** With regard *to*, as suggested by. (Fr. *à propos de.*) *absol.*: By the way. 1761. **B.** *adj.* To the point or purpose; pertinent, happy 1691. **C.** *sb.* † A pertinent occurrence 1783; pertinency 1860.

1. They] arrived very àpropos ADDISON. **2.** But a-propos! Hast thou seen the girl SMOLLETT. **B.** A tale extremely a. POPE. **C.** To describe with a. 1860.

Apse (æps). Pl. **apses** (æ·psīz). 1822. [– L. *apsis*, *absis* – Gr. ἀψίς, var. of ἁψίς, arch, vault, perh. f. ἅπτειν to join, fit; cf. the earlier APSIS and also *base*, *basis*.] **1.** *Arch.* A semi-circular or polygonal recess, arched or dome-roofed in a building, *esp.* at the end of the choir, aisles, or nave of a church. Cf. APSIS 3. 1846. **2.** *Astr.* = APSIS 2. 1822.

† **A·psid.** Also **abside.** 1670. [– It. *abside*, or Fr. *abside* (Arch.), *apside* (Astr.) – L. *apsid-*, *absid-*, stem of *apsis*, *absis*; see prec.] = APSE, APSIS –1743.

Apsidal (æ·psidăl), *a.* 1846. [f. L. *apsis*, *apsid-* + -AL[1].] **1.** *Astr.* Of or belonging to the apsides 1859. **2.** *Arch.* Of the form or nature of an apse 1846.

‖ **Apsis** (æ·psis). Pl. **apsides** (æpsəi·dīz, usu. in Eng. æ·psidīz). 1601. [L., see APSE.] † **1.** Circumference; orbit of a planet –1706. **2.** *Astr.* One of the two points in the elliptic orbit of a planetary body at which it is respectively at its greatest and least distance from the body about which it revolves; the aphelion or perihelion of a planet, the apogee or perigee of the moon 1658. **3.** *Arch.* = APSE 1. Hence (*a*) The bishop's throne in ancient churches. (*b*) A reliquary.

2. *Line of apsides*: the line joining the apsides.

Apsychical (æpsəi·kikăl), *a. rare.* 1678. [f. A- *pref.* 14 + PSYCHICAL *a.*] **1.** Unspiritual. **2.** Not controlled by the mind 1878.

Apt (æpt), *a.* ME. [– L. *aptus*, pa. pple. of *apere* fasten, attach. Cf. Fr. *apte.*] Const. *to, for,* or *inf.* **1.** Fitted (materially), fitting (*rare*) 1791. **2.** Suited, fitted, adapted († *to*, or *for*); fit (*arch.*) ME. **3.** *ellipt.* Suited to its purpose; becoming appropriate 1563; *esp.* of language, thoughts, etc.: Expressive, apposite 1590. **4.** Having an habitual tendency (*to* do); habitually liable; prone 1528. **5.** Susceptible to impressions; ready to learn. Mod. const. *at.* 1535.

2. Places apte to make cites ME. A. for any bodily exercise 1700. **3.** Pray the good woman take some apter time DEKKER. In all the play There is not one word a. *Mids. N.* v. i. 65. The prompt reply or the a. retort DISRAELI. **4.** For fat is wondrous a. to burn BUTLER *Hud.* III. i. 1048. So a. to quarell *Rom. & Jul.* III. i. 34. **5.** The aptest scholar that ever was DE FOE.

† **Apt**, *v.* 1540. [f. prec., partly through OFr. *apter* adapt.] **1.** To make fit, adapt (*to*) –1672. **2.** *intr.* (for *refl.*) To suit 1602. **3.** *trans.* To incline, dispose *to* –1641.

1. A song wel apted too a melodious noiz 1575. **2.** Here occasion apteth, that [etc.] 1602.

Apteral (æ·ptĕrăl), *a. rare.* 1833. [f. Gr. ἄπτερος wingless + -AL[1].] **1.** Wingless; *Zool.* = APTEROUS. **2.** *Arch.* Having no columns along the sides.

A·pteran, *a.* 1852. [f. as prec. + -AN.] *Zool.* Wingless. As *sb.* One of the *Aptera*.

A·pteroid. 1836. [f. as prec. + -OID.] *Zool.* A bird whose wings are merely rudimentary.

A·pterous, *a.* 1775. [f. as prec. + -OUS.] **1.** *Zool.* Wingless; *esp.* belonging to the *Aptera*, a sub-order of Insects including lice and springtails. **2.** *Bot.* Of seeds, etc.: Having no membranous expansions; opp. to *alate* 1830.

Apteryx (æ·ptĕriks). 1813. [mod.L. – Gr. ἀ- A- *pref.* 14 + πτέρυξ wing.] *Ornith.* A New Zealand bird, about the size of a goose, with merely rudimentary wings and no tail, called by the natives Kiwi.

Aptitude (æ·ptitiud). 1548. [– (O)Fr. *aptitude* – late L. *aptitudo* (Boethius), f. *aptus*; see -TUDE and ATTITUDE.] **1.** The quality of being fit for a purpose or position, or generally; fitness, suitableness 1643. **2.** Natural tendency or propensity 1633. **3.** Natural capacity *for* any pursuit 1789; *esp.* intelligence, quick-wittedness 1548.

1. That sociable and helpful a...between man and woman MILT. **2.** [The] nature and aptitudes [of children] LOCKE. **3.** A. for mechanical inventions MORSE. The general idea..he had acquired with great a. DICKENS.

Aptly (æ·ptli), *adv.* 1525. [f. APT *a.* + -LY[2].] In an apt manner (see APT 1, 3, 5).

Aptness (æ·ptnes). 1538. [f. as prec. + -NESS.] The state or quality of being apt (see APT 3, 4, 5).

A scholar of any a. 1612.

Aptote (æ·ptōᵘt). 1589. [– late L. *aptotus* – Gr. ἄπτωτος without cases (πτῶσις case), indeclinable.] *Gram.* A noun that has no distinction of cases; an indeclinable noun. Hence **Apto·tic** *a.* uninflected. (Applied to languages without inflexions.)

Apulmo·nic, *a. rare.* 1874. [f. A- *pref.* 14 + PULMONIC.] Having no lungs.

Apyre·tic, *a.* 1842. [f. A- *pref.* 14 + PYRETIC; cf. Fr. *apyrétique.*] *Path.* Free from fever.

Apyrexy (æ·pireksi). 1656. [– mod.L. *apyrexia* (also used) – Gr. ἀπυρεξία absence of fever; partly from Fr. *apyrexie* (XVI).] *Path.* The period of intermission in a fever. Hence **Apyre·xial** *a.* (*rare*).

Apyrous (ăpəiᵊ·rəs, æ·pirəs), *a.* 1782. [f. Gr. ἄπυρος without fire, unsmelted (f. ἀ- A- *pref.* 14 + πῦρ, πυρ- fire) + -OUS. Cf. Fr. *apyre.*] Not altered by exposure to fire.

‖ **Aqua** (ēⁱ·kwă, æ·kwă). ME. The Latin word for *water*, used in Pharmacy and Chemistry, with sense of: Liquid, solution.

‖ **Aquafortis** (ēⁱkwă,fǭ·ɹtis). 1601. [L., = strong water.] The early scientific, and still the pop. name of the Nitric Acid of commerce, a powerful solvent and corrosive. † Also of other powerful solvents –1607. Also *fig.* Hence **A:quafo·rtist**, one who makes etchings or engravings by means of a.

Aquamarine (ēⁱ:kwă,mărī·n). 1727. [– L. *aqua marina* sea-water, whence also (Fr.) AIGUE-MARINE.] **1.** A bluish-green variety of beryl. **2.** Hence as *adj.* and *sb.* Bluish-green (colour); sea-colour(ed 1846.

†‖ **A:qua mira·bilis.** 1741. [L.] 'The wonderful water, prepared of cloves, galangals, cubebs, mace, cardomums, nutmegs, ginger, and spirits of wine, digested twenty-four hours, then distilled.' J. –1818.

Aquapuncture (ēⁱ:kwă,pʊ·ŋktiur). 1876. [f. L. *aquā* with water + PUNCTURE *sb.*; cf. Fr. *aquapuncture.*] *Med.* Puncture of the skin by means of a fine jet of water from a force-pump.

‖ **Aqua regia** (ēⁱ:kwă,rī·dʒiă). Also **aqua regis.** 1610. [L., = royal water.] A mixture of nitric and hydrochloric acids, so called because it can dissolve the 'noble' metals, gold and platinum.

‖ **Aquarelle** (ækwăre·l). 1869. [Fr. – It. *acquerella* water-colour, f. *acqua* :– L. *aqua* water.] A kind of painting or illuminating with Chinese ink and thin transparent water-colours. Also, the design so produced. Hence **Aquare·llist**, an artist in a.

Aquarian (ăkwēᵊ·riăn). 1586. [f. L. *aquarius* pertaining to water (in pl. masc. *Aquarii* name of a heretical sect) + -AN.] **A.** *adj.* Of, or pertaining to, an aquarium (*rare*) 1865. var. **Aqua·rial. B.** *sb.* **1.** One of a sect of early Christians, who used water instead of wine in the Lord's Supper 1586. **2.** One who keeps an aquarium 1857.

Aquarium (ăkwēᵊ·riɒm). Pl. **-iums, -ia.** 1854. [subst. use of neut. sing. of L. *aquarius* (see next), after VIVARIUM. L. *aquarium* meant 'watering-place for cattle'.] An artificial pond, or a tank (usu. with glass sides), in which aquatic plants and animals are kept alive for observation and study. Also, recently, a place of entertainment, containing such aquariums.

‖ **Aquarius** (ăkwēᵊ·rɒs). ME. [L., = water-carrier, subst. use of *aquarius* of water, f. *aqua* water; see -ARY.[1]] *Astr.* A constellation, giving its name to the eleventh sign of the zodiac, which the sun enters on the 21st of January.

Aquarius is the butlere of goddes and yeuyth them a water potte ME.

A-quarter (ăkwǭ·ɹtəɹ), *advb. phr.* 1849. [A *prep.*[1] 5.] *Naut.* On the quarter, *i.e.* 45° abaft the beam.

Aquatic (ăkwæ·tik). 1490. [– (O)Fr. *aquatique* or L. *aquaticus* (varying with *aquatilis* AQUATILE); see AQUA, -ATIC.] **A.** *adj.* † **1.** Watery, rainy –1686. **2.** Living or growing in or near water 1642. **3.** Of pastimes: Taking place in or upon the water 1866.

B. *sb.* **1.** An aquatic plant or animal (*arch.*); one given to aquatic pastimes 1669. **2.** A water-drinker (*rare*). FRANKLIN. **3.** *pl.* Pastimes conducted in or upon the water 1865.

Hence † **Aqua·tical** *a.* of aquatic nature; having to do with water. **Aqua·tically** *adv.*

Aquatile (æ·kwătil, -əil). *arch.* 1622. [– L. *aquatilis*; see prec., -ILE.] *adj.* = AQUATIC *a.* **2.** *sb.* = AQUATIC *sb.* 1. 1638.

Aquatint (æ·kwă,ti:nt), **aqua-tinta** (æ:-kwă,ti·ntă), *sb.* 1782. [– Fr. *aquatinte*, It. *acquatinta*, repr. L. *aqua* water, It. *tinta* dyed; see TINT.] Engraving on copper by the use of a resinous solution and nitric acid, which produces effects resembling those of Indian-ink or water-colour drawing; also, the design so produced. Also *attrib.* Hence **Aquatint**, *v.* to engrave in a. **Aquati·nter.**

Aquavalent (ăkwæ·vălĕnt). 1881. [f. L. *aqua* water + *-valent*, as in *uni-*, *equivalent.*] *Chem.* The molecular proportion between an anhydrous salt and the water of its cryohydrate.

‖ **Aqua-vitæ** (ēⁱ:kwa,vəi·tī). 1471. [L.; = water of life; cf. Fr. *eau de vie*, Ir. *uisge bheatha*, USQUEBAUGH.] **1.** A term of alchemy applied to unrectified alcohol; occ. applied, in commerce, to ardent spirits of the first distillation. **2.** Hence, *pop.* Any form of ardent spirits taken as a drink, as brandy, etc. 1547. **3.** *attrib.* 1634.

2. That curst restriction On Aquavitæ BURNS.

Aqueduct (æ·kwĭdɒkt). 1538. [– L. *aquæductus*, *aquæ ductus*, i.e. *aquæ* gen. of *aqua* water, *ductus* conveyance. Cf. Fr. *aqueduc* (XVI), † *aqueduct* (XVI–XVII), perh. the immediate source.] **1.** An artificial channel for the conveyance of water from place to place; a conduit; *esp.* an elevated structure of masonry so used. Also *fig.* **2.** The similar structure (also called *aqueduct-bridge*) by which a canal is carried over a river, etc. 1791. **3.** *Phys.* Name of small canals, chiefly in the head of mammals 1709.

3. The facial nerve..traversing..a canal termed the Aqueduct of Fallopius MIVART.

†**Aqueity.** [– med.L. *aqueitas* the nature of water; see AQUA, -ITY.] The watery principle. B. JONS.

†**Aque·nch**, *v.* [OE. *ācwenćan*; see A- *pref.* 1, QUENCH] **1.** To quench, put out –1482; to satisfy ME. *intr.* To go out –1485. **2.** *fig.* To put an end to –1578.

Aqueo-, (ēⁱ:kwi,o), comb. f. AQUEOUS; as in *aqueo-igneous*, by the action of super-heated water.

Aqueous (ēⁱ·kwi,əs), *a.* 1643. [f. med.L. *aqueus* (cf. L. *terreus* earthy) + -OUS; see -EOUS.] **1.** Of, or of the nature of, water; watery; diluted with water 1646. **2.** Connected with, or relating to water 1731. **3.** *Geol.* Produced by the action of water 1802.

1. *Aqueous humour* of the eye, a fluid, nearly pure water, contained in the space between the cornea and the lens. **3.** The a. rocks, sometimes called the sedimentary LYELL. Hence **A·queously** *adv.* in, or by means of, water (*rare*).

† **Aquerne.** [OE. *ācweorna*, later *ācwern*, of unknown origin.] A squirrel –ME.

Aquiferous (ăkwi·ferəs), *a.* 1836. [f. L. *aqui-*, comb. f. *aqua* water: see -FEROUS.] Conveying or yielding water.

† **A·quilege.** 1599. [– med.L. *aquilegia*, of unkn. origin. Cf. It., Pg. *aquilegia* columbine.] Columbine.

Aquilegia (ækwilī·dʒⁱă). [mod. use of med.L. *aquilegia*; see prec.] A genus of ranunculaceous plants having pentamerous flowers with spurred petals; = COLUMBINE *sb.*[2]

Aquiline (æ·kwilin, -əin), *a.* 1646. [– L. *aquilinus*, f. *aquila* eagle, prob. after Fr. *aquilin*; see -INE[1].] **1.** Of or belonging to an eagle 1656. **2.** Eagle-like; *esp.* of the nose: Curved like an eagle's beak, hooked 1646.

† **Aquilon.** ME. [– (O)Fr. *aquilon* – L. *aquilo*, *-ōn-* north wind.] The north or north-north-east wind. SHAKS.

A-qui·ver, *adv.* 1883. [A *prep.*[1] 11.] In a quiver, trembling.

Aquo·se, *a. rare.* 1727. [– L. *aquosus*, f. *aqua* water; see -OSE[1].] Watery.

Aquosity (ăkwǫ·sĭti). 1528. [– late L. *aquositas*, f. as prec.; see -ITY. Cf. Fr. *aquosité.*] Moist or watery quality; † *concr.* moisture, humour –1720.

What better philosophical status has 'vitality' than a. HUXLEY.

Ar (āɹ). Name of the letter R.

Ar, obs. f. ARE (see BE *v.*), and EAR *v.*

† **Ar-**, *pref.*[1] The orig. WGer. form of the prefix, reduced in OE. to *a-*. See A- *pref.* 1 and Æ- *pref.* Cf. ARISE.

Ar-, *pref.*[2] = L. *ad-* bef. *r-*, reduced in OF. to *a-*, and later often re-spelt *ar-* after L., and so in Eng. Hence most words from OF. in *ar-* are now written *arr-*, e.g. *arrange*, etc. See also AD- 2.

-ar[1], *suff.* **1.** of *adjs.* repr. L. *-arem* (*-aris*, *-are*) 'belonging to', cogn. w. *-alem*, and used where *l* preceded. See -AL[1]. In Eng. words adopted from OF. orig. *-er*, but later assim. to L. with *-ar*, e.g. L. *scholarem*, OF. *escolier*, AFr. *escoler*, ME. *scoler*, now *scholar*. **2.** of *sbs.* repr. L. *-are*, *-ar*, neut. of adjs. in *aris*, meaning 'thing pertaining to'.

-ar[2], *suff.*, occas. repr. of L. *-arius*, *-arium* (usu. repr. by -ER, -ARY). Generally, a refash. of *-er* from OFr. *-ier*, after the prec., or after mod.Fr. in *-aire*, as *bursar*, ME. *burser*, F. *boursier*, and *vicar*, F. *vicaire*. The Sc. *notar*, etc., are from the F. forms in *-aire*.

-ar³, *suff.*, occ. var. of -ER, -OR, suffix of agent, and -ER suffix of comparative. Common in n. dial., and in mod.Eng. in *beggar, liar*, etc.

Arab (æ·răb). 1634. [– Fr. *arabe* – L. *Arabs* – Gr. Ἄραψ, Ἀραβ- – Arab. *'arab.*] **1.** A native of Arabia; a member of any of the Arabic-speaking peoples tracing their descent to the 7th c. inhabitants of Arabia. **2.** An Arab horse 1880. **3.** (orig. *City, street Arab.*) A homeless little wanderer; a child of the street 1848. **4.** *adj.* Of or pertaining to Arabia or the Arabs 1816.

3. City Arabs..are like tribes of lawless free-booters 1848. 4. The delicate A. arch of her feet TENNYSON.

‖ **Araba** (ără·bă). Also **aroba.** 1845. [Pers. – Arab. *'araba* wheeled carriage.] A wheeled carriage used in the East.

Arabesque (æræbe·sk). 1656. [– Fr. *arabesque* – It. *arabesco*, f. *arabo* Arab; see -ESQUE.] **A.** *adj.* **1.** Arabian, Arabic 1842; *esp.* carved or painted in arabesque (see *sb.* 2) 1656. **2.** *fig.* Strangely mixed, fantastic 1848.

B. *sb.* [the adj. used *absol.*] † **1.** The vulgar Arabic language –1796. **2.** Mural or surface decoration in colour or low relief, composed in flowing lines of branches, leaves, and scroll-work fancifully intertwined. Also *fig.* 1786.

The arabesques of Raphael and the Renaissance, founded on Græco-Roman work, include representations of living creatures, and to this variety the term is now usually applied. Moorish and Arabic non-figurative work, the type generally known in the Middle Ages, is now distinguished as Moorish Arabesque, or Moresque.

2. *fig.* His manner of writing is—a wild complicated Arabesque CARLYLE. Hence **Arabe·squed** *ppl. a.* ornamented in a. **Arabe·squely** *adv.* in the style of the Arabs, or of arabesques.

Ara·bia. The country so named; *fig.* Spices 1711.

Arabian (ărē¹·biăn). ME. [First as sb., f. OFr. *arabi* (see ARABY) or L. *Arabus* or *Arabius* – Gr. Ἀράβιος + -AN, -IAN.] **A.** *adj.* Belonging to Arabia 1606.

Arabian bird: the phœnix, *fig.* a unique specimen. Oh Anthony, oh thou A. bird *Ant. & Cl.* III. ii. 12.

B. *sb.* A native of Arabia; also, one of an Arabian sect (3rd c.) holding that the soul died and rose with the body ME.

Arabic (æ·răbik), *a.* ME. [– OFr. *arabic* (mod. *arabique*) – L. *Arabicus* – Gr. Ἀραβικός.] **1.** Of or pertaining to Arabia or its language 1650; *esp.* in *Gum arabic*, exuded by certain species of Acacia, and *Arabic acid*, obtained from it. 1616. **2.** *absol.* The language of the Arabs ME.

1. *Arabic numerals*: the figures 1, 2, 3, 4, etc. 2 Those English (or rather European) nouns ..derived from Arabic, as *alchemy, alcohol*, etc. EARLE. Hence **Ara·bical** *a.* **Ara·bicism,** an Arabic idiom or peculiarity. **Ara·bicize** *v.* to make like Arabic.

Arabin (æ·răbin). 1840. [f. ARAB(IC + -IN¹.] *Chem.* The pure soluble principle in gum arabic and the like. Hence **Arabino·se,** sugar derived from a. **Arabi·nic, Arabino·sic** *a.*

‖ **Arabis** (æ·răbis). 1706. [– med.L. *arabis* – Gr. ἀραβίς (Dioscorides), subst. use of fem. of Ἄραψ Arabian.] *Bot.* A genus of cruciferous plants, named prob. from growing on sandy or stony places.

Arabist (æ·răbist). 1753. [f. ARAB + -IST; cf. Fr. *arabiste.*] A student of Arabic, or follower of the medical system of the Arabs.

Arable (æ·răb'l), *a.* 1576. [– (O)Fr. *arable* or L. *arabilis*, f. *arare* to plough; see -ABLE.] Capable of being ploughed; fit for tillage; opp. to *pasture-* or *wood-land.* Also quasi-*sb.* Arable land 1576.

If the tenant conuert arable land into wood COKE.

Araby (æ·răbi). ME. [– OFr. *ar(r)abi*, prob. f. Arab. *'arabī*, adj. of *'arab.* As the name of the country (*sb.* 3) *Araby* is a different word, – (O)Fr. *Arabie* – L. *Arabia* – Gr. Ἀραβία.] **A.** *adj.* Arabian, Arabic (*arch.* and *poet.*) 1502. **B.** *sb.* † **1.** An Arab –1587. † **2.** An Arab horse. ME. only. **3.** Arabia ME.

† **Ara·ce,** *v.* ME. [– AFr. *aracer*, OFr. *aracier*, also *esrachier* :– L. *eradicare* pull up by the roots; see ERADICATE.] To pull up by the roots; to tear away –1530. var. † **Ara·che.**

Araceous (ărē¹·ʃəs), *a.* [f. mod.L. *Araceæ*, f. L. *arum* – Gr. ἄρον; see -ACEOUS.] *Bot.* Belonging to the N.O. *Araceæ*, as the Cuckoo-pint or Wake-robin (*Arum maculatum*).

Arach; see ORACH.

‖ **A·rachis.** [mod.L. – Gr. ἄραχος, ἄρακος, ἀρακίς, some leguminous plant.] *Bot.* A genus of leguminous plants, including one known as the Ground Nut. Hence **Arachi·dic,** as in *Arachidic Acid* ($C_{20}H_{40}O_2$), obtained from the oil of the Ground Nut.

Arachnean (æræknī·ăn), *a. rare.* 1854. [f. Gr. ἀράχναιος (f. ἀράχνη spider or its web) + -AN.] Like a spider's web, gossamer.

Arachnid (ăræ·knid). 1869. [– Fr. *arachnide* or mod.L. *arachnida*, n. pl., f. Gr. ἀράχνη spider; see -ID³.] *Zool.* A member of the *Arachnida.* ‖ **Ara·chnida,** *sb. pl.* [mod.L.], a class of the *Arthropoda*, comprising spiders, scorpions, and mites; distinguished by having eight legs, by lacking wings and antennæ, and by breathing by means of tracheal tubes or pulmonary sacs. Hence **Ara·chnidan** *a.* of or belonging to the *Arachnida*; *sb.* an arachnid. **Arachni·dean, -ian** *a.* and *sb.* = prec. **Arachni·dial** *a.* [f. next] of or pertaining to the *Arachnidium.* ‖ **Arachni·dium** [mod.L.], the apparatus by which the spider produces its web. **Ara·chnidous** *a.* of the nature of the *Arachnida.*

Arachnoid (ăræ·knoid). 1836. [– mod.L. *arachnoides* – Gr. ἀραχνοειδής like a cobweb; see prec., -OID. Cf. Fr. *arachnoïde.*] **A.** *adj.* **1.** *Bot.* Covered with or formed of cobweb-like hairs or fibres 1857. **2.** *Phys.* Of or pertaining to the arachnoid. (See B.) 1782. **3.** *Ent.* Resembling the *Arachnida* 1852.

B. *sb.* The delicate serous membrane or membranous sac lining the *dura mater*, and enveloping the brain and spinal cord 1839.

Hence **Arachnoi·dal** *a.* of the nature of, or pertaining to, the arachnoid. **Arachnoi·deal, -ean, -eous** *a.* unnecessary vars. of ARACHNOID, -AL.

Ara:chnolo·gical, *a.* Of, or pertaining to, arachnology. **Arachno·logist,** a student of, or proficient in, arachnology. **Arachno·logy** [f. Gr. ἀράχνη spider + -LOGY], the department of Zoology relating to spiders, or to the *Arachnida.*

Arad (ēᵊ·răd). 1853. [f. ARUM + -AD 1 d.] *Bot.* An araceous plant, as the Wake-robin.

Aræometer, areo- (ēᵊri,ǫ·mītəɹ). 1706. [– Fr. *aréomètre*, f. Gr. ἀραιός thin + *-mètre* -METER. Cf. *pycnometer* (f. Gr. πυκνός thick, dense).] An instrument for measuring the specific gravity of fluids; a hydrometer. Hence **Aræome·tric, -al** *a.* of or pertaining to aræometry. **Aræo·metry** [Gr. μετρία], the art or science of estimating the specific gravity of fluids by the use of the a.

Aræostyle (ărī·ostəil). Also **areo-.** 1706. [– L. *aræostylus* (Vitruvius) – Gr. ἀραιόστυλος, f. ἀραιός few, rare + στῦλος pillar; cf. Fr. *aréostyle.*] *Arch.* **A.** *adj.* Of columned buildings: Having the distance between the columns equal to four or more diameters of the column. **B.** *sb.* A building, or style of building, in which the columns are so arranged.

Aræosystyle (ărī:osi·stəil). 1834. [– Fr. *aréosystyle* (Perrault, 1673), f. Gr. ἀραιός rare, few + σύστυλος (Vitruvius) with columns close together; see SYSTYLE.] *Arch.* An alternatively very wide and very narrow intercolumniation.

† **Aræo·tic,** *a.* 1634. [– Gr. ἀραιωτικός of or for rarefying, f. ἀραιοῦν rarefy, f. ἀραιός rare; see -IC, -OTIC.] Tending to make thin the humours of the body. Also as *sb.*

† **Ara·ge,** *v.* 1470. [– OFr. *arager, -ier*, f. *à* to + *rage* RAGE *sb.*] To enrage –1568.

Aragonite, arr- (æ·răgŏnəit). 1803. [f. *Aragon* or *Arragon* in Spain + -ITE¹ 2 b.] *Min.* A carbonate of lime, crystallizing in orthorhombic prisms and many derived forms.

Aragonspath, Aragon Spar, = prec.

‖ **Araguato.** 1852. [Sp., Pg. *araguato.*] The 'howling monkey'.

‖ **Araignée** (are·nʸe). 1706. [Fr.; = spider's web.] *Mil.* A military mine constructed with branching galleries.

Arain. *Obs.* exc. *dial.* ME. [– (O)Fr. *araigne* :– L. *aranea* spider.] A spider.

† **Arai·se,** *v.* ME. [A- *pref.* 1; cf. *rise, arise.* Cf. also AREAR.] **1.** To raise, lift up –1557; to raise from the dead –1601; to raise (money, troops, a siege, etc.) –1548. **2.** To arouse –1494.

1. A medicine..powerfull to a. King Peppin SHAKS.

Arak, var. of ARECA, and obs. f. ARRACK.

A-rake (ărē¹·k), *adv.* 1883. [A *prep.*¹ 11.] On the rake; inclined.

Aramæan (ærămī·ăn), *a.* 1834. [f. Gr. Ἀραμαῖος + -AN. Cf. Fr. *araméen.*] Belonging to the country or language of Aram; Syrian, Syriac. As *sb.* A native of Aram.

Aramaic (ærămē·ik), *a.* 1834. [f. Gr. Ἀραμαῖος, f. *'ᵃrām*, Heb. name of Syria; see -IC.] Of Aram; *spec.* applied to the northern branch of the Semitic family of languages, including Syriac and Chaldee. Often used *absol.*, sc. *language.* vars. † **A·ramite,** † **Arami·tic.** Hence **Arama·ism,** an A. idiom or peculiarity.

Araneidan (ærănī·idăn), *a.* 1835. [f. mod. L. *Araneida*, the typical family of *Arachnida*, f. L. *aranea* spider; see -ID³, -AN.] *Zool.* Of or belonging to the *Araneida* or spiders. As *sb.* A spider. **Arane·iform** *a.* having the shape of a spider. **Araneo·logist** = *arachnologist.*

Araneose (ărē¹:ni,ōᵘ·s), *a.* 1880. [– L. *araneosus* full of or like cobwebs, f. *aranea* spider, cobweb; see -OSE¹.] = ARACHNOID. var. **Ara·neous.**

‖ **Arango** (ăræ·ŋgo). Pl. **-oes.** 1715. A bead made of rough carnelian, formerly imported from Bombay for re-exportation to Africa.

† **A-ra·nk,** *adv.* ME. [A *prep.*¹ 11.] In a rank or row –1570.

Araphoro·stic, arapho·stic, *a.* 1828. [Incorr. f. eccl.Gr. ἄρραφος without seam, f. ἀ- A- *pref.* 14 + ῥάπτειν sew.] Unsewed, seamless, as shoes, etc.

† **Ara·se,** *v.* 1523. [– OFr. *araser* raze, f. *à ras*, f. *ras* :– L. *rasus.* Cf. ERASE.] To raze, level with the ground. Also (? erron.) to erase. –1553.

Aration (ărē¹·ʃən). *arch. rare.* 1663. [– L. *aratio*, f. *arat-*, pa. ppl. stem of *arare* to plough; see -ION.] Ploughing; tillage.

Araucaria (ærǭkēᵊ·riă). 1833. [mod.L., fem. sing. (sc. *arbor* tree) f. *Arauco*, name of a province of Chile; see -ARY¹ 3.] *Bot.* A genus of lofty coniferous trees, native to the southern hemisphere, one species of which (*A. imbricata*, called also 'Monkey-puzzler') is now cultivated in Great Britain. Hence **Arauca·rian** *a.* of or belonging to the genus Araucaria; *sb.* a species of this or an allied genus.

A·rbalest, -balist, -blast. *Obs.* exc. *Hist.* [Late OE. *arblast*, ME. *arblaste, arbelest*, later *alblast*, and (w. assim. to *arrow*) *arwe-blast, arow-blast* – OFr. *arbaleste, arbe-* (mod. *arbalète*) :– late L. *arcubalista*, f. *arcus* bow; see ARC, BALLISTA.] **1.** A cross-bow, consisting of a steel bow fitted to a wooden shaft, furnished with special mechanism for drawing and letting slip the bowstring, and discharging arrows, bolts, stones, etc. **2.** = *Arbalester* 1450. **3.** A mathematical instrument, formerly used to take the altitude of the stars 1816.

1. A quarel..shotte out of Arbalaste CAXTON. Unbend thy arblast, and come into the moonlight SCOTT. Hence **A·rbalester, -balister, -blaster,** a soldier armed with an a.; a cross-bowman (*Obs.* exc. *Hist.*). † **A·rbalestre, -ter, -blaster,** = ARBALEST; also, the missile shot from the a. **Arbale·strier, alblastrer** (*Obs.* exc. *Hist.*) = *Arbalester.* **A·rbalestry,** the art or practice of shooting with an a.

† **A·rber, e·rber.** ME. [– OFr. *erbier* (mod. *herbier*), of unkn. origin.] The wind-pipe or weasand; occ. extended to the whole 'pluck'. *To make the erber* (hunting phr.): to take out the 'pluck', the first stage in disembowelling. (See Sir W. Scott in Notes to *Sir Tristram*, p. 268, where it is wrongly explained.)

Arbiter (ā·ɹbitəɹ). 1502. [– L. *arbiter* (whence Fr. *arbitre*).] **1.** *gen.* One whose opinion or decision is authoritative in a matter of debate; a judge. **2.** *spec.* One who is chosen by the parties in a dispute to decide the difference between them; an arbitrator, an umpire 1549. Also *transf.* or *fig.* **3.** One who has a matter under his sole control 1628.

1. The late Mr. Fox (no mean a. in literary taste) T. F. DIBDIN. **2.** *fig.* Twilight..short A. Twixt Day and Night MILT. *P.L.* IX. 50. **3.** Use..which is the a. of language REID.

† **A·rbitrable,** *a.* 1531. [f. L. *arbitrari* to judge, decide + -BLE.] Subject to the decision of an arbiter –1650.

Arbitrage (ā·ɹbitrʒdʒ). 1480. [– (O)Fr. *arbitrage*, f. *arbitrer*; see ARBITRE *v.*, -AGE.] **1.** Exercise of the functions of an arbitrator; decision by arbitration (*arch.*). **2.** Authoritative decision or determination (*arch.*) 1601. **3.** *Comm.* The traffic in Bills of Exchange drawn on sundry places, and bought or sold in sight of the daily quotations of rates in the several markets (see ARBITRATION of Exchange). Also, the similar traffic in Stocks. [In this sense from mod.Fr. and pronounced (arbitra·ʒ).] 1881. Hence **A·rbitragi:st,** one who transacts arbitrage business.

Arbitral (ā·ɹbitrăl), *a.* 1609. [– (O)Fr. *arbitral* or late L. *arbitralis*, f. *arbiter* ARBITER; see -AL¹.] **1.** *Sc. Law.* Of or pertaining to arbiters or arbitration. **2.** Subject to the exercise of will 1662.

Arbitrament, -ement (aɹbi·trămĕnt). ME. [– OFr. *arbitrement* – med.L. *arbitramentum*; see ARBITRATE, -MENT.] † **1.** Free choice –1810. **2.** The power to decide for others; absolute control (*Obs.* exc. as fig. of 3.) 1534. **3.** The deciding of a dispute by an ARBITRATOR. Also *fig.* and *transf.* 1549. **4.** The award of an arbitrator; sentence accepted as authoritative ME. † **5.** Friendly agreement, compromise –1625.

1. To stand or fall Free in thine own A. it lies MILT. *P.L.* VIII. 641. **2.** I committe to your charge and a., that thing LD. BERNERS. **3.** *fig.* The a. of Swords *Hen. V*, IV. i. 168, of Time 1863, of war 1870. **4.** To renounce their a. and sentence 1642.

Arbitrary (ā·ɹbitrări), *a.* (*sb.*) 1574. [– L. *arbitrarius*, f. *arbiter* (perh. after Fr. *arbitraire*); see -ARY¹.] **1.** Dependent upon will or pleasure. (*Obs.* in gen. use.) –1768. **2.** *Law.* Relating to, or dependent on, the discretion of an arbiter; discretionary, not fixed 1581. **3.** Based on mere opinion or preference; *hence*, capricious 1646. **4.** Unrestrained in the exercise of will, absolute; *hence*, despotic 1642. **5.** *sb.* [sc. *number*, *term*, etc.] 1879.

1. The same things were a., and might have been otherwise WHITGIFT. **2.** The fines on admission.. even if a., must be reasonable SCRIVEN. **3.** Our estimation of birth is entirely a. and capricious JOHNSON. **4.** Acts of Will and Tyranny, which make up an A. Government 1642. var. † **Arbitra·rious.** Hence **A·rbitrarily** *adv.* capriciously; despotically; var. † **Arbitra·riously. A·rbitrariness,** capriciousness; despotism.

Arbitrate (ā·ɹbitreˢt), *v.* 1590. [– *arbitrat-*, pa. ppl. stem of L. *arbitrari* examine, give judgement, f. *arbiter*; see -ATE³.] **1.** *gen.* To decide. *Obs.* or *arch.* **2.** *trans.* To give an authoritative decision with regard to, determine (*arch.*) 1605. **3.** To act as arbitrator or umpire (*in*, *between*) 1619. **4.** *trans.* To settle by, or submit to, arbitration 1592.

2. But certaine issue stroakes must a. *Macb.* V. iv. 20. An equal poise of hope and fear Does a. the event MILT. *Comus* 411. **4.** Let them a. the differences 1647. Hence **A·rbitrated** *ppl. a.* settled by arbitration; *spec.* determined by 'Arbitration of Exchange'.

Arbitration (āɹbitrēˢ·ʃən). ME. [– (O)Fr. *arbitration* – L. *arbitratio*, f. *arbitrat-*; see prec., -ION.] † **1.** Uncontrolled decision –1651. **2.** The settlement of a question at issue by one to whom the parties agree to refer their claims in order to obtain an equitable decision 1634.

1. The a. of War, and Peace HOBBES. **2.** *Arbitration-bond*..a bond entered into by two or more parties to abide by the decision of an arbitrator BLACKSTONE. *Arbitration of Exchange* (cf. Fr. *arbitrage*): The determination of the rate of exchange to be obtained between two countries or currencies when the operation is conducted through a third or several intermediate ones, in order to ascertain the most advantageous method of drawing and remitting bills.

Arbitrator (ā·ɹbitreˢtəɹ). ME. [– late L. *arbitrator*, f. as prec.; see -OR 2. Cf. OFr. *arbitrateur*.] **1.** = ARBITER 2. † **2.** Hence *fig.* of that which brings about a definite issue –1606. **3.** = ARBITER 3. 1579.

2. That old common A., Time, Will one day end it *Tr. & Cr.* IV. iii. 225. **3.** God is the a. of success in war WHISTON. Hence **A·rbitra:torship.**

† **A·rbitre,** *v. rare.* 1494. [– (O)Fr. *arbitrer* – L. *arbitrari* ARBITRATE.] Earlier f. ARBITRATE –1548.

† **A·rbitrer, -or.** ME. [– AFr. *arbitrour*, OFr. *arbitreor* :– late L. *arbitrator* ARBITRATOR.] Earlier f. ARBITRATOR –1814.

Arbitress (ā·ɹbitrĕs). ME. [– OFr. *arbitresse*, fem. of *arbitre* ARBITER; see -ESS¹.] A female ARBITER (senses 2, 3).

While over head the Moon Sits A. MILT. *P.L.* I. 784. var. **Arbitra·trix.**

† **Arbitry.** ME. [Two words: 1. *Arbitre* (*e* mute), – OFr. *arbitre* :– L. *arbitrium*; 2. *Arbitrie*, *-y*, later – L. *arbitrium*.] **1.** Power to choose or act –1649. **2.** Arbitration –1609. **3.** Decision, award –1615.

Arblast, -er, vars. of ARBALEST, -ER, -RE.

Arbor¹ (ā·ɹbəɹ). 1659. [– Fr. *arbre* tree, principal axis, assim. in sp. to L. *arbor*.] *Mech.* **a.** The main support or beam of a machine (*e.g.* of a crane); **b.** The axle or spindle on which a wheel revolves. (Cf. *axle-tree.*)

‖ **Arbor**² (ā·ɹbǫɹ). 1669. L. for 'tree', used as part of names in *Bot.*, *Chem.*, etc.; as in *Bot.* **arbor Judæ,** the Judas tree (*Cercis siliquastrum*); in *Chem.* **arbor Dianæ,** the arborescent appearance formed on introducing mercury into a solution of nitrate of silver; **arbor Saturni,** the similar precipitate formed by putting zinc into a solution of acetate of lead.

Arbora·ceous, *a.* 1848. [f. L. *arbor* tree + -ACEOUS.] Tree-like or wooded.

A·rbor Day. 1872. [ARBOR².] A day set apart, orig. in Nebraska, U.S.A., for the planting of trees.

Arboreal (aɹbōᵊ·rĭăl), *a.* 1667. [f. L. *arboreus* (f. *arbor* tree) + -AL¹.] **1.** Pertaining to, or of the nature of, trees; vars. **A·rboral, A·rborary, Arbo·rical** (*rare*). **2.** Connected with, haunting, or inhabiting trees 1834; var. **Arbo·rean.**

Arboreous (aɹbōᵊ·rĭəs), *a.* 1646. [f. as prec. + -OUS.] **1.** Abounding in trees 1664. **2.** = ARBOREAL 1646. **3.** = ARBORESCENT 1753.

Arborescence (āɹbŏre·sĕns). 1856. [f. next; see -ENCE.] Tree-like formation. Also *fig.*

Arborescent (āɹbŏre·sent), *a.* 1675. [– *arborescent-*, pres. ppl. stem of L. *arborescere*, f. *arbor* tree; see -ESCENT; cf. Fr. *arborescent*.] **1.** Tree-like in growth or size; having a woody stem. **2.** Branching like a tree 1679; *spec.* in *Arch.* 1849.

1. A. grass, very like a bamboo DARWIN. Hence **Arbore·scently** *adv.*

Arboret¹ (ā·ɹbŏret). *arch.* 1596. [f. L. *arbor* tree + -ET.] A little tree, a shrub.

† **A·rboret**². 1604. [– L. *arboretum* (next).] A shrubbery; arbour.

‖ **Arboretum** (āɹborī·tŏm). Pl. **-a.** 1838. [L., = place grown with trees.] A place devoted to the cultivation and exhibition of rare trees; a tree-garden.

Arbo·ricole, *a. rare.* 1874. [– Fr. *arboricole*, f. L. *arbor* tree + *-cola* inhabiting.] Inhabiting or haunting trees.

Arboriculture (ā·ɹbŏriˌkʊ:ltiŭr). 1834. [f. as prec. + L. *cultura* tending, after *agriculture*.] The cultivation of trees and shrubs for use and ornament. Hence **A:rboricu·ltural** *a.* **A:rboricu·lturist.**

A·rboriform, arbo·-, *a.* 1848. [f. as prec. + -FORM.] = ABORESCENT 2.

Arborist (ā·ɹbŏrist). 1578. [orig. – Fr. *arboriste*; later f. as prec. + -IST.] † **a.** A keeper of a 'herber', a herbalist. **b.** A scientific student or cultivator of trees.

Arborization (ā:ɹbŏrəizēˢ·ʃən). 1794. [f. L. *arbor* tree; see -IZATION.] The production of a tree-like appearance, as (*Min.* and *Chem.*) in dendritic silver ore, or the markings of agates, etc.; (*Anat.*) by the distension or injection of capillary vessels.

Arborize (ā·ɹbŏrəiz), *v.* 1847. [f. L. *arbor* tree + -IZE.] To make tree-like. Perh. only in **A·rborized** *ppl. a.*

Arborous (ā·ɹbŏrəs), *a.* [f. late L. *arborosus* tree-like (Dioscurides); see -OUS.] Of, belonging to, or consisting of trees. MILT.

† **Arbor vine** (J.), **arbor** (? *arbour*) **wind.** 1551. The Sarsaparilla.

‖ **Arbor vitæ** (ā·ɹbǫɹ vəi·tī). 1664. [L., = tree of life.] **1.** *Bot.* An evergreen shrub of the genus *Thuja*, N.O. *Coniferæ*. **2.** *Phys.* The arborescent appearance of a longitudinal section of the cerebellum 1800.

† **A·rbory.** 1600. [After wds. in -ORY, or -RY.] = ARBOUR –1695.

Arbour, -or (ā·ɹbəɹ). ME. [orig. *erber* – AFr. *erber*, OFr. *erbier* (mod. *herbier*), f. *erbe* herb + *-ier* :– L. *-arium*; see -ARIUM. Normal phonetic change gave (*h*)*arber*, (*h*)*arbour*, and the sp. *arbour* was furthered by assoc. w. L. *arbor* tree.] † **1.** A garden lawn, or green; a garden of herbs or flowers –1578. † **2.** An orchard. [Cf. *orchard*, and Fr. *verger*. Orchards were usu. formed on grass.] –1580. † **3.** Trees or shrubs, trained on trellis-work; espaliers –1648. **4.** A bower or shady retreat, usu. of lattice-work covered with climbing shrubs and plants ME.; † a covered alley or walk –1712.

4. A litel herber that I have, That benched was on turves fressh ygrave CHAUCER. Those hollies of themselves a shape As of an a. took, A close, round a. COLERIDGE. Yon flourie Arbors, yonder Allies green, Our walks at noon, with branches overgrown MILT. *P.L.* IV. 626. Hence **A·rboured** *ppl. a.* embowered; furnished with arbours.

Arbuscle (ā·ɹbɒs'l). 1657. [– L. *arbuscula*, dim. of *arbor*, *arbos* tree; see -CULE.] **a.** A dwarf tree, a tree-like shrub. **b.** A tuft of feathery cilia. Hence **Arbu·scular** *a.* of or pertaining to arbuscles; tufted.

† **Arbu·st.** *rare.* [– Fr. *arbuste* shrub – L. *arbustum* plantation.] A dwarf tree, a shrub. EVELYN. Hence † **Arbu·stive** *a.* shrubby; trained to a tree.

Arbute (ā·ɹbiŭt). *arch.* or *poet.* 1551. [– L. *arbutus* (next).] = ARBUTUS.

The thin-leav'd A. Hazle Graffs receives DRYDEN.

‖ **Arbutus** (ā·ɹbiutŏs). 1551. [L.] A genus of evergreen shrubs and trees (N.O. *Ericaceæ*), including the species *Arbutus unedo*, or Strawberry Tree, cultivated for ornamental purposes.

Arc (āɹk). ME. [– (O)Fr. *arc* :– L. *arcus* bow, arch, curve.] **1.** Part of a curve; also *transf.* or *fig.* 1570. **2.** *spec.* in *Astr.* The part of a circle which a heavenly body appears to pass through above (*diurnal arc*) or below (*nocturnal arc*) the horizon. The earliest use in Eng. Also *fig.* ME. **3.** A band contained between parallel curves, or anything of this form, e.g. the rainbow (Fr. *arc-en-ciel*), the arc of a quadrant, etc. 1642. † **4.** An arch. (Cf. Fr. *arc de triomphe.*) –1731. **5.** *Electr.* The luminous bridge formed between two carbon poles, when they are separated by a small air space, and a current of electricity is sent through them. Also *attrib.* in *a. lamp*, *light*. 1821. **6.** *transf.* in *Phys.* Circuit 1855.

2. Parfourmed hath the sonne his ark diourne CHAUCER. **4.** Turn arcs of triumph to a garden-gate POPE.

Arc, obs. f. ARK.

‖ **Arcabucero** (āɹkābupē·ro). [Sp.] = HARQUEBUSIER. LONGF.

Arcade (aɹkēˢ·d), *sb.* 1731. [– Fr. *arcade* – Pr. *arcada* or It. *arcata*, f. Rom. **arca* ARCH *sb.*; see -ADE.] † **1.** An arched opening or recess in a wall –1823. **2.** 'A continued arch' (J.); a passage; a walk formed by a succession of arches having a common axis, and supported on columns or shafts. Also used of an avenue of trees, etc.; and of any covered avenue, *esp.* one with rows of shops, etc., on one or both sides 1731. **3.** *Arch.* A series of arches on the same plane, either open or closed: 'In mediæval architecture, an ornamental dressing to a wall, consisting of colonnettes supporting moulded arches.' Gwilt. (= Fr. *arcature.*) 1795.

1. A small a. or receptacle for holy water WARTON. **2.** A garden, with trim lawns, green arcades and vistas of classic statues THACKERAY.

Arcade (aɹkēˢ·d), *v.* 1805. [f. the sb.] To furnish with, or form into, an arcade. Hence **Arca·ding** *vbl. sb.* arcades as ornament.

Arcadian (aɹkēˢ·diăn), *a.*¹ and *sb.* 1590. [f. L. *Arcadius* (f. Gr. Ἀρκαδία in the Peloponnesus) + -AN.] **A.** *adj.* Belonging to Arcadia, taken as the ideal region of rural felicity; ideally rural or rustic 1667. **B.** *sb.* An ideal rustic. Hence **Arca·dianism,** pastoral simplicity. **Arca·dianly** *adv.*

Arca·dian, *a.*[2] 1870. [f. ARCADE *sb.* + -IAN.] Of, pertaining to, or furnished with arcades.

Arcady (ā·ɹkădi). *poet.* 1590. [– L. *Arcadia* – Gr. Ἀρκαδία; cf. Fr. *Arcadie.*] Arcadia; see ARCADIAN[1].

Arcane (aɹkēⁱ·n), *a.* 1547. [– (O)Fr. *arcane* or L. *arcanus*, f. *arcēre* shut up, f. *arca* chest.] Hidden, secret.

The A. Mysteries of Atheism CUDWORTH.

|| **Arcanum** (aɹkēⁱ·nðm). Usu. in pl. **-a.** 1599. [L., n. sing. of *arcanus* ARCANE, used subst. In XVII–XVIII the pl. was occas. treated as sing. with pl. *arcanas.*] **1.** A hidden thing; a profound secret. **2.** *Alchem.* One of the great secrets of nature; *hence*, a marvellous remedy, an elixir 1646.

1. The mysterious arcana of political intrigue R. F. BURTON. **2.** The Philosophers stone, potable gold, or any of those Arcana's SIR T. BROWNE. Hence **Arca·nal** *a.*

|| **Arc-boutant** (ā:r,butaṅ·). 1731. [Fr.] *Arch.* An arched or flying buttress.

Arch (āɹtʃ), *sb.* ME. [– (O)Fr. *arche* :– Rom. **arca*, n. pl. taken as fem. sing., f. L. *arcus* ARC.] **I.** = L. *arcus.* † **1.** = ARC 1, 2. –1831. **2.** A curved structure of firm material, either bearing weight or merely ornamental ME. **3.** *transf.* Anything having the curves or structures of 1, 2; *esp.* the rainbow 1590. **4.** Curvature in the shape of an arch 1855. **5.** An arched roof, a vault; *fig.* the heavens 1606. **6. Court of Arches,** or briefly *Arches*: the eccles. court of appeal for the province of Canterbury, formerly held at the church of St. Mary-le-Bow (or 'of the Arches'), so named from the arches that supported its steeple 1297.

1. An A. of the Horizon SIR T. BROWNE. **2.** 'Tis the last keystone That makes the a. B. JONS. **3.** The circled arches of thy brows GREENE. The Queene o'th Skie, whose watry A., and messenger, am I *Temp.* IV. i. 71. **4.** The delicate Arab a. of her feet TENNYSON. **5.** This vaulted A. *Cymb.* I. vi. 33. **6.** Cited to appear in the Arches at Bow Church FOXE.

II. *pl.* (= L. *arca.*) Archives 1600.

Comb. etc.: **a.-brick, -stone,** a wedge-shaped brick or stone used in the construction of arches; **-buttress** = ARC-BOUTANT; **archways** = ARCHWISE; **-work,** structure consisting of arches.

Arch (āɹtʃ), *v.* ME. [f. prec.; cf. OFr. *archer.*] **1.** To furnish with an arch. **2.** To form into an arch, to curve. *trans.* 1625. *absol.* and *intr.* 1732. Also with *over.* † **3.** To put *together* so as to be mutually supporting, like the stones of an arch. So *to arch up.* –1662. **4.** *trans.* To overarch 1795.

2. Arched like the back of a frightened Cat BUCKLAND. Build on the wave, or a. beneath the sand POPE. **4.** The blue blocks that a. the source of the Arveiron TYNDALL.

Arch (āɹtʃ), *a.* (*sb.*) 1547. [The prefix ARCH- used independently as adj.] **1.** Chief, prime, pre-eminent. (Now rare without the hyphen.) **2.** [From assoc. with *wag, knave*, etc., and hence with *fellow, face*, etc.] Clever, cunning, waggish. Now usu. of women and children: Slyly saucy, pleasantly mischievous 1662. **3.** quasi-*sb.* A chief (one) 1605.

1. We cannot helpe it though we can, which is the A. infirmity in all morality 1647. **2.** The archest chin Mockery ever ambush'd in M. ARNOLD. **3.** The Noble Duke. . My worthy A. and Patron *Lear* II. i. 61.

Arch- (āɹtʃ; exc. in *archangel*), *prefix*; repr. Gr. ἀρχι-, comb. f. ἀρχός chief. In OE. at first translated by *héah-* high, but later adopted from L. as *arće-, ærće-, erće-*, ME. *erche-, arche-*. From these *arch-* later became a living formative. (In mod. literary words from Gr. the prefix is ARCHI- q.v.). In pronunciation established compounds tend to have the main stress on *arch-*, *esp.* when prefixed to a name, as *A·rchbishop Cra·nmer.* **1.** In titles: meaning, 'Chief, principal, -in-chief; superior, -master'; as ARCHBISHOP, ARCHDEACON, ARCHDUKE; *esp.* in titles of offices in the Holy Roman or German empire, as *arch-chamberlain*, etc. 1693. **2.** In descriptive appellations: meaning, 'One pre-eminent as; greatest, chief, leading', as *arch-mystagogue*, etc. In mod. use *esp.* with terms of odium: meaning, 'Out-and-out, worst of, ringleader of'; as *arch-agitator*, etc., often with a specific reference to the Devil. 1548. **3.** As prec., with sense of 'First in time, original', as *arch-father.* Mostly *arch.* 1541. **4.** Of things: with senses: **a.** 'Chief, main, prime', as *arch-mock* (*Oth.* IV. i. 71); **b.** 'Primitive, original', as † *arch-christendom. spec.* **a.-house,** archducal house (of Austria); † **-sea,** archipelago; **-see,** archiepiscopal see. **5.** Adjectives: as † *arch-chemic.* MILT. *P. L.* III. 609.

-arch, repr. Gr. -αρχος, -άρχης ruling, rel. to ἀρχή rule, ἄρχειν begin, take the lead, as in μόναρχος MONARCH, τέτραρχος TETRARCH, ἐθνάρχης ETHNARCH. The corresp. abstract sbs. end in *-archy*, repr. Gr. -αρχεία, -αρχία government, leadership; see -Y[3].

Archæan (aɹkī·ăn), *a.* 1881. [f. Gr. ἀρχαῖος + -AN.] *Geol.* Of or belonging to the earliest geological period.

Archæo- (ā:ɹki,o), – Gr. ἀρχαιο-, comb. f. ἀρχαῖος ancient, primitive (f. ἀρχή beginning). Formerly, and still occas., spelt *archaio-*.

archæo-geo·logy, that of ancient periods of the world's history; **-li·thic** [Gr. λίθος] *a.*, of or pertaining to the most ancient stone implements used by prehistoric man; **-sto·matous** [Gr. στόμα] *a.*, having the primitive orifice of invagination of the wall of the embryo persistent as a mouth; **-zo·ic** [Gr. ζωή] *a.*, pertaining to the era of the earliest living beings on our planet.

Archæography (āɹki,ǫ·grăfi). 1804. [f. ARCHÆO- + -GRAPHY.] Systematic description of antiquities. Hence **A:rchæogra·phical** *a.*

Archæologic (ā:ɹki,o,lǫ·dʒik), *a.* 1731 [– Gr. ἀρχαιολογικός; see ARCHÆOLOGY and -IC.] Of or pertaining to archæology. Hence **A:rchæolo·gical** *a.* **A:rchæolo·gically** *adv.*

Archæo·logist. 1824. [f. next; see -IST.] A professed student of archæology. vars. **Archæo·loger, A:rchæolo·gian.**

Archæology (āɹki,ǫ·lŏdʒi). 1607. [– mod.L. *archæologia* – Gr. ἀρχαιολογία, f. ἀρχαῖος ancient + -λογία -LOGY.] **1.** Ancient history generally; systematic description or study of antiquities. **2.** *spec.* The scientific study of the remains and monuments of the prehistoric period.

2. A. displays old structures and buried relics of the remote past TYLOR.

|| **Archæopteryx** (āɹki,ǫ·ptĕriks). 1859. [f. ARCHÆO- + Gr. πτέρυξ wing.] *Palæont.* The oldest known fossil bird, having a long vertebrate tail.

Archaic (aɹkē·ik), *a.* 1832. [– Fr. *archaïque* – Gr. ἀρχαϊκός, f. ἀρχαῖος ancient; see -IC.] Marked by the characteristics of an earlier period; primitive, antiquated 1846; *esp.* of language: Belonging to an earlier period, though still retained by individuals, or for special purposes, poetical, liturgical, etc. 1832. Hence **Archa·ical** *a.* (*rare*), **-ly** *adv.*

Archaism (ā·ɹke,iz'm). 1643. [– mod.L. *archaismus* – Gr. ἀρχαϊσμός, f. ἀρχαΐζειν copy the ancients in language, etc., f. ἀρχαῖος ancient; see -ISM.] **1.** The retention or imitation of what is old or obsolete; archaic style. **2.** An archaic word or expression 1748. Hence **A·rchaist,** an antiquary; one who employs archaism. **Archai·stic** *a.* of or pertaining to an archaist; imitatively archaic; affectedly antique.

Archaize (ā·ɹke,əiz), *v.* 1850. [– Gr. ἀρχαΐζειν; see prec., -IZE.] To imitate the archaic; to render archaistic.

Archangel (ā·ɹk,ēⁱ·ndʒĕl). OE. [– AFr. *archangele* – eccl.L. *archangelus* – eccl.Gr. (LXX) ἀρχάγγελος; see ARCH-, ANGEL.] **1.** An angel of the highest rank. Also *fig.* **2.** *Herb.* **a.** Name of several species of Dead-Nettle and allied plants (*Lamium, Galeopsis, Galeobdolon, Stachys*); **b.** formerly of the Black Stinking Horehound (*Ballota nigra*). 1551. **3.** A fancy pigeon 1867.

1. The feast of S. Michael the Ark-angell. 1642. Hence **Archange·lic, -al,** *a.* **Archa·ngelship.**

Archbishop (ā·ɹtʃ,bi·ʃəp; see ARCH-). OE. [prob. a substitution of *arch-* for *héah* in OE. *héah-bisćop.*] The chief bishop: the highest dignitary in an episcopal church, superintending the bishops of his province; a metropolitan.

We shall see him For it, an Arch-byshop *Hen. VIII*, III. ii. 74. Hence **Archbi·shopess** (*nonce-wd.*), the wife of an a. **Archbi·shophood, Archbi·shopship. Archbi·shopling. Archbi·shoply** *a.*

Archbi·shop, *v.* 1692. [f. prec.] To make or call archbishop. In phr. *To archbishop it*: to act as archbishop.

Archbi·shopric. OE. [f. ARCHBISHOP *sb.* + OE. *rīce* region; see BISHOPRIC.] The see, jurisdiction, rank, or office, of an archbishop.

Arch-buttress; see ARCH *sb.*

Arch-butler, -chamberlain, etc.; see ARCH- 1.

A·rch-cha·nter. *Hist.* ME. [f. ARCH- + CHANTER, after med.L. *archicantor* (also in Eng. use).] A precentor.

Archdeacon (ā·ɹtʃ,dī·kən; see ARCH-). [OE. *arće-, erće-diacon* – eccl.L. *archidiaconus* (Jerome) – eccl.Gr. ἀρχιδιάκονος; see ARCHI- 1, DEACON.] The chief deacon: *orig.* the chief of the attendants on a bishop, whose duties gradually placed him next in rank to the bishop. In *Eng. Ch.* the archdeacon is appointed by the bishop, superintends the rural deans, and holds the lowest eccl. court, with the power of spiritual censure.

Which archdeacons are termed in law the bishops eies 1577. Hence **Archdea·conate,** the position of a. **Archdea·coness,** the wife of an a. **Archdea·conry,** the jurisdiction, rank, office, or residence, of an a. **Archdea·conship.**

A·rchdea·n. *Hist.* ME. [ARCH- 1.] The chief of the deans. Sc. for ARCHDEACON. –1646. Hence † **Archdea·nery,** the jurisdiction, rank, or office of an a.

Archdiocese (ā·ɹtʃ,dəi·ŏsīs). 1844. [ARCH- 4.] The see or jurisdiction of an archbishop.

Archduchess (ā·ɹtʃ,dɒ·tʃĕs). 1618. [– Fr. *arche-, archiduchesse*; see ARCH- 1, DUCHESS.] The wife of an archduke; or *spec.* a daughter of the Emperor of Austria.

Archduchy (ā·ɹtʃ,dɒ·tʃi). 1680. [– earlier Fr. *archeduché* (now *archi-*); see ARCH- 4, DUCHY.] The territory subject to an archduke. var. **Archdu·kedom.**

Archduke (ā·ɹtʃ,diū·k, ā·ɹtʃ,diū:k; see ARCH-). 1530. [– OFr. *archeduc* (now *archi-*) :– Merovingian L. *archidux, -duc-* (*c* 750); see ARCH- 1, DUKE.] The chief duke: *formerly* title of the rulers of Austrasia, Lorraine, Brabant, and Austria; *now* titular dignity of sons of the Emperor of Austria. Hence **Archdu·cal** *a.*

† **Arche.** ME. [– (O)Fr. *arche* :– L. *arca*; see ARK.] = ARK *sb.* 2, 3. Also *transf.* –1532.

Arched (āɹtʃt, -tʃĕd), *ppl. a.* 1581. [f. ARCH *v.* + -ED[1].] Furnished with, formed into, or consisting of, an arch or arches 1598. † **b. A viol,** a musical instrument somewhat resembling a hurdy-gurdy (PEPYS *Diary* 5 Oct. 1664).

1. The right arched-beauty of the brow *Merry W.*

Archegay (ā·ɹtʃĭgāi). *Hist.* 1523. [– OFr. *archegaie, archigaie*, var. of *arcigaie, azagaye*; see ASSAGAI. Erron. disyllabic in W. Morris.] An iron-pointed wooden dart; an assagai.

|| **Archegonium** (āɹkĭgōᵘ·niðm). Pl. **-a.** 1854. [mod.L., dim. of Gr. ἀρχέγονος, f. ἀρχε- = ἀρχι- (see ARCHI-) + γόνος race. Occ. **archegon.**] *Bot.* The female organ in Cryptogams, corresponding to the pistil in flowering plants. Hence **Archego·nial** *a.*

Archelogy (aɹke·lŏdʒi). 1856. [– mod.L. *archelogia*, f. Gr. ἀρχή beginning; see -LOGY.] The scientific study of principles.

† **A·rchemastry.** 1477. [f. ARCHI- 1 + MASTERY.] Supreme skill; mastery of applied science, or applied mathematics –1594. Hence † **A·rchemaster,** a supreme master.

A·rch-e·nemy. 1550. [ARCH- 2.] A chief enemy; *spec.* the arch-fiend Satan.

Archer (ā·ɹtʃəɹ). ME. [– AFr. *archer*, OFr. *archier* (mod. *archer*) :– Rom. **arcarius*, f. L. *arcus* bow, ARC; see -ER[2].] **1.** One who shoots with bow and arrows, *esp.* in war; a bowman. Also *fig.* and *attrib.* † **2.** An arrow. (Cf. *arbalester.*) –1485. † **3.** Name of the bishop in Chess 1656. **4.** The ninth zodiacal constellation, *Sagittarius* 1594. **5.** *Ichthyol.* A fish (*Toxotes jaculator* Cuvier), which shoots water at insects resting near.

1. If wee can doe this, Cupid is no longer an A. *Much Ado* II. i. 401. Hence **A·rcher-ess, -ship.**

Archery (ā·ɹtʃəri). ME. [– OFr. *archerie*, f. *archier* archer; see -ERY 2.] **1.** The practice or art of shooting with bow and arrow; skill as an archer. Also *fig.* **2.** *collect.* An archer's weapons; bows, arrows, etc. 1440. **3.** *collect.* A company of archers 1465. † **4.** A feudal service (see quot.) 1691.

1. Sir Boy let me see your Archerie *Tit. A.* IV. iii. 2. **4.** *Archery* was a Service of keeping a Bow for the Use of the Lord [etc.] BLOUNT.

Arches (ā·ɹtʃīz). 1626. [Cf. *arch-sea*, ARCH- 4.] A seamen's term for the Archipelago.

Arches-court; see ARCH *sb.* 6.

Archetypal (aɹke·tipăl, ā·ɹkĭtəipăl), *a.* 1642. [f. L. *archetypum* ARCHETYPE + -AL[1].] Of the nature of, constituting, or pertaining to, an archetype; primitive, original.

(In Platonic philosophy, *archetypal* is applied to the idea or form as present in the divine mind prior to creation, and still cognizable by intellect, independently of the *ectypal* object.)

A. forms of language FARRAR. Hence **Archety·pally** *adv.* var. † **Archety·pical.**

Archetype (ā·ɹkĭtəip). Also † **archi-**, † **arch-**. 1605. [– L. *archetypum* – Gr. ἀρχέτυπον, subst. use of n. of adj., 'first moulded as a model', f. ἀρχε- (var. of ἀρχι-) + τύπος model, TYPE. Cf. Fr. *archétype* (OFr. *arquetipe*).] **1.** The original pattern from which copies are made; a prototype. **2.** *spec.* **a.** in *Minting.* A coin of standard weight. ? *Obs.* **b.** in *Compar. Anat.* An assumed ideal pattern of the fundamental structure of each great division of organized beings 1849.

1. The House of Commons, the a. of all the representative assemblies which now meet MACAULAY. **2.** The vertebrated a. MURCHISON.

Archetypist (ā·ɹkĭtəipist). 1881. [f. prec. + -IST.] One who studies early typography.

‖ **Archeus** (aɹkī·ŏs). *Hist.* 1641. [mod.L. *archæus*, f. Gr. ἀρχαῖος ancient.] The Paracelsian immaterial principle which produces and regulates the activities of the animal and vegetable economy; vital force. Also *attrib.* 1798. Hence † **Arche·al** *a.*

Arch-fiend (ā·ɹtʃ,fī·nd). 1667. [ARCH- 2.] A chief of fiends; Satan.

Arch-flamen (ā·ɹtʃ,flē[i]·men). ME. [– med.L. *archiflamen* = *archiepiscopus*; see ARCHI-, FLAMEN.] A chief flamen or priest; an archbishop.

Bishop Valentine! thou venerable A. of Hymen LAMB

Arch-foe (ā·ɹtʃ,fō[u]·). 1615. [ARCH- 2.] Arch-enemy; *spec.* the Devil.

A·rch-he·retic. 1528. [ARCH- 1, 2.] A chief or first heretic; a founder or leader of heresy. So **Arch-heresy,** fundamental or extreme heresy.

Archi- (ā:ɹki-), *pref.*, – L. *archi-*, Gr. ἀρχι-; see ARCH-. The form used in words taken in modern times from Gr. or L., in compounds modelled on these, and occ. in adjs. whose sbs., being of earlier date, have *arch-*, as *archdeacon, archidiaconal.*

1. = ARCH-; chief, first in authority or order. **a.** in *sbs.*, as ‖ **archidida·scalus** [Gr. ἀρχι-διδάσκαλος], head-master of a school; whence **archididasca·lian, -ine** *a.*; **archi-master,** see *Archemaster*; **architypo·grapher** [mod.L. *architypographus* in Laudian Statutes], chief printer, superintendent of printing office. **b.** in *adjs.*, as ARCHIDIACONAL, etc. **2.** In *Biol.* and *Anthrop.*, meaning 'archetypal' or 'primitive'; as **a·rchiblast,** the epiblast; **archine·phron,** the primitive kidney, whence **archine·phric** *a.*; **archiptery·gium,** the primitive fin or wing, whence **archiptery·gian** *a.* Also **archili·thic, archizo·ic;** see ARCHÆO-.

Archiater (ăɹki,ē[i]·təɹ). 1634. [– late L. *archiatrus, archiater* – Gr. ἀρχίατρος, f. ἀρχι- + ἰατρός physician. Cf. Fr. *archiatre.*] The chief physician, *esp.* the king's or court physician.

† **A·rchical,** *a.* 1651. [f. Gr. ἀρχικός, f. ἀρχή + -AL[1].] **1.** Governmental –1692. **2.** Of the nature of a first principle. CUDWORTH.

Archidiaconal (ā:ɹki,dəi,æ·kŏnăl), *a.* 1651. [– med.L. *archidiaconalis*; see ARCHI-, DIACONAL *a.*] Of, pertaining to, or holding the position of, an archdeacon. So **Archidia·conate,** the office or order of archdeacons (*rare*).

†‖ **Archido·xis.** 1643. [mod.L., f. Gr. ἀρχι- ARCHI- + δόξις opinion.] A work of Paracelsus; a collection of philosophical secrets.

Archiepiscopacy (ā:ɹki,ĭpi·skŏpăsi). 1642. [f. eccl.L. *archiepiscopus* – Gr. ἀρχιεπίσκοπος (Athanasius, *c* 320) archbishop + -ACY.] **a.** The system of church government by archbishops. † **b.** = *archiepiscopate* 1662. So **A:rchiepi·scopal** *a.* of, pertaining to, or of the nature of, an archbishop. **Archiepi·scopalship. A:rchiepi:scopa·lity,** archiepiscopal character. **A:rchiepi·scopate,** an archbishop's tenure of office; also = ARCHBISHOPRIC.

Archi·gony. 1876. [f. Gr. ἀρχι- (see ARCHI- 2) + -γονία begetting.] = ABIOGENESIS.

Archil (ā·ɹtʃil, ā·ɹkil). 1483. [var. of ORCHIL.] A name of various species of lichens, also called Orchil and Orchilla-weed (*Roccella tinctoria*, etc.), which yield a violet dye, and the chemical test substance litmus. Also, the colouring-matter prepared from these lichens.

Archilochian (ăɹkilō[u]·kiăn), *a.* 1751. [f. L. *Archilochius* (f. Gr. Ἀρχίλοχος) + -AN.] Pertaining to, or derived from, Archilochus, the alleged inventor of iambic metre.

Archimage (ā·ɹkimē[i]dʒ). 1553. [– Gr. ἀρχίμαγος chief of the magi; see ARCHI-, MAGE, MAGUS, and cf. Fr. *archimage.*] A chief magician; a great wizard.

Dismiss. . the false a., Dissimulation SCOTT.

Archimandrite (ăɹkimæ·ndrəit). 1591. [– Fr. *archimandrite* or eccl.L. *archimandrita* – eccl.Gr. ἀρχιμανδρίτης, f. ἀρχι- ARCHI- + μάνδρα enclosure, stable, monastery; see -ITE[1] 1.] In *Gr. Ch.* The superior of a monastery, or the superintendent of several; an *abbot*, or *father provincial.*

Archimedean (ăɹkimī·dīăn, -midī·ăn), *a.* Also **-ian.** 1813. [f. late L. *Archimedeus* (f. next) + -AN.] Of, pertaining to, or invented by Archimedes.

Archimedean Screw or *Archimedes' Screw*: an instrument for raising water, formed by winding a tube into the form of a screw around a long cylinder.

‖ **Archimedes** (ăɹkimī·dīz). Also **Archimede** (ā·ɹkimīd). 1630. [Gr. proper name.] A Syracusan mathematician, famous for discoveries in applied mechanics, etc., and for the saying that with a point to stand upon he could move the world. (Used connotatively.)

Archimime (ā·ɹkiməi:m). Also **arch-.** 1658. [– L. *archimimus* – Gr. ἀρχίμιμος; see ARCHI-, MIME *sb.*] A chief buffoon or jester; the chief mimic who in Roman funeral processions imitated the deceased.

Arching (ā·ɹtʃiŋ), *vbl. sb.* 1598. [f. ARCH *v.* + -ING[1].] The action of the vb. ARCH; *concr.* structure consisting of arches; arched curve. *ppl. a.* Forming an arch, or arched curve 1677.

Archipelago (ăɹki,pe·lăgo[u]). Pl. **-os, -oes.** 1502. [– It. *arcipelago* (XIII), f. Gr. ἀρχι- ARCHI- + πέλαγος sea. No such word appears in ancient or med. Gr. It is an Italian formation.] **1.** The Ægean Sea, between Greece and Asia Minor. *Hence* **2.** Any sea or sheet of water, studded (like the Ægean) with many islands; *transf.* a group of islands 1600.

2. These broken lands and Islands being very many in number, do seeme to make there an Archipelagus HAKLUYT. var. † **Archipe·l.** Hence **A:rchipela·gian, A:rchipela·gic** *adjs.*

† **Archisy·nagogue.** 1582. [– eccl.L. *archisynagogus* – Gr. ἀρχισυνάγωγος (in N.T.); see ARCHI- 1, SYNAGOGUE.] The ruler of a synagogue –1753.

Architect (ā·ɹkitekt). 1563. [– Fr. *architecte* – It. *architetto*, or their source, L. *architectus* – Gr. ἀρχιτέκτων, f. ἀρχι- ARCHI- + τέκτων builder.] **1.** A master-builder. *spec.* One whose profession it is to prepare plans of edifices, and exercise a general superintendance over their erection. *Naval Architect*: One who takes this part in the construction of ships. **2.** One who designs and frames any complex structure; *esp.* the Creator 1659. **3.** One who so plans or constructs as to achieve a desired result; a builder-up 1588; *transf.* of things 1835.

1. One pulls down his house and calls architects about him JOHNSON. **2.** The great A. of nature CHALMERS. The a. of the Iliad GROTE. **3.** Chiefe A. and plotter of these woes *Tit. A.* V. iii. 122. Hence **A·rchitective** *a.* pertaining to architecture; fitted for construction. † **A·rchitector** = ARCHITECT 1; a superintendent. **A·rchitectress,** a female a.

Architectonic, -al (ā:ɹki,tektǫ·nik, -ăl). 1595. [– L. *architectonicus* (Vitruvius) – Gr. ἀρχιτεκτονικός; see prec., -IC, -AL[1].] **A.** *adj.* **1.** Of or pertaining to architecture; serviceable for construction 1608. **2.** Constructive 1595. **3.** Directive, controlling. (So in Gr.) 1678. **4.** *esp.* in *Metaph.* Pertaining to the systematization of knowledge 1801.

1. A. skill [of birds] G. WHITE. **4.** The a. impulse of reason, which seeks to refer all science to one principle 1877. Hence **A:rchitecto·nically** *adv.* in relation to architectonics; with architectural fitness.

B. *sb.* **Architectonic(s:** the science **a.** of architecture 1660; **b.** (*Metaph.*) of the systematic arrangement of knowledge 1838.

Architectural (ăɹkite·ktiŭrăl), *a.* 1762. [f. ARCHITECTURE + -AL[1].] Of, relating to, or according to, architecture. Hence **Archite·cturali:st,** a professed student of, or connoisseur in, architecture. **Architecturaliza·tion,** adaptation to the purposes of architecture. **Archite·cturali:ze** *v.* to adapt to architectural purposes or design. **Archite·cturally** *adv.*

Architecture (ā·ɹkitektiŭr), *sb.* 1563. [– Fr. *architecture* or L. *architectura*; see ARCHITECT, -URE.] **1.** The art or science of constructing edifices for human use, specialized as *Civil, Ecclesiastical, Naval,* and *Military.* Occas. regarded merely as a fine art. (See quots.) **2.** The action or process of building (*arch.*) 1646. **3.** *concr.* Architectural work; structure 1611. **4.** A special method or style of structure and ornamentation 1703. **5.** *transf.* or *fig.* Construction generally 1590.

1. Marine A. 1800. A., as distinguished from mere building, is the decoration of construction G. SCOTT. **3.** The ruins of their a. are the schools of modern builders JOHNSON. **4.** Many other architectures besides Gothic RUSKIN. Hence **A·rchitecture** *v.* to design as architect. KEATS.

Architrave (ā·ɹkitrē[i]v). 1563. [– Fr. *architrave* – It. *architrave*, f. *archi-* ARCHI- + *trave* :– L. *trabs, trab-* beam.] *Arch.* **1.** The lowest division of the entablature, the main beam that rests upon the abacus on the capital of a column; the epistyle. **2.** Collective name for the parts (lintel, jambs, and their mouldings) that surround a doorway or window. Also *attrib.* 1663. **3.** Ornamental moulding round the exterior of an arch. Also *attrib.* 1849.

1. Doric pillars overlaid With Golden A. MILT. Hence **A·rchitraved** *ppl. a.* furnished with an a.

† **Architricline.** ME. [– (O)Fr. *architricline* (also OFr. *archedeclin*) – eccl.L. *architriclinus* – Gr. ἀρχιτρίκλινος (*John* 2:8, 9), f. ἀρχι- ARCHI- 1 + τρίκλινον dining room with three couches.] The ruler of a feast -1493.

Archive (ā·ɹkəiv, -kiv). 1603. [– Fr. *archives* – L. *archiva, archia* – Gr. ἀρχεῖα magisterial residence, public office, n. pl. of adj. ἀρχεῖος governmental, f. ἀρχή government. The sp. *archifs* may be – Fr. (XVI) *archif*; cf. late L. *archivum* (Tertullian).] **1.** A place in which public records or historic documents are kept. Now only in *pl.* 1645. **2.** A historical record or document so preserved. Chiefly in *pl.* 1638. **3.** *transf.* and *fig.* in both senses 1603.

1. Lubeck, wher the Archifs of their ancient Records is still HOWELL. **2.** Some rotten a., rummaged out of some seldom-explored press LAMB. **3.** So expert was he, a living a. in that business CARLYLE. Hence **A·rchival** *a.* **A·rchivist,** a keeper of archives.

Archivolt (ā·ɹkivō[u]lt). 1731. [– Fr. *archivolte* or It. *archivolto* (whence med.L. *archivoltum*), f. *arco* :– L. *arcus* ARC + *volto* (see VAULT *sb.*[1]).] *Arch.* The under curve of an arch, from impost to impost; the band of mouldings which ornaments this curve.

A·rchlet. 1862. [f. ARCH *sb.* + -LET.] A little arch.

Archlute (ā·ɹtʃ,liū·t). 1727. [– Fr. *archiluth*, It. *archiliuto*; see ARCH-, LUTE *sb.*[1]] A long and large lute, having its bass strings lengthened, and each row doubled either with a little octave or a unison.

Archly (ā·ɹtʃ,li), *adv.* 1662. [f. ARCH *a.* + -LY[2].] In an arch manner (see ARCH *a.*).

A. the maiden smiled LONGF.

Archness (ā·ɹtʃ,nės). 1709. [f. ARCH *a.* + -NESS.] The quality of being arch (see ARCH *a.*).

With a provoking a. in her looks RICHARDSON.

Archology (aɹkǫ·lŏdʒi). 1825. [f. Gr. ἀρχή beginning, origin + -LOGY.] **a.** Doctrine of the origin of things. **b.** Science of government.

Archon (ā·ɹkǫ̆n). 1659. [– Gr. ἄρχων ruler, subst. use of pres. pple. of ἄρχειν to rule.] **1.** The chief magistrate, or, after the time of Solon, one of the nine chief magistrates, of Athens. **2.** A ruler or president 1735. **3.** A power subordinate to the Deity, held by Gnostics to have made the world 1751.

2. We might establish a Doge, a lord A., a regent BOLINGBROKE. Hence **A·rchonship,** the office, or tenure of office, of an a.; so **A·rchontate. Archo·ntic** *a.* of or pertaining to an a.; *sb.* one of the Gnostics, who held that the world was created by *archontes* (ἄρχοντες); see ARCHON 3.

A·rch-pre·late. 1594. [ARCH- 1.] Chief prelate; archbishop.

A·rch-pre·sbyter. Also **archi-.** 1562. [– late L. *archipresbyter* – Gr. ἀρχιπρεσβύτερος see ARCHI-, PRESBYTER.] = ARCHPRIEST. Hence † **A:rchpre·sbytery,** full-blown presbyterianism. MILT.

Archpriest (ā·ɹtʃ,prī·st). 1485. [– OFr. *archeprestre* (mod. *archiprêtre*) :– late L. *archipresbyter* (see prec.); later assim. to ARCH-, PRIEST *sb.*] A chief priest; *spec.* a kind of vicar to the bishop, acting also as dean of the cathedral; *later*, a rural dean. Hence †**Archprie·sthood,** †**Archprie·stship,** the position or office of an a.

Arch-sea, Arch-see; see ARCH- 4.

A·rch-trai·tor. 1539. [ARCH- 2.] Chief traitor; *spec.* Satan, Judas Iscariot.

A·rch-vi·llain. [ARCH- 2.] Chief villain, ringleader of villainy. *Meas. for M.* v. i. 57.

Archway (ā·ɹtʃ,weⁱ). 1802. [f. ARCH *sb.* + WAY.] **1.** An arched passage. **2.** An arched entrance 1808.

† **A·rchwife.** [ARCH- 2.] A masterful wife. CHAUCER.

A·rchwise, *adv.* 1577. [f. ARCH *sb.* + WISE *sb.*[1]] In the form of an arc, arch, or vault.

-archy; see -ARCH.

Arcifinious (āɹsifi·niəs), *a. rare.* 1859. [f. L. *arcifinius* (f. *arx, arc-* defence or *arcēre* to ward off + *finis* boundary) + -OUS.] Having a frontier which forms a natural defence.

Arciform (ā·ɹsifǭɹm), *a.* 1839. [f. L. *arcus* bow + -FORM.] Bent like a bow, bow-shaped, as certain nerve-fibres.

Arcograph (ā·ɹko,grɑf). 1822. [f. as prec. + -GRAPH.] An appliance for drawing an arc of a circle without using a central point; a cyclograph.

Arctation (āɹktēⁱ·ʃən). 1656. [– med.L. *arctatio*, f. *arctat-*, pa. ppl. stem of L. *arctare*, prop. *artare* to constrict (ART *v.*[1]); see -ION.] *Med.* The action of drawing close together; constriction.

Arctic (ā·ɹktik). [ME. *artik* – OFr. *artique*– L. *ar(c)ticus* – Gr. ἀρκτικός, f. ἄρκτος bear, the Great Bear, pole-star; from XVII refash. after L. *arct-*; see -IC.] **A.** *adj.* **1.** Of or pertaining to the north pole, or north polar regions; northern. **2.** *fig.* with reference to extremeness or cold 1670.

1. *Arctic pole*: the north pole of the heavens or earth. *Arctic Circle* of the earth: the fixed parallel of 66° 32′ North, which separates the North Temperate and North Frigid Zones. In the latitude in which astronomy was first cultivated, the great bear just swept the sea, and did not set, whence the boundary circle [= *Arctic Circle* of the heavens (*obs.*)] obtained its name 1834.

B. *sb.* [the adj. used *absol.*] The north pole or north polar regions; the arctic circle. Also *fig.* 1569.

Arctitude (ā·ɹktitiud). 1828. [– med.L. *arctitudo* tightness, f. L. *ar(c)tus* compressed; see -TUDE.] Tightness, straitness; cf. ARCTATION.

Arctogæal (āɹkto,dʒī·ăl, -gī·ăl), *a.* 1870. [f. mod.L. *Arctogæa* (f. Gr. ἄρκτος Arctic + γαῖα earth) + -AL[1].] Of or belonging to the *Arctogæa*, or arctic regions of the earth.

‖ **Arcturus** (āɹktiūᵊ·rǒs). ME. [L. – Gr. ἀρκτοῦρος, f. ἄρκτος bear (see ARCTIC) + οὖρος guardian; so called from its situation at the tail of the Great Bear.] The brightest star in Bootes; formerly, the whole constellation, and occ. the Great Bear itself.

Canst thou guide A. with his sons *Job* 38 : 32.

Arcuate (ā·ɹkiu,ĕt), *a.* 1626. [– L. *arcuatus*; see next, -ATE[2].] Curved like a bow, arc-shaped, arched. So **A·rcual, A·rcuated** *adjs.* Hence **A·rcuately** *adv.*

Arcuation (āɹkiu,ēⁱ·ʃən). 1696. [– Fr. *arcuation* or L. *arcuatio* (Frontinus), f. *arcuat-*, pa. ppl. stem of *arcuare* to curve, f. *arcus* ARC; see -ION.] **1.** A curving into the shape of an arch; incurvation. **2.** *Hort.* A method of raising trees, by bending down twigs and pegging them into the ground to take new root. ? *Obs.* 1727. **3.** The use of the arch in building; arched work 1856.

A·rcubalist, -ister, = ARBALEST, -ESTER.

Arcubos, -use, obs. ff. HARQUEBUS.

-ard, *suffix* – OF. *-ard, -art* – Ger. *-hart, -hard*, 'hardy'. In ME. in words from OFr., as *bastard*, and names of things, as *placard*; later, an Eng. formative, as in *drunkard*, etc., meaning 'one who does to excess, or does what is discreditable'. In some words it has replaced *-ar, -er*, as in *stander, standard* (tree). Occ. now written *-art*, as in *braggart*.

‖ **Ardass.** ? *Obs.* 1701. [– Fr. *ardasse* – Pers. *ardan* raw silk.] A very fine sort of Persian silk. Hence **Ardassine,** a fabric made from it.

‖ **A·rdeb.** 1861. [Arab. *'irdabb, 'ardabb.*] An Egyptian dry measure (185 litres).

†‖ **Ardelio, -on.** 1621. [– Fr. *ardélion* or L. *ardelio.*] A busybody –1653.

Ardency (ā·ɹdĕnsi). 1549. [f. next; see -ENCY.] **1.** Burning quality 1634. **2.** *fig.* Warmth of feeling or desire; intense eagerness, zeal. 1549.

2. With a great a. of spirit, he pierced Gods ear LATIMER.

Ardent (ā·ɹdĕnt), *a.* [late ME. *ardaunt* – OFr. *ardant* (mod. *ardent*) :– *ardent-*, pres. ppl. stem of L. *ardēre* to burn; see -ANT, -ENT.] **1.** Burning, red-hot; fiery, parching. **2.** Inflammable. *Obs.* exc. in *ardent spirits*, with reference to their fiery taste. 1471. **3.** Glowing like fire; flaming, fierce 1603. **4.** *fig.* Glowing with passion or desire; eager, zealous ME.

1. A. feuers HOLLAND. 2. Spirits of wine, or any a. spirit BREWSTER. 3. A. eyes POPE. 4. Ardaunt in auarice CHAUCER. *Ardent*, said of a vessel when she . . comes to the wind quickly SMYTH. Their . . ryght ardaunt courage CAXTON. Hence **A·rdently** *adv.*

† **A·rder.** 1524. [prob. – ON. *arðr* plough, – L. *aratrum.*] **1.** Ploughing; *esp.* the fallowing –1688. **2.** Land ploughed up and left fallow –1668.

Ardour, ardor (ā·ɹdəɹ). ME. [– OFr. *ardour* (mod. *ardeur*) :– L. *ardor*, f. *ardēre* burn. The sp. *ardor*, assim. to L., has been in use since XVI.] **1.** Fierce or burning heat; *concr.* fire, flame 1645. † **2.** *poet.* An effulgent spirit. (Cf. *Heb.* 1 : 7.) 1667. **3.** *fig.* Heat of passion or desire; warmth of emotion, eagerness, enthusiasm. Const. *for.* (Formerly used of evil passions, but now only of generous impulses.) ME.

1. The excessive ardours of the sun C. COTTON. 2. The wingèd saint . . from among Thousand Celestial ardors . . up springing light MILT. *P.L.* v. 249. 3. The Ardeur and brennyng of lecherye CAXTON. A martial ardor 1769. The bright ardours of boyhood 1847.

Arduous (ā·ɹdiu,əs), *a.* 1538. [f. L. *arduus* steep + -OUS; see -UOUS.] **1.** High, steep, difficult to climb; also *fig.* 1713. **2.** Hard to achieve; difficult, laborious, severe 1538. **3.** Of the activity: Strenuous, energetic, laborious 1753.

1. To forgive is the most a. pitch human nature can arrive at STEELE. 2. An a. battle POPE, task 1775, enterprise MACAULAY. 3. An a. climber TYNDALL. Hence **A·rduous-ly** *adv.*, **-ness.**

A·rdurous, *a. rare.* [? for *ardorous.*] Ardent. CARY.

† **Are, A re** (ā·rē·), *sb.*[1] 1450. [A + RE *sb.*[1]] *Mus.* Name of the note A in Aretino's 1st, 4th, and 7th hexachords, in which it coincided with the second lowest note, sung to the syllable *re.*

Are to plead Hortensio's passion *Tam. Shr.* III. i. 74.

‖ **Are** (ar), *sb.*[2] 1819. [Fr., – L. *area.*] The unit of superficial measurement in the Fr. metric system; a square of which the side measures ten metres, equal to 119·6 sq. yards.

Are (āɹ, ăr, 'r, r), *v.* Pl. pres. Ind. of BE. Part of the orig. substantive vb.; cf. AM.

Area (ēᵊ·riă). Pl. **areas,** occ. **areæ.** 1538. [– L. *area* vacant piece of level ground.] **1.** A level piece of ground not built over or occupied; a clear space within a building, as the arena of an amphitheatre, etc. **2.** An enclosed court, *spec.* a sunken court, which gives access to the basement of dwelling-houses; often *attrib.* 1649. **3.** Superficial extent. (Formerly also of cubic content.) 1570. **4.** A particular extent of (*esp.* the earth's) surface; a region, tract 1845; *Biol.* a limited part of the surface of any organism 1851. **5.** *fig.* Scope, range, extent 1627. † **6.** A bed or border in a garden. (So in L.) –1669. **7.** A bald place on the head. (So in L.) 1706.

1. A floor or a. of goodly length 1651. The a. or platform of the old stage CIBBER. Comfortable a. seats 1884. 2. Windows which opened to the a. below STEELE. *Area-sneak*: a thief who steals into kitchens through area-gates. 3. The a. of a triangle 1570. 4. The a. over which a language is spoken LATHAM. The germinative a. 1880. 5. The whole a. of life 1852.

† **Area·ch,** *v.* [OE. *arǣcan*, f. A- *pref.* 1 + *rǣcan* REACH *v.*[1]] **1.** *trans.* To reach, get at (*esp.* with a weapon) –1513; *fig.* to obtain –1596; to hand, deliver –1530. **2.** *intr.* To reach, extend (*to*). Also *fig.* –1541.

Aread, arede, areed (ărī·d), *v. arch.* [OE. *arēdan*, f. A- *pref.* 1 + *rēdan*; see READ. The reg. conjugation is *area·d, are·d, are·d.*] † **1.** *trans.* To divine –1600; to make known, utter –1642. **2.** To guess (*arch.*) ME. **3.** To interpret, solve (*arch.*) OE. ** Later senses formed on READ. **4.** *trans.* To counsel 1559. Also *intr.* or *absol.* **5.** To decide, adjudge 1593.

2. Rightly he ared the Maid's intent SOUTHEY. 3. So is thy dream areded W. MORRIS. 4. I arede therfore . . all people to be wise 1559. 5. We may best areede who is most credible 1593.

† **Area·d,** *sb.* 1590. [f. the vb.] Counsel –1601.

† **Area·dy,** *a.* ME. [f. READY; see A- *pref.* 6.] Prepared; in readiness –1480. Hence † **Area·dily** *adv.* † **Area·diness.**

Areal (ēᵊ·ri,ăl), *a.* 1676. [– late L. *arealis*, f. *area* AREA; see -AL[1].] Of, pertaining to, or of the nature of, an area. Hence **Area·lity,** condition in respect of area.

† **Area·r,** *v.* [OE. *arǣran*, f. A- *pref.* 1 + *rǣran* REAR *v.*] **1.** To raise, set up –1627; also *fig.* **2.** To raise (a person) *against* –1611. **3.** *refl.* and *intr.* –ME.

A-rea·r, *adv.* [A *prep.*[1] 5 + REAR *sb.*] In the rear.

† **Area·son.** ME. [– OFr. *aresoner* (mod. *arraisonner*), earlier *araisnier* :– Rom. **adrationare*; see ARRAIGN *v.*[1], REASON *v.*] By-form of ARRAIGN *v.*; to address words and *esp.* questions to; call to account –1594.

‖ **Areca** (æ·rĭkă). 1599. [– Pg. *areca* – Malayalam *aḍekka* = Canarese *aḍike*, Tamil *aḍaikay.*] Name of the tree and fruit of a genus of palms, of which *A. catechu* yields a nut which the natives roll up in betel-leaves and chew.

A-ree·k, *adv.* [A *prep.*[1] 11.] Reeking. SWIFT.

Arefaction (ærĭfæ·kʃən). ? *Obs.* 1576. [– Fr. *aréfaction* or med.L. *arefactio*; see next, -FACTION.] The action or process of drying; dried condition.

Arefy (æ·rĭfəi), *v.* ? *Obs.* 1542. [f. L. *arefacere* f. *arēre* to dry; see -FY. Cf. *liquefy.*] *trans.* and *intr.* To dry up, parch.

Arena (ărī·nă). Pl. **arenas.** 1627. [– L. *arena*, prop. *harena* sand, sandy place.] **1.** The central part of an amphitheatre, in which the combats take place; orig. strewn with sand. Also, the whole amphitheatre; *fig.* A battle-field 1814. **2.** Any sphere of public or energetic action 1798. **3.** *Med.* Sand or gravel deposited from the urine 1706.

1. The thronged a. shakes with shouts for more BYRON. The a. of controversy 1863. 2. The a. of authorship 1857.

Arenaceo- (ærĭnēⁱ·ʃi,o), comb. f. L. *arenaceus* (see next); = sandy, as in *a.-argillaceous*, of the nature of sandy clay.

Arenaceous (ærĭnēⁱ·ʃəs), *a.* 1646. [f. L. *arenaceus*, f. *arena* + -OUS; see -ACEOUS.]

Having the appearance of sand; sandy; largely composed of sand or quartz grains. Also *fig.*

‖ **Arenaria** (ærīnēᵊ·riă). 1806. [mod.L., subst. use of fem. of L. *arenarius*; see next. Cf. Fr. *arénaire*.] The Sandwort; a genus of small herbs (N.O. *Caryophyllaceæ*) allied to chickweed.

Arena·rious, *a.* ? *Obs.* 1758. [f. L. *arenarius*, f. *arena* sand, + -OUS; see -ARIOUS.] = ARENACEOUS.

Arenation (ærīnēⁱ·ʃən). ? *Obs.* 1717. [– L. *arenatio* (Vitruvius) plastering (with sand), f. *arena* sand; see -ATION.] *Med.* Application of hot sand to the body as a remedy.

Are·ndalite. 1868. [f. *Arendal* in Norway + -ITE[1] 2 b.] *Min.* = EPIDOTE.

Arendator; see ARR-.

Arenicolite (ærīni·kŏləit). 1864. [f. mod.L. *arenicola* (cf. Fr. *arénicole*) sand-worm (f. L. *arena* sand + *-cola* inhabiting) + -ITE[1] 2 a.] A worm-hole made orig. in sand, and preserved in a sandstone rock.

Arenicolous (-ŏləs), *a.* 1851. [f. as prec. + -OUS.] Inhabiting sand.

Arenilitic (ăre:nili·tik), *a.* 1799. [f. L. *arena* sand + -LITE + -IC.] Of or pertaining to sandstone.

Arenose (æ:rīnōᵘ·s), *a.* 1731. [– L. *arenosus*, f. *arena* sand; see -OSE[1].] Sandy. var. † **A·renous.**

Arenos·o-, comb. f. L. *arenosus*, Eng. *arenose*.

Areo-, f. Gr. Ἄρεος of Ares or Mars; *esp.* in *Astr.*; as **A:reoce·ntric** *a.*, having Mars as centre. **Areo·graphy,** description of the physical features of Mars; whence **Areo·grapher, Areo·graphic** *a.* **Areo·logy,** scientific investigation of the substance of Mars.

‖ **Areola** (ărī·ŏlă). Pl. **areolæ.** 1664. [L., dim. of *area*.] A very small area. **1.** A small space marked out on a surface by intersecting lines, as the space between the veins of a leaf or the nervures of an insect's wing. **2.** An interstice in the tissue of any organized substance 1848. **3.** A circular spot; the coloured circle about a nipple, or a vesicle, or pustule 1706. **4.** *Biol.* **a.** A slightly depressed spot on any surface 1872. **b.** The cell-nucleus of a plant 1862. Hence **Are·olar** *a.* consisting of areolæ; *spec.* in *areolar* (or *connective*) *tissue*: the mixture of fibrous and elastic tissue, which underlies the skin. Also, of or pertaining to a small area. **Are·olate, Are·olated** *ppl. adjs.* marked by, or consisting of, areolæ. **A:reola·tion,** division into areolæ. **Are·olet,** a small areola. var. **A·reole.**

Areometer, var. of ARÆOMETER.

Areo·pagist, rare var. of next.

Areopagite (æri,ǫ·păgəit). ME. [– L. *areopagites* – Gr. ἀρειοπαγίτης; see AREOPAGUS, -ITE[1] 1.] A member of the court of Areopagus.

Areopagi·tic. 1649. [– late L. *areopagiticus*, – Gr.; see prec., -IC.] **A.** *adj.* Of or pertaining to the Areopagus or its court. **B.** *sb.* A speech imitating the oration of Isocrates addressed to the court of Areopagus. So **Areopagi·tical** *a.*

‖ **Areopagus** (ærī,·ǫpăgŏs). 1642. [L. – Gr. Ἄρειος πάγος the hill of Ares.] A hill at Athens where the highest judicial court held its sittings; *hence*, the court itself, and *transf.* any important tribunal.

Areo·pagy. 1646. [f. L. *Areopagus* + -Y[3].] A secret tribunal.

Areostyle, -systyle, areotic; see ARÆ-.

Arere, obs. var. of AREAR *v.*; earlier f. ARREAR.

Arest, obs. f. ARREST, and ERST.

† **Are·t, are·tt(e,** *v.* ME. [– OFr. *areter, aretter*, f. *à* + *reter* :– L. *reputare*; see REPUTE. Erron. latinized as *arrectare*, whence the sp. *arect, arrect*.] **1.** *trans.* To reckon –1485; to ascribe *to* –1549; to charge *upon* –1602. **2.** To indict a person (*of*) –1641. ¶ **3.** To commit a charge to. (A false use of Spenser's.) –1625.

Aretaics (ærītē·iks), *sb. pl.* [f. Gr. ἀρετή virtue + -IC; cf. SPONDAIC.] The science of virtue. J. GROTE.

‖ **Arête** (arēt). 1862. [Fr. :– L. *arista* ear of corn, fish-bone or spine. Cf. ARRIS.] A sharp ascending ridge or edge of a mountain. The local name in Fr. Switzerland, now technical with climbers.

Arew(e, obs. f. ARROW, AROW, and ARUE.

Arfvedsonite. 1837. [f. *Arfvedson* a chemist + -ITE[1] 2 b.] *Min.* A ferruginous variety of hornblende, occurring in black crystals; soda-hornblende.

Argaile, argal, obs. vars. of ARGOL.

A·rgal, *conj. adv.* 1602. Perversion of L. *ergo* 'therefore'; hence *subst.* a clumsy piece of reasoning.

He drownes not himselfe, A., he . . shortens not his owne life *Haml.* V. i. 21. Mr. Buckle's argument is as absurd an a. [etc.] 1861.

‖ **Argala** (ā·ɹgălă). Better **argee·lah.** 1754. [Hind. *hargilā*.] The adjutant-bird (*Ciconia Argala*).

‖ **Argali** (ā·ɹgăli). 1779. [Mongol.] *Zool.* The wild or rock sheep of Asia.

‖ **Argan.** 1809. [– Arab. *arjān*, in Barbary pron. *argān*.] An evergreen tree (N.O. *Sapotaceæ*), found in Morocco, furnishing an oil from its seeds.

Argand (ā·ɹgænd). 1790. A lamp invented by Aimé Argand (1755–1803) about 1782, having a cylindrical wick, which allows air to pass to both inner and outer surfaces of the flame; also, a ring-shaped gas-burner made on the same principle.

‖ **Argema** (ā·ɹgīmă). 1661. [L., = Gr. ἄργεμον, -ος, f. ἀργός white; cf. ALBUGO.] *Med.* A small white ulcer or speck on the margin of the cornea. var. **Argemon.**

Argent (ā·ɹdʒĕnt). 1500. [– (O)Fr. *argent* – L. *argentum* silver.] **A.** *sb.* **1.** The metal silver (*arch.* or *poet.*) 1530. † **2.** Silver coin; hence *gen.* cash –1742. **3.** *Her.* The silver of a coat of arms; the white colour in armorial bearings 1562.

1. *Spume of a.* (L. *argenti spuma*): litharge of silver. **3.** Called Siluer, and blased by the name of A. 1562.

B. *adj.* Of, or resembling, silver; silvery white 1590; *esp.* in *Her.* 1591.

The a. moon H. COLERIDGE. The a. Eagle that he bare HARINGTON. Hence **Arge·ntal** *a.* of silver; as in *Argental Mercury*, the *Amalgam* of Dana. **Arge·nteous** *a.* silvery. **Argenti·ferous** *a.* yielding silver. **Argenti·fic** *a.* producing silver. **Arge·ntify** *v.* to turn into silver.

Argentan (ā·ɹdʒĕntæn). 1857. [– Fr. *argentan* – L. *argentum*.] An alloy of nickel, copper, and zinc; German silver.

Argentate (ā·ɹdʒĕnte t), *sb.* 1880. [f. L. *argentum* + -ATE[4].] *Chem.* A combination of a base with argentic oxide, as in *A. of Ammonia*, fulminating silver.

Argentate, *a.* 1880. [– L. *argentatus*, f. *argentum* silver; see -ATE[2]; cf. Fr. *argenté*.] Silvery, or shining white with a tinge of grey.

Argentic (aɹdʒe·ntik), *a.* 1868. [f. L. *argentum* + -IC.] *Chem.* Containing silver in chemical composition; as *A. Chloride*, AgCl, etc.

Argentine (ā·ɹdʒĕntəin). 1537. [– (O)Fr. *argentin, -ine*, f. *argent* silver + *-in* -INE[1].] **A.** *adj.* Of, made of, or containing silver. **2.** Silvery 1578.

1. An antick deaurate with letters a. 1537. **2.** Celestial Dian, goddess a. *Per.* V. i. 251.

B. *sb.* **1.** A material simulating silver: **a.** Electro-plate. **b.** The silvery lamellæ on the scales of fish, used in making artificial pearls 1839. **2.** *Zool.* A genus of small fishes, of the family *Salmonidæ*, with silvery scales; see 1 b. Also used of the *Scopelus pennanti*, now called the Pearlside. 1769. † **3.** *Herb. Argentine Thistle*, the Cotton Thistle (*Onopordium acanthium*) 1578. **4.** *Min.* Slate-spar 1794.

Argentite (ā·ɹdʒĕntəit). 1837. [f. L. *argentum* + -ITE[1] 2 b.] *Min.* Silver-glance or argyrose, a native sulphide found traversing granite, etc.

Arge·nto-, comb. f. L. *argentum* (see -O-); = 'Having silver as a constituent'.

Argento·meter. 1879. [See prec., -METER.] An instrument for measuring the strength of silver solutions.

Argentous (aɹdʒe·ntəs), *a.* 1869. [f. L. *argentum* + -OUS.] *Chem.* Containing silver in composition (in twice the proportion contained in the compounds called argentic), as *A. Chloride*, Ag_2Cl; *A. Oxide*, Ag_4O.

Argentry (ā·ɹdʒĕntri). 1622. [– (O)Fr. *argenterie*; see ARGENT, -ERY, -RY.] Silver plate. *Obs.* exc. *fig.*

Pawning his own a. and jewels HOWELL.

† **A:rgent-vi·ve.** 1453. [– Fr. *argent vif*, obs. var. of (O)Fr. *vif-argent* (XIII); cf. L. *argentum vivum* (Vitruvius).] Quicksilver –1662.

Argh, *a.* [OE. *arg, earg* = OFris. *erg*, OHG., G. *arg*, ON. *argr*, :– Gmc. **argaz*.] **1.** Cowardly, fearful. (Still in north. dial.) OE. **2.** Inert, lazy, reluctant. (Still in north. dial.) OE.

Argh(e, *v.* [OE. *argian, eargian*, f. prec.] To be timid; to hesitate from fearfulness. (Still in Sc.)

Argil (ā·ɹdʒil). 1530. [– OFr. *argille*, mod. *argile* :– L. *argilla* – Gr. ἄργιλλος clay.] Clay, *esp.* potter's clay. Proposed at one time as a name for alumina.

Argilla·ceo-, comb. f. next.

Argillaceous (āɹdʒilēⁱ·ʃəs), *a.* 1731. [f. L. *argillaceus* (f. *argilla* clay) + -OUS; see -ACEOUS.] Of the nature of clay; largely composed of clay; clayey.

Argilli·ferous, *a.* 1800. [f. L. *argilla* clay + -FEROUS.] Yielding clay.

Argillite (ā·ɹdʒiləit). 1795. [f. as prec. + -ITE[1] 2 b.] *Min.* Argillaceous schist, clay slate. Hence **Argilli·tic** *a.*

Argillo- (aɹdʒi·lo), comb. f. ARGILLOUS, as in **a.-calcareous** *a.* calcareous with an admixture of clay; **-calcite,** a clayey lime.

Argillous (aɹdʒi·ləs), *a. rare.* ME. [– OFr. *argillus* (mod. *argileux*) :– L. *argillosus*; see -OUS.] Clayey. var. † **A:rgillo·se.**

† **Argin(e.** *rare.* 1589. [– It. *argine* embankment.] An embankment or rampart in front of a fort.

A·rgle, *v.* Still *dial.*; also in **argle-bargle, argol-bargol.** 1589. [prob. alt. of ARGUE, with *-le* as in *haggle*.] **1.** To dispute about. **2.** *intr.* To bandy words, wrangle 1823.

Argol[1] (ā·ɹgǫl). ME. [ME. *argoile* (Chaucer) – AFr. *argoile*, of unkn. origin.] The tartar deposited from wines, and adhering to the sides of the casks as a crust; crude bitartrate of potassium, which, when purified, becomes *cream of tartar*.

‖ **Argol**[2], **-al** (ā·ɹgəl). 1856. [Mongol.] Dried cow-dung used as fuel in Tartary.

Argon (ā·ɹgǫn). 1894. [– Gr. ἀργόν, n. of ἀργός idle, inert, for ἀεργός, f. ἀ- A- *pref.* 14 + ἔργον work.] *Chem.* An inert gas occurring in very small quantities in the air.

Argonaut (ā·ɹgŏnǫt). 1596. [– L. *argonauta* – Gr. ἀργοναύτης sailor (ναύτης) in the ship Argo.] **1.** One of the legendary heroes who sailed with Jason in the Argo in quest of the Golden Fleece. **2.** Name of a genus of cephalopod molluscs of the octopod type, *esp.* of the 'paper nautilus', formerly believed to sail on the surface of the sea 1835. Hence **Argonau·tic** *a.* of or pertaining to the Argonauts; *sb.* an Argonaut; a poem concerning the Argonauts.

† **Argosi·ne.** *rare.* 1559. [In the two forms *Argosie, Argosine*, prob. – It. *Raguseo, Ragusino* Ragusan; for *Arg-* see next.] ? A Ragusan –1645.

Argosy (ā·ɹgŏsi). 1577. [Earliest forms *ragusye, argose, -ea, arguze* – It. *ragusea*, fem. adj. used subst. (sc. *nave* or *caracca*) ship or carrack of Ragusa.] *Hist.* and *Poet.* A merchant-vessel of the largest size and burden; *esp.* those of Ragusa and Venice. Also *transf.* and *fig.*

Argosies with portly saile Like Signiors and rich Burgers on the flood *Merch. V.* I. i. 9.

† **A·rgot**[1]. Also **argo.** ME. [– OFr. *argot* (mod. *ergot*) cock's spur; see ERGOT *sb.*] **a.** The spur of a cock; the analogous part on the feet of other animals. **b.** A spur left in pruning a tree –1708.

‖ **Argot**[2] (argo). 1860. [Fr., of unkn. origin.] The jargon, slang, or peculiar phraseology of a class, *orig.* that of thieves and rogues. Hence **Argo·tic** *a.*

Argue (ā·ɹgiu), *v.* ME. [– (O)Fr. *arguer* :– L. *argutari* prattle, prate, frequent. of *arguere* make clear, prove, assert, accuse. Whilst L. *argutari* is the formal origin of the French and English words, the sense-development of these is that of L. *arguere*.] **I.** † **1.** To convict. Const. *of.* –1660. † **2.**

trans. To accuse, call in question. Const. *of.* –1692. **3.** To prove or evince; to indicate 1494.

1. Which of you shal a. me of sinne *John* 8:46. **2.** Nor would we a. the definitive sentence of God SIR T. BROWNE. **3.** Not to know mee argues your selves unknown MILT. *P.L.* iv. 831. So bad a death, argues a monstrous life 2 *Hen. VI*, III. iii. 30.

II. 1. *intr.* To bring forward reasons in support of or against a proposition; to discuss; to reason; *hence*, to raise objections, dispute. Const. *with, against* an opponent; *for, against* a proposition; † *of, about* a matter. ME. **2.** *trans.* To discuss the pros and cons of; to examine controversially 1494. **3.** To maintain, by adducing reasons, *that* [etc.] 1548. **4.** To use as an argument (*arch.*) 1626.

1. His philosophy and faculty of arguing GLANVILL. More ready to a. than to obey BACON. Of good and evil much they argu'd then MILT. *P.L.* II. 562. **2.** The sayd causes warre well and sufficiently argued 1494.

Phrases. *To a. away, off*, etc.: to get rid of by argument 1713. *To a. into* or *out of*: to persuade by argument into, or out of, a course of action, etc. Hence **A·rguable** *a.* capable of being argued. **A·rguer. A·rguing** *vbl. sb.* † accusation; argument.

Argufy (ā·ɹgiufəi), *v. colloq.* 1751. [Illiterate f. ARGUE. Cf. *speechify*.] **1.** *intr.* To prove something; *hence*, to signify. **2.** To dispute, wrangle 1800. **3.** *trans.* To worry with argumentation 1771.

† **Argu·itively,** *adv. rare.* 1665. [repr. med.L. *arguitivus* (*-ive*, XIV), f. *arguit-* pa. ppl. stem of L. *arguere* ARGUE; see -IVE, -LY².] In a way that proceeds by argument.

Argument (ā·ɹgiumĕnt). ME. [– (O)Fr. *argument* – L. *argumentum* (also used); see ARGUE, -MENT.] **1.** Proof, token. (Passing from *clear proof* to *proof presumptive*; cf. ARGUE 3.) (*arch.*) **2.** *Astr.* and *Math.* The angle, arc, etc., on which the calculation of another quantity depends ME. **3.** A statement or fact advanced to influence the mind, or to support a proposition; *spec.* in *Logic*, the middle term of a syllogism. Also *fig.* Const. † *to, for*, and later *against*. ME. (In certain phrases borrowed from the schools the L. form *argumentum* is used, *esp.* in *argumentum ad hominem*.) **4.** A connected series of statements intended to establish (or subvert) a position; a process of reasoning; argumentation ME. **5.** Statement of the pros and cons of a proposition; discussion; debate 1494; † *transf.* subject of contention –1614. **6.** Theme, subject (*arch.*) 1570. **7.** The summary of the subject-matter of a book; *fig.* the contents 1535.

1. It is..no great a. of her folly *Much Ado* II. iii. 242. **3.** To plеade my cause before him, and to fyll my mouth with argumentes *Job* 23:3. The arguments for and against..trial by jury Cox. **4.** The successive steps of the a. 1877. **5.** In a. with men a woman ever Goes by the worse MILT. *Sams.* 903. Sheath'd their swords for lack of a. *Hen. V*, III. i. 21. **6.** It would be a. for a weeke 1 *Hen. IV*, II. ii. 100. He grew the A. of all Tongues CLARENDON. **7.** If I would..try the a. of hearts, by borrowing *Timon* II. ii. 187. Hence †**Argume·ntal** *a.* argumentative. †**A·rgumentize,** to conduct an a.

† **A·rgument,** *v.* ME. [f. the *sb.* or – (O)Fr. *argumenter* – L. *argumentari*; see prec.] **1.** *intr.* To argue –1637; to furnish proof *that* 1558. **2.** *trans.* To make the subject of argument 1746. Hence † **Argume·ntable** *a.* that may be argued; argumentative. **A·rgumenta·tor,** a reasoner.

Argumentation (ā:ɹgiumĕntēⁱ·ʃən). 1491. [– (O)Fr. *argumentation* – L. *argumentatio*, f. *argumentari*; see prec., -ATION.] **1.** The action of inferring a conclusion from propositions premised; methodical employment or presentation of arguments; formal reasoning. **2.** Interchange of argument, debate 1538. **3.** = ARGUMENT 4. 1548.

1. The eloquence and a. of the bar SCOTT. **2.** But what a. can a man hold with him CLARENDON. **3.** What a misfashioned a. is this 1548.

Argumentative (āɹgiume·ntǎtiv), *a.* 1642. [– OFr. *argumentatif, -ive* or late L. *argumentativus* (Donatus), f. *argumentari*; see prec., -ATIVE.] † **1.** Of the nature of an argument (*for*); of weight as evidence (*of*) –1691. **2.** Controversial, logical 1647. **3.** Addicted to argumentation; capable of arguing 1667. **3.** A strong, capacious, a. mind GIBBON. Hence **Argume·ntative-ly** *adv.*, **-ness.**

‖ **Argumentum**; see ARGUMENT.

Argus (ā·ɹgŏs). ME. [L. – Gr. Ἄργος.] **1.** A mythological person fabled to have had a hundred eyes. *Hence*, a very vigilant watcher. (After the death of Argus, his eyes were transferred by Hera to the tail of the peacock.) **2.** A genus of pheasants, natives of Asia, esp. *A. giganteus*, which is as large as a turkey 1768. **3.** A butterfly of the genus *Polyommatus* 1827.

1. Fayre pecocks..full of A. eyes SPENSER.

Comb.: **a.-eyed** *a.*, watchful or sharp-sighted; **-shell,** a species of porcelain-shell; **-snake,** one marked by rows of round ocellated red spots.

† **Arguta·tion.** 1641. [f. *argutat-*, pa. ppl. stem of *argutari*; see ARGUE, -ION.] Cavilling, cavil –1681.

Argute (aɹgiū·t), *a.* ME. [– L. *argutus*, pa. pple. of *arguere* make clear; see ARGUE.] † **1.** Of taste: Sharp. **2.** Shrill 1719. **3.** Of persons, etc.: Quick, keen, subtle, shrewd, *esp.* in small matters 1577. Hence **Argu·te-ly** *adv.*, **-ness.**

Argyll (aɹgəi·l). 1822. [f. proper name.] A vessel of metal, like a small coffee-pot, for serving up gravy hot.

Argyr-, argyro- (ā·ɹdʒir-, -ro), repr. Gr. ἀργυρο- comb. f. ἄργυρος silver.

Argyra·nthemous, Argyra·nthous [Gr. ἄνθος, ἀνθεμίς] *a.*, *Bot.* having silvery white flowers. **Argyra·spid** [L. *argyraspides*, Gr. ἀργυράσπιδες], in *pl.* the silver-shielded; a corps of the Macedonian army. ‖ **Argu·ria,** *Med.* silver-poisoning. **Argy·ric** [Gr. ἀργυρικός] *a.*, *Chem.* = ARGENTIC. **A·rgyrite, Argyro·se,** *Min.* = ARGENTITE. **Argyroce·phalous** [Gr. κεφαλή] *a.*, having a shining white head. **Argyroce·ratite** [Gr. κέρατ-], *Min.* = CERARGYRITE.

Arh-; see ARRH-.

‖ **Aria** (ā·riꞁă). 1742. [It.; see AIR.] *Mus.* An air, melody, or tune; *esp.* a more elaborate accompanied melody sung by a single voice in the older operas, etc., as dist. from simple airs or songs.

Arian, -ize. *Ethnol.* See ARYAN.

Arian (ēᵊ·riăn), *a.* 1532. [– eccl. L. *Arianus*, f. *Arius, Arīus* – Gr. Ἄρειος, Ἄρεῖος.] Of, pertaining to, or holding the doctrine of, Arius, a presbyter of Alexandria in the 4th c., who denied that Christ was *consubstantial* with God 1642. As *sb.* One holding this doctrine.

Our first Teutonic version of the Scriptures was by an A. missionary, Ulfilas STANLEY. Hence **A·riănism,** the A. doctrine or heresy. **A·rianize** *v.* to follow the doctrine of Arius; to convert to Arianism. **A·rianizer.**

-arian (ēᵊ·riăn) *suffix*, f. L. *-arius* + -AN, first appearing in the 16th c., as in names of sects (*Disciplinarian*) and holders of religious tenets (*Trinitarian*); hence gen. (*humanitarian*).

Aricine (æ·risəin). 1847. [f. *Arica* in Peru + -INE⁵.] *Chem.* An alkaloid.

Arid (æ·rid), *a.* 1652. [– Fr. *aride* or L. *aridus*, f. *arēre* be dry or parched; see -ID¹.] **1.** Dry, parched, withered. *Hence*, barren, bare 1656. **2.** *fig.* Uninteresting, jejune 1827. Hence **A·ridly** *adv.*, **-ness.**

1. A. sands BAKER. **2.** A. studies 1846.

Aridity (ări·dĭti). 1599. [– Fr. *aridité* or L. *ariditas*; see prec., -ITY.] **1.** Arid state or quality, parched condition, dryness, barrenness: *spec.* (*Med.*) of the body. **2.** *fig.* Lack of interest; in the theological sense, want of unction or tenderness 1692.

2. The excessive a. of scholasticism LECKY.

† **Ariel**¹. ME. A word from the Vulgate (after Ἀριήλ of the LXX, etc.). rendered 'altar'.

(Generally in O.T. the word occurs as a man's name; also an appellation of Jerusalem = 'lion of God'; in Milton as the name of an angel, in Shaks. of 'an Ayrie spirit'; in *Astron.* of a satellite of Uranus.)

Ariel² (ēᵊ·riꞁĕl). 1832. [Arab. *'aryal* (var. of *ayyil* stag), applied in Syria to the gazelle.] A species of the gazelle found in Western Asia and Africa.

‖ **Aries** (ēᵊ·riꞁīz). ME. [L., = ram.] The ram; a zodiacal sign, which the sun enters on the 21st of March.

Arietation (æ:ri-, ēᵊ:riꞁĕtēⁱ·ʃən). *arch.* 1625. [– L. *arietatio*, f. *arietat-*, pa. ppl. stem of *arietare* to butt like a ram, f. *aries, ariet-* ram; see -ION.] **1.** The action of butting like a ram; *hence*, the striking with a battering-ram, etc. **2.** *transf.* and *fig.* Battering, clashing, concussion 1625.

‖ **Arietta** (ariꞁe·ttă). 1742. [It.; dim. of ARIA.] *Mus.* A short air. var. ‖ **Arie·tte.** [Fr.]

Aright (ărəi·t), *adv.* [OE. *on riht, ariht*; see A *prep.*¹ 9, RIGHT *sb.*¹] **1.** In a right manner; justly, correctly. † **2.** Straightway. (Cf. RIGHTS.) –1460. **3.** Right: Exactly (*arch.*) ME. † Straight –1611. **4.** On the right (hand) (*arch. rare*) 1795.

1. A generacion that set not their herte a. *Ps.* 77:8. **4.** A., aleft, The..foemen scatter SOUTHEY. Hence † **Ari·ght** *v.* to make right. **Ari·ghtly,** †**Ari·ghts** *advs.*

Aril (æ·ril). 1794. [– mod.L. *arillus* (Fr. *arille*, It. *arillo*, Sp., Pg. *arilo*), of unkn. origin; med.L. *arilli* = dried grape-stones.] *Bot.* (See quot.)

The..arillus is an accessory seed-covering, more or less incomplete, formed between the time of fertilization and the ripening of the seed, by a growth from the apex of the funiculus, at or just below the hilum GRAY. Hence **A·rillary** *a.* of or pertaining to the a. **A·rillate, A·rillated, A·rilled** *ppl. adjs.* furnished or covered with an a. **Ari·lliform** *a.* **A·rillode,** a false a., originating at or near the micropyle.

† **A·riolate,** *v. rare.* 1652. [– *ariolat-*, pa. ppl. stem of L. *ariolari*, prop. *hariolari* foretell, f. *hariolus* sooth-sayer; cf. OFr. *hariole, harioler*.] To divine, foretell from omens. Hence † **Ariola·ter, -or;** vars. † **A·riole,** † **A·rioler,** † **A·riolist.** † **Ariola·tion.**

Ariose (ariꞁōᵘ·s), *a.* 1742. [– It. *arioso*; see next.] *Mus.* Melodious; song-like.

‖ **Arioso** (ariꞁōᵘ·so), *a.* 1742. [It.; = *airy*, f. *aria*.] *Mus.* Ariose, melodious. Used of instrumental music, it describes a sustained vocal style; of vocal music, an air of the character both of air and recitative, which requires rather to be *said* than *sung*. Hence used *advb*, as a direction, and *subst.* as piece of such music.

A-ri·ot, *adv.* 1851. [A *prep.*¹ 11.] In riot.

-arious, *comp. suffix*, forming adjs., f. L. *-arius, -a, -um* 'connected with' + -OUS (as if – L. *-ariosus*). The reg. Eng. repr. of *-arius* is -ARY¹.

A-ri·pple, *adv.* 1855. [A *prep.*¹ 11.] In a ripple.

Arise (ărəi·z), *v. Pa. t.* **arose**; *Pa. pple.* **arisen.** [OE. *ārīsan* (Northumb. *arrīsa*) = OS. *ārīsan*, OHG. *ur-, ar-, irrīsan*, Goth. *us-, urreisan*; see A- *pref.* 1, RISE *v.* Almost replaced by *rise* in all senses exc. those in III.] **I. 1.** To get up from sitting or kneeling, to stand up (*arch.*); † hence *transf.* and *fig.*: To adjourn (as a court), to stand on end (as hair) –1649. **2.** To get up † from a fall –1667; from sleep or rest (*arch.*) OE. **3.** To come above the horizon (of the sun, etc.); *transf.* of the day, morning. Now *arch.* and *poet.* OE. **4.** To rise from the dead. Now *poet.* OE. **5.** To rise from inaction; *esp.* in hostility or rebellion (*against*). Now *poet.* OE. **6.** To rise in agitation, to boil up. Now *poet.* OE. **7.** *transf.* Of sounds: To come up so as to be audible ME.

1. A., let us go hence *John* 14:31. **2.** Awake, a., or be for ever fall'n MILT. *P.L.* I. 330. A., a.! the morning is at hand KEATS. **3.** A. faire Sun and kill the enuious Moone *Rom. & Jul.* II. ii. 4. **4.** Many bodies of the saints which slept arose *Matt.* 27:52. **5.** Aryse o Lorde God, lift vp thine honde *Ps.* 9:12. **6.** A wind arose and rush'd upon the South TENNYSON. **7.** And there arose a great cry *Acts* 23:9.

II. To go or come higher. **1.** To go or come up, ascend on high, mount. Now *poet.* OE. † **2.** To rise with its summit or surface; to grow higher, to swell up –1664; to rise in rank, etc. –1756; in price or amount –1714; to attain to, reach –1798.

1. The duste arose with the wynde 1450.

III. To spring up, come above ground, into existence. **1.** † To spring forth from its source. *transf.* To take its rise, originate. OE. **2.** To be born, come into the world of action OE. **3.** Of things: To spring up, be raised, built, etc. (*poet.* or *rhet.*) OE. **4.** To spring, originate, or result *from*, † *of* ME. **5.** *gen.* To come into existence or notice OE.

2. There arose no prophet more in Israel like vnto Moses *Deut.* 24:10. **4.** Some sodaine mischiefe may a. of it SHAKS. Comfort arose from the reflection 1793. **5.** Questions which arose in the Privy Council MACAULAY. Those Thoughts which a. . in the Mind of Man ADDISON. Hence † **Ari·se** *sb.* arising.

‖ **Arista** (ări·stă). Pl. **-æ.** 1691. [L.] The awn or beard of grain or grasses; *hence* used of similar bristle-like processes. Hence **Ari·state** *ppl. a.* awned, bearded.

Aristarch (æ·ristăɹk). 1621. [– L. *Aristarchus* – Gr. Ἀρίσταρχος, a severe Greek critic of the Homeric poetry.] A severe critic. Hence **Arista·rchian** *a.* severely critical.

† **Aristi·ppus.** 1627. [Name of a Gr. philosopher, luxurious in his living.] A cant name for canary wine.

Aristo- (æ·risto), comb. f. Gr. ἄριστος best; as in *a.-democratical*, having a democratic constitution limited by aristocratic elements.

Aristocracy (æristǫ·krăsi). 1561. [– (O)Fr. *aristocratie* – (through med.L. translations of Aristotle) Gr. ἀριστοκρατία, f. ἄριστος best; see -CRACY.] Contrasted earlier with *monarchy*; now with *democracy*. **1.** *lit.* The government of a state by its best citizens. Also *fig.* **2.** That form of government in which the sovereign power lies with those who are most distinguished by birth and fortune; oligarchy 1577; a state so governed 1603. **3.** An oligarchy 1611. *Hence* **4.** The class to which such a ruling body belongs; the nobles; *pop.* all those who by birth or fortune rank distinctly above the rest of the community. Also *fig.* 1651. **5.** = *aristocraticism* 1822.

1. A truer A., or Government again by the Best CARLYLE. **2.** The republic of Venice is an a. 1751. **4.** Our a. and gentry date, on the whole, from the days of Henry the Eighth ROGERS.

Aristocrat (æ·ristoˌkræ:t, ări·stŏkræt). 1789. [– Fr. *aristocrate* (a word of the French Revolution), not on Gr. analogies but extracted f. *aristocratie*, *-ique*; see -CRAT.] A member of an aristocracy; *strictly*, one of an oligarchy; *hence*, one of a patrician order, a noble; *occ.* one who favours an aristocratic form of government (opp. to *democrat*).

Their excellencies, the *aristocrats* of Venice A. YOUNG. In came that fierce A., Our pursy woollen-draper COLERIDGE.

Aristocratic (æ:ristoˌkræ·tik), *a.* 1602. [– Fr. *aristocratique* – Gr. ἀριστοκρατικός; see ARISTOCRACY, -IC.] **1.** Of or pertaining to an aristocracy; attached to or favouring aristocracy. **2.** Befitting an aristocrat; grand, stylish 1845.

1. The so-called a. party, the landlords G. DUFF. **2.** The principal tradesmen. . deemed it more 'aristocratic' DISRAELI. Hence **A:ristocra·tical** *a.* oligarchical; of or belonging to the higher classes; *sb.* a partisan of aristocracy. **A:ristocra·tically** *adv.* **A:ristocra·ticalness,** a quality or style. **A:ristocra·ticism,** adherence to a. principles or custom. **Aristo·cratism,** haughty exclusiveness. **Aristo·cratize** *v.* to make a.; to favour aristocracy.

‖ **Aristolochia** (æ:ristolōᵘ·kiă). ME. [– med.L. *aristologia* (also Sp. and It.), Fr. *aristoloche*, XVI *aristolochie* – L. *aristolochia* – Gr. ἀριστολοχία, -εια f. ἀριστόλοχος well-born (from its repute in promoting child-birth).] *Bot.* A genus of shrubs, including *A. clematitis*, the Common Birthwort.

Aristo·logy. 1835. [f. Gr. ἄριστον breakfast, luncheon + -LOGY.] The art or science of dining. Hence **A:ristolo·gical** *a.* **Aristo·logist.**

Aristotelian (æ:ristotī·liăn). 1607. [f. L. *Aristotelius*, *-eus* (– Gr. Ἀριστοτέλειος) + -AN; see -IAN, -EAN.] *adj.* Of or pertaining to Aristotle, the Greek philosopher, or to his system. *sb.* One who follows, or is skilled in, the philosophy of Aristotle. var. **A:ristote·lean.** [f. L. *Aristoteleus*, Gr. Ἀριστοτέλειος.] Hence **Aristote·lianism,** the system or any doctrine of Aristotle. **A:ristote·lic,** † **-al** *a.* = ARISTOTELIAN. **Aristo·telism** = *Aristotelianism*. **Aristo·telize** *v.* to lean towards or teach the system of Aristotle.

Aristulate (ări·stiŭleⁱt), *ppl. a.* [f. mod.L. *aristula*, dim. of *arista* ARISTA + -ATE.²] *Bot.* Bearing a diminutive awn.

Arithmancy (æ·ripˌmænsi). 1577. [contr. f. *arithmomancy* (see ARITHMO-).] Divination by numbers. Hence **Arithma·ntical** *a.*

Arithmetic (ări·þmĭtik), *sb.* ME. [Earliest forms *arsmetike*, *-metrike*, *arismetrik* – OFr. *arismetique* – Rom. **arismetica* for L. *arithmetica* – Gr. ἀριθμητική (sc. τέχνη art) 'art of counting', f. ἀριθμεῖν reckon, f. ἀριθμός number. Assoc. w. L. *ars metrica* 'measuring art' led to forms of the type of *ar(i)smetric*, which were later (XVI) conformed, through the stage *arithmetric*, to the orig. L. and Gr.] **1.** The science of numbers; the art of computation by figures. **2.** Arithmetical knowledge, computation 1607. **3.** A treatise on computation 1623.

1. These roguish Arsmetrique gibbets or flesh-hookes, and cyphers or round oos NASHE. **2.** But now 'tis oddes beyond Arithmetick *Cor.* III. i. 245.

† **Arithme·tic(k.** 1652. [– Fr. *arithmétique*.] *adj.* = ARITHMETICAL. –1767. *sb.* An arithmetician –1711.

Arithmetical (æriþme·tikăl), *a.* 1543. [f. L. *arithmeticus* (– Gr. ἀριθμητικός) + -AL¹; see ARITHMETIC.] Of, pertaining to, or connected with arithmetic; according to the rules of arithmetic. As *sb.* A number in an a. progression 1798. Hence **Arithme·tically** *adv.*

A. progression, series: one of which the terms differ by a constant difference, positive or negative. So *a. proportion*.

Arithmetician (ări:þmĭti·ʃăn, æ:riþ-). 1557. [– Fr. *arithméticien*, f. L. *arithmetica*; see ARITHMETIC, -ICIAN.] One skilled in arithmetic.

Arithmo-, comb. f. Gr. ἀριθμός number.

Arithmo-cracy [Gr. -κρατία], rule by a mere numerical majority; whence **-cra·tic** *a.*; **-gram** [Gr. γράμμα], a number expressed by the letters of a word, name, or phrase; **-graphy** [Gr. -γραφία], representation of a number by letters; **-lo·gical** [Gr. -λογικός] *a.*, pertaining to the scientific treatment of numbers; **-logy** [Gr. -λόγια], a treatise on numbers, or statement bearing on them; **-ma:ncy** [Gr. -μαντεία], divination by numbers; arithmancy; **-meter** [Gr. -μέτρον], an instrument for working out arithmetical problems.

-arium, *suffix* of sbs. – L. *-arium* 'thing connected with or employed in, place for', orig. neut. of adjs. in *-arius*. The reg. Eng. repr. of *-arium* is *-ary*; see -ARY¹.

Ark (ăɹk), *sb.* [OE. *ærc* (*earc*), corresp. to OFris. *erke*, OHG. *arca*, *archa*, ON. *ǫrk*, *ark-*, Goth. *arka* :– L. *arca* chest, box, coffer.] **1.** A chest, coffer, close basket, etc.; *esp.* in *north. dial.* a bin for meal, etc. OE. **2.** *spec.* in *Jew. Hist.* The wooden coffer containing the tables of the law, kept in the Holiest Place of the Tabernacle. Also called *Ark of the Covenant*, *Ark of Testimony*. OE. Also *fig.* **3.** The large floating covered vessel in which Noah was saved at the Deluge; hence *fig.* a place of refuge OE. **4.** *transf.* A ship, boat, etc.; *spec.* in U.S., a large flat-bottomed river boat used to transport produce 1475. † **5.** An enclosure for catching or confining fish.

1. She toke an arke of bul-rushes *Ex.* 2:3. **2.** Therein an A., and in the A. his Testimony MILT. *P.L.* XII. 251. *To touch* or *lay hands on the ark*: to treat irreverently what is held to be sacred (2 *Sam.* 6:6). **3.** There is sure another flood toward, and these couples are comming to the Arke *A.Y.L.* v. iv. 36. *Comb.*: **a.-full**; **-net,** a kind of fish-trap (cf. *eel-ark*); **-shell,** a species of bivalve mollusc. Hence † **Ark,** *v.* to shut up in an ark.

Arkansite. *Min.* [f. *Arkansas*, U.S.A., + -ITE¹ 2 b.] A variety of BROOKITE.

Arkite (ā·ɹkəit). 1774. [f. ARK + -ITE¹ 1.] *adj.* Of or pertaining to Noah's ark. *sb.* An inmate of the ark.

Arkose (aɹkōᵘ·s). 1839. *Geol.* A sandstone containing felspar and quartz.

Arksutite (ā·ɹksutəit). 1868. [f. *Arksut* in Greenland + -ITE¹ 2 b.] *Min.* A white, vitreous fluoride of lime, soda, and alumina.

Arle (ăɹl), *v. north.* 1609. [f. next. Cf. Fr. *arrher* (XVI), med.L. *arr(h)are* affiance.] To give earnest-money to or for.

Arles (ăɹlz). *north. dial.* ME. [app. repr. med.L. **arrhula*, dim. of L. *arr(h)a*; see ARRHA. Cf. OFr. *ere*, pl. *erres*, *arres* (mod. *arrhes* XVI) :– L. *arr(h)a*.] Money given to bind a bargain; *esp.* that given when a servant is hired; earnest-money 1540; *fig.* an earnest, a foretaste ME. var. **Arles-penny.**

† **A·rling.** [OE. *eorðling* 'agricola', f. *eorðe* earth.] A bird; the wheatear –1753.

Arm (ăɹm), *sb.*¹ [OE. *arm* (*earm*) = OFris. *arm*, *erm*, OS., OHG. (Du., G.) *arm*, ON. *armr*, Goth. *arms* :– Gmc. **armaz* (whence Finn. *armas*).] **I.** The limb. **1.** The upper limb of the human body, from the shoulder to the hand; the part from the elbow downwards being the *fore-arm*. **2.** *fig.* Might, power, authority OE.; a prop, a stay ME.; and generally 1597. **3.** The fore limb of an animal 1607; in *Falconry*, the leg of a hawk from the thigh to the foot 1575; the flexible limbs or other appendages of invertebrate animals 1822. **4.** A sleeve 1797.

1. Smot him þoru þe riht arum ME. She stript it from her Arme *Cymb.* II. iv. 101. **2.** I haue broken the arme of Pharaoh *Ezek.* 30:21. *Secular arm*: the authority of a temporal (opp. to an eccl.) tribunal. Sir Lancelot, my right arm (= main stay) TENNYSON. I saw the new moon, late yestreen, Wi' the auld moon in her a. *Sir Patrick Spens.* **4.** The right a. lined with fur H. WALPOLE.

II. Things resembling arms. **1.** A narrower portion of anything projecting from the main body, as an *arm of the sea*, of a machine, etc. OE. **2.** One of the branches into which a main trunk divides, as an arm of a tree, a river, a nerve, etc. ME. **3.** One of two lateral (and usu. horizontal) parts, which answer to each other, as (*Naut.*) the parts of an anchor which bear the flukes; the parts of the yard extending on either side of the mast (see YARD-ARM); in machines, the parts of the balance; in levers, the part from the fulcrum to the point of application of the power or weight 1659. **4.** One of the two rails of a chair, sofa, etc., on which the sitter's arms may rest. See ARM-CHAIR. 1633.

1. That a. of the sea. . now called the Humber DE FOE.

Phrases. **a. Arm-in-arm** (improp. *arm-and-arm*): said of two persons, when one interlinks his arm with the other's; hence *fig.* in close communion. **To give** or **offer one's arm (to)**: to allow *or* invite a person to walk arm-in-arm with one, or lean on one's a. **A child** or **infant in arms**: one too young to walk. **With open arms:** with eager welcome. **b. At arm's** † **end, length:** as far away from one as the arm can reach; *hence*, away from familiarity, at a distance; *spec.* in *Law*, without fiduciary relations. **To work at arm's length:** awkwardly or disadvantageously.

Comb.: **a.-bone,** the *humerus*; **-coil,** an armlet; † **-gaunt** *a.*, ? with gaunt limbs; † **-great** *a.*, as large round as an a.; † **-labour,** manual labour; **-piece,** armour to protect the a.; **-strong,** *a.*, strong of a.

Arm, *sb.*² Usu. in *pl.* **Arms** (ăɹmz). ME. [– (O)Fr. *armes* repr. L. *arma* n.pl. (no sing.).] **I.** *pl.* Things used in fighting. **1.** Defensive covering, etc., for the body; armour, mail. Now *poet.* **2.** Instruments of offence used in war; weapons ME.; *sing.* a particular kind of weapon 1861.

2. *Fire-arms*: those for which gunpowder is used. *Small-arms*: those not requiring carriages, opp. to *artillery*. *Stand of arms*: a complete set for one soldier. A well-balanced a. 1877. *Man of arms*, later *man-at-arms*: one practised in war; a fully armed knight.

II. Elliptical senses. (Only *pl.* exc. in 4.) **1.** The exercise of arms; fighting, war, etc. ME. **2.** The practice or profession of arms 1450. **3.** Deeds or feats of arms. Now *poet.* ME. **4.** *sing.* and *pl.* Each kind of troops of which an army is composed; the infantry, cavalry, artillery, and engineers; orig. the two first 1798.

1. Success in arms 1780. *To appeal to arms*; see APPEAL *v.* **2.** Since first I follow'd Armes SHAKS. **3.** Arms and the man I sing DRYDEN. *A passage, assault, of* (or *at*) *arms*; see PASSAGE, ASSAULT. **4.** About 12,000 of all arms GLEIG.

III. Transf. and fig. senses. (Usu. *pl.*) **1.** in *Law*. Anything that a man, in his anger, takes into his hand to cast at, or strike another 1641. **2.** Instruments of defence or attack possessed by animals; the ARMATURE or ARMOUR of plants 1711. **3.** *fig.* (from 2) of things immaterial ME.

3. The intellectual arms of Reason SIR T. BROWNE.

IV. Heraldic Arms. Heraldic insignia or devices, borne originally on the shields of knights or barons to distinguish them (hence called ARMORIAL bearings), which later became hereditary. Also the ensigns of countries, corporations, etc. ME. *collect.* as *sing.* 1590.

The lawful holder of Arms has in them a true estate in fee 1864. *In arms with*: quartered with. *To bear arms*: to show armorial bearings. Also *to grant* or *assign arms*. *Coat of Arms*: see ARMOUR *sb.* *College of Arms*: the Heralds' College, where armorial bearings are granted. *King at Arms*: a chief herald.

Phrases: **To arms!** take to your arms, be ready to fight. **In arms:** armed, ready to fight; also *fig.* **To take up arms:** to arm oneself, rise in hostility; also *fig.* **To bear arms:** to serve as a soldier. **To turn one's arms against:** to make war upon. **To lay down arms:** to surrender. **Under arms:** in battle array; so, **to lie upon their arms. Stand to your arms!** i.e. in order of battle with arms presented.

Arm (āɹm), *v.*[1] ME. [– (O)Fr. *armer* :– L. *armare*, f. *arma*; see prec.] **1.** *lit.* To furnish with arms, *esp.* (in early use) with armour; *now*, with weapons. **2.** Hence, *transf.* and *fig.*: To *arm* **a.** with tools or appliances; **b.** with qualities, offensive or defensive ME; **c.** (an animal) with natural organs of offence or defence 1607; **d.** (a thing) with necessary appendages, etc. 1534; **e.** to prepare (for action, etc.) 1590. **3.** *intr.* for *refl.* To arm oneself ME. **4.** *trans.* To plate (*with*), or furnish with a protective covering ME. **5.** To furnish (a magnet) with an armature 1664.

1. To a. a man of war 1716, the population GLEIG, the heels of fighting cocks STRUTT. **2. b.** Arme me, Audacitie, from head to foote *Cymb.* I. vi. 19. **d.** First you must a. your hook WALTON. **e.** Arme your selfe To fit your fancies to your Fathers Will *Mids. N.* I. i. 117. **3.** Arme, arme, and out *Macb.* V. v. 46.

Arm (āɹm), *v.*[2] 1538. [f. ARM *sb.*[1]] †**1.** To put one's arms or arm round (*rare*) 1611. **2.** To give one's arm to 1612. †**3.** *intr.* To project like an arm 1538.

‖ **Armada** (aɹmē·dă). 1533. (**-ado**). [Early forms also *armado* (see -ADO), *-ade*, *-ata* – Sp. *armada* :– Rom. *armata* army; see -ADE.] **1.** A fleet of ships of war. **2.** *spec.* The 'Invincible Armada' sent by Philip II of Spain against England 1588. **3.** An armament 1728.

3. Nor was the naval unworthy of the land a. LYTTON. Hence **Armadi·lla**, a small fleet of ships of war; a small war-vessel.

Armadillo (āɹmădi·lo). 1577. [– Sp. *armadillo*, dim. of *armado* armed man :– L. *armatus*, pa. pple. of *armare* ARM *v.*[1]] **1.** Name of several species of burrowing animals (order *Edentata*), peculiar to South America; encased in bony armour, within which they roll themselves into a ball when attacked. **2.** *transf.* A genus of small terrestrial Crustacea (order *Isopoda*), having the power of rolling themselves into a ball 1847.

Armageddon (āɹmăge·dŏn). 1811. [*Rev.* 16:16 (A.V.); the R.V. has *Harmagedon*.] The site of the last decisive battle on the Day of Judgement; hence, a final contest on a grand scale.

Armament (ā·ɹmămĕnt). 1699. [– L. *armamentum*, in cl. L. only pl., f. *armare*; see ARM *v.*[1], -MENT; cf. (O)Fr. *armement*.] **1.** A force (*esp.* naval) equipped for war. Also *fig.* **2.** Munitions of war; *spec.* the great guns on board a man-of-war 1721. **3.** Equipment for resistance or action of any kind 1870. **4.** The process of equipping for war 1813.

1. That boundless A. of Mechanisers and Unbelievers threatening to strip us bare CARLYLE. **4.** With the a. of the navy, Hawkins had not much to do 1868.

†**Armame·ntary.** *rare.* 1731. [– L. *armamentarium* armoury; see prec., -ARY[1].] An armoury, an arsenal; *transf.* (in L. form) a case of (surgical) apparatus.

Armature (ā·ɹmătiŭɹ). 1542. [– Fr. *armature* – L. *armatura*, f. *armat-*, pa. ppl. stem of *armare*; see ARM *v.*[1], -URE.] **1.** Arms, armour (*esp.* defensive) 1669. **b.** *fig.* esp. in Theol. lang. 1542. †**2.** Armed troops. (So in L.) –1765. **3.** The art of protecting with armour, etc. 1611. **4.** *transf.* Protective covering of animals or plants; occ., apparatus of attack 1662. **5. a.** *Magnetism.* A piece of soft iron or steel placed in contact with the poles of a magnet, which preserves and increases the magnetic power 1752. †**b.** The coating of tinfoil on a Leyden jar. **6.** Iron framing used to consolidate a building 1846. **7.** *Electr.* That part of a dynamo or electric motor carrying the conductors, consisting usually of a number of separate coils of wire on a laminated core of soft iron. Also *attrib.* and *Comb.* 1884.

1. *fig.* Not the armour of Achilles, but the A. of St. Paul SIR T. BROWNE.

A·rm-chai·r. Also **armed-chair.** 1633. [f. ARM *sb.*[1] q.v.] A chair with arms.

Armed (āɹmd, ā·ɹmĕd), *ppl. a.*[1] ME. [f. ARM *v.*[1] + -ED[1].] **1.** *lit.* Furnished with arms or armour. **2.** *transf.* and *fig.* Furnished (see ARM *v.*[1] 2, 5) 1585. **3.** *Her.* Having the claws or talons of a different tincture from that of the adjoining parts; *also*, represented with claws, teeth, etc. 1572.

1. *Armed demonstration, neutrality*, when the power making the demonstration or remaining neutral is fully equipped for war. *Armed to the teeth* (intensive phr.) COBDEN.

Armed, *ppl. a.*[2] 1625. [f. ARM *sb.*[1] + -ED[2].] Having, or fitted with, arms.

Armenian (aɹmī·niăn). 1598. [f. L. *Armenia*, Gr. Ἀρμενία, f. OPers. *Arminâ* (the Armenian name is Hayasdan or Hayq); see -AN, -IAN.] *adj.* Of or pertaining to Armenia or the Armenians 1727. *sb.* A native of Armenia; an adherent of the Armenian Church 1598.

1. *Armenian bole*: a pale red earth from Armenia. *Armenian stone*: a blue carbonate of copper, formerly used as an aperient, etc. var. †**Arme·niac** *a.*; whence, by corruption, *bole ammoniac*.

Armer (ā·ɹməɹ). 1611. [f. ARM *v.*[1] + -ER[1].] One who arms.

Armet (ā·ɹmĕt). 1507. [– (O)Fr. *armet* (XIV).] A globular iron helmet, with visor, beaver, and gorget, which replaced the basinet in 15th c.

Armful (ā·ɹmful). 1579. [f. ARM *sb.*[1] + -FUL.] As much as both arms, or one, can hold; a heap.

A·rm-ho:le. ME. [f. ARM *sb.*[1]] **1.** An armpit (*arch.*). Also *fig.* **2.** The similar cavity in other animals (*arch.*) 1607. **3.** The hole in a garment through which the arm is put 1775.

Armiger (ā·ɹmi,dʒəɹ). 1762. [– L. *armiger* bearing arms, f. *arma* ARM *sb.*[2] + *-ger*, *gerere* to bear; see -GEROUS.] An esquire; *orig.* one who attended a knight to bear his shield, etc.; later, one entitled to bear (heraldic) arms. Hence **Armi·geral** *a.* of squires. **Armi·gerous** *a.* entitled to bear (heraldic) arms.

Armil (ā·ɹmil). 1480. [Partly – (O)Fr. *armille* :– L. *armilla*, partly a more recent adaptation f. Latin. See next.] **1.** = ARMILLA 1. **2.** One of the insignia of royalty, put on at the coronation 1485. **3.** = ARMILLA 4. 1837.

‖ **Armilla** (aɹmi·lă). 1706. [L., = bracelet, hoop, dim. of *armus* shoulder.] **1.** A bracelet; now *esp.* in *Archaeol.* **2.** A coronation garment 1721. **3.** An iron ring, hoop, or brace, in which the gudgeons of a wheel move 1706. **4.** An ancient astronomical instrument, consisting of a circular hoop fixed in the plane of the equator (*Equinoctial A.*), sometimes crossed at right angles by another in the plane of the meridian (*Solstitial A.*) 1797.

Armillary (ā·ɹmilări, aɹmi·lări), *a.* 1664. [– mod.L. *armillaris*; see prec., -ARY[2]. Cf. Fr. *armillaire* XVI.] Of or pertaining to bracelets or hoops. As *sb.* = ARMILLA 4. 1841.

Armillary Sphere: a skeleton celestial globe, consisting merely of metal rings representing the equator, ecliptic, tropics, arctic and antarctic circles, and colures, revolving on an axis, within a wooden horizon.

†**A·rming,** *sb.* [OE. *earming*, f. *earm* poor + -ING[3]. Cf. NITHING.] A poor or miserable creature –1605.

Arming (ā·ɹmiŋ), *vbl. sb.* ME. [f. ARM *v.*[1] + -ING[1].] **1.** The action of arming; †*concr.* arms, armour. **2.** Any defensive or protective covering; *spec.* on a ship 1466. **3.** The equipment of anything with that which strengthens, or fits for a purpose; *concr.* the part thus furnished; *spec.* the tallow at the bottom of the sounding-lead; the armature of a magnet. Often *attrib.* 1552. **4.** Furnishing with heraldic devices 1598.

4. *attrib.* in **arming-press,** a bookbinder's machine used in stamping and lettering the covers of books.

Arminian (aɹmi·niăn), *a.* 1618. [f. *Arminius*, Latinized f. *Harmensen*.] Of, belonging to, or following the doctrine of, James Arminius or Harmensen, a Dutch Protestant theologian, who opposed Calvin, *esp.* on predestination. Arminius died in 1609. As *sb.* An adherent of the doctrine of Arminius 1618.

The A...is condemn'd for setting up free will against free grace MILT. The Arminians believe it [predestination] is conditional; the Calvinists, that it is absolute WESLEY. Hence **Armi·nianism,** the A. doctrines, or adherence to them. **Armi·nianize** *v.* to make A.; to teach Arminianism; whence **Armi·niani:zer,** one who teaches Arminianism.

Armipotent (aɹmi·pŏtĕnt), *a.* ME. [– L. *armipotens*, *-ent-*, f. *arma* arms + *potens* powerful.] Mighty in arms: orig. of Mars. Hence **Armi·potence** (*rare*).

Armistice (ā·ɹmistis). 1707. [– Fr. *armistice* or mod.L. *armistitium*, f. *arma* arms + *-stitium* stoppage, after *solstitium* SOLSTICE.] A cessation from arms; a short truce. Also *fig.* 1841.

A·rmless, *a.*[1] ME. [f. ARM *sb.*[1] + -LESS.] Without arm or branch.

A·rmless, *a.*[2] 1619. [f. ARM *sb.*[2] + -LESS.] Without weapons, unarmed.

Armlet (ā·ɹmlĕt). 1535. [f. ARM *sb.*[1] + -LET.] **1.** An ornament, etc., worn round the arm. (Cf. *bracelet*, worn at the wrist.) **2.** A small arm of the sea or of a river (see ARM *sb.*[1] II. 1) 1538. **3.** Armour for the arm 1706.

‖ **Armoire** (ar,mwar). 1571. [Fr., closet, cupboard, press.] An AMBRY.

Armoniac, obs. f. AMMONIAC.

Armor(e, Armorer, obs. ff. ARMOUR, -ER.

Armorial (aɹmōᵊ·riăl), *a.* 1576. [f. ARMORY + -AL[1]; cf. Fr. *armorial* (XVII).] Pertaining to heraldic arms. As *sb.* A book containing coats of arms 1753.

‖ **Armorica** (aɹmǫ·rikă). ME. [– L. *Armoricae* (Caesar, the northern provinces of Gaul), f. Gaulish *are-* (= L. *præ* in front of) + *mor* sea.] Name of the part of Gaul now called Bretagne or Brittany. **Armo·ric** *a.* of Armorica or its people; *absol.* its language. **Armo·rican** *a.* = *Armoric*; *sb.* an inhabitant of Armorica.

Armoried (ā·ɹmŏrid), *ppl. a.* 1866. [f. ARMORY + -ED[2].] Decked with escutcheons.

Armorist (ā·ɹmŏrist). 1586. [f. ARMORY + -IST.] One skilled in heraldry, or in blazoning arms.

Armory (ā·ɹmŏri). 1489. [– OFr. *armoierie* (mod. *armoiries* pl.), f. *armoier* to blazon, f. *arme* ARM *sb.*[2]; see -Y[3].] **1.** Heraldry. **2.** Armorial bearings (*arch.*) 1500. †**3.** Ensigns of war 1523.

Armour (ā·ɹməɹ). [ME. *armur(e)* – (O)Fr. *armure*, earlier *armëure* :– L. *armatura* ARMATURE. From XIV assim. to words ending in -URE.] **1.** *collect. sing.* Defensive covering for the body; mail. †**2.** (with a *pl.*) A suit of mail –1751. **3.** *collect. sing.* with *pl.* The whole apparatus of war, offensive and defensive. (*Obs.* exc. in *Law.*) ME. †Often = *arms* in obs. phrases –1577. †**4.** = ARM *sb.*[2] II. 1. –1602. **5.** *fig.* now only from sense 1. ME. **6.** *transf.*, *Naut.* †**a.** = ARMING *vbl. sb.* 2. **b.** The steel or iron sheathing of a ship of war. See ARMOUR-PLATE. 1466. **7.** A diver's watertight suit; (cf. 2.) 1822. **8.** *Nat. Hist.* Protective or defensive covering of animals or plants; †*abstr.* protection, etc. 1605. **9.** Heraldic insignia ME. ¶ For ARMER or ARMOURER 1550.

1. Arms on A. clashing MILT. *P.L.* VI. 209. **3.** The people..were up in a. against the King HOLINSHED. **5.** Let vs put on the Armoure of lyght TINDALE *Rom.* 13:12. **6.** A belt of a...to protect broadside guns 1870. **9.** *Coat armour* = 'coat of arms', orig. a vest of silk, etc., embroidered in colours, worn over the armour of a knight, to distinguish him. Cf. ARM *sb.*[2] IV.

Comb.: **a.-bearer,** one who carried a warrior's armour; a squire; see 1 *Sam.* 14:14; **-fish,** *Cataphractus americanus*; **-proof,** as impenetrable as a., or ?proof against arms; **-wise,** *adv.* Hence **A·rmour** *v.* to put a. on. **A·rmoured** *ppl. a.* clad in a.; also *transf.*, esp. of war-vessels; cf. ARMOUR-CLAD. **A·rmourless** *a.*

A·rmour-cla:d, *ppl. a.* 1869. [f. prec.] Clad in, or protected by, armour. *Ellipt.* as *sb.* A warship protected by a sheathing of iron or steel. Cf. *ironclad*.

Armourer (ā·ɹmərəɹ). ME. [– AFr. *armurer*, (O)Fr. *armurier*, f. *arm(ë)ure* ARMOUR; in med.L. *armurarius* (XIV); see -ER[2].] **1.** A maker of armour; now, a manufacturer of arms. **2.** One who equipped men-at-arms in their mail. Also *fig.* Now *Hist.* ME. **3.** An official who has charge of the arms of a ship, regiment, etc. 1753. ¶Confused with *armure* by CHAUCER.

2. The Armourers accomplishing the Knights *Hen. V*, IV. Cho. 12. The A. of my heart *Ant. & Cl.* iv. iv. 7.

A·rmour-pla:te. 1864. One of the metal pieces or plates of which armour is composed; *esp.* one of the plates of iron or steel used to cover the sides of warships. Hence **A·rmour-pla:ted** *ppl. a.* **A·rmour-pla:ting** *vbl. sb.* (used *concr.* for 'armour-plates').

Armoury, -ory (ā·ɹməri). ME. [– OFr. *armoi(e)rie* ARMORY, with assim. to ARMOUR (cf. the early forms *armurie, armery*); see -Y[3].] **1.** Armour collectively (*arch.*). †**2.** An armed force –1532. **3.** A place where arms are kept, an arsenal. Also *fig.* 1538. **4.** The workshop of an armourer; a place where arms are manufactured (U.S.) 1841. **5.** The craft of the armourer 1718.

1. Celestial Armourie, Shields, Helmes, and Speares MILT. *P.L.* IV. 553. **3.** The goodliest weapons of his armorie *Tit. A.* IV. ii. 11. *fig.* A book of Apothegms is an a. of thought SELDON.

Armozeen (āɹmŏzī·n). 1599. [– Fr. *armoisin*, in XVI *tafetas armoisy, armezin*, – It. *ermesino* – mod. Gr. χερμεζί – Arab. *ḳirmizī*; see CRIMSON, KERMES.] A stout plain silk, usu. black, used for clerical gowns, etc.

A·rmpi:t. ME. [f. ARM *sb.*[1] + PIT *sb.*] **1.** The hollow under the arm where it is jointed to the trunk. **2.** The analogous cavity in other animals. Cf. ARM-HOLE. (*arch.*) 1601. †**3.** *fig.* The axil of a plant 1601.

Armure, -rer, -rie, obs. ff. ARMOUR, etc.

Army (ā·ɹmi). ME. [– (O)Fr. *armée* :– Rom. *armata* (X), subst. use of pa. pple. fem. of *armare* ARM *v.*[1] in the senses 'armed force', 'army', 'navy', 'fleet'. See -Y[5].] †**1.** An armed expedition by sea or land –1525. **2.** *gen.* An armed force (by sea or land); a host. *Obs.* exc. as in *land-army*, etc. 1460. **3.** *spec.* †**a.** A naval armament, an armada, a fleet –1786. **b.** A land force; a body of men armed for war, and organized in divisions and regiments under officers, and a commander-in-chief or general 1557. **4.** *transf.* A vast assemblage, a host 1500. *fig.* (from 3.) A marshalled host 1593. **5.** (*fig.* or *transf.* from 2, 3, 4.) A body of men organized, or striving for the advancement of a cause, as the *Salvation Army*, the *Blue Ribbon Army* 1543.

2. He sent a navall armie etc. KNOLLES. **3. a.** A true Discourse of the Armie [*i.e.* 'Spanish Armada'] ..assembled in the hauen of Lisbon 1588. **b.** *Standing Army*: an army of professional soldiers kept permanently on foot, not raised on each special occasion. *The Army*: the whole military service of a state (first so named *c* 1647). **4.** A whole a. of waiters 1888, of words COKE. Armies of Pestilence *Rich. II*, III. iii. 87. **5.** The noble armye of Martyrs do prayse the 1543.

Comb.: **a.-corps,** a main division of an a. in the field; **-list,** an official list of all the commissioned officers of the Army; **-worm,** the larva of the cotton-moth.

Arn(e. Now *dial.* 1791. [perh. = *alrn, allern*, OE. *ælren*; see ALDERN.] The alder tree.

Arnatto, var. of ANATTA.

†**A·rnement.** ME. [alt. of OFr. *arrement* :– L. *atramentum* ink, blacking; cf. med.L. *arna-, arnementum* black horse-salve.] Ink, or materials for making it –1586.

Arnica (ā·ɹnikă). 1753. [mod.L., of unkn. origin.] **1.** A genus of Composite plants, including *A. montana* or Mountain Tobacco, which has medicinal properties. **2.** A medicine (*esp.* a tincture) prepared from the plant 1788.

2. Stiffish cock-tail, taken in time, Is better for a bruise than a. BROWNING. Hence **A·rnicin,** *Chem.* the bitter active principle of a. **A·rnicine,** an alkaloid found in a.

Ar'n't, contr. for *are not*; cf. AIN'T, AN'T.

Arnotto, var. of ANATTA.

Arnut, obs. f. EARTH-NUT.

A-roa·r, *adv.* 1461. [A *prep.*[1] 11.] In a roar.

Aroid (ēᵊ·roid). 1830. [f. ARUM + -OID. The N.O. *Araceæ* is also called *Aroideæ*.] *Bot.* A plant allied to the Arum; an arad. Hence **Aroi·deous** *a.*

Aroint, aroynt (ăroi·nt). 1605. [Origin unkn.] **1.** In *Aroint thee!* (? verb in the imperative, or interjection): Avaunt! Begone! **2.** Used by Mr. and Mrs. Browning as a vb.: To drive away with an execration 1850.

1. Aroynt thee, witch *Macb.* I. iii. 6. Also *Lear* III. iv. 129. (The orig. sources of the word.) **2.** That Humbug, whom thy soul aroints BROWNING.

Arolla (ărǫ·lă). 1881. [Latinized f. Swiss-Fr. *arolle*.] French Swiss name for the *Pinus cembra*.

Aroma (ărōᵘ·mă). ME. [– L. *aroma* – Gr. ἄρωμα, -ματ- spice; earlier *aromat* (XIII–XVII), – OFr. *aromat* (mod. *-ate*) – L. pl. *aromata*. Pl. **aromas,** rarely **aro·mata.**] †**1.** Spice; usu. in *pl.* –1753. **2.** The distinctive fragrance of a spice, plant, etc.; *gen.* an agreeable odour 1814. **3.** *fig.* A subtle pervasive quality or charm 1851.

3. The pure Parisian a. TROLLOPE.

Aromatic (æromæ·tik), *a.* ME. [– (O)Fr. *aromatique* – late L. *aromaticus* – Gr. ἀρωματικός; see AROMA, -IC.] **1.** Yielding aroma; spicy, fragrant, sweet-smelling. **2.** *Chem.* Epithet of a group of organic compounds, consisting of benzene and its homologues 1869. **3.** *sb.* 1494.

1. Die of a rose in a. pain POPE. **3.** While Ma'am the Aromatics blended, To gain the scent which she intended COMBE. Hence **Aroma·tical** *a.*, **-ly** *adv.*

Aromatization (ărōᵘ:mătəizēⁱ·ʃən). 1603. [– Fr. *aromatisation* or med.L. *aromatizatio*; see AROMA, -IZE, -ATION.] The action or process of rendering aromatic; aromatic flavouring.

Aromatize (ărōᵘ·mătəiz), *v.* 1480. [– (O)Fr. *aromatiser* – late L. *aromatizare* – Gr. ἀρωματίζειν to spice; see AROMA, -IZE.] To render aromatic or fragrant; to flavour or season with spice. Also *fig.* Hence **Aro·matizer.**

†**A-roo·m,** *adv.* ME. [orig. *on rūm, on rūme*; see A *prep.*[1], ROOM.] To or at a distance; aside, off –1530.

A-roo·t, *adv.* [A *prep.*[1] 11.] On root; *hence* firm. CHAUCER.

Aroph. 1657. [Said to be a contr. for *aroma philosophorum*.] Name of various Paracelsian medicinal preparations.

Arose (ărōᵘ·z), pa. t. of ARISE.

Around (arau·nd). ME. [In earliest use perh. after OFr. *a la reonde* 'in the round'; later f. A- *pref.* 2; cf. Fr. *en rond* in a circle, *au rond de* round about (XVI).] **A.** *adv.* (Often with *all.*) †**1.** In circumference; in a round –1596. **2.** On or along the circuit (of a globular body) 1596. **3.** *gen.* On every side ME. **4.** In U.S.: = ROUND 1816. **5.** In U.S.: = ABOUT. **a.** All about, at random. **b.** Somewhere near. 1776. **B.** *prep.* **1.** On or along the circuit ME. **2.** So as to surround; about 1816. **3.** On all sides of 1667. Also *fig.* **4.** In U.S.: At random through, about 1828.

A. 3. The signs of the time were all a. BUCKLE. **4.** Enough to go a. 1883. **5.** She..must be pleasant to have a. 1870. **B. 1.** Nor war nor battle's sound was heard the world a. MILT. **2.** With his martial cloak a. him WOLFE. **4.** Born a. three o'clock 1888.

Arousal (ărau·zăl). 1854. [f. next + -AL[1] 2.] The action of arousing, or being aroused.

Arouse (ărau·z), *v.* 1593. [f. A- *pref.* 11 + ROUSE *v.*, after *rise, arise*, etc.] **1.** To raise or stir up from sleep or inactivity. **2.** To stir into activity (emotions, etc.) 1728. **3.** *intr.* (for *refl.*) To wake up 1822.

1. Grasping his spear, forth issu'd to a. His brother COWPER. **2.** No suspicion was aroused MERIVALE. Hence **Arou·se** *sb.* an alarum (*rare*). **Arou·ser. Arou·sing** *ppl. a.*

A-row·, *adv.* ME. [A *prep.*[1]] **1.** In a row, rank, or line. †**2.** In succession –1598.

1. Till home they walk arowe SIDNEY.

‖ **Arpeggio** (arpe·ddʒⁱo). 1742. [It., f. *arpeggiare* play on the harp, f. *arpa* HARP.] *Mus.* The employment of the notes of a chord in rapid succession instead of simultaneously; a chord thus treated. Hence **Arpe·ggio** *v.* to play or sing as an a.

‖ **Arpent.** 1580. [(O)Fr. *arpent* :– Gallo-Rom. **arepennis*, whence med.L. *arpentum* (*Lex Bajuvariorum* VIII).] An obs. Fr. measure of land, a hundred square perches, varying with the value of the perch from about an acre and a quarter to about five-sixths of an acre. Hence ‖ **Arpenteu·r** (Fr.), a land-surveyor. A. YOUNG.

Arquated, obs. var. of ARCUATED.

Arquebus, etc.; see HARQUEBUS.

Arquerite (ā·ɹkwĕrəit). [f. (1842) *Arqueros* in Chile + -ITE[1] 2 b.] *Min.* A native amalgam of silver.

Arquifoux, var. of ALQUIFOU.

Arr, *sb.* ME. [– ON. *ǫr(r)* scar; cf. Da. *ar.*] A wound, scar. Still north. dial.

†**Arr,** *v.*[1] ME. [Cf. OE. *erre, eorre, ierre* anger, LG. *arren* vex, f. *arre* anger.] To anger, vex, worry –1651.

†**Arr,** *v.*[2] 1483. [Echoic.] To snarl as a dog –1603.

‖ **Arracacha** (ærăkā·tʃă). 1823. [Native S.-Amer. Indian name.] *Bot.* A genus of umbelliferous plants, with tuberous roots, including *A. esculenta*, which is used for food.

Arrach, obs. f. ORACH.

Arrack (ăræ·k, æ·răk). 1602. [ult. – Arab. *'araq* sweat, juice, esp. in *'araq at-tamr* (fermented) juice of the date. Aphet. to RACK *sb.*[6]] In Eastern countries any spirituous liquor of native manufacture; *esp.* that distilled from the fermented sap of the coco-palm, or from rice and sugar, fermented with the coco-nut juice. Also *attrib.*

Arragonite; see ARA-.

Arrah (æ·ră), *int.* 1705. [Anglo-Ir. – Ir. *ara.*] An expletive, expressing emotion or excitement.

Arraign (ărēⁱ·n), *v.*[1] [ME. *arayne* – AFr. *arainer, areiner*, OFr. *arais-, areisnier* – Rom. **adrationare*, f. *ad* AR- + *ratio* account, REASON *sb.*] †**1.** *trans.* To call to account; to interrogate, examine –1447. **2.** *esp.* To call to answer on a criminal charge; to indict. Hence *gen.* To accuse, charge with fault. ME. **3.** To impeach, call in question, find fault with (actions, measures, etc.) 1672. Also *absol.*

2. Thou art here accused and arraigned of High Treason *Wint. T.* III. ii. 14. **3.** To a. the abuses of public and private life GIBBON. Hence **Arrai·gn** *sb.* arraignment. **Arrai·gner.**

†**Arrai·gn,** *v.*[2] 1528. [– AFr. *arraigner, arainer*, alt. of *aramer* = OFr. *aramier, aramir* :– med.L. *arramire* (Lex Salica) guarantee, decide, f. *ad* AR-[2] + Frank. *hramjan* appoint a place or time.] *Law.* To appeal to, claim, demand; in phr. *arraine* (i.e. *arrame*) *an assize*.

Arraignment (ărēⁱ·nmĕnt). 1548. [– OFr. *araisnement*, f. *araisnier*; see ARRAIGN *v.*[1], -MENT.] **1.** The act of arraigning, or being arraigned; accusation before a tribunal, indictment, charge. **2.** Hostile criticism 1595.

1. The a. of the prisoners 1864. **2.** An a. of their proceedings 1722.

Arrand, obs. f. ERRAND, ARRANT.

Arrange (ărēⁱ·ndʒ), *v.* ME. [– OFr. *arangier, arengier* (mod. *arranger*), f. *a* AD- + *rangier* RANGE *v.*[1] Rare till mod. times; not in BIBLE 1611, SHAKS., MILT., or POPE.] **1.** To draw up in ranks or in line of battle. **2.** To put (the parts) into order; to adjust 1802; *refl.* to prepare oneself 1865. **3.** *Mus.* To adapt (a composition) for instruments or voices for which it was not written 1838. **4.** To place in some order, dispose 1791; *intr.* to fall into place 1805. **5.** To settle (claims, differences, etc.), to adjust 1837. **6.** *intr.* To come to an agreement or understanding 1796. **7.** To plan, or settle details, beforehand 1786. **8.** *intr.* (*simply*, or with *inf.* or *subord. cl.*) To settle details with other persons concerned 1849.

1. Arranged in supreme regimental order CARLYLE. **2.** A mechanism previously arranged PALEY. **4.** The parts in the two dramas were differently arranged FREEMAN. **5.** The quarrel..was arranged SEELEY. **6.** We cannot [now] a. with our enemy BURKE. **7.** Every step..was calculated and arranged 1837. **8.** To a. about my passport HAWTHORNE. Hence **Arra·nger.**

Arrangement (ărēⁱ·ndʒmĕnt). 1727. [– (O)Fr. *arrangement*; see prec., -MENT.] **1.** The action of arranging (see ARRANGE *v.* 2). **2.** Arranged condition, order 1743; style or mode of disposition 1785. **3.** *concr.* A structure or combination of things for a purpose, etc.; hence loosely, like *affair*, etc. 1800. **4.** *Mus.* The act of arranging a composition (see ARRANGE *v.* 3); *concr.* a piece so arranged 1849. **5.** A settlement of mutual relations, claims, or matters in dispute 1855; *euphem.* an affair of gallantry 1751. **6.** Disposition of measures for a particular purpose 1786.

2. In my new a., I ought to have placed this piece [etc.] T. WARTON. **3.** That lace a. which you call a cap 1881. **5.** An a. that would please everybody MACAULAY. **6.** The arrangements for the flight MACAULAY.

Arrant (æ·rănt), *a.* ME. [var. of ERRANT, which, from its use in *arrant thief*, etc., became an intensive, 'notorious, downright'. For the vowel-change cf. *arrand* = *errand*, etc.] †**1.** Wandering, itinerant; *esp.* in *knight, bailiff arrant*, now ERRANT. –1647. **2.** In *arrant thief* [= robber]: *orig.* an outlawed robber roving about the country, a highwayman; *hence*, a public, notorious, professed robber, a common thief ME. **3.** Hence, notorious, downright, unmitigated ME.; *transf.* of things 1639. **4.** Without opprobrious force: Thorough, genuine, 'regular' 1570. †**5.** Good-for-nothing, rascally –1761.

2. Every servant an a. thief as to victuals and drink SWIFT. **3.** A. dunce GREENE, knaue SHAKS., asse BURTON, cowards DE FOE, Atheism BENTLEY, nonsense RICHARDSON, trifling BUCKLE. **4.** With the air of an a. old bachelor W. IRVING. **5.** So a. a critic of the modern Poets as..to damn them without a hearing POPE. Hence **A·rrantly** *adv.* abominably.

Arras (æ·răs). ME. [– *arras* in AFr. *draps d'Arras* 'cloths of Arras', name of a town in Artois.] **1.** A rich tapestry fabric, in which figures and scenes are woven in colours. **2.** A hanging screen of this formerly placed round the walls of rooms 1598. Also *fig.* Also *attrib.*

1. My suit of A. with the story of the Nativity and Passion BACON. **2.** I will ensconce mee behinde the A. *Merry W.* III. iii. 97. *attrib.* Our dim a.-picture of these University years CARLYLE. Hence **A·rrased** *ppl. a.* covered with a.

Arrasene (ærăsī·n). 1881. [f. ARRAS.] A material of wool and silk, used in embroidery.

‖ **Arrastre** (ărɑ·stre). 1881. [Sp., f. (ult.) L. *rastrum* harrow.] An apparatus for grinding ores by dragging a heavy stone round on a circular bed.

Arras-wise, erron. f. *arris-wise*; see ARRIS.

Array (ărēⁱ·), *v.* [ME. *aray(e* – AFr. *araier*, OFr. *areer* :– Rom. **arredare* put in order, f. L. *ad* AR-² + Gmc. **ræð-* prepare; see READY.] **1.** To set or place in order of readiness, *esp.* for battle. Also *fig.* **2.** *Law.* To array a panel, a jury 1591. †**3.** To put in order for a purpose; prepare –1485; *spec.* of food –1513; of a house, etc. –1450. **4.** To furnish the person with raiment (= arrayment), to attire; *now*, to dress up with display ME. **5.** *transf.* and *fig.* To attire ME.; to adorn, set off 1652. †**6.** *ironically*, To give a dressing to, thrash; rout –1530; to put into a plight, afflict –1600; to disfigure, dirty –1575.

1. This place is..fit..to a. an host of men upon 1576. *fig.* To a. themselves against Science BUCKLE. **4.** Take vp thy chyldren and aray them 1523. I drinke, I eate, a. my self, and liue *Meas. for M.* III. ii. 26. **5.** Arraye youe withe iustice EARL RIVERS. Pearld dew arraies As yet the virgin-meads 1652. Hence **Array·er**, one who arrays; *spec.* in *Hist.* (= *Commissioner of Array.*) **Array·ment**, accoutrement; RAIMENT.

Array (ărēⁱ·), *sb.* [ME. *arai, aray(e* – AFr. *arai* – OFr. *arei* (mod. *arroi*), f. AFr. *araier*, OFr. *areer*; see prec.] **1.** Arrangement in line or ranks. *esp.* martial order. Also *fig.* †**2.** A display of military force –1553. **3.** The calling forth of a military force, as the militia, etc. 1640. **4.** *concr.* A military force. *Hist.* The militia of a county or city. 1643. **5.** An imposing series 1814. **6.** *Law.* The order of impanelling a jury; the panel 1579. **7.** A state of special preparation, as for war, festivities, etc. Now *poet.* ME. †**8.** Plight; state of affairs –1568. **9.** Outfit, attire. Now *poet.* ME. Also *fig.* and *transf.*

1. Place thy men-at-arms In battle 'ray GREENE. Wedged together in the closest a. GIBBON. **3.** The form of the *Commission of Array* was settled in parliament *anno* 5 Hen. 4. TOMLINS. **4.** The whole a. of the city of London was under arms MACAULAY. **5.** An a. of powerful Doric cities GROTE. **6.** The Jurors names are ranked in the pannel one vnder another, which..ranking..is called the a. COKE. **7.** To be redy in their moost defensible arraye 1484. *In evil array*: in a bad condition. **9.** Thou Wolfe in Sheepes a. SHAKS. Hence **Array·al**, muster of a force; array.

†**Arrea·r**, *adv.* [ME. *arere* – OFr. *arere, ariere* (mod. *arrière*) :– med.L. *adretro*, f. L. *ad* AR-² + *retro* backward, behind.] Backward –1591; behind –1600; overdue (now *in arrear*) –1768.

Arrear (ărīᵊ·ɹ), *sb.* ME. [The prec. adv. used *absol.*: 'that which is behind'.] **I.** *In arrear.* **1.** Backward. *In arrear of*: behind 1845. **2.** Behind in the discharge of duties or liabilities. So *In arrears.* Cf. the earlier ARREARAGES, now U.S. 1620.

2. I am two or three letters in a. 1831.

II. Without *in.* **1.** The rear, *esp.* of a train or procession (*arch.*) 1627. †**2.** A portion held back 1768. **3.** That wherein one has fallen behind; *esp.* a debt remaining unpaid 1658; in *pl.* outstanding liabilities; debts 1648.

3. To you..I owe a long a. of thanks DICKENS. To pay the late Arrears of the Army 1648. Hence †**Arre·ar** *v.* to keep back; *intr.* to fall back, retreat.

Arrearage (ărīᵊ·rėdʒ). [ME. *arerage* – OFr. *arerage-s* (mod. *arrérage*), f. *arere*; see ARREAR *adv.*, -AGE. Cf. *avant-age*, ADVANTAGE.] †**1.** Indebtedness, debt –1637. With pl. *In arrearages*: in arrears –1642. **2.** *gen.* State of being in arrear 1576. **3.** *concr.* That which is in arrear; an outstanding balance 1466; something still in reserve 1594. **4.** *pl.* = ARREAR 3. ME.

†**Arrea·r-guard**, and ‖ **Arrière-guard.** 1489. [– Fr. † *arrière-guarde* (now *-garde*); naturalized in XVI–XVII, but now spelt partly as Fr. Aphet. as *ryere-, rere-* REAR. See also next.] = REARGUARD.

†**Arrea·r-ward.** 1589. [f. ARREAR *adv.* + WARD *sb.*] = prec.

Arrect, later corrupt f. † ARET *v.* to impute.

†**Arre·ct**, *v.* 1529. [– *arrect-*, pa.ppl. stem of L. *arrigere* raise up, f. *ad* AR-² + *regere* straighten.] To set upright; to direct upwards, lift up –1556.

Arrect (ăre·kt), *ppl. a.* 1646. [– L. *arrectus*, pa.pple. of *arrigere*; see prec.] Set upright, pricked up (as the ears of a horse); *fig.* intent, on the alert.

†**Arre·ctary.** [– L. *arrectarius* whence *arrectaria* (Vitruvius), upright posts; see prec., -ARY¹.] An upright post. BP. HALL.

‖ **Arrenda·tor.** [med.L., = leaseholder, f. *arrendare* for *arrentare*; see ARRENT, -OR 2.] One who rents or farms at a yearly rent.

Arrenotokous (ærĭnǫ·tŏkəs), *a.* 1877. [f. Gr. ἀρρενότοκος (f. ἄρρην male + -τοκος begetting) + -OUS.] Used of the parthenogenetic females which produce male young. Hence **Arreno·toky.**

Arrent (ăre·nt), *v.* 1598. [– Fr. *arrenter*, also OFr. *arentir*, f. *à* to + *rente* RENT *sb.*¹ Anglo-L. *arrentare* (XIII) is f. Fr.] To let out or farm at a rent; *spec.* to allow the enclosure of forest land 'with a low hedge and small ditch' under a yearly rent. Hence **Arre·ntable** *a.* **Arrenta·tion**, the action, or privilege, of arrenting.

†**Arre·ption.** *rare.* 1612. [f. *arrept-*, pa.ppl. stem of L. *arripio* snatch away, f. *ad* AR-² + *rapere* seize; see -ION. Cf. late L. *adreptio.*] A sudden carrying off –1633.

†**Arrepti·tious**, *a.* 1641. [f. eccl.L. *arreptitius* inspired (f. as prec.) + -OUS; see -ITIOUS¹.] **1.** Liable to raptures, ecstatic, mad –1656. **2.** Hastily caught up; hurried 1653.

1. Odd arrepititious frantic extravagancies HOWELL.

Arrest (ăre·st), *v.* ME. [– OFr. *arester* (mod. *arrêter*) :– Rom. **arrestare*, f. *ad* AR-² + L. *restare* stop behind, REST *v.*²] †**1.** *intr.* To stop –1483; to stay, rest –1538. **2.** *trans.* (and *refl.*) To cause to stop; to stop the course of (a person or animal, a thing in motion, motion, etc.) ME. †**3.** *refl.* To stop (Fr. *s'arrêter*); to tarry –1563. †**4.** *trans.* and *refl.* To keep our minds, ourselves, fixed upon –1667. **5.** *gen.* To catch, lay hold upon (*Obs.* exc. *fig.*) 1481. **6.** *esp.* To lay hold upon, or apprehend by legal authority ME.; *transf.* of property (now only in Sc. and Admiralty Law) 1598. **7.** *fig.* To take as security 1588. **8.** *trans.* To catch and fix (the sight, attention, etc.) 1814; to catch and fix the attention of (a person) 1835. ¶ *catachr.* To wrest 1593.

2. In the pursuit of greatness he was never arrested by the scruples of justice GIBBON. Its progress is arrested 1879. *To arrest judgement*: to stay proceedings, after a verdict, on the ground of error. **4.** We may a. our thoughts upon the divine mercies JER. TAYLOR. **5.** We cannot a. sunsets RUSKIN. **6.** I A. thee of High Treason *Hen. VIII*, I. i. 201. The Roecliff was arrested in a cause of collision 1869. **7.** We a. your word *L.L.L.* II. i. 160. *Meas. for M.* II. iv. 134. **8.** Arrested and held by the interests of the story 1835. Hence **Arre·stable** *a.* **Arresta·tion**, stopping; apprehension by legal authority (more or less Fr.). **Arre·sted** *ppl. a.* stopped; seized by legal warrant. **Arre·stee**, the person in whose hands property is attached by arrestment (see ARRESTMENT 3). **Arre·ster**, he who or that which arrests, *esp.* by legal authority; *Sc. Law*, one who uses ARRESTMENT (more formally ARRESTOR). **Arre·sting** *vbl. sb.* stopping; apprehending by legal authority; *ppl. a.* that arrests the attention. **Arre·stingly** *adv.*

Arrest (ăre·st), *sb.*¹ ME. [– OFr. *areste* stoppage, and *arest* (mod. *arrêt*) act of arresting, f. the vb.] †**1.** The act of standing still; stoppage, halt, delay –1598; continuance; abiding-place ME. only. **2.** The act of stopping anything in its course; stoppage, check ME. **3.** The act of laying hold of; seizure (*lit.* and *fig.*) ME. **4.** *spec.* The apprehending of one's person, in order to be forthcoming to answer an alleged or suspected crime 1440. **5.** Custody, imprisonment. Also *fig.* ME. *transf.* Of a ship 1848. †**6.** A judgement, decree, order, or sentence (*prop.* Fr.; now *arrêt*). Also *fig.* –1721.

1. † *In arrest*; in rest, as a lance. † *At arrest*: at attention. **2.** Some Checke or A. in their Fortunes BACON. An a. of the vital processes 1879. *Arrest of Judgement*: see ARREST *v.* 2 (quots.). **3.** The first arrests of sleep LAMB. **5.** The Forty hath decreed a month's a. BYRON. *Under (an) arrest*: under legal restraint, arrested. **6.** He sends out Arrests On Fortinbras, which he (in breife) obeyes *Haml.* II. ii. 67.

Arrest, *sb.*² ? *Obs.* 1639. [– early mod. Fr. † *areste* (XIV–XVI *arreste*) :– L. *arista*; see ARÊTE.] **1.** Mangy tumours on the hind-legs of a horse; called also *rat-tails.* **2.** in *pl.*: The small bones of a fish 1742.

Arrestive (ăre·stiv), *a.* 1850. [f. ARREST *v.* + -IVE.] **1.** Tending to arrest, arresting. **2.** *Gram.* Used of conjunctions such as *but* 1863.

Arrestment (ăre·stmĕnt). 1474. [– OFr. *arestement* or med.L. *arestamentum*; see ARREST *v.*, -MENT.] **1.** The action of stopping; *concr.* the result of stopping 1836. **2.** Apprehension of a person by legal authority. (Chiefly *Sc.*) Also *fig.* 1474. **3.** Seizure of property by authority of law; attachment. *Esp.* in *Sc. Law.* 'A process by which a creditor may attach money or moveable property, which a third party holds for behoof of his debtor' 1581.

‖ **Arrêt** (ărē·; ăre·t). 1650. [Fr.; see ARREST *sb.*¹] = ARREST *sb.*¹ 6.

‖ **Arrha** (æ·ră). Pl. **-æ.** 1573. [L. *arr(h)a* (Gellius) short for *arr(h)abo* (Plautus) – Gr. ἀρραβών earnest-money. See ARLES.] Earnest-money, a part of the purchase-money given to bind a bargain; *fig.* a pledge. Hence **A·rrhal** *a.*

Arrhizal (ărəi·zăl), *a.* Also **arh-.** 1880. [f. Gr. ἀ- **A-** *pref.* 14 + ῥίζα root + -AL¹.] *Bot.* Rootless. var. **Arrhi·zous.**

Arrhythmic, -al (ări·þmik, -ăl), *a.* Also **arh-.** 1880. [A- *pref.* 14.] Not rhythmic; *spec.* in *Path.* of the pulse. Hence **Arrhy·thmically** *adv.* var. **Arrhy·thmous.**

Arrhythmy (æri·þmi). 1844. [– Gr. ἀρρυθμία, f. ἄρρυθμος lacking rhythm; see A- *pref.* 14, RHYTHM.] Want of rhythm or measure.

Arride (ărəi·d), *v.* 1599. [– L. *arridere* smile upon, f. *ad* AR-² + *ridere* to laugh, smile.] †**1.** To smile at, laugh at, scorn –1656. **2.** To gratify. ? *Obs.* 1599.

2. His humour arrides me exceedingly B. JONS. Hence † **Arri·dent** *a.* smiling; gratifying.

‖ **Arrière** (aryę̄·r). Mod.Fr. form of ARREAR (OF. *arere*), used in combs., partly refash.

arriere-band [cf. ARRIÈRE-BAN], a rear-division of an army; **-fee** or **fief**, a sub-fief; **-supper**, a late supper; † **-tenant**, the tenant of a mesne lord, a sub-tenant; † **-vassal**, the holder of an arriere-fief.

‖ **Arrière-ban** (æ·riər-bæ·n, aryę̄r-bañ·). 1523. [– Fr. *arrière-ban*, OFr. *ariereban*, alt. of *arban, herban* = Frank. **hariban* (OHG. *heriban* call-up for military service), f. *hari, heri* army + *ban* proclamation, BAN *sb.*¹] *prop.* The order of a (Frankish or French) king summoning his vassals to the military service due by holders of fiefs; the body of vassals thus summoned or liable to be summoned. *Corruptly*, the summoning of the *arrière-vassals*.

‖ **Arrière-pensée** (aryę̄rpaṅse). 1824. [Fr., 'behind thought'.] Mental reservation.

Arris (æ·ris). 1677. [Corruptly – early mod.Fr. *areste* sharp ridge, ARÊTE.] The sharp edge formed by the angular contact of two plane or curved surfaces; *e.g.* the edges of a prism, or those that separate the flutings in a Doric column. var. **Aris,** *dial.* **Arridge.**

Comb.: **a.-fillet,** a piece of timber of a triangular section, used to raise the slates against a chimney-shaft or a wall; **-gutter,** a V-shaped wooden gutter fixed to the eaves of a building; **-ways, -wise** *adv.* ridge-wise.

Ar(r)ish (æ·riʃ). Also **ersh.** 1597. [dial. var. of EDDISH.] Stubble; a stubble-field.

† **Arrivage.** ME. [– OFr. *arivage* (mod. *arr-*), landing, landing-place, f. *ariver*; see ARRIVE, -AGE.] **1.** Landing, arrival –1627; a landing-place –1542. **2.** That which befalls one 1603.

Arrival (ărəi·văl). ME. [– AFr. *arrivaile*, f. *arriver* ARRIVE; see -AL¹.] **1.** The coming to shore, landing. **2.** *gen.* The act of arriving (see ARRIVE *v.* 4) 1518; *transf.* of things 1712. **3.** The coming to a position, state of mind, etc. **4.** One that arrives or has arrived 1847.

1. They set apart the sixth day of August, after their a., for fasting and prayer C. MATHER. **2.** Demand of yonder Champion The cause of his arriuall heere in Armes *Rich. II*, I. iii. 8. **2.** *For arrival*: (a cargo) to be delivered when the ship arrives.

† **Arri·vance.** 1604. [f. ARRIVE *v.* + -ANCE.] The act or fact of arriving; arrivals –1646.

Arrive (ărəi·v), *v.* ME. [– OFr. *ariver* (mod. *arriver*) :– Rom. **arripare* come to land, f. *ad* AR-² + *ripa* shore; cf. RIVER.] **1.** To † bring, or come to shore or into port; to land. *intr.* Of things 1755. **2.** *trans.* (by omission of prep.) To come to, reach (*arch.*) 1587. † **3.** To bring, convey –1667. **4.** *intr.* To come to the end of a journey, to some definite place, upon the scene. Const. *at, in, upon,* † *into,* † *to.* ME. *transf.* Of things 1651. **5.** *trans.* (by omission of prep.) To come to, reach (*arch.*) 1647. **6.** *intr.* To come to as the result of continuous effort; to attain, achieve, compass. Const. † *to, at,* † *inf.* ME. **7.** *intr.* To come to by growth, lapse of time, etc.; to reach. Const. † *to, at.* 1599. Of time and temporal states: To come, so as to be present 1748. **8.** To come about, happen 1633; † *trans.* to happen to –1659.

1. The schype arryvyth at the haven purposyd 1538. *Sold to arrive*: (a cargo) sold for delivery on arrival in port. **2.** Ere he a. the happy Ile MILT. *P.L.* II. 409. **4.** Before Harold could actually a. GEO. ELIOT. A policeman arrived upon the scene 1888. The ladder now arrived TYNDALL. **6.** To a. at any employment 1671, at a knowledge of a law of nature 1850, at a conclusion H. SPENCER. **7.** Arrived at years of discretion ADDISON. At length the hour arrived SMOLLETT. **8.** What they had long hoped would a. TRENCH. Hence † **Arri·ve** *sb.* landing, arrival. **Arri·ver.**

‖ **Arroba** (ărōᵘ·bă). 1598. [– Sp. *arroba* – Arab. *arrub'*, i.e. *al-rub'* 'the quarter', the weight being ¼ of the Sp. quintal; see AL-¹.] **1.** A weight used in Spain and Sp. America, of the standard value of 25 Sp. or 25·36 Eng. pounds, but varying locally. **2.** A Sp. liquid measure, varying from 2·6 to 3·6 gallons 1633.

Arrogance (æ·rŏgăns). ME. [– (O)Fr. *arrogance* – L. *arrogantia*, f. *arrogant-*, pres. ppl. stem of *arrogare*; see ARROGATE, -ANCE.] The taking of too much upon oneself as one's right; undue assumption of dignity, authority, or knowledge; aggressive conceit, presumption, or haughtiness.

Their a. was soon humbled by misfortune GIBBON.

Arrogancy (æ·rŏgănsi). 1529. [f. prec.; see -ANCY.] The quality or state of being arrogant; † a piece of arrogance –1649.

Arrogant (æ·rŏgănt), *a.* (*sb.*) ME. [– (O)Fr. *arrogant* – L. *arrogant-*; see ARROGANCE, ARROGATE, -ANT¹.] **1.** Making or implying unwarrantable claims to dignity, authority, or knowledge; aggressively conceited or haughty, overbearing. † **2.** *sb.* [sc. *person.*] –1668. Hence **A·rrogant-ly** *adv.*, **-ness** (*rare*).

Arrogate (æ·rogeⁱt), *v.* 1530. [– *arrogat-*, pa. ppl. stem of L. *arrogare* claim for oneself, f. *ad* AR-² + *rogare* ask; see -ATE³.] **1.** *Rom. Law.* To adopt as a child. (See ADROGATE.) 1649. **2.** To claim and assume as a right that to which one is not entitled; to appropriate without just reason, or through self-conceit, insolence, or haughtiness. Const. *to* and *refl. pron.*, or *simple obj.* 1537. **3.** To assume without foundation 1563. **4.** To ascribe *to* (another) without just reason 1605.

2. To themselves all glory a., to God give none MILT. *P.R.* IV. 315. And a. a praise that is not ours ROWE. **4.** To antiquity we a. many things, to ourselves nothing COLERIDGE. Hence **A·rroga:tingly** *adv.* **A·rrogator,** one who adrogates; one who advances pretentious claims.

Arrogation (ærogēⁱ·ʃən). 1590. [– L. *arrogatio*, f. *arrogat-*; see prec., -ION. Cf. OFr. *arrogacion.*] **1.** = ADROGATION. **2.** Unwarrantable assumption 1594.

‖ **Arrondi** (arŏṅdi), *ppl. a.* 1727. [Fr., pa. pple. of *arrondir* make round.] *Her.* Rounded (by shading), as parts of a coat of arms.

‖ **Arrondissement** (arŏṅdis,maṅ). 1807. [Fr., f. *arrondiss-*, *arrondir*; see prec., -MENT.] **1.** The action of rounding off an outline (*rare*) 1815. **2.** An administrative sub-division of a French department 1807.

† **Arrou·nd,** *v.* 1625. [f. AR- *pref.*² + ROUND *v.*¹] To flow round –1652.

† **Arrou·se,** *v.* 1480. [– OFr. (now dial.) *arrouser* (mod. *arroser*) :– Gallo-Rom. *arrosare* for cl.L. *arrorare*, after *ros* (*ror-*) dew.] To bedew, sprinkle, water –1635.

Arrow (æ·roᵘ), *sb.* [Late OE. *ar(e)we* – ON. **arw-*, nom. *ǫr* (gen. sing., pl. *ǫrvar*), rel. to Goth. *arhwazna* arrow, f. Gmc. base **arχw-* :– Indo-Eur. **arkw-*, whence L. *arcus* bow, ARC. The native OE. form was *earh.*] **1.** A slender pointed missile shot from a bow, usu. feathered and barbed; occ. used of a *bolt*, or *quarrel*. Also *fig.* **2.** *Surveying.* An iron pin (orig. a real arrow) used to stick in the ground at the end of a chain 1753. **3.** Anything arrow-shaped 1834. **4.** The constellation *Sagitta* 1727. † **5.** *Geom.* The *sagitta*, or versed sine of an arc –1751. **6.** The leading shoot of a plant or tree 1580. **7.** *Fortif.* A work in communication with the covert-way, placed at the salient angle of the glacis 1816.

1. I will shoot three arrowes. .as though I shot at a marke 1 *Sam.* 20:20. *fig.* The Slings and Arrowes of outragious Fortune *Haml.* III. i. 58. **3.** The spire is surmounted by an a. 1888. **6.** The cane-fields then in a. 1833.

Comb.: **a.-loop, -slit,** a narrow loop-hole or slit for shooting through; **-plant,** a species of pine; **-smith,** a maker of iron arrow-heads; **-snake,** *Acontias jaculus*; **-stitch,** the triangular stitch used in securing the ends of whalebone in stays; † **-stone,** a belemnite; **-wise,** *adv.* **Broad Arrow,** *lit.* one having a broad arrow-head; the arrow-head-shaped mark, used by the British Board of Ordnance, and placed on government stores; in *Her.* = PHEON. Hence **A·rrow** *v.* to shoot arrows (*rare*); to shoot into blossom, as the sugar-cane. **A·rrowed** *a. poet.* made into an a.; provided with arrows.

Arrow, vulgar corruption of *e'er a, ever a.*

A·rrow-grass. 1792. Eng. name of the endogenous genus *Triglochin*, referring to the 3-barbed appearance of the burst capsule.

A·rrow-head. 1483. **1.** The pointed part of an arrow, made separately from the shaft; *esp.* those of flint, jade, etc., as *elf-arrows*, found among prehistoric remains. **2. Broad arrow-head. a.** *prop.* a kind of arrow-head. **b.** *transf.* = *Broad Arrow.* **c.** *fig.* Any mark like these 1865. **3.** A direction-mark 1836. **4.** *Bot.* The genus *Sagittaria*, of which *S. sagittifolia* has arrow-head-shaped leaves 1597. *attrib.* 1875. Hence **A·rrow-hea:ded** *a.* shaped like an arrow-head; *spec.* = CUNEIFORM.

A·rrow-root. 1696. [Perversion of Aruak *aru-aru* 'meal of meals', by assimilation to ARROW and ROOT *sb.*, the tubers having been used to absorb poison from arrow and other wounds.] **1.** *Bot.* A plant; orig. *Maranta arundinacea*, a herb with fleshy tuberous rhizomes, found in the West Indian Isles; also, other species of *Maranta*. **2.** *Comm.* A pure nutritious starch, prepared from the tubers of *Maranta* (and from many other plants) 1811. **3.** The food prepared from this starch 1848.

A·rrow-wood. 1848. An American name for species of *Viburnum* (*V. dentatum, pubescens*, etc.) with long straight stems used by the Indians for the shafts of their arrows.

Arrowy (æ·roᵘ,i), *a.* 1637. [f. ARROW + -Y¹.] Consisting of, or abounding in, arrows 1671. **2.** Like an arrow, in shape, motion, etc. 1637.

1. Sharp sleet of a. showers MILT. *P.R.* III. 324. **2.** A. minarets 1877, Rhone BYRON. A. words, each one hitting its mark GEO. ELIOT.

‖ **Arroyo** (ăroi·o). 1850. [Sp., = stream.] A rivulet or stream; *hence*, the bed of a stream, a gully. (*in U.S.*)

'Arry (æ·ri). 1874. [Vulgar for *Harry.*] Used humorously for: A low-bred fellow (who 'drops his *h*'s') of lively temper and manners. Hence **'A·rryish** *a.* vulgarly jovial.

Arse (āɹs). *Obs.* in polite use. [OE. *ærs* (*ears*) = OFris. *ers*, MLG. *ars, ers*, MDu. *aers, e(e)rs* (Du. *aars, naars*), OHG. *ars* (G. *arsch*), ON. *ars, rass* :– Gmc. **arsaz* :– Indo-Eur. **órsos*, whence Gr. ὄρρος rump.] The fundament, buttocks, or rump of an animal OE.; *transf.* or *fig.* the bottom; the fag end, tail ME.

Phr. *Arse upwards*: in good luck.

Comb.: † **a.-foot,** a dabchick, or penguin; **-gut,** the rectum, also *fig.*; **-smart,** the plant Water-pepper (*Polygonum hydropiper*); † **-ward** *adv.* and *a.* backward; perverse, perversely; whence † **-wardly** *adv.*

A·rsedine. 1472. [Etymology and correct form unknown.] A gold-coloured alloy of copper and zinc; 'Dutch gold'.

Arsen- (ā·ɹsĕn), short for ARSENIC, used **1.** in *Comb.*, as in *Arsen-dimethyl*, $As_2(CH_3)_4$ **2.** in derivatives, with var. **Arseni-** (aɹsī·ni).

A·rsenate or **Arse·niate,** a salt of arsenic acid, e.g. *Sodium arsenate.* **A·rsenetted** *ppl. a.* combined chemically with arsenic. **Arse·niate** *a.* mixed or treated with arsenic (*rare*). **Arse·niated** *ppl. a.* = *arseniate.* **A·rsenide,** a primary combination of arsenic with another element, or an organic radical. **A·rsenite,** a salt of arsenious acid, as *Arsenite of lead*, etc.; *Min.* = *arsenolite* (*see* ARSENO-).

Arsenal (ā·ɹsĭnăl). 1506. [Early forms *arse-, arzenale, archynale* – Fr. *arsenal*, † *archenal* or its source It. † *arzanale*, (mod.) *arsenale*, f. Venetian It. *arzanà*, ult. (w. unexplained loss of *d*) – Arab. *dār-ṣinā'a*, f. *dār* house, *ṣinā'a* art, mechanical industry, f. *ṣana'a* make, fabricate.] **1.** A dock equipped for the reception, construction, and repair of ships; a dockyard. *Hist.* **2.** A public establishment for the manufacture and storage, or for the storage alone, of arms and ammunition 1579. Also *fig.*

Arsenate, -etted, -iate, etc.; see ARSEN-.

Arsenic (ā·ɹsnik), *sb.* ME. [– (O)Fr. *arsenic* – L. *arsenicum* – Gr. ἀρσενικόν, var. of ἀρρενικόν yellow orpiment, lit. male (f. ἄρρην male) – (with etymologizing alt. to express its powerful properties) Arab. *al-zarnīḵ* (*zirnīḵ*), i.e. *al* AL-², *zarnīḵ* (*zirnīḵ*) – Pers. *zarnīḵ*, f. *zar* gold.] **1.** Name of a chemical element, and of some of its compounds, which are strong poisons. † **a.** orig. *Yellow Arsenic* or ORPIMENT, the trisulphide of arsenic (As_2S_3) –1634. † **b.** *Red Arsenic* or REALGAR, the *disulphide* (As_2S_2), the σανδαράκη of the Greeks –1751. **c.** in pop. use: *White Arsenic*, the trioxide of arsenic (As_2O_3), native (as arsenolite) and manufactured 1605. **d.** *Chem.* and *Min.* The element; a brittle semi-metallic substance, steel-grey, crystallizing in rhombohedrons, and volatilizing without fusion, with an odour of garlic. It links metals and non-metals. Symbol As. 1812. *fig.* Poison 1598. **2.** *attrib.* = Of arsenic, arsenical. *Arsenic bloom*, a. trioxide in native crystals. *Arsenic glass*, the same in a vitreous mass obtained from the powder by re-sublimation.

1. c. *Flowers of a.*: the trioxide of a. sublimed.

Arsenic (aɹse·nik), *a.* 1801. [f. the sb.] *Chem.* Of or belonging to arsenic; in *Chem.* combining as a pentad. *Arsenic anhydride* = arsenic pentoxide.

Arsenic- (aɹse·nik), in derivation; as in **Arse·nicane,** Davy's name for arsenious chloride. **Arse·nicate** *v.* to mix or treat with arsenic. **Arse·nicated** *ppl. a.* **Arse·nicism,** disease produced by arsenic, also called *Arseni·asis.* **Arse·nicite,** *Min.* = PHARMACOLITE. **Arse·nicized** *ppl. a.* treated or impregnated with arsenic. **Arsenico·phagy,** *Med.* the eating of arsenic, as by the Tyrolese.

Arsenical (aɹse·nikăl), *a.* 1605. [f. ARSENIC + -AL¹; cf. Fr. *arsénical* (XVII).] Of, of the nature of, or containing arsenic; pertaining to or effected by arsenic.

Arsenide, -ite; see ARSEN-.

Arsenio- (aɹsī·nio), comb. form of next, as in **arse·nio·si·derite,** a fibrous yellowish-brown mineral, containing arsenic acid, sesquioxide of iron, and lime.

Arsenious (aɹsī·niəs), *a.* 1818. [f. ARSEN(IC) + -IOUS.] Of the nature of, or containing, arsenic; in *Chem.* applied to compounds in which arsenic combines as a triad, as *Arsenious oxide.* var. **A·rsenous.**

Arseniuret (aɹse·niŭrĕt). 1834. [f. as prec. + -URET.] *Chem.* Replaced by ARSENIDE. Hence **Arse·niuretted** *a.* combined with arsenic, chiefly in *Arseniuretted hydrogen,* for which Watts uses *arsenetted* (see ARSEN-).

Arseno- (ā·ɹsĕno), comb. f. ARSENIC, *arsenous* (see ARSENIOUS), in comps. and derivs. **A:rsenocro·cite** = *arseniosiderite* (see ARSENIO-). **Arse·nolite** [Gr. λίθος], white arsenic as a native mineral (Dana). **A:rsenopy·rite** [Gr. πυρίτης], native arsenio-sulphide of iron, called also Mispickel (Dana).

‖ **Arsheen** (āɹʃī·n). 1734. [Russ. *arshin.*] A measure of length used in Russia and Turkey.

Arsine (ā·ɹsəin). [f. ARS(ENIC) + -INE⁵, after *amine.*] *Chem.* A compound having the structure of an amine, with arsenic instead of nitrogen; i.e. *Arseniuretted hydrogen* (AsH_3), and any derivative such as *Trimethyl arsine* $(CH_3)_3As$. Hence **Arsi·nic** *a.*

‖ **Arsis** (ā·ɹsis). ME. [– late L. *arsis* – Gr. ἄρσις lifting, raising, f. αἴρειν raise; opposed to THESIS. By Gr. writers applied to the raising of the foot in beating time, which marked the unaccented syll., by later L. writers (followed by Bentley) referred to the raising of the voice, which marked the accented syllable.] **1.** (See above.) **2.** In mod. use: The strong syllable in Eng. metre, the strong note in barred music; thus identical with the mod. meaning of L. *ictus* 1834. ‖ **3.** In Mus. *Per arsin*: By descent of voice or sound from higher to lower pitch. *? Obs.* 1706.

Arsmetik, -tric, -trik, obs. ff. ARITHMETIC.

† **A·rsmetry.** 1594. Corruption of *arsmetrick,* after *geometry.*

† **A·rson¹.** ME. [– OFr. *arçun, arzon* (mod. *arçon*) :– Rom. **arcio, -ōn-,* dim. of L. *arcus* bow, ARC.] **1.** A saddle-bow –1623. **2.** Occ., a saddle –1460.

Arson² (ā·ɹsən). 1680. [– legal AFr., OFr. *arson* :– med.L. *arsio, -ion-,* f. *ars-,* pa. ppl. stem of *ardēre* to burn.] The act of wilfully and maliciously setting fire to another man's house, ship, forest, etc.; or to one's own, when insured, with intent to defraud the insurers.

A·rsy-ve·rsy. *Obs.* in polite use. 1539. [f. ARSE + L. *versus* turned, with -Y¹ added to both elements to make a jingle.] *adv.* Backside foremost; perversely, preposterously. *adj.* Contrary, preposterous 1659.

Art (āɹt), *sb.* ME. [– (O)Fr. *art* :– L. *ars, art-,* f. base **ar-* put together, join, fit.] **I.** Skill. Sing. *art*; no pl. **1.** *gen.* Skill as the result of knowledge and practice. **2.** Human skill (opp. to *nature*) ME. **3.** The learning of the schools; see II. 1. † **a.** *spec.* The *trivium,* or any of its subjects –1573. **b.** *gen.* Learning, science (*arch.*) 1588. † **4.** *spec.* Technical or professional skill –1677. **5.** The application of skill to subjects of taste, as poetry, music, etc.; *esp.* in mod. use: Perfection of workmanship or execution as an object in itself 1620. **6.** Skill applied to the arts of imitation and design, *Painting, Architecture,* etc.; the cultivation of these in its principles, practice, and results. (The most usual mod. sense of *art* when used simply.) 1668.

1. Golde, or siluer, or stone grauen by arte, and mans deuice *Acts* 17:29. **2.** A. may err, but nature cannot miss DRYDEN. **3. b.** So vast is a., so narrow human wit POPE. *Words* or *terms of art*: words peculiar to a particular art or pursuit. **5.** A. more frequently appears in fiddling and dancing, then in noble deeds 1675. We mean by a. . also a law of pure and flawless workmanship M. ARNOLD. **6.** Sacred and Legendary A. MRS. JAMESON (*title*).

II. Anything wherein skill may be attained. Sing. *an art*; pl. *arts.* **1.** Chiefly in pl. Certain branches of learning, which are of the nature of instruments for more advanced studies, or for the work of life. Applied in the Middle Ages to the *trivium* (containing *grammar, logic,* and *rhetoric*), and the *quadrivium* (containing *arithmetic, geometry, music,* and *astronomy*); called also the *free* or *liberal* arts. Hence the 'faculty' of arts in the Universities, and the degrees of 'Bachelor' and 'Master of Arts'. ME. † *sing.* Any one of these subjects –1450. **2.** A body of rules for practice. Often opp. to *science.* 1489. *esp.* A craft, business, or profession ME.; a guild of craftsmen 1832. **3.** An occupation in which skill is employed to gratify taste or produce what is beautiful 1597. **4.** An acquired faculty of any kind; a knack 1637.

1. He being a Master in all the seuen liberall Arts, is not so ignorant in grammar FULKE. **2.** So that the Arte and Practique part of Life must be the Mistresse to this Theorique *Hen. V,* I. i. 51. **3.** *The Arts* (specifically) = the Fine Arts.

III. Conduct. Studied conduct or action; address; artfulness 1600; an artful device; wile, trick, etc. (chiefly in *pl.*) 1597.

Phrases: *Art and part* (*Sc. Law* and *gen.*): orig. *to be concerned in (either) by art* (in contriving it), *or by part* (taken in executing it): whence, *to have* art or (and) part in; corruptly *To be* art or part in (*be* for *have,* or = to be *of* art, etc. in); *To be* art *and* part in: to be accessary in both ways or, *loosely,* to be accessary. *Industrial, mechanical, useful arts*: those in which the hands and body are more concerned than the mind. *Fine Arts*: see FINE ART.

Comb. **1.** passing into adj. **a.** = produced by an artist, composed with conscious artistry: said esp. of poetry and music, opp. to *popular* or *folk,* as *a. ballad, song.* **b.** = designed to produce an artistic effect, as *a. china, needlework, pottery.* **2.** Chiefly attrib. from sense II. 3, as *a.-critic, -master, -school, -teacher,* etc.

† **A·rt,** *v.*¹ ME. [– L. *artare* draw close, contract, f. *artus* confined.] To cramp, limit –1496; to constrain *to do* –1553.

† **Art,** *v.*² 1602. [f. ART *sb.*] **1.** To instruct in arts, or in an art 1660. **2.** To artificialize (*rare*) 1627. **3.** To obtain by art (*rare*) 1602. **4.** phr. *To art it*: to use art or artifice –1655.

Art (ăɹt, ăɹt, 'ɹt), *v.*³ 2nd sing. pres. ind. of BE, part of the orig. substantive vb.; cf. AM.

Artefact; see ARTIFACT.

Artemisia (ăɹtĭmi·ziă). ME. [L. *artemisia* – Gr. ἀρτεμισία wormwood, f. Ἄρτεμις the goddess Diana.] *Bot.* A genus of plants (N.O. *Compositæ*), of bitter or aromatic taste, including the Common Wormwood, Mugwort, and Southernwood.

† **A·rter.** 1622. [– early Fr. *artre* (XVI) a wood-worm (mod. *artison*), – Pr. *arta* scab, scurf.] A wood-worm.

† **Arte·riac.** 1661. [As adj., – late L. *arteriacus,* – Gr. ἀρτηριακός; as sb., – L. *arteriace* – Gr. ἀρτηριακή; see ARTERY, -AC.] *adj.* Of or pertaining to the windpipe. *sb.* A remedy for disease of the windpipe.

Arterial (aɹtiᵊ·riăl), *a.* 1541. [– Fr. † *arterial* (mod. *artériel*); see ARTERY, -AL¹.] **1.** Of, or of the nature of, an artery. **2.** Resembling an artery in having a main channel and branches; esp. of main roads or lines of transport 1831.

1. The scarlet blood is commonly known as a. HUXLEY. **2.** *Arterial drainage*: a system of drains ramifying like an artery. (A term objected to on the ground of the direction of the flow.) var. **Arte·rious.** Hence **Arte·rialize** *v.* to convert venous into a. (blood) by exposure to oxygen in the lungs; to furnish with an a. system. **Arte:rializa·tion,** arterializing.

Arterio- (aɹtiᵊ·rio) [– Gr. ἀρτηριο-], comb. f. ARTERY, ARTERIAL.

arterio·graphy [Gr. -γραφία], systematic description of the arteries; **-logy** [Gr. -λογία], scientific study of, or a treatise upon, the arteries; **-tomy** [Gr. -τομία], cutting into or opening an artery, esp. for blood-letting; that part of anatomy which treats of the dissection of arteries; whence **-tomist.**

Arte·riole. 1839. [– Fr. *artériole,* dim. of *artère* ARTERY.] A minute or ultimate artery.

‖ **Arteritis** (ăɹtĕrəi·tis). 1836. [f. L. *arteria* + -ITIS.] *Path.* Inflammation of an artery.

Artery (ā·ɹtəri), *sb.* ME. [– L. *arteria* – Gr. ἀρτηρία, prob. f. base **ar-* raise; cf. AORTA, ARSIS. See -Y³.] † **1.** The trachea or windpipe. (L. *arteria aspera.*) –1661. **2.** One of the tubes forming part of the system of vessels by which the blood is conveyed from the heart ME. Also *attrib.* Also *fig.* **3.** *transf.* A main channel in a ramifying system of communication 1860. † **4.** A ligament –1658.

Among the ancients, the arteries were regarded as air-ducts, ramifying from the trachea. Mediæval writers supposed them to contain 'spiritual blood', or 'vital spirits' (cf. ANIMAL SPIRITS), an error which survived Harvey's discovery for some time.

1. [The Lungs]. . through the Artire, throat and mouth, maketh the voice BACON. **3.** The great arteries of inland commerce MAURY. Hence **A·rtery** *v.* to furnish with, or as if with, arteries.

Artesian (aɹtī·ʒăn), *a.* 1830. [– Fr. *artésien,* f. OFr. *Arteis* (mod. *Artois*), name of an old French province.] Of or pertaining to Artois, or resembling the wells first made there, in which a perpendicular boring into a synclinal fold of the strata produces a constant supply of water rising spontaneously.

Artful (ā·ɹtful), *a.* 1613. [f. ART *sb.* + -FUL.] † **1.** Learned, wise –1681. **2.** Having practical skill; dexterous, clever (*arch.*) 1697. **3.** Skilful in adapting means to ends, adroit; *whence,* wily; crafty, deceitful 1739. **4.** Performed according to the rules of art; artistic (*arch.*) 1615. **5.** Produced by art, artificial (opp. to *natural*) 1706. **6.** Of actions, etc.: Skilfully adapted for a purpose; *whence,* cunning, crafty 1705.

2. A. hands POPE. **3.** A. and designing men BEWICK. **4.** Thyrsis! whose a. strains have oft delayed The huddling brook MILT. *Comus* 495. The a. distresses of a romance 1779. **6.** This is a very a. dodge DICKENS. Hence **A·rtfully** *adv.* with skill; craftily; **-ness.**

Arthritic (aɹþri·tik), *a.* (*sb.*) [Late ME. *artetik* – OFr. *artetique* – med.L. *arteticus,* alt. of L. *arthriticus* – Gr. ἀρθριτικός; later assim. to the L.–Gr. form; see -IC.] **1.** Of or pertaining to diseased joints; *spec.* gouty. † **2.** Good against gout, etc. –1752. **3.** *sb.* † **a.** Gout. **b.** A gouty person. ME.

Arthri·tical, *a.* (*sb.*) ? *Obs.* 1528. [f. prec. + -AL¹.] **1.** = prec. † **2.** Of the nature of a joint 1646. † **3.** *sb.* A remedy for affections of the joints 1671.

‖ **Arthritis** (aɹþrəi·tis). 1544. [L. *arthritis* – Gr. ἀρθρῖτις, f. ἄρθρον joint, f. **ar-* fit (cf. L. *artus* limb, ARTICLE); see -ITIS.] *Path.* Inflammation of the joints; *spec.* gout. Hence **A·rthritism,** the disposition in which affections of the joints are liable to occur.

Arthro-, comb. f. Gr. ἄρθρον joint.

Arthro-dy·nic [Gr. ὀδύνη] *a., Path.* of or pertaining to *Arthrodynia,* i.e. pain in the joints, chronic rheumatism; **-graphy** [Gr. -γραφία], systematic description of the joints; **-pathy** [Gr. -πάθεια], painful affection of the joints; ‖ **-sia** [mod.L.] = ARTHRITIS; **-sis** [L. – Gr.], connection by a joint; **-stome** [Gr. στόμα], the mouth of the *Arthropoda* (L. Agassiz); **-zoic** [Gr. ζωικός] *a., Zool.* the sixth series of the *Metazoa* (Huxley).

‖ **Arthrodia** (aɹþrōᵘ·diă). 1634. [Gr. ἀρθρωδία, f. ἀρθρώδης well-articulated. See -IA¹.] *Phys.* Articulation in which the surfaces of the bones are either plane, or but slightly convex and concave respectively; *e.g.* the shoulder-joint. Hence **Arthro·dial, Arthro·dic** *adjs.*

Arthrology (aɹþrǫ·lŏdʒi). 1644. [f. ARTHRO- + -LOGY.] **1.** A scientific treatise on the joints 1859. † **2.** Finger speech 1644.

‖ **Arthropoda** (aɹþrǫ·pŏdă), *sb. pl.* 1870. [mod.L., f. Gr. ἄρθρον joint + πούς ποδ- foot; see -A 4. Sing. **a·rthropod**; also pl. **-pods.**] *Zool.* Animals with jointed feet; a name for the more highly organized *Annulosa* or *Articulata,* comprising Insects, Spiders, Crustacea, and Myriapoda, in respect of their antennæ, wings, or legs. Hence **Arthro·podal, Arthro·podous** *adjs.* of or belonging to the *Arthropoda.*

Artiad (ā·ɹti,ăd). 1870. [f. Gr. ἄρτιος even + -AD 1 a.] *Chem.* An element or radical of even equivalence, *e.g.* a dyad or tetrad.

Artichoke (ā·ɹti,tʃoᵘk). 1531. [– northern It. *arti-, arciciocco,* for *arcicioffo,* alt. of **alcarcioffo* (cf. mod.It. *carcioffo*) – OSp. *alcarchofa* (mod. *alcachofa*) – Arab. *al-ḵaršūfa,* i.e. *al* AL-², *ḵaršūfa* artichoke.] **1.** A composite plant (*Cynara scolymus*), allied to the thistles; its eatable parts are the fleshy bases of the involucral leaves or scales of the flower, and its receptacle when freed from the bristles, etc. Also *fig.* **2. Jerusalem Artichoke:** a species of Sunflower (*Helianthus tuberosus*), having edible tuberous roots 1620.

2. From this *girasol* (i.e. in the It. name *Girasole Articiocco*) we have made Jerusalem, and from the Jerusalem a. we make Palestine soup PEACOCK.

Article (ā·ɹtik'l), *sb.* ME. [– (O)Fr. *article* – L. *articulus*, dim. of *artus* joint, f. base **ar-* join (cf. ARM, ART).] † **1.** A joint –1693. **2.** A nick of time which joins two periods, a juncture; the critical moment ME. **3.** [cf. L. *articulus*, the parts jointed on; whence *transf.* the component parts.] The separate clauses of any summary of faith ME.; of a statute 1523; each count of an indictment ME. **4.** Each head or point of an agreement or treaty; hence **a.** in *pl.* a formal agreement ME. **b.** Terms, conditions (*arch.*) 1650. † **5.** A clause in a will; a legacy –1761. **6.** *gen.* A paragraph, section, or distinct item ME. **7.** A literary composition *in* a journal, magazine, encyclopædia, etc., but treating a topic independently 1712. † **8.** A particular piece of business, a matter, or concern; a subject –1793; an item in an account, list, etc. –1774. **9.** A distinct part or portion; a piece, a particular 1741. **10.** *ellipt.* (= article of trade, etc.): A commodity; a piece of goods or property, etc. 1804. † **11.** *Arithm.* The number 10; each round number between units and hundreds –1751. **12.** *Gram.* A name for the adjs. *a, an, the* 1530.

2. In the A. of the Setting of the Sun 1665. In the article of death 1782. 3. The Thirty-nine Articles [of the Church of England] BROUGHAM. The Famous act of the six articles 1711. **Lords of the Articles:** *Sc. Hist.* a standing committee of the Scottish Parliament, who drafted and prepared the measures submitted to the House. **The Articles of War:** regulations made for the government of the military and naval forces of Great Britain and the United States. And charge him with what articles they lusted FOXE. **4. a.** Articles of Separation FIELDING, of capitulation WELLINGTON. *Articles of Apprenticeship*: terms of agreement between an apprentice and his employer. *Articles of Association*: rules, conditions, etc., upon which a commercial agreement is founded. 7. Charles Lamb's articles, signed 'Elia' 1822. Leading articles THACKERAY. 8. A soul of great a. (= moment) *Haml.* v. ii. 122. Wealth, which is the great A. of Life STEELE. *In the article of*: under the head of. 9. *An article of*: a thing coming under the head of. 10. Lady Selina was just the a. he wished for 1856.

Article (ā·ɹtik'l), *v.* 1447. [f. prec.] † **1.** *trans.* To formulate in articles, specify; with *cl.*, to state *that* –1592. **2.** To set forth in articles *against* 1494; *absol.* to bring charges *against* 1530. **3.** *absol.* To indict 1604. † **4.** To arrange by treaty, or stipulations. *trans.* –1682; *intr.* with *subord. cl.* or *inf.* –1762; also *with* (a person), *for* (a thing) –1770. **5.** To bind by articles of apprenticeship 1820. **6.** To furnish with articles (of faith) (*rare*) 1826.

2. All his. .follies were articled against him JER. TAYLOR. The Lords. .began to a. against the Protector 1611. 3. Articled for an ecclesiastical offence 1868. 4. I will a. with them to do so WESLEY. 5. Articled to an attorney 1820. Hence **A·rticled** *ppl. a.* (in senses 1, 5, 6). **A·rticler,** one who draws up articles or charges.

Articular (aɹti·kiŭlăɹ), *a.* ME. [– L. *articularis*, f. *articulus* joint; see ARTICLE, -AR[1].] Of, or pertaining to, the joints. var. **Arti·culary. 2.** *Gram.* Of the nature of an ARTICLE (*sb.* 12) 1750. Hence † **Arti·cularly** *adv.* article by article.

‖ **Articulata** (aɹti:kiulē·tă), *sb. pl.* 1834. [L., n. pl. (sc. *animalia*) of *articulatus* jointed; see next, -A 4.] *Zool.* Cuvier's third great sub-kingdom of animals, embracing invertebrate animals with an external skeleton, having the body and limbs composed of segments jointed together, as Insects, Crustacea, etc. (Cf. ANNULOIDA, ARTHROPODA.)

Articulate (aɹti·kiŭlĕt), *a.* (*sb.*) 1569. [f. L. *articulatus*, f. *articulus* ARTICLE; see next, -ATE[2].] **1.** United by a joint 1610; composed of jointed segments 1607; *Zool.* of the type of the ARTICULATA 1855. **2.** Distinctly jointed or marked 1664. **3.** Of sound: Divided into distinct and significant parts; *fig.* speaking intelligibly 1586. **4.** Hence *transf.* Distinct 1626. † **5.** Formulated, set forth in articles –1726. † **6.** Consisting of tens. See ARTICLE *sb.* 11. –1646. **7.** *sb. Zool.* One of the AR-TICULATA 1874.

3. Beasts. .created mute to all articulat sound MILT. *P.L.* IX. 557. *Articulate-speaking*: using articulate speech. 4. A. hearing 1626, Apparitions H. MORE, Thoughts CARLYLE. var. **Arti·culated** *ppl. a.* (exc. in sense 6.) Hence **Arti·culate-ly** *adv.*, **-ness.**

Articulate (aɹti·kiŭlēˈt), *v.* 1553. [– *articulat-*, pa. ppl. stem of L. *articulare*, f. *articulus* ARTICLE; see -ATE[3].] **1.** To attach by a joint. (Usu. in *pass.*) 1616. **2.** To connect by, or mark with, apparent joints. (Usu. *pass.*) 1644. **3.** *intr.* (for *refl.*) To form a joint *with* 1832. **4.** *trans.* To divide (vocal sound) into distinct and significant parts 1594; to pronounce distinctly, express in words, utter 1691; *intr.* to utter words; to speak distinctly; *often* to pronounce 1642. **5.** To formulate or specify in an article or articles. ? *Obs.* 1562. † **6.** *trans.* and *intr.* To charge *against* –1603. † **7.** To arrange by articles or conditions –1676. † **8.** To come to terms, capitulate –1643.

2. Reticulated or articulated 1879. 4. To interpret and a. the deep dumb wants of the people CARLYLE. He had so great a weakness in his tongue, that he could not a. COTTON.

Articulation (aɹti:kiulē·ʃən). 1541. [– Fr. *articulation* or L. *articulatio*, f. as prec.; see -ION.] **1.** The action of jointing; the state of being jointed; mode of jointing or junction 1597. **2.** A joint: **a.** The structure whereby two bones, or parts, are connected, whether stiffly, or so that one moves in or on the other 1615. **b.** *Bot.* The place at which a leaf, etc., separates from the plant; *also*, a knot or joint 1658. **3.** A segment of a jointed body 1664. **4.** Articulate voice 1615; utterance, speech 1711; an articulate sound, *esp.* a consonant 1764. **5.** Articulate quality (*rare*) 1785.

2 a. To form a kind of ball and socket a. KIRBY. 4. Overgreat distance confoundeth the a. of sounds BACON. 5. The definiteness and a. of imagery COLERIDGE. Hence **Articula·tionist,** one who teaches deaf-mutes.

Articulator (aɹti·kiŭlēˈtəɹ). 1777. [f. ARTICULATE *v.* + -OR 2.] **1.** One who articulates words. **2.** *techn.* One who articulates bones, and mounts skeletons 1865. Hence **Arti·culatory** *a.* (sense 1). Occ. = ARTICULAR 1.

‖ **Arti·culus.** 1877. [L.] Occas. scientific term for *joint.* Pl. **articuli.**

Artifact (ā·ɹtifækt). Also **arte-.** 1821. [f. *arti-*, comb. f. L. *ars, art-* + *factus*, pa. pple. of *facere* make.] An artificial product.

‖ **Artifex** (ā·ɹtifeks). 1657. [L.] Artificer.

Artifice (ā·ɹtifis). 1534. [– (O)Fr. *artifice* – L. *artificium*, f. *ars, arti-* ART + *fic-*, var. of *fac-* of *facere* make.] † **1.** The action of an artificer, construction, workmanship, *esp.* mechanic art –1682. † **2.** The product of art –1688; an artificial substance 1677. † **3.** Mode or style of workmanship –1756. † **4.** Constructive skill –1777. **5.** Human skill 1857. **6.** Skill in expedients; address, trickery 1618. **7.** An ingenious expedient, a manœuvre, device, trick. (The ordinary sense now.) 1656.

1. The skill of A. or Office mean MILT. *P.L.* IX. 39. 4. Does it not counterwork the a. of nature? HUME. 7. He condemned Rhetorick, as being used rather as an A., than an Art 1660.

Artificer (aɹti·fisəɹ). ME. [– AFr. *artificer* (cf. med.L. *artificiarius*), prob. after OFr. *artificien*; see prec., -ER[2].] **1.** One who makes by art or skill; *esp.* a craftsman. **2.** *Mil.* A soldier mechanic attached to the ordnance, artillery, and engineer service 1804. † **3.** *gen.* Maker, manufacturer –1751. **4.** *transf.* Contriver, inventor. (Cf. ARCHITECT.) 1605. † **5.** One who practises any art; a savant. (Cf. ARTIST.) 1635. † **6.** An artful person; a trickster –1621.

1. A base a. NASHE. 4. A. of fraud. .the first That practised falshood under saintly shew MILT. *P.L.* IV. 121. Hence **Arti·ficership,** workmanship.

Artificial (āɹtifi·ʃăl). ME. [– (O)Fr. *artificiel* or L. *artificialis*, f. *artificium*; see ARTIFICE, -AL[1].] **A.** *adj.* **I.** Opp. to *natural.* **1.** Made by or resulting from art or artifice; not natural. **2.** Made by art in imitation of, or as substitute for, what is natural or real 1577. **3.** Factitious; *hence*, feigned, fictitious 1650. **4.** Affected 1598.

1. To give an a. stimulus to population MC-CULLOCH. A. Teares SHAKS., hunger 1834, light 1879. 2. A list of a. flies FRANCIS. 4. Frivolous and a. 1849.

† **II.** Displaying art or skill. (All *Obs.*) **1.** Skilfully made –1738; skilful –1682. **2.** Scholarly –1628. **3.** Workmanlike –1656. **4.** Artful, deceitful –1702.

1. The a. structure of the eye 1738. 2. Scholastique and artificiall men DONNE.

† **III.** Of or pertaining to art. (All *Obs.*) **1.** According to the rules of art –1753. **2.** Technical –1809.

B. *sb.* [the adj. used *absol.* in *pl.*] Artificial things; products of art 1611.

Phrases: *Artificial horizon*: a level reflecting surface, such as that of a fluid at rest, or a mirror laid horizontally on the earth's surface, used in taking altitudes. *Artificial grasses*: such as do not grow spontaneously in a locality, but are sown. *Artificial lines*: lines on a sector representing the logarithmic sines and tangents. *Artificial numbers*: logarithms. *Artificial system* or *classification* (in *Nat. Hist.*): a system based on arbitrary, limited, and unimportant characters, and serving chiefly as an index.

Hence **Artifi·cialism,** an a. principle or practice. **Artifi·cialize** *v.* to make a. **Artifi·cially** *adv.* **Artifi·cialness,** the quality of being a., opp. to naturalness.

Artificiality (ā:ɹtifiʃi,æ·lĭti). 1763. [f. prec. + -ITY.] **1.** The quality or state of being artificial. **2.** With *pl.* An artificial thing or characteristic 1848.

† **Artifi·cious,** *a.* 1530. [– (O)Fr. *artificieux* or L. *artificiosus*; see ARTIFICE, -OUS, -IOUS.] Displaying constructive skill; affected; artful –1679. Hence † **Artifi·ciously** *adv.*

† **A·rtilize,** *v.* 1744. [Rendering Fr. † *artialiser* (Montaigne after *naturaliser*).] To make artificial –1778. Cf. ARTIZE.

† **Arti·ller,** *sb.* ME. [– OFr. *artiller, -ier*, f. *artiller* provide or equip with engines of war; see ARTILLERY, -ER[2].] A maker of artillery; *spec.* a bowyer –1483.

Artillerist (aɹti·lĕrist). 1778. [f. next + -IST.] One who studies the principles of gunnery; a gunner.

Artillery (aɹti·lĕri), *sb.* ME. [–(O)Fr. *artillerie*, f. *artiller*, alt. (after *art*) of OFr. *atillier* equip, arm, prob. by-form of *atirier*, f. *à* AD- + *tire* order; see TIER[1], -ERY.] † **1.** Warlike munitions, implements of war –1794. **2.** Engines for discharging missiles; formerly, catapults, slings, arbalests, bows, etc. 1476; now, large guns, ordnance 1533. † **3.** Missiles discharged in war –1867. **4.** The science and practice of Gunnery (formerly of Archery) 1545. **5.** That branch of an army which manages the cannons in war 1786. **6.** *fig.* (with reference to 1, 2, 3.) 1599. **7.** Thunder and lightning (*poet.*) 1596.

2. Ionathan gaue his a. vnto his ladde 1 *Sam.* 20:40. Artillerie, th' infernall instrument, New brought from hell to scourge mortalitie With hideous roaring, and astonishment DANIEL. 7. Heauen's Artillerie SHAKS.

Comb.: **a.-company,** a company † of archers, or of a. (sense 5); **-park,** the place in which the a. is encamped, or collected; **-train,** a number of pieces of ordnance mounted on carriages and fitted out for marching. Hence **Arti·llerying** *vbl. sb.* firing of a. CARLYLE. **Arti·lleryman,** one who serves a gun; one who belongs to the a. **Arti·lleryship,** the skilful management of cannon; artillery practice.

Artiodactyl(e (ā:ɹti,o,dæ·ktil). 1849. [f. Gr. ἄρτιος even + δάκτυλος finger, toe.] *Zool. adj.* Having an even number of toes. *sb.* [sc. *ungulate animal.*]

Artisan (āɹtizæ·n). 1538. [– Fr. *artisan* – It. *artigiano* :– Rom. **artitianus*, f. L. *artitus*, pa. pple. of *artire* instruct in the arts, f. *ars, art-* ART; see -AN; cf. *partisan.*] † **1.** One who practises or cultivates an art; an artist –1795. **2.** One occupied in any industrial art; a mechanic, handicraftsman, artificer 1538. Also *fig.* Also *attrib.* 1859.

2. The meanest a. . .contributes more to the accommodation of life than the profound scholar JOHNSON.

Artist (ā·ɹtist). 1581. [– (O)Fr. *artiste* = It. *artista*, f. *arte* ART; see -IST.] **A.** *sb.* **I.** † **1.** A learned man, a Master of Arts (see ART *sb.* II. 1) –1753. † **2.** *gen.* One who pursues some practical science 1677; *spec.* a medical practitioner –1761; an astrologer or alchemist; *later*, a chemist –1686.

2. The Tuscan A. [*i.e.* astronomer] MILT. *P.L.* I. 288.

II. † **1.** A follower of a pursuit in which skill comes by study or practice; *hence*, a proficient; a practical man, opp. to a *theorist* –1793. † **2.** A follower of a manual art; a mechanic, etc. –1815. **3.** One who makes his craft a 'fine art'. Cf. ARTISTE. 1849.

1. I will give you more directions concerning fishing; for I would fain make you an A. WALTON. 3. A famous pilau, made by my a. [*i.e.* cook] CURZON.

III. 1. *gen.* One who cultivates one of the fine arts, which please by perfection of execution. (Formerly extended to all the *arts* presided over by the *Muses*.) 1581. **2.** *spec.* One skilled in † **a.** music –1712; **b.** dramatic art (see ARTISTE) 1714; **c.** now *esp.* one who practises the arts of design; or, pop. and more usually, one who cultivates painting as a profession 1747.

1. The true poet is always a true a. 1855. 2. He judged her [the actress] as a woman, not an a. C. BRONTË. She's a perfect Hebe; and if I were an a., I would paint her GEO. ELIOT.

† **IV.** One who practises artifice; a schemer –1813.

B. *adj.* Artistic, skilful 1603.

Hence **A·rtistdom**, the class or estate of artists. **Artist-like** *adj.* artistic; *adv.* artistically; var. **A·rtistly** *adv.* **A·rtistry**, the occupation or characteristics of an a.; artistic ability.

Artiste (arti·st). 1832. [Fr.; see ARTIST; re-introduced in consequence of the limited sense now given to *artist*.] = ARTIST II. 3, III. 2 a, b.

A·rtistess. [f. ARTIST + -ESS[1].] A female artist. H. WALPOLE.

Artistic, -al (aɹti·stik, -ăl), *a.* 1753. [f. ARTIST + -IC, -ICAL.] Of or pertaining to artists or art; befitting an artist. Hence **Arti·stically** *adv.* tastefully; from an a. point of view.

† **A·rtize,** *v.* [f. ART *sb.* + -IZE; see ARTILIZE *v.*] *intr.* To exercise an art. *trans.* To artificialize. FLORIO.

Artless (ā·ɹtlės), *a.* 1589. [f. ART *sb.* + -LESS.] **1.** Devoid of art or skill, unpractised, ignorant; devoid of the fine or liberal arts, uncultured 1599. **2.** Constructed, or designed, without art; clumsy; inartistic 1695. **3.** Unartificial, natural, simple 1672. **4.** Simple-minded, sincere, ingenuous 1714.

1. The artlesse tongue of a tedious dolt NASHE. A shadowy life—a., joyless, loveless RUSKIN. 2. Brogues, a kind of a. shoes JOHNSON. 3. Such A. beauty lies in Shakespears wit DRYDEN. 4. Imitation is a kind of a. flattery BUDGELL. Hence **A·rtless-ly** *adv.*, **-ness.**

Art-like. 1630. *adj.* In accordance with, or resembling, art 1651. *adv.* According to the rules of art 1630.

† **A·rtly,** *adv.* 1576. [f. ART *sb.* + -LY[2]; cf. LOVELY *adv.*] With art; skilfully –1662.

Artocarpad (āɹtokā·ɹpăd). 1834. [f. mod. L. *artocarpus* bread-fruit tree (f. Gr. ἄρτος bread + καρπός fruit) + -AD 1 d.] *Bot.* A tree belonging to the *Artocarpaceæ*, or Bread-fruit group. **Artoca·rpeous, -pous** *a.* of or pertaining to this group.

† **Arto·latry.** 1626. [f. Gr. ἄρτος bread + λατρεία worship; see -LATRY.] The worship of bread –1658.

Arto·phagous, *a. rare.* 1816. [f. Gr. ἀρτόφαγος (f. as prec.) + -OUS; see -PHAGOUS.] Bread-eating.

Artotyrite (āɹtotəi·rəit). 1586. [– late L. *artotyritæ* (Augustine) – eccl. Gr. ἀρτοτυρῖται, f. Gr. ἀρτότυρος bread and cheese; see -ITE[1] 1.] *Eccl. Hist.* One of a sect who celebrated the Eucharist with bread and cheese.

Artou, artow, obs. contr. of *art thou.*

A·rts-man. *arch.* 1551. [f. *art's* + MAN; cf. *craftsman*, etc.] One skilled in an art or in arts.

† **A·rts-ma:ster.** 1589. [f. as prec. + MASTER.] **1.** A teacher of art, or of an art or craft –1740. **2.** One who is master of a craft; a chief artificer –1624.

Arty (ā·ɹti), *a. colloq.* 1901. [f. ART *sb.* + -Y[1].] Contemptuous or joc.: Of artistic pretensions.

‖ **Arum** (ēᵊ·rɒm). Pl. **-s.** 1551. [L. – Gr. ἄρον.] **1.** *Bot.* A genus of plants (N.O. *Araceæ*), with a large spathe, enclosing a fleshy spadix, as the Wake-robin, Cuckoo-pint, or Lords and Ladies (*A. maculatum*) **2.** *attrib.*, as in **Arum lily** (*Richardia æthiopica*) 1599.

Arundinaceous (ărɒ:ndinē[i]·ʃəs), *a.* 1657. [f. L. *arundinaceus*, f. (*h*)*arundo*; see -ACEOUS.] Reed-like, reedy. var. **Arundi·neous** (*rare*).

Aruspex, and derivatives; see under HAR-.

A·rval, -el, -ill. Now *dial.* 1459. [app. – ON. *ervi-ǫl* funeral-feast, f. *arfr* (OE. *erfe*) inheritance + *ǫl* ALE, banquet.] A funeral feast. Also *attrib.*

Arval (ā·ɹvăl), *a.* 1656. [– L. *arvalis*, f. *arvum* arable land; see -AL[1].] Of or belonging to ploughed land: *esp.* in *Arval Brethren* (= L. *Fratres Arvales*), a college of priests in Ancient Rome, who offered sacrifice to the field-Lares to secure good crops.

-ary[1], *suffix* of adjs. and sbs., – L. *-arius, -arium.* In ME. *-arie*, later *-arye.* **A.** *adjs.* repr. (or after) L. *-arius* 'connected with, pertaining to'; as *arbitrary.* **B.** *sbs.* **1.** repr. (or after) L. *-arius* 'a man (or male) belonging to or engaged in'; as *adversary, January* (mensis). **2.** repr. (or after) L. *-arium* 'a thing connected with or employed in, a place for'; as *aviary, granary.* **3.** repr. L. *-aria* (Fr. *-aire*); as *fritillary.*

-ary[2], *suffix* of adjs.; occas. – L. *-aris* 'of the kind of, belonging to', as *military.* The reg. Eng. repr. is -AR[1].

Aryan, Arian (ēᵊ·riăn, ā·riăn). 1601. [f. Skr. *āryas* (Vedic *āria*) noble, applied earlier as a national name. Cf. L. *Ariāna, -ē* eastern region of the Persian kingdom (*Ariāni, -ēni* its unhabitants), Gr. Ἄριοι Medes (Herodotus), Ἀριανή (Strabo), Ἀριανοί; also Av. *Airyana*, whence mod. *Iran.* Cf. Fr. *arien*, G. *arisch*, sb. pl. *Arier.* See -AN.] **A.** *adj.* Applied to the family of languages, which includes Sanskrit, Zend, Persian, Greek, Latin, Celtic, Teutonic, and Slavonic; also called *Indo-European, Indo-Germanic*, and occ. *Japhetic*; or restricted to the Asiatic portion of these, as the only members of the family known historically to have called themselves by the name. *absol.* The original Aryan language 1847.

B. *sb.* A member of the Aryan family; one belonging to, or descended from, the ancient people who spoke the parent Aryan language 1851.

The region of the Arianes, all scorched and senged with the parching heate of the Sunne HOLLAND.

Aryanize (ēᵊ·riănəiz, ā·riăn-), *v.* 1858. [f. prec. + -IZE.] To make characteristically Aryan. Hence **Aryanized** *ppl. a.* made Aryan in language (though not of Aryan race).

Aryteno- (æritī·no), comb. form of next.

Arytenoid (æritī·noid). 1727. [– mod.L. *arytænoides* – Gr. ἀρυταινοειδής, f. ἀρύταινα funnel f. ἀρύτειν draw off; see -OID.] *Phys. adj.* Funnel-, pitcher-shaped: applied *spec.* to two pyramidal cartilages of the larynx which regulate the vocal chords, and to parts connected with them. As *sb.* [sc. *cartilage, muscle.*] 1849. var. **Arytæ·noid.** Hence **A:rytenoi·dal** *a.* belonging to the a. cartilages, etc.

As (æz, ăz, əz), *adv.* (*conj.* and *rel. pron.*) OE. [Reduced form (XII) of *ase* or *als*, which are divergent developments of *alse*:– OE. *alswā* (*ealswā*); see ALSO and cf. OFris. *asa, as(e), is* and G. *als* as, than, reduced form of *also* (which survives in the sense 'therefore').]

A. In a main sentence, as Antecedent or Demonstrative Adverb. † **1.** *As . . . so*: In that quantity . . . (in which) . . . –1532; in that way . . . (in which) . . . ME. only. **2.** *As . . . as*: In that degree . . . (in which) . . . Expressing the *Comparative of Equality*: *as* good *as* gold, etc. ME. **3.** With relative cl. elliptically absent: *as* = *equally* ME.

2. He was as covetous as cruel W. WOTTON. 3. I hear quite as well where I am 1888. *As lief, as soon* (as not).

B. In a subord. sentence, as a Relative or Conjunctive Adverb, introducing a clause:

I. Of quantity or degree. (Preceded by *adj.* or *adv.*) **1.** With antecedent *as*: . . . In which degree (expressing the *Comparative of Equality*; cf. A. 2); As if, as though (*arch.*) ME. **2.** With antecedent *so* in the same sense as 1. ME. **3.** With antecedent *as* (*so*) suppressed: Emphatic ME.; Concessive = Though, however ME. † **4.** After Comparatives = Than –1824.

1. Will serve as well as I were present there MARLOWE. 2. No country suffered so much. . as England MACAULAY. 3. Momentarie as a sound *Mids. N.* I. i. 144. Bad as his Actions were. . would there not [etc.] 1742. 4. I rather like him as otherwise SCOTT.

II. Of quality or manner. (Preceded by a *verb.*) * *With antecedent expressed.* † **1.** With antecedent *as*: . . . in the way that ME. only. **2.** With antecedent *so*, or *such, same*, etc.: . . . in the manner that . . . (*arch.*) ME. **3.** With the clauses transposed for emphasis; *as . . . so*: in the way that . . . (in that manner) ME.; even as, just as; both . . . and (*arch.*) 1602. ** *With antecedent not expressed.* **4.** = with antecedent *so* omitted: . . . in the manner that . . .; to the same extent as; even as; . . . as on the other hand; whereas; whilst 1523. **5.** = mod. As if, as though (*arch.*) ME. **6.** With the subord. cl. abbreviated: As if, as it were OE. † With numbers = About –1523. **7.** With subj. or obj. repr. subord. cl.: The same as, like ME.; in the character, capacity, or *rôle* of 1523. **8.** Used to introduce elliptical or parenthetical clauses, e.g. *as a rule*, etc. ME. **9.** Introducing clauses used to attest a statement, or to adjure any one by his faith, hopes, etc.: In such a manner as befits the prayer, † wish, belief, etc. that . . . ME.

2. So doe, as thou hast said *Gen.* 18:5. 3. As she brews so let her bake 1614. 4. General amicable *As-you-were* between Austria and Bavaria CARLYLE. The oath, as it stands, is [etc.] 1882. If I had been present, as I was not, I should [etc.] 1888. 5. I heard the wrack As earth and sky would mingle MILT. *P.R.* IV. 447. *As it were*: As if it were so, in some sort; She has thought fit, as it were, to mock herself STEELE. 6. God dealeth with you as with sonnes *Heb.* 12:7. 7. Yee shall bee as Gods, knowing good and euill *Gen.* 3:5. The fact is assumed as a hypothesis 1837. *As who*: Like one who, as if one (*arch.*); † as being he who. 8. This war was, as usual, no less feeble in its operations than [etc.] HUME. 9. This sweares he, as he is a Prince SHAKS.

III. Of time and place. **1.** When, while, whenever ME. † **2.** Where. ME. only.

1. They wander, grazing as they go DRYDEN.

IV. Of reason. It being the case that; inasmuch as; since ME.

As you are not ready, we must go without you 1888.

V. Of result or purpose. † **1.** With finite vb. (Now repl. by *that*, through *as that.*) So . . . as: in such manner . . . that –1777; *Such . . . as*: of that kind . . . that –1671. **2.** With inf. (Still in use.) 1590. * *With* so *wanting, or conjoined with* as *in the subord. cl.* † **3.** = mod. *so that* (through *so as that*) –1797.

2. Be so good as to come 1888.

VI. Introducing an attrib. cl.; after *such, same*, etc. **1.** After *such* (OE. *swylc* containing *swá*, so), and after *same* (an adv. followed by *swá* in OE.), *as* = That, who, which ME. **2.** With *such* omitted, or replaced by *that, those*, 'as' becomes a relative pron. = That, who, which. Still in dial. use. ME. **3.** In parenthetic clauses, affirming or commenting on a word 1550; also = A thing or fact which 1552. **4.** = Such as, of the kind of; for instance. (App. ellipt. = *such* as . . . *is.*) ME. † **5.** Added to *there, then, thither*, etc. (earlier to *where, when*, etc.) to make them conjunctive –1808.

1. Such a one as was the glory of the land of Israel A.V. *Transl. Pref.* 3. I haue vs'd thee (Filth as thou art) with humane care *Temp.* I. ii. 346. Yff. . we shoulde warre with them (as God defende) 1552. 4. A prelat, as an abott or a priour WYCLIF.

VII. Introducing dependent sentences or clauses. **1.** A noun sentence, after *say, know*, etc. Also *as that, as how.* (Replaced by *that.*) 1483. † **2.** Contracted interrog. sentences: *As how?* (arch.) *As why?* (illiterate.) –1801. † **3.** Formerly bef. an inf. cl., where now a pple. is used, as in 'Speaking of volcanoes, I [etc.]'.

1. I believe as how your man deals with the devil SMOLLETT.

VIII. Prefixed to preps. and advs. **1.** With preps. = *as far as, so far as*. (In *as in, as by, as after*, etc., *as* was pleonastic.) ME. **2.** With advs. and advb. phrases. Of time: in *as then, as now*, etc., *as* is restrictive. In literary Eng. *as yet* (still in use) = up to this time ME. † Of place: *as here*, etc. –1532.

1. My only doubt was as to the mode HELPS. **2.** He could not get John punished as then 1653.

Phrases: **1.** *As much* has the special sense of: The same; what practically amounts to that, so; as in 'I thought as much'. **2.** *As well* has the special senses: **a.** (with following *as*) Just as much ..as; equally..with, in the same way..as; both.. and; like; in addition to, besides. **b.** (*ellipt.*) Just as much, no less; also. **c.** (*absol.*) As well as not; *hence* (deferentially) better. **3.** *As good as*: Practically.

‖ **As** (æs), *sb.* 1601. [L. *as*. Cf. ACE.] A Roman copper coin, originally weighing twelve ounces, after the first Punic war reduced to two ounces, during the second to one, and by the *Lex Papiria* (B.C. 191) to half an ounce.

As, obs. f. ACE, ASS, and ASH.

As-, *prefix*[1], assim. f. L. *ad-*, bef. *s-*. Orig. adopted from OFr. as *a-*; but refash. later.

As-, *prefix*[2], var. of OFr. *es-* :- L. *ex-*, as in *as-cape* (now *es-cape*), *as-tonish* (still used).

‖ **Asafœtida** (æsăfe·tidă). ME. [– med.L. ('stinking asa'), i.e. *āsa* (– Pers. *azā* mastic), *fœtida*, fem. of *fœtidus* FETID.] A concreted resinous gum, with a strong alliaceous odour, procured from the *Narthex asafœtida*, etc.; used in cookery, and as an antispasmodic in medicine. Also, the plant itself 1607.

A-sa·le, *adv.* 1553. [A *prep.*[1] + SALE.] On sale, for sale.

‖ **Asarabacca** (æ:sără,bæ·kă). 1551. [Syncopated f. L. *asarum* hazel-wort, – Gr. ἄσαρον + *bacc(h)ar* (Plin.), – Gr. βάκκαρ, βάκχαρ, a Lydian name for the same plant, or *bacc(h)aris* – βάκκαρις unguent made from it, βάκχαρις sowbread.] *Herb.* The plant *Asarum europæum*, used now as an ingredient in cephalic snuffs.

Asarin (æ·sărin). 1834. [f. L. *asarum* (see prec.) + -IN[1].] *Chem.* A crystallizable, aromatic, camphor-like substance obtained from the root of asarabacca; also called *Camphor of Asarum*. var. **A·sarone.**

Asbestos, asbestus (æzbe·stǫs, -ʊs). ME. [Earliest forms *asbeston, abiston, albestone* – OFr. *abeston, albeston* – L. – Gr. ἄσβεστον, acc. of ἄσβεστος, f. Gr. ἀ- A- *pref.* 14 + σβεστός, f. σβεννύναι quench. The present form dates from XVII.] † **1.** The unquenchable stone. (A distorted reference to the action of cold water on quick lime.) –1750. † **2.** An (alleged) incombustible flax (see 3) –1734. **3.** A mineral of fibrous texture, capable of being woven into an incombustible fabric; AMIANT or AMIANTUS. In *Min.* applied to all fibrous varieties of Hornblende or Amphibole, and of Pyroxene, as well as to *Amiantus*. 1607. Also *fig.* Also *attrib.* var. **Asbest** (*arch.*). Hence **Asbe·stic** *a.* of the nature of a. **Asbe·stiform** *a.* having the form or appearance of a. **Asbe·stine, Asbe·stous** *a.* of, pertaining to, or having the properties of a.; incombustible. **Asbe·stoid** *a.* resembling a.; *sb.* (*Min.*) = BYSSOLITE; so **Asbestoi·dal** *a.*

Asbolan, asbolite (æ·zbolæn, -əit). 1837. [f. Gr. ἀσβόλη soot; see -AN 2, -ITE[1] 2 b.] *Min.* A kind of wad containing oxide of cobalt; also called *Earthy Cobalt*.

Asboline (æ·zbolәin). 1863. [f. as prec. + -INE[4].] An acrid volatile oil obtained from soot.

Ascan (æ·skăn), *a.* 1876. [f. mod.L. ASCUS + -AN.] *Bot.* Of or belonging to an *ascus*, as *ascan spores*.

† **Asca·pe**, *v.* ME. form of ESCAPE (see AS-[2]) –1523.

‖ **Ascarides** (ăskæ·ridīz), *sb. pl.* ME. [mod. L. – Gr. ἀσκαρίδες, pl. of ἀσκαρίς. Occas. sing. **ascarid.**] *Zool.* A genus of intestinal worms; thread-worms.

† **Asce·nce.** 1450. [– OFr. *ascense* – med. L. *ascensa*, fem. sing. of pa. pple. of L. *ascendere*; see ASCENSION and cf. *defence*.] Earlier equiv. of ASCENT, ASCENSION.

Ascend (ăse·nd), *v.* ME. [– L. *ascendere*, f. *ad* AS-[1] + *scandere* climb.] **1.** *intr.* (occas. with *up*) To go or come up; to mount, soar; to rise, be raised 1514. **2.** Of planetary bodies, etc.: **a.** *spec.* To come above the horizon. **b.** *gen.* To move towards the zenith. **3.** To rise by growth or construction. Only *poet.* 1667. **4.** To slope upwards 1832. **5.** *trans.* To walk up, climb; *hence*, to reach the top of ME. **6.** To go up into or get up on; to mount. *Obs.* exc. *poet.*, and in 'to ascend the throne'. 1593. **7.** *intr.* To proceed from the inferior to the superior; to rise in thought, feeling, station, etc. 1549. **8.** To rise in pitch 1597. **9.** To go back in time, or in genealogical order 1574.

1. Voice always ascends, the vibration moving most naturally upwards DE FOE. **2.** All mild ascends the Moon's more sober light POPE. **3.** Where Apennine ascends GOLDSM. **5.** *To ascend* a river: to go along it towards its source. **9.** Inheritance may..not lyneally a. 1574. Hence **Asce·ndable** *a.* (*rare*), that may be ascended. **Asce·nder.**

Ascendancy, -ency (ăse·ndĕnsi). 1712. [f. next; see -ANCY.] The state or quality of being in the ascendant; paramount influence, domination. Constr. *over*. (The spellings are equally common.)

He would not submit to the a. of France MACAULAY. var. **Asce·ndance, -ence.**

Ascendant, -ent (ăse·ndĕnt). ME. [– (O)Fr. *ascendant* – *ascendant-*, pres. ppl. stem of L. *ascendere*, used subst.; see ASCEND, -ANT[1]. The prevalent sp. is now *-ant*.] **A.** *adj.* **1.** *gen.* Rising; tending upwards 1591; *spec.* in *Phys.* and *Bot.* = ASCENDING *ppl. a.* 3. 1611. **2.** *Astr.* Rising towards the zenith; *spec.* in *Astrol.* Just above the eastern horizon 1594. **3.** *fig.* Superior; predominant 1634.

1. Rooted and a. strength like that of foliage RUSKIN. **3.** To make a. all that is rational..in us 1806.

B. *sb.* [the adj. used *absol.*] **1.** *Astrol.* The point of the ecliptic, or degree of the zodiac, which at any moment (*esp.* at the birth of a child) is just rising above the eastern horizon; the horoscope ME. Hence *fig.* 1654. **2.** *gen.* = ASCENDANCY. Const. *over*. 1596. † **3.** An upward slope; a flight of steps. Also *fig.* –1641. † **4.** One who ascends –1701. † **5.** A summit or peak –1676. **6.** One who precedes in genealogical order; an ancestor; a relative in the ascending line 1604.

1. Min ascendant was Taur, and Mars therinne CHAUCER. *The house of the ascendant*: 5 degrees of the zodiac above and 25 below the ascendant. *The lord of the ascendant*: any planet within the house of the ascendant. **2.** Strong minds have undoubtedly an a. over weak ones CHESTERFIELD. **In the ascendant:** supreme, dominant. (Erron.: Rising, ascending.) Hence **Ascende·ntal** *a.* of the nature of ascent (*rare*).

Asce·ndible, *a. rare.* [– L. *ascendibilis*; see ASCEND, -IBLE.] = *Ascendable* (see ASCEND *v.*).

Ascending (ăse·ndiŋ), *vbl. sb.* 1482. [f. ASCEND *v.* + -ING[1].] The action of the vb. ASCEND; ascent, ascension.

attrib. in *Ascending Latitude*: the latitude of a planet when ascending. *A. Node*: the point in a planet's orbit where it crosses the ecliptic in ascending.

Asce·nding, *ppl. a.* 1616. [f. ASCEND *v.* + -ING[2].] **1.** Rising, mounting up 1667. **2.** Sloping upwards; acclivitous 1616. **3.** Directed upwards: *spec.* in *Phys.* of structures that pass, or serve as a passage, from a lower to a higher part of the body; and in *Bot.* of a stem which gradually curves to an erect position 1713. **4.** Going backwards in genealogical order 1703. Hence **Asce·ndingly** *adv.* with upward motion.

Ascension (ăse·nʃən). ME. [– (O)Fr. *ascension* – L. *ascensio*, f. *ascens-*, pa. ppl. stem of *ascendere* ASCEND; see -ION.] **1.** *gen.* The action of ascending (see ASCEND *v.*) 1574. **2.** *spec.* The ascent of Jesus Christ to heaven on the fortieth day after His resurrection. Occ. = *Ascension-day*. ME. **3.** *Astr.* The rising of a celestial body ME. † **4.** *Alch.* Distillation, evaporation; *concr.* a fume –1817. **5.** Upward slope (*arch.*) 1447.

2. *Ascension-day*: the day on which the ascension into heaven took place, and on which it is commemorated; Holy Thursday. **3.** *Right Ascension* of the sun or a star: the degree of the equinoctial or celestial equator, reckoned from the first point in Aries, which rises with it in a right sphere, or which comes with it to the meridian; the arc of the equator intercepted between this degree and the first point of Aries; celestial longitude. *Oblique Ascension* of a star: the arc of the equator intercepted between the first point of Aries and the point of the equator which rises with the sun or star in an oblique sphere.

Ascensional (ăse·nʃənăl), *a.* 1594. [f. prec. + -AL[1].] Of or belonging to ascension, or ascent.

A. Difference in *Astr.*: the difference between the right and oblique ascension of the sun or a star.

Asce·nsionist. 1863. [f. as prec. + -IST, after Fr. *ascension(n)iste*.] One who makes ascents.

Ascensive (ăse·nsiv), *a.* 1646. [– med.L. *ascensivus* (*-ive*, XIV), f. L. *ascens-* (see ASCENSION) + -IVE.] **1.** Given to moving upwards; rising, progressive. **2.** *Gram.* Augmentative, intensive 1857. var. † **Asce·ntive.**

Ascent (ăse·nt). 1600. [f. ASCEND *v.*, after *descend, descent*.] **1.** *gen.* The act of ascending; upward movement 1614. Also *fig.* (see ASCEND 7) 1607. **2.** *esp.* The act of climbing or travelling up 1753. Also *fig.* **3.** A going back in time or in genealogical order; † *concr.* a single step backward in genealogy 1628. **4.** Method or way of ascending 1600; *concr.* a way up; upward slope; a flight of steps, etc. 1611. † **5.** An eminence –1742.

1. To him with swift a. he up return'd MILT. *P.L.* x. 224. **2.** The a. of the Simplon DICKENS. **4.** With one a. Accessible from Earth MILT. *P.L.* v. 545.

Ascertain (æsəɹtē[i]·n), *v.* [ME. *acertein, -ain*, – OFr. *acertain-*, tonic stem of *acertener* (later *ass-, asc-*, and so in Eng.), f. *a* AD- + *certain* CERTAIN.] † **1.** *trans.* To make (a person) certain; to assure; *loosely*, To inform, apprise. Const. *simply*, with *of*, or *subord. cl.* –1789. *refl.* To make oneself certain –1731. **2.** *trans.* To make (a thing) certain to the mind (*arch.*) 1494; † to establish as a certainty –1810. **3.** To find out or learn for a certainty; to make sure of, get to know. (The only current use.) 1794. † **4.** To ensure, secure (*to* a person) –1823. † **5.** To bring or deliver certainly, destine or doom (a person) *to* –1667. † **6.** To make (a thing) certain, or definite; to decide, fix, limit –1789.

1. Who may..Be ascertained that Two and Two make four CHURCHILL. **2.** [This] would a. it not to be the production of Johnson BOSWELL. **3.** Legal measures for ascertaining the culprit GEO. ELIOT. **6.** Some effectual method for correcting, enlarging, and ascertaining our language SWIFT. Hence **Ascertai·nable** *a.* that may be ascertained (senses 3, 6). **Ascertai·nableness. Ascertai·nably** *adv.* **Ascertai·ned** *ppl. a.* † fixed; known. **Ascertai·ner.**

Ascertainment (æsəɹtē[i]·nmĕnt). 1657. [f. prec. + -MENT; cf. OFr. *acertenement*.] The process or result of ascertaining. **1.** Reduction to certainty; exact determination (*arch.*). **2.** Finding out, discovery 1799.

Ascescent, -ency, erron. vars. ACESCENT, -ENCY.

Ascetic (ăse·tik). 1646. [– med.L. *asceticus* or Gr. ἀσκητικός, f. ἀσκητής monk, hermit (Philo), f. ἀσκεῖν to exercise; see -IC.] **A.** *adj.* **1.** Of or pertaining to the Ascetics, or to the exercise of rigorous self-discipline; severely abstinent, austere. **2.** = ASCETICAL 1. 1822.

1. A. discipline BURKE, gloom TENNYSON.

B. *sb.* **1.** *Eccl. Hist.* One of those who in the early church retired into solitude, to exercise themselves in meditation and prayer, and in the practice of rigorous self-discipline by celibacy, fasting, and toil 1673. **2.** *gen.* One who is extremely rigorous in self-denial 1660. **3.** *pl.* An ascetical treatise 1751.

1. The Ascetics, who obeyed and abused the rigid precepts of the gospel GIBBON.

Asce·tical, *a.* 1617. [f. prec. + -AL[1].] **1.** Pertaining to, or treating of, the spiritual exercises by which perfection and virtue may be attained, as in *Ascetical Theology*. **2.** = ASCETIC *a.* 1. 1836. Hence **Asce·tically** *adv.*

Asceticism (ăse·tisiz'm). 1646. [f. as prec. + -ISM.] The principles or practice of the Ascetics.

Ascham (æ·skăm). 1860. [f. *Ascham*, author of *Toxophilus*.] A sort of cupboard or case to contain implements of archery.

Ascians (æ·ʃiănz), *sb. pl.* 1635. [f. med.L. *Ascii* (– Gr. ἄσκιοι, f. ἀ- A- *pref.* 14 + σκιά shadow) + -AN.] Inhabitants of the torrid zone, who twice a year have the sun directly overhead, and then cast no shadows.

Ascidian (ăsi·diăn), *a.* 1835. [f. mod.L. *Ascidia* (see ASCIDIUM, -A 4) + -AN.] *Zool.* Of or pertaining to the Ascidia (or Ascidiæ), a group belonging to the tunicate Mollusca 1856. As *sb.* [sc. *animal.*] Hence **Asci:dia·rium,** the aggregate mass of organisms in compound Ascidians. **Asci·dioid** *a.* resembling the Ascidia. **Asci:diozo·oid,** one of the organisms forming an ascidiarium.

‖ **Ascidium** (ăsi·diŏm). Pl. **-a.** 1766. [mod. L. – Gr. ἀσκίδιον, dim. of ἀσκός leather bag, wine-skin.] **1.** *Zool* (Also *Ascidia*, pl. *-æ.*) A genus of tunicate molluscs, having the enveloping tunic elastic and leathery. **2.** *Bot.* A pitcher-shaped leafy appendage 1830. Hence **Asci·diate, Asci·diform** *adjs.* shaped like an a.

Ascigerous (ăsi·dʒĕrəs), *a.* 1829. [f. mod.L. ASCUS + -GEROUS.] *Bot.* Bearing or producing asci (see ASCUS).

Ascitan (ăsəi·tăn, æ·sităn). 1727. [f. late L. *Ascitæ* (Augustine) – Gr. ἀσκός wine-skin, + -AN; see -ITE[1] 1.] *Eccl. Hist.* One of a heretical sect (2nd c.), who used to dance round an inflated wine-skin, in reference to *Matt.* 9:17.

† **Asci·te,** earlier f. ACCITE *v.*

‖ **Ascites** (ăsəi·tīz). ME. [late L. – Gr. ἀσκίτης dropsy, f. ἀσκός wine-skin.] *Path.* A collection of serous fluid in the peritoneal cavity; dropsy of the abdomen. Hence **Asci·tic, -al** *a.*

Ascititious (æsiti·ʃəs), *a.* 1628. [f. *ascit-* = *adscit-*, pa. ppl. stem of L. *adsciscere* + -ITIOUS[1].] = ADSCITITIOUS (now more common).

Asclepiad[1] (ăsklī·piæ̆d). 1656. [– late L. *asclepiadeus* – Gr. ἀσκληπιάδειος, f. Ἀσκληπιάδης name of a Greek poet.] *Gr. and L. Pros.* A verse, invented by Asclepiades, consisting of a spondee, two (or three) choriambi, and an iambus. Also *attrib.* Hence **Ascle:piade·an** *a.*

Ascle·piad[2]. 1859. [f. next + -AD 1 d.] *Bot.* A plant of the order *Asclepiadaceæ*; see next. Hence **Ascle:piada·ceous** *a.* of or belonging to this order. **Ascle:piade·ous** *a.* of the genus *Asclepias.*

‖ **Asclepias** (ăsklī·piæ̆s). 1578. [L. – Gr. ἀσκληπιάς, f. Ἀσκληπιός Aesculapius.] *Bot.* A genus of plants, giving its name to a N.O., including the Milkweed, Swallow-wort, etc.

Asco- (æ:sko), comb. f. ASCUS, used in *Bot.*: **asco-go·nium** [cf. *archegonium*], the spirally coiled organ from which the asci are produced; **-myce·tal, -myce·tous** *a.* of or belonging to the *Ascomycetes*, or fungi, in which spores are formed asexually in the interior of asci; **-phorous** [Gr. -φορος], *a.*, producing asci; **-spore,** a spore developed in an ascus.

Ascribe (ăskrəi·b), *v.* ME. [– L. *ascribere* enrol, etc., f. *ad* AS-[1] + *scribere* write In the earlier form *ascrive* (XIV–XVII), – OFr. *ascriv-*, stem of *ascrire* – L. *ascrivere.*] † **1.** *trans.* To annex or add in writing, to subscribe –1649; to dedicate *to* –1563; to enrol in a class –1680; to appoint –1624. **2.** To enter *to*, or to the credit of, in an account; to assign, impute, refer, as due *to* ME. **3.** To reckon or count *to*, as a characteristic, etc. (*rarely* as a material possession); to claim for ME. † **4.** To count –1601. † **5.** with *compl.* To consider as. *refl.* To pretend *to be.* –1580.

2. We usually *ascribe* good, but *impute* evil JOHNSON. Others ascribed the whole disaster to the use of small notes HT. MARTINEAU. **3.** Ascribing..All 'holiness unto the Lord' 1880. Hence **Ascri·bable** *a.* that may be ascribed; attributable.

† **Ascri·pt,** *ppl. a.* 1564. [– L. *ascriptus*, pa. pple. of *ascribere* (see prec.).] Enrolled; appointed –1610.

Ascription (ăskri·pʃən). 1597. [– L. *ascriptio*, f. *ascript-*, pa. ppl. stem of *ascribere*; see ASCRIBE *v.*, -ION.] † **1.** The act of ascribing (see ASCRIBE 1, 2, 3). **2.** *concr.* The declaration thus made 1845.

1. The theoretical a. of English law to immemorial unwritten tradition MAINE.

Ascriptitious (æskripti·ʃəs), *a. rare.* 1652. [f. L. *ascripticius*; see ASCRIPT and -ITIOUS[1]. Cf. *adscriptitious.*] † **1.** Appended to a list 1658. **2.** Merely ascribed to. (Cf. *fictitious.*) 1652.

† **Ascry·,** *v.* [ME. *ascrie* – AFr. *ascrier (see AS-[2]) = OFr. *escrier* (mod. *écrier*), f. *es* :– L. *ex* + *crier* CRY. Cf. ESCRY *v.*] **1.** To call forth, out, or upon –1450; *esp.* to challenge –1523. **2.** *intr.* To shout, exclaim –1528. **3.** *trans.* = DESCRY; *hence* to espy; inform upon –1559. Hence † **Ascry·** *sb.* outcry, clamour.

‖ **Ascus** (æ·skŏs). Pl. **-i.** 1830. [mod.L. – Gr. ἀσκός bag, sac.] *Bot.* A membranous tubular cell, *esp.* the sac-like cell at the end of the branches of the hyphæ in certain fungi, etc., in which the reproductive sporules or sporidia develop.

-ase, suffix taken from the ending of DIASTASE and used in naming enzymes, as *lactase, maltase, urase*, etc.

A-sea (ăsī·), *adv.* 1858. [A *prep.*[1]] On the sea; to the sea.

A-see·the, *adv.* 1879. [A *prep.*[1] 11.] Seething.

A-seity (ē[i]:sī·ĭti, ăsī·ĭti). 1691. [– med.L. *aseitas*, f. L. *a* from + *se* oneself + *-itas* -ITY; cf. SEITY.] *Metaph.* Underived or independent existence.

Aselline (ăse·lǝin), *a. rare.* 1855. [f. L. *asellus* little ass + -INE[1].] Of or pertaining to a little ass, or to the two stars in Cancer called *Aselli.*

Aseptic (e[i]se·ptik), *a.* 1859. [f. A- *pref.* 14 + SEPTIC.] Not liable to putrefy; preventing putrefaction. Also as *sb.* Hence **Ase·pticism.**

Asexual (e[i]se·ksiuăl), *a.* 1830. [A- *pref.* 14.] *Biol.* Not sexual, without sex. In *Bot.* formerly of cryptogams; cf. AGAMIC. Hence **Ase:xua·lity,** a. condition, absence of sex.

† **Asfa·st, as fast,** *adv. phr.* ME. only. [After (O)Fr. *aussitôt.*] Formerly in the special sense of: As fast as might be, straightway (Fr. *aussitôt*).

Ash (æʃ), *sb.*[1] [OE. *æsc* = OS. *ask* (Du. *esch*), OHG. *ask*, ON. *askr* :– Gmc. *askiz.] **1. a.** A forest tree, indigenous to Europe, Western Asia, and North Africa; having silver-grey bark, pinnate foliage, a peculiar winged seed or samara called the 'ash-key', and tough close-grained wood valuable for implements. **b.** The tribe of trees *Fraxineæ*, N.O. *Oleaceæ*, including the Common Ash (*Fraxinus excelsior*) and the Manna or Flowering Ashes (*Ornus europæa* and *rotundifolia*). OE. **2.** The timber of the ash-tree ME. † **3.** The ashen shaft of a spear; a spear –1700.

1. The warlike beech; the a. for nothing ill SPENSER *F.Q.* I. i. 9. **3.** My grained A. *Cor.* IV. v. 114.

Comb.: **a.-key,** the winged two-celled seed or samara of the ash-tree; **-leaf,** an early potato with leaves like ash-leaves. **Ground Ash,** an ash sapling; an umbelliferous herb with pinnate leaves, *esp.* the ASHWEED, and Wild Angelica. **Mountain Ash,** the Rowan-tree or Quickbeam (*Pyrus aucuparia*); occas. the Aspen (*Populus tremula*), called also *Quaking Ash.* **Wild Ash,** occas. the Mountain Ash; also the *Ornus.*

Ash (æʃ), *sb.*[2]; commonly in *pl.* **ashes** (æ·ʃėz). [OE. *æsce, æxe* = MLG. *asche*, Du. *asch*, OHG. *asca* (G. *asche*), ON. *aska*; cf. Goth. *azgo.*] **1.** The powdery residue, chiefly earthy or mineral, left after the combustion of any substance. *pl.* OE. *collect. sing.* ME. *simple sing.* ME. Also *transf.* or *fig.* **2.** That which remains of a human body after (*orig.*) cremation or (*transf.*) total decomposition; hence *poet.* for 'mortal remains' ME. **3.** Dust of the ground. (Hence applied to man's mortal constitution.) OE. **4.** Death-like pallor; the colour of wood ashes ME. **5.** A symbol of grief or repentance OE.

1. Sprinkle sordid ashes all around DRYDEN. A charring ember, smouldering into a. 1868. My heart is within me As an a. in the fire SWINBURNE. *Volcanic ash*: the powdery matter ejected from volcanoes. *Black ash*: a mixture of carbonate of soda and sulphide of calcium formed in manufacturing soda from salt. *To lay in ashes*: to burn to the ground; Whole kingdoms laid in ashes ADDISON. **2.** I commende..thy body to the grounde,..asshes to asshes, dust to dust *Bk. Com. Pr.* E'en in our ashes live their wonted fires GRAY. **b.** *The Ashes*: the symbolical remains of English cricket taken back to Australia. **3.** Lord, what shall Earth and Ashes do? WESLEY. **4.** The lip of ashes, and the cheek of flame BYRON. **5.** Repents..not in ashes, and sackecloath, but in new Silke, and old sacke 2 *Hen. IV*, I. ii.

Comb.: **a.-bin,** a receptacle for ashes, etc.; **-fire,** a low fire of ash and cinders; **-furnace,** one used in glass-making; **-heap; -hole; -leach,** a hopper or tub in which wood-ashes are placed that the alkaline salts may be dissolved from them; **-like** *a.*; **-oven** (= *-furnace*); **-pan; -pit; -tub** (= *-bin*).

Ash (æʃ), *v.*[1] *dial.* [f. ASH *sb.*[1]] To flog with an ash-stick. Cf. *To birch.*

Ash (æʃ), *v.*[2] 1645. [f. ASH *sb.*[2]] To strew with ashes.

† **Asha·ke,** *v.* [OE. *āsceacan*, f. A- *pref.* 1 + *sceacan* SHAKE.] To shake off; *fig.* to dispel –ME.

A-sha·ke, *adv.* 1856. [A *prep.*[1] 11.] Shaking.

Ashame (ăʃē[i]·m), *v.* OE. [A- *pref.* 1; see next.] † **1.** *intr.* To feel shame –1566. **2.** *trans.* To put to shame 1591.

Ashamed (ăʃē[i]·md), *pred. a.* [OE. *āscamod*, pa. pple. of *āscamian* feel shame; see A- *pref.* 1, SHAME *v.*, -ED[1].] **1.** Affected with shame; abashed or put to confusion; disconcerted. Const. *of*, † *on*, † *for* ME.; with *subord. cl.* ME.; with *inf. phr.* 1647. **2.** With *inf. phr.*: Reluctant through fear of shame *to.* With a negative: Prevented by fear of shame from. ME. Rarely *attrib.*

1. In Milton, the Devil is never described a. but once ADDISON. A. of sitting idle JOHNSON, to be seen TENNYSON. **2.** I am aschamyd to begge WYCLIF *Luke* 16:3. Hence **Asha·medness.**

Ashen (æ·ʃĕn), *a.*[1] ME. [f. ASH *sb.*[1] + -EN[4].] **1.** Of or pertaining to an ash-tree 1562. **2.** Made of the wood of an ash ME.

Ashen (æ·ʃĕn), *a.*[2] 1808. [f. ASH *sb.*[2] + -EN[4].] **1.** Of ashes. Also *fig.* 1850. **2.** Ash-coloured, deadly pale 1808.

2. The a. hue of age SCOTT.

Ashery (æ·ʃĕri). 1859. [f. ASH *sb.*[2] + -ERY.] **a.** A place where potash or pearl-ash is manufactured. **b.** An ash-pit.

Ashet (æ·ʃėt). *north. dial.* 1552. [– Fr. *assiette.*] A dish, or platter.

A-shi·ne, *adv.* 1840. [A *prep.*[1] 11.] Shining.

A-shi·pboard, *adv.* 1598. [A *prep.*[1] 1.] On board ship.

A-shi·ver, *adv.* 1840. [A *prep.*[1] 11.] In a shiver.

Ashlar (æ·flǝɹ). [ME. *as(s)heler* – OFr. *aisselier* – L. *axilla*, dim. of *axis, assis*, board, plank.] **1.** A square hewn stone for building purposes or for pavement (? so called as resembling a wooden beam); also used as a missile. Called also *Ashlar-stone.* **2.** Masonry of hewn stone, usu. in thin slabs, used as a facing to rubble or brick wall. Also *attrib.* 1823.

1. A. stones of the Bastille continue thundering through the dusk CARLYLE. *Ashlar-work*: masonry constructed of square hewn stones; opp. to *rubble-work. Ashlar-rafter, -piece* = *ashlaring.* Hence **A·shlared** *ppl. a.* covered with a.; cf. 2. **A·shlaring** *vbl. sb.* the short upright quartering fixed in garrets between the rafters and the floor, to cut off the angles formed by the rafters. Also, ashlar masonry.

Ashling (æ·fliŋ). 1883. [f. ASH *sb.*[1] + -LING[1].] An ash sapling.

Ashore (ăʃō[ə]·ɹ), *adv.* 1586. [f. A *prep.*[1] + SHORE *sb.*[1], after earlier ALAND.] **1.** To the shore; to land. **2.** On shore, on land 1631.

1. I must be getting a. now W. BLACK. **2.** He behaves himself a. as if he were still on board STEELE

Ash-We·dnesday. ME. [f. ASH *sb.*[2] + WEDNESDAY.] The first day of Lent; so called from the custom introduced by Pope Gregory the Great of sprinkling ashes on the heads of penitents on that day.

Ashweed (æ·ʃwīd). 1578. [f. ASH *sb.*[1]] *Herb.* The Goutweed (*Ægopodium podagraria*).

Ashy (æ·ʃi), *a.* ME. [f. ASH *sb.*[2] + -Y[1].] **1.** Consisting of ashes 1483. **2.** Covered or sprinkled with ashes ME. **3.** Ash-coloured, deadly pale 1541. **4.** quasi-*adv.* 1592.

Eyebrows..you can see are a.-blond CARLYLE.

Asian (ē[i]·ʃ[i]ăn). 1563. [– L. *Asianus* – Gr. Ἀσιανός; see -IAN.] = ASIATIC.

Asiarch (ē[i]·ʃi,ăɹk). 1753. [– late L. *asiarcha* – Gr. ἀσιάρχης; see -ARCH.] Director of religious rites, etc., in Asia Minor under the Romans. (Cf. *Acts* 19:31.)

Asiatic (ē[i]ʃi,æ·tik), *a.* 1631. [– L. *asiaticus* – Gr. ἀσιατικός; see -IC.] Of or pertaining to Asia or its inhabitants; formerly applied to literary style. As *sb.* A native of Asia. Hence **Asia·tically** *adv.* in A. manner, in accordance with A. customs. **Asia·ticism,** an A. phrase or practice. **Asia·ticize** *v.,* improp. **A·siatize,** to make A., to conform to A. customs.

It is A. prose, as the Ancient Critics would have said; prose somewhat barbarously rich M. ARNOLD.

Aside (ăsəi·d). [ME. *on syde, a syde*, i.e. ON, *prep.*, A *prep.*[1], SIDE *sb.*[1]] **A.** *adv.* **I.** Of motion. **1.** To one side; out of the way, away. **2.** Into seclusion or privacy, apart 1450. **3.** Away from one's person; off, down 1596. **4.** Out of thought or use 1440.

1. To..slip a. from difficulty BURKE. **2.** But soft, a.; heere comes the King *Haml.* v. i. 240. **3.** Let us lay a. every weight *Hebr.* 12:1. **4.** *To lay* or *set a.*: (*fig.*) to put away, dismiss; He often laid a. decorum 1798. *Law. To set a.* (a verdict, etc.): to quash it.

II. Of direction. **1.** Off from the direct line ME. **2.** Sidewise, obliquely ME.; var. † **Asi·den.**

1. They are all gone a., they are together become filthy *Ps.* 14:3.

III. Of position. † **1.** On one side, off –1610. **2.** Apart from the general company; in privacy ME. **3.** *A. from*: apart from. *U.S.* 1818.

2. *To speak a., i.e.* apart, so as to be (supposed) inaudible to the general company, or, on the stage, to the other players.

B. *prep.* [by omission of *of.*] **1.** At the side of 1615. † **2.** Past, beyond –1663.

C. *sb.* [the *adv.* used *attrib.*] **1.** Words spoken aside, or in an undertone, so as to be (supposed) inaudible to some person or persons present 1727. **2.** An indirect or side effort 1877.

2. The asides of many writers possess a more lasting..influence than their deliberate..labours 1877.

A-si·mmer, *adv.* 1849. [A *prep.*[1] 11.] On the simmer.

† **Asine·go.** 1606. [– Sp. *asnico*, dim. of *asno.*] **1.** A little ass –1685. **2.** A fool, dolt –1714.

2. An asinico may tutor thee; Thou..Asse SHAKS.

Asinine (æ·sinəin), *a.* 1610. [– L. *asininus*, f. *asinus* ass; see -INE[1].] **1.** Of or pertaining to asses 1624. **2.** Like an ass; obstinate, stupid 1610.

1. Her a. dayrie 1624. **2.** A. employ COWPER. Hence **Asini·nity,** stupidity.

Asiphonate (ăsəi·fəne[i]t), *a.* 1859. [f. A- *pref.* 14 + SIPHONATE.] *Zool.* Having no respiratory siphon. As *sb.* An acephalous mollusc so characterized.

-asis, *suff.*, L. *-ăsis*, Gr. *-ασις*, forming names of diseases, really nouns of state or process, as *elephantiasis, psoriasis*, etc.

‖ **Asitia** (ăsi·ʃ[i]ă). 1853. [mod.L. – Gr. *ἀσιτία* want of appetite, f. *ἀ-* A- *pref.* 14 + *σῖτος* food; see -IA[1].] *Path.* Loathing of food.

Ask (ɑsk), *v.* [OE. *āscian, ācsian, āhsian, āxian* = OFris. *āskia*, OS. *ēscon*, OHG. *eiscōn* :– WGmc. **aiskōjan*. The standard form *ask* resulted from metathesis of *aks-, ax* (now only *dial.*).] † **I.** *trans.* To call for – ME.

II. 1. To call upon for information or an answer: **a.** *trans.* With the thing asked as object OE.; † *at* (still *dial.*), † *to, of* a person ME.; **b.** With the person asked as object OE.; with the thing asked as second object OE.; *of* (arch.), *about* (a matter), *after* or *for* (a person) OE. **2.** With no object expressed: To inquire † *of, about, after* (a thing or person), *for* (a person) OE.

1. a. To a. what I wanted STEELE. To a. a question, the price, a name (*mod.*). A farmer of whom I asked the way 1888. **b.** Aske my dogge *Two Gent.* II. v. 36. Aske mee if I am a Courtier *All's Well* II. ii. 38. Aske him his name *Rich. II*, I. iii. 9. **2.** To ask *for* a person; to ask to see; formerly = to ask *after*. A. for this great Deliverer now, and find him Eyeless in Gaza at the Mill with slaves MILT. *Sams.* 40.

III. 1. To make request for: **a.** *trans.* With the thing asked as object; *simply* ME.; *of, from* a person ME.; *to do* or *be done to* ME.; **b.** *trans.* With the person asked as object ME.; *to do* or *for* (a thing) ME. **2.** To make request: With no object ME.; *for* (a thing) ME.

1. a. I axe no more 1570. *To a. a price*: to a. so much as the price. To a. another favour of [anyone] BURNS. **b.** I a. Mr. Blifil pardon FIELDING. I asked him to accompany me TYNDALL. I might aske you for your Commission *A.Y.L.* IV. i. 138. **2.** Aske and it shalbe giuen you *Matt.* 6:7. I'll ..a. for leave DICKENS. *To ask for*: to act so as to incur.

IV. Pregnant senses and special uses. † **1.** To investigate –1612. **2.** To ask as by right, call for, demand; *esp.* in *To ask an account* ME. **3.** To make proclamation in church, etc., calling on any who have claims or objections to put them forward; *esp.* in *To ask* (now *To publish*) *the banns* 1450. **4.** *ellipt.* To ask to come, invite 1834. **5.** *fig.* Predicated of things: Need, call for ME.

4. We ought to a. him to dinner 1888. **5.** To give a Milton birth ask'd ages more COWPER.

Ask (ɑsk), *sb.* ME. [app. worn down from OE. *āþexe* newt, cogn. w. OHG. *egidehsa* (G. *eidechse* lizard).] A newt or eft; *Sc.* and *north.* occ. also the lizard. See also ASKER[2].

Askance (ăskɑ·ns), *adv.* 1530. [Early forms *a scanche, a sca(u)nce*, suggest a Fr. origin; but cf. It. *a, di, per scancio* obliquely. The source remains unknown.] **1.** Sideways, askew, asquint; with a side meaning **2.** *ellipt.*, quasi-*adj.* Turned sideways 1593.

1. To look at, eye, view askance; to look at with disdain, envy, jealousy, and now *esp.* with mistrust. **2.** Whom the grand foe, with scornful eye a., Thus answerd MILT. *P.L.* VI. 149.

† **Aska·nce,** *v.* [f. prec.] To turn aside. SHAKS. *Lucr.* 637.

† **Aska·nce(s,** *conj. adv.* late ME. [Of unkn. origin; not rel. to ASKANCE.] **1.** As though –1580. **2.** *ellipt.* As if saying –1572.

Askant (ăskɑ·nt), *adv.* 1695. [Later var. of ASKANCE, perh. infl. by *asquint, aslant.*] = ASKANCE. ¶ In SHAKS. *Haml.* (Qos.) IV. vii. 167 *ascaunt* is read, but the folios have *aslant.*

† **A·skapart.** ME. Name of a race of warriors living near Arabia; also of a giant assailed by Sir Bevis of Southampton –1735.

Asker[1] (ɑ·skəɹ). ME. [f. ASK *v.* + -ER[1].] **1.** One who asks (questions, favours, gifts, alms, etc.). † **2.** A prosecutor; an exactor, oppressor –1483.

A·sker[2]. *dial.* 1674. [f. ASK *sb.*, with suff. of unkn. origin.] A newt.

Askew (ăskiū·). 1573. [f. A *prep.*[1] + SKEW *sb.*[2], *a.* and *adv.*] **A.** *adv.* Obliquely, to one side, awry. **B.** *adj.* Made or standing awry; skew 1859. **C.** † *sb.* A sidelong glance 1655.

adv. Lattice blinds all hanging a. DICKENS. *To look askew*: i.e. sidelong, out at the corners of one's eyes; *fig.* to look as if pretending not to see; to reflect *upon. adj.* A. arches 1859, bridges 1862.

Asking (ɑiskiŋ), *vbl. sb.* OE. [f. ASK *v.* + -ING[1].] **1.** The act of putting a question. † **b.** A question –ME. **2.** Praying, begging ME.; a petition, a prayer, etc. (*arch.*) ME. † **3.** A price asked –1637. † **4. a.** A calling for justice. **b.** Exaction. –1480. **5.** The publication of banns of marriage. *fam.* 1727. Hence **A·skingly** *adv.* **Askle·nt, ascle·nt** *adv.* Sc. f. ASLANT.

† **Askoye·, askoy·ne,** *adv.* ME. [Of unkn. origin; synon. w. ASKANCE, ASKEW.] Sidewise, askance. (Always with *look.*) –1552.

Aslake (ăslē[i]·k), *v.* [OE. *aslacian*; see A- *pref.* 1, SLAKE *v.*] † **1.** *intr.* To become slack; to grow less –1587. **2.** To cool (*arch. rare*) 1810. **3.** To mitigate, assuage, abate (*arch.*) ME.

Aslant (ăslɑ·nt). [ME. *o slant, on slent*; see A *prep.*[1], SLANT *sb.*[1]] *adv.* On the slant, in a sloping direction, obliquely. quasi-*adj.* Slanting 1790. *prep.* Across in a slanting direction 1602.

prep. There is a Willow growes a. a Brooke SHAKS.

Asleep (ăslī·p), *adv.* and *pred. a.* ME. [= OE. *on slæpe*; see A *prep.*[1] 11, SLEEP *sb.*] **1.** In a state of sleep; *fig.* at rest, dormant, idle 1590. **2.** Into a state of sleep ME.; *fig.* of inactivity or quiescence 1545. **3.** *fig.* Dead ME. **4.** *transf.* Of the limbs; Benumbed. Formerly also = Stunned. ME. **5.** *Naut.* The sail just bellying out (opp. to *flapping*) 1867.

1. *fig.* Their pride and mettall is asleepe SHAKS. **2.** By whispering winds soon lull'd a. MILT. *L'Allegro* 116. **3.** David..fell on sleepe and was laide vnto his fathers *Acts* 13:36. **4.** Leaning long upon any part maketh it numme, and, as we call it, asleepe BACON.

Aslope (ăslōᵘ·p), *a.* and *adv.* ME. [Earlier than SLOPE *sb.*[1], *v.* (*c*1600); of unc. origin.] *adj.* Inclined, slanting. *adv.* On the incline, aslant, crosswise, athwart. Also *fig.*

While the first drizzling show'r is borne a. SWIFT.

A-slu·g, *adv.* 1619. [A *prep.*[1] 11.] Sluggishly.

A-smea·r, *adv.* 1861. [A *prep.*[1] 11.] Smeared.

A-smou·lder, *adv.* 1880. [A *prep.*[1] 11.] Smouldering.

A-sno·rt, *adv.* 1850. [A *prep.*[1] 11.] Snorting.

A-soa·k, *adv.* 1609. [A *prep.*[1] 11.] Soaking.

Asomatous (ăsōᵘ·mătəs), *a.* 1731. [– late L. *asomatus* – Gr. *ἀσώματος* (f. *ἀ-* A- *pref.* 14 + *σῶμα, σωματ-* body) + -OUS.] Unembodied, incorporeal.

A-sou·th, *adv.* 1809. [A *prep.*[1] 5.] In the south.

Asp[1] (ɑsp). [OE. *æspe* = OHG. *aspa* :– Gmc. **aspōn*, and OE. *æps* (for **æsp*), ON. *ǫsp* :– Gmc. **aspō*. Superseded by ASPEN.] **1.** A poplar (*Populus tremula*), with greyish bark and spreading branches, the leaves of which are especially tremulous. Also *attrib.* **2.** The wood of this tree 1551.

1. Cherry and quaking a...belted the little brook 1848.

Asp[2] (ɑsp). ME. [– OFr. *aspe* or its source L. *aspis* (formerly used, with pl. *aspisses*) – Gr. *ἀσπίς, ἀσπιδ-*. See ASPIC[1].] *Zool.* **1.** A small, venomous, hooded serpent, found in Egypt and Libya; the *Naje Haje*. **2.** Also a species of Viper (*Vipera aspis*), and *poet.* any venomous serpent 1712.

1. The venym of eddris, *that ben clepid aspis*, vndur her lippis WYCLIF *Rom.* 3:13.

‖ **Aspalathus** (ăspæ·lăþŏs). 1601. [L. – Gr. *ἀσπάλαθος*.] A genus of African shrubs (N.O. *Leguminosæ*); the fragrant wood of some.

A sweete smell like cinamon, and a. *Ecclus.* 24:15.

‖ **Aspalax** (æ·spălæks). 1860. [L. – Gr. *ἀσπάλαξ*, also *σπάλαξ*.] *Zool.* A genus of Rodentia, resembling the mole.

Asparagine (ăspæ·radʒəin). 1813. [f. ASPARAGUS + -INE[5].] *Chem.* A nitrogenous crystallizable compound contained esp. in asparagus. It is primary malic diamide $C_4H_4O_3(NH_2)_2$.

Asparaginous (æspăræ·dʒinəs), *a.* 1832. [irreg. f. ASPARAGUS + -INE[1] + -OUS.] Allied to or like asparagus.

Asparagus (ăspæ·răgəs). OE. [– L. *asparagus* – Gr. *ἀσπάραγος*, Attic *ἀσφάραγος*. In polite use the L. form has supplanted the various altered or deriv. forms that have been current: (i) *sparagus*, a med.L. form, whence It. *sparagio*, G. *sparge(n, spargel*, Fr. † *esperage*, † *esparge* (mod. *asperge*), Eng. (ii) *a)sperage, sparage* (XV–XVII); (iii) *sparrow-grass* (XVII), *sparagras*, alt. of *sparagus* by assoc. with *grass*. 'The corruption of the word into *sparrow-grass* is so general that *asparagus* has an air of stiffness and pedantry' (Walker, 1791).] A plant (*Asparagus officinalis*, N.O. *Liliaceæ*), the vernal shoots of which form a delicacy of the table. *Bot.* The genus of which this is a species.

I will have Sparagus every meale all the yeare long BROME. A hundred of Sparrowgrass PEPYS. *Comb.* **a.-beetle,** a small beetle (*Crioceris asparagi*), that feeds upon the foliage of the a.

Aspara·mic, Aspa·ramide = ASPARTIC, ASPARAGINE.

A-spa·rkle, *adv.* 1840. [A *prep.*[1] 11.] Sparkling.

Aspartic (ăspā·ɹtik), *a.* 1847. [Formed arbitrarily, with regard mainly to euphony, on *asparagus*; see -IC.] *Chem.* Of or pertaining to asparagine; *esp.* in *Aspartic acid*, $C_4H_7NO_4$.

Aspect (æ·spekt). ME. [– L. *aspectus*, f. *aspect-*, pa. ppl. stem of *aspicere* look at, f. *a-* AD- + *specere* look.] **I. 1.** † The action of looking at; contemplation; gaze, view –1810; a look, a glance (also *fig.*) 1590. † **2.** Mental looking; regard, respect –1673.

1. That the basilisk killeth by a. BACON. Some other Mistresse hath thy sweet aspects *Com. Err.* II. ii. 113.

II. 1. *Astrol.* The relative positions of the planets as they appear to an observer on the earth's surface at a given time. (*prop.* The way in which, from their relative positions, they look upon each other.) ME. **2.** A looking, facing, or fronting, in a given direction; exposure 1667; the side or surface which fronts in any direction 1849. **3. Bearing;**

reference *to* 1509. **4.** A phase 1824. **5.** *Gram.* A verbal form used to express action or being in respect of its inception, duration, or completion 1853.

1. Frendly aspectys of planetes CHAUCER. Aspects In Sextile, Square, and Trine, and Opposite MILT. *P.L.* x. 658. **2.** The setting Sun.. with right a. Against the eastern Gate of Paradise MILT. *P.L.* IV. 541. **3.** Divers things..which I hope have a public a. CROMWELL. **4.** Two aspects of one..thought 1870.

III. 1. The look which one wears; countenance, face 1590. **2.** The appearance presented to the eye 1594; to the mind 1704. † **3.** *concr.* A thing seen; an appearance –1722.

1. Thy martial face and stout aspect MARLOWE. Of..vinegar a. SHAKS. **2.** The physical a. of the country GREEN. The superficial aspects of Buddhism 1883. Hence **Aspe·ctable, -ible** *a.* (now *rare*), visible; fit or fair to look upon. † **Aspe·ctful** *a.* benignant.

† **Aspe·ct,** *v.* 1548. [– L. *aspectare*, frequent. of *aspicere* (see prec.). Cf. *respect, suspect.*] **1.** To look for, expect –1584. **2.** To look at, behold; watch –1698. **3.** Of a planet: To look upon another in one of the 'Aspects' –1671. **4.** To look on with favour (*rare*) 1663. **5.** *intr.* To look; to have a bearing –1651. Hence **Aspe·ctant** *a. Her.* facing each other. **A·spected** *ppl. a.* † **1.** (*aspe·cted*). Looked at. † **2.** *pple.* or *adj.* Looked at by a planet. **3.** *adj.* Having an aspect.

† **Aspe·ction.** 1646. [– L. *aspectio*, f. *aspect-*; see prec., -ION. Cf. OFr. *aspection.*] The act of looking at, watching –1652.

Aspen (a·spĕn). ME. [f. ASP[1] + -EN[4].] *adj.* **1.** Of or belonging to the asp; see ASP[1]. **2.** *fig.* Tremulous; timorous ME. *sb.* = ASP[1] 1596.

1. Lyk an a. leaf he quok for ire CHAUCER. **2.** A. fear CHAPMAN

† **A·sper, a·spre,** *a.* ME. [– OFr. *aspre* (mod. *âpre*) :– L. *asper* rough, harsh.] **1.** Rough, rugged –1681. **2.** Harsh in sound or taste –1639. **3.** Harsh to the feelings; cruel –1578. **4.** Of persons: Harsh –1630. **5.** Hardy; mettled, savage –1503.

‖ **Asper** (æ·spəɹ), *sb.*[1] [L. *asper* (sc. *spiritus*); see prec.] *Gr. Gram.* The rough breathing; the sign (ʽ) above an initial vowel, or over ρ, = Roman *h*; thus ὡς = *hōs*, ῥάβδος = *rhabdos*.

Asper (æ·spəɹ), *sb.*[2] 1589. [– Fr. *aspre*, app. – Turk. – med. Gr. ἄσπρον – L. *asper* (*nummus*) newly minted (coin).] A silver Turkish coin (120 aspers = 1 piastre); now a 'money of account'.

Asperate (æ·spĕrĕt), *ppl. a.* 1623. [– L. *asperatus*, pa. pple. of *asperare*, f. *asper* rough; see -ATE[2].] Roughened, rough. Hence **A·sperate** *v.* to make rough, rugged, or harsh.

Asperge (ăspə̄·ɹdʒ), *v.* 1547. [– Fr. *asperger* or L. *aspergere*, f. *ad* AS-[1] + *spargere* sprinkle.] To sprinkle, besprinkle.

Asperges (ăspə̄·ɹdʒīz). *Liturg.* First word of *Asperges me hyssopo et mundabor*, Thou shalt purge me with hyssop and I shall be clean (*Ps.* 50 (51): 9), the recitation of which accompanies the sprinkling of altar and people with holy water before the principal Mass on Sundays, used for the ceremony.

Aspergill (æ·spəɹdʒil). Also ‖**Aspergillum** (æspəɹdʒi·lŏm). 1649. [mod.L. *aspergillum*, f. L. *aspergere* (see ASPERGE *v.*) + *-illum* dim. suffix as in *vexillum.*] *R.C.Ch.* A kind of brush used to sprinkle holy water; see ASPERGES. (The L. form is the more usual.) Hence **Aspergi·lliform** *a.* shaped like an a., as the stigmas of some grasses.

‖ **Aspergi·llus.** 1847. [See prec.] *Biol.* A genus of microscopic fungi, resembling the holy-water sprinkler in appearance.

Asperifoliate, -ous (æ:spĕrifōᵘ·liĕt, -liəs), *a.* 1686. [f. mod.L. *asperifolius* (f. *asper* + *folium* leaf) + -ATE[2], -OUS.] *Bot.* Having rough leaves, formerly *spec.* of the *Boragineæ*.

Asperity (ăspe·riti). [– (O)Fr. *aspérité* or L. *asperitas*, f. *asper* rough; see -ITY.] **1.** Unevenness of surface, roughness; *concr.* in *pl.* sharp or rough excrescences 1491. **2.** Roughness of savour, tartness (*arch.*) 1620. **3.** Harshness of sound (*arch.*) 1664. **4.** Of style: Lack of polish, ruggedness (*arch.*) 1779. **5.** *fig.* Harshness to the feelings; *hence*, hardship, difficulty. (The earliest sense; *arch.* exc. in **b.** Bitter coldness, rigour.) ME. **6.** Harshness of temper; crabbedness, acrimony; in *pl.* harsh, embittered feelings 1664.

1. The asperities of the Moon HY. MORE. **3.** Our language, of which the chief defect is ruggedness and a. JOHNSON. **5.** The nakedness and a. of the wintry world JOHNSON. **6.** A. of reply JOHNSON.

† **A·sperly,** *adv.* ME. [f. ASPER *a.* + -LY[2].] Harshly; fiercely, bitterly –1531.

Aspermous (ăspə̄·ɹməs), *a.* 1853. [f. Gr. ἄσπερμος (f. ἀ- A- *pref.* 14 + σπέρμα seed) + -OUS.] *Bot.* and *Phys.* Without seed. var. **Aspe·rmatous.** Hence **Aspe·rmatism,** lack of seed, impotence.

† **Aspe·rn(e,** *v. rare.* 1513. [– L. *aspernari*, f. *a* = *ab* away from + *spernari* despise.] To spurn.

† **A·sperness.** [f. ASPER *a.* + -NESS.] Bitterness. CHAUCER.

A·sperous, *a.* 1547. [– late L. *asperosus*, f. *asper* rough; see -OUS.] **1.** Rough, rugged. (Now techn.) † **2.** Rough-tasted 1670. † **3.** Harsh –1653. Hence **A·sperously** *adv.* (*rare*).

Asperse (ăspə̄·ɹs), *v.* 1490. [– *aspers-*, pa. ppl. stem of L. *aspergere*; see ASPERGE.] **1.** To besprinkle, bespatter *with*. **2.** To sprinkle, scatter 1607. † **3.** To intermingle –1607. **4.** To bespatter *with* damaging imputations, etc. In 17th c.: Injuriously and falsely to charge *with*. 1611. **5.** To slander, defame, traduce, vilify 1647.

1. She dide a. the place with the waters CAXTON. **4.** The calumnies with which the Jews had aspersed him PALEY. **5.** A libel tending to a. or vilify the house of Commons 'JUNIUS'. To a. a man's character 1868. Hence **Aspe·rsed** *ppl. a.* **1.** Besprinkled; *spec.* in *Her.* strewed or powdered with small charges. **2.** Calumniated, defamed. † **Aspe·rsive** *a.* defamatory † **-ly** *adv.*

Aspersion (ăspə̄·ɹʃən). 1553. [– L. *aspersio*, f. *aspers-*; see prec., -ION. Cf. (O)Fr. *aspersion.*] **1.** The action of besprinkling, or of sprinkling or scattering. **2.** That which is sprinkled 1610. **3.** The action of casting damaging imputations, or false and injurious charges; defamation 1633. **4.** A damaging report; a calumny, slander 1596.

1. A. may answer the true end of baptism BURNET. **3.** Who by aspersions throw a stone At the head of others, hit their own G. HERBERT. **4.** The a. of his being a great usurer FULLER.

‖ **Aspersoir** (asperswar). 1851. [Fr.; see next.] An aspergillum.

‖ **Aspersorium** (æspəɹsōᵊ·riŏm). 1861. [med.L.: see ASPERSE, -ORIUM.] A vessel for holding the holy water used in ceremonial sprinkling.

Asphalt (æ·sfælt, æsfæ·lt). Also **asphaltum,** esp. in scientific use. [ME. *aspaltoun*, *aspalt* – OFr.; *aspallto* (XVI) – It. *aspalto*; later the Gr. and L. forms were used; in recent times *asphalt(e* – Fr. *asphalte* (XVI), ult. – late L. *asphalton*, *-um* – Gr. ἄσφαλτον, *-os* of alien origin.] **1.** A smooth, hard, brittle, black or brownish-black resinous mineral consisting of a mixture of different hydrocarbons; called also *mineral pitch, Jews' pitch*, and in the O.T. *slime* ME. Also *attrib.* **2.** A composition of bitumen, pitch, and sand, or made from natural bituminous limestones, used to pave streets and walks, etc. Mostly *attrib.* 1847.

1. Cressets fed With Naphtha and Asphaltus MILT. *P.L.* I. 729. A whole lake of a. is said to exist in..Trinidad KIRWAN. **2.** *Artificial asphaltum*: a mixture of coal-tar with sand, chalk, or lime. Hence **Aspha·lt** *v.* to cover or lay with a. **Aspha·lter,** one who lays down a. **Aspha·ltic** *a.* of the nature of, or containing, a., as in *Asphaltic Pool*: the Dead Sea MILT. **Aspha·ltite** *a.* asphaltic.

Asphaltene (æ:sfæltīn). 1837. [– Fr. *asphaltène*, f. *asphalte* (prec.); see -ENE.] *Chem.* An oxygenated hydro-carbon, supposed to be the solid constituent of asphalt.

Asphe·terism. 1794. [f. Gr. ἀ A- *pref.* 14 + σφέτερος, after σφετερισμός.] The doctrine that there ought to be no private property; communism. **Asphe·terize** *v.* to practise aspheterism (*rare*).

Asphodel (æ·sfodĕl). 1597. [– L. *asphodilus*, *-elus* – Gr. ἀσφόδελος; see AFFODILL, DAFFODIL.] *Bot.* **1.** A genus of liliaceous plants, including the White Asphodel or King's Spear. **b.** By the poets made an immortal flower, and said to cover the Elysian meads. (Cf. Homer *Odyss.* XI. 539.) 1634. *attrib.* (occ. = 'Elysian'.) 1831. **2.** With qualifications: **a.** Bog, English, or Lancashire A. (*Narthecium ossifragum*), common on moorlands. **b.** False A., in America, a species of Tofieldia. **c.** Scotch A. (*Tofieldia palustris*), a British subalpine plant.

1. b. The dead are made to eat Asphodels about the Elysian meadows SIR T. BROWNE. The a. meadows of their youth RUSKIN. Hence **Asphode·lian** *a.*

‖ **Asphyxia** (æsfi·ksiă). 1706. [mod.L. – Gr. ἀσφυξία, f. ἀ- A- *pref.* 14 + σφύξις pulsation; see -IA[1]; cf. SPHYGMO-.] **1.** *lit.* Stoppage of the pulse. **2.** The condition of suspended animation produced by a deficiency of oxygen in the blood; suffocation. Also *fig.* 1778.

2. Lingering a. of soul O. W. HOLMES. Hence **Asphy·xial** *a.* of, pertaining to, or characterized by, a.

Asphyxiate (æsfi·ksi,eⁱt), *v.* 1836. [f. prec. + -ATE[3].] To affect with asphyxia, to suffocate. Hence **Asphy:xia·tion,** the action of producing asphyxia, or condition of being asphyxiated.

Asphyxiator (æsfi·ksi,eⁱtəɹ). 1882. [f. prec. + -OR 2.] An asphyxiating agent; an apparatus for extinguishing fire by the agency of carbonic acid gas, etc.

Asphyxy (æsfi·ksi). 1784. [– Fr. *asphyxie*; see ASPHYXIA, -Y[3].] = ASPHYXIA. Hence **Asphyxy** *v.* to asphyxiate. (Chiefly in pa. pple.)

Aspic[1] (æspik). 1530. [– (O)Fr. *aspic*, var. of OFr. *aspide* (see ASP[2]), prob. infl. by *piquer* to sting.] **1.** By-form of ASP[2], chiefly *poet.* Also *attrib.* Also *fig.* 1649. **2.** *transf.* A piece of ordnance which carries a 12-pound shot. (? Fr.)

1. Showing the aspic's bite TENNYSON. A. poison LAMB. The Aspicke of invadeing feare 1649.

Aspic[2] (æ·spik). 1604. [– Fr. *aspic* (XVI) – Pr. *aspic*, *espic* – med.L. (*lavandula*) *spica*; see SPICA.] The Great Lavender or Spike (*Lavandula spica*).

Aspic[3] (æ·spik). 1789. [– Fr. *aspic* (XVIII), a use of *aspic* serpent (see ASPIC[1]), due to comparison of the various colours of the jelly with those of the serpent.] A savoury meat jelly, made of and containing meat, fish, game, hard-boiled eggs, etc. Also *attrib.*

Aspidistra (æspidi·stră). 1822. [mod.L., f. Gr. ἀσπίς, ἀσπιδ- shield, (with ref. to the shape of the leaves) + *-istra*, after *Tupistra.*] A plant of the liliaceous genus so named (of China and Japan), kept in dwelling rooms.

Aspirant (ăspəiᵊ·rănt, *occas.* æ·spirănt). 1738. [– Fr. *aspirant* or L. *aspirant-*, pres. ppl. stem of *aspirare*; see ASPIRE *v.*, -ANT.] *adj.* = ASPIRING 1814. *sb.* One who aspires; one who, with steady purpose, seeks advancement, privilege, or advantage 1738.

sb. The way to greatness was left clear to a new set of aspirants MACAULAY. The A. to the Mysteries WARBURTON.

Aspirate (æ·spirĕt). 1669. [– L. *aspiratus*, pa. pple. of *aspirare*; see ASPIRE *v.*, -ATE[1], -ATE[2].] **A.** *ppl. adj.* Aspirated.

B. *sb.* **1.** A consonantal sound which is followed by or blended with the sound of H 1727. **2.** The simple sound of the letter H, or its equivalent the *spiritus asper* (ʽ). *Esp.* applied to the initial *h-*. 1725.

1. That the aspirates [in Sanskrit]..are real mutes or contact sounds..is beyond question WHITNEY. **2.** A Middlemarch mercer of polite manners and superfluous aspirates GEO. ELIOT.

Aspirate (æ·spireⁱt), *v.* 1700. [– *aspirat-*, pa. ppl. stem of L. *aspirare*; see ASPIRE *v.*, -ATE[3].] **1.** To pronounce with a breathing; to prefix H to a vowel, or add H or its supposed equivalent to a consonant sound. Also *absol.* **2.** To draw out a gas or vapour from a vessel; cf. ASPIRATOR 1880.

1. Our *w* and *h* aspirate DRYDEN. ¶ Erron. *asperate*, after *spiritus asper*.

Aspiration (æspireⁱ·ʃən). ME. [– (O)Fr. *aspiration* – L. *aspiratio*, f. as prec.; see -ION.] **I.** (From ASPIRE.) † **1.** Inspiration –1535. **2.** The action of breathing; a breath, sigh. *techn.* The drawing in of air in, or as in, breathing. 1607. **3.** The action of aspiring; steadfast desire for something above one 1606.

3. That spirit of his In a. lifts him from the earth *Tr. & Cr.* IV. v. 16.

II. (From ASPIRATE.) **1.** The action of aspirating; see ASPIRATE *v.* ME. **2.** An aspirated sound or letter; the letter H or its equivalent; the breathings (ʽ) and (ʼ) in Greek; = ASPIRATE *sb.* 1550.

2. What is no substantial letter but a bare a. FULLER. ¶ Erron. *asperation*; see prec. ¶.

Aspirator (æ·spireⁱtəɹ). 1863. [f. ASPIRATE *v.* + -OR 2.] He who or that which aspirates, breathes, or blows upon; *spec.* **a.** an apparatus for drawing a stream of air or gas through a tube; **b.** an instrument for evacuating pus from abscesses by means of an exhausted receiver; **c.** a kind of winnowing machine. Hence **Aspi·ratory** *a.* of or pertaining to aspiration (*rare*).

Aspire (ăspəiᵊ·r), *v.* 1460. [– (O)Fr. *aspirer* or L. *aspirare* breathe upon, have an ambition, etc., f. *ad* AS-¹ + *spirare* breathe.] † **1.** *trans.* To breathe *to* or *into*, to inspire –1633; *intr.* to exhale (*rare*) –1750. **2.** *intr.* To have a fixed desire or ambition for something at present above one; to seek to attain, to pant, long. Const. *to*; *after, at*, † *for*; with *inf.*; *absol.* 1460. † *trans.* To be ambitious of, aim at –1816. **3.** *intr.* To rise up, as smoke, etc.; hence *gen.* to mount up, tower, rise high, become tall. Also *fig.* 1585. † *trans.* To mount up to, reach, attain. Also *fig.* –1596.

2. Woman oght to be repressed. . if she a. tc any dominion KNOX. Wilt thou a. to guide the heauenly Car *Two Gent.* III. i. 153. **3.** Orgilio sees the golden pile a. JOHNSON. *trans.* That gallant spirit hath aspir'd the clouds *Rom. & Jul.* III. i. 122.

Aspirin (æ·spirin). 1899. [– G., orig. tradename, f. *a(cetylirte* acetylated + *Spir(säure* spiræic (= salicylic) acid + -IN.¹] Acetylsalicylic acid, used as an analgesic and antipyretic; an aspirin tablet.

Aspiring (aspəiᵊ·riŋ). 1565. [f. ASPIRE *v.* + -ING¹, -ING².] *vbl. sb.* Aspiration 1584; † upward tapering 1634. *ppl. a.* **1.** Of lofty aim, ambitious 1577. **2.** Rising, tapering upward 1565. *fig.* 1579.

1. Two able and a. prelates MACAULAY. Hence **-ly** *adv.*, **-ness.**

A·spish, *a.* 1608. [f. ASP² + -ISH¹.] Of or pertaining to asps.

Asplenium, *Bot.*; see SPLEENWORT.

Asport (æspōᵊ·rt), *v.* 1621. [– L. *asportare* carry away, f. *as-* = *abs-* = *ab-* + *portare* carry.] To carry away, remove feloniously.

Asportation (æspoɹtēⁱ·ʃən). 1502. [– L. *asportatio*; see prec., -ATION.] The action of carrying off; in *Law*, felonious removal of property.

A-spou·t, *adv.* 1870. [A *prep.*¹ 11.] Spouting.

A-spraw·l, *adv.* 1878. [A *prep.*¹ 11.] Sprawling.

A-sprea·d, *adv.* 1879. [A *prep.*¹ 11.] Spread out.

Asprete, obs. f. ASPERITY.

A-sprou·t, *adv.* 1880. [A *prep.*¹ 11.] Sprouting.

† **Aspy·,** *sb.* ME. [– AFr. **aspier* = OFr. *espier*; see ESPY *sb.*] = SPY *sb.* –1467.

A-squa·t, *adv.* 1748. [A *prep.*¹ 11.] Squatting.

Asquint (ăskwi·nt), *adv.* (and *a.*). ME. [Perh. f. A- *pref.* 11 + a LG. or Du. form now repr. by Du. *schuinte* obliquity, slant, f. *schuin* oblique, = Fris., LG. *schüns.* The source of SQUINT *v.*] **1.** (To look) to one side; obliquely, out at the corners of the eyes ME. Also *transf.* and *fig.* **2.** (To look) with suspicion, askance (*arch.*) ME.; with bias (*arch.*) 1605; furtively (*arch.*) 1727; † to cast a passing glance –1650. **3.** *esp.* (To look) obliquely through defect in the eyes, so that they look in different directions ME. Also *fig.* **4.** With other verbs (*rare*). Off to one side. ? *Obs.* 1645. **5.** quasi-*adj.* (Only in pred. or after the sb. *eye.*) 1643.

A-squi·rm, *adv.* 1866. [A *prep.*¹ 11.] Squirming (U.S.).

Ass (æs). [OE. *assa, asa* – OCelt. **as(s)in* (W. *asyn* = MIr. *assan*, Corn. *asen*, Bret. *azen*) – L. *asinus.*] **1.** A quadruped of the horse kind, but smaller, with long ears, tuft at end of tail, and black stripe across the shoulders. Called also *donkey* in familiar use (in Scotland *cuddie*). **b.** *fig.* 'Beast of burden' 1614. **c.** In fables and proverbs, the type of clumsiness, ignorance, and stupidity. **2.** Hence *transf.* An ignorant fellow, a conceited dolt 1578.

1. He shall but beare them, as the Asse beares Gold *Jul. C.* IV. i. 21. A braying a. COWPER. **c.** An unlettered king is a crowned a. FREEMAN.

Phrases: **1.** *To make an ass of*: to treat as an ass, stultify. *To make an ass of oneself*: to behave absurdly. **2.** *Asses' Bridge* or *Pons Asinorum*: a name given to the fifth proposition of the first book of Euclid's Elements. **3.** *Astr.* The *Two Asses*: the stars γ and δ of the constellation Cancer, on either side of the nebula *Præsepe* (the *Crib*).

Ass, *v. nonce-wd.* To call ass 1592; to act the ass 1647.

Assafœtida, var. of ASAFŒTIDA.

Assagai, assegai (æ·săgai). 1625. [– Fr. † *azagaie* (Rabelais; mod. *zagaie, sagaie*) or its source Pg. *azagaia* (Sp. *-aya*) – Arab. *az-zaġāyah*, i.e. AL-², *zaġāyah*, Berber word for spear. Cf. ARCHEGAYE.] A slender spear or lance of hard wood, usu. pointed with iron, used in battle. Orig. the native name of a Berber weapon adopted by the Moors; in English use commonly the missile weapon of the South African tribes. **b.** *attrib.* **Assagai tree, wood,** a large South African tree (*Curtisia faginea*, N.O. *Cornaceæ*). Hence **A·ssagai, asse-** *v.* to pierce with an a.

‖ **Assai** (assāi·), *adv.* [It.] *Mus.* A direction: Very: as in *adagio assai* = very slow.

Assail (ăsēⁱ·l), *v.* [ME. *asaile, ass-* – *asaill-*, tonic stem of OFr. *asalir* (mod. *assaillir*) :– med.L. *assalire* (f. L. *assilire*), f. *ad* AS-¹ + *salire* to leap.] To leap upon or at. **1.** To attack **a.** by physical means; **b.** with hostile action or influence 1564; **c.** by speech or writing 1593. **2.** To address with reasoning or argument 1440. **3.** To approach with the intention of mastering (anything arduous) 1680. *fig.* Of states physical, emotional, or mental ME. **4.** Of things: To dash against, encounter 1667. † **5.** To tempt, try –1564; to woo –1611. **6.** *absol.* quasi-*intr.* in prec. senses ME. † **7.** To venture on, ASSAY –1595; *intr.* to endeavour, ASSAY –1606.

1. To a. one another like brute Beasts STEELE. **b.** Virtue may be assail'd, but never hurt MILT. *Comus* 589. Let crowds of Critics now my verse a. POPE. She assailed her husband on the subject of taking work 1833. **3.** New pangs of mortal fear our minds a. DRYDEN. **4.** No rude noise mine ears assailing COWPER. **5.** Beauteous thou art, therefore to be assail'd SHAKS. *Sonn.* xli. **6.** Though troubles a. NEWTON. Hence **Assai·l** *sb.* assault (*arch.*). **Assai·lable** *a.* open to assault, or hostile criticism. †**Assai·lableness. Assai·ler,** one who assails. **Assai·lment,** the action of assailing; power of assailing.

Assailant (ăsēⁱ·lănt). 1532. [f. after Fr. *assaillant*; see prec., -ANT.] *adj.* Assailing (*arch.*) 1592. *sb.* **1.** He who, or that which, assails or attacks 1532. **2.** A hostile critic 1665.

1. So shall we passe along, And neuer stir assailants SHAKS. **2.** The assailants of the syllogism MILL.

Assamar (æ·sămāɹ). 1863. [f. L. *assum* roast + *amarus* bitter.] *Chem.* Reichenbach's name for the bitter substance produced when gum, sugar, starch, gluten, meat, bread, etc., are roasted in the air till they turn brown.

Assapanick. 1706. [Amer. Ind.] *Zool.* The flying squirrel of Virginia and Maryland.

Assart (ăsā·ɹt), *v.* 1523. [– AFr. *assarter, -ier, -ir*, OFr. *essarter* :– med.L. *ex(s)artare*, f. *ex* EX-¹ + *sart-* (as in L. *sartura* for *sarritura* weeding), pa. ppl. stem of *sar(r)ire* to hoe, weed. See ESSART.] *Law.* To grub up trees and bushes from forest-land, so as to make it arable. Also *absol.*

Assart (ăsā·ɹt), *sb.* 1598. [– AFr. *assart*, f. the vb. See ESSART.] **1.** A piece of land converted into arable by assarting 1628. **2.** The action of assarting 1598. Also *attrib.* So † **Assa·rtment.**

A·ssary. 1727. [– Gr. ἀσσάριον, or L. *assarius* = AS.] A Roman copper coin, translated by 'farthing' in N.T.

Assassin (ăsæ·sin). 1531. [– Fr. *assassin* or med.L. *assassinus* – Arab. *ḥaššāš*in, acc. pl. of *ḥaššāš* hashish-eater. For the adoption of the pl. form cf. *Bedouin.*] **1.** *lit.* A hashish-eater, *Hist.* (in *pl.*) Certain Moslem fanatics in the time of the Crusades, who were sent forth by their Sheikh, the 'Old Man of the Mountains', to murder the Christian leaders 1603. **2.** Hence: One who undertakes to put another to death by treacherous violence. (Used chiefly of the murderer of a public personage.) 1531. Also *fig.* Also *attrib.*

1. The assassins. . before they attacked an enemy, would intoxicate themselves with. . an inebriating electuary, called *hashish* J. WOLFF. **2.** *fig.* Lord Byron was the a. of his own fame DIBDIN. *attrib.* The a. spear DISRAELI. var. †**Assa·ssinant.**

† **Assa·ssin(e,** *v.* 1647. [– Fr. *assassiner*; see prec.] To assassinate. Also *fig.* –1788.

† **Assa·ssinate,** *sb.* 1600. [In sense 1, app. – Fr. *assassinat* – med.L. *assassinatus*; sense 2 is unexplained.] **1.** Assassination. Also *fig.* –1755. **2.** = ASSASSIN 2. Also *fig.* –1737.

Assassinate (ăsæ·sineⁱt), *v.* 1618. [– *assassinat-*, pa. ppl. stem of med.L. *assassinare*; see ASSASSIN, -ATE³.] **1.** To kill by treacherous violence. Also *absol.* † **2.** To attack by an assassin –1706. **3.** *fig.* To destroy or wound by treachery 1626.

1. Brutus and Cassius. . conspired to a. him 1618. **3.** Your rhimes a. our fame DRYDEN. Hence †**Assa·ssinacy,** assassination. **Assa·ssinative** *a.* disposed to a. (*rare*). **Assa·ssinator,** an assassin. **Assa·ssinatress,** a female assassin. †**Assa·ssinous** *a.* of the nature of assassins MILT.

Assassination (ăsæ:sinēⁱ·ʃən). 1605. [f. as prec.; see -ION.] The action of assassinating; the taking the life of any one by treacherous violence, *esp.* by a hired emissary or volunteer. Also *fig.*

If th' A. Could trammell vp the Consequence, and catch With his surcease, Successe *Macb.* I. vii. 2.

Assa·tion. ?*Obs.* 1605. [– Fr. *assation* or med.L. *assatio*, f. *assat-*, pa. ppl. stem of late L. *assare*, f. L. *assum* roast; see -ION.] Roasting or baking.

Assault (ăsǭ·lt), *sb.* [ME. *asaut* – OFr. *asaut* (mod. *assaut*) :– Rom. **assaltus* (for L. *assultus*), f. **assalire* ASSAIL. Spelt with *l* from XV.] **1.** *gen.* An onset with hostile intent; an attack with blows or weapons. **2.** The sudden charge of an attacking force against the walls of a city or fortress; a storm ME. **3.** An unlawful attack upon the person of another. (In *Law* a menacing word or action may constitute an *assault*; the term *battery* being added when an actual blow is inflicted.) 1447. **4.** An attack upon institutions, opinions, or customs 1449. **5.** *transf.* and *fig.* 1508. **6.** *esp.* An attack by spiritual enemies. (The earliest use in Eng.) ME. † **7.** A wooing –1611.

1. In which a., we lost twelue hundred men SHAKS. **Assault (of** or **at arms)**: an attack made upon each other by two fencers, etc., as an exercise or trial of skill; a display of hand-to-hand military exercises. **2.** *To make, give, a., to win, gain, take, carry by a.* **3.** If one lifts up his cane, or his fist, in a threatning manner at another; or strikes at him, but misses him; this is an a. BLACKSTONE. **4.** Assaults upon the prerogative of parliament CLARENDON. **5.** The sharpe assautes of deth FISHER. **7.** Inuincible against all assaults of affection *Much Ado* II. iii. 120.

Assault (ăsǭ·lt), *v.* 1450. [Earlier *assawte* – OFr. *assauter* :– Rom. **assaltare* (for L. *assultare*), f. *ad* AS-¹ + *saltare*, frequent. of *salire* leap. Spelt with *l* from XVI.] **1.** To make a violent hostile attack by physical means upon; to commit an assault upon the person of (see ASSAULT *sb.* 3). Also *fig.* or *transf.* **2.** = ASSAIL *v.* 3. (*arch.* or *Obs.*) 1551. **3.** = ASSAIL *v.* 5. 1667. **4.** To come upon, attack, invade, as disease. (*arch.* or *Obs.*) 1594. **5.** To tempt, try. (*arch.* or *Obs.*) 1529. **6.** *absol.* chiefly in sense 1. 1489.

1. Naked as I am I will a. thee *Oth.* V. ii. 258. Assaulting the constable DE FOE. *To a. a city* or *fortress*: to storm it. **5.** Satan ceaseth not to a. our faith ABP. SANDYS. Hence **Assau·ltable** *a.* **Assau·lter.**

† **Assau·t,** *adv.* (*adj.*) ME. [– Fr. *à saut.*] In phr. *To go* or *be assau(l)t*: to seek the male, to rut –1601.

Assay (ăsēⁱ), *sb.* Also aphet. SAY, and refash. ESSAY, q.v. ME. [– OFr. *assai, assay*, var. of *essai*; see ESSAY *sb.* Aphet. SAY *sb.*²] **1.** The trying, in order to test the virtue, fitness, etc. (of a person or thing). *Obs.* exc. as fig. of 3. † **2.** 'Trial', tribulation –1671; experiment –1768; experience ME. only. **3.** *spec.* The trial of metals, by touch, fire, etc.; the determination of the quantity of metal in an ore or alloy; or of the fineness of coin or bullion ME. **4.** The substance to be assayed 1837. **5.** The trial of weights, measures, quality of bread, etc., by legal standard. Now *Hist.* 1601. **6.** Tasting (*arch.*) 1477; † *fig.* a foretaste –1605. **7.** The act of tasting the food or drink before giving it to an exalted personage. Now *Hist.* 1547. **8.** An endeavour (*arch.*) ME.; † best effort –1797. † **9.** An assault –1705; a first tentative effort –1677; a sample –1675. **10.** † **a.** Approved quality, proof, etc., of metal, etc. –1596. **b.** Standard of fineness in the precious metals 1820.

1. A great a. of the human soul RUSKIN. **2.** My way must lie Through many a hard a. MILT. *P.R.* I. 263. **7.** *Cup of assay*: a small cup with which a. of wine, etc., was taken. **8.** A. of disobedience BACON. **9.** Galling the gleaned Land with hot Assayes SHAKS.

Phr.: **At all assays.** (Also *at all, every, assay.*) † At every trial, or time of need; hence: At all events; always –1658. † (Armed, ready) *at all assays*: ready for every event –1603. *Comb.*: **a.-master,** the master of an assay-house; **-ton,** a weight of 29166⅔ milligrams.

Assay (ăsēⁱ·), *v.* ME. [– OFr. *assaier*, var. of (O)Fr. *essayer*; see ESSAY *v.*] **1.** To put to the proof, try; to test. *Obs.* exc. as fig. of 3. † *intr.* To make trial (*of*) –1576. † **2.** To try by touch (*lit.* and *fig.*) ME. **3.** To make an assay (see ASSAY *sb.* 3) 1440. Also *fig.* **4.** With *of.* To try by tasting; *spec.* to taste first (see ASSAY *sb.* 7). Now *Hist.* ME. † **5.** To practise by way of trial –1725. † **6.** To examine for the sake of information –1622; to inquire –1664; to learn or know by experience –1597. † **7.** To try with afflictions –1596, temptations –1614, force –1676. † **8.** To assail with words, or arguments –1603; with love-proposals –1598. **9.** To attempt, try to do ME.; *intr.* † to set oneself (*to do*) –1669; to do one's best, endeavour ME.; † to venture –1678.

1. I shall. .his strength as oft a. MILT. *P.R.* II. 233. **2.** Crist .bad him [Seynt Thomas] assaye his woundes ME. **3.** To a. it for lead 1818. **5.** Let him tempt and now a. His utmost subtlety MILT. *P.R.* I. 143. **9.** The King's strength was failing, but he assayed to show himself in the usual kingly state FREEMAN. Hence **Assay·able** *a.* **Assay·ing** *vbl. sb.* the action of proving or trying; *spec.* the trial of metals; † *Mus.* a preliminary flourish.

Assayer (ăsēⁱ·ər). ME. [– AFr. *assaior, -our*, f. *assayer* ASSAY *v.*] **1.** One who tries, or finds out by trial. **2.** One who assays metals 1618. **3.** An officer who tastes food before it is served to a prince or lord (L. *prægustator*). (In this sense prob. confused with ASSEOUR, 'he who sets the table'.) ME.

† **Assea·l,** *v.* ME. [ME. *asele* – OFr. *enseeler*: see A- *pref.* 10, ENSEAL. Later assim. to SEAL *sb.*², *v.*¹] To set one's seal to –1492; to seal up. Also *fig.* ME. only.

† **Assecu·re,** *v.* 1594. [– med.L. *assecurare*, f. L. *as-* = *ad-* + *securus* SECURE.] To make secure; to assure –1597. Hence † **Assecu·rance.** † **Assecura·tion.**

† **Assecu·tion.** 1630. [f. *assecut-*, pa. ppl. stem of L. *assequi* obtain; see -ION. Cf. OFr. *assecucion.*] The action of obtaining, acquirement –1726.

Assegai, var. of ASSAGAI.

† **Assei·ze,** *v. rare.* [f. AS- *pref.*¹ + SEIZE.] To seize. MARLOWE.

Asself (ăse·lf), *v.* 1632. [irreg. f. AS- *pref.*¹ + SELF.] To take to oneself, appropriate.

Assemblage (ăse·mblėdʒ). 1704. [f. ASSEMBLE *v.*¹ + -AGE, partly through Fr. *assemblage.*] **1.** A bringing or coming together; the state of being collected 1730. **2.** The joining of two things. *Obs.* exc. in *Carpentry.* 1727. **3.** A number of persons gathered together. (Less formal than *assembly.*) 1741. **4.** A collection of things 1704.

1. The first a. of the thegns at York FREEMAN. **3.** An a. of all ages and nations H. WALPOLE. **4.** An a. of bare poles 1833. var. † **Assembla·tion.**

† **Asse·mblance**¹. 1485. [– OFr. *assemblance* assemblage; see ASSEMBLE *v.*¹, -ANCE.] Assemblage, assembling –1596.

† **Asse·mblance**². 1485. [– OFr. *assemblance* in the sense of *resemblance*; see AS-¹, SEMBLANCE.] Semblance, show –1597. var. † **Asse·mblant.**

Assemble (ăse·mb'l), *v.*¹ [ME. *asem(b)le* – OFr. *asembler* (mod. *ass-*) :– Rom. **assimulare*, f. L. *ad* AS-¹ + *simul* together.] Occ. strengthened by *together.* **1.** To bring together into one place, company, or mass; to collect, convene; † *formerly*, to heap up ME. † **2.** To unite (*to* or *with*) –1483; to couple (sexually) ME. only. **3.** *intr.* To come together into one place or company; to congregate, meet ME. † **4.** *esp.* To meet in fight –1513.

1. To a. on yche side soudiours ynoch ME. These proverbs. .I assembled FRANKLIN. **3.** The Parliament assembled in November 1860. *refl.* All the men of Israel assembled themselves unto king Solomon 1 *Kings* 8:2.

† **Asse·mble,** *v.*² 1483. [– OFr. *as(s)embler* in the sense of *resemble*; cf. ASSEMBLANCE².] To compare; to resemble –1550.

Asse·mble, *sb.* 1883. [ASSEMBLE *v.*¹ 3, in the imperative.] *Mil.* The second beat of the drum, or other signal, ordering soldiers to strike tents and stand to arms. Cf. ASSEMBLY.

† **Asse·mblement.** 1470. [– (O)Fr. *assemblement*; see ASSEMBLE *v.*¹, -MENT.] An assembly, assemblage –1645.

Assembler (ăse·mblər). 1635. [f. ASSEMBLE *v.*¹ + -ER¹.] **1.** One who collects or convenes. **2.** One who takes part in an assembly, *e.g.* in the Westminster Assembly of Divines 1647.

Assembly (ăse·mbli). ME. [– OFr. *asemblee*, subst. use of fem. pa. pple. of *asembler*; see ASSEMBLE *v.*¹, -Y⁵.] **1.** = ASSEMBLAGE 1. † **2.** The coming together of two persons or things –1483; hostile meeting, attack –1535. **3.** A gathering of persons, a concourse, throng ME. **4.** *esp.* A gathering of persons for deliberation and decision; a deliberative body, a legislative council ME. **5.** A congregation 1600. **6.** A social gathering, either private, as a modern 'reception' or 'at-home', or public, as in the 18th century 1590. † **7.** = ASSEMBLAGE 4. –1699. **8.** A military call by drum or bugle. Cf. ASSEMBLE *sb.* 1727.

3. If there bee any in this A., any deere Friend of Cæsar's *Jul. C.* III. ii. 19. **4.** *Assembly* or *General Assembly*: the name given to the legislature in some of the United States of America. *General A.* of the Church of Scotland: the representative body which meets annually to direct its affairs. *National A.* of France: the popularly-elected branch of the legislature. *Westminster A.* of Divines, appointed by the Long Parliament in 1643, to aid in settling the government and liturgy of the Church of England (whence *The Assembly's Catechism*). **6.** He will find admittance into all the crowded Balls and Assemblies FOOTE.

Comb.: **a.-man,** a member of an A. (sense 4); **-room,** a room in which assemblies (sense 6) were formerly held, and in which balls, etc., are now given.

Assent (ăse·nt), *v.* ME. [– OFr. *as(s)enter* :– Rom. **assentare* (L. *-ari*) f. *ad* AS-¹ + *sent-* of *sentire* feel, think.] **1.** *intr.* To give the concurrence of one's will, to agree *to*, to comply with (*arch.*, exc. as said of the sovereign *assenting* to a measure, or as in 4). Replaced by *consent.* † *trans.* (ellipt.) To agree to –1675. † **2.** *intr.* To agree together, determine. Const. *to, into.* –1470. *trans.* To agree upon (a thing) –1591. † **3.** *intr.* To submit, yield (*to*) –1636. **4.** To give or express one's agreement with a statement or matter of opinion. Const. *to*, † *with*, † *unto.* (The mod. use as distinguished from CONSENT.) ME. † **5.** *refl.* in prec. senses –1485.

1. The Lords passed a resolution to which the King assented 1863. **4.** Assenting to the premises, we reject the conclusion F. HALL. Damn with faint praise, assent with civil leer POPE. Hence † **Asse·ntant** (repl. by ASSENTIENT) *ppl. a.* assenting; agreeing; *sb.* one who assents or consents to. **Asse·nter,** one who assents or consents. **Asse·ntingly** *adv.* **Asse·ntive** *a.* inclined to assent. **Asse·ntiveness.**

Assent (ăse·nt), *sb.* ME. [– OFr. *as(s)ent, as(s)ente*, f. the vb.] **1.** The concurrence of the will, compliance with a desire (*arch.* and repl. by *consent*, exc. as in next). **2.** Official, judicial, or formal sanction; the action or instrument that signifies such sanction ME. † **3.** Accord –1718. † **4.** Opinion –1559. **5.** Agreement with a statement, or matter of opinion; mental acceptance. (The mod. use as distinguished from CONSENT.) 1534.

2. I will nothyng graunt withowt the under shreves a. J. PASTON. **3.** Made kyng by a. of the britons CAXTON. Phr. *By* or *with one assent*, *common assent.* **5.** Our a. to the conclusion being grounded on the truth of the premises MILL. The deliberate *assent and consent* of a parliament STUBBS. var. **Asse·ntment** (*arch. rare*).

† **Asse·nt,** *pa. pple.* [app. pa. pple. of *asend v.*, OE. *asendan* (A- *pref.* 1, *sendan* send).] Sent forth; sent for. GOWER.

Assenta·neous, *a.* [f. med.L. *assentaneus* + -OUS; cf. CONSENTANEOUS.] Inclined to assent, deferential. LANDOR.

Assenta·tion. 1481. [– Fr. *assentation* (COTGR.), f. *assenter* ASSENT *v.*; see -ATION.] The (obsequious or servile) expression or act of assent.

Abject flattery and indiscriminate a. degrade CHESTERF. Hence **Assenta·tious** *a.*

Assentator (æsĕntēⁱ·təɹ). 1531. [– L. *assentator*, f. *assentat-*, pa. ppl. stem of *assentari* ASSENT *v.*; see -OR 2.] One who assents to or connives at. Hence **Asse·ntato:rily** *adv.* (*rare*).

Assentient (ăse·nʃĕnt). 1851. [– *assentient-*, pres. ppl. stem of L. *assentiri*; see ASSENT *v.*, -ENT.] *ppl. a.* Assenting, accordant. *sb.* An assenter 1859.

Assentor (ăse·ntǫɹ). 1880. [Specific legal form of *assenter*; see -OR 2.] An assenter; *spec.* used of those who, in addition to the proposer and seconder, subscribe the nomination-paper of a candidate in an election.

† **Asseour.** ME. only. [– AFr. *asseour* = OFr. *asseor* (mod. *asséeur*) assessor (of taxes, etc.), = med.L. *assidator*, see ASSESS *v.*, ASSIZE.] An officer who used to set the king's table for dinner. Cf. ASSAYER 3 and ASSEWER.

Assert (ăsə̄·ɹt), *v.* 1604. [– *assert-*, pa. ppl. stem of L. *asserere* claim, affirm, f. *ad* AS-¹ + *serere* join. Cf. med.L. *assertare* affirm.] † **1.** To set free (*rare*). (Cf. L. *asserere in libertatem.*) –1699. † **2.** To take the part of; to champion, protect. Cf. 4. –1814. **3.** To claim as belonging *to* (*arch.*) 1652; † to lay claim to –1791. **4.** To vindicate a (disputed) claim to (anything) 1649. **5.** To declare formally and distinctly, aver, affirm 1604. † **6.** To affirm the existence of –1724; to bespeak (*rare*) –1823; to state –1677.

2. That I may a. th' eternal Providence, And justifie the wayes of God to men MILT. *P.L.* I. 25. **4.** To a. one's rights 'JUNIUS'. *To assert oneself*: to insist upon the recognition of one's rights or claims, and take means to secure them. **5.** It is not directly asserted, but it seems to be implied FREEMAN. Common sense asserts the existence of a reality H. SPENCER. Hence † **Asse·rt,** assertion (*rare*). **Asse·rtable, -ible** *a.* capable or worthy of being asserted. **Asse·rtative** *a.* (*rare*) = ASSERTIVE. **Asse·rted** *ppl. a.* claimed, maintained; affirmed. **Asse·rter.**

Assertion (ăsə·ɹʃən). 1449. [– (O)Fr. *assertion* or L. *assertio* declaration, f. as prec.; see -ION.] † **1.** The action of setting free –1707. **2.** The action of maintaining or defending a cause; vindication (*arch.*) 1532. Insistence upon a right or claim 1660. **4.** The action of positively stating; declaration, averment 1449; a positive statement, a declaration 1531.

2. Flinching from the a. of his daughter's reputation SCOTT. **3.** An a. of her right of arbitrary taxation GREEN. The haughty and defiant *self-assertion* of Dante LOWELL. **4.** Looseness of a. CHURCH. A sweeping, unqualified a. HAZLITT.

Assertive (ăsə̄·ɹtiv), *a.* 1562. [– Fr. *assertif, -ive* – med.L. *assertivus*; see ASSERT, -IVE.] Of the nature of, or characterized by, assertion; declaratory affirmative; dogmatic, positive. Hence **Asse·rtive-ly** *adv.*, **-ness.**

Assertor (ăsə̄·ɹtǫr, əɹ). 1566. [– L. *assertor*; in sense 3, f. ASSERT *v.* + -OR 2.] † **1.** (In L. senses) One who liberates, or lays claim to, a slave –1678. **2.** A champion, vindicator, advocate 1647. **3.** One who makes a positive statement 1646.

Assertorial (æsəɹtōᵊ·riăl), *a.* 1863. [f. next + -AL¹; see -ORIAL.] *Logic.* Of the nature of assertion, affirming that a thing *is*; opp. to *problematical*, and *necessary* or *apodictical.* var. **Asserto·rical.** Hence **Asserto·rially** *adv.*; var. **Asserto·rically.**

Assertory (ăsə̄·ɹtəri), *a.* 1617. [– med.L. *assertorius*, f. *assert-*; see ASSERT, -ORY².] **1.** Assertive, affirmative 1639. **2.** *Logic.* = ASSERTORIAL 1837.

1. *Assertory oath*: one taken in support of a present statement, as opp. to a *promissory oath.*

Asservilize (asə̄·ɹvilǝiz), *v. rare.* 1877. [f. As- *pref.*[1] + SERVILE + -IZE.] To make servile. var. † **Asse·rvile.**

Assess (ăse·s), *v. Aphet.* CESS, SESS. 1447. [– OFr. *assesser*, f. *assess-*, pa. ppl. stem of L. *assidēre* sit by, etc., in med.L., to levy tax, etc., f. *ad* As-[1] + *sedēre* sit. See ASSIZE.] **1.** To fix the amount of (taxation, fine, etc.) to be paid by a person or community. **2.** To determine the amount of and impose *upon* 1495. **3.** To impose a fine or tax upon; to tax, fine. Const. *in, at* the amount. 1494. Also *fig.* **4.** To estimate officially the value of (property or income) for taxation 1809.

2. A forced loan was assessed upon the whole kingdom GREEN. **3.** John Hampden was assessed twenty shillings COX. **4.** To a. a person's annual income 1842. Hence †**Asse·ss(e** *sb.* = ASSESSMENT. **Asse·ssable, -ible** *a.* capable of being assessed, liable to assessment. **Asse·ssably** *adv.* rateably.

Assessed (ăse·st), *ppl. a.* 1552. [f. ASSESS *v.* + -ED[1].] **1.** Fixed by assessment 1796. **2.** Subject to taxation, taxed, fined 1552.

1. *Assessed taxes*: those on inhabited houses, male servants, carriages, dogs, hair-powder, armorial bearings, windows, etc.

Assession (ăse·ʃǝn). 1447. [Sense 1, – L. *assessio* session; sense 2, – med.L. *assessio* assessment; see ASSESS, -ION.] **1.** A sitting beside or together; a session 1560. † **2.** = ASSESSMENT ME. only. Hence **Asse·ssionary** *a.* pertaining to a. or assessors. ? *Obs.*

Assessment (ăse·smĕnt). 1540. [f. ASSESS *v.* + -MENT.] The action of assessing; the amount assessed. **1.** The determination of the amount of taxation, etc., to be paid 1548. **2.** The scheme of charge or taxation 1700. **3.** The amount of charge so determined upon 1611. **4.** Official valuation of property or income for the purposes of taxation; the value assigned to it 1540. **5.** *fig.* Estimation 1626. **6.** *attrib.* 1870.

1. The assessment of..fines 1548. **5.** In the comparative a. of Hellenic forces GROTE.

Assessor (ăse·sǝɹ). ME. [– OFr. *assessour* (mod. *-eur*) – L. *assessor*; sense 3 – med.L. *assessor* assessor of taxes; see ASSESS, -OR 2.] **1.** One who sits beside; *hence*, one who shares another's position, rank, etc. 1667. **2.** One who sits as assistant or adviser to a judge or magistrate; *esp.* an assistant skilled in technical points of law, commercial usage, navigation, etc. [The earliest sense in Eng.] ME. **3.** One who assesses taxes; one who assesses income or property for taxation 1611. **4.** *transf.* or *fig.* in prec. senses 1625.

1. Whence to his Son, Th' A. of his Throne, he thus began MILT. *P.L.* VI. 670. **2.** The body of unlearned assessors, termed..Jurymen BENTHAM. Hence **Assesso·rial** *a.* of or pertaining to an a. or assessors; var. †**Asse·ssory.** **Asse·ssorship,** the office, position, or function of an a.

† **Asse·th(e,** *sb.* ME. [– OF. *a(s)set* (pronounced *ase-þ*), orig. the same word as *assez* adv. :– late L. *ad satis.* The word had no connection in Eng. with *assets.*] Satisfaction; amends –1494. Hence † **Asse·the** *v.* to satisfy.

Assets (æ·sĕts). 1531. [– legal AFr. *assets*, earlier *asetz* (Britton), OFr. *asez* (mod. *assez* enough) :– Rom. **assatis*, i.e. L. *ad* to, *satis* enough, sufficiency; orig. in legal phr. *aver asetz* have sufficient (sc. to meet claims).] **1.** *Law.* Orig.: Sufficient estate or effects; *esp.* 'Goods enough to discharge that burthen, which is cast upon the executor or heir, in satisfying the testator's or ancestor's debts and legacies' (COWELL). **2.** Extended to: Any property or effects liable to be applied as in sense 1. (Now a *collective plural.*) **3.** *Law* and *Comm.* Effects of an insolvent debtor or bankrupt, applicable to the payment of his debts; and by extension: All the property of a person or company which may be made liable for his or their debts. (In this sense used as *pl.*, with sing. *asset.*) Also *fig.* 1675.

1. Unlesse that he hath A. by discent in Fee simple 1574. **2.** *Assets in hand*: effects in the hands of executors which are applicable to discharge the testator's debts. He left not assids enough to bury him COLLIER. **3.** A very doubtful asset 1888.

Assever (ăse·vǝɹ), *v. arch.* 1581. [– L. *asseverare*; see next.] To asseverate. Hence † **Asse·vering** *ppl. a.* solemnly affirmative.

Asseverate (ăse·vĕrēit), *v.* 1791. [– *asseverat-*, pa. ppl. stem of L. *asseverare*, f. *ad* As[1]- + *severus* grave, SEVERE; see -ATE[3].] To affirm solemnly, assert emphatically, avouch, aver.

They asseverated that they saw no child 1791. Hence † **Asse·verantly** *adv.* **Asse·veratin:gly** *adv.* **Asse·verative, Asse·veratory** *adjs.* of, pertaining to, or characterized by asseveration.

Asseveration (ăse:vĕrēi·ʃǝn). 1556. [– L. *asseveratio*, f. *asseverat-*; see prec., -ION.] **1.** The action of asseverating 1564. **2.** That which is asseverated; a solemn or emphatic declaration or assertion 1556. **3.** Emphatic confirmation; an oath 1602.

1. With more or lesse a., as they [things] stand.. prooued more or lesse BACON. **3.** With many choice asseverations DICKENS.

† **Assew·er.** 1478. [app. a conflation of ASSEOUR and SEWER *sb.*[2], and used in the senses of both.] An officer who used to set the table for a banquet, or who himself carried in and arranged the dishes; a sewer –1483.

A·ss-head. 1550. [See ASS 2 and HEAD.] A stupid fellow. Hence **A·ss-hea:ded** *a.* stupid.

Assibilate (ăsi·bilēit), *v.* 1844. [– *assibilat-*, pa. ppl. stem of L. *assibilare* hiss at, f. *ad* As-[1] + *sibilare* hiss; see -ATE[3].] To give a sibilant sound to. Hence **Assi:bila·tion,** pronunciation with a sibilant sound.

Assidæan, -ean-, ian (æsidī·ăn). ME. [f. Gr. Ἀσιδαῖοι (Heb. *ḥ*[a]*sīdīm* the pious, the godly) + -AN.] **a.** orig.: One of the Jews who under the leadership of Mattathias, opposed the attempts of Antiochus Epiphanes to introduce idolatry among them. (1 *Macc.* 2:42.) **b.** later: A member of a Jewish sect professing peculiarly intimate communion with God; more usu. *Chasidim.*

† **A·ssident.** 1753. [– *assident-*, pres. ppl. stem of L. *assidēre*; see ASSESS, -ENT.] *adj.* Usually, but not always, accompanying (a disease). *sb.* [sc. *symptom.*] Hence † **A·ssidence** (*rare*).

† **Assi·dual,** *a.* ME. [– OFr. *assiduel* or med.L. *assidualis*, f. L. *assiduus*; see ASSIDUOUS, -AL[1].] **1.** = ASSIDUOUS 1. 1651. **2.** = ASSIDUOUS 3. –1678. Hence † **Assi·dually** *adv.* constantly.

† **Assi·duate,** *a.* 1494. [– *assiduat-*, pa. ppl. stem of late L. *assiduare* apply constantly; see ASSIDUOUS, -ATE[2].] Constantly exercised –1658. Hence † **Assi·duately** *adv.*

Assiduity (æsidiū·ĭti). 1605. [– L. *assiduitas*, f. *assiduus* (next); see -ITY. Cf. (O)Fr. *assiduité.*] Constant or close attention to the business in hand, unremitting application, perseverance. **2.** Persistent endeavour to please (*arch.*) 1630; *esp.* in *pl.* constant attentions 1683. † **3.** Frequency –1668.

1. To fail in a purpose for want of a. GEO. ELIOT. **2.** The obsequiousnesse and a. of the Court 1630.

Assiduous (ăsi·diu,ǝs), *a.* 1538. [– L. *assiduus*, f. *assidēre* sit by the side of, attend or apply oneself to, f. *ad* As-[1] + *sedēre* sit; see -OUS. Cf. OFr. *assiduos.*] **1.** Constant in application to the business in hand, persevering, sedulous 1660. **2.** Obsequiously attentive (*arch.*) 1725. **3.** Of actions: Unremitting, persistent 1538.

1. To be a. in our prayers JER. TAYLOR. **2.** Few can be a. without servility JOHNSON. **3.** To wearie him with my a. cries MILT. *P.L.* XI. 310. Hence **Assi·duously** *adv.* **Assi·duousness,** assiduity.

† **Assie·ge,** *v.* [ME. *asege* – OFr. *asegier* (mod. *assiéger*) :– Rom. **assedicare*, f. L. *ad* As-[1] + **sedicum* SIEGE.] To besiege, beset. Hence † **Assie·ge, Assie·gement** *sbs.* a siege.

Assientist (æsi,e·ntist). 1713. [f. next + -IST; cf. Fr. *assientiste.*] A party to an Assiento contract; a shareholder in an Assiento company.

‖ **Assiento, asiento** (ăsye·nto, æsi,e·nto). 1714. [Sp.] A contract, or convention between the King of Spain and other powers, for furnishing the Spanish dominions in America with negro slaves. *spec.* That made between Great Britain and Spain at the peace of Utrecht.

‖ **Assiette** (asye·t). 1869. [Fr. = seat, site.] *Bookbinding.* A composition laid on the cut edges of books before gilding them.

A·ssify, *v.* 1804. [f. ASS + -FY.] To make an ass of (*joc.*).

Assign (ăsǝi·n), *v.* ME. [– OFr. *asi(g)ner* (mod. *assigner*) :– L. *assignare*, f. *ad* As-[1] + *signare* SIGN *v.*] **I. 1.** To allot (*to*); to appoint, apportion, make over. **2.** To transfer or formally make over to another. In *Eng. Law* the appropriate word to express the transference of *personal* property. ME. **3.** To allot or appoint *to* a person, or for a purpose ME. † **4.** To prescribe (a course of action) –1607. **5.** To appoint, designate, for an office, duty, or fate. *Obs.* exc. in *Law.* ME. **6.** To settle or authoritatively determine (a time or period) ME. **7.** To lay down as a thing ascertained 1664.

1. The work which here God hath assign'd us MILT. **3.** The Lords assigned us five very worthy lawyers BP. HALL. **5.** If the founder has..assigned any other person to be visitor BLACKSTONE. **6.** A hell to the duration of which no period is assigned 1883.

II. To point out exactly, designate, specify ME.; *spec.* in *Law* 1672.

The special locality which Jewish tradition has assigned for the place STANLEY.

III. To ascribe, attribute, or refer 1541; to ascribe (a reason) *to* or as accounting *for* 1489; to allege, suggest (as a reason, etc.) 1665.

To a. a motive to behaviour 'JUNIUS', a supposition of forgery PALEY. Hence **Assi·gner,** one who assigns; see the vb.

† **Assign,** *sb.*[1] **1.** [f. ASSIGN *v.*] Command 1633. **2.** [f. SIGN *sb.*] A sign, portent 1601.

Assign (ăsǝi·n), *sb.*[2] 1450. [– AFr., (O)Fr. *assigné* pa. pple.; see ASSIGNEE. For the muted *-é* cf. ASTRAY, COSTIVE, DEFILE *sb.*, TAIL *a.*, TROVE.] † **1.** = ASSIGNEE 1. –1714. **2.** = ASSIGNEE 2. Esp. in *heirs and assigns.* 1450. † **3.** An appurtenance SHAKS.

Assignable (ăsǝi·năb'l), *a.* 1659. [f. ASSIGN *v.* + -ABLE.] **1.** That may be assigned 1809, specified 1659, referred as belonging *to* 1673, alleged as accounting for 1659. Hence **Assi:gnabi·lity. Assi·gnably** *adv.*

‖ **Assignat** (æ·signæt, asinyā·). 1790. [Fr. – L. *assignatum*, pa. ppl. of *assignare* ASSIGN *v.*] Paper money issued by the revolutionary government of France, on security of the state lands. Cf. ASSIGNATION 4.

Assignation (æsignēi·ʃǝn). ME. [– (O)Fr. *assignation* – L. *assignatio*, f. pa. ppl. stem of *assignare* ASSIGN *v.*; see -ION.] **1.** The action of allotting; apportionment 1600. **2.** The action of legally assigning (see ASSIGN *v.* 2). Also **a.** formal declaration of transference; **b.** the transferred interest. (Now usu. ASSIGNMENT.) 1579. † **3.** The setting apart of certain revenue to meet a claim. Also **a.** the mandate granting the money; **b.** the amount set apart. –1747. **4.** Paper currency; a bill, an *assignat* 1674. † **5.** Appointment to office –1656; prescription, order –1605. **6.** The arrangement of a particular time and place (*esp.* for an interview); an appointment, tryst 1660. **7.** Attribution as belonging or due *to* 1603.

1. Not a Matter of Choice, but of divine A. 1716. **6.** Compelled to make assignations with as much secrecy as two young lovers 1854.

Assignee (æsinī·). ME. [– (O)Fr. *assigné*, pa. pple. of *assigner* ASSIGN *v.*, used subst. See ASSIGN *sb.*[2], -EE[1].] *ppl. a.* Assigned, appointed 1494. *sb.* **1.** One who is appointed to act for another; a deputy, agent, or representative ME. **2.** One to whom a right of property is legally transferred 1467.

2. *Assignees in bankruptcy*: those to whom the management, realization, and distribution of a bankrupt's estate is committed, on behalf of the creditors. Hence **Assignee·ism,** the practice of appointing assignees. **Assignee·ship.**

Assignment (ăsǝi·nmĕnt). ME. [– OFr. *assignement* – med.L. *assignamentum*, f. L. *assignare* ASSIGN *v.*; see -MENT.] **1.** The action of appointing as a share, allotment 1460. **2.** Legal transference of a right, etc. (cf. ASSIGN *v.* 2); the document effecting or authorizing it 1592. † **3.** = ASSIGNATION 3. –1678; **b.** = ASSIGNATION 4. –1708. **4.** The allotting of convicts as unpaid servants to colonists 1843. † **5.** Appointment to office; setting apart for a purpose –1600; appointment, command –1744. **6.** = ASSIGNATION 7. 1704. **7.** Statement (of a reason) 1651; specification 1646.

1. A. of lands to the veterans MERIVALE. **6.** By his a. of definite functions to definite organs LEWES.

Assignor (æsinǭ·ɹ). 1668. [f. ASSIGN *v.* + -OR 2.] *Law.* One who assigns a right or property. (Correlative with *assignee.*)

Assimilable (ăsi·milăb'l), *a.* 1646. [– med.L. *assimilabilis,* f. L. *assimilare*; see ASSIMILATE *v.*, -ABLE.] **1.** That may be appropriated as nourishment 1667. **2.** That may be likened *to* 1847. Also as *sb.* 1646. Hence **Assi:milabi·lity.**

† **Assi·milate.** 1671. [– L. *assimilatus,* pa. pple.; see next, -ATE [1, 2].] *pple.* Likened. *sb.* That which is like.

Assimilate (ăsi·mileⁱt), *v.* 1578. [– *assimilat-*, pa. ppl. stem of L. *assimilare,* f. *ad* AS-[1] + *similis* like, SIMILAR; see -ATE [3].] **I.** To make or be like. **1.** To cause to resemble 1628. Const. *with.* (Influenced by II.) 1849. To make alike 1785. **2.** *intr.* To be or become like *to* 1837; also with *with.* (See 1.) 1768. **3.** To adapt *to* (*arch.*) 1664. *intr.* (for *refl.*) To conform *to* (*arch.*) 1792. **4.** To liken, compare, class. Const. *to, with.* 1616. † **5.** To be like, take after –1661.

1. To a. our law in this respect to the law of Scotland BRIGHT. **2.** Which revenues..do always a., or take the same nature, with the antient revenues BLACKSTONE. **4.** Marcus Aurelius mournfully assimilated the career of a conqueror to that of a simple robber LECKY.

II. To absorb and incorporate. **1.** To convert into a substance of its own nature; to absorb into the system, incorporate. Also *fig.* 1578. **2.** *intr.* To become absorbed or incorporated into the system. Also *fig.* 1626. ¶ Occas. for ASSIMULATE, q.v.

1. Aliment that is easily assimilated, and turned into blood ARBUTHNOT. **2.** *fig.* I am a foreign material, and cannot a. with the Church of England J. H. NEWMAN. Hence **Assi·milative** *a.* of, characterized by, or tending to assimilation; that may be or has been assimilated. **Assi·milator,** he who or that which assimilates. **Assi·milatory** *a.* assimilative. vars. † **Assi·mile, Assi·milize.**

Assimilation (ăsi:milēⁱ·ʃən). Also **-ulation.** 1605. [– Fr. *assimilation* or L. *assimilatio,* f. *assimilat-* ; see prec., -ION.] **1.** The action of making or becoming like; the state of being like; similarity, likeness. **2.** Conformity *with* (*arch.*) 1677. **3.** Comparison 1855. **4.** Conversion into a similar substance; *esp.* the conversion by an animal or plant of extraneous material into fluids and tissues identical with its own. (By some restricted to the final stage.) Also *fig.* 1626.

1. Wisdom..is..an a. to the Deity 1660. **4.** A... is the ultimate term of nutrition TODD. *fig.* Which, by a bland a., incorporated into politics the sentiments which beautify and soften private society BURKE.

† **Assi·mulate,** *v.* 1630. [f. *assimulat-, assimulare,* var. of *assimilare* in sense of *simulare*; see ASSIMILATE *v.*] = ASSIMILATE –1652.

Assinego, var. of ASINEGO.

† **Assinuate,** *v.* Corrupt f. INSINUATE.

‖ **Assise** (asī·z). 1882. [Fr. = layer (of rock); see ASSIZE.] *Geol.* A formation consisting of parallel beds of rock agreeing in their organic remains.

Assish (æ·siʃ), *a. rare.* 1587. [f. ASS + -ISH[1].] Stupid. Hence **A·ssishness.**

Assist (ăsi·st), *v.* 1514. [–(O)Fr. *assister* – L. *assistere,* f. *ad* AS-[1] + *sistere* take one's stand.] † **1.** *intr.* To take one's stand *to* or towards; *fig.* to stand *to* (an opinion) –1646. *trans.* To stand near, or by; to attend –1650. † **2.** *trans.* To join. Also *absol.* –1610. **3.** *intr.* To be present (*at*) as a spectator (now treated as Fr.), or as taking part 1626. **4.** To aid, help; to second, to succour, to promote 1547. *absol.* and *intr.* 1514. Const. † *to, in,* or *inf.*

2. The King, and Prince, at prayers, let's a. them *Temp.* I. i. 57. **3.** To a. at a solemn Masse 1626. The dinner at which we have just assisted THACKERAY. **4.** To a. the rebellious Gauls 1683, a friendless person STEELE, digestion (*mod.*). To a. in the murder of her husband BROOME. Hence **Assi·ster, -or** (legal var.), he who assists (senses 3, 4). **Assi·stful** *a.* ? *Obs.* **Assi·sting** *ppl. a.* † bordering; † attendant; giving aid. **Assi·stless** *a. poet.* helpless.

Assistance (ăsi·stăns). ME. [Early form *assistence* – med.L. *assistentia* presence, assistance, f. L. *assistere* (prec.); see -ENCE; later infl. by Fr. *assistance.*] **1.** Presence, attendance (*Obs.* exc. as Fr.) 1520. **2.** *collect.* (rarely *pl.*) Persons present, bystanders. (*Obs.* exc. as re-adopted from Fr.) 1491. **3.** The action of helping or aiding; *also,* the help afforded, aid, relief. Formerly often in *pl.* ME. † **4.** *collect.* (rarely *pl.*) A body of helpers; see ASSISTANT *sb.* 3. –1692.

1. His sumptuous burial..solemnized with so great an a. of all the University MILTON. **3.** By the..assystence of almyghty god TREVISA. **4.** After them the Court of A. 1692.

Assistant (ăsi·stănt). ME. [Early form *assistent* – med.L. *assistens, -ent-* present, helping; later infl. by Fr. *assistant*; see ASSIST *v.*, -ENT, -ANT.] **A.** *adj.* † **1.** Standing or remaining by, present –1677. **2.** Present to help; auxiliary (*to*) ME.

2. Animals a. to man 1858. The Assistant-Surgeon's Tent 1844.

B. *sb.* † **1.** One who is present; one who takes part. Usu. in *pl.* –1781. **2.** A helper; a promoter; *also,* a means of help, an aid 1541. **3.** *spec.* **a.** A deputy-judge. **b.** An official auxiliary to the Father-General of the Jesuits. **c.** *Court of Assistants*: certain senior members who manage the affairs of the City of London Companies 1611.

2. Numbers and rhymes..as assistants to memory MRS. CHAPONE. Hence **Assi·stantship.**

Assith, -ment, obs. ff. ASSYTH, -MENT.

Assize (ăsəi·z). [ME. *asise, assyse* – OFr. *as(s)ise* subst. use of fem. of *assis,* pa. pple. of *aseeir* (mod. *asseoir* sit, settle, assess :– L. *assidēre*; see ASSESS *v.*] † **1.** A sitting of a consultative or legislative body. **2.** The decree or edict made at such a sitting. Now *Hist.* ME. † **b.** Hence *gen.* Ordinance, regulation –1523. † **3.** *esp.* Ordinances regulating weights and measures, and the weight and price of articles of general consumption (*assisæ venalium*); rule of trade ME. **4.** The statutory regulation of the price of bread and ale by the price of grain 1447. **5.** The standard so ordained; *hence,* customary or prescriptive standard ME. † **6.** *Hence*: Measurement (Now SIZE.) –1624. Extent (of things immaterial) –1655. **7.** Orig. used of: All legal proceedings of the nature of inquests or recognitions ME.; hence, an action to be so decided; also the writ by which it is instituted 1574. **8.** Hence (usu. in *pl.*): The sessions held periodically in each county of England, for the purpose of administering civil and criminal justice, by judges acting under certain special commissions. ME. Also *attrib.* ME. **9.** In Scotland: A trial by jury ME.; the jury or panel 1513. † **10.** Judgement, sentence –1643. **11.** With *great, last,* etc.: The Last Judgement ME. † **12.** *transf.* The office of judge, censorship –1675. † **13.** Fixation of imposts. (See EXCISE.) 1642.

2. By..the a. of arms, it was provided that every man's armour should descend to his heir BLACKSTONE. † *Rent of assise*: a fixed rent. **3.** The act of 51 Henry III (1266) is called the a. of bread and of ale 1821. **5.** Convicted for selling bread under the a. 1710. **7.** The *Grand* or *Great Assize,* the assizes of *Mort d'ancestre, Novel disseisin,* etc. **11.** Till summon'd to the last a. COMBE.

† **Assi·ze,** *v.* ME. [– AFr. *assiser,* f. *assise* (prec.); cf. Anglo-L. *assisare* assess, fix.] **1.** To place ME. only. **2.** To ordain, decide ME. only; to assess –1624. **3.** To regulate according to a standard –1638. Hence **Assi·zement,** the action of assizing; statutory inspection.

Assizer, -or (ăsəi·zəɹ). [ME. *assisour* – AFr. *assisour,* f. *assiser*; see prec., -OUR.] **1.** *Eng. Hist.* One of those who constituted the assize or inquest. **2.** *Sc. Law.* A juryman. (*Obs.* exc. *Hist.*) ME. **3.** An officer who had charge of the Assize of Weights and Measures, or who fixed the Assize of Bread and Ale 1751.

† **Asso·bre,** *v.* [f. AS- *pref.*[1] + SOBER.] To make or become sober. GOWER.

Associable (ăsōᵘ·ʃiăb'l), *a.* 1611. [– Fr. *associable,* f. *associer* to ASSOCIATE; see -ABLE.] † **1.** Companionable COTGR. **2.** That may be associated in thought (*with*) 1855. **3.** *Phys.* Liable to be affected by sympathy with other parts. Hence **Asso:ciabi·lity. Asso·ciableness.**

Associate (ăsōᵘ·ʃi,ĕt). ME. [– L. *associatus,* pa. pple. of *associare,* f. *ad* AS-[1] + *socius* sharing, allied; see -ATE[1], -ATE[2].] **A.** *ppl. a.* = ASSOCIATED. **1.** Joined in companionship, function, or dignity. **2.** Allied, confederate 1600. **3.** United in the same group or category; concomitant 1750.

1. A president and six a. judges BROUGHAM. **3.** The Mouth..Jaws, and A. Parts 1880.

B. *sb.* [the adj. used absol.] **1.** One who is united to another by community of interest, etc.; a partner, comrade, companion 1533. **2.** Companion in arms, ally 1548. **3.** One who shares an office or position of authority with another; a colleague, coadjutor. *spec.* One of the officers of the Superior Courts of Common Law in England, formerly directed by *writ* to *associate* themselves with the judges in taking the assizes. (Abolished in 1879.) 1552. **4.** One who is frequently in company with another, on equal and intimate terms; a companion, mate 1601. **5.** One who belongs to an association with a status subordinate to that of a full member or 'Fellow' 1812. **6.** A thing placed or found in conjunction with another 1658.

4. No mean Cumrades, no base associates WEEVER. **5.** Associates of the Academy of Sciences BREWSTER. Hence **Asso·ciateship.**

Associate (ăsōᵘ·ʃi,eⁱt), *v.* ME. [– *associat-*, pa. ppl. stem of L. *associare*; see prec., -ATE [3].] **1.** *trans.* To join, join *with, in*; to link together, unite, confederate; to elect as ASSOCIATE (see the *sb.* 5) 1806. **2.** *trans.* To join (things together, or one *with* another). (Mostly *refl.* or *pass.*) 1578. **3.** *intr.* To combine for a common purpose, to join or form an association 1653. **b.** To have intercourse (*with*) 1644; to make oneself a partner in (a matter) 1881. † **4.** To escort, attend –1657; to consort with –1590; of things: (cf. 2) to accompany –1691.

1. None but Papists are associated against him SWIFT. **2.** Faults..associated with transcendent merit JOHNSON. To a. rose-leaves with hell-fires M. CONWAY. **3.** When bad men combine, good men must a. BURKE. A. with men much older than yourself CHATHAM. *refl.* I a. myself with that answer (*mod.*). Hence **Asso·ciative** *a.* of, pertaining to, or characterized by association. **Asso·ciatively** *adv.* **Asso·ciator, -er,** he who or that which joins in association. **Asso·ciatory** *a.* having the quality of associating.

Asso·ciated, *ppl. a.* 1611. [f. prec. + -ED[1].] **1.** Joined in companionship, action or purpose, dignity or office, allied. **2.** Connected in thought 1748. **3.** Combined (*with*); occurring in combination 1830.

3. *A. movements*: those coincident or consensual, but unconnected, with the essential act calling them forth.

Association (ăsōᵘ:ʃi-, ăsōᵘ:si,ēⁱ·ʃən). 1535. [– Fr. *association* or med.L. *associatio*; see ASSOCIATE *v.*, -ION.] **1.** The act of associating, or the being associated (see ASSOCIATE *v.* 3); confederation, league 1535. **2.** A body of persons associated for a common purpose; the organization formed to effect their purpose; a society; *e.g.* the British Association for the Advancement of Science, etc. 1659. † **3.** A document setting forth the common purpose of a number of persons, and signed by them –1855. **4.** Fellowship, intimacy 1660. **5.** Conjoining one person or thing with another 1774. **6.** *Law.* The appointment of additional legal colleagues; the writ appointing them. (Cf. ASSOCIATE *sb.* 3.) 1613. **7.** The mental connection between an object and ideas (*e.g.* of similarity, contrariety, contiguity, causation). (*Association of ideas.*) 1690. **8.** An idea linked in the mind with some object of contemplation, and recalled in connection with it 1810.

1. *Deed of a.*: the document setting forth the particulars of a proposed limited liability company. **4.** The nobility would be profaned by my a. SMOLLETT. **7.** Words being arbitrary must owe their powers to a. JOHNSON. **8.** Pleasant associations with a place 1862. **A. football,** the kind played (according to the rules of the Football Association, 1863) with a round ball, which must not be handled. Cf. SOCCER.

Associationism (ăsōᵘ:ʃi,ēⁱ·ʃəniz'm). 1882. [f. prec. + -ISM.] The doctrine that mental and moral phenomena may be accounted for by association of ideas. var. **Asso:cia·tionalism. Asso:cia·tionist, -alist,** one who belongs to an association; one who holds the doctrine of association of ideas.

Assoil (ăsoi·l), *v.* ME. [– AFr. *as(s)oilier, -ir,* f. OFr. *assoil-*, tonic stem of *asoldre* (mod. *absoudre*) :– L. *absolvere* ABSOLVE.] **1.** To absolve from sin, pardon. Const. *of, from* (*arch.*) ME. **b.** from purgatory (*arch.*) 1483. † **2.** To absolve from any ecclesiastical sentence –1691. **3.** To set free (*of, from* obligations, etc.) –1650. **4.** To pronounce not guilty. Const. *of, from* (*arch.*) 1528. **5.** To release; to discharge. Const. *of, from* (*arch.*) ME. † **6.** To unloose the knot of, solve. (Cf. SOIL *v.*) –1696. † **7.** To refute –1721. **8.** To purge, atone for (*arch.*) 1596. † **9.** To discharge (an obligation) (*rare*) 1596. † **10.** To get rid of (a thing) (*rare*) 1596. ¶ **11.** *Catachr.* for SOIL, *sully* 1845.

1. God remitting whomsoever the Priest assoileth 1638. **4.** The houses did a. the army from all suspicion CROMWELL. **5.** Death's mild curfew shall from work a. MRS. BROWNING. Hence † **Assoi·l** *sb.* solution (*rare*). **Assoi·ler,** absolving (from excommunication). **Assoi·lment,** the action of assoiling, or being assoiled; † discharge (of a duty); † solution, reconciliation (of conflicting statements). ¶ *Catachr.* for: Defilement.

Assoilzie (ăsoi·lyi, asoi·li, retaining Fr. *l mouillé*), Scotch f. ASSOIL *v.*

'God a. her!' ejaculated old Elspeth SCOTT.

† **Assoi·n(e,** *sb.* ME. only. [Early var. of *essoyn* ESSOIN *sb.*; see AS- *pref.*[2], and cf. A- *pref.* 9.] An excuse put in for non-appearance.

† **Assoi·n(e,** *v.* [ME. *as(s)oyne*, early var. of *essoyne*; see ESSOIN *v.* and prec.] To put in an excuse for non-appearance of –1646; *intr.* to excuse oneself, decline –1470.

Assonance (æ·sŏnăns). 1727. [– Fr. *assonance*, f. L. *assonare* (of Echo) answer to, f. *ad* AS-[1] + *sonare* SOUND *v.*[1]. See -ANCE.] **1.** Correspondence of sound between words or syllables. **2.** *Pros.* The correspondence or rhyming of one word with another in the accented vowel and those which follow, but not in the consonants, as in OFr., Sp., and other versification 1823. **3.** A word or syllable answering to another in sound 1882. **4.** *transf.* Rough correspondence 1868.

2. In the Roland such assonances occur 1879. **4.** A. between facts seemingly remote LOWELL. var. **A·ssonancy** (sense 1). ? *Obs.*

Assonant (æ·sŏnănt). 1727. [– Fr. *assonant*, f. as prec.; see -ANT.] *adj.* Characterized by assonance. *sb.* [sc. *word.*] 1862. Hence **Assona·ntal, Assona·ntic** *adjs.* of or pertaining to assonance.

Assonate (æ·sŏnei̊t), *v.* 1656. [Formed after ASSONANT, -ANCE; see -ATE[3].] To correspond in sound, *esp.* in vowel-sound.

As soon, assoo·n, *adv.* ME. See AS, and SOON. *Assoon* had also the special meaning: Immediately. (Fr. *aussitôt.*) –1585.

Assort (ăsǭ·ɹt), *v.* 1490. [– OFr. *assorter* (mod. *assortir*), f. *à* (see AS-[1]) + *sorte* SORT *sb.*[2]] **1.** To distribute (things, *rarely* persons) into groups, as being of like nature or intended for the same purpose; to classify. **2.** To group *with* 1833. **3.** *intr.* To fall into a class; to be of a sort, match *well* or *ill with* 1800. **4.** *intr.* To consort *with* 1823. **5.** To furnish with an assortment 1611.

1. Assorting some parcels on the counter 1803. **2.** He would..a. it with the fabulous dogs..as a monstrous invention DICKENS. **3.** His *muse* assorts ill with the personages of the Christian mythology 1800. **4.** To a. with fisher-swains LAMB. Hence **Asso·rtedness.**

Assortment (ăsǭ·ɹtmĕnt). 1611. [f. prec. + -MENT, after Fr. *assortiment.*] **1.** The action of assorting; assorted condition; classification. **2.** A group of things of the same sort 1759. **3.** An assorted set, whether of varieties of the same thing, or of different things 1791.

3. Such as the sample is, will the entire a. be 1869.

† **Asso·t,** *v.* [ME. *as(s)ote* – OFr. *as(s)oter* (mod. *assoter*) f. *à* (see AS-[1]) + *sot* fool, SOT.] To become or act like a fool; to become infatuated. *trans.* To make a fool of –1741. Hence † **Asso·te** *pa. pple.* SPENSER.

Assua·de, *v. rare.* 1806. [f. AS- *pref.*[1], after *persuade.*] To present as advice.

Assuage (ăswē[i]·dʒ), *v.* [ME. *aswage, asuage* – OFr. *as(s)ouagier* :– Rom. **assuaviare*, f. *ad* AS-[1] + *suavis* sweet.] **1.** *trans.* To soften, mitigate, appease, allay (passion, pain, disease, appetite). **2.** To pacify (the excited person) ME. **3.** *gen.* To abate (*esp.* anything swollen) (*arch.*) ME. † **4.** *intr.* To become less violent –1722. **5.** *gen.* To grow less; to abate, subside ME.

1. To a. religious animosities BUCKLE, human misery MILMAN, hunger DRYDEN, thirst COMBE. **2.** Kindling pity, kindling rage At once provoke me, and asswage ADDISON. **4.** His sorwe gan aswage CHAUCER. **5.** As the deluge assuaged MOTLEY. Hence **Assua·gement. 1.** The action of assuaging; or the being assuaged. **2.** An assuaging medicine or application. **Assua·ger,** he who, or that which, assuages.

Assuasive (ăswē[i]·siv). ? *Obs.* 1708. [f. AS- *pref.*[1] after *persuasive*, but confused in sense with ASSUAGE; cf. ASSUADE, SUASIVE.] *adj.* Soothingly persuasive. *sb.* [sc. *medicine* or *application.*] 1829.

Music her soft a. voice applies POPE.

Assubjugate (ăsɒ·bdʒ[i]ŭge[i]t), *v.* 1606. [f. AS- *pref.*[1] + SUBJUGATE, perh. after earlier *assubject* (XVI).] To reduce to subjection. So † **Assubje·ct.**

† **Assuefa·ction.** 1644. [f. L. *assuefacere* habituate + -TION; see -FACTION. Perh. partly through Fr. *assuéfaction* (COTGR.).] The action of accustoming; becoming or being used to a thing; habituation –1682.

Forget not how a. unto anything minorates the passion from it SIR T. BROWNE. So † **A·ssuetude.**

Assume (ăsiū·m), *v.* 1436. [– L. *assumere* take up, adopt, usurp, f. *ad* AS [1] + *sumere* take. Cf. Fr. *assumer.*] **1.** To take to be with one; to adopt, take 1581. *esp.* To receive up into heaven. (The earliest use in Eng.; cf. ASSUMPTION 1.) (*arch.*) † **2.** To adopt, elect, to some position. (So in L.) –1670. † **3.** To take into the body (food, etc.). (So in L.) –1657. **4.** To take upon oneself (a garb, etc.) 1447. **5.** To take to oneself formally (the insignia of office, etc.); to undertake (an office) 1581. **6.** To lay claim to, usurp 1548. **7.** To pretend to possess; to simulate 1602; (with *inf.*) to pretend 1714. **8.** To suppose 1598. **9.** *Logic.* To add the minor premiss to a syllogism 1628.

1. To a. as a partner in business 1868. **4.** Then should the Warlike Harry..A. the Port of Mars *Hen. V*, Prol. 6. **5.** Mr. Speaker assumed the Chair 1640. **6.** Murray assumed to himself the praise of all that was done BURNET. **7.** A. a vertue, if you haue it not *Haml.* III. iv. 160. Sage saws assuming to inculcate content LAMB. **8.** Assuming the truth of the history PALEY. Hence **Assu·mable** *a.* that may be assumed. **Assu·mably** *adv.* **Assu·med** *ppl. a.* usurped; pretended; taken for granted. **Assu·medly** *adv.* presumably. **Assu·mer.** **Assu·ming** *vbl. sb.* assumption; pretension. **Assu·mingness.**

† **A·ssument.** *rare.* 1731. [– L. (Vulg.) *assumentum* patch sewn on (Mark 2:21), f. *assuere* sew on; see -MENT.] Something tacked on.

† **Assu·mmon,** *v.* 1450. [f. AS- *pref.*[1] + SUMMON *v.*] To summon –1607.

Assumpsit (ăsɒ·msit). 1612. [L. = 'he has taken upon himself', 3rd pers. sing. pret. of *assumere* ASSUME.] **1.** An undertaking; *spec.* in *Law.* **a.** A promise or contract, oral or in writing not sealed, founded upon a consideration; **b.** An action to recover damages for breach or non-performance of such a contract. † **2.** An assumption 1628.

† **Assu·mpt.** 1447. [– L. *assumptus*, pa. pple. of *assumere* ASSUME.] *pa. pple.* Used as pa. pple. of the vb. ASSUME –1587. *sb.* An assumption –1638.

† **Assu·mpt,** *v.* 1530. [– *assumpt-*, pa. ppl. stem of L. *assumere*; see next.] **1.** = ASSUME *v.* 1, 2. –1629. **2.** To put on, assume –1611.

Assumption (asɒ·mʃən). ME. [– OFr. *asompsion* (mod. *assomption*) or L. *assumptio*, f. *assumpt-*, pa. ppl. stem of *assumere* ASSUME; see -ION.] **1.** The action of receiving up into heaven; ascent to or reception into heaven; *esp.* the reception of the Virgin Mary into heaven, with body preserved from corruption (*R.C. Ch.*); the feast held annually on the 15th of August in honour of the event. **2.** Incorporation, inclusion; adoption (*arch.*) 1617. † **3.** The taking of food, etc., into the body –1645. **4.** The taking upon oneself of a form or character; taking of office or position 1646; the form or character assumed 1871. **5.** *Law.* A promise or undertaking, either oral or in writing not sealed 1590. **6.** Appropriation 1754. **7.** Unwarrantable claim, usurpation 1647; arrogance 1606. **8.** The taking of anything for granted as the basis of argument or action 1660; a supposition, postulate 1628. **9.** *Logic.* The minor premiss of a syllogism 1588.

1. The A. of Elias 1627. **4.** The a. of the Bachelor's degree 1866. **6.** *Arms of assumption* = *assumptive arms.* The a. of the whole legislative authority MACKINTOSH. **7.** His usual air of haughty a. SCOTT. **8.** Hold! says the Stoick, your assumption's wrong DRYDEN. Hence **Assu·mptious** *a.* given to a. (*rare*). **Assu·mptiousness.**

Assumptive (ăsɒ·mtiv), *a.* 1611. [– L. *assumptivus*; see ASSUMPT, -IVE.] Characterized by being assumed. **2.** Of the nature of an assumption 1650. **3.** Apt to assume; appropriative; arrogant 1829.

1. *Assumptive arms* in *Her.*: those assumed by any one, formerly with, now without, sanction. Hence **Assu·mptively** *adv.*

Assurance (ăʃū[ə]·răns). ME. [– (O)Fr. *assurance*, earlier *aseürance*, f. as next; see -ANCE.] **1.** A promise making a thing certain; an engagement, pledge, or guarantee. *esp.* Terms of peace. *Obs.* exc. *Hist.* 1513. † **2.** A marriage engagement –1641. **3.** A declaration intended to give confidence 1609. **4.** *Law.* The conveyance of lands or tenements by deed; a legal evidence of the conveyance of property 1583. **5.** The action of insuring or securing the value of property in the event of its being lost, or of securing the payment of a specified sum in the event of a person's death; insurance. (Techn., life-*assurance* is now differentiated from fire- and marine-*insurance.*) 1622. † **6.** = *Assuredness* –1603. **7.** Security 1559. **8.** Subjective certainty; in *Theol.* certainty of salvation; confidence, trust ME. **9.** Self-confidence; steadiness, intrepidity 1594. **10.** Hardihood, presumption, impudence 1699.

1. Plight me the full a. of your faith *Twel. N.* I. v. 192. **3.** He was..sincere in the assurances he..gave MCCARTHY. **4.** The Touchstone of Common Assurances and Conveyances (*title*) 1648. **7.** To sende..unto a place of most assuraunce all ..prisoners 1576. **8.** But yet Ile make a. double sure *Macb.* IV. i. 83. **10.** Quote authors they had never read, with an air of a. BENTLEY. Hence † **Assu·rancer,** one who makes great professions. **Assu·rant,** one who takes out a policy of insurance. † **Assu·rantly** *adv.* confidently.

Assure (ăʃu[ə]·ɹ), *v.* ME. [– (O)Fr. *assurer*, earlier *aseürer* :– Rom. **assecurare*, f. *ad* AS-[1] + L. *securus* SECURE.] **1.** † To render safe; to secure –1614; † to make sure of –1674; to make safe *from* or *against* risks. esp. *To assure life.* (Cf. ASSURANCE 5.) ME. **2.** To establish securely 1474. † **3.** To make sure the possession or reversion of; to convey by deed –1670. † **4.** To betroth –1581. **5.** To ensure (an event) 1622; to make certain (a thing doubtful) (*arch.*) 1682. † **6.** To guarantee. Const. *to* a person, † *absol.*, or with *subord. cl.* ME. **7.** To give confidence to, encourage ME. † *refl.* and † *intr.* To have confidence –1641; to venture –1513. **8.** To make (a person) sure or certain (*of*, or *that*) ME. *refl.* and *pass.* To feel certain 1484. **9.** To tell (a person) confidently as a thing that he may trust (*that*, or *of*) 1513. † **10.** To state positively –1617.

1. If they could be assured against any unpleasant consequences 1884. **2.** As weak States each other's Pow'r a. DRYDEN. **3.** And with my proper blood A. my soul to be great Lucifers MARLOWE. **5.** Yet is not the Success for Years assur'd DRYDEN. **7.** Youre humanité Assureth us and giveth us hardynesse CHAUCER. **8.** Thy words a. me of kind success MARLOWE. A. yourself, sir..that [etc.] SCOTT. **9.** He assured us of his own willingness to go 1888. Hence † **Assu·re** *sb.* assurance. **Assu·ringly** *adv.*

Assured (ăʃū[ə]·ɹd). ME. [f. prec. + -ED[1].] *ppl. a.* † **1.** Made safe; secure –1614. **2.** Made certain ME. † **3.** Pledged –1672; betrothed –1590. **4.** Certified 1574; satisfied, confident 1523. **5.** Self-possessed; in a bad sense: Presumptuous 1475. As *sb.* (occ. with pl. in -**s**). A person whose life or goods are insured 1755. Hence **Assu·redness,** assurance.

Assuredly (ăʃū[ə]·rėdli), *adv.* ME. [f. prec. + -LY[2].] **1.** Certainly; in very truth. **2.** With confidence 1508.

1. It will almost a. rain 1758. Yours a., W. Burleigh 1578. **2.** Trust thereto a. 1557.

Assurer (ăʃ[ə]ū·rəɹ). 1607. [f. ASSURE *v.* + -ER[1].] **1.** He who, or that which, gives assurance. **2.** = ASSUROR 1827. **3.** One who insures his life. (A recent use.) 1865.

† **Assu·rge,** *v.* 1556. [– L. *assurgere* rise up, f. *ad* AS-¹ + *surgere* rise.] To arise –1670.

Assurgent (ăsɒ̄·ɹdʒĕnt), *a.* 1578. [– *assurgent-*, pres. ppl. stem of L. *assurgere*; see prec., -ENT.] Ascending; in *Bot.* rising obliquely. **2.** Seeking ascendancy 1881. As *sb.* He who, or that which, rises up 1791. Hence **Assu·rgency.**

Assuror (ăʃūᵊ·rǫɹ). 1622. [f. ASSURE *v.*; see -OR 2.] One who assures or insures any one's life or property; an underwriter. (A legal form of ASSURER.)

Assyrian (ăsi·riăn). 1591. [f. L. *Assyrius*, Gr. Ἀσσύριος + -AN.] *adj.* Of Assyria; *absol.* its language. *sb.* A native of Assyria 1815. var. † **Assy·riac** *a.*

Assyriology (ăsi:riˌǫ·lŏdʒi). 1865. [f. L. *Assyria* – Gr. Ἀσσυρία + -LOGY.] The study of the language, history, and antiquities of Assyria. Hence **Assyriolo·gical** *a.* pertaining to A. **Assyrio·logist, Assy·riologue,** a student of A.

Astacian (ăstēⁱ·ʃⁱăn). [– L. *astacus* – Gr. ἀστακός lobster + -IAN.] *Zool.* A crustacean of the lobster kind. **A·stacite, Asta·colite,** a fossil crustacean, resembling a lobster or crayfish.

A-starboard (ăstā·ɹbōᵊɹd), *adv.* 1627. [A *prep.*¹ 5.] *Naut.* On or towards the starboard side. *To put the helm a-starboard*: to bring the rudder to the port side, making the vessel turn to the left.

A-sta·re, *adv.* 1855. [A *prep.*¹ 11.] Staring; prominent.

† **Asta·rt,** *v.* ME. [A- *pref.* 1.] **1.** *intr.* To start up –1596; to happen, fall out (*orig.* with *dat.* of person; hence *trans.*), to befall –1579; to start off, escape –1541. **2.** *trans.* (*orig.* with *dat.*) To escape, avoid –1575.

A-sta·rt, *adv.* 1721. [A *prep.*¹ 11.] With a start, suddenly.

† **Asta·te,** early var. of ESTATE.

Astatic (ăstæ·tik), *a.* 1832. [f. Gr. ἄστατος unstable + -IC. Cf. Fr. *astatique.*] *Electro-Magn.* Having no tendency to remain in a fixed position.

Astatic needle: one so situated as to be unaffected by the earth's magnetism. Hence **Asta·tically** *adv.*

A-stay (ăstēⁱ·), *adv.* 1867. [A *prep.*¹ 11.] *Naut.* Used of an anchor when, in heaving in, the cable is at an acute angle, in a position like that of one of the ship's stays. Cf. A-PEAK.

† **A-stay·s,** *adv.* 1622. [f. A *prep.*¹ 11 + STAY *sb.*¹; cf. *abackstays.*] = ABACK –1671.

Astee·r, *adv. Sc.* 1535. [f. A *prep.*¹ 11. + *stere*, var. of STIR *sb.*¹] Stirring; in commotion.

Asteism (æ·stiˌiz'm). 1589. [– late L. *asteismus* – Gr. ἀστεισμός refined, witty talk, f. ἀστεῖος polite, f. ἄστυ city.] *Rhet.* Genteel irony, polite and ingenious mockery.

A·stel. ME. [– OFr. *astele, astelle* :– late L. *astella*, alt. of **astula* for L. *assula* splinter, shaving.] † **1.** A slip of wood; a splinter; split wood –1472. **2.** *Mining.* A board, or ceiling of boards, over the men's heads in a mine, to protect them (Weale).

Aster (a·stəɹ). 1603. [– L. *aster* – Gr. ἀστήρ star.] † **1.** A star. *Obs.* as Eng. –1706. **2.** *Bot.* A large genus of the N.O. *Compositæ*, with radiated flowers, including the indigenous British Sea Starwort or Michaelmas Daisy (*A. tripolium*) 1706. **3. China Aster:** a flower (*Callistephus chinensis*) resembling the asters proper 1794. Hence **Astera·ceous** *a.*

-aster (æstəɹ), – L. *-aster*, suffix of sbs. and adjs., expressing incomplete resemblance, hence generally pejorative; in Eng. used only in words from L. or Rom., e.g. *poetaster.*

‖ **Aste·ria.** 1646. [L.] A precious stone mentioned by Pliny; either the *Asteriated saphhire* or the Cymophane.

† **Aste·rial,** *a.* 1686. [f. Gr. ἀστέριος starry (f. ἀστήρ star) + -AL¹.] **a.** Of or connected with the stars 1708. **b.** Star-like; asteriated.

‖ **Asterias** (ăstīᵊ·riĕs). Pl. **-æ.** 1794. [mod. L. – Gr. ἀστερίας kind of dog-fish, *Squalus stellaris.*] *Zool.* A genus of Echinoderms, containing the common Five-rayed Star-fish, with allied species. **Aste·rialite,** a fossil star-fish. **A·sterid, Asteri·dian,** an animal belonging to the *Asteridæ* or star-fish family.

Asteriated (ăstīᵊ·riˌeⁱtĕd), *ppl. a.* 1816. [f. Gr. ἀστέριος starry + -ATE² + ED¹.] Radiated; with rays diverging from the centre, as in a star.

‖ **Asterion** (ăstiᵊ·riǫn). OE. [L. – Gr. ἀστέριον kind of plant, f. ἀστήρ star.] † **a.** *Herb.* Name of an unknown plant –1614. **b.** in *Phys.* 'The point behind the mastoid process, where the parietal, occipital, and temporal bones meet' 1878.

Asterisk (æ·stĕrisk). 1612. [– late L. *asteriscus* – Gr. ἀστερίσκος, dim. of ἀστήρ star. Cf. Fr. *astérisque.*] **1.** A little star 1682. **2.** *transf.* Anything shaped or radiating like a star; *spec.* in *Eastern Ch.* a star-shaped instrument placed above the chalice and paten to prevent the veil from touching the elements 1708. **3.** *esp.* The figure of a star (*) used in writing and printing **a.** as a reference to a footnote, **b.** to indicate an omission, **c.** to mark words and phrases as conjectural, obscure, etc., **d.** as a dividing mark, etc. 1612.

3. The A. divides each verse of a Psalm into two parts 1824. Hence **A·sterisk** *v.* to mark with an a.

Asterism (æ·stĕriz'm). 1598. [– Gr. ἀστερισμός, f. ἀστήρ star; see -ISM.] **1.** A cluster of stars; a constellation. † **2.** *loosely*, A star, or anything star-shaped –1743. **3.** Three asterisks placed thus (⁂) to direct attention to a particular passage. *Rarely*, a single asterisk so used. 1649. **4.** *Min.* (Also *asterismus.*) An appearance of light in the shape of a six-rayed star, as in star sapphire 1879. Hence **Asteri·smal** *a.* of or pertaining to asterisms. † **Asteri·stic** *a.* starry (*rare*).

† **A·sterite.** ME. [– late L. *asterites* – Gr. ἀστερίτης. The L. form is more usual.] A gem known to the ancients; cf. ASTERIA, ASTRION.

Astern (ăstɜ̄·ɹn), *adv.* (*prep.*). 1627. [f. A *prep.*¹ + STERN *sb.*²] *Naut.* **1.** In or at the stern 1675; hence, in the rear 1627. **2.** Of motion: To the rear, backward; stern foremost 1681. **3.** *prep.* At the stern of (a ship) 1675.

Asternal (ăstɜ̄·ɹnăl), *a.* 1847. [f. A- *pref.* 14 + STERNUM + -AL¹.] Not joined to the breast-bone.

Asteroid (æ·stĕroid). 1802. [– Gr. ἀστεροειδής, f. ἀστήρ star; see -OID.] **A.** *adj.* Star-shaped, star-like 1854. **B.** *sb.* **1.** One of the numerous minute planetary bodies revolving round the sun between the orbits of Mars and Jupiter; called also *planetoids* and *minor planets* 1802. † **2.** A meteor –1849. **3.** Hence, a kind of fire-work 1875. Hence **Asteroi·dal** *a.*; var. † **Asteroi·dical.**

Asterophyllite (æ:stĕroˌfi·ləit). 1847. [f. Gr. ἀστήρ, ἀστερο- star + φύλλον leaf + -ITE¹ 2 b.] *Palæont.* A fossil plant, with leaves arranged in whorls, found in the coal formations of Europe and America.

‖ **Asthenia** (æsþīnəi·ă). Occ. **a·stheny.** 1830. [mod.L. – Gr. ἀσθένεια weakness, f. ἀσθενής weak.] *Path.* Lack of strength, diminution of vital power, debility. **Astheno·logy,** scientific consideration of diseases arising from debility. **Astheno·pia** [Gr. ὤψ, ὦπα], weakness of sight. Hence **Asthe·nic, -al** *a.* of, pertaining to, or characterized by a.

Asthma (æ·sþmă, æ·smă). ME. [Earliest form (after med.L.) *asma* – Gr. ἆσθμα hard breathing, f. ἄζειν breathe hard.] Difficulty of breathing; *spec.* a disease of respiration, marked by intermittent paroxysms of difficult breathing, with a wheezing sound, constriction in the chest, cough, and expectoration.

Asthmatic (ăsþmæ·tik), *a.* (*sb.*) 1542. [– L. *asthmaticus* – Gr. ἀσθματικός, f. ἆσθμα, -ματ-; see -IC. Cf. Fr. *asthmatique.*] **1.** Affected with or suffering from asthma. **2.** Of or pertaining to, or good against, asthma 1620. **3.** *fig.* Wheezy 1853. **4.** *sb.* One suffering from asthma 1610. Hence **Asthma·tical** *a.*, **-ly** *adv.*

Astigmatic (æstigmæ·tik), *a.* 1849. [f. as next + -IC.] *Phys.* Pertaining to or characterized by astigmatism.

Astigmatism (ăsti·gmătiz'm). 1862. [f. Gr. ἀ- A- *pref.* 14 + στίγμα, -ματ- point + -ISM.] A structural defect in the eye, viz. unequal curvature of the cornea, which prevents the rays of light from being brought to a common focus on the retina.

† **Asti·pulate,** *v.* 1548. [– *astipulat-*, pa. ppl. stem of L. *astipulari*; see AS- *pref.*¹, STIPULATE *v.*] *intr.* To make an agreement or stipulation; to assent (*to*) –1652; *trans.* to assent to 1658. Hence † **Asti:pula·tion,** bargain; assent; a confirming statement.

† **Asti·r,** *v.* [OE. *astyrian*; see A- *pref.* 1, STIR *v.*] To stir up, move –1567.

Astir (ăstɜ̄·ɹ), *adv.* 1823. [A *prep.*¹ 11.] Stirring; *esp.* out of bed; *gen.* in motion; in excitement.

All kings and kinglets..are a.; their brows clouded with menace CARLYLE.

† **Astite, as tite,** *adv.* Chiefly *north.* ME. As soon. Also, as quickly as possible, immediately (Fr. *aussitôt*). –1674.

Astomatous (ăstǫ·mătəs), *a.* 1855. [See next.] Having no mouth; as in *Zool.* the *Astomata*, a division of the Protozoa, comprising the *Gregarinidæ* and *Rhizopoda.*

Astomous (æ·stŏməs), *a.* 1857. [f. Gr. ἄστομος mouthless (f. ἀ- A- *pref.* 14 + στόμα, -ματ- mouth) + -OUS.] Having no mouth; as in *Bot.* those Mosses in which the urn does not open by the detachment of the operculum.

† **Astone, astun** (ăstɒ·n), *v.* ME. [– OFr. *estoner* (mod. *étonner*) :– Gallo-Rom. **extonare*, f. L. *ex* EX-¹ + *tonare* to thunder. See ASTOUND *v.*, STUN *v.*] **1.** To stun –1612; to daze (the eyes) CHAUCER. **2.** To strike mute with amazement; to astonish –1677. **3.** *intr.* To be amazed. (Cf. G. *erstaunen.*) ME. only. Hence † **Astoned, Astunned** *ppl. a.* † **Asto·ning** *vbl. sb.* = ASTONISHING.

Astonied (ăstǫ·nid), *ppl. a.* ME. [pa. pple. of † *astonie*, obscure var. of ASTONE; see next.] † **1.** Stunned; made insensible, benumbed, paralysed –1611. Of the teeth: set on edge ME. **2.** Dazed (*arch.*); dismayed (*arch.*); amazed (*arch.*) ME.

Astonish (ăstǫ·niʃ), *v.* 1530. [First in (Sc.) pa. pple. *astonist*, prob. extension, with -ISH², of pa. pple. of † *astonie*, † *astony* (XIV–XVII); see prec., ASTOUND *ppl. a.*] † **1.** To stun; to deprive of sensation, as by a blow –1635; to set the teeth on edge –1656. † **2.** To stun mentally; to drive stupid, bewilder –1600. † **3.** To dismay –1601. **4.** To amaze, surprise greatly 1611.

1. I astonysshe with a stroke upon the head 1530. **3.** Such dreadfull Heraulds to a. *Jul. C.* I. iii. 56. **4.** The people were astonished at his doctrine *Matt.* 7:28. Hence † **Asto·nishable** *a.* calculated to a. **Asto·nishedly** *adv.* **Asto·nisher.**

Astonishing (ăstǫ·niʃiŋ), *vbl. sb.* 1530. [f. prec. + -ING¹.] † Deprivation of sensation; dismaying (*arch.*); surprised wonder. Hence **Asto·nishing-ly** *adv.*, **-ness.**

Asto·nishment. 1576. [f. as prec. + -MENT.] † **1.** Insensibility –1656. † **2.** Loss of sense or wits; mental prostration –1725. **3.** Loss of presence of mind, coolness, or courage (*arch.*) 1586. **4.** Amazement due to the sudden presentation of anything unlooked for or unaccountable 1594. **5.** An object of such amazement 1611.

2. *Wine of astonishment*: stupefying wine *Ps.* 60:3. **3.** They stricken were with great a., And their faint hearts with senselesse horror queld SPENSER. **4.** Thou in our wonder and a. Hast built thy selfe a livelong monument MILT. *On Shaks.* **5.** Thou shalt become an a., a prouerbe, and a by-worde *Deut.* 28:37.

Astony (ăstǫ·ni), *v. arch.* ME. [var. of ASTONE.] **1.** *trans.* = ASTONE –1646. **2.** *intr.* (? or *absol.*) (*rare*). E. B. BROWNING.

Astoo·p, *adv.* 1644. [A *prep.*¹ 11.] In an inclined position.

Astound (ăstau·nd), *ppl. a. arch.* ME. [Phonetic development of ASTONED; see next.] † **1.** Stunned –1596. **2.** Confounded; amazed (*arch.*) 1440. Hence † **Astou·ndedness.**

Astound (ăstau·nd), *v.* [prob. f. pa. pple. † *astound*, † *astouned*, earlier † *astoned*, † *astuned* (XIII), f. AFr. **astoné*, **astuné*, for OFr. *estoné* (see A- *pref.* 9), f. *estoner*; see ASTONE.] † **1.** To deprive of consciousness, stupefy –1727. **2.** To shock with alarm, surprise, or wonder 1634.

2. These thoughts may startle well, but not a. The virtuous mind MILT. *Comus* 210. Hence **Astou·ndingly** *adv.* **Astou·ndment.**

† **A·stracism.** *rare.* 1590. [Perversion of contemp. ASTERISM.] An asterism; an asterisk –1695.

A-stra·ddle, *adv.* 1703. [A *prep.*[1] 11.] In a straddling position. *A-straddle of*: bestriding.

Astragal (æ·străgăl). 1563. [– L. *astragalus* (partly through Fr. *astragale*) – Gr. ἀστράγαλος huckle-bone, (pl.) dice, moulding of a capital.] **1.** *Phys.* The ball of the ankle-joint; the huckle-bone; = ASTRAGALUS 1. Hence in *pl.* (as in Gr.): Dice, which were orig. huckle-bones 1727. **2.** *Arch.* A small moulding, of semicircular section, placed round the top or bottom of columns. Also *attrib.* 1563. **3.** *Gunnery.* A ring or moulding encircling a cannon about six inches from the mouth 1656.

Astragalomancy (ăstræ·gălo,mæ:nsi). 1652. [f. ASTRAGALUS + -MANCY.] Divination by means of dice or huckle-bones.

‖ **Astragalus** (ăstræ·gălŏs). 1541. [L. – Gr.; see ASTRAGAL.] **1.** *Phys.* The ball of the ankle-joint, the upper bone of the foot, on which the tibia rests. **2.** *Bot.* An extensive genus of leguminous plants, including *A. verus*, which produces gum tragacanth, and three British species known as Milk-vetch 1548.

† **Astrai·n,** *v.* ME. [– *astreign-*, stem of OFr. *astreindre* :– L. *astringere* ASTRINGE.] To bind –1594.

A-strai·n, *adv.* 1856. [A *prep.*[1] 11.] On the strain.

Astrakhan (æstrăkæ·n). 1766. The skin of still-born or very young lambs from Astrakhan in Russia, the wool of which resembles fur.

Astral (æ·străl), *a.* (*sb.*) 1605. [– late L. *astralis*, f. *astrum* star; see -AL[1]. Cf. Fr. *astral.*] **1.** Of, connected with, or proceeding from the stars. **2.** Star-shaped, star-like 1671. **3.** *sb.* An astral lamp 1860.

1. A. showers SIR F. PALGRAVE. *Astral spirits*, those formerly supposed to live in the heavenly bodies, represented as fallen angels, souls of dead men, etc. **2.** *A. lamp*: one resembling an Argand lamp, with the oil in a flattened ring, and so contrived that uninterrupted light is thrown upon the table below it.

A-stra·nd, *adv.* 1810. [A *prep.*[1] 11.] Stranded.

† **Astray·,** *v.* ME. [– AFr. *astraier, OFr. *estraier* (see A- *pref.* 9); see next. Aphet. to STRAY *v.*]

Astray (ăstrēⁱ·), *adv.* or *a.* [ME. *o straie*, *astraie* – AFr. **astraié*, OFr. *estraié* (see A- *pref.* 9), pa. pple. of *estraier* :– Rom. **extravagare*, f. L. *extra* out of bounds + *vagari* wander. For the loss of *-é* cf. ASSIGN *sb.*[2], TROVE, etc. The aphet. STRAY is now used as adj.] **1.** Out of the right way, wandering. **2.** Away from the right 1535.

1. And lead these testie Riuals so a. *Mids. N.* III. ii. 358. **2.** They go astraie and speake lyes *Ps.* 62[:]3.

‖ **Astre.** 1500. [– OFr. *astre*, *aistre* (mod. *âtre*) – late L. *astracus* tile, pavement (Oribasius), med.L. *astracum* paved floor.] A hearth, a home. Hence **Astrer,** a peasant householder, residing at the hearth where he was bred.

† **Astre·an,** *a. rare.* [f. Gr. ἀστραῖος starry + -AN.] Of or belonging to the stars. HOWELL.

Astrict (ăstri·kt), *v.* 1513. [– *astrict-*, pa. ppl. stem of L. *astringere* ASTRINGE.] **1.** To bind up, compress; *hence*, to render costive 1548. **2.** To bind by moral or legal obligation 1513. **3.** To restrict, limit *to* 1588. **4.** *Sc. Law.* To restrict in tenure.

3. The mind is thus astricted to certain necessary modes or forms of thought SIR W. HAMILTON. Hence **Astri·cted** *ppl. a.* confined, restricted; *spec.* in *Sc. Law* of lands held on such terms that the tenant must take grain grown upon them to be ground at a particular mill, paying a toll called *multure* or *thirlage*.

Astriction (ăstri·kʃən). 1536. [–(O)Fr. *astriction* or L. *astrictio*, f. *astrict-*; see prec., -ION.] **1.** The action of binding, or drawing close together, *esp.* the soft organic tissues; the state of being thus bound; constriction; constipation 1568. † **2.** Astringency –1750. † **3.** Obligation, bond –1643. **4.** Restriction; *spec.* in tenure; see ASTRICTED 1619.

4. In Norway there is no a. to mills 1836.

Astrictive (ăstri·ktiv), *a.* (*sb.*) 1555. [f. as prec. + -IVE; cf. Fr. *astrictif.*] † **1.** Binding (*lit.* and *fig.*) –1659. **2.** Astringent, styptic 1562. **3.** *sb.* An astringent 1657. Hence **Astri·ctively** *adv.*

Astride (ăstrəi·d). 1664. [A *prep.*[1] 11.] **1.** *adv.* With the legs stretched wide apart, or so that one leg is on each side of some object between. Also *transf.* and *fig.* **2.** *prep.* Bestriding 1713.

1. The way in which the impudent little beggar stands a., and sticks his little feet out THACKERAY.

Astringe (ăstri·ndʒ), *v.* 1523. [– L. *astringere*, f. *ad* AS- *pref.*[1] + *stringere* bind, draw tight.] **1.** To bind together, draw close; to constrict; *hence*, to constipate 1562; † *intr.* to become constricted. HOLLAND. † **2.** To bind morally or legally; to oblige –1752.

2. Your Grace is not astringed or bounden to any charge 1523.

Astringency (ăstri·ndʒĕnsi). 1601. [f. next; see -ENCY.] **1.** Astringent quality. † **2.** Astricted state 1669. **3.** *fig.* Harshness 1823.

1. The a. of tea is due to the tannin present 1881.

Astringent (ăstri·ndʒĕnt). 1541. [– Fr. *astringent* – L. *astringent-*, pres. ppl. stem of *astringere* ASTRINGE; see -ENT.] *adj.* **1.** Having power to draw together or contract the organic tissues; binding, constrictive, styptic. **2.** *fig.* Severe, stern 1820. † **3.** Constipated 1662. **4.** *sb.* [sc. *medicine* or *substance.*] 1626.

4. Blood is stanched..by astringents BACON. Hence **Astri·ngently** *adv.*

Astringer, var. of AUSTRINGER.

‖ **A·strion.** ME. [L., dim. of Gr. ἀστήρ star.] A kind of precious stone; perh. the star sapphire. Cf. ASTERIA, ASTROITE.

Astro- (æ·stro), repr. Gr. ἀστρο-, comb. f. ἄστρον.

astro-a·lchemist, one who mingled astrology and alchemy; **-chronolo·gical** *a.*, pertaining to the chronology of the heavenly bodies; **-litho·logy,** the scientific study of meteoric stones; **-ma·gical** *a.*, pertaining to star-divination; † **-phano·meter** [Gr. φανός], = ASTROMETER; † **-phile,** a lover of the stars; **-photo·meter,** an apparatus for measuring the intensity of a star's light; **-photome·trical** *a.*; **-phy·llite** [Gr. φύλλον], an orthorhombic mineral of yellow colour and micaceous composition, occurring sometimes in stellate groups; **-phy·sical** *a.*, relating to stellar physics; **-theo·logy,** that part of theology which may be deduced from a study of the stars; a religious system based upon the observation of the heavens.

Astrognosy (ăstrǫ·gnŏsi). 1871. [– mod.L. *astrognosia*, f. Gr. ἀστρο- ASTRO- + -γνωσία = γνῶσις knowledge; see -Y[3].] Knowledge of the stars, *esp.* the fixed stars.

Astrogony (ăstrǫ·gŏni). 1869. [f. ASTRO- + Gr. -γονία production.] The doctrine of the generation of the stars. var. **Astro·geny.** Hence **Astrogo·nic** *a.*

Astrography (ăstrǫ·grăfi). 1740. [f. ASTRO- + -GRAPHY.] The science of describing the stars; the mapping of the heavens.

Astroite (æ·stro,əit). 1601. [– L. *astroites* – Gr. ἀστροΐτης; see ASTRO-, ITE[1] 2 b.] **1.** = ASTRION. † **2.** Any star-shaped mineral or fossil –1728. **3.** *Zool.* A species of madrepore 1708.

Astrolabe (æ·strŏlēⁱb). ME. [– OFr. *astrelabe* – med. L. *astrolabium* – Gr. ἀστρόλαβον, subst. use of neut. of adj. ἀστρόλαβος startaking.] An instrument formerly used to take altitudes, and to solve other problems in astronomy.

The chief types of the astrolabe were: *a.* A portable ARMILLA. *b.* A planisphere. *c.* A graduated brass ring, with movable index turning upon the centre.

His almagest..his astrylabe CHAUCER. Hence **Astrola·bical** *a.*

Astrolatry (ăstrǫ·lătri). 1678. [f. ASTRO- + -LATRY.] The worship of the stars.

† **A·strologe.** ME. [– Fr. *astrologe*, corrupt. of *aristoloche* ARISTOLOCHIA.] The herb ARISTOLOCHIA –1706.

Astrologer (ăstrǫ·lŏdʒəɹ). ME. [– OFr. *astrologue* and *astrologien*, based on L. *astrologus* astronomer, star-diviner – Gr. ἀστρολόγος; see -LOGER.] † **1.** An observer of the stars, a practical astronomer. (Orig. distinguished from *astronomer* as *practical* from *speculative.*) –1676. † **2.** The cock ME. only. **3.** One who professes (judicial) astrology (see ASTROLOGY 1 b) 1601.

1. An A. expert in his art, foretelleth an eclipse of the Sunne 1625. **2.** The cok, commune a. CHAUCER. vars. † **A·strolog, -logue; Astro·loga:ster** *? Obs.*; † **Astrolo·gian.**

Astrologic (æstrolǫ·dʒik). 1569. [– Fr. *astrologique* or late L. *astrologicus* – Gr. ἀστρολογικός; see ASTROLOGY, -IC.] **1.** *adj.* Of or belonging to astrology or astrologers 1648. † **2.** *sb. pl.* Matters or facts of astrology –1671. Hence **Astrolo·gical** *a.* astronomical; pertaining to astrology; var. **Astro·logous. Astrolo·gically** *adv.*

Astro·logize, *v.* 1733. [f. Gr. ἀστρολόγος (see ASTROLOGER) + -IZE.] To examine by astrology; *intr.* to practise or study astrology (*rare*).

Astrology (ăstrǫ·lŏdʒi). ME. [– (O)Fr. *astrologie* – L. *astrologia* astronomy – Gr. ἀστρολογία, f. ἀστρολόγος astronomer; see ASTRO-, -LOGY.] **1.** *gen.* Practical astronomy; the application of astronomy, *esp.* (in later usage) to the prediction of events natural and moral. It was of two kinds: † **a.** *Natural A.*: the calculation and foretelling of natural phenomena, as tides and eclipses, etc. (*Obs.* since 17th c.). **b.** *Judicial A.*: the art of judging of the occult influences of the stars upon human affairs; astromancy. (The only meaning since 17th c.) † **2.** = ASTRONOMY –1807.

1. Naturall A., when it keepes it selfe within its due bounds is lawfull BP. HALL. Judicial A. judicially condemned (*title*) 1652.

Astromancy (æ·stromæ:nsi). *rare.* 1652. [– Gr. ἀστρομαντεία; see ASTRO-, -MANCY.] Divination by the stars; astrology (in mod. sense). Hence **A·stroma:ncer** (*rare*). **Astroma·ntic** *a.* of or pertaining to a.; *sb.* an astromancer.

Astro-meteorology (æ:stro,mī:tiŏrǫ·lŏdʒi). 1862. [f. ASTRO- + METEOROLOGY.] The investigation of the (alleged) influence upon the weather, climate, etc., of planetary phenomena, such as sun-spots, comets, planetary conjunctions, etc.; also, the (pretended) prognostication of the weather. Hence **A:strome:teorolo·gical** *a.* **A:strome:teoro·logist.**

Astrometer (ăstrǫ·mĭtəɹ). 1830. [f. ASTRO- + -METER.] An instrument for measuring the apparent relative magnitude of the stars.

Astronomer (ăstrǫ·nŏməɹ). [Late ME. *astronomyer*, f. *astronomy*, after earlier † *astronomyen* ASTRONOMIEN; see -ER[1].] One who studies astronomy. † **b.** An astrologer –1611.

A. Royal: official title of the a. who has charge of one of the royal, or national, observatories of Great Britain. **b.** Astronymers and enchaunteris ..that disseyven mennus wittis WYCLIF 2 *Chr.* 33:6.

Astronomic (æstronǫ·mik), *a.* 1712. [– Fr. *astronomique* or L. *astronomicus* – Gr. ἀστρονομικός; see ASTRONOMY, -IC.] Of or belonging to astronomy.

Astrono·mical, *a.* 1556. [f. as prec.; see -ICAL.] Connected with, bearing upon, dealing with astronomy. (Cf. an *Astronomical* Society with an *astronomic* fact.) Also *ellipt.* as *sb. pl.* 1706.

Astronomical year: one determined by a. observations, apart from conventional reckoning. *ellipt.* A. Numbers or Astronomicals PHILLIPS, 1706. See Sexagesimal Fractions. Hence **Astrono·mically** *adv.*

† **Astronomien, -an.** ME. [– OFr. *astronomien*, f. *astronomie* ASTRONOMY + *-ien* -IAN. Cf. *astrologian.*] Early word for ASTRONOMER (including *astrologer*).

Astronomize (ăstrǫ·nŏməiz), *v.* 1682. [f. ASTRONOMY + -IZE.] *intr.* To pursue astronomy; to act or speak astronomically.

Thales..astronomising as he walked 1848.

Astronomy (ăstrǫ·nŏmi). ME. [– (O)Fr. *astronomie* – L. *astronomia* (Seneca) – Gr. ἀστρονομία, f. ἀστρονόμος astronomer, ἀστρονομεῖν observe the stars; see ASTRO-, -NOMY.] The science which treats of the constitution, relative positions, and motions of the heavenly bodies, including the earth. † **b.** Astrology –1728.

Astronomye, whiche is of all clergye the ende CAXTON. **b.** Not from the stars do I my judgment pluck, And yet methinks I have astronomy SHAKS. *Sonn.* xiv.

A·strophel. [perh. perversion of *astrophyllum* 'star-leaf'.] Name of an unknown plant. SPENSER.

Astroscope (æ·strŏskoᵘp). 1675. [f. ASTRO- + -SCOPE.] An old instrument composed of two cones, having the constellations, etc., delineated on their surface. Hence † **Astro·scopy.**

† **Astru·ctive,** *a. rare.* [var. of CONSTRUCTIVE, after L. *astruere* build on to.] Constructive. BP. HALL.

A-strut (ăstrɒ·t), *adv.* ME. [A *prep.*[1] 11.] **1.** Sticking out; puffed up (*arch.*). † **2.** Stubbornly –1460. **3.** On the strut, strutting.

Astucious (ăstiū·ʃəs), *a.* Also **-tious.** 1823. [– Fr. *astucieux*, f. *astuce, astucie* astuteness + *-eux* -OUS.] Astute. Hence **Astu·ciously** *adv.* **Astu·city,** astuteness.

Astute (ăstiū·t), *a.* 1611. [– Fr. † *astut* or L. *astutus*, f. *astus* craft, cunning.] Of keen penetration, *esp.* as to one's own interests; subtle, sagacious; wily.

The a. fickleness of a barbarian BOSW. SMITH. Hence **Astu·tely** *adv.* **Astu·teness** (occ. *astutia*).

Astylar (ăstəi·lăɹ), *a.* 1842. [– Gr. ἄστυλος without pillars (f. ἀ- A- *pref.* 14 + στῦλος pillar) + -AR[1].] Without columns or pilasters.

Asty·llen. 1849. [Origin unkn.] *Mining.* A small dam in an adit or level.

A-su·dden, *adv.* 1875. [A *prep.*[1]] Of a sudden.

Asunder (ăsɒ·ndəɹ), *adv.* [OE. *onsundran, -um*, ME. *asundre, o sundere*, f. A *prep.*[1]; cf. SUNDER *a.*] † **1.** In or into a position apart –1548. **2.** Of two or more things: Apart from each other in position, direction, or thought ME. **3.** Of one thing: In two, in pieces; *esp.* with *break, rend*, etc. 1450.

2. Wide a. as pole and pole FROUDE. My Chaffe And Corne shall flye a. SHAKS. Freres and feendes been but litel a. CHAUCER. Hence **Asu·nderness.**

† **Asu·nder,** *v.* [OE. *asundrian*; see A- *pref.* 1, SUNDER *v.*] To put asunder, divide –1593.

A-swa·rm, *adv.* 1882. [A *prep.*[1] 11.] Swarming.

† **A-swa·sh,** *adv.* 1530. [A *prep.*[1] 11.] **1.** Crosswise, aslant –1611. **2.** With scorn –1611.

A-sway·, *adv.* 1858. [A *prep.*[1] 11.] Swaying.

A-swea·t, *adv.* 1879. [A *prep.*[1] 11.] Sweating.

A-swi·m, *adv.* 1663. [A *prep.*[1] 11.] Swimming.

A-swi·ng, *adv.* 1876. [A *prep.*[1] 11.] Swinging.

† **Aswi·the, as swithe,** *adv.* ME. only. [f. AS + *swithe* quickly; cf. ASSOON, ASTITE.] As quickly. Also, immediately.

A-swoon (ăswū·n), *adv.* [Late ME. *aswowne*, alt. of *iswow(e)n*, OE. *ġeswōgen*, pa. pple. of **swōgan*; see SWOON *v.*, A- *pref.* 6.] In a swoon or faint. Hence **Aswoo·ned** *ppl. a.* **A-swou·nd** *adv.* (*arch.*).

† **Aswou·gh, aswow(e,** *adv.* (or *ppl. a.*) [Either developed f. ME. *on swough, on swowe* in a swoon (see A *prep.*[1]), or = *iswowe* for *iswowen*; see A-SWOON.] = A-SWOON –1460.

† **Asy·le.** [–(O)Fr. *asile* – L. *asylum* ASYLUM.] Early f. ASYLUM (in senses 1, 2, 3).

Asyllabical (æsilæ·bikăl), *a.* 1751. [A- *pref.* 14.] Not constituting a syllable.

Asylum (ăsəi·lŏm). Pl. **-ums** (also, exc. in sense 3, **-a**). ME. [– L. *asylum* – Gr. ἄσυλον refuge, subst. use of n. of ἄσυλος inviolable, f. ἀ- A- *pref.* 14 + σύλη, σῦλον right of seizure.] **1.** A sanctuary for criminals and debtors, from which they cannot be forcibly taken without sacrilege. **2.** *gen.* A secure place of refuge or shelter 1642. **3.** *abstr.* Inviolable shelter; protection 1725. **4.** A benevolent institution affording shelter and support to some class of the afflicted, the unfortunate, or destitute; *esp.* (pop.) a 'lunatic asylum' 1776.

1. Romulus..set up a sanctuarie or lawlesse church, called A. HOLLAND. **2.** The *A.* for superstition SIR E. DERING. **3.** The Right of A. 1725. **4.** Asyla for [lepers] PENNANT.

Asymbo·lic, -al, *a.* 1660. [A- *pref.* 14.] Not symbolic(al.

† **Asy·mmetral,** *a.* 1630. [f. Gr. ἀσύμμετρος + -AL[1].] **a.** Incommensurable. **b.** ASYMMETRICAL. –1706.

Asy:mmetra·nthous, *a.* [f. as prec. + Gr. ἄνθος flower + -OUS.] *Bot.* Having asymmetric flowers.

Asymme·tric, -al, *a.* 1690. [A- *pref.* 14.] Not symmetrical, with the parts not arranged correspondingly. var. † **Asy·mmetrous** (*rare*). Hence **Asymme·trically** *adv.*

Asymmetroca·rpous, *a.* [f. Gr. ἀσύμμετρος + καρπός fruit + -OUS.] Having asymmetric fruit.

Asymmetry (ăsi·mĕtri). 1652. [– Gr. ἀσυμμετρία; see A- *pref.* 14, SYMMETRY.] **1.** *Math.* The relation of two quantities which have no common measure. ? *Obs.* **2.** Want of symmetry or proportion 1664.

Asymptote (æ·simtŏᵘt). 1656. [– mod.L. *asymptota* (sc. *linea* line) – Gr. ἀσύμπτωτος, subst. use (sc. γραμμή line) of adj., 'not falling together', f. ἀ- A- *pref.* 14 + σύν with, SYN- + πτωτός apt to fall.] *Math.* A line which continually approaches a given curve, but does not meet it within a finite distance. A rectilinear asymptote may be considered as a tangent to the curve when produced to infinity. Also *fig.* and *attrib.* **Asy·mptosy,** the quality of being asymptotic. HOBBES. Hence **Asympto·tic(al** *a.* **Asympto·tically** *adv.*

Asynartete (ăsi·naɹtīt). 1830. [– Gr. ἀσυνάρτητος not connected, f. ἀ- A- *pref.* 14 + συναρτᾶν knit together.] *Pros.* **1.** *adj.* Not connected; consisting of two members having different rhythms. **2.** *sb.* [sc. *verse.*] Hence **Asy:narte·tic** *a.*

Asynchronism (ăsi·ŋkrŏniz'm). 1875. [A- *pref.* 14.] Non-correspondence in time. **A-sy·nchronous** *a.* not coinciding in time.

‖ **Asyndeton** (ăsi·ndĭtŏn). 1589. [mod.L. – Gr. ἀσύνδετον, n. of ἀσύνδετος unconnected, f. ἀ- A- *pref.* 14 + σύνδετος bound together.] *Rhet.* A figure which omits the conjunction. **Asynde·tic** *a.* not connected by conjunctions.

A...as thus: I saw it, I said it, I will sweare it PUTTENHAM.

Asyntactic (æsintæ·ktik), *a.* 1880. [– Gr. ἀσύντακτος disorganized, ungrammatical, irregular + -IC (after *syntactic*).] Loosely put together, ungrammatical.

‖ **Asystole** (ăsi·stŏli). 1870. [mod.L., f. A- *pref.* 14 + SYSTOLE.] *Path.* Cessation of the functional contraction of the heart. **Asy·stolism** [= Fr. *asystolie*], the symptoms of a.

At (æt, ăt), *prep.* [OE. *æt* = OFris. *et*, OS. *at*, OHG. *az*, ON., Goth. *at*, Gmc. prep. and verbal prefix, rel. to L. *ad.*] **I.** Local position. **1.** Expressing primarily the relation of a thing to a point of space which it touches; hence, indefinitely, the *place* where it is, in the sense of *close to, near, by, in*, etc. OE. **2.** With proper names of places, *esp.* of towns (exc. one's own town, or capital), and small islands OE. **3.** *At* a person (L. *apud*): In contact with, *esp.* (*ellipt.*) applying to, pestering, assailing ME. Also (*ellipt.*) with possessive case: At a person's (house). Fr. *chez*, G. *bei*. 1562. **4.** Expressing some practical connection: e.g. *at* school (cf. *in* school) OE. **5.** Assisting or present at OE. **6.** Expressing the point or part, side or direction, where anything is, or is applied OE. **7.** Of distance: e.g. *at* arm's length 1526. **8.** Referring an attribute to a particular part: e.g. cut *at* elbows OE. **9.** Defining the point *at* which anything enters or issues, and hence = *through* or *by* OE. **10.** Determining the source *at* which we seek anything; e.g. *to ask*, etc., at. *Obs.* or *dial.* (repl. by *of, from*) exc. in *at the mouth* or *hands of*. OE. **11.** With verbs of motion: † *to* –1601; † *esp.* into personal contact with –1678; even to, as far as: e.g. *to come* (arch.), *arrive, land* at ME.; to reach (through obstacles), *esp.* in *to come, get* at 1530. **12.** Hence, of motion *towards*; often *against* ME. **13.** Of motion to attain or acquire (*lit.* and *fig.*) 1590.

1. To deliver..materials at the spot 1787. **2.** At St. Helena, at the Lakes, (formerly also *at*, now *in*, London, Ireland). **3.** They are at me for a subscription (*mod.*). We met at her father's (*mod.*). **5.** He had been at the battle THACKERAY. **6.** With a dog at his heels (*mod.*). An infant at the breast (*mod.*). **9.** He entered at the front door (*mod.*). **11.** He..commanded None should come at him *Wint. T.* II. iii. 32. Stooping down to get at his ear DICKENS. **12.** *To run, rush, go, have, throw, shoot, etc.* at; *to stare, shout, swear, etc.* at; *to hint, etc.* at. **13.** Drowning men catch at straws *Provb.* Setting your cap at him JANE AUSTEN.

II. Of action, position, state, condition, manner. **1.** With things put for the activities of which they are the objects, centres, or instruments: e.g. *at meat* = eating; *at the bar*; *at sword's point*; *assault-at-arms*, etc. OE. **2.** With actions, as *at work* 1440; *at it*: hard at work 1606. **3.** After many verbs of action: *to work, toil* at; *to tear* at, etc. ME. **4.** Connecting adjs. of occupation and proficiency, or their sbs., with a thing or action OE. **5.** Of posture, position: *at gaze, at bay* 1535. **6.** Of state, or condition of existence: e.g. *at peace, at a loss*, etc. ME. **7.** Of mutual relations: e.g. *at one, at daggers drawn* ME. **8.** Of manner, measure, extent, etc.: e.g. *at large, at random* ME. **9.** Of conditioning circumstance: e.g. *at peril, at a disadvantage*, etc. ME. **10.** Of relation to some one's will or disposition: e.g. *at his discretion*, etc. ME.

4. In agility and skill at his weapons MACAULAY.

III. Of relative position in a series, degree, rate, value. **1.** Defining special point in a series at which one begins, stops, etc.; *esp.* with superlatives ME. **2.** Of rate or degree, *at* which a thing is done ME. **3.** Of price or value ME. **4.** = *according to* ME.

1. Johnson at his very best TREVELYAN. **2.** She ..worked at high pressure 1882. **3.** To set at nought their counsel 1888. **4.** By land or by water at their choice MACAULAY.

IV. Of time, order, occasion, cause, object. **1.** Introducing the time or occasion ME.; the age *at* which one is ME.; distance in time, interval ME. **2.** Of the number of times, turns, etc. ME. **3.** Of order: e.g. *at first*, etc. OE. **4.** Introducing the occasion, and *hence* the cause of a fact, action, or emotion ME.

1. Late at Night DRYDEN. At the Restoration Hyde became chief minister MACAULAY. At riper years MARLOWE. At three Months after date 1716. **2.** To complete the business at two sittings 1888. **4.** They bee caryed aboute like babes at euery blast of doctrine 1574. Impatient at the delays KANE.

V. Phr. See *at* ALL, *at any* RATE, *at* STAKE, AT HOME, AT ONCE, AT ONE.

VI. † With the infinitive mood: e.g. nothing *at* do, nothing ADO –1470.

VII. † **1.** With preps. –1594. **2.** With advbs. *Obs.* or *dial.* 1440.

At, 'at (ăt). ME. [Worn-down f. *that*; rare after 1500, but still *dial.*] **1.** *adv.* or *conj.* = 'that'. **2.** *rel. pron.* That; who, which; what ME.

At-, *pref.*[1] :– OE. *æt-*. The prep. AT in composition, 'at, close to, to', freq. in OE., and occas. in ME., but now lost exc. in *atwi·te*, surviving as *twit*.

† **At-,** *pref.*[2] :– OE. *æt-*. Repr. earlier OE. *op-*, 'away, from'.

At-, *pref.*[3]; assim. f. L. *ad-*, bef. *t*. Erron. refash. of *a-* in many non-Latin words, as *a(t)tame*, etc. See AD- *pref.* 1.

‖ **Atabal** (atăba·l). 1672. [– Sp. *atabal* – Arab. *at-ṭabl*, i.e. *al* AL-[2], *ṭabl* drum.] A kettle-drum or tabour used by the Moors.

Atacamite (ătæ·kăməit). 1837. [f. *Atacama* in Chile + -ITE[1] 2 b.] *Min.* A bright green ore, an oxychloride of copper.

Atactic (ătæ·ktik), *a.* 1842. [f. Gr. ἄτακτος not arranged + -IC; cf. ASYNTACTIC.] Of language: Not syntactic.

Ataghan (æ·tăgan). 1813. var. of YATAGHAN, q.v.

† **Ata·ke,** *v.* ME. only. [A- *pref.* 1.] To overtake; get at.

† **Atala·ntis.** 1709. Brief title (prob. after Bacon's *New Atlantis*) of a romance satirizing the movers of the Revolution of 1688; hence *gen.* a secret or scandalous history –1789.

† **Ata·me,** *v.* Also **att-.** [A- *pref.* 1.] To tame, subdue –1530.

Ataraxy (æ·tăræksi). Also **ataraxia.** 1603. [– Fr. *ataraxie* – Gr. ἀταραξία impassiveness.] Freedom from disturbance of mind or passion; stoical indifference.

Ataunt (ătǭ·nt), *adv.* ME. [In sense 1 – (O)Fr. *autant* as much; in sense 2, f. A- *pref.* + TAUNT *a.*] † **1.** As much as possible, thoroughly –1520. **2.** *Naut.* With all sails set. (Also *ataunto, all-a-taunto.*) 1622.

Atavic (ătæ·vik), *a.* 1866. [– Fr. *atavique*, f. L. *atavus*; see next, -IC.] Of or pertaining to a remote ancestor. var. **Atavi·stic.**

Atavism (æ·tăviz'm). [– Fr. *atavisme*, f. L. *atavus* great-grandfather, grandfather, f. *at-* beyond + *avus* grandfather. See -ISM.] Resemblance to more remote ancestors rather than to parents; tendency to reproduce the ancestral type in plants and animals. **b.** *Path.* Recurrence of the disease or constitutional symptoms of an ancestor after the intermission of one or more generations.

Some mysterious a.—Some strange recurrence to a primitive past BAGEHOT.

Ataxy (ătæ·ksi, æ·tæksi). Also in sense 2 as L. *ataxia.* 1615. [– mod.L. *ataxia* – Gr. ἀταξία, f. ἀ- A- *pref.* 14 + τάξις order; see -Y[3].] † **1.** Irregularity, disorderliness –1733. **2.** *Path.* Irregularity of the animal functions, or of the symptoms of disease.

1. A mere a., or confused chaos 1634. **2.** *Locomotor ataxy*: inability to co-ordinate the voluntary movements. Hence **Ata·xic** [not on Gr. analogies] *a.* characterized by a. *Ataxic fever*: malignant typhus.

Atchison (æ·tʃisən, ē[i]·tʃi-). *Obs.* exc. *Hist.* 1605. [Sc. pronunc. of Atkinson, assay-master of the Edinburgh Mint in James VI's reign.] A copper coin coated with silver = two-thirds of an English penny, or eight pennies Scots –1773.

‖ **Ate** (ē[i]·ti). 1587. [Gr. ἄτη.] Infatuation; personified by the Greeks as goddess of mischief and rash destruction.

Not by myself but vengeful Ate driven POPE.

Ate (et, *occas.* ē[i]t), pa. t. of EAT *v.*

-ate, *suffix*[1], formerly *-at*, forming sbs. derived from L. sbs. in *-atus* (*-ato-* and *-atu-*), *-atum, -ata.* **1.** In OFr., L. *-atus, -atum* became *-é*, refash. later, and adopted in Eng., as *-at*, with *-e* added in Eng., after 1400, to mark the long vowel. In meaning words in *-ate* are chiefly: **a.** Sbs. denoting office or function, or the persons performing it, as *episcopate, syndicate.* **b.** Participial nouns, as *legate* 'one deputed', *mandate* 'a thing commanded'. **c.** Chemical terms, denoting salts formed by the action of an acid on a base, as *nitrate*, etc. **2.** In some words *-ate* = F. *-ate*, – L. or It. *-ata*, as in *pirate*, etc.

-ate, *suffix*[2], formerly *-at*, forming ppl. adjs. from L. pa. pples. in *-atus, -ata, -atum* by dropping the termination, e.g. *desolatus, desolat,* subseq. *desolate.* Hence many causative verbs, to which, for a time, the ppl. adjs. served as pa. pples., afterwards becoming obs. or simple adjs. (But cf. *situate* = *situated.*) **2.** L. ppl. adjs. in *-atus* were also formed on nouns, etc., when no other part of the vb. was required. Hence *caudate, insensate, apiculate,* etc. **3.** Words like *delegate, reprobate,* etc., orig. adj., are also used subst.; see -ATE[1].

-ate, *suffix*[3], a verbal formative, used to English L. vbs. in *-are*, and to form Eng. vbs. on other L. words or elements. This use originated in the formation of vbs. from the ppl. adjs. in *-ate* mentioned under -ATE[2]. Cf. *separate, fascinate, isolate, felicitate, capacitate,* etc.

-ate, *suffix*[4], in *Chem.*; see -ATE[1] 1 c.

Atechnic (ăte·knik). 1869. [f. A- *pref.* 14 + TECHNIC.] *adj.* Not having technical knowledge. *sb.* [sc. *person.*]

‖ **Ate·knia.** 1874. [mod.L. – Gr. ἀτεκνία, f. τέκνον child.] Childlessness.

Atelectasis (ætĭle·ktăsis). 1859. [mod.L. – Gr. ἀτελής imperfect + ἔκτασις extension.] *Path.* Imperfect dilatation, *esp.* of the lungs of newly-born children.

Atelene (æ·tĭlīn), *a.* 1859. [f. Gr. ἀτελής imperfect.] *Crystallog.* Imperfect; wanting regular forms in the genus.

‖ **Atelier** (atəlye). 1840. [Fr.] A workshop; an artist's or sculptor's studio.

Atellan (ăte·lăn). Also **Att-.** 1621. [– L. *Atellanus*, f. *Atella* in Campania.] **1.** *adj.* Of or pertaining to Atella, or its licentious farces; *hence*, farcical, ribald 1647. **2.** *sb.* A dramatic composition of this kind 1621.

Atelo- (æ·tĭlo), comb. f. Gr. ἀτελής imperfect, as **atelo-glo·ssia,** malformation of the tongue; **-gna·thia,** of the jaws; **-mye·lia,** of the spinal marrow; **-sto·mia,** of the mouth.

A-temporal (ăte·mpŏrăl), *a.* 1870. [A- *pref.* 14.] Timeless.

Ater-; see ATTER-.

Athalamous (ăþæ·lăməs), *a.* 1847. [f. Gr. ἀ- A- *pref.* 14 + θάλαμος bed + -OUS.] *Bot.* Of lichens: Having no conceptacles on the thallus.

Athamantin (æþămæ·ntin). 1863. [See -IN[1].] *Chem.* A crystalline substance, $C_{24}H_{30}O_7$, of rancid soapy odour and bitter taste, procured from the roots and seeds of *Athamanta oreoselinum.*

Athamaunte, obs. f. ADAMANT.

Athanasian (æþănē[i]·ʃiăn). 1586. [f. *Athanasius* (A.D. 293–373), bishop of Alexandria in the reign of Constantine; see -IAN.] *adj.* Of or pertaining to Athanasius. *sb.* An adherent of the doctrines of Athanasius. **Athana·sianism,** the principles or doctrines of the Athanasian Creed. **Athana·sianist,** an adherent of this Creed.

Athanasian Creed: that beginning '*Quicunque vult*', which has been attributed to Athanasius.

Athanasy (ăþæ·năsi). 1870. [– late L. *athanasia* – Gr. ἀθανασία, f. θάνατος death.] Deathlessness, immortality.

Athanor (æ·pănǭɹ). 1471. [– Arab. *attannūr* the furnace.] *Alch.* A digesting furnace used by the alchemists, in which a constant heat was maintained by means of a self-feeding apparatus. Also *fig.*

Atheism (ē[i]·þiˌiz'm). 1587. [– Fr. *athéisme* (XVI), f. Gr. ἄθεος without God, denying God, f. ἀ- A- *pref.* 14 + θεός god; see -ISM.] Disbelief in, or denial of, the existence of a God. *Also*, Godlessness (*practical* atheism).

A little or superficial knowledge of philosophy may incline the mind of man to a. BACON.

Atheist (ē[i]·þiˌist). 1571. [– Fr. *athéiste* or It. *atheista*; see prec., -IST.] **1.** One who denies or disbelieves the existence of a God. **2.** One who denies God morally 1577. **3.** *attrib.* Atheistic, impious 1667.

1. The Atheistes which say..there is no God GOLDING. **2.** When the Priest Turns A., as did Ely's Sons MILT. *P.L.* I. 495. **3.** The A. crew MILT. Hence **Athei·stic, -al** *a.* of or befitting an a.; involving atheism; of the nature of an a., godless, impious. **Athei·stically** *adv.* **Athei·sticalness.** ? *Obs.*

Atheize (ē[i]·þiˌəiz), *v.* 1678. [See prec., -IZE.] **1.** *intr.* To speak, write, or act as an atheist. **2.** *trans.* To render atheistic. Hence **A·theizer.**

† **A·thel,** *sb.*[1] [OE. *æþelu, -o* = OS. *aðali, eðili*, OHG. *adal, edili* (Du., G. *adel*) noble descent, ON. *aðal* family, race, kind. Cf. ETHEL *sb.*] Ancestry; *spec.* noble ancestry; *hence*, honour, might –ME.

† **A·thel,** *a.* and *sb.*[2] [OE. *æþele* = OFris. *ethele*, OS. *eðili*, OHG. *edili* (Du., G. *edel*) – Gmc. **aþaliz.* Cf. † ETHEL.] *adj.* Noble, illustrious –ME.; excellent, fine –ME. *sb.*[2] One who is noble; a lord, chief –1515.

Atheling (æ·þeliŋ). *Obs.* exc. *Hist.* [OE. *æþeling* = OFris. *etheling*, OHG. *ediling, adalung* :- WGmc. **aþelinga*, f. **aþal* race, family; see ATHEL *sb.*[1], -ING[3].] A member of a noble family, a prince, lord, baron; in OE. poetry often used in pl. for 'men'; later restricted to a prince of the blood royal, *esp.* the heir apparent to the throne.

‖ **Athenæum** (æþĭnī·ŏm). Also **-eum.** Mod. pl. **-æums.** 1727. [– late L. *Athenæum* – Gr. Ἀθήναιον, subst. use of n. of adj. 'pertaining to Ἀθήνη', goddess of wisdom.] **1.** *Gr. Antiq.* The temple of Athene in ancient Athens, in which professors taught, and orators and poets rehearsed their compositions. (Similar institutions were established at Rome and Lyons.) **2. a.** A literary or scientific club 1864. **b.** A literary club-room, reading-room, etc. 1822. **c.** A periodical devoted to literature, art, etc., e.g. *The Athenæum*, published in London.

Atheological (ē[i]:þiˌoˌlǫ·dʒikăl), *a.* 1641. [A- *pref.* 14.] Opposed to theology. **Atheolo·gian,** one destitute of theology. **Atheo·logy,** opposition to theology.

Atheous (ē[i]·þiˌəs), *a.* 1612. [f. Gr. ἄθεος + -OUS.] † **1.** Atheistic –1792. **2.** Not dealing with the existence of a God; opp. to the negative *atheistic* 1880.

1. Suffers the Hypocrite or a. Priest To tread his Sacred Courts MILT. *P.R.* I. 487.

Atherine (æ·þərəin). 1770. [– mod.L. *atherina* – Gr. ἀθερίνη kind of smelt; see -INE[3].] Name of various species of smelt.

Athermancy (ăþə̄·ɹmănsi). 1863. [f. as next + -CY.] Athermanous quality.

Athermanous (ăþə̄·ɹmănəs), *a.* 1863. [f. Gr. ἀ- A- *pref.* 14 + θερμαν-, stem of θερμαίνειν to heat + -OUS.] *Physics.* Not permeable by radiant heat.

‖ **Atheroma** (æþĕrō[u]·mă). 1706. [L. – Gr. ἀθήρωμα, f. ἀθήρη = ἀθάρη groats; see -OMA.] *Path.* **a.** An encysted tumour containing matter resembling oatmeal-gruel. **b.** Fatty degeneration of the arterial coats. Hence **Athero·matous** *a.*

† **Athe·ticize,** *v. rare.* [irreg. f. Gr. ἀ- A- *pref.* 14 + θετικός affirmative + -IZE.] To set aside 1701.

† **Athi·nk,** *v.* ME. only. [Worn-down f. *ofthink*; see A- *pref.* 3, OFF- *pref.* 1] impers. *It athinks me*; it repents me.

Athirst (ăþə̄·ɹst), *ppl. a.* [Worn-down f. OE. *ofþyrst* (see A- *pref.* 3), short form of *ofþyrsted*, pa. pple. of *ofþyrstan* suffer thirst. Cf. AHUNGERED.] Suffering from, or oppressed by, thirst; *fig.* eager, longing (*for*) 1480.

fig. My soule is a thurste for God *Ps.* 42:1.

Athlete (æ·plīt). 1528. [– L. *athleta* – Gr. ἀθλητής, f. ἀθλεῖν contend for a prize. Before 1750 always, and occas. afterwards, in L. form.] **1.** A competitor in the physical exercises that formed part of the public games in ancient Greece and Rome. **2.** One who by special training has acquired great physical strength; one who exhibits feats of strength and activity; a physically powerful man 1827. *fig.* 1759.

2. *fig.* Athletes of debate LOWELL. Hence **A·thletism.**

Athletic (ǣþle·tik). 1605. [– Fr. *athlétique* or L. *athleticus* – Gr. ἀθλητικός; see prec., -IC.] **A.** *adj.* **1.** Pertaining to an athlete, or to the contests in which an athlete engages. Also *fig.* 1636. **2.** Of the nature of, or befitting, an athlete; muscular, robust 1659.

† **B.** *sb.* **a.** = ATHLETICS. **b.** An athlete –1817.

a. Art of Activity, which is called a. BACON. var. **Athle·tical.** ? *Obs.* Hence **Athle·tically** *adv.* **Athle·ticism,** the practice of, or devotion to, athletic exercises; training as an athlete.

Athle·tics. 1727. [ATHLETIC *a.* used in pl. (see -IC 2). Cf. L. *athletica.*] The practice of physical exercises by which muscular strength is increased.

Athlothete (æ·ploˌþīt). 1850. [– Gr. ἀθλοθέτης, f. ἆθλον prize + θέτης one who places.] The awarder of prizes, judge, or steward in the public games.

At home, at-home (ǣtˌhō[u]·m). OE. [See AT and HOME.] *advb. phr.* **1.** At one's home; prepared to receive visitors 1829. **2.** (As opp. to ABROAD): **a.** Near at hand. **b.** In one's own country OE. **3.** At ease, as if in one's own home. Hence *fig.* Thoroughly conversant *with*, practised *in* 1840. **4.** *sb.* A reception of visitors during certain stated hours, when the visitors may call and leave as they please 1745.

1. The President makes it a point to be 'at home' on Sunday afternoons 1883. **2.** No newes so bad abroad as this at home *Rich. III*, I. i. 134. **3.** Never..at home in our island MACAULAY.

A-thri·ll, *adv.* 1879. [A *prep.*[1] 11.] Thrilling.

A-thro·b, *adv.* 1857. [A *prep.*[1] 11.] Throbbing.

A-throng (ăþrǫ·ŋ), *adv.* ME. [A *prep.*[1] 11.] In a throng; thronged.

Athwart (ăþwǭ·ɹt). 1470. [A *prep.*[1] + *thwart* adv., prob. after ON. *um þvert* 'over in a transverse direction'.] **A.** *adv.* **1.** Across from side to side, transversely; usu. in an oblique direction 1611. *Naut.* From side to side of a ship 1762. **2.** Across the course (of anything) 1594; *fig.* perversely, awry 1596.

B. *prep.* [the adv. with obj. expressed.] **1.** From side to side of, transversely over, across 1470. † **2.** To and fro over, all over. (Only in north. dial.) –1662. **3.** *Naut.* Across. or transversely to the course of 1693. **4.** Across the direction of; hence *fig.* into the notice of 1622. **5.** Across the course of 1667; *fig.* in opposition to 1644.

1. Nor neuer lay his wreathed arms a. His louing bosome *L.L.L.* IV. iii. 135. **3.** *To run athwart*: to run into sidewise. **4.** Ye sweep a. my gaze COLERIDGE. *Comb.*: **a.-hawse,** said of a ship's position across the stem of another ship at anchor; **-ship** *a.*, **-ships** *adv.*, from side to side of the ship; **-wise,** athwart.

Athymy (æ·þimi). 1853. [– Gr. ἀθυμία.] *Path.* Despondency.

-atic, *suffix*, forming adjs. (= Fr. *-atique*), – L. *-aticus*, a case of the suffix *-icus*, 'of, of the kind of' (see -IC), appended to pa. ppl. stems of verbs; as in *erratic*; also used with sbs., e.g. *aquatic*, etc. In *aromatic, idiomatic, problematic*, and the like, the suffix represents Gr. -ατικός, f. noun stems in -ατ-. Cf. -AGE.

-atile, *suffix*, forming adjs. (= mod.Fr. *-atile*), – L. *-atilis*, consisting of the suffix *-ilis* (see -ILE), denoting possibility or quality', appended to ppl. stems in *-at-* of vbs. in *-are*, as *volatile*; also with sbs. as *aquatile*.

A-ti·lt, *adv.* 1562. [f. A *prep.*[1] 11 + TILT *v.*[1]] **1.** Tilted up, and just ready to fall over. Also *fig.* **2.** In phr. *To run* (or *ride*) a-tilt: i.e. in an encounter on horseback with the thrust of a lance. Now usu. *fig.* Const. *at, with, against.* [*a-* is here obscure.] 1591.

2. Breake a Launce, and runne a-Tilt at Death 1 *Hen. VI*, III. ii. 51.

Atimy (æ·timi). 1847. [– Gr. ἀτιμία.] Public disgrace; *spec.* deprivation of civil rights.

A-ti·ngle, *adv.* 1855. [A *prep.*[1] 11.] Tingling.

-ation (-ēi·ʃən), the form of the compound suffix -T-ION (*-s-ion, -x-ion*), which forms nouns of action from L. pples. in *-atus* of vbs. in *-are*, Fr. vbs. in *-er*, and their English representatives. See -TION. In Eng., nouns in *-ation* number more than 1500 in modern use. A few have no Eng. vb., e.g. *constellation*, etc.; the great majority have a vb. in *-ate*, e.g. *cre-ate, -ation*, etc.; some are formed on Gr. vbs. in -IZE (= L. *-izare*, Fr. *-iser*), e.g. *organize, -ation*, etc.; the remainder have a vb. without suffix, derived through Fr., e.g. *alter-ation, caus-ation*, etc. The latter are pop. referred to the Eng. vbs. *alter, cause*, etc.; and *-ation* thus becomes a living Eng. suffix, and is applied to words not of Fr. origin, as in *starvation*, etc. Words in which *-ation* is merely added to the vb. are synonymous with the vbl. sb. in *-ing*, and tend to replace it, as *vexation, vexing*, etc.

A-tiptoe (ăti·ptōu), *adv.* 1576. [A *prep.*[1] 11.] On the tips of one's toes.

-ative, – Fr. *-atif, -ative*, L. *-ativus*, consisting of *-ivus* (see -IVE) appended to ppl. stems in *-at-* of vbs. in *-are*, e.g. *demonstrative*, and by extension *talkative*; also *authoritative*, from the sb. AUTHORITY.

Atlantad (ætlæ·ntăd), *adv.* 1825. [f. as next + -AD II.] *Phys.* Towards the atlas (vertebra); towards the upper part of the body.

Atlantal (ætlæ·ntăl), *a.* 1803. [f. Gr. ἄτλας, ἀτλαντ- (see ATLAS *sb.*[1]) + -AL[1].] *Phys.* Of or belonging to the atlas; belonging to the upper part of the body.

Atlantean (ætlæ̆ntī·ăn), *a.* 1667. [f. L. *Atlanteus*, f. *Atlant-* (cf. prec.) + -AN; see -EAN.] Pertaining to, or having the strength of, Atlas. With A. shoulders MILT. *P.L.* II. 306.

‖ **Atlantes** (ætlæ·ntīz), *sb. pl.* 1706. [Gr. Ἄτλαντες, pl. of Ἄτλας; see ATLAS *sb.*[1] Cf. med.L. *atlantes* columns.] *Arch.* Figures or half-figures of men used instead of columns to support an entablature.

Atlantic (ætlæ·ntik), *a.* (*sb.*) ME. [– L. *Atlanticus* – Gr. Ἀτλαντικός, f. Ἄτλας, Ἀτλαντ-; see ATLAS *sb.*[1]] Of or pertaining to Mount Atlas in Libya (see ATLAS *sb.*[1]). Hence applied to the sea near the western shore of Africa, and later to the whole ocean lying between Europe and Africa on the east and America on the west. 1601. *fig.* Far-reaching, distant; *transf.* in U.S.: Eastern 1650. † **2.** = ATLANTEAN –1652. † **3.** Of the size of an atlas JOHNSON. **4.** *sb.* The Atlantic ocean; also *fig.* ME.

4. Down on the Earth it in Atlanticks rain'd KEN.

Atlanto- (ætlæ·nto), comb. f. ATLAS *sb.*[1] (sense 2), as in *atlanto-axial*.

Atlas (æ·tlăs), *sb.*[1] Pl. **atlases.** 1589. [– L. *Atlas* – Gr. Ἄτλας, -αντ-; name of a god, who was supposed to hold up the pillars of the universe, also of the mountain in Libya that was fabled to support the heavens. Hence the fig. uses.] **1.** One who supports a great burden; a mainstay. **b.** *Arch.* (See ATLANTES.) **2.** *Phys.* The uppermost cervical vertebra, which supports the skull, being articulated above with the occipital bone. (So in Gr.) 1699. **3.** A collection of maps in a volume. [This use, found first in Mercator, is said to be derived from a representation of Atlas supporting the heavens forming a frontispiece to early atlases.] 1636. **4.** A similar volume containing illustrative plates, etc., or a conspectus of a subject arranged in tabular form; *e.g.* 'an anatomical atlas', 'an ethnographical atlas' 1875. **5.** A large square folio resembling a volume of maps; an *a.-folio*. **6.** A large size of drawing-paper 1712.

1. The A., and sustainer of the whole state of Holland 1618. **3.** Atlas; or a Geographic Description of the World, by Gerard Mercator and John Hondt (*title*) 1636. *Comb.* **a.-beetle,** a gigantic olive-green lamellicorn beetle (*Chalcosoma atlas*).

Atlas (æ·tlăs), *sb.*[2] ? *Obs.* 1687. [– (ult.) Arab. *atlas* smooth, bare; smooth silk cloth; cf. G. *atlas*.] A silk-satin made in the East.

Atlas (æ·tlăs), *v.* 1593. [f. ATLAS *sb.*[1]] To prop up, like Atlas.

A·tlo-, atloi·do-, comb. ff. ATLAS, formed on imperfect analogy; see ATLANTO-. So **Atloide·an** *a.* = ATLANTAL.

Atmido·meter. 1830. [f. Gr. ἀτμίς, -ιδ- vapour + -METER.] = ATMOMETER.

Atmology (ætmǫ·lŏdʒi). 1837. [f. Gr. ἀτμός vapour + -LOGY.] *Physics.* The science of the laws and phenomena of aqueous vapour. Hence **Atmo·logist,** one skilled in a. **Atmolo·gical** *a.*

Atmolysis (ætmǫ·lisis). 1866. [f. as prec. + -LYSIS.] *Physics.* The (partial) separation of gases of unequal diffusibility. **A·tmolyse, -ze** *v.* to perform a. **A·tmolyser, -zer,** an instrument for effecting a.

Atmometer (ætmǫ·mĭtəɹ). 1815. [f. Gr. ἀτμός + -METER.] *Physics.* An instrument for measuring evaporation from a moist surface.

Atmosphere (æ·tmŏsfīəɹ), *sb.* 1638. [– mod.L. *atmosphæra*, f. Gr. ἀτμός vapour + σφαῖρα ball, SPHERE.] **1.** The spheroidal gaseous envelope surrounding any of the heavenly bodies. **b.** *esp.* The whole body of terrestrial air. **2.** *transf.* A gaseous envelope surrounding any substance 1863. **3.** † A supposed outer envelope of effective influence surrounding various bodies –1750. **b.** *Magnetic Atmosphere*, the sphere within which the magnet acts. **c.** *fig.* Mental or moral environment 1797. **4.** The air in any particular place, *esp.* as affected by heat, cold, purifying influences, etc. 1767. **5.** A pressure of 14·7 lb. on the square inch, which is that of the atmosphere on the earth's surface 1830.

1. There is an Atmosphæra, or an Orb of Gross Vaporous Air immediately encompassing the Body of the Moon WILKINS. **3. c.** He lives in a perfect a. of strife, blood, and quarrels SCOTT. **4.** The suffocating a. . . of a small apartment 1767. Hence **A·tmosphere** *v.* to surround like, or as with, an a.

Atmospheric, -al (ætmŏsfe·rik, -ăl), *a.* 1661. [f. prec.; see -IC, -ICAL.] **1.** Of the nature of, or forming, the atmosphere 1664. **2.** Existing, taking place, or acting in the air 1666. **3.** Caused, produced, or worked by the action of the atmosphere 1661.

2. Small a. tides 1835. **3.** The a. engine of Newcomen 1822. *Atmospheric engine*, a steam-engine in which the piston was forced down by the pressure of the atmosphere, after the condensation of the steam that caused it to rise. *Atmospheric line*, the equilibrium-line on the indicator-card of a steam-engine. *Atmospheric pressure*: see ATMOSPHERE 5. *Atmospheric railway*, one worked by the propulsive force of compressed air or by the formation of a vacuum; a pneumatic railway. Hence **Atmosphe·rically** *adv.*

Atmosphe·rics, *sb. pl.* 1913. [pl. of prec.; see -IC 2.] Interfering sounds in aerial communication due to electric disturbance in the atmosphere.

‖ **Atoll** (ătǫ·l, æ·tǫl). 1625. [– Maldive *atolu*, said to be rel. to Cingalese *ätull* interior.] A coral island consisting of a ring-shaped reef enclosing a lagoon. *Comb.* and *attrib.* 1842.

Such sunken islands are now marked by rings of coral or atolls standing over them DARWIN.

Atom (æ·təm). ME. [– (O)Fr. *atome* – L. *atomus* smallest particle (in med.L. smallest division of time) – Gr. ἄτομος, subst. use of adj. 'indivisible'.] *Scientific. **1.** A hypothetical body, so small as to be incapable of further division; and thus held to be one of the ultimate particles of matter 1477. **2.** In Nat. Phil. *Physical Atoms*: the supposed ultimate particles in which matter actually exists (without reference to divisibility) 1650. **3.** *Chemical Atoms*: **a.** The smallest particles in which the elements combine, or are known to possess the properties of a particular element 1819. **b.** The smallest known quantity of a chemical compound 1847. ** In popular use. **4.** A particle of dust, or a mote in the sunbeam (*arch.*) 1605. **5.** A very minute portion, a particle, a jot 1630. **6.** Anything relatively very small; an atomy 1633. Also *attrib.* *** Of time. [In eccl.Gr. ἄτομος (1 *Cor.* 15:22) = 'twinkling of an eye'.] † **7.** The smallest mediæval measure of time = $\frac{15}{94}$ of a second. ME. only.

1. That the universe was formed by a fortuitous concourse of atoms SWIFT. **2.** Atoms are endowed with powers of mutual attraction TYNDALL. **4.** Rays of light Peopled with dusty atoms BYRON. **5.** There was not an a. of water SIR J. ROSS. *To smash, shiver*, etc., *to* or *into atoms*. Casting atomes of Scripture, as dust before mens eyes HOBBES. **6.** The smallest ant or a. G. HERBERT. Hence † **A·tom** *v.* to atomize. **Atoma·re,** an area supposed to be formed by a combination of ultimate atoms. **A:tomecha·nics,** the mechanics of atoms. **A·tomless** *a. poet.* without leaving an a.

Atomic (ătǫ·mik), *a.* (*sb.*) 1678. [– mod.L. *atomicus*; see prec., -IC.] **1.** Of or pertaining to atoms 1692. **2.** Concerned with atoms 1678. **3.** Adhering to the atomic philosophy 1691. **4.** Minute 1809. **5.** Simple, elemental 1881. † **6.** *sb.* An adherent of the atomic philosophy. CUDWORTH.

1. *Atomic weight* in *Chem.*: the weight of an atom of an element (or radical), as compared with that of an atom of hydrogen, taken as unity; also the sum of the weights of the atoms of a compound. *A. volume* of a body: the space occupied by a quantity of it proportional to its atomic weight. **2.** *A. philosophy*: the doctrine taught by Leucippus, Democritus, and Epicurus: see ATOMISM. *A. theory* in *Chem.*: the doctrine that elemental bodies consist of a aggregations of indivisible atoms of definite relative weight; that the atoms of different elements unite with each other in fixed proportions; and that the latter determine the fixed proportions in which elements and compounds enter into chemical combination with each other. **4.** A. globules 1809. Changes almost a. ROGERS. var. **Atoma·tic** *a.* (*rare*). Hence **Ato·mical** *a.*, **-ly** *adv.*

Atomicity (ætŏmi·sĭti). 1865. [f. prec. + -ITY.] *Chem.* The combining capacity of an element (or radical), *i.e.* the number of atoms of hydrogen, or other monovalent element, with which one of its atoms normally combines. Now usu. called *valency*.

Atomism (æ·tŏmiz'm). 1678. [f. ATOM + -ISM.] **1.** Atomic philosophy; the doctrine of the formation of all things from indivisible particles endued with gravity and motion; var. † **Ato·micism.** **2.** Individualism 1836.

Atomist (æ·tŏmist). 1610. [f. as prec. + -IST.] **1.** One who holds the principles of atomism; var. **Atomi·cian** (*rare*). **2.** A student or exponent of the *atomic theory* (see ATOMIC *a.* 2) 1869. Hence **Atomi·stic, -al** *a.* of or pertaining to atomists or atomism; consisting of separate atoms. **Atomi·stically** *adv.*

Atomization (æ:tŏməizēi·ʃən). 1871. [f. next + -ATION.] The process of reducing to minute particles, *spec.* in *Med.* of reducing liquids to a fine spray.

Atomize (æ·tŏməiz), *v.* 1678. [f. ATOM + -IZE.] † **1.** To hold the atomic philosophy. **2.** To reduce to atoms, or to an atom; to belittle 1845. Hence **A·tomizer,** *spec.* an instrument for reducing liquids to a fine spray.

Atomology (ætǒmǫ·lŏdʒi). 1678. [f. Gr. ἄτομος ATOM + -LOGY.] The science of atoms.

Atomy[1] (æ·tǒmi). 1597. [f. ANATOMY, taken as *an atomy*; cf. *natomy*. Now mostly joc.] **1.** An anatomical preparation; *esp.* a skeleton 1728. **2.** An emaciated or withered living body 1597. *fig.* or *transf.* of things 1848.
You starved bloodhound!..Thou a., thou! SHAKS.

Atomy[2] (æ·tǒmi). 1591. [prob. – *atomi*, pl. of L. *atomus* ATOM, but assoc. w. prec.] **1.** An atom, a mote 1595. **2.** A mite, a pigmy 1591.
1. To count Atomies SHAKS. **2.** Drawne with a teeme of little Atomies Ouer mens noses *Rom. & Jul.* I. iv. 57.

Atonal (æ̆-, eᶦtōᵘ·năl), *a.* 1922. [A- 14.] *Mus.* Having no reference to a key or tonic.

At once (æ̆t,wɒ·ns), *advb. phr.* [ME. *at ones* (XIII), f. AT *prep.* + gen. of ONE; cf. NONCE.] † **1.** At one stroke, etc.; once for all; in (or into) one heap; together –1579. **2.** At one and the same time ME. **3.** In one and the same act, position, etc.; equally, both 1588. **4.** Immediately 1531.

At one (æ̆t,wɒ·n), *adv.* (passing into *adj.*) *phr.* [ME. *at one* (*aton, a-ton, at-on*); cf. ATONEMENT.] **1.** In concord or friendship; opp. to *at variance*, etc. Sometimes = Reconciled (*arch.*). ME. **2.** Into a state of harmony or unity of feeling, as *to bring, make*, etc., *at one* (*arch.*) ME. **3.** Of one mind ME. † **4.** Together. SPENSER.
1. So beene they both atone SPENSER *F.Q.* II. i. 29. *Comb.* **at-oneness** (*rare*).

Atone (ătōᵘ·n), *v.* 1555. [Back-formation from ATONEMENT. Not used in A.V., though *atonement* was used by Tindale (see next, sense 3).] **1.** *trans.* To set at one, reconcile. *Obs.* exc. as etymol. archaism 1593. † **b.** To compose (differences) –1702. † **2.** *intr.* To come into unity or concord –1607. **3.** *trans.* To reconcile, to appease 1617. **4.** *absol.* To make reconcilement or propitiation **a.** *for* the offender 1682; **b.** *for* the offence (= to make amends) 1665. **5.** *trans.* (*for* omitted) To expiate 1665. † **6.** *trans.* To join in one –1672. *fig.* To harmonize 1691. *intr.* 1649.
1. The king and parliament will soon be atoned MILT. To a. a broil 1565. **2.** He and Auffidius can no more a. Then violent'st contrariety *Cor.* IV. vi. 72. **3.** So heaven, atoned, shall dying Greece restore POPE. **4. b.** Nothing can a. for the Want of Modesty STEELE. **5.** To a. sin BARROW. **6.** *fig.* To a. our ideas with our perceptions A. HARE. Hence **Ato·nable, ato·neable** *a.* that may be atoned for. **Ato·ne** *sb.* † reconciliation; expiation (*arch.* with mod. sense). **Ato·ner.**

Atonement (ătōᵘ·nmĕnt). 1513. [f. phr. AT ONE in harmony (XIII) + -MENT, after med.L. *adunamentum* (VIII), f. *adunare* unite, and earlier ONEMENT, as used in *make an onement* be reconciled, *set at onement* reconcile.] † **1.** The condition of being *at one* with others; concord, agreement –1623. † **2.** The action of setting at one, or being set at one, after discord; reconciliation –1685; appeasement –1622. **3.** *spec.* in *Theol.* Reconciliation or restoration of friendly relations between God and sinners 1526. **4.** Propitiation by reparation of wrong or injury; amends, expiation 1611; *Theol.* propitiation of God by expiation of sin 1611. ¶ *Atonement* is variously used by theologians in the sense of *reconciliation, propitiation, expiation*. (Not so applied in any version of the N.T.)
1. What a. .is there betwixt light and darkness 1554. **2.** He desires to make attonement Beweene the Duke of Glouster, and your Brothers *Rich. III*, I. iii. 36. **3.** The office to preache the a. TINDALE 2 *Cor.* 5:18. **4.** The best A. he can make for it ADDISON. The High-Priest..having made an A. for the Sins of the People ADDISON. *Comb.* **a.-money,** money paid in expiation of sins. Hence **Ato·nementist,** one who holds the Calvinistic doctrine of the atonement.

Atonic (ătǫ·nik). 1727. [f. A- *pref.* 14 + TONIC, partly (esp. *Philol.*) through Fr. *atonique*. In *Path.*, f. ATONY.] **A.** *adj. Pros.* Unaccented; *usu.* not bearing the stress or syllabic accent 1878. **2.** *Path.* Wanting tone, or nervous elasticity 1792.
2. We live in..an a. age 1861.
B. *sb.* **1.** *Pros.* A word or element of speech not having an accent. (Used *spec.* in Gr. Gram. of ὁ, ἡ, οἱ, αἱ, ἐν, ἐς, εἰς, ἐκ, ἐξ, εἰ, οὐ, ὡς.) 1727. **2.** *Med.* A remedy having power to allay excitement 1864.

Atony (æ·tŏni). 1693. [– (O)Fr. *atonie* or late L. *atonia* debility – Gr. ἀτονία.] *Path.* Want of tone; enervation, languor. Also *fig.*
Ennui is..an intellectual a. 1847.

Atop (ătǫ·p). 1655. [A *prep.*[1] 1.] **1.** *adv.* On or at the top 1658; with *of* 1672. **2.** *prep.* [*of* omitted.] On the top of 1655.
1. A black mass a-top, and a metallic mass at bottom 1779.

-ator (ēᶦtəɹ), suffix formed by combination of the *-ā*-stem of L. vbs. in *-āre* + *-tor*, e.g. *creator* CREATOR; a few, like *senātor*, were formed otherwise. The earliest exx. in Eng. came through Fr. forms in *-ateur* († *-our*, etc.). Since the 17th cent. used in names of instruments, and from the 19th widely extended; e.g. *escalator, incubator, perambulator, ventilator.*

† **Atou·r,** *sb.* ME. [– (O)Fr. *atour* f. OFr. *atorner* equip, f. *torner* (mod. *tourner*) to TURN.] **1.** Attire, array –1475. **2.** Military equipment or preparation –1480.

Atour (ătūᵘ·r). *Sc.* ME. [app. f. AT *prep.* + *our, ower*, Sc. f. OVER.] **A.** *prep.* **1.** Over. **2.** In defiance of (an obstacle, etc.) 1535.
1. *By and atour*: in addition to; By and attour her gentle havings SCOTT.
B. *adv.* Over and above, besides ME.

Atrabilarian (ætrăbilēᵊ·riăn). 1678. [f. med.L. *atrabilarius* (see ATRABILIOUS, -ARY[1]) + -AN.] *adj.* = ATRABILARIOUS. *sb.* A hypochondriac.

Atrabila·rious, *a.* 1684. [f. as prec. + -OUS.] **1.** Of or pertaining to black bile. **2.** Atrabilious, hypochondriacal; acrimonious. vars. † **Atrabila·r,** † **-ai·re,** † **Atrabila·ric,** † **Atrabi·lary.**

† **A·trabile.** 1594. [– Fr. *atrabile* – L. *atra bilis*; see ATRABILIOUS.] *lit.* Black bile, an imaginary fluid, supposed anciently to be the cause of melancholy; *hence*: Melancholy, spleen.

Atrabi·liary, *a.* 1725. [– mod.L. *atrabiliarius*, f. L. *atra bilis* (see next) + *-arius* -ARY[1].] **1.** Of or pertaining to black bile; applied to the renal or suprarenal glands, and to the arteries supplying them. **2.** = ATRABILIOUS.

Atrabilious (ætrăbi·liəs), *a.* 1651. [f. L. *atra bilis* black bile, tr. Gr. μελαγχολία MELANCHOLY; see -IOUS.] Affected by black bile or 'choler adust'; melancholy; splenetic.
My a. censures CARLYLE. vars. **Atrabi·liar,** † **Atrabi·lous.** Hence **Atrabi·liousness.**

Atrament (æ·trămĕnt). ME. [– L. *atramentum* blacking, ink, f. *ater* black.] Blacking, ink; any similar black substance. Hence **Atrame·ntal** *a.* ink-. **Atrame·ntous** *a.* inky, black.

† **Atre·de,** *v. rare.* [f. AT- *pref.*[2] + REDE *v.*] To outdo in counsel. CHAUCER.

A-tre·mble, *adv.* 1856. [A *prep.*[1] 11.] Trembling.

† **Atre·n,** *v.* ME. [f. AT- *pref.*[2] + OE. *rennan.*] *intr.* To run away (with *dat.* = from).
Men may the wise atrenne, and nought atrede CHAUCER.

‖ **Atresia** (ătrī·ʃᶦă). 1866. [f. A- *pref.* 14 + Gr. τρῆσις perforation + -IA[1].] *Path.* Occlusion of a natural channel of the body.

A·trial, *a.* 1869. [f. L. ATRIUM + -AL[1].] *Phys.* Of or belonging to the *atrium.*

A-trip (ătri·p), *adv.* 1626. [A *prep.*[1] 11.] *Naut.* **1.** Of yards: Swayed up, ready to have the stops cut for crossing. Of sails: Hoisted from the cap, sheeted home, and ready for trimming. **2.** Of an anchor: Just raised perpendicularly from the ground in weighing 1796.

‖ **Atrium** (ēᶦ·triŏm). 1577. [L.] **1.** A court. **a.** The central hall of a Roman house. **b.** A portico in front of the principal doors of churches, etc. **2.** *Phys.* **a.** That part of the auricle into which the veins pour the blood. **b.** In the Tunicata: A large cavity into which the intestine opens. 1870.

Atro- (æ·tro), comb. f. L. *ater* black, as in *atrosanguineous* of a dark blood-red colour.

† **Atro·ce,** *a.* [– (O)Fr. *atroce* – L. *atrox, atroc-* (see next).] Atrocious. NORTH.

Atrocious (ătrōᵘ·ʃəs), *a.* 1669. [– L. *atrox, atroc-* fierce, cruel; see -IOUS.] **1.** Excessively and wantonly savage or cruel; heinously wicked. † **2.** Stern, fierce; extremely violent –1733. **3.** *colloq.* Very bad, execrable (*mod.*).
1. A. criminals 1772, acts DARWIN. **2.** A. Symptoms CHEYNE. **3.** An a. pun (*mod.*). Hence **Atro·ciously** *adv.* **Atro·ciousness.**

Atrocity (ătrǫ·sĭti). 1534. [– (O)Fr. *atrocité* or L. *atrocitas*; see prec., -ITY.] **1.** Savage enormity, horrible wickedness. **2.** Fierceness, sternness, implacability (*arch.*) 1635. **3.** An atrocious deed 1793. **4.** *colloq.* A very bad blunder, violation of taste or good manners, etc. 1878.
3. The deeds known as 'the Bulgarian atrocities' MCCARTHY. **4.** Atrocities in spelling 1878.

A·trophous, *a.* 1877. [f. next + -OUS.] Characterized by atrophy. var. **Atro·phic.**

Atrophy (æ·trŏfi), *sb.* 1620. [– Fr. *atrophie* or late L. *atrophia* – Gr. ἀτροφία lack of food, f. τροφή nourishment.] A wasting away of the body, or any part of it, through imperfect nourishment; emaciation.
Pining a. MILT. *fig.* By fatal a. of purse 1782.

Atrophy (æ·trŏfi), *v.* 1865. [f. prec.; cf. Fr. *atrophier* (XVI).] *lit.* and *fig.* **1.** *trans.* To starve. **2.** *intr.* To become atrophied or abortive 1865. Hence **A·trophied** *ppl. a.*; var. **Atro·phiated.**

Atropine (æ·tropəin). 1836. [f. mod.L. *atropa* deadly nightshade, fem. f. Gr. Ἄτροπος 'Inflexible', name of one of the Fates; see -INE.[5]] *Chem.* and *Med.* A poisonous alkaloid found in the Deadly Nightshade and the seeds of the Thorn-apple. var. **Atro·pia. Atro·pic** *a.* of or pertaining to a., as in *Atropic acid.* **A·tropini:sm, A·tropism,** poisoning by a. **A·tropini:zed** *ppl. a.* poisoned by a.

Atropous (æ·trŏpəs), *a.* 1839. [f. Gr. ἄτροπος not turned + -OUS.] *Bot.* Of ovules: Not inverted, erect. var. **A·tropal.**

Atrous (ēᶦ·trəs), *a. rare.* [f. L. *ater* black + -OUS.] *Nat. Hist.* Jet-black.

A-try (ătrəi·), *adv.* 1611. [A *prep.*[1] 11.] *Naut.* Of a ship in a gale: Kept by a judicious balance of canvas with her bows to the sea.

Attach (ătæ·tʃ), *v.* ME. [In I, II, – OFr. *atachier* (mod. *attacher*) = It. *attaccare*, Sp. *atacar*; in III, IV, – alteration, by prefix-substitution, of OFr. *estachier* fasten, fix = Pr., Sp. *estacar*; – Gmc. **stakōn*, f. **stak-* STAKE *sb.*[1]]
The sense development was: **1.** In OFr. 'to fasten' (recently adopted in Eng.). **2.** To '*attach* by some tie to the control of a court', hence to 'arrest, seize'. **3.** Fr. *attacher*, subseq. *attaquer*, after It. *attaccare*, gave Eng. ATTACK, and occas. (in 17th c.) *attach.*

I. 1. *Law.* To place or take under the control of a court; to arrest or seize by authority of a writ of attachment: **a.** a person; **b.** property, goods ME. † **2.** To accuse –1653. † **3.** To seize, lay hold of. Also *fig.* –1681.
1. Euery shiriffe..shall attache the saide offenders 1531. He was attached of heresy BP. BURNET. **b.** France..hath attach'd Our Merchants goods at Burdeux SHAKS. **3.** Attach'd with weariness *Temp.* III. iii. 5.

† **II.** To attack –1666.

III. 1. To tack on; to fasten or join (*to*) by tacking, tying, sticking, etc. 1802. **2.** To join on (e.g. a person *to* a company, etc.). Often *refl.* 1700. **3.** To join in sympathy or affection *to*. Often in pass. *To be attached to.* 1765. **b.** *esp.* To win the attachment of 1811. **4.** To fix *to*, as a name, description, or other adjunct 1812; *refl.* to fasten itself on, stick *to* 1861. **5.** To attribute 1837.
1. The means of attaching the doublet to the hose SCOTT. **2.** A Bedouin who had attached himself to us 1873. **3.** How she attached her little brothers to her 1833. **b.** Incapable of attaching a sensible man JANE AUSTEN. **4.** The liability which English law attaches to contracts BOWEN. **5.** The importance they attached to their own services PRESCOTT.

IV. *intr.* (for *refl.*) **1.** To fall, or come *upon*, and adhere to 1780. **2.** To be incident *to*, † *on* 1791. **3.** To come into legal operation in connection with anything 1818.
3. The wife's right to dower accordingly attached 1844. Hence † **Atta·ch** *sb.* arrest; *fig.* an attack of disease, etc.; an attachment; a thing attached. **Atta·cher,** one who attaches.

Attachable (ătæ·tʃăb'l), *a.* 1579. [f. prec. + -ABLE.] **1.** Liable to arrest or seizure. **2.** Capable of being tacked on as an adjunct *to* anything 1856. **3.** Capable of attachment 1865.

|| **Attaché** (ătæ·ʃe). 1835. [Fr., pa. pple. of *attacher* ATTACH.] A junior official attached to the staff of an ambassador, etc.; a naval or military representative of his government in a foreign country. **b.** *A. case*, a small leather case for carrying papers 1904.

Attached (ătæ·tʃt), *ppl. a.* 1552. [f. ATTACH *v.* + -ED[1].] **1.** Arrested 1611; † seized (with sickness, etc.) –1619; joined functionally 1859; joined by taste, affection, or sympathy *to*, affectionate 1793; incident *to* 1852. **2.** Fastened by a material union *to* 1841; *Zool.* stationary, as opp. to 'free' 1854; *Arch.* joined to a wall, etc., not 'detached' 1879. Hence **Atta·chedly** *adv.*

Attachment (ătæ·tʃmĕnt). 1447. [– (O)Fr. *attachement*; see ATTACH *v.*, -MENT.] **1.** The action of attaching (see ATTACH *v.* 1); now *esp.* of arrest for contempt of court; the writ commanding it 1468. **2.** The taking of property into the actual or constructive possession of the judicial power 1592. † **3.** Arrest, confinement –1606. **4.** The action of fastening on, or being fastened on or to; connection 1817. **5.** Affection, devotion, fidelity 1704. **6.** A fastening, tie, or bond 1801. **7.** An adjunct 1797.

1. If he does not appear, an a. is issued against him DE LOLME. **2.** *Foreign attachment*: 'legal seizure of the goods of foreigners, found in some liberty (*e.g.* the City of London) to satisfy their creditors within such liberty'. **5.** The lover's eye discovered the object of his a. SCOTT. **7.** Compass a. to the Theodolite 1876.

Attack (ătæ·k), *v.* 1600. [– Fr. *attaquer* – It. *attaccare* (see ATTACH), as in *attaccare battaglia* join battle.] *trans.* in all senses. **1.** To fasten or fall upon with force or arms; to assail, assault. (The common military term.) Also *absol.* **2.** To set upon with hostile action or words, so as to overthrow, injure, or bring into disrepute 1643. **3.** To assail with temptations 1673. **4.** To enter upon a work of difficulty 1871. **5.** Of disease: To seize upon, begin to affect 1677. **6.** To begin to act upon destructively, to begin to waste, decompose, or dissolve 1842.

1. The strong towns he successively attacked GIBBON. **2.** Who attacks the liberty of the press 'JUNIUS'. **5.** Rheumatism. .attacks indiscriminately the young and old F. A. KEMBLE. **6.** White ants .attacking the wood-work of houses 1842. Hence **Atta·ckable** *a.* assailable. **Atta·cker.**

Attack (ătæ·k), *sb.* 1667. [f. prec., or – Fr. *attaque* (– It. *attacco*).] **1.** The act of attacking (see ATTACK *v.* 1). The common military term; opp. to *defence*. **b.** *ellipt.* for: Point of attack, attacking force 1709. **2.** *fig.* The offensive part in any contest; *e.g.* the bowling in *Cricket*, etc. 1822. **3.** An assault with hostile or bitter words 1751. **4.** *fig.* The commencing of operations on a work of difficulty. So (*joc.*) upon dinner, etc. 1812. **5.** An access of disease; a fit or bout of illness 1811. **6.** The commencement of destructive or dissolving action by a physical agent 1842. **7.** *Mus.* [after It. *attacca*.] The action or manner of beginning a piece, passage, or phrase, in respect of precision and clarity; also *gen.*, brilliance of style, courageous rendering 1880.

1. The dire a. Of fighting Seraphim MILT. *P.L.* VI. 248. **3.** The a. upon a rising character JOHNSON. **5.** Attacks of overpowering giddiness SEELEY.

Attain (ătē^i·n), *v.* [ME. *ateyn(e, ateine* – AFr. *atain-, atein-*, OFr. *ataign-, ateign-*, stem of *ataindre, ateindre* (mod. *atteindre*) :– L. *attingere* touch on, reach, f. *ad* AT- *pref.*[3] + *tangere* touch.] † **I.** *trans.* **1.** To touch, hit –1475; to touch upon, treat of –1448. † **2.** To catch in an offence, convict, condemn, ATTAINT –1400.

II. *trans.* † **1.** To overtake, come up with, catch –1622. **2.** To reach by motion, gain (a point aimed at) 1585; (an age or time) 1826. **3.** To reach, arrive at, by continuous effort ME. **4.** To come into the possession of (not now used of a material thing) (*arch.*) ME. † **5.** To 'get at', find out –1666.

2. We quickly shall a. the English shore 1585. Had attained his sixteenth year 1826. **3.** Reason is not. .borne with us. .but attayned by Industry HOBBES. **4.** He attained the Crowne and Scepter of the Realme MORE.

III. *intr.* **1.** To get (*to*) ME. **2.** To live on (*to* a time or age) 1535. **3.** To succeed in reaching. Cf. II. 3, 4. ME. † **4.** = II. 5, but with *to, unto* –1628.

1. Nor nearer might the dogs a. SCOTT. **2.** He has attained to years of discretion 1888. **3.** Infallibility. .being what no man can a. vnto PRIDEAUX.

† **IV.** (cf. L. *attinere*.) To stretch, reach (*to*) –1530; to pertain *to* (ME. only).

Hence **Attai·nable** *a.* **Attai·nableness. Attai·ner. Attai·ning** *vbl. sb.*

† **Attai·n,** *sb.* 1599. [f. the vb.] = ATTAINMENT –1665.

Attainder (ătē^i·ndəɹ). 1473. [– AFr. *attainder, atteinder* (XIV), subst. use of inf. *atteinder*, (O)Fr. *atteindre* ATTAIN; see -ER[4].] **1.** The action or process of attainting: *orig.* as in ATTAIN *v.* I. 2; later, the legal consequences of judgement of death or outlawry, in respect of treason or felony, viz. forfeiture of estate real and personal, corruption of blood, so that the condemned could neither inherit nor transmit by descent, and generally, extinction of all civil rights and capacities. Through erron. assoc. with OFr. *teint, taint* TAINT, the second of these was looked upon as the essence of ATTAINDER. **b.** Act of Attainder 1587. † **2.** *fig.* Condemnation; dishonouring allegation –1593; stain of dishonour –1752.

1. *Bill* or *Act of Attainder*: one introduced or passed in the English parliament (first in 1459) for attainting any one without a judicial trial. All attainders are now abolished 1844. **2.** Th' Attaindor of his sland'rous Lippes *Rich. II*, IV. i. 24. vars. † **Attai·ndrie** COKE, † **Attai·ndure.**

Attainment (ătē^i·nmĕnt). ME. [f. ATTAIN *v.* + -MENT.] **1.** The action or process of attaining, reaching, or acquiring by effort (no *pl.*) 1549. **2.** That which is attained; *esp.* a personal accomplishment 1680.

1. Dost thou ayme at the a. of wisedome? HEALEY. **2.** A man of good attainments 1736. A low standard of a. PATTISON.

Attainor (ătē^i·nəɹ, -ǭ:ɹ). [– AFr. *atteignour*, f. *atteign-*; see ATTAIN *v.*, -OUR.] *Law.* One of the twenty-four jurors in the process of ATTAINT.

† **Attai·nt,** *ppl. a.* ME. [– OFr. *ataint, ateint*, pa. pple. of *ataindre* ATTAIN; later infl. in meaning by TAINT *v.*] **1.** Convicted, attainted. Used *orig.* as pa. pple. of ATTAIN, subseq. of ATTAINT *v.*; also as adj. –1768. **2.** Affected with sickness, passion, etc.; infected –1500. **3.** Exhausted. [Cf. F. *éteint*.] –1485.

Attaint (ătē^i·nt), *v.* ME. [f. ATTAINT *ppl. a.* (cf. *to convict*), used as pa. pple. before *attainted*. Its senses are thus due partly to *attain*, partly also to later association with TAINT *v.*, L. *tingere*; cf. the aphetic TAINT.] † **1.** = ATTAIN *v.* I. 1, II. 5. –1530. † **2.** To convict –1768. † **3.** *Old Law.* To convict a jury of having given a false verdict; to bring an action to reverse a verdict so given –1667. **4.** To subject to ATTAINDER (sense 1) ME. **5.** To accuse *of* crime or dishonour (*arch.*) 1586. **6.** To touch, strike, or affect, as a disease, or other bodily or mental affection 1534. † **7.** (Cf. TAINT.) To infect –1631. **8.** (= TAINT.) To infect with corruption, poison, etc. 1580; *fig.* to sully 1596.

4. To be attainted is, that his Blood be held in Law as stained and corrupted HOBBES. **5.** Rebecca. .being attainted of sorcery. .doth deny the same SCOTT. **7.** Attaynted With coveytous and ambycyon SKELTON. **8.** When secret Vlcers shall a. thy breath QUARLES. Lest she with blame her honour should a. SPENSER. Hence **Attai·ntment,** conviction, attainder. **Attai·nture** = ATTAINDER; *fig.* stain.

Attaint (ătē^i·nt), *sb.* 1523. [– OF. *ateinte, atainte* pa. pple. fem. used subst.; see ATTAINT *ppl. a.*] **1.** The act of touching; *spec.* a hit in tilting (*arch.*) 1525; † *fig.* a dint (of misfortune, etc.) 1655. **2.** *Vet. Surgery.* A blow on the leg of a horse caused by overreaching 1523. **3.** *Old Law.* The conviction of a jury for giving a false verdict; a legal process for reversing the verdict and convicting the jurors. (This was done by a grand jury of twenty-four.) 1528. **4.** = ATTAINDER 1603. **5.** *fig.* Imputation or touch of dishonour; stain 1592.

1. Both the others failed in the a. SCOTT. Thou. . maiest without a. o're-looke The dedicated words SHAKS.

† **Attal,** var. of ETTLE *v.*

† **Atta·me,** *v.* [ME. *atame* – OFr. *atamer* :– late L. *attaminare* touch, attack, defile; see AT- *pref.*[3], CONTAMINATE.] **1.** *trans.* To cut into –1494; to broach (a cask, etc.) –1440. **2.** To attack, meddle with –1450; to begin (ME. only).

Attar (æ·tăɹ). Also **atar,** and OTTO. 1798. [– Pers. (Arab.) *ʻaṭār*, f. *ʻiṭr* perfume (*ʻiṭr-gul* essence of roses). Earlier OTTO.] A fragrant, volatile, essential oil obtained from the petals of the rose; fragrant essence (of roses). *Attar-gul* (= Pers. *ʻiṭr-gul*) 'essence of roses' is occas. used.

† **Atta·sk,** *v.* [A- *pref.* 11 (*at-*).] To blame. *Lear* I. iv. 366.

† **Atta·ste,** *v.* ME. [– OFr. *ataster*, f. *a* AD- + *taster* TASTE *v.*] To taste, experience. *trans.* –1559. *absol.* –1460.

Atte, obs. f. AT; also = ME. *at þe*, at the.

Atteal (æ·tīl). 1600. *Ornith.* A kind of duck of the Orkney and Shetland isles.

Attemper (ăte·mpəɹ), *v.* ME. [– OFr. *atemprer* (mod. *attremper*) :– L. *attemperare* adjust, accommodate, f. *ad* AT- *pref.*[3] + *temperare*; see TEMPER *v.*] **1.** To qualify, modify, or moderate by admixture; to temper. **2.** To modify the temperature of ME. **3.** To moderate, assuage (passion or harshness); to soothe, appease (persons) ME. **4.** To restrain. Also *refl.* ? *Obs.* ME. **5.** To regulate ME. **6.** To make fit or suitable *to*. Also *refl.* ME. **7.** To attune 1579. **8.** To temper (metal) 1869.

1. The love attempered the sorow CAXTON. **2.** A. the air with a fire of charcoal EVELYN. **6.** God often attempers Himself. .to the condition of men PUSEY. **7.** High airs, attemper'd to the vocal strings POPE. Hence **Atte·mperament, -perment,** the bringing to a proper temper; mixture in due proportions.

† **Atte·mperance.** ME. [– OFr. *atemprance* f. *atemprer*; see prec., -ANCE.] **1.** Moderation –1560. **2.** = *Attemperament* (see ATTEMPER) –1555. **3.** Harmony 1481. **4.** Natural constitution. CHAUCER.

† **Atte·mperate,** *ppl. a.* ME. [– L. *attemperatus*, pa. pple. of *attemperare*; see ATTEMPER, -ATE[2].] Temperate; well-regulated; well-proportioned –1534. Hence † **Atte·mperately** *adv.*

Attemperate (ăte·mpĕrē^i t), *v.* 1561. [f. prec.] † **1.** = ATTEMPER 5, 6. –1711. **2.** = ATTEMPER 2. 1605. Hence **Atte:mpera·tion,** the action of attempering or regulating. **Atte·mperator,** that which attempers; *spec.* in *Brewing*, an arrangement for regulating the temperature of the fermenting wort, etc. † **Atte·mperature,** attempered condition.

† **Atte·mpre,** *a.* ME. [– OFr. *atempré*, pa. pple. of *atemprer* ATTEMPER.] Temperate, mild –1555. Hence † **Atte·mprely** *adv.*

Attempt (ăte·mt), *v.* 1513. [– OFr. *attempter*, latinized form of *atenter* (mod. *attenter*) :– L. *attemptare*, f. *ad* AT- *pref.*[3] + *temptare* TEMPT.]

I. 1. To make an effort or endeavour to do or accomplish some action. **2.** *ellipt.* To try to accomplish or attain (any action or object of activity, *esp.* one attended with risk or danger); to venture upon 1534. † **3.** To try to use or in use –1770.

1. Him he attempts with studied arts to please DRYDEN. To a. the conversion of the English GREEN. **2.** Courage and Hardiness to a. the Seas RAY.

II. † **1.** To try with afflictions –1650. **2.** To try to seduce, or entice; to tempt (*arch.*) 1513. † **3.** To try to obtain or attract –1749. † **4.** To try to move (by entreaty, etc.) –1673.

2. God. .Hinder'd not Satan to a. the minde of Man MILT. *P.L.* X. 8. **4.** Deare sir, of force I must a. you further, Take some remembrance of vs as a tribute *Merch. V*, IV. i. 421.

III. † **1.** *intr.* (with *indirect pass.*) To make an attack, or assault *upon*. Fr. *attenter sur*. *Obs.* (Now 'to make an attempt upon' or as 2.) –1697. **2.** *trans.* To try to take by force, master, or overthrow; to attack: **a.** an enemy, fortress, etc.; also *fig.* and *transf.* (*arch.*) 1562; † **b.** to try to ravish or seduce –1741.

1. We look to be attempted upon euery day CROMWELL. † *To a. nothing upon* = Fr. *rien attenter sur*. **2. b.** The Judges. .who attempted Susanna 1610. *To a. the life of*: to try to take the life of. Hence **Atte·mpter,** one who attempts anything; † an assailant; † one who attempts the virtue of a woman; † a tempter. **Atte·mptingly** *adv.*

Attempt (ăte·mt), *sb.* 1534. [f. prec. vb.] **1.** A putting forth of effort to accomplish what is uncertain or difficult; a trial, endeavour; enterprise, undertaking 1548; *esp.* futile endeavour 1605. † **2.** The thing attempted, aim –1790. **3.** † **a.** An attack, onset –1665. **b.** A personal assault on a person's life, a woman's honour, etc. (Now usu. 'an attempt upon the life of', etc.) 1593. † **4.** Temptation, seduction –1667.

1. If God be favourable vnto our attemptes UDALL. They haue awak'd, And 'tis not done: th'a., and not the deed, confounds vs *Macb.* II. ii. 11. *To make an a.*: to try (*to do*). **3. a.** Hee Prepares for some a. of Warre *Macb.* III. vi. 39. **b.** The Maid will I..make fit for his a. *Meas. for M.* III. i. 267. var. † **Attempta·tion. Atte·mptless** *a.* without attempting.

Attemptable (ăte·mtăb'l), *a.* also † **-ible.** 1611. [f. ATTEMPT *v.* + -ABLE.] That may be attempted. Hence **Atte:mptabi·lity.**

† **Atte·mptive,** *a. rare.* 1603. [irreg. f. ATTEMPT *v.* + -IVE.] Given to attempts; venturous.

This great nation..A., able, worthy, generous DANIEL.

Attend (ăte·nd), *v.* Aphet. TEND. [– OFr. *atendre* (mod. *attendre* wait for) :– L. *attendere*, f. *ad* AT- *pref.*[3] + *tendere* stretch.] To stretch to; *hence*, to direct the mind or energies to; to watch over; to wait for, expect. **I. 1.** To turn one's ear to, listen to. *trans.* (*arch.*) ME. *intr.* (Const. *to, unto.*) 1447. **2.** To turn the mind to, regard, consider. † *trans.* –1775. *intr.* with *to* 1678. **3.** To turn the energies to, look after. † *trans.* –1798. *intr.* with *to*, † *upon*, † *inf.*, or † *subord. cl.* ME.

1. My tale A. SCOTT. O Lord, a. vnto my crie *Ps.* 17:1. **2.** To a. to the justice of the case only McCULLOCH. **3.** To a. tasks POPE, to one's work 1833.

II. 1. To direct one's care to; to TEND, guard. *trans.* (*arch.*) ME. *intr.* with *to* 1796. **2.** *trans.* To apply oneself to the care or service of; *esp.* to minister to (the sick), to pay professional visits to (a patient) 1572. **3.** To wait upon 1469; *intr.* to be in waiting 1514; with *on, upon*, † *of* 1499. **4.** To follow, escort, or accompany, for the purpose of rendering services. (Used *spec.* in relation to royal personages.) *trans.* 1653. *intr.* with *on, upon*; and *absol.* 1591. **5.** *Mil.* and *Naut.* To follow closely upon for hostile purposes. (*trans.*, and *intr.* with *to.*) 1674. **6.** Of things: To follow closely upon, to accompany. (Now only of things immaterial.) *trans.* 1615. *intr.* with *on, upon* 1606. † **7.** *causal.* To follow up, conjoin –1775. **8.** To present oneself at a meeting, etc., in order to take part in the proceedings. *trans.* e.g. to *attend* church, a *place* of worship 1646. *intr.* Const. *at* the place. 1660.

1. They a. their lamps KANE. To a. to all the services NELSON. **2.** Hired nurses who attended infected people DE FOE. **3.** Summoned to a. the King MACAULAY. **4.** The Portuguese infanta.. was attended by a numerous train of nobles PRESCOTT. Trip Audry, I a. *A.Y.L.* v. i. 66. **5.** If this is so, a force is necessary to a. [the Enemy] NELSON. **6.** Our food was attended with some ale FIELDING. Destruction and misery a. on wicked doings 1847. **7.** I have..attended them with brief observations BACON. **8.** To a. lectures 1770, a funeral, school, at the City Temple (*mod.*).

III. 1. *trans.* To look out for, await 1475; † *ellipt.* with *cl.* to wait to see or learn –1699. † **2.** *fig.* Of things: To be reserved for, await –1734. † **3.** To expect –1692. † **4.** *intr.* To tarry, wait –1768.

1. Here I a. The king—and lo! he comes SMOLLETT. They must a. the moving of the waters 1642. Attended what would be the Issue TEMPLE. Hence **Atte·ndedness** (*rare*).

Attendance (ăte·ndăns). ME. [– OFr. *attendance*; see ATTEND *v.* and -ANCE.] † **1.** = ATTENTION 1. –1790. † **2.** = ATTENTION 2. –1674. **3.** The action or condition of attending (see ATTEND II. 4); ministration, assiduous service ME. **4.** Waiting the leisure, convenience, or decision of a superior 1461. **5.** The action or fact of being present at a meeting, etc., or when summoned 1460. † **6.** Waiting –1664; expectation –1641. † **7.** A body of attendants, retinue –1779. **8.** The body of persons present at any proceedings 1835.

3. Phr. *In attendance.* Reputation for..good a. on his customers DE FOE. **4.** *To* † *wait, dance*, a. = 'to attend' (usu. contemptuous). **5.** The number of attendances recorded 1888. *Comb.* **a.-officer,** one whose duty it is to see that children attend school.

† **Atte·ndancy.** Also **-ency.** 1594. [f. prec.; see -ANCY, -ENCY.] **1.** Attention 1679. **2.** The giving of attendance 1594. **3.** = ATTENDANCE 7. 1586. **4.** Attendant relation 1626. **5.** An adjunct 1654. **6.** Expectation 1646.

Attendant (ăte·ndănt). ME. [– (O)Fr. *attendant*; see ATTEND, -ANT.] **A.** *adj.* † **1.** Attentive –1649. **2.** Waiting upon, in order to do service; ministrant 1485. Const. † *to, on, upon.* ME. † **3.** *Law.* Dependent on; owing service to –1641. **4.** Accompanying; closely consequent. Const. *on, upon.* 1617. **5.** Present at a meeting, etc. (see ATTEND II. 8) 1588.

2. Other Suns..With thir a. Moons thou wilt descrie MILT. *P.L.* VIII. 149. **4.** *Attendant Keys* in *Mus.*: the keys or scales on the fifth above, and fifth below (or fourth above) any key-note or tonic, considered in relation to the key or scale on that tonic. A. circumstances 1888.

B. *sb.* **1.** One who attends (see ATTEND II. 4); a servant, satellite, companion 1555. *transf.* or *fig.* 1667. **2.** 'One that waits the pleasure of another' (J.) 1684. **3.** An accompaniment, close consequent 1607. **4.** One who is present at a meeting, etc. (see ATTEND II. 8) 1641. **5.** *Law.* (See *adj.* 3.)

1. Sin..and her black a., Death MILT. *P.L.* VII. 547. **3.** The laugh, the jest, attendants on the bowl POPE. Hence **Atte·ndantly** *adv.*

Attender (ăte·ndəɹ). 1461. [f. ATTEND *v.* + -ER[1].] **1.** One who gives heed; an observer 1660. **2.** He who (or that which) waits upon, *esp.* to render service 1461. **3.** = ATTENDANT *sb.* 4. 1704. **Atte·ndress,** a waitress. FULLER.

† **Atte·ndment.** *rare.* ME. [– OFr. *atendement* expectation, f. *atendre* ATTEND, see -MENT.] **1.** Sense, meaning. **2.** A thing that attends; *pl.* surroundings 1646.

Attent (ăte·nt), *ppl. a.* 1482. [– L. *attentus*, pa. pple. of *attendere* ATTEND.] Intent, attentive (*to, upon*).

Myne eares shall be attente vnto prayer 2 *Chr.* 7:15. Hence **Atte·ntly** *adv.*

† **Atte·nt,** *sb.* [ME. *atent(e* – OFr. *atente* (mod. *attente*), subst. use of fem. pa. pple. of *atendre* ATTEND. In OFr. confused w. *entente*, whence sense 2.] **1.** Attention; heed –1652. **2.** Intention, aim –1450. Hence † **Atte·ntful** *a.*

Atte·ntat(e. ? *Obs.* 1622. [– (O)Fr. *attentat* (XIV), or med.L. *attentatum*, f. pa. ppl. stem of *attentare* to attempt, attack, var. of *attemptare* to ATTEMPT. See -ATE[1].] † **1.** A criminal attempt or assault –1721. **2.** An attempt to gain an unauthorized advantage in law, e.g. after an inhibition is decreed 1701.

Attention (ăte·nʃən). ME. [– L. *attentio*, f. *attent-*, pa. ppl. stem of *attendere*; see ATTEND, -ION; cf. Fr. *attention* (XVI). Used by Chaucer in transl. from L., then not till *c.* 1600.] **1.** The action, fact, or state of attending or giving heed; earnest direction of the mind, consideration, or regard. The mental faculty of attending. **2.** Practical consideration, notice 1741. **3.** Attending to the comfort and pleasure of others; ceremonious politeness, courtesy. Often in *pl.* 1752. † **4.** A consideration (*rare*) 1784. **5.** *Mil.* A cautionary word used as a preparative to any particular exercise or manœuvre 1820.

1. The tongues of dying men Inforce a. *Rich. II*, II. i. 6. A. is that state of mind which prepares one to receive impression 1762. *To pay* or *give a. To attract, call, draw, arrest, fix*, etc. *a.* **2.** They have a. to everything, and always mind what they are about CHESTERF. **3.** *To pay a.* or *one's attentions to*: to court. **5.** *To come to a.*: to assume a prepared military attitude; so *to stand at a.*

Attentive (ăte·ntiv), *a.* 1570. [– (O)Fr. *attentif, -ive*, f. *attente*; see ATTENT *sb.*, -IVE.] **1.** Steadily applying one's mind, or energies; intent, heedful, observant 1577. **2.** Giving watchful heed to the wishes of others; polite, courteous 1570.

1. Diligent and a. at their workes 1622. **2.** Very a. to the ladies 1888. Hence **Atte·ntive-ly** *adv.*, **-ness.**

Atte·nuable, *a.* ? *Obs.* [f. L. *attenuare*; see ATTENUATE *v.*, -BLE.] That may be attenuated. SIR T. BROWNE.

Attenuant (ăte·niu,ănt), *a.* 1603. [– Fr. *atténuant* (XVI) – *attenuant-*, pres. ppl. stem of L. *attenuare*; see next, -ANT[1].] Having the property of thinning; *spec.* in *Med.* of thinning the secretions. As *sb.* [sc. *drug, agent.*] 1725. var. † **Atte·nuative.**

Attenuate (ăte·niu,eit), *v.* 1530. [– *attenuat-*, pa. ppl. stem of L. *attenuare*, f. *ad* AT- *pref.*[3] + *tenuare*, f. *tenuis* thin; see -ATE[3].] **1.** To make thin or slender (*e.g.* by natural or artificial shaping, starving, physical decay, etc.). **2.** To make thin in consistency, to separate the particles of a substance, to rarefy 1594. *spec.* in *Med.* To make thinner (the humours or concretions of the body) 1533. **3.** *fig.* To reduce in intensity, force, amount, or value; † to extenuate 1530. **4.** *intr.* To become slender, thinner, or weaker 1834.

1. They crucifie the soul of man, a. our bodies BURTON. **2.** Salt, for example, may a. earth 1762. **3.** To a. power 1530, numbers 1645, authority 1850, appetites LECKY. Hence † **Atte·nuater, -or** = ATTENUANT *sb.*

Attenuate (ăte·niu,ĕt), *ppl. a.* 1626. [– L. *attenuatus*, pa. pple. of *attenuare*; see prec., -ATE[2].] **1.** Slender, thin; tapered, reduced to thinness 1848. **2.** Rarefied; refined 1626.

1. The a. hands 1864. **2.** Such a rare and a. substance, as is the spirit of living creatures BACON.

Attenuation (ăte:niu,ēi·ʃən). 1594. [– Fr. *atténuation* or L. *attenuatio*, f. *attenuat-*; see prec., -ION.] **1.** The making thin or slender; diminution of thickness; emaciation 1631. **2.** Diminution of density 1594. **3.** The process of weakening, as if by dilution 1868.

3. The gradual 'attenuation' of disease germs 1882.

A·tter, *sb.* [OE. *ātr, ātor, āttor* = OS. *ettar*, OHG. *eitar* (G. *eiter*), ON. *eitr.*] † **1.** Venom, *esp.* that of reptiles –ME. † **2.** Gall; also *fig.* –ME. **3.** Corrupt matter, pus. Still in *Sc.* and *north. dial.* ME. Hence † **A·tter** *v.* to envenom; also *fig.*; to mix with gall.

A·ttercop. [OE. *āttorcoppe*, f. *āttor* (see prec.) + *-coppe* head; see COB *sb.*[4], COBWEB, COP *sb.*[3]] † **1.** A spider –1691. **2.** *fig.* A venomous person 1505. **3.** Misapplied to: A spider's web 1530.

Atte·rmine, *v.* ? *Obs.* ME. [– OFr. *aterminer* – late L. *atterminare*, f. *ad* AT- *pref.*[3] + *terminare*; see TERMINATE *v.*] To settle the term of; *esp.* to adjourn payment of (a debt) till a day fixed.

† **Atte·rr,** *v.* 1598. [– Fr. *atterrer* (XV), f. phr. *à terre* to the ground.] To bring to the ground, humble –1614.

† **A·terrate,** *v.* 1673. [f. It. *atterrare* 'to fill or dam vp with earth' (Florio, 1598), f. *a* to + *terra* earth. Cf. OFr. *aterrir* in same sense.] To fill up with (*esp.* alluvial) earth –1757. Hence † **Atterra·tion.**

A·ttery, a·ttry, *a.* OE. [f. ATTER *sb.* + -Y[1].] † **1.** Venomous –ME. † **2.** Mixed with gall (*lit.* and *fig.*) –ME. † **3.** Malignant –1535. **4.** Purulent 1868.

Attest (ăte·st), *v.* 1596. [– Fr. *attester* – L. *attestari*, f. *ad* AT- *pref.*[3] + *testari* to witness.] **1.** *trans.* To bear witness to, affirm the truth or genuineness of; to testify, certify. **b.** formally by signature or oath 1665. **2.** *transf.* Of things: To be evidence of, vouch for 1599. **3.** *intr.* To testify *to* 1672. **4.** *trans.* To call to witness (arch.). (So in Fr.) 1606. **5.** To put (a man) on his oath, or solemn declaration 1685.

1. The merit of the English bowmen..is strongly attested by Froissart 1875. **b.** I will assert nothing here, but what I dare a. SWIFT. **4.** But I a. the gods, your full consent Gaue wings to my propension *Tr. & Cr.* II. ii. 132. Hence **Atte·stable** *a.* **Atte·ster, -or**; var. **Attesta·tor. Atte·stive** *a.* furnishing evidence (*rare*). **Atte·stment,** testimony (*rare*).

Attest (ăte·st), *sb.* 1606. [f. prec. vb.] **1.** Evidence, testimony. **2.** Attesting signature, attestation 1649.

1. Th' a. of eyes and eares *Tr. & Cr.* v. ii. 122.

Attestant (ăte·stănt). 1880. [f. ATTEST *v.* + -ANT[1].] *ppl. adj.* Bearing witness. *sb.* One who attests (by signature).

Attestation (ætestēi·ʃən). 1547. [– Fr. *attestation* or late L. *attestatio*, f. *attestat-*, pa. ppl. stem of *attestari*; see ATTEST *v.*, -ION.] **1.** The act of bearing witness; the testimony borne; evidence, proof 1598. **b.** Formal confirmation by signature, oath, etc.; *esp.* the verification of the execution of a deed or will by signature in the presence of witnesses 1674. † **2.** The act of calling to witness –1741. **3.** The administration of an oath, *e.g.* of the oath of allegiance to a recruit 1812.

1. b. The last requisite to the validity of a deed is the a., or execution of it in the presence of witnesses BLACKSTONE.

Atte·stative, *a.* 1832. [f. L. *attestat-* (see prec.) + -IVE; see -ATIVE.] Of the nature of, or pertaining to, attestation.

Attic (æ·tik), *a.* and *sb.*[1] 1599. [– L. *Atticus* – Gr. Ἀττικός of Attica.] **1.** Of or pertaining to Attica, or to its capital Athens; Athenian. *Formerly* = Greek. **2.** Having characteristics peculiarly Athenian; *hence*, of style, etc.: Pure, classical 1633. **3.** *sb.* A native of Attica, an Athenian (author) 1699.

1. No Atticke eloquence is so sweete DEKKER. **2.** Well, but Addison's prose is A. prose M. ARNOLD. *Attic salt* or *wit* (L. *sal Atticus*): refined, delicate, poignant wit. *Attic faith*: inviolable faith. *Attic base* in *Arch.*: a base consisting of an upper and lower torus divided by a scotia and two fillets, used for Ionic, Corinthian, and occ. for Doric columns. *Attic order*: a square column of any of the five orders. vars. † **A·ttical, -an,** *adjs.* (*rare*).

Attic (æ·tik), *sb.*[2] (orig. *adj.*). 1696. [– Fr. *Attique*; see prec. and sense 1.] **1.** A small order (column and entablature) placed above another order of much greater height constituting the main façade. (Usually an Attic order, with pilasters; whence the name.) **2.** *attrib.* quasi-*adj.* in *Attic storey*: orig. the space enclosed by such a structure; *hence*, the top storey of a building, under the beams of the roof, where there are more than two storeys 1724. **3.** The highest storey of a house, or a room in it; a garret. Hence *joc.* the brain. 1817.

2. The Rustic and A. Stories are 12 feet high each DE FOE. **3.** A small lodging in an a. MACAULAY.

† **Atti·ce,** *v.* 1450. [– OFr. *atisier* (mod. *attiser*) :– Rom. **adtitiare*, f. **titium* for L. *titio* fire-brand.] To stir up, instigate; to gain over, entice –1557.

Atticism (æ·tisiz'm). 1612. [– Gr. Ἀττικισμός; see ATTIC *a.*, -ISM. Cf. Fr. *atticisme* (XVI).] **1.** Siding with, or attachment to, Athens 1628. **2.** The peculiar style and idiom of Greek as used by the Athenians; *hence*, refined, elegant Greek, and *gen.* a refined amenity of speech, a well-turned phrase 1612.

Atticist (æ·tisist). 1835. [– Gr. Ἀττικιστής; see -IST.] One who affected Attic style.

Atticize (æ·tisəiz), *v.* 1610. [– Gr. Ἀττικίζειν; see -IZE.] **1.** *intr.* To side with or favour Athens 1753. **2.** To affect Attic style; to conform to Athenian (or Greek) habits, modes of thought, etc.

† **Atti·nge,** *v.* 1639. [– L. *attingere* touch on; see ATTAIN.] To touch upon, come in contact with –1742. Hence † **Atti·ngency,** effective contact.

‖ **Attirail, attiral.** *Obs.* 1611. [Fr., f. OFr. *atirier*; see ATTIRE *v.*, -AL[1].] Apparatus, gear –1790.

Attire (ătəiə·ɹ), *v.* See also aphet. TIRE *v.*[3] [ME. *atire* – OFr. *atir(i)er* arrange, equip, f. OFr. phr. *a tire*, Pr. *a tieira* in succession or order, of unkn. origin.] † **1.** To put in order. † **2.** To prepare, fit out –1440. **3.** To equip: † **a.** for war: To arm –1593. **b.** with dress, etc.: To dress, adorn. (Now only literary and usu. *refl.* and *pass.*) ME. **c.** To dress (the head, *mostly* of women) (*arch.*) ME.

3. a. A palfray of prise, prudly atyrit ME. **b.** To greet her thus attired TENNYSON. **c.** Shee painted her face, and tyred her head, and looked out at a window 2 *Kings* 9:30. Hence **Atti·red** *ppl. a.*; *spec.* in *Venery* and *Her.* furnished with horns. **Atti·rement,** outfit, dress; † furniture, † decoration.

Attire (ătəiə·ɹ), *sb.* ME. [f. ATTIRE *v.*; aphet. TIRE *sb.*[1]] † **1.** Equipment for war –1440. † **2.** Personal adornment. Also (with *pl.*) an ornament. –1642. **3.** Dress, apparel; † (with *pl.*) a dress ME. † **4.** Head-dress; *spec.* of women. Also aphet. TIRE. (Erron. conn. w. *tiara.*) –1611. **5.** *Venery* and *Her.* The 'headgear' of a deer 1562. **6.** *fig.* Anything which clothes or adorns; the external surroundings of anything immaterial 1610. † **7.** In plants: The parts within the corolla, as the stamens, and the florets of the disc in Composite flowers –1751.

3. Having neither..nor attyre to clothe their backes 1553. **5.** The Heralds call the Horns of a Stag..his A. BRADLEY. **6.** Earth in her rich a. MILT. *P.L.* VII. 501.

Attiring (ătəiə·riŋ), *vbl. sb.* ME. [-ING[1].] **1.** The action of fitting out, accoutring, dressing. **2.** Dress, trappings; head-dress; personal ornament. Also *fig.* 1552. **3.** = ATTIRE *sb.* 5. 1678.

Comb.: † **A.-house, -room** = *Tiring-house, -room*, the room where players dress themselves for the stage; **a.-room,** a dressing-room, generally.

Attitude (æ·titiud). 1668. [– Fr. *attitude* – It. *attitudine*, Sp. *attitud* fitness, disposition, posture :– late L. *aptitudo, -din-* APTITUDE. Orig. a technical term of the Arts of Design, taking the place of *aptitude*, XVIII; thence extended into general use.] **1.** In *Fine Arts*: The disposition of a figure in statuary or painting; *hence*, the posture given to it. (Now merged in 2.) **2.** A posture of the body proper to or implying some action or mental state 1725. Also *fig.* **3.** Settled behaviour or manner of acting, as representative of feeling or opinion 1837. **4.** *Attitude of mind*: habitual mode of regarding anything 1862.

1. The business of a painter in his choice of attitudes DRYDEN. **2.** *To strike an a.*: to assume it theatrically. *fig.* The mien and attitudes of truth JOHNSON. **4.** The allegorical a. of mind 1881. Hence **Attitu·dinal** *a.* pertaining to attitudes. **A:ttitudina·rian,** one who studies or practises attitudes. **A:ttitudina·rianism,** the excessive use of attitudes.

Attitudinize (ætitiū·dinəiz), *v.* 1784. [f. It. *attitudine* + -IZE.] *intr.* To study or practise attitudes excessively; to pose. Also *fig.*

Don't attitudinise JOHNSON. *fig.* In every line that he wrote Cicero was attitudinising for posterity FROUDE. Hence **Attitu:diniza·tion,** the practice of attitudes. **Attitu·dinizer.**

Attle (æt'l). 1849. [etym. uncertain; cf. ADDLE.] *Mining.* 'Refuse; impure off-casts in the working of mines' (Weale).

Attollent (ătǫ·lĕnt). 1713. [– *attollent-*, pres. ppl. stem of L. *attollere* elevate, f. *ad* AT- *pref.*[3] + *tollere* raise. See -ENT.] *adj.* Lifting up; *spec.* of certain muscles. (Usu. in L. form, *attollens*). *sb.* [sc. *muscle.*]

Attomy, Attonce, Attone, obs.; see ATO-.

Attorn (ătǿ·ɹn), *v.* 1458. [– OFr. *atorner, aturner* assign, appoint, (whence law L. *attornare*), f. *a* AD- + *torner* to TURN.] **1.** *trans.* To turn over to another; to assign, transfer 1649. **2.** *intr.* (for *refl.*) In *Feudal Law*: To transfer oneself (*i.e.* one's homage and allegiance) from one lord to another; to do homage to, as lord. Also *fig.* 1611. **3.** *Mod. Law.* To agree formally to be the tenant of one into whose possession the estate has passed 1458. So *to attorn tenant.* 1844.

1. To a. a vassal's service to some other 1649, one's allegiance 1691. **3.** Tenant who attorns under any mistake may defend against lessor WHARTON.

Attorney (ătɒ·ɹni), *sb.*[1] [ME. *aturne, atorne* – OFr. *atorné, aturné*, subst. use of pa. pple. of *atorner*; see prec.] † **1.** One appointed to act for another; an agent, deputy, commissioner. In later times only *fig.* –1642. **2.** (*Attorney in fact, private attorney.*) One duly appointed or constituted (by *Letter* or *Power of Attorney*) to act for another in business and legal matters, either *generally*, or in some *specific* act 1466. Also *fig.* **3.** (*Attorney-at-law, public attorney.*) A properly-qualified legal agent practising in the courts of Common Law (as a *solicitor* practised in Chancery); one who conducts litigation in these courts, preparing the case for the barristers, who plead in open court. (Often used as almost = knave, or swindler. In U.S. the distinction between *attorney* and *counsel* does not exist. The title was abolished in England by the Judicature Act of 1873.) ME. **4.** *transf.* An advocate, mediator. ? *Obs.* 1537. **5.** Specific title of the law officer, or clerk, of various courts or councils 1494.

1. I will attend my husband..And will haue no atturney but my selfe *Com. Err.* V. i. 100. **2.** None may appear in Gods service by an Atturney FULLER. **3.** Johnson observed, that 'he did not speak ill of any man behind his back, but he believed the gentleman was an a.' BOSWELL. **4.** Be the Atturney of my loue to her SHAKS. **5.** *The King's Attorney*: now ATTORNEY-GENERAL. *Mr. Attorney*, the style used in speaking to or † *of* him.

Attorney-General. † **1.** *gen.* A legal representative acting under a general power of attorney; opp. to *a. special* or *particular*. Pl. *attorneys general.* –1717. **2.** *spec.* *Attorney-General, Attorney General*: a legal officer of the state empowered to act in all cases in which the state is a party. In England, Ireland, etc., and in U.S., the first ministerial law-officer of the government. In the duchies of Lancaster and Cornwall, and county palatine of Durham, the title of his or her Majesty's attorney. Pl. (better): *Attorney-Generals.* 1533. Hence **Attorney-generalship.**

Atto·rney, *sb.*[2] 1461. [– OFr. *atornée*, subst. use of fem. pa. pple. of *atorner* ATTORN *v.*] The † **1.** action of appointing a legal representative, procuration. (? *Hence*, 'by attorney'.) –1635. Now only used in, **2.** *Letter* or *Warrant of Attorney*: a legal document by which a person appoints one or more persons to act for him as his attorney or attorneys. *Power of A.*: the authority so conferred, the document itself.

Atto·rney, *v.* [f. the sb.] To perform by attorney. *Wint. T.* I. i. 30.

Atto·rneydom. 1881. [-DOM.] The body of attorneys collectively. (*Contemptuous.*)

Atto·rneyism. 1837. [-ISM.] The practice of the 'rascally attorney'. (*Vituperative.*)

Atto·rneyship. 1591. [-SHIP.] **1.** The acting as an attorney for another; proxy. **2.** The profession and practice of an attorney; also = *Attorney-generalship* 1611.

Attornment (ătǿ·ɹnmĕnt). 1531. [– OFr. *atornement*, f. *atorner*; see ATTORN, -MENT.] **1.** A turning over; transference or assignment 1650. **2.** *spec.* The transference of his homage, etc., by a tenant to a new feudal lord; *hence*, legal acknowledgement of the new landlord 1531.

† **Attour,** var. of ATOUR *adv.* and *prep.*

† **Attou·rne,** *v.* ME. [alt. of *return* by prefix-substitution.] = RETURN –1470.

Attract (ătræ·kt), *v.* 1540. [– *attract-*, pa. ppl. stem of L. *attrahere*, f. *ad* AT- *pref.*[3] + *trahere* draw.] Only *trans.* † **1.** To draw in; to absorb –1652; to inhale –1667. † **2.** To pull, drag in –1677. **3.** To draw to itself by invisible influence: **a.** Said of physical forces 1627. **b.** Said of influencing the will and action of men and animals 1568. **c.** Said of presenting conditions favourable, *e.g.* to parasites, disease, criticism, etc. 1771. **4.** Hence, without material movement: **a.** To excite towards oneself the pleasurable emotions of a person, who thus 'feels drawn' to one 1601. **b.** To draw forth, and fix upon oneself the attention, or notice, of others 1692.

3. a. Jet and amber attracteth straws SIR T. BROWNE. **b.** A great capital attracts great talent HELPS. **c.** Conditions which a. fever 1888. **4. a.** Adornd and lovely to a. Thy love MILT. *P.L.* X. 152. **b.** A wife..Made to a. his eyes, and keep his heart DRYDEN. Hence † **Attra·ct** *sb.* attraction; chiefly in *pl.* charms. **Attra·ctable** *a.* capable of being attracted; whence **Attra:ctabi·lity. Attra·ctableness. Attra·ctingly** *adv.*

Attraction (ătræ·kʃən). 1533. [– Fr. *attraction* or L. *attractio*, f. *attract-*; see prec., -ION.] † **1.** Absorption; the taking in of food –1621. † **2.** Inhalation –1638. † **3.** *Med.* The action of drawing humours, etc.; *concr.* an application that so draws, a poultice, etc. –1656. † **4.** Pulling –1578. **5.** The action of a body in drawing to itself, by some physical force, another to which it is not materially attached; the force thus exercised 1607. *fig.* Personal influence, figured as magnetic 1750. **6.** The action of causing men or animals to come to one by influencing their appetites, etc. 1742. **7.** The action of drawing forth interest, affection, sympathy; the power of so doing 1767. **8.** An attracting quality 1608. **9.** A thing or feature which 'draws' people; *esp.* any interesting or amusing exhibition 1862.

5. The Sunnes a Theefe, and with his great a. Robbes the vaste Sea *Timon* IV. iii. 439. *Magnetic attraction*: the action of a magnet in drawing and attaching iron to itself. *Electric a.*: the similar action of electrified bodies upon other substances. *A. of gravity* or *gravitation*: that which exists between all bodies, and acts at all distances, with a force proportional to their masses, and inversely proportional to the square of their distance apart. *Molecular a.*: that which takes place between molecules, and acts only at infinitely small distances. *A. of cohesion*: that by which the particles composing a body are kept together. *A. of adhesion*: that by which certain substances, when brought into contact, stick together. *Capillary a.*: that whereby a liquid is drawn up through a hair-like tube. *Chemical a.* = AFFINITY. **6.** The a. of the disaffected to his standard 1888. **8.** She had new Attractions every time he saw her STEELE. Hence **Attra·ctionally** *adv.* † **Attra·ctionist,** one who accounted for phenomena by a theory of a. **Attra·ctionless** *a.*

Attractive (ătræ·ktiv). 1540. [– Fr. *attractif, -ive* – late L. *attractivus,* f. as prec.; see -IVE.] **A.** *adj.* † **1.** Absorptive –1713. † **2.** *Med.* Drawing humours –1786. **3.** Having the property of ATTRACTION (sense 5). Also *fig.* 1602. **4.** Having the quality of ATTRACTION (sense 6) 1590. **5.** Having the quality of attracting attention, etc.; interesting, engaging, pleasing, alluring. (Now the most frequent use.) 1602.

5. Interesting and a. for those who love to hear an old man's stories of a past age SCOTT. Hence **Attra·ctively** *adv.* **Attra·ctiveness.**

B. *sb.* † **1.** *Med.* A medicament which 'draws' –1786. † **2.** That which draws like a magnet. Also *fig.* –1652. † **3.** An ATTRACTION (sense 9) –1765. † **4.** A quality that attracts; *esp.* an attractive personal quality. (Now repl. by ATTRACTION.) –1805.

Attractor (ătræ·ktəɹ). 1641. [f. ATTRACT + -OR 2.] **1.** That which attracts 1646. **2.** One who draws by sympathy, etc. 1641.

Attrahent (æ·trăhĕnt). 1661. [– *attrahent-,* pres. ppl. stem of L. *attrahere*; see ATTRACT, -ENT.] *adj.* That attracts, attracting. *sb.* [sc. *agent.*]

The motion of steel to its a. GLANVILL.

† **Attra·p,** *v.*[1] 1524. [– Fr. *attraper,* f. *à* AT- *pref.*[3] + *trappe* TRAP *sb.*[1]] To catch in, or as in, a trap –1681.

† **Attra·p,** *v.*[2] 1580. [f. A- *pref.* 11 + TRAP *v.*[2]] Usu. in pa. pple. **attrapped.** Furnished with trappings –1693.

† **Attrecta·tion.** 1615. [– L. *attrectatio,* f. *attrectat-,* pa. ppl. stem of *attrectare* to touch, handle.] Touching, handling –1663.

Attributable (ătri·biŭtăb'l), *a.* 1665. [f. ATTRIBUTE *v.* + -ABLE.] Capable of being attributed, *esp.* as owing to, produced by.

How much is a. to that cause MILL.

† **A·ttribute,** *ppl. a.* ME. [– L. *attributus,* pa. pple. of *attribuere*; see next.] Attributed; assigned, given –1599.

Attribute (æ·tribiut), *sb.* ME. [– (O)Fr. *attribut* or L. *attributum,* subst. use of n. pa. pple. of *attribuere,* f. *ad* AT- *pref.*[3] + *tribuere* allot. Cf. TRIBUTE.] **1.** A quality ascribed to any person or thing, one which is in common usage assigned to him; hence, *occas.,* an epithet or appellation in which the quality is ascribed. † **2.** Distinguished quality or character; credit, reputation. (Cf. *quality,* etc. in 'a person of *quality*', i.e. '*quality* worth naming'.) –1690. **3.** A material object recognized as symbolic of any office, or actor; *spec.* in *Painting,* etc.: A conventional symbol added to identify the personage represented 1596. **4.** An inherent or characteristic quality 1836. (Sir W. Hamilton's distinction (*Metaph.* viii. (1870) I. 151) is hardly historical.) **b.** in *Logic,* That which may be predicated of anything; *strictly* an essential and permanent quality 1785. **5.** *Gram.* An attributive word; a predicable. *esp.* in *Sentence Analysis*: = Attributive adjunct, *i.e.* an adj., or a word, phr., or cl. equivalent to an adj.

1. Mercy is..an a. to God himselfe *Merch. V.* IV. i. 195. **2.** It takes From our achievements..The pith and marrow of our a. *Haml.* I. iv. 22. **3.** The club is an a. of Hercules 1727. *Merch. V.* V. iv. 191. **4.** The attributes and acts of God, as far as they are revealed to man BACON. Beauty was an a. of the family SCOTT. **b.** Every a. is..an universal REID.

Attribute (ătri·biut), *v.* 1523. [– *attribut-,* pa. ppl. stem of L. *attribuere*; see prec.] **1.** To assign, give, concede *to* any one, as his right (*arch.* or *Obs.*). **b.** To ascribe in praise 1563. **2.** To ascribe *to* as belonging or proper 1538. **3.** To ascribe as an attribute belonging, proper, or inherent 1534; as an effect *to* the cause 1530. **4.** To ascribe *to* an author as his work 1599. **5.** To assign in one's opinion to its proper time and place 1567.

2. God attributes to place No sanctity, if none be thither brought By men MILT. *P.L.* XI. 836. † *To attribute (much),* etc.: to ascribe great importance *to.* **3.** Attributed folly to God 1611. I cannot a. this honour to any desert in me 1626. Hence **Attri·buter** (*rare*).

Attribution (ætribiū·ʃən). 1467. [– (O)Fr. *attribution* – L. *attributio,* f. as prec.; see -ION.] **1.** Bestowal (in fact) (*arch.* or *Obs.*). **2.** Ascription in statement 1649. **3.** The assigning of a quality as belonging or proper to anything 1651. **4.** The ascribing of an effect to a cause, of a work to its (supposed) author, date, place, or of date and place to a work 1665. † **5.** *Rhet.* Giving of epithets 1589. **6.** *Logic.* Predication of an attribute 1860. **7.** Anything ascribed in one's opinion, *e.g.* appellation, credit, sense of a word, etc. ? *Obs.* 1596. † **8.** An attribute 1589. **9.** Authority or function granted (to a ruler, delegate, etc.). (From mod.Fr.) 1796.

3. The a. of sexes to plants WHEWELL. **7.** Such a. should the Dowglas haue, As not a Souldiour.. Should go so generall currant through the world 1 *Hen. IV,* IV. i. 3. **9.** Trials for homicide were only a small part of its attributions GROTE.

Attributive (ætri·biutiv). 1606. [– Fr. *attributif, -ive,* f. *attribut*; see ATTRIBUTE sb., -IVE.] **A.** *adj.* † **1.** Characterized by attributing. SHAKS. **2.** *Logic.* That assigns an attribute to a subject 1849. **3.** *Gram.* That expresses an attribute 1840. **4.** So-assigned, so-ascribed. Cf. *putative,* and ATTRIBUTION 4. 1866. **B.** *sb.* A word that denotes an attribute. (Now usu. limited to adjs. and their equivalents.) 1750. Hence **Attri·butive-ly** *adv.,* **-ness** (*rare*).

Attrist (ătri·st), *v.* ? *Obs.* 1680. [– Fr. *attrister,* f. *à* AT- *pref.*[3] + *triste* sad :– L. *tristis.*] To sadden.

Attrite (ătrəi·t), *ppl. a.* 1625. [– L. *attritus,* pa. pple. of *atterere,* f. *ad* AT- *pref.*[3] + *terere* rub. Cf. TRITE.] **1.** Ground down by friction. ? *Obs.* 1654. **2.** Having ATTRITION (sense 4) 1625. Hence **Attri·ted** *ppl. a.* worn down by friction. Also *fig.* **Attri·tive** *a.* characterized by attrition (*rare*). **Attri·tor. Attri·tus,** matter produced by attrition.

Attrition (ătri·ʃən). ME. [– late L. *attritio,* f. *attrit-,* pa. ppl. stem of *atterere*; see prec., -ION.] **1.** The act or process of rubbing one thing against another 1601. Also *fig.* **2.** Rubbing away, wearing or grinding down, by friction 1601. **3.** *Surg.* **a.** Excoriation, abrasion. **b.** Comminuted fracture 1543. **4.** An imperfect sorrow for sin, not amounting to *contrition* or utter crushing, and having its motive, not in love of God, but in fear of punishment. (*Scholastic Theol.*) ME.

2. Contact with English society exercises a constant a. on the system of castes MAX-MÜLLER.

Attroopment (ătrū·pmĕnt). *rare.* 1795. [– Fr. *attroupement,* f. *attrouper,* f. *à* + *troupe* TROOP *sb.*] A tumultous troop or crowd.

Attune (ătiū·n), *v.* 1596. [f. AT- *pref.*[3] + TUNE *v.*] **1.** To bring into musical accord. Const. *to.* Also *fig.* **2.** To bring (a musical instrument) to the right pitch; to tune. Also *fig.* 1728. **3.** To make tuneful 1667.

1. *fig.* The mind attuned to grace FREEMAN. **3.** Joy lift her spirit, joy a. her voice COLERIDGE. Hence **Attu·ne** *sb.* harmony (*rare*). **Attu·nement.**

A-tu·mble, *adv.* 1881. [A *prep.*[1] 11.] In tumbling condition.

A-twain (ătwē̆ⁱ·n), *adv. arch.* ME. [A *prep.*[1] 6. Cf. A-TWO.] **1.** In two. **2.** Asunder 1870.

Atwee·l, *phr. Sc.* 1768. Perh. contr. f. *wat weel* = 'wot well'; aphet. *'tweel.*

Atween (ătwī·n). *arch.* and *dial.* ME. [f. A *prep.*[1] 5 + *-twene, -tween,* stem of BETWEEN, on analogy of *afore, before, among, bimong.* Cf. ATWIXT.] *prep.* Between. † *adv.* Between whiles –1596.

† **Atwi·nd,** *v.* [f. AT- *pref.*[2] + OE. *windan* to WIND.] To escape (with *dat.* = from) –ME.

A-twi·st, *adv.* 1754. [A *prep.*[1] 11.] Twisted, askew.

† **Atwi·te,** *v.* [f. AT- *pref.*[1] + OE. *wītan.* Aphet. TWIT, formerly *twite.*] To reproach, blame, taunt, twit –1530.

A-twi·tter, *adv.* 1833. [A *prep.*[1] 11.] In a twitter.

Atwixt (ătwi·kst), *prep. arch.* or *dial.* ME. [f. A *prep.*[1] 5 + *-twix(t,* stem of BETWIXT; cf. ATWEEN. Aphet. 'TWIXT.] Between.

A-two (ătū·), *adv. arch.* and *dial.* [OE. *on twā, on tū,* i.e. ON, TWO. Cf. A *prep.*[1] 6.] **1.** In or into two parts (*arch.*). † **2.** Apart, asunder –1450.

Atypic (ăti·pik), *a.* [A- *pref.* 14.] Not typical, not conformable to the ordinary type.

‖ **Aubade** (oba·d). 1678. [Fr. – Sp. *albada,* f. *alba* (= Fr. *aube*) dawn.] A piece of music to be played or sung at dawn; an open-air morning serenade; hence, any morning concert.

The crowing cock..Sang his a. LONGF.

‖ **Aubain** (obæ̃n). 1882. [Fr.; in med.L. *Albanus.*] A non-naturalized foreigner subject to the right of *aubaine.*

‖ **Aubaine** (obę·n). 1727. [Fr.; see prec.] A right of French kings, whereby they claimed the property of every non-naturalized stranger who died in their country. Abolished in 1819.

Aube, obs. f. ALB.

‖ **Auberge** (obe·rʒ). 1615. [Fr. (XVI), the southern var. of northern Fr. *héberge.*] An inn. Hence ‖ **Aubergi·ste,** keeper of an a. † **Aube·rgical** *a.*

‖ **Aubergine** (obɛrʒi·n). 1794. [Fr. *aubergine* – Cat. *alberginia* – Arab. *al-bādinjān* – Pers. *bādingān* – Skr. *vātiṃgaṇa.*] The fruit of the Egg-plant, *Solanum esculentum.*

‖ **Aubin** (obeñ). 1753. [Fr., earlier *haubby* – Eng. HOBBY *sb.*[1]] A kind of broken gait, between an amble and a gallop.

Auburn (ǭ·bəɹn), *a.* [Early forms *aborne* (XV), *alborne* (XVI) – OFr. *alborne, auborne* :– med.L. *alburnus* whitish, f. L. *albus* white. In XVI–XVII often written *abron, abroune, abrown,* and so assoc. w. *brown.*] *orig.* Of a yellowish- or brownish-white colour; *now,* of a golden- or ruddy-brown colour. quasi-*sb.* 1852.

Abourne or blounde CAXTON. The rays..lit up her pale red hair to a. GEO. ELIOT.

Au·chlet. *Sc.* 1796. [f. *aucht* EIGHT + -LET *dim.,* or LOT a part (Jamieson).] The eighth part of a boll; cf. *firlot,* the fourth part.

Aucht, Sc. form of AUGHT and EIGHT.

† **Au·ctary.** 1580. [– L. *auctarium* surplus weight or charge, f. *auct-*; see next, -ARY[1], -ARIUM.] Augmentation –1653.

Auction (ǭ·kʃən), *sb.* 1595. [– L. *auctio* increase, public sale in which bids are increased, f. *auct-,* pa. ppl. stem of *augēre* increase; see -ION.] † **1.** Increase, growth –1696. **2.** A public sale in which each bidder offers more than the last previous bid, the article put up being sold to the highest bidder. Called in Scotl. and north of Engl. a *roup.* (In U.S. 'to sell or put up *at* auction' is common; in Engl. the constr. is 'to sell *by*' or 'put up *to*' auction.) 1595. **3.** A public sale of analogous character 1673. † **4.** The property put up to auction 1732.

2. Auction bridge: see BRIDGE *sb.*[2] **3.** *Dutch auction*: one in which property is offered at a high price, the price being gradually lowered till some one buys it. Hence **Au·ction** *v.* to sell by a. 1807.

Auctioneer (ǭkʃəniᵊ·ɹ), *sb.* 1708. [f. prec. + -EER.] One who conducts sales by auction. Hence **Auctionee·r** *v.* to sell by auction.

‖ **Auctor** (ǭ·ktǫɹ). 1875. [L.; see AUTHOR.] *Rom. Law.* The person who warrants the right of possession; *hence,* a vendor.

Auctor, obs. f. AUTHOR.

† **Aucto·rizate, autor-.** 1548. [f. med.L. *auctorizatus,* pa. pple. of *auctorizare*; see AUTHORIZE, -ATE[2].] *pa. pple.* Authorized. *adj.* Of established authority 1558.

Aucuba (ǭ·kiŭbă). 1819. [Jap.] *Bot.* A hardy evergreen diœcious shrub (*A. japonica,* N.O. *Cornaceæ*), with laurel-like leaves usually blotched with pale yellow.

A...introduced by Mr. John Grœfer in 1783 REES.

Aucupate (ǭ·kiŭpeⁱt), *v.* ? *Obs.* 1630. [– *aucupat-,* pa. ppl. stem of L. *aucupari* (f. *avis* bird, *capere* to catch).] *lit.* To go a bird-catching; *fig.* (as in L.) to lie in wait for, gain by craft.

Audacious (ǭdēⁱ·ʃəs), *a.* 1550. [– L. *audax, -ac-* bold, f. *audēre* dare; see -ACIOUS.] **1.** Daring, confident, intrepid. *transf.* of things 1609. **2.** Unrestrained by, or defiant of, decorum and morality; presumptuously wicked, shameless 1591.

1. Big was her voice, a. was her tone:—The maid becomes a youth DRYDEN. A. Ornaments B. JONS. **2.** Like an a. profligate, as he was 1825. Hence **Auda·ciously** *adv.* **Auda·ciousness,** boldness; reckless daring; effrontery.

Audacity (ǭdæ·sĭti). ME. [– med.L. *audacitas*, f. as prec.; see -ITY.] **1.** Boldness, intrepidity; confidence. **b.** Daring originality 1859. **2.** Boldness combined with recklessness; venturesomeness 1531. **3.** Open disregard of decorum or morality; effrontery, shamelessness 1545.

1. b. Happy a. of language 1878. **2.** The desperate a. of his [Clive's] spirit MACAULAY. **3.** His Excellency was shocked at her a. LIVINGSTONE.

Audible (ǭ·dĭb'l), *a.* (*sb.*) 1529. [– late L. *audibilis*, f. L. *audire* hear; see -BLE.] *adj.* **1.** Able to be heard. † **2.** Able to hear (*rare*) 1603. **3.** *sb.* [the adj. used *absol.*] A thing capable of being heard 1626.

1. The ioyes of heauen are..to mans eares not a. MORE. Hence **Audibi·lity, Au·dibleness,** audible capacity. **Au·dibly** *adv.* so as to be heard, aloud.

Audience (ǭ·dĭĕns). ME. [– (O)Fr. *audience*, refash. after L. of † *oiance* :– L. *audientia*, f. *audient-*, pres. ppl. stem of *audire* hear; see -ENCE.] **I.** Audience (*abstractly*). *No pl.* **1.** The action of hearing. **2.** The state of hearing, or being able to hear; hearing ME. **3.** Judicial hearing ME. **4.** Formal hearing, reception at a formal interview; see II. 1. ME.

1. *To give audience*: to give ear. **2.** † *In (open, general) a.*: so that all may hear. He said, in open a.: 'This is your place' MALORY. **3.** *Court of Audience* or *A. Court*: an eccl. court, at first held by the Archbishop, afterwards by his auditors. That of Canterbury is now merged in the Court of Arches. **4.** The ambassador had a. of her majesty 1888.

II. An audience. *With pl.* **1.** A formal interview granted (*esp.* by a sovereign) to an inferior for conference or the transaction of business. Const. *of*, *with*. 1514. **2.** The persons within hearing; an auditory ME.; *transf.* the readers of a book 1855. **3.** A court, either of government or justice, in Sp. America; also, the territory administered by it. (Sp. *audiencia.*) 1727.

1. *Audience of leave*: farewell interview. **2.** Fit a. find, though few MILT. *P.L.* VII. 31.

† **Au·diencer, -ie·r.** 1611. [– (O)Fr. *audiencier* – med.L. *audientiarius*, f. as prec.; see -ER² 2.] 'An Officer in the Chancerie, that examines..all letters patents, etc...receives the fees of the seale', etc. (Cotgr.) –1752.

Audient (ǭ·dĭĕnt). 1612. [– *audient-*, pres. ppl. stem of L. *audire* hear; see -ENT. As sb., – late L. *audiens* (Cyprian) catechumen.] *adj.* Listening 1839. *sb.* A listener; *spec.* (in *Eccl. Hist.*) a hearer of the gospel, not yet a member of the church.

Audiometer (ǭdi,ǫ·mĭtəɹ). 1879. [f. L. *audire* + -METER.] An application of the telephone for measuring minute differences of hearing.

Audiphone (ǭ·difoᵘn). 1880. [irreg. f. L. *audire* hear + *-phone*; cf. Fr. *audiphone*, *audio-*.] An instrument which, placed against the upper teeth, enables the deaf to hear more distinctly.

Audit (ǭ·dit), *sb.* ME. [– L. *auditus* hearing, f. *audit-*, pa. ppl. stem of *audire* hear; in med.L. *auditus* (*compoti*) audit (of an account).] **1.** *gen.* A hearing; *esp.* a judicial hearing of complaints, a judicial examination (*arch.*) 1598. **2.** Official examination of accounts with verification by reference to witnesses and vouchers. Auditing was orig. *oral*; cf. Matt. 20:19–30; Luke 16:2–7.) ME. *fig. Esp.* the Day of Judgement 1548. **3.** A periodical settlement of accounts between landlord and tenant; *hence*, receipts, revenue 1489. **4.** A balance-sheet as prepared for the auditor (*arch.*) 1550.

1. With his orisons I meddle not, for hee appeals to a high a. MILT. **2.** *fig.* One who..is hasting continually to his final a. HERVEY. **3.** A Nobleman that had the greatest Audits, of any Man in my Time BACON. **4.** An auditt of the time I have spent 1619.

Comb.: **a. ale,** ellipt. *audit*, ale of special quality brewed (at certain Colleges in the English Universities), orig. for use on the day of a.; **-house, -room,** a building or room appendant to a cathedral, used for the transaction of business.

Audit (ǭ·dit), *v.* 1557. [f. prec.] **1.** *trans.* To make an official systematic examination of (accounts). † **2.** *gen.* To calculate –1667. † **3.** *intr.* To draw up an account –1712.

1. Auditors generall..to Audite..thaccompts of all other officers 1557. **3.** Let Hocus a.; he knows how the money was disbursed ARBUTHNOT. Hence **Au·dited** *ppl. a.* submitted to audit.

Audition (ǭdi·ʃən). 1599. [– L. *auditio*, f. *audit-*, pa. ppl. stem of *audire* hear; see -ION. Cf. (O)Fr. *audition*.] **1.** The action, power, or faculty of hearing; listening. **b.** A trial hearing of an applicant for employment as a vocalist, etc. 1881. **2.** Something heard; cf. *vision* 1762.

1. Quite beyond his limit of a. TYNDALL.

Auditive (ǭ·ditiv), *a.* 1611. [– (O)Fr. *auditif*, *-ive*, f. as prec.; see -IVE.] = AUDITORY *a.* 1.

Auditor (ǭ·ditəɹ). ME. [– AFr. *auditour*, (O)Fr. *auditeur* – L. *auditor*, f. as prec., see -OR 2.] **1.** A hearer, listener ME. **2.** One who learns by oral instruction; a disciple; in *Eccl. Hist.* a catechumen; cf. AUDIENT *sb.* **3.** An official whose duty it is to receive and examine accounts of money in the hands of others, who verifies them by reference to vouchers, and has power to disallow improper charges ME. **4.** One who listens judicially and tries cases, as in the Audience Court (see AUDIENCE 3) 1640.

1. What, a Play toward? Ile be an a. *Mids. N.* III. i. 81. **3.** Call me before th' exactest Auditors And set me on the proofe *Timon* II. ii. 165.

Auditorial (ǭditōᵊ·riăl), *a.* 1859. [Sense 1: f. AUDITORY *a.* + -AL¹; sense 2: f. AUDITOR + -IAL.] **1.** = AUDITORY *a.* **2.** Of or pertaining to auditors or an audit 1883. Hence **Audito·rially** *adv.* by means of hearing or listening.

Auditorium (ǭditōᵊ·riə̆m). 1727. [– L. *auditorium*, n. of adj. used subst.; see AUDITORY *a.*, -ORIUM.] **1.** The part of a public building occupied by the audience: in ancient churches, the nave. ‖ **2.** The reception room of a monastery 1863.

Auditorship (ǭ·ditəɹʃi:p). 1779. [-SHIP.] The office or position of an auditor.

Auditory (ǭ·ditəri), *a.* 1578. [– late L. *auditorius*, f. *auditor*; see AUDITOR, -ORY².] **1.** Pertaining to the sense or organs of hearing; received by the ear. **2.** Belonging to the AUDITORIUM 1740.

1. Three small bones in the A. Organ..Incus, Malleus, and Stapes SIR T. BROWNE. var. **Audi·tual.**

Auditory, *sb.* ME. [– L *auditorium*; see prec. -ORY¹.] **1.** An assembly of hearers. **2.** A place for hearing; an AUDITORIUM 1548. † **3.** A philosophical school –1774. † **4.** The office of an auditor of accounts 1611.

Auditress (ǭ·ditrĕs). 1667. [-ESS¹.] A female auditor.

Adam relating, she sole a. MILT. *P.L.* VIII. 51.

‖ **Au fait** (o fē·), *advb. phr.* 1748. [Fr.] In phr. *To be au fait in* or *at*: to be well instructed in, thoroughly conversant with. *To put a person au fait of* (= F. *mettre au fait de*): to instruct thoroughly in.

† **Auf(e.** 1621. [– ON. *álfr* (cogn. w. OE. *ælf*). See ELF *sb.*] An elf's child, a changeling left by the fairies; *hence*, a misbegotten, deformed, or idiot child. The earlier form of OAF. –1750.

† **Auge,** *sb.* 1594. [– OFr. *auge*, – Arab. *awj* height.] **1.** = APOGEE 2, 3. –1679. **2.** = APOGEE 1. 1594. **3.** = APSIS 1. 1601.

Augean (ǭdʒī·ăn), *a.* 1599. [f. L. *Augeas*, Gr. Αὐγείας + -AN.] Abominably filthy; *i.e.* like the stable of Augeas, King of Elis, which contained 3,000 oxen, and had been uncleansed for 30 years, when Hercules, by turning the river Alpheus through it, purified it in one day.

Augelite (ǭ·dʒiləit). 1868. [f. Gr. αὐγή lustre + -LITE.] *Min.* A hydrous phosphate of alumina.

Auger (ǭ·gəɹ). [OE. *nafogār*, f. *nafu* NAVE *sb.*¹ + *gār* javelin, spear, piercer, borer; corresp. to OS. *nabugēr*, OHG. *nabugēr*, ON. *nafarr*. For loss of initial *n* cf. *adder*, *apron*, *umpire*.] **1.** A carpenter's tool for boring holes in wood, etc., having a long shank with a cutting edge and a screw point, and a handle fixed at right angles to the top of the shank, by means of which the tool is turned round by hand. **2.** An instrument for boring in the earth, having a stem which may be lengthened as the perforation extends 1594.

1. Item three naugers 1572. Your Franchises..confin'd Into an Augors boare *Cor.* IV. iv. 87. *Comb.*: **a.-hole.** the hole drilled by an a.; **-shell,** the shell of the molluscous genus *Terebra*.

‖ **Auget, -ette** (oʒe, ǭdʒe·t). 1816. [Fr., dim. of *auge* trough.] **a.** A wooden pipe containing the powder used in exploding a mine. **b.** The priming tube used in blasting 1881.

Augh! (ǭχ), *int. Sc.* = faugh!

Aught, *sb.*¹ [OE. *ǣht* (= OHG. *ēht*, Goth. *aihts*), f. *āgan* own, possess, pa. t. *āhte*. Sc. *aucht* (āuχt) is still a living word.] **1.** Possession; property OE. † **2.** *esp.* Live stock –ME.

Aught (ǭt), *sb.*² (*pron.*), *adv.*, *adj.* [OE. *āwiht*, *āwuht*, *āuht*, *āht*, corresp. to OFris. *āwet*, *āet*, OS. *ēowiht*, OHG. *eowiht*, *iewiht*; WGmc. compd. of AY *adv.* and WIGHT *sb.*] **1.** *sb.* (*pron.*) Anything whatever; anything. † **2.** *adj.* (Attrib. use of prec. Cf. *naught* = worthless.) Anything worth, something worth; worthy, doughty –ME. **3.** *adv.* [The accus. of the sb. used advb.] To any extent, in any respect, at all ME.

1. For aught I know GOLDSM. **3.** Nor aught suspect the doom COWPER.

Augite (ǭ·dʒəit). 1804. [– L. *augites* – Gr. αὐγίτης, f. αὐγή lustre; see -ITE¹ 2 b.] *Min.* An aluminous variety of PYROXENE, greenish, brownish, or pure black in colour, consisting chiefly of silica, magnesia, iron, and lime, and occurring mostly in igneous rocks. Hence **Augi·tic** *a.* of, pertaining to, or characterized by, a.

Augment (ǭ·gmĕnt), *sb.* ME. [– (O)Fr. *augment* or late L. *augmentum*, f. *augēre* to increase; see -MENT.] † **1.** Increase, augmentation –1696. **2.** *Gram.* The prefixed vowel (in Skr. *ă*, in Gr. ἐ) which marks the past tenses of the vb. in early Aryan languages. (Occ. used of other prefixes, *e.g.* the *ge-* of German pa. pples.)

In Gr., the ἐ, when separate, is called the *syllabic augment*; when it goes to form a long vowel or diphthong, the *temporal augment*. Hence **Au·gmentless** *a.*

Augment (ǭgme·nt), *v.* ME. [– (O)Fr. *augmenter* or late L. *augmentare*; see prec.] **1.** *trans.* To make greater in size, number, amount, degree, etc.; to increase 1460. **2.** *intr.* To become greater in size, etc. ME. † **3.** *trans.* To add to the resources of –1601. † **4.** *trans.* and *refl.* To raise in estimation or dignity –1655. **5.** *Her.* (*trans.*) To make an honourable addition to (a coat of arms) 1655. † **6.** To multiply (mathematically) –1593.

1. Hou our Navye may be mayntaynyd, and augmentyd 1460. **2.** The rains a. DRYDEN. **5.** The Armes of London were augmented with the addition of a Dagger FULLER. Hence **Augme·ntable** *a.* capable of †increasing, or being increased. **Augme·ntedly** *adv.* **Augme·nter,** he who or that which augments; *spec.* a magnifying glass.

Augmentation (ǭgmĕntēⁱ·ʃən). 1463. [– OFr. *aument-*, *augmentacion* (mod. *-tion*), – late L. *augmentatio*, f. *augmentat-*, pa. ppl. stem of *augmentare*; see prec., -ATION.] **1.** The action or process of augmenting (see AUGMENT *v.* 1, 2, † 4). **2.** Augmented state or condition; increase 1533. **3.** That by which anything is augmented; an addition 1576. **4.** *Her.* An honourable addition to a coat of arms 1662. **5.** *Med.* 'The period between the commencement and height of a fever' (Mayne). **6.** *Mus.* The repetition of a subject (*esp.* in fugues) in notes double or quadruple those of the original 1597. **7.** *Sc. Law.* Increase of clerical stipend obtained by an action (*Process of A.*) in the Court of Teinds 1653.

1. To the avmentacion of his lif loode 1463. The excessive a. of their numbers MCCULLOCH. **2.** The result was an a. of the revenue 1825. **3.** The new Mappe, with the a. of the Indies *Twel. N.* III. ii. 85.

Augmentation Court, Court of Augmentation(s, or ellipt. *The Augmentation*: a court established by 27 Hen. VIII, so called because, by the suppression of monasteries, it augmented the revenues of the Crown. Dissolved by 1 Mary, sess. 2, cap. 10. **Augmenta·tioner,** an officer of this court.

Augmentative (ǭgme·ntătiv), *a.* (*sb.*) 1502. [– (O)Fr. *augmentatif*, *-ive* or med.L.

augmentativus, f. as prec.; see -IVE.] **1.** Having the property of augmenting; in Metaph. = AMPLIATIVE. **2.** *Gram.* Augmenting in force the idea conveyed, said of suffixes, etc., of derivative words, and words with augmentative *affixes* 1641. **3.** *sb.* An augmentative formative or word 1804.

2. For the word *wizard*, from *witch*, see the Section on A. forms LATHAM. var. **Augme·ntive** (less usual). Hence **Augme·ntatively** *adv.*

Augrim(e, -isme, -ym(e, obs. ff. ALGORISM.

Augur (ǭ·gəɹ), *sb.* 1549. [– L. *augur*; sp. *augure* (XVI–XVII) from Fr.] **1.** *Rom. Hist.* A religious official, who interpreted omens derived from the flight, singing, and feeding of birds, the appearance of the entrails of sacrificial victims, etc., and advised upon the course of public business in accordance with them. **2.** Hence: A soothsayer, diviner, or prophet generally 1593.

1. Augures, that by observation of the birds of the air..made men believe they knew things to come HOOPER. **2.** A. accursed! denouncing mischief still POPE. vars. † **Au·gurer,** † **Au·gurist.** Hence **Au·gurate, Au·gurship,** the office, or term of office, of an a. **Au·gurous** *a.* presaging (*rare*).

Augur (ǭ·gəɹ), *v.* 1549. [– prec., after L. *augurari*; cf. (O)Fr. *augurer*.] **1.** *trans.* To prognosticate from signs or omens; to divine, forebode, anticipate 1601. Of things: To portend, give promise of 1826. **2.** *intr.* (or with *subord. cl.*) To take auguries; to conjecture from signs and omens 1808. **3.** *trans.* (also with *in*) To usher in with auguries; to inaugurate 1549.

1. It seems to a. genius SCOTT. **2.** Do we a. from them [cock-sparrows], as the Romans did from chickens 1840. To a. *well* or *ill*: to have *good* or *bad* anticipations *of*, *for*; Of things: to give *good* or *bad* promise. All augured ill for Alpine's line SCOTT. var. † **Au·gurize.**

Augural (ǭ·giŭrăl), *a.* 1513. [– L. *auguralis*; see AUGUR *sb.*, -AL[1].] **1.** Of or pertaining to augurs or augury. **2.** Significant of the future; lucky or ominous 1600.

1. The a. gate 1598, staff of Romulus 1770. **2.** Aristotle saith that sternutation was an a. signe GALE.

† **Au·gurate,** *v.* 1623. [– *augurat-*, pa. ppl. stem of L. *augurari*; see AUGUR *v.*, -ATE[3].] **1.** *intr.* To perform the duties of augur 1678. **2.** = AUGUR *v.* 1. 1652. **3.** = AUGUR *v.* 3. 1623. Hence † **Augura·tion,** augury; *gen.* prognostic, token.

† **Au·gure.** [– (O)Fr. *augure* – L. *augurium*.] = AUGURY, q.v.

Augurial (ǭgiuə·riăl), *a.* 1513. [– late L. *augurialis*; see AUGURAL, -IAL.] Pertaining to augury.

Augury (ǭ·giŭri). ME. [– OFr. *augurie* or L. *augurium*; see AUGUR *sb.*, -Y[3].] **1.** The art of the augur; divination. **2.** An augural observation, or rite 1742. **3.** An omen drawn by augury; a significant token of any kind 1612. **4.** *fig.* Presentiment, anticipation 1783; presage, promise 1797.

We defie Augury..If it be now, 'tis not to come; if it bee not to come, it will bee now *Haml.* v. ii. 230. **2.** The priests took the auguries and gave the signal for onset STUBBS. **4.** He resigned himself..with a docility that gave little a. of his future greatness PRESCOTT. var. † **Au·gurism.**

August (ǭgʊ·st), *a.* 1664. [– (O)Fr. *auguste* or L. *augustus* consecrated, venerable.] **1.** Inspiring mingled reverence and admiration; magnificently impressive; stately, solemnly grand; venerable, revered 1664. **2.** Venerable from birth or position; dignified, eminent, majestic. (Occas. perfunctory.) 1673.

1. The funeral was..the saddest and most a. that Westminster had ever seen MACAULAY. **2.** And made obeisance to that a. Assembly 1720. var. † **Augu·stious.** Hence **Augu·st-ly** *adv.*, **-ness.**

August (ǭ·gʊst), *sb.* OE. [– L. *Augustus*.] The eighth month of the year, named after Augustus Cæsar, the first Roman emperor. Hence **Au·gust** *v.* to ripen.

† **Augu·stal,** *a.* 1658. [– L. *augustalis* Augustan, f. *Augustus* (*Cæsar*); see -AL[1].] Of or pertaining to the emperor Augustus, or to his worship; imperial –1730.

Augustan (ǭgʊ·stăn, ǭ-, ǫ̆-), *a.* (and *sb.*) 1645. [– L. *Augustanus*, f. as prec.; see -AN.] **1.** Connected with the reign of Augustus Cæsar, the palmy period of Latin literature 1704. **2.** Hence, Of the palmy period of purity and refinement of any national literature; and *gen.* Classical 1819. **3.** Of Augsburg (Augusta Vindelicorum), where in 1530 Luther and Melanchthon drew up their confession of Protestant principles 1645. **4.** *sb.* A writer of the Augustan age (of any literature) 1882.

2. The reign of queen Anne is often called the A. age of England 1819. **3.** Som embracing..the Augustane and som the Helvetian Confession HOWELL. var. † **Auguste·an** *a.* CUDWORTH.

Augustin(e (ǭgʊ̆·stin, ǭ·gʊ̆stin), *sb.* (and *a.*) ME. [– (O)Fr. *augustin* Austin friar – *Augustinus* (354–430), Bishop of Hippo Regius, and one of the Doctors of the Church.] An Augustinian monk. See also AUSTIN.

Augustinian (ǭgʊsti·niăn), *a.* (and *sb.*) 1602. [f. *Augustinus* Augustine (see prec.) + -IAN.] **1.** Of or pertaining to St. Augustine or his doctrines, chief of which were immediate efficacy of grace and absolute predestination. *sb.* An adherent of his doctrines 1674. **2.** Belonging to (*sb.* one of) the order of Augustines 1602. **3.** Adhering to (*sb.* an adherent of) Augustine the Bohemian 1645. Hence **Augusti·nianism, Augu·stinism,** the doctrines of St. Augustine and his followers.

Auh (ǭh), *int.* expressing disgust 1732.

Auk (ǭk). 1678. [– ON. *álka* (Sw. *alka*, Da. *alke*).] A northern sea-bird, with short wings used only as paddles; strictly applied to the Great A. (*Alca impennis*), Little A. (*Mergulus melanoleucus* or *alle*), Razor-bill (*Alca torda*); but dial. also to the guillemots.

Auk(e,- ly, -ness, -ward, obs. ff. AWK, etc.

Aularian (ǭlē°·riăn). 1695. [f. med.L. *aularius* pertaining to a University hall or college, f. med.L. *aula* college, + -AN; see -ARIAN.] *adj.* Of or belonging to a hall. *sb.* A member of a hall at Oxford or Cambridge. var. **Au·lary** *a.* (*rare*).

Auld (ǭld, *Sc.* ăld), *a. dial.* [Sc. form repr. OE. (Anglian) *ald* OLD.] = OLD; as in *auld lang syne*, 'old long-since' (used subst.); *Auld Reekie*, 'Old Smoky', a sobriquet of Edinburgh; *auldfarrand*, 'favouring' the old, having the manners or sagacity of age; *auldwarld*.

Aulete (ǭ·līt). 1850. [– Gr. αὐλητής.] A flute-player. Hence **Aule·tic** *a.*

Aulic (ǭ·lik). 1701. [– Fr. *aulique* or L. *aulicus* – Gr. αὐλικός, f. αὐλή court; see -IC.] **A.** *adj.* Of or pertaining to a court; courtly. *Aulic Council*: in the old German Empire the personal council of the Emperor; it heard appeals from Germanic states, and was dissolved, with the Empire, in 1806. Later the name of a council at Vienna, managing the war-department of the Austrian Empire.

B. *sb.* The ceremony observed in the Sorbonne in granting the degree of doctor of divinity, when, after a harangue from the Chancellor, the new doctor received his cap and presided at a disputation. Hence † **Au·licism,** a courtly phrase.

Auln-, ault- (in various words); see AL-.

Aum (ǭm). 1502. Mod.Eng. var. of AAM.

Aumail (ǭmē°·l). *rare.* [refash. of AMEL *sb.*, after Spenser's *aumayld*; see AMELED.] Enamel.

Aumbry(e, -brie, arch. spellings of AMBRY.

‖ **Aumil** (ǭ·mil, ā·mil). 1800. [Urdu (ult. Arab.) *'āmil* operator, agent.] A native collector of revenue in India; also called AMILDAR. Hence by confusion Aumildar (with same sense).

‖ **Aumônière.** 1834. [Fr.] = ALMONER[2].

† **Au·ncel.** ME. [– AFr. *auncel*, earlier *aunser* (XIII–XV), = Anglo-L. *auncella*, *a(u)nser*, of unkn. origin.] A kind of balance and weight formerly used in England –1691.

Aunc-, aund- (in various words); see AN-.

‖ **Aune** (ōn). 1706. [Fr.; see ALNAGE.] An ell; an obs. Fr. cloth measure.

Aunt (ānt). ME. [– AFr. *aunte*, OFr. *ante* (mod. *tante*) :– L. *amita*.] **1.** The sister of one's father or mother. Also, an uncle's wife, *aunt-in-law*. **b.** (in U.S.) Any benevolent and generally helpful woman; cf. Sp. *tia* 1861. † **c.** A title for the 'sister university', used by alumni of Oxford or Cambridge –1701. † **2.** An old woman; a gossip 1590. † **3.** A procuress; a prostitute –1678.

1. *Merry W.* IV. ii. 76. **c.** PEPYS *Corr.* 1701. Hence **Au·nthood, Au·ntship,** the relationship of a. **Au·ntly** *a.*

Aunt Sally: a game in which the figure of a woman's head with a pipe in its mouth is set up, and the player, throwing sticks from a certain distance, tries to break the pipe.

† **Au·nters,** *adv.* ME. [f. *aunter*, *aventure*, ADVENTURE; the *-s* (orig. wanting) may be genitival; cf. *per adventure* and *per-hap-s*.] In any case; perhaps –1807.

Auntie, aunty (ā·nti). 1792. [f. AUNT + -Y[6].] Familiar f. *aunt*. In U.S.: A term often used in addressing elderly women.

‖ **Au pair** (*o* pę̄r). 1897. [Fr., = on equality.] Applied to an arrangement between two parties by which mutual services are rendered without consideration of money payment.

‖ **Aura** (ǭ·ră). ME. [L. – Gr. αὔρα breath, breeze.] **1.** A gentle breeze, a zephyr. **2.** A subtle emanation from any substance, *e.g.* the odour of flowers 1732. Also *fig.* **3.** *Electr.* † **a.** = Electrical ATMOSPHERE. **b.** The current of air caused by the discharge of electricity from a sharp point, *e.g.* from those of the electrical whirl 1863. **4.** *Path.* A sensation, as of a current of cold air rising from some part of the body to the head, a premonitory symptom in epilepsy and hysterics 1776.

Hence **Au·ral** *a.*[1]

Aural (ǭ·răl), *a.*[2] 1847. [f. L. *auris* ear + -AL[1].] **1.** Of or pertaining to the organ of hearing. **2.** Received or perceived by the ear. **Au·rally** *adv.*

Aurantiaceous (ǭræ:ntiˌē·ʃəs), *a.* 1837. [f. mod.L. *aurantiaceæ*, f. *aurantium*, latinized f. ORANGE; see -ACEOUS.] Of or belonging to the N.O. *Aurantiaceæ*, including the orange, etc.

‖ **Aurata** (ǭrē·tă). 1520. [– L. *aurata*, pa. pple. fem. (used subst.) of *aurare* to gild, f. *aurum* gold.] A gold-coloured fish; prob. the Golden Maid, a variety of Wrasse.

Aurate (ǭ·reᶦt). 1838. [f. L. *aurum* + -ATE[4].] *Chem.* A compound of auric acid with a base.

Aurated (ǭ·reᶦtėd), *ppl. a.*[1] 1864. [f. L. *auratus* (see AURATA) + -ED[1].] Like or containing gold; gold-coloured, gilded. † In *Chem.* Combined with auric acid.

Au·rated, *ppl. a.*[2] 1843. [A bad form of AURITED.] *Conchol.* Having ears, as in the pecten.

Aureate (ǭ·riˌĕt), *a.* ME. [– late L. *aureatus*, f. *aureus* golden, f. *aurum* gold; see -ATE[2].] Golden, gold-coloured 1450. † Also *fig.* var. † **Au·real.**

Aureity (ǭrī·Iti). 1824. [– med.L. *aureitas*, f. *aureus* golden, + *-itas* -ITY.] The properties peculiar to gold.

Aurelia (ǫrī·liă, ǭ-, ǫ̆-). 1598. [– It. *aurelia* silk-worm in its cocoon, subst. use of fem. of *aurelio* golden (Florio).] **1.** *Ent.* The chrysalis of an insect, *esp.* of a butterfly. (Now *rare.*) 1607. † **2.** The Gold-flower (*Heliochrysum stœchas*) 1598. **3.** *Zool.* A genus of phosphorescent marine animals of the class *Acalephæ* 1876.

Aure·lian. 1778. [f. prec. + -AN.] *adj.* Of or pertaining to an aurelia; *gen.* golden 1791. *sb.* A lepidopterist 1778.

‖ **Aureola** (ǭrī·ŏlă). 1483. [L., fem. (sc. *corona* crown) of *aureolus* adj. dim. of *aureus* golden, f. *aurum* gold.] **1.** *Mediæval* and *R.C.Ch.* The celestial crown won by a martyr, virgin, or doctor, as victor over the world, the flesh, or the devil; the several degrees of glory of these. **2.** = AUREOLE 2. 1727. **3.** = AUREOLE 3. 1871.

Aureole (ǭ·riˌōᵘl). ME. [– (O)Fr. *auréole* – L. *aureola*; see prec.] **1.** = AUREOLA 1. **2.** *Art.* Properly: The gold disc surrounding the head (or ? figure) in early pictures; *hence*, applied by some to **a.** The radiant circle of light depicted around the head 1848; by others to **b.** The oblong glory, or *vesica*, with which divine figures are surrounded 1851. **c.** *fig.* A glorifying halo 1852. **3.** *transf.* An actual halo of radiating light; *esp.* that seen in eclipses; also in wider sense 1842.

2. c. The a. of young womanhood O. W. HOLMES. **3.** An inseparable a. of sweet sound MRS. BROWNING.

Aureolin (ǭ·rīŏlin, ǭrī·ŏlin). 1879. [f. L. *aureolus* (see above) + -IN[1].] A transparent yellow pigment.

‖ **Au revoir** (o:rəvwā·r). 1694. [Fr., = until we meet again.] Good-bye till we meet again.

Auric (ǭ·rik), *a.* 1838. [f. L. *aurum* + -IC.] Of or pertaining to gold. In *Chem.* used of compounds in which gold is trivalent.

Aurichalcite (ǭrikæ·lsəit). 1844. [f. (by Böttger, 1839) L. *aurichalcum*, erron. spelling of *orichalcum* – Gr. ὀρείχαλκον 'mountain copper'. See -ITE 2 b. So called because when reduced it yields brass.] *Min.* A cuprous hydrozincite, of pale green, verdigris, or sky-blue colour.

Auricle (ǭ·rik'l). 1653. [– L. *auricula*, dim. of *auris* ear; see -CULE.] **1.** The external ear of animals. Formerly limited to the lower lobe of the human ear. *transf.* An 'ear' or ear-hole 1859. **2.** An ear-shaped process; a lobe; *esp.* in *Bot.* and *Conch.* (Cf. AURICULATE.) 1665. **3.** Name of the two upper cavities of the heart which receive blood from the veins and lungs respectively 1664. **4.** A kind of ear-trumpet 1864.

Auricomous (ǭri·kŏməs), *a.* 1864. [f. L. *auricomus* (f. *aurum* gold + *coma* hair) + -OUS.] Of or pertaining to golden hair.

‖ **Auricula** (ǭri·kiŭlă). 1655. [L.; see AURICLE.] **1.** = AURICLE 1. 1691. **2.** (See quot.). **3.** *Bot.* A species of Primula, also called Bear's-ear, named from the shape of its leaves 1655. **4.** A genus of pulmoniferous molluscs, found chiefly in brackish swamps 1843.

2. In the Echinoida, ambulacral plates of the oral margin of the corona are produced into five perpendicular perforated processes, which arch over the ambulacra and are called the auriculæ HUXLEY.

Auricular (ǭri·kiŭlăɹ). 1542. [– late L. *auricularis*, f. *auricula*; see prec., -AR¹.] **A.** *adj.* **1.** Of or pertaining to the ear 1649. **2.** Perceived by the ear; audible 1579; † hearsay –1626. **b.** *esp.* (in *auricular confession*): Told privately in the ear 1542. **3.** Pertaining to the auricle of the heart 1870. **4.** Shaped like an auricle 1857.

2. You shall..by an A. assurance haue your satisfaction *Lear* I. ii. 99. A. traditions BACON. The practice of a. confession brought with it an entire science of casuistry HALLAM. *Auricular witness* (F. *témoin auriculaire*); one who relates what he has heard. Hence **Auri·cularly** *adv.* in one's ear, in a whisper; by means of auricles.

B. *sb.* An auricular organ or part. *spec.* **a.** A tuft of feathers covering the orifice of a bird's ear. **b.** The little finger, as the one most easily inserted in the ear: Fr. *doigt auriculaire* 1797.

Auriculate (ǭri·kiŭlĕt), *ppl. a.* 1713. [f. L. *auricula* AURICLE + -ATE².] Furnished with auricles or earlike appendages. **1.** *Bot.* Of leaves: Having at the base a pair of small, blunt, ear-shaped projections. **2.** *Conch.* Having an ear-shaped process on one or both sides of the *umbones*, as in certain bivalves 1854. var. **Auri·culated.** Hence **Auri·culately** *adv.*

Auriculo- (ǭri·kiŭlo), comb. f. AURICLE, as in *a.-temporal*, *-ventricular*, etc.

Auri·culoid, *a.* 1856. [f. L. *auricula* AURICLE + -OID.] Shaped like an auricula or auricle.

Auriferous (ǭri·fĕrəs), *a.* 1727. [f. L. *aurifer* gold-bearing + -OUS; see -FEROUS.] Containing or yielding gold. *lit.* and *fig.* Hence **Auri·ferously** *adv.*

‖ **Au·rifex.** 1862. [L.] A worker in gold.

Aurific (ǭri·fik), *a.* 1667. [f. L. *aurum* gold; see -FIC.] Producing gold.

Aurification (ǭ:rifikēi·ʃən). 1881. [– Fr. *aurification*; see AURIFY, -FICATION.] Working in gold; *spec.* the stopping of a tooth with gold.

Auriform (ǭ·rifǭɹm), *a.* 1816. [f. L. *auris* ear + -FORM.] Shaped like an ear.

Aurify (ǭ·rifəi), *v.* 1652. [– med.L. **aurificare* turn into gold, f. L. *aurum* gold + *-ficare* -FY.] *trans.* and *intr.* To turn into gold.

‖ **Auriga** (ǭrəi·gă). ME. [L.] A charioteer. † **a.** *fig.* Leader. **b.** *Astr.* The Wagoner. † **c.** *Phys.* The fourth lobe of the liver. † **d.** *Med.* A bandage for the sides. **Auriga·tion,** the action or art of driving a chariot.

†‖ **Auri·go.** ME. [– *aurigo*, var. spelling of late L. *aurugo* jaundice.] Jaundice –1795.

Aurigraphy (ǭri·grăfi). [– med.L. *aurigraphia*, f. *aurum* gold; see -GRAPHY.] A writing or graving in gold (Dicts.).

Aurilave (ǭ·rilē¹v). 1874. [f. L. *auris* ear + *lav-* in *lavare* to wash.] An instrument for cleansing the ear.

Aurin (ǭ·rin). 1869. [f. L. *aurum* gold + -IN¹.] *Chem.* A red colouring matter produced by heating phenol with certain acids.

Auriphrygiate (ǭrifri·dʒi,ĕt), *ppl. a.* 1814. [– med.L. *auriphrygiatus*, f. *auriphrygium* gold fringe; see -ATE², ORPHREY.] Embroidered or fringed with gold. SOUTHEY.

† **Auripi·gment.** ME. [– L. *auripigmentum* (also used); see ORPIMENT.] Now ORPIMENT –1741.

Auriscope (ǭ·riskoᵘp). 1853. [f. L. *auris* ear + -SCOPE.] *Med.* An instrument for examining the ear. **Auri·scopy,** the use of the a.

Aurist (ǭ·rist). 1678. [f. L. *auris* ear + -IST.] *Med.* A specialist in regard to diseases of the ear.

Aurited (ǭrəi·tėd, ǭ·ritėd), *ppl. a.* [f. earlier *aurite* (– L. *auritus* eared) + -ED¹.] Furnished with ears or auricles; auriculate.

Aurivorous (ǭri·vŏrəs), *a.* 1783. [f. L. *aurum* gold + -VOROUS.] Gold-devouring.

Auro- (ǭ·ro), comb. f. L. *aurum*, as in **a.-ce·phalous** *a.*, having a gold-coloured head; **-chlo·ride,** a chloro-aurate; **-plumbi·ferous** *a.*, containing lead mixed with gold; **-tellu·rite,** SYLVANITE.

‖ **Aurochs** (au·rǫks, ǭ·rǫks). 1766. [G., early var. of *auerochs* (OHG. *ūrohso*, f. *ūr* = OE. *ūr*, etc., of unkn. origin, + *ohso* Ox).] Historically and properly, an extinct species of Wild Ox (*Bos Urus* Owen, *B. primigenius* Boj.) described by Cæsar as *Urus*. Since this became extinct, the name has been erron. applied to the European Bison (*Bos Bison* Gesn., *B. bonasus* Linn.), still extant in Lithuania.

Aurora (ǭrōᵊ·ră). 1483. [L.; occas. in Fr. form *aurore*.] **1.** The rising light of the morning; the dawn. **2.** *personified*, The (Roman) goddess of the dawn, rising with rosy fingers from the saffron-coloured bed of Tithonus 1587. **3.** *fig.* The early period; *poet.* 'rise', 'dawn', 'morn' 1844. **4.** A luminous atmospheric phenomenon, now ascribed to electricity, occurring near, or radiating from, the earth's northern or southern magnetic pole, and visible from time to time by night over more or less of the earth's surface; pop. called the Northern (or Southern) Lights, merry-dancers, streamers, etc. (Now the ordinary prose meaning of *Aurora*, which is used generically, with Eng. pl. *auroras*, without any thought of 'dawn'.) 1621. **5.** A rich orange colour, as of the sky at sunrise 1791. **6.** Name of a monkey (*Chrysothrix sciurea*), a sea-anemone, and of various flowers 1774.

2. Zephyr with A. playing MILT. *L'Alleg.* 19. **4.** Lit up by auroræ and long lingering twilights LOCKYER.

Comb. etc.: **A. australis, borealis, septentrionalis:** the Southern and Northern Lights, the latter orig. described by Gassendi under the appellation of 'northern dawn' (see sense 4). **A.-parrot,** *Psittacus Aurora*; **-pole,** one of the two points on the earth's surface which form the centres of the luminous circles of the aurora borealis and australis; **-snake.**

Auroral (ǭrōᵊ·răl), *a.* 1552. [In XVI – Fr. *auroral* or med.L. *auroralis*; in mod. use f. prec. + -AL¹.] **1.** Of or pertaining to the dawn, eastern; *fig.* of the first period of anything. **2.** Like the dawn; dawning, roseate, rosy 1827. **3.** Of or pertaining to the aurora (borealis) 1828. **4.** Like the aurora in its coruscations 1871.

1. The French a. 'biscuit de Rheims' BADHAM. **2.** The a. light of Tasso CARLYLE. **4.** A. flashings of wit PALGRAVE. Hence **Auro·rally** *adv.* (senses 2, 4).

Aurorean (ǭrōᵊ·rĭăn), *a.* 1819. [f. AURORA + -EAN.] Belonging to dawn, or like it in hue.

At tender eye-dawn of a. love KEATS.

Aurous (ǭ·rəs), *a.* 1862. [f. L. *aurum* + -OUS.] Of or containing gold; *Chem.* of compounds in which gold is univalent, e.g. aurous iodide, AuI.

Aurulent (ǭ·riŭlĕnt), *a.* 1731. [– late L. *aurulentus*, f. *aurum* gold; see -ULENT.] Gold-coloured.

‖ **Aurum** (ǭ·rŏm). 1500. [L.] Gold.

a. fulminans = FULMINATE of gold; **a. mosaicum** or **musivum,** bisulphide of tin, known also as *bronze-powder*; † **a. potabile,** 'drinkable gold', gold held in a state of minute subdivision in some volatile oil, formerly taken as a cordial.

Auscultate (ǭ·skɒltē¹t), *v.* 1881. [– *auscultat-*, pa. ppl. stem of L. *auscultare* (see next); see -ATE³.] *trans.* To listen to; *spec.* in *Med.* to examine by auscultation. var. **Auscu·lt.**

Auscultation (ǭskɒltēi·ʃən). 1634. [– L. *auscultatio*, f. *auscultat-*, pa. ppl. stem of *auscultare* hear with attention; see -ION. Cf. Fr. *auscultation.*] **1.** The action of listening or hearkening. **2.** *Med.* The action of listening, with ear or stethoscope, in order to judge by sound the condition of heart, lungs, or other organs 1833.

2. The whole doctrine of a. as a means of diagnosis 1833. **Auscu·ltative** *a.* of the nature of, or pertaining to, a. **Auscu·ltatory** *a.* of or pertaining to listening, or (*Med.*) to a.

Auscultator (ǭ·skɒltē¹təɹ). 1831. [In sense 2, – L. *auscultator* hearer; in sense 1, f. AUSCULTATE; see -OR 2.] **1.** *Med.* One who practises auscultation 1833. ‖ **2.** Title formerly given in Germany to a young lawyer who has passed his first public examination, and is thereupon employed by Government, but without salary or fixed appointment. (Now *referendar.*)

‖ **Auspex** (ǭ·speks). Pl. **auspices.** 1598. [L. *auspex*, *-spic-*; see AUSPICE.] *Rom. Antiq.* One who observed the flight of birds, to take omens thence; *hence*, a director, protector.

† **Au·spicate,** *a.* 1603. [– L. *auspicatus* auspicious, pa. pple. of *auspicari*, see next, -ATE².] Started with good auspices; fortunate –1657.

Auspicate (ǭ·spikē¹t), *v.* 1603. [– *auspicat-*, pa. ppl. stem of L. *auspicari*; see AUSPEX, -ATE³.] † **1.** *trans.* To give omen of, prognosticate. **2.** *intr.* To augur, predict 1848. **3.** *trans.* To initiate with an auspicious ceremony; to give a fortunate start to 1611. **4.** To handsel, signalize (one's entrance upon) 1652. **5.** *trans.* and † *intr.* To begin 1652.

3. To a. his Temporall affaires with Spirituall deuotions SPEED. **4.** The..acts, by which [this new Government] auspicated its entrance into function BURKE. Hence † **Auspica·tion,** the taking of auspices (*rare*).

Auspice (ǭ·spis), now usu. in pl. **auspices** (ǭ·spisėz). 1533. [– Fr. *auspice* or L. *auspicium* action of an AUSPEX, f. *avis* bird + **spic-* look.] **1.** An observation of birds for omens; a sign or token given by birds. **2.** *gen.* Any divine or prophetic token; prognostic; *esp.* indication of a happy future 1660. **3.** Prosperous lead; patronage, favouring direction; *esp.* in phr. *Under the auspices of* 1637.

2. A life which had opened under the fairest auspices MACAULAY. **3.** Under the auspices of religion and piety BURKE. Hence **Auspi·cial** *a.* of or pertaining to auspices or augury; auspicious.

Auspicious (ǭspi·ʃəs), *a.* 1601. [f. prec. + -OUS.] **1.** Ominous, *esp.* of good omen, betokening success 1614. Of persons: Predicting good 1702. **2.** Favouring, conducive to success 1610. Of persons: Propitious, kind 1601. **3.** Favoured by fortune, prosperous 1616.

1. A. planets YOUNG. **2.** Calme Seas, a. gales *Temp.* V. i. 314. **3.** For five a. years 1804. Hence **Auspi·cious-ly** *adv.*, **-ness.**

† **Au·spicy.** 1603. [– L. *auspicium* AUSPICE.] The drawing of omens from birds –1687.

‖ **Auster** (ǭ·stəɹ). ME. [L.] The south wind; *hence*, the south.

Austere (ǭstīᵊ·ɹ), *a.* ME. [– (O)Fr. *austère* – L. *austerus* – Gr. αὐστηρός severe.] **1.** Sour or bitter and astringent; harsh to the taste 1541. **2.** Harsh to the feelings generally; stern; rigorous, judicially severe ME.; grim in warfare ME. **3.** Severe in self-discipline, strict, abstinent ME. **4.** Grave, sober 1667. **5.** Severely simple; without any luxury 1597.

1. Sloes a. COWPER. **2.** They would be gentle, not a. BROWNING. **3.** An a. life PRIESTLEY. **4.** Eve.. With sweet austeer composure thus reply'd MILT. *P.L.* IX. 272. **5.** This a. repast HOOKER. Hence **Auste·rely** *adv.*, **-ness.**

Austerity (ǭste·rĭti). ME. [– (O)Fr. *austérité* – L. *austeritas*; see prec., -ITY.] **1.** Harshness to the taste, astringent sourness 1634. **2.** Harshness to the feelings; stern or severe treatment or demeanour; judicial severity ME.; *transf.* rugged sternness (*arch.*) 1713. **3.** Severe self-discipline; abstinence, asceticism 1590; *esp.* in *pl.* ascetic practices 1664. **4.** Severe simplicity; lack of luxury 1875.

2. Notwithstanding the a. of the Chair BURKE. **3.** To protest For aie, a., and single life *Mids. N.* I. i. 90. The austerities of an anchorite 1851.

Austin (ǭ·stin). ME. [Reduction of AUGUSTIN(E – (O)Fr. *Augustin*, transf. use of the proper name *Augustin*.] = AUGUSTINIAN. var. † **Au·stiner.**

Austral (ǭ·străl), *a.* ME. [– L. *australis*; see AUSTER, -AL[1].] Belonging to the south, southern; *also*, influenced by the south wind, warm and moist.

A. magnetism is the imaginary magnetic matter which prevails in the southern regions of the Earth 1881. *Austral signs*: the six signs of the zodiac from *Libra* to *Pisces*.

Australasian (ǭstrălēi·ʃiăn). 1766. [f. *Australasia* – Fr. *Australasie* (f. L. *Australis* + *Asia*) + -AN; orig. a name for one of 3 divisions of the *Terra Australis* (De Brosses): now = Australia and its adjoining islands.] *adj.* Of or belonging to Australasia. *sb.* A native or colonist of Australasia.

Australene (ǭ·strălīn). 1863. [f. L. *australis* + -ENE.] *Chem.* The chief constituent of English turpentine-oils, prepared from the turpentine of *Pinus australis*; also called *austraterebenthene*.

Australian (ǭstrēi·liăn). 1693. [– Fr. *australien*, f. L. *australis*, in *Terra Australis*, now *Australia*.] *sb.* † **1.** A native of the *Terra Australis*, including Australasia, Polynesia, and 'Magellanica'. **2.** A native of, later also a colonist or resident in, the island-continent of Australia. *adj.* Of or belonging to Australia 1814. Hence **Austra·lioid** *a.*, also **Au·straloid**, of the ethnological type of the aborigines of A.

† **Au·strian,** *a. rare.* [f. L. *auster*, *austr*- south + -IAN.] Southern. QUARLES. var. † **Au·strine.**

Austringer (ǭ·strindʒəɹ). Also **astr-, ostr-.** 1486. [erron. spelling of *ostringer*; see OSTREGER.] A keeper of goshawks.

Austromancy (ǭ·stromænsi). 1656. [f. L. *Auster* south wind + -MANCY.] Divination from observation of the winds.

† **Autæ·sthesy.** 1642. [f. Gr. αὐτ(ο-) AUTO- + αἴσθησις perception; see -Y.[3]] Self-consciousness –1652.

Autantitypy (ǭtænti·tĭpi). [f. AUTO- + ANTITYPY.] Ultimate incompressibility in body. SIR W. HAMILTON.

Autarch (ǭ·taɹk). 1865. [Back-formation f. AUTARCHY, after *anarch*, *monarch*.] = AUTOCRAT.

Autarchy[1] (ǭ·tăɹki). 1691. [– mod.L. *autarchia* (Milton, after *monarchia*), f. Gr. αὐτ(ο-) AUTO- + -αρχία ruling, f. ἄρχειν to rule.] **1.** Absolute sovereignty, despotism 1692. **2.** Self-government 1691.

Autarchy[2], **autarky** (ǭ·tăɹki). [– Gr. αὐτάρκεια, f. αὐτάρκης self-sufficient, f. αὐτ(ο-) AUTO- + ἀρκεῖν suffice.] Self-sufficiency.

† **Autexousy.** *rare.* [f. Gr. αὐτεξούσιος possessing free-will; see -Y[3].] Free-will. So † **Autexou·sious** *a.* exercising freewill. CUDWORTH.

Authentic (ǭþe·ntik). [ME. *au(c)tentik* – OFr. *autentique* (mod. *authentique*) – late L. *authenticus* – Gr. αὐθεντικός principal, genuine.] **A.** *adj.* † **1.** Of authority, authoritative; entitled to obedience or respect –1849. † **2.** Legally valid –1723. Of persons: Legally or duly qualified –1610. **3.** Entitled to belief, as being in accordance with, or as stating fact; reliable, trustworthy, of established credit. (The prevailing sense; often opp. to, occas. identified with, *genuine*. See sense 6.) ME. † **4.** Original, first-hand; opp. to *copied* –1822. **5.** Real, actual, genuine. (Opp. to *pretended*.) (*arch.*) 1490. **6.** Really proceeding from its reputed source or author; genuine. (Opp. to *counterfeit*, *forged*, etc. Cf. note, sense 3.) 1790. † **7.** Own, proper –1649. **8.** *Mus.* **a.** Of eccl. modes: Having their sounds comprised within an octave from the final; also of a melody: composed in an authentic mode 1730. **b.** Of a cadence: Having the tonic chord immediately preceded by the dominant 1873. Opp. to PLAGAL.

1. The bible, Whiche is a booke autentyke and credible ME. An a. writer 1710. **2.** Under autenticke seales 1466. **3.** If some stanch Hound, with his authentick Voice Avow the recent Trail SOMERVILLE. Some of the authentickest annalists HOWELL. **4.** Joves a. fire MILT. *P.L.* IV. 719. **5.** A faint a. twilight CARLYLE. **7.** [For justice] to put her own a. sword into the hands of an unjust.. man MILT. var. **Authe·ntical** *a.* Hence **Authe·ntically** *adv.* † **Authe·nticly** *adv.*

B. *sb.* † **1.** An authoritative document –1602; an original document –1655. **2.** The *Authentics*: a collection of the New Constitutions of Justinian (translated authentically from the Gr.) 1614. † **3.** An authority (*rare*) 1713. † **4.** *Mus.* = Authentic mode see A. 8); var. † **Au·thent.** 1609.

Authenticate (ǭþe·ntikeit), *v.* 1653. [f. med.L. *authenticare*, f. late L. *authenticus*; see prec., -ATE[3].] **1.** *trans.* and *refl.* To invest with authority 1733; to give legal validity to; establish the validity of 1653. **2.** To establish the title to credibility of a statement, or of a reputed fact 1654. **3.** To establish the genuineness of 1852.

1. They want antiquity to a. their ceremonies NORTH. **2.** To a. a hypothesis 1664, a conclusion 1856. Hence **Authe·nticator.**

Authentication (ǭþe:ntikēi·ʃən). 1788. [–med.L. *authenticatio*, f. *authenticat*-, pa. ppl. stem of *authenticare*; see prec., -ION.] The action of authenticating; the condition of being authenticated.

The use of seals for the a. of contracts 1847.

Authenticity (ǭþenti·sĭti). 1657. [f. AUTHENTIC + -ITY.] The quality of being authentic, **1.** as being authoritative or duly authorized. **2.** as being true in substance 1762. **3.** as being genuine; genuineness 1760. **4.** as being real, actual; reality 1851.

3. With regard to the a. of the these fragments of our Highland poetry HUME. vars. † **Authe·nticalness,** † **Authe·nticness** (senses 1, 2, 3).

¶ Some writers, esp. on the Christian evidences, confine *authenticity* to sense 2, and use *genuineness* in sense 3.

Author (ǭ·þəɹ). [ME. *autour* – AFr. *autour*, OFr. *autor* (mod. *auteur*) – L. *auctor*, f. *augēre*, *auct*- increase, promote, originate. The latinized spellings *aucto(u)r* were usual XV–XVI; *aucthor*, *autho(u)r* appear XVI, with the graphic variant *th* for *t*, which finally influenced the pronunciation.] **1.** *gen.* The person who originates or gives existence to anything: **a.** An inventor, constructor, or founder. Now *obs.* of things material; exc. as in b. ME. **b.** (*of all*, etc.) The Creator ME. **c.** He who gives rise to an action, event, circumstance, or state of things ME. † **d.** The prompter or instigator –1656. **2.** *spec.* One who begets; a father, an ancestor. (Still used in *Author of his being*; cf. 1 c.) ME. **3.** *esp.* and *absol.* One who sets forth written statements; the writer or composer of a treatise or book. (Now usu. includes *authoress*.) ME. *ellipt.* An author's writings 1601. **4.** An authority, an informant. (Usu. with *poss. pron.* 'my author'.) *? Obs.* ME. **5.** *attrib.* 1711.

1. a. One Robert Creuequer, the authour of the Castle 1576. **b.** A. and maker of all thynges FISHER. **c.** The.. A. of their variance *Ant. & Cl.* II. vi. 138. **2.** Old Walter Plumer (his reputed a.) LAMB. **3.** No a. ever spar'd a brother GAY. I will read politicke Authours *Twel. N.* II. v. 175. **4.** I wold se a better a. therof than such an heretyque as Luther MORE. Hence † **Au·thor** *v.* to originate, cause; to declare, say. **Autho·rial, auto-** *a.* pertaining to an a. of books. **Autho·rially** *adv.* **Au·thoring** *vbl. sb.* book-writing. (FIELDING.) **Au·thorish** *a.* (*rare*)., **Au·thorism,** the position or character of a writer of books. **Au·thorling,** a petty a. **Au·thorly** *a.*

Authoress (ǭ·þŏrės). 1478. [f. prec. + -ESS[1].] A female author: **a.** an originator, causer; **b.** a leader; **c.** a mother; **d.** *esp.* a female literary composer. (Now used only when sex is emphasized; see AUTHOR 3.)

Authoritarian (ǭþǫ:ritēə·riăn), *a.* 1879. [f. AUTHORITY + -ARIAN; cf. *trinitarian*.] Favourable to the principle of authority. As *sb.* One who supports this principle 1883.

Authoritative (ǭþǫ·riteitiv), *a.* 1605. [f. as prec. + -ATIVE. Cf. med.L. *auctoritativus*.] **1.** Of authority, exercising or assuming power; imperative, dictatorial. **2.** Possessing authority; entitled to obedience or acceptance 1653. **3.** Proceeding from a competent authority 1809.

1. He was diligent and in acting a. NORTH. **2.** An a. canon of faith J. TAYLOR. **3.** An a. declaration of pardon 1853. Hence **Autho·rita:tive-ly** *adv.*, **-ness.**

Authority (ǭþǫ·riti, ǭ-, ǫ-). [ME. *autorite* f. (O)Fr. *autorité* – L. *auctoritas*; see AUTHOR, -ITY.] **1.** Power or right to enforce obedience; moral or legal supremacy; the right to command, or give an ultimate decision. **2.** Derived or delegated power; authorization ME. **3.** Those in authority. (Formerly in *sing.* = Government; now usu. abst. in *sing.*, concr. in *pl.*) 1611. **4.** Power to influence the conduct and actions of others; personal or practical influence ME. **5.** Power over the opinions of others; authoritative opinion; intellectual influence ME. **6.** Title to be believed; authoritative statement; weight of testimony. Occas.: Authorship, testimony. ME. **7.** The quotation or book acknowledged, or alleged, to settle a question or give conclusive testimony ME. **8. a.** The author of an accepted statement. **b.** An expert in any question. 1665.

1. Proud man, Drest in a little briefe authoritie *Meas. for M.* II. ii. 118. *In authority*: in a position of power. **2.** By what auctorite dost thou these things, and who gaue the this auctorite COVERDALE *Mark* 11:28. **3.** A. has thought fitt..to prosecute the offenders LUTTRELL. The Mozambique authorities LIVINGSTONE. **4.** With your Lordship's Interest and A. in England ADDISON. **5.** The auctority of the ancients CAXTON. **6.** On the a. of the evening papers (*mod.*). **7.** By turning o'er authorities SHAKS. **8.** Historians in a season of faction are not the best authorities PRESCOTT. A great utilitarian a. BLACKIE.

Authorization (ǭ:þŏrəizēi·ʃən). 1610. [f. AUTHORIZE + -ATION. Cf. Fr. *autorisation*.] The conferment of legality; formal warrant or sanction.

A. does away the fraud: what is authorized is legalized BENTHAM.

Authorize (ǭ·þŏrəiz), *v.* [ME. *autorize*, - (O)Fr. *autoriser* – med.L. *auctorizare*; see AUTHOR, -IZE.] **I.** † **1.** To set up or acknowledge as authoritative –1620. † **2.** To give legal force to –1692. **3.** To give formal approval to; to sanction, countenance ME.; to justify 1603. † **4.** To vouch for –1646.

3. The gentlest..of philosophers..authorised the persecution of Christianity MILL. If Human Strength might a. a Boast COWLEY. **4.** A womans story, at a Winters fire, Authoriz'd by her Grandam SHAKS.

II. 1. To endow with authority; to commission 1494. **2.** † *refl.* To found one's authority *upon* 1581. **3.** To give legal or formal warrant to (a person) *to do*; to empower, permit authoritatively 1571. **4.** Of things: To give satisfactory ground to 1794.

1. Did manyfestly auctoryse his sonne UDALL. **3.** We..by warrant herof authoriss you to procede LD. BURLEIGH. **4.** Past experience authorises us to infer..MILL. Hence **Au·thori:zable** *a.* † having the faculty of authorizing; capable of being authorized. **Au·thorizer,** one who authorizes.

Authorized (ǭ·þŏrəizd), *ppl. a.* ME. [f. prec. + ED[1].] **1.** Possessed of authority; thoroughly established; highly esteemed. **2.** Placed in (*obs.*) or endowed with authority 1483. **3.** Legally or duly sanctioned or appointed 1480.

1. Received and a. opinions COLERIDGE. **3.** *Authorized Version* of the Bible: a popular appellation of the version of 1611, which did not explicitly claim to be 'authorized'.

Authorless (ǭ·þəɹlės), *a.* 1713. [-LESS.] **1.** Anonymous. **2.** Without originator; uncreated 1862. **3.** Void of authors 1879.

Authorship (ǭ·þəɹʃip). 1710. [-SHIP.] **1.** Occupation or career as a writer of books. **2.** The dignity of an author 1782. **3.** Literary origin or origination 1825. **4.** *gen.* Origination of an action, state of affairs, etc. 1884.

1. The trade of a. COLERIDGE. **4.** The a. of the riots at Aston Park 1884.

‖ **Auto** (ɑu·to). 1727. [Sp. and Pg. :– L. *actus*.] **1.** A play 1779. **2.** = AUTO-DA-FÉ 1727.

Auto (ǭ·to), short for AUTOMOBILE *sb.*, after Fr. 1899.

Auto- (ǭ·to), repr. Gr. αὐτο- 'self, one's own, by oneself, independently', comb. f. αὐτός self. In Eng., to a certain extent, a living element, prefixable esp. to scientific terms denoting action or operation, and occas. to others, in combs. which are virtually nonce-words.

auto-ca·rpous [Gr. καρπός] *a.*, *Bot.* '(a fruit) consisting of pericarp alone having no adnate parts' (Gray); var. **-ca·rpian**: **-ce·phalous** [Gr. κεφαλή] *a.*, *lit.* having a head or chief of its own; independent or archiepiscopal or patriarchal jurisdiction; **-clave** [L. *clavus* nail or *clavis* key], a French stew-pan with a steam-tight lid; **-dida:ct** [Gr. δίδακτος], one who is self-taught; **-dyna·mic** [Gr. -δύναμος] *a.*, *Physics*, operating by its own power, as the *Autodynamic elevator*, a machine for raising weights, worked by a falling column of water; **-facture,** self-making; **-gamy** [Gr. -γαμία], *Bot.* self-fertilization; **-ga·mic** *a.*, characterized by, or fit for, autogamy; **-genous** [Gr. -γενής], self-produced, independent; *spec.* **a.** in *Phys.* of parts of the skeleton developed from independent sources of ossification; **b.** in *Path.* of the essential elements of morbid tissues; **c.** of a process of soldering, by melting and so joining the ends of metal; vars. **-ge·neal, -ge·nic; -geny, -gony,** a mode of spontaneous generation, opp. to *plasmogeny*; **-latry** [Gr. λατρεία], self-worship; **-logy,** scientific study of oneself; **-math** [Gr. -μαθής], *rare*, an autodidact; **-metry** [Gr. -μετρία], self-measurement, self-estimation; measurement of the parts of a figure in terms of its entire height; **-metric** *a.*; **-molite** [f. Gr. μολεῖν], *Min.* a variety of GAHNITE; **-mo·rphic** [Gr. -μορφος] *a.*, characterized by automorphism; **-mo·rphic-ally** *adv.*; **-mo·rphism,** the ascription of one's own characteristics to another; **-noe·tic** [Gr. νοητικός] *a.*, self-perceiving; **-nym** [Gr. ὄνυμα = ὄνομα], a book published under the author's real name; **-pa·thic** [Gr. παθικός] *a.*, of or pertaining to disease inherent in a living being itself; **-phag-ous** [Gr. φαγος, f. φαγεῖν] *a.*, self-devouring; **-phagy,** sustenance of life by absorption of the tissues of the body; **-phoby** [Gr. -φοβία], *joc.*, fear of referring to oneself; **-phony** [Gr. -φωνία], *Med.* observation of the resonance of the practitioner's own voice in auscultation; **-phonic** *a.*; **-ophtha·lmoscope** [Gr. ὀφθαλμός + σκοπός], = *Autoscope*; **-plasty** [Gr. -πλαστος], *Surg.* repair of wounds, etc., by means of tissue taken from other parts of the same body; **-pla·stic** *a.*; **-psorin** [Gr. ψώρα], *Med.* a patient's own virus administered homœopathically in cases of itch, smallpox, etc.; **-sche·diasm** [– Gr. αὐτοσχεδίασμα], something extemporized or done off-hand; **-schedia·stic, -al** *a.*; **-sche·diaze** *v.*; **-scope** [Gr. -σκοπός], an instrument for the self-examination of the eye; **-scopy,** the use of the autoscope; **-sty·lic** [Gr. στῦλος] *a.*, *Phys.* of skulls having the mandibular arch suspended by its own proper pier, the quadrate; **-suggestion** = SELF-SUGGESTION 1890; **-tomic** [Gr. -τομός] *a.*, self-intersecting. **b.** Used in names of self-acting mechanisms, as *a.-coherer* **c.** Short for AUTOMOBILE in *autobus*, *-car*.

Autobiographer (ǭ:to,bəiǫ·grăfəɹ). 1829. [AUTO-.] One who writes the story of his own life.

Autobiographic (ǭ:to,bəi,ŏgræ·fik), *a.* 1850. [f. next + -IC.] **1.** Of the nature of autobiography. **2.** Of the character of an autobiographer 1864. Hence **Au:tobiogra·phical** *a.* (1829) belonging to autobiography; also = AUTOBIOGRAPHIC 1, 2. **Au:tobiogra·phically** *adv.*

Autobiography (ǭ:to,bəi,ǫ·grăfi, -bi,ǫ·g-). 1809. [f. AUTO- + BIOGRAPHY. Cf. Fr. *autobiographie.*] The writing of one's own history; the story of one's life written by himself.

What would we give for such an A. of Shakspeare CARLYLE.

Autochthon (ǭtǫ·kþǫ̆n, -ǭn). Pl. **autochthons,** or L. **autochthones** (ǭtǫ·kþǫ̆nīz). 1646. [– Gr. αὐτόχθων, f. αὐτο- AUTO- + χθών earth, soil.] **1.** One sprung from the soil he inhabits; a 'son of the soil'. **2.** Hence in *pl.*: The earliest known dwellers in any country; aborigines 1741. **3.** Original inhabitants or products 1837.

1. There was therefore never any A... but Adam SIR T. BROWNE. Hence **Auto·chthonal, Autochtho·nic, Auto·chthonous** (1805), *adjs.* native to the soil, aboriginal; in *Path.* remaining confined in the part in which it first arose, as a thrombus. **Auto·chthonism,** birth from the soil of a country, or aboriginal occupation of it.

Autochthony (ǭtǫ·kþǫ̆ni). 1846. [f. prec. + -Y³.] Autochthonous condition.

Autocracy (ǭtǫ·krăsi). 1655. [– Gr. αὐτοκράτεια (see next); in mod. use after *autocrat.* † **1.** Self-sustained power –1755. Of states: = AUTONOMY. **2.** Absolute government 1855. Also *transf.* **3.** *Med.* The controlling influence of the vital principle over disease 1864.

2. The religious a. of the Pope MILMAN. The a. of philosophic bodies 1860.

Autocrat (ǭ·tŏkræt). 1803. [– Fr. *autocrate* (a word of the French Revolution) – Gr. αὐτοκρατής, f. αὐτός AUTO- + κρατε-, κράτος power.] A monarch of uncontrolled authority; an absolute, irresponsible governor. (*Autocrat of all the Russias*, a title of the Czar.)

The Russian noble is..a serf to his a., and an a. to his serf H. SPENCER. Hence **Autocra·tic, -al,** *a.* despotic, absolute. **Autocra·tically** *adv.* **Au·tocratshi:p.**

Autocrator (ǭtǫ·krătǫɹ). ? *Obs.* 1789. [– late L. *autocrator* the Emperor – Gr. αὐτοκράτωρ one's own master, f. αὐτός AUTO- + κράτωρ ruler.] = AUTOCRAT. † **Autocrato·ric, -al** *a.*

Autocratrix (ǭtǫ·krătriks). 1762. [Latinized fem. of prec.; see -TRIX.] A female autocrat; the title of empresses of Russia, first assumed by Catherine II.

‖ **Auto-da-fé, -de-fé** (au·to,dă,fē:, dĕ,fē:). Pl. **autos-da-fé;** improp. **auto-da-fés.** 1723. [– (through Fr.) Pg. *auto-da-fé* 'act (i.e. judicial sentence) of the faith'. The Sp. form is *auto de fe.*] **1.** A judicial 'act' or sentence of the Inquisition. **2.** The execution of the sentence; *esp.* the public burning of a heretic 1727.

Autogiro (ǭ:to,dʒəiᵊ·ro). 1925. Also **-gyro.** [– Sp. *autogiro*; see AUTO-, GIRO, GYRE *sb.*] Trade-name of a type of flying machine that can descend vertically by means of a windmill revolving freely on its own shaft.

Autograph (ǭ·tŏgrɑf). 1640. [– Fr. *autographe* or late L. *autographum* – Gr. αὐτόγραφον, subst. use of n. of αὐτόγραφος; see AUTO-, -GRAPH.] **1.** That which is written in one's own handwriting; one's own manuscript. *abstr.* One's own handwriting 1858. **2.** A person's own signature. Hence *attrib.* 1791. **3.** A copy produced by autography 1868. *adj.* Written in the author's own handwriting 1832; var. † **Auto·graphal** *a.*

Au·tograph, *v.* 1818. [f. prec. sb.] **1. a.** To write with one's own hand. **b.** To reproduce by autography. **2.** To write one's autograph on or in 1837.

Autographic, -al (ǭtogræ·fik, -ăl), *a.* 1868. [f. AUTOGRAPH; see -IC, -ICAL.] Of or pertaining to autography; of the nature of an autograph; written in the author's own handwriting. Hence **Autogra·phically** *adv.* in autograph, by means of autography.

Autography (ǭtǫ·grăfi). 1644. [f. AUTOGRAPH + -Y³.] **1.** The action of writing with one's own hand; the author's own handwriting. **2.** Reproduction of the form of anything by an impression of the thing itself; nature printing; *esp.* a process in lithography by which a writing or drawing is transferred from paper to stone 1864. † **3.** = AUTOBIOGRAPHY 1661. **4.** Autographs collectively 1788.

1. Every expert would here detect the a. of the son of Jesse SPURGEON.

† **Autoki·nesy.** [– Gr. αὐτοκινησία self-motion.] Spontaneous motion. CUDWORTH. Hence † **Au:tokine·tical** *a.*

† **Au·toma.** 1625. Erron. sing. of *automata* (see AUTOMATON) –1669.

† **Au·tomate.** 1649. [– Fr. *automate* – L. *automaton, -um*; see AUTOMATON.] *sb.* = AUTOMATON –1751. *adj.* = AUTOMATIC 1818. var. † **Auto·matary** *a.*

Automatic, -al (ǭtŏmæ·tik, -ăl), *a.* 1586. [f. Gr. αὐτόματος (see AUTOMATON) + -IC, -ICAL; cf. Fr. *automatique.*] Of the nature of, or pertaining to, an automaton. **1.** *lit.* Self-acting, having the power of motion or action within itself 1812. **2.** Going by itself; *esp.* of machinery and its movements, which produce results otherwise done by hand, or which simulate human or animal action 1802. **3.** Of animal actions: Not accompanied by volition or consciousness, mechanical 1748. **4.** Not characterized by active intelligence 1843. **5.** Relating to automatons 1860.

1. In the universe, nothing can be said to be a. SIR H. DAVY. **2.** A Sewing Machine with a. tension (*mod.*). **3.** The winking of the eyes is essentially a. BAIN. **4.** Mechanical and a. acts of devotion MILMAN. Hence **Automa·tically** *adv.* **Auto:mati·city,** *a.* condition or nature.

Automatism (ǭtǫ·mătiz'm). 1838. [– Fr. *automatisme* (Descartes), f. *automate* AUTOMATON; see -ISM. Cf. Gr. αὐτοματισμός that which happens of itself, chance.] **1.** The quality of being automatic, or of acting mechanically only; involuntary action. *Hence*, the doctrine attributing this quality to animals. **2.** Mechanical, unthinking routine 1882. **3.** The faculty of independently originating action or motion. (From the orig. sense of *automaton.*) 1876. Hence **Auto·matist,** one who holds the doctrine of a. (sense 1).

Auto·matize, *v. rare.* 1837. [– Fr. *automatiser*, f. *automate* AUTOMATON; see -IZE.] To reduce to an automaton.

Automaton (ǭtǫ·mătǫ̆n). Pl. **-ata, -atons.** 1611. [– L. *automaton, -um* – Gr. αὐτόματον, subst. use of n. of αὐτόματος.] **1.** *lit.* Something which has the power of spontaneous motion or self-movement 1625. Thus applied to: **2.** A living being viewed materially 1645. **3.** A piece of mechanism having its motive power so concealed that it appears to move spontaneously; now usu. applied to figures which simulate the actions of living beings, as clock-work mice, etc. 1611. **4.** A living being whose actions are purely involuntary or mechanical 1678. **5.** A human being acting mechanically in a monotonous routine 1796.

1. [It] doth move alone, A true a. BEAUM. & FL. **2.** These living Automata, Human bodies BOYLE. **3.** Another a. strikes the quarters EVELYN. **5.** [Slaves]..a set of scarcely animated automatons 1796.

Automatous (ǭtǫ·mătəs), *a.* 1646. [f. Gr. αὐτόματος (see prec.) + -OUS.] **1.** Acting spontaneously; having power of self-motion 1769. **2.** Of the nature of an automaton 1646.

1. I am not a.: I need to be wound up 1808.

Automobile (ǭtomǭᵘ·bil, -mŏbī·l). Chiefly *U.S.* 1886. [– Fr. *automobile* adj. (1876); see AUTO-, MOBILE.] **A.** *adj.* Self-propelling. **B.** *sb.* A motor vehicle. Also as vb.

Autonomic, -al (ǭtonǫ·mik, -ăl), *a.* 1659. [f. AUTONOMY + -IC, -ICAL.] Self-governing.

Reason is thus ever autonomic; carrying its own law within itself 1854. Hence **Autono·mically** *adv.*

Autonomist (ǭtǫ·nŏmist). 1865. [f. as prec. + -IST.] An advocate of autonomy. Also *attrib.*

Autonomize (ǭtǫ·nŏməiz), *v.* 1878. [f. as prec. + -IZE.] To make autonomous.

Autonomous (ǭtǫ·nŏməs), *a.* 1800. [f. Gr. αὐτόνομος (see next) + -OUS.] **1.** Of or pertaining to an autonomy. **2.** Possessed of autonomy; self-governing. In *Metaph.*: see AUTONOMY 1 c. 1804. **3.** *Biol.* **a.** Conforming to its own laws only. **b.** Independent, *i.e.* not a mere form or state of some other organism. 1861.

2. If the [Irish] nation was to become a. 1804. **3.** The view that they [lichens] are a. organisms. 1882.

Autonomy (ǭtǫ·nŏmi). 1623. [– Gr. αὐτονομία, f. αὐτόνομος (f. αὐτο- AUTO- + νόμος law); see -Y³.] **1.** Of a state, institution, etc.: The right of self-government, occ. specialized as political, local, or administrative. **b.** Personal freedom 1803. **c.** *Metaph.* Freedom (of the will); the Kantian doctrine of the self-determination of the will, apart from any object willed; opp. to *heteronomy* 1817. **2.** *Biol.* Autonomous condition (see AUTONOMOUS 3) 1871. **3.** A self-governing community 1840.

3. All those autonomies wherewith the world was filled..one after another, stoop and disappear 1840.

Autopsy (ǭ·tǫpsi, -ǫ·psi). 1651. [– Fr. *autopsie* or mod.L. *autopsia* – Gr. αὐτοψία, f. αὐτόπτης eye-witness; see AUTO-, OPTIC, -Y³.] **1.** Seeing with one's own eyes; personal observation. **2.** Dissection of a dead body, so as to ascertain by actual inspection *esp.* the cause or seat of disease; post-mortem examination 1678. Also *fig.*

1. The defect of a. may be compensated by sufficient testimony of a multitude DE QUINCEY. **2.** *fig.* This a. of a fine lady's poem MISS BRADDON.

Autoptic, -al (ǭtǫ·ptik, -ăl), *a.* 1651. [– Gr. αὐτοπτικός; see prec., -IC, -AL¹.] Of, or of the nature of, an eyewitness; based on personal observation. Hence **Auto·ptically** *adv.* **Autopti·city,** a. quality or nature.

Autor, -ial, -ity, etc., obs. ff. AUTHOR, etc.

Autotheism (ǭtoþī·iz'm). 1582. [f. eccl. Gr. αὐτόθεος very God (f. αὐτο- AUTO- + θεός God) + -ISM; cf. αὐτοθεότης Godhead itself.] **1.** The doctrine of God's self-subsistence, *esp.* that of the Second Person of the Trinity. **2.** Self-deification 1619.

1. Calvin's a. signifies..That God the Son is not *Deus de Deo*, God from God BLOUNT. So **Autothe·ist** (in both senses).

Autotype (ǭ·tŏtəip). 1853. [f. AUTO- + -TYPE.] **1.** A 'type' or true impress of the thing itself; a reproduction in facsimile. **2.** A process of permanent photographic printing, which reproduces works of art in monochrome; a facsimile produced by it. Also *attrib.* or as *adj.* 1869.

1. The outward and visible a., of the spirit which animates it [the utterance] KINGSLEY. Hence **Au·totype** *v.* to reproduce by a. process.

Autotypography (ǭ:to,tipǫ·grăfi). [f. AUTO- + TYPOGRAPHY.] A process by which drawings made on gelatine are transferred to soft metallic plates, which may be used for printing.

Autumn (ǭ·tŏm). [ME. *autumpne* – OFr. *autompne* (mod. *automne*), later directly – L. *autumnus.*] **1.** The third season of the year, or that between summer and winter, reckoned astronomically from the descending equinox to the winter solstice; i.e. in the northern hemisphere, from September 21 to December 21. Pop., it comprises, in Great Britain, August, September, and October; in North America, September, October, and November; in the southern hemisphere it corresponds in time to the northern spring. *poet.* The fruits of autumn, harvest 1667. **2.** *fig.* A season of maturity, or of incipient decay 1624.

1. Though she chide as loud As thunder, when the clouds in Autumne cracke *Tam. Shr.* I. ii. 96. On [Thir Table's] ample square..All A. pil'd MILT. *P.L.* V. 394. **2.** The.. a. of a form once fine LANGHORNE.

Comb.: **A.-bells,** *Gentiano Pneumonanthe*; **-fly,** *Conops Calcitrans* Linn.

Autumn (ǭ·tɒm), *v.* 1771. [– L. *autumnare* bring on autumn, in med.L., ripen.] To bring or come to maturity.

Autumnal (ǭtɒ·mnăl), *a.* 1574. [– L. *autumnalis*; see AUTUMN *sb.*, -AL[1].] **1.** Of, belonging or peculiar to, autumn 1636. **2.** Maturing or blooming in autumn 1574. **3.** *fig.* Past the prime (of life) 1656.

1. *Autumnal Equinox*: the time when the sun crosses the equator as it proceeds southward. *A. point*: the point at which the celestial equator is intersected by the ecliptic as the sun proceeds southward; the first point in Libra. *A. signs*: *Libra, Scorpio,* and *Sagittarius. A. star*: Sirius. Thick as A. Leaves MILT. *P.L.* I. 302. **3.** Melissa.. verged on the a. DICKENS. So † **Autu·mnian.** Hence **Autu·mnally** *adv.*

Autumnity (ǭtɒ·mnĭti). ? *Obs.* 1599. [– L. *autumnitas*; see AUTUMN *sb.*, -ITY.] Autumn quality or conditions. **Au·tumnize** *v.* to make autumnal (in appearance) (*rare*).

Autunite (ǭ·tɒnəit). 1868. [f. *Autun* in France + -ITE[1] 2 b.] *Min.* A hydrous phosphate of lime and uranium, of citron or sulphur-yellow colour; also called *lime-uranite.*

Au·turgy. Also **-ergy.** 1651. [– Gr. αὐτουργία, f. αὐτο- AUTO- + ἔργον work; see -Y[3].] Self-action; working with one's own hand.

‖ **Auxesis** (ǭksī·sis). 1577. [Late L. – Gr. αὔξησις increase, amplification.] *Rhet.* Amplification; hyperbole.

By this figure, the orator doth make..of thistles, mighty oaks PEACHAM. Hence **Auxe·tic,** †**-al** *a.* amplifying. **Auxe·tically** *adv.*

Auxiliar (ǭgzi·liăɹ). *arch.* 1583. [– L. *auxiliaris*; see next, -AR[1].] *adj.* AUXILIARY, helpful (*to*). *sb.* An AUXILIARY; something which helps 1670.

adj. A. to divine [purposes] WORDSW.

Auxiliary (ǭgzi·liări). 1601. [– L. *auxiliarius*, f. *auxilium* help, f. **aug-* augment; see -ARY[1]. Cf. Fr. *auxiliaire.*] **A.** *adj.* Const. *to.* **1.** Helpful, assistant, giving support or succour 1603. **b.** in *Grammar*: see B. 3. Formerly applied to any subordinate or formative elements of language, *e.g.* prefixes, prepositions. 1677. **2.** Subsidiary to the ordinary 1687.

1. Calling upon the a. name of Jesus 1686. A. cohorts MERIVALE. **2.** A. Seamen, are such as have another Trade besides, wherewith to maintain themselves, when they are not employed at sea PETTY. *Auxiliary scales* in *Mus.*: the six keys or scales, consisting of any key major, with its relative minor, and the relative keys of each WEBSTER.

B. *sb.* A helper, assistant, confederate, ally; *also,* that which is a source or means of help 1656. **2.** *Mil.* (usu. in *pl.*) Foreign or allied troops in the service of a nation at war 1601. **3.** *Gram.* A verb used to form the tenses, moods, voices, etc., of other verbs 1762. **4.** *Math.* A quantity introduced to simplify or facilitate some operation, as in equations, etc.

1. He Rains and Winds for Auxiliaries brought COWLEY. **2.** The third [sort of soldiers] are Auxiliaries, which serue for pay 1601. **3.** After the verb *to be*, the next in importance among the auxiliaries is the verb *to have* 1835. var. † **Auxi·liatory** *a.* and *sb.*

† **Auxi·liate,** *v.* 1656. [– *auxiliat-*, pa. ppl. stem of L. *auxiliari* to help f. *auxilium*; see prec., -ATE[3].] To help.

Av-. From the Norman Conquest to *c* 1625, the letter *u* had the phonetic value of both *u* and *v*, and *v* was merely the initial *shape* of *u*. Hence *Au-* was commonly written for *Av-*. Such words are here entered under AV-.

Ava, ava' (ăvā·), *phr. Sc.* 1768. [Worn-down f. *of all.*] Of all; at all.

‖ **Ava** (ā·vă), *sb.* 1831. Native name in the Sandwich Islands of a species of Cordyline yielding an intoxicating liquor; the liquor itself; and *gen.* any intoxicant spirit.

Avadavat. Corrupt f. AMADAVAT. [Itself a corruption of *Ahmadabad.* Yule.]

Avail (ăvē[i]·l), *v.* ME. [Engl. formation on VAIL *v.*[1] (of equal date), app. on the analogy of pairs like *amount, mount* (the second of which is aphetic).] **1.** *intr.* To have efficacy for the accomplishment of a purpose; to be of use, afford help. **2.** To be of value, or advantage ME. **3.** *trans.* (at first with *dat.*) To be of use or advantage to; to profit; to help ME. **4.** esp. *To avail oneself of* (in Shaks., ellipt., *To avail of*): **a.** to profit by 1603. **b.** to use 1768. **5.** *causal.* To give (a person) the advantage of; hence, *ellipt.* to inform, assure *of.* (Only in U.S.) 1785. † **6.** *intr.* To do well, profit –1563. † **7.** *trans.* To be equivalent to –1598.

1. This labor..too no great purpose avayleth 1583. **2.** Whilst counsel auayled 1583. **3.** What avails it me to oppose them RICHARDSON. **4. a.** I..availed myself of my position to [etc.] TYNDALL. **5.** To a. government of information T. JEFFERSON. Hence **Avai·ler. Avai·lment,** the fact of being beneficially effective.

Avail (ăvē[i]·l), *sb.* ME. [app. f. the vb. (VAIL *sb.*[1] is later); cf. AFr. *avail.*] **1.** Beneficial effect; advantage. *arch.* or *Obs.* exc. as in quots. **2.** Assistance, aid. *Obs.* exc. as in quots. 1450. **3.** Value, estimation. *Obs.* or *arch.* 1513. **4.** *concr.* (chiefly *pl.*) Profits or proceeds; remuneration or perquisites. Cf. VAILS. (Still common in U.S.) 1449.

1. Taking a. of the cover 1871. † *To have at avail*: i.e. at an advantage. **2.** *Of a.*: of advantage in accomplishing a purpose, effectual. *Of no a., without a.*; ineffectual. *Of little a.*: to little purpose. **3.** The Marchaunt..Doth ioy for gaine of his auailes 1568. Hence † **Avai·lful** *a.* of much a. (A desirable word.)

Availability (ăvē[i]·lăbi·lĭti). 1803. [f. next + -ITY; see -ILITY.] **1.** Available quality. **b.** *spec.* in U.S. That qualification in a candidate which makes his success probable apart from substantial merit 1848. **2.** *concr.* That which is available 1867.

1. b. He was..nominated for his a.,—that is, because he had no history LOWELL.

Available (ăvē[i]·lăb'l), *a.* 1451. [f. AVAIL *v.* + -ABLE.] **1.** Capable of producing a desired result (*arch.* or *Obs.*) 1502. **b.** *Law.* Valid 1451. **2.** Of advantage (*to, unto*) (*arch.*) 1474. **3.** Capable of being turned to account; *hence,* at one's disposal, within one's reach 1827.

1. And all charges by him lawfully made..shall be good and in a. in law BLACKSTONE. **3.** Lenders.. wish..to have their assets as a. as they can ROGERS. Hence **Avai·lableness,** † efficacy; = AVAILABILITY 1, 1 b. **Avai·lably** *adv.*

‖ **Aval.** 1880. [Fr., f. phr. *à val* at the bottom; see AVALE *v.*] An endorsement (*lit.* a writing 'at the bottom') on a bill, etc., guaranteeing payment of it.

Avalanche (æ·vălɑnʃ, ævălɑ·nʃ). 1789. [– Fr. *avalanche*, of Romansh origin, alt., by blending w. *avaler* descend, of Alpine Fr. dial. *lavanche* (cf. Pr. *lavanca*, It. *valanga*), of unkn. origin.] **1.** A large mass of snow, mixed with earth and ice, loosened and descending swiftly down a mountain side. Also *transf.* and *fig.* Also *attrib.*

Ye avalanches, whom a breath draws down BYRON. Such an a. of forgeries CARLYLE.

† **Ava·le,** *v.* ME. [– (O)Fr., *avaler* f. phr. *à val* down (cf. AVAL) :– L. *ad vallem.* Cf. AMOUNT *v.*] **1.** *intr.* To come, go, or get down; to dismount, alight –1596. **2.** Of things: To sink, flow, or sail down –1596. **3.** *trans.* To cause to descend, fall, or sink; to lower; to send downwards –1770. **4.** To lower (the visor of a helmet); *hence,* to doff (hat, etc.) –1557. Also *fig.*

3. Phœbus gan auaile His weary waine SPENSER. Hence † **Ava·ling,** descent; declivity.

Avance, obs. f. ADVANCE.

‖ **Avania** (avănī·ă). 1687. [In form corresp. to It. *avania*; as AVENY = OFr. (XIII) *avenie, aveinie,* (also mod.) *avanie* – med. Gr. ἀβανία, perh. – Arab. *'awān* contempt.] An imposition by the (Turkish) government; *spec.* (as applied by Christians) an extortionate exaction or tax levied by the Turks. See also AVENY. Hence **Avanious** *a.* extortionate.

Avant, obs. f. AVAUNT.

‖ **Avant-** (ăvɑ·nt, avań). 1600. [Fr. :– L. *abante,* f. *ab* + *ante.* See AVAUNT. In early words worn down to *vant-, van-,* and occ. to *vaw-, va-.*] In a few combs., partly French, partly hybrid:

† **ava·nt-, avaw·mbrace** (oftener VAMBRACE), armour for the front of the arm; **-courier,** one who runs or rides before; a herald; *esp.* (in *pl.*) the scouts, skirmishers, or advance-guard of an army; **-fosse** [Fr.], the ditch on the outer side of a counterscarp, dug at the foot of the glacis; **-guard,** *Obs.* and **-garde** [Fr.], the vanguard or van of an army; † **-lay,** the laying on of fresh hounds to intercept a deer already chased by others; † **-mure,** the outer wall of a fortress, etc.; † **-ward,** aphet. VAWARD (common in Shaks.), VANWARD, = *avant-garde.*

Avantage, obs. f. ADVANTAGE.

Avant-courier, *v.* [f. the sb.] To herald.

† **Ava·nters, avancers,** *sb. pl.* ME. [– AFr. *avanters* (pl.), f. *avant* in front; see AVAUNT *adv.*] Part of the numbles of a deer –1486.

Avanturine, var. AVENTURINE.

Avarice (æ·văris). ME. [– (O)Fr. *avarice* – L. *avaritia,* f. *avarus* greedy; see -ICE.] Inordinate desire of getting and hoarding wealth; cupidity. Also *fig.*

To me a. seems not so much a vice, as a deplorable piece of madness SIR T. BROWNE. *fig.* The worst a. is that of sense POPE.

Avaricious (ævări·ʃəs), *a.* 1474. [–(O)Fr. *avaricieux,* f. *avarice* AVARICE + *-ieus, -ieux,* -IOUS.] Immoderately desirous of wealth; grasping. Also *fig.*

Queen Elizabeth was a. with pomp H. WALPOLE. var. † **Ava·rous.** Hence **Avari·ciously** *adv.*; var. † **Ava·rously. Avari·ciousness.**

Avast (ăvā·st), *phr.* 1681. [– Du. *hou' vast, houd vast* 'hold fast', with first syll. assim. to A- *prep.*[1]] *Naut.* Hold! stop! stay! cease!

'A. heaving,' said Gascoigne MARRYAT.

Avatar (avătā·ɹ, æ·vătāɹ). 1784. [– Skr. *avatāra* descent, f. *áva* off, away, down + *tar-* pass over.] **1.** *Hindu Myth.* The descent of a deity to the earth in an incarnate form. **2.** Incarnation 1815. **3.** Manifestation or presentation to the world as a ruling power or object of worship 1859. **4.** *loosely,* Manifestation, phase 1850.

1. The ten Avatars or descents of the deity, in his capacity of Preserver SIR W. JONES. **2.** A third a. of this singular emanation of the evil principle [Bonaparte] SCOTT. **3.** The a. of Mathematics MASSON, of art 1883. **4.** Wit and sense are but different avatars of the same spirit L. STEPHEN.

† **Avau·nt,** *sb.*[1] ME. [f. AVAUNT *v.*[1]] A vaunt; boasting, vain-glory –1553. *To make avaunt*: to boast; = AVAUNT *v.*[1]

† **Avau·nt,** *sb.*[2] [The adv. used subst.; cf. *alarm,* etc.] The order to be off –1711.

To give her the a. SHAKS.

† **Avau·nt,** *v.*[1] ME. [– OFr. *avanter, avaunter,* f. *a* intensive + *vanter*; see VAUNT *v.*] **1.** *trans.* To boast of (an action);

to praise (a person) –1556. **2.** *refl.* To vaunt oneself –1580. *intr.* in same sense –1576. Hence † **Avau·nter.** † **Avau·ntry,** boasting.

† **Avau·nt,** *v.*[2] ME. [f. AVAUNT *adv.* and *int.*] **1.** *intr.* To advance –1596. **2.** *trans.* To raise, ADVANCE –1605. **3.** To be off, depart –1601.

Avaunt (ăvǭ·nt, ăvā·nt), *adv., int.,* etc. ME. [– AFr. *avaunt,* (O)Fr. *avant* before, onward, :– Rom. *abante,* f. L. *ab* from + *ante* before.] † **A.** *adv.* Forward, to the front –1440. **B.** *int.* orig. and lit.: Onward! go on! *Hence,* Begone! away! 1485. **C.** *prefix.* Fore-. See AVANT-, VANT-, VAN-.

int. A., she cried, offensive to my sight POPE.

Ave (ēⁱ·vi). ME. [– L. *avē,* taken as imper. sing. of *avēre* be or fare well.] **A.** *int.* Hail!—Farewell! **B.** *sb.* **1.** A shout of welcome, or farewell 1603. **2.** Short for AVE MARIA, q.v. ME. **3. a.** The time of ringing the Ave-bell. **b.** The beads on a rosary, one for each Ave repeated. 1463.

A. And 'Ave, Ave, Ave,' said, 'Adieu, adieu' for evermore TENNYSON. **B. 2.** *Ave-bell:* that rung at the hours when Aves are to be said.

† **Ave·ll,** *v.* 1530. [– L. *avellere* tear away.] To pull up or away –1651.

Avellan (ăve·lăn, æ·vĕlăn). ME. [– L. *Avellanus* of Avella in Campania.] *adj.* Of Avella; filbert-, hazel-; cf. L. *Avellana nux.* *sb.* A filbert- or hazel-nut ME. *attrib.* in *Her.* of a cross like four filberts joined together 1611.

Ave Maria. [L. and It.], and **Ave Mary** (ēⁱvi,mēᵊ·ri). ME. [See AVE.] The *Hail Mary!* the angelic salutation to the Virgin (*Luke* 1:28), combined with that of Elizabeth (*v.* 42), used devotionally, with the (more recent) addition of a prayer to the Virgin, as Mother of God; so named from its first two words. **b.** = AVE *sb.* 2, 3 a. 1599.

The Eng. pronunc. of the L. is ēⁱ·vi,mărəi·ă, but ā·ve,mări·a, after It., is common; some poets have mā·ri,ă after L.

Avenaceous (ævĭnēⁱ·ʃəs), *a.* 1775. [f. L. *avenaceus* (f. *avena* oats) + -OUS; see -ACEOUS.] Of the nature of, or belonging to, oats; in *Bot.* belonging to the *Avenæ* or Oat-grasses, including the cultivated oats.

† **A·venage.** 1594. [– (O)Fr. *avénage,* f. *aveine* (mod. *avoine*) :– L. *avena* oats.] A payment in oats made to a landlord.

† **A·venant.** ME. only, exc. 2. [– OFr. *avenant,* pres. pple. of *avenir* arrive, succeed, befit, :– L. *advenire,* f. *ad* AD- + *venire* come.] *adj.* **1.** Convenient. **2.** Comely; pleasant –1481. *sb.* That which suits one; convenience, purpose.

Ave·ner. *Obs.* exc. *Hist.* ME. [– AFr. *avener,* OFr. *avenier* :– med.L. *avenarius,* subst. use of L. *avenārius* adj., f. *avena* oats; see -ARY¹.] A chief officer of the stable, who had charge of the provender for the horses. Hence † **Ave·nary, -ery,** the office of the a.

Avenge (ăve·ndʒ), *v.* ME. [– OFr. *avengier,* f. *a* intensive + *vengier* (mod. *venger*) :– L. *vindicare* VINDICATE.] **1.** To take vengeance, inflict retributive punishment, exact satisfaction, or retaliate, on behalf of (a person, a right, etc.); to vindicate. Const. *on, upon, of* (arch.), † *against,* † *over* the offender; *of, against* the offence (*arch.*). *intr.* (refl. pron. omitted) To take vengeance 1535. **2.** *trans.* To take vengeance, etc., on account of (a wrong or injury, or the feelings caused by it) ME. † **3.** To take vengeance upon –1666.

1. A., O Lord, thy slaughtered saints MILT. Thou shalt a. thy right NEALE. **2.** To a. even a look that threatened her with insult BURKE. Hence **Ave·nge** *sb.* execution of vengeance (*arch.*). † **Ave·ngeance, Ave·ngement,** vengeance. **Ave·ngeful** *a.* vengeance-taking, full of vengeance. **Ave·ngingly** *adv.*

¶ At no period is *avenge* absolutely restricted to the idea of just retribution, as distinguished from *revenge,* although the restriction is largely prevalent.

Avenger (ăve·ndʒəɹ). ME. [f. prec. + -ER¹.] **1.** He who avenges (the injured or the injury) 1535. † **2.** He who takes vengeance on (the offender). Cf. AVENGE *v.* 3. –1667.

1. Time, the a. BYRON. **2.** With fury driv'n By his A. MILT. *P.L.* x. 241. Hence **Ave·ngeress.**

Ave·niform, *a.* [f. L. *avena* + -FORM.] Oat-like.

Avenin (ăvī·nin). 1863. [f. as prec. + -IN¹.] The nitrogenous principle of the oat.

Avenous (ăvī·nəs), *a.* 1881. [f. A- *pref.* 14 + L. *vena* vein + -OUS. *Avenious* is an erron. form.] Veinless.

Avens (æ·vĕnz). ME. [– OFr. *avence* = med.L. *avencia,* of unkn. origin.] *Herb.* Pop. name of the Wood A., or Herb Bennet (*Geum urbanum*), and Water A. (*Geum rivale*); also applied to the Mountain A. (*Dryas octopetala*).

Aventail, -ayle (æ·vĕntēⁱl). ME. [– AFr. **aventail* = OFr. *esventail* air-hole (see A- *pref.* 9), f. *esventer,* (whence ME. *avent*), mod. *éventer,* :– Rom. **exventare,* f. L. *ex* EX-¹ + *ventus* wind; see -AL¹.] The mouthpiece of a helmet.

Aventine (æ·vĕntəin). 1625. [– L. *Aventinus* (sc. *mons*) one of the seven hills of Rome.] *fig.* A secure position (*obs.*).

† **Ave·ntre,** *v.* 1557. [prob. alt. (after Fr. *ventre* belly) of **afeutre* (= ME. *fewter*) – OFr. *afeutrer* set (a spear) in the rest.]

He dressed his shelde, and they auentred their speres 1557.

† **Ave·nture.** 1672. [– OFr. (see ADVENTURE *sb.*), used spec. in Eng. law-books of death by accident pure and simple; opp. to *mesaventure.*]

Aventurine, -in (ăve·ntiŭrin). Also **avant-.** 1811. [– Fr. *aventurine* – It. *avventurino,* f. *avventura* chance; so called from its accidental discovery. See ADVENTURE, -INE¹.] **1.** A brownish-coloured glass flecked with gold-coloured spangles, manufactured first at Murano. Also called *Artificial a., A. glass, Gold flux.* **2.** *trans.* A variety of quartz, spangled with yellow scales of mica 1858.

A. felspar or **sunstone,** a mixture of oligoclase and orthoclase spangled with yellowish crystals.

Avenue (æ·vĭniu), *sb.* 1600. [– Fr. *avenue,* subst. use of fem. pa. pple. of *avenir;* see AVENANT, VENUE.] † **1.** The action of coming to 1639. **2.** *gen.* A way of approach; a passage or path of entrance or exit. (Formerly a military term.) Now chiefly *fig.* 1600. **3.** The chief approach to a country-house, usu. bordered by trees; *hence* any broad roadway marked by objects at regular intervals. Occ. of the trees alone. (The current literal sense.) 1654. **4.** A fine wide street (*esp.* in U.S.) 1858. **5.** The ambulacrum in sea-urchins 1841.

2. To watch..this a. to India 1800. *fig.* New avenues of wealth GREEN. **3.** Let them read for *avenue,* the principal walk to the front of the house EVELYN. **4.** Northumberland A. (*mod.*). Hence **A·venue** *v.* to make into an a.; to form avenues in.

† **A·veny.** 1676. [– OFr. *avenie.*] = AVANIA, q.v.

Aver (ē·vəɹ), *sb.*¹ [OE. *eafor,* ME. *aver, haver* draught-horse, tenant's obligation to transport goods, whence AFr. *aver,* Anglo-L. *av(e)ra, affrus.*] A draught-horse; now *Sc.* and *north. dial.* old horse, nag.

An auld jaded aver to ride upon SCOTT.

† **Aver,** *sb.*² ME. [– OFr. *aveir, aver* (mod. *avoir*) chattels, subst. use of *aveir* have :– L. *habēre.*] Possessions, property, estate; farm-stock, cattle.

Aver (ăvə·ɹ), *v.* ME. [– (O)Fr. *avérer,* f. *a-* AD- + *veir, voir* :– L. *verus* true.] † **1.** *trans.* To declare true –1646. † **2.** To prove true, confirm –1678. **3.** *Law.* To prove or justify a plea; to offer to justify an exception pleaded; to make an averment 1490. **4.** To assert as a fact 1509. **5.** To assert the existence or occurrence of 1611.

4. What one author avers upon the subject, another denies 1839. Which..I do averr to be a Calumny BENTLEY. **5.** Chronicles aver many stranger accidents MILT. Hence **Ave·rrable** *a.* capable of being † verified, or asserted. † **Ave·rral,** averment.

Aver-, in some compound terms pertaining to feudal usage, appears to be connected with AVERAGE *sb.*¹:

† **aver-corn,** ? corn paid as a feudal due or in lieu of service; † **averland,** ? land subject to average; † **averpenny,** ? money paid in lieu of average; † **-silver,** ? = *averpenny.*

A·verage, *sb.*¹ 1489. [– med.L. *averagium,* f. OE. *aferian* (*auerian*) supply with horse-transport, f. **afor, eafor* nag; see AVER *sb.*¹] *Old Law.* Some kind of service due by tenants to the feudal superior. Explained in Law Dicts., since Sir J. Skene, as 'service done by the tenant with his beasts of burden'.

Average (æ·vĕrĕdʒ), *sb.*² 1491. [Earlier forms *auerays, averi(d)ge* – Fr. *avarie* (pl. *-ies*) damage to ship or cargo – It. *avaria* – Arab. *'awārīya* damaged goods, pl. of *'awār* damage at sea, loss. Perh. the use of the Fr. pl. induced phonetic association with -AGE (through *-i(d)ge*) and esp. with *damage.*] * Maritime. † **1.** *orig.* A duty charged upon goods; a customs-duty or the like –1760. **2.** Any charge over and above the freight incurred in the shipment of goods, and payable by their owner. (Still in *petty average.*) 1491. **3.** *spec.* The expense or loss to owners, arising from damage at sea to the ship or cargo 1622. **4.** The incidence of any such charge, expense, or loss; *esp.* the equitable distribution of such expense or loss among all the parties interested 1598. ** Transf. **5.** The determination or statement of an arithmetical mean; a medial estimate. (Now only in *at, on, an a.*) 1735. **6.** The arithmetical mean so obtained; the medium amount, the ruling quantity, rate, or degree; the 'common run' 1755.

4. *Particular average* is the incidence of the partial loss or damage of ship, cargo, or freight, through *unavoidable accident,* upon the individual owners (or insurers) of the interests affected. *General a.* is apportionment of loss caused by *intentional* damage to ship, or sacrifice of cargo, etc., and of expense incurred, to secure the general safety of ship and cargo; in which case contribution is made by the owners, etc., in proportion to the value of their respective interests. **5.** Earthquake-shocks occur, on an a., about three times a week HUXLEY. **6.** The month's a. of wrecks has been.. three a day MAURY. The hotel is..above the a. 1867.

Comb.: **a.-adjuster, -stater,** one whose profession it is to adjust claims and liabilities in a case of General Average, and to make up an **a.-statement** showing the same. Hence **A·verager,** an a.-adjuster.

† **Average,** *sb.*³ 1537. [Of. unkn. origin; med.L. *averagium* and OFr. *average* have no such sense. Cf. ARRISH.] The pasturage of arable land after harvest.

Average (æ·vĕrĕdʒ), *a.* 1770. [attrib. use of AVERAGE *sb.*², in sense 5.] **1.** Estimated by average. **2.** Equal to what would be the result of taking an average; medium, ordinary; of the usual standard 1803.

1. The a. price of corn 1770. **2.** A modern drawing of a. merit RUSKIN. Hence **A·veragely** *adv.*

Average (æ·vĕrĕdʒ), *v.* 1821. [f. AVERAGE *sb.*² in sense 5; cf. to *square,* etc.] **1.** *trans.* To estimate, by dividing the aggregate of a series by the number of its units (*at*); to form an opinion as to the prevailing standard of 1831. **2.** *ellipt.* for: To average itself at; to be on an average 1821. **3.** *ellipt.* for: To do, take, etc., on an average 1822.

2. The sale of the book..averaged a thousand copies a year MASSON. **3.** So much this surgeon averaged upon each day for about twenty years DE QUINCEY.

Averin (ēⁱ·vərĕn). *Sc.* 1768. [etym. unkn.] The cloudberry or knoutberry (*Rubus chamæmorus*).

A·verish, *v. dial.* [f. AVERAGE *sb.*³] To consume the eddish, arrish, or average.

Averment (ăvə·ɹmĕnt). ME. [– AFr., OFr. *aver(r)ement;* see AVER *v.,* -MENT.] **1.** The action of proving, by argument or evidence. **2.** *Law.* Formal offer to prove or justify a plea; the proof or justification offered, verification 1514. **3.** Assertion, affirmation 1633. **4.** A positive statement, assertion, or declaration 1629.

2. *Averment*..general..concludes every plea, etc.,..with these words, *and this he is ready to verify* TOMLINS. **3.** Noise and bold a. SCOTT.

Avern (ăvə̄·ɹn). 1599. [– Fr. *Averne* the infernal regions, Hades, or L. *Avernus* (sc. *lacus*) = Gr. ἄορνος (λίμνη) the birdless (lake), f. ἀ- A- *pref.* 14 + ὄρνις bird.] A lake in Campania, the effluvium from which was said to kill birds flying over it. **b.** The infernal regions.

Avernal (ăvə·ɹnăl). 1578. [– L. *avernalis;* see prec., -AL¹. Cf. Fr. *avernal* (Cotgr.).] *adj.* Of the nature of, or belonging to, Avernus; infernal. *sb.* An inhabitant of Avernus, a devil. var. **Ave·rnian** *a.*

Averroist (ævĕrōᵘ·ist). Also **Averrh-.** 1753. One of a sect of peripatetic philosophers who appeared in Italy before the restoration of learning, and adopted the leading tenets of Ibn Roshd or Averrhoes, an Arabian philosopher born at Cordova, viz. that the soul is mortal, or that the only immortal soul is a universal one, from which particular souls arise, and into which they return. Hence **Averro·ism.**

Averruncate (ævĕrɒ·ŋkeˈt), *v.* ? *Obs.* 1623. [f. *averruncat-*, pa. ppl. stem of L. *averruncare* avert, f. *a* AB- + *verruncare* to turn; see -ATE[3] and cf. ABERUNCATE.] **1.** *prop.* To avert, ward off 1663. **2.** *improp.* To root up, to prune 1623. Hence **Averrunca·tion** (in both senses).

Averruncator (ævĕrɒŋkeˈ·təɹ). 1842. [f. prec. in sense 2 + -OR 2.] A pair of pruning shears, or a knife-blade working within a hook, mounted on a pole and worked by a string or wire; used for cutting off the higher branches of trees.

Aversation (ævəɹseˈ·ʃən). *arch.* 1600. [– L. *aversatio*, f. *aversat-*, pa. ppl. stem of *avertari*; see AVERSE, AVERT, -ION.] † **1.** The act of turning away –1673. † **2.** Estrangement –1659. **3.** = AVERSION 4 (*arch.*) 1613. **4.** = AVERSION 5. 1730.

3. Auersation towards Society BACON.

Averse (ăvɜ̄·ɹs), *a.* 1597. [– L. *aversus*, pa. pple. of *avertere* AVERT.] † **1.** Turned away or in the reverse direction, averted –1703; quasi-*adv.* –1814. † **2.** Lying on the opposite side 1667. † **3.** Behind 1646. **4.** Turned away in mind or feeling; actuated by repugnance; habitually opposed, disinclined 1597. Const. *from, to.* (The use of *to*, condemned by Johnson, is explained by the analogy in sense to words like *hostile*, etc. Shaks. does not use the word.) With *inf.* Unwilling 1646. † **5.** Of things: Adverse –1683. † **6.** *sb.* The hinder part (so L. *aversum*); the reverse of a coin –1658.

1. The tracks a. a lying notice gave DRYDEN. **4.** That Law..which leads the Willing, and compels the A. HARRIS. As men auerse from war *Mic.* 2:8. What Cat's a. to fish GRAY. A. to declare herself openly 1777. Hence † **Ave·rse** *v.* to turn away. **Ave·rsely** *adv.* in the reverse direction; backwardly; with aversion. **Ave·rseness** = AVERSION 4.

Aversion (ăvɜ̄·ɹʃən). 1596. [– Fr. *aversion* or L. *aversio*; see prec., -ION.] † **1.** The action of turning away oneself, one's eyes, etc.; in *Rhet.* = APOSTROPHE[1] 1. –1668. † **2.** The action of averting –1684. † **3.** Estrangement (*from*) –1691. **4.** An averted state of mind or feelings; a mental attitude of opposition or repugnance; an antipathy 1651. Const. † *towards*, † *against*, *from*, *to* (*for*), *infin.* See AVERSE 4. 1626. **5.** An object of dislike or repugnance 1678.

4. There are among Brute Creatures many natural Aversions and Antipathies STEELE. Nature..has put into Man a desire of Happiness, and an a. to Misery LOCKE. A. from war 1771. **5.** 'The Excursion', Writ in a manner which is my a. BYRON.

Avert (ăvɜ̄·ɹt), *v.* ME. [Partly – OFr. *avertir* :– Rom. **avertire* for L. *avertere* (f. *a* AB- + *vertere* to turn); partly direct from L.] **1.** *trans.* To turn away. *fig.* To estrange (*arch.*) 1532. **2.** *intr.* (refl. pron. omitted.) To turn away (*arch.*) 1483. **3.** *trans.* To turn away (the face, eyes, thoughts) 1578. **4.** To turn away anything about to befall, *esp.* things threatened; to ward off 1612. † **5.** To oppose –1667. ¶ **6.** *catachr.* for EVERT and REVERT.

1. *fig.* Appease Zeus and the averted Gods L. MORRIS. **3.** Therefore beseech you T'auert your liking a more worthier way *Lear* I. i. 214. **4.** Any expedient which might a. the danger MACAULAY. Hence **Ave·rted** *ppl. a.*, turned aside; unpropitious (*arch.*). **Ave·rtedly** *adv.* **Ave·rter. Ave·rtible, -able** *a.*

Avertiment, obs. f. ADVERTISEMENT.

Avian (ēˈ·viăn), *a.* 1870. [f. L. *avis* + -AN.] Of or pertaining to birds. var. **A·vine.**

Aviary (ēˈ·viări). 1577. [– L. *aviarium*, f. *avis* bird; see -ARY[1].] A large cage, house, or enclosure, in which birds are kept.

Lincolnshire may be termed the a. of England, for the wild fowl therein FULLER. Hence **A·viarist.**

Aviation (ēˈvi,ēˈ·ʃən). 1887. [– Fr. *aviation* (1869), irreg. f. L. *avis* bird + -ATION.] Flying in an aeroplane. So **A·viator,** † (*a*) a flying machine 1891, (*b*) the pilot of an aeroplane 1896 (so **-tress, -trix**).

‖ **Avicularium** (ăvikiulēᵊ·riɒm). Pl. **-a.** 1856. [mod.L., f. *avicula*, dim. of *avis* bird; see -CULE, -ARIUM.] *Zool.* A small, snapping, prehensile process, shaped like a bird's head with a movable mandible, found on the cells of many Polyzoa. **Avicula·rian** *a.*

Aviculture (ēˈ·vikɒltiuɹ). 1880. [f. L. *avis* bird + *cultura* CULTURE.] Rearing of birds; bird-fancying.

Avid (æ·vid), *a.* 1769. [– Fr. *avide* or L. *avidus*, f. *avēre* long for; see -ID[1].] Greedy. Const. *of, for*, etc.

The human heart is a. of pleasure and gain 1769. vars. **Avi·dious,** † **A·vidous.** Hence **A·vidly** *adv.*, var. **Avi·diously.**

Avidity (ăvi·diti). 1449. [– Fr. *avidité* or L. *aviditas*, f. *avidus*; see prec., -ITY.] **1.** Extreme eagerness, greediness. *transf.* of things 1646. **2.** *ellipt.* Greediness of gain, graspingness 1662.

1. To read with a. TYNDALL.

† **A-vie·,** *adv.* 1509. [f. A *prep.*[1] 11 + VIE *sb.*] In emulation –1644.

† **Aview·,** *v.* Also **advewe, -view.** 1494. [f. A- *pref.* + VIEW *v.*] To view officially; to reconnoitre; in Spenser simply = to view –1596.

Avifauna (ēˈ·vi,fǭ:nă), *sb.* 1874. [f. L. *avis* bird + FAUNA.] The Fauna of a district so far as concerns birds.

Avignon Berry (ăvi·nyǫ̆n). 1727. [f. *Avignon* in France.] The fruit of the *Rhamnus infectorius*, etc., used for dyeing yellow, and for making *sapgreen*.

† **Avi·le,** *v.* ME. [– OFr. *aviler* (mod. *avilir*) :– Rom. **advilare*, f. L. *ad* AD- + *vilis* VILE.] To make vile; degrade; hold cheap; vilify –1670. Hence † **Avi·lement.**

‖ **Avion** (avyoṅ). 1898. [Fr., f. L. *avis* bird, + *-on* in *ballon*.] A (French) aeroplane.

Avis(e, etc., obs. f. ADVICE, ADVISE, etc.

† **Avi·sion.** ME. [– OFr. *avision*, f. *a* = L. *ad* AD- + VISION.] A dream; a monition (given in a dream) –1525.

Aviso (ăvəi·zo). Pl. **-os,** † **-o's.** 1634. [– Sp. *aviso* advice, intelligence, advice-boat, :– Rom. **advisum*; see ADVICE; XVI–XVII also ADVISO.] † **1.** Intelligence; a notification –1654. **2.** An ADVICE-BOAT 1714.

Avital (ăvəi·tăl, æ·vităl), *a.* ? *Obs.* 1611. [f. L. *avitus* of a grandfather (*avus*) + -AL[1].] Ancestral, ancient.

Avives (ăvəi·vz), *sb. pl.* ? *Obs.* 1616. [– Fr. *avives*, also OFr. *vives* (XIV, see VIVES), ult. – Arab. *ad-dī'ba*, lit. the she-wolf.] A swelling of the parotid glands in horses; the strangles; also called VIVES.

‖ **Avizandum, avis-** (ævizæ·ndɒm). 1861. [– med.L., n. gerund of *avizare, avisare* consider; see ADVISE.] Consideration. *To take a case into* or *to a.* is for a judge to take it for consideration out of court.

‖ **Avocado** (ævokā·do). 1697. [– Sp. *avocado* advocate (whence Fr. *avocat*), substituted by popular perversion for Aztec *ahuacatl*, more closely repr. by Sp. *aguacate*; further corrupted, through *avigato*, to *alligator* (*pear*) XVIII.] The fruit of a W. Indian tree (*Persea gratissima*); a large pear-shaped fruit, called also *Alligator Pear*.

Avocat(e, obs. f. ADVOCATE.

† **A·vocate,** *v.* 1543. [In sense 1, – *avocat-*, pa. ppl. stem of L. *avocare*, f. *a, ab* away + *vocare* to call; in sense 2, after Fr. † *avoquer* (see AVOKE), later *advoquer* (whence ADVOKE), – L. *advocare*; see ADVOCATE *v.*] **1.** To call away, withdraw (*from*) –1752. **2.** To call to a higher tribunal; = ADVOCATE *v.*[1] 2. –1679.

1. Avocated and called away from sin BECON. **2.** Seeing now..the cause avocated to Rome 1649. Hence **Avo·cative** *a.* calling off or away; *sb.* anything which calls away.

Avocation (ævokēˈ·ʃən). 1529. [– L. *avocatio*, f. *avocat-*, pa. ppl. stem of *avocare* call away, f. *a* AB- + *vocare* to call.] **I. 1.** The calling away (of a person) from an employment; diversion of the thoughts (*arch.*) 1617. **2.** The condition of being called away; distraction 1646. **3.** That which calls one away from an occupation. *Hence*, A minor occupation, a by-work (πάρεργον). 1642. **4.** *improp.* Ordinary employment, usual occupation, vocation, calling 1660.

1. I could be larger, but for a sudden auocation to business HOWELL. **3.** Heaven is his vocation, and therefore he counts earthly employments avocations FULLER. **4.** Found, even in the midst of his most pressing avocations, time for private prayer MACAULAY. The common avocations of life 1761.

II. [– L. *advocatio.*] = ADVOCATION 2. 1529. His unjust a. of the cause to Rome FROUDE.

Avocatory (ăvǫ·kătəri), *a.* (*sb.*) 1666. [– med.L. *avocatorius*, f. as AVOCATE *v.*; see -ORY[2].] **1.** Recalling, that recalls. **2.** *sb.* (in L. form) Avocatory letter or mandate 1689.

Letters avocatory: letters by which a sovereign recalls his subjects from a foreign state with which he is at war, or bids them desist from illegal proceedings.

Avocet, -set (æ·vose:t). 1766. [– Fr. *avocette* (Buffon) – It. *avosetta*, of unkn. origin.] One of the Wading birds (*Grallatores*), allied to the Snipes and Stilts, distinguished by its flexible upturned beak.

Avoid (ăvoi·d), *v.* ME. [– AFr. *avoider* = OFr. *esvuidier, evuider* (see A- *pref.* 9), f. *es-* EX-[1] + *vuide* empty, VOID.] Formerly strengthened with *out, away*. **I.** † **1.** *trans.* To make void or empty; to free or rid (*of*) –1601. **2.** To make void or of no effect. In *Law*, to defeat (a pleading); to invalidate (a sentence, etc.). ME. † **3.** *intr.* (for *refl.*) Of benefices: To become void, or fall vacant –1726.

1. A-voyd þou thi trenchere 1500. **2.** To a. a feoffment COKE, a deed BLACKSTONE, a purchase 1858.

II. † **1.** To empty out, remove –1641; to eject by excretion, to void –1691; to get rid of, put an end to –1685. † **2.** To get rid of, send away (a person *from, out of* a place) –1643. † **3.** *intr.* To move or go away, withdraw; to retire, retreat –1763. Const. *from, out of, forth of* –1611. † **4.** *trans.* To depart from, quit (a place); to dismount from (a horse) –1660.

1. To a. and end controversies BAXTER. **2.** *refl.* A. thee, Fiend SCOTT. **4.** Ye commaunded them to auoyde your Court CAXTON.

III. 1. To leave alone; to have nothing to do with. (The usual current sense—cf. II. 4.) ME. **2.** To escape, evade; to keep out of the way of 1530. † **3.** To prevent, obviate –1831.

1. Never have to do with hym, if thou mayst avoyde hym PALSG. Avoiding Scylla, he fell into Charybdis 1888. **2.** T'auoid the Censures of the carping World *Rich. III*, III. v. 68. Hence † **Avoi·d** *sb.* the withdrawal of dishes after meals. **Avoi·dable** *a.* liable to be made or become void (? *Obs.*); † to be avoided; capable of being avoided. **Avoi·dably** *adv.* **Avoi·der,** one who avoids. **Avoi·dless** *a.* (*poet.*) inevitable; indefeasible.

Avoidance (ăvoi·dăns). ME. [f. prec. + -ANCE.] † **1.** The action of emptying a vessel, etc.; *hence*, a clearing away, removal; ejection, excretion –1661; an outlet –1625. **2.** Voidance, invalidation. (*Esp.* in *Law.*) 1628. † **3.** The action of vacating a benefice, etc. 1642. **4.** The becoming vacant, vacancy; also *ellipt.* the right to fill up the vacancy 1462. † **5.** Dismissal, removal –1650. † **6.** Withdrawal, exit –1635. **7.** The action of avoiding anything unwelcome, or shunning a person 1610.

1. Fountaines, Running..from the Wall, with some fine Auoidances BACON. **2.** The a. of the marriage MILMAN. **4.** A learned Vintner and worthie to haue the next auoydance of Bacchus his chaire PLAT. **7.** Some things may be yeelded for the..a. of others misconstruction BP. HALL.

Avoirdupois (æ:vəɹdəpoi·z). ME. [ME. *aver-, avoirdepeis, -pois*, – OFr. *aveir de peis* 'goods of weight', i.e. *aveir, avoir*, ME. *aver* AVER sb.[2], *de* of, *peis, pois* (mod. *poids*) weight. The substitution of meaningless *du* for *de* was established XVII.] † **1.** Merchandise sold by weight –1691. **2.** (In full *avoirdupois weight*) The standard system of weights used, in Great Britain, for all goods exc. the precious metals, precious stones, and medicines 1485. **3.** Weight. (U.S.) 1597.

The A. pound contains 7000 grains. The cwt. contains in U.S. 100, in G.B. 112 lb., and the ton of 20 cwt. differs accordingly. In the pound, ounce, and dram there is no difference.

3. The weight of an hayre will turne the Scales betweene their Haber-de-pois 2 *Hen. IV*, II. iv. 276.

† **Avo·ke,** *v.* 1529. [In sense 1, – L. *avocare*, after *revoke*, etc. In sense 2, – Fr. †*avoquer* – L. *advocare*. See ADVOKE, ADVOCATE *v.*] **1.** To call away (*rare*) –1639. **2.** = ADVOKE, ADVOCATE *v.*¹ 2. 1529.

† **A·volate,** *v.* 1673. [– *avolat-*, pa. ppl. stem of L. *avolare*, f. *a*, *ab* AB- + *volare* to fly; see -ATE³.] To fly off, escape, exhale, evaporate –1709. Hence † **Avola·tion.**

Avolitional (ævoli·ʃənăl), *a.* 1855. [A *pref.* 14.] Not volitional.

Avoset, var. of AVOCET.

Avouch (ăvau·tʃ), *v.* ME. [– OFr. *avochier* – L. *advocare* ADVOCATE *v.*². See AVOW *v.*¹, VOUCH *v.*] † **1.** To appeal or refer for confirmation to some warrant or authority –1718; to certify by reference to vouchers 1540; to establish upon testimony –1678. **2.** To give one's own warrant; to guarantee. *intr.* 1532. *trans.* 1548. **3.** To declare as a thing one can prove, or upon which one offers his own express testimony as a personal witness; to affirm, assert. (Formerly also of matters of inference or opinion.) 1494. **4.** To acknowledge (or claim) solemnly as one's own, AVOW (*arch.*) 1579. **5.** To acknowledge an act of a subordinate agent (*arch.*) 1553; to own to (any act) as one's own (*arch.*) 1606. **6.** To acknowledge (a charge), confess, avow 1649. **7.** To acknowledge and support or justify (combining 4 with 2); to make good (*with*) 1599.

1. † *To avouch a thing upon one*: to call or cite him as warrant for it. Auouching of him [God] as a witnesse vnto their lye 1619. **2.** I can a. for her reputation DE FOE. **3.** Loe how plainly Saint Augustine auoucheth Purgatorie BEDELL. **4.** Thou hast auouched the Lord this day to be thy God *Deut.* 26:17. **5.** He for whom thou dost this villanie . will not a. thy fact DANIEL. **6.** To a. oneself a coward SCOTT. **7.** And will a. his saying with the sword MARLOWE. Hence † **Avou·ch** *sb.* (*arch.*) guarantee. *Haml.* I. i. 57. **Avou·chable** *a.* able to be avouched. **Avou·ched** *ppl. a.* vouched for; avowed. **Avou·cher. Avou·chment,** guarantee; declaration.

‖ **Avoué** (avu,e). 1851. [Fr. :– L. *advocatus*; = Eng. AVOWE, ADVOWEE.] A patron.

† **Avou·r(e,** *sb.*¹ *rare.* ME. [erron. for *avourie*, AVOWRY.] = AVOWRY 2.

† **Avou·re,** *sb.*² [for AVOWER.] (Legal) Avowal. SPENSER.

Avouter(e, etc., obs. f. ADULTER, etc.

Avow (ăvau·), *v.*¹ ME. [– (O)Fr. *avouer* acknowledge, hence recognize as valid – L. *advocare* appeal to, invoke. See ADVOCATE *v.*, AVOUCH. Aphet. VOW *v.*²] **1.** To own or acknowledge (a person) as one's own. † **2.** To own (the deeds of an agent); to sanction –1651. **3.** To declare (as a thing one can vouch for); to affirm, maintain ME. **4.** To own, admit, or confess (facts, etc., that one might conceal or deny). Const. as in 3. ME. **5.** *refl.* and *pass.* To confess one's identity 1465. **6.** *Law.* To justify or maintain (*spec.* a distress) 1528.

1. His Father. .avowed him for his Son NORTH. † *To a.* (*oneself*) *on* or *upon*: to claim the authority of. **3.** De Clerieux. .aduowed his report to be true for them both 1596. **4.** Many a man thinks, what he is ashamed to a. JOHNSON. **5.** A. yourself, and prove the charge 1769. Hence † **Avow·** *sb.*¹ avowal (*rare*). **Avow·able** *a.* **Avow·ableness. Avow·er,** one who avows. † **Avow·ment,** avowal.

† **Avow** (ăvau·), *v.*² ME. [– OFr. *avoer*, *avouer* vow, f. *a* AD- + *vouer*; see VOW *v.*¹] **1.** *trans.* To put (one) to a vow or oath (*to* or *to do*); to dedicate by a vow (*to*) –1583. **2.** *intr.* (from *refl.*) To take a vow (*to* or *to do*) –1603. Hence **Avow** *sb.*² a vow; † a votive offering.

Avowal (ăvau·ăl). 1732. [f. AVOW *v.*¹ + -AL¹] Acknowledgement; unconstrained admission.

A plain a. of his sentiments PRESCOTT.

Avowance (ăvau·ăns). 1603. ? *Obs.* [f. AVOW *v.*¹ + -ANCE.] **1.** The action of the avowant 1642. **2.** Public acknowledgement.

Avowant (ăvau·ănt). 1529. [f. AVOW *v.*¹ + -ANT.] In *Law*, A challenger; a person making AVOWRY or cognizance.

† **Avowé.** ME. [– (O)Fr. *avoué* :– L. *advocatus*; see ADVOCATE *sb.*, ADVOWEE.] An advocate, or patron; *esp.* a patron saint –1490.

Avowed (ăvau·d), *ppl. a.* ME. [f. AVOW *v.*¹] **1.** Acknowledged, owned. **2.** Self-acknowledged 1651.

1. A. brutality 1659. **2.** An a. enemy to American independency 1792. Hence **Avow·ed-ly** *adv.*, **-ness.**

Avowry (ăvau·ri). [ME. *avoerie*, – AFr. *avowrie*, OFr. *avoerie*, f. *avoeor* (f. *avoer* AVOW *v.*¹ + -OR 2) + *-ie*; see -Y³, -RY.] † **1.** The function of an *avoué*, ADVOWEE, advocate or patron; patronage, protection. **2.** Advocacy, protection or authority *personified*: a protector, a patron; *esp.* a patron saint. (Occ. *attrib.*) ME. † **3.** Advowson 1660. **4.** (From AVOW *v.*¹, in its legal sense): The avowal of an act done; *esp.* the plea whereby one who distrains for rent *avows* the act and justifies it 1531. † **5.** (Due to both vbs. AVOW): A vowing, solemn declaration, or oath –1593.

4. He is said to make *avowry* if he justifies in his own right. .and to make *cognisance* if he justifies in the right of another DIGBY.

Avowter(e, -trie, -tresse, etc., obs. ff. ADULTER, etc.

† **Avoy·,** *int.* ME. only. [– OFr. *avoï*, of unkn. origin.] Exclam. of surprise, fear, remonstrance.

‖ **Avoyer** (avwa,ye, ăvoi·əɹ). 1586. [Swiss-Fr. *avoyer* – OFr. *avoié* (XIV), corresp. to Fr. *avoué*.] Till 1794, the Fr. title of the chief magistrate of some of the Swiss Cantons.

Avulse (ăvɒ·ls), *v.* 1765. [– *avuls-*, pa. ppl. stem of L. *avellere*, f. *a* AB- + *vellere* to pluck.] To pluck off, tear away.

Avulsion (ăvɒ·lʃən). 1622. [– Fr. *avulsion* or L. *avulsio*, f. as prec.; see -ION.] **1.** The action of plucking out or tearing away; forcible separation. **2.** A part torn off 1678. **3.** *Law.* The sudden removal of land, by change in a river's course, or by the action of flood, to another person's estate; distinguished from *alluvion* 1864.

1. By a. or division of the Sea. .Sicily was. . severed from Italy 1622.

Avuncular (ăvɒ·nkiŭlăɹ) *a.* 1831. [f. L. *avunculus* maternal uncle, dim. of *avus* grandfather, + -AR¹; cf. Fr. *avunculaire*.] Of, belonging to, or like, an uncle. (*joc.*) Of a pawnbroker; see UNCLE 1859.

Love. . Paternal or a. LANDOR

Avu·nculize, *v.* [f. as prec. + -IZE.] To act like an uncle. FULLER.

Avys(e, -ness, etc., obs. ff. ADVICE, -ISE, etc.

Aw- was frequently written in ME. for AU-, and in Sc. for AV-. For such forms see AU-, AV-.

Aw, obs. f. AWE, OWE, OUGHT.

Awa, Sc. f. AWAY.

Await (ăwē^i·t), *v.* ME. [– AFr. *awaitier* = OFr. *aguaitier*, f. *a* AD- + *waitier* (mod. Fr. *guetter*) WAIT.] † **1.** To keep watch, watch for; *esp.* to waylay –1671. † **2.** *trans.* To watch for a chance of doing, contrive, plot (harm) *to* ME. † **3.** To look at, notice ME.; *intr.* to take note ME. † **4.** *intr.* with *on*, *inf. phr.*, or *subord. cl.* To keep watch, take care, endeavour –1603. † **5.** To attend. *trans.* –1641. *intr.* with *on*, *upon*, or *absol.* –1742. † **6.** *intr.* To wait *upon* to do business –1489. **7.** To wait for (an event or person). *trans.* ME. (This and 8 are the only current senses.) † *intr.* To wait –1821; with *for* –1608. **8.** To be in store, be reserved, for 1593.

5. On whom three hundred gold-capt youths a. POPE. **7.** Gabriel sat. .awaiting night MILT. *P.L.* IV. 550. **8.** What fates a. the Duke of Suffolke 2 *Hen. VI*, I. iv. 35. Hence † **Awai·t** *sb.* ambush; a snare; watch, watchfulness; caution. **Awai·ter,** † one who lies in wait; † an attendant; one who awaits. **Awai·ting** *vbl. sb.* † ambush; † attendance; waiting, expectation (*arch.*).

Awake (ăwē^i·k), *v.* Pa. t. **awo·ke,** formerly also **awa·ked.** Pa. pple. **awo·ke** and **awa·ked.** [From two verbs: 1. OE. *āwæcnan* (earlier *on-*, see A- *pref.* 2), pa. t. *āwōc*, pa. pple. *āwacen*. OE. had already a weak pa.t. *āwæcnede*, whence mod.E. *awaken*, *awakened*. 2. OE. *āwacian*, pa. t. *āwacode*, in sense = *āwæcnan*, repr. in mod. Eng. by *awake*, *awaked*. All these forms in OE. were intr., but in early ME. *awake* took on the trans. sense of ME. *awecche*. Later, *awoke* and its pa. pple. were referred to *awake* as strong equivalents of *awaked*. There has been some tendency, esp. in later times, to restrict the strong pa. t. and pa. pple. to the orig. intr. sense, and the weak inflexion to the trans. sense, but this has never been fully carried out. See WAKE *v.*]

I. *intr.* **1.** To come out of the state of sleep; to cease to sleep. Cf. AWAKEN 1. **2.** *fig.* To rise from a state resembling sleep, as death, indifference, inaction; to become active or vigilant 1450. **3.** To be or keep awake (*rare*) 1602.

1. Hee awoke out of his sleepe *Judg.* 16:20. And Jacob awaked out of his sleepe *Gen.* 28:16. **2.** A.! A.! English Nobilitie! Let not slouth dimme your Honors 1 *Hen. VI*, I. i. 78. My Lute a. WYATT. *To awake to*: to become alive to.

II. *trans.* (replacing ME. *awecche*.) **1.** To arouse from sleep ME. **2.** *fig.* To rouse from a state resembling sleep; to make active ME.

1. No dreadful Dreams awak'd him with affright DRYDEN. His disciples. .awoke him *Matt.* 8:25. **2.** He will a. my mercie *K. John* IV. i. 26. Hence **Awa·ker** = *Awakener*.

Awake (ăwē^i·k), *pred. a.* ME. [Clipped form of pa. pple. *awaken* (see prec.) used as an adj.] **1.** Roused from sleep, not asleep ME. **2.** *fig.* In activity; vigilant, on the alert 1618.

1. She still beheld Now wide awake, the vision of her sleep KEATS. **2.** Grudge his own rest, and keep the world a. DRYDEN. He was awake to the dangers FROUDE.

Awaken (ăwē^i·k'n), *v.* [OE. *onwæcnan*, *āwæcnan* (see A- *pref.* 2), *āwæcnian*. See AWAKE, WAKEN. In sense 4 *awaken* is still preferred to *awake*.] **1.** *intr. lit.* = AWAKE *v.* I. 1. **2.** *transf.* and *fig.* = AWAKE *v.* I. 2. 1768. **3.** *trans. lit.* To rouse from sleep 1513. **4.** *transf.* and *fig.* To rouse into activity; to stir up; kindle (desire, anxiety, etc.); in *Theol.* to arouse to a sense of sin 1603.

2. Just awakening, and darkly feeling after God WESLEY. **3.** Satan. .his next subordinate Awak'ning MILT. *P.L.* V. 672. **4.** To a. . .their Piety and Industry HOBBES. Hence **Awa·kenable** *a.* **Awa·kener,** he who or that which awakens. **Awa·kening** *vbl. sb.* a rising or an arousing from sleep or its semblance; *ppl. a.* rising as if from sleep; fitted to arouse; rousing. **Awa·kenment.**

Awalt (ā·wəlt), *adv. Sc.* 1799. [Origin unkn.] Of a sheep: Lying helplessly on its back.

A-wane (ăwē^i·n), *adv.* ME. [A *prep.*¹ 11.] † In want; on the wane.

Awanting (ăwǭ·ntiŋ), *ppl. a.* 1661. [Erron. for the phr. *a wanting* (see A *prep.*¹ 12, 13). Cf. *amissing*.] Wanting.

Award (ăwǭ·ɹd), *v.*¹ ME. [– AFr. *awarder*, var. of ONFr. *eswarder* (see A- *pref.* 9), OFr. *esguarder* consider, ordain :– Rom. **exwardare*, f. L. *ex* EX-¹ + **wardare* WARD *v.*] † **1.** *trans.* To decide after deliberation–1725. **2.** To determine upon and appoint by judicial sentence 1533. **3.** To adjudge (*to* a person) 1523. † **4.** To sentence, appoint (*to do*) –1650. † To sentence, consign (*to* custody, etc.) –1648.

2. An umpire. .awarded that the local board should pay. .200*l.* 1884. **3.** A pound of that same marchants flesh is thine, The Court awards it, and the law doth give it *Merch. V.* IV. i. 300. Hence **Awa·rdable** *a.* rightly or lawfully to be awarded. **Awa·rder.** † **Awa·rdment** = AWARD *sb.* † **Awa·rdship,** the action of an awarder, arbitration.

† **Awa·rd,** *v.*² 1534. [f. A- *pref.* 11 + WARD *v.*] **1.** To guard. **2.** To ward off –1783.

Award (ăwǭ·ɹd), *sb.* ME. [– AFr. *award*, f. *awarder*; see AWARD *v.*¹] **1.** A sentence or decision after examination, *esp.* that of an arbitrator or umpire; the document embodying it. **2.** That which is awarded or assigned, as payment, penalty, etc. 1596. † **3.** Custody, wardship. (Cf. WARD *sb.*) –1570.

1. Sette attone by the adward off the Kyng PASTON. **2.** The balance of the Geneva A. 1882.

Aware (ăwē^ə·ɹ), *pred. a.* OE. [ME. *awar*, for earlier *iwar* (A- *pref.* 6), OE. *ġewær* = OS. *giwar* (MDu. *ghewāre*), OHG. *ga-*, *giwar* (G. *gewahr*); WGmc. f. **ʒa-* Y- + **war-* WARE *a.*] † **1.** Watchful, on one's guard –1542. **2.** Informed, cognizant, conscious, sensible ME. † **3.** *ellipt.* with *be* omitted. (Be) on your guard, (be)ware. (Cf. *Soft! Quick!*) –1590.

1. *To be a. of* to be on one's guard against. Are you all a. of. .evil-speaking? WESLEY. **2.** Arnan loked, and was a. of Dauid *1 Chron.* 22:21. Are you a. that your friends are here? 1885. Hence **Awa·redom.** H. WALPOLE. **Awa·reness,** the quality or state of being a. † **Awa·ring** *vbl. sb.* perception.

† **Awa·rn,** *v.* [A- *pref.* 11.] To warn. SPENSER.

A-wash (ăwǫ·ʃ), *adv.* (*pred. a.*) 1833. [A *prep.*[1] 11.] **1.** Flush with the surface of the water, so that it just washes over. **2.** Washing about, at the mercy of the waves 1870.

2. The rising water set everything a. READE.

A-wa·ste, *adv.* [A *prep.*[1] 11.] Wasting. E. B. BROWNING.

A-wa·tch, *adv.* [A *prep.*[1] 11.] On the watch E. B. BROWNING.

A-wa·ve, *adv.* [A *prep.*[1] 11.] On the wave, waving. BROWNING.

Away (ăwēⁱ·), *adv.* [Late OE. *aweġ*, for earlier *onweġ* (see A *prep.*[1] 2, A- *pref.* 2), orig. two words 'on (the or one's) way', (hence) 'from such-and-such a place'. See ON, WAY *sb.*] **I.** Of motion in place, removal. **1.** On (his or one's) way; on. **2.** From this (or that) place, to a distance OE. **3.** Off, aside; also *fig.* as in to *fall away* ME. **4.** Out of one's possession; *e.g.* with *put, give, take, throw*, etc. ME. **5.** From existence; to death, to an end, to nothing ME. **6.** Hence used with trans. vbs., as '*boil, kiss* away', and '*explain, analyse* away'; also with intr. vbs., as 'to sigh away one's life', making them trans. 1661.

1. Come a. death *Twel. N.* II. iv. 55. **2.** The bride's going-away dress 1884. A. went Gilpin COWPER. **3.** To lay work a. LONGF. **5.** Man dieth, and wasteth a. *Job* 14:10.

II. Of action. [From I.] **1.** Onward in time, on, continuously, e.g. *to work away* 1562. **2.** Straightway, without hesitation or delay; chiefly colloq., as in *Fire away! Say away!* and U.S. and Eng. dial. *Right away* 1535.

III. Of position. [From senses I. 2–5.] **1.** In the other direction ME. **2.** Added to *where, there, here*, = about. (Now *dial.*) 1564. **3.** In another place; at a distance; off 1712. **4.** Gone (from a place); absent; wanting ME. **5.** Gone (from existence); destroyed, consumed; dead; fainted. (Now chiefly *dial.*) ME.

1. I turned a. from this despicable troop STEELE. **3.** I shall not be able to stay a. 1712. **4.** I called, but found him a. 1885.

IV. Elliptical (vb. suppressed). **1.** = Go away ME. **2.** = Go or get away *with*, take away 1526. **3.** = Get on or along *with*, put up with 1477. **4.** *And away* (= and going away again), in *once and away* (now *once in a way*) = once but not continuously 1583. ¶ **5.** Formerly erron. for WAY.

1. A., get thee downe *Exod.* 19:24. **2.** Awaye with him, crucify him *John* 19:15. **3.** That saucy fleer I cannot a. with RICHARDSON. **4.** Short hints and a., may please a Scholar 1655. var. † **Away·s** (with advb. gen. *-s*). Hence † **Away·ward** *adv.* turned away; away; var. **-wards**; quasi-*adj.* averted, wayward. *Comb.* **a.-going** *ppl. a.*

Awe (ǭ), *sb.*[1] [ME. *aȝe* – ON. *agi* :– **aȝon*, f. Gmc. **aȝ-*. The Scand. word displaced the native *eie, eȝe*, OE. *eġe* (:– **aȝiz*, whence Goth. *agis* fear).] † **1.** Terror, dread –1784. **2.** Dread mingled with veneration, as of the Divine Being OE. **3.** Solemn and reverential wonder, tinged with latent fear, inspired by what is sublime and majestic in nature 1756. **4.** Power to inspire fear or reverence OE. † **5.** Anger, fierceness, rage –ME. † **6.** A cause of dread; a restraint –1657.

1. His voice Shook the delinquent with such fits of a. COWPER. **2.** There is an a. in mortals' joy, A deep mysterious fear KEBLE. **3.** She pointed with a. to a mighty object HT. MARTINEAU. **4.** Shall Rome stand vnder one mans a.? *Jul. C.* II. i. 52. *Comb.*: † **a.-bound** *a.* bound by a.; submissive, obedient; **-stru·ck** *a.* struck with, or overwhelmed by, a.

Phrases. *To stand in awe of*: to dread; *later*, to entertain a profound reverence for. (Orig. 'Awe stood to men', later, 'Awe stood men (*dat.*)', inverted into 'men stood awe', 'men' being erron. taken as a nom. case, 'in' was inserted to restore the sense.) *To hold* or *keep in awe* (*of*): to restrain or control by fear (of). *Haml.* v. i. 238.

Hence **Awe·less, aw·less** *a.* without dread, undaunted; irreverent; † that inspires no awe. **Awe·lessness. Awe·some, aw·some** *a.* reverential; inspiring awe, appalling, weird. (Chiefly *Sc.*)

Awe, *sb.*[2] 1503. [Etym. and orig. form unkn.] One of the float-boards of an undershot water-wheel, on which the water acts.

Awe (ǭ), *v.* ME. [f. AWE *sb.*[1]] **1.** To inspire with dread, terrify, daunt; to control by the influence of fear. (Orig. *impers.*) **2.** To influence or control by profound respect or reverential fear 1611. **3.** To inspire with reverential wonder combined with latent fear 1753. † **4.** To reverence (*rare*) 1632.

1. Shall quips, and sentences.. awe a man from the careere of his humour *Much Ado* II. iii. 250. **2.** He was not awed by the sanctity of the place GIBBON. Hence **Aw·ed** *ppl. a.* awe-struck; † dreaded. **Aw·ing, aweing** *vbl. sb.* and *ppl. a.*

Awearied (ăwiᵊ·rid), *ppl. a.* 1604. [A- *pref.* 11.] Wearied, weary.

Aweary (ăwīᵊ·ri), *pred. a.* 1552. [A- *pref.* 11.] Tired, weary. Const. *of.*

I ginne to be a. of the Sun *Macb.* v. v. 49.

A-weather (ăwe·ðəɹ). 1599. [A *prep.*[1] 5.] *Naut. adv.* Towards the weather or windward side, in the direction from which the wind blows; *esp.* in *helm a-weather*; opp. to *a-lee. prep.* Short for *a-weather of.*

† **Awe-band.** 1536. [f. AWE *sb.*[1]] A curb, check, restraint; 'a band for tying black cattle to the stake' (Jamieson).

A-week (ăwī·k), *adv.* 1547. [A *prep.*[1] 8; cf. *a-day.*] In every week, weekly.

Aweel (ăwī·l), *conj. adv. Sc.* 1800. [Weakened f. *ah well!* cf. Fr. *eh bien.*] Well!

Aweigh (ăwēⁱ·), *adv.* 1627. [A *prep.*[1] 11.] *Naut.* Of an anchor: Just raised perpendicularly from the ground; = *a-peak, a-trip.*

A-we·st, *adv.* 1809. [A *prep.*[1] 5.] In the west; westward.

Awe-strike (ǭ·ˌstrəi:k), *v.* 1832. [f. AWE-STRUCK by analysis.] To strike with awe. Hence **Awe·-stri:cken** *ppl. a.* = AWE-STRUCK.

Awe-struck (ǭ·ˌstrɒ:k), *ppl. a.* 1634. [f. AWE *sb.*[1] + *struck* pa. pple.] Struck with awe.

Awful (ǭ·ful), *a.* OE. [f. AWE *sb.*[1], continuing the sense of OE. *eġefull*. Occas. compared *awfuller, -est.*] **1.** Causing dread; terrible, appalling. **2.** Worthy of, or commanding, profound respect or reverential fear OE. **3.** Solemnly impressive; sublimely majestic 1660. **4.** *slang.* Frightful, very ugly, monstrous; and *hence* as a mere intensive = Exceedingly great, bad, etc. 1834. † **5.** Terror-stricken; timorous –1748. **6.** Profoundly respectful or reverential 1593.

1. A. massacres GREEN. **2.** Cato's character.. is rather a. than amiable ADDISON. **4.** An a. scrawl 1870, duffer 1873, time 1885. **5.** A weak and a. reverence for antiquity WATTS. Hence **Aw·fully** *adv.* dreadfully; sublimely, majestically; *slang*, very (cf. Gr. δεινῶς); with a feeling of awe. **Aw·fulness,** the quality of inspiring awe; the being full of awe (*arch.*).

† **Awha·pe,** *v.* [ME. *awhaped*, pa. pple., prob. f. A- *pref.* 1 + (*h*)*wappen* to beat; see WAP *sb.* and *v.*] To amaze –1591.

A-whee·ls, *adv.* [A *prep.*[1] 1.] On wheels. B. JONS.

Awhile (ăhwəi·l), *adv.* [OE. *āne hwīle*, ME. *ōne hwīle*, obl. case of A *adj.*[2] and WHILE *sb.*, reduced to *a while* and finally written as one word.] (For) a short time, (for) a little.

A. she paused, no answer came SCOTT.

¶ Improp. written together, when *while* is purely a sb.

After awhile they seemed [etc.] 'OUIDA'.

† **A-whiles, a wiles,** *advb. phr.* [A- *pref.* 11 (or A *prep.* 1).] At times 1546.

A-whi·r, *adv.* 1865. [A *prep.*[1] 11.] Whirring.

A-whi·rl, *adv.* 1883. [A *prep.*[1] 11.] Whirling.

† **Awi·de,** *adv.* 1609. [f. WIDE, after *afar*, etc.] Wide, widely –1642.

A-wi·ng, *adv.* 1823. [A *prep.*[1] 11.] On the wing.

A-wi·nk, *adv.* 1883. [A *prep.*[1] 11.] Winking.

† **Awk** (ǭk), *a.* ME. [– ON. *afugr, ǫfugr* turned the wrong way, back foremost. For the phonetic development cf. *hafoc*, HAWK.] **1.** In the wrong direction, backhanded –1634. **2.** Untoward, perverse –1655. **3.** Awkward to use, clumsy –1674. **4.** *adv.* –1694. **5.** *sb.* –1674. Hence † **Aw·kly** *a.* perverse. † **Aw·kly** *adv.* in the wrong direction; *hence*, unluckily; perversely, awkwardly. † **Aw·kness.**

Awkward (ǭ·kwəɹd), *adv.* and *a.* ME. [f. AWK *a.* + -WARD, *i.e.* 'in an awk direction'; cf. *forward*. The adjectival use is later.] † **A.** *adv.* In the wrong direction, or way. **a.** Upside down; hindside foremost. **b.** In a backward direction, with a back stroke. **c.** Asquint. **d.** Occ. = AWALT, q.v. –1589.

B. *adj.* **1.** Turned the wrong way, backhanded; not straightforward, oblique. Still *dial.* 1513. † **2.** Froward, perverse –1755. † **3.** Untoward, unfavourable (*lit.* and *fig.*) –1663. **4.** Of things: Ill-adapted for use; clumsy in operation 1695. Of persons: Clumsy in action, bungling 1530. **5.** Ungraceful, ungainly; uncouth 1606. **6.** Of things: Embarrassing, inconvenient 1709. Of persons: Embarrassed 1713. **7.** Of things: Not easy to deal with; *euphem.* for 'rather dangerous' 1860. Of persons: Dangerous to meddle with 1863.

2. I haue an aukward pride in my nature FIELDING. **3.** With a. winds and with sore tempests driven MARLOWE. **4.** A., unmanageable instruments 1783. Clumsy, aukward, unhandy people SWIFT. **5.** Vulcan with aukward grace his office plies POPE. The son an aukward booby GOLDSM. **6.** He was beginning to feel a. with his Whig friends L. HUNT. **7.** There is an a. step here 1881. An 'awkward customer' 1863. Hence **Aw·kwardish** *a.* **Aw·kwardly** *adv.* † wrongly; clumsily; in a bungling way; inelegantly; embarrassingly; dangerously. **Aw·kwardness.**

Awl (ǭl). [OE. *æl* = OHG. *ala* (MHG. *ale*, G. *ahle*), ON. *alr*, of unkn. origin.] **1.** A small tool, having a slender, tapering, sharp-pointed blade, with which holes may be pierced; a piercer, pricker, bodkin. **2.** *esp.* That used by shoemakers. Cf. also BRADAWL (used by carpenters). OE. Also *fig.* **3.** *transf.* A sharp spine, or boring organ ME.

2. The Cobler kept him to his nall B. JONS. *To pack up one's awls*: cf. ALL *sb.* (Perh. a pun.)

Comb.: **a-bird,** the Green Woodpecker (*Picus viridis*); **-shaped** *a.* subulate; **-wort,** a plant (*Subularia aquatica*) so named from its leaves.

Awm(e, obs. f. AAM, AUM, AIM.

Awmbrie, -y, awmery, obs. ff. AMBRY.

Awmous, Sc. f. ALMOUS.

Awn (ǭn), *sb.* ME. [– ON. *agn-*, obl. stem of *ǫgn* (Sw. *agn*, Da. *avn*), corresp. to late OE. *æġnan* (pl.), also *eġenu* husk, chaff, OHG. *agana* (G. *ahne*), Goth. *ahana* chaff.] The spinous process, or 'beard', that terminates the grain-sheath of barley, oats, etc.; extended in *Bot.* to any similar growth. Hence **Aw·ned** *ppl. a.*[1] furnished with an a. **Aw·nless** *a.* without awns. **Aw·ny** *a.* bearded, bristly (*rare*).

Awn (ǭn), *v.*[1] 1807. [f. prec. sb.] To get rid of the awns. Cf. *to shell* (peas).

Awned, *ppl. a.*[2] 1881. [Badly f. AWN(ING + -ED[2].] Awninged.

Awning (ǭ·niŋ). 1624. [Of unkn. origin.] **1.** A roof-like covering of canvas, etc., used as a shelter from sun, rain, etc.; *esp.* above the deck of a vessel. **2.** *transf.* **a.** *Naut.* That part of the poop-deck which is continued forward beyond the bulkhead of the cabin. **b.** *gen.* A shelter. 1764. Hence **Aw·ninged** *ppl. a.* furnished with an a. **Aw·ningless** *a.*

A-wo·bble, *adv.* 1881. [A *prep.*[1] 11.] Wobbling.

† **Awo·nder,** *v.* ME. [prob. worn-down f. OE. *ofwundrian*; cf. *athirst.*] **1.** *impers.* It astonishes (one). **2.** *intr.* To be astonished –1513. **3.** *pa. pple.* Amazed –1513.

A-work (ăwɜ̄·ɹk), *adv.* ME. [A *prep.*[1] 11.] At work, in activity.

Maystres.. to set them awerke CAXTON.

† **Awo·rry,** *v.* [OE. *awyrġan*, f. A- *pref.*[1] + *wyrġan* strangle (see WORRY *v.*). Cf. OHG. *irwurgen*, G. *erwürgen* strangle.] To strangle; to worry –ME.

† **Awo·rth,** *adv.* ME. [A *prep.*[1] 9.] In *To take a.*: to take (a thing) in honour, or at its worth; *hence*, to bear patiently, to disregard –1537.

A-wrack (ăræ·k), *adv.* 1627. [A *prep.*[1] 11.] In a state of wreck.

† **A-wrea·k,** *v.* [OE. *awrecan*; see A- *pref.* 1, WREAK.] **1.** To punish (an offence, etc.) –1481. **2.** To condemn –ME. **3.** To avenge or revenge –1586.

A-wreck (ăre·k), *adv.* 1878. [A *prep.*[1] 11.] In a wrecked condition.

Awrong (ărǫ·ŋ), *adv.* ME. [A *prep.*[1] 9.] Wrong, in a wrong way.

Awry (ărəi·). [Late ME. *on wry, awrie*, f. A *prep.*[1] 9 + WRY.] **A.** *adv.* **1.** Away from the straight; to one side; unevenly, crookedly, askew ME. **2.** *fig.* Out of the right course or place; amiss 1494.

1. *To look awry*: to look ASKANCE or ASQUINT. **2.** Much of the Soul they talk, but all awrie MILT. *P.R.* IV. 313. *To go, run, step, tread, walk awry*: (of persons) to do wrong; (of things) to go wrong. *To tread the shoe awry*: to fall from virtue. Cf. Fr. *faux pas.* Where he trod his holy sandals a. FULLER.

B. *adj.* (usu. *pred.* Cf. WRY.) **1.** Out of the right course or position; disordered, disarranged; crooked, distorted 1658. **2.** *fig.* Perverted, wrong 1581. *ellipt.* quasi-*vb.* 1613.

2. Nothing more awry from the Law of God.. then that a Woman should give Laws to Men MILT.

Ax, obs. or dial. f. ASK *v.*

Axal (æ·ksăl), *a.* 1823. [irreg. f. AXIS + -AL[1].] = AXIAL.

Axe (æks), *sb.*[1] Also **ax.** [OE. *æx (eax), æces* = OFris. *axa*, OS. *akus* (Du. *aaks*), OHG. *ackus* (G. *axt*), ON. *øx*, Goth. *aqizi* :- Gmc. **akwizjō*, **akuzjō*.] **1.** A tool for hewing, cleaving, or chopping trees, wood, ice, etc.; consisting of a squarish head, now usu. of iron with a steel edge, fixed by means of a socket upon a handle or helve of wood. Also called (*esp.* when light) *a hatchet.* OE. **b.** PICKAXE, q.v. **2.** In olden warfare: A battle-axe ME. **3.** The headsman's axe. Hence *fig.* execution. 1450. **b.** *The a.*: the cutting down of expenditure in public services; a body for doing this 1922. **4.** In *Archæol.* applied to double-edged or wedge-shaped stone implements 1851.

2. The Lochaber ax is only a slight alteration of the old English bill JOHNSON. The two-handed axe of Harold FREEMAN. **3.** Gave to the cruel ax a darling son YOUNG. **b.** The Geddes axe 1923.

Comb.: **a.-man**, a woodman; a warrior armed with a battle-axe; **-stone,** a greenish variety of jade or nephrite, used in S. America, etc., for making stone hatchets.

Phrases. *To put the axe in the helve*: to solve a doubt. *To send the axe after the helve* (= the better *To send the helve after the hatchet*). *To have axes to grind* (U.S. politics): to have private ends to serve. [In ref. to a story told by Franklin.]

Axe, *sb.*[2] *Obs.* exc. *dial.* [OE. *eax, æx,* = OFris. *axe*, OS., OHG. *ahsa*, also ON. *ǫxull* (see AXLE) :- Gmc. **axsō* fem. See AXIS[1], AXLE.] = AXLE, AXIS.

Axe, *v.* Also **ax.** 1677. [f. AXE *sb.*[1]] **1.** To shape or trim with an axe. **2.** To remove (officials, etc.) to save expenditure; to cut down (expenditure) by means of 'the axe' 1923.

1. The..stretchers in returns, which are not axed, are dressed upon the rubbing-stone 1823. **2.** Under the Geddes recommendations fifteen hundred officers had been axed 1923.

Axed (ækst). 1830. [f. AXE *v.* or *sb.*[1]] **1.** *ppl. a.* Shaped or dressed with an axe. **2.** *adj.* Furnished with an axe or axes 1879.

2. The axed fasces of the lictors FARRAR.

† **Axes, axesse, axez, axis, axys,** obs. ff. ACCESS, 'attack, fit, ague'.

This axes hath made hym so weake PALSGR.

Axial (æ·ksiăl), *a.* 1849. [f. AXIS + -AL[1]. Cf. Fr. *axial.*] **1.** Forming, or of the nature of, an axis. **2.** Of, or belonging to, an axis 1859. **3.** Round, or about, an axis 1862.

1. A true or a. root HENFREY. **2.** A. inclination [of the planets] PROCTOR. **3.** The earth's a. rotation TYNDALL. Hence **Axia·lity,** a. quality. **A·xially** *adv.* in the direction of the axis, from pole to pole.

Axiferous (ǣksi·fĕrəs), *a.* 1842. [f. AXIS + -FEROUS.] *Bot.* Consisting of an axis only, without leaves or appendages.

A·xiform, *a.* 1847. [f. as prec. + -FORM.] In the shape of an axis.

Axifugal (æksi·fiūgăl), *a.* 1740. [f. AXIS, after CENTRIFUGAL.] = CENTRIFUGAL; in *a. force*: tendency to fly from the axis of rotation.

Axil (æ·ksil). 1794. [– mod.L. use of L. *axilla* armpit.] *Bot.* The upper angle between a leaf or petiole and the stem from which it springs; also that between a branch and the trunk.

Axile (æ·ksəil), *a.* 1845. [f. AXIS + -ILE.] Belonging to the axis. Used in *Bot.* of an embryo having the same direction as the axis of the seed.

‖ **Axilla** (æksi·lă). Pl. **-æ.** 1616. [L., = armpit, dim. of **acsla*, *āla* wing.] **1.** An armpit. **2.** = AXIL 1830.

Axillar (æ·ksilăɹ), *a.* (*sb.*) 1541. [f. AXILLA + -AR[1], after Fr. *axillaire.*] **1.** = AXILLARY 1. 1651. **2.** = AXILLARY 2. 1831. **3.** *sb.* An axillary vein 1541.

Axillary (æ·ksilări), *a.* 1615. [f. as prec. + -ARY[2].] **1.** Pertaining or adjacent to the armpit. **2.** *Bot.* Situated in, or growing from, the axil 1786.

1. The a. artery 1791. A. feathers DARWIN. **2.** A. leaves REES.

Axin (æ·ksin). 1873. *Chem.* An oleaginous and waxy product, yielded by the large Mexican cochineal (*Coccus axinus*), and used as an ointment. Hence **Axi·nic** *a.*

Axine (æ·ksəin). 1826. [f. AXIS[2] + -INE[1].] *Zool. adj.* Of or pertaining to the group of stags of which the Spotted Axis is the type. *sb.* One of this group.

Axi·niform, *a.* 1852. [f. Gr. ἀξίνη axe + -FORM.] Shaped like an axe-head.

Axinite (æ·ksinəit). 1802. [f. as prec. + -ITE[1] 2 b.] *Min.* One of Dana's epidote group of unisilicates, consisting chiefly of silica, alumina, lime, and iron, with acute-edged crystals somewhat like an axe-head.

Axinomancy (ǣksi·no,mænsi). 1601. [– L. *axinomantia* – Gr. ἀξινομαντεία, f. ἀξίνη axe; see -MANCY.] Divination by means of an axe-head.

Axiolite (æ·ksi,oləit). 1879. [f. AXIS + -LITE.] *Min.* Elongated lenticular and curved zones of brownish glass, exhibiting crystallization or fibrous structure at right angles to a median line, as in a rhyolite. **A:xioli·tic** *a.*

Axiom (æ·ksiəm). 1485. [– Fr. *axiome* or L. *axioma* – Gr. ἀξίωμα what is thought fitting, self-evident principle (Aristotle), f. ἄξιος worthy.] **1.** A proposition that commends itself to general acceptance; a well-established or universally-conceded principle; a maxim, rule, law. In Bacon, An empirical law 1626. † **2.** *Logic.* A proposition (true or false) –1742. **3.** *Logic* and *Math.* A self-evident proposition, not requiring demonstration, but assented to as soon as stated 1600.

1. Which A., though received by most, is yet certainly false HOBBES. Empirical rules (Bacon would call them *axioms*) SIR W. HAMILTON. **3.** The a. that the whole is greater than its part H. SPENCER.

Axiomatic (æ:ksiŏmæ·tik), *a.* 1797. [– Gr. ἀξιωματικός, f. ἀξίωμα, -ματ-; see prec., -ATIC.] **1.** Of the nature of an AXIOM (sense 3); self-evident. **2.** Characterized by axioms; axiomatical 1812. **3.** Full of maxims, aphoristic 1834.

1. A. truths H. SPENCER. **2.** He gave an a. form to the Science SIR H. DAVY. **3.** The most a. of English Poets SOUTHEY.

A:xioma·tical, *a.* 1588. [f. as prec. + -AL[1]; see -ICAL.] † **1.** *Logic.* Pertaining to, or of the nature of, an AXIOM (sense 2) –1679. **2.** Of or relating to AXIOMS (sense 3) 1676. **3.** = AXIOMATIC 1. 1678. **4.** = AXIOMATIC 3. 1738. Hence **A:xioma·tically** *adv.*

Axis[1] (æ·ksis). Pl. **axes** (æ·ksīz). 1549. [– L. *axis*, rel. to Skr. *ákshas*, Gr. ἄξων, OSl. *osĭ*, Lith. *aszìs*, and OE. *æx* axle (cf. † *axtree* XIII–XVII) = OFris. *axe*, MLG., MDu. *asse* (Du. *as*), OHG. *ahsa* (G. *achse*) :- Gmc. **axsō* fem. See AXE *sb.*[2], AXLE.] **I.** Axis of rotation. **1.** The axle of a wheel. ? *Obs.* 1619. *fig.* The 'pivot' on which a matter turns. **2.** *Phys.* A tooth or process on the second cervical vertebra, upon which the head is turned; the vertebra itself 1694. **3.** The imaginary straight line about which a body (*e.g.* the earth) rotates; the prolongation of that of the earth on which the heavens appear to revolve 1549. † **4.** *fig.* A central prop, which sustains any system –1646. **5.** The geometrical line, by the revolution of a superficies about which, globes, cylinders, cones, etc., are said to be generated 1571.

1. The a. of the revolt was the religious question MOTLEY. **4.** The Atlas or maine a., which supported this opinion, was daily experience SIR T. BROWNE.

II. Axis of symmetry. **1.** The straight line about which the parts of a body or system are symmetrically arranged 1796. **2.** *Geom.* Any line in a regular figure which divides it into two symmetrical parts; in a conic section, the line from the principal vertex or vertices, perpendicular to the tangent at that point; in a curve, a straight line which bisects a system of parallel chords (called *principal axis* when it cuts them at right angles) 1734. **3.** *Cryst.* An imaginary line drawn between the centres of opposite faces or edges, or the apices of opposite angles 1817. **4.** *Optics.* A ray passing through the centre of the eye or of a lens, or falling perpendicularly on it; the line which passes through the centres of the lenses in a telescope; the straight line from the eye to the object of sight 1701. **5.** *Phys. and Zool.* (With 5, 6, and 7 cf. III.) The central core of an organ or organism; the central skeleton or nervous cord; the central column of a whorled shell 1741. **6.** *Bot.* **a.** The central column of the inflorescence. **b.** The main stem and root. 1786. **7.** *Physiogr.* and *Geol.* A central ridge; the central line in a valley 1830.

1. *Axis of a balance*: the line upon which it turns. *A. of oscillation* (of a pendulum, etc.): a horizontal line passing through the centre of the oscillation, and perpendicular to its plane. *A. of polarization*: the central line round which the prismatic rings or curves are arranged. *Neutral a.* (of a girder): the line where there is neither compression nor tension (Brewster). **2.** *Transverse a.* (in the ellipse and hyperbola): that which passes through the two foci; *conjugate a.*: that which bisects the transverse one at right angles. (The axes of an ellipse are also called *major* and *minor.*) **4.** *A. of incidence*: the line passing through the point of incidence perpendicularly to the refracting surface. *A. of refraction*: the continuation of the same line through the refracting medium. *A. of double refraction*: the line on both sides of which double refraction takes place, but along which it does not exist. **7.** *Anticlinal a.*: the line along which two opposite planes of stratification meet in a ridge. *Synclinal a.*: the line along which they meet in a depression.

III. A straight line from pole to pole (cf. I. 3), or from end to end, of any body. **1.** *gen.* e.g. *Axis of the equator*: the polar diameter of the earth; see I. 3. *Axis of the ecliptic, of the horizon*: a diameter of the sphere passing through these circles at right angles. 1796. **2.** *spec.* An imaginary line uniting the two poles of a magnet 1664. **3.** A main line of motion, growth extension, direction 1818.

IV. Axis of reference. *Analyt. Geom.* Each of the two intersecting lines, by reference to which the position of a *locus* is determined 1855.

Comb. **a.-cylinder** (or **-band**), the central fibre of a nerve tube.

Axis[2] (æ·ksis). 1601. [L. (Pliny).] *Zool.* Buffon's name for an Indian deer (*Cervus axis*) known by sportsmen as the Hog-deer.

Axle (æ·ks'l). 1596. [Not in OE.; found in 13th c. in *axle-tree* (synonymous with the native *ax-tree*), f. ON. *ǫxull* masc.; thence taken and used in place of OE. *æx, eax*; see AXE *sb.*[2]] **1.** The centre-pin or spindle upon which a wheel revolves, or which revolves along with it. (In carriages, used to include the axle-tree or axlebar.) 1634. *fig.* (Cf. 'pivot'.) 1635. **2.** The imaginary line about which a planet, etc. (or, anciently, the heaven) revolves. Also *poet.* the pole, the sky or heaven. *Obs.* exc. *poet.* (Replaced by AXIS.) 1596.

1. The gilded car of day His glowing a. doth allay In the steep Atlantic stream MILT. *Comus* 96. *fig.* Mov'd..as upon the a. of discipline MILT. **2.** Since earth on a. ran E. B. BROWNING.

Comb.: **a.-bar**, an iron bar serving the purpose of an axle-tree; **-box**, in a locomotive engine or railway carriage, the box, usu. of cast iron, within which the end of the axle revolves; **-guards,** the part of the frame in which the a.-box slides up and down as acted on by the springs; **-journal, -neck,** the polished end of the a. which revolves under the bearing in the a.-box; **-nail, -pin**, one of the two nails or pins used to fasten a cart to the axle-tree; **-shaft,** a driving shaft forming an extension of the a. of a wheel. Hence **A·xled** *a.* furnished with an a.

† **A·xle-too:th.** 1483. [f. Da. *axel* molar + TOOTH; cf. Da. *axel-tand.*] A molar tooth, a grinder.

Axle-tree (æ·ks'l,trī). [ME. *axel-tre* – ON. *ǫxultré*, f. *ǫxull* :- **axsulaz*, f. * *axsō* (see AXE *sb.*[2]), ult. replacing the native *ax-tree* (see AXLE[1]).] (Now restricted to sense 1.) **1.** The fixed bar, etc., on the rounded ends of which the opposite wheels of a carriage revolve. † **2.** The spindle or AXLE of any wheel; the 'axle' in the *Wheel-and-axle* –1664. *fig.* (Cf. *pivot, axis.*) –1674. † **3.** = AXLE 2. –1633.

1. *Axle-tree arms*: the ends which project beyond the wheels. **3.** Strong as the A. In which the Heauens ride *Tr. & Cr.* I. iii. 65. Hence **A·xle-treed** *a.* furnished with an a.

Axminster (æ·ksminstəɹ). 1818. [Name of a town in Devonshire.] Used attrib. in *A. carpet* or *rug*, and absol.: a seamless carpet formerly made at A., having a thick soft pile.

Axoid (æ·ksoid). 1876. [f. AXIS + -OID.] A curve generated by the revolution of a point round an advancing axis, *e.g.* the cycloid.

Axoide·an, *a.* 1840. [f. AXIS, on imperfect analogy.] = AXIAL.

Axolotl (æ·ksǒlǫt'l). 1786. [Nahuatl, f. *atl* water + *xolotl* servant.] *Zool.* A batrachian reptile (*Siredon pisciforme*, family *Proteidæ*) found in Mexican lakes, resembling the salamander in appearance, but retaining through life the gills of its young state.

Axonometry (æksǒnǫ·mėtri). 1865. [f. Gr. ἄξων, ἀξον- axis + -METRY.] Measurement of axes.

Axophyte (æ·ksǒfəit). 1857. [f. as prec. + -PHYTE.] *Bot.* A plant that has an axis or stem. var. **Axo·nophyte.**

Axotomous (æ̆ksǫ·tǒməs), *a.* 1834. [f. as prec. + -TOMY + -OUS.] *Min.* Having a cleavage perpendicular to the axis.

Axunge (æ·ksɒndʒ). 1541. [– Fr. †*axunge* (mod. *axonge*) – L. *axungia* axle-tree grease, f. *axis* axle + *ung-* of *ungere* to grease.] The internal fat of the kidneys, etc.; *esp.* goose-grease, lard; also *gen.* fat, grease. Hence **Axu·ngious** *a.* lard-like.

Ay-, formerly interchangeable with *ai-* in many words: e.g. *ayd(e*, etc. For such see AI-. It also interchanged with EI-, EY-; and occ. with A-, EA-, E.

Ay, aye (ē[i]), *adv.* [ME. *ai, ei* (*aȝȝ* Orm) – ON. *ei, ey* = OE. *ā* (ME. *ā, ō, oo*), OS. *eo*, OHG. *eo, io* (G. *je*), Goth. *aiws* age, eternity :– Gmc. **aiwaz*, rel. to L. *ævum* age, Gr. ἀεί, ἀιϝεί ever, αἰϝών ÆON.] **1. a.** Ever, continually; **b.** on all occasions. (Now only in *Sc.* and *north. dial.*). **2.** With *comp. degree.* (Still in *Sc.*) ME.

1. And ay the ale was growing better BURNS. Phrases. *For ay:* for ever. Also *for ever and ay;* in ME. *for ay and o.* (Only *poet.* in Eng.). † *In aye:* for ever

Ay (ē[i]), *int.* (*sb.*) ME. [Natural exclam. of surprise, sorrow or pity; *ay me* (XVI) is prob. modelled on OFr. *aimi* or It. *ahimè*, Sp. *ay de mi.*] **1.** = Ah! O! (Northern exclam. of surprise, invocation, earnestness.) **2.** *Ay me!* = Alas! Ah me!—an exclam. of regret, sorrow, pity 1591. **3.** *sb.* 1607.

2. Ay me! how dread can look the Dead E. B. BROWNING.

Ay, var. of AYE, yes.

‖ **Ayah** (ai·ă) 1782. [Anglo-Ind., – Pg. *aia*, fem. of *aio* a tutor.] A native Indian nurse or lady's maid.

Aye, ay (ai, əi), *interj.* (*adv.*), *sb.* 1576. [In earliest use spelt *I* (XVI–XVIII), later *ai, ay*, and *ey*; *aye* not common before XIX. Prob. the pron. *I* used as a formula of assent in answer to a question; cf. OE. *nić* 'not I', used as a negative answer (whence *niććan* deny); also the use of OFr. *je* I, as in *oje*, for *o je* 'that (say) I', yes, beside *na je* no.] *int.* (*adv.*?) **1.** An affirmative response to a question: Yes, even so. Common in dial. and nautical language; the formal word used in voting 'yes' in the House of Commons; but arch. for 'yes' in mod. educated language. **2.** Indicating assent to a previous statement, and preliminary to a further one 1598. **3.** *sb.* An affirmative answer or vote; in *pl.* (ellipt.) those who so vote 1589.

1. If you say I, syr, we will not say no 1576. **2.** I, so I do B. JONS. I; but you doe us wrong 1640. **3.** The ayes proved 138 and the noes 129 MARVELL.

Aye, var. of AY *adv.* ever.

A-year, *phr.* = in the year, per annum; see A *prep.*[1] 8.

Aye-aye (ai·ai:). 1781. [– Fr. *aye-aye* – Malagasy *aiay.*] *Zool.* A quadrumanous animal (*Cheiromys madagascariensis*), of the size of a cat, found only in Madagascar; it is classed with the Lemurs, but in many points approaches the Rodentia.

A-yelp (ă,ye·lp), *adv.* [A *prep.*[1] 11.] Yelping. E. B. BROWNING.

Ayen(e, etc., obs. f. AGAIN, etc.

† **Aye·nbite.** ME. [f. *ayen* (see AGAIN-) + BITE *sb.*; ME. tr. of L. *remorsus.*] Remorse.

Ay-green (ē[i]·grī:n). 1562. [= *Evergreen*; see AY *adv.*] *Herb.* The house-leek.

† **Ayie·ld,** *v.* [OE. *aġieldan*, f. A- *pref.* 1 + YIELD *v.*] To yield up –1450.

Ayme, obs. f. *Ay me!*

† **Ayne,** *a.* 1483. [– Fr. *aîné* – OFr. *ainz, ains né* 'earlier born'; cf. EIGNE. The final vowel muted as in ASSIGN *sb.*[2]] First-born, eldest, EIGNE.

Ayo·nd, ayo·nt, *prep. dial.* 1724. [A- *pref.* 2; cf. *beyond.* (*Ayont* is Sc. and north. dial.)] Beyond, on the other side of.

Ayre, -ie, -y, obs. ff. HEIR, AERIE.

Ayrshire (ē[ə]·ɹʃəɹ), *a.* and *sb.* 1856. A breed of horned cattle named from the shire of Ayr, and esteemed for dairy farming.

Azalea (ăzē[i]·liă). Pl. **-as.** 1753. [– mod.L. *azalea* (Linnæus) – Gr. ἀζαλέα, subst. use of fem. of ἀζαλέος dry, so called because it flourishes in dry soil.] *Bot.* A genus of shrubby plants (N.O. *Ericaceæ*), growing in sandy soil, and blooming profusely, with showy and mostly fragrant flowers. The one British species (*A. procumbens*) is by some made a distinct genus, *Loiseleuria.*

Azarole (æ·zărō[u]l). 1658. [– Fr. *azerole* (†*azarole*) – Sp. *azarolla, acerola* – Arab. *az-zu'rūra*; see AL-[2].] The fruit of the Neapolitan Medlar, a species of Hawthorn (*Cratægus azarolus*); also, the tree itself, occ. called, after Fr., **Azerolier.**

Azedarac (ăze·dăræk). 1753. [– Fr. *azédarac* – Sp. *acedaraque* – Arab. *'āzād - dirakt*, i.e. Pers. *'āzād* free, *dirakt* tree.] *Bot.* **1.** A lofty tree (*Melia azedarach*), with bipinnate leaves, a native of the East Indies; called also Bead-tree, Pride of India, False Sycamore, and Holy-tree. **2.** *Pharm.* The bark of the root of this tree, used in medicine 1853.

† **A·zimene,** *a.* 1647. *Astrol.* Weak and lame degrees –1819.

Azimuth (æ·zimɒþ). ME. [– (O)Fr. *azimut*, corresp. to It. *azzimutto*, Pg. *azimuth*, med.L. *azimuth* (XIV) – Arab. *as-sumūt*, i.e. AL-[2], *sumūt*, pl. of *samt* way, direction, point of the compass (see ZENITH).] **1.** An arc of the heavens extending from the zenith to the horizon which it cuts at right angles; the quadrant of a great circle of the sphere passing through the zenith and nadir, called an *azimuth circle.* **2.** The angular distance of any such circle from a given limit, *e.g.* a meridian 1626. **3.** *transf.* and *fig.* Horizontal angle, or direction; point of the compass 1667.

2. *Magnetic azimuth*: the arc intercepted between the magnetic meridian and the great circle. *A compass*: a minutely divided mariner's compass, fitted with vertical sights, used for taking the magnetic a. of a heavenly body. *A. dial*: one whose gnomon is perpendicular to the plane of the horizon. *A. mirror*: an instrument placed on the glass cover of a mariner's compass and used for taking azimuths.

Azimuthal (æ·zimiū:þăl), *a.* 1654. [f. prec. + -AL[1].] **1.** Of or pertaining to the azimuth; used in taking azimuths. **2.** In a horizontal circle 1863.

2. *Azimuthal error* (of a transit instrument): its deviation from the plane of the meridian. Hence **Azimu·thally** *adv.*

Azo- (æ·zo-). *Chem.* Short comb. f. AZOTE, nitrogen. Used **1.** *gen.* of compounds containing nitrogen; **2.** *spec.* of compounds in which nitrogen is substituted for another element; and *particularly*, of compounds derived from the aromatic hydrocarbons, which contain nitrogen combined in a peculiar way, constituting the *azo-* and *diazo-* compounds, or *azo-* derivatives.

1. **Azohu·mic,** nitrogenized humic (acid); **Azoli·tmin,** the principal colouring matter of litmus; **Azole·ic,** an acid formed by treating oleic with nitric acid. **2.** **Azopa·raffins,** formed from the paraffins by substituting 1 atom of nitrogen for 3 of hydrogen: as *azo-methane*, etc.; **Azobenzene, azotoluene.**

Azoic (ăzō[u]·ik), *a.* 1854. [f. Gr. ἄζωος (f. ἀ- A- *pref.* 14 + ζωή life) + -IC. Cf. ZOIC.] Having no trace of life; in *Geol.* Containing no organic remains, as *Azoic period.*

Azonic (ăzǫ·nik), *a.* 1795. [f. Gr. ἄζωνος (f. ἀ- A- *pref.* 14 + ζωνή zone) + -IC.] Not confined to a zone.

Azoology (æ:zo,ǫ·lǒdʒi). 1817. [f. Gr. ἄζωος (see AZOIC) + -LOGY.] The science of inanimate nature.

Azorite (æ·zorəit). 1868. [f. *Azores* + -ITE[1] 2 b.] *Min.* A white mineral crystallizing in minute octahedrons, occurring in albitic rock.

Azote (æ·zō[u]t). 1791. [– Fr. *azote*, improperly f. Gr. ἀ- A- *pref.* 14 + ζωή life.] Lavoisier's name for *nitrogen*, as unable to support life.

Hence: † **A·zotane,** Davy's name for Chloride of Nitrogen. **A·zotine,** a residuum of melted wool, rich in nitrogen, resulting from the action of superheated steam on cotton and woollen rags. † **A·zotite,** a nitrite. †**Azo·tous** *a.* nitrous. † **Azo·turet,** a nitride. **Azoto·meter,** an apparatus for measuring nitrogen.

A·zoth. 1477. [Arab. *az-zāwūk.*] *Alch.* **a.** Mercury. **b.** The universal remedy of Paracelsus.

Azotic (ăzǫ·tik), *a.* 1791. [f. AZOTE + -IC; cf. Fr. *azotique.*] *Chem.* Of, pertaining to, or chemically compounded with, azote. † *A. air* or *gas*: nitrogen. † *A. acid*: nitric acid. *fig.* Deadening.

Azotize (æ·zǒtəiz), *v.* 1804. [f. as prec. + -IZE.] To nitrogenize; *hence*, to deprive of oxygen. **A·zotized** *ppl. a.* nitrogenous.

Aztec (æ·ztek). 1787. [– Fr. *Aztèque* or Sp. *Azteca* – Nahuatl *aztecall* 'north-men', f. *aztlan* north.] An Indian of the Nahuatlan tribe, which founded the empire of Mexico.

‖ **Azulejo** (ɑþulē·ho). 1854. [Sp., f. *azul* blue.] A kind of Dutch glazed tile painted in colours.

A·zuline. 1864. [app. – Sp. *azulino* bluish, f. *azul* blue; see AZURE, -INE[1]; cf. AZURINE.] A shade of blue.

Azure (æ·ʒəɹ, ē[i]·ʒ[i]ŭɹ). [ME. *asur(e), azur(e)* – OFr. *asur*, (also mod.) *azur* – med.L. *azzurum, azolum* – Arab. *al-lāzaward*, f. (with *al* AL-[2]) Pers. *lāžward* LAPIS LAZULI.] **A.** *sb.* **1.** The semi-precious stone lapis lazuli. **2.** A bright blue pigment or dye; *ellipt.* a fabric dyed of this colour ME. **3.** *Her.* Blue, represented in engravings by horizontal lines ME. **4.** The clear blue of the unclouded sky 1481. **5.** The unclouded vault of heaven 1667.

1. A broche of golde and asure CHAUCER. **4.** The colour of Asure lyke unto the heuen whan it is pure and clere CAXTON. **5.** Not like those steps On Heavens A. MILT. *P.L.* I. 297.

B. *adj.* **1.** *Her.* Blue 1450. **2.** Coloured like the unclouded (southern) sky; cerulean 1505. **3.** *fig.* Clear, cloudless 1827.

2. Her a. veins SHAKS. He rides his a. Carr DRYDEN. *Comb.*: **a.-spar,** lazulite; **-stone,** the lapis lazuli or lazulite. Hence **A·zure** *v.* to dye, or colour a. vars. **Azu·rean** *a.* (*rare*); **A·zured** *ppl. a.* (*arch.*). **Azu·reous** *a.* (*rare*). † **A·zurn** *a.* MILT.

Azurine (æ·ziŭrəin,-in). 1600. [– Fr. *azurin*; cf. It. *azzurrino*, med.L. *azurinus*; see -INE[1].] **1.** *adj.* Blue; pale blue, inclining to grey (Littré). **2.** *sb.* The blue Roach (*Leuciscus cæruleus*) 1832.

Azurite (æ·ziŭrəit). 1868. [f. AZURE + -ITE[1] 2 b.] *Min.* Blue carbonate of copper, an ore allied to malachite.

Azury (æ·ʒəri, ē[i]·ʒ[i]ŭri), *a.* 1600. [f. AZURE + -Y[1]; cf. f. Fr. *azuré* (XV).] Blue, bluish. ? Hence † **A·zury** *sb.* azure hue or colour.

Azygos, -ous (æ·zigəs). 1646. [– Gr. ἄζυγος, f. ἀ- A- *pref.* 14 + ζυγόν yoke; see -OUS.] **1.** *adj.* Fellowless, unpaired; used techn. of organic parts not existing in pairs. **2.** *sb.* [sc. *organic part.*] Hence **A·zygously** *adv.* singly.

Azyme (æ·zim, -əim). 1582. [– eccl.L. *azymus* adj., *azyma* sb. pl. – eccl. Gr. ἄζυμος, τὰ ἄζυμα *sb. pl.*, f. ἀ- A- *pref.* 14. + ζύμη leaven. Cf. Fr. *azyme* adj., *azymes* sb. pl.] The Jewish passover cake of unleavened bread; also, in *pl.* the feast of unleavened bread. Hence **A·zymous** *a.* unleavened.

Azymite (æ·zimǝit). 1727. [– med.L. *azymita* – med.Gr. ἀζυμίτης, f. ἄζυμος; see prec., -ITE[1] 1.] One who administers the Eucharist with unleavened bread; a name given by the Gr. Ch. to the Roman Catholics and others.

B

B (bī). The second letter of the Roman alphabet, corresponding to, and in form derived from, the Gr. *Beta*, and Heb. *Beth*; repr. the sonant labial mute, or lip-voice stop consonant. *Pl.* Bees, B's, *Bs*.

II. Used to indicate serial order, with the value of *second*, as (b., *b.*) the left-hand page or *verso* of a leaf, the second column of a page. Also *spec.*: **1.** *Mus.*: In England the 7th note of the scale of C major, called H in Germany, where B means the English B flat (= Bb, Fr. *B rond*), a semitone lower than B. **2.** In *Law*, etc., B is put for a second or another person or thing. **3.** *Alg.* (see A. II. 5.).

III. *Abbreviations.* **1.** B. (*Mus.*) Bass, Basso. B (*Chem.*) Boron. b., *b.*, born. B. (in *Academical degrees*) Bachelor, or L. *baccalaureus*, as B.A. (or A.B.) Bachelor of Arts, etc. B. (b.) in *Cricket* 'Byes', b. bowled by. B.B.C. British Broadcasting Corporation (*orig.* Company); B.C. Before Christ; B. and S. Brandy and soda; B.V. (M.), the Blessed Virgin (Mary), *Beata Virgo Maria*.

2. *B.* (or *B. flat*), joc. for *bug* (*Cimex lectularius*).

† **Ba,** *v. rare.* ME. [A nursery word, suggestive of OFr. *baisier* kiss, or *baer, beer* gape.] To kiss, as a child –1529.

Baa (bā), *v.* 1586. [Echoic.] To bleat.

He's a Lambe indeed, that baes like a Beare (*Cor.* II. i. 12). Hence **Baa** *sb.* the bleat of a sheep or lamb. **Baa-lamb,** a lamb (nursery-word).

‖ **Baal** (bēi·ăl). Pl. **Baalim.** ME. [Heb. *ba'al* owner, lord.] The chief male deity of the Phœnician and Canaanitish nations; *transf.* false god.

Peor and Baalim Forsake their temples dim MILT. Hence **Ba·alish** *a.* of or belonging to B.; idolatrous. **Ba·alism,** the worship of B.; idolatry. **Ba·alist,** a worshipper of B.; *transf.* a worshipper of false gods or idols; var. **Ba·alite** *a.* (All applied in 17th c. to the R.C. worship.)

Bab, earlier f. BABE (now dial.).

Bab, dial. f. BOB *sb.*[1], a bait for eels.

Ba·ba[1], var. of *pa·pa*, papa.

‖ **Ba·ba**[2]. 1864. [Fr. – Pol.] A light plum-cake.

Ba·bacoote. 1880. [– Malagasy *babakoto.*] A species of lemur (*Lichanotus brevicaudatus*).

Babbie, babby, Sc. and n. dial. f. BABY.

Ba·bbit, *v.* 1875. [See next.] To line with babbit-metal. Hence **Ba·bbiting,** a fitting of babbit-metal.

Babbit-metal. 1875. [f. I. *Babbitt* (1799–1862), Amer. inventor.] A soft alloy of tin, antimony, and copper, used in journal-bearings, etc., to diminish friction.

Babblative (bæ·blătiv). 1583. [f. BABBLE *v.* + -ATIVE.] Given to babbling.

Babble (bæ·b'l), *v.* ME. [– MLG. (Du.) *babbelen* (whence Sw. *babbla*, Da. *bable*), if not a parallel native imit. formation; cf. Fr. *babiller* prattle, L. *babulus* fool; see -LE.] **1.** *intr.* To utter inarticulate or indistinct sounds, like a child. **2.** To talk childishly, to prattle; to talk incoherently, or foolishly; to utter meaningless words ME. **3.** To talk excessively; to chatter 1510. Also *transf.* of streams, birds, hounds, etc. **4.** *trans.* To utter with meaningless iteration; to prate ME. **5.** To reveal by chattering. Cf. *blab.* 1562.

2. A long tongu'd babling Gossip *Tit. A.* IV. ii. 150. **3.** Echo babling by the mountain's side SIR W. JONES. **5.** Who heareth all, And all bableth 1562. Hence **Ba·bblement,** † **Ba·blery,** idle or unseasonable chatter. **Ba·bblingly** *adv.* **Ba·bblish** *a.* full of idle talk; var. **Ba·bbly.**

Babble (bæ·b'l), *sb.* 1460. [f. the vb. Cf. Fr. *babil.*] **1.** Inarticulate speech, as of infants 1688. **2.** Idle, foolish, or unseasonable talk 1460. **3.** Confused murmur, as of a stream 1616.

1. The babes, their b. TENNYSON. **3.** This Sack has fill'd my head so full of bables, I am almost mad BEAUM. & FL.

Babbler (bæ·bləɹ). 1530. [f. the vb. + -ER[1].] **1.** A foolish or idle talker, a chatterer. **2.** A prating gossip; a blabber 1580. **3.** A hound that gives tongue too freely 1732. **4.** Name for the Long-legged Thrush, on account of its note 1839.

2. For who will open himselfe to a Blab or a B. BACON. var. † **Ba·belard.**

Babe (bēib). ME. [Contemporary and synon. w. BABY. *Babe*, not *baby*, is used in the Bible.] **1.** An infant. † **2.** = BABY *sb.* 2. –1595. **3.** *fig.* (see below) 1526.

3. *Babes in Christ*: newly-made converts to Christianity. Even babes in Christ are in a sense perfect WESLEY. Hence **Ba·behood,** infancy. **Ba·belet,** a tiny babe. † **Ba·beship.** **Ba·bish** *a.* infantile, silly (*arch.*). † **Ba·bishly** *adv.* † **Ba·bishness.**

Babel (bēi·bĕl). ME. [– Heb. *bābel* Babylon – Akkadian *bāb ili*, tr. Sumerian *kā-dingir-ra* 'gate of god'.] **1.** The city and tower, described in *Gen.* 11, where the confusion of tongues took place; hence **a.** a lofty structure; **b.** a visionary scheme. **2.** A scene of confusion; a confused assemblage 1625. **3.** A confused turbulent medley of sounds 1529.

1. Therfor was callid the name of it B., for there was confoundid the lippe of all the erthe WYCLIF *Gen.* 11:9. **2.** The whole b. of sectaries joined against the church SWIFT. Hence **Ba·beldom,** noisy confusion. † **Ba·belish** *a.* noisily confused. **Ba·belism,** noisy confusion of speech; strange utterance. **Ba·belize** *v.* to make a b. of.

Ba·bery. ME. [perh. orig. f. *babwynrie* BABOONERY; in later use, f. BABE, BABY *sb.* 4.] Grotesque ornamentation in architecture and books; grotesque absurdity.

‖ **Babillard** (babilyā·r, bæ·bilaɹd) 1802. [Fr., f. *babiller* prattle (see BABBLE *v.*, -ARD); cf. BABBLER 4.] The CHATTERER, a small bird.

Babingtonite (bæ·biŋtŏnəit). 1837. [f. Dr. *Babington* + -ITE[1] 2 b.] *Min.* A bisilicate of iron and lime, with manganese and magnesia, found in greenish-black crystals in Norway, and elsewhere.

† **Ba·bion.** 1599. [– Fr. *babion* (XV), alt. of *babouin* BABOON.] A baboon; an ape; applied to persons –1624.

Babiroussa, -russa (bābirū·sā). 1696. [f. Malay *bābi* hog + *rūsa* deer.] *Zool.* A species of wild hog (*Babirussa alfurus*) found in the islands of Eastern Asia. The upper canine teeth, in the male, pierce the lip and grow upwards and backwards like horns. Also called Hog-deer, Indian Hog, Horned Hog.

† **Ba·bish,** *v.* 1460. [– *baubiss-*, lengthened stem of OFr. *baubir* mock, ridicule; see -ISH[2]. So OFr. *babuise* mockery.] To scoff at, scorn; to treat as mere children –1549.

Bable, old sp. of BABBLE.

‖ **Baboo, babu** (bā·bu). 1782. [Hind. (– Hindi) *bābū.*] *orig.* = our *Mr.* or *Esquire*; hence, a native Hindu gentleman; also, a native clerk who writes English; occas. used of a Bengali with a superficial English education.

Baboon (băbū·n). ME. [– OFr. *babuin* gaping figure, manikin, baboon (mod. *babouin*) or med.L. *babewynus*. Perh. f. (O)Fr. *baboue* muzzle, grimace.] † **1.** A grotesque figure (? of a *baboon* in sense 2) used in architecture, etc. –1592. **2.** A member of one of the divisions of the *Simiadæ* or Monkeys, distinguished by a long dog-like snout, large canine teeth or tusks, capacious cheek-pouches, and naked callosities on the buttocks; they are mostly inhabitants of Africa ME. **3.** *fig.*; cf. *ape* 1500.

2. His forehead low as that of a b. MACAULAY. *Comb.* **b.-bird,** *Threnœdus militaris*, with a note like that of a b. Hence **Baboo·nery,** a colony of baboons (cf. *rookery*); baboonish condition, or behaviour. **Baboo·nish** *a.* baboon-like.

‖ **Babouche** (băbū·ʃ). 1695. [Fr. *babouche* – Arab. *bābūj* – Pers. *pāpūš*, f. *pā* foot + *pūš* covering.] A Turkish or oriental slipper.

‖ **Babui·na.** 1882. [fem. of mod.L. *babuinus*, = Fr. *babouine.*] A female baboon.

Baby (bēi·bi), *sb.* ME. [*Babe* and *baby* appear about the same time and are prob. both deriv. of a reduplicated form **baba* (cf. ME. † *baban* XIII and later † *babbon* XVI), similar to MAMA, PAPA.] **1.** An infant of either sex. (Formerly = *child*; now, usually, an infant 'in arms'.) † **2.** A doll, puppet –1721. † **3.** The small image of oneself reflected in the pupil of another's eye; hence, *to look babies* –1682. **4.** *pl.* Pictures in books: cf. BABERY. Still in *n. dial.* 1598. Also *fig.*

Comb. **1.** passing into *adj.* = young; small or diminutive of its kind, as *b. car, grand, jib* 1873. **2. b.-farmer,** one who takes infants to nurse for payment, whence *baby-farming*, etc.; **-house,** a doll's house; **-jumper,** a frame suspended by an elastic attachment, so that a young child secured in it may exercise its limbs; **-like** *a.* infantile; *adv.* as a baby does. Hence **Ba·byhood,** the period or condition of infancy; babies collectively; babyishness. So **Ba·bydom** (*rare*). **Ba·byish** *a.* childish, simple, silly. **Ba·byish-ly** *adv.*, **-ness. Ba·byism,** babyhood; babyishness; babyish phrase or action. **Babyo·latry** (*nonceωd.*), baby-worship. **Ba·byship,** babyhood; the personality of a baby.

Baby (bēi·bi), *v.* 1742. [f. prec.] To treat as a baby.

Babylon (bæ·bilən), *sb.* ME. [– L. *Babylon* – Gr. Βαβυλών – Heb. *bābel.*] The capital of the Chaldee Empire; also, the mystical Babylon of the Apocalypse; whence, used polemically of the papal power, and rhetorically of any great and luxurious city.

The approach..to mighty Babylon [= London] BYRON. Hence **Babylo·nic** *a.* = BABYLONIAN *a.* † **Babylo·nical** *a.* of or belonging to B.; hence *fig.* **a.** Romish, popish; **b.** Babel-like, tumultuous. † **Babylo·nically** *adv.* **Ba·bylonism,** † *fig.* popery; a Babylonian word or phrase. **Ba·bylonize** *v.* to make Babylonian.

Babylonian (bæbilōu·niăn). 1564. [f. L. *Babylonius* – Gr. Βαβυλώνιος + -AN; see -IAN.] **1.** *adj.* Of or belonging to Babylon; hence *fig.* **a.** huge; † **b.** popish; **c.** (cf. *Rev.* 17:4) scarlet. 1637. **2.** *sb.* An inhabitant of Babylon; hence *fig.* † **a.** papist; **b.** astrologer. 1564.

Babylonish (bæbilōu·niʃ), *a.* 1535. [-ISH[1].] **1.** Of, belonging to, or made at Babylon. **2.** *fig.* † **a.** Popish; **b.** Babel-like, confused in language. 1590.

1. A costly Babilonish garment *Josh.* 7:21. **2.** A B. dialect, Which learned pedants much affect BUTLER *Hud.* I. i. 93.

‖ **Bac** (bæk). 1672. [(O)Fr. *bac* – Du. *bak*; see BACK *sb.*[2]] **1.** A flat-bottomed French ferry-boat; a ferry. **2.** In *Brewing* and *Distilling*; see BACK *sb.*[2]

‖ **Bacalao** (bækălā·o). 1555. [Sp.] Cod-fish.

Baccalaurean (bækălǭ·riăn), *a.* 1845. [f. med.L. *baccalaureus* (see next) + -AN.] Befitting a bachelor.

Baccalaureate (bækălǭ·rīˌĕt). 1625. [– Fr. *baccalauréat* or med.L. *baccalaureatus*, f. *baccalaureus*; see BACHELOR, -ATE[1].] **1.** The University degree of bachelor. **2.** = BACHELOR 1696. **3.** quasi-*adj.* in *B. sermon*: a farewell discourse to a graduating class. *U.S.* 1864.

‖ **Baccara, -at** (bakără). 1866. [– Fr. *baccara.*] A game at cards played for money between a banker and punters.

Baccate (bæ·keit), *a.* 1830. [– L. *baccatus*, f. *bacca* berry, pearl; see -ATE[2].] **1.** Bearing berries; bacciferous 1836. **2.** Berry-like 1830. So **Ba·ccated** *ppl. a.* † set with pearls; berry-bearing.

Bacchanal (bæ·kănăl). 1536. [– L. *bacchanalis*, f. *Bacchus*, Gr. Βάκχος god of wine; see -AL[1]. Cf. Fr. *bacchanal.*] **A.** *adj.* **1.** Of or pertaining to Bacchus or his worship 1550. **2.** Riotously drunken, roystering 1711.

B. *sb.* **1.** A devotee of Bacchus; a Bacchant or Bacchante 1590. **2.** A drunken reveller 1812. **3.** (Usu. *pl.*) A festival in honour of Bacchus. [L. *Bacchanalia.*] 1616. **4.** An orgy 1536. **5.** A dance or song in honour of Bacchus 1606. **6.** A scene of revelry painted or sculptured 1753.

1. The riot of the tipsie Bachanals *Mids. N.* V. i. 48. **4.** At their debauches and bacchanals BURKE. **5.** Shall we daunce now the Egyptian Backenals? SHAKS.

‖ **Bacchanalia** (bækănēi·liă), *sb. pl.* 1633. [L., n. pl. of *bacchanalis*; see prec. and -AL[1] 2. Formerly treated in Eng. as sing., with pl. *-as.*] **1.** The festival held in honour of Bacchus 1753. **2.** Drunken revelry; an orgy 1633. † **3.** A drinking-song; cf. BACCHANAL *sb.* 5. 1651. † **4.** = BACCHANAL 6. 1662.

Bacchanalian (bækănēi·liăn), *a.* (*sb.*) 1565. [f. L. *bacchanalis* BACCHANAL + -AN.] **1.** Of, connected with, or relating to Bacchanals 1622. **2.** Marked by, connected with, or given to drunken revelry 1565. **3.** *sb.* A drunken reveller, a tippler 1617.

2. B. writers JOHNSON, tones H. STANLEY. Hence **Bacchana·lianism, Ba·cchanalism,** b. practices, drunken revelry. **Bacchana·lianly** *adv.*

Bacchanalize (bæ·kănăləiz), *v.* 1656. [– Fr. *bacchanaliser*; see BACCHANAL and -IZE.] **1.** *intr.* To indulge in revelry. **2.** *trans.* To turn into drunken revelry.

Bacchant (bæ·kănt). 1699. [– Fr. *bacchante*; see next.] **1.** *sb.* A priest, priestess, or votary of Bacchus; *hence,* a drunken reveller. **2.** *adj.* Bacchus-worshipping, wine-loving 1800. Hence **Baccha·ntic** *a.* of or pertaining to the bacchants.

Bacchante (băkɑ·nt, bæ·kănt, băkæ·nti). 1797. [– Fr. *bacchante* – *bacchant-*, pres. ppl. stem of L. *bacchari* celebrate the feast of Bacchus; in L. only in fem. pl. *bacchantes.* The first pronunc. is after Fr.; the third after It., favoured by the frequent pl. (of both genders) *Bacchantes* (-æ·ntīz) after L.] **1.** *sb.* A priestess or female votary of Bacchus. **2.** *attrib.* as *adj.*; cf. BACCHANT 1821.

Bacchar, baccar (bæ·kăɹ). 1551. [– L. *bacc(h)ar, bacc(h)aris* (also used) – Gr. βάκκαρις, βάκχαρις ('a Lydian wd.').] *Bot.* A plant variously identified. (*Baccharis* is now applied to an American genus of *Compositæ.*)

Baccharis..in englishe sage of hierusalem TURNER.

Bacchic (bæ·kik), *a.* 1669. [– L. *bacchicus* – Gr. βακχικός of Bacchus; see -IC.] **1.** Of or pertaining to Bacchus or his worship. **2.** Frenzied like a votary of Bacchus; riotously drunken, jovial 1699. † **3.** (*absol.* as) *sb.* A drinking-song 1676. † **Ba·cchical** *a.*

‖ **Bacchius** (băkəi·ɒ̆s). 1589. [L. *bacchius* – Gr. βακχεῖος (sc. πούς).] A metrical foot of three syllables, one short and two long.

‖ **Bacchus** (bæ·kɒ̆s). 1496. [L. – Gr. Βάκχος.] The god of wine; *hence,* wine.

Bacciferous (bæ̆ksi·fĕrəs), *a.* 1656. [f. L. *baccifer* + -OUS; see -FEROUS. Cf. Fr. *baccifère.*] Berry-bearing, producing berries.

Bacciform (bæ·ksiʃǫɹm), *a.* 1839. [f. L. *bacca* berry + -FORM.] Berry-shaped.

Baccivorous (bæ̆ksi·vŏrəs), *a.* 1661. [f. as prec. + -VOROUS.] Berry-eating.

Baccy (bæ·ki). 1833. *colloq.* f. *bacca, bacco,* clipped forms of TOBACCO; see -Y⁶.

Bacharach (ba·χăraχ, bæ·kăræk). 1620. A town on the Rhine giving its name to a wine formerly esteemed. var. **Back-rac(k.**

† **Bache.** OE. [ME. *bache, bæch(e),* OE. *beće*; see BECK *sb.*¹] The vale of a stream or rivulet –1494.

Bachelor (bæ·tʃĕləɹ). [ME. *bacheler* – OFr. *bacheler* young man aspiring to knighthood :– Rom. **baccalaris.* Ult. source and connections doubtful.] **1.** A young knight who followed the banner of another; a novice in arms. [Hence the suggested derivation from *Bas Chevalier.*] Hence, **b.** *Knight Bachelor,* a simple knight; the full title of a gentleman who has been knighted 1609. † **2.** A junior member, or 'yeoman', of a trade-guild, or City Company –1809. **3.** A man or woman who has taken the first degree at a university. [In this sense latinized as *baccalarius,* and altered by a pun to *baccalaureus.*] ME. **4.** An unmarried man (of marriageable age) ME. † **5.** A single woman. B. JONS.

4. His wife!..I haue heard him sweare he was a bachiler DEKKER.

Comb. **Bachelor's** or **Bachelors' Buttons:** *Herb.* any of various flowers of round or button-like form; orig. the double variety of *Ranunculus acris*; also the Tansy.

Hence **Ba·chelordom,** the estate or body of bachelors collectively. **Ba·chelorhood,** the state or quality of a b. **Ba·cheloriːsm,** a habit or peculiarity of a b. **Ba·chelorly** *a.* bachelor-like.

Ba·chelorshiːp. 1591. [-SHIP.] **1.** The state of being a bachelor, *i.e.* unmarried. † **2.** The state or position of a knight bachelor 1611. **3.** The standing of a Bachelor of Arts, etc. 1656.

† **Ba·chelry.** ME. [– OFr. *bachelerie,* f. *bacheler*; see BACHELOR, -RY.] **1.** The quality of a young knight; prowess. **2.** Bachelors collectively: **a.** Young knights as a class. (Cf. *chivalry.*) –1656. **b.** A body of unmarried men –1615.

Bacillary (bæ·silări), *a.* 1865. [f. L. *bacillus* little rod + -ARY¹. Cf. Fr. *bacillaire.*] Of, pertaining to, or consisting of little rods. So **Baci·lliform** *a.* rod-shaped.

‖ **Bacillus** (băsi·lɒ̆s). Pl. **bacilli.** 1883. [mod. use of late L., dim. of *baculus* rod, stick.] *Nat. Hist.* A genus of *Schizomycetes,* microscopic vegetable organisms of the lowest grade among what were called *Infusoria.* Dist. from *Bacterium* by its larger size and mode of reproduction. First described by Müller *ante* 1850.

Bacin, bacinet, obs. ff. BASIN, BASINET.

Back (bæk), *sb.*¹ [OE. *bæc* = OFris. *bek,* OS. *bak,* (M)LG., MDu. *bak,* OHG. *bah,* ON. *bak* :– Gmc. **bakam.*] **I. 1.** *properly.* The convex surface of the body of man and vertebrated animals which is adjacent to the spinal axis, and opposite to the belly. It extends from the neck and shoulders to the extremity of the backbone. **2. a.** In man, the hinder surface of the body, that which is turned upon those who are left behind OE. **b.** that part of the body which is the special recipient of clothing ME. **c.** the part which bears burdens OE. **d.** In animals, the upper surface opposite to that on which they move or rest ME.

2. The Army broken, And but the backes of Britaines to be seen *Cymb.* v. iii. 6. Borrow..of thy backe and thi belly LATIMER. Wrongs more then our backe can beare *Tit. A.* IV. iii. 48.

II. *transf.* **1.** That side or surface of any object which is opposite to the face or front, or side approached or contemplated; *e.g.* the convex side of the hand; the under side of a leaf; the convex part of a book; the thick edge of a knife ME. **2.** The side of any object away from the spectator, the other or farther side 1645.

1. He put his name at the b. of a bill SHERIDAN. **2.** Passing by the b. of the Goodwin Sand 1704.

III. Parts of things having relation, or analogous in position, to the back. † **1.** *pl.* Clothes –ME. † **2.** A back-plate –1695. Also *fig.* **3.** The hind part; *e.g.* of a garment, a chair, etc. 1530. **4.** The rear of an armed force (*arch.*) 1597. † **5.** A following; backing –1662.

3. A chair without a b. 1670. **4.** He leaues his backe vnarm'd 2 *Hen. IV,* I. iii. 79.

IV. 1. *fig.* The surface of a river, the waves, etc., as bearing burdens 1610. **2.** The ridge of a hill, † of the nose 1615. **3.** The keel and kelson of a ship 1692.

1. I saw him beate the surges vnder him, And ride vpon their backes *Temp.* II. i. 115. **3.** A..ship with her b. broken 1883.

Phrases: **a.** With preps. *At the b. of*: behind, close behind, as in supporting, pursuing, etc. *Behind the b. of*: (*emphatic for*) behind; in the absence of. **b.** With verbs. *To break the b. of*: (*fig.*) to overburden; to finish the hardest part of. *To put* or *set up the b.*: to arch it as angry cats do; to anger. *To turn the b.*: to flee; *to turn the b. upon*: to abandon. *To be* or *lie on one's b.*: to be laid up, to be afflicted.

attrib.: **ba·ckache,** pain in the back 1601.

Back (bæk), *sb.*² 1682. [– Du. *bak,* LG. *back* large dish; cf. med.L. *bacca 'vas aquarium'* (Isidor).] A tub, trough, vat; *esp.* as used by brewers, etc.

Back (bæk), *a.* 1490. [BACK *sb.*¹ used attrib.; also partly BACK *adv.* used ellipt.; cf. BACK-.] **1.** Situated at the back, behind, or away from the front; remote, as in *b. blocks* (Australia), *settlement*; mean, obscure, as in *b. slum.* (¶ The superl. BACKMOST is still in use.) **2.** In arrear; behindhand 1525. **3.** Reversed, as in *b. current, b. smoke* 1857.

Back (bæk), *v.* ME. [f. BACK *sb.*¹] **1.** To cover the back; to put a back to 1793; to form the back of 1826. **2.** (Cf. BACK *sb.*¹) To support physically, materially (*esp.* by a bet), or morally 1548; in *Sporting,* of dogs: To follow the lead of a dog that points 1860. **3.** To mount, ride on (a horse) 1592. **4.** To write at the back of (a bill, cheque, etc.); to print on the back 1768. **5.** *trans.* To set, lay, or incline back; *esp.* by reversing the action; as, to back a boat, a locomotive engine, etc. 1707. **6.** *intr.* To move back, or in the reverse direction, as the wind 1486. **7.** To lie with the back *on* 1891.

1. To b. a book 1885. The chalk cliffs which b. the beach HUXLEY. **2.** A troup of Demi-lances to b. them 1548. Phr. *To b. an anchor, rope,* or *chain*: to reinforce with another. Which Godly course Augustine backeth 1612. *To b. a horse. To b. the field*: to bet on the rest of the horses, against the favourite. To b. one's opinion with a wager BYRON. Phr. *To b. up*: to support or second; esp. in *Cricket,* of a fielder or batsman. **5.** *To b. a sail, a yard*: to lay it aback so that the wind may retard the ship. Phr. *To b. the oars.* **6.** Phr. *To b. out*: to move out backwards without turning; *fig.* to retreat out of a difficulty. *To b. down,* to descend as one does from a ladder. Also *fig.*

Back (bæk), *adv.* ME. [Aphetic f. ABACK.] **1.** Toward the rear (often with the vb. omitted); away from the front, or from the actual or ordinary position ME. **2.** Away from an engagement or undertaking 1783. **3.** Backward in time 1711. **4.** In the reverse direction, so as to return to a former place, or condition 1535; in reversal of action or change of any kind (often with AGAIN) 1607. Also. *ellipt.* **5.** In return, requital, retaliation 1599. **6.** At a point or distance behind ME. **7.** In a state of check 1535. **8.** In time past, ago 1796. **9.** Behindhand, in arrear 1875.

1. B. with that leg 1590. B., beardless boy SCOTT. The angel of the Lord rolled b. the stone *Matt.* 28:2. To force b. a bolt 1885. **2.** To go b. from one's word MACAULAY. **3.** B. to the days of Solomon STEELE. **4.** The whole country fell b. into heathenism FREEMAN. *ellipt.* To be b. = Fr. *être de retour.* **5.** To answer b. 1885. Hence *b.-answer, -chat, -talk,* implying rudeness or insolence. **7.** The Lord hath kept thee b. from honour *Num.* 24:11. **8.** Dug up, a few years b. SOUTHEY.

Phrase. *B. and forth*: backwards and forwards, to and fro. *Back of*: back from, behind. (In U.S.)

Back-, *in comb.* is used in many relations, substantive, adjective, and adverbial (rarely verbal), and the combs. are usually self-explanatory. The use of the hyphen is often optional, especially when *back* can be viewed as an adj.

Special Combs.: **b.-bar,** a bar in the chimney to hang a vessel on; **-casing** *Mining,* a temporary shaft-lining of bricks, in front of which the permanent lining is built; **-chain,** a chain that passes over a cart-saddle to support the shafts of a cart; **-draught,** a draught of air backward, a hood for producing this in a fire; **-flap, -fold** (= *back-shutter*); **-hair,** the long hair at the back of a woman's head; **-lining,** in *Archit.,* the piece of a sash-frame parallel to the pulley-piece and next to the jamb on either side; **-links,** the links in a parallel motion which connect the air-pump rod to the beam; **-painting,** the method of painting mezzotinto prints, pasted on glass, with oil colours; **-paternoster,** the Lord's Prayer repeated backwards as a charm, *fig.* a muttered curse; **-pressure,** in the steam-engine, the resistance of the atmosphere or waste-steam of the piston; **-rest,** a guide attached to the slide-rest of a turning-lathe, to steady the work; **-rope** (of a horse) = BACKBAND; *Naut.,* one leading inboard from the martingale; **-shift,** in *Coal-Mining,* the second shift or set of hewers for the day; **-shutter,** the part of a shutter which folds up behind; **-stop,** in *Cricket* = LONG-STOP; **-sweep,** in *Shipbuilding,* that which forms the hollow of the top-timber; **-swimmer,** the hemipterous insect *Notonecta*; **-tack** (*Sc. Law*), a lease of land given by the mortgagee of it to the mortgagor on condition of payment of rent till redeemed; **†-timber** (*joc.* for) clothing; **†-trick,** ? a caper backwards in dancing (*Twel. N.* I. iii. 131); **-word** (in *Lancs.*) withdrawal from a promise or from an accepted invitation, also *dial.* a rude answer; **-wort** (*Herb.*), old name for the Comfrey (*Symphytum officinale*).

† **Backare, baccare,** *interj. phr.* 1553. [perh. joc. f. BACK *adv.* + *-are,* L. inf. ending.] Back! give place! *Tam. Shr.* II. i. 72.

Backband (bæ·kbænd). 1523. [f. BACK *sb.*¹ + BAND.] A broad leather strap, or iron chain, passing over a cart-saddle, and serving to support the shafts.

† **Ba·ckbear,** *sb.* 1598. [f. BACK *sb.*¹ 2 c + BEAR *v.*] In *Forest Laws*: The act of carrying on the back venison killed illegally –1667.

† **Ba·ck-berend,** *adj.* (*pr. pple.*) [OE. *bæc-berende,* f. *bæc* back + *berende,* pr. pple. of *beran* BEAR *v.*] Bearing on the back: long used as a law-term to describe a thief caught thus carrying off stolen property.

Backbite (bæ·kbəit), *v.* ME. [– MSw. *bakbīta,* f. *bak* back + *bīta* bite.] To detract from the character of, to traduce, speak ill of. Also *absol.* or *intr.*

People will b. one another to any extent rather than not be amused HELPS. Hence **Ba·ckbiːter,** a secret calumniator.

† **Ba·ckblow.** 1642. [f. BACK *sb.*¹ and *adv.* + BLOW *sb.*¹] A blow struck at the back or from behind. Also *fig.* (Cf. AFTER-CLAP.)

fig. So many back-blows of fortune 1649.

Back-board (bæ·kbōᵊɹd). OE. [f. BACK *sb.*¹] † **1.** = LARBOARD. Only in OE. **2.** A board placed at, or forming, the back of anything, *e.g.* of a cart 1761. **3.** A board attached to the rim of a water-wheel, to prevent the water from running off the floats into the interior of the wheel 1864. **4.** A board held or strapped across the back to straighten the figure 1794. Hence **Ba·ckboa:rd** *v.* to subject to the use of a b.

Backbone (bæ·kbōᵘ·n). ME. [f. BACK *sb.*¹ 1 + BONE. Still occas. hyphened.] **1.** The vertebral column, the spine. **2.** *transf.* A main support or axis, or chief substantial part, *e.g.* the b. of a bicycle 1684. **3.** *fig.* The main element; mainstay 1849. **4.** Strength of character, stability of purpose, firmness 1865.

1. Phr. *To the backbone*: completely; English to the b. 1864. **2.** The Cordilleras, or b. of America 1865. **3.** The b. of our subject EARLE. **4.** A character destitute of b. 1865.

Ba·ckcast, *sb. n. dial.* 1818. [f. BACK *adv.* + CAST *sb.*] A throw back; a reverse.

Ba·ck-cast, *ppl. a.* 1580. [f. BACK *adv.* + CAST pa. pple.] Cast backwards.

Back-door (bæ·kˌdōᵊ·ɹ). 1530. [f. BACK *a.* + DOOR.] **1.** A door at the back of a building, etc.; a secondary or private entrance. **2.** *fig.*; also *attrib.* = Unworthily secret 1611.

2. The backe doore..Of the vnguarded hearts SHAKS.

Backed (bækt). ME. [f. BACK *sb.*¹, *v.* + -ED², -ED¹.] **1.** *adj.* Having a back, background, or backing; *esp.* in *comb.*, as *broad-backed.* **2.** *pple.* and *a.* Supported at the back, etc. (See the vb.) 1589.

Backen (bæ·k'n), *v.* 1649. [f. BACK *a.* + -EN⁵; cf. *lessen.*] To put, keep, or throw back; to retard. Now *rare.* † **2.** *intr.* To draw back 1748.

Back-end (bæ·kˌe·nd). 1617. [f. BACK *a.* + END. Cf. FORE-END.] **1.** The hinder of two ends. **2.** The later part of a season; (absol.) of the year: The late autumn 1820.

Backer (bæ·kəɹ), *sb.* 1583. [f. BACK *v.* + -ER¹.] **1.** A supporter; *esp.* one who bets on a horse or event, or supports by money or credit. **2.** *Archit.* A narrow slate at the back of a broad square one where it begins to get narrow 1823.

† **Ba·cker,** *a. compar.* 1564. [f. BACK *a.* + -ER³.] Farther back, hinder. So *superl.* † **Ba·ckermost.**

Backet (bæ·kėt). *Sc.* 1789. [– (O)Fr. *baquet*, dim. of *bac* BACK *sb.*²] Shallow wooden trough.

Backfall (bæ·kfǭ:l). 1676. [f. BACK *adv.* and *sb.*] † **1.** A grace in old English music. **2.** A fall on the back in wrestling. Often *fig.* 1838. **3.** A lever in the coupler of an organ 1880.

Back-fire (bæ·kfəiᵊɹ), *sb.* 1897. [BACK *adv.*, BACK-.] A premature explosion in the cylinder of a gas or oil engine, tending to drive the piston in a direction reverse to that in which it should travel. Also as *vb.*, and said of the engine. So **Ba·ck-firing** *vbl. sb.*

Back-forma·tion. 1887. [J. A. H. Murray (cf. *aphesis*). Hence G. *rückbildung.*] Formation of a seeming root-word from a word which might be (but is not) a derivative of it, as *burgle* from *burglar.*

Backfriend (bæ·kfre:nd). 1472. [f. BACK *sb.* or *adv.*] † **1.** A pretended friend; an unavowed enemy –1827. **2.** A backer 1599.

Backgame (bæ·kgēⁱ:m). 1718. = next.

Backgammon (bækgæ·mən). 1645. [f. BACK *adv.* + an earlier form of GAME *sb.* (see GAMMON *sb.*³).] **1.** A game played on a board consisting of two tables (usu. hinged together), with draughtsmen whose moves are determined by throws of the dice. **2.** *spec.* A victory in which the winner has borne all his men off, before the loser has carried all his men to his own table 1883.

Background (bæ·kgraund). 1672. [f. BACK *a.*] **1.** The ground or surface lying behind the objects which occupy the *foreground*; *esp.* as represented in any of the Arts of Design 1752. Also *fig.* **2.** Retirement, obscurity 1779.

1. Ranger retires to the b. WYCHERLEY **2.** Keep your madness in the b. SHERIDAN. Hence **Ba·ckground** *v.* to form a b. to E. B. BROWNING.

Back-hand (bæ·kˌhæ:nd). 1657. [f. BACK *adv.*] **A.** *sb.* **1.** The hand turned backwards in making a stroke, as (at *Tennis*) in taking balls at the left hand, *hence* the left-hand play or court. Hence *fig.* **2.** Handwriting with the letters sloped backwards 1885. **B.** *attrib.* = BACK-HANDED 1695.

Back-handed (bæ·khæ:ndėd), *a.* 1813. [f. the *sb.* + -ED².] **1.** With the back of the hand. **2.** Directed backwards, or with the hand or arm crossing the body, as a sword-cut; sloping backwards, as handwriting. **3.** *fig.* † **a.** Backward, remiss; **b.** Indirect 1800.

3. b. A back-handed reminder DICKENS. Hence **Backha·ndedness.**

Ba·ck-hander. 1803. [f. as prec. + -ER¹ 1.] **1.** A blow with the back of the hand. Also *fig.* **2.** An extra glass of wine out of turn, the bottle being passed back 1854. **3.** A back-handed stroke or blow 1890.

2. I will take a b., as Clive don't seem to drink THACKERAY.

Backing (bæ·kiŋ), *vbl. sb.* 1596. [f. BACK *v.* + -ING¹.] The action of BACK *v.* **1.** The action of supporting at the back. **2.** The mounting of a horse; the breaking in of a colt to the saddle 1607. **3.** Retardation 1649. **4.** Motion backward, *esp.* of the wind 1686. **5.** *techn.* **a.** *Printing.* 'Perfecting' a sheet by printing it also on the back. **b.** *Bookbinding.* Preparing the back with glue, etc., before putting on the cover. 1846. **6.** That which backs; a body of supporters; that which forms a back or hinder part 1793.

1. Call you that b. of your friends? a plague vpon such b. SHAKS.

Back-lash (bæ·klæʃ). 1815. [f. BACK *adv.* + LASH *sb.*¹] *Mech.* The jarring reaction or striking back of a wheel or set of wheels in a piece of mechanism, when the motion is not uniform or when sudden pressure is applied. Also *transf.* and *fig.* var. **Ba·ck-lashing.**

Back-log (bæ·kˌlǫg). 1684. [BACK *a.*] A large log placed at the back of a wood fire to keep it in. Also *fig.* Something in reserve 1883.

Backmost (bæ·kmōst), *a. superl.* 1782. [f. BACK *a.*; after *foremost*, etc.] Most to the back, hindmost. var. **Ba·ckermost.**

Back-piece (bæ·kpīs). 1586. [f. BACK *sb.* or *a.*] **1.** A piece of armour protecting the back. Also *fig.* **2.** The piece which forms the back 1838.

Back-plate (bæ·kplēⁱt). 1656. [f. as prec.] **1.** A plate of armour for the back. **2.** A plate placed at or forming the back 1772.

† **Ba·ck-ra:cket.** 1608. [f. BACK *adv.*] The return of a ball in tennis; *fig.* a 'tu quoque'.

Backs, *sb.* (*pl.*) 1535. *Leather-trade.* The thickest and best-tanned hides.

Back-set (bæ·kset), *sb.* 1721. [f. BACK *adv.* + SET *sb.*¹] **1.** A setting back; a reverse, relapse. (orig. Sc.) **2.** An eddy or counter-current 1882.

Ba:ckse·t, *v.* 1573. [f. as prec. + SET *v.*] † **1.** To set upon in the rear. **2.** (in U.S.) To re-plough in the autumn prairie-land ploughed in the spring 1883.

Ba·ck-se·ttler. 1809. [f. *back-settlement*; see BACK *a.* 1.] One who lives in the back settlements of a colony or new country.

Backsheesh, var. of BAKSHEESH.

Backside. 1489. [f. BACK *a.* Now pronounced as two words, exc. in sense 3.] **1.** The hinder or back part; the back, the rear. **2.** The back premises; also, the privy. Now *dial.* 1541. **3.** (bæ·ksəid). The posteriors or rump 1500. † **4.** = BACK *sb.* II. 1. –1720. † **5.** *fig.* The reverse side; the opposite –1695.

5. Just the very b. of Truth CONGREVE.

Backsight (bæ·kˌsəi·t). 1860. [f. BACK *adv.* and *a.*] **a.** In *Surveying*, a sight or reading taken backwards, or towards the point of starting. **b.** The sight of a rifle nearer the stock.

Back-slang (bæ·kˌslæ·ŋ). 1860. [f. BACK *adv.*] Slang in which every word is pronounced backwards; as *ynnep* for *penny.*

Backslide (bæ·ksləi·d), *v.* 1581. [f. BACK *adv.* + SLIDE *v.*] To *slide back*, in a fig. sense; to fall away, *esp.* in religious faith and practice; to relapse. Hence **Ba·cksli·der,** an apostate.

† **Ba·ck-sta:ff.** 1627. [f. BACK *sb.*] A quadrant for taking altitudes at sea, so named because the observer turned his back to the sun.

Backstairs (bæ·kstēᵊ·ɹs). 1627. [f. BACK *a.*] **1.** Stairs at the back of a house; a secondary staircase 1654. **2.** *esp.* The private stairs in a palace, used for other than state visitors 1627; also *fig.* **3.** *attrib.* Of, pertaining to, or employing underhand intrigue at court. (Occ. *backstair.*) 1697.

3. A b. influence and clandestine government BURKE.

Backstay (bæ·kstēⁱ). 1626. [f. BACK *a.* or *sb.*] **1.** *Naut.* (often *pl.*) Long ropes, slanting a little abaft, extending from the upper mastheads to the sides of the ship; used to second the shrouds in supporting the masts. **2.** *gen.* A stay or support at the back; *e.g.* in *Printing*, a leather strap to check the carriage of a printing-press 1864.

Backster (bæ·kstəɹ). 1867. A flat piece of wood or cork, strapped on the feet for walking over loose beach.

Backster, obs. f. BAXTER.

Back-stitch (bæ·ksti:tʃ). 1611. [f. BACK *adv.*] A method of sewing in which, for every new stitch, the needle enters behind, and comes out in front of, the end of the previous one. Hence **Backstitch** *v.* to sew thus.

Back-stroke (bæ·kˌstrōᵘ:k). 1674. [f. BACK *adv.* and *a.*] A stroke in return; a recoil; also, a backhanded stroke.

Back-sword (bæ·kˌsōᵊ·ɹd). *arch.* 1611. [f. BACK *sb.*] **1.** A sword with only one cutting edge. **2.** A single-stick; *hence* **b.** fencing exercise with it 1699. **3.** A fencer with back-sword or single stick 1672. Hence **Back-swo·rding. Back·swo·rdman.**

Ba·ck-wa·rd, *sb.* ME. [f. BACK *a.*] Rear-guard, rearward –1580.

Backward (bæ·kwəɹd). ME. [Aphetic f. † ABACKWARD, f. ABACK + -WARD.] **A.** *adv.* **1.** In the direction of one's back, as with *lean, push*, etc.; **b.** With the face to the rear, as with *go, ride, walk* ME. † **2.** Of position: Toward the back of a place (*arch.*); commonly *back, to, at, the back* –1812. **3.** In the direction which is ordinarily behind one, or from which one is moving (*arch.*); commonly *back, behind* ME. **4.** In the direction from which one has come. (Not properly used of persons or animals.) ME. **5.** In the direction of retreat. (Usu. *back.*) ME. **6.** *fig.* Towards a worse state. (More usu. *back.*) 1583. **7.** Towards or in the past (*arch.*; commonly *back*) 1562. **8.** In the reverse direction or order 1520; *fig.* the wrong way 1552.

3. *To look, turn the head, b.* **4.** Like as an arowe.. returneth not bacwarde 2 *Esdras* 16:16. *B. and forward*: to and fro; also *fig.* **5.** Let them be driuen b., and put to shame *Isa.* 1:4. **8.** What is Ab speld b. with the horn on his head *L.L.L.* v. i. 50. Phr. *To ring the bells b.*: to ring them beginning with the bass bell, in order to give the alarm, etc.

B. *adj.* [attrib. (often ellipt.) use of the *adv.*] **1.** Directed to the rear 1552. **2.** Directed in the opposite way; of or pertaining to return 1604. **3.** Reversed 1725. † **4.** Perverse, unfavourable –1605. † **5.** Placed towards or at the back –1819. **6.** Turning or hanging back from action; reluctant; shy, bashful 1599. **7.** Behindhand, late; *esp.* of the season or crops 1616. **8.** Reaching into the past 1650.

2. Their b. course *Oth.* I. iii. 38. **6.** Perish the man, whose mind is b. now *Hen. V*, IV. iii. 72. **7.** A very b. scholar HUME. Hence **Ba·ckward·ly** *adv.*, **-ness.**

C. *sb.* † **1.** *lit.* The hinder part of the body 1627. **2.** *poet.* The past portion (of time) 1610.

2. The dark b. and abisme of Time *Temp.* I. ii. 50.

† **Ba·ckward,** *v.* 1594. [f. the adj.] To put or keep back, retard –1660.

Backwardation (bækwəɹdēⁱ·ʃən). 1850. [f. prec. vb., after *retardation*, etc.] *Stock Exchange.* The percentage paid by a seller of stock for the privilege of postponing delivery till the next account or to any other future day. So † **Backwardiza·tion.**

Backwards (bæ·kwəɹdz). 1513. [f. BACKWARD with advb. gen. *-s.*] **A.** = BACKWARD *adv.* † **B.** = BACKWARD *a.* (*rare*) –1683.

Backwash (bæ·kwǫʃ), *sb.* 1876. [f. BACK *adv.*] The motion of a receding wave; a backward current.

Ba·ckwash, *v.* 1775. [Cf. prec. sb.] **1.** To affect with backwash 1882. **2.** To clean the oil from wool after combing.

Backwater (bæ·kwǭ:təɹ). ME. [f. BACK *a.* or *adv.*] † **1.** Water flowing in from behind –1577. **2.** Water dammed back in its course, or that has overflowed in time of flood 1629.

3. Water dammed back for any purpose 1792. 4. A piece of water without current, parallel to a river, and fed from it at the lower end by a backflow 1863. 5. A creek or arm of the sea parallel to the coast, separated by a narrow strip of land from the sea, and communicating with it by barred outlets 1867. 6. A backward current of water 1830. 7. The swell of the sea thrown back from contact with a solid body; *e.g.* with the paddles of steamboats. Also *attrib.* 1838.

6. A kind of b., or eddying swirl CARLYLE. 7. The b. cast from the paddles 1865.

Back-way (bæ·kwēⁱ). 1577. [f. BACK *a.*] A way at, or to the back; *hence*, a bypath.

Backwoods (bæ·kwu:dz). 1834. [f. BACK *a.*] Wild, uncleared forest land; *e.g.* that of North America. Also *attrib.* Hence **Ba·ckwoodsman**, a settler in the backwoods.

Bacon (bēⁱ·kən). ME. [– OFr. *bacon, -un* = Pr. *bacon* – Frankish *bako* ham, flitch = OHG. *bahho*, f. Gmc. **bakkon*, rel. to **bakam* BACK *sb.*[1]] 1. The back and sides of the pig, cured by salting, drying, etc. Formerly also = *pork.* † 2. The carcase of a pig; *rarely* a live pig –1768. † 3. A rustic, a chaw-bacon 1596.

3. On Bacons, on, what ye knaues? Yong men must liue 1 *Hen. IV*, II. ii. 93.

Phr. *To save one's b.*: to escape bodily injury or loss. Hence **Ba·coner**, a pig fit for being made into b.

Baconian (beⁱkōᵘ·niăn), *a.* and *sb.* 1812. [f. Lord *Bacon* + -IAN.] 1. Pertaining to Lord Bacon; of, an adherent of, his experimental and inductive system of philosophy. 2. Pertaining to, an advocate of, the theory that Lord Bacon wrote the works attributed to Shakespeare 1886. Hence **Baco·nianism.**

Bacony (bēⁱ·kəni), *a.* 1878. [f. BACON + -Y[1].] Like bacon; fatty; *esp.* in a state of fatty degeneration, as *b. liver.*

Bacterial (bæktīᵊ·riăl), *a.* 1871. [f. BACTERIUM + -AL[1].] *Biol.* Of or pertaining to bacteria. vars. **Bacte·rian, Bacte·ric.**

Bactericidal (bæktīᵊrisəi·dăl), *a.* [f. BACTERIUM + -CIDE + -AL[1].] *Biol.* Destructive to bacteria.

Bacteriology (bæktīᵊri,ǫ·lŏdʒi). 1884. [f. BACTERIUM + -LOGY.] The science of bacteria. Hence **Bacte:riolo·gical** *a.* 1886. **Bacte:rio·logist,** a student of b. **Bacte:rio·scopy,** microscopic investigation of bacteria.

Bacterium (bæktīᵊ·riŏm). Pl. **-a.** 1847. [mod.L. – Gr. βακτήριον, dim. of βάκτρον stick, staff.] A genus of *Schizomycetæ*, microscopic unicellular rod-shaped vegetable organisms, found in all decomposing animal and vegetable liquids. Hence **Bacteri·tic** *a.*, marked by the (morbid) presence of bacteria. **Ba·cteroid** (better *bacterioid*), of the nature of, or allied to, bacteria.

Bacule, var. of BASCULE.

Baculine (bæ·kiŭləin), *a.* 1710. [f. L. *baculum, -us* rod, stick + -INE[1].] Of or pertaining to punishment by caning, etc.

Baculite (bæ·kiŭləit). 1822. [f. as prec. + -ITE[1] 2 b.] *Palæont.* A genus of fossil cephalopods, with chambered cylindrical shells.

Baculo·metry. [f. as prec. + -METRY.] Measurement of distances or lines by means of a staff or staves. (Dicts.)

Bad (bæd), *a.* (and *sb.*). [ME. *badde* (2 syll.), perh. repr. OE. *bǣddel* hermaphrodite (cf. *bǣdling* sodomite), with loss of *l* as in *much(e, wench(e* for OE. *mycel, wencel.* Compared *badder, baddest* to 18th c.; though Shaks. has only *worse, worst*, taken over from *evil, ill*, after *bad* acquired that sense.] **A.** *adj.* **I.** In a privative sense. 1. Of defective quality or worth. 2. Incorrect 1688. 3. *Law.* Not valid 1883. 4. Unfavourable; that one does not like ME.

1. Mete and drynke . . it was ful poure and badde CHAUCER. A b. correspondent 1873. *B. air* 1884. *B. coin* debased, false coin. *B.* (i.e. irrecoverable) *debts. To go b.*: to decay. *With b. grace*: unwillingly. 2. To speak b. French 1767. B. form 1885. *B. shot*: a wrong guess. 3. The claim is b. 1883. 4. The good fortune as the badde GOWER. In a b. sense 1751.

II. In a positive sense. 1. Immoral, wicked ME. 2. Offensive, disagreeable 1515. 3. Injurious, dangerous. Const. *for.* 1653. 4. In ill health, in pain 1748.

1. Corrupted by b. books 1767. 2. B. colour 1515, weather NELSON, temper MACAULAY. *B. blood*: angry feeling. 3. B. for his eyes ADDISON. A b. fall 1855. 4. B. with my gout RICHARDSON.

B. quasi-*sb.* 1. *absol.* That which is bad 1591. 2. *sb.* (with *pl.*) A bad thing or (*rarely*) person 1592.

1. T'exchange the b. for better *Two Gent.* II. vi. 13. (To go) *to the b.*, i.e. to ruin; (to be, etc.) *to the bad*, i.e. in deficit. Hence **Ba·ddish** *a.* rather bad.

Bad, badd, obs. ff. BADE, BODE.

Badder, obs. compar. of BAD.

Badderlocks. *Sc.* 1789. [perh. for *Balderlocks*; cf. *balderherb* (see BALDER).] An edible sea-weed (*Alaria esculenta*).

Bade, pa.t. of BID *v.*; obs. f. BODE *sb.* and *v.*

Badge (bædʒ), *sb.* ME. [In AFr. *bage* (XIV), OFr. (XV), Anglo-L. *bagia* (cf. Eng. *bagy* XV, Sc. *bawgy, badgie, bagie* XVI); of unkn. origin.] 1. A distinctive device, emblem, or mark, orig. = *cognizance* in *Her.*, but now worn as a sign of office, employment, membership of a society, etc. 2. *gen.* A distinguishing sign 1526. Also *transf.* and *fig.* 3. *Naval Arch.* A sort of ornament near the stern of small vessels, containing either a sash or the representation of one 1769.

1. B. of a gentylman PALSGR. 2. For suffrance is the b. of all our Tribe *Merch V.* I. iii. 111. *Comb.* **b.-man,** a licensed beggar or almsman. Hence **Ba·dgeless** *a.* without b. or cognizance.

Badge (bædʒ), *v.*[1] ME. [f. prec. sb.] To mark with, or distinguish by, a badge.

† **Badge,** *v.*[2] 1552. [Origin unkn.; possibly back-formation from BADGER *sb.*[1]] To deal as a badger (see BADGER *sb.*[1]); *hence*, to regrate –1772.

Badger (bæ·dʒəɹ), *sb.*[1] 1500. [Origin unkn.; cf. BADGE *v.*[2]] One who buys corn and other commodities and carries them elsewhere to sell; a cadger, hawker, or huckster. Still *dial.* (Explained in 17th c. as a 'forestaller'.)

Badger (bæ·dʒəɹ), *sb.*[2] 1523. [perh. f. BADGE *sb.* + -ARD, with allusion to the white mark on the animal's forehead (but *badge* is not recorded in this sense).] 1. A plantigrade quadruped (*Meles vulgaris*) intermediate between the weasels and the bears; it is a nocturnal, hibernating animal, digging for itself a burrow, which it defends fiercely against attack. Called earlier *brock* and *bauson*; also *gray.* 2. (in *U.S.*) Nickname of inhabitants of Wisconsin 1856. 3. **a.** An artificial fly; **b.** a brush (for painting or shaving) made of badger's hair. 1787.

1. *Cape-* or *Rock-b.*: the daman (*Hyrax capensis*). *Honey-b.*: the ratel (*Ratellus mellivorus*). *Badger* (in Australia): the wombat.

Comb.: **b.-baiting, -drawing,** the sport of setting dogs to draw out a b. from its (artificial) hole; hence *badger-baiter*; **-dog** (= Ger. *dachshund*); **-fly** (= BADGER 3 a); **-legged** *a.*, having legs of unequal length, as the b. was thought to have. Hence **Ba·dgerly** *a.* badger-like; greyish-haired.

Badger (bæ·dʒəɹ), *v.* 1794. [f. prec. sb.] 1. To bait like a badger; *hence*, to subject (one who cannot escape from it) to persistent worry or persecution. 2. *dial.* [f. BADGER *sb.*[1]] To beat down in price 1875. Hence **Ba·dgerer,** a badger-dog; *dial.* a cheapener. **Ba·dgering** *vbl. sb.* persecution; *dial.* beating down the cost.

‖ **Badiaga** (bădyā·gă, bædi,āgă). 1753. [Russ. *badyaga.*] A species of alga, the powder of which takes away the livid marks of bruises.

‖ **Badian** (bā·diăn). 1847. [– Fr. *badiane*, – Pers. and Urdu *bādyān* fennel, anise.] The Chinese or Star Anise, *Illicium anisatum.*

Badigeon (bădi·dʒən). 1753. [– Fr. *badigeon*, of unkn. origin.] A mixture of plaster and freestone ground together, used by builders, etc., or of sawdust and glue, used by joiners, for filling up defects in their work, or giving a surface to it.

‖ **Badinage** (badina·ʒ, bæ·dinėdʒ). 1658. [Fr., f. *badiner* joke, trifle (with), f. *badin* – mod. Pr. *badin* fool, f. *badar* gape :– Rom. **batare* gape; see -AGE.] Light raillery, or humorous banter. Hence **Badinage** *v.*, to banter playfully.

† **Badiner,** *v.* 1697. [– Fr. *badiner*; see prec.] To banter. Hence ‖ **Badi·nerie:,** raillery. † **Badineu·r,** one who banters.

† **Ba·dling.** [OE. *bǣdling*, f. *bǣddel*; see BAD, -LING[1].] A womanish man –1600.

Badly (bæ·dli), *adv.* ME. [f. BAD *a.* + -LY[2].] 1. Defectively. 2. Unsuccessfully ME. 3. Incorrectly 1836. 4. Immorally, improperly 1440. 5. So as to cause pain, danger, disgrace, or harm 1799. 6. *colloq.* with 'need, want' = Much, greatly (*mod.*). 7. *dial.* Unwell 1783.

‖ **Badmash, bud-** (bʊdma·ʃ). 1843. [Pers. and Urdu, f. Pers. *bad* evil + *ma'aš* manner or style of living.] One following evil courses; a 'bad lot'.

Badminton (bæ·dmintən). 1853. [The Duke of Beaufort's country seat.] 1. A kind of claret-cup. 2. A game resembling lawn-tennis, played with shuttle-cocks 1874.

Badness (bæ·dnės). ME. [f. BAD *a.* + -NESS.] 1. Inferior quality or condition; incorrectness; invalidity 1539. 2. Evil quality or condition; wickedness; noxiousness ME.

Bæ- in OE. and EE. words; see BA-.

Bætyl (bī·til). *rare.* [– L. *bætulus* – Gr. βαίτυλος.] A sacred meteoric stone.

Baff, *sb. Sc.* 1800. [perh. – OFr. *baffe* slap in the face.] A blow with anything flat or soft, *e.g.* the palm of the hand, a soft ball, etc. Also vb. 1858.

† **Baff,** *v.* ME. [perh. – LG., (M)Du. *baffen*, MDu. *beffen* bark.] To bark or yelp; also *transf.* –1599.

Baffle (bæ·f'l), *v.* 1548. [In senses 1–2 perh. alt. f. Sc. *bauchle* (XV) disgrace, of unkn. origin. In senses 'foil, etc.' perh. rel. to Fr. *bafouer* (XVI) subject to ridicule, alt. f. OFr. *beffer* mock; cf. Fr. † *beffler* (Rabelais) mock, deceive.] † 1. To subject (*esp.* a perjured knight) to public disgrace or infamy –1660. † 2. *gen.* To treat with contumely –1693. † 3. To gull, cheat –1726. † 4. *intr.* To juggle –1733. † 5. To bewilder, confound –1704. † 6. To bring to nought –1812. 7. To defeat any one in his efforts; to frustrate, to foil 1675. 8. *intr.* To struggle ineffectually 1860.

1. He by the heels him hung upon a tree And bafful'd so, that all which passed by The picture of his punishment might see SPENSER *F.Q.* VI. vii. 27. 3. To cheat and b. the poor man DE FOE. 6. To b. Reproach with Silence STEELE. 7. **b.** To check, turn, or disperse in its course, by an opposing force or obstacles 1748. Hence **Ba·ffled** *ppl. a.* disgraced MILT.; foiled. **Ba·fflement,** the action of baffling; being baffled. **Ba·ffling-ly** *adv.*, **-ness.**

Baffle (bæ·f'l), *sb.* 1628. [f. prec. *v.*] † 1. Affront –1692. † 2. A shuffle 1783. † 3. Discomfiture –1745. 4. Baffled state 1843. 5. = *baffle-plate* 1881.

attrib.: *b.-plate*, = BAFFLER 3; also, a plate hindering or regulating the passage of fluid through an outlet or inlet, or the direction of sound.

Baffler (bæ·fləɹ). 1606. [f. as prec. + -ER[1].] † 1. A juggler; a trifler –1677. 2. He who or that which BAFFLES (in various senses) 1677. 3. A contrivance used in stoves and furnaces, for changing the direction of the heated air 1861.

Baffy (bæ·fi). 1888. [f. BAFF *sb.* + -Y[6].] *Golf.* A short wooden club for lofting. Also *b. spoon.*

Baft. 1598. [– Hind. – Pers. *bāfta* textile, woven.] A coarse and cheap fabric, usually of cotton.

Baft (bɑft). [OE. *beæftan*, f. *be*, by, at + *æftan* behind. Cf. AFT.] **A.** *adv.* 1. Behind; now only *Naut.*: Astern, aft, abaft (*arch.*). † 2. Of time: After (*rare*) ME. **B.** † *prep.* [orig. the adv. with dat. of reference.] Behind, to the rear of –ME.

Bag (bæg), *sb.* [poss. – ON. *baggi* bag, pack, bundle, of unkn. origin. Cf. OFr. *bague* (mod. † *bagues*, pl.) baggage, thought to be rel. to ON. *baggi.*] 1. *gen.* A receptacle of flexible material open only at the top (where it can be closed); a pouch, a small sack. 2. *spec.* = Money-bag, purse ME. † 3. *poet.* in *pl.* Bagpipes –1790. 4. A silken pouch to hold the back-hair of a wig; cf. BAG-WIG 1702. 5. A measure of quantity, varying with the commodity 1679. 6. = Mail-bag; mail 1702. 7. *Sporting.* = Game-bag; *hence*, the quantity killed on one occasion 1486. Also *fig.* 8. *transf.* An udder, a dug 1579. 9. A sac (in the body of an animal) containing honey, poison, etc. (Usu. *fig.*) 1529. 10. *pl.* The stomach.

(*N. dial.* and *Sc.*) **11.** *Coal-Min.* A cavity filled with gas or water 1733. **12.** *pl.* (colloq.) trousers 1860.

2. *John* 12:6. **9.** *Mids. N.* III. i. 171.

Phrases. *B. of bones*: an emaciated living person. *To give* (one) *the b. to hold*: to engage any one while slipping away, to leave in the lurch. *To let the cat out of the b.*: to disclose the secret. **B. and baggage:** all belongings; *orig.* as in *to march out (with) b. and baggage*, i.e. without surrender of anything; now used to express the completeness of the departure.

Comb.: **b.-fox,** a fox brought alive in a bag to be turned out before the hounds; **-muff,** a muff containing a pouch; **-rod,** a fishing-rod which can be carried in pieces in a case; **-sleeve,** one tight at the wrist and baggy above; **-wolf** (cf. *-fox*). Hence **Ba·gful.**

Bag (bæg), *v.*[1] ME. [f. the sb.] **1.** *intr.* To bulge; *Naut.* to sag 1440; to hang loosely, as clothes 1824. † **2.** *intr.* To be pregnant –1603. **3.** *trans.* To cause to swell or bulge 1583. **4.** To put into a bag or bags 1573. **5.** To put game killed into a bag; *also*, to kill game 1814. **6.** *colloq.* To catch, seize, steal 1818.

1. Bagging to leeward MARRYAT. **4.** To b. Hops 1711. **6.** Led up..for bagging fowles HUGHES. Hence **Ba·gger,** † *spec.* a miser.

Bag, *v.*[2]; also **badge.** 1697. [Origin unkn.] To cut corn, pease, or beans, with a 'bagging' hook. So **Ba·gging** *vbl. sb.* reaping corn, pease, and beans thus 1677.

‖ **Bagasse** (băgæ·s). 1854. [Fr. *bagasse* (XVIII) – mod.Pr. *bagasso.*] The refuse products in sugar-making. *Comb.* **b.-burner,** a furnace for burning b.

Bagatelle (bæ:găte·l). 1637. [– Fr. *bagatelle* – It. *bagatella*, dim. of (dial.) *bagata* little property, prob. f. *baga* (see BAGGAGE). Now scarcely naturalized in sense 1; sense 2 is purely Eng.] **1.** A trifle, a thing of no value or importance 1645. **b.** A piece of verse or music in a light style 1827. **2.** A game played on a table having a semicircular end at which are nine numbered holes. The balls are struck from the other end with a cue. 1819.

Baggage (bæ·gėdʒ). ME. [– (O)Fr. *bagage* f. *baguer* tie up, or f. *bagues* (pl.) bundles, packs; see BAG *sb.*, -AGE.] Usually *collective* in senses 1–4 (formerly occas. with pl.). **1.** The collection of property in packages that a traveller takes with him on a journey; luggage. (The regular term in U.S.; in Great Britain usu. called 'luggage'.) **2.** *spec.* The portable equipment of an army; = L. *impedimenta* 1489. † **3.** *fig.* Burdensome matters –1757. † **4.** Rubbish, refuse –1661; pus –1610; *fig.* trash, 'rot' –1579. † **5.** A worthless or vile fellow –1601. **6.** A good-for-nothing woman, a strumpet 1596. **7.** Used joc. of any young woman, *esp.* with *artful, pert*, etc. 1672.

1. Indians..to cary b. 1578. **2.** *Bag and b.*: see BAG. **4.** To read such beastly b. FULKE. **7.** I believe the b. loves me CONGREVE.

† **B.** *adj.* (from attrib. use of the sb. in sense 4; cf. *trumpery.*) † **1.** Rubbishy –1625. † **2.** Trashy, despicable –1640. † **3.** Good-for-nothing, scurvy –1670. † **4.** Purulent –1597.

Comb.: **b.-check,** a ticket for luggage on U.S. railways; **-man,** or **-master,** one who has charge of the b.; **-room,** a luggage-office; **-smasher** (*joc.*), railway-porter (U.S.).

Hence **Ba·ggaged** *ppl. a.* (*nonce-wd.*), packed up BYRON. † **Ba·ggagely** *a.* rubbishy. **Ba·ggager,** one who carries or has charge of b.

† **Bagge,** *v.* ME. only. [orig. unkn.] To look askew; to leer, ogle.

Bagged (bægd), *ppl. a.* ME. [f. BAG *v.* and *sb.* + -ED[1], [2].] † **1.** Big with young –1616. **2.** Enclosed in, or as in, a bag; encysted 1572. **3.** Hanging slack, or in bags 1618. **4.** Having bags 1861.

Ba·gging, *sb.*[1] 1750. [perh. orig. a vbl. sb. expressing the act of carrying food in a bag; hence transf.] Used in n. dial. for food eaten between meals; now, *esp.* in Lancs. a substantial afternoon tea.

Bagging (bæ·giŋ), *sb.*[2] 1732. [f. BAG *sb.* + -ING[1]; cf. *sacking*, etc.] Coarse woven fabric out of which bags are made.

Baggit (bæ·git). 1848. [perh. Sc. form of BAGGED, sense 1.] A salmon that is in spawn.

Baggy (bæ·gi), *a.* 1831. [f. BAG *sb.* + -Y[1].] **1.** Puffed out; hanging loosely. **2.** *fig.* Of language: Inflated 1866. Hence **Ba·ggily** *adv.* **Ba·gginess,** baggy state.

† **Ba·gle.** ME. [– ON. *bagall* – L. *baculum* staff, rod; in form *baghel* – OIr. *bachdl.*] The staff or crozier of a bishop –1557.

Bagman (bæ·gmæ̆n). 1531. [f. BAG *sb.* + MAN.] **1.** One who carries a bag 1531. **2.** *spec.* A commercial traveller, who shows samples and solicits orders for his principal, etc. (*derog.*) 1765. **3.** A bag-fox 1875.

‖ **Bagne** (banʸ). 1863. Fr., – It. *bagno* (next).] = BAGNIO 2.

Bagnio (bæ·nyo). 1599. [– It. *bagno* :– L. *balneum* bath.] † **1.** A bath, a bathing-house; *esp.* one with appliances for sweating, cupping, etc. –1820. **2.** An oriental prison for slaves 1599. **3.** A brothel. (Cf. STEW.) 1624.

Bagpipe (bæ·gpəip), *sb.* ME. [f. BAG *sb.*[1] + PIPE *sb.*[1]] **1.** A musical instrument of great antiquity, consisting of an air-tight wind-bag, and one or more reed pipes into which the air is pressed by the performer. Now often in *pl.*

Formerly a favourite rural Eng. instrument; now chiefly used in the Scottish Highlands, and in Ireland. The Highland bagpipe is a greased leathern bag covered with flannel, inflated through a valved mouth-tube, and having three *drones* or bass pipes, and a *chanter* for the tenor or treble.

2. *fig.* A wind-bag; a long-winded speaker 1603. Hence **Ba·gpi:per.**

Ba·gpipe, *v.* 1769. [from the shape the sail assumes.] *Naut.* Of the mizzen: To lay it aback, by bringing the sheet to the mizzen-shrouds.

† **Ba·gpu·dding.** 1598. [f. BAG *sb.*[1]] A pudding boiled in a bag –1817.

Bag-reef (bæ·g,rī·f). 1867. [f. BAG *v.*] *Naut.* A fourth or lower reef of fore-and-aft sails.

Baguette (băge·t). 1727. [– Fr. *baguette*, in *Arch.* – It. *bacchetta*, dim. of *bacchio* :– L. *baculum* staff.] A small moulding of semi-circular section, like an astragal.

Bag-wig (bæ·g,wi:g). (Also as two wds.) 1717. An 18th c. wig with the back-hair enclosed in a bag.

Bah (bā), *int.* 1817. [prob. after Fr. *bah* in same sense.] An exclam. of contempt.

‖ **Bahar, barr(e** (băhā·ɹ). 1753. [– Hind. *bhār* – Skr. *bhāra* load, burden.] A measure of weight used in India and China, varying in different places from 223 to 625 lbs.

‖ **Bahu·t.** [repr. It. *bautta* domino.] A dress for masquerading. BERRY.

Baign(e, obs. f. BAIN.

‖ **Baignoire** (be·nwar, -wǭɹ). 1873. [Fr., = bath-tub.] A box at the theatre on the same level as the stalls.

Bail (bēⁱl), *sb.*[1] ME. [In senses 1 and 2, – OFr. *bail* power, custody, jurisdiction, delivery, f. *bailler* take charge of, receive, deliver :– L. *bajulare* bear a burden, manage f. *bajulus* carrier. The other senses are English.] † **1.** Custody, jurisdiction –1596. † **2.** Delivery ME. only. † **3.** The friendly custody of a person otherwise liable to be kept in prison, upon security given for his appearance at a time and place assigned –1809. † **4.** Temporary release from imprisonment on finding sureties or security to appear for trial; *also*, release –1768. **5.** Security so given 1495; also *fig.* **6.** The person or persons who thus become sureties 1593. Also *fig.*

1. His body is undyr your bayle ME. **3.** *Admitted to b.* if the offences were bailable SELDEN. So *let to b.* **5.** Put to sufficient baill 1495. *To give leg b.* (joc.): to be beholden to one's legs for release, to run away. **6.** I'll go b. for that THACKERAY.

Comb.: **b.-bond,** the bond entered into by a b.; **-piece,** a slip of parchment containing the recognizance which is handed to the court.

Bail, *sb.*[2] [ME. *beyle*, ring, hoop, prob. – ON. *beygla*, f. *beygja* = OE. *bēgan, byġan* bend, bow.] **1.** A hoop; a half-hoop for supporting the cover of a wagon, the tilt of a boat, etc. 1447. **2.** The hoop-handle of a kettle, etc. 1463.

Bail, bayle (bēⁱl), *sb.*[3] [– OFr. *bail, baile*, app. f. *bailler* enclose, shut. Cf. BAIL *v.*[2], BAILEY.] **1.** *pl.* Outer line of fortification, formed of stakes; palisades 1523. **2.** The wall of the outer court of a feudal castle; *hence*, the courts themselves. See BAILEY. † **3.** *pl.* The bulwarks of a boat –1603. **4.** A bar or pole to separate horses in an open stable 1844. **5.** *Austral.* A framework for securing the head of a cow while she is milked 1885.

Bail, *sb.*[4] 1575. [perh. – OFr. *bail* cross-beam, possibly from a transf. use of L. *bajulus* carrier (see BAIL *sb.*[1]).] † **1.** A cross-bar. **2.** In *Cricket*, each of the two pieces of wood laid across the stumps 1770.

Bail, *sb.*[5] 1466. [– Fr. *baille* bucket :– Gallo-Rom. **bajula* f. L. *bajulus* carrier; see BAIL *sb.*[1]] *Naut.* A bucket or scoop for bailing water from a boat.

Bail (bēⁱl), *v.*[1] 1548. [– OFr. *bailler* deliver, etc.; see BAIL *sb.*[1]] **1.** 'To deliver (goods) in trust, upon a contract expressed or implied that the trust shall be faithfully executed on the part of the bailee'. Blackstone. [See BAILMENT, BAILOR, BAILEE.] 1768. **2.** To admit to bail, to liberate on bail. Said of the magistrate (*arch.*). 1548. Also † *fig.* and *gen.* **3.** To procure the liberation of (any one) by becoming bail for him. Also *fig.* 1587. **4.** *fig.* To be security or pledge for 1587.

1. If cloth be..bailed to a taylor to make a suit of cloathes BLACKSTONE. **3.** I offer to b. the fellow out 1859. Hence **Bailed** *ppl. a.* released on bail.

Bail, *v.*[2] 1600. [app. – OFr. *baillier* enclose, shut, see BAIL *sb.*[3]] **1.** To confine (*rare*). **2.** *To bail up* (in Australia): **a.** To secure a cow's head in a bail while she is milked; **b.** (Said of bushrangers) To 'stick up' and disarm before robbing; also *intr.* To disarm oneself by throwing up the arms 1880.

1. My friends heart let my poore heart bale SHAKS.

Bail, *v.*[3] 1613. [f. BAIL *sb.*[5]; see BALE *v.*[3]] To lade water out of a boat, etc., with buckets (formerly called bails), or other vessels. **a.** To b. *the water* (out). **b.** To b. *the boat* (out) 1840. **c.** *absol.* 1624.

† **Bai·lable,** *a.*[1] 1502. [– OFr. *baillable.*] Deliverable.

Bailable (bēⁱ·lăb'l), *a.*[2] 1554. [– OFr. *baillable*; see BAIL *v.*[1], -ABLE.] **1.** Entitled to be released on bail. **2.** Admitting of bail, as a *b. offence* 1649.

Bailage (bēⁱ·lėdʒ). 1669. [f. BAIL *v.*[1] + -AGE.] A duty upon delivery of goods.

† **Bai·l-dock, ba·le-dock.** 1624. [f. BALE *sb.*[3] barrier; see DOCK.] At the Old Bailey, London, (formerly) 'a small room taken from one of the corners of the court, and left open at the top; in which, during the trials, are put some of the malefactors' (*Scots Mag.*) –1823.

† **Baile, bayle,** *int.* 1529. [perh. imper. of Fr. *bailler* 'Deliver (blows)!'] A call to combatants to engage –1530.

Bailee (bēⁱ:lī·). 1528. [f. BAIL *v.*[1] + -EE[1].] One to whom a BAILMENT (sense 1) is made.

Bai·ler[1]. 1883. [f. BAIL *v.*[3] + -ER[1].] He who or that which bails water out, *esp.* a machine to lift and throw out water from a pit, etc.

Bai·ler[2]. 1881. [f. BAIL *sb.*[4] + -ER[1] 1.] *Cricket.* A ball that hits the bails.

Bailey (bēⁱ·li). [ME. *bail(l)y*, var. *baile*, prob. – OFr. *bail, baille*, enclosed court (whence med.L. *ballium, ballia*), f. *bailler* enclose, of unkn. origin. See BAIL *sb.*[3], BAIL *v.*[2]] **1.** The external wall of a feudal castle; more widely, any circuit of walls which surrounded the keep. **2.** Later: The outer court of a feudal castle; also, any court within the circuits of walls. Hence *outer, inner* 1845. **3.** Retained in proper names: e.g. the *Old Bailey* in London, the seat of the Central Criminal Court, so called from the ancient *bailey* of the city wall between Lud Gate and New Gate, within which it lay 1570.

Bailie (bēⁱ·li). [ME. *bail(l)i* – OFr. *bailli*, later form of *baillis* (nom.), *bailif* (see next).] *Obs.* in England. † **1.** = BAILIFF 1. –1662. **2.** *In Scotland.* † **a.** *formerly*, The chief magistrate (= sheriff) of a barony –1754; **b.** *now*, A municipal magistrate (= Eng. alderman) 1484. † **3.** = BAILIFF 2. –1668. † **4.** = BAILIFF 3. –1730. Hence **Bai·liery, -ary,** = BAILIWICK 1, 2. So **Bai·lieship,** the office of b.

Bailiff (bēⁱ·lif). [ME. *baillif* – OFr. *baillif*, obl. case of *baillis* (mod. *bailli*) :– med.L. *bajulivus* (*ballivus*), adj. deriv. of L. *bajulus* carrier, (hence) manager, administrator. Cf. BAIL *sb.*[1]] **1.** One charged with administrative authority in a certain district, the chief officer of a hundred; the 'chief magistrate', as in High B. of Westminster, a 'custodian', as in B. of Dover Castle. **2.** A sheriff's deputy, who executes writs, etc., distrains, and arrests ME. **3.** An agent who collects rents, or a steward who manages an estate, for the landlord; one who superintends the husbandry of a farm for its owner or tenant 1531.

1. The quene sent in hast to the Baillifs of wynchestre CAXTON. **2.** Then a Processe-seruer (a Bayliffe) *Wint. T.* IV. iii. 102. Hence **Bai·liffry** (*rare*), a *Bailiery*. **Bai·liffship,** the office of b. **Ba·lival** *a.* of or pertaining to a b. or his office.

† **Bai·liffwick.** 1509. [f. prec. + -WICK.] **1.** The district under the jurisdiction of a bailiff –1766. **2.** = BAILIFFSHIP. –1570. **3.** Stewardship 1605.

Bailiwick (bē̆ⁱ·li,wik). 1460. [f. BAILIE + -WICK.] **1.** A district under a bailie or bailiff. In *Eng. Hist.* it includes *sheriffdom*; also *transf.* **2.** = prec. (sense 2). *Hist.* † **3.** = prec. (sense 3). –1601. var. **Bailliage.**

† **Baillie, bailly.** [– OFr. *baillie* jurisdiction, f. *baillir* have under one's jurisdiction, etc.; cf. med.L. *bajulia* tutelage, etc.; see BAILIFF, -Y³.] **1.** The jurisdiction, or office of a BAILIE or BAILIFF; delegated authority; stewardship –1738. **2.** *gen.* Jurisdiction, charge –1475. **3.** A BAILIWICK ME. only.

Bailment (bē̆ⁱ·lmĕnt). 1554. [– OFr. *baillement*, f. *bailler* bail, give, deliver; see BAIL *v.*¹, -MENT.] **1.** Delivery for a specific purpose; delivery in trust, upon a contract expressed or implied, that the trust shall be faithfully executed 1602. **2.** The action of bailing a person accused. Also the record of the same.

‖ **Bailo** (bai·lo). Occ. **baile.** 1682. [It. :– L. *bajulus*. See BAIL *sb.*¹ and BAILIFF.] The Venetian 'Resident' at the Ottoman Porte.

Bailor (bē̆ⁱ:lǭ·ɹ). 1602. [f. BAIL *v.*¹ + -OR 2; cf. *bailee.*] *Law.* One who makes a BAILMENT (sense 1).

Bailsman (bē̆ⁱ·lzmæ̆n). 1862. [f. BAIL *sb.*¹] One who gives bail for another, a bail.

Bain (bē̆ⁱn). Now *dial.* ME. [– ON. *beinn* straight, direct, ready to serve.] **A.** *adj.* **1.** Willing –1674. **2.** Limber –1674. **3.** Direct; short (*n. dial.*) 1864. **B.** as *adv.* **1.** Willingly –1513. **2.** Near, 'handy' (*n. dial.*) 1700.

† **Bain,** *sb.* 1475. [– Fr. *bain* :– L. *balneum* bath.] **1.** A quantity of water, etc., placed in a vessel, in which one may bathe –1641; the vessel itself –1543; *abstractly*, a bath –1563. **2.** = BAGNIO 1. –1693. **3.** A hot or medicinal spring –1655. **4.** in *pl.* Stews –1599. **5.** *Chem.* An apparatus for heating gradually through the medium of water, sand, etc. Cf. BATH. –1657.

† **Bain,** *v.* ME. [– Fr. *baigner* :– L. *balneare.*] **1.** To bathe; to drench –1602. Also *fig.* **2.** *intr.* To bathe oneself (*lit.* and *fig.*) –1573.

‖ **Bain-marie** (bæ̃nmari). 1822. [Fr., tr. med.L. *balneum Mariæ*, tr. med.Gr. *κάμινος Μαρίας* furnace of Maria, a supposed Jewish alchemist.] A flat vessel to hold hot water, in which other vessels are placed for heating food, etc.

‖ **Bairam** (bairā·m, bai·răm). 1599. [Turk. and Pers.] The name of two Mohammedan festivals—the *Lesser B.*, lasting three days, which follows the fast of Ramadan, and the *Greater B.*, seventy days later, lasting four days.

Bairn (bēᵊɹn, in Sc. bern). [Sc. form of ME. *barn*, repr. OE. *bearn* = OS., OHG., ON., Goth. *barn* :– Gmc. **barnam*, f. **bar*, var. of stem of **beran* BEAR *v.*¹] A child; a son or daughter. (Expressing relationship.)

Mercy on's, a Barne?..A boy or a childe I wonder *Wint. T.* III. ii. 70. Hence **Bai·rnie,** little child. **Bai·rnish** *a.* childish. **Bai·rnishness, Bai·rnliness,** childishness. **Bai·rnly** *a.* childish; child-like; also, † as *adv.* **Bai·rn-team, -time,** also **Barm-team,** brood of children, offspring; posterity.

†‖ **Baisemain.** 1656. [(O)Fr.] A kiss of the hands; in *pl.* respects –1748.

Bait (bē̆ⁱ·t), *v.*¹ [– ON. *beita* hunt or chase with dogs or hawks (= OE. *bǣtan*, OHG. *beizen*, G. *beizen*), causal of *bíta* BITE *v.* Senses 8–10 prob. from the *sb.*] † **1.** To set on to bite or worry (*lit.* and *fig.*). **2.** To set on dogs to bite or worry a chained or confined animal; † to hunt with dogs ME. Also *fig.* **3.** To attack with endeavour to bite or tear 1553. Also *absol.* **4.** *fig.* To harass with persistent attacks ME. **5.** *trans.* To give food and drink to (a horse, etc.), *esp.* on a journey ME. Also (*refl.* and) *intr.* **6.** *intr.* Of travellers: To stop at an inn for rest and refreshment; *hence*, to make a short stay ME. Also *fig.* † **7.** *intr.* (and *refl.*) To feed –1633. Also † *fig.* **8.** To furnish (a hook, etc.) with a bait ME. Also *fig.* **9.** To lay (a place) with bait 1623. **10.** To offer bait to; to tempt 1590.

2. Are these thy Beares? Wee'l bate thy Bears to death 2 *Hen. VI*, V. i. 148. **4.** To b. a Secretary of State MACAULAY. **6.** To b. here a few days longer SHERIDAN. *fig.* For evil news rides post, while good news baits MILT. *Sams.* 1538. Hence **Bai·ted** *ppl. a.* (senses 2, 9). **Bai·ter. Bai·ting** *vbl. sb.* and *ppl. a.*

Bait, *v.*² *Falconry.* See BATE *v.*¹

Bait (bē̆ⁱt), *sb.* ME. [– ON. *beit* (neut.) pasture, *beita* (fem.) food, cogn. w. OE. *bāt*; in part f. BAIT *v.*¹] **1.** Food placed on a hook or in a trap, in order to allure fish or other animals ME.; worms, fish, etc., to be thus used 1496. Also *fig.* **2.** Food, refreshment; *esp.* a feed for horses, or slight repast for travellers, upon a journey. Still *dial.* a snack taken between meals. Also † *fig.* 1570. **3.** A halt for refreshment or rest 1579. **5.** Setting dogs to worry other animals 1450.

1. Let your b. fall gently upon the water WALTON. *fig.* A doore without locke, is a baite for a knaue TUSSER. Hence **Bai·tless,** without food (*rare*).

Baize (beⁱz), *sb.* 1578. [Early form *baies* = Fr. *baies* fem. pl., subst. use of *bai* reddish brown, BAY *sb.*⁷; so named presumably from its orig. colour. The pl. was early taken as a sing., with sp. with *z* XIX.] **1.** A coarse woollen stuff, having a long nap. Also *attrib.* **2.** A curtain, table cover, etc., of baize 1862. Hence **Baize** *v.* to cover or line with b.

‖ **Bajocco** (ba,yǭ·kko). Pl. **-cchi.** 1547. [It., f. *bajo* brown.] A small Italian copper coin (now obs.) worth about a halfpenny.

† **Ba·julate,** *v. rare.* 1613. [– *bajulat-*, pa. ppl. stem of L. *bajulare* carry; see BAIL *sb.*¹, -ATE³.] To carry, *esp.* as a BADGER *sb.*¹ FULLER.

Bake (bē̆ⁱk), *v.* [OE. *bacan*, str. vb. = OHG. *backan*, ON. *baka*, – Gmc. **bak-* :– Indo-Eur. **bhog-*, whence Gr. *φώγειν* roast, parch. The weak pa.t. *baked* appeared before 1400; the weak pa. pple. *baked*, in XVI, and is alone used by SHAKS.] **1.** To cook by dry heat acting by conduction and not by radiation, as in an oven, etc., or on a heated surface; primarily used of preparing bread. (In transf. uses not sharply separated from *roast.*) **b.** *fig.* To ripen with heat 1697. **2.** To harden by heat ME. **3.** To harden as frost does 1572. † **4.** To cake –1684. **5.** *intr.* (for *refl.*) To undergo baking 1605.

3. Th'earth When it is bak'd with frost *Temp.* I. ii. 256. **5.** These apples b. badly (*mod.*).

Comb., *bake* (= *baking* vbl. sb.) attrib., as **b.-board; -house; -stone.** Hence **Bake** *sb.* In *Sc.* A biscuit; the act, process, or result, of baking. **Ba·ken** *ppl. a.* (*arch.*). **Ba·king** *vbl. sb.* attrib. *b.-powder*, a substitute for yeast, used in making bread.

Bakelite (bē̆ⁱ·kĕləit). 1913. [– G. *bakelit*, f. the name of L. H. *Baekeland* its inventor + -ITE¹ 4.] A proprietary name of a synthetic resin formed by the condensation of phenols and formaldehyde, used as a plastic and for insulating purposes.

† **Ba·ke-meat.** ME. [f. *bake* = *baken*; also *baken, baked m.*] Pastry, a pie –1700.

Baker (bē̆ⁱ·kəɹ). [OE. *bæcere*, f. *bacan*; see BAKE, -ER¹.] **1.** One who bakes; *spec.* one whose business it is to make bread. **2.** A small portable tin oven. In U.S. **3.** An artificial salmon fly 1867.

Comb.: **b.-feet, -legs, -knees, baker's knee,** names of deformities incident to bakers; **-legged, -kneed,** *a.*; **baker's salt,** a name for commercial carbonate of ammonia, used instead of yeast. Phr. *Baker's dozen*: thirteen. Hence **Ba·kerdom,** condition of a b. **Ba·kership,** skill as a b. **Ba·kery,** craft or business of baker: a baker's establishment.

‖ **Baksheesh, bakhshish** (bæ·k,ʃīʃ). 1755. [ult. – Pers. *bakšīš*, ‹ f. *bakšīdan* give.] Oriental for a 'tip'. Hence **Bak·sheesh** *v.* to 'tip'. Also *absol.*

Bal. 1600. [– Cornish *bal* 'collection of mines'.] A mine. Also *attrib.*, as in *b.-girl*, etc.

Balaam (bē̆ⁱ·lăm). 1648. **1.** Name of the prophet (*Numb.* 22–4), used connotatively. Hence **Balaam** *v.* to make a B. of. **Ba·laamite,** one who follows religion for gain; **Balaamitical** *a.* **2.** (In journalistic slang) Trumpery paragraphs reserved to fill up the columns of a newspaper, etc. **B.-box** (or **-basket**), a receptacle for such matter.

‖ **Balachong** (bæ·latʃǫŋ). 1697. [– Malay *bālachān.*] A condiment for rice, made of putrid shrimps or small fishes pounded up with salt or spices, and then dried.

Balaclava (bælăklā·vă). [Site of Crimean battle in 1854.] *B. helmet* (*cap*), a woollen covering for the head and shoulders worn esp. by soldiers on active service 1892.

Baladine (bæ·lădīn). 1599. [– Fr. *baladin* (XVI)–Pr. *baladin* – *balada* dance; see BALLAD.] † **1.** A theatrical dancer; a mountebank –1676. **2.** A female public dancer BROWNING. † **3.** A ballad-maker or -singer 1604.

Balalaika (bælăləi·kă). 1788. [Russ., of Tatar origin.] Instrument of guitar kind, used esp. in Russia.

Balance (bæ·lăns), *sb.* ME. [– (O)Fr. *balance* :– Rom. **bilancia*, f. late L. *bilanx*, *bilanc-* (in *libra bilanx* balance having two scales), f. *bi-* BI-² + *lanx* scale.] **1.** An apparatus for weighing, a beam poised so as to move freely on a central pivot, with a scale pan at each end. † **2.** *sing.* One scale of a balance; *pl.* scales. (The *pl.* was occ. *balance.* See *Merch. V.* IV. i. 255.) –1655. **3. a.** The constellation *Libra.* **b.** The seventh sign of the Zodiac ♎, into which the sun enters at the autumnal equinox 1488. **4.** Any apparatus used in weighing 1829. **5.** *Watch-making.* A contrivance which regulates the speed of a watch, etc. 1660. **6.** *Naut.* The operation or result of reefing with a *balance-reef*; see below 1762. **7.** *fig.* The balance of reason, justice, or opinion ME.; † one scale of the balance –1635. **8.** The wavering balance of Fortune or chance ME. † **9.** *Hence*, Hesitation, doubt –1683; risk –1685. **10.** Power to decide ME. **11.** A weight which produces equilibrium; a counterpoise. Also *fig.* 1601. **12.** Equilibrium 1642. **13.** General harmony between the parts of anything; *esp.* in the Arts of Design 1732. **14. a.** Physical equipoise 1667; **b.** Equipoise of mind, etc.; sanity 1856. **15.** The preponderating weight; the net result 1747. **16.** The process of finding the difference, if any, between the Dr. and Cr. sides of an account; the tabular statement exhibiting this; the result 1588; *gen.* a comparative reckoning (*rare*) 1719. **17.** An equality between the total of the two sides of an account. Cf. 12. 1652. **18.** The difference between the Dr. and Cr. sides of an account 1622. **19.** *Comm. slang*: The remainder 1864.

1. He had a b. in his hand R.V. *Rev.* 6:5. **2.** A pair of Balance FULLER. **7.** A Moth wil turne the ballance, which Piramus which Thisby is the better *Mids. N.* V. 324. **8.** Mens lives hang in the ballance 1612. **10.** Henry viii held the b. with..a stronger hand 1760. **12. Balance of power** (*in Europe*): such an adjustment of power that no single state is in a position to interfere with the independence of the rest. **14.** If my mind had retained its b. KANE. **15.** The b. of evidence appears in favour of the due execution BROUGHAM. **16.** *To strike a b.*: to determine the exact difference, if any, between the two sides of an account (*lit.* and *fig.*). **Balance of trade**: the estimation of the difference of value between the exports and imports of a country; the difference in favour of, or against, the country. **18.** *B.* (*of indebtedness*): the difference between the amounts which two parties mutually owe each other. *B.* (*in hand*): the sum remaining over after realizing all assets and discharging all liabilities. *B.* (*due*): the sum still outstanding on an account.

Comb.: **b.-beam,** the beam of a b., *also* the beam keeping a drawbridge balanced aloft; **-bob,** a heavy lever ballasted at one end, and attached at the other to the pump-rod; **-fish,** *Squalus zygæna*; **-knife,** a table-knife with a handle which keeps the blade from touching the cloth; **-master, -mistress,** an acrobat; **-reef,** the closest reef of a lower fore-and-aft sail, used to steady the ship in stormy weather, whence *balance-reefed*; **-sheet,** a tabular statement of assets and liabilities; **-step** (= GOOSE-STEP); **-yard** = *balance-beam*.

Balance (bæ·lăns), *v.* 1579. [–(O)Fr. *balancer* f. *balance*; see prec.] **1.** *trans.* To weigh (a matter); to ponder 1694. **2.** To weigh two things, considerations, etc., against each other 1596. **3.** To counterpoise one thing *by*, *with*, or *against* another 1624. **4.** To bring to or keep in equilibrium 1634. **5.** To poise, keep steady or erect 1840; also *refl.* and *intr.* **6.** *trans.* To equal in weight, counterpoise. Also *absol.* to balance (each other) 1727. **7.** *Hence*: To neutralize the effect of, make up for 1593. **8.** *intr.* To waver, deliberate 1655. **9.** *Dancing*: To *set to* a partner 1775. **10.** *trans.* To add up the Dr. and Cr. sides of an account, and ascertain the difference, if any, between their amounts 1588. **11.** To equalize the two sides of an account by making proper entries; hence **b.** accounts are said (intr.) *to b.* (i.e. themselves); or an entry is said *to b. the account*, or an opposite entry 1622. **12.** *Hence*: To settle (an account) by paying an amount due 1740. **13.** *Naut.* To reef with a balance-reef; see BALANCE *sb.*

2. Truth is determined by balancing probabilities 1875. **5.** Strong men. . balancing chests of drawers . . upon their heads DICKENS. **6.** Do these scales b. (*mod.*). **7.** To ballance the Protestants, the Jesuits were set on foot FULLER. **8.** A disposition to b. and temporize MERIVALE. **10.** To compute and b. my gain and my loss SWIFT. **12.** A cheque for £30 to b. his account 1877. Hence **Ba·lanceable** *a.* **Ba·lanced** *ppl. a.*, poised; in equipoise; well arranged or disposed. **Ba·lancement** (*rare*), equipoise.

Balancer (bæ·lănsəɹ). ME. [f. prec. + -ER¹.] † **1.** One who weighs with a balance (*rare*) –1611. **2.** An acrobat 1510. **3.** One who maintains the balance of power 1731. **4.** Something which helps to preserve the balance; *spec.* the *halteres* or *poisers* in two-winged flies 1753.

‖ **Bala·ndra.** 1845. [It., Sp., Pg., whence Fr. *balandre* (now *bélandre*); see BILANDER.] A small coasting vessel.

Balanid (bæ·lănid). 1836. [f. L. *balanus* – Gr. βάλανος acorn + -ID³.] *Zool.* A member of the *Balanidæ* or Acorn-shells.

Balaniferous (bælăni·fĕrəs), *a.* 1881. [f. as prec. + -FEROUS.] Acorn-bearing.

Balanite (bæ·lănəit). 1598. [– L. *balanites* – Gr. βαλανίτης acorn-shaped, f. βάλανος acorn; see -ITE¹ 2 b.] † **1.** A kind of precious stone. **2.** A fossil balanid 1835.

Balanoid (bæ·lănoid). 1869. [f. as prec. + -OID.] *adj.* Acorn-shaped. *sb.* A balanid.

Balas (bæ·lăs). ME. [–(O)Fr. *balais* – med.L. *balascus* -*cius* – Arab. *balaḵš* f. Pers. *Badaḵšān*, a district of Persia near Samarkand, where found.] A delicate rose-red variety of the spinel ruby. Now usu. *b.-ruby*.

† **Ba·latron, -oon.** *rare.* 1623. [– L. *balatro*, -*ōn*- buffoon; see -OON.] A buffoon –1678. Hence **Balatro·nic** *a.*

‖ **Balausta** (bălǭ·stă). 1842. [mod.L. (Linn.); see next.] *Bot.* The fruit of the pomegranate.

Balaustine (bălǭ·stin). Also **-in, -ian.** 1671. [– L. *balaustium* (whence It. *balaustio*) – Gr. βαλαύστιον (in same sense); the suffix *-ine* (*-in, -ian*) is unexpl.] The flower of the wild pomegranate, used when dried as an astringent. var. † **Balau·sty.**

Balbu·tient, *a.* 1642. [– *balbutient*-, pres. ppl. stem of L. *balbutire* stammer.] Stammering.

‖ **Balbuties** (bælbiū·fi,īz). 1655. [mod.L., f. *balbutire*; see prec.] *Med.* Stuttering; lisping.

† **Balcon.** *rare.* 1635. [– Fr. *balcon*; see BALCONY.] = BALCONY –1665.

Balcone·tte. 1876. [f. next + -ETTE.] A miniature balcony.

Balcony (bæ·lkŏni). 1618. [– It. *balcone* (whence also Fr. *balcon*, Sp. *balcón*), prob. f. Gmc. *balkon beam, BALK *sb.*, with augm. suffix; see -OON. Till *c*1825 bælkōᵘ·ni, though bæ·lkŏni occurs once in Swift.] **1.** A platform projecting from the wall of a house or room, supported by pillars, brackets, or consoles, and enclosed by a balustrade. **2.** The similar structure at the stern of large ships 1666. **3.** In theatres: † A stage-box; *now*, The open part above the dress circle 1718.

1. The Maids to the Doors and the Balconies ran, And said, lack-a-day! he's a proper young man SWIFT. Hence **Ba·lconied** *ppl. a.* furnished with a b.

Bald (bǭld), *a.* [ME. *balled*(*e*), MSc. *bellit* hairless, having a white blaze, prob. an OE. formation with suffix *-ede* (as in *healede* ruptured, *hoferede* hunch-backed) on a base **ball*- meaning orig. 'white patch'. See BALL *sb.*³, BALLARD.] † **1.** ? Rotund ME. only. **2.** Lacking hair on some part of the head where it naturally grows ME.; also *fig.* **3.** Without hair (feathers, etc.) on other parts of the body ME. Also *transf.* (see quots.) **4.** Streaked or marked with white. [Cf. Welsh *ceffyl bál* (F. *cheval belle-face*).] 1690. **5.** *fig.* Bare of meaning or force ME. **6.** Bare of ornament and grace 1589. **7.** Undisguised 1854.

2. His heed was ballid, and schon as eny glas CHAUCER. Occasion's b. behind; Slip not thine opportunity MARLOWE. **4.** Now Ierkin, you are like to lose your haire, & proue a b. Ierkin *Temp.* IV. 238. Thy b., awful head, O sovran Blanc *c*1800. **5.** Balde sermons 1593, some b. truism COLERIDGE. **6.** B. Latine 1693, prose 1851, the b. street TENNYSON. **7.** A b. egotism 1870.

Comb.: *b.-faced, -nosed* (sense 4). Also **b.-coot,** the Coot (*Fulica atra*), so called from its white frontal plate, destitute of feathers: *fig.* = *bald-head*; **-head,** one who has a b. head: *transf.* a kind of pigeon: whence *bald-headed*; **-pate,** one who has a b. head; *transf.* a kind of duck; also used *attrib.* = BALD *a.*; whence *bald-pated*; **-rib,** a joint of pork cut nearer the rump than the spare-rib; (*joc.*) a lean bony person. Hence † **Bald** *v.* to make b. (*lit.* and *fig.*). **Ba·ldly** *adv.*

Bald, early and north. f. BOLD.

Baldachin, -quin (bæ·ldăkin). 1598. [– It. *baldacchino*, f. (with suffix *-ino* -INE¹) *Baldacco*, It. form of *Bagdād* name of a city on the Tigris, where the stuff was made. See BAUDEKIN.] **1.** A rich stuff, orig. woven with woof of silk and warp of gold; rich brocade. **2.** A structure in the form of a canopy, either borne on columns, suspended from the roof, or projecting from the wall, placed above an altar, throne, or doorway; orig. made of the stuff described in sense 1. 1645.

Ba·lden, *v.* 1883. [f. BALD *a.* + -EN⁵.] To make or become bald.

Balder, -ur. [ON. *Baldr*, cogn. w. OE. *baldor* hero, f. *bald*; see BOLD.] A Scandinavian deity, whose name occurs in: **B.-herb** (*Amaranthus hypochondriacus*); **B. Brae, Balder's Brae, Baldeyebrow** (*Anthemis cotula*). See also BALDMONEY and BADDERLOCKS.

Balderdash (bǭ·ldəɹdæʃ), *sb.* 1596. [Of unkn. orig. Cf. med.L. *balductum* posset, *-a* pl. curd, used in Eng. for 'balderdash', 'trashy' XVI.] † **1.** ? Froth –1599. † **2.** A jumbled mixture of liquors, *e.g.* of milk and beer, beer and wine, etc. –1693. **3.** *transf.* A senseless jumble of words; trash 1674.

2. Beer or buttermilk, mingled together. . To drink such b. B. JONSON. [App. the primary sense is 1 or 2.]

Baldmoney (bǭ·ldmɒni). ME. [etym. unkn. Not = *Balder's Money*.] *Herb.* † **1.** Gentian –1597. **2.** Mew (*Meum athamanticum*) 1598.

Ba·ldness. ME. [f. BALD *a.* + -NESS.] **1.** Absence of hair, *esp.* from the head. Also *fig.* **2.** *transf.* Lack of natural covering 1863. **3.** Poverty of style; lack of ornament; bareness 1774.

Baldric (bǭ·ldrik). ME. [Earliest ex., ME. *baudry*, – OFr. *baudrei*; the later forms corr. to early MHG. *balderich*; of obscure origin, doubtfully referred to L. *balteus* belt.] **1.** A belt or girdle, often richly ornamented, worn pendent from one shoulder across the breast, and used to support a sword, bugle, etc. **2.** *fig.* The zodiac, as a gem-studded belt 1596. † **3.** A necklace –1577. † **4.** The leather-gear, etc., for suspending the clapper of a church bell –1742. Hence **Baldric-wise** *adv.*

† **Bale,** *a.* [OE. *balu* :– Gmc. **balwaz*; see next.] **1.** Actively evil –ME. **2.** Sorrowing –ME.

Bale (bēⁱl), *sb.*¹ [OE. *balu* (*bealu*) = OFris., OS. *balu*, OHG. *balo*, ON. *bǫl* :– Gmc. **balwam*, n. of adj. **balwaz*, repr. also in Goth. *balwawesei* wickedness.] Usu. *poet.* Marked obs. *c*1600, and rare thence till 19th c. **1.** Evil, *esp.* as active; fatal, dire, or malign, quality or influence; woe, mischief, harm, injury; in early use often = death, infliction of death. **2.** Evil as suffered; torment, pain, woe ME. **3.** Misery, grief ME.

Bale, *sb.*² [OE. *bǣl* = ON. *bál* great fire, cogn. w. Skr. *bhālas* lustre, Gr. φαλός shining, bright. In ME. and mod.Eng. – ON. *bál*. Much confused w. BALE *sb.*¹ Cf. BALE-FIRE.] † **1.** *gen.* A great consuming fire; a bonfire –1600. **2.** *spec.* **a.** A funeral pile or pyre. (*Obs.* exc. in W. MORRIS.) OE. **b.** A signal- or beacon-fire. *Sc.* (*arch.*) 1455. **3.** *fig.* 1568.

Bale (bēⁱl), *sb.*³ ME. [prob. – MDu. *bale* (Du. *baal*) – OFr. *bale* (later and mod. *balle*); ult. identical w. BALL *sb.*¹] **1.** A large bundle or package, orig. more or less round in shape; now, *spec.* one closely pressed, done up in canvas, etc., and corded or hooped, for transportation. **2.** A varying measure of quantity 1502. † **3.** The set of dice –1822.

Comb. **b.-goods,** merchandise in bales: opp. to *case-goods*. Hence **Bale** *v.*¹ to make up into a bale or bales.

† **Bale,** *v.*² *rare.* ME. only. [– OFr. *baler* (mod. *baller*) :– late L. *ballare* dance (Augustine) – Gr. βάλλειν in the sense 'dance'. See BALL *sb.*²] To dance.

Bale, *v.*³ 1692. [Later sp. of BAIL *v.*³]

Bale, obs. sp. of BAIL *sb.*¹ and *v.*¹; improp. f. BAIL *sb.*²

† **Baleare,** *a.* 1576. [f. L. *Balearis*.] = *Balearic*. Hence **Balea·rian** *a.* and *sb.*, and **Balea·ric** *a.* [L. *Balearicus*] of or pertaining to, *sb.* a native of, Majorca, Minorca, Ibiza, etc. (= L. *Baleares Insulæ*), in the Mediterranean Sea. *Balearic Crane*: the Crowned Crane.

Baleen (bălī·n) [– OFr. *baleine* whale (so in ME.) :– L. *balæna*.] †**1.** A whale –1601. **2.** ? The Sea bream ME. **3.** Whalebone. Also *attrib.* ME.

Bale-fire (bēⁱ·lfəiᵊɹ). OE. [f. BALE *sb.*² (occas. confused with BALE *sb.*¹) + FIRE. Till lately Sc. only.] **1.** A great fire in the open air. In OE. *spec.* the fire of a funeral pile. **2.** A signal- or beacon-fire. (App. first used by SCOTT.) 1805. **3.** A bonfire, *feu de joie* 1800.

1. The fires of death, The bale-fires flash on high BYRON.

Baleful (bēⁱ·lful), *a.* [OE. *bealu-full*, f. BALE *sb.*¹ Chiefly literary.] **1.** Full of active evil. **2.** *subjectively*: † **a.** Full of pain or suffering –1579. **b.** Unhappy; sorrowful (*arch.*) ME.

1. B. weedes SHAKS., Envy SMOLLETT, prejudices 1863. **2.** B. spirits barr'd from realms of bliss 1812. Hence **Ba·leful-ly** *adv.*, **-ness.**

Ba·leless, *a. arch.* [OE. *bealulēas*; see BALE *sb.*¹ and -LESS.] Harmless, innocent.

† **Baleys,** *sb.* ME. [– OFr. *baleis*, nom. sing. (or acc. pl.) of *balei* (mod. *balai*).] A rod; also, a birch, as used in flogging –1517. Hence **Baleys** *v.* to flog (still *dial.*).

† **Balinger** (bæ·lindʒəɹ). *Hist.* ME. [– AFr. *balenger* = med.L. *balingaria*, *-gera* whale-boat, *-arius* kind of warship, (O)Fr. *baleinier* whaler, f. *baleine* :– L. *balæna* whale.] A kind of sloop; acc. to Adm. Smyth, without forecastle.

† **Bali·ster, -ester.** 1489. [– OFr. *balestre* arbalester, = med.L. *balistarius*, *balestarius*, f. *bal*(*l*)*ista*, *bal*(*l*)*esta*; see -ER².] A crossbowman –1613.

‖ **Balistraria** (bælistrēᵊ·riă). 1845. [– med.L. *ballistraria* (in sense 1), fem. of the formally identical late L. *ballistarius*, *-trarius* one who discharges the *ballista*.] *Archit.* **a.** A cruciform opening in the walls of a fortress, through which arbalests were discharged. **b.** A room in which arbalests were kept.

‖ **Balize** (bălī·z). 1847. [– Fr. *balise* (XV), of unkn. origin.] A pole, surmounted by a barrel, or the like, raised as a beacon at sea.

Balk, baulk (bǭk), *sb.* [Late OE. *balc* – ON. *bálkr* partition :– **balkuz*, rel. to OFris. *balca*, OS., OHG. *balco* (Du. *balk*, G.

balken), ON. *bjálki* :– Gmc. **balkon*, **belkon* beam.] † **1.** A ridge, or mound –ME. † **2.** An isthmus; a bar of sand, etc. –1633. **3.** A ridge between two furrows (L. *porca*), or a strip of ground left unploughed OE. **4.** A piece missed in ploughing ME. † **5.** *fig.* A blunder –1717; † an omission –1775. † **6.** A stumbling-block, obstacle –1747. **7.** *fig.* A check or defeat 1660; a disappointment 1733. **8.** *transf.* The part of a billiard table behind a transverse line (the 'baulk-line') near one end, within the D or half-circle of which a player whose ball is in hand must place it to make his stroke 1800. **9.** A roughly squared beam of timber ME. **10.** A tie-beam of a house. A loft above was called 'the balks'. Now chiefly *north.* ME. **11.** The beam of a balance. Now *dial.* ME. **12.** *dial.* Stakes surrounded by netting or wicker work for catching fish 1836. **13.** The stout rope by which fishing nets are fastened one to another in a fleet. (In Cornw. *balch.*) 1847.

3. Narrow balks that intersect the fields 1821. **5.** *To make a balk*: to blunder. **7.** There cannot be a greater b. to the tempter SOUTH. **8.** *To make a baulk*: to bring one's own and the red ball within the baulk, when the opponent's ball is in hand. **11.** Unto the tubbes hangyng in the balkes CHAUCER.

Balk (bǭk), *v.*[1] ME. [f. prec. sb.] † **1.** *trans.* (and *absol.*) To make balks in ploughing –1611. **2.** To miss or omit intentionally; † to pass by –1783; to ignore 1440; to refuse (*e.g.* drink offered) 1587; to avoid (a duty, etc.) 1631; to let slip 1601. **3.** *intr.* To stop short, swerve. *Esp.* of a horse: To jib, refuse to go on, to shy. 1481. **4.** *trans.* To miss unintentionally –1710. **5.** To place a balk in the way of; to check 1589; to disappoint 1590; to frustrate 1635. † **6.** *trans.* and *absol.* To quibble, chop logic, bandy words –1653.

2. I never..balked an invitation out to dinner JOHNSON. To b. an opportunity DRYDEN. **3.** If he balked, I knew I was undone DE FOE. His horse balked at a leap 1862. **5.** An enemy who is baulked and defeated, but not overcome DE FOE. Balk'd of his prey POPE. Hence **Balked** *ppl. a.* † ridged; † ? heaped up (1 *Hen. IV*, I. i. 69); checked; disappointed. **Ba·lker**[1], one who balks, or makes or frequents balks. **Ba·lkingly** *adv.*

Balk, *v.*[2] ? *Obs.* 1603. [prob. – Du. *balken* bray, bawl, shout, cogn. w. OE. *bælcan* shout, vociferate.] To signify to fishing-boats, by shouting or signals from the heights, the direction taken by shoals of herrings or pilchards. Hence **Ba·lker**[2], one who does this; a huer, or conder.

† **Ba·lkish,** *a.* 1577. [f. BALK *sb.* + -ISH[1].] In ridges; uneven.

Balky (bǭ·ki), *a.* 1856. [f. as prec. + -Y[1].] Given to balking (as a horse).

Ball (bǭl), *sb.*[1] [ME. *bal* (inflected *balle, balles*) – ON. *ball-, bǫllr* (OSw. *baller*, Sw. *båll*) :– Gmc. **balluz*, rel. to **ballōn* (whence OHG. *balla*).] **1.** *gen.* A globular body. **2.** *spec.* Any planetary body, *esp.* the earth, the globe ME. † **3.** The golden orb borne together with the sceptre –1715. **4.** A globular body to play with, as in football, tennis, golf, cricket, etc. (Perh. the earliest Eng. sense.) ME. **b.** A game played with a ball ME. **c.** A throw, toss, or delivery of the ball, *esp.* in *Cricket* 1483. **5.** A missile (orig. spherical) projected from an engine of war. In artillery, a solid as dist. from a hollow projectile. ME. **6.** *Pyrotechny* and *Mil.* A globular case filled with combustibles; e.g. *fire-, smoke-, stink-balls* 1753. **7.** A small globe of wood, etc., used in voting by BALLOT 1580. **8.** *Ball of the eye*: **a.** orig. the pupil; **b.** now, the eye itself within the socket ME. **9.** A rounded mass of any substance ME. **10.** *Med.* A bolus. Now only in *Vet. Med.* 1576. **11.** (f. Fr. *balle*) A BALE 1583. **12.** A kind of small cushion used by printers for inking the type 1611. **13.** Any rounded protuberant part of the body; *esp.* of the thumb and great toe 1483. **14.** The central hollow of the palm of the hand or sole of the foot (*obs.*); the central part of an animal's foot 1601.

1. He rolleth vnder foot as dooth a bal CHAUCER. **2.** This Terrestrial b. *Rich. II*, III. iv. 41. **3.** The Scepter, and the B. *Hen. V*, IV. i. 277. **4.** *Cricket*: *No ball*, one unfairly bowled. *Wide ball*, one not properly within the batsman's reach. **5.** Mineral and stone..to found their Engins and their Balls Of missive ruin MILT. *P.L.* vi. 518. To load with b. MACAULAY. **7.** One black b. in three excludes DICKENS. **8.** His sightless balls SCOTT. **9.** Balls of cowslips HERRICK.

Phrases, etc. *fig.* from games: *To catch* or *take the b. before the bound*: to anticipate opportunity. *To have the b. at one's feet* or *before one*: to have a thing in one's power. *To keep the b. up* or *rolling*: to keep the conversation, etc., from flagging. *To take up the b.*: to take one's turn in conversation, etc. *The b. is with you*: it is your turn. **B. and socket**: a joint formed of a rounded end partly enclosed in a cup or socket, which is strong and yet moves freely. *Three (golden) balls*: the sign of a pawnbroker; supposed by some to be taken from the ensign of the Medici family.

Comb.: **b.-bear·ing(s**, a contrivance for lessening friction by means of small loose metal balls, used for the bearings of axles; **-cartridge**, a gun- or pistol-cartridge containing a bullet; **-clay**, very adhesive clay, as that brought up in lumps sticking to a ship's anchor; **-cock**, a self-regulating cistern-tap turned on and off by the rising or falling of a hollow floating ball; **-flower** (*Arch.*), an ornament like a ball within three or four petals of a flower, often inserted in a hollow moulding; **-mine**, iron-ore found in nodules; **-stamp**, an American ore-crushing machine; **-stone**, a rounded lump of ironstone or limestone; **-tap** (= *ball-cock*); **-thistle**, the Globe Thistle, also a species of Echinops; **-valve**, one opened or closed by the rising or falling of a valve which fits a cup-shaped opening in the seat; † **-vein**, iron ore in nodules; **-weed**, *Centaurea nigra.*

Ball (bǭl), *sb.*[2] 1632. [– (O)Fr. *bal* dance, f. † *baler*, † *baller* to dance, – late L. *ballare* – Gr. βάλλειν in the sense 'to dance'; cf. βαλλίζειν dance (Sicily and Magna Græcia).] † **1.** A dance or dancing 1633. **2.** A social assembly for the purpose of dancing 1632. Also *attrib.*, as *ball-room* (1752).

2. Balls..the perdition of precious houres JER. TAYLOR. Phr. *To give, go to, a b. To open the b.*: (*fig.*) to commence operations.

† **Ball,** *sb.*[3] 1523. [prob. Celtic – base **ball-*, meaning orig. 'white patch', cf. Welsh *bāl* in *ceffyl bāl* horse having a white streak on his forehead, Ir. and Gael. *bal* spot, mark.] white streak or spot; ? a bald place. **2** ? A white-faced horse; hence, a horse's name 1573.

Ball (bǭl), *v.* 1593. [f. BALL *sb.*[1]] **1.** *trans.* To round or swell out. **2.** To make or wind into a ball 1658. **3.** *intr.* To gather (itself) into a ball 1713. **4.** To clog, or become clogged, with balls (of snow, etc.) 1828.

4. The pony stumbled through the..snow..getting its feet balled 1863.

Ballad (bæ·lăd). 1492. [– (O)Fr. *ballade* – Pr. *balada* dance, song or poem to dance to, f. *balar* dance; see BALL *sb.*[2]] In 16th and 17th c. *-ad* became *-at(e, -et* (cf. *salad, sallet*), and in Sc. *-ant.* Cf. BALLET. See also BALLADE. † **1.** A song to accompany a dance –1616. **2.** A light, simple song of any kind; now *spec.* a sentimental or romantic composition, each verse of which is usu. sung to the same melody 1492. † **3.** A popular song, often scurrilous or personal –1825. † **4.** A posy. (Cf. L. *cantilena.*) –1601. **5.** A simple spirited poem in short stanzas, narrating some popular story. (This sense is mod.) 1712.

2. We do nought togyder, But prycked balades synge 1500. **3.** Who makes a ballet for an ale-house doore 1602. **4.** Spend, and god shall send..saith tholde ballet J. HEYWOOD. **5.** The grand old b. of Sir Patrick Spence COLERIDGE.

Comb.: **b.-monger**, one who sells ballads; *contemptuously*, ballad-maker (Shaks.); **-farce, -opera**, a play into which popular songs are introduced.

Hence **Ba·llader**, a writer of ballads or † scurrilous verses. **Balla·dic**, † **-al** *a.* of the nature of, or pertaining to, ballads. † **Balladie·r**, a street b.-singer. **Ba·lladism**, the characteristic quality of ballads. **Ba·lladist**, a ballader. **Ba·lladize** *v.* to make, or turn into, a b. **Ba·lladry**, b. poetry; composition in the b. style. (Formerly *depreciative.*)

Ba·llad, *v.* ? *Obs.* 1592. [f. prec. sb.] **1.** To write or compose ballads. **2.** *trans.* To make the subject of (scurrilous) ballads 1606.

Ballade (bălɑ·d). ME. [Early (and mod. Fr.) form of *ballad* differentiated in application.] **1. a.** *strictly*, A poem consisting of one or more triplets of seven- or (later) eight-lined stanzas each ending with the same line as refrain, and (usu.) an envoy. **b.** A poem divided into stanzas of equal length, usu. of seven or eight lines. † **c.** *occas.* One of these stanzas. **2.** *collect.* Poetry of this form ME. **3.** *Mus.* **a.** A composition of poetic character, usu. for piano. **b.** = BALLAD 2. 1863.

Ballan (bæ·lăn). 1769. [Of unkn. origin.] *Zool.* A kind of Wrasse (*Labrus maculatus*).

Ballarag, obs. f. BULLYRAG.

† **Ba·llard.** ME. [f. BALL *sb.*[3] + -ARD. Cf. BALD.] A bald-headed person.

Ballast (bæ·lăst), *sb.* 1530. [Early XVI *balast, ballace* (AL. *ballastum* 1462), prob. – LG. or Scand. (*a* 1400), in OSw., ODa. *ballast*, also *barlast*, which last has been assumed to be the orig. form and derived from (i) *bar* 'bare', mere, or (ii) *barm* hull (of a ship) + *last* burden.] **1.** Any heavy material, as gravel, sand, etc., placed in a ship's hold, to sink her to such a depth as to prevent her from capsizing when in motion. **2.** *fig.* That which tends to give stability in morals, politics, etc. 1612. † **3.** *transf.* Load, freight –1646. **4.** Gravel, broken stone, slag, etc., used to form the bed of a railroad. Also applied to burnt clay. 1837.

1. *In ballast*: **a.** in the hold. **b.** Of ships: Laden with b. only. **c.** Of materials: In the capacity of b. **2.** Solid and sober natures, have more of the b., then of the saile BACON. *Comb.*: **b.-ports**, square holes cut in the sides of merchantmen for taking in b.; **-shovel** (*Min.*), a round-mouthed shovel.

Ballast (bæ·lăst), *v.* 1538. [f. prec. sb.] **1.** To furnish (a ship) with ballast. **2.** *transf.* To steady 1596; also *fig.* † **3.** To load (*with* cargo –1666. **4.** *transf.* and *fig.* To weight (*arch.*) 1566. **5.** To fill in or form with BALLAST (sense 4) 1864. ¶ **6.** Confused w. BALANCE *v.* 1611.

2. Deliberation..to b. the impetuosity of the people A. YOUNG. **4.** To b. my purse SCOTT. Hence **Ba·llastage,** toll paid for the privilege of taking ballast. **Ba·llaster**, one who supplies ships with ballast. **Ba·llasting** *vbl. sb.*; *concr.* and *fig.* = BALLAST *sb.*

Ballat, -ry, obs. ff. BALLAD, -RY.

Ballatoo·n. 1828. [Russ.] A Russian lumber-boat.

Balled (bǭld), *ppl. a.* 1591. [f. BALL *v.*[1] and *sb.*[1] + -ER[1], -ER[2].] **a.** Formed into a ball. † **b.** Cleared of lumps; cf. *shelled peas.*

Baller (bǭ·ləɹ). 1668. [f. BALL *v.*[1] and *sb.*[2] + -ER[1].] **1.** One who forms into balls 1865. † **2.** One who goes to balls. PEPYS.

Ballerina (bælərī·nă). 1792. [– It., fem. of *ballerino* dancing-master, f. *ballare* dance; see BALL *sb.*[2], BALE *v*[2]., -INE[1].] A danseuse, esp. one in a leading role.

‖ **Ballet** (ba·le, *rarely* bæ·let). 1667. [– Fr. *ballet* – It. *balletto*, dim. of *ballo* BALL *sb.*[2]] **1.** A theatrical representation, consisting of dancing and pantomime, originally employed to illustrate foreign dress and manners, but now mainly an exhibition of skill in dancing. † **2.** A dance–1829.

1. Not a Balette or Masque, but a play DRYDEN. *Comb.*: **b.-master, -mistress,** one who arranges and directs the dancing of the b.

Ballet (bæ·let), *sb.*[2] 1727. [f. BALL *sb.*[1] + -ET.] *Her.* A little ball.

Ballet, -ette, obs. ff. BALLAD.

Balling (bǭ·liŋ), *vbl. sb.* 1713. [f. BALL *v.* + -ING[1].] **1.** Formation into a ball or balls; occas. *attrib.*, as in *b.-machine* (for winding twine), etc. **2.** The throwing of (snow-) balls 1865.

† **Ba·llised,** *ppl. a.* 1624. [perh. for *pallised* (cf. *palysyd* (XV) = *palisadoed*), after Fr. *palissé* surrounded with pales.] Surrounded with a railing or balustrade. WOTTON.

Ba·llist. *rare.* ME. [– L. *ballista.*] = next.

‖ **Ballista** (băli·stă). Also (less well) **balista.** Pl. **-æ,** occas. **-as.** 1598. [L., f. (ult.) Gr. βάλλειν throw.] An ancient military engine, resembling a bow stretched with cords and thongs, used to hurl stones, etc.; in med.L. also for: Arbalest.

Balli·stic, *a.* 1775. [f. prec. + IC.] Of or pertaining to the throwing of missiles; projectile.

The b. power of our weapons 1879. *Ballistic pendulum*: an instrument for determining the relative velocity of projectiles

Balli·stics, *sb. pl.* 1753. [f. as prec.; see -IC 2.] The science of projectiles.

‖ **Ballium** (bæ·liˌǒm). 1798. [med.L. – OFr. *bail, baille.*] = BAIL *sb.*[3], BAILEY.

Ba·llock. *Obs.* in polite use. [OE. **balluc (bealluc)*, dim. f. Gmc. **ball-* BALL *sb.*[1]] A testicle.

† **Ballon.** *rare.* 1753. [– Fr. † *balon* (mod. *ballot*); see BALE *sb.*[3]] A bale, as of paper.

Balloon (bălū·n), *sb.* 1634. [– Fr. *ballon* or It. *ballone*, augm. of *balla* BALL *sb.*[1]; see -OON.] † **1.** A large inflated leather ball, struck to and fro by the arm protected by a bracer of wood –1801. † **2.** The game played with this –1820. † **3.** *Pyrotechny.* = *shell* or *bomb* –1753. **4.** *Archit.* A globe crowning a pillar, pier, etc. 1656. **5.** *Chem.* A large globose glass vessel, with one or more short necks, used to receive the products of distillation, etc. 1727. **6.** An air-tight envelope of silk, etc., usually globose or pear-shaped, which, when inflated with light gas, rises in the air; *esp.* one with a car attached to carry human beings for purposes of observation, etc. 1783. *fig.* Anything inflated and empty 1812. **7.** *Hort.*: **a.** A method of training fruit trees in which the branches form the shape of a balloon. **b.** A balloon-shaped trellis. **8.** The outline containing words represented in comic papers as issuing from the mouth of any one 1844.

2. That wondrous match at ballon SCOTT. **6.** The hollow b. of popular applause CARLYLE.

Comb.: **b.-brasser** (cf. Fr. *brassart*, the wooden bracer worn by b.-players); **-fish,** one of the Diodontes, so named because they distend their bodies with air.

Hence (besides nonce-words): **Balloo·ner,** an aeronaut; *Naut.* a. b.-like sail. **Balloo·nery, -nry. Balloo·ning** *vbl. sb.* aeronautics. **Balloo·nist,** an aeronaut.

Ballot (bæ·lət), *sb.*[1] 1549. [– It. *ballotta*, dim. of *balla* BALL *sb.*[1]] **1.** A small ball used for secret voting; hence, a ticket, etc., so used. **2.** The method of secret voting; orig. by means of small balls placed in an urn or box; an instance of this; the votes thus recorded 1549. **3.** A method of drawing lots by taking small balls, etc., from a box; hence *gen.* lot drawing 1680.

1. To convey each Man his bean or b. into the Box MILT. **2.** To try the result of a b. MACAULAY. **3.** The b. for the militia WELLINGTON. *Comb.*: **b.-box,** a box used for the balls in a b.; *fig.* secret voting; **-paper,** the voting-paper used in a b. Hence **Ba·llotage,** in France, the second b., to decide between the two candidates that have come nearest to a legal majority. **Ballotee·r,** an advocate of the b. † **Ba·llotin,** an officer in charge of a b.-box. **Ba·llotist,** an advocate of the b.

Ba·llot, *sb.*[2] 1865. [– Fr. *ballot* (cf. BALON), dim. of *balle*; see BALE *sb.*[3], -OT[1].] A small bale, of 70 to 120 lbs.

Ballot (bæ·lət), *v.* 1549. [– It. *ballottare*, f. *ballotta* BALLOT *sb.*[1]] † **1.** *trans.* To vote upon secretly, as by depositing small balls in an urn or box –1691. **2.** *intr.* To give a secret vote (*for, against*) 1580. **3.** To select by the drawing of lots 1785.

2. *To b. for*: to select, elect, or reject, by secret voting. **3.** *To b. for*: to select by lot. To b. for another day for one's resolution 1884. Hence † **Ballota·tion,** voting by ballot. **Ba·lloter.**

† **Ballo·te.** 1551. [– Fr. *ballote* – L. *ballote* – Gr. βαλλωτή.] *Herb.* The Black Stinking Horehound.

‖ **Ballottement** (bălǫ·tmĕnt). 1839. [Fr.] *Med.* A mode of diagnosing pregnancy.

† **Ba·llow,** *sb.* [Only in loc. cit.] = BATON 1. Ice try whither your Costard or my B. be the harder *Lear* IV. vi. 247. Fo. (1623.)

Bally (bæ·li), *a.* and *adv. slang.* 1887. A euphemism for *bloody* (BLOODY A. 8, B. 2), used as a vague intensive of general application.

Ballyhoo (bæ·lihū), orig. *U.S.* 1901. [Said to be orig. the name of a Central Amer. wood, of which some schooners were made that were failures, and hence applied to badly rigged vessels.] A barker's speech; advance publicity; blarney.

Balm (bām), *sb.* [ME. *basme, bame*, later *baume* – OFr. *basme, bame*, later refash. after L. to *bausme, baume* :– L. *balsamum* BALSAM. Further assim. to L. produced *balsme, baulme, balm.* For the mod. pron. cf. *calm, palm, psalm.*] **1.** An aromatic substance, exuding naturally from various trees of the genus *Balsamodendron.* † **2.** An aromatic preparation for embalming the dead –1618. **3.** Fragrant oil or ointment 1447; also *fig.* **4.** Aromatic ointment used for soothing pain or healing wounds (*arch.*) ME. Also *transf.* or *fig.* **5.** A tree yielding balm; one of the genus *Balsamodendron*, N.O. *Amyridaceæ* ME. **6.** Name of some fragrant garden herbs (N.O. *Labiatæ*); esp. Balm Gentle or Balm-mint (*Melissa officinalis*) and Bastard Balm (*Melittis melyssophyllum*). Also Field Balm (*Calamintha nepeta*). 1440.

4. As B. to fester'd wounds MILT. *Sams.* 186. **5.** Let not their precious balms break my head *Ps.* 141:5. *Phrases*: **Balm of Gilead** (also *Balm of Mecca*), a gold-coloured oleo-resin exuded from the tree *Balsamodendron gileadense*, or perh. *B. opobalsamum*, once esteemed as an antiseptic and vulnerary. **b.** *American B. of G.*: a resin obtained from the *Icica carana.* (The Heb. word *tsŏri* (see *Gen.* 37: 25) was identified with *resin* by the Vulg. 'Balm' began with Coverdale.) **Balms of Gilead Fir**: the N. American species yielding Canada Balsam.

Balm (bām), *v. arch.* ME. [app. – prec. sb.] **1.** To embalm (*arch.*). **2.** † To anoint, or mix, with balm, etc. –1600; to smear with something sticky 1530. **3.** To soothe, alleviate (pain, etc.) (*arch.*) ME.

Balm-apple: see *Balsam-apple* in BALSAM *sb.*

Ba·lm-cri:cket. 1783. [Earlier *baum-cricket*, partial tr. of G. *baumgrille*, alt. after *balm.*] The cicada.

The balm-cricket carols clear In the green that folds thy grave TENNYSON. (Taken by Tennyson from Dalzel *Analec. Maj.* II. 187.)

Balmoral (bælmǫ·răl). 1864. [f. *Balmoral* Castle.] Name for: **a.** A variety of Scotch cap. **b.** A kind of figured woollen petticoat. **c.** A kind of boot lacing in front.

Balmy (bā·mi), *a.* 1500. [f. BALM *sb.* + -Y[1]; in sense 7, var. of BARMY.] **1.** Yielding balm 1667. † **2.** Resinous 1782. **3.** Fragrant 1500. **4.** *fig.* Soft and soothing 1604. **5.** Of wind, air, weather, etc. (combining 3 and 4): Deliciously mild, fragrant, and soothing 1704. **6.** Of healing virtue 1746. **7.** *slang.* Soft, weak-minded, idiotic 1851. Also BARMY 1896.

3. B. breath *Oth.* V. ii. 16, firs 1824. **4.** B. slumbers *Oth.* II. ii. 259, sleep YOUNG. **5.** The b. zephyrs POPE. Hence **Ba·lmify** *v.* **Ba·lmily** *adv.* **Ba·lminess.**

Ba·lneal, *a.* 1645. [f. L. *balneum* bath + -AL[1].] Of or pertaining to a (warm) bath or bathing.

Balneary (bæ·lniări). 1646. [– L. *balnearium* (cl. in pl. only) bathing-place, subst. use of *-arius* adj. f. *balneum* bath; see -ARY[1].] A bath or bathing-place; a medicinal spring.

Balnea·tion. ? *Obs.* [– med.L. *balneatio*, f. *balneat-*, pa. ppl. stem of late L. *balneare*; see -ION.] Bathing.

Balneo·graphy. 1879. [f. L. *balneum* bath + -GRAPHY.] A description of, or treatise upon, baths. **Balneo·logy** [see -LOGY], scientific medical study of bathing, etc.; whence **Ba:lneolo·gical** *a.* **Balneothe·rapy** [Gr. θεραπεία], treatment of disease by baths or medicinal springs.

‖ **Balneum** (bæ·lniŏm). 1471. [L.] **1.** A bath or bathing 1652. **2.** *Alch., Chem.*, and *Cookery.* = BAIN MARIE. (Occas. *balneo.*)

† **Balow·, baloo·.** 1611. [app. a nursery word of unkn. origin.] **1.** *int.* An utterance used in lulling to sleep 1724. **2.** *sb.* **a.** A lullaby. **b.** A song and tune containing this word. 1611.

‖ **Balsa** (bæ·lsă). 1778. [Sp., = raft.] A raft or fishing-float, used chiefly on the Pacific coasts of S. America.

Balsam (bǫ·lsăm), *sb.* [OE. *balsam, -zam, -zama* or *-e*, – L. BALSAMUM. In ME. replaced by *basme, baume* from OFr. (see BALM *sb.*), and spec. by the L. form, or It. *balsamo.*] **1.** = BALM *sb.* 1. **2.** An aromatic oily or resinous medicinal preparation, for healing wounds or soothing pain 1579. Also *fig.* † **3.** *transf.* in *Alch.* A healthful preservative essence, oily and softly penetrative, conceived by Paracelsus to exist in all organic bodies –1753. † **4.** = BALM *sb.* 2; *fig.* a preservative –1753. **5.** *Chem.* Compounds, insoluble in water, consisting of resins mixed with volatile oil 1673. **6.** = BALM *sb.* 7. OE. **7.** A flowering plant of the genus *Impatiens*, esp. *I. balsamina*; also *I. noli-tangere* 1741.

1. *True Balsam*, or *B. of Mecca* (the earliest known sort): *Balm of Gilead*, q.v. The discovery of America . . gave also *B. of Acouchi, of Copaiba, of Peru, of Tolu*, and *Canada B.* **2.** Is this the Balsome, that the vsuring Senat Powres into Captaines wounds *Timon* III. v. 10. **4.** Noble Acts are the Balsom of our Memories SIR T. BROWNE.

Comb.: **B. Apple** (or *Balm Apple*): name of species of *Momordica* (*M. balsamina, M. charantia*), gourd-like plants with highly coloured fruits, also called *Apple of Jerusalem*, and Male B. Apple. Also used, improp., of the common garden B. ('Female' B. Apple).

Hence **Balsama·tion,** the process of embalming. **Balsami·ferous** *a.* yielding b. **Ba·lsamy** *a.* balmy.

Balsam (bǫ·lsăm), *v.* 1666. [f. prec. sb.] **1.** To anoint with balsam; to heal, salve. Also *intr.* (for *refl.*). **2.** To embalm (*rare*) 1855.

Balsamic (bǫlsæ·mik, bæl-). 1605. [f. BALSAM *sb.* + -IC; cf. Fr. *balsamique* (XVII).] **A.** *adj.* **1.** Of the nature of, or yielding, balsam 1676. **2.** Balmy 1714. **3.** Soothing, restorative 1605. **4.** Of, pertaining to or full of, BALSAM (sense 3) 1644. **5.** *fig.* Soothing, healing, balmy 1667. **B.** *sb.* = BALM *sb.* 4, BALSAM *sb.* 2. 1713. Hence **Balsa·mical** *a.* **Balsa·mically** *adv.* var. **Ba·lsamous** *a.*

† **Ba·lsamine.** 1578. [– Fr. *balsamine* – med.L. **balsamina*, subst. use of fem. of L. *balsaminus*, f. BALSAMUM; see -INE[1].] Book name for: **a.** *Balsam Apple*; **b.** the plant *Impatiens balsamina.*

‖ **Ba·lsamum.** OE. [L. – Gr. βάλσαμον, perh. of Semitic orig. (cf. Arab. *balasān*). See BALSAM.] **1.** = BALM *sb.* 1. **2.** = BALM *sb.* 2–4. ME. **3.** *Alch.* = BALSAM *sb.* 3. ME. **4.** = BALSAM *sb.* 6. ME. Also *attrib.*

Balter, bolter (bǭ·ltəɹ, bōᵘ·(l)təɹ), *v.* Now *dial.* ME. [Senses 1–2: prob. – ON.; cf. Da. *baltre, boltre* wallow, welter, tumble. Senses 3–4: chiefly midl. dial.; also *boulter* (XVII), mod. *bawter, bolter*; in *Macbeth* IV. i. 123 *blood-bolter'd* matted with blood; perh. frequent. of BALL *v.*] † **1.** To tumble about, *e.g.* in dancing –1500. **2.** *trans.* To tread clumsily (*dial.*). **3.** To mat (the hair) 1693. **4.** *intr.* (for *refl.*) To form tangled knots or clots 1601. Hence **Ba·lter** *sb. dial.* a clot.

Baltimore (bǭ·ltimōᵊɹ). Also **B.-bird, -oriole.** An American bird (*Icterus baltimorii*) of the Starling family; so named because its colours (orange and black) are those of the coat of arms of Lord Baltimore, formerly proprietor of Maryland.

Baluster (bæ·lŏstəɹ). 1602. [– Fr. *balustre*, – It. *balaustro*; so named from It. *balausta, balaustra* 'blossom of the wild pomegranate' (L. *balaustium*, Gr. βαλαύστιον), which a baluster resembles in shape. See BANISTER.] **1.** A short pillar of circular section, slender above and bulging below; usu. one of a series called a *balustrade.* Also, a similar pillar used in a window. **2.** A slender upright post supporting a rail; in *pl.* a railing, a balustrade 1633. **3.** (Usu. in *pl.*) The uprights which support the handrail of a staircase; also, the whole structure. Now usu. BANISTER(S. 1732. **4.** *collect. sing.* A balustrade (*arch.*) 1644. **5.** *Class. Arch.* 'The lateral part of the volute of an Ionic capital' (Gwilt). Hence **Ba·lustered** *ppl. a.* furnished with, or enclosed by, balusters.

Balustrade (bæ:lŏstrēⁱ·d). 1644. [– Fr. *balustrade*, after It. *balaustrata*, Sp. *balaustrada.*] A row of balusters surmounted by a rail or coping. Hence **Ba:lustra·ded** *ppl. a.* **Ba:lustra·ding,** b.-work.

Bam (bæm), *v. slang.* 1707. [abbrev. of contemporary BAMBOOZLE.] To hoax, cozen 1738. Also *absol.* or *intr.* Hence **Bam** *sb.* a hoax or imposition.

‖ **Bambino** (bambī·no). 1761. [It., dim. of *bambo* silly.] A child, a baby; *spec.* an image of the child Jesus in swaddling clothes.

Bambocciade. 1868. [– Fr. *bambochade*, It. *bambocciata* child, simpleton, f. *bamboccio*, f. *bambo* (see prec.); a nickname of the painter Peter de Laer.] A painting of rustic and grotesque scenes.

Bamboo (bæmbū·). 1598. [In early forms *bambus, -os, -ous* (XVI) – Du. *bamboes* (whence G. *bambus*), mod. L. *bambusa*, alt., with unexpl. *b-* and *-s*, of Pg. (– Malay) *mambu* (also in Eng. use XVII–XVIII). *Bamboo* was deduced from *bambos*, which was taken as a pl.] A genus of giant grasses (genus *Bambusa*), common in tropical countries. Also the stem of any of these used as a stick, etc. *Comb.* **b.-coolie,** one that carries loads suspended on bamboos. Hence **Bamboo·** *v.* to beat with a b.

Bamboozle (bæmbū·z'l), *v.* 1703. [Included by Swift in 'Tatler' No. 230 (see quot.); prob. of cant origin; cf. Sc. *bum-*, *bombaze* perplex (XVII) and the contemporary short form BAM (*bamb.*] **1.** To deceive by trickery, hoax, cozen. Also *absol.* or *intr.* **2.** To mystify 1712.

1. Certain Words invented by some pretty Fellows, such as Banter, Bamboozle..some of which are now struggling for the vogue SWIFT *Tatler* No. 230 ¶ 7. Hence **Bamboo·zle** *sb.* bamboozling. **Bamboo·zlement,** mystification. **Bamboo·zler.**

Bambusa; see BAMBOO.

Ban (bæn), *v.* [OE. *bannan* summon; curse, denounce = OFris. *banna*, MLG., MDu. *bannen*, OHG. *bannan*, ON. *banna* :- Gmc. **bannan* proclaim under penalty, f. **ba-*, repr. by Gr. φάναι, L. *fari* speak. See BAN *sb.*[1]] † **I.** To summon by proclamation. (Chiefly, to arms.) –ME.

II. 1. To curse, imprecate damnation upon (*arch.*) ME. Also *intr.* **2.** *trans.* and *absol.* To chide, address with angry language (*dial.*) ME. **3.** To anathematize (*arch.*) ME. **4.** To interdict, proscribe 1816.

1. And some men b. the, & some men blesse 1460. **4.** To whom the goodly earth and air Are bann'd and barr'd BYRON.

Ban (bæn), *sb.*[1] ME. [In earliest uses 'proclamation, summons to arms', partly aphetic of ME. *iban*, OE. *ġebann* (cf. OHG. *ban*, ON. *bann*), partly – OFr. *ban* – Gmc. **bann-* of **bannan* BAN *v.*, whence late L. *bannus, bannum*; in the sense 'proclamation of marriage' only pl. BANNS. The later senses 'anathema, curse', and 'denunciation, prohibition' (XV) are prop. a separate word, f. BAN *v.*] **1.** A summons by public proclamation, chiefly to arms; an edict. ‖ **2. a.** The gathering of the (French) king's vassals for war; the whole muster; orig. = *arrière-ban*. **b.** In France now the *ban* is the younger part of the population liable to serve, the *arrière-ban* the reserve; in Prussia, the first and second *bans* were the two divisions of the Landwehr. ME. ‖ **3.** Sentence of banishment; whence 'to keep', or 'break his b.' 1873. **4.** Proclamation of marriage; always in *pl.*, now spelt BANNS, q.v. **5.** A formal eccl. denunciation; anathema, interdict 1481. Also *fig.* **6.** *gen.* A curse, supposed to have supernatural sanction and power to harm 1602. **7.** The utterance of a curse 1596. **8.** A formal and authoritative prohibition; an interdict 1667. **9.** Sentence of outlawry; *esp.* 'Ban of the (Holy Roman) Empire' 1674. **10.** *fig.* Practical outlawry, denunciation by society or public opinion 1839.

4. Beneath the b. of Pope and Church SCOTT. **6.** With Hecats B., thrice blasted, thrice infected *Haml.* III. ii. 269. **8.** To taste it under banne to touch MILT. *P.L.* IX. 925. **10.** Opinions which are under the b. of society MILL.

‖ **Ban** (bæn), *sb.*[2] 1614. [– Pers. *bān* lord, master, introduced by the Avars who ruled in Slavonic countries subject to Hungary.] The viceroy of certain military districts in Hungary, Slavonia, and Croatia, who takes the command in time of war. Hence, **Banate, Bannat,** the district under the jurisdiction of a b. **Banal** *a.* of or pertaining to a b.; *sb.* a Banate.

Banal (bēⁱ·năl, bæ·-), *a.* 1753. [– (O)Fr. *banal*, f. *ban* BAN *sb.*[1]; see -AL[1].] **1.** Of or belonging to compulsory feudal service. **2.** (From the intermediate sense of, Open to the use of all the community): Commonplace, trivial 1864.

Banality (bănæ·lĭti). 1861. [– Fr. *banalité*; see prec., -ITY.] **1.** Anything trite or trivial; a commonplace **2.** Triteness, triviality 1878.

Banana (bănā·nă). 1597. [– Sp., Pg. *banana*, given as the native name in the Congo.] **1.** A tree (*Musa sapientum*) cultivated largely in tropical countries; it grows to a height of 20 feet 1697. **2.** The fruit of this tree, growing in clusters of angular, finger-like berries containing a highly nutritious pulp 1597. Also *attrib.*

Comb. **b.-bird,** a gregarious West Indian bird (*Xanthornus icterus*).

Banausic (bănǭ·sik), *a. rare.* 1876. [– Gr. βαναυσικός of or for mechanics.] Proper for a mechanic.

Banbury. *a*1535. A town in Oxfordshire, England, once noted for its Puritan zeal, now for its cakes.

‖ **Banc** (bæŋk). 1727. [AFr. = 'bench'; see BANK *sb.*[3]] *Law.* Bench; in phr. *in banc* = in BANCO.

‖ **Banco** (bæ·ŋko), *a.* [It.; = bank.] The bank money of account in certain places, as dist. from (depreciated) *currency*. Retained in calculating exchanges with foreign countries.

‖ **Banco** (bæ·ŋko), *sb.* 1768. [Law L., abl. of *bancus*; see BANK *sb.*[2] and cf. BANC.] In phr. *in banco* = on the bench : used of sittings of a superior Court of Common Law as a full court.

Band (bænd), *sb.*[1] [– ON. *band* = OFris., OS. *band*, OHG. *bant* (Du., G. *band*) :- Gmc. **bandam*, f. base **band-* of **bindan* BIND; superseded OE. *bend* (BEND *sb.*[1]) in the sense 'fetter' and repl. mainly by BOND *sb.*[1] in the fig. sense 'restraint, binding agreement'. Now assoc. with BAND *sb.*[2]] **1.** Anything with which a person is bound; a shackle, chain, fetter, manacle (*arch.*). Also *fig.* **2.** A string or tie with which any loose thing is bound ME.; in *Bookbinding*, one of the cords or straps crossing the back of a book, to which the quires or sheets are attached 1759. **3.** A hinge of a door or gate ME. **4.** A connecting piece by which the parts of a whole are held firmly together ME. **5.** A leading-string, strap, or chain (*lit.* and *fig.*) ME. † **6.** *Logic.* The copula (*rare*) –1628. **7.** An obligation which operates as a tie, restraint, or bond ME. **8.** A uniting force or influence (now BOND) 1483. **9.** An agreement, or promise, binding on him who makes it (now BOND) ME. **10.** Security given; a deed legally executed, binding on him who delivers it (now BOND) 1521. † **11.** A league –1649. † **12.** Binding quality or power –1619. † **13.** A state of union 1631.

1. Euery ones bands were loosed *Acts* 16:26. *fig.* Bunden faste With bandes of syn HAMPOLE. **4.** The bands of life *Rich. II*, II. ii. 71. **7.** To joyne in Hymens bands *A.Y.L.* V. iv. 136. **10.** His word is as good as his b. FULLER.

Band (bænd), *sb.*[2] [– (O)Fr. *bande*, earlier *bende* (cf. BEND *sb.*[2]) = Pr., Sp., It., med.L. *benda* – Gmc. **bendōn* (OHG. *binda*), f. **bendan*, **bindan* BIND *v.* The var. BEND *sb.*[2] – OFr. *bende*, is retained in *Her.*] **1.** A strip of any material flat and thin, used to bind together, clasp, or gird 1483. **2.** *esp.* A flat strip of a flexible substance (*e.g.* leather, india-rubber, etc.), used to bind round an object 1611. **3.** A flat strip or strap used to confine a dress at the waist, etc., or to encircle and confine a hat, cap, or other article of apparel 1552. **4.** *spec.* **a.** The neckband or collar of a shirt, orig. used to make it fit closely round the neck. Hence, a collar or ruff. 1568. Hence, **b.** A pair of strips (now called *bands*) hanging down in front, as part of clerical, legal, or academical dress 1700. **5.** A strip of linen, etc., to swathe the body; a bandage 1568. **6.** *Mech.* A flat strap, belt, etc., passing round two wheels or shafts, by which motion is communicated from the one to the other 1705. † **7.** A side or flitch (of bacon). [The earliest use in Eng., f. OFr. *bande* side.] ME. **8.** Anything having the appearance of a band in sense 1. 1823. **9.** A more or less broad stripe crossing a surface 1470; **b.** (*pl.*) a fault in flannel and serge cloth, when stripes occur across the piece. **10.** *Ent.* A transverse stripe of colour, also called *fascia* 1841. **11.** *Geol.* A stratum with a band-like section 1837.

Comb.: **b.-case** = BANDBOX; **-collar** (cf. 4 above); **-fish,** a fish of the genus *Cepola*; **-pulley,** a flat-faced wheel, fixed on a shaft and driven by a b.; **-saw,** an endless saw, consisting of a steel belt with a serrated edge running over wheels; **-string,** a string for fastening bands (see above, 4); **-wheel,** one to which motion is communicated by a band running over it.

Band (bænd), *sb.*[3] 1490. [– (O)Fr. *bande* = Pr., Sp., It., med.L. *banda*, prob. of Gmc. origin and assoc. w. med.L. *banda* scarf, *bandum* banner (cf. Goth. *bandwa* sign; see BANNER), also company, crowd. The var. *bende* (– OFr. *bende*, see BEND *sb.*[3]) was in regular use from late XV to early XVII.] **1.** An organized company; a troop. **2.** A confederation of persons having a common purpose 1657. **3.** A company of persons or animals in movement 1601. **4.** A company of musicians; now usu. of players upon various wind and percussion instruments; applied also to various sections of an orchestra, as *the string b.*, etc., and sometimes loosely to the entire orchestra 1660.

1. The 'black bands' who still Ravage the frontier BYRON. *Trained* or *train-band*; see TRAIN-BAND. **3.** Hee diuided the..camels two bands *Gen.* 32:7.

Comb: **b.-master,** the leader of a b. of musicians; **-stand,** a structure for the use of a b. of musicians.

Band (bænd), *sb.*[4] 1513. [Origin unkn.] A ridge of a hill; in the Lake district, *esp.* a long narrow sloping offshoot from a higher hill.

Band (bænd), *v.*[1] 1488. [– (O)Fr. *bander*, f. *bande*; see BAND *sb.*[2]] **1.** To bind with a band or bands. † **2.** To furnish or cover with a band or bandage –1855. **3.** To mark with stripes 1853. **4.** To join or form into a company 1530.

4. Certaine of the Iewes banded together *Acts* 23:12. Hence **Ba·nded** *ppl. a.*; *spec.* in *Her.* with a band differing in colour from the garb. **Ba·nder,** a confederate.

† **Band,** *v.*[2] 1580. [Short f. BANDY *v.*] = BANDY *v.*

† **Band(e.** 1420. [var. of *bonde*, ME. form of BOUND *sb.*[1]] = BOUND, limit –1523.

Bandage (bæ·ndėdʒ), *sb.* 1599. [– Fr. *bandage*, f. *bande*; see BAND *sb.*[2], -AGE.] **1.** *Surg.* A strip of woven material used to bind up a wound, sore, etc. **b.** *abstr.* = *Bandaging vbl. sb.* **2.** A strip of flexible material used for binding or covering up, *esp.* the eyes 1715. **3.** A strip of material used to bind together any structure (*arch.*) 1766.

2. Tie the controversy with bandages of argument MAURICE. Hence **Ba·ndage** *v.* to tie or bind up with a b. (*lit.* and *fig.*). **Ba·ndager. Ba·ndaging** *vbl. sb.* the action or art of applying bandages; material for bandages. **Ba·ndagist,** a maker of bandages.

† **Bandalore.** 1790. [Origin unkn.] A toy containing a coiled spring, which caused it, when thrown down, to rise again to the hand –1864.

Bandanna, -ana (bændæ·nă). 1752. [prob. through Pg. *bandana*, f. Hind. (cf. *bāṅdhnū* mode of dyeing in which the cloth is tied in different places to prevent parts of it from receiving the dye.] A coloured silk handkerchief with spots left white or yellow by this process. Now used also of cotton handkerchiefs, in which the pattern is produced by chemical agency. Also *attrib.*

Bandbox (bæ·ndbǫks). 1631. [f. BAND *sb.*[2] + BOX *sb.*[2]] A slight box of cardboard or thin chip, for collars, hats, caps, and millinery; orig. made for the bands or ruffs of the 17th c.

‖ **Bandeau** (bæ̆ndō·). Pl. **-eaux.** 1790. [– Fr. *bandeau*, OFr. *bandel*, dim of *bande*; see BAND *sb.*[2], -EL[2].] **a.** A narrow band or fillet for the hair. **b.** A bandage for the eyes. **c.** A fitting-band inside a woman's hat 1908.

That b...was worn by every woman at court 1790.

† **Ba·ndel, bandle.** 1598. [– OFr. *bandele*, *-elle*, fem. f. *bandel*; see prec.] A swaddling-band –1603. Hence **Ba·ndelet,** a small band, streak, or fillet; in *Archit.* small flat moulding, encircling a column.

‖ **Banderilla** (banderi·lʸă). [Sp., dim. of *bandera* banner.] A little dart, ornamented with a banderole, which bull-fighters stick into the neck and shoulders of the bull. Hence **Ba:nderille·ro,** the bull-fighter who uses banderillas.

Banderol(e, bandrol, bannerol (bæ·ndĕrŏl, -ōᵘl, bæ·nĕrŏl). 1562. [– Fr. *banderole*, earlier *banerolle* – It. *banderuola*, dim. of *bandiera* BANNER.] **1.** A long narrow flag or streamer. **2.** A ribbon-like scroll bearing a device 1622. **4.** *Archit.* A flat band with an inscription. **5.** = BANNEROL.

1. The..lances bore gay bandaroles W. IRVING.

Bandicoot (bæ·ndikūt). 1789. [Corrupt. f. Telugu *pandikokku* 'pig-rat'.] **1.** An Indian rat (*Mus malabaricus* or *giganteus*), as big as a cat, and very destructive. **2.** A genus of insectivorous Australian marsupials (*Parameles*), resembling the above 1831.

Banding (bæ·ndiŋ), *vbl. sb.* 1575. [f. BAND *v.*[1] + -ING[1].] **1.** Combining in parties. **2.** Formation of, or marking with, bands or stripes 1859.

Banding-plane: one used for cutting out grooves and inlaying strings and bands.

Bandit (bæ·ndit). Pl. **bandi·tti** (the more usual), **ba·ndits.** 1593. [– It. *bandito*, pl. *-iti*, subst. use of pa. pple. of *bandire* ban = med.L. *bannire* proclaim, proscribe, BANISH.] *lit.* One who is proscribed or outlawed; *hence*, a lawless desperate marauder. *collect. sing.* A company of bandits 1706. Also *attrib.*

The banditti do you call them?..I am sure we call them plain thieves in England 1602. An adventurer had assembled a banditti WELLINGTON.

Bandle (bæ·nd'l). 1623. [– Ir. *bannlamh* cubit, f. *bann* measure + *lamh* hand, arm.] An Irish measure of two feet in length.

Bandlet (bæ·ndlĕt). 1727. [syncop. f. *Bandelet.*] A small band, fillet, or streak; in *Arch.* = *Bandelet.*

†‖ **Ba·ndo.** 1598. [– It. (and Sp.) *bando.*] A public proclamation –1642.

Bandog (bæ·ndǫg). ME. [f. BAND *sb.*[1] 5 + DOG.] *orig.* A (ferocious) dog tied or chained up; hence, a mastiff, bloodhound. Also *fig.*

To speak b. and Bedlam: i.e. furiously and madly.

Bandoleer, -ier (bændŏlīə·ɹ). 1577. [– Du. *bandelier*, or its source Fr. *bandoulière*, dial. *bandroulière*, prob. f. *banderole* BANDEROL(E; cf. It. *bandoliera*, Sp. *-era.*] † **1.** A broad belt, worn over the shoulder and across the breast, by which a wallet might be suspended –1767. **2.** *esp.* A belt of this kind worn by soldiers; *orig.* to support the musket, and carry cases containing charges for it; *later*, a shoulder-belt for cartridges 1596. **3.** By transference: in sing. One of the cases; hence used in *pl.* as = prec.

Bandoline (bæ·ndŏlin). 1856. [– Fr. *bandoline*, f. BANDEAU + L. *linere* bedaub, anoint.] A gummy preparation for fixing the hair.

† **Ba·ndon, -oun,** *sb.* ME. [– OFr. *bandon* jurisdiction, control :– Rom. *bando, -ōn-, f. *bandum, var. of med.L. *bannum* BAN *sb.*[1]; see ABANDON *adv.*] Jurisdiction, dominion, control –1611.

† **Ba·ndon,** *v.* ME. Aphet. f. ABANDON *v.*

Bandore[1] (bĕndōə·ɹ, bæ·-). 1566. [Also *bandora* XVI–XVII. Immed. origin doubtful; the nearest forms are Du. *bandoor*, Sp. *bandurria*, It. *pandora*, *-ura* – late L. *pandurium* – Gr. πανδοῦρα PANDORA. See BANJO.] A guitar- or lute-like instrument, used as a bass to the cithern. Cf. PANDORA[2], PANDORE.

† **Bando·re**[2]. 1712. [Corruption of Fr. *bandeau.*] A widow's head-dress –1719.

Bandsman (bæ·ndzmæ̆n). 1842. **a.** A member of a (musical) band. **b.** *Mining.* A man having to do with the band or flat rope by which coal, etc., is hoisted 1852.

Ba·ndster. 1794. [f. BAND *sb.*[1] + -STER; cf. *maltster.*] One who binds sheaves.

‖ **Bandu·rria.** [Sp.] = BANDORE[1]. LONGF.

Bandy (bæ·ndi), *v.* 1577. [poss. – Fr. *bander* 'to bandie at Tennis', 'to bandy or oppose himself against' (Cotgrave), corr. to It. *bandare* 'to side or bandy' (Florio), and Sp. *bandear* 'to bandy, follow a faction, .. to become factious' (Minsheu), perh. f. *bande*, *banda* side (see BAND *sb.*[3]). If the immediate source is Fr., the extension of the stem by means of *-y* may be paralleled in *occupy*, Fr. *occuper.*] **1.** To throw or strike to and fro, as balls in tennis, etc. (Usu. *fig.*) Also *absol.* † **2.** To toss aside or away –1667. **3.** To toss from side to side 1596. **4.** To toss about 1600; to discuss from mouth to mouth 1642. **5.** To give and take; to exchange 1589. † **6.** To band together, league. *trans.* and *intr.* –1818. **7.** *intr.* To contend 1588.

1. Kingdoms..be no balles for me to bandie HOLINSHED. **4.** Bandied about thus from pillar to post BARHAM. **5.** Phr. *To b. words*: to argue pertinaciously. Do you b. lookes with me *Lear* I. iv. 92. **7.** That Law may b. with nature..was an error MILT.

Bandy (bæ·ndi), *sb.*[1] 1578. [Obscurely rel. to prec.] † **1.** A way of playing tennis, no longer known –1607. † **2.** A stroke with a racket, a ball so struck; a return at tennis –1655. **3.** = HOCKEY. 1693. **4.** A club curved at its lower end, used in this game 1629. var. (sense 3), **Bandy-ball.**

Bandy (bæ·ndi), *sb.*[2] 1761. [– Telugu *baṇḍi*, Tamil *vaṇḍi.*] A carriage, buggy, or cart, used in India.

Bandy (bæ·ndi), *a.* 1552. [See the senses.] **1.** Of legs: Curved laterally with the concavity inward. [perh. attrib. use of BANDY *sb.*[1] 4.] Also short for *bandy-legged.* 1687. **2.** Marked with bands; cf. BAND *sb.*[2] 9 b. 1552. **3.** Full of bands [f. BAND *sb.*[3] 4.] Hence **Ba·ndiness. Ba·ndy-legged** *a.* (both from sense 1).

Bane (bēⁱn), *sb.* [OE. *bana* = OFris. *bona*, OS., OHG. *bano*, ON. *bani* :– Gmc. *banon; cf. Goth. *banja*, ON., OE. *ben* :– *banjō; ulterior connections uncertain.] † **1.** A slayer or murderer –1691. **2.** That which destroys life; *esp.* poison. (Now only *fig.*, referred to 4; and in *comb.*, as HENBANE, etc.) ME. † **3.** Murder, death, destruction –1655. **4.** that which causes ruin or woe; the curse. (Now the usual sense.) 1577. **5.** Ruin, harm, woe. Chiefly *poet.* ME. **6.** The rot in sheep 1859.

1. Let Rome herselfe be b. vnto herselfe *Tit. A.* v. iii. 73. **2.** B. and antidote ADDISON. **4.** Theoretic plans..the b. of France BURKE.

Bane, *v. arch.* 1578. [f. BANE *sb.*] † **1.** To kill: said *esp.* of poison –1596. **2.** To harm, hurt, poison 1587.

2. For what shall heal, when holy water banes KEBLE.

Baneberry (bēⁱ·nberi). 1755. [f. BANE *sb.* + BERRY *sb.*[1]] A plant, *Actæa spicata* (N.O. *Ranunculaceæ*); also, its fruit.

Baneful (bēⁱ·nfŭl), *a.* 1579. [f. BANE *sb.* + -FUL.] **1.** Life-destroying; poisonous 1593. **2.** Pernicious 1579.

1. The old serpent's b. breath 1593. **2.** B superstition 1832. Hence **Ba·neful-ly** *adv.*, **-ness.**

Banewort (bēⁱ·nwɒɹt). 1578. [f. BANE *sb.* + WORT.] Any poisonous plant (*dial.*); *spec.* the Lesser Spearwort (*Ranunculus flammula*), reputed to poison sheep; also, the Deadly Nightshade.

Bang (bæŋ), *v.*[1] 1550. [imit.; perh. immed. – Scand. (cf. ON. *bang* hammering, *banga* hammer); LG. has *bangen*, *bangeln* beat.] **1.** To strike violently with a resounding blow; to thump, thrash. **2.** *intr.* To strike violently or noisily; to bump or thump. Of a door To slam. 1713. **3.** Hence: To make a violent noise 1840. **4.** To knock about; to drub, defeat. *lit.* and *fig.* 1604. **b.** *Comm.* To beat down 1884. **5.** *colloq.* To outdo 1808. **6.** Used advb. *esp.* with *come*, *go*, in the senses of: **a.** with a violent blow; **b.** with a sudden clap; **c.** all of a sudden (Fr. *tout d'un coup*).

1. An..anvil bang'd With hammers TENNYSON. *To b. off* (a gun, a tune, etc.), *To b.* (a door). **4.** To b. the market by heavy sales 1884. **5.** This bangs Bannagher *Irish Provb.* Hence **Ba·nger,** he who or that which bangs; *slang*, an astounding lie. **Ba·nging** *vbl. sb.* and *ppl. a.*; *fig.* (*colloq.*) 'thumping'.

Bang, *v.*[2] 1882. [f. BANG *sb.*[2]] To cut (the front hair) square across.

Their hair banged low over their foreheads (*mod.*).

Bang (bæŋ), *sb.*[1] 1550. [f. BANG *v.*[1]] **1.** A heavy resounding blow. **2.** A sudden violent or explosive noise 1855. **3.** Impetus, go 1774.

2. The steps..were let down with a b. THACKERAY.

Bang (bæŋ), *sb.*[2] 1880. [Hair cut 'bang' off; cf. BANG-TAIL.] The front hair cut square across the forehead. (Orig. in U.S.)

Bang, *sb.*[3], obs. f. BHANG.

Ba·ngle, *v.* Now *dial.* 1567. [Origin unkn.] **1.** Orig. of hawks: To beat about in the air, instead of making direct for the quarry. **2.** *intr.* To flap, hang loosely 1622.

1. *To bangle (away)*: to fritter away. **2. Bangled** (also **bangle**) **ear,** one hanging loosely, like a spaniel's.

Bangle (bæ·ŋg'l). 1787. [– Hind. *bangrī*, *bangrī*, orig. coloured glass bracelet.] A ring-bracelet or anklet. Hence **Ba·ngled** *ppl. a.* wearing bangles.

† **Ba·ngster.** Now *dial.* 1570. [f. BANG *v.* + -STER.] A bully; a winner –1824.

Ba·ng-tai·l. 1870. [f. BANG *v.*[2] + TAIL *sb.*[1] Cf. *dock-tailed.*] A (horse's) tail cut horizontally across; hence **Bang-tailed** *ppl. a.*

Ba·ng-up, *adj. slang.* Also **banged-up.** 1812. [Cf. BANG *v.*[1] 6 c; so *slap-up.*] Quite up to the mark.

Banian (bæ·niăn). 1599. [– Pg. *banian* – Gujarati *vāṇiyo* (pl. *vāṇiyān*) man of the trading caste :– Skr. *vāṇija* merchant.] **1.** A Hindu (*esp.* Gujarati) trader. **2.** In Bengal: A native broker attached to a firm or the like: now called *sircar* 1687. **3.** A loose gown, jacket, or shirt of flannel. (Orig. *attrib.* from sense 1.) 1725. **4. Banian-** or **Banyan-tree,** now often **Banyan**: the Indian Fig Tree (*Ficus religiosa* or *indica*), the branches of which drop shoots to the ground, that take root and support their parent branches; thus, one tree will often cover much ground. [The appellation was orig. given by Europeans to an individual tree of this species growing near Gombroon on the Persian Gulf, under which the Banian settlers had built a pagoda.]

1. The religion of the Banians not permitting them to eat any thing that hath had life 1676. *Comb.* **b.-day** (*Naut.*), one on which no meat is served out (see prec. quot.).

Banish (bæ·niʃ), *v.* ME. [– OFr. *baniss-*, lengthened stem (see -ISH[2]) of *banir* (mod. *bannir*) :– Rom. *bannire – Gmc. *bannjan, f. *bann- BAN *sb.*[1]] † **1.** *orig.* To proclaim as an outlaw. **2.** To condemn by public edict or sentence to leave the country; to exile ME. **3.** *gen.* To send or drive away, expel, dismiss 1450. † **4.** To empty. Cf. AVOID *v.* –1573.

1. Sycorax..from Argier..was banish'd *Temp.* I. ii. 266. **3.** To die, is to be banisht from my selfe *Two Gent.* III. i. 171. B. squint suspicion MILT. *Comus* 413. Hence **Ba·nisher,** he who or that which banishes.

Banishment (bæ·niʃmĕnt). 1507. [f. prec. + -MENT.] **1.** The action of banishing; a state of exile. **2.** *gen.* Enforced absence; dismissal 1535.

1. The B. of that worthy Coriolanus *Cor.* IV. iii. 22.

Banister (bæ·nistəɹ). Also **bannister.** 1667. [Later form of † *barrister* (XVII), alt. of BALUSTER, partly by assoc. w. BAR *sb.*[1]] = BALUSTER 3. Also as *collect. sing.*

He comes down stairs..thumping the banisters all the way SHERIDAN.

Banjo (bæ·ndʒo). Also **banjore, banjer.** 1790. [– Negro slave pronunc. *banjō·*, *banjo·re* of BANDORE[1].] A stringed musical instrument, played with the fingers, having a head and neck like a guitar, and a body like a tambourine. **Ba·njoist,** one who plays a b.

Banjulele (bændʒŭlēⁱ·li). 1925. [f. prec., after UKULELE.] A stringed musical instrument of a type between a banjo and a ukulele.

Bank (bæŋk), *sb.*[1] ME. [– ON. *banki (OIcel. *bakki*, ridge, bank; ODa. *banke*; Sw. *backe*, Da. *bakke* hillock, ascent), :– Gmc. *baŋkon, rel. to *baŋkiz BENCH.] **1.** A raised shelf or ridge of ground. **2.** A high ground, fell. Still *dial.* ME. **b.** *Hence*, A hillside, a brae; a 'hanger' ME. † **3.** An earthwork, an embankment –1611. **4.** A shelving elevation in the sea or the bed of a river. Also, a bed of oysters or the like. 1605. **5.** A long flat-topped mass: *e.g.* of cloud, snow, etc. 1626. **6.** *Mining.* **a.** 'The face of the coal at which miners are working' 1862. **b.** 'An ore-deposit or coal-bed worked by drifts above water-level' 1881. **7.** The sloping margin of a river or stream; the ground bordering upon a river ME. Also *fig.* † **8.** The sea-coast or shore –1592. **9.** A raised edge of a pond, lake, etc.; also *Mining*, the ground at the pit-mouth. ME. **10.** Lateral inclination when rounding a curve. Cf. BANK *v.*[1] 7. 1913.

1. I know a banke where the wilde time blowes *Mids.N.* II. i. 249. **4.** But here, vpon this Banke and Schoole of time Wee'ld iumpe the life to come *Macb.* I. vii. 7. **5.** A b. of clouds BACON, of mist R. DANA, of fog 1848. **7.** Tyber trembled vnderneath her bankes *Jul. C.* I. i. 50. **8.** From Englands banke Droue backe againe 2 *Hen. VI*, III. ii. 83.

Comb.: **Bank cress** (*Herb.*), the Hedge-mustard (*Sisymbrium officinale*); **b.-engine,** the engine at a pit's mouth; **-fish,** cod from Newfoundland Bank, whence *-fishing, -fishery*; **-hook,** a large fishing-hook attached by a line to the b. of a stream; **-jug,** the Willow Warbler, or Willow Wren; **-manager,** the superintendent at a pit's mouth; **-martin, -swallow,** the Sand-martin; **-smack,** a Newfoundland fishing-smack.

Bank (bæŋk), *sb.*[2] ME. [– (O)Fr. *banc* bench, (= Pr. *banc*, Sp., It. *banco*), Rom. deriv. of Gmc. **baŋk-* BANK *sb.*[1], BENCH.] † **1.** A long seat for several, a bench; a platform. (Cf. *mountebank.*) –1680. † **2.** A seat of justice; = BENCH. Cf. BANCO *sb.* –1768. **3.** The bench occupied by rowers of each oar in a galley 1599. **4.** *catachr.* A rank of oars 1614. **5.** *Printing.* The table on which the sheets are laid 1565.

2. *Bank-royal*: King's Bench. *Common Bank*: Common Pleas.

Bank (bæŋk), *sb.*[3] 1474. [– Fr. *banque*, or its source It. *banca*, also *banco* :– med.L. *bancus, banca* – Gmc. **baŋk-*; cf. BANK *sb.*[1], [2].] **1.** The table of a dealer in money. Now *Hist.* 1567. † **2.** The place of business of a money-dealer –1649. † **3.** A sum of money, an amount (It. *monte*) –1758. **4.** In games of hazard, the amount which the banker has before him 1720. † **5.** A joint stock or capital –1790. † **6.** A capital so contributed for lending to the poor; a loan-bank; whence the pawnbroker's establishment (Fr. *mont-de-piété*) –1633. **7.** In modern use: An establishment for the custody of money received from, or on behalf of, its customers. Its essential duty is to pay their drafts on it; its profits arise from the use of the money left unemployed by them. *fig.* 1642.

Banks (in England) are—**a.** *Private Banks*, carried on by one or not more than ten persons in partnership. Cf. sense 2. **b.** *Joint-Stock Banks*, of which the capital is subscribed by many shareholders. Cf. sense 5. Of these the greatest is.. **c.** *The Bank of England*, shortly 'The Bank', which manages the service of the public debt, receives and accounts for the revenue when collected, and issues legal tender notes to an amount automatically regulated. Its banking business does not differ from that of other banks.

4. He had seen his friend..break the b. three nights running THACKERAY. **5.** No Banke or Common Stocke, but euery Man..Master of his owne Money BACON. **7.** I defined a b. to be an institution for the transfer of debts B. PRICE. † *In bank*: at one's banker's: *fig.* in store.

Comb.: **B. annuities,** a techn. term for certain British government funds; usu. 'consols'; **b.-cheque,** an order to pay issued on a b.; **-court,** the weekly meeting of the Governor and Directors of a joint-stock b.; *also*, the general court of proprietors; **-credit,** a credit opened for any person at a bank, so that he can draw for the amount; **-money** (cf. BANCO *a.*); *also*, money in the b.; **-paper,** bank-notes in circulation; bills of exchange accepted by a banker; **-post,** a kind of writing-paper used in foreign correspondence; **-rate,** the rate per cent. per annum at which the Bank of England will discount bills of exchange having not more than 95 days to run; **-stock,** the capital stock of the Bank of England, orig. £1,200,000. **B. of deposit,** one that receives lodgements of money. **B. of issue** or **circulation,** one which issues its own notes or promises to pay. **Savings-b.,** one to take charge of the savings of the poor, or of small sums of money.

Bank (bæŋk), *v.*[1] 1590. [f. BANK *sb.*[1]] **1.** To border, edge, hem in as a bank; † *intr.* to border *upon* 1598. **2.** To confine within a bank. Also *fig.* 1622. **3.** *Watch-making*: **a.** To confine the movement of the escapement. **b.** *intr.* To impinge against the banking-pins. † **4.** To coast. SHAKS. **5.** *trans.* To pile *up* 1833; *intr.* (for *refl.*) to rise *up* into banks 1870. **6.** To cover up (a fire) with fresh fuel, so as to make it burn slowly 1860. **7.** *trans.* To incline (an aeroplane or car) laterally in rounding a curve. Also *intr.* 1911.

Bank, *v.*[2] 1727. [f. BANK *sb.*[3]] **1.** *intr.* To keep a bank. **2.** *intr.* To keep an account with a banker 1833. **3.** *trans.* To deposit in a bank. Also, to convert into current money. 1864. **4.** *intr.* To form a bank at a gaming-table 1826.

3. If Parliament were to b. this whole estate 1868. **4. b.** To counter or rely *upon* 1883. Hence **Ba·nkable** *a.* receivable at a bank, as 'bankable securities'.

Bank-bill. 1696. [f. BANK *sb.*[3] + BILL *sb.*[3]] **a.** In U.S., and formerly in England, a BANK-NOTE. **b.** A bill drawn by one bank on another; a *banker's draft.* **c.** *Bank Post Bill*: a bill, usu. at seven days' sight, issued by the Bank of England for transmission by post.

Bank-book. 1714. [f. BANK *sb.*[3] + BOOK.] A book furnished by a banker to each customer, containing a transcript of his account; a *Pass-book.* (Also called *Banker's book.*)

† **Ba·nker**[1]. ME. [– AFr. **banker*, **banquer* = ONFr. *bankier, banquier*, f. *banc* (BANK *sb.*[2]); see -ER[2] 2.] A covering for a bench or chair –1660.

Banker[2] (bæŋkəɹ). 1534. [– (O)Fr. *banquier* (cf. It. *banchiere*, Anglo-L. *bancarius*), f. *banque*; see BANK *sb.*[3], -ER[2] 2.] **1.** One who keeps or manages a BANK *sb.*[3]; in *pl.* a joint-stock banking company. **2.** One who keeps the bank in a gambling-house; the dealer, in some games of chance 1826. **3.** A gambling game of cards 1891.

1. *Bankers' Books*, Books of Account, etc., extracts from which are evidence in a British Court of Law. Hence **Ba·nkerdom,** the banking interest. **Ba·nkeress,** a female b.; a banker's wife.

Banker[3] (bæ·ŋkəɹ). 1666. [f. BANK *sb.*[1] + -ER[1].] **1.** A ship employed in cod-fishing on the Bank of Newfoundland. (Cf. Fr. *banquier.*) **2.** A labourer who makes banks of earth, ditches, etc. 1795. **3.** *Hunting.* A horse which can jump on and off banks too wide to be cleared. (Cf. *fencer.*) **4.** (*Australia*). A river full to the brim 1888.

Ba·nker[4]. 1677. [f. BANK *sb.*[2]; in senses a, b, perh. a perversion of It. *banco* (a statuary's) bench.] **a.** A wooden bench for dressing bricks. **b.** A stone bench used by masons. **c.** (*Local.*) A pile of Purbeck stone from the quarry.

Banket (bæ·ŋkėt). 1886. [– Du. *banket* sweetmeats, etc., – (O)Fr. *banquet*; see BANQUET.] *South African Mining.* (See quot.) Also *attrib.*, as *b.-reef*, etc.

What is known as the *Main Reef Series* comprises half-a-dozen parallel beds of conglomerate —locally called 'Banket' from its resemblance to the sweetmeat known in English as 'almond-rock' T. REUNERT.

Ba·nk-full, *a.* 1581. [f. BANK *sb.*[1]] Full to the bank.

Bank ho·liday. 1871. [see BANK *sb.*[3] + HOLIDAY.] A day on which banks are legally closed. (Bills payable on these days are paid next day.)

Banking (bæ·ŋkiŋ), *vbl. sb.* 1735. [f. BANK in various senses + -ING[1].] **1.** The business of a banker. Also *attrib.* **2.** The construction of banks 1753. **3.** Embankment 1853. **4.** Fishing on the Newfoundland (or other) Bank 1842. **5.** In *Watchmaking*: Limitation of the motion of the balance, by the *banking-pins* or *screw* 1870. **6.** *B.-ground* (in U.S.): a place where logs are brought to a river bank 1880.

Ba·nking-house. 1809. A mercantile firm engaged in banking.

Bank-note. 1695. [See BANK *sb.*[3] and NOTE *sb.*[2]] A promissory note given by a banker: *formerly*, one payable at a fixed date and to a specified person; *now*, one payable to bearer on demand, and circulating as money.

Bankrupt (bæ·ŋkrɒpt), *sb.* 1533. [In XVI *banke rota* – It. *banca rotta* lit. 'bench or table broken'. Later infl. by Fr. *banqueroute*, and further by L. *ruptus* broken. The transference to the agent (in sense 2) is Eng. only.] † **1.** = BANKRUPTCY. Chiefly in the phrase 'to make b.' (Fr. *faire banqueroute*). –1712. **2.** Any person, whose effects, on his becoming insolvent, are administered and distributed for the benefit of all his creditors, under the Bankruptcy Laws. **b.** *pop.* One who is unable to meet his liabilities, whether he is in the Bankruptcy Court or not 1580. **3.** *transf.* One without resources 1586.

Formerly only a trader could be made a *bankrupt*; other persons became *insolvent.* The distinction was abolished in 1869.

2. † *To play the bankrupt*: to become insolvent; *often*, to play false with the money of others, and *fig.* to prove false to a trust. These modern languages will, at one time or other, play the b. with books BACON. Hence † **Ba·nkruptly** *adv.*

Ba·nkrupt, *v.* 1552. [app. f. the sb. (in sense 1). Not in It. or Fr.] † **1.** To fail; = the early phr. 'to make bankrupt. See BANKRUPT *sb.* 1. –1689. **2.** *trans.* To make (any one) bankrupt 1616. † **3.** To beggar, exhaust the resources of (*lit.* and *fig.*) –1748.

3. Make rich the ribs, but bankerout the wits SHAKS.

Ba·nkrupt, *a.* 1566. [conn. w. the sb. in sense 2; in Eng. only.] **1.** Under legal process because of insolvency; insolvent 1570. **2.** *fig.* † Discredited –1612; at the end of one's resources 1589; stript bare *of*, or now wanting *in* (a property or quality) 1589.

2. To be out of fashion, is to bee banquerupt 1601. I shall make your wit b. *Two Gent.* II. iv. 42. B. of intelligence 1651.

Bankruptcy (bæ·ŋkrɒ̆ᵗpsi). 1700. [f. BANKRUPT + -CY, with *-t* retained. Successively termed *bankrupting, bankruptism, bankrupture, bankruptship*, and finally *bankruptcy.*] **1.** The state of being, or fact of becoming, bankrupt. Also *attrib.* **2.** *fig.* Utter wreck, or loss of (a quality) 1761.

2. A general b. of reputation BURKE.

‖ **Ba·nkshall.** 1673. [prob. Bengali *bankaśālā* 'hall of trade'.] **a.** A warehouse. **b.** The office of a harbour master, or port authority.

Banksia (bæ·ŋksiă). 1803. [f. name of Sir Joseph *Banks*; see -IA[1].] An Australian genus of shrubs with dense spikes of flowers.

Ba·nk-si·de. 1596. [f. BANK *sb.*[1]] **1.** The sloping side of a bank. **2.** The margin of † sea, lake, or river 1618.

Ba·nksman. 1598. [f. BANK *sb.*[1]] An over-looker above ground at a coal mine.

Ba·nky, *a.* Now *dial.* 1601. [f. as prec. + -Y[1].] Full of banks; of or pertaining to, or inclined like, a bank; hilly.

Banner (bæ·nəɹ), *sb.* [ME. *baner(e* – AFr. *banere*, OFr. *baniere* (mod. *bannière*) for **bandiere* :– Rom. **bandaria*, f. med.L. *bandum* standard, f. Gmc. base repr. in Goth. *bandwa, bandwo* sign. See BAND *sb.*[3]] **1.** *prop.* A piece of stout taffeta or other cloth, attached by one side to the upper part of a staff, and used as a standard. (Chiefly *Hist.*) Also *fig.* **2.** An ensign or flag bearing some device, carried in a procession. (Sometimes restricted to an ensign other than an ordinary flag.) ME. Also *fig.* **3.** *transf.* The company ranged under a banner. Now *Hist.* ME. † **4.** = BANDEROLE 2. *Hen. V*, IV. ii. 60. **5.** *Bot.* The vexillum of a papilionaceous flower 1794.

1. Terrible as an armie with banners *S. of S.* 6:4. Our glorious *semper eadem*, the b. of our pride MACAULAY. The star-spangled b. KEY. **2.** A b. with the strange device, Excelsior LONGF.

Comb.: **b.-cry,** a cry summoning men to join a b., a slogan; **-screen,** a fire-screen hung by its upper edge.

Banner (bæ·nəɹ), *v.* 1667. [f. BANNER *sb.*] To furnish, or decorate, with banners.

A Bannered Host, Under spread ensigns marching MILT. *P.L.* II. 885. Hence **Ba·nnered** *ppl. a.* furnished with, or blazoned on, a banner.

Ba·nnerer. Now *Hist.* ME. [– AFr. *banerer* = OFr. *-ier*, f. *banere* BANNER; see -ER[2] 2.] **1.** A standard-bearer. **2.** = BANNERET 1484.

Banneret (bæ·nĕrėt). [ME. *baneret* – OFr. *baneret* (mod. *banneret*) f. *baniere* BANNER + *-et* :– L. *-atus* -ATE[1].] **1. a.** Orig., a knight able and entitled to bring vassals into the field under his own banner; commonly used as a title of rank. (This sense was mainly Fr.) **b.** Subseq., a title and rank conferred for deeds done in the king's presence on the field of battle; thus, a rank and order of knighthood 1548. Hence *knight-banneret*, opp. to *knight-bachelor* 1475. **2.** An official in Swiss cantons and Italian republics 1689. **3.** Confused with BANNERER 1494.

1. b. Sir Ralph Sadleir..the last Knyht B. of England 1635.

Bannerette (bæ:nĕre·t). Also **banneret.** ME. [– OFr. *banerete*, dim. of *baniere* banner; see -ETTE.] A small banner.

Ba·nnerman. *Sc. arch.* 1500. [f. BANNER *sb.*] A standard-bearer.

Bannerol (bæ·nĕrōᵘl, -ǒl). 1548. Var. of BANDEROLE; *esp.* A banner borne at the funerals of great men, and placed over the tomb.

† **Banni·tion.** 1644. [– med.L. *bannitio*, f. *bannire*; see BANISH, -TION.] Banishment, expulsion –1758.

Bannock (bæ·nək). [OE. *bannuc* (once); perh. orig. – OBrit. word repr. by Bret. *bannach, banne* drop, bit, Cornish *banna* drop.] In Scotland and north of England, a large cake, usually of barley- or pease-meal, round or oval in form, and flattish, but thicker than 'scone' or oat-cake.

Comb. **b.-fluke** (also *bannet-*), *Sc.* the turbot.

Banns (bænz), *sb. pl.* ME. [In XIV *bane*, pl. *banes*, later *baines*, from XVI *bann(e)s*. Pl. of BAN *sb.*¹, after med.L. pl. *banna.*] **1.** Public notice given in church of an intended marriage, in order that those who know of any impediment thereto may lodge objections 1440. † **2.** Proclamation or prologue of a play –1609.

1. Our bans thrice bid GAY. Phrases. *To † bid, ask, publish, put up the b. To forbid the b.*: to make a formal objection to the intended marriage. Also *fig.*

Banquet (bæ·ŋkwět), *sb.* 1483. [– (O)Fr. *banquet* (whence also G., Du. *banket*), dim. of *banc* bench (BANK *sb.*²), corresp. to It. *banchet-, to* dim. of *banco.*] A sumptuous entertainment of food and drink; now usu. a ceremonial or state feast, followed by speeches. Also *transf.* and *fig.* 1495. † **2.** A slight repast between meals. Occas. called *running b.* –1657. **3.** A course of sweetmeats, fruit, and wine; a dessert. *Obs.* in gen. use. 1523. † *collect.* Sweetmeats –1700. † **4.** A wine-drinking carousal –1719. See also BANQUETTE.

1. The Lord Mayor..gave a b. to her Majesty's Judges 1885. **2.** Besides the running B. of two Beadles [*i.e.* a whipping] *Hen. VIII*, v. iv. 69.

Banquet (bæ·ŋkwět), *v.* 1514. [– Fr. *banqueter*, f. as prec.] **1.** *trans.* To entertain at a banquet 1538. **2.** *intr.* To take part in a banquet; to carouse; also *fig.* 1514. **3.** To take a BANQUET (senses 2, 3) 1564.

2. Born but to b., and to drain the bowl POPE. The minde shall b., though the body pine *L.L.L.* I. i. 25.

Banqueteer. 1821. [f. as next + -EER.] = BANQUETER 2.

Banqueter (bæ·ŋkwětəɹ). 1542. [f. BANQUET *v.* + -ER¹.] † **1.** The giver of a banquet –1637. **2.** A guest at a banquet 1549.

‖ **Banquette** (baŋke·t). 1629. [– Fr. *banquette* – It. *banchetta*, dim. of *banca* bench, shelf.] **1.** A raised way running along the inside of a parapet, or bottom of a trench, on which soldiers stand to fire at the enemy. **2.** A raised footway or side-walk 1842. **3.** The long low bench behind the driver in a French 'diligence' 1859.

Banshee (bæ·nʃī). 1771. [– Ir. *bean sidhe*, OIr. *ben síe*, i.e. *ben* woman, *side* fairies.] A supernatural being supposed by the Scotch and Irish peasantry to wail under the windows of a house where one of the inmates is about to die.

Banstickle (bæ·nstik'l). 1450. [prob. f. OE. *bān* bone + *sticels* sting.] The Three-spined Stickleback.

Bant, *v.*; see BANTING.

Bantam (bæ·ntăm). 1749. [app. f. name of a district (*Băntăn*) of n.w. Java, but the fowls are not native there.] A small variety of the domestic fowl; the cocks are spirited fighters; also *fig.* in reference to size or 'cockiness' 1782.

B. battalion, a battalion of men of less than standard height. *B.-weight*, a boxer weighing not more than 8 st. 6 lb.

Banter (bæ·ntəɹ), *sb.* 1690. [Of unkn. etym. Treated as slang in 1688.] **1.** Wanton or humorous ridicule; *now usually*, good-natured raillery, pleasantry 1702. **2.** A jest (*arch.*) 1700.

1. I have done my utmost for some years past to stop the progress of *Mobb* and *Banter* SWIFT.

Banter (bæ·ntəɹ), *v.* 1676. [See prec.] **1.** To make fun of; to ridicule; to rally, chaff. Now usually of good-humoured raillery. **2.** To impose upon, orig. in jest; to cheat, bamboozle (*arch.*) 1688. **3.** *absol.* or *intr.* (in prec. senses) 1688.

1. B. him, b. him, Toby. 'Tis a conceited old Scarab D'URFEY. Hence **Ba·nterer. Ba·nteringly** *adv.*

Banting (bæ·ntiŋ). 1864. Name of a London cabinet-maker, given to his method of reducing obesity by avoiding fat, starch, and sugar in food. Hence **Ba·ntingism, Ba·ntingize** *v.*, and, by back-formation, **Bant** *v.*

Bantling (bæ·ntliŋ). 1593. [perh. corruptly – G. *bänkling* bastard (f. *bank* bench, BANK *sb.*²); cf. BASTARD; see -LING¹.] A young or small child, a brat. (Formerly = *bastard*). Also *fig.*

Lo their precious Roman b., lo the colony Camulodune TENNYSON.

Banxring (bæ·ŋksriŋ). 1824. [– Javanese *bangsring.*] A squirrel-like insectivore.

Banyan, the prevailing spelling of BANIAN 4.

‖ **Banzai** (bænzəi·). 1904. [Jap., '10,000 years'.] A cheer used in greeting the emperor, etc.

Baobab (bēⁱ·o,bæb). 1640. [acc. to Prosper Alpinus (1592) an Ethiopian tree; prob. the name is from some dialect of Central Africa.] A tree (*Adansonia digitata*), with an enormously thick stem, found throughout tropical Africa, and long naturalized in India. Called also Monkey-bread, and Ethiopian Sour Gourd. The fibres of the bark are used for ropes and cloth.

Baphomet (bæ·fomet). 1818. [– Fr. *baphomet* – med.L. *baphomet* for *Mahomet.*] **a.** A medieval form of Mahomet. **b.** Alleged name of the idol which the Templars were accused of worshipping. Hence **Baphome·tic** *a.*

Baptism (bæ·ptiz'm). [ME. *baptem(e)* – OFr. *ba(p)teme, -esme* (now *baptême*), semi-pop. – eccl.L. *baptismus, -um* (also *baptisma*) – eccl. Gr. βαπτισμός ceremonial washing, βάπτισμα baptism, f. βαπτίζειν BAPTIZE. Refash. after L. and Gr.] The action or ceremony of baptizing; application of water to a person by immersion, pouring, or sprinkling, as a religious rite, symbolical of purification or regeneration, and betokening initiation into the Church. Also *fig.* (in various senses.)

Name of b.: see *Baptismal name*. The b. of bells and ships ABP. SANDYS. The b. of blood in martyrdom [*i.e.* death by violence of unbaptized martyrs] 1860. var. † **Baptiza·tion.**

Baptismal (bæpti·zmăl), *a.* 1641. [– med.L. *baptismalis*; see prec., -AL¹.] Of, pertaining to, or connected with baptism.

Baptismal name: the Christian name given at baptism. Hence **Bapti·smally** *adv.*

Baptist (bæ·ptist). ME. [– (O)Fr. *baptiste* – eccl.L. *baptista* – eccl.Gr. βαπτιστής, f. βαπτίζειν; see BAPTIZE, -IST.] **1.** One who baptizes; *esp.* John, the forerunner of Christ. **2.** One who immerses himself, or is immersed (*rare*) 1775. **3.** One of a body of Protestants holding that baptism ought to be administered only to believers, and by immersion; at first called, by opponents, ANABAPTISTS 1654. Also *attrib.*

1. *Baptist's day*: the 24th of June.

Baptistery, -try (bæ·ptistəri, -tri). 1460. [– OFr. *baptisterie* (mod. *baptistère*) – eccl.L. *baptisterium* – eccl.Gr. βαπτιστήριον, f. βαπτίζειν.] **1.** That part of a church (or, earlier, a building contiguous to the church), in which baptism is administered. **2.** A receptacle, in Baptist places of worship, containing water for the baptismal rite 1835. **3.** = BAPTISM 1851.

Bapti·stic, *a.* 1884. [f. BAPTIST (sense 3) + -IC] = BAPTIST *attrib.* Hence † **Bapti·stical** *a.* of or belonging to baptism (*rare*).

Baptize (bæ̆ptəi·z), *v.* ME. [– (O)Fr. *baptiser* – eccl.L. *baptizare* – Gr. βαπτίζειν, dip, immerse; in eccl. use, baptize.] **1.** To administer baptism to; to christen. Also *absol.* Also *fig.* (in reference to initiation, spiritual agency, etc.) **2.** To give a name to, as in baptism 1549.

1. *fig.* Sorrow had baptized her O. W. HOLMES. **2.** Ile be new baptiz'd; Henceforth I neuer will be Romeo *Rom. & Jul.* II. ii. 50. Hence **Bapti·zer.**

‖ **Baquet** (bake). 1786. [– (O)Fr. *baquet*; see BACKET.] A small tub or trough.

Bar (bāɹ), *sb.*¹ [– (O)Fr. *barre* :– Rom. **barra*, of unkn. origin.] **I. 1.** A piece of wood, metal, or other rigid material, long in proportion to its thickness, and frequently used as a barrier, fastening, or obstruction. **2.** A narrow four-sided block of metal or material as manufactured, *e.g.* of iron or soap; an ingot 1595. **3.** A small slip of silver fixed transversely below the clasp of a medal 1864. **4.** A straight strip or stripe, narrow in proportion to its length, a broad line; *e.g.* of colour ME. **5.** *Her.* An honourable ordinary, formed like the fesse, but narrower, and including the fifth part or less of the field 1592. **6.** *Farriery.* **a.** (usu. *pl.*) The transverse ridges of a horse's palate. **b.** The recurved ends of the crust of a horse's hoof, meeting in the centre of the sole 1617.

1. *Bar*, a drilling or tamping-rod RAYMOND. Every Bolt and B...with ease Unfast'ns MILT. *P.L.* II. 877. **5.** *B. sinister*: pop., but erron., the heraldic sign of illegitimacy: see BATON, BEND.

II. 1. That which forms an enclosure, or obstructs entry or egress ME. **2.** A barrier closing the entrance to a city; *subseq.*, the gate replacing this, as in *Temple Bar*, etc. ME. **3.** A bank of sand, silt, etc., across the mouth of a river or harbour, which obstructs navigation 1586. **4.** *Mus.* A vertical line (now commonly called the *bar-line*) drawn across the stave to mark the metrical accent; hence, that which is included between two bars 1665. **b.** = BASS-BAR, FRET *sb.*³ **5.** *Law.* A plea which arrests an action or claim at law 1495; also *fig.*

2. A house without the Barres at Aldgate 1645. **4.** Phr. *Double b.*: two parallel vertical lines, marking the close of a section. **5.** *In b. (of)*: as a sufficient reason (against).

III. 1. *Law.* The barrier or wooden rail at which prisoners are stationed for arraignment, trial, or sentence ME.; *fig.* a tribunal, *e.g.* that of public opinion ME. **2.** Hence: **a.** Court; *esp.* in *At (the) b.*: in open court ME. **b.** A (particular) court of law, as, the Exchequer b. 1559. **3.** *In the Inns of Court.* A partition separating the seats of the benchers from the rest of the hall, to which students, after they had attained a certain standing were 'called'. *Obs.* (After 1600, *bar* was assumed to mean the b. in a court of justice, within which King's Counsel and Sergeants-at-Law have places, but not ordinary barristers.) **4.** Barristers collectively, or *spec.* those practising in a particular court, circuit, or county 1559. **5.** The profession of a barrister 1632. **6.** *In legislative assemblies.* The rail dividing from the body of the house a space near the door to which non-members may be admitted for business purposes 1577. **7.** *In an inn, etc.* A counter, over which drink or food is served out to customers; *also*, the space behind this, and sometimes the whole apartment 1592.

1. When self is at the b., the sentence is not like to be impartial GLANVILL. **2.** *Trial at b.*: a trial before the full court in which the action is brought; in England, the Queen's Bench Division. **3.** *To be called to the b.*: to be admitted a barrister. *To be called within the b.*: to be appointed King's Counsel. **6.** A deputation..heard at the b. of the Commons 1849.

Comb.: **b.-boat,** one marking the position of a b.; **-diggings,** shallows of a stream worked for gold; **-iron,** iron wrought into bars; **-keeper,** one who keeps a b., or keeps guard at a barrier; **-line** (see II. 4 above); **-shot,** a shot consisting of two half cannon balls joined by an iron bar; **-silver,** silver in bars; so **-tin; -tracery,** Gothic window-tracery, resembling a b. of iron twisted into various forms; **-ways, -wise** *adv. Her.* horizontally across the field.

Bar, *sb.*² 1724. [– Fr. *bar, bars* – Du. *baars* (cf. G. *barsch*). See BARSE, BASE *sb.*⁵, BASS *sb.*¹] A fish, *Sciæna aquila*, the MAIGRE.

Bar, *sb.*³ (= G. *berg*); see BARMASTER, BARMOTE.

Bar (bāɹ), *v.* Pa. t. and pple. **barred.** [ME. *bare, barre* – (O)Fr. *barrer*, f. *barre* BAR *sb.*¹.] **1.** To make fast by a bar or bars; to fasten up with bars. **2.** To fasten in by means of bars. Also *transf.* and *fig.* 1460. **3.** To close by some barrier 1596. **4.** To obstruct; to arrest or stop 1578. **5.** To hinder, prohibit *from*; to debar *of* 1551. **6.** To stop, hinder 1559. **7.** To exclude from consideration 1481. **8.** To object to 1611. **9.** To mark with a bar or bars ME. **10.** To make into bars 1712.

1. Shut the doores and barre them *Neh.* 7:3. **4.** What villaine Boy, bar'st me my way in Rome? *Tit. A.* I. i. 291. To b. a person from his action 1726. To b. dower 1854, a right 1884. **7.** Nay but I barre tonight *Merch. V.* II. ii. 208. **8.** † *To b. the dice*: to declare the throw void. **10.** *To b. a vein* (*Farriery*): to tie it above and below a part which is to be operated on.

Bar (bāɹ), *prep.* 1714. [f. BAR *v.*; prob. after *except*, etc.; cf. BARRING.] Excluding from consideration, except.

‖ **Baragouin** (ba:ragwe·n̄, -gwin). 1613. [Fr. *baragouin*, f. Bret. *bara* bread + *gwin* wine.] Unintelligible speech; jargon, double-Dutch. Hence **Baragoui·nish** *a.*

Baralipton (bærăli·ptǫn). 1653. [A mnemonic vocable invented by the Scholastic philosophers, and used first in med.L.] A mnemonic wd. representing the first indirect mood of the first syllogistic figure, in which a particular affirmative conclusion is drawn from two universal affirmative premisses.

‖ **Barathrum** (bæ·răþrɒm). 1520. [L. – Gr. βάραθρον.] A pit, gulf. Hence **a.** A pit at Athens, into which criminals condemned to death were thrown 1849. **b.** The abyss, hell 1520. **c.** An insatiable extortioner or glutton (so in It.) 1609.

Barb (bāɹb), *sb.*¹ ME. [–(O)Fr. *barbe*:– L. *barba* beard.] † **1.** The beard of a man (*rare*) –1618. **2.** A similar appendage in animals 1468. **3.** A piece of white plaited linen, worn over or under the chin, as by nuns ME. **4.** *Veter. Surg.* in *pl.* Folds of the mucous membrane under the tongue of horses and cattle, protecting the orifices of the ducts of the submaxillary glands; the disease caused by their inflammation 1523. **5.** *Her.* A sepal (*pl.* the calyx) of a flower 1572. **6.** One of the lateral processes from the shaft of a feather, which bear the barbules 1836. **7.** Little ridges produced in metal-working, *e.g.* by engravers; bur 1842. **8.** A sharp process curving back from the point of a weapon (*e.g.* an arrow), rendering its extraction difficult ME. Also *fig.* **9.** *Bot.* A hooked hair 1864.

8. *fig.* The malice of a good thing is the b. that makes it stick SHERIDAN.

Barb, *sb.*² 1566. [corrupt f. BARD *sb.*².] A covering for the breast and flanks of a war-horse –1630.

Barb (bāɹb), *sb.*³ 1636. [– Fr. *barbe* – It. *barbero*, of BARBARY.] Occas. *attrib.* **1.** A horse of the breed imported from Barbary and Morocco, noted for speed and endurance. Also called BARBARY. **2.** A black or dun pigeon, orig. introduced from Barbary 1725.

Barb (bāɹb), *v.* 1483. [– Fr. † *barber* (Cotgr.), in OFr. *barbier*, f. *barbe* beard. See BARB *sb.*¹] † **1.** To shave or trim the beard of –1693. Also *absol.* or *intr.* (for *refl.*) **2.** *transf.* To clip; to mow 1483. Also † *fig.* **3.** To furnish with barbs 1611. Also *fig.* **4.** To pierce with, or as with, a barb 1803.

3. Arrows barbd with fire MILT. *P.L.* VI. 546. She barbs with wit those darts too keen before SHERIDAN.

Barbadoes (baɹbē̆ⁱ·doᵘz). Name of an island in the West Indies, referred to Pg. *las barbadas* 'bearded', epithet of the Indian fig-tree growing there; formerly 'the Barbadoes'.

Phrases, etc. **B.-cherry**, the tart fruit of the *Malpighia urens*. **B. leg**, a form of elephantiasis incident to hot climates. **B. nuts**, the purgative seeds or fruit of the *Jatropha curcas*, or *Curcas purgans*. **B. pride**, a plant (*Poinciana pulcherrima*), used for fences. **B. tar**, a greenish petroleum. **B.-water**, a cordial flavoured with orange- and lemon-peel. Also † **Barbadoes** *v.* to transport to B.

Barbal (bā·ɹbăl), *a.* 1650. [f. L. *barba* + -AL¹.] Of or belonging to the beard.

† **Ba·rbar.** [ME. *barbar, barbre* – (O)Fr. *barbare* or its source L. *barbarus* (also used XVI); see BARBAROUS.] **A.** *sb.* = BARBARIAN –1723. **B.** *adj.* = BARBAROUS –1726.

Barbara (bā·ɹbără). 1589. [A Latin word (= barbarous things), taken as a mnemonic term, for its three *a*'s: 'A' indicating a universal affirmative proposition.] A mnemonic term designating the first mood of the first syllogistic figure, in which both premisses and the conclusion are universal affirmatives.

Barbaresque (baɹbăre·sk), *a.* 1804. [– Fr. *barbaresque* – It. *barbaresco*, f. *Barbaria* BARBARY; see -ESQUE.] **1.** Of or pertaining to Barbary 1824. **2.** Barbarous in style, *esp.* in reference to art 1823. **3.** as *sb.* A native of Barbary 1804.

2. Architecture . . b., rich in decoration, at times colossal in proportions, but unsymmetrical DE QUINCEY.

Barbarian (baɹbē̆ᵊ·riăn). 1549. [– Fr. *barbarien* or L. **barbarianus*, extended forms (after *chrétien*, *christianus* CHRISTIAN) of (O)Fr. *barbare*; see BARBAR, -IAN.] **A.** *sb.* **1.** *orig.* A foreigner. **2.** *Hist.* **a.** A non-Hellene. **b.** A non-Roman. **c.** A non-Christian. **d.** A non-Italian. **3.** A rude, wild, uncivilized person 1613. **4.** An uncultured person 1762. † **5.** A native of Barbary. [See BARBARY.] –1709.

1. I shall be vnto him that speaketh, a B., and he that speaketh shal be a B. vnto me 1 *Cor.* 14 : 11. 2. I would they were Barbarians . . not Romans *Cor.* III. i. 238. 4. Cromwell, though himself a b., was not insensible to literary merit HUME.

B. *adj.* **1.** Non-Hellenic, non-Roman (*most usual*), non-Christian 1549. **2.** Uncivilized, savage, rude 1591. † **3.** Of or belonging to Barbary –1699.

1. Bought and solde . . like a B. slaue *Tr. & Cr.* II. i. 51.

Barbaric (baɹbæ·rik), *a.* 1490. [–(O)Fr. *barbarique* or L. *barbaricus* – Gr. βαρβαρικός, f. βάρβαρος foreign.] **1.** = BARBARIAN *a.* 2. 1490. **2.** Pertaining or proper to barbarians or their art 1667. **3.** = BARBARIAN *a.* 1. 1849.

2. B. Pearl and Gold MILTON. Hence **Barba·rically** *adv.*

Barbarism (bā·ɹbăriz'm). 1579. [–(O)Fr. *barbarisme* – L. *barbarismus* – Gr. βαρβαρισμός, f. βαρβαρίζειν (behave or) speak like a foreigner; see -ISM.] **1.** The use of words or expressions not in accordance with the classical standard of a language; *hence*, rudeness of language. **b.** A foreign or non-classical word or idiom 1589. **2.** Barbarous social or intellectual condition; opp. to *civilization* 1584. Also with *a* and *pl.* (Only in Eng.) 1645. † **3.** BARBARITY –1665.

1. A b., then, is a fault of style originating in rudeness and ignorance; but a solecism is [one] originating in affectation and over-refinement 1801. 2. Plundering and other barbarismes HOWELL.

Barbarity (baɹbæ·riti). 1570. [f. L. *barbarus* + -ITY; not in L. or Fr.] † **1.** = BARBARISM 2. –1819. **2.** Barbarous cruelty; inhumanity. (The usual sense.) 1685. Also with *a* and *pl.* **3.** = BARBARISM 1. ? *Obs.* 1706. **4.** Barbarism of style in art. Also with *a* and *pl.* 1644.

2. With breach of faith, with cruelty and b. DE FOE.

Barbarize (bā·ɹbărəiz), *v.* 1644. [In sense 1, – late L. *barbarizare* (Boethius) – Gr. βαρβαρίζειν; in senses 2, 3, f. as BARBARISM 2 and 3, + -IZE.] **1.** *intr.* To speak or write like a barbarian. **2.** *trans.* To render barbarous 1648. **3.** *intr.* To fall into barbarism 1824.

2. The hideous changes which have since barbarized France BURKE.

Barbarous (bā·ɹbărəs), *a.* 1526. [f. L. *barbarus* (– Gr. βάρβαρος non-Greek, foreign, esp. w. ref. to speech) + -OUS.] **1.** Of language: **a.** *orig.* Not Greek; *subseq.* not Greek or Latin; *hence*, not classical or pure. Hence, **b.** Unpolished; pertaining to an illiterate people. **2.** Of people: Foreign in speech; *orig.* non-Hellenic; *then*, not Roman; *occas.* not Christian 1542. **3.** Uncultured, unpolished; rude, savage. (Opp. to *civilized.*) 1538. **4.** Cruelly savage, or harsh 1588. **5.** Harsh-sounding, coarsely noisy 1645. † **6.** = BARBARIC 2. –1700.

2. The b. people shewed vs no little kindnesse *Acts* 28 : 2. 3. *Twel. N.* IV. i. 52. 4. The b. aspect of war MOZLEY. 5. A b. noise MILT. **6.** B. gold DRYDEN. Hence **Ba·rbarous-ly** *adv.*, **-ness.**

Barbary (bā·ɹbări). ME. [In I. – OFr. *barbarie* or L. *barbaria, -ies* land of barbarians, f. *barbarus*; see BARBAROUS, -Y³; in II. ult. – Arab. *Barbar*; see BERBER.] **I.** † **1.** Foreign nationality; heathenism. *concr.* Non-Christian lands. *attrib.* = Paynim. –1629. † **2.** Barbarity –1635. † **3.** Uncultivated speech. Also *attrib.* –1608. **II.** The Saracen countries along the north coast of Africa. (The surviving sense.) 1596. Also *attrib.*, esp. in **Barbary ape, horse,** etc. Also † *ellipt.* = BARB *sb.*³

Barbastel(le (bāɹbăste·l, bā·ɹbăstel). 1791. [– Fr. *barbastelle* (Buffon) – It. *barbastelo* barbastelle bat.] A dark brown bat (*Plecotus barbastellus*), found in France and Germany.

Barbate (bā·ɹbeⁱt), *a.* 1853. [– L. *barbatus* bearded, f. *barba* beard; see -ATE².] Bearded; furnished with a small hairy tuft or tufts.

† **Ba·rbated,** *a. rare.* 1782. [f. as prec. + -ED¹.] Barbed, as an arrow; barbate –1802.

Barbecue (bā·ɹbĭkiū), *sb.* 1697. [– Sp. *barbacoa* – Haitian *barbacòa* framework of sticks set on posts.] **1.** A rude framework, used in America for sleeping on, and for smoking or drying meat over a fire. **2.** An ox, hog, etc., roasted whole 1764. **3.** (in U.S.) An open-air social entertainment, at which animals are roasted whole 1809. **4.** An open floor on which coffee-beans, etc., may be dried 1855.

1. His Couch or Barbecu of Sticks DAMPIER. 3. I am invited to dinner on a barbicu FOOTE.

Barbecue (bā·ɹbĭkiū), *v.* 1661. [f. prec. sb.] **1.** To dry or cure on a barbecue; see the sb. 1, and 4. **2.** To broil or roast (an animal) whole on a huge gridiron.

2. B. your whole hogs to your palate LAMB.

Barbed (bāɹbd), *ppl. a.*¹ 1526. [f. BARB *v.*, *sb.*¹ + -ED¹,².] † **1.** Bearded (*rare*) 1693. † **2.** Wearing a BARB (sense 3) –1601. **3.** *Her.* Having a calyx 'coloured proper' 1611. **4.** Furnished with a barb or barbs 1611.

4. Can'st thou fill his skinne with b. yrons *Job* 41 : 7.

Barbed (bāɹbd, bā·ɹbėd), *ppl. a.*² 1509. [f. BARB *sb.*² + -ED².] Barded (see BARD *v.*¹).

Barbel (bā·ɹbĕl). ME. [– OFr. *barbel* (mod. *barbeau*) :– late L. *barbellus* (cf. med.L. *barbulus*), dim. of *barbus* barbel, f. *barba* beard.] **1.** A large European freshwater fish (*Barbus vulgaris*), named from the fleshy filaments which hang from its mouth. **2.** A fleshy filament hanging from the mouth of certain fishes 1601. Hence **Ba·rbelled, -eled,** *ppl. a.* furnished with barbels. **Ba·rbelling, -eling** *vbl. sb.* fishing for b.

† **Ba·rbeled, -bled,** *ppl. a.* ME. [f. (O)Fr. *barbelé* barbed; see -ED².] Barbed –1480.

Barbellate (bā·ɹbĕleⁱt), *a.* 1847. [f. mod.L. *barbella*, dim. of *barbula* little beard, + -ATE².] *Bot.* Furnished with *barbellæ* or short stiff hairs.

Barbellulate (baɹbe·liŭleⁱt), *a.* 1847. [f. mod.L. *barbellula*, dim. of *barbella*; see prec.] *Bot.* Furnished with *barbellulæ* or minute conical spines.

Barber (bā·ɹbəɹ), *sb.* [– AFr. *barber, barbour*, OFr. *barbeor* :– med.L. *barbator*, f. L. *barba* beard; see -ER².] **a.** One whose business it is to shave or trim the beard, and cut and dress the hair. (Now usu. *hairdresser.*) Formerly the barber was also a surgeon and dentist. **b.** *fig.* A curtailer. B. JONS. Also *attrib.*, as in † **b.-monger,** a frequenter of the barber's shop, a fop.

For Barbers they use their women CAPT. SMITH.

Phrases. *Barber's chair*, one common to all his customers, † *fig.* a drab. *Barber's music*, discordant music, like that formerly produced by waiting customers in a barber's shop. *Barber's pole*, a pole painted spirally with red and white stripes, used as a barber's sign. Hence **Ba·rber** *v.* (*rare*) to trim.

Barberry, berberry (bā·ɹbĕri, bɔ̄·ɹbĕri). ME. [XV *barbere*, – OFr. *berberis*, corresp. to It. *berberi*, Sp. *berberis*, med.L. *barbaris*; assim. early to *berry.*] *Bot.* **1.** A shrub (*Berberis vulgaris*), with spiny shoots, and pendulous racemes of small yellow flowers, succeeded by oblong, red, sharply acid berries; the bark yields a bright yellow dye. Also the genus *Berberis.* **2.** The berry of this tree 1533. Also *attrib.*

Barbery (bā·ɹbəri), ME. [– Fr. † *barberie* barber's craft, f. *barbier* BARBER + *-ie* -Y³; see -ERY.] † **1.** A barber's shop. **2.** The barber's art or craft 1540.

Barbet (bā·ɹbėt). 1753. [– Fr. *barbet*, f. *barbe* beard; see -ET.] **1.** A little dog with long curly hair 1780. † **2.** Name of a worm with tufts of white filaments, which feeds on aphides 1753. **3.** A family of birds, found in warm countries, having a short conical bill, with tufts of bristles at its base. (In Fr. *barbu.*) 1824.

‖ **Barbette** (baɹbe·t), *sb.* 1772. [Fr., dim. of *barbe* beard; see -ETTE.] A platform within a fortification, on which guns are raised for firing over the parapet. *Guns en barbette, b. gun* or *battery*: those so mounted as to fire over the parapet; similarly in ironclad ships. Hence *attrib.*, as in *b.-cruiser, -turret.*

Barbican (bā·ɹbikăn). ME. [–(O)Fr. *barbacane*, = med.L. *barbacana, barbi-*, of unkn. origin.] An outer defence to a city or castle, *esp.* a double tower erected over a gate or bridge. † **2.** A temporary wooden tower. CAXTON. † **3.** A loophole in the wall of a castle or city 1600.

Ba·rbicanage. 1691. [– Anglo-L. *barbicanagium*; see prec., -AGE.] Tribute paid for the maintenance of barbicans.

Barbicel (bā·ɹbisĕl). 1869. [– It. and mod.L. *barbicella*, dim. of *barba* beard; cf. PEDICEL.] One of the minute hooked filaments which interlock the barbules of a bird's feathers.

Barbi·gerous, *a.* 1731. [f. L. *barbiger* bearded + -OUS; see -GEROUS.] Bearded.

‖ **Ba·rbiton, -os.** 1545. [L. *barbiton, -os* – Gr. βάρβιτον, -ος.] A many-stringed instrument; a lute or lyre. Hence † **Ba·rbitist,** a player on the b.

Barble, obs. f. BARBEL.

Barbotine (bā·ɹbŏtin). 1865. [– Fr. *barbotine*.] A paste of kaolin clay used to ornament pottery.

Barbre, obs. f. BARBARY.

‖ **Barbula** (bā·ɹbiŭlă). 1688. [L., dim. of *barba*.] **1.** A small beard. ? *Obs.* **2.** The inner row of fringes in the peristome of mosses 1866.

Barbule (bā·ɹbiŭl). 1835. [– prec.; see -ULE.] **1.** = BARBEL 2. **2.** One of the processes fringing the barbs of a feather 1835. **3.** *Bot.* = BARBULA 2. 1881.

Barcarole, -olle (bā·ɹkărōᵘl). 1779. [– Fr. *barcarolle* – Venetian It. *barcarola*, rel. to *barcarolo* gondolier, f. It. *barca* BARQUE.] ‖ **1.** An Italian boatman 1854. **2.** A song sung by Venetian gondoliers; a piece of music composed in imitation of such songs 1799.

† **Barcelo·na.** 1795. [– *Barcelona*, in Spain.] A handkerchief or neckerchief of soft twilled silk –1833.

‖ **Barco·ne.** [It., augm. of *barca* BARQUE; cf. -OON.] A vessel used for freight in the Mediterranean. var. **Barcon** (Webster).

Bard (bāɹd), *sb.*[1] ME. [– Gael., Ir. *bárd*, W. *bardd* :– OCelt. **bardos* (whence Gr. βάρδος, L. *bardus*). Orig. a term of contempt, but idealized by Scott.] **1.** An ancient Celtic order of minstrel-poets, who composed and sang (usually to the harp) verses celebrating the achievements of chiefs and warriors. In Welsh *spec.* A poet who has been recognized at the Eisteddfod. **2.** In early Lowland Scotch: A strolling musician or minstrel 1449. **3.** Used of the Old English *gleeman*, Scandinavian *scald*, etc. 1623. **4.** *poet.* A 'singer'. (Chiefly after Lucan.) 1667.

2. Feinzied fooles, bairdes, rynners about . . after sundrie punishments, may be hanged 1609. The last of all the bards was he Who sung of Border minstrelsy SCOTT. 4. That wild rout that tore the Thracian b. In Rhodope MILT. *P.L.* VII. 34.

Bard, *sb.*[2] Now *Hist.* 1480. [– (O)Fr. *barde*, ult. – Arab. *barḏa'a* saddle-cloth, stuffed saddle. Corruptly BARB *sb.*[2]] **1.** (Usu. *pl.*) A covering of armour for the breast and flanks of a war-horse; occas. an ornamental covering of velvet or the like. **2.** *pl.* Plate-armour, as formerly worn by men-at-arms 1551.

Bard (bāɹd), *sb.*[3] 1725. [– Fr. *barde*, transf. from prec.] A thin slice of bacon used to cover a fowl, etc.

Bard (bāɹd), *v.*[1] 1521. [– Fr. *barder*, f. *barde* BARD *sb.*[2] and [3].] **1.** To arm or caparison with bards. (Chiefly in pa. pple.) **2.** To cover with slices of bacon 1665.

† **Bard,** *v.*[2] 1641. [app. by confusion of BARB *v.* and BEARD.] = BARB *v.* 2. –1693.

† **Barda·sh.** 1548. [– Fr. *bardache* – It. *bardascia* – Pers. *bardagī* captive, prisoner.] A catamite –1721.

† **Barde·l(le.** *rare.* 1603. [– Fr. *bardelle*, dim. of *barde* BARD *sb.*[2]; see -EL[2].] A pack-saddle –1753.

Bardic (bā·ɹdik), *a.* 1775. [f. BARD *sb.*[1] + -IC.] Of, pertaining to, or of the character of, bards. So **Bardish** (bā·ɹdiʃ) *a.* of or belonging to bards. (*Somewhat depreciatory.*) **Bardism** (bā·ɹdiz'm), the system, doctrine, or principles of bards. **Ba·rdling,** an inexperienced poet; a poetaster; var. **Ba·rdlet.**

†‖ **Bardocucu·llus.** 1611. [L.] A Gallic peasant's cloak, with a hood, worn also by monks.

Ba·rdship. 1787. [f. BARD *sb.*[1] + -SHIP.] The office, dignity, or personality of a bard.

Bare (bēᵊɹ). [OE. *bær* = OFris., OS., (O)HG. *bar*, MDu. *baer*, Du. *baar*, ON. *berr* :– Gmc. **bazaz* :– Indo-Eur. **bhosós*.] **A.** *adj.* **1.** Without covering, naked. **2.** = BAREHEADED (*arch.*) ME. **3.** *fig.* Open to view OE. **4.** Of natural objects: Without the covering which they have at other times OE. **5.** Stripped of hair, wool, flesh, etc.; bald ME. **6.** Unfurnished, uncovered, unarmed ME. † **7.** Defenceless –1551. † **8.** Desolate –1642. **9.** Destitute, needy; scantily furnished ME. Hence, **10. a.** Empty ME.; **b.** † Worthless –1596; **c.** Bald, unadorned ME.; † **d.** Simple, unpolished –1603. **11.** Without addition, mere, simple ME. † **12.** Sheer, absolute, very –ME.

1. Make b. the legge *Isa.* 47: 2. In his b. shirt 1866. 3. B. in thy guilt MILT. *Sams.* 902. 4. The Country . . being eaten b. 1720. 6. To lie upon b. boards 1722. Their b. hands *Oth.* I. iii. 175. B. Liueries SHAKS. *Bare poles* (Naut.): masts with no sails set. 8. SHAKS. *Lucr.* 1741. 9. As b. as Job BALE. B. of saintliness 1883. 10. A b. treasury DRYDEN. B. excuses SHAKS. 11. The b. Necessaries of Life ADDISON. A b. majority 1844. *B. contract* (Law): an unconditional promise or surrender.

B. *adv.* With numeral adjs.: BARELY (*arch.*) –1716.

† **C.** *sb.* † **1.** A naked part of the body. Also *fig.* –1611. † **2.** A bare space or place –1706.

Comb. **b.-bone,** a lean skinny person.

Bare (bēᵊɹ), *v.* [OE. *barian* (f. *bær*) = OFris. *baria*, OHG. *gibarōn*, ON. *bera*; see prec.] **1.** To make or lay bare, expose to view; to unsheathe. **2.** *fig.* To disclose, make manifest ME. **3.** To strip. Const. *of, from.* 1440.

1. Have bar'd my Bosome to the Thunder-stone *Jul. C.* I. iii. 49. 3. To b. a garden LIVINGSTONE.

Bareback (bēᵊ·ɹbæk), *a. adv.* 1562. = BAREBACKED 2.

Bare-backed (bēᵊ·ɹbækt), *a.* 1628. [See BARE *a.* 6.] **1.** With the back bare 1831. **2.** Without saddle; also with *ride* as *adv.* 1628.

‖ **Bareca, -ka** (barē·kă). 1773. [– Sp. *bareca, barrica*; see BREAKER[2], BARRICO.] A small cask or keg, a BREAKER.

Barefaced (bēᵊ·ɹfēⁱst), *a.* (in use occas. advb.). 1590. **1.** With the face uncovered: *hence* **a.** beardless, also *fig.*; **b.** without mask. **2.** Avowed, open 1605. **3.** Hence: Audacious, shameless 1674.

2. B. and open tyranny 1766. 3. A b. orphan DICKENS, lie MRS. STOWE. Hence **Ba·refaced-ly** *adv.*, **-ness.**

Barefoot (bēᵊ·ɹfut). [OE. *bærfōt*, ON. *berfœttr*. See BARE *a.*] With the feet bare: **a.** as *adj.*, passing (with vbs. of motion) into **b.** *adv.*

b. Who waitth for dead men shoen, shall go long barefoote J. HEYWOOD. Hence **Ba·re-foo:ted** *a.*

‖ **Barege** (bare·ʒ). 1811. [Fr. *barége*, f. *Barèges*, a village of Hautes-Pyrénées, France.] **1.** A gauze-like, silky dress-fabric, orig. made at Barèges 1851. **2.** A mineral water obtained at Barèges. Hence **Baregin(e,** a glairy organic substance found in many mineral waters after exposure to the air.

Ba·rehead, *a.* and *adv. arch.* ME. = next.

Bare-headed (bēᵊ·ɹhe:dėd), *a.* and *adv.* 1530. [f. prec.; cf. *barefoot(ed.*] With the head uncovered, *esp.* as a token of respect. Hence **Bare-headedness.**

Barely (bēᵊ·ɹli), *adv.* OE. [f. BARE *a.* + -LY[2].] **1.** Nakedly 1483. **2.** Without concealment or disguise OE. † **3.** Unconditionally; wholly; positively –ME. **4.** Merely, only (*arch.*) 1577. **5.** Only just; *hence*, not quite, with difficulty 1494. **6.** Scantily; baldly 1535.

2. When the question is put b. before them 1875. 4. Not b. in word, but truly in deed HANMER. 5. B. time to get out of the way 1805.

Ba·reness. 1552. [f. BARE *a.* + -NESS.] **1.** Nakedness. **2.** Destitution, scantiness; baldness (*lit.* and *fig.*) 1580; † leanness –1596.

Baresark (bēᵊ·ɹsāɹk). 1840. [lit. = 'bare shirt'; see BERSERKER.] **1.** *sb.* (also *attrib.*) A BERSERKER. **2.** *adv.* In a shirt only, without armour.

† **Ba·rful,** *a.* [f. BAR *sb.*[1] + -FUL.] Full of hindrances. *Twel. N.* I. iv. 41.

Bargain (bā·ɹgėn), *sb.*[1] ME. [– OFr. *bargaine, -ga(i)gne* fem., *bargaing* m.; see BARGAIN *v.*] † **1.** Discussion between two parties as to terms; chaffering –1596. **2.** An agreement between two parties settling the part of each in a transaction between them; a compact ME. **b.** Occas., the compact in relation to one of the parties only, *e.g.* a 'bad b.' 1502. **3.** That which is acquired by bargaining; a purchase qualified as *good*, etc.; *without qualification*, an advantageous purchase ME. **4.** *transf.* A (bad or unfortunate) 'business' (*arch.*) ME. † **5.** Contention for the mastery; battle. *north.* –1606. Also *fig.*

1. † *To beat a (the) b.*: to haggle. 2. So clap hands, and a bargaine *Hen. V*, v. ii. 134. 3. Picked up as a b. 1882.

Phrases. **B. and sale** (*Law*): a kind of conveyance, in which the legal owner agreed with the purchaser for the sale to him of his interest, and the purchaser paid, or promised to pay, the money for the land. *Dutch* or *wet b.*: one concluded by the parties drinking together. *Into,* † *to, the b.*: over and above what is agreed; besides. † *To sell any one a b.*: to make a fool of him SHAKS. *To strike* († *up*) *a b.*: to come to terms over a purchase. *To make the best of a bad b.*: to make the best of adverse circumstances.

Hence **Ba·rgainee·**, the party with whom an agreement of bargain and sale of land is made. **Ba·rgainer,** one who bargains; † = *Bargainor*. **Ba:rgaino·r,** the party making an agreement of bargain and sale of land.

Ba·rgain, *sb.*[2] Now *dial.* 1602. [perh. = prec.] A small farm-holding.

Bargain (bā·ɹgėn), *v.* ME. [– OFr. *bargaignier* trade, dispute, hesitate (mod. *barguigner* hesitate) = Pr. *barganhar*, It. *bargagnare*, med.L. *barcaniare*, prob. – Gmc. **borȝanjan*, extended form of **borȝan* (OHG. *borgēn* look after, in MHG., G. give or take on loan, BORROW); but the vowel *-a-* of the first syll. is unexpl.] **1.** *intr.* To haggle over terms, negotiate. **2.** To arrange terms; to strike a bargain *with* (a person) *for* 1483. **3.** *trans.* To agree to buy or sell; to contract for. *Obs.* exc. in *To bargain and sell.* 1488. † **4.** *Sc.* To contend –1513.

1. Judas bargaining with the priests 1859. 2. I . . have bargained to be landed in France 1787. Phr. *To bargain for*: *fig.* to arrange for beforehand; to count on, expect.

Bargander, obs. f. BERGANDER.

Barge (bāɹdʒ), *sb.* ME. [– (O)Fr. *barge*, perh. :– med.L. **barica*, f. Gr. βᾶρις Egyptian boat; cf. BARQUE.] **1.** A small sea-going vessel with sails; *spec.* one next in size above a BALINGER. Now *Hist.* **2.** A flat-bottomed freight-boat or *lighter*, chiefly for canal- and river-navigation 1480. † **3.** *vaguely*, A rowing-boat; *esp.* a ferry-boat. (Used for L. *linter.*) –1601. **4.** *spec.* The second boat of a man of war; a long narrow boat for the use of the chief officers 1530. **5.** A vessel of state, propelled by oars (or towed); an ornamental house-boat 1586. **6.** (in *U.S.*) A large carriage 1881.

4. A b. properly never rows less than ten [oars] FALCONER. 5. *Ant. & Cl.* II. ii. 196. *Comb.*: **Barge-man,** one who has charge of, or rows in, a b. **Barge-master,** the owner of a b. **Barge-pole,** esp. in colloq. phr. *would not touch with a b.-p.*, regard with loathing. Hence **Barge** *v.* to carry by b.; also *intr.* (*slang*) to lurch or bump heavily *into*, *against*, etc., to intrude *in*.

Ba·rge-board. 1833. [See next.] A board running along the edge of the gable of a house, to conceal the barge-couples, etc.

Ba·rge-cou:ple. 1562. [With *barge-* in this, prec., and next, cf. med.L. *bargus* (Du Cange) a kind of gallows = cl.L. *furca*.] *Archit.* Two beams mortised and tenoned together to increase the strength of a building.

Ba·rge-course. 1668. [See prec.] A portion of the roof of a house carried slightly beyond the wall at the gable-end, to keep out rain, etc.

Bargee (bāɹdʒī·). 1666. [f. BARGE *sb.* + -EE (used irreg.).] A bargeman.

Ba·rge-stone. 1833. [See BARGE-COUPLE.] In *pl.*: Stones forming the sloping line of a gable.

Bargh (bāɹf). *dial.* 1674. [mod. north. form of BARROW *sb.*[1] In sense 3 app. infl. by G. *berg-* mining-.] **1.** A detached low ridge 1823. **2.** A road up a steep hill 1674. **3.** A mine 1693.

Barghest (bā·ɹge:st). 1732. [Origin unkn.] A goblin, in the shape of a large dog, fabled to portend death or misfortune.

† **Ba·r-goose.** 1598. [app. short f. *barnacle-goose*.] The barnacle-goose –1647.

† **Ba·ria.** Also **barya.** 1812. [f. BARIUM, after *strontia*, f. *strontium*; see -IA[1].] *Chem.* = BARYTA –1819.

Baric (bēᵊ·rik), *a.*[1] 1869. [f. BARIUM + -IC.] *Chem.* Of barium; containing barium in composition.

Baric (bæ·rik), *a.*[2] 1881. [f. Gr. βάρος weight + IC.] Of or pertaining to weight, *esp.* that of the air; barometric.

Barilla (bări·lă, bări·lʸa). 1622. [– Sp. *barrilla*, dim. of *barra* bar.] **1.** A maritime plant (*Salsola soda*) growing largely in Spain, Sicily, and the Canary Islands. **2. a.** An impure alkali produced by burning dried plants of this and allied species; used in making soda, soap, and glass. **b.** Also, an impure alkali made from kelp.

Baring (bēᵊ·riŋ), *vbl. sb.* 1601. [f. BARE *v.* + -ING[1].] **1.** The action of laying bare. **2.** That which is removed in this process; the top soil.

Barish (bēᵊ·riʃ), *a.* 1661. [f. BARE *a.* + -ISH[1].] Somewhat bare.

Barite (bēᵊ·rəit). [f. BARIUM + -ITE[1] 2 b.] *Min.* Dana's name for BARYTES.

Baritone: see BARYTONE. The spelling with *i* is now usual, esp. when applied to the voice.

Barium (bēᵊ·riŏm). 1808. [f. BAR(YTA + -IUM (H. Davy, 1808), as in ALUMIUM f. ALUMINA.] *Chem.* A white metallic element, not found native, but as the basis of baryta.

Bark (bāɹk), *sb.*[1] [ME. *bark* – *bark-*, obl. stem of OIcel. *bǫrkr* (Sw., Da. *bark*), perh. rel. to BIRCH. The native word is RIND *sb.*[1]] **1.** The rind or outer sheath of the trunk and branches of trees; *spec.* that used in dyeing, tanning, etc., spent bark, tan. † **2.** The rind, husk, or shell of fruit and grains –1661. **3.** *gen.* An outer covering or husk. Now *dial.* 1601. **4.** *dial.* and *slang.* The skin 1758. **5.** *fig.* Outside (*arch.*) ME. **6.** *spec.* in *Med.* (also *Jesuits'* or *Peruvian Bark*); The bark of the Cinchona tree, from which quinine is procured 1704.

1. He is no friend to the tree, that strips it of the b. FULLER. *Comb.*: **b.-bed,** a hot-bed made of spent b.; **-bound** *a.*, hindered in growth by tightness of the b.; **-heat,** that of a b.-bed; **-louse,** a kind of aphis, infesting the b. of trees; **-pit,** a pit filled with b. and water in which hides are steeped; **-worm** = *bark-louse.*

Bark, barque (bāɹk), *sb.*[2] 1475. [– (O)Fr. *barque*, prob. – Pr. *barca* :– late L. *barca* (so Sp., It.), of which a collateral form **barica* may be repr. by BARGE.] **1.** *orig.* Any small sailing vessel; now rhet. or poet. for any sailing vessel; = BARGE 1. Also *fig.* **2.** A rowing boat; now only poetically and vaguely 1598. **3.** *spec.* A sailing vessel of particular rig; in 17th c. used of the *barca-longa*; *now* of a three-masted vessel with fore- and main-masts square-rigged, and mizen-mast fore-and-aft rigged. (Freq. spelt *barque.*) 1601.

1. The skarfed barke puts from her natiue bay *Merch. V.* II. vi. 15. My spirit's b. is driven, Far from the shore SHELLEY.

Bark (bāɹk), *sb.*[3] 1562. [f. BARK *v.*[1], preceded by OE. (*ge*)*beorc*, ME. *berk.*] **1.** The sharp explosive cry of dogs; also, that of foxes, squirrels, etc. **2.** *transf.*; *e.g.* the sound of cannon-fire; *colloq.* a cough. 1871.

Bark (bāɹk), *v.*[1] [OE. *beorcan*, pa. t. **bearc*, pa. pple. *borcen* :– **berkan*, perh. metathetic var. of Gmc. **brekan* BREAK.] **1.** *intr.* To utter a sharp explosive cry. (Orig. of dogs, hence of other animals.) **2.** *fig.* To speak or cry out angrily or aggressively ME. **3.** *mod. colloq.* To cough. **4.** *trans.* To utter with a bark; to break out with 1440.

1. Harke, harke, bowgh, wawgh; the watch-Dogges barke *Temp.* I. ii. 383. **2.** Phr. *To bark against* (or *at*) *the moon*: to clamour to no effect.

Bark (bāɹk), *v.*[2] ME. [f. BARK *sb.*[1]] **1.** *intr.* (with *over*) To form a bark. **2.** *trans.* To treat with bark; to tan ME. **3.** To strip off the bark from 1545. Also *fig.* **b.** *transf.* To scrape the skin (*esp.* from the shins and joints) 1850. **4.** To enclose with or as with bark 1633.

3. *fig.* Would barke your honor from that trunke you beare, And leaue you naked *Meas. for M.* III. i. 72. Phr. *To b.* (a squirrel, etc.): to shoot at the bark beneath it and kill it by concussion.

† **Ba·rkary.** 1594. [– med.L. *barcarium*, *-ia*, *bercarium*, *-ia* for *berbicaria* sheepfold, f. *berbica* sheep = cl.L. *berbex*, *vervex* wether.] A sheepfold –1641.

Barkentine, var. of BARQUENTINE.

Barker (bā·ɹkəɹ), *sb.*[1] ME. [f. BARK *v.*[1] + -ER[1].] **1.** One who or that which barks; a dog. **2.** *fig.* A noisy assailant 1483. **b.** One who cries wares at a cheap shop or show; now chiefly *U.S.* 1700. **3.** The Spotted Redshank (*Totanus fuscus*) 1802. **4.** *slang.* A pistol 1815.

Ba·rker, *sb.*[2] ME. [f. BARK *v.*[2] + -ER[1].] † **1.** A tanner –1609. **2.** One who barks trees 1611.

Ba·rkey. *colloq.* 1847. [f. BARK *sb.*[2] + *-ey* = -Y[6].] A little bark.

Barking (bā·ɹkiŋ), *vbl. sb.*[1] ME. [f. BARK *v.*[1] + -ING[1].] **1.** The utterance of barks; *transf.* harsh coughing 1813. **2.** *fig.* Angry outcry 1549.

Ba·rking, *vbl. sb.*[2] ME. [f. BARK *v.*[2] + -ING[1].] **1.** Tanning 1440. **2.** Cutting off the bark from trees; ring-barking 1545.

2. *Barking-irons*: tools used for barking trees.

Ba·rking, *ppl. a.* 1552. [f. BARK *v.*[1] + ING[2].] Uttering barks. Also *transf.* and *fig.*

Barking-bird, the *Pteroptochus tarnu*, so named from its voice; **b.-iron** (*slang*), a pistol. Hence **Ba·rkingly** *adv.*

Barky (bā·ɹki), *a.* 1590. [f. BARK *sb.*[1] + -Y[1].] Covered with, or of the nature of, bark.

The b. fingers of the Elme *Mids.N.* iv. i. 48.

Barley (bā·ɹli). [OE. *bærlic* adj. (first as sb. in 'Peterborough Chronicle' an. 1124), f. OE. *bære*, *bere* barley (cf. BARN, BEAR *sb.*[2]) + *-līċ* -LY[1]; cf. ON. *barr* barley, Goth. *barizeins* of barley.] A hardy awned cereal (genus *Hordeum*); used for food, and for making malt liquors and spirits. **a.** The plant ME. **b.** The grain. *French, Pearl, Pot barley.* OE.

Comb.: **b.-bird,** name given locally to the wryneck, siskin, greenfinch, and occas. the nightingale, which appear about the time of barley-sowing; **-bree, -broth,** strong ale; **-candy** (=*barley-sugar*); † **-hat** (cf. BARLEY-CAP, -HOOD); **-milk,** a gruel of b., or b.-meal; **-mow,** a stack of b.; † **-sick,** *a.* intoxicated; **-straw** (*fig.*), a trifle; **-sugar,** a confection made from sugar, formerly by boiling in a decoction of b.; **-water,** a demulcent drink, made by the decoction of pearl b.

Ba·rley, *int. Sc.* and *n. dial.* 1814. [perh. corrupt f. Fr. *parlez*, Eng. *parley.*] Parley, truce; a term used in children's games.

Barley-break (bā·ɹli,brēⁱk). 1557. [Origin unkn.] An old country game, resembling *Prisoner's Bars*, played by six persons (three of each sex) in couples; one couple had to catch the others, who were allowed to 'break', and change partners, when hard pressed.

† **Ba·rley-ca:p.** 1598. [f. BARLEY.] In phr. *To have on*, etc., *a barley-cap*: to be tipsy; hence *barley-cap* = tippler.

Barley-corn (bā·ɹli,kǭɹn). ME. [See CORN.] **1.** = BARLEY. **b.** Personified as *John Barleycorn*; esp. as providing malt liquors 1620. **2.** A grain of barley 1588. **3.** A grain of barley as a measure of length, ⅓, formerly also ¼, of an inch 1607. **4.** *Building.* A little planed cavity between the mouldings of joiner's work 1753.

1. John Barleycorn, Thou king o' grain BURNS.

Ba·rley-hoo:d. 1529. [-HOOD, or HOOD *sb.*; cf. BARLEY-CAP.] A fit of drunkenness, or of ill humour brought on by drinking.

† **Ba·rling.** 1611. [– Sw. *bärling* pole.] A pole. DE FOE.

† **Barm,** *sb.*[1] [OE. *barm* (*bearm*) = OFris., OS., OHG. *barm*, ON. *barmr*, Goth. *barms* :– Gmc. **barmaz*, f. *bar-*, rel. to **beran* BEAR *v.*[1]] A bosom, a lap.

Barm (bāɹm), *sb.*[2] [OE. *beorma* :– **bermon*, prob. orig. a Com. LG. word; cf. OFris. *berme*, *barm*, LG. *barm*, *barme*, *borme* (whence G. *bärme*, Sw. *barma*, Da. *bärme*).] The froth that forms on the top of fermenting malt liquors; used to leaven bread, and to ferment other liquors; yeast, leaven. Also *transf.* or *fig.* Hence **Barm** *v.* (*arch.*) to leaven; to rise in fermentation.

Barmaid (bā·ɹmēⁱd). 1772. [f. BAR *sb.*[1]] A female who serves at a tavern or hotel bar.

Barman (bā·ɹmæ̆n). 1714. [f. BAR *sb.*[1]] **1.** One who prepares (metal) bars. **2.** One who serves at the bar of a public-house 1837.

Barmaster (bā·ɹmā:stəɹ). 1662. [Earlier *barghmaster* – G. *bergmeister*, f. *berg-* mining-. Cf. BARMOTE.] A local judge among miners.

Barmecide (bā·ɹmĭsəid). 1713. Patronymic of a family of princes at Bagdad, one of whom put a succession of empty dishes before a beggar, pretending that they contained a sumptuous repast—a fiction which the beggar humorously accepted. (See, 'Arabian Nights'.) Hence, one who offers imaginary food or illusory benefits. Often *attrib.* Hence **Barmeci·dal** *a.*

Ba·rming. *Sc. rare.* 1823. [perh. f. *barm v.* (see BARM *sb.*[2]) + -ING[1].] The formation of barm on a fermenting liquor; *fig.* the accruing of interest on money.

Barmkin (bā·ɹmkin). *north. arch.* ME. [perh. corruption of *barbican.*] The battlement of the outer fortification of a castle; a turret or watchtower on the outer wall.

Barmote (bā·ɹmōᵘt). 1653. [Earlier *barghmote*, f. Ger. *berg-* mining- + *mote*, var. of MOOT *sb.*; cf. BARMASTER.] A local court amongst miners.

Barmy (bā·ɹmi), *a.* 1535. [f. BARM *sb.*[2] + -Y[1].] Full of barm. Also *fig.* Also = BALMY *a.* 7.

Like b. beer HOGG.

Barn (bāɹn), *sb.* [OE. *bern*, *beren*, earlier *berern*, f. *bere* (BEAR *sb.*[2], BARLEY) + *ern*, *ærn* (= OFris. *ern*, ON. *rann*, Goth. *razn*) house, f. base **ras-* of REST *v.*[1]] A covered building for the storage of grain; also of hay, straw, flax, etc.

Comb. etc.: **b.-floor,** the floor of a b., *hence* what is there stored; **-gallon,** two imperial gallons (of milk); **barn(s)man,** a thresher; **-owl,** a bird of prey (*Strix flammea*), also called White, Church, and Screech Owl; **-stormer,** a strolling player; **-swallow,** the common house-swallow; **-yard,** the enclosure round a b., a farm-yard. Hence † **Barn** *v.* to garner.

Barn(e, obs. f. BAIRN.

Barnabite (bā·ɹnăbəit). 1706. [f. *Barnabas* the apostle + -ITE[1] 1.] A member of a religious order named from the Church of St. Barnabas at Milan.

Barnaby (bā·ɹnăbi). 1595. [– Fr. *Barnabé* – eccl.L. *Barnabas.*] By-form of Barnabas; whence **B.-day, B. bright,** or **long B.,** St. Barnabas' Day, 11 June, in Old Style reckoned the longest day; **B.-thistle,** the *Centaurea solstitialis*, which flowers about June 11.

Barnacle (bā·ɹnăk'l), *sb.*[1] [ME. *bernacle*, *barnackle*, alt. of AFr. *bernac*, of unkn. origin.] **1.** A kind of bit or twitch for the mouth of horse or ass; later, *spec.* an instrument consisting of two hinged branches placed on the nose of a restive horse. **2.** An instrument of torture similarly applied. Also *fig.* 1625. **3.** *colloq.* in *pl.* = SPECTACLES. [Prob. from their bestriding the nose.] 1571. Hence **Ba·rnacle** *v.*[1] to apply a barnacle to (a horse) 1861.

Barnacle (bā·ɹnăk'l), *sb.*[2] ME. [orig. *bernak*, *-ek(ke)*, corresp. to med.L. *bernaca*, *-eca*, the app. source of Fr. *bernaque*, mod. Pr., Pg. *bernaca*, Sp. *berneca*; *barnacle* (XV) is paralleled by Fr. *barnacle*, *bernacle*, † *bernicle*, but may be of independent origin; ult. source unkn. The name was orig. applied to the bird, not to the shell.] **1.** A species of wild goose (*Anas leucopsis*), allied to the Brent Goose, found in the arctic seas (where alone it breeds), and visiting the British coasts in winter. (Formerly fabled to be produced out of the fruit of a tree, or to grow upon the tree attached by its bill (whence called *Tree Goose*), or to be produced out of a shell. **b.** Now often *Bernacle Goose* 1768. **2.** Name of the pedunculate genus of Cirripides, which attach themselves to objects by a long fleshy foot-stalk. Occas. used of sessile Cirripides; see ACORN-SHELL. (From this the B. Goose was supposed to be produced.) 1581. **3.** *fig.* A companion that is difficult to shake off 1607. Hence **Ba·rnacle** *v.*[2] to affix strongly 1863.

Barnacled (bā·ɹnăk'ld), *ppl. a.* 1691. [f. prec. + -ED[2].] **a.** Covered with barnacles. **b.** *colloq.* Wearing spectacles.

† **Ba·rnage.** ME. [f. *barn*, var. of BAIRN, + -AGE.] Infancy –1513.

† **Ba·rnard.** 1532. [app. var. of late ME. *berner*, one who waited with hounds to intercept a hunted animal.] A swindler's decoy; a lurking scoundrel –1608.

Barn dance. 1892. orig. *U.S.* A dance danced in a barn; *spec.* a dance in which partners advance side by side and then dance a waltz or schottische step.

Barn-door. 1547. The large door of a barn. (Used joc. of a target too large to be missed, and, in *Cricket*, of a player who blocks every ball.) *attrib.* Reared at the b.-door 1685.

Ba·rney. 1865. [Origin unkn.] **a.** Cheating. (*slang*). **b.** *Mining.* A small car attached to a rope and used to push cars up a slope.

Barnumize (bā·ɹnəməiz), *v.* 1851. [f. P. *Barnum* (1810–91), U.S. showman, + -IZE.] To exhibit with a lavish display of puffing advertisements. **Ba·rnumism,** boastful 'tall talk'.

Barograph (bæ·rŏgraf). 1865. [f. Gr. βάρος weight + -GRAPH.] A barometer, actuating mechanism which records automatically the atmospheric pressure. **Ba·rogram,** the record traced by a b.

Baroko, -oco (bărōᵘ·ko). 1581. *Logic.* A mnemonic word, repr. the fourth mood of the second syllogistic figure, in which a particular negative conclusion is drawn from a universal affirmative major premiss and a particular negative minor.

Barology (bărǫ·lŏdʒi). 1859. [f. Gr. βάρος weight + -LOGY.] The science of weight.

Ba:romacro·meter. 1847. [f. Gr. βάρος weight + μάκρος length + -METER.] An instrument for taking the weight and length of new-born infants.

Barometer (bărǭ·mĭtəɹ). 1665. [f. Gr. βάρος weight + -METER.] An instrument for measuring the weight or pressure of the atmosphere, and hence for forecasting the weather, ascertaining the height of an ascent, etc. Also *fig.*

(The common barometer is a straight glass tube, 34 inches long and closed at the top, filled with mercury, and inverted in an open cup of the same liquid. The *siphon barometer* is a curved tube, with the mercury in the shorter limb exposed to the air; it is adapted as the *wheel barometer* by putting on the mercury in the shorter limb a float with a cord attached, which passes over a pulley, and moves an index.)

fig. Interest is the true b. of the state HUME.

Comb. **Barometer-gauge:** an appliance resembling a b., attached to the receiver of an air-pump, to indicate the rarity of the air within. Hence **Barome·tric, -al** *a.* of the nature of, pertaining to, or indicated by, a b. **Barome·trically** *adv.*

Ba:rome·trograph. 1847. [f. as prec. + -GRAPH.] = BAROGRAPH. So **Ba:rometro·graphy,** the part of science which treats of the barometer.

Barometry (bărǫ·mĕtri). 1713. [f. BAROMETER + -Y³; see -METRY.] The art or science of barometric observation.

Barometz (bæ·rŏmets). 1791. [– Russ. *baranets,* dim. of *baran* ram.] The creeping root-stock and frond stalks of a woolly fern (*Cibotium barometz*) turned upside down; once thought to be half-animal, and called the Scythian Lamb.

Baron (bæ·rən). Early ME. [– AFr. *barun,* (O)Fr. *baron,* acc. of *ber* = Pr. *bar,* acc. *baron* :– med.L. *baro, -ōn-* man, male, warrior; identified by scholiasts and others with L. *baro* simpleton, dunce (Cicero, etc.), but of unkn. origin.] **1.** *Hist.* Orig., one who held, by military or other honourable service, from the king, or other superior; subseq. restricted to the *King's barons,* and later to the *Great Barons,* who were summoned by writ to Parliament; *hence,* a lord of Parliament; a peer. **2.** The lowest rank or order of nobility ME. † **3.** Formerly applied to the freemen of London, York, etc.; applied till the 18th c. to the freemen of the Cinque Ports, and, till 1832, to the burgesses returned by these ports to Parliament. **4.** Title of the judges of the Court of Exchequer ME. **5.** *Law* and *Her.* (conjoined with *feme, femme*): Husband 1594. **6.** A foreign title (giving no rank in England), *e.g.* Baron Rothschild. ‖ **7.** In foreign use applied in respect to any man, also to Christ and the saints ME.

2. Boþe kniȝt and barun. .erl. .and king ME. **3.** Foure Barons Of the Cinque-Ports *Hen. VIII,* IV. i. 48. **4.** Barons of the Exchequer. .because Barons of the realm were used to be employed in that office 1751. **7.** Ioseph, þat god barune 1300.

Phr. *Baron of beef* [origin unkn.]: two sirloins left uncut at the backbone. *Comb.* **b.-court:** see COURT-BARON.

Hence **Ba·ronism** (*rare*), feudalism. **Ba·ronist** (*rare*), an adherent of the Barons' party. ‖ **Baronne·tte,** a baron's daughter; occ. a baronet's wife. **Ba·ronship,** the position of a b.

Baronage (bæ·rŏnėdʒ). [ME. *barnage* – OFr. *barnage,* med.L. *barnagium, baronagium*; see prec., -AGE.] **1.** The barons collectively; the nobles, lords, peerage. **b.** *ellipt.* A list of the barons; a 'Peerage'. † **2.** A barony –1480. **3.** The dignity of a baron 1614.

1. The Judges. .were the B. of England SELDEN.

Baroness (bæ·rŏnės). ME. [– OFr. *baronesse* (Anglo-L. *baronissa, -essa*); see BARON, -ESS¹.] **a.** The wife of a baron. **b.** A lady holding the title in her own right.

Baronet (bæ·rŏnėt), *sb.* ME. [– Anglo-L. *baronettus*; see BARON, -ET.] † **1.** *orig.* A word meaning *young, little,* or *lesser baron.* Used of gentlemen, not barons by tenure, summoned to the House of Lords by Edward III. In Ireland, the holder of a small barony. Often = BANNERET. –1662. **2.** *now,* A titled order, the lowest that is hereditary, ranking next below a baron, having precedence of all orders of knighthood, except that of the Garter. A baronet is a commoner. 1614.

They consist of *Baronets of England* (now of *Great Britain*) instituted in 1611; *Baronets of Scotland* (or of *Nova Scotia*) instituted in 1625; *Baronets of Ireland* instituted in 1619. Of the two latter there have been no new creations since 1707 and 1801 respectively. Hence **Ba·ronete:ss,** the wife of a b. **Barone·tical** *a.*

Baronet (bæ·rŏnet), *v.* Pa. t. and pple. **-eted.** 1733. [f. prec. sb.] To raise to the rank of baronet. (Usu. in *pass.*)

Baronetage (bæ·ronėtėdʒ). 1720. [f. BARONET *sb.* + -AGE.] **1.** The rank of baronet 1760. **2.** The order of baronets 1876. **b.** A book giving a list of the order, with other particulars 1720.

Baronetcy (bæ·rŏnėtsi). 1812. [f. as prec. + -CY.] A baronet's rank or patent. So **Ba·ronethood, Ba·ronetship.**

Baronial (bărōᵘ·niăl), *a.* 1767. [f. BARONY + -AL¹.] Of or pertaining to a baron or the barons; befitting the rank of a baron.

Barony (bæ·rŏni). ME. [– OFr. *baronie* (mod. *baronnie*), in med.L. *baronia*; see -Y³.] **1.** The domain of a baron. **b.** In Ireland: A division of a county 1596. **c.** In Scotland: A large freehold estate (even though owned by a commoner). 1843. † **2.** The baronetage –1596. **3.** The rank or dignity of baron; baronship 1788. var. **Ba·ronry** (in senses 1, 3). ? *Obs.*

Baroque (bărǫ·k), *a.* 1818. [– Fr. *baroque* (in earliest use of pearls) – Pg. *barroco,* Sp. *barrueco,* of unkn. origin; as applied to architecture (orig. that of Francesco Borromini) – It. *barroco.*] Irregularly shaped; grotesque, odd; *spec.* of a florid style of late Renaissance architecture prevalent in the 18th c. Also *ellipt.* as *sb.*

Baroscope (bæ·rŏskoᵘp). 1665. [f. Gr. βάρος weight + -SCOPE.] **1.** A kind of barometer. **2.** An instrument designed to show that bodies in air lose as much weight as that of the air they displace 1881. Hence **Barosco·pic, -al** *a.*

Barouche (bărū·ʃ). 1813. [– G. dial. *barutsche* – It. *baroccio* (Sp. *barrocho*) for **biroccio* 'two-wheeled' – late L. **birotium,* f. L. *birotus,* f. *bi-* BI- + *rota* wheel.] A four-wheeled carriage with a half-head behind which can be raised or let down, having a seat in front for the driver, and seats inside for two couples to sit facing each other.

Barque (bāɹk). Var. of BARK *sb.*²

Barquentine, bark- (bāɹkĕntīn). 1693. [f. BARK *sb.*² after BRIGANTINE.] A small bark; *spec.* now: A vessel having the foremast square-rigged, and the main- and mizen-masts fore-and-aft-rigged.

† **Barr,** *v.* 1653. [var. of † *bary* – OFr. *barier* (mod. *barrir*) – L. *barrire.*] To utter the cry of an elephant.

Barrable (bā·răb'l), *a.* 1788. [f. BAR *v.* + -ABLE.] That can be legally stayed.

† **Ba·rracan.** 1638. [– Fr. *barracan* (Cotgr.), *bouracan* – Arab. *burru-, barrakân* cloak of camlet; cf. BARRAGAN.] A fabric: orig. coarse camlet; still in Spain 'a water-proof cloth of coarse wool or goat's hair' (Marsh). Used vaguely by European writers.

Barrace (bæ·răs). *Obs.* exc. *Hist.* ME. [– OFr. *barras,* f. *barre* BAR *sb.*¹ + *-as,* augmentative suffix :– L. *-aceus.*] **1.** A barrier or outwork in front of a fortress. **2.** The lists 1513. **3.** Hence: Contention (cf. BARRAT) 1470.

Barrack (bæ·răk), *sb.* 1686. [– Fr. *baraque* – It. *baracca* or Sp. *barraca* soldier's tent, of unkn. origin.] **1.** A temporary hut or cabin. Still in *n. dial.* **b.** A straw-thatched roof, sliding on four posts, under which hay is kept. (In U.S.) 1848. **2.** A set of buildings used as a place of lodgement or residence for soldiers. Properly in *pl.* (collect.) 1697.

1. He lodged in a miserable hut or b. GIBBON.

Barrack (bæ·răk), *v.*¹ 1701. [f. prec. sb.] **1.** To provide with or locate in barracks. **2.** *intr.* To lodge in barracks 1834.

Ba·rrack, *v.*² 1890. [alt. of native Austral. *borak* sb., in phr. *to poke borak* poke fun.] *intr.* To shout derisively so as to disconcert players; *trans.* to shout at thus.

Barracoon (bærăkū·n). 1851. [– Sp. *barracón,* augm. of *barraca*; see BARRACK *sb.*, -OON.] An enclosure, in which negro-slaves, etc., are temporarily detained.

Barracuda, -coota, -couta (bærăkū·dă, -ū·tă). 1678. [– Amer. Sp. *barracuda,* of unkn. origin.] A voracious fish (*Sphyræna barracuda*) found in West Indian seas.

Ba·rragan, -on. 1787. [– Sp. *barragan*; see BARRACAN, of which this is a modern revival, in the Spanish form, for trade purposes.] A kind of fustian.

Barrage (bā·rėdʒ). 1859. [– Fr. *barrage,* f. *barrer*; see BAR *v.*, -AGE.] **1.** The action of barring; the formation of an artificial bar in a river, etc., to increase the depth of water; the bar thus formed. **2.** (bæ·rāʒ, -ėdʒ). A barrier of continuous artillery or machine-gun fire concentrated on a given area; also *creeping* or *moving b.*, and *b. fire* 1917.

‖ **Barranca** (bāræ·ŋkă). 1884. [Sp., used in U.S.] A deep ravine with precipitous sides.

Barrandite (bæ·răndəit). 1868. [Named, in 1867, after *Barrande,* a Bohemian geologist; see -ITE¹ 2 b.] *Min.* A phosphate of alumina and iron occurring in spheroidal concretions in Bohemia.

† **Ba·rras.** 1640. A coarse linen fabric, orig. from Holland –1714.

† **Ba·rrat.** ME. [– (O)Fr. *barat,* OFr. *barate* (fem.) deceit, fraud, trouble, etc., f. *barater* – ON. *barátta* contest, fighting; see BARRATOR.] **1.** Deception, fraud –1503. **2.** Trouble –1552. **3.** Contention –1496. Hence † **Ba·rrat** *v.* to quarrel.

Barrator, -er (bæ·rătəɹ). ME. [– AFr. *baratour,* OFr. *barateor* cheat, trickster, f. *barater* (= Pr., OSp., Pg. *baratar,* It. *barattare*) :– Rom. **prattare* exchange, cheat – Gr. πράττειν do, perform, manage, practise (sometimes dishonestly). See prec.] **1.** [f. AFr. *baratour.*] One who buys or sells eccles. preferment, or offices of state. **2.** A judge who takes bribes 1864. **3.** A ship's master who commits BARRATRY (sense 3) 1847. † **4.** [f. BARRAT *sb.*] One who fights; *esp.* a hired bully –1583. † **5.** A brawler –1714. **6.** One who vexatiously raises, or incites to, litigation ME. Hence † **Ba·rratous** *a.* quarrelsome.

Barratrous (bæ·rătrəs), *a.* 1842. [f. BARRATRY + -OUS.] In *Marine Law*: Of the nature of barratry. **Ba·rratrously** *adv.*

Barratry (bæ·rătri). ME. [– OFr. *bar(a)terie* (= Pr. *barataria*) deceit, f. *barat*; see BARRAT, -ERY.] **1.** The purchase or sale of eccles. preferment, or of offices of state. **2.** *Sc. Law.* The acceptance of bribes by a judge 1773. **3.** *Marine Law.* Fraud, or gross and criminal negligence, on the part of the master or mariners of a ship, to the prejudice of the owners, and without their consent 1622. **4.** The offence of habitually moving or maintaining lawsuits or quarrels 1645.

Barred (bāɹd), *ppl. a.* ME. [f. BAR *v.* and *sb.* + -ED¹, -ED².] **1.** Secured or shut with bars 1593. **2.** Having, or furnished with, a bar or bars 1571. **3.** Ornamented with bars, as *b. owl* ME.

Barrel (bæ·rĕl), *sb.* ME. [– (O)Fr. *baril* = Pr. *baril,* It. *barile* (med.L. *barriclus, barillus, barile*); plausibly taken by Diez to be a deriv.

of *barra* BAR *sb.*[1]] **1.** A cylindrical wooden vessel, generally bulging in the middle and of greater length than breadth, formed of curved staves bound together by hoops, and having flat ends; a cask. **2.** A measure of capacity for both liquids and dry goods, varying with the commodity ME. **3.** By metonymy: Intoxicating liquor. Cf. 'the bottle'. ME. † **4.** *abstr.* Brand, quality –1789. **5.** A revolving cylinder or drum, round which a chain or rope is wound; as, the b. of a windlass; the b. of a watch, containing the mainspring; the revolving b. of a musical box, barrel-organ, etc. 1500. **6.** A (usually hollow) cylinder forming part of various objects; *e.g.* of a pump, engine-boiler, bell, feather 1629. **7.** The metal tube of a gun, through which the shot is discharged. Hence in *single b.*, etc., of the whole weapon. 1648. **8.** The belly and loins of a horse, ox, etc. 1703. **9.** *Phys.* The cavity of the ear situated within the tympanic membrane 1706.

Comb.: **b.-bird,** dial. name of the Long-tailed Tit; **-bulk,** a measure equal to five cubic feet; **-drain,** a cylindrical brick drain; **-ful; -head,** (either) flat end of a b.; **-organ,** orig., a musical instrument of the organ type, with a pin-studded revolving barrel or cylinder acting mechanically on the keys; now, an instrument in which the notes are produced by metal tongues struck by pins fixed in the barrel; also as vb.; **-pen,** one with a split cylindrical shank to take a wooden holder; **-sewer** (cf. *-drain*); **-vault,** one with a semi-cylindrical roof; whence **-vaulted.**

Barrel (bæ·rĕl), *v.* 1466. [f. prec. sb.] **1.** To put or pack in a barrel or barrels. **2.** *gen.* To store up 1589.

Barrelled, -eled (bæ·rĕld), *ppl. a.* 1494. [f. BARREL + -ED[1,2].] **1.** Packed or stowed away in a barrel or barrels. **2.** Shaped like a barrel 1853. **3.** Having a barrel or barrels; chiefly in *comb.*, as *single-b.* 1704.

Barren (bæ·rĕn). Comp. *barrener, -est.* [ME. *barain* – AFr. (fem.) *barai(g)ne*, OFr. *barhaine, bra-, brehai(g)ne* (mod. *bréhaigne*), of unkn. origin.] **A.** *adj.* **1.** Of a woman: Bearing no children. **2.** Of animals: Not pregnant at the usual season ME. **3.** Of plants, etc.: Without fruit or seed ME. **4.** Of land: Unproductive. So of mines, etc. ME. **5.** Void of vital germs 1871. **6.** *fig.* Bare of interest, arid ME. **7.** Unprofitable 1549. **8.** Of persons: Unresponsive, dull 1590. **9.** *Const.* in all prec. senses with *of.*

1. To live a b. sister all your life *Mids. N.* I. i. 72. **4.** B. mines 1776, soil MILL. **6.** A list of b. names GROTE. **7.** B. praise DRYDEN. **8.** B. Spectators *Haml.* III. ii. 46. **9.** Hearts b. of kindness STEELE. Hence † **Ba·rren,** † **Ba·rrenize** *vbs.* to make b. or sterile. **Ba·rrener,** a cow not in calf for the year. **Ba·rrenly** *adv.*, **-ness.**

B. *sb.* [the adj. used *absol.*] † **1.** [sc. *woman* or *animal.*] ME. **2.** A tract of barren land; *spec.* in N. America **a.** plains on which grow small trees and shrubs, but no timber, as *oak-barrens*, etc.; **b.** in Nova Scotia and New Brunswick, open marshy spaces in the forest 1784.

Barrenwort (bæ·rĕnwɒɹt). 1597. [f. BARREN + WORT.] *Herb.* Name of the genus *Epimedium*, esp. of *Epimedium alpinum* (N.O. *Berberidaceæ*).

Barret (bæ·rėt). 1828. [– Fr. *barrette* – It. *baretta* (mod. *berretta*); see BIRETTA.] A little flat cap; *esp.* the BIRETTA.

Barricade (bærikē̆ⁱ·d). 1642. [– Fr. *barricade*, f. *barrique* – Sp. *barrica* cask, f. stem of *barril* BARREL; see -ADE. The first barricades in Paris (*la journée des barricades*, 1588) were composed of barrels filled with earth, paving-stones, etc.] **1.** = BARRICADO 1. **2.** *transf.* and *fig.* Any barrier obstructing passage 1735. **3.** *Naut.* = BARRICADO 4. 1769.

1. The world has heard of the Barricades of Paris 1670.

Barrica·de, *v.* 1592. [f. prec., after Fr. *barricader.*] **1.** To block with a barricade. Also *transf.* and *fig.* **2.** To shut in with or as with a barricade 1657.

1. B. al the streets 1592. **2.** B. mee with these Bulwarkes against myne enemyes 1657.

Barricado (bærikēⁱ·do), *sb.* Pl. **-oes, -os.** 1590. [Earlier form of BARRICADE; see -ADO.] **1.** A hastily formed rampart of barrels, wagons, stones, or anything at hand, thrown up to obstruct an enemy's advance. **2.** *transf.* and *fig.* = BARRICADE 2. 1611. †**3.** A natural frontier. MILT. **4.** *Naut.* 'A strong wooden rail, supported by..stanchions, and extending, as a fence, across the foremost part of the quarter-deck' (Falconer) 1675.

2. Many were drowned in the river, which proved a b. to the French 1693.

Barricado (bærikēⁱ·do), *v.* 1598. [f. prec. sb.] **1.** To close or block with (or as with) a barricade 1611. **2.** To fortify or defend with barricades. Also *fig.* 1601. **3.** To shut up, bar in securely (*lit.* and *fig.*) 1598. **4.** To preclude *from* (*lit.* and *fig.*) 1611.

3. I barricado'd myself round with the chests DE FOE

Barrico (bărī·ko). Pl. **-oes.** 1607. [– Sp. *barrica* cask; see BARECA.] A keg.

Barrier (bæ·riəɹ), *sb.* [ME. *barrer(e* – AFr. *barrere*, (O)Fr. *barrière* :– Rom. **barraria*, collect. f. **barra* BAR *sb.*[1]; see -IER.] **1.** *gen.* A material obstruction of any kind which bars advance or prevents access. **a.** *orig.* A palisade or stockade erected to defend a gate, etc. **b.** *transf.* a fortress, etc., which commands the entrance into a country 1600. **c.** A fence or railing to prevent access to any place 1570. **d.** The *carcer* or starting-place in the ancient race-course 1600. **e.** In continental towns: The gate at which custom duties are collected 1825. **f.** *Coal-mining.* A breadth of coal left against an adjoining royalty, for security against water or foul air 1851. **2.** *spec.* in *pl.* The palisades enclosing the ground where a tournament, etc., was held; the lists. Also, a low fence running down the centre of the lists. 1581. **3.** Any natural obstacle which bars access 1703. **4.** Anything immaterial that keeps separate and apart 1702.

2. At length the barriers were opened, and five knights advanced slowly into the area SCOTT. **4.** He..erects a b. between himself and his reader GODWIN.

Comb.: **b.-gate,** a heavy gate closing the opening through a b.; **-reef,** a wall of coral rock, separated from the land by a deep channel; **-treaty,** one fixing the frontier of a country, *esp.* 'The Treaty of the Barriers' signed at Antwerp in 1715. Hence **Ba·rrier** *v.* to close or shut with a b. **Ba·rriered** *ppl. a.* furnished with or confined by a b. or barriers.

Barring (bā·riŋ), *vbl. sb.* ME. [f. BAR *v.* + -ING[1].] The action of BAR *v.*

Barring-out: shutting the school-room against the master, etc., a mode of schoolboy rebellion.

Barring (bā·riŋ), *prep.* 1481. [Prepositional use of pres. pple. of BAR *v.* 7 exclude, except; see -ING[2].] Excluding from consideration, except.

Barrister (bæ·ristəɹ). 1532. [Earliest form *barrester*, obscurely f. BAR *sb.*[1], perh. after † *legister* lawyer, or *minister.*] A student of law, who has been called to the bar, and practises as advocate in the superior courts of law. Formally *barrister-at-law.*

Revising barrister: one appointed to revise the list of persons qualified to vote for Members of Parliament. Hence **Barriste·rial** *a.* **Ba·rristership. Barrista·tion,** the action of a b. (*nonce-wd.*)

Barrow (bæ·roᵘ), *sb.*[1] [OE. *beorg* = OFris., OS., OHG. (Du., G.) *berg* :– Gmc. **berȝaz* (cf. ON. *berg, bjarg* n. rock, precipice, Goth. *bairgahei* hill country. See BOROUGH.] **1.** A mountain, hill, or hillock. (Still in local use, as in Cadon B. in Cornwall, Whitbarrow in Lancs., etc.) **2.** A grave-mound, a tumulus OE. **3.** *dial.* A mound or heap 1869.

2. Grassy barrows of the..dead TENNYSON.

Barrow (bæ·roᵘ), *sb.*[2] [OE. *barg* (*bearg*) = OFris., MDu. *barch* (Du. *barg*), OS., OHG. *bar(u)g*, (G. dial. *barch*), ON. *bǫrgr* :– Gmc. **barzuz* or **barzwaz*; not known outside Gmc.] **1.** A castrated boar. Still *dial.* † **2.** A badger (*rare*). (? misprint for *bauson*). 1552.

Barrow (bæ·roᵘ), *sb.*[3] [OE. *bearwe* :– **barwōn*, f. **bar-* **ber-* BEAR *v.*[1] See BIER.] **1.** A contrivance for the carrying of a load; a frame, having shafts or trams by which it is carried, and sometimes four legs; a stretcher; a bier; a hand-barrow ME. **2.** A modification of this, having a wheel or wheels; a wheelbarrow; a costermonger's barrow ME. **b.** The contents of a barrow 1598. **3.** *Saltmaking.* A conical basket for draining wet salt 1686.

Comb.: **b.-man, -woman,** one employed in wheeling a b.; **-tram,** the shaft of a b.; **-way** (*Mining*), a tramway on which the barrow-men put the tubs of coal. Hence **Ba·rrow** *v.* to transport in a b.

Ba·rrowist. 1589. *Hist.* A follower of Henry Barrowe, one of the founders of Congregationalism, executed for nonconformity in 1593.

Barrulet (bæ·riŭlėt). Also **-ette.** 1562. [dim. of assumed AFr. **barrule*, dim. of Fr. *barre* BAR *sb.*[1]; see -LET, -ULE.] *Her.* The fourth part of a *bar.*

Barruly (bæ·riŭli), *a.* 1562. [– AFr. *barrulé*; see prec., -Y[5].] *Her.* Crossed by barrulets. var. **Ba·rrulety** *a.* (Dicts.)

Barry (bā·ri), *a.* 1486. [– Fr. *barré* barred, striped, f. *barrer* BAR *v.*; see -Y[5].] *Her.* (A field) Divided horizontally into equal parts by bars of two colours alternating.

Barse. Still *dial.* [OE. *bærs, bears* (:– **bars*) = OS. *bars*, MDu. *ba(e)rse*, Du. *baars*, MHG. *bars*, G. *barsch.* See BAR *sb.*[2], BASE *sb.*[5], BASS *sb.*[1]] Name of a fish, subseq. corrupted to BASE and BASS(E.

Bart., abbrev. of BARONET, written after the name, and supplementary to the prefixed *Sir*, also given to a Knight.

Barter (bā·ɹtəɹ), *v.* ME. [Form and meaning suggest deriv. from OFr. *barater* (see BARRATOR), but connecting links are wanting.] **1.** To give (a commodity) for something (not being *money*) taken as of equivalent value. Const. *for*, † *with* a thing, *with* a person 1440. **2.** *fig.* **a.** To exchange 1602. **b.** To dispose of for a consideration, usu. an unworthy one 1664. **3.** *intr.* To trade by exchange of commodities 1485.

1. To b. ware for ware PALSGR. **2.** To b. blowes 1602. E'en liberty itself is barter'd here GOLDSM. Hence **Ba·rterer. Ba·rtering** *vbl. sb.*

Barter (bā·ɹtəɹ), *sb.* 1592. [f. prec. vb.] **1.** The act or practice of trafficking by exchange of commodities; truck. Also *fig.* **2.** Goods to be bartered 1740. **3.** *Arith.* The computation of the comparative values of different commodities; the method of computing this. var. † **Ba·rtery** (in senses 1, 2).

Barth. Still *dial.* 1573. [Origin unkn.] A sheltered place for cattle.

Bartholomew (baɹþǫ·lŏmiū). Also **Bartlemy** (bā·ɹt'lmi), **Bartelemy, Bart'lemy.** 1552. [Partly – eccl.L. *Bartholomæus*, Gr. βαρθολομαῖος, partly – Fr. *Barthélemy.*] **a.** Name of one of the twelve apostles, whose festival is held on the 24th of August (*B.-day, -tide*). **b.** On this day, in 1572, took place the massacre of the Protestants in France. **c.** On the same day in 1662, the English Act of Uniformity (*B. Act*) came into force. **d.** Used of a fair (*B. Fair*) held annually from 1133 to 1855, at West Smithfield; and hence of articles sold at it, e.g. *B.-baby, -boar, -pig*, etc.

Bartisan, bartizan (bā·ɹtizæn). *Hist.* or *Arch.* 1801. [A seventeenth-century form of BRATTICING revived by Sir Walter Scott.] A battlemented parapet at the top of a castle or church; *esp.* a battlemented turret projecting from an angle at the top of a tower, etc.

Barton (bā·ɹtən). [OE. *bere-tūn*, lit. 'barley enclosure', f. *bere* barley (BEAR *sb.*[2]) + *tūn* (TOWN). Cf. BARN.] † **1.** A threshing-floor OE. only. **2.** A farm-yard. (The regular mod. sense.) 1552. **3.** A demesne farm 1587. † **4.** A pen for poultry –1783.

Bartram, obs. f. BERTRAM.

‖ **Bartsia** (bā·ɹtsiă). 1753. [Named by Linnæus after *Bartsch* of Königsberg; see -IA[1].] *Bot.* A genus of *Scrophulariaceæ*, including *B. odontites.*

Ba·rvel, -ell. 1878. [perh. phonetic corruption of *barm-fell* leather apron; see BARM *sb.*[1]] A leather apron.

Barwood (bā·ɹwud). 1788. [prob. so named from its being sent over in bars; cf. *logwood.*] The red wood of *Baphita nitida*, imported from the Gaboon, etc., used chiefly for dyeing purposes, and also for violin bows, etc.

Baryce·ntric, *a.* [f. Gr. βαρύς heavy + CENTRIC. Cf. *geocentric.*] Of or pertaining to the centre of gravity.

Baryphony (bări·fŏni). [f. as prec. + φωνή speech.] *Med.* Difficulty of speech.

Baryta (bărəi·tă). 1809. [f. BARYTES, with *-a* after *soda*, etc.] *Chem.* † Barium monoxide; barium hydroxide, $Ba(OH)_2$. var. † **Ba·ryt** [– Fr. *baryte.*] 1794.

Barytes (bărəi·tīz). 1789. [f. Gr. βαρύς heavy + *-ites*, the L. suffix corresp. to Gr. -ιτης; see -ITE[1] 2 b. Named in ref. to its great weight.] † **1.** = BARYTA. (Occas. *attrib.*) –1854. **2.** Native sulphate of barium, heavy spar 1789. Hence **Bary·tic** *a.* of, pertaining to, or containing baryta or barium.

Barytine, Barytite, synonyms of BARYTES.

Baryto- (bărəi·to), comb. f. BARYTA, as in **B.-ca·lcite,** a carbonate of barium and calcium. **B.-cele·stite,** a sulphate of barium and strontium.

Barytone, -itone (bæ·ritōᵘn). 1609. [Of the voice, – It. *baritono* – Gr. βαρύτονος deep-sounding (f. βαρύς deep + τόνος pitch); in Gr. gram., – late L. *barytonos* – Gr. βαρύτονος not oxytone.] **A.** *sb.* **1.** The male voice of barytone compass, ranging from lower A in the bass clef to lower F in the treble clef. **2.** A singer having such a voice 1821. **3.** A musical instrument of deep sound: † **a.** a kind of bass viol; **b.** the smaller bass saxhorn in B♭ or C. 1685. **4.** *Gk. Gram.* A barytone word: see B. 2.

B. *adj.* **1.** Of the voice: Having a compass intermediate between bass and tenor. **b.** Suited for a barytone voice. **c.** Possessing a barytone voice. 1729. **2.** *Gr. Gram.* Not having the acute accent on the last syllable 1828.

Basal (bēⁱ·săl), *a.* (*sb.*) 1828. [f. BASE *sb.*[1] + -AL[1].] **1.** Pertaining to, situated at, or forming the base. **2.** *fig.* Fundamental 1865. **3.** *sb.* A basal part; *spec.* one of the basal plates encircling the stem of the crinoids 1877.

1. *Basal plane* and *cleavage* in *Crystallog.*: one parallel to the lateral or horizontal axis. Comb. *b.-nerved*, with nerves all springing from the base of the leaf. Hence **Ba·sally** *adv.*

Basalt (băsǭ·lt, bæ·sǫlt). 1601. [orig. in L. form; – L. *basaltes*, var. of *basanites* – Gr. βασανίτης (sc. λίθος stone), f. βάσανος touch-stone.] *Min.* A kind of trap rock; a greenish- or brownish-black igneous rock, composed of augite or hornblende containing titaniferous magnetic iron and crystals of feldspar, often lying in columnar strata, as at the Giant's Causeway in Ireland, etc. (Pliny's *basaltes* was prob. Syenite.) Also *attrib.* **2.** A black porcelain invented by Wedgwood 1832.

The B. is only Lava, which has flowed beneath the sea DARWIN. Hence **Basa·ltic,** † **Basa·ltine** *adjs.* of, consisting of, of the nature of, or resembling b. **Basa·ltiform, Basa·ltoid** *adjs.* having the form of b. † **Basa·ltin(e,** *Min.* a kind of basaltic hornblende.

Basan, bazan (bæ·zăn). 1714. [– (O)Fr. *basane* – Pr. *bazana* – Sp. *badana* (cf. med.L. *bedana*, Anglo-L. *basana*) – Arab. *biṭāna* lining.] Sheep-skin tanned in bark; distinguished from *roan*, which is tanned in sumach.

Basanite (bæ·sănəit). 1794. [– L. *basanites* (see BASALT), f. Gr. βάσανος touch-stone + *-ites* -ITE[1] 2 b.] A velvet-black siliceous quartz, used for testing the purity of gold, etc., by means of the mark left after rubbing the metal upon it.

† ‖ **Bas bleu** (bā,blö). 1801. [Fr. tr. of Eng. BLUE-STOCKING.] A blue-stocking, a literary lady –1821.

Basculation (bæskiŭlēⁱ·ʃən). 1881. [– Fr. *basculer* see-saw (f. *bascule*, see next) + -ATION.] *Surg.* The movement by which retroversion of the uterus is remedied.

Bascule (bæ·skiul). 1678. [– Fr. *bascule*, earlier *bacule* see-saw, f. stem of *battre* beat + *cul* posteriors.] An apparatus acting on the principle of the lever, whereby one end is raised when the other is depressed; *esp.* in **Bascule-bridge,** a drawbridge balanced by a counterpoise which rises or falls as the bridge is lowered or raised.

Base (bēⁱ·s), *sb.*[1] ME. [– (O)Fr. *base* or L. *basis*; see BASIS.] **1.** The bottom of any object, considered as its support, or that on which it rests. **2.** *fig.* Fundamental principle, foundation 1500. **3.** *Archit.* **a.** The plinth and mouldings between the bottom of the shaft and the top of the pedestal, or between the shaft and the pavement ME. **b.** The plinth and mouldings which project at the bottom of the wall of a room. **c.** The lowest course of masonry in a building. **4.** A pedestal 1440. **5.** *Gunnery*, The protuberant rear-portion of a cannon, between the knob and the base-ring. **6.** *Bot.* and *Zool.* That extremity of a part or organ by which it is attached to the trunk 1831. **7.** *Her.* The lower part of a shield 1611. **8.** *Geom.* That line or surface of a plane or solid figure on which it is considered to stand 1570. **9.** *Fortification.* The imaginary line which connects two salient angles 1721. **10.** *gen.* The principal ingredient 1471. **11.** *Dyeing.* A substance used as a mordant, by which colours are fixed 1791. **12.** *Mod. Chem.* The electro-positive compound body which combines with an acid to form a salt, the correl. of ACID, including, but wider than ALKALI 1810. **13.** *Gram.* The form of a word to which suffixes are attached 1875. **14. a.** The line from which runners start, or which serves as a goal, in a race. **b.** The fixed line or goal in hockey, etc. **c.** The fixed points or stations in rounders or baseball. 1695. **15.** *Mil.* The line or place relied upon as a stronghold and magazine, and from which the operations of a campaign are conducted. Also *transf.* 1860. **16.** *Surv.* A line on the earth's surface or in space, of which the exact length and position are accurately determined, and which is used as a base (sense 8) for observations and computations 1834. **17.** *Math.* The number from which a system of numeration or logarithms proceeds 1874.

1. The extent of the b. of the great pyramid JOHNSON. **15.** The territory on which these resources are spread is called the 'base of operations' KINGLAKE.

Comb.: **b.-burner,** a furnace or stove in which the fuel is supplied to the fire automatically from a hopper as the lower stratum is consumed; **-line,** *Mil.* that on which all magazines and means of supply for an army are established (cf. 15, 16); in *Gunnery*, a line traced round a cannon at the rear of the vent; **-ring,** a moulding on the breech of a cannon between the b. and the first reinforce.

Base (bēⁱs), *sb.*[2] Also **prisoner's base.** 1440. [prob. for *bars*, pl. of BAR *sb.*[1] For the form, cf. BASS *sb.*[1]] A game played by two sides, who occupy contiguous 'bases' or 'homes'; any player running out from his base is chased by one of the other side, and, if caught, made a prisoner.

† *To bid base*: to challenge SHAKS. *Ven. & Ad.* li.

† **Base** (bēⁱs), *sb.*[3] *Hist.* 1548. [app. use of BASE *sb.*[1] 'bottom'.] ***sing.* 1.** ? The housing of a horse –1667. ****pl.* *bases* (cf. *skirts*). **2.** A pleated skirt, appended to the doublet, and reaching from the waist to the knee; also an imitation of this in mailed armour –1821. **3.** The skirt of a woman's outer petticoat or robe –1697. **4.** An apron –1663.

† **Base,** *sb.*[4] 1450. *Mus.* The spelling of BASS *sb.*[5], till the 19th c.

Base, *sb.*[5] Now *dial.* 1440. [var. of BARSE, now BASS *sb.*[1]; see also BAR *sb.*[2]] = BASS *sb.*[1]

† **Base,** *sb.*[6] 1544. [app. corrupt – Fr. † *barce, berche* (Cotgr.) in same sense.] The smallest kind of cannon used in 16–17th centuries –1692.

Base (bēⁱs), *a.* ME. [– (O)Fr. *bas* :– med.L. *bassus* (explained by Isidore as 'thick, fat', by Papius as 'short, low'), found in cl.L. as a cognomen.] **1.** Low; of small height (*arch.*). In *Bot.* denoting lowly growth; e.g. *B. Broom*, *B. Rocket.* 1578. † **2.** Low-lying; *esp.* geographically or topographically –1851. **3.** Of sounds: Not loud; deep, BASS 1450. **4.** *fig.* Of lowly condition, plebeian (*arch.*) 1490. **5.** Illegitimate. ? *Obs.* exc. in BASE-BORN. 1570. **6.** Low in the natural scale 1534. **7.** Low in the moral scale; reprehensibly cowardly, selfish, or mean; opp. to *high-minded* 1535. **8.** Degraded or degrading, menial 1594. **9.** *Law.* Servile, as opp. to *free* 1523. **10.** Of inferior quality: mean, poor, shabby, etc. 1561. Of language: Debased 1549. **11.** Worthless 1607. **12.** Debased, counterfeit, as coin, etc. 1528.

2. B. Egypt watered..with Nilus HOLLAND. **4.** Borne of basse parentage CAXTON. **6.** Ciuet is of a baser birth then Tarre *A.Y.L.* III. ii. 69. B. vermine, such as Rats 1680. **7.** B., fearefull, and despayring Henry 3 *Hen. VI*, I. i. 178. A most b. piece of flatterie RALEIGH. **9.** *B. tenure, estate, fee*: *orig.* tenure by *b. service*, such as a villain owed to his lord; *later*, such tenure in fee simple as may determine on the fulfilment of a contingent qualification or limitation. See also B.-COURT. **11.** *B. metals*: those not classed as *noble* or *precious.* **12.** B. money MACAULAY.

† **Base,** *v.*[1] ME. [Partly aphet. f. *abase v.*; partly – OFr. *baissier* (mod. *baisser*) :– Rom. **bassiare*, f. *bassus* BASE *a.*] **1.** To lower –1626. **2.** To lessen in amount or value; to debase (metals) –1626.

Base (bēⁱs), *v.*[2] 1587. [f. BASE *sb.*[1]] **1.** To make a foundation for. **2.** To place *on* or *upon* a foundation or logical basis; to secure. (So Fr. *baser.*) 1841.

2. These [bank-]notes were based on gold ROGERS.

Baseball (bēⁱ·sbǭl). 1850. [f. BASE *sb.*[1] 14.] The national field-game of the United States; so called from the bases or bounds (usu. four in number) which mark the circuit to be taken by each player of the in-side after striking the ball. Also, the ball used in the game.

Base-born (bēⁱ·s,bǭɹn), *a.* 1591. [f. BASE *a.* 4, 5.] **1.** Of humble birth, plebeian 1593. **2.** *fig.* Of base origin or nature 1591. **3.** Illegitimate 1645.

1. Ten-thousand base-borne Cades SHAKS.

Base-court (bēⁱ·s,kōᵊɹt). 1491. [f. BASE *a.* 2 + COURT; in sense 1 – Fr. † *basse-court* (mod. *basse-cour*).] **1.** The lower or outer court of a castle or mansion, occupied by the servants; the court in the rear of a farm-house, containing the out-buildings. **2.** A court of justice that is not of record; *e.g.* a court baron 1542.

Basedow's disease; see BRONCHOCELE.

† **Ba·selard.** ME. [– OFr. *baselard, -arde* = med.L. *base-, basilardus*, etc.; of unkn. origin.] A dagger or hanger, worn at the girdle –1788.

Baseless (bēⁱ·slės), *a.* 1610. [f. BASE *sb.*[1] + -LESS.] **a.** Without base or foundation; groundless. **b.** *Mil.*; cf. BASE *sb.*[1] 15. 1862.

The baselesse fabricke of this vision *Temp.* IV. i. 151. Hence **Ba·selessness.**

‖ **Basella** (băse·lă). 1761. [mod.L., of unkn. origin. Cf. Fr. *baselle.*] *Bot.* A genus of climbing plants (N.O. *Chenopodiaceæ*); the Malabar Nightshade.

Basely (bēⁱ·sli), *adv.* 1500. [f. BASE *a.* + -LY[2].] † **1.** In a low tone –1577. **2.** In humble rank of life; illegitimately (? *Obs.*) 1583. **3.** Dishonourably, disingenuously 1550. † **4.** At small value or esteem –1651.

Basement (bēⁱ·smėnt). 1730. [prob. – Du. † *basement* foundation (Kilian), in WFlem. *bazement*, perh. – It. *basamento* base of a column, etc., f. *basare*, f. *base* BASE *sb.*[1]; see -MENT, and cf. (O)Fr. *soubassement.*] **1.** The lowest or fundamental portion of a structure 1793. **2.** *fig.* Groundwork; *attrib.* = fundamental 1818. **3.** *spec.* The lowest storey (not a cellar) of a building, *esp.* when sunk below the ground level 1730. **4.** The action of basing; the being based; cf. *debasement* 1836.

1. *Basement-membrane*: a fine transparent layer lying between the epithelium and the fibro-vascular layer of mucous membranes.

Baseness (bēⁱ·snės). 1552. [f. BASE *a.* + -NESS.] The quality or condition of being BASE; an instance of this 1598.

I once did hold it..A basenesse to write faire *Haml.* V. ii. 34. We alledged..the b. of his metal SWIFT.

Basenet, -ette, vars. of BASINET.

† **Bash,** *v.*[1] ME. [aphet. f. ABASH *v.*] **1.** *trans.* To disconcert, dismay, abash –1594. **2.** *intr.* To be daunted; to be abashed –1610.

Bash (bæʃ), *v.*[2] 1641. [ult. imit.; perh. a blend of *bang* and ending of *dash, smash*, etc.] To strike with a smashing blow 1790.

† **Basha·lic(k.** 1682. Early f. PASHALIK –1703.

Bashaw (băʃǭ·). 1534. [var. of PASHA.] **1.** The earlier form of PASHA. **2.** *fig.* A grandee; a haughty imperious man 1593.

1. With all the insolence of a basha FIELDING.

Bashful (bæ·ʃfŭl), *a.* 1548. [f. BASH *v.*[1] + -FUL.] † **1.** Wanting in self-possession, daunted –1709. **2.** Shrinking from publicity, shy; sensitively modest; excessively self-conscious, sheepish 1548. **3.** Of things, etc.: Characterizing or characterized by extreme sensitiveness or modesty 1595.

2. I pity b. men COWPER. **3.** Hence bashfull cunning *Temp.* III. i. 81. Hence **Ba·shfully** *adv.*

Ba·shfulness. 1534. [f. prec. + -NESS.] † **1.** *Bashfulness of*: a timid or reverential shrinking back from –1674. **2.** The quality of being BASHFUL (sense 2) 1539.

2. Haue you no modesty, no maiden shame, No touch of bashfulnese? *Mids. N.* III. ii. 286.

‖ **Bashi-bazouk** (bæ:ʃi,bǎzū·k). 1855. [– Turk. *başı bozuk* 'wrong-headed' (*baş* head, *bozuk* out of order).] A mercenary soldier belonging to the irregular troops of the Turkish empire; notorious for their lawlessness and savage brutality. Also *fig.*

† **Ba·shless,** *a.* 1578. [f. BASH *v.*[1] + -LESS.] Shameless; bold.

† **Ba·shment.** ME. [aphet. f. ABASHMENT.] Discomfiture, shame –1610.

Basi- (bēi·si), comb. f. BASE, BASIS, in sense of 'pertaining to, situated at, or forming, the base of': e.g. **b.-branchial, -cranial, -facial, -hyal, -temporal,** pertaining to, situated at, or forming, the base or posterior part of the branchial arch (in fishes), the skull, the face, the hyoid bone, the temples. Often used *ellipt.*; e.g. the *basihyal* (bone).

Basial (bēi·ziǎl), *a.* [f. L. *basium* kiss + -AL[1].] Of or pertaining to kissing.

Basic (bēi·sik), *a.* 1842. [f. BASE *sb.*[1] + -IC; cf. Fr. *basique*.] **1.** Of, pertaining to, or forming a base: *spec.* in *Archit.* and *Chem.* **2.** Having the base in excess 1854. **a.** *Chem.* (A salt) Having the amount of the base atomically greater than that of the acid, or exceeding in proportion that of the related neutral salt 1854. **b.** *Min.* (An igneous rock) Having relatively little silica 1877. **c.** Applied to a process of steel manufacture, in which phosphorus is eliminated by the use of non-siliceous materials for the lining of the converters; hence, the steel thus produced 1880. See also MONOBASIC, BIBASIC, TRIBASIC.

Basicerite (beⁱsi·sĕrəit). 1877. [f. Gr. βάσις base + κέρας horn + -ITE[1] 3.] *Animal Physiol.* The second segment of the antenna of an Arthropod.

Basicity (beⁱsi·sĭti). 1849. [f. BASIC *a.* + -ITY.] *Chem.* The power of combining with bases possessed by an acid, dependent on the number of atoms of hydrogen replaceable by a metal which are contained in it.

‖ **Basidium** (bǎsi·diǒm). 1858. [mod.L. dim., f. Gr. βάσις + -ιδιον dim. ending.] *Bot.* Name given to the cells of the fructification in some fungi, which bear the spores. Hence **Basi·diospore,** *Bot.* a spore borne at the extremity of a b.

Basifugal (beⁱsi·flugǎl), *a.* 1875. [f. L. *basis* BASE *sb.*[1] + *-fugus* fleeing + -AL[1], after *centrifugal*.] *Bot.* Tending away from the base, as *b. growth* (of a leaf, etc.). Hence **Basi·fugally** *adv.*

‖ **Basigynium** (bēⁱsi,dʒi·niǒm). 1880. [mod. L., f. Gr. βάσις BASE *sb.*[1] + γυνή female + -IUM.] *Bot.* The pedicel or stalk bearing the ovary.

Basil[1] (bæ·zil). 1481. [– OFr. *basile* – med.L. *basilicum* – Gr. βασιλικόν, n. of adj. 'royal'.] *Herb.* **1.** Popular name of a genus (*Ocymum*, N. O. *Labiatæ*) of aromatic shrubby plants, including the culinary herbs Common or Sweet B. (*O. basilicum*), and Bush or Lesser B. (*O. minimum*). **2.** A book-name for: Wild B. (*Calamintha acinos*, or *C. clinopodium*), Field or Cow B. (*Saponaria vaccaria*); also B.-balm, -thyme 1578.

† **Ba·sil**[2]. *rare.* 1565. [– OFr. *basile* (see prec.), applied, through confusion of forms, to the BASILISK; similarly mod.Fr. *basilic* (= plant, serpent).] **1.** = BASILISK 2. 1565. † **2.** An iron round the ankle of a prisoner. (Perh. a distinct wd.) –1755.

Basil[3], **bazil** (bæ·zil). 1674. [app. an Eng. corrupt. of (O)Fr. *basane*; see BASAN.] = BASAN, q.v. Also *attrib.*

Basil, *sb.*[4] and *v.*, corrupt f. BEZEL.

Basilar (bæ·silǎɹ), *a.* 1541. [– mod.L. *basilaris*, irreg. f. *basis*; see BASE *sb.*[1]] Of, pertaining to, or situated at the base, *esp.* at that of the skull. So **Ba·silary.**

Basilic, -al (bǎsi·lik, -ǎl), *a.* 1541. [– (O)Fr. *basilique* or L. *basilicus* – Gr. βασιλικός royal. See -IC, -ICAL.] **1.** Kingly (*rare*) 1728. **2.** *Phys.* Specific epithet of the large vein of the arm starting from the elbow and discharging into the axillary vein. [So called from its supposed importance.] 1541.

Basilic (bæ·sĭlik), *sb. arch.* 1703. [– Fr. *basilique* – L. *basilica*; see next.] = BASILICA 1, 2.

Basilica (bǎsi·likǎ). Pl. **-as,** *rarely* **-æ.** 1541. [– L. *basilica* – Gr. βασιλική (sc. οἰκία, στοά), subst. use of fem. of βασιλικός royal, f. βασιλεύς king.] **1.** *Anc. Hist.* Orig., a royal palace; thence, an oblong building or hall, with double colonnades and a semicircular apse at the end, used for a court of justice and place of public assembly. **2.** A building of this type, used for Christian worship; improp. applied to churches generally. In Rome applied spec. to the seven principal churches founded by Constantine. 1563. † **3.** The basilic vein; see BASILIC *a.* 2. –1751. **4.** (*neut. pl.*) = BASILICS, q.v.

2. The application of the name of B. to the small burial-chapels in the Catacombs is a mistake 1874. Hence **Basi·lical** *a.*[2], **Basi·lican** *a.* of, pertaining to, or resembling a b. **Basi·licanism,** adherence to the basilican type of church. **Basi·licate** *a.* shaped like a b.

† **Basilicock.** ME. = BASILISK 1. –1583.

Basi·licon, -um. 1541. [– L. *basilicum* or Gr. βασιλικόν, subst. use of n. adj.; see BASILICA.] Name of ointments supposed to possess sovereign virtues. ¶ See also BASIL[1].

Basilics (bǎsi·liks), *sb. pl.* 1751. [tr. L. *basilica* (also used) – Gr. βασιλικά, subst. use of n. pl. of adj. βασιλικός; see BASILICA.] A digest of the laws of Justinian, etc., translated from Latin into Greek, by command of the emperors Basil and Leo.

Basilidian (bæsili·diǎn). 1586. [f. L. *Basilides*, Gr. Βασιλίδης + -IAN.] **1.** *adj.* Of, pertaining to, or derived from Basilides, an Alexandrian Gnostic of the 2nd century. **2.** *sb.* One of his followers.

Basili·scan, *a. rare.* 1600. [f. L. *basiliscus* BASILISK + -AN.] Pertaining to a basilisk. So **Basili·scine.**

Basilisk (bæ·zilisk, bæ·s-). Also (from Sp.) **basilisco.** ME. [– L. *basiliscus* – Gr. βασιλίσκος kinglet, kind of serpent, golden-crested wren, dim. of βασιλεύς king; acc. to Pliny, the name is due to a crown-like spot on the reptile's head.] **1.** A fabulous reptile, also called a *cockatrice*, alleged to be hatched by a serpent from a cock's egg; its breath, and even its look, was said to be fatal. [So called from a crown, 'combe or coronet', on its head.] Also *fig.* (often *attrib.*) **2.** *transf.* A large brass cannon, throwing a shot of about 200 pounds weight. (Cf. SHAKS. *Hen. V*, v. ii. 17.) 1549. **3.** *Zool.* A small American lizard of the family *Iguanidæ*, having on its head a hollow crest which can be inflated at will 1813. † **4.** The Golden-crested Wren or Kinglet (*Regulus cristatus*) 1753. † **5.** The star Regulus in Leo –1751.

1. Make me not sighted like the Basilisque *Wint. T.* I. ii. 389. **2.** The Basilisks, That, roaring, shake Damascus turrets down MARLOWE. **3.** The green and golden b. SHELLEY. Hence **Basili·skian** *a.*

Basin (bēi·s'n). [ME. *ba(s)cin, -ine* – OFr. *bacin* (mod. *bassin*) :– med.L. *ba(s)cinus* (cf. *bacchinon* wooden vessel, Gregory of Tours, VI), f. med.L. *bacca* 'vas aquarium' (Isidore), perh. of Gaulish orig.] **1.** A circular vessel of greater width than depth, used for holding water for washing and other liquids. **b.** The quantity held by a basin 1834. **2.** A similar dish for any purpose 1525. **3.** The scale-dish of a balance ME. † **4.** *pl.*? Cymbals –1609. **5.** *spec.* A concave tool used in the manufacture of convex glasses 1727. † **6.** *Phys.* **a.** The pelvis; **b.** A funnel-shaped cavity situated between the anterior ventricles of the brain –1771. **7.** A hollow depression, natural or artificial, containing water 1712. **8.** A dock constructed in a tidal river or harbour, in which by means of flood-gates the water is kept at a constant level 1709. Also *transf.* **9.** A land-locked harbour; a bay 1725. **10.** *Phys. Geog.* The tract of country drained by a river, or which drains into a particular lake or sea 1830. **11.** *gen.* A circular or oval valley or hollow 1854. **12.** *Geol.* A circumscribed formation in which the strata dip inward from all sides to the centre; the deposit, *esp.* of coal, lying in such a depression 1821.

1. Basons and ewers, to laue her dainty hands *Tam. Shr.* II. i. 350. A b. of tea 1834. **7.** And in a b. black and small Receives a lofty waterfall WORDSW. **9.** The harbor of Quebec..a b. two miles across THOREAU. **10.** The hydrographical b. of the Thames LYELL. Hence **Ba·sined** *ppl. a.* placed or contained in a b. **Ba·sinful,** the content of a b.

Basinet, basnet (bæ·sinĕt, bæ·snĕt). Now *Hist.* ME. [– OFr. *bacinet*, dim. of *bacin* BASIN. See -ET.] A small, light, steel headpiece, in shape somewhat globular, and closed in front with a ventail or visor.

Basiophthalmite (bēi:si,ǫfþæ·lməit). 1877. [f. Gr. βάσις BASE *sb.*[1] + ὀφθαλμός eye + -ITE[1] 3.] *Anim. Phys.* The lowest joint of the eye-stalk of Crustacea.

Basipodite (beⁱsi·pǒdəit). 1870. [f. Gr. βάσις BASE *sb.*[1] + πούς, ποδ- foot + -ITE[1] 3.] *Anim. Phys.* The second segment of the leg of an Arthropod.

Basis (bēi·sis). Pl. **bases.** 1571. [– L. *basis* – Gr. βάσις stepping, step, pedestal; see BASE *sb.*[1]] **1.** (Literal senses, now rarely used.) = BASE *sb.*[1] 1, † 3, 6, † 8. † **2.** A pedestal –1686. **3.** The main constituent 1601. **4.** A foundation, support (of anything immaterial) 1605. **5.** That on which anything is reared, and by which its constitution or operation is determined 1601. **6.** = BASE *sb.*[1] 15 (*lit.* and *fig.*) 1833.

2. Cæsar..That now on Pompeyes B. lye[s] along *Jul. C.* III. i. 115. **3.** Salt, the B. of all Natural Productions 1665. **4.** Great Tyrrany, lay thou thy b. sure *Macb.* IV. iii. 32. **5.** The b. of Exchange MALYNES, of mutual compensation BURKE.

Basi·solute, *a.* 1847. [f. L. *basis* BASE sb.[1] + *solutus* unbound, free.] *Bot.* Of leaves: Prolonged at the base below the point of origin.

Bask (bɑsk), *v.* ME. [Of doubtful origin, but usu. referred to ON. **baðask* (later *baðast*), refl. of *baða* BATHE. Cf. BUSK *v.*[1]] † **1.** *intr.* (also *refl.*) To bathe, *esp.* in warm water, etc., whence *transf.* to swim in blood, etc. –1530. **2.** *trans.* Chiefly *refl.*; = 3. 1600. **3.** *intr.* To expose oneself to, or disport oneself in a flood of warmth; to lie enjoying the heat 1697. Also *fig.*

2. A foole, Who laid him downe, and bask'd him in the Sun *A.Y.L.* II. vii. 15. **3.** Basking in the sunshine of unmerited fortune BURKE.

† **Bask,** *a.* ME. [– ON. *beiskr* bitter, acrid.] Bitter, acrid –1808.

† **Baske,** *v.* 1642. [var. of BASH *v.*[2]; cf. Da. *baske*.]

Basket (bɑ·skĕt), *sb.* ME. [In Anglo-L. *baskettum* (XIII–XV), AFr., OFr. *basket* (XIII), of unkn. origin.] **1.** A vessel of wickerwork, made of plaited osiers, cane, rushes, etc. **b.** taken as the type of daily provisions; also, of alms 1535. **2.** A basketful 1725. **3.** A wicker-work guard for the hilt of a sword-stick; *ellipt.* a basket-hilt sword or stick 1773. **4.** The over-hanging back compartment on the outside of a stage coach (*arch.*) 1773. **5.** *Mil.* A gabion 1753. **6.** The vase of a Corinthian capital, with its foliage, etc. (Gwilt) 1753. **7.** A wickerwork or wire screen used in hat-making.

1. Looke, heere is a b., he may creepe in heere *Merry W.* III. iii. 137. **b.** Blessed shal be thy baszkett, & thy stoare COVERDALE *Deut.* 18:5. *To be left in the b.*: to remain unchosen (like the worst apples, etc.). *The pick of the b.*: *i.e.* of the lot. **4.** It has shook me worse than the b. of a stage-coach GOLDSM.

Comb.: **b.-beagle,** a small dog used to hunt a b.-hare; **-boat,** a boat of b.-work; in India, a circular b., covered with skins; **-button,** a metal button with a basket-pattern on it; **-fish,** a star-fish of the genus *Astrophyton*, with five rays divided into curled filaments; **-hare,** one turned out of a b. to be coursed; **-hilt,** a b. shaped hilt of a sword; hence **b.-hilted; -osier,** the *Salix forbyana*; **-work,** structure composed of interlaced osiers, twigs, etc., or carved in imitation of this. Hence **Ba·sketful, Ba·sketing.** (Cf. *matting.*) **Ba·sketry,** b.-work, or -ware.

Basket (bɑ·skĕt), *v.* 1583. [f. prec. sb.; cf. *to bag.*] **1.** To put into, or hang up in, a basket. Also *fig.* **2.** To throw into the waste-paper basket; also *fig.* 1867.

Ba·sket-ball. 1893. A game played with a large inflated ball, the object being to score by casting it into a basket fixed ten feet above the ground at one's opponents' end.

Ba·sking, *ppl. a.* 1742. [f. BASK *v.* + -ING².] That basks or suns himself.

Basking-shark: the largest species of shark (*Selachus maximus*), called also Sun-fish; so named from its habit of lying on the surface of the water.

Basnat, -et, -ette, -ite, vars. of BASINET.

Bason, var. of BASIN.

Bason (bēⁱ·s'n), *sb.* 1727. [Origin unkn.] *Hat-making.* A bench with a plate of iron or stone flag fitted in it, and a little fire underneath, on which formerly the first part of the felting process was performed. Hence **Ba·son** *v.* to harden the felt on the b.

Basque (bask). 1817. [– Fr. *Basque* – L. *Vasco* (pl. *Vascones*, Juvenal, Pliny), whence GASCON.] **A.** *sb.* **1.** A native of Biscay; name of the ancient race inhabiting both slopes of the Western Pyrenees, who speak a language of non-Aryan origin in 1835. **2.** The language of this race 1860. **3.** The continuation of a lady's bodice, forming a kind of short skirt. (? A distinct wd.) 1860. **B.** *adj.* Of or pertaining to the Basques 1817. Hence **Basqued** *ppl. a.* (sense 3). † **Ba·squish** *a.* and *sb.* Basque (language).

Basquine (baskī·n). 1819. [– Fr. *basquine* – Sp. *basquiña* f. *basco, vasco* Basque.] A rich outer petticoat worn by Basque and Spanish women.

Bas-relief, Bass-relief (ba:s,rīlī·f, bā:rĭlī·f). 1667. [Earlier *basse relieve* – It. *basso rilievo*; alt. later after Fr. *bas-relief.*] **1.** Low relief; sculpture or carved work in which the figures project less than one half of their true proportions from the background 1696. **2.** *concr.* A sculpture, etc., in low relief 1667.

Bass, basse (bæs), *sb.*¹ ME. [Late ME. (XV) alt. of (dial.) BARSE; see also BAR *sb.*²] **1.** The Common Perch (*Perca fluviatilis*), or an allied freshwater species 1440. **2.** A voracious European marine fish (*Labrax lupus*) of the Perch family; called also Sea-wolf and Seadace. Also an allied species (Sea-bass) caught off N. America. 1530.

1. *Black Bass*: a Perch (*Perca huro*) found in Lake Huron.

Bass (bæs), *sb.*² 1691. [alt. of BAST *sb.*¹ by suppression of *t*, as in *bast mat, bast tree.*] **1.** The inner bark of the lime or linden; *loosely*, any similar fibre. Also *attrib.* **b.** A fibre obtained from certain palms used for brushes, ropes, etc. 1881. **2.** *ellipt.* A mat, a hassock, a flat plaited bag, etc., made of this 1706.

Bass (bæs), *sb.*³ 1686. [perh. for *bas-* or *base-coal*, as in *base coin.*] *Mining.* Shale stained dark by vegetable matter.

Bass (bæs), *sb.*⁴ 1849. [Name of manufacturers.] Ale or beer (India Pale Ale or Bitter Beer) made by Messrs. Bass and Co. of Burton-on-Trent.

Bass (bēⁱs), *a.* and *sb.*⁵ [orig. identical in form and still in pronunc. with BASE *sb.*⁴; from XVI assim. in form to It. *basso.*] **A.** *adj.* † **1.** Low in sound, soft –1513. **2.** Low in the musical scale 1533. **3.** Of, pertaining to, or suited to the bass part (see B. 1) 1552. Hence in *comb.*, as BASS-VIOL, etc.

3. *B. voice*: that ranging from E♭ below the b. stave to F above it. *B. clef*: see CLEF¹.

B. *sb.* **1.** The lowest part in harmonized musical composition; the deepest male voice, or lowest tones of an instrument, which sound this part 1450. Also = THOROUGHBASS. **2.** A singer or instrument (or a string) having such a voice, part, or compass; *spec.* a bass tuba (see TUBA), BASS-VIOL, DOUBLE-BASS 1591.

1. *Comb.*: **b.-baritone,** a voice higher than bass, yet of bass and not tenor quality; a singer having such a voice.

Bass, *v. nonce-wd.* [f. BASS *sb.*⁵] To utter with bass sound.

The Thunder..did base my Trespasse *Temp.* III. iii. 99.

Bass-bar (bēⁱ·sbāɹ). 1838. [f. BASS *sb.*⁵] *Mus.* An oblong piece of wood fixed lengthwise within violins, etc., to resist the pressure of the left foot of the bridge.

Basset (bæ·sėt), *sb.*¹ 1616. [– Fr. *basset*, f. *bas* low; see BASE *a.*, -ET.] A short-legged dog used in unearthing foxes and badgers.

† **Basset** (bæ·sėt), *sb.*² 1645. [– Fr. *bassette* – It. *bassetta*, fem. of *bassetto*, dim. of *basso*; see BASE *a.*, -ET.] A game at cards, resembling Faro. Hence **B.-table. Ba·sset** *v.*¹ to play at b.

Basset (bæ·sėt), *sb.*³ 1636. [Origin unkn.] *Geol.* The edge of a stratum showing at the surface of the ground; an outcrop. Also *attrib.* Hence **Ba·sset** *v.*² to crop out at the surface. **Ba·sseting** *vbl. sb.* the outcrop.

Basset-horn (bæ·set,hǭɹn). 1835. [– G., partial tr. of Fr. *cor de bassette* – It. *corno di bassetto* (*bassetto*, see BASSET *sb.*²).] *Mus.* A tenor clarinet of extra compass.

‖ **Bassette** (base·t) [– Fr. *bassette* – It. *bassetto*; see next], and **Bassetto** (basse·tto). [It., see BASSET sb.²] *Mus.* A small bass-viol.

Bass-horn. [See BASS *a.* 3.] *Mus.* A modification of the bassoon, much deeper in its tones.

‖ **Bassia** (bæ·siă). 1863. [Named after Fernando *Bassi*; see -IA¹.] *Bot.* A genus of tropical trees (N.O. *Sapotaceæ*), from the seeds of which a butter-like oil is pressed. Hence **Ba·ssic** *a.*

Bassinet. Also **bassinette.** 1578. [– Fr. *bassinet*, dim. of *bassin*; see BASIN, -ET.] **1.** (bæ·sinėt.) Var. of BASINET. † **2.** *Herb.* Name of species of Ranunculus and Geranium, and of the Marsh Marigold –1727. **3.** (bæ:sine·t.) An oblong wickerwork basket, hooded at one end, used as a cradle for babies, or a perambulator 1854.

‖ **Basso** (ba·sso). 1817. [It.; see BASSET *sb.*²] *Mus.* = BASS *a.* 3, *sb.*⁵ 1, 2. Hence **b. cantante,** a high bass voice, between b. profundo and baritone; **b. continuo** = THOROUGHBASS; **b. ostinato** = GROUND-*bass*; **b. profondo,** usu. **profundo,** a deep bass voice, having a compass of about two octaves above D below the bass stave; also, a singer having such a voice; **b. ripieno,** a bass part used only occ. in a grand chorus.

Bassoon (băsū·n). 1727. [– Fr. *basson* – It. *bassone*, augm. of *basso* low; see BASSET *sb.*², -OON.] *Mus.* **1.** A wooden double-reed instrument, with a compass of about three octaves, used as a bass to the oboe. **2.** An organ-stop similar in tone to a b. **Bassoo·nist.**

‖ **Ba·sso-relie·vo, -rilie·vo.** Pl. **-os.** 1676. [It.; see BAS-RELIEF.] = BAS-RELIEF.

Bassorin (bæ·sŏrin). 1830. [f. *Bassora* + IN¹.] A chemical principle found in Bassora and other gums, insoluble but swelling to a gelatinous state in water.

Bass-viol (bēⁱ·s,vəi·əl). 1590. [See BASE *a.* 3.] A viol da gamba for playing the bass part in older concerted music; a violoncello.

Bass-wood (ba·s,wud). 1824. [f. BASS *sb.*²] The American Lime or Linden (*Tilia americana*); also, its wood. Also *attrib.*

Bast (bast), *sb.*¹ [OE. *bæst*, corresp. to (M)Du., (O)HG., ON. *bast* :- Gmc. **bastaz, -am*, of unkn. origin. See BASS *sb.*²] The inner bark of the lime or linden; also, any flexible fibrous bark (cf. BASS *sb.*²). Also *attrib.* **2.** A rope, mat, etc., made of bast; cf. BASS *sb.*² 1450.

† **Bast,** *sb.*² and *a.* ME. [– OFr. *bast* (mod. *bât*) – Pr. *bast* – med.L. *bastum* pack-saddle; see BASTARD, BATMAN.] **A.** *sb.* Bastardy –1494. **B.** *adj.* Bastard –1572.

†‖ **Basta** (ba·stă), *int.* 1596. [It., = it is enough.] Enough!

Bastard (ba·stăɹd). ME. [– OFr. *bastard* (mod. *bâtard*) = Pr. *bastard*, It., Sp., Pg. *bastardo* :- med.L. *bastardus*, commonly held to be f. *bastum* (see BAST *sb.*², BAT *sb.*³) + *-ardus* -ARD; cf. OFr. *fils de bast* (see BAST sb.²), illegitimate son.] **A.** *sb.* **1.** One begotten and born out of wedlock; an illegitimate or natural child. Also *fig.*

By the civil and canon laws, and since 1926 by the law of England, a child born out of wedlock is legitimated by the subsequent marriage of the parents.

† **2.** A mongrel –1602. **3.** A sweet Spanish wine, resembling muscadel; any sweetened wine. *Hist.* ME. † **4.** Anything of inferior quality or unusual make; *e.g.* a kind of cloth –1523; a cannon –1753; a size of paper –1774. **5.** A large sail used in the Mediterranean. (So Fr. *bâtard.*) 1753. **6.** *Sugar-refining.* A coarse brown sugar made from the refuse syrup of previous boilings; also, a mould into which sugar is drained. (So Fr. *bâtard.*) 1859.

1. Fame being a b. or *filia populi*, 'tis very hard to find her father FULLER. **3.** Anon sir, Score a Pint of B. in the Halfe Moone 1 *Hen. IV*, II. iv. 30.

B. *adj.* **1.** Born out of wedlock ME. **2.** Mongrel, hybrid. ? *Obs.* ME. **3.** *fig.* Illegitimate, unauthorized 1558. **4.** *fig.* Not genuine; spurious; debased 1552. **5.** Having the appearance of; an inferior kind of; as, *b. diamonds, B. Alkanet*, etc. 1530. **6.** Of abnormal shape or irregular (*esp.* large) size; *spec.* applied: **a.** to a file intermediate between the coarse and fine cuts 1677; **b.** in *Printing*, to (*a*) a fount of type cast on a larger or smaller body than that to which it usually belongs, (*b*) an abbreviated title on the page preceding the title-page of a book; † **c.** to swords, guns, etc. –1753.

3. Usurie..is the B. use of money BACON. *B. branch* or *slip*: one springing of its own accord from the root of a tree, or where not wanted. **5.** *B.-wing*: *Zool.* three or four quill-like feathers placed at a small joint in the middle of a bird's wing, taken as the analogue of the thumb in mammals.

† **Ba·stard,** *v.* 1549. [f. prec. sb.] *trans.* To BASTARDIZE –1658. Also *fig.*

† **Ba·stardice, -ise.** 1579. [– Fr. *bastardise* (mod. *bât-*), f. *bastard*; see BASTARD *sb.*, -ICE.] Bastardy; falsity –1611.

Bastardism (ba·stăɹdiz'm). ? *Obs.* 1589. [f. BASTARD *sb.* + -ISM.] = BASTARDY 1.

Bastardize (ba·stăɹdəiz), *v.* 1587. [f. BASTARD *sb.* + -IZE.] **1.** *trans.* To declare or stigmatize as bastard 1611. † **2.** To beget bastard issue (*Lear* I. ii. 144). **3.** To deteriorate 1587. Also *intr.* Hence **Ba·stardiza·tion.**

† **Ba·stardly,** *a.* 1552. [f. BASTARD *sb.* + -LY¹.] **1.** Of bastard sort; unauthorized; counterfeit; debased –1785. **2.** = BASTARD *a.* 5. –1610.

Bastardy (ba·stăɹdi). 1486. [– AFr., OFr. *bastardie* (med.L. *bastardia* XII); see BASTARD *sb.*, -Y³.] **1.** The condition of a bastard; illegitimate birth. Also *fig.* **2.** Begetting of bastards, fornication; also *fig.* 1577.

Baste (bēⁱst), *sb.* Also **bast.** 1850. *Card-playing.* Var. of BEAST.

Baste (bēⁱst), *v.*¹ ME. [– OFr. *bastir* baste :- Frankish **bastjan* = OHG., MHG. *besten* lace, sew, f. Gmc. **bastaz* BAST *sb.*¹ For the sense, cf. Sp. *bastear, embastar*, It. *imbastire.*] *trans.* To sew together loosely; hence † **a.** To quilt; **b.** To tack together temporarily with long loose stitches. Also *transf.* or *fig.*

fig. To b. up a story hastily or clumsily SCOTT.

Baste (bēⁱst), *v.*² 1509. [Origin unkn.] **1.** To moisten (a roasting joint, etc.) with melted fat, gravy, etc. Also *transf.* or *fig.* † **2.** To perfuse as with a liniment –1735. **3.** To mark (sheep) with tar (*north.*).

Baste (bēⁱst), *v.*³ 1533. [perh. a fig. use of prec.] *trans.* To beat soundly, cudgel. Also *fig.*

Baste (bēⁱst), *v.*⁴ 1850. [f. BASTE *sb.*] *Card-playing.* Var. of BEAST *v.*

Bastel-house (bæ·stĕlhaus). 1544. [f. *bastel*, var. of BASTILE.] A fortified house.

Basten (bæ·stĕn), *a.* [OE. *bæsten*; see BAST *sb.*¹, -EN⁴.] Made of bast.

‖ **Bastide** (ba·stid, bastī·d). 1523. [– OFr. *bastide* – Pr. *bastida* (med.L. *bastida* XIII); see next.] **1.** *Obs.* exc. *Hist.* A fortlet. ‖ **2.** A country-house in southern France.

Bastille, -ile (bastī·l, ba·stil), *sb.* ME. [– (O)Fr. *bastille*, refash. f. contemp. *bastide* (see prec.) – Pr. *bastida*, subst. use of fem. pa. pple. of *bastir* build. Cf. med.L. *bastile* XIV, *-illa.*] **1.** A tower or bastion of a castle; a small fortress. **2.** *spec.* In siege operations: **a.** A wooden tower on wheels. **b.** One of a series of huts, defended by entrenchments, for the accommodation of the besieging troops. ME. **3.** Name of the prison-fortress built in Paris in the 14th and destroyed in the 18th century 1561. **4.** Hence: A prison 1790.

3. That rock-fortress..which they name B., or Building, as if there were no other building CARLYLE.

Bastille, -ile (bastī·l, ba·stil), *v.* 1480. [f. OF. *bastiller*, f. *bastille*; see prec.] † **1.** To fortify (a castle) –1500. **2.** [f. prec. sb.] To confine in a bastille 1742.

Basti·llion. *Hist.* 1549. [– OFr. *bastillon*, dim. of *bastille*; see prec.] A small fortress or castle; a fortified tower.

† **Ba·stiment.** 1598. [– Sp. *bastimento*, f. *bastir* build; see -MENT.] **1.** Military supplies –1622. **2.** A building, a wall 1679.

Bastinade, -onade (bæstinēi·d, -ōnēi·d), *sb.* (*arch.*) 1660. [refash. of BASTINADO after Fr. *bastonnade*; see -ADE, -ADO.] = BASTINADO *sb.* 1–3.

Bastina·de, -ona·de, *v. arch.* 1601. [f. prec. sb.] To BASTINADO.

Bastinado (bæstinēi·do), *sb.* 1577. [– Sp. *bastonada*, f. *baston* stick, cudgel; see BATON, -ADO.] **1.** A blow with a stick or cudgel; *esp.* one upon the soles of the feet. **2.** A cudgelling (*arch.*) 1594. **3.** *spec.* An Eastern method of punishment, by beating with a stick the soles of the culprit's feet 1726. **4.** A stick, staff, truncheon, etc. 1598.

Bastina·do, *v.* Also **-onado.** 1614. [f. prec. sb.] **1.** To beat with a stick (*arch.*). **2.** *spec.* To beat or cane on the soles of the feet 1688.

Bastion (bæ·stiən). 1598. [– Fr. *bastion*, earlier *bastillion* (see above) – It. *bastione*, f. *bastire* build.] A projecting part of a fortification, consisting of an earthwork in the form of an irregular pentagon, having its base in the main line, or at an angle, of the fortification; its 'flanks' are the two sides which spring from the base, and are shorter than the 'faces' which meet in the frontal angle. Also *transf.* and *fig.* Hence **Ba·stioned** *ppl. a.* furnished with or defended by a b. or bastions. **Ba·stione·t,** a small b.

Ba·stite, 1837. [f. *Baste* in the Harz Mountains + -ITE[1] 2 b.] *Min.* A bronze- or green-ish-coloured impure foliated serpentine; Schiller-spar.

Basto (ba·sto). 1675. [– Sp. (*el*) *basto* (whence Fr. *baste*) (ace of) clubs. See BASTE *sb.*] The ace of clubs in quadrille or ombre.

† **Baston.** ME. [ME. *baston* – OFr. *baston*; see BATON.] **1.** A staff or stick used as a weapon or as a symbol of office –1756. **2.** A stanza or verse. (Transl. of *staff, stave.*) ME. only. **3.** *Her.* = BATON 3. –1660. **4.** *Old Law.* One of the Warden of the Fleet's men, who attended the king's courts with a red staff, to take into custody such as were committed by the court. (Cf. *tip-staff*, etc.) –1671. **5.** *Archit.* A torus. (So F. *bâton.*) –1847.

Bastonite. [f. *Bastoigne* in Luxembourg + -ITE[1] 2 b.] *Min.* A variety of LEPIDOMELANE

Basyl(e (bēi·sil, bæ·sil). 1863. [f. BASE *sb.*[1] 12 + -YL.] *Chem.* A body that unites with oxygen to form a base. Hence **Ba·sylous** *a.*

Bat (bæt), *sb.*[1] 1575. [alt. of ME. *backe*, *bakke* – Scand. word repr. in MSw. *aftan|-bakka*, *nat|bakka* evening or night-bat, MDa. *nat(h)|bakke*; the change from *k* to *t* may have been due to assoc. w. med.L. *blatta*, *blacta*, *batta*.] A member of the Mammalian order of *Cheiroptera*, and *esp.* of the family *Vespertilionidæ*; consisting of mouse-like quadrupeds (whence the names *Rere-mouse*, *Flittermouse*) having the fingers extended to support a thin membranous wing which stretches from the side of the neck by the toes of both pairs of feet to the tail; they were formerly classed as birds. They are all nocturnal.

The curious formation of a b., a mouse with wings BOSWELL.

Comb.: **b.-shell,** a species of volute; **b.-tick,** an insect parasitical on bats. Also in many adjs., as **b.-blind, -eyed, -minded,** etc.

Bat (bæt), *sb.*[2] ME. [Senses 1–4, – late OE. *batt* club, perh. partly – (O)Fr. *batte*, f. *battre* beat, strike; senses 5–6, 7–9 of unkn. origin, prob. diff. words.] **1.** A stick, a club, a staff for support or defence (*arch.*). † **2.** ? A balk of timber –1686. **3.** The wooden implement with rounded handle and flattened blade used in cricket. (The most common mod. sense.) 1706. **b.** Short for *batter*, *batsman* 1859. **4.** Harlequin's sword of lath. [From Fr.] 1859. † **5.** A lump, piece ME. only. **6.** *esp.* A piece of a brick having one end entire 1519. **7.** Shale interstratified between seams of coal, etc. Cf. BASS *sb.*[3] 1686. **8.** A felted mass of fur, etc., in hat-making; often spelt BATT 1836. **9.** A sheet of cotton wadding for quilts; batting. **10.** A blow. Cf. BAT *v.* ME.

1. Make you ready your stiffe bats and clubs *Cor.* I. i. 165.

‖ **Bat, bât** (bā, bāt, bæt), *sb.*[3] ME. [– OFr. *bat*, earlier *bast*; see BAST *sb.*[2]] **1.** A pack-saddle. Only in *comb.*, as † **b.-needle,** a packing needle; **bât-horse** (Fr. *cheval de bât*), a sumpter-beast; **bât-mule. 2.** In *bat-money*: An allowance for carrying baggage in the field. Occas. confused w. BATTA. 1793.

Bat (bæt), *v.*[1] ME. [f. BAT *sb.*[1], or – (O)FR. *battre* beat, strike. See BATE *v.*[1].] **1.** To strike with or as with a bat; to cudgel, beat. **2.** To hit a ball with a bat. Also *absol.* 1773.

Bat, *v.*[2] 1615. [var. of BATE *v.*[1] and [2].] **1.** *intr.* To bate or flutter as a hawk. **2.** *trans.* (*dial.* and in U.S.) *To b. the eyes*: to blink 1847.

† **Ba·table,** *a.* 1453. [Short f. DEBATABLE; cf. BATE *sb.*[1]] Debatable –1610.

‖ **Batardeau** (batardo·). 1767. [Fr.: formerly *bastardeau*, dim. of OFr. *bastard*, of doubtful origin.] **a.** A coffer-dam. **b.** A wall built across the moat or ditch surrounding a fortification.

Batata (bătā·tă, bătēi·tă). 1577. [– Sp. *batata* – Taino *batata*; see POTATO.] A plant (*Batatas edulis*, N.O. *Convolvulaceæ*), called also Spanish or Sweet Potato.

Batavian (bătēi·viăn). 1598. [f. L. *Batavia*, f. *Batavi*, a people who dwelt on Betawe, an island between the Rhine and the Waal. See -AN.] **A.** *adj.* Of or pertaining to the ancient Batavi. **b.** Pertaining to Holland or the Dutch. 1796. **B.** *sb.pl.* **a.** The ancient Batavi. **b.** The Dutch or Netherlanders (*rare*). 1598.

Batch (bætʃ). [ME. *bac(c)he* :- OE. **bæćće*, f. *bacan* BAKE; cf. OE. *ġebæć* baking, thing baked, and for the formation *wæćće* WATCH, *wacan* WAKE *v.*] † **1.** The process of baking –1551. **2.** *concr.* A baking; the quantity produced at one baking 1461; † *ellipt.* the bread itself 1648. Also *fig.* † **3.** *fig.* and *transf.* Sort, lot –1705. **4. a.** The quantity of dough for one baking. **b.** The quantity of corn sent at one time to the mill 1549. **5.** *transf.* A quantity produced at one operation, *e.g.* a brewing (*arch.*) 1713. **6. a.** An instalment 1833. **b.** A set 1598.

2. Thou crusty b. of Nature, what's the newes *Tr. & Cr.* V. i. 5. **3.** One..o' your owne b. B. JONS. **5.** A b. of beer 1713, of soup 1878. **6.** A b. of prize-money 1833, of visitors 1793.

Bate (bēit), *v.*[1] ME. [– OFr. *batre* (mod. *battre*) beat, fight :- Rom. **batere* for L. *batuere*. Cf. BATTLE.] † **1.** To contend with blows or arguments –1440. **2.** *Falconry.* To beat the wings impatiently and flutter away from the fist or perch. (F. *se battre.*) ME. Also † *fig.* **b.** To flutter downwards 1590.

2. *fig.* Come, civil night..Hood my vnman'd blood, bayting in my Cheekes *Rom. & Jul.* III. ii. 14. Hence **Ba·ter,** a hawk that bates.

Bate (bēit), *v.*[2] ME. [aphet. f. ABAT EV.[1]] † **1.** To beat down or away –1601. **2.** To lower, let down; *fig.* to cast down, humble ME. Also † *intr.* **3.** To beat back or blunt the edge of (*lit.* and *fig.*) 1535. † **4.** To reduce –1691; † *intr.* to decrease –1596. **5.** To lessen in force or intensity. Now chiefly in *To b. one's breath.* ME. **6.** To strike off or take away (a part of) 1440; *ellipt.* to deprive (a person) *of* 1823. † **7.** To omit, except –1704.

1. B. the earth from about the roots of olives HOLLAND. **2.** Bating nor heart nor hope S. ROGERS. (Cf. 6.) **3.** Which shall b. his sythes keene edge *L.L.L.* I. i. 6. **4.** These greefes and losses have so bated mee *Merch. V.* III. iii. 32. **6.** I will not b. a penny 1602. *To bate an ace*; see ACE 3. Phr. † *To bate of*: to make a lessening of. † **Ba·teless** *a.*

Bate (beit), *v.*[3] 1875. [rel. to BATE *sb.*[4]] *Tanning.* To steep in bate; see BATE *sb.*[4]

† **Bate,** *sb.*[1] ME. [f. BATE *v.*[1]; or short f. DEBATE *sb.*] Contention, discord –1690.

At (the) b.: at strife. Hence † **Ba·teful** *a.* full of strife.

Bate (bēit), *sb.*[2] *dial.* 1450. [f. BATE *v.*[2]] † **1.** Depression 1686. **2.** Deduction, abatement 1450.

Bate (bēit), *sb.*[3] *n. dial.* 1664. [Origin unkn.] The grain of wood or stone.

Bate (bēit), *sb.*[4] 1804. [Goes with BATE *v.*[3] Cf. Sw. *beta* maceration, G. *beize* tanner's ooze, *beizen* soak, steep, cogn. w. BAIT *v.*[1]] *Tanning.* An alkaline lye, used to make the hides supple; a vat containing it; the process of steeping in it.

‖ **Bateau** (bato). Pl. **bateaux** (batōz). [Fr., = boat.] A light river-boat; *esp.* the long tapering boats with flat bottoms used by the French Canadians. erron. **Batteau.**

Batell (bæ·tl), var. of BATTEL.

† **Batement.** 1677. Aphetic of ABATEMENT.

Bat-fowl (bæ·t,fau:l), *v.* 1440. [app. f. BAT *sb.*[2] + FOWL *v.*] **1.** To catch birds at night by dazing them with a light, and knocking them down or netting them. † **2.** *slang.* To swindle, to victimize the simple –1608. Hence **Ba·t-fow·ler, Ba·t-fow·ling** *vbl. sb.* (in both senses).

† **Ba·tful,** *a.* 1549. [f. *bat-* (see BATTEN *v.*); freq. in Drayton.] = BATTABLE –1612.

Bath (baþ), *sb.*[1] Pl. **baths** (bāðz). [OE. *bæþ* = OFris. *beth*, OS. *bað*, (O)HG. *bad*, ON. *bað* :- Gmc. **baþam.*] **1.** The action of immersing the body, or a part of it, in, or surrounding it with, water, vapour, hot air, mud, or the like. Also *transf.* **2.** A quantity of water or other liquid for bathing OE. **3.** *fig.* and *transf.* Any enveloping medium producing effects analogous to those of bathing ME. **4.** A receptacle, apartment, or building containing a series of apartments, for bathing; (the last usu. *pl.*) 1591. **5.** A place for undergoing medical treatment by bathing, etc. Usu. in pl. Cf. BATH[2] 1. 1562. **6.** *Chem.* A contrivance for producing a steady heat at high temperature, or at a temperature not exceeding that of boiling point, as a sand-b., a water-b. 1599. **7.** *Photography.* A solution in which photographic plates or prints are immersed; the vessel holding the solution 1861. **8.** *Metallurgy.* A mass of molten material in a furnace 1881. **9. Order of the Bath:** a high order of British knighthood. (So called from the bath which preceded installation.) 1603.

1. *transf.* His head all over in a b. of sweat MANDEVILLE. **3.** A b. of blisse CHAUCER, of sunshine 1871. Sleepe..sore Labors B. *Macb.* II. ii. 38. **4.** The Lambeth Baths (*mod.*). **5.** Matlock Bath (*mod.*).

Attrib. and *comb.* as **bathroom,** a room for bathing in; **b. salts,** a toilet preparation for softening and perfuming bath-water; **b. towel.**

Bath (baþ), *sb.*[2] OE. [Same word as prec., orig. a dat. pl. *baðum*, whence as an indecl. sb. *Baðum, Baðon* (latinized *Bathonia*), reduced through *Baþen, Bathe*, to *Bath* in XVII.] A city in the west of England, so called from its hot springs. Also *attrib.*

Comb. etc.: **B.-brick,** a preparation of calcareous earth moulded in form of a brick, made at Bridgwater; used for cleaning polished metal. **B. bun,** a large fruit bun with sugared top. **B.-chair,** a large chair on wheels for invalids. (Both these are often written without a capital B.) **B.-metal,** an alloy, consisting of 3 or 4 oz. of zinc to one pound of copper. **B. oolite, B.-stone,** a building stone from the oolite formation near Bath. **B.-post,** a sort of letter-paper.

Bath (bæþ), *sb.*[3] ME. [– Heb. *baṯ*; Vulg. *batus*, LXX βάτος.] A Hebrew liquid-measure, about eight and a half gallons.

Bath (baþ), *v.* 1660. [f. BATH *sb.*[1]; cf. to *tub*, etc.] To subject to a bath. Different from *bathe* in having a distinct reference to a vessel for bathing, and in being always literal.

To London and saw the bath-ing..of the Knights of the Bath EVELYN.

Bathe (bēið), *v.* [OE. *baþian* = Du. *baden*, OHG. *badōn* (G. *baden*), ON. *baða* :- Gmc. **baþōn*, f. **baþam* BATH *sb.*[1]] **1.** *trans.* To immerse, as in a bath; to plunge or dip ME. **2.** To apply liquid so as to wet or moisten copiously; to lave, perfuse, suffuse OE. **3.** To envelop, or encompass, like the air, etc. 1816. **4.** *intr.* To take a bath; earlier also, to bask OE. Also in transf. and fig. uses 1576.

1. The moder batheth the chylde TREVISA. **2.** To b. the eye with vinegar and water 1877. The river bathed the foot of the walls GIBBON. Bathed in sweat 1746, in tears BURKE. Phr. *To bathe in blood*: usu. *fig.* to express the great quantity shed. **3.** The babe..Lies bathed in joy EMERSON. Hence **Bathe** *sb.* an act of bathing (intr.) 1831. **Ba·ther.** one who takes a bath, esp. in sea or river. So **Ba·thing** *vbl. sb.*; the action of the v., sense 4; *attrib.* in *bathing dress*, MACHINE (1 b), etc.

Bathetic (bаþe·tik), *a.* 1834. [f. *bathos*, after *pathos, pathetic.*] Characterized by bathos; absol. *The b.* = BATHOS.

Bathometer (bǎþǫ·mǐtəɹ). 1875. [f. Gr. βάθος depth + -METER.] A spring balance for ascertaining the depth of water without measuring the sounding line.

Bathos (bē̆ⁱ·þǫs). 1727. [– Gr. βάθος depth. First made Eng. in sense 2 by Pope.] **1.** Depth; bottom 1758. **2.** *Rhet.* Ludicrous descent from the elevated to the commonplace; anti-climax 1727. **3.** Hence *gen.* A come-down 1814.

Bathukolpian (bæþiukǫ·lpiăn), *a. rare.* 1825. [f. Gr. βαθύκολπος (f. βαθύς deep + κόλπος bosom) + -IAN.] Deep-bosomed. var. **Bathuko·lpic.**

‖ **Bathybius** (băþi·biʊs). 1868. [mod.L., f. Gr. βαθύς deep + βίος life.] *Zool.* Huxley's name for a gelatinous substance found at the bottom of the Atlantic Ocean, and at first supposed to be a formless mass of living protoplasm, but now regarded as an inorganic precipitate.

Bathymetric, -al (bæþime·trik, -ăl), *a.* 1862. [f. Gr. βαθύς deep + -METRIC; see -ICAL.] Of or pertaining to the measurement of depth, *spec.* to the vertical range of distribution of plants and animals in the sea. Hence **Bathyme·trically** *adv.*

Bathymetry (băþi·mĕtri). 1864. [f. as prec. + -METRY.] The art or science of measuring depths (in the sea). WEBSTER.

Bating (bē̆ⁱ·tiŋ), *prep.* 1568. [Absolute use of pres. pple. of BATE *v.*² 7; cf. *barring, excepting.*] Leaving out of account.

Batiste (bătī·st). 1697. [– Fr. *batiste* = *Baptiste*, its original maker, of Cambray (Littré).] The French word for *cambric*; applied in commerce to a fabric of the same texture, made of cotton as well as linen. Often *attrib.*

† **Ba·tler,** in mod. edd. of SHAKS. **Batlet.** *rare.* [f. BATTLE *v.*⁴ + -ER¹; or poss. dim. f. BAT *sb.*⁴ + -LET.] A beetle for battling clothes. *A.Y.L.* II. iv. 49.

‖ **Batman**¹ (bæ·tmăn). 1599. [– Turk. *bātmān, batmān, -man* (whence also Russ. *batmán*).] An oriental weight varying according to the locality.

Batman² (bæ·tmæn, † bā·mæn). 1755. [f. BAT *sb.*³] **1.** A man in charge of a bat-horse and its load 1809. **2.** An officer's servant.

‖ **Baton** (bæ·tən, ‖ batoṅ). 1548. [– Fr. *bâton* (earlier *baston*, see BASTON), = Pr., Sp. *baston*, It. *bastone* :– Rom. **basto, -on-*, f. **bastare* drive with a stick (cf. L. *burdubasta* donkey-driver, Petronius), f. late L. *bastum* stick.] **1.** A staff or stick used as a weapon –1829; also *gen.* a stick 1801. **2.** A staff of office; *e.g.* a Marshal's b. 1590. **3.** *Her.* An ordinary, in breadth the fourth part of a BEND, broken off short at each end, so as to have the figure of a truncheon; used in Eng. coats of arms only in the form of the *baton sinister*, the badge of bastardy (pop. *bar sinister*) 1816. **4.** *Mus.* The wand used in beating time. (Often pronounced as Fr.) 1867. **5.** See BATTEN.

4. Phr. *Under* ——*'s baton*, conducted by —— Hence **Ba·ton** *v.* to strike with a b.; formerly, to cudgel. **Ba·toned** *ppl. a.* furnished with, or bearing, a b.; in *Her.* marked with, or bearing, the b. of bastardy.

Batoon (bătu·n), *sb. arch.* 1562. [– Fr. *bâton*; see -OON. Now superseded by BATON.] = BATON 1, 2, 3, 5. Hence **Batoo·n** *v.* (*arch.*) = BATON *v.*

‖ **Batrachia** (bătrē̆ⁱ·kiă), *sb. pl.* 1847. [mod.L. – Gr. βατράχεια (sc. ζῷα animals), n. pl. of adj. f. βάτραχος frog; see -IA².] *Zool.* **a.** One of Brongniart's four orders of Reptiles. **b.** Now, restricted to an order of the class Amphibia, containing those animals only, as frogs and toads, which subsequently discard the gills and tail of their larval state. (The sing. is BATRACHIAN.) Hence **Batra·chian** *a.* of or pertaining to the B., *esp.* frogs and toads; *sb.* an animal of the order B.

Batrachite (bæ·trăkəit). 1837. [– L. *batrachites* – Gr. βατραχίτης, f. βάτραχος frog; see -ITE¹ 2 b.] **a.** A stone resembling a frog in colour. **b.** A fossil batrachian.

Batracho-, comb. f. Gr. βάτραχος frog: **Ba·trachoid** *a.*, frog-like. **Ba:trachomyo·machy** [ad. Gr., f. βάτραχος + μῦς + -μαχία], the battle of the frogs and mice, a mock heroic poem, possibly of the Homeric age. **Batracho·phagous** [Gr. -φάγος] *a.*, frog-eating. **Ba:trachopho·bia** [Gr. -φοβία], dread of or aversion to frogs, toads, etc.

Batsman (bæ·tsmæ̆n). 1756. [f. *bat's* (BAT *sb.*²)] One who handles the bat at cricket.

Batt, var. of BAT *sb.*² 8.

‖ **Batta**¹ (bæ·tă). 1680. [– Indo-Pg. *bata* = Canarese *bhatta* rice.] *Anglo-Ind. orig.* Subsistence money. Hence, extra pay during a campaign, and *spec.* An extra allowance, which became a constant addition to the pay of officers serving in India.

‖ **Batta**² (bæ·tă). 1680. [– Hind. *baṭṭa, bāṭṭa.*] *Anglo-Ind.* In Indian Banking, agio; discount on coins not current, or of short weight.

† **Ba·ttable,** *a.*¹ 1570. [f. *bat-* (see BATTEN *v.*) + -ABLE.] Fattening; fertile in pasture –1641.

† **Battable,** *a.*² 1601. [– OFr. *batable, batt-*, f. *battre* beat, or f. BAT *v.*¹; see -ABLE.] That may be beaten out, malleable.

† **Battailant.** 1591. [– Fr. *bataillant*, pres. pple. of *batailler*; see BATTLE *v.*¹, -ANT.] **1.** *adj.* Combatant SPENSER. **2.** *sb.* A combatant 1620.

Battailous (bæ·tĕləs), *a. arch.* ME. [– OFr. *bataillos, -eus*, f. *bataille*; see BATTLE *sb.*, -OUS.] Fond of fighting, ready for battle.

Battalia (bătā·lyă). *arch.* 1594. [– It. *battaglia* BATTLE *sb.*] **1.** *Mil.* Order of battle. (Usu. with *in, into.*) 1613. † **2.** = BATTLE *sb.* 6, 7. (Cf. BATTALION 1.) –1750. Also *fig.* (cf. 'host').

1. Friedrich draws out in b. CARLYLE.

Batta·lia pie. 1664. [Earliest form *beatille* – Fr. *béatilles*, in med.L. *beatillæ* 'small blessed articles', as samplers worked by nuns, etc., dim. of L. *beatus*. *Battalia* is due to pop. etym.] 'Tit-bits, as cocks' combs, sweetbreads, etc. in a pie.'

Battalion (bătæ·liən). 1589. [– Fr. *bataillon* – It. *battaglione*, augm. of *battaglia* BATTLE *sb.*] **1.** *gen.* A large body of men in battle array; one of the large divisions of an army. † **b.** = BATTLE 7. –1656. **2.** *spec.* A body of infantry (or engineers) composed of several companies, and forming part of a regiment. (The number of battalions in a regiment varies greatly.) 1708.

1. Providence is on the side of the strongest battalions *Provb.* Hence **Batta·lion** *v.* (*rare*) to form into a b.

Battel, batell (bæ·t'l), *sb.* 1594. [In med.L. *batelli, -illi, batellæ* (pl.), of unkn. orig.; perh. connected w. BATTLE *v.*³, BATTLE *a.*] Now only in *pl.* **battels, batells,** except attrib. In the University of Oxford (and formerly elsewhere), a provision of food taken by a member of a college; hence, the accounts of the costs of such provisions, and other college charges, for an individual; also, such college accounts in general.

Ba·ttel, *v.* 1570. [See prec., and cf. BATTLE *v.*³] **1.** In Univ. of Oxford: To have a kitchen and buttery account in college. † **2.** (?) To put into a common stock –1606.

Ba·tteler. *Obs.* exc. *Hist.* 1604. [f. prec.; cf. BATTLE *v.*] One who battels in college; formerly, an order of students in Oxford below Commoners.

Batten (bæ·t'n), *sb.*¹ 1658. [Earliest forms *bataunt, batent, batant* (XV) – OFr. *batant*, subst. use of pres. pple. of *battre* beat; see -ANT. For loss of final *t* cf. next.] **1.** *Carp.* and *Build.* A piece of squared timber, not more than 7 inches broad and 2½ inches thick, used for flooring, etc.; a scantling. **2.** *spec.* A bar or strip nailed or glued across parallel boards, to hold them together, or prevent warping; a ledge, a clamp 1663. **3.** *Naut.* A narrow strip nailed to the masts and spars to prevent them from chafing; one used to fasten down the edges of the tarpaulin fixed over the hatchways; also, a wooden bar from which hammocks are slung 1769.

Comb. **b.-door,** a door formed of narrow boards, held together by battens. Hence **Ba·ttening** *sb.* the application of, or a structure formed with, battens.

Batten (bæ·t'n), *sb.*² 1831. [– Fr. *battant* (of same meaning). Loss of *t* as in prec.] A movable bar in a silk-loom which closes the weft.

Batten (bæ·t'n), *v.*¹ 1591. [– ON. *batna* improve, get better, f. **bat-* (cf. OE. *ġebatian* get better); see -EN⁵. Cf. BATTLE *v.*³] **1.** *intr.* To improve in condition; *esp.* (of animals) to thrive, grow fat by feeding. **b.** To glut oneself *on*; to gloat *in* 1602. **c.** *fig.* To thrive (*esp.* to the detriment of another) 1605. **2.** To grow fertile (as soil); to grow rank (as a plant) 1855. † **3.** *trans.* To improve, fatten up (The pa. pple. *battened* belonged orig. to the intr. sense; cf. *well-read*, etc.) –1790.

1. It makes her fat you see. Shee battens with it B. JONS. *fig.* Battening vampyre-like on a People next door to starvation CARLYLE. Hence **Ba·ttener.**

Batten (bæ·t'n), *v.*² 1775. [f. BATTEN *sb.*¹] To furnish or strengthen with battens.

To b. down (chiefly *Naut.*): to fasten down with battens.

Batter (bæ·təɹ), *v.*¹ ME. [– AFr. *baterer*, f. OFr. *batre* (mod. *battre*) beat; cf. BAT *v.*¹] **1.** *trans.* (and *absol.*) To strike with repeated blows so as to bruise or shatter. **2.** *transf.* and *fig.* To subject (persons, etc.) to crushing or persistent attack 1578. **3.** To beat out of shape, as (in *Printing*) the surface of type 1697. † **4.** [f. BATTER *sb.*¹] To beat into a batter –1622. † **5.** *Sc.* To paste, to fix (as with paste) –1756.

1. Or with a logge B. his skull *Temp.* III. ii. 98. The Ramme that batters downe the wall *Tr. & Cr.* I. iii. 206. **3.** Boats..battered by exposure to ice and storm KANE. Hence **Ba·tterable** *a.* **Ba·tterer.**

Batter (bæ·təɹ), *v.*² ME. [Origin unkn.] *Archit. intr.* Of walls, etc.: To incline from the perpendicular.

Batter (bæ·təɹ), *sb.*¹ 1546. [ME. *bature, batour, bat(e)re* – AFr. *batour* = OFr. *bateüre* action of beating, f. *batre*; see -ER² 3.] **1.** A mixture of two or more ingredients beaten up with a liquid for culinary purposes. Also *transf.* **2.** *Sc.* Flour and water made into paste 1530. **3.** A heavy bruising blow (*rare*) 1823. **4.** A cannonade of heavy ordnance 1859. **5.** *Printing.* A bruise on the face of printing type, etc, (Cf. BATTER *v.*¹ 3.) 1824. Also *attrib.*

Ba·tter, *sb.*² 1743. [f. BATTER *v.*²] The slope of a wall, terrace, or bank from the perpendicular.

Batter-rule, an instrument consisting of a plumb-line and a frame, used for setting a wall, etc. at the proper slope or b.

Ba·tter, *sb.*³ 1824. [f. BAT *v.*¹ + -ER¹.] One who bats, *esp.* in *Cricket.*

Battering (bæ·təriŋ), *vbl. sb.* 1542. [f. BATTER *v.*¹ + -ING¹.] **1.** The action of the vb., *esp. Mil.* **2.** Bruising or defacement thus caused 1558.

Comb.: **b.-charge,** the full charge of powder for a cannon; **-engine** = RAM; **-train,** a number of cannon intended for siege purposes.

Battering-ram. 1611. [f. prec. + RAM *sb.*¹ 3.] An ancient military engine employed for battering down walls, consisting of a beam of wood, with a mass of iron at one end, sometimes shaped like a ram's head.

Battery (bæ·təri). 1531. [– (O)Fr. *batterie*, f. *battre* beat :– L. *battuere*, later *battere*; see -ERY.] **1.** The action of battering or assailing with blows; also *transf.* or *fig.*; *spec.* in *Law*, an unlawful attack upon another by beating, etc., including technically the least touching of another's person or clothes in a menacing manner. † **b.** A bruise –1639. **2.** A number of guns placed in juxtaposition for combined action; in *Mil.*, the smallest division of artillery for tactical purposes 1555. **3.** The platform or fortified work, on or within which artillery is mounted (sometimes including the artillery there mounted) 1590. Also *transf.* or *fig.* **4.** *Mining.* The set of stamps that work in one mortar of a stamp-mill 1881. **5.** (from 2) A combination of simple instruments. **6.** *Electr.* A number of Leyden jars so connected that they may be charged and discharged simultaneously 1748. Also *fig.* **7.** *Galvanism.* A series of cells, each containing the essentials for producing voltaic electricity, connected together. Also used of a single voltaic cell. 1801. **8.** *Optics.* A combined series of lenses or prisms 1867. **9.** Apparatus for preparing or serving meals. [= F. *batterie de cuisine*; ? from next sense.] 1819. **10.** Metal, or articles of metal, wrought by hammering 1502. **11.** *Mining.* **a.** A bulkhead of timber. **b.** The plank closing the bottom of a coal-chute. RAYMOND. **12.** *Mus.* The percussion section of an orchestra.

1. Ile haue an action of B. against him *Twel. N.* IV. i. 36. 2. *Horse batteries*, those in which the gunners are carried partly on the carriages, partly on horses; *Field Batteries*, those in which they are carried wholly on the carriages. *Garrison batteries*, bodies of artillerymen serving heavy guns in forts, etc.

Phrases, etc. *B.-wagon*: one carrying tools and materials for repair of the b. *Cross-batteries*: two batteries playing upon the same point from different directions. *Enfilading b.*: one which sweeps the whole line attacked. *Floating b.*: a heavily armed and armoured vessel for bombarding fortresses. *In b.*: (a gun) projecting in readiness for firing through an embrasure or over a parapet. *Masked b.*: one screened from the enemy's view.

Batting (bæ·tiŋ), *vbl. sb.* 1611. [f. BAT *v.*[1], *sb.*[2] + -ING[1].] **1.** The action of using or striking with a bat: † **a.** in *Laundry-work* –1798. **b.** in *Cricket* 1773. **c.** in cleaning raw cotton by hand 1819. **2.** Cotton fibre prepared in sheets for quilts, etc.; cf. BAT *sb.*[2] 9. 1875.

Battle (bæ·t'l), *sb.* [ME. *batai·le* – (O)Fr. *bataille* :- Rom. **battalia*, for late L. *battualia* military or gladiatorial exercises, f. *battuere* beat.] **1.** A hostile encounter between opposing forces; a fight. **2.** A single combat, a duel ME. Also applied to animals. **3.** (Without article or pl.): Fighting, war ME. † **4.** A war –1557. **5.** *fig.* Strife, struggle for victory ME. **6.** An army, or one of its main divisions, in battle array; = BATTALION (*arch.*) ME. † **7.** The main body of an army or naval force; = BATTALIA 2, BATTALION 1 b. (More fully 'great' or 'main b.') –1596. † **8.** = BATTALIA 1. –1596.

1. *Pitched b.*, one of which the ground has been chosen beforehand by both sides. *Soldier's b.*, one which is decided by the courage and energy of the soldier. 2. *Trial by b.*: the legal decision of a dispute by single combat. **B. royal,** a fight (*spec.* a cockfight) in which several combatants engage; a general engagement; hence *fig.* a general squabble. The race is not to the swift, nor the b. (= victory) to the strong *Eccles.* 9:11. 5. Their mouthes are softer then butter, and yet haue theyr batell in their mynde COVERDALE *Ps.* 55:21. 6. What may the Kings whole Battaile reach vnto 1 *Hen. IV*, IV. i. 129. 7. A Vanguard . . a Battaile of 400 . . ships, and a Reare RALEIGH.

Phrases. *To offer, refuse, accept b.*; *to join b.*; also, *to do b.*; *to give b.*, to attack. *Line of b.*: the position of troops drawn up in b. array; the line formed by ships of war in an engagement. Hence *line-of-battle ship*, one large enough to take part in a main attack; formerly, one of 74 guns and upwards.

Comb.: **b.-cry, -word,** a war-cry, a slogan; **-field, -ground,** the field or ground on which a b. is fought; **-piece,** a painting of a b., a passage describing a b.; **-wise** *adv.* in manner or order of b.

Battle, battel (bæ·t'l), *a. Obs.* exc. *dial.* 1513. [Earliest in Sc. XVI; prob. f. **bat-* as in BATTEN *v.*[1], with suffix -LE 1 as in *brittle*, etc. Cf. BATTLE *v.*[3]] **1.** Of grass, etc.: Improving to sheep and cattle; fattening. **2.** Hence, of land: Rich, productive (prop. in pasture) 1540.

Battle (bæ·t'l), *v.*[1] ME. [– (O)Fr. *batailler* fight, f. *bataille* BATTLE *sb.*] **1.** *intr.* To fight. (Now usu. *fight.*) **b.** *fig.* To maintain a (defensive) struggle, e.g. *with* or *against* bigotry, etc. 1502. † **2.** *trans.* and *refl.* To embattle ME. only. **3.** To assail in battle. Also *fig.* ME.

1. Whiles Lyons Warre, and battaile for their Dennes SHAKS. His virtues battling with his place SWIFT. They *b. it* beyond the wall BYRON. Hence **Ba·ttled** *ppl. a.*[1] ranged in battle-array; *poet.* fought.

† **Ba·ttle,** *v.*[2] ME. [– OFr. *bataillier*, *bateillier* furnish w. ramparts, etc., (med.L. *batellare* XIII); cf. also *bateilleïs* crenelated, embattled; app. rel. to *bataille* BATTLE *sb.* See BATTLEMENT.] To fortify or furnish with battlements. (Usu. in *pass.*) –1618. Hence **Ba·ttled** *ppl. a.*[2] embattled; † crenelated. **Ba·ttling** *vbl. sb.* embattling; *concr.* battlements.

† **Battle, battel** (bæ·t'l), *v.*[3] 1548. [app. a deriv. of BATTLE *a.*; cf. the synon. BATTEN *v.*[1]] *trans.* † **1.** *trans.* To feed, or nourish –1662. † **2.** To fertilize –1662. † **3.** *intr.* To grow fat, to thrive –1721. † **4.** To become fertile –1578. Hence † **Ba·ttled** *ppl. a.*[3] fattened; manured.

† **Battle,** *v.*[4] 1570. [frequent. of BAT *v.*[1] see -LE 3); cf. BATTING, BATLER.] To beat (clothes) with a wooden beetle during washing, or when dried.

Battle-axe, -ax (bæ·t'l,æ:ks). ME. [BATTLE *sb.*] **1.** A kind of axe used as a weapon of war in the Middle Ages. **2.** A halberd or bill 1709.

Battledore (bæ·t'ldō°ɹ), *sb.* ME. [perh. – Pr. *batedor* beater (cf. Sp. *batidor*), f. *batre* beat (cf. BATTERY), infl. by BATTLE *v.*[4]] **1.** A beetle used in washing, also for mangling linen clothes; hence applied to other similarly shaped instruments. **2.** An instrument like a small racket used in playing with a shuttlecock 1598. **b.** The game of *b. and shuttlecock* 1719. **3.** A horn-book; so called from its usual shape. *Obs.* exc. *dial.* 1693.

Phrase. **Battledore barley**: a cultivated barley (*Hordeum zeocriton*) with short broad ears. Hence [f. sense 2] **Ba·ttledore** *v.* to toss or fly to and fro.

Battlement (bæ·t'lmĕnt), *sb.* [Earliest form *batelment* (XIV), an Eng. formation (+ -MENT) on OFr. *bataillier*; see BATTLE *v.*[2] and cf. EMBATTLE *v.*[2]] **a.** An indented parapet at the top of a wall, orig. used for purposes of defence, subseq. for architectural decoration. The raised parts are *cops* or *merlons*, the indentations *embrasures* or *crenelles*. **b.** *loosely* for 'embattled roof'. 1595. **c.** *fig.* The towering summits of the mountains, the roof of the heavens 1667.

Thrown by angry Jove Sheer o're the Chrystal Battlements MILT. *P.L.* I. 742. Hence **Ba·ttlement** *v.* to furnish or decorate with battlements. **Ba·ttlemented** *ppl. a.* having battlements.

Battler[1] (bæ·tləɹ). ME. [– OFr. *batailleor*, *bataillier* warrior, f. *bataillier* BATTLE *v.*[1], see -ER[2]. In mod. use f. BATTLE *v.*[1] + -ER[1].] One who fights; a fighter.

† **Ba·ttler**[2]. *rare.* 1650. [f. BATTLE *v.*[4] + -ER[1].] **1.** One who beats with a bat or battledore –1720. **2.** A small bat for playing at ball. **3.** = BATLER.

Battleship (bæ·t'lʃip). 1884. Short for *line-of-battle ship* (1705): see BATTLE *sb.* phr.

Battology (bætǫ·lŏdʒi). 1603. [– mod.L. *battologia* – Gr. βαττολογία, f. βάττος stammerer; see -LOGY.] A needless repetition in speaking or writing. Hence **Battolo·gical** *a.* **Batto·logist. Batto·logize** *v. trans.* and *intr.*

‖ **Battue** (batū·). 1816. [Fr., pa. pple. fem. of *battre* used subst.] **1.** The driving of game from cover (by beating the bushes, etc.). **2.** *transf.* **a.** A thorough beat up or search. **b.** Wholesale slaughter, *esp.* of unresisting crowds.

‖ **Batture** (‖ batū·r, bătiū°·ɹ). 1856. [Fr.] A river- or sea-bed elevated to the surface.

‖ **Battuta** (battū·tă). 1819. [It.] *Mus.* The beating of time.

Batty (bæ·ti), *a.* 1590. [f. BAT *sb.*[1] + -Y[1].] **1.** Belonging to a bat. **2.** *slang.* Crazy 1922.

Batz (bæts). 1625. [– G. † *batze* (mod. *batzen*); prob. taken as a pl., *bats*, whence as sing. *bat* XVII–XVIII.] A small coin worth four kreuzers, formerly current in Switzerland and South Germany.

Baubee, -ie, vars. of BAWBEE.

Bauble (bǭ·b'l). ME. [ME. *babel*, *babulle* – OFr. *babel*, *baubel* child's toy, plaything, of unkn. orig. (cf. Anglo-L. *baubellum* XII–XIII).] † **1.** A stick with a mass of lead fixed or hung at one end, used for weighing, etc. –1570. † **2.** A child's toy –1814. **3.** A showy trinket, or gewgaw ME. **4.** The baton of the Court Fool or jester ME. **5.** *transf.* or *fig.* A foolish matter, or † person 1579; a paltry thing 1634.

3. Paltrie cap . . a b. *Tam. Shr.* IV. iii. 82. 4. Such is a fole and well worthy a babyll 1509. That fooles bable, the Mace 1676. Hence † **Bau·bling** *a.* paltry.

Bauch, baugh (bāχ, bāχʷ, bāf), *a. Sc.* 1560. [perh. – ON. *bágr* uneasy; mod.Icel. poor, hard up; cf. also *bagr* awkward, clumsy.] Weak, poor, pithless; sorry, shaky. ¶ The north. Eng. dial. is *baff*, as in *baff week*, 'hard-up week'.

Bauchle, bach le(bā·χʷ'l). *Sc.* 1787. [Origin unkn.] **1.** An old shoe down at the heel. **2.** A shambler, a ne'er-do-well.

Baud(e, obs. f. BAWD.

Baudekin, baudkin (bǭ·dĭkin, bǭ·dkin). *Obs.* exc. *Hist.* ME. [– OFr. *baudekin* – med.L. *baldachinus*; see BALDACHIN.] = BALDACHIN I.

† **Bau·dery.** [– OFr. *bauderie* gaiety, jollity, f. *baud* gay, sprightly; see BAWDSTROT.] Gaiety, mirth. CHAUCER.

Baudrons (bǭ·drənz). *Sc.* 1450. [Origin unkn. Cf. BAWD *sb.*[2]] Sc. name for the cat.

† **Bau·frey.** *rare.* 1639. [perh. = BELFRY.] A beam.

‖ **Bauge** (bōʒ). 1847. [mod. Fr.] A drugget made at Bauge in Burgundy.

Bauk, obs. f. BALK.

Bauld, dial. f. BOLD.

Baulk, var. of BALK, *esp.* in Billiards.

Bauson (bǭ·sən). *arch.* [ME. *bausen*, *bauson* subst. use of *bausand*; see next.] **1.** *sb.* A badger; see BADGER *sb.*[2] **b.** A fat or pertinacious person 1607. **2.** *adj.* = BAUSOND 1587.

Bau·sond, *a. Obs.* or *dial.* ME. [ME. *bausand* – OFr. *bausant* piebald (sb. piebald horse) = Pr. *bausan* (whence It. *balzano*, whence mod.Fr. *balzan*) :- Rom. **balteanus* 'belted', striped, f. L. *balteus* BELT. For a similar application see BADGER.] Of animals: Having white spots on a black or bay ground; *esp.* (now) having a white patch on the forehead, or a white stripe down the face.

Bauxite. 1872. [– Fr. *bauxite*, f. Les *Baux*, near Arles, France; see -ITE[1] 2 b.] Var. BEAUXITE.

‖ **Bavardage** (bavardā·ʒ). 1835. [Fr., f. *bavarder* chatter, f. *bavard* talkative, f. *bave* saliva.] Idle talk.

† **Ba·varoy.** 1714. [prob. – Fr. *bavarois* Bavarian.] A surtout –1788.

Bavian, obs. f. BABION.

Bavin (bæ·vin), *sb.* 1528. [Origin unkn.] **1.** A bundle of brushwood, etc., bound with only one withe; in *Mil.* a fascine. **2.** Impure limestone. (? a different wd.) 1839.

1. *attrib.* **b. wits,** wits having a quick and short-lived blaze 1 *Hen. IV*, III. ii. 61. Hence † **Ba·vin** *v.* to bind up into bavins.

Bawbee (bǭbī·). *Sc.* 1542. [Named after the laird of Sille*bawby*, mint-master under James V.] A Scotch coin of base silver, orig. three, later six, pennies of Scotch money, or a half-penny English; *hence*, a half-penny, a copper.

Bawble, obs. f. BAUBLE.

Bawcock (bǭ·kǫk). 1599. [– Fr. *beau coq* 'fine cock'.] Fine fellow, good fellow.

Good B. bate thy rage *Hen. V*, III. ii. 25.

Bawd (bǭd), *sb.*[1] ME. [abbr. f. BAWDSTROT.] A procurer or procuress; since *c* 1700 only fem., and applied to a woman keeping a place of prostitution. Also *fig.* Hence **Baw·dily** *adv.* **Baw·diness,** † dirtiness; lewdness. **Baw·dship.** (Cf. *lordship.*)

† **Bawd,** *sb.*[2] *dial.* 1592. [perh. = *bad*, *badde* (XIV) cat, or short f. BAUDRONS. Cf. Eng. use of *puss*, and Sc. use of *malkin*, for both hare and cat.] A hare.

† **Bawd,** *v.*[1] 1529. [f. BAWDY *a.*[1]] To dirty.

Bawd, *v.*[2] *arch.* or *Obs.* 1651. [f. BAWD *sb.*[1]] To pander; also *fig.*

Bawdry (bǭ·dri). *arch.* ME. [f. BAWD *sb.*[1] + -RY.] **1.** The practice of a bawd. † **2.** *gen.* Unchastity –1651. **3.** Lewdness in speech or writing; obscene talk, etc. 1589.

† **Bawdstrot.** ME. [– OFr. *baudetrot*, *baudestroyt* 'pronubus', 'pronuba' (XIII), which seems to be f. *baud* lively, gay (– Gmc. **bald-* BOLD) + the word repr. by AFr. *trote* TROT *sb.*[2], hag; relation to BAWDY *a.*[1] is undetermined.] A BAWD, male or female –1483.

† **Baw·dy,** *a.*[1] ME. [Origin unkn.] Soiled, dirty –1621. Hence † **Baw·dy** *v.* to make dirty.

Bawdy (bǭ·di), *a.*[2] 1513. [f. BAWD *sb.* + -Y[1].] **1.** Of, pertaining to, or befitting a bawd. (Usu. of language.) **2.** quasi- *sb.*, esp. in *To talk b.*: Lewd language, obscenity. *Comb.* **b.-house,** a brothel.

Bawhorse, obs. f. *bât-horse*: see BAT *sb.*[3]

Bawke. *dial.* 1880. [perh. var. of BACK *sb.*[2]] *Mining.* A bucket for raising coal.

Bawl (bǭl), *v.* 1556. [corresp. in form and meaning w. med.L. *baulare* bark, of imit. origin; but cf. Icel. *baula* (Sw. *bǫla*) low, as an ox.] † **1.** *intr.* To bark or howl as a dog –1753. **2.** *gen.* To shout protractedly at the top of one's voice; to bellow. Often with *out.* 1570. **3.** *trans.* To utter with bawling 1597.

1. At my blunte behauour barke ye or ball ye J. HEYWOOD. 3. To b. out, My Beloved; and the

Words Grace! Regeneration! Sanctification! *Tatler* No. 66, ¶ 1. Hence **Bawl** *sb.* a loud prolonged rough cry. **Baw·ler**, one who bawls, *esp.* a preacher. **Baw·ling** *vbl. sb.*; *spec.* in *Hunting*, the giving tongue too loudly.

Bawn (bǫn). 1537. [– Ir. *bábhún*, MIr. *bódhún*, f. *bó* cow + *dún* fortress.] A fortified enclosure; the fortified court or outwork of a castle.

1. Our Englishe men assauted the..baon of the castell 1537.

† **Baw·rel, baw·ret.** 1706. [Origin unkn.] The female and male of a kind of hawk. (Dicts.)

Bawsint, bawson, etc., var. BAUSON, -OND.

Ba·xter. *Obs.* exc. *dial.* [OE. *bæcestre*, fem. of *bæcere*, f. *bacan* BAKE; see -STER.] A baker: fem. ME.; masc. or fem. OE.

Bay (bēi), *sb.*[1] ME. [– (O)Fr. *baie* :– L. *baca* berry. See BAYBERRY.] † **1.** A berry, *esp.* that of the laurel or bay-tree –1866. **2.** Short for *Bay-tree* or *Bay Laurel* (*Laurus nobilis*), called also Sweet Bay; also applied to other laurels 1530. **b.** (Cf. BAY *sb.*[2] 3.) **3.** Usu. in *pl.* Leaves or sprigs of this tree, *esp.* as a wreath for a conqueror or poet; hence *fig.* the fame attained by these 1564.

2. I have seen the wicked in great power, spreading himself like a green bay tree *Ps.* 37:35. **3.** A poet's garland made of bays GREENE. *Comb.* **b.-rum,** an aromatic liquid, obtained by distilling rum in which bay-leaves have been steeped.

Bay (bēi), *sb.*[2] ME. [– (O)Fr. *baie* – (O)Sp. *bahia*, recorded first by Isidore of Seville (VII) and perh. of Iberian origin.] **1.** An indentation of the sea into the land with a wide opening. **2.** A recess in a range of hills, etc. 1853. **3.** in U.S.: **a.** An arm of a prairie extending into, and partly surrounded by, woods. **b.** A piece of marshy ground covered with Bay-trees 1848.

1. My affection hath an vnknowne bottome, like the B. of Portugall *A.Y.L.* IV. i. 211.

Comb.: **b.-duck,** (east Eng.) name of the Sheldrake; **-floe, -ice,** new-formed ice, such as first appears in sheltered water; **Bay-state,** pop. name (in U.S.) for the State of Massachusetts.

Bay (bēi), *sb.*[3] ME. [– (O)Fr. *baie*, f. *bayer*, earlier *baer*, *beer* gape, stand open (mod. *béant* wide open) :– med.L. *batare* (c. 800), of unkn. origin.] **1.** An opening in a wall; *esp.* the space between two columns. **2.** 'The division of a barn or other building, generally from fifteen to twenty feet in breadth' (Gwilt). Of a house: The space lying under one gable, or between two party-walls. 1557. **3.** Applications of 'recess': e.g. *horse-bay*, the stall for a horse; *sick-bay*, part of the forepart of a ship's main-deck, used as a hospital 1582. **4.** = Applications of 'intervening space', as *bay* in plastering, of joists, of roofing 1823. **5.** An internal recess formed by causing a wall to project outwardly, for the reception of a window, etc.

Bay (bēi), *sb.*[4] ME. [In phr. (hold, keep) *at bay*, † *at a bay* – OFr. *bai*, or aphet. f. ME. ABAY (*at abay* being apprehended as *at a bay*) – OFr. *abai* (mod. *aboi* in phr. *être* and *mettre aux abois* be and bring to bay; cf. OFr. *tenir a bay*, It. *stare* and *tenere a bada*); the Fr. sbs. are f. *bayer*, *abayer* BAY *v.*[1]] **1.** The deep prolonged barking of a dog when hunting 1530. **2.** *esp.* The chorus raised by hounds in conflict with the quarry; *hence*, the final conflict with the quarry ME. **3.** Used of the position of a hunted animal, when obliged to turn and defend itself: *To stand, be at, turn to, b.* ME.; also *fig.* **4.** Of the action of the hunted animal: *To hold or keep at (a) b.* (the hounds) 1532.

1. Dogs..all bristle and b. C. BRONTË. **3.** To fight to the last and die at b. FROUDE. **4.** By Riding..keep Death as it were at a B. 1711.

Bay (bēi), *sb.*[5] 1440. [Origin unkn. See BAY *v.*[3]] † **1.** Obstacle. **2.** An embankment or dam 1581.

Bay (bēi), *sb.*[6] 1863. [Short for *bay-antler*, earlier *be-* or *bes-antlier*, f. OFr. *bes* second + ANTLER.] The second branch of a stag's horn.

Bay (bēi·), *sb.*[7] *Obs.* exc. *Hist.* 1581. [– (O)Fr. *baie*, or its Du. repr. *baai*, f. *bai* adj. (see next); see BAIZE.] Baize. Usu. in pl., whence BAIZE, q.v.

Bay (bēi), *a.* (and *sb.*) ME. [– (O)Fr. *bai* :– L. *badius* (Varro) chestnut-coloured (only of horses), rel. to OIr. *buide* yellow.] **1.** A reddish brown colour; used esp. of horses. **2.** as *sb.*, *ellipt.* for 'bay horse' 1535.

Bay (bēi), *v.*[1] ME. [aphet. f. OFr. *abaiier*, or f. synon. *baiier* (mod. *aboyer*) = It. (*ab*)*baiare*, f. imit. base **bai-*; infl. by BAY *sb.*[4]] **1.** To bark, prop. of a hound or mastiff. **2.** *fig.* (see quots.) ME. **3.** To assail with barking ME. Also *fig.* **4.** To utter by baying 1591. **5.** To pursue, or drive to bay, with barking 1590. **6.** To bring to bay, hold at bay 1575.

2. What moves Ajax thus to b. at him *Tr. & Cr.* II. iii. 99. **3.** I had rather be a dog, and b. the moon Than such a Roman *Jul. C.* IV. iii. 27. **4.** To b. a welcome KANE.

Bay (bēi), *v.*[2] 1649. [f. the sb. in 'at bay'; see BAY *sb.*[4]] **1.** *intr.* To turn to, stand at, bay. **2.** *trans.* To stand at bay against (*rare*) 1848.

Bay (bēi), *v.*[3] 1598. [Connected w. BAY *sb.*[5], either as source or (prob.) as deriv.] To obstruct, dam (water).

‖ **Bayadère** (bāyădē·r, -dīə·ɹ). 1598. [Fr. – Pg. *bailadeira*, f. *bailar* dance, obsc. rel. to med.L. *ballare*; see BALE *v.*[2]] A Hindu dancing girl.

The southern Bayadère, who differ considerably from the nâch girls of northern India HEBER.

Bayard (bēi·ăɹd), *a.* and *sb.*[1] *arch.* ME. [– OFr. *baiard*, f. *bai*; see BAY *a.*, -ARD.] **1.** Bay-coloured; *absol.* a bay horse. **2.** Name of the bay-coloured magic horse given by Charlemagne to Rinaldo; *whence* **a.** Mock-heroic for any horse ME. **b.** Taken as the type of blindness, or blind recklessness ME. **3.** *Hence*: A self-confident ignoramus 1529.

2. Who is so blind as Bold Bayarde 1609. **3.** Being a b., who never had the soul to know, what conversing means MILT. Hence † **Bay·ardism,** ignorant presumption. † **Bay·ardly** *a.* bayard-like (sense 3).

† **Bay·ard,** *sb.*[2] 1642. [– Fr. *bayard*, *-art*, *bart*, OFr. *baiart* (earlier *beart*, *baart*).] A hand-barrow used for heavy loads.

Bayberry (bēi·be:ri). 1578. [f. BAY *sb.*[1] 2.] **1.** The fruit of the bay-tree. **2.** In U.S., the fruit of the Wax-myrtle (*Myrica cerifera*); also, the plant 1860. **3.** In Jamaica, the fruit of the Bayberry Tree, *Eugenia acris*, a species of Pimento 1756.

Bayed (bēid), *ppl. a.* 1848. [f. BAY *sb.*[3] + -ED[2].] Having a bay, formed as a bay or recess.

Bayness (bēi·nės). 1570. [f. BAY *a.*[1] + -NESS.] The quality of being bay-coloured.

Bayonet (bēi·ŏnet). 1692. [– Fr. *baïonnette*, earlier *bayonnette*, said to be f. *Bayonne*, France, the orig. place of manufacture (cf. *bayonnettes de Bayonne*, Tabourot Des Accordes, d. 1590); see -ET.]

†‖ **1.** A short flat dagger –1707. **2.** A stabbing instrument of steel for fixing to the muzzle of a musket or rifle. See also *Sword-bayonet*. 1704. **b.** *abst.* Military force 1774. **3.** *pl.* Soldiers armed with bayonets 1780. **4.** *Mech.* A pin which plays in and out of a hole, and serves to engage and disengage portions of machinery, a clutch 1798.

2. Under the rule of the b. 1879. **3.** On the demand of 40,000 Irish bayonets BURKE. *Comb.*, etc.: *Spanish Bayonet*, a species of Yucca, found in N. America; **b.-clutch,** a clutch with two prongs for engaging and disengaging machinery; **-joint,** one in which the two parts cannot be separated by a simple longitudinal movement 1812. Hence **Bay·oneted** *ppl. a.* armed or fitted with a b.

Bayonet (bēi·ŏnet), *v.* 1700. [f. prec. sb.] **1.** To stab with a bayonet. **2.** To drive or coerce at or as at the point of the bayonet 1790.

2. To sabre and to b. us into a submission BURKE.

Bayou (bəi·ū). 1766. Also **bayeau, bio.** [– Amer. Fr. – Choctaw *bayuk*.] In southern U.S., a stream or channel with little current, aften forming an inlet or outlet to a river or lake.

Bay-salt (bēi·sǫ:lt). 1465. [f. BAY *sb.*[2]] Salt, obtained in large crystals by slow evaporation; orig., from sea-water by the sun's heat.

Bay-window (bēi·wi·ndoᵘ). ME. [f. BAY *sb.*[3]] A window forming a bay in a room, and projecting outwards from the wall; often called a *bow*-window.

Baywood (bēi·wud). 1869. Mahogany from the Bay of Campeachy.

Bayz, var. of BAIZE.

Bazaar, bazar (băzā·ɹ). 1599. [Earlier *bazar(r)o*, prob. – It. – Turk. – Pers. *bāzār* market.] **1.** An Oriental market-place or market, usually consisting of ranges of shops or stalls. **2.** A fancy fair for the sale of useful and ornamental articles, usually on behalf of a charitable or religious object 1816.

2. *Soho Bazaar* 1816. A b. is the clergyman's.. ultimate hope 1876.

Bdellatomy (delæ·tŏmi). 1868. [f. Gr. βδέλλα leech + -TOMY.] *Med.* The practice of cutting leeches to empty them of blood while still sucking.

‖ **Bdellium** (de·liŏm). ME. [– L. *bdellium* (Pliny, Vulg.) – Gr. βδέλλιον (Dioscorides), used in versions of the O.T. later than LXX to render Heb. *bᵉḏōlaḥ*.] **1.** Name of several trees or shrubs of the N.O. *Amyridaceæ*, chiefly of the genus *Balsamodendron*, yielding a gum-resin resembling impure myrrh. **2.** The gum-resin itself 1585. **3.** As tr., in the Eng. Bible, of Heb. *bᵉdōlaḥ*; see above ME.

3. Ther is foundun bdelyum and the stoon onychyrus WYCLIF *Gen.* 2:12. Cf. *Num.* 11:7.

Bdellometer (delǫ·mĭtəɹ). 1839. [– Fr. *bdellomètre*, f. Gr. βδέλλα leech + *-mètre* -METER.] *Med.* An instrument proposed as a substitute for leeches, and showing the amount of blood drawn.

Be (bī), *v.* [OE. *bēon*, f. stem **beu-**.

An irreg. and defective vb., the full conjugation of which is made up of the surviving inflexions of four bases, viz. (1) the original Aryan subst. vb. with stem **es-**, Skr. *as-*, Gr. ἐσ-, L. *es-*, *'s-*, Gmc. **es-*, *'s*; (2) the vb. with stem **wes-**, Skr. *vas-*, Gmc. *wes-*, Goth. *wisan* to remain; (3) the stem **beu-**, Skr. *bhu-*, Gr. φυ-, L. *fu-*, OE. *bēon* to become; (4) the old perfect formation Gmc. **ar-* (:– **or*), of unkn. origin. Of the stem *es-*, OE. possessed only the present tenses, all the other parts being supplied from the stem *wes-*, pa. t. *was*, pl. *were*. *Bēon* be, 'to become, come to be', at first served merely as a future tense to the vb. *am-was*, thus constituted, but as parts of *am-was* became obs., it took their place, and now it gives its name to the whole verb *am-was-be*. In OE. the pres. Indic. of *am* had two pl. forms, (1) *sind*, *sindon* (= Goth. and G. *sind*, L. *sunt*, Skr. *sánti*), and (2) *earon*, *aron* (= ON. *eru*). Of these *sind*, *-on* was replaced in southern Eng. bef. 1250 by *beth*, *ben*, *be*; while *aron*, *aren*, *are* survived in the north, and spread south, till early in 16th c. *are* appeared in standard Eng. *Be* was in concurrent use till the end of the century (see Shaks., and Bible of 1611), and still occurs as an archaism. But the regular mod. Eng. pl. is *are*. For the history of the inflexions see O.E.D. s.v.]

1. To have place in the realm of fact, to exist; *also*, to live. **2.** To come into existence, come about, happen, take place OE. **3.** To be the case or the fact, *esp.* in *So be*, *Be it that* = suppose that ME. **4.** To continue, remain ME. **5.** With adv. or prepositional phrase: stating *where* or *how*, i.e. in what place or state a thing is. [= Sp., Pg. *estar* as dist. from *ser*.] OE. **6.** To belong, pertain, befall: with *dat.* or *to* = have. Now only in exclams. or wishes (with *be* often omitted). ME. **7.** With adj., sb., or adjective phrase; acting as simple copula: stating *of what sort* or *what* a thing is. **a.** To exist as the subject of some predicate OE. **b.** To exist as the thing known by a certain name; to be identical with OE. **c.** To signify, amount to, mean ME. **d.** *ellipt.* To be good for, 'stand'. *Obs.* or *dial.* 1749. **8.** With pples. and infins., serving as an auxiliary and forming periphrastic tenses. **a.** With *pa. pple.*: in *trans. vbs.*, forming the passive voice OE.; in *intr. vbs.*, forming perfect tenses (now largely displaced by *have*) OE. **b.** With the present pple.: with *active* signification OE.; with *passive* signification, as 'our house was building' (= mod. 'was being built') 1551. **c.** With the dat. infin., making a future of appointment or arrangement; hence of necessity, obligation, or duty (now replaced by *have*) ME. (The same constr. is used in the sense 'to be proper or fit (to)'.)

1. Troy is no more DRYDEN. God is, nay alone is CARLYLE. **2.** When is it to be 1887. **3.** And be it indeed that I haue erred *Job* 19:4. **4.** Phr. *Let be* (arch.): leave as it is; leave off; *Sc.* omit. Ile..not be all day neither *All's Well* II. i. 94. Don't be long (*mod.*). **5.** Your book is here 1887. There is a cow in the garden (*mod.*). I had been to see Irving (*mod.*). To be off; to be in debt, at one's ease (*mod.*). Is your father well *Gen.* 43:27.

6. O well is the, happie art thou COVERDALE *Ps.* 127:2. Success (be) to your efforts (*mod.*). **7. a.** Then are they glad *Ps.* 108:30. **b.** My selfe am Naples *Temp.* I. ii. 434. **c.** Is it nothing to you, all ye that passe by *Lam.* 11:2. I'll tell you what it is, you must leave (*mod.*). **8. a.** Mony ben calle(d ME. They are rested in their bataylis LD. BERNERS. **b.** Leat vs be trudgeing 1562. **c.** Uneasy..about their being to go back again DE FOE. † *To be to seek*: to have to seek. They are not to compare with these (*mod.*).

Phrases. *I were better* (*best, as good*), orig. *me were better* = it were better for me. Now *had better* is used, after *had rather*, etc. Cf. HAVE, RATHER. *He came here Monday was a week*, i.e. he came here on the Monday a week before Monday last. Here the phrase became a mere adjectival clause. *Was* is now generally omitted: I was in town Monday (was) three weeks. *To be about to*: see ABOUT. *What one would be at*: what one aims at. *To be for*: **a.** to be bound for; **b.** to be on the side of; **c.** to desire (*dial.*).

Be-, *prefix* :- OE. *be-*, weak form of the prep. and adv. *bī-* (*biǵ*) BY. The original meaning was 'about', weakened in preps. and advs. into *at* or *near*. Still (*esp.* in senses 2, 6, 7) a living element.

1. Forming derivative vbs., with sense of 'around': **a.** on all sides, as in BESET, BESMEAR, etc.; **b.** from side to side (within a space), in or through all its parts, thoroughly, as in BESTIR, *bejumble*, etc. **2.** Forming intensive vbs., with sense of 'thoroughly, soundly, conspicuously, to excess, ridiculously', as in *bemuzzle, bewidow*, etc. **3.** Forming derivative vbs. with privative meaning 'off, away', as in BEDEAL, BEREAVE. **4.** Making vbs. trans., by adding a prepositional relation: primarily 'about', whence *against, at, for, to, on, upon, over*, as in BESPEAK, speak about (or for, to), BEMOAN, moan about (or over), etc. **5.** Forming trans. vbs. on adjs. and sbs., taken as complements of the predicate, meaning To make: as BEFOUL, BEDIM, BEFOOL, BESOT. In mod. use, nearly all contemptuous. **b.** To style, dub, etc., as in *bemadam, be-Roscius*, etc. **6.** Forming trans. vbs. on sbs. used in an instrumental relation; the primary idea being: **a.** To surround, cover, or bedaub with, as in BECLOUD, BEDEW. Thence **b.** To affect in any way, as in BENIGHT, BEGUILE, BEFRIEND. In both sets there is often the notion of 'thoroughly, to excess'. **c.** In sense of 'bereave of', as in BEHEAD, BELIMB, etc. (No longer in living use.) **7.** Forming ppl. adjs., which unite the prec. senses, esp. 6 and 2, in the notion of 'covered or furnished with', usu. in an overdone way. In mod. use (e g. with Carlyle) *be-* is often merely rhet., expressing depreciation, raillery, etc.; cf. *booted* and *bebooted*, etc. This is now the most freq. use of *be-*.

Beach (bītʃ), *sb.* 1535. [Early forms also *bache, bayche, baich*. Perh. identical with OE. *bæće, beće* brook, stream (cf. BACHE, BECK *sb.*[1]), with transf. meaning '(pebbly) river valley', a word surviving in many place-names, as *Bache*, Sand*bach*, Wis*bech*.] **1.** (Usu. *collect.*, formerly occas. with *pl.*): The water-worn pebbles of the sea-shore; shingle. **2.** The shore of the sea, the strand; *spec.* the part lying between high- and low-water-mark. (This is prob. Shakespeare's sense.) Also *transf.* In *Geol.* An ancient sea-margin. 1596.

1. Rowling pebble stones, which those that dwell neere the sea do call Bayche GERARD. **3.** The Pibbles on the hungry b. *Cor.* V. iii. 58.

Comb.: **b.-comber**, a long wave rolling in from the ocean (U.S.); also, a settler on the Pacific islands, living by pearl-fishery, etc., or loafing about wharves and beaches (whence *beach-combing* ppl. a.); **-grass**, a reedy grass (*Arundo arenaria*) growing on the sea-shore; **-man**, one who earns his living on the b.; **-master**, an officer in charge of the disembarkation of troops; **-wagon**, a light open wagon, with two or more seats. Hence **Bea·chless** *a.* **Bea·chy** *a.* covered with shingle.

Beach (bītʃ), *v.*[1] 1840. [f. prec. sb.] *trans.* To haul or run up on the beach.

† **Beach**, *v.*[2] 1571. [perh. aphet. f. *abeche* (Gower), – OFr. *abechier* (mod. *abecquer*) feed (a bird) f. *à* to + *bec* BEAK.] To give a beakful to (a young bird); hence *spec.* in *Falconry*, to give a little as a whet to appetite.

Beached (bī·tʃėd, bītʃt), *a.* and *pple.* 1590. [f. BEACH *sb.* and *v.*[1] + -ED[1] and [2].] **1.** Having a beach; in early use, Covered with shingle. **2.** Driven or dragged up on the beach (*mod.*).

1. The b. margent of the sea *Mids. N.* II. i. 82.

Beacon (bī·kən), *sb.* [OE. *bēacn* sign, portent, ensign = OFris. *bēcen, bācen*, OS. *bōkan*, OHG. *bouhhan* :- WGmc. **baukna* (cf. BECKON) of unkn. origin.] † **1.** A sign, a portent. † **2.** An ensign –1483. **3.** A signal; *spec.* a signal-fire ME. **4.** Hence *gen.* A signal station, watch-tower 1611. **5.** A conspicuous hill, on which beacons were (or might be) lighted; *e.g.* Dunkery B. on Exmoor, etc. 1597. † **b.** A division of a wapentake; prob. a district bound to furnish a beacon 1641. **6.** Any conspicuous object, as a lighthouse, etc., placed upon the coast or at sea, to warn or direct ME. Also *fig.*

4. Therefore was the name of it called..Mizpah [*marg.* that is a b. or watchtower] *Gen.* 31:49. **6.** Modest Doubt is cal'd The B. of the wise SHAKS.

Beacon (bī·kən), *v.* 1644. [f. prec. sb.] † **1.** *trans.* *To beacon up*: to kindle as a beacon –1651. **2.** To light up, as a beacon-fire does 1803. Also *fig.* **3.** To furnish, or mark the position of, with a beacon or beacons. Occas. with *off, out.* 1821. **4.** *intr.* To shine like a beacon 1821.

2. To b. the dale with midnight fires SCOTT. **3.** To b. out a boundary 1883. **4.** The soul of Adonais, like a star, Beacons from the abode where the Eternal are SHELLEY. Hence **Bea·coned** *ppl. a.* furnished with a beacon.

Beaconage (bī·kənėdʒ). 1607. [f. as prec. + -AGE.] **a.** Toll paid for the maintenance of beacons. **b.** A system of beacons.

Bead (bīd), *sb.* [ME. *bede*, pl. *bedes*, partly aphetic of *ibede* (OE. *ġebed* prayer, see I-[1]), partly generalized from OE. *bedhus* house of prayer; rel. sbs. are OFris. *bede*, OS. *beda* (Du. *bede*), *gibed*, OHG. *beta, gibet* (G. *gebet*), Goth. *bida*; f. Gmc. **beð-* BID.] † **1.** Prayer; *pl.* devotions –1554. **2.** One of a string of small perforated balls forming the *rosary* or *paternoster*, used for keeping count of the number of prayers said ME. **3.** Hence: A small perforated body, of glass, amber, metal, wood, etc., used as an ornament ME. **b.** In *pl.* († occas. in *sing.*) A string of beads for the neck 1500. **4.** *transf.* **a.** A drop of liquid or of molten metal 1596. **b.** A bubble of foam; *spec.* the foam or head upon certain beverages 1753. **c.** The small knob which forms the front sight of a gun 1841. **d.** A string of sponges 1885. **5.** *Archit.* **a.** A small globular ornament, usu. applied in a row like a string of beads. **b.** A narrow moulding of semi-circular section.

1. *To bid a b.*: to offer a prayer. Also *To say one's beads.* **2.** *To tell* or *count one's beads*: to say one's prayers. **3.** *fig.* You minimus..You b., you acorne *Mids. N.* III. ii. 329. **4. a.** Beds of sweate 1 *Hen. IV*, II. iii. 61. The b. of impure silver 1854. **b.** Swimming about among the foam-beads below KINGSLEY. **c.** *To draw a b. upon*: to take aim at (U.S.).

Phrase. *Baily's beads*: a phenomenon observed in total eclipses of the sun, in which, before the beginning and after the end of complete obscuration, the sun's crescent appears as a band of brilliant points, resembling a string of beads.

Comb. I. (f. sense 2, mostly arch., and now often spelt *bede*): **b.-folk**, people (often pensioners) who pray for a benefactor; **-house** (Welsh *Bettws*), *orig.* a house of prayer, *hence* an alms-house, in which prayers are to be offered for the soul of the founder; **-woman** (cf. *b.-folk*). II. **-proof** *a.* (of alcoholic spirits), such that a crown of bubbles (see 4 b) formed by shaking will stand for some time (a fallacious test of strength); **-sedge**, the Bur-reed (*Sparganium ramosum*); **-snake**, a small American snake (*Elaps fulvus*); **-stone**, one used as a bead, or of which beads are made; **-tree**, the AZEDARAC. Hence **Bea·ded** *ppl. a.* worked with beads; edged with bead-like protuberances; furnished with or wearing beads; formed into or like beads; covered with bubbles. **Bea·der**, a tool used in silver chasing to make a b. pattern. **Bea·diness**, beady quality. **Bea·ding**, the formation of beads; bead-work, in trimming, etc.; a bead moulding, etc.; a preparation used to make liquor form beads. **Bea·dy** *a.* beadlike; (of eyes) small, round and glittering; covered with beads (of sweat, etc.); frothy; *Archit.* having a b. moulding.

Bead (bīd), *v.* 1577. [f. prec.] **1.** To furnish with beads, a bead, or beading. **2.** *intr.* To form into a bead or beads 1873. **3.** To string like beads; also *fig.* 1883.

1. Dew, which beaded the webs of the spiders 1856.

† **Bea·d-hook.** [perh. f. OE. *beadu* battle, war. Cf. OE. *beadu wæpen* weapon of battle, etc.] A kind of boat-hook. CHAPMAN.

Beadle (bī·d'l), *sb.* [– OFr. *bedel* (mod. *bedeau*) :- Rom. **bidellus*, of Gmc. origin. Superseded OE. *bydel*, ME. *büdel, bidel* = OHG. *butil* (G. *büttel*) :- Gmc. **buð-*, base of **beuðan*, OE. *bēodan*; see BID *v.*] † **1.** One who makes a proclamation –1644; the crier of a law-court; a town-crier –1691. **2.** A messenger or under-officer of justice OE. **3.** An apparitor or precursor; **a.** *spec.* in the Eng. Universities (conventionally spelt *bedel, -ell*), the name of certain officials, with duties which are now chiefly processional ME.; **b.** the apparitor of a trades guild ME. **4.** An inferior parish officer appointed to keep order in church, punish petty offenders, give notices of vestry meetings, etc. 1594.

4. The unlucky boys with toys and balls were whipped away by a b. STEELE. Hence **Bea·dledom**, stupid officiousness. **Bea·dlehood, Bea·dleism**, the state or dignity of a b. † **Bea·dlery, Bea·dleship**, the office or jurisdiction of a b.

Bead-roll (bī·d,rōᵘl). 1500. [f. BEAD *sb.* + ROLL *sb.*] **1.** *orig.* A list of persons to be specially prayed for (*arch.*). **2.** *transf.* A string of names; a catalogue; a pedigree; a long series 1529. **3.** A rosary 1598.

2. Dan Chaucer..On fames eternall b. worthie to be fyled SPENSER *F.Q.* IV. ii. 32.

Beadsman (bī·dzmæ̆n). [ME. *beode-, bed(e)man*, f. BEAD, repl. by *beadsman* (prob. after *almsman*) in XVI.] **1.** *lit.* A man of prayer; one who prays for the soul of another. **2.** One paid or endowed to pray for others; a pensioner bound to pray for the souls of his benefactors 1528. Hence, later: **a.** An inmate of an almshouse; **b.** in Scotland: A licensed beggar 1788. **3.** A petitioner (*arch.*) 1600. † **4.** = the mod. 'humble servant'. (Cf. 'your petitioners will ever pray'.) –1645.

1. His friend and bedesman, Abbot Eadwine FREEMAN. **2.** The very Beads-men learn to bend their Bowes *Rich. II*, III. ii. 116.

Beagle (bī·g'l). 1475. [– OFr. *beegueule* noisy person, prob. f. *beer* open wide (cf. BAY *sb.*[3]) + *gueule* throat (see GULES).] **1.** The smallest English hound, used for hare hunting when the field follows on foot. **2.** *fig.* A spy or informer; a constable 1559. Hence **Bea·gling** *vbl. sb.* 1889.

1. A physiological peculiarity..enabled the B. to track its prey by the scent HUXLEY.

Beak (bīk), *sb.* ME. [– (O)Fr. *bec* :- L. *beccus* (Suetonius), of Celtic origin.] **1.** The horny termination of the jaws of a bird, consisting of two pointed mandibles; a bird's bill. **2.** The (often horny) extremities of the mandibles of other animals; *e.g.* the turtle, octopus, etc. 1822. † **3.** The snout of quadrupeds –1607. **4.** The elongated head, proboscis, or sucker mouth of certain insects; *e.g.* the weevil, cochineal 1658. **5.** *joc.* The human nose 1854. **6.** *transf.* A beak-shaped projection; a peak 1440. **7.** The projection at the prow of ancient vessels, *esp.* of war galleys; *now* = BEAK-HEAD 1550. **8. a.** A prolongation of the shell of a univalve beyond the aperture, containing the canal. **b.** The projecting apex or *umbo* of each valve, in a bivalve 1851. **9.** *Bot.* A sharp projecting process, as in the seeds of Crane's-bill, etc. 1820. **10.** The spout of a retort, still, etc. 1641. **11.** *spec.* **a.** in *Forging* (see BEAK-IRON). **b.** in *Carpentry*, the crooked end of a hold-fast. **c.** in *Gas-fitting*, a gas-burner with a circular hole $\frac{1}{25}$ of an inch in diameter 1676. **12.** *Archit.* A little pendent fillet left on the edge of the larmier. forming a canal behind to prevent the water from running down the lower bed of the cornice 1734. Hence **Bea·kful**, as much as can be held in a bird's b. **Bea·kless** *a.* **Bea·ky** *a.* furnished with a b.

Beak (bīk), *sb.*[2] *slang.* 1845. [prob. orig. thieves' cant; cf. *harman beck* constable (XVI).] A magistrate.

Beak (bīk), *v.* ME. [– OFr. *bequer, -ier* peck, f. *bec* BEAK *sb.*[1]] **1.** *trans.* To strike or seize with the beak; to push the beak into. Also *intr.*; occas. *fig.* **2.** *intr.* To project with or as with a beak (*rare*) ME.

Beaked (bīkt), *ppl. a.* 1572. [f. BEAK *sb.*[1] + -ED[2].] **1.** Furnished with a beak 1589. **2.** *spec.* **a.** in *Her.* used when the beak of the fowl is of a different tincture from the body 1572. **b.** in *Bot.* Rostrate 1841. **3.** Pointed or hooked 1590.

2. Three herons arg...b. and legged or 1864. **3.** Each b. promontory MILT. *Lycidas* 94.

Beaker (bī·kəɹ). [– ON. *bikarr* = OS. *bikeri*, (M)Du. *bēker*, OHG. *behhari* (G. *becher*) – pop.L. **bicarium*, perh. f. Gr. βῖκος drinking-bowl; see PITCHER.] **1.** A large drinking vessel with a wide mouth, a goblet. (Now literary.) **b.** The contents of a beaker 1819. **2.** An open-mouthed glass vessel, with a lip for pouring, used in scientific experiments 1877.

1. Stimulated by . . beakers of Badminton DISRAELI.

Beak-head (bī·k,hed). 1580. [f. BEAK *sb.*[1]] **1.** *Naval Arch.* **a.** = BEAK 7. **b.** A small platform at the fore part of the upper deck. **c.** The part of a ship in front of the forecastle, fastened to the stem, and supported by the main knee. **2.** *Archit.* An ornament shaped like a bird's beak used in Norman mouldings 1849.

Bea·k-iron. 1667. [alt. f. BICKERN.] The pike of a blacksmith's anvil.

† **Beal,** *sb.*[1] ME. [app. var. of BOIL *sb.*[1]; cf. ME. *beel.*] A pustule –1783.

‖ **Beal** (bēl, bⁱēl), *sb.*[2] [Gael. *béul* mouth.] The mouth of a river or valley. SCOTT.

Beal, *v.* Now *Sc.* or *dial.* 1611. [f. BEAL *sb.*[1]] To gather, suppurate.

Be-all (bī·ǭl), *sb. phr.* 1605. That which constitutes the whole. *Macb.* I. vii. 5.

Beam (bīm), *sb.* [OE. *bēam* = OFris. *bām*, OS. *bām, boom* (M)Du. *boom* (see BOOM *sb.*[2]), OHG. *boum* (G. *baum*) :– WGmc. *bauma; rel. obscurely to Goth. *bagms*, ON. *baðmr* tree.] † **1.** A tree; only in OE., exc. in HORNBEAM, etc. † **2.** The roodtree or cross. (Cf. *Acts* 5:30.) –1720. **3.** A large piece of squared timber, long in proportion to its breadth and thickness; *orig.* the squared timber of a whole tree. The current sense. OE. Also *fig.* (see *Matt.* 7:3). **4.** The wooden cylinder in a loom, on which the warp is wound before weaving; also called *fore-b.* The similar roller on which the cloth is wound as it is woven; also called *back-b.* OE. **5.** The great timber of the plough, to which all the other parts of the plough-tail are fixed OE. **6.** The transverse bar of a balance, from the ends of which the scales are suspended; also, the balance. Often *fig.* ME. † **7.** The pole of a chariot –1697. † **8.** A large bar of metal –1613. **9.** The shank of an anchor. **10.** In the steam-engine, etc.: A heavy iron lever, having a reciprocating motion on a central axis, one end of which is connected with the piston rod from which it receives motion and the other with the crank or wheel-shaft; also called *working-* and *walking-beam* 1758. **11.** The main trunk of a stag's horn which bears the antlers 1575. **12.** *Naut.* One of the horizontal transverse timbers holding a ship together 1627. **13.** *Hence*, The greatest breadth of a ship 1627. **14.** Hence designating the side of a vessel or sideward direction 1628. **15.** A ray or pencil of light; also *fig.* OE. **b.** In full *wireless b.*, wireless waves sent as a beam, i.e. undispersed, by reflection from a parabolic mirror 1924.

3. A rush will be a beame To hang thee on *John* IV. iii. 129. **4.** The shaft of his speer was as the beem of websters WYCLIF 1 *Sam.* 17:7. **6.** Deceivable and untrue Beams and Scales 1503. *The common b., the King's b.* (*Hist.*): the public standard balance kept by the Grocers' Company of London. *To kick* or *strike the b.*: (of one scale of a balance) to be greatly outweighed. **14.** *Lee* or *weather b.*: the side away from or towards the wind. *On the* (*starboard or larboard*) *b.*: at some distance on the (right *or* left) side of a ship, at right angles to the keel. *Abaft* or *before the b.*: behind *or* before an imaginary line drawn across the centre of the ship. *B. sea*: one rolling against the ship's side. **B.-ends,** the ends of a ship's beams. *To be*, or *be laid, on the b.-ends*: to have them touching the water, so that the vessel is in danger of capsizing; *fig.* to be utterly at a loss, hard up. **15.** How farre that little candell throwes his beams *Merch. V.* v. i. 90. A B. of truth 1674, of comfort 1742.

Comb.: **b.-bird** (*dial.*), the Spotted Flycatcher; **-centre,** the central pin on which the b. of a steam-engine works; **-compass,** an instrument consisting of a b. with sliding sockets, for drawing large circles; **-line,** that which shows the junction of the upper sides of the beams with the ship's sides; **-trawl** *v.* to fish with a trawl-net kept open by a b.

Hence **Beamed** *ppl. a.* having a horn of the fourth year, as a stag. **Bea·mer,** one who works with a b. **Bea·mful** *a.* luminous. **Bea·mily** *adv.* radiantly. **Bea·miness,** radiance. **Bea·mish** *a. arch.* Shining brightly. **Bea·mless** *a.* without beams; also *fig.* **Bea·mlet,** a little b.; var. † **Bea·mling.**

Beam (bīm), *v.* ME. [ME. *beme, beem* (*bemyng* XIV, *bemed* XV; then not until XVII), from the sb. Not certainly attested in OE., which had, however, the sense 'beam of light' in *byrnande bēam, fȳren bēam* pillar of fire (tr. Vulg. *columna lucis*), *lēohtbēamed* having bright rays, *sunnebēam* sunbeam. For the sense development, cf. L. *radius* RAY *sb.*[1], SHAFT *sb.*[1]] **1.** *trans.* To throw out or radiate (beams of light); to emit in rays. Also *fig.* **2.** *intr.* To shine radiantly (*lit.* and *fig.*) 1640. **3.** To stretch (cloth) over a beam; to use a beam in *Tanning* 1605. **4.** To smile radiantly 1893.

1. The genial Sun. . Beams forth ungentle influences SHENSTONE. **2.** Her. . countenance beamed with smiles W. IRVING. Hence **Bea·ming** *vbl. sb.* radiance; the use of a beam. **Bea·mingly** *adv.*

Bea·m-tree. 1800. [Short f. *Whitebeam* (*tree*), so called from the white under-surface of its leaves.] A tree (*Pyrus aria*) related to the Apple, Pear, and Wild Service.

Beamy (bī·mi), *a.* ME. [f. BEAM *sb.* + -Y[1].] **1.** Emitting beams of light; radiant. **2.** Massive as a (weaver's) beam 1698. **3.** Antlered 1697. **4.** Of a ship: Broad in the beam 1882.

1. B. eyes SHELLEY. **2.** Lords of the biting axe and b. spear HEBER. **3.** B. stags DRYDEN.

Bean (bīn). [OE. *bēan* = MDu. *bōne* (Du. *boon*), OHG. *bōna* (G. *bohne*), ON. *baun* :– Gmc. *baunō.] **1.** A smooth, kidney-shaped, laterally flattened seed, borne in long pods by a leguminous plant, *Faba vulgaris*. **2.** The plant that bears this seed OE. **3.** The plant and seed of the allied genus *Phaseolus*, including the French, Kidney, or Haricot Bean (*P. vulgaris*), and Scarlet Runner (*P. multiflorus*) 1548. **4.** Name of the seeds of other plants resembling the common bean ME. **5.** Any object like a bean in shape; e.g. small coals 1561. **6.** In literary and proverbial uses (see quots.) ME.

1. Beanes. . are harde of digestion, and make troblesum dreames TURNER. **3.** *Navy b.*: the dried haricot. *Pea b.*: a small variety of it. **4.** **Egyptian or Pythagorean B.,** the seed of the Lotus (*Nelumbium speciosum*); **B. of St. Ignatius,** seed of *Strychnos amara*. See also COFFEE 3, TONKA 1. **6.** No rich man. . dredeth God The worth of a b. ME. To convey each man his b. or ballot into the box MILT. Alwaie the bygger eateth the beane 1562. **7.** *slang.* (A piece of) money; *not a b.*, no money whatever 1903.

Slang phrases. *To be full of beans*, to be full of energy and in high spirits (cf. BEANY *a.*). *To give* (a person) *beans*, to deal severely with, punish heavily; so *to get beans*. *Old b.*: familiar form of address.

Comb.: **b.-brush,** the stubble of beans; **-caper,** Eng. name of the S. Afr. genus *Zygophyllum*, plants with flower-buds used as capers; **-crake,** the corncrake; **-dolphin,** the aphis of the bean; **-fly,** a pale purple insect, found on beans; **-goose,** a goose (*Anser segetum*), so called from the aspect of its bill; **-mouse,** the Long-tailed Field-mouse; **-pole, -stick,** *fig.* a lanky fellow; **-stalk,** the stem of the b.-plant; **-straw,** the dried stems of the b.-plant; **-tree,** a name of various trees bearing podded seeds, as the carob, laburnum, catalpa, etc.; **-trefoil,** a bushy shrub, *Anagyris fœtida*: also, the laburnum; **-vine,** *Phaseolus diversifolius*.

Hence **Bea·ny** *a. slang*, spirited, fresh.

Bea·n-feast. 1806. [From *beans* being a prominent dish.] An annual dinner given by employers to their work-people. Hence **Bea·no** (*slang*, orig. Printers' abbrev.), also, a merry time or spree.

Bear (bēᵊɹ), *sb.*[1] [OE. *bera* = MDu. *bere* (Du. *beer*), OHG. *bero* (G. *bär*) :– WGmc. *bero; rel. to ON. *bjǫrn* :– *bernuz.] **1.** A heavily-built, thick-furred plantigrade quadruped, of the genus *Ursus*, belonging to the *Carnivora*, but having teeth partly adapted to a vegetable diet.

The best-known species are the Brown Bear of Europe (*U. arctos*), the White or Polar B. (*U. maritimus*), the Grizzly B. (*U. horribilis* or *ferox*), and Black B. (*U. americanus*) of N. America, and the Syrian B. (*U. syriacus*), mentioned in the Bible. There are fossil remains of larger species.

2. *fig.* A rough, unmannerly, or uncouth person 1579. **3.** *Astr.* Name of two constellations, the 'Great Bear' and 'Lesser Bear' ME. **4.** In New South Wales, the *Phaseolarctos*, a marsupial animal, called by the natives *Koala* or 'Biter' 1847. **5.** **Sea-bear:** a species of seal 1847. **6.** A rough mat for wiping boots on; a block covered with shaggy matting for scrubbing decks 1795. **7.** A machine for punching holes 1869. **8.** *Stock Exchange.* A speculator for a fall; *i.e.* one who sells stock for future delivery expecting that meanwhile prices will fall. *Formerly*, The stock contracted to be delivered. 1709.

1. You must not sell the skin till you have shot the b. 1858. **2.** *To play the b.*: to behave rudely and roughly. **8.** *To sell a B.*, 'to sell what one hath not' BAILEY.

Comb.: **bear('s)-breech,** Brank-ursine; **b.-dog,** one used in hunting or baiting bears; **bear's-ear,** the AURICULA; **b.-garden,** a place set apart for the baiting of bears, etc. *fig.* a scene of strife and tumult; **bear's-garlic,** *Allium ursinum* or Ramsons; **-grease,** the fat of the b., used esp. in cosmetic preparations; **b.-hound** (= *-dog*); **-leader,** a travelling tutor, cf. sense 2; **-play,** rough tumultuous behaviour; **-warden** = BEARWARD.

Hence **Bea·rish** *a.* b.-like; rough; surly; *Stock Exchange*, belonging or tending to a fall in prices. **Bea·rish-ly** *adv.*, **-ness.** **Bea·r-like** *a.* and *adv.* after the manner of a b.

Bear (bīᵊɹ), *sb.*[2] [OE. *bære, bere*, see BARLEY.] Barley: the orig. Eng. name, retained only in the north; hence *spec.* the six- (or four-) rowed variety (*Hordeum hexastichon* or *tetrastichon*), till lately chiefly grown there.

Bear (bēᵊɹ, bīᵊɹ), *sb.*[3] *Obs.* or *dial.* [ME. *bere, beer.* Connection with LG. *büre* (G. *bühre*) cannot be made out.] A case for a pillow.

Bear (bēᵊɹ), *v.*[1] *str.* Pa. t. **bore.** Pa. pple. **borne** (bōᵊɹn), **born** (bǫɹn). [OE. *beran* = OS., OHG. *beran*, ON. *bera*, Goth. *bairan* f. Gmc. *ber- :– Indo-Eur. *bher-, as in Skr. *bhárati*, Arm. *berem*, Gr. *φέρειν*, L. *ferre*.]

I. 1. To support and remove; to carry; now restricted in prose to the carrying of something weighty. Also *fig.* **2.** *refl.* To carry oneself; behave, acquit oneself ME. **3.** To carry about with or upon one, to wear; to have OE. **4.** To wield (power, sway, etc.); to hold (an office) ME. **5.** *fig.* To entertain (a feeling) ME.

1. Boren aboute wiþ windis WYCLIF. Borne senseless from the lists SCOTT. *fig.* To b. tale or tidynges HULOET. Phr. *To b. in mind. To b. witness, record, testimony. To b. away, off*: to carry off as a winner. *To b. out*: to back up, confirm. *To b.* (*any one*) *company, a hand*: to bring, give, lend it. † *To b. in hand*: to maintain (a statement); to pretend (*Cymb.* v. v. 43); to delude (*Much Ado* IV. i. 305). † *To b. it*: to carry the day. **3.** Apt to b. arms G. FERRERS. To b. a fair face 1550, seven per Cent. Interest 1719, a firm front SOUTHEY, a very high rental ROGERS. **5.** One beryth malyce agayn another STARKEY.

II. 1. *trans.* To sustain, support (a weight or strain) OE. Also *absol.* or *intr.* Also *fig.* (Formerly also *b. out.*) **2.** To sustain successfully; *fig.* to stand (a test, etc.); to admit of 1523. Also † *intr.* (for *refl.*) **3.** To sustain (anything painful or trying); to endure; to tolerate OE. **4.** To hold (*up*), to support, keep *up* ME. † **5.** *trans.* To uphold (any one in a course of action). Also *refl.* and *intr.* –1697. **6.** To hold up, hold on top or aloft ME. **7.** To have written or inscribed upon it 1503. **8.** *fig.* To purport (*that*) (*arch.*) ME.

1. Proportionate. . to the stress it was likely to b. SMEATON. *fig.* There shall no poore neighbour. . bere no losse MORE. Phr. *To b. a part*: to take a part in. **2.** To b. criticism DRYDEN, ornament RUSKIN. **3.** The wrongs I b. from Atreus' son POPE. This Railer is not to be born 1704. I cannot b. antimacassars (*mod.*). Phr. *To b. hard, or heavily* (L. *ægre ferre*): to endure with a grudge. *To b. with*: to put up with. **4.** *To b. a rein up*: to hold in check by means of a bearing rein. A manly voice. . Bare burthen to the music well SCOTT. **5.** Phr. *To b. up*: to uphold (a principle); to keep up the spirits of (a person); also *intr.* (for refl.). **7.** A Pillar. . bare this inscription, *Sacred to Diana* STANLEY. To b. an effigy 1853.

III. 1. *trans.* To move onward by pressure; to push, force, drive; *esp.* in phr. *To b. down*: to overthrow, vanquish ME. **2.** *intr.* To press (laterally) *on*, to come with force against (*arch.*) 1450. **3.** Transferred to downward pressure; with *down, on* 1674. **4.** *intr.* To exert or transmit pressure *upon, on, against*; to rest *upon*; also, to thrust (as an arch against its piers) 1677. **5.** To tend to affect; to have reference to, touch 1672. **6.** To thrust, pierce *through* –1485. **7.** *intr.* To press; to move with effort or with persistence in some direction. Also with *back, away, on, down*, etc. 1593. **8.** To extend in a particular direction 1601.

9. Chiefly *Naut.*: To lie off in a certain direction from a given point. (Cf. BEARING.) 1594. 10. Of cannon: To lie so as to cover 1692.

1. Borne backward Talbot turns SOUTHEY. His ..zeal bore down all opposition MACAULAY. 5. To point out how the argument bears on the general question PALEY. Phr. *To bring to b.*: to cause to act (*against, upon,* etc.). *To b. in,* pass. *to be borne in*: to be forced in *upon* (the mind). 7. Stand backe; roome, beare backe *Jul. C.* III. ii. 172. B. a little to the right (*mod.*). Phr. *Naut. To b. away*: to sail away. *To b. down* (*upon* or *towards*): to sail with the wind (towards). *To b. off*: to sail so as to keep clear (of land, etc.). *To b. up*: to put the helm up so as to put the ship before the wind. *To b. up for* (a place): to sail towards. *To b. down upon*: to proceed (*esp.* with force) against. 8. Possession Bay bore due west SIR J. ROSS. 9. Our after-guns ceased to b. NELSON.

IV. 1. To bring forth, produce, yield OE. Also *absol.* **2.** To give birth to OE. Also *absol.*

¶ Since *c* 1775 the pa. pple. *born* is used only in sense IV. 2, and there only in the pass., when not followed by *by* and the mother. In all other cases *borne* is used.

1. The Oakes beare Mast *Timon* IV. iii. 422. India, black Ebon and white Ivory bears DRYDEN. *absol.* An apple that bears well (*mod.*). 2. Sarray non childre ne bar ME.

Bear (bēᵊɹ), *v.*[2] 1842. [f. BEAR *sb.*[1] 8.] *intr.* To speculate for a fall on the Stock Exchange. *trans.* To produce a fall in the price of (stocks, shares, or commodities).

Bearable (bēᵊ·răb'l), *a.* 1550. [f. BEAR *v.*[1] + -ABLE.] That may be borne; endurable. Hence **Bea·rableness. Bea·rably** *adv.*

Bea·rance. 1725. [f. BEAR *v.*[1] + -ANCE.] **1.** Endurance (*arch.*). **2.** A bearing (in mechanism) 1834.

Bea·r-baiting, *vbl. sb.* 1475. [f. BEAR *sb*[1].] The sport of setting dogs to attack a bear chained to a stake; also *fig.*

An old way of Recreating, Which learned Butchers call Bear-Baiting BUTLER *Hud.*

Bearberry (bēᵊ·ɹberi). 1625. [f. BEAR *sb.*[1]] **a.** A procumbent shrub, *Arctostaphylos uva-ursi* (Family *Ericaceæ*), bearing astringent berries; also *A. alpina* (Black Bearberry). **b.** (occas). The Arbutus. † **c.** (erron.) = BARBERRY.

Bearbine, -bind (bēᵊ·ɹbəin). 1732. [f. OE. *bere* BEAR *sb.*[2] + *bindan* BIND.] **a.** The Lesser Field Convolvulus; **b.** the hedge convolvulus; **c.** a species of Polygonum (*P. Convolvulus*).

Beard (biᵊɹd), *sb.* [OE. *beard* = OFris. *berd*, MDu. *baert* (Du. *baard*), OHG., G. *bart* :- WGmc. **barða*, rel. to OSl. *brada*, L. *barba* beard.] **1.** The hair that grows upon the chin, lips, and adjacent parts of a man's face; now usu. excluding the moustache. **2.** The similar growth on the face of other animals; *e.g.* the goat, lion, etc. ME. **3.** *Zool.* **a.** The appendages to the mouth of some fishes. **b.** The rows of gills in some bivalves, *e.g.* the Oyster. **c.** The byssus of certain shell-fish, *e.g.* the *Pinna*. **d.** Two small processes situated above the antlia of moths and butterflies; the similar part in some *Diptera*, *e.g.* the Gnat. 1753. **4.** *Ornith.* **a.** The bristles at the base of the beak in the Barbet (*Bucco*), etc. **b.** The vane of a feather. 1802. **5.** Specific name of: The freshwater Shrimp, the Hake, and a kind of pigeon 1611. **6.** *Bot.* The awn of grasses; prickles, bristles, or hair-like tufts found on plants; also quasi-*fig.* 1552. † **7.** The barb of an arrow, fish-hook, etc. -1793. **8.** *Printing.* **a.** That part of the type above and below the face, which allows for ascending and descending letters. **b.** The horizontal bases and tops added to the letters. 1823. **9.** *Obs.* or *dial.* The brim or margin of a vessel. [f. ON. *barð*.] ME.

1. † *In spite of or maugre any one's b.*: in defiance of his purpose. *To one's b.*: to one's face, openly. *Comb.* **b.-grass**, the genus of grasses *Polypogon*; **-moss**, a British lichen (*Usnea barbata*); **-tree**, the Hazel. Hence, **Bea·rdless** *a.* without a b.; *fig.* immature. **Bea·rdlessness. Bea·rdlet**, a tiny awn. **Bea·rdy** *a.* bearded.

Beard (biᵊɹd), *v.* ME. [f. prec. sb.] † **1.** To become bearded -1672. **2.** *trans.* To cut or strip off the beard of (*e.g.* oysters) ME. **3.** To oppose openly and resolutely; to set at defiance, thwart, affront. [Partly from the idea of taking a lion by the beard.] 1525. **4.** To furnish with a beard ME.

3. To b. the lion in his rage SMOLLETT.

Bearded (biᵊ·ɹdėd), *ppl. a.* ME. [f. BEARD *sb.* + -ED[2].] **1.** Having a beard; *spec.* in B. Eagle, Tit, Titmouse, etc. 1530. Also *transf.* **2.** Of a comet, etc.: Having a train (*arch.* or *poet.*).

Beardie (biᵊ·ɹdi). 1828. [f. BEARD *sb.* + *-ie* = -Y[6].] Chiefly *Sc.* The Loach (*Cobitis barbatula*).

Bearer (bēᵊ·rəɹ). ME. [f. BEAR *v.*[1] + -ER[1].] **1.** *gen.* He who or that which bears, carries, or brings; a carrier, messenger, etc. **b.** One who helps to carry a corpse to the grave; a pall-bearer 1633. **c.** In India: A palanquin-bearer 1766; also, a body-servant 1811. **2.** The actual holder or presenter of a cheque, draft, or order to pay money 1683. **3.** *Her.* One who bears heraldic arms 1610. **4.** The possessor or holder of rank, office, or of any personal quality 1597. **5.** That in, or by means of, which anything is carried; *e.g.* a bier 1847. **6.** He who or that which supports or sustains 1483; *spec.* in *Printing*, a kind of packing used to lessen the pressure of the types 1846. **7.** She who, or that which, brings forth or produces; *spec.* a fruit-yielding tree. ME.

1. Bearers of burdens 2 *Chron.* 2:18. In behalf of this young man, the b. PEPYS. 7. The Tree is a great Bearer 1719.

† **Bea·rherd.** 1589. [f. BEAR *sb.*[1] + HERD *sb.*[2]] The keeper of a bear, who leads him about for exhibition -1860. vars. **Bearard, Berard, Beareheard, Berrord** (all in Shaks.).

Bearing (bēᵊ·riŋ), *vbl. sb.* ME. [f. BEAR *v.*[1] + -ING[1].] **1.** (f. BEAR *v.*[1] I.) The action of the vb. **2.** The carrying of oneself (with reference to the manner); deportment; demeanour ME. **3.** *Her.* A single charge or device 1562. † **4.** (f. BEAR *v.*[1] II.) Upholding -1552. **5.** Supporting, endurance 1526. **6.** A material support; a supporting surface; supporting power ME. **7.** *Carpentry.* The length of a beam between two supports, span 1677. **8.** (f. BEAR *v.*[1] III.) A straining in any direction; thrust, pressure 1591. **9.** Tendency to exert influence; aspect 1785. **10.** *Mech.* (usu. in *pl.*) Those parts of a machine which bear the friction; the block or supports on which a shaft or axle turns, and also the part of the shaft or axle resting on these supports 1791. **11.** The direction in which any point lies from a point of reference, *esp.* as measured in degrees from a quarter of the compass. In *pl.* the relative positions of surrounding objects. 1635. **12.** The direction of any line on the earth's surface in relation to a meridian 1802. **13.** *Naut.* The widest part of a vessel below the plank-shear 1627. **14.** (f. BEAR *v.*[1] IV.) The action of bringing forth; birth. Also in comb. *child-bearing.* ME. **15.** The action of producing leaves, flowers, and *esp.* fruit 1583. **16.** A crop 1838.

1. The b. of Armes 1598, a grudge (*mod.*). 2. His b. towards women 1873. 5. Insolent beyond b. 1815. 9. The legal bearings of the case 1867. 11. Phr. *To take one's bearings*: to determine one's position with reference to surrounding objects; also *fig.* 16. Rich mellow bearings WORDSW.

Comb.: † **b.-cloth**, a child's christening robe; **-door** (*Coal-Mining*), one of the main doors for ventilation.

Bearing (bēᵊ·riŋ), *ppl. a.* ME. [f. BEAR *v.*[1] + -ING[2].] **1.** That bears (see the vb.) 1500. † **2.** Of food: Sustaining -1633. **3.** Bringing forth ME.

Comb. **b.-rein**, a short fixed rein which passes from the bit to the saddle, and keeps the horse's head up and its neck arched; also *fig.*

† **Bea·rleap, -lep(e.** ME. [f. ME. *beren* BEAR *v.*[1] + LEAP *sb.*[2]] A carrying basket -1677.

Bear's-foot. 1551. [f. BEAR *sb.*[1]] *Herb.* **1.** Pop. name of species of Hellebore, *esp.* of the Black Hellebore (*H. fœtidus*). **2.** Also of Bear's-breech or Acanthus, of Lady's Mantle, and of Monkshood 1552.

Bearskin (bēᵊ·ɹ,skin). 1677. [f. as prec.] **1.** The skin of a bear used as a wrap or garment. Also *fig.* **2.** The tall cap worn by the Guards in the British Army 1863. **3.** A shaggy woollen cloth used for overcoats. **4.** See BEAR *sb.*[1] 8.

4. *Bearskin jobber*, early name of the 'bear' on the Stock Exchange (prob. in allusion to the proverb 'To sell the bear's skin before one has caught the bear').

Bearward (bēᵊ·ɹwǭɹd). ME. [f. as prec. + WARD *sb.*] **1.** The keeper of a bear, who leads it about for exhibition; also *fig.* † **2.** The constellation Bootes, or its chief star Arcturus, just behind *Ursa Major* -1577.

Beast (bīst), *sb.* ME. [- OFr. *beste* (mod. *bête*) :- pop.L. *besta*, f. L. *bestia*. *Beast* displaced *deer* and was itself displaced by *animal* in the gen. sense.] **1.** A living being, an animal. (Used as tr. Gr. ζῷον, or L. *animal*.) **2.** A quadruped, as dist. from man, and also from birds, reptiles, fishes, etc. (The current literary use.) ME. **3.** A domesticated animal, used as part of the farm stock or cattle [F. *bestiaux, bétail*] ME. **b.** An animal used in riding, driving, etc.; a draught animal ME. **4.** *fig.* A human being swayed by animal propensities ME. **5.** A brutal, savage, irrational man. (Now expressive of disgust, or merely aversion.) ME. **6.** In *Card-playing.* [orig. *beste* as in 17th c. Fr. Mod.F. *bête* also as var. BASTE *sb.*] An obs. game, resembling *Nap.* **b.** A penalty at this game; also at Ombre and Quadrille. -1751.

1. Þe nedder..was mast wis of ani best ME. 2. Beasts, Birds, Fishes, and Insects RAY. *Wild b.*: an animal not domesticated, formerly esp. a beast of the chase, now esp. a ferocious animal from abroad. **b.** *The Beast*: Antichrist (*Rev.* 13:18). 3. *Luke* 10:34. 5. Also of things. Phr. *a beast of..*a beastly 1862.

Comb. **b.-fly**, the gad-fly. Hence **Bea·sthood,** the rank, condition, or nature of beasts. **Bea·stie** (orig. *Sc.*), an endearing form of BEAST. **Bea·stily** [as if f. *beasty* adj.] *adv.* bestially SHELLEY. † **Bea·stish** *a.* = BEASTLY. † **Bea·stlihead** = BEASTHOOD, BEASTLINESS (Spenser). **Bea·stlike** *a.* and *adv.*

Beast (bīst), *v.* 1646. [f. prec. sb.] See also BASTE *v.*[4] † **1.** To treat as a beast. **2.** *pass.* To fail to win at Ombre, or to incur a forfeit 1653.

Beastliness (bī·stlinės). ME. [f. BEASTLY + -NESS.] Beastly quality; resemblance to a beast; *concr.* = 'beastly stuff'.

Beastlings, var. of BEESTINGS.

Beastly (bī·stli), *a.* ME. [f. BEAST *sb.* + -LY[1].] † **1.** Of the nature of a BEAST (sense 1) -1526. **2.** Of the nature of a BEAST (sense 2) (*arch.*) ME. † **3.** Brutish, irrational -1703. **4.** Like a beast in conduct ME. **5.** Abominable; disgusting, or offensive, *esp.* from dirtiness 1603.

2. See more of this b. fable BEDWELL. 4. The b. vice of drinking to excess SWIFT. 5. That b. hole, London BROUGHTON.

Beastly, *adv.* ME. [f. as prec. + -LY[2].] † **1.** In a beastly manner -1652. **2.** Added to an adj.: Abominably, offensively. (In society slang, often merely = Exceedingly.) 1561.

Beat (bīt), *v.*[1] Pa. t. **beat** (bīt). Pa. pple. **beaten** (bī·t'n), **beat.** [OE. *bēatan* = OHG. *bōzan*, ON. *bauta* :- Gmc. **bautan*, the base of which may be rel. to **fu-* of L. *confutare* strike down, CONFUTE.] **I. 1.** To strike with repeated blows. **2.** *intr.* To strike repeated blows (*on, at*) ME. **3.** Said of the action of the feet upon the ground in walking, etc. Often *fig.* OE. **4.** To punish by beating; to thrash OE. † **5.** To batter, bombard -1664. **6.** Of physical agents: To dash against, strike violently, assail (*poet.*) OE. Also *intr.* with *on, upon, against*; also *absol.* OE. † **7.** Said of the impact of sounds -1677. † **8.** To hammer at (a subject), to thresh out; to discuss, reason about -1659. † **9.** *intr.* To insist with iteration *on* or *upon* -1633. **10.** To overcome, to conquer in any contest, *at* doing anything; to master, to excel. (Cf. *thrash.*) 1611. Also *absol.* † **11.** To strike *together* the eyelids (= BAT), or the teeth; also *intr.* -1617. **12.** To flap (the wings) *with force*; also *intr.* (*absol.*) ME. **13.** *intr.* Of the heart: To strike against the breast; *hence*, to throb, pulsate. (Said also of the pulse, etc. and *fig.* of passions.) ME. **14.** *intr.* Hence **a.** Of a watch, etc. **b.** *Mus.* To sound in pulsations; see BEAT *sb.*[1] 6. 1614.

1. *To b. the breast*: i.e. in sign of grief. *To b. the air, the wind*: to fight to no purpose or against no opposition. 3. *To b. the streets*: to walk up and down. *To b. a path* or *track*: to tread it hard or bare by frequent passage; *hence*, to open up a way. 6. The Sunne beat vpon the head of Ionah *Jonah* 4:8. 10. 'This beats me altogether', mused the lawyer J. PAYN. You may b. the Latine *into their heads* 1612.

II. 1. *trans.* To force or impel (a thing) by striking, hammering, etc. 1607. Also *fig.* **2.**

To drive by blows (a person) *away, off, from, into*, etc. ME. **3.** To break, crush, or overthrow by hard knocks; to batter 1570. **4.** = ABATE, or BATE. Now only in *b. down.* 1592. **5.** *Naut.* (*intr.*) To strive or make way against wind or current 1677. Also *trans.* of the ship or of the mariners. **6.** *Venery.* (*intr.*) **a.** To run hither and thither. **b.** To take to the water, and go up stream; also *trans.* 1592. **7.** To affect the state or condition of by beating: **a.** to hammer, forge ME.; **b.** to pound, pulverize ME.; to mix; to make into a batter; to switch or whip (an egg, etc.). Also with *up.* 1486. **8.** To strike (cover) in order to rouse or drive game; to scour (a wood) in hunting ME. Also *intr.* or *absol.* Also *fig.* esp. with *about.* 1709. **9.** Of a drum: **a.** *intr.* = To sound when beaten 1656; **b.** *trans.* To express by its sound when beaten 1636; **c.** *intr.* = To be beaten 1816.

1. *fig. To b.* (a thing) *into one's head, mind*, etc. **2.** He's beat from his best ward *Wint. T.* I. ii. 33. **5.** *To b. about*: to tack against the wind. **7.** *To b. a carpet* (mod.) They shall beate their swords into plough-shares *Isa.* 2:4. **8.** To b. the jungle 1872. fig. *To b. about the bush*: *lit.*, as in I. 12; *fig.* to make a cautious or roundabout approach. *To b. up (for) recruits, to beat up the town for recruits*, etc. *To b. up the quarters of*: to visit unceremoniously (*colloq.*). **9.** The Drums beat to Arms 1758. The drums of Limerick beat a parley MACAULAY. Before the assembly beats THACKERAY. Phr. *To b. time*: to mark musical time by beating a drum, by tapping, by striking the air with a baton, etc.; also *fig.* to keep time with.

Comb. With adverbs. **B. about**: (see II. 5). **B. away: a.** *intr.* to go on beating; **b.** *trans.* to drive away by blows. **B. back: a.** to force back by beating; **b.** to drive back by force; **c.** to cause to rebound. **B. down: a.** to drive downward by beating; **b.** to break down by heavy blows; **c.** *fig.* to overthrow (an institution, opinion, etc.); **d.** to force down by haggling (cf. II. 4); **e.** *intr.* to come down with violence, like rain, the sun's rays, etc.; **f.** (see II. 4); **g.** to reduce by beating. **B. in: a.** to knock in by beating; **b.** to drive in by force; **c.** to smash or batter in by blows; **d.** to inculcate; **e.** (see II. 4). **B. off: a.** to drive away from by blows, attacks, etc.; **b.** (see II. 4). **B. on:** (see I. 2). **B. out: a.** to trace out a path by treading it first (cf. II. 3); **b.** to knock or force or shape out by beating; **c.** to drive out by force or fighting; **d.** to hammer out into a bulge, to extend by hammering; **e.** to thresh (corn); **f.** to hammer out, or get to the bottom of (a matter, laboriously); **g.** (in U.S.) to exhaust; **h.** to measure out by beats. **B. up: a.** to tread up by much trampling; **b.** to bring to equal consistency by beating; **c.** *to b. up quarters*, etc. (see II. 8).

Phrases. *To b. the bounds*; to trace out the boundaries of a parish, striking certain points with rods, etc.

Beat (bīt, bēⁱt), *v.*[2] 1534. [conn. w. BEAT *sb.*[3], q.v.] To slice off the rough sod from uncultivated or fallow ground: cf. BEAT *sb.*[3]

Beat (bīt), *sb.*[1] 1615. [f. BEAT *v.*] **1.** A stroke or blow. **2.** *Fencing.* A particular blow struck upon the adversary's sword or foil 1753. **3.** A stroke upon a drum, the striking of a drum with the sound produced; the signal thus given; also in *drum-b.* Occas. *fig.* 1672. **4.** The movement of the hand or baton, by which the rhythm of a piece of music is indicated; also, the different divisions of a bar or measure with respect to their relative accent 1880. **5.** A recurring stroke; a measured sequence of strokes or blows, or sounds thereby produced 1795. **6.** A throbbing or undulating effect taking place in rapid succession when two notes not quite of the same pitch are sounded together 1733. **7.** *Mus.* Name given to a melodic grace or ornament of uncertain identity 1803. **8.** The round of a watchman, etc. on duty. [prob. f. BEAT *v.*[1] I. 3.] 1825. **9.** A tract ranged over in pursuit of game 1875. **10.** In sailing: One of the transverse courses in beating to windward 1880. **11.** *Physics* and *Wireless Telegr.* Each of the pulsations of amplitude produced when two oscillations of different frequencies occur simultaneously in the same system 1918.

5. Phr. *In* or *out of b., off the b.*: making a regular or irregular succession of strokes. **11.** *Comb.*: **b.-note,** a note whose frequency equals the difference in the frequencies of two oscillators.

Beat (bīt, *dial.* bet), *sb.*[2] 1450. [perh. f. BEAT *v.* = 'a quantity to be beaten at once'. Cf. *stack*, etc.] A bundle of flax or hemp made up ready for steeping.

Beat (bīt, bēⁱt), *sb.*[3] [In Devonsh. *bait, bate, beat*, pronounced (bĕt). But historically *beat(e* is the proper form. See BEAT *v.*[2]] The rough sod of moorland, or the matted growth of fallow-land, which is sliced off and burned before plowing the land.

Comb. **b.-axe** (in Devonsh. *dial.* bidax, bidix), the axe or adze used in paring off b.

Beat (bīt), *ppl. a.* ME. Short f. BEATEN; as *adj.*: Overcome by hard work or difficulty; common in *dead-b.* (*lit.* and *fig.*)

Beaten (bī·t'n), *ppl. a.* ME. Used adjectively in many senses of BEAT *v.*, q.v. **1.** Trodden, hard, bare, or plain. Often *fig.* 1477. † **2.** Trite –1756. † **3.** Inured *to* –1700. **4.** Worked by hammering ME.; whence, pure gold being most malleable: Fine, of pure quality; also *fig.* 1535. **4.** Conquered 1562. **5.** Exhausted 1681. **6.** Scoured for game 1883.

Beater (bī·təɹ). 1483. [f. BEAT *v.* + -ER[1].] **1.** A person who beats (see BEAT *v.*); *spec.* a man employed in rousing and driving game 1825. **2.** An instrument for beating; used in many specific senses 1611.

Beath (bīð), *v.* Still *dial.* [OE. *beðian* foment :– Gmc. **baþian*, rel. to *baþian* BATHE.] **1.** To foment. **2.** To heat unseasoned wood in order to straighten it 1496.

Beatific, -al (bīˌăti·fik, -ăl), *a.* 1605. [– Fr. *béatifique* or L. *beatificus*, f. *beatus* blessed; see -FIC, -AL[1].] Making blessed; imparting supreme happiness.

Beatific vision: a sight of the glories of heaven. Hence **Beati·fically** *adv.*

Beatification (biˌæ:tifikēⁱ·ʃən). 1502. [– (O)Fr. *béatification* or eccl.L. *beatificatio*, f. *beatificat-*, pa. ppl. stem of eccl.L. *beatificare*; see next.] **1.** The action of making, or the being made, blessed. **2.** *R.C.Ch.* An act of the Pope, declaring a deceased person to be in the enjoyment of heavenly bliss, and granting a form of worship to him (the first step towards canonization) 1626.

Beatify (biˌæ·tifəi), *v.* 1535. [– (O)Fr. *béatifier* or eccl.L. *beatificare*, f. *beatus* blessed; see -FY.] **1.** To make supremely happy or blessed. **2.** To declare supremely blessed 1677. **3.** *R.C.Ch.* To pronounce to be in enjoyment of heavenly bliss; see BEATIFICATION 2. 1629.

2. To b. wealth BARROW. var. **Beati·ficate.**

Beating (bī·tiŋ), *vbl. sb.* ME. [f. BEAT *v.* + -ING[1].] **1.** The infliction of repeated blows; *spec.* punishment by blows; the dashing of waves against the shore; the flapping of wings; rousing of game, etc. **2.** A defeat in a contest 1883. **3.** *Naut.* Sailing against the wind 1883. **4.** A pulsating or throbbing movement 1601.

5. The b. of a watch 1801, of the heart HUXLEY.

Beatitude (biˌæ·titiūd). 1491. [– (O)Fr. *béatitude* or L. *beatitudo* (Cicero), f. *beatus* happy, blessed; see -TUDE.] **1.** Supreme blessedness or happiness. **2.** An ascription of special blessedness; *esp.* (in *pl.*) those pronounced by Christ in the Sermon on the Mount 1526. **3.** = BEATIFICATION 2. (*lit.* and *fig.*) 1837.

Beau (bōᵘ), *a.* and *sb.* ME. [In ME. – (O)Fr. *beau* :– L. *bellus*. The adj., in ME. quite naturalized, and pronounced as in *beauty, Beaulieu* (biu·li), became obs. in XVI. The sb. is a reintroduction from mod.Fr., whence its pronunc.] † **A.** *adj.* **1.** Beautiful. **2.** Used in addressing relations, friends, etc.: = 'fair' (fair sir), 'dear' (dear sir), etc. –1513.

B. *sb.* Pl. **beaux, beaus** (bōᵘz). **1.** A man who attends excessively to dress, mien, and social etiquette: a fop, a dandy 1687. **2.** The attendant or suitor of a lady 1720.

1. You're a perfect Woman, nothing but a b. will please you T. BROWN. Hence **Beau** *v.* to act the b. to. **Beau·ish** *a.* after the manner of a b.; dandified.

† **Beauclerk** (bōᵘ·klāɹk). ME. [– (O)Fr. *beau* + *clerc*; see prec., CLERK.] A scholar. (Surname of Henry I.) –1856.

Beaufet, Beaufin; see BUFFET *sb.*[3], BIFFIN.

‖ **Beau garçon** (bo garsoṅ). 1665. [Fr.] An exquisite, a fop.

Beau-ideal (bōᵘ:əidī·ăl). 1801. [– Fr. *beau idéal* the ideal Beautiful. In Eng. *ideal* tends to be taken as the sb.] † **1.** The Beautiful, or beauty, in its ideal perfection –1801. **2.** That type of beauty or excellence in which one's ideal is realized, the perfect type or model 1820.

‖ **Beau-monde** (bo·mōṅ·d, bōᵘˌmǫ·nd). 1714. [Fr., 'fine world'.] The fashionable world, society.

† **Beau·pe·re.** ME. [f. OFr. *beau* + *père* father, or in sense 2 *per, peer* (mod. *pair*) equal. See BEAU. In OFr. used politely of every one whom one called 'father'; but about XVI distinctive for 'father-in-law' or 'stepfather'. See also BEL.] **1.** A term of courtesy, used *esp.* to or of an eccles. 'Father' –1599. **2.** Good fellow, fellow, companion –1610.

† **Beau·pers, bewpers.** 1592. [Origin unkn.] A fabric, app. linen; used for flags –1720.

Beau-pot (bōᵘ·pǫt). 1761. [alt. f. orig. BOUGH-POT.] A vase for cut flowers.

† **Beausire.** ME. [– (O)Fr. *beau* fair, *sire* sir, lord. In OFr. a form of respectful address; cf. BEAU, BEAUPERE, BEL, BELSIRE.] Fair sir, a form of address –1513.

Beauteous (biū·tiəs), *a.* 1440. [f. BEAUTY + -OUS, after *bounteous, plenteous.*] Distinguished by beauty, beautiful. (*Literary.*)

England is beauteous. . flour of londes all aboute CAXTON. Hence **Beau·teous-ly** *adv.*, **-ness.**

Beautification (biū:tifikēⁱ·ʃən). 1640. [f. BEAUTIFY; see -FICATION, and cf. *amplify, -fication*, etc.] The action of beautifying; embellishment.

Beautiful (biū·tiful), *a.* 1526. [f. BEAUTY + -FUL.] **A.** Full of beauty, possessing the qualities which constitute beauty; pleasing to the senses or intellect. Used colloq. of anything that a person likes very much, *e.g.* 'a b. ride'.

Beautifull for situation, the ioy of the whole earth is mount Sion *Ps.* 48:2. B. weather HAWTHORNE. A b. operation in surgery 1887.

B. quasi-*sb.* **1.** = Beautiful one 1535. **2.** That which is beautiful. *The beautiful*: beauty in the abstract. 1756.

Hence **Beau·tiful-ly** *adv.*, **-ness.**

Beautify (biū·tifəi), *v.* 1526. [f. as prec. + -FY.] To render, or grow, beautiful.

To beautifie the house of God HIERON. Hence **Beau·tifier.**

Beauty (biū·ti). [ME. *bealte, beute, beaute* – AFr. *beute*, OFr. *bealte, beaute* (mod. *beauté*) :– Rom. **bellitas, -at-*, f. L. *bellus*; see BEAU, -TY.] **1.** That quality or combination of qualities which affords keen pleasure to the senses, *esp.* that of sight, or which charms the intellectual or moral faculties. **2.** The abstract quality personified 1667. **3.** A beautiful person or thing; esp. a beautiful woman. (Often ironical.) 1483. **b.** *collect.* The beautiful women, etc. 1611. **4.** A beautiful feature or trait; an ornament, grace 1563.

1. Beauties ensigne yet Is Crymson in thy lips *Rom. & Jul.* V. iii. 94. We ascribe b. to that which is simple; which has no superfluous parts; which exactly answers its end EMERSON. **2.** Such a lord is Love, And B. such a mistress of the world TENNYSON. **3.** A celebrated B. ADDISON. **b.** The b. of Israel is slaine vpon thy high places 2 *Sam.* 1:19. **4.** The concealed beauties of a writer ADDISON.

Comb.: with reference to face massage, etc., as *b. doctor, parlour* (orig. *U.S.*), *specialist*; **b.-sleep,** the sleep secured before midnight; **-spot,** (*a*) a patch placed on a lady's face to heighten its beauty 1657; (*b*) a locality conspicuous for its beauty 1919.

Hence **Beau·tiless** *a.* void of b.

Beau·ty, *v. arch.* ME. [f. prec. sb.] To render beautiful.

Beauxite (bōᵘ·zəit). 1868. [f. *Beaux* or *Baux* in France; see -ITE[1] 2 b.] *Min.* A hydrous oxide of alumina and iron, used as a source of aluminium.

Beaver[1] (bī·vəɹ). [OE. *beofor, befor* = (M)LG., (M)Du. *bever*, OHG. *bibar* (G. *biber*), ON. *bjórr* :– Gmc. **bebruz* :– Indo-Eur. **bhebhrús*, redupl. deriv. of **bhru-* brown.] **1.** An amphibious rodent, with a broad, oval, flat, scaly tail, palmated hind feet, coat of soft fur, and hard incisor teeth with which it cuts down trees; remarkable for its skill in constructing huts for its habitation, and dams for preserving its supply of water. **2.** The fur of the beaver ME. Also *fig.* and *attrib.* **3.** A hat made of beaver's fur, or some imitation of it 1528. **4.** A felted cloth, used for overcoats, etc. 1756. **5.** A kind of glove 1816.

3. Mr. Holden sent me a bever, which cost me 4£ 5s. PEPYS. *In beaver* (Univ. slang): in a tall hat, etc., not in cap and gown.

Comb.: **b.-rat,** the musquash or MUSK-RAT; **-stones,** the two small sacs in the groin of the b., from which the substance 'castor' is obtained. Hence **Bea·vered** *ppl. a.* wearing a b. (hat). **Bea·vertee:n,** a cotton twilled cloth, in which the warp is drawn up into loops, forming a pile, which is left uncut; cf. *velveteen.* **Bea·very,** a place in which beavers are kept.

Beaver[2] (bī·vəɹ). *Obs.* exc. *Hist.* [– OFr. *baviere,* orig. child's bib, f. *baver* slaver, f. *beve* saliva :– Rom. *baba.] The lower portion of the face-guard of a helmet, when worn with a visor; but occas. serving the purposes of both. Also *fig.*

Then saw you not his face? O yes, my Lord, he wore his b. up *Haml.* I. ii. 230.

† **Beba·r,** *v.* ME. [See BE- 1.] To bar about; to debar –1649.

‖ **Bebeeru, bibiru** (bĭbīᵊ·ru). 1851. [Native name.] The Greenheart Tree of Guiana (*Nectandra rodiæi* or *leucantha*). **Bebee·ria, Bebee·rine,** also **beber-, bibir-,** an alkaloid resembling quinine, yielded by this tree.

Beblee·d, *v. arch.* ME. [BE- 2.] To cover with blood, make bloody.

Beble·ss, *v.* 1598. [BE- 2.] To bless profusely.

Bebli·ster, *v.* 1575. [BE- 1.] To blister badly.

Bebloo·d, *v.* 1580. [BE- 5.] = BEBLEED.

† **Beblo·t,** *v.* ME. [BE- 2.] To blot all over; also *fig.* –1580.

Beblu·bbered, *ppl. a.* 1583. [BE- 2.] Befouled with tears; also † with blood.

Becall (bĭkǭ·l), *v.* ME. [BE- 4.] † **1.** To challenge –1500. **2.** To call names 1683.

Becalm (bĭkā·m), *v.* 1559. [BE- 2.] **1.** To make calm; to quiet; *fig.* to assuage, tranquillize 1613. **2.** *Naut.* To shelter from, or deprive (a ship) of, wind; usu. in pass. 1595.

1. What power becalms the innavigable seas POPE. 2. The fleet was becalmed off the Godwin Sands MACAULAY.

Because (bĭkǭ·z, -kǫ·z), *adv.* and *conj.* [ME. *bi cause,* i.e. *bi* BY, CAUSE, after OFr. *par cause de* by reason of. Orig. often followed by a subord. cl. introduced by *that* or *why.*] **A.** *adv.* **1.** Followed by *that* or *why*: For the reason that (*arch.*). **2.** Followed by *of* and subst.: **a.** By reason *of,* on account *of* ME. † **b.** For the sake *of,* for the purpose *of* –1523. † **3.** Followed by *to* with inf. = In order *to* –1546.

B. *conj.* [from A. 1.] **1.** For the reason that; inasmuch as, since ME. **2.** In order that, so that, that. (Common *dial.*) 1485.

1. We wonder b. we are ignorant and we fear b. we are weak BUCKLE.

‖ **Be:ccabu·nga.** 1706. [mod.L. – Ger. *bachbunge,* f. *bach* brook + *bunge* :– OHG. *bungo* bulb.] *Bot.* The BROOKLIME, q.v.

‖ **Beccaccia** (bekka·ttʃa). [It.] A woodcock. BROWNING.

‖ **Beccafico** (bekkăfī·ko). 1621. [It., f. *beccare* peck + *fico* FIG.] A small migratory bird of the genus *Sylvia,* much esteemed as a dainty in the autumn, when it has fattened on figs and grapes.

† **Becco.** 1604. [– It. *becco* goat.] A cuckold –1623.

‖ **Bechamel** (be·fămel). 1796. [f. the Marquis de *Béchamel,* steward of Louis XIV.] *Cookery.* A fine white sauce thickened with cream.

Bechance (bĭ,tʃɑ·ns), *v.* 1527. [BE- 2.] **1.** *intr.* To happen, chance. **2.** (with dat. obj.) To befall (a person) 1530.

1. All happinesse b. to thee in Millaine SHAKS.

† **Becha·nce,** *adv.* 1548. [f. BY *prep.*] By chance –1570.

Becharm (bĭ,tʃā·ɹm), *v.* ME. [BE- 5.] To hold by a charm.

‖ **Bêche-de-mer** (bēʃ də mɛ̄r). 1814. [Quasi-Fr. of Eng. origin, for *biche de mer* – Pg. *bicho do mar* 'worm of the sea'.] The Trepang.

Bechic (be·kik, bī·kik). 1661. [– Fr. *béchique* or late L. *bechicus* – Gr. βηχικός, βήξ cough.] **A.** *adj.* Tending to cure or relieve a cough 1678. **B.** *sb.* [sc. *medicine.*] 1661.

Beck (bek), *sb.*[1] ME. [– ON. *bekkr* :– *bakkiz, rel. to *bakiz, whence OE. *beće,* OS. *beki,* OHG. *bah* (G. *bach*). See BACHE.] A brook or stream; *spec.* a brook with a stony bed or rugged course.

Beck (bek), *sb.*[2] ME. [f. BECK *v.*] **1.** A nod, or other mute signal, indicating assent, command, etc. Also *transf.* **2.** A bow, a curtsey, a nod, etc. Chiefly *Sc.* ME.

1. With a b. of the head or hand, as we beckon to servants DE FOE. Phr. *To be at the b. and call of.*

Beck (bek), *sb.*[3] 1828. [app. erron. for BACK *sb.*[2]] = BACK *sb.*[2]

Beck (bek), *v.* ME. [Short f. BECKON *v.*; cf. *ope, open.*] **1.** *intr.* To make a mute signal, or significant gesture, as by nodding, etc. *trans.* To express by a beck 1821. **2.** *trans.* (obj. orig. *dat.*) To make a mute signal to; to beckon 1486. **3.** *intr.* To nod, bow; to curtsey. Chiefly *Sc.* 1535.

2. When gold and siluer becks me to come on SHAKS.

Be·cker, becket. *dial.* 1602. [Origin unkn.] Sea-bream.

Becket (be·kėt), *sb.* 1769. [Origin unkn.] *Naut.* A contrivance, usu. a loop of rope with a knot on one end and eye at the other, or a large hook, or a wooden bracket, used for confining ropes, tackle, oars, spars, etc., and also for securing the tacks and sheets of fails. Hence **Be·cket** *v.* to fasten by or furnish with beckets.

Beckon (be·k'n), *v.* [OE. *bēcnan,* (*bīecnan*) = OS. *bōknian,* OHG *bouhnen* :– WGmc. *bauknian f. *baukna BEACON.] **1.** *intr.* To make a mute signal with the head, hand, finger, etc.; now *esp.* in order to bid a person approach. **2.** *trans.* (obj. orig. *dat.*): To make a significant gesture of head or hand to; hence, to summon or bid approach ME.

1. I beckon'd with my Hand to him, to come back DE FOE. 2. Iago becons me; now he begins the story *Oth.* IV. i. 134. **Be·ckon** *sb.* a significant gesture of head, hand, etc., *esp.* one indicating assent or command.

† **Becla·p,** *v.* ME. [BE- 1.] To catch or lay hold of suddenly –1530.

Beclaw·, *v.* 1603. [BE- 1.] To scratch or tear all over with claws or nails.

Beclip (bĭkli·p), *v.*[1] *arch.* [OE. *beclyppan,* f. BE- 1 + *clyppan*; see CLIP *v*[1].] † **1.** To embrace –1669. **2.** To wrap round, encircle OE. † **3.** To lay hold of; to catch, overtake –1557.

Beclog (bĭklǫ·g), *v.* ME. [BE- 1.] To encumber with a sticky substance.

† **Beclo·se,** *v.* [orig. OE. *beclȳsan,* f. BE- 1 + *clȳsan* shut up; subseq. refash. after CLOSE.] To shut up or in; to imprison –1677.

Beclothe (bĭklōᵘ·ð), *v.* Pa. t. and pple. **beclothed, beclad.** 1509. [BE- 1.] To clothe about.

Becloud (bĭklau·d), *v.* 1598. [BE- 6.] To cover or obscure with clouds. Also *fig.*

To b. unpleasant facts GEO. ELIOT.

Become (bĭkʌ·m), *v.* Pa. t. **became**; Pa. pple. **become.** [OE. *becuman* = OFris. *bicuma,* MLG., (M)Du. *bekomen,* OHG. *biqueman* (G. *bekommen*) obtain, receive, Goth. *biquiman*; :– Gmc. *bi- BE- + *kweman COME.] † **1.** *intr.* To come (to a place), to arrive; later, to go –1737. Also † *transf.* † **2.** To happen; to befall –1655. **3.** To come to be (something or in some state) ME. **4.** To come into being 1598. **5.** To accord with; to befit (obj. orig. *dat.*) ME. **6.** *impers.* (now usu. with *it*). † **a.** (*absol.,* with *to, for,* or *clause.*) Replaced by 'it is becoming'. –1591. **b.** with *object.* (orig. *dat.*) To befit ME. **7.** Hence, To look well (on or with), to set out ME.; hence, To look well in (a dress, etc.) 1660.

1. *transf.* It becomes to be loved on its own account SYD. SMITH. 2. His wife looked backe.. she became a pillar of salt *Gen.* 19:26. 5. Soft stilnes and the night Become the tutches of sweet harmonie *Merch V.* V. i. 57. 6. Fonder of hunting than became an Archbishop FREEMAN. 7. She will b. thy bed *Temp.* III. ii. 112. To b. a gown HELPS. Phr. *B. of* (after 'what'): *orig.* = 'come out of, result from; *now,* replaces 'where is it become', etc. (= 'where went it, has it gone') in reference to the later locality, position, or fate of a thing.

† **Beco·med,** *ppl. a.* [f. BECOME (sense 7) + -ED[1].] Befitting. *Rom. & Jul.* IV. ii. 26.

Becoming (bĭkʌ·miŋ), *vbl. sb.* (and *ppl. a.*) 1600. [f. BECOME *v.* + -ING[1].] **1.** The action of befitting; that which befits or graces (*rare*). **2.** A coming to be 1853. **3.** *ppl. a.* Befitting 1565.

3. Within the limits of b. mirth *L.L.L.* II. i. 67. *The becoming*: decorum; that which is coming into existence. Hence **Beco·ming-ly** *adv.,* **-ness.**

Becripple (bĭkri·p'l), *v.* 1660. [BE- 2.] To make lame.

Becrow·n, *v.* 1583. [BE- 2.] To crown.

Becu·rl, *v.* 1614. [BE- 2.] To cover or deck out with curls.

Bed (bed), *sb.* [OE. *bed(d)* = OFris. *bed(d),* OS. *bed, beddi,* MDu. *bedde* (Du. *bed*), OHG. *betti* (G. *bett*), Goth. *badi* :– Gmc. *baðjam.] **I.** The sleeping-place of men or animals. **1.** A permanent structure or arrangement for sleeping on, or for the sake of rest. It consists for the most part of a sack or mattress, stuffed with something soft or springy, often raised upon a bedstead, and covered with sheets, blankets, etc. The name is given both to the whole structure, and to the stuffed sack or mattress. Also *fig.* **2.** *transf.* As the place of conjugal union, and of procreation and childbirth ME. **3.** Any sleeping place ME. **4.** *fig.* The grave ME.

1. He was in his b. and a slepe on a fethyr bedde CAXTON. *B. and board*: entertainment with lodging and food. Of a wife: full connubial relations. 2. False to his B. *Cymb.* III. iv. 42. George..the eldest son of this second b. CLARENDON. 4. As we hollowed his narrow b. WOLFE.

II. 1. A level or smooth piece of ground in a garden, usu. somewhat raised; also the plants which grow in it OE. **2.** The bottom of a lake or sea, or of a watercourse 1586. **3.** An extended base, a matrix 1633. **4.** A level surface on which anything rests, *e.g.* the level surface in a printing press on which the form is laid 1846. **5.** Hence *techn.*:

a. *Gunnery.* The portion of a gun-carriage on which the gun rests. **b.** *Archit.* and *Building.* The surface of a stone, or brick, which lies in the mortar; the under side of a slate. **c.** *Mech.* Any solid foundation, framework, or support, upon which to rest a superstructure. **d.** *Carpentry.* A support or rest, *e.g.* for a ship on the stocks, etc. **e.** *Railway-making.* The layer of stone, etc., upon which the rails are laid.

1. Beds of violets blue MILT. 2. The b. of the Adriatic LYELL.

III. 1. A layer or stratum; a horizontal course; *spec.* in *Geol.* 1616. **2.** A layer of reptiles, shell-fish, etc., covering a space or tract of ground 1608.

1. The lowest 'bed' of the Lias LYELL. 2. A b. of oysters 1688.

Phrases, etc. *To bring to b.,* formerly = put to b.; now usu. pass., to be delivered of a child; also *fig.* (See ABED.) *To die in one's b.*: to die at home or of natural causes. *To keep one's b.*: to remain in b. through sickness, etc. So *To leave one's b.*: to recover. *To make a b.*: to put one in order after use. *To lie* or *sleep in the b. one has made* (cf. prec.): to accept the natural results of one's own conduct. *To make up a b.*: to extemporize sleeping accommodation. *To take to one's b.*: to become confined to b. through sickness or infirmity.

Comb., etc.: **b.-key,** an iron tool for screwing and unscrewing the nuts and bolts of a bedstead; **-moulding** (*Archit.*), 'the mouldings under a projection, as the corona of a cornice' (Gwilt); **-pan,** a warming-pan; a chamber utensil constructed for use in b.; **-piece, -plate** (*Mech.*), the foundation or support of any mechanical structure; **-post,** a post of a b.; **-rock** (*Geol.*), the solid rock underlying superficial formations; also *fig.* bottom, lowest level; **-screw,** one used for holding together the posts and beams of a wooden bedstead; also, a machine for lifting heavy bodies, often used in launching vessels; **-sore,** a soreness of the skin produced by long lying in b.; **-stone,** a large heavy stone used as the foundation and support of girders, etc., in building; also, the lower stone in an oil-mill, on which the runners roll; † **-swerver,** one unfaithful to the marriage-bed (*Wint. T.* II. i. 93); † **-vow,** promise of fidelity to the marriage-bed; **-way** (*Geol.*), an appearance of stratification in granite; **-winch, -wrench,** = *bed-key*; † **-work,** work that is or can be done in bed, easy work *Tr. & Cr.* I. iii. 203.

Bed, *v.* Pa. t. and pple. **bedded.** [OE. *beddian,* f. *bed(d* BED.] † **1.** *intr.* To prepare a bed –ME. **2.** To put to bed; to furnish with a bed ME. **3.** To take (a wife) to bed (*arch.*) 1548. **4.** *intr.* To go to bed ME. **5.** To provide (animals) with litter 1480. **6.** *intr.* Of an animal: To make its lair 1470. **7.** To plant in or as in a garden bed 1671. **8.** To EMBED

1586; *intr.* to rest *on* 1875. **9.** *Building.* To lay (bricks, etc.) in position in cement or mortar 1685. **10.** *Masonry.* To dress the face of a stone (cf. BED *sb.* II. 5 b) 1793. **11.** To spread with a bed of anything. Cf. *to carpet.* 1839. **12.** To lay (*e.g.* oysters) in a bed or beds 1653. **13.** *intr.* To form a compact layer 1615.

4. O then we'll wed, and then we'll b. CAREY. **5.** To rub, feed, and b. a horse WESLEY. Phr. *To bed up*: to lie up in strata *against*.

Bedabble (bĭdæ·b'l), *v.* 1590. [BE- 1.] To wet with dirty liquid, or so as to make dirty.

Bedad (bĭdæ·d), *int. Irish.* 1710. [For *by dad*, substituted for *by God* (see BEGAD), after earlier †*adad* (XVII–XVIII).] An asseveration.

† **Beda·ff,** *v.* [f. BE- 5 + DAFF *sb.*] To befool. CHAUCER.

† **Beda·ggle,** *v.* 1580. [f. BE- 2 + DAGGLE.] To bemire the bottom of (dress) –1660.

Bedangled (bĭdæ·ng'ld), *ppl. a.* 1601. [BE- 1.] Beset with things dangling about one.

Bedarken (bĭdā·ɹk'n), *v.* [BE- 1.] To involve in darkness. Also *fig.*

Bedash (bĭdæ·ʃ), *v.* 1564. [BE- 1.] **a.** To dash against. **b.** To injure by dashing. **c.** To cover with dashes of colour, etc.

Bedaub (bĭdǭ·b), *v.* 1553. [BE- 1.] **1.** To daub over, to plaster 1558. Also *fig.* **2.** To bedizen 1581. Also *fig.*

1. They all bedawbed their faces with mire 1683.

Bedawee·, -wi, -wy, pl. **bedawee·n, -win,** forms of BEDOUIN, -S.

Bedazzle (bĭdæ·z'l), *v.* 1596. [BE- 2.] To dazzle thoroughly. So **Beda·zzlement.**

Bedchamber (be·dˌtʃē¹:mbəɹ). ME. [f. BED *sb.* + CHAMBER.] A room intended for holding a bed; *arch.*, and displaced by *bedroom*, exc. in reference to the royal bedchamber.

The Ladies of the Bed-chamber 1702.

Bed-clothes (be·d-klōᵘðz), *sb. pl.* (The sing. is obs.) ME. [f. BED *sb.* + CLOTHES.] Sheets, blankets, etc., for a bed.

Bedder (be·dəɹ). 1612. [f. BED *v.* or *sb.*] **1.** One who puts to bed; one who litters cattle. **2.** An upholsterer. Now *dial.* 1803. **3.** The lower stone in an oil-mill 1611. **4.** A bedding-out plant 1862.

Bedding (be·diŋ), *vbl. sb.* OE. [f. BED *sb.* and *v.* + -ING¹.] **1.** (conn. w. BED *sb.*) The articles which compose a bed, *esp.* the mattress, etc., and the bedclothes. **b.** Anything used to sleep on or in (*arch.*) ME. **c.** Litter 1697. **2.** A foundation 1611. **3.** Arrangement of rocks, etc., in beds or layers 1860. **4.** (conn. w. BED *v.*) A putting to bed; *esp.* of a bride 1859. **5.** Planting flowers in beds; also called *bedding out* 1862.

Comb.: **b.-moulding** = *Bed-moulding*; **-stone,** a straight piece of marble used to try the rubbed side of a brick.

Bede, *sb.*¹ ME. form of BEAD *sb.*, prayer. Now *arch.* So **bedehouse, bedesman,** etc.

Bede (bīd), *sb.*² [Origin unkn.] A miner's pickaxe. RAYMOND.

Bedeck (bĭde·k), *v.* 1566. [BE- 1.] To deck about, to cover with ornament.

So bedecked, ornate, and gay MILT. *Sams.* 712.

Bedeguar (be·dĭgāɹ). Also **-gar, -gaur.** 1578. [– Fr. *bédegar* (1425) – Pers. name quoted in an Arab. text, *bād-āwar*(*d* lit. 'wind-brought'.] † **1.** A white spiny plant, perh. the Milk Thistle (*Silybum marianum*) –1601. **2.** A kind of gall on rose-bushes produced by an insect *Cynips rosæ* 1578.

Bedel, bedell, archaic forms of BEADLE, q.v. So **Bedelry,** etc.

† **Bede·lve,** *v.* [OE. *bedelfan*, f. BE- 1 + *delfan* DELVE.] **1.** To dig about OE. only. **2.** To bury –1513.

Bedeman, obs. f. BEADSMAN.

Bede·ne, *adv.* Now *dial.* [ME. *bidene*; *bid-* is unexplained; *-ene* = ME. adv. *æne*, *ene*, OE. *ǣne* once, at once, in one, together.] = ANON; occ. a mere expletive, or a rime word.

Bedevil (bĭde·v'l), *v.* 1768. [BE- 5, 6.] **1.** To treat diabolically. **2.** To possess with, or as with, a devil 1831. **3.** To torment, worry 1823. **4.** To 'play the devil with'; to transform mischievously or bewilderingly 1800.

1. My poor..Muse..be-deviled with their..ribaldry BYRON. **4.** To b. the registration DISRAELI. Hence **Bede·villed, -iled** *ppl. a.* **Bede·vilment.**

Bedew (bĭdiū·), *v.* ME. [BE- 6.] *pass.* To be wetted with dew; hence *active*, To cover with or as with dew. Also *transf.* and *fig.*

The moisture which bedews a cold metal or stone when we breathe upon it HERSCHEL.

Bedfellow (be·dfe:loᵘ). 1478. [f. BED + FELLOW.] One who shares a bed with another; also *fig.*

† **Bed-fere, -ifere.** ME. [f. BED *sb.* + FERE *sb.*¹; see YFERE.] = prec. –1656.

Bedfordshire (be·dfǒɹdʃəɹ). 1665. Name of an English county; joc. for *bed.*

Be·dgown. 1762. [See GOWN.] **1.** A woman's night-gown. **2.** A kind of jacket worn by working women in the north 1827.

Be·d-hea·d. ME. [HEAD *sb.*] The upper end of a bed.

Bedight (bĭdəi·t), *v. arch.* Pa. pple. **bedight, -ed.** ME. [BE- 2 + DIGHT.] To equip, array, bedeck. (Now *poet.*)

Bedim (bĭdi·m), *v.* 1566. [BE- 5.] To make dim.; *esp.* the eyesight 1583. Also *fig.*

Bedi·p, *v.* [OE. *bedyppan*, f. BE- 2 + *dyppan* DIP *v.*] To dip, immerse.

Bedizen (bĭdəi·z'n, -di·z'n), *v.*; also **bedizzen.** 1661. [f. BE- 2 + DIZEN.] All Eng. orthoepists have (əi). To dress out, *esp.* with vulgar finery; also *fig.* Hence **Bedi·zenment.**

Bedlam (be·dləm). [ME. *Bedlem* = *Bethlem, Bethlehem.*] † **1.** Bethlehem in Judea –1616. **2.** The Hospital of St. Mary of Bethlehem, used since 1547 as an asylum for the insane. **3.** Hence, A madhouse 1663. Also *fig.* † **4.** An inmate of a lunatic asylum, a madman; *spec.* one of the discharged, but often only half-cured, patients, licensed to beg, wearing as a badge a tin plate on their left arm –1701. Also *attrib.*, and *adj.* 1535.

2. Phr. *Jack or Tom o' B.*: a madman. **3.** 'Twas both an hospital and b. 1699. **4.** She roar'd like a B. SWIFT. Plaine b. stuffe MILT. Hence **Be·dlamite** *sb.* an inmate of B.; a lunatic; *adj.* lunatic.

Be·d-ma:ker. 1465. [f. BED *sb.* + MAKER.] **1.** One who constructs beds 1500. **2.** One who makes beds after they have been slept in 1465.

† **Bedo·te,** *v.* ME. [f. BE- 5 + DOTE *sb.*¹ or *v.*] To cause to dote, befool –1583.

Bedouin (be·duˌīn), *sb.* (and *a.*) ME. [– OFr. *beduin* (mod. *bédouin*), ult. (through med.L.) – Arab. *badwiyyūn* (nom. pl.), *badwiyyīn* (obl. pl.) inhabitants of the desert (*badw*).] **a.** An Arab of the desert. **b.** *transf.* A gipsy. (Cf. *City Arab.*) 1863. Also *attrib.* Hence **Be·douinism.**

Bedrabble (bĭdræ·b'l), *v.* 1440. [BE- 2.] To make dirty with rain and mud.

Bedraggle (bĭdræ·g'l), *v.* 1727. [BE- 2.] **a.** To wet (skirts, etc.) so that they drag or hang limp. **b.** 'To soil clothes by suffering them, in walking, to reach the dirt' (J.).

Bedral, bederal (be·d(ĕ)răl). *Sc.* 1815. [app. corrupt. f. BEADLE.] A church officer, often acting as clerk, sexton, and bell-ringer.

Bedrench; see BE- 2.

Bedrid (be·drid), *a.*, orig. *sb.* [ME. *bedred*(*e*), repr. OE. *bedreda, -rida* sb. and adj. paralysed (man), agent-noun f. *bedd* BED + **rid-*, short base of *rīdan* RIDE.] **1.** Confined to bed through sickness or infirmity. Now usu. *Bedridden.* **2.** *fig.* Worn out 1621.

1. To her decrepit, sicke, and b. Father *L.L.L.* I. i. 139. var. **Be·dri:dden,** the *-en* being due to the analogy of ppl. adjs.

† **Be·drip.** [OE. *bed-rīp*, f. *bed-* (see BEAD) + *rip*: lit. 'reaping by request'; called also *bēnrīp*, f. *bēn* prayer.] A service which some tenants owed to their lord, viz. at his request to reap his corn at harvest-time –ME.

Bedroom (be·drūm). 1590. [ROOM *sb.*] **1.** Room in bed (*Mids. N.* II. ii. 51). **2.** A room used to contain a bed; a sleeping apartment. (Replacing BEDCHAMBER.) 1616. Hence **Be·droomed** *a.* having a b.

Bedrop (bĭˌdrǫ·p), *v.* ME. [BE- 4.] **1.** To wet with drops. **2.** *pa. pple.* Sprinkled as with drops; *fig.* interspersed ME.

Bedside (be·dsəi:d). ME. [For *bed's side.*] Place or position by a bed; *esp.* by way of attendance on one confined to bed (so *b. manner* of a doctor 1869).

Bedspread (be·dspred). orig. *U.S.* 1848. [SPREAD *sb.* II. 2; cf. Du. *bed*(*de*)*sprei.*] A light thin covering to spread over the clothes on a bed.

† **Bedstaff** (be·dstɑf). Pl. **staffs, staves.** 1576. A stick used in some way about a bed. Formerly handy as a weapon; hence, prob., the phr. *in the twinkling of a b.* –1845.

Say there is no virtue in cudgels and bedstaves BROME.

Bedstead (be·dsted). 1440. [STEAD *sb.* 6.] Strictly, the place occupied by a bed; but long ago transferred to the framework of a bed.

Be·dstock. *n. dial.* 1483. [STOCK *sb.*¹ II. 2.] A BEDSTEAD, or its front and back parts.

Be·dstraw. ME. [STRAW.] † **1.** The straw formerly used as bedding –1637. **2.** A genus of plants (*Galium*, N.O. *Rubiaceæ*), one of which (*G. verum*) is known as *Our Lady's B.* 1527.

Bedtick (be·dtik). 1569. [TICK *sb.*²] A bag or case, into which feathers, etc., are put to form a bed. Hence **Be·dti:cking,** the materials of which bedticks are made; also *attrib.*

Bedtime (be·dtəim). ME. [TIME.] The hour for going to bed. Also *fig.*

Between our after supper, and bedtime *Mids.N.* v. i. 34.

Bedub (bĭdʌ·b), *v.* 1657. [BE- 2.] † **a.** To adorn. **b.** To denominate.

Bedull, bedung, bedust; see BE- *pref.*

Bedward, -wards (be·dwǒɹd, -z), *adv.* ME. [See -WARD(S: orig. *to bedward.*] Towards bed or † bedtime.

Bedwarf, bedye; see BE- *pref.*

Bee¹ (bī). [OE. *bēo* = OFris. *bē*, MLG., MDu. *bīe* (Du. *bij*), OHG. *bīa* (G. dial. *beie*), ON. *bý*:– Gmc. **bīōn.*] **1.** A genus of insects of the Hymenopterous order, living in societies composed of one queen, or perfect female, a few males or 'drones', and an indefinite number of undeveloped females or 'neuters' (which are the workers), all having four wings; they produce wax, and collect and store up honey. **2.** Applied to a group of allied insects, e.g. Humble B., Mason B., Carpenter B., etc. OE. **3.** (orig. in U.S.): A meeting of neighbours to unite their labours for the benefit of one of their number; as a *quilting-b.*, etc. *Hence*: A gathering for some object, e.g. a *spelling-b.* 1809.

2. The Humble Bees are larger than the Bees 1861. **4.** I made a b.; that is I collected..the most expert..of the settlers to assist at the raising GALT.

Phr. To have *a b. in one's bonnet*: *i.e.* a craze on some point, a screw loose. (Cf. *maggot.*) *Comb.*: **b.-bird,** the Spotted Fly-catcher, also a humming-bird; **-cell,** one of the cells of the comb; **-cuckoo,** an African bird (*Cuculus indicator*), which indicates the nests of wild bees; **-eater,** a genus of birds (*Merops*) which devour bees; **-fly,** a two-winged fly resembling a b., *esp.* certain of the *Bombylidæ* and *Syrphidæ*; **-glue,** the substance with which bees fill up crevices, and fix the combs to the hives, propolis; **-gum,** U.S. local name for a b.-hive; **-hawk,** the Honey Buzzard; also a clear-wing hawk-moth (*Sesia furciformis*); **-line,** a straight line between two points on the earth's surface, such as a b. was supposed to take in returning to its hive; **-master,** a keeper of bees; so **-mistress**; **-nettle,** species of Dead-nettle much visited by bees; **-orchis,** a plant (*Ophrys apifera*) with a flower in part resembling a b.; **-tree,** one in which bees have hived; **-wine,** nectar of a flower.

Bee² (bī). [OE. *bēag, bēah* ring = ON. *baugr*, OHG. *bouc* :– Gmc. **baugaz*, f. **bauȝ-* strong grade of **beuȝ* **bauȝ-* **buȝ-* BOW *v.*¹] † **1.** A ring or torque of metal –1552. **2.** *Naut.*: *bee*, a hoop of metal; *bee-block*, a piece of hard wood, bolted to the outer end of the bowsprit, to reeve the fore-mast stays through 1860.

Bee·bread. [OE. *bēo-brēad* = MHG. *bīe brōt* (G. *bienenbrot*). The mod. word is prob. a new combination.] † **1.** *orig.* In OE.: Honeycomb with the honey in it. **2.** Pollen, or honey and pollen, consumed by the nurse-bees 1657. **3.** Used of plants yielding nectar, as the White Clover and Borage.

Beech (bītʃ). [OE. *bēće* = MLG. *bōke*, *bōke* (wk. fem.):– Gmc. **bōkjōn*, rel. to **bōkō* (str. fem.), whence OE. *bōc*, which survives with shortened vowel in BUCKMAST, BUCKWHEAT. Cogn. w. L. *fagus* beech, Gr. φαγός, φηγός edible oak.] **1. a.** A forest tree indigenous to Europe and Western Asia, having fine thin smooth bark and glossy oval leaves, and bearing triquetrous nuts (called *mast*); it has several varieties, as the Purple, Copper, and Fern-leaved Beech. **b.** The genus *Fagus*, N.O. *Corylaceæ*, including the Common Beech (*F. sylvatica*). **c.** The wood of this tree. Often *attrib.* 1607. **2.** Applied to other trees resembling the beech of Europe.

Comb.: **b.-drops,** a North American plant, *Epiphegus*, N.O. *Orobanchaceæ*, parasitic upon the roots of the b.; **-fern,** *Polypodium phegopteris*; **-finch,** local name of the Chaffinch; **marten,** see MARTEN; **-mast,** the fruit of the b.; **-oil,** oil extracted from b.-mast; **-owl,** local name of the Tawny Owl; **-wheat** = BUCKWHEAT.

Beechen (bī·tʃĕn), *a. arch.* and *poet.* [OE. *bēćen*; see prec., -EN[4].] **1.** Of, pertaining to, or derived from the beech. **2.** Made of the wood of the beech 1663. ¶ Replaced by BEECH *attrib.*

A b. bowl, A maple dish WORDSW.

Beechy (bī·tʃi), *a.* 1612. [f. BEECH + -Y[1].] Of, characterized by, or abounding in, beeches.

Beef (bīf), *sb.* Pl. **beeves,** in U.S. **beefs.** ME. [– AFr., OFr. *boef*, *buef* (mod. *bœuf*) :– L. *bos*, *bov-* ox. See COW.] **1.** The flesh of an ox, bull, or cow, used as food. **2.** *transf.* (see quots.) 1661. **3.** An ox, or any animal of the ox kind; *esp.* a fattened beast, or its carcase. Usu. in *pl.* (*arch.* or *techn.*) ME.

1. What say you to a peece of Beefe and Mustard *Tam. Shr.* IV. iii. 23. **2.** Ling. . is counted the beefe of the Sea LOVELL. Chelmsford. . showed less b. about him 1862.

Comb.: † **b.-brained** *ppl. a.* thick-headed; **-head,** a thick-head; **-tea,** the juice extracted from b., used as a food for invalids; **-witted** *a.* (= *beef-brained*); hence **-wittedness.** Hence **Bee·finess,** beefy quality; also *transf.* **Bee·fing, bee·fin** (*dial.*), an ox for slaughter. **Bee·fy** *a.* abounding in, or like, b.; fleshy; stolid.

Beef-ea:ter. 1610. [f. BEEF + EATER; cf. OE. *hlāf-æta*, lit. 'loaf-eater', a menial servant. Not conn. w. *buffet*.] **1.** An eater of beef; *contemptuously*, a well-fed menial. (Properly *beef-eater*.) **2.** One of the Yeomen of the Guard; also of the Warders of the Tower of London 1671. **3.** *Ornith.* A genus of African birds (*Buphaga*), called also Oxpeckers 1836.

Beefing, see BIFFIN, a kind of apple.

Beef-steak (bī·f‚stē[i]·k). 1711. A thick slice of beef, cut from the hind-quarters of the animal. Also *attrib.*

Beef-steak Club, a society founded by Lord Peterborough; the members wear a gridiron upon their buttons.

Beef-wood (bī·fwud). 1756. [f. BEEF + WOOD.] **1.** The timber of an Australian tree (*Casuarina*), so called from its red colour 1836. **2.** Also applied to other trees, e.g. in N. S. Wales to *Stenocarpus salignus*; in Queensland to *Banksia compar* (both N.O. *Proteaceæ*), etc.

Beehive (bī·həiːv). ME. [f. BEE *sb.*[1] + HIVE *sb.*] A receptacle used as a home for bees; usually made of thick straw work in the shape of a dome.

Beele. Now *dial.* 1671. [app. a var. of BILL *sb.*[1]] A pick-axe with both ends sharp. Hence **Beeleman.**

Beelzebub (bi‚e·lzĭbʊb). [OE. *Belzebub*, ME. *Beelzebub*, *Belsabub* – Vulg. *Beelzebub*, tr. (i) Heb. *ba'al zᵉbūb* Lord of Flies, Philistine God (2 Kings 1:2) and (ii) Gr. Βεελζεβούβ of the N.T. (Matt. 12:24). Milton made Beelzebub one of the fallen angels.] The Devil; a devil; also *transf.*

Been, *pa. pple.* of BE *v.* Also, obs. f. *be*, pres. infin., and pres. indic. pl.

Been, obs. pl. of BEE *sb.*[1] var. of BEIN *a.*

Beënt (bī·ĕnt), *a.* 1865. [f. BE *v.* + L. *suffix* -ENT.] *Metaph.* That is or exists; existing (in the most abstract sense); also used subst. (tr. Ger. *seiend* = the Hegelian *pure being*.)

Beer (bīᵊɹ), *sb.*[1] [OE. *bēor* = OFris. *biār*, *bier*, MLG., MDu. *bēr*, OHG. *bior* (Du., G. *bier*), a WGmc. word (whence prob. ON. *bjórr*) – monastic L. *biber* drink, f. L. *bibere*. Prob. reinforced from LG. on the introduction of hopped liquor.] **1.** An alcoholic liquor obtained by the fermentation of malt (or other saccharine substance), flavoured with hops or other bitters. Formerly distinguished from *ale* by being hopped; but now generic, including ale and porter. See ALE. **2.** Applied to other fermented liquors, as *nettle beer*, etc. OE.

1. Buttered beer: see ALE. **Small beer:** weak b.; *fig.* small things, as in *To think no small b. of oneself*. Phr. *To be in b.*: to be intoxicated.

Comb.: **b.-engine,** a machine for drawing or pumping up beer from the casks to the bar; **-garden,** one attached to an inn for the consumption of b.; **-house,** one licensed for the sale of b. only; **-money,** an allowance to servants instead of b.; **-vinegar,** vinegar made from b. (cf. BEEREGAR). Hence **Bee·riness,** beery quality or condition. **Bee·rishly** *adv.* in beery fashion.

† **Beer** (bī·əɹ), *sb.*[2] *rare.* ME. [f. BE *v.* + -ER.[1]] One who is; *spec.* the Self-existent, the great *I Am* –1602.

Beer, *sb.*[3] 1712. [The same wd. as BIER.] *Weaving.* A (variable) number of ends in a warp.

Beeregar (bīᵊ·rĭgăɹ). ? *Obs.* 1500. [f. BEER *sb.*[1] + *egre* EAGER = Fr. *aigre*; after *vinegar*, *alegar*.] Sour beer; vinegar made from beer.

Beery (bīᵊ·ri), *a.* 1861. [f. BEER *sb.*[1] + -Y[1].] Belonging to, or abounding in beer; affected by beer; beer-like.

Beest (bīst). [OE. *bēost* = NFris. *bjast*, *bjüst*, (M)Du. *biest*, OHG. *biost* (G. *biest*, as in *biestmilch*); WGmc., of unkn. origin. See next.] The first milk drawn from a mammal, *esp.* a cow, after parturition.

Beestings (bī·stiŋz). [OE. **bēsting* (late WS. *bȳsting*), f. synon. *bēost*; see prec.] **1.** = prec. † **2.** A disease caused by imbibing beestings. L. *colostratio*. 1607.

Bees-wax (bī·z‚wæːks). 1676. [f. BEE[1] + WAX.] The wax secreted by bees as the material of their combs. Hence **Bee·swax** *v.* to rub or polish with b.

Beeswing (bī·z‚wiŋ). 1860. [f. BEE + WING.] The second crust, consisting of shining filmy scales of tartar, formed in port and some other wines after long keeping; so called from its appearance; *ellipt.*, old wine showing beeswing. Hence **Bee·s-winged** *a.* so old as to show b.

Beet (bīt). [OE. *bēte* = MLG. *bēte* (LG. *beete*, whence G. *beete*), MDu. *bēte* (Du. *beet*), OHG. *bieza* (G. dial. *biessen*), early WGmc. – L. *bēta*, perh. of Celtic orig. Unrecorded between OE. and late ME., when its currency was prob. due to LG.] **1.** A plant or genus of plants (N.O. *Chenopodiaceæ*), having a root used for food, and also for yielding sugar. There are two species, the Common or Red (*Beta vulgaris*), and the White (*B. cicla*). Formerly used chiefly in pl. 'beets', like *beans*, etc.

Comb.: † **B.-raves** [– Fr. *bette-rave* 'beet', lit. 'beet-turnip'], the small red b.; **-root,** the root of the b.; also *attrib.*

Beet, bete (bīt), *v.* Now *dial.* [OE. *bētan* (older *bœ̄tan*) amend = OS. *bōtian* (MLG. *bōten*, MDu. *boeten*), OHG. *buozen* (G. *büssen*), ON. *bœta*, Goth. *bōtjan* :– Gmc. **bōtjan*, f. **bōt-*, see BOOT *sb.*[1] Repl. by BOOT *v.*] **1.** *trans.* To mend, make good. **2.** To relieve ME. **3.** To make, kindle, put on (a fire) OE. **4.** To mend (a fire). Still in *Sc.* ME.

4. Nyght and day greet fuyr they under betten CHAUCER.

Beetle (bī·t'l), *sb.*[1] [OE. *bētel* (WS. *bietel*) :– Gmc. **bautilaz*, f. **bautan* BEAT *v.*[1] + *-il-* -LE 1.] **1.** An implement with a heavy head, and a handle or stock, used to drive wedges, ram paving stones, etc.; a mall. Also *fig.* **2.** The type of heavy dullness 1520.

1. *Three-man b.*: one that requires three men to lift it; see 2 *Hen. IV*, I. ii. 255. **2.** Tendre wyttes. . be made as dull as a betell 1520. *Comb.* **b.-head,** the monkey of a pile-driving engine.

Beetle (bī·t'l), *sb.*[2] [OE. *bitula*, *bitela*, f. **bit-*, short base of *bītan* BITE *v.*; see -LE 1.] **1.** The class name for coleopterous insects, having the upper pair of wings converted into hard wing-cases (elytra) that close over the back, and protect the lower or true wings. **2.** In pop. use applied *esp.* to those that are large and black, and including the **Black-beetle** or COCKROACH, which is not a beetle OE. **3.** A type of blindness; whence *fig.* 1548.

1. The poore B. that we treade vpon *Meas. for M.* III. i. 79. **2.** Beetles blacke approach not neere *Mids. N.* II. ii. 22. **3.** They that had charge to guyde other, were poore blinde betels themselves TOMSON.

Beetle (bī·t'l), ? *a.* ME. [Of unkn. origin. First in *bytell browet*, *bitelbrowed* (XIV) having bushy, shaggy, or prominent eyebrows; later (XVI) *betle browes*, *beetil brow* was used of the human brow and the brow of a mountain.] **1.** In **Beetle-browed:** 'Having prominent brows', Johnson (but *brow* in ME. was always = eyebrow, not = forehead); having 'black and long' (1782), or 'shaggy, bushy, or prominent' eyebrows (ME.) Usu. reproachful, and occas. simply = Lowering, scowling. Cf. *supercilious*. Also *fig.* **2. a.** (qualifying *brows*) 1532. **b.** Of the brow of a mountain: Prominent, or perh. tree-clad 1580.

2. I rather would a husband wed With a beetill brow than a beetell hed *Prov.* var. **Bee·tled** *a.* (in sense 2).

Beetle (bī·t'l), *v.*[1] 1602. [f. BEETLE *a.* 2 b. App. used as a nonce-wd. by Shaks.] **1.** *intr.* To 'lift up beetle brows' (Sidney), scowl; in mod. use, 'to overhang'; but prob. used by Shaks. with some reference to eyebrows. **2.** *fig.* To hang threateningly 1859.

1. The dreadfull summit of the Cliffe, That beetles o'er his base into the Sea *Haml.* I. iv. 71.

Beetle (bī·t'l), *v.*[2]; also (*Sc.*) **bittle.** 1608. [f. BEETLE *sb.*[1]] To beat with a beetle, in order to thresh, crush, or flatten; also, *techn.*, to emboss fabrics by pressure from figured rollers.

Beeves (bīvz). Pl. of BEEF; now usu. poet. for 'oxen'.

Befall (bĭfǭ·l), *v.* Pa. t. **befell (-fel).** Pa. pple. **befallen.** [OE. *befeallan* = OFris. *befalla*, OS., OHG. *bifallan*; see BE- 2, FALL *v.*] † **1.** *intr.* To fall. (Chiefly *fig.*) –1649. **2.** To fall *to*; to pertain; be fitting ME. **3.** To happen ME. † **4.** To become *of* –1590.

2. '*Reddite Caesari*,' seide god, 'pat to cesar byfalleþ' LANGL. **3.** Lest peraduenture mischiefe b. him *Gen.* 42:4. So b. my soule, As this is false *Com. Err.* V. i. 208. Phr. † *Fair*, *foul befall*.

Befeather, Befetter, etc.: see BE- *pref.*

† **Befile,** *v.* [OE. *befȳlan*, f. BE- 1 + *fȳlan* FILE *v.*[2] Repl. by BEFOUL.] To make foul; to defile –1532.

Befit (bĭfi·t), *v.* 1460. [f. BE- 2 + FIT *v.*; repl. earlier *besit*.] **1.** *trans.* To be fit for; to agree with; to become. **2.** To be proper to, as a duty or task; to be right for 1602. † **3.** To fit out *with* –1759.

1. Any businesse that We say befits the houre *Temp.* II. i. 289. **2.** It us befitted To beare our hearts in greefe *Haml.* I. ii. 2. Hence **Befi·ttingly** *adv.*

Beflatter, Beflower, Befoam, Befog, † **Befold**; see BE-.

Befool (bĭfū·l), *v.* ME. [BE- 5.] **1.** To dupe. **2.** To treat as a fool, call fool 1612.

1. The old Rumpers were befoold by Cromwel 1673. **2.** Who is hee, whom Salomon doth so often be-foole in his Prouerbs HIERON.

Before (bĭfōᵊ·ɹ). [OE. *beforan* = OFris. *befora*, OS. *biforan*, OHG. *bifora* (G. *bevor*), f. Gmc. *bi-* BY + **forana* from the front (f. **fora* FOR).] **A.** *adv.* **1.** Of motion: Ahead, in front. **2.** Of position or direction: In front, in or on the fore side ME. **3.** In time previous, earlier, sooner; *hence*, beforehand; in the past ME.

1. I am sent with broome b. *Mids. N.* V. i. 397. **2.** Had he his hurts b.? *Macb.* V. vii. 75. **3.** When the But is out we will drinke water. not a drop b. *Temp.* III. ii. 2. Phr. *Long b.*, *the week b.*, etc.

B. *prep.* **1.** Of motion: Ahead of OE.; driven in front of 1598; *hence*, with causal force 1535. **2.** Of position or direction: In front of OE. **3.** In front of so as to be in the sight of; under the cognizance of OE. **4.** In the (mental) view of (*arch.*) OE. **5.** Open to the knowledge of ME. **b.** Claiming the attention of 1711. **6.** In front of one; in prospect. **a.** Open to ME. **b.** Awaiting 1807. **7.** Preceding in order of time OE. **8.** Earlier than (a date or event) ME. **9.** Previous to the expiration of a future space of time 1865. **10.** In precedence of; in advance of ME. **11.** In preference to ME. **12.** In comparison with 1711.

1. Theyr gyde. . to go b. them 1526. The leaf b. the wind KINGSLEY. Our enemies shall falle b. us 2 *Hen. VI*, IV. ii. 37. **2.** When many meats are set b. me HOOKER. *B. the mast*: used of common sailors who are berthed in the forecastle in front of the foremast. **3.** The proceedings b. the police court 1883. **4.** Though this be not theft b. the world 1583. **5.** *B. God!* = As God knows. **b.** The problem b. us BUCKLE. **6. a.** The World was all b. them, Where to choose, Their place of rest MILT. *P.L.* XII. 646. **7.** Brave men were living b.

Agamemnon BYRON. 9. Some day b. long TROLLOPE. 11. They would die b. yielding 1887. 12. So shows..My spirit b. Thee TENNYSON.

C. *Conj.* or *conjunctive adv.* **1.** Of time: Previous to the time when ME. **2.** Rather than 1596.

D. 1. quasi-*adj.* = Anterior ME. **2.** quasi-*sb.* 1850.

1. Punisht for b. breech of the King's Lawes SHAKS.

Beforehand (bĭfōᵊ·ɹhænd), *adv.* (*a.*) ME. [Cf. AFr. *avant main*, OFr. *avant la main* (*les mains*).] **1.** In advance; *spec.* in reference to payment in advance. † **2.** Before this or that –1520. † **3.** *adj.* Prepared (*rare*) 1704.

1. To pay a yeere or two yeeres rent before hande 1583. *To be b. with*: to anticipate; to forestall in action. *To be b. with the world*: to have money in hand for future contingencies (*arch.*).

Befo·resaid, *ppl. a.* ME. Now *arch.* = AFORESAID.

Befo·retime, *adv.* ME. [Cf. later *aforetime* (XVI).] In former time. Hence † **Beforetimes** *adv.*

Befo·rtune, *v. rare.* 1591. [BE- 6 + FORTUNE *sb.*] *intr.* To befall.

As much, I wish all good b. you *Two Gent.* IV. iii. 41.

Befoul (bĭfau·l), *v.* ME. [BE- 5.] To make foul, cover with filth.

Befriend (bĭ,fre·nd), *v.* 1559. [BE- 6.] To act as a friend to, to help, favour; to further.

Befringe (bĭ,fri·ndʒ), *v.* 1611. [BE- 1.] To furnish or adorn with (or as with) a fringe. Befringed with gold FULLER.

Befur (bĭfɒ·ɹ), *v.* 1859. [BE- 2, 6 + FUR *v.*, *sb.*] To cover with furs.

Beg (beg), *v.* [ME. *begge*, contemp. w. *beggare*, prob. :– OE. *bedecian*, deriv. (cf. Goth. *bidagwa* beggar) of Gmc. **beð-*, base of BID; for the same development of *c* after *d* cf. **Badecan tūn*, *Badechitone*, Bagington, **Badecan healh*, *Badegenhall*, Bagnall.] **1.** *trans.* To ask (bread, money, etc.) in alms; *intr.* to ask alms; *esp.* to live by asking alms ME. **2.** To ask as a favour: *intr.* to ask humbly or supplicatingly, entreat ME. **3.** In *B. pardon, excuse, leave*, etc.: often a courteous mode of asking what is expected, or even of taking as a matter of course 1600. **4.** To take for granted without warrant; *esp.* in *To b. the question* 1581.

1. Yet haue I not seene the righteous forsaken, nor his seede begging bread *Ps.* 37:25. They which begge must not choose 1617. 2. I have three favours to b. of you H. WALPOLE. I must..begge for pardon 1649. He begg'd of me to steale 't *Oth.* V. ii. 229. 3. *Mod.* In reply to your letter I b. leave to say..; hence *ellipt.* I beg to say...

Phrases. † *To beg a person*: to petition the Court of Wards for the custody of a minor, an heiress, or an idiot, as feudal superior, etc.; hence also *fig. To b.* (any one) *for a fool*: to set him down as a fool. *To b. off* (trans. and intr. for refl.): to obtain by entreaty the release of (any one) from a penalty, etc. Hence **Be·ggable** *a.* capable of being begged.

† **Beg,** *sb.* 1686. [Osmanli *beg* = BEY; cf. BEGUM.] A bey. *Beg beg* = BEGLERBEG.

Begad (bigæ·d), *int. colloq.* 1742. [Minced form of *by God*; cf. †*agad*, EGAD, GAD *sb.*⁴, BEDAD.] So † **Begar** (bigā·ɹ) SHAKS.

Begem (bĭ,dʒe·m), *v.* 1800. [BE- 6.] To set about or stud with gems.

Beget (bĭge·t), *v.* Pa. t. **bego·t,** *arch.* **bega·t.** Pa. pple. **bego·tten.** [First in north. texts, with *g* repl. *ġ*, *ȝ* of the native forms OE. *beġietan*, ME. *biȝete*, corresp. to OS. *bigetan* seize, OHG. *bigeȥȥan* receive = Goth. *bigetan* find; see BE- 1, GET (XIII, 'procreate', after ON. *geta*).] † **1.** To acquire (usu. by effort) –1602. **2.** To procreate, generate; occas. said of both parents ME. † **b.** = GET (with child) –1611. **3.** *Theol.* Applied to the relationship of the Father to the Son in the Trinity ME. **4.** *fig.* and *transf.* To call into being 1581.

1. *Haml.* III. ii. 8. 2. He that begetteth a foole, doth it to his sorrow *Prov.* 17:21. 4. His eye begets occasion for his wit *L.L.L.* II. i. 69. Hence **Bege·ttal** (*rare*). **Bege·tter,** a procreator; also *fig.*

† **Bege·t,** *sb.* ME. only. [f. BEGET *v.*] **1.** The action of acquiring; *concr.* gain; spoils of war. **2.** Procreation; *concr.* progeny.

Beggar (be·gəɹ), *sb.* [ME. *begger*, *beggar*, f. BEG *v.* + -ER¹. The sp. *-ar* is a survival of the ME. var. Cf. LIAR.] **1.** One who asks alms, *esp.* habitually. **2.** *transf.* One in needy circumstances ME. † **3.** One who begs a favour; a suppliant. (The regular form of this and 4 would be *begger*.) –1601. † **4.** One who begs the question –1694. **5.** = BEGHARD ME. **6.** = Mean or low fellow ME. Also used playfully (cf. *rogue*, etc.) 1833.

1. A certaine begger named Lazarus *Luke* 16:20. *Sturdy b.*: an able-bodied man begging without cause, and often with violence. 6. A good-hearted little b. HUGHES.

Comb.: † **beggar's bush,** a bush under which a b. finds shelter (name of a tree near Huntingdon, formerly a rendezvous for beggars), *fig.* beggary; **beggar's-lice,** the plant called Clivers, also (in U.S.) certain boraginaceous plants, whose fruit or seeds stick to the clothes; **b.-tick** (in U.S.), the plant *Bidens frondosa*; **b.-weed,** a name of several plants, so called because they indicate poverty of soil, or beggar the land.

Hence **Be·ggardom,** mendicancy; mendicants as a body. **Be·ggarhood,** the condition of a b.; people in this condition. **Be·ggarism,** practice characteristic of a b.; extreme poverty.

Beggar (be·gəɹ), *v.* 1528. [f. prec. sb.] **1.** To make a beggar of; to impoverish. Also *fig.* **2.** To exhaust the resources of, outdo 1606.

1. [Conscience] beggars any man that keepes it *Rich. III*, I. iv. 145. 2. Phr. *To b. description, compare*, etc. *Comb.* **Beggar-my-neighbour:** a game at cards. Hence **Be·ggarer.**

Beggarly (be·gəɹli), *a.* 1526. [f. BEGGAR + -LY¹.] **1.** In the condition of, or befitting a beggar; indigent, mean 1545. **2.** *fig.* Destitute of meaning or value 1526. **3.** Sordid 1577.

1. Ragged, old, and beggerly *Tam. Shr.* IV. i. 140. 2. B. Arguments CLARENDON. 3. Beggerly thankes *A.Y.L.* II. v. 29. Hence **Be·ggarliness.** So **Be·ggarly** *adv.* indigently; suppliantly.

Beggary (be·gəri). ME. [f. BEGGAR *sb.* + -Y³.] **1.** The condition of a beggar; extreme poverty. Also *fig.* † **2.** The action or habit of begging –1764. **3.** *concr.* Beggars as a class; a place where they live 1615. † **4.** Beggarly stuff –1644.

1. Nought But beggery, and poore lookes *Cymb.* V. v. 10. 4. The Jewish b. of old cast Rudiments MILT.

† **Be·gged, -eth.** [f. BEG *v.* Orig. *beggeth*, after 'a hunteth', from OE. *huntað* sb. 'hunting' Skeat.] In phr. *To go a-begged*: to go a-begging. CHAUCER.

Begging (be·giŋ), *vbl. sb.* ME. [f. BEG *v.* + -ING¹.] **1.** The action or habit of asking earnestly; *spec.* of asking alms. **2.** *To go* (or *have been*) *a begging*: **a.** to go about begging 1535; **b.** *fig.* (said of offices, etc., in need of men to fill them; things finding no purchaser; and the like.) 1593.

2. Benefices went a begging HOWSON.

Beghard (be·gāɹd). [– med.L. *Beghardus*, f. OFr. *Bégard*, *-art*, MDu. *Beggaert*, MHG. *Beghart*, f. stem of *Beguina*, etc.; see BEGUINE, -ARD.] A member of one of the lay brotherhoods which arose in the Low Countries in the 13th c., in imitation of the female BEGUINES. Many were simply idle mendicants: see BEGGAR sb. 5.

Be-gi·ft, *v.* ME. [BE- 6.] † **1.** To entrust. **2.** To present with gifts 1590.

Begi·ld, *v.* 1594. [BE- 1.] To cover with, or as with, gold.

Begin (bĭgi·n), *v.* Pa. t. **began** (bĭgæ·n), pa. pple. **begun** (bĭgɒ·n). [OE. *beġinnan* = OFris *biginna*, OS., OHG. *biginnan* (Du., G. *beginnen*), WGmc. f. *bi-* BE- + Gmc. **ginnan*, in comps. meaning 'begin', of unkn. origin. An alternative pa. t. *begun* was current till early 19th c.] **1.** *intr.* To set oneself *to do* something, commence or start OE.; also *absol.* and with preps., as *at, by, from, with* ME. **b.** To start speaking 1563 (esp. *poet.*). **c.** *To b. on, upon*: to set to work upon, start to deal with 1808. **2.** *trans.* To set about doing, start upon OE. **3.** To start (a thing) on its course, bring into being or action, be the first to do or practise ME. **4.** *intr.* To enter upon its career, come into existence, arise, start ME.

1. Then began men to call vpon the Name of the Lord *Gen.* 4:26. You alwaies end ere you b. *Two Gent.* II. iv. 32. *To b. with*, († *withal*), advb. phr.: at the outset. 2. Proud Nimrod first the savage chace began POPE. 3. And than a newe [world] shal beginne GOWER. Phr. *To b. the world*: to start in life.

Beginner (bĭgi·nəɹ). ME. [f. prec. vb. + -ER¹.] **1.** One who begins; an originator, founder. **2.** *spec.* One beginning to learn; a tyro 1470.

2. A band of raw beginners BYRON.

Beginning (bĭgi·niŋ), *vbl. sb.* ME. [f. as prec. + -ING¹.] **1.** The action or process of entering upon existence or upon action, or of bringing into existence; commencing, origination. **2.** The point of time at which anything begins; *absol.* the time when the universe began to be ME. **3.** Origin, source, fount ME. **4.** The first part ME. **5.** The rudimentary stage; the earliest proceedings. Often in *pl.* ME.

1. A line hath his b. from a point 1570. 2. In the bigynnyng God made of nouȝt heuene and erthe WYCLIF *Gen.* 1:1. 4. Who hast safely brought us to the b. of this day *Bk. Com. Pr.* 5. Great fortunes acquired from small beginnings A. SMITH. Hence **Begi·nningless** *a.* uncreate.

Begird (bĭgɜ̄·ɹd), *v.* Pa. t. and pple. **begirt.** [OE. *begyrdan*, f. *bi-* BE- 1 + *gyrdan* GIRD *v.*¹] **1.** To gird about or round. Also *fig.* **2.** To encompass *with*. Also *fig.* OE. † **3.** *spec.* To besiege –1791.

Begirdle (bĭgɜ̄·ɹd'l), *v.* 1837. [BE- 1.] To encompass like a girdle.

Begirt (bĭgɜ̄·ɹt), *v.* 1608. [f. BE- 1 + GIRT *v.*] To surround, enclose.

‖ **Beglerbeg** (be·gləɹbeg). 1594. [– Turk., 'bey of beys'; cf. BEG (of which *begler* is the pl.).] The governor of a province of the Ottoman Empire, in rank next to the grand vizier.

Begloom (bĭ,glū·m), *v.* 1799. [BE- 5 + GLOOM *sb.*¹] To render gloomy.

Begnaw (bĭnǭ·), *v.* Pa. pple. **begnawn.** [OE. *begnagan*, f. BE- 1 + *gnagan* GNAW.] To gnaw at; to corrode; to nibble.

Bego·, *v. Obs.* exc. in *pa. pple.* **begone.** [OE. *begān*, OS. *bigangan*, OHG. *bigān*, Goth. *bigaggan*; see BE-¹, GO.] † **1.** To go about, inhabit; to cultivate –ME. † **2.** To go about hostilely; to beset, overrun –1602. † **3.** To dress –1513. **4.** To beset as an environment. Now only in *woe-begone*, and the like. (Orig. 'him was wo begone', i.e. to him woe had closed round.) ME.

† **Bego·d,** *v. rare.* 1576. [BE- 6.] To make a god of –1716.

Begone (bĭgǫ·n), *ppl. a.*; see BEGO 4.

Begone (bĭgǫ·n), *v. arch.* ME. [imper. *be gone* treated as one word, like BEWARE.] Go away, depart, take yourself off. Later established as one word and sometimes const. as an inf. (cf. *beware*).

Angrily ordered to b. CARLYLE.

Begonia (bĭgōᵘ·niă). 1751. [Named by Charles Plumier (d. 1706), French botanist, after Michel Begon (d. 1710), French patron of botany; see -IA¹.] A genus of plants, having flowers without petals, but with coloured perianths, and often richly-coloured foliage, cultivated as ornamental plants.

Begorra (bĭgǫ·ră), *int.* 1839. Ir. var. of BEGAD, BEGAR.

Begotten (bĭgǫ·t'n), *ppl. a.* ME. [pa. pple. of BEGET *v.*] † **1.** Gotten –1523. **2.** Procreated. (Usu. with *only-*, *first-*.) Also *absol.* ME.

Begrace (bĭ,grē̆·s), *v.* 1530. [BE- 5.] To address as 'your grace'.

† **Begra·ve,** *v.* [OE. *bi-*, *begrafan*, corresp. to OHG. *bigraban* (G. *begraben*) bury, Goth. *bigraban* dig (a ditch) round; f. BE- 1 + *grafan* dig, GRAVE *v.*¹] **1.** To bury –1528. **2.** To engrave ME.

Begrease, begrim, begroan, etc.; see BE- *pref.*

Begrime (bĭ,grəi·m), *v.* 1553. [f. BE- 2 + GRIME *v.*] To blacken or soil with grime.

My name..is now begrim'd and blacke As my own face *Oth.* III. iii. 387.

† **Begri·pe,** *v.* [OE. *begrīpan*, = OHG. *begrīfan* (G. *begreifen*), f. BE- 2 + *grīpan* seize; see GRIPE *v.*¹] **1.** To catch hold of; to seize and hold fast –1485. **2.** To take in, contain ME.

Begrudge (bĭ,grɒ·dʒ), *v.* [f. BE- 4 + GRUDGE *v.*] To grumble at; *esp.* to envy (one) the possession of; to give reluctantly, to be reluctant.

To begrutch the cost of a school C. MATHER.

Begru·tten, *ppl. a. Sc.* 1805. [f. BE- 4 + *grutten*, pa. pple. of GREET *v.*²] Swollen in face by much weeping.

† **Be·gster.** Also **beggestere.** [f. BEG *v.* + -STER; cf. *trickster.*] A beggar. CHAUCER.

† **Begua·rd,** *v.* 1605. [f. BE- 6 + GUARD *sb.*] To adorn with 'guards' or facings -1640.

Beguile (bǐgəi·l), *v.* ME. [f. BE- 2 + GUILE *v.*; cf. MDu. *begīlen*, AFr. *degiler.*] **1.** To over-reach with guile. Also *absol.* **2.** To deprive *of* by fraud, to cheat out *of* ME. † **3.** To cheat (hopes, etc., or a person in them); to disappoint, to foil -1670. **4.** To win the attention of by wiling means; to charm; to wile on, or into any course 1593. **5.** To divert attention in some pleasant way from; to wile away 1588.

1. To b. this crafty fish WALTON. **2.** Let no man b. you of your reward *Col.* 2:18. **3.** Thou hast beguil'd my hopes *Two Gent.* V. iv. 37. **5.** By sports like these are all their cares beguil'd GOLDSM. Hence **Begui·lement. Begui·ler. Begui·lingly** *adv.*

Beguine (begi·n, be·gin). 1483. [- (O)Fr. *béguine* (MDu., MHG. *begīne*), in med.L. *Beguina*, said to be f. name of Lambert (le) *Bègue* (i.e. the Stammerer), a priest of Liège (XII), founder of the community, but this is disputed.] A name for members of certain lay sisterhoods which began in the Low Countries in the 12th c., who devoted themselves to a religious life, but took no vows, and might go away and marry. They are still represented in the Netherlands. Hence **Be·guinage,** an establishment of, or house for, beguines.

‖ **Begum** (bī·gǫ̆m). 1634. [- Urdu (Pers.) *begam* - E. Turk. *bīgam* princess, fem. of *big* prince, of which the Osmanli form is BEG *sb.*] A Moslem queen, or lady of high rank in Hindustan.

Begun (bǐgʊ·n), *ppl. a.* 1483. [pa. pple. of BEGIN.] That has begun, or has been begun.

Begunk (bǐgʊ·ŋk), *v. Sc.* 1821. [Origin unknown.] To delude, take in. Hence **Begu·nk** *sb.* a befooling trick.

Behalf (bǐ,hā·f). ME. [BIHALVE, orig. a phr., *be healfe*, and subseq. a prep., became a sb., by the mixture of *on his halve* and *bihalve him*, both meaning 'by or on his side', in *on his bihalve*; see HALE I. 2 b.] **1.** *On b. of*: † **a.** (*lit.*) On the side of -1502; (*fig.*) On (one's own) part or side -1538. **b.** On the part of (another). (With the notion of official agency.) ME. † **c.** As concerns. Also, *on this b.*, etc. -1674. **d.** In recent use *on b. of* is often found in the sense of *in b. of* (2 b). 1791. **2.** *In b. of*: † **a.** In the name of -1606. **b.** In the interest of. (With the notion of interposition.) 1598. **c.** *In this* or *that b.*: in respect of this or that; in this or that matter, or aspect (*arch.*). Cf. 1 c. 1458.

1. b. Things which a servant may do on b. of his master BLACKSTONE. **2. a.** And rob in the behalfe of charitie *Tr. & Cr.* V. iii. 22. **b.** Speaking in B. the Trading Interest 1719. **c.** More could be said in that b., but [etc.] 1658.

Beha·ng, *v. Obs.* exc. in *pa. pple.* **Behung.** [OE. *behōn*, f. BE- 1 + *hōn* HANG.] To hang (a thing) about *with*.

† **Beha·p(pen,** *v.* 1450. [f. BE- 2 + HAPPEN.] To befall. With *dat. obj.* -1714.

Behave (bǐ,hē^i·v), *v.* Pa. t. **behaved.** 1440. [f. BE- 2 + HAVE (with the early pronunc. of the stressed form preserved); cf. MHG. *sich behaben* maintain oneself, (now) conduct oneself, behave.] **1.** *refl.* To bear, comport, or conduct oneself; to act: **a.** with *adv.* or phr. (Formerly a dignified expression, but now usually as in b.) **b.** Without qualification: To conduct oneself with propriety. (Now chiefly said of children.) 1691. Also *transf.* of things. † **2.** To handle, conduct, regulate -1607. **3.** *intr.*: in same senses as 1 a. and b. 1719.

1. To b. oneself with gallantry STEELE, with insolence 1715. **b.** B. yourself (*mod.*). **2.** *Timon* III. v. 22. **3.** He behaved like a man of sense MACAULAY. *To b. towards* or *to*: to act in regard *to*. Hence **Beha·ved** *ppl. a.* (usu. with *adv.*, as *well-*, etc.). **Beha·ving** *vbl. sb.* conduct.

Behaviour (bǐ,hē^i·viəɹ), *sb.* 1490. [Early forms *behavour, behaver*, later *-your, -iour*, on the anal. of *haver, havour, haviour*, vars. of *aver* possession infl. by *have*; see AVER *sb.*², HAVIOUR, †HAVOUR. Cf. *demeanour.*] **1.** Manner of conducting oneself; bearing, manners. † **b.** 'Person'. *John* I. i. 3. **c.** *absol.* Good manners 1591. **2.** Conduct; course of action *towards* or *to* others 1515. † **3.** Handling, disposition *of* (anything); bearing (*of* body) -1589. **4.** *transf.* Of things 1674.

1. In clennes of lyfe and in a gentyll behauer BALE. **c.** Strong aversion to b. DE FOE. **2.** *To be* (or *stand*) *on* or *upon one's b.*, or *one's good b.*: to be placed on a trial of conduct or deportment; hence, to behave one's best. **4.** The b. of the vessel during her maiden voyage 1882. Hence † **Beha·vioured** *a.* mannered.

Behaviourism (bǐhē^i·vyəriz'm). *Psychol.* 1913. [f. prec. sb. + -ISM.] A theory and method of psychological investigation based on the objective study of behaviour. Hence **Beha·viourist,** one who practises this method; **-i·stic** *a.*

Behead (bǐ,he·d), *v.* [OE. *behēafdian*, f. BE- 3 (priv.) + *hēafod* HEAD.] *trans.* To deprive of the head or top part. Also *fig.*

To bee byhedded at Pountfreit MORE. Hence **Behea·dal.**

Behemoth (bǐhī·mǫþ, -ǭþ). ME. [- Heb. *b^ehēmôṯ* pl. (of intensity, 'great or monstrous beast') of *b^ehēmāh* beast, held to be - Egyptian *p-ehe-mau* water-ox. Cf. Russ. *begemót* hippopotamus.] An animal: prob. the hippopotamus; also a general term for one of the largest and strongest animals. Cf. LEVIATHAN.

Lo! bemoth that I made with thee WYCLIF *Job* 40:15. B. biggest born of Earth MILT. *P.L.* VII. 471.

Behest (bǐ,he·st), *sb.* [OE. *behǣs* + parasitic *t* :- Gmc. *bixaissi-, abstr. sb. f. *bixaitan, f. *bi- BE- + *xaitan bid, call; see HIGHT *v.*¹, HEST.] † **1.** A vow, promise -1634. **2.** A command, injunction ME.

1. Breken his biheste CHAUCER. **2.** Us he [God] sends upon his high behests MILT. *P.L.* VIII. 238. Hence † **Behe·st** *v.* to vow, promise.

† **Behi·ght,** *v.* [OE. *bi-, behātan* = OHG. *biheizzan*, f. *bi-* BE- + *hātan*, see HIGHT *v.*¹. The pa. t. *behight* (*behite*) was ult. taken as present, with pa. t. and pple. *behighted.*] **I. 1.** To vow, promise -1621. **2.** To hold out hope of (life, etc.) -1571. **3.** To assure (one) of the truth of a statement. (Cf. mod. *I promise you.*) -1513.

1. The trayteresse..That al behoteth, and nothing halt CHAUCER. **3.** Litel whil it last, I you biheete CHAUCER.

II. Improper uses by the archaists. **1.** *trans.* To grant, deliver. SPENSER. **2.** To bid, ordain. SPENSER. **3.** To call, to name -1652. **4.** To bespeak 1615. Hence † **Behi·ght** *sb.* a promise.

Behind (bǐhəi·nd), *adv., prep.* (*sb.*) [OE. *bi-, behindan* = OS. *bihindan*, lit. at a place in the rear; f. *bi* BY + *hindan*. See HIND *a.* The use as prep. originated in an OE. dat. of reference, *behindan him* 'in the rear *as to him*'.] **A.** *adv.* **1.** In a place whence the others have gone; *fig.* in the position, condition, or state which a person or thing has left ME. **b.** In the past 1526. **2.** In the rear of anything moving; following ME. **3.** *fig.* (from 1.) In reserve; still to come ME. **4.** *fig.* (from 2.) **a.** Of progress; *hence* of rank, order, etc. ME. **b.** *esp.* In arrear ME. **5.** At the back; in the rear ME. Also *fig.* **6.** Backwards ME. **7.** To the back, into the rear ME.

1. We shall abyde bihynde ME. To leave this world behinde DONNE. **b.** As in the winters left b. TENNYSON. **2.** *To come b.*: to follow. *To fall b.*: to fall into the rear. **3.** But stronger evidence is b. MACAULAY. **4. a.** B. with no one in kind speeches MISS BURNEY. **b.** B. with my landlord 1614. **6.** Run, Nor look b. 1692. **7.** Go b. and look 1887.

B. *prep.* **1.** In a place, or (*fig.*) condition, state, or time left by (one) ME. **2.** In the rear of (one moving); after ME. **b.** Inferior to, in progress, order, etc. 1526. **3.** Later than (the set time) 1600. **4.** In the space lying to the rear of, on the back side of ME. Also *fig.* **5.** On the farther side of; beyond ME.; *fig.* hidden by 1866. **6.** Backward from (oneself) ME. **7.** To the back side of ME. Also *fig.*

1. He left b. him myself and a sister *Twel. N.* II. i. 20. **2. b.** B. her years LAMB. **4.** *B. fortifications*, etc.: inside of, so as to be defended by them. **5.** B. the Mountain DRYDEN. *B. the scenes*: in the rear of the scenery of a theatre; *hence*, out of sight, in private. **7.** Get thee b. mee, Satan *Matt.* 26:23. *To go b.*: to press an inquiry into what is not avowed. Phr. *B.* (*one's*) *back*: emphatic for *b.* (*one*) in all senses, *esp.* 'in one's absence'.

C. as *sb.* (*colloq.* and *vulgar*): The back side (of the person or of a garment); the posteriors.

Behindhand (bǐhəi·nd,hænd), *adv.* (and *a.*) 1530. [f. BEHIND *prep.* + HAND, after *beforehand.*] **1.** In arrears financially, in debt. (Const. *with.*) **2.** Behind time, late, too late; behind the times 1549. **3.** In a state of backwardness (*in*); ill prepared (*with*) 1542. **4.** *attrib.* Backward, tardy. *Wint. T.* V. i. 151.

1. Something b. with the world SWIFT. **3.** B. in politeness STERNE.

† **Behi·ther,** *adv.* and *prep.* 1521. [See BE-, and cf. *behind*, etc. (A word worth reviving.)] **A.** *prep.* **1.** On this side of. (L. *cis, citra.*) -1711. **2.** Short of, save -1671. **B.** *adv.* On the nearer side 1650.

1. A..seat 2 miles b. Cliefden EVELYN.

Behold (bǐhō^u·ld), *v.* [OE. *bihaldan* = OFris. *bihalda*, OS. *bihaldan*, (Du. *behouden*), OHG. *bihaltan* (G. *behalten*), f. BE- 2 + *haldan* HOLD. The sense of watching is Eng. only.] † **1.** *trans.* To hold by, retain -1525. † **2.** *intr.* To hold on *by*, belong *to*; *trans.* to concern -ME. † **3.** To regard (with the mind), consider; *intr.* to have regard *unto, to* -ME. **4. a.** To hold in view, to watch (*arch.*) OE. Hence **b.** To see: the current sense ME. † **5.** *intr.* To look -1795. † **6.** *intr.* To look or face; *trans.* to face -1677. † **7.** To look upon *as* -1662.

4. a. From far B. the field POPE. **b.** I neuer yet beheld that speciall face, Which I could fancie *Tam. Shr.* II. i. 11.

Beho·ld, *int.* 1535. Imper. of prec. vb.; = Lo!

B., I will send my messenger *Mal.* 3:1.

Beholden (bǐhō^u·ld'n), *ppl. a.* ME. [orig. pa. pple. of BEHOLD *v.*] **1.** Attached or obliged (*to* a person). † **2.** In duty bound (*to do* something) -1502.

1. The more b. is the lorde unto hym CAXTON. † **Beholdenness,** a mistake for *Beholdingness*, q.v.

Beholder (bǐhō^u·ldəɹ). ME. [f. BEHOLD *v.* + -ER¹.] One who beholds, a watcher, spectator.

Beholding (bǐhō^u·ldiŋ), *vbl. sb.* ME. [f. as prec. + -ING²; in sense 1, alt. f. BEHOLDEN by suffix-substitution to express active meaning.] **1.** The action of looking at; sight; † consideration. **2.** The thing beheld (*arch.*) ME. ¶ Johnson's sense 'Obligation' is a blunder.

Beho·lding, *ppl. a.* 1483. [f. as prec. + -ING².] † **1.** Under obligation. (Orig. an error for BEHOLDEN.) In late use: Dependent. -1719. **2.** Gazing 1593. Hence † **Beho·ldingness,** obligation; dependence.

Behoof (bǐhū·f). [OE. *behōf*, in phr. *tō.. behōfe* for (one's) use or needs (cf. *behōflić* useful, necessary), = OFris. *bihōf*, (M)Du. *behoef*, MHG. *behuof* (G. *behuf*), WGmc. f. *bi- BE- + *xōf- var. of the base of *xafjan HEAVE.] **1.** Use, benefit. Chiefly in *to, for, on* (*the*) *b. of.* (*In, on b. of*, are due to confusion with *behalf.*) *pl.* rare. ME. † **2.** Duty (*rare*) 1594. † **3.** ? A douceur SPENSER.

1. To the use and b. of A and his heirs BLACKSTONE.

Behove, behoove (bǐhō^u·v, -hū·v), *v.* [OE. *behōfian* = OFris. *bihōvia*, MLG. *behōven*, MDu. *behoeven*, f. prec.] † **1.** *trans.* To have use for or need of -1670. **2.** † To be physically of use or needful *to*; (only in 3 *pers.*) -1667; to be incumbent ME.; to befit, be due *to*; to belong 1470. **3.** quasi-*impers.* (the subject being a clause). Now ordinarily with *it* (*arch.*). ME. **4.** As a personal verb: = must needs, ought, have. (Due to confusion of acc. and nom. Now only *Sc.*) ME.

3. It behooves the more weakly..to be more cautious 1756. It behoveth, that the son of man must die TINDALE. Hence † **Beho·vable** *a.* useful, incumbent. **Beho·veful, -hoo·veful** *a.* (*arch.*) useful; expedient; needful. † **Beho·vefully** *adv.* † **Beho·vely** *a.* of use.

Beige (bē^iʒ). 1858. [- Fr. *beige* (OFr. *bege*), of unkn. origin.] A fine woollen dress-material, originally left in its natural colour but now dyed. **b.** A yellowish-grey shade, like that of unbleached wool. Also *adj.* and *Comb.*

Beild, var. of BIELD *sb.* and *v.*

Bein (bīn), *a.* and *adv.* Now *dial.* ME. [ME. *bene*, of unkn. origin. The sp. *bein, bien*, are mod. Sc. for *been*, the regular repr. of ME. *bene.*] **A.** *adj.* † **1.** Pleasant, kindly; nice. (L. *amœnus, almus, benignus.*) -1513. **2.**

Comfortable 1533. **3.** Well-to-do 1548. **B.** *adv.* Pleasantly ME.

Being (bī·iŋ), *vbl. sb.* ME. [f. BE + -ING[1].] **1.** Existence, material or immaterial; life 1596. **2.** Existence in some relation of place or condition 1526. † **b.** Standing (in the world) –1818. † **c.** Livelihood –1731. **3.** Substance, constitution, nature ME.; essence 1530. **4.** *gen.* That which exists or is conceived as existing 1628; (with qualifications) God 1600; a human being 1751.

1. The house had no corporate b. FREEMAN. A legacy to a person in b. POWELL. **2.** During his b. a Bishop BURNET. **3.** Our very b. is none of ours 1659. **4.** Beings that had no other existence but in their own minds LOCKE. The Supreme B. SCRIVENER. This mean, incorrigible b. MAR. EDGEWORTH. Hence **Be·ingless** *a.* non-existent.

Being (bī·iŋ), *ppl. a.* 1458. [f. BE + -ING[2].] **1.** Existing, present; *esp.* in *The time b.* **2.** *absol.* = It being the case that, seeing 1528.

† **Bei·sance.** 1556. Aphet. f. OBEISANCE, ABAISANCE –1650.

† **Beja·de,** *v.* 1620. [BE- 2.] To tire out –1641.

Bejan (bī·dʒən). *Sc.* 1642. [– Fr. *béjaune*, for *bec jaune* 'yellow-beak', i.e. fledgeling.] A 'yellow beak' or freshman: a term adopted from the University of Paris.

† **Beja·pe,** *v.* ME. [f. BE- 2 + JAPE *v.*] To play a trick on; to befool –1500.

Beje·suit. 1644. [f. BE- 5 + JESUIT.] To work upon by, or subject to, Jesuits.

Bejewel (bĭ,dʒ[i]ū·ĕl), *v.* 1557. [BE- 6.] To deck with or as with jewels; to spangle.

Beknave (bĭnē[i]·v), *v.* 1525. [BE- 5.] To call 'knave'.

† **Beknow·,** *v.* ME. [BE- 2.] To recognize –1560; to confess –1580.

Phr. *To be beknown*: to be aware *of*; *hence*, to confess. Hence **Beknow·n** *ppl. a.* (*arch.*) known.

‖ **Bel,** *a.* ME. [ME. *bele* – OFr. *bel* (m.), *bele* (fem.) :– L. *bellus, bella*; see BEAU. Naturalized in ME., but after 1600 consciously French.] † Fair, fine, beautiful –1678. Used also as a formative prefix in *belsire, belfader*, etc. Cf. *good* in *goodsire*, etc., and mod.F. *bonpapa*, etc.

Belabour (bĭlē[i]·bəɹ), *v.* 1596. [BE- 4.] † **1.** To labour at; to ply –1686. **2.** To buffet with all one's might 1600. Also *fig.*

1. To b. the earth with culture BARROW. **2.** The tempest which belaboured him 1600.

† **Bel-accoil, -accoyle.** ME. [– OFr. *bel acoil* fair welcome; see ACCOIL *v.*] Kindly greeting, welcome –1596.

Belace (bĭlē[i]·s), *v.* 1648. [f. BE- 2, 6 + LACE *v.* and *sb.*] **1.** To adorn with lace. † **2.** To beat with stripes –1857.

Bela·ce, *v.* '*Sea Term.* To fasten; as to belace a rope.' Johnson. [a mistake for BELAGE, made first in Bailey's folio, 1730.]

† **Bela·ge,** *v.* 1678. [app. orig. a misprint or misreading of BELAY; cf. BELACE.] *Naut.* To make fast any running rope.

Belam, *v.* 1595. [BE- 2 + LAM *v.*] To thrash.

† **Belamou·r.** 1595. [Fr., f. *bel* BEL + *amour* love.] **1.** A loved one of either sex –1603. **2.** A look of love 1610. **3.** Name of some flower. SPENSER.

† **Be·lamy.** ME. [– OFr. *bel ami* (nom. sing. *amis*) good friend; see BEL.] Fair friend (*esp.* as a form of address) –1689.

† **Bela·p,** *v.* ME. [BE- 1.] To clasp; to surround –1562.

Belate (bĭlē[i]·t), *v.* 1642. [f. BE- 5 + LATE *a.*] To make late, delay.

Belated (bĭlē[i]·tėd), *ppl. a.* 1618. [f. prec. + -ED[1].] **1.** Overtaken by lateness of the night; *hence*, benighted. **2.** Coming or staying too late; behind date 1670.

1. B. shepherd swains 1789. **2.** Who contested this b. account BURKE. Hence † **Bela·tedness.**

Belaud (bĭlǭ·d), *v.* 1849. [BE- 2.] To load with praise.

Belay (bĭlē[i]·), *v.* [OE. *beleċġan* = OFris. *bilega*, Du. *beleggen*, OHG. *bileggen* (G. *belegen*). From XVI *belay* appears as a new formation. The naut., now the only current, sense seems to be modelled on Du. *beleggen* (whence G. *belegen* in the same sense).] † **1.** *trans.* To surround, enclose, etc. (a thing) *with* –1606. † **2.** *spec.* To beset with armed men; to beleaguer –1698; to waylay –1760. **3.** *Naut.* To coil a running rope round a cleat, belaying pin, or kevel, so as to secure it. (The only current sense.) 1549. Also *transf.*

3. Mak fast and b. 1549. *B. there*, stop! (Smyth). Hence **Belaying** *vbl. sb.*; chiefly *attrib.*, as in *belaying-cleat, -pin.*

Belch (beltʃ, belʃ), *v.* [Either shortening of OE. *belċettan, beal-*, or repr. an OE. **belċan*, rel. to *bealcan, bælcan*, repr. in ME. by *balke, belke* (see BALK *v.*[2], BELK *v.*).] **1.** *intr.* To void wind noisily from the stomach, to eructate. (Now *vulgar.*) **2.** To ejaculate; to vent with vehemence (L. *eructare*). In later use confined to the utterance of offensive things, or to furious vociferation. OE. **3.** To emit by belching. Also *fig.* 1561. **4.** To vomit (*lit.* and *fig.*) 1558. **5.** To eject, throw out; *esp.* of volcanoes, and *hence* of cannons, etc. 1580.

2. To b. out blasphemies against God 1612. **3.** Belching the soure crudities of yesterdayes Poperie MILT. **5.** Strombolo. . belched out fire and smoke *a*1733.

Belch, *sb.* 1513. [f. prec. vb.] An eructation. Also *fig.* **b.** *slang.* Poor beer 1706.

Belcher (be·lʃəɹ). 1812. [f. Jim *Belcher* (1781–1811), a pugilist.] Any particoloured handkerchief, *esp.* one with blue ground and white spots, worn round the neck.

Beldam, -dame (be·ldəm). 1440. [An Eng. formation, f. BEL + DAM *sb.*[2], earlier DAME, as in BELFATHER, BELSIRE.] † **1.** A grandmother (or more remote ancestress). Also *fig.* –1863. **2.** An aged woman. (In 16th c. used in addressing nurses.) 1580. **3.** *esp.* A hag; a witch; a virago (of any age) 1586.

1. To show the beldame daughters of her daughter SHAKS. *Lucr.* 953. **3.** That accursed b. whom she caused to work upon me SCOTT.

Beleaguer (bĭlī·gəɹ), *v.* 1589. [– Du. *belegeren*, f. *be-* BE- 1 + *leger* camp; see LEAGER *sb.*[1], *v.*] To surround (a town, etc.) with troops so as to prevent ingress and egress, to invest. Also *transf.*

Antwerpe. . then by him beleaguered 1598. Hence **Belea·guerer. Belea·guerment.**

† **Belea·ve, -eve,** *v.* [OE. *belǣfan*, corresp. to Goth. *bilaibjan* :– Gmc. **bi-* BE- + **laiƀjan*; see LEAVE *v.*[1]] **1.** *trans.* To let or cause to remain behind, to abandon –1627. **2.** *intr.* [taking place of BELIVE: = Ger. *bleiben.*] To remain behind, survive, continue –1480. Hence † **Belea·ving** *vbl. sb.* that which is left.

† **Belee,** *v. rare.* [f. BE- 6 + LEE *sb.*] To place (a ship) so that the wind is cut off from her.

fig. I. . must be be-leed and calm'd *Oth.* I. i. 30.

Belemnite (be·lėmnəit). 1646. [– mod.L. *belemnites* (also used) – Gr. βέλεμνον dart; see -ITE[1] 2 a.] *Palæont.* A fossil common in rocks of the Secondary formation; a straight, smooth, cylindrical object, a few inches long, convexly tapering to a point, formerly known, from its shape and supposed origin, as *thunderbolt, thunderstone*, etc. It is the internal bone of an animal allied to the cuttle-fish. Also, this extinct animal. Hence **Belemni·tic** *a.*

† **Bele·per,** *v.* 1623. [BE- 5.] To afflict with or as with leprosy –1649.

‖ **Bel-esprit** (be·lespri·). 1638. [Fr.] A clever genius, a brilliant wit.

A beauty and a bel esprit MAR. EDGEWORTH.

Beletter (bĭle·təɹ), *v.* 1655. [BE- 6.] † **1.** To serve with letters. **2.** *nonce-wd.* To decorate with letters (e.g. F.R.S., etc.) 1883.

† **Be·lfather.** 1440. [f. BEL + FATHER, after *belsire, beldam(e).*] Grandfather –1483.

Belfry (be·lfri). [ME. *berfrei* – OFr. *berfrei*, later *belfrei, be(l)froi* (mod. *beffroi*), in med.L. *bel-, berfridus*, etc., – Frankish **berȝfriđ-* (= MHG. *ber(c)vrit* siege-tower),]prob. f. **berȝan* protect + **friþuz* peace; see FRITH *sb.*[1]] † **1.** A wooden tower, usually movable, formerly used in besieging fortifications. Prob., at first, a mere shed or pent-house. –1530. **2.** A shed to shelter cattle, carts, produce, etc. 1553. **3.** A bell-tower 1440. **b.** The room of the church tower in which the bells are hung 1549. † **c.** The part of the floor under the tower, where the ringers stand –1659. **4.** *Naut.* An ornamental framing, with a covering, under which the ship's bell is hung 1769.

‖ **Belga** (be·lgă). 1926. [L., fem. of *Belgus* Belgian (sc. *pecunia*).] A Belgian unit of exchange (= five Belgian francs).

† **Belga·rd.** [– It. *bel guardo.*] A loving look. SPENSER.

Belgium (be·ldʒə̆m). 1602. **a.** Latin name of the territory occupied by the Belgæ; **b.** a name for the Netherlands; **c.** title of the new kingdom established by the separation of the provinces watered by the Meuse and Scheldt from the kingdom of the Netherlands. **Belgia** = prec. b. **Belgian** (be·ldʒăn) *a.* of or pertaining to Belgium; as *sb.* † **a.** one of the ancient Belgæ of southern England; † **b.** a Low German; **c.** a native of modern Belgium; **d.** a kind of canary. **Belgic** (be·ldʒik) *a.* of or pertaining to the Netherlands; *sb.* a Low German.

Belial (bī·liăl). ME. [– Heb. *b[e]liyya'al* worthlessness, wickedness, f. *b[e]lī* without + *ya'al* use, profit. In later use treated as a proper name.] The spirit of evil personified; used by Milton as the name of one of the fallen angels. Also *attrib.*

B. came last, then whom a Spirit more lewd Fell not from heaven MILT. *P.L.* I. 490.

Belibel; see BE- 2.

† **Belie** (bĭləi·), *v.*[1] [OE. *bi-, beliċġan*, = OHG. *biligan* (G. *beliegen*), f. *bi-* BE- 1 + *liċġan* LIE *v.*[1]] **1.** To lie around, encompass –1627; *spec.* to beleaguer –ME. **2.** To lie near; to pertain or belong *to* –1522.

Belie (bĭləi·), *v.*[2] [OE. *beleogan* = OFris. *biliuga*, OHG. *biliugan* (G. *belügen*); see BE- 4, LIE *v.*[2]] Always *trans.* † **1.** To deceive by lying. **2.** To tell lies about; *esp.* to calumniate by lies ME. † **3.** To allege falsely –1659. **4.** To misrepresent 1601; † to disguise –1810. † **5.** To contradict as a lie or a liar –1649. **6.** To be false or faithless to 1698. **7.** To show to be false; to falsify (expectations, etc.) 1685. † **8.** ? To fill with lies. *Cymb.* III. iv. 38.

2. To b. the subjects of the King HUME. **3.** To belye divine Authority MILT. **4.** A declar'd Papist, If his own letter to the Pope belye him not MILT. **6.** He grossly belied his faith FREEMAN. Hence **Beli·er.**

Belief (bĭlī·f). [Early ME. *bileafe*, repl. OE. *ġelēafa* (see BELIEVE). The loss of the final syll. resulted in the unvoicing of the final consonant.] **1.** The mental action, condition, or habit, of trusting to or confiding in a person or thing; trust, confidence, faith. (*Faith*, orig. = fidelity, fealty, used in 14th c. to translate L. *fides*, has ultimately superseded 'belief' in this sense.) **b.** *absol.* Trust in God; the virtue of faith (*arch.*) ME. **2.** Mental assent to or acceptance of a proposition, statement, or fact, as true, on the ground of authority or evidence; the mental condition involved in this assent 1533. **3.** The thing believed; in early use, *esp.* a religion. Now often = opinion, persuasion. ME. **b.** Intuition, natural judgement 1838. **4.** A creed. *The B.*: the Apostles' Creed (*arch.*) ME.

1. A stedfast byleue of God FISHER. **b.** The war of B. against Unbelief CARLYLE. **2.** My only defence shal be beleefe of nothing SIDNEY. We talked of b. in ghosts BOSWELL. Statements unworthy of b. (*mod.*). Phr. *B. in* (a thing): persuasion of its existence. **3.** It is my b. that. . 1714. Hence † **Belie·fful** *a.*

Believable (bĭlī·văb'l), *a.* ME. [f. BELIEVE + -ABLE.] Capable of being believed. Hence **Belie:vabi·lity. Belie·vableness.**

Believe (bĭlī·v), *v.* [Late OE. *belȳfan, belēfan*, repl., by prefix-substitution, earlier *ġelēfan* (WS. *ġeliefan*) = OFris. *gĕleva*, OS. *gilōbian* (Du. *gelooven*), OHG. *gilouben* (G. *glauben*), Goth. *galaubjan* :– Gmc. **ȝalaubjan* hold dear, cherish, trust in, f. **ȝa-* Y- + **laub-* dear, see LIEF. The hist. form is *beleeve*. *Believe* is prob. after *relieve.*] **I.** *intr.* **1.** To have confidence or faith *in*, and consequently to rely upon. Const. *in*, and (in theol. lang.) *on*. Also *absol.* † **2.** To give credence *to*. Repl. by II. 1, 2. –1647. **3.** *ellipt.* To believe *in* (a person or thing), i.e. in its existence or occurrence 1716.

1. I Beleue in God the father almightie *Bk. Com. Pr.* To b. in human nature MOZLEY, universal suffrage 1888. *absol.* Be not afraid, onely beleeue *Mark* 5:36. **3.** A strong disposition to b. in miracles 1716.

II. *trans.* **1.** To give credence to (a person in making statements, etc.). Obj. orig. *dat.* ME.

2. To give credence to (a statement) ME. 3. With cl. or inf. phrase: To hold it as true *that* . . ., to think ME. † 4. To hold as true the existence of. (Now expressed by I. 3.) –1732.

1. A man. .who deserves to be believed CLARENDON. 2. Beleeving lies Against his Maker MILT. *P.L.* X. 42. 3. Our Conqu'ror whom I now Of force b. Almighty MILT. *P.L.* I. 144. 4. To b. a God SWIFT. Hence **Belie·ving** *vbl. sb.* the having faith; confidence; the acceptance of a statement as true; *ppl. a.* that believes, or has faith. **Belie·vingly** *adv.*

Believer (bĭlī·vəɹ). 1549. [f. prec. + -ER[1].] One who believes. **a.** One who has faith in the doctrines of religion; *esp.* a Christian. **b.** *gen.* One who believes *in* (or *of*) anything 1600.

Thou diddest open the kyngdome of heauen to all beleuers *Bk. Com. Pr.* A b. in the rights and power of the crown GREEN.

Beli·ght, *v.* Now *dial.* ME. [f. BE- 2 + LIGHT *v.*[2]] To light up.

Belike (bĭləi·k). 1533. [orig. *by like* (varying w. *of like*), i.e. BY, LIKE *a.* used as sb. 'probability, likelihood', prob. after the earlier *by* or *of liklyhode* XV.] **A.** *adv.* To appearance, probably; possibly. var. † **Beli·kely.** † **B.** *adj.* Like, likely (*to do* something) –1805.

† **Beli·me,** *v.* 1555. [f. BE- 6 + LIME *sb.*[1]] To cover, or entangle, as with bird-lime –1674.

Belittle (bĭli·t'l), *v.* 1796. [orig. Amer., f. BE- 5 + LITTLE *a.*] **1.** To diminish in size. **2.** To dwarf 1850. **3.** To depreciate 1862.

3. The *Times* in 1809 belittled the victory of Talavera 1881. Hence **Beli·ttlement.**

† **Beli·ve, bilive, blive,** *v.* [OE. *belīfan* = OS. *bilīban*, OHG. *bilīban* (G. *bleiben*), Goth. *bileiban*, of which *belǣfan* (see BELEAVE) is the factitive form, f. Gmc. **bi-* BE- + **līban* remain.] *intr.* To remain –1483.

Belive (bĭləi·v), *adv.* [ME. *bi life*, i.e. *bi* BY + *life, live* dat. sing. of *lif* LIFE lit. 'with life'; cf. QUICK, and mod. *look alive.*] **1.** With speed, eagerly. (Still *Sc.*) ME. † **2.** At once –1563. Hence **3.** Soon; anon. (Still *Sc.*) 1616.

† **Belk,** *v.* [dial. f. BELCH esp. in senses to boil, to throb; see also BALK *v.*[2]] To throb.

Bell (bel), *sb.*[1] [OE. *belle* = MLG., MDu. *belle* (Du. *bel*); a word of the LDu. area, perh. rel. to BELL *v.*[4]] **1.** A hollow body of cast metal, usu. of the form of an inverted deep cup with a recurving brim, which rings, by the vibration of its whole circumference, when struck by a clapper, or hammer suspended within. **2.** *spec.* A bell rung to tell the hours; the bell of a clock ME. **b.** *Naut.* The bell which is struck on shipboard, every half-hour, to indicate the number of half-hours of the watch which have passed; a period of half-an-hour thus indicated 1836. **3.** *transf.* Applied to any object or part shaped like a bell; hence BLUE-B., HAREBELL, etc. 1610. **4.** *Archit.* The naked vase or corbeille of the Corinthian or Composite capitals 1848. **5.** *Mus.* (usu. in *pl.*) An instrument consisting of a number of long metal bars or tubes of various lengths, which when struck with a hammer give out sounds resembling those of different-sized bells. = CARILLON 3.

Phrases. *To bear the b.*: to take the first place (cf. BELL-WETHER). *To bear* or *carry away the b.*: to carry off the prize (perh. a golden or silver bell given as a prize in races, etc.). The two phrases have been confused. *By b. and book, book and b.* (*i.e.* those used in the service of the mass): a mediæval oath. *To curse by b., book, and candle*: referring to a form of excommunication, which ended 'Doe to the book, quench the candle, ring the b.!' Also used as a summary of the terrors of excommunication; and joc. of the accessories of a religious ceremony. For *b. the cat* see BELL *v.*[5] *As sound as a b.*: see SOUND *a.*

Comb., etc.: **b.-animalcules, -animals,** the *Vorticellidæ*, infusoria having a b.-shaped body on a long flexible stalk; **-binder,** the large Wild Convolvulus or Bindweed; **-boat,** one with a b. which rings as the vessel is moved by the waves, and thus gives warning; so **-buoy; -crank,** a kind of lever for communicating motion from one bell-wire to another lying at right angles to it; also *attrib.*; **-founder,** a caster or maker of bells; **-gable,** one in which bells are hung; **-glass,** a b.-shaped glass, used to protect plants; **-hanger,** one whose business it is to put up bells, bell-wires, etc.; **-heather,** the cross-leaved heath, *Erica tetralix*; **-jar,** a b.-shaped glass jar used in chemical and physical laboratories; **-moth,** a group of the family *Tortricidæ*, named from their outline when at rest; **-pepper,** a species of Capsicum (*C. grossum*), named from the shape of the fruit; **-polype** (= *bell-animalcule*); **-pull,** a handle or cord attached to a b.-wire; **-ringer,** one who rings a church or town b.; **-roof,** one shaped like a b.; **-rope,** the rope by which a b. is rung; **-stone,** the part of a column between the shaft and the abacus (cf. 4); **-tent,** one resembling a b. in shape; **-tower; -trap,** a bell-shaped stench-trap.

Bell, *sb.*[2] 1594. [perh. – prec., from its shape.] The strobile of the hop plant. So **Bell** *v.*[1], to be, begin to be, in b. 1574.

Bell, *sb.*[3] Now chiefly *Sc.* and *dial.* 1483. [Origin unkn.; cf. synon. Du. *bel*, and MDu. *bellen* bubble up; cf. BELL *v.*[3]] A bubble.

Bell, *sb.*[4] 1510. [f. BELL *v.*[4]] The cry of a stag or buck at rutting time.

† **Bell** (bel), *v.*[2] Pa. pple. **bollen.** ME. [May repr. OE. *belgan*, pa. pple. *bolgen* swell.] *intr.* To swell up (like a boil) –1664. Also *fig.*

Bell, *v.*[3] Now *dial.* 1598. [Goes with BELL *sb.*[3]] *intr.* To bubble.

Bell (bel), *v.*[4] [OE. *bellan*, corresp. to OHG. *bellan* (G. *bellen*) bark, bray; cf. ON. *belja* and BELLOW.] **1.** *intr.* To bellow, roar. **2.** *spec.* Of the cry of deer in rutting time 1486. **3.** *trans.* To bellow forth 1596.

Bell, *v.*[5] 1721. [f. BELL *sb.*[1]] **1.** *trans.* To furnish with a bell 1762. **2.** To cause to bulge out 1870.

1. *To b. the cat*: to hang a bell round the cat's neck, so as to be warned of its approach, as the mice proposed to do in the fable, and *esp.* to undertake the perilous part in any movement.

‖ **Belladonna** (be:lăˌdǫ·nă). 1597. [mod. L. – It. *bella donna* lit. 'fair lady'; said to be so named because in Italy a cosmetic was made from it.] **1.** *Bot.* The specific name of the Deadly Nightshade (*Atropa b.*), occas. used as Eng. **2.** *Med.* The leaves and root of this plant, and the drug thence prepared, the active principle of which is *atropine* 1788.

1. Bella-donna. .so called because the Italian ladies make a cosmetic from the juice 1757. **Belladonna Lily,** *Amaryllis belladonna*, a native of the Cape of Good Hope.

Bellarmine (be·lăɹmīn). Now *Hist.* 1719. A glazed drinking-jug with capacious belly and narrow neck, orig. designed as a burlesque likeness of Cardinal Bellarmine.

Jugs, Mugs, and Pitchers, and Bellarmines of State D'URFEY.

Bell-bird (be·lbəɹd). 1848. [f. BELL *sb.*[1]] A name given to two birds, the *Procnias carunculata* or Campanero of Brazil, and the *Myzantha melanophrys* of Australia, both having a bell-like note.

Belle (bel). 1622. [– Fr. *belle*, fem. of BEL, BEAU.] **A.** *adj.* † **1.** Handsome 1668. **2.** In Fr. phrases, occas. used in Eng., as *b. assemblée* brilliant gathering; *b. dame* belle; *b. passion* the tender passion 1698. **B.** *sb.* A handsome woman; a reigning beauty 1622.

sb. The b. of all Paris last winter 1860.

Belled (beld), *ppl. a.* 1833. [f. BELL *sb.* or *v.* + -ER[1], -ER[2].] **1.** Furnished with a bell or bells. Often in comb. **2.** Bell-flowered. Often in comb. 1850.

Belleric, beleric (bĕle·rik), *a.* and *sb.* 1757. [– Fr. *belleric* – (ult.) med.Arab. *balīlaj* – Pers. *balīlah.*] The fruit of *Terminalia bellerica*, or Bastard Myrobalan, imported from India for use as a dye.

‖ **Belles-lettres** (be:l le·tr), *sb. pl.* 1710. [Fr.; 'fine letters', parallel to *beaux arts*; embracing grammar, rhetoric, and poetry.] Elegant literature or literary studies; formerly = 'the humanities', *literæ humaniores.* Now = 'literature'; and *esp.* applied to light literature, or the æsthetics of literary study. Hence **Belle·trist, -lettrist,** one devoted to belles-lettres. **Belletri·stic** *a.* of or pertaining to belles-lettres.

Bell-flower (be·lˌflauəɹ, -flauəɹ). 1578. [f. BELL *sb.*[1]] Any plant of the genus *Campanula*, having bell-shaped blossoms.

Be·ll-house. *arch.* and *dial.* OE. [f. BELL *sb.*[1]] = BELFRY 4.

† **Be·llibone.** *rare.* 1579. [perh. for Fr. *belle bonne* or *belle et bonne* fair and good, or humorous perversion of BONNIBEL.] A bonny lass.

† **Be·llic, -al,** *a.* 1513. [– OFr. *bellique* – L. *bellicus*; see next.] Of or pertaining to war; warlike –1680.

Bellicose (be·likōᵘs), *a.* ME. [– L. *bellicosus*, f. *bellicus* war-like, f. *bellum* war; see -OSE[1].] Inclined to war or fighting; warlike.

Our godis aboue. .In Albione hes plantit. .The perfite pepill, bald and bellicois 1535. Hence **Be:llico·sely** *adv.* **Bellico·sity.** var. † **Be·llicous.**

Bellied (be·lid), *ppl. a.* 1475. [f. BELLY *v.* or *sb.* + -ED[1], [2].] **1.** Having a belly. Often in comb., e.g. *big-b.* **b.** Corpulent 1532. Also *fig.*

1. The Colt. . Sharp headed. Barrel belly'd, broadly backed DRYDEN. **B. b.** B. monks 1532.

Belligerence (beli·dʒĕrĕns). 1814. [f. BELLIGERENT; see -ENCE.] The carrying on of hostilities; also = next.

Belli·gerency. Also **-ancy.** 1863. [f. as prec.; see -ENCY.] The position or status of a belligerent.

Belligerent (beli·dʒĕrĕnt). 1577. [Earlier *belligerant* – *belligerant-*, pres. ppl. stem of L. *belligerare*, f. *belliger* waging war, f. *bellum*; subseq. irreg. assim. to *gerent-*, pres. ppl. stem of L. *gerere*; see -GEROUS, -ENT.] **A.** *adj.* **1.** Waging regular recognized war. Also *fig.* or *transf.* 1809. **2.** *attrib.* Of or pertaining to belligerents 1865. **B.** *sb.* A nation, party, or person waging regular war 1811. Also *fig.* or *transf.* 1839.

Belling (be·liŋ), *vbl. sb.* 1440. [f. BELL *v.*[4] + -ING[1].] **1.** The roaring of animals. **2.** *spec.* The cry of deer in rutting time; hence *ellipt.* the rutting season. Occas. *attrib.* 1513.

Belli·potent, *a.* 1635. [– L. *bellipotens, -ent-*, f. *bellum* war + *potens* mighty; see POTENT.] Mighty in war. (*Obs.* in serious use.)

Bellman (be·lmæ̆n). ME. [f. BELL *sb.*[1]] **1.** A man who rings a bell; *esp.* a town-crier. (Formerly a bellman also acted as night-watchman, and called the hours.) † **2.** He who 'bears the bell'; the best (*rare*) 1617.

1. The b. came by. .and cried 'Past one of the clock, and a cold, frosty, windy morning' PEPYS.

Be·ll-me·tal. 1541. An alloy of about 4 parts of copper to one of tin, of which bells are made. Also *attrib.*

Bell-metal ore, stannite, which has the appearance of bell-metal.

Bellon (be·lən). 1794. [Origin unkn.] Lead-colic.

Bellona (belōᵘ·nă). 1605. [L., f. *bellum.*] **1.** Name of the goddess of war; also *transf.* **2.** One of the asteroids.

Bellona's Bridegroom, lapt in proofe *Macb.* I. ii. 54.

Belloot, belote (bĕlū·t, bĕlōᵘ·t). 1866. [– Sp. *bellota* acorn.] The edible acorn of *Quercus ballota*, in N. Africa and Spain. **Bellote Oak:** the tree which bears it.

Bellow (be·loᵘ), *v.* [ME. *belwe*, of uncertain origin; possibly OE. (Anglian) **belgan*, (W.S.) **bielgan* (:– **balʒjan*), late *bylgan*, rel. to OE. *bellan* BELL *v.*[4]] **1.** *prop.* To roar as a bull. **2.** Used of other animals 1486. **3.** Of human beings: To cry in a loud and deep voice; to roar (*depreciative* or *joc.*); also to roar from pain 1602. Also *trans.* **4.** Of thunder, cannon, etc.: To make a loud hollow noise; to roar ME. Also with *obj.* 1706.

1. Iupiter Became a Bull, and bellow'd *Wint. T.* IV. iv. 28. 2. The croaking Rauen doth b. for Reuenge *Haml.* III. ii. 264. 3. Not fit for that liberty which. .they bellowed for MILT. *trans.* To b. out blasphemies 1581. 4. A soun As lowde as beloweth wynde in helle CHAUCER. Hence **Be·llower.**

Be·llow, *sb.* 1779. [f. prec. vb.] The roar of a bull. Also *transf.* of human beings, cannon, thunder, a storm, etc.

Bellows (be·loᵘz, be·ləs), *sb.* OE. [ME. *belwes, belows*, pl. of *belu, below*, prob. repr. OE. pl. *belga, belgum*, of *bel(i)ġ, bæl(i)ġ* BELLY, abbr. of *blǣstbel(i)ġ* 'blowing-bag' = ON. *blástrbelgr*; cf. G. *blasebalg.*] An instrument or machine constructed to furnish a strong blast of air. In its simplest form, it consists of an upper and lower board joined by flexible leather sides, enclosing a cavity, and furnished with a valve opening inwards, through which air enters, filling and expanding the cavity, and with a nozzle, through which the air is forced out when the machine is compressed. Used to blow a fire, to supply air to an organ, etc. Often, with reference to the two halves or handles, called *a pair of b.*, rarely, as sing., *a bellows*. Also *fig.* **2.** The expansible part of a camera 1884. **3.** *Hydrostatic Bellows*; see HYDROSTATIC.

1. Thou..like a b., swell'st thy face DRYDEN. *fig.* My voice is not a b. unto ire KEATS.

Comb. **b.-fish,** *Centriscus scolopax*, from its shape.

† **Be·llows,** *v. rare.* 1605. [f. prec.] To blow (with bellows) –1748.

† **Bellrags.** 1548. *Herb.* A water plant, *Nasturtium amphibium* (Britten).

Bell-tongue, var. of BILTONG.

† **Be·lluine,** *a.* 1618. [– L. *belluinus*, f. *bellua* beast; see -INE[1].] Pertaining to or characteristic of beasts; brutal –1731.

The animal and b. life ATTERBURY.

Bell-wether (be·lweðəɹ). ME. [f. BELL *sb.*[1]] **1.** The leading sheep of a flock, on whose neck a bell is hung 1440. **2.** *fig.* A leader. (Mostly *contempt.*) ME.

Bellwort (be·lwɒɹt). 1884. [f. BELL *sb.*[1]] Any plant of the N.O. *Campanulaceæ*. Also, in U.S., a name for the genus *Uvularia*.

Belly (be·li), *sb.* [OE. *beliġ*, var. of *bæl(i)ġ*, WS. *biel(i)ġ*, *byl(i)ġ* = MDu. *balch*, OHG. *balg*, ON. *belgr*, Goth. *balgs* :– Gmc. **balʒiz* bag, sack, f. **balʒ-*, **belʒ-* be inflated, swell; cf. BELLOWS. The sense 'belly' is Eng. only.] † **1.** A bag, purse, pod, husk OE. only. † **2.** The body –ME. **3.** That part of the human body which lies between the breast and the thighs, and contains the bowels; the abdomen. (The ordinary mod. sense.) ME. **4.** The under part of the body of animals 1440. **5.** That part of the body which receives food; the stomach with its adjuncts ME. **6.** The bowels ME. **7.** The womb 1440. **8.** The 'inside' of the body 1491. **9.** The interior (of things material and immaterial) 1535. **10.** The bulging part, *e.g.* of a bottle, a vein of ore, a muscle, etc. 1591. **11.** A concave surface, *e.g.* the belly of a sail 1607. **12.** The front, inner, or lower surface of anything, as opp. to the *back*; e.g. the upper plate of the sounding box of a violin, etc.; the sound-board of a piano 1790.

3. The Iustice in faire round b. *A.Y.L.* II. vii. 154. **4.** A..Serpent on his b. prone MILT. *P.L.* X. 514. **5.** The b. is not filled with fair words *Prov.* Whose God is their bely *Phil.* 3:19. Evyll beastes, and slowe belies *Tit.* 1:12. To work for the Backs and Bellies of the People 1719. **8.** Ionas in the bely of the fysh *Jonah* 2:1. **9.** Out of the bely off hell I cried *Jonah* 2:2.

Comb.: **b.-ache,** the colic in the bowels; **-bound** *a.*, constipated; **-brace,** a cross-brace passing beneath the steam-boiler of a locomotive; † **-cheat** (*slang*), food; also, an apron; † **-doublet,** one covering the b.; **-fretting,** pain in a horse's b.; also, the galling of a horse's b. with a girth; **-gut,** a slothful glutton; **-guy** (*Naut.*), a tackle applied half-way up sheers; **-pinched** *a.*, pinched with hunger; † **-slave,** a glutton; **-stay** (*Naut.*), a stay used half-mast down.

Belly (be·li), *v.* 1606. [f. prec.] **1.** To cause to swell out. **2.** *intr.* To bulge or swell out 1624. † **3.** To become corpulent –1772.

3. I begin to b., I think SHADWELL.

Be·lly-band. 1523. [f. BELLY *sb.* + BAND *sb.*[2]] **1.** The band which passes round the belly of a horse in harness, to check the play of the shafts. **2.** *Naut.* A strip of canvas stitched across a sail, to strengthen it 1860. **3.** The piece of string on the face of a kite to which the ball of twine is attached.

† **Be·lly-cheer,** *sb.* 1549. [f. BELLY *sb.* + CHEER *sb.*] **1.** The gratification of the belly –1650. **2.** *concr.* Viands –1699. † **Be·lly-cheer** *v. intr.* to feast.

Bellyful (be·li͵ful). 1535. [f. BELLY *sb.* + -FUL.] **1.** One's fill of food 1573. **2.** A sufficiency; as much as one cares to take 1535.

1. I never once had my belly-full, even of dry bread SMOLLETT. **2.** Bellyfulls of Sermons 1705.

Belly-god (be·li͵gǫ:d). 1540. [f. BELLY *sb.* + GOD. Cf. *Phil.* 3:19, 'whose God is their belly'.] One who makes his belly his god; a glutton.

† **Be·lly-piece.** 1591. [f. BELLY *sb.* + PIECE *sb.*] **1.** The peritoneum –1659. **2.** An apron 1689. **3.** The piece forming the belly of a violin, etc. 1609.

Be·lly-ti:mber. 1607. [f. BELLY *sb.* + TIMBER *sb.*[1]] Food. (Not now in serious use.)

† **Belo·ck,** *v.* [BE- 2.] Intens. of LOCK. *Meas. for M.* V. 210.

Belomancy (be·lomænsi). 1646. [f. Gr. βέλος dart + -MANCY.] Divination by means of arrows.

Belong (bǐlǫ·ŋ), *v.* [prob. intensive (see BE-) f. ME. *longen*, used in the same sense; see LONG *v.*[2]] **1.** *intr.* To go along with, as an adjunct, function, or duty; to pertain *to*. Also *impers.* or with subject *it*. **2.** To pertain, concern, or relate *to* (*arch.*) ME. **3.** To be the rightful possession of. Const. *to*; occas. w. *indirect obj.* ME. **b.** To be a property or attribute of 1662. **4.** To be connected with; to form a part or appendage of ME.

1. Wee know what belongs to a Watch *Much Ado* III. iii. 40. Here..it doth not well b. To speak KEATS. **2.** All that belongs to this *Cymb.* V. v. 147. **3.** Property belonging to another state 1852. If motion doth b. to it 1662. **4.** To b. to a parish CAXTON, to the Lady Oliuia SHAKS., to a period 1875, to the rank and file 1884.

Belonging (bǐlǫ·ŋiŋ), *vbl. sb.* 1603. [f. prec. + -ING[1]. Perh. the pl. *belongings* was orig. taken from pr. pple., = 'things belonging'.] Usu. in *pl.* only. **1.** Circumstances connected with a person or thing. **2.** Goods, effects 1817. **3.** Relatives 1852. **4.** A thing forming a part, appendage, or accessory of another 1863.

1. Thy selfe and thy belongings Are not thine owne so proper *Meas. for M.* I. i. 30. **2.** Collecting their belongings 1871. **3.** To be trouble enough to one's belongings DICKENS.

Belonite (be·lŏnəit). 1879. [f. Gr. βελόνη needle + -ITE[1] 2 b.] *Min.* A mineral variety occurring in microscopic needle-shaped crystals.

Belo·rd, *v.* 1586. [BE- 5.] **1.** To address as 'my lord'. **2.** To act the lord over.

Belove (bǐlɒ·v), *v.* [f. BE- 2 + LOVE *v.*[1]] † **1.** *intr.* To be pleasing ME. only. **2.** To love. Now only in *pass.* ME.

Beloved (bǐlɒ·vėd, -lɒ·vd). ME. [f. prec. + -ED[1].] **A.** *ppl. adj.* Loved. (Often *well-*, etc.). Dearly b. brethren *Bk. Com. Pr.*

B. *sb.* (cf. *dear*.) One who is beloved 1526.

What is thy beloued more then another beloued? *S. of S.* 5:9.

Below (bǐlōᵘ·). [f. *be* BY + LOW *a.*, on the model of ALOW *adv.*[1], †*on lau*, and BENEATH.] **A.** (without obj.) *adv.* **1.** *gen.* In or to a lower position, lower down; also *fig.*; *hence*, later in a book or writing; at the foot of the page 1694. **2. a.** Under heaven; on earth (*arch.* or *poet.*) 1574. **b.** Under the earth; in Hades, in hell 1610. **c.** On a lower floor; in or into the cabin or hold of a ship 1598.

1. The child..leaped..into the flood b. GOLDSM. *fig.* The judgment of the Court b. 1884. **2.** Man wants but little here b. GOLDSM. Or Phœbus Steeds are foundered Or Night kept chain'd b. *Temp.* IV. i. 31.

B. (with obj.) *prep.* **1.** Lower in position than 1575. Also *fig.* **2.** Lower on a slope than; farther down a valley or stream than; nearer (what is considered) the bottom of a room than 1603. **3.** Deeper than. Also *fig.* 1849. **4.** Underneath 1605. **5.** Lower in a graduated scale than; hence *fig.* lower in rank, dignity, or station than 1601; inferior to 1711. **6.** = BENEATH 1637.

1. B. the snow-line 1849. *B.-stairs* (now usu. *downstairs*): on or to the floor b., *esp.* the ground-floor. **2.** B. the gangway sat a strong Radical party 1885. **3.** At a small depth b. the surface 1849. **5.** B. par 1788, Zero 1849, the average 1884. *fig.* To dress b. oneself LAMB. **6.** A compiler..who thinks no fact b. his regard HALLAM.

† **Be·lsire.** ME. [f. BEL + SIRE; cf. *beldame*.] A grandfather; an ancestor –1631.

† **Be·lswagger.** Also **belly-.** 1592. [perh. a contr. of *belly-swagger* 'one who swags his belly'; see SWAG *v.*, -ER[1].] A swaggering gallant or bully; a whoremonger, pimp –1775.

Belt (belt), *sb.* [OE. *belt*, corresp. to OHG. *balz*, ON. *belti* (Sw. *bälte*, Da. *bælte*) :– Gmc. **baltjaz*, **baltjōn* – L. *balteus*, *-um*, of Etruscan origin (Varro).] **1.** A broadish flat strip of leather, etc., used to gird the person, and to support articles of use or ornament; **b.** *esp.* one worn as a mark of rank or distinction ME. Also *fig.* **2.** *transf.* A broadish strip or stripe, or a continuous series of objects, engirdling something 1664. **3.** *Mech.* A broad flat strap, passing round two wheels or shafts, and communicating motion from one to the other 1795. **4.** A broadish flexible strap. (The idea of girdling here begins to be lost.) 1672. **5.** A tract or district long in proportion to its breadth 1808. **b.** *Arch.* 'A course of stones projecting from the naked, either moulded, plain, or fluted' (Gwilt). **c.** *Naval Arch.* A series of thick iron plates running along the water-line in armoured vessels 1885.

1. The champion's b. THACKERAY. *fig.* Within the b. of rule *Macb.* V. ii. 17. Phr. *To hit below the b.*: *fig.* to act unfairly in any contest. **2.** A b. of ice SOUTHEY, of Scotch firs 1834. The body of Jupiter is surrounded by several parallel faint substances called Belts 1787. **5.** A range or b. about forty degrees broad, across the old continent 1808. *Great* and *Little Belts*: two channels leading to the Baltic.

Comb.: **b.-lacing,** thongs for lacing together the ends of machine belts; **-saw** (= *band-saw*; see BAND *sb.*[2]); **-wise** *adv.* in the manner of a b.

Belt (belt), *v.* ME. [f. BELT *sb.*] **1.** To gird with or as with a belt; to fasten on with a belt. Also *refl.* **2.** To thrash with a belt. Cf. *to strap*. 1649. **3.** 'To shear the buttocks and tails' of (sheep) 1523.

1. *transf.* They b. him round with hearts undaunted WORDSW. **3.** Belting of sheep, is the dressing of them from filth HOLME.

Beltane (be·ltěn). ME. [– Gael. *bealltainn* (= OIr. *belltaine*, Manx *boaltinn*, *boaldyn*), Celtic name of the first of May.] **1.** The first day of May (reckoned since 1752 according to Old Style); Old May-day. The quarter-days anciently in Scotland were Hallowmas, Candlemas, Beltane, and Lammas. ‖ **2.** An ancient Celtic anniversary celebration on May-day, when great bonfires were kindled on the hills 1772.

2. For him thy b. yet may burn BYRON. *attrib.* The shepherd lights his b. fire SCOTT.

Belted (be·ltėd), *ppl. a.* 1483. [f. BELT *v.*, *sb.* + -ED[1], [2].] **1.** Wearing, or girded with, a belt; *spec.* as the cincture of an earl or knight; fastened on by means of a belt. **2.** Furnished with a belt or belts; marked by bands of colour 1785.

1. A prince can mak a b. knight BURNS. **2.** B. cruisers 1884. *B. cattle*: a Dutch breed of black cattle with a broad band of white round the middle.

Belting (be·ltiŋ), *vbl. sb.* 1567. [f. BELT *v.*, *sb.* + -ING[1].] **1.** The action of the vb. **2.** *concr.* Belts collectively, or the material for making them; also, a belt.

† **Belue.** *rare.* 1474. [– OFr. *belue* – L. *belua* great beast.] A great beast; *spec.* a whale –1572.

‖ **Beluga** (bǐlū·gă). 1591. [In sense 1 – Russ. *belúga*, in sense 2 – *belúkha*, f. *belo-* white + *-uga*, *-ukha* augm. suffixes.] **1.** The Great or Hausen Sturgeon (*Acipenser huso*), found in the Caspian and Black Seas. **2.** The white Whale (*Delphinapterus leucas*), an animal of the Dolphin family, found in herds in the Northern Seas 1817.

Belute (bǐlᵉū·t), *v.* 1760. [BE- 6 + LUTE *sb.*[2]] To cover with mud.

Belvedere (belvǐdīᵊ·ɹ). 1596. [– (partly through Fr. *belvédère*) It. *belvedere* lit. 'fair sight', f. *bel*, *bello* beautiful + *vedere* (subst. use of infin.) sight.] **1.** *Archit.* A raised turret or lantern on the top of a house, or a summer-house erected on an eminence, commanding a fine view. **2.** *Hort.* A plant, *Kochia scoparia* (N.O. *Chenopodiaceæ*), also called *Summer Cypress* 1597.

1. Apollo B., a..statue of Apollo..placed..in the B. of the Vatican 1834.

Belzebub, var. of BEELZEBUB.

‖ **Bema** (bī·mă). 1683. [– Gr. βῆμα step, pace; hence, a raised place to speak from.] **1.** *Eccles. Antiq.* The altar part or sanctuary in ancient churches; the chancel. **2.** *Gk. Antiq.* The platform from which Athenian orators spoke 1820.

Bemad (bǐmæ·d), *v.* 1605. [f. BE- 2 + MAD *v.*] To make mad.

Unnatural and bemadding sorrow *Lear* III. i. 38.

Bemangle, bemask, bemaster, bemaul, bemazed, etc.; see BE-.

† **Beme,** *sb.* [OE. *bēme*, WS. *bīeme*, *bȳme*.] A trumpet –1500. Hence † **Beme** *v.* to blow on a trumpet; also *transf.*

† **Bemea·n**, *v.*[1] ME. [f. BE- 2 + MEAN *v.*] To signify –1502.

Bemean (bǐmī·n), *v.*[2] 1651. [f. BE- 5 + MEAN *a.*[1], prob. after DEMEAN *v.*[2]] To render mean, to abase.

† **Bemee·t**, *v.* 1605. [BE- 2.] To meet with. *Lear* v. i. 20.

† **Beme·te**, *v.* [OE. *bemetan*, f. BE- 2 + *metan* METE *v.*[1]; in Shaks. prob. an independent re-formation.] To measure. *Tam. Shr.* IV. iii. 113.

Bemire (bǐməiᵊ·ɹ), *v.* 1532. [f. BE- 6 + MIRE *sb.*] To befoul with, or plunge in, mire; *pass.* to sink in the mire (*lit.* and *fig.*).

I was filthily bemired SWIFT. Doubt..bemires the soul WESLEY.

Bemist (bǐmi·st), *v.* 1598. [BE- 6 + MIST *sb.*[1]] To involve in, or as in, mist.

Bemoan (bǐmōᵘ·n), *v.* [f. BE- 4 + MOAN *v.*, repl. ME. *bemene*, OE. *bemǣnan.*] To lament (*trans.* and *intr.*).

The children of Israel..bemoaning the ruines of Sion WALTON.

Bemo·ck, *v.* 1607. [f. BE- 2 + MOCK *v.*] To flout.

To gird the Gods—Bemocke the modest Moone *Cor.* I. i. 261.

† **Bemoi·l**, *v.* 1596. [f. BE- 2 + MOIL *v.*] To bemire. *Tam. Shr.* IV. i. 77.

† **Bemol.** [ME. *bemol* – med.L. *b mollis* 'softened B'. Later reinforced by Fr. *bémol* (XVI).] **1.** Name given to B♭, when first introduced into the scale. **2.** By extension: **a.** A flat 1609. **b.** A semitone 1626.

Bemonster (bǐmǫ·nstəɹ), *v.* 1605. [BE- 5.] **1.** To make monstrous. **2.** To regard as, or call a monster 1692.

† **Bemou·rn**, *v.* [OE. *be-*, *bimurnan*; see BE- 2, MOURN.] To lament (*trans.* and *intr.*) –1622.

Bemouth, bemud, bemuddle, bemuffle, etc.; see BE-.

Bemuse (bǐmiū·z), *v.* 1735. [f. BE- 2 + MUSE *v.*] To make utterly muddled, as with drink. ¶ *joc.* To devote entirely to the Muses. POPE.

A parson much be-mus'd in beer POPE.

Ben (ben). *Sc.* and *north.* ME. [Sc. and north. Eng. var. (unexpl.) of ME. *bin, binne* :– OE. *binnan* (= OFris. *binna,* (M)LG., (M)Du., (M)G. *binnen*), f. *be* BY + *innan* within; see IN and cf. BUT.] **A.** *adv.* Within, towards the inner part; *esp.* in or into the parlour, etc., from the kitchen. (The words *but* and *b.* had reference originally to houses with only one outer door, opening into the kitchen.) **b.** *But and b.*: in the outer and inner apartment, in both (or all) parts of the house ME. **B.** *prep.* In or into the inner part of 1684. **C.** *adj.* Inner 1774. **D.** *sb. ellipt.* The inner room 1791.

‖ **Ben** (ben), *sb.*[2] 1788. [– Gael. *beann* = OIr. *benn* (Ir. *beann*), W. *ban* prominence, peak, height.] A mountain-peak, *e.g.* Ben Nevis.

Ben (ben), *sb.*[3] 1559. [– North African regional pronunc. of Arab. *bān.*] The winged seed of the Horseradish tree (*Moringa pterygosperma*); also called *b.-nut.* Hence *Oil of B.* 1594.

Ben, obs. pres. indic., subj. pl., and inf. of BE *v.*

† **Bena·me**, *v. Obs.* (*arch.* in pa. pple.) Pa. t. and pple. **benamed, benempt, benempted.** [OE. *benemnan*; see BE- 2, NAME *v.*] † **1.** To declare solemnly –1615. † **2.** To name. SPENSER. **3.** To name, describe as 1580.

Bench (benᵗʃ), *sb.* [OE. *benć* = OFris. *benk,* OS. *banc,* OHG. *bank* (Du., G. *bank*), ON. **benkr* (Icel. *bekkr*) :– Gmc. **baŋkiz*; cf. BANK *sb.*[1] and *sb.*[2]] **1.** A long seat, usually of wood or stone, with or without a back. **2.** The seat on which judges sit in court; the judge's seat or seat of justice; hence, the office of a judge, the judicial status (as opp., e.g., to *bar*) ME. **b.** The place where justice is administered as †*The (Court of) Common B.*, (*The Court of) King's or Queen's B.* (since the Judicature Act of 1873, a division of the High Court of Justice) ME. **c.** A court of justice 1589. **d.** The judges or magistrates collectively, or the judge or magistrate sitting in the seat of justice 1592. **3.** A seat where persons sit side by side in some official capacity 1742. **b.** *transf.* The dignity of occupying such a seat. **c.** The persons collectively who occupy such a seat 1600. **4.** Anything similar in form to a long seat (sense 1): † **a.** a footstool; **b.** the table at which carpenters, etc. work; **c.** a banker's counter ME. **5.** *transf.* A collection of dogs as exhibited at a show on benches 1883. **6.** = BANK *sb.*[1] 1. 1450. **7.** Any conformation of earth, stone, etc. which has a raised, and flat surface 1730. **8.** *Law.* See FREE BENCH.

1. Thy benches of Yuorie *Ezek.* 27:6. **2.** To be raised to the b. 1887. **d.** The b...smiled 1592. **3.** The b. of bishops 1771, the Treasury b. 1812. **6.** Vpon a b. couered with greene torves we satte 1551. **7.** A b. or layer of coal RAYMOND.

Comb.: **b.-clamp,** a vice with sliding side used to force together the parts of work; **-holdfast, -hook,** an iron hook, sliding in a socket, by which a plank may be gripped; **-plane,** a joiner's plane for working on a flat surface; **-shears,** shears used by copper- and zinc-workers; **-show** (see 5); **-stop, -strip,** a strip of wood or metal fixed on a carpenter's b. to rest his work against; **-table,** a low stone seat on the inside of walls, or round the bases of pillars, in churches, cloisters, etc.; **-warrant,** one issued by a judge, as opp. to a *justice's* or *magistrate's warrant.*

Hence **Be·nchlet,** a little b., a stool.

Bench (benʃ), *v.* ME. [f. prec. sb.] **1.** *trans.* To furnish with benches. **2.** To seat on a bench. Also *refl.* and *intr.* 1605.

1. I-benchede newe with turvis CHAUCER. **2.** Whom I..Haue bench'd, and rear'd to Worship SHAKS.

Bencher (be·nʃəɹ). 1534. [f. as prec. + -ER[1].] **1.** One who sits on a bench (or thwart). **2.** *esp.* A magistrate, judge, assessor, senator, alderman, etc. (*arch.*) 1571. **3.** *spec.* One of the senior members of the Inns of Court 1582.

1. O, the benchers phrase: *pauca verba* B. JONS. Hence **Be·nchership,** the position of a b. in an Inn of Court.

Be·nch-mark. 1864. A surveyor's mark, cut in rock, or other durable material, to indicate the starting or other point in a line of levels for the determination of altitudes over the face of a country. It consists of a broad arrow with a horizontal bar through its apex, thus ⩚. When below sea-level, the mark is inverted.

Bend (bend), *sb.*[1] [OE. *bend* fem. (also m., n.), corresp. to Goth. *bandi* :– Gmc. **bandjō*, f. **band-* **bend-* BIND; later coinciding w. *bende* – OFr. *bende*, BAND *sb.*[2] Now replaced by BAND *sb.*[1], BOND exc. in naut. use.] † **1.** A band, bond, fetter. *pl. collect.* Bonds, imprisonment. –ME. † **2.** = A clamp; a connecting piece –1596. **3.** *Naut.* A knot, used to unite one rope to another, or to something else, as the *cable b.*, *fisherman's b.*, etc. (The only extant sense.) 1769.

Bend (bend), *sb.*[2] OE. [app. originally Eng., as a sense of the prec. wd. Later, identified w. OFr. *bende* (mod. Fr. *bande*); see BAND *sb.*[2]] † **1.** A thin flat strip adapted to bind round. *Archit.* a scroll or riband. –1799. **2.** *Her.* An ordinary drawn from the dexter chief to the sinister base of the shield, containing the fifth, or, if charged, the third, part of the field in breadth. *B. sinister*: a similar ordinary drawn in the opposite direction: one of the marks of bastardy. Cf. BATON. ME. **3.** A shape or size in which ox- or cow-hides are tanned into leather, forming half of a 'butt' 1600.

2. *In b.*: placed bendwise. *Parted per b.*: divided bendwise. **3. B.-leather** (orig. *north.*): the leather of a b., *i.e.* the stoutest kind of leather; sole-leather. Hence **Be·ndlet,** var. † **Be·ndel,** a smaller b. † **Be·ndly, Be·ndwise,** *advs.* in the position or direction of a b.

† **Bend,** *sb.*[3] 1475. [– OFr. *bende* = (O)Fr. *bande* (see BAND *sb.*[3]). Eng. *bend(e* (a var. of *band*) was in regular use from late XV to early XVII.] = BAND *sb.*[3] –1611.

Bend (bend), *sb.*[4] 1529. [Late deriv. of BEND *v.*] **1.** The action of the vb. BEND; bending; bent condition. † **2.** Inclination of the eye in any direction 1601. **3.** Turn of mind, bent 1591. **4.** *concr.* A thing of bent shape; the bent part, *e.g.* of a river, a road 1600. **5.** *Naut.* (*pl.*) The wales of a ship 1626.

1. A wave just on the b. HAWTHORNE. **2.** That same eye whose b. doth awe the world *Jul. C.* I. ii. 123. **4.** The perfection of fishhooks in shank, b. [etc.] 1883.

Bend (bend), *v.* *pa. t.* and *pple.* **bended, bent.** [OE. *bendan*, = ON. *benda* :– Gmc. **bandjan*, f. **band-*; see BAND *sb.*[1]] † **1.** To put in bonds OE. only. **2.** *spec.* To bring into tension by a string (a bow, etc.). Also *fig.* OE. **3.** *Naut.* To tie, fasten on, make fast ME. † **4.** To bring into the shape of a bow; to arch –1655. **5.** To bow, curve, crook, inflect. Used only of things which possess some rigidity. Now the main sense. ME. **6.** *intr.* To assume or receive a curved form, or one in which one part is inclined at an angle to the other ME. **7.** *spec.* Of persons: To bend the body, to stoop, *e.g.* in submission; to bow ME. Also *fig.* **8.** *trans.* To cause to bow, stoop, incline, or relent 1538. **9.** *trans.* To turn away from the straight line; to deflect, turn 1513. Also *fig.* **10.** *intr.* To incline in any direction; to trend 1572. † **11.** *trans.* To direct, aim, bring to bear *against, upon, at* –1801. Also † *fig.* **12.** *fig.* (*intr.*) To direct oneself, turn (*arch.*) ME.; *trans.* to direct or turn (one's steps, etc.) 1579. **13.** To direct, turn, or incline (the eyes, or ears), in the direction of anything seen or heard 1581.

2. Sone there were good bowes ibent 1500. *fig.* They b. their tongue like their bow for lies *Jer.* 9:3. I am settled, and b. up Each corporal agent to this terrible feat *Macb.* I. vii. 79. **3.** *To b. the cable*: to fasten it to the ring of the anchor. *To b. a sail*: to make it fast to its proper yard or stay. **4.** *To b. the brows*: (*orig.*) to arch the eyebrows; (*later*) to knit the brow; to scowl. **5.** On knees down bent GOWER. **6.** Their knees b. so, that they are apt to trip 1815. **7.** I bent down to go in SWIFT. The sonnes also of them that afflicted thee, shall come bending vnto thee *Isa.* 60:14. **8.** The spirit of the rustic gentry was not to be bent MACAULAY. *To b. the head or face*: to lower it by bending the neck. **11.** They bent their guns at the frigate CROMWELL. *To be bent*: to be intent, determined. **12.** Thence we came: And..Thither we b. againe *All's Well* III. ii. 57. **13.** And to my cries..Thine ear with favor b. MILT.

Hence **Be·ndable** *a.* **Be·nded** *ppl. a.* the orig. pa. pple., now semi-arch., and used chiefly in *on bended knees*, etc. **Be·ndsome** *a.* flexible.

† **Be·nded,** *a.* ME. [f. BEND *sb.*[2] + -ED[2].] *Her.* = BENDY –1572.

Bender (be·ndəɹ). 1496. [f. BEND *v.* + -ER[1].] **1.** He who or that which bends. **2.** A pair of pliers. † **3.** A flexor muscle –1668. **4.** *slang.* A sixpence 1836.

† **Be·nding,** *vbl. sb.* [f. BEND *sb.*[2] + -ING[1].] Decoration with bends or stripes. CHAUCER.

Bendy (be·ndi), *a.* 1486. [– OFr. *bendé* (mod. *bandé*); see BEND *sb.*[2], -Y[5].] *Her.* Of a shield: Divided into an even number of bends, coloured alternately.

† **Bene.** [OE. *bēn* = ON. *bœn* :– **bōniz*; see BOON *sb.*[1]] Prayer, boon; *esp.* prayer to God –ME.

Beneaped (bǐnī·pt), *ppl. a.* 1692. [f. BE- 6 b + NEAP *sb.*[2]] Left aground by a neaping spring tide.

Beneath (bǐnī·þ). [OE. *biniþan, bineoþan*, f. *bi* BY + *niþan, neoþan* below, down, orig. from below; f. Gmc. **niþ-* (as in NETHER). For the formation cf. BEN, BUT.] **A.** *adv.* **1.** *gen.* In a lower position; = BELOW *adv.* **1.** ME. **2.** = BELOW *adv.* 2a, b. ME. **3.** Directly below, underneath ME.

2. Hell from b. is mooued for thee *Isa.* 14:9. **3.** It droppeth as the gentle rain from heaven Upon the place b. *Merch. V.* IV. i. 186.

B. (with obj.) *prep.* (Now usu. *under*, or *below*, exc. in sense 7, and fig. uses of 4.) † **1.** *gen.* In a position lower than. Now usu. BELOW *prep.* 1. OE. **2.** Directly down from; under, underneath ME. **3.** Immediately under; underneath; hence, concealed by 1611. **4.** Under, as overborne by pressure; often *fig.* ME. † **5.** = BELOW *prep.* 2. –1704. **6.** *fig.* = BELOW *prep.* 5. OE. **7.** Unworthy of. Better BELOW. 1849.

2. Lands that lye b. another Sun DRYDEN. **3.** The waters b. the earth *Deut.* 5:8. **4.** Our Country sinks b. the yoake *Macb.* IV. iii. 39. **7.** So farre b. your soft and tender breeding *Twel. N.* V. i. 332.

‖ **Benedicite** (benǐdəi·siti). ME. [L., 2nd pl. imper. of *benedicere* wish well to, bless, f. *bene* well + *dicere* say. In ME. abbrev. to *benste.*] **A.** *interj.* **1.** Bless you! **2.** Bless us! Good gracious! ME. **B.** *sb.* **1.** Invocation of a blessing 1610. **2.** *esp.* The blessing asked at table. (The earliest sense in Eng.) ME. **3.** The canticle in the Book of Common Prayer, known also as 'The Song of the Three Children' 1661.

Benedict (be·nĭdikt). 1576. [– L. *benedictus*, pa. pple. of *benedicere*; see prec., and BENEDICTUS.] † **A.** *adj.* Blessed, benign; *spec.* in *Med.* mildly laxative –1693. † **b.** *Priest b.*: = BENET, exorcist. **B.** *sb.* Also **benedick.** A newly married man; *esp.* an apparently confirmed bachelor who marries. [From the character of that name. See *Much Ado* v. iv. 100.]

Benedictine (benĭdi·ktin). 1602. [– Fr. *bénédictine* or mod. L. *benedictinus*, f. *Benedictus* of Nursia, abbot of Monte Cassino; see -INE.[1]] **A.** *adj.* Of or belonging to St. Benedict or the order founded by him 1630. **B.** *sb.* **1.** One of the order of monks, also known, from their dress, as 'Black Monks', founded by St. Benedict about the year 529. 1602. **2.** A kind of liqueur 1882.

Benediction (benĭdi·kʃən). ME. [– (O)Fr. *bénédiction* – L. *benedictio*, f. *benedict-*, pa. ppl. stem of *benedicere*; see BENEDICT, -ION.] **1.** The utterance of a blessing; solemn invocation of blessedness upon a person; devout expression of a wish for the happiness, prosperity, or success of a person or an enterprise: **a.** *gen.* ME.; **b.** as officially pronounced, *esp.* at the consecration of an abbot 1638; **c.** as pronounced at the conclusion of divine worship 1549; **d.** as an expression of thanks; *spec.* as grace before or after meals 1671; **e.** as a service in the R.C.Ch. 1812. **2.** Blessedness 1483.

1. a. Hold your hand in b. o're me *Lear* IV. vii. 58. **d.** The thought of our past years in me doth breed Perpetual b. WORDSW. **2.** As if my Trinkets had..brought a b. to the buyer *Wint. T.* IV. iv. 614. Hence **Benedi·ctional**, a book of forms of b.; var. **Benedi·ctionary. Benedi·ctory** *a.* of or pertaining to the utterance of b.

Benedictive (benĭdi·ktiv), *a.* 1660. [f. L. *benedict-* (see prec.) + -IVE.] **1.** Tending to bless. **2.** *Gram.* A form of the Optative Mood in Skr., also called the 'precative' 1841.

‖ **Benedi·ctus.** 1552. [First word of (i) *Benedictus qui venit* or (ii) *Benedictus Dominus Deus Israel.*] **1.** The fifth movement in the service of the Mass, beginning with the words 'Benedictus qui venit' 1880. **2.** The hymn of Zacharias (Luke 1:68), used as a canticle in the Book of Common Prayer 1552.

Benedi·ght. *Obs.* or *arch.* ME. [– L. *benedictus* (see prec.) w. assim. to DIGHT *v.*] Blessed.

Benefaction (benĭfæ·kʃən). 1662. [– late L. *benefactio*, f. *bene facere* benefit (someone), pa. ppl. stem *fact-*; see FACT, -ION.] **1.** A doing good, beneficence; a benefit or blessing. **2.** *esp.* The bestowal of money for a charitable purpose; a gift, bounty, endowment 1674.

2. She was liberal in her benefactions to convents and colleges PRESCOTT.

Benefactor (benĭfæ·ktəɹ). 1494. [– late L. *benefactor*; see prec., -OR 2.] **1.** One who renders aid to others, or to a cause or institution. **2.** A well-doer 1603.

1. A b. of learning BACON. **2.** *Meas. for M.* II. i. 50. Hence **Benefa·ctorship**, the office or action of a b. **Benefa·ctory** *a.* of or pertaining to a b.; beneficial. **Benefa·ctress**, a female b.

Benefic, -al (bĭne·fik, -ăl), *a.* 1600. [– L. *beneficus*, f. as prec.; see -FIC, -AL[1].] **1.** *Astrol.* Of favourable influence. **2.** *gen.* Beneficent, kindly 1641.

Benefice (be·nĭfis). ME. [– OFr. *benefice* (mod. *bénéfice* profit, perquisite) – L. *beneficium* favour, support, f. (after *beneficus* BENEFICENT) *bene* well + *fic-* var. of *fac-* in *facere* do, make.] † **1.** A kindness, favour; a grace or indulgence –1677. **2.** Favourable influence or operation; advantage, protection. Now *Hist.* ME. † **3.** Beneficial property or action (as of natural causes) –1652. **4.** Land granted in feudal tenure; a fief. (Only as tr. L. *beneficium.*) 1753. **5.** *esp.* An ecclesiastical living ME.

2. *B. of clergy*; see BENEFIT 3 b. **4.** Benefices.. were grants of Roman provincial land to be holden..on condition of military service MAINE. **5.** Then he dreames of another b. *Rom. & Jul.* I. iv. 81. Hence **Be·nefice** *v.* to endow or invest with a church living. **Be·neficed** *ppl. a.* holding a b.

Beneficence (bĭne·fĭsĕns). 1531. [– L. *beneficentia*, f. *beneficus*; see BENEFIC, -ENCE.] **1.** Doing good, active kindness. **2.** *concr.* A benefaction 1654.

1. Law itself is only b. acting by a rule BURKE.

† **Bene·ficency.** 1576. [f. as prec.; see -ENCY.] The quality of being beneficent –1682.

Beneficent (bĭne·fisĕnt), *a.* 1616. [– L. *beneficent-*, whence *beneficentior*, compar. of *beneficus*. Cf. *magnificent.*] Doing good, performing kind deeds. (Replacing *beneficial* in this sense.)

A b. genius 1879. That b. luminary the Sun 1772. So **Bene:fice·ntial** *a.* of or pertaining to beneficence. **Bene·ficently** *adv.*

Beneficial (benĭfi·ʃăl), *a.* 1494. [– (O)Fr. *bénéficial* or late L. *beneficialis*, f. *beneficium*; see BENEFICE, -AL[1].] † **1.** = BENEFICENT –1658. **2.** Of benefit 1494. **3.** *Law.* **a.** Of or pertaining to a benefice; beneficed. Now *Hist.* 1592. **b.** Of or pertaining to the usufruct of property; enjoying the usufruct 1844.

2. These beneficiall Newes *Oth.* II. ii. 7. **3. b.** A b. owner 1844, interest KEBLE. Hence **Bene·fi·cial·ly** *adv.*, **-ness.**

Beneficiary (benĭfi·ʃ'ări). 1611. [– L. *beneficiarius*, f. *beneficium*; see BENEFICE, ARY[1]. Cf. Fr. *bénéficiaire.*] **A.** *adj.* Holding, held as, or pertaining to the holding of a benefice: *spec.* feudatory 1626.

B. *sb.* **1.** The holder of a fief; a feudatory 1611. **2.** The holder of an eccles. living 1641. **3.** A debtor to another's bounty 1662.

2. Your Beneficiaries the Priests MILT. **3.** Content to be a b. of society—to receive favors and confer none HOLLAND.

Beneficiate (benĭfi·ʃiĕ[i]t), *v.* 1871. [f. Sp. *beneficiar* to benefit from a mine; see -ATE[3].] *Min.* To reduce (ores). Hence **Beneficia·tion.**

[**Beneficience, -ficiency, -ficient**, erron. ff. of BENEFICENCE, etc., orig. misprints.]

Benefit (be·nĭfit), *sb.* [Late ME. *benfe(e)t* – AFr. *benfet*, OFr. *bienfet, -fait* :– L. *benefactum* good deed, f. *bene facere* do well; cf. BENEFICE.] † **1.** A thing well done; a good deed –1811. **2.** A kind deed; a favour, gift (*arch.*) ME. **3.** Advantage, profit, good. (The ordinary sense.) 1512. **b.** *Law.* The advantage of belonging to a privileged order which was exempted from the jurisdiction or sentence of the ordinary courts of law: in *B. of Clergy, B. of Peerage*; see CLERGY, PEERAGE 1488. **c.** Pecuniary profit 1592. **4.** Hence **a.** A theatrical performance the receipts from which are given to a particular actor, etc. 1709. † **b.** A prize in a lottery; a winning ticket –1715. † **c.** A BENEFICE (sense 5), an endowment –1719. **d.** The pecuniary assistance, etc. to which an insured person is entitled 1895.

2. Her [Fortune's] benefits are mightily misplaced *A.Y.L.* I. ii. 37. **3.** To labour for the b. of mankind JOHNSON. The b. of the doubt 1887, of the contract 1885. **4.** She was going to have a b. and appear as Ophelia THACKERAY.

Benefit (be·nĭfit), *v.* 1549. [f. prec. sb.] **1.** *trans.* To do good to, to be of advantage or profit to; to improve, help forward. **2.** *intr.* (for *refl.*) To receive benefit 1613.

1. A system..which injures our interests without benefiting those of the colonies LUBBOCK. Hence **Be·nefiter**, he who confers, or derives benefit.

† **Bene·me**, *v.* [OE. *be-, binæman, -nēman.* ME. *beneme* may also be a var. of BENIM *v.*] To deprive (with *gen.*); to take away –1562.

Benempt, obs. pa. t. and pple. of BENAME.

† **Beneplacit.** *rare.* 1643. [– eccl. L. *beneplacitum* (e.g. Vulg., *Eph.* 1:9) good pleasure, f. *bene* well; see PLACITUM.] Good pleasure, gracious purpose.

Benet (be·nĕt), *sb.* [ME. *benet* – AFr. *benet*, OFr. *beneeit* :– L. *benedictus* blessed; see BENEDICT.] The third of the four lesser orders in the R.C.Ch., one of whose functions was the exorcizing of evil spirits.

Benet (bĭne·t), *v.* 1602. [BE- 6.] To cover as with, or catch in, a net. Usu. *fig.*

† **Beneurous**, *a.* [– OFr. *beneurous* (mod. *bienheureux*).] Happy, blessed. CAXTON.

Benevolence (bĭne·vŏlĕns). ME. [– (O)Fr. *bénévolence* (OFr. also *beni-*) – L. *benevolentia*, f. *benevolent-*; see BENEVOLENT, -ENCE.] **1.** Disposition to do good, kindness, generosity, charitable feeling (towards mankind). † **2.** Affection, goodwill (towards another) –1817. **3.** *concr.* An act of kindness; a gift of money; a charitable contribution ME. **4.** A sum of money, disguised as a gift (*donum*), demanded by the sovereign from his subjects without the consent of parliament 1473.

1. Sauer of vs by thy beneuolence CHAUCER. **2.** † *To do one's b.*: to lend one's friendly offices. I..will be glad to do my b. *Merry W.* I. i. 32. **4.** The B. proves..an occasion of so much discontent..that it had better it had never been set up PEPYS 1661.

† **Bene·volency.** 1540. [f. as prec.; see -ENCY.] The quality of being benevolent; also *concr.* a gift of money –1766.

Benevolent (bĭne·vŏlĕnt), *a.* 1482. [– OFr. *benivolent* – *benevolent-*, pres. ppl. stem of L. *bene velle* wish well; see -ENT.] **1.** Desirous of the good of others, of a kindly disposition, charitable, generous. **2.** Well-wishing *to, unto* (= L. *bene volens*) 1502.

1. Beloued old man! b. as wise POPE. *transf.* The b. Heat of the Sun HALE. Hence **Bene·volently** *adv.* † **Bene·volous** *a. Astrol.* auspicious.

Bengal (bengǭ·l). Name of a province of Hindustan. Hence **1.** Applied to piece goods imported from Bengal in the 17th c. 1680. **2.** *Comb.* etc., as **B. light,** a firework producing a steady and vivid blue-coloured light, used for signals; **B. root,** the root of the Yellow Zedoary; **B. silk, B. stripes,** striped ginghams formerly imported from Bengal; **B. tiger,** the tiger proper, which abounds in Lower Bengal.

Bengali, Bengalee (bengǭ·li). 1613. [An Eng. formation on BENGAL (in early Eur. use *Bangala, Bemgala, Bengala*). The native name of the language is *baŋgabhāṣā* language of Baŋga, i.e. Bengal.] **A.** *adj.* Of or belonging to Bengal. **B.** *sb.* A native of Bengal; the language of Bengal.

Be·nic, *a.* 1873. [f. BEN *sb.*[3] + IC.] *Chem.* Obtained from oil of ben.

Benight (bĭnəi·t), *v.* 1560. [f. BE- 6 + NIGHT *sb.*] **1.** To be overtaken by, or (*active*) to involve in, the darkness of night. Also *refl.* 1654. **2.** To involve in darkness, to cloud (*lit.* and *fig.*) 1610. **3.** To blind 1621.

1. I am like to be benighted, for the day is almost spent BUNYAN. **2.** Whom Error doth b. 1692.

Benign (bĭnəi·n), *a.* ME. [– (O)Fr. *bénigne* fem., *bénin* m. :– L. *benigna, -us* prob. for *benigenus*, f. *bene* well + *-genus* born. For the formation cf. MALIGN, for the sense L. *gentilis* GENTLE.] **1.** Of a kind disposition, gracious; † meek. **2.** Exhibiting or manifesting kindly feeling; bland, gentle, mild ME. Also *transf.* of things. **3.** *Med.* † **a.** Of medicines: Gentle in operation –1735. **b.** Of diseases: Not malignant 1743.

1. Charity is benyngne WYCLIF. **2.** *transf.* ffful lusty was the weder and benigne CHAUCER. Hence **Beni·gnly** *adv.*

Benignancy (bĭni·gnănsi). 1876. [f. next; see -ANCY.] Benignant quality or manner.

Benignant (bĭni·gnănt), *a.* 1782. [f. BENIGN or L. *benignus*, after *malignant*; see -ANT.] Cherishing or exhibiting kindly feeling towards inferiors or dependants; gracious, benevolent (with a suggestion of condescension). Also *transf.* of things.

1. Your b. sovereign BURKE. The b. or malignant character of our natal star 1844. Hence **Beni·gnantly** *adv.*

Benignity (bĭni·gnĭti). [– (O)Fr. *bénignité* or L. *benignitas, -tat-*, f. *benignus*; see BENIGN, -ITY.] **1.** Kindly feeling; kindness of disposition, or of manner. (Now attributed to superiors or those who are venerable.) **b.** *concr.* A kindly or generous deed 1534. **2.** Of things (*arch.*). See BENIGN 2, 3.

1. O God..Thow be my sheld, for thy benignite CHAUCER. **b.** Ample grants and benignities 1590.

† **Beni·m**, *v.* [OE. *be-, biniman* = OHG. *bineman*, Goth. *biniman*, f. *bi-* BE- 2 + *niman* NIM.] **1.** *trans.* To take away –1494. **2.** To deprive; (without constr.) to rob; to spoil, ravish –1480.

2. Euer he that was strengest bynome hym that was feblyst CAXTON.

Benison (be·nisən). [ME. *bene(y)sun* – OFr. *beneiçun, beneis(s)on* :– L. *benedictio, -ōn-* BENEDICTION.] **1.** Blessing, beatitude. **2.** Benediction ME.

1. The bountie, and the benizon of Heauen *Lear* IV. vi. 228. Her patriot Dead have b. E. B. BROWNING. 2. I have slept sound under such a b. SCOTT.

Benjamin[1] (be·ndʒǎmin). 1580. [alt. of early var. *benjoin* of BENZOIN, by assoc. with the name *Benjamin.*] **1.** Gum benzoin. **2. Benjamin tree: a.** *Styrax benzoin*, which yields benzoin; **b.** *Benzoin oderiferum* or *Lindera benzoin*, a N. American shrub with tonic bark; called also *Benjamin-bush*, and in U.S. *Benjamin*; **c.** *Ficus benjamina*. 1640.

Be·njamin[2]. 1817. [f. a tailor's name.] A form of overcoat for men.

Bennet[1] (be·nět). [ME. *herbe beneit*, tr. med. L. *herba benedicta*, said to put the devil to flight.] In Herb. Bennet, the common Avens, *Geum urbanum* (N.O. *Rosaceæ*). Used also of the Hemlock, and the Wild Valerian.

Be·nnet[2]. Earlier f. BENT; see BENT *sb.*[1] 2.

† **Be·nnet**[3]. 1731. A fish of the African seas –1784.

Benorth (bǐnǭ·ɹþ). [OE. *be northan*, f. BE- + *norþan* adv. from the north; cf. *biforan.*] **A.** † *adv.* To the north –1535. **B.** *prep.* North of. Now only *Sc.* ME.

Benshi, -shie, var. of BANSHEE.

Bent (bent), *sb.*[1] ME. [repr. OE. *beonet* in place-names, e.g. *Beonetlēah* (Bentley), perh. 'meadow of stiff grass'; corresp. to OS. *binet*, OHG. *binuz* (G. *binse*):–WGmc. **binut-* of unkn. origin.] **1.** A name given to grass of a reedy habit; also to various grass-like reeds, rushes, sedges, etc. With *pl.* 'bents'. Also *collect.* **2.** The stiff flower-stalk of grasses. (Also *bennet.*) 1577. **3.** The name of the genus *Agrostis*. More fully *B. grass*. 1796. **4.** A place covered with grass, as opp. to a wood; a bare field, unenclosed pasture-land, a heath. In ME. the stock poetic wd. for 'field' (of battle), L. *campus*. ME. **5.** ? A hill-side, slope. (Only in southern writers.) ME.

4. [Three lords] upon the b. did breathlesse bide *Flodden F.* ix. 84. *To flee, go, take to the b.*: to escape to the open country.

Bent (bent) *sb.*[2] 1521. [prob. f. BEND *v.* on the analogy of pairs like *descend/descent, extend/extent.*] **1.** A curved position or form; curvature. Also *fig.* (Now *rare.*) 1541. † **2.** A curved part, a bend; a bow –1677. † **3.** Bowing, stooping –1713. **4.** The condition of being deflected in some direction; a turn, twist, inclination; cast (of the eye); set (of a current), etc. Usu. *fig.* 1534. **b.** *esp.* Mental inclination; propensity, bias. The usual mod. sense. 1586. † **5.** That towards which an action, etc. is directed; aim, purpose –1798. † **6.** Impetus. Fr. *élan*. –1742. **7.** Degree of tension of a bow; *hence* limit of capacity, etc. Now only in *To the top of one's b.*, or the like. 1594.

4. They weare their faces to the b. Of the King's lookes *Cymb.* I. i. 13. Bents, and Propensities, and Inclinations, will not do the Business SOUTH. The whole b. of their actions MILT. 7. They foole me to the top of my b. *Haml.* III. ii. 401.

Bent (bent), *ppl. a.* ME. [f. BEND *v.*] **1.** Constrained into a curve, as a strung bow; deflected from the straight line. † **2.** Wound up for action; couched for a spring; levelled as a weapon –1675. † **3.** Determined, devoted, set –1740. **4.** Directed in a course, bound 1697.

1. The Bente Mone CHAUCER. *B. brow*: † an arched eyebrow; a knit brow. 4. Saylors homeward b. DRYDEN.

Comb. **b.-lever**, a lever whose arms form an angle with each other.

Benthamism (be·nþǎmiz'm). 1840. The philosophical system of Jeremy Bentham, 1748–1832, who taught that the aim or end of life is happiness, identified by him with pleasure, and that the highest morality is the pursuit of the greatest happiness of the greatest number. So **Bentha·mic** *a.* of or according to Bentham. **Be·nthamite** *sb.* an adherent of B.; *a.* = benthamic.

Benthos (be·nþǫs). *Biol.* 1891. [– Gr. βένθος depth (of the sea).] The flora and fauna of the bottom of the sea. Hence **Be·nthic, -o·ic, -o·nic** *adjs.*

Be·ntinck. 1867. [f. Captain *Bentinck.*] **1.** *pl.* Triangular courses, now superseded by storm stay-sails; also used in U.S. as try-sails. **2. B.-boom,** one which stretches the foot of the foresail in many small square-rigged merchantmen. **B. shrouds:** shrouds extending from the weather-futtock staves to the opposite lee-channels; not now used.

Benting (be·ntiŋ), *vbl. sb.* 1672. [f. BENT *sb.*[1] + -ING[1].] **1.** The going after bents. *B.-time*: the time when pigeons, etc. are reduced to feed on bents; also *transf.* **2.** The seeding stalks of the plantain (herb) 1807.

Benty (be·nti), *a.* 1597. [f. BENT *sb.*[1] + -Y[1].] **1.** Of, of the nature of, or pertaining to BENT. **2.** Covered with BENT 1700.

† **Benu·mb,** *ppl. a.* [ME. *benomen*, pa. pple. of *benimen* deprive (see BENIM), in phr. 'to be benome(n) the power of one's hands, etc.' whence *benum* v. (see next). Repl. by *be-num(b)ed* XVI.] –1530.

Benumb (bǐnɒ·m), *v.* 1485. [Earlier *benome, benum* pa. pple., f. prec.; for the sp. *benumb* cf. *dumb, limb*, etc. Cf. NUMB *v.*] **1.** To make insensible, torpid, or powerless; *occas.* to stupefy or stun 1530. **2.** To deaden (the mental powers, will, feelings) 1485. Also *fig.* Hence **Benu·mbed** *ppl. a.* (replacing *benome(n)*). **Benu·mbedness. Benu·mbment.**

Benzene (benzī·n, be·nzīn). 1835. [orig. *benzine*, f. BENZOIC + -ENE.] *Chem.* An aromatic hydrocarbon, phenyl hydride, C_6H_6, a colourless liquid obtained from coal-tar oil: = BENZOL 1.

attrib. **b. ring,** the arrangement of the six carbon atoms in the formula of the b. molecule.

Benzine (benzī·n, be·nzīn). 1885. [f. as prec. + -INE[5].] An inflammable liquid, petroleum ether, prepared from natural petroleum, and used as a solvent. Hence as vb., to clean with b.

Benzo-, bef. a vowel **benz-.** [f. BENZOIC.] A formative of the names of substances belonging to, or derived from, the benzene series.

Be·nzamide, C_7H_7NO, the amide of benzoic acid. **Be·nzil, -ile,** a yellowish crystalline substance, $C_{14}H_{10}O_2$, formed bythe action of oxidizing agents on benzoin. **Benzi·lic acid,** $C_{14}H_{12}O_3$; a salt of which is **Be·nzilate. Be·nzin(e,** earliest name of BENZENE. **Be·nzoate,** a salt of benzoic acid; hence **Be·nzoated** *a.* **Be·nzone,** the ketone of benzoic acid (diphenyl ketone). **Benzoyl** (be·nzo,il), the hypothetical radical, C_7H_5O, of benzoic acid, etc.; hence **Benzoy·lic** *a.* **Be·nzyl,** the hypothetical radical $C_6H_5.CH_2$, contained in *Benzyl alcohol*, etc.; hence **Benzy·lic** *a.* **Be·nzylene,** a hypothetical diatomic radical, C_7H_6, found in chlorobenzyl; hence **Benzyle·nic** *a.*

Benzo·ic, *a.* 1791. [f. BENZOIN + -IC.] *Chem.* Of or derived from benzoin; as **B. acid,** $C_7H_6O_2$, a monobasic acid of the Aromatic series, existing in large quantity in gum benzoin.

Benzoin (be·nzo,in, -zoin). 1558. [In XVI *benjoin* (see BENJAMIN[1]), etc. – Fr. *benjoin*, repr. Sp. *benjui*, Pg. *beijoim*, It. *benzoi*, for **lobenzoi*, **lobenjui* (*lo-* being taken for the definite article) – Arab. *lubān-jāwī* 'incense from Sumatra (Java)'.] **1.** A resinous substance obtained from the *Styrax benzoin*, a tree of Sumatra, etc.; now termed for distinction *Gum b.*; also, by pop. corruption BENJAMIN. **2.** *Bot.* A genus of *Lauraceæ*, including the Benzoin Laurel 1866. **3.** *Chem.* Bitter-almond-oil camphor; a constituent of gum-benzoin; it is a ketone, $C_{14}H_{12}O_2$, of the di-phenyl group, and crystallizes in shining prisms 1863. Hence **Be·nzoinate** *v.* to impregnate with b.

Benzol, -ole (be·nzǫl, -zōᵘl). 1838. [f. BENZOIC + the -OL of ALCOHOL. The sp. -OLE prob. refers to L. *oleum.*] **1.** *Chem.* (Benzol) Liebig's name for *benzine*, now replaced by Hoffmann's BENZENE. Also in comb. 1869. **2.** *Min.* (Benzole) Dana's name for native benzine or benzol.

Benzoline (be·nzǒlīn, -lin). 1874. [f. BENZOL + -INE[5].] **1.** *Chem.* Earlier name for AMARINE. **2.** A commercial name for impure benzene, and often for other inflammable liquid hydrocarbons, *esp.* coal-tar naphtha. Also, for a light hydrocarbon obtained from petroleum, and used to burn in lamps.

Bepaint (bǐpē·nt), *v.* 1555. [f. BE- 1 + PAINT *v.*] To paint over; to paint obtrusively; to colour.

Else would a maiden blush b. my cheeke SHAKS.

Bepelt, bepinch, beplaster, etc.; see BE-.

Beplumed (bǐ,plū·md), *ppl. a.* 1582. [BE- 7.] Furnished with feathers.

Bepommel, bepowder, bepraise, beprose, bepuff, etc.; see BE-.

Bequeath (bǐ,kwī·ð), *v.* [OE. *becweþan*, f. BE- 4 + *cweþan* say (see QUOTH). An old word, kept alive in wills.] † **1.** To say; to mean -ME. † **2.** To assign, give as an attribute –1674. **3.** † **a.** To make over, assign –1611. **b.** To leave by will. (The only surviving sense.) OE. Also *fig.* † **4.** To commit *to, unto*; to commend –1718. † **5.** *gen.* To give, yield –1674.

3. **a.** B. to Death your numnesse *Wint. T.* V. iii. 102. **b.** Bequeathing it as a rich Legacie Vnto their issue *Jul. C.* III. ii. 141. **4.** The judges to the common urn b. Their votes DRYDEN. **5.** A niggards purse shall scarce b. his master a good dinner 1608. Hence **Beque·athable** *a.* **Beque·thal,** the action of bequeathing. **Beque·ther. Beque·athment,** the action of bequeathing; a bequest.

† **Beque·th,** *sb.* [ME. *byquide*, OE. *bīcwide, biġcwide* byword, proverb, f. *bī-*, emphatic form of *bi-* BE- + *cwide* saying. Later assim. in sp. to the verb.] **1.** Byword, proverb. (Only in OE.) **2.** Bequest, testament –1642. Also *fig.*

Bequest (bǐ,kwe·st). [ME. *bequeste, -quyste*, f. (after BEQUEATH) BE- + †*quiste*, repr. OE. *-cwiss* (only in comps.), repl. *cwide* saying, testament (see prec.). For the parasitic *-t* cf. BEHEST.] **1.** The action of bequeathing; gift by will, etc. **2.** *concr.* A legacy 1496.

1. B. in a primitive state of society, was seldom recognized MILL. Hence † **Beque·st** *v.* to bequeath.

Beqwete, -qweth(e, etc. obs. ff. BEQUEATH.

† **Berai·n,** *v.* ME. [f. BE- 4 + RAIN *v.*] **1.** To rain upon –1582. **2.** To besprinkle as with rain –1567.

Berate (bǐrē·t) *v.* 1548. [f. BE- 2 + RATE *v.*[2] *Obs.*, exc. in U.S.] To rate vehemently; to scold.

† **Bera·ttle,** *v.* 1553. [f. BE- 2 + RATTLE *v.*[1]] To rattle away upon, or at; to fill with din –1602.

Beray·, *v. arch.* 1530. [f. BE- 2 + RAY *v.*[2] 4 (aphet. f. ARRAY *v.*, see 6). By mod. writers usu. mis-spelt *bewray.*] **1.** To disfigure, defile (with dirt, etc.). **2.** *fig.* To asperse 1576.

Berber (bɔ̄·ɹbəɹ). 1842. [See BARBARY.] **A.** *sb.* An Arab name for the aboriginal people west and south of Egypt; now applied to any member of the great N. African stock to which belong the aboriginal races of Barbary and the Tuwariks of the Sahara. **B.** *adj.* Of or pertaining to the Berbers or their language; applied (often *absol.*) to one of the three great sub-divisions of the Hamitic group 1854.

† **Be·rber.** *Sc.* 1440. [– OFr. *berbere*, in med. L. *berberis*. See BARBERRY.] = BARBERRY.

From *Berberis* (*berberid-*) also; **Be·rberal** *a. Bot.*, of or related to the Barberry, or genus *Berberis*. **Berberida·ceous,** belonging to the N.O. *Berberidaceæ*, of which the barberry is the type. **Berberi·deous,** belonging to the tribe Berberideæ, which includes the barberry. **Berbe·ria, Be·rberine,** a yellow bitter principle obtained from the barberry, etc.

Berberia = BERIBERI, a disease.

Berceaune·tte. 1885. [Tradesman's pseudo-etymological perversion of *bassinette*, which has no connection with Fr. *berceau.*]

† **Be·rcelet.** ME. [Dissimilated form of OFr. *berseret* (in Anglo-L. *bercelettus, canis berserettus*), f. *berser* shoot with the bow, hunt, in med.L. *bersare*. Thence It. *bersaglio* archer's butt, *bersagliere* rifleman, G. *birschen* hunt.] A hunting dog –1679.

Berdash, var. of BURDASH.

Bere, obs. f. BEAR, BEER, BIER, BIRR, BOAR.

Bereave (bǐrī·v), *v.* [OE. *berēafian* = OFris. *birāvia*, OS. *birōbon* (Du. *beroven*), OHG. *biroubōn* (G. *berauben*), Goth. *biraubōn* :– Gmc. **biraubōjan*; see BE- 3, REAVE *v.*[1]] **1.** To deprive, rob, strip, dispossess *of*. Since c1650 mostly of immaterial possessions, *life, hope*, etc., exc. in reference to the loss of relatives. (In the former case *bereft*, in the latter *bereaved*, is more usual.) **2.** To rob, plunder (a possessor); to leave destitute, orphaned, or widowed ME. † **3.** To remove by violence –1718.

1. Madam, you have bereft me of all words *Merch. V.* III. ii. 177. The accident which had bereaved the father of his child D'ISRAELI. All joy was bereft me SCOTT. **3.** Thy life, Echechus! next the sword bereaves POPE. Hence **Berea·ved,** occ. **Berea·ven** (poet.), *ppl. a., spec.* deprived by death of a near relative, etc. **Berea·vement,** the state or fact of being bereaved. **Berea·ver.**

Bereft (bĭre·ft), *ppl. a.* 1531. [Developed normally f. OE. *berēafod* (see prec.); *bereaved* is a new formation.] **1.** Forcibly deprived *of*; void *of* 1586. † **2.** Taken away 1531. **3.** Deprived of a near relation, bereaved (*rare*) 1828.

Berenice's hair (berĕnəi·sīz hēᵊɹ). 1601. [f. *Berenice*, wife of Ptolemy Euergetes, king of Egypt, *c* 248 B.C., whose hair, stolen from the temple of Venus, was said to have been afterwards placed in heaven as a constellation.] The name of a small constellation situated near the tail of Leo; formerly of the star Canopus.

Beresite (be·rĭsəit). 1849. [f. *Beres(owsk* + -ITE¹ 2 b.] *Min.* A fine-grained granite from Beresowsk in the Ural.

‖ **Beret, berret** (berę, be·rėt). 1850. [– Fr. *béret* Basque cap – s.w. Fr. dial. *berret*, Pr. *berret*; see BIRETTA.] A round flat cap worn by the Basque peasantry; also a clerical biretta, and a cap named from it.

Berg (bəɹg). 1823. [Short for ICEBERG.] A (floating) mountain or mass of ice. Hence **Be·rgy** *a.*

Berg, obs. f. BARROW *sb.*¹

Be·rgamask. 1590. [– It. *bergamasco* of Bergamo.] † **1.** *B. dance*: a rustic dance, framed in imitation of the people of Bergamo in Italy. *Mids. N.* v. 360. **2.** A native of Bergamo 1602.

Bergamot¹ (bɔ̄·ɹgămǫt). 1696. [f. *Bergamo*, in Italy.] **1.** A tree (*Citrus bergamia*); from the rind of the fruit a fragrant oil is prepared, called Essence of Bergamot. Also *attrib.* **2.** The essence itself 1766. † **3.** Snuff scented with bergamot –1785. **4.** A kind of mint (*Mentha citrata*). **Wild B.** (in U.S.), *Monarda fistulosa.* 1858. **5.** A woven tapestry of mixed flock and hair, first produced at Bergamo 1882.

Bergamot² (bɔ̄·ɹgămǫt). 1616. [– Fr. *bergamotte* – It. *bergamotta* – Turk. *begarmud*, f. *beg* prince, BEG² + *armud* pear; cf. G. *fürstenbirne.*] A fine kind of pear. Also *attrib.*

Berga·nder. 1544. [perh. f. ME. *berȝ* shelter, burrow (see BERRY *sb.*²) + GANDER; cf. synon. *burrow-duck*, Da. *grav-gaas.*] *Ornith.* An old name of the Sheldrake, *Tadorna vulpanser*, which breeds in rabbit-holes or burrows.

Be·rgeret. ME. [– Fr. *bergerette*, f. *berger* shepherd.] A pastoral.

‖ **Bergfall** (be·rχᵞfal, bɔ̄·ɹgfǭl). 1856. [G., = fall of a mountain.] The ruinous fall of a mountain peak, an avalanche of stones.

Bergmannite (bɔ̄·ɹgmănəit). 1811. [f. *Bergmann*, a mineralogist, + ITE¹ 2 b.] *Min.* A Natrolite, red or white in colour, found in Norway.

Bergomask, = BERGAMASK.

Bergylt, berguylt (bɔ̄·ɹgilt). 1809. [Referred by Jamieson to ON. *berg* rock; cf. synon. *bergle.*] **1.** The name of a fish, the Black Goby, in Shetland. **2.** The Norwegian haddock or Sea Perch (*Sebastes norvegicus*) 1838.

‖ **Be·ribe·ri.** 1879. [Sinhalese; redupl. of *beri* weakness. So Fr. *béribéri.*] *Med.* An acute disease, prevalent in India, generally presenting dropsical symptoms, with paralytic weakness of the legs.

Berime, berhyme (bĭrəi·m), *v.* 1589. [BE- 4]. To compose rimes about; often, to lampoon. *A.Y.L.* III. ii. 186.

Berkeleian (bāɹklī·ăn). 1804. [f. *Berkeley*, Bishop of Cloyne (died 1753), who denied the objective existence of the material world. See -AN.] **A.** *adj.* Of or originating with Berkeley. **B.** *sb.* A follower of Berkeley. Hence **Berkelei·anism, Be·rkeleyism,** the philosophical opinions held by Berkeley and his followers.

Berlin (bɔ̄·ɹlin, bəɹli·n). 1731. [The name of the capital of Prussia, used *attrib.*, and transferred to things coming thence.] **1.** An old-fashioned four-wheeled covered carriage, with a seat behind covered with a hood. [Also *Berline* from Fr.] **2.** Short for 'Berlin wool' 1881. **3.** Short for 'Berlin Glove': A knitted glove (of Berlin wool) 1836.

Comb., etc.: **B. black,** a black varnish used for coating the better kinds of ironware; **B. blue** = PRUSSIAN blue; **B. castings,** ornamental objects of **B. iron,** a very fusible quality of iron, suitable for casting figures and delicate objects; **B. warehouse,** a shop for B. wool, etc.; **B. wool,** a fine dyed wool used for knitting, tapestry, etc.; **B. work,** worsted embroidery.

Berlin, -ling, var. of BIRLINN. SCOTT.

†‖ **Berli·na, -ino.** [It.] Pillory. B. JONS.

Berm (bɔ̄ɹm). 1729. [– Fr. *berme* – Du. *berm*, prob. rel. to ON. *barmr* brim.] **1.** A narrow space or ledge; *esp.* in *Fortif.* a space, from 3 to 8 feet wide, sometimes left between the ditch and the base of the parapet. **2. Berm-bank,** the bank of a canal opposite the towing path. [? Only in U.S.] 1854.

Bermuda (bəɹmiū·dă, -miū·dă). 1640. A group of islands in the N. Atlantic; *hence*, a variety of cigar, or rolled tobacco. **B. grass,** name in U.S. of *Cynodon dactylon.*

Bernacle, -icle, bernak(e, vars. of BARNACLE.

Bernardine (bɔ̄·ɹnăɹdin), *a.* (*sb.*) 1676. [– mod.L. *Bernardinus*; see -INE¹.] **1.** Of or pertaining to St. Bernard (abbot of Clairvaux in 1115), or to the Cistercian order, patronized by him. **2.** *sb.* A monk of this order.

† **Berne.** [OE. *beorn*, earlier *biorn* (:– **bern*) 'warrior', hence 'man', *vir*, ἀνήρ.] A warrior; later, poet. for 'man' –1528.

Bernoo, bernous, vars. of BURNOUS.

Bero·b, *v.*; see BE- 2.

‖ **Beroe** (be·ro,ī). 1769. [– L. *Beroë* – Gr. Βερόη, a daughter of Oceanus.] *Zool.* A genus of small, gelatinous, marine animals classed by Huxley among the Cœlenterata.

† **Bero·gue,** *v.* 1673. [BE- 5.] To call (one) a rogue –1733.

Berret, berretta, obs. ff. BERET, BIRETTA.

Berried, *a.* 1794. [f. BERRY *sb.*¹ + -ED².] **1.** Bearing berries. **2.** Formed as or consisting of a berry; baccate 1824. **3.** Bearing eggs; 'in berry', as a hen lobster carrying her eggs 1868.

1. Red-berried holly 1871.

Berry (be·ri), *sb.*¹ [OE. *beri(ġ)e*, cogn. w. OS. *beri*, MDu. *bēre*, (M)Du. *bezie* (Du. *bes*), OHG. *beri* (G. *beere*), ON. *ber*, Goth. *basi*, f. Gmc. **basj*- **bazj*-.] **1.** Any small globular or ovate juicy fruit, not having a stone; in OE. *esp.* the grape; in Sc. and n. Eng. the gooseberry. **b.** *loosely*, A coffee bean 1712. **2.** *Bot.* A many-seeded inferior pulpy fruit, the seeds of which are scattered throughout the pulp, as the grape, gooseberry, and currants 1809. **3.** The eggs in the roe of a fish; the eggs of a lobster 1768.

Be·rry, *sb.*² ME. [f. *beorġe*, dat. of OE. *beorg* hill, whence BARROW *sb.*¹] A mound, hillock, or barrow. Now *dial.*

† **Be·rry** *sb.*³ 1486. [Cf. BURROW *sb.*³] A (rabbit's) burrow –1685. Also *transf.*

Be·rry, *v.*¹ Now *dial.* [ME. *berien, bery*, – ON. *berja* strike, beat, thresh = OHG., MHG. *berren*; repr. in OE. only by pa. pple. *ġebered.*] **1.** To beat, thrash. **2.** To thresh (corn, etc.) 1483. **3.** To beat (a path, etc.).

Berry (be·ri), *v.*² 1865. [f. BERRY *sb.*¹] **1.** *intr.* To come into berry; to swell. **2.** To go gathering berries 1871.

Berserk, -er (bɔ̄·ɹsəɹk, -əɹ). 1822. [– Icel. *berserkr*, acc. *berserk*, prob. f. *bern-*, *björn* BEAR *sb.*¹ + *serkr* coat, SARK, but otherwise explained as f. *berr* BARE *a.*, whence Eng. BARESARK.] A wild Norse warrior, who fought on the battle-field with a frenzied fury known as the 'berserker rage'; often a lawless bravo. Also *fig.* and *attrib.*

Berskin, obs. f. BEARSKIN.

Berstel, obs. f. BRISTLE.

Berth (bɔ̄ɹþ). 1622. [Early vars. *birth*, *byrth*; prob. f. BEAR *v.*¹ + -TH¹, with ref. to the nautical sense of the verb 'sail in a certain direction'.] **1.** *Naut.* Convenient sea-room. Also *transf.* and *fig.* **2.** Hence, The place where a ship lies when at anchor or at a wharf 1706. **3.** *Naut.* 'A place on board a ship for a mess to put their chests, etc.'; whence, A room where any number of the officers or ship's company mess and reside 1706. **b.** *fig.* (*Naut.*) Proper place (for a thing) 1732. **c.** *transf.* An allotted place in a barracks, a coach, etc. 1813. **4.** A situation, a place, an appointment. (Usu. a 'comfortable' one.) 1720. **5.** A sleeping-place in a ship; a long box or shelf on the side of a cabin, or of a railway carriage, for sleeping in 1796.

1. Giving the apparent phantom what seamen call a wide b. SCOTT. **3.** The best b. in the coach SCOTT. **4.** An officer's b. R. DANA. You have a good warm b. here MISS BURNEY. *Comb.*, **b.-deck,** the deck on which the passengers' berths are arranged.

Berth (bɔ̄ɹþ), *v.*¹ 1667. [f. prec. sb.] **1.** To moor or place (a ship) in a suitable position. Also *refl.* of the ship or sailors. **2.** To allot a berth to. Usu. in *pass.* 1845. **3.** To provide with a situation 1865.

3. Comfortably berthed in the City Chamberlainship 1865.

Berth, *v.*² 1574. [perh. f. Icel. *byrði* board (side) of a ship.] To cover or make up with boards. (Chiefly in Ship-building.)

Bertha, berthe (bɔ̄·ɹþă, bɔ̄ɹþ). 1856. [– Fr. *berthe*, anglicized as *bertha*, a use of the proper name, Fr. *Berthe*, Eng. *Bertha.*] A deep falling collar, attached to the top of a low-necked dress.

Berthage (bɔ̄·ɹþėdʒ). 1881. [f. BERTH *v.*¹ + -AGE.] Accommodation for mooring vessels.

Berthierite (bɔ̄·ɹþiərəit). 1827. [f. *Berthier*, a naturalist + -ITE¹ 2 b.] *Min.* A sulphide of antimony and iron, occurring native in elongated masses.

Berthing (bɔ̄·ɹþiŋ), *vbl. sb.*¹ 1800. [f. BERTH *v.*¹ + -ING¹.] The action of placing a ship in a berth.

Be·rthing, *vbl. sb.*² 1706. [f. BERTH *v.*² + -ING¹.] The upright planking of the sides, etc., of a ship; *esp.* that outside above the sheer-strake.

‖ **Bertillonage** (bęrtiyonā·ʒ). 1892. [f. Alphonse *Bertillon* (1853–1914) + -AGE.] A system of identifying criminals by measurements, finger prints, etc.

† **Be·rtram.** 1578. [– G. *bertram*, corruption of L. PYRETHRUM.] Pellitory of Spain.

† **Beru·n,** *v.* [OE. *berinnan* = OHG., Goth. *birinnan*, f. *bi-* BE- 4 + *rinnan* RUN *v.*] To run or flow round –1515.

Beryl (be·ril). ME. [– (O)Fr. *beryl*, *beril* (mod. *béryl*) :– L. *beryllus* – Gr. βήρυλλος, prob. of foreign origin.] **A.** *sb.* **1.** A transparent precious stone of a pale-green colour passing into light-blue, yellow, and white; distinguished only by colour from the emerald. Varieties are the *aquamarine*, which is of pale bluish-green, and the chrysoberyl, and perh. the chrysoprase, which are yellow. So *beryl-stone.* Also † *fig.* **2.** *Min.* A mineral species including not only the beryl, but also the emerald, a variety of the beryl, distinguished by the presence of oxide of chromium. Beryl is a silicate of aluminium and glucinum. 1837. † **3.** *transf.* A fine kind of crystal or glass –1625. † **4.** A mirror –1576. **5.** The colour of the beryl (pale sea-green) 1834.

B. *attrib.* and as *adj.* **1.** Of beryl; also *formerly*, Of crystal 1594. **2.** *adj.* Beryl-like in colour, clear pale green 1857. Hence **Be·ryl-line** *a.* b.-like.

Beryllia (bĕri·liă). 1873. [f. BERYLLIUM, after *magnesia*, *magnesium*, etc.; see -IA¹.] *Chem.* The oxide of beryllium or glucinum; GLUCINA.

Beryllium (bĕri·liŏm). 1863. [f. BERYL + -IUM.] *Chem.* A metallic element formerly called GLUCINUM. Symbol Be.

Berylloid (be·riloid). [f. L. *beryllus* BERYL + -OID.] *Crystallog.* A geometrical solid consisting of two twelve-sided pyramids put base to base, as in the beryl.

Berzelianite (bəɹzī·liănəit). [f. name of J. J. *Berzelius* (1779–1848), Swedish chemist and mineralogist; see -ITE¹ 2 b.] *Min.* A native selenide of copper, silver white with metallic lustre. **Berze·liite,** an anhydrous arsenate of lime and magnesia; Kühnite.

Bes-, repr. OFr. *bes-* :– L. *bis* 'twice, in two ways, doubly'; in Romanic, 'secondarily, in an inferior way'; whence, 'improperly, unsymmetrically, not right or straight, awry, aslant'. Found in Eng. as *bes-*, *be-*, *bez-*.

Besai·el, besaile. *Obs.* exc. *Law.* [Late ME. *beayell* (– AFr.), *bysayeul* – OFr. *besayel* (mod. *bisaieul*), f. *bes-* BES- + *ayel* grandfather; see AIEL.] A great-grandfather. **b.** *Law.* In *Writ of besaile*, a writ which formerly lay for the heir where his great-grandfather died seised of land in fee-simple, and a stranger entered the day of his death, or abated after his death.

Besai·nt (bǐsēⁱ·nt). 1603. [BE- 5.] To make a saint of.

Besand(e, -saunt(e, obs. ff. BEZANT.

Bes-antler, var. of BEZ-ANTLER.

Bescatter (bǐˌskæ·təɹ), *v.* 1574. [BE- 1.] **a.** To besprinkle *with*. **b.** To scatter about.

Bescratch, -scrawl, -screen, -scribble, -scumber, etc.; see BE-.

Besee·, *v. arch.* [OE. *bi-*, *besēon* = OS., OHG. *bisehan*, Goth. *bisaihwan*, f. *bi-* BE- + *sēon* SEE *v.*] **I.** † **1.** *intr.* To look about; to see; also *fig.* –ME. † **2.** To see to; *hence*, to use (*well* or *ill*) –1596. † **3.** To provide, arrange ME. only. **II.** Later uses of the pa. pple. **Beseen.** † **1.** Seen; as in *well-beseen*, good looking –1542. **2.** Appearing; furnished ME.

Beseech (bǐsī·tʃ), *v.* Pa. t. and pple. **besought** (bǐsǭ·t). ME. [f. *bi-* BE- 2 + ME. *secen, sechen, seken* SEEK. In contrast to the simple verb, in which the northern *seek* has displaced the southern *seech*, in the compound *beseech* has become the standard form.] † **1.** To seek after, try to get. **2.** To beg earnestly for ME. **3.** To supplicate ME. **4.** To ask earnestly (*arch.*) ME.

2. I b. your worship's name *Mids. N.* III. i. 183. **3.** I b. thee, shew me thy glory *Ex.* 33:18. I pray and b. you. . to accompany me *Bk. Com. Pr.* **4.** To b. for food SOUTHEY. Hence † **Besee·ch** *sb.* (*rare*) beseeching. **Besee·cher,** a petitioner, *esp.* to the king or his courts. **Beseeching-ly** *adv.*, **-ness. Besee·chment,** beseeching.

Beseek(e, obs. f. BESEECH.

Beseem (bǐsī·m), *v.* ME. [BE- 2.] † **1.** To seem, look. (Mostly in 3rd pers.) –1779. Also *impers.* **2.** To suit in appearance; to become, befit ME. **3.** *absol.* To be seemly ME.

2. A prison may well b. his holiness MARLOWE. Sad pause and deep regard b. the sage SHAKS. *Lucr.* 277. **3.** To treat thee as beseems MILT. Hence **Besee·ming-ly** *adv.*, **-ness. Besee·mly** *a.* seemly; whence **Besee·mliness.**

Beset (bǐse·t), *v.* Pa. t. and pple. **beset.** [OE. *besettan* = OFris. *bisetta*, OS. *bisettian* (Du. *bezetten*), OHG. *bisezzan* (G. *besetzen*), Goth. *bisatjan* :– Gmc. **bi-* BE- 1, 4 + **satjan* SET *v.*] **I.** *trans.* **1.** To set about, surround *with*. Now only in pa. pple. **2.** To surround with hostile intent; to assail (a person); to invest (a place); to occupy (a road, passage, etc.) ME. Also *fig.* **3.** *gen.* To close round; hem in 1534.

1. A tiara beset with pearls DE QUINCEY. **2.** The lioness. . beset by men and hounds POPE. *fig.* The sinne which does so easily b. us *Heb.* 12:1. Beset with contradictions FREEMAN. **3.** Completely beset [by ice] KANE.

II. To set (in fig. sense), to bestow. All *trans.* † **1.** To set or place (one's mind, trust, etc.) *on* or *upon*; = SET *v.* –1627. † **2.** To employ (one's wit, money, etc.). Cf. *bestow*. –1560. † **3.** To bestow (*esp.* in marriage), to allot, transfer –1599. † **4.** To set in order –1500. † **5.** To become. Cf. Sc. *set*, Fr. *seoir*. –1598.

1. This worthi man ful wel his witte bisette CHAUCER. Hence **Bese·tter. Bese·tting** *ppl. a.* (*esp.* in *besetting sin*).

Besetment (bǐse·tmĕnt). 1830. [f. prec. + -MENT.] **1.** The fact of besetting; *concr.* that which besets one. **2.** A condition of being beset 1853.

† **Besew, beshade, beshadow, beshame, beshear,** etc.; see BE-.

Beshine (bǐʃəi·n), *v.* [OE. *bi-*, *bescīnan* = OFris. *bischīna*, OS., OHG. *biscīnan*, Goth. *biskeinan* :– Gmc. **bi-* BE- 1 + **skīnan* SHINE.] To shine about or upon; to illumine. Obs. bef. 1600, but revived by Carlyle. Hence **Besho·ne** *ppl. a.*

Beshrew (bǐʃrū·), *v. arch.* ME. [f. BE 2 + SHREW *v.*] † **1.** To make wicked; to deprave –1556. † **2.** To curse, or blame greatly, as the cause of misfortune –1682. **b.** Now only in *Beshrew me, thee*, etc.: 'Devil take, hang'; also, 'plague on', and often playful. [Perh. ellipt. Cf. (*I*) *thank you.*]

Beshroud, † **beshut,** etc.; see BE-.

Beside (bǐsəi·d). [Early ME. *biside, bisiden*, repr. OE. *be sīdan*, i.e. *be* BY, dat. sing. of *sīde* SIDE. Cf. the orig. synon. BIHALVE.] **A.** *adv.* **1.** † By the side, by one's side; hard by (*arch.*). **2.** In addition. (Now usu. BESIDES.) ME. **3.** Otherwise, else. (Now usu. BESIDES.) 1588. † **4.** On or to one side. (Now ASIDE.) –1604. † **5.** By, past. *To go b.*: to pass on one side, to miss. –1592.

1. Some on horsys and some besyde ME. **2.** My selfe, and diuers Gentlemen b. SHAKS. **3.** We talk'd Of thee and none b. 1816.

B. *prep.* **1.** *lit.* By the side of; *hence*, hard by ME. **b.** *fig.* Side by side with in rank, or for comparison 1513. **2.** In addition to. (Now usu. BESIDES.) ME. **3.** Other than, else than. (Now usu. BESIDES.) ME. † **4.** Outside of, out of, away from, past –1663. Also *fig.*

1. The thefe that honge on the crosse besyde our lorde 1526. Seint Gyles b. Holbourne ME. *fig.* Besyde Latyne our langage is imperfite 1513. **4.** *To go b.*: to pass by, miss. *To look b.*: to overlook, miss. (*fig.*) *B. oneself*: out of one's wits; cf. Fr. *hors de soi*, Ger. *ausser sich*. Enough to put him quite b. his patience SHAKS. B. the purpose MORE, my Scope RAY, the real issue FROUDE. At Durham, b. all expectation, I met an old friend JOHNSON.

Besides (bǐsəi·dz). ME. [f. BESIDE + -S *suffix*; prob. a northern substitute for the southern *-en* of *besiden.*] **A.** *adv.* † **1.** = BESIDE A 1. –1450. **2.** In addition, as well 1564; moreover 1596. **3.** Other than that mentioned, else 1596. † **4.** Now ASIDE –1660.

2. Hast thou here any b.? *Gen.* 19:12. B., they were indemnified for it BURKE. **3.** Robbers, who break with all the world b., must keep faith among themselves BURKE.

B. *prep.* † **1.** = BESIDE B 1. –1677. **2.** Over and above, in addition to, as well as. (This and 3 are the ordinary current senses.) 1535. **3.** Other than, else than: in neg. and interrog. sentences = 'except, excluding' ME. † **4.** = BESIDE B 4. –1702. Also *fig.*

2. Besydes all this, betwene you and us there is a great gulfe set *Luke* 16:26. **3.** The Jews. . for ever unsainting all the world b. themselves SOUTH.

Besiege (bǐsī·dʒ), *v.* [ME. *bi-*, *by-*, *besege*, f. (by substitution of prefix BE-) ME. *assiege*; see ASSIEGE.] To sit down before (a town, etc.) with armed forces in order to capture it; to lay siege to, beleaguer, invest. Also *fig.* and *transf.*

Antigonus besieged the city for ten months THIRLWALL. When forty winters shall b. thy brow SHAKS. *Sonn.* ii. To b. the doors of the bakers 1789. To b. Heaven with supplications 1867. Hence † **Besie·ge** *sb.* siege. **Besie·ged** *ppl. a.* invested by hostile forces; *absol.* the people besieged. **Besie·gement,** the action of besieging; the being besieged. **Besie·ger. Besie·gingly** *adv.* (*rare*).

Besilver, besing, etc.; see BE-.

† **Besi·t,** *v.* [OE. *besittan* sit about, besiege, f. BE- 1 + SIT; see BESET.] **1.** To encamp about, besiege ME. only. **2.** To sit properly upon (as a dress); to fit, suit. Cf. F. *seoir*. –1614.

Beslabber, var. of BESLOBBER.

Beslave (bǐˌslēⁱ·v), *v.* 1615. [BE- 5.] To make a slave of; to call 'slave'; to pollute with slavery.

Beslaver (bǐˌslæ·vəɹ), *v.* 1589. [f. BE- 4 + SLAVER *v.*] **1.** To slaver upon or over. **2.** *fig.* To cover with fulsome flattery 1861.

Beslobber (bǐˌslǫ·bəɹ), *v.* ME. [f. BE- 1, 4 + SLOBBER.] To wet or befoul with saliva (= to BESLAVER), or with liquid food escaping from the mouth; to kiss like a drivelling child; *fig.* = prec. 2.

Beslubber (bǐˌslɒ·bəɹ), *v.* ME. [BE- 1 + SLUBBER *v.*] To wet and soil with a thick liquid; to bedaub.

Besmear (bǐˌsmīᵊ·ɹ), *v.* [OE. *bismierwan*, f. *bi-* BE- 1 + *smierwan* SMEAR *v.*] To smear over or about; to cover (and soil) *with* any greasy or sticky substance. Also *fig.*

Besmering and dawbing eche other with dirte and myer 1535.

Besmirch (bǐˌsmə̄·ɹtʃ), *v.* 1602. [f. BE- 2 + SMIRCH *v.*] To soil, discolour, as with smoke, soot, or mud; *fig.* to dim the lustre of.

Besmoke (bǐˌsmōᵘ·k), *v.* ME. [BE- 4.] To fill, or act on, with smoke, to fumigate.

† **Besmo·ttered,** *ppl. a.* [Origin unascertained.] Bespattered as with mud. CHAUCER.

Be-smut (bǐˌsmɒ·t), *v.* 1610. [BE- 1 + SMUT *v.*] To blacken with smut; also *fig.*

Be-smu·tch, *v.* 1831. [f. BE- 1 + SMUTCH *v.*] To besmirch.

Besnow (bǐˌsnōᵘ·), *v.* [OE. *bisnīwian*, f. BE- 1 + *snīwian* SNOW *v.*] To cover with or as with snow.

† **Beso·gne.** 1615. [– obs. Fr. *bisogne*, '*bisongne*, a filthie knaue, or clowne; a raskall, bisonian, base humoured scoundrell' (Cotgrave), – It. *bisogno*; see BESONIO.] **a.** A raw recruit. **b.** = BEZONIAN. –1658. So † **Beso·gnier.**

Besoi·l, *v.* ME. [BE- 1.] To sully; also *fig.*

Besom (bī·zəm), *sb.*[1] [OE. *besema, besma* = OFris, *besma*, OS. *besmo* (Du. *bezem*), OHG. *besamo* (G. *besen*) :– WGmc. **besmo.*] † **1.** A bundle of rods or twigs used for birching –ME. **2.** An implement for sweeping, usu. a bunch of broom, etc. tied round a handle; a broom. (In lit. Eng. 'broom' is now the generic name, 'besom' specific.) OE. **3.** *fig.* Any agent that sweeps away or cleanses ME.

3. Swepe thy soul clene wyth the besome of the drede of God ME.

Besom, *sb.*[2] *Sc.* 1816. A low woman.

Be·som, *v.* ME. [f. BESOM *sb.*[1] Cf. *to brush.*] † **1.** *intr.* To sweep with violence ME. only. **2.** To sweep (*away, out*, etc.) 1791. Hence **Be·somer,** one who uses a besom.

† **Beso·nio, beso·gnio.** 1603. [var. of BISOGNIO.] **a.** A raw soldier. **b.** (term of contempt) A needy beggar; a base worthless fellow. –1820.

† **Beso·rt,** *v.* [f. BE- + SORT *sb.* or *v.*] To assort or match with; to befit. *Lear* I. iv. 272. ? Hence † **Beso·rt** *sb.* suitable company. *Oth.* I. iii. 238.

Besot (bǐsǫ·t), *v.* 1581. [f. BE- 5 + SOT *sb.* or *v.*, after earlier ASSOT; cf. BEDOTE.] **1.** *trans.* To cause to dote *on*; to infatuate *with*. **2.** To stupefy in mind or morally 1615. **3.** To make a sot of. (Said of narcotics.) Also *absol.* 1627.

2. Besotted with words HAZLITT. **3.** Pleasure. . has an opiate in it; it stupefies and besots YOUNG. Hence **Beso·tted-ly** *adv.*, **-ness.**

Besought (bǐsǭ·t), pa. t. and pple. of BESEECH.

Besouth (bǐsau·þ), *prep.* Now *Sc.* ME. [Late ME. *besowth*, f. BE- + SOUTH; cf. BENORTH.] On or to the south of.

Bespangle (bǐˌspæ·ŋg'l), *v.* 1593. [BE- 6.] To besprinkle with or as with spangles. var. **Bespa·nkle.**

[Stars] to. . b. a canopy over our heads WOLLASTON.

Bespatter (bǐˌspæ·təɹ), *v.* 1644. [BE- 1.] **1.** To spatter over or about 1674. **2.** *fig.* To asperse (*with* abuse, etc.). Usu. in a bad sense. 1644. **3.** *spec.* To slander 1653.

1. Bespattered with mud THIRLWALL.

† **Bespaw·l,** *v.* 1602. [f. BE- 4 + SPAWL *v.* (sense 1).] To bespatter with saliva; also *fig.* –1647.

Bespeak (bǐˌspī·k), *v.* Pa. t. **bespoke,** and (*arch.*) **-spake.** Pa. pple. **bespoken, bespoke.** [OE. *bisprecan* = OFris. *bispreka*. OS. *besprekan* (Du. *bespreken*), OHG. *bisprehhan* (G. *besprechen*); see BE- 1 and 4, SPEAK.] † **1.** *intr.* To call out, complain *that* OE. only. † **2.** To exclaim: orig. by way of remonstrance; later, simply, to speak –1791. † **3.** *trans.* To speak against –ME. † **4.** To speak about; to discuss –1489. **5.** To speak for; to arrange for, engage beforehand; to order (goods) 1583. **6.** To address (a person). Now *poet.* 1590. **7.** To speak of, indicate 1628; to augur 1719.

2. Until their Lord himself bespake, and bid them go MILT. **5.** To b. a lodging 1602, a play STEELE, one's custom 1712, a friendly reception for oneself COBBETT. **7.** But her house Bespake a sleepy hand of negligence WORDSW. Circumstances that b. war HAWTHORNE. Hence **Bespea·k** *sb.* a bespeaking; *esp.* of a play; *hence*, a benefit night, when the actor's friends, etc., choose the play. **Bespea·ker.**

Bespecked, bespeckle, bespew, bespeed, etc.; see BE-.

† **Bespe·te,** *v. arch.* [ME. *bespeten*, f. BE- 1 + *speten*, OE. *spǣtan* SPIT *v.*[2]] = BESPIT. CHAUCER.

Bespice, bespill: see BE-.

Bespi·t, *v. arch.* ME. [See BE- 1.] *trans.* To spit upon. Rarely *intr.* with *upon*.

Besplash, bespot; see BE-.

Bespou·t, *v.* 1575. [f. BE- 4 + SPOUT *v.* (intr.).] To besprinkle by spouting (*lit.* and *fig.*).

Woe for the age,. . quack-ridden, bespeeched, bespouted CARLYLE.

Bespread (bĭ͵spre·d), *v.* [ME. *bi-, bespred(en*, f. *bi-* BE- 4, 1 + *spreden* SPREAD *v.*] **1.** To spread *with*. **2.** Of things: To spread over 1641. **3.** To spread out 1557.

2. Mats bespreading the floor 1779.

Bespre·ng, *v.* Obs. exc. in pa. pple. **besprent.** [OE. *besprengan*, f. BE- 1 + *sprengan* sprinkle :– Gmc. **spraʒʒjan*, causative of **spreʒʒan* SPRING *v.*[1]] **1.** *trans.* To sprinkle over; to strew *with* –1606. **2.** To sprinkle (things) about –1820. var. † **Bespri·ng.**

Besprent (bĭ͵spre·nt), *ppl. a.* ME. [pa. pple. of ME. *besprenge*; see prec.] **1.** Besprinkled, strewed *with*. **2.** Scattered about 1567.

1. Knot-grass dew-b. MILT. *Comus* 542. Flower-b. meadows WORDSW.

Besprinkle (bĭ͵spri·ŋk'l), *v.* [ME. *besprengil*, **besprenkel*, f. BE- 1 and 4 + *sprenkel*, freq. of *sprengen* asperse.] *trans.* To sprinkle all over *with*. Also *fig.*

The walls were besprinkled with holy water GIBBON. Hence **Bespri·nkler.**

† **Bespurt,** † **bespurtle, besputter,** † **besquirt;** see BE- 4.

Bessemer (be·sĭmər). 1856. [f. name of inventor, Sir Henry *Bessemer* (1813–98).] **B. process:** a process for decarbonizing and desiliconizing pig-iron so as to convert it into steel or malleable iron, by passing air through the molten metal. Hence **B. iron, steel,** briefly *Bessemer*; also *attrib.*

Best (best), *a.* and *adv.* [OE. *betest*, adv. *betost, betst* = OFris., OS. (Du.) *best*, OHG. *bezzist-o* (G. *best*), ON. *bezt-r, bazt-r*, Goth. *batist-s* :– Gmc. **batist-az*, superl. of **bat-*; see BETTER, -EST.] **A.** *adj.* Superl. of GOOD. Most good (*Goodest* is not a Gmc. form.) **I. 1.** Excelling all others in quality. **2.** Of persons: Most kind. Of persons and things: Most advantageous; most appropriate. OE. **3.** Largest, most; *esp.* in *best part* 1538.

1. Of many good, I thinke him b. *Two Gent.* I. ii. 102. The b. people in the town (*mod.*). **2.** Which of your brothers is b. to you? 1887. *I, you,* etc. *had b.* (formerly *me were b.*, later *I were b.*): it would be b. for me, etc. See BETTER.

II. *absol.* (rarely passing into a *sb.*) **1.** *pl.* The best people OE. **2.** *sing.* The best thing, point, circumstance, element ME. **3.** With possessive. *One's best*: **a.** The best one can (do) ME. **b.** Best state, point, or condition 1571. **c.** Best clothes 1790.

2. Bad is the b. 1693. All these I better in one generall b. SHAKS. *Sonn.* xci. **3.** He did his b. to seem to eat POPE. It exhibits man at his b.

Phrases, etc. *To put one's b. foot* or *leg foremost*: to do one's b. to get on. With *verbs*: *To have the b. of it*: to have the advantage in a contest, or a transaction, and *hence*, the least possible loss; so *To make the b. of it*. With *preps.*: † *At the b., at b*: in the best possible manner or condition. *At b.*: (taken) in the most favourable aspect, making every allowance. *For the b.*: aiming at, tending to, the b. result. *To the b.*: to the utmost effort or extent (of one's power, etc.).

B. *adv.* Superl. of WELL. **1.** With *vbs.* In the most excellent way, in the highest degree; in the most suitable manner, with the greatest advantage, to the fullest extent OE. **2.** With *adjs.* and *pples.* written with the hyphen, as *b.-bred, b.-conditioned*, i.e. *best condition* + *-ed* ME. **3.** With *agent-nouns*, as *b.-wisher*.

1. Who b. bear his mild yoke, they serve him b. MILT. **2.** The b.-laid schemes o' mice an' men BURNS. The b.-natured fellow alive 1863.

Best, *v. colloq.* 1863. [f. prec.; cf. *to worst*.] To get the better of.

† **Bestad, -stadde,** *v.* 1579. Earlier f. BESTED *pa. pple.* Used only in pass.; but by Spenser made a pa. t. and active pple. = BESET.

Bestain (bĭ͵stēⁱn), *v.* 1559. [f. BE- 1 + STAIN *v.*] To mark with stains.

† **Besta·nd,** *v.* [OE. *bestandan* = Goth. *bestandan*, f. *bi-* BE- 1 + *standan* STAND *v.*] **1.** To stand by or near; *esp.* to stand by (the dead), to mourn for. Also *absol.* –ME. **2.** To stand round in hostility, to beset –1485.

Bestar (bĭ͵stā·ɹ), *v.* 1612. [BE- 6.] To spangle or adorn as with stars. Hence **Besta·rred** *ppl. a.*; *spec.* decorated with the star of an order.

Bestead (bĭ͵ste·d), *v.* Pa. t. **besteaded.** Pa. pple. **bested, bestead.** 1581. [f. BE- 2 + STEAD *v.*] **1.** *trans.* To assist. **2.** To avail 1589.

1. Better able by his purse. . to b. his neighbours, than they him 1627. **2.** Thou vain Philosophy! Little hast thou bestead CLOUGH.

† **Bestea·l,** *v.* [OE. *bestelan*, f. BE- 4 + *stelan* STEAL *v.* (intr.).] *intr.* (and *refl.*) To steal or move stealthily (*away* or *on*) –1597.

Bested, bestead (bĭste·d), *pa. pple.* [ME. *bistad*, f. *bi-* BE- 2 + *stad* – ON. *staddr*, pa. pple. of *steðja* place, w. later assim. to native *sted* STEAD.] † **1.** Placed ME. only. † **2.** Settled ME. only. **3.** Beset *by*, † *with* ME. **4.** Situated, circumstanced (with *ill*, etc.) ME. † **b.** (Without an adv.) Hard pressed –1587.

3. Bestad with dethe on euery syde 1493. **4.** I never saw a fellow worse bestead 2 *Hen. VI*, II. iii. 56.

Bestial (be·stiăl), *sb.* [– OFr. *bestial* – med. L. *bestiale*, subst. use of n. sing. of late L. *bestialis* (see next); earlier ME. *bestaile* – OFr. *bestaille* – med. L. *bestialia*, n. pl. of *bestialis*.] **1.** A collective term for domestic animals, kept for food or tillage. Since 17th c. displaced in Eng. by *cattle*, but in Sc. still in use. **2.** A single beast; (with *pl.*) ME.

Bestial (be·stiăl), *a.* [– OFr. *bestial* – late L. *bestialis*, f. L. *bestia* BEAST; see -IAL.] **1.** Of or belonging to the lower animals, *esp.* quadrupeds. **2.** *transf.* Like a beast; brutish, irrational; barbarous ME. **3.** *esp.* Like a beast in indulging the animal instincts; depraved, lustful, cruel, brutal, beastly, obscene 1447.

1. A Satyr; of Shape, part Humane, part B. STEELE. **2.** Bestiall ignorance 1615. **3.** Thy faythfull felowe is bestiall dronkennes BARCLAY. Hence **Be·stialism,** the condition of beasts. **Be·stially** *adv.*

Bestiality (bestiæ·lĭti). [– (O)Fr. *bestialité*, see prec., -ITY.] **1.** The state or quality of being BESTIAL. † **2.** Unnatural connection with a beast –1765.

Bestialize (be·stiăləiz), *v.* 1684. [f. BESTIAL *a.* + -IZE.] To change into the form or nature of a beast; to brutalize, debase.

He bestializes man and humanizes beasts 1845.

† **Be·stian,** *a.* 1652. [f. L. *bestia* BEAST + -AN.] Of or belonging to the 'Beast' of the Apocalypse (cf. BEAST) –1701. **Be·stianism,** the power of the Beast. **Be·stianize,** to be a follower of the Beast.

Bestiary (be·stiări). 1625. [Sense 1 – L. *bestiarius*; sense 2 – med.L. *bestiarium*; f. L. *bestia* BEAST; see -ARY[1].] † **1.** A beast-fighter in the Roman amphitheatre. **2.** A treatise on beasts, as written during the Middle Ages 1840.

Besti·ck, *v.* 1623. [f. BE- 1 and 4.] **1.** To cover all over. Also *fig.* **2.** To transfix 1667.

Bestill; see BE- 1.

Bestir (bĭ͵stɔ̄·ɹ), *v.* [f. BE- 2 + STIR, not continuous w. OE. *bestyrian* heap up.] To stir up. **a.** *refl.* To busy oneself ME. **b.** *trans.* To rouse into activity 1549.

B. the and hardiliche fight ME. Bestyre youre werye handes COVERDALE.

Best man (be·st mæ·n). 1814. [orig. Sc.] The groomsman at a wedding.

Bestorm (bĭ͵stǫ·ɹm), *v.* 1651. [f. BE- 1 + STORM *v.*] To storm on all sides.

Bestow (bĭ͵stōᵘ·), *v.* [ME., f. BE- 2 + OE. *stow* place, STOW *sb*[1].] **1.** To place, locate; to dispose of (*in* some place) (*arch.*). **2.** To stow away (*arch.*) ME. **3.** To lodge, put up (*arch.*) 1577. Also *refl.* † **4.** To settle or give in marriage. Also *refl.* –1714. **5.** To apply, to employ (*in* an occupation); to devote *for* a purpose ME.; *esp.* † to lay out (money) –1631; † *refl.* to acquit oneself –1606. **6.** *trans.* (and *absol.*) To confer as a gift 1535.

1. How should I b. him? Shall I put him into the basket againe? *Merry W.* IV. ii. 48. **5.** The boy . . bestowes himselfe Like a ripe sister *Two Gent.* III. i. 87. **6.** In bestowing, madam, he was most princely *Hen. VIII*, IV. ii. 56. The importance that wealth can b. MAR. EDGEWORTH. Hence **Bestow·able** *a.* capable of being bestowed. **Bestow·al,** location; gift. **Bestow·ed** *ppl. a.* (often with *well-, ill-*). **Bestow·er. Bestow·ment,** bestowal; a gift.

Bestraddle, bestraw, etc.; see BE- *pref.*

† **Bestrau·ght,** *v.* and *ppl. a.* 1547. [alt., by prefix-substitution, of *distraught*; cf. *astraught* (XVI).] **1.** as *pa. t.* Distracted, bereft (*of* wits) 1580. **2.** *pa. pple.* and *adj.* Distraught 1547.

Bestreak, bestream; see BE-.

Bestrew (bĭ͵strū·), *v.* Also **bestrow** (bĭ͵strōᵘ·). Pa. pple. **bestrewed; bestrewn, bestrown.** [OE. *bestrēowian*, f. BE- 1 + STREW.] **1.** To strew *with*. Also *transf.* and *fig.* **2.** To strew or scatter about 1667. **3.** To lie scattered over 1718.

1. The dewy turf with flowers bestrewn WORDSW. **2.** So thick bestrown Abject and lost lay these, covering the Flood MILT. *P.L.* I. 311. Hence **Bestrew·ment** (*rare*).

Bestride (bĭ͵strəi·d), *v.* Pa. t. **bestrode**; also **bestrid.** Pa. pple. **bestridden**; also **-strid, -strode.** [OE. *bestrīdan*; see BE- 4, STRIDE *v.*] **1.** To sit upon or across with or as with the legs astride. **2.** To stand over with the legs astride. Also *fig.* 1601. Also *transf.* of things (e.g. a rainbow, bridge). **3.** To stride across. Also *fig.* 1600.

1. The pressed nostril, spectacle-bestrid COWPER. **2.** He doth b. the narrow world like a Colossus *Jul. C.* I. ii. 135. When I bestrid thee in the warres, and tooke Deepe scarres to saue thy life *Com. Err.* V. i. 192.

Bestrow, -n, vars. of BESTREW, -N.

† **Bestru·t,** *ppl. a.* 1603. [f. BE- 5 + †*strut a.* distended (XVI), f. (perh. orig. pa. pple.) STRUT *v.*[1]] Swollen –1648.

Bestuck, pa. t. and pple. of BESTICK.

Bestu·d; see BE- 1.

‖ **Bestuur** (bĕstü·r). 1885. [Du.; f. *besturen* govern.] Administration; i.e. in the Dutch-speaking parts of S. Africa.

Bet (bet), *sb.* 1592. [perh. aphetic f. ABET in the sense 'instigation, support (of a cause), the vb. being then derived from the sb. See BET *v.*] The staking of money or other value on the event of a doubtful issue; a wager; also, the sum of money or article staked.

An even b. (fig.): a balance of probabilities.

Bet (bet), *v.* Pa. t. and pple. **bet;** also **betted.** 1597. [The verb and sb. appear at the end of XVI, and it is uncertain which is prior; but see prec.] To stake or wager in support of an affirmation or on the issue of a forecast. Also *absol.*

Iohn of Gaunt. . betted much Money on his head 2 *Hen. IV.* III. ii 50. He enjoys it [gambling] that looks on and bets not EARLE. *You b.* (*slang*, U.S.): certainly.

† **Bet,** *adv.* (and *a.*) [OE. *bet* = OFris. *bet*, OS. *bat, bet*, OHG. *baz* (G. *bass*), ON. *betr* :– Gmc. **batiz* adv.; *bet* was superseded by BETTER about 1600.] *adv.* **1.** The earlier form of BETTER –1586. **2.** As predicate after *be* –1634. **3.** *absol.* and quasi- *sb. The bet*: the advantage –1592.

† **Bet** *adv.*[2] ME. [Origin and meaning doubtful. In *go bet* perh. = go better, i.e. go quicker (Skeat).] In *Go b.* –1617.

Beta (bī·tă). ME. [– L. *beta*, Gr. βῆτα.] **1.** The second letter of the Greek alphabet B, β. **2.** Used to mark: *esp.* **a.** *Astron.* The second star in a constellation. **b.** *Chem.* The second isomerous modification of an organic compound. **c.** *Beta rays* or *β-rays*, the second of three types of rays emitted by radioactive substances, with great penetrative power 1904.

Betaine (bī·te͵əin). 1879. [irreg. f. L. *beta* BEET + -INE[5].] *Chem.* A base ($C_5H_{11}NO_2$) found in beet and mangel-wurzel.

Betake (bĭtēⁱ·k), *v. str.* Pa. t. **betook.** Pa. pple. **betaken.** [f. BE- 2 + TAKE; in ME. functioning as a var. of BETEACH.] † **1.** = BETEACH 2, 3, 4. –1649. **2.** *refl.* To commit oneself, have recourse *to* any kind of action 15.. **3.** *refl.* To resort, turn one's course, go 1612.

1. Nowe to the Devil I the b. SKELTON. **2.** That defence thou hast, b. thee to't *Twel. N.* III. iv. 240. *To b. oneself to one's heels*: to run away. **3.** Whither shall I b. me, where subsist? MILT. *P.L.* X. 922.

† **Betea·ch**, *v.* [OE. *betǣcan*, f. *be-* BE- 2 + *tǣcan* show, TEACH. Cf. prec.] **1.** To point out OE. only. **2.** To hand over, give up, yield –1513. **3.** To entrust, give in charge *to* –1513. **4.** To commit or commend *to* (God, the Devil, etc.) –1685. **5.** To TEACH –ME.

† **Beteela.** 1598. [app. identified w. Pg. *beatilha* 'linen to make white veils for women', Sp. *beatilla* 'sort of fine thin linen'. See BATTALIA PIE.] A kind of East Indian muslin –1727.

† **Beteem**, *v.* 1565. [XVI-XVII *beteem(e)*, app. rel. to † *teem* (rare, XVI) think fit, and OS. *teman* (MDu. *temen, tamen*, Du. *betamen*), OHG. *zeman* (G. *ziemen*), but precise relationship cannot be established.] **1.** To think fit –1647. **2.** To grant, concede –1674. **b.** To allow *Haml.* I. ii. 141.

Betel (bī·t'l). 1553. [– Pg. *betel* – Malayalam *veṭṭila*.] The leaf of a plant, which is wrapped round parings of the areca nut and a little lime, and chewed in India, etc. as a masticatory 1585. **b.** Also the shrubby plant (*Piper betle*, or *Chavica betel*, N.O. *Piperaceæ*) which yields the leaf 1553.

Betel nut: the nut of the Areca Palm (see ARECA); so misnamed because chewed with the b. leaf. Hence *b.-tree*, Areca catechu.

† **Bete·ll**, *v.* [OE. *betellan*, f. BE- 1 + *tellan* TELL.] To speak for; to declare; to lay claim to; to calumniate –1567.

Bête noire (bęt nwār). 1850. [Fr. = black beast.] An insufferable person or thing.

Beth(e, = shall be, is, are, be (ye); see BE *v.*

Bethel (be·þĕl). 1617. [– Heb. *bêṯ-'ēl*, f. *bêt* house of + *'ēl* God.] **1.** A place where God is worshipped; the pillar that marks it. (See *Gen.* 28 : 17.) **2.** *transf.* A chapel or meeting-house 1840.

Bethink (bĭþi·ŋk), *v.* Pa. t. and pple. **bethought** (bĭþǭ·t). [OE. *biþenćan* = OFris. *bithanka, bithenzia*, OS. *bithenkian*, OHG. *bidenken* (Du., G. *bedenken*), Goth. *biþagkjan*; Gmc., f. **bi-* BE- 4 + **þaŋkjan* THINK.] **1.** *trans.* To think of or about; to recollect. *Obs.* exc. w. cl. † **2.** To conceive –ME.; to consider –1647; to contrive –1593. † **3.** To regret, grudge –1696. † **4.** *refl.* To take thought; to recollect oneself –1649. **5.** To reflect; *also*, to call to mind ME. **6.** To resolve. (Fr. *s'aviser.*) ME. **7.** *intr.* To reflect, think (*arch.*) ME. **8.** *pass.* *To be bethought*: to bethink oneself (in senses 4, 5, 6) ME.

3. I can never b. any pains. . in the service of my country LOCKE. **4.** If they shall bethinke themselues. . and repent 1 *Kings* 8:47. **5.** I will bethinke me: come againe to morrow *Meas. for M.* II. ii. 145. **6.** It may be I shall otherwise bethinke me *Jul. C.* IV. iii. 251. Hence † **Bethou·ght** *pple.* and *a.* purposed; minded (with *ill-*, etc.).

Bethlehem, Bethlem: see BEDLAM.

† **Be·thlehemite.** Also **Bethlemite.** 1721. [– AL. *Bethlehemita* (XIII); see -ITE[1].] One of an order of monks existing in England in the 13th c.; they wore a five rayed star, in memory of the star of Bethlehem. BAILEY.

Bethumb, bethump, bethwack: see BE-.

Bethwine (be·þwəin). 1609. [Origin. unkn.] Local name of: **a.** The Great Hedge Convolvulus (*C. sepium*). **b.** The Bearbind (*Polygonum convolvulus*). **c.** The Traveller's Joy (*Clematis vitalba*).

Betide (bĭtəi·d), *v.* ME. [f. BE- 2 + TIDE *v.*[1]] **1.** *intr.* To happen, befall. Only in 3rd pers. and often *impers.* Also, with *dat. obj.*; occas. *to, unto.* † **2.** To become *of* (rarely *on*) –1675. † **3.** To fall to as a possession –1587. † **4.** To befit (any one) –1566. ¶ *catachr.* To bode 1799.

1. B., b., whatever b., Haig shall be Haig of Bemerside *Pop. Rhyme.* But woe b. the wandering wight SCOTT.

† **Beti·me, bitime**, *v.* ME. only. [f. *bi-*, BE- 2 + *time(n* happen; see TIME *v.*] *intr.* To betide. In *L.L.L.* IV. iii. 382 *be time* should be read, as in the Folio of 1623.

† **Beti·me**, *adv.* [ME. *bi-, by-time*, i.e. *by time.*] In good time; early in the day –1630. To businesse that we loue, we rise b. *Ant. & Cl.* IV. iv. 20.

Betimes (bĭtəi·mz), *adv.* ME. [f. BETIME + -S.] **1.** At an early time, period, or season. **2.** *spec.* Early in the morning 1481. **2.** In good time ME. **3.** In a short time, speedily ME.

1. He must learn b. to love truth HELPS. **2.** Not to bee a bedde after midnight, is to be vp b. *Twel. N.* II. iii. 2. **3.** He tyres b., that spurs too fast b. SHAKS.

Betitle, betoil; see BE-.

Betoken (bĭtōᵘ·k'n), *v.* [OE. **bitācnian* = OFris. *bitēknia*, Du. *beteekenen*, OHG. *bizeihhanōn* (G. *bezeichnen*); see BE- 2; TOKEN *v.*] † **1.** To signify; to express in words –1612. † **2.** To be a type of –1667. **3.** To be a sign, or omen of; to presage ME. **4.** To point to, indicate 1486.

2. In the Cloud a BOW. . Betok'ning peace from God and Cov'nant new MILT. *P.L.* XI. 867. **3.** Like a red morn, that ever yet betoken'd Wreck to the seaman SHAKS. *Ven. & Ad.* 453. **4.** With looks Betokening rage CARY. Hence **Beto·kener.**

‖ **Beton** (be·toṅ, be·tən). 1819. [– Fr. *béton*, OFr. *betun* = Pr. *betun* cement :– L. *bitumen* mineral pitch, BITUMEN.] A concrete, composed of sand, lime, and hydraulic cement.

Beto·ngue, *v.* 1639. [BE- 6.] To flout.

Betony (be·təni). ME. [– (O)Fr. *betoine* – pop.L. **betonia* for *betonica*, in Pliny *vettŏnica*, said by him to be a Gaulish name of a plant discovered by a Spanish tribe named Vettones.] *Bot.* **1.** *prop.* A plant (*Stachys betonica*), formerly credited with medicinal and magical virtues. **b.** Applied also to: **St. Paul's B.** (*Veronica serpyllifolia*); **Water-B.** (*Scrophularia aquatica*).

† **Beto·rn**, *ppl. a.* ME. [BE- 1.] Torn; tattered –1599.

Betoss; see BE- 1.

† **Betraise, -traish**, *v.* ME. [f. BE- 2 + *traïss-*, lengthened stem of OFr. *traïr*; see BETRAY.] A by-form of BETRAY, chiefly north. **1.** = BETRAY 1. –1558. **2.** To deceive (the trustful) –1501; to entrap (the unsuspecting) –1583.

Betrap (bĭ,træ·p), *v.*[1] [OE. *betreppan, -træppan*; see BE- 1, TRAP *v.*[1]] To catch in a trap, circumvent, enclose. Also *fig.*

† **Betra·p**, *v.*[2] 1509. [f. BE- 1 + TRAP *v.*[2]] To furnish with trappings (*lit.* and *fig.*) –1597.

Betray (bĭ,trēⁱ·), *v.* ME. [f. BE- 2 + †*tray* (XIII) – OFr. *traïr* (mod. *trahir*) :– Rom. **tradire* for L. *tradere* deliver up.] **1.** To give up to, or place in the power of an enemy by treachery. **2.** To be or prove false to (a trust or him who trusts one); to disappoint the hopes or expectations of ME. Also *fig.* † **3.** *loosely*, To disappoint –1704. **4.** To lead astray, as a false guide; to mislead, seduce, deceive (the trustful) ME. **5.** To reveal with breach of faith (a secret) 1735. **6.** To reveal against one's will the existence, identity, real character of (a person or thing desired to be kept secret) 1588. **7.** To reveal incidentally; to exhibit, show signs of (a thing which there is no attempt to keep secret) 1697.

1. Verely I saye vnto you, that one of you shall betraye me *Matt.* 26 : 21. **2.** To b. a cause BURKE. **4.** Pride and self-confidence b. man to his fall PUSEY. **5.** To b. a patient's confidence 1798. **6.** I do b. my selfe with blushing *L.L.L.* I. ii. 138. **7.** A temple. . which betrayed great antiquity BRYANT. Hence **Betray·al** (senses 1, 2, 6). **Betray·er.** **Betray·ment** = *Betrayal.*

Betread, betrend, betrim; see BE-.

Betroth (bĭ,trōᵘ·ð, -trǫ·þ), *v.* [ME. *betrouþe, betreuþe*, f. BE- 6 + *trouþe, treuþe* TRUTH, later assim. to TROTH.] **1.** To engage (a woman) in contract of marriage, to plight one's troth to (*arch.*). **2.** To affiance (usu. the woman to the man) 1566. **3.** *fig.* Said of God and his Church or people. Also, of the relation of a bishop to a church before consecration. 1611. † **4.** *transf.* **a.** To pledge –1670. **b.** To espouse (a cause) –1674.

1. If a man wish to b. a maiden LINGARD. **2.** The lovers were soon after betrothed 1798. **3.** I will b. thee vnto me for euer *Hosea* 2 : 19. **4.** What is hee for a foole that betrothes himselfe vnto vnquietnesse *Much Ado* I. iii. 49. Hence **Betro·thal**, the act of betrothing; the being betrothed; affiance. **Betro·thment** = *Betrothal.*

† **Betru·st**, *v.* 1440. [f. BE- 2 + TRUST *v.*] To trust (a person); to entrust –1748.

†‖ **Be·tso.** 1641. [It. *bezzo.*] A small brass coin in Venice.

Better (be·təɹ), *a.*, (*sb.*), and *adv.* [OE. *betera* (m. adj.) = OFris. *betera*, OS. *betiro* (Du. *beter*), OHG. *bezziro* (G. *besser*), ON. *betri*, Goth. *batiza* :– Gmc. **batizon*, f. **bat-*, rel. to BET *adv.*[1], BEET *v.*, BOOT *v.*[1]] **A.** *adj.* The compar. of GOOD, q.v.: more good. **1.** Of superior quality. **2.** Of persons: Kinder. Of persons and things: More profitable, useful, or suitable for a purpose; more desirable. ME. **3.** More; larger, greater 1580.

1. I could haue b. spared a b. man 1 *Hen. IV*, v. iv. 104. People of the b. Sort DE FOE. **2.** Some b. Messenger *Two Gent.* I. i. 159. Oh excellent deuise, was there euer heard a better *Two Gent.* II. i. 145. **3.** Vntill nine and b. 1630. The b. half of his estate SWIFT. *B. half*: orig. *my b. half*, the more than half of my being; said of a very close friend; *esp.* (after Sidney) used for 'my husband' or 'wife'; now, joc. appropriated to the latter. *I, we, you, he*, etc. *had b.* (orig. *me, us*, etc. *were betere* or *bet*), = it would be more advantageous for me, etc. Now replaced by *I had b.* = I should have or hold it better, to do, etc. See HAVE. *To be b. than one's word*: to do more than one has promised.

II. *absol.* **1.** Something better; that which is better 1635. **2.** *sb.* with possessive pron.: One's superior ME.

1. I never look'd for b. at his hands SHAKS. **2.** His b. doth not breath vpon the earth SHAKS. Who cals? Your betters Sir *A.Y.L.* II. iv. 68. Prudence got the b. of his pride THIRLWALL.

B. *adv.* [The orig. form was BET, q.v.] **1.** In a more excellent way ME. **2.** In a superior degree ME. † **b.** Rather –1801. **3.** In the predicate, after *be*, the adv. and adj. run together. **4.** With *adjs.* and *pples.*, usually written with the hyphen, as *b.-advised, b.-humoured*, i.e. (*better humour*) + *-ed*, etc. 1609.

1. I drinke b. than I syng 1530. **2.** Where-by it [sage] prospereth the b. 1577.

Phrases. *To be b.*: to be improved in health, *esp.* after an illness. (In north. use, to be well again.) *To get b.*: to amend, recover. *To think b. of*: **a.** (a thing): to reconsider it and decide more wisely. **b.** (a person): to form a better opinion of him. *B. off*, comp. of *well off*: see OFF.

Better, -or (be·təɹ), *sb.* 1609. [f. BET *v.* + -ER.[1]] One who makes bets.

Better (be·təɹ), *v.* late ME. [f. BETTER *a.*; not continuous w. OE. *ġebeterian.*] **1.** To make better; *esp.* morally, or in health or worldly condition. **2.** To do better than 1548. **3.** *intr.* To grow better, improve 1832.

1. Love betters what is best WORDSW. Girls marry merely to 'b. themselves' 1792. **2.** Each day still b. others happinesse SHAKS. Hence **Be·ttering** *vbl.sb.* making better; becoming better.

Betterment (be·təɹmĕnt). 1598. [f. prec. + -MENT; orig. U.S.] **1.** Making or becoming better; being better; improvement. **2.** *spec.* Improvement of property. (In U.S.) 1809. † **3.** = BETTERNESS 1. 1678.

Betterness (be·təɹnės). ME. [f. as prec. + -NESS.] **1.** The quality of excelling; superiority. **2.** *spec.* Fineness of the precious metals above the standard 1530.

Betting (be·tiŋ), *vbl. sb.* 1599. [f. BET *v.* + -ING[1].] The making of bets, wagering.

Comb., as **b.-book**, a book in which bets are entered; **-man**, a better, *usually* a professional gambler.

‖ **Be·ttong.** 1839. [Native name (N.S.W.).] A species of kangaroo rat, about the size of a hare.

Bettor. † **1.** Aphet. f. ABETTOR 1671. **2.** Var. of BETTER *sb.*

Betty (be·ti), *sb.* [dim. of *Bet*, abbrev. of *Elizabet, -beth.*] **1.** A female familiar name, now chiefly rustic or homely. Hence, **2.** Given in contempt to a man who occupies himself with a woman's duties. (So MOLLY.) **3.** A pear-shaped bottle covered with straw; called by chemists a *Florence flask.* (? Only in U.S.) 1725. **4.** Cant name for a short crowbar; called now a *Jemmy* 1700.

4. Ruffians, who, with Crows and Betties, Break Houses 1707. Hence (sense 2), **Be·tty** *v.* to fuss about (*colloq.*).

Betulin (be·tiŭlin). 1879. [f. L. *betula* birch + -IN[1].] *Chem.* A resinous substance extracted from the bark of the birch-tree (*Betula alba*).

† **Betu·mbled**, *ppl. a.* [f. BE- 7 + TUMBLE *v.*] Disordered. SHAKS. *Lucr.* 1037.

Between (bĭ,twī·n), *prep.* and *adv.* [OE. *betwēonum* (beside *betwēon* and *betwēonan*), f. Gmc. **bi* BY + **twēon* :– **twixnai* (cf. OFris. *twine*; Goth. *tweihnai* two each), formation with *-n*-suffix on **twix-* (whence OE. *twēo*, OS. *tweho*, OHG. *zweho* doubt, difference), ult. rel. to TWO.]

A. *prep.* **1.** Of a point: In the space which separates two points; in the direct line which joins two points. Also *fig.* ME. **2.** Of time, quantity, or degree: Intermediate to two others OE. **3.** Expressing the relation that motion along a line bears to two points on opposite sides of it ME. **4.** Expressing the relation of the continuous space which separates or connects two points ME. **5.** Hence *transf.* of objective relations uniting two (or more) parties; also, of subjective relations involving comparison ME. **6.** Expressing motion from one body or place to another 1598. **7.** Expressing reciprocal action or relation between two agents OE. **8.** Used of relation to two (or more) things or parties acting conjointly or participating in action OE. **9.** Expressing the relation of a line to two spaces which it separates. Also *transf.* OE. **10.** The only word expressing the relation of a thing to many surrounding things severally and individually OE.

1. I lie b. that sun and thee SHAKS. *fig.* B. hope and fear BURTON. *B. wind and water*: along the line where anything is submerged in water, etc., *esp.* on the load-line of a ship. **2.** B. one and two in the morning BOSWELL. Forty and Fifty ADDISON, frost and thaw JANE AUSTEN. **3.** The salt rheume that ran betweene France and it *Com. Err.* III. ii. 132. **4.** The lang Scots miles That lie b. us and our hame BURNS. **5.** A marriage, an alliance, a coalition b. [etc.]. **7.** I will put enmitie betweene thee and the woman *Gen.* 3:15. **8.** To take the bit b. his teeth DRYDEN. *B. ourselves*: as a matter not to be communicated to others. We brought home six brace b. us JANE AUSTEN. They had it b. them (*mod.*). **9.** There was but a ston wal hem be-tweene CHAUCER. Phr. *B. the bark and the tree.* **10.** B. the prior, the boatmen, and a little offering to St. Patrick, he had not as much money left [etc.] SOUTHEY.

B. *adv.* (Mostly the prep. with obj. understood.) **1.** Of place: In an intermediate position or course (*lit.* and *fig.*) OE. **2.** Of time: In the interval, at intervals ME.

1. *To go b.*: to act as a medium or mediator: see GO-BETWEEN.

C. quasi-*sb.* **1.** Anything occupying an intermediate position; an interval of time 1611. **2.** An intermediate size of sewing-needle 1862.

Between-decks (bǐ,twī·n,deks), *adv.* and *sb.* 1725. [Also 'TWEEN-DECKS; cf. Du. *tussendek*, G. *zwischendeck*.] **A.** *adv.* In the space between the decks of a ship. **B.** *sb.* The space itself 1769.

Betwee·nity. 1760. [Formed playfully by H. Walpole, after *extremity*, etc.] Intermediateness of kind, quality, or condition; anything intermediate.

Between-whiles (bǐ,twī·n,hwəilz). 1678. [WHILE *sb.*] At intervals.

Betwixt (bǐ,twi·kst), *prep.* and *adv.* [ME. *bitwixte*, OE. *betwēohs, betwēox, betwyx* corresp. to OFris. *bituischa, bituiskum*; f. Gmc. **bi* BY + **twisk-*, repr. also by OFris. *twiska*, OS. *twisc*, OHG. *zwiski* two each, twofold, f. **twa* TWO + **-isk-* -ISH[1]. See BETWEEN.] **A.** *prep.* **1.** = BETWEEN. Still in dial. use. OE. **2.** Of more than two: in early use = AMONG OE.

† *B. and* (prob. ellipt. for *b. this and..*) *n. dial.*: between this (or that) and.., until. ME.

B. *adv.* = BETWEEN 1, 2. ME.

B. and between (colloq.): in an intermediate position; neither one thing nor the other.

Beudantite (biū·dăntəit). [f. *Beudant*, name of a French mineralogist + -ITE[1] 2 b.] *Min.* A mineral occurring in modified acute rhombohedrons, containing sesquioxide of iron and oxide of lead, with phosphoric or arsenic acid, or both.

‖ **Beurré** (bǫre). 1741. [Fr., 'buttered, buttery'.] A mellow variety of pear. Also *attrib.*

Bevel (be·vĕl). 1562. [– OFr. **bevel*, Fr. *béveau, bi-, bu-, beau-* (XVI), f. OFr. *baïf* openmouthed, f. *baer*; see BAY *sb.*[3] Cf. OFr. *bever* give bias to.] **A.** *adj.* **1.** *Her.* Of a line: Broken so as to have two equally acute alternate angles, thus ‾/_. **2.** Oblique; *esp.* at more than a right angle; sloping, slant 1600.

2. I may be straight though they themselues be beuel SHAKS. *Sonn.* cxxi.

B. *sb.* **1.** A common joiner's and mason's tool, consisting of a flat rule with a movable tongue stiffly jointed to one end, for setting off angles 1611. **2.** A slope from the right angle, an obtuse angle; a slope from the horizontal or vertical; a surface or part so sloping. (Occ. used techn. for *b.-angle.*) 1677.

2. The brethren o' the mystic level May hing their head in waefu' b. BURNS.

Comb., etc.: **b.-angle,** any angle exc. 90° or 45°; **-gear, -gearing,** gear for conveying motion by means of b.-wheels from one shaft to another at an angle with it; **-joint,** a sloping joint for uniting pieces of timber end to end; **-wheel,** a toothed wheel whose working face is oblique with the axis.

Be·vel, *v.* 1677. [f. prec. sb.] **1.** *trans.* To cut to a slope; to reduce (a square edge) to a more obtuse angle; often with *off, away*, etc. **2.** *intr.* To recede in a slope from the right angle; to slant 1679.

2. Their houses are very ill built, the walls b., without one right angle in any apartment SWIFT.

Bevelled, beveled (be·vĕld), *ppl. a.* 1757. [f. the vb.] **a.** Made or cut to a bevel; sloped off. **b.** *spec.* in *Archit.*; in *Crystallog.*: Replaced by BEVELMENT; in *Her.* = BEVEL A I.

Be·velling, beveling, *vbl. sb.* 1769. [f. as prec. + -ING[1].] A cutting to an oblique angle; the slant so given; a bevelled portion: *esp.* in *Shipbuilding*. Used also in comb., as **b.-board** (*Shipbuild.*), **-machine** (*Bookbind.*).

Be·velment. 1804. [f. as prec. + -MENT.] The process of bevelling; *spec.* in *Crystallog.*, the replacement of the edge of a crystal by two similar planes equally inclined to the adjacent faces.

Be·ver (bī·vəɹ), *sb.* 1451. [– AFr. *bever*, OFr. *beivre* drinking, drink, subst. use of *beivre* (mod. *boire*) :– L. *bibere* drink.] † **1.** Drink. † **2.** A potation; a time for drinking –1626. **3.** A small repast between meals. Chiefly *dial.* (in *pl.* at Winchester). 1500. Hence † **Be·ver** *v.*[1] to partake of b.

Bever (be·vəɹ), *v.*[2] Now *dial.* 1470. [frequent. of OE. *beofian* tremble; see -ER[5]. Cf. LG. *beveren*, Du. *bibberen* tremble.] To tremble, shake.

Beverage (be·vĕrēdʒ). [– OFr. *bevrage, beuvrage* (mod. *breuvage*) :– Rom. **biberaticum*, f. L. *bibere* drink; see BEVER *sb.*, -AGE.] **1.** Drink; *esp.* a liquor which is in common use. † **2.** Drinking, a draught –1697. **3.** *spec.* A name applied locally to various drinks; as, lemonade, small cider, etc. 1721. **4.** A drink, or drink-money. Now *dial.* 1721.

1. Tea..that elegant and popular b. BOSWELL.

Bevil(e, bevilled, vars. of BEVEL, -ELLED.

‖ **Bevue** (bevü). 1716. [Fr., f. *bé-, bes-* pejorative + *vue* VIEW *sb.*] An error of inadvertence.

Bevy (be·vi). ME. [Of unkn. origin.] **1.** The proper term for a company of maidens or ladies, of roes, of quails, or of larks. **2.** *transf.* A company; *rarely*, a collection of objects 1603.

1. A Beavie of fair Women, richly gay MILT. *P.L.* XI. 582. **2.** What a beavy of beaten slaves are here BEAUM. & FL.

Bewail (bǐwēᵢ·l), *v.* ME. [BE- 4.] **1.** *trans.* To wail over, *esp.* over the dead. Also *refl.* **2.** To lament loudly, mourn. Also *refl.* ME. **3.** *intr.* To utter lamentations ME.

2. Bewaylynge ay the day that they were borne CHAUCER. Hence **Bewai·lable** *a.* proper to be bewailed. **Bewai·led** *ppl. a.* lamented; † expressed by wailing. **Bewai·ler. Bewai·lingly** *adv.* **Bewai·lment.**

Beware (bǐwēᵊ·ɹ), *v.*[1] ME. [orig. *be war*, i.e. BE imper., inf., or pres. subj., and *war* WARE *a.*; used mostly only where *be* (not *am*, etc.) is the appropriate form, but formerly also inflected † *bewared*, † *bewaring*. Cf. BEGONE.] **1.** To be cautious or on one's guard; to take heed. Const. *simply*; with *of*, † *from*, † *with*; † with infin.; with cl.; with simple obj. † **2.** To have a care of. Const. with *of*; with simple obj.; with infin. or cl. (*arch.*). –1713. † **3.** To take warning by –1605. **4.** As an inflected vb. 1598.

1. B. of all, but most b. of Man POPE. Since I am a dog, b. my phangs *Merch. V.* III. iii. 72. **2.** Now, bishop, b. thy purse 1600. **4.** I had beward'd if I had foreseen MILT. We b. to ask only for high things EMERSON.

Bewa·re, *v.*[2] ME. [f. BE- 2 + WARE *v.*[2] spend (north.).] To lay out (money, etc.) –1472.

Bewash, bewed; see BE-.

Beweep (bǐwī·p), *v.* [OE. *bewēpan*, f. BE- 4 + *wēpan* WEEP.] **1.** To weep for, weep over. **2.** To wet with or as with tears 1420. † **3.** *intr.* To weep ME. only.

1. I all alone beweepe my out-cast state SHAKS.

† **Bewe·nd,** *v.* [OE. *bewendan* = OS. *biwendian*, OHG. *biwentan*, Goth. *biwandjan*, f. *bi-* BE- 1 + *wendan* WEND *v.*] *trans.* To turn round or away. Also *refl.*, and *intr.* (for *refl.*). –ME.

Bewest (bǐwe·st). [OE. *be westan*, f. BE- *pref.* + *westan* from the west; cf. *be-east*, BENORTH.] *adv.* and *prep.* On or to the west (of). Now only *Sc.*

Bewet; see BE-.

Bewet, bewit (biū·ĕt), *sb.* 1486. [app. – (AFr. or OFr.) **beuette*, unrecorded dim. of OFr. *buie* collar, bond, fetter :– pop.L. **boja* for L. *boiæ* (pl.) collar for the neck.] *Falconry.* A ring or slip of leather for attaching the bell to a hawk's leg.

† **Bewho·re,** *v.* 1604. [BE- 5.] To call whore; to make a whore of –1623.

† **Bewie·ld,** *v.* [ME. *bewelden*, f. BE- 2 + *welden* WIELD.] To hold in hand, handle, wield. *refl.* To use one's limbs. –1577.

Bewig (bǐwi·g), *v.* 1774. [BE- 6.] To furnish with a wig. Hence **Bewi·gged** *ppl. a.* **a.** Wearing a wig. **b.** Ruled by red-tape.

A paltry Baden, a bewigged Prussia 1851.

Bewilder (bǐwi·ldəɹ), *v.* 1684. [f. BE- 2 + WILDER.] **1.** *lit.* To lose in pathless places (*arch.*) 1685. **2.** *fig.* To perplex, confound; to cause mental aberration 1684.

1. Bewildered in the enormous extent of the town JOHNSON. **2.** The bewilder'd soul BEATTIE. Hence **Bewi·ldered** *ppl. a.* at a loss for a way; *fig.* confused mentally; *transf.* pathless. **Bewi·ldered-ly** *adv.*, **-ness. Bewi·lderingly** *adv.*

Bewilderment (bǐwi·ldəɹmĕnt). 1820. [f. prec. + -MENT.] **1.** Bewildered state. **2.** An inextricable confusion or medley of objects 1844.

1. Thought was arrested by utter b. GEO. ELIOT.

Bewit (*Falconry*), var. of BEWET.

Bewitch (bǐwi·tʃ), *v.* [ME. *bewicchen*, f. BE- 2 + *wicchen* WITCH *v.*] **1.** To affect (*esp.* to injure) by witchcraft or magic. Occ. with *into*, etc. **2.** *fig.* To influence as if by witchcraft; to fascinate, charm. Now usu. of pleasing influences. 1526.

1. Looke how I am bewitch'd *Rich. III*, III. iv. 70 **2.** I am bewitcht with the rogues company 1 *Hen. IV*, II. ii. 18. Hence **Bewi·tcher. Bewi·tchery** = BEWITCHMENT. † **Bewi·tchful** *a.* having power to b. **Bewi·tching** *vbl. sb.* fascination; *ppl. a.* fascinating. **Bewi·tching-ly** *adv.*, **-ness.**

Bewi·tchment. 1607. [f. prec. + -MENT.] **1.** The fact or power of bewitching. **2.** The being bewitched 1810.

1. I will counterfet the b. of some popular man *Cor.* II. iii. 108.

† **Bewo·nder,** *v.* 1580. [f. BE- 4 + WONDER *v.*] **1.** *trans.* To fill with wonder –1600. **2.** To wonder at, admire –1628.

† **Bewo·rk,** *v.* Pa. pple. **bewrought.** [OE. *bewyrćan*, f. BE- 1 + *wyrćan* WORK *v.*] **1.** To work round about. **2.** To embroider –1637.

Bewrap (bǐræ·p), *v.* [ME., f. BE- 1 + WRAP *v.*] To wrap up, cover. Also *fig.*

Bewray (bǐrēᵢ·), *v. arch.* [ME., f. BE- 2 + WRAY *v.*] † **1.** To accuse, malign ME. only. † **2.** To expose (a person) by divulging his secrets, etc. *Hence*, To reveal (the doer of an act). –1603. **3.** To divulge (secrets) prejudicially ME. † **4.** To reveal, make known –1611. † **5.** To betray (a fugitive) –1628. **6.** = BETRAY 6. 1535. † **7.** = BETRAY 7. –1763.

3. None shulde issue out to b. their enterprice LD. BERNERS. **4.** Write downe thy mind, b. thy meaning so *Tit. A.* II. iv. 3. **6.** Thy speach bewrayeth the COVERDALE *Matt.* 26:73. Hence **Bewray·er** (*arch.*). † **Bewray·ingly** *adv.* † **Bewray·ment.**

Bewray, erron. f. BERAY.

† **Bewrea·k,** *v.* [ME., f. BE- 2 + WREKE *v.*] To avenge; to wreak –1586.

Bewrought, pa. pple. of BEWORK.

† **Bewry·,** *v.*[1] [OE., f. BE- 1 + WRY *v.*[1]] To cover up or over –1513.

† **Bewry,** *v.*[2] [f. BE- 2 + WRY *v.*[2]] To distort.

Bey (bēᵢ), *sb.* 1599. [– Osmanli *bey*, mod. pronunc. of BEG *sb.*] A Turkish governor of a province or district; also a title of rank.

Bey, *v.* [OE. *bēġan* (WS. *bīeġan*) = OS. *bōgian*, OHG. *bougen*, ON. *bǿygja*, Goth. *baugjan*, causal of Gmc. **beuȝ- *bauȝ- *buȝ-*, see BOW *v.*[1]] *trans.* and *intr.* To bend.

‖ **Beylic, -lik** (bēᵢ·lik). 1733. [– Osmanli *beglik, beylik*.] The jurisdiction of a bey.

Beyond (bǐ,yǫ·nd), *adv.* and *prep.* [OE. *beġ(e)ondan*, f. *be* BY + *ġ(e)ondan* from the farther side :– Gmc. **jandana*, f. **jand-*

YOND.] **A.** *adv.* **1.** On the farther side, farther away. **2.** In addition (*rare*) 1886.

1. B., a line of heights TENNYSON.

B. *prep.* **1.** On the farther side of OE.; past, further on than ME. **2.** To the farther side of, past OE. Also *fig.* **3.** Towards the farther side of, past. (With *look*, etc.) 1597. **4.** Of time: Past, later than 1597. **5.** *fig.* Outside the limit or sphere of, past 1535. **6.** More than in amount or degree 1500. **7.** In addition to; in neg. and interrog. sentences almost = Except. Cf. BESIDES. 1449.

1. *B. seas*: out of the country; abroad. **2.** B. your depth POPE, the line of rectitude WASHINGTON. † *To go b.*: to circumvent. **3.** *To look b.*: to misconstrue; you looke b. him quite 2 *Hen. IV*, IV. iv. 67. **4.** Which shall..remain B. all date SHAKS. **5.** B. the reach of mercie SHAKS. So, *b. belief, doubt, endurance, question*, etc. *To be b. a person* (colloq.): to pass his comprehension. **6.** An amount..b. their value 1885. Delight b. the bliss of dreams MILT. *Comus* 813. *B. measure* (advb. phr.): excessively. **7.** Somewhat b. and above all this HOOKER.

C. quasi-*sb.* That which lies on the other side or farther away; that which lies beyond our present life or experience 1581.

They are the All, with no b. MARTINEAU. *The back of b.*: any very out-of-the-way place.

† **Beza·n,** *sb.* [– Du. *bezaan* (*besane*, also *mesane* in Kilian) – Fr. *misaine*; see MIZEN.] App. a small sailing vessel. PEPYS.

Bezant, byzant (be·zănt, bĭza·nt). ME. [– OFr. *besant*, nom. *besanz* :– L. *Byzantius* (sc. *nummus* coin), adj. of *Byzantium*, Gr. Βυζάντιον, the modern Istanbul (Constantinople), where it was first coined.] **1.** A gold coin first struck at Byzantium, and in England varying in value between the sovereign and half-sovereign, or less. There were also silver Bezants worth from a florin to a shilling. Used by Wyclif to translate both *talentum* and *drachma*. **2.** The gold offered by the kings of England at the sacrament, or at festivals 1667. **3.** *Her.* A gold roundel representing the above coin plain and unstamped. Also *attrib.* 1486.

Bez-antler (bēⁱ-, bēⁱz,æ·ntləɹ). Also **bay antler.** 1598. [– AFr. *besantouiller, f. OFr. *bes-* BES- + *andouiller* ANTLER.] The second branch of a deer's horn.

Bezanty (bĭzɑ·nti), *ppl. a.* Also **bezantee.** 1486. [– AFr. *besanté*; see BEZANT, -Y⁵.] *Her.* Charged with or formed of bezants.

Bezel (be·zĕl). 1611. [– OFr. **besel* (mod. *béseau, bizeau*; cf. Sp. *bisel*); origin unkn.] **1.** A slope, a sloping edge or face; *esp.* that of a chisel, etc. (usu. *basil*). **2.** The oblique sides or faces of a cut gem 1839. **3.** 'The groove and flange by which the crystal of a watch or the stone of a jewel is retained in its setting' 1616. Hence **Be·zel** *v.* to grind or cut to an edge; to bevel.

‖ **Bezesteen** (be·zĕstīn). 1656. [ult. – Turk. *bezestān*, orig. Pers. for 'clothes-market'.] An exchange, bazaar, or market-place in the East.

‖ **Bezetta** (bĭze·ta). 1863. [Corrupt f. It. *pezzetta*, dim. of *pezza* a PIECE of cloth.] A pigment prepared by dipping linen rags in certain colouring matters.

Bezique (bĕzī·k). 1861. [– Fr. *bésigue*, also *bésy*, perh. – Pers. *bāzīgar* juggler, *bāzī* game.] A game of cards, in which the knave of diamonds and queen of spades together form 'Bezique'.

Bezoar (bī·zoᵊɹ, be·zo,aɹ). 1477. [Many forms repr. Fr. *bezahar(d)*, OFr. *bezar* (mod. *bézoard*), Sp. *bezar*, mod.L. *beza(h)ar* – med. Arab. *bādizahr, bāzahr* – Pers. *pādzahr*, f. *pād* protector + *zahr* poison.] † **1.** *gen.* An antidote –1750. **2.** *spec.* **a.** A calculus or concretion found in the stomach or intestines of some animals, chiefly ruminants, formed of layers of animal matter deposited round some foreign substance. Often called *b.-stone*. (The ordinary current sense.) 1580. † **b.** Other alleged stones or concretions –1634. † **c.** Various medicinal preparations –1807. † **3.** *transf.* The wild goat of Persia, the best-known source of the calculus (2 a) –1781; var. **b.-goat;** so **b. antelope.**

Bezoardic, -artic (bezo,ā·ɹdik, -ā·ɹtik). 1670. [– mod.L. *bezoardicus, -articus*; see prec., -IC.] **A.** *adj.* Of the nature of, or pertaining to, bezoar. **B.** *sb.* An antidote 1671.

† **Bezonian** (bĭzōᵘ·nian). 1592. [f. It. *bisogno*, Sp. *bisoño* + -AN, -IAN. See BISOGNIO.] = BESONIO –1843.

Be·zzle, *v.* Now *dial.* 1604. [– AFr. *besiler* = OFr. *besillier*, Pr. *besillar* maltreat, ravage, destroy, of unkn. origin. See EMBEZZLE.] *trans.* To make away with (drink, one's money, the property of others); *intr.* to guzzle, to revel.

‖ **Bhang, bang** (bæŋ). 1598. [orig. – Pg. *bangue*, later assim. to Pers. *bang* and Urdu etc. *bhāng, bhang, bhung* :– Skr. *bhaṅgā* hemp.] Indian Hemp, the leaves and seed capsules of which are chewed or smoked, or eaten in sweetmeats, or sometimes an infusion of them is drunk. The name is occas. given to *hashish* (see HASHISH).

‖ **Bheesty, bheestie** (bī·sti). 1781. [– Hind. – Pers. *bihištī* a person of paradise.] In India, the servant who supplies an establishment with water, which he carries in a skin slung on his back.

Bi- *pref.*¹, the early OE., and the ordinary ME., form of the prefix BE-, q.v.

Bi- *pref.*², – L. *bi-* (earlier *dui-*, cogn. w. Gr. δι-, Skr. *dvi-*) 'twice, doubly, having two, two-', which is in Latin a prefix of adjs., occas. of sbs., rarely of vbs. *Bi-* is used in Eng. to form:—

I. Adjs., with the sense:—**1.** Having or furnished with two —, two- —, as **bi-angular, -ate, -ated, -ous,** having two angles; **bibracteate,** having two bracts; **bicallose, -ous,** having two callosities; † **bicapited, bicapitate; bicapsular; bicavitary,** having two cavities; **bicentral; bichord; biciliate; bicoloured, biconsonantal; bicorporal, -ate, -ated, -eal,** having two bodies; **bifacial; biglandular; bimarginate, bimembral, bimuscular; binodal,** having two nodes; **binuclear,** having two nuclei; **biovulate; bipetalous; bipupillate,** having two pupil-like markings; **biradiate; birainy,** having two rainy seasons; **bispinous; bistipuled; bitentaculate; bituberculate, -ated; bivaulted. 2. Doubly** —; — in two ways or directions; on both sides; as **biconic, -al,** conical in two directions; **biconvex,** etc. **3.** *Bot.* and *Zool.* Twice over, re-; *i.e.* having characteristically divided parts which are themselves similarly divided, as BILACINIATE, etc. **4.** Lasting for two —; occurring or appearing every two —; as BIENNIAL, **bi-hourly, -monthly, -weekly. b.** Occurring or appearing twice in a —; as in **bi-diurnal, -monthly, -quarterly, -weekly, -winter, -yearly.** (*Semi-* would avoid the ambiguous usage; e.g. *semi-monthly*; cf. *half-yearly*.) **5.** Joining two —; as BI-ACHROMIAL, etc. **6.** Occ. as in **bimanual,** employing two hands; BISERIATE, etc.

II. Advbs., vbs., and sbs.; *esp.* sbs. formed after L. analogies, in which *bi-* = 'double, two'; as **bi-millionaire,** the man who is worth two millions of money; **binomenclature; biprong.**

III. *Chem.* Sbs. and adjs., in which *bi-* = having two equivalents of the acid, base, etc., named; as *bicarbonate of soda*, etc. Now superseded by *di-*.

Biacid (bəi,æ·sid), *a.* 1864. [BI- *pref.*² III.] *Chem.* Of a base: Capable of combining with an acid in two different proportions.

Biacuminate (bəi,ăkiū·minĕt), *a.* 1880. [See BI- *pref.*² I. 1, 2.] *Bot.* Two-pointed.

Biannual (bəi,æ·niuăl). 1877. [See BI- *pref.*² I. 4, 4 b.] **A.** *adj.* Half-yearly. **B.** = BIENNIAL *sb.*

Biarticulate; see BI- *pref.*² I. 1.

Bias (bəi·ăs). 1530. [– (O)Fr. *biais* = Pr. *biais*, Cat. *biax, biaix* :– late L. *bifax, -fac-* looking two ways, f. L. *bi-* BI-² + *facies* face, after Gr. διπρόσωπος.] **A.** *adj.* † **1.** Oblique –1688. **b.** *spec.* in dress (cf. B 1): Cut across the texture 1883. **2.** Swelled as the bowl on the biased side. *Tr. & Cr.* IV. v. 8.

1. *On the b.*: diagonally.

B. *sb.* **1.** An oblique or slanting line. Now only of a gore, cut across the texture of a woven fabric. 1530. **2.** *Bowls.* The construction or form of the bowl causing it to swerve when rolled; the curved course in which it runs; the allowance made for this deviation 1570. Also *fig.* **3.** *transf.* An inclination, leaning, bent; predisposition *towards*; predilection; prejudice 1572. † **4.** Set course –1799. **5.** A swaying influence, impulse, or weight 1587.

2. A bowl may lie still for all its Byass SOUTH. *fig.* Which set a B. vpon the Bowle, of their owne Petty Ends BACON. **3.** Our natural b. to evil HARE. **4.** *To put out of* or *off one's b.*: to put out, disconcert. **5.** The Bribery and Byass of Sense and Flesh STANHOPE.

C. *adv.* **1.** Obliquely, aslope. *Obs.* exc. of dress. 1575. † **2.** Off the straight, awry –1633.

Bias (bəi·ăs), *v.* 1622. [f. prec. sb. In inflexions, often spelt *biasses, biassed*, etc.; but the single *s* is more regular.] **1.** To give bias to (a bowl) 1662. Also *transf.* and *fig.* † **2.** *intr.* To swerve from the right line –1687.

1. Men whom no Advantages can byass BURNET. Such exercises as..biased the mind to military pursuits STRUTT.

Bias(s)ed (bəi·ăst), *ppl. a.* 1611. [See prec.] Having a bias; *esp.* unfavourably inclined.

Bib (bib), *v.* ME. [perh. – L. *bibere* drink; but perh. independently imit. (cf. the var. *beb* XV, surviving in Yorks. dial.).] *trans.* and *intr.* To drink; tipple.

Folks kept bibbing beer BROWNING. Hence **Biba·tion,** bibbing. **Bi·bber** (freq. in comb., as *wine-b.*).

Bib (bib), *sb.*¹ 1580. [perh. f. BIB *v.*] **a.** A cloth placed under a child's chin for cleanliness, *esp.* at meals. **b.** A similar cloth worn by adults, often as the upper part of an apron 1687.

Best b. and tucker: best clothes (of girls, women, or men).

Bib (bib), *sb.*² 1674. [f. BIB *sb.*¹] The whiting-pout (*Gadus luscus*).

Bibacious (bi-, bəibēⁱ·ʃəs), *a.* 1676. [f. L. *bibax, -aci-* + -OUS; see -ACIOUS.] Given to drinking; bibulous. So **Biba·city,** addiction to drinking.

Bibasic (bəibēⁱ·sik), *a.* 1847. [See BI- *pref.*² I. 1.] *Chem.* Having two bases.

B. acid: one which contains two atoms of displaceable hydrogen, and can therefore form two series of salts. Now usu. DI-BASIC.

Bibb (bib). 1779. [var. of BIB *sb.*¹] *Naut.* A bracket under the trestle-tree of a mast, resembling in position a child's bib.

Bibble (bi·b'l), *v.* 1529. [frequent. of BIB *v.*; see -LE.] † **1.** *trans.* and *intr.* To keep drinking –1583. **2. a.** *intr.* To dabble with the bill like a duck. **b.** *trans.* To drink with a dabbling noise. 1552. Hence **Bi·bbler.**

Bibble-babble (bi·b'l,bæ·b'l). 1532. [reduplic. of BABBLE; cf. *tittle-tattle*, etc.] Idle talk; prating.

Bibitory (bi·bitəri), *a. rare.* 1696. [– med. L. *bibitorius*, f. *bibit-*, pa. ppl. stem of L. *bibere* drink; see -ORY².] Of or pertaining to drinking; *spec.* in *B. muscle* = 'rectus internus oculi'.

Bible (bəi·b'l). ME. [– (O)Fr. *bible* = Pr. *bibla*, Sp. *biblia*, It. *bibbia* – eccl. L. *biblia*, n. pl. taken in Rom. as fem. sing., – Gr. (τά) βιβλία 'the books'. The Gr. sing. βιβλίον, dim. of βίβλος, βύβλος papyrus, scroll, roll, book (of Sem. orig.) lost its dim. sense and became the ordinary word for 'book' before its application (as in LXX) to the Hebrew and Christian sacred scriptures.]

1. The Scriptures of the Old and New Testament. (Occas. used for the Old Testament.) ME. **b.** A copy of the Scriptures 1468. **2.** Hence *fig.* A textbook, an authority; a sacred book 1804. † **3.** *transf.* A large book, a tome –1629. † **4.** A library. –1483.

1. As þe bibul sais ME. Certaine bookes which we call the B. or Olde Testament GOLDING. **b.** License ..for the sale of his Bibles COVERDALE. The 'Breeches B.' (see Geneva *Gen.* 3:7), the 'Vinegar B.' **2.** The poets who have contributed to the B. of existing England sentences of guidance EMERSON. **3.** Men myght make of hem a b. xxᵗⁱ. foote thykke CHAUCER.

Comb.: **B.-oath,** one taken upon the B.; **-reader, -woman,** one employed to read the B. from house to house. Hence **Bi·blic, -al** *a.* of, relating to, or contained in, the B. **Bi·blically** *adv.* **Bi·blicism,** adherence to the letter of the B. **Bi·blicist** one who adheres to the letter of the B. **Bi·blicize** *v.* to subject to the B. **Bi·blism,** adherence to the B. as the sole rule of faith; whence **Bi·blist.**

Bible-Chri·stian. 1766. **1.** A Christian according to the Scriptural standard. **2.** One of a sect founded in 1815 by W. O. Bryan, a Wesleyan preacher in Cornwall 1860.

Bible-cle·rk. 1626. **a.** A student of the Bible. **b.** *spec.* One of a class of students in certain colleges at Oxford, having the duty of reading the lessons in chapel, and of saying grace in Hall.

Biblico- (bi·bliko), comb. f. BIBLIC, -AL, as in **b.-literary** *a.*, relating to the literature of the Bible; **b.-poetic,** etc.

Biblio- (bi·bli,o), repr. Gr. βιβλίο-, stem and comb. f. βιβλίον book.

Biblio-cla·sm [Gr. -κλασμος], destruction of books, or of the Bible; so **-cla·st; -gno:st** [Gr. γνώστης], one who knows books and bibliography; **-gony** [Gr. -γονία], the production of books; **-klept** [Gr. -κλέπτης], a book-thief; **-kle:pto-ma·niac**, a book-thief regarded as insane; **-latry** [Gr. -λατρεία], book-worship; excessive reverence for the mere letter of the Bible; so **-later, -latrist, -latrous** *a.*; **-mancy** [Gr. μαντεία], divination by books, or by verses of the Bible; **-ma·nia** [Gr. μανία], a rage for collecting books; so **-ma:ne, -ma·niac** *sb.* and *a.*, **-mani·acal** *a.*, **-ma·nian** *a.* and *sb.* **-manism, -manist; -pegy** [Gr. -πηγία, f. πηγνύναι], book-binding as a fine art; so **-pe·gic** *a.*, **-pegist, -pegi·stic(al** *a.*; **-phagist** [Gr. -φάγος], a devourer of books; so **-pha·gic** *a.*; **-pho·bia** [Gr. -φοβία], aversion to books; **-po·esy** [Gr. ποιησία], the making of books; **-taph** [Gr. ταφος], one who buries books under lock and key; so **-ta·phic** *a.*, **-taphist.**

Bibliographer (bibli,ǫ·grăfəɹ). 1656. [f. Gr. βιβλιογράφος (see BIBLIO-, -GRAPH) + -ER[1]; see -GRAPHER.] † **1.** One who writes or copies books -1761. **2.** One who writes about books, their authorship, printing, publication, etc. 1815. var. **Bi·bliograph.**

Bibliographic, -al (bi·bliogræ·fik, -ăl), *a.* 1802. [f. as prec. + -IC, -ICAL.] Of, relating to, or dealing with bibliography. Hence **Bi:blio-gra·phically** *adv.*

Bibliography (bibli,ǫ·grăfi). 1678. [– Fr. *bibliographie* or mod. L. (*bibliographia* list or account of books on a particular subject), – Gr. βιβλιογραφία; see BIBLIO-, -GRAPHY.] † **1.** The writing of books. **2.** The systematic description and history of books, their authorship, printing, publication, editions, etc. 1814. **3.** A book containing such details 1838. **4.** A list of the books of a particular author, printer, country; the literature of a subject 1869. Hence **Biblio·graphize** *v.* to write a b. of.

Bibliology (bibli,ǫ·lŏdʒi). 1807. [f. BIBLIO- + -LOGY.] **a.** Book-lore; bibliography. **b.** Biblical literature, doctrine, or theology 1859. Hence **Bi:bliolo·gical** *a.*, of or pertaining to b. **Biblio·logist**, a student of b.

Bibliophil(e (bi·bli,ofil). 1824. [– Fr. *bibliophile*; see BIBLIO-, -PHIL(E).] A lover of books; a book-fancier; also as *adj.* **Bi:blio-phi·lic** *a.* of or pertaining to a b. **Biblio·-philism**, the principles and practice of a b. **Biblio·philist**, a b. **Biblio·philous** *a.* addicted to bibliophily. **Biblio·phily**, love of books, taste for books.

Bibliopole (bi·bliŏpōᵘl). 1775. [– L. *bibliopola* – Gr. βιβλιοπώλης, f. βιβλίον book + πώλης seller, dealer.] A dealer in books, a bookseller. **Bibliopo·lar, -po·lic, -po·lical** *a.* of or belonging to booksellers; hence **Bi:bliopo·lically** *adv.* **Biblio·polism**, the principles or trade of bookselling. **Biblio·-polist**, a bookseller; whence **Bi:bliopoli·-stic** *a.* **Biblio·poly, Bi·bliopo:lery**, bookselling.

Bibliothec (bibli,ǫ·þĕk), *a.* and *sb.* 1641. [f. next.] Belonging to a library or librarian; *sb.* a librarian.

‖ **Bibliotheca** (bi:bli,o,þī·kă). [L. – Gr. βιβλιοθήκη, f. βιβλίον + θήκη repository; used by Jerome for the BIBLE: hence OE. *biblio-þece* the BIBLE.] **a.** (in OE.) The Scriptures, the Bible. **b.** *mod.* A collection of books, a library. **c.** A bibliographer's catalogue. Hence **Bi:bliothe·cal** *a.* belonging to a library. **Biblio·thecary** *sb.* † a library; a librarian; *adj.* of or belonging to a library or librarian. So **Bibliotheca·rian** *a.* and *sb.*

‖ **Bibliothèque.** 1549. [Fr. (see prec.); formerly naturalized, but now treated as French.] = BIBLIOTHECA b.

‖ **Biblus, -os** (bi·blŏs, -ǫs). 1656. [L. – Gr. βίβλος.] The papyrus; its inner bark.

Bibulous (bi·biŭləs), *a.* 1675. [f. L. *bibulus*, f. *bibere* drink, + -OUS; see -ULOUS.] **1.** Absorbent of moisture. **2.** Addicted to drinking 1861. **3.** Relating to drink 1858.
1. B. paper 1827. Hence **Bi·bulously** *adv.*

Bicalcarate (bəikæ·lkăreⁱt), *a.* 1876. [f. BI- *pref.*[2] I. 1 + CALCARATE.] Furnished with two spurs.

Bicameral (bəikæ·mĕrăl), *a.* 1832. [f. BI- *pref.*[2] I. 1 + CAMERA 2 + -AL[1].] Having two (legislative) chambers. So **Bica·merist**, an advocate of two chambers.

Bicarbide, -onate, -uret, etc.: see BI- *pref.*[2] III.

Bicarinate (bəikæ·rineⁱt), *a.* 1872. [BI- *pref.*[2] I. 3.] *Bot.* Furnished with two keels or axial ridges.

Bicaudal; see BI- *pref.*[2] I. 3.

† **Bi·cched,** *ppl. a.* ME. [f. BITCH *sb.*[1] + -ED.[2]] Cursed -1533. *B. bones*: dice.

Bice (bəis). ME. [– (O)Fr. *bis* dark grey = Pr. *bis*. It. *bigio*, of unkn. origin.] † **A.** *adj.* Brownish grey. **B.** *sb.* (also *attrib.*) **1.** Short for *blewe bis* 'blue b.': a dull blue, often loosely identified with azure ME. **2.** The pigment which yields this colour, prepared from smalt; also a green pigment (*green b.*) made by adding yellow orpiment to smalt 1548.

Bicentenary (bəise·ntĭnări, -sĕntī·nări). 1862. [BI- *pref.*[2] I. 4.] **A.** *adj.* Consisting of or relating to two hundred (*years*, as if confused with *bicentennial*). **B.** *sb.* Used for: The two hundredth anniversary.

Bicentennial (bəisĕnte·niăl). 1883. [BI- *pref.*[2] I. 4.] **A.** *adj.* Occurring every two hundred years; lasting two hundred years. **B.** *sb.* = BICENTENARY (and etymologically more correct).

Bicentral; see BI- *pref.*[2] I. 1.

Biceps (bəi·sĕps). 1634. [– L. *biceps*, *-cipit-*, two-headed, f. *bi-* BI- *prep.*[2] I. 1 + *-ceps*, rel. to *caput*, *capit-* head.] **A.** *adj.* Having two heads or summits; *spec.* of muscles. **B.** *sb.* A muscle with two heads or tendinous attachments; *spec.* the flexor muscle on the front of the upper arm (often taken as the type of physical strength); also, that of the thigh.

Bichlo·ride. 1810. [BI- *pref.*[2] III.] *Chem.* A compound in which two equivalents of chlorine are combined with a metal, etc.

Bichromate (bəi,krōᵘ·mĕt). 1854. [See BI- *pref.*[2] III.] *Chem.* A salt containing two equivalents of chromic acid, e.g. *B. of potash*; whence **Bichro·mated, -matized** *ppl. a.*

Bicipital (bəisi·pităl), *a.* 1646. [f. L. *bicipit-* (see BICEPS) + -AL[1].] **1.** = BICEPS *a.* **2.** Of or pertaining to the biceps (muscle) 1831.

Bici·pitous, *a.* 1646. [f. as prec. + -OUS.] Having two heads or terminal extremities, as *b. serpents*.

Bicker (bi·kəɹ), *sb.*[1] 1458. [Sc. f. BEAKER.] A (wooden) bowl or dish for containing liquor. Formerly, a drinking cup.

Bicker (bi·kəɹ), *sb.*[2] [ME. *biker*, *beker*, of unkn. origin.] **1.** Skirmishing; an encounter; exchange of blows. **2.** *Sc.* A street or school fight with stones, etc. 1470. **3.** Quarrel; angry altercation ME. **4.** Noise as of contention, rattle of light guns, sound of a stream brawling over stones, etc. 1870. **b.** *Sc.* A short rapid run. BURNS.

Bicker (bi·kəɹ), *v.* [Goes w. BICKER *sb.*[2], which occurs somewhat earlier.] **1.** To skirmish; to fight. † **2.** *trans.* To attack with repeated strokes -1550. **3.** *intr.* To quarrel, wrangle 1450. **4.** *transf.* Applied to the making of any rapidly repeated noisy action, such as the brawling of a stream over stones, the pattering of rain, etc. 1748. **b.** *Sc.* To make a short quick run 1792. **5.** *poet.* Of flame and light in quick movement: To flash, quiver, glisten. Cf. *flicker*. 1667.
3. Though their Merchants b. in the East Indies MILT. **4.** At the crook of the glen, Where bickers the burnie SCOTT. **5.** She saw Dust, and the points of lances b. in it TENNYSON. Hence **Bi·ckerer,** a skirmisher. **Bi·ckerment,** bickering.

Bickern (bi·kəɹn). 1547. [– Fr. *bigorne* – Pr. *bigorna*, f. L. *bicornis* two-horned, f. *bi-* BI- *prep.*[2] I. 1 + *cornu* horn. See BEAK-IRON.] *orig.* An anvil with two projecting taper ends; *later* (see BEAK-IRON) used of: One such taper end of an anvil.

Bicolligate (bəikǫ·ligeⁱt), *a.* 1847. [BI- *pref.*[2] I. 2.] *Ornith.* Of the anterior toes of birds: United by a basal web.

Biconjugate (bəikǫ·ndʒiŭgĕt), *a.* 1847. [BI- *pref.*[2] I. 2.] Twice paired: applied *e.g.* in *Bot.* to a petiole that forks twice.

Bicorn (bəi·kǭɹn). 1823. [– L. *bicornis* two-horned.] **A.** *adj.* Having two horns or horn-like processes. **B.** *sb.* [sc. *animal.*] vars. **Bi·corned, Bico·rnous, Bi:cornu·te** *a.*

Bicrenate (bəi,krī·neⁱt), *a.* 1835. [See BI- *pref.*[2] I. 3.] *Bot.* Of (leaf-) margins: Crenate or scalloped, with the scallops themselves crenate.

Bicrescentic, -cristate; see BI- *pref.*[2] I. 2.

Bicru·ral, *a.* 1847. [See BI- *pref.*[2] I.] Two-legged.

Bicuspid (bəikɒ·spid). 1836. [f. L. *bi-* BI- *pref.*[2] I. 1 + *cuspis*, *-id-* CUSP.] **A.** *adj.* Having two cusps or points. **B.** *sb.* A premolar tooth in man. var. **Bicu·spidate** *a.*

Bicycle (bəi·sik'l), *sb.* 1868. [– Fr. *bicycle*, f. *bi-* BI- *prep.*[2] II + Gr. κύκλος circle, wheel, CYCLE.] A machine for riding, consisting of a saddle-seat surmounting two wheels, to which the rider communicates motion by means of pedals. Hence **Bicy·clic** *a.* of or connected with bicycles. **Bi·cyclism,** the practice or art of bicycling. **Bi·cyclist,** one who rides a b. **Bicy·cular** *a.* of the nature of a b. or pertaining to bicycling.

Bi·cycle, *v.* 1869. [f. prec.] To ride on a bicycle. Hence **Bi·cycler, Bi·cycling.**

Bid (bid), *v. str.* Pa. t. **bad, bade** (bæd), **bid.** Pa. pple. **bidden, bid.** [Two OE. verbs are merged. **A.** The present forms repr. OE. str. v. *biddan*, pa. t. *bæd*, *bǣdon*, pa. pple. *beden* ask, entreat, demand = OFris. *bidda*, *bidia*, OS. *biddian*, MDu. *bidden*, OHG. (G.) *bitten*, ON. *biðja*, Goth. *bidjan* :– Gmc. **biðjan*, f. base **beð-*, repr. by OE. *ġebed* prayer, see BEDE sb. The present meanings combine those of this verb with those of OE. *bēodan*, pa. t. *bēad*, *budon*, pa. pple. *boden* offer, proclaim, announce, command, decree = OFris. *biada*, OS. *biodan*, (M)Du. *bieden*, OHG. *biotan* (G. *bieten*), ON. *bjóða*, Goth. *biudan*, repr. Indo-Eur. **bheudh-* **bhudh-* (whence Gr. πεύθεσθαι, πυθέσθαι ascertain). OE. *biddan* had already acquired the sense 'command', and the similarity of several of the ME. forms of the two verbs furthered their unification.]

A. Senses from OE. *bēodan*, ME. *bede*. **1.** *trans.* To offer. *Obs.* in gen. sense. **2.** *trans.* To offer (a certain price) *for* ME.; *intr.* (*ellipt.*) to make an offer (*for* a thing) 1611. Often *fig.* † **3.** To proclaim, announce, threaten -1603.
1. That spirit which had bidden defiance to..the House of Valois MACAULAY. **2.** Who bids five shillings for this lot? 1887. Phr. *To b. against*: to compete with in offers. To b. for the Irish vote 1887. Phr. *To b. up*: to raise the price by successive bidding. *To b. fair* (intr.): to offer with reasonable probability, seem likely. **3.** *To b. the banns*: to proclaim them (but cf. B. 1). To b. a truce to thought SOUTHEY.

B. Senses from OE. *bidden*. **1.** *trans.* To ask pressingly, beg, entreat, pray OE; also † *intr.* -1458. **2.** To ask (any one) to come, to invite (*to* a feast, etc.) (*arch.* but common *dial.*) ME. **3.** To command, enjoin, order. (Still literary and colloq. in the north; but in the south expressed by *tell.*) OE. † **4.** To bid not to do, forbid -1622.
1. I bidde god I neuere mot haue Ioye CHAUCER. To haue of God what yᵗ he bedde ME. Phr. To b. a *bene*, *bede*, *prayer*, etc.: *orig.* to pray; *later* 'to move the people to join in prayer', as in BIDDING PRAYER. *To b. welcome*, *adieu*, *farewell*, *good-bye*, *good morning*. (Now used without analysis, 'bid' being merely = 'say, utter, express'.) **2.** I made a feast; I bad him come TENNYSON. **3.** Thou.. bad'st me bury Loue *Rom. & Jul.* IV. v. 83. He will not stand when he is bidden *Much Ado* III. iii. 32.
Hence **Bid** *sb.* the offer of a price, the amount offered; *spec.* at an auction. **Bi·ddable** *a.* ready to do what is bidden, docile. **Bi·ddance,** invitation. **Bi·dder,** one who bids (*esp.* in senses A. 2, B. 2, 3).

† **Bi·d-ale.** 1462. [f. BID *v.* B. 2 + ALE. Cf. BRIDAL.] An 'ale' for the benefit of some person, to which a general bidding was given -1733.

Bi·dcock. [Earlier var. of BILCOCK, of unkn. origin.] The Water-rail. DRAYTON.

Bidden, pa. pple. of BID and BIDE.

Bidding (bi·diŋ), *vbl. sb.* ME. [f. BID *v.* + -ING[1].] **1.** A bid. † **2.** Request, entreaty ME. only. † **3.** Praying; prayer -1440. **4.** Invitation, summons 1810. **5.** A command, order, injunction ME.
3. *Bidding of beads, beads-bidding; bidding of prayers, bidding prayer.* The orig. sense was 'praying of prayers', *i.e.* praying; cf. BID *v.* B. 1. In the 16th c., when *bid* in the sense of 'pray' was becoming obsolete, the 'bidding of prayers'

became 'the directing or injoining of prayers'. Hence 'the form of bidding prayers' or 'prayer' (= *precationem hortandi*), whence, by a later misunderstanding, 'the bidding-prayer', as if this exhortation were itself a kind of prayer qualified by 'bidding'.

Biddy[1] (bi·di). [Pet-form of *Bridget*.] Used in U.S. for an Irish maid-servant.

Bi·ddy[2]. *Obs.* exc. *dial.* [perh. a use of prec.; cf. the dial. use of *Betty* and *Molly* for the hedge-sparrow, and *Jenny* for the *wren*. Cf. CHICKABIDDY.] A chicken, a fowl. *Twel. N.* III. iv. 128.

Bide (bəid), *v.* [OE. *bīdan* = OS. *bīdan*, OHG. *bītan*, ON. *bīða*, Goth. *beidan*. Now mostly ABIDE, exc. in north. Eng. and Sc.] **1.** *intr.* To remain in expectation, to wait. (Chiefly north., and *poet.*) **2.** To remain or continue *in* some state or action (*arch.*) OE. **3.** To stay (*esp.* when others go) (*arch.*) OE. **4.** Of things: To remain, be left ME. **5.** To sojourn, dwell (*arch.*) ME. **6.** *trans.* To await. Now only in *To b. one's time*. OE. **7.** To await in resistance, to face, encounter. Cf. ABIDE. ME. **8.** To endure, suffer, undergo. Cf. ABIDE. Now *dial.* ME. **9.** To tolerate, put up with. Cf. ABIDE. ME.

1. 'B. a wee, b. a wee,' said Cuddie SCOTT. **3.** Who bides at home, nor looks abroad EMERSON. **5.** The spirit who bideth by himself In the land of mist and snow COLERIDGE. **9.** I never could b. the staying still in ae place SCOTT.

Bident (bəi·dĕnt). 1675. [– L. *bidens, -dent-* having two teeth, two-pronged.] **1.** An instrument or weapon with two prongs. **2.** A two-year-old sheep (*rare*) 1881. So **Bide·ntal** *a.* belonging to a b. **Bide·ntate, -tated** *a.* having two teeth or tooth-like processes; var. † **Bide·nted. Bide·ntial** *a.* two-pronged.

‖ **Bide·ntal,** *sb.* 1692. [L.] A place struck by lightning, consecrated, and enclosed. Also *fig.*

Bidet (bidę, bide·t). 1630. [– Fr. *bidet*, of unkn. origin.] **1.** A small horse. **2.** 'A vessel on a low narrow stand, which can be bestridden' for bathing purposes 1785.

Bidigitate: see BI- *pref.*[2] I. 1.

Biding (bəi·diŋ), *vbl. sb.* ME. [f. BIDE *v.* + -ING[1].] **1.** Expectation; tarrying. **2.** Stay, dwelling ME. † *concr.* A dwelling –1687.

2. I'll lead you to some b. *Lear* IV. vi. 228. *Comb.* **b.-place.**

‖ **Bidri, bidree, bidry** (bi·dri). 1794. [Urdu *bidrī*, f. *Bidar* or *Bedar* a town in India.] An alloy of copper, lead, tin, and zinc, used as a ground for inlaying with gold and silver, in the manufacture of *Bidri-* or *Biddery-ware*.

† **Bi·dstand.** [One who *bids* traveller *stand* and deliver.] A highwayman. B. JONS.

Bield (bīld), *sb.* Now *dial.* [OE. *beldu* (WS. *bieldu*) = OHG. *baldī*, Goth. *balþei* boldness, confidence :– Gmc. **balþjōn*, f. **balþaz* BOLD.] **1.** Boldness. **2.** Confidence; *hence*, comfort ME. **3.** Help; defence ME. **4.** Cheer, sustenance. (Only Sc.) 1513. **5.** Shelter; a place of shelter. (Only Sc. and n. dial.) 1450.

5. Better a wee bush than nae b. BURNS.

Bield (bīld), *v.* Now *dial.* [OE. *beldan* (WS. *bieldan*) = OS. *beldian*, OHG. *belden*, Goth. *balþjan* :– Gmc. **balþjan*, f. **balþaz*; see prec.] **1.** To make bold. **2.** *intr.* To have confidence ME. **3.** To defend, shelter. *Sc.* and *n. dial.* ME. **4.** *intr.* To find refuge or protection; to lodge, dwell ME.

3. That..bielded me as if I had been a sister SCOTT.

Biennial (bəi,e·niăl). 1621. [f. L. *biennis* of two years, *biennium* space of two years; see BI- *pref.*[2] I. 4, ANNUAL.] **A.** *adj.* **1.** Existing or lasting for two years; *esp.* of plants. **2.** Taking place once in every two years 1750. **B.** *sb. Bot.* A plant which springs from seed and vegetates one year, and flowers, fructifies, and perishes the next 1770. Hence **Bie·nnially** *adv.*

‖ **Bienséance** (byæṅ,se,āṅs). 1788. [Fr., f. *bien* + *séant*, f. *seoir* to befit.] Decorum.

†‖ **Bienvenue.** ME. [Fr., f. *bien* well + *venue* coming. Formerly as freq. in Eng. use as *adieu*.] **1.** Welcome –1629. **2.** A fee exacted from a new workman 1793.

Bier (bīᵊɹ). [OE. *bēr* (WS. *bǣr*) = OFris. *bēre*, OS., OHG. *bāra* (G. *bahre*) :– WGmc. **bērō*, f. **beran* BEAR *v.*[1] The sp. with *ie* dates from *c*1600.] **1.** A framework for carrying; a handbarrow; a litter, a stretcher. Now *Hist.* **2.** The movable stand on which a corpse is placed before burial; that on which it is carried to the grave OE. **3.** *transf.* A sepulchre 1513.

Comb.: † **b.-balk,** a balk in a field where there is a right of way for funerals; † **-right,** an ordeal in which a person, accused of murder, was required to approach the corpse, and clear himself on oath.

Bifacial, bifanged; see BI- *pref.*[2] I.

Bifarious (bəifēᵊ·riəs), *a.* 1656. [f. L. *bifarius* two-fold, double + -OUS.] **1.** Twofold, ambiguous (*arch.*). **2.** *Bot.* Ranged in two rows 1846. Hence **Bifa·riously** *adv.*

Bifer (bəi·fəɹ). [– L. *bifer*, f. *bi-* BI- *pref.*[2] + *-fer*; see -FEROUS.] A plant which produces flowers or fruit twice a year. So **Bi·ferous** *a.*

Biffin (bi·fin). 1794. [Also *beefin*, dial. pronunc. of BEEFING; for the suffix cf. *golding, jenneting, sweeting, wilding*.] **1.** A (Norfolk) cooking apple. **2.** A baked apple, flattened in the form of a cake 1822. vars. **Beefen, -in, -ing, beaufin** (a fabricated spelling, as if f. Fr. *beau* + *fin*).

Bifid (bəi·fid, bi·fid), *a.* [– L. *bifidus*, f. *bi-* BI- *pref.*[2] + **fid-*, base of *findere* cleave.] Divided into two parts by a cleft or notch. **Bi·fidly** *adv.* **Bi·fidate** *a.* (a bad var.). **Bifi·dity.**

Bifilar (bəifəi·lăɹ), *a.* 1870. [f. BI- *pref.*[2] I. 1 + FILAR.] Fitted with two threads; *spec.* applied to apparatus for measuring minute distances or angles, minute forces, etc.

Gauss's b. magnetometer 1870.

Bifistular (bəifi·stiŭlăɹ), *a.* 1870. [See BI- *pref.*[2] I. 1.] Having two tubes.

Biflorous (bəi,flōᵊ·rəs), *a.* 1794. [f. mod. L. *biflorus*, (f. *bi-* BI- *pref.*[2] + *flos, flor-* flower) + -OUS.] Bearing two flowers or blooms. var. **Biflo·rate.**

Bifold (bəi·fōᵘld), *a.* 1609. [See BI- *pref.*[2] + -FOLD.] Double, twofold.

Bifoliate, bifoliolate; see BI- *pref.*[2] I.

Biforate (bəifōᵊ·rĕt bi·fōreⁱt), *a.* 1842. [f. BI- *pref.*[2] I. 2 + L. *foratus* pierced.] Having two perforations.

Biforine (bi·fōrəin). 1842. [f. L. *biforis* having two doors or openings (f. *bi-* BI- *pref.*[2] + *foris* door) + -INE[1].] *Bot.* An oval sac found in the pulpy part of some leaves, which discharges its contents by an opening at each end.

Biforked (bəi·fǫɹkt), *a.* 1578. [BI- *pref.*[2] I. 1.] Having two forks, branches, or peaks.

Biform (bəi·fǭɹm), *a.* 1816. [– L. *biformis* f. *bi-* BI- *pref.*[2] + *forma* shape, form.] Having, or partaking of, two forms. var. **Bi·formed.** Hence **Bifo·rmity.**

Bifront (bəi·frɒnt), *a.* 1598. [– L. *bifrons, -front-* f. *bi-* BI- *pref.*[2] + *frons* forehead, face.] Having two faces or aspects; double; *absol.* = Janus. vars. **Bifro·ntal, Bifro·nted.**

Bifurcate (bəi·fɒɹkeⁱt), *v.* 1615. [f. *bifurcat-*, pa. ppl. stem of med.L. *bifurcare*, f. L. *bifurcus* two-forked, f. *bi-* BI- *pref.*[2] + *furca* FORK; see -ATE[3].] To divide into two forks, branches, or peaks. *trans.* and *intr.* So **Bifu·rcate** *a.* = BIFORKED. **Bifurca·tion,** division into two forks or branches; the point of division; the branches, or one of them.

Big, *sb. Obs.* exc. *dial.* 1573. [Origin unkn.] **1.** A teat. **2.** A boil 1601.

Big (big), *a.* ME. [Of unkn. origin; perh. Scand.] † **1.** Of great strength or power. L. *validus, potens*. –1599. † **2.** Of things: Strong; stiff; forceful; violent, vehement –1604. **3. a.** Of great size, bulk, or extent; large 1552. **b.** *esp.* Grown, grown up 1552. **c.** 'Having comparative bulk, greater or less' 1547. **4.** Far advanced in pregnancy. Const. *with*, occas. *of*. 1535. Also *transf.* and *fig.* **5.** Loud 1581. **6.** Important. (Colloq. or joc. for *great*.) 1577. **7.** Pompous; *esp.* in *To talk, look b.* 1570.

1. Bigge Mars SHAKS. **2.** Farewell the bigge Warres *Oth.* III. iii. 349. **3.** The biggest and the fattest Bishoprick MILT. He run away Till I am bigger *Cor.* V. iii. 128. Statues..bigger than life HOGARTH. **4.** Their women bygg with childe *Hos.* 13:16. B. with the fate Of Cato and of Rome ADDISON. **6.** Pompey surnam'd the b. *L.L.L.* V. ii. 555. **7.** Nay, looke not b., nor stampe, nor stare *Tam. Shr.* II. ii. 230.

Comb.: **b.-bellied** *a.* corpulent; pregnant; **-horn,** a species of sheep inhabiting the Rocky Mountains. Also in various collocations with specific force, as **b. drum, game, foe; b. daisy,** the Ox-eye daisy, etc.; **b. dog,** a watch-dog; also *fig.*; **b. trees,** the Sequoias or Wellingtonias of the Sierra Nevada.

Big, bigg (big), *v. Obs.* exc. *n. dial.* [ME. – ON. *byggja* inhabit, build.] *trans.* To build. Also *transf.* and *fig.*

God..sal..bigge þe cites of Jude *E.E.Ps.* 68:36. Hence **Bi·gging** *vbl. sb.* † dwelling; building; a building. *n. dial.*

Big, var. of BIGG barley.

‖ **Biga** (bəi·gă). 1850. [L.] *Rom. Antiq.* A two-horsed chariot.

† **Bi·gam(e.** ME. [– (O)Fr. *bigame*; see BIGAMY.] **A.** *adj.* Having at the same time two wives or husbands. **B.** *sb.* One so married. In *Eccl. Law* applied to one who marries a second time. –1502. var. ‖ **Bi·gamus.**

Bigamist (bi·gămist). 1631. [f. BIGAMY + -IST.] A man or woman living in BIGAMY (senses 1, 2).

Bigamous (bi·găməs), *a.* 1864. [f. BIGAMY + -OUS.] Living in bigamy; involving bigamy. Hence **Bi·gamously** *adv.* so as to commit or involve bigamy.

Bigamy (bi·gămi). ME. [– (O)Fr. *bigamie*, f. *bigame* – late L. *bigamus*, f. L. *bi-* BI- *pref.*[2] + Gr. -γαμος *married*.] **1.** The crime of having two wives or husbands at once. Also *fig.* 1635. **2.** *Eccl. Law.* Marriage of, or with, a widow (*or* widower). Now *Hist.* ME.

1. Lamech, that broute in first bigamie CAPGRAVE. **2.** Our laws certainly allow [b.] FIELDING.

Bigarreau, -roon (bi·gărōᵘ; -rū·n). 1675. [– Fr. *bigarreau* – mod. Pr. *bigarreu*, f. *bigarra* variegate. The form *-oon* is of Eng. origin.] The large white heart-cherry, which has one side yellow, and the other red.

† **Bi·gate,** *a.* (*sb.*) 1600. [– L. *bigatus*; see -ATE[2].] (A coin) bearing the figure of a biga.

Bigeminal (bəi,dʒe·minăl), *a.* 1836. [Earlier *bigeminate*, f. BI- *pref.*[2] I. 3 + L. *geminus* twin; see -AL[1].] Existing or arranged in pairs; *spec.* in *Phys.* of the *corpora quadrigemina* of the brain. var. **Bige·minate** *a.* Also **Bige·minated** *ppl. a.* (Chiefly in *Bot.*)

Bigener (bəi·dʒĭnəɹ). 1835. [– L. *bigener*, f. *bi-* BI- *pref.*[2] + *genus, gener-* kind.] A cross between two genera. Hence † **Bige·nerous** *a.* hybrid.

Bigential (bəi,dʒe·nʃăl), *a.* 1846. [f. BI- *pref.*[2] I. 1 + L. *gens, gent-* race + -IAL.] Composed of or containing two races or peoples.

Bigg, big (big). *Sc.* and *dial.* 1450. [– ON. *bygg* barley (Da. *byg*, Sw. *bjug*), corresp. to OE. *bēow* grain, OS. *beo, bewod* harvest.] The four-rowed barley. (*Barley* is generic; *bear* interchanges locally, now with *barley*, now with *bigg*.)

Biggen (bi·g'n), *v.* Now *dial.* 1643. [f. BIG *a.* + -EN[5].] **1.** To make or become big. **2.** To recover strength after confinement (*dial.*) 1674.

Bi·gger, *a.*, compar. of BIG (see -ER[3]). Also *sb.* One who is bigger.

Biggin[1] (bi·gin). 1530. [– Fr. *béguin*, f. *beguine* BEGUINE.] **1.** A child's cap; *fig.* infancy 1609. **2.** A hood for the head, a night-cap; the coif of a Serjeant-at-law 1562.

2. Hee whose Brow (with homely Biggen bound) Snores out the Watch of Night 2 *Hen. IV*, IV. v. 27.

Bi·ggin[2]. 1803. [f. the inventor's name.] A kind of coffee-pot with a strainer.

Bi·ggish, *a.* 1626. [f. BIG *a.* + -ISH[1].] Rather big.

Bi·ggonet. Sc. 1725. [dim. of BIGGIN[1]; cf. OFr. *beguinet* in same sense.] A woman's cap or head-dress.

Bight (bəit). [OE. *byht* (:– *buxtiz*); cf. (M)LG. *bucht* (whence Du. *bocht*, G. *bucht*, Sw., Da. *bugt*) :– **buʒ-*, short stem of **beuʒ-* see BOW *v.*[1]] **1.** A bending or bend; *esp.* an angle, hollow, or fork in the human or animal body; a corner. **2.** *esp.* The loop of a rope, as opp. to the ends 1622. **3.** *Geog.* An indentation in a coast line, a recess of a bay, a bend in a river, etc. 1481. Also *fig.* **4.** The space between two headlands, a slightly-receding bay; *spec.* in the Bights of Benin and Biafra; also *transf.* a bay-like segment 1555.

1. B. of the Elbow RAY. 4. A b. of meadow STEVENSON.

† **Bi·gly,** *a.* ME. [f. BIG *v.* + -LY¹.] Habitable; pleasant –1803.

Bigly (bi·gli), *adv.* ME. [f. BIG *a.* + -LY².] † **1.** With force or violence –1556. **2.** Loudly, boastfully, pompously 1532.

Bigness (bi·gnės). 1494. [f. BIG *a.* + -NESS.] **1.** Large size or bulk; also *fig.* **2.** Size, bulk 1529.

1. B. with the bulk of mankind is the nearest synonym for greatness HARE. 2. The b. of a large pea 1826.

‖ **Bignonia** (bignōᵘ·niă). 1835. [f. Abbé *Bignon*, librarian to Louis XIV + -IA¹] *Bot.* A genus of plants, N.O. *Bignoniaceæ*, with showy trumpet-shaped flowers. Hence **Bignonia·ceous, Bigno·nial** *adjs.*

Bigot (bi·gət, -ǫt). 1598. [– Fr. *bigot* (XV), of unkn. origin.] † **1. a.** A hypocrite. **b.** A superstitious person. –1664. **2.** A person obstinately and unreasonably wedded to a creed, opinion, or ritual 1661. Also *transf.* **3.** *attrib.* or as *adj.* 1623.

2. A dogmatist in religion is not a long way off from a b. WATTS. 3. Old b. zeal against Christians 1844.

Bigoted (bi·gətėd), *a.* 1645. [f. prec. (In XVII *bigo·tted.*)] Obstinately and blindly attached to some creed, opinion, or party, and intolerant towards others.

A b. Jacobite 1759. So nursed and b. to strife BYRON. Hence **Bi·gotedly** *adv.* var. † **Bigo·tic** *a.* So † **Bigo·tical** *a.*, whence **Bigo·tically** *adv.*

Bigotry (bi·gətri). 1674. [f. BIGOT + -RY, partly through Fr. *bigoterie.*] The condition of a bigot; obstinate and blind attachment *to* a creed, etc.; *concr.* a specimen of bigotry 1715. var. † **Bi·gotism.**

Bigwig (bi·gwig). 1792. [f. BIG + WIG, from the large wigs formerly worn by people of importance.] A man of high official standing, or of note or importance. (*humorous* or *contemptuous.*) Hence **Bi·gwigged** *ppl. a.*; **Bigwi·ggedness, Bigwi·ggery, Bigwi·ggism,** official display of importance.

† **Biha·lve, -en, -es,** *adv.* and *prep.* [OE. *be healfe*; see BEHALF.] Beside –ME.

‖ **Bijou** (bi·ʒu). Pl. **bijoux.** 1838. [Fr. – Breton *bizou* finger-ring, f. *biz* (cf. W. *bys*) finger.] A jewel, a trinket; a 'gem' among works of art. Also *attrib.* Hence ‖ **Bijou·terie,** bijoux collectively.

Bijugate (bəi·dʒⁱugeⁱt), *a.* 1725. [f. BI- *pref.*² I. 1 + L. *jugatus* yoked; see -ATE².] **1.** Of a coin: Bearing two heads side-facing, one overlapping the other. **2.** Two-paired. var. **Bi·jugous.**

Bike (bəik), *sb.*¹ *n. dial.* ME. [ME. *bike* (= AL. *bica, byka* XIII), of unkn. origin.] **1.** A nest of wasps, hornets, or wild bees. **2.** *fig.* A swarm of people; a 'crew' 1552.

Bike, *sb.*², *v.* Colloq. abbrev. of BICYCLE.

‖ **Bikh.** 1830. [Hindi, Nepali *bikh*, Bengali *bish* poison :– Skr. *visha* poison.] The poison of various Aconites, esp. *Aconitum ferox*; also the root or plant.

Bilabiate (bəilēⁱ·bi‚ĕt), *a.* 1794. [BI- *pref.*² I. 1.] Two-lipped. var. **Bila·bial.**

Bilaciniate (bəilăsi·ni‚ĕt), *a.* [See BI- *pref.*² I. 3.] *Bot.* Of leaves: Doubly laciniate.

Bilamellate, -ated (bəilæ·meleⁱt, -ēⁱtėd), *a.* 1846. [BI- *pref.*² I. 1.] Having or consisting of two small thin plates. var. **Bila·mellar.**

Bilaminate, -ated (bəilæ·mineⁱt, -ēⁱtėd), *a.* 1839. [BI- *pref.*² I. 1.] Having or consisting of two thin plates. var. **Bila·minar.**

Biland, var. of BYLAND.

Bilander (bi·lăndəɹ, bəi·-). 1656. [– Du. *bijlander* (Flem. *billander*), f. *bij* BY + *land* LAND, whence Fr. *bélandre*; see -ER¹, and BALANDRA.] A kind of hoy with a trapezoidal mainsail; used in Holland for coast and canal traffic.

Like bilanders to creep Along the coast DRYDEN.

Bilateral (bəilæ·tĕral), *a.* 1775. [BI- *pref.*² I. 6.] Of, pertaining to, or affecting two sides; disposed on opposite sides of an axis. *Law.* Pertaining to or affecting two parties 1818. Hence **Bila·terally** *adv.* on both sides. **Bila·teralism, Bilatera·lity, Bila·teralness,** b. condition.

Bilberry, bill- (bi·lbəri). 1577. [prob. of Norse origin; cf. Da. *böllebær*, f. *bölle* bill-berry + *bær* BERRY.] **1.** The fruit of a dwarf hardy shrub (*Vaccinium myrtillus*); the berry, called also WHORTLEBERRY and BLAEBERRY, is of a deep blue black. Also the plant. Used also *attrib.* **2.** Used of other species of *Vaccinium*; e.g. the Great B. (*V. uliginosum*) 1640.

1. There pinch the Maids as blew as Bill-berry *Merry W.* V. v. 49. Hence **Bi·lberrying** *vbl. sb.* gathering bilberries.

Bilbo¹ (bi·lboᵘ). 1592. [orig. *Bilbo blade*, f. *Bilboa*, Eng. form of *Bilbao* name of a town in Spain, famous for its swords.] A sword noted for the temper of its blade. Now *Hist.* 1598. **b.** A humorous term for the sword of a bully 1676. Also *attrib.*

At drawn b. SCOTT.

Bilbo². Pl. **bilboes** (bi·lboᵘz). 1557. [Origin unkn.; commonly referred to *Bilbao* (see prec.) but without evidence.] A long iron bar, with sliding shackles to confine the ankles of prisoners, and a lock to fasten one end of the bar to the floor.

Me thought I lay Worse then the Mutines in the Bilboes *Haml.* V. ii. 6.

Bilboquet (bilboke·t). 1616. [– Fr. *bilboquet*, OFr. *bille-boquet*, of unkn. origin.] † **1.** A cord with two sticks fastened to it, used by gardeners to square out beds –1688. **2.** The plaything called Cup-and-ball; also, the game 1743.

Bilcock (bi·l‚kǫk). 1678. [Later var. of BIDCOCK, of unkn. origin.] The Water-rail.

Bile (bəil). 1665. [– Fr. *bile* – L. *bilis.*] **1.** The fluid secreted by the liver, and poured into the duodenum, as an aid to the digestive process. It is bitter, yellowish or green in colour, and of a complex structure. (Formerly called *choler*, and in early physiology one of the 'four humours'.) **b.** Excess or derangement of the bile 1803. **2.** *fig.* Anger, peevishness. Cf. CHOLER, GALL, SPLEEN. 1836.

1. Black b.: see ATRABILE. **b.** I am..quite free both from gout and b. PITT. *Comb.* **b.-stone,** a calculus formed in the gall-bladder.

Bile, obs. f. BOIL tumour.

† **Bi·lewhit,** *a.* OE. [OE. *bilewit.* Has been doubtfully referred to *bil-* in G. *billig* (OHG. *billīch*) just, reasonable, and WIT, but connections are wanting.] Mild, clement; innocent –ME.

Bilge (bildʒ), *sb.* 1513. [prob. obscure var. of BULGE, used in the same senses.] **1.** The bottom of a ship's hull, on which the ship would rest if aground; also the lowest internal part of the hull. **b.** Bilge-water 1829. **c.** *slang.* Nonsense, 'rubbish' 1921. **2.** The belly of a cask, etc. 1513.

Comb.: **b.-free** *a.* (of a cask), stowed so that the b. does not come in contact with the floor; **-piece** = BILGE-KEEL; **-pump,** a pump to draw off the b.-water; **-ways,** cradles, placed under the bottom, to conduct the ship into the water whilst launching. Hence **Bilged** *ppl. a.* broad-bottomed. **Bi·lgy** *a.*

Bilge, *v.* 1557. [f. the sb.] **1.** *trans.* To stave in a ship's bottom. **2.** *intr.* (for *refl.*) To suffer fracture in the bilge; to spring a leak. Also *fig.* 1728. **3.** *trans.* and *intr.* To bulge 1807.

Bi·lge-keel. 1850. The timber fastened under the bilge of boats, etc., to keep them upright when on shore, or to reduce rolling.

Bi·lge-water. 1706. The foul water that collects in the bilge of a ship.

Bili- (bəili), comb. f. L. *bilis* bile, used esp. in the names of bile-pigments; as *bili-cyanin, -rubin, -verdin*, etc. Hence also **Bilia·tion,** the secretion of bile. **Bili·ferous** *a.* † **Bi:lifica·tion,** making bile. † **Bi·lify** *v.* to form bile.

Bi·liary, *a.* 1731. [– Fr. *biliaire*, f. *bile* BILE + *-aire* -ARY².] **1.** Of or pertaining to the bile. **2.** = BILIOUS 2. 1837.

1. The b. duct 1731. B. organs CARLYLE.

‖ **Bilimbi** (bili·mbi). 1772. [Tamil.] An Indian tree (*Averrhoa bilimbi*, N.O. *Oxalidaceæ*), which yields a juice used in the cure of skin-diseases; also its fruit.

† **Bi·liment.** 1553. [aphet. f. ABILIMENT, HABILIMENT.] **1.** *gen* = HABILIMENT –1790. **2.** *spec.* in 16th c.: Attire or ornaments for a woman's head or neck. So *B. lace.*

Bilin (bəi·lin). 1849. [f. BILE + -IN¹.] A gummy pale yellow mass, once considered to be the principal constituent of the bile.

Bilinear (bəili·nĭăɹ), *a. rare.* [See BI- *pref.*² 6.] Of, pertaining to, or contained by, two (straight) lines. MANSELL.

Bilingual (bəili·ŋgwăl), *a.* 1847. [f. L. *bilinguis* (f. *bi-* BI- *pref.*² + *lingua* tongue) + -AL¹.] **1.** Having, or characterized by two languages 1862. **2.** *spec.* Of inscriptions, etc.: Inscribed simultaneously in parallel versions in two languages. Also quasi-*sb.*

2. The inscriptions were b., in Assyrian characters as well as Greek GROTE. Hence **Bili·ngually** *adv.* **Bili·nguist,** one who speaks two languages. vars. **Bili·nguar, Bili·nguous.**

Bilious (bi·liəs), *a.* 1541. [– L. *biliosus*, f. *bilis* BILE; see -OUS; cf. Fr. *bilieux* (XVII).] † **1.** = BILIARY 1. –1697. **2.** Affected by, or arising from excess or derangement of the bile 1651. **3.** Choleric, peevish, ill-tempered 1561.

2. Rise in the morning as b. as a Bengal general DISRAELI. 3. The outpouring of a b. cynicism 1866. Hence **Bi·liously** *adv.* **Bi·liousness,** bilious quality or condition; *fig.* ill-temper.

Biliteral (bəili·tĕrăl), *a.* 1787. [BI- *pref.*² I. 1.] Consisting of two letters; as quasi-*sb.* a linguistic root consisting of two letters.

The so-called biliterals are..the result of phonetic decay SAYCE. Hence **Bili·teralism,** a b. condition of language.

Bilk (bilk), *sb.* 1633. [app. f. earlier BILK *v.*] **1.** *Cribbage.* A balking or spoiling of an adversary's score in his crib 1791. † **2.** A statement having nothing in it –1733. **3.** A 'take in' 1664. **4.** A person who bilks; a cheat 1790.

2. Bilk! what's that? Why, nothing: a word signifying Nothing; and borrowed here to express nothing B. JONS. 4. Johnny W—lks, Thou greatest of bilks SHERIDAN.

Bilk (bilk), *v.* 1651. [perh. alt. f. BALK, with symbolic 'thinning' of the vowel.] **1.** *Cribbage.* To balk any one's score in his crib. **2.** To balk (hope, etc.); to cheat, deceive, betray 1672. **3.** To 'do out' *of*; to defraud; to evade payment of 1672. **4.** To elude, evade, give the slip to 1679.

2. Hopes often bilkt OLDHAM. 3. His skill..In bilking tavern bills COWPER.

Bill (bil), *sb.*¹ [OE. *bil* = OS. *bil*, OHG. *bill* (MHG. *bil*; but G. *bille* fem., axe) :– WGmc. **bilja.*] † **1.** A kind of sword mentioned in OE. poetry. **2.** An obsolete weapon carried by soldiers and watchmen, varying in form from a concave blade with a long wooden handle, to a kind of concave axe with a spike at the back and its shaft ending in a spear-head; a halberd ME. **3.** Short for BILLMAN 1495. **4.** An implement having a long blade with a concave edge (cf. BILL-HOOK), used for pruning, cutting wood, etc. OE. † **5.** A pickaxe –1483.

2. Wer't with the Speare, or Browne B., or the Pike DRAYTON. The watchmans browne bil 1589. 3. A strong guard of bills and bows SCOTT.

Bill, *sb.*² [OE. *bile*, not elsewhere in Gmc.] **1.** The horny BEAK of certain birds, *esp.* when slender or weak. † **2.** *transf.* The beak, muzzle, or snout of other animals (cf. BEAK) –1625. **3.** A beak-like projection, as in *Portland B., Selsea B.* ME. **4.** *Naut.* The point of the fluke of an anchor 1769.

2. How she holds vp the Neb, the Byll to him *Wint. T.* I. ii. 183. **4. B.-board,** a board for the b. of the anchor to rest upon. *Comb.* **B.-fish** (*Belone truncata*), a sea-fish of N. America. Also called Sea-pike, Silver Gar-fish, etc.

Bill (bil), *sb.*³ [– AFr. *bille* or Anglo-L. *billa* (XIII), prob. unexpl. alt. of med. L. *bulla* BULL *sb.*²] **1.** A written document (orig. sealed); a letter, note, memorandum (cf. BILLET *sb.*). *Obs.* exc. in *Law* and *Comm.* † **b.** A papal 'bull' –1500. † **c.** A lampoon –1587. † **d.** A deed –1613. † **2.** A (written) petition to a person in authority –1728. **3.** The draft of an Act of Parliament submitted to the legislature for discussion and adoption as an 'Act'. (*Private bills* are still introduced in the form of petitions.) 1512. † **4.** *Law.* A written statement of a case; a pleading (*esp.* by a plaintiff), e.g. a *b. of complaint* in Chancery; an indictment –1788. **b.** *Sc. Law.* Any summary application by way of petition to the Court of Session. † **5.** A written list, an inventory –1605. † **b.** *Med.* A prescription –1754. **c.** *Naut.* A list of persons appointed to duties 1830. **d.** *Typog.* A list of the quantities of each letter required for a fount 1824.

6. A note of charges for goods delivered or services rendered; a *b. of parcels* ME. † **7.** A label. *A.Y.L.* I. ii. 131. **8.** A poster, a *handbill* 1480. **9.** (More fully **B. of Exchange**) A written order by the drawer to the 'drawee' to pay a certain sum on a given date to the drawer, or to the 'payee' 1579. † **b.** Loosely used for: A promissory note. Cf. BANK-BILL, EXCHEQUER-BILL. –1721.

3. We knew..that the B. must remain a B., and could never become an Act of Parliament GLADSTONE. **4.** *To find a true b., to ignore the b.*, said of a Grand Jury, in criminal Assizes, finding that there is, or is not, sufficient evidence for the case to go before the judge and an ordinary jury. **5. b.** Like him that took the Doctor's B. And swallow'd it instead o' th' Pill BUTLER *Hud.* I. I. 603. **6.** Well, now, Master Snip, let me see your b. B. JONS. **8.** He set vp his bils here in Messina, and challenged Cupid at the flight *Much Ado* I. i. 39. **9.** *Accommodation B.*: see ACCOMMODATION.

Phrases: **B. of fare,** a list of dishes to be served at a banquet, or which may be ordered (at stated prices) at a restaurant; often *fig.* a programme; **b. of health,** an official certificate given to the master of a vessel, stating whether at the time of sailing any infectious disease existed on board or in the port (hence a *clean b.*, *suspected* or *touched b.*, *foul b.*); **b. of lading,** an official detailed receipt given by the master of a vessel to the person consigning goods, by which he makes himself responsible for their safe delivery to the consignee; † **b. of mortality,** an official return, published periodically, of the deaths (later, also of the births) in a certain district; **b. of sale,** a written instrument effecting a transfer of personal property; *spec.* a document given as security for money borrowed, authorizing seizure of the property on default; **b. of sight,** permission from the custom-house officers to land goods for inspection in their presence, when it is not possible to enter them accurately; **b. of store,** a custom-house licence for a vessel to carry stores for a voyage custom-free; also, for British goods to be brought back into the United Kingdom within five years from the time of exportation. Also *b. of attainder, attorney* (= letter of attorney), *credit, exceptions, indictment, review, rights*, etc., see these words.

Comb. **b.-head** (sense 6), paper ruled for a tradesman's bills, having his name, etc. printed at the top.

Bill, *sb.*[4] *rare.* [For *beel, beeal*, dial. f. BELL, BELLOW.] Bellowing; the boom of the bittern.

Bill (bil), *v.*[1] 1440. [f. BILL *sb.*[1]] *trans.* To work at or on with a bill; to hoe, hack, chop, lop.

Bill, *v.*[2] ME. [f. BILL *sb.*[2]] † **1.** *intr.* To peck –1678. **2.** To stroke bill with bill (as doves) 1592. **3.** *transf.* To caress 1606.

2. Like two silver doves that sit a-billing SHAKS. **3.** What, billing againe? *Tr. & Cr.* III. ii. 60.

Bill, *v.*[3] ME. [f. BILL *sb.*[3]] † **1.** *trans.* To enter (in a bill, book, etc.) –1656. † **2.** To enter in a list –1633. † **3.** To make the subject or object of a bill; to lampoon; to indict; to petition –1728. **4.** To announce by bill 1694. **5.** To plaster over or crowd with bills 1851.

4. At the Opera to-night Flick und Flock is 'billed' 1871. **5.** To b. a town 1884.

Bi·llage, *sb.* and *v.* A var. of BILGE.

Bi·llard. *Obs.* or *dial.* 1661. [Earlier form of BILLET *sb.*[3], both from Scarborough; ult. origin unkn.] The Coal-fish; cf. BILLET *sb.*[3]

Billbe·rgia, bilbe·rgia. 1858. [f. *Billberg*, botanist + -IA[1].] A genus of epiphytes (N.O. *Bromeliaceæ*), natives of S. America.

Billed, *ppl. a.* ME. [f. BILL *sb.*[1] and [2] + -ED[2].] Furnished with a bill; having a beak, spike, etc. (Usu. in comb., as *broad-b.*, etc.)

Billet (bi·lėt), *sb.*[1] [– AFr. *billette* or Anglo-L. *billetta*, dim. of *billa* BILL *sb.*[3] See -ET.] † **1.** A short written document –1555; a note 1579; † a pass –1823. **2.** *Mil.* An official order requiring the addressee to board and lodge the soldier bearing it. **b.** The quarters so assigned 1858. **c.** *fig.* A post, berth 1870.

1. The Lady..writ this B. to her Lover STEELE **2. B.-master,** the official who makes out billets. Phr. *Every bullet has its b.* (*i.e.* its appointed destination): only those are killed whose death Providence has ordained.

Bi·llet, *sb.*[2] 1440. [– (O)Fr. *billette* and *billot*, dims. of *bille* tree-trunk, length of round timber – med. L. *billa, billus* branch, trunk, prob. of Celtic origin (cf. Ir. *bile* sacred tree, large tree); see -ET.] **1.** A piece of wood cut to a proper length for fuel; billet-wood. **2.** A (thick) stick used as a weapon 1603. **3.** A small bar of metal 1670. **4.** *Archit.* A Norman moulding, consisting of short cylindrical pieces placed lengthwise at intervals in a hollow moulding. Also *attrib.* 1835. **5.** *pl.* The excrements of a fox. ¶ Senses belonging doubtfully to this or the prec. wd. **6.** *Her.* A bearing of the shape of a rectangle placed on end 1592. **7.** *Saddlery.* **a.** A strap which enters a buckle. **b.** A loop which receives the end of a buckled strap. 1481.

2. Or they shall beat out my braines with billets *Meas. for M.* IV. iii. 58. *Comb.*: **b.-head,** a piece of wood at the bow of a whale-boat, round which the harpoon line runs; **b.-moulding** = sense 4.

Bi·llet, *sb.*[3] 1769. [Earlier BILLARD, q.v.] A coal-fish, when one year old.

Billet (bi·lėt), *v.* 1599. [f. BILLET *sb.*[1]] † **1.** *trans.* To enter in a list; to enrol –1629. **2.** To assign quarters to; *spec.* to quarter (troops) by billet *in, at, on, upon, with* 1599.

2. Go where thou art Billited *Oth.* II. iii. 386.

‖ **Billet-doux** (bi:ledū·). 1673. [Fr.] A love-letter. (Now *joc.*)

He..writes the billets doux to a miracle DRYDEN.

Billeté, -etté, -etty (bi·lėti). 1572. [– Fr. *billeté*, f. *billet*; see BILLET *sb.*[2] 6, -Y[5].] *Her.* Charged with billets.

Bill-hook (bi·l,huk). 1611. [f. BILL *sb.*[1]] A heavy thick knife or chopper with a hooked end, used for pruning, etc.

Billiards (bi·lyăɹdz), *sb. pl.* Sing. only in comb. 1591. [– Fr. *billard* name of the game and the cue, f. *bille*; see BILLET *sb.*[2], -ARD. In Eng. only the name of the game, and made pl. like *bowls*, etc.] A game played with balls on a rectangular table having a smooth cloth-covered horizontal surface, the balls being knocked about, according to rules, by means of cues.

Let it alone, let's to billards *Ant. & Cl.* II. v. 3. *Comb.*: **b.-cloth,** fine green woollen cloth used for covering billiard-tables; **-marker,** a person who marks the scores in b.; *also*, an apparatus for registering results; **-table,** the table on which the game is played; in England usu. 12 ft. by 6, covered with b.-cloth, surrounded by a cushioned ledge, and provided with six pockets at the corners and sides.

Billingsgate (bi·liŋsgėⁱt). [ME. *Billingesgate* (Ekwall), f. personal name.] **1.** A gate of the city of London; the fish-market near it, noted for vituperative language. Also *attrib.* **2.** Violent abuse 1676. † **3.** A foul-mouthed person, a scold –1790.

2. Philosophers and Divines, who..write in learned Billinsgate SHAFTESB.

Billion (bi·lyən). 1690. [– Fr. *billion*, arbitrarily f. *million* MILLION, by substitution of BI- *pref.*[2] for *mi-*.] **1.** In Great Britain; A million millions. (= Fr. *trillion.*) **2.** In U.S. (as in France, where the system of numeration is based on groups of threes, not of sixes): A thousand millions. Hence **Billionai·re,** the possessor of property worth a b. of money. **Bi·llionth** *a.* the ordinal adj. corresponding to 'billion'; *sb.* the billionth part.

Billman (bi·lmæn). 1530. [f. BILL *sb.*[1]] A soldier or a watchman armed with a bill; a labourer using a bill.

Billon (bi·lən). 1727. [– (O)Fr. *billon* (orig.) ingot, (now) bronze or copper money, f. *bille* (see BILLET *sb.*[2]); see -OON.] An alloy of gold or silver with copper, tin, or other base metal, in which the latter predominates.

Billot (bi·lət). [– (O)Fr. *billot* wooden block, dim. of *bille*; see BILLET *sb.*[2]] **1.** Obs. f. BILLET *sb.*[2] **2.** Bullion in the bar before being coined 1846. (Dicts.)

Billow (bi·loᵘ), *sb.* 1552. [– ON. *bylgja* billow (Sw. *bölja*, Da. *bölge*), f. Gmc. **bulʒ-* **belʒ-* swell, Cf. BELLY.] † **1.** The swell produced on the sea, a river, etc., by wind or tide –1614. **2.** *prop.* A great swelling wave of the sea; often used as = WAVE, and hence poetically for 'the sea'. 1552. Also *fig.* and *transf.*

2. Why now blow winde, swell B., And swimme Barke SHAKS. *transf.* Billows of armed men 1854.

Bi·llow, *v.* 1597. [f. prec. sb.] *intr.* To rise in billows; to surge, swell. Also *fig.*

A laugh..billowed and broke through the whole school 1865.

Billowy (bi·loᵘi), *a.* 1615. [f. BILLOW *sb.* + -Y[1].] **1.** Characterized by billows. **2.** Of, pertaining to, or of the nature of billows 1791. Also *transf.*

1. Crests and troughs of a b. sea GEIKIE.

Billy (bi·li). 1795. [f. *Billy*, for *Willie*, pet form of *William*.] A name for: **a.** a slubbing machine; **b.** a highwayman's club; **c.** an Australian bushman's tea-pot. Cf. JACK, JEMMY, etc.

Billyboy (bi·liboi), 1855. [Origin unkn. Cf. GEORDIE.] 'A Humber or East-coast boat, of river-barge build, and a try-sail.' SMYTH.

Billycock (bi·likǫk). 1862. [Said to be f. name of *William Coke*, nephew of Thomas William Coke, Earl of Leicester (1752–1842).] A kind of bowler hat.

Billy-goat (bi·ligōᵘt). 1861. [f. *Billy* (a male name) + GOAT.] A male goat (*colloq.*).

Bilobed (bəilōᵘ·bd), *ppl. a.* 1756. [BI- *pref.*[2] I. 1.] Having, or divided into, two lobes. vars. **Bilo·bate, Bi·lobated.**

Bilo·bular, *a.* 1859. [BI- *pref.*[2] I. 1.] Having, or divided into, two small lobes.

Bilocation (bəilokēⁱ·ʃən). 1858. [BI- *pref.*[2] II.] The fact or power of being in two places at the same time.

Bilocellate (bəilǫ·sėleⁱt), *a.* 1880. [f. BI- *pref.*[2] I. 1 + L. *locellus* small compartment, dim. of *loculus*, dim. of *locus* place, + -ATE[2].] Having two minute cells.

Bilocular (bəilǫ·kiŭlăɹ), *a.* 1783. [BI- *pref.*[2] I. 1.] Having, divided into, or consisting of two cells. var. **Bilo·culate.**

Biloquist (bi·lŏkwist). 1810. [BI- *pref.*[2] II.] One who can speak with two different voices. So **Bilo·quial** *a.*

‖ **Biltong** (bi·ltǫŋ). 1815. [S.Afr. Du., f. Du. *bil* buttock + *tong* tongue.] (Tongue-like) strips of lean meat dried in the sun.

Bima·culate, -ated, *a.* 1769. [BI- *pref.*[2] I. 1.] Marked with two spots.

‖ **Bimana** (bi·mănă, bəi-), *sb. pl.* 1839. [mod.L. n. pl. of **bimanus* (sc. *animalia*), Buffon's *bimane*, f. L. *bi-* two + *manus* hand.] *Zool.* Two-handed animals: Cuvier's name for an order of Mammalia, of which man is the only species. Hence **Bi·manal, Bi·manous** *adjs.* two-handed; of or belonging to the *B.* **Bi·mane,** one of the *B.*

Bimarginate, bimembral; see BI- *pref.*[2] I. 1.

Bimedial (bəimī·diăl), *a.* (and *sb.*) 1570. [BI- *pref.*[2] I. 1.] *Geom.* The sum of two medial lines; a medial line being the geometric mean between two lines commensurable only in power.

Bimestrial (bəime·striăl), *a.* 1846. [f. L. *bimestris* (f. *bi-* BI- *pref.*[2] I. 4 + *mensis* month) + -AL[1].] Lasting two months; occurring every two months.

Bimetallic (bəimĭtæ·lik), *a.* 1876. [– Fr. *bimétallique*, first used by M. Cernuschi in 1869, and in Eng. form in 1876; see BI- *pref.*[2] I. 1.] Of, pertaining to, or using a double standard of currency, i.e. one based upon the two metals gold and silver, as opp. to a monometallic currency.

In point of fact the world is already b.; but it is an unregulated and haphazard bimetallism which prevails among us H. H. GIBBS.

Bimetallism (bəime·tăliz'm). 1876. [f. as prec. + -ISM.] The system of allowing the unrestricted currency of two metals (*e.g.* gold and silver) at a fixed ratio to each other, as coined money. So **Bime·tallist,** an advocate of b. Also *attrib.* or as *adj.*

Bimillenary (bəimi·lĭnări). 1850. [f. BI- *pref.*[2] I. 4 + MILLENARY.] Properly an adj.: Of or pertaining to two thousand, two thousand strong; but taken to express: A space of two thousand years (better *bimillennium*).

Bimodulus (bəimǫ·diŭlŏs). 1881. [See BI- *pref.*[2] II.] *Math.* The double of the modulus of a system of logarithms. Hence **Bimo·dular** *a.*

Bimonthly, bimuscular; see BI- *pref.*[2] I. 4.

Bin (bin), *sb.* [OE. *bin(n), binne* – OBrit. **benna* (W. *ben* cart); or – med. L. *benna* (Festus, recording a Gaulish word), whence Fr. *banne*, It. dial. *benna* hamper, Du. *ben*, G. *benne* body of a cart.] **1.** *gen.* A receptacle (*orig.* of wicker- or basket-work) 1570. † **2.** *spec.* A manger –ME. **3.** A hutch, for corn, meal, bread, etc. Also, later, for dust, coal, etc. ME. **4.** A partitioned stand for storing wine in bottle; *transf.* wine from a particular bin 1758.

3. A little b. best fits a little bread HERRICK. **4.** A b. reserved for banquests TENNYSON. Hence **Bin** *v.* to stow in a b.

Bin, obs. and dial. f. *been,* pa. pple. etc. of BE *v.*

Bin-, *pref.,* treated as euphonic f. BI- *pref.*[2], used before vowels. Not L.: app. it originated in Fr. *binocle,* prob. formed from L. *bini.* Thence extended in Eng., esp. to chemical compounds (see BI- *pref.*[2] III), as *binacetate,* etc.

Binal (bəi·năl), *a.* 1658. [– med. L. *binalis* twin, f. L. *bini* two together, a pair; see -AL[1].] Twin, double, twofold.

Binary (bəi·nări). 1460. [– late L. *binarius,* f. *bini* two together; see -ARY[1], [2].] **A.** *adj.* Of, pertaining to, characterized by, or compounded of, two; dual 1597.

B. system (of classification): one by which each group or sub-group is divided by dichotomy till individuals (or genera) are reached. In *Mus. B. measure*: that which has two beats to a bar. *B. form*: the form of a movement which is divided into two sections. In *Astron. B. stars* or *system*: two stars or suns, one of which revolves round the other, or both of which revolve round a common centre. In *Chem.* and *Min. B. compound*: one consisting of two elements. *B. theory*: that which considers all acids as compounds of hydrogen with a radical, and all salts as similar compounds with a metal replacing hydrogen. In *Math. B. arithmetic*: a method of computation in which the b. scale is used. *B. scale*: the scale of notation whose radix is 2, in which, therefore, 1 of the denary scale is 1, 2 is 10, 3 is 11, 4 is 100, etc. *B. logarithms*: a system for use in musical calculations, in which 1 is the logarithm of 2, and the modulus is 1·442695.

B. *sb.* **1.** A combination of two things; a pair, 'two'; duality. ? *Obs.* 1460. **2.** *Astron.* A binary star or system. Cf. A. 1868.

Binate (bəi·neⁱt), *a.* 1807. [– mod. L. *binatus* (cf. late L. *combinatus*), f. L. *bini* two together; see -ATE[2].] Arranged in couples. **Bi·nately** *adv.* in pairs.

Binaural (binǭ·răl), *a.* 1881. [f. BIN- + AURAL.] Of, pertaining to, or used with both ears, as the *b. stethoscope.*

Bind (bəind), *v.* Pa. t. and pple. **bound.** [OE. *bindan,* pa. t. *band, bundon,* pa. pple. *bunden* = OFris. *binda,* OS. *bindan,* (M)Du. *binden,* OHG. *bintan* (G. *binden*), ON. *binda,* Goth. *bindan,* f. Indo-Eur. base **bhendh-* (Skr. *bandh* bind).] **1.** *trans.* To make fast with a tie; to tie up ME. Also *fig.* **2.** *esp.* To make fast with bonds; to make a captive OE. Also *fig.* **3.** To tie (a knot *obs.*); hence *fig.* to conclude (a bargain), to make (any contract) fast or sure ME. **4.** To make costive 1597. **5.** To bandage (the body, etc. *with* something) OE. **6.** To cover with dressings and bandages. Usu. with *up.* ME. **7.** To fasten round, to gird, wreathe, encircle OE. **8.** To secure with a border; also *fig.* ME. **9.** To tie so as to hold together; to fasten together; to unite OE. Also *fig.* Also *intr.* (for *refl.*) To cohere 1674. **10.** To tie or restrain, *e.g.* by a covenant, oath, etc. ME. **11.** To constrain with legal authority 1463. **12.** To subject to a specific legal obligation 1462. **13.** To attach *to,* by ties of duty, gratitude, etc. 1530.

1. Fast binde fast finde J. HEYWOOD. *fig.* To b. men to their kind 1866. **2.** To open the preson to them that are bounde *Isa.* 61:1. To b. the conscience 1634. **3.** To b. the bargain 1677. **6.** B. vp my Wounds *Rich. III,* v. iii. 177. **9.** Hee that bindeth sheaues *Ps.* 129:7. To b. the loose sand 1887. Phr. *To b. up*: i.e. together into one volume. *transf.* To b. the chariot to the swift beast *Micah* 1:13, a rug across the shoulders 1720, two countries together 1855. **12.** To b. over to keep the peace DICKENS. *I dare,* or *will be bound*: I feel certain. *To be bound*: to be under obligation, moral or legal, *to do.* As mariage binds *A.Y.L.* v. iv. 59.

Bind (bəind), *sb.* OE. [f. BIND *v.*] **1.** Anything used to bind; a band or tie; *spec.* in *Mus.,* a straight (or curved) line placed under (or over) notes of the same pitch, to indicate that the sound is to be sustained. Cf. TIE *sb.* 6 b. **2.** A twining or climbing stem, *esp.* of the hop-plant. **b.** = BINE. ME. **3.** Hence, † **a.** Honeysuckle or WOOD-BINE. **b.** = BINDWEED (*Convolvulus* and *Polygonum*). 1440. **4.** Indurated clay 1799. **5.** A measure of quantity in salmon and eels 1477. **6.** Capacity, limit. *Sc.* 1551.

Binder (bəi·ndəɹ). OE. [f. BIND *v.* + -ER[1].] **1.** *gen.* One who binds. (See the vb.) **2.** *spec.* **a.** A bookbinder 1556. **b.** One who binds sheaves 1611. **3.** Anything used to bind; a band, bandage, etc. Also *fig.* 1695. **4.** A connecting piece; *esp.* in *Carpentry,* a tie-beam or binding joint; in *Ship-building,* a principal part of a ship's frame, such as keel, transom, stem, etc. 1642. **5.** In various techn. uses: *esp.* **a.** A band of straw, etc. for binding sheaves; **b.** A detachable cover for unbound magazines, etc. † **6.** *Med.* Anything which BINDS the bowels –1678. † **7.** A cement –1751.

Bindery (bəi·ndəri). 1828. [f. prec. (see -ERY 2), orig. U.S. after Du. *binderij.*] A bookbinder's workshop.

Binding (bəi·ndiŋ), *vbl sb.* ME. [f. BIND *v.* + -ING[1].] **1.** The action of the vb. BIND in various senses. **2.** The state of being bound ME. **3.** *concr.* A bond, band, bandage; a fastening ME. **4.** *spec.* **a.** The strong cover of a book, which holds the sheets together, etc. 1647. **b.** A protective covering for the raw edges of a fabric; braid, etc. 1598. **c.** *Archit. & Shipbuilding.* A band of masonry and brickwork; a connecting timber, etc. 1626.

Bi·nding, *ppl. a.* ME. [f. as prec. + -ING[2].] **1.** That binds together or up; causing or tending to cohere; astringent, styptic. **2.** *fig.* Obligatory, restrictive, coercive 1611.

1. Byndynge frost and colde, blesse ȝe to the Lord WYCLIF *Dan.* 3:69. *Comb.*: **b.-joist,** a joist resting on the wall-plates and carrying other joists; **-plate,** one of the iron plates used to strengthen a puddling-furnace; **-screw,** a screw used in various instruments for clamping or adjustment. Hence **Bi·nding-ly** *adv.,* **-ness.**

Bindweed (bəi·nd,wīd). 1548. [f. BIND *v.* + WEED *sb.*[1].] *Bot.* **1.** Name for the species of the N.O. *Convolvulus*; as *C. sepium, C. arvensis,* etc. **2.** Used also vaguely of species of *Smilax, Honeysuckle, Tamus,* etc. **3.** **Black, Corn, or Ivy B.,** *Polygonum convolvulus*; **Blue B.,** Bittersweet or Woody Nightshade.

Bindwith (bəi·nd,wiþ). 1797. [f. BIND *v.* + WITHE.] *Clematis vitalba* or Traveller's Joy.

Bine (bəin). 1727. [Adoption as a literary form of a var. of synon. dial. *bind*; see BIND *sb.* 2.] A flexible shoot of a shrub, a climbing stem; *esp.* of the hop, whence *White-b.,* etc.

Binervate (bəinə·ɹveⁱt), *a.* 1842. [BI- *pref.*[2] I. 1; see -ATE[2].] Having two nerves (in *Bot.* and *Ent.*).

Bing (biŋ), *sb.*[1] ME. [Senses 1, 2 = ON. *bingr* heap (Sw. *binge* heap); senses 3-4 are unexpl., but cf. Da. *bing* bin; in Eng. *bing* has been used dial. for *bin* since XV.] **1.** A heap or pile 1513. **2.** *spec.* A heap of metallic ore, of alum; 8 cwt. of lead ore 1815. **3.** = BIN. Now *dial.* ME. **4.** The kiln of a furnace in which charcoal is burnt in metal-smelting 1658.

1. Potato-bings BURNS. **2.** *B. ore,* or *b.*: the best lead ore. Hence **Bing** *v.* to pile or put up in a b.

†‖ **Bing,** *sb.*[2] 1701. [Chinese *bing,* dial. form of *ming.*] A kind of tea.

Binge (bindʒ), *sb.* 1854. [prob. sl. use of dial. *binge* vb. soak (a wooden vessel).] *slang.* A drinking-bout; a spree. Also vb.

Bi·ngo. 1861. [prob. f. *b.* of *brandy* + ST)INGO.] Brandy (*slang*).

Bink (biŋk). *Sc.* and *n. dial.* ME. [Later f. ME. *benk,* north. and Sc. var. of BENCH *sb.*] **1.** = BENCH 1, 2, 6, 7. **2.** A shelf; also, a dresser 1535.

Binnacle (bi·năk'l). 1622. [In XVII *bitakle, biticle, bittacle* – Sp. *bitácula, bitácora,* or Pg. *bitacola,* corresp. to Pr. *abitacle,* It. *abitacolo,* Fr. *habitacle* – L. *habitaculum* habitation, f. *habitare* inhabit.] A box on the deck of a ship near the helm, in which the compass is placed. Also *attrib.*

Binny (bi·ni). [Origin unkn.] *Ichthyol.* The barbel of the Nile (*Barbus bynni*).

Binocle (bi·nǒk'l). 1696. [– Fr. *binocle* (XVII), f. L. *bi-* BI- *pref.*[2] + *oculus* eye.] A field- or opera-glass having tubes for both eyes.

Binocular (binǫ·kiŭlăɹ). 1713. [f. L. *bini* two together + *oculus* eye, after OCULAR; cf. prec., and Fr. *binoculaire.*] **A.** *adj.* **1.** Having two eyes ? *Obs.* So **Bino·culate** *a.* **2.** Performed by or adapted to both eyes 1738. **B.** *sb.* (Short for *b. glass.*) A BINOCLE. Also, applied to a microscope. 1871. Hence **Bino·cula·rity,** b. quality; simultaneous employment of both eyes. **Bino·cularly** *adv.*

Binomial (bəinōᵘ·miăl). 1557. [f. Fr. *binôme* or mod. L. *binomium,* f. *bi-* BI- *pref.*[2] + Gr. νόμος part, portion + -AL[1]. See BINOMY.] **A.** *adj.* **1.** *Math.* Consisting of two terms; see B. 1570. **2.** = BINOMINAL 1656.

1. *B. theorem*: the formula by which any power of a binomial may be found without performing the successive multiplications.

B. *sb.* An algebraic expression consisting of two terms joined by + or – (formerly only +) 1557.

Binominal (bəinǫ·minăl), *a.* 1880. [f. L. *binominis* (f. *bi-* BI- *pref.*[2] + *nomen, nomin-* name) + -AL[1].] Having two names, *esp.* those of genus and species in scientific nomenclature.

Binominated (bəinǫ·mineⁱtėd), *a.* 1857. [f. BI- *pref.*[2] + L. *nomen* name, *nominatus* named; cf. *nominated.*] Having two names. So **Bino·minous** *a.*

† **Bi·nomy.** 1571. [– mod.L. *binomium* (also used), f. *bi-* BI- *pref.*[2] + Gr. νόμος part, portion; cf. BINOMIAL.] = BINOMIAL *sb.* –1670.

Binotonous (bəinǫ·tŏnəs), *a.* 1802. [f. L. *bini* (see BIN-) + *tonus* TONE, note + -OUS, app. after *monotonous.*] Consisting of two notes, as a *b. cry.*

Binous (bəi·nəs), *a.* 1832. [f. L. *bini* (see BIN-) + -OUS.] = BINATE.

Binoxalate, Binoxide; see BIN-.

Binuclear, -ate; see BI- *pref.*[2] I. 1.

Bio- (bəi·o, bəi,ǫ·). Gr. βιο-, comb. f. βίος 'life, course or way of living' (as opp. to ζωή 'animal life, organic life'). In mod. scientific wds. extended to mean 'organic life'.

Bio-bibliogra·phical *a.,* dealing with the life and writings of an author. **Bi·oblast** [Gr. βλαστός], *Biol.* a minute mass of amorphous protoplasm having formative power. **Bioce·ntric** *a.,* treating life as a central fact. **Bioche·mic, -al** *a.,* pertaining to the chemistry of life. **Biodyna·mic, -al** *a.,* of or relating to biodynamics. **Biodyna·mics,** the doctrine of vital force, or of the action of living organisms. **Bi·ogen,** the substance of the soul, the 'od' of Reichenbach. **Bio·gnosy,** generic term for the life-sciences. **Biokine·tics,** the doctrine of the successive changes through which organisms pass in development. **Bioly·tic** *a.,* life-destroying. **Biomagne·tic** *a.,* of or pertaining to animal magnetism. **Bioma·gnetism,** animal magnetism. **Bio·meter,** a measurer of life. **Bio·metry,** the calculation of the average duration and expectation of life. **Biophysio·logist,** an investigator of the physiology of living beings. **Bi·oscope,** a view of life; that which affords it. **Biosta·tic, -al** *a.,* of or pertaining to biostatics. **Biosta·tics,** the doctrine of structure as adapted to act, as opp. to *biodynamics* or *biokinetics.*

Biocellate (bəi,ǫ·sėleⁱt), 1847. [f. BI- *pref.*[2] I. 1 + OCELLATE.] Marked with two small eye-like spots, as a wing, etc.

Biogenesis (bəio,dʒe·nėsis). 1870. [f. BIO- + Gr. γένεσις birth.] The theory that living matter always arises by the agency of pre-existing living matter. Hence **Bioge·nesist,** one who holds the theory of b.

Biogeny (bəiǫ·dʒĭni). 1870. [f. BIO- + -GENY.] **1.** The history of the evolution of living organisms 1879. Hence **Biogene·tic** *a.* of or pertaining to b. **Bio·genist.** **2.** = BIOGENESIS 1870.

Bi·ograph. 1897. [U.S. trade name; see -GRAPH.] An earlier form of cinematograph.

Biographer (bəiǫ·grăfəɹ). 1715. [f. BIOGRAPHY + -ER[1] 4, replacing *biographist.*] A writer of biographies, or of a life. var. **Bio·graphist.**

Biographic, -al (bəi,ogræ·fik, -ăl), *a.* 1738. [f. BIOGRAPHY: see -IC, -ICAL.] Of or of the nature of biography. **Biogra·phically** *adv.*

Biographize (bəi,o·grăfəiz), *v.* 1800. [f. as BIOGRAPHY + -IZE.] To write a biography of.

Biography (bəiǫ·grăfi). 1661. [– Fr. *biographie* or mod.L. *biographia,* med.Gr. βιογραφία; see BIO-, -GRAPHY.] **1.** The history of the lives of individual men, as a branch of literature. **2.** A written record of the life of an individual 1791. Also *transf.* of an animal or plant.

1. In all parts of B... Plutarch equally excell'd DRYDEN.

Biologic, -al (bəiˌolǫ·dʒik, -ăl), *a.* 1859. [f. BIOLOGY + IC, -ICAL.] Of, relating to, or of the nature of biology. Hence **Biolo·gically** *adv.*

Biologist (bəiˌǫ·lŏdʒist). 1813. [f. as prec. + -IST.] One who studies biology.

Bio·logize, *v.* 1862. [f. as prec. + -IZE.] † **1.** To mesmerize –1874. **2.** To cultivate biology; to deal with biologically. *intr.* and *trans.*

Biology (bəiǫ·lŏdʒi). 1813. [– Fr. *biologie* (Lamarck, 1802) – G. *biologie* (Gottfried Reinhold, 1802). See BIO-, -LOGY.] † **1.** The study of human life and character. **2.** The science of physical life, dealing with organized beings or animals and plants, their morphology, physiology, origin, and distribution; occas. = PHYSIOLOGY 1819. † **3.** = ELECTRO-BIOLOGY –1874.

Bioplasm (bəi·oˌplæzm). 1872. [f. BIO-, after *protoplasm.*] *Biol.* Prof. Beale's term for: The germinal matter of all living beings; living protoplasm. Hence **Biopla·smic** *a.*

Bioplast (bəi·oˌplæst). 1877. [f. BIO-, after prec. and PROTOPLAST.] *Biol.* 'A small separate portion of Bioplasm generally less than the thousandth of an inch in diameter.' Hence **Biopla·stic** *a.*

Biordinal (bəiǭ·ɹdinăl). 1853. [f. BI- *pref.*[2] II + ORDINAL.] *Math.* **A.** *adj.* Of the second order. **B.** *sb.* A linear differential equation of the second order; see ORDINAL 1881.

Biotaxy, etc: see BIO- *pref.*

Bio·tic, *a. rare.* 1600. [– late L. *bioticus* – Gr. βιωτικός, f. βίος life. In mod. use – Fr. *biotique.*] † **1.** Of or pertaining to (common) life, secular. **2.** Of animal life; vital. So **Bio·tical.** 1874.

Biotite (bəi·ŏtəit). 1862. [f. *Biot,* French mineralogist, + -ITE[1] 2 b.] *Min.* Hexagonal or magnesia mica.

Bipalmate, biparietal; see BI- *pref.*[2]

Bi·parous, *a.* 1731. [f. BI- *pref.*[2] 2 + -PAROUS.] Producing two at once (in time or place).

Bipartible (bəipă·ɹtib'l), *a.* 1847. [f. L. *bipartire* bisect; cf. late L. *partibilis* divisible; see PART *v.*, -IBLE.] Divisible into two parts. var. **Bipa·rtile.**

Bipartient (bəipă·ɹtiĕnt). 1678. [– *bipartient-*, pres. ppl. stem of L. *bipartire* divide into two; see BI- *pref.*[2], PART *v.*, -ENT.] **A.** *adj.* That divides into two parts. **B.** *sb.* A number which divides another into two equal parts 1819.

Bipartite (bəipă·ɹtəit), *a.* 1506. [– L. *bipartitus,* pa. pple. of *bipartire*; see prec.] **1.** Divided into or consisting of two parts 1574. **b.** Divided between or shared by two 1618. **c.** *Bot.* Divided into two parts nearly to the base 1864. **2.** *Law.* Drawn up in two corresponding parts, one for each party 1506. var. **Bipa·rted.** Hence **Bipa·rtitely** *adv.* **Biparti·tion,** division into two parts (action or result).

Bipe·ctinate, -ated, *a.* 1836. [f. BI- *pref.*[2] I. 1 + PECTINATE.] Having two margins toothed like a comb.

Biped (bəi·pĕd). 1646. [– L. *bipes, -ped-,* f. *bi-* BI- + *pes* foot.] **A.** *sb.* A two-footed animal. **B.** *adj.* Two-footed 1793.

Bipedal (bəi·pīdăl), *a.* ME. [– L. *bipedalis*; see prec., -AL[1]; in mod. use f. prec. + -AL[1].] † **1.** Two feet long ME. only. **2.** Biped 1607. **3.** Of, pertaining to, or caused by a biped 1833. Hence **Bipeda·lity,** the quality of being two-footed.

Bipe·ltate, *a.* 1846. [f. BI- *pref.*[2] I + L. *peltatus* armed with a *pelta*; see PELTA, -ATE[2].] Having a defence like a double shield.

Bipennate, -ated (bəipe·nei̇t, -ei̇tĕd), *a.* 1713. [f. BI- *pref.*[2] I + PENNATE, -ATED.] Two-winged.

Bipinnate (bəipi·nei̇t), *a.* 1794. [f. BI- *pref.*[2] I + PINNATE, -ATED.] **1.** Doubly or subordinately pinnate. So **Bipi·nnated** *a.* **2.** *Zool.* Having feathery appendages in opposed pairs 1856.

Bipinnatifid (bəipinæ·tifid), *a.* 1830. [f. BI- *pref.*[2] I. 3 + PINNATIFID.] *Bot.* Of leaves: Pinnatifid, with the pinnæ themselves similarly divided. So **Bipinnatipa·rted, -pa·rtite, -sect, -se·cted.**

Biplane (bəi·plēⁱn). 1908. [f. BI- *pref.*[2] II + PLANE *sb.*[3] 1 e(*b*). Cf. Fr. *biplan.*] An aeroplane having two planes or main supporting surfaces, one above the other.

Bipolar (bəipōᵘ·lăɹ), *a.* 1810. [f. BI- *pref.*[2] I + POLAR.] Having two poles or opposite extremities. Also *fig.* Hence **Bipola·rity.**

Bi·pont, bipo·ntine, *a.* [– med.L. *Bipontium* 'two bridges', *-inus*; see -INE[1].] Of editions of the classics, etc.: Printed at Zweibrücken (*Bipontium*) in Bavaria, in the late 18th c.

Bipunctate (bəipɒ·ŋktei̇t), *a.* 1864. [f. BI- *pref.*[2] I. 1 + PUNCTATE.] Having or marked by two punctures or points. var. **Bipu·nctual.** (Dicts.)

Biquadrate (bəiˌkwǫ·dreⁱt). 1706. [f. BI- *pref.*[2] + QUADRATE.] *Math.* The square of the square (power or root); = BIQUADRATIC. Hence **Biqua·drate** *v.* to raise to the fourth power.

Biquadratic (bəiˌkwǫ̆dræ·tik). 1661. [f. BI- *pref.*[2] + QUADRATIC.] *Math.* **A.** *adj.* Pertaining to the biquadrate, or fourth power of a number. 1668. **B.** *sb.* **a.** The fourth power of a number. **b.** A biquadratic equation.

B. equation: an equation in which the unknown quantity is raised to the fourth power. *B. parabola*: a curve of the third order, having two infinite legs tending the same way. *B. root*: the square root of the square root.

Biquintile (bəiˌkwi·ntəil, -il). 1647. [f. BI- *pref.*[2] I + QUINTILE.] *Astrol.* An aspect of the planets, when they are distant from each other twice the fifth part of a great circle,—that is, 144 degrees.

Biradiate, -ated; see BI- *pref.*[2] I.

Bira·mous, *a.* [f. BI- *pref.*[2] I. 1 + L. *ramus* branch + -OUS.] Two-branched. HUXLEY.

Birch (bɜ̄ɹtʃ), *sb.* [OE. *birće, bierće* = MLG. *berke,* OHG. *birihha, birka* (G. *birke*) :– Gmc. **berkjōn*; rel. to OE. *berc, beorc* = Du. *berk,* ON. *bjǫrk* :– Gmc. **berkō.*] **1.** A genus of hardy northern forest trees (*Betula*), having smooth tough bark and slender branches. **a.** *esp.* The common European species (*B. alba*); also called Lady Birch, Silver B., White B. The Weeping or Drooping B. (*B. pendula*) is a variety. **b. Dwarf-B.** (*B. nana*); **Paper B.** or **White B.** of America (*B. papyracea*); **Cherry B.** (*B. lenta*), also called **Sweet Mahogany** or **Mountain B. c.** The wood of this tree ME. **d.** The pl. *birks* in the north signifies a grove of birches 1724. **2.** A bunch of birch-twigs used for flogging; a birch-rod 1648. **3.** A canoe made of the bark of *B. papyracea* 1864.

1. Byrche..serueth..for betynge of stubborne boyes TURNER. Shadows of the silver birk Sweep the green that folds thy grave TENNYSON.

Comb.: **b. camphor,** a resinous substance obtained from the bark of *B. nigra*; **b. oil,** an oil extracted from the bark of the b., and used in the preparation of Russia leather, to which it gives its smell; **b.-rod** = BIRCH 2; **b.-water,** the sap obtained from the b. in spring; **b.-wine,** wine prepared from b.-water. Hence **Birch** *v.* to punish with a b.-rod; to flog.

Birchen (bɜ̄·ɹtʃ'n), *a.* 1440. [f. prec. + -EN[4].] Of or pertaining to BIRCH 1, 2; composed of birch.

Canoe-men, in their b. vessels 1865.

Bird (bɜ̄ɹd). [OE. *brid* (surviving in dial.), late Northumb. *bird*; of unkn. origin and without cognates.] **1.** *orig.* The young of the feathered tribes; a chicken, eaglet, etc.; a nestling. Still in n. dial. Also † *transf.* and *fig.* **b.** A maiden, a girl. [At first confused with *burde* BURD; but later taken as fig. sense of 1 or 2.] ME. **2.** Any feathered vertebrate animal; a member of the second class (*Aves*) of the great Vertebrate group. (Now used generically in place of FOWL.) ME. **3.** *Sport.* A game bird; *spec.* a partridge. Also *fig.* 1596. **4.** *fig.* (See quotes.) 1588.

1. He..cheryssheth vs, as the egle her byrdes 1526. **b.** The B. is dead That we haue made so much on *Cymb.* IV. ii. 197. **2.** The bryddes of the aier have nestes TINDALE *Matt.* 8:20. **3.** Am I your B., I meane to shift my bush *Tam. Shr.* V. ii. 46. Reports say the birds are very wild 1887. **4.** *Arabian b.* = phœnix. A little b. has whispered a secret to me 1833. There must be such queer birds however B. TAYLOR.

Phr. *Birds of a* (= *one*) *feather*: those of like character. *To get the* (*big*) *b.,* to be hissed.

Comb.: **1.** With defining word, as **b. of Jove,** the eagle; **b. of Juno,** the peacock; **b. of paradise,** one of the family *Paradiseidæ*, remarkable for the beauty of their plumage; **b. of passage,** any migratory b.; **b. of Washington,** the American Eagle (*Falco leucocephalus*); **b. of wonder,** the phœnix. **2.** † **b.-bolt,** a blunt-headed arrow, used for shooting birds; **-call,** an instrument for imitating the note of birds, in order to attract them; **B-** (or **bird's**) **cherry,** a wild fruit tree or shrub (*Prunus padus*); **-fly,** a fly (*Ornithomyia*) which lives under the plumage of birds; **-mouthed** *a.,* having a mouth like a b.; *hence,* unwilling to speak out (*obs.*); **-organ,** a small organ used in teaching birds to sing; **-pepper,** kinds of capsicum; **-seed,** canary-seed, hemp, millet, plantain, etc.; **-spit,** a spit for roasting birds on, † *fig.* a rapier; **-witted** *a.,* lacking the faculty of attention. **3.** (Comb. of *bird's*): **a.** *gen.* as **bird's-beak moulding,** one which in section forms an ovolo or ogee with or without a fillet under it followed by a hollow; **-mouth,** an interior or re-entrant angle cut out of the end of a piece of timber. **b.** *esp.* in plant-names; *e.g.* **Bird's bread,** the small Yellow Stone-crop (*Sedum acre*); **Bird's eggs,** the Bladder Campion; **Bird's tare,** a species of Arachis; **Bird's tongue,** the Greater Stitchwort (*Stellaria holostea*), the Common Maple, Scarlet Pimpernel, Ornithoglossum, etc. (from the shape of their leaves); also the fruit of the ash-tree.

Hence **Bi·rdikin, Bi·rdlet, Bi·rdling,** a little b.

Bird (bɜ̄ɹd), *v.* 1576. [f. prec.] *intr.* To catch or shoot birds.

Bird-cage (bɜ̄·ɹdˌkēⁱdʒ). 1490. [f. BIRD *sb.* + CAGE *sb.*] **1.** A cage for a bird or birds. **2.** *Sporting.* The paddock at Newmarket 1884.

1. The Bird-Cages in St. James's Park. [Hence *Birdcage Walk.*] 1691.

† **Birde.** [ME. app. short for **ȝebirde* :– OE. *ġebyrd, -o* birth.] **1.** Birth; offspring ME. only. **2.** Family, nation ME. only.

Birder (bɜ̄·ɹdəɹ). 1481. [f. BIRD *v.* + -ER[1].] † **1.** A fowler –1622. **2.** A breeder of birds 1827. **3.** A wild cat (*local*) 1864.

Birdie (bɜ̄·ɹdi). 1792. [f. BIRD *sb.* + -IE, -Y[6].] **1.** A dear little bird. **2.** *Golf.* The fact of doing a hole in one under the par score 1921.

Bi·rd-lime, *sb.* 1440. [LIME *sb.*[1]] A glutinous substance spread upon twigs, by which birds may be caught. Also *fig.* and *transf.* Also *attrib.*

Hence **Bi·rd-lime** *v.* to smear or catch with (or as with) b. **Bi·rd-limy** *a.*

Bird's-eye. Also **bird-eye.** 1597. **1.** *sb.* A name of several plants with small round bright flowers, as the *Bird's-eye Primrose* (*P. farinosa*), Germander Speedwell, species of *Adonis* (usu. *Pheasant's eye*), Robert's Geranium, etc. **2.** A manufactured tobacco in which the ribs of the leaves are cut along with the fibre 1861. **3.** *attrib.* Of or belonging to a bird's eye; as in *Bird's-eye view*: a view of a landscape from above, such as a bird would have; *fig.* a résumé of a subject 1762. **4.** *attrib.* Marked as with bird's eyes; spotted; as *Bird's-eye limestone, maple,* etc. 1665.

Bird's-foot, bi·rd-foot. 1578. Applied to objects having the shape of a bird's foot, as **a.** A small yellow vetch (*Ornithopus*); **b.** A small fern (*Cheilanthes radiata*); **c.** = Bird's-foot Trefoil.

Bird's-foot Trefoil or *Lotus*: a yellow leguminous plant (*Lotus corniculatus*), a native of Britain. *Bird's-foot star, sea-star*: an echinoderm related to the star-fish.

Bi·rd's-nest, bird-nest, *sb.* 1597. **1.** (Usu. two wds.): The nest of a bird; *spec.* the edible nest of certain species of swallow found in the Chinese Sea. Also *attrib.* 1599. **2.** A CROW'S NEST, q.v. 1867. **3.** A name of plants: **a.** The Wild Carrot; **b.** *Monotropa hypophitys*; **c.** = Bird's-nest Orchid.

Bird's-nest fern, a name given to some exotic ferns from their habit of growth; **Bird's-nest Orchid** (*Neottia nidus-avis*), a plant, wild in Britain, entirely of a brown feuillemort colour. Hence **Bi·rd's-ne·sting, bird-nesting** *vbl. sb.* the action or occupation of searching for birds' nests; whence **Bi·rd's-ne·st** *v. intr.*

Bireme (bəi·rīm). 1600. [– L. *biremis,* f. *bi-* BI- *pref.*[2] I. 1 + *remus* oar.] **A.** *adj.* Having two banks of oars. **B.** *sb.* [sc. *galley.*]

Biretta (bire·tă). Also **beretta, birretta.** 1598. [– It. *berretta,* †*bar(r)etta* or Sp. *birreta,* fem. dims. corresp. to Pr. *beret* BERET, based on late L. *birrus, -um* hooded cape or cloak, perh. of Celtic orig.] The square cap worn by clerics of the R.C.Ch.; that of priests being black, of bishops purple, of cardinals red.

Birgand(er, obs. f. BERGANDER.

Birk, -en, -in, north. ff. BIRCH, BIRCHEN.

Birkie (bɜ̄·ɹki, *Sc.* bė·rkie). 1724. [Origin unkn.] **A.** *sb.* Joc. term for a man 'with a mind of his own'; occas. = 'strutting fellow', often simply = 'fellow', 'carle'. **2.** *Cards.* = 'Beggar-my-neighbour' 1777. **B.** *adj.* Mettlesome 1821.

Birl (bɜ̄ɹl, *Sc.* bir'l), *v. Sc.* 1724. [Echoic; cf. *pirl, whirl.*] To revolve or cause to revolve rapidly and with characteristic noise; to spin.

Birle (bɜ̄ɹl), *v. Obs.* exc. *dial.* [OE. *byrelian*, ON. *byrla*, f. *byrele* cup-bearer, perh. rel. to *beran* BEAR *v.*[1]] **1.** To pour out (drink, *to* or *for* any one). **2.** To ply *with* drink ME. **3.** *intr.* To carouse; *trans.* to drink and pass (the cup). (Pseudo-*arch.*) 1800.

Bi·rlie, bi·rley. *Sc.* 1609. Corrupt f. BYRLAW, used in comb.

‖ **Birlinn** (biᵊ·rlin). 1595. [Gael.] A large rowing boat, used by the chieftains in the Western Islands of Scotland.

Birmingham (bɜ̄·ɹmiŋhæ̆m). A town in Warwickshire, in England. See ANTI-BIRMINGHAM. Also **Birminghamize** *v.*, to make up artificially. Cf. BRUMMAGEM.

Birostrate, -ated, Birotate; see BI- *pref.*[2] I. 1.

Birr (bɜ̄ɹ, *Sc.* bėrr). ME. [– ON. *byrr* favouring wind. Sense 3 is prob. echoic.] † **1.** A strong (carrying) wind ME. only. **2.** Momentum, impetus; rush ME.; emphatic utterance 1825. **3.** An energetic whirring sound 1837.

2. What the Scotch call the B...the emphatic energy of his pronunciation LD. COCKBURN. **3.** The b. of the moorcock SMILES. Hence **Birr** *v.* to emit a b.

Birretta, var. of BIRETTA.

Birse (bəɹs, *Sc.* bėrs), *sb.* [OE. *byrst* BRISTLE. Now only Sc.] = BRISTLE. Also *fig.*

Birsle (bə·ɹs'l, *Sc.* bė·rs'l), *v. Sc.* 1513. [Origin unkn., and etymological form uncertain; the mod. Sc. is *birsle*, but XVI Eng. had *brissill*, and XVII north.-dial. *brusle.*] To toast hard; also *fig.*

† **Birt, burt.** 1552. [Also in form *bret* XV; of unkn. origin.] A Turbot –1783.

Birth (bɜ̄ɹþ), *sb.* ME. [– ON. *byrð* birth, descent, corresp. to Goth. *gabaurþs* :– East Gmc. **ʒaburþiz*, f. **ʒa-* Y- + **bur-* **ber-*, see BEAR *v.*[1], -TH[1]. WGmc. forms with *-d* are OE. *ġebyrd*, OS. *giburd*, OHG. *giburt* (G. *geburt*).] **1.** The bearing of offspring. **a.** Giving birth ME. **b.** The being born, nativity ME. Also *fig.* of things. **2.** That which is born; offspring; young (of animals) (*arch.*) ME. Also *fig.* of things. **3.** Parentage, lineage, descent ME. *spec.* Noble lineage 1595. † **4.** Nature, kind, sex –1592. **5.** Conditions involved in birth ME. † **6.** *Astrol.* Nativity SHAKS. **7.** *Theol.* in *New b.*: regeneration 1535.

1. a. Two children at one b. 2 *Hen. VI*, IV. ii. 147. **b.** The birthe of Cryst our thraldom putte vs fro CHAUCER. Phr. *To give b. to*: to bear (offspring). The b. of an idea 1875. **2.** *fig.* Innouations, which are the Births of Time BACON. **3.** She is no equall for his b. *Much Ado* II. i. 172. **5.** An Athenian by b. JOWETT. **7.** Baptism confers a new b. MANNING.

attrib.: **b. control,** the artificial restriction of b., esp. the use by married persons of contraceptive methods; **b. mark,** a mark on the skin dating from b.; **b. rate,** the ratio of the number of births to the population. Hence † **Bi·rthdom,** birthright.

Bi·rth, *v. rare.* ME. [f. prec.] *intr.* To have birth.

Birth, obs. f. BERTH.

Birthday (bɜ̄·ɹþdēⁱ). ME. [f. BIRTH + DAY.] **1.** The day on which any one is born; *transf.* that of origin or commencement 1580. **2.** The anniversary of the day of birth; occas. *spec.* of that of the sovereign ME. Also *attrib.*

1. The Anniversary of the B. of this Glorious Queen STEELE. **2.** This is my B.; as this very day was Cassius born *Jul. C.* V. i. 71. *B. suit*: bare skin.

Birthnight (bɜ̄·ɹþnəit). 1628. [f. as prec. + NIGHT.] **1.** The night on which any one is born 1671. **2.** The night annually kept in memory of any one's birth 1628. † **3.** *spec.* The evening of a royal birthday –1730.

1. The Angelic Song in Bethlehem field, On thy birth-night MILT. *P.R.* IV. 506.

Birthplace (bɜ̄·ɹþplēⁱs). 1607. [f. as prec. + PLACE.] The place where a person (or *fig.* a thing) is born.

The b. of valour BURNS *Farew. Highlands.*

Birthright (bɜ̄·ɹþ,rəit). 1535. [f. as prec. + RIGHT.] Right by birth; the rights, privileges, etc. to which one is entitled by birth. *spec.* The rights of the first-born. Also *fig.*

Sell me this daye thy byrth-right *Gen.* 25:31. The laws of the land are the b. of every native COLERIDGE.

Birthwort (bɜ̄·ɹþ,wɒɹt). 1551. [f. as prec. + WORT.] *Bot.* The genus of shrubs ARISTOLOCHIA.

‖ **Bis,** *adv.* 1819. [Fr. and It. – L. *bis* twice.] Encore, again: used **a.** in *Mus.* as a direction to repeat a phrase or passage. **b.** Twice; to call attention to the occurrence of a number, word, etc., twice, as 'p. 175 (*bis*)'.

Bis-, *pref.*[1] The prec. adv. used occas. bef. *s, c*, or a vowel, in place of BI- *pref.*[2] as in *bisalternate*, etc.

Bis-, *pref.*[2], *Chem.* abbrev. of BISMUTH, used in comb.

Bis; see BICE, BYSS.

Bisaccate; see BI- *pref.*[2] I.

† **Bisa·nnual,** *a.* and *sb.* 1725. [BIS-[1].] = BIENNIAL.

‖ **Biscacha** (bis,kɑ·tʃă). Also **biz-, vis-.** 1837. [– Sp. *biscacho.*] *Zool.* A species of the *Chinchillidæ*, a burrowing rodent of S. America.

Biscayan (bi·skeⁱăn), *a.* 1634. [f. *Biscay* + -AN.] Belonging to, or characteristic of, the province of Biscay; also as *sb.*, an inhabitant or native of Biscay. So **Biscayen** [– Fr. *biscaïen*], **a.** A long heavy musket, first used in Biscay; **b.** One of its balls.

† **Bi·scot,** *sb.* 1662. [f. SCOT = payment. Prefix undetermined.] A fine formerly imposed on owners of marsh-lands for failure to repair banks, ditches, etc. –1790.

† **Biscotin.** 1727. [– Fr. *biscotin* – It. *biscottino* dim. of *biscotto*, corresp. to Fr. *biscuit.*] A sweet biscuit made of flour, sugar, eggs, etc.

Biscuit (bi·skėt). ME. [Early forms *besquite, byscute, bisket* – OFr. *bescoit, -cuit, biscut* (mod. *biscuit*) :– med.L. **biscoctus* twice baked (sc. *panis* bread), f. *bis* twice + *coctus*, pa. pple. of *coquere* cook. From XVI to XVIII spelt *bisket*, as still pronounced.] **1.** A kind of crisp dry bread more or less hard, made generally in thin flat cakes. The essential ingredients are flour and water, or milk, without leaven. In U.S., a small soft cake, usually fermented. **2.** *Pottery.* Pottery-ware fired once, but not glazed, or embellished; also *fig.* 1791.

1. As drie as the remainder bisket After a voyage *A.Y.L.* II. vii. 39. var. **B. bread.** Hence **Bi·scuiting** *vbl. sb.* (sense 2).

Biscutate (bəi,skiū·teⁱt), *a.* 1838. [f. BI- *pref.*[2] I. 6 + SCUTATE.] Having two shields; resembling two bucklers.

‖ **Bise** (biz, bīz). ME. [Fr., of unkn. etym.] A keen dry N. or NNE. wind, prevalent in Switzerland and its neighbourhood.

Bise, obs. f. BICE.

Bisect (bəise·kt), *v.* 1646. [f. BI- *pref.*[2] + *sect-*, pa. ppl. stem of L. *secare* cut, after *intersect.*] **1.** To cut into two equal parts. (The usual sense.) **2.** To divide into any two parts 1789. **3.** *intr.* To fork 1870.

1. Borneo is nearly bisected by the equator 1879.

Bisection (bəise·kʃən). 1656. [f. as prec. + -ION, after *section.*] **1.** Division into two (usually equal) parts. **2.** Forking 1870. Hence **Bise·ctional** *a.*, **-ly** *adv.*

Bisector (bəise·ktəɹ, -tǫɹ). 1864. [f. as prec. + -OR 2.] One who or that which bisects; a bisecting line.

Bisectrix (bəise·ktriks). 1854. [f. as prec. + -TRIX.] = prec.; *spec.* in biaxial polarization, the line bisecting the angle between the two axes of polarization (= *linea bisectrix*).

Bisegment (bəise·gmĕnt). 1847. [f. BI- *pref.*[2] II + SEGMENT.] One of the two equal parts into which a line, etc., is divided.

Biseptate, biserial, biseriate, biserrate; see BI- *pref.*[2]

‖ **Biset** (*bize*, bi·zėt). 1834. [– Fr. *biset*, f. *bis* dark-grey.] The wild rock-pigeon.

Bisetous (bəisī·təs), *a.* 1842. [f. BI- *pref.*[2] I + L. *seta* + -OUS.] Having two *setæ* or bristles. var. **Biseto·se.**

† **Bi·sexed,** *a.* 1606. [f. BI- *pref.*[2] I. 2 + SEX + -ED[2].] Of both sexes –1646. So **Bise·xous** *a.*

Bisexual (bəise·ksiuăl, -ʃⁱuăl), *a.* 1824. [BI- *pref.*[2] I. 1.] Of two sexes; *spec.* having both sexes in the same individual.

The..tradition..that the original man..was b. COLERIDGE.

Bish, var. of BIKH.

Bishop (bi·ʃəp), *sb.* [OE. *biscop*, corresp. to OFris., OS. *biskop*, (M)Du. *bisschop*, OHG. *biscof* (G. *bischof*), ON. *biskup* – pop.L. **biscopus*, for eccl.L. *episcopus* – Gr. ἐπίσκοπος overseer (whence Goth. *aipiskaupus*), f. ἐπί EPI- + -σκοπος looking (see -SCOPE).] **1.** A spiritual superintendent or overseer in the Christian Church. **a.** In N. T. versions, tr. ἐπίσκοπος, used either descriptively, or as a title. In Acts 20: 28 (where applied to the πρεσβύτεροι of Ephesus) replaced in some versions by 'overseers'. Also applied to Christ. (Occas. used in non-episcopal churches of the pastor or chief elder.) ME. **b.** *spec.* In the episcopal churches: A clergyman consecrated for the spiritual government of a diocese, ranking next below an archbishop (where these exist). (The sense in which the wd. passed into all the Gmc. langs.) OE. † **2.** *transf.* Any chief priest, *e.g.* a *pontifex maximus*, Moslem caliph, etc. –1647. **3.** One of the pieces in the game of chess, having the upper part shaped like a mitre; formerly called *archer* 1562. **4.** The Lady-bird 1674. **5.** A sweet drink, compounded of wine, oranges or lemons, and sugar; mulled and spiced port 1738. **6. a.** A bustle (*U.S.*) 1860. **b.** A child's smock (*n. dial.*) 1874.

1. a. In the language of the New Testament the same officer in the Church is called indifferently 'bishop' ἐπίσκοπος and 'elder' or 'presbyter' πρεσβύτερος 1868. **b.** *Bishop in partibus* (*infidelium*) in R.C.Ch., a titular bishop, whose diocese is in the possession of infidels. Bischops.. shulden not amersy pore men WYCLIF. **5.** That liquor called b., which Johnson had always liked BOSWELL.

Comb.: **Bishop's Bible,** the version published in 1568 under the direction of Abp. Parker; **bishop's length** (*Painting*), a certain size of canvas. **b.** Plant-names: **bishop's cap,** the genus *Mitella* or Mitrewort; **bishop's elder** = *bishop-weed*; **bishop's hat,** *Epimedium alpinum*; **bishop's leaves,** Water Figwort (*Scrophularia aquatica*); **bishop's weed, b.-weed,** the genus AMMI; also *Ægopodium*; **bishop('s wort,** Wood Betony, *Stachys betonica*; also Devil-in-a-bush, *Nigella damascena.*

Bi·shop, *v.*[1] *arch.* [OE. *bisċeopian* exercise the office of a bishop, f. prec.] **1.** To administer confirmation to; to confirm (*arch.* or *obs.*). **2.** To make a bishop of 1549. **3.** To let (milk, etc.) burn while cooking. In allusion to the proverb 'The bishop has put his foot into it'. (*n. dial.*) 1863.

[If the porage be burned..we say the bishop hath put his foote in the potte..because the bishops burn who they lust TINDALE.]

Bi·shop, *v.*[2] 1727. [f. *Bishop*, personal name.] **1.** To file down the teeth of (a horse) so as to make him look young. **2.** To murder by drowning (cf. BURKE *v.*) 1840.

Bishopdom (bi·ʃəpdəm). [OE. *bisċeopdōm*; in later use, f. BISHOP *sb.* + -DOM.] † **1.** = BISHOPHOOD –1635. **2.** Episcopal order; *concr.* bishops collectively 1641.

Bi·shopess. 1672. [-ESS[1].] The wife of a bishop (*nonce-wd.*); a she-bishop (*joc.*) 1854.

Bishophood (bi·ʃəphud). [OE. *bisċeophād*; see -HOOD.] The office, dignity, or rank of a bishop.

Bishoplike (bi·ʃəp,ləik). **A.** *adj.* Like a bishop; † episcopal OE.; var. **Bi·shoply** *a.* **B.** *adv.* After the manner of a bishop 1555.

Bishopric (bi·ʃəprik). [OE. *bisċeopriċe*, f. *bisċeop* + *riċe* realm, province.] **1.** The province of a bishop; a diocese. **2.** The office or position of a bishop ME. † **3.** Overseership. (tr. Gr. ἐπισκοπή.) –1592.

3. His Bishopricke [*marg.* office: or, charge] let another take *Acts* 1: 20.

Bishopstool (bi·ʃəp,stūl). [OE. *bisċeopstōl* bishop's seat; see STOOL.] The throne, seat, or see of a bishop. *Obs.* since 13th c., but revived by historians.

Bisie, obs. f. BUSY.

Bisk (bisk), *sb.* 1647. [– Fr. *bisque*, of unkn. origin.] A rich soup made by boiling down birds, etc.; *spec.* crayfish soup.

Bisk, var. of BISQUE[1].

Bismar (bi·smăɹ). 1805. [– Da. *bismer*, ON. *bismari* steelyard; in LG. *besemer*, Sw. *besmar*; of Slav. origin.] **1.** A steelyard used in Orkney, Shetland, etc. **2.** The fifteen-spined stickleback (*Gasterosteus spinachia*), from its supposed resemblance to the steelyard 1805.

† **Bisme.** 1513. [aphet. f. *abisme* ABYSM.] A deep pit –1663.

† **Bi·smer,** *sb.* [OE. *bīsmer* = OS., OHG. *bismer* ridicule, f. *bī* BY + *smer* mockery, cf. *smerian* smile contemptuously, *smearcian* (see SMIRK).] **1.** Disgrace; mockery; scorn –1460. **2.** A person worthy of scorn; a pander or bawd –1535. Hence † **Bi·smer** *v.* to treat with scorn.

Bismethyl; see BIS- *pref.*[2]

‖ **Bismi·llah.** 1813. [Arab.] In the name of Allah; a Moslem exclam.

Bismite (bi·smait, biz-). [f. BISM(UTH) + -ITE[1] 2 b.] *Min.* The native oxide of bismuth; bismuth-ochre.

Bismite, bismoke, etc.; see BE-.

Bismuth (bi·smǝþ, biz-). 1668. [– mod.L. *bisemutum* (Georg Agricola, 1530), latinization of G. *wismut*, of doubtful origin.] One of the elementary bodies; a reddish white metal, found native, and also in combination. (Chemically, a triad and a pentad, used in the arts and in medicine. Symbol Bi.)

Comb.: **b.-blende** = EULYTIN; **-glance** = *Bismuthinite*; **-ochre** = BISMITE; **-silver,** Ag_6Bi a native compound of b. and silver. Hence **Bi·smuthal** *a.* of or pertaining to b. **Bi·smuthate**, a salt of bismuthic acid. **Bismuthic** *a.* combined with b. as a pentad, as *bismuthic oxide* Bi_2O_5. **Bi·smuthide** (*Chem.*), a primary compound of b. with another element or an organic radical; (*Min.*) a family of minerals of the b. type. **Bi·smuthine**, a compound of b. having the structure of an amine; also = **Bismu·thinite** (*Min.*), native sulphide of b., or *b.-glance*, a lead-grey lustrous mineral, isomorphous with stibnite. **Bi·smuthous** *a.* combined with b. as a triad, as *bismuthous oxide* Bi_2O_3. **Bi·smutite, Bismuthite** (*Min.*), the native hydrous carbonate of b., Bi_2C, of various forms and colours.

† ‖ **Biso·gnio, bisogno.** 1591. [– It. *bisogno* 'need, want; also, a fresh needy souldier. *Bisogni*, new leuied souldiers such as come needy to the war' (Florio). See BESOGNE, BEZONIAN.] = BESONIO –1636.

Bison (bai·sǝn, bi·sǝn, bi·zǝn). ME. [In the present form first in A.V. (*Deut.* 14:5 margin), earlier in L. pl. *bisontes* of *bison* (whence Fr. *bison*) – Gmc. **wisand-*, **wisund-* (OE. *wesend*, OHG. *wisant*, *-unt*, ON. *visundr*).] **1.** *orig.* A European Wild Ox (*Bos bison* Gesn., *B. bonasus* Linn.), still existing in Lithuania. (Occas., but erron., called the *Aurochs.*) **2.** The N. American species *B. americanus*, pop. 'Buffalo', now found chiefly in the region of the Rocky Mountains 1774.

Bispinose, -ous; see BI- *pref.*[2] I. 1.

Bisque[1] (bisk). 1656. [– Fr. *bisque*, of unkn. origin.] *Tennis.* Odds given to a player in the form of a point to be scored once during the set at any time he may elect. In *Croquet*: An extra turn allowed to a weaker player.

Phr. *To give one fifteen*, etc. *and a b.*: to give him long odds, to 'leave him nowhere'.

Bisque[2]. 1664. [f. BISCUIT.] **1.** ? BISCUIT (bread). **2.** In *Pottery*, = BISCUIT 2; also, unglazed white porcelain.

Bisque, var. of BISK, soup.

† **Bisse·xt.** ME. [– late L. *bi(s)sextus* (sc. *dies* day), f. *bi-* BI- *pref.*[2] I + *sextus* sixth.] *prop.* The intercalary day in leap-year (see next); also = BISSEXTILE. –1618.

Bissextile (bise·kstil). 1581. [– late L. *bi(s)sextilis* (sc. *annus* year) year of the *bissextus*; see prec., -ILE.] **A.** *adj.* Containing the *bissextus* which the Julian calendar inserts every fourth year after the *sixth* day before the calends of March, or 24th of February 1594. *B. day* (= L. *bissextus dies*; see above). **B.** *sb.* Leap-year.

† **Bi·sson,** *a.* [OE. (late Northumb.) *bisene*; of unkn. origin.] **1.** Blind –1559. *Occas.*, purblind –1607. **2.** ? Blinding. *Haml.* II. ii. 529.

Bist, obs. or dial. = *art*; see BE *v.*

Bistipuled; see BI- *pref.*[2] I.

Bistort (bi·stǭɹt). 1578. [– Fr. *bistorte* or med.L. *bistorta* 'doubly twisted', f. *bis* twice + *torta*, pa. pple. fem. of *torquēre* twist.] **1.** A species of Polygonum (*P. bistorta*) having a root twisted upon itself; also called *Snakeweed.* See ADDERWORT. **2.** *Surgery.* = BISTOURY 1655.

Bistoury (bi·stǝri, bi·sturi). 1748. [– Fr. *bistouri* (Paré), earlier *bistorie* dagger, of unkn. origin.] *Surgery.* A scalpel; made in three forms, straight, curved, or curved and probe-pointed.

Bistre (bi·stǝɹ). Also **bister.** 1727. [– Fr. *bistre*, of unkn. origin.] A brown pigment prepared from soot; the colour of this. Also *attrib.* **Bi·stred** *ppl. a.* stained with or as with b.

† **Bi·sulc.** 1650. [– L. *bisulcus* two-furrowed, two-cleft, f. *bi-* BI- *pref.*[2] I + *sulcus* furrow.] **A.** *adj.* Cleft in two; *spec.* having a cloven hoof 1661. **B.** quasi-*sb.* A cloven-hoofed animal 1693. So **Bisu·lcate, Bisu·lcated, Bisu·lcous** *adjs.* in same sense.

Bit (bit), *sb.*[1] [OE. *bite* = OFris. *bit, bite*, OS. *biti* (MDu. *bēte*, Du. *beet*), OHG. *biʒ* (G. *biss*), ON. *bit* (Sw. *bett*, Da. *bid*) :– Gmc. **bitiz*, f. **bit-*, **bītan* BITE *v.*] † **1.** The act or action of biting; a BITE –1653. Also *fig.* and *transf.* **2.** What one bites, victuals 1719. **3.** The biting part of anything; the blade, edge, or cutting end of a tool; *spec.* the movable boring-piece of a drill, or a similar tool for use with machines, etc.; the cutting-iron of a plane, the jaws of tongs, pincers, etc. 1594. **4.** The part of a key which engages with the levers of the lock 1644. **5.** The mouthpiece of a horse's bridle, consisting of the metal *b.-mouth*, and adjacent parts, to which the reins are attached ME.

1. An idle servant..good at b., and nothing else 1635. **2.** A b. and a sup KINGSLEY. **5.** *To draw b.*: to stop one's horse by pulling at the reins; *fig.* to slacken speed. *To take the b. in his teeth* (of a horse): *i.e.* so that it cannot hurt the mouth; hence, to be beyond restraint; also *fig.* Hence **Bi·tted** *ppl. a.* (sense 5).

Bit, *sb.*[2] [OE. *bita* = OFris. *bita*, OS. **bito* (MDu. *bēte*, Du. *beet*), OHG. *bizzo* (MHG. *bizze*, G. *bissen*), ON. *biti* :– Gmc. **biton*, f. **bit-*, **bītan* BITE *v.*] † **1.** A bite or mouthful –1665. Hence **2.** Morsel (of food) ME. **3.** A small piece, a fragment 1606. **4.** A small portion, a little (of anything) 1740. **5.** *colloq.* A jot, a whit. Also *advb.* 1675. **6.** Of money: **a.** *Thieves' slang.* Money 1607. **b.** In the Southern States of N. America, etc., a small silver coin forming a fraction of the Spanish dollar, or of its value in current money 1683. **c.** *colloq.* A small piece of money. In slang = fourpence. 1829.

2. Dainty bits make rich the ribs *L.L.L.* I. i. 26. **3.** Bits of linen 1718, glass or china 1838. *By bits* 1624. **4.** *A b. of one's mind* (colloq.); see PIECE *sb.* 2. An interesting b. 1879. To stop for a b. GODWIN. 'Bits of children' = poor little children. A b. of a coward 1885. *To do one's b.*: to do one's proper share, orig. in the war of 1914–18. **5.** It isn't changed a b. TROLLOPE.

† **Bit,** *sb.*[3] [OE. *byt(t)* = ON. *bytta*, MDu., MLG. *butte* (Du. *but*, LG. *but*, *büt* water-bucket, cask) :– late L. *buttis*; see BUTT *sb.*[2]] A leathern bottle; the uterus; a fire-bucket –1467.

Bit (bit), *v.* 1583. [f. BIT *sb.*[1]] To put the bit into the mouth of; to accustom to the bit. Also *fig.*

Bit, pa. t. and pple. of BITE *v.*

Bitake, etc., ME. f. BETAKE, etc.

Bitch (bitʃ), *sb.* [OE. *bićće*, rel. obscurely to ON. *bikkja* (connected by some with Lappish *pittja*), of which there is a synon. *grey|baka.*] **1.** The female of the dog; also of the fox, wolf, and occas. of other beasts. **2.** Applied to a (lewd) woman. ME.

† **Bitch,** *v.* 1675. [f. BITCH *sb.* 2.] To frequent lewd women.

Bite (bait), *v.* Pa. t. **bit.** Pa. pple. **bitten;** also **bit** (*arch.*). [OE. *bītan*, pa.t. *bāt*, *biton*, pa. pple. *biten* = OFris. *bīta*, OS. *bītan* (Du. *bijten*), OHG. *bīzan* (G. *beissen*), ON. *bíta*, Goth. *beitan* :– Gmc. **bītan.*] **1.** *trans.* To cut into, pierce, or nip with the teeth (incisors or canines). Also *intr.* or *absol.* **2.** To wound or lacerate with the teeth OE. Also *fig.* Also *absol.* and *intr.* ME. **3.** To sting as a serpent, or an insect that sucks blood ME. † **4.** To nibble, to eat. *trans.* and *intr.* or *absol.* –1640. **5.** *intr.* To seize or snap *at* (bait) 1653. Also *fig.* **6.** *trans.* To cut into or penetrate, as a sharp-edged weapon. Also *fig.* Also *absol.* OE. **7.** *trans.* and *intr.* To cause a sharp smarting pain (to): as a blister, etc. ME. **8.** *trans.* and *absol.* To affect painfully or injuriously with intense cold. Cf. *frost-bitten.* 1552. **9.** To corrode, or eat into 1623. **10.** *trans.* and *intr.* To grip or take hold, either by penetration or friction: used of the action of a plough, an anchor, a skate on ice, etc. 1523. Also *fig.* † **11.** *trans.* To speak sharply or injuriously against (cf. *backbite*). Also *intr.* –1683. **12.** (*colloq.*) To 'take in'. Now only in *pass.* 1709.

•**1.** The appulle that Adam bett 1500. **2.** The dog..went mad, and bit the man GOLDSM. **3.** Saynt machaire Kylde a flee that bote hym CAXTON. **6.** I haue a Sword; and it shall b. vpon my necessitie *Merry W.* II. i. 136. **8.** Freize, freize, thou bitter skie that dost not bight so nigh as benefitts forgot *A.Y.L.* II. vii. 184. **9.** *To b. in* in *Engraving*: to eat out etched lines with an acid. **12.** 'The biter bit' 1887.

Phrases. *To b. the dust, ground*, etc.: to fall in death, to die. *To b. the lip*: to restrain the expression of anger or mirth. So † *To b. one's tongue.* † *To b. the thumb at*: to put the thumb nail into the mouth, 'and with a ierke..make it to knack' (Cotgr.); to give the 'fico', to insult.

Bite (bait), *sb.* 1499. [f. BITE *v.* Replacing BIT *sb.*[1] and[2] in various senses.] **1.** The act or action of cutting, piercing, or wounding, with the teeth; also *transf.* and *fig.* **b.** The corrosive action of acid upon the metal plate in etching 1875. **2.** The biting of food; *concr.* food to eat, as in *b. and sup* 1562. **3.** *Angling.* The seizure of the bait by the fish 1653. **4.** A piece bitten off (usu. to eat); a mouthful 1535. **5.** A wound made with the teeth 1736. **6.** The grip or hold of an edge surface in mechanical contrivances. Also *fig.* 1865. **7.** *Typogr.* A black left in printing through the accidental covering of the form by the frisket 1677. † **8.** *slang.* **a.** A deception; a 'sell'. (Cf. BITER 2.) –1726. **b.** A sharper –1846.

1. His bark is worse than his b. *Mod. Prov.* **4.** Never make two bites of a cherry SCOTT. † **8. a.** What were then called bites and bams, since denominated hoaxes and quizzes SCOTT. Hence **Bi·teable, bi·table** *a.* (*rare*). **Bi·teless** *a.* that does not bite.

Biter (bai·tǝɹ). ME. [f. BITE *v.*] **1.** One who or that which bites. **2.** *spec.* A hoaxer, a sharper. (*Obs.* exc. in 'the biter bit'.) 1680.

Bite·rnate; see BI- *pref.*[2] 3.

† **Bite-sheep.** 1553. [Cf. G. *beißschaf.*] A pun upon *bishop* –1683.

Your Bishops are bite-Sheep 1683.

Bitheism; see BI- *pref.*[2] II.

Biting (bai·tiŋ), *vbl. sb.* ME. [f. BITE *v.* + -ING[1].] **1.** The action of the vb. Also *fig.* † **2.** The wound made by a bite; the part bitten –1669. **3.** *Biting in* (cf. BITE *v.* 9).

Bi·ting, *ppl. a.* ME. [f. BITE *v.* + -ING[2].] **1.** That bites. **2.** That causes pain or smart (*lit.* and *fig.*). In names of plants: Acrid, pungent 1597.

2. B. weather DICKENS. Too bitter, too byting, too satiricall 1611. So b. a calamity FIELDING. Hence **Bi·tingly** *adv.*

Bi·tless. 1605. [f. BIT *sb.*[1] 5 + -LESS.] Not having a bit.

Bi-tri- (bai,trai), *pref.* compounded of BI- *pref.*[2] and TRI-, expressing a possibility of either conformation specified; as in **bitripartite**, divided into two or three parts.

Bitt, usu. in *pl.* **bitts** (bits). [XIV (in Sandahl), prob. orig. a LG. sea term; cf. synon. LG., Du. *beting*, †*beeting* (whence G. *beting*, Sw. *beting*, Norw. *beiting*, Da. *beding*), f. Gmc. **bit-*, repr. also by MHG. *bizze* wooden peg, ON. *biti* cross-beam.] *Naut.* One of the posts fastened in pairs in the deck or decks of a ship, for fastening cables, belaying ropes, etc.

The chief pair, the *riding bitts*, are used for fastening the cable while the ship rides at anchor; others are the *topsail-sheet bitts, carrick-bitts, windlass bitts*, etc. Hence **Bitt** *v.* to coil or fasten (a cable) upon the bitts.

Bittacle, obs. f. BINNACLE.

Bitten (bi·t'n), *ppl. a.* 1599. [f. BITE *v.*] **1.** Cut into, pierced, or wounded with the teeth; *fig.* infected 1613. Often in comb. † **2.** *actively.* Biting. (Cf. *fair-spoken.*) (*rare*) 1616.

Bitter (bi·təɹ), *a.* and *sb.*[1] [OE. *biter*, corresp. to OS., OHG. *bittar* (Du., G. *bitter*), ON. *bitr*, Goth. (with variation of vowel) *baitrs*; prob. f. **bit-*, base of **bītan* BITE *v.*] **A.** *adj.* **1.** Obnoxious, or irritating to the gustatory nerve; having the characteristic taste of wormwood, quinine, or the like; the opposite of *sweet*; causing 'the proper pain of taste' (Bain). Also *fig.* **2.** *transf.* Attended by pain or suffering; grievous OE. **3.** Hence, of a state: Full of affliction; mournful, pitiable 1485. **4.** Expressing or betokening intense grief or misery ME. † **5.** Causing suffering; cruel, severe –1635. **6.** Virulent OE. **7.** Of words (or the person who utters them): Stinging, harsh, cruelly reproachful, virulent ME. **8.** Of wind, weather, etc.: Keen, cutting, bitingly cold 1600.

1. When I was sick, you gaue me b. pils *Two Gent.* II. iv. 149. B. truths COLERIDGE. **2.** A b. moment SCOTT. *To the b. end*: to the last extremity, to death. But see BITTER *sb.*[2] **3.** All our b. griefe *Tit. A.* V. iii. 89. **4.** Esau..cried with a great and exceeding b. cry *Gen.* 27:34. **6.** A b. partisan MACAULAY. **7.** A b. Foole *Lear* I. iv. 150. In b. terms ADDISON. **8.** Freize, thou b. skie *A.Y.L.* II. vii. 184.

B. quasi-*sb.*[1] **1.** That which is bitter; bitterness (*lit.* and *fig.*) OE. **2.** A bitter medicinal substance: now usu. BITTERS, q.v. 1711. Hence † **Bi·tterful** *a.* full of bitterness. **Bi·tterish** *a.* somewhat b. **Bi·tterly** *adv.*

Bitter (bi·tər), *adv.* [OE. *bitere, bitre*, f. BITTER *a.*] = Bitterly (*arch., poet.*, and *dial.*).

Bitter-, *a.* and *adv.* in *comb.*

1. Advb. and parasynthetic, as *b.-pungent, -tasted*, etc. **2.** (*adj.*) In names of plants and other productions, denoting **a.** a bitter variety of the plant, etc., as **b. almond, b. beer; b.** a distinct plant or substance, as **b.-apple** (= *bitter-gourd*); **-cress,** a book-name for the genus *Cardamine*, and esp. *C. amara*; **-cucumber** or **-gourd,** the Colocynth (*Citrullus colocynthus*); **b. earth,** magnesia; **-fitch** (= *bitter-vetch*); **b. herb,** *Erythræa centaurium*; **-king,** a tree, *Soulamea amara*, of the Eastern Archipelago; **-nut,** the Swamp Hickory, *Carya amara*, of North America; † **-salt,** Epsom salts; **-spar,** *Min.* a variety of dolomite; **-vetch,** a book-name for species of *Lathyrus* and *Vicia* formerly *Orobus*; † **-weed,** species of poplar, also a N. American species of wormwood; **-wood,** the timber of an American genus of trees *Xylopia*, also the trees; **-wort,** species of gentian, esp. *G. amarella*.

Bitter, *sb.*[2] 1627. [f. BITT + -ER[1].] *Naut.* A turn of the cable round a bitt.

When a..rope is paid out to the bitter-end, no more remains to be let go SMYTH. (Hence perh. *bitter end*: but cf. BITTER *a.* 2.)

Bitter (bi·təɹ), *v.* [ME. *bitt(e)re(n)* :– OE. *biterian*, f. *biter* BITTER *a.*] *trans.* To make bitter; also † *fig.*

Bitterbump, var. of BUTTERBUMP, bittern.

Bi·ttering, *sb.* 1864. [f. BITTER *a.* + -ING[1].] = BITTERN *sb.*[2] 2.

Bittern (bi·təɹn), *sb.*[1] [Earliest forms *botor, butor, bittor, -er* – OFr. *butor* – Rom. **butitaurus*, f. L. *butio* bittern + *taurus* bull (used by Pliny of a bird that bellows like an ox; cf. synon. Fr. *taureau d'étang, boeuf de marais* 'marsh ox', G. *meerochs, meerrind* 'sea-ox'). Forms with final *n* (XVI) are perh. due to assoc. with *hern* HERON.] **1.** A genus of grallatorial birds (*Botaurus*), allied to the herons, but smaller. *spec.* The species *B. stellaris*, a native of Europe. It utters a 'boom' during the breeding season, whence its names *mire-drum*, and *bull of the bog*.

As a Bitore bombleth in the Myre CHAUCER.

Bittern (bi·təɹn), *sb.*[2] 1682. [perh. dial. f. *bittering.*] **1.** The lye which remains after the crystallization of common salt from sea-water, etc. Also *attrib.* **2.** An old trade name for a mixture of quassia and other drugs employed in adulterating beer; called also *bitterin(g)* 1775.

Bitterness (bi·təɹnės). [OE. *biternes.*] The quality or state of being bitter: **a.** to taste; **b.** to the mind or feelings; **c.** anguish of heart; **d.** animosity, acrimony; **e.** intensity of cold. **f.** † *concr.* Anything bitter –1790.

In the bitternesse of my soule *Isa.* 38:15. The bittrenesse of the aloe tre 1477. The bitternesse.. of the Winter MARKHAM.

Bitters (bi·təɹz), *sb. pl.* 1713. [f. BITTER *sb.*[1]] Bitter medicines generally, as quinine, etc.; *spec.* alcoholic (or other) liquors, impregnated with the extract of gentian, quassia, orange peel, or the like, and used as stomachics, etc. (Also in *sing.*)

Bitter-sweet (bi·təɹ,swīt). ME. **A.** *adj.* Sweet with an admixture or aftertaste of bitterness; also *fig.* **B.** *sb.* **1.** A thing which is bittersweet (*lit.* and *fig.*) ME. **2.** A kind of apple ME. **3.** *Herb.* The Woody Nightshade, *Solanum dulcamara* 1568.

† **Bi·tter-swee:ting.** [f. prec. + -ING[1].] The Bittersweet Apple. *Rom. & Jul.* II. iv. 83.

Bi·ttock. *n. dial.* 1802. [f. BIT *sb.*[2] + -OCK.] A little bit.

Bittor, -our, obs. ff. BITTERN, *sb.*[1]

Bitts, *sb. Naut.*; see BITT *sb.*

† **Bitume,** *v.* [f. *bitume*, obs. f. BITUMEN.] To smear or spread with bitumen. SHAKS.

Bitumen (bi·tiŭmėn, bitiū·mėn). 1460. [– L. *bitumen, -min-.*] **1.** Orig., a kind of mineral pitch found in Palestine and Babylon, used as mortar, etc.; Jew's pitch. **2.** Generic name of native hydrocarbons more or less oxygenated, including naphtha, petroleum, asphalt, etc. **3.** A pigment prepared from asphalt 1855. Also *attrib.* Hence **Bitu·minate** *v.* to cement with b.; to convert into or impregnate with b. **Bitumini·ferous** *a.* yielding b. **Bitu·minize** *v.* to convert into, or impregnate with, b.; to varnish with b.; whence **Bitu:miniza·tion. Bitu·minoid** *a.* resembling b.

Bituminous (bitiū·minəs), *a.* 1620. [– Fr. *bitumineux* – L. *bituminosus*; see prec., -OUS.] **a.** Of the nature of, consisting of, or containing bitumen. **b.** *spec.* as in *b. coal, limestone, schist, shale*; *cement, mastic* 1830. Also *fig.*

The Plain, wherein a black b. gurge Boiles out from under ground, the mouth of Hell MILT. *P.L.* xii. 41.

Bivalent (bi·vălėnt), *a.* 1869. [f. BI- *pref.*[2] III + *valent-*, pres. ppl. stem of L. *valēre* be worth, have power.] *Chem.* Combining with two atoms of an element or radical; also *divalent*. Hence **Bi·valency,** the property of being b.

Bivalve (bəi·vælv). 1661. [f. BI- *pref.*[2] I + VALVE.] **A.** *adj.* † **1.** Having two folding parts 1677. **2.** *Zool.* Having two shells united by a hinge 1661. **3.** *Bot.* Having two valves 1737. vars. **Bi·valved, Biva·lvous, Biva·lvular. B.** *sb.* **1.** *pl.* Folding-doors. *Hist.* 1832. **2.** *Zool.* A mollusc having a shell consisting of two halves joined together by an elastic ligament at the hinge, so as to open and shut like a book; e.g. the oyster, mussel, etc. Also the shell of such animal. 1683. **3.** *Bot.* A bivalve seed-vessel.

Bivaulted; see BI- *pref.*[2] I.

Biventer (bəive·ntəɹ). 1706. [f. BI- *pref.*[2] II + L. *venter* belly.] *Phys.* A muscle having two bellies; *esp.* the digastric muscle. Hence **Bive·ntral** *a.*

Bive·rb. *rare.* 1831. [f. BI- *pref.*[2] II + L. *verbum* word.] A name composed of two words. **Bive·rbal** *a.* relating to two words; punning (*rare*).

Bivial (bi·viăl), *a.* 1877. [f. BIVIUM + -AL[1].] *Phys.* Of or pertaining to the *bivium*.

Bivious (bi·viəs), *a.* 1644. [f. L. *bivius* (f. *bi-* two + *via* way) + -OUS.] Having or offering two ways.

‖ **Bivium** (bi·viŏm). 1877. [L., a place where two ways meet; see prec.] The two hinder ambulacra of Echinoderms.

Bivocal (bəivōᵘ·kăl). 1813. [f. BI- *pref.*[2] II + VOCAL.] A combination of two vowels, a diphthong. **Bivo·calized** *ppl. a.* placed between two vowels.

Bivouac (bi·vwæk, bi·vu,æk). 1706. [– Fr. *bivouac* (†*bivac*, †*biwacht*), prob. – Swiss-G. *beiwacht* lit. 'extra watch' (BY, WATCH), said to have been used in Aargau and Zürich to denote a patrol of citizens to assist the ordinary town watch.] **1.** *Mil.* Orig., a night-watch by a whole army under arms, to prevent surprise; now, a temporary encampment under improvised shelter or none; also, the place of this. **2.** A camping out 1853.

Bivouac, *v.* 1809. [f. prec.] *Mil.* Of troops: To remain, *esp.* during the night, in the open air, without tents, etc. Also *transf.*

The Carrousel, where about 2000 Prussians are bivouacked 1815.

Biw-; see BEW-, BYW-.

‖ **Bixa** (bi·ksă). 1879. [Native name in Central America.] A genus of small trees, from the fruits of one of which (*B. orellana*) the dye anatta is prepared. **Bixin,** the colouring principle of anatta.

Biz. 1865. Colloq. abbrev. of BUSINESS.

Bizant, Bizantine, obs. ff. BEZANT, BYZANTINE.

Bizarre (bizā·ɹ, as Fr. biza·r'), *a.* 1648. [– Fr. *bizarre* (formerly) handsome, brave – Sp., Pg. *bizarro* handsome, brave (cf. It. *bizzarro* angry) – Basque *bizarra* beard; (cf. Sp. *hombre de bigote* lit. 'moustached man', man of spirit).] Eccentric, whimsical, odd; grotesque, irregular.

Her attire seemed as bizare as her person 1648. B. tulips 1843. Hence ‖ **Biza·rrerie,** b. quality.

Bizcacha, var. of BISCACHA.

Bizel, obs. f. BEZEL.

Bizygomatic (bəi:zigomæ·tik), *a.* 1878. [f. BI- *pref.*[2] I. 5 + ZYGOMATIC.] Joining the two zygomatic arches.

Blab (blæb), *sb.*[1] ME. [contemp. w. †*blabber* babble, chatter, and synon. †*lab*. *Blab, blabber* and the foll. forms point to an imit. Gmc. base **blab-*; OHG. *blabbizōn* (MHG. *blepzen*), Icel. *blabbra* (Da. *blabbre*).] **1.** One who does not control his tongue; a babbler, or tell-tale; used also of the tongue. **2.** Loose chatter ME. Also in *comb.*

1. To be..avoided as a b. MILT. *Sams.* 491.

Blab, *sb.*[2] *Obs.* exc. *dial.* 1656. [var. of BLEB, BLOB.] A bubble; a blister. Hence **B.-lipped** = Blabber-lipped (see BLABBER *a.*).

Blab, *v.*[1] 1535. [f. BLAB *sb.*[1]] † **1.** *trans.* To utter with open mouth; usually with *out*. Also *absol.* –1598. **2.** *trans.* To open one's mouth about; to reveal indiscreetly 1583. **3.** *intr.* To talk indiscreetly, to betray secrets 1601. **4.** *trans.* (*transf.*) To bewray 1597.

2. He blabb all, and not sticke to tell 1589. To b. out a secret 1869. **3.** Mum's the Word, I never b. 1747. **4.** Beaufords red sparkling eyes b. his hearts mallice *2 Hen. IV*, III. i. 154. Hence **Bla·bber** *sb.*

† **Blab,** *v.*[2] 1601. [f. BLAB *sb.*[2]] To make swollen (the cheeks) –1719.

† **Bla·bber,** *a.* 1483. [First in comb. *blabyr-lypped*. Cf. BLOB, BLUBBER, BUBBLE, expressing the sense of swelling or inflation.] Swollen, protruding; said of the lips and cheeks –1800.

† **Blabber,** *v.* [ME. *blaberen*; see BLAB *sb.*[1]] **1.** *intr.* To make sounds with the lips and tongue as an infant (cf. sense 3); to babble, mumble –1800. **2.** *intr.* To chatter –1483. Also *trans.* **3.** To move the tongue between the lips in mockery –1629. Hence † **Bla·bberer.**

Black (blæk), *a.* [OE. *blæc, blac-*, corresp. to OS. *blac* ink, OHG. *blah-, blach-* (in comps.); cf. ON. *blakkr* dusky, black, dun; of unkn. origin. (In ME. confused with *blāc* pale, wan; see BLEAK *a.*). *Black* has superseded SWART in gen. use as a colour-name.] **1.** As a colour pertaining to objects, even in full light: Absorbing all light; 'of the colour of night' (J.); 'of the colour of soot or coal'; 'of the darkest possible hue'; swart. **b.** Having a very dark skin, as Negroes or Negritos; *loosely*, swarthy OE. **c.** *fig.* Of or pertaining to the Negro race 1852. **2.** Characterized in some way by this colour OE. **3.** Characterized by absence of light ME. **4.** Soiled, dirty ME. **5.** *fig.* Having dark purposes, malignant; deadly; baneful, disastrous, sinister 1583. **6.** *fig.* Foul, iniquitous, atrocious 1581. **7.** *fig.* Dismal, gloomy, sad 1659. **b.** Of the countenance, the 'look' of things: Clouded with anger; threatening, boding ill 1709. **8.** *fig.* Indicating disgrace, censure, etc. Cf. BLACK BOOK, LIST, etc. 1612.

1. B. velvet 1536, Chimney-sweepers SHAKS., hair 1611, port-wine 1859. c. The b. blood..in my veins STEVENSON. 2. The blak dowglass BARBOUR. How if she be Blacke and Witty? *Oth.* II. i. 133. 3. The blacke winter night GOWER. The heauen was blacke with cloudes 1 *Kings* 18:45. 5. That b. Name, Edward, b. Prince of Wales *Hen. V*, II. iv. 56. A b. augury BYRON. 6. B. ingratitude 1738. A. b. lie 1839. 7. B. despair 1809, looks 1840. *To look b.*: to look angrily (*at* or *upon*).

Phrases. **B. and blue**: discoloured by beating, etc., so as to have b. and blue or livid bruises. **B. and tan** (of a terrier dog): having the back b., and tan (yellowish brown) upon the face, flank, and legs. Also *ellipt.* as *sb.* **B. and white**: **a.** *adj.* Having a surface diversified with b. and white. **b.** *sb.* Black characters upon white paper; writing. Phr. *In b. and white*: in writing or in print. **c.** *Art.* (A sketch, etc. in) black tint on white paper, or with white colour used.

Comb. (For such as **b. cattle, coal, draught,** etc. see CATTLE, COAL, etc.) **b.-band,** an earthy carbonate of iron found in the coal measures, and containing coaly matter; † **b. canon,** a canon regular of St. Augustine; **b. character** = BLACK-LETTER; **-coat,** parson (*depreciative*); **B. Country,** a name given to parts of Staffordshire and Warwickshire blackened by the coal and iron trades; **b.-fellow,** an Australian aboriginal; **-heart** (for *black* HEART-*cherry*), a dark sort of cultivated cherry; **b. note** *Mus.*, a note with a solid (black) head, as a crotchet (opp. to *white note*); **b. quarter,** a disease of cattle (= BLACK-LEG 1); **b. rent,** black mail, an illegal tribute; **-seed,** the b. Medick; **b. strap** (or **stripe**), an inferior port wine, also a mixture of rum and treacle; **b. sugar** (*Sc.*), liquorice juice; **B. Watch**: see WATCH *sb.* II. 8; **-wort,** the Comfrey. Hence **Bla·ckish** *a.* somewhat b. **Bla·ckly** *adv.*

Black, *sb.* ME. [The adj. used absol.] **1.** Black colour or hue. Also in pl. **2.** A black paint, dye, or varnish, as *lamp b.*, *Brunswick b.*, etc. 1573. **3.** A black speck; *spec.* the smut in wheat, a flake of soot, etc. ME. † **4.** The dark spot in the centre of the eye –1648. **5.** Black fabric or material; as black clothing, funereal hangings, etc. 1608. **6.** = Black man or woman: **a.** A Negro, Negrito, etc. 1625. † **b.** One of a band of poachers who went about their work with blackened faces. *attrib.* in *black-act* (9 Geo. I. xxii). –1809.

1. Knowe what whyte is, and it is soone perceyued what blacke is 1526. 3. If you see a b. on my nose, tell me so DICKENS. 5. Neither are all that weare blackes his mourners 1636. 6. a. The mouth of the Riuer [Gambra] where dwell the Blackes, called Mandingos PURCHAS.

Black (blæk), *v.* ME. [f. BLACK *a.*] † **1.** *intr.* To be or become black –1460. **2.** *trans.* To make black; now *esp.* to put black colour on ME.; to clean and polish with BLACKING 1557. **3.** *fig.* To sully; to defame. (Usu. *blacken.*) 1440.

2. Causing his shoos to be blacked 1684. The Russian censor who blacks out all matter that is displeasing to the Government GEN. GORDON.

Blackamoor (blæ·kămūᵊɹ, -mōᵊɹ). 1547. [= *Black Moor* (also used); the connecting *a* is unexplained. Cf. BLACK-A-VISED.] **1.** A Negro; any very dark-skinned person. (Now a nickname.) Also *attrib.* **2.** *attrib.* Quite black 1813.

1. The Negro's, which we call the Blacke-Mores RALEIGH. 2. Some b. rook 1856.

Black art. 1590. [prob. after LG. *swarte kunst*, G. *schwarze kunst*; cf. L. *niger* black, fig. wicked, and med.L. var. *nigromantia* of *necromantia* NECROMANCY.] **1.** Magic, necromancy. † **2.** *Thieves' slang.* Lock-picking –1608.

Black-a-vised (blæ·kăvəi:st), *a. n. dial.* Also **-viced, -vized.** 1758. [f. BLACK *a.* and Fr. *vis* face; perh. orig. *black-à-vis*, or *black o' vis.*] Dark-complexioned.

Black-ball, bla·ckball, *sb.* 1847. **1.** A composition used by shoemakers, etc., and also for taking rubbings of brasses and the like; a *heel-ball.* **2.** A black ball of wood, etc., dropped into the urn to express an adverse vote; *hence*, an adverse secret vote 1869.

Blackball (blæ·kbǫl), *v.* 1770. [See prec.] **1.** To exclude from a club, etc., by adverse votes, recorded by placing black balls in the ballot-box, or in other ways. **2.** To exclude from society, taboo 1840. **3.** To blacken with black-ball 1818.

1. I shall make a note to b. him at the Athenæum DISRAELI. Hence **Bla·ckballer.**

Blackberry (blæ·kberi). [OE. (pl.) *blaceberian.*] **1.** The fruit of the bramble (*Rubus fruticosus*), and its varieties. Also *attrib.* **2.** The bramble 1579. **3.** Now, in the north, the Black Currant (*Ribes nigrum*), formerly in some localities the Bilberry 1567.

1. If Reasons were as plentie as Black-berries [etc.] 1 *Hen. IV*, II. iv. 265. Hence **Bla·ckbe:rrying** *vbl. sb.* the gathering of blackberries. Cf. NUTTING.

Blackbird (blæ·kbəɹd). 1486. [The only BIRD in an earlier sense (before crows and rooks were included) which is *black.*] **a.** A species of thrush (*Merula turdus*, L.). In N. America the name is given to other birds, e.g. the *Gracula quiscala*, and *Oriolus* (*Agelaius*) *phœniceus*. **b.** *loosely* = Songster.

Black board, bla·ckboard. 1823. A large wooden board, or the like, painted black, and used in schools, etc. to draw or write upon with chalk.

Black book. 1479. **1.** An official book bound in black 1624. **2. a.** *Black Book of the Exchequer*: a book kept in the Exchequer Office, containing an official account of the royal revenues, etc. 1479. **b.** *Black book of the Admiralty*: an ancient code of rules for the government of the navy, compiled in the reign of Edw. III. 1769. **3.** An official return prepared in the reign of Henry VIII, containing the reports of the visitors upon the abuses in the monasteries 1581. **4.** A book recording the names of persons who have incurred censure or punishment 1592. **5.** A book of necromancy 1842.

4. *To be in (any one's) black books*: to be out of his favour.

Bla·ck-browed, *ppl. a.* 1590. Having a dark brow or front; frowning, scowling.

Black cap, bla·ck-cap, bla·ckcap. **1.** *Black cap*: spec. that worn by English judges when in full dress, and assumed when passing sentence of death upon a prisoner 1838. **2.** One who wears a black cap 1856. **3.** *Blackcap*: A bird having the top of the head black, as the Blackcap Warbler, *Curruca* (or *Motacilla*) *atricapilla*. Also, in U.S., *Parus atricapillus*, the Blackcap Tit or Chickadee. 1678.

Blackcock (blæ·kˌkǫk). 1427. The male of the Black Grouse or BLACK GAME.

Black death; see DEATH.

Black dog. 1706. † **1.** A cant name for a base silver coin –1724. **2.** *fig.* Depression of spirits; ill-humour 1826.

Black drop. 1823. **1.** *Med.* A dark-coloured medicine, chiefly opium, with vinegar and spices. **2.** *Astron.* A dark drop-like appearance observed at solar transits of Venus and Mercury 1869.

Blacken (blæ·k'n), *v.* [f. BLACK *a.* + -EN[5].] **1.** *intr.* To become black (*lit.* and *fig.*). **2.** *trans.* To make black or dark (*lit.* and *fig.*) 1552.

1. To b. into cynicism MORLEY. 2. Calumnies, tho' they do not burn, yet b. DRUMM. OF HAWTH. The Birds..blackening all the air KINGSLEY. Hence **Bla·ckener.**

Black eye. 1604. **1.** An eye of which the iris is very dark-coloured 1667. Hence **Black-eyed** *a.* **2.** A discoloration of the flesh around the eye produced by a blow 1604.

Bla·ck-face. 1844. A black-faced sheep or other animal.

Bla·ck-faced, *a.* 1592. **1.** Having a black or dark-coloured face. Also *fig.* 1594. **2.** Of things: Dark, gloomy 1592.

Black fish. 1754. **1.** A name of several varieties of Eng. and Amer. fishes; *e.g.* the Black Ruff (a kind of perch), *Centrolophus pompilus* (a kind of mackerel), *Tautoga americana* (a species of wrasse). **2.** A small species of whale 1796. **3.** A name given to salmon just after spawning; whence **Black-fisher.** **Black-fishing,** the taking of these; in Scotland, *esp.* by torchlight at night. 1808.

Black flag. 1593. A flag of black cloth, used with reference to death or deadly purpose; *e.g.* as a sign that no quarter will be given or asked, as the ensign of pirates, and as a signal of the execution of a criminal. Also in *pl.* used of the pirates of the Chinese Sea, etc.

Black foot. 1842. One of a tribe of N. Amer. Indians.

Black friar. 1500. One of the Dominican friars, so called from the colour of their dress. Hence in *pl.*, the quarters of these friars, in London or elsewhere. 1583.

Black game. 1678. Black Grouse (*Tetrao tetrix*), of which the male is called BLACKCOCK, and the female *grey hen.*

Blackguard (blæ·gāɹd). 1532. [orig. meaning and application unknown.] **A.** *sb.* † **1.** The scullions and kitchen-knaves of a royal or noble household, who had charge of pots and pans, etc. –1678. † **b.** The servants and camp-followers of an army. Also *fig.* –1702. † **2.** A guard of attendants, black in person, dress, or character –1705. † **3.** The vagabond or criminal class of a community –1768; *esp.* the shoeblacks –1736. † **4.** A guard black in person, dress, or character. Also *fig.* Cf. 2. –1745. † **5.** A street shoe-black; a 'city Arab' –1785. **6.** One of the criminal class; hence, an unprincipled scoundrel. (A highly opprobrious term.) 1736. **7.** A kind of snuff. Also called *Irish b.* 1792.

1. Ye have lyen among the Pots, black and sooty, as the black guard of an army TRAPP. 4. Satan..placed his Black Guards there 1696. 5. The little b. who gets very hard His halfpence for cleaning your shoes SWIFT. 6. And cheat like ony unhang'd b. BURNS.

B. *attrib.* or *adj.* † **1.** Of or pertaining to the shoe-black or street Arab class –1822. **2.** Blackguardly 1784.

2. I have heard him use language as b. as his action BYRON.

Hence **Bla·ckguardism,** blackguardly conduct or language. **Bla·ckguardly** *adj.* characteristic of a b., ruffianly, low; *adv.* after the manner of a b. **Bla·ckguardry** (*rare*) = BLACKGUARD *sb.* 3.

Blackguard (blæ·gaɹd), *v.* 1786. [f. prec. sb.] **1.** *intr.* To act the blackguard (senses 3, 6). **2.** *trans.* To treat as a blackguard; to abuse or revile in scurrilous terms 1823.

Black-head (blæ·khed). 1658. **1.** A name of certain black-headed birds. **2.** = COMEDO 1885.

Black-hole, Black Hole. 1758. (Beside obvious application to any black hole:) **1.** *Mil.* The punishment cell in a barracks; the guard-room. (The name has become historic in connection with the Black Hole of Fort William, Calcutta, into which 146 Europeans were thrust for a whole night in 1756, of whom only 23 were alive next morning.) **2.** *gen.* A place of confinement for punishment 1831.

Blacking (blæ·kiŋ), *vbl. sb.* 1571. [f. BLACK *v.* + -ING[1].] **1.** The action of making black 1609. † **2.** Lamp-black 1594. **3.** Any preparation for making black; *esp.* for giving a shining black surface to boots and shoes 1571.

Black Jack, bla·ck-jack. 1513. **1.** A large leather beer-jug, coated with tar. ? *Obs.* 1591. **2.** Mining term for zinc sulphide or blende 1747. **3.** *U.S.* A kind of oak (*Quercus nigra*) 1856. † **4.** *Sc.* A black leather jerkin; see JACK –1820. **5.** The mustard beetle 1886.

Black lead, black-lea·d, bla·cklead. 1583. † **1.** A black ore of LEAD. **2.** Name of the mineral plumbago or graphite, consisting of almost pure carbon with a little iron; it is chiefly used in the form of pencils, and as a polish for iron-work. (The name preceded the knowledge of its composition.) 1583. **b.** A pencil of this substance 1656. Also *attrib.* Hence **Black-lea·d** *v.* to colour or rub with, or draw in, black-lead.

Bla·ck-leg, -legs. 1722. **1.** A disease in cattle and sheep which affects the legs. (Better *black-legs.*) **2.** A turf swindler; a sharper generally 1771. **3.** Opprobrious term for: A workman willing to work for a master whose men are on strike 1865. Hence **Bla·ck-leg** *v.*, to take the place of a worker on strike. **Black-le·ggery, -le·gism,** profession or practice of a b.

Bla·ck-letter, black letter, bla·ckletter. **1.** A name (dating from *c* 1600) for the type used by the early printers, a form of which is still in regular use in Germany, and, as 'Gothic' or 'Old English', in occasional use in England. **2.** Anything printed in this type 1811. **3.** *attrib.* (Usu. w. hyphen, or as one wd.) 1791.

1. The Seven champions in the black-letter ARBUTHNOT. *Black letter day*: an inauspicious day; as distinguished from *e.g.* a saint's-day, marked in the calendar with red letters.

Black list. 1692. **1.** A list of persons who have incurred suspicion, censure, or punishment; cf. BLACK *a.* 8. **2.** *fig.* A list of bad cases 1853. **Bla·ck-list** *v.* to enter in a black list.

Black mail. 1552. Also **black-mail, blackmail.** [See MAIL *sb.*[2]] **1.** *Hist.* A tribute formerly exacted from small owners in the border districts of England and Scotland, by freebooting chiefs, in return for immunity from plunder. **2.** Hence, Any payment extorted by intimidation 1840. † **3.** *Law.* Rent reserved in labour, produce, etc., opp. to 'white rents', reserved in white money or silver –1768.

1. The boldest of them will never steal a hoof from any one that pays black-mail to Vich Ian Vohr SCOTT. Hence **Black-mai·l** *v.* to levy black mail upon; to extort money from by intimidation or the unscrupulous use of an official or social position, or of political influence or vote. **Black-mai·ler.**

Black Maria. 1874. A prison van for the conveyance of prisoners.

Black mark. 1845. A mark made against the name of a person who has incurred censure, penalty, etc. Also *fig.*

Black Monday; see MONDAY.

Black Monk. ME. See MONK.

Black moor, more; see BLACKAMOOR.

Bla·ck-mouth. 1642. A black-mouthed person or animal; *fig.* a slanderer. So † **Black-mou·thed** *a.* having a black mouth; also *fig.*

Bla·ck-neb. *dial.* 1802. [See NEB, beak.] **1.** Name for black-billed birds, as the Crane and the Common Crow. † **2.** *Sc.* A person of democratic sympathies at the time of the French Revolution –1864.

Bla·ckness. ME. [f. BLACK *a.* + -NESS.] The quality or state of being black.

The spots of Heauen, More fierie by nights Blacknesse *Ant. & Cl.* I. iv. 13.

Black ox; see OX 4 b.

† **Bla·ck-pot.** 1590. A beer-mug (cf. BLACK JACK); a toper –1818.

Black Prince. 1563. **1.** A name given to the eldest son of Edw. III. [The explanations current are guess-work.] † **2.** The prince of darkness, the devil 1589.

Black pudding. (Also hyphened.) 1568. A sausage made of blood and suet.

Black Rod. 1632. Short for *Gentleman Usher of the Black Rod*, so called from his symbol of office. The chief Gentleman Usher of the Lord Chamberlain's department of the royal household, and also usher to the House of Lords, and to the Chapter of the Garter. Also, a similar officer in colonial legislatures.

Black salts. 1880. Impure potassium hydrate. Hence **Bla·ck-salter,** a maker of this.

Black sheep; see SHEEP *sb.* 2 c.

Bla·ckshirt. 1923. [tr. It. *camicia nera.*] = FASCIST.

Blacksmith (blæ·ksmiþ). 1483. A smith who works in iron or black metal, as opp. to a 'whitesmith' who works in tin.

Black-snake. 1688. **1.** A name for dark-coloured snakes; as in U.S. the *Coluber constrictor* and *C. alleghaniensis*; in Jamaica the *Natrix atra*. **2.** *U.S.* A long whip-lash 1883.

Bla·ck-tail. 1661. † **1.** An unkn. sea fish; the *melanurus* of ancient writers. **2.** A name for varieties of the perch 1734.

Bla·ck-thorn. ME. **1.** A common thorny shrub, bearing white flowers before the leaves and very small dark purple plums; the Sloe (*Prunus spinosa*). **b.** A walking-stick made of the stem of this 1849. Also *attrib.* **2.** *U.S.* A hawthorn (*Cratægus tomentosa*) 1864.

Bla·ck-wash. 1818. **1.** *Med.* A lotion of calomel and lime-water. **2.** Any composition used for washing over and blackening 1861. Hence **Bla·ckwash** *v.* to wash with a black liquid; *fig.* to calumniate.

Bla·ckwater. † **1.** A dark-coloured stream 1678. **2.** A disease of cattle 1800. **3.** *B. fever*, a tropical disease characterized by dark-coloured urine 1884.

Bla·ck-wood, blackwood. 1631. A name given to various trees and their dark-coloured timber.

Blacky (blæ·ki), *sb. colloq.* [f. BLACK *a.* + -Y.[6]] Also **-ie, -ey.** 1815. A Black, Negro. Cf. DARKY.

Bla·cky, *a.* 1594. [f. BLACK *a.* + -Y[1].] Blackish.

Blad, *sb.*[1] *Sc.* 1715. [f. BLAD *v.*] A firm flat blow.

Blad, *sb.*[2] *Sc.* Also **blaud.** 1527. [perh. same as prec., or f. BLAD *v.*; cf. *dad* beat, thump, and *dad* large piece, 'thumping' piece.] A fragment, piece, lump.

Blad, *v. Sc.* 1524. [prob. echoic.] To slap heavily.

Bladder (blæ·dəɹ). [OE. *blǣdre*, later *blæddre* = OS. *blādara*, MLG., MDu. *blāder* (Du. *blaar*), OHG. *blātara* (G. *blatter*), ON. *blāðra* :– Gmc. **blǣdrōn*, f. **blǣ-* BLOW *v.*[1] + *-dro-*, instr. suff. corresp. to L. *-trum*, Gr. *-trā*, *-tron*, Skr. *-tram*.] **1.** *orig.* The musculo-membranous bag which receives the urinary fluid; the *urinary b.* **b.** Any membranous bag in the animal body; usu. defined, as *gall-*, *air-*, *swimming-b.* 1661. † **2.** A boil, blister, pustule –1607. **3.** The prepared bladder of an animal, used as a float, as part of a bagpipe, etc. ME. **4.** A vesicle, a bubble 1702. **5.** *fig.* Anything inflated and hollow; a 'wind-bag' 1579. **6.** *Bot.* An inflated pericarp 1578; a hollow vesicle, as in various seaweeds 1789. Also *attrib.*

3. Boyes that swim on bladders *Hen. VIII*, III. ii. 359. 5. Prick the b. of our pride SANDERSON. Them that are . . bladders full of winde 1579.

Comb.: **b.-campion,** *Silene inflata*, named from the inflated calyx; **-fern,** a fern of the genus *Cystopteris*; **-green,** a pigment obtained from the Common Buckthorn, sap-green; **-kelp,** = *bladder-wrack*; **-nose,** a species of seal; **-nut,** the fruit of *Staphylea pinnata*, contained in b.-like pods; also the shrub; **-pod,** the *Physolobium*, a species of *Leguminosæ*; the American B.-pod is *Vesicaria shortii*; **-seed,** the *Physospermum*, named from the loose outer coating of the undeveloped fruit; **-senna,** the *Colutea arborescens*, with distended pods; **-tangle, -weed,** = *bladder-wrack*; **-wort,** a genus of water-plants, *Utricularia*, with small bags on roots, stems, and leaves, filled with air; **-wrack,** a species of sea-weed (*Fucus vesiculosus*), with air-bladders in the fronds. Hence **Bla·dderet** (*Phys.*), a small b.; a vesicle. **Bla·ddery** *a.* of the nature of a b. (*lit.* and *fig.*); abounding in bladders or vesicles.

Bladder, *v.* 1440. [f. prec.] † **1.** *intr.* To swell out like, or into, a bladder –1543. † **2.** *trans.* To inflate –1649. **3.** To put into a bladder, as 'bladdered lard'.

Blade (blēⁱd). [OE. *blæd*, pl. *bladu*, = OFris. *bled*, OS. (Du.) *blad*, OHG. *blat* (G. *blatt*), ON. *blað* leaf, blade of rudder, knife, etc. :– **blaðam*, perh. pa. ppl. formation (Indo-Eur. **-tos*) on the base **blō-* BLOW *v.*[2]] **1.** The leaf of a herb or plant; *esp.* the leaves of grass and cereals; also, the whole plant before the ear appears. Cf. 2. 1450. **2.** *Bot.* The broad, thin, expanded part of a leaf or petal; the lamina 1835. **3.** The broad, flattened part of any instrument or utensil, as a spade, bat, paddle, oar OE. **4.** The thin cutting part of an edged tool or weapon; often put poetically for the whole weapon, etc. ME. Also *fig.* **5.** The *shoulder-blade* or scapula ME. **6.** *Archit.* The principal rafter of a roof 1851. **7.** A gallant, a free and easy fellow; 'fellow'. (Now colloq. or slangy: in lit. use, a reminiscence of last century.) 1592.

1. First the b., then the eare, after that the full corne in the eare *Mark* 4:28. Phr. *In the b.*: i.e. not yet in the ear. 4. The haft also went in after the b. *Judges* 3:22. And by his syde he baar a rusty b. CHAUCER. 7. A b. whom I took for a decent tailor COBBETT. A knowing b. DICKENS. A keen Yorkshire b. 1882. *Comb.*: **b.-bone,** the shoulder-b., the corresponding bone of animals and 'joint' of meat; **-fish,** a Ribbon-fish (*Trichiurus lepturus*). Hence **Bla·dy** *a.* characterized by a b., or blades; blade-like.

Blade (blēⁱd), *v.* 1440. [f. prec. sb.] **1.** To take off the BLADES (sense 1). *dial.* **2.** To provide with a (cutting) blade 1440. **3.** *intr.* To put forth blades 1601.

Bladed (blēⁱ·dėd), *ppl. a.* 1578. [f. as prec. + -ED.] **1.** Lanceolate. **2.** Having a blade or blades 1590. **3.** ? Not yet in full ear *Macb.* IV. i. 55. **4.** Stripped of the blades 1611. **5.** *Min.* Having a structure characterized by long narrow plates.

Blae (blē, bliə, blī·), *a.* (*sb.*) Now *Sc.* and *n. dial.* [ME. *blo, bloo*, in north. dial. *bla*, *blaa* – ON. *blár*; see BLUE.] **A.** *adj.* **1.** Blackish blue; livid; also, bluish grey, lead-coloured. **2.** Bleak, sunless 1513. **B.** *sb.* A kind of soft slate 1724.

Blaeberry (blēⁱ·beri, bliə·-). 1562. [f. BLAE + BERRY.] Sc. and north. name of the BILBERRY, fruit and plant.

‖ **Blague** (blag), *sb.* 1837. [Fr.] Humbug. Hence ‖ **Blague** *v.* to tell lies.

Blain (blēⁱn). [OE. *blegen* = MDu. *bleine* (Du. *blein*), LG. *bleien* :– WGmc. **blezen* (cf. OHG. *blehinougi* blear-eyed); cf. CHILBLAIN.] **1.** A blister, botch, pustule. Cf. CHILBLAIN. **2.** A bladder growing on the root of the tongue of beasts against the windpipe 1727. Hence **Blain** *v.* to affect with blains.

Blake, *a. Obs.* exc. *dial.* ME. [ME. *blāk* :– OE. *blāc* pale; see BLEAK *a.*] **1.** Pallid, wan; of a sickly hue. **2.** Yellow (*local*) 1691. Hence † **Blake** *v.* to become pale.

Blame (blēⁱm), *v.* ME. [– OFr. *blamer*, earlier *blasmer* (mod. *blâmer*) :– pop.L. *blastemare*, for eccl.L. *blasphemare* revile, reproach – Gr. βλασφημεῖν (dial. βλαστ-) BLASPHEME.] **1.** *trans.* To find fault with. † **2.** To reprove –1559. † **3.** To bring into disrepute –1611. † **4.** To accuse (*of*, *with*) –1649. **5.** To lay the blame on ME.

1. Goe girle, I cannot b. thee now to weepe *Tam. Shr.* III. ii. 27. 5. She has nobody to b. for it but herself ADDISON. Phr. *To b.*: in 16–17th c. *to* was taken as *too*, and *blame* as = blameworthy. The King mine Vnkle is too b. for it *Rich. III*, II. ii. 13. Hence **Bla·meable, bla·mable** *a.* **Bla·meably, bla·mably** *adv.* **Bla·mer.**

Blame (blēⁱm), *sb.* ME. [– OFr. *blame*, f. *blamer*; see prec.] **1.** The action of censuring; imputation of demerit on account of a fault; reproof; reprehension. † **2.** A charge –1581. **3.** Blameworthiness; fault (*arch.*) ME. **4.** Responsibility for anything wrong ME.

1. The contrary to Fame and Applause, to wit, B. and Derision 1709. 3. Holy and without b. *Ephes.* 1:4. 4. He took all the b. on himself MORLEY. Hence **Bla·meful** *a.* blaming, fully meriting b. **Bla·meful-ly** *adv.*, **-ness. Bla·meless** *a.* uncensured; undeserving of b. **Bla·meless-ly** *adv.*, **-ness. Bla·meworthy. Bla·meworthiness.**

Blancard (blæ·ŋkăɹd). 1848. [– Fr. *blancard* ((O)Fr. *blanchard*), f. *blanc* white.] A linen cloth woven in Normandy, the thread of which is half bleached before it is woven.

Blanch (blanʃ), *sb.* 1601. [– BLANCH *a.* (or its French source), and *v.*] † **1.** White paint (esp. for the face) –1610. † **2.** A white spot on the skin –1609. **3.** *Min.* 'Lead ore mixed with other minerals'. Raymond.

Blanch, *a. Obs.* exc. *Hist.* ME. [– (O)Fr. *blanche*, fem. of *blanc* white; see BLANK *a.*] † **1.** White, pale, as *b. sauce*, etc. –1586. **2.** *Her.* White, argent 1697. **3.** *Blanch*, Sc. *blench*; more fully *b. farm*, *blench ferme*: Rent paid in silver; in Sc. writers any nominal quit-rent 1602.

Blanch (blanʃ), *v.*[1] ME. [– (O)Fr. *blanchir*, f. *blanc*, fem. *blanche* white; see prec.] **1.** To make white, whiten: now chiefly by depriving of colour; to bleach; *spec.* to make (metals) white. Also *fig.* **2.** *Cookery.* To whiten almonds, etc., by taking off the skin; *hence*, to scald in order to remove the skin ME. **3.** To whiten plants by depriving them of light 1669. **4.** To palliate, to 'white-wash'. (Now only with *over*.) 1549. **5.** *intr.* To turn white; to bleach; to pale 1768.

1. Age had blanched his hair MERIVALE. The famine blanches your lips RUSKIN. 4. To b. and varnish her deformities MILT. 5. As when the rolling breakers boom and b. on the precipices TENNYSON. Hence **Bla·ncher.**

Blanch, *v.*[2] 1572. [var. of BLENCH, *v.*[1]] † **1.** To bilk –1602. † **2.** To blink (a fact); to pass without notice –1671. **3.** *intr.* To start back (*arch.*) 1572. **4.** *trans.* To turn off, aside, away; to head back (deer) 1592.

3. 'Tis no time to b. 1572. Hence **Bla·ncher**[2], one who heads back (deer), etc.

† **Blanch,** *v.*[3] 1572. [app. worn down from BLANDISH (like *blench*, XIV–XV, from BLEMISH *v.*).] *intr.* = BLANDISH *v.* 2. –1612.

Bookes will speake plaine, when Counsellors B. BACON.

Blanchimeter (blanʃi·mĭtəɹ). 1847. [f. BLANCH *v.*[1] + -METER.] An instrument for measuring the blanching power of chloride of lime and potash; a chlorometer.

Blancmange (blămā·nʒ, -mǫ·nʒ, -mā·ṅʒ). [Earliest form *blancmanger* – (O)Fr. *blanc-manger*, f. *blanc* white + *manger* food, subst. use of *manger* eat. The second element was shortened to *-mange* XVIII.] An opaque jelly made formerly with isinglass, etc., now usu. with corn-flour boiled with milk. Also *fig.* (cf. *flummery*).

Blancmanger that made he with the beste CHAUCER. To make Blomange of Isinglass 1769.

Bland (blænd), *sb.* 1703. [– ON. *blanda* (fem.) mixture of fluids; cf. OE. *bland* (neut.) mixture; see BLEND *v.*[2]] In Orkney and Shetland, a beverage made of buttermilk and water.

Bland (blænd), *a.* 1661. [– L. *blandus* soft, smooth.] **1.** Smooth and suave; mildly soothing or coaxing; gentle. **2.** Of things: soft, mild; genial, soothing; not irritating; not stimulating 1667.

1. With b. words at will MILT. *P.L.* ix. 855. **2.** The air was b. 1872. Hence **Bla·nd-ly** *adv.*, **-ness.**

† **Blanda·tion.** *rare.* 1605. [f. BLAND *a.* + -ATION.] Flattery; an illusion.

Blandi·loquence. *rare.* 1656. [– L. *blandiloquentia*; see BLAND *a.*, ELOQUENCE.] Smooth speech, flattering talk. So **Blandi·loquent, -loquous** *adjs.* (*rare*).

Blandish (blæ·ndiʃ), *v.* ME. [– OFr. *blandiss-*, lengthened stem (see -ISH[2]) of *blandir* :– L. *blandiri*, f. *blandus* BLAND.] **1.** To flatter gently by words or actions, to coax; to cajole. **2.** *intr.* (*absol.*) To use blandishments ME. † **3.** *trans.* To offer blandly (cf. *to smile thanks*) –1638.

3. Though they [flowers] sometime b. soft delight DRUMM. OF HAWTH. Hence **Bla·ndisher.**

Blandishment (blæ·ndiʃmĕnt). 1591. [f. prec. + -MENT.] **1.** Gently flattering speech or action; cajolery. **2.** *fig.* Attraction, allurement. *concr.* Anything that pleases or allures. 1594.

1. Strange..blandishments of words BACON.

Blank (blæŋk), *a.* ME. [– (O)Fr. *blanc* :– Rom. ***blancus* – Gmc. **blaŋkaz* (OHG. *blanc*) white, shining, corresp. to OE. *blanca* steed, ON. *blakkr* pale, sb. horse.] **1.** † White; pale, colourless –1821. **2.** Of paper: Left white; not written upon, or marked; said also of orders, cheques, and documents left with an empty space for special signature or instruction 1547. **3.** *gen.* Empty, without contents, void 1748. **4.** *fig.* Void of interest, result, or expression 1553. **5.** (Looking) nonplussed; as in *To look b.* 1542. **6.** Of emotions: Prostrating the faculties 1634. **7.** *gen.* Pure, downright, sheer, absolute (with neg. or priv. force) 1839.

1. The blanc Moone MILT. *P.L.* x. 656. **2.** A b. Passport 1708. Bills drawn *in b.* (*i.e.* without names specified) 1861. **3.** B. darkness HOOD, space 1856. **4.** A b. day 1832. **5.** Upon this I looked very b. ADDISON. **6.** Countenances of b. dismay DICKENS. **7.** B. atheism 1871. *B. verse*: verse without rhyme; *esp.* the iambic pentameter or unrhymed heroic.

Comb., etc. (in sense 2): **b. acceptance, cheque,** one not having the amount filled in; **b. bar,** a plea in bar, to compel the plaintiff in an action of trespass to assign the certain place where the trespass was committed; **b. charter,** a document given to the agents of the crown in Richard II's reign, with power to fill it up as they pleased; hence *fig.* liberty to do as one likes; **b. indorsement,** a bill in which the indorsee's name is omitted. Also (in sense 3): **b.-cartridge,** one containing no ball; **-door** (*Archit.*), an imitation of a door; **-tyre,** a tyre without a flange; **-tooling** = blind-blocking; see BLIND *a.*; **-window,** an imitation window. Hence **Bla·nk-ly** *adv.*, **-ness.**

Blank (blæŋk), *sb.* ME. [f. prec., in absolute or elliptical uses of the adj.] † **1.** A small French coin, orig. of silver, later of copper, worth 5 deniers; also a silver coin of Henry V, current in the parts of France then held by the English –1629. **2.** The white spot in the centre of the target; hence *fig.* anything aimed at, the range of such aim 1554. **b.** 'Level line mark for cannon, as point-b., equal to 800 yards' (Smyth). † **3.** A nonplus –1580. **4.** A lottery ticket which does not gain a prize, as *to draw a b.* 1567. **5.** A blank space in a document 1570. **b.** Provisional words printed in italics (instead of blank spaces) in a bill before Parliament 1817. † **6.** A blank form (*e.g.* a blank charter) –1780. **b.** An empty form; nothing at all 1700. **7.** *fig.* A vacant space, place, or period 1601. **8.** Blank verse 1589. **9.** *Mech.* A piece of metal, cut and shaped, and ready for finishing; *esp.* in *Coinage*, the disc of metal before stamping 1596. **10.** The $\frac{1}{230400}$ of a grain 1680. **11.** A domino without points on either or both of its divisions. **12.** A dash written in place of an omitted letter or word. Cf. DASH.

2. As level as the cannon to his b. Transports his poisoned shot *Haml.* IV. i. 42. Also *Oth.* III. iv. 128. **4.** When one has drawn a b. W. IRVING. **7.** And what's her history? A blanke, my lord SHAKS.

Blank (blæŋk), *v.* 1483. [f. prec.] † **1.** *trans.* = BLANCH *v.*[1] –1652. **2.** To nonplus. Cf. BLANK *a.* 5. (*arch.*) 1548. **3.** To frustrate; disconcert (plans, etc.) (*arch.*) 1566. † **4.** To turn away. (Cf. BLANCH *v.*[2] 4.) –1659. **5.** To render blank or void; to veil from sight 1763. b. To indicate by a dash (——) 1789. ¶ c. Blank (printed ——, but read 'blank') = 'damn', or the like 1873. † **6.** *intr.* To blench; to shrink back –1642.

2. Which fairly blanked the bold visage of Adam Woodcock SCOTT. **5.** Night..blank'd half the Globe CHURCHILL. **c.** B. him! that is just like him C. READE.

Blanket (blæ·ŋkėt), *sb.* ME. [– OFr. *blancquet* (AL. *blanchettum, -ketum, -chetta* XIII), var. of *blanchet*, f. *blanc* white; see BLANK *a.*, -ET.] † **1.** An undyed woollen stuff used for clothing –1440. **2.** A large oblong sheet of soft loose woollen cloth, used chiefly as a bed-covering; also for throwing over a horse, and, by savages, for clothing ME. Also *fig.* **3.** *Printing.* A woollen cloth used to deaden and equalize the pressure of the platten 1824. **4.** *transf.* A layer of blubber in whales 1885.

2. A rascally Slaue, I will tosse the Rogue in a B. 2 *Hen. IV*, II. iv. 241. *fig.* The B. of the darke *Macb.* I. v. 54. *A wet b.*: a person or thing that throws a damper over everything. *Born on the wrong side of the b.*: i.e. illegitimate.

Bla·nket, *v.* Pa. t. and pple. **-eted.** 1605. [f. the sb.] **1.** To cover with or as with a blanket. **2.** *Yachting.* To take the wind out of the sails of a yacht by passing to windward of it 1884. **3.** To toss in a blanket 1609. Hence **Bla·nketed** *ppl. a.* covered with or as with a blanket; in U.S. used *spec.* of cattle having a broad belt of white round the middle.

† **Blanketee·r.** 1755. [f. BLANKET + -EER.] **a.** One who uses a blanket. **b.** *pl.* A body of operatives who met at the Blanket Meeting in Manchester, on 10th March, 1817, provided with blankets, etc., in order to march to London and call attention to their grievances. –1833.

Blanketing (blæ·nkėtiŋ), *sb.* 1577. [f. as prec. + -ING[1].] **1.** Material for blankets; supply of blankets 1677. **2.** The action of the vb. (senses 2, 3) 1577.

Blare (blēᵊɹ), *v.* [Late ME. *blere*, early mod. *blear, blare*, Sc. *bleir* (XVI) – (M)Du. *bleren* and MLG., MDu. *blaren*; of imit. origin.] **1.** *intr.* To roar with prolonged sound in weeping, as a child; to bellow as a calf. Now *dial.* **2.** To sound a trumpet, to trumpet. (Now the ordinary wd. in this sense.) 1782. **3.** *trans.* To utter in blaring 1859.

2. Blairing like trumpeters at a fair COWPER. Hence **Blare** *sb.*[1] the weeping of a child, the bellowing of calves; the noise of trumpets, etc.

Blare, *sb.*[2] 1867. [ME. *blare* (Sandahl, XIII), perh. of Scand. origin; cf. OSw. *blaar* (pl.) tow.] A paste of hair and tar for caulking the seams of boats.

Blarney (blā·ɹni), *sb.* 1819. [f. *Blarney*, a village near Cork. The saying is that whoever kisses the 'Blarney stone' in the castle will ever after have a cajoling tongue and the art of flattery.] Smoothly flattering or cajoling talk (*colloq.*). Hence **Bla·rney** *v.* (*trans.*) to assail with b.; (*intr.*) to use flattering speech.

† **Blas.** [ME. *blas*, for *bles* (:– OE. *blǣs*), by blending with ME. *blase*, BLAST.] **1.** A blast, breath. ME. only. **2.** A supposed flatus or influence of the stars, producing changes of weather 1662.

‖ **Blasé** (bla·ze), *a.* 1819. [Fr.] Exhausted by enjoyment, disgusted with it; used up.

Blason, obs. f. BLAZON.

Blaspheme (blasfī·m), *v.* [ME. *blasfeme* – OFr. *blasfemer* (mod. *blasphémer*) – eccl.L. *blasphemare* revile, blaspheme – Gr. βλασφημεῖν, f. βλάσφημος evil-speaking. See BLAME *v.*] **1.** *intr.* To talk profanely. **2.** *trans.* To utter impiety against (God or anything sacred) ME. **3.** *gen.* To speak evil of, revile, calumniate ME.

2. Blaspheming God, and cursing men on earth 2 *Hen. VI*, III. ii. 372. **3.** So they b. the muse TENNYSON. Hence **Blasphe·mer.**

† **Blasphe·me,** *a.* and *sb.*[1] ME. only. [– OFr. *blasfeme* (mod. *blasphème*) – eccl.L. *blasphemus* – Gr. βλάσφημος; see prec.] **A.** *adj.* Blasphemous. Hence † **Blasphemely** *adv.* **B.** *sb.* A blasphemer.

† **Blasphe·me,** *sb.*[2] ME. [ME. *blasfeme*, *-pheme* – OFr. *blasfeme* (mod. *-phème*) – eccl. L. *blasphemia* BLASPHEMY.] Early f. BLASPHEMY –1583.

In b. of the goddis CHAUCER.

Blasphemous (bla·sfīməs), *a.* 1535. [f. eccl.L. *blasphemus* (see BLASPHEME *a.* and *sb.*) + -OUS; cf. OFr. *blasfemeus, -phemeus*, AFr. *-phemous.*] **1.** Uttering profanity. † **2.** Abusive, defamatory –1610.

1. O argument b., false and proud MILT. *P.L.* v. 809. **2.** You bawling, b., incharitable dog *Temp.* I. i. 43. Hence **Bla·sphemous-ly** *adv.*, **-ness.**

Blasphemy (bla·sfīmi). [ME. *blasfemie*, *-phemie* – OFr. *blasfemie* – eccl.L. *blasphemia* – Gr. βλασφημία slander, blasphemy. See -Y[3].] **1.** Profane speaking of God or sacred things; impious irreverence. Also *fig.* 1605. † **2.** *gen.* Evil speaking, defamation –1656. † **b.** *transf.* A thing evil spoken of 1609.

1. B. against the Almighty BLACKSTONE, *fig.* against learning BACON.

Blast (blast), *sb.* [OE. *blǣst* = OHG. *blāst*, ON. *blástr* (perh. the immed. source in ME.) :– Gmc. **blǣstaz*, f. **blǣs-*; see BLAZE *v.*[2]] **1.** A blowing or strong gust of wind. **2.** A puff of air through the mouth or nostrils; a breath (*arch.*) ME. **3.** The blowing of a trumpet or other wind-instrument; hence, the sound so produced; any similar sound. Also *fig.* ME. **4.** A strong current of air produced artificially 1618. **b.** *spec.* That used in iron-smelting, etc. 1697. † **5.** The sudden stroke of lightning –1751. **6.** A sudden infection (formerly attributed to the breath of a malignant power, foul air, etc.). **a.** Blight; also an insect which causes it. **b.** *transf.* and *fig.* Any blasting influence, a curse 1547. **c.** A flatulent disease in sheep. **7.** An explosion 1635; the quantity of explosive used 1885. **8.** *Sc.* A smoke (of tobacco). Cf. *Counterblast.*

1. Snows, and Bitter Blasts DRYDEN. **2.** The b. of thy nostrils *Ex.* 15: 8. **3.** Loud as the trumpet's b. HAN. MORE. Phr. † *At one b.* (L. *uno flatu*): at the same time. **4.** To give very strong and lasting Blasts for Iron Forges 1697. *In b.*, *at* or *in full b.*: at work. *Out of b.*: stopped. **6. b.** Resistless as the blasts of pestilence JOHNSON.

Comb.: **b.-fan,** a fan for producing a b. of air; **-hearth,** a hearth for reducing lead-ore; **-hole,** the hole by which water enters a pump; **-pipe,** in a locomotive, a pipe conveying the steam from the cylinders into the funnel and so increasing the draught.

Blast (blast), *v.* ME. [f. the sb.] **1.** † *intr.* To blow violently –1768; † *trans.* to blow (*out, forth, abroad*); to proclaim –1631. † **2. a.** *intr.* To blow (on a trumpet, etc.). **b.** *trans.* To blow (a trumpet, etc.). **c.** To din or denounce (any one) by trumpeting. –1858. **3.** To blow (up), inflate. Also *intr.* (for *refl.*) *Obs.* exc. *dial.* 1578. **4.** To blow up by explosion 1758. **5.** To blow or breathe on balefully, to blight 1532. Also *transf.* and *fig.* † **6.** To wither under a blight –1630. **7.** To curse. Often in imprecations. 1640. Also *absol.*

5. O fairest flower, no sooner blown but blasted MILT. Blasted or stricken with a planet 1580, with lightning 1634. To b. the Memory..of King William STEELE. He saw; but blasted with excess of light, Clos'd his eyes in endless night GRAY. **6.** Tell Beauty how she blasteth RALEIGH. **7.** Calling on their Maker to curse them..b. them, and damn them MACAULAY. Hence **Bla·sted** *ppl. a.* a low expression of reprobation and hatred. **Bla·ster,** one who or that which blasts.

-blast [– Gr. βλαστός sprout, shoot, germ], used techn., esp. in Biology, in sense of 'germ, embryo', as in *epiblast, mesoblast*, and *hypoblast.*

‖ **Blastema** (blæstī·mă). Pl. **blaste·mata.** 1849. [Gr. βλάστημα sprout.] **1.** *Biol.* The primary formative material of plants and animals; protoplasm. Now *spec.*: The initial matter out of which any part is developed.

2. *Bot.* The budding or sprouting part of a plant 1880. Hence **Blaste·mal, Blastema·tic** *adjs.* of or pertaining to b.

Bla·st-fu·rnace. 1706. A furnace in which a blast of air is used; *spec.* the common furnace for iron-smelting.

Bla·stide. 1880. [irreg. f. Gr. βλαστός sprout, bud + -IDE for -OID.] *Biol.* 'The clear space in each segment of a dividing impregnated ovum, which precedes the appearance of a nucleus'. (*Syd. Soc. Lex.*)

Blasting (blɑ·stiŋ), *vbl. sb.* 1460. [f. BLAST *v.* + -ING[1].] † **1.** The production of blasts; flatulence –1579. **2.** Withering or shrivelling up caused by atmospheric, electric, or unseen agency 1535. **3.** Blowing rocks to pieces; also its result 1824. var. **Bla·stment** (sense 2).

Blasto- (blæsto), repr. Gr. βλαστο-, stem and comb. form of βλαστός sprout, germ. Used techn. in the sense of 'germ' or 'bud'.

Blastoca·rpous [Gr. καρπός] *a.*, *Bot.* of the nature of a seed which germinates before escaping from the pericarp. **Bla·stocœle** [Gr. κηλίς spot], the germinal spot. **Bla·stocheme** [Gr. ὄχημα vehicle], a Medusa in which a generative body is developed in the radiating canals. **Bla·stochyle** [Gr. χυλός juice], the mucilaginous fluid in the embryonal sac of plants. **Bla·stocœle** [Gr. κοῖλος hollow], the central cavity which forms in the ovum after segmentation. **Blastoco·lla** [Gr. κόλλα glue], *Bot.* the gummy substance which coats certain buds. **Bla·stocyst** [Gr. κύστις bladder], **Blastocy·stinx** [Gr. κυστιγξ little bladder] = BLASTODERM. **Bla·stodisc,** the germinal disc of the ovum of birds. **Blastoge·nesis,** reproduction by buds. **Blasto·geny,** Haeckel's term for the germ-history of persons. **Blasto·graphy,** the scientific description of the buds of plants. **Bla·stomere** [Gr. μέρος part], each of the segments into which the impregnated ovum at first divides. **Bla·stophor** [Gr. -φορος], a portion of the spermatophore which remains to carry spermatoblasts; whence **Blasto·phoral** *a.* **Bla·stophore,** *Bot.* Richard's name for the part of the embryo with a large radicle which bears the bud. **Blasto·phyly** [Gr. φυλή tribe], Haeckel's name for the tribal history of persons. **Bla·stopore** [Gr. πόρος passage], the orifice produced by the invagination of a point on the surface of a blastule, or blastosphere, to form the enteron. **Bla·stosphere,** a name for the impregnated ovum, when, after segmentation, it has acquired a blastocœle and blastoderm. **Blastostro·ma** [Gr. στρῶμα a stratum], the germinal area. **Bla·stostyle** [Gr. στῦλος pillar], a stalk upon which gonophores are developed in the Hydrozoa.

Blastoderm (blæ·stodɜɹm). 1859. [f. BLASTO- + Gr. δέρμα skin.] *Embryol.* A disc of cells found in the early segmentation of a fertilized ovum (as differentiated from *blastula*, a hollow ball of cells, and *morula*, a solid ball). Hence **Blastoderma·tic, Blastode·rmic** *adjs.*

Bla·stule. 1882. [f. Gr. βλαστός sprout, shoot + -ULE.] A small germ; a blastophore.

Blasty (blɑ·sti), *a.* 1583. [f. BLAST *sb.* + -Y[1].] Characterized by blasts of wind. † **2.** Causing blight 1667.

Blatant (blēi·tănt), *a.* Also **blattant.** 1596. [First used by Spenser in *the blat(t)ant beast* (*F.Q.* v. xii. 37, etc.) to describe the thousand-tongued monster produced by Cerberus and Chimæra and symbolizing calumny 1596; perh. alt. after adjs. in -ANT of Sc. *blatand* (G. Douglas), pres. pple. of *blate* BLEAT, and assoc. w. *blatter* speak volubly (XVI) – L. *blat(t)erare* babble, f., like synon. *blat(t)ire*, imit. base.] **1.** In 'the blat(t)ant beast': see above. **2.** *fig.* Noisy; offensively or vulgarly clamorous; bellowing 1656; clamorous 1790. **3.** Loud-voiced 1791; loud 1816.

1. 'The blattant beast,' quoth he, 'I doe pursew' SPENSER *F.Q.* VI. i. 7. **2.** Up rose a b. Radical BAGEHOT. Not the less Hear I the b. appetite demand Due sustenance COWPER. Hence **Bla·tancy. Bla·tantly** *adv.*

Blate (blēit, *dial.* blĕt, bliət), *a.* *Sc.* and *n. dial.* [Found in Sc. late in XV. Corresp. phonetically to OE. *blāt* pale, ghastly, but the difference in sense is unexplained.] † **1.** Pale, ghastly. (In OE.) † **2.** Void of feeling –1548. † **3.** Spiritless –1560. **4.** Undiscerning 1513. **5.** Bashful, backward, sheepish 1600.

5. When I was beardless, young, and b. BURNS.

Blate (blēit), *v. rare.* 1666. [Sc. var. of BLEAT (sense 2); see BLATANT.] To babble, prate.

Blatera·tion (blætərēi·ʃən). Also **blatt-.** 1656. [– late L. *blateratio*, f. L. *blaterare* babble; see -TION.] Babbling chatter.

† **Blateroo·n.** Also **blatt-.** 1645. [– It. *blaterone*, f. *blaterare* babble; see -OON.] A babbler.

Blather; see BLETHER.

Blatherskite; see BLETHERSKATE.

‖ **Bla·tta.** 1601. [L.] **1.** Generic name of the Cockroach. **2.** Purple; purple silk 1658. Hence † **Bla·ttean** *a.* purple.

Blatter (blæ·təɹ), *v.* 1555. [– L. *blaterare* babble; partly echoic.] *intr.* To speak or prate volubly. Also *trans.*

Noe matter tho' Ignorance b. folly DANIEL. Hence **Bla·tter** *sb.* a volley of clattering words, or sound of rapid motion. **Bla·tterer.**

† **Blau·nner.** ME. [Also *blaundener, blaundemer*, prob. – AFr. **blaunc et ner* black and white.] A species of (? white) fur used to line hoods, etc. –1460.

‖ **Blauwbok** (blău·bǫk). 1786. [Du. *blaauwbok*, f. *blaauw* blue + *bok* buck.] *S. Afr.* A large Antelope (*A. leucophæa*), with bluish hair.

Blay, bley (blēi). Also (*rare*) **blea.** [OE. *blǣġe* = MLG., MDu. *bleie* (Du. *blei*), G. *blei(h)e* :– WGmc. **blaijjo*, of unkn. origin. See BLEAK *sb.*] A fish, the bleak.

† **Blayk(e,** *a.* [ME. *bleik* :– ON. *bleikr* shining, pale; see BLEAK *a.*] **a.** Pale. **b.** Yellow. –1570.

Blaze (blēiz), *sb.*[1] [OE. *blæse, blase* :– Gmc. **blasōn*; cf. MHG. *blas* torch, rel., through the gen. sense 'shining', to BLAZE *sb.*[2]] † **1.** A torch –1535. **2.** A bright glowing flame or fire OE. Also *fig.* **3.** Brilliant light; a glow of colour 1564. **4.** *fig.* **a.** Splendour, brilliant display 1579. **b.** Clear or full light 1748.

2. *In a b.*: in flames. *Blazes* pl.: referring to the flames of hell, used in: *The blazes! Like blazes*: furiously. *To (the) blazes*: to the deuce. His rash fierce b. of Ryot *Rich. II*, II. i. 33. **3.** Dark, amid the b. of noon MILT. *Sams.* 80. **4.** A b. of jests JOWETT. The b. of publicity 1869.

Blaze (blēiz), *sb.*[2] 1639. [Of unc. origin, but identical in meaning with ON. *blesi* white spot on a horse's forehead, MDu. *blesse* (Du. *bles*), G. *blässe, blesse*; cf. synon. OHG. *blassa* (MHG. *blasse*) and OHG. *blas/ros*, MLG. *blasenhengst* horse with a blaze; also MHG. *blas* bald, G. *blass* pale, and parallel formations with *r*, as MLG. *blare*, Du. *blaar* cow with a blaze, MDu. *blaer* bald.] **1.** A white spot on the face of a horse or ox. **2.** *transf.* A white mark made on a tree, *esp.* by chipping off bark; also, a track indicated by such marks. (First in U.S.) 1737.

Blaze (blēiz), *v.*[1] ME. [f. BLAZE *sb.*[1] Not in OE., or any Gmc. language.] **1.** *intr.* To burn with a bright fervent flame. Also *fig.* **2.** *trans.* To cause to blaze (*rare*) 1485. **3.** *intr.* To shine like flame or fire. Also with *forth.* ME. Also *trans.* with cognate obj. 1667. **4.** *intr.* To shine or be conspicuous. Also with *out.* ME.

1. *To b. up*: to flash into a blaze. *fig.* Stein.. blazed up, and there was an exchange of hot words SEELEY. *To b. out*: to exhaust in a blaze of excess (*arch.*); *intr.* to go out with a flare. **3.** Eyes That sparkling blaz'd MILT. *P.L.* 1. 194. Phr. *To b. away*: to fire continuously with guns, etc.: *fig.* to work enthusiastically (*colloq.*). Cf. *fire away.* Hence **Bla·zer**[1], one who or that which blazes; a jacket, usually of wool and bright-coloured, often with a badge, worn esp. at sports. **Bla·zing** *ppl. a.*; in *Venery*: Of scent, very strong; as opp. to a *cold scent.* **Bla·zingly** *adv.*

Blaze (blēiz), *v.*[2] ME. [– MLG., MDu. *blāzen* blow = OHG. *blāsan* (G. *blasen*), ON. *blása*, Goth. *uf/blesan* to puff up :– Gmc. **blǣsan* (cf. BLAST *sb.*), extension of **blǣ-*; see BLOW *v.*[1]] † **1.** To blow (e.g. with a musical instrument); to puff –1535. **2.** *trans.* To proclaim (as with a trumpet), to make known 1450. **b.** with *abroad.* (The prevalent use.) 1552. † **3.** To BLAZON –1628. **4.** (Mixing senses 2 and 3.) † **a.** To celebrate –1635. † **b.** To portray –1642.

2. b. Fearing..that I should b. it abroad in his lifetime BOSWELL. **3.** What Herald [can] b. their Arms without a blemish? F. GREVILLE. Hence **Bla·zer**[2], one who proclaims.

Blaze, *v.*[3] 1812. [f. BLAZE *sb.*[2]] To mark (trees) with white by chipping off bark, etc. Also to indicate (a spot or path) by such marks.

Blazed (blēizd), *a.* 1685. [f. BLAZE *sb.*[2] + -ED[2].] Having a blaze on the face.

Blazing star. 1460. [-ING[2].] † **1.** A comet –1762. **2.** *fig.* Cynosure, 'star' (*arch.*) 1460. † **3.** = BLAZE *sb.*[2] 1. 1705. **4.** Popular name of three N. Amer. plants: *Alteris farinosa, Chamælirium luteum*, and *Liatris squarrosa.*

Blazon (blēi·z'n), *sb.* ME. [– (O)Fr. *blason* orig. shield (whence Sp. *blason*, Pg. *brasão*, It. *blasone*) = Pr. *blezon, blizon*; of unkn. origin.] † **1.** A shield used in war. ME. only. **2.** *Her.* A shield in heraldry; coat of arms; a banner bearing the arms ME. **3.** Heraldic description or representation of armorial bearings 1610. **4.** (cf. BLAZE *v.*[2]) A description or record, *esp.* of virtues or excellencies 1577. **5.** Divulgation, publication 1602.

2. St. George's b. red SCOTT. **3.** The earliest b. of a Royal Banner..occurs in the Roll of Caerlaverock 1864. **4.** The b. of sweet beauties best SHAKS.

Blazon (blēi·zən), *v.* 1513. [f. prec.; see BLAZE *v.*[2]; with sense 2 cf. mod.Fr. *blasonner*, med.L. *blazonare.*] **1.** To describe in proper heraldic language. Also *absol.* 1586. **2.** To depict according to the rules of heraldry 1570; *fig.* to illuminate 1699. **3.** To adorn as with blazonry 1813. Also *fig.* **4.** = BLAZE *v.*[2] 4. 1513. **5.** To publish boastfully 1534. **6.** = BLAZE *v.*[2] 2. Also with *forth, out.* Often in a bad sense. 1577.

1. To b. the arms painted in the glass windows WARTON. **2.** Having his armes verie excellentlie blazoned in fine coulored glasse 1593. **3.** Walls.. blazoned all with feats of pride SCOTT. **4.** To b. the kingly attributes and virtues 1863. **5.** I wold neuer blasen loue with my tongue LD. BERNERS. **6.** To b. out their blames SPENSER. Hence **Bla·zoned** *ppl. a.* (senses 2, 6). **Bla·zoner, a** herald; one who records with commendation; one who proclaims. **Bla·zonment,** blazoning; proclaiming.

Blazonry (blēi·zənri). 1622. [f. BLAZON + -RY.] **1.** The description or depicting of heraldic devices. **2.** Armorial bearings 1649. Also *fig.* **3.** *fig.* Brilliant or artistic display 1814.

2. The old impresa or arms, b. of the house and family DRUMM. OF HAWTH. var. † **Bla·zure.**

-ble, – (O)Fr. *-ble* :– L. *-bilem*, nom. *-bilis*, suffix forming verbal adjs., with the sense 'given to, tending to, like to, fit to, able to'. The most numerous of the *-ble* words are those in *-able.* In Fr., all pres. pples. in *-ant* (now the universal form of pres. pple.) may give rise to an adj. in *-able.* But in Eng. *-ible* is preferred wherever there was or might be a L. *-ibilis*; while *-able* is used for words of distinctly Fr. or Eng. origin. Hence the distractions of English usage. See -ABLE, -IBLE. An *e* mute before *-able must* be retained after *c, g*, as *peaceable, changeable*, etc., and it is usually retained in monosyllables, as *tameable*, etc.; otherwise its retention is more or less optional. In words from Eng., a final consonant is usu. doubled before *-able*, when doubled in the pres. pple., as *clubbable*, etc.

Adjs. in *-bili-, -ble*, were orig. active (and neuter) as well as passive; but the majority of the former remain only (if at all) with a passive force, as in *credible, audible*, which is also the only use of *-able* as a living formative, e.g. *eatable, likeable*, etc.

Blea (blī), *sb. rare.* 1730. [perh. f. *blea*, BLAE *a.* in the sense 'livid, pale'.] The young wood of a tree under the bark; the alburnum.

Blea, *v. Obs.* exc. *dial.* 1568. [prob. echoic. (Pronunc. blē, bliə, blī.)] *intr.* To bleat as a lamb; to cry piteously as a child.

Bleach (blītʃ), *sb.*[1] [Sense 1 = OE. *blǣċe* leprosy, f. *blǣċ* pale (see BLEACH *a.*); sense 2 f. the *v.*] † **1.** A disease of the skin 1601. **2.** An act of bleaching.

† **Bleach,** *sb.*[2] 1500. [perh. the southern form of BLECK, or :– OE. **blæċċe*, f. *blæc* BLACK.] Any substance used for blacking –1611.

† **Bleach,** *a.* [ME. *bleche*, prob. :– OE. *blæċ*, var. of *blāc*; see BLAKE *a.*] = BLEAK *a.* 1, 2. –1655.

Bleach (blītʃ), *v.*[1] [OE. *blǣċan* = ON. *bleikja* :– Gmc. **blaikjan*, f. **blaik-* shining, white, pale; see BLEAK *a.*] **1.** To whiten (linen, etc.) by washing and exposure or by chemical processes ME. Also *fig.* **2.** To blanch, *esp.* by exposure 1583. **3.** *intr.* To become white or colourless 1611. Also *fig.*

1. When..Maidens b. their summer smockes *L.L.L.* v. ii. 916. **3.** Bones of travellers bleaching amongst the yellow sand 1865. Hence **Blea·cher,** one who or that which bleaches. **Blea·chery,** a place where bleaching is done.

† **Bleach,** *v.*[2] 1611. [f. BLEACH *sb.*[2]] To blacken.

Bleak (blīk), *sb.* 1496. [prob. – ON. *bleikja* = OHG. *bleicha* :– Gmc. **blaikjōn*, f. **blaik-* white (see BLEAK *a.*). For the phonology cf. *weak*. The OE. word was *blǣġe* BLAY.] A small river-fish, called also the Blay (*Leuciscus alburnus*); also an allied sea-fish.

Bleak (blīk), *a.* 1538. [Obscurely rel. to BLAKE *a.*, †BLEACH *a.*, †BLAYK(E) *a.* – ON. *bleikr* shining, white = OE. *blāc* (see BLOKE *a.*), OS. *blēk*, OHG. *bleih* (G. *bleich*) :– Gmc. **blaikaz*; see BLEACH *v.*[1] For the phonology cf. *weak* (= ON. *veikr*).] **1.** Pallid, wan; of a sickly hue. Still *dial.* 1566. **2.** Bare of vegetation; exposed; now often wind-swept 1538. **3.** Cold, chilly 1595. **4.** *fig.* Cheerless 1719.

2. Our lodgings, standing b. upon the sea *Per.* III. ii. 14. **3.** The b. air MILT. *P.R.* II. 72. Hence **Blea·kish** *a.* **Blea·k-ly** *adv.*, **-ness.** So **Blea·ky** *a.*, inclining to b. (in senses 2, 3).

†**Bleak** (blīk), *v.* ME. [Three formations.] I. **1.** = BLEACH *v.*[1] 1, 2. –1612. **2.** *intr.* = BLEACH *v.*[1] 3. 1606. II. To chill or ? make livid with cold 1605. III. = BLEACH *v.*[2] 1611.

Blear (blīᵊɹ), *a.* late ME. [Now chiefly in *blear-eyed* (ME. *blere-eied*), with which cf. LG. *blarroged*, *blerroged*, and MHG. *blerre* blurred vision; the verb is recorded earlier (XIII); immed. source and ult. origin unkn.] **1.** Of the eyes or sight: Dim from water or other superficial affection. Also *fig.* **2.** *transf.* Dim, misty, indistinct in outline 1634.

1. Her eyes grew watery and b. THACKERAY. **2** To cheat the eye with b. illusion MILT. *Comb.*: **b-eyed** *a.* having b. eyes, or wits; **-witted,** having the mental faculties dimmed. Hence **Blea·rness,** blearedness (of the eyes). **Blea·ry** *a.* more or less b.

Blear (blīᵊɹ), *v.*[1] ME. [See prec.] † **1.** *intr.* To have watery or inflamed eyes. (Said also of an albino.) –1570. **2.** *trans.* To dim (the eyes) with tears, rheum, or inflammation ME. **b.** To blur (the face) as with tears ME.

2. He..bleared his eyes with books LONGF. **b.** The Heaven weeps and blears itself, in sour rain CARLYLE.

Phr. (*fig.*) *To b. the eyes*: to deceive, hoodwink *Tam. Shr.* V. i. 120. Hence **Blea·redness. Blea·ring** *vbl. sb.* being bleared; the action of making blear; *transf.* the guttering of a candle.

† **Blear,** *v.*[2] [ME. *blere* to insult by shouting, offensive gestures, or both; prob. the same word as BLARE *v.*] *intr.* To protrude the tongue in mockery –1605.

Bleat (blīt), *v.* [OE. *blǣtan* = OHG. *blāzen*, Du. *blaten*; of imit. origin. Cf. BLEA *v.*] **1.** *intr.* To cry as a sheep, goat, or calf. Also *trans.* (with cognate obj.) 1719. **2.** *transf.* Used contemptuously of the human voice 1563.

1. Lambs, that did..b. the one at th' other *Wint. T.* I. ii. 68. Hence **Blea·ter.**

Bleat (blīt), *sb.* 1505. [f. the vb.] The cry of a sheep, goat, or calf; *transf.* any similar cry.

A Calfe..Much like to you, for you haue iust his b. *Much Ado* V. iv. 51.

Bleb (bleb), *sb.* 1607. [var. of earlier BLOB.] **1.** A small swelling on the skin; also on plants. **2.** A bubble of air in water, glass, etc. 1647. **3.** A vesicular body 1775. Hence **Bleb** *v.* to furnish with blebs. **Ble·bby** *a.* full of blebs or bubbles.

Bleck, *sb.* Now *dial.* [ME. *blek(e)* – ON. *blek* ink (Sw. *bläck*, Da. *blæck* ink) :– **blak-* BLACK.] **1.** Black fluid substance; *spec.* †ink; †shoemakers' black; black grease round an axle, etc. **2.** Soot or smut, a smut 1590. Hence **Bleck** *v.* (now *dial.*) to blacken; also *fig.*

Blee (blī). *arch.* [OE. *blēo(h)*, *blīo(h)* = OFris., OS. *blī*, north. Fris. *bläy*.] **1.** Hue (*arch.*). **2.** Complexion; visage (*arch.*) ME.

1. Eyes so grey of b. E. B. BROWNING. **2.** His daughter bright of b. 1834.

Bleed (blīd), *v.* Pa. t. and pple. **bled.** [OE. *blēdan* = OFris. *blēda*, MLG. *blōden*, ON. *blœða* :– Gmc. **blōþjan*, f. **blōðam* BLOOD.] **I.** *intr.* **1.** To emit, discharge, or lose blood. **2.** To lose blood from wounds; to die by bloodshed ME. Also *fig.* **3.** Of plants: To emit sap when wounded 1674. **4.** Said of blood, etc.: To drop, ooze forth ME. **5.** With cognate obj.: To emit as blood ME. Also *fig.*

1. Least he should bleede to death *Merch. V.* IV. i. 258. *fig.* O my heart bleedes To think oth' teene that I haue turn'd you to *Temp.* I. ii. 63. **2.** Cæsar must b. for it *Jul. C.* II. i. 171. *To b. well*: Of corn, etc.: to give a large yield (*dial.*). Of persons: to lose or part with money to an extent that is felt. **5.** Shee did..I would faine say, b. Teares *Wint. T.* V. ii. 96.

II. *trans.* **1.** To draw or let blood from, *esp.* surgically ME. **2.** To extort money from (*colloq.*) 1680.

2. By Jove, sir, you've bled that poor woman enough THACKERAY. Hence **Blee·der,** one who draws blood; *Med.* a person subject to hæmophilia.

Bleeding (blī·diŋ), *ppl. a.* ME. [f. prec. + -ING[2].] **1.** In senses of the vb. **2.** *fig.* and *transf.* Said of nations devastated by war, etc. 1668.

1. Whose sonnes lye scattered on the b. ground SHAKS. With b. hearts HOOKER. **2.** Greece, b. and exhausted 1863.

Comb.: **b.-heart,** pop. name for plants; *e.g.* the Wallflower, *Dicentra formosa*, and a variety of Cherry; **b. root** = BLOOD-ROOT.

Blemish (ble·miʃ), *v.* ME. [– OFr. *blemiss-*, extended stem (see -ISH[2]) of *blemir*, *blesmir* render pale, injure, prob. of Gmc. origin.] † **1.** To hurt, damage, deface –1607. † **2.** To dim (the eye-sight) –1677. **3.** To mar, injure the working of ME. **4.** To impair the perfection of 1460. **b.** To impair morally; to sully ME. **c.** To discredit, disable. *Obs.* exc. in *Law.* ME.

3. To b. the peace 1625. **4. b.** To b. reputation 1735. **c.** To b. oneself by pleading one's own insanity BLACKSTONE. Hence **Ble·misher. Ble·mishment,** damage; flaw; impairment.

Blemish (ble·miʃ), *sb.* 1526. [f. the vb.] **1.** Physical defect or disfigurement, *e.g.* the scar of a broken knee in a horse; a stain 1535. **2.** *transf.* A defect or flaw generally 1555. **3.** *fig.* A moral defect; a fault, blot, slur 1526.

1. Speaking thicke (which Nature made his b.) 2 *Hen. IV*, II. iii. 34. **3.** Some stain or b. in a name of note TENNYSON. Hence **Ble·mishless** *a.*

Blemmatrope (ble·mătrōᵘp). 1876. [f. Gr. βλέμμα look, glance + τρόπος turning.] An apparatus for illustrating the various positions of the eye.

† **Blench,** *sb.* [f. BLENCH *v.*[1]] **1.** A trick. ME. only. **2.** A side glance. SHAKS.

Blench, *a.* Sc. form of BLANCH *a.*

Blench (blenʃ), *v.*[1] OE. [In sense 1: OE. *blenćan* = ON. *blekkja* impose upon :– Gmc. **blaŋkjan*, which has the form of a causative verb. corresp. to †*blenk*, north. var. of BLINK *v.*] † **1.** To deceive, cheat –ME. **2.** *intr.* To start aside, so as to elude anything; to shy; to flinch ME. **3.** *trans.* To elude; to flinch from; to blink ME. † **4.** To disconcert, turn aside –1640. **5.** *intr.* Of the eyes: To lose firmness of glance, to quail 1775.

2. Sometimes you doe b. from this to that *Meas. for M.* IV. v. 5. **5.** That..influence at which the eyes of eagles have blenched BURKE. Hence **Ble·ncher,** he who or that which turns or frightens away, *e.g.* a scarecrow; one who flinches.

Blench, *v.*[2], var. of BLANCH *v.*[1], q.v.

Blencorn, var. of BLEND CORN; see BLEND(E.

† **Blend,** *v.*[1] [OE. *blendan* blind, deceive = OFris. *blenda*, MLG. *blenden*, OHG. *blenten* (G. *blenden*) :– Gmc. **blandjan*, causative formed on *blind-* BLIND *a.*] To make blind; to dazzle. Also *fig.* –1600.

Blend (blend), *v.*[2] [prob. of Scand. origin and due to *blend-* pres. stem., *blĕnd-* pa. stem of ON. *blanda* mix = OE., OS., Goth. *blandan*, OHG. *blantan* mix; see BLAND *sb.*] **I.** *trans.* **1.** To mix, to mingle; *esp.* to mix (spirits, teas, wines, etc.), so as to produce a certain quality. † **2.** To mix or stir up (a liquid); hence occas. to render turbid, spoil; occas., to agitate, trouble; to disturb (joy, peace, beauty, weather) –1596. **3.** To mingle closely *with* 1591. **4.** To mix (components) so that their individuality is obscured in the product; now the most frequent *trans.* use 1601.

3. To b. realty with personalty 1788. **4.** Rider and horse,—friend, foe,—in one red burial blent BYRON.

II. *intr.* **1.** To mix, mingle; *esp.* so as to form a uniform mixture ME. **2.** To pass imperceptibly into each other, *esp.* in reference to colour 1822.

1. All motions, sounds, and voices..B. in a music of tranquillity WORDSW. Hence **Blend** *sb.* a blending. **Ble·nder,** one who or that which blends. **Ble·nding** *vbl. sb.* and *ppl. a.*

† **Blend(e.** Also **bland.** ME. Obs. pa. pple. of BLEND *v.*[2] As *adj.* = BLENDED –1679. *Comb.*: **blend corn, blencorn,** wheat and rye sown and grown together; **b.-water,** a urinary disease of cattle.

Blende (blend). 1683. [– G. *blende* (cf. *blendendes erz* 'deceptive ore'), f. *blenden* deceive (see BLEND *v.*[1]); so called because, while often resembling galena (hence its name *pseudogalena*), it yielded no lead.] *Min.* Sulphide of zinc. Hence **Ble·ndous, Ble·ndy** *adjs.* pertaining to or containing b.

Blenheim (ble·nėm, -im). Name of the Duke of Marlborough's house, near Woodstock; used in **a.** *Blenheims*, a breed of spaniels 1851; **b.** *B. Orange*, a golden-coloured apple 1879.

† **Blenk,** v. OE. **1.** = BLENCH *v.*[1] 1, 2, 4. –ME. **2.** To blanch. Cf. BLENCH *v.*[2] –1600. **3.** = BLINK 1, 3, 4. –1625.

† **Blenk,** *sb. north.* Earlier f. BLINK.

Blennioid (ble·niˌoid). 1865. [irreg. f. BLENNY + -OID.] **A.** *adj.* Allied to the BLENNY. **B.** *sb.* [sc. *fish.*]

Blenno-, blenn-, – Gr. βλέννος, βλέννα, mucus, comb, form.

Blennoge·nic, Blenno·genous *a.*, generating mucus. **Ble·nnoid** a. resembling mucus. **Blennorrha·gia. Blenno·rrhœa,** discharge of mucus; hence **-rrha·gic, -rrho·ic** *a.*

Blenny (ble·ni). 1774. [– L. *blennius*, var. of *blendius* (Pliny) – Gr. βλέννος slime, in ref. to the mucous coating of its scales.] A genus of small spiny-finned fishes, the scales of which are coated with mucus.

Blent, *ppl. a.* [f. BLEND *v.*[2]] Mingled.

Blepharo- (ble·făro) – Gr. βλέφαρον eyelid, comb. form.

Blephari·tis, inflamation of the eyelids, **Ble·pharoplast·ty,** the operation of supplying any deficiency caused by wound or lesion of the eyelid; hence **Ble·pharopla·stic** *a.* **Ble·pharospasm,** spasm of the orbicular muscle of the eyelids. **Ble·pharostat,** an instrument for fixing the eylid during operations.

Blere, obs. f. BLEAR.

‖ **Bles-bok** (ble·sbǫk). 1824. [S. Afr. Du., f. Du. *bles* BLAZE *sb.*[2] + *bok* goat.] A South African antelope, the *Gazella albifrons*.

Bless (bles), *v.*[1] [OE. *blētsian*, *blēdsian*, *blœ̄dsian*, f. *blōd* BLOOD. Not in other Gmc. langs. The orig. meaning was thus 'to mark or consecrate with blood'. (See *Exod.* 12:23.) But the word was chosen at the Eng. conversion to render L. *benedicere* 'to praise', which was itself used as tr. Heb., in the sense 'to bend the knee, worship'.

The pa. t. and pple. are usu. spelt *blessed*, though pronounced (blest), exc. occas. in verse, or liturgical reading. As an adj. *blest* is now archaic, but is frequent in verse, and traditional phrases.]

1. To consecrate by a spoken formula or charm, or, later, by a prayer. **2.** *spec.* To sanctify (and protect) by making the sign of the cross. esp. *refl.* and *absol.* To cross oneself (*arch.*) OE. † **3.** To guard, keep *from* (evil) –1650. Also †*refl.* **4.** To call holy; to adore (God) as holy OE. **5.** To pronounce words that confer divine favour OE.; to invoke blessings upon ME. **6.** To confer well-being upon; to make happy, to prosper; *orig.* said of God OE. **7.** *refl.* To account or call themselves supremely happy *with, in, that* 1611. ¶ In ME. *bless to*, app. after *benedicere alicui*. **8.** Exclamatory uses: **a.** in sense 3, as *God b. me!* ellipt. *b. me! b.* (also *save*) *the mark* (see MARK *sb.*[1]). **b.** in sense 7, as (*God*) *b. you!* 1588. ¶ **9.** In many senses *bless* is euphemistic or ironical for curse, etc. 1812.

1. Phr. *To b. food*, to ask God's blessing upon it (cf. 5). **2.** *Not to have a penny to b. oneself with*: in allusion to the cross on the silver penny (cf. Ger. *Kreutzer*), or to the practice of crossing the palm with a piece of silver. **3.** The bellmans drowsy charm To b. the doors from nightly harm MILT. *Pens.* 83. **4.** Then God be blesst, it is the blessed Sunne *Tam. Shr.* IV. v. 18. **5.** Then shal the Busshop blisse the children, thus saying *Bk. Com. Prayer.* The Fatherless..and the Stranger b. his unseen Hand in their prayers STEELE. **6.** It [mercy] is twice blest, It blesseth him that giues, and him that takes *Merch. V.* IV. i. 186. **7.** The nations shall blesse themselues in him *Jer.* 4:2. **8.** B. us! What a word on A title-page is this MILT. *Sonn.* xi. 5. *To b. oneself*: to ejaculate 'God b. me!', etc. Hence **Ble·sser.**

† **Bless,** *v.*² 1526. [– Fr. *blesser* injure, wound.] To wound; to thrash –1612.

Tarry, thou knave..I shall make these hands b. thee 1575.

† **Bless,** *v.*³ 1596. [Mainly Spenserian; perh. a use of prec.] To brandish; also to brandish round (an object *with* a weapon).

Blessed, blest (ble·sėd, blest), *ppl. a.* ME. [f. BLESS *v.*¹ See note under BLESS *v.*¹] **1.** Consecrated, holy. **2.** Adorable ME. **3.** Happy, fortunate ME.; beatified 1475. Also *absol.* The beatified saints ME. **4.** Pleasurable, blissful 1458. **b.** Of plants and herbs: Endowed with healing virtues, as *b. thistle, Carduus benedictus* 1563. **5.** = 'cursed' or the like (cf. BLESS *v.* 9) 1806. **6.** As quasi-*adv.* Blessedly 1600.

1. The B. Sacrament 1688. **2.** Oure blessyd lorde Iesu 1493. **3.** She desires no isles of the blest, no quiet seats of the just TENNYSON. **4. b.** The blest infusions That dwell in vegetives *Per.* III. ii. 35. Hence † **Ble·ssedful** *a.* full of blessing. † **Ble·ssedhede,** beatitude. **Ble·ssedly, ble·stly** *adv.* **Ble·ssedness,** the state of being blessed, *esp.* with divine favour, as in *single blessedness* (*Mids. N.* I. i. 78); hence used *joc.* for the unmarried state.

Blessing (ble·siŋ), *vbl. sb.* OE. [f. BLESS *v.*¹ + -ING¹.] † **1.** The action of the vb. (senses 1, 2) –1563. **2.** Authoritative declaration of divine favour; benediction; and hence **b.** Invocation of divine favour. OE. **3.** Favour and prospering influence of God. (So now 'to ask a b.') OE. **4.** Anything that makes happy or prosperous; a boon ME. † **b.** A present (tr. Heb.) –1611. **5.** Grateful adoration ME.

2. All the blessings Of a glad father, compasse thee about *Temp.* V. i. 179. **3.** With God's B. he will recover 1881. **4.** Eminence, Wealth, Soueraignty; which, to say sooth, are Blessings SHAKS. **b.** I pray thee, take a b. of thy seruant 2 *Kings* 5:15.

Blest, pa. t. and pple. of BLESS *v.*¹

Blet (blet), *v.* 1835. [– (by Lindley) Fr. *blettir*, f. *blet* soft, said of fruit.] *intr.* To become 'sleepy', as an over-ripe pear.

Blether, blather (ble·ðəɹ, blæ·-), *v. Sc.* and *n. dial.* [ME. *blather* – ON. *blaðra*, f. *blaðr* nonsense. *Blether* is the Sc. and north. form. The etymological form *blather* is usual in U.S.] **1.** *intr.* To talk nonsense loquaciously 1524; *trans.* to babble 1810. **2.** *intr.* To cry loudly (*dial.*) 1863. Hence **Ble·ther, bla·ther** *sb.* voluble nonsense.

Ble·therskate, bla·therskite. *dial.* and *U.S. colloq.* 1650. [f. BLETHER *v.* + SKATE *sb.*¹, in Sc. used contempt. Popularized in U.S. by the Sc. song *Maggie Lauder*, during the War of Independence.] A talker of blatant nonsense.

Jog on your gait, ye b. *Maggie Lauder* i.

Ble·tonism. 1812. [f. a Mr. *Bleton.*] The supposed 'faculty of perceiving subterraneous springs and currents by sensation'.

Blewits (blˈū·ˌits). 1830. [prob. f. BLUE.] An edible mushroom.

† **Bleymes.** 1725. [– Fr. *bleime*, f. *blêmir* in OFr. meaning 'wound', 'injure'; see BLEMISH.] An inflammation in the foot of a horse between the sole and the bone.

Blick (blik). 1881. [– G. *blick* sheen.] The brightening or iridescence appearing on silver or gold at the end of the cupelling or refining process (Raymond).

Blight (bləit), *sb.* 1611. [perh. for earlier **blēht*, repr. formally OE. *blǣċþu, blǣċþ|rust*, rel. to *blǣċe* (all applied to skin diseases); see BLEACH *sb.*¹] **1.** *gen.* Any atmospheric or invisible influence that suddenly blasts, nips, or destroys plants, or affects them with disease; a diseased state of plants so originating 1669. **2.** *spec.* **a.** Diseases in plants caused by fungoid parasites, as mildew, rust, or smut 1611. **b.** An aphis, destructive to fruit-trees 1802. **3.** *fig.* Anything which withers hopes or prospects, or checks prosperity 1852.

3. The withering b. of Turkish rule 1884.

Blight (bləit), *v.* 1695. [f. prec.] **1.** *trans.* To affect with blight. **2.** *fig.* To affect balefully, nip in the bud 1712.

2. Deprivation of rank..which blights so many prospects 1832. Hence **Bli·ghtingly** *adv.*

Blighter (bləi·təɹ). 1822. [f. prec. + -ER¹.] **1.** A thing that blights. **2.** A contemptible fellow; sometimes *joc.* 1896.

Blighty (bləi·ti). *Army slang.* 1915. [– Hind. *wilāyatī* foreign, pronounced *bilātī* in vulgar Urdu.] England, home; in the war of 1914–18, applied to a wound that secured return to England.

† **Blin,** *v.* [OE. *blinnan* = **bilinnan*, f. BE- *pref.*² 2 + *linnan* LIN *v.*] *intr. and trans.* To leave off, stop –1765.

Blind (bləind), *a.* [OE. *blind* = OFris., OS. *blind*, OHG. *blint* (G. *blind*), ON. *blindr*, Goth. *blinds* :– Gmc. **blindaz.*] **1.** Without the sense of sight. **b.** *absol.* A blind person, *esp.* as *pl.* The blind as a class OE. **c.** (*attrib.*) Of, pertaining to, or for the use of the blind as a class: as *b. asylum* (mod.). **2.** *fig.* and *transf.* Lacking in intellectual, moral, or spiritual perception OE. **3.** *fig.* Undiscriminating; inconsiderate, heedless, reckless ME. **b.** Purposeless 1873. **4.** *fig.* Acting without intelligence or consciousness 1692. **5.** *transf.* Dark, obscure (*arch.*) OE.; † having its light cut off –1705. **6.** Dim; indistinct ME.; of a letter, indistinctly or imperfectly addressed 1864. **7.** Out of sight, secret, obscure. With *b. alley* cf. 10. **b.** Of a way or path: Difficult to trace 1593. **8.** Covered from sight 1513. **9.** Having no openings for light or passage 1603. **10.** Closed at one end. So *b. alley*; cf. 7. 1668. **11.** Of plants: Without buds or eyes, or without a terminal flower 1884.

1. Galileo, frail and b. 1859. **b.** If the blinde lead the blinde, both shall fall into the ditch *Matt.* 15:14. **2.** Blynde jugement of men WYCLIF. *B. side*: the unguarded, also, formerly, the unpresentable side. **3.** B. prejudice HAZLITT, speed DICKENS, fury MACAULAY. **4.** B. chance BENTLEY. **5.** *B. lantern*: a dark lantern. **6.** *B. man, officer, reader*, a post-office official who deals with 'b. letters'. **7.** To..some b. change-house SCOTT. **b.** The b. mazes of this tangled wood MILT. *Comus* 181. **9.** A b. wall, hedge, window, door (*mod.*). Phr. *B. story*, one without point.

Comb.: **b. area** (*Archit.*), a clear space around the basement wall of a house; **b.-axle** = *dead-axle*; **-beetle**, a name for beetles which fly against people, esp. by night; also, a small beetle found in rice; **-blocking** (*Bookbinding*), impressions on book-covers produced by heated blocks, etc., without gold-leaf; **-coal**, non-bituminous coal which burns without flame; **-fish**, the *Amblyopsis spelæus*; **-gallery** (see sense 9); **-hazard, -hookey**, games at cards; **-level** (*Mining*), one notyet connected with other workings; **-shaft**, a winze; **-shell** (*Artillery*), one containing no powder, also one that fails to explode; **-spot**, the spot on the retina which is insensible to light; **-story** (*Archit.*), a triforium below the clerestory of a cathedral, admitting no light; **b. tooling** = *blind-blocking*. Hence **Bli·ndish** *a.* **Bli·ndling** *sb.* a b. person. **Bli·ndly** *adv.* in a b. way; without an opening. **Bli·ndness** (*lit.* and *fig.*).

Blind (bləind), *v.* [ME. *blind(e)*, f. prec., repl. †*blend* (which survived into XVI); see BLEND *v.*¹] **1.** To make blind; to render insensible to light or colour. Also *fig.* **2.** To hide; to make difficult to trace ME. **3.** To deprive (things) of light 1643. **b.** To eclipse 1633. **4.** *Gunnery.* To provide with blindages 1850. **5.** *intr.* To be or become blind or dim ME.

1. Blinded of one eye 1875. This great light blyndeth my sight PALSGR. *fig.* How jealousy blinds people SHERIDAN. **3. b.** Thy sweet eyes.. b. the stars. Hence **Bli·nded** *ppl. a.* (senses 1, 4); also, having the window-blinds drawn down. **Bli·nder,** he who or that which blinds; a blinker for a horse. (U.S.). **Bli·ndingly** *adv.*

Blind (bləind), *sb.* 1644. [f. BLIND *v.* or *a.*] **1.** Anything which obstructs the light or sight; *esp.* a screen for a window made of woven material mounted on a roller 1702. **2.** A blinker for a horse 1711. **3.** A blindage 1644. † **4.** Any means or place of concealment –1697. **5.** *fig.* A pretence, a pretext, to conceal one's real design 1664.

1. *Venetian blinds*: those made of light laths fixed on strips of webbing. **5.** Her constant care of me was only a b. STEELE. Hence **Bli·ndage,** a screen or the like used in fortification, sieges, etc.. to protect from the enemy's firing; a mantelet, **Bli·ndless** *a.*

Blindfold (bləi·ndfōᵘld), *v.* ME. [Superseded *blindfelle* (XIII–XVI), OE. *ġeblindfellian* strike blind, f. BLIND *a.* + FELL *v.*; superseded XVI by *blindfold.* The pa.t. and pa. pple. *blindfelled, -feld* was altered (XIV) to *blindfold* by assoc. w. FOLD *v.*¹] † **1.** To strike blind –1440. **2.** To cover the eyes, *esp.* with a bandage ME. **3.** *fig.* To darken the mind 1581.

Blindfold, *a.* 1450. [See prec.] **1.** Having the eyes bandaged so as to prevent vision 1483. **2.** *fig.* With the mind blinded; without forethought, reckless. Cf. BLIND *a.* 3. 1450.

2. The b. blows of ignorance DRYDEN. Hence **Bli·ndfold** *sb.* a bandage over the eyes (*lit.* and *fig.*). **Bli·ndfoldly** *adv.* (*rare*).

Blind gut. 1594. [See BLIND *a.* 10.] The *cæcum.*

† **Bli·nd-head.** 1662. A cover for a retort; a retort with such a cover –1743.

† **Blindman.** ME. Now written as two wds. *Much Ado* II. i. 205.

Blind-man's-buff (bləi:nd mænz bʊ·f). 1590. [Earlier *-man-*; see BUFF *sb.*¹] A game in which one player is blindfolded, and tries to catch and identify any one of the others, who, on their part, push him about. Also *fig.*

fig. Government by Blind-man's-buff CARLYLE.

Blind man's holiday. 1599. The time just before candles are lighted.

Bli·nd-nettle. OE. [f. BLIND *a.* 11, as wanting sting.] *Herb.* The Dead-nettle; also the Hemp-nettle and Hedge Nettle.

Blind-worm (bləi·nd,wɔ̄ɹm). 1450. [So called from the smallness of its eyes; cf. Du. *blindworm*, Da. *blindorm*, and G. *blindschleiche* (OHG. *blintslīhho*, OS. *blindeslīko*).] The Slow-worm (*Anguis fragilis*). Formerly used also of the Adder.

Blink (bliŋk), *v.* [Partly later form of synon. †*blenk* (XIV), var. of BLENCH *v.*¹; partly – (M)Du. *blinken* shine, glitter; cf. Da. *blinke*, Sw. *blinka* wink, twinkle.] † **1.** To deceive (*rare*). ME. only. † **2.** *intr.* = BLENCH *v.*¹ 2 (*rare*). ME. only. **3.** To twinkle with the eye or eyelids; to glance; to look with glances; to wink for an instant 1590. **4.** To cast a sudden or momentary gleam of light; to shine unsteadily or dimly 1786. **5.** To shut the eyes to; to shirk, pass by, ignore: *orig.* a sporting phrase 1742. **6.** To turn (milk, beer, etc.) slightly sour 1616. *intr.* 1648. ¶ **7.** To cause to blink. LANDOR. (Pseudo-arch.)

3. On him she..blinkit bonnilie 1729. A..setter ..blinking at the blaze 1863. **4.** Ev'ry star that blinks aboon BURNS. **5.** Dogs b. their coveys BYRON. Hence **Blinked** *ppl. a.* affected with a blink. **Bli·nking** *vbl. sb.*; *spec.* in *Brewing*: giving a sharp taste to beer by letting the wort stand; *ppl. a.*, winking, etc.; also (*slang*) used as a substitute for a strong expletive.

† **Blink,** *sb.*¹ ME. [f. BLINK *v.* 1.] **1.** A trick; = BLENCH *sb.* ME. only. **2.** *pl.* Boughs thrown to turn aside deer from their course; also feathers, etc., on a thread to scare birds –1625.

Blink (bliŋk), *sb.*² ME. [f. BLINK *v.* 3–4.] **1.** A momentary gleam of light; a slight flash; a twinkling gleam; also *poet.* glimmer 1717. Also *fig.* **2.** A (bright) glance; a glimpse. (Chiefly *Sc.*) 1594. **3.** *transf.* An instant, the twinkling of an eye; = Ger. *Augenblick.* (Chiefly *Sc.*) 1813. **4.** = ICE-BLINK: a shining whiteness about the horizon produced by reflection from distant masses of ice. Also, loosely, a large mass or field of ice. 1772.

1. Like blue-bottle flies in a b. of sunshine SCOTT. **3.** Bide a b. SCOTT. **4.** The b. from packs of ice, appears of a pure white 1818. Hence **Blinks** *sb. Herb.* Blinking Chickweed, *Montia fontana.*

Blink (bliŋk), *a.* 1590. [f. BLINK *v.*] **1.** Of the eyes: Habitually blinking. Hence **Blink-eyed** *a.* **2.** Of milk: Slightly sour 1883.

Blinkard (bli·ŋkărd). 1510. [f. BLINK *v.* + -ARD.] **1.** One who habitually blinks or winks. **2.** *fig.* One who lacks mental perception 1523. **3.** *attrib.*, or *adj.*, usu. *fig.* 1529.

Blinker (bli·ŋkəɹ). 1636. [f. as prec. + -ER¹.] **1.** One who blinks; a purblind person.

2. *pl.* Spectacles for directing the sight in one direction only, so as to cure squinting, or to protect the eyes; = GOGGLES 1732. **b.** Leather screens attached to a horse's bridle on each side to prevent his seeing in any direction except straight ahead 1789. **3.** The eye (*slang*) 1816.

2. Bigots who but one way see Through blinkers of authority 1732. Hence **Bli·nker** *v.* to put blinkers on; *fig.* to hoodwink.

Blirt (blɔ̄ɹt), *v. n. dial.* 1721. [Echoic, nearly identical with BLURT, with *bl-* as in *blow, blast, blash*, etc., and *-irt* as in *spirt, squirt*, etc., expressing the forcible emission of liquid.] To burst into tears; disfigure with tears. Hence **Blirt** *sb.* a gust of wind and rain. *Naut.*

Bliss (blis), *sb.* [OE. *bliss, bliþs* = OS. *blizza, blīdsea, blītzea* :- Gmc. **bliþsjō*, f. **blīþiz* BLITHE.] † **1.** Blitheness of aspect. (Only in OE.) **2.** Blitheness; gladness; enjoyment; *esp.* the beatitude of heaven. Hence, paradise. *concr.* A cause of delight. OE.

2. Blisse of þe bodi WYCLIF. O only blest, and Author of all b. DRUMM. OF HAWTH. Far other once beheld in b. MILT. *P.L.* i. 607. *concr.* Womman is mannes Ioye and al his blis CHAUCER.

Blissful (bli·sfŭl), *a.* ME. [f. BLISS *sb.* + -FUL.] **1.** Full of or fraught with bliss. † **2.** Beatified; sacred –1534. † **3.** Having power to bless 1598.

1. B. bride of a b. heir TENNYSON. The b. Seat MILT. Hence **Bli·ssful-ly** *adv.*, **-ness.**

Bli·ssom, *a.* 1668. [– ON. *blœsma*, in same sense.] Of a ewe: In heat.

Bli·ssom, *v.* ME. [f. as prec.] **1.** *trans.* Of a ram: To tup. In *pass.* said of the ewe. **2.** *intr.* To be lustful ME.

Blister (bli·stəɹ), *sb.* [ME. *blister, blester*, perh. – OFr. *blestre, blostre, bloustre* swelling, pimple, app. vars. of *bloste* clod of earth, pimple, tumour.] **1.** A thin vesicle on the skin, containing serum, caused by friction, a burn, a vesicatory, or the like. **2.** A swelling, containing fluid or air, on a plant, metal, a painted surface, etc. 1597. **3.** *Med.* Anything applied to raise a blister 1541.

Comb.: **b.-beetle, -fly,** an insect used for raising blisters, *spec.* the Spanish fly (*Cantharis vesicatoria*); **-copper,** copper having a blistered surface, obtained during smelting; **-plant,** a name for *Ranunculus acris, R. sceleratus*, etc.; **-steel,** steel having a blistered surface, obtained during the process of converting iron into shear-steel, etc. Hence **Bli·stery** *a.*

Blister (bli·stəɹ), *v.* 1496. [f. prec.] **1.** *trans.* To raise blisters on. Also *fig.* and *transf.* Also *absol.* 1541. **2.** *intr.* To be or become covered with blisters 1496.

1. Bled, cupped, or blistered SCOTT. *fig.* This tyrant whose sole name blisters our tongue *Macb.* IV. iii. 12.

Blite (bləit). ME. [– L. *blitum* – Gr. βλίτον.] *Herb.* Name for plants of the N.O. *Chenopodiaceæ*: esp. Wild Spinach (*C. bonus-henricus*), *Amaranthus blitum*, species of *Atriplex*, and the genus *Blitum* (STRAWBERRY *blite*). Formerly also for Garden Spinach.

Blithe (bləið), *a.* (*sb.* and *adv.*) [OE. *bliþe* = OFris. *blī(d-)*, OS. *blīði* (Du. *blijde, blij*), OHG. *blīdi* cheerful, friendly, ON. *blīðr*, Goth. *bleiþs* :- Gmc. **blīþiz*, the orig. sense of which, 'mild, gentle, merciful', is shown in ON. and Goth.; of unkn. origin. Cf. BLISS.] **A.** *adj.* † **1.** Exhibiting kindly feeling to others –1570. **2.** Jocund, gay, sprightly, merry. (Now mostly of things.) OE. **3.** Of men; Joyous, cheerful; glad, happy, well-pleased. Since 16th c. chiefly *poet.* OE.

2. Buxom, b., and debonair MILT. *Allegro* 24. B. sounds of festal music 1855. **3.** Bardolph, be blythe SHAKS. **Bli·the-ly** *adv.*, **-ness. Bli·thesome** *a.*

B. *sb.* † **1.** A blithe one; cf. *fair*. 1548. † **2.** Compassion, good-will; mirth, delight –1585. Hence **Bli·theful** *a.* **Bli·thefully** *adv.*

C. *adv.* † **a.** Benignantly. **b.** Blithely. OE.

Blithering (bli·ðəriŋ), *ppl. a. colloq.* 1889. [f. *blither*, var. BLETHER.] Senselessly talkative; as an intensive, 'consummate', and hence, contemptible.

Blizzard (bli·zăɹd). orig. *U.S.* 1829. [Of unkn. origin.] **1.** A sharp blow or knock; a shot. Also *fig.* **2.** A furious blast of frost-wind and blinding snow 1870.

2. Those fearful blasts known as 'blizzards' which send the..dry snow whirling in icy clouds 1881.

† **Bloat** (blōᵘt), *a.*[1] [ME. *blote*, perh. = ON. *blautr* 'soaked, wet'; or from a parallel form **blót*. With sense 2 cf. ON. *blautr fiskr*. i.e. 'soft fish'.] † **1.** ? Soft with moisture. ME. only. **2.** *B. herring*: a bloater: see BLOAT *v.*[1] –1661.

Bloat (blōᵘt), *a.*[2] [ME. *blout* (XIII), *blowt* = ON. *blautr* soft. See also BLOAT *a.*[1]] † **1.** *Blowte, bloute*: ? Soft, flabby; puffy –1603. **2.** *Bloat*: Puffed, swollen, *esp.* with self-indulgence. (In mod. writers an echo of Shaks.: see quot.) 1638.

1. Let the blowt king tempt you againe to bed *Haml.* III. iv. 182. [So all the Quartos, exc. Qo. 1.]

Bloat, *v.*[1] 1611. [app. f. BLOAT *a.*[1]] *trans.* To cure (herrings) by a process which leaves them soft and only half-dried. (*Bloated* herrings are opposed to *dried* or *red* herrings.) Hence **Bloa·ted** *ppl. a.*[1] half-dried in smoke.

Bloat, *v.*[2] 1677. [app. f. BLOAT *a.*[2]] **1.** To blow out, swell, make turgid. Also *absol.* **2.** *intr.* To swell 1735.

Bloa·ted, *ppl. a.*[2] 1664. [f. prec. + -ED[1].] **1.** Swollen, puffed up, *esp.* with self-indulgence; of things, overgrown, of excessive size. **2.** Swollen with pride; puffed up, pampered 1731.

1. B. wassailers KEATS, armaments DISRAELI. **2.** A b. aristocracy 1868. Hence **Bloa·tedness.**

Bloa·ter. 1832. [f. BLOAT *a.*[1], after *deader*, etc.; see -ER[1] 1.] A bloat or bloated herring.

Blob (blǫb), *sb.* 1536. [Like the earlier *bluber, blober*, BLUBBER, and the later synon. BLEB (XVII), containing the symbolical consonent-combination *bl—b*; cf. BUBBLE.] **1.** A bubble. Now *n. dial.* **2.** A pimple. *n. dial.* 1597. **3.** A globule of liquid or viscid substance 1725. **4.** A small rounded mass of colour 1863.

3. A honey b. [yellow gooseberry] GALT. A b. of ink 1857, jelly 1866. Hence **Blo·bby** *a.*

Blobber (blǫ·bəɹ), *a.* 1593. [Later var. of BLABBER, perh. infl. by BLOB.] Of the lips: Thick, swollen, protruding. Hence **b.-lipped** *a.*

Hanging b. lips but pout for Kisses DRYDEN.

Blobber, obs. and dial. f. BLUBBER *sb.* and *v.*

Block (blǫk), *sb.* [ME. – (O)Fr. *bloc* – (M)Du. *blok*, (M)LG. *block* (whence G. *block*; cf. southern G. *bloch* :- OHG. *bloh*); of unkn. origin.] **1.** A log of wood; part of the trunk of a tree. Often used in similes as a type of inertia or stupidity. **2.** A large solid piece of wood: **a.** One of which the top or surface is used for various operations: *e.g.* for chopping on, *esp.* by butchers; for beetling or hammering on; for mounting, or dismounting from, a horse, etc. 1485. **b.** The piece of wood on which the condemned were beheaded 1541. **c.** A falcon's perch 1844. **3.** A piece of wood or other substance on which something is moulded or shaped: *spec.* **a.** A mould for a hat 1575. Hence **b.** *fig.* Shape, fashion (of hat) 1580. **4.** *Mech.* A pulley or system of pulleys mounted in a case; used to increase the mechanical power of the ropes running through them; employed esp. for the rigging of ships, and in lifting great weights 1622. **5.** A piece of wood which acts as a support 1801. **6.** A piece of wood on which lines, letters, or figures are engraved, in order to be printed from it, or to be stamped by pressure 1732. **7.** *gen.* Any solid mass of matter with an extended surface 1530. **b.** A large quantity of anything dealt with at once. Hence *In b.*: wholesale; = Fr. *en bloc*. 1876. **8.** A lump of wood, stone, etc., that bars one's way; *fig.* an obstacle. Now only in *stumbling-b.* 1500. **9.** *spec.* A mass of rock or stone in its unhewn state 1847. **b.** A piece prepared for building purposes; also, the bricks which children build with 1854. **10.** A compact mass of buildings, with no intervening spaces; (*esp.* in U.S. and Canada) the quadrangular mass of buildings included between four streets, etc. **b.** A space of ground bounded by four streets. 1851. **11.** *fig.* A blockhead; a hard-hearted person 1553. **12.** (from BLOCK *v.*) A blocking up, *e.g.* of traffic or progress 1864. **13.** *Cricket.* The position in which a batsman blocks balls; the *centre* of the wicket; hence *b.-hole* (or *b.*) a mark made in the ground to indicate the *centre* 1845. **14.** *attrib.* or *adj.* Taken in the block 1864.

1. Sitting patient on a big b.—huge stump of a tree-root FROUDE. **2.** He laid down his head upon the b. CLARENDON. **3.** We have blockes for all heads DEKKER. *Barber's b.*: a wooden head for a wig. **7.** A b. of tin 1758, of masonry 1813, of ice TYNDALL. **b.** Large blocks of the Stock for future delivery 1876. **9.** *Erratic b.*: a boulder transported by physical agencies far from its native site. **10.** American towns are built in blocks FREEMAN. **11.** You Blockes, you stones, you worse than senslesse things *Jul. C.* I. i. 40. *A chip of the* (*same* or) *old b.*: a piece of the same stuff; a descendant taking after a parent or ancestor. *As deaf* (etc.) *as a b.*: see 1. *To cut blocks with a razor*: (any incongruous application of abilities or means). **12. B. system** (on *Railways*): a system in which the line is divided into sections, with signals, so worked that no train is allowed to pass into any section till it is wholly clear.

Comb.: **b.-battery,** in gunnery, a wooden battery for two or more small pieces mounted on wheels; **-furnace,** a bloomery (BLOOM *sb.*[2]); **-letters,** printing-types cut out of wooden blocks; **-printing,** printing from wooden blocks, as in the BLOCK-BOOKS, now also used for printing calico, etc.; so **-printed** *a.*; **-ship,** a ship moored to block the entrance to a harbour; **-tin,** see TIN.

Hence **Blo·ckage,** a blocked (up) state. **Blo·ckish** *a.* of the nature of a b.; obtuse; roughly blocked out, rude. **Blo·ckish-ly** *adv.*, **-ness.**

Block (blǫk), *v.* 1570. [f. prec., or – Fr. *bloquer*, f. *bloc* BLOCK *sb.*] **1.** *trans.* To obstruct or close with obstacles (a passage). Also *fig.* 1645. **2.** To shut *up* or *in* by obstructing ingress or egress 1630. **3.** *spec.* To blockade (usu. with *up*) 1591. **4.** To obstruct the course of 1865. **5.** *Cricket.* To stop (a ball) with the bat; also *absol.* 1773. **6.** *Parliament.* To prevent or postpone the passage of a bill; *spec.* to give notice of opposition to a bill, so that it cannot be taken after half-past twelve (midnight) 1884. **7.** *trans.* To shape on, or stamp with, a block 1622. **8.** To mark out roughly; to plan. Now usu. with *out*; also *in.* 1585. **9.** To cut *out* into blocks, *e.g.* coal 1863. **10.** To support or fit with blocks of wood 1881.

2. Our little harbor was..blocked in by heavy masses [of ice] KANE. **6.** The term 'blocking' is a colloquial expression recognized in this House 1884. **8.** Pictures blocked in roughly 1884.

Blockade (blǫkēⁱ·d). 1693. [f. BLOCK *v.* + -ADE, prob. after *ambuscade*; contemp. with G. *blockade*.] **1.** The shutting up of a place, blocking of a harbour, line of coast, frontier, etc., by hostile forces or ships, so as to stop ingress and egress 1693. **2.** *transf.* A party of blockade-men. **3.** *fig.* 1742.

1. *Paper b.*: one declared by a belligerent to exist, but not effective. *To raise a b.*: to withdraw the investing forces, or compel them to withdraw. *To break a b.*: to enter a blockaded port by force. *To run a b.*: to enter or leave a blockaded port by eluding the blockading force.

Comb.: **b.-man,** a coastguardsman; **-runner,** a vessel which attempts to run into a blockaded port; the owner, master, or one of the crew of such a vessel.

Blocka·de, *v.* 1680. [f. prec. sb.] **1.** *trans.* To subject to a blockade as an incident of war. **2.** *transf.* and *fig.* To obstruct 1732.

2. Huge bales of British cloth b. the door POPE. Hence **Blocka·der,** one who blockades; a blockading vessel.

Blo·ck-book. 1727. † **a.** A book of wooden tablets. **b.** A book printed from engraved wooden blocks.

Blo·cker. 1609. [f. BLOCK *v.*] One who blocks; *spec.* in *Shoemaking* and *Bookbinding*.

Blockhead (blǫ·khed). 1549. [f. BLOCK *sb.* + HEAD *sb.*] † **1.** A wooden head, a wooden block for hats or wigs –1698. **2.** Hence, an utterly stupid fellow 1549. † **3.** as *adj.* Block-headed, stupid –1719.

2. Block-heads and dull-pated Asses 1668. Hence **Blo·ckhea:ded** *a.* stupid, obtuse. **Blo·ckhea:dedness. Blo·ckhea:dish** *a.* **Blo·ckheadism.** † **Blo·ckheadly** *a.*

Blockhouse (blǫ·khaus). [– (M)Du. *blokhuis*, whence Fr. †*blocquehuys* (mod. *blocus*).] **a.** *orig.* A detached fort blocking a strategical point. **b.** Later: An edifice constructed chiefly of timber, loopholed and embrasured for firing. 1512. **c.** *slang.* A prison 1624. **d.** A house of squared logs of timber 1857. Also *transf.* and *fig.*

a. The b. of Tilberie GERARD. **d.** The Backwoodsman who begins by building a b. 1878.

Blo·cking, *vbl. sb.* 1585. [f. BLOCK *v.* + -ING[1].] **1.** The action of the vb. BLOCK 1637. **2.** The product of this action 1585. **3.** *Carpentry.* See BLOCK *v.* 10. 1823.

Blocking course (or **blocking**): the plain course of stone which surmounts the cornice at the top of a Greek or Roman building; also a projecting course of stone or brick at the base of a building.

† **Blo·ckwood.** 1581. = LOGWOOD 2. –1667.

Bloke (blō^{u}k), *sb. slang.* 1851. [Shelta.] Fellow.

† **Blok(e, bloc,** *a.* [The normal Eng. repr. of OE. *blāc* shining :– Gmc. **blaikaz*; see BLEAK *a.*] Pale; also black, dark. ME. only.

† **Blo·man.** ME. only. [f. *blo* adj. blackish-blue + MAN.] A black man, Negro.

Blond, blonde (blǫnd). 1481. [–(O)Fr. *blond*, fem. *blonde* :– med. L. *blundus, blondus* yellow, perh. of Gmc. origin. Revived as Fr. XVII; whence the final *e* when applied to a woman.] **A.** *adj.* Prop. (of the hair): Light auburn; *loosely*, light-coloured, fair. **b.** *Blond(e lace*: see B 2. 1771. **B.** *sb.* **1.** A person with blond hair; one with 'fair' hair and complexion; *esp.* a woman, in which case spelt *blonde* 1822. **2.** (More fully *blonde lace*): A silk lace of two threads, twisted and formed in hexagonal meshes; orig. of unbleached silk, but now white or black. Usu. written *blonde*, as in Fr. (sc. *dentelle*). 1755. Also *attrib.*

Comb. **b.-metal,** a clay ironstone of the coal measures. Hence **Blo·ndness.**

Blood (blɒd), *sb.* [OE. *blōd* = OFris., OS. *blōd* (Du. *bloed*), OHG. *bluot* (G. *blut*), ON. *blóð*, Goth. *blōþ* (Crim.-Goth. *plut*) :– Gmc. **blōðam*, of unkn. origin.] **I. 1.** The red liquid circulating in the arteries and veins of man and the higher animals; extended, later, to the corresponding liquid, coloured or colourless, in animals of lower organization. **2.** *fig.* and *transf.* Applied to liquids or juices in some way resembling it; e.g. to a blood-like juice; to the sap of plants, etc. ME. **3.** Blood shed; hence, bloodshed; manslaughter, murder, death OE. **b.** The guilt of bloodshed OE.

1. *Flesh and b.*: = 'humanity', as opp. to 'deity or disembodied spirit'. See FLESH. † *To let b.* (in Surg.): to bleed; also *transf.* to shed the b. of. † *God's b.!* † *Christ's b.!* †*'S blood!* † *Blood!*: forcible ejaculations not now in use. **2.** Go, sucke the subtle b. o' th' Grape *Timon* IV. iii. 432. **3.** An Affront that nothing but B. can expiate ADDISON. **b.** His b. be on vs, and on our children *Matt.* 27:25.

II. † **1.** The vital fluid; *hence*, the vital principle; life –1740. **2.** The supposed seat of emotion, passion; whence, Passion, temper mood, disposition; *emphatically*, mettle, anger ME. **3.** The supposed seat of animal appetite; hence, the fleshly nature of man 1597.

2. When you perceiue his b. enclin'd to mirth 2 *Hen. IV*, IV. iv. 38. Phr. *To breed bad* (or *ill*) *b. In cold b.*: not in the heat of passion. **3.** The strongest oathes, are straw To th'fire ith' b. *Temp.* IV. i. 53. *In b.*: full of life; *out of b.*: not vigorous. (Hunting phrases.)

III. 1. The typical part of the body which children inherit from their parents and ancestors ME. **2.** Hence, Blood-relationship, and *esp.* parentage, lineage, descent; also: Family, kin, race, stock, nationality ME. **3.** *concr.* Persons of any specified blood or family collectively; blood-relations, kindred, family, race ME. **4.** *esp.* Offspring, child, near relative, one dear as one's own offspring ME. **5.** Blood worth mention, good blood; good parentage or stock. Cf. BIRTH (*sb.*[1]) ME. Also *attrib.*

1. *Blue blood*: tr. Sp. *sangre azul* claimed by certain families of Castile, as being uncontaminated by Moorish, Jewish, or other admixture; prob. founded on the blueness of the veins of people of fair complexion. *Fresh b.*: a new strain or stock not related by b. to the family; also *fig.* [God] hath made of one b. all nations of men *Acts* 17:26. **2.** *B. royal* or *the b.*: royal race or family. *Whole b.*: race by both father and mother, as opp. to *half-b.*, by one parent only. Hence concr. *half-b.*: one whose b. is half of one race and half of another. B. is thicker than water *Provb.* **3.** By that one Deed Enobles all his B. DRYDEN. *To run in the* († *a*) *b.*: *i.e.* in a family or race. **4.** (*Own*) *flesh and b.*: near kindred. See FLESH. **5.** The highest pride of b. MACAULAY. In horses. . there is nothing like b. 1846. *To restore in* or *to b.*: to re-admit to forfeited privileges of birth and rank those under sentence of 'corruption of b.'; see ATTAINDER.

IV. † **1.** A living being –ME. **2.** 'A hot spark' (J.); a 'fast' or foppish man. *arch.* 1562. **b.** *Univ.* and *Public School slang.* One of those who are held to set the fashion in dress and manners.

2. A. .celebrated 'b.' or dandy about town THACKERAY. *Young b.*; now, a youthful member of a party, who brings to it youthful vigour.

† **V.** A disease in sheep and in swine –1787.

Comb.: **b.-baptism,** the martyrdom of early Christians who had not been baptized; **-bath,** a bath in warm b.: also, a massacre; † **-boltered** *ppl. a.*, clotted with b.; *esp.* having the hair matted with b.; [see BALTER]; **-fine,** one paid as whole or part compensation for murder; **-flower,** genus *Hæmanthus*; † **-hunter,** one who tracks murderers; **-pudding,** a black pudding; **-ripe** *a.*, (of fruit) so ripe that the juice has become b.-coloured, hence **-ripeness**; **-sausage,** a black pudding; **-tree** (Bot.), *Croton gossypiifolium*; **-vein,** a moth (*Bradyepetes amataria*); **-wood,** name of several trees, *e.g.* in Jamaica *Gordonia hæmatoxylon*, in Australia various species of *Eucalyptus*, etc.

Hence † **Bloo·ding** *sb.* a black pudding. **Bloo·dless** *a.* without b., *hence* lifeless; pallid from want of b.; unattended by bloodshed. **Bloodless-ly** *adv.*, **-ness. Bloo·d-like** *a.* like b.; like a blood (horse).

Blood (blɒd), *v.* 1593. [f. prec.] **1.** *trans.* To cause blood to flow from; *esp.* in *Surg.* to BLEED 1633. **2.** To wet or smear with blood. ? *Obs.* 1593. **3.** *Venery.* To give a hound its first taste, or sight and smell of the blood of the game it is to hunt. Also *fig.* 1781. † **4.** To raise the blood of, *i.e.* to exasperate; esp. soldiers at the beginning of a fight –1677.

1. They had scruples about eating an animal not blooded in their own way LIVINGSTONE. **2.** To b. the points of spears DRYDEN. **3.** Blooded to fox BECKFORD.

Blooded (blɒ·dėd), *a.* ME. [f. BLOOD *v.* or *sb.* + -ED.] † **1.** Stained with blood –1637. **2.** Having (*hot, cold,* etc.) blood 1805. **3.** Of horses: Of good breed 1858.

Bloo·d-guilty, *a.* 1597. [f. BLOOD + GUILTY.] Responsible for bloodshed. Hence **Blood-gui·ltiness.** So **Blood-gui·ltless** *a.*

Bloo·d-hea:t. 1812. The ordinary heat of blood in the healthy human body, viz. 98·6° Fahr. Also *fig.*

Bloo·dhound. ME. A large, very keen-scented dog (*Canis sanguinarius*), formerly much used in tracking large game, stolen cattle, and fugitives. Also *fig.* of men. Also *attrib.*

Bloo·d-le·tter. [OE. *blōd lǣtere.*] He who or that which lets blood. So **Bloo·d-letting,** phlebotomy; also *fig.*

Bloo·d-mo:ney. 1535. **a.** A reward for bringing about the death of another; *e.g.* money paid to a witness who gives evidence leading to conviction on a capital charge. **b.** Money paid the next of kin as compensation for the slaughter of a relative.

Blood-red, Bloo·d-re:d, *a.* ME. Red like blood.

Bloo·d-rela·tion. 1846. [See RELATION.] A person related by birth; a kinsman. var. **Bloo·d-re·lative.** HAWTHORNE.

Bloo·d-root. 1578. Pop. name of plants: *esp.* the Tormentil; Crimson Crane's Bill, and Red Puccoon (*Sanguinaria canadensis*) of N. America.

Bloodshed (blɒ·dˌʃed), *sb.* (*a.*) 1500. [f. the phr. *to shed blood.* Superseded *blood-shedding* (XIII).] **1.** The shedding of blood; slaughter 1536. † **2.** An act of blood-shedding. (With *pl.*) –1677. **3.** The shedding or parting with one's own blood; *orig.* said of the death of Christ. ? *Obs.* 1500. † **4.** = BLOOD-SHOT *sb.* and *adj.* –1702.

1. The long b. of the Civil Wars J. R. GREEN. Hence **Bloo·dshe:dder.**

Bloodshot (blɒ·dˌʃǫt). 1607. [For earlier † BLOOD-SHOTTEN. See SHOOT *v.*] **A.** *adj.* Of the eye: Over-shot or suffused with blood 1618. Also *fig.* and *transf.* 1851. † **B.** *sb.* [The adj. used *absol.*] **1.** An effusion of blood, caused by inflammation of the conjunctiva –1671. **2.** Any effusion of blood 1611.

† **Blood-shot** (blɒ·dʃǫt), *v.* 1578. [f. BLOODSHOT *a.*] To make bloodshot –1643.

Bloo·d-sho:tten, *a.* (*sb.*) *arch.* 1507. [Instrumental comb. f. *shotten* pa. pple. of SHOOT *v.*] **A.** *adj.* Earlier f. BLOODSHOT: now *arch.* † **B.** *sb.* = BLOOD-SHOT *sb.* 1578.

Blood-spavin; see SPAVIN.

Bloo·d-stain, *sb.* 1838. [f. BLOOD + STAIN *sb.*] A stain made by blood. So **Bloo·d-stained** *a.* stained with blood (*lit.* and *fig.*).

Blood-stone (blɒ·dstō^{u}n). 1551. **1.** A name given to certain precious stones spotted or streaked with red; esp. a green jasper or quartz with small spots of red jasper; also the *heliotrope* of Pliny. **2.** Hematite. (Dicts.)

1. The bloodstone stoppeth blood 1551.

Bloo·d-strange. 1578. [Origin unkn.] *Herb.* An obs. name of the Mousetail (*Myosurus minimus*).

† **Bloo·d-suck,** *v.* 1541. [f. BLOOD + SUCK, perh. back-formation f. next.] *trans.* To suck blood from; said of leeches. Also *fig.* –1592.

Blood-sucker (blɒ·dsɒ:kəɹ). ME. [f. BLOOD + SUCKER.] **1.** An animal which sucks blood; *esp.* the leech. † **2.** One who draws or sheds the blood of another –1659. **3.** *fig.* An extortioner; a sponger 1668.

3. While there is a silver sixpence left, these bloodsuckers will never be quiet SWIFT.

Bloodthirsty (blɒ·dþɔ̄:ɹsti), *a.* 1535. [Coverdale, after Luther's *blutdürstig.*] Thirsting for blood; eager for bloodshed.

Blood-vessel (blɒ·dve:sĕl). 1694. One of the tubes (veins or arteries) which convey the blood throughout the animal system.

Bloo·d-warm, *a.* 1577. As warm as blood; see BLOOD-HEAT. Also *fig.*

Blood-wite (blɒ·dwəit). Also (erron.) **-wit.** [OE. *blōdwīte*, f. *blōd* blood + *wīte* punishment. See WITE, WYTE.] A penalty for bloodshed: **a.** in *OE. Law*, A fine to be paid to the alderman or king, in addition to the *were-gild* ME. **b.** *gen.* A penalty for murder 1881.

Blood-worm (blɒ·dwɒ̆ɹm). 1741. **a.** A small bright-red earthworm used by anglers. **b.** The scarlet larva of a genus of crane-flies (*Chironomus*) found in rain-water cisterns, etc.

Blood-wort (blɒ·dwɒɹt). ME. [WORT[1].] A name of plants having red roots or leaves, or supposed to stanch or to draw blood; *e.g.* the Bloody Dock (*Rumex sanguineus*), the Dwarf Elder (*Sambucus ebulus*); also Burnet (*Sanguisorba officinalis*), and genus *Hæmodorum.*

Bloody (blɒ·di). [OE. *blōdiġ* = OFris. *blōdich*, etc.; see BLOOD *sb.*, -Y[1].] **A.** *adj.* **1.** Of the nature of, composed of, resembling, or pertaining to blood. **2.** Covered, smeared, stained, with blood; bleeding OE. **3.** Of animals: Having blood in the veins ME. **4.** Accompanied by or involving bloodshed; sanguinary ME. **5.** Of thoughts, words, etc.: Concerned with, portending, decreeing, bloodshed ME. **6.** Bloodthirsty; blood-guilty 1563. **7.** Blood-red 1591. **8.** In low Eng., an epithet expressing detestation; often merely intens., *esp.* with a neg., as 'not a b. *one*'. [Prob. from the advb. use.] 1840.

1. In great agony he swet blody droppes 1526. **2.** Dirty b. spots HY. MORE. *B. grave*; the grave of one who has been murdered. † *B. hand* in *Forest-law*: one kind of trespass in the King's forest, in which a man is found there in any way imbrued with blood; cf. RED-HAND(ED); in *Her.*, the armorial device of Ulster, borne by baronets. **4.** A b. deed *Macb.* II. iv. 23, battle ADDISON. **5.** I do begin to haue b. thoughts *Temp.* IV. i. 220. **6.** B. Queen Mary DICKENS. Hence **Bloo·dily** *adv.* **Bloo·diness.**

B. *adv.* † **1.** Bloodily ME. **2.** As an intensive: Very. . . and no mistake; abominably, desperately. Colloq. to c 1750; now low Eng. [Probably f. *blood, 'sblood* (see BLOOD *sb.* I. 1) + -Y[1]; cf. WOUNDY *adv.*, f. WOUNDS.]

2. The doughty Bullies enter b. drunk DRYDEN. This is a b. positive old fellow FIELDING.

Comb.: **a.** † **b. flux** (formerly *flix*), dysentery; **b. nose beetle,** *Timarcha*; † **b.-water,** *hæmaturia.* **b.** In names of plants, as **b. finger,** the Foxglove; **b. man's finger,** the same; also the Arum or Wake-Robin; **b. dock** (*Rumex sanguineus*); **b. twig,** the Dogwood (*Cornus sanguinea*).

Bloody (blɒ·di), *v.* 1530. [f. the adj.] *trans.* To make BLOODY; also *fig.*

Bloody-bones (blɒ·diˌbō^u:nz). Formerly **-bone.** 1550. Usu. in *Rawhead and Bloody-bone(s*, as the name of a bugbear to terrify children; also *fig.* 'bugbear, terror'.

Bloom (blūm), *sb.*¹ [ME. *blom, blome* – ON. *blóm* flower, blossom, and *blómi* prosperity, pl. flowers, corresp. to OS. *blōmo*, MDu. *bloeme* (Du. *bloem*), OHG. *bluomo, -ma* (G. *blume*), Goth. *blōma* :– Gmc. *blōmon, -ōn, f. *blō- BLOW *v.*² For the OE. synonym, see BLOSSOM.] **1.** The blossom or flower of a plant. (Expressing florescence as the culminating beauty of the plant.) **b.** *collect.* Blossom, flowers ME. Also *transf.* of persons (cf. 'flower'). **2.** *fig.* Prime, perfection ME. **3.** The crimson tint of the cheek; flush, glow. Also *fig.* 1752. **4.** The delicate powdery deposit on fruits like the grape, plum, etc., when fresh-gathered, and on certain plant-leaves. (? from prec.) 1639. **b.** *fig.* Freshness, delicate beauty 1777. **c.** In various special senses: *e.g.* the yellowish deposit on well-tanned leather, the powdery appearance on newly struck coins, etc. 1825. **5.** A fine variety of raisin 1841.

1. The fruytes of the holy goost..be more lyke.. to be called blomes and floures than fruytes 1526. Sight of vernal b. MILT. *P.L.* III. 43. *In b.*: in flower, flowering. **b.** He was Engelondes blome ME. **2.** His Maie of youth, and bloome of lustihood *Much Ado* V. i. 76. **3.** Miss Bath had.. recovered..her b. FIELDING. **4. b.** *To take the b. off*: to deprive (a thing) of its first freshness or beauty. Hence **Bloo·mless** *a.* **Bloo·my** *a.*

Bloom (blūm), *sb.*² [OE. *blōma*, identical in form w. prec., but prob. a different word.] **1.** A mass of iron after having undergone the first hammering. *spec.* An ingot of iron or steel, or a pile of puddled bars, brought into the form of a thick bar, and left for further rolling when required for use 1674. ¶ **2.** Improp. The ball or mass of iron from the puddling furnace 1865. Hence **Bloo·mery, -ary,** the first forge in an iron-works through which the metal passes after melting, and in which it is made into blooms.

Bloom (blūm), *v.*¹ [ME. *blomen*, f. BLOOM *sb.*¹] **1.** *intr.* To bear flowers; to blossom. **2.** *fig.* and *transf.* To come into, or be in, full beauty or vigour; to flourish ME. **3.** *trans.* To bring into bloom; to cause to flourish. Chiefly *fig.* (*arch.*) 1592. **4.** *intr.* To glow 1860. **5.** *trans.* To give a BLOOM to 1821. **6.** *techn.* To cloud a varnished surface 1859.

2. The daughter begins to b. before the mother can be content to fade JOHNSON. **3.** The Tree of Life..blooming Ambrosial Fruit MILT. *P.L.* IV. 219.

Bloom, *v.*² 1875. [f. BLOOM *sb.*²] To hammer or squeeze the ball or mass of iron from the puddling-furnace into a bloom; to shingle.

Bloomed (blūmd, *poet.* -ėd), (*ppl.*) *a.* 1505. [f. BLOOM *sb.* and *v.*] In bloom. Also *fig.*

Bloomer¹ (blū·məɹ). 1730. [f. BLOOM *v.*¹] **1.** A plant that blooms (in some way). **2.** A floriated letter 1899. **3.** [= *blooming* error.] A bad mistake (*slang*) 1889.

Comb. **b.-pit,** a tan-pit in which hides are treated with a strong infusion of tanning liquor.

Bloo·mer². *Hist.* 1868. [f. Mrs. Amelia Jenks *Bloomer* (1818-94) of N.Y.] More fully *B. costume, dress*: A style of female dress consisting of a short skirt and long loose trousers gathered closely round the ankles. **b.** Loose trousers or knickerbockers worn by women cyclists, etc.; 'rational dress' 1869. Hence **Bloo·merism,** the principles of Mrs. Bloomer as to female dress.

Bloo·ming, *ppl. a.* ME. [f. BLOOM *v.*¹ + -ING².] With sense 2 cf. ON. *blómandi* blooming, flourishing.] **1.** That blooms 1664. **2.** *fig.* In the bloom of health, beauty, youth; flourishing ME. **b.** Bright, shining 1513. ¶ **3.** *slang.* Full-blown; often = BLOODY (sense 8) or the like. Cf. BLESSED (5). 1882.

2. His b. bride 1774. **b.** Her b. mantle torn TENNYSON. **3.** Oh, you b. idiot 1882. Hence **Bloo·mingly** *adv.*

Blooth, var. of BLOWTH, bloom.

Blore (blōᵊɹ), *sb. arch.* 1440. [app. conn. w. *blow, blast*; perh. partly echoic (an 'expressive word', J.).] **a.** A violent blowing; also *fig.* **b.** *transf.* The air. CHAPMAN.

Blore, *v.* Now *dial.* 1440. Var. of BLARE, q.v.

Blossom (blǫ·səm), *sb.* [OE. *blōstm, blōs(t)ma*, corresp. to WFris. *blossum*, (M)Du. *bloesem*, MLG. *blōs(s)em*; cf. ON. *blómstr*; gen. referred to the same base as BLOOM *sb.*¹] **1.** 'The flower that grows on any plant, previous to the seed or fruit'. (J.) Orig. the generic wd. for 'flower'. See BLOOM, FLOWER. **a.** A single flower (with *pl.*) OE. **b.** *collect.* The mass of flowers on a fruit-tree, etc. ME. Also *fig.* (by *simile.*) 1789. **2.** *fig.* Anything compared to the preceding ME. **3.** *techn.* **a.** *Mining.* The decomposed outcrop of a vein or a coal-bed. **b.** The colour of a horse whose hairs are white mixed with sorrel or bay, peach-colour; a horse so coloured.

1. a. The braunches ful of blosmes softe CHAUCER. *fig.* He prest the b. of his lips to mine TENNYSON. **2.** The bloosme of comely courtesie SPENSER. My babe, my b. TENNYSON. Nipt in the blossome BP. HALL.

Comb. **b.-faced** *a.* having a red bloated face; so **-nosed.** Hence **Blo·ssomless** *a.* **Blo·ssomy** *a.*

Blossom (blǫ·səm), *v.* [OE. *blōstmian*, ME. *blosme(n)*, f. prec.] *intr.* To put forth blossoms, bloom, flower. Also *transf.* and *fig.*

Fruites that blossome first, will first be ripe SHAKS.

Blot (blǫt), *sb.*¹ ME. [prob. of Scand. origin; cf. Icel. *blettr* blot, stain, Da. dial. *blat* spot, blot.] **1.** A spot or stain of ink, mud, etc. **b.** An obliteration 1704. **c.** *transf.* Any dark patch; also, a blemish or disfigurement 1578. **2.** *fig.* A moral stain; a disgrace, a fault ME. **b.** Imputation of disgrace 1587.

1. Inky blottes and rotten Parchment bonds *Rich. II*, II. i. 64. **2.** O indignity, O b. To honour and religion MILT. *Sams.* 411. Hence **Blo·tless** *a.*

Blot, *sb.*² 1598. [prob. – Du. *bloot* naked, exposed, but the use of this word, subst. and in this sense, is found only in Eng.] **a.** In *Backgammon*: An exposed piece, liable to be taken; also, the action of exposing a piece. **b.** *fig.* An exposed point in one's procedure; a fault or failing; also, a mark, butt 1649.

a. *To hit a b.*: to take an exposed piece. **b.** Here the critic has hit a b. 1887.

Blot (blǫt), *v.* 1440. [f. BLOT *sb.*¹] **1.** *trans.* To spot or stain with ink, tears, etc.; to blur. Also *absol.* **b.** *intr.* To become blotted 1860. **2.** To cover with worthless writing; to disfigure (*arch.*) 1494. **b.** To paint coarsely 1844. **3.** *fig.* **a.** To cast a blot upon; to tarnish (*arch.* or *Obs.*) 1566. † **b.** To stigmatize, calumniate –1611. **4.** To obliterate, efface. (Usu. with *out.*) 1530. **5.** *fig.* To efface, obscure, eclipse 1592. **6.** To dry with blotting-paper 1854.

1. Evene as he [my pen] goth he doth b. 1447. **2.** The vnpleasant'st words That euer blotted paper *Merch. V.* III. ii. 253. **3.** Vnknit that thretaning vnkinde brow..It blots thy beautie *Tam. Shr.* V. ii. 139. **4.** My name be blotted from the booke of Life *Rich. II*, I. iii. 202. Repent yee ..that your sins may be blotted out *Acts* 3:19.

Blotch (blǫtʃ). 1604. [Partly alt. of synon. † *plotch* (XVI-XVII), by assoc. w. BLOT *sb.*¹ and BOTCH *sb.*¹, partly blending of these.] **1.** A discoloured patch on the skin; a pustule, boil, or botch. **2.** A large irregular spot or blot of ink, colour, etc. 1768. Also *fig.* and *transf.* **3.** = BLOT (of ink). *north.* and *Sc.* 1863.

2. The snow fell in large blotches 1807. Hence **Blo·tchy** *a.*

Blotch (blǫtʃ), *v.* 1604. [f. prec.] **1.** *trans.* To mark with blotches. **2.** = BLOT *v.*¹ *north.*

† **Blote, blot.** 1657. [*Blote, blot* in *flyeblotes* (XVII), app. a dial. var. of unrecorded *blowth, f. BLOW *v.*¹ (III. 2) + -TH¹. Cf. *treut* (XV) for *truth.*] The egg or larva of flies, etc.

Blotter (blǫ·təɹ). 1591. [f. BLOT *v.*] **1.** One who or that which blots, *esp.* a sorry writer 1601. **2.** A thing used for drying wet ink-marks, as a blotting-pad 1591. **3.** *Comm.* A waste-book; also, a rough copy of a letter. CRAIG.

Blottesque (blǫte·sk), *a.* 1880. [f. BLOT *v.* + -ESQUE, after *grotesque*, etc.] **a.** Of painting: Characterized by blotted touches heavily laid on. **b.** quasi-*sb.* A daub 1882. Hence **Blotte·squely** *adv.* with b. effect.

Blotting (blǫ·tiŋ), *vbl. sb.* 1440. [f. BLOT *v.* + -ING¹.] The action of the vb.; *concr.* a blot, smear, obliteration.

Phr. *B. out*: obliteration of writing, etc.; also, effacement, destruction.

Comb.: **b.-book,** a book consisting of leaves of b.-paper; also, a waste-book; **-case,** a cover enclosing b.-paper; **-pad,** a pad consisting of sheets of b.-paper joined at the edges; **-paper,** a bibulous unsized paper, used to absorb superfluous ink.

Blouse (blauz). 1828. [– Fr. *blouse* (blūz), of unkn. origin.] **1.** A short loose garment of cotton or silk, resembling a shirt, worn on the upper part of the body; prop. applied (as an alien term) to the blue blouse of the French workman. **b.** A woman's loose bodice usu. worn tucked into the skirt at the waist 1870. **2.** *transf.* A French workman 1865. Hence **Bloused** *ppl. a.* wearing a b.

Blow (blōᵘ), *v.*¹ Pa. t. **blew.** Pa. pple. **blown.** [OE. *blāwan*, pa. t. *blēow*, pa. pple. *blāwen*, = OFris. *blā, OHG. *blā(h)an*, repl. by wk. OHG. *blājan* (G. *blähen* blow up, swell); f. Indo-Eur. base *bhlā-, repr. also by L. *flare.*] **I. 1.** *intr.* The proper verb naming the motion or action of the wind, or of an aerial current. **2.** To send out a strong current of air, *e.g.* from the mouth, or from bellows OE. **3.** To breathe hard, pant, puff ME. **4.** Of whales, etc.: To eject water and air from the blow-holes; to spout 1725. **5.** To utter noisy breath; to brag (chiefly *dial.*); to storm (chiefly *colloq.*) ME. **6.** (causal of 2.) ME. **7.** (causal of 3.) To cause to pant: usu. of horses 1651. **8.** *trans.* To emit a current of air, breath, etc.) with the mouth; also to force (a current of air) *through, into, upon*, by other means. Also *fig.* ME. **b.** To smoke (tobacco); also *intr.* (*dial.*) 1808. † **9.** To utter; also with *out.* Usu. in a bad sense: To utter boastfully, angrily, etc. –1652. **10.** *trans.* To drive or carry by means of a current of air; also *fig.* ME. **b.** *intr.* To be driven or carried by the wind 1842. **11.** *trans.* (*fig.*) To proclaim, blaze *abroad*, †*out*, etc. ME.

1. Heark how it rains and blows WALTON. *To b. great guns*: to blow a violent gale. *To b. up*: to rise, increase in force. **2.** *To b. hot and cold*: to be inconsistent or vacillating. (See Æsop's Fables.) **5.** He brags and he blaws o' his siller BURNS. **6.** To blowe smithes bellowes 1577. **7.** To be well blown in the pursuit 1859. **8.** Good thoughts are blown into a man by God HOBBES. *To b. off*: (*trans.*) to allow (steam, etc.) to escape forcibly with a blowing noise; also *fig.* to get rid of in a noisy way; *intr.* (for *refl.*) of steam, gas, etc.: to escape forcibly. **10.** What winde blew you hither, Pistoll *2 Hen. IV*, V. iii. 90. *To b. over*: (of storms, etc.) to pass over a place without descending upon it; to come to an end; also *fig.* of misfortune, danger, etc.

II. 1. To make (a wind-instrument) sound by blowing air into it OE. **b.** To sound (a blast) *on* or *with* an instrument ME. **c.** To sound the signal of (an advance, etc.) *on* an instrument ME. **d.** Predicated of the instrument 1593. **2.** *intr.* Of a wind-instrument: To give forth a sound by being blown ME. Of the blower: To sound a blast ME. Of the blast: To sound 1599. **3.** To direct a current of air against so as to cool, warm, or dry ME. **4.** *esp.* To direct a current of air into (a fire), in order to make it burn. Also with *up.* ME. † **5.** *fig.* To excite, inflame, fan (passion, discord, etc.). Usu. with *up.* –1776. **6.** *trans.* To clear of matter by sending air through 1532. **7.** *trans.* To inflate, puff up; to shape by inflation. Const. *up, out.* ME. † **8.** *fig.* To puff *up* with pride or vanity. Also *absol.* –1718. **9.** *trans.* To shatter, destroy, etc., by means of explosion. Const. with adverbs of direction, esp. *up.* 1599. **10.** *intr.* To undergo explosion; to erupt. Usu. with *up.* 1694.

1. B. ye the cornet in Gibeah *Hosea* 5:8. *To b. one's own trumpet*: to brag. **d.** Sonorous mettal blowing Martial sounds MILT. *P.L.* I. 540. **2.** Trumpet, b. loud *Tr. & Cr.* I. iii. 256. Let the mournful martial music b. TENNYSON. **4.** *To b. the coals* or *the fire* (fig.): to fan the flame of discord. *To b. out*: to extinguish by a current of air; also *intr.* The glass blew in, the fire blew out TENNYSON. In *Metallurgy. To b. in, out*: to put a blast furnace in, out of, operation. **6.** To b. the nose 1532. So *to b. eggs, gaspipes*, etc. **7.** To b. bladders A. YOUNG, soap-bubbles TYNDALL. **8.** Kunnynge blowith, charite edifieth WYCLIF 1 *Cor.* 4:19. **9.** To b. up mines 1599. *To b. any one's brains out*: to shoot him through the head (with fire-arms). *To b. up* (fig.): † to destroy; to scold (*colloq.*). **10.** *To b. out* (Mining): to go off like a gun, but without shattering the rock.

III. 1. To expose, inform upon. Now *slang.* 1575. Also *absol.* **2.** Said of flies, etc.: To deposit their eggs. [App. old natural history, unconnected with the notion of blowing or inflating meat.] †*trans.*, and †*absol.* or *intr.* –1771. **b.** *trans.* To fill (a place) with eggs. Cf. FLY-BLOWN. 1588. **3.** To curse, 'confound', 'hang'. *vulgar.* (With pa. pple. *blowed.*) 1835.

1. D—n me, if I don't blow. . I'll tell Tom Neville L. HUNT. 2. b. These summer flies Haue blowne me full of maggot ostentation *L.L.L.* v. ii. 409.

Phr. **To blow upon**: To take the bloom off; to make hackneyed; to defame; also to inform upon.

Blow (blōu), *v.*[2] Pa. t. **blew.** Pa. pple. **blown.** [OE. str. vb. *blōwan*, pa. t. *blēow*, pa. pple. *blōwen*, corresp. to wk. vbs. OFris. *blōia*, OS. *blōjan* (MDu., Du. *bloeien*), OHG. *bluojan, bluoen* (G. *blühen*); all f. Gmc. **blō-*, repr. also by BLADE, BLOOM *sb.*[1], BLOSSOM.] **1.** *intr.* = BLOSSOM *v.* 1. **2.** *fig.* To bloom; to attain perfection 1610. **3.** To cause to blossom (*lit.* or *fig.*) ? *Obs.* 1645.

1. I know a banke where the wilde time blows *Mids. N.* II. i. 249. 2. Wit in Northern Climates will not b. DRYDEN.

Blow (blōu), *sb.*[1] 1460. [Of unkn. origin.] **1.** A stroke; a violent application of the fist or of any instrument to an object. Also *fig.* Cf. 'stroke'. 1605. **2.** *fig.* A severe disaster; a sudden and severe shock 1678. **3.** 'An act of hostility' (J.). Usu. in *pl.* 1593.

1. Well strooke, there was b. for b. *Com. Err.* III. i. 56. A most poore man, made tame by Fortunes blows *Lear* IV. iv. 225. 3. Their controversie must either come to blowes, or be undecided HOBBES.

Phrases. *At a (one) b.*: by one stroke; suddenly; at once. *To strike a b.* (fig.): to take vigorous action.

Blow (blōu), *sb.*[2] 1660. [f. BLOW *v.*[1]] **1.** A blowing; a blast. **a.** of the wind. **b.** of whales 1851. **c.** of a wind-instrument; of the nose 1723. **2.** *fig.* A boast; boastfulness 1684. **3.** The oviposition of flesh-flies, etc. 1611. **4.** *Metallurgy.* A single *heat* of the Bessemer converter; the quantity of metal dealt with at one time 1883.

1. *To get a b.*: to expose oneself to the action of a resh breeze.

Blow-, in *comb.*

1. With adverbs, denoting actions; as **b.-out,** a quarrel; also, a 'good feed' (*slang*); **-up,** an explosion; *fig.* a disturbance. **2.** With sb., qualified by *blow-* (= 'blowing', or 'that blows', or 'is blown'); as **b.-ball,** the globular seeding head of the dandelion, etc.; also *fig.*; **-cock,** a tap by which to blow off steam; **-gun** = BLOW-PIPE 2; **-line** (*Angling*), a fishing-line of the lightest floss silk, used with the living fly; **-post,** a system of conveying letters, etc., by pneumatic tubes; **-tube** = BLOW-PIPE 2; also a tube used in glass-blowing; **-valve,** the shifting valve of a condensing engine. **3.** With sb., as object after *blow* (= 'one who blows'); as **b.-bottle, -bowl,** a sot; † **-point,** a game.

Blow (blōu), *sb.*[3] 1710. [f. BLOW *v.*[2]] **1.** A state of blossoming; bloom 1759. Also *fig.* **2.** A display of blossoms, or (*fig.*) of anything brilliant 1710. **3.** Manner, style, or time of blossoming. Also *fig.* 1748. **4.** Blossom 1797.

1. The wood-anemone was in b. 1759. 2. A b. of tulips ADDISON. 3. Flowers of richer. . b. MILLER.

Blo·wen. *slang.* Also **blowing.** 1812. [Slang, of unkn. origin.] A wench, trull.

Blower[1] (blōu·əɹ). [OE. *blāwere*, f. *blāwan* BLOW *v.*[1] + -ER[1].] **1.** *gen.* One who or that which blows. **2.** *spec.* A marine animal which blows (see BLOW *v.*[1] I. 4); *e.g.* a whale 1854. **3.** A contrivance for producing a current of air; *e.g.* a plate of metal fixed before a fire 1795. **4.** An escape of gas through a fissure in a coal-mine; the fissure itself; a current of air escaping through a fissure in a glacier 1822. **5.** *fig.* A boaster (*dial.* and in *U.S.*) 1863.

1. The best b. of horn ME. 5. General Grant. . is not one of the 'b.' generals 1863.

Blower[2]. 1796. [f. BLOW *v.*[2] + -ER[1].] A plant which blooms.

Blowess, var. of BLOWSE.

Blow·-fly. 1852. [See BLOW *v.*[1] III. 2.] Pop. name of the Flesh-fly.

Blow-hole (blōu·hōul). 1691. [See BLOW *v.*[1] I. 4.] **1.** Each of the two holes (constituting the nostrils) at the top of the head in cetaceans, through which they breathe or blow 1787. † **2.** = AIR-*hole* 1691. **3.** A hole through which air or gas escapes; *spec.* for the escape of steam or foul air from underground passages, etc. 1875. **4.** A hole in the ice to which whales and seals come to breathe.

1. The blow-holes are two in number in many, but in others only one 1787.

Blowing (blōu·iŋ), *vbl. sb.*[1] OE. [f. BLOW *v.*[1] + -ING[1].] **1.** *gen.* The action of the vb. **2.** Breathing; hard breathing; *esp.* of animals ME. **3.** The oviposition of flesh-flies; †*concr.* the egg of a flesh-fly or other insect. 1558. **4.** **Blowing up:** an explosion; *colloq.* a scolding.

Comb.: **b.-cylinder,** the air-cylinder of a blast-engine; **-engine** = *blowing-machine*; **-furnace,** a blast-furnace used in glass-working; **-iron, -pipe, -tube** (*Glass-working*), an iron tube used in blowing glass; **-machine,** any machine for producing a blast of air.

Blowing, *vbl. sb.*[2] ME. [f. BLOW *v.*[2] + -ING[1].] The action of the vb. **b.** † A bloom or blossom. Also *fig.*

Blow·ing, *ppl. a.*[1] ME. [f. BLOW *v.*[1] + -ING[2].] That blows; *esp.* windy.

B. adder, snake, a snake of Virginia, that extends and inflates the surface of its head before it bites.

Blow·ing, *ppl. a.*[2] OE. [f. BLOW *v.*[2] + -ING[2].] In bloom, blossoming.

Blown (blōun), *ppl. a.*[1] ME. [pa. pple. of BLOW *v.*[1]] **1.** Fanned, driven or tossed by the wind 1552. **2.** Out of breath 1674. † **3.** Stale; tainted –1640. **4.** Whispered, hinted. *Oth.* III. iii. 182. **5.** Inflated; formed by inflation ME. Also *fig.* (*arch.*) 1483.

Blown, *ppl. a.*[2] OE. [pa. pple. of BLOW *v.*[2]] In bloom; that has blossomed. Cf. FULL-BLOWN.

Blow-pipe, blowpipe. 1685. [f. BLOW *v.*[1]] **1.** A tube through which a current of air, etc., is blown into a flame to increase the heat, for the purpose of fusing metals, etc.; esp. employed in chemical experiments, analysis, etc. Also *attrib.* **b.** *Glass-blowing.* A tube by which the molten glass is blown into shape. **2.** A long tube through which American Indians propel arrows or darts by force of the breath 1825.

Blowse, -sed, -sy; vars. of BLOWZE, etc.

Blowth. Now *dial.* 1602. [f. BLOW *v.*[2] + -TH[1].] Blowing; blossom, bloom.

Blowy (blōu·i), *a.* 1830. [f. BLOW *v.*[1] + -Y[1].] Windy.

Blowze (blauz). 1573. [Of unkn. origin.] † **1.** A beggar's trull; a wench –1719. **2.** 'A ruddy fat-faced wench' (J).

1. Calls his b., his queene HERRICK. Hence **Blow·zy** *a.* like a b.; coarse, rustic; of hair, etc., frowzy, slatternly.

Blowzed (blauzd), *a.* 1748. [As if pa. pple. of *to blowze* = 'to make blowzy'; cf. prec.] Rendered blowzy in the face. So **Blow·zing** *a.* tending to be blowzy.

† **Blub,** *v.* 1559. [var. of dial. *blob* vb.; cf. BLOB *sb.* In sense 2, short for BLUBBER *v.*] † **1.** To swell, puff out. *trans.* and *intr.* –1684. **2.** = BLUBBER *v.* 3. 1873. Hence † **Blub** *a.* swollen, protruding; chiefly in *Comb.*

Blubber (blɒ·bəɹ), *sb.* [Late ME. *blober, bluber*, perh. of imit. origin; cf. LG. *blubbern* bubble, G. *blubbern* bubble, splutter.] † **1.** The boiling of the sea. ME. only. **2.** A bubble upon water. Now *dial.* ME. **3.** A jelly-fish or Medusa 1602. **4.** The fat of whales, etc., from which train-oil is obtained 1664. **5.** The action of blubbering 1825.

4. In a large whale the b. will weigh thirty tons 1870. 5. All in a b. of tears CARLYLE.

Comb.: **b.-guy,** a guy, suspended between the fore and main masts of a whaler, to assist in securing and supporting the carcase of a whale; **-lamp,** one which burns b.-oil; **-spade,** a spade-like knife used by whalers. Hence **Blu·bbery** *a.* (sense 4).

Blu·bber, *a.* 1667. [var. of earlier BLABBER, BLOBBER; prob. infl. by BLUB, BLUBBER *sbs.*] Swollen, protruding; *esp.* said of the lips. (Often hyphened, as *b.-lipped*, etc.)

Blubber (blɒ·bəɹ), *v.* [f. BLUBBER *sb.*] † **1.** *intr.* To bubble, bubble up; to make a bubbling noise –1750. **2.** *trans.* To utter or cry *out* with copious tears and sobs 1590. **3.** *intr.* To weep effusively. (Much used in ridicule for 'weep'.) ME. **4.** To wet profusely or disfigure with weeping. Also *fig.* 1584.

2. She. . sobbing, blubbers forth her sins GAY. 3. Phœbe Mayflower blubbered heartily for company SCOTT. Hence **Blu·bbered** *ppl. a.* flooded with tears; said of the eyes, cheeks, face; also, later, swollen with weeping. **Blu·bberer. Blu·bberingly** *adv.*

Blu·cher. 1831. [f. Field-Marshal von *Blücher* (1742-1819). Properly (blüxyĕr), but pop. pronounced (blu·tʃəɹ) or (blū·kəɹ).] A strong leather half-boot.

Bludgeon (blɒ·dʒən). 1730. [Of unkn., perh. cant, origin.] A short stick or club, with one end loaded or thicker than the other, used as a weapon. Hence **Blu·dgeon** *v.* to strike with a b.

Blue (blū, bliū), *a.* [ME. *bleu, blew(e)* – (O)Fr. *bleu, -e* :– Rom. **blavus* – Gmc. **blæwaz*, whence OE. *blǣ-hǣwen, blǣwen* blue, ON. *blár* dark-blue, livid, whence BLAE. The pronunc. (bliū) belongs to dictionaries.] **1.** Of the colour of the sky and the deep sea, or a hue resembling it. **b.** Of a flame or flash without red glare; *esp.* in phr. *To burn b.*, as a candle is said to do as an omen of death, or as indicating the presence of ghosts or of the Devil 1594. **c.** Taken as the colour of constancy. Hence *true b.* (fig.) 1500. **2.** Livid, leaden-coloured ME. **3.** *fig.* Affected with fear, discomfort, anxiety, etc.; low-spirited; *esp.* in *To look b.* 1550. **4.** *transf.* Belonging to the political party which has chosen blue for its colour. (In England usu. the Conservative party.) 1835. **5.** Of women: Learned, pedantic. See BLUE-STOCKING. (Usu. *contemptuous.*) 1788. **6.** *fig.* As the colour of plagues and things hurtful. Cf. BLUE DEVIL. 1742. **7.** *colloq.* Obscene 1840.

1. The b. sky bends over all COLERIDGE. The skyish head Of blew Olympus *Haml.* v. i. 277. His b. blade 1809. The b. distance DICKENS. Heere My blewest vaines to kisse *Ant. & Cl.* II. v. 29. 2. B. meagre hag MILT. *Comus* 434. 3. *B. funk* (slang): extreme nervousness. 4. To vote b. 1868. *True b.*: (see above 1 c) spec. used of the Scottish Presbyterian or Whig party, in contradistinction to the royal *red*. 5. They are all so wise, so learned, and so b. MAR. EDGEWORTH.

Phrases (*colloq.*). *Till all is b.*: said of the effect of drinking on the eyesight. *By all that's b.*; cf. Fr. *parbleu* (euphem. for *pardieu*).

Comb. **1.** Used descriptively and distinctively, in forming the names of **a.** *Animals*, as **b.-back,** a species of bird; **-breast,** the Blue-throated Redstart; **b. bull,** the Nyl-gau or Nhilgai of India; **b. cat,** a Siberian cat valued for its fur; **b. cocks,** the *Salmo albus*; **b. fox,** a variety of the Arctic fox, and its fur; **b. hawk,** (*a*) the Peregrine Falcon; (*b*) the Ring-tailed Harrier (*Circus cyaneus*), also called *b. glede* and *b. kite*; **b.-head,** a worm used as bait; **b. poker,** a duck, the Pochard; **b.-poll** = *blue cocks*; **-rock,** a kind of pigeon; **-throat,** a bird, the *Sylvia suecica*; **b. tit** = BLUE-CAP 4; **b.-wing,** a genus of ducks. **b.** *Plants*, as **b.-berry,** various species of *Vaccinium*; **-blaw, -cup** = BLUEBOTTLE 1; **b. chamomile** or **b. daisy,** the Sea Starwort, etc.; **b.-gage,** a kind of plum; **-grass** (*U.S.*), various species of *Carex*; also = WIRE-GRASS 1; **b. gum (tree),** the *Eucalyptus globulus* of Australia; **b.-hearts,** *Buchnera americana*; **b. rocket,** *Aconitum pyramidale*; **b. tangles,** *Vaccinium frondosum*; **b.-weed,** Viper's Bugloss, *Echium vulgare*. **c.** *Minerals*, as **b. asbestos** = CROCIDOLITE; **b.-billy,** the residuum of cupreous pyrites after roasting with salt; **b. copper, b. malachite,** = AZURITE; **b. copperas, b. stone, b. vitriol,** sulphate of copper (see VITRIOL); **b. felspar, b. spar,** = LAZULITE; **b. iron** = VIVIANITE; **b. slipper,** Gault clay (*local*).

2. Special combs. or phrases. † **b. apron,** one who wears a b. apron, a tradesman; **b. blanket,** the banner of the Edinburgh craftsmen; *fig.* the sky; **b. blood** (see BLOOD III. 1.); **b. dahlia,** anything rare or unheard of; **b. disease,** *Cyanosis*; **b. fire,** a b. light used on the stage for weird effect; hence *attrib.* sensational; **b. heat,** a heat of about 550° Fahr., at which ironwork assumes a bluish tint; **b. jacket,** a sailor (*esp.* as opp. to a marine); **b. jaundice** = *blue disease*; **b. laws,** severe Puritanic laws said to have been enacted in the 18th c. at New Haven, Connecticut, U.S.; **b. light,** a pyrotechnical composition which burns with a b. flame, used also at sea as a night-signal; **b. line** (in *Tennis*), the service-line (so coloured); **b. mantle,** dress, and title, of one of the four pursuivants of the English College of Arms; **b. Monday,** (*a*) the Monday before Lent; (*b*) a Monday spent in dissipation by workmen; **b. moon** (*colloq.*), a rarely recurring period; **b.-mould,** the mould on cheese so coloured, consisting of a fungus, *Aspergillus glaucus*; **b. ointment,** mercurial ointment; **Blue Peter,** a b. flag with a white square in the centre, hoisted as the signal of immediate sailing; hence, in *Whist*, the signal or call for trumps; **b. pill,** a mercurial antibilious pill; **b. pot,** a black-lead crucible; **b. ruin** (*slang*), (bad) gin; **b. water,** the open sea.

Blue, *sb.* ME. [The adj. used absol. or ellipt.] **1.** Blue colour. (With *pl.*) **2.** A pigment of a blue colour, usually defined, as *cobalt*, etc. *b.* 1862. **b.** *spec.* A powder used by laundresses 1618. **3.** Blue clothing or dress 1482. **4.** Ellipt., for blue animals, objects, or substances, indicated by the context 1787. **5.** The sky; the sea 1647. **6.** = *Blue Squadron*, one of the three 17th c. divisions of the English fleet 1703. **7.** *pl.* Applied to companies of troops, wearing blue 1766. **8.** The colour worn by a party, faction, or class; hence, *transf.* a member of such party, etc. Also *true b.* See BLUE *a.* 1 c, 5. 1755. **9.** Short for 'blue-stocking' 1788. **10.** *Archery.* The second ring from the centre of the target 1882.

1. The b. of distance, however intense, is not the b. of a bright blue flower RUSKIN. **4.** The potatoes were salmons and blues 1845. Bits of old Nankin 'blue' 1884. **5.** Where one may float between b. and b. GEO. ELIOT. **8.** *Dark Blues*: Oxford men or Harrow boys. *Light Blues*: Cambridge men or Eton boys. *To win his b., to be a B.*: to be chosen to represent his University (or School) in rowing, cricket, etc. *An old B.*: one who has figured in an inter-University contest. *Blue-coat boy*: a scholar of Christ's Hospital.

Phr. *The blues* (for '*blue devils*'): depression of spirits (*colloq.*).

Blue, *v.* 1606. [f. the adj.] **1.** To make blue. **2.** To treat (linen) with BLUE (see BLUE *sb.* 2 b) 1862. **† 3.** *intr.* To blush (*slang*). SWIFT. Hence **Blu(e)·ing** *vbl. sb.* a making blue; in U.S., laundresses' blue.

Bluebeard (blū·bīᵊɹd). 1822. A personage of popular mythology, so called from the colour of his beard. References are frequent in literature to the locked turret-chamber, in which hung the bodies of his murdered wives.

The B. chamber of his mind, into which no eye but his own must look CARLYLE.

Blue bell, blue·-bell. 1578. [See BELL *sb.*[1]] **1.** A species of *Campanula* (*C. rotundifolia*). Called also the 'hair-bell' or 'harebell'. (Usu. blū͵be·l, or as two wds.) **2.** In the south of Eng.: (blū·bel) a bulbous-rooted plant, *Scilla nutans* (*Hyacinthus non-scriptus* Linn.) 1794.

Blue·-bird. 1688. **1.** A small perching bird (*Motacilla sialis* Linn., *Sylvia sialis* Wilson), common in U.S. in early spring. Its upper part is sky-blue. **2.** ? A species of albatross (*Diomedea fuliginosa*) 1731.

Blue-black. 1823. **A.** *adj.* Black or dark with a tinge of blue 1853. **B.** *sb.* A pigment of this colour.

Blue bonnet, -bo·nnet. 1682. [Cf. BLUE-CAP.] **1.** *spec.* A broad round flat cap of blue woollen material, formerly in general use in Scotland. **2.** *transf.* A blue-bonneted peasant or soldier 1818. **3.** Sc. name of species of *Centaurea*, as the Bluebottle 1863. **4.** *dial.* = BLUE-CAP 4.

Blue book, blue·-book. 1715. [Cf. BLACK-BOOK.] A book bound in blue; now *spec.* one of the official reports of Parliament and the Privy Council, issued in a blue paper cover. **b.** *U.S.* A printed book, containing the names, places of birth, salaries, etc., of all persons holding office under the government.

Blue·bottle. 1551. [Cf. BOTTLE *sb.*[4]] **1.** The Blue Corn-flower (*Centaurea cyanus*). Also used of other blue flowers. **2.** A nickname for a beadle or a policeman 1597. **3.** *B. fly*: a fly (*Musca vomitoria*) with a large bluish body; the Blow-fly.

Blue·-cap. 1596. [Cf. BLUE-BONNET.] **1.** A cap of blue material; the 'blue bonnet' of Scotchmen. Also *attrib.* 1674. **† 2.** *transf.* A Scotchman –1663. **3.** *dial.* A salmon in its first year; so called because it has a blue spot on its head 1677. **4.** The Blue Titmouse (*Parus cæruleus*) 1804. **5.** = BLUE BONNET 3. 1821.

Blue coat, blue·-coat. 1593. **1.** Formerly the dress of servants, etc.; hence of almoners and charity children 1600. **2.** One who wears a blue coat; *e.g.* an almsman, a beadle; a soldier or sailor 1593. Also *attrib.* **3.** (= *Blue coat boy*): A scholar of a charity school wearing the almoner's blue coat; *esp.* a scholar of Christ's Hospital 1665. Hence **Blue·-coated** *a.*

Blue devil. 1616. [See BLUE *a.* 3, 6.] **1.** A baleful demon (cf. BLUE *a.* 3, 6). **2.** *fig.* in pl. *Blue devils*: **a.** Depression of spirits 1787. **b.** The apparitions seen in *delirium tremens* 1822.

Blue eye. 1552. **† a.** = BLACK EYE 2. **† b.** A blueness round the eye from weeping, etc. **c.** An eye of which the iris is blue. Hence **Blue·-eyed** *a.*, now in sense c.

Blue-eyed grass: *Sisyrinchium bermudianum.*

Blue·-fish. 1734. **a.** A species of *Coryphæna*, found about the Bahamas, etc. **b.** *Temnodon saltator*, a salt-water fish of the mackerel order, but larger.

Blue gown, blue·-gown. 1787. **† 1.** The dress of an almoner, in Scotland of a king's bedesman or licensed beggar. BURNS. **2.** One who wears this dress. Also *attrib.* 1816.

Blu(e)ism. 1822. The characteristics of a blue-stocking.

Blue·-John. 1672. **† 1.** = AFTER-WORT. Hence *fig.* –1683. **2.** The blue fluor-spar found in Derbyshire 1772.

Blue·ly, *adv.* 1647. [f. BLUE *a.* + -LY[2].] **1.** With a blue colour or tinge. **† 2.** Badly; only in *To come off b.* –1783.

Blueness (blū·nės). 1491. [f. BLUE *a.* + -NESS.] The quality of being BLUE (senses 1, 2, 5, 7).

Blue·-nose. (Chiefly in U.S.) 1837. **1.** A purplish potato grown in Nova Scotia. **2.** A nickname for a Nova Scotian 1837. **3.** A kind of clam shell-fish 1883.

Blue ri·bbon, riband. 1651. **1.** A ribbon of blue silk worn as a badge of honour; *esp.* the blue ribbon of the order of the Garter. **2.** The greatest distinction, the first place or prize 1848. **3.** A small strip of blue ribbon, worn as a distinctive badge by certain teetotallers 1878.

3. *Blue Ribbon Army*: the association of such teetotallers. Hence **Blue-ribboner, -ism, -ist, -ite.**

Blue-stocking (blū·stǫ:kiŋ). [First found in the 17th c. (see 1 a). In its transferred sense, it dates from the assemblies which met at Montagu House in London about 1750 in order to substitute for card-playing literary conversation, etc. At these a principal attendant was Mr. Benjamin Stillingfleet, who habitually wore blue worsted instead of black silk stockings. In reference to this the coterie was dubbed by Admiral Boscawen 'the Blue Stocking Society'.] **1.** *attrib.* Wearing blue worsted stockings; *hence*, not in full dress, in homely dress. (*contemptuous.*) **a.** Applied to the 'Little Parliament' of 1653. **b.** Applied depreciatively to the assemblies at Montagu House, their frequenters, etc. 1757. **c.** Hence, Of women: Having or affecting literary tastes; learned 1804. **2.** *sb.* = *Blue Stocking Lady.* (Now obsolescent.) 1790. **3.** The American Avocet (*Recurvirostra americana*). BARTLETT.

1. a. That Blew-stocking Parliament, Barebone Parliament 1683. **b.** He [Mr. Stillingfleet] has left off his old friends and his blue stockings MRS. MONTAGUE (1757). Hence **Blue-stockingism.**

Bluet, -ett. ME. [In 1 – Fr. †*bluette*, fem. dim. of *bleu* blue, in med.L. *bluetum*, *bluettum*; in 2 – Fr. *bleuet*, *bluet* masc. dim. of *bleu*; see -ET, -ETTE.] **† 1.** A bluish woollen cloth. **2.** The Corn Bluebottle (*Centaurea cyanus*). In U.S., *Oldenlandia cærulea*, also a Bilberry (*Vaccinium angustifolium*). 1727.

Blueth. *nonce-wd.* Blueness. H. WALPOLE.

Blue water. 1834. The deep sea, the open sea.

Bluey (blū·i). 1802. [f. BLUE *a.* + -Y[1].] **A.** *adj.* More or less blue; also as *adv.* **B.** *sb.* (in Australia): A bushman's bundle, generally wrapped in a blue blanket.

Bluff (blɒf), *a.* 1627. [orig. naut., perh. of LDu. origin, but no suitable form is known and Du. †*blaf* (Kilian, 1599) broad and flat (of the face) appears to be isolated.] **1.** Presenting a broad flattened front. **2.** *fig.* **a.** 'Big, surly, blustering' (J.); later, rough, blunt 1705. **b.** Good-naturedly blunt 1808.

1. B. headland COWPER, bows [of a steamer] 1861. **2. a.** I maul'd you, when you look'd so b. SWIFT. **b.** B. downright honesty. Hence **Blu·ffly** *adv.*, **-ness.**

Bluff (blɒf), *sb.*[1] 1737. [f. BLUFF *a.*] A cliff or headland with a broad precipitous face. (First used in U.S.)

Bold bluffs, that mark the limits of an ancient shore GEIKIE. Hence **Blu·ffy** *a.* full of bluffs; rather bluff.

Bluff, *sb.*[2] 1777. [Goes w. BLUFF *v.*] **1.** A blinker for a horse. **2.** *slang.* An excuse; ?a blind 1851. **3.** The action of bluffing in the game of *poker*; see BLUFF *v.*[1] *Hence*, challenging or confident language or demeanour, 'tried on' in the hope of intimidating an opponent. (First used in U.S.) 1848.

3. The offer was only a b. 1884.

Bluff, *v.* 1674. [– Du. *bluffen* brag, boast, and *bluf* bragging, boasting. The obs. dial. *bluff* blindfold (superseded by *bluft*) appears to be unrelated.] **1.** *trans.* To blindfold or hoodwink. **2.** In the game of *poker*: To impose upon (an opponent) as to the strength of one's hand, by betting heavily upon it, or the like, so as to induce him to throw up the game. (Of U.S. origin.) Hence *transf.* 1864. **3.** *intr.* To attempt the imposition described in 2. 1882.

2. *To b. off*: to frighten off by bluffing. Hence **Blu·ffer.**

Bluish (blū·iʃ), *a.* ME. [f. BLUE *a.* + -ISH[1].] Somewhat blue; *esp.* in comb., as *b.-green*, etc. Hence **Blu·ish-ly** *adv.*, **-ness.**

Blunder (blɒ·ndəɹ), *v.* [prob. of Scand. origin; cf. MSw. (Norw.) *blundra* shut the eyes, frequent. of the base found in ON. (Sw.) *blunda*, ODa. *blunde*, rel. to BLIND; but the sense-development is not clear.] **I. † 1.** *trans.* To mix up confusedly; to derange; to make (water) turbid –1638. **2.** To confound (in one's mind) stupidly 1699.

II. 1. *intr.* To move blindly or stupidly; to flounder, stumble. Often with *on, into, against.* ME. Also *fig.* **† 2.** *intr.* To deal blindly and stupidly –1471. **3.** *trans.* To utter thoughtlessly, stupidly, or by a blunder. Usu. with *out.* 1483. **4.** *intr.* To make a stupid and gross mistake in doing anything 1711. **5.** *trans.* To mismanage, make a blunder in 1805.

1. The horses had to b. their way along a bright rushing river 1880. *To b. upon*: to come upon by a 'fluke'. **4.** The soldier knew some one had blunder'd TENNYSON. **5.** To b. a siege WELLINGTON. Hence **Blu·nderer. Blu·nderingly** *adv.*

Blunder (blɒ·ndəɹ), *sb.* ME. [app. f. the vb.] **† 1.** Confusion, clamour –1774. **2.** A gross mistake 1706.

2. Another mistake, not to call it a b. DE FOE.

Blunderbuss (blɒ·ndəɹbɒs). 1654. [alt., by assoc. w. *blunder*, of Du. *donderbus*, f. *donder* THUNDER + *bus* gun (orig. box, tube, cf. G. *büchse*).] **1.** A short gun with a large bore, firing many slugs, and doing execution at short range without exact aim. (No longer used in civilized countries.) **2.** *transf.* A blustering noisy talker (*obs.*); a blunderhead 1685. Also *attrib.*

Blu·nderhead. 1697. [prob. alt. f. earlier DUNDERHEAD; cf. prec.] A blundering muddle-headed fellow. Hence **Blu·nderhea:ded** *a.*, **Blu:nderhea·dedness.**

Blunge (blɒndʒ), *v.* 1830. [app. of symbolic origin, combining *plunge* w. words in *bl-*, as *blend*, etc.] *Pottery.* To mix (clay, etc.) up with water.

Blunger (blɒ·ndʒəɹ). 1830. [f. prec. + -ER[1].] An appliance for blunging; formerly a wooden instrument, with a cross handle at the top; now an apparatus driven by power.

† Blu·nket. 1440. [Earliest and most frequent form *blunket*, connection of which with OFr. *blancquet* BLANKET is unlikely.] **A.** *adj.* Grey, greyish blue –1783. **B.** *sb.* [sc. *fabric.*] ? = BLANKET *sb.* 1. –1600.

Blunt (blɒnt). ME. [The earliest evidence suggests a Scand. source and a possible neuter formation (as in SCANT, THWART, WIGHT *a.*) on the base of ON. *blundr* dozing, sleep (used as a nickname), *blunda* close the eyes (Norw. *blunde* doze). Cf. BLUNDER.] **A.** *adj.* **1.** Dull; said orig. of the sight, whence of the perceptions, etc. **2.** Not sharp; without edge or point. (Now the leading literal sense.) ME. **b.** *transf.* to the effect 1656. Also *fig.* **† 3.** Barren, bare –1599. **4.** Rude, unpolished (*arch.*) 1477. **† b.** Unfeeling, unsparing. SHAKS. **5.** Abrupt of speech or manner; plain-spoken; curt 1590.

1. Ill can your blunter feelings guess the pain CAMPBELL. **2.** If the yron be b. *Eccles.* 10:10. A b. pencil 1753, hatchet 1885. **b.** A b. stroke COWLEY. **5.** By his b. bearing he will keepe his word *Hen. V*, IV. vii. 185. Hence **Blu·ntish** *a.* **Blu·nt-ly** *adv.*, **-ness.**

B. *sb.* † **1.** A foil for fencing –1694. **2.** A size of needles 1833. **3.** *slang.* Ready money 1812.

Blunt, *v.* ME. [f. BLUNT *a.*] **1.** To dull, or make less sharp. Also *intr.* **2.** To make dull (the feelings or faculties) 1597.

1. Cupid now..blunts the point of ev'ry dart SWIFT. 2. B. not his Loue..By seeming cold SHAKS.

Blur (blɔ̄ɹ), *sb.* 1548. [Priority of sb. or vb. cannot be determined; perh. rel. to BLEAR, but Levins's 'Manipulus Vocabulorum' (1570) has 'blirre, *deceptio*, blirre, *fallere*'.] **1.** A smear which partially obscures 1601. **2.** *fig.* A moral stain, a blemish 1548. **3.** An indistinct blurred appearance 1860.

1. He that clenses a blot with blotted fingers makes a greater blurre QUARLES. 2. This b. to youth SHAKS. *Lucr.* 222. 3. The..nebulous b. of Orion EMERSON. Hence **Blu·rry** *a.*

Blur (blɔ̄ɹ), *v.* 1581. [See prec.] **1.** To obscure or sully by smearing with ink, etc. **b.** *intr.* To make blurs 1622. **2.** *fig.* To stain, sully, blot, or blemish; to disfigure, befoul 1593. **3.** To make indistinct or dim. Also *fig.* 1611. **4.** *transf.* To dim (the senses, etc.) 1620.

1. A full paper blurred over with falsehoods FULLER. 2. Such an Act That blurres the grace and blush of Modestie *Haml.* III. iv. 41. 3. One low light..Blurr'd by the creeping mist TENNYSON. 4. Feare..blurres your senses 1620.

Blurb (blɔ̄ɹb). orig. *U.S.* 1924. [Of unkn. origin.] A publisher's commendatory advertisement of a book.

Blurt (blɔ̄ɹt), *v.* 1573. [prob. imit.] **1.** *intr.* To emit the breath eruptively from the mouth; to snort in sleep. Also *trans.* with *out.* Now *dial.* 1611. † **2.** *intr.* To puff in scorn, to pooh –1654. Also *trans.* **3.** *trans.* (usu. with *out*) : To utter abruptly, or impulsively; to burst out with 1573. *absol.* MILT.

2. All the world will b. and scorn at us 1596. 3. To b. out the broad staring question of, Madam will you marry me GOLDSM.

Blurt (blɔ̄ɹt), *sb.* 1580. [f. the vb.; cf. BLIRT.] † **1.** An eruptive emission of breath from the mouth, *esp.* in contempt –1611. **2.** An abrupt impulsive outburst 1865.

† **Blurt,** *int.* 1592. [The vb.-stem used without constr.] 'Pooh!' 'a fig for!' –1606.

Blush (blɒʃ), *v.* Pa. t. and pple. **Blushed, blusht.** [OE. *blyscan* (glossing L. *rutilare* glow red), corresp. to MLG. *bloschen*, LG. *blüsken*; rel. in meaning and no doubt ult. in form to MDu. *blōzen, blo̅zen* (Du. *blōzen*) to blush; cf. OE. *āblysian* to blush, *āblysnung* redness of confusion, and *blysa* torch, *blysian* to blaze.] † **1.** *intr.* To shine forth; also, to cast a glance. (in allit. ME. poetry.) **2.** *intr.* To become red in the face, (usu. from shame or modesty); to colour up 1450. **b.** *trans.* To exhibit, make known by blushing. Chiefly *poet.* 1592. **c.** To turn *into, out of*, by blushing 1636. **3.** *fig.* To be ashamed 1530. **4.** *transf.* To become or be red, or roseate 1679. **5.** *trans.* To make red 1593.

2. She changed colour and blussyd as rudy as a rose LD. BERNERS. **b.** He b. you Thanks *Wint. T.* IV. iv. 595. 3. I do not b. to own, that I am out of fashion BOLINGBR. 5. Ne're returneth, To b. and beautifie the cheeke againe 2 *Hen. VI*, III. ii. 167. Hence **Blu·sher.** **Blu·shingly** *adv.*

Blush (blɒʃ), *sb.* (*a.*) ME. [f. the vb.] † **1.** A gleam –1661. **2.** A glance. *Obs.* exc. in *at, on*, etc. (*the*) *first b.* ME. **3.** A look, appearance. Now *dial.* 1620. **4.** The reddening of the face, caused by shame, modesty, etc. 1593. **5.** *transf.* A rosy colour or glow; a flush of light or of colour 1590. **6.** *adj.* Of the colour of a blush 1633.

2. Vidimus. And that not..'at a b.', passing by; but had a full sight BP. ANDREWES. 3. Without any b. of absurdity 1620. 4. Put off your Maiden Blushes *Hen. V*, v. ii. 253. *To put to the b.*: to put to shame. 5. Light's last blushes ting'd the distant hills LYTTELTON. *Comb.* **b.-rose,** a rose of a very delicate pink. Hence † **Blu·shet,** little blusher. B. JONS. **Blu·shful** *a.* full of blushes; blush-coloured, rosy. **Blu·shful-ly** *adv.*, **-ness.** **Blu·shless** *a.* unblushing. **Blu·shy** *a.* blush-coloured; suffused with blushes.

Bluster (blɒ·stəɹ), *v.* [ult. imit.; there is a formal analogue in LG. *blustern, blistern* flutter. In sense I may be a different word.]

† **I.** The ME. vb. *intr.* To wander blindly or aimlessly. Cf. BLUNDER *v.* 3.

II. The mod. vb. **1.** *intr.* To blow boisterously or with stormy violence: said of wind. Also said of water agitated by wind or flood. 1530. Also *fig.* **b.** To blow about, dishevel (*rare*) 16.. † **2.** *intr.* To breathe hard 1530. † **3.** *trans.* To utter with stormy violence and noise. Usu. with *out* or *forth.* –1604. **4.** *intr.* To storm or rage boisterously; to hector 1494. **b.** *trans.* To force, or drive, by blustering 1661.

1. When to land B. the winds and tides the selfsame way TENNYSON. 4. Boswell blustered, but nothing could be got JOHNSON. Hence **Blu·sterer,** one who or that which blusters. **Blu·steringly** *adv.*

Bluster (blɒ·stəɹ), *sb.* 1583. [f. prec. vb.] **1.** Boisterous blowing; a rough and stormy blast. Also *fig.* **2.** The boisterous blast of a wind instrument, etc. 1724. **3.** Boisterous inflated talk 1704.

1. The skies..threaten present blusters SHAKS. 3. Mirabeau has much more of b.; a noisy, forward, unresting man CARLYLE. Hence **Blu·sterous, -strous** *a.* boisterous, stormy; truculent. **Blu·stery** *a.* boisterously blowing; noisily self-assertive.

† **Bo,** *a.* (*pron.*) [OE. *bēġen, bā, bū* corresp. to Goth. *bai* (masc.), *ba* (n.), f. Gmc. **ba-* :– **bo-*, as in Gr. ἀμ-φο-, L. *am-bo.*] The earlier word for BOTH.

† **Bo,** *conj.* ME. The neuter or common form of prec. used with *and.*

Bo, boh (bōᵘ), *int.* ME. [A combination of consonant and vowel esp. suited to surprise or startle. Cf. L. *boare*, Gr. βοᾶν cry aloud.] An exclam. to surprise or frighten.

Phr. *To say* or *cry 'bo' to a goose*, (also occas.) *a battledore*: to open one's mouth, speak.

Boa (bōᵘ·ă). Pl. **boas** (occas. in L. form **boæ**). ME. [– mod.L. use by Linnæus ('Systema Naturæ' I. iii. 1083) of L. *boa* (Pliny), of unkn. origin.] **1.** *Zool.* A genus of large non-venomous serpents native to tropical S. America, which kill their prey by constriction. Pop. any large serpent of similar habits, *e.g.* the Python of the Old World. **2.** A snake-like coil of fur or feathers worn by women round the neck 1836.

Boa-constrictor (bōᵘ·ă kǫnstri·ktəɹ). 1809. [f. prec. + L. *constrictor* squeezer.] A large Brazilian serpent of the genus *Boa*, erron. supposed by Linnæus to be the largest species; pop., any great crushing snake, whether a Boa or a Python. Also *fig.*

fig. A great logical boa constrictor 1848.

‖ **Boanerges** (bōᵘănə̄·ɹdʒīz), *proper name.* ME. [– Gr. βοανεργές (*Mark* 3:17), perh. ult. – Aram. **bᵉnê rᵉgěš* 'sons of thunder'.] The name given by Christ to the two sons of Zebedee. Hence, as a sing. (pl. *-es, -esses*), a loud vociferous preacher or orator.

Boanthropy (bo,æ·nþrǒpi). 1864. [f. Gr. βοάνθρωπος (f. βοῦς ox + ἄνθρωπος man) + -Y³.] A form of madness in which a man believes himself an ox (see *Daniel* 4:33).

Boar (bō̆ᵊɹ). [OE. *bār* = OS. *bēr-swīn*, (M)Du. *beer*, OHG. *bēr* (G. *bär*) :– WGmc. **baira* (cf. Lombardic *sonor-pair* BOAR of the SOUNDER).] The male of the swine, whether wild or tame (but uncastrated). **b.** The flesh of the animal 1460. **c.** *spec.* **Wild Boar:** usual name of the wild species (*Sus scrofa*) ME. **d.** *fig.* applied to persons ME.

Comb.: **boar's ear** (corruption of *bear's ear*): = AURICULA 3; **boar's foot,** a plant, *Helleborus viridis.*

† **Boar,** *v.* 1528. [f. prec.] Of swine: To be in heat –1607.

Board (bōᵊɹd), *sb.* [OE. *bord*, combining two words; (i) a str. n. = OFris., OS. *bord* (Du. *boord* board, *bord* shelf, plate), MHG., G. *bort* board, ON. *borð* board, etc. (Sw., Da. *bord* table, ON. *fótborð*, Goth. *fōtubaurd* footstool) :– Gmc. **borðam*, f. gradation-var. of **breð-* (OE., OS. *bred*, OHG. *bret*, G. *brett* board, plank); (ii) a str. m. = OS. *bord*, MDu. *bort* (Du. *boord*) border, edge, ship's side, ON. *borð* margin, shore, ship-board (Sw., Da. *bord* ship-board) :– Gmc. **borðaz.* The OE. words were reinforced in ME. by the uses of Fr. *bord* edge, rim, side of a ship, and by the uses of the ON. words, prob. in this group of senses, as well as in that of 'table' (barely evidenced in OE.) and the derived sense of 'maintenance at table', 'supply of provisions'.] **I.** A board of wood, etc. [OE. *bord* (i).] **1.** A piece of timber sawn thin, usually rectangular, and of greater length than breadth; a thin plank. (A *board* is thinner than a *plank*, and is generally less than 2½ inches in thickness.) **b.** *spec.* in *pl.* The stage of a theatre. Cf. STAGE. 1779. **2.** A tablet, *e.g.* a *black b.*, *paste-b.*, *spring-b.*, *notice-b.*, etc. ME. **b.** *spec.* One on which games are played, as *chess-b.*, *backgammon-b.*, etc.; also the frame used for scoring at cribbage. Often *fig.* 1474. **3.** A kind of thick stiff paper, formed by pasting or squeezing layers of paper together, as *pasteboard, cardboard, mill-b.*, etc. **4.** *Bookbinding.* Pieces of strong pasteboard covered with paper and used for the covers of books. So *In cloth boards*: in boards covered with cloth. 1533.

1. Ships are but boords *Merch. V.* I. iii. 32. **b.** To go upon the boards GARRICK. 2. *To keep one's name on the boards*: to remain a member of a college (at Cambridge). **b.** There is scarce any thing but pawns left upon the b. CLARENDON. 4. The bookseller..had not one in boards LOCKHART.

II. A table [Cf. ON. *borð.*] † **1.** *gen.* A table –1470. **2.** *spec.* A table used for meals; now, always, one spread for a repast. Chiefly *poet.*; but see BED *sb.* I. 1. ME. **3.** *transf.* Food served at the table; daily meals provided according to stipulation; the supply of daily provisions; entertainment. Often joined with *bed* or *lodging.* ME. **4.** A table at which a council is held; *hence* a council-meeting 1575. **b.** Hence: The persons who meet at a council-table, as *B. of Control, B. of Trade, B. of Guardians*, etc. 1613. **5.** Any piece of furniture resembling a table, as *sideboard* a side table ME.

1. *Above b.*: open, openly; cf. I. 2b, and see ABOVE-BOARD. *To sweep the b.* (at cards): to take all the cards, to pocket the stakes. 2. † *God's b.*: the Communion table in a church. Fful ofte tyme he hadde the bord bigonne (*i.e.* taken precedence at table) CHAUCER. 3. He payth for hys borde wykely xxd. MARG. PASTON. 4. **b.** 'Bow to the b.,' said Bumble. Oliver..seeing no b. but the table, fortunately bowed to that DICKENS.

† **III.** [OE. *bord* (ii).] A shield –1535.

IV. [OE *bord* (ii); lost in ME. and replaced by Fr. *bord.*] A hem, an edge, a coast. *Obs.* exc. in *seaboard.* OE.

V. A ship's side. [OE. *bord* (ii): reinforced by OFr. *bord.*] **1.** *Naut.* The side of a ship. (See ABOARD.) Now only in phrases, as *over (the) b.*, *weather-b.*, etc. OE. † **2.** (*poet.* in OE.) A ship –ME. **3.** *Naut.* Sideward direction (in reference to the ship's course); the course of a ship when tacking. Cf. TACK. 1533.

1. They came within b. MALORY. *By the b.*: (down) by the ship's side, overboard, as *To slip by the b. To come, go*, etc., *by the b.*: to fall overboard, to go for good and all. *To try by the b.*: to try boarding. Also *fig. On b.*: on one side, close alongside (*of* a ship or shore); also as *prep.*, short for *on b. of.* Also, in common use: On or in a ship, boat, etc.; into or on to a ship. (Ellipt. for *on ship-b.*) Also *transf.* (in U.S.). In or into a railway train, tram-car, etc. *To lay (a ship) on b.*: to place one's own ship alongside of (it). *To run on b.* (*of*), *to fall on b.* (*of*): *lit.* to run against, fall foul *of* (a ship); *fig.* to make an attack, fall, *upon* (a person or thing). *B. on b.*, (corruptly) *b. and b., b. by b.*: side by side. [*On b.* is app. an expansion of ABOARD, taken from Fr. *à bord*, short for *au bord du vaisseau*, in which *bord* 'ship's side' comes to be equal to 'ship' itself.] 3. *To make boards*: to tack. *To make short boards*: to tack frequently.

Comb.: **b.-measure,** superficial measure applied to boards; **-money** = BOARD-WAGES; **-nail,** a spike or large brad; **-rule,** a scale for finding the superficial area of a b. without calculation.

Board (bōᵊɹd), *v.* 1460. [f. prec. sb.: cf. ABORD *v.* and Fr. *border.*] **1.** *trans.* **a.** To come close up to or alongside (a ship), usually for the purpose of attacking. **b.** In later use, To go on board of or enter (a ship), usually in a hostile manner. Also *absol.* (in sense b.) 1494. **2.** *trans.* To go on board of 1597. *transf.* (in U.S.) To enter (a railway train, etc.); to enter in a hostile way 1879. **3.** *fig.* To approach, address, assail; to make advances to. Cf. ACCOST. 1547. **4.** *intr.* Of a ship: To tack 1627. † **5.** *trans.* To border on; *intr.* to lie close *by* –1636. **6.** To cover or furnish with boards 1530. **7.** To provide with daily meals; now generally to provide with both food and lodging at a fixed rate 1599. **8.** *intr.* To be supplied with food, or food and lodging, at a fixed rate; to live with a family as one of its members for a stipulated charge 1556. **9.**

causal. To place at board. Also with *out.* 1655.

1. b. In boarding the San Nicholas..we lost about seven killed NELSON. 6. The floors were roughly boarded over HOWELLS. To have books boarded BUCKLE. 8. He had engaged to b. with the family W. IRVING. Hence **Boa·rdable** *a.* that can be boarded, as a ship; *fig.* approachable. (Dicts.)

Boarder (bōᵊ·ɹdəɹ). 1530. [f. BOARD *v.* + -ER¹.] **1.** One who has his food, or food and lodging, at the house of another, or lives with a family as one of its members, at a fixed rate. *spec.* A boy who boards and lodges at a school. **2.** One who boards an enemy's ship 1769.

Boa·rding, *vbl. sb.* 1546. [f. BOARD *v.* + -ING¹.] **1.** *Naut.* The action of coming close up to, or of entering (a ship), usually in a hostile manner. **2.** The action of covering with boards; boards collectively, a structure of boards 1552. **3.** *Currying.* The treatment of leather with a graining-board 1870.

Comb.: **b.-house,** one in which persons board; **-out,** the obtaining of stated meals at another person's house; the placing of destitute children in families where they are treated as members; **-school,** one in which pupils are boarded as well as taught.

† **Boa·rd-school. 1.** A boarding-school 1740. **2.** A school under the management of a School-board, as established by the Elementary Education Act of 1870. Also *attrib.* –1903.

Boa·rd-wages, board wages. 1539. Wages allowed to servants to keep themselves in victual.

Boar-fish (bōᵊ·ɹfiʃ). 1836. A fish (*Capros aper, Zeus aper*) akin to the Mackerel, having a turned-up snout.

Boarish (bōᵊ·riʃ), *a.* 1550. [f. BOAR *sb.* + -ISH¹.] Of, pertaining to, or resembling, a boar; sensual; cruel. (Formerly often confused with *boorish.*)

A grosse and borish opinion MILT. Hence **Boa·rish-ly** *adv.*, **-ness.**

Boast (bōᵘst), *sb.* [ME. *bost* – AFr. *bost,* of unkn. origin.] † **1.** Loud noise of the voice, outcry. ME. only. † **2.** Speaking big, menace –1637. **3.** Proud or vainglorious speech; vaunt, brag ME. † **b.** Pomp, vainglory –1440. **4.** 'A cause of boasting, an occasion of pride, the thing boasted' (J.) 1593.

4. It is my b., that I was the first Minister who looked for it [merit] 1792. Hence **Boa·stful** *a.* full of boasting; given to boasting. **Boa·stful-ly** *adv.*, **-ness.** † **Boa·stive** *a.* (*rare*) boastful. **Boa·stless** *a.* (*rare*).

Boast (bōᵘst), *v.*¹ [ME. *bost* – AFr. **boster,* f. *bost*; see prec.] † **1.** To threaten. *intr.* and *trans.* –1756. **2.** *intr.* To vaunt; to brag *of, about,* glory *in* ME. Also *refl.* ME. **3.** *trans.* To extol; to brag of ME. **4.** To display vaingloriously or proudly (*arch.*) 1590. **5.** *fig.* To possess as a thing to be proud of 1697.

2. B. not thy selfe of to morrow *Prov.* 27:1. 3. Who boast'st release from hell MILT. *P.R.* I. 409. We..but b. we know POPE. 4. Would steer too nigh the Sands, to b. his Wit DRYDEN. Hence **Boa·sted** *ppl. a.* vaunted. **Boa·ster¹,** one who boasts. **Boa·stingly** *adv.*

Boast, *v.*² 1823. [Origin unkn.] **1.** *Masonry.* To pare stone with a broad chisel and mallet. **2.** *Sculpture.* To shape roughly before putting in details. Hence **Boa·ster²,** a broad chisel for boasting.

Boat (bōᵘt). [OE. *bāt,* str. m., corresp. to ON. *beit,* str. n. (:– **bait-,* not repr. elsewhere, but perh. rel. to BITT). ON. *bátr* was from Eng.; from Eng. or Scand. the word was adopted into LG. and Du., thence into G. (*boot*) and Fr. (OFr. *batel,* Fr. *bateau*).] **1.** A small open vessel, usually propelled by oars, though sometimes by a sail. **b.** Extended to fishing vessels, mail packets, and small steamers. (Sometimes also to large ocean steamers.) 1571. **2.** A vessel or utensil like a boat in shape, as a *sauce-b.*, an *incense-b.* 1684.

1. To hazard our liues in one small B. 1 *Hen. VI,* IV. vi. 33. White Star Line..the Boats are uniform and vary little in point of speed 1880.

Phrases. *To take b.*: to embark in a b. *To be in the same b.* (fig.): to be in the same case. *To sail in the same b.* (fig.): to act together.

Comb.: **b.-cloak,** a large cloak worn by officers on duty at sea; **-hook,** an iron hook and spike fixed at the end of a pole, used in pulling a boat towards, or pushing it off from, any fixed object; **-house,** a house communicating with the water, in which boats are kept; **-insect,** the BOAT-FLY; **-shell,** the genus *Cymba* of molluscs; **-slide,** a double inclined plane (with rollers) over which a boat may be drawn, thus avoiding the lock; **-tail,** a genus of birds, *Quiscalinæ*; **-train,** a railway train timed to meet a b.

Boat (bōᵘt), *v.* 1610. [f. prec. sb.] **1.** To place, or carry, in a boat 1613. † **2.** *intr.* To take boat 1610. **3.** To go in a boat, to row; to conduct a freight-boat (*U.S.*) 1673.

1. *To b. the oars,* is to cease rowing and lay the oars in the boat SMYTH. 3. We boated to Antwerp RAY. Hence **Boa·table** *a.* navigable by boat. (Orig. U.S.) **Boa·tage,** carriage by boat; a charge paid on such carriage; † boats, etc. collectively. **Boa·ter,** a canal-boat man; one who boats for pleasure; a hard straw hat worn by men.

Boa·t-bill. 1776. [See BILL *sb.*²] A genus of birds (*Cancroma*) belonging to the Heron tribe; esp. *C. cochlearia,* so called from the shape of its bill.

Boa·t-fly. 1753. A water-bug (*Notonecta glauca*), whose body resembles a boat.

Boatful (bōᵘ·tful). Pl. **boatfuls,** formerly **boatsful.** 1652. [f. BOAT *sb.* + -FUL.] The quantity or number which fills a boat.

Boating (bōᵘ·tiŋ), *vbl. sb.* (and *ppl. a.*) 1610. [f. BOAT *sb.* and *v.*] † **1.** Boats collectively. Cf. *shipping.* 1610. **2.** The action of going by boat, or of rowing; now *esp.* rowing as an amusement 1788. Also *attrib.* † **3.** A punishment in ancient Persia, in which the offender was tied in a boat, and left to perish 1753. **4.** *ppl. a.* Addicted to boating 1884.

† **Boa·tion.** 1646. [– mod.L. *boatio* (Levins), f. L. *boare* bellow; see -ION.] Bellowing.

[To] assist this mugiency or b. SIR T. BROWNE.

Boatman (bōᵘ·tmæ̆n). 1513. **1.** A man who manages a boat. **2.** = BOAT-FLY. 1841. Hence **Boa·tmanship,** the art of managing a boat.

† **Boa·tsman.** 1549. **1.** A boatswain –1622. **2.** = BOATMAN 1. –1684.

Boatswain (bōᵘ·tswēⁱn, usu. bōᵘ·s'n). 1450. [Late OE. *bātsweġen,* f. *bāt* boat + ON. *sveinn* SWAIN.] **1.** An officer in a ship who has charge of the sails, rigging, etc., and whose duty it is to summon the men to their duties with a whistle. **2.** The Arctic Skua (*Cataractes parasiticus*) 1835.

Comb.: **boatswain's-mate,** a boatswain's deputy or assistant; **b.-bird,** a tropical bird (*Phaeton æthereus*) so called from its whistle.

Boa·t-woman. 1843. A woman who manages a boat.

Bob (bǫb), *sb.*¹ ME. [First recorded in north. texts (sense 1); of unkn. origin.] **1.** A bunch or cluster. *north.* Still Sc. for a nosegay. **2.** †A rounded mass at the end of a rod, etc.; a knob –1659. *spec.* The weight on a pendulum, a plumb-line, the arm of a steelyard (*dial.*); a beam, etc. in a pumping engine (*dial.*) 1752. † **3.** A pendant; an ear-drop –1773. **4.** A knot or bunch of hair; also, a short bunch or curl; cf. *bob-curl.* Often short for **b.-peruke, -periwig, -wig,** a wig having the bottom locks turned up into bobs or short curls. 1685. **5.** A horse's tail docked short 1711. **6.** A knob, knot, or bunch of coloured ribbons; a weight on the tail of a kite 1761. **7.** A bunch of lob-worms threaded on worsted, used to catch eels 1660. **8.** A knob-like body 1615. † **9. a.** The larva of a beetle used as bait for fish. **b.** A beetle: chiefly in *comb.*, as *black-b.*, *blind-b.* (also *fig.*). –1792. **10.** The refrain of a song (? as if a pendant to each stanza) 1606.

3. My cousin Con's necklaces, bobs, and all GOLDSM. 4. A decent powdered doctor's b. MAR. EDGEWORTH. 10. *To bear a b.*: to join in the chorus.

Comb.: **b.-curl,** ? a short curl like a tassel; **-jerom,** a bob-wig; **-pendulum, -balance,** one with a b. or bobs; **-periwig, -peruke, -wig:** see 4.

† **Bob,** *sb.*² 1528. [f. BOB *v.*¹; cf. OFr. *bobe* deception.] A trick; a bitter jest –1682.

Bob (bǫb), *sb.*³ 1571. [f. BOB *v.*²] † **1.** A blow with the fist –1721. † **2.** *fig.* A rap; often a bitter jibe –1734. **3.** A tap 1611.

Dry b.: a blow that does not break the skin (*lit.* and *fig.*).

Bob (bǫb), *sb.*⁴ 1550. [f. BOB *v.*³] **1.** An act of bobbing. **2.** Sc. name of some dances 1550. **3.** A curtsy 1825.

Bob (bǫb), *sb.*⁵ 1671. [perh. conn. w. BOB *sb.*⁴] *Bell-ringing.* A term for certain changes in the working of the methods by which long peals of changes are produced. (See Grove *Dict. Music* s.v. *Change.*)

Bob (bǫb), *sb.*⁶ 1879. [app. spec. use of BOB *sb.*¹ 2.] An apparatus for polishing burnished metal surfaces, consisting of a disc or discs of leather or cloth, revolving rapidly on a spindle.

Bob (bǫb), *sb.*⁷ 1721. A pet form of *Robert.* Hence, perh., **dry-bob,** a boy (at Eton) who takes to land-sports; **wet-b.,** one who takes to boating; **light-b.,** a soldier of the light infantry, etc.

Bob (bǫb), *sb.*⁸ *slang.* 1812. [Slang, of unkn. origin.] A shilling.

Bob, *a.* 1790. [*Bob* in *bobtail* taken as an adj.; cf. BOBBISH.] **1.** Cut short (as a horse's tail). **2.** *slang.* ? Lively, 'nice' 1721.

† **Bob,** *v.*¹ [ME. *bobbe* – OFr. *bober* befool; cf. *bobu* stupid, and Sp. *bobo* fool (see BOOBY).] **1.** To make a fool of, deceive, cheat –1725. **b.** To take by deception *Oth.* v. i. 16. **2.** To mock, flout. ME. only.

1. *To b. (out) of*: to cheat (out) of; You shall not b. vs out of our melody *Tr. & Cr.* III. i. 75.

Bob (bǫb), *v.*² [prob. of symbolic origin; cf. BUFFET *sb.*¹] † **1.** To buffet –1605. **2.** To strike with anything knobbed ME. **3.** To rap or tap 1745. **4.** To cause to rap or bounce *against, at,* etc. 1612.

Bob (bǫb), *v.*³ ? ME. [prob. same word as prec., of symbolic origin.] **1.** *intr.* To move up and down; *hence,* to dance; to move to and fro. **2.** *intr.* To move up or down with a bob or slight jerk; *spec.* to curtsy. With cognate obj., *To b. a curtsy.* 1794. **3.** *trans.* To move (a thing) up or down with a slight jerk. Cf. BOB *v.*² 4. 1685.

1. A postilion..bobbing up and down on the off-horse HAWTHORNE. *To b. for apples, cherries,* etc.: to snatch with the mouth at apples, etc. floating on water, or dangling from a string. 2. The end of the pole bobbed up and struck me 1887.

Comb. **b.-fly,** in angling, a second artificial fly that bobs on the water, to indicate the position of the end-fly.

Bob (bǫb), *v.*⁴ 1614. [f. BOB *sb.*¹ 7.] *intr.* To fish (*for* eels) with a bob. Also *fig.*

Bob, *v.*⁵ 1822. [BOB *sb.*¹ 5.] **1.** *trans.* To dock (a horse's tail). **2.** To cut (the hair) short so that it hangs level above the shoulders 1918.

Bob (bǫb), *adv.* 1673. The stem of BOB *v.*² or ³, used to denote sudden action.

‖ **Bobac** (bōᵘ·bæ̆k). 1774. [Pol.] A burrowing squirrel, the Polish Marmot. var. **Boback.**

Bobadil (bǫ·bădil). 1771. A thrasonical character in Ben Jonson's *Every Man in Hum.*; hence, a braggart who pretends to prowess. Hence **Bobadi·lian, Bo·badilish** *adjs.* **Bo·badilism.**

† **Boba·nce.** ME. [– OFr. *bobance* arrogance, pomp.] Boasting –1534.

Bobbed (bǫbd), *a.* 1658. [f. BOB *sb.*¹ + -ED².] Furnished with a BOB (in various senses); formed into a bob; cut short.

Bobber (bǫ·bəɹ). 1837. [f. BOB *v.*³, ⁴ + -ER¹.] **1.** He who or that which bobs up and down or in and out; *spec.* a float used in angling, also the *bob-fly.* **2.** One who bobs for eels 1882. **3.** *dial.* and *slang.* A mate or chum 1860.

Bobbery (bǫ·bəri). *slang.* 1816. [Anglo-Ind. repr. Hindi *Bāp re* O father!, an exclam. of surprise or grief.] Noisy disturbance, row.

Bobbin (bǫ·bin), *sb.* 1530. [– Fr. *bobine,* † *bobin,* of unkn. origin.] **1.** An article round which thread or yarn is wound, for use as required, in weaving, sewing, etc. **a.** A small pin of wood, with a notch, used in lace-making. **b.** A wooden or metal cylinder, perforated so as to revolve on a spindle, having a flange at one or both ends, used in the processes of spinning, warping, weaving, etc. **c.** A small spool, placed within the shuttle, in some sewing machines. **d.** An ordinary reel or spool. **e.** A reel round which wire is coiled in electrical instruments 1870. **2.** A fine cord or narrow braid in haberdashery 1578. **3.** A rounded piece of wood attached to a latch-spring 1820.

Comb.: **b.-lace,** lace made on a pillow with bobbins; **-winder,** a contrivance for winding thread, etc. on a b. Hence **Bo·bbin** *v.* to wind on bobbins.

Bobbinet, var. of BOBBIN-NET.

Bo·bbing, *vbl. sb.* 1526. [f. BOB *v.* + -ING¹.] **1.** Beating, striking; also *fig.* giving a rap. (See BOB *sb.*³ 2.) **2.** Movement up and down, etc.; dancing, curtsying. (See BOB *v.*³) 1776. **3.** Fishing for eels with a bob 1653.

Bobbin-net, bobbinet (bǫ·binˌne:t, bǫ·binet). 1832. [f. BOBBIN + NET.] A kind of machine-made cotton-net, originally imitating bobbin-lace.

Bobbish (bǫ·biʃ), *a. dial.* and *slang.* 1813. [Cf. BOB *a.*, BOB *v.*³; see -ISH¹.] Well, in good spirits. Hence **Bo·bbishly** *adv.*

Bobby (bǫ·bi), *sb.* [See BOB *sb.*⁷, -Y⁶.] **1.** Pet form of *Bob.* (See BOB *sb.*⁷) **2.** [Hence, after Mr. (later Sir) *Robert* Peel, who introduced the new Police Act in 1828.] A slang nickname for a policeman. See also PEELER. 1851.

Bob-cherry. A children's game; see BOB *v.*³ 1 (quots.).

† **Bobet,** *sb.* ME. [f. BOB *sb.*³ or *v.*²; cf. *buffet.*] A cuff –1530.

Bobolink (bǫ·bǒliŋk). Also **boblincoln,** etc. 1796. [app. at first *Bob Lincoln,* or *Bob o' Lincoln,* echoic of the bird's call.] A North American singing-bird (*Dolichonyx oryzivorus*). Called also *Reed-bird* and *Rice-bird.*

Bob-sled, Bob-sleigh. 1848. [f. BOB (uncertain in what sense) + SLED, SLEIGH.] A sled or sleigh, made of two short sleds or sleighs coupled together; used in drawing logs, etc. (U.S.) Now also a long sleigh used in Alpine sport by a 'crew' of tobogganers.

Bobstay. 1758. [f. BOB (uncertain in what sense) + STAY *sb.*¹] *Naut.* A rope used to draw down the bowsprit of a ship and keep it steady. Also *attrib.*

Bob-tail. 1577. [f. BOB *sb.*¹ + TAIL *sb.*¹] **A.** Two words (bǫ·b tēⁱ·l): The tail (of a horse) cut short. **B.** *attrib.* (bǫ·bteⁱl). Having a bobtail 1605. **C.** *sb.* (bǫ·bteⁱl). **1.** [sc. *horse,* or *dog.*] 1676. † **b.** An arrow 'big toward the hede'. ASCHAM. † **2.** *transf.* A contemptible fellow 1619. **3.** *collect. Tag-rag and bob-tail,* or *tag, rag, and bob-tail*: the rabble 1645.

Bobtail (bǫ·btēⁱl), *v.* 1577. [f. prec.] To dock the tail of; *fig.* to curtail. Hence **Bobtailed** *a.* with tail cut short.

Bob-white (bǫ·bˌhwəit). 1864. The common partridge of N. America (*Odontophorus virginianus*), so called from its note.

Bob-wig; see BOB *sb.*¹ 4.

Boc, boc-land, etc.; see BOOK *sb.*

‖ **Bocage.** 1644. [Fr. *bocage,* OFr. *boscage* BOSCAGE.] Woodland; var. of BOSCAGE.

‖ **Bocal** (boka·l, bōᵘ·kăl). 1847. [Fr. *bocal* – It. *boccale* – late L. *baucalis* earthenware vessel for cooling liquids in – Gr. βαύκαλις.] A glass bottle or jar with a short wide neck. (Dicts.)

Bocardo, bokardo (bǫkā·ɹdo). 1509. **1.** *Logic.* A mnemonic word, representing a mood of the third syllogistic figure in which a particular negative major premiss (O), and a universal affirmative minor (A), give a particular negative conclusion (O). † **2.** The name of the prison in the old North Gate of the city of Oxford, pulled down in 1771. † **3.** A prison –1709.

1. B., which..was the opprobrium of the scholastic system of reduction SIR W. HAMILTON. **2.** Wee haue set Dunce [Duns Scotus] in B. 1535.

Bocasin (bǫ·kăsin). 1485. [– Sp. *bocaci, bocacin* cotton stuff used for lining (so Fr. †*boccasin* (Cotgrave), mod.Fr. *boucassin*) – Turk. *boğası.*] A fine buckram.

‖ **Bocca** (bo·kkă, bǫ·kă). 1799. [It.; = 'mouth'.] **1.** A circular opening in a glass-furnace, through which the melting-pots are inserted and withdrawn. **2.** The mouth of a volcano 1881.

‖ **Boccarella** (bokkăre·llă, bǫkare·lă). 1799. [It., dim. of prec.] A smaller opening on each side of the bocca in a glass-furnace.

‖ **Boche** (bǫʃ). 1914. [Fr. (sl.) 'bad lot', 'rascal', 'German', held to be shortening of *tête* (*de*) *boche,* in which *boche* is for *caboche* hard skull (see CABBAGE *sb.*¹).] French soldiers' name for a German.

Bock, bock-land, etc.; see BOOK *sb.*

† **Bo·ckerel, bo·ckeret.** 1653. [Origin unkn.; cf. BAWREL, BAWRET.] Names of the male and female of a long-winged hawk.

Bockey (bǫ·ki). 1860. [– Du. *bakje,* dim. of *bak* trough, tray.] A bowl made from a gourd. (New York.)

Bocking (bǫ·kiŋ). 1759. [f. *Bocking* in Essex.] A coarse woollen drugget or baize.

† **Bo·cstaff, -stave.** [OE. *bōcstæf* = OS. *bōkstaf,* OHG. *buohstap* (G. *buchstabe*), ON. *bókstafr,* f. *bōc* writing tablet, BOOK + *stæf* staff, letter; see STAFF *sb.*¹ Repl. by *letter* XIII.] A letter (of the alphabet).

Bodd-; see BOD-.

Bode (bōᵘd), *sb.*¹ [OE. *boda* messenger = OFris. *boda,* OS. *bodo,* OHG. *boto* (G. *bote*), ON. *boði* :– Gmc. **buðon,* f. **buð-,* weak grade of **beuðan* BID.] One who proclaims; a herald, a messenger. Resuscitated from 12th c. by some recent writers on OE. history.

Bode (bōᵘd), *sb.*² [OE. *bod* (chiefly north. for *ġebod*) n. = OFris. *bod,* OS. *gibod,* OHG. *gibot* (G. *gebot*), ON. *boð* :– Gmc. **ʒaboðam,* f. **buð-*; see prec.] † **1.** Behest –ME. † **2.** Message –1637. † **3.** Premonition, omen –1632. **4.** Foreboding (*arch.*) 1587. **5.** A bid. Still in n. dial. ME.

† **Bode,** *sb.*³ [ME. *bod, bode,* either f. BIDE *v.*, on the anal. of *abide, abode,* or aphet. f. ABODE *sb.*] Biding, tarrying, delay. *But b.*: without delay. –1593.

Bode (bōᵘd), *v.* [OE. *bodian* = OFris. *bodia,* f. *boda* messenger; see BODE *sb.*¹] † **1.** To proclaim; *absol.* to preach (the gospel) –ME. † **2.** To decree, command (a person) *that* –ME. **3.** To announce beforehand, predict, presage (*arch.*) OE. **4.** Of things: To portend ME.; *esp.* (with *well* or *ill*) To give *good* or *bad* promise 1700. **5.** To forebode (usu. *evil*) 1740.

3. There are croakers in every country, always boding its ruin FRANKLIN. **4.** This boades some strange erruption to our State *Haml.* I. i. 69. Hence **Bo·der,** one who or that which bodes. **Bo·dingly** *adv.* var. † **Bo·den.**

Bode = bude, pa. t. of BUS *v.*

Bodeful (bōᵘ·dful), *a.* 1813. [mod.; f. BODE *sb.*² + -FUL.] Full of presage, ominous.

‖ **Bodega** (bodī·gă). 1876. [Sp., wine-shop :– L. *apotheca* (whence also Fr. *boutique* shop) – Gr. ἀποθήκη store.] A wine-shop in Spain; adopted as a name for a cellar or shop for the sale of wines only.

Bodement (bōᵘ·dmĕnt). 1605. [f. BODE *v.* + -MENT.] **1.** An omen, presage, **2.** Foreboding 1642. **3.** Prediction, prognostication 1826.

2. Bodements sweet of immortality 1820.

Bo·den, *ppl. a. Sc.* Also **bodin.** ME. [Occurs in the Scottish Acts from 1429 in the sense of 'accoutred, armed'; the form is that of the pa. pple. of BID *v.* Form and meaning are unexplained.] † **1.** Accoutred, armed –1828. **2.** Fitted out, prepared; dressed. Usu. with *well* or *ill.* ME.

1. Bodin in effeir of war SCOTT.

Bo·deword. Now *n. dial.* ME. [f. BODE *sb.*²] † **1.** Behest. ME. only. † **2.** Message –1700. **3.** Presage 1832.

Bodge, *sb.*¹ 1589. [f. BODGE *v.*; cf. BOTCH *sb.*²] A clumsy patch; a botched piece of work. Now *dial.*

† **Bodge,** *sb.*² [Origin unkn.] A measure of oats; app. about half a peck. B. JONS.

Bodge, *v.* 1552. [Altered f. BOTCH *v.*; cf. *grudge* from *grutch.*] To patch clumsily. Now *dial.* Hence **Bo·dger**¹.

Bo·dger². 1736. [perh. var. of BADGER *sb.*¹] ? A pedlar. Now *dial.*

Bodice (bǫ·dis). 1566. [orig. *bodies,* pl. of *body* (see BODY II. 2), retaining the earlier (unvoiced) sound of *-s,* as in *dice, ice, pence.*] **1.** *Formerly,* An inner garment for the upper part of the body, strengthened with whalebone; a corset, stays; freq. called *a pair of bodies* (*bodice*) = 'a pair of stays' 1618. Also *fig.* **2.** The upper part of a woman's dress, a tight-fitting outer vest (cf. BODY *sb.*); also, an inner vest worn over the stays. Now, the upper part of any dress, down to the waist. 1566.

1. A pair of new blewish Bodice 1706. **2.** Nothing but her vpper bodies FLETCHER.

Bodied (bǫ·did), *ppl. a.* 1547. [f. BODY + -ED².] **1.** Having a body or trunk; usu. in comb., as *big-b.*, etc. **b.** Having substance, strength, etc. 1611. **2.** Made corporeal or material; embodied 1646.

1. Ill-fac'd, worse b., shapelesse euery where *Com. Err.* IV. ii. 20. **2.** Like the b. heaven in clearness BROWNING.

† **Bo·dikin, Bodikie.** Also **bodkin.** 1598. [dim. of BODY; see -KIN.] **1.** A diminutive body, a particle 1668. **2.** (*God's, ods*) *bodikins! bodkins!* (*bodlikins!*). An oath: God's dear body! –1753.

Bodiless (bǫ·dilės), *a.* ME. [f. BODY + -LESS.] **1.** Having no body; incorporeal, unsubstantial. **2.** Wanting the trunk 1587.

1. This Bodilesse Creation extasie Is very cunning in *Haml.* III. iv. 138.

Bo·dilize, *v. nonce-wd.* [After *spiritualize.*] To make material. SOUTHEY.

Bodily (bǫ·dĭli), *a.* ME. [f. BODY + -LY¹.] † **1.** Of the nature of body; corporeal, physical; as opp. to *spiritual* –1674. **2.** Of or belonging to the body or physical nature of man ME. † **b.** Real, actual *Cor.* I. ii. 5. † **3.** Solid; of or pertaining to a solid –1601.

2. The fear..of corporeall hurt, which we call *B. Fear* HOBBES. † *B. oath*: = CORPORAL *oath.* Hence **Bo·diliness.**

Bodily (bǫ·dĭli), *adv.* ME. [f. as prec. + -LY².] † **1.** In the manner of, or with regard to, the body; (often = 'unspiritually') –1685. **2.** In the flesh; in person 1440. **3.** *transf.* 'Body and all'; all together, in one mass, as a whole 1793.

2. Christ..b. present 1640. **3.** A portrait..cut out b. from the walls 1877.

Bodken, -kin, obs. vars. of BAUDEKIN.

Bodkin (bǫ·dkin). ME. [orig. *boidekyn* (three syll.), perh. of Celtic origin (cf. W. *bidog,* Gael. *biodag* dagger); *-kin* suggests a dim. formation.] † **1.** A short pointed weapon; a dagger, lancet, etc. –1657. **2.** A small pointed instrument used for piercing holes in cloth, etc. 1440. **3.** A long pin used by women to fasten up the hair 1580. **4.** An instrument with a knobbed point, having a large eye, for drawing tape or cord through a hem, loops, etc. 1714. **5.** *Printing.* An awl-like tool used to pick out letters from set-up type 1846. **6.** *transf.* (*colloq.*) A person wedged in between two others where there is room for two only; *esp.* in *To ride* or *sit b.* 1638.

1. When he himselfe might his Quietus make With a bare B. *Haml.* III. i. 76. **6.** While the pressed b., punched and squeezed to death, Sweats in the midmost place 1798. Hence **Bo·dkin, Bo·dkinize** *v.* to squeeze in as a b. (sense 6).

Bodkin (*Ods bodkins!*), var. of BODIKIN.

Bodkin, bodkin-work, var. of BAUDEKIN.

Bodle (bǫ·d'l). *Sc.* 1650. ['Said to have been denominated from a mint-master of the name of *Bothwell*' (Jamieson). Cf. ATCHISON, BAWBIE, *Bradbury.*] A Scotch copper coin = one-sixth of an English penny; the smallest coin.

Not that I cared a brass b. for his benison SCOTT.

Bodleian (bǫdlī·ăn, bǫ·dliˌăn). 1663. [f. Sir Thomas *Bodley* (1545–1613), who in 1597 refounded the Library.] **A.** *adj.* Of or pertaining to Sir T. Bodley or the Library bearing his name. **B.** quasi-*sb.* The Oxford University Library; also colloquially called **Bodley.** Also *fig.* and *transf.*

† **Bo·drag(e.** 1537. [prob. Irish; cf. *buaidhreadh* molestation, disturbance, *buadre* tumult.] A hostile incursion –1596.

Body (bǫ·di), *sb.* [OE. *bodiġ* str. n., corresp. to OHG. *botah* str. m. corpse (MHG. *botich,* mod. Bavarian dial. *bottech* body of a chemise), superseded in G. by *leib* (see LIFE) and *körper*; perh. an alien word in OE. and OHG.] **I. 1.** The physical or material frame of man or of any animal; the whole material organism. (In *Biol.* occas. used of plants.) **2.** Short for 'dead body', corpse ME. **3.** Used symbolically of the bread in the sacrament of the Lord's Supper ME.

1. He shold come fyght with hym b. for b. CAXTON. A struggle to keep b. and soul together 1887. **2.** The lyon stode by the b. 1 *Kings* 13:24.

II. 1. The main portion of the animal frame; the trunk OE. **b.** The main stem, trunk, stock of a plant or tree 1523. Also *fig.* **2.** The part of a dress which covers the body; also the part of a woman's dress above the waist, as dist. from the skirt 1585. **3.** The main, central, or principal part OE. **b.** *Naut.* The hull of a ship; various sections of this 1691. **4.** The main portion of a collection or company; the majority; the bulk of anything 1599. † **5.** A retort. (With some reference to *spirit.*) –1800. **6.** *Type-founding.* The breadth of the shank of the type, as opp. to its thickness; hence, size of type 1824.

1. All heade and veri litel b. 1600. Phr. *The B. of Christ (fig.)*: the Church of which Christ is the head. **3.** The b. of a land SHAKS., of a tree DE FOE, of true religion BURKE. **4.** The b. of a discourse *Much Ado* I. i. 287, the Empire 1678.

III. Personal being, individual. **1.** The material being of man, taken for the whole; the person. Chiefly legal. ME. **2.** An individual, of either sex. (Now familiar, with a tinge of compassion.) ME.

1. A warrant..to bring without delay the b. of the same prisoner 1652. *Heir of the b.*: an heir who is a direct descendant. **2.** It shall be given away to some poor b. WALTON.

IV. 1. *Law.* An artificial 'person' created by law; a corporation. Always with defining adj., as *b. corporate*, etc. 1461. **2.** A society, association, league, fraternity 1689. **3.** An organized collection of fighting men; a force. (The most general term so applied.) 1597. **4.** (loosely) A collective mass of persons or things 1593. **5.** A pandect (cf. L. *corpus juris*); a textbook 1593.

1. The king is a b. politick, for that a b. politique never dieth MILT. (*B. politic* means also an 'organized society'.) **The b. politic:** the nation in its corporate character; the state. (Orig. with reference to the *headship* of the sovereign.) **3.** A b. of horse 1769. **4.** The entire b. of the Scripture HOOKER. A b. of opinion 1874. **5.** A b. of laws BENTLEY.

V. Transferred to matter generally. **1.** A material thing ME. **2.** *Geom.* A solid 1570. **3.** Amount; bulk; quantity 1650. **4.** *Chem.* and *Min.* Any kind of 'substance', simple or compound, solid, liquid, or gaseous 1594. **5.** *abstractly.* Matter 1668. † **6.** Reality, as opp. to shadow, etc. –1702. **7.** Substance or substantial quality 1645. Also *fig.* **8.** Fundamental constituent 1787. † **9.** *Metaph.* An entity; an agent or cause of phenomena –1660.

1. *Heavenly bodies*: *now*, the masses of matter that exist away from the earth, the sun, moon, planets, comets, etc.; *orig.* the seven 'bodies celestial' of the astro-alchemists, viz. the sun, moon, and five old planets, to which answered seven ancient metals, called 'the seven bodies terrestrial'. A b...may be defined, the external cause to which we ascribe our sensations MILL. **3.** A b. of igneous rock MURCHISON, of air HUXLEY. **4.** Crystallized bodies, such as nitre BREWSTER. *Simple bodies*: the chemical elements; *Compound bodies*: the substances formed by their combination. **6.** The verie Age and Bodie of the Time *Haml.* III. ii. 26. **9.** Night and Day are bodies 1660. Voice is a B., for it maketh that which is heard; in a word, whatsoever is, is a B. and a Subject STANLEY.

Comb.: **b.-chamber,** the outer and largest chamber of a shell occupied by the b. of the animal; **-cloth,** a cloth to cover horses, etc.; **-coat,** one fitting closely to the body, † a dress-coat; **-colour,** a colour that has b., as opp. to a tint or wash; a colour rendered opaque by the addition of white; **-hoop,** one securing the arris pieces of a made mast; **-lifter** = *body-snatcher*; **b.-line bowling** (*Cricket*), fast bowling delivered persistently on the leg side; **-louse,** a species of louse (*Pediculus corporis*) which infests the body of the uncleanly; **-plan,** in *Shipbuilding*, an end elevation of a ship, showing the breadth, contour of the sides, timbers, etc.; **-snatcher,** one who secretly disinters dead bodies for the purpose of dissection; **-tube,** the main tube forming the body of an organ-pipe; **-whorl,** the last and largest whorl of a shell, containing the b. of the mollusc.

Body (bǫ·di), *v.* 1449. [f. prec.] *trans.* **1.** To furnish with a body; to embody. † **2.** To give body to (*lit.* and *fig.*) –1657. † **3.** To draw up or form (troops, etc.) into a body. (Also *intr.* for *refl.*) –1653.

Phr. *To b. forth*: to represent to oneself as in bodily form; to exhibit in outward reality; to typify.

Body-guard (bǫ·di,gāːɹd). 1735. [Cf. Fr. *garde du corps*, G. *leibwache*.] **1.** A guard for the person (*esp.* of a sovereign); a retinue or escort. **2.** A soldier of the body-guard 1861.

Bodyhood (bǫ·dihud). 1674. [f. BODY *sb.* + -HOOD.] The quality of having a body or of being body.

Bœhmenism (bō·mĕniz'm). 1656. The doctrines taught by Jacob Bœhme, a German mystic and theosophist (1575–1624); so **Bœhmenist, Bœhmenite.** var. **Behmenism.**

Bœ·otarch. 1822. [– Gr. βοιωτάρχης, f. Βοιωτία Bœotia + -αρχης ruler.] A chief magistrate of the Bœotian league.

Bœotia (bi,ōᵘ·ʃ'ă). 1786. [See prec.] A district of ancient Greece proverbial for the stupidity of its inhabitants; hence *fig.* **Bœ·otize** *v.* to become or make Bœotian.

Bœotian (bi,ōᵘ·ʃ'ăn). 1598. [f. prec. + -AN.] **A.** *adj.* Of Bœotia; dull, stupid; var. **Bœo·tic. B.** *sb.* A native of Bœotia; a thick-head 1649.

‖ **Boer** (būᵊɹ). Formerly **boor.** 1824. [Du. *boer* 'farmer', the same word as BOOR.] A Dutch colonist in S. Africa engaged in agriculture or cattle-breeding.

Bog (bǫg), *sb.*[1] 1505. [– Gael. (and Ir.) *bogach*, f. *bog* soft (in comps. 'bog', as *bog-bhuine, bogluachair* bulrush).] A piece of wet spongy ground, consisting chiefly of decayed moss and other vegetable matter, too soft to bear the weight of any heavy body upon its surface; a morass or moss. **b.** (without *pl.*) Bog-land, boggy soil 1687. Also *fig.* (Cf. *fog.*) 1614.

That Serbonian B...Where Armies whole have sunk MILT. *P.L.* II. 592. *fig.* A b. of uncertainty DICKENS.

Comb. **a.** In names of plants growing in bogs: as *B. Asphodel, Cinquefoil, Pimpernel*, etc.; **b. bean, b. nut,** or **b. trefoil,** also called BUCKBEAN; **b. berry,** the Cranberry; **b. moss,** various species of Sphagnum; **b. myrtle,** Sweet Gale (*Myrica gale*); **b. orchis,** *Malaxis paludosa*; **b. pink,** Lady's Smock (*Cardamine pratensis*); **b. rush,** *Schœnus nigricans*; **b. violet** = BUTTERWORT (*Pinguicula*). **b.** Special comb.: **b.-blitter, -bluiter, -bumper,** the Bittern; **-butter,** a fatty hydrocarbon found in the peat-bogs of Ireland; **-earth,** earth composed of, or largely mixed with, peat; **b. fir** = *bog-pine*; **b. iron, b. iron ore,** a brittle porous variety of brown hæmatite found in bogs; **-jumper,** (*local*) the Bittern; **-land,** marshy land; *joc.*, Ireland, hence **-lander; b. manganese,** the hydrated peroxide of manganese; **-mould** = *bog-earth*; **b. oak,** the wood of oak preserved in a black state in peat-bogs, etc.; **b. ore** = *bog iron ore*; **-pine,** pine-wood found in peat-bogs; **-spavin,** an encysted tumour on the inside of the hock of a horse; **-timber, -wood,** the trunks of trees found in peat-bogs. Hence **Bo·gginess,** boggy quality. **Bo·ggy** *a.* of the nature of, or characterized by, b.; swampy; *transf.* flabby.

† **Bog, bogge,** *sb.*[2] 1527. [perh. var. of BUG *sb.*[1]] A bugbear, a source of dread –1676.

Bog (bǫg), *v.* 1603. [f. BOG *sb.*[1]] **1.** To sink or entangle in a bog. Also *fig.* **2.** *intr.* (for *refl.*) To sink and stick in a bog 1800.

1. Bogged up to the saddle-girths SCOTT.

Bogey (bōᵘ·gi). 1892. Also **bogy, bogie.** [f. (Colonel) *Bogey*, an imaginary partner.] *Golf.* The score that a good player should do a hole or a course in. (Cf. PAR *sb.*[1] 4.)

Bogey, var. of BOGIE, BOGY.

Boggard, -art (bǫ·găɹd, -ăɹt). 1570. [A north. and midl. word rel. to BOGGLE *v.*, BOGLE, and BOG *sb.*[2]] **1.** = BOGLE. † **2.** An object at which a horse boggles –1725.

Boggle (bǫ·g'l), *v.* 1598. [prob. f. dial. *boggle* (see BOGY, BOGEY), as if orig. 'to see a boggle or spectre'.] **1.** *intr.* To start with fright, shy; to be startled *at.* **2.** To raise scruples, stickle (*at, about, over*, etc., or *to do*) 1638. **3.** 'To play fast or loose' (J.); to palter 1613. **4.** To bungle, fumble 1853.

1. You b. shrewdly, euery feather starts you *All's Well* v. iii. 232. **2.** To b. at an oath 1876. **3.** Are ye not afraid to b. thus with God Almighty DRUMM. OF HAWTH. **4.** To b. at a lock 1853. Hence **Bo·ggler.**

Boggle (bǫ·g'l) *sb.* 1660. [f. prec.] The act of boggling; scruple (1667); a bungle (1834).

Boggle. north. Eng. var. of Sc. BOGLE.

Bo·g-house. *dial.* and *vulg.* 1705. A privy, 'a house of office' J.

Bogie (bōᵘ·gi). Also **bogy, bogey.** 1817. [A north. dial. word, of unkn. etym. Not conn. w. BOGY.] **1.** *n. dial.* A low strong truck upon four small wheels, also called *trolley*. Hence *gen.* the truck used by plate-layers on a railway. **2.** A low truck running on two or more pairs of wheels and attached to the fore-part of a locomotive engine or the ends of a long railway-carriage by a central pivot, on which it swivels freely in passing curves 1844. Also *attrib.*

Bogie, var. of BOGEY, BOGY.

Bogle (bōᵘ·g'l). *north. Eng.* **boggle.** 1505. [Sc. *bogle*, north. Eng. *boggle*: see BOGY.] **1.** A phantom causing fright; a goblin, bogy, or spectre. **2.** *fig.* and *transf.* A bugbear (not a phantom); a mere phantom 1663.

Bo·g-trot, *v.* 1734. [Back-formation f. next.] *intr.* To trot over, or live among, bogs.

Bog-trotter (bǫ·g-trǫːtəɹ). 1682. [f. BOG *sb.* + TROTTER.] † **1.** One accustomed to trot over bogs –1755. **2.** *spec.* Applied to the wild Irish in the 17th c. 1682.

Bogus (bōᵘ·gəs), (*sb.*[1]) *a.* 1827. [orig. U.S. Appears first in 1827 applied to an apparatus for coining false money; of unkn. origin.] † **1.** *sb.* An apparatus for counterfeit coining. **2.** *adj.* Counterfeit, spurious, sham 1852.

2. B. transactions 1857. A b. Company..instead of paying dividends..goes into Liquidation 1877.

Bogus (bōᵘ·gəs), *sb.*[2] *U.S.* [Origin unkn.] A liquor made of rum and molasses.

Bogy, bogey (bōᵘ·gi). Also **bogie.** Pl. **bogies.** 1836. [orig. as proper name (*Bogey* and *Old Bogey* the Devil), presumably rel. to synon. BOG *sb.*[2], north. dial. BOGGARD, -ART, Sc. BOGLE, north. Eng. BOGGLE (all recorded from XVI), and further to BUG *sb.*[1], but the connections of the group are uncertain.] **1.** As quasi-proper name: The devil. **2.** A bogle 1857. **3.** *fig.* A bugbear; an object of terror 1865.

1. The people are all naughty and Bogey carries them all off THACKERAY. See also BOGEY, BOGIE.

Bohea (bohī·). 1701. [– Fuhkien Chinese *Bu-i*, local var. of *Wu-i*.] **A.** *adj.* Of the Wu-i hills, whence black tea first came to England; applied also to similar tea grown elsewhere 1704. **B.** *sb.* **1.** = *B. tea.* The name orig. of the finest kinds of black tea, now of the poorest. 1701. **2.** An infusion of this tea 1706.

2. Richardson's goddess who fed on muffins and b. THACKERAY.

Bohemia (bohī·miă). 1449. **1.** A kingdom of central Europe, forming part of the Austrian empire. **2.** Gipsydom; see BOHEMIAN *sb.* 2. 1871. **3.** The community of social Bohemians, or their district. So Fr. *la Bohème.* [f. BOHEMIAN *sb.* 3.] 1861.

3. B. had no name in Philip's young days THACKERAY.

Bohemian (bohī·miăn). 1579. [f. prec. + -AN; see -IAN.] **A.** *sb.* **1.** A native of Bohemia 1603. **b.** A Bohemian Protestant or Hussite. FULKE. **2.** A gipsy. [Fr. *bohème, bohémien.*] 1696. **3.** A gipsy of society; *esp.* an artist, literary man, or actor, who leads a vagabond or irregular and unconventional life. (Used with much latitude, with or without reference to morals.) 1848.

3. She was of a wild, roving nature, inherited from father and mother, who were both Bohemians, by taste and circumstances THACKERAY.

B. *adj.* 1. Of or belonging to Bohemia. **2.** Of or pertaining to the gipsies 1848. **3.** Of, or characteristic of, social Bohemians 1861.

Comb.: **B. chatterer,** or **waxwing,** a bird of passage (*Ampelis* or *Bombycilla garrula*); **B. glass,** a fine kind of glass, orig. made in Bohemia, in which potash is the alkali used. Hence **Bohe·mianism,** the conduct and manners of a B.

† **Boiette.** [– Fr. *boëtte, boëte*, obs. var. of Fr. *boîte* box; see BOIST.] A casket. LD. BERNERS.

‖ **Boiguacu.** [Tupi *boiguaçú*, f. *boi, boya* serpent + *guaçú, goaçú* big.] Native name of the Boa Constrictor or other large boa.

Boil (boil), *sb.*[1] [OE. *bȳl* and *bȳle* = OFris. *bēle, beil*, OS. *būla* (Du. *buil*), OHG. *būlla* bladder (G. *beule*):– WGmc. **būlja, -jo*, f. **būl-* (cf. Goth. *ufbauljan* puff up, and Icel. *beyla* hump :– **baulj-*). The ME. form was *bile*. Cf. BEAL *sb.*[1]] A hard inflamed suppurating tumour; a furuncle. *transf.* A blister on a painted surface 1840. Also *fig.*

Holy Job healed of his biles 1737.

Boil (boil), *sb.*[2] 1440. [f. BOIL *v.*] **1.** An act of boiling. **2.** The state of boiling, or being at boiling point; also *transf.* and *fig.* 1813. **3.** That which is boiled 1755.

2. The coffee was near the b. 1870. **3.** I put the linen..into a b. of soap 1755.

Boil (boil), *v.* ME. [– AFr. *boiller*, OFr. *boillir* (mod. *bouillir*) :– L. *bullire* bubble, boil, f. *bulla* bubble (see BULL *sb.*[3]).] **1.** *intr.* Of a liquid: To bubble up in agitation through the action of heat upon the lowest portions of the liquid, which become gaseous and escape; also said of the vessel containing the liquid. **b.** To reach the boiling point, to turn from the liquid into the gaseous state ME. **2.** *transf.* To move with an agitation like that of boiling water; to bubble, to seethe ME. **3.** *fig.* Said of passions, persons in a passion, etc. ME. **4.** *trans.* To cause to bubble with heat (see 1); to bring to the boiling point; *esp.* said of food; said also of the containing vessel ME. Also *intr.* (for *refl.*) **5.** To subject to, cook, cleanse, produce, etc., by, boiling ME. Also *intr.*

1. The fire causeth the waters to boyle *Isa.* 64:2. Phr. *To b. over*: to bubble up and run over the side of the vessel. **2.** The billows b. POPE. **3.** Resentment was boiling in his sullen, unsociable mind HUME. **5.** A Cook they hadde..To boille the chiknes with the Marybones CHAUCER. Martyrs.. were stoned..or boiled in oil TENNYSON. *To b. away* (intr.): to evaporate in boiling. *To b. down*: to lessen the bulk of by boiling; *fig.* to condense. Phr. *To b. the pot*: to supply one's livelihood. So *to keep the pot boiling*: also = to keep anything going. Cf. POT. Hence **Boiled** *ppl. a.* brought to the state of ebullition; subjected to, cooked, cleansed, etc. by, boiling. (In *Cymb.* I. vi. 125 *boiled stuff* = harlots.) *ellipt.* Boiled beef or mutton. *colloq.*

Boiler (boi·ləɹ). 1540. [f. prec. + -ER[1].] **1.** One who boils (anything). **2.** A vessel in which any liquid is boiled 1725. **b.** *spec.* In a steam-engine, the large vessel, usually of wrought-iron plates riveted together, in which the water is converted into steam; the tank attached to a kitchen grate; the vessel in which clothes are boiled 1757. **3.** What makes anything boil, as in *pot-b.*, a piece of work done *to boil the pot.* **4.** A vegetable, etc., suited for boiling 1812.

Comb. etc. (in sense 2 b) as **b.-alarm,** an apparatus for indicating lowness of water in a b.; **-feeder,** an apparatus for supplying a b. with water; **-float,** one which by its rising or falling turns the feed-water off or on; **-iron, -plate,** rolled iron of ¼ to ½-inch thickness, used for making steam-boilers, etc.; **-man,** one who attends to a b.; **-protector,** a coating to prevent the escape of heat from a b.; **-tube,** one of the tubes by which heat is diffused through the water in a b.

Boilery (boi·ləri). 1628. [– Fr. *bouillerie* distillery, f. *bouillir* BOIL *v.*; see -ERY.] A place for boiling anything, *e.g.* salt or sugar. Usu. in comb., as *sugar-b.*

Boiling (boi·liŋ), *vbl. sb.* ME. [f. BOIL *v.* + -ING[1].] **1.** The action of the vb. (senses 1–5). **2.** That which is boiled or being boiled, a decoction; a quantity boiled at one time; hence *the whole b.* (slang): 'the whole lot' 1674.

Comb.: **b.-furnace,** a reverberatory furnace sometimes employed in the decarbonization of cast iron; **-house,** a boilery; **-heat, -point, -temperature,** the temperature at which anything boils; *spec.* that at which water boils (at the sea-level 212 °Fahr., 100 °Cent.); *fig.* a high degree of excitement, etc. Hence **Boi·lingly** *adv.*

Boist. [ME. *boist(e* – OFr. *boiste* (mod. *boîte*) – med.L. *buxida* – Gr. πυξίς, -ιδ- box; see PYX.] † **1.** A box, a casket (= Box *sb.*[2] 1) –1633. **2.** A rude hut (*dial.*) 1840.

Boisterous (boi·stərəs), *a.* 1474. [var. of †*boisteous*, later by-form of †BOISTOUS, *-uous* (XIII, see next), of unkn. origin.] † **1.** Rough, coarse, as *e.g.* food. CAXTON. † **2.** Of rough, strong, or stiff texture; unyielding –1700. † **3.** Bulky, big and cumbrous –1642. † **4.** Painfully rough *Rom. & Jul.* I. iv. 26. † **5.** Coarse-growing, rank MILT. *Sams.* 1164. † **6.** Acting roughly; violent 1695. **7.** Rough, as opp. to 'calm' 1576. **8.** Of persons and actions: † **a.** Violently fierce, truculent –1791. **b.** Too rough or clamorous. (Orig. in a bad sense.) 1568. **c.** Abounding in rough but good-natured activity bordering upon excess 1683.

2. The leathern out-side, boistrous as it was, Gave way DRYDEN. **3.** His boystrous club SPENSER. **6.** A b. and bestial strength MILT. **7.** The boyst'rous Seas DRAYTON. **8. c.** Their b. Mirth STEELE. Hence **Boi·sterous-ly** *adv.*, **-ness.**

† **Boi·stous,** *a.* ME. [Of unkn. origin (see prec.).] **1.** Of persons, etc.: Rough, unpolished –1547. **2.** = BOISTEROUS 2, 3, 6, 7, 8. –1578. Hence † **Boi·stous-ly** *adv.*, † **-ness.**

Boke, *v.* Now *dial.* 1601. [app. var. of POKE *v.*] *intr.* and *trans.* To butt, to poke.

Bolar (bōᵘ·lăɹ), *a.* 1676. [f. BOLE *sb.*[2] + -AR[1].] Consisting of, or of the nature of, bole. var. † **Bo·lary.**

‖ **Bolas** (bō·las), *sb. pl.*; also as sing. with *pl.* **bolases.** 1843. [Sp., Pg., pl. of *bola* ball; see BULL *sb*[2].] A missile, used by the Patagonians and others, consisting of two or more balls or stones connected together by strong cord; these are swung round the head and discharged so as to wind round and entangle cattle, etc.

† **Bolbanac, bolbonac.** 1578. *Herb.* The plant 'Honesty' (*Lunaria biennis*) –1640.

† **Bold,** *sb.* [OE. *bold* (also *botl*) = OFris. *bold* house, OS. *bodal*, ON. *ból*, f. Gmc. **bu*dwell (see BUILD) + instr. suff. *-þla-*.] A dwelling –ME.

Bold (bōᵘld), *a.* [OE. *bald* (WS. *beald*) = OS. *bald* (Du. *boud*), OHG. *bald* (MHG. *balt*, surviving in G. adv. *bald* soon), ON. *ballr* dangerous, fatal :– Gmc. **balþaz.*] **1.** Stout-hearted, daring, fearless. Often = *brave. absol.* A bold man. Now only pl. *the b.* ME. quasi-*adv.* Boldly 1593. **2.** Of words, actions, etc.: Showing or requiring courage ME. **3.** In bad sense: Audacious, presumptuous; opp. to 'modest' ME. **4.** † Strong, big. Of grain, etc.: Well-filled ME. † **5.** Confident (*in*), sure (*of*) –1616. **6.** *fig.* Showing daring, vigour, or licence of conception or expression 1667. **7.** Striking to the eye; firmly marked, pronounced 1678. **8.** *Naut.* Of a coast: Rising steeply from water; used also of the deep water close to such a shore; also, generally, of any broad, steep, or projecting rock. Of a ship: Broad and bluff in the bows. 1628. Also in *comb.*

1. The righteous are bolde as a lyon *Prov.* 28:1. B.-following where your fathers led BURNS. **2.** A b. design MILT., task POPE, belief JOWETT. *To make (so) b., to be (so) b.*: to venture, presume so far as (*to do* a thing). **3.** Ane deuill of hell, Is na compair to the iniquitie, Of bald wemen DOUGLAS. A b. young woman 1887. **5.** Be b. in vs, weele follow where thou lead'st *Tit. A.* v. i. 13. **6.** A b. expressive phrase POPE. **7.** A good b. hand SHERIDAN. **8.** At Honfleur..they can ride in b. water 1787. Hence **Bo·ld-ly** *adv.*, **-ness.**

† **Bold,** *v.* [OE. *baldian* = OHG. *baldēn*, f. prec.] **1.** *intr.* To be or become bold –1706. **2.** *trans.* To make bold, encourage –1605.

† **Bold-beating,** *a.* Confusion of *bold-faced* and *brow-beating. Merry W.* II. ii. 28.

Bo·lden, *v.* Now *dial.* 1526. [f. BOLD *a.* + -EN[5].] **1.** To make bold, encourage. *refl.* To make bold (*to do*). **2.** *intr.* To take courage 1864.

1. These..b. us likewise and spur us on 1709.

Bold-face (bōᵘ·ld,fēⁱs). 1692. One who has a bold face; an impudent person; also *attrib.* A Sauce-box, and a Bold-face RICHARDSON. Hence **Bo·ld-faced** *ppl. a.*

Bole[1] (bōᵘl). ME. [– ON. *bolr*; cf. MHG. *bole* (G. *bohle*) plank; perh. rel. to BALK.] The trunk of a tree. *transf.* Anything of a cylindrical shape like the trunk of a tree, as a roll, a pillar, etc.

The shadow of the b. of the tree FISHER.

Bole[2] (bōᵘl). ME. [– late L. *bolus*; see BOLUS.] **1.** The name of several kinds of fine, compact, earthy, or unctuous clay, usually coloured yellow, red, or brown by the presence of iron oxide 1641. **b.** *spec.* **B. armeniac,** † *armoniak*, etc.: an astringent earth brought from Armenia, and formerly used as an antidote and styptic ME. † **2.** A large pill, a BOLUS; also *fig.* –1725.

Bole[3] (bōᵘl). *Sc.* 1728. Also **boal.** [Origin unkn.] **a.** A small square recess in the wall of a room for holding articles. **b.** An unglazed aperture in a wall for admitting air or light; sometimes closed with a shutter.

Open the b. wi' speed, that I may see if this be the right Lord Geraldin SCOTT.

Bole[4]. 1670. [= AL. *bola* (XIII); of unkn. origin.] A place where in ancient times lead ores were smelted –1785.

Bolection (bole·kʃən). 1708. [Origin unkn.] *Archit.* A moulding which projects before the face of the work decorated, as a raised moulding round a panel.

‖ **Bolero** (bolēᵊ·ro, -īᵊ·ro). 1787. [Sp.] A lively Spanish dance; also the music for it.

Boletus (bolī·tŏs). 1601. [– L. *boletus* – Gr. βωλίτης, perh. f. βῶλος lump; see BOLUS.] *Bot.* A large genus of fungi, having the under surface of the pileus full of pores. Hence † **Bole·tic** *a. Chem.* Of or pertaining to B., as *Boletic acid.*

Bolide (bǫ·ləid). 1852. [– Fr. *bolide* – L. *bolis, -id-* – Gr. βολίς missile.] A large meteor; usually one that explodes; a fire-ball.

Bolk, *v.* Now *dial.* [Late XIV *bolke*, var. of *balke* (BALK *v.*[2]), *belke* (BELK *v.*); see BELCH *v.*] **1.** = BELCH 1–3. **2.** *intr.* To vomit; to retch ME.; also *trans.* **3.** *fig.* and *transf.* To eject (as a volcano) 1513. **4.** *intr.* To heave or throb, like a confined gas, etc. 1561. **5.** To flow in gulps 1550. Hence † **Bolk** *sb.* a belch.

Boll (bōᵘl), *sb.*[1] ME. [– MDu. *bolle*, Du. *bol* round object; corresp. to OE. *bolla* BOWL *sb.*[1]] † **1.** Earlier f. BOWL *sb.*[1], q.v. † **2.** A bubble. ME. only. **3.** *spec.* A rounded seed-vessel or pod, as of flax or cotton 1500. † **4.** A round knob –1660. † **5.** The Adam's apple.

Comb. **b.-worm,** an insect that destroys the cotton b. or pod.

Boll (bōᵘl), *sb.*[2] ME. [– ON. *bolli* (cf. *blótbolli* sacrificial bowl) = OE. *bolla* BOWL *sb.*[1]; cf. prec.] A measure of capacity for grain, etc., containing in Scotland 6 imperial bushels, but in the north of England varying from the 'old b.' of 6 to the 'new b.' of 2 bushels. Also a measure of weight = 140 pounds.

Bollandist (bǫ·lăndist). 1751. [f. Jean *Bolland* (1596–1665), a Flemish Jesuit + -IST.] *pl.* The Jesuit writers who continue the *Acta Sanctorum*, begun by John Bolland.

Bollard (bǫ·lăɹd). [ME. *bollarde* (XIV in Sandahl); not again recorded until 1844. Perh. f. ON. *bolr* BOLE[1].] *Naut.* A wooden or iron post, on a ship, a quay, etc., for securing ropes to. Also *attrib.*, as in *b.-timber*, one of two large oak timbers bolted to each side of the stem, and supporting the bowsprit.

† **Bo·llen,** *ppl. a.* ME. [pa. pple. of BELL *v.*[2]] Swollen; puffed up –1609.

Here one, being thronged, bears back, all b. and red SHAKS. *Lucr.* 1417. vars. † **Boln, bolne.**

Bolling (bōᵘ·liŋ), *sb.* 1691. [f. BOLE[1] + -ING[1].] A pollard (tree).

‖ **Bolli·to.** 1753. [It., = 'boiled'.] The calcined materials for glass-making, frit.

Bologna (bǒlō·nʸă). 1563. A town in Italy, anciently called Bononia. Hence **Bolo·gnan, Bono·nian** *a.*; also **B. bottle, flask, phial,** an unannealed bottle, which may be dropped upon a brick floor without breaking, but will burst in pieces if scratched; **B. phosphorus,** a phosphorescent preparation of B. stone and gum; **B. sausage,** a large kind of sausage first made at B.; **B. spar, stone,** native sulphate of baryta found near B., having phosphorescent properties.

Bolometer (bolǫ·mĭtəɹ). 1881. [f. Gr. βολή beam of light + -METER.] An electrical instrument of great sensitiveness for measuring radiant heat. Hence **Bolome·tric** *a.*

Bolshevik (bǫ·lʃĭvik), *sb.* and *a.* 1917. [– Russ. *bol'shevik*, f. *ból'she*, compar. of *bol'shóĭ* big.] A member of that part of the Russian Social-Democratic Party which took Lenin's side in the split that followed the second congress of the party in 1903, seized power in the 'October' Revolution of 1917, and was subsequently renamed the (Russian) Communist Party; *transf.* an extreme revolutionary. So **Bo·lshevist** *sb.* and *a.* (abbrev. **Bo·lshy, -ie**). **Bo·lshevism, Bo·lshevize** *v.*

Bolster (bōᵘ·lstəɹ), *sb.* [OE. *bolster* cushion = (M)Du. *bolster*, OHG. *bolstar* (G. *polster*), ON. *bolstr* :– Gmc. **bolstraz*, perh. for **bolxstraz*, f. **bolʒ* **belʒ-* swell; cf. BELLY.] **1.** A long stuffed pillow or cushion used to support the sleeper's head in a bed; now restricted to the under-pillow. **2.** Applied to things of the nature of a pad: † **a.** A surgical pad or compress –1813. † **b.** A ridge of padding on a saddle –1753. † **c.** A padding in a garment –1753. **d.** *Naut.* in *pl.* Small cushions of tarred canvas, also pieces of timber, used to prevent chafing between ropes and other parts of the ship 1769. **3.** Applied to parts of mechanism which form a support or base: **a.** A block of wood fixed on a siege-gun carriage, on which the breech rests during transport. **b.** The transverse bar over the axle of a wagon. Also, the principal cross-beam of a railway-truck or carriage body. 1686. **c.** The part of the pier on which a truss-bridge rests. **d.** The spindle-bearing in the rail of a spinning-frame 1825. **e.** A horizontal cap-piece laid upon the top of a post or pillar, to shorten the bearing of the beam of a string-piece supported by it. **f.** In the centering of an arch, each of the transverse pieces which lie across the ribs and support the voussoirs. **g.** The plate or block of a punching-machine on which the metal to be punched is laid 1677. **4.** Applied to things of the nature of a supporting or strengthening ridge: **a.** The projecting shoulder of a knife, chisel, etc., which abuts upon the handle 1827. **b.** The metallic end of the handle of a pocket-knife. **c.** A raised ridge on the wrest-plank of a piano to give bearing to the strings by raising them. **5.** *Archit.* One of the rolls forming the sides of an Ionic capital; cf. BALUSTER 1876.

Bolster (bōu·lstəɹ), *v.* 1508. [f. prec. sb.] **1.** *trans.* To support with a bolster 1610. **2.** *transf.* and *fig.* To prop *up* 1508. **b.** *fig.* To uphold or bear out (evil-doers, crime, etc.). Also with *up*. 1523. **c.** Now usually: To give fictitious support to. Usually with *up*, occas. *out*. 1581. **3.** To pad, or stuff out with padding. 1530. Also *fig.* † **4.** *spec.* in *Surg.* To furnish with a pad or compress. Also *fig.* –1766. **5.** ? *intr.* To lie on the same bolster. *Oth.* III. iii. 399. **6.** To belabour with bolsters 1871.

1. Bolstered up in bed 1873. **2. c.** To b. up the credit of the government WELLINGTON. **3.** Revenues bolstered out with secular dignities 1616. Hence **Bo·lstered** *ppl. a.* **Bo·lsterer,** a supporter. (Usu. in a bad sense.) **Bo·lstering** *vbl. sb.* the action of the vb.; *concr.* padding; in *Surg.* a pad.

Bolt (bōult), *sb.*[1] [OE. *bolt* arrow = MLG. *bolte, -en* bolt, fetter, (M)Du. *bout*, OHG. *bolz* (G. *bolzen*) arrow, bolt for a door; of unkn. origin.] **1.** An arrow; *esp.* a stout and short arrow with thickened head, called also *quarrel*. Often *fig.* **2.** A thunderbolt 1535. **3.** An appliance for fastening a door, viz. a cylindrical or other piece of iron, etc. moving longitudinally through staples on the door, so that its end can be shot or pushed into a socket in the door-post or lintel. **b.** That part of a lock which springs out and enters the staple. ME. **c.** In breech-loading rifles, a sliding part resembling a door-bolt which is moved back and forth to open and close the bore; a corresp. part in a Lewis gun. † **4.** An iron for fastening the leg; a fetter –1688. **5.** A stout metal pin with a head, used for holding things fast together. See CLINCH, RING, etc. 1626. **6.** *transf.* A roll of woven fabric, usually of a definite length, as 30 yards, 28 ells, 40 feet. ME. **7.** A bundle (of osiers, reeds, etc.) of a certain size 1725. **8.** Wood in special size for cleaving into laths 1688. **9.** Name of the Globe-flower, and Marsh Marigold 1597; also of species of BUTTERCUP 1640.

2. *A b. from the blue* (BLUE *sb.* 5): a complete surprise. **3.** Forc't Vertue is as a b. overshot; it goes neither forward nor backward MILT.

Comb.: **b.-cutter,** one who cuts bolts; a machine for cutting bolts, or threads on bolts; **-hole,** a hole through which a b. passes; **-iron,** round bar iron; **-strake** (*Naut.*), certain strakes of plank which the beam fastenings pass through; **-threader,** a machine for cutting screw-threads on bolts.

Bolt (bōult), *sb.*[2] 1550. [f. BOLT *v.*[2]] **1.** A sudden spring or start. **2.** The act of breaking away; (*U.S. colloq.*) breaking away from a political party 1835. **3.** Bolting food 1835.

† **Bolt, boult,** *sb.*[3] ME. [f. BOLT *v.*[1]] A flour-sieve, a boulter –1611.

Bolt, boult (bōult), *v.*[1] ME. [– OFr. *bulter* (mod. *bluter*), earlier *buleter*, presumably for **bureter* (cf. *buretel*, mod. *bluteau* sieve) = It. *burattare*; of unkn. origin. The sp. *bolt* has arisen by assoc. w. BOLT *sb.*[1]] **1.** To sift; to pass through a sieve or bolting-cloth. Also *transf.* and *fig.* **2.** *fig.* To examine by sifting; to search and try ME.

1. To b. the bran From the pure flour POPE. The fan'd snow, that's bolted By th' Northerne blasts *Wint. T.* IV. iv. 375. **2.** I must first b. myself before I can censure them BURKE.

Bolt (bōult), *v.*[2] ME. [f. BOLT *sb.*[1]] † **1.** To spring back; to spring or start *up, upright* –1813. **2.** To spring suddenly † *upon, in, into* 1666; to dart *forth, forward, out* 1513. **3.** To dart *off* or *away* 1611. *spec.* Of a horse: To break away from the rider's control 1820. **b.** *transf.* To break away from a political party (*U.S. politics*) 1884. **4.** To discharge like a bolt; to shoot; to expel ME. **5.** To blurt *out* or *forth* 1577. **6.** *colloq.* To swallow hastily and without chewing, to gulp *down* 1794. **7.** *trans.* = *bolt from* in sense 3. (*U.S. politics.*) 1884. † **8.** To fetter; also *fig.* –1606. **9.** To secure (a door, etc.) with a bolt 1580. **10.** To fasten together or furnish with bolts 1727.

2. I think to b. upon you at Bath JOHNSON. Forth he bolted from the bush 1834. **3.** My donkey bolted about every five minutes 1877. **5.** The Rudest Head will b. a Paraphrase DANIEL. **6.** He bolted the alcohol SCOTT. **8.** To b. vp change *Ant & Cl.* V. ii. 6. **10.** I have ordered her [a ship] to be new bolted NELSON.

Bolt, *adv.* ME. [f. BOLT *sb.*[1] and *v.*[2]] **1.** In † *b. up, b. upright* the sb. = 'as a bolt'. Hence **Bolt-upri·ghtness. 2.** The vb. stem used *advb.* = 'bolting, with one bolt, straight' 1845.

Boltel (bōu·ltĕl). 1463. [Origin unkn.] A plain round moulding; a shaft of a clustered pillar.

Bolter[1], **boulter** (bōu·ltəɹ). 1440. [f. BOLT *v.*[1] + -ER[1].] **1.** One who sifts meal, etc. **2.** A piece of cloth used for sifting; a sieve; a bolting-machine. Also *fig.* Also, the fabric thus used. 1530.

Bo·lter[2]. 1840. [f. BOLT *v.*[2] + -ER[1].] **1.** One that bolts or runs; *esp.* a horse that bolts. **2.** One who bolts from his party (*U.S.*) 1883.

2. To whom a 'scratcher' or a 'b.' is more hateful than the Beast 1883.

Bolt-head, bolt's-head. 1475. [f. BOLT *sb.*[1]] **1.** The head of a BOLT (senses 1, 5). **2.** *Chem.* A globular flask with a long cylindrical neck, used in distillation 1610.

Bo·lt-hole. 1839. [BOLT *v.*[2]] **1.** *Mining.* A short connecting heading or opening. **2.** = *bolting-hole* (BOLTING *vbl. sb.*[2]) 1851.

Bolting, boul- (bōu·ltiŋ), *vbl. sb.*[1] ME. [f. BOLT *v.*[1] + -ING[1].] The act of sifting, *lit.* and *fig.*; *concr.* siftings. † **b.** The private arguing of law cases for practice –1670.

Bo·lting, *vbl. sb.*[2] 1692. [f. BOLT *v.*[2] + -ING[1].] The action of the vb., in various senses. *Comb.* **b.-hole,** a hole by which to bolt; *fig.* a means of escape.

Bo·ltless, *a.* [f. BOLT *sb.*[1] + -LESS.] Without a bolt or bolts as *b. lightning* (*poet.*).

Bo·ltonite. *Min.* [f. *Bolton*, Mass. + -ITE[1] 2 b.] A silicate of magnesium, found near Bolton, Mass.

Bolt-rope (bōult,rōup). [ME. *bolt(e)rop* (Sandahl, XIV). The first element is unexpl. Cf. *leech-rope* (LEECH *sb.*[3]).] *Naut.* A rope sewn all round the edge of the sail, to prevent it from tearing.

Boltspreet, -sprit, obs. var. of BOWSPRIT.

Bolus (bōu·lŏs). Pl. **boluses.** 1603. [– late L. *bolus* = Gr. βῶλος clod, lump of earth.] **1.** *Med.* A large pill. (Often contemptuous.) **2.** A small rounded mass of anything 1782. **3.** = BOLE[2] 1. 1682.

1. Physic him to death with pills and boluses 1832. Your Home Rule b. W. BLACK.

‖ **Bom, boma.** 1864. Native name in Congo, W. Africa, of a huge non-poisonous snake, in Brazil applied to the largest boas.

Bomb (bǫm), *sb.* 1588. [– Fr. *bombe* – It. *bomba*, prob. f. L. *bombus* – Gr. βόμβος booming, humming, of imit. origin.] † **1.** tr. Sp. *bomba de fuego* 'a ball of fire' 1588. **2.** A hollow iron projectile, usually spherical, charged with an explosive fired by concussion or a fuse; formerly = SHELL *sb.* III. 2 b; now usu. a hand-grenade (e.g. *Mills b.*) or an explosive shell dropped by aircraft 1684. **b.** *Whale-fishery.* A harpoon with an explosive charge in its head 1883. † **3.** A small war-vessel carrying mortars for throwing bombs. More fully *b.-ketch, -vessel*, etc. –1804. *Volcanic b.*: a roundish mass of lava thrown out of a volcano. *Comb.* **b.-lance** = 2 b.

Bomb (bǫm), *v.* 1688. [f. prec.] Formerly, to bombard; now, to attack with bombs.

† **Bo·mbace, -ase.** 1553. [– OFr. *bombace* – med.L. *bombax, -ac-*, alt. of *bombyx* silk – Gr. βόμβυξ; see BOMBASINE.] **1.** Raw cotton –1609. **2.** Cotton-wool; *fig.* padding –1662.

Bombard (bǒ·m-, bǫmbā·ɹd), *sb.* ME. [– (O)Fr. *bombarde*, in med.L. *bombarda*, prob. f. L. *bombus*; see BOMB.] **1.** The earliest kind of cannon, usually throwing a stone ball or a very large shot. **2.** = BOMB *sb.* 3. † **3.** A leather jug for liquor; a black-jack –1635. † *fig.* A toper 1617. **4.** An early variety of bassoon. Also BOMBARDO. ME.

1. Springalles, bombardes, bowes, and other artillary LD. BERNERS. **3.** That huge B. of Sacke *1 Hen. IV*, II. iv. 497. *Comb.*: † **b.-man,** a pot-boy; † **b.-phrase** (tr. L. *ampulla*), bombast.

Bombard (bǒmbā·ɹd), *v.* 1598. [– Fr. *bombarder*, f. *bombard*; see prec.] † **1.** *intr.* To fire off bombards –1695. **2.** *trans.* To batter with shot and shell. Also *fig.* 1686. **3.** *Cookery.* To stuff (a fillet of veal) 1769.

2. *fig.* Milton..bombarding Salmasius with foul epithets M. PATTISON. Hence **Bomba·rdment,** continuous attack upon a place with shot and shell.

Bombardier (bǫm-, bǫmbăɹdiə·ɹ). 1560. [– Fr. *bombardier*; see BOMBARD *sb.*, -IER.] **1.** A soldier in charge of a bombard; an artilleryman (*arch.*) **2.** *spec.* † **a.** Formerly: One of the master-gunner's men, employed about the mortars and howitzers –1769. **b.** Now: A non-commissioned officer in the artillery 1844. † **3.** A bomb-ship 1686.

Comb. **b. beetle,** a genus of beetles (esp. *Brachinus crepitans*) which when irritated eject fluid with a sharp report and blue vapour.

‖ **Bomba·rdo.** [It.] = BOMBARD *sb.* 4.

Bo·mbardon, -o·ne. 1856. [– It. *bombardone*, augmentative f. prec.] *Mus.* A brass instrument of the trumpet-kind, in tone resembling an ophicleide; also a brass reed-stop on the organ.

Bombasine (bǫm-, bǫmbăzī·n). 1555. [– (O)Fr. *bombasin* – med.L. *bombacinum*, for *bombycinum* (Isidore), n. of *bombycinus* (Pliny), f. *bombyx, -ic-* – Gr. βόμβυξ silkworm, silk; see -INE[1].] † **1.** = BOMBACE 1. –1580. **2.** A twilled dress-material, composed of silk and worsted, cotton and worsted, or worsted alone. In black, much used in mourning. 1572. Also in *comb.*

In Sorrow's dismal crape or bombazeen 1789.

Bombast (bǫ·m-, bǫmbă·st), *sb.* 1568. [var., with parasitic *t*, of BOMBACE.] † **1.** Raw cotton; cotton-wool –1665. Also *attrib.* **2.** Cotton-wool used as padding or stuffing for clothes, etc. *Obs.* exc. *Hist.* 1572. Also † *fig.* **3.** *fig.* Inflated or turgid language; fustian 1589. Also *transf.*

2. Iacks quilted with b. to resist arrowes 1601. **3.** Another soars, inflated with b. BYRON. Hence **Bomba·stic, -al** *a.* of the nature of b.; turgid; given to the use of bombastic language. **Bomba·stically** *adv.* † **Bo·mbastry,** bombastic composition SWIFT.

Bombast, *v. arch.* 1565. [f. prec., q.v.: in the vb. stress is oftener on the last syllable.] † **1.** To stuff or pad with cotton-wool, etc. –1820. **2.** *fig.* and *transf.* To stuff, inflate, *esp.* with bombastic language 1566.

2. That doth..bumbast his labours with high swelling and heaven-disimbowelling words FLORIO.

Bo·mbast, *ppl. a.* 1575. [f. BOMBACE *v.*; later = sb. used *attrib.*] † **1.** Stuffed, padded, puffed out –1656. **2.** *fig.* Puffed, empty, inflated. Of language: Bombastic. 1604.

2. A bumbast circumstance, Horribly stufft with Epithites of warre *Oth.* I. i. 13. Forty b. lines GIBBON. So † **Bombastly** *adv.* H. WALPOLE.

Bombax (bǫ·mbæks). 1834. [med.L. *bombax*, alt. f. L. *bombyx*; see BOMBACE, BOMBASINE.] A genus of tropical trees (N.O. *Sterculiaceæ*), which bear a fruit containing seeds surrounded by a silky fibre; esp. *B. ceiba*, the Silk-cotton tree of W. Indies.

Bombazeen, -zin(e, var. of BOMBASINE.

Bombed (bǫmd, bǫ·mbĕd), *ppl. a. rare.* [– Fr. *bombé*, f. *bombe* BOMB *sb.*] Rounded, convex. BROWNING.

Bombic (bǫ·mbik), *a.* 1816. [irreg. f. L. *bombyx, -ic-* (see BOMBYX) + -IC.] Of or pertaining to the silk-worm; as in *b. acid*, an acid secreted by the silk-worm.

Bombilate (bǫ·mbileⁱt), *v.* [f. *bombilat-*, pa. ppl. stem of med.L. *bombilare* buzz, f. L. *bombus*; see BOMB *sb.*, -ATE³.] *intr.* To hum, buzz. So **Bombilation.**

Bo·mbinate, *v.* 1880. [f. *bombinat-*, pa. ppl. stem of med.L. *bombinare* buzz, f. L. *bombus* (see BOMB *sb.*); see -ATE³.] To buzz. Hence **Bombina·tion.**

[RABELAIS II. vii, Questio subtilissima, utrum chimera in vacuo bombinans possit comedere secundas intentiones.]

† **Bo·mb-ketch.** 1693. [See BOMB and KETCH.] A small ketch-rigged vessel, carrying one or two mortars for bombarding –1830.

Bo·mb-proof. 1755. [See PROOF *a.*] **A.** *adj.* Strong enough to resist bombs or shells. **B.** *sb.* [sc. *shelter* or *structure.*] 1809.

Bo·mb-shell. 1708. = BOMB 2. Also *fig.*

‖ **Bombus** (bǫ·mbŏs). 1753. [L.; see BOMB *sb.*] **1.** *Med.* A humming noise in the intestines, ears, etc. **2.** *Entom.* The genus containing the humble-bees.

† **Bombycine** (bǫ·mbisin), *a.* 1599. [– L. *bombycinus* adj.; see BOMBASINE.] **1.** Silken, silk; as *sb.*, a silk fabric –1736. **2.** Of cotton, of paper made of cotton, as a *b. MS.* 1886.

† **Bombycinous** (bǫmbi·sinəs), *a.* 1656. [See prec. and -OUS.] **1.** Made of silk, silken (Dicts.) **2.** Of a pale yellow colour, like the silk-worm before it spins –1820.

† **Bomby·lious,** *a.* 1713. [f. Gr. βομβυλιός buzzing insect + -OUS.] Buzzing, humming, like a large bee.

‖ **Bombyx** (bǫ·mbiks). ME. [L. – Gr. βόμβυξ; see BOMBACE.] **1.** The silk-worm. † **2.** Raw silk. ME. only. **3.** *Entom.* A genus of moths, including the Silk-worm moth (*Bombyx mori*). Occas. any moth of the sub-order *Bombycina.* 1847.

‖ **Bon** (boṅ), *a.* Fr. = 'good'. adopted in ME. in the form *bon, bone,* BOON, q.v.; also used in several Fr. phrases.

Bon-accord (bǫnăkǭ·ɹd). *Sc.* Agreement good-fellowship; an expression of good will. **Bon-chrétien** (boṅ-kretyæṅ). [Fr. = 'good Christian'.] A name given to one or two kinds of pears. **Bon mot** (boṅ mo, pl. mōz). [Fr. = 'good saying'.] A clever or witty saying. **Bon-ton** (boṅ-toṅ). *arch.* Good style, good breeding; polite society; the fashionable world. **Bon-vivant** (boṅ vivaṅ); *fem.* **bonne vivante** (bon vivāṅt). One fond of good living; a gourmand. Cf. BONNE.

‖ **Bona fide.** 1542. [L., 'with good faith', abl. of *bona fides.*] **A.** *adv.* In good faith; genuinely.

The same to procede bona fide, without fraude 1542.

B. *adj.* (orig. with agent nouns.) Acting or done in good faith; genuine 1788.

A bona fide purchaser for valuable consideration 1788. The bona fide poor 1882.

‖ **Bona fides** (bōᵘ·nă fəi·dīz). 1845. [L.] Good faith, freedom from intent to deceive.

† **Bonaght.** 1568. [Irish]. A tribute formerly levied by Irish chiefs for the maintenance of soldiers –1827.

The barbarous practices of coshering and b. HALLAM.

† **Bona(ire,** *a.* [ME. *bonure, -er(e), -air(e)* – OFr. *bonaire,* short f. *de bon aire* gentle, friendly, tame (orig. spec. of dogs, falcons, etc.); see DEBONAIR.] **1.** Well-bred, courteous, complaisant –1696. As quasi-*adv.* = *bonairly.* Hence † **Bonairly** *adv.*, courteously, meekly. † **Bonairness,** † **Bonairty,** gentleness, courtesy.

† **Bonally, bonaillie** (bonæ·li, -*e*·li). *Sc.* 1470. [– (O)Fr. *bon* good + *aller* go; cf. *boon voyage,* BOON *a.*] Good speed, farewell; as in 'to drink his b.'

‖ **Bonanza** (bonæ·nză). *U.S. colloq.* 1878. [Sp.; = fair weather, prosperity, f. L. *bonus.*] **1.** *Mining.* A body of rich ore. Used *esp.* of the great silver mines on the Comstock lode. Also *fig.* **2.** *attrib.* as in **b. farm,** one which is 'a mine of wealth'; one on a large scale with all modern appliances; so **b. farmer** 1883.

1. The 'boss', the 'railroad king', and the b. Crœsus 1878.

Bonapartism (bōᵘ·năpaɹti:z'm). 1815. Attachment to the government and dynasty founded in France by Napoleon Bonaparte.

Bonapartist (bōᵘ·năpaɹtist). Also **Buonapartist.** 1815. **A.** *sb.* An adherent of Bonapartism. **B.** *adj.* Adhering to Bonaparte or Bonapartism 1869.

‖ **Bo·na-ro·ba.** 1597. [– It. *buonaroba,* f. *buona* good + *roba* dress.] A wench; a wanton.

‖ **Bona·sus, bona·ssus.** 1572. [L. *bonasus* – Gr. βόνασος.] *Zool.* The BISON. See also AUROCHS.

† **Bonave·nture.** 1500. [– It. *bonaventura,* f. †*bona* (mod. *buona*) good + *ventura* fortune.] **1.** A kind of boat or ship –1614. **2.** 'The old outer mizen, long disused.' Smyth.

‖ **Bon-bon** (bo·ṅ,boṅ, bǫ·n,bǫ·n). 1818. [Fr.; cf. *goody.*] **1.** A confection made of sugar. † **2.** A dainty –1842. Hence ‖ **Bonbonnière,** a small fancy box to hold sweets.

Bonce (bǫns). 1862. [Origin unkn.] A large marble; a game played with such marbles.

† **Bonchief.** [ME. *bonchef,* an Eng. (perh. AFr.) formation, f. *bon*(see BON), after *meschef* MISCHIEF.] Good fortune –1563.

Bond (bǫnd), *sb.*¹ [ME. *bond,* a phonetic var. of BAND *sb.*¹, preserving more the connection with *bind, bound.*] **1.** That with which one is bound; a shackle, chain, fetter, manacle (*arch.*, and only in *pl.*). *abstr.* Imprisonment, custody. (Latterly only in *pl.*) (*arch.*) ME. **2.** That with which a thing is tied down, or together; e.g. the withe which ties up a faggot, etc. Cf. also 9. ME. † **b.** Formerly, 'string, band, tie' –1674. † **3.** A bandage –1670. **4.** A restraining force; a uniting tie ME. **5.** An agreement or engagement binding on him who makes it. **b.** A covenant between two or more persons. ME. **6.** *Eng. Law.* A deed by which A (the *obligor*) binds himself, his heirs, executors, or assigns to pay a certain sum to B (the *obligee*), or his heirs, etc. 1592. **b.** *Sc. Law,* A mortgage 1862. **7.** A document of this nature issued by a government or public company borrowing money: now = *debenture* 1651. **8.** Surety 1632. **9.** Techn.: **a.** *Bricklaying* and *Masonry.* A method of disposing the bricks or stones in a wall, etc., by which the whole is bound into one compact mass; also a brick or stone placed lengthways through a wall to bind and strengthen it, a binder. **b.** *Carpentry.* The jointing of two or more pieces of timber together; also in *pl.* the timbers used for strengthening the wall of a building. **c.** *Slating.* The distance between the lower edge of an upper slate and the nail of the one below it. 1677.

1. Altogether such as I am, except these bonds *Acts* 26:29. † *Our Lady's bonds*: pregnancy; accouchement. **4.** The tight bonds of an old order MORLEY. The b. of right or law 1592. Charitie, the verie bonde of peace and all vertue *Bk. Com. Prayer.* Phr. *Bond(s of wedlock, matrimony.* **5.** O Kingis word suld be a kingis bonde 1500. *To put under bonds*: to order to find bail. **6.** † *Single* or *simple b.*: one by which the obligor binds himself to a payment absolutely and unconditionally. *Penal b.*: one with a condition attached that the deed shall be made void by some stated performance or observance, the sum named being only a penalty in case of default. Goe with me to a Notarie, seale me there Your single b. *Merch. V.* I. iii. 146. **7.** Bonds of turnpike commissioners POWELL. **9. a.** *English b.*, the method in which the bricks are placed in alternate courses of headers (bricks laid endwise towards the face of the wall) and stretchers (bricks laid lengthwise); *Flemish b.*, that in which each course consists of alternate headers and stretchers.

Phrases. *In b.*: (goods liable to customs-duty) stored in bonded warehouses, till it suits the importer to pay the duty and take possession. The importer on entering the goods pledges himself by b. to redeem them. So *to take out of b.*, *release from b.*

Comb.: (sense 4) *b.-friend*; (sense 6) *b.-creditor, -debt*; (sense 9) *b.-piece*; **b.-stone** = BONDER¹; **b.-timber,** horizontal pieces, built in walls, to strengthen them. See also under BAIL *sb.*¹ Hence **Bo·nd-less** *a.*

Bond (bǫnd), *sb.*² and *a.* [Late OE. *bonda* – ON. *bóndi* occupier and tiller of the soil (cf. HUSBAND), for *bóandi*, subst. use of pres. pple. of East Norse *bóa* = OIcel. *búa,* f. Gmc. **bū-* (see BOOTH, BOWER *sb.*¹).] **A.** *sb.* † **1.** Householder; husband. (Only in OE.) † **2.** Peasant, churl (ranking below *burgess*) –1450. † **3.** Base vassal, serf [tr. med.L. *nativus*]; a slave; also *fig.* –1618.

2. When I soughte silver. . Of baron, burges, or of bande 1450. **3.** I liue her b., which neither is my foe, Nor frend T. WATSON.

B. *adj.* **1.** In a state of serfdom or slavery; in bondage (*to*). Also *fig.* (*arch.*) ME. † **2.** Of or pertaining to slaves; servile –1567.

1. Whether wee bee b. or free 1 *Cor.* 12:13.

‖ **Bond,** *sb.*³ 1884. [Du., = 'league' (G. *bund*), f. *binden* bind.] In reference to the Dutch-speaking population of S. Africa: A league or confederation. Hence **Bondsmen.**

Bond (bǫnd), *v.* 1677. [f. BOND *sb.*¹] **1.** *trans.* in *Building*: To bind together so as to give solidity; to hold together by bond-stones, clamps, etc. **2.** *intr.* To hold together so as to give solidity 1836. **3.** *trans.* To encumber with bonded debt; to mortgage 1883. **4.** To put into bond (see BOND *sb.*¹) 1809.

3. They said the road. . was too heavily bonded 1883.

Bondage (bǫ·ndėdʒ). [ME. *bondage* – AL. *bondagium* (XIII), f. BOND *sb.*² Influenced later by BOND *sb.*¹] † **1.** Tenure in villenage; the service rendered by a *bonde* or BOND –1651. **2.** The condition of a serf or slave; servitude, serfdom, slavery ME. **b.** *transf.* The condition of being bound or tied up; that which binds (*poet.*) 1597. **3.** *fig.* Subjection to some bond, binding power, influence, or obligation 1450. † **b.** Binding force. *Cymb.* II. iv. 111.

2. To love B. more than Liberty MILT. *Sams.* 270. **3.** The b. of sin and vice COVERDALE. Hence † **Bo·ndage** *v.* to reduce to b.

Bondager (bǫ·ndėdʒəɹ). *Sc.* 1837. [f. prec. + -ER¹.] In Scotland and Northumberland, a female outworker, supplied by each cotter on a farm, as a condition of his tenancy

Bonded (bǫ·ndėd), *ppl. a.* 1597. [f. BOND *sb.*¹ + -ED².] **1.** Held, pledged, or confirmed by bond. **2.** Put into bond. (See BOND *sb.*¹) 1809.

1. That strong b. oth SHAKS. **2. B. store, warehouse,** one in charge of Custom-house officials, in which goods may be kept in bond.

Bonder¹ (bǫ·ndəɹ). 1845. [f. BOND *v.* + -ER¹.] **1.** *Building.* A binding stone or brick. **2.** A person who puts goods into bond, or owns goods in bond.

‖ **Bonder**² (bǫ·ndəɹ). [erron. formation from Norw. *bonde,* pl. *bönder.*] A Norwegian peasant farmer or petty freeholder. **Bonderman.**

Bo·ndhold. *Obs.* exc. *Hist.* 1611. [f. BOND *sb.*² + HOLD *sb.*¹, after *copyhold,* etc.] Tenure in bond service, or of bond-land; a sort of *copyhold.*

Bo·ndholder¹. *Obs.* exc. *Hist.* 1539. [f. as prec. + -ER¹.] A tenant in bond service, or of bond-land.

Bondholder² (bǫ·ndhōᵘ:ldəɹ). 1844. [f. BOND *sb.*¹ 6.] A person who holds a bond or bonds granted by a private person or by a public company or government.

Bonding (bǫ·ndiŋ), *vbl. sb.* 1677. [f. BOND *v.* + -ING¹.] **1.** The action of the vb. **2.** The storing of goods in bond; hence **b.-house, -warehouse.**

Bond-land. [OE. *bondeland,* f. *bonda* BOND *sb.*²] Land held by bondage tenure; a form of copyhold land.

Bondmaid, -maiden (bǫ·ndmeⁱd, -mēⁱd'n). *arch.* 1526. [f. BOND *a.*; cf. BONDMAN 2.] A slave girl. So **-servant, -service.**

Bondman (bǫ·ndmæ̆n). *arch.* ME. [f. BOND *sb.*² (cf. *husband*); but subseq. influenced by BOND *sb.*¹] **1.** = BOND *sb.*² 2. *Obs.* exc. *Hist.* **2.** A villein; a serf, slave ME. Hence **Bo·ndmanship.** So **Bo·ndwoman.**

Bo·ndslave. 1561. = BONDMAN, -WOMAN.

Bondsman (bǫ·ndzmæ̆n). 1735. [f. BOND *sb.*¹, with genitival *'s*; in sense 2 used as a var. of BONDMAN.] **1.** One who becomes surety by bond 1754. **2.** = BONDMAN 2. 1735.

‖ **Bonduc** (bǫ·ndɒk). 1696. [– Fr. *bonduc* – Arab. *bunduk* hazel-nut, filbert, Pers. *funduk* hazel-nut – Gr. ποντικόν (κάρυον).] A tropical leguminous shrub of two species (*Guilandina bonduc* and *G. bonducella*) bearing respectively yellow and lead-coloured seeds, also called Nicker-nuts.

Bone (bōᵘn), *sb.* [OE. *bān* = OFris., OS. *bēn* (MDu., LG. *been*), OHG. (G.) *bein,* ON.

bein :– Gmc. **bainam*.] **1.** The general name for each of the distinct parts which unitedly make up the skeleton of vertebrate animals; differentiated as, *ankle-*, *blade-*, *jaw-b.*, etc. **2.** *pl.* The bones of the body collectively, the skeleton; hence, the bodily frame, body, person (*joc.*) ME. **b.** = 'mortal remains' OE. **3.** The bony substance of the body. (Used as *collect. sing.*) OE. Also *fig.* **4.** The material of the bones, which consists of animal matter, *ossein*, and salts of carbonate and phosphate of lime in varying proportions 1471. Also *transf.* (see WHALEBONE). **5.** Anything made of bone, ivory, etc. **a.** *pl.* Dice ME. **b.** *pl.* Pieces of bone struck or rattled, to make rude music 1590. **c.** *pl.* Bobbins made of trotter bones, for weaving bone-lace. *Twel. N.* II. iv. 46. **d.** A strip of whalebone used in stays, etc.; also *attrib.* 1595. **6.** A bone (or part of one) with flesh on it, a fragment of meat. Often in comb. as *aitch-b.*, etc. ME. Also *fig.* **7.** *transf.* A callous growth on the legs of horses, becoming as hard as bone; as in *b.-spavin*, etc. **8.** *fig.* The hard framework of anything, e.g. of a ship 1634. **9.** *Min.* The slaty matter intercalated in coal-seams 1880.

1. Fie how my bones ake *Rom. & Jul.* II. v. 27. By these tenne bones (*i.e.* the fingers) 2 *Hen. VI*, I. iii. 193. Phr. *Hard*, or *dry, as a b.* **2.** Night hangs vpon mine eyes, my Bones would rest *Jul. C.* v. v. 41. She'll never live to make old bones 1873. **b.** Cvrst be he yt moves my bones *Inscr. over Shakespeare's Grave.* **3.** Art thou not of my b., and of my flesh? 2 *Sam.* 19:13. *To the b.*: through the flesh, so as to touch the bone; *fig.* to the inmost part. So *In the b.* **5. b.** *Mids. N.* IV. i. 33.

Phrases. (sense 6) *A b. to pick* or *gnaw*: something to occupy one as a bone does a dog; a 'nut to crack'. *To have a b. to pick with one*: to have something disagreeable to settle with a person. *B. of contention, discord*, etc.: some thing that causes contention, discord, etc. *To make bones of* or *about*: to make objections or scruples about. So *Without more bones*, etc. referring to bones found in soup, etc. as an obstacle to its being swallowed.

Comb. etc.: **b.-ash**, the mineral residue of bones burnt in contact with air, chiefly phosphate of lime; **-bed** (*Geol.*), a stratum abounding with bones of animals; **-black**, animal charcoal; **-breaker**, a name of the Osprey (L. *ossifraga*, Ger. *beinbrecher*); also *attrib.*; **-brown**, a pigment obtained by roasting bones, etc. till uniformly brown; **-cave**, one in which are found bones of animals; **-charcoal** = *bone-black*; **-dog**, a kind of Dog-fish; **-dust**, bones ground for manure; **-earth** = *bone-ash*; **-fever**, 'phlegmonous inflammation of the hand and arm, often seen in workers in b.'; **-fish**, a species of whale, valued for its whalebone; **-manure** = *bone-dust*; **-nippers** (*Surg.*), cutting forceps used in the removal of b.; **-shaker**, the bicycle as originally made (*joc.*); **-spavin**, a bony excrescence on the inside of a hock of a horse's leg; **-spirit**, a crude ammoniacal liquor obtained from b.; † **-work**, work done with b. bobbins. Hence **Boned** *ppl. a.* having bones; chiefly in comb., as *big-b.*, etc.; manured with b.; stiffened with whalebone; deprived of the bones. **Bo·neless** *a.* without bones; destitute of b.; *fig.* wanting backbone.

Bone (bōun), *v.*[1] 1494. [f. BONE *sb.*] † **1.** *intr.* ? To throw out spicules of bone. PEPYS. **2.** *trans.* To take out the bones from; also *fig.* 1494. **3.** To manure with bones; to stiffen with whalebone 1871.

Bone (bōun), *v.*[2] *slang.* 1819. [Origin unkn.] *trans.* To take into custody; to lay hold of; to steal.

Bone, *v.*[3] See BONING *vbl. sb.*[2]

† **Bone-ace.** 1611. [Origin unkn.] A game at cards in which the player who turns up the highest of the third cards dealt obtains the 'bone' or half the stake; also, the ace of diamonds, the highest card in this game –1726.

Bone-lace. 1574. [f. BONE *sb.* 5 c.] Lace, usually of linen thread, made by knitting upon a pattern, with bobbins originally made of bone.

Boneset (bōu·nse:t). 1670. [prob. f. BONE + SET *v.*] † **a.** The Common Comfrey, *Symphytum officinale* (*rare*). **b.** A North American plant, *Eupatorium perfoliatum*, valued for its medicinal properties; thorough-wort.

Bone-setter (bōu·nse:təɹ). 1470. One who sets broken or dislocated bones; a surgeon; now *spec.* one who makes a calling of treating fractures, without being a surgeon. So **Bone-setting** *vbl. sb.* and *ppl. a.*

Bonetta, var. of BONITO.

† **Bo·ne-wort.** [OE. *bānwyrt*; see BONE, WORT[1].] Name of plants supposed to be bone-healing, as the common Daisy, Golden-Rod, etc. –1736.

Bonfire (bǫ·nfəiəɹ), *sb.* 1483. [f. BONE *sb.* 1 + FIRE. In Sc. *bane-fire.*] † **1.** A great fire in which bones were burnt in the open air –1684. † **2.** A funeral pyre. (tr. L. *pyra, rogus* in 16–17th c.) –1658. **3.** A fire in which heretics or proscribed books were burnt 1581. **4.** A large fire kindled in the open air: **a.** (orig.) on certain anniversaries. These were orig. *bone-fires* in sense 1. 1493. **b.** (In mod. use) in celebration of a victory or the like, or for amusement, or combined amusement and utility 1530.

1. Ere I die, those foul idolaters Shall make me bonfires with their filthy bones MARLOWE. **4. b.** Celebrate the victorie with bonefiers in euerie town RALEGH. Hence **Bo·nfire** *v.* (*rare*) to illuminate with bonfires; *intr.* to make bonfires.

† **Bo·ngrace.** 1530. [– Fr. *bonnegrace* (Cotgrave); see BON, GRACE.] **1.** A shade worn on the front of women's bonnets to protect the complexion –1636. **2.** A broad-brimmed hat –1815.

‖ **Bonhomie** (bonomī). Also **bonhommie.** 1803. [Fr., f. *bonhomme* good man, good-natured fellow.] Good nature; the quality of being a good fellow.

‖ **Bonhomme** (bono·m). 1526. [Fr.; see prec. In med.L. *Bonus homo* (XIII).] † **1.** A member of an order of begging friars who came over to England in the 13th c. –1697. † **2.** A name given to the Albigenses 1751. ‖ **3.** A peasant. *Jacques B.*: the French peasant. 1851.

Boniface (bǫ·nifeis). 1803. [Proper name.] Name of the jovial innkeeper in Farquhar's *Beaux' Stratagem* 1707; thence generic as the proper name of innkeepers.

Boniform (bǫ·nifǭɹm), *a.* 1677. [– mod.L. *boniformis*, used as tr. Plato's ἀγαθοειδής.] Having the form of good; akin to the Good. Used by Hy. More to denote a faculty cognizant of moral goodness.

Bonify (bǫ·nifəi), *v.* 1603. [– Fr. *bonifier* improve, f. *bon* good + *-fier* -FY. Cf. med.L. *bonificare.*] † **1.** To benefit. **2.** To make good, turn into good 1678. So **Bonifica·tion,** †bettering; the paying of a bonus.

Boning (bōu·niŋ), *vbl. sb.*[1] 1495. [f. BONE *v.* + -ING[1].] **1.** The removing of bones from meat, fish, etc. **2.** The applying of bones to land as manure 1875.

Bo·ning, *vbl. sb.*[2] 1785. [Origin unkn.] *Surveying*, etc. The process of judging of the straightness of a surface or line by the eye, as by looking along the tops of two straight edges, or along a line of poles; also *attrib.*, as in *b. rod*, etc.

Bonitarian (bǫnitēə·riăn), *a.* 1861. [f. late L. *bonitarius* (cited only in Greek sp.; f. L. *bonitas* + *-arius* -ARY[1]) + -AN.] Beneficial; having beneficial possession without legal title. So **Bo·nitary.**

‖ **Bonito** (bǫnī·to). 1599. [Sp. *bonito* = Fr. *bonite* (XVI), of unkn. origin.] The striped tunny; a fish about three feet long, common in tropical seas. Also *transf.* var. **Bone·ta.**

† **Bo·nity.** 1585. [– L. *bonitas* 'goodness', a sense lost from BOUNTY, see -ITY.] Goodness –1790.

Bon mot; see BON.

‖ **Bonne** (bon). 1529. [Fr., fem. of *bon* good; as sb. a nurse.] † **A.** *adj.* Good. **B.** *sb.* A (French) nursemaid 1771.

Phrases. **Bonne-bouche** (bon buʃ). *Pl.* **bonnes bouches.** In Fr. 'A pleasant taste in the mouth': in Eng. = 'dainty morsel'. † **Bonne mine** (bon min). Good appearance. *To make a bonne-mine* (Mil.): to show oneself in force.

† **Bo·nnering,** *vbl. sb.* 1613. [f. Bishop *Bonner* + -ING[1].] Burning for heresy –1627.

Bonnet (bǫ·nėt), *sb.* [– OFr. *bonet* (mod. *bonnet*), short for *chapel de bonet* hat made of 'bonet', in med.L. *bonetus, -um*, of unkn. origin.] **1. a.** A head-dress of men and boys. In Eng. replaced by *cap*, but retained in Sc.; hence, occas. = 'Scotch cap'. **b.** A head-dress of women out of doors; usually without a brim, and covering no part of the forehead 1499. **c.** *Her.* The velvet cap within a coronet. **2.** *Naut.* An additional piece of canvas laced to the foot of a sail to catch more wind ME. **3.** *Fortif.* A portion of the works at any salient angle, raised to protect from enfilade fire and ricochet 1700. **4.** The second stomach of ruminants 1782. **5.** *techn.* Applied to a protective covering or defence: **a.** The cowl at the top of a lighthouse, chimney, etc. **b.** A wire covering over the chimney of a locomotive engine or steamer (chiefly in U.S.); **c.** A covering over the cage in mines; **d.** A cap for a safety lamp; **e.** An iron plate covering the openings in the valve-chambers of a pump. 1862. **f.** The protecting hood over the machinery of a motor vehicle 1902. **6.** = BLUE-BONNET 3. **7.** A thing or person used to put a good face on underhand proceedings. Also *fig.* 1833.

1. Off goes his b. to an Oyster-wench *Rich. II*, I. iv. 31. *To vail* (or *vale*) *the b.*: to take it off in respect. **7.** His look and bearing are..those of a b. at a fashionable hell 1833.

Phr. *To have a bee in one's b.*: see BEE[1].

Comb.: **b.-headed** *a.* (*Archit.*), of a window in which the outside of the arch is more splayed than the jambs; **-limpet**, a gasteropodous mollusc, so called from the shape of the shell; **-macaque, -monkey**, a monkey (*Macacus sinicus*), so called from the arrangement of the hairs on its head; **-piece**, a gold coin of James V of Scotland, on which the king is represented wearing a b.; **-shape**, the frame-work of a b. Hence **Bo·nnetless** *a.*

Bonnet (bǫ·nėt), *v.* 1607. [f. the sb.] † **1.** *intr.* To take the bonnet off in respect. SHAKS. **2.** To put a bonnet on 1858. **3.** To crush down a person's hat over his eyes 1837.

3. The Students hustled and 'bonnetted' a new Professor 1882.

Bonnibel (bǫ·nibe:l). *arch.* 1579. [perh. f. Fr. *bonne et belle*; cf. BELLIBONE.] Fair maid.

† **Bo·nnilass(e.** 1546. Now two wds.: Bonny lass –1579.

Bonny (bǫ·ni), *a.* 1529. [Of doubtful origin, perh. to be referred to OFr. *bon*, fem. *bone* good.] **1.** Pleasing to the sight, comely, expressing homely beauty. Now Sc. and north. and midl. Eng. **2.** † **a.** Of fine size 1600. **b.** Looking well, plump (*dial.* and *colloq.*) 1749. † **3.** Smiling, bright –1820.

1. Honest men and b. lasses BURNS. **3.** Then sigh not so, but let them goe And be you blithe and bonnie SHAKS. Hence **Bo·nnily** *adv.* **Bo·nniness.**

† **Bonny,** *sb.* 1671. [perh. rel. to BUNNY[1], earlier *bony* (XV).] *Mining.* A bed of ore, not forming, nor communicating with, a vein.

Bonny-clabber (bǫ·ni,klæ·bəɹ). *Anglo-Irish.* 1631. [– Ir. *bainne clabair* (*bainne* milk, *clabair* thick sour milk).] Milk naturally clotted on souring; = Sc. *loppert* or *lappert* milk.

Bonspiel (bǫ·nspīl, -spėl). *Sc.* 1565. [prob. of LG. origin; cf. WFlem. *bonespel* child's game.] † **1.** A set match. **2.** *spec.* A 'grand curling-match' between two clubs or districts 1772.

‖ **Bontebok** (bǫ·ntĕbǫk). 1786. [S. Afr. Du., f. *bont* pied + *bok* BUCK *sb.*[1]] A S. African Antelope (*Damalis pygarga*, Gray) also called Pied Antelope.

Bon-ton; see BON.

Bonus (bōu·nǒs). 1773. [prob. joc. or ignorant application of L. *bonus* m., for *bonum* n. good thing. Prob. orig. Stock Exchange slang.] A boon or gift over and above what is normally due. **a.** A premium for services rendered or expected; occas. = *douceur, bribe*. Also *fig.* and *attrib.* **b.** An extra dividend paid out of surplus profits; a portion of the profits of an insurance company distributed 'pro rata' to the policy-holders 1808.

Bon-vivant; see BON.

Bonxie (bǫ·ŋksi). 1802. Shetland name of the Skua Gull.

Bony (bōu·ni), *a.* 1535. [f. BONE *sb.* + -Y[1].] **1.** Of, pertaining to, of the nature of, bone or bones; consisting or made of bones. **2.** Abounding in bones; having large or prominent bones 1598. *Comb.* **b.-pike**, an American ganoid fish. Hence **Bo·niness.**

Bonze (bǫnz). 1588. [– Fr. *bonze* or Pg. *bonzo* (mod.L. *bonzus, bonzius*), prob. – Jap. *bonzō* or *bonzi* – Chin. *fan seng* religious person, or Jap. *bō-zi* – Chin. *fa-sze* teacher of the law.] A term applied by Europeans to the Buddhist clergy of Japan, and occas. of China, etc. Hence **Bo·nzery**, a Buddhist monastery.

Boo, booh (bū), *int.* (*sb.*) 1801. [Echoic.] An expression of contempt or aversion.

Boo (bū), *v.* 1816. [f. prec.] To low as a cow; to utter 'boo!'; to hoot.

Boob. *U.S. slang.* 1912. = BOOBY 1.

Booby (bū·bi), *sb.* 1599. [prob. (with -Y⁶) – Sp. *bobo* (used in both senses) :– L. *balbus* stammering, stuttering.] **1.** A dull, heavy, stupid fellow, *esp.* a dunce. Also *attrib.* **2.** A species of Gannet, esp. *Sula fusca* 1634.

Comb.: **b.-hatch** (*Naut.*), a smaller kind of companion which lifts off in one piece; **-hutch** (*dial.*), a small clumsy cart; **-prize,** a prize (of no value) awarded to the last or lowest scorer; **-trap,** a kind of practical joke in vogue among schoolboys and others. Hence **Boo·byish** *a.* awkwardly silly. **Boo·byism.**

Boodh, boodha, etc.: see BUDDHA, etc.

Boodle (bū·d'l). *U.S.* 1833. [– Du. *boedel*, *boel* the whole of one's possessions (*de heele boel*), disorderly mass, corresp. to OFris. *bōdel* movable goods, LG. *bödel* (*de ganse bödel*). Cf. CABOODLE.] **1.** Crowd, lot: often *whole kit and boodle.* **2. a.** Counterfeit money 1858. **b.** Money or means for corrupt dealing in public affairs 1884.

2. b. 'Sinews of war'..'soap' and other synonymes for campaign b. are familiar 1884.

Boohoo·, *int.* and *sb.* 1525. A word imitative of noisy weeping or laughter. Also as vb.

Book (buk), *sb.* [OE. *bōc* fem., corresp. to OFris., OS. *bōk* fem. and n. (Du. *boek*), OHG. *buoh* mostly n. (G. *buch*), ON. *bók* fem. (cf. Goth. *bōka* letter of the alphabet) :– Gmc. **bōks* usually taken to be a derivative of **bōkā* BEECH, the wood of the tree being the material of the tablets on which runes were inscribed.] **1.** A writing; a written charter or deed. *Obs.* exc. *Hist.* † **2.** A (written) narrative, record, list, register –1681. **3.** *gen.* A collection of sheets of paper or other substance, blank (cf. 8), written, or printed, fastened together so as to form a material whole; *esp.* such a collection fastened together at the back, and protected by covers; also, a literary composition long enough to make one volume, as dist. from a *tract*, *pamphlet*, *essay*, etc. Also *fig.* ME. † **4.** 'Benefit of clergy' –1710. † **5.** Book-learning, scholarship, lessons, reading. In later use only *pl.* –1680. **6.** A main subdivision of a large treatise ME. **7.** The libretto of an opera, etc. 1768. **8.** A volume in which to keep records of commercial transactions, minutes, etc. Also, one containing such records. 1498. **9.** *Betting.* A betting-book 1856. **10.** *Whist.* The first six tricks taken by either side. **11.** A packet of gold-leaf.

1. The witnesses, that subscribed the booke of the purchase *Jer.* 32:12. **2.** This is the booke of the generations of Adam *Gen.* 5:1. **3.** Books, as well printed as in Manuscript TINDAL. *fig.* Our life..Findes..bookes in the running brookes *A.Y.L.* II. i. 16. The b. of Knowledge MILT. Blotting your names from Bookes of Memory SHAKS. **5.** My sonne profits nothing..at his Booke *Merry W.* IV. i. 15. **6.** The *B. of Genesis.* The sixth booke of Euclide 1635. **8.** *A merchant's books*: his account books. So *cash-b.*, etc.

Phrases. **1.** *B. of God*: God's b., the Bible. *B. of life*, (*the living*): the list of those who shall inherit eternal life (cf. *Phil.* 4:3: *Rev.* 20:12). **2.** *By* (*the*) *b.*: in set phrase. *In a person's good* (or *bad*) *books*: in favour (or disfavour) with him (see also BLACK BOOK 4). *Without* († *one's*) *b.*: without authority; also *lit.* from memory. **3.** *To be upon the books*: to have one's name entered in the official list of members, etc.: hence, *to take one's name off the books. To bring to b.*: to cause to show authority; to investigate (a statement, etc.). *To close the books* (of a business): to make no further entries (for a time). *To shut the books*: to suspend business operations. *To speak like a b.*: i.e. with precise information. *To take a leaf out of* (a person's) *b.*: to follow his example.

Comb.: **b.-crab,** = *-scorpion*; **-credit, (-debt),** an amount credited, (debited), to a person's account in a ledger; **-ends,** a pair of (ornamental) props or supports used to keep a row of unshelved books upright; **-holder,** one who or that which holds a b., † *spec.* a theatrical prompter; **-louse,** an insect, *Psocus pulsatorius*, destructive to books; **-mark,** a book-plate; also = **-marker,** anything inserted between the leaves of a b. to mark a place; **-mate,** school-fellow, fellow-student; **-muslin,** a fine kind of muslin folded like a b. when sold in the piece, also *ellipt.* a dress of this; **-oath,** one sworn on the Bible; **-packet,** one which may be sent by b.-post; **-post,** the system under which books and printed matter may be sent through the post-office; **-postage, -rate,** the price charged for carriage by b.-post; **-scorpion,** an insect, *Chelifer cancroides*, resembling a scorpion, found in old books; **-slide,** an expanding stand for books; **-work,** study of textbooks; **-wright,** a maker of books.

Book (buk), *v.* [OE. *bōcian*; f. prec.] **1.** *trans.* To grant or assign (land) by charter; see BOOK *sb.* 1. *Obs.* exc. *Hist.* **2.** To enter in a book; to record, register ME. Also *fig.* **3.** To enter in a list 1548. **4.** To engage for oneself by payment (a seat or place). Also *absol.* 1826. **b.** To enter (a person's name, etc.) for a seat or place; to issue railway tickets to; *refl.* to take one's ticket 1841. **c.** To enter and pay for the transmission of (goods, etc.) by any conveyance 1829. **5.** *transf.* To engage (a person) as a guest or the like (*colloq.*) 1872.

2. Not eager to b. fresh orders 1883. **4.** Sam Weller booked for them all DICKENS. **5.** I shall b. you for that evening 1887.

Bookbinder (bu·kbəindəɹ). ME. One who binds books. So **Boo·kbindery** (*U.S.*), a bookbinding establishment; **Bookbinding** *vbl. sb.*

Bookcase (bu·kˌkeˈs). 1742. A case for books; a set of bookshelves shut in by doors.

† **Book-case.** 1552. A law case found on record –1726.

Book-craft. *arch.* OE. Book-learning, literary skill; authorship.

Booker (bu·kəɹ). [OE. *bōcere* = OHG. *buohhāri*, Goth. *bōkareis* (see -ER¹); in mod. sense formed anew on BOOK *v.*] † **1.** A writer of books –ME. **2.** A book-keeper 1863.

Boo·kery. 1599. [See -ERY 2.] † **1.** Study of books. **2.** A collection of books 1812.

Boo·k-fell. *Obs.* exc. *Hist.* OE. [FELL *sb.*¹] A skin prepared for writing upon; a vellum or parchment manuscript.

Boo·kful, *sb.* 1599. As much as fills a book.

† **Boo·kful,** *a.* Full of book knowledge. POPE.

Bookie (bu·ki). *colloq.* 1885. [See -IE, -Y⁶.] = BOOKMAKER 3.

Booking (bu·kiŋ), *vbl. sb.* 1643. [f. BOOK *v.* + -ING¹.] The entering in a book, *esp.* in order to engage a seat or place; also the issuing of tickets, entitling to the same 1884.

Comb.: **b.-clerk,** the clerk who books passengers or goods for conveyance, or who sells tickets at a b.-office; **-office,** one where places are booked for a coach, etc., or goods for transit; also a ticket-office.

Bookish (bu·kiʃ), *a.* 1567. [f. BOOK *sb.* + -ISH¹.] **1.** Of or belonging to a book or books; literary. **2.** Studious 1570; knowing books only 1593.

2. A b. man, who has no knowledge of the world ADDISON. Hence **Boo·kish-ly** *adv.*, **-ness.**

Book-keeper (bu·kˌkīpəɹ). 1555. One who keeps the accounts of a business, public office, etc. So **Boo·k-keeping,** the art of keeping books or accounts.

Bookland. *Obs.* exc. *Hist.* OE. Land taken from the *folcland* or common land, and granted by *bōc* or charter to a private owner; later, all land exc. *folcland.* Hence *Buckland* (place-name).

Book-latin. [OE. *bōc-lēden.*] Latin; later, book-language.

Boo·k-lea:rned, *a.* ME. Learned in books or book-knowledge. (Now disparaging.)

Whate'er these booklearn'd blockheads say DRYDEN. Hence **Book-learnedness.** So **Boo·k-lea:rning,** learning derived from books (merely).

Boo·kless, *a.* 1735. Unscholarly (*poet.*); destitute of books 1788.

Booklet (bu·klėt). 1859. [-LET.] A tiny book. So **Boo·kling.**

Boo·k-lore. [OE. *bōclār* (see LORE *sb.*¹); revived XIX.] Knowledge gained from books.

Book-maker (bu·kmēˈkəɹ). 1515. † **1.** A printer and bookbinder –1711. **2.** One who composes or compiles a book. (Often disparaging.) 1533. **3.** One who keeps a betting-book. Cf. BOOK *sb.* 9. 1862. So **Boo·k-ma:king.**

Bookman (bu·kmæ̆n). 1583. A scholar.

You two are book-men: Can you tell [etc.] SHAKS.

Book-plate (bu·kplēˈt). 1791. A label, usually pasted inside the covers of a book, bearing a device indicating ownership, place, etc.

Boo·k-rea:d, *ppl. a.* 1591. Well-read in books.

Bookseller (bu·kˌse:ləɹ). 1527. A vender of books. So **Boo·kse:lling** *vbl. sb.*; also *attrib.* or *adj.*

Boo·k-ways, boo·kwise, *adv.* 1696. [See -WAYS.] In the form of a book.

Boo·k-wi:se, *a.* 1616. Book-learned.

Book-worm (bu·kˌwɔ̄ɹm). 1599. **1.** *lit.* The larva of various beetles, esp. *Anobium hirtum*, destructive to books 1855. **2.** *fig.* One who is always poring over books 1599.

2. Perverted and spoiled by a whoreson b. B. JONS.

Boo·ky, *a. colloq.* 1880. [-Y¹.] Bookish.

† **Booly.** 1596. [– Ir. *buaile*; deriv. of *bo* cow, or – L. *bovile.*] A temporary fold used by the Irish who wandered about with their herds in summer; a company of such people and their cattle –1846. Hence † **Booling.** SPENSER.

Boom (būm), *sb.*¹ 1500. [f. BOOM *v.*¹] A loud, deep, resonant sound, as of a cannon, a large bell, etc.: the cry of the bittern.

The dull b. of the disturbed sea RUSKIN.

Boom (būm), *sb.*² 1645. [– Du. *boom* 'tree, beam, pole'; taken from Du. in senses in which *beam* was not used.] *Naut.* **1.** A long spar run out to extend the foot of a particular sail; as *jib.-b.*, etc. 1662. *pl.* That part of the deck where the spare spars are stowed 1762. † **2.** A pole set up to mark the course of the channel or deep water. (Dicts.) **3.** A bar or barrier consisting of connected spars, pieces of timber, etc., stretched across a river or harbour mouth to obstruct navigation 1645. **4.** A fixed line of floating timber across a river or round an area of water to retain floating logs. (*N. Amer.*) 1702.

3. The sea-works and booms were traced out by Marquis Spinola HOWELL.

Comb.: **b.-iron,** an iron ring fitted on the yard-arm, through which the studding-sail b. slides when rigged out or in; **-jigger,** a tackle for rigging the top-mast studding-sail booms out or in; **-sail,** one which is set to a b. instead of to a yard; **-sheet,** one fastened to a b.; **-spar,** 'a spar of a larger kind' (Smyth).

Boom (būm), *sb.*³ *U.S.* 1879. [prob. application of BOOM *v.*¹ w. ref. to sense 2.] **1.** A start of commercial activity; a rapid advance in prices; a rush of activity in business or speculation. **2.** The effective launching of anything upon the market, or upon public attention; an impetus given to any enterprise; a vigorously worked movement in favour of a candidate or cause 1879.

2. The Grant 'B.' may be succeeded by the Sherman 'B.' SALA.

Boom (būm), *v.*¹ 1440. [ult. imit.; perh. orig. – Du. *bommen.*] **1.** *intr.* To hum or buzz, as a bee or beetle; to make a loud deep resonant sound, as a cannon, a large bell, etc.; also the word to express the cry of the bittern; *trans.*, usually with *out* 1837. **2.** *intr.* To rush with violence, as a ship making all the way she can 1617.

1. Unless I get home, Ere the curfew bome BARHAM. **2.** The first of them booming by himself before the wind 1617.

Boom (būm), *v.*² 1627. [f. BOOM *sb.*²] **1.** *Naut. trans.* **a.** *To b. out*: to extend (the front of a sail) with a boom. **b.** *To b. off*: to push off with a pole. Cf. Du. *boomen.* **2.** To furnish (a river, etc.) with a boom to retain floating timber; to collect (logs, etc.) in a boom. (*N. Amer.*) 1879. **3.** Cf. BOOMING *vbl. sb.* 2.

Boom (būm), *v.*³ *U.S.* 1879. [f. BOOM *sb.*³] **1.** *intr.* To go off with a BOOM; to burst into sudden activity; to make rapid (commercial) progress, to advance vigorously. **2.** *trans.* To give a BOOM to; to push, puff, write up. Also *absol.* 1879.

1. Every one says business is booming 1879 **2.** The *World* is booming Mr. Conkling for..Senator 1884.

Boomer¹ (bū·məɹ). 1883. [f. BOOM *v.*³] One who booms an enterprise. *U.S. slang.*

Boo·mer². 1881. Australian name of the male of the largest species of Kangaroo.

Boomerang (bū·məræŋ). 1827. [Native name; *wo-mur-rāng* is recorded as a Port Jackson word, *būmarin* as Kamilaroi.] An Australian missile weapon: a curved piece of hard wood, with a sharp edge along the convexity of the curve. It can be thrown so as to hit an object in a different direction from that of projection, or so as to return to or behind the starting-point. Also *fig.*

Like the strange missile which the Australian throws, Your verbal b. slaps you on the nose HOLMES.

Booming (bū·miŋ), *vbl. sb.* 1774. [f. BOOM *v.*[1], [2], [3] + -ING[1].] **1.** The action of the vb. BOOM[1]. **2.** The accumulation and sudden discharge of a quantity of water (in placer mining) 1880. **3.** See BOOM *sb.*[3], BOOM *v.*[3] 1881. **Boo·mingly** *adv.* with a b. noise.

Boon (būn), *sb.*[1] ME. [– ON. *bón* (Sw., Da. *bön*) :– Gmc. **bōniz*, whence also OE. *bēn* BENE. Sense-development prob. infl. by BOON *a.*] † **1.** A prayer, petition, request –1623. † **2.** A command couched in the form of a request –1593. **3.** *transf.* The matter prayed for or asked (*arch.*) ME. **4.** A favour, a gift; in 17th c. a gratuity; but now only *fig.* or *arch.* 1460. **5.** A blessing, an advantage, a thing to be thankful for. (The usual current sense.) 1767. **6.** An unpaid service due by a tenant to his lord. Now *dial.* 1634. ¶ **7.** Modern archaists confuse with BOON *a.*

1. The kyng assentede to his bone CHAUCER. **2.** SHAKS. 3 *Hen. VI*, III. ii. 46. **3.** Cousin, you must grant me my b. SCOTT. **7.** For b. or bale 1874. Hence **Boo·nless** *a.*

Boon, *sb.*[2] ME. [Origin unkn. See BUN *sb.*[1]] The stalk of flax or hemp after the fibre has been removed.

Boon (būn), *a.* ME. [– (O)Fr. *bon* :– L. *bonus* good; in gen. Eng. use XIV–XVII, surviving in senses 3 and 4.] † **1.** Good, goodly –1686. † **2.** Fortunate, prosperous: *esp.* in *b. voyage*, prosperous journey, also *fig.* good success. –1657. **3.** Gracious, bounteous, benign; = L. *almus* (*poet.*) 1612. **4.** In *b. companion*, lit. 'good-fellow', also occ. used predicatively: Jolly, convivial 1566.

1. Seint Iulian! lo, bon hostelle CHAUCER. **3.** Flours..which..Nature b. Powrd forth profuse MILT. *P.L.* IV. 242. **4.** Hight'nd as with Wine, jocund and b. MILT. *P.L.* IX. 793.

Boon, *v. Obs.* or *dial.* ME. [f. BOON *sb.*[1]] † **1.** To ask as a boon. † **2.** *intr.* To do boon-work (see BOON *sb.*[1] 6) 1691. **3.** *trans.* To repair (public roads). Now *dial.* 1783.

Boopic (bo,ǫ·pik), *a. rare.* 1854. [f. Gr. βοῶπις (f. βοῦς ox + ὤψ eye) + -IC.] Ox-eyed.

Boor (būɹ). 1430. [– LG. *būr* or Du. *boer*; the word is repr. by OE. *ġe|būr*, *nēahġebūr* NEIGHBOUR. Cf. BOR, BOWER *sb.*[5]] **1.** A husbandman, peasant. *Obs.*, exc. as in 3. **2.** A Dutch or German peasant (Ger. *bauer*) 1581. **b.** A Dutch colonist in Guiana, S. Africa, etc. (In S. Africa now BOER.) 1824. Also *transf.* **3.** A rustic (and therefore coarse); a clown 1598. Also *fig.*

1. A countrie Boore, a goodlie proper swayne 1592. **2.** Germany hath her Boores, like our Yeomen FULLER. **3.** As to manners a mere b. or clown DE FOE. *Comb.* **Boor's Mustard** [–early mod. G. *Baurensenfe*] *Herb.*, name given to *Thlaspi arvense*. Hence **Boo·rish** *a.* (and † quasi-*sb. A.Y.L.* v. i. 54). **Boo·rish-ly** *adv.*, **-ness.**

Boose (būz), *sb. north.* 1440. [Late ME. repr. OE. **bōs*, whence *bōsiġ* BOOSY.] A cow- or horse-stall; a crib. var. **Boo·sy.**

Boose, var. of BOOZE.

† **Boost,** *sb.*[1] Also *north.* **bost.** ME. A var. of BOIST box, pyx –1651.

Boost (būst), *sb.*[2] *U.S. colloq.* 1858. [f. BOOST *v.*] A lift, a shove up.

Boost (būst), *v. U.S. colloq.* 1848. [Origin unkn.] *trans.* To hoist; to push up from behind. Also *fig.* Hence **Boo·ster** (*Electr.*), a machine for raising voltage.

Boot (būt), *sb.*[1] [OE. *bōt* = OFris. *bōte*, OS. *bōta*, (M)Du. *boete*, OHG. *buoza* (G. *busse*), ON. *bót*, Goth. *bōta* :– Gmc. **bōtō* remedy, advantage, f. **bōt-* **bat* (see BETTER, BEST).] † **1.** Advantage; profit; avail, use –1693. **2.** The making good or mending of anything; the means of doing so; repair; remedy, relief OE. **3.** Compensation paid for injury or wrong-doing; amends. (Only in OE., and *Hist.*, as OE. *bōt*, ME. *bote.*) In comb., as *man-bote*, etc. **4.** Expiation of sin; sin-offering; penance. *Obs.* (exc. *Hist.*).

Phr. *To b.*: to the good, into the bargain; For two books that I had and 6*s.* 6*d.* to b. I had my great book of songs PEPYS. Apply [thy daies] To better b. SPENSER. **2.** Anon he yaf the sike man his boote CHAUCER. *Saint George to b.! Grace to b.!* i.e. to our help. *None other b.*: no alternative.

† **Boot,** *sb.*[2] 1593. [app. a use of prec., influenced by BOOTY. Cf. BOOT *sb.*[1] 3.] Booty, spoil, *esp.* in phr. *To make b.* SHAKS.

Boot (būt), *sb.*[3] [ME. *bote* – ON. *bóti* or its source, OFr. *bote* (mod. *botte*); in AL. *bota* (XII), *botta*; of unkn. origin.] **1.** A covering for the foot and lower part of the leg, usually of leather. (At first used only by riders.) † **2.** A greave –1609. **3.** An instrument of torture formerly used in Scotland to extort confessions 1513. **4.** Part of a coach; an uncovered space on or by the steps on each side, where attendants sat, facing sideways; later, a low outside compartment in front or behind. Now *Hist.* 1608. **b.** The receptacle for parcels, etc. under the seats of the guard and coachman 1781.

1. Get on thy boots, wee'l ride all night SHAKS. **3.** Shall I draw him on a Scotch pair of boots, Master, and make him tell all? VANBRUGH.

Phrases. *The b. is on the other leg*: the case is altered, the responsibility is on the other party. *To have* († *wish*) *one's heart in one's boots*: to be in extreme fear (cf. 'the heart sinks'). † *Over shoes, over boots*: used of reckless persistence in any course. *Boot and saddle* [perversion of Fr. *boute-selle* 'place saddle'; see BOUTE-SELLE], the signal to cavalry for mounting.

Comb.: **b.-black,** a shoe-black (chiefly *U.S.*); † **-catcher,** a servant at an inn who pulled off the guests' boots; **-closer,** one who sews together the upper leathers of boots; **-hook,** one for pulling on boots; **-hose, -stocking,** an over-stocking which covers the leg like a jack-boot; **-jack,** a contrivance for pulling off boots; **-last** = *boot-tree*; **-lick** *v.* to toady; *sb.* a toady (*U.S. slang*); **-stretcher, -tree,** a shaped block inserted into a b. to stretch it.

Boot (būt), *v.*[1] [ME. *bote, boote*, f. BOOT *sb.*[1], repl. *bete* BEET *v.*] † **1.** *trans.* To make better –1481. † **2.** To make good, make up –1530. **3.** To profit, avail (Only in 3rd pers.) ME. **b.** with sense 'it matters' 1752. † **4.** To benefit, enrich. *Ant. & Cl.* II. v. 71.

3. It boots not to look backwards ARNOLD. What boots thy wealth SOUTHEY. **b.** What boots it which prevails 1752.

Boot (būt), *v.*[2] 1468. [f. BOOT *sb.*[3]] **1.** *trans.* To put boots on (another or oneself); *intr.* (for *refl.*) to put on one's boots 1597. **2.** *trans.* To torture with the BOOT (*sb.*[3] 3) 1580. **3.** *Mil. slang.* To beat, formerly with a jack-boot, now with a waist-belt 1802.

1. Boote, boote, Master Shallow 2 *Hen. IV*, v. iii. 140.

Booted (bū·tėd), *ppl. a.* 1552. [f. BOOT *v.*[2] + -ED[1].] **1.** Having boots on; formerly 'equipped for riding', *esp.* in *booted and spurred*. Also *fig.* **2.** *transf.* Clothed or covered as to the legs 1601.

Bootee (būtī·). [f. BOOT *sb.*[3] + -EE[2].] A high-low boot for ladies; an infant's wool boot.

‖ **Boötes** (bo,ō·tīz). 1656. [L. – Gr. βοώτης.] *Astron.* A constellation, the Wagoner, situated at the tail of the Great Bear.

Booth (būð), *sb.* [ME. *bōþ* (cf. AL. *botha, bothus* XII) – Old East Norse **bōð* (Sw., Da. *bod* stall, shop) = OIcel. *búð* dwelling, f. East Norse *bóa* = OIcel. *búa* dwell; see BOND *sb.*[2], BOWER *sb.*[1]] **1.** A temporary dwelling covered with boughs, canvas, or other slight material (*arch.*). **2.** *spec.* A covered stall at a market, fair, etc. See also TOLL-BOOTH. ME. *Comb.* **polling-b.,** a temporary structure for voting purposes at an election.

† **Boot-hale,** *v.* 1598. [f. BOOT *sb.*[2] + HALE *v.*] **1.** *intr.* To carry off booty –1670. **2.** *trans.* To spoil, pillage, plunder –1625.

Bootikin, bootakin (bū·tĭkin, -ăkin). 1727. [dim. of BOOT *sb.*[3] Cf. *mannikin.*] **1.** A soft boot or mitten made of wool and oiled skin, worn as a cure for the gout 1767. **2.** A small kind of boot; a knitted legging with feet, worn by children 1844. **3.** = BOOT *sb.*[3] 3. 1727.

† **Boo·ting,** *vbl. sb.*[1] ME. [f. BOOT *v.*[1] + -ING[1].] Relieving, healing, helping; payment to the good; service, avail –1591.

† **Boo·ting,** *vbl. sb.*[2] 1572. [f. BOOT *sb.*[2] or *v.*[2] + -ING[1].] **1.** Booty; = BUTIN –1600. **2.** Plundering; cf. *freebooting.* HOBBES.

Booting (bū·tiŋ), *vbl. sb.*[3] 1678. [f. BOOT *v.*[3] + -ING[1].] **a.** Torture with the BOOT (*sb.*[3] 3). **b.** Punishment by being booted (see BOOT *v.*[2] 3).

Boot-leg. [BOOT *sb.*[3]] The upper part of a tall boot 1634. **b.** *attrib.* (*U.S.*) with reference to illicit trading in liquor, etc., orig. as conveyed hidden in a boot-leg 1889. Hence **Boo·t-legger, -legging** *vbl. sb.* and *ppl. a.* **Boot-leg** *v.*

Bootless (bū·tlės), *a.*[1] [OE. *bōtlēas*, f. BOOT *sb.*[1] + -LESS.] † **1.** Not to be expiated by a 'bote'; see BOOT *sb.*[1] 3. (In OE. law.) † **2.** Without help or remedy –1659. **3.** To no purpose; unprofitable 1559. **4.** quasi-*adv.* ME.

3. Bootlesse prayers *Merch. V.* III. iii. 20. Hence **Boo·tless-ly** *adv.*, **-ness.**

Boo·tless, *a.*[2] ME. [f. BOOT *sb.*[3] + -LESS.] Without boots.

Boots (būts). 1623. [pl. of BOOT *sb.*[3], used as sing.] **1.** The servant in hotels who cleans the boots 1798. **2.** (*slang.*) The youngest officer in a regiment, junior member of a club, etc. 1806. **3.** In comb. = 'Fellow'; as *lazy-b.*, etc. 1623.

Boo·t-to:pping. 1767. *Naut.* **a.** The act of cleaning the upper part of a ship's bottom, and covering it with a mixture of tallow, sulphur, etc. **b.** 'Sheathing a vessel with planking over felt' (Adm. Smyth) 1867.

Booty (bū·ti), *sb.*[1] 1474. [First as *botye, buty* (Caxton) – MLG. *būte, buite* exchange, distribution (whence G. *beute*), rel. to ON. *býta* deal out, exchange, of doubtful origin. See BUTIN.] **1.** *orig.* Plunder or profit acquired in common and so divisible. **a.** Spoil of war. **b.** That taken by thieves 1567. † **2.** A prize of war, etc. (With *pl.*) –1823. **3.** *loosely.* Plunder, spoil; a prize 1580.

1. Phr. *To play b.*: to join with confederates in order to victimize another player; hence, to play or act falsely so as to gain a desired object. Hence: *Booty* = playing b.

† **Boo·ty,** *sb.*[2] 1577. Erron. used for BOOT *sb.*[1]

Booze, boose (būz), *sb. colloq.* Mod. sp. and pronunc. of BOUSE, BOWSE *sb.*[1]

Booze, boose (būz), *v.* Var. of BOUSE, perh. dial. Hence **Boo·zer.**

Boozy (bū·zi), *a.* 1529. [f. BOOZE *sb.* + -Y[1].] **1.** Affected by drinking. **2.** Given up to boozing 1592. Hence **Boo·ziness.**

Bo-peep (bō:pī·p). 1528. [f. BO *int.* + PEEP *v.*] A nursery play with a young child, in which the nurse alternately hides, and peeps out unexpectedly, and hides again as suddenly. Also *fig.* and *attrib.*

He playeth b. with the scripture TINDALE.

Bor (bǭɹ), *sb. dial.* 1677. [perh. repr. OE. (*ġe*)*būr*; see BOOR.] An East Anglian form of address = Neighbour, gossip, etc.

Bor-, *Chem.*, short for BORON, in comb.; e.g. **Bor-ethyl** $3(C_2H_5)B$, **Bor-methyl** $3(CH_3)B$.

‖ **Bora** (bō·ra). 1864. [Local form (Venice, Trieste) of It. *borea* – L. *boreas* north wind.] A severe north wind which blows in the Upper Adriatic.

†‖ **Bora·chio.** 1583. [Sp. *borracha*, It. *borraccia*, leathern bag for wine, Sp. *borracho* drunkard.] **1.** A goatskin bag used in Spain for wine, etc. –1775. **2.** A drunkard –1729.

Boracic (boræ·sik), *a.* 1801. [f. *borac-*, stem of med.L. *borax* (see BORAX) + -IC.] *Chem.* Like, pertaining to, or derived from borax. *B. acid* is now called *Boric acid.* Hence **Bo·racite,** native borate of magnesia.

† **Bora·cium.** 1808. [f. as prec. + -IUM.] *Chem.* Davy's name for BORON, at that time taken for a metal.

Borage (bɒ·rėdʒ). ME. [– (O)Fr. *bourrache* – med.L. *bor(r)ago*, *-agin-*, perh. – Arab. *'abū 'āraḳ* 'father of sweat', the Arabian physicians using the plant as a diaphoretic.] A genus of plants, giving its name to a natural order (*Boraginaceæ*). The common British species (*Borago officinalis*), which has bright blue flowers, and stem and leaves covered with prickly hairs; formerly a cordial, and still used in *cool tankard*, claret cup, etc. Also *attrib.*

Hence..'I B. always bring Courage' SIR W. HOOKER. *Comb.* **b.-wort,** any boraginaceous plant.

Boraginaceous (boræ:dʒinē·ʃəs), *a.* [f. med.L. *borago* (see prec.) + -ACEOUS.] *Bot.* Of or pertaining to the order *Boraginaceæ*; see prec.

Boragineous (bǫrădʒi·nīəs), *a.* [f. as prec. + -EOUS.] *Bot.* Of or pertaining to the *Borageineæ*, containing the genus *Borago*; *loosely* = prec.

‖ **Bora·sco, -a·sque.** 1686. [– Fr. *bourrasque*, It. *burrasca* and Sp. *borrasca* – L. *boreas*; see BORA.] A violent squall of wind.

‖ **Borassus** (boræ·sǒs). 1798. [mod.L. – Gr. βόρασσος palm-fruit.] *Bot.* A genus of palms, with two species, of which *B. flabelliformis* yields palm-wine and palm-sugar.

Borate (bōᵊ·reⁱt). 1816. [f. BORON + -ATE⁴.] *Chem.* A salt of boric acid.

Borax (bōᵊ·ræks). [ME. *boras* – OFr. *boras* – med.L. *borax* (whence Eng. sp., XVI, and mod. Fr.) – Arab. *būraḳ* – Pers. *būrah*.] **1.** A native salt; the acid borate of sodium or biborate of soda ($Na_2B_4O_7$): when pure, a whitish crystal, or white powder, also imported as tincal.

B. beads, beads made of b., used in blowpipe analysis to distinguish the metallic oxides, and test minerals by the characteristic colours they give in the flame.

Bo·rborygm. Also **-mus.** 1719. [– (ult.) Gr. βορβορυγμός.] *Med.* A rumbling in the bowels. Hence **Borbory·gmic** *a.*

Bord, obs. f. BOARD.

Bordage (bǫ·ɹdėdʒ). ME. [– OFr. *bordage* (= med.L. *bordagium*), still in local use in France, f. (O)Fr. *borde* small farm, cot – Gallo-Rom. **borda* – Frankish **bord* BOARD *sb.* See -AGE.] The tenure of a BORDAR; the services due from him. *Hist.*

Bordar (bǫ·ɹdăɹ). 1776. [– AL. *bordarius* = (O)Fr. *bordier*, f. *borda*; see prec., -ER².] *Feudal Syst.* A villein of the lowest rank, who rendered menial service for a cottage, held at the will of his lord. (In Domesday Book *bordarius*.)

Bordeaux (bǫɹdōᵘ·). 1570. A city in the south of France; hence, the wine of B., claret.

† **Bo·rdel.** ME. [– (O)Fr. *bordel* cot, small farm, brothel; in med.L. *bordellum, -us*; dim. of OFr. *borde*, med.L. *borda*; see BORDAGE, -EL². Superseded by BROTHEL.] **1.** A brothel –1850; prostitution ME. only. **2.** A good-for-nothing. (Erron. for BROTHEL 1.) CAXTON. Also *attrib.* Hence † **Bo·rdeler,** a keeper or ? frequenter of brothels. var. † **Borde·llo.**

Border (bǫ·ɹdəɹ), *sb.* [ME. *bordure* – (O)Fr. *bordure* – Rom. deriv. of **bordare*, f. **bordus* – Gmc. **borðaz*; see BOARD, -ER² 3.] **1.** A side, edge, brink, or margin; a limit or boundary; the part lying along the boundary or outline. **2.** A frontier; *pl.* the marches, the border districts ME. **b.** The frontier line 1535. **3.** A strip of ground forming a fringe to a garden. Also *attrib.* ME. **4.** A defined edging, of distinct material, colour, shape, pattern, etc. ME. **5.** *fig.* A limit, boundary, verge. (Transferred to time, etc.) 1728.

2. Wolves of war, They kept their b. well SOUTHEY. *Over the b.*: across the frontier line. Phr. *The B., the Borders*: the district adjoining the boundary between England and Scotland; An emphatic B. motto, Thou shalt want ere I want SCOTT. **5.** On the borders of eternity HERVEY.

Comb.: **b.-line,** boundary strip of land; *fig.* extreme verge; also *attrib.* verging on the indecent, insanity; **B.-pricker, -rider,** a mounted freebooter living on the B.; **B.-side,** the district about the B.; **B.-warden,** Warden of the Marches; **B.-warrant,** a writ issued on one side of the B. for the apprehension of a person on the other side.

Border (bǫ·ɹdəɹ), *v.* ME. [f. prec.] **1.** *trans.* To put a border to. Also *fig.* **2.** To form a border to; to bound 1570; † *fig.* to keep within bounds (*Lear* IV. ii. 33). **3.** To lie on the borders of, adjoin 1649. **4.** *intr.* To lie on the border, be contiguous *on, upon* 1535. † **5.** *trans.* To cut up (a pasty) 1513.

3. Lands bordering the Mediterranean LYELL. **4.** Hill tribes, bordering on cultivated countries. Phr. *To b. on* or *upon* (fig.): to resemble closely, verge on; This borders on the common-place 1839.

Borderer (bǫ·ɹdərəɹ). 1494. [f. BORDER *v.* and *sb.* + -ER¹.] **1.** One who dwells near a border, *esp.* that of England and Scotland. **2.** One who borders *on* or dwells close *to* or *by*; a next neighbour. Formerly said of a country. Also *fig.* 1538.

2. Borderers upon the Roman world SELDEN. Borderers on the savage state HAZLITT.

Bo·rder-la:nd. (Also as one and as two wds.) 1813. A land or district on or near a border; *esp.* that between England and Scotland. Also *fig.*

A neutral strip of borderland GROTE. The b. of old romance LONGF.

† **Bord-land.** ME. *Feudal Syst.* Prob. land held in *bordage tenure* –1664.

† **Bord-lode.** [See LODE.] Prob. some service, *e.g.* haulage of timber, due by the BORDAR.

† **Bo·rdman.** [Found first in L. form, *bordmannus*, etc., a synonym of *bordarius*, see BORDAR.] A bordar, a cottier. (Dicts.)

† **Bordrage,** var. BODRAGE, hostile incursion.

Bordure (bǫ·ɹdiŭɹ). 1460. [Earlier f. BORDER, q.v.] **1.** *Her.* A bearing that goes all round and parallel to the boundary of a shield, always a fifth part of the field in breadth. **2.** = BORDER. (An occas. var.) 1664.

Bore (bōᵊɹ), *sb.*¹ ME. [Partly f. BORE *v.*¹; OE. *bor* gimlet, ON. *borr* borer, f. Gmc. **boraz* (see BORE *v.*¹); in ME. (sense 1) prob. – ON. *bora* bore-hole = OHG. *boro* auger (wk. fem. :– Gmc. **borōn*).] **1.** That which is bored; a hole made by boring; an aperture (*arch.*) **2.** *spec.* The cylindrical perforation of a tube, gun, etc. Also attrib., as in *smooth-b.*, etc. 1572. **b.** Hence, the diameter of a tube; the calibre of a gun; also *fig.* and *transf.* 1583. **3.** *transf.* The tubular outlet of a geyser 1863. † **4.** An instrument for boring 1677.

Comb. **b.-hole,** = sense 1. Now more usual.

Bore (bōᵊɹ), *sb.*² 1766. [Of unkn. origin; some of the earliest exx. (1766–8) make ref. to *French bore* (connoting dullness or lack of interest), which has not been explained.] † **1.** The malady of *ennui*; a fit of ennui or sulks; a dull time. **2.** A thing which bores; an annoyance 1778. **3.** A tiresome or uncongenial person 1812.

1. Your last letter. . without that d—d French *b.* 1766. **2.** Reproof's a b. 1778. **3.** He says the country girls are bores THACKERAY.

Bore (bōᵊɹ), *sb.*³ ME. [Absence of earlier evidence makes the origin very doubtful, but deriv. from ON. *bára* wave, billow, is appropriate for form and meaning.] † **1.** ? Billow (*rare*). **2.** A tide-wave of unusual height, caused either by the meeting of two tides, or by the rushing of the tide up a narrowing estuary. Cf. EAGRE. 1601.

The Bristol Channel is very subject to the B. LYELL.

Bore (bōᵊɹ), *v.*¹ [OE. *borian* = MLG., MDu. *boren*, OHG. *borōn* (G. *bohren*), ON. *bora* :– Gmc. **borōn*, f. **boraz*; see BORE *sb.*¹] **1.** *trans.* To pierce, make a hole in or through; in mod. use *esp.* to pierce as with an auger. Also with *through.* **2.** *trans.* To hollow out evenly (a cylinder, gun, etc.) 1753. **3.** *absol.* and *intr.* To make a hole (mod. use limited as in 1). In *Mining*, to sink a bore-hole, as *to b. for coal*, etc. ME. **b.** To advance as by boring; also *fig.* 1697. **c.** *trans.* and *intr.* Of a horse: To thrust the head straight forward 1731. **4.** *trans.* To make (a hole, tunnel, etc.) by boring (mod. use as in 1, 3) 1523. † **5.** To gull; ? = BOURD *v.*¹ 2. –1622.

3. b. They take their Flight. . boring to the West DRYDEN.

Bore (bōᵊɹ), *v.*² 1768. [app. f. BORE *sb.*²] *trans.* To weary by tedious conversation or by failure to interest.

A man. . has no unlimited privilege of boring one DE QUINCEY.

Bore, pa. t. and obs. pa. pple. of BEAR *v.*¹

Boreal (bōᵊ·rĭăl), *a.* 1470. [– (O)Fr. *boréal* or late L. *borealis*, f. L. *boreas*; see next.] **1.** Northern; of or pertaining to the north, or to the north wind. **2.** Belonging to the 'boreal province' of the Mollusca 1854.

1. *B. signs*: the six signs of the Zodiac from *Aries* to *Virgo*. *B. dawn* (rare): the *Aurora Borealis.*

Borea·lis. Short for AURORA *borealis.* BURNS.

Boreas (bōᵊ·rĭæs). ME. [– L. *Boreas* – Gr. Βορέας north wind.] The north wind; the god of the north wind. Now only in *Mythol.*, and as a personification. Hence **Bo·rean** *a.*

Borecole (bōᵊ·ɹkōᵘl). 1712. [– Du. *boerenkool* 'peasant's cabbage', f. *boer* BOOR + *kool* COLE¹.] A loose and open-headed kind of cabbage, also called Kale.

Boredom (bōᵊ·ɹdəm). 1852. [f. BORE *sb.*² + -DOM.] **1.** = BOREISM 1864. **2.** The state of being bored; ennui 1852. **3.** Bores as a class 1883.

† **Bo·ree.** 1676. [– Fr. *bourrée* a rustic dance belonging orig. to Auvergne.] A kind of dance –1730.

Boreism (bōᵊ·riz'm). Also **borism.** 1833. [f. BORE *sb.*² + -ISM.] The behaviour of bores; the practice of being a bore.

Borel, var. of BORREL, BUREL.

Borer (bōᵊ·rəɹ). 1483. [f. BORE *v.*¹ + -ER¹.] **1.** One who bores; *esp.* a horse that bores 1872. **b.** A name given to the Myxine or Hag-fish; also to the *Teredo* or shipworm, and to various insects that bore through wood, etc. 1789. **2.** An instrument for boring 1572.

Boric (bōᵊ·rik), *a.* 1869. [f. BORON + IC.] *Chem.* Of or pertaining to boron; containing boron in comb.; as *B. acid*, formerly called *boracic acid* (H_3BO_3).

Boride (bōᵊ·rəid). 1863. [f. as prec. + -IDE.] *Chem.* A primary compound of boron with a metallic element.

Boring (bōᵊ·riŋ), *vbl. sb.*¹ 1440. [f. BORE *v.*¹ + -ING¹.] The action of the vb.; also *concr.* a hole made by boring.

Comb.: **b.-bar,** the suspended bar which carries the bit for boring cannon; **-gauge,** one for limiting the action of the boring tool to the required depth.

Boring (bōᵊ·riŋ), *vbl. sb.*² 1868. [f. BORE *v.*² + -ING¹.] The action of BORE *v.*² Hence **Bo·ringly** *adv.*

† **Bo·ring,** *vbl. sb.*³ [f. BOREE, as 'chasing' from *chassé* sb.] A step in dancing. SHERIDAN.

‖ **Bo·rith.** ME. [Eccl. L. – Heb. *bōrîṯ*, rendered in A.V. 'sope'.] A plant yielding an alkali for cleansing.

Born (bǫɹn), *pple.* and *a.* [Form of the pa. pple. (OE. *boren*) of BEAR *v.*¹, differentiated from BORNE since *c* 1600; *born* is now no longer assoc. w. *bear*, the phr. *to be born* being an independent intr. vb. equiv. to Fr. *naître*, L. *nasci*; *borne* is retained in literary use for 'carried', 'endured'.] **A.** Senses of *to be born.* **1.** To be brought forth as offspring. (See BEAR *v.*) **2.** *fig.* **a.** Of things: To come into existence (chiefly *poet.* and *rhet.*). **b.** in *Theol.* of persons, *To be b. of God*: to become a child of God; *to be b. again*: to become or be regenerate. ME. **3.** To be . . . by the conditions of one's birth, as *to be b. a poet, an Englishman, lucky*, etc. OE. **4.** Of qualities, etc., *To be born in, with*: to be implanted at birth 1710.

B. Pa. pple. used attrib. **1.** Said of persons: **a.** generally = that (ever) was b. 1550; **b.** qualified or qualifying as *a b. orator, b. free, eldest-b., Danish-b., gently-b., free-b.*, etc. ME. **2.** Of qualities, etc.: Innate, inherited 1742.

1. Goodliest man of men since b. MILT. *P.L.* IV. 324. **b.** Pet son (her last-b.?) of the Scarlet Woman CARLYLE. Phr. *(One's) b. days*: one's lifetime. *colloq.*

Borne (bōᵊɹn), *ppl. a.* 1600. [See BEAR *v.*] Carried, sustained, endured, etc. Also used *attrib.*

Borne, obs. f. BOURN.

Borneo (bǫ·ɹniₒo). 1876. An island in the Indian Archipelago. Also *attrib.* Hence **Borneene** (bǫ·ɹniₗin), **Borneol** (bǫ·ɹniₒǫl), organic compounds chiefly obtained from the B. camphor tree (*Dryobalanops camphora*); **Bornesite** (bǫ·ɹnĭsəit), a volatile substance obtained from Borneo rubber latex.

Boro- (bōᵊ·ro). *Chem.* Comb. f. BORON:

boroflu·oride, a compound of fluoride of boron with a metallic fluoride; **borotu·ngstate,** a salt formed by the combination of boric and tungstic acids with the same base; **borogly·ceride,** a compound of boric acid with glycerine, used as an antiseptic; also in *Min.*, **boroca·lcite,** native borate of calcium.

Boron (bōᵊ·rǫn). 1812. [f. BOR(AX + CAR-B)ON.] One of the elementary bodies; a non-metallic solid, not fusible at known temperatures. It is obtained as a greenish brown powder (*amorphous b.*); and as crystals (*adamantine b.*). Symbol B.

Borough (bɒ·roᵘ, bɒ·rŏ). [OE. *burg, burh* = OFris. *burch*, OS. *burg* (MDu. *burch*, Du. *burg*; see BURGOMASTER), OHG. *burg* (G. *burg*), ON. *borg*, Goth. *baurgs* :– Gmc. **burgs*, rel. to **berȝan* protect, shelter; see BORROW *v.*¹, BURROW *sb.*¹, BURY *v.* The Sc. form is BURGH.] † **1.** A fortress, castle, or citadel –ME. † **b.** A court, a manorhouse –ME. † **2.** A fortified town; a town possessing municipal organization; any inhabited place larger than a village. (The three notions were orig. co-extensive.) –1483. **3.** A town possessing a municipal corporation and special privileges conferred by royal charter. Also a town which sends representatives to parliament. (Less dignified than a CITY.) ME. See also BURGH. † **4.** A property held by BURGAGE, and formerly qualifying for the parliamentary vote. Cf. BOROUGH-HOLDER. 1715. † **5.** The portion of a city lying outside the wall. Cf. Fr. *bourg*. –1523. See also BOURG, BURG.

3. Edward VI created fourteen boroughs HALLAM. *The B.*: esp. that of Southwark.

Phrases. *To own a b., to buy a b.*: to possess or to buy the power of controlling the election of a member of parliament for a b. *Close b., pocket b.*, a b. owned by some person. *Rotten b.*: one which had so decayed as no longer to have a real constituency.

Comb., etc. † **a.** Obs. law terms used *Hist.*: **burgh-bote** [OE. *burh-bōt*], a tax for the repair of fortresses; **burgh-breche** [OE. *burh-bryce*], close-breaking, burglary; **burgh-mote, borough-moot** [OE. *burhġemōt*], the judicial assembly of a b. † **b. borough-folk** [OE. *burh-folc*], the people of a town; **burh-were,** *pl.* **-weren** [OE. *burhwaru, -ware, -waran*], the people of a town, the townsmen.

Borough, obs. f. BURROW.

Borough-English (bɒ·rŏ,i·ŋgliʃ). ME. [f. AFr. *tenure en Burgh Engloys*, tenure in (an) English borough. In AL. *tenementum in burgo Anglico*.] A custom in parts of England, by which the youngest son inherits the lands and tenements.

Borough-holder (bɒ·rŏ,hōᵘ:ldəɹ). 1712. In Yorkshire: A person who holds property by burgage tenure; see BOROUGH 4. Also explained as = BORSHOLDER.

† **Borough-man.** [OE. *burhman*; see BOROUGH.] A townsman, citizen, burgess. **b.** In Yorkshire: = BOROUGH-HOLDER.

Borough-master (bɒ·rŏmā:stəɹ). 1494. † **1.** A Dutch or Flemish burgomaster; used also transf. **2.** The owner of a BOROUGH (3). BENTHAM.

Boroughmonger (bɒ·rŏmɒ:ŋgəɹ). 1794. One who trades in parliamentary seats for boroughs. (Freq. in discussions on electoral reform up to 1832). Hence **Bo·rough-monger** *v. rare.* **Bo·roughmongering** *vbl. sb.* and *ppl. a.* **Bo·roughmongery,** the arts and practices of a b.

Borough-reeve (bɒ·rŏrīv). OE. **a.** A governor of a town or city; substantially = PORTREEVE. *Hist.* **b.** The chief municipal officer in certain unincorporated English towns, before the Municipal Corporations Act, 1835.

Bo·rough-town. *arch.* [Cf. OE. *burhtūn* enclosure surrounding a castle (as in *Burton*).] A town which is a borough. Still in occ. use in Ireland.

Borrachio var. of BORACHIO.

Borrel, borel (bǫ·rĕl), *a. arch.* ME. [Conjectured to be an attrib. use of *borel* BUREL 'coarse clothing'.] **1.** Belonging to the laity (*arch.*). **2.** Unlearned, rude; rough (*arch.*) 1513.

2. A coarse, ignorant, b. man like me SCOTT.

Bo·rrow, *sb. Obs.* exc. *Hist.* [OE. *borg* = OFris., OS. *borg*, MHG. *borc* pledge, :– Gmc. **borȝ-*, rel. to OE. *beorgan* = OS., OHG. *bergan* (Du., G. *bergen*), ON. *bjarga*, Goth. *bairgan* :– Gmc. **berȝan*; see next.] **1.** A pledge; a guarantee, bail; suretyship; ransom. Still in *Sc. Law.* **2.** Of persons: A surety; bail, deliverer from prison –1819. **3.** (f. BORROW *v.*¹) A borrowing. *Wint. T.* I. ii. 39.

2. Retain as borrows my two priests SCOTT.

Comb.: (in sense 1) **b.-breach** (OE. *borh-bryċe*), breach of covenant; **b.-roll,** a mortgage-roll.

Borrow (bǫ·roᵘ), *v.*¹ [OE. *borgian* = OFris. *borgia*, MLG., MDu. *borgen*, OHG. *borgēn* (G. *borgen*), f. Gmc. **borȝ-* (whence OE. *borg*, see prec.), rel. to **berȝan*; see BOROUGH, prec.] **1.** *trans.* **a.** To take (a thing) on security given for its safe return; **b.** To take (a thing) on credit on the understanding of returning it or an equivalent; *hence*, to obtain the temporary use of. Const. *of*, occ. *from*, † *at*. **c.** *Arith.* In *Subtraction*, To transfer to the minuend mentally the equivalent of a unit of the next higher denomination, paying back for this at the next step in the process 1594. **2.** *fig.* To render oneself indebted for; to make temporary use of. Const. *from, of*, † *at*. ME. (See also LOAN-WORD.) † **3.** To be surety for; to ransom –1783. † **4.** To give safety to; to rescue; to protect –1522.

1. Let vs borowe money of the kinge vpon vsury COVERDALE 2 *Esdr.* 5:3. **2.** To b. example LATIMER, behauiours from the great SHAKS., Music and Poetry 1763, illustrations 1847. Hence **Bo·rrower.**

Borrow (bǫ·roᵘ), *v.*² 1622. [perh. orig. 'to shelter'; see BURROW.] *Naut.* (*intr.*) To approach closely either to land or wind.

Borrowed (bǫ·roᵘd), *ppl. a.* 1440. [f. BORROW *v.*¹ + -ED¹.] **1.** Taken on loan. **2.** *transf.* and *fig.* Not one's own; assumed 1571.

Borrowing (bǫ·roᵘiŋ), *vbl. sb.* ME. [f. BORROW *v.*¹ + -ING¹.] The action of the vb. (senses 1, 2); *concr.*, that which is borrowed.

B. days: the last three days of March (Old Style), said in Scottish folk-lore to have been borrowed by March from April, and supposed to be specially stormy. Called also *borrowed days*. **Bo·rrowingly** *adv.*

Borsholder (bǭ·ɹshōᵘ:ldəɹ). *Hist.* ME. [AFr., AL. *borgesaldre* (OFr. also *borghes-*, AL. also *-drus*) repr. ME. *borȝes*, gen. sing. of *borh* BORROW *sb.* + ALDER *sb.*²] The chief of a frankpledge; later, a petty constable.

Borstal (bǭ·ɹstăl). 1902. Name of a town in Kent applied orig. to the system adopted there for reforming 'juvenile adult' offenders.

Bort (bǭɹt). 1622. [– Du. *boort*.] Coarse diamonds, and small fragments of good diamonds, used as an abrasive.

Borzoi (bǫ·ɹzoi). 1887. [– Russ. *borzói* swift (the Russ. word for the dog is *borzáya*).] The Russian or Siberian wolf-hound.

Boscage, boskage (bǫ·skėdʒ). [ME. *boskage* – OFr. *boscage* (mod. *bocage*) wooded country, thicket :– Gallo-Rom. **boscaticus*, f. **boscos*; see BUSH *sb.*¹, -AGE.] **1.** A mass of growing trees or shrubs; a thicket, grove; sylvan scenery. † **2.** The pictorial representation of wooded landscape; also, of branches, foliage, etc. –1679. † **3.** *Law.* A piece of wood-land (CAXTON); a tax on windfalls (MANWOOD); mast for domestic animals 1672.

1. The sombre boskage of the wood TENNYSON.

‖ **Bosch**¹ (bǫʃ, ‖ bos). 1786. [Du.] = BUSH *sb.*¹ 8.

Comb.: **b.-bok,** a S. Afr. antelope, the Bush-buck; **-man** = BUSHMAN (in Du. *boschjesman*); **-vark,** a species of wild pig in S. Africa.

Bosch², bosh (bǫʃ). 1879. [In full, *Bosch butter*, i.e. artificial butter made at 'sHertogenbosch or 'Bosch' (Bois-le-duc) in Holland.] An imitation butter; BUTTERINE.

Bosh (bǫʃ), *sb.*¹ 1679. [Origin unkn.] **1.** *pl.* In a blast-furnace, the lower part of the shaft (formerly *four* walls), sloping downwards from the belly to the hearth. **2.** *Mining.* A trough for cooling bloomery tools, hot ingots, etc. 1881.

† **Bosh** (bǫʃ), *sb.*² 1726. [Origin unkn.] An outline, rough sketch –1751. Hence † **Bosh** *v.*¹ to cut a dash; to flaunt.

Bosh (bǫʃ), *sb.*³ *slang* or *colloq.* 1834. [– Turk. *boş* empty, worthless.] **1.** Stuff; trash; foolish talk or opinions. **2.** *int.* Stuff and nonsense! 1852.

1. This firman is *bosh*—nothing MORIER. Hence **Bosh** *v.*² to spoil; to humbug.

Bosh; see BOSCH².

Bosk (bǫsk). [ME. *bosk(e)*, var. of *busk* BUSH *sb.*¹ In mod. literary use a back-formation from *bosky*.] **1.** A bush. Now *dial.* **2.** A thicket of bushes, etc.; a small wood 1814.

Planted with..little bosks and trim hedges 1885.

Bosket, bosquet (bǫ·skėt). 1737. [– Fr. *bosquet* – It. *boschetto*, dim. of *bosco* wood; cf. BOUQUET, BUSKET.] A plantation in a garden, park, etc., of small trees; a thicket.

Bosky (bǫ·ski), *a.*¹ 1593. [f. BOSK + -Y¹.] Consisting of or covered with bushes or underwood; bushy. (Also *transf.*)

My boskie acres *Temp.* IV. i. 81. Hence **Bo·skiness.**

Bosky (bǫ·ski), *a.*² *dial.* or *slang.* 1730. [perh. joc. use of prec.] Tipsy.

Bosom (bu·zəm), *sb.* [OE. *bōsm* = OFris. *bōsm*, OS. *bōsom* (Du. *boezem*), OHG. *buosam* (G. *busen*) :– WGmc. **bōsm-*, perh. for **bōχsm-*, f. **bōȝ-*; see BOUGH.] **A. 1.** The breast of a human being; also *transf.* **b.** The enclosure formed by the breast and the arms. Now only *arch.* ME. **2.** *fig.* (See quots.) OE. **3.** *transf.* That part of the dress which covers the breast; also the space between the breast and its covering, *esp.* as a receptacle for money or letters ME. **4.** A curved recess; a cavity, hollow interior; a sinus. [Cf. L. *sinus*.] **b.** *Mech.* The depression round the eye of a millstone 1813. **5.** The interior, the midst; also *fig.* 1489. **6.** *fig.* The breast considered as the seat of thoughts and feelings; hence 'inward thoughts', desire ME. † **7.** Transferred to a person. (Cf. *hand, heart, head*, etc.) –1756.

1. Within my b...My boding heart pants SHAKS. *In Abraham's b.* (fig.): in the abode of the blessed dead. *Wife of one's b.*: orig. a Hebraism, but in Eng. use influenced by sense 6. Hence, *To take to one's b.*: to marry. **2.** The b. of the ground SHAKS., of a river DRYDEN, lake 1816, stormy sea WORDSW. To put money in ones b. BARET. **4.** The b. of a bay 1685, sail 1872. **5.** fig. *In the b. of one's family, of a church*, etc. **6.** *Friend of one's b.*: cf. BOSOM FRIEND. Emptying our bosomes, of their counsell sweld *Mids. N.* I. i. 216. You shal haue your bosome on this wretch *Meas. for M.* IV. iii. 139. They come home to Mens Businesse and Bosomes BACON. *Comb.* **b.-staff,** an instrument used in testing the straightness of the faces of millstones (see 4 b).

B. as *adj.* Private, confidential, intimate 1640.

Bosom (bu·zəm), *v.* ME. [f. prec.] † **1.** *intr.* To belly. **2.** *trans.* To put into the bosom 1598. **3.** *trans.* To take to the bosom, embrace. Also *fig.* 1605. **4.** *transf.* and *fig.* To embosom 1632. **5.** *fig.* To hide (a secret) in the bosom; to keep in mind. Also with *up*. 1606.

4. Towers..Bosom'd high in tufted trees MILT. *Alleg.* 78. **5.** Bosome vp my counsell SHAKS.

Bosomed (bu·zəmd), *ppl. a.* 1650. [f. BOSOM *sb.* and *v.* + -ED.] **a.** Having a bosom, shaped like the bosom; bellied (as a sail). **b.** Enclosed, hidden; confined in the bosom, bated (breath).

Bo·som frie·nd, bosom-friend. 1590. [f. BOSOM 6. Cf. G. *busenfreund*.] A specially intimate or dear friend. Also † *transf.*

Bo·somy. 1611. [f. BOSOM *sb.* + -Y¹.] Full of sheltered hollows.

Boson, obs. f. BOATSWAIN.

Boss (bǫs), *sb.*¹ [ME. *boce, bose, boos* – OFr. *boce* (mod. *bosse*) :– Rom. **bokja* or **botja*, of unkn. origin. See BOTCH *sb.*¹] **1.** A protuberance on the body of an animal or plant; a convex or knob-like process. **2.** *Geol.* Applied to masses of rock protruding through strata of another kind 1598. **3.** A round prominence in hammered or carved work; *e.g.* a raised ornament in bookbinding; one of the metal knobs on each side of the bit of a bridle (Fr. *bossette*); a metal stud ME. **b.** *spec.* The convex projection in the centre of a shield ME. Also *transf.* and *fig.* **c.** *Archit.* An ornamental projection in a vault at the intersection of the ribs 1823. **d.** *Mech.* 'The enlarged part of a shaft, on which a wheel is keyed, or at the end, where it is coupled to another'. *Shipbuilding.* The projecting part of the stern-post of a screw steamer, which is pierced for the shaft of the propeller to pass through. (Cf. Fr. *bosse* nave of a wheel.) 1869. **4.** A sort of die used by cutlers 1831. Also *attrib.*

3. In the afternoon I..saw some silver bosses put upon my new Bible PEPYS. **b.** As brood as is the boos of a bokeler CHAUCER. *fig.* Yonder woodland isle, the central b. Of Ocean COWPER.

† **Boss**, *sb.*[2] 1520. [Of unkn. origin. Connection with (O)Fr. *buse* (OFr. also *buise*) conduit is phonologically difficult.] 'A water conduit, running out of a gor-bellied figure' (Bailey): chiefly in 'the B. of Billingsgate' –1657.

Boss, *sb.*[3] 1542. [perh. – MDu. *bosse*, *busse*, Du. *bos*. *bus* box.] A plasterer's tray, a hod.

Boss (bǫs), *sb.*[4] Now *dial.* 1695. [perh. alt. f. BASS *sb.*[2] but cf. Du. *bos* bottle of straw.] A seat of straw; a hassock.

Boss (bǫs), *sb.*[5] 1822. [orig. U.S., – Du. *baas* master.] *U.S.* A master; a business manager, any one who has a right to give orders. In Eng. = 'swell, top-sawyer'. (*Workmen's slang* or *joc.*) **b.** In U.S. politics, a manager or dictator of a party organization 1882. **c.** *attrib.* Of persons: Master, chief. Of things: champion. 1860.

Boss (bǫs), *v.*[1] ME. [f. BOSS *sb.*[1]] † **1.** *intr.* To project –1542. **2.** To fashion in relief; to beat or press *out* into a raised ornament, to emboss ME. **3.** To furnish with bosses 1626.
3. Thence to the clasp-makers to have it [my Chaucer] clasped and bossed PEPYS.

Boss (bǫs), *v.*[2] *U.S.* 1856. [f. BOSS *sb.*[5]] *trans.* To be the master or manager of; to control, direct.

Bossage (bǫ·sėdʒ). 1704. [– Fr. *bossage*, f. *bosse* BOSS *sb.*[1]; see -AGE.] *Archit.* **1.** A stone laid in its place uncut and projecting, to be afterwards carved 1730. **2.** 'Rustic work, which seems to advance before the naked of a building, by reason of indentures or channels left at the joints' (Gwilt). Also *attrib.* 1704.

Bossed (bǫst), *ppl. a.* 1536. [f. BOSS *v.*[1] and *sb.*[1] + -ED.] **1.** Made to project 1541. **2.** Embossed; also, portrayed in relief 1536. **3.** Furnished with bosses 1586.
3. Turky cushions bost with pearle *Tam. Shr.* II. i. 355.

Bosselated (bǫ·sėlēⁱtėd), *ppl. a.* 1873. [f. Fr. *bosselé*, pa. pple. of *bosseler*, f. *bosse* BOSS *sb.*[1]; see -ATE[3], -ED[1].] *Phys.* Formed into small protuberances.

Bosset (bǫ·sėt). 1859. [– Fr. *bossette*; see BOSS *sb.*[1], -ET.] A small protuberance or knob.

Bossism (bǫ·siz'm). *U.S.* 1881. [f. BOSS *sb.*[5] + -ISM.] The system in which political parties are controlled by bosses.

Bossy (bǫ·si), *a.*[1] 1543. [f. BOSS *sb.*[1] + -Y[1].] **1.** Swelling in, or like, a boss; projecting in rounded form. **2.** Having bosses or prominences 1812. Hence **Bo·ssiness**, the quality of being b.

Bossy (bǫ·si), *a.*[2] orig. *U.S. colloq.* 1882. [f. BOSS *sb.*[5] + Y[1].] Given to acting like a boss.

‖ **Bostangi** (bǫstæ·ndʒi). 1694. [Turk. *bostancı*, lit. 'keeper of the garden'.] A Turkish guard of the palace.

Bo·ston. 1820. [– Fr. *boston* – *Boston* in Massachusetts.] A game at cards, allied to whist, of which the technical terms refer to the siege of Boston in the American War of Independence.

Bostrychoid, -al (bǫstrikoi·d, -ăl), *a.* 1875. [f. Gr. βόστρυχος curl or lock of hair, see -OID, -AL[1].] *Bot.* Having the form or character of a ringlet.

‖ **Bostryx** (bǫ·striks). 1880. [– Gr. βόστρυξ, var. of βόστρυχος, see prec.] *Bot.* 'An uniparous helicoid cyme' (Gray).

Boswellian (bǫzwe·liăn), *a.* 1825. [f. James *Boswell* (1740–94), friend and biographer of Dr. Johnson; see -IAN.] Resembling Boswell as a biographer. Also **Bo·swellism**, the manner of Boswell as a biographer. **Bo·swellize** *v.* to write in Boswell's style.

Bot, bott (bǫt). Usu. in *pl.* 1523. [prob. of LDu. origin and introduced as a farming term; cf. Du. *bot*, WFris. *botten* (pl.), WFlem. *botse*, NFris. *galboten* liver-worm, WFris. *botgalle* disease caused by these.] A parasitical worm or maggot; now restricted to the larvæ of flies of the genus *Œstrus*. Prop. the larva of *Œ. equi*, inhabiting the digestive organs of the horse; but applied also to those of *Œ. bovis* and *Œ. ovis*. *The botts* (as sing.): the disease caused by these parasites.
Comb.: **b.-bee, -fly**, an insect of the genus *Œstrus*, whose eggs produce the bots; **-hole**, a hole in a hide made by a b. in escaping.

Bot, OE. form of BOOT *sb.*[1]

Botanic (bŏtæ·nik). 1656. [– Fr. *botanique* or late L. *botanicus* – Gr. βοτανικός, f. βοτάνη plant; see -IC.] **A.** *adj.* Pertaining to botany. (Now mostly disused, exc. in early names of institutions, etc., as 'The B. Gardens'.) † **B.** *sb.* **1.** A botanist –1676. **2.** Chiefly in *pl.* = BOTANY –1758.

Botanical (bŏtæ·nikăl), *a.* 1658. [f. as prec; see -ICAL.] Concerned with the study or cultivation of plants; pertaining to botany. Hence **Bota·nically** *adv.*

Botanist (bǫ·tănist). 1682. [– Fr. *botaniste*; see prec., -IST.] One who studies botany.
That diligent b. Bellonius SIR T. BROWNE.

Botanize (bǫ·tănəiz), *v.* 1767. [– mod.L. *botanizare* – Gr. βοτανίζειν gather plants.] **1.** *intr.* To seek for plants for botanical purposes; to study plants botanically. **2.** *trans.* To explore or examine botanically 1861.
1. To b. in the woods 1775. 2. To b. an island 1861. Hence **Bo·tanizer. Bo·tanizing** *vbl. sb.* and *ppl. a.*

Botano-, repr. Gr. βοτανο-, comb. f. βοτάνη plant. Hence in 17th c. many compounds, formed after those in ASTRO-. † **Botano·loger,** a botanist. † **Botano·logy,** botany. **Bo·tanoma:ncy,** divination by plants.

Botany (bǫ·tăni). 1696. [f. BOTANIC after analogy of sbs. in -Y[3] rel. to adjs. in -IC, as *astronomy* and *astronomic*.] **1.** The science which treats of plants. **2.** Short for 'Botany Bay'. Usu. *attrib.*, as *B. wool*, now used of all Australian wool; *B. yarn*, yarn made of this.

Botany Bay. 1812. [So named by Captain Cook on account of the great variety of plants found there.] Name of a place in N.S. Wales, formerly a convict settlement; hence = 'transportation'; also *fig.*

Botargo (botā·ɹgo). Pl. **-oes, -os.** 1598. [– It. *botargo*, *botarga* (now *bottarga*) – med. Arab. *buṭārḵa* salted fish roe – Coptic *outarakhon*, f. *ou-* indef. art. + *tarīkhion* pickle.] A relish made of the roe of the mullet or tunny.
Drinking great draughts of claret, and eating b., and bread and butter PEPYS.

Botch (bǫtʃ), *sb.*[1] [– ONFr. *boche*, var. of OFr. *boce*; see BOSS *sb.*[1]] † **1.** = BOSS *sb.*[1] 1. –1519. **2.** A boil, ulcer, or pimple. Now *dial.* ME. **3.** An eruptive plague, as 'the b. of Egypt' (*arch.*) ME.

Botch (bǫtʃ), *sb.*[2] 1605. [f. BOTCH *v.*] **1.** A botched place or part. Also *fig.* **2.** A bungled piece of work 1648. Also *fig.*
1. To leaue no Rubs nor Botches in the Worke *Macb.* III. i. 133. *fig.* Every Epithet is..a B., which does not add to the thought DENNIS.

Botch (bǫtʃ), *v.* [Of unkn. origin; perh. transf. use of BOTCH *sb.*[1], or obscurely rel. to synon. dial. BODGE *v.*] **1.** To patch, mend. Now only: To repair clumsily. Often with *up*. Also *absol.* **2.** To spoil by clumsy work; to bungle 1530. **3.** *fig.* To put or stitch together clumsily; to construct or compose in a bungling manner. Often with *up, together*. 1561.
1. I labour and b...and produce at last a base caricature SCOTT. 2. To b. a block of marble HAWTHORNE. Hence **Bo·tchedly** *adv.*

Botcher[1] (bǫ·tʃəɹ). ME. [f. prec. vb.] **1.** A mender, or patcher; *esp.* a cobbler, or a tailor who does repairs. **2.** A clumsy maker up *of*; a bungler 1440.
1. Though but a b., which is something less than a tailor COWPER. Hence † **Bo·tcherly** *adj.*, *adv.* **Bo·tchery,** a botcher's work.

Bo·tcher[2]. 1801. A young salmon, a grilse.

† **Bo·tchy,** *a.*[1] ME. [f. BOTCH *sb.*[1] + -Y[1].] Pertaining to, or of the nature of, a botch; covered with botches, as *a b. core* –1768.

Botchy (bǫ·tʃi), *a.*[2] [f. BOTCH *sb.*[2] + -Y[1].] Full of bungling work. Hence **Bo·tchily** *adv.*

Bote, ME. form of BOOT *sb.*[1], still in occas. use in legal senses of OE. *bōt*: Repair; estovers; compensation; expiation.

‖ **Bo·terol.** [– Fr. *bouterolle* the tip of a scabbard, etc.] *Her.* Some kind of charge borne on a shield.

Both (bōᵘþ), *a., pron., adv., conj.* [ME. *bāþe*, *bōþe* (gen. *bāþre*, *bōther*) – ON. *báðir* m., *báðar* fem., *báði*, *bæði* n. = OFris. *be(i)the*, *be(i)de*, OS. *beðia*, OHG. *bēde* (G. *beide*); extended form of the base found in OE. *bēġen* m., *bā*, *bū* fem. and n., Goth. *bai* m., *bā* n., and in L. *ambō*. See BO *a.*] **A.** *adj.* **1.** The one and the other; = 'the two, and not merely one of them'. Const.: **a.** *absol.* (occas. † *the b.*). **b.** in *apposition* with a pl. sb. or pronoun: *Both* is placed after the vb. *be* (occas. also after *become, seem,* etc.) and after an auxiliary vb. ME. **c.** in *attrib.* relation to a pl. sb. (or two sbs. or pronouns, or a sb. and pron., coupled by *and*): *Both* precedes the sb., or defining wd. (if any), but for emphasis, liveliness, etc., may follow the sb. ME. **d.** in *attrib.* relation to a pl. pronoun: *Both* follows the pron. (but *both which* still occurs; *both of* is the mod. constr.) ME. **e.** with *of*: *Both of* is now used before pronouns instead of *both* (see d) 1590. **2.** = 'the two', as in *between both* (arch.) 1443.
1. **a.** B. were Tories MACAULAY. **b.** We are b. men of the world DICKENS. They have b. gone (*mod.*). **c.** Laughter holding both his sides MILT. Fare you well, Gentlemen b. SHAKS. **d.** They b. speak of your death 1816. In b. which [epistles] I stir vp your pure minds 2 *Peter* 3:1. **e.** You b. of you remember me SHAKS. **2.** The argument was supported, for some time, between b. GOLDSM.

B. *adv.* (*conj.*) **1.** Preceding two (or more) homogeneous wds. or phrases, coupled by *and*, *both* adds emphasis by an implied contrast. Thus *B...and* is nearly = *not only.. but.* (As *b...and* = L. *et..et*, *b.* is often classed as a conj.; but cf. EVEN.) OE. **2.** In the case of two sbs., subjects of the same pl. vb., *b.* may follow, instead of preceding (as in 1). In this case *b.* is often = *too*, or *also*. ME.
1. B. now and evermore *Bk. Com. Prayer.* B. man and bird and beast COLERIDGE. 2. Malice marres logike and charitie b. 1600.
Comb.: † **b.-hands**, a factotum (cf. *one's right hand*).

Bother (bǫ·ðəɹ), *v. colloq.* 1718. [Of Anglo-Ir. origin, but no plausible Ir. source can be adduced; perh. an Ir. pronunc. of POTHER.] † **1.** To bewilder with noise –1853. **2.** *trans.* To pester, annoy, worry. Also *refl.* 1745. **b.** In the imperative as a mild imprecation 1850. **3.** *intr.* and *absol.* To give trouble to others or to oneself; to make a fuss 1774.
3. Make money; and don't b. about the universe CARLYLE. Hence **Bo·thersome** *a.* troublesome.

Bother (bǫ·ðəɹ), *sb.* 1803. [f. prec. vb.] † **1.** ? Blarney, humbug, palaver –1822. **2.** Petty trouble, worry; fuss 1823.
2. We had a little b. with him at first M. SCOTT.

Botheration (bǫðərēⁱ·ʃən). *colloq.* 1801. [f. prec. + -ATION.] The act of bothering; petty vexation; often used as an exclam.
The pipe that allayeth b. G. MEREDITH.

Bothrenchyma (bǫþre·ŋkimă). 1835. [f. Gr. βόθρος pit + ἔγχυμα infusion; cf. PARENCHYMA.] *Bot.* Pitted tissue.

Bothy, Bothie (bǫ·þi). *Sc.* 1771. [Obscurely rel. to Ir., Gael. *both*, *bothan*, perh. cogn. w. BOOTH.] A hut or cottage; *spec.* a one-roomed building in which unmarried farm-labourers (or masons, quarrymen, etc.) lodge together. Also *attrib.*

Botling (bǫ·tliŋ). 1613. [Cf. Du. *bot* stumpy.] The chub or chevin (*Cyprinus cephalus*).

Boté, -ée, -y (bǫ·tone, -i). 1572. [– OFr. *botoné* (mod. *boutonné*) covered with buds; see BUTTON, -Y[5].] *Her.* Ornamented with three bud-like projections resembling a trefoil leaf.

Bo-tree (bōᵘ·trī). 1861. [repr. Sinhalese *bogaha*, f. *bo* (:– Pali, Skr. *bodhi* perfect knowledge), more fully *bodhitharū* (*taru* tree, + *gaha* tree).] The *Ficus religiosa* or pipal tree, allied to the Banyan.

Botrycymose (bǫ:tri,səimōᵘ·s), *a.* 1880. [f. Gr. βότρυς cluster of grapes + CYMOSE.] *Bot.* Racemes cymosely aggregated. GRAY.

Botrylle (bǫtri·l). *rare.* 1835. [– mod.L. *botryllus* (oftener used), f. Gr. βότρυς (see prec.)] *Zool.* A genus of tunicate molluscs, giving its name to the family *Botryllidæ*. Hence **Botry·llian** *a.*

Botryoid, -al (bǫ·tri,oid, -ăl), *a.* 1747. [– Gr. βοτρυοειδής, f. βότρυς cluster of grapes; see -OID, -AL[1].] Resembling a cluster of grapes.

Botryolite (bǫ·tri,oləit). 1850. [f. Gr. βότρυς (prec.) + -LITE.] *Min.* A radiated spheroidal variety of datolite.

Botryose (bǫ·tri,ō^{u}·s), *a.* 1880. [f. as prec. + -OSE^{1}.] *Bot.* Bearing flowers in clusters, which develop successively from the base upward.

Bottine (bǫ·tīn). 1513. [– Fr. *bottine*, dim. of *botte*; see BOOT *sb.*^{3}, -INE^{4}.] **1.** A buskin, partly covering the leg. **2.** A half-boot, worn by ladies and children 1866.

† **Bo·ttle,** *sb.*^{1} [WS. metathetic var. of OE. (Angl.) *bold*; see BOLD *sb.*] A dwelling.
[In place-names, as *Harbottle*, etc.]

Bottle (bǫ·t'l), *sb.*^{2} ME. [– OFr. *botele, botaille* (mod. *bouteille*) :– med.L. *butticula*, dim. of late L. *buttis* BUTT *sb.*^{2}] **1.** A vessel with a narrow neck for holding liquids; orig. of leather. **b.** A bottleful. Cf. GLASS. Often *attrib.* 1687. Also *fig.* **2.** *transf.* The practice of drinking 1709.

1. Ye were wonte to drynke Of a lether bottell SKELTON. *A three-b. man*: one who drinks three bottles of wine at a sitting. *To bring up on the b.*: to rear an infant by means of a feeding-b. **2.** *Over a b.*: see OVER *prep.* I. 3.

Comb.: **b.-boy,** an apothecary's boy; **-chart,** a chart of ocean surface currents compiled from data obtained by means of bottles thrown from ships and subseq. picked up at a distance; † **-coaster,** a stand on which decanters were passed round the table; **-fish,** the *Saccopharynx ampullaceus*, a fish which can inflate its body so as to resemble a leathern b.; **-glass,** the coarse kind of which common bottles are made; also *attrib.*; **-gourd,** a flask-shaped gourd (*Lagenaria vulgaris*); **-green** *a.*, of the colour of b.-glass; as *sb.* this colour; **-heath,** *Erica tetralix*; **-imp,** one supposed to inhabit a b.; **-jack,** one for roasting, shaped like a b.; **-neck,** a narrow outlet for traffic; **-nest** (= *bottle-tit*); **-ore,** bladder-wrack (*Fucus vesiculosus*); †**-slider, -slide** (= *bottle-coaster*); **-tit, -tom,** the Long-tailed Tit (*Parus caudatus*), from the shape of its nest; **-washer,** one who or that which washes bottles; also (*joc.*) a factotum. Hence **Bo·ttleful,** as much as a b. will hold.

Bottle (bǫ·t'l), *sb.*^{3} ME. [– OFr. *botel*, dim. of *botte* bundle – MLG., MDu. *bote* bundle of flax, prob. f. Gmc. *but- strike; cf. BUTT *v.*^{1}] A bundle of hay or straw.

To look for a needle in a b. of hay: see NEEDLE *sb.*

Bottle (bǫ·t'l), *sb.*^{4} 1573. [Corruption of *boþel* BUDDLE *sb.*^{1}; also special use of BOTTLE *sb.*^{1}] Pop. name of plants, as BLUE-BOTTLE; **White B., Yellow B.,** *Chrysanthemum segetum* (= BUDDLE), etc.

Bottle (bǫ·t'l), *v.* 1622. [f. BOTTLE *sb.*^{2}] **1.** To put into a bottle for the purpose of storing. Often with *up.* 1641. **2.** *fig.* To store up as in bottles; to keep under restraint (wrath, etc.); to shut *up, in, down, out.*

1. *To b. off*: to transfer (liquors) from the cask into bottle. **2.** Twenty years of wrath bottled up 1853.

Bottle-brush. 1713. [f. BOTTLE *sb.*^{2}] **1.** A brush for cleaning bottles, with bristles diverging on all sides. **2.** *Bot.* Pop. name of the Horse-tail and Mare's-tail 1851.

Bottled (bǫ·t'ld), *ppl. a.* 1594. [f. BOTTLE *sb.*^{2} and *v.* + -ED.] † **1.** Like a bottle, swollen –1769. **2.** Kept in or as in a bottle 1660.

Bottle-head. 1654. [f. BOTTLE *sb.*^{2} + HEAD.] **1.** var. of BEETLE-HEAD (see BEETLE *sb.*^{1}); a stupid fellow (*arch.*). **2.** The Bottle-nosed Whale (so-called) 1819.

Bottle-holder (bǫ·t'l,hō^{u}:ldəɹ). 1753. [f. as prec.] One who holds a bottle; *spec.* one who waits on a pugilist at a prize-fight; *fig.* a second, a supporter.

Bottle-nose (bǫ·t'lnō^{u}:z). 1635. [f. as prec.] **1.** A nose resembling a bottle, a swollen nose. (Usu. written as two wds.) **2.** The Bottle-nosed Whale: a name given to various Dolphins, *esp.* the genus *Hyperoödon* 1668. † **3.** The Puffin (*dial.*) 1678. Hence **Bo·ttle-nosed** *a.* having a bottle nose.

Bo·ttler. ME. [f. BOTTLE *sb.*^{2} and *v.* + -ER.] † **1.** A bottle-maker. ME. only. **2.** One who bottles liquor 1878.

Bottom (bǫ·təm). [OE. *botm* (*boþm*) = OS. *bodom* (Du. *bodem*), corresp. w. variation of suffix (cf. OE. *bytme, byþme, byþne* bottom, keel) to ON. *botn*, and parallel to OE. *bodan*, corresp. to OHG. *bodam* (G. *boden* ground, earth) :– Gmc. **buþm-*, **buþn-*, rel. to L. *fundus.* Sense 7 is from Du.] **1.** The lowest part of anything, considered as a material thing; the under surface; the base. Applied *spec.* to the keel of a ship, the circular end of a cask, etc. **b.** The sitting part of a man, the posteriors (*colloq.*) 1794. **2.** The ground or bed under the water of a lake, sea, or river OE. † **3.** A deep place; an abyss –1759. **4.** Low-lying land, a valley; an alluvial hollow ME. **5.** The lowest point or locality, the foot (see quots.) ME. **6.** *transf.* The furthest point, or inmost part of a recess, bay, or the like 1603. **7.** *Bottom* (*of a ship*): generally, as in 1; *spec.* the part of the hull which is below the wales; also, the hull; *hence*, a ship, boat, etc. 1522. Also *fig.* † **8.** Dregs, sediment –1703. † **9.** That on which anything is built or rests; the foundation –1674. Also *fig.* **10.** The fundamental character, essence, reality 1577. † **11.** A pecuniary basis; capital, resources; *hence*, financial stability –1787. **12.** Staying power 1774. † **13.** A clew on which to wind thread; also a skein or ball of thread. Also *fig.* –1754.

1. Every tub (vat) must stand on its own b. *Provb.* **2.** Phr. *To go to the b., to touch b., to have no b.* (Often *fig.*) **3.** In the Carpathian b. DRYDEN. **5.** The b. of a hill KINGSLEY, the heart 1549, a page, a list, a class, a table, etc. (*mod.*). **7.** Goods imported in foreign bottoms 1883. **9.** *To stand on one's own b.*: to be independent. **10.** *At* (*the*) *b.*: in reality. *To be at the b. of*: to be the real author or source of. **12.** [He] died all game and b. BYRON.

Comb.: **b.-heat,** that supplied to plants through the soil; **-ice,** that which forms on the b. of a river or sea; **-lift,** the deepest lift of a mining-pump, or the lowest pump; **-moraine,** débris dropped from icebergs on the b. of the sea; **-up, -upwards,** *adv.* Hence **Bo·ttomless** *a.*, without a b. (*b. pit*, hell); baseless; inexhaustible.

Bottom (bǫ·təm), *v.* 1544. [f. prec.] **1.** *trans.* To put a bottom to. † **2.** *fig.* To find a foundation for; to serve as a bottom for; to establish firmly –1685; *intr.* (for *refl.*) to rest as upon a foundation (*lit.* and *fig.*) –1790. † **3.** To wind (as a skein) –1612. **4.** *trans.* To reach the bottom of, to empty. Also *intr.* 1808. Also *fig.*

2. *To b. upon*: to base, found, ground upon; also *refl.* **4.** *fig.* To b. an enquiry SMILES. Hence **Bo·ttomer,** one who puts a bottom to anything; a draught in which the cup is emptied.

Bottomed (bǫ·təmd), *ppl. a.* 1559. [f. BOTTOM *sb.* and *v.* + -ED.] **1.** Having a bottom; usu. in comb., as *full-b.* **2.** Founded, based, grounded; mostly *fig.* 1645.

Bo·ttommost, *a. superl.* 1861. [f. BOTTOM *sb.* as *adj.* + -MOST; cf. *topmost.*] Lowest.

Bottomry (bǫ·təmri). 1622. [– Du. *bodemerij* (also *bomerij*; cf. BUMMERY), f. *bodem* BOTTOM in the sense 'ship's hull, ship'; see -RY.] A species of contract of the nature of a mortgage, whereby the owner or the master of a ship borrows money at a stipulated interest or premium to enable him to carry on or complete a voyage, and pledges the ship as security for repayment. If the ship is lost, the lender loses his money. Also *attrib.* as *b.-bond*, etc. Hence **Bo·ttomry** *v.* to pledge (a ship) as security for money lent.

Botulism (bǫ·tiuliz'm). 1887. [f. L. *botulus* sausage + -ISM, after G. *botulismus.*] Poisoning caused by eating foods, esp. preserved meats, containing *Bacillus botulinus.*

† **Bouche,** *sb.*^{1} 1440. [– Fr. *bouche*, lit. 'mouth'.] **1.** Rations granted by a king or noble to his household, his attendants on a military expedition, etc. Only in phr. *to have b. of* (*in*) *court.* –1662. **2.** Mouth; *esp.* in *ball, bullet in* (*en*) *b.* –1650.

† **Bouch(e,** *sb.*^{2} ME. [app. var. of BOTCH *sb.*^{1}, confused w. BOUGE *sb.*^{1}] A hump, swelling –1538.

Bouche (buʃ), *sb.*^{3} 1862. [prob. f. BOUCHE *v.*] A metal plug which is drilled to form the vent of a cannon. var. **Bush** (*sb.*^{2}).

Bouche, *v.* 1781. [prob. – Fr. *boucher* plug.] To insert the BOUCHE (*sb.*^{3}) into (a cannon).

‖ **Bouchées** (bu·ʃē), *sb. pl.* [Fr., lit. 'mouthfuls', f. *bouche* mouth.] *Cookery.* Small baked confections, patties.

† **Boucher.** 1450. [var. of ME. *bouger* purser (f. BOUGE *sb.*^{1}); cf. BOUGE *sb.*^{2} for BOUCHE *sb.*^{1}] A treasurer, cashier, bursar –1583.

Boud. Now *dial.* 1440. [Origin unkn.; perh. repr. OE. *budda*, ME. *bod(d)e* in *scharnboddes* dung-beetles.] A weevil; an insect or worm which breeds in malt, etc.

Boud, = behoved; see BUS *v.*

‖ **Bou·derie.** *rare.* [Fr., f. *bouder* pout, sulk; see -ERY.] Pouting. THACKERAY.

‖ **Boudoir** (bu·dwar). 1781. [Fr. 'place to sulk in', f. as prec.] A room where a lady may retire to be alone, or to receive her intimate friends. Occas. used of a man's 'den'. Hence **Boudoire·sque** *a.* of the kind proper to a b.

† **Bou·ffage.** [– OFr. *boufage* food.] A satisfying meal. SIR T. BROWNE.

‖ **Bouffe** (buf). [Fr. – It. *buffa*, fem. of *buffo* comic, back-formation from *buffone* clown.] Short for *Opéra b.*; see OPERA.

‖ **Bougainvillæa** (būgē^{i}nvilī·ă, commonly -vi·liă). Also **-ea, -ia.** 1866. [f. *Bougainville*, French navigator, 1729–1811.] A genus of tropical plants of the order *Nyctaginaceæ*, having flowers almost concealed by large leafy bracts.

Bouge, *sb.*^{1} *Obs.* or *dial.* ME. [–(O)Fr. *bouge* :– L. *bulga* leathern sack, bag, of Gaulish origin. See BULGE *sb.*, BUDGET.] † **1.** = BULGE *sb.* 1. –1600. † **2.** = BULGE *sb.* 2. –1483. **3.** = BILGE *sb.* 2. 1741. **4.** A cowrie (*rare*) 1875. var. **Bowge.**

† **Bouge,** *sb.*^{2} 1461. Perverted f. BOUCHE *sb.*^{1} 1. Also, provisions. B. JONS.

† **Bouge,** *v.* ME. [Partly differentiated var. of BOUGE *sb.*^{1}] **1.** = BILGE *v.* 1. –1600. **2.** = BILGE *v.* 2. 1577. **3.** = BULGE *v.* 3. –1851.

Bouget (bū·dʒėt). 1592. [Early spelling of BUDGET.] *Her.* A representation of an ancient water vessel.

Bough (bau), *sb.* [OE. *bōg, bōh* = MLG. *bōch, būch* (LG. *boog*), MDu. *boech* (Du. *boeg* shoulders, chest of a horse, bows of a ship), OHG. *buog* shoulder, forearm (G. *bug* horse's hock or point of shoulder, bow of a ship), ON. *bógr* shoulder :– Gmc. **bōʒuz*, rel. to Gr. πῆχυς forearm, cubit.] † **1.** The shoulder of an animal –ME. **2.** A limb, leg. *Sc.* 1550. **3.** A limb of a tree. (Only in Eng.) OE. **4.** *transf.* A gallows; cf. *tree* 1590.

4. *Legal Provb.* 'The father to the b., the son to the plough': meaning that in Kent, in Gavelkind, attainder for felony does not deprive a man's children of the succession to his property. Hence † **Bough** *v.* to strip of boughs; to send out boughs. **Boughed** *ppl. a.* having boughs, as *dark-b.*; stripped of boughs.

Bough-pot (bau·pǫt). *arch.* 1583. [f. BOUGH *sb.*; cf. BEAU-POT.] A pot, etc. for holding boughs for ornament; a flower-pot; also, in 19th c., a bouquet.

'We have made her a bow-pot.' 'Say a bouquet ..'tis more genteel.' THACKERAY.

† **Bought,** *sb.*^{1} 1460. [Late ME., prob. – LG. *bucht* (see BIGHT); later assoc. w. *bout*, aphet. f. *about*; see BOUT *sb.*] † **1.** A bend or curve, *esp.* in the animal body. Cf. BIGHT 1, 3. –1675. † **2.** A loop, a fold, a turn or involution –1648. var. **Bout.**

Bought, bught (bauχt, bvχt), *sb.*^{2} 1513. [Origin unkn.] A sheep-fold; *spec.* a pen for ewes at milking-time.

† **Bought,** *v.*^{1} 1521. [f. BOUGHT *sb.*^{1}] *trans.* and *intr.* To bend, wind, fold; to link –1832.

Bought, bucht, *v.*^{2} *Sc.* 1724. [f. BOUGHT *sb.*^{2}] **1.** To pen or fold (sheep). **2.** *gen.* To fence in.

Bought (bǭt). 1599. [pa. pple. of BUY *v.*] var. **Bou·ghten,** used chiefly *dial.*, and in U.S. of purchased as opp. to home-made things.

‖ **Bougie** (bu·ʒi). 1754. [–(O)Fr. *bougie* (orig. the wax itself), f. name of a town *Bougie* (Arab. *Bujiya*) in Algeria.] **1.** A wax-candle, a wax-light 1755. **2.** *Surg.* A thin flexible instrument made of waxed linen, indiarubber, etc., for exploring, dilating, etc., the passages of the body.

‖ **Bouillabaisse** (bu^{l}yabę·s). 1863. [Fr. – mod. Pr. *bouiabaisso.*] A Provençal dish of fish stewed in water or white wine.

Bouilli (bu·^{l}yi). 1664. [– Fr *bouilli*, subst. use of pa. pple. of *bouillir* BOIL *v.*; cf. BULLY *sb.*^{4}] Boiled or stewed meat, *esp.* beef.

‖ **Bouillon** (bu·^{l}yoṅ). 1656. [Fr. – *bouillir* BOIL *v.*] **1.** Broth, soup. **2.** A saline bath, in which wool is steeped previous to dyeing 1791. **3.** An excrescence of flesh in the foot of a horse.

Bouk. Now *Sc.* and *dial.* [OE. *būc* = OFris., MLG. *būk*, OHG. *būh*, ON. *búkr* :- Gmc. **būkaz.*] † **1.** The belly –1486. **2.** The trunk of the body; hence, the body ME. **3.** = BULK. *Sc.* and *dial.* 1697.

Boul, bool. Now *Sc.* and *n. dial.* 1513. [perh. – MDu. *bōghel* (Du. *beugel*, G. *bügel*) rel. to Gmc. **beuʒan*; see BOW *v.*[1], -EL[1].] **1.** Anything bent into a curve; a curvature 1513. **2.** A curved handle 1560.

Boulangerite (bulɑ·ndʒərəit). 1868. [f. *Boulanger*, French mineralogist + -ITE[1] 2 b.] *Min.* A native sulphide of antimony and lead.

Boulder, bowlder (bōu·ldəɹ), *sb.* 1617. [Short f. BOULDER-STONE.] **1.** A rounded water-worn stone, larger than a pebble; a cobble. **2.** *Geol.* A large weather-worn mass of stone, frequently carried by natural forces to a distance from the parent rock; an erratic block 1813. **3.** *transf.* A lump or mass of some material. Also *attrib.* = 'big, lumpy'. 1861.

1. The Bastille..its ashlars and boulders tumbling down continuously CARLYLE. **3.** Boulders of native copper DANA.

Comb.: **b.-clay**, a clayey deposit of the ice-age, containing boulders; **-drift, -formation**, a formation consisting of mud, clay, etc., containing boulders; **-head**, a kind of sea-wall; **-period**, the Glacial Period, in which b.-formations were being produced.

Boulder-stone (bōu·ldəɹstōun). [ME. *bulder ston* (Havelok), of Scand. origin; cf. Sw. dial. *bullersten, buldurstajn*; perh. orig. a stone that causes a rumbling noise in water (cf. Sw. *buller* sb., *bullra* v. rumble).] = BOULDER *sb.* 1, and (later) 2.

Bouldery (bōu·ldəri), *a.* 1859. [f. BOULDER *sb.*[1] + -Y[1].] Marked by the presence of boulders.

† **Boule**[1]. 1449. [app. a var. of BOLL *sb.*[2], BOWL *sb.*[1]] A measure of lead ore –1670.

Boule[2] (būl); see BUHL.

‖ **Boulevard** (buləvar, bulvar). *rarely* **-vart.** 1772. [Fr. *boulevard*, †*boullewerc* – G. *bollwerk*; see BULWARK.] A broad street or promenade, planted with rows of trees, as *esp.* in Paris. (Orig. the Fr. word meant the horizontal portion of a rampart; hence the promenade laid out on a demolished fortification.) Hence ‖ **Boulevardier** (bulvardye), one who frequents a b.

‖ **Bouleversement** (bulvęrsmaṅ, bulvə̄·ɹsmĕnt). 1814. [Fr., f. *bouleverser* turn as a ball.] A turning upside down, a violent upsetting.

Boulimy, var. of BULIMY.

† **Boultel.** 1460. [– OFr. *buletel* (mod. *bluteau*), f. *buleter*; see BOLT *v.*[1]] A kind of cloth for sifting; a sieve (= BOLTER[1] 2); hence, degree of fineness –1660.

Boultell, var. of BOLTEL.

Boulter (bōu·ltəɹ). 1602. [Origin unkn.] A long fishing-line with many hooks. var. **Bulter.**

† **Boun** (baun), *v.* ME. [f. *boun*, older f. BOUND *ppl. a.*[1] Revived by Sir W. Scott.] **1.** *trans.* To make or get ready –1866. **2.** *intr.* To set out, go –1805.

Bounce (bauns), *sb.*[1] 1523. [See BOUNCE *v.*] **1.** A sounding knock 1529. † **2.** The burst of noise produced by an explosion; the explosion itself –1766. **3.** A leap, a bound 1523. **4.** (from 2.) A boastful lie; swagger 1714.

2. He speakes plaine Cannon fire, and smoake, and b. SHAKS. **4.** The whole story is a b. DE QUINCEY.

Bounce (bauns), *sb.*[2] 1709. The Dogfish (*Scyllium canicula*).

Bounce (bauns), *v.* [First in ME. *bunsen* beat, thump; later senses appear in *v.*, *sb.* and *int.* in early XVI; possibly of LDu. origin (cf. LG. *bunsen* beat, thwack; Du. *bons* thump), but perh. of independent imit. origin.] † **1.** *trans.* and *intr.* To thump, knock loudly –1801. † **2.** *intr.* To make a noise of explosion, go 'bang' –1719. **3.** *intr.* To talk big, bluster; to swagger 1626. **4.** *trans.* To talk big at; to bully. *colloq.* To blow up, scold. 1626. **5.** *intr.* To bound like a ball; to throw oneself about 1519. **6.** To throw oneself, burst, unceremoniously *into*, *out of* 1679. **7.** *trans.* To discharge from employment. *U.S.* 1884.

3. *To b. out* (*with*): to blurt out roundly. Let him b. at his customers if he dares JOHNSON. **4.** To b. opponents out of territory 1883. **5.** I saw the porpus, how he bounced and tumbled SHAKS. **6.** The inn-keeper's wife bounced into the room 1883.

Bounce (bauns), *int.* and *adv.* 1523. [See prec.] **A.** *int.* **a.** Imitating the sound of a gun. **b.** Expressing sudden violent movement.

Bownce would hee say SHAKS.

B. *adv.* With a BOUNCE (senses 1, 2, 3) 1604.

Bownce goes the guns DEKKER.

Bouncer (bau·nsəɹ). 1762. [f. BOUNCE *v.* + -ER[1].] **1.** One who bounces (sense 3 of the vb.). **2.** A bully, a swaggering liar 1833. **3.** A large specimen of its kind; a thumping lie 1805.

3. She was a b. (*colloq.*) 1887.

Bouncing (bau·nsiŋ), *ppl. a.* 1579. [f. as prec. + -ING[2].] That bounces. Often also (like 'whopping', etc.) used with the sense of 'big', *esp.* 'big rather than elegant'.

A b. head of, I believe, Cleopatra H. WALPOLE. *Comb.* **B.-Bet,** the Soap-wort (*Saponaria officinalis*). Hence **Bou·ncingly** *adv.*

Bound (baund), *sb.*[1] ME. [– AFr. *bounde*, OFr. *bun(n)e, bone, bunde, bonde*, earlier *bodne* :- med.L. *bodina*, earlier *butina*, of unkn. origin. Cf. BOURNE *sb.*[2]] † **1.** A landmark. ME. only. **2.** The boundary line of a territory, etc.; *gen.* a limit or boundary ME. **3.** *pl.* The territory near a boundary; a border-land; also land within certain limits, a district ME. Also *sing.* 1 *Hen. IV*, v. iv. 90. **b.** In *Tin-mining.* The area taken in by a miner 1696. **4.** *fig.* A limit to things immaterial, e.g. duration, feeling, etc. ME. Also in *comb.* = BOUNDARY.

2. The utmost bounds of the West 1839. *To beat the bounds*: see BEAT *v.* **4.** Thou hast apoynted him [man] his boundes, he can not go beyond them COVERDALE *Job* 14:5.

Bound (baund), *sb.*[2] 1553. [– (O)Fr. *bond*, f. *bondir* BOUND *v.*[2]] An elastic spring upward or onward. (*Leap* is used only of animals.)

To take before the b.: to be beforehand with.

Bound (baund), *ppl. a.*[1] [ME. *būn, boun* – ON. *búinn*, pa. pple. of *búa* prepare. The final *d* of *bound* (XVI) may be purely phonetic, but is prob. in part due to assoc. with BOUND *ppl. a.*[2]] † **1.** Ready, prepared. Of persons: Dressed. –1853. **2.** Prepared or purposing to go, starting, directing one's course, destined ME. **3.** With inf., = about (to), going (to). Only *dial.*

1. Bowne on hor best wise in hor bright wedis ME. Also *Haml.* III. iii. 41. **2.** B. on we know not what errand HERSCHEL. Phr. *Homeward b.*, *outward b.*

Bound (baund), *ppl. a.*[2] ME. [pa. pple. of BIND *v.*; shortened from BOUNDEN.] **1.** Made fast by a tie, confined; bandaged; also *fig.* 1552. † **2.** Kept fast in bonds or in prison –1611. **3.** Constipated 1530. **4.** Tied in the same bundle; intimately connected; also *fig.* 1611. **5.** Of books: Provided with a binding. Const. *in.* 1708. **6.** Under obligations (of duty, contract, etc.) 1470. **b.** With inf.: Compelled; under necessity (*esp.* logical or moral); fated, certain; also in *U.S.* determined (*sc.* to go, etc.) ME.

1. A synnar bund with the band of syn 1552. **4.** *B. up in* or *with*: (*fig.*) having common interests *with*, 'wrapped *up' in*, dependent upon; His life is bound vp in the lads life *Gen.* 44: 30. **6.** Whoever owned land, was bound to military service FROUDE. **b.** The best horse is b. to win 1883.

Bound (baund), *v.*[1] ME. [f. BOUND *sb.*[1]] † **1.** *trans.* To limit; to confine within bounds; to mark (*out*) the bounds of –1762. Also *fig.* ME. **2.** *trans.* To form the boundary of 1601; † to enclose, contain –1606.

1. He shall..b. his Reign With earth's wide bounds MILT. *P.L.* xii. 370. Views bounded by narrow ideas of expediency 1850. **2.** He crossed the little river Rubicon, which bounded his province FROUDE. *To b. on* (intr.): to abut upon, adjoin.

Bound (baund), *v.*[2] 1593. [– (O)Fr. *bondir* resound, (later) rebound :- Rom. **bombitire*, for late L. *bombitare*, var. of *bombilare*; see BOMBILATE, BOMBINATE.] † **1.** To recoil, rebound –1633. **2.** *intr.* To spring upwards, leap; to advance with leaps. Also *fig.* 1592. † **3.** *trans.* To make (a horse) leap –1599.

2. He leaps, he neighs, he bounds *Ven. & Adon.* 265. Like a roe I bounded o'er the mountains WORDSW.

Bound, *v.*[3] *rare.* Var. of BOUN *v.* SPENSER.

Boundary (bau·ndări). 1626. [alt. of (dial.) *bounder* (XVI), f. BOUND *v.*[1] + -ER[1]; perh. after *limitary*.] That which serves to indicate the limits of anything; the limit itself. **b.** In cricket, etc., the limits of a match enclosure 1889; a hit to this 1896.

The simple Ideas we receive from Sensation and Reflection are the Boundaries of our Thoughts LOCKE. *Comb.*: **b.-line,** an established line marking the limits of a town, state, etc.; **-rider** (Australia), one who rides round the fences of a station and repairs them when broken.

Bounded (bau·ndĕd), *ppl. a.* 1600. [f. BOUND *v.*[1] + -ED[1].] That has bounds or limits; that has its limits marked. **b.** *fig.* Limited, circumscribed 1709. † Also, improp. for BOUND, BOUNDEN –1819.

b. The b. level of our mind POPE. Hence **Bou·ndedness,** the quality of being b.; limited range.

Bounden (bau·ndĕn), *ppl. a.* ME. [pa. pple. (OE. *bunden*) of BIND *v.*; see BOUND *ppl. a.*[2]] † **1.** = BOUND, in literal senses –1856. **2.** Made fast in bonds or in prison (*arch.*) ME. Also *fig.* **3.** Under obligation (legal or moral); compelled (*arch.*) ME. **4.** Obliged, beholden, indebted (*to*). The usual modern sense. 1530. **5.** *esp.* in *b. duty* (occas. found as *bound and duty*) 1530.

2. Her b. thrall SPENSER. **4.** I am much b. to your Maiesty *John* III. iii. 29. **5.** Our b. duty and seruice *Bk. Com. Prayer.*

Bounder (bau·ndəɹ), *sb.*[1] 1505. [f. BOUND *v.*[1] + -ER[1]; but see sense 3.] **1.** One who sets or marks out bounds (*lit.* and *fig.*) 1570. † **2.** One who occupies a bound of tin-ore ground –1708. **3.** A boundary; a landmark; prob. a corruption of BOUNDURE [cf. *border*], taken as *bounder* 'that which bounds'. Now *dial.* 1505.

3. They..builded it for a b. and a testimony GRINDAL. Hence † **Bou·nder** *v.* to bound.

Bounder, *sb.*[2] *slang.* 1890. [f. BOUND *v.*[2] + -ER[1], perh. assoc. w. *bounce* and *bumptious*.] A would-be stylish person kept at or beyond the bounds of society, or found irrepressible by it.

† **Bou·nding,** *vbl. sb.*[1] 1543. [f. BOUND *v.*[1] + -ING[1].] **1.** The action of the vb. Also with *out.* –1614. **2.** Abuttal; boundary –1750. **3.** *fig.* A limiting or confining –1658.

Bounding (bau·ndiŋ), *vbl. sb.*[2] 1617. [f. BOUND *v.*[2] + -ING[1].] A leaping or springing.

Boundless (bau·ndlės), *a.* 1592. [f. BOUND *sb.*[1] + -LESS.] Without limits; unbounded.

My bounty is as boundlesse as the Sea *Rom. & Jul.* II. ii. 133. Hence **Bou·ndless-ly** *adv.*, **-ness.**

Bou·ndly, *a.* ? Finite: opp. to *boundless.* Or ? Bounden. KEATS.

† **Bou·ndure.** 1634. [f. BOUND *sb.*[1] Cf. *closure.*] A bounding, limitation; limit –1654.

Bounteous (bau·ntiəs), *a.* [Late ME. *bountevous* (later *bounteous* XV), f. OFr. *bontif, -ive* benevolent (f. *bonté* BOUNTY), after *plentevous* PLENTEOUS.] **1.** Full of goodness; in mod. use, always: Full of goodness to others, beneficent; munificent ME. **2.** Of things: Proceeding from bounty; liberal, ample, abundant 1542.

1. Colleges on b. Kings depend DRYDEN. **2.** A b. crop DRYDEN. Hence **Bou·nteous-ly** *adv.*, **-ness.**

Bountiful (bau·ntifŭl), *a.* 1508. [f. BOUNTY + -FUL.] **1.** Of persons: Full of bounty; graciously liberal, generous. **2.** Of things: Characterized by bounty, abundantly yielding; also, ample, plenteous 1538.

1. *Lady B.*, a character in Farquhar's *Beaux' Stratagem*; hence, the great lady in a neighbourhood. **2.** That's a b. answere that fits all questions *All's W.* II. ii. 15. Hence **Bou·ntiful-ly** *adv.*, **-ness.**

Bou·ntihead. *arch.* 1596. [f. BOUNTY + -HEAD.] Bounteousness.

Bounty (bau·nti). ME. [– (O)Fr. *bonté* :- L. *bonitas, -tat-*, f. *bonus* good; see -TY[1].] † **1.** Goodness in general, worth, virtue; in *pl.* virtues; also high estate –1623. † **b.** Valour –1530. † **2.** Of things: Good quality, excellence –1592. † **3.** Kindness; an act of kindness (occas. *ironical*) –1651. **4.** Goodness shown in giving, munificence ME. **b.** An act of generosity; a gift, gratuity ME. **5.** *esp.* A gift bestowed by the sovereign, or by the state, as a gratuity given to recruits on enlistment, money paid to merchants for the encouragement of any branch of industry, etc. 1719. **b.** *transf.* and *fig.* A premium or reward 1868.

4. Bountie and largesse is befallyng for kynges UDALL. The b. of Providence JOHNSON. **5.** *Queen Anne's B.*: a provision made in the reign of Queen Anne 'for the Augmentation of the Maintenance of the Poor Clergy'. The Parliamentary b. upon the exportation of corn ADAM SMITH.

Comb.: **b.-jumper,** *U.S.* a recruit who enlisted for the b., and soon deserted to enlist again.

Bouquet (bukē·, bu·ke). 1716. [– Fr. *bouquet* (earlier, clump of trees), f. dial. var. of OFr. *bos, bois* wood; cf. BUSH *sb.*[1], BOSKET, BUSKET, -ET.] **1.** A bunch of flowers, a nosegay; also *fig.* **2.** The perfume exhaled from wine 1846. **3.** *transf.* **a.** A bunch of flavouring herbs. **b.** A large flight of rockets. **c.** The flight of pheasants breaking cover from the central point at which the beaters meet; this central spot itself. 1846.

2. The 'b.' is something different from the odour of wine 1865. Hence **Bouque·ted** *a. rare*, furnished with a b. or bouquets.

‖ **Bouquetin** (bukətæ̃n, bū·kĕtin). 1783. [Fr., OFr. *boc estaign* – MHG. *steinbock*.] The ibex.

Bour, obs. f. BOOR and BOWER.

† **Bou·rage,** *rare.* [perh. error for OFr. *bourgage* (mod. *bourgade*); see BOURGADE, -AGE.] The Borgo in Rome. LD. BERNERS.

Bourbon (burbǫ·n), *sb.* 1768. [f. *Bourbon l'Archambault*, France.] **1.** A member of the family which long held the thrones of France and Naples, and until 1930 that of Spain; also *fig.* and *attrib.* **2.** *transf. U.S.* A nickname for 'a Democrat behind the age and unteachable'. 1884. **3.** The former name of the island of Réunion; whence **B. Palm,** a name of the genus *Latania.*

1. Muleteers are typical Bourbons, They learn nothing and they forget nothing TRISTRAM. Hence **Bou·rbonism,** adhesion to the B. dynasty, or to the B. party in U.S. politics; **Bou·rbonist,** a supporter of the B. dynasty.

† **Bourd,** *sb.* ME. [– (O)Fr. *bourde* lie, cheating, = Pr. *borda*; of unkn. origin.] A jest; jesting –1606. In a bad sense: Mockery –1602. So † **Bourd** *v.* to say things in jest or mockery; † *trans.* to mock. † **Bou·rder,** a mocker.

† **Bourdis.** ME. [– OFr. *bordis*, earlier *behordeïs* shock of lances, f. *behorder, -ir* joust, f. *behort* lance; of unkn. origin.] Tilting –1450.

† **Bou·rdon**[1], **burdoun.** ME. [– (O)Fr. *bourdon* pilgrim's staff :– med.L. *burdo, -on-* staff, identified by Du Cange with *burdo* mule.] **1.** A pilgrim's staff –1652. **2.** A stout staff; occ. a spear or spear-shaft –1550.

Bourdon[2], **burdoun** (bū°·ɹdǫn). ME. [– (O)Fr. *bourdon* drone :– Rom. **burdo, -on-*, of imit. origin.] † **1.** The low undersong or accompaniment to a melody. [See BURDEN.] –1596. **2.** A bass stop in an organ, usu. of 16 ft. tone; also the drone of a bagpipe 1861.

‖ **Bourg** (bur, bū°ɹg). 1450. [– (O)Fr. *bourg* :– med.L. *burgus* BOROUGH.] A town or village under the shadow of a castle (*Hist.*); a continental town.

‖ **Bourgade** (burga·d). 1601. [Fr., f. *bourg*; see prec., -ADE.] A village or straggling unwalled town. (In 17th c. used as English.)

Dispersed into pettie villages and burgades HOLLAND.

‖ **Bourgeois** (burʒwā), *sb.*[1] and *a.* 1564. [– (O)Fr. *bourgeois*, earlier *burgeis*; see BURGESS.] **A.** *sb. orig.* A (French) citizen or freeman of a burgh, as distinguished from a peasant and a gentleman; *now* a member of the mercantile or shop-keeping middle class of any country 1674.

B. *adj.* Of, belonging to, or characteristic of the (French) middle classes; also in *comb.* 1564.

A regular b. physiognomy THACKERAY. Hence ‖ **Bourgeoisie** (burʒwazī), the body of freemen of a French town; the French (or other) middle class.

Bourgeois (bɒɹdʒoi·s), *sb.*[2] 1824. [Conjectured to be f. the name of a printer; but perh. referring to its intermediate size.] A size of type between Long Primer and Brevier, as in:

Bourgeois type

Bourlaw, var. of BYRLAW, whence **bourlawmen.** *Sc.*

Bourn, bourne (bō°ɹn), *sb.*[1] ME. [south. Eng. var. of BURN *sb.*[1] Orig. pronounced like *burn.*] A small stream, a brook.

Sundry smal brookes or boornes LAMBARDE.

Bourne, bourn (bō°ɹn), *sb.*[2] 1523. [– (O)Fr. *borne*, earlier *bodne*; see BOUND *sb.*[1] The mod. use is due to Shakespeare.] † **1.** A boundary (between fields, etc.) –1790. **2.** A bound, a limit (*arch.*) 1606. **3.** The point aimed at; destination, goal. (Somewhat *poet.*; often *fig.*) 1602. ¶ *incorrectly* for: Domain. KEATS.

1. One that fixes No borne 'twixt his and mine *Wint. T.* I. ii. 134. **3.** The vndiscouered Countrey, from whose Borne No Traueller returnes *Haml.* III. i. 79. [More probably *Borne* means here the 'frontier or pale' of a country.] Hence **Bourn** *v. rare*, to set a limit or bounds to. **Bou·rneless, bournless** *a. rare*, boundless.

Bournonite (bū°·ɹnǒnəit). 1805. [f. Count *Bournon*, its discoverer, + -ITE[1] 2 b.] *Min.* Antimonial sulphide of lead and copper; a brittle opaque mineral with metallic lustre.

Bournous, obs. f. BURNOUS.

Bourock (bū·rək). *Sc.* 1807. [perh. dim. of *boor* BOWER; see -OCK.] A little cot; a small heap of stones.

‖ **Bourse** (burs, bū°ɹs). 1845. [Fr., = purse; see BURSE.] An exchange, or place of meeting for merchants; the money-market (of a foreign town). Used *esp.* of the Paris Stock-Exchange.

Bourtree (bū^e·ɹtri). Now *Sc.* and *n. dial.* 1450. [Origin unkn.] The Elder-tree (*Sambucus nigra*).

Bouse, bowse (būz, bauz), *v.*[1] [ME. *bouse* (once in XIV), surviving as *bouse, bowse* (bauz); re-adopted in XVI from the same source, MDu. *būsen* (Du. *buizen*) drink to excess, whence the usual mod. pronunc. (būz) and the corresp. sp. BOOZE, BOOSE.] **1.** *intr.* = BOOZE *v.* Also *trans.* † **2.** *Falconry.* Of a hawk: To drink much –1682. Hence **Bou·ser.**

Bouse, bowse (baus), *v.*[2] 1593. [Origin unkn.] *trans.* To haul with tackle. Also *absol.*

Bouse, bowse (būz, bauz), *sb.*[1] ME. [ME. *bous* (once XIV), re-adopted in XVI from orig. source; see BOUSE, BOWSE *v.*] **1.** *colloq.* Drink, liquor. **2.** A carouse 1786.

Bouse (baus, būs), *sb.*[2] 1653. [Origin unkn.] Lead ore in its rough state.

‖ **Boustrophedon** (baustrofī·dǫn, bū-), *adv.* and *a.* (*sb.*) 1783. [Gr., f. βου-στρόφος ox-turning.] (Written) alternately from right to left and from left to right, like the course of the plough; as in some ancient inscriptions. Hence **Boustrophedo·nic** *a.*

Bousy (bū·zi, bau·zi), *a.*[1] 1529. Earlier form of BOOZY.

Bout (baut), *sb.* 1541. [var. of BOUGHT *sb.*[1], assoc. w. BOUT *adv.*[2]] † **1.** A circuit; a roundabout way –1655. **b.** The going and returning of the plough: also *attrib.* 1601. **2.** A round at any kind of exercise, a turn of work 1575. **3.** A round at fighting; a contest 1591. **b.** Used of a fit of drinking 1670. **c.** A turn of illness 1839.

2. *This, that b.*: i.e. occasion, turn, time. **3.** A b. at cudgels 1726, at altercation FIELDING. **c.** A severe b. of influenza 1887.

† **Bout,** *adv.*[1] and *prep.*[1] OE. [ME. *boute(n* :– OE. *būtan* (*būta, būte*) adv., prep., conj., orig. *be-ūtan* adv. and prep. 'without' = OS. *bi-ūtan, būtan*, OHG. *bi-ūʒan*; f. *bi* BY + *ūtan, ūtana* (= Goth. *ūtana*) from without.] **A.** *adv* Outside; out –ME. **B.** *prep.* **1.** Outside of –ME. **2.** Without, not having: *esp.* in *bouten ende.* (Still in Sc. in form *bot*, BUT q.v.) –1500. Also *absol.* –1674. **3.** Except, more than –ME.

Bout (baut), *adv.*[2] and *prep.*[2] [ME. *bute(n* aphet. f. *abute(n*, as *'bout* of ABOUT.] **A.** *prep.* In senses of ABOUT. (Not in literary prose.) **B.** *adv.* In *'bout ship* = put about the ship, alter her course 1830.

† **Bouta·de, bouta·do.** 1614. [– Fr. *boutade*, f. *bouter* thrust; for *boutado*, see -ADO.] A sally, a sudden outburst or outbreak –1704.

† **Boutefeu.** 1598. [– Fr. *boutefeu* linstock, incendiary, f. *bouter* put + *feu* fire.] An incendiary, a firebrand; also *attrib.* –1754.

A great Boutifleu & firebrand in the Church WOOD.

† **Bou·te-selle.** *rare.* 1628. [– Fr. *boute-selle*, f. *bouter* put + *selle* saddle.] A trumpet-call; = *Boot and saddle*; see BOOT *sb.*[3] –1658.

‖ **Bouts-rimés** (bu·rime·), *sb. pl.* 1711. [Fr., = rhymed endings.] Rhymed endings, given to a versifier to make verses to them in the order given.

Bovate (bō^u·ve^it). 1688. [– med.L. *bovata*, f. L. *bos, bov-* ox; see -ATE[1].] An ox-gang, or as much land as one ox could plough in a year; varying from 10 to 18 acres.

Bove, *adv.* and *prep.* [ME. *bove(n)* :– OE. *bufan*, f. *bi-* BY + *ufan* above, f. Gmc. **uf-* UP.] † **1.** (In OE. and early ME.) Early f. ABOVE. **2.** In mod. Eng. *'bove, bove*, shortening of ABOVE, in verse 1591.

Bovey (bɒ·vi). 1760. [Name of a parish near Exeter.] *B. coal*: a lignite or brown coal of Miocene age found at Bovey and elsewhere.

Bo·vid, *a.* [f. L. *bos, bov-* ox + ID[3].] Of or pertaining to the ox family, or *Bovidæ* of Zoologists, a family of Ruminants, having simply rounded horns, and no lachrymal sinuses.

Bo·viform, *a.* [f. as prec. + -FORM.] Ox-shaped. CUDWORTH.

Bovine (bō^u·vəin), *a.* 1817. [– late L. *bovinus*, f. as prec. + -INE[1].] Belonging to, or characteristic of, the ox tribe. Also *ellipt.* = b. animal. **2.** *fig.* Sluggish; stupid; cf. *bucolic* 1855.

2. Where b. rustics used to doze O. W. HOLMES.

Bow (bō^u), *sb.*[1] [OE. *boga* bow, rainbow, arch = OFris. *boga*, OS. *bogo* (Du. *boog*), OHG. *bogo* (G. *bogen*), ON. *bogi* :– Gmc. **buʒon*, f. **buʒ*, short stem of **beuʒan* (cf. BOW *v.*[1]).] **1.** *gen.* A thing bent or curved; a bend, a bent line ME. **2.** *spec.* A rainbow. (Mostly contextual or poet.) OE. **3.** An arch (of masonry). Now *dial.* OE. **4.** A weapon for shooting arrows, etc., consisting of a strip of elastic wood, steel, etc., with a string stretched between its two ends, by means of which the arrow is impelled ME. **b.** *transf.* A bowman (in *pl.*) 1511. † **5.** A yoke for oxen –1721. **b.** *pl.* = SADDLE-BOW. **6.** *Mus.* A rod of elastic wood with a number of horsehairs stretched from end to end; used for playing on stringed instruments. (It was formerly curved, like an archer's bow.) 1580. † **7. a.** The iris of the eye 1611. **b.** The eye-brow 1729. † **8.** An arc of a circle –1674. † **9.** A sort of quadrant formerly used to take altitudes at sea –1706. **10.** An instrument for drawing curves, *esp.* of large radius 1706. **11.** A ring or hoop of metal, etc. forming a handle. Cf. BAIL *sb.*[2] 1611. **12.** *Archit.* The part of any building which projects from a straight wall 1723. † **13.** A bow's length, as a measure; chiefly in *fig.* phrases –1649. **14. a.** A single-looped knot. **b.** A double-looped knot into which ribbons, etc. are tied (the usual sense). **c.** A necktie, etc. tied up in such a knot. Hence *b.-knot.* 1671. Also *attrib.*

2. A dewie Cloud, and in the Cloud a B. MILT. *P.L.* xi. 865. **3.** After the scole of Stratford atte Bowe CHAUCER. **4.** The b. of Ulysses, which none but its master could bend 1830. **b.** There was among these a thirtie bowes with a bagpipe HOLINSHED. **7.** The Bows her Eyes above 1729.

Phrases. (f. sense 4) *To have two* (*many*, etc.) *strings to one's b.*: to have two (or many) resources or alternatives. *To draw the long b.*: to exaggerate, lie.

Comb.: **b.-arm,** the arm that holds the b. (in archery or in violin-playing); **-bender,** ? a b.-bearer; **-bent,** bent like a b. MILT.; **-boy,** a boy with a b. (*esp.* Cupid); **-brace** = BRACER[2]; **-drill,** a drill turned by means of a b. and string; **-fin,** a fish (*Amia calva*); **-houghed** *a.* having crooked hips; **-instrument,** one played with a b.; **-knot** (see sense 14); **-pen, -pencil,** a b.-compass with a pen or pencil; **-pin,** a key to fasten the b. of an ox-yoke; **-saw,** one with a narrow blade stretched in a strong frame; **-wood,** the wood of the Osage Orange (*Maclura aurantiaca*).

Bow (bau), *sb.*[2] 1656. [f. BOW *v.*[1] II. 1.] An inclination of the body or head in salutation, and in token of respect, reverence, submission, etc.; an obeisance.

To make one's b.: to retire, leave the stage.

Bow (bau), *sb.*[3] 1626. [– LG. *boog*, Du. *boeg* (whence Sw. *bog*, Da. *boug*); see BOUGH. Not rel. to BOW *sb.*[1] or *v.*[1]; but pop. assoc. with the latter and infl. by its pronunciation.]

Naut. **1.** The rounded fore-end of a ship or boat. Also in *pl.* 'bows', i.e. the 'shoulders' of a boat. **2.** *transf.* The rower nearest to the bow (*colloq.*) 1830.

1. Phr. *On the b.*: within 45° of the point right ahead.

Comb.: **b.**†**-chase, -chaser,** a cannon in the b. of a ship, to fire upon any object ahead of her; **-fast,** a hawser at the b. to secure a vessel to a wharf (see FAST); **-grace, -grease,** a junk-fender placed round the bows and sides to prevent injury from floating ice, timber, etc.; **-oar,** the oar nearest the b.; *transf.* = 2 above; **-pieces,** the ordnance in the bows.

Bow (bau), *v.*[1] Pa. t. and pple. **bowed** (baud). [OE. *būgan*, corresp. to MLG. *būgen*, MDu. *būghen* and, with a different grade in the pres. stem, OHG. *biogan* (G. *biegen*), ON. **bjuga*, Goth. *biugan* :- Gmc. **beuʒan*; cf. BOW *sb.*[1]] **I.** Intrans. uses. (Occas. trans. by ellipsis.) **1.** To assume a bent shape, bend. Now *dial.* † **2.** To turn aside, off, or away; to retreat –1580. † **b.** To bend one's course, go. (Occas. = flee.) –ME. † **3.** To curve –1756. † **4.** To lower the head and body, *esp.* in condescension (*arch.*) ME. **5.** To bend the neck under a yoke; *hence*, to become a subject; to submit OE. **6.** To bend the body, knee, or head, in token of reverence, respect, or submission; to make obeisance. (Also with *down.*) OE. **7.** To incline the body or head (*to*) in salutation, polite assent, acknowledgement, etc. 1651. **b.** *trans.* To express by bowing 1606.

1. Like an Asse, whose backe with Ingots bowes *Meas. for M.* III. i. 26. **4.** She bow'd upon her hands..She bow'd down And wept in secret TENNYSON. **5.** To b. to the inevitable 1862. **6.** Shall I b. to the stock of a tree HOOKER. **7.** He bowed to Homer, and sat down by him *Tatler*, No. 81. **b.** To b. one's assent 1887. *To b. in* or *out*: to usher *in* or *out* with a b. or bows; so *to b. up* or *down* (stairs, etc.).

II. Causative. **1.** *trans.* To cause to bend; to inflect, curve, crook (*arch.* and *dial.*) ME. esp. *To b. the knee*: i.e. to bend it in adoration or reverence ME. Also † *fig.* † **2.** To incline, turn, direct; *fig.* to influence –1705. **3.** To bend to crush (anything) downwards; to lower (often *fig.*) ME. **4.** To cause to stoop, (as a load does) 1671.

2. *To b. the ear, the eye*: to turn with attention, bending the head downwards; B. downe thine eare, O Lord, heare me *Ps.* 86:1. **4.** With sickness and disease thou bow'st them down MILT. *Sams.* 698. Hence † **Bow·able** *a.*; *fig.* complaisant.

Bow (bōu), *v.*[2] 1838. [f. BOW *sb.*[1] 6.] *trans.* and *intr.* To use the bow (on a violin, etc.).

Bow-backed (bōu·bæ:kt), *a.* 1470. **a.** (f. BOWE *ppl. a.*) Crook-backed. **b.** (f. BOW *sb.*[1]) Having the back arched, as an angry cat.

Bow-bearer (bōu·bēə:rəɹ). 1538. [f. BOW *sb.*[1]] **1.** One who carries a bow 1600. **2.** An under-officer in a forest, who looked after trespasses affecting vert and venison.

Bow-bell, -bells. 1600. The bells of Bow Church, *i.e.* St. Mary-le-Bow, in Cheapside, London. Cf. ARCH. Hence 'within the sound of Bow-bells' = 'within the City bounds'; this church being nearly in the centre of the City. Also *attrib.*

Bow-compass (bōu·kɒ:mpăs), **-compasses** (-ėz). 1796. [f. BOW *sb.*[1]] A pair of compasses with the legs jointed so that the points can be bent inwards; any compasses made for drawing small circles. (Usu. called *bows.*)

Bowdlerize (bau·dləɹəiz), *v.* 1838. [f. Dr. T. *Bowdler*, who in 1818 published an expurgated edition of Shakespeare.] To expurgate (a book, etc.) by omitting or altering words or passages considered indelicate; to castrate.

† **Bow·-draught.** ME. [f. BOW *sb.*[1] + DRAUGHT *sb.*, from the phrase *to draw a bow.*] A bowshot –1716.

Bow-dye. 1659. [f. *Bow* near Stratford in Essex.] A scarlet dye; also as *adj.* Hence **Bow-dye** *v.* **Bow-dyer.**

† **Bowe,** *ppl. a.* [ME. *bowe* :- OE. *bogen*, pa. pple. of *būgan* BOW *v.*[1]] Bent, crooked –1500.

Bowel (bau·ėl), *sb.* [ME. *buel, bouel* – OFr. *buel, boel, bouel, boiel* (mod. *boyau*) :- L. *botellus* pudding, sausage (Martial), small intestine, dim. of *botulus* sausage.] **1.** An intestine. Now only in *Med.* † **b.** Any internal organ of the body –1782. **2.** *pl.* The intestines ME. **b.** The inside of the body; also *fig.* Cf. *womb*, etc. (rarely *sing.*) 1532. **3.** *transf.* (Taken as the seat of the tender emotions, hence) Pity, feeling, heart. Chiefly *pl.* (*arch.*) Cf. HEART, BREAST. ME. **4.** The interior of anything 1548. † **5.** Offspring. [Cf. L. *viscera.*] –1682.

1. b. These two bowels, especially the liuer 1620. **2.** The bowelles ben cominly called the guttes TREVISA. **3.** Bloody Bonner..full (as one said) of guts, and empty of bowels FULLER. So *bowels of compassion, pity*, etc. **4.** The bowels of the earth 1593. **5.** Thine owne bowels which do call thee, sire *Meas. for M.* III. i. 29. Hence **Bow·elless** *a.* without bowels; unfeeling.

Bowel (bau·ėl), *v.* ME. [f. prec.] To disembowel.

Bowelled (bau·ėld), *ppl. a.* 1589. [f. BOWEL *sb.* and *v.* + -ED.] **a.** Disembowelled. **b.** Having bowels or recesses.

Bower (bauəɹ, bau·əɹ), *sb.*[1] [OE. *būr*, corresp. to OS. *būr* (LG. *buur*), OHG. *būr* (G. *bauer* birdcage), ON. *bur* :- Gmc. **būraz, -am*, f. *bū-* dwell. For the present sp. (ME. *bour*) cf. *flower, tower.*] **1.** A dwelling. In early use *lit.* A cottage; later *poet.* for 'abode'. **b.** A fancy rustic cottage 1810. **2.** An inner apartment, opp. to *hall*; *hence*, a bedroom (*arch.* and *poet.*) OE. **b.** *esp.* A boudoir. Now only *poet.* OE. **3.** A shady recess, arbour 1523. **4.** A structure raised by the bower-bird 1869.

1. The Apartments of Rosamond's B. ADDISON. The bowr of earthly blisse MILT. **2.** Merily masking both in bowre and hall SPENSER. **b.** Love-lorn swain in lady's b. SCOTT. Hence **Bo·wery** *a.* b.-like; leafy.

Bower (bōu·əɹ), *sb.*[2] 1440. [f. BOW *sb.*[1] and *v.*[2] Cf. BOWYER.] † **1.** A maker of bows –1733. **2.** One who plays with a bow on a stringed instrument 1668.

Bower (bau·əɹ), *sb.*[3] 1580. [f. BOW *v.*[1]] **1.** One who bows (see BOW *v.*[1]) 1630. † **2.** That which causes to bend; *esp.* a muscle –1611.

Bower (bau·əɹ), *sb.*[4] 1652. [f. BOW *sb.*[3] + -ER[1].] The name of two anchors, the *best-b.* and *small-b.*, carried at the bows of a vessel; also the cable attached to either. Called also *b.-anchor, b.-cable.* Also *fig.*

† **Bow·er,** *sb.*[5] 1430. [– Du. *boer*; cf. BOOR. For the sp., see BOWER *sb.*[1]] = BOOR 1. –1563.

† **Bow·er,** *sb.*[6], **bow·ess.** *rare.* 1460. [f. BOUGH *sb.* + -ER[1], prob. after BRANCHER[2].] *Falconry.* A young hawk, when it first leaves the nest and clambers on the boughs –1706.

Bower (bau·əɹ), *sb.*[7] 1871. [– G. *bauer* (see BOOR) knave at cards.] In Euchre the name of the two highest cards—the knave of trumps, and the knave of the same colour, called *right* and *left b.* respectively.

Bower (bauəɹ, bau·əɹ), *v.* 1592. [f. BOWER *sb.*[1]] **1.** To embower; to enclose (*lit.* and *fig.*). † **2.** *intr.* To lodge. SPENSER. Hence **Bow·ered** *ppl. a.* embowered; furnished with bowers.

Bower-bird (bauə·ɹ,bɔ̄ɹd), 1847. The name given to several Australian birds of the Starling family, which build bowers or runs, adorning them with feathers, bones, shells, etc., and using them not as nests, but as places of resort.

† **Bowery** (bau·əri), *sb. U.S.* 1809. [– Du. *bouwerij* husbandry, farm, f. *bouwen* cultivate; see BOOR, -ERY.] A farm; a plantation. Hence 'the Bowery' in New York City. –1876.

Bowess; see BOWER *sb.*[6]

Bowet (bau·ėt, *Sc.* bū·ėt). 1440. [app. – med.L. *boeta* box or pyx as housing for a candle, hence 'lantern'; relation to OFr. *boiste* cannot be made out. See BOIST.] A small lantern.

McFarlane's buat [i.e. the moon] SCOTT.

Bowge, var. of BOUGE, bag, wallet; also obs. f. BOUGE *v.*, BULGE *v.*

Bow-hand (bōu·hænd). 1588. [f. BOW *sb.*[1]] The hand which holds the bow, i.e. in *Archery*, the left hand, in *Violin-playing*, the right. † (*Wide*) *on the bow-hand*: wide of the mark, out.

Bowie[1] (bau·i, bō·wi). *Sc.* 1538. [perh. dim. of Sc. *bowe* = BOLL *sb.*[1]; see -Y[6].] A shallow tub; a wooden milk-bowl.

Bow·ie[2]. Short for BOWIE-KNIFE.

Bowie-knife (bōu·i,nəif). 1842. [f. Colonel James *Bowie* (killed 1836).] A large long-bladed knife, curved and double-edged near the point, carried as a weapon in the wilder parts of the United States.

Bowing (bau·iŋ), *vbl. sb.*[1] ME. [f. BOW *v.*[1] + -ING[1].] **1.** The action of the verb; † *concr.* a curved or bent part; a joint –1681. **2.** The action of inclining the body or head in salutation, etc.; also *attrib.*, as in *b. acquaintance* 1616.

Bowing (bōu·iŋ), *vbl. sb.*[2] 1838. [f. BOW *v.*[2] + -ING[1].] **1. a.** The playing of (a violin, etc.) with a bow; the method of handling the bow. **b.** The particular manner in which a phrase or passage is to be executed, and the signs by which such a manner is usually marked. **2.** *Hat-making.* The process of distributing the fibres for felting by means of the bow 1842.

Bowl (bōul), *sb.*[1] [OE. *bolla, bolle*, corresp. to OS. *bollo* cup (Du. *bol* round object; see BOLL *sb.*[1]), OHG. *bolla* bud, round pod, globular vessel; f. **bul-* **bel-* **bal-* swell; cf. BALL *sb.*[1]] **1.** A vessel to hold liquids. Usually hemispherical or nearly so. **b.** *esp.* as a drinking vessel; whence *the b.*, conviviality OE. Also *fig.* and *transf.* **2.** *transf.* A bowlful 1530. **3.** The more or less bowl-shaped part of anything; *e.g.* of a cup or flagon, tobacco-pipe, spoon, etc. ME. † **4.** *Naut.* A round space at the head of the mast for the men to stand in –1800.

1. Bryngeth eek with yow a bolle or a panne ful of water CHAUCER. *Comb.* **b.-barrow,** a prehistoric mound of the shape of an inverted b.

Bowl (bōul), *sb.*[2] [– (O)Fr. *boule* :- L. *bulla* BULL *sb.*[2]] **1.** A sphere, globe, ball. *Obs.* in lit. Eng. –1670. **2.** *spec.* **a.** in the game of *bowls* (3): A body of hard wood, made slightly oblate on one side and prolate on the other, so as to run with a BIAS (q.v.). Also applied to those of wood, used in skittles, nine-pins, etc. ME. Also *fig.* **b.** *Sc.* A marble 1826. **3.** *pl.* A game played with bowls: **a.** on a bowling-green; † **b.** in a bowling-alley 1495. **4.** The roller or anti-friction wheel in a knitting-machine on which the carriage traverses.

1. The six Boules of his [the Medici] Arms 1670. **2.** Which set a Bias vpon the Bowle, of their owne Petty Ends BACON. **3.** The captains and commanders were..at bowls upon the Hoe at Plymouth OLDYS. *Comb.* † **b.-alley,** a skittle-alley.

Bowl (bōul), *v.* 1440. [f. BOWL *sb.*[2]] **1.** *intr.* To play at bowls; to roll a bowl, etc. along the ground. **2.** *trans.* To cause to roll 1580. **b.** To carry on wheels, i.e. in a carriage, etc. 1819. **3.** *intr.* To move by revolution; to move on wheels (esp. *to b. along*); also *transf.* of a ship 1759. **4.** *intr.* To deliver the ball at cricket (orig. by trundling along the ground) 1755. **5.** *trans.* in various constructions. **a.** To b. *the ball.* **b.** To b. *a batsman* (*out*): to get him out by bowling the bails off. **c.** To b. *the wicket* (*down*). 1746. Hence *fig.* (*colloq.* or *slang*).

1. Sir, challenge her to boule SHAKS. **2.** Children bowling their hoops 1887. **3.** The carriage bowls along COWPER. We bowled through..Overton 1872.

Bowlder, var. of BOULDER *sb.*[1]

Bow-legged (bōu·legd), *a.* 1552. [f. *bow-legs* + -ED[2].] Having outwardly bent legs. (In HULOET = *knock-kneed.*)

Bowler[1] (bōu·ləɹ). 1500. [f. BOWL *v.* + -ER[1].] **1.** One who plays at bowls. **2.** The player who bowls at cricket 1755.

Bowler[2] (bōu·ləɹ). [f. BOWL *sb.*[1] or *v.*[2] + -ER[1].] † **1.** A deep drinker. **2.** The workman who shapes the bowl of a spoon 1879.

Bowler[3]. 1861. [f. name of John *Bowler*, hat-manufacturer of Nelson Square, London.] A hard low-crowned stiff felt hat. Cf. BILLYCOCK.

Bow·less, *a.* Without a bow (in various senses).

Bowline (bōu·lin). ME. [(In ONFr. and AFr. *boeline* XII–XIII) – MLG. *bōlīne*, MDu. *boechlijne*, f. *boeg* BOW *sb.*[3] + *lijne* LINE *sb.*[2]] **I. 1.** A rope passing from about the middle of the perpendicular edge on the weather side of the square sails (to which it is fastened by subdivisions called 'bridles') to the larboard or starboard bow, for the purpose of keeping the edge of the sail steady when sailing on a wind. **2.** Short for *b.-knot* 1823.

On a b.: said of a ship when close-hauled, so as to

sail close to the wind. *Comb.*: **b.-bridle** (see 1); **-knot,** a knot used in fastening the b.-bridles to the cringles.

II. In *Ship-building.* A longitudinal curve representing the ship's fore-body cut in a vertical section.

Bowling (bōᵘ·liŋ), *vbl. sb.* 1535. [f. BOWL *v.* + -ING[1].] **1.** Playing at bowls; the action of rolling a ball, etc. **2.** *Cricket.* The action of delivering the ball 1755.

Comb.: **b.-alley,** an alley for playing at bowls or skittles; **-crease,** the line from behind which the bowler delivers the ball in cricket; **-green,** a smooth level green for playing bowls upon.

Bowman[1] (bōᵘ·mæ̆n). ME. [f. BOW *sb.*[1]] One who shoots with a bow; *esp.* a fighting man armed with a bow.

Bowman's root: a name of: *Gillenia trifoliata, Euphorbia corollata,* and *Isnardia alternifolia.*

Bowman[2] (bau·mæ̆n). 1829. [f. BOW *sb.*[3]] *Naut.* = BOW *sb.*[3] 2.

Bowne, obs. f. BOUN.

Bow-net (bōᵘ·ˌnet). OE. [f. BOW *sb.*[1]] **1.** A trap for lobsters, etc., viz. a cylinder of wickerwork closed at one end and having a narrow funnel-shaped entrance at the other; also called, a bow-weel. **2.** A net attached to a bow of wood, etc., used by fowlers 1875.

Bowse, bowsie, var. of BOUSE, BOUSY.

† **Bow·ser.** 1534. [alt. of AFr. *bourser* = OFr. *boursier* (see BURSAR) or var. of *bowger,* f. *bowge* BOUGE *sb.*[1]] A treasurer, bursar. Hence **Bow·sery,** a bursary. –1631.

Bowshot (bōᵘ·ʃǫt). ME. [f. BOW *sb.*[1]] The length an arrow can be shot from a bow.

Bowsprit (bōᵘ·sprit). [ME. *boghespret(e), bow-* (later *bowsprit(e)*) – (M)LG. *bōgsprēt,* MDu. *boechspriet*; see BOW *sb.*[3], SPRIT *sb.*[1]] **1.** A large spar or boom running out from the stem of a vessel, to which (and the jib-boom and flying jib-boom) the fore-mast stays are fastened. †**2.** *fig.* The human nose (*joc.*) –1691.

† **Bow·ssen,** *v.* 1602. [– Cornish *beuzi* 'to immerge, drown'.] To immerse in a holy well –1865.

† **Bowstaff.** Pl. **bowstaves.** ME. [f. BOW *sb.*[1] 4.] A stick to be made into a bow –1720.

Bow-street (bōᵘ·strīt). 1812. A street in London near Covent Garden in which the principal metropolitan police-court is situated: hence **Bow-street officer, -runner,** etc., a police officer.

Bow-string, bowstring (bōᵘ·striŋ). 1486. [f. BOW *sb.*[1]] **1.** The string of a bow; also *fig.* **2.** As used in Turkey for strangling offenders 1603.

Comb.: **b.-bridge,** a bridge consisting of an arch and horizontal tie, to resist the horizontal thrust; hence **-girder; b. hemp,** plants of the genus *Sanseviera,* N.O. *Liliaceæ,* of the fibres of which bow-strings are made. Hence **Bow·string** *v.* to strangle with a bow-string. **Bow·stringer.**

Bowtel(l, var. of BOLTEL.

Bow-window (bōᵘ·wi·ndoᵘ). 1753. [f. BOW *sb.*[1]] **1.** A bay-window segmentally curved on plan. (Erron. taken as generic, *e.g.* in 'square bow windows'.) **2.** *slang.* A big belly. Hence **Bow·-wi:ndowed** *ppl. a.* (in both senses).

Bow-wow, *int.* and *sb.* 1576. [Echoic.] **1.** (bau·wau·) An imitation of the barking of a dog. **2.** as *sb.* Also *fig.* 1832. **b.** *attrib.* (bau·-wau), as in *bow-wow theory,* the theory that human speech originated in imitation of animal sounds 1864. Also quasi-*adj.* Dog-like, barking, snarling 1838. **3.** *transf.* A dog (*joc.* or *nursery*) *a*1800. Hence **Bow·wow·** *v.* to bark; *fig.* to growl.

Bowyer (bōᵘ·iəɹ). ME. [f. BOW *sb.*[1] + -IER, -YER. Cf. BOWER *sb.*[2]] **1.** One who makes, or trades in, bows. **2.** A bowman 1440.

Box (bǫks), *sb.*[1] [OE. *box* – L. *buxus* – Gr. πύξος.] *Bot.* **1.** A genus (*Buxus*) of small evergreen trees or shrubs of the N.O. *Euphorbiaceæ*; specially *B. sempervirens,* the Common or Evergreen Box-tree. A dwarfed variety (*Dwarf* or *Ground Box*) is used for the edgings of flower-beds. OE. **2.** BOX-WOOD ME. Also *attrib.*

1. The wood of boxe is yelowe and pale TURNER. *Comb.*: **b.-berry,** the fruit (and plant) of the wintergreen of America (*Gaultheria procumbens*); **-elder, -alder,** a N. Amer. tree, the Ash-leaved Maple (*Acer negundo*); **-holly,** Butcher's broom (*Ruscus aculeatus*); **-thorn,** shrubs of the genus *Lycium,* esp. *L. barbarum.*

Box (bǫks), *sb.*[2] [Late OE. *box,* prob. – **bux-,* for late L. *buxid-,* stem of *buxis,* var. of L. *pyxis,* prop. box of box-wood. Cf. PYX, BOIST.] **I. 1.** A case or receptacle usually having a lid. Also *fig.* **2.** *esp.* A money-box ME. **b.** *transf.* The money contained in such a box; a fund for a special purpose ME. **3.** = CHRISTMAS-BOX 1593. **4.** A box under the driver's seat on a coach; hence, the driver's seat 1625. **5.** A box and its contents; hence, a measure of quantity ME.

1. Take this boxe of oile in thine hand 2 *Kings* 9:1. *fig.* Thou damnable b. of enuy thou *Tr. & Cr.* v. i. 29. **4.** Our coachmen so drunk, that they both fell off their boxes EVELYN.

II. A compartment partitioned off. **1.** A seated compartment in a theatre. In *pl.* **a** part of the auditorium. 1609. **b.** *transf.* The occupants of the boxes; *esp.* the ladies 1700. **2.** A compartment in the public room of a coffee-house, etc. 1712. **3.** = JURY-BOX, WITNESS-BOX 1822. **4.** A stall for a horse, etc., in a stable, or a railway truck. Also *horse-b.* 1846.

1. b. The boxes and the pit Are sovereign judges of this sort of wit DRYDEN. **4.** *Loose b.*: one in which the animal is free to move about.

III. A box-like shelter, as a sentry's b. 1714. **2.** A small country-house; *e.g.* a *shooting-b.* 1714.

IV. Technical. **1.** The case in which the needle of a compass is placed 1613. **2.** A metal cylinder in the nave of a cart or carriage wheel, which surrounds the axle. **b.** A journal-box, a bearing. (Cf. BUSH *sb.*[2]) 1711. **3.** The piston of a pump; the case containing the valve 1626. **4.** *Printing.* One of the cells into which a type-case is divided 1696.

Phrase. *To be in the* († *a*) *wrong b.*: to be in a wrong position, out of the right place. (The allusion is lost.)

Comb.: **b.-barrow,** one with upright sides and front; **-beam,** an iron beam with a double web; **-chronometer,** a marine chronometer with gimbal arrangements like a ship's compass; **-cloth,** a thick close-woven cloth for riding garments, etc.; **-coat,** a heavy overcoat for driving; **-coupling,** an iron collar used to connect two shafts, etc.; **-crab,** one of the genus *Calappa,* which when at rest resembles a b.; **-drain,** one of quadrangular section; **-fish,** the trunk-fish, *Ostracion*; **-girder,** an iron girder resembling a b., the sides being fastened together by angle-irons; **-iron,** a smoothing iron with a cavity to contain a heater; also *attrib.*; **-keeper,** an attendant at the boxes in a theatre; **-metal,** a metallic alloy of copper and tin, or of zinc, tin, lead, and antimony for bearings; **-office,** an office in a theatre, etc. for booking seats (orig. for hiring a box); **-pleat** a double pleat in cloth; so **-pleated** *ppl. a.,* **-pleating** *vbl. sb.*; **-slater** (*Zool.*), the genus *Idothea* of Isopods; **-sleigh,** one with a b.-like body; **-tortoise, -turtle,** one of the genus *Pyxis,* which by means of a movable door or lid can shut itself up in a sort of b.; *joc.* a reticent person; **-wallah** (*Anglo-Ind.*), a native itinerant pedlar in India. Hence **Bo·xful** *a.*

Box (bǫks), *sb.*[3] [Origin unkn.] † **1.** A blow. Now only as in 2. –1727. **2.** *spec.* A slap or cuff on the ear or side of the head 1440.

A B. oth' Ear for a Prologue, you know D'URFEY.

Box (bǫks), *v.*[1] 1477. [f. BOX *sb.*[2]] **1.** To furnish or fit with a box 1481. † **2.** To cup –1543. **3.** To put into, or as into, a box; often with *up, in* 1586. **4.** To lodge a document in a Law Court 1868. **5.** To fit compactly as in a box; *techn.* to fit with a scarf joint 1794. **6.** To make a cavity in the trunk of (a tree) for the sap to collect 1720. **7.** *slang.* To overturn in his box (*e.g.* a watchman) 1851.

Box (bǫks), *v.*[2] *Naut.* 1519. [– Sp. *bojar* (*boxar*) sail round (e.g. *bojar el mundo, la isla*) – MLG. *bōgen* bend, bow, f. base of BOW *sb.*[1], *v.*[1]] *To b. the compass*: to repeat the names of the 32 points of the compass in order and backwards; *fig.* to go completely round. *To b. about*: to sail up and down, often changing the direction.

Box (bǫks), *v.*[3] 1519. [f. BOX *sb.*[3]] **1.** *trans.* orig. To beat, thrash; *later,* to cuff; *now* usu., to strike (the cheek, ear, etc.) with the hand. **2.** *intr.* To fight with fists; now mostly of practice with boxing-gloves 1567. **3.** *trans.* To fight (another) with fists 1694.

1. I've a good mind to b. your ears 1876. **2.** To leap, to b., to wrestle, and to run COWPER.

Box-calf. 1904. [Named *c* 1890 by Edward L. White, of White Bros. & Co., Massachusetts, U.S.A., after Joseph *Box,* bootmaker, of London.] Chrome-tanned calf-skin having a grain of rectangularly crossed lines.

Boxen (bǫ·ksĕn), *a. arch.* 1566. [f. BOX *sb.*[1] + -EN[4].] **1.** Of or pertaining to the box-tree or box-trees 1578. **2.** Made of or resembling box-wood 1566.

1. B. Groves DRYDEN. **2.** A B. Haut-Boy 1710.

Boxer[1] (bǫ·ksəɹ). 1871. [f. BOX *v.*[1] + -ER[1].] One who puts things up in boxes.

Bo·xer[2]. 1848. [f. BOX *v.*[3] + -ER[1].] One who boxes; a pugilist.

With cap.: A member of a Chinese nationalist secret society (*li ho chuan* 'righteous-harmony-boxers') 1900.

Box-haul (bǫ·ksˌhǫl), *v.* 1769. [f. BOX *v.*[2] + HAUL *v.*] To veer a ship round on her heel.

Boxia·na. 1819. [irreg. f. BOXING *vbl. sb.*[2]; see -AN I.] Notes about boxing. MOORE.

Boxing (bǫ·ksiŋ), *vbl. sb.*[1] 1519. [f. BOX *v.*[1] and *sb.*[2] + -ING[1].] **I.** From the vb. **1.** The putting into, or providing with, a box 1607. **b.** *Law.* The lodgement of pleadings in court 1863. † **2.** Cupping. Hence *b.-glass*: a cupping-glass. –1610. **3.** *Naut.* = BOX-HAULING 1769. **II.** From the sb. **1.** A structure of boxes 1845. **2.** *Shipbuilding.* A scarf joint 1850. **3.** The cases, one on each side of a window, into which the shutters fold 1823.

Boxing (bǫ·ksiŋ), *vbl. sb.*[2] 1711. [f. BOX *v.*[3] + -ING[1].] The action of fighting with fists.

Bo·xing-day. 1849. The first week-day after Christmas-day, observed as a holiday, on which Christmas-boxes are given.

Bo·x-tree. [OE. *boxtrēow.*] = BOX *sb.*[1] 1.

Bo·xwood. 1652. [f. BOX *sb.*[1]] **1.** The wood of the box-tree; much used by turners, wood-engravers, and makers of mathematical instruments. **2.** The tree or shrub itself 1768.

American B., *Cornus florida,* having heavy close-grained wood; **Jamaica B.,** *Tecoma pentaphylla.*

Boy (boi), *sb.* ME. [Early vars. point to an AFr. **abuié,* **embuié,* (see A- *pref.* 10), pa. pple. of OFr. *embuier* fetter :– late L. **imboiare,* f. *in* IM-[1] + L. *boia,* pl. *boiæ* fetters – Gr. βοεῖαι (δοραί) ox-hides, f. βοῦς ox. For muting of *-é* cf. ASSIGN *sb.*[2]] † **1.** A servant, esp. one in a humble position –1601. **b.** *spec.* in *boot-b., link-b., post-b., pot-b.* **c.** A native personal servant 1609. † **2.** A male person of the lower orders. †**3.** Used, like *fellow,* as a vague term of abuse for a male person, and to an inferior –1607. **4.** A male child late ME. **5.** A male of any age or condition, esp. unmarried (*dial.*) 1730. **6.** Used familiarly as a form of address, esp. with *my, old, dear* 1601. **7.** A member of a fraternity or group 1590.

4. The very boyes will learn to talk and swear WALTON. **5.** Our Irish boys 18.. So *Cornish, Western boys.* **6.** To sea, boys, and let her goe hang *Temp.* II. ii. 56.

Phrases, etc. *The old b.*: the devil. *Yellow boys*: guineas. **Boy-bishop,** the boy elected by his fellows to play the part of bishop from St. Nicholas' Day to Innocents' Day. **Boy scout**: see SCOUT *sb.*[2] Hence **Boy·ism,** the nature of a b.; a puerility.

Boy (boi), *v.* 1568. [f. the sb.] To play the boy; to call (one) 'boy'; to represent (a woman's part) on the stage (*Ant. & Cl.* v. ii. 220); to furnish with boys. (Nonce-usages.)

‖ **Boyar, boyard** (boˌyā·r, boi·ăɹd). 1591. [– Russ. *boyárin,* pl. *boyáre* grandee.] A privileged order of Russian aristocracy, next in rank to a *Knyaz* or 'prince', abolished by Peter the Great. Erron. applied in Eng. newspapers to Russian landed proprietors. (The Eng. *boyar* app. represents the pl.; *boyard* is an erroneous Fr. spelling.) Hence **Boy·ardism.**

‖ **Boyau** (boi·o). 1847. [Fr.; see BOWEL.] *Fortif.* A branch of a trench; a zig-zag; a trench in rear of a battery, forming a communication with the magazine; a small gallery of a mine.

Boycott (boi·kǫt), *v.* 1880. [f. Capt. C. C. *Boycott* (1832–97), who was a victim of such treatment as agent for the estates of the earl of Erne, Co. Mayo, Ireland, at the hands of the tenants.] *trans.* To combine in refusing to hold relations of any kind with (a neighbour), on account of political or other differences, so as either to punish him, or coerce him into abandoning his position. The word was first used to describe the action instituted by the Irish Land League towards those who incurred its hostility. Also *transf.* and *fig.* Hence **Boy·co:tter, Boy·co:tting** *vbl. sb.*, **Boy·co:ttism**; also **Boy·cott** *sb.* = *Boycotting*; (U.S.) an application of boycotting. (Now also written without capitals.)

Boydekyn(ne, obs. f. BODKIN.

Boyer (boi·əɹ). 1618. [– Du. *boeier* smack.] A sloop of Flemish construction, with a raised work at each end.

Boyhood (boi·hud). 1745. [f. BOY *sb.* + -HOOD.] **a.** The state of being a boy; the time of life during which one is a boy; also *fig.* the early period. **b.** Boys collectively. **c.** Boyish feeling.

Look at him, in his b.,..and in his manhood SWIFT.

Boyish (boi·iʃ), *a.* 1548. [f. BOY *sb.* + -ISH¹.] **1.** Of or pertaining to boys or boyhood. **2.** Boylike; puerile 1579.

1. My b. daies *Oth.* I. iii. 132. **2.** B. vanities MACAULAY. Hence **Boy·ish-ly** *adv.*, **-ness.**

Boy's love. 1863. Southernwood, *Artemisia abrotanum*, also called *Lad's love.*

‖ **Boyuna** (bo,yū·nă). [Tupi *boi-una.*] A harmless snake of Ceylon. GOLDSM.

‖ **Boza, bosa** (bōᵘ·ză). 1656. [Turk. *bōza.*] An Egyptian drink, made of millet-seed fermented and certain astringents; also an inebriating preparation of darnel-meal, hempseed, and water. vars. **Booza, bouza, boosa.**

Brab (bræb). 1698. [– Pg. *braba* (var. of *brava*) wild, in *palmeira braba* the Pg. name.] The Palmyra palm (*Borassus flabelliformis*).

Brabant (brăbæ·nt). 1840. [f. the name of the Duchy.] A name applied (in error) to a base Flemish coin of the 13th c.

Brabble (bræ·b'l), *v. Obs.* or *arch.* exc. *dial.* 1500. [prob. ult. imit., but perh. immed. – (M)Du. *brabbelen* jabber; possibly, however, a blend of BRAWL *v.* and BABBLE *v.*] **1.** *intr.* To dispute obstinately; to cavil. **2.** To quarrel about trifles; *esp.* to squabble 1530. Hence **Bra·bblement,** † cavilling; contentious uproar (*dial.*). **Bra·bbler.** (Both *arch.*)

Bra·bble, *sb.* 1566. [f. prec.] † **1.** A quibble –1674. † **2.** A frivolous action at law –1677. **3.** A paltry or noisy quarrel 1566; † a brawl, or petty war –1622. **4.** Discordant babble 1861.

3. To make a Nationall Warre of a Surplice B. MILT.

Braccate (bræ·keᶦt), *a.* 1847. [– L. *brac(c)atus*, f. *brac(c)æ* trousers; see -ATE².] *Ornith.* Having the legs fully covered with feathers.

‖ **Braccio** (bra·ttʃo). Pl. **braccia.** 1760. [It., lit. 'an arm'.] An It. measure of length; = 2 ft.

† **Brace,** *sb.*¹ ME. [– (O)Fr. *bras* :– L. *bracchium*; cf. next.] An arm, esp. an arm of the sea, etc. –1530.

B. of St. George = med.L. *brachium Sancti Georgii*: the Bosporus or the Hellespont.

Brace (brēᶦs), *sb.*² ME. [– OFr. *brace* two arms or their extent (mod. *brasse* fathom) :– L. *bracchia*, pl. of *bracchium* arm (whence Fr. *bras*) – Gr. βραχίων. Partly f. BRACE *v.*¹] **I.** Sense 'pair of arms'. † **1.** Armour for the arms. (At first 'a pair of brace'.) –1611. † **b.** A state of defence, *Oth.* I. iii. 24. † **2.** A measure of length, orig. repr. the length of the extended arms –1710. **3.** A carpenter's tool, having a crank handle, and a pad to hold a bit for boring 1567.

II. That which clasps, connects, or fastens. Cf. BRACE *v.*¹ 3. **1.** A clasp, buckle, clamp, or the like 1440. **2.** One of a pair of straps of webbing, used to support the trousers 1816. **3.** A leathern thong which slides up and down the cord of a drum, and regulates the tension of the skins 1596; *transf.* tension –1697. **4.** One of the straps by which the body of a carriage is suspended from the springs 1720. **5.** *Naut.* One of the metal straps secured with bolts and screws to the stern-post and bottom planks of a ship 1850. **6.** A bandage securing a decoy-bird 1768. **7.** A sign } used in writing or printing, chiefly to unite together two or more lines, words, staves of music, etc. In *pl.* (occas. but erron.) = square brackets [ ]. 1656.

2. It broke, and..Carried away both stays and braces. (A pun on BRACE *sb.*³) 1816. **3.** The laxness of the tympanum when it has lost its b. or tension 1697.

III. Two things taken together; a pair, a couple. Often = *two.* Used *orig.* of dogs; later, generally, *esp.* of game. ME.

B. of howndys 1440. A b. of Deere 1570, of Partridges 1741, pistols 1832, twins TENNYSON, of vulgar demagogues 1863.

IV. That which makes rigid or steady; see BRACE *v.*¹ 6. **1.** A band of metal used for support, e.g. in mounting bells 1730. **2.** *Building* and *Mech.* A timber or scantling used in a roof, etc., to stiffen the assemblage of pieces composing it; a piece of timber or iron used to strengthen the framework of a vessel, bridge, pier, etc. 1530.

V. *Mining.* The mouth of a shaft 1881.

Brace (brēᶦs), *sb.*³ 1626. [– Fr. *bras* (*de vergue*) of same meaning, assim. to BRACE *sb.*²] *Naut.* A rope attached to the yard of a vessel for the purpose of trimming the sail. Also *attrib.*

Brace (brēᶦs), *v.*¹ ME. [– OFr. *bracier* embrace, f. *brace* (BRACE *sb.*²); later senses directly f. the sb.] † **1.** To embrace –1570. **2.** To encompass; also, *causally*, to make to surround 1513. **3.** To clasp, gird ME. **4.** To make tense; to stretch 1440. **5.** To string up (nerves, etc.), give tone to. Also with *up.* 1736. Also *fig.* **6.** To render firm or steady by binding tightly 1785. **b.** To fix, render firm 1849. Also *fig.* **7.** To couple together 1826.

2. Bigge Bulles of Basan b. hem about SPENSER. **3.** To b. armor on BRYANT. **4.** Their gluttony.. Brac'd like a drum her oily skin SWIFT. **5.** They gave you toils, but toils your sinews b. SHENSTONE. *To b. one's heart, energies*, etc.: to summon up resolution for a task. Hence **Braced** *ppl. a.* in various senses; *Her.* interlaced; var. *brased.*

† **Brace,** *v.*² 1447. [prob. a use of BRACE *v.*¹ (*esp.* sense 5).] To bluster; to assume a defiant attitude; chiefly in *to face and b.* –1563.

Brace (brēᶦs), *v.*³ 1669. [f. BRACE *sb.*³ Cf. Fr. *brasser.*] To move or turn (a sail) by means of braces.

Phrases. *To b. about*: to turn the yards round for the contrary tack; *to b. by*, to b. (the yards) in contrary directions on the different masts; *to b. in*, to lay (the yards) less obliquely athwartships; *b. round* = *brace about*; *to b. to*, to ease the lee- and draw in the weather-braces; *to b. up*, to put (the yards) into a more oblique position. Also *absol.* in these uses.

Bracelet (brēᶦ·slėt). ME. [– (O)Fr. *bracelet*, dim. of *bracel* :– L. *bracchiale*, f. *bracchium* arm; see BRACE *sb.*¹ -EL², -ET.] **1.** An ornamental ring or band worn on the arm or wrist. † **2.** Any ornament of similar shape –1684. **3.** A handcuff 1816. **4.** A piece of armour covering the arm 1580. **5.** *Her.* = BARRULET.

2. About Christian's neck the Shepherds put a B. BUNYAN.

Bracer¹ (brēᶦ·səɹ). 1579. [f. BRACE *v.*¹ + -ER¹.] That which clamps, binds, etc.; a cincture, bandage, brace. **2.** That which braces; *hence* † a tonic (common in 18th c.) 1740.

Bracer². ME. [– OFr. *brasseüre*, f. *bras* arm (see BRACE *sb.*¹) + *-eüre* -URE.] The portion of a suit of armour covering the arm. Also a guard for the wrist in archery, etc.

† **Bracery.** 1540. *Eng. Law.* [aphet. f. EMBRACERY.]

Braces; see BRACE *sb.*²

Brach (brætʃ). *arch.* [ME. *braches* pl. – OFr. *braches, -ez*, pl. of *brachet*, dim. of *brac*, acc. *bracon* :– Rom. *braccus*, *bracco – Frankish **brak* (cf. OHG. *brakko* (G. *bracke*)). The sing. *brach* is a back-formation.] A kind of hound which hunts by scent; in later Eng. use, always fem. *fig.* A term of abuse; cf. BITCH. B. JONS.

Brachelytrous (brĕke·litrəs), *a.* 1847. [f. mod.L. *brachelytra* n. pl.; see -A 4 (f. Gr. βραχύς short + ἔλυτρον case) + -OUS.] Pertaining to the *Brachelytra*, a division of beetles with short wing-sheaths.

Brachet (bræ·tʃėt). *arch.* ME. [– (O)Fr. *brachet*, dim. of *brac*; see BRACH, -ET.] **1.** = BRACH. **2.** = BRATCHET 2.

Brachial (bræ·kiăl, brēᶦ·kiăl), *a.* 1578. [– L. *brachialis*, f. *brachium* arm; see -AL¹; cf. Fr. *brachial.*] **1.** Belonging to the arm; chiefly in *Phys.*, as in *b. vein, artery, nerve,* etc. Rare exc. techn. Also as quasi-*sb.* **2.** Of the nature of, or resembling, an arm 1835.

2. The mouth, surrounded by four b. appendages 1836.

Brachiate (bræ·ki,eᶦt, brēᶦ·ki,ĕt), *a.* 1835. [– L. *brachiatus* with boughs or branches, f. *brachium* arm; see -ATE².] *lit.* Having arms; in *Bot.* having branches in pairs running out nearly at right angles with the stem and crossing each other alternately.

Brachiferous (brĕki·fĕrəs), *a.* 1877. [f. L. *brachium* arm + -FEROUS.] *Zool.* Arm-bearing. So **Brachi·gerous** *a.*

Brachio-cephalic (bræ:ki,o,sifæ·lik), *a.* 1836. [– mod.L. *brachiocephalicus*, f. Gr. βραχίων arm + κεφαλή head; see -IC.] *Anat.* Pertaining to both arm and head: used chiefly of blood-vessels.

Brachiopod (bræ·ki,opǫd). Pl. **-pods, also -poda.** 1836. [– mod.L. *brachiopoda* n. pl. (see -A 4), f. Gr. βραχίων arm + πούς, ποδ- foot.] *Zool.* A bivalve mollusc, having, on each side of the mouth, a long spiral arm, used in procuring food. Also *attrib.* Hence **Brachio·podist,** one versed in the study of brachiopods. **Brachio·podous** *a.*

Brachisto-, comb. f. Gr. βράχιστος, superl. of βραχύς short, hence:

‖ **Brachi:sto-ce·phali,** men or races with the shortest skull; **-ce·phaly,** the quality of having the shortest type of skull; **-chrone** [Gr. χρόνος], the curve in which a body descending to a given point under the action of gravity will reach it in the shortest time.

‖ **Brachium** (brēᶦ·kiŏm, bræ·kiŏm). 1731. [L.] *Biol.* In Mammalia, the upper arm from the shoulder to the elbow.

Brachman, obs. f. BRAHMIN.

Brachy-, comb. f. Gr. βραχύς short, hence: **Bra:chy-catale·ctic** *a.*, *Pros.* wanting one foot or two syllables; **-ceral, -cerous** (sĕr) [Gr. κέρας] *a.*, *Ent.* Having short horns or antennae; **-dia·-gonal** *a.*, *Cryst.* pertaining to the shorter lateral axis of a rectangular prism; also as *sb.*; **-dome,** *Cryst.* a prism whose face is parallel to the brachydiagonal axis; **-elytrous,** see BRACHELYTROUS; **-me·tropy,** near- or short-sightedness; **-pinacoid, -koid** [Gr. πίναξ] *a.*, *Cryst.* pertaining to either of the two planes which in the Orthorhombic system are parallel to the vertical and brachydiagonal axes respectively; **-pleu·ral** [Gr. πλευρά] *a.*, having short ribs; **-pterous** [Gr. πτερόν] *a.*, short-winged, as some diving-birds; **-typous** [Gr. τύπος] *a.*, *Min.* of a short form.

Brachycephalic (bræ:ki,sĭfæ·lik), *a.* Also **-kephalic.** 1849. [f. BRACHY- + Gr. κεφαλή head + -IC.] *lit.* Short-headed: used in *Ethnology* of skulls in breadth at least four-fifths of the length; opp. to DOLICHOCEPHALIC. var. **Brachyce·phalous.**

Skulls with a cephalic index of 0·8, or more, are B. HUXLEY. So **Brachycephales, -cephali** [mod.L.], men with b. skulls. **Brachyce·phalism, Brachyce·phaly,** the condition of being b.

Brachygraphy (brĕki·grăfi). 1590. [– Fr. *brachygraphie*, f. as BRACHY- + -GRAPHY.] = STENOGRAPHY. Also *attrib. Obs.* exc. as a name of old systems. Also *fig.*

Brachylogy (brĕki·lŏdʒi). 1623. [– late L. *brachylogia* – Gr. βραχυλογία, f. as BRACHY- + -LOGY.] Laconism; *concr.* a condensed expression.

Brachyurous, -ourous (brĕki,ūᵊ·rəs), *a.* 1828. [f. mod.L. *brachyura* n. pl. (see -A 4), f. BRACHY- + Gr. οὐρά tail + -OUS.] *Zool.* Pertaining to the *Brachyura*, a tribe of Decapod Crustacea, including the crab, etc., characterized by the non-development of the abdomen or tail. So **Brachyu·rul, -ou·ral** *a.*, **Brachyu·ran, -ou·ran** *a.* and *sb.*

Bracing (brēᶦ·siŋ), *vbl. sb.* 1536. [f. BRACE *v.*¹ + -ING¹.] **1.** The action of the vb. **2.** An appliance for tying, fastening, supporting, or strengthening (*lit.* and *fig.*) 1849.

Bracing, *ppl. a.* 1750. [f. BRACE *v.*² + -ING².] That braces, girds, etc. Now chiefly of the air or climate; formerly of tonics.

Brack (bræk), *sb.*¹ [In I – ON. *brak* = OE. *ġebræc*, OS. *gibrak*, creaking noise, f. Gmc. **brekan* BREAK *v.*; in II, a parallel form to BREAK *sb.*¹] **I.** ME. † **1.** Noise, outcry –1513. **II.** mod. † **1.** A breach, rupture –1669; *fig.* a quarrel –1608. **2.** A flaw in cloth 1552. † **3.** A fragment –1674. † **4.** Fault in mining 1747.

† **Brack,** *sb.*[2] *rare.* 1530. [prob. identical w. prec.; cf. connection of L. *rupes* and *rumpere* break, and BREAK *sb.*[1]] A cliff, crag, or rock.

Brack, *sb.*[3] 1734. [f. G. *bracken* to sort goods.] The system of official sorting in vogue at Baltic ports.

† **Brack,** *sb.*[4] 1482. [app. shortened f. BRACKEN[1].] Bracken –1675.

Brack, *a.* and *sb.*[5] 1513. [– MLG., MDu. *brac* (LG., Du. *brak*), of unkn. origin.] **A.** *adj.* Salt, brackish. ? *Obs.* † **B.** *sb.* Salt water, brine; the sea. DRAYTON.

Brack (bræk), *v.* 1858. [– G. *bracken*; see BRACK *sb.*[3]] To sort (goods, produce, etc.) (at the Baltic ports). Hence **Bra·cker,** a government sorter.

Bracken[1] (bræ·k'n). [north. ME. *braken* – ON. **brakni* (whence Sw. *bräken*, Da. *bregne*).] A fern; *spec. Pteris aquilina*, the 'Brake'. In southern writers often collective. Also *attrib.*

The commune Ferne or brake, which the northerne men call a bracon TURNER. *Comb.* **b.-clock,** the Rose-beetle (*Phyllopertha horticola*).

† **Bra·cken**[2]. 1652. [– Gael. and Ir. *breacan*, f. *breac* chequered.] A tartan plaid –1828.

Bracket (bræ·kėt). 1580. [Earliest forms *brag(g)et* – Fr. *braguette* codpiece, or Sp. *bragueta* codpiece, bracket, corbel, dim. of Fr. *brague* mortice, pl. breeches, lashing – Pr. *braga* pl. breeches; ult. – L. *braca*, pl. *bracæ* breeches.] **1.** In *Building*, a piece of stone, wood, or metal projecting from a wall, and having a flat upper surface which serves to support a statue, the spring of an arch, a beam, shelf, etc.; usu. decorated, and sometimes merely a decoration. See CORBEL and CONSOLE. **b.** A small (ornamental) shelf for the wall of a room 1635. **2.** In *Carpentry, Shipbuilding*, etc.: A support consisting of two pieces of wood or metal joined at an angle. Also *attrib.* 1627. **3.** One of the two cheeks of a gun-carriage 1753. **4.** A (decorative) metal pipe projecting from the wall of a room, to support and supply the gas lamps or burners 1876. **5.** One of two marks [ ] or ( ), and in *Math.* also { }, used for enclosing a word or words, a portion of a formula, or the like, so as to separate it from the context. Occas. used (improp.) of the 'vinculum' and the 'brace' (cf. BRACKET *v.*); hence *brackets* (fig.), 'the position of being bracketed equal'. 1750.

1. The angel b. of an oriel window 1859. **5.** [ ] Brackets or Crochets 1750. On a shorter course Regnard may earn brackets 1883. *Comb.*: **b.-burner, -light,** = sense 4; **-crab,** a windlass attached to a wall or post; **-shelf.**

Bra·cket, *v.* 1861. [f. prec.] **1.** To provide with brackets; to enclose within brackets 1870 **2.** To connect by means of a brace; hence to mention together as equal, or as having something in common.

Bra·cketing, *vbl. sb.* 1823. [f. prec. + -ING[1].] **1.** The action of the vb. 1869. **2.** *Archit.* A skeleton, consisting of wooden ribs nailed to the ceiling, joists, and battening, to support a cornice, cove, or other moulding.

Brackish (bræ·kiʃ), *a.* 1538. [f. BRACK *a* + -ISH[1].] **1.** Of a somewhat salt taste; partly fresh, partly salt. **2.** *fig.* and *transf.* **a.** Spoilt by mixture. **b.** Nauseous. **c.** Nautical. 1611.

1. The southern wind with b. breath MARLOWE. **2.** The [English] language..b. with the mixture of vulgar Irish SPEED. Hence **Bra·ckishness.**

Bra·ckmard. *Obs.* exc. *Hist.* 1653. [– Fr. *braquemart.*] = CUTLASS.

† **Bra·cky,** *a.*[1] 1593. [f. BRACK *sb.*[5] + -Y[1].] = BRACKISH –1603.

Bra·cky, *a.*[2] 1618. [f. *brack*, var. of BRAKE *sb.*[1], [2] + -Y[1].] **a.** Abounding in bracken. **b.** Of the nature of a thicket.

Bract (brækt). 1770. [– L. *bractea* (also used), var. of *brattea* thin plate of metal, gold leaf.] **1.** *Bot.* A small modified leaf, or scale, growing below the calyx of a plant, or upon the peduncle of a flower. Also *attrib.* **2.** A similar appendage found among Hydrozoa 1878. Hence **Bra·cteal** *a.* pertaining to, or like, bracts. **Bra·cted** *ppl. a.* furnished with bracts. **Bra·cteiform** *a.* b.-shaped. **Bra·cteolate, bracte·olate** *a.* furnished with bracteoles. **Bra·cteole,** a small b. **Bracteo·se** *a.* full of, or with conspicuous, bracts. **Bra·ctlet,** a minute or secondary b.

Bracteate (bræ·kti,ĕt). 1845. [– L. *bracteatus*; see prec., -ATE[2].] **A.** *adj.* **1.** *Bot.* Having or bearing bracts. **2.** Formed of metal beaten thin; applied to coins, medals, etc. **B.** *sb.* A bracteate coin or medal; also *attrib.* 1845.

Brad (bræd). ME. [Later var. of BROD.] **1.** A thin flattish nail of the same thickness throughout, but tapering in width, having a small lip on one edge, instead of a head. **2.** *pl.* Halfpence; money (*slang*) 1812. Hence **Brad** *v.* to fasten with brads.

Bradawl (bræ·dǭl). 1823. [f. prec. + AWL.] A small boring tool, a sprig-bit.

Bradoon, obs. f. BRIDOON.

† **Bradypepsy** (bræ·dipe:psi), **-pe·psia.** 1598. [– Gr. βραδυπεψία, f. βραδύς slow + πέψις cooking, digestion.] Slowness of digestion –1710.

Bradypod, -pus (bræ·dipǫd, -pɒs). 1833. [– Gr. βραδύπους, -ποδ- slow-footed, f. βραδύς slow + πούς foot.] One of the family of edentate mammals represented by the Sloth. Hence **Brady·podal** *a.*

Brae (brē[i], *dial.* brē, brī[ə], brī). Now *Sc.* and *n. dial.* [ME. *brā* – ON. *brá* eyelash = OE. *brǣw* eyelid, OFris. *brē*, OS., OHG. *brāwa* (G. *braue*) eyebrow; the sense-development is parallel to that of BROW *sb.*[1]] **1.** The steep bank bounding a river valley. **2.** A steep, a slope, a hill-side (= *hill* in Ludgate Hill) ME. vars. (*dial.*) **brea, breea.**

Brag (bræg), *sb.* ME. [Earliest is the adj. (XIII–XVII) meaning (i), coupled at first with *bold*, 'spirited, brisk, mettlesome', and (ii) 'boastful'; sb. and v. (XIV), in earliest exx. often w. *boast*, denote arrogant, boastful, or pompous behaviour. Of unkn. origin. The similar Fr. words, *braguer* vaunt, brag and *brague* ostentation, are recorded only some three centuries later than the Eng. words.] † **1.** The bray of a trumpet 1513. **2.** Arrogant or boastful language; boasting ME. † **3.** Show; pompous demeanour –1632. **4.** *concr.* That which is boasted of 1538. **5.** A braggart 1671. **6.** A game at cards, essentially = 'poker' 1734.

2. Cesars Thrasonicall bragge of I came, saw, and ouercame SHAKS. **4.** Beauty is nature's b. MILT.

† **Brag** (bræg), *a.* and quasi-*adv.* ME. [See BRAG *sb.*] **1.** Brisk, mettlesome, valiant –1610. **2.** Boastful (*of*) –1655. **3.** as quasi-*adv.* Boastfully –1579.

Brag (bræg), *v.* ME. [See BRAG *sb.*] † **1.** *intr.* Of a trumpet: To sound loudly; also, to make a loud sound (with a trumpet); *trans.* to sound (a trumpet). ME. only. **2.** *intr.* and *refl.* To talk boastfully, boast oneself. Const. *of, about.* ME. **3.** *trans.* **a.** To challenge; also, to bully. Now *dial.* 1551. **b.** To overawe by boasting (*mod.*). **4.** To vaunt, lay boastful claim to 1588. **5.** To boast. With *subord. cl.* 1563.

2. If I see a Man boast and b. himself, I cannot but deem him a Proud Man 1543. **4.** He brags his seruice *Cymb.* v. iii. 93. Hence **Bra·gger. Bra·ggery,** bragging; † rabble (*rare*).

Braggadocio (brægădō[u]·ʃio), *sb.* (and *a.*) 1590. [f. *r*-less form of BRAGGART (as in *Bragadisme*, *Two Gent.* II. iv. 164) + *-occio* It. augm. suffix.] See SPENSER *F. Q.* II. iii. **1.** An empty idle boaster; a swaggerer 1594. **2.** Empty vaunting 1734. Also *attrib.*

1. He..had much of the sycophant, alternating with the b. CARLYLE. **2.** Half blunder, half b. SOUTHEY. Hence † **Braggado·cian** *a.* of the nature of a b.; *sb.* = BRAGGADOCIO.

Braggart (bræ·gă.ɪt). 1577. [– Fr. *bragard*, f. *braguer* (see BRAG *sb.*) + var. of -ARD.] **A.** *sb.* A vain bragger. **B.** *adj.* Vainly boastful 1613. Hence **Bra·ggartism,** the practice of a b. **Bra·ggartly** *adv.*

Bragget (bræ·gėt). ME. [– early W. *bragaut*, *bracaut* (mod. *bragawd*) = Ir. *bracát* :– OCeltic **bracātā*, f. **brac-*, repr. by L. *bracē* kind of grain.] A drink made of honey and ale fermented together; latterly of sugar and spice and ale. *attrib.* in *Braggot Sunday.*

Bra·gless, *a.* [f. BRAG *sb.* + -LESS.] Without brag. *Tr. & Cr.* v. ix. 5.

† **Bra·gly,** *adv.* 1759. [f. BRAG *a.* + -LY[2].] Briskly –1717.

Brahm, Brahma (brām, brā·mă). 1785. [– Skr. *Brahmā* m., *Brahma* n. the creator, base *brahman*.] **a.** The supreme God of post-Vedic Hindu mythology. **b.** In the later pantheistic systems, the Divine reality, of which all else is only a manifestation. Hence **Bra·hmahood,** the state of Brahma; absorption into the divine essence.

Brahma, shortened f. BRAHMAPOOTRA.

Brahman, etc.; see BRAHMIN, etc.

Brahmapootra (brāmăpū·tră). 1851. A variety of domestic fowl, brought from Lakhimpur on the River Brahmaputra, in 1846; now abbrev. *Brahma.*

Brahmic (brā·mik), *a.* 1582. [f. Skr. *brahma*, comb. f. BRAHMAN + -IC.] Pertaining to the Indian society called Brahmo Somāj, or to the older Brahma Sabhā.

Brahmin, Brahman (brā·min, -măn). 1481. [– Skr. *brâhmaṇas* one of the caste, f. *brahmaṇ* (nom. *brahmā* priest; forms in *-in* are as early as XVI.] A member of the highest or priestly caste among the Hindus. Also *fig.*

Other peple whiche ben callyd..bragman whiche ben fayrer than they to fore named CAXTON.

Comb.: **B.-beads,** the corrugated seeds of *Elæocarpus*, used by the Brahmins and others as necklaces; **-ox,** a humped variety of the ox. Hence **Brahminee·**, a female b. **Brahmi·nic, -al, -ma·nic, -al,** *a.* **Brahmi·nicide, -ma·nicide,** one who has killed, or the act of killing, a B. **Brah·minism, -manism,** the principles and practice of Brahmins.

Brahminee (brā·minī), *a.* Also **Brahminy.** 1811. [f. BRAHMIN, after anal. of native Indian words like BENGALEE, BENGALI.] Pertaining to the Brahmin caste; appropriated to the Brahmins. *B. bull* = Brahmin ox; *B. duck*, the *Casarca rutila*; *B. fig-tree*, the Banyan; *B. kite*, the *Haliastur indicus.*

Brahmism (brā·miz'm). 1813. [f. BRAHM + -ISM.] † **a.** The religion of Brahma. **b.** The tenets of the 19th c. Indian society called Brahma Sabhā, or of the later Brahmo Somāj. In the last sense also **Brahmoism.**

Braid (brē[i]d), *sb.* [f. BRAID *v.*[1]] † **1.** A sudden movement (*lit.* and *fig.*); a start; a strain –1626. Also † *fig.* † **2.** *transf.* A moment –1657. † **3.** An adroit turn; a trick –1570. **4.** Anything plaited or interwoven; *esp.* A plait of human hair 1530. **b.** A string or band confining or entwined in the hair 1576. **5.** A woven fabric of silken, woollen, cotton, gold, or silver thread in the form of a band, used for trimming or binding dress 1706.

4. b A chain of gold ye sall not lack Nor b. to bind your hair SCOTT.

† **Braid,** *a. rare.* [Of doubtful meaning and origin; cf. BRAID *sb.* 3, whence *braidie* (+ -IE, -Y[1]) deceitful.] ? Deceitful. *All's Well* IV. ii. 73.

Braid (brē[i]d), *v.*[1] [OE. *breġdan* = OFris. *breida*, *brīda*, OS. *bregdan* (Du. *breien*), OHG. *brettan*, ON. *bregða* :– Gmc. **breȝđan*, of unkn. origin.] † **1.** *trans.* To make a sudden movement with (the hand, foot, etc.); to brandish; to deal (a blow); to draw (a sword, etc.); to jerk, snatch, wrench, fling, etc., with a sudden effort –1505. † **2.** *intr.* To start, as out of a sleep, etc.; to break forth abruptly into speech, or crying –1603. † **3.** *intr.* To change suddenly or abruptly –ME. **4.** To twist in and out, interweave, plait; to embroider; to make by plaiting. (Now *poet.* or *dial.*, exc. as used of the hair in the sense 'to arrange in braids'.) OE. Also *transf.* **5.** [f. BRAID *sb.* 4 b.] To bind (the hair) with a ribbon or the like 1793. **6. a.** To trim with braid. **b.** To outline (a design for point-lace work) by means of braid. **c.** To manufacture braid. 1848.

2. ffor verray wo out of his wit he breyde CHAUCER. **5.** To pull the thorn thy brow to b. SCOTT. Hence **Brai·ding** *vbl. sb.* braids collectively; braided work.

† **Braid,** *v.*[2] ME. [aphet. f. ABRAID *v.*[2] or UPBRAID.] To upbraid, reproach –1608.

Braid, obs. and Sc. f. BROAD.

Braider (brē[i]·dəɹ). 1866. [f. BRAID *v.*[1] + -ER[1].] One who or that which makes or applies braids.

Braidism (brē^{i}·diz'm). 1882. *Med.* Applied to a process of inducing sleep or trance, orig. called MESMERISM, to which Dr. James Braid, who first scientifically applied and explained it in 1842, gave the name HYPNOTISM, q.v.

Brail (brē^{i}l), *sb.* 1450. [– OFr. *brail, braiel* :– med. L. *bracale* waist-belt, f. *braca*; see BRACKET.] **1.** *pl.* Small ropes fastened to the edges of sails to truss them up before furling. **2.** A girdle for confining a hawk's wing 1828. **3.** *pl.* The feathers about a hawk's rump 1486.

Brail (brē^{i}l), *v.* 1625. [f. BRAIL *sb.*] *trans.* **1.** To haul *up* (sails) by means of brails. **2.** To confine (a hawk's wings) with a brail 1643.

Braille (brē^{i}l), 1871. [f. the name of Louis *Braille*, French inventor, 1809–52.] A system of embossed printing or writing for the blind, in which the characters are represented by tangible points or dots.

Brain (brē^{i}n), *sb.* [OE. *brægen* = MLG. *bragen, bregen,* (M)Du. *brein* :– WGmc. **braȝna*.] **1.** The convoluted mass of nervous substance contained in the skull of man and other vertebrates. Formerly restricted to the anterior portion (L. *cerebrum*), as opp. to the posterior portion (L. *cerebellum*); but now used of the entire organ, and extended to the analogous organs of invertebrates. When mere cerebral substance is meant, the pl. is used. **2.** Taken as the seat of sensation, the organ of thought, memory, or imagination. (Usually pl., exc. in dignified language.) ME. **3.** *fig.* Intellectual power, intellect, sense, thought, imagination. (Often pl.) ME.

1. Betwene the brayne and Cerebellum 1578. He haue my braines tane out and butter'd *MerryW.* III. v. 7. Phr. *To dash, knock out, blow out (any) one's brains.* **2.** Was that plan the conception of any one b. ? STUBBS. **3.** The uncommon gift of brains CHURCHILL.

Phrases. **a.** (sense 2) *To beat, busy, cudgel, drag, puzzle one's brains*: to exert oneself in thinking or contriving. *To have* anything *on the b.*; to be crazy about. *To turn one's b.*: to render giddy, hence *fig.* to render vain or imprudent. **b.** (sense 3) *To suck* (or *pick*) *a person's brains*: to elicit and appropriate the results of his thought.

Comb.: **b.-box, -case, -pan,** the skull; **-cell,** one of the cells forming the tissue of the b.; **-coral,** coral resembling in form the convolutions of the b.; **-fag,** brain weariness; **-fever,** a term for inflammation of the brain, and fevers with brain complications; **-stone** = *brain-coral*; **-tunic,** a membrane enveloping the b.; **-wave,** *colloq.*, a sudden inspiration or bright thought; **-worm,** a worm infesting the b.; *fig.* a wriggling disputant MILT.

Hence **Brai·nish** *a. arch.* passionate, headstrong. **Brai·nless** *a.* devoid of b.; that has had the b. removed; †insane; irrational; wanting intelligence or self-control. **Brai·nless-ly** *adv.*, **-ness.** † **Brai·nlet,** the cerebellum. **Brai·ny** *a.* having brains; acute, clever.

Brain (brē^{i}n), *v.* ME. [f. the sb.] **1.** *trans.* To dash (any one's) brains out; to kill by dashing out the brains. Also *fig.* SHAKS. † **2.** To conceive in the brain. *Cymb.* V. iv. 147. **3.** To furnish with a brain 1882.

1. Most cruelly murder'd, by being brain'd like an Ox WOOD. Hence **Brained** *a.*, as *addle-brained.*

Brainsick (brē^{i}·nsik), *a.* 1483. [f. BRAIN *sb.*] **1.** Diseased in the brain or mind; addle-headed, mad, frantic. **2.** Proceeding from a diseased mind 1571. Hence **Brainsick-ly** *adv.*, **-ness.**

Braird (brē^{ə}rd), *sb. Sc.* 1450. [Same word as BRERE.] The first shoots of grass, corn, etc. Hence **Braird** *v.* to sprout.

Braise (brē^{i}z), *v.* 1797. [– Fr. *braiser*, f. *braise* live coals; cf. BRAZIER[2].] To cook *à la braise*; i.e. to stew in a tightly closed pan (prop. with hot charcoal above and below). Hence **Braise** *sb.* braised meat. **Brai·ser** [partly – Fr. *braisière*]. var. **Braize.**

Brake (brē^{i}k), *sb.*[1] [perh. shortening of BRACKEN, this being apprehended as a pl. form; cf. *chick, chicken.*] Fern, bracken.

Brake (brē^{i}k), *sb.*[2] 1440. [OE. *bracu* (recorded in gen. pl. *fearnbraca* beds of fern, in ME. *fernebrake*), corresp. to MLG. *brake* branch, twig, tree-stump (whence OFr. *bracon* branch); perh. reinforced in ME. from LG. (cf. *busk unde brake* 'bush and brake').] A clump of bushes, brushwood, or briers; a thicket. Also *attrib.*

So thick entwin'd, As one continu'd b., the undergrowth Of shrubs MILT. *P.L.* iv. 175.

Brake (brē^{i}k), *sb.*[3] ME. [Identical w. MLG. *brake* or ODu. *braeke*, Du. *braak* flax-brake, f. Du. *breken* BREAK *v.*] **1.** A toothed instrument for braking flax or hemp 1450. **2.** A baker's kneading-machine 1440. **3.** A heavy harrow for crushing clods; a *b.-harrow* 1785. **4.** An instrument for peeling the bark from willows 1824.

Brake (brē^{i}k), *sb.*[4] ME. [Origin unkn. Held by some to be obscurely rel. to Fr. *braquer* (*un canon* point a canon, *le timon* turn the rudder), but evidence is wanting.] A lever or handle for working a machine; *e.g.* †the winch of a crossbow (whence, a cross-bow, etc.), the handle of a pump, part of an apparatus for boring coal. *Comb.* **b.-pump,** a pump worked by a b.

† **Brake,** *sb.*[5] 1430. [perh. – ODu. *braeke* (see BRAKE *sb.*[3]), occurring in the sense of a nose-ring for a draught-ox.] A bridle or curb –1753.

Brake, *sb.*[6] 1529. [Origin unkn.] † **1.** A cage; a trap; *fig.* a difficulty –1640. **2.** A framework intended to hold anything steady, *e.g.* a horse's foot while being shod 1609. **3.** An instrument of torture. *Hist.* 1530. † **4.** A turner's lathe –1609.

2. *To set one's face in a b.*: to assume an immovable expression of countenance.

Brake, break (brē^{i}k), *sb.*[7] 1772. [prob. a use of BRAKE *sb.*[4] or [5].] An apparatus for retarding or arresting the motion of any mechanism, as a vehicle, engine, etc.; *esp.* a device including a block or shoe, a lever, or band applied to the rim of a wheel, etc., or a shoe or ratchet applied to the track or roadway.

Comb.: **b.-compartment, -van,** the compartment or the carriage which contains the b. apparatus; **-wheel,** the wheel by which the brakes are worked. Hence **Bra·keless** *a.*

Brake, *v.*[1] ME. [f. BRAKE *sb.*[3]] **1.** To beat and crush flax, hemp, etc. **2.** To break (clods) with a harrow 1800. **3.** To knead (dough) 1832.

† **Brake,** *v.*[2] 1530. [f. BRAKE *sb.*[6] 3.] To torture on the rack.

Brake, *v.*[3] 1857. [f. BRAKE *sb.*[4]] *intr.* To attend to a winding engine.

Brake, *v.*[4] 1868. [f. BRAKE *sb.*[7]] To apply a brake to; also *transf.*

† **Brake,** *v.*[5] ME. [perh. repr. OE. **bracian*, f. *bræc* phlegm, mucus, saliva, = MLG. *brēke*; cf. ODu. *bracken*, MLG., Du. *braken* vomit; rel. to BREAK *v.* (cf. G. *sich (er)brechen*).] *trans.* and *intr.* To spew, vomit –1768.

Brake (brē^{i}k), arch. pa. t. of BREAK.

Brakesman (brē^{i}·ksmǣn). 1851. [f. BRAKE *sb.*[4] and [7].] **1.** *Coal-mining.* A man who attends to the winding-machine. **2.** The man in charge of the brake-apparatus of a railway-train; in U.S. (*brakeman*) the guard.

Braky (brē^{i}·ki), *a.* 1636. [f. BRAKE *sb.*[1] or [2] + -Y[1].] Overgrown with brushwood or fern.

Bramah (prop. bræ·mă, often brā·mă). 1836. [f. Joseph *Bramah* (1749–1814).] Attrib. use of proper name, = 'invented by Bramah'; as *B.-key, -lock, -pen*; **Bramah's press,** a hydraulic press of enormous power.

Bramantip. 1870. *Logic.* A mnemonic word, repr. the first mood of the fourth syllogistic figure, in which two universal affirmative premisses yield a particular affirmative conclusion.

Bramble (bræ·mb'l). [OE. *bræmbel*, later form of *brǣmel, brēmel*, f. the base repr. in OE. *brōm* BROOM; cf. OS. *brāmalbusc*, north. G. *brommelbeere*; see -EL.] A rough prickly shrub; *spec.* the blackberry bush (*Rubus fruticosus*) OE.

Their defenceless Limbs the brambles tear DRYDEN.

Comb.: **b.-berry,** the fruit of the b.; a blackberry; **-brand,** a fungus (*Aregma rubi*) which appears on the b.; **-flower,** the blossom of a b.; also the Dogrose (*Rosa canina*); **-rose,** the white trailing dogrose. Hence **Bra·mbled** *ppl. a.* covered with brambles. **Bra·mbly** *a.*

Brambling (bræ·mbliŋ). 1570. [= G. *brämling*, prob. f. WGer. **brām-* BRAMBLE.] The Mountain Finch (*Fringilla montifringilla*).

† **Brame.** [prob. – It. *brama* strong desire.] Longing. SPENSER.

Bran[1] (bræn). [ME. *bran, bren* – (O)Fr. *bran* bran, (now) excrement, muck, filth, †*bren*, = Pr., OSp., It. dial. *bren*; of unkn. origin. The Celtic words quoted as the source are from Fr. and Eng.] **1.** The husk of wheat, barley, oats, etc., separated from the flour after grinding; *techn.*, the coarsest portion of this. Also *fig.* and *transf.* 1577. † **2.** Scurf in the hair –1580.

1. In stide of flour yet wol I yeue hem bren CHAUCER.

† **Bran**[2]. 1610. [prob. special use of BRAN[1], suggested by the L. phr. *eiusdem farinæ.*] Sort, class, quality –1672.

Bran (bræn), *v.* [f. BRAN *sb.*[1]] *trans.* To 'clear' maddered goods by boiling in bran-water.

Brancard (bræ·ŋkăɹd). 1592. [– Fr. *brancard* litter, stretcher.] A horse-litter.

Branch (branʃ), *sb.* ME. [– (O)Fr. *branche* = Pr., Sp. *branca* claw, It. *branca* claw, paw, Rum. *brîncă* hand, paw :– late L. *branca* (*branca ursina* 'bear's foot', acanthus), of unkn. origin.] **1.** A portion or limb of a tree or other plant growing out of the stem or trunk, or out of one of the boughs. (*A branch* is smaller than a bough and larger than a shoot or spray.) **2.** *transf.* Anything analogous to a limb of a tree, in relation to the trunk ME. **3.** *fig.* **a.** One of the portions into which a family or race is divided according to the differing lines of descent from a common ancestor; hence a division, a group ME. **b.** A child, descendant; cf. *scion.* Now only *joc.* 1535. **4.** *fig.* A consequence of a principle; an effect of a cause 1526. **5.** *fig.* A division; a subdivision; a department 1509. **6.** *fig.* A component portion of an organization or system 1696. **7.** *fig.* A local and subordinate office of business 1817. **8.** The certificate of competency given by the Trinity House to pilots 1865. **9.** *attrib.* Having the character of a branch, as *b.-line* (of railway), *b. bank, -office*, etc.

1. As the sprai cometh out of the braunche, the braunche out of the bouȝ PECOCK. **2.** A b. of Mount Atlas 1603, of the aorta 1831, of the Great Northern 1878. **3. a.** Minyans..a b. of the Greek nation THIRLWALL. **5.** Fidelity..a b. of naturall Justice HOBBES. A b. of the prerogative CLARENDON, of Trade STEELE, learning SWIFT, revenue HUME, of a statute 1542, of discourse 1783, of a will 1818. **6.** *B. of the legislature*, one of the houses or chambers into which the legislative body is divided.

Phr. *To destroy (anything) root and b.*: to destroy both the thing itself and all its effects; orig. suggested by the wording (derived from *Mal.* 4:1) of the London Petition of 11 Dec. 1640, for the total abolition of episcopal government. Hence *Root-and-b. petition, bill, party*; also gen. *root and b. policy*, a radical and destructive policy.

Comb.: **b.-building** *a.*, building in branches; **-chuck** (*Mech.*), a chuck having four branches, and furnished with screws; **-coal,** anthracite (local); **-pilot,** one who holds a Trinity House certificate; **b. wines** (Pg. *vinos de ramo*), wines made for home consumption; **-work,** ornamental figured patterns. Hence **Bra·nchery,** branches in the mass. **Bra·nchless** *a.* **Bra·nchlet,** a little branch; in *Bot.* a smaller b. growing from a larger one.

Branch, *v.* ME. [f. prec. sb.] **I.** *intr.* **1.** To put forth branches; occas. with *forth, out.* Also *transf.* and *fig.* **2.** To spring out, as a branch or branches; to strike off in a new path; now chiefly with *out, off,* occas. *away* ME.

1. What subject does not b. out to infinity? BURKE. **2.** The Foss Way..branched off from the Eastern gate FREEMAN.

II. *trans.* **1.** To divide (anything) into branches 1700. Also *fig.* **2.** To embroider with work representing flowers or branches 1596.

2. A dress All branch'd and flower'd with gold TENNYSON.

Branched (branʃt), *ppl. a.* ME. [f. BRANCH *sb.* and *v.* + -ER[1] and [2].] **1.** Provided with branches (*lit.* and *fig.*). Often in *comb.* **2.** Adorned with a figured pattern. Cf. BRANCH *v.* II. 2. 1509.

Brancher[1] (bra·nʃəɹ). 1610. [f. BRANCH *v.* + -ER[1].] That which puts forth branches.

Brancher[2]. ME. [– AFr. **brancher*, (O)Fr. *branchier*, orig. adj., f. *branche* BRANCH + *-ier* -ER[2].] A young hawk, etc., when it first leaves the nest and takes to the branches.

‖ **Branchiæ, branchia** (bræ·ŋki,ī, bræ·ŋkiă), *sb. pl.* ME. [L. *branchia*, pl. *-iæ* – Gr. βράγχια gills; see -A 4, -Æ.] The organs of respiration in fishes, etc.; gills. Hence **Bra·nchial** *a.* pertaining to, of the nature of, or resembling gills. **Bra·nchiate, -ated** *a.* having gills. **Branchi·ferous** *a.* bearing gills. **Bra·nchiform** *a.* like gills.

Branching (bra·nʃiŋ), *vbl. sb.* 1578. [f. BRANCH *v.* + -ING[1].] The action of the vb.; *concr.* a collection of branches. Also *fig.*

Bra·nching, *ppl. a.* ME. [f. as prec. + -ING[2].] **1.** That branches. **2.** Spreading, ramifying, diverging; also, rambling 1720. **3.** Antlered 1667.

Branchio- (bræ:ŋki,o), also erron. **brancho-**, comb. f. Gr. βράγχια gills:
branchio-a·nal *a.*, pertaining to the branchiæ and anus; **-ca·rdiac** *a.*, belonging to the gills and heart; **-ga·steropod,** *pl.* **-poda, -pods,** a gasteropod which breathes air through water; also, any gasteropod; **-pa·llial** *a.*, pertaining to the gills and mantle of molluscs; **-pari·etal** *a.*, pertaining to the gills and wall of the atrium (of molluscs).

Branchiopod (bræ·ŋki,ǒpǫ:d). Pl. **-opods, -opoda** (-ǫ·pǒda). 1826. [– mod.L. *branchiopoda* (sc. *crustacea*), f. BRANCHIO- + Gr. πούς, ποδ- foot; see -A 4.] *lit.* 'Gill-footed',—one of the Crustacean order distinguished by having the gills upon the feet. Also *attrib.* Hence **Branchio·podous** *a.*

Branchiostegal (bræŋki,ǫ·stĭgăl), *a.* 1749. [f. BRANCHIOSTEGE + -AL[1].] **1.** Pertaining to the membrane which protects a gill chamber; covering the gills. **2.** quasi-*sb.* for *b. ray* 1849.

Branchiostegan (bræŋki,ǫ·stĭgăn). 1847. [f. mod.L. *branchiostegi* (cf. next) + -AN.] A member of the *Branchiostegi*, an old order of fishes having free gills covered by a membrane.

Branchiostege (bræ·ŋki,ostī:dʒ), *a.* 1748. [– Fr. *branchiostège*, f. BRANCHIO- + Gr. στέγειν cover.] Covering the gills. Hence **Branchio·stegi:te,** the membrane covering the gills; **Branchio·stegous** *a.* = BRANCHIOSTEGAL.

Branchiostomous (bræŋki,ǫ·stǒməs), *a.* 1881. [f. BRANCHIO- + Gr. -στομος mouthed + -OUS.] Having the gills in connection with the mouth.

Branchireme (bræ·ŋkirī:m). 1835. [f. L. *branchiæ* gills + *remus* oar.] An organ in branchiopods both for respiration and for locomotion.

Branchy (bra·nʃi), *a.* ME. [f. BRANCH *sb.* + -Y[1].] Bearing branches; full of, or consisting of branches. Also *transf.* Hence **Bra·nchiness.**

Brand (brænd), *sb.* [OE. *brand* = OFris., (M)Du. *brand*, OHG. *brant* (G. *brand*), ON. *brandr* :– Gmc. **brandaz*, f. **bran-* **bren-* BURN *v.*[1]] † **1.** Burning –ME. **2.** A piece of wood that is or has been burning on the hearth; *poet.* a torch, a linstock; also *fig.* and *transf.* OE. **3.** The mark made by burning with a hot iron 1552; hence **b.** *fig.* a mark (usu. of infamy) 1597; **c.** a trade-mark 1827. **4.** A branding-iron 1828. **5.** (*transf.* from 3 c.) A class of goods 1854. **6.** A kind of blight in plants; called also BURN (cf. Ger. *brand*) 1639. **7.** † The blade of a sword, etc. –ME.; hence a sword. [perh. from its flashing in the light.] OE.

2. The brands of one of their fires were still smoking W. IRVING. *A b. from the burning* (see *Zech.* 3:2): a person delivered from imminent danger. *God's b.*: the lightning. *Phœbus' b.*: the burning rays of the sun. (With a blending of sense 7.) **3.** The b. of error HOOKER. **7.** Th' Eastern side..Of Paradise..Wav'd over by that flaming B. MILT. *P.L.* xii. 643.

Brand (brænd), *v.* ME. [f. prec.] **1.** *trans.* To burn with a hot iron, whether for marking or cauterizing; also *fig.* **2.** To mark indelibly, as a proof of ownership, a sign of quality, etc.; to impress (a device, etc.) by way of brand 1587. **b.** *fig.* To impress indelibly on one's memory 1602. **3.** *fig.* To stamp with infamy 1625.

2. Thou wouldest that God should at leastwise brond him with the broade arrow GOLDING. **3.** They..intended by some Vote to B. him, and make him odious CLARENDON.

Bra·nded, *ppl. a. Obs.* exc. *dial.* 1561. [north. var. of *brended*, BRINDED.] Brindled.

Bran-deer. Adaptation of G. *brandhirsch*, a stag with dark-brown breast. GOLDSM.

† **Bra·ndenburgh.** 1676. [f. *Brandenburg* in Prussia.] A morning gown –1691.

† **Bra·ndenburgs.** 1753. [See prec.] *pl.* The ornamental facings to the breast of an officer's coat –1691.

Bra·nder, *sb.*[1] 1860. [f. BRAND *v.* + -ER[1].] One who brands.

Bra·nder, *sb.*[2] Now *Sc.* and *n. dial.* 1450. [var. of BRAND-IRON.] A gridiron. Hence **Bra·nder** *v.* to cook on the b., grill. Prob. also, 'To arrange cross-bars in the form of a gridiron'; whence **Bra·ndering** *vbl. sb.* the covering (of joists) with battens for plastering.

Brand-goose; see BRANT *sb.*

Brandied (bræ·ndid), *ppl. a.* 1833. [f. BRANDY *sb.* + -ED[1].] Mixed, treated, or fortified with brandy.

Bra·ndi:ron. *Obs.* exc. *dial.* ME. [f. BRAND + IRON.] **1.** A gridiron; used also of andirons, a stand for a kettle, a trivet. See BRANDER *sb.*[2] **2.** In Spenser and Quarles: A sword.

Bra·ndise. Now *dial.* [OE. *brandīsen*, f. *brand* burning + *īsen* iron; but the history of the word between *c*1000 and XIX is uncertain.] Perh. = BRAND-IRON.

Brandish (bræ·ndiʃ), *v.* ME. [– (O)Fr. *brandiss-*, lengthened stem of *brandir* :– Rom. **brandire*, f. **brand-* blade of a sword, prob. the same word as BRAND *sb.*] **1.** To wave about (a sword, etc.) by way of threat or display, or in preparation for action. Also *fig.* **b.** To flourish about (the limbs, the head, etc.) (*arch.*) ME. Also *absol.* **2.** *intr.* (for *refl.*) = to be brandished 1649. † **3.** *trans.* To dart forth (rays of light); *occ.*, to irradiate –1656. † **b.** *intr.* To glitter, gleam.

1. I shall b. my sword before them *Ezek.* 32:10. *fig.* Lawes which they so impotently b. against others MILT. Hence **Bra·ndish** *sb.* an act of brandishing. **Bra·ndisher.**

† **Bra·ndle,** *v.* 1606. [– (O)Fr. *branler* (cf. BRANLE), with parasitic *-d-* as in *spindle*; but cf. OFr. *brandeler* shake.] To shake. Also *intr.* –1655.

Brandling (bræ·ndliŋ). 1651. [f. BRAND sb. + -LING[1].] **1.** A red worm, used as bait by anglers. **2.** *dial.* A salmon parr 1730.

Brand-mark (bræ·nd-mā:ɹk). 1655. The mark left by a branding-iron; also *fig.*

Brand-new, bran- (bræ·nd-, bræ·n,niū·), *a.* 1570. [f. BRAND *sb.*; cf. Shakespeare's *fire-new*. Now usu. *bran-*.] Quite new, perfectly new.

† **Bra·ndon.** *rare.* 1647. [– (O)Fr. *brandon*, f. OFr. **brant* torch, f. Gmc.; see BRAND *sb.*] A torch (*lit.* and *fig.*).

Brandreth (bræ·ndrěþ). ME. [– ON. *brandreið* grate, f. *brandr* BRAND *sb.* + *reið* carriage, vehicle.] **1.** A gridiron; an iron tripod or trivet. Now *dial.* **2.** A framework of wood, as a stand for a cask, or for a hayrick; a substructure of piles to support a house; a rail round a well 1483.

Brandy (bræ·ndi), *sb.* 1657. [Earlier *brand(e)wine*, then *brandy wine*, whence ellipt. *brandy*; – Du. *brandewijn* (whence G. *branntwein*), f. *branden* burn, distil + *wijn* WINE.] Prop. an ardent spirit distilled from wine or grapes; but also a name for other similar spirits.

Comb.: **b.-ball,** a kind of sweet; † **-cherry** = cherry brandy; so **-peach,** etc.; **-snap,** wafer-like gingerbread.

Brandy-bottle (bræ·ndi-bǫ:t'l), *sb.* 1676. **1.** A bottle (for) containing brandy; also *fig.* **2.** *Bot.* The Yellow Water-lily (*Nuphar luteum*) 1846.

Brandy-pawnee (bræ:ndi,pǭ·ni). 1816. [f. BRANDY + Hind. *pānī* water; a camp wd.] Brandy-and-water.

Bra·ngle, *sb. Obs.* exc. *dial.* 1600. [f. BRANGLE *v.*] A brawl, wrangle.

Bra·ngle, *v. Obs.* or *arch.* 1553. [perh. f. *brangle* (XVI–XVIII) shake, etc., infl. in meaning by WRANGLE, and perh. by BRABBLE-BRAWL, with which it is nearly synonymous.] *intr.* To wrangle. Hence **Bra·nglement.** † **Bra·ngler.**

Brank, *sb. dial.* 1577. [Origin unkn.] Buck-wheat.

† **Brank** (bræŋk), *v.*[1] *Sc.* 1574. [app. f. *brank*, sing. of BRANKS.] To bridle, restrain; to put in the branks. Also *fig.* –1664.

† **Brank,** *v.*[2] *Sc.* and *dial.* ME. [Origin unkn.] **1.** *intr.* Of horses: To prance –1513. **2.** Of persons: To strut; to prank 1550.

† **Brank(e.** [– OFr. *branc* (*de l'espée*) sword-blade = Prov. *brenc.*] A sword. CAXTON.

Branks (bræŋks). Rare sing. **brank**; also as sing. *a branks.* 1595. [perh. alt. f. *bernaks*, pl. of ME. *bernak* (– OFr. *bernac*) bridle; see BARNACLE *sb.*[1]] **1.** A scold's bridle; an instrument of punishment, consisting of an iron framework for the head, having a sharp metal gag which restrained the tongue. **2.** A sort of wooden muzzle, used as a bridle 1675. **3.** The mumps 1794.

Brank-ursine (bræŋk,ǒ·ɹsin). 1551. [– Fr. *branche* (dial. *branque*) *ursine*, in med.L. *branca ursina* 'bear's claw' see BRANCH, URSINE.] Bear's breech, Acanthus. Erron. used of the Cow-parsnip (*Heracleum sphondylium*).

† **Bra·nle,** *sb.* 1581. [– Fr. *branle*, f. *branler*; see next.] **1.** Wavering, ? confusion. **2.** One of several dances of French origin; the music for it –1820.

† **Bra·nle,** *v. rare.* [– Fr. *branler* shake; see BRANDLE.] To agitate, toss about. JER. TAYLOR.

Bran-new; see BRAND-NEW.

Branny (bræ·ni), *a.* 1533. [f. BRAN *sb.*[1] + -Y[1].] Consisting of, abounding in, or resembling bran.

† **Bra·nsle.** 1596. [– Fr. *bransle* (XVI), a graphical var. of *branle* BRANLE.] = BRANLE *sb.* 1, 2. –1829.

Brant (brænt), *sb.* (Also BRENT, q.v.) 1544. [Of unkn. origin.] The smallest species of wild goose (*Bernicla brenta*). Formerly confounded with the Barnacle-goose. Also **Brant-goose.**

Brant (brænt). [OE. *brant* high, steep, corresp. to ON. **brantr*, whence OIcel. *brattr*, Sw. *brant*, Da. *brat*. Still north. dial. In Sc., BRENT.] **A.** *adj.* **1.** Lofty, steep, sheer. † **2.** Of the forehead: Unwrinkled –1483. † **B.** *adv.* Straight, straight up; steeply –1544.

† **Bra·ntcorn.** 1578. [– MDu. *brantkoren* (G. *brantkorn*); cf. BRAND *sb.* 6.] Smut (*Uredo segetum*) –1646.

Brant-fox (bræ·nt,fǫks). 1864. [– G. *brandfuchs*, perh. from the colour.] A variety of fox, having much black in its fur. (Dicts.)

† **Bra·ntle.** [var. of BRANDLE.] = BRANLE *sb.* 2. PEPYS.

Bra·nular, *a. rare.* [A spurious formation from BRAIN.] Pertaining to or affecting the brain. I. TAYLOR.

Braquemard, var. of BRACKMARD.

Brasen, obs. f. BRAZEN.

‖ **Bra·sero.** 1652. [Sp.] = BRAZIER[2].

Brash (bræʃ), *sb.*[1] Chiefly *dial.* 1573. [Sc. and north. dial., perh. imit.] † **1.** An attack; a bout. *Sc.* and *n. dial.* –1724. **2.** A slight attack of sickness; *esp.* one arising from a disorder of the alimentary canal. Hence *teething-b.*, *weaning-b.* 1785. **3.** An eruption of fluid; as *water-b.*, pyrosis; a sudden dash of rain 1811.

Brash, *sb.*[2] 1722. [Of unkn. origin.] A mass of fragments, as of rubble, crushed ice, hedge-clippings, etc.

Brash (bræʃ), *a.*[1] Now *U.S.* [perh. echoic.] Fragile, brittle: used chiefly of timber.

Brash, *a.*[2] *dial.* 1824. [perh. expressive form of *rash*.] Rash, impetuous.

† **Brash,** *v.* 1565. [f. BRASH *sb.*[1] 1.] To assault; to breach. Also *fig.* –1638.

Brashy (bræ·ʃi), *a.*[1] [f. BRASH *sb.*[2] + -Y[1].] Broken, crumbly, fragmentary.

Bra·shy, *a.*[2] *Sc.* 1805. [f. BRASH *sb.*[1] 3 + -Y[1].] Showery.

Brasier(e, obs. f. BRAZIER.

Brasil, -sile, -sill, obs. ff. BRAZIL.

Brasque (brɑsk). 1871. [– Fr. *brasque* – It. dial. *brasca* coal-ash.] 'A lining for crucibles and furnaces; generally, a compound of clay, etc. with charcoal dust' (Raymond).

Brass (brɑs), *sb.* [OE. *bræs* = OFris. *bres* (*bras-penning* copper penny), MLG. *bras* metal; of unkn. origin.] **1.** *Hist.*: Any alloy of copper with tin or zinc (and occas. other base metals). **b.** In mod. use: A yellow-coloured alloy of copper and zinc, usu. containing about one part in three of zinc. (BRONZE, the Italian word for brass, is now used to distinguish the ancient alloy of copper and tin.) **c.** A type of hardness, imperishableness, insensibility, etc. ME. † **d.** *transf.* Copper –1617. **e.** Iron pyrites in coal. Cf. BRAZIL[2]. 1879. **f.** in *Organ-building*: A composition of lead and tin 1852. **2.** Elliptically: **a.** A sepulchral tablet of brass 1613. **b.** A bearing for a shaft 1731. **c.** Musical instruments of brass ME. **3.** Money. † **a.** Copper or bronze coin –1775. **b.** Money in general (*slang* or *dial.*) 1597. **4.** *fig.* Effrontery, impudence, unblushingness 1642.

1. c. Mens euill manners liue in Brasse, their Vertues We write in Water SHAKS. **4.** His face is of brasse, which may be said either ever, or never to blush FULLER.

Comb.: **b. band**, one with wind instruments of b.; **b. farthing**, emphatic = *farthing*; **b.-foil, -latten**, Dutch leaf made by beating out b. very thin; **b. plate**, a plate of b., bearing an inscription; also, a monumental b. (2 a); **b. rule**, a strip of b., type-high, used to separate lines or columns of type; **-smith; -work, -worker.**

Brass (brɑs), *v.* 1859. [f. prec.: cf. *to tin.*] To coat with brass 1865; *fig.* to cover with effrontery.

Brassage (bræ·sėdʒ). 1806. [– Fr. *brassage*, f. *brasser* mix, stir (melted metals), brew :– pop. L. **braciare*, f. L. *brace* kind of grain; see BRAGGET.] A mint-charge to cover the cost of coining money.

Brassard (brăsā·ɹd). Also **brassart.** 1830. [– Fr. *brassard*, f. *bras* arm; see BRACE *sb.*[1], -ARD.] **1.** Armour for the upper arm. *Hist.* **2.** A badge worn on the arm 1870.

Bra·ssate. 1863. [f. BRASS(IC) + -ATE[4].] *Chem.* A salt of brassic acid.

Brasse (bræs). 1847. [perh. var. of *brassem* – Du. *brasem* BREAM.] A kind of perch.

Brassed (brɑst), *ppl. a.* ME. [f. BRASS *sb.* + -ED[2].] Made of, or overlaid with brass.

Brass(e)y (bræ·si). 1888. [var. of BRASSY.] *Golf.* A brass-shod club.

‖ **Brassica** (bræ·sikă). 1832. [L.; = cabbage.] *Bot.* A genus of cruciferous plants, containing the cabbage, the turnip, rape, etc. Hence **Bra·ssic** *a.*

‖ **Brassière** (bræ·siēᵊɹ). 1912. [Fr.] A woman's underbodice worn to support the breasts.

Brassy (brɑ·si), *a.* 1583. [f. BRASS *sb.* + -Y[1].] **1.** Of or covered with brass. **2.** Of the nature or appearance of brass 1789. **3.** *fig.* **a.** Hard as brass 1596; **b.** unblushing 1576; **c.** debased yet pretentious 1586; **d.** strident and artificial in tone 1865.

3. b. A b. impudence 1690. **c.** A b. age TENNYSON. **d.** That hard, b., overstretched style M. ARNOLD. Hence **Bra·ssiness.**

Brast, *v.*, north. f. BURST.

Brat (bræt), *sb.*[1] Now *dial.* [OE. (late Northumb.) *bratt* cloak – OIr. *bratt* (Ir., Gael. *brat*) mantle.] **1.** † **a.** (in OE.) A cloak. **b.** in *midl.*, *w.*, and *n. dial.* A pinafore or apron. **c.** A rag. **2.** A jacket for a sheep's back 1862. † **3.** Rubbish 1656. **4.** *Sc.* The skin which forms on porridge, rice pudding, etc. 1795.

Brat (bræt), *sb.*[2] 1505. [perh. shortening of Sc. *bratchart* (mod. BRATCHET), perh. f. *brat* rugged garment; see prec.] A child (usu. implying insignificance). *fig.* Offspring, product.

I should be glad to hear how the little b. doth CROMWELL. Hence **Bra·tling**, a little b. **Bra·ttery**, a nursery. (*contemptuous.*)

Brat, *sb.*[3] 1759. [var. of BRET (XV), also BIRT, BURT.] The turbot.

Brat, *sb.*[4] 1856. [Cf. BRAT[1] 3.] *Mining.* A thin bed of coal mixed with pyrites or carbonate of lime.

Bratchet (bræ·tʃėt). 1600. [app. same wd. as BRACHET.] **1.** = BRACH. **2.** A little brat. (*contemptuous* or *playful.*)

‖ **Brattach** (bra·tăx). 1828. [Gael. (and Ir.) *bratach* standard, banner, flag, f. *brat* cloth; see BRAT *sb.*[1]] An ensign or banner.

Brattice (bræ·tis), *sb.* ME. [– AFr. *breteske*, etc., OFr. *bretesque*, *-esche* (mod. *bretèche*), – med.L. *brittisca* (IX), f. OE. *brittisć* BRITISH.] **1.** A temporary breastwork, parapet, or gallery of wood, for use during a siege. (*Hist.*) **2.** (dial. also *brattish*): A partition, generally of deal 1851. **3.** In form *brattish*: A shelf; also a seat with a high back (*n. dial.*).

Comb. **b.-cloth** (sense 2): stout tarred cloth used in mines instead of wooden bratticing.

Brattice, *v.* 1862. [f. prec.] In *To b. up*: to line the sides of a shaft, etc., with planking.

Bratticing (bræ·tisiŋ). 1866. [f. BRATTICE *v.* (or *sb.*) + -ING[1].] **1.** Brattice-work in a coalpit 1866. **2.** *Archit.* See BRATTISHING.

Brattishing (bræ·tiʃiŋ). 1593. Var. of BRATTICING, used in *Archit.*: A cresting of open carved work on the top of a shrine. Also *dial.* in other senses.

Braunite (brau·nəit). 1839. [f. K. *Braun* of Gotha + -ITE[1] 2 b.] *Min.* An anhydrous oxide of manganese, a brittle dark brownish-black mineral occurring both crystallized and massive.

† **Brava·de.** 1579. [– Fr. *bravade* – It. *bravata*; see BRAVE *a.*, -ADE.] = BRAVADO –1833.

† **Brava·de**, *v. arch.* 1634. [f. prec.] **1.** *intr.* To assume a bold and defiant look –1667. **2.** *trans.* To defy 1676.

Bravado (brăvēⁱ·do, -ā·do), *sb. pl.* **-oes**, or **-os.** 1599. [– Sp. *bravata*, f. *bravo* BRAVO *sb.*[1], with alt. of suffix (see -ADO).] **1.** Boastful or threatening behaviour; ostentatious display of courage or boldness. (Now usu. in sing. without *a*: occas. with *a* or in *pl.*) † **2.** A swaggering fellow. Cf. BRAVO. –1825.

1. A sort of b.—an air of affected unconcern JANE AUSTEN. **2.** The Hectors & bravadoes of the House PEPYS. Hence **Brava·doism** (*rare*).

Brave (brēⁱv), *a.*, *sb.*, *int.* 1485. [– Fr. *brave* – It. *bravo* bold, or Sp. *bravo* courageous, savage :– Rom. **brabus*, for L. *barbarus* BARBAROUS, through **brabarus*.] **A.** *adj.* **1.** Courageous, intrepid, stout-hearted (as a good quality). absol. *The brave* (now only pl.) 1697. **2.** Finely-dressed; = Sc. BRAW; splendid, showy, handsome. (Now app. a literary revival.) 1568. **3.** *loosely*, Capital, fine (*arch.*) (Cf. BRAW *a.*) 1577. **4.** quasi-*adv.* = BRAVELY. (Now *poet.*) 1596.

1. High hopes of living to be b. men and worthy Patriots MILT. None but the b. deserves the fair DRYDEN. The b. of other lands TENNYSON. **2.** The lilies which are braver than Solomon 1593. **3.** O that's a braue man, hee writes braue verses, speakes braue words *A.Y.L.* III. iv. 43. Braue punishments *Much Ado* v. iv. 130. Hence **Bra·vely** *adv.*, **-ness.**

B. *sb.* [in sense 1, directly from Fr. *brave.*] **1.** A brave man, a warrior: since 1800 *esp.* a warrior among the N. American Indians 1601. **b.** A bully; a hired assassin (*arch.*) 1598. **2.** A bravado (*arch.*) 1590.

1. A Blackfoot b. 1841. **2.** Life's braves should somehow be made good BROWNING.

C. *interj.* [Cf. BRAVO.] Capital! Bravo! Now *dial.* 1593.

Brave (brēⁱv), *v.* 1546. [– Fr. *braver*, f. *brave* (see prec.), after It. *bravare*.] **1.** *trans.* To treat with bravado; to challenge, defy. **2.** To meet or face with bravery; to encounter, defy. (The ordinary current sense.) 1776. † **3.** To make brave 1593. † **4.** To make splendid, adorn –1625. † **5.** To boast –1652.

1. Ossa and Pelion that so b. the sky HEYWOOD. **2.** To b. danger 1832, severe weather 1876. **4.** Thou [the tailor] hast brau'd manie men SHAKS.

II. *intr.* (and const. *to b. it*) † **1.** To boast, vaunt. *To b. it*: to act the bravo. –1817. † **2.** To dress splendidly –1632. Hence **Bra·vingly** *adv.*

Bravery (brēⁱ·vĕri). 1548. [– Fr. *braverie* or It. *braveria*; see BRAVE, -ERY.] † **1.** The action of braving or acting the bravo; daring, defiance; bravado –1814. **2.** Daring, courage, fortitude (as a good quality). (The ordinary current sense.) 1581. **3.** Display, show; splendour 1570. *concr.* Fine clothes; = Sc. BRAWS. 1563. † **b.** A fine thing; an adornment –1657. † **4.** Mere show –1681. † **5.** A gallant, a beau; also *collect.* grandees, chivalry –1670.

1. Ere long thou shalt lament These braveries MILT. *Sams.* 1243. **2.** Lancelot, the flower of b. TENNYSON. **3.** The brauerie of this world.. likened is, to flowre of grasse TUSSER.

Bravissimo; see BRAVO *sb.*[2]

Bravo (brā·vo), *sb.*[1] Pl. **-oes** (**-os**). 1597. [– It. *bravo*. Long naturalized, whence the pronunc. (brēⁱvo) in some Dicts.] **1.** A daring villain, a hired soldier or assassin; a reckless desperado. † **2.** = BRAVADO (*rare*) –1713.

1. I have been three Nights together dogged by Bravoes STEELE.

Bravo (brā·vo), *int.* and *sb.*[2] 1761. [– Fr. – It. *bravo* fine, splendid. The superl. *bravissimo* is also used.] Capital! Well done! Hence, as *sb.* A cheer.

‖ **Bravura** (bravū·ră). 1788. [It., f. *bravo* BRAVE; see -URE.] **1.** Display of daring or defiance; brilliancy of execution; attempt at brilliant performance 1813. **2.** A passage or piece of music requiring elaborate execution, written to task the artist's powers. Also *transf.* 1788.

2. A short b. of John Paul Richter..I call it a b., as being intentionally a passage of display and elaborate execution DE QUINCEY. **3.** attrib., as *b. player*, *singer*, *singing*, *song.*

Braw (brǭ). *Sc.* 1563. [var. of *brawf* BRAVE; cf. *ca'* = *calve*, etc.] **A.** *adj.* **1.** = BRAVE *a.* 2. 1724. **2.** = BRAVE *a.* 3. 1565. **B.** *sb. pl.* = BRAVERY 3; fine clothes 1724.

Brawl (brǭl), *sb.*[1] 1460. [f. BRAWL *v.*] **1.** A noisy turbulent quarrel, a row. † **2.** Clamour –1611.

† **Brawl**, *sb.*[2] 1521. [– Fr. *branle*, as BRANLE *sb.*] **1.** A particular pace or movement in dancing –1531. **2.** A kind of French dance; the music for it –1842.

2. Will you win your loue with a French braule *L.L.L.* III. i. 9.

† **Brawl**, *sb.*[3] 1725. A blue and white striped cloth made in India –1788.

Brawl (brǭl), *v.* [Late ME. *brawle*, *braule*, *bralle* – OPr. *braular*, Pr. *bralhar*, *braulhar*, *brailhar* (whence (O)Fr. *brailler*); ult. rel. to stem of Fr. *brailler*, see BRAY *v.*[1]] **1.** *intr.* To wrangle, to squabble. (At first, perh. simply 'to contend'.) † *trans.* To scold, revile –1649. **2.** *intr.* To raise a clamour ME. *trans.* To utter clamorously 1563. **3.** *intr.* Of a stream: To make a noise of conflict in its rapid course over stones, etc. 1600.

1. Gyue thou place to hym that brawleth or chideth CAXTON. **2.** *To b. in Church*, to indulge in any speaking other than as prescribed in the Prayer Book. **3.** Shallowest brookes b. the most SPURGEON. Hence **Braw·ler. Braw·lingly** *adv.*

Brawn (brǭn), *sb.* ME. [– AFr. *braun*, OFr. *braon* fleshy part, esp. of the hind leg – Gmc. **brādon* (OHG. *brāto*, G. *braten* roast flesh; cf. synon. OE. *brǣde*, and *brǣdan* roast).] **1.** Fleshy part, muscle, *esp.* of the arm, leg, and thumb. Also *transf.* and *fig.* † **2.** The muscle or flesh of animals as food –1656. **3.** *spec.* The flesh of the boar; *esp.* (in recent use) collared, boiled, and pickled or potted. [Cf. *bacon*, a deriv. of *back.*] ME. **4.** *transf.* A boar (or swine) as fattened for the table (*dial.*). Cf. BACON. ME. **5.** Hardened or thickened skin; also *fig.* L. *callum.* 1578.

1. Hise lymes grete, hise brawnes harde and stronge CHAUCER. **3.** Is a man therefore bound.. at noon to B., or Beefe ?MILT. *Comb.* **b.-fallen** *a.* shrunken in flesh.

Brawn (brǭn), *v.* 1571. [f. prec.] **1.** To make or become hard; also *fig.* **2.** *trans.* To fatten (a boar) 1655. † **3.** *intr.* To grow fat. (Of a boar.) 1580.

Brawned (brǭnd), *ppl. a.* 1505. [f. BRAWN *sb.* and *v.* + -ED.] **1.** Muscular, brawny. **2.** Hardened, callous: mostly *fig.* 1583. † **3.** Fattened as a boar –1601.

Brawner (brǭ·nəɹ). 1708. [f. BRAWN *v.* + -ER[1].] A boar fattened for the table.

Brawniness (brǭ·ninės). 1645. [f. BRAWNY + -NESS.] Muscularity; †insensibility.

Brawny (brǭ·ni), *a.* 1420. [f. BRAWN *sb.* + -Y[1].] **1.** Characterized by muscle or muscular strength 1599. **2.** Callous (*lit.* and † *fig.*). Also in *comb.*

1. A brawney arme 1644. **2.** A b. conscience 1638.

Braxy (bræ·ksi), *sb.* and *a. Sc.* 1785. [prob. from 'the *bracks*'; cf. *poxy*.] **1.** Splenic apoplexy in sheep 1791. **2.** as *adj.* Characterized by this disease, as *b.-sheep, mutton*; also *absol.* the flesh of a b. sheep 1785.

Bray (brēi), *sb.* ME. [f. BRAY *v.*[1], or – OFr. *brai, brait* cry, f. *braire* (next).] † **1.** Outcry; a shriek –1596. **2.** The cry of some animals, *esp.* the ass 1650. **3.** *transf.* Any loud harsh sound 1593.

2. No brayes of asses nor of bulls 1650. **3.** The b. of rusty bolts SCOTT, of horns 1884.

Bray (brēi), *v.*[1] [– (O)Fr. *braire* cry (now only of the ass) :– Rom. **bragere*, perh. of Celtic origin.] † **1.** *intr.* To utter a loud harsh cry –1613. **2.** Of animals: formerly the cry of horses, oxen, deer, etc.; now *esp.* of the ass ME. **b.** *contemptuously* of the human voice 1635. **3.** *transf.* Of wind, thunder, etc. (now *esp.* of the trumpet): To make a loud harsh jarring sound ME. **4.** *trans.* To utter harshly. Often with *out.* ME.

2. Stags pitifully b. DRYDEN. **b.** None ever brayed so learnedly 1692.

Bray (brēi) *v.*[2] [– AFr. *braier*, OFr. *breier* (mod. *broyer*) – Gmc. **brekan* BREAK *v.*] **1.** To beat small; to bruise, pound; usu. in a mortar. Also *fig.* **2.** Techn.: † **a.** To crush flax or hemp with a brake. [Fr. *broyer le chanvre.*] –1530. **b.** To pound and scour (woollen cloth) 1879.

1. *fig.* Though thou shuldest b. a foole with a pestell in a morter like otemeell, yet wil not his foolishnesse go from him COVERDALE *Prov.* 27:22. Hence **Bray·ing** *vbl. sb.*[2]

Braye. 1512. [– Fr. *braie* = med.L. *braca* dike, embankment; of unkn. origin.] A military outwork. *False b.* (– Fr. *fausse braie*): an advanced parapet surrounding the main rampart. *Hist.*

Brayer[1] (brēi·əɹ). 1598. [f. BRAY *v.*[1] + -ER[1].] One who brays; *esp.* an ass.

Bray·er[2]. 1688. [f. BRAY *v.*[2] + -ER[1].] *Printing.* A wooden pestle used to rub down and temper the ink.

Bray·er[3]. 1770. [Of unkn. origin.] Part of a compound lever for raising or depressing the upper grindstone in a corn-mill.

Braze (brēiz), *v.*[1] 1552. [In XVI, f. *brass* after *glass, glaze*; not continuous with OE. *brasian*, f. *bræs* BRASS.] **1.** *trans.* To make of, or cover with, brass. **2.** *fig.* To make hard like brass, harden 1602.

Braze (brēiz), *v.*[2] 1581. [Sense 1 – OFr. *braser* burn; sense 2 – Fr. *braser* solder; f. *braise* hot coals; see BRAZIER[2].] † **1.** To expose to the action of fire. **2.** To solder (with an alloy of brass and zinc) 1677.

Brazen (brēi·z'n), *a.* [OE. *bræsen*, f. *bræs* BRASS; see -EN[4].] **1.** Made of brass; strong as brass ME. **2.** *transf.* and *fig.* Like brass. (Often after Homer's οὐρανὸς χάλκεος, etc.) 1596. **3.** *fig.* Hardened in effrontery 1573.

1. A brassin ymage 1552. Inuiron'd with a B. wall SHAKS. **2.** The brasen sky SPENSER. **3.** B. mendacity 1869. Phr. *Brazen age*: the third mythological age of mankind. Hence **Bra·zen-ly** *adv.*, **-ness.**

Brazen (brēi·z'n), *v.* 1555. [f. the adj.] **1.** *trans.* With *out*: to face impudently. So *to b. it out.* **2.** *trans.* To make bold or reckless 1884.

1. He would talk saucily, lye, and b. it out 1712.

Brazen-face. 1573. [f. BRAZEN *a.* 3.] **1.** As two wds.: An unabashed countenance. **2.** As one wd.: A brazen-faced person 1598. Hence **Bra·zen-faced** *a.* unblushing, impudent. **Bra·zen-facedly** *adv.*

Brazier[1] (brēi·ziəɹ, -ʒiəɹ). ME. [prob. f. BRASS *sb.* by analogy with *glass, glazier.*] One who works in brass. Hence **Bra·ziery,** brazier's work; also *concr.*

Brazier[2] (brēi·ziəɹ, -ʒiəɹ). 1690. [– Fr. *brasier*, f. *braise* hot coals; cf. BRAISE *v.*] A large flat pan or tray for holding burning charcoal, etc.

Brazil[1] (brăzi·l). [Late ME. *brasile* – med.L. *brasilium, -illum*; in Fr. *brésil*, Pr. *bresil*, Sp. Pg. *brasil*, It. *brasile*. As the name of the country (so-called from the wood), f. Sp., Pg. *brasil.*] **1.** Orig., the red wood of an East Indian tree (*Cæsalpinia sappan*), from which dyers obtain a red colour. Later, the similar wood of a S. American species (*C. echinata*), and also other species, all valuable to the dyer. Now usu. called **Brazil-wood.** Also *attrib.* **b.** Taken as a type of hardness: hence *as hard as b.* Pronounced (bræ·zil, bræ·z'l). 1635. † **2.** The dye-stuff and dye yielded by this wood –1669. Also *attrib.* **3.** A country of S. America, also called 'the Brazils' 1555. Also *attrib.* and in *comb.* **4. Brazil-nut:** A triquetrous nut, the seed of *Bertholletia excelsa* (N.O. *Lecythidaceæ*) 1830. Hence **Brazi·lian** *a.* and *sb.*

1. b. Are my bones b., or my flesh of oak QUARLES. **3.** The Portuguese nam'd it Brazile, from the red wood of that name W. ROGERS.

Brazil[2] (bræ·zil). *dial.* Also (perh. better) **brassil, brazzle.** 1747. [prob. f. BRASS *sb.*] **1.** Iron pyrites (*midl. dial.*). **2.** Coal containing much pyrites 1853. ¶ *As hard as b.*: occas. referred to this wd.

Braziletto (bræzile·to). 1656. [– Sp., Pg. *brasilete*, Pg. *brasileto*, dim. of *brasil* Brazil-wood.] Species of dyewood, inferior to Brazil-wood, imported from Jamaica (*Cæsalpinia brasiliensis* and *crista*; now referred to the genus *Peltophorum*).

Brazilin (bræ·zilin). 1863. [f. BRAZIL[1] + -IN[1].] The red colouring-matter of Brazil-wood.

Breach (britʃ), *sb.* ME. [– (O)Fr. *brèche* = Pr. *breca* :– Gallo-Rom. **brecca* – Frankish **breka*, f. Gmc. **brekan* BREAK *v.* Superseded ME. *brüche*, OE. *bryće* (ult. connected), with which there is no continuity.] † **1.** The action of breaking; the fact of being broken; breakage, fracture –1676. **2.** The breaking of waves on a coast or over a vessel 1601. **3.** The breaking of any legal or moral bond or obligation; violation, infraction ME. † **4.** An irruption *into*, an infringement *upon* –1751. **5.** A breaking of relations (*of* union or continuity) 1625. Also *absol.* **6.** A broken or injured spot, place, or part; a disrupted place, gap or fissure; *esp.* a gap in a fortification made by a battery ME. Also *fig.* † **7.** Surf made by the sea breaking over rocks –1707. † **8.** A break in a coast; a bay, harbour 1611. † **9.** An interval; a division marked by intervals –1590. **10.** A condition of ruptured relations 1745.

2. *Clear b.*, the waves rolling clean over without breaking.. *.Clean-b.*, when..every object on deck is swept away ADM. SMYTH. **3.** Nuptial breaches *Lear* I. ii. 162. Phr. *B. of contract, promise, trust.* **5.** B. of friendes BARET. **6.** *To stand in the b.* (often *fig.*). **8.** Asher continued on the sea shore and abode in his breaches [WYCL. hauens] *Judges* 5:17.

Phrases: (sense 3) **b. of arrestment,** illegal disposal of property which has been attached; **b. of close,** trespass; **b. of (the) peace,** a violation of the public peace by an affray, riot, or other disturbance; **b. of pound,** breaking into a pound without warrant; **b. of prison,** escape of a prisoner from confinement; **b. of privilege,** a violation of the rights of a privileged body; **b. of promise,** *spec.* = b. of promise to marry.

Breach (britʃ), *v.* 1547. [f. the sb.] **1.** *trans.* To make a breach in; to break through. Also *fig.* † **2.** *intr.* To cause a breach; to separate –1641. **3.** *Naut.* Of whales: To leap out of the water 1843.

1. The English had breached the fort JAS. MILL.

Breachy (brī·tʃi), *a.* 1800. [f. BREACH + -Y[1].] **1.** Of cattle: Apt to break fences, and get out of enclosures. **2.** Having breaches.

Bread (bred), *sb.* [OE. *brēad* = OFris. *brād*, OS., (M)LG. *brōd*, OHG. *brōt* (G. *brot*), ON. *brauð* :– Gmc. **brauðam*, of unkn. origin. Superseded the orig. name repr. by *hlāf* LOAF *sb.*[1] before 1200.] † **1.** (Only in OE.) Bit, piece, morsel (of food). **2.** An article of food prepared by moistening, kneading, and baking meal or flour, usu. with the addition of yeast or leaven OE. † **3.** (with *pl.*) A loaf, a roll –1643. **4.** Taken as a type of ordinary food. (Perh. from the Lord's Prayer.) ME. Also *fig.* **5.** Means of subsistence 1719. **6.** *attrib.* Of bread; about or for bread, as *b. riots* 1783.

2. Better is halfe a lofe than no b. HEYWOOD. **4.** *B. of idleness*: food not worked for; so *B. of affliction*, etc. † *Full of* b.: full-fed. **4.** He meant no harm in scribbling..'twas..his b. BYRON.

Phrases. *To break b.*: **a.** to partake of b. or food; **b.** (from N. T.) to dispense b., or *fig.* the b. of life; also to administer or join in the Communion. *To know on which side one's b. is buttered*: to know where one's interest lies. *To take the b. out of one's mouth*: to take away his livelihood, to take from a person what he is on the point of enjoying. *B. buttered on both sides*: great good fortune.

Comb.: **b. and butter,** b. spread with butter; the means of living; also *attrib.* boyish, girlish, *esp.* school-girlish; **b. and cheese,** *fig.* for plain fare, living; **black b.,** a coarser dark kind, made of rye, etc.; **-meal,** meal for household or brown b.; occ. = rock-meal (Ger. *berg-mehl*); **-root,** *spec.* a species of Psoralea (*P. esculenta*), and *Camassia esculenta* or Quamash; also the root itself.

Bread (bred), *v.* 1727. [f. BREAD *sb.*] **a.** *Cookery.* To dress with bread-crumbs. **b.** To clean by rubbing with bread.

Bread(e, var. of BREDE.

Brea·d-basket. 1552. **1.** *lit.* A basket for holding or handing round bread. **2.** *slang.* The stomach 1753.

Brea·d-corn. ME. Grain for making bread, *e.g.* rye.

Brea·d-crumb. 1769. **a.** (Prop. two wds.) A crumb of bread; *esp.* (in *pl.*) crumbs for dressing fish, etc. **b.** The soft part of bread, as opp. to the crust. Hence **Brea·d-crumb** *v.*, to cover with b.-c.

Breaden (bre·d'n), *a.* 1579. [f. BREAD *sb.* + -EN[4].] Made or consisting of bread. † *B. god*: *polemical* for the consecrated host. var. † **Brea·dy.**

Brea·d-fruit. 1697. The farinaceous fruit of a tree; *esp.* of *Artocarpus incisa* of the South Sea Islands, etc., having a whitish pulp of the consistency of new bread.

Breadless (bre·dlės), *a.* ME. [f. BREAD *sb.* + -LESS.] Without bread; without food.

Brea·dness. 1866. [f. BREAD *sb.* + -NESS.] In discussions on Transubstantiation: The quality of being bread.

Bread-stitch, var. of *brede-stitch*; see BREDE *sb.*[2]

Bread-stuff (bre·dstɒf). 1793. Material for bread; grain, flour: now usu. in *pl.*

Breadth (bredþ). 1523. [f. †*brēde* BREDE *sb.*[2] (OE. *brǣdu* = OFris. *brēde*, OHG. *breitī*, ON. *breidd*, Goth. *braidei* :– Gmc. **braidjōn*, abstr. sb. f. **braið-* BROAD) + -TH[1]. The new formation provided a parallel to *length*; cf. WIDTH.] **1.** Measure or distance from side to side; width, extent across. Also *fig.* **2.** A piece (of cloth, etc.) of the full breadth; a width 1584. **3.** Extent, length 1595. **4.** *fig.* Largeness (of mind, sentiment, or view), liberality, catholicity; also, wide display of a quality 1847. **5.** *Art.* A broad effect 1788.

1. *To a hair's b.*: to a nicety *Merry W.* IV. ii. 4. **3.** The b. of his great voyage *Per.* IV. i. 37. **4.** To attack with a b. of calumny 1852. **5.** B., or that quality of execution which makes a whole.. predominate over the parts 1811. Hence **Brea·dthless** *a.* **Brea·dthways, -wise** *adv.* in direction of the b.

Bread-tree (bre·dtrī). 1786. Occas. name of the Bread-fruit tree; also of *Gardenia edulis, Encephalartos caffer.*

Bread-winner (bre·dˌwinəɹ). 1818. **1.** One who supports himself and those dependent upon him by his earnings 1821. **2.** The tool, art, or craft with which any one earns his living 1818.

1. The stay and bread-winner of some widowed mother or sister 1863. **2.** 'I'se gang hame,—and then get my bread-winner' [a fiddle] SCOTT.

Break (brēik), *v.* Pa. t. Late ME. **brake,** now *arch.*, gave place to **broke** (brōᵘk) early in 16th c. Pa. pple. **broken** (brōᵘk'n), and in verse **broke.** [OE. *brecan* = OFris. *breka*, OS. *brekan* (Du. *breken*), OHG. *brehhan* (G. *brechen*), Goth. *brikan* :– Gmc. **brekan*; IE. base **bhreg-*, whence also L. *frangere* (*fregi, fractum*) break.] **I. 1.** *trans.* To sever into parts by force, to part by violence. Also *intr.* (for *refl.*) Often with *in pieces, asunder,* etc. **2.** *trans.* and *intr.* To burst ME.; to lay open the surface of 1499; to crack ME.

1. A threefold rope is not easily broken BP. BARLOW. To b. windows STEELE, a battle-axe SCOTT. *intr.* If both [points] breake, your gaskins fall *Twel. N.* I. v. 24.

Spec. uses. To cut up; to tear (a fox) in pieces. You can carve, breake up this capon *L.L.L.* IV. i. 58. † To wreck: The ships were broken 1 *Kings* 22:48. To destroy the completeness of; to divide, part: To b. a bottle 1808, the set 1887. Cf. *To b.*

bulk. † To dissolve, disband; also *intr.* In phrases *To b. bread*: see BREAD. *To b. a lance with*: to enter the lists against. **2.** The berry breaks before it staineth SHAKS. I will breake thy pate acrosse *Com. Err.* II. i. 78. *To b. Priscian's head*: to violate the rules of grammar. *intr.* Said of † a bell, and hence of a boy's voice PEPYS.

II. 1. To disable, destroy cohesion, solidity, or firmness; to crush, shatter; to overwhelm, ruin, destroy OE. *intr.* To relax 1530. **2.** To crush in spirit; to tame. Now also *to b. in.* 1474.

1. Phr. *To b. the leg, or arm*: i.e. the bones of the limb. *To b. on the wheel*: to dislocate on a wheel (a form of torture). *fig. To b. the neck of a journey*, etc.: to get through the worst of it. *To b. the (one's) heart*: to overwhelm with sorrow. The frost breaketh (*intr.*) 1530. Thou breakest the proude *Ps.* 88. Of waves, etc. *trans.* and *intr.* ME. *To b. the bank*: to make the bank, or at a gaming-table the 'banker', stop payment. Also *intr.* (for *refl.*) *Merch. V.* III. i. 120. *intr.* His health was breaking fast TREVELYAN. **2.** To b. the spirit of the army MACAULAY. About breaking of my horses to the coach PEPYS.

III. To do violence to, fail to keep sacred or intact OE.

The laws have been shamefully broken 'JUNIUS'. So, *To b. the Sabbath, the King's peace, an indenture, contract, oath*, etc. *To b. a marriage*: to annul it.

IV. 1. To lay open by breaking; often with *open* OE. † **2.** To enter by force or violence. (Now *To b. into*, q.v.) –1768. **3.** To escape violently or suddenly from ME. **4.** Of light, sound, etc.: To penetrate 1599. **5.** To reveal († one's mind), disclose (news, etc.); now implying caution and delicacy; to utter 1450. **6.** To open, begin 1588.

1. Hunger broke stone wals *Cor.* I. i. 210. **2.** John Wesley broke a house WESLEY. **3.** To b. prison SPENSER, bounds 1887, cover 1859. **4.** What beam shall b. my night BYRON. **5.** I have some news to b. HOOD. To b. a comparison *Much Ado* II. i. 152, a sigh GOLDSM. **6.** Phr. *To b. the balls* (*Billiards*): to make the opening stroke.

V. 1. To rupture union or continuity; to disrupt; to stop for the time ME. **2.** To alter abruptly the direction of (a line); also *intr.* 1616.

1. *fig.* To b. the bonds of modesty 1578, a spell MACAULAY. To b. the enemy's ranks MASSINGER, the enemy's line 1769. *absol.* They broke twice and fled like sheep 1781. *intr.* The clouds are breaking DISRAELI. To b. the thread of these Speculations ADDISON. Phr. *To b. one's fall, journey*. To b. one's sleep SHAKS., silence STERNE, one's fast ME. To b. the monotony of the plain 1877. **2.** Phr. *To b. joint*: said of bricks, etc., when the lines of junction are discontinuous. *To b. sheer*: see SHEER *sb.*[1] *To b. away, off. To b., b. in, b. back*: said of the ball or the bowler at *Cricket*.

VI. 1. To sever by breaking; also *intr.* to cease from relation *with*, quarrel *with* ME. **2.** To cashier (an officer) 1695.

1. Thou shalt breake his yoke from off thy necke *Gen.* 27:40. Phr. *To b. (any one) of a practice* or *habit*. Charles broke with his Parliament 1859. To b. with the past FREEMAN. **2.** Three other colonels are broke 1695.

VII. *intr.* **1.** To escape from restraint; to issue forth OE. **2.** To burst out of darkness, begin to shine. Const. *on, upon*. (Cf. IV. 4.) 1535. **3.** To make a forcible entrance *into* a place ME.

1. To b. from the trammels of a notion RUSKIN. Cries..broke from them 1833. Phr. *To b. into arms, rebellion, weeping, a laugh*. To b. from concealment STEELE. **2.** Let me goe, for the day breaketh *Gen.* 32:26. So of *morning, daylight*, and by confusion *darkness, clouds*. **3.** The Lacedemonians afterwards brake into Attica HOBBES.

Phrases. *To b. bulk*: to begin to unload. *To b. (the) ground* (cf. I. 2): **a.** To plough up for the first time. See also *To b. up*. **b.** Of an army: To begin digging trenches. Also *fig. To b. the ice*: to make a beginning. *To b. square* or *squares*: to violate the regular order, do harm. *To b. wind*: to void wind from the stomach or bowels.

Comb.: **To b. away. a.** *trans.* To remove by breaking. Also *intr.* (for *refl.*) **b.** *intr.* To start away with abruptness and force. Also *fig.* **To b. down. a.** *trans.* To demolish, destroy. **b.** To decompose. **c.** To crush in strength, health, courage, etc. **d.** *intr.* (for *refl.*) To fall broken; to prove of no avail. **To b. forth. a.** *intr.* To make a rush forward. **b.** Of flame, war, disease, etc.: To burst out. **c.** To break loose. **d.** To burst into utterance. **To b. in. a.** *trans.* = II. 2. **b.** *intr.* To enter forcibly or abruptly. **c.** To infringe *upon*; to interrupt unexpectedly. **d.** To burst *upon*. **To b. off. a.** *trans.* To put an abrupt end to. **b.** *intr.* To leave off abruptly. **c.** *trans.* To sever by breaking. **d.** *intr.* To detach oneself abruptly *from*. **e.** To sever connection (*with*). **f.** *trans.* To draw off sharply. † **g.** *intr.* To begin. **To b. out. a.** *trans.* To force out by breaking. **b.** *intr.* To burst from restraint, or concealment. Said of persons and things. Cf. *To b. out (in* or *into* boils, etc.); to *b. out, into*, or *in* feeling or action. **To b. through.** [f. Branch VII. Prop. the analysis is *to b. through-a-fence*, not *to b.-through* a fence.] **a.** *trans.* To penetrate by breaking. **b.** To transgress. Also *absol.* **To b. up. a.** To disintegrate (*trans.* and *intr.*). **b.** *trans.* To open up (ground). **c.** Of frost, † an epidemic: To give way. **d.** To fail physically. † **e.** *trans.* To burst open, open forcibly.

Break-. The verb-stem in *comb.* forming sbs. or adjs.

I. With verb + object. **1.** Forming *sbs.*, as **b.-bones,** the Ossifrage or Osprey; **-bulk,** a captain that abstracts part of his cargo; **-wind** *dial.*, a disease of sheep. **2.** Forming *adjs.*, as **-axe,** that breaks axes, as in **Break-axe Tree,** *Sloanea jamaicensis*; **-bone,** bone-breaking, as in **b.-bone fever,** the *dengue*; **-covert,** that breaks covert. **II.** With the vb. used attrib. = *breaking*; as **b.-piece, -iron.**

Break (brē^{i}k), *sb.*[1] ME. [f. prec. vb.] **1.** An act of breaking; fracture. **2.** *Cricket.* A twist of the ball on touching the ground 1866. **3.** *Billiards* and *Croquet*. A consecutive series of successful strokes; the points thus scored 1865. **4.** A broken place, gap, or opening: wider than BREACH ME. **5.** An interruption of continuity 1627. **a.** *spec.* 'the sudden termination or rise in the decks of some merchant ships' 1725; **b.** marks [– – –] used in print or writing to indicate abrupt pauses 1733. **6.** *Mus.* The point of separation between the different registers of a voice 1883. **7.** An irregularity, roughness, knot, etc. 1756. *spec.* in *Archit.* 1685. **8.** A portion of ground broken up for cultivation; a tract distinct in appearance 1674.

1. *B. of day* or *morn*: the first appearance of light. So *B. of June*: the beginning of June. **5. b.** In modern wit all printed trash is Set off with num'rous breaks – – – and dashes — SWIFT.

Break, *sb.*[2] Also **brake.** 1831. [perh. identical with BRAKE *sb.*[6]] **1.** A large carriage-frame with no body, used for breaking in young horses. **2.** A large wagonette 1874.

Breakable (brē^{i}·kăb'l), *a.* 1570. [f. BREAK *v.* + -ABLE.] Capable of being broken.

Breakage (brē^{i}·kėdʒ). 1813. [f. BREAK *v.* + -AGE.] **1.** The action or fact of breaking. **2.** The results of breaking; loss or damage caused by breaking 1848. **3.** A break 1871. **4.** *Naut.* The leaving of empty spaces in stowing the hold 1867.

Breakage[2], var. f. BRAKEAGE.

Brea·k-back, *a.* 1556. [Cf. BREAK-NECK.] That breaks the back; crushing.

Break-down (brē^{i}·kdaun, also brē^{i}:k dau·n). 1832. [f. *to break down* (see BREAK *v.*).] **1.** The act of breaking and falling down; a collapse (*lit.* and *fig.*). Also *attrib.*, as in *break-down gang*, etc. **2.** A riotous dance, in the style of the Negroes. (U.S.; but freq. in Eng.) 1864.

Breaker[1] (brē^{i}·kəɹ). ME. [f. BREAK *v.* + -ER[1].] **1.** One who breaks, crushes, or destroys; often with defining sb., as HOUSE-BREAKER, etc. 1514. **2.** One who violates a law, oath, convention, etc. ME. **3.** One who subdues, tames, or trains 1552. **4.** That which breaks 1661; *spec.* the name of machines for crushing the stems of flax or hemp, and for performing the first operation in carding cotton, etc. 1817. **5.** A heavy ocean-wave which breaks, esp. in passing over reefs or shallows 1684.

1. A b. of idols CARLYLE. **5.** *Breakers ahead!* 'the common pass-word to warn..of broken water in the direction of the course'.

Breaker[2] (brē^{i}·kəɹ). 1833. [– Sp. *bareca*, var. of *barrica*, f. stem. repr. in BARREL; cf. BARRICO. For the perversion of form, cf. GROUPER.] A small keg.

Breakfast (bre·kfăst). 1463. [f. phr. *break (one's) fast*; see BREAK, FAST *sb.*[1]] **1.** That with which a person breaks his fast in the morning; the first meal of the day. **2.** Occas.: A meal 1526.

1. That men shoulde go to masse as well after sowper as before brekefast MORE. **2.** The wolves will get a b. by my death DRYDEN.

Breakfast (bre·kfăst), *v.* 1679. [f. prec.] **1.** *intr.* To take the first meal of the day. **2.** *trans.* To provide with breakfast 1793.

Breaking (brē^{i}·kiŋ), *vbl. sb.* OE. [f. BREAK *v.* + -ING[1].] **1.** The action of BREAK *v.* **2.** A piece of land newly broken up. (*U.S.*) 1883.

Comb.: **b.-up** = BREAK-UP; **-crop,** the first crop on newly broken ground; **-frame,** a machine for drawing out the slivers in spinning wool.

Break-neck (brē^{i}·kne:k). 1562. [f. BREAK *v.* II. 1 + NECK.] **A.** *adj.* Likely to break the neck; headlong (of speed, etc.); precipitous. † **B.** *sb.* 'A fall in which the neck is broken; a steep place endangering the neck' (J.); *fig.* destruction, ruin –1653.

Brea·k-off, *sb.* **1.** The action of breaking off: *esp.* discontinuance of relations 1860. **2.** The metal work of the stock of a gun into which the breech of the barrel fits 1804.

Breakstone (brē^{i}·kstō^{u}n). 1688. [tr. L. *saxifraga*.] Herbalists' name for Saxifrages, and some other plants.

Break-up, *sb.* 1795. [f. *to break up*.] The action or fact of breaking up; disruption, separation into parts, disintegration (*lit.* and *fig.*); *e.g.* decay of animal functions; change from fine weather, or from frost; dispersal or dissolution of a society, system, etc.

Breakwater (brē^{i}·kˌwǭtəɹ). 1721. [f. BREAK *v.* + WATER.] **1.** Anything that breaks the force of the waves at a particular place, *esp.* a mole, pier, or the like, erected to form or protect a harbour 1769. **2.** A groyne or barrier on the beach to retain shingle 1721.

Bream (brīm), *sb.* late ME. [– OFr. *breme, bresme* (mod. *brème*) – Frankish **brachsima* = OS. *bressemo*, OHG. *brahsema* (G. *brachsen, brassen*).] **1.** A freshwater fish (*Abramis brama*), called also Carp-bream, distinguished by its yellowish colour and its high arched back. Also its genus (*Abramis*, family *Cyprinidæ*). **2.** Used also of some acanthopterygious sea-fishes, of the genus *Pagellus* (family *Sparidæ*), and genus *Labrus* (family *Labridæ*), as the Sea Bream (*P. centrodontus*), Spanish Bream (*P. erythrinus*) 1460.

Bream (brīm), *v.* 1626. [prob. of LG. origin and rel. to BROOM *sb.* (cf. Du. *brem* broom, furze).] To clear (a ship's bottom) of shells, sea-weed, ooze, etc., by singeing it with burning reeds, furze, or faggots. Cf. BROOM *v.*

Breards (bri^{ə}ɹdz), *sb. pl. Sc.* 1733. [The same as BRAIRD, *sb.* in sense of 'short ends or points'.] The short flax recovered from the first tow by a second hackling.

Breast (brest). [OE. *brēost* (freq. in pl.) = OFris. *briast*, OS. *briost*, ON. *brjóst* :– Gmc. **breustam*; parallel to a fem. cons.-stem **brusts*, repr. by (M)LG., (M)Du. *borst*, OHG., G. *brust*.] **1.** Each of the two soft protuberances situated on the thorax in females, in which milk is secreted for the nourishment of their young; the mamma; also the mammilla in males. **b.** Hence *fig.* Source of nourishment 1611. **2.** The front of the thorax or chest. (In OE. usu. in pl., for dual.) OE. **b.** The part of a garment or armour covering the breast 1651. **c.** The bosom 1650. † **3.** Occas. = the thorax or chest –1766. **4.** The corresponding part in the lower animals ME. **5.** *fig.* and *transf.* The seat of the affections and emotions; the repository of consciousness; the heart; *hence*, the affections, private thoughts and feelings. (Usu. pl. in OE.) OE. † **6.** *transf.* The place of the lungs; *hence*, breath, voice in singing –1711. † **7.** A broad even front of a moving company –1807. **8.** Used of analogous surfaces or parts of things. † In *military* use, a breastwork. ME. **9.** Techn.: **a.** *Archit.* The part of a wall between a window and the floor; also, the part of a chimney between its flues and the rooms; † the *torus* in a column. **b.** *Mining.* The face of a working; also, that side of the hearth of a shaft-furnace which contains the metal-notch. RAYMOND.

1. Come to my Womans Brests And take my Milke for Gall *Macb.* I. v. 48. Past the b. 1647. Put to the B. STEELE. **2.** You must cut this flesh from off his b. *Merch. V.* IV. i. 252. **5.** What his Brest forges, that his Tongue must vent *Cor.* III. i. 258. *To make a clean b.*: to make a full disclosure. **6.** *Twel. N.* II. iii. 19. **7.** *In, of, on (a) b.* = ABREAST. *Obs.* **8.** The b. of the battle ME., of Heaven SHAKS., earth 1814, a hill 1872.

Comb.: **b.-backstays** (*Naut.*), long ropes to support the masts against an oblique headwind (cf. BACKSTAY); **-band,** a band passing round the breast; also *spec.* = *breast-rope*; **-collar,** a broad pulling strap passing round the b. of a horse; **-drill,** one against which the workman bears his b. while drilling; **-fast,** a large rope or chain, used to confine a ship's broadside to a wharf, quay, etc.; **-height,** the interior slope of a parapet; **-hooks,** large pieces of compass-timber fixed within and athwart the bows of a ship; **-knees** *sb. pl.*, timbers placed in the forward part of a vessel across the stem to unite the bows on each side; **-knot,** a knot or bow of ribbon, etc. worn on the b.; **-pain,** a disease in horses; **-pang,** the *Angina pectoris*; **-pump,** an instrument for drawing milk from the b. by suction; **-rail** (*Naut.*), the upper rail of the balcony, etc.; **-rope** (*Naut.*), a rope for securing the yard-parrels; a rope for supporting the leadsman while sounding; **-strap** (*Harness*), a strap fixed at one end to the collar and supporting the pole of the vehicle; **- weed,** *Saururus cernuus*; **-wimble,** a gimlet or auger upon which the b. presses in working; **-wood,** young shoots of fruit trees trained on espaliers or against walls. Hence **Brea·stwise** *adv.*

Breast (brest), *v.* 1573. [f. prec.] **1.** To oppose the breast to; to meet in full opposition 1599. † **2.** To defend in front or with a breastwork –1624. **3.** To apply the breast to 1820.

1. *To b. a fence, horse*, etc.: to mount by springing so as to bring the breast over. **3.** As swift As bird on wing to b. its eggs again KEATS. Hence **Brea·sted** *ppl. a.* having a breast; *esp.* in comb., as *big.-b.*

Breast-beam (bre·st,bīm). 1790. **1.** *Naut.* One of the beams at the fore-part of the quarter-deck, and after-part of the forecastle 1850. **2.** The horizontal beam in front of a loom 1790. **3.** The front cross-beam of the frame of a locomotive.

Breast-board (bre·stbōᵊɹd). 1649. **1.** The mould-board of a plough. **2.** *Rope-making.* A loaded carriage to which the yarn-ends are attached at the foot of the rope-walk.

Breastbone (bre·stbōᵘn). OE. The bone running down the front of the thorax, and articulated by cartilages with the ribs; the sternum.

Breast-high (bre·st,həi). 1580. **A.** *adj.* As high as the breast 1677. **B.** *adv.* **1.** To the height or depth of the breast 1580. **2.** Said in *Hunting* of a strong scent which the hounds can follow at a racing pace with heads erect 1858.

Breasting (bre·stiŋ), *vbl. sb.* 1817. [f. BREAST *sb.* and *v.* + -ING¹.] **1.** The action of BREAST *v.* **b.** *concr.* A covering for the breast, breast-work. **2.** *techn.* The curved channel in which a breast-wheel works.

Breast-plate (bre·stplēⁱt). ME. **1.** A piece of armour, or any plate, worn on the breast. **2.** A folded piece of embroidered linen worn on the breast of the Jewish high-priest, and adorned with twelve precious stones, representing the twelve tribes. Cf. *Exod.* 28, 39. 1581. **3.** Techn.: **a.** *Mech.* A plate in which the butt end of a drill is inserted when the breast is applied in boring. **b.** A strap or straps passing across the breast of a riding-horse. 1667.

Brea·st-plough. 1725. A sort of plough pushed by the breast, used for paring turf. Hence **Brea·st-plough** *v.*

Breastsummer, bressummer (brɒ·seməɹ). 1611. [f. BREAST *sb.* + SUMMER *sb.*²] A summer or beam extending horizontally over a large opening, and sustaining the whole superstructure of wall, etc.; *e.g.* the beam over a shop-front, and the like.

Breast-wheel (bre·st,hwīl). 1759. A water-wheel, in which the water is admitted to the float-board nearly on a level with the axle.

Breastwork (bre·stwɒ̈ɹk). 1642. **1.** *Fortif.* A fieldwork thrown up breast-high for defence; a parapet. Also *fig.* **2.** *Naut.* A sort of balustrade which terminates the quarter-deck and poop at the fore ends 1769.

Breath (breþ). [OE. *brǣþ* odour, exhalation :– Gmc. **brǣþaz* :– Indo-Eur. **bhrētos*, f. **bhrē-* burn, heat. The sense 'air in the lungs or mouth' was taken over from OE. *ǣþm* and *anda* (ME. *ethem* and *ande, onde*).] † **1.** Odour –ME. **2.** An exhalation or vapour from heated objects, etc.; steam, smoke, reek –1667. **b.** (cf. 3.) The air exhaled from anything, or impregnated with its exhalations. Also *fig.* 1625. **c.** A whiff 1873. **3.** The air exhaled from the lungs, orig. as smelt or seen; hence generally, The air received into and expelled from the lungs in the act of respiration. Now the main sense. ME. Also *transf.* **4.** A puff; now usu. *of air* or *of wind*; but orig. used absol. ME. **5.** The faculty of breathing. Hence, spirit, life. ME. **6.** A single respiration 1483. **7.** Power of breathing, free or easy breathing; *esp.* in *out of b.* 1590. **8.** Time for breathing; exercise of the respiratory organs. Also *fig.* 1594. **9.** *transf.* Whisper, utterance, speech; will expressed in words ME. **10.** *Phonology.* Voiceless expiration of air, forming a hiss, whish, puff, etc. Also *attrib.* 1867.

2. Like gentle breaths from rivers pure MILT. **b.** The B. of Flowers BACON. **3.** *To draw b.* DRYDEN. *To spend b.* BERKELEY. So *To waste b.* The b. is not the flute BROWNING. **4.** A summer night without a b. SHELLEY. Summers b. SHAKS. So 'b. of morn'. The b. of popular applause 1703. **5.** The b. of life WYCLIF, of the nostrils *Gen.* 7:22. *To catch* or *hold one's b.*: to check suddenly or suspend the act of respiration. **6.** Phr. *In* (*with*) *one* or *the same b., at a b.* **7.** *To take b.*, to recover free breathing. **9.** A b. can make them, as a b. has made GOLDSM. Princes and lords are but the b. of kings BURNS. *Below* or *under one's b.*: in a low voice. *Bated b.*, breathing subdued or restrained under the influence of awe, etc. **10.** *B. consonant*, a consonant formed by the breath in the mouth without the action of the vocal cords, as k, t, p, etc.

Breathe (brīð), *v.* [ME. *brethe*, f. *breth* BREATH; not formed in OE.] **I.** *intr.* † **1.** To exhale, steam, evaporate –1670. † **2.** To emit odour, to smell –1712. *fig.* To be redolent *of* 1697. **3.** To exhale air from the lungs ME. **b.** To exhale and inhale, to respire. (The ordinary current sense.) ME. **c.** To bring (*to, into* a state) by breathing 1816. **4.** To live, exist ME. Also *fig.* **5.** To take breath (see BREATH 7); *fig.* to pause, take rest 1577. **6.** *transf.* To give forth audible breath; to speak, sing, etc. 1598. **7.** Of air, etc.: To blow softly. (Cf. 3.)1610.

1. A warmth breathes out of her *Per.* III. ii. 94. **2.** All Arabia breathes from yonder box POPE. **3. b.** When we b., sleep, move HOOKER. **4.** A better fellow does not b. 1873. **6.** As I wake, sweet music b. MILT. *Penser.* 151. **7.** The low wind hardly breathed for fear TENNYSON.

II. *trans.* **1.** To exhale, to emit by expiration (*out*); *fig.* to send *into*, communicate by breathing ME.; *transf.* of things 1647. **2.** To inhale and exhale (air, etc.), to respire; *esp.* to inhale. Also *fig.* 1588. **3.** To give utterance to, in various senses (see quots.) 1535. **4.** *trans.* and *refl.* To let breathe; to give a breathing space to; to recreate 1563. **5.** To excite the respiratory organs of: *hence* † to exercise briskly; to put out of breath, exhaust ME. **6.** To give breath to (a wind instrument); to blow 1721.

1. To b. new life into any one MORLEY. Phr. *To b. one's last*: to expire. **2.** Free as the air we b. 1887. **3.** I would not b. (= whisper) it to another (*mod.*). Breathing (= uttering with vehemence) vengeance SPENSER. Language breathing (= manifesting) the eloquence of truth S. ROGERS. **4.** To b. oneself 1563, horses 1596.

Phrases. *To b. through* (sense I. 4): to animate, inform. *To b. again* (sense I. 5): (*fig.*) to be relieved in mind. *To b. freely*: to be at ease, in one's element. *To b. upon* (fig.): to infect; to tarnish (as if with breath); to taint. *To b. a vein*: to lance it so as to let blood. ? *Obs.*

Hence **Brea·thable** *a.* fit or agreeable to b.

Breathed, *ppl. a.* ME. [f. BREATHE *v.* and BREATH *sb.*] **1.** From the vb. (*now* brīðd, brī·ðėd). **1.** In (good) wind; *esp.* in *well-b.*, etc. *fig.* †*Lust-b.* (in Shaks.): breathing lust. **2.** Winded, exhausted 1599. **3.** Exhaled, respired; uttered in a breath, whispered 1579.

1. As swift As b. Stags SHAKS. **3.** No . . b. spell MILT.

II. From the sb. (*now* breþt). **1.** Having breath; as in *long-b.*: long-winded, or -lived 1555. **2.** *Phonology.* Uttered with breath only; surd; cf. SONANT 1877.

Breather (brī·ðəɹ). ME. [f. BREATHE *v.* + -ER¹.] **1.** He who or that which breathes. **2.** A spell of exercise taken to stimulate the breathing, etc. Also, that which puts out of breath. 1836.

1. Breathers of this world SHAKS., of an ampler day TENNYSON. **2.** To take a 'b.' 1884.

Breathful (bre·þful), *a.* 1583. [f. BREATH + -FUL.] Full of breath or air; having life; redolent.

Breathing (brī·ðiŋ), *vbl. sb.* ME. [f. BREATHE *v.* + -ING¹.] **1.** Respiration; a single act of respiration. **b.** A short time 1625. **c.** Wind 1667. **d.** *fig.* Influence 1587. † **2.** Time to breathe, pause –1687. **3.** = BREATHER 2. 1755. **4.** Utterance 1606. **5.** Aspiration (*after*), longing (*for*) 1652. **6.** Of the wind: Gentle blowing 1635. † **7.** Ventilation; a vent, air-hole –1697. **8.** The opening of a vein in order to let blood 1612. **9.** *Gram.* An aspiration, an aspirate: *spec.* (Gr. πνεῦμα, L. *spiritus*), in Gr. grammar, (ʽ) or 'rough breathing', and (ʼ) or 'smooth breathing', indicating respectively the presence or absence of the aspirate. See ASPER *sb.*¹, ASPIRATE.

1. Forsake mee not . . in my last b. HIERON. **4.** Hide not thine eare at my b. *Lam.* 3:55. **6.** There's not a b. of the common wind That will forget thee WORDSW.

Comb.: **b.-fit,** pause, rest; **-hole,** a hole or vent for air; **-part, -place,** a place or opening for b.; a pause; **-pore,** a minute opening for the passage of air, a spiracle; **-space,** room or time to breathe; so **-spell, -time, -while.**

Brea·thing, *ppl. a.* ME. [f. as prec. + -ING².] In the senses of the vb. **b.** *fig.* Life-like (cf. Vergil's *spirantia signa, æra*) 1697. Hence **Brea·thingly** *adv.*

Breathless (bre·þlės), *a.* ME. [f. BREATH + -LESS.] **1.** Without breath: **a.** Without respiration. **b.** Lifeless 1595. † **c.** *Gram.* Unaspirated 1668. **2.** Breathing with difficulty, panting; exhausted 1450. Also *fig.* **b.** Holding one's breath, as with awe, etc. 1802. **3.** Unstirred by a breath of wind 1815.

2. B. and spent 1709. **b.** A nun B. with adoration WORDSW. Hence **Brea·thless-ly** *adv.*, **-ness.**

Breathy (bre·þi), *a.* 1528. [f. as prec. + -Y¹.] **1.** Of, pertaining to, or of the nature of breath. **2.** Of the voice: Having the sound of breathing in it. Hence **Brea·thiness,** b. quality.

Breccia (bre·ttʃă, bre·tʃiă). 1774. [It., = 'gravel or rubbish of broken walls', cogn. w. (O)Fr. *brèche* – Gmc. **brekan* BREAK *v.*] *Geol.* A composite rock consisting of angular fragments of stone, etc., cemented, *e.g.* by lime: occas. opp. to *conglomerate*.

Osseous or *bone b.*: one containing fossil bones. Hence **Bre·cciated,** *a.*, formed into a b., of the structure of a b.

† **Breck.** ME. [A parallel form of BREAK *sb.*¹, or directly f. *brec-* stem of BREAK *v.*] A breach, blemish.

Bred. Now *dial.* [OE. *bred* = OHG. *bret* (G. *brett*) :– Gmc. **breðam*, var. of **borðam* BOARD *sb.*] A board; a tablet.

Bred (bred), *ppl. a.* Pa. pple. of BREED *v.*; used chiefly in *comb.*, as *country-, ill-, thorough-b.*

† **Brede,** *sb.*¹ [OE. *brǣde*, f. *brǣdan* roast; see BREDE *v.*¹ Cf. the synon. derivative **brādon*; see BRAWN *sb.*] Roast meat. (Cf. SWEETBREAD.) –1535.

Brede, *sb.*² Now *n. dial.* [OE. *brǣdu* = OFris. *brēde*, OHG. *breitī* (G. *breite*), ON. *breidd*, Goth. *braidei*, f. Gmc. **braid-*; see BROAD.] Breadth, width.

Brede (brīd), *sb.*³ *arch.* 1640. [var. of BRAID *sb.* Cf. BREDE *v.*³] = BRAID *sb.* 4. *Comb.* **b.-stitch.**

A curious B. of Needle-work DRYDEN.

† **Brede,** *v.*¹ [OE. *brǣdan* = OFris. *brēda*, OS. *brādan* (MLG. *brāden*), OHG. *brātan* (G. *braten*) :– Gmc. **brǣdan* :– **brǣ-*, **brē-* burn, heat, warm; see BREATH, BROOD.] *trans.* To roast, broil, toast –1509.

Brede, *v.*² Now *dial.* [OE. *brǣdan* = OS. *brēdian*, OHG., G. *breiten*, ON. *breiða*, Goth. *-braidjan* :– Gmc. **braið-*; see BROAD, BREDE *sb.*²] **1.** *trans.* To broaden. **2.** *trans.* and *intr.* To spread out ME.

† **Brede,** *v.*³ ME. [var. of BRAID *v.*; cf. BREDE *sb.*³] To intertwine.

† **Bree** (brī), *sb.*¹ Now *n. dial.* [OE. *brǣw* eyelid, OFris. *brē*, OS., OHG. *brāwa* (G. *braue*) eyebrow, ON. *brá* eyelash; cf. BRAE. Not allied to BROW.] † **1.** The eye-lid –ME. **2.** The eye-brow ME. † **3.** An eye-lash –1656.

Bree (brī), *sb.*² Now *Sc.* [ME. *bre* repr. OE. *brīw*, *brīġ* = MLG., MDu. *brī* (Du. *brij*), OHG. *brīo* (G. *brei*) :– Gmc. **brīwaz.*] † **1.** A thick pottage made of meal, etc. –ME.

2. Broth, juice. Also *fig.* ME. † **3.** *fig.* Water, the sea ME. only.

2. *Barley-b.*: malt liquor. *Herring-b.*: herring-brine.

Breech (brītʃ), *sb.* [OE. *brōc*, pl. *brēć*, corresp. to OFris. *brōk*, pl. *brēk*, OS. *brōk* (Du. *broek*), OHG. *bruoh* (G. † *bruch*), ON. *brók*, pl. *broekr* :– Gmc. **brōks*, fem. const. stem.] † **1.** A garment covering the loins and thighs –1642. **b.** Now always in pl. **Breeches** (bri·tʃėz), or *a pair of breeches*. (*Breeches* come only just below the knee, but *dial.* (and *joc.*) *breeches* includes *trousers*.) ME. **2.** The part covered by this garment; the buttocks. ? OE. Also *transf.* **3.** *techn.* **a.** *Gunnery.* The part of a cannon, or other firearm, behind the bore 1575. **b.** *Ship-building.* The outside angle formed by the knee-timber. SMYTH.

1. b. They sewed figge leaues together, and made themselues breeches BIBLE (Genev.) *Gen.* 3:7.

Phr. *To wear the breeches* († *breech*): to be master, said of a wife.

Comb.: (sense 3) **b. action,** the mechanism at the b. of a gun; **-block,** a movable steel block by which the end of the barrel in certain fire-arms is closed; **-pin, -plug,** a pin or plug closing the b. end of a gun; **-screw,** a cylinder of iron with a screw, which presses the vent piece into its place when the gun is loaded; (sense 2) **breeches-ball,** a ball of composition for cleaning breeches; **Breeches Bible,** the Geneva Bible of 1560, so named on account of the rendering of *Gen.* 3:7, already occurring in Wyclif; **breeches-buoy,** a life-buoy with suspended canvas support resembling breeches.

Breech (britʃ, brītʃ), *v.* 1468. [f. prec.] **1.** To cover or clothe with, or as with, breeches; to put (a boy) into breeches. Also *fig.* † **2.** To flog –1821. **3.** *Naut.* To secure (a cannon) by a breeching 1757.

1. *fig.* Their Daggers Vnmannerly breech'd with gore SHAKS. **2.** The bois must be britch[t] 1573.

Breeching (brī·tʃiŋ), *vbl. sb.* 1515. [f. BREECH *v.* and *sb.* + -ING[1].] **1.** The action of the vb. (sense 1). † **2.** A flogging –1613. Also *attrib.* **3.** A leather strap passing round the breech of a shaft-horse, and enabling him to push backwards. Also *attrib.* 1515. **4.** Coarse wool on the buttocks of sheep 1799. **5.** *Naut.* A stout rope attached by a thimble to the cascabel of a gun, and securing the gun to the ship's side. Hence *b.-bolt, -loop.* 1627. **6.** The parts forming the breech of a gun 1802.

2. Aristarchus' eyes, Whose looks were as a b. to a boy MARLOWE.

Breech-loader (brī·tʃ,lōᵘdəɹ). 1858. A fire-arm which is loaded at the breech. So **Bree·ch-loading** *vbl. sb.* this method of loading (fire-arms). *attrib.* That is loaded at the breech.

Breed (brīd), *sb.* 1553. [f. BREED *v.*] † **1.** Breeding, birth; extraction –1632. **2.** Race, stock, strain; a line of descendants perpetuating particular hereditary qualities. (Abstract and concrete.) 1553. **b.** *gen.* A species, a set 1588. † **3.** Offspring; *esp.* a litter, etc. Now BROOD. Also *fig.* –1802.

2. Rammes of the b. of Bashan *Deut.* 32:14. Too good for such a b. 1843. **b.** The b. of wits so wondered at *L.L.L.* v. ii. 266. **3.** A breede of barraine mettall *Merch. V.* I. iii. 135.

Breed (brīd), *v.* Pa. t. and pple. **bred.** [OE. *brēdan* = OHG. *bruotan* (G. *brüten*) :– WGmc. **brōdjan*, f. **brōd-* BROOD *sb.*] **I.** *trans.* (and *absol.*) **1.** Of a female parent: To cherish (brood) in the womb or egg; to hatch from the egg; to produce (offspring). **2.** *absol.* To be pregnant. (Now chiefly *dial.*) 1629. **3.** *absol.* Of animal species: To have offspring; to propagate their species ME. Also *fig.* **4.** *trans.* Said of countries, etc. (without reference to parental action) ME. **5.** To give rise to, engender, develop, produce, be the source of ME. † **6.** with *compl.* To make (to do something) –1625. **7.** To take charge of or promote the engendering of (animals); to raise (cattle) ME. Also *absol.* **8.** To train up physically or mentally 1523.

1. Neither thou in begetting him, nor his mother in breeding him GOLDING. **3.** *fig.* Shee speakes, and 'tis such sence That my Sence breeds with it *Meas. for M.* II. ii. 142. **4.** Waters that b. Trouts WALTON. Dirt breeds fever KINGSLEY. *To b. bad blood*: see BLOOD. **5.** Shee is young, wise, faire.. And these b. honour *All's Well* II. iii. 140. **8.** To b. a bullock to the plough DRYDEN. Bred in All Souls in Oxford FULLER, to the Church SOUTHEY, a smith FRANKLIN.

II. *intr.* (for *refl.*) **1.** To come into being, as a continued process; hence, to be engendered or produced ME. † **b.** To grow, as animal structures, etc. –1688. **2.** *fig.* To originate, make their appearance ME.

Phrases. *Born and bred*, or *bred and born*: here *bred* has usu. sense I. 7, though formerly sense I. 1. † *To b. out*: to degenerate *Timon* I. i. 259. *To b. in and in*: to b. always with near relatives. *Comb.* † **Bree·d-bate,** one who breeds bate, or strife.

Breeder (brī·dəɹ). 1531. [f. prec. vb. + -ER[1].] That which, or one who, produces, breeds, or † brings up.

Breeding (brī·diŋ), *vbl. sb.* ME. [f. as prec. + -ING[1].] **1.** Bringing to the birth; hatching; production of young. Hence (vulgarly), †extraction –1606. **2.** *fig.* Origination, production, development 1549. **3.** The bringing up of the young; formerly in sense of 'education' 1577. **4.** The results of training as shown in manners and behaviour; usu. = 'good manners' 1596. Also *attrib.*

4. Men of parts and b. BERKELEY.

† **Bree·dling.** [f. as prec. + -LING[1].] One born and bred in a place. PEPYS. [Taken by Macaulay for a proper name.]

Breek (brīk). ME. N.Eng. and Sc. var. of BREECH *sb.* Now only in pl. **breeks** = trousers. Hence **Bree·kless** *a.*

Breeze (brīz), *sb.*[1] [OE. *briosa*, of unkn. origin.] **1.** A gad-fly; *esp.* of the genera *Œstrus* (BOT-FLY) and *Tabanus* (*arch.* or *dial.*). Also *fig.* So **b.-fly.** † **2.** Used vaguely of other insects –1483.

Breeze (brīz), *sb.*[2] 1565. [prob. – OSp., Pg. *briza* (Sp. *brisa*) north-east wind (cf. It. *brezza*, dial. *brisa* cold wind), whence also Fr. *brise*.] † **1.** *orig.* A north or north-east wind –1706. † **2.** The cool wind that blows from the sea by day on tropical coasts –1839. **b.** By extension, the counter-current that blows from the land by night 1700. **3.** A gentle or light wind: a current of air lighter than a *wind*. In naut. use = wind in general. 1626. **4.** *fig. colloq.* **a.** A disturbance, row 1785. **b.** A breath of news, whisper 1879. Also in *comb.*

2. b. From land a gentle b. arose by night DRYDEN. **4. a.** The cession would create a b. in the Konkan WELLINGTON. Hence **Bree·zeless** *a.*

Breeze (brīz), *sb.*[3] 1726. [– Fr. *braise*, earlier *brese* burning charcoal, hot embers, half-burnt coal (*braise de boulanger* baker's breeze); cf. BRAISE.] Small cinders and cinder-dust, used in burning bricks, etc.; small coke and coke-dust.

Breeze, *v. rare.* 1682. [f. BREEZE *sb.*[2]] *intr.* To blow gently, as a breeze.

Phr. *To b. up* (Naut.): (of a wind) to freshen; also *impers.* Of a noise: To rise on the breeze.

Breezy (brī·zi), *a.* 1718. [f. BREEZE *sb.*[2] + -Y[1].] **1.** Exposed to breezes. **2.** Attended by breezes, windy; *fig.* fresh; airy 1753.

1. The b. shore POPE, elms WORDSW. **2.** B. verse LOWELL. Hence **Bree·zily** *adv.*, **Bree·ziness.**

‖ **Bregma** (bre·gmă). Pl. **bre·gmata.** 1578. [Gr. βρέγμα front of the head.] The region of the skull where the frontal and the two parietal bones join; the sinciput. Hence **Bregma·tic** *a.*

Brehon (brī·hǫn). Now *Hist.* 1581. [– Ir. *breathamh*, in OIr. *brithem*, f. *breth* judgement.] An ancient Irish judge.

B. law, the code of law which prevailed in Ireland before its occupation by the English.

Breithauptite (brəi·t,hauptəit). [f. *Breithaupt*, mineralogist + -ITE[1] 2 b.] Antimonial nickel, a native alloy of these two metals (NiSb) found in the Harz Mountains.

‖ **Bre·kekeke·x.** 1607. Gr. βρεκεκεκέξ, echoic of the croaking of frogs.

‖ **Breloque** (brəlo·k). 1856. [Fr.] A small ornament fastened to a watch-chain.

† **Bre·mber.** [OE. *brember*, var. of *brembel*, BRAMBLE.] By-form of BRAMBLE.

Breme (brīm), *a.* Still *dial.* [I. OE. *brǣme*, *brēme* celebrated. II. Of unkn. origin.] **I.** † **1.** Celebrated (only in OE.); *hence*, fine, famous –ME. † **2.** Brilliant; clear, loud, distinct –1617. **II.** † **1.** Fierce, wroth –1818. **2.** Of the sea, etc.: Raging, rough; usu. echoed from Spenser. In n. dial. *brim.* ME.

Bren(e, obs. f. BRAN, BURN.

Brended, obs. f. BURNT.

† **Bre·ndice.** *rare.* [– It. *brindisi* a toast, health – G. *bring dir's* (i.e. *ich bringe dir's zu*), whence also Fr. *brinde* (XVI), *bringue* (Cotgr.), Swiss Fr. *brinda, bringa*.] A bumper. DRYDEN.

Bre·nnage [– OFr. *brenage*, f. *bren* BRAN + *-age* -AGE, or med.L. *brennagium*.] *Old Law.* A payment in, or in lieu of, bran, made by tenants to feed their lord's hounds.

Brent, *a.* Phonetic var. of BRANT, q.v.

Brent, *sb.* Also **Brent-goose.** = BRANT *sb.*

Brepho-, comb. f. Gr. βρέφος babe; only in nonce-wds., as **Brepho·latry** baby-worship, etc.

Brerd. Now *dial.* [OE. *brerd* brim, margin; cf. OHG. *brort, brord* prow, margin, lip, also OE. *brord* point, prick, ON. *broddr* shaft, spike; see BRAIRD, BROD.] The topmost surface or edge; brim. Hence † **Bre·rd-full** *a.* brim-full.

Brere (briᵊɹ). Original form of BRIER (*dial.* and *poet.*).

Bressomer, bressumer, var. of BREAST-SUMMER.

Brest, obs. f. BREAST, BURST.

Bret, *sb.* 1460. [Origin unkn.] † **1.** = BIRT –1671. **2.** = BRIT 1725.

Bre·tessé, bretessee, bretessy. 1572. [– Fr. *bretessé* bratticed; see -Y[5].] *Her.* Having embattlements on each side.

† **Bre·t-full,** *a.* ME. [var. of BRERD-*full*.] Brim-full –1616.

Brethren (bre·ðrėn), special pl. of BROTHER.

Brethrenism. The principles and system of the (*Plymouth*) *Brethren*.

Brett. Short f. BRITZKA, a four-wheeled carriage.

Brettice, brettis, common var. of BRATTICE.

Bretwalda (bretwǭ·ldă). [OE., varying w. *Brytenwalda*, f. *Brettas* (see BRITISH), *Bryten* (see BRITAIN) + **wald-* (see WIELD).] *Hist.* A title given in the O.E. Chronicle to King Egbert, and (retrospectively) to seven earlier Old English kings, and occas. assumed by later ones: = 'lord of the Britons', or 'of Britain'. (See Freeman *N.C.* I.)

Breu-, see BREV-, BREW-.

Breve (brīv), *sb.* ME. [var. of BRIEF *sb.* in various senses.] **1.** A letter of authority; *spec.* a pope's letter; = BRIEF *sb.* 1, 2. **2.** *Music.* A note of the value of two semibreves, now written white and either oblong or oval, with one or two strokes on each side; rarely used in mod. music 1460. † **3.** *Gram.* A short syllable –1751. **4.** *Print.* The mark ˘ placed over a vowel to signify that it is short. **5.** [Fr. *brève*.] The Ant-thrush, so named from its short tail.

1. The pope had sent two breves to Garnet 1862.

† **Breve,** *v.* [ME. *breven*, app. – ON. *bréfa* write – med.L. *breviare*, f. *breve* note, dispatch; see BRIEF *sb.*] **1.** *trans.* (and *absol.*) To set down in writing –1560. **2.** To recount, tell –1448. Hence † **Bre·vement, brievement,** the action of the vb.; *concr.* an entry.

Brevet (bre·vėt), *sb.* ME. [– (O)Fr. *brevet*, f. *bref, brief* BRIEF *sb.*; see -ET.] † **1.** An authoritative message in writing; *esp.* a Papal Indulgence –1754. **2.** An official document granting certain privileges; *spec.* in the Army, one conferring nominal rank on an officer, but giving no right to extra pay 1689. Also *transf.* and *fig.* Also *attrib.*

2. The Duke de Chartres..holds this Employment by a b. only 1721. Hence **Bre·vetcy,** b. rank (Dicts.)

Brevet (bre·vėt), *v.* 1839. [f. prec.] To raise to a certain rank by brevet; also *fig.* Hence **Bre·veted** *ppl. a.*

Brevi- (bre·vi-), comb. f. of L. *brevis* 'short'.

Breviped [L. *pes, ped-*] *a.*, having short feet (or legs); *sb.* [sc. *bird*]; **-pen** [L. *penna*] *sb.*, a short-winged bird; **-pennate** *a.*, short-winged; **-rostrate** [L. *rostrum*] *a.*, having a short beak.

Breviary (brī·viări). 1547. [– L. *breviarium* summary, abridgement, f. *breviare* abridge; see ABBREVIATE *v.*, -ARY[1].] **1.** A brief statement, epitome. ? *Obs.* **2.** R.C. Ch. The book containing the 'Divine Office' for each day, which those who are in orders are bound to recite 1611. Also *fig.*

† **Bre·viate,** *a.* 1509. [– L. *breviatus*, pa. pple. of *breviare* shorten, f. *brevis* short; see BRIEF *a.*, -ATE².] Abbreviated; short –1656.

Breviate (brī·viět), *sb.* 1581. [f. prec. adj. used subst.] **1.** A brief statement; a summary, compendium. Also *fig.* † **2.** A brief missive; a note –1748. † **3.** A lawyer's brief –1734.

1. A B. of all Luthers doctrine 1581. **3.** As well-fee'd Lawyer on his B. BUTLER *Hud.* II. ii. 612.

† **Bre·viate,** *v.* 1526. [f. as prec. (see -ATE³), or aphet. f. ABBREVIATE *v.*] **1.** To abbreviate –1637. **2.** To abridge; *spec.* to abstract for counsel's instruction –1679. Hence † **Bre·viature,** an abbreviation.

Brevier (brĭvīᵊ·ɹ). 1598. [– Du. or G. *brevier* – med.L. use of L. *breviarium* BREVIARY; so called because used in printing breviaries; cf. *canon*, *pica*, etc.] The name of the type in size between Bourgeois and Minion, as in

Brevier Type.

Breviloquence (brĭvi·lŏkwěns). *rare.* 1656. [– L. *breviloquentia*, f. *brevis* short + *loquentia* speaking.] Brevity of speech; laconism. So **Brevi·loquent** *a.* laconic.

‖ **Brevi· manu.** 1808. [L.] *Law.* Summarily.

Bre·vit, *v.* Now *dial.* 1600. [Origin unkn.] To forage; to beat about for game.

Brevity (bre·vĭti). 1509. [– AFr. *breveté*, (O)Fr. *brièveté*, f. *bref*, fem. *brève*; see BRIEF *a.*, -ITY.] **1.** Shortness, esp. as used of time 1542. **2.** The being short in speech or writing; terseness 1509. **3.** Shortness in other relations (*rare* and *forced*) 1597.

2. Since Breuitie is the Soule of Wit..I will be breefe *Haml.* II. ii. 90. **3.** 2 *Hen. IV*, II. ii. 135.

Brew (brū), *v.* [OE. *brēowan* = OFris. **briuwa*, OS. *breuwan* (Du. *brouwen*), OHG. *briuwan*, *brūwan* (G. *brauen*, *bräuen*), ON. *brugga* :– Gmc. **breu(w)an*.] **1.** *trans.* Properly: To make (ale, etc.) by infusion, boiling, and fermentation. Also *fig.* **b.** To convert (barley, malt, etc.) into a fermented liquor ME. Also *absol.* † **2.** To mix (liquors) –1641. **3.** *transf.* To make by mixing, as punch; or by infusion, as tea 1626. **4.** To concoct, contrive, cause ME. **5.** *intr.* To be in process of mixing, concocting, etc. ME.

1. She brewes good Ale *Two Gent.* III. i. 304. **b.** O Willie brew'd a peck o' maut BURNS. **4.** To b. bale ME., bitternesse LANGL., some notable matter GOLDING, a storm FALCONER, plagues SOUTHEY.

Comb.: **b.-house,** a brewery.

Brew, *sb.* 1510. [f. the vb.] The action of brewing; the beverage, etc. brewed.

Brewage (brū·ėdʒ). 1542. [f. BREW *v.* + -AGE; prob. conn. in origin w. Fr. *breuvage* BEVERAGE.] **1.** A concocted beverage; a decoction; something that has been *brewed*. Also *fig.* **2.** The process of brewing 1776. **3.** A boiling (*e.g.* of salt) 1550.

1. Malmsey, or some well spic't bruage MILT.

Brewer (brū·əɹ). ME. [f. as prec. + -ER¹.] **1.** One who brews; *spec.* one whose trade is to make malt liquors. **2.** A concocter of 1563.

Brewery (brū·əri). 1658. [prob. – Du. *brouwerij* (whence G. *brauerei*); earlier *brewhouse* XIV.] **1.** A place or establishment for brewing; formerly called a BREWHOUSE. † **2.** The process or trade of brewing –1796.

Brewing (brū·iŋ), *vbl. sb.* 1467. [f. BREW *v.* + -ING¹.] **1.** The action, process, or occupation described under BREW (various senses). *fig.* Concoction 1545. **2.** The quantity brewed at once 1626. **3.** *Naut.* A collection of black clouds betokening a storm. Also *attrib.*

1. Great brewyng, small drinke 1562. **b.** I have an *Edinburgh* article in b. ALFORD.

Brewis (brū·ĭs). [ME. *browes*, *brewes*, etc., – OFr. *broez*, *brouez* (mod. *brouet*), f. *breu* :– Rom. **brodo* – Gmc. *broþam* BROTH. Cf. BROSE.] **1.** Broth (*dial.*). **2.** Bread soaked in broth or dripping ME.

1. Mountains of beef, and oceans of b. SCOTT. **2.** Drops o' fat on Owdham breawis 1857.

Brewster (brū·stəɹ). ME. [f. BREW *v.* + -STER; cf. *baxter*.] **1.** *orig.* A woman that brews. **2.** A brewer. *N. Eng.* and *Sc.* ME. **B. Sessions,** sessions for the issue of licences to trade in alcoholic liquors.

Brewsterite (brū·stěrəit). 1843. [f. Sir David *Brewster* + -ITE¹ 2 b.] A zeolitic mineral, belonging to the hydrous silicates, white in colour, and of uneven fracture.

Briar; see BRIER.

Briareus (brəi,ēᵊ·riŭs, brəi·ărĭus). 1606. Proper name of a hundred-handed giant of Gr. mythology; often used connotatively.

A gowtie B., many hands and no vse *Tr. & Cr.* I. ii. 30. Hence **Briarean** (-ī·ăn, -ēᵊ·riăn), of or relating to B.; hundred-handed. Also quasi-*sb.*

Bribable, bribeable (brəi·băb'l). 1829. [f. BRIBE *v.* + -ABLE; see also -BLE.] **A.** *adj.* Capable of being bribed. **B.** *sb.* [sc. *person.*] 1867. Hence **Bribabi·lity, bribe-,** venality.

Bribe (brəib), *sb.* ME. [f. BRIBE *v.*] † **1.** A thing stolen; robbery; plunder –1509. **2.** 'A reward given to pervert the judgment or corrupt the conduct' (J.) 1535. Also in *comb.*, as *b.-broker*. †**3.** (*perh.*) Rascally behaviour 1560.

2. His sonnes..tooke bribes, and peruerted iudgement 1 *Sam.* 8:3. His rise hath been his giving of large bribes PEPYS.

Bribe (brəib), *v.* ME. [– OFr. *briber*, also *brimber* beg, be a mendicant; of unkn. origin.] † **1.** *trans.* To take dishonestly; to extort –1643. Also † *absol.* **2.** To influence corruptly, by a consideration, the action of 1528. Also *absol.* **3.** To purchase by bribery 1718. **4.** *fig.* To gain over by some influence 1595.

2. To b. a trustee..is..to suborn him to be guilty of a breach or an abuse of trust BENTHAM. He fawned, bullied, and bribed indefatigably MACAULAY.

Bri·beless, *a.* 1608. [f. BRIBE + -LESS.] Free from bribes; incorruptible.

Briber (brəi·bəɹ). ME. [– AFr. *bribour*, OFr. *bribeur*, *brimbęur* beggar, vagabond; later f. the verb; see -ER¹.] † **1.** A strolling vagrant –1600. † **b.** Hence: Scoundrel, wretch –1550. † **2.** A thief; a taker of blackmail; an extortioner –1587. † **3.** An official who exacts or accepts bribes –1611. **4.** One who offers or gives a bribe 1583. † **5.** A thing that bribes. *Timon* III. v. 61.

Bribery (brəi·bəri). ME. [– OFr. *briberie*, *brimberie* mendicancy; see BRIBE *v.*, -ERY.] † **1.** Theft, robbery –1567. † **2.** Extortion –1589. **3.** The exaction or taking of a bribe (*arch.*) 1549. **4.** The offer or acceptance of bribes; *spec.* the application of such means to gain votes at an election 1570.

1. He knew of bribryes mo Than possible is to telle in yeres two CHAUCER. *Comb.* **b.-oath,** an oath administrable to a voter at a parliamentary election, declaring that he has not received a bribe for his vote.

‖ **Bric-à-brac** (bri·kăbræ:k). Also as one wd. 1840. [Fr., f. phr. † *à bric et à brac* at random.] Old curiosities, knick-knacks, antiquarian odds and ends, such as furniture, plate, china, etc. Also *attrib.*, and quasi-*adj.* (*joc.*)

Brick (brik), *sb.* 1416. [Late ME. *brik(e)*, *breke*, prob. introduced by Flemish workmen, – MLG., MDu. *bricke*, *brike*, Du. dial. *brik*, WFlem. *brijke*; whence also (O)Fr. *brique*, which prob. reinforced the adoption from LDu.; of unkn. origin.] **1.** A substance formed of clay, kneaded, moulded, and hardened by baking with fire, or sun-dried; used in building. **2.** A block of this substance, of a definite size and shape; usually rectangular († pl. *brick*) 1525. **b.** A similar block or slab of sand and lime, concrete, etc. 1875. **3.** *transf.* Any brick-shaped block, *e.g.* a b. of tea, of bread, etc. 1827. **4.** *fig.* (*colloq.*) A good fellow 1840. **5.** as *adj.* **a.** Of brick. **b.** Brick-shaped. 1440.

2. Goe to, let vs make bricke, and burne them thorowly *Gen.* 11: 3. **4.** Robert was no end of a b. 1870.

Phrases. *Like bricks, like a b.*: vigorously, with good will. *To drop a b.*: to commit an indiscretion (*slang*).

Comb.: **b.-box,** a box of wooden bricks for a child to build with; **-bread, -loaf** (see 3); **-burner,** one who attends to a b.-kiln; **-nog, -nogging,** a method of building in which a timber framework is filled in with brickwork; **-press,** a machine for consolidating the moulded clay; **-setter,** = BRICKLAYER; **-tea,** tea leaves pressed into the shape of a small b.; **-trimmer,** an arch of brickwork for receiving the hearth of a fireplace; **-yard,** a place where bricks are made.

Brick (brik), *v.* 1648. [f. the sb.] Mostly in comb. with advbs. **1.** To line, face, or pave with brick; to imitate brickwork on a plaster surface 1825. **2.** *intr.* To work with (load, make, etc.) bricks 1884.

1. *To b. up*: to close up with brickwork. *To b. over*: to cover with brick.

Brickbat (bri·kbæt). 1563. [See BRICK *sb.* and BAT *sb.*²] A piece (prop. less than one half) of a brick; a typical missile.

She sent a b. after him FOXE.

Brick-dust (bri·kdɒst). 1664. **1.** Powdered brick. **2.** A tint as of brick-dust 1807. Also *attrib.*

Brick-earth (bri·k,ɜ·ɹþ). 1667. Clay suitable for making bricks; in *Geol.* an earth lying below the surface soil in the London basin.

Bri·ck-field. 1801. A field in which bricks are made.

Brick-kiln (bri·k-kil). 1481. A kiln or furnace for burning bricks.

Bricklayer (bri·klēⁱ:əɹ). 1485. One who lays the bricks in building.

Bricklayer's itch: a cutaneous disease produced on the hands of bricklayers through contact with lime. So **Bri·cklaying,** the craft of building with brick.

Brickle (bri·k'l), *a.* Now *dial.* 1460. [Doublet of ME. *brüchel*; cf. *mickle*, *much*; f. (ult.) Gmc. **brekan* BREAK *v.*] Liable to break; brittle. Also *fig.* Hence † **Bri·ckleness.**

Bri·ckmaker. 1465. One whose trade is to make bricks. So **Bri·ckmaking.**

† **Brickwall,** *sb.* 1580. [Perversion of BRICOLE.] = BRICOLE *sb.* 2. So † **Bri·ckwall** *v.* to cause to rebound.

Bri·ckwork, brick work. 1580. **1.** Builders' work in brick. **2.** Bricklaying 1677. **3.** *pl.* A place where bricks are made 1703.

Bri·cky, *a.* 1596. [f. BRICK *sb.* + -Y¹.] **a.** Made or built of brick. **b.** Full of or abounding in bricks. **c.** Brick-red. Hence **Bri·ckiness.**

Bricole (bri·kəl, brikōᵘ·l) *sb.* 1525. [– (O)Fr. *bricole* – Pr. *bricola* or It. *briccola*, of unkn. origin.] **1.** An ancient military engine for throwing stones or bolts. **2.** In *Tennis*: The rebound of a ball from the wall of a tennis court, a side-stroke against the wall; also *fig.* an indirect unexpected stroke or action. Similarly in *Billiards*. Cf. BRICKWALL. 1598. **3.** Harness worn by men in drawing guns, where horses cannot be used 1864. Hence † **Bri·cole** *v.* to cause to rebound.

Brid, var. of BIRD, BRED, BURD.

Bridal (brəi·dăl), *sb.* (*a.*) [Late OE. *brȳdealu*, f. *brȳd* BRIDE (in attrib. use 'marriage', 'wedding') + *ealu* ALE, i.e. ale-drinking.] **1.** A wedding feast; a wedding. Now chiefly *poet.* **2.** Used attrib., after adjs. in *-al*, as *nuptial*, etc. 1440. **b.** Also as adj.: = Of or pertaining to a bride, worn by a bride; bride-like 1748.

1. The bridalis of Crist and of the Chirche WYCLIF *Song of Sol.* **2.** The b. day SPENSER, chamber SHAKS., bed 1714. Hence **Bri·dalty,** wedding (*rare*).

Bride (brəid), *sb.*¹ [OE. *brȳd* = OFris. *brēd*, *breid*, OS. *brūd* (Du. *bruid*), OHG. *brūt* (G. *braut*), ON. *brúðr*, Goth. *brūþs* :– Gmc. **brūðiz*, of unkn. origin.] **1.** A woman about to be married or very recently married. Also *fig.* † **2.** A bridegroom –1598.

1. Ripe to be a B. *Rom. & Jul.* I. ii. 11. *fig.* I will shew thee the B., the Lambes wife *Rev.* 21 : 9.

In combination, **Bride-** had orig. the force of 'bridal, wedding'; the sense 'bride' is modern. Hence: **b.-bed** (*arch.*); † **-belt,** the zone worn by a virgin; **-bowl** = BRIDE-CUP; **-cake**; **-chamber,** the room in which a wedding is celebrated; **-couple,** a newly-wedded pair; **-door,** the door of the BRIDEHOUSE; **-knot,** a wedding favour; † **-leader,** = the later BRIDEMAN; † **-mother,** one who acts the part of mother at a wedding; **-price,** money paid for a bride; † **-squire** = BRIDEMAN; **-stake,** a pole set up to dance round at a wedding; **-weed,** a bride's dress or veil; **-wort,** Meadow-sweet.

Bride (brəid), *sb.*² ME. [– (O)Fr. *bride* bridle, bonnet-string, ult. f. Gmc. **breʒd-*; see BRIDLE *sb.*] † **1.** A bridle, rein. Also *fig.* ME. only. **2.** The network which connects the patterns in lace; also, a bonnet-string 1869.

† **Bride** (brəid), *v.* 1530. [f. BRIDE *sb.*¹] **1.** *intr.* To act the bride. (Also with *it.*) –1652. **2.** *trans.* To wed –1658.

Bride-ale, bridale (brəi·d,ēⁱ:l). OE. [The analytical form of BRIDAL *sb.*] An ale-drinking at a wedding.

Bri·de-cup. *arch.* 1554. [f. *bride-* = wedding: see BRIDE *sb.*¹] **a.** A bowl handed round at a wedding. **b.** A spiced cup prepared at night for the bride-couple. Also *fig.*

Bridegroom (brəi·dgrūm). [OE. *brȳdguma* = OS. *brudigomo* (Du. *bruidegom*), OHG. *brūtigomo* (G. *bräutigam*), ON. *brúðgumi*; the second element OE. *guma* man, assim. to GROOM *sb.*] A man about to be, or just, married. Also *fig.*

He that hath the bryde is the brydegrome *John* 3:29. *fig.* For me the Heavenly B. waits TENNYSON.

Bri·dehouse. Now *dial.* 1550. [f. as BRIDECUP.] The house where a wedding is held.

Bri·de-lace. Now *Hist.* 1575. [f. as prec.] **1.** A piece of lace used to bind up the sprigs of rosemary formerly worn at weddings –1663. **2.** *pl.* The striped ribbon-grass, or Lady's Garters.

† **Bri·delope.** OE. [Late OE. *brȳdlōp*, perh. – ON. *brúðhlaup*; see LOPE.] The oldest Teut. name for wedding: *lit.* 'the bridal run', in conducting the bride to her new home. ? Only in OE.

Bri·deman. Now *dial.* 1613. [f. as BRIDECUP, or f. BRIDE *sb.*[1] 2.] † **1.** = BRIDEGROOM. **2.** Now = BRIDESMAN. (Formerly called also *brideleader*, because he led the bride to the bridegroom.) 1663.

Bridesmaid (brəi·dzmēɪd). 1552. [orig. *bridemaid*, f. *bride-* (see BRIDE *sb.*[1]); the *s* is 19th c.] A young unmarried woman or girl attending the bride at a wedding.

Bridesman (brəi·dzmæ̆n). 1808. [Altered from the earlier BRIDEMAN, q.v.] = BEST MAN, GROOMSMAN.

Bridewell (brəi·dwĕl). 1552. [From *Bride Well*, i.e. (*St.*) *Bride's Well* in London, near which stood a royal lodging, given by Edward VI for a hospital, and converted later into a house of correction.] A house of correction for prisoners; a gaol, prison. Also *fig.* and *attrib.*

Bridge (bridʒ), *sb.*[1] [OE. *bryċġ* = OFris. *brigge, bregge*, OS. *bruggia*, MDu. *brugghe* (Du. *brug*), OHG. *brucca* (G. *brücke*), ON. *bryggja* (whence north. Eng. dial. *brig* XII) :– Gmc. **bruʒjō*.] **1.** A structure forming or carrying a road over a river, a ravine, etc., or affording passage between two points at a height above the ground. (For the different kinds, as *chain-b.*, etc., see the first element of the compound.) **2. a.** A gangway for boats. **b.** A landing-stage, jetty, or pier. Now *dial.* ME. **3.** A narrow ridge of rock, sand, or shingle, across the bottom of a channel 1812. **4.** *Naut.* A raised platform, extending from side to side of a ship, for the officer in command. **5.** *Phys.* The upper bony part of the nose. Also the curved central part of a pair of spectacles, etc. 1450. **6.** *Mus.* **a.** In a violin, etc.: A thin upright piece of wood over which the strings are stretched, and which transmits their vibrations to the body of the instrument 1607. **b.** The ridge on a piano sound-board. **c.** The transition from the first to the second subject in sonata form; called also *b. passage*. **7.** In various specific and technical uses: *esp.* **a.** In a furnace or boiler: A low vertical partition which retains the fuel in its place, and deflects the flame, etc. 1838. **b.** *Electric b.*: a contrivance for measuring electrical resistance 1881.

1. Phr. *B. of boats*: a roadway supported by boats moored abreast across a body of water. *A gold* or *silver b.*; an easy and attractive way of escape.

Comb.: **b.-board,** a board into which the ends of the steps of wooden stairs are fastened (Gwilt); † **-bote,** a tax for the repair of bridges; **-deck** (see 4); **-head,** a fortification covering the end of a. b. nearest the enemy = Fr. *tête de pont*; **-islet,** a portion of land which becomes insular at high water; **-man** = BRIDGEMASTER; **-money** = *bridge-bote*; **-rail,** a rail having the form of a reversed U; **-stone,** a flag spanning a gutter, etc.; **-train,** a company of Military Engineers equipped with material and appliances for b.-building; **-tree,** a splinter-bar; also, the beam which supports the spindle of the runner in a grain mill; **-way,** the way formed by a b.; also, the waterway beneath it.

Bridge, *sb.*[2] 1886. [Said to have been played in Constantinople and the Near East, *c* 1870, and the name may be, therefore, of Levantine origin; the source of the earliest (seemingly Russian) form *biritch* is unknown.] A game resembling dummy whist, in which in each deal the dealer's partner is dummy, his hand being exposed and played by the dealer.

Auction b., a variety in which the right to name trumps, etc. goes to the player who undertakes to make the highest score. *Contract b.*, a form of this.

Bridge (bridʒ), *v.*[1] [OE. *bryċġian*, f. *bryċġ* BRIDGE *sb.*[1]] **1.** To make a bridge over; to span with a means of passage. **b.** To span as with a bridge 1872. Also *fig.* **2.** To form (a way) by means of a bridge 1667.

1. An arch of ice..bridging a fissure KANE. **2.** Xerxes..Over Hellespont Bridging his way MILT.

† **Bridge,** *v.*[2] ME. [aphet. f. ABRIDGE.] To abridge. Also *absol.* –1526.

Bri·dge-house. ME. A house connected with a bridge; *spec.* the house with its officers, etc., formerly connected with the care and repair of London Bridge.

Bri·dgemaster. 1502. An officer having control of a bridge; formerly, in some boroughs, a member of the corporation; a *bridgeman*.

Bridgetin (bri·dʒĕtin). 1533. [– med.L. *Brigittinus*, f. *Brigitta* Bridget + *-inus* -IN[2], -INE[4], as in BEGUINE.] One of a religious order founded by St. Bridget in the 14th century.

Bridgeward (bri·dʒ,wǭːɹd), *sb.* OE. [WARD *sb.*] **1.** The warden or wardship of a bridge. **2.** The main ward of a key.

† **Bri·dgewater.** 1552. A woollen cloth formerly made at Bridgewater –1607.

Bridging (bri·dʒiŋ), *vbl. sb.* 1839. [f. BRIDGE *v.*[1] or *sb.*[1] + -ING[1].] **1.** The action of BRIDGE *v.*[1] **2.** Bridges viewed as work 1884. **b.** *Carpentry.* A bridging piece 1850.

Comb.: **b.-floor,** a floor having bridging joists; **-joist,** a joist of a flooring resting upon the binding-joists below, and supporting the boarding above; **-piece,** a piece placed between two opposite beams to prevent their nearer approach.

Bridle (brəi·d'l), *sb.* [OE. *brīdel* (:– **briġdel*), corresp. to OFris. *brīdel*, (M)Du. *breidel*, OHG. *brittil*; WGmc. deriv. of **breʒd-*; see BRAID, -LE.] **1.** The head-gear, consisting of a head-stall, bit, and rein, by which a horse, etc., is controlled and guided. Also *fig.* **2.** *fig.* A restraint, curb, check ME. **3.** = BRANKS 1. 1623. **4.** The gesture of bridling (see BRIDLE *v.* 3) 1748. **5.** Anything resembling a bridle in form or use: *esp.* **a.** *Naut.* A mooring-cable or 'fast' 1626. **b.** *Firearms.* The plate inside a gun-lock, which holds the sear and tumbler in position 1844.

1. *fig.* Giving the b. to a desperate man NORTH. **2.** A brydel of lawe..& also a brydell of the drede of God 1530.

Comb.: **b.-arm** (cf. *bridle-hand*); **-bridge** (cf. *bridle-path*); **-cable,** a cable attached to the middle of a ground cable; **-gate,** one leading into a b.-path; **-hand,** the left hand, which holds the b. in riding; **-path, -road, -way,** a path fit for the passage of a horse, but not of vehicles; **-port,** a port in a ship's bow through which bridles (see 5a) may be run or chase-guns fired; **-rein,** a rein attached to the bit.

Bridle (brəi·d'l), *v.* [OE. *brīdlian*, f. prec.] **1.** To put a bridle on (a horse); to furnish with a bridle ME. **2.** *fig.* To curb, check, hold *in* OE. **3.** *trans.* and *intr.* To throw up the head and draw in the chin (as a horse does when reined in), expressing pride, vanity, or resentment. Now usu. *To b. up.* 1460.

1. To be taught to saddle and b. 1833. **2.** Rise.. And b. in thy headlong wave MILT. *Comus* 887. Forts..to b. Rochelle HUME. **3.** Everybody bridled up at this remark DICKENS. Hence **Bri·dler,** one who bridles; † a bridle-maker.

Bridoon (bridū·n). 1753. [– Fr. *bridon*, f. *bride* BRIDE *sb.*[2]; see -OON.] The snaffle and rein of a military bridle, which acts with or independently of the bit.

Brief (brīf), *sb.* [ME. *bref, brefe* – AFr. *bref*, OFr. *brief* :– L. *breve*, n. of *brevis* short, brief. See next.] † **1.** A writing issued by official or legal authority; a royal mandate; a writ, a summons. (tr. L. *breve* in legal senses.) –1641. **2.** A letter of the pope, less ample and solemn than a *bull*, and differing from it in form. More fully called *apostolical* or *papal b.* 1460. **3.** A letter patent issued by the sovereign as Head of the Church, licensing a collection in the churches throughout England for a specified object; a *Church B.* or *Kings' Letter. Obs.* in practice. 1588. † **4.** A letter, dispatch, note –1652. † **5.** An abridgement, epitome –1691. Also *fig.* † **6.** A list; an invoice, memorandum –1849. **7.** *Law.* A summary of facts and points of law, drawn up for counsel in charge of a case 1631. † **8.** *Mus.* = BREVE *sb.* 2. –1658.

3. Briefes for a gathering towards the erecting of a colledge 1588. **6.** *Mids. N.* V. i. 42. **7.** *To hold a b.*: to be retained as counsel *for*. *To take a b.*: to accept the conduct of a case. Hence **Brie·fless** *a.* holding no briefs, unemployed. **Brie·flessness.**

Brief (brīf). [Late ME. *bref* – AFr. *bref* = OFr. *brief* (mod. *bref*) :– L. *brevis* short, brief.] **A.** *adj.* **1.** Of short duration. **2.** Concise ME. **b.** Curt in manner (*rare*). SCOTT. **3.** Short, curtailed, limited in space. (Less usual.) 1668. Also † *fig.* ¶ **4.** Rife; as an epidemic disease (*dial.*) (Of obscure origin.) 1595.

1. Out, out, breefe Candle *Macb.* V. v. 23. † *To be b.*, i.e. expeditious *Tr. & Cr.* IV. v. 237. **2.** Breefe Chronicles *Haml.* II. ii. 548. *To be b.*: to speak concisely. **3.** *fig. Cymb.* V. v. 165.

B. quasi-*sb.* **a.** *In b.*: in few words. With ellipsis of 'to speak': To sum up. ME. † **b.** *The b.*, used *absol.* like *the short* –1601. **C.** quasi-*adv.* **a.** Shortly, quickly; in few words 1557. **b.** In brief 1600.

Hence **Brie·fly** *adv.* shortly, in few words; † within a short time. **Brie·fness,** † celerity (*Lear* II. i. 20); brevity.

† **Brief,** *v.*[1] 1601. [f. prec.] To shorten, abridge –1655.

Brief (brīf), *v.*[2] 1837. [f. BRIEF *sb.*, sense 7.] **1.** To reduce to the form of a counsel's brief. **2.** To put (instructions) into the form of a brief *to* a barrister. Also *fig.* 1864. **3.** To give a brief to (a barrister); to retain 1862.

Brier, briar (brəiᵊɹ, brəi·əɹ), **brere** (brīᵊɹ), *sb.*[1] [OE. (Anglian) *brēr*, (WS.) *brǣr*, of unkn. origin; for the vocalism cf. *friar, quire*.] **1.** Any prickly, thorny bush or shrub; now usu. a wild rose bush. **2.** Brier-bushes collectively ME. **3.** A twig, or † thorn of a brier ME. **4.** *fig.* (*pl.*) Vexations 1509.

1. Sweet is the Rose, but growes upon a brere SPENSER.

Comb.: **Sweet B.,** a species of wild Rose (*R. rubiginosa*) with fragrant leaves; **Austrian B.,** *R. lutea*; **Green B.,** *Smilax retundifolia*; **Sensitive B.,** the genus *Schronkia*. **B.-rose, -tree,** the Dog-rose. Hence **Bri·ered, bri·ared** *ppl. a.* entangled in or covered with briers. Also *fig.* **Bri·ery, bri·ary** *a.* full of or consisting of briers; *fig.* vexing.

Brier, briar (brəi·əɹ), *sb.*[2] 1868. [In earliest exx. *bruyer* – (O)Fr. *bruyère* heath :– Gallo-Rom. **brūcaria*, f. **brūcus* – Gaulish **brūko*; assim. in form to prec.] The White Heath (*Erica arborea*), the root of which is used for making tobacco-pipes; also a pipe of this wood. So **B.-root, -wood.**

Brieve (brīv). 1609. [var. of BRIEF *sb.*] *Sc. Law.* A writ or precept issued from Chancery in the Sovereign's name, directing trial to be made of certain points specified.

Brig (brig). 1720. [Shortening of BRIGANTINE.] **a.** = BRIGANTINE 1. **b.** A vessel with two masts square-rigged like a ship's fore- and main-masts, but carrying also on her main-mast a lower fore-and-aft sail with a gaff and boom. (The changes in rig have accompanied the shortened name only.) 1769. **c.** A 'hermaphrodite brig'; = BRIGANTINE 3. *Comb.* **b.-schooner,** a hermaphrodite b., or brigantine.

Brig, north. f. BRIDGE.

Brigade (brigēɪ·d), *sb.* 1637. [– (O)Fr. *brigade* – It. *brigata* troop, company, f. *brigare* be busy with, f. *briga* strife, contention; see -ADE.] † **1.** A crew of people –1650. **2.** *gen.* A large division of troops 1649. **b.** *spec.* A subdivision of an army, formerly two regiments or squadrons; but now of variable composition. In the British Army, at present used only of the Horse and Field Artillery. **3.** A band of persons more or less organized; e.g. a *fire-b.*, etc. 1806.

2. a. Thither..A numerous Brigad hasten'd MILT. *P.L.* I. 675. *Comb.* **b.-major,** a staff officer attached to a brigade, who assists the brigadier in command.

Brigade (brigēɪ·d), *v.* 1805. [f. prec.] **1.** *trans.* To form into a brigade or brigades. **2.** *loosely,* To form (people) as if into a brigade; to combine 1859.

Brigadier (brigădiᵊ·ɹ). 1678. [– Fr. *brigadier*, f. *brigade*; see prec., -IER.] **1. B.-General:** A military officer in command of a brigade; the rank was abolished after the war of 1914–18, being superseded by *colonel-commandant*, which was replaced by *b.* in 1928. † **2.** *B-wig*: a full wig tied back in two curls –1818.

Brigand (bri·gănd). ME. [– (O)Fr. *brigand* – It. *brigante*, orig. foot-soldier, subst. use of pres. pple. of *brigare* contend; see BRIGADE.] † **1.** A light-armed, irregular foot-soldier –1795. **2.** One who lives by pillage and robbery: a bandit; *esp.* a member of one of the gangs infesting districts of Italy, Spain, Turkey, etc. ME. Also *attrib.* Hence **Bri·gandish** *a.* **Bri·gandishly** *adv.* **Bri·gandism.**

Brigandage (bri·gănděd3). 1600. [– Fr. *brigandage*; see prec., -AGE.] **1.** The practice of brigands; highway-robbery, freebooting, pillage. **2.** Brigands collectively 1875.

1. The b. of the Free Companies SCOTT.

† **Bri·gander.** ME. [– AL. *brigandera* (XV), var. of *brigandina* BRIGANDINE.] **1.** = BRIGANDINE 1. –1611. **2.** A soldier wearing a brigander 1525.

Brigandine, brigantine (bri·găndīn, -tīn). [– (O)Fr. *brigandine*, or its source It. *brigantina*, in med.L. *brigandina*, *-tina*; see BRIGAND, -INE[3].] Body armour composed of iron rings or plates, sewed upon, and covered with, canvas, linen, or leather; at first worn in two halves; loosely = 'coat of mail, corslet' 1456. Also *attrib.*

Put on the brigandines *Jer.* 46:4. MILT. *Sams.* 1120.

Brigantine[1] (bri·găntīn). 1525. [– OFr. *brigandine* (mod. *brigantin* after It.), or its source It. *brigantino*, f. *brigante*; see BRIGAND, -INE[3].] **1.** *orig.* A small vessel equipped both for sailing and rowing, employed for purposes of piracy, espionage, landing, etc. Only *Hist.* **2.** Applied (loosely) to other similar vessels. Still *poet.* and *rhet.* 1552. **3.** A two-masted vessel, with a brig's foremast, square-rigged, and a schooner's main-mast, fore-and-aft-rigged 1695.

Brigantine[2], var. of BRIGANDINE.

Bright (brəit). Comp. *brighter*, *-est*. [OE. *beorht*, Anglian *berht*, late Northumb. *breht* = OS. *ber(a)ht*, OHG. *beraht*, *-eht*, ON. *bjartr*, Goth. *bairhts* :- Gmc. **berχtaz*.) **A.** *adj.* (The opposite to *dull*.) **1.** Shining; emitting, reflecting, or pervaded by much light. **b.** *fig.* Lit up with happiness, gladness, or hope 1751. † **2.** Clear to the mind –1741. **3.** Of persons: 'Resplendent with charms' (J.); fair (*arch.*) ME. **4.** Of vivid colour ME. **5.** Of sounds: Clear, shrill ME. **6.** Illustrious, splendid. (L. *clarus*). OE. **7.** Lively, brilliant, vivacious; opp. to *dull* 1605. **8.** Quick-witted, clever; keen. (Used chiefly of one's inferiors or children.) 1741.

1. A b. starre SHAKS., swerde ME., evening POPE, transparent Æther STEELE. 3. Angels are b. still, though the brightest fell *Macb.* IV. iii. 22. 4. The brightest Bay DRYDEN. Strange b. birds HEMANS. 6. The wisest, brightest, meanest of mankind Pope. 7. B. and Iouiall SHAKS. B. thoughts O. W. HOLMES. 8. A b. specimen! (Ironical.) (*mod.*). A b. look-out R. DANA. Hence **Bri·ghtly** *adv.*

B. *sb.* Brightness, light. *arch.* (*poet.*) ME. Dark with excessive b. MILT. *P.L.* III. 380.

Bright (brəit), *adv.* [OE. *beorhte*, f. the adj., with adverbial *-e*, lost *c* 1400.] **1.** = Brightly. **2.** *Comb.*, as *b.-burning*, etc. 1588.

† **Bright,** *v.* [OE. *beorhtian*, f. *beorht* bright.] **1.** *intr.* To shine bright –ME. **2.** *trans.* To make bright –1686.

Brighten (brəi·t'n), *v.* [f. BRIGHT *a.* + -EN[5].] **1.** *trans.* To make bright 1583. Also *fig.* **2.** *intr.* To become bright; to shine ME. Also *fig.* (see BRIGHT *a.*).

1. To b. up the skies DRYDEN. Joy Bright'ns his crest MILT. *P.L.* IX. 634. 2. The boy's eyes.. Brighten'd BYRON.

Brightness (brəi·tnės). [OE. *beorhtnes*, *brehtnis*; see -NESS.] The quality of being bright (see BRIGHT *a.*).

Bright's Disease. [f. Dr. R. *Bright* (1827).] *Med.* 'A generic term including several forms of acute and chronic disease of the kidney usually associated with albumen in the urine'; granular degeneration of the kidneys.

Bri·ghtsome, *a. arch.* 1558. [f. BRIGHT *a.* + -SOME[1].] Partaking of brightness, bright-looking. (Vaguer than *bright*.)

† **Bri·gous,** *a.* ME. [– AFr. **brigous* = OFr. *brigeus*, med.L. *brigosus*; see next, -OUS.] Of or pertaining to strife; contentious –1519. var. † **Bri·gose.**

‖ **Brigue** (brig), *sb.* ME. [– (O)Fr. *brigue* – It. *briga* (in med.L. *briga*, XIII); see BRIGADE.] † **1.** Strife, contention –1678. ‖ **2.** Intrigue, faction. [From mod.Fr.] *Obs.* (exc. casually). 1701.

† **Brigue** (brig), *v.* ME. [Sense 2 – Fr. *briguer* (XVI) or f. prec. (in med.L. *brigare* brawl XIV). For sense 1, cf. BRIKE.] † **1.** To ensnare, beguile. ME. only. **2.** *intr.* To intrigue; to canvass –1808.

† **Brike.** ME. only. [– ONFr. *brique*, var. of *briche*, *brice*, trap.] A trap, a snare; a dilemma.

Brill (bril), *sb.* 1481. [Also *brell*, *prylle* (XV), *prill* (XVII), *pearl* (XVII–XIX); of unkn. origin.] A flat-fish (*Rhombus vulgaris*), allied to the Turbot.

‖ **Brillante** (brilla·nte), *a.* [It.] *Mus.* Gay, showy, and sparkling in style.

Brilliance (bri·lyăns). 1755. [f. BRILLIANT; see -ANCE.] Intense or sparkling brightness, radiance, or splendour. Also *fig.*

The b. of a lamp HOWELLS. B. of mind 1842.

Brilliancy (bri·lyănsi). 1747. [f. as prec.; see -ANCY.] The quality of being brilliant; shining quality.

She is full of b. MISS MITFORD. The comparative b. of two colours 1887.

Brilliant (bri·lyănt), *a.* (*sb.*) 1681. [– Fr. *brillant*, pres. pple. of *briller* shine – It. *brillare*, of unkn. origin.] Brightly shining, glittering, sparkling, lustrous. Also *fig.* of qualities, actions, and persons.

fig. A man of solid though not b. parts MACAULAY. A b. circle of noblemen and gentlemen MACAULAY. Hence **Bri·lliant-ly** *adv.*, **-ness.**

† **B.** as *sb.* = BRILLIANCY –1694.

Bri·lliant, *sb.* 1690. [– Fr. *brillant* adj. used subst.; see prec.] **1.** A diamond of the finest cut and brilliancy. Also *attrib.* and in *comb.*

(The *brilliant* differs from the *rose* in having horizontal faces on its upper and under sides, called the *table* and the *collet* respectively, which are surrounded and united by facets. The French brilliant consists of two truncated pyramids placed base to base.)

† **2.** A kind of silken fabric 1719. **3.** A firework 1875. **4.** The smallest type used in Eng. printing, being a size less than 'diamond'. (Cf. *pearl*, *ruby*, etc.) 1875.

Brilliant type.

Bri·lliant, *v. rare.* 1752. [f. BRILLIANT *a.*] To cut as a brilliant.

† **Brim,** *sb.*[1] [OE. *brim* surf, (poet.) the sea = ON. *brim*, prob. f. *brem-* roar, rage; see BRIM *v.*[1]] The sea; also 'flood', water –1596.

Brim (brim), *sb.*[2] [ME. *brimme*, *brymme*, of unc. etym., corresp. in sense to MHG. *brem* (G. *bräme*, *brähme*), ON. *barmr* edge; cf. MLG. *vorbrēmen*, G. *verbrähmen* provide with a border or edge.] † **1.** *orig.* The border, margin, edge, or brink, as of the sea or of any piece of water –1597; also, of other things (*arch.* or *dial.*) 1525. Also † *fig.* **2.** Now *esp.* The edge, margin, or lip of a cup, bowl, basin, or the like 1562. **3.** The upper edge or surface of water (*arch.* or *poet.*) 1552. **4.** The marginal rim of a hat 1592.

1. Let thy love hang at thy hearts bottome, not at the tongues brimme LYLY. 2. A molten Sea of ten cubites, from b. to b. 2 *Chron.* 4:2. 3. The feet of the Priestes..were dipped in the brimme of the water *Josh.* 3:15. Hence **Brim-full, brimful** (prop. pronounced (bri·m,fu·l); erron. (bri·mful), after *mindful*, etc.), full to the brim; on the point of overflowing. **Brimfully** *adv.* (*rare*). **Bri·mless** *a.*

Brim (brim), *v.*[1] [In XV *brymme*, in XVI and mod. dial. *breme*, repr. OE. *bremmen*, roar, rage = OS. *bremmia*, OHG. *breman* (MLG., MHG. *brimmen*, *brummen*, MLG. *brammen*); f. Gmc. **brem-*, an echoic element prob. repr. by L. *fremere*.] **1.** *intr.* Of swine: To be in heat, rut, copulate. **2.** *trans.* Said of a boar 1552.

Brim (brim), *v.*[2] 1611. [f. BRIM *sb.*[2]] **1.** To fill to the brim. Also *absol.* Also *fig.* and *transf.* **2.** *intr.* To be or become brim-full 1818. † **3.** To provide with a brim 1623.

1. Arrange the board and b. the glass TENNYSON.

‖ **Brimborion, -um.** 1653. [Fr., earlier *breborion*, perversion of med.L. *breviarium* BREVIARY.] A thing without use or value; trash, nonsense.

Brimmed (brimd, bri·mėd), *ppl. a.* 1606. [f. BRIM *v.*[2] and *sb.*[2]] **1.** Filled to the brim; brim-full 1624. **2.** Having a brim, as a hat, etc. Chiefly in *comb.*, as *broad-b.*, etc. 1606.

Brimmer (bri·məɹ), *sb.* 1652. [f. BRIM *v.*[2] + -ER[1].] **1.** That which fills to the brim. **2.** A brimming goblet 1663. † **3.** A hat with a brim –1670.

2. Boy! Fill a B., Nay fuller yet COWLEY.

Bri·mming, *ppl. a.* 1667. [f. BRIM *v.*[2] + -ING[2].] **1.** That rises to the brim of its vessel, basin, or bed. Also *fig.* **2.** Of a vessel: Full to overflowing 1697. Also *advb.*

1. The b. stream MILT. 2. A b. pail DRYDEN. Hence **Bri·mmingly** *adv.*

Brimse. Now *dial.* 1579. [prob. – ON. *brims*; cf. OHG. *primissa*, G. *bremse*, and without *-s* OS. *bremmia*, G. *breme*; prob. f. Gmc. **brem-*; see BRIM *v.*[1]] A gadfly; = BREEZE *sb.*[1]

Brimstone (bri·mstən). ME. [prob. f. OE. *bryne* (= ON. *bruni*) burning (f. **burn-* BURN *v.*[1]) + STONE.] **1.** Formerly the common vernacular name for SULPHUR. Now used chiefly when referring to its inflammable character, and to the use in *Gen.* 19:24 and *Rev.* 19:20. Also *fig.* **2.** A virago, spitfire. 1751. **3.** *B. Butterfly*: a butterfly with wings of a sulphur colour, *Gonepteryx rhamni* 1827.

Comb.: **b. match**, one having its end dipped in b.; **b. moth**, one of sulphur colour, *Rumia cratægata*; **b.-wort**, Sulphur-wort, *Peucedanum palustre* (and *officinale*). Hence **Bri·mstony** *a.*

Brinded (bri·ndėd), *a. arch.* ME. [Earlier *brended* (XV), f. †*brende* (Lydgate), prob. of Scand. origin (cf. ON. *bröndóttr* brindled, f. *brandr* burning, and *brandkrossóttr* brindled, with a white cross on the forehead).] Of a tawny or brownish colour, marked with bars of a different hue; *gen.* streaked, spotted; brindled.

The b. Cat SHAKS., lioness SHELLEY.

Brindle (bri·nd'l). 1676. [Deduced from next.] **A.** *adj.* = BRINDED, BRINDLED. **B.** *sb.* **a.** Brindled colour. **b.** A brindled dog. 1696.

Brindled (bri·nd'ld), *a.* 1678. [alt. of BRINDED, prob. by assoc. w. *grizzled*, *speckled*.] 'Streaked, tabby, marked with streaks' (J.).

Brine (brəin), *sb.* [OE. *brine* = MDu. *brine* (Du. *brijn*), of unkn. origin.] **1.** Water saturated, or strongly impregnated, with salt; salt water. **2.** The water of the sea; the sea. (Usu. *poet.*) 1598. **3.** = Briny tears (*poet.*) 1592.

2. On the level b. Sleek Panope with all her sisters played MILT. *Lycidas*. 3. I should be well seasoned, for mine eyes lye in b. DEKKER.

Comb.: **b.-gauge**, a salinometer; **-pan**, a shallow iron vessel in which b. is evaporated; **-pump**, a pump used to remove b. from a steamer's boilers; **-seeth**, a salt boilery; **-shrimp, -worm**, *Cancer Salinus* (Linn.), a small shrimp or worm which peoples reservoirs of b.; **-smeller**, one who prospects for beds of salt; **-valve**, a valve in a boiler which is opened to allow the escape of b.

Brine (brəin), *v.* 1552. [f. BRINE *sb.*] To treat with brine.

To b. Fields 1677, wheat 1722, hides 1883.

Bring (briŋ), *v.* Pa. t. and pple. **brought** (brǭt). [OE. *bringan* (pa. t. *brōhte*, pple. *brōht*) = OFris. *bringa*, OS., OHG. *bringan* (Du. *brengen*, G. *bringen*), Goth. *briggan* :- Gmc. **breŋʒan*.] **1.** To cause to come along with oneself; to fetch. In sense the causal of *come*. **2.** To escort (a person) on his way. Now *dial.* 1450. **3.** *fig.* To cause one to have; to procure 1450. † **4.** To deduce, infer –1713. **5.** To prefer or lay (a charge, etc.); to set on foot (an action at law); to adduce (a statement, etc.) OE. **6.** † **a.** = *Bring forth* –1795. **b.** = *Bring in* 1535. **7.** *fig.* To cause to come *from*, *into*, *out of*, *to*, etc., or *to be* or *do* something; to cause to become (see quots.) ME. **8.** To cause to come (to a certain course of action, etc.); to induce, persuade 1611. **9.** *Naut.* To cause to come or go into a certain position or direction, as *to the wind* (see WIND).

1. To b. Trophies home DRYDEN, ships to land 1565. What brings him here? 1887. Phr. *To b. an answer, word, tidings.* 2. *Gen.* 18:16. 3. *fig.* Those lines..brought tears into the Duchess's eyes THACKERAY. The loss that brought us pain TENNYSON. 5. To b. an action BLACKSTONE. *To b. home*: see HOME. 6. b. So much money as [a thing] will b. BUTLER *Hud.* II. i. 466. 7. To b. into hatred HOOKER, into difficulties BUTLER, in question 1818; to b. [a man] to himself (= to his senses) CHAUCER. So *to b. to an end, head, issue, to bearings, to nought, shame, to remembrance, to bed* (see BED); *to b. to bear, boil, to pass.*

Combined with adverbs. **B. about. a.** To cause to happen, effect. **b.** To turn round; *fig.* to convert. **c.** = *bring round.* **B. down. a.** To cause to fall to the ground; to kill or wound (a flying bird, etc.). **b.** To cause (punishments, etc.) to alight *on, upon.* **c.** *fig.* To humble. **d.** To lower (price); to simplify. **e.** To continue (information, etc.) to a later date (cf. *Bring up*). **f.** *To bring down the house*, etc.: to evoke applause which suggests the downfall of the building. **B. forth. a.** To give birth to, bear, yield. † **b.** To utter; advance *Isa.* 41:21. † **c.** To bring to public view. *Macb.* III. iv. 125. **B. forward.** *Book-keeping.* To carry on a sum from the bottom of one folio to the top of another. **B. in. a.** To introduce (customs, etc.). **b.** To bring (money) into the purse or pocket. **c.** To introduce (a bill, etc.). **d.** To introduce (into consideration); to adduce. **e.** Of a jury: *colloq.* to find (guilty, etc.). **B. off. a.** To bring away from; *esp.* by boat from a ship, wreck, the shore 1656. **b.** To rescue, acquit (*arch.*). **B. on.** † **a.** To conduct; to advance the growth of. **b.** To cause (illness, etc.). **c.** To introduce (a subject, etc.). **d.** *techn.* To join, weld together. **B. out. a.** To utter. **b.** To bring into prominence; to develop. **c.** To introduce (a young lady, a company, a loan, etc.). **d.** To produce (a play, etc.); to publish (a book). **B. over.** To cause to come to one's own side or party. **B. round.** To restore from a fainting-fit or an attack of illness. **B. through.** *spec.* To treat successfully through the stages of an illness. **B. to. a.** *Naut.* To tie, bend. **b.** To cause to come to a standstill. Also *intr.* (for *refl.* or *absol.*). † **c.** To cause to acquiesce. **d.** To restore to consciousness or to health. **B. under.** To subdue. **B. up. a.** To raise, rear, build up; to raise to a point or amount, etc. **b.** To rear; to educate. **c.** To bring before a tribunal or for examination. **d.** *Naut.* To bring to anchor, or to a standstill. Also *intr.*, whence 'to stop, pull up'. **e.** To bring under notice or consideration (*esp.* a by-gone matter). **f.** To vomit (*colloq.*). **g.** *B. up the rear* (*arrear*): see REAR.

Bringer (bri·ŋəɹ). ME. [f. prec. + -ER[1].] One who or that which brings (see BRING *v.*).

The first b. of vnwelcome newes 2 *Hen. IV*, I. i. 100.

Brinish (brəi·niʃ), *a.* 1580. [f. BRINE *sb.* + -ISH[1].] 1. Of the nature of brine; saltish; of or pertaining to the sea 1588. 2. *fig.* Bitter 1580.

‖ **Brinjal, -jaul** (bri·ndʒǫl). 1611. [Anglo-Ind., (ult.) – Pg. *berinjela* = Sp. *berenjena*; see AUBERGINE.] The fruit of the Egg-plant (*Solanum melongena*).

‖ **Brinjarry** (brindʒā·ri). *Anglo-Ind.* 1793. [– Urdu *banjārā*, prob. based on Skr. *vaṇij* (*baṇij*) trader, trade.] A travelling grain and salt merchant of the Deccan.

Brink (briŋk). [ME. *brink, brenk* – ON. **brenkōn* (in OIcel. *brekka* slope), corresp. to MLG. *brink* edge of a field, (brow of) a hill (whence G. dial. *brink* hill), MDu. *brinc* (Du. *brink* grassland), of unkn. origin.] 1. The edge, margin, or border of a steep place, *e.g.* a precipice, chasm, grave. (The specific current sense.) 2. The edge of the land bordering a piece of water: formerly = 'bank, shore, brim'; now *esp.* when this is steep ME. 3. = BRIM 4. Now *dial.* ME. 4. *gen.* A margin, border, edge (*arch.*) ME. 5. *fig.* The very verge of some state, time, event, or action (see quots.) ME.

2. A ryall cite vpon the brinke of twede CAXTON. 5. The b. of eternity BARROW, of destruction DE FOE, ruin SWIFT, absurdity JOHNSON.

Briny (brəi·ni), *a.*[1] 1608. [f. BRINE *sb.* + -Y[1].] Of or pertaining to brine or to the sea; saturated with salt.

The b. Flood 1697. B. marshes 1799.

Briny, *a.*[2] (? *sb.*) 1602. [Cf. OE. *bryne* burning, also *burning* (XVII–XVIII), *briming* (XIX) phosphorescence of the sea.] Phosphorescent, ? phosphorescence.

‖ **Brio** (brī·o). 1855. [It.] Liveliness, go.

Brionine, Briony, vars. of BRYONIN(E), BRYONY.

‖ **Briquette, briquet** (brike·t, bri·kėt). 1883. [Fr., dim. of *brique* BRICK; see -ETTE.] 1. A block of artificial stone. 2. A brick-shaped block of artificial coal 1884.

Brisk (brisk), *a.* 1592. [prob. – Fr. *brusque* BRUSQUE, but connection of sense is not clear. W. *brysg*, Gael. *brisg*, Ir. *brisc* are from Eng.] 1. Sharp or smart in regard to movement (in a praiseworthy sense). 2. In allied senses, chiefly unfavourable, and mostly obs. (See quots.) 1601. † 3. Spruce –1603. 4. Of liquors: Effervescent. Of the air: Fresh, keen. 1597.

1. Young b. fellows DE FOE. A b. cannonade 1855, traffic 1833, gale 1759, fire 1837. 2. Briske and giddy-paced times *Twel. N.* II. iv. 6. A b. (= 'sharp') letter 1700. Hence **Bri·skish** *a.* **Bri·skly** *adv.* **Bri·skness.** † **Bri·sky** *a.* *Mids. N.* III. i. 97.

Brisk (brisk), *v.* 1592. [f. prec.] 1. To make brisk. Now with *up.* 1628. Also *intr.* (for *refl.*) 2. *trans.* † To smarten *up* –1710. Also *intr.* (for *refl.*) 1637.

1. I like a cup to briske the spirits FELTHAM. *To b. up* (intr.): to come up briskly. *To b. about* (intr.): to move about briskly.

Brisket (bri·skėt). 1450. [– AFr. **brusket*, **brisket*, vars. of OFr. *bruschet*, **brischet*, *bruchet*, *brichet* (mod. *bréchet*), perh. – ON. *brjósk* (Norw., Da. *brusk* cartilage, gristle; see -ET.] The breast of an animal, the part covering the breast-bone, esp. as a joint.

Brisling (bri·sliŋ). 1902. [– Norw., Da. *brisling* sprat.] A small Norw. fish of the herring family resembling a sardine.

Bristle (bri·s'l), *sb.* [ME. *brüstel*, *bristel*, *brestel*, pointing to OE. **brystel*, **byrstel*, corresp. to OS. **brustil*, (M)Du. *borstel*, deriv. of the base repr. by OE. *byrst* bristle, OS. *brusta*, OHG. *burst* (in MHG., G. *borste*), ON. *burst*, *bursti*. See -EL[1].] 1. *prop.* One of the stiff hairs that grow on the back of the hog and wild boar. 2. *gen.* Any short, stiff, pointed or prickly hair ME. 3. In plants: A seta 1731.

Comb.: **b.-fern,** *Trichomanes radicans*; **-grass,** the genus *Setaria*; **-moss,** the genus *Orthotrichum*.

Bristle (bri·s'l), *v.*[1] 1480. [f. prec. sb. See BRUSTLE *v.*] I. *intr.* 1. Of hair, quills, etc.: To be, become, or stand, stiff and bristly. 2. Of animals: To raise the bristles, as a sign of anger or excitement. b. Of persons: To show fight. Also with *up.* 1549. 3. To be or become bristly. Also *fig.* 1600.

2. Don't b. up like a hedgehog 1861. 3. France.. bristles with bayonets 1837. To b. with difficulties 1875.

II. *trans.* 1. To erect stiffly (hair, etc.) like bristles: chiefly in anger. Also with *up.* 1595. Also *fig.* 2. To furnish with bristles 1678.

1. Now..Doth dogged warre b. his angry crest *K. John* IV. iii. 149.

Bri·stle, *v.*[2] Now *dial.* 1483. [*Brissle*, *bristle* (XV–XIX, with unrounded vowel, as in BRISK *a.*), later *brussle*, *brustle* – OFr. *brusler* (mod. *brûler*) burn.] To make or become crisp with heat.

Bristletail (bri·s'ltēil). 1706. A wingless insect (*Machilis maritima*) having bristly caudal appendages.

Bristly (bri·sli), *a.* 1591. [f. BRISTLE *sb.* + -Y[1].] 1. Set with bristles or short stiff hairs; setose. Also *fig.* 2. Of the nature of or like bristles 1592. Hence **Bri·stliness.**

Bristol (bri·stəl). 1. A city of England upon the Lower Avon, giving its name to various products. 2. Short for 'Bristol-stone'; see 3. 1618. 3. *attrib.*, as **B.-board,** a kind of paste-board with a smooth surface; **-brick,** a brick of siliceous material, used for cleaning cutlery; **-diamond, -gem, -stone,** transparent rock-crystal found in the Clifton limestone near Bristol; also *attrib.*; **-fashion** (*Naut.*), in good order; **B. milk,** rich sherry.

Brisure (brizü·r, bri·ʒ[i]ŭɹ). 1623. [– Fr. *brisure* fracture.] 1. *Her.* A difference. 2. *Fortif.* A break in the general direction of a rampart or parapet 1706.

Brit, Britt (brit), *sb.*[1] 1602. [Origin unkn.] Local name of the young of the Herring and Sprat; also the spawn of these. Also *transf.*

Brit, Brett, *sb.*[2] [OE. *Bret* (pl. *Brettas*), based on L. *Britto* (pl. *Brittones*) or OCelt. **Britto* or **Brittos.*] A. A Briton: the ordinary name in the OE. Chronicle; now *Hist.* B. *adj.* British.

Britain (bri·t'n), *sb.* [ME. *Bretayne* – OFr. *Bretaigne* (mod. *-agne*) :– L. *Brittania*, *-annia*, f. *Brit(t)anni* = Gr. Βρετ(τ)ανοί, Πρετ(τ)ανοί. OE. *Breoten*, *Breten*, *Bryten* Britain – L. *Brittones*; cf. BRITON.] The proper name of the whole island containing England, Wales, and Scotland, with their dependencies; more fully called Great Britain; now also used for the British empire as a whole.

Britain, after the OE. period, was for long used only as a historical term; but in 1604 James I was proclaimed 'King of Great Britain'; and this name was adopted for the United Kingdom at the Union in 1707. *North B.* for Scotland is still occ. in (postal) use. *Greater B.* = 'Great B. and the colonies' dates from 1868.

† 2. The duchy of Brittany or Bretagne in France; also called Little Britain –1622.

† **Britain,** *a.* and *sb.* 1547. [– L. *Brit(t)annus*, *Brittanus* Briton, British. Cf. prec.] A. *sb.* 1. An ancient Briton –1702. 2. A Breton –1618. B. *adj.* 1. Ancient British –1641. 2. British, in the mod. sense. **B. Crown,** a gold coin struck by James I, orig. = 5*s.*, subseq. 5*s.* 6*d.* 3. Breton 1645. vars. † **Bri·tainer, Bri·taner.**

Britannia (britæ·niă). OE. [– L. *Britannia*, also *Brittannia*, *Brittānia* (Bede), corresp. to Gr. Βρεττανία (Diodorus Siculus); see BRITAIN *sb.*] The Latin name of Britain; a name for Britain personified as a female; the figure on coins, etc., emblematic of Britain. Also *attrib.*

Comb. **B.-metal,** an alloy of tin and regulus of antimony, resembling silver.

Britannic (britæ·nik), *a.* 1641. [– L. *Britannicus*.] Of Britain, British. Used in *His* or *Her B. Majesty.* Hence **Brita·nnically** *adv.* in British fashion; in reference to Great Britain.

† **Brita·nnic,** *sb.* 1567. [– L. *britannica* (*herba*).] *Herb.* The Water-dock (*Rumex hydrolapathum*) –1601.

† **Bri·tany.** 1579. [– L. *Britannia.*] 1. Britain, Great Britain –1662. 2. The French province of Bretagne: 'Little Britany', commonly spelt Brittany.

Brite, *v.* Now *dial.* 1669. [Cf. ON. *brjóta*, corresp. to OE. *brēotan* to break, burst. See BRITTLE.] *intr.* Of grain, etc.: To become over-ripe and shatter.

Briticism (bri·tisiz'm). 1883. [f. *Brit(ish)*, or a possible *Britic*, after *Gallicism*, *Scotticism*; see -ISM.] A phrase or idiom characteristic of the English of Great Britain. vars. **Bri·tishism, Bri·tticism.**

British (bri·tiʃ), *a.* (*sb.*) [OE. *Brettisc*, *Brittisc*, *Bryttisc*, f. *Bret*; see BRIT, BRETT *sb.*[2], -ISH[1].] 1. Of or pertaining to the ancient Britons. † b. Welsh 1662. 2. Of or belonging to Great Britain or its inhabitants; see BRITAIN. Now chiefly used in political or imperial connection. ME. † 3. Breton 1602. 4. *ellipt.* as *sb. pl.* British people, soldiers, etc. 1641.

1. A road acknowledged to be B. 1870. 2. A stony B. stare TENNYSON. *Comb.*: **B. crown,** a gold coin of the reign of Charles I; **B. Empire** (see EMPIRE *sb.* 5) 1604; **B. gum,** a commercial name of dextrin.

Britisher (bri·tiʃəɹ). 1829. [f. BRITISH + -ER[1]; cf. *foreign-er.*] A British subject (as dist. from an American citizen). (App. of U.S. origin, but disclaimed by U.S. writers.)

Briton (bri·t'n, -ən), *sb.* (*a.*) [– (O)Fr. *Breton* – L. *Britto*, *-on-*, corresp. to OCelt. **Britto*, **Brittones*, whence W. *Brython.*] A. *sb.* A native of Britain: a. One of the ancient Britons. † b. A Welshman. c. Since the Union: A native of Great Britain, or of the British empire. *North B.*: a Scotchman. 2. A Breton. var. † **Bri·toner.**

1. Britons, hold your own TENNYSON. Hence **Bri·toness** (*rare*).

† B. *adj.* = British –1605.

Brittle (bri·t'l), *a.* [ME. *britul*, *britil*, *bretil*, f. *bryt-* (as in OE. *ġebryttan* break in pieces), f. Gmc. **brut-*, weak grade of **breutan*; cf. OE. *brēotan* break up = ON. *brjóta*; see BRITE, -LE 1, and BROTEL.] Liable to break; fragile; † friable ME. † b. Perishable, mortal –1777. Also *fig.*

1. The ice being b., cracks and snaps HUXLEY. *fig.* A second Eve..As beauteous, not as b. as the first DRYDEN. *Comb.* **b.-star,** a name for species of starfish of the genus *Ophiocoma*. Hence **Bri·ttlely** *adv. rare.* ? *Obs.* **Bri·ttleness.**

Britzka, britzska (bri·tskă, Pol. bri·tʃka). 1832. [– Pol. *bryczka*, dim. of *bryka* goods wagon.] An open carriage with calash top and space for reclining when used for a journey. vars. **Britschka, britzschka, britska.**

Broach (brōᵘtʃ), *sb.* ME. [– (O)Fr. *broche* spit :– Rom. *brocca spike, subst. use of fem. of L. *brocc(h)us* (as in *brocchi dentes* projecting teeth). See BROOCH.] **1.** A pointed rod of wood or iron. Still *dial.* **2.** *esp.* A spit ME. † **3.**? A taper: occas. explained as a spike on which to stick a candle –1504. **4.** A piece of tough pliant wood, pointed at each end, used by thatchers ME. **5.** A church spire; now, a spire which does not rise from within parapets 1501. **6.** *Venery.* 'A start of the head of a young stag' 1575. **7.** A general name for tapered boring-bits for enlarging or smoothing holes, sometimes used for burnishing, as in watchmaking; a similar tool used in dentistry; an instrument for broaching casks. Also, the pin in a lock which enters the barrel of the key. 1753. **8.** A narrow pointed chisel used by masons. **9.** (f. the vb.) A perforation 1519.

Phr. † *A b., on b.*: with a perforation or tap; esp. *to set a (on) b.*: to tap and set running; also *fig.* (Now ABROACH.)

Broach, *a. rare.* 1721. [sb. used attrib.] Like a broach or spit; in *Archit.* broach-shaped.

Broach (brōᵘtʃ), *v.*[1] ME. [– (O)Fr. *brocher* :– Rom. deriv. of the sb.] † **1.** *trans.* To pierce, thrust through –1631. † **2.** *spec.* To spur –1530. Also † *absol.* † **3.** To spit (meat) for roasting –1623. † **b.** *gen.* To spit –1704. **4.** To pierce, as a cask, etc., so as to draw the liquor; to tap ME. Also *transf.* and *fig.* **5.** To give publicity to; to give out; to begin conversation or discussion about, introduce. (The chief current sense.) 1579. **6.** *techn.* To chisel stone with a BROACH (sense 8) 1544.

3. b. Bringing Rebellion broached on his sword SHAKS. **4.** We broached a vessel of ale PEPYS. Blood was ready to be broach'd BUTLER *Hud.* I. ii. 489. **5.** To broch a newe and straunge doctrine TOMSON.

Broach (brōᵘtʃ), *v.*[2] 1705. [Origin unkn.] *Naut.* **1.** *intr.* in *To b. to* (said of the ship): to veer suddenly so as to turn the side to windward, or to meet the sea. **2.** *trans.* To cause (the ship) to veer to windward 1762.

Broacher (brōᵘ·tʃəɹ). 1587. [f. BROACH *v.* + -ER[1].] **1.** One who BROACHES. † **2.** A spit –1725.

1. A b. of more newes then hogsheads 1628. **2.** On five sharp broachers rank'd the roast they turn'd DRYDEN.

Broad (brǭd), *a.* (*sb.*) [OE. *brād* = OFris., OS. *brēd* (Du. *breed*), OHG. *breit*, ON. *breiðr*, Goth. *braiþs* :– Gmc. **braiðaz*, of which no cognates are known.] **1.** Extended in the direction measured from side to side; wide. Opp. to *narrow.* † **b.** *B. gold, money*; see BROAD-PIECE. **2.** Less definitely: Of great extent, wide, ample, spacious OE. **3.** Wide open; fully expanded OE. **b.** *esp.* Of day, daylight, etc. ME. **4.** Plain, obvious; emphatic, explicit ME. **b.** Most apparent; main. (Opp. to 'minute'.) 1860. **5.** Of language (or the speaker): **a.** Plainspoken (often in a bad sense); unreserved 1588. † **b.** Vulgar –1589. **c.** Loose, indecent 1580. **6.** Of pronunciation: Perhaps orig.: With wider or lower vowel-sounds; but commonly used of any strongly-marked dialectal or vulgar pronunciation, *e.g.* 'B. Yorkshire', 'B. Cockney'. *B. Scotch*: the Lowland Scotch. **7.** Unrestrained 1602. † **8.** Widely diffused *Macb.* III. iv. 23. **9.** Having a wide range; inclusive, general 1871. **10.** Characterized by breadth of opinion or sentiment; catholic, tolerant. (Cf. BROAD CHURCH.) 1832. **11.** *Art.* Characterized by artistic breadth. Cf. BREADTH 5. 1862.

1. The braid..way of deadly syn 1552. **2.** The hole brode worlde 1526. In ample space under the broadest shade MILT. **3.** The worldes b. eye DEKKER. B. day light 1579, sunshine LOCKE, noon-day SHELLEY. **4.** A b. hint BENTLEY. **b.** The b. facts 1860, outlines HUXLEY. **5. c.** Without any b. speeches or uncomly jests NORTH. **7.** Prankes..too b. to beare with *Haml.* III. iv. 2. B. mirth JOWETT.

Phrase. *It's as b. as it's long* (or *as long as it's b.*): it comes to the same thing either way. Hence **Broa·dish** *a.* **Broa·dness,** breadth; coarseness. **Broa·dway, -ways, -wise** *adv.* laterally.

B. *sb.* [mostly ellipt.] † **1.** Breadth: only in *in, on, o, a brode*; now replaced by ABROAD *adv.* –1456. **2.** The broad part (of the back, etc.) 1741. † **3.** = BROAD-PIECE –1763. **4.** In East Anglia, a piece of fresh water formed by the broadening out of a river 1787.

C. *adv.* [OE. *brāde*, ME. *brode.*] **1.** In a broad way; widely, fully; far OE. **2.** Outspokenly, unreservedly ME. **3.** With a broad pronunciation 1532.

1. *B. awake, b. waking*: fully awake. **2.** † *To laugh b.*: to laugh without restraint, grossly.

Comb.: **b. bean** (see BEAN 1); **-bill,** a name of birds having broad bills, *esp.* the Shoveller and Spoonbill; **-blown** *a.*, full-blown; **-eyed** *a.*, having large eyes, with eyes wide open; **-glass,** window-glass; **-leaf** (*Bot.*), a tree (*Terminalia latifolia*) found in Jamaica; **-seed** (*Bot.*) the genus *Ulospermum.*

Broa·d-arrow, -head; see ARROW.

Broa·d-axe. ME. An axe with a broad head, used for hewing timber (*U.S.*), formerly in war.

Broa·d-brim. *colloq.* 1797. **a.** A hat with a broad brim. **b.** A Quaker, as one who wears such a hat. **Broa·d-brimmed** *a.* 1688.

Broadcast (brǭ·dkɑst). 1767. [f. BROAD *adv.* and CAST *pa. pple.*] **A.** *adj.* Of seed, etc.: Scattered over the whole surface. Of sowing: Performed by this method. Also *fig.* **B.** *adv.* Only in *To sow, scatter, throw,* etc. *b.* (*lit.* and *fig.*) 1814. **C.** *sb.* **1.** Broadcast sowing 1796. **2.** Broadcasting by wireless telephony 1922.

Broa·dcast, *v.* 1813. [f. as prec. + CAST *v.*] **1.** *trans.* To scatter (seed, etc.) broadcast. Also *fig.* **2.** To disseminate (audible matter) from a wireless transmitting station 1921.

Broad Church. 1853. [See BROAD *a.* 10.] Designating members of the Church of England who take its formularies and doctrines in a broad sense, and allow wide limits to orthodoxy.

It [another party in the Church of England] is called by different names; Moderate, Catholic, or Broad Church, by its friends; Latitudinarian or Indifferent by its enemies. Its distinctive character is the desire of comprehension. Its watch-words are Charity and Toleration 1853. Hence **Broad-Churchism, Broad-Churchman.**

Broadcloth, broad cloth (brǭ·dklǫþ). 1420. [In *Act* 1 *Rich. III*, viii, an. 1482, 'broad cloths', two yards within the lists, are distinguished from 'streits', one yard wide.] Fine, plain-wove, dressed, double width, black cloth, used chiefly for men's garments. (The term now implies quality rather than width. But cloths of less than 54 inches wide are not doubled.) Also *attrib.*

Broaden (brǭ·d'n), *v.* 1726. [f. BROAD *a.* + -EN[5].] **1.** *intr.* To become broad or broader 1727. **2.** *trans.* To make broad or broader; to widen, dilate 1726.

1. Low walks the sun, and broadens by degrees THOMSON. **2.** With broaden'd nostrils..The..heifer snuffs the..gale 1726.

Broad-faced (brǭ·dfē¹st), *a.* 1607. **1.** Having a broad face. † **2.** *fig.* Undisguised, as *b. treason* –1678.

Broad gauge. 1864. The wider distance at which the rails are laid on some railways. (The ordinary gauge is 4 ft. 8½ in.) Often *attrib.* Hence **Broa·d-gauged** *a.*

Broa·d-leaved, *a.* Also **-leafed.** 1552. Having broad leaves; in *Bot.* = L. *latifolius.*

Broadly (brǭ·dli), *adv.* 1580. In a broad manner (see BROAD *a.*).

Broad pendant, pennant; see PENDANT.

† **Broad-piece.** 1678. The 20 shilling-piece ('Jacobus' and 'Carolus'), so called as being broader and thinner than the guinea.

Broad seal, *sb.* 1536. The Great Seal of England. Also *transf.* Also as *v. trans.* B. JONS.

Broadsheet (brǭ·d,ʃīt). 1705. A large sheet of paper printed on one side only.

Broadside (brǭ·dsəid), *sb.* 1591. [Formerly two wds.] **1.** *Naut.* The side of a ship above the water between the bow and the quarter. Also *attrib.* and *transf.* **2.** The whole array, or the simultaneous discharge, of the artillery on one side of a ship of war 1597. **3.** = BROADSHEET 1575.

1. *B. on, b. to,* († *a b.*) (Naut.): with the side of the vessel turned fully to the object considered; transversely. **2.** Feare wee broad-sides? No, let the Fiend giue fire 2 *Hen. IV*, II. iv. 196.

Broa·dside, *adv.* 1870. With the side turned full (*to* a point, etc.).

Broa·dsider. *nonce-wd.* One who collects (printed) broadsides. BURTON.

Broadsword (brǭ·dsōᵊɹd). 1565. 'A cutting sword with a broad blade' (J.). Also *attrib.* **b.** *transf.* (*pl.*) Men armed with broadswords 1855.

Broa·dway. 1613. [Now usu. two wds.] A wide open road, as opp. to a narrow lane or byway. As a compound, now used as the proper name of a street, as in New York, Hammersmith, etc. **b.** *attrib.* Applied by Dryden to divines of the English Church who were for widening its basis 1687.

Brob (brǫb). 1874. [prob. related to North dial. '*brob* to prick with a bodkin' (Grose), cf. BRAD, BROD, BROG.] 'A peculiar spike, driven alongside the end of an abutting timber, to prevent its slipping.' RAYMOND.

Brobdingnag (brǫ·bdiŋnæ:g). Also erron. **brobdignag.** 1727. Swift's name in *Gulliver's Travels* for an imaginary country where everything was on a gigantic scale. Hence *attrib.*: Of, or pertaining to, that country; immense; gigantic. Hence **Brobdingna·gian** *a.* = BROBDINGNAG; *sb.* an inhabitant of B., a giant; erron. vars. **-digna·gian, -naggian.**

Brocade (brokē¹·d). 1563. [In XVI *brocardo*, XVII *brocado* – Sp., Pg. *brocado*, with blending of Fr. *brocart* – It. *broccato*, lit. 'embossed stuff', f. *brocco* twisted thread; see -ADE.] A textile fabric woven with raised figures, orig. in gold or silver; in later use, any kind of stuff flowered with a raised pattern; also a cloth of gold and silver made in India. Also *fig.* Also *attrib.*

Stiff in Brocard, and pinch'd in stays PRIOR. Hence **Broca·de** *v.* to work with a raised pattern. **Broca·ded** *a.* worked or woven like b.; ornamented with b.; dressed in b.

Brocage, var. of BROKAGE.

Brocard[1] (brōᵘ·kăɹd). 1624. [– Fr. *brocard* or med.L. *brocardus*, appellative use of the latinized form of Burchart, name of a bishop of Worms (XI), author of 'Regulæ Ecclesiasticæ' in 20 books.] **1.** *Law.* An elementary principle or maxim. Also *gen.* ‖ **2.** Biting speech. [Fr.] 1837.

1. *Dolus latet in generalibus* is a b. of the civilians 1862.

Brocard[2], obs. f. BROCADE.

‖ **Brocatelle** (brǫkăte·l). 1669. [Fr., earlier *brocatel* – It. *broccatello* gold tinsel, dim. of *broccato*; see BROCADE.] **1.** An imitation of brocade, usually of silk or wool, for upholstery, etc., now also for dresses. Also *attrib.* **2.** = next 1756.

‖ **Brocatello** (brǫ:kate·lo). Also **-tella, -telli.** 1752. [It. *brocatello di Siena*, which is coloured like brocade; see prec.] A kind of variegated marble, clouded and veined white, grey, yellow, and red, yellow usually prevailing.

Broccoli, brocoli (brǫ·kŏli). 1699. [– It. *broccoli*, pl. of *broccolo* cabbage sprout or head, dim. of *brocco* shoot; see BROACH *sb.*] A cultivated form of the cabbage (*Brassica oleracea botrytis asparagoides*): in its origin a more robust variety of the cauliflower.

Broch, brogh, brough. 1654. [n.e. Scottish, – ON. *borg* (= OE. *burh*; see BOROUGH, BURGH).] *Archæol.* A prehistoric structure, peculiar to the Orkney and Shetland Isles, and adjacent mainland of Scotland, being a sort of round tower, having an outer and an inner wall of dry stone, the interstitial space containing little chambers for human habitation, while the open centre might be used for cattle.

Brochantite (brǫ·ʃăntəit). 1865. [f. *Brochant* de Villiers, a French mineralogist, + -ITE[1] 2 b.] *Min.* A hydrous sulphate, occurring in thin, rectangular, green crystals.

† **Broche,** *v.* 1480. Obs. spelling of BROACH *v.* = Fr. *brocher* to stitch, brocade –1834. Hence **Broched** *ppl. a.* brocaded, embroidered.

Brochure (brǫʃū·r). 1765 [– Fr. *brochure* lit. 'stitching', f. in *brocher* to stitch; see prec., -URE.] A short printed work, of a few leaves stitched together; a pamphlet.

Brock (brǫk), *sb.*[1] [OE. *broc(c)* – OBrit. **brokkos* (W., Corn., Bret. *broch*, Ir., Gael. *broc*, OIr. *brocc*).] **1.** A badger, usually qualified as *stinking*. **2.** A stinking or dirty fellow; a 'skunk' 1600. Also *attrib.*

Brock, *sb.*[2] ? *Obs.* 1515. [Shortening of BROCKET.]

† **Brock,** *v. rare.* ME. [Referred by some to *bruk-, wk. grade of Gmc. *brek- (see BREAK *v.*), as in G. *brocken* crumble, OHG. *brohhōn*, but the sense-history is obscure.] *app.* To give mouth, speak querulously. CHAUCER.

Brocket (brǫ·kėt). ME. [– AFr. **broquet* (cf. AL. *brokettus* XIII), f. *broque*, dial. var. of *broche* BROOCH; cf. Fr. *brocard* young roe (XV), and synon. *daguet*, † *dagard* (f. *dague* dagger, stag's first antler).] **1.** A stag in its second year with its first horns (see BROACH *sb.* 6). **2.** A genus of deer of Brazil, having short prongs for horns 1837.

† **Bro·ckish,** *a. rare.* 1546. [f. BROCK *sb.*[1] 2 + -ISH[1].] Like a brock; beastly, dirty –1553.

Brod (brǫd), *sb.* Now *dial.* [ME., app. – ON. *broddr* = OE. *brord* spike. Mainly *Sc.* Cf. PROD, BROB, BROG.] † **1.** A sprout. ME. only. **2.** A goad, prick ME. **3.** A prick from a goad 1549. **4.** [Cf. AL. *broddum* brad-nail XIII.] A round-headed nail made by blacksmiths. Hence **Brod** *v.* † to sprout; to goad, prod, prick (*n. dial.*).

† **Bro·dekin, brodkin.** 1481. [– Fr. *brodequin*, earlier *broissequin* – Du. *brosekin*. See BUSKIN.] A half-boot; a buskin –1725.

Bro·derer. ME. Earlier form of BROIDERER, retained as the name of one of the London City Companies.

Brog (brǫg), *sb. dial.* 1781. [Of unkn. origin. Cf. BROB, BROD.] **1.** A pricking or boring instrument; a bradawl (*Sc.*); also, an awl 1808. **2.** A prick with a bradawl, etc: 1808. **3.** A short stick, *esp.* one to stick in the ground 1781.

Brog (brǫg), *v. dial.* 1678. [f. prec.] **1.** To prick, prod; to push an awl *through* 1774. **2.** To insert brogs into (see BROG *sb.* 3) 1875. **3.** To BROGGLE for eels, to sniggle (*dial.*) 1678.

‖ **Brogan** (brōᵘ·găn). 1846. [Ir., dim. of *brōg* shoe; see BROGUE *sb.*[2]] A coarse stout sort of shoe.

† **Bro·gger.** 1460. [var. of *broker* (XIV–XV); thus AFr. *brogour* beside *brocour*; cf. *brogge* (XVI) BROGUE *sb.*[1]] An agent; a jobber, *esp.* a corrupt jobber of offices; a BROKER –1720. Broggers of Corn and Forestallers of Markets 1641.

Broggle (brǫ·g'l), *v. n. dial.* 1653. [freq. f. BROG *v.*] To fish for eels with a brog; to sniggle.

† **Brogue** (brōg), *sb.*[1] Now *Sc.* [Origin unkn.] An escheat; a cheat –1791.

Brogue (brōᵘg), *sb.*[2] 1586. [– Ir., Gael. *brōg* (OIr. *bróc*) – ON. *brók*; see BREEK, BREECH.] **1.** A rude shoe, of untanned hide, worn in the wilder parts of Ireland and the Scotch Highlands. **b.** (In full *b. shoe.*) A strong shoe, esp. for country and sports wear 1906. † **2.** *pl.* Hose, trousers –1845. **3.** *Fishing brogues*, waterproof leggings with feet 1880.

Brogue (brōᵘg), *sb.*[3] 1705. [perh. same wd. as prec.] A strongly-marked dialectal pronunciation or accent; now esp. that of the English speech of Ireland.

Charles Morgan. .having much of the Irish B. in his Speech 1705. Hence **Brogue** *v.* to utter with a b.

† **Broid,** *v.* ME. [var. of BRAID *v.*; cf. BROIDEN.] To plait, interweave –1624.

Broiden, *ppl. a.* ME. [A pa. pple. of BRAID *v.* (cf. ABRAID, *abroiden*), and thus a doublet of *browden*, which was the normal form.] Interwoven, braided. (More usu.) *fig.* Skilfully contrived.

Broider (broi·dəɹ), *v. arch.* 1450. [Later form of *broudre*, *brouder* (XV), taken as = Fr. *broder*, *brouder* stitch, embroider, of which the regular Eng. repr. was *broude*, BROWD. The *-oi-* is due to assoc. w. BROID *v.*] To work in needlework upon cloth; to embroider. (Usu. in pa. pple.) Also *transf.* and *fig.*

Theyr noble actes. .Freshly were browdred in these clothes royall 1513. The Hyacinth with rich inlay Broiderd the ground MILT. *P.L.* IV. 702. Hence **Broi·derer. Broi·dery,** embroidery.

Broil (broil), *sb.*[1] 1525. [Earliest forms *breull, bruill*, f. BROIL *v.*[2]] A confused disturbance, tumult, or turmoil; a quarrel. Also in *comb.*

Prosper this Realme, keepe it from Ciuill Broyles SHAKS.

Broil, *sb.*[2] 1583. [f. BROIL *v.*[1]] **1.** A great heat; a very hot state. **2.** Broiled meat 1822.

Broil (broil), *v.*[1] ME. [Earliest forms (Sc.) *brulȝe, broille, brule, bruyle* – OFr. *bruler, bruller*, earlier *brusler* (mod. *brûler*) burn :– Rom. **brustulare*, perh. f. Gmc. **brun-* **bren-* BURN *v.*[1] + L. *ustulare* burn up.] † **1.** *trans.* To burn –1568. **2.** *spec.* To cook (meat) by placing it on the fire, or on a gridiron over it; to grill ME. **3.** To scorch; to make very hot 1634. **4.** *intr.* To be subjected to great heat, to be very hot 1613; also *fig.* 1561.

2. He cowde roste, sethe, broille, and frie CHAUCER. **3.** I was. .half broiled in the sun 1718.

Broil, *v.*[2] ME. [– AFr. *broiller*, (O)Fr. *brouiller*, earlier *brooillier* :– Rom. **brodiculare*, f. **brodicare*, f. **brodum*, whence OFr. *breu* (see BROSE); cf. IMBROGLIO.] † **1.** To mix confusedly –1631. † **2.** To involve in confusion or disorder; to set by the ears, embroil –1642. **3.** *intr.* To be or to engage in a BROIL 1567.

Broiler[1] (broi·ləɹ). 1671. [f. BROIL *v.*[1] + -ER[1].] **1.** One who or that which broils; also said of a very hot day (cf. *scorcher*). **2.** *spec.* A chicken for broiling 1886.

Broi·ler[2]. 1660. [f. BROIL *v.*[2] + -ER[1].] One who stirs up or engaged in broils.

Broi·ling, *vbl. sb.* 1440. [f. BROIL *v.*[1] + -ING[1].] Exposing to scorching heat; *spec.* grilling. Hence **Broi·lingly** *adv.*

† **Bro·kage, brocage.** ME. [– AFr. *brocage*, in AL. *brocagium*; see BROKER, -AGE.] = BROKERAGE. *esp.* **a.** The corrupt jobbing of offices; the bribe unlawfully paid for any office. **b.** Trafficking in match-making, etc. **c.** 'The trade of dealing in old things' (J.). –1755.

Broke, var. BROKEN, surviving in predic. use of sense 7. 1851.

Broke (brōᵘk), *v.* 1496. [Back-formation from BROKER. Cf. BROKING.] † **1.** *intr.* To bargain –1625. † **2.** *trans.* To retail 1599. **3.** *intr.* To act as broker 1652.

Broken (brōᵘ·k'n), *ppl. a.* ME. Used esp. in the following senses of BREAK *v.* **1.** Separated forcibly into parts; in fragments; in pieces. **2.** Rent, ruptured, burst ME. **3.** Of organic structures: **a.** Having the bone fractured; **b.** having the surface ruptured ME. **4.** Shattered, as *b. water, a b. wave* 1793. **5.** Crushed or exhausted by labour, etc.; enfeebled 1490. **6.** Crushed in feelings by misfortune, remorse, etc.; humbled, contrite 1535. **7.** Reduced or shattered in worldly estate; bankrupt 1593. **8.** Reduced to obedience, tamed, trained. Often with *in.* 1805. **9.** Violated, transgressed, not kept intact 1605. **10.** Having the ranks broken; routed 1810. **11.** Having continuity or uniformity interrupted 1599. **12.** Fragmentary, disconnected, disjointed, in patches; *esp.* **a.** of sound, voice, etc.: Uttered disjointedly, interrupted 1530; **b.** of language: With the syntax incomplete 1599. **13.** Produced by breaking, severed ME. **14.** Of colours: Reduced in tone by the addition of other colours 1882. † **15.** Of music: Arranged for different instruments, 'part' (music); concerted –1626.

1. Three b. oars DE FOE. *B. bread, meat*, etc.: fragments left after a meal, etc.; extended to drink, as *b. ale*, etc. **2.** Old and b. apparell 1641. **3.** B. limbs SHAKS., Shins ADDISON. **6.** A b. and a contrite hert COVERDALE *Ps.* **7.** The kings growne bankrupt like a b. man *Rich. II*, II. i. 257. **B. man.** *Sc. Law and Hist.* One under sentence of outlawry, or living the life of an outlaw. **B. clan,** one having no chief able to find security for their good behaviour. **11.** B. sleep ADDISON. **12.** The fruits of b. hours QUARLES. **a.** Her voice. .b. with sobs 1853. **b.** Breake thy minde to me in b. English *Hen. V.* V. ii. 265. **13.** *B. number*: a fraction. A b. tale BYRON.

Comb.: **b.-bellied, -bodied** (*dial.*), affected with hernia, ruptured; **-kneed** (*Farriery*), having the knees damaged by stumbling, etc.; also *fig.* Hence **Bro·ken-ly** *adv.*, **-ness.**

Broken-backed (brōᵘ·k'n,bæ·kt), *a.* ME. **1.** Having a broken back; formerly, hunch-backed. Also *transf.* and *fig.* **2.** *Naut.* The state of a ship so loosened in her frame as to droop at both ends 1769.

Broken-hearted (brōᵘ·k'n,hā·ɹtėd), *a.* 1526. Having the spirits crushed by grief or despair. Broken-hearted widows MACAULAY. Hence **Broken-hea·rted-ly** *adv.*, **-ness.**

Broken wind, broken-wind. 1838. *Farriery.* An incurable disease of horses, caused by the rupture of the air-cells, which disables them from bearing fatigue. Hence **Broken-wi·nded** *a.* affected with broken wind. Also *fig.*

Broker (brōᵘ·kəɹ). [Late ME. *broco(u)r* – AFr. *brocour*, beside *abrocour* (cf. AL. *brocator*, *abrocator*), corresp. to Pr. *abrocador* broker, *abrocatge* brokerage, beside *brocatge* charge on wine; of unkn. origin.] † **1.** A retailer; *contemptuously*, Pedlar, monger –1730. **2.** A dealer in second-hand furniture and apparel; a pawnbroker 1583. **3.** One employed as a middleman to transact business or negotiate bargains; often specialized, as *bill-, cotton-, pawn-, ship-, wool-b.* Formerly also = 'jobber, agent, factor, commission-agent'. ME. † **4.** A go-between in love affairs; a hired match-maker; a pimp, bawd; a pander –1694. **5.** A middleman generally; an interpreter, messenger, commissioner 1530. **6.** A person licensed to sell or appraise household furniture distrained for rent 1818.

1. But B. of anothers wit MARSTON. **2.** A Houndsditch man, sir. One of the deuils neere kinsmen, a b. B. JONS. **4.** *Two Gent.* I. ii. 41. **5.** Two false knaues neede no b. HEYWOOD.

Brokerage (brōᵘ·kərėdʒ). 1466. [f. prec. + -AGE; repl. BROKAGE.] **1.** The business or action of a broker. **2.** The commission paid to a broker on the business done by him 1622.

† **Bro·kerly.** 1592. [f. as prec. + -LY[1, 2].] **A.** *adj.* Like a broker; huckstering –1611. **B.** *adv.* By the agency of a broker 1593.

† **Bro·kery.** 1583. [f. as prec. + -Y[3]; see -ERY.] **1.** = BROKERAGE 1. –1641. **2.** A broker's wares; anything second-hand or stale –1634. **3.** Rascally dealing –1654.

Broking (brōᵘ·kiŋ), *vbl. sb.* 1569. [f. BROKE *v.* + -ING[1].] **1.** The broker's trade. † **2.** Lending of money upon pawns; fraudulent dealing –1619.

Brolly (brǫ·li). 1874. Colloq. altered f. UMBRELLA.

Brom-; see BROMO-.

†‖ **Bro·ma**[1]. 1555. [Sp.] A ship-worm.

‖ **Broma**[2] (brōᵘ·mă). 1811. [Gr. βρῶμα food.] **1.** *Med.* Any food that is masticated. **2.** A preparation of chocolate (so called from *theobroma*, the name of the Cacao plant) 1858.

Bromal (brōᵘ·măl). 1875. [f. BROMINE + -AL[2].] A compound analogous to chloral, produced by the action of bromine on alcohol.

Bromate (brōᵘ·meᶦt). 1836. [f. BROMIC + -ATE[4].] A salt of bromic acid.

Bromatology (brōᵘmătǫ·lŏdʒi). 1811. [f. Gr. βρῶμα, -ματ- food + -LOGY.] **1.** A discourse on food. **2.** The science of food.

Brome[1] (brōᵘm). 1827. [– Fr. *brome* – Gr. βρῶμος stink.] *Chem.* The French name of BROMINE, formerly used in English.

Brome[2] (brōᵘm). 1759. [– *Bromus*, Bot. name of the genus – Gr. βρόμος (also βρῶμος) oats.] *Bot.* A genus of oat-like grasses (*Bromus*). Also **B.-grass.**

Bromeliaceous (bromīːliēᶦ·ʃəs), *a.* 1882. [See -ACEOUS.] *Bot.* Pertaining to the natural order *Bromeliaceæ*, which includes the Pine-apple.

Bromic (brōᵘ·mik), *a.* 1828. [f. BROMINE + -IC.] *Chem.* Containing bromine in combination.

bromic acid ($HBrO_3$), the acid which forms bromates; **b. silver** = BROMYRITE.

Bromide (brōᵘ·məid). 1836. [f. BROMINE + -IDE.] **1.** *Chem.* A primary compound of bromine with an element or organic radical. **2.** (orig. *U.S. slang.*) A commonplace bore, trite remark, conventionalism 1906.

‖ **Bromidrosis** (brōᵘːmidrōᵘ·sis). 1866. [f. Gr. βρῶμος stink + ἱδρώς sweat; see -OSIS.] *Med.* A disorder of the sweat glands attended by offensive perspiration.

Bro·minated, *a.* 1875. [f. BROMINE + -ATE[3] + -ED[1].] Charged or compounded with bromine.

Bromine (brōᵘ·min, -məin). 1827. [f. Fr. *brome* (see BROME[1]) + -INE[5]; cf. IODINE.] *Chem.* A non-metallic element discovered by

Balard in 1826; a reddish-black heavy liquid, with a strong irritating smell, and highly poisonous. Symbol Br. Also *attrib.*

Bromism (brōᵘ·miz'm). 1867. [f. BROMINE + -ISM.] *Med.* The condition produced by misuse of bromine or a bromide.

Bro·mite. 1850. *Min.* = BROMYRITE.

Bromize, -ise (brōᵘ·məiz), *v.* 1853. [f. BROMINE + -IZE.] To treat, compound, impregnate, or infuse with bromine; in *Photogr.*, to prepare (a plate) with bromine or a bromide.

Bromlite (brǫ·mləit). 1835. [f. *Bromley* Hill in Cumberland + -ITE[1] 2 b.] *Min.* = ALSTONITE.

Bromo- (brōᵘ·mo), bef. a vowel **brom-.** *Chem.* Comb. f. BROMINE, as in: **bro:mace·tic acid,** a compound of bromine and acetic acid ($C_2H_3BrO_2$), forming salts called **broma·cetates**; **broma·rgyrite** = BROMYRITE; **bromhy·drin,** a class of compounds 'produced by the action of tribromide or pentabromide of phosphorus on glycerin' (Watts); **bro·moform,** a compound analogous to chloroform ($CHBr_3$).

† **Bro·muret.** 1878. [f. BROMINE + -URET.] *Chem.* The earlier name for a BROMIDE.

Bromyrite (brōᵘ·mirəit). 1854. [f. BROMINE, after *argyrite*; see -ITE[1] 2 b.] *Min.* The native bromide of silver, an isometric yellow, amber, or green splendent mineral; also called *Bromargyrite, bromic silver.*

‖ **Bronchia** (brǫ·ŋkiă), *sb. pl.* 1674. [Late L. – Gr. n. pl. βρόγχια, f. βρόγχος windpipe. Formerly occas. treated as sing., w. pl. *bronchiæ.*] The branches of the bronchi within the lungs. Hence **Bro·nchial, Bro·nchic** *a.* pertaining to the bronchi or bronchia. **Bro·nchially** *adv.*

Bronchio- (brǫ·ŋki,o), bef. a vowel **bronchi-.** *Med.* Comb. f. BRONCHIA, as in: **bronchia·rctia** [L. *ar(c)tus*], contraction of the bronchial tubes; **bro:nchie·ctasis** [Gr. ἔκτασις], dilatation of the bronchial tubes; **bronchio-cri·sis** [Gr. κρίσις], paroxysmal attacks resembling whooping-cough occurring in tabes; **-pneumo·nia,** inflammation of the lungs, beginning in the bronchial membrane; **-pu·lmonary** *a.*, pertaining to the bronchi and lungs.

Bronchiole (brǫ·ŋki,ōᵘl). 1866. [– mod. L. **bronchiola*, dim. of *bronchia.*] A minute bronchial tube.

‖ **Bronchitis** (brǫŋkəi·tis). 1814. [mod.L., f. *bronchi, bronchia* + -ITIS.] *Med.* Inflammation of the bronchial mucous membrane. Hence **Bronchi·tic** *a.*

Broncho- (brǫ·ŋko), bef. a vowel **bronch-.** *Med.* Comb. f. BRONCHUS, as in: **bro·nchadene** [Gr. ἀδήν], one of the bronchial glands; **broncha·rctia** [L. *ar(c)tus*], contraction of a bronchus; **broncho-pneumo·nia** = *bronchio-pneumonia* (see BRONCHIO-); **-lith,** a calcareous deposit in a bronchial gland; **-rrhœ·a,** a kind of chronic bronchitis, etc.

Bronchocele (brǫ·ŋkŏsīl). 1657. [– Gr. βρογχοκήλη tumour in the throat, f. βρόγχος BRONCHUS + κήλη tumour; cf. Fr. *bronchocèle.*] *Med.* A swelling of the thyroid gland; goitre.

Bronchophony (brǫŋkǫ·fŏni). 1834. [– Fr. *bronchophonie.*] *Med.* The sound of the voice heard in the bronchi by means of the stethoscope; *esp.* the increased vocal resonance heard in certain diseased conditions of the lungs. Hence **Bronchopho·nic** *a.* var. **Broncho·phonism.**

Bronchotome (brǫ·ŋkŏtōᵘm). 1837. [f. BRONCHO- + -TOME[1].] *Surg.* A knife, or a pair of scissors, used for bronchotomy.

Bronchotomy (brǫŋkǫ·tŏmi). 1706. [f. BRONCHO- + -TOMY. Cf. Fr. *bronchotomie.*] *Surg.* The operation of making an incision in the wind-pipe; a generic term, including *thyrotomy, laryngotomy,* and *tracheotomy.* Hence **Broncho·tomist,** one who performs b.; (*joc.*) a cut-throat.

‖ **Bronchus** (brǫ·ŋkǫs). Pl. **-chi** (*improp.* **-chæ**). 1706. [– late L. *bronchus*; see BRONCHIA.] *Phys.* Each of the two main branches of the trachea.

‖ **Bronco** (brǫ·ŋko). 1883. [Sp., = 'rough, rude'.] An untamed or half-tamed horse, or a cross between the horse and a mustang. (*Western U.S.*)

† **Bro·nstrops.** 1617. [app. a further corruption of *bawstrop*, corrupt form of BAWDSTROT.] A bawd –1661.

‖ **Bronte·on.** 1849. [Gr. βροντεῖον.] In the Greek theatre, a number of brazen vessels with stones in them placed under the floor, to imitate thunder.

Brontology (brǫntǫ·lŏdʒi). 1731. [f. Gr. βροντή thunder + -LOGY.] That part of meteorology which treats of thunder.

‖ **Brontosaurus** (brǫntosǭ·rǫs). [mod.L. (1879), f. Gr. βροντή thunder + σαῦρος lizard.] A huge dinosaurian reptile.

Brontothere (brǫ·ntoþīᵊɹ). 1877. [f. as prec. + θηρίον wild beast.] *Palæont.* An extinct genus of ungulate mammals, having affinities to the elephant and also to the tapir.

Bronze (brǫnz), *sb.* 1721. [– Fr. *bronze* – It. *bronzo* (whence med.L. *bronzium, brontium*, in It. documents), prob. – Pers. *birinj, pirinj* copper.] **1.** A brown-coloured alloy of copper and tin, sometimes also containing a little zinc and lead. Formerly included under the term BRASS, q.v. 1739. **2.** (with *pl.*) A work of art, as a statue, etc., executed in bronze 1721. † **3.** *fig.* Unblushingness. (Cf. *brass.*) –1823. **4.** (More fully *b. powder*): A metallic powder (usu. brass, copper, or tin) used in painting, printing, etc. 1753. **5.** A colour like that of bronze 1817. **6.** *attrib.* Made of bronze 1839; bronze-coloured 1828.

1. *Aluminium b.*: see ALUMINIUM. *Phosphor-b.*: an alloy of b. or copper with a little phosphorus added, which increases its tenacity. **2.** How little gives thee joy or pain; A print, a b., a flower, a root PRIOR. **3.** Imbrown'd with native b., lo! Henley stands POPE. **6.** The b. coinage (*mod.*). *Comb.*: **b. age** = *bronze period*; **b. man** (*Archæol.*), a man living in the b. period; **b. period** (*Archæol.*), the prehistoric period (preceded by the Stone, and succeeded by the Iron Period) during which weapons, etc. were made of b.; **b. powder** = sense 4; **b. wing,** a Pigeon (*Phaps chalcoptera*) found in Australasia. Hence **Bro·nzy** *a.* tinged with b. colour.

Bronze (brǫnz), *v.* 1645. [f. prec., or – Fr. *bronzer.*] **1.** *trans.* To give a bronze-like appearance to, by any mechanical or chemical process. **2.** *fig.* To render unfeeling or shameless; to harden, steel 1726. **3.** To make bronze-coloured 1792. **4.** *intr.* To become like bronze 1880.

3. The..veteran..bronz'd by many a summer sun ROGERS.

Bronzed (brǫnzd), *ppl. a.* 1748. [f. prec. + -ED[1].] In senses of the vb. 1–3.

Bronzed Skin, *supra-renal melasma* or Addison's disease.

Bro·nzite. 1816. [f. BRONZE *sb.* + -ITE[1] 2 b.] *Min.* A bronze-coloured variety of diallage.

Broo. *Sc.* 1440. [– OFr. *breu* = Pr. *bro*; see BROSE.] = BREE *sb.*[2] 2.

Brooch (brōᵘtʃ). [ME. *broche*; the same wd. as BROACH. Occas. pronounced (brūtʃ).] **1.** An ornamental fastening, consisting of a safety pin, with the clasping part variously fastened and enriched. Now mainly a (female) ornament. † **2.** Formerly, a necklace, a bracelet, a trinket, etc. –1676. Also † *fig.*

2. *fig.* He is the B. indeed, And Iemme of all our Nation *Haml.* IV. vii. 94. Hence **Brooch** *v. rare,* to adorn as with a b.

Brood (brūd), *sb.* [OE. *brōd*, corresp. to MDu. *broet* (Du. *broed*), OHG. *bruot* (G. *brut*), f. Gmc. **brōd-*, dental deriv. of **brō-* warm, heat.] **1.** Progeny, offspring, young; *esp.* of animals that lay eggs. **b.** Family. (Now usu. *contemptuous.*) ME. **c.** *fig.* Of things inanimate 1597. **2.** The cherishing of the fœtus in the egg or the womb; hatching, breeding (*arch.*) ME. † **b.** Hence: Parentage, extraction. SPENSER. **c.** *attrib.* = 'breeding'; as in *b. class*, etc. Often hyphened. 1526. **3.** A race, a kind. Now *contemptuous*; = 'swarm, crew, crowd'. 1581. **4.** *spec.* The spat of oysters in its second year 1862. **5.** *Min.* The heavier kinds of waste ore (*Cornwall*) 1880.

1. The Serpents B. DRYDEN. A B. of Ducks ADDISON, of silk-worms 1760. **b.** A b. of daughters GEO. ELIOT. **c.** The b. of Folly without father bred MILT. *Penser.* 96. **3.** A. b. of petty despots FREEMAN. *Comb.* **b.-hen,** a breeding-hen; also, † the Pleiades.

Brood (brūd), *v.* ME. [f. prec.] **I.** *trans.* (mostly *arch.* or *poet.*) **1.** To sit on eggs so as to hatch them. **2.** To cherish (young brood) under the wings, as a hen does; often *fig.* 1571. **3.** *fig.* To hatch (products or projects) 1613. **4.** To cherish in the mind, to nurse (wrath, etc.). Now usu. *to b. on* or *over.* 1571.

3. Hell, and not the heavens, brooded that design FULLER. **4.** To b. hope JOHNSON.

II. *intrans.* **1.** To sit as a hen on eggs; to sit or hover with outspread wings 1588. **2.** *fig.* To sit *on*, or hang close *over*; to hover over. Said esp. of *night, silence, mist, storm-clouds,* and the like. 1697. **3.** To mediate moodily *on* or *over*; to dwell closely upon in the mind 1751. **b.** To meditate (*esp.* in a morbid way) 1826. **4.** *transf.* **a.** To breed interest 1678. **b.** To lie as a cherished nestling, etc. 1679.

1. Birds sit brooding in the snow *L. L. L.* V. ii. 933. Also MILT. *P. L.* I. 21. **2.** Perpetual Night.. In silence brooding on th' unhappy ground DRYDEN. **3.** To b. On dark revenge SCOTT. **4. b.** The Injury..had long been brooding in his mind DRYDEN.

Broo·dy, *a.* 1513. [f. BROOD *sb.* + -Y[1].] **1.** Apt or inclined to breed. Now *dial.* **2.** Of a hen: Inclined to sit 1523. Hence **Broo·diness.**

Brook (bruk), *sb.* [OE. *brōc*, corresp. to LG. and HG. words meaning 'marsh, bog', MLG. *brōk*, (M)Du. *broek*, OHG. *bruoh* (G. *bruch*); of unkn. origin.] A small stream; *orig.* a torrent. Also *transf.*

These rivers are fed by numberless brooks MORSE. *Comb.* **B. ouzel** or **B. runner,** the Water-rail. Also in many plant-names.

Brook (bruk), *v.* [OE. *brūcan* = OFris. *brūka*, OS. *brūkan* (Du. *bruiken*), OHG. *brūhhan* (G. *brauchen* use, want, need), Goth. *brūkjan*, Gmc. deriv. of **brūk-* make use of :– IE. **bhrug-*, whence L. *frui* enjoy.] **1.** *trans.* To enjoy the use of, profit by; to possess, hold. *Obs.* exc. *Sc.* and *arch.* † **2.** To make use of (food); later, to digest, to bear on the stomach –1598. Also *fig.* **3.** To put up with [cf. 2]. Now chiefly in neg. constructions. 1530.

1. † *To b. a name* (*well*): to act consistently with it, do it credit. **3.** Heav'n..Brooks not the works of violence and war MILT. *P.L.* VI. 274.

Brookite (bru·kəit). 1879. [f. H. J. *Brooke*, mineralogist, + -ITE[1] 2 b.] *Min.* Native titanic anhydride.

Brooklet (bru·klėt). 1813. [f. BROOK *sb.* + -LET.] A little brook. So † **Broo·ket.**

Brooklime (bru·k,ləim). 1450. [orig. *brokelemk* (OE. *hleomoce* = MLG. *lōmeke*), whence *brooklem, lyme* (XVI).] A species of Speedwell (*Veronica beccabunga*); also Lesser Brooklime (*V. anagallis*).

Brool (brūl). 1837. [– G. *brüll* (poet. for *gebrüll*), f. *brüllen* roar.] A low deep humming sound; a murmur. Also *fig.*

List to the b. of that royal forest-voice CARLYLE.

Broom (brūm), *sb.* [OE. *brōm*, corresp. to MLG. *brām*, MDu. *brāme* (Du. *braam*), OHG. *brāmo, brāma*; cf. also MLG. *brēme*, MDu. *bremme*, OHG. *brāmma* brier, and forms s.v. BRAMBLE.] **1.** A shrub, *Sarothamnus* or *Cytisus scoparius* (N. O. *Leguminosæ*), bearing yellow papilionaceous flowers. Also the genus to which this belongs, and the allied genus *Genista*, including the White Broom, and Giant or Irish Broom, etc. **2.** Any one of various other plants used for sweeping, or fancied to be akin to the broom proper; as BUTCHER'S BROOM, SPANISH BROOM, q.v. **3.** Any implement for sweeping, a besom; orig. one made of twigs of broom, heather, etc., fixed to a handle. Cf. BESOM *sb.*[1] 2. ME. Also *fig.* and *transf.*

Comb.: **b.-bush,** *Parthenium hysterophorus*; **-cod,** the seed-vessel of the b.; **-cypress,** *Kochia scoparia*; **-grass,** *Andropogon scoparius*; **-heath,** *Erica tetralix*; **-sedge,** a species of coarse grass; **-scuires,** squatters in the New Forest, and elsewhere, who live by tying heath into brooms; **-tail** (of a horse), a long bushy tail; **-weed,** a tropical American plant (*Corchorus siliquosus*), from the leaves of which a drink is prepared.

Broom (brūm), *v.* 1627. [f. prec. sb.] **1.** *trans.* To sweep with a broom 1838. **2.** To BREAM a ship (Dicts.) 1627.

Broo·m corn. 1817. [f. (in U.S.) BROOM + (Indian) CORN.] The U.S. name of the Common Millet, *Sorghum vulgare*, of which the panicles are made into brooms, etc.; also the *Sorghum saccharatum* of the East.

Broomrape (brū·mrēⁱp). 1578. [tr. med.L. *Rapum genistæ* broom tuber.] A large genus of parasitic herbs (*Orobanche*), which attach themselves to the roots of broom and other plants, having a leafless fleshy stem furnished with pointed scales. First applied to *O. major*.

Broomstaff (brū·mstaf). *arch.* Also **-stave.** *rare.* Pl. **-staffs, -staves.** 1613. The staff or handle of a broom, a broomstick.

Broomstick (brū·mstik). 1683. Same as BROOMSTAFF.

To marry over the b.: to go through a *quasi*-marriage ceremony, in which the parties jump over a b.; = *to jump the besom.*

Broomy (brū·mi), *a.* 1649. [f. BROOM *sb.* + -Y [1].] **1.** Covered with broom. † **2.** Of or pertaining to a broom or besom. SWIFT. **3.** Broom-like (*rare*) 1807.

1. The b. banks of Nith BURNS.

Broose. *Sc.* 1786. [Sc. pronō. *brz*, *brūz*; of unkn. origin.] A race by the young men present at country weddings in the north, the course being from the bride's former home to the bridegroom's house. (A survival from primitive marriage-customs. Cf. BRIDE-LOPE.)

Brose (brōᵘz). 1657. [mod. Sc. form of BREWIS; see also BROO.] A dish made by pouring boiling water (or milk) on oatmeal (or oat-cake) seasoned with salt and butter.

Pease b.: a similar dish of pease-meal. *Athole b.*: a mixture of whisky and honey.

† **Bro·tel, brotle,** *a.* [ME. *brotil, brutil*, f. *broten* broken, pa. pple. of OE. *brēotan* (see BRITE *v.*). In use *brotel* appears as one of the various forms of *britil, bretil*, BRITTLE, and it may have been of later analogical formation. Cf. BRICKLE.] Brittle; mortal –1529. Also *fig.* Hence † **Bro·telness.**

Broth (brǫþ), *sb.* [OE. *broþ* = OHG. *brod*, ON. *broð* :- Gmc. **broþam*, f. (**bro*-) **bru*-, base of BREW.] A decoction; *esp.* that in which meat is boiled; also a thin soup made from this and vegetables, as Scotch 'broth'. Also *fig.* and *transf.*

I am sure. .you love B. better than Soup STEELE. Phr. *A b. of a boy*: the essence of what a boy should be.

Brothel (brǫ·þ'l), *sb.* [Late ME. *broþel* worthless fellow, prostitute, f. OE. *ā*|*broþen* gone to ruin, pa. pple. of *brēoþan* deteriorate, degenerate (cf. *brieþel* worthless), of unkn. origin. For a similar formation cf. BROTEL, BROTLE. In the present sense (XVI), short for † *brothel-house*, by assoc. w. earlier BORDEL, which it superseded.] † **1.** A worthless abandoned fellow –1594. † **2.** A prostitute –1606. **3.** Short for *brothel's house, b.-house*; superseding BORDEL: A house of ill-fame 1593. Also *attrib.*

2. A company of concubins and brothels 1606. **3.** Keep thy foote out of Brothels *Lear* III. iv. 99. *Comb.* **b.-house** = sense 3. Hence † **Bro·theller,** a whoremonger. † **Bro·thelling,** whoring. † **Bro·thelry,** harlotry; also, a place of prostitutes.

Brother (brɒ·ðəɹ), *sb.* Pl. **brothers, brethren** (breð·rèn). [OE. *brōþor* = OFris. *brōther*, *brōder*, OS. *brōthar*, (M)Du. *broeder*, (M)LG. *brōder*, OHG. *bruodar* (G. *bruder*), ON. *bróðir*, Goth. *brōþar* :- Gmc. **brōþar* :- IE. **bhrāter*, whence Skr. *bhrātṛ*, Gr. φράτηρ, L. *frater*.] **1.** A male being related to others (male or female) as the child of the same parents or parent. In the latter case, he is more properly called a *half-b.*, or *b. of the half blood*. **b.** A kinsman, as uncle, nephew, cousin. (A Hebraism.) ME. **c.** One who is as a brother 1795. **2.** One of the same clan, city, fatherland; fellow-man, fellow-creature OE. **3.** A fellow-Christian; a co-religionist generally. (Pl. *brethren.*) OE. **4.** A fellow-member of a guild, corporation, or order; hence, one of the same profession, trade, society, or order. (Pl. *brethren.*) ME. **b.** Vaguely: One in the same case or position; a comrade, fellow. (Pl. usu. *brothers.*) ME. **5.** *esp.* A fellow-member of a religious order (cf. *frater, frère, friar*) 1500. **6.** *fig.* Of things ME. **7.** *attrib.* Bef. other sbs. (often hyphened) = *fellow-*. *Brother-man*: a man and brother. 1503. Also of things 1822.

1. His borne broder ME. **b.** *Gen.* 13:8. **c.** My friend, the b. of my love, My Arthur TENNYSON. **2.** Adams sonnes are my brethren *Much Ado* II. i. 67. **3.** The soul of our dear b. here departed *Bk. Com. Prayer*. *The Brethren*: in N. T. the members of the early Christian churches. Also adopted by some modern sects who reject orders in the church, e.g. the 'Brethren', or 'Plymouth Brethren'. **4. b.** Your B. Kings SHAKS. A b. to dragons, and a companion to owles *Job* 30:29. **6.** That April morn, Of this the very b. WORDSW. *Comb.*: **B.-consanguinean,** one born of the same father; **-uterine,** one born of the same mother.

Bro·ther, *v.* 1573. [f. prec.] **1.** To make a brother of; to admit to brotherhood; to address as brother. **2.** To be a brother to 1600.

Brother-german (brɒ:ðəɹ,dʒɜ·ɹmăn). Pl. **brothers-german** († **brethren-**). ME. [f. BROTHER *sb.* + GERMAN *a.*[1] 2.] A brother through both parents. (In early times used also as = 'brother-uterine'.)

Brotherhood (brɒ·ðərhud), also † **brotherhead.** [Not in OE.: prob. f. BROTHERRED, assim. to the *-hede* class through *brothered(e).*] **1.** The relation of a brother, or of brothers mutually. Also in spiritual sense. ME. **2.** Brotherliness, friendly alliance ME. † **3.** The rank of a 'brother' in a corporation. *Tr. & Cr.* I. iii. 104. **4.** An association of brothers; a fraternity or guild; also the brethren collectively ME. Also *fig.* of things 1728. **5.** Community of feeling uniting man and man 1784.

1. The b. of blood was not to wear out PUSEY. **4.** There is a b. of you, but I will breake it 1555. *fig.* A b. of lofty elms WORDSW. **5.** The common b. of man D'ISRAELI.

Brother-in-law (brɒ·ðərinlǭ:). ME. [app. 'in law' = *in Canon Law*; *esp.* with reference to intermarriage; see -IN-LAW.] *prop.* The brother of one's husband or wife, the husband of one's sister. Occas., the husband of one's wife's (or husband's) sister.

Brotherly (brɒ·ðəɹli), *a.* [OE. *brōþorlić*; see -LY [1].] Of or pertaining to a brother; also, characteristic of a brother, kind, affectionate. Hence **Bro·therliness. Bro·therly** *adv.*

† **Bro·therred.** [OE., f. *brōþor* + *-rǣden* condition; see -RED.] = BROTHERHOOD, q.v. –1542.

Brothership (-ʃip). [OE., f. as prec. + -SHIP.] **a.** Brotherly fellowship. **b.** A fraternity or guild-brotherhood 1866.

Bro·therwort. ME. Wild Thyme.

Brough. Now *Sc.* and *north.* 1496. [var. of BROCH.] A luminous ring round a shining body; a halo.

Brougham (brūm, brū·əm, brōᵘ·əm). 1851. [f. name of Henry Peter, Lord *Brougham* (1778–1868).] A one-horse closed carriage, with two or four wheels, for two or four persons.

Brought (brǭt). Pa. pple. of BRING *v.*

Brow (brau), *sb.*[1] [OE. *brū* :- Gmc. **brūs* :- IE. **bhrūs*, whence also Gr. ὀφρύς, Skr. *bhrus.*] † **1.** The eye-lash, L. *cilium*. Only in OE. † **2.** The eye-lid, L. *palpebra*. Usu. *pl.* –1500. **3.** 'The arch of hair over the eye' (J.). Usu. *pl.* Now EYE-BROW. ME. **4.** *pl.* The prominences of the forehead above the eyes. Now poet. = next sense. 1588. **5.** The forehead. (L. *frons.*) 1535. Also *fig.* **b.** *esp.* as the seat of the facial expressions of joy, sorrow, resolution, etc. (*poet.*) 1593. **6.** The projecting edge of a cliff or hill, standing over a steep. (From sense 3; though now occ. assoc. w. sense 5.) ME. **7.** *Coal-mining.* A gallery in a coal-mine running across the face of the coal.

3. *To knit, bend one's brows*: to frown. The charm of married brows TENNYSON. **4.** Did not they Put on my Browes this wreath of Victorie? *Jul. C.* V. iii. 82. **5.** Men of more b. then brain FULLER. Thy calm clear b., Wherein is glass'd serenity of soul BYRON.

Comb.: **b.-ague,** 'strictly supra-orbital neuralgia of malarious origin' (now = *Megrim*); **-antler,** the lowest tine of a stag's horn; **-point** = *brow-antler*; **-post** (*Archit.*), a cross-beam; **-snag, -tine** = *brow-antler*; **-stone** (cf. *brow-post*). Hence **Browed** *a.* having a b. or brows; chiefly in *comb.*, as *dark-browed*. † **Bro·wless** *a.* unabashed.

Brow (brau), *sb.*[2] 1867. [app. – Norw. *bru*, ON. *brú* bridge.] *Naut.* Old name for a ship's gangway.

Brow, *v. rare.* 1634. [f. BROW *sb.*[1]] To form a brow to, be on the brow of.

1. The hilly crofts That b. this bottom glade MILT.

Browbeat (brau·bīt), *v.* Pa. t. **browbeat,** Pa. pple. **browbeaten.** 1581. [f. BROW *sb.*[1] + BEAT *v.*] To bear down with stern, arrogant, or insolent looks or words; to bully. Also *fig.*

He browbeat the informers against us FIELDING. Hence **Brow·beater.**

† **Browd,** *v.* ME. [– OFr. *brouder* (mod. *broder*); see BROIDER, EMBROIDER.] **1.** *trans.* To broider, embroider –1503. **2.** To braid. CHAUCER.

† **Brow·et.** ME. [– (O)Fr. *brouet*, dim. of *breu* :- Rom. **brodo*; see BROO, BREWIS.] Soup or broth of the juice of boiled meat, thickened –1500.

Brow·is. Now *dial.* [ME. *broys, browis, browes* (whence mod. Sc. BROSE), later *brewis, brewes*; see BREWIS.] † **1.** = BREWIS –1658. **2.** A kind of BROSE; as the *browis* of the Sheffield Cutlers' Feast 1839.

Brown (braun), *a.* [OE. *brūn* = OFris., OS. *brūn* (Du. *bruin*), OHG. *brūn* (G. *braun*), ON. *brúnn* :- Gmc. **brūnaz* (whence Fr., Pr. *brun*, It. *bruno*). Reinforced in ME. from (O)Fr. *brun.*] **1.** Dusky, dark. (Now only poet.) **b.** *fig.* Gloomy, serious. See BROWN STUDY. **2.** Name of a composite colour produced by a mixture of red, yellow, and black ME. **3.** Of persons: Having the skin of a brown or dusky colour; dark-complexioned; tanned OE. † **4.** Of steel, etc.: Burnished. [Cf. Fr. *brunir.*] –1802.

1. Umbrage broad, And b. as Evening MILT. *P.L.* ix. 1088. **2.** *B. ant. bear, owl*; *b. willow*; *b. hæmatite*, etc. **3.** The b. Indian GOLDSM. Phr. *To do b.*: 'to do thoroughly', suggested by roasting; to cheat. *slang.*

Comb.: **b. coal,** lignite, etc.: **b. gannet, b. gull,** the Booby (*Sula fusca*); **b. gum,** the inspissated juice of *Eucalyptus resinifera*; **-heart,** a species of tree in Guiana; **-hen,** the female of the Black Grouse (*Tetrao tetrix*); **-holland** (see HOLLAND); **b. jolly,** corrupt. f. BRINJAL; **b. rust,** a disease of wheat caused by a parasitic fungus (*Trichobasis rubigo vera*); **-spar** (Min.), a variety of dolomite; also used of ankerite, magnesite, chalybite, etc.; **b. stout,** a superior kind of porter; **b. sugar,** unrefined or partially refined sugar; **-thrasher,** the (American) Ferruginous Thrush, called also the Brown Thrush (*Turdus rufus*); **b. ware,** a common kind of pottery. Hence **Brow·nish** *a.* **Brow·nness.**

Brown, *sb.* ME. [The adj. used absol.] **1.** Brown colour 1607. **b.** A pigment of a brown colour, as *Vandyke b.* 1549. **2.** Ellipt. (see quots.) ME. **b.** *slang.* A copper coin 1812.

1. The browns and greens of the heather W. BLACK. **2.** The b. [of roast meat] BURTON. March b. [fly] KINGSLEY.

Brown (braun), *v.* ME. [f. BROWN *a.*] **1.** *intr.* To become brown. **2.** *trans.* To make brown; to roast brown; to give (by a chemical process) a dull brown lustre to gun-barrels, etc. 1570.

Brown Bess. 1785. Familiar name given in the British Army to the old flint-lock musket, which had a brown walnut stock.

Brown bill, brown-bill. 1589. [See BILL *sb.*[1] 2.] A kind of halberd painted brown, once used by foot-soldiers and watchmen.

Brown Bills levied in the City Made Bills to pass the Grand Committee BUTLER *Hud.*

Brown bread. 1489. Any bread of a darker colour than white bread. Now *spec.* applied in England to bread made of unboulted flour, or whole meal. Also *attrib.*

Brown George. 1688. **1.** † A loaf of coarse brown bread. **b.** A hard coarse biscuit. † **2.** A kind of wig –1840. **3.** A brown earthenware vessel. Cf. BLACK JACK. 1861.

Brownian (brau·niăn), *a.* 1871. [f. Dr. Robert *Brown*, who first described the movement, see -IAN.] *B. movement*; the irregular oscillatory movement of microscopic particles suspended in a limpid fluid.

Brownie (brau·ni). 1513. [dim. of BROWN; = 'a wee brown man'; see -IE.] **1.** A benevolent goblin, supposed to haunt old houses, *esp.* farm-houses, in Scotland, and occ. to do household work while the family slept. **2.** A junior member of the Girl Guides 1916.

Brow·ning, *sb.* 1905. An automatic pistol invented by J. M. *Browning* of Utah, U.S.A. (1884–1926).

Browning (brau·niŋ), *vbl. sb.* 1769. [f. BROWN *v.* + -ING [1].] **1.** The process of making or becoming brown 1791. **2.** *Cookery.* A preparation for colouring gravy, etc., brown.

Brow·nism. 1617. [f. the surname *Brown* + -ISM.] **1.** The system of church-government advocated *c* 1581 by the Puritan Robert Brown, and adopted by the Independents. **2.** *Med.* The BRUNONIAN system. So **Brow·nist.**

Brown study. 1532. [orig. f. BROWN in sense of 'gloomy'.] A state of mental abstraction or musing: now *esp.* an idle reverie.

Brownwort (brau·nwɒɹt). ? *Obs.* OE. *Herb.* The Water Betony (*Scrophularia aquatica*), and perh. other species of *Scrophularia.*

Brow·ny, *a. rare.* 1582. [f. BROWN *a.* + -Y[1].] Inclining to brown.

† **Brow·sage.** 1610. [f. BROWSE *v.* + -AGE.] **1.** The browsing of cattle; *concr.* that on which they browse –1688. **2.** The right of browsing 1611.

Browse (brauz), *sb.*[1] 1523. [In XVI *brouse* – OFr. *brost* bud, young shoot, later *broust* (mod. *brout*), prob. of Gmc. origin; but the loss of *t* in Eng. is unexplained.] **1.** Young shoots and twigs of shrubs, trees, etc., used as fodder for cattle. **2.** That which is or can be browsed 1552. **3.** The action of browsing 1810. Hence **B.-wood.**

1. Their gotes upon the brouzes fedd SPENSER. **2.** Th' unworthy browze Of buffaloes DRYDEN.

Browse, *sb.*[2] 1875. *Min.* [Origin unkn.] A variety of slag.

Browse, browze (brauz), *v.* [Late ME. *brouse, bruse* (XV) – OFr. *broster* (mod. *brouter*) to crop, f. *brost*; see BROWSE *sb.*[1]] **1.** *intr.* and *absol.* To feed *on* the leaves and shoots of trees and bushes: said of goats, deer, cattle. (Also carelessly used for *graze.*) 1542. Also *fig.* and *transf.* **2.** *trans.* To crop and eat (leaves, twigs, etc.) 1523. **3.** *causal.* To feed (cattle) *on* (twigs, etc.) 1550.

1. Cattell forsaking the..pastures to broose vpon leaues and boughes T. TAYLOR. **2.** Trees..perpetually browsed down by the cattle DARWIN. Hence **Brow·ser,** ? one who feeds the deer in winter time; an animal which browses.

Browsing (brau·ziŋ), *vbl. sb.* 1580. [f. prec. + -ING[1].] The action of the vb.; also *concr.* shoots and leaves; browsing-ground.

‖ **Bruchus** (brū·kɒs). ME. [L. – Gr. βροῦχος 'a wingless locust'.] **1.** = BRUKE. **2.** A genus of rhynchophorous beetles, the larvæ of which are destructive to pease, etc. Hence **Bru·chian,** one of the genus *B.*

Brucine (brū·sain). 1823. [From *Brucea antidysenterica* + -INE[5].] *Chem.* A poisonous vegetable alkaloid existing in false Angostura bark, and in Nux Vomica. var. ‖ **Bru·cia.**

Brucite (brū·səit). 1868. [f. A. *Bruce*, an American mineralogist + -ITE[1] 2 b.] *Min.* A native hydrate of magnesia.

Bru·ckle, *v.* Now *dial.* 1648. [prob. a frequentative of Sc. *bruik*; see -LE.] To begrime.

† **Bruges.** 1517. Name of a city of Flanders, used *attrib.* in *B. satin*, and occas. elliptically.

Bruin (brū·in). 1481. [– Du. *bruin*, the Du. form of BROWN used as the name of the bear in *Reynard the Fox.*] Applied, as a proper name, to the Brown Bear. (But now often used without capital B.)

Bruise (brūz), *sb.* 1441. [f. the vb.] † **1.** A breaking; a breach –1530. **2.** An injury to the body by a blunt or heavy instrument, causing discoloration but not laceration of the skin; a contusion 1541. **b.** Of a plant, fruit, etc. 1678.

One arm'd with metal, th' other with wood, This fit for b., and that for blood BUTLER *Hud.*

Bruise (brūz), *v.* [OE. *brȳsan* crush, ME. *brüse, brise, brese,* with which coalesced *brüse, broyse, brose,* later *bruise* – AFr. *bruser*, OFr. *bruisier* (mod. *briser*) break, smash, of unkn. origin.] **1.** *trans.* 'To crush by any weight' (J.). But now: To injure by a blow which discolours the skin but does not lacerate it, and breaks no bones; to contuse. Also *transf.* † **2.** [f. Fr.] To break (*in pieces, down*), to smash –1611. **3.** *fig.* (to senses 1, 2, 4) ME. **4.** To beat small, crush, bray, grind down ME.

1. It shal b. thy head, and thou shalt b. his heele *Gen.* 3:15. **2.** As yron brusseth and breaketh all thinges COVERDALE *Dan.* 2:40. **3.** An Iron Rod to b. and breake Thy disobedience MILT. *P.L.* v. 884. **4.** Pot-herbs..bruis'd with Vervain DRYDEN.

Hence **Bruised** *ppl. a.*; of blood: extravasated.

Bruiser (brū·zəɹ). 1586. [f. BRUISE *v.* + -ER[1].] **1.** One who bruises or crushes. **2.** A prize-fighter 1744. **3.** *Hunting slang.* One who rides recklessly 1830. **4.** A concave tool used in grinding lenses or specula 1777.

2. Bear-garden bruisers H. WALPOLE.

† **Brui·sewort.** OE. *Herb.* A plant supposed to heal bruises, *esp.* the Common Daisy –1830.

Bruit (brūt), *sb.* 1450. [– (O)Fr. *bruit*, subst. use of pa. pple. of *bruire* roar :– Rom. **brūgere*, alt. of L. *rugire* roar, by assoc. w. **bragere* BRAY *v.*[1]] **1.** Noise, din, clamour (*arch.*). **2.** Report noised abroad, rumour (*arch.*) 1494. † **3.** Renown –1609. ‖ **4.** *Med.* Any sound heard in auscultation; e.g. *bruit de souffle.* [Fr.]

1. The b. of arms MERIVALE. **2.** An uncertain b. from Barbadoes of some disorder there EVELYN.

Bruit (brūt), *v.* 1525. [f. the sb.] **1.** *trans.* To noise, report, rumour. Often with *abroad, about.* 1528. Also *intr.* KEATS. **2.** *trans.* To speak of, make famous 1553.

1. I finde thou art no lesse then Fame hath bruited 1 *Hen. VI*, II. iii. 68.

Bruke. Now *dial.* ME. [– L. *brucus, bruchus*; see BRUCHUS.] **1.** A locust without wings; ? the larva of the locust. **2.** A field-cricket (*north.*) 1847.

Brum. 1881. Contr. of BRUMMAGEM; *attrib.* 'counterfeit, not genuine'.

‖ **Brumaire** (brümę̄·r). 1803. [Fr., f. *brume* fog + *-aire* -ARY[1]; see BRUME.] The second month (Oct. 22 to Nov. 20) in the calendar of the French Republic, introduced in 1793.

Brumal (brū·măl), *a.* 1513. [– L. *brumalis*, f. *bruma* winter; see -AL[1].] Belonging to winter; wintry.

The brumall Solstice SIR T. BROWNE.

Brume (brūm). 1808. [– Fr. *brume* fog :– L. *bruma* (prec.).] Fog, mist, vapour.

The drifting b. LONGF.

Brummagem (brɒ·mĕdʒĕm). 1681. **A.** *sb.* **1.** A local vulgar form of *Birmingham.* Hence (contemptuously) An article made at Birmingham: *spec.* **a.** A counterfeit coin; **b.** a spur. 1834. **2.** *Eng. Hist.* = 'Birmingham (i.e. counterfeit) Protestant'. See ANTI-BIRMINGHAM. 1681.

B. *attrib.* or *adj.* **1.** Made at Birmingham. **b.** With allusion to counterfeit groats, plate, etc.: Counterfeit, sham; cheap and showy 1637. **2.** *Hist.* Of or pertaining to the 'Birminghams' of 1680; see A 2. 1681.

1. b. I coined heroes as fast as Brumingham groats T. BROWN. B. jewellery 1861.

Brumous (brū·məs), *a.* 1850. [– Fr. *brumeux* – late L. *brumosus* rainy (Isidore), f. *bruma*; see BRUME, -OUS.] Foggy, wintry.

† **Brunel, -elle.** 1597. [abbrev. of *Brunella*, the L. name now less correctly written *Prunella.*] The plant Self-heal.

Brunette (brune·t, brüne·t). 1712. [– (O)Fr. *brunette*, fem. of *brunet*, f. *brun* BROWN; see -ETTE.] **A.** *sb.* A girl or woman of a dark complexion 1713. **B.** *adj.* Of dark complexion, brown-haired; nut-brown. Also *absol.* the colour. 1712.

† **Bru·nion.** 1706. [– Fr. *brugnon.*] A nectarine. (Dicts.)

Brunonian (brunōᵘ·niăn), *a.* 1799. [f. *Bruno*, Latinized f. the name *Brown* + -IAN.] Applied to a system or theory of medicine founded by Dr. John Brown (1735–1788), according to which all diseases arise either from deficiency or excess of excitement, and must be treated with stimulants or sedatives. **b.** *sb.* One who holds this theory.

Brunswick (brɒ·nzwik). 1480. [– LG. *Brunswik* (G. *Braunschweig*), f. gen. of *Brūn* Bruno (the founder) + *wik* WICK[2].] **1.** The name of a town and province of Germany. † **2.** Hence the name of a textile fabric 1480. **B. black,** a black varnish made of turpentine and asphalt or lamp-black; **B. green,** a green pigment consisting of oxychloride of copper.

Brunt (brɒnt), *sb.* ME. [Origin unkn.] † **1.** A sharp blow –1485. † **2.** An onset, violent attack. (Often with *bear*, etc.) –1821. **3.** Shock; violence (of an attack) 1573. **4.** The chief stress; crisis. (Formerly *chief b.*) [perh. influenced by *burnt* (in Sc. *brunt*).] 1769. † **5.** A sudden effort, or outburst –1670.

3. The first b. of the enemy's attack WELLINGTON. The b. of their argument JOWETT. **4.** The b. of the danger seems past CARLYLE.

Brunt (brɒnt), *v. rare.* 1440. [f. BRUNT *sb.*] † **1.** *intr.* To make an assault or attack –1690. **2.** *trans.* To bear the brunt of (*rare*) 1859.

Brunt, obs. and dial. pa. t. and pple. of BURN *v.*

Brush (brɒʃ), *sb.*[1] [ME. *brusche* – AFr. *brousse*, OFr. *broce, brosse* (whence Fr. *broussaille*) :– Rom. **bruscia*, perh. f. L. *bruscum* excrescence on the maple (Pliny).] **1.** Loppings of trees or hedges; cut brushwood (now in U.S.). **b.** A faggot of such brushwood ME. **2.** The small growing trees or shrubs of a wood; a thicket of small trees or underwood. (Esp. in U.S., Canada, and Australia.) 1440. † **3.** Stubble –1790.

Comb.: **b.-kangaroo,** a species inhabiting the Australian b.; **-turkey,** an Australian bird (*Talegalla lathami*).

Brush (brɒʃ), *sb.*[2] ME. [– OFr. *broisse*, (also mod.) *brosse*, perh. to be identified with prec.; cf. BROOM.] **1.** A utensil consisting of a piece of wood or other material, set with small tufts or bunches of bristles, hair, etc., for sweeping or scrubbing dust and dirt from a surface; and generally any utensil for brushing or sweeping. (*Brushes* are of many shapes and materials. They are named according to their use, as *clothes-, hat-, hairbrush*, etc.) **2.** An instrument consisting of a bunch of hairs attached to a handle, for applying moisture, colours, etc., to a surface 1483. **b.** The painter's art or skill 1687. **3.** Any brush-like bunch or tuft; *spec.* the tail of the fox 1581. **4.** *Entom.* A brush-like organ on the legs of bees, etc. 1828. **5.** *Electr.* A brush-like discharge of sparks. **b.** A piece of metal terminating in metallic wires, or strips of carbon or copper, used for securing good metallic connection between two portions of an electrical instrument 1789. **6.** *Optics.* Bright or dark figures accompanying certain phenomena observed in polarized light, which suggest the idea of brushes 1817. **7.** (f. BRUSH *v.*[2]) An application of a brush 1822. **8.** A graze, *esp.* on a horse's leg 1710. **9.** *attrib.* Brush-like 1675.

2. b. Bretheren of the b. STERNE. **3.** The squirrel, flippant..whisks his b. COWPER. **7.** He..gives his beaver a b. SCOTT.

Comb.: **b.-grass,** *Andropogon gryllus*; **-ore, -iron-ore,** an iron ore found in the Forest of Dean; **-wheel,** (*a*) a wheel which turns another by means of bristles, cloth, leather, etc., fixed on their circumferences; (*b*) a circular revolving b. used for polishing, etc. Hence **Bru·shless** *a.*

Brush (brɒʃ), *sb.*[3] ME. [f. BRUSH *v.*[1]] **1.** A forcible rush, a hostile encounter; now *esp.* a short but smart encounter. Hence *At a* (*the first*) *b.* Also *fig.* **2.** ? A slight attack of illness. (Cf. BRASH.) SWIFT.

1. A smart b. with the Spaniards KINGSLEY.

Brush (brɒʃ), *v.*[1] ME. [– OFr. *brosser* go through brushwood, f. *brosse* BRUSH *sb.*[1]] † **1.** *intr.* To rush with force or speed, usu. into collision –1650. † **2.** To force with a rush –1470. **3.** To burst away with a rush, decamp 1690. **4.** *intr.* (cf. BRUSH *v.*[2]) To move briskly *by, through, against* anything, grazing it or sweeping it aside in passing 1674.

3. He brush'd apace On to the abbey BYRON. **4.** A pretty young thing..brushing by me ADDISON.

Brush (brɒʃ), *v.*[2] 1460. [f. BRUSH *sb.*[2]] **1.** *trans.* To pass a brush briskly across (a surface) so as to remove dirt or dust, or to smooth the surface. **2.** To rub softly as with a brush in passing; to graze lightly or quickly 1647. Also *intr.* **3.** To remove (dust, etc.) with a brush, to sweep (away). Also *transf.* and *fig.* To sweep away as with a brush. 1631. **4.** To injure by grazing 1691.

1. A brushes his hat a mornings *Much Ado* III. ii. 41. *To b. up*: to brighten up by brushing; also *fig.* to revive one's acquaintance with anything. *To b. (a thing) over*: to paint lightly; also *fig.* **3.** It is..time to b. this nonsense away 1884. Hence **Bru·sher,** one who brushes or uses a b.; also *techn.* in various trades. **Bru·shing** *vbl. sb.*; whence **brushing-machine,** a name of machines acting as brushes for smoothing, dressing flax, etc.

Brushite (brɒ·ʃəit). 1880. [f. Prof. *Brush* of Yale, U.S.; see -ITE[1] 2 b.] *Min.* A hydrous phosphate of lime.

Brushwood (brʊ·ʃwud). 1613. [f. BRUSH sb.[1]] **1.** Cut or broken twigs or branches 1637. Also *fig.* **2.** Small growing trees or shrubs; thicket, underwood 1732.

Brushy (brʊ·ʃi), *a.*[1] 1719. [f. BRUSH sb.[1] + -Y[1].] Covered with brush.

Bru·shy, *a.*[2] 1673. [f. BRUSH sb.[2] + -Y[1].] Brush-like; bushy, shaggy.

† **Brusk,** *a.* 1486. [Origin unkn.] *Her.* The colour *tawny* or *orange* –1688.

Brusk(e, obs. f. BRUSQUE.

Brusque (brʊsk, brüsk), *a.* 1601. [– Fr. *brusque* lively, fierce, harsh – It. *brusco* sour, tart, sour-looking, a use of the sb. = Sp., Pg. *brusco* butcher's broom (a spiny bush):– Rom. **bruscum*, perh. blend of L. *ruscum* butcher's broom with **brucus* heather (see BRIAR). Cf. BRISK.] † **1.** Tart. (= It. *brusco.*) **2.** Somewhat rough or rude in manner; blunt, offhand 1651.

2. He was brusk, ungracious, scowling, and silent DISRAELI. Hence **Bru·sque-ly** *adv.*, **-ness.**

Brusque, *v.* 1826. [f. prec.] To treat brusquely or in an off-handed way.

To b. it: to assume a brusque manner.

‖ **Brusquerie** (brüskəri). 1752. [Fr.] Bluntness, abruptness of manner.

Erring, if at all, ever on the side of b. RUSKIN.

Brussels (brʊ·sělz). Name of the capital of Belgium: hence, **1.** Short for 'Brussels carpet' 1845. **2.** *attrib.*, as **B. carpet,** a carpet having a back of stout linen thread and an upper surface of wool; **B. lace,** a costly kind of pillow-lace made in B.; **B. sprout** (usu. *pl.*), the bud-bearing Cabbage (*Brassica oleracea gemmifera*), producing buds like small cabbages in the axils of its leaves 1748.

† **Bru·stle,** *v.*[1] [Early ME. *brustlien*, var. of *brastlien* OE. *brastlian*; of echoic origin.] *intr.* To crackle, rustle –1755.

† **Bru·stle,** *v.*[2] 1648. [var. of BRISTLE *v.*] **1.** *intr.* To bristle as hair. **2.** To bristle *up*, raise the mane 1656. **3.** *esp.* Of birds: To raise the feathers; hence *fig.* To show off, bluster –1800.

† **Bru·sure.** ME. [– OFr. *briseüre* (mod. *brisure*), f. *briser* break; see -URE.] **1.** Bruising or crushing; a bruise –1494. **2.** Breaking, breach; ruin –1506.

‖ **Brut** (brūt). 1450. [= MWelsh *brut*, mod.W. *brud* 'chronicle', a transf. use of *Brut* = *Brutus*, as in the *Brut* of Layamon.] A chronicle of British history from the mythical Brutus downward.

† **Brut,** *v.* 1577. [perh. – Fr. *brouter* (see BROWSE *v.*); but cf. *bret*, *brit* (XVI), perh. – OE. *brēotan* (see BRITE *v.*).] **1.** To browse –1699. **2.** *trans. dial.* To break *off* (young shoots).

Brutal (brū·tăl), *a.* 1450. [– (O)Fr. *brutal* or med.L. *brutalis*, f. L. *brutus* BRUTE + -AL[1].] **1.** Of or belonging to the brutes, as opp. to man; of the nature of a brute; animal (*arch.*). **2.** Pertaining to or resembling the brutes: **a.** in irrationality 1510; **b.** in sensuality 1534; **c.** in coarseness 1709. **3.** Inhuman; coarsely cruel, savage 1641.

2. a. A sort of b. Courage DE FOE. **b.** The slaves of b. appetite SMOLLETT. **c.** [Tyrconnel's] b. manners MACAULAY. **3.** The cruel and b. abominations of slavery MORLEY. Hence **Bru·talism,** b. state. **Bru·tally** *adv.*

Brutality (brutæ·liti). 1549. [f. prec. + -ITY; cf. Fr. *brutalité*.] **1.** The condition of the brutes 1711. **2.** The quality of being brutal (see BRUTAL 2) 1549. **3.** Inhumanity; an inhuman action 1633.

1. From b. to reason and speech 1863. **3.** The Brutallity of the Turkish Troops 1693.

Brutalize (brū·tăləiz), *v.* 1704. [f. as prec. + -IZE; cf. Fr. *brutaliser*.] **1.** To live or become like a brute 1716. **2.** *trans.* To render brutal or inhuman 1704. **3.** To treat brutally 1879.

1. If possible we b. more and more H. WALPOLE. Hence **Bru:taliza·tion.**

Brute (brūt), *a.* and *sb.*[1] 1460. [– Fr. *brut*, *brute* = Sp., It. *bruto* – L. *brutus* heavy, stupid, dull.] **A.** *adj.* (Often *sb.* used *attrib.*) **1.** Of animals: Wanting in reason, as *b. beasts*, = the 'lower animals'. **2.** Of human beings and their attributes: Brute-like, brutish; stupid; unreasoning; sensual 1535. **b.** Rude, wanting in sensibility 1555. **3.** Of things: Irrational, unconscious, senseless; merely material; *esp.* in *b. matter, force* 1540.

2. A b. conjugality MILT. **b.** This b. Libel MILT. **3.** A tendency to prevail over b. force BUTLER. Hence **Bru·te-ly** *adv.*, **-ness.**

B. *sb.* **1.** One of the lower animals as distinguished from man 1611. **b.** The animal nature in man 1784. **2.** A man resembling a brute in want of intelligence, cruelty, coarseness, etc. Now (*colloq.*) often merely a term of reprobation. 1670.

1. My Image not imparted to the B. MILT. *P.L.* VIII. 441. **b.** Exalt the b. and sink the man BURNS. **2.** The b. of a cigar required relighting GEO. ELIOT. Hence **Bru·tehood.**

† **Brute,** *sb.*[2] 1513. [In sense 1, a var. of *Brett* or *Britt*, influenced by the *Brutus* myth; in 2, = *Brut, Brutus*.] **1.** A Briton, a Welshman –1586. **2.** The legendary Trojan Brutus, first king of Britain. **b.** A Brutus, a hero of British, Welsh, or Arthurian story. **c.** Hence, generally, a hero, 'brave', 'worthy'. –1599.

Brutify (brū·tifəi), *v.* 1668. [f. BRUTE + -FY.] To make or become brute-like; to brutalize.

Hopeless slavery effectually brutifies the intellect MILL. Hence **Bru:tifica·tion.**

Brutish (brū·tiʃ), *a.* 1494. [f. BRUTE + -ISH[1].] **1.** Of or pertaining to the brutes 1534. **2.** = BRUTAL 2. 1555. † **3.** Rude, rough; savage –1773. † **4.** = BRUTE *a.* 3. Of thunder: Striking blindly. [after L. *brutum fulmen*.] –1640.

1. Wandring Gods disguis'd in b. forms Rather then human MILT. *P.L.* I. 481. **2.** Slowe and brutysshe wyttes 1555. B. Lusts and Appetites STEELE. Hence **Bru·tish-ly** *adv.*, **-ness.**

Brutism (brū·tiz'm). 1687. [f. as prec. + -ISM.] The behaviour or condition of a brute.

Brutus (brū·tŏs). 1851. In full *Brutus wig*. A rough-cropped head was so called by the French, after Brutus.

Bry-, in obs. words; see BRI-.

Bryology (brəi,ǫ·lŏdʒi). 1863. [f. Gr. βρύον moss + -LOGY.] That branch of botany which treats of mosses. Also, the mosses (collectively) of any country or place. Hence **Bryolo·gical** *a.*, **-ly** *adv.* **Bryo·logist.**

† **Bry·on.** 1579. [– Fr. *bryon* or L. *bryon* – Gr. βρύον moss.] A kind of moss –1601.

Bryo·nia, L. form of BRYONY.

Bryonin (brəi·ŏnin). 1836. [f. BRYONY + -IN[1].] The bitter principle of the root of *Bryonia dioica*.

Bryony (brəi·ŏni). OE. [– L. *bryonia* (Pliny) – Gr. βρυωνία.] **1.** *prop.* Name of the plant-genus Bryonia (N.O. *Cucurbitaceæ*); and *spec.* the common wild species (*B. dioica*), occas. called Red, or White B. **2. Black B.**: Lady's Seal, *Tamus communis* (N.O. *Dioscoreaceæ*) 1626. **3. Bastard B.**: *Cissus sicyoides*.

Comb. **b.-vine** = sense 1.

‖ **Bryozoa** (brəiŏzōᵘ·ă), *sb. pl.*; sing. **-zoon** (-zōᵘ·ǫn). 1847. [mod.L., f. Gr. βρύον moss + ζῷα, pl. of ζῷον animal.] *Zool.* A phylum of small colonial aquatic animals forming tuft-like or moss-like aggregate masses, each individual having a distinct alimentary canal. Hence **Bryozo·an** *a.*, *sb.*

Brys-, Bryt-, in obs. forms; see BRI-.

Brython (bri·þǫn). 1884. [– W. *Brython* Britons :– OCelt. **Brittones*, pl. of **Britto*; see BRITON.] A Briton of Wales, Cornwall, or ancient Cumbria. Hence **Brytho·nic** *a.*

Buat, var. of BOWET, *Sc.*, a lantern.

Bub (bʊb), *sb.*[1] 1671. [prob. echoic.] **1.** Drink, *esp.* strong beer (*slang*). **2.** A mixture of meal and yeast with warm wort and water, used to promote fermentation 1880.

Bub, *sb.*[2] Contr. of BUBBY[1], [2].

† **Bub,** *v.*[1] *rare.* 1563. [Short for BUBBLE *v.*] To throw up in bubbles.

† **Bub,** *v.*[2] *rare.* 1719. [Short for BUBBLE *v.* 3.] ? To bribe, or ? to cheat.

Bubal, -ale (biū·băl). 1461. [– L. *bubalus* (– Gr. βούβαλος); cf. BUFFALO.] Used to render L. *bubalus*: **a.** (early) with uncertain meaning (antelope or buffalo). **b.** (mod. *Zool.*) A species of antelope (*Antilope bubalus*).

Bubble (bʊ·b'l), *sb.* 1481. [prob. imit. like the parallel Du. *bobbel*, G. dial. *bobbel*, *bubbel*; perh. in part a modification of the earlier BURBLE *sb.*] **1.** A thin vesicle of water or other liquid, filled with air or gas. Often = *soap-bubble*. Also a quantity of air or gas occluded within a liquid; *spec.* the air left in the spirit-level. Occ. a cavity produced by occluded air in a solid that has cooled from fusion. † **2.** *transf.* A hollow globe or bead of glass produced by blowing –1667. **3.** *fig.* Anything fragile, unsubstantial, or worthless; *esp.* a delusive commercial or financial scheme, as the *South Sea B.* 1599. Also *attrib.*, as *b. company*, etc. 1635. **4.** The process of bubbling; the sound made by bubbling; a state of agitation 1839. † **5.** One who is bubbled; a gull –1807.

1. The Earth hath bubbles, as the Water ha's *Macb.* I. iii. 79. **3.** The b. Reputation *A.Y.L.* II. vii. 152. **4.** *A b. of a sea* (Naut.). *Comb.* **b.-shell,** a sort of mollusc.

Bubble (bʊb'l), *v.* ME. [As prec.; parallel forms are Du. *bobbelen*, G. dial. *bobbeln*, *bubbeln*, Sw. *bubla*, Da. *boble*; cf. earlier BURBLE *v.*] **1.** *intr.* To form bubbles (as boiling water, etc.); to rise in bubbles; to emit the sounds due to bubbles forming and bursting. Also *fig.* **2.** *intr.* To make a sound as of bubbles in boiling or running water. Also *trans.* (*rare.*) 1602. **3.** *trans.* To delude with bubbles (sense 3); to cheat, humbug. Now *rare.* 1675.

1. Water, bubbling from this fountain P. FLETCHER. Phr. *To b. over, up* (with fun, etc.): *fig.* from the bubbling of a pot on the fire. **2.** At mine ears Bubbled the nightingale TENNYSON.

Bu:bble-and-squea·k. 1785. [From the sounds made in cooking the dish.] Meat and cabbage fried up together.

† **Bu·bble-bow, -boy.** 1727. [app. f. BUBBLE *v.* 3 + BEAU, as if 'Beau-befooler'.] A lady's tweezer case –1807.

Bubbler (bʊ·bləɹ). 1720. [f. BUBBLE *v.* + -ER[1].] † **1.** A swindler –1728. **2.** A fish of the Ohio river, so called from the noise it makes.

Bubbly (bʊ·bli), *a.* 1599. [f. BUBBLE *sb.* + -Y[1].] Full of bubbles. (In *Sc.* = blubbering.)

Bu·bbly-jock. *Sc.* 1814. [The first element is imit. of the bird's cry (cf. *gobbler*), the second is *jock* JACK.] A turkey-cock.

Bu·bby[1]. Now *dial.* 1686. [Cf. dial. G. *bübbi* teat.] A woman's breast.

Bubby[2]. 1848. [perh. childish pronunc. of *brother*; or = G. *bube* boy.] A little boy. (*U.S.*, *colloq.*)

Bubo (biū·bo). Pl. **buboes.** ME. [– L. *bubo*, *-on-* owl, med.L. swelling – Gr. βουβών groin, swelling in groin.] An inflamed swelling in glandular parts of the body, *esp.* the groin or arm-pits. Also *attrib.* Hence **Bu·boed** *ppl. a.* affected with buboes. **Bubo·nic** *a.* attended with the appearance of buboes.

Bubonocele (biubǫ·nŏsīl). 1615. [– mod.L. (Bacon) – Gr. βουβωνοκήλη, f. as prec. + κήλη rupture.] Inguinal hernia.

† **Bu·bukle.** Confusion of BUBO and CARBUNCLE. *Hen. V*, III. vi. 108.

Buccal (bʊ·kăl), *a.* 1831. [f. L. *bucca* cheek, mouth + -AL[1].] Of or pertaining to the cheek.

‖ **Bucca·n, buca·n, bouca·n,** *sb.* 1611. Also **bocan.** [– Fr. *boucan* barbecue (Tupi *mukem, mocaém*, whence Pg. *moquém*).] **1.** A wooden framework on which meat was roasted or smoked over a fire. (*S. Amer.*) **2.** (in form *bocan*) = BARBECUE *sb.* 4. 1857. **3.** Boucaned meat. [prop. Fr.] 1860. Hence **Bu·ccan** *v.* to roast or smoke (meat) upon a b.

Buccaneer, -ier (bʊkănīᵊ·ɹ), *sb.* 1661. [– Fr. *boucanier*, f. *boucaner* cure flesh on a *boucan* or barbecue (prec.); see -EER.] † **1.** *orig.* One who dries and smokes flesh on a *boucan*. The name was first given to the French hunters of St. Domingo. –1761. **2.** (From the subsequent habits of these.) One of the piratical rovers who infested the Spanish coasts in America 1690. **3.** A filibuster 1846. Hence **Buccanee·rish** *a.*

Buccaneer (bʊkănīᵊ·ɹ), *v.* 1795. [f. prec.] **a.** = To buccan. **b.** To act as a buccaneer.

Buccinal (bʊ·ksinăl), *a.* 1846. [f. L. *buc(c)ina* curved trumpet + -AL[1].] Shaped or sounding like a trumpet.

Buccinator (bʊ·ksineⁱtəɹ). 1671. [– L. *buc(c)inator*, f. *buc(c)inare* blow the *buc(c)ina*, or curved trumpet.] *Anat.* A flat thin muscle which forms the wall of the cheek.

So **Bu·ccinatory** *a.* pertaining to a trumpeter or trumpeting.

‖ **Buccinum** (bɒ·ksinǒm). 1601. [L. (Pliny), from a supposed resemblance to a trumpet.] *Zool.* The genus of gasteropod Molluscs represented by the Whelk. Hence **Bu·ccinoid** *a.* b.-like.

‖ **Bucellas** (biuse·lăs). 1836. [Name of a village near Lisbon.] A Portuguese white wine.

Bucentaur (biuse·ntǭɹ, biu·sentǭɹ). 1612. [– Fr. *bucentaure* (simulating *centaure* CENTAUR) = It. *bucentoro*, f. (Venetian) **bucio int' oro* 'barge in gold'.] *Hist.* The state barge in which on Ascension Day the Doge of Venice went to wed the Adriatic by dropping a ring into it. Also, a large ship 1623.

Bucephalus (biuse·fălǒs). 1799. [– L. *Bucephalus* – Gr. Βουκέφαλος name of Alexander the Great's charger, f. βοῦς ox + κεφαλή head.] The name of Alexander the Great's charger; (*joc.*) any riding-horse.

‖ **Buchu** (bɒ·ku, bu·ku). 1731. Native Cape name of the plant formerly called *Diosma crenata*; now assigned to species of *Barosma*.

Buck (bɒk), *sb.*[1] [(i) OE. *buc* male deer = MDu. *boc* (Du. *bok*), OHG. *boc* (G. *bock*), ON. *bukkr, bokkr* :– Gmc. **bukkaz*; (ii) OE. *bucca* he-goat = ON. *bokki* my good fellow, old buck :– **bukkon*.] **1.** The male of: **a.** † the goat –1551; **b.** the deer, *esp.* the fallow-deer OE.; **c.** the reindeer, the chamois, the hare, the rabbit, and in S. Africa (after Du. *bok*) any animal of the antelope kind 1674. **2.** *transf.* **a.** A dashing fellow; a dandy 1725. **b.** A man: used of S. Amer. Indians. *B. nigger:* a Negro man. (*U.S.*)

1. a. *To blow the buck's horn* (Chaucer): to have his labour for his pains. b. The b. is called..the fifth year *a b. of the first head*; and the sixth, *a great b.* GOLDSM. 2. a. I remember you a b. of bucks when that coat first came out to Calcutta THACKERAY.

† **Buck,** *sb.*[2] 1577. **1.** = BUCKWHEAT –1807. **2.** = BUCK-MAST; beech-mast –1727.

Buck, *sb.*[3] *arch.* and *dial.* 1530. [f. BUCK *v.*[1]] † **1.** ? A washing tub, a vat in which to steep clothes in lye. **2.** Lye in which linen, yarn, etc., is steeped in buck-washing or bleaching 1560. **3.** A quantity of clothes, etc. put through the process of bucking; a 'wash' 1532.

Buck (bɒk), *sb.*[4] 1851. [Origin unkn.] A basket used to catch eels. Also *attrib.*

Buck, *sb.*[5] 1691. [perh. a form of BOUK.] The body of a cart. (*dial.*)

Buck, *sb.*[6] *U.S.* 1860. [f. Du. *zaag-boc* (G. *sägebock*) or shortly *boc* (*bock*) = goat; cf. Fr. *chèvre*.] A frame on which wood is cross-cut; a saw-buck.

Comb. **b.-saw,** a heavy frame-saw used with a b.

Buck, *v.*[1] Now *dial.* [ME. *bouken, bowken* :– OE. **būcian*, corresp. to MHG. *būchen* (G. *beuchen*), LG. *būken*, Sw. *byka*, Da. *byge*, f. Gmc. **buk-*.] **1.** To steep or boil in an alkaline lye in buck-washing, or bleaching. **2.** To drench, soak 1494.

Buck (bɒk), *v.*[2] 1530. [f. BUCK *sb.*[1]] To copulate with; said of male rabbits, etc.

Buck (bɒk), *v.*[3] 1859. [f. BUCK *sb.*[1]] To leap vertically from the ground, drawing the feet together like a deer, and arching the back. Also trans. *To b. off.* Cf. BUCK-JUMP.

Buck (bɒk), *v.*[4] *U.S.* 1865. [perh. f. BUCK *sb.*[6]] *trans.* To lay across a log.

Buck (bɒk), *v.*[5] 1683. [Cf. Du. *boken, boocken* beat or strike (Hexham).] To break ore small with a bucker.

Buck, *v.*[6] *dial.* or *colloq.* 1854. [f. BUCK *sb.*[1] 2.] In *b. up*: To dress up; to make haste; to make or become vigorous or cheerful; *esp.* in *imper.* Buck up!

Buck-bean (bɒ·kbīn). 1578. [tr. Flem. *bocks boonen* 'goat's beans'.] *Herb.* A water plant (*Menyanthes trifoliata*) common in bogs in Britain; it bears racemes of pinkish white flowers.

Buckeen (bɒkī·n). *Anglo-Irish.* 1793. [f. BUCK *sb.*[1] + *-een*, Ir., Gael. *-in*, dim. suff. Cf. SQUIREEN.] A young man belonging to the inferior gentry of Ireland, or a cadet of the poorer aristocracy, having no profession, and aping the habits of the wealthy.

Bu·cker[1]. 1884. [f. BUCK *v.*[3]] A horse that bucks.

Bu·cker[2]. 1653. [f. BUCK *v.*[5]] *Mining.* A hammer for bucking ore.

Bucket (bɒ·kėt), *sb.*[1] ME. [– AFr. *buket, buquet* tub, pail (AL. *bo-, bukettum* XIII), perh. f. OE. *būc* belly, pitcher; see -ET.] **1.** 'The vessel in which water is drawn out of a well.' **b.** 'The vessel in which water is carried, particularly to quench a fire.' (J.)

Buckets are now chiefly of wood, and vary in shape. In England and U.S. they are round pails with arched handles; in Scotland, four-sided vessels for carrying salt, coal, etc.

2. The piston of a lift-pump 1634. **3.** One of the compartments on the circumference of a water-wheel, which retain the water while they descend; one of the metal cups on the endless band of a grain-elevator, etc. 1759. **4.** *transf.* A leathern socket or rest for a whip, or for a carbine or lance 1833.

1. Like a deepe Well, That owes two Buckets, filling one another *Rich. II*, IV. i. 185. *To kick the b.*: see BUCKET[2].

Comb.: **b.-engine,** a machine having buckets attached to an endless chain running over sprocket-wheels, so as to utilize the power of a small stream of water with a good fall; **-lift,** a set of iron pipes attached to a lift-pump; **-pump,** a lift-pump; **-well; -wheel,** a contrivance for raising water, consisting of buckets fixed round a wheel, or attached to a rope passing round a wheel, which fill at the bottom and empty themselves at the top.

Bu·cket, *sb.*[2] 1570. [perh. – OFr. *buquet* 'balance'.] A beam or yoke on which anything may be hung, as, in Norfolk, a pig by its heels. Hence (?) *To kick the b.*: (*slang*) to die.

Bucket (bɒ·kėt), *v.* 1621. [f. BUCKET *sb.*[1]] **1.** *trans.* To lift (water) in buckets. Also *fig.* 1649. **2.** To pour buckets of water over 1621. **3.** *slang.* To swindle 1812. **4.** To ride (a horse) hard; to pump (take it out of him by bucketfuls) 1856. **5.** *Rowing. intr.* To hurry the forward swing of the body; also *trans.* 1869.

5. A..tendency to b. the recovery 1882.

Bu·cket-shop. *U.S.* 1882. [orig. a place where liquor was obtainable in buckets, etc., supplied by customers. Hence transf.] An unauthorized office used orig. for smaller gambling transactions in grain, and subseq. extended to offices for other descriptions of gambling and betting on the stocks, etc.

Bu·ckety. *Sc.* ['A corruption of buckwheat' (Jamieson).] Paste used by weavers in dressing their webs.

Bu·ck-eye. 1789. [f. BUCK *sb.*[1] + EYE.] *Bot.* **1.** The American Horse-chestnut (*Æsculus glabra*). **2.** *U.S. colloq.* A native of Ohio, the 'Buckeye State'.

1. Called buck-eye..from the hilum of the fruit having the appearance of a stag's eye 1841.

Buck-eyed, *a.* 1847. *Farriery.* Having bad or speckled eyes; said of horses.

Buck-horn (bɒ·khǭrn). Also **Buck's horn.** 1447. [f. BUCK *sb.*[1]] † **1.** The horn of a buck. **b.** The horn of a goat used for blowing a blast. –1548. **2.** The material of a buck's horn; also *attrib.* horny 1613. **3.** From its hardness: Dried whiting or other fish 1602.

Buck-hound (bɒ·khaund). 1530. [f. as prec.] A smaller variety of staghound. *Master of the Buckhounds*, an officer of the Royal Household.

Buckie (bɒ·ki). *Sc.* 1596. [Sense 1: origin unkn.; sense 2: app. f. BUCK *sb.*[1]] **1.** The whorled shell of any mollusc; *e.g.* a whelk. Cf. BUCCINUM. **2.** A perverse or refractory person 1719.

Bucking (bɒ·kiŋ), *vbl. sb.*[1] 1483. [f. BUCK *v.*[1] + -ING[1].] Steeping or boiling yarn, clothes, etc., in a lye, in the old process of bleaching, or in buck-washing; the quantity so treated.

Comb.: **b.-keir,** a large wooden vat used in b.; **-washing,** the annual purification of family linen by means of buck.

Bu·cking, *vbl. sb.*[2] 1875. [f. BUCK *v.*[5] + -ING[1].] *Mining.* The bruising of ore with a bucker.

Buckish (bɒ·kiʃ), *a.* 1515. [f. BUCK *sb.*[1] + -ISH[1].] **1.** Like or characteristic of a he-goat; lascivious; ill-smelling. **2.** Foppish 1806.

Bu·ck-jump. 1878. [f. BUCK *sb.*[1]] A leap like that of a buck. *esp.* A jump of a horse that bucks (see BUCK *v.*[3]). Of American or Australian origin. Hence **Bu·ck-jump** *v.* = BUCK *v.*[3] **Buck-jumper.**

Buckle (bɒ·k'l), *sb.* ME. [– (O)Fr. *boucle* :– L. *buccula* cheek-strap of a helmet, dim. of *bucca* cheek, boss of a shield.] **1.** A rim of metal, with a hinged tongue carrying one or more spikes, for securing a belt, strap, etc., which passes through the rim, and is pierced by the spike or spikes. Often defined, as *shoe-b.*, etc. † **2.** The drop of an ear-ring. (Fr. *boucle d'oreille.*) 1674. † **3.** The state of hair when crisped and curled –1789.

Comb.: **b.-covering,** a certain step in dancing; so, *to cover the b.*; **-plates,** plates of iron buckled or bent concave; **-wig,** see BUCKLE *v.* 5.

Buckle (bɒ·k'l), *v.* ME. [f prec. sb.; **in** sense 6, after Fr. *boucler*.] **1.** *trans.* To fasten with a buckle. **2.** *trans.* To equip, prepare (for battle, etc.). Chiefly *refl.*, and now only *fig.* 1570. Also *intr.* (for *refl.*) **3.** *trans.* To join closely; *intr.* (for *refl.*) to close; to grapple, engage. Now *dial.* 1535. **4.** *trans.* To unite in marriage (*joc.* or *dial.*) Cf. *splice.* 1724. Also *intr.* † **5.** To fasten in curl –1796. **6.** *trans.* To warp, crumple, bend out of its plane. Now chiefly techn.: To bend a bar or surface (under longitudinal pressure) into a double curve. 1525. *intr.* To bend under pressure 1597. Also † *fig.*

1. Nailynge the speres, and helmes bokelynge CHAUCER. *To b. in* (fig.): to enclose. *A.Y.L.* III. ii. 140. 2. *To b. to*: to apply oneself vigorously. 4. Dr. R. who buckles beggars for a tester and a dram of Geneva SCOTT. 6. Reason doth b. and bowe the mind unto the nature of things BACON. To b. a saw 1854.

Comb.: † **b.-beggar** (Sc.), a hedge-priest.

Bu·ckler, *sb.*[1] 1650. [f. prec.] One who or that which buckles.

Buckler (bɒ·klәɹ), *sb.*[2] [ME. *boc(e)ler* – OFr. *bocler* (mod. *bouclier*), orig. adj. in *escu boucler* shield having a boss, f. *boucle* boss; see BUCKLE *sb.*, -ER[2].] **1.** A small round shield; in England 'used not so much for a shield as for a warder to catch the blow of an adversary' (Fairholt). Also (erron.) Any kind of shield. Also *attrib.* **2.** *fig.* Protection, protector ME. **3.** Techn.: **a.** *Naut.* A wooden shutter placed against the inside of a hawse-hole to prevent the water from coming in. A *Blind B.* has no aperture; a *Riding B.*, used at anchor, has a hole in the middle for the passage of a cable. 1832. **b.** *Anat., Zool.*, etc. Applied to the hard protective covering of parts of the body of the armadillo, the ganoid fishes, and some crustacea; *spec.* the anterior segment of the shell of the trilobites 1828.

1. A swerd and a bocler baar he by his side CHAUCER. 2. A b. of impenetrable indifference C. BRONTË.

Comb.: **b.-fern,** the genus *Aspidium*; **-head,** the fossil fish *Cephalaspis*; **-mustard,** *Biscutella auriculata*; **-thorn,** *Rhamnus paliurus aculeatus.* Hence **Bu·cklered** *ppl. a.* furnished with bucklers.

Buckler (bɒ·klәɹ), *v.* 1590. [f. prec.] **1.** *trans.* To act as a buckler to; to shield, defend. † **2.** To ward or catch (blows) 3 *Hen. VI*, I. iv. 50.

1. 'Tis not the king can b. Gaveston MARLOWE.

† **Bu·ck-mast.** 1425. [OE. **bōc-mæst*; see BEECH, MAST *sb.*[2]] Beech-mast –1607.

† **Bucko·ne.** 1625. [– It. *boccone*, f. *bocca* mouth.] A mouthful –1659.

‖ **Buckra** (bɒ·krā). 1794. [– Surinam *bakra* master.] A white man (in Negro talk).

Buckram (bɒ·krăm), *sb.* [ME. *boker(h)am* – AFr. *bukeram*, OFr. *boquerant* (mod. *bougran*), corresp. to Pr. *bocaran*, Sp. *bucaran*, It. *bucherame*, obscurely f. *Bukhara*, name of a town in Turkestan. For the change of final *n* to *m* cf. *grogram, megrim, vellum.*] † **1.** A kind of fine linen or cotton fabric –1553. **2.** A kind of coarse linen or cloth stiffened with gum or paste ME. † **b.** A lawyer's bag –1622. **3.** *fig.* Stiffness; a starched manner 1682. **4.** *attrib.* and quasi-*adj.* Of, or like, buckram 1537; *fig.* stuck up; that has a false appearance of strength 1589.

2. Foure Rogues in Buckrom let driue at me SHAKS. 3. A fine..unaffected lad, no pride or b. CORNWALLIS. 4. A wondrous b. style,—the best he [Johnson] could get CARLYLE.

Buckram (bɒ·krăm), *v.* 1783. [f. prec.] *trans.* To pad or stiffen with buckram; to give

to anything a starched pomposity or a false appearance of strength.
Written by Walpole, and buckram'd by Mason 1784.

† **Bu·ckra·ms.** 1578. [perh. f. BUCK *sb.*[1] 1. a + *rams*, var. RAMSON.] A name for Ramsons or Wild Garlic –1783.

† **Buck's-beard.** 1551. [tr. Gr. τραγοπώγων.] Goats-beard; Salsify.

Buck's-horn. 1450. **a.** *Senebiera coronopus*, Swine's Cress. **b.** The Virginia Sumach (*Rhus typhina*). Also **Buck's horn Plantain, Buck's horn Weld.** So called from the appearance of their leaves or branches.

Buck's-horn, var. of BUCK-HORN.

Buck-shot (bʊ·kˌʃɒt). 1447. [f. BUCK *sb.*[1]] † **1.** The distance at which a buck may be shot (*rare*). **2.** A kind of shot, larger than *swan-shot*, used in shooting deer and large game. Also *attrib.* 1776.
Comb. **b.-rule,** a political nickname for government (of Ireland) upheld by a constabulary with loaded rifles.

Buckskin (bʊ·kskin). 1433. [f. BUCK *sb.*[1]] **1.** The skin of a buck. **2.** Leather made from buckskin; also from sheepskin 1804. Also *attrib.* **3.** Breeches (and perh. gloves) made of buckskin 1481. † **4.** A nickname of the American troops during the Revolutionary war; hence, a native American –1823.

Bu·ck-stall. 1503. [f. BUCK *sb.*[1] + STALL *sb.*; cf. also STALL *v.* III.] A net for catching deer. (*Hist.*)

Buckthorn (bʊ·kþǭɹn). 1578. [f. BUCK *sb.*[1] + THORN, tr. mod.L. *cervi spina* 'stag's thorn'.] The shrub *Rhamnus catharticus*; its berries yield sap-green, and are a strong cathartic.

Bu·ck-tooth. 1753. [f. as prec.] A large projecting tooth. Also *attrib.*

† **Bu·ck-wa:shing.** 1598. [f. BUCK *sb.*[3]] The process of washing very dirty linen, by boiling it in an alkaline lye (BUCK *sb.*[3]), and afterwards beating and rinsing it in clear water –1879. So **Buck-washer**; also dial. **buck-wash.**

Buckwheat (bʊ·kˌhwīt). 1548. [– MDu. *boecweite* (Du. *boekweit*), MLG. *bōkwēte* (LG. *bookweeten*), f. *boek*, *bōk* (see BEECH) + *weite* WHEAT.] **1.** A species of Polygonum (*P. fagopyrum*). The seed is in Europe used as food for horses, cattle, and poultry; in N. America its meal is made into buckwheat cakes. Also *attrib.* **2.** Applied also to *P. convolvulus*, and to *P. tartaricum* 1548.

Bucolic (biukǫ·lik). 1531. [– L. *bucolicus* – Gr. βουκολικός, f. βουκόλος herdsman, f. βοῦς ox; see -IC.] **A.** *adj.* **1.** Of or pertaining to herdsmen or shepherds; pastoral 1613. **2.** Rural, rustic, countrified. (Partly *joc.*) 1846. var. **Buco·lical,** whence **Buco·lically** *adv.*
1. Mingling b. details and sentimental effusions SYD. SMITH.

B. *sb.* [Cf. L. *Bucolica*, Gr. Βουκολικά.] **1.** *pl.* Pastoral poems: rarely in *sing.* 1531. **2.** = Bucolic poet 1774. **3.** A rustic (*joc.*) 1862. **4.** *pl.* Agricultural pursuits (*rare*) 1865.
1. [Virgil's] bucolikes ELYOT.

Bucra·ne. Also **bucra·nium.** 1854. [– Fr. *bucrane* (*-crâne*) and late L. *bucranium* – Gr. βουκράνιον f. βοῦς ox + κρανίον skull.] *Archit.* A sculptured ornament representing an ox-skull.

Bud (bʊd), *sb.* [Late ME. *bodde*, *budde*, of unkn. origin.] *Bot.* A little projection found at the axil of a leaf, forming the rudiment of a branch, cluster of leaves, or blossom. Hence, applied to a flower (or leaf) at any stage of growth until fully opened. **b.** *Zool.* A similar growth in animals of low organization, which develops into a new individual 1836. Also *transf.* and *fig.*
So longe it is called the budde of a rose, as it is not a perfyte rose *Pilgr. Perf.* (W. de W. 1531). *fig.* Now will Canker-sorrow eat my b. [Arthur] *K. John* III. iv. 82.
Phr. *In b.* (said of plants): budding. *In the b.*: not yet developed. *To nip* or *crush in the b.*: *fig.* to repress or destroy (a project, etc.) in its beginnings.
Comb.: **b.-germ** (*Zool.*) = **b.**; **-rudiment,** the cell in the embryo, from which the b. is developed.

Bud (bʊd), *v.*[1] ME. [f. BUD *sb.*[1]] **1.** *intr.* **a.** To put forth buds. **b.** with *out*: To come or push out, as a bud. **2.** *fig.* To begin to grow; to develop 1566. **3.** *trans.* To put forth as buds; to produce by gemmation; also *fig.* 1591. **4.** To cause to bud; also *fig.* 1604. **5.** *Gardening.* To ingraft by inserting a bud of a shrub or tree under the bark of another stock. Also *absol.* 1663.
1. The rose is budding fain SCOTT. **2.** Many vices b. out of this one *a*1593. Budding honours SHAKS. Hence **Bu·dder** KEATS. **Bu·dding** *vbl. sb.* and *ppl. a.* that buds; in b.; also *fig.*

Bud, *v. Sc.* = must; see BUS *v.*

Buddha (bu·dă, bu·dˌha). 1681. [– Skr. *buddha* enlightened, awakened, pa. pple. of *budh* awake, know, perceive.] The title given by the adherents of BUDDHISM to the founder of their faith, Sākyamuni, Gautama, or Siddārtha, who flourished in Northern India in the 5th century B.C. Sākyamuni is regarded as only the latest of a series of Buddhas, which is to be continued indefinitely.
Hence **Bu·ddhahood,** the condition of a B. **Bu·ddhaship,** the office of a B. **Bu·ddhism,** the religious system founded by B. **Bu·ddhist** *sb.*, a follower of B.; *adj.* relating to Buddhism (vars. **Bu·ddhic, -i·stic, -al** *a.*). † **Bu·ddhite** *sb.* and *a.*

Bu·ddle, boo·dle, *sb.*[1] ME. [Origin unkn.] The Corn-marigold.

Buddle (bʊ·d'l), *sb.*[2] 1531. [Origin unkn.] *Mining.* A shallow inclined vat in which ore is washed.

Buddle (bʊ·d'l), *v.* 1693. [f. prec.] To wash (ore) by means of a buddle.

Buddleia (bʊdlī·ă, bʊ·dliă). 1885. [mod.L., f. the name of Adam *Buddle* (died 1715); see -IA[1].] Any plant of the genus of shrubs of this name, bearing clusters of yellow or violet flowers.

Bu·ddy, *a. rare.* 1598. [f. BUD *sb.* + -Y[1].] Full of buds; like a bud.

Bude (biūd). 1807. [f. *Bude* in Cornwall.] **B.-burner,** a gas-burner invented at Bude by Sir G. Gurney, consisting of two or three concentric argand rings. **B.-light,** 'a light obtained by directing a stream of oxy-hydrogen gas on a quantity of pounded egg shells.'

Bude = *behoved*; see BUS *v.*

Budge (bʊdʒ), *sb.*[1] ME. [Early forms (dissyl.) *bugee*, *bugeye*, *buggy*, *bog(e)y*, in AL. *buggetum*, of unkn. origin.] A kind of fur, consisting of lamb's skin with the wool dressed outwards. *Comb.* **b.-bachelor,** one of a company in gowns trimmed with b., who took part in the procession on Lord Mayor's Day (see BACHELOR 2). For *b.-doctor*, see BUDGE *a.*

† **Budge,** *sb.*[2] 1606. Later sp. of BOUGE *sb.*[1] A leather bag. Cf. BUDGET.

† **Budge,** *sb.*[3] *slang.* 1673. [Origin unkn.] A sneaking thief –1751.

† **Budge,** *a.* 1634. [attrib. use of BUDGE *sb.*[1] Thus *budge doctor* would be originally one who wore budge fur.] **1.** Solemn in demeanour, pompous, formal –1781. **2.** *dial.* Brisk –1800.
Those b. doctors of the Stoic fur MILT. *Comus* 707.

Budge (bʊdʒ), *v.* 1590. [– (O)Fr. *bouger*, prob. = Pr. *bolegar* disturb oneself, It. *bulicare* bubble up :– Rom. **bullicare* bubble, f. L. *bullire*, f. *bulla* bubble; see BULL *sb.*[2]] **1.** With neg.: *intr.* To stir; to move from one's place. **2.** *trans.* To stir 1598.
1. Not a soul will b. to give him place GOLDSM. **2.** Three men..could not b. it 1883. Hence **Bu·dger.**

Bu·dge-ba:rrel. 1627. [f. BUDGE *sb.*[2] = BOUGE *sb.*[1] + BARREL *sb.*] A small powder-barrel, having a leather cover with a long neck drawing together like the mouth of a bag.

Budgerigar (bʊ:dʒěrigā·ɹ). 1847. [Native Australian (Port Jackson), f. *budgeri* good + *gar* cockatoo.] The Australian grass parakeet.

Budgerow (bʊ·dʒərōᵘ). *Anglo-Ind.* 1727. [Earlier † *bazara* (XVI) – Hindi, Bengali *bajrā.*] A lumbering keelless barge, formerly much used on the Ganges.

Budget (bʊ·dʒėt). 1432. [– OFr. *bougette*, dim. of *bouge* leather bag :– L. *bulga*; see BULGE *sb.*, -ET.] **1.** A pouch, bag, wallet, usu. of leather. Now *dial.* **2.** *spec.* † **a.** A leather or skin bottle –1786. **b.** A boot in a carriage, for carrying luggage. ? *Obs.* 1794. **c.** A leathern socket for the butt of a cavalry carbine. Cf. BUCKET *sb.*[1] 4. 1816. **3.** *transf.* The contents of a bag or wallet; a bundle, a collection or stock 1597. **b.** A title for a journal (*i.e.* a b. of news, etc.): e.g. *Pall Mall B.* **4.** A statement of the probable revenue and expenditure for the ensuing year, with financial proposals founded thereon, annually submitted by the Chancellor of the Exchequer for the approval of the House of Commons. Sometimes put for the condition of the national finances as thus disclosed; also for the financial measures proposed. Hence, any analogous statement, estimate, or proposals. 1733. † **5.** *Her.* = BOUGET 1766. **6.** (See MUM-BUDGET, a phr. enjoining silence.) *Merry W.* v. ii. 7.
1. Staff, b., bottle, scrip he wore SCOTT. **3.** A B. of Paradoxes DE MORGAN (*title*). **4.** The time was now come for opening the *b.*, when it was incumbent on him to state the finances, debts, and calls of government H. WALPOLE. *Comb.*: **b.-bar,** a bar of timber on which rests the boot of a carriage; **-gut,** the cæcum. Hence **Bu·dgetary** *a.* pertaining to a b. **Budgetee·r,** one who makes up a b. (in sense 3 or 4). **Bu·dgeter,** one who carries a wallet; † a charlatan; a strolling player.

Bu·dget, *v.* 1618. [f. prec.] *trans.* † **a.** To put in a wallet; to store *up.* **b.** *To b. for*: to provide for in a b.

† **Bu·dgy,** *a. rare.* 1598. [f. BUDGE *sb.*[1] + -Y[1].] Of or like lamb's fur.

Bu·dlet. [f. BUD *sb.* + -LET.] A secondary bud springing from another bud. DARWIN.

Budmash, var. of BADMASH, 'bad character.'

Buff, *sb.*[1] *Obs.* exc. in BLIND-MAN'S-BUFF. ME. [– OFr. *buffe* BUFFET[1]; cf. Du. *bof.*] A blow, stroke, buffet.
Phr. **To stand buff:** to stand firm, not to flinch.

Buff (bʊf), *sb.*[2] 1552. [prob. – Fr. *buffle* BUFFALO. Cf. BUFFLE *sb.*] † **1.** A buffalo, or other large species of wild ox –1706. † **2.** (More fully *buff-leather*): *prop.* Leather made of buffalo-hide; but usu. a very stout kind of leather made of ox-hide, dressed with oil, having a fuzzy surface, and a dull whitish-yellow colour –1756. **b.** Military attire; a military coat made of buff; = BUFF-COAT. Also the dress of sergeants and catch-poles. 1590. **3.** *colloq.* (somewhat *arch.*) The bare skin. *In b.*: naked. 1654. **4.** = *buff-stick* or *-wheel*; see *Comb.* 1831. **5.** Buff colour; a dull light yellow. *Blue and b.*, formerly the Whig colours. 1788. **6.** *The Buffs*: a name given, from the colour of their facings, to the old 3rd regiment of the line (later the East Kent Regiment) 1806. **7.** *Pathol.* = BUFFY COAT. 1739.
2. b. In b. and bandoleer for King Charles SCOTT. *Comb.*: **b.-jerkin,** a military jerkin of b.-leather; **-stick, -wheel,** a stick or wheel, covered with b.-leather or other soft material, for polishing metal.

† **Buff,** *sb.*[3] *colloq.* 1708. [Cf. the later BUFFER[4].] Fellow, 'buffer' –1764.

Buff (bʊf), *a.* 1695. [f. BUFF *sb.*[2] 2.] **1.** Of or like buff-leather. **2.** Of the colour of buff-leather; a light brownish yellow 1762. See also BUFF *sb.*[2] 5, 6.
2. The dress..of a Cavalier..b. with blue ribbands H. WALPOLE.

Buff, *v.*[1] Now *dial.* ME. [prob. echoic; cf. PUFF, BUFF *sb.*[1]] **1.** *intr.* **a.** To stutter. **b.** To explode into a laugh, or the like. **2.** *trans.* To cause to burst out by sudden force. B. JONS. **3.** *intr.* To act and sound as a soft inflated body does when struck 1550. **4.** *intr.* and *trans.* To strike a soft inflated body (with this effect) 1600.

Buff, *v.*[2] 1885. [f. BUFF *sb.*[2]] **a.** To polish with a buff. **b.** To impart the velvety surface usual in buff leather for belts, etc.

Buffalo (bʊ·fălo). Pl. **buffaloes.** 1588. [prob. immed. – Pg. *bufalo* (mod. *bufaro*), corresp. to It. *bufalo* (whence Fr. *buffle*), Sp. *búbalo*, *búfalo* :– late L. *bufalus* (Fortunatus), L. *bubalus* – Gr. βούβαλος antelope, wild ox. Cf. BUFF *sb.*[2]] **1.** The name of: *esp.* **a.** *Bos bubalus*, originally a native of India. It is tamed in India, Italy, and elsewhere. 1588. **b.** *B. caffer*, the Cape Buffalo of S. Africa 1699. **c.** *pop.* The American BISON 1789. **2.** A fresh-water fish resembling the Sucker 1789. **3.** = *buffalo-robe*; see *Comb.* (*colloq. U.S.* and

Canada) 1856. **4.** Short for *b.-horn*: used by cutlers.

Comb.: **b.-bag** (cf. *buffalo-robe*); **-berry,** the edible scarlet fruit of *Shepherdia argentea*, found on the Upper Missouri; **-bird,** an insessorial bird (*Textor erythrorhynchus*) which accompanies herds of buffaloes in S. Africa; **-chips,** *pl.*, the dried dung of the American bison, used as fuel; **-clover,** a species of clover (*Trifolium pennsylvanicum*) found in the prairies; **-fish** = sense 2; **-grass,** a grass (*Sesleria dactyloides*) found in the prairies; **-nut,** a N. American shrub (*Pyrularia oleifera*), or its fruit; **-robe,** a cloak or rug made of the skin of the American bison dressed with the hair on.

Buff coat, bu·ff-coat. 1633. [See BUFF *sb.*[2]] **1.** A stout coat of buff leather, *esp.* one worn by soldiers. Also *fig.* **2.** One who wears a buff coat; a soldier 1670. **3.** = BUFFY COAT.

Buffed (bɒft), *a.* 1640. [f. BUFF *sb.*[2] + -ED[2].] **a.** Clad in buff. **b.** Coated or covered with buff, having a buffy coat.

† **Bu·ffer**[1]. ME. [f. BUFF *v.*[1]] A stammerer.

Buffer[2] (bɒ·fəɹ). 1835. [app. f. BUFF *v.*[1] 3.] *Mech.* A mechanical apparatus for deadening the force of a concussion, as fixed at the front and back of railway carriages, etc. Extended also to contrivances which sustain without deadening the concussion. (Formerly called *buffing apparatus*.) Also *fig.* and *attrib.*

Comb.: **b.-state,** a neutral state lying between two others and serving to render less possible hostilities between them.

Bu·ffer[3]. 1854. [f. BUFF *v.*[2]] **a.** One who buffs knives, plate, etc. **b.** = BUFF *sb.*[2] 4. **c.** A machine for polishing daguerreotype plates.

Bu·ffer[4]. *slang.* 1749. [Senses 2 and 3 prob. based on BUFF *v.*[1] (senses 1 a, 3); sense 1 is a different word; cf. †*bufe* (cant) dog (XVI), *bugher* barking dog (XVII).] **1.** A dog. **b.** *transf.* A pistol; = BARKER 4. 1812. **2.** *Sc.* and *dial.* A foolish fellow 1808. **3.** A fellow: usu. slightly contemptuous 1749.

1. Here be a pair of buffers will bite as well as bark SCOTT.

Buffet (bɒ·fėt), *sb.*[1] ME. [– OFr. (now dial.) *buffet*, dim. of *bufe*, of imit. origin.] A blow; *esp.* one given with the hand. † *Pl.* Fisticuffs (*rare*). Also *transf.* and *fig.* (Cf. BLOW, STROKE.)

The vile Blowes and Buffets of the World SHAKS.

Buffet (bɒ·fėt), *sb.*[2] ME. [– OFr. *bufet* stool, bench, table, of unkn. origin.] **1.** A low stool; a footstool. Now *Sc.* and *n. dial.* var. **Bu·ffet-stool. 2.** A hassock (*dial.*) 1877.

Buffet (bɒ·fėt), *sb.*[3] 1718. [– mod.Fr. *buffet* = OFr. *bufet* BUFFET *sb.*[2]] **1.** A sideboard or side-table for china, plate, etc. **2.** A cupboard in a recess for china and glasses 1720. ‖ **3.** (bü·fe). A refreshment bar 1869. var. **Beaufet.**

Buffet (bɒ·fėt), *v.* Pa. t. and pple. **-eted.** ME. [– (O)Fr. *buffeter*, f. *buffet* BUFFET *sb.*[1]] **1.** To beat, strike, *esp.* with the hand; to cuff, knock about. **b.** To beat back, contend with (waves, etc.) 1601. Also *fig.* **2.** *intr.* To deal blows, fight, struggle 1599. Also *fig.* **3.** *trans.* To drive, force, or produce, by buffeting 1734. **4.** *trans.* To muffle (bells). [perh. a distinct wd.] 1753.

1. Bang'd and buffeted into Reason BENTLEY. **2.** To b. resolutely with hardships W. IRVING. **3.** To b. one's way to riches and fame 1865. Hence **Bu·ffeter** (*rare*), one that buffets.

† **Bu·ffin.** 1572. [Origin unkn.] A coarse cloth in use for gowns in Elizabeth's time; a gown of this. Also *attrib.* –1632.

† **Bu·ffle,** *sb.* 1511. [– Fr. *buffle* – It. *bufalo*; see BUFFALO, BUFF *sb.*[2]] **1.** = BUFFALO 1 a, b. –1738. Also *attrib.* **2.** = BUFFLEHEAD. [After Fr. *buffle*.] –1710.

Bu·ffle, *v.* 1610. [perh. echoic; conn. w. some sense of BUFF; or ? misprint for *bustle*. '*Buffle* to puzzle' in Dicts. is a bogus wd., founded on this misprint.]

Bu·fflehead. 1659. [f. BUFFLE *sb.*] A fool, blockhead.

Buffle-headed (bɒ·f'lhe:dėd), *a.* 1654. [f. prec. + -ED[2].] † **1.** Having a head like a buffalo's –1713. **2.** *transf.* and *fig.* **a.** Large-headed. **b.** Foolish.

2. So fell this buffle-headed gyant 1654.

‖ **Buffo** (bu·ffo). 1764. [– It. *buffo* puff of wind, buffoon, f. *buffare* (see next).] **A.** *sb.* A comic actor, a singer in a comic opera. **B.** as *adj.* Comic, burlesque.

Buffoon (bɒ̆fū·n), *sb.* 1549. [– Fr. *bouffon* – It. *buffone* – med.L. *buffo* clown (Aldhelm, VIII), f. Rom. **buffare* puff (prob. w. allusion to puffing out the cheeks as a comic gesture), of imit. origin. See -OON.] † **1.** A pantomime dance. *Sc.* (*rare*). **2.** 'A man whose profession is to make sport by low jests and antick postures' (J.); a clown; a jester, fool (*arch.*) 1585. **3.** *transf.* A low jester; a wag, a joker (implying contempt or disgust) 1598. Also *attrib.*

3. Age was authoritie Against a b., and a man had, then..reverence payd unto his yeares B. JONS. Hence **Buffoo·nish,** † **Buffoo·nly** *a.* † **Bu·ffoonize, Bu·ffonize** *v.*

Buffoon (bɒ̆fū·n), *v. arch.* 1638. [f. prec.] **1.** *trans.* To turn into ridicule; to burlesque. **2.** *intr.* To play the buffoon 1672.

Buffoonery (bɒ̆fū·nəri). 1621. [– Fr. *bouffonnerie*; see BUFFOON, -ERY.] The practice of a buffoon; low jesting or ridicule, farce.

Flatterie and Buffonrie swayed all in the Roman Senate 1621.

Buffy (bɒ·fi). 1782. [f. BUFF *sb.*[2] and *a.* + -Y[1].] **1.** Of a colour approaching to buff 1842. **2.** *Phys.* Applied to blood having a buff or BUFFY COAT 1782.

Buffy Coat. 1800. *Phys.* A layer of a light buff colour forming the upper part of the clot of coagulated blood under certain conditions.

† **Bu·fo.** [– L. *bufo* toad.] The black tincture of the alchemists. B. JONS.

Bu·fonite. 1766. [f. L. *bufo, -on-* + -ITE[1] 2 b.] = TOADSTONE[1], q.v.

Bug (bɒg), *sb.*[1] [ME. *bugge*, rel. to BOG *sb.*[2], BOGGARD, BOGLE, BOGY, of unkn. origin. Connection w. W. *bwg, bwgan* ghost, hobgoblin, *bwgwl* fear, threat, cannot be made out. Survives only in BUGBEAR.] An (imaginary) object of terror; a bugbear, bogy; a scarecrow. **b.** A self-important person 1771. *Big bug* (orig. U.S.): a person of great importance 1827.

Warwicke was a Bugge that feared vs all SHAKS.

Bug (bɒg), *sb.*[2] 1622. [Origin unkn.] **1.** A name given vaguely to various insects, *esp.* beetles, etc., also to grubs, larvæ of insects, etc. Now chiefly *dial.* and *U.S.*; *esp.* with defining wd., as *harvest b.*, etc. 1642. **2.** *spec.* The *Cimex lectularius*, more fully *bed-* or *house-b.*, a blood-sucking hemipterous insect. Also, any Hemipteran or Heteropteran. 1622.

1. The b. which breeds the butterfly SHAFTESB. **2.** As safe as a b. in a rug 1798. *Comb.* **b.-bane, -wort,** *Cimicifuga fœtida* and allied plants, used to drive away bugs; **-hunter,** *slang*, an entomologist.

Bugaboo (bɒ·găbū:). 1740. [prob. of dial. origin; cf. W. *bwcibo* the Devil, Corn. *buccaboo*.] A bogy; a bugbear.

No b. tales POE.

Bugbear (bɒ·gbēᵊɹ). 1580. [app. f. BUG *sb.*[1] + BEAR *sb.*[1]] † **1.** A sort of hobgoblin (? in the shape of a bear) supposed to devour naughty children; hence, generally, any imaginary being invoked by nurses to frighten children –1842. **2.** *transf.* An object of (needless) dread; an imaginary terror 1580. Also *attrib.*

1. Meare bugge-beares to scare boyes NASHE. **2.** All that thinke originall sinne a bugbeare 1642. Hence † **Bu·gbear** *v.* to frighten with bugbears.

Bugger (bɒ·gəɹ). ME. [– MDu. *bugger* – (O)Fr. *bougre* † heretic, (arch.) sodomite, (colloq.) 'chap':– med.L. *Bulgarus* Bulgarian, heretic (the Bulgarians being so regarded as belonging to the Greek Church), spec. Albigensian.] **1.** A heretic: used esp. of the Albigenses. (*Hist.*) **2.** One who commits buggery; a sodomite. In decent use only as a legal term. 1555. **b.** A coarse term of abuse; also, in Eng. dial. and in U.S., = 'chap', 'customer', etc. Hence **Bu·gger** *v.* to commit buggery with. Also *absol.*

Buggery (bɒ·gəri). ME. [– MDu. *buggerie* (OFr. *bougerie*). See prec., -Y[3].] † **a.** Abominable heresy. **b.** Sodomy. Now only as a technical term in criminal law.

† **Bu·ggess.** 1699. [– *Bugis*, name given to the dominant race among the Malays.] A name formerly used in the Indian Archipelago for a native soldier in European service –1811.

Buggy (bɒ·gi), *sb.* 1773. [Origin unkn.] A light one-horse (or two-horse) vehicle for one or two persons. The American buggy has four wheels; the English (or Indian) buggy two; in India there is a hood.

I asked for a two-horse b. and driver B. TAYLOR.

Comb.: **b.-boat,** a boat made so that wheels can be fastened to it, for use on land; **-cultivator, -plough,** a plough having a seat for the ploughman to ride on.

Bu·ggy, *a.* 1714. [f. BUG *sb.*[2] + -Y[1].] Infested with bugs.

Bugle (biū·g'l), *sb.*[1] ME. [– OFr. *bugle* :– L. *buculus*, dim. of *bos* ox.] **1.** † **a.** = BUFFALO 1 a. **b.** A young bull (*dial.*). **2.** *Mus.* Short for BUGLE-HORN. **a.** A hunting-horn, made originally of the horn of a bugle or wild ox. **b.** A military instrument of brass or copper, resembling the trumpet, but smaller; used as the signal-horn for the infantry. ME.

1. The B...is lyke to an oxe and is a fyers beest TREVISA. **2. b.** Comb. *b.-blast, -call, -clang, -man.*

Bugle (biū·g'l), *sb.*[2] ME. [– late L. *bugula* (whence Fr. *bugle*, Sp. *bugula*, It. *bugola*).] The Eng. name of plants of the genus *Ajuga*, esp. *A. reptans*. (Occas. confounded with *Buglossa*.)

Bugle (biū·g'l), *sb.*[3] 1579. [Origin unkn.] A tube-shaped glass bead, usually black, used to ornament wearing apparel. Also *attrib.*

Adam and Eve in B.-work..upon Canvas STEELE.

Bu·gle, *v.* 1862. [f. BUGLE *sb.*[1] 2.] **a.** *intr.* To sound a bugle. **b.** *trans.* To give forth (a sound) as a bugle; also (*nonce-use*) to summon by bugle.

Bu:gle-ho·rn. ME. [f. BUGLE *sb.*[1]] The horn of a bugle or wild ox, used † **a.** as a drinking vessel –1519. **b.** as a musical instrument, whence = BUGLE *sb.*[1] 2.

b. Two squyers blewe..with ij grete bugles hornes CAXTON.

Bugler (biū·gləɹ). 1840. [f. as prec. + -ER[1].] One who plays on a bugle; *spec.* a soldier who sounds orders on a bugle.

Bu·gle-weed. 1860. [f. BUGLE *sb.*[2]] *Bot.* An American plant, *Lycopus virginicus*, occas. used as a remedy for spitting of blood.

Bugloss (biū·glǫs). 1533. [– Fr. *buglosse* or L. *buglossus* – Gr. βούγλωσσος lit. 'ox-tongued', f. βοῦς ox + γλῶσσα tongue.] *Bot.* A name of several boraginaceous plants, *esp.* the *Small, Corn,* or *Field B.* (*Lycopsis arvensis*); Viper's B. (*Echium vulgare*), and other species of *Echium*; also of *Helminthia echioides*, Prickly Ox-tongue. *Comb.* **B. Cowslip,** the lungwort.

† **Bug-word, bug's-word.** 1562. [f. BUG *sb.*[1]] A word meant to frighten. Usu. in *pl.* Swaggering or threatening language. –1734.

A Rebellion; O no, that's a bug word NORTH.

Buhl (būl). Also **Boule,** q.v. 1823. [Germanized f. *Boule*, a French wood-carver in the reign of Louis XIV.] Brass, tortoise-shell, etc., worked into ornamental patterns for inlaying; work inlaid with buhl. Also *attrib.*

Build (bild), *v.* Pa. t. and pple. **built,** *poet.* and *arch.* **builded.** [OE. *byldan* (cf. *bylda* builder), f. *bold* dwelling, house, var. of *botl*. See BOLD *sb.*, BOTTLE *sb.*[1]] **1.** *trans. Orig.* To construct for a dwelling. *Hence*, To erect, construct; whence, To construct by fitting together of separate parts. **2.** *absol.* To erect a building or buildings. Of birds, etc.: To construct nests, etc. ME. **3.** *transf.* To construct as by building 1598. **4.** *fig.* To construct, frame, raise, by gradual means. Often with *up*. 1440. **5.** *lit.* and *fig.* To work up *into*. Also with *up*. ME. **6.** *fig.* **a.** *trans.* To found (hope, etc.) *on* a basis 1528. **b.** *absol.* To found one's confidence, establish an argument, etc. *on*; to rely confidently *on* (*obs.* or *arch.*) 1573.

1. Roome was not bylt on one day 1562. *To b. a fire*: to pile the fuel. *To b. a railroad* (only in U.S.), *a gun, a nest.* **2.** Our ayerie buildeth in the Cedars top *Rich. III*, I. iii. 264. *Phr. To b. up*: to obstruct (a doorway, etc.) by building. *To b. in*: to enclose by buildings. **3.** Built as it were to make a good Boxer BENTLEY. A crystal built up from particles of silica TYNDALL. **4.** *To b. up* (the Church, an individual) = to EDIFY. To b. the lofty rhyme MILT., an everlasting name TENNYSON. 6. He that builds upon the people builds upon the sand 1674.

Build (bild), *sb.* ME. [f. prec.; cf. BUILT *sb.*] † **1.** A building. ME. only. **2.** Building; style of construction, make (*lit.* and *fig.*) 1667.
2. The b. of ships PEPYS. A patriot of the old Roman b. 1833.

Builder (bi·ldəɹ). ME. [f. as prec. + -ER[1].] One who builds. Also *fig.* (As the name of a trade, *builder* now = the master artisan, who is instructed by the architect, and employs the manual labourers.)
The builders..of Babel on the Plain MILT.

Building (bi·ldiŋ), *vbl. sb.* ME. [f. as prec. + -ING[1].] **1.** The action of the vb. BUILD (*lit.* and *fig.*) † **b.** Build (*e.g.* of a ship). **2.** That which is built; a structure, edifice ME.
2. By much slouthfulnesse, the b. decayeth *Eccles.* 10: 18. *Comb.*: **b.-lease,** a lease of land for building upon; **-society,** one in which the members contribute to a fund for lending money to any member who wishes to build (or purchase) a house; **-term,** the duration of a *building-lease.*

† **Built,** *sb.* 1615. [f. BUILD *v.*; cf. *gilt, f. gild.*] Style of construction, build –1794.

Buirdly (bü·rdli), *a. Sc.* ME. [prob. var. of Sc. *buirly* BURLY.] Large and well-made; stalwart; stately; sturdy, stout.

Bukk-; see BUCK-.

‖ **Bukshi, bukshee** (bɒ·kʃī). 1615. [– Pers. *bakšī* giver, f. *bakšīdan* give; see BAKSHEESH.] The Paymaster-General of the army in native Indian states; in the Anglo-Indian army a *Paymaster.*

Bulb (bɒlb), *sb.* 1568. [– L. *bulbus* = Gr. βολβός onion, bulbous root. Cf. Fr. *bulbe.*] † **1.** An onion –1712. **2.** *Bot.* The underground spheroidal portion of the stem of an onion, lily, or the like. **b.** A bulbil 1845. **3.** A bulb-like dilatation, *e.g.* of a hair, a glass tube, etc. 1715. **4.** The glass bulb-shaped container of the incandescent filament used for producing electric light in a glow lamp 1882.
2. Bulbs are in reality underground stems in the state of buds CARPENTER. Hence **Bulbed** *a.* b.-shaped, having a b. **Bulbi·ferous** *a.* producing bulbs. **Bu·lbiform** *a.* b.-shaped.

Bulb (bɒlb), *v.* 1681. [f. prec.] *intr.* To swell into a bulb-like form; to form a bulb-shaped root.

Bulbar (bɒ·lbăɹ), *a.* 1878. [f. BULB *sb.* + -AR[1].] Of or pertaining to a bulb; *esp.* to the bulb of the spinal cord.

Bulbil (bɒ·lbil). Also **bulbel.** 1831. [– mod.L. *bulbillus*, dim. of *bulbus.*] **a.** A small bulb formed at the side of an old one. **b.** A small solid or scaly bud, which detaches itself from the stem, becoming an independent plant. So **Bu·lblet** (in sense b).

† **Bu·lbine.** 1548. [L. *bulbinē*, Gr. βολβίνη.] A bulbous plant mentioned by Pliny; *Gagea lutea* (Turner) –1611.

Bu·lbo-, comb. f. L. *bulbus.*

Bulbous (bɒ·lbəs), *a.* 1578. [– L. *bulbosus*; see BULB *sb.*, -OUS; in mod. use f. BULB *sb.*; cf. Fr. *bulbeux.*] **1.** Of, pertaining to, or of the nature of, a bulb. **2.** Having bulb-like roots 1578. **3.** Bulb-shaped; swollen 1783.
3. A bottle belly and a b. nose SOUTHEY. vars. **Bulba·ceous, Bulbo·se.**

Bulbul (bu·lbul). 1784. [– Pers. – Arab. *bulbul*, of imit. origin.] **1.** A species of the genus *Pycnonotus*, belonging to the Thrush family; sometimes called the nightingale of the East. **2.** *transf.* A sweet singer; also *attrib.* 1848.
1. The fighting B...said to be enamoured of the rose 1797.

Bulbule (bɒ·lbiul). 1836. [– late L. *bulbulus*; see BULB, -ULE.] A little bulb.

† **Bulchin.** ME. [Sense a – MDu. *bul(le)tjen*, later var. of *bul(le)kin*; sense b – MDu. *boeletjen*, later var. of *boelekijn* darling; see BULKIN, BULLY *sb.*[1]] **a.** A bull-calf –1727. **b.** Used as a term of contempt, or endearment –1638.

Bulge (bɒldʒ), *sb.* [– OFr. *boulge*, (also mod.) *bouge* :– L. *bulga* leathern sack, bag, of Gaulish origin.] † **1.** A wallet or bag, *esp.* one made of hide; = BOUGE *sb.*[1] 1 –1623. **2.** A bulging 1741. **3.** = mod. BILGE 1. 1622. Hence **Bu·lgy** *a.* swollen. **Bu·lginess.**

Bulge (bɒldʒ), *v.* 1563. [f. prec.] † **1.** = BILGE *v.* 1. –1821. † **2.** *refl.* and *intr.* Of a ship: To strike (*on* or *against*) so as to damage the bilge –1807. **3.** *intr.* To form a protuberance, to swell out 1677. **4.** *trans.* To make protuberant 1865.
2. It bulged on a rock, and the waves rushed in fast COLERIDGE. 4. A purse bulged with Austrian florin notes 1866.

‖ **Buli·mia,** mod.L. form of BULIMY. Hence **Buli·mic** *a.* indicating b.; voracious. **Buli·mious** *a.* having a voracious appetite.

‖ **Bulimus** (biulǝi·mɒ̆s). Pl. **bulimi.** 1830. [mod.L. – Gr. βούλιμος, perh. taken as adj. with sense 'bulimious'.] A genus of terrestrial gasteropods. Hence **Buli·miform** *a.*

Bulimy (biū·limi). ME. [– mod.L. *bulimia* – Gr. βουλιμία, f. βοῦς ox + λιμός hunger; see -Y[3]. Cf. Fr. *boulimie.*] *Med.* 'A morbid hunger, chiefly occurring in idiots and maniacs..the so-called canine hunger'. Also *fig.*

Bulk (bɒlk), *sb.*[1] 1440. [Sense 1 – OIcel. *búlki* cargo; senses 2, 3 perh. at first alt. f. BOUK; senses 4, 5 prob. transf. use of 1 or 2.] † **1.** A heap –1725. **b.** The cargo of a ship; a cargo as a whole; the whole lot (of a commodity) 1575. † **2.** The belly; the trunk, the body –1718. **b.** A huge frame (cf. 4); also *fig.* 1587. † **3.** *transf.* The hold of a ship; cf. Ger. *bauch* –1678. **4.** Magnitude in three dimensions; volume, *esp.* great volume 1449. **5.** A mass. Often *esp.* a large mass. 1641. **6.** Greater part, or number; the main body 1711.
1. b. *To break b.* (see BREAK *v.*). *In b.* (of fish, etc.): lying loose in heaps, without package. *To load* (a ship) *in b.*: to put the cargo in loose, *e.g.* wheat, salt, etc. *To sell in b.*: to sell the cargo as it is in the hold; to sell in large quantities. 2. His B. too weighty for his Thighs is grown DRYDEN. b. The b. of Ajax POPE. 4. They [gold and silver] possess great value in small b. MCCULLOCH. 6. The b. of a people ADDISON.

Bulk (bɒlk), *sb.*[2] 1586. [perh. – ON. *bálkr* partition, low wall; but cf. OE. *bolca* gangway of a ship; perh. rel. to BALK *sb.*] A framework projecting from the front of a shop; a stall. SHAKS.

Bulk (bɒlk), *v.* 1540. [f. BULK *sb.*[1]] **1.** *intr.* To be of bulk; to present an appearance of size (*lit.* and *fig.*) 1672. **2.** *trans.* To pile in heaps, as fish for salting. Cf. BULK *sb.*[1] 1. 1822. **3.** *Comm.* To ascertain the bulk of 1883.
1. To b. large in the world's eye CARLYLE. Phr. *To b.* (*up*): to swell up. 2. To b. pilchards 1822. 3. Indian teas are 'bulked' by Her Majesty's Customs 1883. Hence **Bulked** *ppl. a.* having bulk.

Bulker (bɒ·lkəɹ). 1857. [f. BULK *v.* 3 + -ER[1].] One who ascertains the bulk of goods.

Bulkhead (bɒ·lkhed). 1626. [f. BULK *sb.*[2]] **1.** One of the upright partitions serving to form the cabins in a ship or to divide the hold into watertight compartments. Also *transf.* **2.** *Mining.* 'A tight partition..in a mine for protection against water, fire, gas.' 1881. **3.** The roof of a projecting stall; the stall itself. Cf. BULK *sb.*[2] 1722.
1. *Collision b.*: the foremost b. in a vessel. Hence **Bu·lkhea:ded** *ppl. a.* furnished with bulkheads.

† **Bu·lkin.** 1583. [Sense a – MDu. *bul(le)kin* (see BULL *sb.*[1]); sense b – MDu. *boelekijn* darling; see -KIN, BULCHIN.] **a.** A bull-calf. **b.** Used as a term of endearment. –1616.

Bulky (bɒ·lki), *a.* 1687. [f. BULK *sb.*[1] + -Y[1].] Of large bulk, voluminous; occupying (too) much space.
Too b. for the post JOHNSON. Hence **Bu·lkily** *adv.* **Bu·lkiness.**

Bull (bul), *sb.*[1] [Late OE. *bula* (in place-names), ME. *bole* – ON. *boli*, corresp. to MLG. *bulle*, MDu. *bulle, bolle* (Du. *bul*).] **1.** The male of any bovine animal; also of the buffalo, etc. **2.** The male of other large animals, as the elephant, alligator, whale, etc. 1615. **3.** *Astron.* The constellation and sign Taurus 1509. **4.** *Stock-Exchange* [see BEAR *sb.*[1]]. One who endeavours by speculative purchases, or otherwise, to raise the price of stocks. *Bull* was orig. a speculative purchase for a rise. 1714. Also *attrib.* **5.** *attrib.* **a.** Male ME. **b.** Of or pertaining to a bull, bull-like 1814.
1. Bulls aim their horns, and Asses lift their heels POPE. *Bulls of brass, brazen bulls*, as those that guarded the golden fleece, and Phalaris' bull (proverbial as an engine of torture). 5. a. A b. elk 1863, whale 1880. d. A b. neck 1830.
Phrases. *A b. in a china shop*: a symbol of one who produces reckless destruction. *To take the b. by the horns*: to meet a difficulty with courage. *Comb.*: **b.-bat,** the American Goatsucker (*Caprimulgus americanus*); **-boat,** a boat made of hides stretched on a frame; **-comber,** a dung-beetle (*Typhœus vulgaris*); **-feast,** a b.-baiting (Eng.); a b.-fight (Sp.); **-foot** (*Bot.*), Colt's-foot (*Tussilago*); **-hoof** (Bot.), *Murucuja ocellata*; **b.-of-the-bog,** the bittern, from its booming cry; **-poll,** the Turfy Hair-grass (*Aira cæspitosa*); **-pup,** a young bull-dog; **-ring,** the arena for a b.-fight (Sp.); the place where bulls were baited (Eng.); the ring to which a b. was fastened; **-roarer,** a flat slip of wood fastened by one end to a thong for whirling it round, a 'whizzer'; **-rope** (*Naut.*), a hawser let through a block on the bowsprit end to the buoy, to keep the buoy clear of the stem; † **-seg** (*dial.*), **-stag,** a bull gelded when past his prime; **-toad,** ? = -FROG; **-whacker** (Amer.), a bullock-driver in the Western states. **b.** *Comb.* with gen. *bull's*: **bull's-nose** (*Archit.*), 'the external or other angle of a polygon, or of any two lines meeting at an obtuse angle' (Gwilt); **bull's pizzle,** the penis of the bull, formerly used as an instrument of flagellation.

Bull (bul), *sb.*[2] ME. [– (O)Fr. *bulle* – L. *bulla* bubble, round object, in med.L. seal, sealed document. See BOWL *sb.*[2]] **1.** A seal attached to a document; *esp.* the leaden seal attached to the Pope's edicts. **2.** A papal or episcopal edict or mandate ME. **3.** Applied to a non-ecclesiastical edict 1696.
2. Indulgences, Dispenses, Pardons, Bulls, The sport of Winds MILT. *P. L.* III. 492. **Bullantic** *a.* (*rare*), of, pertaining to, or used in papal bulls.

† **Bull,** *sb.*[3] *rare.* 1561. [– (O)Fr. *bulle* :– L. *bulla*; see prec.] A bubble.

Bull (bul), *sb.*[4] 1630. [Origin unkn.] † **1.** A ludicrous jest (cf. BULL *v.*[3]) –1695. **2.** A self-contradictory proposition; in mod. use, an expression involving a ludicrous inconsistency unperceived by the speaker. The epithet *Irish* is a late addition. [Not conn. w. the Pope's *bulls*, or 'one Obadiah Bull'.]
2. Dumbe Speaker! that's a B. BROME.

Bull (bul), *sb.*[5] 1523. [Origin unkn.] One of the main bars of a harrow. Also *attrib.*

Bull. Short for JOHN BULL, BULL'S-EYE (7).

Bull-. 1450. [usu. = BULL *sb.*[1]; but cf. BOLL *sb.*[1], which may be the etymon in some of the words.] Comb. f. as in:
bull-brier, an American brier, from the root of which the Indians make bread; **-oak,** an oak within which bulls take shelter; **-plum,** a sloe (*Prunus spinosa*), cf., however, BULLACE; **-sedge,** the reed-mace; **-weed,** *Centaurea nigra*; **-wort,** *Ammi majus*, or Bishop-weed.

Bull (bul), *v.*[1] ME. [f. BULL *sb.*[1]] † **1. a.** *trans.* Of a bull: To gender with (the cow). **b.** Of the cow: To take, or desire, the bull. –1736. **2.** *Stock-Exchange.* To try to raise the price of (stocks, etc.) 1842.

† **Bull,** *v.*[2] 1563. [f. BULL *sb.*[2]] To insert in a Papal bull; to affix the Papal seal to –1670.

† **Bull,** *v.*[3] 1532. [– OFr. *boler, bouler* deceive; cf. *bul* (Cursor M.) – OFr. *bole, boul* deceit.] To make a fool of, to mock; to cheat (*out of*) –1674.

‖ **Bulla** (bu·lă, bɒ·lă). Pl. **bullæ.** 1847. [L.; see BULL *sb.*[3]] **1.** *Pathol.* A vesicle containing watery humour and causing an elevation of the skin 1876. **b.** *Phys.* 'The tympanic element of the temporal bone, when, as in the dog, it forms a..bubble-like appearance' 1872. **2.** *Zool.* A genus of deep-water molluscs, with thin and fragile shells 1847.

Bullace (bu·lės). ME. [– OFr. *buloce*, (also mod.) *beloce* sloe :– Rom. **bullucea*, f. **bulluca*, perh. of Gaulish origin.] **1.** A wild plum (*Prunus insititia*) larger than the sloe. **2.** The tree bearing the plum 1616; var. **B.-tree.**
1. Boollesse, black and white TUSSER.

Bullary (bu·lări). Also **-ery.** 1674. [– med.L. *bullarium* (also used), f. *bulla* (BULL *sb.*[2]); see -ARY[1], -ARIUM.] A collection of papal bulls.

Bullate (bu·lēⁱt, bɒ·lēⁱt), *a.* 1819. [– med.L. *bullatus*; see BULL *sb.*[2], -ATE[2].] **1.** *Bot.* Having blisters; inflated: said of leaves, in which the surface rises above the veins. **2.** *Phys.* Having *bullæ* or puffy excrescences on the surface 1872.

Bu·llated, *ppl. a.* 1698. [f. as prec. + -ED[1].] † **1.** *Rom. Ant.* Furnished with a *bulla* worn round the neck. **2.** = BULLATE 1707.

Bull-bait (bu·lˌbēⁱt). ? *Obs.* 1656. [f. BULL *sb.*[1] + BAIT *sb.* 5.] = BULL-BAITING.

Bu·ll-baiter. 1802. [f. as prec. + BAITER.] One who baits bulls.

Bu·ll-baiting, *vbl. sb.* 1580. [f. as prec. + BAITING.] The action of baiting bulls with dogs. (Cf. BULL-DOG.)

† **Bu·ll-beggar.** 1584. [Origin unkn.] A bogy; a scarecrow; a bugbear –1851.

Beggers will needes be somewaies bulbeggers 1588.

Bull-bitch. 1681. The female of the bull-dog.

Bull-dog. (Also † **bold-dogge.**) Often as one word, *esp.* in *transf.* uses. 1500. [f. BULL *sb.*[1] + DOG, either because used in bull-baiting, or perh. from the shape of the head.] **1.** A dog with large bull-head, short muzzle, strong muscular body of medium height, and short smooth hair, formerly much used for bull-baiting. Also *transf.* of persons. Also *attrib.* **2.** † A sheriff's officer; one of the Proctor's attendants at Oxford and Cambridge (*colloq.*) 1698. **3.** *transf.* Applied joc. to firearms; in mod. use, a kind of revolver. Cf. BARKER. Also *attrib.* 1700. **4. a.** A gad-fly (Amer.). **b.** An ant (Australian). 1865. **5.** In *Iron-works.* 'A refractory material used as furnace-lining, got by calcining mill-cinder' 1881.

1. The courage of bull-dogs and game-cocks seems peculiar to England HUME. **3.** He whips out his Stiletto and I whips out my bull-dog FARQUHAR.

Bull-doze, -dose (bu·l₁dōᵘz). *U.S.* 1876. [f. BULL *sb.*[1] + DOSE *sb.* ('as if to give a dose fit for a bull' but this is doubtful).] **A.** *sb.* ? A severe dose (of flogging). **B.** *vb.* **a.** ? To flog severely. **b.** To coerce by violence. Hence **Bull-dozer,** one who bull-dozes; also, a large pistol.

† **Bu·lled,** *ppl. a.*[1] ME. [f. BULL *sb.*[2] or *v.*[2]] Having a seal attached –1610.

† **Bulled,** *ppl. a.*[2] [perh. = *bolled* swollen.] B. JONS.

Buller (bu·ləɹ), *sb. Sc.* 1513. [prob. echoic; cf. Sw. *buller* noise, roar, Da. *bulder* tumbling noise; MHG., G. *bollern* make a noise.] A roaring noise (of waves, etc.); the boiling of an eddy or torrent. Also *fig.* Cf. *The Buller(s of Buchan.* Hence **Bu·ller** *v. Sc.* to bellow.

Bullescence (bule·sěns). 1880. [f. L. *bulla* bubble, after BULLATE; see -ESCENT, -ENCE.] *Bot.* The condition of being BULLATE 1.

Bullet (bu·lět), *sb.*[1] 1557. [– Fr. *boulet, boulette,* dim. of *boule* ball; see -ET.] **1.** A small round ball. (Now *transf.* from 3.) 1578. **2.** A cannon-ball (of metal or stone). Now *Hist.* 1557. **3.** A ball of lead, etc., used in firearms of small calibre; now often conical. Formerly also collective (cf. BALL *sb.*[1]). 1579. Also *fig.* **4.** † **a.** The missile from a sling; also *attrib.* **b.** The angler's plumb. 1587.

1. Upon the braunches [of the burdock] there groweth small bullets or rounde balles LYTE. **3.** *fig.* Paper bullets of the braine *Much Ado* II. iii. 249.

Phr. *Every b. has its billet* (see BILLET *sb.*[1]). *Comb.* **b.-shell,** a shell used with small-arms. Hence **Bu·lleted** *ppl. a.* bullet-shaped; furnished with bullets.

† **Bu·llet,** *sb.*[2] *rare.* 1612. [Sense 1, perversion of *billet*; sense 2 – It. *bulletta.* See BULLETIN.] **1.** = BILLET *sb.*[1] 2. **2.** A slip of paper on which the voter wrote the name of the candidate he supported. 1615.

Bullet-head. 1690. [f. BULLET *sb.*[1]] **a.** A head round like a bullet. **b.** A person with such a head; in U.S. *fig.* a 'pig-headed' person. Hence **Bu·llet-hea:ded, -hea·dedness.**

He aint No more'n a tough old bullethead LOWELL.

Bulletin (bu·lětin). 1651. [– Fr. *bulletin* – It. *bullettino, boll-* safe-conduct, pass, f. *bulletta* passport, dim. of *bulla* BULL *sb.*[2]] † **1.** A short note or memorandum. **b.** A warrant or appointment to an office. –1673. **2.** A short report of public news, issued by authority; *esp.* a report sent from the seat of war by a commander for publication at home 1791. **3.** An official statement as to the health of an invalid 1765.

2. 'False as a b.' became a proverb in Napoleon's time CARLYLE. Hence **Bu·lletin** *v.* (*trans.*) to make known by b.

Bullet Tree, var. *Bully Tree* (BULLY *sb.*[3]).

Bu·ll-fight. 1753. A sport practised esp. in Spain, in which a bull is engaged by horsemen (*picadores*) armed with lances, and by men on foot (*chulos*) having darts and cloaks, and is finally dispatched by a swordsman (*espada*). Hence **Bu·ll-fi:ghter.**

Bullfinch[1] (bu·lfinʃ). Also **bulfinch.** 1570. [f. BULL *sb.*[1] + FINCH.] One of a genus of birds (*Pyrrhula*), allied to the Grosbeaks, having handsome plumage and a short, hard, rounded beak. Also in *comb.*

Bullfinch[2] (bu·lfinʃ). 1832. [perh. corrupt f. *bull-fence.*] A quickset hedge with a ditch on one side, too high and strong to be cleared. Hence **Bu·llfinch** *v. intr.* to leap a horse through such a hedge. var. **Bullfincher.**

Bu·llfist. 1611. [f. BULL *sb.*[1] + † *fist* stink.] The puff-ball.

Bu·ll-fro:g. 1738. [f. BULL *sb.*[1]] A large American frog (*Rana pipiens*), which has a voice not unlike a bull's.

Bu·llhea:d. 1450. **1.** A small fish with a large head; the *Miller's Thumb.* **2.** A tadpole. Still *dial.* 1611. † **3.** A mass of curled or frizzled hair worn over the forehead; also called *bull-tour* –1688. **4.** A blockhead 1624.

Bullheaded (bu·lhe:dėd), *a.* 1818. Broad-headed; *fig.* blindly impetuous, blockheaded. Hence **Bu:llhea·dedness.**

Bu·llimong. ME. [perh. f. BULL *sb.*[1] + ME. *imong* :– OE. *ġemang, ġemong* mixture.] **1.** A mixture of grain (as oats, pease, and vetches) sown together, for feeding cattle. Cf. DREDGE *sb*[2], MASLIN.[2], and L. *farrago.* Also *attrib.* † **2.** = BUCKWHEAT –1706.

Bullion[1] (bu·liən). ME. [– AFr. *bullion* (XIV), which appears to mean 'mint', var. of (O)Fr. *bouillon* :– Rom. **bullio, -on-* boiling, f. L. *bullire* BOIL *v.*; see -ION.] **1.** ?Melting-house or mint; but in 16th c. 'place of exchange'. **2.** Gold or silver in the lump; also applied to coined or manufactured gold or silver considered as raw metal 1451. Also *fig.* **b.** Solid gold or silver (as opp. to imitations). Often *fig.* Also *attrib.* 1596. † **3.** Impure gold or silver –1820. **4.** Any metal in the lump 1590.

2. The B. of neighbour Kingdoms brought to receive a Stamp from the Mint of England CLARENDON. All silver money should be taken only as b. SWIFT. **3.** *fig.* The drossie B. of the Peoples sinnes MILT. Hence † **Bu·llioner,** a dealer in b. **Bu·llionist,** one who advocates a metallic currency.

† **Bu·llion**[2]. 1463. [app. – Fr. *boulon* (spelt *bouillon* in Cotgrave), f. *boule* ball; see -OON.] A knob or boss of metal; a convex ornament on a book, girdle, harness, or ring –1707. Also *attrib.*

Bullion[3] (bu·liən). 1594. [– Fr. *bouillon* in same senses; see BULLION[1].] † **1.** More fully *b.-hose*: Trunk-hose, puffed out at the upper part, in several folds –1632. **2.** A fringe made of twists of gold or silver thread; also, a twist of such fringe. Also *attrib.* [Now occas. assoc. w. BULLION[1].] 1662.

2. All in a blaze of scarlet and b. and steel THACKERAY.

Bullish (bu·liʃ), *a.*[1] 1566. [f. BULL *sb.*[1] + -ISH[1].] **1.** Of or pertaining to, resembling or having the nature of, a bull. **2.** *Stock-Exchange,* etc. Tending to or aiming at a rise in the price of stocks or merchandise 1882.

2. B. about cotton 1884. Hence **Bu·llishly** *adv.*

† **Bullish,** *a.*[2] *rare.* 1641. [f. BULL *sb.*[4] + -ISH[1].] Having the nature of a bull (BULL *sb.*[4]) –1660.

† **Bulli·tion.** 1620. [– late L. *bullitio,* f. *bullit-,* pa. ppl. stem of L. *bullire* boil; see -ION.] Bubbling or boiling –1791.

Bullock (bu·lək), *sb.* [Late OE. *bulluc,* dim. of BULL *sb.*[1]; see -OCK.] **1.** Orig. a young bull, or bull calf; now always, a castrated bull, an ox. **2.** *Loosely,* A bovine beast generally. Now *dial.* 1535.

2. 'Yes, she's a purty cow..one of these days she'll make a nice b.' 1875.

Comb. **a. Bullock's Eye,** the common House-leek; **Bullock's Heart,** the fruit of *Anona reticulata*; **Bullock's Lungwort,** the Great Mullein. **b. b.-puncher** (*Austral.*), a bullock-driver.

Bu·llock, *v.* Now *dial.* 1716. [Perversion of BULLY *v.*] = BULLY *v.*

Bu·ll's-eye. 1825. The eye of a bull (cf. Fr. *œil de bœuf*); hence **1.** A boss of glass, or the central protuberance formed in making a sheet of blown glass 1832. **2.** *Naut.* A thick disc of glass inserted in the side or deck of a ship, etc., to light the interior 1825. **3.** A lens, hemispherical or plano-convex 1839. **4.** A glass of similar shape inserted in the side of a lantern; the lantern itself; also *attrib.* 1851. **5.** *Naut.* A small pulley in the form of a ring, having a rope round the outer edge, and a hole in the middle for another to slide in 1769. **6.** *Archit.* A small circular opening or window 1865. **7.** The centre of a target; also, a shot which hits it; also *fig.* 1833. **8.** A circular ornament of gold lace 1879. **9.** A globular sweetmeat 1825. **10.** 'A little dark cloud, reddish in the middle', common about the Cape of Good Hope, supposed to portend a storm; hence, the storm itself 1753. **11.** *slang.* A crown-piece 1690.

4. Policemen, with their Bull's-eyes 1851.

Bu:ll-te·rrier. 1848. A dog of a cross breed between a bull-dog and a terrier.

Bu·ll-trou:t. 1653. [f. BULL *sb.*[1]] A large fish of the Salmon tribe (*Salmo eriox*).

Bully (bu·li), *sb.*[1] 1538. [prob. – (M)Du. *boele* lover (MHG. *buole,* G. *buhle*) used as a term of endearment or reproach, of which the dims. *boelekijn* and *boeltje(n)* are repr. by BULKIN and BULCHIN.] **1.** Sweetheart, darling: orig. used of either sex. Later, of men only. Often as a sort of title, as in Shaks., 'b. Bottom', etc. Now *arch.* Also *attrib.*, as in *b.-boy* 1609. **2.** *dial.* Brother, companion, mate 1825. **3.** A blustering gallant; a swashbuckler; now *esp.* a person (or animal) who makes himself or herself a terror to the weak or defenceless 1688. **b.** A hired ruffian (*arch.*) 1730. **4.** *spec.* One who protects and lives on prostitutes 1706.

1. From heartstring I loue the louely B. SHAKS. **3.** Where London's column, pointing at the skies Like a tall b., lifts the head, and lyes POPE. **4.** The b. and the bawd, who fatten on their misery 1750.

Bully (bu·li), *sb.*[2] 1865. [perh. f. prec.] **1.** *Eton football.* A scrimmage. **2.** *Hockey.* Putting the ball in play; hence as *v. trans.* and *intr.* 1886.

Bu·lly, *sb.*[3] Also **bullet.** 1657. [Origin unkn.; cf. *bully,* dial. var. of BULLACE.] *attrib.* in *B. Bay, B.-berry Tree, B. Tree,* genera of the order *Sapotaceæ,* also a species of *Mimusops.*

Bully (bu·li), *sb.*[4] 1800 (*bouillie beef*). [– Fr. *bouilli*; see BOUILLI. Used as a label of tinned army rations of beef in the Franco-Prussian war of 1870–1.] In full, *b. beef*: tinned beef, esp. as used in the British army.

Bully (bu·li), *a.* 1681. [perh. arising from attrib. use of BULLY *sb.*[1]] **1.** Of persons: Worthy, jolly, admirable. **2.** *U.S.* and *Colonies.* First-rate, crack 1855. **b.** as an exclam., *esp.* in 'B. for you !' = bravo! 1864. **3.** Like or characteristic of a bully 1727.

2. The cook will give you a b. dinner 1855. **3.** A b. imposition of sheer physical ascendancy G. MEREDITH.

Bully (bu·li), *v.* 1710. [f. BULLY *sb.*[1]] **1.** *trans.* To act the bully towards; to intimidate, overawe. **2.** To drive by bullying; with *away, into, out of, to* 1723. **3.** *intr.* and *absol.* To bluster, use violent threats; to swagger 1744.

1. To b. the servant 1802. **2.** To b. away customers DE FOE.

Bullyrag (bu·liræg), *v. dial.* and *colloq.* Also **ba·llyrag.** 1807. [Origin unkn.] † **a.** To intimidate. **b.** To abuse.

b. Irish tenantry..ballyragging their member 1879.

† **Bully-rock, bully-rook.** 1598. [perh. f. ROOK *sb.*[1] (XVI) cheat; cf. also *bully-rake* (RAKE *sb.*[4] XVII).] = BULLY *sb.*[1] 1, 3. –1827.

What saies my Bully Rooke? *Merry W.* I. iii. 2.

Bulrush (bu·lrɒʃ). 1440. [perh. f. BULL *sb.*[1], in the sense 'large', 'coarse', as in BULL-FINCH, -FROG, *-trout.*] A book-name for *Scirpus lacustris*; but pop. applied to *Typha latifolia,* the 'Cat's Tail', and in the Bible to the Papyrus of Egypt. Also *fig.* with reference to its fragility.

She tooke for him an arke of bul-rushes *Ex.* 2:3 *fig.* We leane on the b. of our oune merits 1646.

Bulse (bɒls). *arch.* 1708. [– Pg. *bolsa* :– med.L. *bursa.* Cf. BURSE.] A package of diamonds or gold-dust.

Bultell(e, var. of BOULTEL.

Bulwark (bu·lwǫ̈ɹk), *sb.* ME. [– MLG., MDu. *bolwerk* (= MHG. *bol(e)werk*, G. *bollwerk*, whence Fr. BOULEVARD); ult. f. words repr. by BOLE[1], WORK *sb.*] **1.** A substantial defensive work of earth, etc.; a rampart, a fortification. Now *arch.* or *poet.* **b.** A breakwater, mole, sea-wall, etc. Also *fig.* 1555. **2.** *transf.* and *fig.* A powerful defence or defender 1577. **3.** The raised woodwork running along the sides of a vessel above the level of the deck. Usu. *pl.* 1804.

2. To destroy their Fleete: which..are their Walls and Bulwarks CLARENDON.

Bulwark (bu·lwǫ̈ɹk), *v.* 1450. [f. prec.] **1.** *trans.* To furnish with bulwarks. *intr.* To throw up bulwarks (*lit.* and *fig.*). **2.** *trans.* To serve as a bulwark to 1610.

2. Friends bulwarked him about BROWNING.

Bum (bɒm), *sb.*[1] ME. [Late ME. *bom*, of unkn. origin.] **1.** The posteriors. Also *transf.* **2.** *colloq.* Short for BUMBAILIFF (like Fr. *cul* for *pousse-cul*) 1691.

† **Bum,** *sb.*[2] and *int.* 1552. [imit.; cf. BUB *sb.*[1], BUMBO.] A child's word for drink –1598.

Bum, *v.*[1] Now *dial.* 1450. [var. of BOOM *v.*[1]] *intr.* To hum loudly.

I..'eerd un a bummin' awaäy loike a buzzard-clock TENNYSON.

† **Bum,** *v.*[2] 1579. [Of echoic origin.] *trans.* (or *absol.*) To strike, beat, thump –1622.

Bum, *v.*[3] 1833. To act as a bumboat woman.

Bum-; see BOM-.

Bumaloe, Bumaree; see BUMM-.

Bumbailiff (bɒ·mbē̆i·lif). 1601. [f. BUM *sb.*[1]; so called because he attacks from the rear; cf. Fr. *pousse-cul* 'push-bum'.] 'A bailiff of the meanest kind; one that is employed in arrests' (J.).

A confounded pettifogging bum-bailiff THACKERAY.

† **Bumbard, -art.** 1505. [f. *bumb* BUM *v.*[1] + -ARD.] A bumble-bee, a drone; also *fig.* –1614.

Bu·mbarge. 1839. [alt. of *bumboat* by substitution of BARGE.]

Bumbaste *v.* Now *dial.* 1571. [app. f. BUM *sb.*[1] + BASTE *v.*[3]; but see next.] To beat on the posteriors; hence, to beat soundly.

Bumbaze (bɒmbē̆i·z), *v.* Chiefly *Sc.* 1725. [app. f. obs. *baze* stupefy, with *bum-* as a meaningless intensive or redupl. prefix.] To confound, bamboozle.

Bu·mbelo, bu·mbolo. 1854. [– It. *bombola.*] A glass flask for subliming camphor.

Bu·mble, *sb.*[1] Now *dial.* 1597. [f. BUMBLE *v.*[1]] A bumble-bee. Also, a bittern (*local*).

Bu·mble, *sb.*[2] Now *dial.* 1648. [Of symbolic origin; cf. BUNGLE, JUMBLE, FUMBLE.] **1.** A jumble. **2.** A blunderer; an idler 1786. ¶ **3.** Associated with this is the name of the beadle in Dickens's *Oliver Twist* (see BUMBLEDOM) 1856.

† **Bumble,** *v.*[1] ME. [frequent. of ME. *bumme, bumbe, bombe*; see BOOM *v.*[1], BUM *v.*[1], -LE.] **1.** *intr.* To boom; to buzz –1868. **2.** *trans.* To blame –1781.

1. As a Bitore bombleth in the Myre CHAUCER.

Bu·mble, *v.*[2] Now *Sc.* 1532. [See BUMBLE *sb.*[2]] *intr.* To blunder. *trans.* To do in a bungling manner.

Bumble-bee (bɒ·mb'lbī·). 1530. [f. BUMBLE *v.*[1] + BEE[1].] A large bee of the genus *Bombus*; a humble-bee.

Bumbledom (bɒ·mb'ldəm). 1856. [f. *Bumble*, name of the beadle in Dickens's *Oliver Twist* + -DOM.] Stupid officiousness and pomposity; beadledom in its glory.

Bumble - puppy (bɒ·mb'lpɒpi). 1801. [Origin unkn.] **a.** Nine-holes. **b.** Whist played unscientifically. Cf. BUMBLE *v.*[2]

Bu·mbo. 1748. [perh. – It. *bombo* child's word for a drink. Cf. BUM *sb.*[2]] A drink composed of rum, sugar, water, and nutmeg, or the like.

Bumboat (bɒ·mbōᵘt). 1671. [app. var. of contemp. *dirt-boat*, by substitution of BUM *sb.*[1]] † **1.** A scavenger's boat, employed to remove filth from ships lying in the Thames –1685. **2.** A boat carrying provisions, vegetables, etc., to ships. (Orig. the 'dirt-boats' did this.) 1769. Also *attrib.*, as *b. man, woman*, etc.

Bumkin, bumpkin (bɒ·mkin). 1632. [– Du. *boomken* (also *boompje*), f. *boom* tree, boom + *-ken* -KIN.] *Naut.* 'A short boom projecting from each bow of a ship, to extend the lower edge of the foresail to windward.' Also applied to similar booms.

‖ **Bummalo.** 1673. [Also *bumbalo, -eloe*, which has been referred to Marathi *bombīl(a).*] A small fish (*Harpodon nehereus*) found off Southern Asia.

Bummaree (bɒmărī·). 1786. [Origin unkn.] A middleman in the fish trade at Billingsgate.

Bu·mmer. *U.S. slang.* 1865. [perh. based on G. *bummler*, f. *bummeln* loaf about.] An idler, loafer. So **Bu·mmerish** *a.*

† **Bu·mmery.** 1663. [– Du. *bommerye, bodmerij*; see BOTTOMRY.] = BOTTOMRY –1836.

Bump (bɒmp), *sb.*[1] 1592. [The sb. and v. appear about the same time; perh. of Scand. origin; cf. MDa. *bumpe* strike with the fist.] **1.** A heavyish blow, rather dull in sound; a sudden collision 1611. **2.** *Boating.* The impact of the stem of a boat against the stern or side of another 1861. **3.** A protuberance such as is caused by a knock; an irregular prominence 1592. **4.** *transf.* One of the prominences on the cranium associated by phrenologists with special faculties or propensities; also, the faculties, etc. (*colloq.*) 1815. **5.** A variation of air pressure causing irregularity in an aeroplane's motion 1914.

Bump, *sb.*[2] 1528. [Imitative.] The cry of the bittern.

Bump, *sb.*[3] [Origin unkn.] **a.** A kind of matting. **b.** Cotton threads loosely twisted together, used for candle-wicks, also woven into sheets.

Bump, *v.*[1] 1566. [Goes with BUMP *sb.*[1]] **1.** *trans.* To strike heavily, knock, thump 1611. **2.** *intr.* To strike with a violent jolt; to move with a bump or bumps 1843. **b.** *intr. Cricket.* Of a ball: To rise abruptly on pitching. Also *trans.* of a bowler. 1888. **3.** *trans. Boat-racing.* To overtake and impinge on. Also *absol.* = 'make a bump'; see BUMP *sb.*[1] 2. 1826. † **4.** To rise in protuberances, to be convex –1603. **5.** *advb.* With a bump, with sudden collision 1806.

1. We bumped ashore a hundred Kegs SCOTT. **2.** She bumped several times..losing her false keel 1860.

Bump, *v.*[2] 1646. [Goes with BUMP *sb.*[2]] To utter the cry of the bittern.

Bumper (bɒ·mpəɹ), *sb.*[1] 1676. [f. *bumping* ppl. a. (XVI) huge, 'thumping' + -ER[1]; cf. *whacker, whacking, whopper, whopping.*] **1.** A cup or glass filled to the brim, *esp.* for a toast. Also *attrib.* **2.** *slang.* Anything unusually large. (Cf. *thumper*, etc.) Also *attrib.* 1859. **3.** *Theatr. slang.* A crowded house 1839. **4.** In *Whist*, etc. Winning two games before the adversaries have scored 1876. **5.** The buffer of a railway carriage (*U.S.*) 1839.

1. Full bumpers crown our blisses 1676. **2.** A b. rubbee crop 1885.

Bumper, *sb.*[2] 1866. [f. BUMP *v.*[2] and *sb.*[2]] In comb. *bog-b.* = BITTERN.

Bu·mper, *v.* 1696. [f. BUMPER *sb.*[1]] **a.** To fill to the brim. **b.** To toast in a bumper. **c.** *intr.* To drink bumpers.

Bumpkin (bɒ·mpkin). 1570. [perh. – Du. *boomken* little tree, or MDu. *bommekijn* little barrel, used fig. for 'squat figure'.] **1.** An awkward country fellow, a lout. **2.** ? A kind of dance 1823. Hence **Bu·mpkinet,** a little b. **Bu·mpkinish, Bu·mpkinly** *adjs.* **Bu·mpkinship** (*joc.*).

Bumptious (bɒ·mpʃəs), *a.* 1803. [joc. f. BUMP *v.*[1], after *fractious*; cf. the fig. uses of *bounce* and *bounder.*] Offensively self-conceited; self-assertive (*colloq.* and *undignified*). Hence **Bu·mptious-ly** *adv.*, **-ness.**

Bumpy (bɒ·mpi), *a.* 1865. [f. BUMP *sb.*[1] or *v.*[1] + -Y[1].] Full of bumps; of a road, etc., jolty; causing bumps.

A b. wicket 1884. Hence **Bu·mpiness.**

Bun (bɒn), *sb.*[1] Now *dial.* [OE. *bune*, origin unkn.] The stalky part of flax or hemp.

Bun (bɒn), *sb.*[2] ME. [Late ME. *bunne*, of unkn. origin. Cf. OFr. *bunette, bagnete, buignon* lump produced by a blow, fritter.] In England, a sweet cake (usu. round and not large); in Scotland, the richest currant bread.

Bun, *sb.*[3] 1587. [Origin unkn. Cf. BUNNY.] **a.** The squirrel. **b.** The rabbit (*dial.*). **c.** A term of endearment.

Bunch (bɒnʃ), *sb.* ME. [Origin unkn.; *hunch* and dial. *clunch* have similar meanings.] † **1.** A protuberance; a hump; a goitre; a tumour –1826. In *pl.* A disease of horses –1775. **2.** A collection or cluster of things of the same kind, as grapes, flowers, keys; also a portion of a dress gathered in folds 1570. **3.** *fig.* A collection 1622.

1. A camell of Arabia hathe two bonches in the backe TREVISA. **3.** She's the best of the b. 1887. *Comb.* **b.-grass,** *Festuca scabrella* of N. America.

Bunch (bɒnʃ), *v.* ME. [f. BUNCH *sb.*] † **1.** *intr.* To bulge (*out*); to form bunches –1807. **2.** *trans.* To make into a bunch; to gather (a dress) into folds; to group (animals) (*U.S.*) 1881.

Bunched (bɒnʃt), *ppl. a.* 1519. [f. BUNCH *sb.* and *v.*] † Having or forming a protuberance; covered with swellings; humped; bulging.

Bunchy (bɒ·nʃi), *a.* ME. [f. BUNCH *sb.* + -Y[1].] **1.** Bulging; full of protuberances; humped. **2.** Like a bunch; having bunches 1824.

2. Bowers Trellised with b. vine TENNYSON. Hence **Bu·nchiness.**

Bunco: see BUNKO.

Buncombe, bunkum (bɒ·ŋkəm). 1850. [f. *Buncombe*, name of a county in N. Carolina, U.S., the member for which, on one occasion, insisted on speaking because Buncombe expected it, and he was *bound to make a speech for Buncombe.*] **1.** *in U.S. use*: **a.** In phrases, such as, *to talk* or *speak for* or *to Buncombe, a bid for buncombe* (i.e. the favour of the electors), and the like 1857. **b.** Political speaking or action not from conviction; political clap-trap 1850. **2.** 'Tall talk'; humbug 1862. Also *attrib.*

1. a. The bill was another bid for b. *N. York Her.* 1859. **b.** Conventions, rights of independence, caucuses, agitation, and whatever else may be implied by the American expression 'bunkum' 1850. **2.** A b. proclamation 1863. Hence **Buncomize** *v.* to talk b.

‖ **Bund** (bɒnd). *Anglo-Ind.* 1813. [Hind. *band*, of Pers. origin.] In India: Any artificial embankment, a dam, dyke, causeway. In Anglo-Chinese ports, *esp.* the embanked quay along the shore.

‖ **Bunder** (bɒ·ndəɹ). *Anglo-Ind.* 1673. [Hind. *bandar*, a Pers. word.] 'A landing-place or quay; a seaport; a harbour; (sometimes a custom-house)' (Col. Yule). *Comb.* **b.-boat,** a boat in use on the Bombay coast for communicating with ships at anchor, etc.

Bundle (bɒ·nd'l), *sb.* ME. [orig. perh. repr. OE. *byndelle* binding, taken in concr. sense, = OS. *bundilin* (Du. *bundel* bundle), OHG. *gi|buntili* (G. *bündel*), but reinforced later by (if not wholly due to) LG., Du. *bundel.*] † **1.** A bandage (*rare*). ME. only. **2.** A collection of things fastened together; a package, parcel ME. **3.** *fig.* A collection, lot; often contemptuous 1535.

1. A b. of papers 1636, of sweet herbs MRS. GLASSE, linen 1802, glass plates BREWSTER. **3.** A b. of calumnies SIR T. BROWNE.

Comb. **b. pillar,** 'a column consisting of a number of small pillars around its circumference' (Gwilt).

Bu·ndle, *v.* 1628. [f. prec.] **1.** *trans.* To tie in, or make *up* into, a bundle 1649. † **2.** *fig.* To gather (*up, together*) into a mass –1690. **3.** *intr.* To pack up one's effects for a journey; hence, to go with all one's incumbrances. Also, of several: To go 'all in a b.' (cf. 4). 1787. **4.** *trans.* To put or send *away, in, off, out*, etc., hurriedly and unceremoniously. Cf. 'pack off'. 1823. **5.** *intr.* To sleep in one's clothes on the same bed or couch *with* (as once was customary with persons of opposite sexes, in Wales and New England) 1781.

4. When he and his are all bundled off to Hades DE QUINCEY. **5.** The custom of bundling.. among Celtic peoples 1878.

‖ **Bundook** (bɒ·nduk). *India.* 1886. [– Hind. *bandūk* –, through Pers., Arab. *bunduk* filbert, musket or cannon ball, firearm; see BONDUC.] A musket.

Bung (bɒŋ), *sb.*[1] ME. [– MDu. *bonghe*, varying with *bomme* and *bonde*, whence MDu. *bonne*, beside Du. *bom*, of doubtful origin.]

1. A stopper; *spec.* a large cork stopper for the mouth of a cask. **2.** *transf.* The bung-hole. (Still *dial.*) 1571. **3.** *Naut.* The master's assistant who superintends the serving of the grog 1863.

Comb.: **b.-hole,** the hole in a cask, which is closed with the b.; **-stave,** that in which is the b.-hole.

† **Bung,** *sb.*² *Thieves' Cant.* 1567. [Origin unkn.] **a.** A purse. **b.** A pick-pocket. *Comb.* **b.-nipper,** a pick-pocket. –1725.

You Cut-purse Rascall, you filthy B. SHAKS.

Bung (bɒŋ), *v.* 1589. [f. BUNG *sb.*¹] *trans.* **1.** To stop with a bung 1616. **2.** *transf.* and *fig.* To close. Now chiefly in pugilistic slang. 1589. **3.** To shut *up*, enclose, as in a bunged cask 1592.

Bungalow (bɒ·ŋgălōᵘ). 1676. [– Gujarati *bangalo* – Hind. *banglā* belonging to Bengal.] A one-storied house, lightly built, with a tiled or thatched roof, orig. in the East. Hence **Bu·ngaloid** *a.*, having the appearance or style of a b.; also as *sb.*

Bungle (bɒ·ŋg'l), *v.* 1530. [prob. symbolic, like synon. and contemp. BUMBLE *v.*²] **1.** *trans.* To make or do in a clumsy manner. Now, usually, To spoil by unskilful workmanship. **2.** *intr.* To work or act unskilfully or clumsily 1549. Hence **Bu·ngler. Bu·nglingly** *adv.*

Bu·ngle, *sb.* 1656. [f. prec.] A clumsy or unskilful piece of work; a botch, muddle.

Bunion (bɒ·nyən). 1718. [Formerly also *bunnian, -on, bunyan, -on* – OFr. *buignon* (mod. dial. *beugnon*), f. *buigne* bump on the head; see BUNNY¹, -OON.] An inflamed swelling on the foot, *esp.* of the bursa mucosa at the inside of the ball of the great toe.

Bunjara, -jarree, var. BRINJARRY.

Bunk (bɒŋk), *sb.*¹ 1815. [Origin unkn.; perh. rel. to BUNKER.] A box or recess serving for a bed; a sleeping-berth. **2.** A piece of wood placed on a lumberman's sled to support the ends of heavy pieces of timber (*U.S.*) 1848.

Bunk, *sb.*² 1914. Abbrev. BUNCOMBE, BUNKUM.

Bunk, *v.*¹ 1840. [f. BUNK *sb.*¹] To sleep in a bunk; *hence*, to camp out. Also, To *b. it* (*colloq.*, chiefly U.S.).

Bunk, *v.*² *colloq.* and *slang.* 1877. [Origin unkn.] To be off. Also as sb. *To do a b.*, to make an escape.

Bunker (bɒ·ŋkəɹ). 1758. [Origin unkn.] **1.** A seat or bench (*Sc.*). **2.** An earthen seat or bank in the fields (*dial.*) 1805. **3.** A receptacle for coal on board ship 1839. **4.** *Golf.* A sandy hollow or other obstruction on the links 1824; also as passive vb., to be hit, etc., into a b.; also *fig.*

Bunko, bunco (bɒ·ŋko), *sb. U.S. slang.* 1876. Also **banco.** [Cf. Sp. *banco* bank, *banca* a card-game.] Swindling by card-sharping, etc. *Comb.* **b.-steerer,** a swindler. Hence **Bu·nko** *v.*

Bunkum; see BUNCOMBE.

† **Bu·nny**¹. ME. [In XV *bony* (cf. obs. XVII dial. (Essex) *boine*) – OFr. *buigne, buyne* (mod. *bigne*) bump on the head, perh. of Gmc. origin (cf. MHG. *bunge* lump). See BUNION.] A swelling as on the joints of animals –1784.

Bu·nny². 1606. [f. BUN *sb.*³ + -Y⁶.] A pet name for a rabbit.

Comb. **B.-hug,** an eccentric rag-time dance. **B. Mouth,** the Common Snapdragon.

Bunny³ (bɒ·ni). *dial.* 1873. [Origin unkn.] A small ravine opening through the cliff line to the sea. Also any small drain, culvert, etc. (*Hampshire.*)

Bunsen (bu·nsĕn, bɒ·nsĕn). 1879. [f. name of R. W. von *Bunsen* (1811–99), German chemist.] **Bunsen('s) burner, lamp,** a gas-burner, in which air is burnt with gas. **Bunsen('s) battery,** a voltaic battery in which the elements are carbon and zinc, and in which nitric and sulphuric acids, or solution of bichromate of potash and sulphuric acid, are employed. **B. cell,** one of the cells of a B. battery.

Bunsenite (bu·nsĕnəit). 1868. [f. BUNSEN + -ITE¹ 2 b.] *Min.* A native protoxide of nickel.

Bunt (bɒnt), *sb.*¹ 1582. [Origin. unkn.] **1.** The bagging part of a fishing-net; the funnel of an eel-trap 1602. **2.** *Naut.* The middle part of a sail. **b.** The middle part of a yard: the *Slings.* 1582.

Phr. *B. fair* (Naut.): before the wind.

Bunt (bɒnt), *sb.*² 1601. [Origin unkn.] *Bot.* **1.** The Puffball (*Lycoperdon bovista*). Now *dial.* **2.** A parasitic fungoid, *Tilletia caries*, or Smutball; also the disease caused by it 1797. Hence **Bu·nted** *ppl. a.* infected with b.

Bunt, *v.*¹ 1611. [f. BUNT *sb.*¹] *Naut.* **1.** To haul up the middle part of (a sail) in furling. **2.** *intr.* Of a sail: To belly 1681.

Bunt, *v.*² Chiefly *dial.* 1825. [Cf. BUTT *v.*] *trans.* and *intr.* To knock, push, butt.

Bu·nter¹. Now *dial.* 1707. [Origin unkn.] A woman who picks up rags about the street; hence, any low vulgar woman.

‖ **Bunter**² (bu·ntər). 1874. *Geol.* Short for *bunter Sandstein*, i.e. 'mottled sandstone', German name for the New Red Sandstone.

Bunting (bɒ·ntiŋ), *sb.*¹ ME. [Origin unkn.] **1.** Name of a group of insessorial birds, the *Emberizinæ*, a sub-family of *Fringillidæ* allied to the larks. **2.** The grey shrimp (*Crangon vulgaris*) 1836. **3.** A term of endearment; cf. Sc. *buntin*, short and thick, plump 1665.

1. I tooke this Larke for a b. *All's Well* II. v. 7. **3.** Bye, baby b. *Nursery rhyme.*

Bu·nting, *sb.*² 1742. [Origin unkn.] An open-made worsted stuff, used for making flags; also, a flag, flags.

Up goes her b. MARRYAT.

Bunting (bɒ·ntiŋ), *ppl. a.* 1584. [f. BUNT *v.*¹ + -ING².] **1.** Of a sail: Bellying 1702. **2.** Swelling, plump; filled out 1584.

Bunting crow (bɒ·ntiŋ krōᵘ·). 1802. [Du. *bonte-kraai*, f. *bont* parti-coloured + *kraai* crow.] The Hooded Crow (*Corvus cornix*).

Buntline (bɒ·ntləin). 1627. [f. BUNT *sb.*¹ + LINE *sb.*²] *Naut.* A rope fastened to the foot-rope of a sail, and passing in front of the canvas, so as to prevent it from bellying when being furled.

Buoy (boi), *sb.* 1466. [prob. – MDu. *bo(e)ye, boeie* (Du. *boei*), perh. – Fr. *boie, buie* chain, fetter :– L. *boia*, esp. pl. *boiæ* – Gr. βοεῖαι (sc. δοραί) straps of ox-leather, f. βοῦς ox.] **1.** A floating object fastened in a particular place to point out the position of things under the water (as anchors, shoals, rocks), or the course for ships; or to float a cable in a rocky anchorage (= *cable-, mooring-b.*). *Bell-b.*, a b. fitted with a bell, to ring with the movement of the water. **b.** That which buoys up a person in the water (= *life-b.*) **2.** *fig.* That which marks out a course, indicates danger, or keeps one afloat 1603. **3.** *attrib.*, as *b.-rope*, etc. 1562.

Buoy (boi), *v.* 1596. [In senses 1–3 – Sp. *boyar* float; see BUOYANT; sense 4 f. the sb.] † **1.** *intr.* To rise to, or float on, the surface of a liquid; to rise, swell (as the sea) –1674. Also † *fig.* **2.** *trans.* To keep from sinking (in a fluid); *transf.* to keep up. (Usu. with *up.*) 1651. **b.** To raise to the surface of a liquid; to bring afloat (*e.g.* a sunken ship) 1616. **3.** *fig.* To keep up, support. (Usu. with *up.*) 1645. **b.** To raise (the spirits, etc.) (Usu. with *up.*) 1652. **4.** To furnish or mark with a buoy or buoys; to mark as with a buoy 1596.

1. *Lear* III. vii. 60. **2.** To b. up a lump of lead BURKE. **b.** I will descend to thee, And b. thee up BEAUM & FL. **3. b.** Hearts sunk down are not to be boyed up FULLER. **4.** The captain sounded and buoyed the bar COOK.

Buoyage (boi·ėdʒ). 1858. [f. BUOY *v.* and *sb.* + -AGE.] The providing of (or with) buoys.

Buoyancy (boi·ănsi). 1713. [f. BUOYANT; see -ANCY.] **1.** Power of floating; tendency to float. Power of supporting a floating body (*rare*). *Hydrost.* Loss of weight due to immersion in liquid; the vertical upward pressure of a liquid on a floating body, which is equal to the weight of displaced liquid. **2.** *fig.* Elasticity of spirit 1819. **3.** Tendency to rise in prices, national revenue, etc. 1883.

2. The reckless b. of young blood 1819. var. **Buoy·ance** (*poet.* or *rhet.*).

Buoyant (boi·ănt), *a.* 1578. [– OFr. *bouyant* or Sp. *boyante* light-sailing, pres. pple. of *boyar* float, f. *boya* BUOY; see -ANT.] **1.** Having the power of floating, tending to float; floating; lightly elastic. Also *fig.* **2.** Having the power of buoying up (BUOY *v.* 2) 1692. Also *fig.*

2. The water under me was b. DRYDEN. *fig.* A man of b. and animated valour 1770. **Buoy·antly** *adv.*

‖ **Buprestis** (bᶦupre·stis). ME. [L. – Gr. βούπρηστις, lit. 'ox-burner'.] **1.** An insect of the ancients, harmful to cattle. **2.** *Zool.* A genus of tropical beetles, brilliant in colouring. Hence the family *Buprestidæ*, occas. called **Bupre·stidans.** 1835.

Bur, burr (bɔ̄ɹ), *sb.* ME. [perh. of Scand. origin; cf. Da. *burre* bur, burdock, Sw. *kard borre* burdock.] **1.** Any rough or prickly seed-vessel or flower-head of a plant: *esp.* the flower-head of the Burdock (*Arctium lappa*); the husk of the chestnut. **b.** The female catkin of the hop before fertilization. [? A different wd.; cf. 4.] 1846. **2.** Any plant which produces burs 1480. **3.** *fig.* Any (thing or person) which clings like a bur 1590. **4.** A knob or knot in a tree; also, one of the buds of the farcy. [But cf. Fr. *bourre* vine-bud, *bourrelet* 'round swelling on a tree'.] 1725. **5.** The rounded knob forming the base of a deer's horn. [Cf. BURL.] 1575. **6.** *dial.* 'The drag-chain and shoe for fastening up a carriage wheel when going down a hill' 1863.

1. I am a kind of Burre, I shal sticke *Meas. for M.* I. iii. 189. **2.** Bur and brake and briar TENNYSON. **3.** Hang off thou cat, thou bur *Mids. N.* III. ii. 260.

Phr. *Bur in the throat*: anything that appears to stick in the throat; 'a lump in the throat'.

Comb.: **b.-flag** = *bur-reed*; **-knot** = sense 4; **-marigold,** the genus *Bidens*; **-oak,** *Quercus macrocarpa* of N. America; **-reed,** the genus *Sparganum*; **-thistle,** *Carduus lanceolatus*; **-weed,** *Xanthium strumarium.*

Bur, *v.* [f. prec.] To remove burs from (wool).

Burberry (bɔ̄·ɹbəri). 1903. Trade name of cloth and clothing made by Burberrys Ltd.

Bu·rble, *sb.*¹ ME. [f. BURBLE *v.*¹] † **1.** A bubble, bubbling –1547. † **2.** A pimple, boil –1622. **3.** A murmurous flow of words 1896.

Burble, *sb.*² *Sc. dial.* 1812. [Goes with BURBLE *v.*²] 'Trouble, perplexity, disorder' (Jam.).

Bu·rble, *v.*¹ ME. [Of imit. origin; cf. Sp. *borbollar* bubble, gush, *barbullar* talk loud and fast, It. *borbugliare.*] † **1.** To bubble; to flow in or with (a sound of) bubbles –1577. **2.** To speak, or say (something), murmurously 1891.

Bu·rble, *v.*² *Sc. dial.* [Of symbolic origin.] To perplex, muddle.

Burbot (bɔ̄·ɹbət). 1475. [ME. *burbot, -but, borbut, -bot*, corresp. to OFr. *barbote* (mod. *bourbotte* (XVII), assoc. w. *bourbe* slime, mud).] A fresh-water fish (*Lota vulgaris*) of the family *Gadidæ*; also called *Eel-pout* or *Coney-fish.*

Burd. [ME. *burde*, of unascertained origin.] A poetic word for 'woman, lady', later = 'young lady, maiden'. *Obs.* exc. in ballads.

Burd, obs. and Sc. f. BIRD, BOARD.

† **Burd-alone,** *a. Sc.* 1572. [perh. f. BURD = BIRD; cf. *Ps.* 102:7.] As a solitary person; all alone –1870.

† **Burda·sh.** 1713. [perh. same as BARDASH (as occas. also spelt).] ? A kind of cravat, or a sash for the waist, worn by men in the time of Queen Anne and George I –1730.

Burden, burthen (bɔ̄·ɹd'n, bɔ̄·ɹð'n). [OE. *byrþen* = OS. *burthinnia* ;– WGmc. **burþinnja*, f. **burþi-* (see BIRTH) + *-*innja* -EN². For the forms cf. *murder*, f. *murther*, etc.] **1.** That which is borne; load. Also *fig.* **2.** A load, as a measure of quantity. Now only the carrying capacity of a ship, stated as so many tons. ME. † **3.** A child, borne in the womb –1667. † **4.** What is borne by the soil; crop –1669. **5.** The bearing of loads, as in *beast of b., ship of b.* (= merchant-ship) ME. **6.** Used in the Eng. Bible as tr. Heb. *massā* 'lifting up (of the voice), oracle' (Gesenius); generally taken in Eng. to mean 'a heavy lot or fate' ME. † **7.** The bass, or undersong; cf. BOURDON² 1. –1833. **8.** The refrain or chorus of a song 1598. **9.** *fig.* The leading idea 1649.

1. Oh! by Thine own sad burthen, borne So meekly KEBLE. *fig.* A greeuous burthen was thy Birth to me *Rich. III*, IV. iv. 167. The b. of any fixed money payment FAWCETT. *B. of proof*, etc.:

(*onus probandi* in Rom. Law) the obligation to prove a controversial assertion, falling upon the person who makes it. **2.** Vessels of from fifteen to thirty tons burthen WELLINGTON. **3.** Let wiues with childe Pray that their burthens may not fall this day *John* III. i. 90. **6.** The burden of Babylon, which Isaiah the sonne of Amoz did see *Isa.* 13:1. **7.** *A.Y.L.* III. ii. 261. **9.** Mercy and justice ..is the burden of the whole Prophetic Teaching STANLEY. Hence **Bu·rdenless** *a.* † **Bu·rdenous, bu·rth-** *a.* burdensome (*lit.* and *fig.*). **Bu·rdensome, bu·rth-** *a.* of the nature of a b. **Bu·rd-, bu·rthensome-ly,** *adv.*, **-ness.**

Burden, burthen (bɔ̄·ɹd'n, -ð'n), *v.* 1541. [f. prec.] **1.** To lay a burden on (*lit.* and *fig.*). † **2.** To charge (a person) *with* (an accusation); to lay as a charge *upon* –1779.

1. Let vs not burthen our remembrances, with A heauinesse that's gon *Temp.* V. i. 199. **2.** This is false he burthens me withall *Com. Err.* V. i. 209. Hence **Bu·rdener.**

Burdened, burthened (bɔ̄·ɹd'nd, bɔ̄·ɹð-), *ppl. a.* 1594. [f. BURDEN *sb.* and *v.* + -ED.] † Imposed as a burden; heavily loaded, oppressed.

May thy Cows their burden'd Bags distend DRYDEN.

Burdock (bɔ̄·ɹdǫk). 1597. [f. BUR + DOCK *sb.*[1]] A coarse weedy plant (*Arctium lappa*, etc.) bearing burs, and large leaves like those of the dock. **b.** Occas. applied to *Xanthium strumarium.* Also *attrib.*

† **Burdon.** ME. [– late L. *burdo, -on-*.] A mule between a horse and she-ass; a hinny –1607.

Bureau (biuˌrō͡ᵘ·, biū͡ᵊ·rō͡ᵘ). *Pl.* **-x, -s.** 1720. [– Fr. *bureau*, orig. woollen stuff, baize (used for covering writing-desks), earlier BUREL.] **1.** A writing-desk with drawers for papers, etc. 1742. **2.** An office, *esp.* for the transaction of public business; a department of public administration. (In this sense often pronounced bürō.) 1720.

2. They have made London a shop, a law-court, a record office, a scientific b. EMERSON.

Bureaucracy (biurǭ͡ᵘ·krăsi, ǫ·krăsi). 1848. [– Fr. *bureaucratie*; see prec., -CRACY.] **a.** Government by bureaux; usually officialism. **b.** Government officials collectively.

The Continental nuisance called 'Bureaucracy' CARLYLE. So **Bu·reaucrat,** a member of a b.; one who endeavours to concentrate power in his bureau; occas. = *bureaucratist.* **Bureaucra·tic** *a.* of or pertaining to b. **Bureaucra·tically** *adv.* **Bureau·cratism,** a bureaucratic system. **Bureau·cratist,** a supporter of bureaucrats and b.

Burel. *Obs.* exc. *Hist.* ME. [– OFr. *burel* (see BUREAU), prob. f. *bure*, var. of OFr. *buire* dark brown :– Rom. **burius* dark red, alt. of L. *burrus* fiery red – Gr. πυρρός red.] A coarse (? brown) woollen cloth (cf. BAIZE); frieze; a garment of this; (plain) clothing.

I wol renne out, my borel for to shewe CHAUCER.

Burette (biure·t). 1483. [– Fr. *burette*, OFr. *buirette* for **buierette*, dim. of *buie* (mod. *buire*).] **1.** A little cruet for oil or vinegar. **2.** A graduated glass tube for measuring small quantities of liquid 1836.

‖ **Burg** (bū͡ᵊɹg, bɔ̄ɹg). 1753. [– (i) med.L. *burgus*, (ii) G. *burg*; see BOROUGH.] **1.** A fortress (BOROUGH 1) or a walled town (BOROUGH 2) of early or mediæval times. **2.** *U.S. colloq.* (bɔ̄ɹg) A town, city 1846.

Burgage (bɔ̄·ɹgėdʒ). ME. [– med.L. *burgagium*, f. *burgus*; see prec., -AGE.] *Law* **1.** A tenure whereby lands or tenements in cities and towns were held of the lord, for a certain yearly rent 1502. **2.** A freehold property in a borough; also, a house, etc., held by burgage tenure –1827. Also *attrib.*

Bu·rgall. (*U.S.*) 1860. [Origin unkn.] A fish (*Ctenolabrus ceruleus*).

‖ **Burgau** (bürgō). 1753. [Fr.] 'The name of several univalve nacreous shells' (Littré).

‖ **Burgaudine.** 1753. [Fr.] Mother of pearl made from the burgau shell.

† **Burge,** *v.* ME. Short f. BURGEON *v.* –1523.

Burgee (bɔ̄ɹdʒī·). 1848. [perh. for **burgee's flag*, i.e. owner's flag; – Fr. *bourgeois* (see BURGESS) in the sense of 'master', 'owner' (cf. '*Le bourgeois d'un navire*, the owner of a ship', Cotgrave).] **1.** A small tapered flag or pennant, three-cornered (or swallow-tailed), used by cutters, yachts, etc. **2.** A size of small coal 1867.

Burgeon (bɔ̄·ɹdʒən), *sb.* [– OFr. *bor-*, *burjon* (mod. *bourgeon*) :– Rom. **burrio, -on-*, f. late L. *burra* wool (whence Fr. *bourre* tag-wool, flock-wool, or long-haired stuff, down covering buds, Pr., Sp., It. *borra*). Cf. BURL *sb.*] **1.** A swelling bud, a young shoot. Recently revived in poetry. **b.** *Zool.* A bud of a zoophyte. Also *fig.* † **2.** *transf.* A pimple 1597.

1. Bounteous with..b. of birth SWINBURNE.

Burgeon (bɔ̄·ɹdʒən), *v.* ME. [–(O)Fr. *bourgeonner*, f. *bourgeon*; see prec.] **1.** *intr.* To bud or sprout; to begin to grow. Also *transf.* and *fig.* **2.** *trans.* To shoot out, put forth as buds. Also *transf.* and *fig.* ME.

1. *fig.* The Prelatism of Episcopacy..began then to b. MILT. **2.** It shal buriown to thee thornes and brembles WYCLIF *Gen.* 3:18.

Burger, -ship; see BURGHER, -SHIP.

Burgess (bɔ̄·ɹdʒės), *sb.* [ME. *burgeis* – OFr. *burgeis* (mod. *bourgeois*) :– Rom. **burgensis*, f. late L. *burgus* BOROUGH + *-ensis* (see -ESE), after **pagensis*, f. *paganus* PAGAN.] **1.** An inhabitant of a borough; *strictly*, one possessing full municipal rights; a citizen. **b.** *spec.* The member of parliament for a borough, corporate town, or University. Used in Virginia, etc. to denote a member of the legislative body called the 'House of Burgesses'. Now techn. and *Hist.* 1472. **2.** *spec.* A magistrate or member of the governing body of a town. Now *Hist.* ME. Also *attrib.*

1. He logyd in a notable burgesse howse LD. BERNERS. **b.** One of the burgesses for the University 1702. **2.** *fig.* The wild burgesses of the forrest SIDNEY.

Burgess-ship (bɔ̄·ɹdʒėsˌʃip). 1467. [See -SHIP.] **1.** The status and privileges of a burgess; the freedom of a borough. Also *fig.* † **2.** ? The position of burgess for a borough –1695.

Burgh (bɒ·rə). *Sc.* ME. [Sc. form of BOROUGH since XIV; cf. BROCH; obs. in ordinary use since XVII.] Orig. = BOROUGH; now used only of a Sc. town possessing a charter. Also *attrib.*

B. and land: town and country. Till each fair b., numerically free Shall choose its members by the *Rule of Three* CANNING. Hence **Bu·rghal** (bɔ̄·ɹgăl) *a.* of or pertaining to a b.

† **Bu·rghal-pe:nny.** ME. only. [f. *burghal* as in † *burghal division* portion (of land) of size suitable for burgage tenure – AL. *burgalis* (XII) (f. *burgus* BOURG + *-alis* -AL[1]) of or for burgage tenure.] *Eng. Law.* ? A municipal tax of some kind.

Burgh-english, obs. f. BOROUGH-ENGLISH.

Burgher (bɔ̄·ɹgəɹ), *sb.* 1568. [– G. or Du. *burger*, f. *burg* BOROUGH; see -ER[1].] **1.** An inhabitant of a burgh, borough, or corporate town; a citizen. Chiefly used of foreign towns. Now *arch.* Also *attrib.* **2.** A member of that section of the Scottish Secession Church which upheld the lawfulness of the burgess oath; also *attrib.* See ANTIBURGHER. 1766.

1. A b. of Antwerp..in a broad Flemish hat 1824.

Burgheristh. Erron. spelling of *burh-riht* 'borough-right' in Domesday Book.

Bu·rgherma:ster. *rare.* = BURGOMASTER.

Burghership (bɔ̄·ɹgəɹʃip). 1568. [f. BURGHER + -SHIP.] The rights and privileges of a burgher.

Burghmaster, erron. f. *bergh-*, BARMASTER. (Dicts.)

Burglar (bɒ·ɹgləɹ). 1541. [– legal AFr. *burgler* = AL. *burg(u)lator* (XII), with corresp. vb. AL. *burg(u)lare* and noun of action AFr. *burglarie*, AL. *burgaria*; app. all derivs. of a base **burg-*, whence OFr. *burgier* pillage, plunder, agent-n. *burgur*.] One who is guilty of burglary. var. † **Bu·rglarer.** Hence **Bu·rglar** *v.* † **Bu·rglarly** *adv.*

Burglarious (bɔ̄ɹglē͡ᵊ·riəs), *a.* 1769. [f. BURGLARY + -OUS; cf. *felonious*.] **1.** Of or pertaining to burglary; addicted to burglary; involving the guilt of burglary. **2.** Burglar-like 1859.

1. The larcenous and b. world SYD. SMITH. Hence **Burgla·riously** *adv.*

Bu·rglarize, *v. U.S.* 1871. [f. BURGLAR + -IZE.] To rob burglariously.

Burglary[1] (bɔ̄·ɹglări). 1532. [– AFr. *burglarie* (AL. *burgaria*); see BURGLAR, -Y[3].] The crime of breaking by night into a house with felonious intent. Also with *a* and *pl.* Also *fig.*

Neither can b. be committed in a tent or booth erected in a market or fair BLACKSTONE.

† **Bu·rglary**[2]. 1533. [– AL. **burglarius* (var. of *burgulator*); see BURGLAR, -ARY[1].] = BURGLAR –1651.

Burgle (bɔ̄·ɹg'l), *v. colloq.* or *joc.* 1872. [Back-formation f. BURGLAR.] *intr.* To follow the occupation of a burglar; *trans.* to break feloniously into the house of; to rob or steal burglariously.

A gentleman of the burgling persuasion DICKENS.

Burgomaster (bɔ̄·ɹgomāːstəɹ). 1592. [– Du. *burgemeester*, f. *burg* BOROUGH, w. assim. to MASTER.] **1.** The chief magistrate (= Eng. *mayor*) of a Dutch or Flemish town. Used loosely for any member of the governing body of a foreign municipality. **2.** A species of gull (*Larus glaucus*) 1678.

1. The only daughter of a burgo-master of Leyden JOHNSON.

Burgonet (bɔ̄·ɹgŏnet). *Hist.* 1563. [– Fr. *bourguignotte*, perh. fem. of *bourguignot* Burgundian, f. *Bourgogne* Burgundy; w. assim. to ending -ET.] **a.** A steel cap, worn esp. by pikemen. **b.** A kind of helmet with a visor. Also *fig. Ant. & Cl.* I. v. 24.

Burgoo (bɔ̄ɹgū·). 1704. [– Arab. *burġul* – Turk. *bulgur*, Pers. *bulġūr*, *barġul* 'bruised grain'.] A thick oatmeal porridge as used by seamen: loblolly.

Burgrave, burggrave (bɔ̄·ɹgrēⁱv). 1550. [– G. *burggraf*, f. *burg* BOROUGH + *graf* (MHG. *grāve*) count.] The governor of a town or castle; later, a noble ruling by hereditary right a town or castle, with the adjacent domain. Hence **Burgra·viate,** the rank or office of b.

† **Burgu·llian.** [Nonce-word of unkn. origin.] A braggadocio. B. JONS.

Burgundian (bɒɹgɒ·ndiăn). 1578. [f. next + -AN.] **A.** *adj.* Belonging to Burgundy (any sense). **B.** *sb.* **1.** An inhabitant of Burgundy. † **2.** (In form *Burgonian*) A kind of ship –1627.

Burgundy (bɔ̄·ɹgŏndi). 1672. [– med.L. *Burgundia* (whence Fr. *Bourgogne*), f. late L. *Burgundii, -iones* (in OE. *Burgendas*), tribe extending from the Main to the Vistula; see -Y[3].] **1.** A kingdom, and later a duchy of the Western Empire, subseq. giving its name to a province of France 1697. **2.** *ellipt.* Wine made in Burgundy 1672. **3.** *attrib.* 1672.

2. At the *Rose* on Sunday, I'll treat you with b. SWIFT. *Comb.* **B. Pitch.** [Obtained near Neufchâtel, once Burgundian territory.] The resinous juice of the Spruce-fir (*Abies excelsa*).

Burh, OE. f. BOROUGH, BURGH, q.v.

Buriable (be·riˌăb'l), *a.* 1598. [f. BURY *v.* + -ABLE.] Capable of being buried (*lit.* and *fig.*).

Burial (be·riăl). [ME. *buriel, biriel*, spurious sing. of *buriels*, OE. *byrġels* = OS. *burgisli* :– Gmc. **burȝisli-*, f. **burȝ-* (see BURY) + **-isli-*, as in OE. *rǣdels* RIDDLE *sb.*[1]; see -ELS, -LE 1.] † **1.** A burying-place –1612. **2.** The act of burying; interment 1453. Also *transf.* and *fig.* **b.** *pl.* Formerly in computations, etc. of mortality: = Deaths 1687. **3.** The depositing of anything under earth or water, or enclosing it in some other substance 1626.

1. *fig. Merch. V.* I. i. 29. **2. b.** A register of births, burials, and marriages BURKE.

Comb.: **b.-aisle,** an aisle in a religious building used for interments, also *fig.*; **-board,** a body appointed by public authority to regulate burials; **-hill, -mound,** a mound erected over a grave, a barrow; **-service,** a religious service accompanying a b.; the part of a liturgy used at a funeral; *esp.* that used in the Ch. of England; **-society,** an insurance society for providing money for the expenses of b.

Burial-ground. 1803. A piece of ground set apart as devoted to the regular interment of the dead; a burying-ground.

That..phrase, which calls The burial-ground God's acre LONGF.

Burial-place. 1633. A place of burial.

† **Bu·riels.** OE. [See BURIAL.] **1.** A burying-place; a tomb –1483. **2.** An interment. ME. only.

Burin (biū͡ᵊ·rin). 1662. [– Fr. *burin*, rel. to It. *burino* (*bulino*), which has been referred to OHG. *bora* boring-tool; see BORE *v.*[1]] **1.** A graver; the tool used by an engraver on copper; also *attrib.* **b.** The style of using the graver 1824. **2.** A triangular tool used by marble-workers.

1. b. A fine specimen of Loggan's bold b. DIBDIN. Hence **Bu·rinist**, an engraver.

Burke (bɔ̄ɹk), *v.* 1829. [f. *Burke*, a criminal executed at Edinburgh in 1829.] **1.** To kill secretly by suffocation or strangulation, or in order to sell the victim's body for dissection, as Burke did. **2.** *fig.* To smother, hush up 1840.

1. As soon as the executioner proceeded to his duty, the cries of 'B. him, B. him—give him no rope'..were vociferated *Times* 2 Feb. 1829. Hence **Bu·rker. Bu·rkism.**

Burl (bɔ̄ɹl), *sb.* ME. [– OFr. *bourle* tuft of wool, dim f. (O)Fr. *bourre*, Sp., Pg. *borra* coarse wool :– late L. *burra* wool. Cf. BURGEON.] **1.** A knot or lump in wool or cloth. † **2.** *transf.* A pimple –1651. † **3.** The bud of a red deer's horn. (Cf. BUR *sb.* 5.) 1611. **4.** A knot in wood (U.S.) 1886.

Burl (bɔ̄ɹl), *v.* 1483. [f. prec.] **1.** To dress (cloth), *esp.* by removing knots and lumps. **2.** To pick out (a lock or flock of wool) 1650. † **3.** To remove burls from the face. HERRICK. Hence **Bu·rler.**

† **Burlace, burlake, burlet,** corrupt ff. *Bourdelais*, a variety of grape, cultivated in 17th c.

Burlap (bɒ·ɹlæp). 1695. [Origin unkn.] Orig. perh. a sort of holland; now a coarse canvas made of jute and hemp, used for bagging; also, a finer material for curtains.

Burlesque (bɒɹle·sk). 1656. [– Fr. *burlesque* – It. *burlesco*, f. *burla* flout, joke, fun, of unkn. origin. See -ESQUE.] **A.** *adj.* † **1.** Droll in look, manner, or speech –1848. **2.** Of the nature of derisive imitation; ironically bombastic, mock-heroic or mock-pathetic 1700.

1. Graham speaks of Fuller as..b. in his manners H. WALPOLE. **2.** B. pictures 1712, authors 1714.

B. *sb.* **1.** That species of composition which excites laughter by caricature of serious works, or by ludicrous treatment of their subjects; a literary or dramatic work of this kind. Also *attrib.* 1667. **2.** Grotesque caricature; *concr.* an action or performance which casts ridicule on that which it imitates, or is itself a ridiculous attempt at something serious; a mockery 1753.

1. Witty burlesques of the noblest performances TUCKER. B. has been driving pantomime off the stage 1869. **2.** A b. upon public worship WESLEY.

Burlesque (bɒɹle·sk), *v.* 1676. [f. prec.] To turn into ridicule by grotesque parody. Also *intr.*

Cervantes has burlesqued the old romances 1804.

Burlesquer (bɒɹle·skəɹ). 1657. [f. BURLESQUE *v.* and *sb.* + -ER¹.] **a.** One who burlesques. **b.** One who acts in burlesques.

† **Burle·tta.** 1748. [– It. *burletta*, dim. of *burla* fun; see -ETTE.] A musical farce –1879.

Burly (bɔ̄·ɹli), *a.* [ME. *borli, burli, -lich*, prob. :– OE. **būrlić* 'fit for the bower'; cf. OHG. *burlīh* exalted, stately, and see BOWER *sb.*¹, -LY¹.] **A.** *adj.* † **1.** Stately, dignified –1664. † **b.** *poet.* Of things: Goodly, noble –1873. **2.** Stout, sturdy, corpulent ME. † **b.** Of a garment, or wool: Thick –1805. **3.** Big; domineering, bluff (*arch.*) 1592. **B.** *adv.* Sturdily, stoutly ME.

3. Wrote against by som b. standard Divine MILT. Hence **Bu·rlily** *adv.* **Bu·rliness.** † **Bu·rly** *v.* to make b. QUARLES.

Burn (bɔ̄ɹn), *sb.*¹ [OE. *burna, burne, burn*, corresp. to OFris. *burna*, MLG. *borne, born*, MDu. *borne* (LG., Du. *born*), repr. a metathetic form of Gmc. **brunnon, -az*, as in OS., OHG. *brunno* (Du. *bron*, G. *brunnen*), ON. *brunnr*, Goth. *brunna*; of unkn. origin.] In OE.: A spring, fountain; a stream or river. In later use: A brook. Now chiefly *north.*

Well watered by a beck or b. 1839.

Burn (bɔ̄ɹn), *sb.*² 1563. [f. BURN *v.*¹] **1.** The act or effect of burning; *esp.* a burnt place on the body 1594. **2.** A mark made by burning, a brand 1563. Also *attrib.*

Burn (bɔ̄ɹn), *v.*¹ *Pa. t.* and *pple.* **burned, burnt.** [(i) OE. *birnan* intr., var. of *brinnan* = OS., OHG., Goth. *brinnan*; (ii) OE. *bærnan* trans., = OS., OHG. *brennan* (G. *brennen* trans. and intr.), ON. *brenna* (intr. and trans.), Goth. *brannjan*; f. Gmc. **bren-* **bran-* **brun-*.] **I.** Intrans. **1.** To be in the state of activity characteristic of fire; to be in combustion. Also *fig.* **2.** Of matter: To be on fire; to be enveloped in flames OE. Also *fig.* ¶*Phys.* Occas. for: To undergo oxidation, as in burning, with evolution of heat 1885. **3.** *gen.* To become or be violently hot OE. **b.** In games: of a person getting very near to a hidden object sought. (Cf. WARM.) Hence *fig.* To approach near to the truth. [Cf. Fr. 'nous brûlons'.] 1821. **4.** Of candles, lamps, etc.: To be in process of combustion so as to give light; hence, to flame, give light, shine. Also *transf.* of the sun, stars, etc. OE. **b.** Of other objects: To appear as if on fire ME. **5.** To suffer the effects of combustion; to be reduced *to* ashes, a cinder, etc., by fire; to be scorched, charred, etc. Often said of food which is overdone. ME. **6.** To suffer death by fire. Now usu. *to be burnt.* 1600.

1. Sometime a fire [Ile be]..and burne *Mids. N.* III. i. 113. *fig.* Let not thine anger burne against thy seruant *Gen.* 44:18. **2.** A place that burns with Fire and Brimstone BUNYAN. **4.** How ill this taper burns *Jul. C.* IV. iii. 275. **b.** The Barge she sat in, like a burnisht Throne, Burnt on the water *Ant. & Cl.* II. ii. 197. **5.** The Capon burnes *Com. Err.* I. ii. 44. **6.** They should all burne for their vilde heresie 1604.

II. Trans. **1.** Of fire: To destroy, consume (any object). Of persons: To cause to be destroyed or consumed by fire. Also *absol.* OE. **b.** *spec.* To make a burnt-offering of (incense, a victim) *to* a deity. Also *absol.* ME. **2.** To put to death by fire, *esp.* as a judicial punishment ME. **3.** To consume for warming or lighting; to keep (a candle, etc.) alight 1712. ¶*Phys.* Occas. for: To consume by oxidation with evolution of heat. **4.** *fig.* To inflame with desire, etc. ME. **5.** Of any heating agency: To produce the effects of combustion upon. (Not used for melting or softening.) Of persons: To expose to the action of fire so as to produce the effects of combustion; *esp.* to treat with fire for a specific purpose, as wood, clay, the soil, etc. 1519. **b.** Hence, To produce (charcoal, bricks, etc.) by burning ME. **c.** *transf.* To produce on (anything) an aspect as of burning. Sometimes said of cold, and of certain manures or crops. ME. **6.** To wound or to cause pain to by the contact of fire, etc.: said both of the fire, and of the person who applies it. Often *refl.* Also *absol.* ME. **b.** To cauterize; to brand 1483. **c.** To wound or cause local pain to, as by fire; *e.g.* by vitriol, a blister, etc., occas. by intense cold. Also *absol.* 1509. † **d.** To infect with sores; *esp.* with venereal disease –1590.

1. They were for burning the body outright SOUTHEY. **b.** The priest..burns the offering with his holy hands POPE. **2.** He was brent for an hereticke 1635. **5. b.** These [earthen vessels] I burnt in the fire DE FOE. **6.** Whan thou shalt go in fyr, thou shalt not be brent WYCLIF *Isa.* 43:2. **c.** The parching air Burns frore, and cold performs th' effect of Fire MILT. *P.L.* II. 595. **d.** Light wenches will burne, come not neere her *Com. Err.* IV. iii. 58.

Phrases. **a.** (sense I. 2) *To b.* (*itself*) *out, to be burnt out*: to burn until extinguished by lack of fuel. So *To b. down, low. To b. up*: to get fairly alight. Also, *to b. red, blue, bright*, etc. **b.** (sense I. 3) fig. *The money*, etc. *burns in one's pocket, burns a hole in one's pocket*, etc., meaning the owner is eager to get rid of it. **c.** *To b. into* (of fire, a caustic, etc.): to eat its way into. Usu. *fig.*: to make an indelible impression upon (a person's mind). **d.** (sense II. I) fig. *To b. one's boats*: to cut oneself off from all possibility of retreat. **e.** (sense II. 3) fig. *To b. daylight*, to b. candles in the daytime, also to waste or consume the daylight. *To b. the* (or *one's*) *candle at both ends*: see CANDLE. **f.** (sense II. 5) † *poet.* Of cattle: *To b.* (the ground) *bare*: to crop it close DRYDEN. fig. *To b. the planks*: to remain long sitting. *To b.* (metals) *together*: to join them by melting their edges, etc. **g.** (sense II. 6) fig. *To b. one's* (*own*) *fingers*: to sustain damage through meddling with something. **h.** *To b. out of house and home*: to drive (a person) out of a place by burning his dwelling. *To b. in*: *fig.* to make indelible *in* a person's mind. Also, to render indelible (the painting upon pottery, etc.) by burning. *To b. the water*: to spear salmon by torchlight.

Burn-. The vb. or vb.-stem in comb. forming sbs. or adjs.

1. With vb. + obj. as **b.-the-wind, burne-win,** *Sc.*, a blacksmith. **2.** With the vb. used *attrib.* = *burning*, as **b.-fire** (*dial.*), perversion of BONFIRE; **-iron,** a branding-iron; **-weed** = THORN-APPLE.

† **Burn,** *v.*² ME. [– OFr. *burnir*, var. of *brunir*, f. *brun* BROWN.] = BURNISH *v.*¹

Burnable (bɔ̄·ɹnăb'l), *a.* 1611. [f. BURN *v.*¹ + -ABLE.] Capable of being burnt by fire.

Bu·rn-beat, *v.* Also **-bait.** 1669. [f. BURN *v.*¹ + BEAT *sb.*³ or *v.*²; pa. pple. *burnbeat.*] To pare off and burn rough turf in order to improve the ground.

Burner (bɔ̄·ɹnəɹ). ME. [f. BURN *v.*¹ + -ER¹.] **1.** One who burns with fire. **2.** One who prepares or produces by burning, as *charcoal-b.* 1463. **3.** That part of a lamp, gas-light, etc., from which the flame comes; often defined, as *Argand, Bunsen*, etc., *b.* 1790.

1. Brenneris of houses and cornes WYCLIF.

† **Bu·rnet,** *a.* and *sb.*¹ ME. [– OFr. *burnete*, var. of *brunete*, dim. of *brun*; see BROWN, -ET; cf. BRUNETTE.] **A.** *adj.* Dark brown. **B.** *sb.* A superior wool-dyed cloth, orig. of dark brown colour ME.

Burnet (bɔ̄·rnėt), *sb.*² ME. [f. prec., from the colour of its flowers.] Any plant belonging to the genera *Sanguisorba* and *Poterium* (N.O. *Rosaceæ*), as the Great or Common Burnet, the Lesser or Salad Burnet, etc. Also, the Burnet Saxifrage, *Pimpinella saxifraga*, resembling these in foliage.

The freckled Cowslip, B., and greene Clouer SHAKS. *Comb.*: **b.-fly, -moth** (*Anthrocera* or *Zygæna filipendulæ*), a greenish black moth with crimson spots on its wings; **-rose,** the Scotch rose (*Rosa spinosissima*); **b. saxifrage** (see above).

Bu·rnettize, *v.* 1867. [f. Sir W. *Burnett*, who patented the process; see -IZE.] To steep canvas, cordage, etc., in a solution of chloride of zinc.

Bu·rnie. *Sc.* 1724. [See -IE, -Y⁶.] Dim. of BURN *sb.*¹

Burning (bɒ·ɹniŋ), *vbl. sb.* ME. [f. BURN *v.*¹ + -ING¹.] The action of the vb. BURN. **I.** *intr.* **1.** See BURN *v.*¹ I. 1, 2, 3 b. † **2.** Heat from disease, or a serpent's bite; the disease itself; *esp.* St. Anthony's fire, and venereal disease –1753. **II.** *trans.* See BURN *v.*¹ II. 1, 2, 5, 6 b.

Burning (bɔ̄·ɹniŋ), *ppl. a.* [f. as prec. + -ING².] That burns in various senses.

Phrases, fig. *B. shame, disgrace*, etc., now perh. 'flagrant, conspicuous'; but often there is a hint of branding, torturing as an inward fire, causing the cheeks to glow, etc. *B. matter, question* (cf. Fr. *question brûlante*, G. *brennende Frage*): one that excites hot discussion or feeling. *B. scent*: very warm scent; *b. chase*: hot, uninterrupted.

Burning Bush. a. 'The bush that burned and was not consumed' (*Exod.* 3), the ensign of the Presbyterian churches of Scotland, assumed in memory of the persecution of the 17th c. **b.** A name of various shrubs or plants, as the Artillery plant, *Pilea serpylliflora*, the *Dictamnus fraxinella*, and (U.S.) the *Euonymus atropurpureus* and *E. americanus.*

Burning-glass (bɔ̄·ɹniŋ-glɑs). 1570. A lens or concave mirror, by the use of which the sun's rays may be concentrated on an object.

Burnish (bɔ̄·ɹniʃ), *sb. rare.* 1647. [f. BURNISH *v.*¹] Burnishing; a burnishing; *spec.* anything laid over a surface to burnish it.

Burnish (bɔ̄·ɹniʃ), *v.*¹ ME. [– *burniss-*, lengthened stem (see -ISH²) of OFr. *burnir*, var. of *brunir*, f. *brun* BROWN.] **1.** To make shining by friction; to furbish; to polish by rubbing with a hard and smooth tool. Also *fig.* **2.** *transf.* To make bright and glossy ME. **3.** Of a stag: To rub the dead skin from his horns [so Fr. *brunir*] 1616. **4.** *intr.* To become bright and glossy; to shine, gleam. Also *fig.* 1624.

1. *fig.* Hye walles & noble, all bournysshed and polysshed with charite 1526. **2.** Fruit burnisht with Golden Rind MILT. *P.L.* IV. 249. **4.** I've seen a snake..B., and make a gaudy show SWIFT.

Bu·rnish, *v.*² Now *dial.* ME. [Origin unkn.] Of the human frame: To grow plump, or stout; to increase in breadth. Also *transf.*

[London] will be found to B. round about, to every point of the compasse FULLER.

Burnisher (bɔ̄·ɹniʃəɹ). 1450. [f. BURNISH *v.*¹ + -ER¹.] He who or that which burnishes; *esp.* a tool, which differs in material and shape according to the purpose and trade.

‖ **Burnous, burnouse** (bɒɹnū·s, -nū·z). 1695. [– Fr. *burnous* – Arab. *burnus* – Gr. *βίρρος* kind of cloak.] A cloak with a hood, as worn by Arabs and Moors; also, by women.
The burnous..is his [the Arab's] garment by day and by night KINGLAKE.

Burnt, burned (bɒ̄ɹnt, bɒ̄ɹnd), *ppl. a.* ME. [f. BURN *v.*¹ q.v.] In various senses of the verb.
Phrases, etc. **Burnt iron** (*Mining*): iron which has been exposed to oxidation until all its carbon is gone. *Burnt taste*, etc.: a taste, etc., as of something burnt. *The burnt child dreads the fire. Comb.* **burnt-ear,** a disease in corn, in which the ear is blackened, owing to the growth of *Uredo segetum*.

Burnt o·ffering, burnt-o·ffering. ME. A sacrifice offered to a deity by burning; *esp.* Jewish animal sacrifice. So **Burnt sacrifice.**

Burr, bur (bɒ̄ɹ), *sb.*¹ ME. [var. of *burrow* (as † *fur* of *furrow*), which is recorded in XV as a gloss on L. *orbiculus* and in sense 5, in the latter sense varying with *brough*. See BROUGH, BURROW *sb.*⁵] **1.** *gen.* A circle. † **2.** A broad iron ring on a tilting spear just behind the place for the hand –1610. **3.** A washer placed on the small end of a rivet before the end is swaged down 1627. **4.** (see BURR-PUMP.) **5.** A circle of light round the moon (or a star); in mod. use, a nebulous disc of light enfolding it 1631.
5. A burre about the moone is..a presage of a tempest 1631.

Burr, bur (bɒ̄ɹ), *sb.*² 1573. [Origin unkn.] A sweetbread.

† **Burr, bur,** *sb.*³ 1573. [Origin unkn.] The external meatus of the ear. (Dr. Johnson's guess 'the lobe or lap of the ear' was unlucky.) –1688.

Burr, bur (bɒ̄ɹ), *sb.*⁴ 1611. [app. the same as BUR *sb.*, but usu. spelt *burr*.] **1.** A rough ridge or edge left on metal or other substance after cutting, punching, etc. **2.** Techn. **a.** short for *b.-chisel, -drill, -saw*; see *Comb.* **b.** A tool used in making screws. 1833.
1. Burr..is caused by the tearing up of the copper by the needle or burin 1876.
Comb. **b.-chisel,** a three-edged chisel for clearing the corners of mortises; **-drill,** a dentist's drill with a serrated or file-cut knob; **-gauge,** a plate with holes of graduated sizes, for determining the sizes of b.-drills; **-saw,** a small circular saw used in turning.

Burr, bur (bɒ̄ɹ), *sb.*⁵ Also **buhr.** 1721. [perh. identical w. BUR *sb.*, being so called from its roughness.] **1.** Siliceous rock suitable for millstones. **b.** A whetstone. **2.** A siliceous boss in calcareous, or other softer, formations; a harder part in any freestone 1839. **3.** A clinker 1823. Also *attrib.*

Burr (bɒ̄ɹ, bɒrr), *sb.*⁶ 1760. [prob. imit., but perh. transf. application of BUR to a 'rough' sound.] **1.** A rough sounding of the letter *r*; *spec.* the rough uvular trill (= French *r grasseyé*), found *esp.* in Northumberland. (The Scotch *r* is a lingual trill.) **b.** Hence, *loosely*, a rough or dialectal utterance 1849. **2.** [= BIRR 3.] Whirr 1818.
1. Along the line of the Cheviots, the Scotch *r* has driven the *burr* a few miles back J. A. H. MURRAY. **b.** Betrayed by his Galilæan b. FARRAR. **2.** The b. of working wheels and cranks 1860.

‖ **Burr, bur,** *sb.*⁷ 1813. [Hind. *baṛ*.] The Banyan-tree (*Ficus indica*); also *attrib.*

Burr, *v.* 1798. [f. BURR *sb.*⁶] *intr.* To pronounce a strong uvular *r*, as is done in Northumberland. Also, *loosely*, to speak with a rough articulation; to utter the syllable *burr* or the like. **2.** To pronounce (*r*) with a burr (or, *loosely*, with a trill) 1868. **3.** *intr.* To make a whirring noise (*mod.*).

Burras-pipe. ? *Obs.* 1676. [f. *burras*, obs. f. BORAX.] A copper box with a spout, having teeth like a saw; used orig. by goldsmiths; occas. also used by surgeons for the application of corrosives by inspersion.

† **Burratine.** [– It. *burattino*.] A puppet. B. JONS.

† **Burree·.** 1719. [– F. *beurré* (lit. 'buttered').] A pear, called also the Butter Pear, from its soft, smooth pulp.

Burrel, app. misprint for BURREE. (Dicts.)

† **Burrel-fly.** 1678. [Origin unkn.] The gadfly –1721.

Burrel-shot. 1706. [Origin unkn.] Case-shot. (Dicts.)

‖ **Burro** (bu·ro). 1800. [Sp.] A donkey.

Burrock (bɒ·rǫk). 1701. [ME. *burrok*, *burrock* (XIV), in med.L. *burrochium* (XII) fish trap; cf. OFr. *bourroiche* fish-trap constructed of osiers.] A small weir or dam in a river where weels are laid for the taking of fish.

Burrow (bɒ·roᵘ), *sb.*¹ ME. [Late ME. *borwȝ*, *borow*, prob. var. of BOROUGH in sense of 'fortified or inhabited place'.] **1.** A hole or excavation made in the ground for a dwelling-place by rabbits, foxes, etc. † **b.** A burrowing –1662. **2.** *transf.* and *fig.* A small hole-like dwelling-place, or place of retreat; a hole 1650.
1. Foxis han dichis or borowis WYCLIF *Matt.* 8:20. **2.** The chief advantage of London is, that a man is always so near his b. BOSWELL *Johnson*.

Bu·rrow, *sb.*² *dial.* or *techn.* [repr. (esp. in Cornwall) of OE. *beorg* hill; see BARROW *sb.*¹ and BERRY *sb.*²] A heap or mound; earlier, a hillock; now, *esp.* a heap of mine refuse, or of burnt sods.

Bu·rrow, *sb.*³ *dial.* 1577. [OE. *beorg*, *beorh*, ME. *bergh* shelter, *f. beorgan* shelter; cf. BORROW *sb.*] Shelter.
Enclosed burrowes where their legions accustomed..to winter 1577.

† **Bu·rrow,** *sb.*⁴ 1634. Var. of BOROUGH, BURGH –1650.

† **Bu·rrow,** *sb.*⁵ 1499. Var. of BURR *sb.*¹, BROUGH –1656.

Burrow (bɒ·roᵘ), *v.* 1602. [f. BURROW *sb.*¹] **1.** *intr.* To make a burrow, *esp.* as a hiding- or dwelling-place 1771. **b.** *fig.* To lodge as in a burrow, hide oneself 1614. **c.** *fig.* To bore under the surface 1804. **2.** *refl.* with *pass. pple.* To hide away in, or as in, a burrow 1602. **3.** *trans.* To excavate 1831.
1. b. To b. in mean lodgings MARRYAT. **c.** Each local body has..to b. its own way GLADSTONE. Hence **Bu·rrower. Burrowing owl,** an American owl (*Noctua cunicularia*) dwelling in burrows.

Burrow-duck. 1678. [f. BURROW *sb.*¹ The bird makes its nest in burrows.] The Sheldrake or Bergander, *Anas tadorna*.

Burrows-town (bɒ·rəstaun). *Sc.* ME. = BOROUGH-TOWN. (Cf. *Borrowston-ness* or *Bo'ness*). Also *attrib.*

Bu·rr-pump, bu·r-pump. 1627. [f. BUR or BURR *sb.*¹] *Naut.* A bilge-pump with the piston so made as not to require a valve.

Burr-stone (bɒ̄·ɹ₁stōᵘn). Also **buhr-, burrh-, bur-.** 1690. [f. BURR *sb.*⁵] A siliceous rock of coarse cellular texture, used for millstones; a piece of this rock.

Bu·rry, *a.* 1450. [f. BUR *sb.* + -Y¹.] **a.** Full of burs. **b.** Rough, prickly.

‖ **Bursa** (bɒ̄·ɹsă). Pl. **bursæ.** 1803. [med.L. *bursa* bag; see PURSE *sb.*] **1.** *Phys.* (more fully *b. mucosa*): A synovial sac interposed between muscles, tendons, or skin, and bony prominences, to lessen friction. **2.** In Germany: A house inhabited by students, under the supervision of a Graduate in Arts 1852. Hence **Bu·rsal** *a.* of or pertaining to a b.; also, fiscal. **Bursa·logy** (better, **Burso·logy**), the doctrine of the *bursæ mucosæ*.

Bursar (bɒ̄·ɹsăɹ). [In sense 1 – (O)Fr. *boursier* or med.L. *bursarius*; see BURSA, -ER²; in sense 2 – Fr. *boursier*.] **1.** A treasurer, *esp.* of a college 1587. **2.** In Scotland: A student who holds a bursary, an exhibitioner 1567. **Bursa·rial** *a.* belonging to a b. or a bursary. **Bu·rsarship,** the office of a b.; also = BURSARY 3.

Bursary (bɒ̄·ɹsəri). 1538. [In sense 1 – med.L. *bursarius*; in sense 2 – med.L. *bursaria* bursar's office; cf. OFr. *bourserie* money coffer, treasury. See prec., -ARY¹.] † **1.** ? = BURSAR 1. **2.** A treasury; the bursar's room in a college, etc. 1585. **3.** In Scotland, an exhibition at a school or university 1733; in England, a scholarship enabling a pupil at an elementary school to proceed to a secondary school 1910.

‖ **Bursch** (burʃ). Pl. **burschen.** 1830. [G. *bursch(e)* (fellow-)student, MHG. *burse* – med.L. *bursa* purse, whence a student living in a *bursa*; see BURSA 2.] A student in a German university.

Burse (bɒ̄ɹs). 1553. [– (O)Fr. *bourse* or med.L. *bursa*, see PURSE; w. sense 3 cf. BOURSE.] **1.** A purse 1570. † **2.** A purse-like sac. HOLLAND. † **3.** A meeting-place of merchants for transaction of business; an Exchange. [So called at Bruges, where the name arose, from the sign of a purse, or three purses, on the front of the house where the merchants met.] –1732. † **b.** *The B.*: (*spec.*) the Royal Exchange, built by Sir Thomas Gresham in 1566, which contained shops –1720. † **4.** *Sc.* A fund or foundation to provide bursaries –1753. **5.** = BURSARY 3. 1560.
3. b. She says, she went to the b. for patterns 1611. Hence **Bu·rsiform** *a.* purse-shaped.

Bursitis (bɒɹsəi·tis). 1857. [f. BURSA 1 + -ITIS.] *Med.* Inflammation of a bursa.

Burst (bɒ̄ɹst), *v.* Pa. t. and pple. **burst.** [OE. *berstan* = OFris. *bersta*, OS., OHG. *brestan* (Du. *bersten*, *barsten*; G. *bersten* from LG.), ON. *bresta* :– Gmc. **brestan*.] **I.** *intr.* † **1.** To break suddenly, snap, crack –1803. **2.** To break suddenly when in a state of tension or expansion, to fly asunder or in pieces. Also *fig.*; now often colloq. with *up*. ME. **3.** *hyperbolically*, To be exuberantly full. Also with *out*. 1563. **b.** Of persons: To be unable to contain oneself. Const. *with*; also with *inf.* 1633. Also † *fig.* of the heart ME. **4.** Of a door. Now usu. *to b. open*: to fly open suddenly 1596.
2. Thus drinke we..tyll we b. 1562. And now a bubble b., and now a World POPE. **3.** Thy presses shall b. out with new wine *Prov.* 3:10. **b.** Ready to b. with..indignation STEELE.
II. *intr. fig.* (With advb. extension.) To break forth into sudden action, activity, or manifestation of an inward force or feeling. Usu. with *out*, *forth*.
She burst out in tears ADDISON. So *To b. into tears, out laughing, into song, speech*, etc.
III. *trans.* (causative). Not in OE. **1.** To break, snap, shatter suddenly. *Obs.* in general sense. ME. **2.** To disrupt, shatter in pieces ME.; to rupture 1712. **3.** To cause (the body) to swell till it bursts; often *refl.* 1530. **4.** *hyperbolically*, To fill to overflowing 1697.
2. Yᵉ new wyne barsteth yᵉ vessels and runneth out COVERDALE *Luke* 5:37. To b. one's sides ARBUTHNOT. Phr. *To b. a blood-vessel*: to cause its rupture by exertion, etc., or simply to suffer the rupture of a vessel.
IV. *intr.* (These uses express more strongly than those of BREAK, branch VII, the notion of sudden violence.) **1.** To issue forth suddenly and copiously by breaking an enclosure or the like. Usu. with an *adv.* ME. Also *transf.* and *fig.* **2.** To rush violently and suddenly *over* ME. **3.** To force a passage impetuously *through* ME. **4.** To break forcibly *into*, come suddenly and impetuously *into*; also with adv. *in*. So *to b. up* (from below). 1563.
1. Blude brist out at voundis vyde BARBOUR. *transf.* The teeres brast out of hir eyghen tuo CHAUCER. *fig.* Defections in Ireland..in the end brast out into open rebellion 1603. **3.** Times when a thankful heart bursts through all forms of prayer NEWMAN. **4.** The first that ever burst Into that silent sea COLERIDGE.
Hence **Burst** *ppl. a.*; also **brast** (*arch.*). **Bu·rsted** *ppl. a.* (now *dial.*). **Bu·rsten** *ppl. a.* (occ. used attrib.). **Bu·rsting charge,** the charge of powder required for bursting a shell or case-shot.

Burst (bɒ̄ɹst), *sb.* [In sense 1 repr. OE. *byrst*; in mod. use from the verb.] † **1.** Damage, harm; loss –ME. **2.** An act of bursting; the result of this act 1611. **3.** A sudden and violent issuing forth 1610. **b.** A sudden opening on the view 1798. **4.** An explosion, outbreak, breaking forth 1649. **5.** A great and sudden manifestation of activity; a spurt 1862. **b.** *Horsemanship.* A hard run 1810. **6.** *colloq.* A 'spree'. Also a big feed. 1881.
2. When beech-buds were near the b. G. MEREDITH. **3.** A b. of flame 1887. A hollow b. of bellowing Like Buls *Temp.* II. i. 311. **b.** A fine b. of country JANE AUSTEN. **4.** Premature bursts [of shrapnel] 1870. A b. of ill humour THIRLWALL. **5.** The b. of creative activity in our literature M. ARNOLD.

† **Burst-cow.** 1646. [f. BURST *v.*] = *burncow*, BUPRESTIS, q.v. –1706.

Burster (bɒ̄·ɹstəɹ). 1611. [f. as prec. + -ER¹.] **1.** He who, or that which, bursts. **2.** In *Australia*: A violent southerly gale 1879.

Burthen, etc.; see BURDEN.

Burton (bɒ̄·ɹt'n). Also **barton.** 1704. [orig. in *Breton* or *Brytton takles* ('Naval Accounts', 1495); presumably a use of *Breton*.] A small tackle consisting of two or three blocks or pulleys used to set up or tighten rigging, or to shift heavy bodies.

† **Bu·ry,** *sb.* OE. [orig. dative of *burh*; see BOROUGH.] A manor-house, or large farm. It survives in many local names. –1656.

Bury (be·ri), *v.* [OE. *byrĝan* (ME. *bürie, birie, berie*) :– WGmc. **burʒjan*, f. **burʒ-* **berʒ-*, base of OE. *beorgan*; see BORROW *sb.*, BURIAL.] **1.** To deposit in the ground, in a tomb, to inter. Hence to commit to the sea, with funeral rites. Also *absol.* Also *fig.* **2.** To put under ground; *esp.* in sign of final abandonment or abrogation 1535. **b.** *fig.* To consign to oblivion 1593. **c.** To consign to a position of obscurity, or inaction; often *refl.* and *pass.* 1711. **3.** *gen.* To cover up with earth or other material ME. **b.** Of things: To cover over out of sight 1737. **4.** To plunge deep *in*, so as to hide 1601. Also *fig.* **5.** *pass.* To be profoundly absorbed *in* ME.

1. Let us b. the Great Duke TENNYSON. *To have buried* (one's relatives) = to have lost them by death. *fig.* He would b. you under a mountain of words JOWETT. **2.** *To b. the hatchet*: to put away strife, as the Red Indians b. a tomahawk on the conclusion of peace. **b.** Giue me a bowl of wine, In this I b. all vnkindnesse Cassius *Jul. C.* IV. iii. 159. **c.** Buried in the country JOHNSON. **3.** I.. buried 3000 pieces of gold LANE. **4.** B. your steel in the bosoms of Gath BYRON. Hence **Bu·ried** *ppl. a.* **Bu·rier,** one who buries; † a grave-digger. **Bu·rying** *vbl. sb.* the action of the vb.; *concr.* a funeral (*Obs.* or *dial.*); *ppl. a.* as in **b. beetle, -sylph,** a clavicorn beetle, which excavates the ground beneath dead moles, mice, etc., so as to b. them as a nidus for its larvæ.

Bu·rying-ground. 1711. BURIAL-GROUND.

Bu·rying-place. ME. A place of burial, a tomb; now usu. = prec.

Bus, 'bus (bɒs), *sb.* Occ. **buss.** 1832. Short for OMNIBUS. Also *colloq.* an aeroplane, motor car. Hence **Bus** *v.* in *to b. it*: To go by b.

Bus, *v.* (*3rd sing.*) *n. dial. Pa. t.* **bud(e.** ME. [contr. f. *behoves, behoved*, chiefly used impers.] † **1.** (It) behoves –1500. **2.** *mod. Sc. Pa. t.* also as *pres.*, with subject: Must, ought.

Busby (bɒ·zbi). 1764. [Origin unkn.; but cf. *buzzwig* (XVIII–XIX); see BUZZ *sb.*³, and cf. BUZZ *sb.*²] † **1.** A large bushy wig –1882. **2.** A tall fur cap, with or without a plume, having a bag hanging out of the top, on the right side; worn by hussars, artillerymen, and engineers; hence, one who wears a busby. Also *b.-bag.*

Buscarl. *Hist.* 1678. Modernized f. 11th c. *butsecarl* – ON. *buzukarl* 'seaman, sailor, mariner'. Cf. BUSS *sb.*¹

Bush (buʃ), *sb.*¹ ME. [(*a*) Early forms *busse, busshe, buysche*, pointing to an OE. **bysć*; (*b*) in north. and east. areas *busk* (from XIII) – ON. *buski*, which survives in north. dial., with Sc. by-form *bus*; cf. BUSKET; (*c*) ME. *bosk* (XIII), surviving dial. (see BOSK, BOSKY), beside *bosh, bossche* (XIV–XV); perh. – OFr. *bos, bosc*, vars. of *bois* wood. Ult. f. Gmc. **busk-*, repr. by OS. *busc* (Du. *bos*), OHG. *busc* (G. *busch*).] **1.** A shrub, *esp.* one with close branches arising from or near the ground; a small clump of shrubs. **2.** In n. dialects extended to *heather, nettles, ferns, rushes*, etc. 1529. † **3.** *collectively.* A thicket; bushy ground. (Now only as in 8.) –1639. † **4.** = AMBUSH, q.v. –1655. **5.** A branch or bunch of ivy (perh. as sacred to Bacchus) hung up as a vintner's sign; *hence*, the sign-board of a tavern 1532. Hence, a tavern 1625. † **6.** *transf.* Anything resembling a bush –1648. † **7.** A bushy tail, *esp.* of a fox. See BRUSH *sb.*² –1610. **8.** (Prob. – Du. *bosch.*) Woodland; applied to the uncleared or untilled districts in the British Colonies, even though not wooded; and hence to the *country* as opp. to the *towns* 1780. Hence, *to take to the b.* 1837.

1. The undergrowth Of shrubs and tangling bushes MILT. *P. L.* IV. 176. **2.** Driven.. to tak the heather-b. for a bield SCOTT. **4.** *Beggar's-b.*: see BEGGAR. **5.** Good wine needs no b. *A.Y.L.* Epil. **6.** Trymme my busshe, barber PALSGR. **8.** The black man loves the b. CARLYLE. Cheaper in Toronto than away in the b. 1864.

Phr. *To beat* (*go*, etc.) *about the b.*: to go indirectly towards an object.

Comb.: **b. antelope,** ? = *bush-buck*; **b. basil,** *Ocymum minimum*; **-bean** (*U.S.*), the Kidney-bean (*Phaseolus vulgaris*); **-buck,** a small African antelope; **-cat,** the Serval; **-creepers,** tropical birds belonging to the family of the Warblers; **-draining,** the draining of land by trenches filled with brushwood; **-goat** = *bush-buck*; **-hog,** a wild pig of S. Africa, the *boschvaark*; **-hook,** a bill-hook (*U.S.*); **-lawyer,** the New Zealand bramble (*Rubus australis*); **-master,** a venomous S. American snake; **-road,** a road through the b.; **-shrike,** Eng. name of the *Thamnophilinæ*; **-syrup,** a syrup obtained from the flowers of *Protea mellifera* in Cape Colony; **-track** = *bush-road*; † **-tree,** the Box; **b. vetch,** *Vicia sepium*; **-wood,** underwood. Hence **Bu·shless** *a.*

Bush (buʃ), *sb.*² 1566. [– MDu. *busse* (Du. *bus*) bush of a wheel (cf. BOX *sb.*² IV. 2, and G. *büchse, rad|büchse*).] The metal lining of the axle-hole of a wheel; hence, the case in which the journal of a shaft revolves. Cf. BOX *sb.*² **b.** A cylindrical metal lining of an orifice; a perforated plug, cylinder, or disc. *Comb.* **b.-metal,** an alloy of copper and tin used for journals.

Bush (buʃ), *v.*¹ ME. [f. BUSH *sb.*¹] † **1.** *trans.* To set in a bush, to place in ambush; *intr.* (for *refl.*) to hide in a bush, lie in ambush. (Cf. BUSH *sb.*¹ 4.) –1623. **2.** To protect or support with bushes. Also *absol.* 1647. **3.** To bush-harrow (ground, etc.) 1787. **4.** *intr.* To grow thick like a bush 1562. Also *transf.*

2. As for netting by night, b. your fields closely 1860. **4.** So thick the Roses bushing round About her glowd MILT. *P. L.* ix. 426.

Bush, *v.*² Now *dial.* ME. [perh. – OFr. *buschier* knock, beat; cf. MDu. *buuschen* (= MHG. *biuschen*) in same sense; relations cannot be made out.] *intr.* To butt; to push.

Bush (buʃ), *v.*³ 1566. [f. BUSH *sb.*²] To furnish with a bush; to line (an orifice) with metal.

† **Bush,** *v.*⁴ 1659. [– Fr. *boucher* in same sense.] To stop an opening –1693.

Bushel (bu·ʃĕl), *sb.*¹ [– OFr. *buissiel, boissiel* (mod. *boisseau*) = Pr. *boissel*; perh. of Gaulish origin.] **1.** A measure of capacity containing 4 pecks or 8 gallons. The *imperial bushel*, used in Gt. Britain, contains 2218·19 cubic inches; the *Winchester bushel*, still used in U.S. and Canada, 2150·4 cubic inches. **b.** *loosely.* A large quantity or number ME. **2.** A vessel used as a bushel measure ME. Also *fig.* (with ref. to Matt. 5:15). 1557.

1. b. Bushels of girls 1873. **2.** Feet.. as broad as a b. TOPSELL. *fig.* Trouth vnder bushell is faine to crepe 1557. Hence **Bu·shelful.**

Bushel, *sb.*² ME. [Cf. BUSH sb.², which, however, occurs a century later.] The bush of a wheel. ? *Obs.*

Bushel (bu·ʃĕl), *v. rare.* 1650. [f. BUSHEL *sb.*¹] To hide under a bushel. Also *fig.*

Bush-fighter (bu·ʃfəi:təɹ). 1760. One accustomed to fight in the bush. So **Bu·sh-fi:ghting** *vbl. sb.* fighting in the bush. Also *fig.*

Bu·sh-hammer. *U.S.* 1884. [prob. – G. *bosshammer*; cf. MHG. *bozen* beat.] A mason's large breaking hammer, often having square ends cut into pyramidal points.

Bush-harrow (bu·ʃhæ:roᵘ), *sb.* 1770. A heavy frame with bars in which bushes are interwoven underneath, used for harrowing grass land or covering in seed. Hence **Bu·sh-ha:rrow** *v.* to use the bush-harrow upon.

Bushman (bu·ʃmăn). 1785. [f. BUSH *sb.*¹ 8, app. after Du. *boschjesman*, as used in S. Africa.] **1.** A tribe of aborigines near the Cape of Good Hope. **2.** A dweller or traveller in the Australian bush 1852.

1. Another species of Hottentots, who have got the name of Boshees-men 1785. Hence **Bu·shmanship,** bush-farming.

Bushment (bu·ʃmĕnt). ME. [In senses 1–3, aphet. f. ABUSHMENT, AMBUSHMENT, q.v. In sense 4, cf. BUSH *sb.*¹] **1.** = AMBUSHMENT 1 (*arch.*). † **2.** = AMBUSHMENT 2. –1550. † **3.** = AMBUSHMENT 3. –1549. **4.** A mass of bushes (?*Obs.*) 1586.

Bush-ranger (bu·ʃ,rēⁱ:ndʒəɹ). 1817. [f. BUSH *sb.*¹ 8.] An escaped convict living in the bush, and subsisting by robbery with violence. So **Bu·sh-ra:nging** *vbl. sb.* the practice of the b.; var. **-ra·ngering.**

Bush-rope (bu·ʃ,rōᵘp). 1814. [f. as prec.] A name of species of *Cissus* or Wild Vine.

Bushwhacker (bu·ʃ,hwæ:kəɹ). *U.S.* 1809. [f. BUSH *sb.*¹ + WHACKER.] *lit.* One who beats bushes; hence **1.** A backwoodsman, a bush-ranger. **2.** In the American Civil War, irregular combatants who took to the woods, and were variously regarded as patriot guerrillas, or as banditti 1862. **3.** An implement used to cut away brushwood 1858.

3. A graduate of the plough.. and the b. EMERSON. Hence **Bu·shwhack** *v.* to act as a b. **Bu·sh-wha:cking** *vbl. sb.* making one's way through bushes; *esp.* the pulling of a boat by means of the bushes along the margin of a stream; bush-fighting.

Bushy (bu·ʃi), *a.* ME. [f. BUSH *sb.*¹ + -Y¹.] **1.** Abounding in bushes; overgrown with bush. **2.** Growing thick like a bush 1611. † **3.** Dwelling among the bushes (*rare*).

2. Each odorous bushie shrub MILT. *P. L.* IV. 696. **3.** The bushie birdes among 1563. Hence **Bu·shily** *adv.* **Bu·shiness.**

Busied (bi·zid), *ppl. a.* 1611. [f. BUSY *v.* + -ED¹.] Attentively occupied, engaged. (The attrib. use is rare.)

The b. monk was tempted but with one Devil 1669.

Busily (bi·zili), *adv.* ME. [f. BUSY *a.* + -LY².] In a BUSY manner.

He shoulde haue resysted.. more besyly 1508. Byrdes besely syngynge 1513.

Business (bi·znės). [OE. *bisiĝnis* (late Northumb., once), f. *bisiĝ* BUSY + -NESS. Shortened to a disyllable since it ceased to be a noun of state.] † **1.** The state of being busily engaged in anything; diligence –1713. † **2.** Activity, briskness –1674. † **3.** Mischievous or impertinent activity –1580. † **4.** Earnestness, importunity –1543. † **5.** Anxiety; uneasiness. (The earliest sense.) –1577. † **6.** Care, attention –1540. † **7.** Trouble; ado –1693. † **8.** Diligent labour –1509. **9.** That about which one is busy; function, occupation ME. **b.** That with which one is concerned at the time; often *spec.* the errand on which one comes 1596. **10.** Stated occupation, profession, or trade 1477. † **b.** Active life. See also *Màn of b.* –1779. **11.** *gen.* Occupation; *esp.* serious occupation, work. Also with *a* and *pl.* ME. **12.** A piece of work, a job. (The pl. is now unusual.) 1557. **b.** *ellipt.* A difficult matter 1843. **13.** A matter that concerns a particular person or thing; const. *of*, or *gen. case.* 1525. **b.** Concern 1759. **c.** *colloq.* A matter with which one has the right to meddle. Also, justifying motive or right of interference, 'anything to do' (*with*). Const. usu. *with*, or infin. 1690. † **14.** A subject of consideration or discussion; the subject of a book, etc. –1699. **15.** *vaguely*, An affair, concern, matter. (Now often indicating contempt or impatience, *esp.* when preceded by a sb. used attrib.) 1605. **16.** Dealings, intercourse (*with*). (*arch.*) 1611. **17.** *Theatr.* Action as opp. to dialogue 1671. **18.** *spec.* (from 13 and 19): Trade, commercial transactions or engagements 1727. **19.** A commercial enterprise as a going concern 1887. Also in *comb.*

2. The businesse of his [a dog's] taile 1616. **6.** Haue thou bisynesse [*curam habe*] of a good name WYCLIF *Ecclus.* 41:15. **7.** Ful mychell besynesse had he or þat he myght his lady wynne CHAUCER. **9.** Because a Thing is every Body's B., it is no Body's B. STEELE. **b.** I asked him his b. (*mod.*). **10.** They make Fooling their B. and their Livelihood 1694. **11.** The b. of the day is done SOUTHEY. Trade.. one of the great businesses of life DE FOE. The b. of a butcher 1878. **12.** A b. of moment BIBLE *Pref.* **13. b.** My b. is with man JOHNSON. **c.** That is no b. of ours KINGSLEY. **15.** This boat b. SOUTHEY. **18.** To do a stroke of b. BURTON, a brisk b. 1884.

Phrases. **a.** (sense 11) *To mean b.*: to be in earnest (*colloq.*). *On b.*: with an errand or purpose relating to b. *A person's b.*: work to be done on his behalf. **b.** (sense 13) *To mind one's own b.*: to refrain from meddling with what does not concern one. Now *colloq.* *To go about one's b.*: to go away. So *To send about one's b.*: to send packing. **c.** *Man of b.* † **1.** One engaged in public affairs. **2.** One engaged in mercantile transactions. **3.** A man skilled in business. **4.** An attorney. Hence **Bu·siness-like** *a.*

Busk (bɒsk), *sb.* 1592. [– Fr. *busc* – It. *busco* splinter, rel. to OFr. *busche* (mod. *bûche*) log – Gmc. **būsk-* piece of wood.] A strip of wood, whalebone, steel, etc., passed down the front of a corset, to stiffen and support it. Applied dial. to the whole corset.

Her bodie pent with buske WARNER.

Busk, *v.*¹ Now *Sc.* and *n. dial.* ME. [– ON. *búask*, refl. of *búa* prepare; see BOUND *ppl. a.*¹ For the ending cf. *bask.*] **1.** *intr.*

(and *refl.*) To prepare oneself; *spec.* to dress. **2.** To set out; to hie, hurry ME. **3.** *trans.* To prepare; to set in order, fit out. Still in *Sc.* ME. **4.** To dress. Still in *Sc.* ME. Also *fig.*
3. Time to b. thy body-clothes SCOTT. **4.** Hedges, busk'd in bravery CAMPBELL.

Busk, *v.*[2] 1665. [– Fr. † *busquer* seek, hunt for – Sp. *buscar*, f. Gmc. **būsk-*; see BUSK *sb.*] *Naut.* **1.** *intr.* Of a ship: To beat about; to tack. **b.** To cruise as a pirate. [Perh. the orig. sense.] 1867. **2.** *fig.* To go about seeking *for*, to seek *after* 1734.

Busk, *v.*[3] 1567. [Of unkn. origin.] *intr.* Of fowls: To shift about restlessly or uneasily.

† **Bu·sket.** *rare.* 1579. [f. *busk* (see BUSH *sb.*[1]) + -ET.] **1.** 'Little bushes of hauthorne.' **2.** = BOSKET 1803.

Buskin (bɒ·skin). 1503. [prob. – late OFr. *bouzequin*, var. of *bro(u)sequin* (mod. *brodequin*), corresp. to Cat., Sp. *borcegui*, Pr. *borzeguim*, It. *borzacchino*; of much disputed origin.] **1.** A covering for the foot or leg reaching to the calf, or to the knee; a half-boot. **2.** *spec.* The high thick-soled boot (*cothurnus*) worn in Athenian tragedy; often opp. to the 'sock' (*soccus*) or low shoe worn in comedy 1570. **b.** Hence *fig.* and *transf.* The tragic vein; tragedy 1579. Also *attrib.*
1. The royal privilege of red shoes or buskins GIBBON. **2.** He..knew all niceties of the sock and b. BYRON. Hence **Bu·skined** *ppl. a.* shod with buskins; concerned with or belonging to tragedy; elevated.

† **Bu·skle,** *v.* 1535. [freqent. of BUSK *v.*[1]; see -LE.] = BUSK *v.*[1] –1642.

Busky (bɒ·ski), *a.* 1570. [f. *busk*, dial. var. of BUSH *sb.*[1], + -Y[1].] Bosky, bushy.
Yon b. hill 1 *Hen. IV*, v. i. 2.

Buss (bɒs), *sb.*[1] ME. [– OFr. *busse*, *buce*, later infl. by MDu. *buisse* (mod. *buis*), parallel to which are OHG. *būzo* (MHG. *būze*), MLG. *butze*, OE. *būtse* in *būtsecarlas* sailors, ON. *búza*, med.L. *bucia*; of unkn. origin.] **1.** A vessel of burden. (*Hist.*) **2.** *spec.* A two- or three-masted vessel of various sizes, used esp. in the Dutch herring-fishery 1471. Also *attrib.*

Buss (bɒs), *sb.*[2] *arch.* and *dial.* 1570. [perh. alt. of earlier † *bass*, rel. to Fr. *baiser*, L. *basium*, *basiare* kiss.] A kiss; kissing.

Buss (bɒs), *v.* *arch.* and *dial.* 1571. [See prec.] *trans.* To kiss. Also *fig.* and *absol.*
We busse our wantons, but our wives we kisse HERRICK.

‖ **Bussu.** 1858. [S. American.] A palm (*Manicaria saccifera*), the spathes of which supply a coarse strong cloth. Hence *b. palm, cloth.*

Bust (bɒst), *sb.*[1] 1691. [– Fr. *buste* – It. *busto*, of unkn. origin.] **1.** A piece of sculpture representing the head, shoulders, and breast of a person. Cf. BUSTO. **2.** The upper front part of the human body; the bosom (*esp.* of a woman) 1727. Also † *transf.* Also *attrib.*
1. Three stone busts of Hermes THIRLWALL. Storied urn or animated b. GRAY.

Bust, *sb.*[2]; see BUSTE.

Bust (bɒst). 1860. Dial. or vulgar pronunc. of BURST *sb.* and *v.*; often *joc.*, *esp.* in U.S. *spec.* 'a frolic, a spree' (Bartlett); cf. BURST *sb.* 6.

Bustard (bɒ·stăɹd). 1460. [perh. – AFr. **bustarde*, blending of OFr. *bistarde* and *oustarde* (mod. *outarde*): – L. *avis tarda* 'slow bird', given by Pliny as Sp.; but the bustard is a swift bird, and the L. term may be a perversion of a foreign word.] **1.** A genus of birds (*Otis*) showing affinities both to the *Cursores* and *Grallatores*. The Great B. (*Otis tarda*) is the largest European bird. **2.** Applied in America to the Canada Goose, *Bernicla canadensis* 1876. **3.** Local var. BUZZARD *sb.*[2], a large moth 1886.
1. The b...Forced hard against the wind a thick unwieldy flight WORDSW.

† **Bust(e.** ME. var. of BOIST *sb.* –1566.

Buster (bɒ·stəɹ). 1839. **1.** Vulgar f. BURSTER. Hence **2.** *slang.* (*U.S.*) **a.** Something that takes one's breath away. **b.** A roistering blade. **c.** A frolic; a spree. 1850.

† **Bu·stian.** 1463. [Late ME. *bostian*, *bustian*, *busteyn*, later *bustian(e)*, perh. alt. f. OFr. *bustan(n)e* kind of stuff made at Valenciennes, perh. after *fustian.*] A foreign cotton fabric –1725.

Bustle (bɒ·s'l), *sb.*[1] 1622. [f. BUSTLE *v.*[1]] **1.** Activity with excitement, noise, and commotion; stir, ado 1634. Also *transf.* **2.** The commotion of conflict; *concr.* a conflict, scuffle (*arch.*) 1622. **3.** *Thieves' cant.* Money 1812.
1. He..could be very busy without b. BYRON. **2.** Divers were killed in the b. 1693.

Bu·stle, *sb.*[2] 1788. [Of unkn. origin.] A pad, or wire framework, worn beneath the skirt of a woman's dress, to expand it behind; a dress-improver.
A waist like a wasp, a magnificent b., and petticoats..puffed out round the bottom MISS MITFORD.

Bustle (bɒ·s'l), *v.* [perh. alt. of † BUSKLE, frequent. of BUSK *v.*[1]; see -LE[1].] † **1.** *intr.* ? = BLUSTER *v.* 1 (*rare*). ME. only. **2.** *intr.* To be fussily or noisily active 1580. † **3.** *intr.* To struggle, scuffle, contend –1712. **4.** *trans.* and *refl.* To bestir, rouse: also with *up*. Now *rare.* 1579. **5.** *trans.* (and *refl.*) To cause to move precipitately; to hurry in a fussy manner 1563.
2. We b. and God works KINGSLEY. **5.** To b. (people) out of the house KINGSLEY. Hence **Bu·stler,** one who displays fussy activity. **Bu·stlingly** *adv.*

† **Bu·sto.** Pl. **-os (-oes, -o's).** 1662. = BUST *sb.*[1] 1. –1863.

† **Bu·sy,** *sb.* [OE. *bisgu*, *bysgu*, f. *bisiġ* BUSY *a.*] Occupation; state of being occupied –ME.

Busy (bi·zi), *a.* [OE. *bisiġ* (ME. *büsi*, *besi*, *bisi*) = MLG., MDu. *besich* (Du. *bezig*), of unkn. origin.] **1.** Occupied with constant attention; actively engaged. (Rare in attrib. use.). **2.** Said of things; *fig.* of passions, etc. OE. **3.** Constantly occupied or in motion ME. **4.** In bad sense: Active in what does not concern one; prying; meddlesome, officious; restless. Cf. BUSYBODY. ME. † **5.** Solicitous, anxious; careful –1483. **6.** Active 1548. † **7.** Elaborate; 'curious' –1615. **8.** Full of stir 1697. **9.** That indicates busyness 1632.
1. B. as a moth over some rotten archive LAMB. **2.** For many days rumour was b. KINGLAKE. **3.** Curiosity, the busiest passion of the idle SCOTT. **4.** A b. and inquisitorial tyranny COLERIDGE. **8.** The b. world of men MORLEY. **9.** The b. hum of men MILT. *Alleg.* 118. So **Busy** *sb.* (*slang*) a detective 1904.

Busy (bi·zi), *v.* [OE. *bisġian*, *bysġian*, f. *bisiġ* BUSY *a.*] **1.** *trans.* To make, or keep busy. **b.** *refl.* (The usual construction.) OE. † **2.** To trouble the body (only in OE.) or mind; to afflict, worry OE. **3.** *intr.* (? for *refl.*) To occupy oneself, take trouble (now *rare*) ME.
1. Thou..busiest all thy wits about it 1587. **b.** B. thee for good or ill BROWNING.

Busybody (bi·zibǫ:di). 1526. [f. BUSY *a.* 4 + BODY.] An officious person; one who meddles in other people's affairs.
Vaine pratling busie bodies 1570.

Busyness (bi·zinės). *rare.* 1868. [f. BUSY *a.* + -NESS.] = BUSINESS 1.

But (bɒt), *prep.*, *conj.*, *adv.* [OE. *būtan* (*beūtan*, *būton*, *būta*) = OS. *biūtan*, *būtan*, OHG. *biūʒan* (MG. *būʒen*); WGmc. comp. of **be*, **bi* BY and **ūtana* from without (see OUT).]

A. *prep.* **1.** Outside of. (OE. and mod.Sc.) **2.** Leaving out, barring, with the exception of, except, save. Clearly a prep. in OE.

B. *adv.* 1. Without, outside 1450. **b.** as *adj.* Outer 1619. **c.** as *sb.* The outer room of a two-roomed house 1724. **2.** In sense: Only ME.
1. Gae b., and wait 1887. **b.** The b. end of a house 1619. **c.** A cosy b., and a canty ben RAMSAY.

C. *conj.* **1.** In a simple sentence; introducing a word or a phrase (rarely a clause): Without, with the exception of, except, save OE. **b.** *elliptically*: Any but, aught but, anything else than, other than, otherwise than. (Often after *ever*, *never.*) 1523. **2.** In a complex sentence; introducing the subordinate clause. **a.** With general sense 'except that'; the full expression being *but that*, often reduced to *but* OE. **b.** With general sense 'if not' OE. **c.** With general sense 'that not', L. *quin.* After negative and questioning constructions. ME. **3.** In a compound sentence, connecting the two co-ordinate members; or introducing an independent sentence connected in sense, though not in form, with the preceding. **a.** On the contrary. = Ger. *sondern.* OE. **b.** Nevertheless, yet, however. = Ger. *aber.* 1535. **c.** After *not only*, *not merely* ME. **d.** However, on the other hand, moreover, yet = Ger. *aber*, L. *autem.* ME.
1. I am one among a thousand; all of them wrong b. I. [Colloq. also, 'b. me.'] J. H. NEWMAN. Last b. one in the class (*mod.*). Phr. *B. now* = just now, only this moment. **b.** I should sinne To thinke b. Noblie of my Grandmother *Temp.* I. ii. 18. It can't b. be obvious to them ADDISON. **2. a.** Nothing would serve him, b. he must imitate Alexander 1701. Phr. *B. that* = Except for the fact that. (Formerly with *that* occas. omitted.) ME. **b.** Beshrew me b. I loue her heartily *Merch. V.* II. vi. 52. It is odds b. you lose STEELE. **c.** Thinke not b. it dooeth brenne my heart LD. BERNERS. It can not be b. offences wyl come CRANMER *Luke* 17:1. Heauen defend, b. still I should stand so 1 *Hen. IV*, IV. iii. 38. Who doubted b. [more logically *that*] the catastrophe was over? CARLYLE. Never doubt b. I'll go 1879. **3. a.** He left not Faction, b. of That was left DRYDEN. **b.** Her face speaks a Vestal, b. her heart a Messalina STEELE. **c.** They not only tell lies, b. bad lies JOWETT. **d.** B. Iesus gave him no answer *John* 19:9. 'Get money; honestly, if you can: b. get money!' 1887.

D. quasi-*sb.* [The adv. used *ellipt.*] See B. 1 c.

E. quasi-*adj.* [The adv. used *attrib.*] See B. 1 b.

Phrases, etc. *B. and*: and also. Now *Sc. B. for* = except for: see B. (sense 1). † *But for*: but because; see FOR. *But that*: see B. (sense 2). *But what* for *but that* is now *dial.* and *colloq.*

But, *sb.* 1571. The conj. *but*, used as a name for itself; *hence*, a verbal objection presented.
'Nay, but me no buts' SCOTT. Hence **But** *v.* (*arch.*) to say or use 'but'.

Butch, *v.* Now *dial.* 1785. [erron. back-formation from BUTCHER.] † *trans.* To cut up. *intr.* To follow the trade of a butcher.

Butcher (bu·tʃəɹ), *sb.* [ME. *bo(u)cher* – AFr. var. of OFr. *bo(u)chier* (mod. *boucher*) = Pr. *bochier*; f. OFr., Pr. *boc* (Fr. *bouc*) he-goat, prob. – OCelt. **bukkos*; see BUCK *sb.*[1], -ER[2].] **1.** One whose trade it is to slaughter large tame animals for food; one who kills such animals and sells their flesh; now, occas., a tradesman who deals in meat. **b.** *fig.* A 'man of blood'; a brutal murderer 1529. † **2.** An executioner; also *attrib.* –1494. **3.** An artificial fly used by anglers for salmon 1867.
1. Itm payd to the Bochsar for a greyt serlyn xvjd. 1525. *fig.* To be b. of an innocent childe SHAKS.
Comb.: **b.-fly,** ? a kind of blow-fly; **butcher's bill,** a sarcastic term for the list of killed in a battle (occas. for the money cost of a war). Hence **Bu·tcherly** *a.* and *adv.*

Butcher (bu·tʃəɹ), *v.* 1562. [f. prec.] **1.** To slaughter in the manner of a butcher (*lit.* and *fig.*). **2.** To inflict torture upon 1642.
1. He, their sire, Butcher'd to make a Roman holiday BYRON. The text is not butchered by misprinting 1850. Hence **Bu·tcherer,** one who butchers.

Bu·tcher-bi:rd. 1668. [f. BUTCHER *sb.*] A name of species of shrike (*Laniadæ*); *Lanius excubitor*, *L. tertius*, *L. cinereus*, etc.

† **Bu·tcher-row.** 1581. [Cf. *Saddlers' Row*, etc.] A shambles, meat-market –1702.

Bu·tcher's broo·m. 1562. [Used by butchers for sweeping their shops.] Common name of *Ruscus aculeatus* (N.O. *Liliaceæ*, tribe *Asparageæ*), also called Knee Holly.

Bu·tcher's mea:t, bu·tcher-mea:t. 1632. Meat sold by butchers, as opp. to poultry, etc.

Butchery (bu·tʃəri), *sb.* ME. [– (O)Fr. *boucherie*; see BUTCHER *sb.*, -Y[3], -ERY.] **1.** A slaughter-house, shambles; a butcher's shop or stall; also *attrib.* (Now chiefly applied to those in public establishments.) Also *fig.* **2.** The trade of a butcher. Now only *attrib.*, as in *b. business.* 1449. † **3.** Butchers collectively –1525. **4.** Cruel and wanton slaughter. Also *fig.* 1561.
1. This house is but a butcherie: Abhorre it SHAKS. **4.** Warres and Butcheries in France 1602.

† **Butin.** 1474. [Earliest *butin*, *butyn* (Caxton) – (O)Fr. *butin*, f. *butiner* plunder,

– MDu. *buyten* seize as booty; see BOOTY.] Spoil, or prey, taken in common; booty –1646.

Butler (bɒ·tləɹ). ME. [– AFr. *buteler*, (O)Fr. *bouteillier* cup-bearer, f. *bouteille* BOTTLE *sb.*[2]; see -ER[2].] **1.** A servant who has charge of the wine-cellar and dispenses the liquor. Formerly also, one who hands round wine. Now usu. the head-servant of a household, who keeps the plate, etc. Also *fig.* **2.** An officer who originally had charge of the wine for the royal table; hence the title of an official of high rank only nominally connected with the supply of wine, etc. (Cf. MARSHAL, etc.) ME.

2. Sir Nicholas Burdel, Chiefe B. of Normandie, was slaine at Pontoise 1587. Hence **Bu·tlership.**

Butlerage (bɒ·tləɹėdʒ). 1491. [f. prec. + -AGE.] **1.** A duty on imported wine paid to the king's butler; prisage. Now *Hist.* **2.** The office, dignity, or department, of a butler 1615.

Butlery (bɒ·tləri). [ME. *boteleryе* – OFr. *botelerie* (mod. *bouteillerie*); see BUTLER, -Y[3], -ERY.] A butler's pantry; a buttery.

Butment (bɒ·tmĕnt). 1624. [f. BUTT *v.*[2] + -MENT.] **1.** *Archit.* = ABUTMENT 3. **2.** An outstanding mass (of rock, etc.) 1865. **3.** A piece of ground abutting on a larger piece 1677.

1. *B. cheeks*: the two solid sides of a mortise.

Butt (bɒt), *sb.*[1] ME. [– MLG. *but*, MDu. *but(te)*, *bot(te)*, whence also G. *but*, *butte*, Sw. *butta* turbot, Da. *bot* flounder; prob. rel. to LG. *but*, MDu. *bot* stumpy (see BUTT *sb.*[3]); cf. HALIBUT.] A name of various flat fish, as sole, fluke, plaice, turbot, etc.

Butt (bɒt), *sb.*[2] ME. [In AL. *butta* (XIII), *bota* (XIV) – AFr. *but*, var. of OFr. *bot*, *bout* = Pr. *bot*, Sp. *bote*, It. *botte* (whence Fr. *botte* butt) ;– late L. *buttis*.] **1.** A cask for wine, ale, etc., holding from 108 to 140 gallons. Later, a measure of capacity = 2 hogsheads, *i.e.* usually in ale measure 108 gallons, in wine measure 126 gallons. **2.** A cask, barrel 1626.

1. Hastely drouned in a Butte of Malmesey MORE. **2.** A water-butt 1823.

Butt (bɒt), *sb.*[3] 1450. [rel. to the base of which BUTTOCK seems to be a deriv. and which is repr. by words meaning 'short and stumpy', as Du. *bot*; see BUTT *sb.*[1]] **1.** The thicker end of anything, *e.g.* of a tool or weapon, a whip-handle, fishing-rod, gun, etc. 1470. **2.** The trunk of a tree, *esp.* the part just above the root 1601. **3.** A buttock. *dial.* and *colloq.* in *U.S.* 1450. **4.** The base of a leaf-stalk; the tip of a branch; also *Sc.* a catkin 1807. **5.** *Iron-work.* One of the blocks out of which iron anvils are formed 1831.

¶ See also BUTT *sb.*[7], BUTT *sb.*[11]

Butt (bɒt), *sb.*[4] ME. [– (O)Fr. *but*, of unkn. origin; perh. infl. by Fr. *butte* rising ground, knoll, (also) target. See BUTT *sb.*[5], BUTTE.] † **1.** A terminal point; a boundary mark, *esp.* in *butts and bounds*; a goal; often *fig.* (see BUTT *v.*[2], quot.) –1726. **2.** A mark for archery practice; prop. an erection on which the target is set up. Hence a mound in front of which the targets are placed for artillery or rifle practice. ME. Also *transf.* and *fig.* † **3.** The length of the shooting-range –1696. **4.** An aim, object 1594. **5.** An object at which ridicule, scorn, or abuse is aimed; *absol.* a person habitually made the object of jokes 1616.

1. Heere is my journies end, heere is my b. *Oth.* V. ii. 267. **2.** The arrow sticks in the B. unto which the marke is fastned BP. REYNOLDS. **5.** The b. and byword of liberalism GLADSTONE. *Comb.* † **b.-bolt,** a strong unbarbed arrow.

Butt (bɒt), *sb.*[5] Now *dial.* 1693. [– (O)Fr. *butte* mound, f *buter*; see BUTTE, BUTT *v.*[1]] A hillock, mound.

Butt, *sb.*[6] 1450. [perh. repr. OE. **butt* (whence BUTTOCK), in AL. *butta*, *buttes* (XII), rel. to LG. *butt*, MDu. *botte*, MHG. *butze*, ON. *butr*, and OE. *bytt* small piece of land.] **1.** A ridge between two furrows of a ploughed field. **2.** Such a ridge when cut short by the irregular shape of the field. (? The orig. sense.) 1523. **3.** *dial.* A small piece of land disjoined from the adjacent lands 1699.

Butt (bɒt), *sb.*[7] 1627. [perh. a sense of BUTT *sb.*[3], or f. BUTT *v.*[2] 3.] **1.** *Naut.* More fully **b.-end, -head**: The end of a plank or plate in a vessel's side which joins on to the end of the next; the plane of juncture, etc. **2.** *Coal-min.* 'A surface [of coal] exposed at right angles to the face' (Raymond).

Phrases, etc. *B. and b.*: with the b. ends together, but not overlaying each other. **B.-strap,** a strip of metal riveted over the joining of two plates in an iron ship. *Comb.*: **b.-hinge** (also *butt*), a hinge composed of two plates the edges of which meet without overlapping; **-joint,** in *Carpentry* (= BUTTING-JOINT).

† **Butt,** *sb.*[8] 1598. [Cf. BUTT *v.*[1] 4.] A promontory, as *The Butt of Lewis.*

Butt (bɒt), *sb.*[9] 1647. [f. BUTT *v.*[1]] A push or thrust with the head or horns; also, a thrust in fencing (*rare*).

† **Butt,** *sb.*[10] 1598. [Late ME. – Fr. *botte* – MLG. *bōte* bundle. Cf. BOTTLE *sb.*[2]] **1.** ? A bundle, pack –1705. **2.** *dial.* A hassock. Hence **b.-woman,** a pew-opener.

Butt (bɒt), *sb.*[11] 1661. [perh. a use of BUTT *sb.*[3] 1 or 3.] The thicker or hinder part of a hide or skin, as *calf-butts*, etc.; the thick leather made from this; sole-leather. (Cf. BEND *sb.*[2] 3.)

Butt (bɒt), *sb.*[12] *dial.* 1796. [Origin unkn.] A short and rudely made cart.

Butt (bɒt), *v.*[1] ME. [– AFr. *buter*, OFr. *boter* (mod. dial. *bouter* put) – Gmc. **buttan*, repr. by MDu. *botten* strike, sprout; infl. in senses 3 and 4 by BUTT *v.*[2]] **1.** *intr.* To strike, thrust, shove (usu. with the head or horns); also *fig.* **2.** *trans.* To strike, *esp.* with the head or horns; to drive or push *away*, *out*, etc., thus 1590. **3.** To come or strike dead against 1875. **4.** *intr.* To run out, jut 1523. ¶ **5.** With assoc. of BUTT *sb.*[4] To aim (*trans.* and *intr.*) 1593. **6.** Used advb., *esp.* with the adv. *full*: Point-blank, violently ME.

1. *To butt in* (orig. *U.S.*), to intrude, meddle. **2.** The beast with many horns butts me away *Cor.* IV. i. 2.

Butt (bɒt), *v.*[2] 1523. [Partly f. BUTT *sb.*[4] 1; partly aphet. f. ABUT.] † **1.** To fix or mark (*out*) the limits of lengthwise; to terminate; to limit, bound. Chiefly in the *passive.* –1727. † **2.** *intr.* = ABUT *v.* 2. Also *fig.* –1798. † **3.** *To b. on, upon*: (of a line) to end in (a point); (of a road) to issue into. (Cf. F. *abouter à.*) Also *fig.* –1678. **4.** *intr.* chiefly *techn.*: To come with one end flat *against*, *on* 1670. **5.** *trans.* To place end *against* a surface; to join end to end 1785. ¶ See also BUTT *v.*[1] 3, 4.

1. Butting it at thends and bounding it at the sides 1592.

Butte (biūt, bɒt). *U.S.* 1838. [– Fr. *butte*; see BUTT *sb.*[5]] In Western U.S.: An isolated hill or peak rising abruptly. var. **Bute.**

Butt-end (bɒ·t e·nd). 1580. [f. BUTT *sb.*[3]] **1.** = BUTT *sb.*[3] 1 (and now more used). **b.** *fig.* The fag end 1594. † **2.** = BUTT *sb.*[3] 2. –1760. **3.** *Naut.* = BUTT *sb.*[7]

Butter (bɒ·təɹ), *sb.*[1] [OE. *butere*, corresp. to OFris., OHG. *butera* (Du. *boter*, G. *butter*); WGmc. – L. *butyrum* – Gr. βούτυρον, prob. of alien origin.] **1.** The fatty substance obtained from cream by churning. *fig.* Unctuous flattery. (Cf. BUTTER *v.*) *colloq.* 1823. **2.** *transf.* Any substance resembling butter in appearance or consistence, as **b. of almonds** = ALMOND-*b.*; **b. of cacao,** a substance obtained from the seeds of the cacao; so **b. of mace, shea b.** (see SHEA), and other *vegetable butters* 1440. **b.** *esp.* in *Chem.*, an old name of several anhydrous chlorides, as **b. of antimony, arsenic, bismuth, tin, zinc** 1641.

1. A grosse fat man.—As fat as B. SHAKS.

Phrases. (*To look*) *as if b. would not melt in one's mouth*: said contemptuously of persons of very demure appearance. *Clarified* or *run b.*: butter melted and potted for culinary use.

Comb.: † **b.-ale** = *buttered ale* (see ALE); **b. and eggs,** pop. name for flowers of two shades of yellow, *esp.* Toadflax (*Linaria vulgaris*), and varieties of *Narcissus*; **b.-back,** a kind of wild duck (*U.S.*); **-bird,** the Bobolink (*U.S.*); **-boat,** a vessel for serving melted b. in; also *fig.*; **-factor,** a tradesman who buys b. from farmers to sell wholesale; **-fish,** the (slimy) Spotted Gunnel; **-flip,** the Avocet (*local*); **-man,** one who makes or sells b.; also *Naut.* a schooner with a certain rig.; **-scotch,** a kind of toffee, made of sugar and b.; **-tree,** name of *Bassia butyracea* and *B. parkii*; **-weed,** a name for *Erigeron canadensis* and *Senecio lobatus*; **-weight,** formerly 18 or more ounces to the pound; *fig.* 'good measure' (*obs.*); **-worker,** a contrivance for pressing the buttermilk out of b.

Butter (bɒ·təɹ), *sb.*[2] 1611. [f. BUTT *v.*[1] + -ER[1].] An animal that butts.

Bu·tter, *sb.*[3] 1874. [f. BUTT *sb.*[3] + -ER[1].] A machine for sawing off the ends of legs or boards, to render them square.

Butter (bɒ·təɹ), *v.* 1496. [f. BUTTER *sb.*[1]] **1.** To spread with butter. Also, To cook or dish up with butter. **2.** *fig.* To flatter lavishly 1816. † **3.** *slang.* 'To increase the stakes every throw or every game' (J.) –1719.

1. Fine words, says our homely old proverb, b. no parsnips LOWELL. *To b. one's bread on both sides*: to be wasteful.

Bu·tter-box. 1600. **1.** A box for holding butter 1756. † **2.** Nickname for a Dutchman –1811.

Butter-bump, bitter-. 1671. [f. *butter*, var. of BITTERN + BUMP *v.*[2]] The Bittern (*local*).

Butterbur (bɒ·təɹbɒ̄ɹ). 1548. [f. BUTTER *sb.*[1] + BUR.] A plant, *Petasites vulgaris*, with large soft leaves, used for wrapping butter in.

Bu·ttercup. orig. *pl.* 1777. [prob. blending of † *butterflower* (XVI, after Du. *boterbloeme*) with *gold-cup* or *king-cup.*] A name of species of Ranunculus bearing yellow cup-shaped flowers, esp. *R. bulbosus*, *R. acris*, and *R. repens.* Called also *butterflower*, *gold-cup*, or *king-cup.*

Bu·tter-fi:ngered, *a.* 1615. That takes hold as if with fingers greased with butter; apt to let things fall or slip. Also *fig.* (*colloq.*) **Bu·tter-fi:ngers,** a butter-fingered person; *esp.* one who fails to hold a catch at cricket.

Butterfly (bɒ·təɹfləi). [Late OE. *buttorfléoge*, f. BUTTER *sb.*[1] + FLY *sb.*[1] Cf. Du. *botervlieg*, G. *butterfliege* and *buttervogel* (-bird). The reason for the name is unkn.] **1.** Any diurnal lepidopterous insect, having knobbed antennæ, and carrying its wings erect when at rest. **2.** *fig.* A vain, gaudily attired person; a giddy trifler 1605. **3.** The guide for the reins on the front of a hansom cab 1883. Also *attrib.*

1. Swich talkyng is nat worth a boterflye CHAUCER. **2.** Wee'l..laugh At gilded Butterflies *Lear* V. iii. 13.

Comb.: **b.-block,** *Naut.*, a small block consisting of two wings containing rollers for a chain to pass over; **-cock** = *butterfly-valve*; **-fish,** the Ocellated Blenny; **-flower,** the genus *Schizanthus*; **b. nut** (*Mech.*) = THUMB-*nut*; **b. orchis,** *Habenaria chlorantha* and *H. bifolia*; **b. plant,** the name of two Orchids, *Oncidium papilio* and *Phalænopsis amabilis*; **b. screw** (*Mech.*), a thumb-screw; **-shaped** *a. Bot.* = PAPILIONACEOUS 2; **-shell,** name of the genus *Voluta* of testaceous molluscs; **-valve,** a kind of double clack-valve, resembling, when open, a butterfly's wings; **-weed,** a name of American plants, esp. *Asclepias tuberosa.*

Butterine (bɒ·tĕrīn). 1874. [f. BUTTER *sb.*[1] + -INE[5].] An imitation butter made from oleo-margarine churned up with milk; now called *Margarine.*

Butteris (bɒ·tĕris). 1573. [unexpl. alt. of earlier *butter* – (O)Fr. *boutoir* horse-shoer's tool, f. *bouter* BUTT *v.*[1] Cf. OFr. *bouterelle*, Fr. *-olle*, *boutereau* names of various instruments.] A farrier's tool for paring a horse's hoofs.

Buttermilk (bɒ·təɹmilk). 1528. The acidulous milk which remains after the butter has been churned out. Also *fig.* and *attrib.*

Butter-nut (bɒ·təɹ,nɒt). 1753. **1.** The large oily nut of the *Juglans cinerea* or White Walnut Tree of N. America. Also, the tree itself. **2.** Name of the genus *Caryocar* of S. America (esp. *C. nuciferum*) and its fruit 1845. **3.** *attrib.* Of a brownish-grey colour, like the butter-nut (sense 1) 1861. **b.** Hence *absol.* 1863.

3. b. A 'Butternut' is..one, in fact, who wears the uniform..of the Southern Army 1863.

Butter-print (bɒ·təɹ,print). 1616. **1.** A stamp for marking butter-pats; an impression from this 1632. † **2.** *fig.* A child (*slang*) –1709.

Butterwort (bɒ·təɹwɒ̄ɹt). 1597. A plant with yellowish-green fleshy leaves (*Pinguicula vulgaris*) common on boggy ground; also the Eng. name of the genus *Pinguicula.*

Buttery (bɒ·tĕri), *sb.* ME. [– AFr. *boterie*, **buterie* (AL. *buteria* XIII, *butria* XV), prob. f. *but* BUTT *sb.*[2]; see -ERY.] A store-room for liquor; also, for provisions generally. **b.** In the colleges at Oxford and Cambridge: The place where ale and bread, butter, etc., are kept 1569.

Comb.: **b.-bar,** a ledge on the top of the b.-hatch; **-book** (at the Universities), the book in which are entered the names and buttery accounts of the members of a college; **-hatch,** the half-door over which the buttery provisions are served.

Buttery (bɒ·tĕri), *a.* ME. [f. BUTTER *sb.*[1] + -Y[1].] **1.** Of the nature of or containing butter. **2.** Like butter in consistence 1719. **3.** Smeared with butter 1796. **4.** *fig.* Given to fulsome flattery (cf. the *sb.*) 1842. Also in *comb.* Hence **Bu·tteriness.**

Bu·tting, *vbl. sb.*[1] 1602. The action of BUTT *v.*[1]

† **Bu·tting,** *vbl. sb.*[2] 1552. [f. BUTT *v.*[2] or *sb.*[7] + -ING[1].] **1.** Bounding, boundary, limit; also *fig.* –1750. **2.** The making of butt-joints 1850.

1. Nature has its buttings and boundings DE FOE.

Bu·tting, *vbl. sb.*[3] 1553. [f. BUT *v.* + -ING[1].] The making use of 'buts'.

Butting-joint 1837. [See BUTT *v.*[2]] *Carp.* A joint formed by the surfaces of two pieces of wood whereof one is perpendicular to the fibres, and the other in their direction, or making an oblique angle with them.

Buttock (bɒ·tək), *sb.* ME. [Formally identical with OE. *buttuc* (once), prob. end ridge of land, rounded slope, dim. of **butt*; see BUTT *sb.*[6], -OCK.] **1.** One of the two protuberances of the rump. Usu. in *pl.* the rump, posteriors. **2.** *Naut.* 'The breadth of the ship astern from the tuck upwards' (Smyth) 1627. **3.** [f. BUTTOCK *v.*] A manœuvre in wrestling 1688.

1. A Barbers chaire that fits all buttockes *All's Well* II. ii. 17. Hence **Bu·ttocked** *a.* having buttocks; defined as *broad-*, *great-*, etc.

Bu·ttock, *v.* 1617. [f. prec.] † **1.** In horse-racing: To overtake (a horse). **2.** In wrestling: To throw by a manœuvre in which the buttock is used 1883.

Button (bɒ·t'n), *sb.* ME. [– (O)Fr. *bouton* :– Rom. **bottone*, rel. to **bottare* thrust, put forth (see BUTT *v.*[1]).] **1.** *gen.* A small knob or stud attached to any object for use or ornament; *esp.* A knob or stud of metal, bone, etc., sewn by a shank or neck to articles of dress, usually for the purpose of fastening one part of the dress to another by passing through a *b.-hole*, but often for ornament: also *transf.* **2.** A bud, or other part of a plant of similar shape, *esp.* a young mushroom 1513. **3.** *transf.* from 1. Used of a knob, handle, catch; the disc of an electric bell. *spec.* An oblong piece of wood or metal, turning on a screw fixed through its centre, used to fasten doors, etc. 1607. **4.** Any small rounded body; *spec.* **a.** (*Chem.*) a globule of metal remaining in the crucible after fusion 1801; **b.** a knob fixed on the point of a fencing foil 1649.

1. Pray you vndo this B. *Lear* V. iii. 309. Phr. *Boy in buttons*: a page. A b. therefore for all worldely differences COVERDALE.

Phr. *To take by the b.*: to BUTTON-HOLE.

Comb. **a.** (chiefly in *pl.*) *bachelor's buttons*, see BACHELOR; used also in comb. of other plants having button-like flowers or seed-vessels. **b. b.-ball,** *Platanus occidentalis* (= *button-wood*); **-blank,** a disc of metal, etc., to be formed into a b.; **-boy,** a page; **-bush,** a North American shrub (*Cephalanthus occidentalis*) having globular flower-heads; **-fish,** the sea-urchin (*Echinus*); **-hook**; **-mould,** a disc of wood, etc., to be covered with cloth to form a b.; **-mushroom** (see sense 2); **-tree,** the genus *Conocarpus*; **-weed,** the genera *Spermacoce* and *Diodia* of tropical *Cinchonaceæ*; also the Knapweed; **-wood,** *Platanus occidentalis* (U.S.); also = *button-bush*; also = *button-tree*. Hence **Bu·ttonless** *a.* **Bu·ttony** *a.*

Button (bɒ·t'n), *v.* ME. [f. prec.] **1.** To furnish or adorn with a button, or buttons. **2.** To fasten with buttons. Often with *up*. ME. **b.** To fasten the clothes of (a person) with buttons. Usu. *refl.*; also *absol.* 1662. Also *fig.* **3.** *intr.* (for *refl.*) To be capable of being fastened (*up*) with buttons 1777.

2. Jack had got Euclid buttoned up inside his jacket 1864. *fig.* As it were, buttoned up, body and soul W. IRVING.

Buttoned (bɒ·t'nd), *ppl. a.* 1534. [f. BUTTON *sb.* and *v.* + -ED.] **1.** Having buttons, adorned with buttons, as *silver-*, *eight-b.*, etc. **b.** Wearing buttons 1813. **2.** Fastened with buttons. Also with *up*. 1826.

Bu·tton-hold, *v.* 1834. [Back-formation f. BUTTON-HOLDER. Superseded by BUTTON-HOLE *v.*] To take hold of (a person) by a button, and detain him in conversation against his will.

Bu·tton-ho:lder. 1806. **1.** One who button-holds. **2.** A case for holding buttons 1870.

Button-hole (bɒ·t'nhōᵘl), *sb.* 1561. **1.** The hole through which a button passes. Also *transf.* **2.** *colloq.* Short for *button-hole flower*, *bouquet* 1879. Also *attrib.* Hence **Bu·tton-hole** *v.* to sew button-holes; also = BUTTON-HOLD (superseding it). **Bu·tton-ho:ler,** one who makes button-holes; one who button-holes; *colloq.* a button-hole flower.

Bu·ttons. 1848. [*pl.* used as sing.] **1.** A boy in buttons, a page (*colloq.*) **2.** A name for the tansy and other plants; see BUTTON *sb.*

Buttress (bɒ·très), *sb.* [ME. *butras*, *-es*, *boterace*, *-as* (cf. AL. *boteracium* XIII) – OFr. *bouterez*, short for *ars bouterez* 'thrusting arch' (cf. Fr. *arc-boutant*), inflexional form of *bouteret*, f. *bouter* BUTT *v.*[1]; the ending was assim. to *-ace*, and thence in XVI to *-ess*.] **1.** A structure of wood, stone, or brick built against a wall to strengthen or support it. Also *fig.* **2.** *loosely*, A prop; a pier or abutment 1609. **3.** A projecting portion of a hill or mountain 1682.

1. A long dead wall, unbroken by porch or b. FREEMAN.

Bu·ttress, *v.* ME. [f. prec.] To furnish, sustain, or strengthen with a buttress. Also *fig.* Occas. with *up*.

To b. it [the ministry] up with the Grenvilles BURKE.

Butty (bɒ·ti). *dial.* 1802. [prob. evolved from the phr. *play* BOOTY (XVI) join with confederates to share 'plunder' with them.] **1.** A confederate, mate. **2.** *Mining.* A middleman, who contracts to raise coal or ore at so much per ton. Also in *comb.* 1845.

Butyl (biū·til). 1868. [f. BUT(YRIC + -YL.] *Chem.* **1.** The monatomic alcohol radical of the tetra-carbon series, C_4H_9; called also *Valyl*, *Tetryl*, and *Quartyl*. **2.** *attrib.* Of butyl, butylic, tetrylic; *esp.* in **b. alcohol,** $C_4H_{10}O$. Hence **Butyla·ctic,** in *Butylactic acid*: the monobasic acid $C_4H_8O_3$, derived from Butyl glycol. **Bu·tylene,** the diatomic hydrocarbon or olefine of the b. series, C_4H_8, also called *Butrene* and *Tetrene*. **Butyle·nic** *a.* **Buty·lic** *a.*

Butyr-, a formative of the names of chemical compounds of the butyric series, and of some minerals. (Cf. BUTYRO-.)

Bu·tyrate, a salt of butyric acid. **Bu·tyrin,** an oily liquid analogous to the acetins, obtained by the action of butyric acid on glycerin. **Bu·tyrone,** the ketone of the butyric series, also called diapropyl ketone $CO.(C_3H_7)_2$.

Butyraceous (biūtirēⁱ·ʃəs), *a.* 1668. [f. L *butyrum* BUTTER + -ACEOUS.] **1.** Of the nature of butter. Also *fig.* **2.** Producing or containing butter 1863.

Butyric (biuti·rik), *a.* 1826. [f. as prec. + -IC.] *Chem.* Of or pertaining to butter, *esp.* in reference to its chemical construction and formation. Hence:

B. acid, the monatomic, monobasic, fatty acid of the BUTYL series, $C_4H_8O_2$, of which there are two modifications, *normal b.* and *isobutyric* acid; the former, occurring in butter, cod-liver oil, etc., is a colourless viscous liquid, with a smell suggestive of both vinegar and rancid butter. Hence **Buty·rically** *adv.*

Bu·tyro-, comb. f. L. *butyrum*. Cf. BUTYR-.

Bu·tyrous, *a.* 1669. [f. L. *butyrum* + -OUS.] Butyraceous.

Buxeous (bɒ·ksiəs), *a.* 1731. [f. L. *buxeus* (f. *buxus* box-tree) + -OUS.] Of or pertaining to box or the box-tree. (Dicts.)

Bu·xerry. Now *Hist.* 1757. [– Hind. *baksāri* 'native of Buxar', i.e. the *Shāhābād* district.] A matchlock-man.

Buxine (bɒ·ksəin). 1836. [f. L. *buxus* box-tree + -INE.[5]] A vegetable alkaloid from the box-tree.

Buxom (bɒ·ksŏm), *a.* [ME. *buhsum*, *ibucsum*, repr. OE. *(*ġe*)*būhsum*, f. (*ġe*)*būgan* bend, BOW *v.*[1] + -SOME[1].] † **1.** Tractable (*to*); meek; gracious, obliging, kindly; prone (with *inf.*). † **2.** Flexible; unresisting (*poet.*) –1700. **3.** Blithe, bright, lively, gay (*arch.*) 1590. **4.** Full of health, vigour, and good temper; plump and comely, 'jolly'. (Chiefly of women.) 1589.

1. I shall be buxome and obedient to justyces 1523. **2.** Wing silently the b. air MILT. *P.L.* II. 842. **3.** A Souldier. . of buxome valour *Hen. V*, III. vi. 28. **4.** A b. dame about thirty SCOTT. Hence † **Bu·xom-ly,** *adv.*, **-ness.**

Buy (bəi), *v.* [OE. *byċġan*, = OS. *buggian*, ON. *byggja* let out, lend, Goth. *bugjan*:– Gmc. **bugjan*, of unkn. origin.] **1.** To get possession of by giving an equivalent, usu. in money; (to obtain by paying a price; to purchase. (Correl. to *sell*.) Also *absol.* **b.** Of things: To be an equivalent price for; to be the means of purchasing 1599. **2.** *fig.* To obtain in exchange for something else, or by making some sacrifice ME. † **3.** ABY *v.* 2; cf. BYE *v.* Often with *dear*. –1615. **4.** To redeem, ransom. *Obs.* exc. in *Theol.*, and now usu. repl. by *redeem*. ME. **5.** To engage by money or otherwise *to* or *to do*; to hire (*arch.*) 1652.

1. To b. some little Cornish borough 1714. . . *To b. into*: to b. a commission in; to purchase stock in, shares in. **b.** Can the world buie such a jewell *Much Ado* I. i. 183. **5.** Nor is [he] with Pray'rs, or Bribes, or Flatt'ry bought DRYDEN.

Phrases and Combs. **B. in:** to collect a stock of by purchase (often opp. to *sell out*); also *absol.*; to b. back for the owner, *e.g.* at an auction when the bids are too low; to b. a commission, stock, shares. **B. off:** to get rid of, to induce (a person) to forgo a claim, opposition, etc., by a money payment. **B. out:** † to ransom; to purchase a person's estate, or interest in any concern, and so to turn (him) out of it; to get rid of (any liability) by a money payment. **Buy over:** to gain over by a payment. **B. up:** to purchase with a view of controlling the supply (a stock, or the *whole* of any commodity). *To be bought and sold*: often *fig.*, usu. To be betrayed for a bribe (*arch.*). Hence **Buy·er.**

Buz, var. of BUZZ in various senses.

Buzz (bɒz), *sb.*[1] 1605. [f. BUZZ *v.*[1]] **1.** A sibilant hum, as that of bees, flies, or other insects 1645. **2.** *transf.* The confused sound made by many people talking or busily occupied; *hence*, stir, ferment 1627. **3.** *fig.* † **a.** A whim, fad: (cf. BEE[1] 5). **b.** A busy rumour 1605.

2. I found the whole. . Room in a Buz of Politics ADDISON. *Comb.* **b.-saw,** a circular saw. *U.S.*

Buzz, *sb.*[2] 1612. [perh. echoic; cf. FUZZ *sb.*[1], FUZZ-BALL, FUZZY.] **1.** A bur. **2.** A downy land-beetle (*Rhizostrogus solstitialis*) used as bait 1760. Also quasi-*adv.*

Buzz, *sb.*[3] Only *attrib.* 1798. [abbrev. of BUSBY.] Epithet of a large bushy wig. Also in comb. *buzz-wig*, one wearing such a wig; a bigwig. Also *transf.*

Buzz (bɒz), *v.*[1] ME. [Earlier *buss*; of imit. origin.] **1.** *intr.* To make a humming sibilant sound like that of bees, etc.; to fly *out*, *in*, etc., with such a sound. **2.** *fig.* To flutter, hover (*about*, *over*) like a buzzing insect 1650. **3.** To mutter, murmur busily. (Usu. contemptuous.) (*arch.*) 1555. **b.** To make the hum produced by many people talking 1832. **4.** *trans.* To tell in a low murmur, to whisper busily (*arch.*) 1583. **5.** To spread as a rumour, with whispering or busy talk 1616. **6.** To utter with, or express by, buzzing 1763.

1. Waspes that buz about his Nose *Hen. VIII*, III. ii. 55. **2.** Boys and wenches buzzing about the cakeshops like flies SWIFT. **5.** A bruit constantly buzzed FULLER. Hence **Bu·zzingly** *adv.*

Buzz, *v.*[2] 1785. [Origin unkn.] To finish to the last drop in the bottle.

Get some more port. . whilst I b. this bottle THACKERAY. var. **Buzza.**

† **Buzz,** *int.* 1602. **a.** An exclam. of impatience. **b.** = 'hey, presto', etc. –1830.

Buzzard[1] (bɒ·zăɹd). ME. [– (O)Fr. *busard* (whence also Du. *buizert*, G. *bussard*), based like OFr. *buson* (whence Fr. *buse*) on L. *buteo*, *-on-*, of unkn. origin; see -ARD.] **1.** A bird of the genus *Buteo*, esp. *B. vulgaris*. Applied also, with defining words, to others of the *Falconidæ*: as **Bald B.,** the Osprey; **Honey B.,** *Pernis apivorus*; **Moor B.,** *Circus æruginosus*. (The buzzard was a useless kind of hawk; hence sense 2.) **2.** *fig.* A worthless, stupid, or ignorant person. Often with *blind*. Now *dial.* ME. **3.** *attrib.* Senseless 1592.

1. An Historian and a Libeller are as different as Hawk and B. NORTH. **3.** A b. idol MILT. Hence **Buzzardet,** a hawk like a b., but with longer legs.

Bu·zzard, *sb.*² *dial.* 1825. [f. Buzz *v.*¹ + -ard.] **1.** A name for moths, cockchafers, etc., that fly by night. **2.** = Buzzer 3. 1878. *Comb.* **b.-clock,** a cockchafer.

Buzzer (bʊ·zəɹ). 1602. [f. Buzz *v.*¹ + -er¹.] **1.** An insect that buzzes. Also *fig.* 1606. † **2.** One who whispers tales. *Haml.* iv. v. 90. **3.** An apparatus for making a loud buzzing noise as a signal; cf. *hooter* 1870.

By, *sb.*¹ [north. OE. *bȳ* – ON. *bœr, býr* (Sw., Da. *by*) habitation, village, town, f. *búa* dwell; cf. Big *v.* Retained in place-names, as *Whitby.*] A place of habitation; a village or town.

By, *sb.*²; see after By *prep.* and *adv.*

By (bəi), *prep., adv.* (*a., sb.*) [OE. *bī,* unstressed *bi, be* = OFris., OS., OHG. *bī, bi* (Du. *bij,* G. *bei*), Goth. *bi* :– Gmc. **bi,* prob. identical with the second syll. of Gr. ἀμφί, L. *ambi-,* OE. *ymb(e)-* around.] **A.** *prep.* **1.** Of position in space. **a.** At the side or edge of; near, close to, beside. **b.** In forms of swearing or adjuration. In Teut. = 'in presence of', 'in touch of', but in ME. use possibly a tr. of Fr. *par,* of instrumentality OE. **c.** By the side of; *hence,* in addition to, beside ME. **d.** In the region or general direction of, towards OE.; *spec.* as in 'North by East', etc., *i.e.* one point towards the east of N., etc. 1682. **e.** On (vaguely). *Obs.* exc. in *by land,* etc. ME. **2.** Of motion. **a.** Alongside of, along, down over, up, over OE. **b.** Through; also expanded into *by way of* ME. **c.** Near to: chiefly in *to come by* (see Come *v.*) ME. **d.** On alongside of, past ME. **e.** At, to, or within the distance of ME. **f.** Expressing the amount of an excess or increase, inferiority or diminution ME. **3.** Of time. **a.** In the course of, at, in, on. Now only in *by day* (L. *interdiu*), and *by night* (L. *noctu*) ME. **b.** During, for. (Now *for.*) 1460. **c.** On or before, not later than; † within. Cf. Betimes. ME. **4.** (*fig.* from 1 a.) **a.** After; with vbs. of *naming,* etc. OE. **b.** According to, in conformity with OE. **c.** According to; as *by retail, by the yard, by the day,* etc. OE. **d.** Indicating succession of groups, quantities, or individuals of the same class, as *two by two, by files, man by man,* etc. ME. **e.** About, concerning, with respect to, in regard to, as concerns OE. **5.** (*fig.* from 2 a.) Indicating the medium, means, instrumentality, or agency OE. **6.** Of circumstance, condition, manner, cause, reason. **a.** The circumstances of an action often pass into the notion of aid or *means,* e.g. in 'to read by candle-light' OE. **b.** The sense of 'means' often passes into that of 'attendant circumstances', and so into the senses of 'manner', 'cause', 'reason' ME. **c.** In *Book-keeping,* placed before Credit entries, the person or account being made creditor *by* the amount entered 1695.

1. Com sit me bye 1485. *Bromley-by-Bow.* You'll stand by me upon Occasion Cibber. **b.** Neither shalt thou sweare by thy head *Matt.* 5:36. So ellipt. *By our Lady.* **c.** If we don't get the horse by the bargain De Foe. **d.** *By the head* (Naut.): deeper in the water forward than abaft. So *by the stern. By the board*: see Board *sb.*V. 1. **2. a.** Moving by the river side 1816. *By the way*: *lit.* in passing along; *fig.* incidentally; *ellipt.,* omitting 'it may be remarked', or the like. **b.** He that cometh not in by the dore *John* 10:1. **e.** A miss by a mile 1880. **f.** He is too moral by half Sheridan. **3. c.** Ready at the door of the hotel by nine Sterne. **4. b.** And tell what rules he did it by Butler *Hud.* i. i. 86. So *by book, by heart, by rote; by your leave, by consent,* etc. **e.** Will doe as did the Foxe by the Kidde Spenser. I know nothing by myself [R.V. against] 1 *Cor.* 4:4. **5.** I did give her a pull by the nose, and some ill words Pepys. *To set by the ears*: to set quarrelling. To live by food *A.Y.L.* ii. vii. 14, by poetry 1880. Send check by bearer 1833. So *by the hands of.* So in *To have children by, be pregnant by.* The walls of it were built by Diocletian 1682. Pipes and alcoholic liquors are superseded by matrimony 1844. **6. b.** He began by banishing 700 families Thirlwall. So in *By way of*: see Way. Phr. *By that*: therefore; Warwickes brother, and by that our foe Shaks.

B. *adv.* [In OE. the adv. may be treated either as prefix to a vb., or as a prep. following its object.] **1.** Of position: Near, close at hand, in another's presence or vicinity. See By- in comb. ME. **2.** Aside, out of the way; out of use or consideration ME. **3.** Of motion: Past a certain point, beyond. Also transf. of time. ME. † **4.** In addition, besides. also –1804.

1. Methinks you sit by very tamely Bp. Berkeley. *Stand by!* (Naut.) = be ready. *Full and by* (Naut.): sailing close-hauled to the wind. **2.** Stand by, or I shall gaul you *John* iv. iii. 95. To lay something by for a rainy day 1807. *To lie (lay) by* (Naut.): = mod. *lie to.* **3.** They marched by in pairs B. Jons.

By, bye, *a.* OE. [attrib. use of prec. *by-* in adv. (The spelling *bye* is now preferred in this use.)] **1.** *gen.* The opposite of *main.* Also *fig.* See By- in *comb.,* and By-path, etc. **2.** *fig.* **a.** Away from the main purpose, incidental, casual; **b.** of secondary importance; **c.** secret, underhand. See By-matter, By-word, etc. OE.

1. The mule preferred the high road to the bye one Southey. **2.** By and idle talke Brome. A bye effect Paley, consideration 1842.

By², **bye,** *sb.* 1567. [ellipt. use of prec. adj.] † A secondary course or matter; a side issue; usually opp. to *main* –1824. See also Bye.

Neither was the main let fall, nor time lost, upon the by North. Phr. **By the by:** by a side way, on a side issue; incidentally. *Obs.* or *arch.* Also quasi-*adj.*: Off the main track, of secondary importance 1615. Also used ellipt., with the omission of 'it may be remarked', or the like 1708.

By- in composition.

A. A ME. var. of the prefix Bi-, Be-, as *bycause* etc.

B. By- (occ. **bye-**): the prep., adv., or adj. in comb.

I. Compounds in which *by-* is a prep., as **by-rote** *a.*

II. Compounds in which *by-* has an advb. force: **a.** with senses 'beside, past'; as *by-stroller, by-flown,* etc. **b.** with sense '*aside,* Side-'; as *by-glance, -thought,* **by-wipe** (= *side-stroke*), etc. **III. 1.** Combs. in which *by* has an adjectival force: **a.** with senses 'at one side', 'out-of-the-way', 'subsidiary'; as in *by-chamber, -window,* etc. **b.** in the sense 'Running alongside and apart', 'devious', 'unfrequented', as *by-alley, -route, -wash,* etc. **c.** in sense 'Side-', as *by-issue,* etc. **d.** *hence,* 'covert', 'underhand', as *by-aim, -payment,* etc. **2.** Incidental, casual, as *by-election, -production* (= Gr. πάρεργον). **3.** Opp. to Main, as *by-feature, -form* (of a word). **4.** Counterfeit, as † **by-fruit,** a gall or the like, † **by-gold,** tinsel.

-by (bi), *suffix,* forming **1.** names of places (north.) from By *sb.*¹, as in *Grimsby,* etc. **2.** personal appellations, derisive or playful, as *idlesby, wigsby,* etc. Perh. formed after personal surnames derived from place-names, as *Littleby,* etc.

By and by (bəi· ənd bəi·, bəi· ən bəi·), *advb. phr.* (and *sb.*) ME. [See By *prep.* 4 d.] † **1.** Of a succession of things: One by one, one after another, in order –1485. † **2.** On and on, continuously –1620. **3.** Straightway, at once –1690. **4.** [Cf. *presently,* and Fr. *bientôt.*] Before long, soon. (The current sense.) 1526. † **5.** Therefore; = L. *continuo* –1631. **6.** *sb.* **a.** Procrastination; **b.** Time coming 1591.

4. To haue slayne the Prophetes before, and byanby Christ 1549.

Byard (bəi·ǎɹd). 1847. [Origin unkn.] *Mining.* A leather strap crossing the breast, used by the men who drag wagons in coal-mines. (Dicts.)

By·bidder. 1880. [See By- III. 1 c.] A person at an auction who bids with the object of raising the prices (*dial.*).

By-blow (bəi·blōᵘ). 1594. [See By- II, III. 1.] **1.** A side-blow or side-stroke (*lit.* and *fig.*). **2.** One who comes into being by a side stroke; a bastard. Also *fig.* 1595. † **3.** A blow that misses its aim –1684.

1. Now and then a by-blow from the Pulpit Milt. **3.** Now also with their by-blows, they did split the very Stones in pieces Bunyan.

† **By-boat.** 1698. [f. By-.] ? An extra boat. Used esp. of the Newfoundland fishery –1796.

† **By·-chop.** [See By-, By-blow, By-slip.] A bastard. B. Jons.

† **Bycoket.** 1464. [– OFr. *bicoquet* ornate military head-dress (etc.), of uncertain etym.] A kind of cap or head-dress (peaked before and behind). ¶Through a series of blunders *a bicocket,* misprinted *abococket,* was turned into Abacot, in which form it appears in mod. dictionaries.

By·-corner; see By- III. 1 a.

Bye (bəi). 1603. [var. of By *prep.* used subst.] **1. a.** *Cricket.* A run scored for a ball which passes the batsman, and is missed by the wicket-keeper and long-stop 1746. **b.** in *Tennis, Boxing,* etc.: The position of an individual who is left without a competitor when the rest have been drawn in pairs 1883. **c.** in *Lacrosse,* etc.: A goal, a starting line 1841. **d.** A by-match or event 1884. **2.** The name of a plot against the government of James I. (Distinguished from the *Main* plot.) 1603.

† **Bye, by,** *v.* ME. [aphet. f. Aby, Abye *v.*] **1.** = Aby *v.* 2, Buy *v.* 3. –1599. **2.** *absol.* = Aby *v.* 4. ME. only. **3.** *intr.* = Aby *v.* 5. –1594.

Bye-bye¹ (bəi·bəi:). [Late ME. *byby byby by* (xv); cf. ON. *bi bi* and *bium bium.*] A sound used to lull a child to sleep; *hence,* 'sleep' or 'bed'.

Bye-bye² (bəi·bəi·). 1709. Colloq. var. of Good-bye.

By·-end; see By- III. 1 c, d.

† **By-fellow.** 1856. [See By- III. 3.] A fellow of a college not on the foundation.

Bygoing (bəi·gōᵘ:iŋ), *vbl. sb.* 1637. [f. By- II. a.] The action of passing by; *esp.* in *In the b.*: in passing.

Bygone, by-gone (bəi·gǫn). ME. [f. By- II. a.] **A.** *ppl. a.* **1.** That has gone by; that has happened in past time; former. † **b.** Ago. Swift. **2.** Deceased. Also *transf.* 1513. **B.** *sb.* **1.** *pl.* Things (*esp.* offences) that are past 1568. **b.** Arrears 1663. **2.** The past (*rare*) 1872.

1. B. shall be b.; the new Era shall begin Carlyle.

† **By·land.** 1577. A peninsula –1630.

Bylander, obs. f. Bilander.

By-lane (bəi·lēⁱ:n). 1587. [f. By- III. 1 b.] A side lane; *also,* a side passage in a mine.

By-law, bye-law (bəi·lǭ). ME. [In sense 1 orig. varying with *birlaw* Byrlaw (xiii) – ON. **býjarlagu,* f. gen. sing. of *býr* habitation, village, town (f. **bū-*; cf. Bower) + **lagu* law; in senses 2 and 3 alt. of this by substitution of By *sb.*¹ town and by assoc. w. By-.] † **1.** Var. of Byrlaw. **b.** Often used spec. of ordinances made by common consent in a Court-leet or Court-baron 1607. **2.** A law or ordinance dealing with matters of local or internal regulation, made by a local authority, or by a corporation or association ME. **3.** A secondary, subordinate, or accessory law 1541.

2. There was likewise a law to restrain the by-laws, or ordinances of corporations Bacon. By lawes wᶜʰ the..Schollers..have made 1523, *Sel. Records Oxford.* **3.** In detail, or what may be called the by-laws of each art Sir J. Reynolds. Hence **By·lawman** = Byrlaw-man.

† **By·live, by·lif(e.** [OE. *bīgleofa,* f. *bīġ, bi* from, etc. (see By) + *līf* Life, *-leofa* living.] That which one lives by; living, sustenance –ME.

By-matter (bəi·mæ:təɹ). 1552. [f. By- III. 1 c, 3.] A side incident; a trivial matter.

Dissenters and Scruplers in by-matters 1674.

Byname, by-name (bəi·nēⁱm), *sb.* ME. [f. By- III. 3.] **1.** A name other than the main one; *esp.* a surname; a sobriquet. **2.** A nick-name 1580.

1. Lions-heart, is..the by-name of K. Richard 1631. **2.** Mr. Welbore Ellis. the butt of Junius, under the by-name of Grildrig Earl Stanhope. Hence **By·name** *v.* to surname, to nickname.

By-pass (bəi·pɑs). 1848. [By- B. III. 1 b, Pass *sb.*¹] **1.** A secondary pipe to allow the free passage of gas, etc.; *esp.* the small tube and pilot light which remains alight when a gas-jet is turned off. **2.** A road diverging from and re-entering a main road, esp. for the relief of congestion 1922. Also as vb.

Bypast, by-past (bəi·pɑst), *ppl. a.* ME. [By- II. a.] Gone by, elapsed; former.

Bypath, by-path (bəi·pɑþ). ME. [f. By- III. 1 b.] A side path; a private or unfrequented path. Also *fig.* (Formerly in a bad sense.)

fig. By-pathes, and indirect crook'd wayes Shaks.

By-play (bəi·plēⁱ). 1812. [f. By- III. 1 c.] Action carried on aside, and often in dumb-show, during the main action. Also *transf.*

By-product (bəi·prǫ:dɒkt). 1857. [f. BY- III. 2, 3.] A secondary product; a substance obtained in the course of a specific process, but not its primary object.

Byre (bəiᵊɹ). [OE. *bȳre*, prob. rel. to BOWER *sb.*[1]] A cow-house.

He had beeves in the b. BARHAM.

† **By·-respe:ct**; see BY- III. 1 c, d.

Byrla·dy, *int.* Still *dial.* 1570. Contr. of *by our Lady*.

† **Byrla·kin.** 1528. Contr. of *by our Lady-kin* –1625.

By·rlaw. *arch.* or *dial.* ME. [– ON. **bȳjarlagu*; see BY-LAW, BYE-LAW.] **1.** The local custom or law of a township, manor, or rural district, whereby disputes as to boundaries, trespass of cattle, etc., were settled without going into the law courts. **2.** *transf.* A district having its own byr-law court, or local law 1850. Hence in Yorkshire place-names, as *Brampton Bierlow*, etc.

By·rlawman. ME. [f. prec.] An officer appointed at a Court-leet for duties connected with the framing and execution of byrlaws. Also called **Bierlaw-grayves** (see GREAVE).

By·rnie. Now *Hist.* ME. [Sc. var. of ME. *brinie* (XII–XV) – ON. *brynja*.] A coat of mail.

By·-road. 1673. [f. BY- III. 1 b.] A road which is not a main road; a little frequented road.

Byronic (bəirǫ·nik), *a.* 1823. [Cf. MILTONIC.] **1.** Characteristic of, or after the manner of, Byron or his poetry. Also *absol.* **2.** quasi-*sb. pl.* [after *philippics*.] Declamation or invective in the style of Byron 1850.

1. A B. youth in a turn-down collar 1856. B. mock heroics FROUDE. So **By·ronism,** the characteristics of Byron or his poetry; imitation of Byron.

By·-room; see BY- III. 1 a.

‖ **Byrsa** (bɔ̄·ɹsă). 1811. [Late L. – Gr. βύρσα hide.] *Med.* A leather skin, to spread plasters upon.

† **By·-slip.** 1612. [f. BY- II. b.] **1.** A trivial fault. **2.** *transf.* A bastard 1670.

†**By·-speech**; see BY- II, III. 1 c.

† **By·-spel, bi·spel.** [ME. *bispell*, OE. *bīspell*, f. *bī* BY + SPELL *sb.*[1] story.] **1.** A parable. **2.** A proverb –1656.

† **Byss,** *sb.* ME. [– OFr. *bysse* – L. *byssus*; see BYSSUS.] = BYSSUS 1; fine linen –1648.

Byssa·ceous, *a.* 1835. [f. BYSSUS; see -ACEOUS.] *Bot.* Composed of fine entangled threads.

Byssi·ferous, *a.* 1835. [f. as prec. + -FEROUS.] *Zool.* Furnished with a byssus.

Byssine (bi·sin), *a.* ME. [– L. *byssinus* – Gr. βύσσινος.] **1.** Made of byssus 1656. **2.** quasi-*sb.* [L. *byssinum*.] = BYSS *sb.*

By·ssoid, *a.* 1857. [f. BYSSUS + -OID.] *Bot.* Like a byssus, byssaceous.

Byssolite (bi·sǒləit). 1847. [f. Gr. βύσσος + -LITE.] An olive-green variety of hornblende.

Byssus (bi·sǒs). ME. [– L. *byssus* – Gr. βύσσος, of Sem. origin. See BYSS.] **1.** An exceedingly fine and valuable textile fibre and fabric known to the ancients; it denoted properly a kind of flax, but was used also of cotton, silk, etc. † **2.** A name for filamentous fungoid growths, which are now more accurately classified –1838. **3.** *Zool.* The tuft of fine silky filaments by which molluscs of the genus *Pinna* and various mussels attach themselves to the surface of rocks; it is secreted by the *byssus-gland* in the foot 1836. **4.** *Bot.* The thread-like stipe of some fungi 1866. † **5.** Asbestos.

1. The fayrest of al [flexe] growyth in Egypte; for therof is Bissus made ryght fayre and whyte as snowe TREVISA.

Bystander (bəi·stæ:ndəɹ). 1619. [f. BY- II. a.] One who is standing by; a spectator.

Such an act, either in Executioner or b., is in no way justifiable DONNE.

By·-street; see BY- III. 1 b.

By-term (bəi·təɹm). 1579. [f. BY- III. 3, 4.] † **1.** A nickname. **2.** In Univ. of Cambridge: A term which is not the main one for entering or for taking degrees 1883.

By·-thing; see BY- III. 2, 3.

By·-time; see BY- III. 2.

By·-turning; see BY- III. 1 b.

By·-view. ? *Obs.* 1731. [f. BY- II. b, III. 1 c, d.] **a.** A side glance or glimpse. **b.** An unavowed or self-interested aim.

No by views of his own shall mislead him ATTERBURY.

By·-walk; see BY- III. 1 b.

Byward (bəi·wǭɹd), *sb.* 1840. [f. BY- III. 1, 3.] A ward or guard which is not the main one; as in the *B. Tower* of the Tower of London.

By-way (bəi·wēⁱ). ME. [f. BY- III. 1 b.] A way other than the highway; a secluded, private, or unfrequented way. Also *transf.* or *fig.*; often depreciatively.

The by-ways and short-cuts to wealth D. JERROLD.

By-west; see BY *prep.* 1 d.

By-wipe; see BY- II. b.

By-word (bəi·wǒɹd). OE. [ME. *bīword*, preceded by late OE. *bīwyrde* = OHG. *bīwurti*, rendering L. *proverbium*; see BY *a.* 2.] **1.** A proverbial saying. **2.** A person or thing that becomes proverbial, as an object of scorn or contempt 1535. **b.** A byname 1598. † **3.** A trick of speech, pet phrase –1710. † **4.** A hint; a word beside the matter in hand –1658.

1. Is it not a by word, like will to like LYLY. **2.** Israel shall be a prouerbe, and a by-word among all people 1 *Kings* 9:7.

By-work (bəi·wǒɹk). 1587. [f. BY- III.] **1.** Work done in by-times; = Gr. πάρεργον; also, work done with ulterior motives. **2.** An accessory work. ? *Obs.* 1587.

Byzantian (bizæ·nʃⁱăn), *a.* and *sb.* 1619. [f. L. *Byzantius* + -AN; see next.] = next.

Byzantine (bizæ·ntəin, bi·zæ̆ntəin). 1599. [– Fr. *byzantin* or L. *Byzantinus*, f. *Byzantium*; see BEZANT, -INE[1].] **A.** *adj.* Belonging to Byzantium or Constantinople. **b.** *spec.* Pertaining to the style of art, *esp.* of architecture, developed in the Eastern division of the Roman Empire. The Byzantine architecture makes special use of the round arch, cross, circle, dome, and rich mosaic work. 1848. **c.** Pertaining to the (style of music of the) Eastern Church.

B. historians: those who lived in the Eastern Empire from the 6th to the 15th c.

B. *sb.* **1.** An inhabitant of Byzantium 1656. **2.** = BEZANT 1. 1599. † **3.** = BEZANT 2. 1605.

2. A Bizantin, which is..six pence sterling HAKLUYT. So also **Byza:ntine·sque** *a.* in the B. style of art. **Byza·ntinism,** the style and method of art developed in the B. empire. **Byza·ntinize** *v. trans.* to make B.

C

C (*sī*), the third letter of the Roman alphabet, was orig. identical with the Greek *Gamma*, Γ, and Semitic *Gimel*, whence its form. In earlier Latin, it functioned both as (g) and (k); but subseq. it stood for the (k) sound only.

When the Roman alphabet was introduced into Britain, C had only the sound (k). The present value of C is the result of developments which took place both in Britain and on the continent during the time covered by the OE. and ME. periods. (See O.E.D.)

In mod. English, C has (1) the 'hard' sound (k) bef. *a*, *o*, *u*, bef. a cons. (exc. *h*), and when final; (2) bef. *e*, *i*, *y* it has the soft sound (s). In all words from OE. and OFr., final *c* is avoided: the (k) sound being written *k*, or *ck*, as in *beak*, *book*, etc. Final *c*, however, is written in mod. words from Latin, Greek, or other langs., and (of late) in the ending *-ic*, as in *sac*, *epic*, *critic*, etc. But where this *c* is followed in inflexion by *e* or *i*, it is changed to *ck*, as in *physicking*, *pic-nicker*, etc. When the (s) sound is final, it must be written *-ce*, as in *trace*, *ice*, etc., and this final *e* is retained in composition bef. *a*, *o*, *u*, as in *trace-able*, etc. (3) *Ci* (rarely *ce*) preceding another vowel has frequently the sound of (ʃ), *esp.* in the endings *-cious*, *-cial*, *-cion*, as *atrocious*, etc. This sound (which is also taken by *t* in the same position) is comparatively modern.

In foreign words, *c* occas. retains the foreign pronunciation, as in It. *cicerone* (tʃitʃerō·ne).

C springs: see CEE (springs): **C clef:** see CLEF[1].

II. Used to denote serial order with the value of 'third', as quire C. *spec.* **a.** in *Music*: The key-note of the 'natural' major scale. Also, the scale which has that note for its tonic. **b.** In *abstract reasoning*, *law*, etc.: Any third person or thing. **C 3:** the lowest grade of physical fitness for military service; hence *fig.*

III. Abbreviations. **1.** C, now rarely c. = L. *centum* a hundred; so CC = 200, CCCC or CD = 400; formerly written ii.c., etc. Also, formerly = cwt. **2.** *Mus.* 'As a sign of time C stands for common time, 4 crotchets in a bar; and ₵ for allabreve time, with 2 or 4 minims in a bar' (Grove). C = Counter-tenor, or Contralto; C.F. = *canto fermo*. **3.** C. = various proper names, as Charles; C = Cardinal (*obs.*); C (*Chem.*) Carbon; C (*Electricity*) current; C. = Centigrade (thermometer); c. chapter; c. century; c. (*Cricket*) caught; *c.* (bef. a date) = L. *circa* about; C.A. Chartered Accountant (*Sc.*); C.B. Companion of the Bath; C.E. Civil Engineer; C.S. Civil Service; C. of E. (sī:əvi ī·) Church of England.

Ca', mod. Sc. f. CALL *sb.* and *v.*, call, drive.

‖ **Caaba** (kā·bă). 1734. [– Arab. *ka'ba* square or cubical house.] The sacred edifice at Mecca, which contains the 'black stone' and is the 'Holy of Holies' of Islam.

This is the C., which is usually called, by way of eminence, *the House* SALE. var. **Kaaba.**

Caam (kām). 1792. [Origin unkn.] The HEDDLES of a loom.

‖ **Cab** (kæb), *sb.*[1] Also **kab.** 1535. [– Heb. *ḳaḇ*, measure of capacity (2 *Kings* 6:25).] A Heb. dry measure; about 2⅞ imperial pints.

† **Cab,** *sb.*[2] 1650. Abbrev. of *cavalier* (or Sp. *caballero*).

Cab (kæb), *sb.*[3] 1827. **1.** Abbrev. of CABRIOLET, but applied more widely; a public carriage with two or four wheels, drawn by one horse, and seating two or four persons. **2.** The covered part of a locomotive, which shelters the drivers 1864.

1. Cabs—or cabriolets..—were not known to us until 1820. 1860. *Comb.*; **c.-rank,** a row of cabs on a stand; **-stand,** a place where cabs are authorized to stand while waiting for hire.

Cab (kæb), *sb.*[4] *slang.* 1876. [Short for CABBAGE *sb.*[2]] A crib used by a pupil in getting up his lessons.

Cab (kæb), *v.*[1] *colloq.* 1858. [f. CAB *sb.*[3]] *intr.* (also *to c. it*): To go in a cab.

Cab, *v.*[2] *slang.* [Short for CABBAGE *v.*[2]] To pilfer; to crib.

‖ **Cabaan, caban** (kăbā·n). 1693. [– Arab. and Pers. *ḳabā'*.] A white cloth worn by Arabs over their shoulders.

Cabal (kăbæ·l), *sb.* 1616. [– Fr. *cabale* – med.L. *cab(b)ala* (It., Sp. *cabala*); see CABBALA.] † **1.** = CABBALA 1. –1663. † **2.** = CABBALA 2. –1763. **3.** A private intrigue of a sinister character formed by a small body of persons 1646. **b.** = Caballing 1734. **4.** A secret meeting, *esp.* of intriguers or of a faction (*arch.*) 1649. **5.** A small body of persons engaged in private machination or intrigue; a junto 1660. **6.** Applied in the reign of Charles II to a small committee of the Privy Council, which was the precursor of the modern *cabinet* 1665. **b.** in *Hist.* applied *spec.* to the five ministers of Charles II, viz. Clifford, Arlington, Buckingham, Ashley, and Lauderdale, who signed the Treaty of Alliance with France in 1672; the initials of their names made up the word *cabal* 1673. Also *attrib.*

3. The c. against Washington BANCROFT. **b.** Centres of c. BURKE. **5.** A c. of artists 1859. **6.** It being read before the King, Duke, and the Caball PEPYS.

Cabal (kăbæ·l), *v.* 1680. [f. prec.] **1.** *intr.* To combine (*together*) for some private end. (Usu. in a bad sense.) **2.** *intr.* To intrigue privately (*against*) 1680. **3.** *refl.* To bring *oneself* by caballing. BURKE.

2. Time has been given to c. to sow dissensions, etc. 1789. Hence † **Cabalist, Caba·ller,** one who cabals. **Caba·lling** *vbl. sb.* petty plotting, intriguing.

Cabala, var. of CABBALA; also = CABAL (*rare*).

Cabalic, -al, -ism, etc.; see CABBALIC, etc.

† **Ca·ball.** 1450. [prob. var. of CAPLE assoc. w. L. *caballus* horse.] A horse –1650.

‖ **Cabalerro** (ka:balʸe·ro). 1877. [Sp., = Fr. *chevalier*, It. *cavaliere*; see CAVALIER.] A (Spanish) gentleman.

Caballine (ka·băləin), *a.* ME. [– L. *caballinus*, f. *caballus* horse; see -INE[1].] Of or belonging to horses; equine.

C. fountain = L. *fons caballinus*, the fountain Hippocrene, fabled to have been produced by a stroke of the foot of Pegasus the winged horse of the Muses; hence = 'fountain of inspiration'.

Caban, cabane, earliest ff. CABIN. Used occ. for local colouring (French or Canadian).

‖ **Cabana** (kăbā·nă). 1864. [f. name of a Spanish exporting house.] The name of a cigar.

‖ **Cabaret** (kæ·bărei). 1655. [– (O)Fr., prob. of Walloon origin and orig. denoting a structure of wood; in med.L. *cabaretus*.] **1.** A drinking-shop. **2.** A restaurant where singing and dancing are provided during a meal; also, the entertainment itself 1915.

1. Sung two or three years ago in cabarets DRYDEN.

Cabbage (kæ·bėdʒ), *sb.*[1] [Earliest forms *cabache, -oche* – (O)Fr. *caboche* head, Picard var. of OFr. *caboce*, of unkn. origin. For the development of the final consonant cf. *knowledge, partridge, sausage, spinach.*] **1.** A plane-leaved cultivated variety of *Brassica oleracea*. Orig. the 'cabbage' was the 'head' formed by the unexpanded leaves of *B. oleracea*; now the name includes the whole species or genus, whether hearting or not, as in *Savoy C.*, *Wild C.*, etc. **2.** Used with epithets of other plants: **Chinese C.,** *Brassica chinensis*; **Dog's C.,** *Thelygonum cynocrambe*, a succulent herb of the Mediterranean; **Kerguelen's Land C.,** *Pringlea antiscorbutica*; **Meadow** or **Skunk C.,** *Symplocarpus fœtidus*; **St. Patrick's C.** = LONDON PRIDE; **Sea C.** = SEA-KALE; **Sea-Otter's C.,** *Nereocystis*. **3.** The terminal bud of palm trees. See CABBAGE-TREE. 1638. † **4.** The burr whence spring the horns of a deer –1611.

1. Take cabaches and cut hom on foure..and let hit boyle 1440.

Comb.: **c. bark,** the narcotic and anthelmintic bark of the **c.-bark tree** or CABBAGE-TREE, *Andira inermis* (N.O. *Leguminosæ*); **c. beetle** = *cabbage flea*; **c. butterfly,** the Large White Butterfly of English gardens and fields, *Pieris brassicæ*, occ. also the small White (*P. rapæ*); **-cole** = sense 1; **-flea,** a minute leaping beetle, *Haltica consobrina*, the larvæ of which destroy c. plants; **-fly,** a two-winged fly (*Anthomyia brassicæ*), the grubs of which destroy the roots of c.; **-head,** see sense 1; *fig.* a brainless fellow; **-lettuce,** a lettuce forming a c.-like head; **-moth,** one of the Noctuina (*Mamestra brassicæ*), the caterpillar of which infests the c.; **-palm,** *Areca oleracea*, a native of the West Indies, etc.; see CABBAGE-TREE; **-plant,** a young seedling of the c.; **-rose,** a double red rose, with large round compact flower (*Rosa centifolia*); **-wood,** (*a.*) the wood of the cabbage-tree, (*b.*) *Eriodendron anfractuosum*, a tree related to *Bombax*; **-worm,** any larva which devours c. Hence **Ca·bbagy** *a. rare.*

Cabbage (kæ·bėdʒ), *sb.*[2] 1663. [Of unkn. origin. Herrick has *carbage* and *garbage* in the same sense, 1648.] **1.** Shreds (or large pieces) of cloth appropriated by tailors in cutting out clothes. † **2.** *slang.* A tailor –1725. **3.** *Schoolboy slang.* A crib; = CAB *sb.*[4]

Ca·bbage, *v.*[1] 1528. [f. CABBAGE *sb.*[1]] † **1.** *intr.* To grow to a head, as the horns of a deer. **b.** To form a head, as a cabbage 1601. **2.** *trans.* See CABOCHE *v.* 1530.

Ca·bbage, *v.*[2] 1712. [f. CABBAGE *sb.*[2] Cf. OFr. *cabas* deceit, theft, Du. *kabassen* pilfer.] To appropriate surreptitiously, as a tailor does shreds. **b.** *Schoolboy slang.* To crib 1837.

Your taylor..cabages whole yards of cloath 1712.

Ca·bbage-tree. 1725. [f. CABBAGE *sb.*[1] 1, 2.] **1.** Any palm tree, whose terminal bud is eaten like the head of a cabbage; *esp.* **a.** The West Indian tree, *Areca* or *Oreodoxa oleracea*, also called *Cabbage-palm* and *Palmetto Royal*. **b.** *Chamærops palmetto* of the Southern U.S. **c.** *Euterpe oleracea* of Brazil. **d.** *Livistona inermis* of N. Australia. **e.** *Corypha australis* of Australia. **2.** Other plants and trees, as the Cabbage-bark Tree, *Andira inermis* of the West Indies; *Cordyline indivisa* of New Zealand. **Bastard** or **Black C. T.,** *Andira inermis* (see above);—of St. Helena: *Melanodendron integrifolium*;—of S. America: the leguminous genus *Geoffroya*. **Canary Island C. T.,** *Cacolia kleinia nervifolia*, a composite plant. **Small Umbelled C. T.,** *Commidendron spurium*.

‖ **Cabbala** (kæ·bălă). 1521. [– med.L. *cabbala* – Rabbinical Heb. *ḳabbālā* tradition, f. *ḳibbel* receive, accept.] **1.** The oral tradition handed down from Moses to the Rabbis of the Mishnah and the Talmud. **b.** Later, the pretended tradition of the mystical interpretation of the Old Testament. **2.** *gen.* † **a.** An unwritten tradition –1692. **b.** Mystery, esoteric doctrine or art 1665.

1. Cabala..is derived fro man to man by mouth only and not by wrytynge FISHER. **2. b.** Doctors in the cabala of political science BURKE. Hence, **Cabba·lic** *a.* of or pertaining to the C. var. **Cabala.**

Cabbalism (kæ·băliz'm). 1590. [f. prec. + -ISM.] **1.** The system or manner of the Jewish Cabbala 1614. **2.** Occult doctrine; mystery 1590. **3.** ? (Cf. CABAL, CABALIST.) 1847.

3. I do not know that there is more Cabalism in the Anglican, than in other Churches EMERSON. var. **Cabalism.**

Cabbalist (kæ·bălist). 1533. [– Fr. *cabaliste*, f. as prec. + -IST; cf. med.L. *cabbalista*.] **1.** One versed in the Jewish Cabbala. **2.** One skilled in mystic arts or learning 1592.

2. Cupid is a casuist, A mystic and a cabalist EMERSON. var. **Cabalist.**

Cabbalistic, -al (kæbăli·stik, -ăl), *a.* Also **cabal-.** 1624. [f. prec. + -IC, or – Fr. *cabalistique*.] Of, pertaining to, or like the Cabbala or cabbalists; having a mystic sense; occult.

Certain..cabalistic signs upon the skull TYLOR. Hence **Cabbali·stically** *adv.*

† **Ca·bbalize,** *v.* Also **cabal-.** 1660. [f. as prec.; see -IZE.] *intr.* To use the manner of the cabbalists; to speak mystically.

Ca·bber. *colloq.* [f. CAB *sb.*[3] + -ER[1].] A cab-horse.

Ca·bbing, *vbl. sb.* 1870. [f. CAB *sb.*[3] + -ING[1].] Cab-driving, cab-letting. Also *attrib.*

Cabble (kæ·b'l), *v.* 1849. [var. of SCABBLE; of unkn. origin.] *Iron-smelting.* To break up flat pieces of partially finished iron for faggoting. Hence **Ca·bbler.**

Ca·bby. *colloq.* 1859. [f. CAB *sb.*[3] + -Y[6].] A cab-driver.

Caber (kē[i]·bəɹ). 1513. [– Gael. *cabar* = Ir. *cabar*, W. *ceibr* beam, rafter.] A pole or spar, usually consisting of the stem of a young pine or fir-tree, used in scaffolding, etc.; and *esp.* in the Highland exercise of *throwing* or *tossing the caber*.

Ca·bful. 1856. [f. CAB *sb.*[3] + -FUL.] As much or as many as a cab will hold.

Cabiai (ka·bi͵ai). 1774. [Fr. – Galibi (or Carib. of French Guiana).] The Capybara (*Hydrochœrus capybara*).

‖ **Cabilliau, cabeliau** (ka·bilyō, kă·bėlyau). 1696. [– Du. *kabeljau*, whence also Fr. *cabillaud*.] Cod-fish; 'also, a dish of cod mashed'.

Cabin (kæ·bin). [Late ME. *cabane* – (O)Fr. *cabane* – Pr. *cabana* = It. *capanna* – late L. *capanna* (according to Isidore, a rustic word), *cavanna*.] † **1.** A booth, hut, (soldier's) tent, or other temporary shelter –1649. **2.** A permanent mud or turf-built hovel, or the like ME. *rhet.* = 'poor dwelling' 1598. † **3.** A cell –1616. † **b.** A small room –1620. † **4.** A natural cave; a wild beast's den –1794. **5.** A compartment in a vessel for eating or sleeping in; an apartment in a ship for officers or passengers ME. Also, † a berth –1769. † **6.** A litter –1631. † **7.** A (political) CABINET –1676.

1. Make me a willow Cabine at your gate *Twel. N.* I. v. 287. **2.** A mud c. here and there 1832. Uncle Tom's Cabin (*title*) 1850. **5.** Keepe your Cabines ..you do assist the storme SHAKS. *Comb.* **c.-boy,** a boy who waits on the officers and passengers on board.

Cabin (kæ·bin), *v.* 1586. [f. the sb.] **1.** *intr.* To dwell, lodge, in, or as in, a cabin (senses 1–4). **2.** *trans.* To lodge, shelter, as in a cabin 1602. **3.** *trans.* To shut up within narrow bounds. (Mostly after Shaks.) 1605.

1. And sucke the Goate, And cabbin in a Caue *Tit. A.* IV. ii. 179. **3.** Now I am cabin'd, crib'd, confin'd, bound in *Macb.* III. iv. 24.

Cabined (kæ·bind), *ppl. a.* 1592. [f. CABIN *sb.* and *v.* + -ED.] Made like a cabin; furnished with a cabin; confined in narrow space; *fig.* confined in action, thought, etc.

Cabinet (kæ·binėt). 1549. [Eng. dim. of CABIN; influenced in senses 3–6 by Fr. *cabinet* – It. *gabinetto* 'closet, press, chest of drawers'.] **I.** (Cf. BOWER 1–3.) † **1.** A little cabin, hut, soldier's tent; a rustic cottage; a lodging, tabernacle; a den of a beast –1640. † **2.** A summerhouse or bower –1737. **3.** A small chamber; a private room, a boudoir (*arch.*) 1565. † **4.** A museum, picture-gallery, etc. –1796. **5.** A case for the safe custody of jewels, letters, documents, etc.; and thus, a piece of furniture, often ornamental, fitted with drawers, shelves, etc., for the preservation and display of specimens 1550. † **6.** *fig.* A secret receptacle, treasure-chamber; *arcanum*, etc. –1667. ¶Short for *Cabinet photograph*.

3. Cabinets shalt thou make in the arke *Gen.* 6 : 14. **5.** The best jewel in the best c. DONNE.

II. In politics. **1.** (cf. I. 3) The private room in which the chief ministers of a country meet; the council-chamber. Now = 'political consultation and action'. 1607. **b.** Those who meet in the cabinet. (Formerly called the *Cabinet Council*, as opp. to the *Privy Council*.) 1644. † **c.** A meeting of this body. Now called a 'Cabinet council', or 'meeting of the Cabinet'. –1805. **2. Cabinet Council: a.** the earlier name of *the Cabinet*; see II. 1 b. 1625. **b.** *now*, A meeting of the Cabinet 1679. **3. Cabinet Counsellor,** a private counsellor; a member of the Cabinet 1611.

1. a. Equally great in the c. as in the field WELLINGTON. **b.** The members of the President's C. 1874.

III. *attrib.*, etc. **1.** Of the cabinet; private, secret 1607. **2.** Fitted for a private chamber, or worthy to be kept in a cabinet. Occ. technical, as in *c. edition*, *c. organ*, *c. photograph*, *c. piano*, etc. 1696. **3.** Fit for cabinet-making, as *c. woods* 1849. **4.** Of or pertaining to the political cabinet, as *c. minister*, etc. 1817.

1. His private C. devotions CLARENDON. **2.** It is quite a c. picture MISS MITFORD. *Comb.* **c.-sized** *a.* of fit size for placing in a c.; (a photograph) of the size larger than a carte-de-visite.

Ca·binet, *v.* 1642. [f. prec.] To enclose in or as in a cabinet.

Ca·binet-ma:ker. 1681. **1.** One whose business it is to make cabinets (sense I. 5), and fine joiner's work. **2.** *casual.* One who constructs a political cabinet 1884.

Cable (kē[i]·b'l), *sb.* [– AFr., ONFr. **cable*, var. of OFr. *chable* (mod. *câble* – Pr. *cable*) :– late L. *cap(u)lum* halter – Arab. *ḥabl*, assoc. with L. *capere* seize, hold; perh., however, immed. – Pr. *cable*, and in any case reinforced by (M)LG., (M)Du. *kabel*, of Rom. origin.] **1.** A strong thick rope, orig. of hemp or other fibre, now also of strands of iron wire. Also *fig.* **2.** *spec.* (*Naut.*) The thick rope to which a ship's anchor is fastened; hence, anything used for the same purpose, as a chain of iron links (*chain cable*) ME. Also *fig.* **b.** = *a cable's length*, 'about 100 fathoms; in marine charts 607·56 feet' (Smyth). **3.** *Telegraphy.* A rope-like line used for submarine telegraphs, containing a core of insulated conducting wires encased in an outer sheathing of strong wire strands. Also **b.** a bundle of insulated wires, passing through a pipe laid underground. 1854. **c.** A CABLEGRAM 1883. **4.** *Arch.*, etc. (also *cable-moulding*): A convex moulding made in the form of a rope 1859.

1. A threfolde c. is not lightly broken *Eccles.* 4:12. **2.** The c. broke, the holding-Anchor lost SHAKS. **3.** Reported by c. to have put into St. Thomas 1880.

Comb.: **c.-bends,** 'two small ropes for lashing the end of a hempen c. to its own part, in order to secure the clinch by which it is fastened to the anchor-ring' (Smyth); **-buoy,** a cask employed to buoy up the c.; **-laid,** *a.*, composed of three main strands, each composed of three smaller strands; **-rope** = sense 1; also c.-laid rope; **-stock,** the capstan; **-tier,** the place in a hold, or between decks, where the cables are coiled away; **-tools,** the apparatus used in drilling deep holes, such as artesian wells, etc.

Cable (kē[i]·b'l), *v.* 1500. [f. the sb.] **1.** To furnish with a cable or cables; to fasten with or as with a cable, to tie *up*. **2.** *Arch.* To furnish (a column) with cable-mouldings (see CABLE *sb.* 4) 1766. **3.** *trans.* and *intr.* To transmit (a message, etc.), or communicate by submarine telegraph 1871.

1. Here I am cabled up above their shot SHIRLEY. **3.** The exciting news cabled from Ireland 1880.

Cablegram (kē[i]·b'lgræm). 1868. [f. CABLE *sb.* + -GRAM, after *telegram*.] A message sent by submarine telegraphic cable.

Cablet (kēⁱ·blėt). 1575. [f. CABLE *sb.* + -ET.] A small cable or cable-laid rope less than 10 inches in circumference.

† **Ca·blish.** 1594. [– AFr. *cablis (OFr. *chaablis*) = Fr. *chablis* (in *bois chablis* XVI), f. OFr. *chaabler* break off branches of trees; in med.L. *cablicium, cablicia* (XIII) wind-fallen wood.] Strictly, windfalls, but explained in 16th c. as = brushwood –1852.

Cabman (kæ·bmæ̆n). 1835. [f. CAB *sb.*[3]] The driver of a public cab.

Cabob (kăbǫ·b). Also **kabob.** 1690. [– Urdu (Pers.) – Arab. *kabāb.*] **1.** An oriental dish of meat roasted in small pieces on skewers; in India = roast meat in general. (Now in *pl.*) 1698. **2.** A leg of mutton stuffed with white herrings and sweet herbs 1690. Hence **Cabo·b** *v.* to cook thus.

‖ **Caboceer** (kæbosīᵊ·ɹ). 1836. [– Pg. *caboceiro*, f. *cabo* head; cf. -EER.] The headman (of a W. Afr. village or tribe).

† **Cabo·che,** *v.* ME. [– Fr. *cabocher*, f. *caboche* head, var. of OFr. *caboce*, see CABBAGE *sb.*[1]] To cut off the head of (a deer) close behind the horns.

Caboched, caboshed, cabossed (kăbǫ·ʃt, kăbǫ·st), *ppl. a.* 1572. [– Fr. *caboché*, pa. pple. of *cabocher*; see prec., -ED[1].] *Her.* Borne (as the head of a stag, bull, etc.) full-faced, and cut off close behind the ears; trunked.

‖ **Cabochon** (kaboʃoṅ·). 1578. [– (O)Fr. *cabochon*, dim. of *caboche* head; see prec., -OON.] A precious stone, as a garnet, etc., when merely polished, without being cut into facets or shaped. Chiefly *attrib.*

Caboodle (kăbū·d'l). orig. *U.S.* 1848. [perh. contr. of *whole kit and boodle*; see BOODLE.] *The whole c.*, the whole lot.

Caboose (kăbū·s). 1769. [– early mod.Du. *cabūse*, var. *combūse* (now *kabuis, kombuis*) = (M)LG. *kabūse*, of unkn. origin.] **1.** The cook-room of merchantmen on deck. **b.** A cooking-oven or fire-place on land 1859. **2.** *U.S.* A van or car on a freight train used by workmen or the men in charge 1881.

‖ **Cabot** (kabo, kæ·bət). 1611. [In sense 1 – OFr. *cabot*, (also mod.) *chabot*, ult. f. L. *caput* head; see -OT[1].] † **1.** The Miller's Thumb. **2.** In the Channel Islands, a half-bushel 1835.

Cabotage (kæ·bŏtėdʒ). 1831. [– Fr. *cabotage*, f. *caboter* coast along, perh. f. † *cabo* (XVI) – Sp. *cabo* CAPE *sb.*[2]] Coasting; coast-pilotage; the coast carrying trade by sea.

‖ **Cabré** (kabre), *a.* [Fr., pa. pple. of *cabrer*; see CAPER *v.*[1]] *Her.* Said of a horse: Capering, rearing on the hind legs.

‖ **Ca·brie, ca·brit.** 1807. [f. Sp. *cabrito*, dim. of *cabra* goat.] The Pronghorn Antelope.

† **Ca·briole.** 1785. [– Fr. *cabriole*, f. *cabrioler*, orig. *caprioler* – It. *capriolare* leap into the air; cf. CAPRIOLE.] **1.** A capriole, a caper (of a horse) 1814. **2.** A kind of small arm-chair 1785. **3.** = CABRIOLET –1801.

Cabriolet (ka·bri,olēⁱ·). 1823. [– Fr. *cabriolet*, f. *cabriole*, so called from its bounding motion; see prec., -ET.] A two-wheeled one-horse chaise with a large hood.

Caburn (kæ·bəɹn). 1626. [Origin unkn.] *Naut.* (*pl.*) 'Spun rope-yarn lines, for worming a cable, seizing, winding tacks', etc. (Smyth).

‖ **Cacafue·go.** 1625. [Sp.] A spit-fire, braggart.

Ca'canny (ka,kæ·ni). 1896. [f. Sc. and north. Eng. phr. *ca' canny*, i.e. CA' 'drive' (see CALL *v.* III), CANNY used advb. 'warily'.] A policy of 'going slow' at one's work for an employer.

Cacao (kăkēⁱ·o, kăkā·o). 1555. [– Sp. *cacao* – Nahuatl *cacauatl* (*uatl* tree). See COCOA.] **1.** The seed of *Theobroma cacao*, N.O. *Byltneriaceæ*, from which cocoa and chocolate are prepared. † **2.** = COCOA –1662. **3.** The **Cacao-tree** 1756. *Comb.* **c.-butter,** a fatty matter obtained from the cacao-nut, used for making pomades, candles, etc.

Caccagogue (kæ·kagǫg). [f. Gr. κάκκη excrement + -αγωγος driving away.] *Med.* An ointment made of alum and honey, and used to promote stool.

† **Cace·mphaton.** *rare.* 1622. [– med.L. – Gr. κακέμφατον, subst. use of n. of κακέμφατος ill-sounding.] An ill-sounding expression.

Cachalot (kæ·ʃălǫt, kæ·ʃălo). 1747. [– Fr. *cachalot* – Sp., Pg. *cachalote*, of unkn. origin.] A genus of whales, belonging to the family *Catodontidæ*, having teeth in the lower jaw.

Cache (kaʃ), *sb.* 1595. [– Fr. *cache*, f. *cacher* to hide.] **1.** A hiding-place; *esp.* a hole or mound made by explorers to hide stores. **2.** The stores so hidden 1830. Hence **Cache** *v.* to store (provisions) underground; said also of animals.

Cachectic, -al (kăke·ktik, -ăl), *a.* 1634. [– Fr. *cachectique* or L. *cachecticus* – Gr. καχεκτικός; see CACHEXY, -IC.] Of or pertaining to cachexy.

† **Cachespell, -pule.** *Sc.* 1526. [– MFlem. *caetsespeel*; cf. Du. *kaatsspel* fives.] **1.** The game of tennis; also *attrib.* –1818. **2.** A tennis-court –1597.

‖ **Cachet** (kaʃę). 1639. [– Fr. *cachet*, f. *cacher* (in the sense of 'press', repr. now in *écacher* crush) :– Rom. *coacticare, for L. *coactare* constrain.] **1.** A seal. **2.** *fig.* Stamp, mark 1840. **3.** *Med.* = CAPSULE 5.

1. *Letter of c.* (Fr. *lettre de cachet*): a letter under the private seal of the French king, containing an order, often of exile or imprisonment.

Cachexy (kăke·ksi). 1541. [– Fr. *cachexie* or late L. *cachexia* – Gr. καχεξία, f. κακός bad + -εξία = ἕξις habit or state.] **a.** A depraved condition of the body, in which nutrition is everywhere defective. **b.** A depraved habit of mind or feeling 1652. Also *fig.*

Cachinnate (kæ·kinēⁱt), *v.* 1824. [– *cachinnat-*, pa. ppl. stem of L. *cachinnare*, of imit. origin; see -ATE[3].] *intr.* To laugh loudly or immoderately.

Cachinnation (kækinēⁱ·ʃən). 1623. [f. L. *cachinnatio*; see prec., -ION.] Loud or immoderate laughter.

The hideous grimaces which attended this unusual c. SCOTT. So **Ca·chinnator. Ca·chinnato:ry** *a.* of, pertaining to, or connected with c.

Cacholong (kæ·tʃŏlǫŋ). 1791. [– Fr. – Mongolian *kashchilon* understood as 'beautiful stone'.] *Min.* A variety of the opal.

‖ **Cachou** (kæ̆ʃū·). 1708. [– Fr. *cachou* – Pg. † *cacho, cachu* – Malay *kāchu.*] **1.** = CATECHU. **2.** A sweetmeat, made of cashew-nut, etc., used by smokers to sweeten the breath.

‖ **Cachucha** (kătʃu·tʃă). Erron. **cachuca.** 1840. [Sp.] A lively Spanish dance.

‖ **Cacique** (kăsī·k). 1555. [– Sp. *cacique, cazique*, of Carib origin; so Fr. *cacique.*] A native chief or prince of the aborigines in the West Indies, etc. Hence **Caci·queship.**

Cack (kæk), *v.* Now *dial.* ME. [– MLG., MDu. *cacken* (Du. *kakken*) – L. *cacare.*] **1.** *intr.* To void excrement. **2.** To void as excrement 1485. So **Cack** *sb.*

† **Cackerel** (kæ·kərĕl). 1583. [– obs. Fr. *caquerel*, also *cagarel*, *-et* (Cotgrave), – Pg. *cagarel, -ello*, also *gagarel.*] **1.** A small fish of the Mediterranean: esp. *Smaris gagarella* (Cuv.), and perh. other small sea-breams –1790. **2.** Dysentery 1659.

Cackle (kæ·k'l), *sb.* ME. [f. the verb.] **1.** A cackler. Now *dial.* **2.** Cackling; as of a hen, etc. 1674. **3.** *fig.* Silly chatter 1676. **b.** A chuckle 1856.

2. The silver goose..by her c., sav'd the state DRYDEN.

Cackle (kæ·k'l), *v.*[1] [prob. – (M)LG., (M)Du. *kākelen*, of imit. origin, but partly f. *kāke* jaw (CHEEK). See -LE.] **1.** *intr.* To make a noise as a hen, *esp.* after laying an egg; also as a goose, or other fowl. **2.** *fig.* Said of persons: **a.** To chatter. **b.** To talk fussily about a petty achievement. **c.** To chuckle, to giggle. 1530. **3.** *trans.* To utter with cackling ME.

1. Some persons are like hens that after laying must be cackling 1660. **2.** Howe these women cackyll nowe they have dyned PALSGR. **3.** To c. satisfaction HOWELLS. Hence **Ca·ckler,** *fig.* a blabber.

Ca·ckle, *v.*[2] 1748. [Origin unkn.] *Naut.* 'To cover a cable spirally with 3-inch old rope to protect it from chafe in the hawse hole' (Smyth).

Caco-, repr. Gr. κακο-, comb. f. κακός bad, evil, used freely in medical terminology to form names of bad states of bodily organs, most of which, however, are not English in form, e.g. *cacogala·ctia* (a condition in which the milk is bad), *cacothymia* (disordered state of mind), etc.

caco-chy·lous [Gr. κακόχυλος] *a.*, *Path.* characterized by bad chyle; **-chy·lia,** depraved chylification; **-chymy** [Gr. κακοχυμία], unhealthy state of the fluids of the body; whence **-chy·mic** *a.*, ill-humoured; *sb.* [sc. person]; also **-chy·mical; -de·mon, -dæ·mon** [Gr. κακοδαίμων] an evil spirit; *Med.* †nightmare; *Astrol.* the (baleful) Twelfth House in a figure of the Heavens; **-doxy** [Gr. κακοδοξία] (*rare*), wrong opinion or doctrine; hence **-do·xical** *a.*; **-epy** [Gr. κακέπεια], bad pronunciation (opp. to *orthoepy*); hence **-epi·stic** *a.*; **-ga·stric** *a.*, having a deranged stomach (*nonce-wd.*); **-genesis** [Gr. γένεσις], morbid or depraved formation; a monstrosity; **-graphy** [Gr. -γραφία], bad writing; incorrect spelling; a bad system of spelling; hence **-grapher, -gra·phic, -al** *a.*; **-logy** [Gr. -λογία], † evil report; bad choice of words; bad pronunciation; **-magician,** an evil magician or sorcerer; **-pla·stic** [f. Gr. κακόπλαστος after *plastic*] *a.*, *Phys.* imperfectly organized, as morbid deposits; **-rhy·thmic, -rrhythmic** [f. Gr. κακόρρυθμος after *rhythmic*] *a.*, in bad rhythm; **-trophy** [f. Gr. κακοτροφία], imperfect or disordered nutrition; **-type** [cf. CALOTYPE], an imperfect description in print.

Cacodorous (kækōᵘ·dŏrəs), *a. rare.* 1863. [f. CACO- + ODOROUS.] Ill-smelling.

Cacodyl (kæ·kodil). 1850. [f. Gr. κακώδης stinking + -YL.] *Chem.* An organic compound of arsenic and methyl, $As(CH_3)_2$ = Kd, also called *Arsendimethyl*, a colourless liquid, of disgusting odour, which takes fire on exposure to the air. Hence **Cacody·lic** *a.* of cacodyl, as in *Cacodylic acid*, KdO_2H.

‖ **Cacoethes** (kæko,ī·þės, -ī·þiz). 1563. [– L. *cacoethes* – Gr. κακόηθες, subst. use of n. of κακοήθης ill-disposed, f. κακός bad + ἦθος ETHOS.] **a.** An evil habit. **b.** A malignant disease. **c.** An itch for doing something, as in the *insanabile scribendi cacoethes* (incurable itch of writing) of Juvenal. Hence † **Cacoe·thic** *a.* malignant (as a disease).

‖ **Cacolet** (kakolę, -let). 1878. [dial. Fr., – mod.Pr. *caco(u)let.*] A military litter in the form either of arm-chairs attached to the pack-saddle of a mule, or of a bed laid along its back.

† **Ca·colike, -leek.** 1582. Perverted f. CATHOLIC, as if conn. w. κακός bad –1626

Cacoon (kăkū·n). 1854. [perh. African.] The bean of a tropical climbing shrub, *Entada scandens* (N.O. *Leguminosæ*), used for making into snuff-boxes, scent-bottles, spoons, etc.

Cacophonous (kæ̆kǫ·fŏnəs), *a.* 1797. [f. Gr. κακόφωνος + -OUS; see next.] Ill-sounding. var. **Cacopho·nic, -al.** Hence **Caco·phonously** *adv.*; var. **Cacopho·nically.**

Cacophony (kæ̆kǫ·fŏni). 1656. [– Fr. *cacophonie* – Gr. κακοφωνία, f. κακόφωνος ill-sounding.] **1.** The quality of having an ill sound; the use of harsh-sounding words and phrases. (Opp. to *euphony.*) **2.** *Mus.* A discordant combination of sounds. Also *fig.* Moral discord. 1789. † **3.** *Med.* A harsh or discordant state of the voice.

1. Avoid c., and make your periods as harmonious as you can CHESTERF.

Cacoto·pia. *nonce-wd.* A place where all is evil; opp. by Bentham to *Utopia* 'nowhere', taken as **Eutopia* 'a place where all is well'.

Cacoxenite (kækǫ·ksėnəit). [f. Gr. κακο- + ξένος stranger + ITE[1] 2 b; so called as being injurious when present in iron ore.] *Min.* A native phosphate of iron, containing also water, peroxide of iron, and phosphoric acid, occurring in radiated tufts.

† **Caco-zea·l.** 1579. [Formed after Gr. κακοζηλία.] **1.** (Also *cacozelon, cacozelia*): Perverse affectation or imitation, as a fault of style –1644. **2.** Perverted zeal 1608.

Cacozyme (kæ·kozəim). [f. CACO- + ZYME.] *Med.* A particle of matter conceived as the active agent in producing infectious disease, either by fermentation or by propagation.

Cactus (kæ·ktŏs). 1607. [– L. *cactus* – Gr. κάκτος cardoon or Spanish artichoke.] † **1.** In ancient Nat. Hist.: The Cardoon. **2.** A genus of succulent plants with thick fleshy stems, and clusters of spines. Now subdivided into about 20 genera, as *Cereus, Echinocactus, Opuntia*, etc., constituting the N.O. *Cactaceæ*. 1767.

† **Cad**[1]. 1657. [Origin unkn.; cf. CADDY[2].] A familiar spirit.

Cad[2] (kæd). 1790. [Short f. CADEE, CADDIE, CADET. Sense 5 is prob. an application of sense 4.] † **1.** An unbooked passenger whose fare the driver of a coach appropriated. **2.** An assistant or confederate of a lower grade 1835. † **3.** An omnibus conductor –1848. **4.** = Sc. CADDIE, sense 2. At Oxford formerly applied contemptuously to townsmen generally. 1831. **5.** *colloq.* An ill-bred vulgar fellow. Now usu., a person (rarely a female) who is lacking in the finer instincts or feelings. 1838.

Cad[3]. Chiefly *dial.* 1651. Var. of CADDIS[2]; called more fully **cod-bait, c.-bait, -bit, -bote, -worm.**

Cadastral (kăda·străl), *a.* 1858. [– Fr. *cadastral*; see next., -AL[1].] Of, pertaining to, or according to a CADASTRE.

C. survey: **a.** *strictly*, a survey of lands for the purposes of a cadastre; **b.** *loosely*, a survey on a scale showing accurately the extent and measurement of every field and plot of land; *e.g.* on the scale of 1:2500 or 25:344 inches to a mile. So *c. map, plan*, etc.

‖ **Cadastre** (kăda·stəɹ). 1804. [– Fr. *cadastre* – mod.Pr. *cadastro* – It. *catast(r)o*, earlier *catastico* – late Gr. κατάστιχον list, register, prop. κατὰ στίχον line by line.] **a.** A register of property to serve as a basis of taxation. **b.** (in mod.Fr. use) A public register of the quantity, value, and ownership of the real property of a country.

Cadaver (kădē̆i·vəɹ). 1500. [– L. *cadaver*, prop. 'fallen thing', f. *cadere* fall; cf. Gr. πτῶμα fall, corpse.] A dead body, *esp.* of man; a corpse. (Now mostly techn.) **b.** A skeleton. SIR T. BROWNE.

Cadaveric (kædăve·rik, kădæ·vĕrik), *a.* 1835. [– Fr. *cadavérique* or f. prec. + -IC.] **1.** Of, pertaining to, or characteristic of, dead bodies. (More techn. than *cadaverous.*) **2.** Caused by contact with a dead body 1871.

1. C. rigidity 1865, alkaloids 1880. **2.** C. warts 1883.

Cada·verine. 1877. [f. CADAVER + -INE[5].] *Chem.* One of the cadaveric alkaloids or Ptomaines.

Cada·verize, *v.* 1651. [f. as prec. + IZE.] To make cadaverous. Hence **Cada·verizable** *a.* capable of being converted into lifeless matter.

Cadaverous (kădæ·vĕrəs), *a.* 1627. [– L. *cadaverosus*; see CADAVER, -OUS. Cf. Fr. *cadavéreux.*] Of or belonging to a corpse; corpse-like; *esp.* of corpse-like pallor.

Some c. smell DERHAM. John Milton..pale, but not c. ELLWOOD. Hence **Cada·verous-ly** *adv.*, **-ness.**

† **Caddesse, cadesse.** 1565. [Origin unkn.] = CADDOW, a jackdaw –1688.

Caddie, cadie (kæ·di). *Sc.* 1634. [orig. Sc. (earliest form *caudie*) – Fr. *cadet*; see CADET.] † **1.** = CADEE, CADET 2, q.v. Also *attrib.* **2.** A lad or man who waits about on the look-out for odd jobs 1730. **b.** *Golf.* A boy (or man) who carries the clubs, etc. 1857. **3.** Lad (*familiar*) 1786.

Caddis[1], **caddice** (kæ·dis). ME. [Sense 1: ME. *cadas, cadace* – OFr. *cadas, cadaz*; sense 2: – (O)Fr. *cadis* serge – Pr. *cadis.* Ult. history unkn.] † **1.** Cotton wool, floss silk, or the like, used in padding –1769. † **2.** Worsted yarn, crewel –1721. Also *attrib.*; also short for *caddis ribbon.* † **3.** A kind of (worsted or ? silk) stuff –1553. **b.** A coarse cheap serge. [mod.Fr. *cadis.*] –1862.

Caddis[2], **caddice** (kæ·dis). 1622. [contemp. w. synon. (dial.) *cadbait, codbait* (see CAD[3]), CADEW, of unkn. origin.] The larva of species of *Phryganea*, which lives in water, and forms for itself a cylindrical case of hollow stems, small stones, etc.; used as a bait by anglers 1651.

Comb.: **c.-bait, -worm**; **-fly,** a Phryganea, as the May-fly. Hence **Ca·ddised** *ppl. a.* furnished with a c.

Caddish (kæ·diʃ), *a. colloq.* 1868. [f. CAD[2] 5 + -ISH[1].] Of the nature of a cad; opp. to gentlemanly. Hence **Ca·ddish-ly** *adv.*, **-ness.**

Caddle, *sb. dial.* 1825. [Origin unkn.] **1.** Disorder, confusion, disturbance. **2.** Bother 1865. Hence **Caddle** *v.* to trouble, disturb.

Ca·ddow[1]. Now *dial.* 1440. [perh. f. *ca, ka* jackdaw (Sc. *kae*) + DAW.] A jackdaw.

Ca·ddow[2]. Now *dial.* 1579. [Cf. CADDIS[1] 3 b.] A rough woollen covering.

Caddy[1] (kæ·di). 1792. [unexpl. alt. of CATTY *sb.*] **1.** A small box for holding tea; usu. *tea-caddy.* **2.** *U.S.* A can with a lid, for water, etc. 1883.

Ca·ddy[2]. 1781. [var. of earlier CAD[1].] A ghost, bugbear.

Caddy, var. of CADDIE. Also as vb. 1908.

Cade (kē̆id), *sb.*[1] ME. [– L. *cadus* wine-jar, measure for liquids, – Gr. κάδος cask, jar, of Sem. origin.] **1.** A cask or barrel. † **2.** *spec.* A barrel of herrings, holding six great hundreds, *i.e.* 720; afterwards 500. –1866.

Cade (kē̆id), *sb.*[2] (*a.*) 1450. [Origin unkn.] **1.** as *adj.* Of the young of animals: Cast by the mother and brought up by hand, as a pet 1475. **2.** as *sb.* A pet lamb or foal 1450; a spoiled child (*dial.*) 1877. **3.** Of fruit: Fallen, cast (*rare*) 1876.

1. It's ill bringing up a c. lamb GEO. ELIOT. Hence **Ca·dish** *a.* tame.

† **Cade,** *sb.*[3] Var. of KED, a sheep-louse.

Cade (kē̆id), *sb.*[4] 1575. [– Fr. (*huile de*) *cade* – Pr. *cade* :– med.L. *catanus* (VII), perh. of Gaulish origin.] A species of Juniper, *Juniperus oxycedrus*, yielding *Oil of Cade*, used in veterinary surgery.

Cade, *v.*[1] ? *Obs.* 1599. [f. CADE *sb.*[1]] To put into a cade.

Cade, *v.*[2] 1755. [f. CADE *sb.*[2]] 'To breed up in softness' (J.).

‖ **Cadeau** (kado). 1845. [Fr.] A gift.

† **Cadee.** 1689. [Phonetic sp. of Fr. *cadet.*] Early form of CADET, CADDIE: A (gentleman) *cadet* in the army –1789.

Cadence (kē̆i·dĕns), *sb.* ME. [– OFr. **cadence* (first recorded XV) – It. *cadenza* – pop.L. **cadentia*, f. *cadent-*, pres. ppl. stem of *cadere* fall. See -ENCE.] **I.** In verse and music. **1.** 'The flow of verses or periods' (J.); rhythm, rhythmical construction, measure. **b.** The beat of music, dancing, marching, etc. 1605. **2.** 'The fall of the voice' (J.) 1589. **b.** Occ., the modulation of the voice; accent 1709. **3.** The rising and (*esp.*) falling of a storm, the sea, etc. 1667. **4.** *Mus.* The close of a musical movement or phrase. Also occ. = CADENZA. 1597. **5.** *Horsemanship.* An equal proportion in all the motions of a horse 1833. **4.** *transf.* Applied to colours 1868.

1. The..golden c. of poesie *L.L.L.* IV. ii. 126. **b.** The occasional boom of the kettle-drum, to mark the c. SCOTT. **2.** A low voice, with a..sweet c. at the end of it STERNE. **3.** Blustring winds..now with hoarse c. lull Seafaring men orewatcht MILT. *P.L.* II. 287.

II. In the L. sense. † **1.** Falling; mode of falling –1667. † **2.** Chance 1601.

1. Now was the Sun in Western c. low MILT. *P.L.* X. 92. Hence **Ca·dence** *v.* (*rare*) to compose metrically. **Ca·denced** *ppl. a.* rhythmical, measured.

Cadency (kē̆i·dĕnsi). 1627. [f. prec.; see -ENCY.] † **1.** = CADENCE II. 2. 1647. **2.** = CADENCE I. 1. 1627. **3.** Descent of a younger branch from the main line of a family; the state of a cadet 1702.

3. *Mark of c.* (Her.): a variation in the same coat of arms intended to show the descent of a younger branch from the main stock.

Cadent (kē̆i·dĕnt), *a.* 1586. [– *cadent-*, pres. ppl. stem of L. *cadere* fall; see -ENT.] **1.** Falling 1605. **2.** *Astrol.* Of a planet: Going down, as *c. houses* in a 'figure of the Heavens' 1586. **3.** Having cadence 1613. **4.** *Geol.* Applied to a division of the palæozoic strata of the Alleghanies, corresponding to the lower middle Devonian 1858.

1. With c. Teares fret Channels in her cheekes SHAKS.

‖ **Cadenza** (kăde·ntsă). 1836. [It.; see CADENCE.] *Mus.* A flourish given to a solo voice or instrument at the close, or between two divisions, of a movement. (Occ. called *cadence.*) **b.** A brilliant solo passage towards the close of the first or last movement of a concerto, in which the main themes are further developed 1879.

Ca·der, cadar. Now *dial.* ME. [– W. *cader* chair.] † **1.** A cradle. ME. only. **2.** A light frame of wood put over a scythe 1679. **3.** (Cf. Fr. *cadre* frame.) A small frame of wood, on which a fisherman keeps his line (*dial.*).

Cadet (kăde·t). 1610. [– Fr. *cadet*, earlier *capdet* – Gascon dial. *capdet* (= Pr. *capdel*) :– Rom. **capitellus*, dim. of *caput, -it-* head; see -ET.] **1.** A younger son or brother. **b.** A younger branch of a family, or a member of it 1690. **c.** The youngest son 1646. **2.** A gentleman who entered the army without a commission, to learn the profession and find a career for himself. **b.** A junior in the East India Company's service. See also CADEE; CADDIE. 1651. **3.** A student in a naval or military college 1775. **b.** A schoolboy receiving military training, esp. to qualify for the O.T.C. Also *attrib.*, as **c. corps.**

3. Watch Sandhurst too, its debts and its Cadets HOOD. Hence **Cade·tship,** the status of a c.; the commission given to a c.; var. **Cade·tcy.**

Cadew (kæ·diu). 1668. Var. of CADDIS[2].

Cadge (kædʒ), *sb.*[1] 1615. [app. var. of CAGE, perh. confused w. CADGE *v.* carry about.] **1.** *Falconry.* A round frame of wood on which hawks are carried for sale. **2.** A pannier.

Cadge, *sb.*[2] *vulgar.* 1812. [f. CADGE *v.*] The action of cadging.

Cadge (kædʒ), *v.* ME. [Origin obscure; connection with ME. and dial. *cagge* fasten, tie (branch I) is improbable; perh. back-formation from CADGER.] **I.** † **1.** *trans.* ? To tie –1627. † **2.** To bind the edge of a garment 1530. **II.** **3.** To carry about (*dial.*) 1607. **4.** To stuff the belly (*dial.*) 1695. **5.** *intr.* To go about as a cadger or pedlar; to go about begging 1812. *trans.* To get by begging 1848.

Cadger (kæ·dʒəɹ). 1450. [orig. carrier, itinerant dealer (first in Sc.), of unkn. origin. Cf. CADGE *v.*] **1.** A carrier; *esp.* one who travels between town and country with butter, eggs, etc., and shop-wares. **2.** A hawker, a street-seller 1840. **b.** One who gets his living by begging or questionable means 1851. **3.** *Falconry.* A man who carries hawks. (Cf. OFr. *cagier.*) 1834.

1. The King's errand lying in the cadger's gate SCOTT.

Ca·dgy, *a. Sc.* and *n. dial.* 1724. [Origin unkn. Cf. Suffolk *kedge* in same sense; also Da. *kaad* wanton, lascivious.] **1.** Wanton; amorous. **2.** Cheerful; glad 1725. Hence **Ca·dgily** *adv.* **Ca·dginess.**

‖ **Cadi** (kāidi, kē̆i·idi). 1590. [– Arab. *al-ḳāḍī*, the judge.] A civil judge among the Turks, Arabs, etc.; usu. the judge of a town or village. Hence **Ca·diship,** the office of a c.

Cadie; see CADDIE.

‖ **Cadilesker** (kădile·skəɹ). 1686. [f. CADI + Turk. *leşger* army.] A chief judge in the Turkish empire, whose jurisdiction originally extended to soldiers.

‖ **Cadjan** (kɑ·dʒăn). *Anglo-Ind.* 1698. [– Malay and Javan. *ḳājāng* palm leaves.] **1.** Coco-palm leaves matted, used for thatch. **2.** A strip of fan-palm leaf prepared for writing on; a document written on such a strip 1707. Also *attrib.*

Ca·dlock, var. of CHARLOCK.

Cadmean (kædmī·ăn), *a.* Also **Cadmian, -mæan.** 1603. [f. L. *Cadmeus* – Gr. Καδμεῖος, f. Κάδμος + -AN.] Pertaining to Cadmus, the fabulous founder of Thebes in Bœotia, and introducer of the alphabet into Greece.

Cadmean victory (Gr. Καδμεία νίκη), a victory involving the victor's ruin; usu. associated with Thebes or the Thebans.

† **Ca·dmia.** 1657. [– L. *cadmia* – Gr. καδμεία or καδμία γῆ Cadmean earth; see CALAMINE.] *Chem.* 'The ancient name of calamine' (Ure); also, a sublimate consisting of oxide of zinc; an ore of cobalt –1837.

Cadmium (kæ·dmiŏm). 1822. [f. CADMIA + -IUM.] *Chem.* A bluish-white metal, occurring sparsely in zinc ores. Symbol Cd. **C. yellow,** an intense yellow pigment, consisting of cadmium sulphide.

† **Cadou·k.** *Sc.* Also **caduac.** 1637. [app. subst. use of the adj. CADUKE.] A casualty, a windfall.

‖ **Cadre** (kadr). 1830. [Fr. – It. *quadro* :– L. *quadrus* square.] **1.** A frame, framework; scheme. **2.** *Mil.* **a.** The permanent establishment forming the framework of a regiment 1851. **b.** The complement of officers of a regiment; the list of such officers 1864.

Caduac; see CADOUK.

Caducary (kădiū·kări), *a.* 1768. [– late L. *caducarius* relating to *bona caduca*; see CADUCOUS 3, -ARY [1].] Subject to, relating to, or by way of escheat or lapse.

‖ **Caduceus** (kădiū·siŏs). Pl. **caducei** (-si,əi). 1591. [L. *caduceus, -eum* – Doric Gr. καρύκειον -ιον, = Attic κηρύκειον subst. use of n. of adj., f. κῆρυξ, κηρυκ- herald.] A herald's wand. *spec.* The wand carried by Mercury, the messenger of the gods; usually represented with two serpents twined round it. (The proper sense in Eng.)

He tooke *Caduceus* his snakie wand, With which the damned ghosts he gouerneth SPENSER. var. † **Ca·duce.** Hence **Cadu·cean** *a.* pertaining to a c.

Cadu·ciary, var. of CADUCARY, after *fiduciary.*

Caducibranchiate (kădiū:sibræ·ŋki,eⁱt), *a.* 1835. [f. L. *caducus* falling + *branchiæ* gills, whence mod.L. *Caducibranchia*, the Batrachians. See -IA [2], -ATE [2].] *Zool.* Of Amphibians: Losing their gills before reaching maturity (like the frog). Also as *sb.*

Caducity (kădiū·sĭti). 1769. [– Fr. *caducité*, f. *caduque* – L. *caducus*, f. *cadere* fall; see -ITY.] **1.** Tendency to fall; transitoriness, frailty 1793. **2.** *esp.* Senility 1769. **3.** *Roman Law.* Lapse of a testamentary gift 1875. **4.** *Zool.* and *Bot.* Quality of being caducous 1881.

1. The..c. of language, in virtue of which every effusion of the human spirit is lodged in a body of death M. PATTISON. **2.** This melancholick proof of my c. CHESTERF.

Caducous (kădiū·kəs), *a.* 1808. [f. L. *caducus* (see prec.) + -OUS.] **1.** *Zool.* and *Bot.* Used of organs or parts that fall off naturally when they have served their purpose; as leaves, the placenta, etc. **2.** = CADUKE 2. **3.** *Roman Law.* Applied to testamentary gifts which lapsed from the donee 1880. var. † **Cadu·ce.**

† **Cadu·ke,** *a.* ME. [– (O)Fr. *caduc* (fem. *-uque*) or L. *caducus*; see prec.] **1.** Liable to fall. **2.** Transitory, perishable –1688; var. † **Cadu·cal** [Cf. AL. *caducalis* transitory]. **3.** Infirm –1541. **4.** Epileptic. ME. only.

2. Euery thynge in this world is c. FISHER.

Cady, var. of CADI, CADDIE.

Cæ-; see also CE-.

Cæcal (sī·kăl), *a.* 1826. [f. CÆCUM + -AL [1].] *Phys.* Pertaining to, or like, the cæcum; having a blind end.

‖ **Cæ·cias.** ? *Obs.* 1653. [L. – Gr. καικίας.] The north-east wind personified.

Cæcilian (sisi·liăn). [f. L. *cæcilia* a kind of lizard + -AN.] One of the *Cæciliadæ*, a family of Amphibia, having the form of serpents; their eyes are very small.

Cæcity, var. of CECITY, blindness.

‖ **Cæcum** (sī·kŏm). Occas. **cecum**; *pl.* **cæca.** 1721. [L., short for *intestinum cæcum* blind gut, tr. Gr. τυφλὸν ἔντερον.] *Phys.* **1.** The blind gut; the first part of the large intestine, which is prolonged into a cul-de-sac. **2.** With pl. *cæca*: Any tube with one end closed, as the *pyloric cæca* in fishes 1753. Hence **Cæ·ciform** *a.* **Cæci·tis,** inflammation of the c.

Cænozoic, var. of CAINOZOIC.

Caen-stone. A lightish-yellow building-stone found near Caen in Normandy.

Cæsar (sī·zăɹ). ME. [The earliest L. word adopted in Gmc. OE. *cāsere*, OFris. *kaiser, keiser*, OS. *kēsar*, OHG. *keisar*, ON. *keisari*, Goth. *kaisar.* See KAISER, CZAR.] **1.** The cognomen of the Roman dictator Caius Julius Cæsar, used as a title of the emperors down to Hadrian (A.D. 138), and subseq. as a title of the heir-presumptive. In mod. use often applied to all the emperors. **b.** The emperor of the Holy Roman Empire; the German KAISER 1674. **2.** *fig.* or *transf.* An autocrat, emperor 1593. **b.** *contextually,* The temporal monarch; the civil power. (See *Matt.* 22:21.) 1601. Also *attrib.*

1. Before whom Cæsars as well as Pontiffs were to quail FREEMAN. **2.** Lead thine own captivity captive, and be C. within thyself SIR T. BROWNE. Hence **Cæ·sardom,** the dominion or dignity of the Cæsars. † **Cæsa·reate, Cæ·sarship,** the imperial dignity.

Cæsarean, Cæsarian (sizēᵊ·riăn). 1528. [– L. *Cæsarianus* or f. *Cæsareus*; see -EAN, -IAN.] **A.** *adj.* Of or pertaining to Cæsar or the Cæsars 1615.

C. birth, operation, section (in *Obstet. Surg.*): the delivery of a child by cutting through the walls of the abdomen, as was done with Julius Cæsar.

B. *sb.* An adherent of Cæsar, of the Emperor (against the Pope), or of an imperial system.

Cæsarism (sī·zăriz'm). 1857. [f. CÆSAR + -ISM.] The system of absolute government founded by Cæsar. **b.** = ERASTIANISM 1876.

Monarchical absolutism, or what I..call modern C. 1857. So **Cæ·sarist,** an imperialist. **Cæ·sarize,** *v. intr.* to play the Cæsar; *trans.* to make like Cæsar or Cæsar's.

Cæsious (sī·ziəs), *a.* 1835. [f. L. *cæsius* bluish-grey + -OUS.] Bluish or greyish green. (Chiefly *Bot.*)

Cæsium (sī·ziŏm). 1861. [– mod.L., n. of L. *cæsius*; see prec., -IUM.] *Chem.* A silvery white metal; named from two blue lines in its spectrum. Symbol Cs.

Cæspitose, cesp- (se:spitōᵘ·s), *a.* 1830. [f. L. *cæspes, -it-* sod, turf + -OSE [1].] *Bot.* Growing in thick tufts or clumps; turfy.

Cæsura (siziūᵊ·ră, sis-). 1556. [– L. *cæsura* lit. cutting, f. *cæs-*, pa. ppl. stem of *cædere* cut; see -URE.] **1.** In Gr. and L. prosody: The division of a metrical foot between two words, *esp.* near the middle of the line 1727. **b.** The lengthening of the last syllable of a word by arsis which sometimes occurs in the cæsura 1678. **2.** In Eng. prosody: A pause about the middle of a metrical line 1556. **3.** *transf.* A formal stop; an interruption 1596.

Cæsu·ral, Cæsu·ric *a.* of or pertaining to a c.

‖ **Café** (kæ·fe). 1816. [Fr., coffee-house.] **1.** A coffee-house, a restaurant; now, a certain class of restaurant. **2.** Coffee, in **c. au lait** (kæ:fe,olēⁱ), coffee with an equal quantity of hot milk; also, the colour of this 1818; **c. noir** (nwăr), lit. black coffee, *i.e.* coffee without milk 1863.

† **Caffa.** 1531. [Origin unkn.] **1.** A rich silk cloth much used in the 16th c. –1641. **2.** A kind of painted cotton cloth made in India –1810.

Caffeic (kĕfī·ik), *a.* 1853. [– Fr. *caféique*, f. *café* COFFEE + *-ique* -IC.] *Chem.* Of or pertaining to coffee; *esp.* in **c. acid** ($C_9H_8O_4$), a substance found in brilliant yellow prisms. So **Ca·ffeidine,** an uncrystallizable base ($C_7H_{12}N_4O$), produced by the action of alkalis on caffeine. **Caffeta·nnate,** a salt of **Caffeta·nnic acid,** an astringent acid found in coffee berries, etc.

Caffeine (kæ·fi,əin). 1830. [– Fr. *caféine*, f. as prec. + *-ine* -INE [5].] *Chem.* A vegetable alkaloid crystallizing in white silky needles, found in the leaves and seeds of the coffee and tea plants, the leaves of guarana, maté, etc.

Caffia·ceous, prop. **Coffeaceous,** *a. rare.* 1865. [See -ACEOUS.] *Bot.* Allied to the genus *Coffea*, of which *C. arabica* is the coffee shrub.

Caffre (kæ·fəɹ). 1599. See also KAFFIR. [Early form of KAFFIR.] ‖ **1.** Infidel; a word applied by the Arabs to all non-Moslems 1680. **2.** *spec.* One of a South African race of Blacks belonging to the Bantu family, and living in *Caffraria*. Also the name of their language, and used *attrib.* 1599. **3.** A native of Kafiristan in Asia; see KAFIR.

Comb.: **C.-bread,** a S. Afr. cycadaceous tree with edible pith; **-corn,** Indian millet, *Sorghum vulgare.*

‖ **Cafila** (kă·filă). 1594. [– Arab. *ḳāfila* convoy of travellers, caravan.] A caravan.

‖ **Caftan** (kaftă·n, kæ·ftăn). 1591. [– Turk. *kaftan*, partly through Fr. *cafetan.*] An oriental garment consisting of a long under-tunic tied at the waist with a girdle.

Jews with their high caps and caftans 1835.

† **Cag** (kæg), *sb.* [1] 1452. [– ON. *kaggi* keg, cask; see KEG.] **1.** A keg –1797. **2.** A small fishing vessel. (Du. *kaag.*) –1667.

Cag, *sb.* [2] Now *dial.* 1604. [Origin unkn.] A stiff point.

Cag, *v. dial.* 1504. [Cf. CAGGY 2.] To offend, insult.

Cage (kēⁱdʒ), *sb.* ME. [– (O)Fr. *cage* :– L. *cavea* stall, cage, coop, etc.]

I. 1. A box or place of confinement for birds or other animals, made wholly or partly of wire, or bars of metal or wood, so as to admit air and light. Also *fig.* † **2.** A lock-up –1850. **3.** Anything like a cage ME.

1. Stone walls do not a prison make Nor iron bars a c. LOVELACE. [The soul's] c. of flesh DANIEL. **2.** 2 *Hen. VI*, IV. ii. 56.

II. Technical.

1. *Mining.* **a.** An enclosed platform for hoisting in a vertical shaft 1851. **b.** The drum on which the rope is wound 1854. **2.** A confining framework; *esp.* **a.** *Carpentry.* A framework of timber, enclosing another work within it, as the c. of a windmill. **b.** One confining the motion of a ball valve. **c.** A strainer over the mouth of a pipe, etc. **d.** A cup with a glass bottom and cover, to hold a drop of water for microscopic examination. 1753. **3.** An iron framework to contain burning combustibles, used to mark an intricate channel, etc. 1837. **4.** *Falconry.* A frame to carry hawks upon. See CADGE *sb.* [1] 1828.

Hence **Ca·geless** *a.* **Ca·geling,** a bird kept in a c. *Comb.* **c.-work,** open work like the bars of a c.; † *Naut.* the upper works of a ship.

Cage (kēⁱdʒ), *v.* 1577. [f. prec.] **a.** To confine in or as in a cage. **b.** To fit as a cage in a mine-shaft 1860.

Caged vp like linnets 1625. Hence **Caged** *ppl. a.* confined in or as in a cage; † closed like a cage, as *caged cloister* SHAKS.

Ca·ggy, *a.* 1848. [Sense 1, see next; sense 2, cf. CAG *v.*] **1.** Unwholesome. **2.** Ill-natured (*dial.*) 1855.

Cagmag (kæ·gmæg), *sb.* (*a.*) *dial.* 1771. [Cf. prec.] **1.** A tough old goose. **b.** Unwholesome meat; offal. **2.** *adj.* Decaying, refuse 1859.

‖ **Cagot** (kago). 1844. [Fr.] Name of an outcast race in southern France; occ. = 'pariah'.

‖ **Cagui** (kă·gi). 1753. [Brazilian.] The fox-tailed monkey.

‖ **Cahier** (ka·ie). 1849. [Fr.; see QUIRE *sb.* [1]] A book of loose sheets tacked together; whence, reports of proceedings, etc. (Hardly in Eng. use.)

Cahoot (kăhū·t). *U.S.* 1829. [Origin unkn.] A company, or partnership. Hence **Cahoo·t** *v.* to act in partnership.

Caic, caïk(e, -jee; see CAÏQUE.

‖ **Caid.** 1860. Same as ALCAYDE.

‖ **Cailleach** (kɑ·lʸăχ). In Scott **cailliach.** 1814. [Gael. *cailleach* old woman.] An old (Highland) woman, a crone.

Caimacam, var. of KAIMAKAM.

Caiman, var. of CAYMAN.

Cain, kain (kēⁱn). *Sc.* and *Ir.* ME. [– Celt. *cáin* 'law', 'rent, tribute, fine'.] **1.** A rent paid in kind. Also *attrib.* and *fig.* **2.** (Ireland) A penalty for an offence 1518.

Cain [2] (kēⁱn). ME. The proper name of the first murderer (*Gen.* 4), used allusively. *To raise C.* (U.S.): to make a disturbance.

Comb. † **C.-coloured,** red or reddish-yellow, the reputed colour of the hair of C. Hence **Cai·nian** = *Cainite.* **Cai·nish** *a.* of the temper of C. **Cai·nism,** the heresy of the Cainites. **Cai·nite,** (*a*) one of a 2nd -c. sect who treated C. and other wicked Scriptural characters as saints; (*b*) a descendant of C.; also *fig.* **Caini·tic** *a.* pertaining to C. or the Cainites.

Ca'ing-whale (kā·,iŋ,hwēⁱl). *Sc.* 1865. [*Ca'ing* (*calling*; see CALL *v.* III.) = driving like a herd.] The round-headed porpoise, which frequents the shores of Orkney, Iceland, etc.

Cainozoic (kainozōᵘ·ik, kēⁱno-), *a.* Also **kainozoic, cænozoic.** 1854. [f. Gr. καινός recent + ζῷον animal + -IC.] *Geol.* Of or pertaining to the third great geological period (also called TERTIARY), or to the remains or formations characteristic of it.

Caipercaillie, var. of CAPER-.

Caique (ka,ī·k). 1625. [– Fr. *caïque* – It. *caicco* – Turk. *kayık.*] **1.** A light skiff propelled by one or more rowers, used on the Bosporus. **2.** A Levantine sailing-vessel 1666.

1. Glanced many a light c. along the foam BYRON. Hence **Cai·quejee, cai·kjee,** rower of a c.

Cair, *v.* [ME. *kayre* – ON. *keyra* drive, etc.] † **1.** *intr.* To go, make one's way (*poet.*) –1470. † **2.** *trans.* To bring. ME. only. **3.** *trans.* and *intr.* To stir about. *Sc.* 1808.

Caird (kēᵊɹd). *Sc.* 1663. [– Gael. *ceard* artificer in metal = Ir. *ceard*, OIr. *cerd.*] A travelling tinker; a gipsy. Hence **Cai·rdman** *sb.*

Cairn (kēᵊɹn). 1535. [Earlier (XVI) as *carne* – Gael. *carn*, corresp. to OIr., W. *carn.*] **1.** A pyramid of rough stones raised: **a.** as a memorial or a sepulchral monument. **b.** as a boundary mark, a landmark on a mountain top, etc., or an indication of a cache 1770. **c.** A mere pile of stones 1699. **2.** The smallest breed of British terrier 1910.

a. *To add a stone to any one's c.*: to do all possible honour to his memory after death. Hence **Cairned** *a.* furnished with a c.

Cairngorm, -gorum (kēᵊ·ɹngōᵊ·ɹm, -gōᵊ·rəm). 1794. [f. the mountain in Scotland (Gael. *Carngorm*, i.e. blue cairn).] (More fully *C. stone*:) A yellow or wine-coloured variety of rock-crystal; much used for ornamenting articles of Highland wear.

Caisson (kēⁱ·sən). Also **caissoon.** 1704. [– Fr. *caisson*, † *casson* large chest – It. *cassone*, subseq. assim. to *caisse* CASE *sb.*²; see -OON.] **1.** *Mil.* **a.** A chest containing explosives, to be buried and fired as a mine. **b.** A chest containing ammunition; a wagon for conveying ammunition. Also *fig.* 1704. **2.** *Hydraul.* **a.** A large water-tight chest used in laying foundations of bridges, etc., in deep water 1753. **b.** A vessel in the form of a boat used as a floodgate in docks 1854. **c.** A machine for raising sunken ships; = CAMEL, q.v. 1811. **3.** *Arch.* 'A sunken panel in ceilings, vaults, and cupolas' (Gwilt).

Comb., etc.: **c. disease,** a disease produced by the sudden variations of atmospheric pressure experienced by men who work in caissons; **-gate** = sense 2 b.

Caitiff (kēⁱ·tif). ME. [– OFr. *caitif* captive, var. of *chaitif* (mod. *chétif* wretched) :– Rom. **cactivus*, alt. of L. *captivus* CAPTIVE by assoc. w. OCelt. **cactos* (= L. *captus*).] **A.** *sb.* † **1.** Orig.: A captive, a prisoner –1603. † **2.** One in a piteous case –1678. **3.** A base, mean, despicable wretch; a villain. Cf. *wretch.* ME.

2. Alas poore Caitiffe *Oth.* IV. i. 109. **3.** The wickedst caitiffe on the ground *Meas. for M.* V. i. 53. Hence † **Caitive** *v.* to make captive.

B. *adj.* † **1.** Captive. ME. only. † **2.** Wretched –1583. **3.** Vile, mean; worthless, miserable ME.

1. He . . ledde caitifte caytif WYCLIF. **3.** Caitiue iudas ME. Hence † **Cai·tifly, -ively** *adv.* † **Cai·tifness, -iveness.**

† **Cai·tifty, -ivetie.** ME. only. [– OFr. *caitivetet* (mod. *chétiveté*) :– L. *captivitas*, *-tat-*; see CAITIFF, -ITY.] Captivity; wretchedness; vileness.

‖ **Cajan** (kēⁱ·dʒăn, kā·dʒan). 1693. [– Malay *kāchang.*] A genus of plants, *Cajanus* (N.O. *Leguminosæ*), and esp. *C. indicus*, cultivated for the seeds or pulse, an article of food, called in India *Dhal, Dhol*, in Jamaica *Pigeon-peas.*

Cajaput, cajeput, var. of CAJUPUT.

Cajole (kădʒōᵘ·l), *v.* 1645. [– Fr. *cajoler.*] **1.** *trans.* To get one's way with, by delusive flattery, specious promises, or the like. Const. *into, from, out of.* **2.** *intr.* or *absol.* To use cajolery 1665.

1. Abused and cajoled, as they call it, by falsities and court-impudence MILT. Hence **Cajo·lement. Cajo·ler. Cajo·lingly** *adv.*

Cajolery (kădʒōᵘ·ləri). 1649. [– Fr. *cajolerie*, f. *cajoler.*] The action or practice of cajoling; persuasion by false arts.

Those infamous cajolleries EVELYN.

‖ **Cajuput** (kæ·dʒəpŏt). 1832. [Ult. – Malay *kayuputih*, i.e. *kayu* wood, *puteh* white.] **1.** *C. tree*: one or more species of *Melaleuca* (N.O. *Myrtaceæ*), esp. *M. minor* (*cajuputi*) 1876. **2.** *C. oil*: the oil obtained from these trees 1832. **3.** Also, *Oreodaphne californica* (N.O. *Lauraceæ*). Hence **Cajuputene, Cajputene,** *Chem.* '$C_{10}H_{16}$, the hydrocarbon of which oil of c. is the hydrate' (*Syd. Soc. Lex.*).

Cake (kēⁱk), *sb.* ME. [– ON. *kaka* (Icel., Sw. *kaka*, Da. *kage*), rel. to G. *kuchen.*] **1.** With pl.: **a.** *orig.* A smallish flattened sort of bread, regularly shaped, and usually turned in baking. **b.** *esp.* in Scotland, *spec.* A thin hard-baked brittle species of oaten-bread 1572. **c.** In England, a sweetened composition of flour and other ingredients, as eggs, milk, dried fruits, nuts, flavourings, etc., often having its surface partly or wholly iced. **2.** As a substance 1579. **3.** Applied to other preparations; e.g. a *fish-cake, potato-cake*, etc. **4.** A flattened mass of any solidified or compressed substance, as soap, coagulated blood, tobacco, etc. 1528. Also *fig.* **5.** *dial.* and *slang.* A stupid fool 1785.

1. b. *Land of cakes*, Scotland. **4.** To create what may be called a c. of custom BAGEHOT.

Phr. *To take the c.*; to rank first; to beat all. † *One's c. is dough*: one's project has failed of success. *Tam. Shr.* I. i. 110. *Cakes and ale*, good things.

Comb.: **c.-bread,** bread made in cakes, or of the quality of c.; **-house,** † one where cakes are sold; one where cakes (sense 4) are stored; **-meal,** 'linseed meal obtained by grinding the cake after the expression of the oil'; **-urchin,** an echinoderm of a discoid shape. Hence **Ca·ky** *a.* like, or of the nature of a c.; weak-minded (*dial.*).

Cake (kēⁱk), *v.* 1607. [f. prec.] **1.** *trans.* To form into a cake or flattish compact mass: also *fig.* (Chiefly *pass.*) **2.** *intr.* (for *refl.*) To form (itself) into a cake. Const. *together.* 1615.

2. The stiff clays . . in dry weather . . c. SIR H. DAVY.

Cal (kæl). 1875. Cornish name of WOLFRAM.

‖ **Calaba** (kæ·lăbă). 1753. [S. Amer.] A tropical evergreen tree (*Calophyllum calaba*), yielding a lamp-oil, and **Calaba-balsam.**

Calabar, var. of CALABER.

Calabar-bean (kælăbā·ɹ bī·n). 1876. [f. *Calabar*, on the Gulf of Guinea.] The seed of *Physostigmum venenosum*, called also the Ordeal-bean, used as a test of witchcraft. Hence **Calabarine,** an alkaloid found in this bean.

Calabash (kæ·lăbæʃ). 1596. [– Fr. *calebasse*, †*cala-* – Sp. *calabaza*; cf. Pers. *k̲arbuz, k̲arbūz* water-melon.] **1.** The name of various gourds or pumpkins 1658. **2.** The fruit of the Calabash-tree of America. Also = *Calabash-tree.* 1596. **3.** The hollow shell of 1 or 2, used as a water-bottle, kettle, or other utensil 1657. Also *transf.* **4.** *U.S.* The head (*joc.*).

Comb., etc.: **c.gourd,** the bottle-gourd (*Lagenaria vulgaris*) = sense 1; **-tree,** a tropical American tree (*Crescentia Cujete*), bearing the fruit called Calabash (sense 2); also, the Baobab tree.

Calaber, calabar (kæ·lăbəɹ). [ME. *calabre* – med.L. *calabris, -ebrum*, presumably f. *Calabria* in Italy.] **1.** The fur of some kind of squirrel; now, commercially, of the grey or Siberian squirrel: also *attrib.* † **2.** The animal itself –1626.

Calaboose (kælăbū·s). *U.S.* 1792. [Negro Fr. *calabouse* – Sp. *calabozo* dungeon.] A common prison (*local*).

‖ **Calade** (kala·d, kălēⁱ·d). 1731. [Fr. – It. *calata* f. *calare* let down – L. *chalare*, f. Gr. χαλᾶν.] The slope of a manège ground, down which a horse is ridden at speed, to supple his haunches. (Dicts.)

‖ **Caladium** (kălēⁱ·diŏm). 1845. [– Malay *kĕlády.*] *Bot.* A genus of plants of the Arum family having starchy corms.

Calamanco (kælămæ·ŋko). 1592. [Of unkn. origin. Cf. Du. *kal(a)mink*, G. *kalmank*, Fr. *calmande.*] **1.** A glossy woollen stuff of Flanders, twilled and chequered in the warp, so that the checks are seen on one side only. Also *attrib.* **b.** *ellipt.* [sc. *garments.*] 1859. **2.** *transf.* Used of wood and plaster buildings 1792.

Calamander (kælămæ·ndəɹ). 1804. [Of unkn. origin; the Sinhalese name is *kalumadīriya.*] An extremely hard cabinet wood of Ceylon and India, the product of *Diospyros quæsita* (N.O. *Ebenaceæ*), specifically akin to ebony.

Calamary (kæ·lămări). 1567. [– med.L. *calamarium* pen-case, n. of L. *calamarius*, f. *calamus* pen – Gr. κάλαμος.] The general name for Cephalopods or Cuttle-fish of the family *Teuthidæ*, esp. of the genus *Loligo*, having a long narrow body flanked by two triangular fins, and with the internal shell a horny flexible pen: *e.g.* the Common C., Squid, or Pen-fish.

‖ **Calambac** (kæ·lămbæk). 1594. [– Sp. *calambac*; in Fr. *calambac, -bar, -bour.*] Aloes-wood or Eagle-wood. (See AGALLOCH.) var. ‖ **Calambou·r.** [Fr.]

Calami·ferous, *a.* 1753. [f. CALAMUS + -FEROUS.] † Culmiferous; bearing reeds, reedy. So **Ca·lamiform** *a.* of the shape of a reed.

‖ **Calamina·ris,** *a.* and *sb.* 1577. [L.; see CALAMINE, -ARY².] Earlier f. CALAMINE. var. † **Calami·nary, -ar.**

Calamine (kæ·lăməin). 1601. [– (O)Fr. *calamine* – med.L. *calamina*, alt. of L. *cadmia* – Gr. καδμία, -εία (sc. γῆ earth), fem. of the adj. of *Cadmus.*] *Min.* An ore of zinc: orig. applied to both the carbonate $ZnCO_3$, and the hydrous silicate Zn_2SiO_4, H_2O, but chiefly, in France and England, to the former. The silicate is distinguished as *Siliceous* or *Electric C.* (See also O.E.D.) Also *attrib.*

Calamint (kæ·lămint). [– (O)Fr. *calament* – med.L. *calamentum*, for late L. *calaminthe* – Gr. καλαμίνθη.] *Bot.* A genus of aromatic herbs, *Calamintha* (N.O. *Labiatæ*), including *C. officinalis, C. nepeta, C. sylvatica*, etc.

† **Calami·strate,** *v. rare.* [– *calamistrat-*, pa. ppl. stem of AL. *calamistrare*, f. L. *calamistrum* curling-iron; cf. (O)Fr. *calamistrer*, which may be the source; see -ATE³.] *trans.* To curl or frizzle (the hair). BURTON. Hence **Ca:lamistra·tion.**

Calamite (kæ·lămait). 1837. [– mod.L. *calamites*, f. CALAMUS; see -ITE¹ 2 b.] **1.** *Palæont.* A fossil plant of the Coal Measures, perh. allied to the *Equisetaceæ* or Mare's-tails, but having a woody stem. **2.** *Min.* A variety of tremolite, occurring in reed-like crystals 1882.

Calamitous (kălæ·mitəs), *a.* 1545. [– Fr. *calamiteux* or L. *calamitosus*; see next, -OUS.] **1.** Fraught with or causing calamity; full of affliction or misery. **2.** Involved in calamity or distress –1752.

1. That c. error of the Jewes, misapprehending the Prophesies of their Messias SIR T. BROWNE. Hence **Cala·mitous-ly** *adv.*, **-ness** (*rare*).

Calamity (kălæ·mĭti). 1490. [– (O)Fr. *calamité* – L. *calamitas*; see -ITY.] **1.** The condition of grievous affliction or adversity; deep distress arising from some adverse circumstance or event. **2.** A grievous disaster or misfortune 1552.

1. Thou art wedded to calamitie *Rom. & Jul.* III. iii. 3. **2.** The bearing well of all calamities MILT.

‖ **Calamus** (kæ·lămŏs). ME. [L. – Gr. κάλαμος.] † **1.** A reed, a cane: vaguely used by early writers –1712. **2. Sweet C.,** *C. aromaticus*: **a.** an eastern aromatic plant (*Exod.* 30:23), taken by some to be the Sweet-scented Lemon Grass of Malabar; **b.** the native Sweet Flag (*Acorus calamus*) ME. **3.** A genus of palms comprising many species, the stems of which form canes or rattans 1836. **4.** A fistular stem without an articulation. var. † **Ca·lamy.**

† **Cala·nder, -re.** 1599. [– (O)Fr. *calandre* – Pr. *calandra* – med.L. *calandrus* – Gr. κάλανδρος.] A species of lark, *Alauda calandra* –1803.

‖ **Calando** (kala·ndo). [It., = 'slackening'.] *Mus.* A direction: Diminishing in tone and rate.

Calash (kălæ·ʃ), *sb.* Also **caleche, calèche.** 1666. [– Fr. *calèche*, †*galèche* (Molière) – G. *kalesche* – Pol. *kolaska* or Czech *kolesa*, f. *kolo* wheel.] **1.** A light carriage with low wheels, having a removable folding hood. In Canada a two-wheeled, one-seated vehicle, with a seat for the driver on the splashboard. **2.** The folding hood of various vehicles, *e.g.* a carriage, a perambulator, etc. 1856. **3.** A woman's hood, supported with hoops, and projecting beyond the face. Formerly much worn. 1774. Also *attrib.*

1. The Canadians . . were riding about in caleches 1866. **3.** That lady in her clogs and c. THACKERAY.

Calastic, *a.* For *chalastic* – Gr. χαλαστικός laxative. BURTON.

‖ **Calathi·dium.** [mod.L., dim. of next.] *Bot.* The flower-head of Compositæ.

‖ **Calathus** (kæ·lăþ*ŏ*s). Pl. **-i.** 1753. [L. – Gr. κάλαθος vase-shaped basket.] **1.** An ancient basket (in sculpture, etc.). **2.** = CALATHIDIUM. Hence **Ca·lathiform** *a.*

Calavance (kæ·lăvæns). ? *Obs.* 1620. [orig. *garvance, caravance* – Sp. *garbanzo* chick-pea.] A name for certain varieties of pulse, as *Dolichos barbadensis*, etc.

Salt fish and calavances MARRYAT.

Cala·verite. 1868. [f. *Calaveras* in California + -ITE[1] 2 b.] *Min.* A bronze-yellow massive telluride of gold, or of gold and silver.

Calc- (kælk). 1875. [– G. *kalk* lime, w. sp. altered after L. *calc-* CALX.] *Min.* and *Geol.* Lime: used *attrib.* or in *comb.* = 'lime-, calcareous', as in C.-SINTER, -SPAR, -TUFF.

‖ **Calcaire** (kalkē·r). 1833. [Fr., adj. (– L. *calcarius*) CALCAREOUS, sb. *Geol.*, limestone.] In *calcaire grossier*, and *c. silicieux* (coarse and siliceous limestone), the French names of two strata of the Paris basin, used by geologists generally.

Calca·neal, Calca·nean, *a.* 1847. [f. L. *calcaneum* (see next) + -AL[1], -AN.] *Phys.* Of or belonging to the heel-bone. Hence **Calca·neo-,** comb. form.

‖ **Calcaneum** (kælkē·ni*ŏ*m). 1751. [L. *calcaneum* the heel.] The bone of the heel.

Calcar[1] (kæ·lkāɹ). 1662. [– It. *calcara* lime-kiln, calcar oven; cf. late L. *calcaria* lime-kiln.] **1.** In *Glass-making*: 'A small furnace, in which the first calcination is made of sand and potash, for the formation of a frit' (Ure). **2.** *Metall.* An annealing oven.

‖ **Calcar**[2] (kæ·lkāɹ). 1836. [L. *calcar* spur.] *Bot.* A hollow spur from the base of a petal. Hence **Ca·lcarate** *a.* spurred.

Calcareo- (kælkē·ri,o). Comb. f. CALCAREOUS, 'containing lime', used **a.** with adjs., as *c.-argillaceous* (composed of clay with a mixture of lime, etc.); **b.** with sbs., as *c.-barite*, 'a white barite from Strontian containing.. 6·6% of lime' DANA.

Calcareous, -ious (kælkē·riəs), *a.* 1677. [f. L. *calcarius* of lime (f. *calx, calc-* lime + *-arius* -ARY[1]) + -OUS; see -ARIOUS. The sp. in *-eous* is erron.] Of the nature of (carbonate of) lime; composed of or containing lime or limestone.

C. spar = CALC-SPAR; *c. tufa* = CALC-TUFF. Hence **Calca·reous-ly** *adv.*, **-ness.**

Calcariferous (kælkări·fĕrəs), *a.* 1853. [In sense 1 f. CALCAR[2] + -FEROUS.] **1.** Bearing spurs. **2.** *catachr.* for *calciferous.* So **Calca·riform** *a.* shaped like a spur; having a calcareous, rhomboidal appearance.

Ca·lcarine, *a.* 1871. [f. CALCAR[2] + -INE[1].] Spur-like.

† **Ca·lcate,** *v. rare.* 1623. [– *calcat-*, pa. ppl. stem of L. *calcare* tread under foot, f. *calx, calc-* heel; see -ATE[3].] To stamp under the heel. Hence **Calca·tion** (*rare*).

‖ **Calcave·lla, Calcave·llos.** 1816. [f. *Carcavelhos* (kārkăve·lʸos) in Portugal.] A sweet white wine brought from Lisbon.

† **Ca·lceate,** *v.* 1656. [– *calceat-*, pa. ppl. stem of L. *calceare* put shoes on (one's) feet, f. *calceus* shoe; see -ATE[3].] To shoe, or put on shoes. Hence **Ca·lceated** *ppl. a.*; var. † **Ca·lceate** *a.* (*rare*).

Calcedon, calcedony, etc.; see CHAL-.

Calceiform (kæ·lsi,ifǭɹm), *a.* 1860. [f. L. *calceus* shoe + -FORM.] *Bot.* Calceolate.

Calceolaria (kæ:lsi,olēᵊ·riă, kælsiŏ-). 1846. [mod.L., f. L. *calceolus* dim. of *calceus* shoe (f. *calx* heel) + *-aria*, fem. of *-arius* -ARY[1].] *Bot.* 'Slipper-flower' or 'slipper-wort'; a genus of *Scrophulariaceæ*, having a flower which suggests its name. Native to S. America.

Calceolate (kæ·lsĭŏleⁱt), *a.* 1864. [f. as prec.; see -ATE[2].] *Bot.* Shaped like a slipper. Hence **Ca·lceolately** *adv.*

Calces, pl. of CALX.

† **Calce·scence.** [f. L. *calx, calc-* lime + -ESCENCE, after *fluorescence.*] Replaced by CALORESCENCE.

Calci-, comb. f. L. *calx* lime. Hence: **calci-ferous** *a.*, yielding or containing (carbonate of) lime; **-fic** *a.*, forming lime; belonging to calcification; **-fica·tion,** conversion into lime; the hardening of a structure, tissue, etc. by the deposit of salts of lime, as in the formation of teeth, and in petrifaction; *concr.* the product of calcifying; **-genous** *a.*, *Chem.* producing a calx, as some metals; **-gerous** *a.*, containing lime; **-mine,** a white or coloured wash for walls; hence **-mine** *v.* to whitewash; **-miner.**

Calcic (kæ·lsik), *a.* 1871. [f. CALCIUM + -IC.] Of or containing calcium.

Calciform (kæ·lsifǭɹm), *a.* 1782. [f. CALCI- + -FORM; in 3, f. L. *calx* heel.] † **1.** Of metals: Oxidized –1812. **2.** Pebble-shaped 1881. **3.** Having a heel-like projection 1881.

Calcify (kæ·lsifəi), *v.* 1836. [f. CALCI- + -FY.] **1.** To convert into lime; to harden by the deposit of lime. **2.** *intr.* To become calcified 1859.

† **Ca·lcinate.** 1610. [– *calcinat-*, pa. ppl. stem of med.L. *calcinare*; see CALCINE, -ATE[1, 2, 3].] *adj.* Calcined. *sb.* [sc. *form* or *product.*] So † **Ca·lcinate** *v.* = CALCINE.

Calcination (kælsinē·ʃən). ME. [– (O)Fr. *calcination* or med.L. *calcinatio*, f. as prec.; see -ION.] **1.** The action or process of calcining. † **b.** Oxidation –1822. **2.** *gen.* A burning to ashes 1616. **3.** A calcined condition or (*concr.*) product –1712.

Calcinatory (kælsi·nătəri, kæ·lsi-). 1611. [f. as prec. + -ORY[2].] *adj.* Serving for calcination. *sb.* [sc. *vessel.*] (Dicts.)

Calcine (kælsəi·n), *v.* ME. [– (O)Fr. *calciner* or med.L. *calcinare* (a term of alchemy), f. late L. *calcina* lime, quick-lime, f. L. *calx, calc-* CALX.] **1.** To reduce by fire to a calx, powder, or friable substance. **b.** To desiccate (air, etc.) by heat 1880. **c.** *fig.* To purify by consuming the grosser part 1634. **2.** *gen.* To burn to ashes 1641. Also *fig.* **3.** *intr.* To suffer calcination 1704.

2. Calcining the cities of Sodom and Gomorrah FARRAR. Hence **Calci·nable** *a.* **Calci·ner,** one who, or that which, calcines; *spec.* a kiln for roasting ore. var. † **Ca·lcinize.**

Calcio- (kæ·lsio-), comb. f. CALCIUM, used in names of minerals.

Calcite (kæ·lsəit). 1849. [– G. *calcit* (Haidinger 1845), f. *calc-* (see CALX) + -ITE[1] 2 b.] *Min.* The native crystallized rhombohedral anhydrous carbonate of lime (calcium carbonate), which exists in a variety of forms: calc-spar, calcareous spar. Also *attrib.*

Ca·lcitrant, *a. rare.* (*pedantic.*) 1866. [– *calcitrant-*, pres. ppl. stem of L. *calcitrare* kick out with the heels, f. *calx* heel; see -ANT.] Kicking; that kicks at any restriction.

Calcitrate (kæ·lsitreⁱt), *v.* 1623. [f. *calcitrat-*, pa. ppl. stem of L. *calcitrare*; see prec., -ATE[3].] *trans* and *intr.* To kick. Hence **Calcitra·tion** (*lit.* and *fig.*).

Calcium (kæ·lsi*ŏ*m). 1808. [f. L. *calx* lime; see CALX, -IUM.] *Chem.* **1.** A chemical element, one of the metals of the alkaline earths, being the basis of lime; a greyish-white metal, ductile and malleable, widely diffused, but found in nature only in composition. Symbol Ca. **2.** *attrib.* = CALCIC 1864.

Calco- (kæ·lko), comb. f. L. *calx, calc-* lime, the regular form of which is CALCI-; *calco-* is after Gk. analogies; see -O-, -I-.

Calcography, improper sp. of CHALC-.

Calc-sinter (kæ·lk,si·ntəɹ). 1823. [– G. *kalk-sinter*, f. *kalk* (see CALC-) + *sinter* slag.] *Min.* A hard crystalline deposit from springs which hold carbonate of lime in solution.

Calc-spar (kæ·lk,spā·ɹ). 1822. [See CALC-.] *Min.* Calcareous spar.

Calc-tuff (kæ·lk,tɒ·f). 1822. [See CALC-.] *Min.* A porous deposit of carbonate of lime, formed by the waters of calcareous springs.

Calculable (kæ·lki*ŭ*lăb'l), *a.* 1734. [f. CALCULATE + -ABLE; cf. Fr. *calculable.*] Capable of being calculated. Of a person: Such that his action in given circumstances can be reckoned upon and estimated 1865.

The least consistent, reliable, and c. of public men 1865. Hence **Ca:lculabi·lity.**

Calcular (kæ·lki*ŭ*lăɹ), *a.* 1831. [f. CALCULUS 3 + -AR[1].] Of or pertaining to a calculus.

† **Ca·lculary,** *sb.* 1674. [f. as next.] A 'congeries of little stony knots' in a pear –1753.

Calculary (kæ·lki*ŭ*lări), *a.* 1660. [– L. *calcularius*, f. *calculus* stone; see CALCULUS, -ARY[1].] *Med.* Of or pertaining to a calculus; gravelly.

Calculate (kæ·lki*ŭ*leⁱt), *v.* 1570. [– *calculat-*, pa. ppl. stem of late L. *calculare*, f. *calculus* stone; see CALCULUS.] **1.** *trans.* To compute mathematically, reckon. *absol.* To perform calculations, to form an estimate 1601. **2.** *ellipt.* To ascertain beforehand the time or circumstances of (an event, etc.) by astrology or mathematics 1593. † **3.** To reckon in 1643. **4.** To think out (*arch.*) 1654. **5.** To arrange, adjust, adapt, or fit *for* a purpose. Const. *for*, or *inf.* with to; now only in *pass.* 1639. Hence, in *pa. pple.* = 'suited'. **6.** *intr.* To count *upon* or *on* 1807. **7.** *U.S. colloq.* To think, opine, suppose, 'reckon'; to intend, purpose 1830.

1. Why Old men, Fooles, and Children c. *Jul. C.* I. iii. 65. **2.** To c. a lunar eclipse DE QUINCEY. **5.** The coach was calculated to carry six regular passengers SCOTT. **6.** To c. on a quiet Sunday 1873. var. † **Ca·lcule** *v.*

Calculated (kæ·lki*ŭ*leⁱtėd), *pa. pple.* and *ppl. a.* 1722. [f. prec. + -ED[1].] **1.** Reckoned, estimated, thought out 1863. **2.** Fitted, suited, apt; proper or likely *to* 1722.

1. To speak with a c. caution GEO. ELIOT. **2.** Disguises not c... to deceive MANSEL.

Calculating (kæ·lki*ŭ*leⁱtiŋ). 1710. [f. as prec. + -ING[1], -ING[2].] *vbl. sb.* The action of the vb. CALCULATE: chiefly *attrib. ppl. a.* That calculates (*esp.* advantage) shrewdly or selfishly 1809.

He was c. and mercenary MAR. EDGEWORTH. Hence **Ca·lcula:tingly** *adv.*

Calculation (kælki*ŭ*lē·ʃən). ME. [– (O)Fr. *calculation* – late L. *calculatio*, f. as prec.; see -ION.] **1.** The action of reckoning; computation. **2.** *concr.* The form in which reckoning is made; its result 1646. **3.** Estimate of probability; forecast 1847.

1. All arithmetic and c. have to do with number JOWETT. **2.** If the first c. is wrong, we make a second JANE AUSTEN. **3.** His. .attack was never the inspiration of courage, but the result of c. EMERSON. vars. † **Ca·lculate,** † **Ca·lcule** *sbs.*

Calculative (kæ·lki*ŭ*lĕtiv), *a.* 1766. [f. CALCULATE + -IVE; see -ATIVE.] Of or pertaining to calculation; given to calculating.

Extraordinary c. powers 1840.

Calculator (kæ·lki*ŭ*leⁱtəɹ). ME. [– L. *calculator*; in mod. use f. as prec. + -OR 2.] **1.** One who calculates; a reckoner. **2.** A set of tables to facilitate calculations; a calculating machine 1784.

1. Nature hates calculators EMERSON. var. † **Ca·lculer.**

Ca·lculatory, *a.* ? *Obs.* 1611. [f. CALCULATE + -ORY[2]; cf. med.L. *calculatorius.*] Of or pertaining to calculation.

Calculifrage (kæ·lki*ŭ*lifrēⁱdʒ). 1879. [– Fr. *calculifrage* adj. 'that breaks calculi'.] *Med.* An instrument for breaking down calculi. Hence **Ca·lculi:fragous** *a.* (medicines) fitted for breaking or reducing calculi.

Ca·lculist. 1829. [f. CALCULUS + -IST.] A mathematician.

Calculous (kæ·lki*ŭ*ləs), *a.* 1605. [f. L. *calculosus* + -OUS; cf. Fr. *calculeux.*] **1.** *Med.* Of or pertaining to a calculus or the stone; diseased with the stone; calculary. † **2.** Stony (as the calculary of a pear) 1671. var. † **Calculo·se.**

Calculus (kæ·lki*ŭ*l*ŏ*s). Pl. **-i, -uses.** 1684. [– L. *calculus* pebble, stone in the body, stone used in calculation.] **1.** *Med.* 'A stone. A generic term for concretions occurring accidentally in the animal body' (*Syd. Soc. Lex.*). Specialized as *renal, vesical*, etc. † **2.** Computation –1817. **3.** *Math.* A method of calculation, as the DIFFERENTIAL, INTEGRAL Calculus, etc. The differential calculus is often spoken of as 'the calculus'. 1672.

3. Science. .with all its calculuses, differential, integral, and of variations CARLYLE.

‖ **Caldarium** (kældēᵊ·ri*ŏ*m). 1753. [L.] A (Roman) hot bath or bath-room.

‖ **Caldera** (kɑldēᵊ·ră). 1865. [Sp., :– late L. *caldaria* pot for boiling, fem. of prec.] *Geol.* A deep cauldron-like cavity on the summit of an extinct volcano.

Caldron, var. of CAULDRON.

‖ **Calean, callean, calleoon.** 1739. [Pers. *ġilyān, ḳalyān* – Arab. *ġalyūn.*] A water-pipe for smoking; the Persian hubble-bubble.

Caleche, calèche; see CALASH.

Caledonian (kælĭdōᵘ·niăn). 1656. [f. *Caledonia*, Roman name of part of northern Britain, in mod. poetry, etc., applied to Scotland, or the Scottish Highlands.] *adj.*

Of ancient Caledonia; of Scotland. *sb.* A native of ancient Caledonia; *joc.* = Scotchman 1768.

Caledonite (kæ·lĭdonəi:t). 1863. [f. as prec. + -ITE¹ 2 b.] Cupreous sulpho-carbonate of lead, found at Leadhills in Lanarkshire and elsewhere.

Calefacient (kælĭfē¹·ʃ¹ĕnt). 1661. [– *calefacient-*, pres. ppl. stem of L. *calefacere*, f. *calēre* be warm; see -FACIENT.] *adj.* Producing warmth. *sb. Med.* [sc. *agent.*] 1661.

Calefaction (kælĭfæ·kʃən). Now *rare.* 1547. [– (O)Fr. *caléfaction* or late L. *calefactio*, f. *calefact-*, pa. ppl. stem of L. *calefacere* make warm; see prec., -ION.] **1.** Making warm (*lit.* and *fig.*); heating. **2.** Heated condition 1634.

Calefactor (kæ·lĭfæktəɹ). 1605. [f. as prec. + -OR 2.] † **1.** He who, or that which, warms. **2.** A small kind of stove 1831.

Calefa·ctory (kælĭfæ·ktəri). 1536. [– late L. *calefactorius* adj., med.L. *-torium* sb.; see prec., -ORY¹ and ².] **A.** *adj.* Adapted for or tending to warming 1711. var. **Calefa·ctive** (now *rare*). **B.** *sb.* **1.** The room in a monastery where the inmates warmed themselves 1681. **2.** A warming-pan; the ball of precious metal containing hot water, on which the priest warmed his hands when administering the eucharist in cold weather; the *pome* 1536. † **3.** = CALEFACIENT *sb.* 1657.

† **Ca·lefy,** *v.* 1526. [– med.L. *cale-*, *calificare* for L. *calefacere*, f. *calēre* be hot; see -FY.] **1.** To warm, heat –1657. **2.** *intr.* To become warm –1658.

‖ **Calembour** (kalaṅbur, kɑ·lĕmbūᵊr). 1830. [Fr.] A pun.

Calendal (kăle·ndăl), *a.* 1839. [f. L. *calendæ* + -AL¹.] Of or pertaining to the Calends.

Calendar (kæ·lĕndăɹ), *sb.* [ME. *kalender* – AFr. *calender*, OFr. *calendier* (mod. *calendrier*) – L. *calendarium* account-book, f. *calendæ* CALENDS, the day on which accounts were due.] **1.** The system according to which the beginning and length of years, and the subdivision of the year, is fixed; as the Babylonian, Jewish, Roman, or Arabic calendar. **2.** A table showing the months, days of the week, and dates of a given year; often also giving other data connected with individual days. Often specialized, as *Gardener's C.*, *Racing C.*, etc. Also a series of more detailed tables; an almanac. ME. † **3.** *fig.* A guide, directory; a model –1602. **4.** A list or register. (Now *fig.*) ME. **b.** *esp.* A list of prisoners for trial at the assizes 1764. **c.** *spec.* A list of documents arranged chronologically with a short summary of their contents 1467. † **5.** *fig.* A record –1718.

1. *Julian C.*, that introduced by Julius Cæsar B.C. 46, in which the ordinary year has 365 days, and every fourth year is a leap year of 366 days, the months having the names, order, and length still retained. *Gregorian C.*, the modification of the preceding with reference to astronomical data and the natural course of the seasons, introduced by Pope Gregory XIII in A.D. 1582, and adopted in Great Britain in 1752. See STYLE. He is the card or c. of gentry *Haml.* V. ii. 114. **4. c.** C. of State Papers (*title*) 1856. **5.** The Kalender of my past endeuours *All's Well* I. iii. 4.

Comb., etc.: **c.-clock,** one which indicates the days of the week or month; **c. month,** one of the twelve months into which the year is divided according to the c.; also the space of time from any date (*e.g.* the 17th) of any month to the corresponding date (the 17th) of the next, as opp. to a lunar month of 4 weeks.

Hence **Calenda·rial, Calenda·rian** *adjs.* (*rare*) of or pertaining to a c. † **Ca·lendarist** (*rare*). † **Ca·lendary** *sb.* = CALENDAR *sb.*; as *adj.* = *Calendarian.* **Cale·ndric, -al** *a.* (*rare*) of the nature of a c.

Calendar (kæ·lĕndăɹ), *v.* 1487. [f. prec.] **1.** To register in a calendar or list. **2.** *spec.* To arrange, analyse, and index (documents) 1859. Hence **Ca·lendarer.**

Calender (kæ·lĕndəɹ), *sb.*¹ 1513. [– Fr. *calandre*, presumably from the verb.] † **1.** = CALENDERER –1782. **2.** A machine in which cloth, paper, etc., is pressed under rollers for the purpose of smoothing or glazing; also for watering or giving a wavy appearance, etc. 1688. Also *attrib.*

1. The c. Will lend his horse to go COWPER.

Ca·lender, *sb.*² 1634. [– Pers. *ḳalandar.*] One of an order of mendicant dervishes in Turkey and Persia.

Ca·lender, *v.* 1513. [– (O)Fr. *calandrer*, of unkn. origin.] To pass through a calender for the purpose of smoothing, glazing, etc. Hence **Cale·nderer,** one whose business it is to c. cloth, etc. **Ca·lendry,** a place where calendering is done.

Calends, kalends (kæ·lĕndz), *sb. pl.* ME. [– (O)Fr. *calendes* – L. *kalendæ* (pl.) first day of the month, when the order of days was proclaimed, f. **kal-* call, proclaim, as in L. *calare*, Gr. καλεῖν.] **1.** The first day of any month in the Roman calendar. (In use till 17th c.) † **2.** The Jewish festival of the new moon –1609. † **3.** *fig.* Prelude. (Also in *sing.*) –1618. **4.** A calendar, record 1470.

3. What is age, but the Calends of death RALEIGH. Phr. *On* (*at*) *the Greek Calends* (L. *ad Græcas kalendas*): joc. for, Never; the Greeks had none.

‖ **Cale·ndula.** 1871. [mod.L. dim. of L. *calendæ* (prec.), intended to express 'little calender, little clock' or perh. 'little weather-glass'.] *Bot.* **1.** Generic name of the Common Marigold, and its congeners. **2.** *Pharm.* A tincture of the flowers used as a hæmostatic. Also *attrib.*

Calendulin (kăle·ndiŭlin). 1859. [f. prec. + -IN¹.] *Chem.* A mucilaginous substance obtained from the common marigold.

Calenture (kæ·lĕntiuᵊɹ). 1593. [– Fr. *calenture* – Sp. *calentura*, f. *calentar* be hot :– Rom. **calentare* f. L. *calēre* be warm.] A disease incident to sailors within the tropics, characterized by delirium in which, it is said, they fancy the sea to be green fields and desire to leap into it. **2.** *fig.* and *transf.* Fever; burning passion, glow 1596.

2. Knowledge kindles Calentures in some DONNE.

† **Ca·lenture,** *v. rare.* 1649. [f. prec. sb.] To infect with the calenture; *fig.* to fire 1678. *intr.* To become hot or inflamed. DANIEL.

Thirst of empire calentur'd his breast MARVELL.

† **Ca·lepin.** 1568. [– Fr. – It. *calepino*, from Ambrosio *Calepino*, of Calepio in Italy, who wrote *the* Latin Dictionary of the 16th c.] A dictionary; *fig.* one's notebook –1662.

Calescent (kăle·sĕnt), *a. rare.* 1804. [– *calescent-*, pres. ppl. stem of L. *calescere* grow warm, f. *calēre* be warm; see -ESCENT.] Growing warm, glowing with heat. Hence **Cale·scence,** increasing warmth or heat.

Calf¹ (kāf). Pl. (and occ. genit. sing., *esp.* in comb.), **calves.** [OE. *cælf* (*ċealf*) = OS. *calf* (Du. *kalf*), OHG. *kálb* (G. *kalb*) :– WGmc. **kalƀa* n., beside ON. *kálfr* m., and Goth. *kalbō* = OHG. *kalba* fem.] **1.** The young (under one year old) of any bovine animal, *esp.* of the domestic cow OE. **b.** *transf.* A dolt; occ. a meek harmless person 1553. **2.** *ellipt.* Leather made from the skin of a calf; *calf-leather* 1727. **3.** The young of other animals; as deer, the elephant, the whale, etc. ME. **4.** *transf.* A small island lying near a larger one; as in 'The Calf of Man' 1833. **5.** An iceberg detached from a coast glacier; a fragment of ice detached from an iceberg 1818.

1. b. Some silly doting brainless calfe DRAYTON. *Essex calf*: a native of Essex.

Comb.: **c.-kill,** a heath-plant (*Kalmia latifolia*); cf. 'lambkill'; **-knee,** knock-knee; **-lick** (*dial.*), a cowlick, a feather; **-love; calves'-snout, calf's-,** ANTIRRHINUM or Snapdragon. Hence **Ca·lfhood. Ca·lfish** *a.* like a c.; raw, untrained. **Ca·lfling.**

Calf² (kāf). ME. [– ON. *kálfi*, of unkn. origin.] The fleshy hinder part of the shank of the leg. Also *transf.*, of a stocking 1659.

ffal longe were his legges and ful lene ylyk a staf ther was no c. ysene CHAUCER. Hence **Ca·lfless** *a.*

† **Ca·lfret.** 1600. [– Fr. *calfreter* (Cotgr.), mod. *calfater*, *calfeutrer* caulk, ult. perh. f. Arab. *ḳallafa* or *kalfaṭa.*] To stop up the seams of (a ship); to caulk –1653.

Calf's-foot, calves-foot. 1450. **1.** *lit.* The foot of a calf; hence *calves-foot jelly* 1620. **2.** *Herb.* The Cuckoo-pint (*Arum maculatum*); see ARUM. [So Fr. *pied-de-veau.*]

Calf-skin. Also **calf's-, calves-, calve-.** 1590. The skin of a calf; a kind of leather made from this. Occ. = *vellum.*

Cali-, erron. f. *calli-*, from Gr. κάλλος beauty; confused with *calo-* from Gr. καλός.

Caliban (kæ·libæn). 1610. [perh. a var. of CANNIBAL, or derived directly from a form of CARIB.] 'A saluage and deformed slaue' in Shakespeare's *Tempest*; whence, a man of degraded bestial nature. Hence **Ca·libani:sm.**

Calibogus (kælibōᵘ·gəs). *U.S.* 1785. [Origin unkn.] A mixture of rum and spruce beer.

Calibrate (kæ·librēⁱt), *v.* 1864. [f. CALIBRE + -ATE³.] To determine the calibre of, as of a thermometer tube; to graduate a gauge of any kind with allowance for its irregularities. Hence **Calibra·tion,** the action of calibrating.

Calibre, caliber (kæ·libəɹ: occas. kăli·br), *sb.* 1567. [– (O)Fr. *calibre* – It. *calibro* or Sp. *calibre* – Arab. *ḳālib* mould for casting metal.] **1.** † **a.** The diameter of a bullet, cannon-ball, etc. **b.** *Hence*, The internal diameter or bore of a gun. (Hence, derivatively, phrases like 'guns of heavy calibre'.) 1588. **c.** *transf.* The diameter of any body of circular section; also, of a tube or hollow cylinder 1727. **2.** *fig.* † **a.** Degree, quality, rank. [The earliest cited sense. prob. from Fr.] **b.** Degree of personal capacity; weight of character. In wider sense: Stamp, degree of merit or importance. 1567. **3.** *pl. calibers.* = CALLIPERS.

1. c. The caliber of these empty tubes REID, of arteries TODD. **2.** Sir Henry Vane, or others of such c. DRUMM. OF HAWTH. The c. of this young man's understanding SCOTT.

Comb., etc.: **c.-rule,** an instrument for determining the c. of a ball from its weight, or vice versa; so **-scale; -compasses, -square:** see CALLIPER. Hence † **Ca·libre, -ber,** *v.* to determine the c. of; to measure with callipers. **Ca·libred** *a.* of or having c.: *esp.* in *comb.*

Ca·liburn, -burno. ME. The name of King Arthur's sword. See EXCALIBUR.

Calic(e, early f. CHALICE.

Caliciform (kæ·lisifǫɹm), *a.* 1849. [f. L. *calix, -ic-* + -FORM.] Cup-shaped. var. (*erron.*) **Calyciform.** So **Cali·cinated** *ppl. a.*

Calicle (kæ·lik'l). 1848. [– L. *caliculus*. dim. of CALIX; see -CULE.] *Biol.* A small cup-like prominence, as in corals. var. (*erron.*) **Calycle.**

Calico (kæ·likо), *sb.* (*a.*) 1540. [In XVI–XVII also *calicut*, from the name of the Indian city (sense 1).] **1.** The name of a city on the coast of Malabar; used *attrib.* in *Calicut-cloth, Calico-cloth.* **2.** Hence: **a.** *orig.* Cotton cloth imported from the East. **b.** Now, in England, plain white unprinted cotton cloth. 1578. **c.** in U.S.; printed cotton cloth, coarser than muslin 1841. **3.** *adj.* Of calico.

Comb.: **c.-printer,** one whose trade is c.-printing; **-printing,** the art or trade of producing a pattern on c. by printing in colours, or other process.

Calicular (kăli·kiŭlăr), *a.* 1658. [f. L. *caliculus*; see CALICLE, -AR¹.] † **1.** ? = *calycular* (see CALYCLE). **2.** *Biol.* Of or pertaining to a calicle 1849. Hence **Cali·cularly** *adv.*

Caliculate (kăli·kiŭlĕt), *a.* 1846. [f. as prec. + -ATE².] Having calicles. var. **Cali·culated.**

Calid (kæ·lid), *a. arch.* 1599. [– L. *calidus.*] Warm, tepid; hot. Hence † **Cali·dity.** (Chiefly *techn.* in *Med.*)

Caliduct (kæ·lidɒkt). 1651. [f. L. *calidus* (prec.) + *-duct*, after *aqueduct.*] A pipe for the conveyance of heat. Cf. Fr. *caliduc.*

Calif, var. of CALIPH.

† **Ca·ligate,** *a.* 1562. [– L. *caligatus*, f. *caliga* (soldier's) half-boot; see -ATE².] Wearing *caligæ* or military boots; *esp.* in *knight c.* –1656.

† **Caliga·tion.** 1615. [– L. *caligatio* darkness, mistiness (Pliny).] *Med.* Dimness or mistiness of sight –1657.

Caliginous (kăli·dʒinəs), *a.* 1548. [f. L. *caliginosus* dark, misty (f. *caligo, -in-*) + -OUS.] Misty, dim, murky; obscure, dark; also *fig.* Now *arch.*

The cave C. COWPER. Hence **Caligino·sity** (*arch.*). † **Cali·ginousness.**

‖ **Caligo** (kăləi·go). 1801. [L.] Dimness of sight.

Caligrapher, -meter, etc.; see CALLI-.

Cali·gulism. *nonce-wd.* A mad extravagance worthy of Caligula, the third Roman Emperor. H. WALPOLE.

‖ **Calin.** 1752. [Fr. – Pg. *calaim.*] The tin of Siam and Malacca, an alloy, of which the Chinese make tea-caddies, etc.

Calipash (kæ·lipæʃ). 1689. [Earliest forms *galley patch, calapatch*; perh. of native W. Indian orig., unless a native alt. of Sp. *carapacho* CARAPACE.] † **a.** The upper shell or carapace of the turtle. **b.** That part next the upper shell, containing a dull green gelatinous substance 1749.

Calipee (kæ·lipī). 1657. [See prec.; not found in any other European lang.] † **a.** The lower shell or plastron of the turtle. **b.** That part next the lower shell, containing a light yellowish gelatinous substance 1679.

Caliper, -compasses; see CALLIPER.

Calipe·va, calli-. 1833. [Origin unkn.] A mullet of the W. Indies, *Mugil liza.*

Caliph, calif (kæ·lif, kē·lif). [–(O)Fr. *caliphe* (med.L. *calipha, -es*) – Arab. *ḵalīfa*, f. *ḵalafa* succeed.] The Moslem title for the chief civil and religious ruler, as successor of Mohammed.

Caliphate (kæ·lifēt). Also **-at.** 1614. [f. prec. + -ATE[1]. Cf. Fr. *caliphat.*] **1.** The rank, dignity, office, or term of office, of a caliph 1734. var. **Ca·liphship** (*rare*). **2.** The dominion of a caliph 1614.

Calippic; see CALLIPPIC.

‖ **Calisaya** (kælisē·ă). 1837. [Sp., perh. f. native S. Amer. name.] In *C. bark*: the best sort of Peruvian Bark, obtained from *Cinchona calisaya.*

Caliver (kæ·livəɹ, kălī·vəɹ). Now *Hist.* 1568. [var. of CALIBRE, prob. first in Fr. phr. *arquebuse* or *pièce de calibre.*] A light kind of harquebus (orig. of a certain calibre), fired without a rest. † **b.** A soldier armed with a caliver –1591.

‖ **Calix** (kæ·liks). Pl. **ca·lices.** 1708. [L., = cup; see CHALICE.] A cup; a cup-like cavity or organ; *e.g.* the body of a Vorticella.

Calixtin, -ine (kali·kstin). 1710. *Eccl. Hist.* [In sense 1 – med.L. *calixtini* (pl.), f. *calix* cup; cf. Fr. *calixtin.*] **1.** One of a section of the Hussites, who claimed the cup as well as the bread for the laity; a Utraquist. **2.** An adherent of George Calixtus (1586–1656), a Lutheran divine and professor, of conciliatory views; a syncretist 1727.

Calk (kǭk), *sb.* 1587. [app. f. (ult.) L. *calc-, calcaneum*, or *calcar*; see CALKIN.] **1.** = CALKIN. **2.** *U.S.* A piece of iron projecting from the heel of a boot, which prevents slipping 1805.

† **Calk,** *v.*[1] ME. [app. short f. † *calcule* (XIV–XVI) – (O)Fr. *calculer* – L. *calculare* CALCULATE.] To calculate; *esp.* astrologically. Also *intr.* or *absol.* –1646.

Calk (kǭk), *v.*[2] 1624. [f. CALK *sb.*] To provide (a shoe) with a calk; to rough-shoe. Hence **Ca·lking** *vbl. sb.*; also *attrib.*, as in **calking-anvil,** an anvil for forming calks; **-tongs,** for sharpening these.

Calk (kǭk, kælk), *v.*[3] 1662. [– Fr. *calquer* in same sense – It. *calcare* – L. *calcare* tread. Also CALQUE.] To copy (a design) by rubbing the back with colouring matter, and drawing a blunt point along the outlines so as to trace them in colour on a surface placed beneath.

Calk, var. of CAULK; obs. f. CAUK *v.*

† **Ca·lker**[1]. 1535. [f. CALK *v.*[1] + -ER[1].] An astrologer; a magician –1662.

Calker[2] (kǭ·kəɹ). *Sc.* 1794. [f. CALK *v.*[2] + -ER[1].] = CALKIN.

Calker[3], var. of CAULKER.

Calkin (kǭ·kin, kæ·lkin). 1445. [Earlier *kakun* – MDu. *kalkoen* or its source OFr. *calcain* :– L. *calcaneum* heel, f. *calx, calc-* heel.] **1.** The turned-down ends of a horseshoe; also a turned edge under the front. **2.** The irons nailed on the heels and soles of shoes or clogs to make them last 1832.

Call (kǭl), *v.* [Late OE. *ceallian* (once) – ON. *kalla* cry, summon loudly, = MLG., (M)Du. *kallen*, OHG. *kallōn* talk, chatter :– **kallōjan*, f. Gmc. **kal-*.]

I. **intr.* **1.** To utter one's voice loudly and distinctly; to shout, cry: often with *out.* Const. *to, after.* OE. Also *fig.* **2.** To make or pay a call. Const. *at, in, on*; also *absol.* (Orig. to call aloud *at a door*; the notion of making a communication to one who answers the door is still essential.) 1593. ***trans.* **3.** To utter, or read over, in a loud voice; to proclaim. Often with *out.* Also *absol.* ME. **4.** To summon by a call; *hence* to cite; to bid (any one) come; † to invite. Also *absol.* ME. Also *fig.* **5.** To convoke, summon ME. **6.** To nominate by a call ME.; to invite (*esp.* to the pastorate of a church) 1560. **7.** To call upon (a person) *to do.* Said *esp.* of the call of God or duty. 1580.

1. Do you hear, my aunt calls DRYDEN. The throstle calls TENNYSON. *fig.* Deepe calleth unto deepe *Ps.* 42: 7. *spec.* (*Cards.*) *To call*: to make a demand (for a card, for a show of hands, etc.). **2.** [Go, knock and c. *Merry W.* IV. v. 9.] To c. at the Alehouses *Much Ado* III. iii. 44. **3.** 'Adsum'!.. the word we used at school when names were called THACKERAY. To c. the odds 1855, a halt 1888. **4.** Not called to the feast LATIMER. To c. a coach TICKELL, *fig.* to penance MILT. C. me early TENNYSON. † = 'call on' *Twel. N.* III. ii. 56. = 'call for', as *to c. a case* (mod.). *To c. a bond*: to give notice that the amount of the bond will be paid. **6.** Paul, called to be an Apostle I *Cor.* 1: 1. **7.** Called to preach the Gospel WESLEY.

II. To name. **1.** To give as name or title to; to speak of as ME. **2.** To call names. Now *dial.* 1633.

1. God called the light, Day *Gen.* 1: 5. The woman whom I was taught to c. mother DE FOE.

III. To drive. *Sc.* **1.** To urge forward (an animal or a vehicle); to turn, drive ME. Also *fig.* **2.** To drive (a nail); to fasten by hammering; to forge 1513. **3.** *absol.* and *intr.* (for *refl.*) To drive. Also *fig.*

1. Some ca' the pleugh BURNS. A puir ca-the-shuttle-body [*i.e.* weaver] SCOTT. **3.** *To ca' canny*, to drive gently and carefully.

Phrases. *To c. attention to*: to invite notice to; to point out. *To c. cousins*: to claim cousinship or kinship *with. To c. names*: to apply opprobrious terms to. *To c. in question*: to summon for trial or examination; to impeach; to cast doubt upon; † to examine; so † *To c. in doubt. To c. into being*: to give life to, make. *To c. into play*: to bring into action. *To c. to account*: to summon (one) to render an account, or to answer for conduct; *hence*, to reprove. *To c. to the bar*: see BAR *sb.*[1] *To c. to (one's) feet, legs*: to bid one stand up; *spec.* in order to speak, sing, etc. *To c. to memory*, etc.: to recollect, recall; also with *back. To c. to witness*, etc.: to appeal to (one) to bear witness, etc.

With prepositions. **C. for. a.** To ask loudly or authoritatively for; *fig.* to require. **b.** To go to or stop at a place and ask *for.* **c.** *Cards. To c. for trumps*: to signal to one's partner to play out trumps. Also *absol.* **To c. on or upon. a.** To call to; to address in a loud voice; to apostrophize the absent. **b.** To invoke, or supplicate (God, etc.). **c.** To appeal to *for*, or *to do*; to make a demand upon. † **d.** To demand (money due). **e.** To pay a short visit to.

With adverbs. **C. back. a.** [sense I. 4.] To recall (*lit.* and *fig.*); to bring back (a thing). **b.** To retract. **C. down. a.** To invoke from above, bring down. † **b.** To decry. **C. forth. a.** *lit.* To cause to come forward. **b.** *fig.* To cause to appear; to summon up (courage). **C. in. a.** To withdraw from the outside, from free action, from circulation. **b.** To summon for assistance or consultation. **c.** To require the payment or repayment of. **C. off.** [See I. 4.] To summon away; *fig.* to divert (the attention). **C. on** Of hands: To challenge. **C. out. a.** To summon forth; *fig.* to evoke. **b.** To challenge to fight (*esp.* a duel). **C. over.** To read aloud (a list of names, *e.g.* in school); hence **C.-over** *sb.* **C. up. a.** To summon from below (*e.g.* from Hades). **b.** To bring into the mind. **c.** To summon before an authority, *spec.* to perform national service; hence **C.-up** *sb.* **d.** To recall.

Call (kǭl), *sb.* ME. [f. prec. vb.] **1.** A loud vocal utterance; a shout, a cry. **2.** The cry of an animal, *esp.* of a bird 1684. **3.** A cry used to attract birds, etc. 1530; a whistle, etc. imitating the note of birds 1654; † a decoy-bird (*lit.* and *fig.*) *John* III. iv. 174. **4.** *Hunting.* A strain blown on the horn to encourage the hounds 1674. **5.** The act of calling at a place on the way 1783; a short formal visit 1862. **6.** Summons, invitation, bidding. Also *fig.* ME. **b.** *Amer. Land Law.* A matter of description, in a survey or grant, calling for a corresponding object, etc., on the land 1864. **7.** Demand, requisition, claim ME. **8.** A requirement of duty, a need, occasion, right 1674. **9.** A spiritual prompting 1650. † **10.** Vocation –1780. **11.** *Comm.* **a.** A demand for the payment of money; *esp.* a notice to a shareholder to pay up a portion of capital subscribed. Also *attrib.* 1709. **b.** On the Stock Exchange: An option of claiming stock at a certain time at a fixed price 1860. **12.** *Sc.* (now *ca', caw.*) Driving. Applied to: Forced respiration; a place where cattle are driven; a pass between hills. 1765.

1. *spec.* A roll-call: A c. of the House [of Commons] 1723. **2.** The parrot's c. TENNYSON. **5.** The baker's punctual c. COWPER. *To make, pay, receive a c.* **6.** Tapsters answering every c. SHAKS. A c. before the curtain (*mod.*). At the c. of Trumpet MILT. *P.L.* VII. 295. *concr.* A silver c. which hung around her neck SCOTT. See also BUGLE-*c.*, TRUMPET-*c.* **7.** The c...for cheap reprints 1832. **8.** I don't know what c. she had to blush so THACKERAY. **9.** We came by a c. of God to serve him here 1650. **11. a.** A c. of fifteen per cent. ADAM SMITH.

Phrases. **a.** with preps., as *At c.*: ready to answer a. c.; immediately available. *Within c.*: within reach of a summons; hence, *within c. of (a place)*: near to (it). **b.** *To have the c.*: to be in chief demand: in *Long Whist*, to be entitled to call honours. **c.** *C. to the bar*: admission to the status of barrister; see BAR *sb.*[1] III. 3.

Comb.: **c.-bell,** a bell for summoning attendance; *spec.* one giving the alarm at a fire-station; **-bird,** a bird for attracting others by its note; **-boy,** a youth employed **a.** (in a theatre) to call the actors when required on the stage, **b.** (on a steamer) to transmit the captain's orders to the engineer, **c.** (in a hotel) to answer the bells; **-day,** in the Inns of Court, the day in each term on which students are called to the bar; **-duck,** a decoy-duck; **-loan,** a loan to be repaid at c.; so **-money; -night,** see *call-day*; **-note,** the note used by a bird, etc., in calling to its mate.

‖ **Calla** (kæ·lă). 1866. [Cf. It. *calla* arum lily.] *Bot.* **1.** A genus of floating marsh plants (N.O. *Orontiaceæ*). **2.** A name erroneously given to the White Arum, Ethiopian or Trumpet Lily, *Richardia æthiopica* (N.O. *Araceæ*), a native of the Cape 1870.

Calla-; see CALA-.

Callæsthe·tic, -ics. [f. Gr. κάλλος beauty + AESTHETIC(S).] Whewell's proposed name for ÆSTHETICS.

Callant (ka·lănt). *Sc.* and *n. dial.* 1716. [– Flem. *kalant* 'customer', 'chap' – north. Fr. dial. *caland*, earlier *calland*, var. of *chaland* customer, etc., f. *chaloir* be warm :– L. *calēre.*] A boy of any age.

Callat, Calle, obs. ff. CALLET, CAUL.

Caller (kǭ·ləɹ), *sb.* 1450. [f. CALL *v.* + -ER[1].] **1.** One who or that which calls, in various senses of the vb.; *esp.* **2.** One who pays a short or complimentary visit. (The chief sense.) 1786.

Caller (ka·ləɹ), *a. Sc.* and *n. dial.* ME. [var. (with assim. of *lv* to *ll*, as in *siller* from *silver*) of ME. CALVER *a.*] **1.** Fresh (as opp. to what is beginning to corrupt); said *esp.* of fish. **2.** Of air, water, etc.: Fresh and cool; well-aired 1513.

1. The..fish-wife..shouting 'C. herrings' 1862.

Ca·llet, *sb.* Now *dial.* 1500. [Origin unkn.] **1.** A lewd woman, trull. **2.** ? = 'scold' 1528. Also *attrib.* Hence **Ca·llet** *v.* to scold. **Ca·llety** *a.* ill-tongued.

Calli-, Gr. καλλι-, comb. f. κάλλος beauty. See also CALI-.

† **Ca·llid,** *a. rare.* 1656. [– L. *callidus* skilful, cunning.] Crafty, cunning.

Callidity (kăli·dĭti). Now *rare.* 1524. [– L. *calliditas, -tat-*; see prec., -ITY.] Craftiness, cunning.

Calligraph (kæ·ligrɑf), *sb.*[1] *arch.* Also **cali-.** 1853. [– Fr. *calligraphe* – med.L. *calligraphus* – Gr. καλλιγράφος; see CALLI-, GRAPH.] One who writes beautifully; *spec.* a professional transcriber of manuscripts; vars. **Calli·grapher, -ist.**

Ca·lligraph, *sb.*[2] 1878. [f. as prec., after *autograph*, etc.] A beautiful specimen of writing. Hence **Ca·lligraph** *v.* to write beautifully or ornamentally. **Calligra·phic, -al,** *a.* of or pertaining to calligraphers or calligraphy. **Calligra·phically** *adv.*

Calligraphy (kæli·grăfi), 1613. [– Gr. καλλιγραφία, f. καλλιγράφος; see prec., -GRAPHY.] **1.** Beautiful writing; elegant penmanship. **2.** Penmanship generally 1645.

Calling (kǭ·liŋ), *vbl. sb.* ME. [f. CALL *v.* + -ING[1].] **I.** The action of the vb. CALL.

The c. of partridges 1693, of Parliament 1848, of simples GALE, of names 1687.

II. Summons, vocation. **1.** A divine call; the inward conviction of such a call 1534. † **2.** Station in life. [Founded on 1 *Cor.* 7:20.] –1691. **3.** Hence, Ordinary occupation, business 1551. *concr.* A body of persons following a profession or trade 1660. Also *attrib.*

1. The conscious warrant of some high c. MILT. A..pastor..diligent in his c. STUBBES. [The sense here includes the *vocatio* or calling of the Bishop, etc., and the professional 'calling'.] **2.** In the same callinge, wherin he was called 1 *Cor.* 7:20. [The mod. sense adds sense 1.] **3.** A ferry-man by my c. T. BROWN.

Ca·lling, *ppl. a.* 1634. [f. as prec. + -ING².] That calls. **b.** *spec.* in names of animals: **C. crab,** a genus of Land-crabs (*Gelasimus*), having one very long claw, which the animal extends, as if beckoning; **C. hare,** a rodent genus (*Lagomys*), having a peculiar call.

Calliope (kălai·ŏpi). *U.S.* 1863. [Gr. καλλιόπη 'beautiful-voiced', Muse of eloquence and heroic poetry.] An instrument consisting of a series of steam-whistles, played by a key-board like that of an organ.

Callipash, Callipee; see CALIPASH, -PEE.

Calliper, caliper (kæ·lipəɹ). 1588. [orig. *calliper compasses,* used for measuring the calibre of a bullet or piece of ordnance; presumably var. of CALIBRE.] **1.** Orig. used attrib., *c. compasses*; afterwards usu. in pl. (*pair of*) *callipers*: A kind of compasses with bowed legs for measuring the diameter of convex bodies; often with a scale attached; also a similar instrument with straight legs and points turned outwards for measuring the bore of tubes, etc. **2.** *transf.* The clip for holding the load in a crane 1769. Hence **Ca·lliper** *v.* to measure with or use callipers.

Callippic (kăli·pik), *a.* 1696. [f. Gr. Κάλλιππος + -IC.] Of or pertaining to Callippus, a Greek astronomer (*c*350 B.C.).

C. cycle or *period*: a cycle proposed by C. as an improvement on the Metonic cycle, consisting of 4 of the latter or 76 years, at the end of which, by omitting one day, he thought that the full and new moon would be brought round to the same day and hour.

Callipygian (kælipi·dʒiăn), *a.* 1800. [f. Gr. καλλίπυγος adj., f. καλλι- CALLI- + πυγή buttocks: the name of a statue of Venus; see -IAN.] Of, pertaining to, or having shapely or finely developed buttocks.

Callis-sand. Now *dial.* 1594. [f. *Callis,* 16th c. form of *Calais.*] A fine white sand, used for blotting ink, scouring, etc.

Callisthenic (kælisþe·nik), *a.* Also **cali-.** 1847. [f. Gr. καλλι- CALLI- + σθένος strength + -IC.] Pertaining to callisthenics. So **Callisthe·nical** *a.* addicted to callisthenics (*rare*).

Callisthe·nics, *sb. pl.* 1847. [f. as prec. + -ICS.] Gymnastic exercises suitable for girls; training calculated to develop the figure and to promote graceful movement. **Callisthe·nium,** a place for the practice of c.

‖·**Callithrix, -trix** (kæ·liþriks). 1607. [– L. *callithrix,* pl. *-triches* (Pliny) – Gr. καλλίτριχος beautiful-haired.] A genus of small Brazilian monkeys.

‖ **Callitriche** (kăli·triki). 1836. [mod.L., f. Gr. καλλίτριχος.] *Bot.* Water Star-wort.

Calloo (kălū·). Also **calaw, callow.** 1792. A species of Arctic duck, *Anas* (*Fuligula, Harelda*) *glacialis,* named from its call.

Callose (kælōᵘ·s), *a.* 1864. [– L. *callosus*; see CALLOUS, -OSE¹.] *Bot.* Having callosities.

Callosity (kălǫ·sĭti). 1578. [– Fr. *callosité* or L. *callositas, -at-*; see CALLOUS, -ITY.] **1.** The condition of being callous; abnormal hardness and thickness of the skin, etc. **2.** *concr.* A callus; a thickened and hardened part of the skin, caused by friction, etc. Also applied to natural thickenings, *e.g.* on the legs of a horse, etc. 1601. **3.** *fig.* = CALLOUSNESS 2. 1658.

Callot(e, -o·tt(e, obs. ff. CALOTTE.

Callous (kæ·ləs), *a.* 1578. [– (partly through Fr. *calleux*) L. *callosus,* f. *callum, callus* hardened skin.] **1.** (Chiefly *Phys.* and *Zool.*) Hardened, indurated; as parts of the skin by friction. Also *Bot.,* of plants. **2.** *fig.* Hardened, unfeeling, insensible 1679.

1. C. and hollow ulcers TIMME. C. hands CONGREVE. **2.** C. to impressions of religion BUTLER, to ridicule ARNOLD. Hence **Ca·llously** *adv.*

Ca·llous, *v.* 1834. [f. prec.] To make callous (*lit.* and *fig.*) Only in **Ca·lloused.**

Callousness (kæ·ləsnĕs). 1660. [f. CALLOUS *a.* + -NESS.] **1.** = CALLOSITY 1, 2. **2.** *fig.* A hardened state of mind or conscience; insensibility 1692.

Callow (kæ·loᵘ). [OE. *calu* = MLG. *kale,* MDu. *kale* (Du. *kaal*), OHG. *kalo* (G. *kahl*) :– WGmc. **kalwa,* prob. – L. *calvus* bald.] **A.** *adj.* † **1.** Bald –ME. **2.** Without feathers; downy 1603. **3.** *fig.* Raw, unfledged 1580. **4.** Of land: **a.** Bare; **b.** (*Ireland*) Low-lying 1677.

2. Yoong c. birds which are not yet fethered HOLLAND. **3.** Young and c. orators H. WALPOLE.

B. *sb.* † **1.** A bald-pate –ME. † **2.** A callow nestling; also *fig.* –1670. **3.** The stratum of vegetable soil lying above the subsoil; the top bed of a quarry (*dial.*) 1863. **4.** (*Ireland*) A low-lying damp meadow 1862. Hence **Ca·llowness. Ca·llowy** *a.*

‖ **Ca·llum.** ME. [L., of which *callus* is a variant.] = CALLUS –1646.

Callus (kæ·lŏs). Also (*erron.*) **callous.** Pl. **calluses.** 1563. [L., var. of the more usual *callum* (prec.).] **1.** = CALLOSITY 2. **2.** *Path.* The bony material thrown out around and between the two ends of a fractured bone in healing 1678. **3.** *Bot.* A hard formation in or on plants 1870. **4.** *fig.* A callous state of feeling, etc. 1692.

Calm (kām), *sb.*¹ [perh. – pop. L. **calma* (cf. med.L. *calmacio, calmus* adj.), alt. of late L. *cauma* (Vulg.) – Gr. καῦμα heat (of the day or the sun), by assoc. w. L. *calēre* be hot; hence also the (later than Eng.) Fr. *calme,* It. *calma.*] Stillness, tranquillity, serenity; freedom from agitation or disturbance. Also *fig.* and *attrib.*

There was a great calme *Matt.* 8:26. = 'want of wind' (usu. in *pl.*): Chained in tropic calms J. WILSON. *fig.* The c. of despotism CALHOUN. A good man's c. WORDSW.

Calm, *sb.*² Now *Sc.* 1535. [Origin unkn.; Cf. CAAM.] **1.** A mould in which metal objects are cast. **2.** The heddles of a loom.

Calm (kām), *a.* [ME. *calme* (XIV) – med.L. *calmus*; see CALM *sb.*¹ Fr. *carme* (XV), *calme* (XVI) is – It. *calmo* – med.L.] Free from agitation or disturbance; still, tranquil, serene; not stormy. Also *transf.* and *fig.*

So shall the sea be calme *Jonah* 1:12. It fell stark C. 1711. C. satisfaction BUTLER, manners and conversation 1641. The calmest life MILT. *P.L.* VI. 461. Hence **Ca·lmly** *adv.* **Ca·lmy** *a. poet. arch.* (rarely *fig.*).

Calm (kām), *v.* ME. [Sense 1 (intr.) perh. – CALM *a.,* both XIV; Fr. *calmer* (trans.) – It. *calmare* (trans.) is XV.] **1.** *intr.* Of the sea or wind: To become calm. *Obs.* exc. w. *down.* Also *fig.* **2.** *trans.* To make calm; to quiet, appease, pacify (*lit.* and *fig.*) 1559. † **3.** To becalm –1753.

1. It..raineth, thundereth, and calmeth 1598. **2.** She calm'd herself SOUTHEY. **3.** *Oth.* I. i. 30. Hence **Ca·lmant** *sb. Med.* = *calmative* sb. **Ca·lmative** *a.* sedative; *sb.* a sedative agent: also *fig.* **Ca·lmer.**

Calmness (kā·mnĕs). 1515. [f. CALM *a.* + -NESS.] The state or quality of being calm; stillness, tranquillity, quietness. Also *transf.* and *fig.*

The sea was returned to its..settled c. DE FOE. C. of speech HOOKER.

Calo-, Gr. καλο-, comb. f. καλός beautiful: occ. interchanging with CALLI-. See -O-, -I-.

Ca·logram. 1868. [f. Gr. κάλως cable.] A suggested substitute for CABLEGRAM.

Calomel (kæ·lŏmĕl). 1676. [– mod.L. *calomel, calomeles* (so in Fr. XVIII), said to be f. Gr. καλός beautiful + μέλας black.] Chiefly *Med.* Mercurous chloride, or protochloride of mercury (Hg_2Cl_2); much used as a purgative; also found native as *horn-quicksilver.*

She dosed them with c. and jalap KINGSLEY.

† **Calor, -our.** 1599. [L. *calor.*] Heat, warmth –1656.

Calorescence (kælŏre·sĕns). 1865. [f. L. *calor*; suggested by *calcescence,* etc. (Incorrect in form, and not expressing the fact.)] *Physics.* Tyndall's name for the change of non-luminous heat-rays into rays of higher refrangibility so as to become luminous. See also CALCESCENCE.

Caloric (kălǫ·rik). 1792. [– Fr. *calorique,* f. L. *calor* heat + *-ique* -IC.] *Physics.* Lavoisier's name for a supposed elastic fluid, to which the phenomena of heat were formerly attributed. (Now abandoned.) **2.** = 'heat'; also *fig.* 1794. *Comb.* **c.-engine,** Ericsson's improved hot-air-engine. Hence **Calo·rically** *adv.* as heat.

Caloricity (kælŏri·sĭti). 1836. [f. CALORIC + -ITY; cf. Fr. *caloricité.*] *Biol.* The faculty in living beings of developing heat so as to maintain a fairly uniform temperature.

Caloriduct (kălǫ·ridɒkt). 1864. [f. L. *calor* heat, after *aqueduct.*] A tube or channel for conducting heat.

Calorie (kæ·lŏri). Also **calory.** 1870. [– Fr. *calorie* (Guillemin), arbitrarily f. L. *calor* heat; cf. -Y³.] *Physics.* (More fully *great* or *major calorie.*) The amount of heat required to raise the temperature of 1 kilogramme (or, in later use, 1 gramme, *lesser calorie*) of water one degree centigrade.

Calorifacient (kălǫ:rifēⁱ·ʃⁱĕnt), *a.* 1854. [f. L. *calor, calori-* heat + -FACIENT.] *Phys.* Heat-producing. var. **Calo·rifi:ant.**

Calorific (kælŏri·fik), *a.* 1682. [– L. *calorificus*; see prec., -FIC.] *Physics.* **1.** Producing heat. **2.** *loosely.* Of or pertaining to heat. var. † **Calori·fical.** Hence **Calori·fically** *adv.* by means of heat.

Calorification (kălǫ:rifikēⁱ·ʃən). 1836. [– Fr. *calorification,* f. as prec.; see -ATION.] *Phys.* The production of heat, *esp.* in living animal bodies.

Calorify (kălǫ·rifəi), *v.* 1841. [f. L. *calor, calori-* heat + -FY.] To make hot. Hence **Calo·rifier,** an air-heater.

Calorimeter (kælŏri·mĭtəɹ). 1794. [f. as prec. + -METER; cf. Fr. *calorimètre.*] An instrument for measuring actual quantities of heat, or the specific heat of bodies. Hence **Calo:rime·tric, -al** *a.* of or pertaining to calorimetry; also, loosely, thermometric. **Calori·metry,** the measurement of heat.

Calorimotor (kălǫ:rimōᵘ·təɹ). 1832. [f. as prec. + MOTOR.] A voltaic arrangement consisting of one or more pairs of very large plates, producing considerable heat effects.

Calorist (kæ·lŏrist). *rare.* 1864. [f. CALORIC + -IST.] One who held heat or caloric to be a material substance.

Calotte (kălǫ·t). ? 1632. [– Fr., dim. of *cale* caul.] **1.** A plain skull-cap; *esp.* that worn by Roman Catholic ecclesiastics, etc.; † the coif of a serjeant-at-law. **2.** A cap-like crest on a bird's head 1874. ‖ **3.** Any thing having the form of a small cap; the cap of a sword-hilt, of a pistol, etc. (Chiefly Fr. uses.) 1886. ‖ **4.** *Arch.* A concavity in the shape of a cup, serving to connect the proportions of a chapel, etc. 1727.

Calotype (kæ·lŏtəip), *sb.* 1841. [f. CALO- + -TYPE.] *Photogr.* The process of producing photographs by the action of light upon silver iodide; also called *Talbotype,* after Fox Talbot its inventor. Hence **Ca·lotype** *v.* to represent by the c. process. **Caloty·pic** *a.* **Ca·loty:pist.**

‖ **Caloyer** (kæ·loyəɹ). 1615. [– Fr. *caloyer* – It. *caloiero* – eccl.Gr. καλόγηρος, f. καλός beautiful + γῆρας, γήρως old age.] A Greek monk, *esp.* of the order of St. Basil.

How name ye yon lone C.? BYRON.

‖ **Calpac, calpack** (kæ·lpæk). 1813. [Turki *qalpāq, qālpāq.*] A felt cap, worn by Turkis, Tartars, etc.; an oriental cap generally. var. **Ka·lpack.**

Calque, var. of CALK *v.*

‖ **Caltha** (kæ·lþă). 1599. [L.] *Bot.* The Marsh Marigold; also its genus.

Caltrop (kæ·ltrǫp), **caltrap.** [Senses 1 and 2: ME. *calketrap* – OFr. *kauketrape,* dial. var. of *cauche-, chauchetrape,* later (mod.) *chaussetrape,* f. *chauchier* (mod. *côcher*) tread + *trappe* trap; ult. identical with sense 3: OE. *calcatrippe,* ME *calketrappe* – med.L. *calcatrippa, -trappa,* whence also OFr. *calcatrepe, cauche-,* AFr. *calketrappe,* Pr. *calcatrepa.*] † **1.** A trap, gin, or snare for the feet –1850. **2.** *Mil.* An iron ball armed with four sharp prongs, placed so that when thrown on the ground it has always one projecting upwards: Used to impede cavalry, etc. 1519. Also *fig.*

3. *Herb.* Now usu. *Caltrops*: A name for various plants that entangle the feet, or suggest the military instrument; as the Star-thistle (*Centaurea calcitrapa*); **Land Caltrops** (*Tribulus terrestris*); **Water Caltrops** (*Potamogeton densus* and *P. crispus*), which entangle swimmers; also for the seed of *Trapa natans*.

Calumba (kălɒ·mbă). 1811. [f. *Colombo* in Ceylon, because supposed wrongly to come from there.] *Med.* The root of *Jateorhiza palmata* (N.O. *Menospermaceæ*), indigenous to the forests of Mozambique, used as a mild tonic and stomachic. Hence **Calu·mbin, Calu·mbic acid,** bitter substances found in Calumba root.

Calumet (kæ·liŭmèt). 1717. [– Fr. *calumet*, dial. var. (with suffix- substitution) of *chalumeau* – late L. *calamellus*, dim. of *calamus* reed – Gr. κάλαμος.] A tobacco-pipe with a bowl of clay, and a long reed stem carved and ornamented with feathers. Used among the Amer. Indians as a symbol of peace.
The French desired to smoak the c. of peace 1754.

Calumniate (kălɒ·mni,eⁱt), *v.* 1554. [– *calumniat-*, pa. ppl. stem of L. *calumniari*, f. *calumnia*; see -ATE[3].] *trans.* To asperse with calumny; to charge falsely and maliciously with something criminal or disreputable; to slander. *intr.* (*absol.*) To utter calumnies 1606.
We must not c. even the Inquisition WHEWELL. Hence **Calu:mnia·tion**, the action of calumniating; a calumny. **Calu·mniator. Calu·mniato:ry** *a.* calumnious. var. † **Ca·lumnize** (*trans.*).

Calumnious (kălɒ·mniəs), *a.* 1490. [– (O)Fr. *calomnieux* or L. *calumniosus*; see next, -OUS.] Of the nature of a calumny or a calumniator; slanderous, defamatory.
A foule mouth'd and c. knaue *All's Well* I. iii. 61. A c. fable 1855. Hence **Calu·mnious-ly** *adv.* **-ness.**

Calumny (kæ·ləmni). 1564. [– L. *calumnia* false accusation (whence Fr. *calomnie*).] **1.** False and malicious misrepresentation, to the injury of another; libellous detraction, slander. **2.** A slanderous report 1611.
1. The Shrug, the Hum, or Ha (these Petty-brands That Calumnie doth vse) SHAKS. **2.** To invent calumnies..requires neither labour nor courage JOHNSON.

‖ **Calva·ria, calva·rium.** ME. [L.; see next.] *Anat.* The part of the skull above the orbits, temples, ears, and occipital protuberance. So **Calva·rial** *a.*

Calvary (kæ·lvări). ME. [– L. *calvaria* skull (f. *calva* scalp, *calvus* bald), tr. in Matt. 27:33, etc., of Aram. *gûlgûltâ* skull, with second *l* elided, rendered in Gr. γολγοθά. Cf. Fr. *calvaire*; see -ARY[2].] **1.** Proper name of the place where Christ was crucified. (In OE. *Headpanstow*.) Also used generically. **2.** [Fr. *calvaire*] in *R.C.Ch.* **a.** A life-size representation of the Crucifixion, on a raised ground in the open air; **b.** A series of representations, in a church or chapel, of the scenes of the Passion 1727.
C. cross, cross C., in *Her.*, a cross mounted on a pyramid of three steps.

Calve (kāv), *v.*[1] [OE. *calfian* (*ċealfian*), f. *cælf* CALF *sb.*[1]] **1.** *intr.* To give birth to a calf. Cf. CALF *sb.*[1] 1, 3. **2.** *trans.* To bring forth ME. **3.** Of a glacier, etc.: To throw off a mass of ice 1837.
2. The cow..caluede not a deed calf WYCLIF *Job* 21:10. **3.** The icebergs 'calved' as they went along 1882. Hence **Ca·lven** [after *shaken*, etc.] *ppl. a.* that has calved. **Ca·lver,** a cow that calves.

Calved (kāvd), *ppl. a.* 1593. [f. *calve(s* (see CALF[2]) + -ED[2].] Having calves.

† **Calver,** *a.* ME. [ME. *calver, -ur, calwar*, presumably adj. use of OE. *calwer* (*ċealer, ċealre*) curds, surviving in *caluer of saulmon* 'escume de saulmon' (Palsgrave), rel. to MLG. *keller*, and f. Gmc. base **kal-* be cold. See CALLER *a.*] An epithet of salmon or other fish. ?'Fresh' (E. Müller); or 'dressed while alive'. –1865.

Ca·lver, *v.* 1651. ? *Obs.* [f. prec.] **1.** To treat or cook as a calver fish; to CRIMP; or, according to others, to cut into slices while fresh, or alive, and pickle. **2.** *intr.* Of fish: To behave when cooked as a calver fish 1651.

Calvinian (kælvi·niăn). 1566. [f. *Calvin* (see next) + -IAN.] *adj.* Of, belonging to, or following the doctrine of, Calvin. † *sb.* = CALVINIST –1691.

Calvinism (kæ·lviniz'm). 1570. [– Fr. *calvinisme* or mod. L. *calvinismus*, f. name of Jean *Calvin*, French Protestant reformer (1509–64). See -ISM.] The doctrines of John Calvin, *esp.* his theological doctrines on grace, in which Calvinism is opp. to ARMINIANISM. **b.** Adherence to these doctrines.
The 'five points of Calvinism' are: (1) Particular election. (2) Particular redemption. (3) Moral inability in a fallen state. (4) Irresistible grace. (5) Final perseverance.

Calvinist (kæ·lvinist). 1579. [f. as prec. + -IST.] An adherent of Calvinism.

Calvini·stic, *a.* 1820. [f. prec. + -IC.] Of or belonging to Calvinism, following the doctrines of Calvin. Hence **Calvini·stical** *a.*, **-ly** *adv.*

Ca·lvinize, *v.* 1659. [f. as prec. + -IZE.] *intr.* To follow Calvin, to teach Calvinism. *trans.* To imbue with Calvinism.

Calvish (kā·viʃ), *a.* 1570. [f. CALF[1] + -ISH[1].] Resembling a calf; doltish, stupid.

Calvity (kæ·lvĭti). *rare.* 1623. [– L. *calvitium*, f. *calvus* bald.] Baldness.

Calx (kælks). Pl. **calces,** † **calxes.** 1460. [– L. *calx* lime, limestone, prob. – Gr. χάλιξ pebble, limestone.] **1.** The powder or friable substance produced by calcining a mineral or metal; formerly taken as the essential substance of the crude mineral. † **2.** Occ. = quick-lime –1834. **3.** *Eton slang.* The goal-line (at football) 1864.

Calybite. [f. Gr. καλύβη little hut + -ITE[1] 1.] One of the early saints who passed their lives in huts.

‖ **Calycanthus** (kælikæ·nþɒs). 1864. [mod. L., f. Gr. κάλυκ- CALYX + ἄνθος flower.] *Bot.* A North American genus of shrubs; esp. *Calycanthus floridus* or Carolina Allspice.

Calycifloral (kæ:lisi,flōᵊrăl, kăli:si-), *a.* 1872. [f. L. *calyx, calyci-* CALYX + *flos, flor-* flower + -AL[1].] *Bot.* Having the stamens and petals inserted in the calyx. So **Calyciflo·rate, Calyciflo·rous** *adjs.*, in same sense.

Calyciform (kæ·lisifǭɹm, kali·si-), *a.* 1831. [f. as prec. + -FORM.] *Bot.* Having the form of a calyx. Also erron. sp. of CALICIFORM cup-shaped.

Calycine (kæ·lisəin, -in), *a.* 1816. [f. as prec. + -INE[1].] Of or belonging to the calyx; resembling a calyx. Hence **Caly·cinal, Caly·cinar,** in same sense.

Calycle (kæ·lik'l). 1731. [– L. *calyculus* (also used), dim. of *calyx*; see CALYX, -ULE.] *Bot.* **1.** A row of bracts round the base of the calyx, resembling a smaller outer calyx. **2.** Erron. f. CALICLE 1794. Hence **Caly·cular** *a.* relating to or composing a c. **Caly·culate** *a.* having a c. † **Caly·culated,** (having fruit) enclosed in a c. var. **Ca·lycule.**

† **Calyon.** ME. only. [– OFr. **caillon* (repr. by *cailloneus* pebbly), dim. of Normandy-Picard (hence mod. Fr.) *caillou* pebble (= OFr. *chail*); cf. the OFr. dims. *caillouel, -let, chaillot*.] Flint or pebble stone.

‖ **Calyptra** (kăli·ptră). 1753. [mod. L. – Gr. καλύπτρα covering, veil.] *Bot.* A hood or cover; *spec.* the hood of the sporecase in mosses. Hence **Caly·ptrate** *a.* having a c.; hooded, operculate. **Caly·ptriform** *a.* calyptra-shaped. **Caly·ptrogen,** the outer zone of the meristem of the youngest part of plants.

Calyx (kæ·liks, kēⁱ·liks). Pl. **calyces** (kæ·lisīz), rarely **calyxes.** 1693. [– L. *calyx*, – Gr. κάλυξ shell, husk, pod, f. base of καλύπτειν hide.] **1.** *Bot.* The whorl of leaves (sepals), usually green, forming the outer covering of a flower while in the bud. Also *transf.* **2.** *Phys.* and *Biol.* Variant sp. of CALIX 1831.
1. The c. is nothing but the swaddling clothes of the flower RUSKIN.

† **Calzoo·ns,** *sb. pl.* 1615. [– Fr. *cal(e)çons*, or its source It. *calzoni* breeches, drawers, (= Sp. *calzones*, Pg. *calções*), ult. f. L. *calceus* shoe, half-boot. See CHAUSSES.] Drawers, hose, trousers –1677.

Cam (kæm), *sb.*[1] Also **camb, camm.** 1777. [– Du. *kam* comb, as in *kamrad* toothed wheel, cog-wheel.] A projecting part of a wheel or other revolving piece of machinery, adapted to impart an alternating or variable motion to another piece, by sliding or rolling contact. Much used where a uniform revolving motion is employed to actuate any kind of non-uniform, alternating, elliptical, or rectilineal movement.

Cam, *sb.*[2] *n. dial.* 1788. [= Sc. *kame, kaim*, – ON. *kambr* COMB, crest, etc. The same word originally as prec. and COMB.] A ridge; a mound of earth; the bank on which a hedge is planted or the like.

Cam, *a.* and *adv.* Now *dial.* Also † **kamme.** 1579. [Implied in earlier *cammed(e)* XIV. The base is Celtic **kambos* (as in *Cambodunum* 'crooked town', Yorkshire), whence W., Gael., Manx, Ir. *cam* crooked, bent, wrong, false.] *adj.* Crooked, twisted. Hence *mod. dial.* Perverse 1600. *adv.* Awry, askew (also *fig.*). Cf. KIM-KAM. 1579.

‖ **Camaieu** (kamayö). 1596. [Fr.; see CAMEO.] **1.** = CAMEO. **2.** A method of painting in monochrome 1727.

Camail. Now *Hist.* 1670. [– (O)Fr. *camail* – Pr. *capmalh*, f. *cap* head + *malh, malhar*; see MAIL *sb.*[1]] **1.** A piece of chain-mail attached to the head-piece, and protecting the neck and shoulders 1826. **2.** A hood worn by the R.C. clergy; also, a blue or purple ornament worn by a bishop over his rochet 1670. Hence **Camailed** *a.* having a c.

Cama·ldolite. Also **Camaldulite, -dulian, -dule, -dolensian.** 1727. [-ITE[1] 1.] A member of the religious order founded by S. Romuald at Camaldoli in the 11th c.

Camara[1] (kæ·mără). 1880. [– Gr. καμάρα (see CAMERA).] *Bot.* **a.** One of the cells of a fruit. **b.** A carpel.

‖ **Camara**[2] (kæ·mără). 1866. [Native name in Guiana.] The hard durable timber of *Dipteryx odorata* (N.O. *Leguminosæ*).

‖ **Camaraderie** (kamara·dəri). 1840. [Fr., f. *camarade* COMRADE; see -ERY.] Comradeship; loyalty to, or partiality for, one's comrades; *esprit de corps.*

‖ **Camarilla** (kæmări·lă, Sp. -i·lʸa). 1839. [Sp., dim. of *camara* CHAMBER.] **1.** A small chamber 1860. **2.** A private cabinet of counsellors; a cabal, clique.

†‖ **Ca·marine.** 1576. [f. *Camarina* (Καμάρινα) in Sicily.] A fetid swamp. Also *fig.* –1681.

‖ **Camas, camash, cammas,** var. ff. QUAMASH (*Camassia esculenta*), a liliaceous plant whose bulbs are eaten by the N. Amer. Indians.

Camber (kæ·mbəɹ), *sb.* Also GAMBER. 1618. [– OFr. *cambre*, f. dial. var. of OFr. *chambre* arched:– L. *camurus* curved inwards.] **1.** The condition of being slightly arched or convex above. *concr.* A flattened arch. **2.** A camber-beam 1677. **3.** 'The part of a dockyard where cambering is performed and timber kept' (Smyth) 1885.
Comb.: **c.-beam,** a beam cut arching in the middle; **-slip,** a piece of board made convex on one or both edges, used as a rule.

Camber (kæ·mbəɹ), *v.* 1627. [– Fr. *cambrer*, f. *cambre* (prec.).] **1.** *intr.* To be or become slightly arched or curved so that the centre is higher than the ends. **2.** *trans.* To bend (a beam, etc.) upwards in the middle; to arch slightly 1852.

Ca·mberwell Beau·ty. 1847. [From *Camberwell*, London.] A species of butterfly, *Vanessa antiopa.*

Cambial (kæ·mbiăl), *a.* 1864. [Sense 1 – Fr. *cambial* (see CAMBIUM 1); sense 2 f. CAMBIUM 3 (cf. Fr. *cambial*); see -AL[1].] **1.** Relating to exchange in commerce. **2.** *Bot.* Pertaining to cambium 1881.

Cambiform (kæ·mbifǭɹm), *a.* 1882. [f. CAMBIUM + -FORM.] *Bot.* Of the form of, or like cambium.

‖ **Ca·mbio.** 1645. [It.:– med.L. *cambium*.] **1.** A bill of exchange. **2.** A place of exchange.

Ca·mbism. *rare.* 1837. [f. after next; see -ISM.] The theory and practice of exchanges.

Cambist (kæ·mbist). 1809. [– Fr. *cambiste* – It. *cambista*, f. *cambio* CHANGE *sb*.] **1.** One skilled in the science of exchanges; one who deals in bills of exchange. **2.** *transf.* As title of a manual of foreign exchanges 1811. Hence **Ca·mbistry.** (Dicts.)

Cambium (kæ·mbiŏm). 1643. [– med.L. *cambium* CHANGE *sb.*; used in sense 2 by *Arnaldus de Villa Nova* (XIII–XIV).] † **1.** Exchange, barter. **b.** A place of exchange. (Dicts.) † **2.** One of the four humours formerly supposed to nourish the body –1800. **3.** *Bot.* A viscid substance lying immediately under the bark of exogens, in which the annual growth of the wood and bark takes place 1671. Also *attrib.*

Camblet, var. of CAMLET.

Camboge, obs. f. GAMBOGE.

Camboose, var. of CABOOSE.

Cambrel (kæ·mbrĕl). Cf. CHAMBREL, GAMBREL. 1450. [Sense 1 is synon. w. † *cambren*, f. W. *cam* crooked (see CAM *a.*) + *pren* wood, stick; sense 2 has a var. CHAMBREL (XVIII–XIX); GAMBREL, used in both senses, is app. to be kept etymol. apart. Connection with *cambren* or with CAMBER *sb.* (sense 2) cannot be determined.] **1.** A bent piece of wood or iron used by butchers to hang carcases on. **2.** The bend of the upper part of a horse's hind leg; the hock. Now *dial.* 1610. Also *attrib.*

‖ **Cambresine** (kæmbrĕzī·n). Also **cambrasine.** 1750. [Fr.] 'A species of fine linen made at Cambray' (Littré); also an eastern fabric.

Cambrian (kæ·mbriăn), *a.* (*sb.*) 1656. [f. *Cambria*, var. of *Cumbria*, latinization of W. *Cymry* Wales :– OCelt. **Kombroges*, f. **kom*- together, COM- + **brog*- border, region; see -IAN.] **1.** Pertaining to Wales, Welsh; *sb.* a Welshman. **2.** *Geol.* A system of Palæozoic rocks lying below the Silurian, in Wales and Cumberland 1836.

Cambric (kē[i]·mbrik). 1530. [f. *Kamerijk* Flemish form of *Cambrai* a town of northern France :– med.L. *Camaracum.*] A kind of fine white linen, orig. made at Cambray in Flanders. (Also an imitation made of hard-spun cotton yarn.) **b.** As the material of handkerchiefs 1886. Also *attrib.*

I would your Cambrick were sensible as your finger *Cor.* I. iii. 95.

Cambuc, var. of CAMMOCK.

Came (kē[i]m). 1688. [app. = CALM[2], 1.] A small grooved bar of lead used for framing the glass in latticed windows: chiefly in *pl.*

Came (kē[i]m), pa. t. of COME *v.*; Sc. f. COMB.

Camel (kæ·mĕl). [OE. *camel* – L. *camēlus*, reinforced in ME. by OFr. *cameil, chameil, -oil* (:– L. *camēlus*) and *camel, chamel* (:– var. **camĕllus*) – Gr. κάμηλος, of Semitic origin.] **1.** A large hornless ruminant quadruped, having a humped back, long neck, and cushioned feet; not found wild, but domesticated in Western Asia and Northern Africa, where it is the chief beast of burden. There are two species, the Arabian or one-humped (including the dromedary), and the Bactrian or two-humped. Also *fig.* **2.** *techn.* A machine for adding buoyancy to vessels, and thus enabling them to cross bars, shoals, etc.; also for raising sunken ships, removing rocks, etc. It consists generally of two or more water-tight chests provided with plugs and pumps. 1716.

Well, therefore, has the C. .been termed 'the Ship of the Desert' 1847. *fig.* A Drayman, a Porter, a very Camell *Tr.& Cr.* I. ii. 271.

Comb.: **c.-bird**, the Ostrich; **-engine** = sense 2; **-gut**, the dried gut of a c. used to furnish strings for musical instruments; **-insect**, a name for members of the genus *Mantis*, from their elongated thorax; **-kneed** *a.*, callous-kneed, like a camel; **-locust** = *camel-insect;* **camel('s)-thorn**, a leguminous plant (*Alhagi camelorum*); **-tree**, *Acacia giraffæ*. Hence **Ca·melcade,** a train of people on camels. **Ca·meldom,** the region of camels. (*nonce-wds.*) **Camelee·r,** a c.-driver; a cuirassier mounted on a c. **Ca·meline** *a.* belonging to a c., or to camels. **Ca·melish** *a.* obstinate as a c.; **Ca·melishness. Ca·melry,** troops mounted on camels; 'a place where camels are laden and unladen'.

Cameleon, obs. f. CHAMELEON.

Camel-hair; see CAMEL'S-HAIR.

Cameline (kæ·mĕlin, kæ·mlin), *sb.*[1] ME. [– OFr. *camelin* – med.L. *camelinum*, subst. use of n. of *camelinus* of a camel; see CAMEL, -INE[1].] *orig.* A kind of stuff supposed to be made of camel's hair; cf. CAMLET. Also, a garment of this 1599.

Cameline (kæ·mĕlǝin), *sb.*[2] ME. [– Fr. *cameline*, earlier *camamine*, f. late L. *chamæmelinus* resembling camomile.] A genus of cruciferous plants; esp. *Camelina sativa.* Also *attrib.* 1578.

† **Camelion.** ME. [As a word app. the same as CHAMELEON, but in XIV taken as made up of *camel* + *lion*, and identified with *camelo-pard.*] A camelopard –1535.

Camellia (kăme·liă, kămī·liă). 1753. [After Josef *Kamel* (latinized *Camellus*), a Jesuit who botanized Luzon; see -IA[1].] A genus of evergreen shrubs belonging to the tea family (*Ternströmiaceæ*), chiefly natives of China and Japan. Also *attrib.*

Camelopard (kæ·mĕlo,pā:ɹd, kăme·lŏpaɹd). ME. [– L. *camelopardus, -pardalis* – Gr. καμηλοπάρδαλις, f. κάμηλος CAMEL + πάρδαλις PARD.] **1.** The GIRAFFE; an African ruminant quadruped with long legs, very long neck, and skin spotted like that of the panther. **2.** *Astr.* A constellation situated between Ursa Major and Cassiopeia 1836.

Camelopa·rdel. 1830. [f. prec.; cf. -EL[2].] *Her.* An animal, figured as a camelopard with the horns of an ibex.

Camelot, obs. f. CAMLET.

Camel's-hair. Also **camel-hair.** ME. **1.** The hair of the camel. (But cf. next.). **2.** The long hairs from the tail of a squirrel, used to make artist's pencils. Also *attrib.* 1771.

Camel-yarn. 1670. [In Da. *kameelgarn*, Du. *kemelshaar*, G. *kamelgarn*, app. from a mistaken notion; cf. CAMLET and MOHAIR.] Yarn made from the wool of the Angora-goat, mohair yarn.

Camenes. *Logic.* A mnemonic word, repr. the second mood of the fourth syllogistic figure, in which the major premiss is a universal affirmative, the minor premiss and the conclusion universal negatives.

Cameo (kæ·mi,o). 1561. [Earliest *cameu* (XV) – OFr. *came(h)u, camahieu* (mod. *camaïeu*), – a type **camahæus* (cf. med. L. *camahutus*, etc.); the form *cameo* – It. *cam(m)eo*, corresp. to med.L. *cammæus*, whence also Fr. *camée.*] A precious stone, as the onyx, agate, sardonyx, etc., having two layers of different colours, in the upper of which a figure is carved in relief, while the lower serves as ground. Also, a shell similarly carved. Also *attrib.*

Camera (kæ·mĕră). 1708. [– L. *camera* vault, arched chamber – Gr. καμάρα object with arched cover; see CHAMBER.] ‖ **1.** In L. sense: An arched or vaulted roof or chamber. Prob. not in Eng. use. **b.** A judge's chamber; hence *in camera*, opp. to 'in open court'. ‖ **2.** [It. or Sp.] A chamber; a council or legislative chamber; a department of the papal curia 1712. **3.** *Optics.* Short for *camera obscura* 1727. **b.** *esp.* That form used in photography 1840.

Ca·mera obscu·ra [L.; lit. 'dark chamber'.] *Optics.* A darkened chamber or box, into which light is admitted through a double convex lens, forming an image of external objects on paper, glass, etc., placed at the focus of the lens. Also *lit.* Dark room. **Ca·mera lu·cida** [L.; lit. 'light chamber'.] *Optics.* An instrument by which the rays of light from an object are reflected by a prism, and produce an image on paper placed beneath the instrument, which can be traced with a pencil.

Ca·meral, *a.* 1762. [– G. *kameral* – med.L. *cameralis*, f. L. *camera* in its late sense 'chamber, bureau'; see -AL[1].] Of or pertaining to the *camera* or chamber; relating to the management of the state property (in Germany). Hence **Ca:merali·stic** *a.*, **Ca:merali·stics** *sb. pl.*

† **Ca·merate,** *v.* 1623. [– *camerat-*, pa. ppl. stem of L. *camerare* vault or arch over, f. *camera*; see CAMERA, -ATE[3].] *trans.* To vault, to arch. Hence **Ca·merated** *ppl. a.* (*Arch.*) arched, vaulted; (*Zool.*) divided into chambers, as some shells; var. **Ca·merate** *a.* **Camera·tion,** (*Arch.*) vaulting, arching; (*Zool.*) division into chambers.

Camerine; see CAMARINE.

Cameronian (kæmĕrō[u]·niăn). 1690. [f. the name *Cameron* + -IAN.] *adj.* Pertaining to Richard Cameron, his tenets, or his followers.

Cameronian Regiment: the old 26th Regiment of Foot, formed originally of Presbyterians who rallied to the cause of William III.

sb. A follower of Richard Cameron, a Scottish Covenanter and field preacher, who rejected the indulgence granted to nonconforming ministers and formally renounced allegiance to Charles II. His followers became the 'Reformed Presbyterian Church of Scotland'.

† **Camery.** 1572. [Origin unkn.] A disease of horses; the *frounce* –1727.

Camestres. 1551. *Logic.* A mnemonic word, repr. the second mood of the second syllogistic figure, in which the major premiss is a universal affirmative, the minor premiss and the conclusion universal negatives.

† **Ca·mis, camus.** [In Spenser, prob. – Sp., Pr. *camisa*; see CHEMISE.] A light loose dress of silk or linen.

Ca:misa·do. *Obs.* or *arch.* 1548. [– Sp. *camisada* lit. 'attack in one's shirt', f. *camisa* shirt; see CHEMISE, -ADO.] *Mil.* **1.** A night attack; orig. one in which the attackers wore shirts over their armour as a means of mutual recognition. Also *fig.* **2.** (*erron.*) The shirt thus worn 1618. var. **Camisa·de.**

By night I wil the cammassado give GASCOIGNE.

† **Camisard, camisar.** 1703. [– Fr. *camisard* – Pr. *camisa* shirt; see CHEMISE, -ARD.] 'Name given to the Calvinist insurgents of the Cevennes, during the persecution which followed the revocation of the edict of Nantes' (Littré). Also *attrib.* –1883.

‖ **Camise, camiss** (kămī·s). In Byron **camese.** 1812. [Arab. *ḳamīṣ* under-tunic; perh. – L. *camisia, camisa*; see CHEMISE.] The shirt worn by Arabs and other Moslems.

Camisole (kæ·misō[u]l). 1816. [– Fr. *camisole* – It. *camiciola* or Sp. *camisola*, dim. of *camicia, camisa* shirt; see CHEMISE.] **1.** Formerly applied to jackets of various kinds. **2.** A woman's underbodice 1894. Hence in attrib. form *cami-* in comb., as *cami-knickers* (1915).

Ca·mister. *Thieves' cant.* 1851. [f. CAMIS in sense of surplice, with termination perh. suggested by *minister.*] A clergyman.

Camlet (kæ·mlĕt), *sb.* ME. [Early forms *chamlett, -lot*, prob. – OFr. *chamelot, camelot*, perh. ult. from Arab. *ḵamlat* nap, pile of velvet, pop. assoc. with camel's hair.] A name orig. for a costly eastern fabric, subseq. for substitutes, made of various combinations of wool, silk, hair, and latterly cotton or linen. Also, a garment of camlet. Also *fig.* and *attrib.*

Stuffs made from the hair of [the Angora goat]. . known among us by the name of *camlet* GOLDSM. Hence **Ca·mlet** *v.* to mark as (watered) c. **Camletee·n, -ine,** an imitation c. **Ca·mleting,** stuff of c.

Cammas, var. of QUAMASH; see CAMAS.

Cammed (kæmd), *a.* Now *dial.* ME. [app. f. CAM *a.*; cf. *wicked.*] † **1.** = CAMOIS –1440. **2.** Crooked, perverse 1746.

Cammock[1] (kæ·mǝk). [OE. *cammoc*, of unkn. origin.] **1.** The plant *Ononis spinosa* (N.O. *Leguminosæ*), also called *Rest-harrow.* **2.** Used dial. of other plants, as St. John's Wort, Ragweed, etc. 1878.

Cammock[2], **cambock** (kæ·mǝk). Now *Sc.* [ME. *kambok*, app. – med.L. *cambuca, -buta* curved stick, crosier, app. of Gaulish origin, cf. **kambos* CAM *a.*] **1.** A crooked staff; *esp.* a hockey-stick, or the like; hence, the game in which it is used. **2.** A crooked piece of wood 1450.

† **Ca·mois, camus,** *a.* (*sb.*) ME. [– (O)Fr. *camus* having a short and flat nose.] **1.** Of the nose: Low and concave. Of persons: Pug-nosed. –1877. Also *fig.* **2.** quasi-*sb.* A person or animal with a camois nose –1751. Hence † **Ca·moised** *a.* having a c. nose. † **Ca·moisly, ca·mously** *adv.* concavely.

Camomile, cham- (kæ·mŏmǝil). ME. [– (O)Fr. *camomille* – late L. *c(h)amomilla*, alt. of *chamæmelon* – Gr. χαμαίμηλον 'earth apple' (χαμαί on the ground, μῆλον apple), so called from the apple-like smell of the blossoms. The sp. *cha-* is chiefly in pharmacy, after Latin.] **1.** A Composite plant, *Anthemis nobilis*, a creeping herb, with downy leaves, and flowers white in the ray and yellow in the disc. The flowers are used in Medicine for their bitter and tonic properties. **b.** A name for the genus *Anthemis*, and pop.

applied to allied plants, esp. *Matricaria chamomilla* (Wild C.); *Blue* or *Purple C.*, the Sea Starwort, etc.

‖ **Camorra** (kămǫ·ră). 1865. [It., of doubtful origin, but perh. – Sp. *camorra* dispute, quarrel.] **1.** A kind of smock-frock or blouse 1869. **2.** A secret society of lawless malcontents in the Neapolitan district. Hence **Camo·rrism,** lawlessness, anarchy. **Camo·rrist,** a member of a c.

‖ **Camouflage** (kæ·muflāʒ), *sb.* 1917. [Fr., f. *camoufler* (thieves' sl.) – It. *camuffare* disguise, deceive, perh. assoc. with Fr. *camouflet* whiff of smoke in the face; see -AGE.] The disguising of any object used in war, by means of paint, smoke-screens, etc., in such a way as to conceal it from the enemy; the disguise used in this way. Also *fig.* Hence **Ca·mouflage** *v.*

Camp, *sb.*[1] Now *dial.* [OE. *camp, comp,* corresp. to OFris. *camp, comp,* MDu. *camp* (Du. *kamp*), OHG. *champf* (G. *kampf*), all masc., ON. *kapp* n. :– Gmc. **kampaz*, an early Gmc. adoption of L. *campus* (see CAMP *sb.*[2]) in the med.L. sense combat, battle, single combat.] † **1.** Martial contest, battle, war –ME. **2. Camp-ball**: An ancient form of football played by large sides 1600.

Camp (kæmp), *sb.*[2] 1528. [–(O)Fr. *camp* – It. *campo* (= (O)Fr. *champ* field, battle-field) :– L. *campus* level field, place for games and military exercises, field of battle, whence Gmc. **kampaz*; see prec.] **1.** The place where a body of troops is lodged in tents or other temporary shelter, with or without intrenchments. (In mod. use, the collection of tents, equipments, etc., is the chief notion.) Also a permanent station for the training of troops in campaigning duties generally. **2.** A body of troops on a campaign. (Earlier *the host.*) 1584. Also *fig.* **3.** The scene of military service; the military life 1725. **4.** *transf.* The temporary quarters of nomads, sportsmen, lumbermen, field-preachers, etc.; an encampment 1560. **5.** A camping out 1865. **6.** The whole body of persons encamped together 1750.

1. The Youth of Rome..pitch their sudden C. before the Foe DRYDEN. **2.** To follow the c. 1706. *Flying c., c. volant*: a body of horse and foot that keeps the field. **3.** Love rules the court, the c., the grove SCOTT.

Comb.: **c.-bed, -bedstead,** one for use in field-service; hence *spec.* a compact folding bedstead; **-chair,** a form of folding chair; **-fever,** any epidemic fever occurring in camps, chiefly typhus; **-fire,** a fire lit in an encampment; hence a military social gathering; **-follower,** one, not a soldier, who hangs on to an army; **-furniture; -seat, -stool,** a light portable folding stool. Hence **Ca·mpish** *a.* savouring of the c. **Ca·mpless** *a.* **Ca·mpward(s** *adv.*

Camp, *sb.*[3] *dial.* 1713. [Of unkn. origin. Cf. CLAMP.] A conical heap of potatoes or turnips, in the open air, covered with straw and earth, for winter storage; a *bury, pie,* or *pit.*

Camp, *v.*[1] Now *dial.* [OE. *campian,* f. *camp* CAMP *sb.*[1]] **1.** To contend; *esp.* at camp-ball. **2.** To scold 1606.

Camp (kæmp), *v.*[2] 1543. [– Fr. *camper,* f. *camp* CAMP *sb.*[2]] **1.** *intr.* To live in a camp or a tent; to encamp; *fam.* to lodge. Often with *out.* **2.** *trans.* To place in camp; to lodge 1549.

1. There Israel camped before the mount *Ex.* 19:2. The messenger..camping at night in the snow THACKERAY. **2.** *Ant.& Cl.* IV. viii. 33.

‖ **Campagna, campagnia** (kampā·nʸa). 1641. [It.; see CAMPAIGN.] † **1.** = CHAMPAIGN (*rare*) –1717. † **2.** A (military) CAMPAIGN (*rare*) –1663. **3.** Now only as proper name 'the Campagna' in Italy; see CAMPANIA.

‖ **Campagnol** (ka·mpănʸǫl). 1835. [Fr., f. *campagne* country.] The Short-tailed Field-mouse.

Campaign (kămpēⁱ·n). 1628. [– Fr. *campagne* – It. *campagna* (used in mil. sense XVI) = (O)Fr. *champagne* :– late L. *campania*; see CHAMPAIGN.] **I.** † **1.** = CHAMPAIGN 1, 3. –1765. **2.** *Mil. orig.* The time for which an army kept the field, without entering into quarters; *now,* A continuous series of military operations, constituting the whole, or a distinct part, of a war 1656. **3.** *Ironworks.* The period during which a furnace is in continuous operation 1871. **4.** *fig.* Any course of action analogous to a military campaign 1770.

4. A reading c. DICKENS, an electoral c. 1888.

II. *attrib.* **a.** Belonging to the open country 1628. **b.** Of, belonging to, or used on, a military campaign 1677.

b. A c.-coat 1677. Hence **Campai·gn** *v.* to serve in, or go on, a c.

Campaigner (kămpēⁱ·nəɹ). 1771. [f. CAMPAIGN *v.* (or *sb.*) + -ER[1].] One who serves in a campaign; *esp.* one who has served in many campaigns; also *fig.*

† **Ca·mpal,** *a.* 1598. [– Sp. (*batalla*) *campal,* in med.L. (*bellum*) *campale*; see CAMP *sb.*[2], -AL[1].] Pertaining to the field –1611.

‖ **Campana** (kămpā·nă). 1613. [Late L. (whence It., Sp. *campana*), bell.] **1.** A church bell 1706. **2.** ? The pasque flower. DRAYTON. **3.** *Arch.* The body of the Corinthian capital; also = GUTTA 1823. Hence **Ca·mpanal** *a.* (*Bot.*) including the *Campanulaceæ* and their allies.

Campane (kămpeⁱ·n). 1662. [–(O)Fr. *campane* – Pr. *campana* :– late L. *campana* bell.] *Her.* A bell. Hence **Campa·ned** *ppl. a.* furnished with bells.

‖ **Campanero** (kæmpănēᵊ·ro). 1825. [Sp., = bell-man; see CAMPANA.] The Bell-bird of S. America.

† **Campa·nia.** 1601. [app. – It. *campagna,* spelt phonetically; cf. synonymous CAMPAGNA, -IA.] **1.** = CHAMPAIGN –1698. **2.** = CAMPAIGN *sb.* 2. –1698.

Campaniform (kămpæ·nifǭɹm), *a.* 1757. [f. late L. *campana*; see -FORM.] *Bot.* Bell-shaped.

‖ **Campani·le.** 1640. [It., f. *campana* bell + *-ile,* see -IL, -ILE. Cf. med. L. *campanile.*] A bell-tower; *esp.* a lofty detached bell-tower; a steeple.

The great C. at Christ-church Oxford H. WALPOLE. Hence **Campani·liform** *a.* shaped like a c.

Campanist (kæ·mpănist). 1872. [– med.L. *campanista*; see CAMPANA, -IST.] One versed in bells.

Campanology (kæmpănǫ·lŏdʒi). 1847. [– mod.L. *campanologia,* f. as prec. + -LOGY.] The subject of bells; the science and art of bell-founding, bell-ringing, etc. Hence **Campano·loger, -logist.**

Campanula (kămpæ·niŭlă). 1664. [– mod. L. dim. of CAMPANA; see -ULE.] *Bot.* A bell-flower; a genus of plants, giving its name to the N.O. *Campanulaceæ.* Hence **Campanula·ceous** *a.* belonging to the N.O. *Campanulaceæ.* **Campa·nular** *a.* bell-shaped. ‖ **Campa:nula·ria,** (*Zool.*) a genus of hydroid Zoophytes having the polype-cells bell-shaped and supported on long footstalks.

Campanulate (kæmpæ·niŭlĕt), *a.* 1668. [f. as prec. + -ATE[2].] *Bot.* and *Zool.* Bell-shaped. var. **Campa·nulated, Campa·nulous.**

Campeachy wood. 1652. [From *Campeachy* on the coast of Yucatan.] = LOGWOOD.

‖ **Campement** (kāṅpəmaṅ). 1821. [Fr.] A detachment whose duty is to mark out the ground for a camp in advance of the army.

Camper (kæ·mpəɹ). 1631. [f. CAMP *sb.*[2], *v.*[2] + -ER[1].] † **1.** A military man; a camp-follower –1691. **2.** One who goes into camp; one who lodges in a tent 1856. Also *camper out.*

Campestral (kămpe·străl), *a. rare.* 1750. [f. L. *campester, -tr-,* f. *campus*; see CAMP *sb.*[2], -AL[1].] Pertaining to fields or open country; growing in the fields. var. † **Campe·strial.**

† **Camp-fight.** 1605. [tr. med. L. *pugna campi.*] In law writers (from 17th c.) the trial of a cause by duel.

Camph-, abbrev. of CAMPHOR, taken as a stem on which to form names of related substances, as **Ca·mphene,** generic name for the hydrocarbons isomeric or polymeric with oil of turpentine ($C_{10}H_{16}$); = TEREBENE. **Ca·mphine** (-əin), an illuminating oil procured by distillation from oil of turpentine. **Ca·mphogen** = CYMENE, $C_{10}H_{14}$; also, loosely, *camphene* or *camphine.* **Ca·mphol** = BORNEOL. **Campho·lic acid,** $C_{10}H_{18}O_2$. **Ca·mphyl,** the radical of Camphol, $C_{10}H_{17}$; whence **Camphy·lic** *a.*

Camphor (kæ·mfəɹ, -ǒɹ). ME. [– OFr. *camphore,* later and mod. *camphre* (AFr. *caumphre*) or med.L. *camphora* – (prob. through Sp. *alcanfor*) Arab. *kāfūr* (whence med. Gr. καφουρά) – Prakrit *kappūram,* Skr. *karpūram.*] **1.** A whitish translucent crystalline volatile substance ($C_{10}H_{16}O$), belonging to the vegetable oils, distilled from *Camphora officinarum* (*Laurus camphora*), and purified by sublimation. It has a bitter aromatic taste and a characteristic smell. † **2.** A tree or plant which yields camphor; esp. *Camphora officinarum* and *Dryobalanops camphora* –1684. Also *attrib.*

2. Here also grew Camphire, with Spiknard, and Saffron BUNYAN. Hence **Ca·mphor** *v.* to camphorate (*rare*). **Camphora·ceous, Ca·mphorous, Ca·mphory** *adjs.* of the nature of c. **Campho·ric** *a.* (*Chem.*) of or pertaining to c.; containing c. in chemical combination.

Camphorate (kæ·mfŏrĕt), *sb.* 1794. [f. as next; see -ATE[1].] *Chem.* A salt of camphoric acid.

Camphorate (kæ·mfŏreⁱt), *v.* 1641. [f. CAMPHOR + -ATE[3].] To impregnate or treat with camphor.

† **Ca·mping,** *vbl. sb.*[1] ME. [f. CAMP *v.*[1] + -ING[1].] **1.** Fighting in CAMP-FIGHT 1481. **2.** Fighting –1587. **3.** Football playing. Also *attrib.* –1567.

Ca·mping, *vbl. sb.*[2] 1572. [f. CAMP *v.*[2] + -ING[1].] The action of CAMP *v.*[2] Also *attrib.*

† **Ca·mpion**[1]. [ME. *campiun* – ONFr. *campiun, -on* = OFr. *champiun, -on*; see CHAMPION.] **1.** One who fights in single combat –1536. **2.** A champion –1651.

Campion[2] (kæ·mpiən). 1576. [tr. of Gr. λυχνὶς στεφανωματική (i.e. 'used for garlands'), on which has been based a derivation from CAMPION[1].] *Herb.* The name of certain plants, species of the genus *Lychnis,* including Rose Campion, *L.* (now *Agrostemma*) *coronaria,* etc. Extended, with a qualification, to allied species, as **Bladder C.,** *Silene inflata,* etc.

Cample (kæ·mp'l), *v.* Now *dial.* 1621. [app. f. CAMP *v.*[1] + -LE.] *intr.* To answer in anger; to wrangle.

Ca·mp-mee:ting. 1809. *U.S.* A religious (usu. Methodist) meeting held in the open air, and often lasting for some days, during which those who attend encamp on the spot.

Campoo (kæmpū·). *Anglo-Ind.* 1803. [app. – Pg. *campo* camp.] A camp; also, † a brigade under European commanders in the Mahratta service.

Camp-shedding, -sheeting. 1819. = next.

Ca·mp-shot. 1691. [Earliest forms *-shide, -shed, -shead,* prob. f. CANT *sb.*[1] + SHIDE.] A facing of piles and boarding along the bank of a river, or at the side of an embankment.

‖ **Campus** (kæ·mpŏs). *U.S.* 1774. [L. *campus* field, plain, level space.] The grounds of a college or university.

Campylospermous (kæ:mpiloˌspə̄·ɹməs), *a.* 1880. [f. Gr. καμπύλος bent + σπέρμα seed + -OUS.] *Bot.* Said of carpels, *e.g.* those of some Umbelliferæ, in which the contained seed produces a longitudinal furrow on the ventral face.

Campylotropous (kæmpilǫ·trǒpəs), *a.* 1835. [f. as prec. + -τροπος turning + -OUS.] *Bot.* Said of the ovule of phanerogamous plants when its nucleus is curved upon itself. var. **Campylo·tropal.**

Camstone (kæ·mstōᵘn). *Sc.* 1791. [Origin unkn.] **a.** A compact, prob. whitish, limestone. **b.** A bluish-white clay used to whiten hearths, etc.

Camus, var. of CAMIS and CAMIS.

Cam-wood (kæ·mwud). 1698. [Said to be – native dial. word *kambi.*] = BARWOOD.

Can (kæn), *sb.* [OE. *canne,* corresp. to MDu. *kanne* (Du. *kan*), OHG. *channa* (G. *kanne*), ON. *kanna*; it is uncertain whether the word is orig. Gmc. or – late L. *canna* (VI).] **1.** A vessel for holding liquids; now of tin or other metal, usually cylindrical in form, with a handle over the top. **b.** A chimney-pot 1833. **2.** *Sc.* A measure 1809. **3.** A vessel of tinned iron, in which fruit, fish, etc., are sealed up air-tight for preservation (chiefly in U.S.) 1874.

1. There weren set sixe stonun cannes WYCLIF *John* 2:6. Hence **Ca·nful.**

Can (kæn), *v.*[1] *irreg. Pa. ind.* **could** [OE. *cunnan* = OFris. *kunna*, OS. *cunnan* (Du. *kunnen*), OHG. *kunnan* (G. *können*), ON. *kunna*, Goth. *kunnan*. This is one of the group of Gmc. preterite-present verbs (see DARE, MAY, SHALL, WIT *v.*[1]). The IE. base **gn- *gnē- *gnō-* appears in L. *gnōscere*, Gr. *γιγνώσκειν* know; the primary meaning of the Gmc. preterite-present verb was 'have learned', 'come to know'.

I. † **1.** To know –1649. **2.** *intr.* To have knowledge *of* (*arch.*) ME.

1. He coulde it by hart 1541. She could the Bible in the holy tongue B. JONS. **2.** The king couthe of venery 1420.

II. With inf., as auxiliary of predication. **1.** To know how (*to do* anything) OE. **2.** To be able; to have the power or capacity. (The current sense.) ME. **3.** Expressing possibility: *can you..?* = is it possible for you to..? 1542. **4.** *ellipt.* 1440.

1. Well couth he tune his pipe SPENSER. **2.** The Egyptians could not drink of the water *Ex.* 7:21. Such language can do no good 1888. **3.** And can you blame them? 1583. Thy way thou canst not miss MILT. *P.L.* III. 735. **4.** I could no more, I was really exhausted 1807. *Cannot but*: see BUT. See also CON.

† **Can**, *v.*[2] (*pa. tense.*) ME. and early mod. Eng. used for GAN, pa. t. of *ginnan* to begin; see GIN *v.* Replaced by *did.*

Can, *v.*[3] 1871. [f. CAN *sb.*[1]] To put in a can or cans; to 'tin', as fruit, beef, etc. Hence **Ca·nner.**

Canaan (kēⁱ·năn). 1637. [– eccl. L. *Chanaan* – eccl. Gr. *Χαναάν* – Heb. *kᵉna'an.*] The ancient proper name of Western Palestine; *fig.* the land of promise, heaven, etc.

Canaanite (kēⁱ·nănəit), *sb.*[1] ME. [f. prec. + -ITE[1] 1.] **1.** A native of Canaan. *fig.* 'No true Israelite'. **2.** (prop. **Cananæan**): One of a Jewish sect fanatically opposed to the Romans; *hence*, a zealot 1611.

2. Simon the Canaanite *Matt.* 10:4. [*R.V.* Cananæan.] Hence **Canaani·tic, Canaani·tish** *adjs.* belonging to Canaan; of or like a C. Also *fig.*

Ca·naanite, *sb.*[2] 1844. [f. as prec. + -ITE[1] 2 b.] *Min.* A variety of pyroxene found near Canaan, Conn., U.S.

Canada[1] (kæ·nădă). [Origin unkn.] The name of a British dominion in N. America, used attrib. in names of plants, animals, products, etc.

C. balsam, a pale balsam derived from *Abies balsamea*, and *A. canadensis*, used in medicine, etc.; **C. rice**, *Hydropyrum esculentum*; **C. turpentine** = *Canada balsam.*

‖ **Cañada**[2] (kănʸă·dă). 1850. [Sp., 'a dale between two mountains', f. *caño* tube, gutter, *caña* reed; see -ADE.] In Western U.S.: A narrow valley or glen; a small cañon.

Canadian (kănēⁱ·diăn). 1805. [f. CANADA[1] + -IAN.] *adj.* Of or belonging to Canada or its people. *sb.* A native or inhabitant of Canada.

†‖ **Cana·glia.** 1605. [It.; see next.] = next –1734.

‖ **Canaille** (kana·ˡy, -ēⁱ·l). 1676. [Fr. – It. *canaglia* lit. 'pack of dogs', f. *cane* dog (:– L. *canis*); for the suffix, cf. -AL[1] 2.] The vile populace; the rabble, the mob.

Let the Canaile wait as they should do 1676.

Canakin, var. of CANNIKIN.

Canal (kănæ·l), *sb.* 1449. [– (O)Fr. *canal*, refash. of earlier *chanel* (see CHANNEL), after L. *canalis* or It. *canale.*] † **1.** A pipe for conveying liquid; also a tube or tubular cavity –1698. **2.** *Phys.* A duct, as the *alimentary canal*, the *semicircular canals* of the ear, etc. (The second current sense.) 1626. † **3.** A CHANNEL; *esp.* a strait –1829. † **4.** A long and narrow piece of water ornamenting a garden or park –1827. **5.** An artificial watercourse uniting rivers, lakes, or seas, for purposes of inland navigation, irrigation, or conveyance of water-power. (The chief mod. sense.) 1673. Also † *fig.* **6.** *Arch.* A groove, fluting, CHANNEL 1727. **7.** *Zool.* The groove in the shells of certain molluscs, for the protrusion of the siphon 1835.

4. Having a Boat on the C. in St. James's Park 1725. *Comb.*: **c.-built** *a.*, of a build adapted to use on a c.

Cana·l, *v. rare.* 1870. [f. prec.] To make a canal through; to furnish with canals.

Canal-bone, -coal, vars. of CANNEL-BONE, *-coal.*

Canalicular (kænăli·kiŭlăɹ), *a.* 1878. [f. CANALICULUS + -AR[1].] *Nat. Hist.* Of, pertaining to, or resembling a canaliculus; minutely tubular.

Canali·culate, *a.* 1828. [f. as prec. + -ATE[2].] *Nat. Hist.* Having a longitudinal groove; minutely channelled. var. **Canali·culated** *ppl. a.*

Ca:nalicula·tion. 1880. [f. as prec.; see -ATION.] A canaliculate formation; a minute grooving.

‖ **Canaliculus** (kænăli·kiŭlŏs). Pl. **-li.** 1563. [L., dim. of *canalis*; see CANAL, -CULE.] † **1.** *Arch.* = CANAL 6. **2.** *Phys.* A small duct, as in bone-structure, etc. 1854. var. **Cana·licule.**

Canaliferous (kænăli·fĕrəs), *a.* 1835. [f. CANAL + -FEROUS.] *Nat. Hist.* Having a canal: said of shells of molluscs.

Canalize (kæ·năləiz), *v.* 1855. [– Fr. *canaliser*; see CANAL, -IZE.] *trans.* **a.** To cut a canal through; to furnish with canals. **b.** To convert (a river) into a canal. Also in *Phys.* and *Pathol.*

This system of canalising Egypt PUSEY. Hence **Ca:naliza·tion.**

‖ **Canard** (kanar, kănā·ɹd). 1850. [Fr.; lit. 'duck'.] An extravagant or absurd story circulated as a hoax; a false report.

Canary (kănēᵊ·ri), *sb.* 1592. [– Fr. *Canarie* – Sp. *Canaria*, in L. *Canaria insula* 'Isle of Dogs', one of the Fortunate Isles, so named from its large dogs (L. *canarius* of dogs, f. *canis* dog). As the name of the bird modelled on Fr. *canari*, †*-ie* – Sp. *canario.*] The name of an island (*Gran Canaria*), and of the group Canary Isles. Hence **1.** A lively Spanish dance, now antiquated. † **2.** = *Canary wine*, a light sweet wine from the Canaries –1848. **3.** = CANARY-BIRD. Occ. *fig.* 1655. ¶ **4.** A malapropism for *quandary. Merry W.* II. ii. 61.

1. A medicine That's able..to make you dance Canari *All's Well* II. i. 77. **2.** Thou lack'st a cup of Canarie *Twel. N.* I. iii. 85.

Comb.: **c.-creeper,** a garden name for *Tropæolum aduncum* (wrongly called *T. canariense*); **-finch** = CANARY-BIRD; **-grass,** *Phalaris canariensis*, which yields canary-seed; **-seed,** the seed of c.-grass, used as food for canaries; **-stone,** a yellow variety of carnelian; **-wood,** the light orange-coloured wood of *Persea indica* and *P. canariensis*, obtained from Brazil.

Cana·ry, *a.* 1854. [prec. used attrib.] Canary-coloured, bright yellow.

† **Cana·ry**, *v.* 1588. [f. CANARY *sb.* 1.] To dance the canary. *L.L.L.* III. i. 12.

Canary-bird. 1576. [See CANARY *sb.*] **1.** An insessorial singing bird, a kind of finch (*Fringilla* or *Carduelis canaria*, family *Fringillidæ*), originally brought from the Canary Islands. The wild bird is green but the cage-breed is mainly yellow. **2.** *Thieves' slang.* A jail bird 1673.

Canaster (kănæ·stəɹ). 1827. [– Sp. *canastro* – med.L. **canastrum* – Gr. *κάναστρον*; cf. CANISTER.] **1.** A rush basket used to pack tobacco in. **2.** A kind of tobacco made of the dried leaves coarsely broken, formerly imported in rush baskets 1827.

‖ **Canaut** (kănǭ·t). *Anglo-Ind.* 1625. [Urdu – Pers. *ḳanāt* wall of a tent.] The side-wall of a tent; a canvas enclosure.

Ca·n-buoy. 1626. [f. CAN *sb.*[1] + BUOY *sb.*] *Naut.* A large cone-shaped buoy, usu. painted of a definite colour for purposes of recognition.

‖ **Cancan** (kaṅkaṅ, kæ·nˌkæn). 1848. [– Fr. *cancan* noise, disturbance (XVI), vulgar noisy dance (XIX), said to be L. *quanquam* although, applied (XVI) to the typical beginning of a wrangle in the Schools.] A kind of dance performed at the public balls of Paris, with extravagant and indecorous gestures.

Cancel (kæ·nsĕl), *sb.* 1596. [(1) – L. *cancelli* (see CANCELLI); (2) f. the vb.] † **I.** *pl.* Prison bars, bounds, confines. Chiefly *fig.* –1667. **II. 1.** The act of cancelling 1884. **2.** *Print.* The suppression and reprinting of a page or leaf. Hence *concr.* **a.** a page so cancelled; **b.** the new page substituted. 1806.

Cancel (kæ·nsĕl), *v.* 1440. [– (O)Fr. *canceller* – L. *cancellare* make lattice-wise, cross out (a writing), f. *cancellus*, pl. *-li* cross-bars; see CANCELLI, CHANCEL.] **1.** To deface or obliterate (writing), properly by drawing lines across it lattice-wise; to cross out. Of deeds, etc.: To annul by so marking, † cutting or † tearing up. **2.** *fig.* To render void 1494. **3.** *gen.* To obliterate; to put an end to 1530. **4.** *Arithm.* To strike out (a figure) by drawing a line through it; *esp.* in removing a common factor or equivalents of opposite signs; also *absol.* 1542. Hence *fig.* To neutralize 1633. **5.** *Print.* To suppress (a page, etc.) after it has been set up or printed off 1738. † **6.** To enclose with lattice-work or rails –1650.

1. A deed may be avoided by delivering it up to be cancelled; that is to have lines drawn over it, in the form of lattice-work or *cancelli* BLACKSTONE. **2.** Shake hands for ever, Cancell all our Vowes DRAYTON. **3.** Canceld from Heav'n and sacred memorie MILT. *P.L.* VI. 379. To c. one's fortunes SHAKS., anxieties BYRON. **4.** *fig.* With publick zeal to c. private crimes DRYDEN. **6.** Cancelling, and railing it with posts FULLER. Hence **Ca·ncellable, cancelable** *a.* **Ca·nceller.**

Cancelee·r, *sb.* 1599. [subst. use of inf. of ONFr. *canceler* swerve, etc., in mod. Fr. *chanceler*; cf. -ER[4].] *Hawking.* The action of a hawk in canceleering; see next. Also *fig.*

Cancelee·r, cancelie·r, *v.* 1633. [f. prec.] Of a hawk: To turn (once or twice) upon the wing, in order to recover herself before striking. *fig.* To digress.

The partridge sprung, He makes his stoop, but, wanting breath, is forced To cancelier MASSINGER.

Cancellarian (kænsĕlēᵊ·riăn), *a. rare.* 1846. [f. med.L. *cancellarius* CHANCELLOR + -AN.] Of, or of the nature of, a chancellor. So **Cancella·riate** (*rare*), chancellorship.

Cancellate (kæ·nsĕlĕt), *a.* 1661. [f. as CANCELLATION + -ATE[2].] Marked with cross lines like lattice-work; reticulated.

Cancellated (kæ·nsĕleⁱtĕd), *ppl. a.* 1681. [f. prec. + -ED[1].] **1.** = prec. **2.** *spec.* Having CANCELLI, as the spongy portion of bones 1836.

Cancellation (kænsĕlēⁱ·ʃən). 1535. [f. *cancellat-*, pa. ppl. stem of L. *cancellare* (see CANCEL *v.*) + -ION; cf. med.L. *cancellatio.*] **1.** The action of the vb. CANCEL. **2.** *etymologically.* The action of marking with cross lines lattice-wise. (*nonce-use.*) 1843.

1. C. of a will 1875, of indebtedness 1878. var. **Ca·ncelment.**

‖ **Cancelli** (kænse·ləi), *sb. pl.* 1642. [L., dim. of *cancer*, pl. *cancri* crossing bars, grating.] **1.** Bars of lattice-work; *spec.* the latticed screen between the choir and body of the church; hence, the CHANCEL. (? In Eng. use.) **2.** *Phys.* The lattice-work of the spongy portion of bones, consisting of thin plates and bars interlacing with each other 1802. ¶ Improperly applied to the interstices between these plates and bars 1845. Hence **Ca·ncellous** *a.* (*Phys.*) having an open porous structure as of network.

Cancer (kæ·nsəɹ), *sb.* ME. [– L. *cancer* crab, creeping ulcer, after Gr. *καρκίνος* crab, *καρκίνωμα* CARCINOMA; see CANKER, CHANCRE.] **1.** A crab. (Now *Zool.*) 1562. **b.** *Med.* An eight-tailed bandage 1753. **2.** *Astron.* **a.** The Zodiacal constellation lying between Gemini and Leo. **b.** The fourth of the twelve signs of the Zodiac (♋), beginning at the summer solstitial point, which the sun enters on the 21st of June ME. **3.** *Pathol.* A malignant growth or tumour, that tends to spread and to reproduce itself; it corrodes the part concerned, and generally ends in death. See also CANKER. 1601. Also *fig.* † **4.** A plant: perh. *cancer-wort* –1609.

2. *Tropic of C.*: the northern Tropic, forming a tangent to the ecliptic at the first point of C. *fig.* Sloth is a C., eating up..Time KEN. *Comb.* (in sense 3) **c.-root,** *Conopholis* (*Orobanche*) *americana* and *epiphegus virginiana*; **-wort,** *Linaria spuria* and *L. elatine*; also the genus *Veronica.*

Cancer (kæ·nsəɹ), *v.* 1774. [f. prec.] To eat into as a cancer. Hence **Ca·ncered** *ppl. a.* affected with cancer.

Cancerate (kæ·nsĕrēit), *v.* 1688. [– *cancerat-*, pa. ppl. stem. of late L. *cancerare*; see CANCER, -ATE[3].] To become cancerous, to grow into a cancer. Hence **Cancera·tion.** (Dicts.)

Cancerin (kæ·nsĕrin). An artificial guano from Newfoundland.

Ca·ncerite, ca·ncrite. 1848. [f. CANCER *sb.* + -ITE[1] 2 a.] *Palæont.* A fossil crab.

Cancerous (kæ·nsĕrəs), *a.* 1563. [f. CANCER *sb.* + -OUS; cf. late L. *cancerosus.*] Of the nature of, or affected with, cancer. Also *fig.* C. tumours 1872. C. close arts H. VAUGHAN. Hence **Ca·ncerously** *adv.* **Ca·ncerousness.**

Cancriform (kæ·ŋkrifǭɹm), *a.* 1826. [f. L. *cancer, -cr-* + -FORM.] **1.** Crab-shaped. **2.** *Pathol.* Looking like cancer 1879.

Cancrine (kæ·ŋkrəin), *a.* 1755. [f. as prec. + -INE[1].] Having the qualities of a crab; crab-like. Applied to (Latin) verse: Palindromic.

Cancrinite (kæ·ŋkrinəit). 1844. [f. *Cancrin,* a Russian statesman + -ITE[1] 2 b.] *Min.* A massive mineral found in the Urals, a silico-carbonate of aluminium and sodium.

Cancroid (kæ·ŋkroid, -oˌid). 1826. [f. L. *cancer, -cr-* crab + -OID; in sense 2 after Fr. *cancroïde.*] **A.** *adj.* **1.** Like the crab in structure. **2.** *Pathol.* Resembling cancer 1859. Also **-ide. B.** *sb.* **1.** A crustacean of the crab family 1852. **2.** A disease resembling cancer 1851. Also **-ide.**

Cand (kænd). 1880. [Local, of unkn. origin.] Fluor spar.

Candareen (kændărī·n). 1615. [Malay *kandūri.*] A Chinese money of account, = 10 cash. As a weight, about 6 grains Troy.

‖ **Candelabrum** (kændĭlēⁱ·brǒm). *Pl.* **-bra.** Also in mod. use **candelabra,** *pl.* **-as.** 1815. [L., f. *candela* CANDLE.] **1.** *Antiq.* A (usu. ornamental) candlestick. **b.** A lamp-stand. 1834. **2.** An ornamental branched candlestick; a chandelier 1815.

Candent (kæ·ndĕnt), *a. arch.* 1577. [– *candent-*, pres. ppl. stem of L. *candēre* be white, glow; see -ENT.] At a white heat; glowing with heat. Also *fig.* (*rare.*)

Lord of the c. lightenings COWPER.

Candescent (kænde·sĕnt), *a. rare.* 1824. [f. as prec.; see -ESCENT.] Glowing with, or as with, heat. Hence **Cande·scence. Cande·scently** *adv.*

Candid (kæ·ndid), *a.* 1630. [– Fr. *candide* or L. *candidus*, f. *candēre* be white, glisten; see -ID[1].] **1.** † White –1805; *fig.* † fortunate –1715; clear 1647. **2.** Free from bias; impartial (*Obs.* or *arch.*) 1635. † **3.** Free from malice; favourably disposed, kindly –1800. **4.** Frank, ingenuous, sincere in what one says 1675.

1. The stones came c. forth, the hue of innocence DRYDEN. This c. and joyful day BENTLEY. His c. stile COWLEY, fame BROWNING. **2.** A c. state of suspense CHATHAM. **3.** Laugh where we must, be c. where we can POPE. **4.** Let us be c., and speak out our mind GOLDSM. Also *ironically*: Save, save, oh! save me from the C. Friend CANNING. Hence **Ca·ndid-ly** *adv.*, **-ness.**

Candidacy (kæ·ndidĕsi). 1864. [f. CANDIDATE; see -ACY.] The position or status of a candidate; CANDIDATESHIP, CANDIDATURE.

Candidate (kæ·ndideⁱt), *sb.* 1613. [– (O)Fr. *candidat* or L. *candidatus* clothed in white, candidate for office (who appeared in a white toga), f. *candidus*; see CANDID, -ATE[1].] **1.** One who offers himself or is put forward by others as aspiring to be elected or appointed to an office, privilege, or position of honour. Const. *for*; † occ. *of.* **2.** *fig.* and *transf.* Aspirant, seeker for 1647; one thought likely or worthy to gain a post, etc. 1766. **3.** *Hist.* One of the *cohors candidatorum* (so called from their white dress) who served as the body-guard of the Roman Emperors after A.D. 237. –1751.

1. A c. for Holy Orders 1704, for a degree 1804. **2.** A c. for Tyburn GOLDSM.

Candidateship (kæ·ndidĕtˌʃip). 1775. [f. prec. + -SHIP.] = CANDIDACY.

Candidature (kæ·ndidĕtiŭɹ). 1851. [f. as prec. + -URE, prob. after Fr. *candidature.*] Standing as a candidate, candidateship.

Candied (kæ·ndid), *ppl. a.* 1600. [f. CANDY *v.* + -ED[1].] **1.** Preserved or encrusted with sugar 1616. *transf.* and *fig.* Covered as with crystallized sugar 1600. **2.** Crystallized, congealed 1641. **3.** *fig.* 'Sugared', glozing 1602.

1. C. ginger VENNER. The winter's candy'd thorn SHENSTONE. **3.** The C. tongue *Haml.* III. ii. 65.

† **Candify,** *sb.* 1727. [perh. subst. use of † *candify, candefy* whiten.] *Herb.* Fuller's Herb or Soapwort.

Candite (kæ·ndəit), *sb.* 1844. [f. *Candy* in Ceylon + -ITE[1] 2 b.] *Min.* A variety of Spinel, dark green or brown to black, also called Ceylonite.

Candle (kæ·nd'l), *sb.* [OE. *candel* – L. *candela,* later *-della,* f. *candēre* glisten. Reinforced in ME. by AFr. *candele,* OFr. *candeile,* var. of *chandeile, -oile* :– L. *candela,* and OFr. *candelle* (mod. *chandelle*) :– L. *candella.*] **1.** A (usually cylindrical) body of wax, tallow, spermaceti, or the like, formed round a wick of cotton or flax, or formerly of the pith of a rush, and used to give artificial light. † **2.** *fig.* (See quots.) –1634. Also *transf.*

1. This C. burnes not cleere *Hen. VIII,* III. ii. 96. There was for euery Saint his c. COTGR. 10,500 cubic feet of 25-candle (= *candle power*) gas to the ton URE. **2.** Nights candles are burnt out *Rom. & Jul.* III. v. 9. The c. of letters DANIEL. Out, out, breefe C. *Macb.* V. v. 23. *Medicated c.*: a candle containing some drug for diffusion by burning.

Phrases. **1.** *Candle, book, and bell*: see BELL *sb.*[1] **2.** *Not able* or *fit to hold a c. to*: not fit even to hold a subordinate position to, not to be compared with. *To hold a c. to the devil*: *orig.* to treat as a saint, and placate with a c.; *now,* to assist an evil person, be active in evil. **3.** *To sell by inch of c.*, etc.: to sell by auction in which bids are received only so long as a small piece of c. burns. Also *fig.* and *transf.* **4.** *The game,* etc. *is not worth the c.*: the enterprise does not justify the labour or expenditure. **5.** *To burn* or *light the c. at both ends*: to be excessively wasteful or extravagant.

Comb.: **c.-bomb,** a small glass bubble filled with water, which, if placed in the flame of a c., explodes; **-fish,** an oily Amer. sea-fish of the salmon-family, used when dried as a c.; † **-fly,** a moth; **-lamp**; †**-mine** (*fig.*), a mine of fat or candle-material; **-nut,** the fruit of the Candleberry tree; **-power,** the illuminating power of a standard spermaceti candle; † **-rush,** the common rush, formerly used for rush-lights; **-shrift,** penance done with candles; **-wick.**

Candle-beam. *Hist.* ME. **1.** A rood-beam 1463. **2.** ? A hanging beam to hold candles.

Candleberry (kæ·nd'lberi). 1753. A name for the fruit and plants of: (*a*) *Myrica cerifera,* whose berries yield bayberry tallow. (*b*) *Aleurites triloba,* which produces the candle-nut of commerce 1866.

Candle-end (kæ·nd'l eːnd). 1547. **1.** The end-piece of a burnt-down candle. **2.** *fig.* A trifle, fragment, scrap. Usu. *pl.* 1626.

Ca·ndle-hoːlder. *rare.* One who lights those who work by night; a candle-bearer. *Rom. & Jul.* I. iv. 38.

Candlelight (kæ·nd'lˌləit). [OE. *candel leoht.*] **1.** The light given by candles; artificial light. **2.** The time during, or at, which candles are lighted; dusk, nightfall 1663.

1. To study by Candle-light ADDISON. He frequently painted candle-lights (= candle-light effects) H. WALPOLE. **2.** The lords satt till after c. LUTTRELL.

Ca·ndle-liːghter. One who, or that which, lights candles; an acolyte; a spill.

Candlemas (kæ·nd'lmæs). [OE. *candel-mæsse,* f. *candel* + *mæsse* MASS *sb.*[1]] **1.** The feast of the purification of the Virgin Mary (or presentation of Christ in the Temple) celebrated with many candles. **2.** The date of this, Feb. 2. A Sc. quarter-day. OE. Also *attrib.*

† **Ca·ndle-rent.** 1611. Rent from house-property (which constantly deteriorates) –1655.

Ca·ndle-snuff. 1552. The burnt wick of a candle. Hence **Ca·ndle-snuːffer,** he who, or that which, snuffs candles.

Candlestick (kæ·nd'lˌstik). [OE. *candel-sticca* the stalk or shaft of a candelabrum.] A support for a candle; formerly including chandeliers, etc. Also *fig.* (See *Rev.* 1:20.)

Set up one. . branching c. of lights BACON.

Ca·ndle-tree. 1691. **1.** = CANDLEBERRY (*a*). Hence *Candle-tree oil.* **2.** *Parmentiera cerifera* (N.O. *Crescentiaceæ*); from the appearance of its fruit 1866.

Ca·ndle-waːster. One who wastes candles by late study or dissipation. *Much Ado* V. i. 18.

Ca·ndle-wood. 1712. **1.** Resinous wood 1753. **2.** A tree which yields such wood, as Californian C., *Fouquiera splendens,* etc.

Can-dock (kæ·ndǫk). 1661. [f. CAN *sb.*[1] + DOCK *sb.*[1]] The Yellow Water-lily. Also, the White Water-lily.

Candour (kæ·ndəɹ). 1610. [– Fr. *candeur* or L. *candor,* f. *cand-* of *candēre* and *candidus* CANDID; see -OUR.] † **1.** Brilliant whiteness –1692. † **2.** Purity, innocence –1704. **3.** Freedom from bias, impartiality (*Obs.* or *arch.*) 1637. † **4.** Freedom from malice, kindliness –1802. **5.** Freedom from reserve in speech; frankness, ingenuousness 1769.

3. Writing thyselfe, or judging others writ, I know not which th' hast most, candor or wit B. JONS. **4.** Sincere, but without c. 1751. **5.** Openness and c. 1876.

Ca·ndroy. 1858. A machine used in preparing cotton cloths for printing.

Candy (kæ·ndi), *sb.*[1] 1769. [– Fr. *candi* in *sucre candi*; see SUGAR-CANDY.] Crystallized sugar, made by boiling and slow evaporation; also any confection made of or with this. (In U.S. including toffee, and the like.)

Comb.: **c.-man,** an itinerant seller of c.; in the north of England, a bum-bailiff (see O.E.D.); **-pull** (*U.S.*), a party of young people at which toffee is made; **-sugar** = SUGAR-CANDY.

† **Ca·ndy,** *sb.*[2] 1597. Obs. f. *Candia* (Crete): used in CANDYTUFT.

‖ **Ca·ndy,** *sb.*[3] 1618. [Mahr. *khaṇḍi.*] A weight used in India, averaging 500 pounds

Candy (kæ·ndi), *v.* 1533. [f. CANDY *sb.*[1], after Fr. *candir,* f. *candi* taken as pa. pple.] **1.** To preserve by boiling with sugar; to encrust with sugar. Also *fig.* **2.** To form into crystals, congeal in a crystalline form 1598. **3.** *transf.* To cover with crystalline substance, as hoar-frost, etc. 1607. **4.** *intr.* To crystallize or congeal, to become encrusted with sugar 1657.

1. Gynger. .candyd with Sugar ELYOT. *fig.* To c. over studies with pleasure FULLER. **2.** To c. [a dropping show'r] SYLVESTER, Sea-salt water 1713, molasses 1880. **3.** Hoary frosts had candy'd all the plaines W. BROWNE. **4.** Preserves c. by long keeping 1888.

Candytuft (kæ·ndiˌtɒft). 1664. [f. CANDY *sb.*[2] + TUFT.] A plant, *Iberis umbellata,* orig. from Crete; by extension, the genus *Iberis* (N.O. *Cruciferæ*).

Cane (kēⁱn), *sb.*[1] [– OFr. *cane,* (also mod.) *canne*; – L. *canna* reed, cane, tube, pipe – Gr. κάννα, κάννη – Assyrian *ḳanū,* Heb. *ḳāne,* both meaning reed.] **1.** The hollow jointed ligneous stem of various reeds or grasses, as Bamboo and Sugar cane; the solid stem of the genus *Calamus* (the Rattan), or some other palms; the stem of the Raspberry and its congeners. **b.** = SUGAR-CANE (hence *c.-sugar*) 1781. † **2.** A dart or lance made of a cane –1700. **3.** A length of a cane stem, used as a walking-stick, or as a rod for beating. Hence, any slender walking-stick. 1590. † **4.** A pipe or tube –1720. **5.** Used of a rod of sealing-wax, sulphur, or glass (solid) 1681.

1. Ther growe in many places [of ynde] canes. . ful of sugre CAXTON. Ribs of split c. (without *pl.*) 1888. **2.** Some flying Parthian's darted C. SEDLEY **3.** Sending the boy down into the cellar. . I followed him with a c., and did there beat him PEPYS.

Comb.: **c.-brake,** (*a.*) a thicket of canes; (*b.*) a genus of grasses, *Arundinaria*; **-gun,** a gun made in the form of a walking-stick; **-harvester; -juice; -killer,** a plant (*Alectra brasiliensis*); **-mill,** a mill for crushing (sugar) cane; **-press; -stripper,** a knife for stripping and topping the sugar-cane; **-trash,** the refuse of sugar-canes.

Cane, *sb.*[2] 1612. [obs. f. KHAN[2].] An eastern inn –1743.

Cane, *sb.*[3] [Origin unkn.] *local.* A weasel. G. WHITE.

Cane, *sb.*[4], var. of CAIN, payment in kind.

Cane, *sb.*[5], obs. f. KHAN[1], an eastern lord.

Cane (kēⁱn), *v.*[1] 1667. [f. CANE *sb.*[1]] **1.** To beat with a cane. **2.** To drive (a lesson) *into* with the cane 1866. **3.** To fit (a chair, etc.) with cane; to furnish with a cane 1696.

2. I had a little Greek caned into me 1866.

Cane, *v.*[2] [Origin unkn.] *dial.* 1483. To form a head, as ale becoming 'mothery'.

† **Ca·nel, canell(e.** [– OFr. *canele* (mod. *cannelle*) – Prov. *canela*, dim. of *cana* CANE *sb.*[1]; cf. med.L. *canella*.] Cinnamon, perh. including Cassia bark –1721.

‖ **Canella** (kănĕ·lă). 1693. [med.L.; see prec.] † **1.** = CANEL. **2.** *Bot.* A genus of plants (N.O. *Canellaceæ*); esp. *C. alba*, or Wild Cinnamon. Also, the inner bark of *C. alba*, or *white cinnamon*; used in medicine, and as a condiment. 1756

Cane·phorus. Also **ca·nephor, cane·-phora.** 1849. [– L. *canephorus* – Gr. κανηφόρος adj. (f. κάνεον basket + -φορος carrying), also as sb.] In ancient Greece, one of the maidens who carried on their heads baskets containing the sacred things used at the feasts of Demeter, Bacchus, and Athena; hence, *Arch.* applied to figures of young persons, of either sex, bearing baskets on their heads.

Canescence (kănĕ·sĕns). *rare.* 1855. [f. as next; see -ENCE.] Dull whiteness.

Canescent (kănĕ·sĕnt), *a.* 1847. [– *canescent-*, pres. ppl. stem of L. *canescere* grow hoary, f. *canus* hoary; see -ESCENT.] Rather hoary; greyish or dull white.

‖ **Canette** (kănĕ·t). 1881. [Fr. dim. of † *cane*, *canne* CAN.] A little (earthenware) can or pot.

Caneva, -as. Obs. f. CANVAS. Also, a woollen fabric made to resemble canvas 1885.

Cangenet. [Perversion or error.] = CANZONET. Shaks.

‖ **Cangia** (ka·ndʒă). 1715. [– It. *cangia*, whence also Fr. *cange*.] A light boat used on the Nile.

Ca·ngica-wood. 1875. A light yellow-brown Brazilian wood, used for cabinet-work.

‖ **Cangue, cang** (kæŋ). 1727. [– Fr. *cangue* – Pg. *canga* – Annamite *gong*.] A broad heavy wooden frame or board worn round the neck like a kind of portable pillory as a punishment in China. Hence **Cangue** *v.*

Can-hook. 1626. [perh. for *cant-hook* (CANT *v.*[2]) a tool for canting over bales, cases etc.] A short rope or chain with a flat hook at each end, used for slinging a cask.

Ca·nicide. 1852. [f. L. *canis* dog + -CIDE.] A dog-killer.

Canicular (kăni·kiŭlăɹ), *a.* (*sb.*) ME. [– late L. *canicularis*, f. *canicula* dog-star, dim. of *canis* dog.]

A. *adj.* **1.** *Canicular days*: the DOG-DAYS, q.v. **2.** Of or pertaining to the dog-days 1577. **3.** *C. year*: the ancient Egyptian year, computed from one heliacal rising of Sirius to the next 1660. **4.** *joc.* Pertaining to a dog 1592.

2. The sun..Afflicts me with c. aspect GREENE.

B. *sb.* † **1.** The dog-star; *pl.* the dog-days –1727. **2.** *joc.* (*pl.*) Doggerel verses 1872.

Canicule (kæ·nikiul). *rare.* 1719. [– Fr. *canicule* or L. *canicula*; see prec.] The dog-days.

Canine (kănəi·n, kæ·nəin), *a.* (*sb.*) 1607. [– Fr. *canin*, *-ine* or L. *caninus*, *-ina*, f. *canis* dog; see -INE[1].] **A.** *adj.* **1.** Of, belonging to, or characteristic of, a dog; having the nature or qualities of a dog 1623; of appetite, hunger, etc.: Voracious 1613. **2.** *Canine tooth*: one of the four strong pointed teeth situated between the incisors and the molars; a cuspidate tooth 1607.

1. The c. race 1870. *C. appetite, hunger*: BULIMY. *C. madness*: hydrophobia. *C. fossa*: (*Anat.*) a depression in the upper jaw-bone behind the c. prominence. *C. prominence* or *ridge*: a ridge on the upper jaw-bone caused by the fang of the c. tooth.

B. *sb.* = Canine tooth (see A. 2). Also *joc.* = 'dog'. var. † **Cani·nal.** Hence **Cani·niform** *a.* shaped like a c. tooth. **Cani·nity,** canine trait; dog nature; sympathy with dogs.

Ca·nion, ca·nnion, canon. 1583. [In form *can(n)ion* – Sp. *cañon* tube, pipe, gun-barrel, 'the cannions of breeches', augm. of *caña*; see CANE *sb.*[1], -OON. In form *canon* – synon. Fr. *canon*: see CANNON *sb.*[2]] *pl.* Ornamental rolls, laid like sausages round the ends of the legs of breeches. Now *Hist.*

Canister (kæ·nistəɹ). 1697. [– L. *canistrum* – Gr. κάναστρον wicker basket, f. κάννα reed; see CANE *sb.*[1]] **1.** A case or box for holding tea, coffee, shot, etc. 1711. **2.** A basket for bread, flowers, etc. [tr. L. or Gr.] 1697. **3.** = *canister-shot* 1801.

2. Full Canisters of fragrant Lillies 1697. *Comb.* **c.-shot,** small bullets packed in cases fitting the bore of a gun. **Ca·nister** *v.* to put in a c.; to fasten a c. to.

Cank (kæŋk), *v. dial.* 1741. [Echoic.] To cackle as geese; to chatter.

Canker (kæ·ŋkəɹ), *sb.* [OE. *cancer* – L.; in ME. reinforced or superseded by ONFr. *cancre*, var. of (O)Fr. *chancre* :– L. *cancrum*, nom. *cancer*; see CANCER, CHANCRE.] **1.** An eating, spreading sore or ulcer; a gangrene. Used as = CANCER till *c* 1700. Now *spec.* A gangrenous affection of the mouth, with fetid sloughing ulcers; *canker of the mouth*, or *water c.* **b.** *Farriery.* A disease of a horse's foot, with a fetid discharge from the frog. **2.** Rust. Now *dial.* 1533. **3.** A disease of plants, *esp.* fruit trees, attended by decay of the bark and tissues 1555. **4.** A canker-worm ME. **5.** The dog-rose (*Rosa canina*). Now *local.* 1582. **6.** *fig.* Anything that frets, corrodes, corrupts, or consumes slowly and secretly 1564.

1. No cankar fretteth flesh so sore 1559. **4.** Cankers in the muske rose buds SHAKS. **5.** 1 *Hen. IV*, I. iii. 176. **6.** Enuie which is the c. of Honour BACON.

Comb.: **c.-berry,** the fruit of the dog-rose; also the plant *Solanum bahamense*; **-bloom,** the blossom of the dog-rose; **-blossom,** a canker (sense 4); also *fig.*; **-rash,** a form of scarlet fever in which the throat is ulcerated; **-rose,** (*a.*) the Dog-rose; (*b.*) the wild poppy (*Papaver rhœas*).

Canker (kæ·ŋkəɹ), *v.* ME. [f. prec.] **1.** To infect or consume with canker; † to corrode. **2.** *fig.* To infect, corrupt; to consume like a canker ME. **3.** *intr.* To become cankered; † to rust; to fester (*dial.*). Also *fig.* 1519.

2. No lapse of moons can c. Love TENNYSON. **3.** So his minde cankers *Temp.* IV. i. 192. Silvering will sully and c. more than gilding BACON.

Cankered (kæ·ŋkəɹd), *ppl. a.* ME. [f. prec. + -ED.] **1.** In the senses of the vb. CANKER. **2.** *fig.* Malignant, envious; spiteful; ill-tempered. (Frequent in 16th c.) 1513.

1. C. sores 1720, gold *Jas.* 5:3, Tulips EVELYN, waters 1679, heresy 1555. **2.** A wicked will..A cankred Grandams will *John* II. i. 194. Hence **Ca·nkered-ly** *adv.*, **-ness.**

Ca·nkerfret, *sb. dial.* 1618. [See next, and the verb.] † **1.** Corrosion by rust. **2.** Copperas. **3.** A blister in the mouth.

† **Ca·nkerfret,** *a.* ME. [f. CANKER *sb.* + *fret*, obs. pa. pple. of FRET *v.*[1]] Eaten away with gangrene; corroded with rust –1603.

† **Ca·nkerfret,** *v.* 1642. [f. CANKER *sb.* + FRET *v.*[1]] *trans.* To eat with canker. *intr.* To become cankered; to rust.

Cankerous (kæ·ŋkərəs), *a.* 1543. [f. CANKER *sb.* + -OUS.] **1.** Of the nature of a CANKER. **2.** Corroding, infectious 1691. Also *fig.*

2. C. fetters E. B. BROWNING. *fig.* A c. regret 1881.

Cankerworm (kæ·ŋkəɹwɔ̄ɹm). 1530. [CANKER *sb.* 4.] A caterpillar that destroys buds and leaves. *spec.* (in U.S.) The larva of the *Geometra brumata* or winter moth. Also *fig.*

That which the locust hath left, hath the cankerworme eaten *Joel* 1:4. *fig.* Lies..are cankerworms, and spoil all causes FROUDE.

Cankery (kæ·nkəri). ME. [f. CANKER *sb.* + -Y[1].] † **1.** Gangrenous. ME. only. **2.** Affected with canker 1669. **3.** *fig.* Crabbed. *Sc.* 1786.

Cann, var. of CON *v.*[2]

‖ **Canna** (kæ·nă), *sb.* 1664. [L.; see CANE *sb.*[1]] *Bot.* A genus of tropical plants (N.O. *Marantaceæ*), with showy flowers and ornamental foliage.

Canna, Sc. form of *cannot.*

Cannabic (kănæ·bik), *a.* 1731. [f. L. *cannabis* hemp (– Gr. κάνναβις) + -IC.] Of the nature of hemp. **Ca·nnabene** (*Chem.*), a volatile, colourless, strong-smelling liquid obtained from Indian hemp. **Ca·nnabin** (*Chem.*), the poisonous resin of the extract of Indian hemp. **Ca·nnabine** *a.* of or pertaining to hemp. ‖ **Ca·nnabis (indica),** Indian hemp; the dried flowering tops of the female plants of *Cannabis sativa.*

Cannach (ka·năχ). *Sc.* Also **canna.** 1803. [– Gael. *cánach.*] The Cotton-grass.

† **Cannel, canel** (kæ·nĕl), *sb.*[1] [ME. *canel*, *kanel* – ONF. *canel* = OFr. *chanel.* See CHANNEL and CANAL.] † **1.** (*canel*) The bed of a stream. Now CHANNEL. ME. only. † **2.** (*canel, cannel*) A gutter. Now KENNEL *sb.*[2], q.v. –1756. † **3.** (*canel*) A pipe; a tap for a cask –1629. † **4.** The neck. ME. only.

Cannel (kæ·nĕl), *sb.*[2] 1538. [Of northern origin, but connection with *candle* (north. dial. *cannle*) cannot be made out.] A bituminous coal, which burns with a bright flame, and is rich in volatile matter: it can be cut and polished like jet. Also called *cannel coal*, and often (since 1700) written *candle-coal.*

† **Ca·nnel-bone.** ME. [See CANNEL *sb.*[1] 4.] The neck-bone; the clavicle; ? the ilium of an animal –1664.

† **Ca·nnellate, -elate,** *a.* 1673. [After It. *cannellato* and Fr. *cannelé*; see next, -ATE[2].] *Arch.* Channelled, fluted –1676.

Cannelure (kæ·nĕliŭɹ). 1755. [– Fr. *cannelure*, f. *canneler*, f. *canne* reed; see CANE *sb.*[1]] A groove, fluting. Hence **Ca·nnelured** *a.*

Cannery (kæ·nĕri). 1879. [f. CAN *v.*[3] + -ERY.] A factory where meat, fruit, etc., are canned.

Ca·nnet. [– Fr. *canette*, dim. of *cane* duck; see -ETTE.] *Her.* A duck, borne as a charge, without feet or bill.

Cannibal (kæ·nibăl). 1553. [First in pl. *Canibales* – Sp. *Canibales*, one of the forms (recorded by Columbus) of the name *Caribes*, a fierce man-eating nation of the West Indies. See CARIB, CALIBAN.] **1.** A man (*esp.* a savage) that eats human flesh; a man-eater. Also *fig.* **2.** An animal that devours its own species 1796. **3.** *attrib.* Pertaining to a cannibal, cannibal-like; bloodthirsty 1596.

1. The Canibals that each others eate *Oth.* I. iii. 143. **3.** He..swarmeth in vile Cannibal words NASHE. Hence **Cannibale·an** (*rare*), **Canniba·lic** *adjs.* of, pertaining to, or characteristic of, a c. **Ca·nnibalish** *a.* savouring of cannibalism. **Cannibali·stic** *a.* addicted to or pertaining to cannibalism. **Cannibali·stically** *adv.* **Ca·nnibally** *adv.* after the manner of a c.; also *fig. Cor.* IV. v. 200.

Cannibalism (kæ·nibăliz'm). 1796. [f. prec. + -ISM.] The practice of eating one's kind. *fig.* Bloodthirsty barbarity.

The political c. of the mob D'ISRAELI. var. **Canniba·lity** (*rare*).

Cannie; see CANNY.

Cannikin, canikin (kæ·nikin). 1570. [– Du. *kanneken*; see CAN *sb.*, -KIN; cf. CATKIN, MANNIKIN.] A small can or drinking vessel.

Cannily (kæ·nili), *adv. Sc.* (and *n. dial.*) 1636. [f. CANNY *a.* + -LY[2].] In a CANNY manner.

Canniness (kæ·ninĕs). *Sc.* 1662. [f. as prec. + -NESS.] Sagacity, cautiousness; gentleness.

Canning (kæ·niŋ), *vbl. sb.* 1872. [f. CAN *v.*[3] + -ING[1].] The preserving of meat, fish, etc., by sealing up in cans; tinning. Also *attrib.*

Cannon (kæ·nən), *sb.*[1] 1525. [– (O)Fr. *canon* – It. *cannone*, augm. of *canna* tube; see CANE *sb.*[1], -OON. In Billiards (sense 6), perversion of CARROM, CAROM (still in U.S.), shortening of CARAMBOLE.] † **1.** A tube –1616. **2.** A piece of ordnance; a gun of a size which requires it to be mounted for firing 1525. (The leading current sense.) Also *collect.*, and as *pl.* **3.** *Mech.* A hollow cylindrical piece capable of revolving independently on a shaft. **4.** A smooth round bit. Also *cannon-bit.* 1596. **5.** The part of a bell by which it is hung; the *ear* 1872. **5.** *Billiards.* A stroke in which the player's ball hits two balls in succession; a *carrom* 1839. Also *transf.*

2. Then a Soldier..Seeking the bubble Reputation Euen in the Canons mouth *A.Y.L.* II. vii. 153.

Comb.: † **c.-basket,** a gabion; **-bone,** the single bones between the knee or hough and fetlock (of a horse, etc.); **-clock,** a c. with a burning-glass so fixed as to fire the priming at noon; **-fodder** [tr. G. *kanonenfutter*; cf. 'food for powder' 1 *Hen. IV*, IV. ii. 72], men regarded as material to be consumed in war; **-lock,** a contrivance for exploding the charge of a c.; **-pinion,** the perforated pinion which carries the minute hand of a watch, and drives the minute wheel; **-royal,** an 8½-inch gun, firing 66 lb. shot. Hence **Ca·nnoned** *a.* furnished with cannon. **Ca·nnonry,** cannonading; artillery.

Ca·nnon, *sb.*[2] 1800. [– Fr. *canon*; see CANION.] A sausage-like curl, properly horizontal.

Ca·nnon, *v.* 1691. [Sense 1 f. CANNON *sb.*[1] q.v.] **1.** To cannonade. **2.** *Billiards.* To make a CANNON (sense 6). Of the ball: To strike and rebound. 1844. **3.** *trans.* To come into rebounding collision with 1864. Also *intr.*

Cannonade (kænǒnē·d), *sb.* 1655. [– Fr. *canonnade* – It. *cannonata*; see CANNON *sb.*[1], -ADE.] A continued discharge of cannon; an attack with cannon. Also *fig.*

Cannona·de, *v.* 1670. [f. prec.] **1.** To batter with cannon; to discharge cannon against. **2.** To discharge cannon continuously 1702.

Ca·nnonarchy. 1841. [f. CANNON *sb.*[1], after words in *-archy.*] Government by cannon.

Ca·nnon-ba:ll. 1663. [See BALL *sb.*[1]] A ball, usu. of iron, to be thrown from a cannon. (Also *collect.* and as *pl.*)

Cannon-ball fruit, the globular woody fruit of a S. American tree, *Couroupita guianensis* (N.O. *Lecythidaceæ*) or **Cannon-ball Tree.**

Cannonee·r. 1562. [– Fr. *canonnier* – It. *cannoniere*; see -EER.] An artilleryman who lays and fires cannon.

Ca·nnon-proof. 1601. [See PROOF *a.*] *sb.* Impenetrability to cannon-shot; cannon-proof armament. *adj.* Proof against cannon 1632.

Ca·nnon-shot. 1580. [See SHOT *sb.*[1]] **1.** The discharge of a cannon 1606. **2.** Shot from or for a cannon 1591. **3.** The range of a cannon 1580.

Cannot (kæ·nǒt), the usual mod. way of writing *can not.*

‖ **Cannula** (kæ·niŭlă). 1684. [L., dim. of *canna* CANE *sb.*[1]] *Surg.* A tubular instrument introduced into a cavity or tumour in order to allow fluid to escape. Hence **Ca·nnular** *a.* tubular.

Ca·nnulate, -ated, *a.* Also (*erron.*) **canu-.** 1684. [f. prec. + -ATE[2], -ED[1].] Tubular; channelled or grooved.

Canny (kæ·ni), *a.* *Sc.* (and *north.*) 1637. [Presumably f. CAN *v.*[1] + -Y[1]; corresp. to *cunning* in its primary sense.] **1.** Sagacious, prudent; cautious. *Sc.* (*arch.*) **b.** *esp.* Cautious in worldly matters. (Perh. from Scott's use.) 1816. † **2.** Wily –1794. **3.** Skilful, 'cunning' (in the old sense) 1768. † **4.** Supernaturally wise. *Sc.* –1816. **5.** Safe to meddle with. Cf. UNCANNY. *Sc.* 1718. **6.** Frugal. *Sc.* (*arch.*) 1725. **7.** Careful or cautious in motion or action; *hence*, quiet, gentle. (The usual sense in mod. Sc.) 1785. **8.** Snug. *Sc.* 1758. **9.** Seemly, comely; good, satisfactory. In N. Lancs. 'of good size'. Not a Sc. sense. 1802. **10.** Also *advb.*, as in *to ca' canny* (see CALL III. 3) 1796.

3. *C. wife*: 'wise woman', midwife (Fr. *sage-femme*); hence *c. moment*: moment of childbirth.

Canoe (kănū·), *sb.* 1555. [In form *canoa* (XVI) – Sp. – Haitian *canoa*; present pronunc. corresp. to later var. *canow*, *canoo* (cf. Carib *canaoua*); present sp. due to Fr. *canoë*.] **1.** A boat in use among uncivilized nations, hollowed out of a tree-trunk, or otherwise rudely constructed, and usually propelled by paddles. **2.** In civilized use: A small light boat or skiff propelled by paddling 1799.

1. The Boate of one tree called the Canoa RALEIGH. **2.** A thousand miles in the Rob Roy Canoe (*title*) 1865. 'Paddle your own c.' *Pop. Song.*

Comb.: **c. birch,** *Betula papyracea*; **c. wood,** the wood of the Tulip tree. Hence **Canoe·ist,** one who paddles a c.

Canoe (kănū·), *v.* 1842. [f. prec.] To paddle a canoe; to move as in a canoe.

Canon[1] (kæ·nən). [OE. *canon* – L. *canon* – Gr. κανών rule; reinforced or superseded by ME. *cano(u)n* – AFr. *canun*, (O)Fr. *canon.*] **1.** A rule, law, or decree of the Church; *esp.* a rule laid down by an eccl. Council. **2.** *gen.* A law, rule, edict; a general rule or axiom of any subject, as canons of descent, etc. 1588; a standard of judgement 1601. † **3.** *Math.* A general rule, formula, table –1798. **4.** The list of books of the Bible accepted by the Christian Church as genuine and inspired. Also *transf.* ME. **5.** The portion of the Mass included between the Preface and the *Pater*, and containing the words of consecration ME. **6.** *Mus.* A species of composition in which the different parts take up the same subject one after another in strict imitation 1597. **7.** 'A Prestation, Pension, or Customary payment upon some religious Account.' From *Rom. Law.* 1633. **b.** A quit-rent 1643. **8.** A chief epoch or era, serving to date from 1833. **9.** A book of the rules of a monastic order 1727. **b.** The list of saints canonized by the Church 1727. **10.** *Print.* A size of type-body equal to 4-line Pica; so called perhaps as being that used for printing the canon of the Mass 1683. **11.** = CANNON *sb.*[1] 5. 1688. Also *attrib.*

1. *The canon* = *Canon law.* *Canon law* (formerly *law canon*: cf. Fr. *droit canon*): ecclesiastical law, as laid down in decrees of the Pope and statutes of councils. Selfe-loue. .the most inhibited sinne in the Cannon *All's Well*, I. i. 158. **2.** Or that the Euerlasting had not fixt His Cannon 'gainst Selfe-slaughter *Haml.* I. ii. 132. The canons of pathology 1806, of taste 1874, of criticism 1879. **6.** Cf. ROUND *sb.*[1] IV. 1a, b. **Ca·non** *v.* *Mus.* to treat in c. fashion 1894.

Canon[2] (kæ·nən). [ME. *canun*, *canoun* – OFr. *canonie* (with ending assim. to *cano(u)n* CANON[1]) – eccl.L. *canonicus* (repr. in OE. *canonic*), subst. use of adj.; see CANONIC.] **1.** *Eccl. Hist.* A clergyman living with others in a clergy-house (*claustrum*), or (later) within the precinct of a cathedral, etc., and ordering his life according to the canons of the church. **2.** A member of an ecclesiastical chapter 1561.

Those who renounced private property were known as *Augustinian* (*Austin*) or *regular*, the others were *secular* canons. *Minor* or *Petty Canon*: a clergyman taking duty in a cathedral, but not a member of the chapter. *Honorary Canon*: a titular member of the chapter, non-residentiary and unpaid.

Cañon (kæ·nʸən, kæ·nyən). 1850. [– Sp. *cañon* tube, etc., augm. of *caña*; see CANE *sb.*[1], and cf. CANION, CANNON *sb.*[2]] A deep gorge or ravine with steep sides, at the bottom of which a river flows. var. **Canyon.**

Canoness (kæ·nǒnės). 1682. [f. CANON[2] + -ESS[1]. Cf. med.L. *canonissa.*] **1.** *Eccl. Hist.* One of a community of women living under a rule, but not under a perpetual vow; hence, a woman holding a prebend or canonry. **2.** *joc.* The wife of a canon 1873.

Canonic (kănǫ·nik). OE. [– Fr. *canonique* or L. *canonicus* – Gr. κανονικός; see CANON[1],[2], -IC.] *adj.* = CANONICAL 1, 2, 3, 5, 6. 1483. **B.** *sb.* **1.** = CANON[2]. OE. **2.** A system of dialectic; = the Epicurean τὸ κανονικόν 1655.

Canonical (kănǫ·nikăl), *a.* (and *sb.*) 1483. [– med.L. *canonicalis*; see prec., -AL[1].] **1.** Prescribed by, or having reference to, canon law. **2.** Of or belonging to the canon of Scripture, or any other sacred canon 1568. **3.** *gen.* Authoritative; orthodox; standard 1553. **4.** *Math.* Furnishing, or according to, a formula (see CANON[1] 3) 1738. **5.** *Mus.* In canon form 1609. **6.** Of or belonging to an eccl. chapter, or to a canon (see CANON[2]) 1579. **7.** *sb. pl.* Canonical robes 1748.

1. *C. hours*: (*a.*) stated times of the day appointed by the canons for prayers, etc.; (*b.*) the hours (from 8 a.m. to 3 p.m.) within which marriage can be legally performed in a parish church in England; also *transf.* *C. obedience*: the obedience to be rendered by inferior clergy to the bishop, and others, according to the canons. **2.** *C. epistles*: *esp.* the seven catholic epistles of James, Peter, John, and Jude. **3.** Wisedome vnder a ragged coate is seldome canonicall 1603. Hence **Cano·nical-ly** *adv.*, **-ness.**

Canonicate (kănǫ·nikět). 1652. [– Fr. *canonicat* or med.L. *canonicatus*; see CANONIC, -ATE[1].] The office of a canon; a canonry.

Canonicity (kænǒni·sĭti). 1797. [f. CANONIC + ITY; cf. Fr. *canonicité.*] Canonicalness, *esp.* the fact of being within the Canon of Scripture.

Canonist (kæ·nǒnist). 1542. [– (O)Fr. *canoniste* or med.L. *canonista*; see CANON[1], -IST.] One skilled in canon law. Hence **Canoni·stic, -al** *a.*

Ca:noniza·tion. ME. [– med.L. *canonizatio*, f. as next; see -ATION; cf. (O)Fr. *canonisation.*] The action of canonizing; *esp.* formal admission into the calendar of saints. Also *fig.*

He sent hym to heauen by his canonyzacyon BALE.

Canonize (kæ·nǒnəiz), *v.* ME. [– med.L. *canonizare*; in late L. admit as canonical or authoritative (= OFr. *canonisier*); see CANON[1], -IZE; cf. Fr. *canoniser.*] **1.** *trans.* To place formally in the canon of saints. Also *fig.* † **2.** To consecrate. ME. only † **3.** To deify –1794. **4.** To admit into the Canon of Scripture. Also *transf.* ME. **5.** To sanction by the authority of the Church ME.

1. *fig.* But women are as it were canonised here TOMSON. **4.** They canonized the Books of the Maccabees 1657. **5.** Canonized doctrines 1635.

Canonry (kæ·nənri). 1482. [f. CANON[2] + -RY.] The benefice of a canon; the status or office of a canon.

His Canonry of X[t] Church HEARNE.

Canoodle (kănū·d'l), *v.* *slang.* (orig. *U.S.*) 1859. [Origin unkn.] *intr.* To indulge in caresses and fondling endearments. Hence **Canoo·dler, -ling.**

Canopic (kănǒᵘ·pik), *a.* 1878. [– L. *Canopicus*, f. *Canopus.*] Of or pertaining to Canopus, a town of ancient Egypt.

Canopic vase: a vase used in Egypt, chiefly for holding the entrails of embalmed bodies.

‖ **Canopus** (kănǒᵘ·pŏs). 1555. [L. – Gr. Κάνωπος.] **1.** The bright star α in the southern constellation Argo. **2.** = Canopic vase 1836.

1. We. .lit Lamps which out-burn'd C. TENNYSON.

Canopy (kæ·nǒpi), *sb.* [Late ME. *canope*, *canape* – med.L. *canopeum* baldacchino, for L. *conopeum*, *-ium* net over a bed, pavilion – Gr. κωνωπεῖον Egyptian bed with mosquito curtains, f. κώνωψ gnat, mosquito.] **1.** A covering suspended over a throne, couch, bed, etc., or held over a person, the Host, etc., in a procession. **2.** *transf.* and *gen.* A covering, an overhanging shade or shelter: used *esp.* of the firmament 1602. Also *fig.* **3.** *Arch.* A roof-like ornamental projection, over a niche, door, window, tomb, etc. 1682.

2. Their shadowes seeme A C. most fatall, vnder which Our Army lies *Jul. C.* v. i. 88. A c. of trees POPE, of perpetual clouds MAURY. Where dwel'st thou? Vnder the C. *Cor.* IV. v. 41. Hence **Ca·nopied** *ppl. a.* covered with, or as with, a c.

Canopy (kæ·nǒpi), *v.* 1600. [f. prec.] To cover with, or as with, a canopy.

Trees. .from heat did canopie the herd SHAKS.

Canorous (kănǒᵊ·rəs), *a* 1646. [f. L. *canorus*, f. *canere* sing, + -OUS.] Singing, melodious, musical; ringing.

A. .c. peal of laughter DE QUINCEY. Hence **Cano·rous-ly** *adv.*, **-ness.**

† **Canstick.** Short f. CANDLESTICK. SHAKS.

Cant (kænt), *sb.*[1] ME. [– MLG. *kant* point, creek, border, *kante* side, edge, (M)Du. *cant* border, side, corner – Rom. **canto* (as in OFr. *cant*, Fr. *chant*, *champ*, Sp., It. *canto* edge, corner, side) for L. *cant(h)us* iron tire.] **I.** sb. senses. † **1.** ? Edge (ME. only); a corner, angle, niche –1688. **2.** One of the side pieces in the head of a cask 1611. **3.** The oblique line or surface which cuts off the corner of a square or cube; an oblique, inclined, or slanting face 1840. **4.** A squared log. *U.S.* 1877. **5.** *Naut.* A piece of wood laid upon the deck of a vessel to support the bulkheads, etc. 1794.

II. f. CANT *v.* **1.** A toss, pitch, or throw, which overturns, etc. 1736. **2.** A sudden movement which tilts up or turns over 1806. **3.** A slope; a deflexion from the perpendicular or horizontal 1847. **4.** *Whale fishing.* A cut made in a whale between the neck and the fins for the cant purchase 1867.

Comb. **c.-block,** one of the large purchase blocks used by whalers to cant the whales round in flensing; † **-ceiling,** a ceiling which slants to meet the wall, as in attics; **-dog,** a hand-spike with a hook; in *U.S.* = *cant-hook*; **-hook,** a lever with an iron catch near the end for canting over timber; **-moulding,** one with a bevelled surface or surfaces; **-purchase,** a purchase formed by a block suspended from the mainmast head, and another block made fast to the c. cut in a whale; **-spar,** a hand-mast pole; **-timbers,** timbers at the two ends of a ship which rise obliquely from the keel.

Cant (kænt), *sb.*[2] Now *dial.* 1541. [Cf. CANT *v.*[1] and CANTLE.] A portion; a share; a parcel; a division.

Cant (kænt), *sb.*[3] 1501. [f. CANT *v.*[3]] **I.** Sporadic uses, f. L. *cantus.* † **1.** Singing –1708. † **2.** Intonation –1763. **II. 1.** A whining manner of speaking 1640. **2.** The secret or peculiar language or jargon of a class, † sect, or subject. (*Depreciative* or *contemptuous.*) 1684. Also *attrib.* **3.** A set form of words repeated mechanically; *esp.* a stock phrase temporarily in fashion 1681.

Also *attrib.* **4.** Affected or unreal phraseology; *esp.* language (or action) implying goodness or piety which does not exist 1709. Also *attrib.* **5.** A person who uses this language 1725.

2. The c. of particular Trades and Employments ADDISON. **3.** Measures, and not men, is the common c. of affected moderation 'JUNIUS'. **4.** My dear friend, clear your mind of c. JOHNSON. Religious phraseology passes into c. ROBERTSON.

Cant (kænt), *sb.*[4] 1705. [Goes with CANT *v.*[4] Perh. aphet. f. *encant – Fr. *encant*, mod. *encan* in same sense.] Sale by auction. Chiefly *Irish.*

Cant (kænt), *a. Sc.* and *n. dial.* ME. [app. same word as mod.Du. *kant* 'neat, clever', thought to have been developed from the sb. *kant* edge, etc.; see CANT *sb.*[1], and cf. CANTY.] Bold, brisk, lusty, hale.

† **Cant,** *v.*[1] ME. [Origin unkn., but perh. rel. to CANTLE.] To divide –1533.

Cant (kænt), *v.*[2] 1542. [f. CANT *sb.*[1]]

I. *trans.* **1.** To give a cant edge to; to bevel. **2.** To slope, tilt up 1711; to turn *over* completely 1850. **3.** To throw off by tilting up 1658. **4.** To pitch; to toss, to throw with a sudden jerk 1685.

1. To c. off corners SMEATON. **2.** To c. a barge 1792. **3.** To c. ballast HOOD. **4.** A sudden yaw.. which canted me overboard 1791.

II. *intr.* **1.** To tilt, turn over; often with *over* 1702. **2.** To lie aslant, slope 1794. **3.** *Naut.* To swing round from a position 1784.

3. In canting the ship got stern way 1784.

Cant (kænt), *v.*[3] 1567. [prob. – L. *cantare* sing, which was applied contemptuously as early as XII to the singing in church services and perh. later to the speech of religious mendicants.] **1.** *intr.* To whine like a beggar; to beg. **2.** *intr.* To use the cant of thieves, etc. 1609; to talk (*dial.*) 1567. Also *trans.* † **3.** To use the current stock phrases –1716. **4.** To affect the cant of a school, party, or subject 1728; *esp.* to affect religious or pietistic cant 1678. Also *trans.* † **5.** *trans.* and *intr.* To sing –1768.

1. [He] bad me c. and whine in some other place JOHNSON. **4.** Don't c. in defence of savages JOHNSON. To set up King Jesus: a phrase much canted 1641.

Cant (kænt), *v.*[4] 1720. [See CANT *sb.*[4]] To dispose of by auction. Chiefly *Irish.*

Can't (kānt), colloq. contr. of *cannot.*

Ca·ntab. 1750. Colloq. abbrev. of CANTABRIGIAN.

Cantabank (kæ·ntăbænk). *rare.* 1834. [– It. *cantambanco*, f. *cantare* sing + *banco* bench; cf. MOUNTEBANK.] A singer on a platform; hence, *contemptuously*, a common ballad-singer.

‖ **Cantabile** (kantā·bile). 1730. [It.] *Mus.* **A.** *adj.* In a smooth flowing style, suited for singing. **B.** *sb.* Cantabile style; a piece of music in this style 1744.

Cantabrigian (kæntăbri·dʒiăn), *a.* and *sb.* 1645. [f. *Cantabrigia*, L. form of *Cambridge*, + -AN.] Of or belonging to Cambridge; a member of the University of Cambridge.

Cantaloup (kæ·ntalūp). Chiefly *U.S.* 1839. [– Fr. *cantaloup* – It. *Cantaluppi*, a former country seat of the Pope near Rome, where, on its introduction from Armenia, it was first grown.] A small round ribbed variety of musk-melon. vars. **Cantalupe, -leup,** etc.

Cantankerous (kæntæ·ŋkərəs), *a. colloq.* 1772. [Earliest literary evidence suggests an Ir. origin; perh. blending of Ir. *cant* (see CANT *sb.*[4]) auction, outbidding, with *rancorous* (cf. also Ir. *cannrán* contention, grumbling).] Ill-conditioned and quarrelsome, perverse, cross-grained.

Hence **Canta·nkerous-ly** *adv.*, **-ness.**

Cantar (kæ·ntăɹ). 1730. [f. It., Sp. *cantaro*, *cantara* :– L. *cantharus.*] A measure of capacity used in countries bordering on the Mediterranean, varying from 74⅘ lb. in Rome to 502⅖ lb. in Syria.

‖ **Cantata** (kantā·tă). 1724. [It. (sc. *aria* air), fem. pa. pple. of *cantare* sing.] Orig., a narrative in verse set to recitative, or recitative and air, for a single voice, with accompaniment; now a choral work, either sacred, resembling a short oratorio, or secular, as a lyric drama set to music but not intended to be acted.

‖ **Cantate** (kæntē·ti, kæntā·te). *c* 1550. [L. *cantate* sing ye, the first word of the psalm.] The ninety-eighth psalm (ninety-seventh in the Vulgate) used as a canticle.

Canta·tion. *rare.* 1623. [– L. *cantatio, -on-* song; late L. spell, incantation, f. *cantat-*, pa. ppl. stem of *cantare* sing; see -ION.] † Singing; incantation.

‖ **Canta·tor.** *rare.* 1866. [L.] A (male) singer.

‖ **Cantatrice** (It. kantatrī·tʃe, Fr. kãntatrīs). 1866. [– Fr. and its It. source, fem. of *cantatore* – L.; see prec., -TRICE.] A female professional singer.

Canted (kæ·ntėd), *ppl. a.* 1649. [f. CANT *sb.*[1] and *v.*[2]] In various senses of CANT *v.*[2]; tilted up; sloping in surface; etc.

Canteen (kæntī·n). 1737. [– Fr. *cantine* – It. *cantina* cellar, perh. f. *canto* corner; see CANT *sb.*[1]] *Mil.* **1.** A sutler's shop in a camp etc., where provisions and liquors are sold to soldiers. Now under regimental control. 1744. **b.** A refreshment-counter, etc., at entertainments and in institutions 1886. ‖ **2.** A small case for carrying bottles. [Fr.] 1737. **3.** A chest fitted with cooking and table utensils, and other articles, used by officers, etc. 1817. **b.** A chest or case of domestic plate or cutlery 1895. **4.** A small tin or vessel for water or liquor, carried by soldiers on the march, travellers, etc. 1744.

Cantel, var. of CANTLE.

Canter (kæ·ntəɹ), *sb.*[1] 1609. [f. CANT *v.*[3] + -ER[1].] **1.** One who uses the cant of thieves, etc.; a rogue, vagabond (*arch.*). **2.** A talker of professional or religious cant 1652.

Ca·nter, *sb.*[2] 1755. [Short for *Canterbury gallop, pace, trot*, a pace such as mounted pilgrims to Canterbury were supposed to have ridden.] A Canterbury gallop; an easy gallop. Also *fig.*

Hermitage *won in a c.* (i.e. without needing to gallop at the finish) 1874.

Canter (kæ·ntəɹ), *v.* 1706. [f. prec.] **1.** *intr.* Of horse and rider: To move in a moderate gallop. Also *transf.* **2.** *trans.* To make (a horse) go at a canter, to ride at a canter 1856. Hence **Ca·nterer.**

Canterbury (kæ·ntəɹbĕri, -bəri), *sb.* ME. [A city of England long famous as the see of the Archbishop and Primate of all England. The shrine of Thomas à Becket (St. Thomas of Canterbury) was at one time an object of pilgrimage. See CHAUCER *Prol.* 16.]

A. *attrib.* Of or pertaining to Canterbury, to the *Canterbury pilgrims*, or to the tales told on the way, as *C. tale* or *story*, later taken as a long tedious story.

C. pace, rack, rate, trot, gallop, etc., the pace, etc., of the mounted pilgrims. A verie old womans fable or Cantorburie tale TURBERV.

B. *sb.* † **1.** A hand-gallop; a CANTER –1729. **2.** A stand with light partitions to hold music, etc. 1849. Hence † **Ca·nterbury** *v.* to canter.

Canterbury Bell(s. 1578. [See BELL *sb.*[1]; app. assoc. with the bells worn on their horses by the pilgrims.] A flowering plant of the genus *Campanula*; orig. a name of *C. trachelium*, erron. transferred to *C. medium*, and, loosely, to other species.

Cantharic (kænþæ·rik), *a.* 1871. [f. CANTHAR(IDES + -IC.] In *Cantharic acid*, a substance of the same composition as cantharidin.

So **Cantha·ridal** *a. Med.*, pertaining to, made with, or caused by cantharides. **Cantha·ridate** *sb.* a salt of cantharidic acid; *v.* to treat with cantharides. **Canthari·dian, -i·dean,** of the nature of, or composed of, cantharides. **Canthari·dic** *a.* of the nature of cantharides, as in *Cantharidic acid.* **Cantha·ridin,** the vesicating principle of cantharides. **Cantha·ridism,** the poisonous action of cantharides. **Cantha·ridize** *v.* to treat with cantharides (*esp.* as an aphrodisiac); also *fig.*

‖ **Cantharides** (kænþæ·ridīz), *sb. pl.* ME. [L., pl. of *cantharis* – Gr. κανθαρίς blister-fly.] **1.** (sing. *Cantharis* in *Entom.*) A genus of coleopterous insects of the family Trachelidæ; the official species (*C. vesicatoria* or Spanish Fly) has golden-green elytra. **2.** The pharmacopœial name of the dried beetle *C. vesicatoria.* Used externally as a vesicant; internally as a diuretic, and † an aphrodisiac.

‖ **Canthus** (kæ·nþŏs). 1646. [L. – Gr. κανθός.] *Phys.* The outer or inner corner of the eye, where the lids meet. Hence, from comb. f. *canth(o-*, **Canthopla·stic** *a.* of or pertaining to **Ca·nthoplasty,** the operation of enlarging the palpebral aperture.

† **Ca·ntic(k,** *sb.* 1483. [– (O)Fr. *cantique* – L. *canticum*; see next.] A song –1669.

Canticle (kæ·ntik'l). ME. [– OFr. *canticle* or its source L. *canticulum*, dim. of *canticum*, f. *cantus* song; see CHANT, -CULE.] **1.** A (little) song; a hymn; *spec.* one of the hymns (mostly from the Scriptures) used in the public services of the Church, as the *Benedicite.* Also *transf.* **2.** *pl.* The Song of Solomon 1526. † **3.** A canto –1647.

1. The sweetest C. is, Nunc dimittis BACON.

‖ **Cantile·na.** 1789. [It. or L.] The plain-song in old church music; the melody in any composition. Also, a ballad.

Cantilever (kæ·ntilīvəɹ). 1667. [Origin unkn.] **1.** *Arch.* A projecting bracket which supports a balcony, a cornice, or the like; also *attrib.* **2.** *Bridge-building.* A projecting arm of great length, two of which, stretching out from adjacent piers, are united by a girder which completes the span; also *attrib.* 1850.

Cantillate (kæ·ntileᶦt), *v.* 1864. [– *cantillat-*, pa. ppl. stem of L. *cantillare* sing low, hum, f. *cantare*; see CHANT, -ATE[3].] To chant; to recite with musical tones. Hence **Cantilla·tion,** musical recitation.

Canting (kæ·ntiŋ), *vbl. sb.*[1] 1769. [f. CANT *v.*[2] + -ING[1].] The action of CANT *v.*[2] Also as *ppl. a.*[1]

Ca·nting, *vbl. sb.*[2] 1567. [f. CANT *v.*[3] + -ING[1].] **1.** The practice of using thieves' cant; the jargon of thieves, beggars, etc. **2.** The use of the jargon of a class or subject; gibberish 1625. **3.** Hypocritical talk 1659.

1. Peddelars Frenche or C. 1567. **3.** *Canting coat*, the Geneva gown DRYDEN.

Ca·nting, *vbl. sb.*[3] *n. dial.* 1651. [f. CANT *v.*[4] + -ING[1].] Sale by auction.

Ca·nting, *ppl. a.*[2] 1625. [f. CANT *v.*[3] + -ING[2].] **1.** In the senses of CANT *v.*[3] **2.** *Her. Canting arms*: = *allusive arms* (see ALLUSIVE). So *c. heraldry, herald, coat.* Hence **Ca·ntingly** *adv.* **Ca·ntingness.**

‖ **Cantinier.** 1721. [Fr.; see CANTEEN, -IER.] A canteen-keeper. (Also *cantinière* fem.)

† **Ca·ntion.** 1579. [– L. *cantio, -on-*, f. *cant-* pa. ppl. stem of *cantare* sing; see CHANT, -ION.] A song –1660; an incantation –1678.

Cantle (kæ·nt'l), *sb.* ME. [– AFr. *cantel* = OFr. *chantel* (mod. *chanteau*) :– med.L. *cantellus*, dim. of L. *cantus*; see CANT *sb.*[1], -EL[2].] † **1.** A corner –1605; a slice –1627. **2.** A segment; a cut of bread, cheese, etc. ME. **3.** A portion (viewed apart) ME. **4.** The hind-bow of a saddle 1592. **5.** The crown of the head. *Sc.* 1822.

2. The huge c. which it used to seem to cut out of the holiday LAMB. **5.** My c. will stand a clour wad bring a stot down SCOTT. Hence **Cantle-wise** *adv.* by cantles. **Ca·ntlet,** a small c.

† **Ca·ntle,** *v.* 1548. [f. prec.] **1.** To cut into portions –1693. **2.** To piece together –1568.

† **Ca·ntling.** *rare.* 1616. [app. f. CANT, CANTLE; but cf. SCANTLING.] **1.** A small cantle 1674. **2.** A support under a cask 1616.

Canto (kæ·nto). Pl. **-os.** 1590. [– It. (Dante), lit. 'song' ;– L. *cantus*; see CHANT.] † **1.** A song, ballad –1710. **2.** One of the divisions of a long poem; so much as the minstrel might sing at one 'fit' 1590. ‖ **3.** *Mus.* The upper part or melody in a composition; anciently the tenor, now the soprano 1789.

‖ **Canto fermo** (ka·nto fe·rmo). 1789. [It.] 'The simple unadorned melody of the ancient hymns and chants of the church' (Grove); plainsong; hence, any simple subject of like character to which counterpoint is added.

Canton (kæ·ntǫn, kæntǫ·n), *sb.*[1] 1534. [– (O)Fr. *canton* – Pr. *canton* :– Rom. **canto, -on-*, f. L. *cantus*; see CANT *sb.*[1]] † **1.** A corner, an angle –1653. **2.** *Her.* A square division less than a quarter, occupying the upper (usually dexter) corner of a shield 1572. † **3.** A quarter; a piece –1686. **4.** A subdivision of a country 1601; a portion of space 1643. **5.** *spec.* **a.** One of the sovereign states of the Swiss confederation 1611. **b.** In France, a division of an arrondissement 1611.

2. The King gave us [the Royal Society] the arms of England to be borne in a c. in our arms

EVELYN. **3.** Hee quarters out his life into foure cantons, eating, drinking, sleeping, and riding 1631. **4.** This little C., I mean this System of our Sun LOCKE. Hence **Ca·ntônâl** *a.* of, pertaining to, or of the nature of, a c. **Ca·ntonalism,** a cantonal system. **Cantoner,** the inhabitant of a c.

† **Ca·nton,** *sb.*² 1594. Var. of CANTO 1, 2. Write loyall Cantons of contemned loue SHAKS.

Canton (kæ·ntǫ̆n, kæ̆ntǫ·n), *v.* Also † **cantoo·n.** 1598. [Partly f. prec., partly – Fr. *cantonner* quarter, It. *cantonnare* canton, quarter.] **1.** To divide or subdivide. **2.** To divide *from* or cut *out* of a whole (*arch.*) 1653. **3.** To quarter (soldiers). (*Pronounced* kæ̆ntǫ·n *and* kæ̆ntū·n.) 1700. Also *fig.* **4.** *intr.* (for *refl.*) To take up cantonments or quarters 1697. **5.** *Her.* To furnish (a shield or cross) with a canton or cantons; to place in a canton 1688.

2. They c. out to themselves a little Goshen in the intellectual world LOCKE. **4.** Orders to c. 1707.

Cantoned (see the vb.), *ppl. a.* 1611. [f. CANTON *sb.* and *v.* + -ED.] **1.** Formed into cantons. **2.** Quartered in cantonments 1790. **3.** *Arch.* Having angles decorated with columns, pilasters, or other similar projections 1727. **4.** *Her.* See CANTON *v.* 5.

† **Ca·ntonize,** *v.* 1606. [f. CANTON *sb.*¹ + -IZE.] **1.** To divide –1807. **2.** *intr.* To form an independent community –1809. **3.** To canton (troops); to locate –1674.

Cantonment (kæ̆ntǫ·nmĕnt, -tū·nment). Also † **cantoonment.** 1756. [– Fr. *cantonnement*; see CANTON *v.*, -MENT.] **1.** The cantoning of troops 1757. **2.** The place of lodging assigned to a section of a force when cantoned out; also (often in *pl.*) a place or places of more permanent encampment for troops, *e.g.* while in winter quarters; in India, a permanent military station 1756. **3.** *transf.* Quarters 1837.

‖ **Cantor** (kæ·ntǫ̆ɹ, -əɹ). 1538. [L., 'singer', f. *cant-*; see CHANT, -OR 2.] † **1.** A singer –1656. **2.** A precentor 1538. **3.** A soloist who sings liturgical music in church or synagogue 1893. Hence **Canto·rial, ca·ntoral** *a.*, pertaining to a c.; used of the north side of a choir, where the precentor sits. **Ca·ntorship.**

‖ **Cantoris** (kæntōᵊ·ris). 1724. [L., gen. of CANTOR.] *C. side, stall,* opposite to DECANI.

Ca·ntred. *Hist.* ME. [app. f. W. *cantref* (f. *cant* hundred + *tref* town, place), w. assim. of second element to Eng. *hundred.*] A district containing a hundred townships. Also **Ca·ntref, -ev** 1606.

Cantrip (kæ·ntrip). *Sc.* Also **-raip.** 1719. [Also *cantrap, -ep, -op,* of unkn. origin.] A spell of necromancy; a witch's trick. Also *joc.* a playful or extravagant act.

‖ **Cantus firmus.** [mod.L.] = Canto fermo.

Canty (kæ·nti), *a. Sc.* and *n. dial.* 1724. [f. CANT *a.* + -Y¹.] Cheerful, lively, brisk. A cantie quean 1775, day BURNS. Hence **Ca·ntily** *adv.* **Ca·ntiness.**

Canuck (kănʊ·k). 1835. [Also *Kanu(c)k* and (occas.) *Canack, Cannacker,* f. *Canada,* perh. after *Polack* Pole.] orig. *U.S.* A (French) Canadian; a Canadian horse or pony. Now in general Canadian colloq. use for any Canadian. Also as *adj.*

Canvas, canvass (kæ·nvăs), *sb.* [ME. *canevas* – ONFr. (and mod.) *canevas,* var. of OFr. *chanevaz* :– Rom. **cannapaceum,* f. **cannapum,* f. L. *cannabis* HEMP.] **1.** A coarse unbleached cloth made of hemp or flax, used for sails, tents, etc. **2.** A covering over the ends of a racing boat 1880. **3.** *spec.* Sail-cloth; *hence,* sails collectively 1609. **4.** *spec.* A piece of canvas primed for painting 1705; an oil-painting; also paintings collectively 1764. Also *fig.* **5.** A clear unbleached cloth woven in regular meshes, used for working tapestry with the needle 1611. Also *attrib.* or *adj.*

1. *Under c.*: in a tent or tents. **3.** *Under c.*: with sails spread. Obliged to reduce our c. SIR J. ROSS. **4.** To fill up a c. 'JUNIUS'. The c. glow'd GOLDSM. *Comb.* **c.-length** (in sense 2), about 15 ft.

Canvas (kæ·nvăs), *v.* Also **-ss.** 1556. [f. prec.; see also CANVASS *v.*] † **1.** *Hawking.* To entangle in a net; also *transf.* and *fig.* –1653. **2.** To cover, line, or furnish with canvas 1556.

2. To c. over a door DICKENS.

† **Canvasa·do, -za·do.** 1581. [Cf. CANVASS *v.*; sense 2 app. infl. by CAMISADO; see -ADO.] **1.** A sudden attack –1599. **2.** = CAMISADO –1617. **3.** ? A stroke in fencing: a countercheck –1605.

Canvas-back. 1605. [f. CANVAS *sb.*] **1.** A back of a garment made of canvas; also *fig.* **2.** A North American duck (*Fuligula valisneriana*), so named from the colour of the back feathers 1813.

2. The canvass-back stands alone 1832.

Canvass, canvas (kæ·nvăs), *v.* 1508. [f. CANVAS *sb.*, in its former spelling *canvass.* The development of sense 6 is not accounted for.] † **1.** *lit.* To toss in a canvas sheet, etc. –1611. † **2.** *transf.* To knock about; to beat, batter –1643. † **3.** *fig.* To buffet in writing; to criticize destructively –1618. **4.** *fig.* To discuss (a subject, etc.); to criticize, scrutinize fully 1530. Also *intr.* 1631. † **5.** ? To bargain with 1688. **6.** *intr.* To solicit, as support, votes, orders, contributions, etc. 1555. **7.** † To sue for (a thing) –1774; to solicit (persons, a district) for votes, custom, orders, etc.; *esp.* to solicit the support of a constituency, by interviewing each elector; to ascertain thus the number of one's supporters 1812.

1. 1 *Hen. VI,* I. iii. 36. **4.** To c. the character of witnesses 1798. **6.** This crime of canvassing or solliciting for Church-Preferment AYLIFFE. **7.** His inability to canvas the Livery in person 1812. Hence **Ca·nvasser** (in all senses); *U.S.* a scrutineer.

Canvass (kæ·nvăs), *sb.* 1608. [f. prec. vb.] † **1.** A shaking up 1611. † **2.** A sudden attack –1627. † **3.** Repulse (*e.g.* at an election, etc.) –1626. † **4.** Full discussion –1687. **5.** The action of personally soliciting votes before an election, and ascertaining the amount of one's support 1691. **6.** A solicitation of support, custom, etc. 1790.

5. Their success on the c. quite astonished them 1788.

Cany (kēⁱ·ni), *a.* 1667. [f. CANE *sb.*¹ + -Y¹.] Of cane; 'full of canes' (J.); cane-like.

Canyon. Also **kanyon.** = CAÑON.

‖ **Canzona** (kantsō·na). 1880. [It.; deriv. f. next.] **1.** = CANZONE. **2.** *Mus.* The setting to music of the words of a canzone; an instrumental piece in the style of a madrigal; † app. = sonata 1880.

‖ **Canzone** (kantsō·ne). 1590. [It., 'song' = (O)Fr. *chanson* :– L. *cantio, -on-*; see CANTION.] In *It.* or *Prov. Lit.*: A song, resembling the madrigal but less strict in style. var. **Ca·nzon** (freq. in 17th c.).

Canzonet (kænzone·t). 1593. [– It. *canzonetta,* dim. of prec.] A little or short song; a vocal solo in more than one movement; now usually, a light airy song.

Caoutchin (kau·tʃin). 1863. [f. CAOUTCHOUC + -IN¹.] *Chem.* A hydrocarbon, $C_{10}H_{16}$, contained in the oils produced by distillation of caoutchouc and gutta-percha.

Caoutchouc (kau·tʃuk, kū·-). 1775. [– Fr. *caoutchouc* – Carib *cahuchu*; in G. *kautschuk.*] India-rubber, or Gum Elastic; the milky resinous juice of certain tropical trees, chiefly the Brazilian *Siphonia elastica* (N.O. *Euphorbiaceæ*), which coagulates on exposure to the air, and becomes elastic, and is waterproof. Also *attrib.* See VULCANITE.

Mineral C. = ELATERITE.

Caoutchoucin (kau·tʃusin). 1863. [f. prec. + -IN¹.] *Chem.* A thin volatile oily liquid, obtained from caoutchouc by dry distillation.

Cap (kæp), *sb.*¹ [OE. *cæppe* – late L. *cappa* (whence Fr. *cape, chape,* Pr., Sp. *capa*), perh. a deriv. of *caput* head; cf. CAPE *sb.*², COPE *sb.*¹]

I. A covering for the head. **1.** A hood. **2.** A head-dress for women, now of muslin, or the like, and ordinarily worn indoors. Cf. MOB-CAP. ME. **3.** A head-dress of cloth, or the like, for men and boys; distinguished from a hat by not having a brim; applied also to many official, professional, and special head-dresses ME. **4.** In names of plants; see FRIAR'S CAP, etc. **5.** Short for CAP-PAPER 1630.

2. Gentlewomen weare such caps as these SHAKS. **3.** He toke of his c. and saluted the duke LD. BERNERS. Spec. uses: = a cardinal's biretta: The Pope expects more windfalls, before he will give any Caps 1666; = *cap of fence*: a helmet 1530; = the raising of the cap in salutation: They shall have cappe and knee, and many gaye good morrowes in this lyfe 1581; *fig.* = top: *Timon* IV. iii. 363.

II. Things of similar shape, position, or use. **1.** A cap-like covering; a top stratum or layer; a cap-like top ME. **2.** A cap-shaped part forming the top or covering the top or end ME. **3.** A cover or case 1688. **4.** = *Gun cap, Percussion cap* 1826. **5.** A part laid horizontally or flat along the top of various structures 1677. **6.** *Arch.* The uppermost part of any assemblage of principal parts 1870. **7.** *Naut.* A collar of wood, used to hold two masts together 1626.

1. The pileus, or c. of [a Fungus] 1762. The c. of a man's knee STERNE. Caps of semi-conglomerate corn-stone MURCHISON. A c. on the crest of the Æggischorn TYNDALL. **2.** The c. of a thimble 1693, of a receiver 1783. Toe-caps of boots 1870. The c. of a magnetic needle 1794, of the lens of a camera 1879. **3.** The c. of a gun = APRON 1704. A *breast-* or *nipple-c.* 1688. The c. of a watch 1884. **5.** A C. or Head over the Door 1688. **7.** *To lower the Flag,* is to pull it down upon the C. 1692.

Phrases. *C. of maintenance*: (*a*) see MAINTENANCE; (*b*) A cap borne before the sovereign of England at the coronation, also before some mayors. *C. of liberty* or *Phrygian bonnet*: the conical cap given in Roman times to slaves on emancipation, used as a republican symbol. *C. and bells*: the insignia of the jester: cf. FOOL'S CAP. *To put on one's thinking c.*: to take time for thinking over. *The c. fits*: what is said suits or is felt to suit. *To set one's c. at* (colloq.): said of a woman who sets herself to gain the affections of a man.

Comb.: **c.-money** (also † *cap*), money collected for the huntsman at the death of the fox; **-sheaf,** the top sheaf of a shock or stook, also *fig.*; **-square,** one of the broad pieces of iron locked over the trunnions of a gun with an iron pin. **Capped, capt** *ppl. a.*

Cap (kæp, kap), *sb.*² *Sc.* 1724. [app. a later Sc. form of COP *sb.*¹] **1.** A wooden bowl used as a drinking vessel. **2.** A measure of quantity: a quarter of a Sc. peck 1879.

Cap (kæp), *v.*¹ 1483. [f. CAP *sb.*¹] **1.** *trans.* To put a cap on. **2.** To cover as with a cap or capping, to cover at the end 1602. **3.** To form a cap to; to crown; to lie on the top of 1808. **4.** To overtop, outdo, beat; also *dial.* to pass the comprehension of 1736. **5.** *intr.* To take off the cap in token of respect. Const. *to.* 1555. Also *trans.* (*to* omitted) 1593.

1. To c. the head VENNER. I had capped the nipples BAKER. **2.** To c. stone-dikes 1853. *To c. a rope*: to cover the end with tarred canvas 1794. **3.** Basalts..capping the hills LYELL. **5.** And c. the fool whose merit is his Place CHURCHILL.

Phrases. *To c. the climax, to c. all*: see sense 4. *To c. an anecdote, proverb, quotation,* etc.: to follow it up with another; to quote alternately in contest. *To c. verses*: to reply to one quoted with another that begins with the final or initial letter of the first or otherwise corresponds with it.

Cap, *v.*² 1589. [– OFr. *caper* seize, app. f. *cape,* see CAPE *sb.*⁴; cf., however, CAPIAS.] † **1.** To arrest –1611. **2.** To appropriate by violence. *Sc.* 1808.

‖ **Capa** (kā·pă). 1787. [Sp.; see CAPE.] A Spanish cape.

Capability (kēⁱ:păbi·lĭti). 1587. [f. next + -ITY.] **1.** The quality of being CAPABLE in various senses. **2.** (usually *pl.*) An undeveloped faculty or property; a condition capable of being turned to use 1778.

2. ['Capability Brown'] got his nickname from his habit of saying that grounds which he was asked to lay out had *capabilities* 1887.

Capable (kēⁱ·păb'l), *a.* 1561. [– Fr. *capable* – late L. *capabilis,* f. *capere* take; see -ABLE.] † **1.** Able to take in; having room for –1775. Also *fig.* † **2.** *absol.* Roomy –1650; comprehensive *Oth.* III. iii. 459. **3.** Open to; susceptible. Const. *of,* also *absol.* 1590. **4.** Having capacity, power, or fitness for. Const. *of,* and † *inf.* 1597. **5.** *absol.* Having general capacity; qualified, gifted, able 1606. † **6.** Having a legal capacity or qualification. Const. *of,* also *absol.* –1818.

1. C. of a bushel of wheate 1601. *fig.* Not c. her eare Of what was high MILT. *P.L.* VIII. 51. **3.** C. of good seed 1612, of wounds SHAKS., of moral improvement BUTLER, of explanation 1794. **4.** C. of better things BP. WATSON, of every wickedness FREEMAN. **5.** A c. witness BLACKIE. **6.** *Lear* II. i. 87. Hence **Ca·pableness. Ca·pably** *adv.*

† **Capa·cify.** [f. as next + -FY.] *rare.* = CAPACITATE. Barrow.

Capacious (kăpēⁱ·ʃəs). 1614. [f. L. *capax, -ac-* (f. *capere* take) + -OUS. See -ACIOUS.] † **1.** Able to take in or hold –1779. **2.** Able to hold much; roomy, spacious 1634. **3.** Qualified for the reception *of* (*arch.*); † of capacity *to do* 1677.

Hence **Capa·ciously** *adv.* **Capa·ciousness.**

Capacitance (kăpæ·sităns). 1916. [f. CAPACITY + -ANCE.] *Electr.* Electrostatic capacity.

Capacitate (kăpæ·siteᶦt), *v.* 1657. [f. CAPACITY + -ATE³.] To endow with capacity *for* or *to do*; to fit; to qualify in law.

Hence **Capacita·tion.**

Capacity (kăpæ·sĭti). 1480. [– Fr. *capacité* – L. *capacitas*; see CAPACIOUS, -ITY.] † **1.** Ability to take in or hold –1702. Also *fig.* **b.** The power of an apparatus to store static electricity; also, any apparatus which gives additional capacity 1777. **2.** Hence, Content: † area; volume 1571. † **3.** A containing space, area, or volume; *esp.* a hollow space –1756. Also *fig.* **4.** Mental receiving power; ability to take in impressions, ideas, knowledge 1485. **5.** Active power of mind; talent 1485. **6.** *gen.* The power, ability, or faculty for anything in particular. Const. *of, for,* or *inf.* 1647. **7.** Capability, possibility 1659. **8.** Position, condition, character, relation 1649. **9.** *Law.* Legal qualification 1480.

1. *Ant. & Cl.* IV. viii. 32. *fig.* A large c. of happiness DE QUINCEY. *C. for heat, moisture,* etc.: the power of absorbing heat, etc **2.** *Measure of c.*: the measure applied to the content of a vessel, and to liquids, grain, etc., which take the shape of that which holds them. **5.** A person of diligence and c. STEELE. **6.** A c. for self-protection BUCKLE. **7.** A c. for infinite division DAUBENY. † *In, into,* or *out of a c.*: i.e. a position which enables or renders capable. **8.** I am . .dead in a natural c. . . dead in a poetical c. . .and dead in a civil c. POPE. *Attrib.* passing into *adj.* That reaches the utmost c., as *c. audience* 1920.

Cap-à-pie (kæpapī·), *adv.* 1523. [– OFr. *cap a pie* (now *de pied en cap*), i.e. *cap* – Pr. *cap* head (see CHIEF), *a* to, *pie* (:– L. *pes, ped-* foot).] From head to foot: in reference to arming or accoutring.

The rest all in bright harnesse capa pe 1556.

Caparison (kăpæ·risən). 1598. [– Fr. † *caparasson* (mod. *-açon*) – Sp. *caparazón* saddle-cloth (cf. Pr. *caparasso* hooded cloak, and med.L. *caparo* old woman's cloak), f. *capa* CAPE *sb.*²] **1.** A covering, often ornamented, spread over the saddle or harness of a horse; housings 1602. **2.** *transf.* Dress and ornaments 1598.

1. To esteeme. .a horse by his trappinges and c. FULBECKE. **2.** *Wint. T.* IV. iii. 27.

Caparison (kăpæ·risən), *v.* 1594. [– Fr. *caparassoner*, f. the sb.] To put trappings on; to deck, harness. Also *fig.*

C. my horse. Caparison'd like a man SHAKS.

† **Capa·x.** ME. [– OFr. *capax* – L. *capax*; see CAPACIOUS.] Of capacity; able and ready to take or receive –1556. var. **Capack(e)s.**

† **Ca·p-case.** 1577. [f. CAP *sb.*¹ or CAPE *sb.*¹, ² + CASE *sb.*²] **1.** A travelling-case, bag, or wallet –1641. **2.** A receptacle; a case (L. *capsa*). Also *fig.* 1597.

Cape (kēᶦp), *sb.*¹ *n. dial.* and *Sc.* ME. [ME. form of COPE *sb.*¹ retained in mod. dial. and Sc. Cf. ONFr. *cape.*] A cloak with a hood; a cloak; a cope.

Cape (kēᶦp), *sb.*² 1565. [– Fr. *cape* – Pr. *capa* (= (O)Fr. *chape*) :– late L. *cappa* (Isidore); see CAP *sb.*¹] † **1.** A Spanish cloak (with a hood) –1580. **2.** The tippet of a cloak 1596. **3.** A short loose sleeveless cloak, fitting round the neck and falling over the shoulders 1758.

Cape (kēᶦp), *sb.*³ ME. [– (O)Fr. *cap* – Pr. *cap* = Sp. *cabo* :– Rom. **capo* for L. *caput* head. Cf. CHIEF.] A piece of land jutting into the sea; a headland or promontory.

The Cape: any familiar headland; *esp.* the Cape of Good Hope in S. Africa. Hence = *Cape Colony*, and ellipt. *Cape* (*colony*) *wine, wool, funds,* etc. *attrib.* **C. elk**, the Eland; **C.-hen**, a small kind of Albatross; **C. jasmine**, *Gardenia florida*; **C. pigeon**, a Petrel; **C. weed**, *Roccella tinctoria* 'a dye lichen, obtained from the Cape de Verde Islands'.

† **Cape**, *sb.*⁴ 1588. [– OFr. *cape* sb. fem. – L. *cape*, imper. of *capere* seize; cf. CAP *v.*²] *Old Law.* The first word and name of a judicial writ relative to a plea of lands and tenements –1706.

† **Cape**, *sb.*⁵ 1650. [var. of CAP *sb.*¹: see II. 1.] Top –1812.

† **Cape**, *v.* 1500. [perh. derived in some way f. Fr. *cap* head of the ship, but no Fr. verb is recorded, and the Eng. analogues *head, head for*, are very much later.] *Naut.* To head, keep a course, bear up. Said of sailors and ship. –1867.

Caped (kēᶦpt), *a.* 1550. [f. CAPE *sb.*² + -ED².] Having a cape; clad in a cape.

Capel¹ (kēᶦ·p'l). 1801. [Origin unkn.] *Min.* A composite stone of quartz, schorl, and hornblende, occurring in the walls of tin and copper lodes.

Capel², var. of † CAPLE, a horse.

Capelet (kæ·pĕlĕt). Also **capellet.** 1731. [– Fr. *capelet*, Picard for *chapelet*, from the resemblance to a wreath.] A wen-like swelling on the heel of a horse's hock, or on the point of the elbow.

Capelin, caplin (kæ·pĕlin, -plin). 1620. [– Fr. *capelan* – Pr. *capelan*; see CHAPLAIN.] A small fish resembling a smelt, found on the coast of Newfoundland; used as a bait for cod.

Capeline (kæ·pĕlin). 1470. [– (O)Fr. *capeline* – Pr. *capelina*, f. *capel* hat (= mod.Fr. *chapeau*).] † **1.** A skull-cap of iron worn by archers in the Middle Ages. **2.** *Surg.* A bandage which forms a kind of cap for the head, or in amputations 1706. **3.** A woollen hood of loose texture, worn by ladies. [Fr.] 1868.

‖ **Capella** (kăpe·lă). 1682. [L., she-goat.] A star of the first magnitude in Auriga.

† **Cape·llane.** 1661. [– med.L. *capellanus*; see CHAPLAIN.] **a.** A keeper of sacred relics. **b.** A chaplain.

Capelo·cracy. [f. Gr. κάπηλος shop-keeper + -CRACY.] The shop-keeping interest. LYTTON.

† **Ca·pe-me:rchant.** Also **Cap-.** 1581. [app. – some foreign title in *cap* or *capo* meaning 'head merchant'.] A supercargo; also the head merchant in a factory. Also *fig.* –1697.

fig. The French. .were the cape-merchants in this adventure [the Crusades] FULLER.

Caper (kēᶦ·pəɹ), *sb.*¹ [In XIV *caperis* (later *capres* – Fr. *câpres* – L.) – L. *capparis* – Gr. κάππαρις. Treated as a pl., hence *caper* sing.] **1.** A shrub (*Capparis spinosa*) of trailing habit, abundant on walls and rocky places in the South of Europe. **2.** (usu. in *pl.*) The flower-buds of the same, used for pickling 1481. **3.** A scented tea 1864.

1. The erbe caperis shal be scatered WYCLIF *Eccles.* 12:5. *Comb.* etc.: *Capucine, Capuchin Capers, English Capers*: the seed-vessels of the Nasturtium (see CAPUCINE), or of the Caper Spurge, used for pickling; also the plants. **C.-bush, -plant, -spurge,** names of *Euphorbia lathyris*; **-tree**, *Busbeckia arborea* of N.S. Wales.

Caper (kēᶦ·pəɹ), *sb.*² 1592. [Shortening of CAPRIOLE *sb.*] A frolicsome leap, as of a kid; a frisky movement; *fig.* a freak.

We that are true Louers, runne into strange capers SHAKS. *To cut a c.* or *capers*: to dance or act fantastically *Twel. N.* I. iii. 129.

Ca·per, *sb.*³ 1657. [– Du. *kaper* privateer, f. *kapen* take away, rob, plunder.] A privateer; the captain of a privateer. Now *Hist.*

Caper (kēᶦ·pəɹ), *v.* 1588. [Cf. CAPER *sb.*²] To dance or leap in a frolicsome manner, to skip for merriment; to prance. Also *fig.*

Dancing and capering like a Kid BOYLE. The Italians. .c. with their voices DOULAND.

Capercailye, capercailzie (kæpəɹkēᶦ·lyi, -kēᶦ·lzi). 1536. [– Gael. *capull coille* great cock (lit. horse) of the wood. The sp. *lz* derives from ME. *lȝ*.] The Wood-grouse (*Tetrao urogallus*); the male is also called Mountain Cock or Cock of the Woods. Formerly indigenous in the Highlands.

† **Caperdew·sie, caperdo·chy.** 1600. [Origin unkn.; cf. CAPPADOCHIO.] The stocks; prison –1663.

Ca·perer. 1693. [f. CAPER *v.* + -ER¹.] **1.** One who capers. **2.** A caddis-fly (*Phryganea*); from its flight 1855.

Capernaite (kăpə̄·ɹneˌəit). 1549. [f. *Capernaum* in Galilee + -ITE¹ 1.] An inhabitant of Capernaum; *hence* (see *John* 6:52) A controversial term for a believer in transubstantiation. Hence **Cape:rnai·tic, -al** *a.* † **Cape·rnize** *v.*

Capernoitie (kæpəɹnoi·ti), *sb. Sc.* 1719. [Origin unkn.] Head, noddle. Hence perh. **Capernoi·ted** *a.* crabbed; slightly muddled with drink.

Ca·pful. 1719. [f. CAP *sb.*¹ + -FUL.] As much as a cap will contain.

A c. of wind (*Naut.*): a light flaw.

Capharnaism (kăfă·ɹneˌi:z'm). 1656. [f. *Capharnaum*, Aram. f. *Capernaum* + -ISM.] The doctrine of the Capernaites.

‖ **Capias** (kæ·piæs). 1467. [L., 'you are to seize', 2nd sing. pres. subj. of *capere* take.] *Law.* A writ or process commanding the officer to take the body of the person named in it, that is, to arrest him; also called *writ of capias.*

The term includes: *C. ad respondendum*, to enforce attendance at court; *C. ad. satisfaciendum*, after judgement, to imprison the defendant, until the plaintiff's claim is satisfied; *C. utlagatum*, to arrest an outlawed person; *C. in Withernam* (see WITHERNAM).

Capibara, var. of CAPYBARA.

Capillaceous (kæpilēᶦ·ʃəs). 1731. [f. L. *capillaceus*, f. *capillus* hair; see -ACEOUS.] Hair-like, thread-like. Cf. CAPILLARY.

‖ **Capillaire** (kæpilē·r). 1754. [Fr. – L. *capillaris*, late L. *capillaris herba* maidenhair fern; see CAPILLARY.] **a.** A syrup of maidenhair fern. **b.** A syrup flavoured with orange-flower water.

† **Capi·llament.** 1681. [– L. *capillamentum* the hair collectively.] **1.** A hair-like fibre, filament, as of a root, or nerve –1785. **2.** *Bot.* A stamen –1751.

Capillarimeter (kăpi:lări·mĭtəɹ). 1874. [f. L. *capillaris* + -METER. Cf. Fr. *capillarimètre.*] An instrument for measuring the strength of wine, etc. on the principle of capillary attraction.

Capillarity (kæpilæ·rĭti). 1830. [– Fr. *capillarité*, f. L. *capillaris*; see next, -ITY.] Capillary quality; *esp.* that of exerting capillary attraction or repulsion. Also, capillary attraction.

Capillary (kăpi·lări, kæ·pilări). 1646. [– L. *capillaris*, f. *capillus* hair, after (O)Fr. *capillaire*; see -ARY².] **A.** *adj.* **1.** Of or pertaining to hair; resembling hair, *esp.* in tenuity 1656. **2.** Having a hair-like bore; as a *c. tube* 1664. **3.** Of, pertaining to, or occurring in, capillaries 1809.

3. *C. Attraction, Repulsion*: see ATTRACTION, REPULSION. var. † **Capi·llar.**

B. *sb.* † **1.** Anything hair-like 1697. **2.** A capillary vessel. Cf. A. 2. *esp.* One of the minute blood-vessels, in which the arterial circulation ends and the venous begins 1667. † **3.** *Bot.* The Maidenhair Fern (*Adiantum capillus-veneris*); also other ferns and allied plants –1751.

† **Capilla·tion.** *rare.* 1646. [– late L. *capillatio, -on-*, f. *capillatus* hairy; see -ION.] Hairy or hair-like condition; hence *concr.* a capillary –1751.

Capi·lliform. 1835. [f. L. *capillus* hair + -FORM.] Hair-shaped.

‖ **Capilli·tium.** 1866. [L., 'the hair collectively'.] *Bot.* Entangled filamentary matter in fungals, bearing sporidia.

Capillo·se. 1843. [– late L. *capillosus*, f. *capillus* hair; see -OSE¹.] *adj.* Full of hair, hairy. *sb.* (*Min.*) = MILLERITE².

Capital (kæ·pităl), *sb.*¹ ME. [– OFr. *capitel* (mod. *chapiteau*) – late L. *capitellum*, dim. of *caput* head; mod. sp. *-al* through assoc. w. CAPITAL *a.*] **1.** The head or top of a column or pillar. **2.** The cap of a chimney, crucible, etc. 1715. ¶ **3.** = CAPITLE. Scott.

1. A c. is only the cornice of a column RUSKIN.

Capital (kæ·pităl), *a.* and *sb.*² ME. [– (O)Fr. *capital* – L. *capitalis*, f. *caput, capit-* head; see -AL¹.]

A. *adj.* **I.** Relating to the head. † **1.** Of or pertaining to the head or top –1688. **2.** Affecting the head or life 1483; punishable by death 1526; † fatal –1701. † **3.** Deadly, mortal –1762. Also *fig.*

1. His [the Serpent's] c. bruise MILT. *P.L.* XII. 383. **2.** A c. sentence CAXTON, verdict 1868, crime 1526. It was c. to preach even in houses HALLAM. **3.** A c. enmyte 1502. *fig.* A c. error PRESCOTT.

II. Standing at the head (*lit.* and *fig.*). † **1.** Of words and letters: Initial –1811. **2.** Chief, head-; important ME.; of ships: 'Of the line' 1688. **3.** In mod. use: First-rate. Often as an exclam. 1762. **4.** Of or pertaining to the original funds of a trader, company, or corporation; principal 1709.

1. *C. letters*: letters of the form and relative size used at the head of a page, or at the beginning of a line or paragraph. **2.** To rase Som C. City MILT. *P.L.* II. 924. My c. secret *Sams.* 394. *C. manor*, one held *in capite*, or directly from the King. **4.** The C. Stock of the Bank of England 1709.

B. *sb.*² [The adj. used ellipt.] **1.** A capital letter. (Cf. A. II. 1.) 1649. **2.** A capital town or city 1667. **3.** A capital stock or fund. **a.** *Comm.* The trading stock of a company, corporation, or individual on which profits or dividends are calculated. **b.** *Pol. Econ.* Accumulated wealth employed reproductively 1630. Also *fig.* **4.** *Fortif.* An imaginary line bisecting the salient angle of a work 1706.

2. Pandæmonium, the high C. of Satan MILT. *P.L.* I. 756. **3.** You began ill. .You set up your trade without a c. BURKE. *Fixed c.*: that which remains in the owner's possession, as machinery, tools, etc. *Circulating, floating c.*: that which is constantly changing hands or form, as goods, money, etc. *To make c. out of* (fig.): to turn to account. *C. levy*, confiscation by the State of a proportion of all property.

Capitalism (kæ·pităli:z'm, kăpi·tăliz'm). 1854. [f. next; see -ISM.] The condition of possessing capital or using it for production; a system of society based on this; dominance of private capitalists.

Capitalist (kæ·pităli:st, kăpi·tălist). 1792. [– Fr. *capitaliste*; see CAPITAL *sb.*², -IST.] One who has capital, esp. one who uses it in business enterprises (on a large scale).

Capitalize (kæ·pitălǝiz, kăpi·t-). 1850. [– Fr. *capitaliser*; see prec., -IZE.] **1.** *trans.* To write or print in capitals, or with initial capital. **2.** To convert into capital 1868. **3.** To compute or realize the present capital value of 1856.

2. The project of capitalizing incomes 1856. Hence **Ca:pitaliza·tion.**

Capitally (kæ·pităli), *adv.* 1606. [f. CAPITAL *a.* + -LY².] **1.** In a manner involving loss of life 1619. **2.** Seriously 1606; eminently 1786; admirably 1750.

1. He was c. impeached THIRLWALL.

‖ **Capitan** (kapita·n, kæpitæ̆·n). 1755. [Sp.] Mostly *attrib.*, as in *C.* (or *Captain*) *Pacha*, chief admiral of the Turkish fleet. Hence ‖ **Capitana** (sc. *nave*), the admiral's ship.

‖ **Capitano** (kapitā·no). 1611. [It.] A captain, headman, or chief.

Capitate (kæ·pitěⁱt), *a.* 1661. [– L. *capitatus*, f. *caput, capit-* head; see -ATE².] *Nat. Hist.* **1.** Having a distinct head. **2.** *Bot.* Having the inflorescence in a head, as in composite flowers 1686. Also **Ca·pitated** *ppl. a.*

Capitation (kæpitēⁱ·ʃǝn). 1614. [– Fr. *capitation* or late L. *capitatio, -on-*, f. as prec.; see -ION.] **1.** The counting of heads or persons. **2.** The levying of a tax by the head, *i.e.* upon each person; a tax, fee, or payment per head. *Comb.* **c. grant,** a grant of so much per head subject to certain conditions.

‖ **Ca·pite** (kæ·piti). 1616. [L., abl. of *caput*, occurring in *tenere in capite* to hold (of the king) in chief; whence *tenant, tenure in capite*, and *capite* in Law Dicts. as the name of a tenure by which land was held immediately of the king or of the crown.

Capitellate (kăpi·teleⁱt), *a.* 1870. [f. next + -ATE².] Furnished with a CAPITELLUM. Cf. CAPITATE.

‖ **Capite·llum.** 1872. [L., dim. of *caput* head (or its dim. *capitulum*); cf. CAPITAL *sb.*¹] A little head; the rounded eminence on the outer surface of the lower end of the humerus.

† **Ca·pitle.** ME. only. [– ONFr. *capitle* = OFr. *chapitle*; see CHAPITLE.] **1.** A chapter of a book. **2.** A summary.

Capitol (kæ·pitǫl). [ME. *capitolie* – OFr. *capitolie, -oile*, later assim. to the source, L. *Capitolium*, f. *caput, capit-* head.] **1.** *lit.* A citadel on the top of a hill. *esp.* The temple of Jupiter Optimus Maximus, on the Saturnian or Tarpeian (subseq. called Capitoline) Hill at Rome; occ. used of the whole Hill. Also *transf.* and *fig.* **2.** *U.S.* The edifice occupied by the congress of the United States. Also, in some states, the state-house. 1843.

1. There the C. thou seest. .On the Tarpeian rock MILT. *P.R.* IV. 47. Hence **Capito·lian, Capi·toline** *a.* of or pertaining to the C.; *Capitoline games*: games in honour of Capitoline Jove.

‖ **Capitoul** (kapitul). 1753. [Fr. – Pr. *capitoul* – med.L. *capitolium* chapter-house, for L. *capitulum*.] A name given to the municipal magistrates of Toulouse.

Capi·tulant. 1839. [– Fr. *capitulant*, pr. pple. of *capituler*; see CAPITULATE *v.*, -ANT.] One who capitulates.

Capitular (kăpi·tiŭlăɹ). 1611. [– late L. *capitularis* in med.L. senses, f. L. *capitulum*; see CHAPTER, -AR¹.]

A. *adj.* **1.** Of or pertaining to an eccl. chapter. **2.** *Phys.* Of or pertaining to a capitulum (see CAPITULUM 1) 1872. **3.** *Bot.* Growing in small heads, as the Dandelion 1846. Hence † **Capi·tularly** *adv.* as a chapter.

B. *sb.* [The adj. used ellipt.] **1.** A member of a chapter 1726. **2.** = CAPITULARY B. 2. 1660. **3.** ? A law or statute of a chapter; also *fig.* 1667. **4.** ? A heading 1846.

Capitulary (kăpi·tiŭlări). 1650. [– late L. *capitularius* in med.L. senses, f. as prec.; see -ARY¹.] **A.** *adj.* Of or pertaining to a chapter 1774. **B.** *sb.* **1.** A member of an eccl. chapter 1694. **2.** A collection of ordinances, *esp.* those made by the Frankish Kings 1650. **3.** A heading 1824.

2. The capitularies of Charle-Magne 1747.

† **Capi·tulate,** *ppl. a.* 1528. [f. as next; see -ATE².] Reduced to heads; stipulated –1600.

Capitulate (kăpi·tiŭleⁱt), *v.* 1580. [– *capitulat-*, pa. ppl. stem of med.L. *capitulare* draw up under distinct heads, f. late L. *capitulum* head of a discourse; in sense 4 through Fr. *capituler*; see CHAPTER, -ATE³.] † **1.** To draw up in chapters or under heads or articles; to specify –1678. † **2.** *intr.* To draw up articles of agreement; to treat, parley –1816. † **3.** *trans.* To make terms about; to arrange for –1661. **4.** To make terms of surrender, to surrender on stipulated terms. (The ordinary use.) *intr.* and *trans.* 1689.

2. We must not c. with mutiny in any shape WELLINGTON. **4.** Want of provisions quickly obliged Trevulci to c. 1769. *fig.* To c. to badges and names EMERSON. Hence **Capi·tulator** (Dicts.).

Capitulation (kapi:tiulēⁱ·ʃǝn). 1535. [– late L. *capitulatio, -on-*, f. as prec.; see -ION; in sense 4, through Fr. *capitulation.*] The action of the vb. CAPITULATE. † **1.** Arranging in chapters or heads 1613. **2.** A statement of heads, summary, enumeration; cf. *recapitulation* 1579. † **3.** The making of terms –1721; *pl.* terms –1728; a covenant, convention, treaty –1843. **4.** The action of capitulating (sense 4) 1650; the instrument containing the terms of surrender 1793.

2. C. is not description STEVENSON. **3.** *Spec. uses.* (*a*) The conditions sworn to by the former German emperors at their election. (*b*) The agreements made by the Swiss cantons with foreign powers respecting the Swiss mercenaries. (*c*) The articles by which the Porte gave immunities and privileges to French subjects, and subseq. to others. **4.** The c. of Metz 1888.

Capitulatory (kăpi·tiŭlătǝ:ri), *a.* [f. prec. + -ORY².] Of or pertaining to CAPITULATION (sense 2).

In their. .c. brass monuments LAMB.

‖ **Capitulum** (kăpi·tiŭlǒm). 1721. [L., dim. of *caput* head.] A little head or knob. **1.** *Phys.* A protuberance of bone received into a hollow portion of another bone 1755. **2.** *Bot.* A close head of sessile flowers 1721. **3.** *Zool.* The part of a barnacle borne by and forming a head to the peduncle 1872.

Capivi, var. of COPAIBA.

Caplan, obs. f. CAPELIN.

Ca·ple, capul. Now *dial.* [ME. *capel* – ON. *kapall* – L. *caballus* nag. Cf. CABALL.] A horse: in ME. chiefly *poetical.*

Caplin, capling (kæ·plin, -liŋ). 1688. [f. CAP *sb.*¹ + -LING¹.] The cap of leather on a flail, through which the thongs pass that connect the swingel and the staff.

Caplin, -ling, var. of CAPELIN.

Capnomancy (kæ·pnomænsi). 1610. [f. Gr. καπνός + -MANCY, perh. through Fr. *capnomancie* (XVI *-tie*).] Divination by smoke.

Capnomor (kæ·pnomǫɹ). 1838. [f. Gr. καπνός smoke, perh. + μόρα, Doric for μοῖρα part.] *Chem.* A colourless transparent oil of peculiar smell, one of the constituents of smoke, obtained from wood-tar.

‖ **Ca·poc,** var. of KAPOK.

† **Capo·che,** *v. trans. rare.* ? 'To strip off the hood' (J.); or joc. use of CABOCHE *v.* BUTLER *Hud.* II. II. 529.

Capon (kēⁱ·pǝn), *sb.* [Late OE. *capun* – AFr. *capun*, var. of (O)Fr. *capon* :– Rom. **cappone*, for L. *capo, -on-*.] **1.** A castrated cock. † **2.** *transf.* A eunuch –1691. **3.** *joc.* One of various fish; *esp.* a red-herring 1640. † **4.** A billet-doux. Cf. Fr. *poulet. L.L.L.* IV. i. 56.

1. In faire round belly, with good C. lin'd *A.Y.L.* II. vii. 154. *Comb.*: **c.-justice,** a magistrate who is bribed by gifts of capons; **-money,** money in commutation of a payment of capons; † **capon's feather,** the Common Columbine (*Aquilegia vulgaris*); † **capon's tail,** a plant, *Valeriana pyrenaica.* Hence **Ca·pon** *v.* to castrate; so **Ca·ponize.** † **Ca·ponet,** a little c.

Caponier (kæpǒnīᵊ·ɹ). 1683. [– Sp. *caponera* (whence Fr. *caponnière*) prop. capon-pen; see prec.] A covered passage across a ditch, serving to shelter communication with outworks, and affording a flanking fire to the ditch.

‖ **Caporal** (kapora·l). 1598. [In sense 2, Fr., short for *tabac de caporal* corporal's tobacco, – It. *caporale*, f. *capo* head, CHIEF.] † **1.** A corporal. (*Sp.*) **2.** A kind of tobacco. (*Fr.*) 1850.

Capot (kăpǫ·t, †kæ·pǝt), *sb.*¹ 1651. [– Fr. *capot*, perh. f. *capoter*, dial. form of *chapoter* castrate; cf. CAPON.] In *Piquet.* The winning of all the tricks by one player. Hence **Capo·t** *v.* to score a c. against; also *transf.*

‖ **Capot** (kapo), *sb.*² 1775. [A masc. form of next.] = CAPOTE.

Capote (kăpōᵘ·t). 1812. [– Fr. *capote* raincloak, dim. of *cape*; see CAPE *sb.*²] A long shaggy cloak or overcoat with a hood; a long mantle, worn by women.

† **Capou·ch,** var. of CAPUCHE.

Cappadine (kæ·pădin, -dīn). 1678. [Origin unkn.] 'A sort of silk flock or waste obtained from the cocoon after the silk has been reeled off.'

† **Cappado·chio.** [Origin unkn.; cf. CAPERDEWSIE, -DOCHY.] = CAPERDEWSIE, q.v.

Cappagh (kæ·pă). 1875. A place near Cork in Ireland; whence *Cappagh* or *Cappah brown*, a brown pigment.

Cap-paper (kæ·pˌpēⁱ:pǝɹ). 1577. [f. CAP *sb.*¹ in different senses.] **1.** A kind of wrapping paper. **2.** A size or kind of writing paper (perh. named from the watermark of a cap) 1854.

Capparid (kæ·părid). [f. L. *capparis* the caper + -ID³.] *Bot.* A plant, one of the *Capparidaceæ.* **Capparida·ceous** *a.* of the natural order Capparidaceæ (erron. f. *Capparaceæ*), of which the Caper is the type.

Cappe·lenite. 1886. [– G. *Cappelenit* (1885), f. D. *Cappelen*; see -ITE¹ 2 b.] *Min.* A silico-borate of yttrium and barium, from Norway.

Capper (kæ·pǝɹ). ME. [f. CAP *sb.* and *v.* + -ER¹.] † **1.** A capmaker –1805. **2.** One who caps (see CAP *v.*) 1587. **3.** *dial.* A person or thing that caps or beats all others; a puzzler 1790.

Cappie (kæ·pi). *Sc.* 1824. [dim. of CAP *sb.*²; see -IE.] **1.** A small drinking vessel. **2.** A kind of beer between table beer and ale.

Capping (kæ·piŋ), *vbl. sb.* 1592. [f. CAP *v.*¹ + -ING¹.] **1.** The action of the vb. CAP in various senses. **2.** Cap-making 1662. **3.** That with which anything is capped or overlaid 1713.

Comb. **c.-plane** (*Joinery*), a plane for working the upper surface of the balustrade on a staircase.

Cappy (kæ·pi), *a.* 1865. [f. CAP *sb.*¹ + -Y¹.] Characterized by, or like, a cap.

Hairless and c. age 1865.

Caprate (kæ·preⁱt). 1836. [f. CAPRIC + -ATE⁴.] *Chem.* A salt of capric acid.

† **Ca·preol(e.** 1578. [– L. *capreolus* (in both senses), dim. of *capreus* roe, f. *caper* goat. With sense 2 cf. OFr. *capreole*, It. *capriolo.*] **1.** A variety of roebuck 1655. **2.** A tendril –1725.

Capreolate (kæ·priŏleⁱt, kăprī·ŏleⁱt), *a.* 1737. [f. as prec. + -ATE².] *Bot.* Furnished with tendrils.

Capreoline (kăprī·ŏlǝin), *a.* 1835. [f. as prec. + -INE¹.] *Zool.* Of or belonging to the genus Capreolus of Cervidæ.

Capric (kæ·prik), *a.* 1836. [f. L. *caper* goat + -IC; cf. Fr. *caprique*.] **1.** Of or belonging to a goat (*nonce-use*) 1881. **2.** *Chem.* *Capric acid* ($C_{10}H_{20}O_2$), a fatty acid obtained from butter, coco-nut oil, fusel oil, etc.: a colourless crystalline body, having a slight odour of the goat.

‖ **Capriccio** (kapri·ttʃo). 1601. [It.; see CAPRICE.] **1.** A prank, trick, caper 1665. † **2.** = CAPRICE 1. –1824. **3.** A thing or work of fancy 1678; *Mus.* a composition more or less free in form and whimsical in style 1696.

‖ **Capriccioso** (kaprittʃō·so), *a.* [It., f. prec. + *-oso* -OUS.] *Mus.* A direction: In a free fantastic style.

Caprice (kăprī·s). 1667. [– Fr. *caprice* – It. *capricchio*, orig. horror (the mod. sense being due to assoc. w. *capra* goat), f. *capo* head (:– L. *caput*) + *riccio* hedgehog (:– L. *ericeus* URCHIN), lit. 'head with the hair standing on end'.] **1.** A sudden turn of the mind without apparent motive; a freak, whim, mere fancy. **b.** Capriciousness 1709. Also *transf.* of things. **2.** = CAPRICCIO 3. 1721.

1. The caprices of woman-kind are not limited by climate or nation SWIFT. **b.** Of less judgement than c. POPE. A c. of language FREEMAN.

Capricious (kăpri·ʃəs), *a.* 1594. [– Fr. *capricieux* – It. *capriccioso*; see prec., -OUS.] † **1.** Humorous, fantastic, full of conceits –1710. **2.** Subject to, or characterized by CAPRICE; whimsical 1605. Also *transf.* of things.

1. The most c. Poet honest Ouid *A.Y.L.* III. iii. 8. **2.** Arbitrary and c. JOHNSON. A c. climate HELPS. Hence **Capri·cious-ly** *adv.*, **-ness.**

Capricorn (kæ·prikǭɹn). ME. [– (O)Fr. *capricorne* – L. *capricornus*, f. *caper, capr-* goat + *cornu* horn, 'goat-horn', after Gr. αἰγόκερως.] **1.** *Astron.* **a.** The Zodiacal constellation of the He-goat. **b.** The tenth sign of the Zodiac, beginning at the most southerly point of the ecliptic, which the sun enters about the 21st of December. † **2.** A goat-horned animal; ? a chamois 1646. **3.** *C. beetle*: any beetle of the genus Cerambyx 1700.

1. As deep as Capricorne MILT. *P.L.* X. 677. *Tropic of C.*: the southern Tropic forming a tangent to the ecliptic as the first point of C.

Caprid (kæ·prid), *a.* 1864. [f. mod.L. *capridæ*, f. L. *caper* goat + -ID³.] *Zool.* Of or belonging to the Capridæ or goat tribe.

Caprification (kæ:prifikēⁱ·ʃən). 1601. [– L. *caprificatio*, f. *caprificat-*, pa. ppl. stem of *caprificare*, f. *caprificus* wild fig tree; see -ION.] **1.** A process of ripening figs by means of the puncture of insects produced on the wild fig, or by puncturing them artificially. ¶ **2.** Erron. used for: Artificial fertilization 1836.

Caprifoil (kæ·prifoil). 1578. [– med.L. *caprifolium* 'goat-leaf', with sp. assim. to *foil, trefoil*.] The Honeysuckle or Woodbine; also, Eng. name for plants of the N.O. *Caprifoliaceæ*.

Caprifoliaceous (kæ:prifōᵘ:li,ēⁱ·ʃəs), *a.* 1852. [f. as prec.; see -ACEOUS.] *Bot.* Belonging to the N.O. *Caprifoliaceæ*.

Capriform (kæ·prifǭɹm), *a.* 1847. [f. L. *caper* goat + -FORM.] Goat-shaped.

Caprine (kæ·prəin, -in), *a.* 1607. [– L. *caprinus*, f. *caper* goat; see -INE¹; cf. (O)Fr. *caprin*.] Of or pertaining to a goat; goat-like.

Capri·nic, *a.* [f. as prec. + -IC.] *Chem.* *C. acid*: older name for CAPRIC acid.

Capriole (kæ·pri,ōᵘl), *sb.* 1594. [– Fr. *capriole* (now *cabriole*) – It. *capriola*, f. *capriolare* leap, f. *capriolo* roe-buck :– L. *capreolus*, dim. of *caper* goat.] **1.** A leap or caper, as in dancing. **2.** *Horsemanship.* A high leap made by a horse without advancing, the hind legs being jerked out together at the height of the leap 1605.

1. Caprioles and pirouettes DE QUINCEY. *fig.* Caprioles of fancy HAWTHORNE.

Capriole (kæ·pri,ōᵘl), *v.* 1580. [f. prec.] To leap, skip, caper. Also *fig.*

Caproic (kăprōᵘ·ik), *a.* 1839. [f. L. *caper* goat + -IC; with *-oic* as in HEXOIC.] *Chem.* *Caproic acid*: a peculiar acid found in butter, etc., a form of the hexoic acids ($C_6H_{12}O_2$).

So **Ca·proate,** a salt of c. acid.

† **Ca·pron.** 1460. [– Fr. *capron*, north. dial. form of *chaperon*; see CHAPERON.] A hood. *Capron hardy*: an impudent fellow –1561.

Capryl (kæ·pril). [f. CAPR-IC + -YL.] *Chem.* Applied to the radical ($C_8H_{17}O$) of caprylic acid. Hence **Ca·prylate,** a salt of caprylic acid.

Capry·lic, *a.* 1845. [f. prec. + -IC.] *Chem.* *Caprylic acid*: one of the octylic fatty acids.

Caps. Printers' abbrev. of *capitals*.

‖ **Capsicum** (kæ·psikǒm). 1725. [– mod.L. (Tournefort), perh. f. L. *capsa* CASE *sb.*²] **1.** A genus of tropical plants (N.O. *Solanaceæ*), characterized by their hot pungent capsules or seeds 1796.

Guinea Pepper (*C. annuum*), and Spur Pepper (*C. frutescens*) produce the chillies of commerce, whence Cayenne pepper.

2. The fruit of the capsicum 1725. Hence **Ca·psicine,** *Chem.* the active principle of the capsules of c.

Capsize (kæpsəi·z), *sb.* 1807. [f. next.] The act of capsizing; an upset. var. **Capsi·zal.**

Capsize (kæpsəi·z), *v.* 1783. [Earlier form *capasise*, perh. to be referred ult. to Sp. *capuzar* sink (a ship) by the head, perh. alteration (by assoc. with *cabo* head) of *chapuzar* dive, duck :– Rom. **subputeare*, f. L. *sub* SUB- + *puteus* well. Cf. BOX *v.*²] *trans.* To upset, overturn. Also *intr.* (for *refl.*).

To c. a boat BYRON, a stool PEACOCK.

Capstan (kæ·pstăn). ME. [– Pr. *cabestan*, earlier *cabestran* (whence Fr. *cabestan*, Sp. *cabestrante*, Sp., Pg. *cabrestante*), f. *cabestre* halter :– L. *capistrum*, f. *capere* seize.] **1.** A cylinder or barrel revolving on a vertical axis, the power being applied by movable bars inserted in horizontal sockets made round the top, and pushed by men walking round; used *esp.* on board ship for weighing the anchor, also for hoisting heavy sails, raising weights, etc.

Phrases. *To rig the c.*, to insert the bars; *to pawl the c.*, to drop the pawls or catches into their sockets so as to prevent recoil; *to surge the c.*, to slacken the rope while heaving.

Comb. **c.-swifter,** a rope passed horizontally through notches in the outer ends of the bars, to steady the men, and to give room for more.

Cap-stone (kæ·pstōᵘn). 1665. **1.** A stone which caps or crowns. **2.** *Geol.* A fossil Echinite of the genus Conulus 1677.

1. The c. of a cromlech 1851, of a quarry SMEATON.

Capsular (kæ·psiŭlăɹ), *a.* 1730. [f. CAPSULE + -AR¹.] Of, pertaining to, or of the nature of a capsule. var. † **Ca·psulary** *a.*

† **Ca·psulate,** *a.* 1668. [f. as prec. + -ATE².] *Bot.* Enclosed in, or formed into, a capsule –1803. So † **Ca·psulated.**

Capsule (kæ·psiul). 1652. [– Fr. *capsule* – L. *capsula*, dim. of *capsa* box; see CASE *sb.*², -ULE.] † **1.** *gen.* A little case –1713. **2.** *Phys.* A membranous integument; a bag or sac 1693. **3.** *Bot.* A dry dehiscent seed-vessel, containing one or more cells 1693. **4.** *Chem.* A shallow saucer, for roasting samples of ores, or for evaporating 1727. **5.** *Med.* A small envelope of gelatine to enclose a dose of medicine 1875. **6.** A metallic cap or cover for a bottle 1858. **7.** A percussion cap; the shell of a metallic cartridge. [Fr.] Hence **Ca·psule** *v.* to furnish or close with a c.

Capsuli-, capsulo-, comb. ff. L. *capsula* CAPSULE; as in

Capsuli·ferous *a.*, bearing capsules. **Ca·psuliform** *a.*, having the form of a capsule. **Capsuli·genous** *a.*, giving origin to capsules. **Ca:psulo-lenti·cular** *a.*, of the capsule of the lens of the eye.

Captain (kæ·ptėn), *sb.* [ME. *capitain* – late OFr. *capitain* (mod. *capitaine*), superseding earlier *chevetaigne* CHIEFTAIN and *chataigne*, *catanie* – late L. *capitaneus* chief, f. *caput*, *capit-* head.] **I. 1.** One who stands at the head of others; a chief or leader. (Now only *fig.* in special senses.) **2.** *esp.* A military leader ME. **3.** A great military leader; an able general; a strategist 1590.

1. Homer, that C. of all poetry 1683. **2.** *Meas. for M.* II. ii. 130. **3.** Foremost C. of his time TENNYSON.

II. The head of a division. **1.** *gen.* An officer holding subordinate command ME. **2.** *spec.* In the army: The officer who commands a company or troop, ranking between the major and the lieutenant 1567. **3.** The officer who commands a man-of-war, ranking, in the British navy, between a rear-admiral or a commodore and a commander. Also, a courtesy title of commanders. 1554. **b.** The chief sailor of a gang having specific duties 1801. **4.** The master or commander of a vessel of any kind 1704. **5.** The superintendent of a mine 1602; the foreman of a workshop 1886; the head boy of a school 1706. **6.** *Cricket*, etc.: The leader of a side, the chief of a club, etc. 1857. **7.** As a term of address (*familiar*). Cf. *governor*. 1607.

3. b. C. of a gun at the Battle of the Nile 1801. **4.** The c. of a slaver MORLEY. **7.** Come Captaine, We must be neat; not neat, but cleanly, Captaine SHAKS.

III. A name for the Grey Gurnard 1810.

Comb. † **c.-pacha:** see CAPITAN. Hence **Ca·ptainess,** a female c. **Ca·ptainless** *a.* † **Ca·ptainry,** captaincy; a district under a c.

† **Ca·ptain,** *a.* 1566. [prec. sb. used attrib.] Chief, head-. –1635.

Captain (kæ·ptėn), *v.* 1598. [f. the sb.] To act as captain to, head. Also *intr.*

Captaincy (kæ·ptėnsi). 1818. [f. CAPTAIN *sb.* + -CY.] **1.** The position or action of a captain. **2.** The district under the rule of a captain (e.g. in Brazil). [Sp.] 1821.

Captain Ge·neral, captain-general. 1514. [Fr. and Sp.] † Chief commander of a force. Also the governor of a Spanish province or colony.

Captain-lieute·nant. 1658. A military officer who commanded a company or troop, with a captain's rank and lieutenant's pay. (The rank is extinct.)

Ca·ptainship. 1465. [See -SHIP.] **1.** The office, position, authority or rank of a captain. **2.** *joc.* The dignity or personality of a captain; cf. *lordship* 1611. **3.** = CAPTAINCY 2. 1680. **4.** 'Skill in the military trade' (J.). 1606.

1. The c. of the Scottish Guards CARTE.

† **Ca·ptate,** *v.* 1628. [– *captat-*, pa. ppl. stem of L. *captare*, frequent. of *capere* seize; see -ATE³.] To catch at, seek after –1671.

Captation (kæ̆ptēⁱ·ʃən). 1523. [– Fr. *captation* or L. *captatio*, *-ōn-*, f. as prec. + -ION.] An endeavour to get, *esp.* by address or art; the making of *ad captandum* appeals.

Popular captations. .in speeches *Eikon Bas.*

Caption (kæ·pʃən). ME. [– L. *captio*, *-ōn-*, f. *capt-*, pa. ppl. stem of *capere* seize; see -ION.] **1.** Seizure, capture (now *rare*). **b.** *Law.* Apprehension by judicial process 1609. † **2.** The action of taking exception; a quibble, sophism. (L. *captio*.) –1734. **3.** *Law.* 'That part of a legal instrument, as a commission, indictment, etc., which shows where, when, and by what authority it is taken, found, or executed' (Tomlins) 1670. **4.** The heading of a chapter, section, illustration, etc., now esp. on a cinema screen 1789. orig. *U.S.*

2. So vain a C. HEYLIN. **4.** Under the c., 'A Budget of Paradoxes' GROSART.

Captious (kæ·pʃəs), *a.* ME. [– (O)Fr. *captieux* or L. *captiosus*, f. *captio* deception, fallacious argument; see prec., -OUS.] **1.** Apt to catch or take one in; fallacious, sophistical 1447. **2.** Disposed to find fault; cavilling, carping ME.

1. A c. question, sir COWPER. **2.** The world is c. COVERDALE. C. of other mens doinges 1561. Nonce uses: = Capacious *All's Well* I. iii. 208; = Taking 1776. Hence **Ca·ptious-ly** *adv.*, **-ness.**

† **Capti·vance.** *rare.* = CAPTIVITY. Spenser.

Captivate (kæ·ptiveⁱt), *v.* 1526. [– *captivat-*, pa. ppl. stem of late L. *captivare*; see CAPTIVE *v.*, -ATE³.] † **1.** To make or hold captive –1825. † **2.** *fig.* To subjugate (the mind, etc.). Const. *to*. –1838. **3.** *esp.* 'To overpower with excellence' (J.); to enslave, fascinate, charm 1525.

1. Thy bragging banners. .Shall all be captivated by this hand 1595. **3.** Hir bewtye captyuated his mynde *Judith* 16:9. Hence **Ca·ptivatingly** *adv.* **Ca·ptivator,** †**-er.**

Captivation (kæptivēⁱ·ʃən). 1610. [– late L. *captivatio*, f. *captivare*; see prec., -ION.] **1.** The action of taking or holding captive; being taken or held captive; now only *fig.* **2.** A fascination. SCOTT.

Captive (kæ·ptiv). ME. [– L. *captivus*, f. *capt-*, pa. ppl. stem of *capere* take, seize; see CAITIFF.]

A. *adj.* **1.** Taken prisoner, *esp.* in war; kept in confinement or bondage. Also *transf.* **2.** *fig.* Captivated, enslaved in will or feeling 1594. **3.** Of or belonging to a captive 1590.

1. The captiue Iewes 2 *Macc.* 8:10. A c. lark, balloon, etc. (*mod.*). **2.** Whose words all eares took captiue *All's Well* v. iii. 17. **3.** His c. state MILT.

B. *sb.* **1.** A person taken prisoner; one taken and held in confinement ME. Also *transf.* **2.** *fig.* One captivated or enslaved by beauty, personal influence, etc. 1732.

1. A man of the captiues of Iudah *Dan.* 2:25.

Captive (kæ·ptiv), *v. arch.* ME. [– (O)Fr. *captiver* – late L. *captivare*, f. *captivus*; see prec.] To take captive (*lit.* and *fig.*). (In MILT. *capti·ve.*)

Their inhabitants slaughtered and captived BURKE.

Captivity (kæpti·vĭti). ME. [– L. *captivitas*, f. *captivus*; see CAPTIVE *a.*, -ITY.] **1.** The condition of a captive; *spec.* that of the Jews at Babylon. **2.** *fig.* The subjection of the reason, will, or affections 1538. † **3.** Captives collectively. (A Hebraism.) 1526.

1. A c. implies a removal of the inhabitants PUSEY. **3.** *To lead c. captive*: now often, to lead one's captors into c. (*Eph.* 4:8); but see also *Judges* 5:12.

Captor (kæ·ptəɹ, -ɔɹ). 1688. [– L. *captor*, f. *capt-*, pa. ppl. stem of *capere* seize; see -OR 2.] One who takes by force a prisoner or a prize. So **Ca·ptress** (*rare*).

Capture (kæ·ptiŭɹ), *sb.* 1541. [– Fr. *capture* – L. *captura*, f. as prec.; see -URE.] **1.** The fact of taking forcibly, or by stratagem, or of being thus taken; *esp.* the seizing as a prize. **2.** The prize, prey, or booty so taken 1706.

2. To bring a dubious c. into port 1750.

Ca·pture, *v.* 1795. [f. prec. sb., repl. CAPTIVE *v.*] To make a capture of (*lit.* and *fig.*).

The value of the property so captured WELLINGTON. Hence **Ca·pturable** *a.* **Ca·pturer.**

Capuche (kapū·ʃ, kăpū·tʃ). 1592. Also **capouch.** [– Fr. *capuche* (now *capuce*) – It. *cappucchio* hood; see next.] The hood of a (Capuchin's) cloak. Hence **Capu·ched** *a.* hooded. †‖ **Capuchon,** a hood.

Capuchin (kæ·piŭtʃin, kæpŭʃī·n), *sb.* Also **-ine.** 1599. [– Fr. *capuchin* (now *capucin*) – It. *cappucchino*, f. *cappucchio* hood, augm. of *cappa* CAPE *sb.*[2]] **1.** A Franciscan friar of the new rule of 1528. So called from the sharp-pointed capuche, first worn by them in 1525. **2.** 'A female garment, consisting of a cloak and hood, made in imitation of the dress of capuchin friars' (J.) 1749.

attrib. **C. monkey,** an American monkey (*Cebus capucinus*) with black hair at the back of the head, looking like a cowl. **C. pigeon,** a sub-variety of the Jacobin pigeon, with a cowl-like arrangement of feathers on the back of the head. **Capuchin's beard,** a variety of endive. **Capuchin capers;** see CAPER *sb.*[1]

†‖ **Capucine** (kapüsīn). 1693. [Fr.; fem. of *capucin*; see prec.] **1.** The Nasturtium. **2.** The dark orange colour of its flowers 1791.

Ca·pulet, var. of – CAPELET.

Caput (kæ·pɒt). 1716. [L.] **1.** Occas. *techn.* for 'head' or 'top', *esp.* in *Anat.* † **2.** Short for CAPUT MORTUUM, q.v. † **3.** The former ruling body or council of the University of Cambridge –1830.

‖ **Ca·put mo·rtuum.** 1641. [L.; = dead head.] † **1.** A skull 1658. **2.** *Alch.* The residuum remaining after distillation or sublimation 1641. **3.** *fig.* Worthless residue 1711.

Capybara (kæpibā·ră). Also **capi-.** 1774. [Native name in Brazil.] The largest extant rodent quadruped (*Hydrochœrus capybara*), nearly allied to the Guinea Pig. Cf. CABIAI.

Car (kāɹ), *sb.* [ME. *carre* – AFr., ONFr. *carre* :– Rom. **carra*, pl. or parallel fem. form of L. *carrum* n., *carrus* m. – OCelt. **karrom* (**karros*), repr. by (O)Ir. *carr*, OW. *carr* (W. *car*), rel. to L. *currus* chariot.] **1.** A wheeled vehicle: orig. used generally, but since 16th c. chiefly poetic and grandiose. **2.** In U.S.: A name for vehicles (as carriages, trucks, wagons, etc.) designed for travelling on railways 1837. In Gt. Britain applied to those of street tramways. **b.** = MOTOR CAR 1: 1896. **3.** The part of a balloon in which aeronauts sit 1794. † **4.** The seven stars of the Great Bear, called also the Plough or Wain –1697.

1. Forty carres (*vehicula*) HOLLAND. Phoebus fiery carre SPENSER. The Carr of Night MILT. The towering c., the sable steeds TENNYSON. The c. of Juggernaut 1853. **2.** The cars of a railway 1850. The cars on the tramways in London 1888.

Ca·rabid, cara·bidan. 1835. [f. mod.L. pl. *carabidæ*, f. L. *carabus* crab; see -ID[3].] *Ent.* One of the *Carabidæ*, a family of large carnivorous beetles.

† **Carabin** (kæ·răbin). 1590. [– Fr. *carabin.*] A mounted musketeer; a carabineer –1735.

Carabineer (kæ:răbinīᵊ·ɹ), **carbineer** (kāɹbinīᵊ·ɹ). 1672. [– Fr. *carabinier*, f. *carabine* CARBINE; see -EER.] A soldier who carries a carbine.

Ca·raboid, *a.* [f. L. *carabus* (see CARABID) + -OID.] *Ent.* Like or related to the genus *Carabus* of beetles.

Caracal (kæ·răkæl). 1760. [– Fr. or Sp. *caracal* – Turk. *karakulak*, f. *kara* black + *kulak* ear.] A feline animal (*Felis caracal*) found in Africa and Asia, supposed to be the 'lynx' of the ancients.

‖ **Caracara** (kărakā·ra). Also **carcara.** 1838. [From its cry.] Name for S. Amer. birds of the *Polyborinæ*, an aberrant subfamily of *Falconidæ*, with affinities toward the Vultures.

Carack, var. of CARRACK.

Caracol (kæ·răkǫl), **caracole** (-koᵘl), *sb.* 1614. [Senses 1 and 2 – Fr. *caracol*, *-cole* snail's shell, spiral; sense 3 – Fr. *caracol*, *-cole*, f. *caracoler*, f. *caracole* spiral.] † **1.** A spiral shell 1622. **2.** *Arch.* A staircase in the form of a helix 1721. **3.** A half-turn to the right or left executed by a horseman 1614.

Ca·racol, caracole, *v.* 1656. [– Fr. *caracoler*; see prec.] To execute a caracol or caracols; *trans.* to make (a horse) caracol.

The Captain. .caracolling majestically THACKERAY. Hence **Ca·racoler, -coller.**

†‖ **Caracoli.** 1753. [perh. – Carib name.] An alloy of silver, copper, and gold, imitating one formerly used in the West Indies.

‖ **Caracore.** 1794. [Also in Fr. *caracore*, Sp. *caracora.*] 'A sort of vessel used in the Philippine Isles' (Littré).

† **Caract, carect,** *sb.* [ME. *caracte*, *carect(e)* – OFr. *c(h)aract* m., *c(h)aracte*, *carecte* fem., perh. ult. – Gr. χαρακτός given, impressed as a mark, taken absol. as = *character.*] A mark, CHARACTER –1655.

Characts, titles, formes *Meas. for M.* v. i. 56. Hence † **Caract** *v.* to mark.

Caracul, kara- (kæ·răkŭl). 1894. [Russ.] A kind of astrakhan fur; cloth imitating this.

Carafe (karā·f). 1786. [– Fr. *carafe* – It. *caraffa*, prob. (through Sp. *garrafa*) – N.-Afr. Arab. *ġarrāfa* big-bellied flask.] A glass water-bottle for the table, bedroom, etc. Also corrupted to *craft*, *croft.*

Carag(h)een, var. of CARRAGEEN.

‖ **Carambola.** 1598. [Pg., of doubtful origin.] The East Indian *Averrhoa carambola* (N.O. *Oxalidaceæ*); also its acid fruit.

Carambole (kæ·rămbōᵘl), *sb.* 1775. [– Sp. *carambola* (whence Fr. *carambole* red ball at billiards), obscure comp. of *bola* ball = (O)Fr. *boule* :– L. *bulla*; see BULL *sb.*[2]] *Billiards.* The stroke otherwise called a CANNON. Hence **Carambole** *v.* to make a cannon.

Caramel (kæ·rămel), *sb.* 1725. [– Fr. *caramel* – Sp. *caramelo*, of unkn. origin.] A black or brown porous substance obtained by heating sugar; burnt sugar. **b.** A kind of candy or sweet. Also *attrib.*

†‖ **Caramoussal, carmousal.** 1587. [– Turk. *kāramusāl*, in Fr. *carmoussal*, It. *carmusali* (Florio), mod.L. *caramussallus.*] A Turkish and Moorish ship of burden, noted in the 17th c.

‖ **Caranx** (kæ·ræŋks). 1836. [mod.L., in Fr. *carangue.*] A genus of fishes of the family *Scomberidæ.*

Ca·rap. 1865. [From the native name.] *C. oil*: an oil yielded by the seeds of *Carapa guianensis.*

Carapace (kæ·răpeⁱs). 1836. [– Fr. *carapace* – Sp. *carapacho*, of unkn. origin.] The upper body-shell of tortoises and of crustaceans. var. **Ca·rapax.**

Carat (kæ·răt). 1552. [– Fr. *carat* – It. *carato* – Arab. *ḳīrāṭ* weight of 4 grains – Gr. κεράτιον fruit of the carob, f. κέρας horn.] † **1.** The bean of the carob-tree 1601. **2.** A measure of weight used for diamonds, etc., originally 3⅓ grains, now 3⅙ grains. It is divided into 4 *carat-grains.* Also *attrib.* 1575. **3.** A proportional measure of one twenty-fourth used in stating the fineness of gold. Also *attrib.* 1555. † **4.** Worth, value; estimate –1680.

2. A Diamond of 10 Carats 1667. **3.** [Gold of] 22 caracts fine HUTTON. **4.** 2 *Hen. IV*, IV. v. 162.

‖ **Caratch** (karā·tʃ). 1682. [– Arab. *ḵarāj* state dues, land tax.] The tribute levied by the Turks on their Christian subjects.

Caravan (kæ·răvæn, kærăvæ·n). 1599. [– Fr. *caravane* – Pers. *kārwān*; in XVI *carouan*, etc., directly – Pers.] **1.** A company of merchants, pilgrims, or others, in the East or northern Africa, travelling together for the sake of security, esp. through the desert. Also *attrib.* **2.** A fleet of Turkish or Russian ships, *esp.* of merchant vessels, with their convoy 1605. **3.** *transf.* A company in motion. Also *fig.* 1667. **4.** A covered carriage or cart (now gen. superseded by VAN *sb.*[3] 1); a house on wheels, as those used by gipsies, showmen, etc. 1674.

1. Trauailing by Carauan, that is, Great Droues of laden Camels 1602. **2.** A C. . .sailing in the vast ocean FULLER. Hence **Caravanee·r,** the leader of an (oriental) c.

Caravanserai, -era, -ary (kærăvæ·nsĕrai, -ĕră, -ĕri). 1599. [ult. – Pers. *kārwān-sarāy* (*serā(y)* dwelling, inn); early forms through Fr. *caravansérai*, etc.] A kind of inn in the East where caravans put up, being a large quadrangular building enclosing a spacious court. Also *transf.* and *fig.*

Caravel (kæ·răvel). 1527. [– Fr. *caravelle* – Pg. *caravela* (whence also Fr. †*carvelle* (XV), It. *caravella*) – Gr. κάραβος horned beetle, crayfish, light ship.] *Naut.* **1.** A kind of ship: **a.** The same as CARVEL, q.v.; **b.** The Portuguese *caravela*, a small ship with lateen sails; **c.** The Turkish war-frigate, called in Italian *caravella.* **2.** The floating mollusc *Ianthina* 1707.

Caraway (kæ·răweⁱ). Also † **carr-.** ME. [The form corresp. most closely to OSp. *alcarahueya* (mod. *alcaravea*) = Pg. *alcaravia* – Arab. *al-karwiya* and *al-karāwiyā* (see AL-[2]); med.L., Fr., It., Sp. *carvi* is repr. by Sc. *carvy*; the ult. source may be Gr. κάρον, κάρεον (L. *carum*, *careum*) cummin.] **1.** An umbelliferous plant (*Carum carui*): its seeds are aromatic and carminative, and yield a volatile oil. † **2.** The seed of the caraway; also a sweetmeat or confection containing caraway-seeds –1712.

2. A dish of Carrawayes 2 *Hen. IV*, v. iii. 3.

Carb-. *Chem.* Comb. f. CARBON, used before vowels, as in:

Ca·rbanil [ANIL], an amido-derivative of the benzene group, cyanate of phenyl, CO = N—C_6H_5, a mobile liquid with a pungent odour. **Ca·rbazol** [AZO- + -OL], an amidophenyl, $2C_6H_4$ = NH, occurring in coal-tar oil, and as a by-product of aniline. **Carbazo·tic acid** [AZOTIC], an earlier name of Picric acid; its salts are **Carba·zotates.**

Carbamide (kā·ɹbămǝid). 1865. [f. CARB- + AMIDE.] *Chem.* Analytical name of UREA. Also **Carba·mic** [see AMIC] *a.*, as in *Carbamic acid*, $CO.NH_2.OH$. **Ca·rbamate,** a salt of carbamic acid.

Carbide (kā·ɹbǝid). 1865. [f. CARB- + -IDE.] *Chem.* A compound of carbon with an element or a metal; earlier *carburet.* **b.** = *calcium c.* 1898.

Carbine (kā·ɹbǝin), **ca·rabine.** 1605. [Earliest *carabine* – Fr. *carabine*, in It., Sp., Pg. *carabina*; orig. the weapon of the †*carabin* (– Fr.) mounted musketeer.] A kind of fire-arm, shorter than the musket, used by mounted soldiers.

Carbinol (kā·ɹbinǫl). [f. CARBON + -OL.] *Chem.* A generic name introduced by Kolbe *c* 1868 for the monatomic alcohols. Simple *Carbinol* is methyl alcohol, $COH.H_3$.

Carbo-. 1810. *Chem.* Comb. f. CARBON, used before consonants.

Carbo-hydrate (kā:ɹbo,hǝi·dreⁱt). 1869. [f. CARBO- + HYDRATE.] *Chem.* An organic compound of carbon with oxygen and hydrogen in the proportion to form water. They are divided into *Sugars proper*, *Glucoses*, and *Amyloses.*

Carbolic (kaɹbǫ·lik), *a.* 1865. [f. CARB- + -OL + -IC.] *Chem.* In **Carbolic acid,** a substance also called *Phenol* or *Phenyl alcohol,* C_6H_5.OH, found in the heavy coal oils and elsewhere. Much used as a disinfectant. Hence **Ca·rbolate,** a salt of carbolic acid. **Ca·rbolize** *v.* to impregnate with carbolic acid.

Carbon (kā·ɹbən). 1789. [– Fr. *carbone* (de Morveau, 1787), f. L. *carbo, -ōn-* coal, charcoal.] **1.** *Chem.* One of the non-metallic elements, occurring uncombined in three allotropic forms—two crystalline (diamond and graphite) and one amorphous (charcoal), and in combination in carbonic acid gas, and all organic compounds (hence called 'the carbon compounds'). Carbon (symbol C) is a tetrad; atomic weight 12. **2.** *Electr.* A pencil of fine charcoal. Two of these are placed with their points close to each other, and a current of galvanic electricity transmitted through them renders the carbon points intensely luminous. 1860.

attrib. etc.: **c. printing, process,** a photographic process producing permanent prints, the shades of which are produced by the c. of lampblack; **C. dioxide,** CO_2, carbonic acid gas; **C. monoxide,** CO, carbonic oxide gas. Hence **Ca·rbonous** *a.*

Carbonaceous (kāɹbǒnē[i]·ʃəs), *a.* 1791. [f. CARBON + -ACEOUS.] Of the nature of, consisting of, or containing carbon. **2.** *Geol.* Coaly 1833.

† **Carbona·do,** *sb.* 1586. [– Sp. *carbonada,* f. *carbon* coal; see CARBON, -ADO.] Fish, flesh, or fowl, scored across and broiled upon the coals. Often *transf.* –1687. var. **Carbona·de.**

Carbona·do, *v. arch.* 1596. [f. prec.] **1.** To score across and broil or grill 1611. **2.** *transf.* To cut, slash, hack 1596.

1. How she long'd to eate. .Toads carbonado'd *Wint. T.* IV. iv. 268. **2.** *Lear* II. ii. 41. var. **Carbona·de** *v.*; whence **Carbona·ded** *ppl. a.*

‖ **Carbonari** (karbonā·ri), *sb. pl.* 1823. [It. pl. of *carbonaro* collier, charcoal-burner, f. *carbone* coal. :– L. *carbo*; see CARBON.] The members of a secret political association formed in the kingdom of Naples early in the 19th c., with the design of introducing a republican government. Hence **Carbona·rism.**

Carbonate (kā·ɹbǒnět), *sb.* 1794. [– Fr. *carbonat* (de Morveau, 1787) – mod.L. *carbonatum*; see CARBON, -ATE[1].] **1.** *Chem.* A salt of carbonic acid. **2.** *ellipt.* Ore containing a large proportion of carbonate of lead 1881.

Carbonate (kā·ɹbǒne[i]t), *v.* 1805. [Sense 1, f. CARBON + -ATE[3]; sense 2, f. prec.: cf. Fr. *carbonater.*] **1.** To CARBONIZE 1831. **2.** *Chem.* To form into a carbonate; also, to aerate 1805. Hence **Carbona·tion,** formation of a carbonate; aeration.

Carbonated (kā·ɹbǒne[i]tėd), *a.* 1797. [f. CARBONATE *v.* + -ED[1].] † Carbonized –1825; † CARBURETTED –1805; chemically combined or impregnated with carbonic acid 1803.

† **Carboned,** *ppl. a.* ? misprint for *carbonaded.* PEPYS.

Carbonic (kaɹbǫ·nik), *a.* 1791. [f. CARBON + -IC; cf. Fr. *carbonique.*] **1.** Of or pertaining to carbon; of or caused by carbonic acid gas. **2.** Of coal; of the Carbonari (BYRON). Also *sb.*

C. acid, formerly known as *fixed air,* and now called **Carbon(ic) dioxide** or **Carbonic anhydride,** CO_2, the gas which is formed in the ordinary combustion of carbon, disengaged from fermenting liquors, given out in the breathing of animals, and known as the choke-damp or foul air of mines, etc. This is still popularly called *c. acid gas,* but the name *C. acid* is applied in chemistry to the compound CH_2O_3 supposed to be formed when carbon dioxide comes in contact with water, of which the carbonates are the salts. **C. oxide** = *carbon monoxide,* CO.

Carboniferous (kāɹboni·fěrəs), *a.* 1799. [f. L. *carbo, -ōn-* + -FEROUS.] Producing coal.

Applied in *Geol.* to the series of strata with which seams of coal are associated, the *C. System* or *Formation,* lying next above the Devonian, and including the Coal Measures, Millstone Grit, and Mountain Limestone; also to the rocks, fossils, etc., of this formation, and to the *C. Age, Era,* or *Period,* during which these strata were deposited, and the vegetation existed that formed the coalbeds.

Carbonify (kaɹbǫ·nifəi), *v.* 1803. [f. as prec. + -FY.] To CARBONIZE. Hence **Carbo·nifica·tion,** conversion into coal.

Carbonize (kā·ɹbonəiz), *v.* 1806. [f. CARBON + -IZE.] **1.** To convert into mere carbon. **2.** To CARBURET (*arch.*) 1808. **3.** To cover with charcoal, lamp-black, etc. Hence **-iza·tion.**

Ca·rbon pa:per. 1895. Thin paper coated on one side with a preparation of lamp-black, used between two papers to make a duplicate copy of what is written on the upper sheet.

Carbonyl (kā·ɹbǒnil). 1869. [f. CARBON + -YL.] *Chem.* The divalent compound radical CO (*carbon monoxide*) considered as a constituent of urea, alloxan, creatin, etc.

Carborundum (kāɹbǒrʊ·ndǒm). 1893. [f. CARBO(N + CO)RUNDUM.] A crystalline compound of carbon and silicon used for polishing and scouring.

Carboxyl (kabɹǫ·ksil). 1869. [f. CARBON + OX(YGEN) + YL.] *Chem.* A name given to the monad group –CO.OH, contained in all the fatty acids; thus *Formic acid* is H—CO.OH.

Carboy (kā·ɹboi). 1753. [ult. – Pers. *ḳar(r)āba* large glass container.] A large globular bottle, of green or blue glass, covered with basket-work for protection, used chiefly for holding acids and other corrosive liquids.

Carbuncle (kā·ɹbʊŋk'l). [– OFr. *charbucle, -buncle, carboucle, -buncle* (now repl. by *escarboucle*) = Pr., Sp. *carbuncle,* It. *carbonchio* :– L. *carbunculus* small coal, carbuncle stone, red tumour, dim. of *carbo* coal; see CARBON, -CULE.] **1.** (Formerly **carbuncle-stone**): A name of various precious stones of a red or fiery colour; anciently of sapphires, spinels or rubies, and garnets; in mod. lapidary work of the garnet when cut *en cabochon.* **2.** *Her.* A charge or bearing supposed to represent a carbuncle with its rays; = ESCARBUNCLE ME. **3.** *Med.* An inflammatory, circumscribed, malignant tumour, caused by inflammation of the skin and cellular membrane. It differs from a boil in having no central core; an anthrax. Also, a red spot or pimple on the nose or face caused by drinking. 1530. Also *attrib.* Hence **Carbu·ncular** *a.* of, pertaining to, resembling, or characterized by carbuncles. **Carbu·nculous** *a.* of, full of, or of the nature of carbuncles.

Carbuncled (kā·ɹbʊŋk'ld), *ppl. a.* 1606. [f. prec. + -ED[2].] **1.** Adorned with carbuncles. **2.** Affected with a carbuncle or carbuncles; spotted, pimpled; red like a carbuncle 1664. Also *transf.*

1. Carbunkled Like holy Phoebus Carre *Ant. & Cl.* IV. viii. 28. **2.** C. and Tun-bellied *Tatler* No. 66.

† **Carbu:ncula·tion.** 1673. [– L. *carbunculatio* disease of trees; see CARBUNCLE, -ATION.] The blasting of the buds of trees or plants by excessive heat or cold –1755.

Carburet (kā·ɹbiŭret), *sb.* 1795. [f. CARB- + -URET.] *Chem.* = CARBIDE, q.v.

Ca·rburet, *v.* 1869. [f. prec.] *trans.* To combine chemically or impregnate with carbon.

Carburetted, -eted (kā·ɹbiŭretėd), *ppl. a.* 1802. [f. prec. + -ED[1].] *Chem.* Combined or impregnated with carbon, as in *C. hydrogen,* the fire-damp of miners, and chief constituent of coal-gas.

Ca·rburettor, -etter. 1866. [f. as prec. + -OR 2, -ER[1].] An apparatus for passing hydrogen, coal-gas, or atmospheric air through or over a liquid hydrocarbon, so as to add illuminating power. **b.** The apparatus for mixing air with petrol vapour for combustion in motor engines 1896.

Carburize (kā·ɹbiŭrəiz), *v.* [f. † *carbure* (repl. by *carburet*) – Fr. *carbure*; see -IZE.] *trans.* To combine with carbon or a carbon compound; used *esp.* of the process of imparting carbon to wrought iron in making cement steel; also = CARBURET *v.* Hence **Carburiza·tion.**

‖ **Carcajou** (ka·rkaʒu). 1774. [– Fr. *carcajou* – some native name not identified.] **1.** The Glutton or Wolverene (*Gulo luscus*). ¶ **2.** Applied erron. to the American Badger, and by Charlevoix to the Canadian Lynx 1839.

Carcake (kā·ɹ,ke[i]k). *Sc.* 1816. [First part as in CARE-SUNDAY.] A small cake baked with eggs, and eaten on Fastern's E'en (Shrove Tuesday) in parts of Scotland.

† **Carcan.** 1534. [– Fr. *carcan* = Pr. *carcan,* med.L. *carcannum,* It. *carcame* – Gmc. **querkbann*; cf. ON. *kverkband* string of a cap going below the chin, f. *kverk* angle below the chin + *band* BAND *sb.*[2]] **1.** An iron collar used for punishment –1777. **2.** = next –1694.

Carcanet (kā·ɹkănet). *arch.* 1530. [f. prec. + -ET.] A collar or necklace, usually of gold or jewelled. Also *transf.* and *fig.*

Carcass, carcase (kā·ɹkăs), *sb.* [– Fr. *carcasse* (XVI); earlier forms *carcays, -as, carkeis, -ois* (XIV–XVII), prop. a distinct word – AFr. *carcois* = OFr. *charcois* (still dial.); in AL. *carcasium, -osium, -oisum* (all XIII); ult. origin of the several forms unkn.] **1.** The dead body of man or beast; now used of the human corpse only in contempt. **2.** A term of contempt or ridicule for the human body, dead or alive 1586. **3.** *fig.* The lifeless shell or husk 1612. **4.** *transf.* The skeleton of a vessel or edifice 1596. **5.** *Mil.* An iron shell, filled with combustibles, and pierced with holes through which the flame blazes; fired from a mortar or gun to set fire to buildings, ships, etc. (Spelt *carcass.*) 1684.

1. The carkeise of Iezebel 2 *Kings* 9 : 37. A c. of meat JEVONS. **2.** To pamper his own carcass SOUTH. **3.** The mere c. of nobility SHENSTONE. **5.** Carcasses, bombs, and red-hot balls 1790. *Comb.* **c.-flooring, -roofing** (*Arch.*), the framework of timber which supports the boarding of the floor or roof (see 4). Hence **Ca·rcassed** *ppl. a.* † dead; having a c.

Ca·rcass, *v.* 1881. [f. prec. sb., sense 4.] *trans.* To put up the carcass of (a building).

Carcel (kā·ɹsěl). 1845. [Name of inventor.] *Carcel lamp,* one in which the oil is pumped up to the wick by clockwork. Called also the *French lamp.*

† **Ca·rceral,** *a.* 1563. [– late L. *carceralis,* f. *carcer* prison; see -AL[1].] Of or belonging to a prison –1696.

Ca·rcerist. *nonce-wd.* [f. L. *carcer* + -IST.] One who advocates prisons. SYD. SMITH.

Carcinology (kāɹsinǫ·lǒdʒi). 1852. [f. Gr. καρκίνος crab + -LOGY.] *Zool.* That part of zoology which treats of crustaceans. Hence **Ca:rcinolo·gical** *a.* **Carcino·logist.**

‖ **Carcinoma** (kāɹsinō[u]·mă). Pl. **-mata.** 1721. [L. – Gr. καρκίνωμα, -ματ-, f. καρκίνος crab; see -OMA. Cf. CANCER.] **1.** *Med.* The disease CANCER. (By some restricted to indolent tumours, or to the early stages only of cancer.) † **2.** *Med.* A disease of the cornea –1753. Hence **Carcino·matous** *a.* characterized by, or of the nature of, c.

‖ **Carcinosis** (kāɹsinō[u]·sis). 1866. [mod.L., f. Gr. καρκίνος crab, cancer, see -OSIS.] *Med.* The production and development of cancer; also = CANCER.

‖ **Carcoon** (kāɹkū·n). *Anglo-Ind.* Also **-koon.** 1803. [Mahratti *kārkūn* clerk – Pers. *kārkun* hard-working; operator, manager.] A clerk.

Card (kāɹd), *sb.*[1] ME. [– (O)Fr. *carde* – Pr. *carda,* f. *cardar* tease, comb :– pop.L. **caritare,* f. L. *carere* card.] **1.** An implement for raising a nap on cloth; *esp.* an iron instrument with teeth, or (later) a wire brush. **2.** A similar instrument used to part, comb out, and set in order the fibres of wool, hemp, etc.; now, a wire brush, consisting of a strip of leather or indiarubber, into which short steel wires are inserted ME. *Comb.* **c.-cloth,** the leather or indiarubber backing of a c.

Card (kāɹd), *sb.*[2] ME. [– (with unexpl. *d*) (O)Fr. *carte* – L. *charta* papyrus leaf, paper (whence Fr. *charte* CHART) – Gr. χάρτης leaf of papyrus, etc.] **1.** One of a pack of small oblong pieces of pasteboard: now called more specifically *playing-cards.* (The earliest sense in Fr. and Eng.) † **2.** A map or plan; = CHART *sb.* –1650. **3.** The circular piece of stiff paper on which the 32 points of the compass are marked 1605. Also *fig.* **4.** *gen.* A flat piece of stiff paper or thin pasteboard, usually rectangular; used to write or draw upon or for other purposes 1610. **5.** *transf.* (*U.S.*) A published note, containing a short statement, request, explanation, or the like 1887. **6.** *Mech.* One of the perforated pasteboards or sheet metal plates in the Jacquard attachments to looms 1831. **7.** *slang* or *colloq.* '*The card*' = 'the correct thing', the TICKET, q.v. 1851.

1. *Playing-cards*: cards used in playing whist and other games. The whist pack consists of 4 suits, each of 13 cards, 10 of which bear respectively 1, 2, 3, etc. (up to 10) pips all of one form, and the remaining 3 have habited figures, 'King', 'Queen', and 'Knave', called COURT (i.e. *coat*) or *picture-cards*. Tell thy cardes, and then tell me what thou hast wonne 1562. *A house of cards* (fig.): any insecure scheme, etc. Phr. *To play cards* or *at cards*. *Sure c.*: an expedient or person sure to bring success. So *knowing, old, queer*, etc. *c.* *To play one's cards well, badly*, etc. *To throw up one's cards*: to abandon a project. *To show one's cards*: to reveal one's plans or strength. *On the cards*: liable to turn up. **2.** *Haml.* v. ii. 114. **3.** All the Quarters that they know I' th' Ship-mans C. *Macb.* I. iii. 17. Reason the c., but Passion is the gale POPE. *To speak by the c.*: to be exact to a point. *Haml.* v. i. 149. **4.** In spec. uses: POST-CARD (in U.S. *postal c.*). So *correspondence-c.* A c. for a party 1876. *Visiting c.*; hence, *To leave a c. on.* *Wedding cards.* *Business c.* Also *birthday, Christmas*, etc. *cards*; *window-c., show-c., pattern-c., sample-c.*

Comb., etc.: **c.-case; -catalogue,** one in which each item is entered on a separate c.; so **c. index** (also as vb.); **-sharper** [SHARP *v.* 4, SHARPER 2], one who makes a trade of cheating at cards; so **-sharping; c. vote,** a vote in which each (trade union) delegate's vote counts as for his constituents.

† **Card,** *sb.*[3] 1658. [– Fr. *carde*; see CARDOON, CHARD[2].] The central leaf-stalk of the artichoke.

Card (kāɹd), *v.*[1] ME. [f. CARD *sb.*[1]] **1.** *trans.* To prepare wool, tow, etc., for spinning by combing out and disentangling with a card. Also with *out*, and *absol.* Also *fig.* and *transf.* † **2.** To stir and mix with cards; to mix –1635. † **3.** To comb or cleanse (of impurities) 1612. **4.** To scratch or tear the flesh with a wool-card or the like, as a method of torture 1556. **5.** *Sc.* 'To scold sharply' (Jamieson).

1. Boþe to karde and to kembe LANGL. **2.** You Tom Tapster. . carde your beere. . halfe smal & halfe strong GREENE. **4.** Carded to death 1827.

Card (kāɹd), *v.*[2] 1548. [f. CARD *sb.*[2]] † **1.** *intr.* To play at cards; to play one's cards. **2.** *trans.* (*U.S.*) To send a message by post-card to. Cf. WIRE *v.* 1875. **3.** To fix on a card, as patterns 1884.

‖ **Cardamine** (kaɹdæ·mini, kā·ɹdămain). 1753. [– Fr. *cardamine* or late L. *cardamina* – Gr. καρδαμίνη, f. κάρδαμον cress.] *Bot.* A genus of cruciferous plants, including the Lady-smock or Cuckoo-flower (*C. pratensis*); Meadow-cress.

Cardamom (kā·ɹdămǫ̆m). 1553. [– (O)Fr. *cardamome* or L. *cardamomum* – Gr. καρδάμωμον, f. κάρδαμον cress + ἄμωμον Indian spice.] A spice consisting of the seed-capsules of species of *Amomum* and *Elettaria* (N.O. *Zinziberaceæ*), natives of the East Indies and China; used as a stomachic and a condiment. (Occas. the plant itself.) Also *attrib.*

Ca·rdboard. 1858. [f. CARD *sb.*[2]] Pasteboard of the thickness of card, for cutting cards from, making boxes, etc. Also *attrib.*

† **Ca·rdecu.** 1605. [– Fr. *quart d'écu* quarter of an *écu*.] An old French silver coin, worth ¼ of the gold *écu*, or 2*s.* 1½*d.* –1819.

‖ **Cardel.** Also **kardel.** 1694. [– Du. *kardeel, quardeel.*] A hogshead used in the Dutch whaling trade.

Carder[1] (kā·ɹdəɹ). 1450. [f. CARD *v.*[1] + -ER[1].] One who or that which cards wool, etc.

† **Ca·rder**[2]. 1530. [f. CARD *v.*[2] + -ER[1].] A card-player –1712.

‖ **Ca·rdia.** 1782. [Gr., = heart.] *Anat.* The upper or cardiac orifice of the stomach, where the œsophagus enters it.

Cardiac (kā·ɹdiæk), *a.* (and *sb.*) 1601. [– Fr. *cardiaque* or L. *cardiacus* – Gr. καρδιακός, f. καρδία heart; see -AC.]

A. *adj.* **1.** Of or pertaining to the heart; var. **Ca·rdial.** **2.** Of medicines: Cordial 1661. **3.** Pertaining to or affected with disease of the heart 1748. **4.** *Anat.* Distinctive epithet of the CARDIA, q.v. 1843. **5.** Heart-shaped (in *cardiac wheel*) 1864.

1. The C. Nerves 1726, arteries 1835. C. action 1883. **3.** C. symptoms KANE. var. † **Cardi·acal.**

B. *sb.* † **1.** An affection of the heart; ? = *cardiac passion*, cardialgia, heartburn –1483. **2.** A cordial. Also *fig.* 1746.

† **Cardiacle.** ME. [– L. *cardiaca* (sc. *passio*) with excrescent *-le* as in TREACLE.] = *Cardiac passion* –1485.

Cardiagraphy, erron. f. *cardiography.*

Cardialgy (kā·ɹdi,ældʒi). 1655. [– mod.L. *cardialgia* (also used) – Gr. καρδιαλγία heartburn, f. καρδία heart + ἄλγος pain; see -Y[3]. Cf. Fr. *cardialgie.*] *Med.* The affection called 'heartburn' (because anciently referred to the heart), consisting of pain and a sensation of heat about the cardiac orifice of the stomach, often accompanying indigestion. Hence **Cardia·lgic** *a.*

Cardigan (kā·ɹdigăn). 1868. [Named after James Thomas Brudenell, seventh Earl of Cardigan, who led the famous charge of the Light Brigade in the Crimean War, 1854.] A knitted woollen over-waistcoat or jacket, with or without sleeves.

Cardinal (kā·ɹdinăl), *a.* ME. [– (O)Fr. *cardinal* or L. *cardinalis*, f. *cardo, cardin-* hinge; see -AL[1].] **1.** *gen.* On which something else hinges, fundamental; chief, principal. **2.** *Zool.* Pertaining to the hinge of a bivalve shell 1836. **3.** [f. CARDINAL *sb.*] Of the colour of a cardinal's cassock; deep scarlet 1879.

1. The cardinall grace, that on which all other graces move 1639. Four c. Angels 1650. In fig. uses: *C. virtues*: in scholastic philosophy, justice, prudence, temperance, and fortitude, the four chief 'natural' virtues; also used in the general sense. *C. numbers* (Arith.): the primitive numbers *one, two, three*, etc., as opp. to the ORDINAL numbers *first, second, third*, etc. *C. points*: **a.** the four intersections of the horizon with the meridian and the prime vertical; the north, south, east, and west points. *C. winds*: the four chief winds which blow from these points. **b.** of the prime vertical: '*Astrol.* The rising and setting of the sun, the zenith and nadir' (Webster); = *cardines* (see CARDO). *C. veins* (Phys.): the venous trunks which transmit the blood in the early embryo from the vertebral column and the parietes of the trunk to the sinus venosus by means of the ducts of Cuvier. In R.C. Ch. *C. bishop, priest*, etc.: tr. L. *episcopus, presbyter*, etc. *cardinalis*; see CARDINAL *sb.* Hence **Ca·rdinally** *adv.* pre-eminently; *joc.* for *carnally* SHAKS.

Cardinal (kā·ɹdinăl), *sb.* OE. [– (O)Fr. *cardinal* – med. L. *cardinalis*; see prec.] **1.** One of the ecclesiastical princes (six cardinal bishops, fifty cardinal priests, and fourteen cardinal deacons) who constitute the pope's council, or the sacred college, and when the papal chair is vacant elect a pope from among themselves. **b.** Title of two of the minor canons of St. Paul's Cathedral, London 1748. **2.** A short cloak worn by ladies, orig. of scarlet cloth with a hood 1745. **3.** *slang.* Mulled red wine 1861. **4.** In *pl.* = the adj. with a sb. pl., as cardinal points, winds, etc. ME.

Comb. (in sense 1): **c.-bird, grosbeak,** a N. American singing-bird (*Cardinalis virginianus*) with scarlet plumage; **cardinal's hat,** the red hat worn by a c., taken for his dignity or office; **c. red,** the scarlet of a cardinal's robes. Hence **Ca·rdinalate,** the office or dignity of a c. **Ca·rdinali:sm,** the institution of cardinals. **Ca·rdinali:st,** a partisan of cardinals or of a c. (Now *Hist.*) † **Ca·rdinali:ze** *v.* to raise to the rank of a c.; *joc.* to make scarlet. **Ca·rdinalship,** the state, office, or tenure of a c.

Cardinal-flower. 1698. [From its colour.] *Bot.* The Scarlet Lobelia (*L. cardinalis*).

Cardines, pl. of CARDO.

Carding (kā·ɹdiŋ), *vbl. sb.* 1468. [f. CARD *v.*[1] + -ING[1].] The action of CARD *v.*[1]; *concr.* the carded product.

attrib. **c. engine, -machine,** a machine for combing wool or cotton, in which a small cylinder set with cards works in connection with smaller cylinders and a hollow shell, also set with cards.

Cardio- (kā·ɹdi,o; with disyllabic endings kā:ɹdi,ǫ·), comb. f. Gr. καρδία heart:

Ca·rdiograph [Gr. γράφος], an instrument which registers the motions of the heart by tracing a curve on paper, etc. So **Cardio·graphy.** **Cardio·logy** [Gr. -λογία], knowledge of, or a treatise on, the heart. **Cardio·meter** [Gr. -μέτρον], an instrument for measuring the force of the heart's action; also *fig.*; hence **-me·trical** *a.* **Cardio·metry** [Gr. μετρία], the measurement of the size of the heart by percussion and auscultation. **Cardio·pathy** [Gr. -παθία], disease of the heart.

Cardioid (kā·ɹdi,oid). 1753. [– Gr. καρδιοειδής heart-shaped, f. καρδία heart; see -OID.] *Math.* A curve something like a heart in shape.

‖ **Carditis** (kaɹdəi·tis). 1783. [mod.L., f. Gr. καρδία heart + -ITIS.] *Med.* Inflammation of the muscular substance of the heart.

‖ **Cardo** (kā·ɹdo). Pl. **cardines** (kā·ɹdinīz). 1571. [L., see CARDINAL.] † **1.** *Astrol.* in *pl.* = CARDINAL *points* –1660. † **2.** *fig.* A hinge –1657. **3.** *Conch.* The hinge of a bivalve shell 1755.

Cardoon (kaɹdū·n). 1611. [– Fr. *cardon*, f. *carde* edible part of the artichoke – mod.Pr. *cardo* :– Rom. **carda*, for L. *cardus, carduus* thistle, artichoke; see -OON.] A composite plant (*Cynara cardunculus*), nearly allied to the Artichoke; cultivated for the fleshy stalks of the inner leaves.

‖ **Cardo·phagus.** Pl. **-gi.** [f. Gr. κάρδος thistle; see -PHAGOUS.] A thistle-eater, *i.e.* donkey. THACKERAY.

‖ **Carduus** (kā·ɹdiu,ǒs). ME. [L.; see CARDOON.] Occ. used for *Carduus benedictus*; esp. *attrib.*

Care (kē̆ɹ), *sb.*[1] [OE. *caru* = OS. *kara*, OHG. *chara* grief, lament, ON. *kǫr* (gen. *karar*) bed of sickness, Goth. *kara* :– Gmc. **karō.*] † **1.** Mental suffering –1718. **2.** Burdened state of mind arising from fear, doubt, or concern about anything; also in *pl.* anxieties, solicitudes OE. **3.** Serious mental attention; concern; caution, pains OE. *Hence*, Regard arising from desire or inclination *to* or *for* ME. **4.** Charge; oversight with a view to protection, preservation, or guidance ME. **5.** An object or matter of care 1590.

1. When one is passed another c. we have, Thus woe succeeds a woe HERRICK. **2.** Fretting C., that kills a Cat 1682. **3.** The busy c. of a noble man UDALL. If any c. for what is here Survive in spirits render'd free TENNYSON. **4.** The c. of all the churches 2 *Cor.* 11:28. Nemo, c. of Mr. Krook DICKENS. **5.** Cares of state JOWETT. *Comb.* **c.-worn** *a.*

Care, *sb.*[2] 1849. [Origin unkn.] The Mountain Ash (*local*).

Care (kēᵊɹ), *v.* [OE. *carian* = OS. *karon*, OHG. *charōn, -ēn*, Goth. *karōn* :– Gmc. **karōjan, -ǣjan*; in later uses f. sb.] † **1.** To sorrow –1530. **2.** To feel concern or interest OE.; to take care or thought 1593. **3.** In neg. and condit. constr.: *Not to care* passes to 'not to mind, be indifferent', and hence 'be disposed *to*'. Const. *for* etc. 1489. **4.** To have a regard or liking *for*, be inclined *to* 1530.

2. As for the Asses. . c. not thou for them for they are founde 1 *Sam.* 9:20. The Lorde careth for us *Ps.* 39:17. **3.** I don't c. what people say 1883. *To c. a pin, a button, a straw, a rap*, etc. I don't c. if I go with you for once 1841. **4.** He never cared to give money GOLDSM. People I c. for 1750.

Ca·re-cloth. *Hist.* 1530. [Origin unkn.] A cloth held over (or placed upon) the heads of the bride and bridegroom as they knelt during the marriage-service.

Careen (kărī·n), *sb.* 1591. [– Fr. *carène*, † *carine* – It. *carena*, dial. repr. of L. *carina* keel.] *Naut.* The position of a ship laid over on one side.

On the c.: turned over on one side for repairing, or by stress of weather, etc.

Careen (kărī·n), *v.* 1600. [f. prec.] *Naut.* **1.** *trans.* To turn (a ship) over on one side for cleaning, caulking, or repairing; to clean, caulk, etc. Also *absol.* and *fig.* **2.** *trans.* To cause (a ship) to heel over 1833. **3.** *intr.* To incline to one side or lie over when sailing on a wind (said of a ship) 1763. Hence **Caree·nage,** the expense of careening; a careening-place (cf. *anchorage*).

Career (kărīᵊ·ɹ), *sb.* 1534. [– Fr. *carrière* – It. *carriera* – Pr. *carreira* :– Rom. **carraria* (sc. *via*) carriage-road, road, f. *carrus* CAR.] † **1.** A race-course; the space within the barrier at a tournament. Also *transf.* –1751. † **2.** Of a horse: A short gallop at full speed. Also a charge, encounter. –1764. Also *fig.* **3.** Hence, A (swift) running, course, as of the sun or a star through the heavens. *abstr.* Full speed, impetus. 1534. Also *fig.* **b.** *Hawking.* A flight of the bird 1727. **4.** A person's course or progress through life (or a distinct portion of life); so of a nation, a party, etc. (Now *esp.*) A profession affording opportunities of advancement. 1803.

2. Mortal combat or carreer with Lance MILT. *P.L.* I. 766. **3.** The Sun in his carriere BARROW. *In full c. fig.* The careere of [a man's] humour *Much Ado* II. iii. 250. **4.** A diplomatic c. 1803. A public c. 1815.

Career (kărīᵊ·ɹ), *v.* 1594. [f. prec.] † **1.** To take a short gallop; to charge; to turn this way and that in running (said of a horse) –1672. **2.** *transf.* and *fig.* To move at full speed 1647.

1. How we Tilt and C. 1672. **Caree·ringly** *adv.*

Carefree (kēᵊ·ɹfrī), *a.* 1854. Free from care.

Careful (kēᵊ·ɹfŭl), *a.* [OE. *carful*; see CARE *sb.*, -FUL.] † **1.** Full of grief –1599. **2.** Full of care; anxious, concerned (*arch.*) OE. **3.** Full of care *for*, taking good care *of* OE. **4.** Applying care, attention, or pains to what one has to do; painstaking; circumspect OE. † **5.** On one's guard against, wary –1579. **6.** Of things: Fraught with sorrow or anxiety (*arch.*) ME.; done with care 1651.

1. A c. widow 1470. **2.** Be not c. therefore for the morrovv (Rhem.) *Matt.* 6:34. **3.** My wife more carefull for the latter-borne *Com. Err.* I. i. 79. **4.** A c. and learned antiquary 1845. **5.** C. of new acquaintance STEELE. **6.** A c. throne FORD, drawing 1883. Hence **Ca·reful-ly** *adv.*, **-ness.**

Careless (kēᵊ·ɹlės), *a.* [OE. *carlēas*; see CARE *sb.*, -LESS.] **1.** Free from care or apprehension. (Now *arch.*, *poet.*, or *nonce-wd.*) **2.** Unconcerned; not solicitous, regardless; having no care *of*, *about*, † *to* OE. **3.** Not taking due care, negligent, thoughtless; inaccurate 1579. **4.** Of things: † Uncared for; artless, *négligé* (*arch.*); (now *esp.*) done, caused, or said heedlessly. 1590. Also as quasi-*adv.*

1. They dwelt carelesse *Judg.* 18:7. **2.** Yet a Boy C. of books WORDSW. **3.** C. writers BERKELEY, eyes WORDSW. **4.** A carelesse Trifle *Macb.* I. iv. 11. To frame the c. rhyme BEATTIE. C. work 1888. Hence **Ca·reless-ly** *adv.*, **-ness.**

† **Carene.** *rare.* 1647. [– med.L. *carena* Lent, forty days' fast.] A forty days' fast; an indulgence from such a fast. ? var. † **Carentane.**

Caress (kăre·s), *sb.* 1647. [– Fr. *caresse* – It. *carezza* :– Rom. **caritia*, f. *carus* dear; see -ESS².] An action of endearment, a fondling touch, a blandishment. Also *fig.*

Solve high dispute With conjugal Caresses MILT. *P.L.* VIII. 56. *fig.* The caresses of faction HUME.

Caress (kăre·s), *v.* 1658. [From the sb., or Fr. *caresser.*] To treat affectionately or blandishingly, to touch, stroke, or pat endearingly; to fondle. Also *transf.* and *fig.* *absol.* 1683.

To c. a fawn 1870. *fig.* Its..echoes c. the ear LOWELL. William was thus busy in half caressing, half coercing, his English subjects FREEMAN. Hence **Care·sser.** **Care·ssingly** *adv.* **Care·ssive** *a.*

Care·ssant, *a. rare.* 1861. [– Fr. *caressant*, pres. pple. of *caresser*; see prec., -ANT.] Caressing.

Care Sunday. *Sc.* 1536. [corresp. to G. *kar* in *kārfreitag* (MHG. *karvritac*) Good Friday, G., MHG. *karwoche* Passion week; same word as CARE *sb.*¹] The fifth Sunday in Lent.

Caret (kæ·rėt, kēᵊ·rėt). 1710. [L., 3rd sing. pres. ind. of *carēre* be without, taken to mean 'is lacking'.] A mark (‸) placed in writing below the line to indicate that something (written above or in the margin) has been omitted in that place.

Ca·re-ta:ker. 1858. [f. CARE *sb.* + TAKER.] One put in charge of any thing or person; *esp.* in Ireland, of an 'evicted farm'.

‖ **Carex** (kēᵊ·rėks). Pl. **carices** (-isiz). ME. [L., = sedge.] *Bot.* A large genus, N.O. *Cyperaceæ*, of grassy-looking plants; a sedge.

Carf. *Obs.* or *dial.* [OE. *cyrf* m. (ME. *kyrf, kerfe*) = ON. *kurfr* m. cut-off piece, f. grade-var. of *ceorfen* CARVE; cf. (M)HG. *kerbe* fem. f. *kerben*. Later form infl. by *carve.*] **1.** Cutting, a cut. † **2.** ? The cut part at the end of a piece of wood –1799.

Carf, obs. pa. t. of CARVE *v.*

Carfax, -fox (ka·ɹfæks, -fǭks) [ME. *carfuks* – AFr. *carfuks* (XIV), for **carrefurkes* = OFr. *carrefurc-s* (mod. *carrefour*) :– pop.L. **quadrifurcus*, f. *quadri-* comb. form of *quatuor* four + *furca* FORK.] **1.** A place where four (or more) roads meet. **2.** Hence, the proper name of such a place, *e.g.* at Oxford 1527.

Ca·rfour, carrefour. 1477. [– Fr. *carrefour*; see prec.] = prec. (Now only as Fr.)

‖ **Ca·rga.** 1622. [Sp., see CARGO¹.] A 'load' as a measure of weight.

† **Ca·rgason, -azon.** 1583. [– Sp. *cargazon*, double augm. of *carga*; see prec., CARGO¹.] **1.** A cargo. Also *fig.* –1882. **2.** A bill of lading. [So Fr. *cargaison*.] 1599.

Cargo¹ (kā·ɹgo). Pl. **cargoes.** 1657. [– Sp. *cargo* (also *carga*), corresp. to (O)Fr. *charge* load; see CHARGE *sb.*] The freight or lading of a ship; a shipload. Also *transf.*

A very rich c. DE FOE. A c. of novels 1806.

† **Ca·rgo**². 1602. [app. a perversion or orig. a misprint of contemp. and synon. CATSO, both first in B. Jonson. Cf. GADSO.] **1.** A contemptuous term for a person. B. JONS. **2.** An exclam. –1615.

Ca·rgoose. 1677. [app. f. CARR²; cf. *carr swallow.*] The Crested Grebe.

† **Cargued, carged,** *a.* 1580. [Origin unkn.] *Naut.* In *High-cargued* or *-carged*, var. *high-charged, high-carved*, of unkn. meaning –1591.

Carib (kæ·rib). *Pl.* (XVI) **caribeis, caribes, cariues.** 1555. [– native *caribe*, understood by Oviedo to mean 'brave and daring'. See CANNIBAL.] One of the native race which occupied the southern islands of the West Indies at their discovery: in early use often connoting *cannibal*. Hence **Ca·ribal** *a.* (after *cannibal*). **Caribbe·an** *a.* and *sb.* used of certain of the West Indian islands, and of the sea between them and the mainland. var. **Caribee·.**

Caribou, -boo (kæribū·). 1774. [– Canadian Fr. *caribou*, presumably from a N. Amer. Indian dialect.] The North-American Reindeer.

Caricature (kæ·rikătiūᵊ:ɹ), *sb.* 1748. [– Fr. *caricature* – It. *caricatura*, f. *caricare* load, burden, exaggerate; see CHARGE *v.*] **1.** In *Art.* Grotesque or ludicrous representation by exaggeration of parts, as in a portrait, etc. Also *transf.* **2.** An exaggerated or debased likeness, or copy, naturally or unintentionally ludicrous 1767. Also *attrib.*

2. A c. of French cookery W. IRVING. The monkey, the c. of our species SMILES.

Caricature (see prec.), *v.* 1749. [f. the sb. Cf. Fr. *caricaturer.*] *trans.* To represent in caricature; to make a grotesque likeness of 1762. *transf.* and *fig.* To burlesque 1749.

He could draw an ill face or c. a good one LYTTELTON. Hence **Ca:ricatu·rish** *a.* **Ca:ricatu·rist.**

Carices, pl. of CAREX.

Caricous (kæ·rikəs), *a.* [f. L. *carica* kind of dry fig + -OUS.] Resembling a fig, as *c. tumour.*

Caries (kēᵊ·ri,īz). 1634. [L.] **a.** *Pathol.* Decay of the bones or teeth. **b.** *Bot.* Decay of vegetable tissue.

‖ **Carillon** (ka·rilʸoṅ, -iˡyoṅ). 1803. [– Fr. *carillon*, alt. of OFr. *car(e)ignon, quarregnon* :– Rom. **quatrinio, -ōn-*, peal of four bells.] **1.** A set of bells so hung and arranged as to be played upon either by hand or by machinery 1836. **2.** A melody played on the bells 1803. **3.** An instrument imitating a peal of bells 1819. Hence ‖ **Carilloneu·r.** [Fr.]

‖ **Carina** (kărəi·nă). 1704. [L., = keel.] *Zool.* and *Bot.* A name of structures of the form of a keel; *esp.* the two petals forming the base of a papilionaceous corolla; also, the median ridge on the sternum of birds. Hence **Cari·nal** *a.* pertaining to the c.

‖ **Carinaria** (kærinēᵊ·riă). 1847. [mod.L. *carinaria*, f. *carina* keel, + *-aria* as in *fritillaria*; cf. -ARY¹ 3.] *Zool.* A genus of Heteropodous Molluscs, having a delicate shell of glassy translucency which protects the heart and liver.

Carinate (kæ·rinět), *a.* 1781. [– L. *carinatus* keel-shaped; see CARINA, -ATE², and next.] *Zool.* and *Bot.* Furnished with a CARINA or ridge; keeled.

Carinate (kæ·rineˡt), *v.* 1698. [– *carinat-*, pa. ppl. stem of L. *carinare* supply with a shell; see CARINA, -ATE³.] To furnish with a carina, keel, or central ridge. Hence **Ca·rinated** *ppl. a.* = prec. **Carina·tion,** a keel-like formation.

Cariosity (kæri,ǫ·sĭti). 1638. [f. as next + -ITY.] *Pathol.* A carious condition, or formation.

Carious (kēᵊ·riəs), *a.* 1530. [– L. *cariosus*, f. CARIES; see -OUS. Cf. Fr. *carieux.*] *Pathol.* Of bones, teeth, etc.: affected with caries. Also *transf.* Hence **Cariousness.**

† **Ca·rity.** 1530. [– L. *caritas*, f. *carus* dear; see -ITY.] Dearness –1656.

Cark (kāɹk), *sb. Obs.* or *arch.* ME. [– AFr. *karke*, repr. northern var. of OFr. *carche, charche*, f. *carchier, charchier* :– Rom. **carcare*, for **carricare* CHARGE *v.*] † **1.** (?) A load (of 3 or 4 cwt.) –1550. † **2.** Charge, responsibility –1580. **3.** A burden of anxiety; anxious solicitude, labour, or toil. (Usu. w. *care.*) ME. † **4.** Care, pains –1603.

3. He woundeth himselfe with his greedy carke 1639.

Cark (kāɹk), *v. Obs.* or *arch.* [– ONFr. *carkier* = OFr. *carchier, charchier*; see prec.] † **1.** *trans.* To burden; *also*, to charge. ME. only. **2.** To burden *with care*; to harass, trouble (*arch.*) ME. **3.** *intr.* To be anxious, fret oneself; to labour anxiously (*arch.*) ME. † **4.** To take thought –1603.

2. Thee nor carketh care nor slander TENNYSON. **3.** A covetous man..carking about his bags BARROW.

Carl, carle (kāɹl), *sb.*¹ OE. [– ON. *karl* man, male, freeman = OHG. *kar(a)l, charlo* :– Gmc. **karlaz*, **karlon*; see CHURL.] **1.** A man of the common people, particularly a husbandman; † a villain. **2.** Hence, a base fellow, a churl ME. *Sc.* A niggard 1542. **3.** = Fellow. *Sc.* 1550. **4.** [By a popular error.] The female or seed-bearing hemp plant; also called *Carl hemp* 1523. Also *attrib.*

1. A stout carl for the nones CHAUCER. **2.** A cross-grained carle 1882. Hence **Ca·rlish** *a.*; **-ness.**

Carl, *sb.*² *dial.* 1688. [cf. CARL *v.*²] **1.** = CARLING². 1875. **2. Carl Sunday** = Carling or Care Sunday.

Carl, *v.*¹ 1602. [perh. f. CARL *sb.*¹] *intr.* (?) To behave like a carl; to snarl. Still *dial.*

Carl, *v.*² *dial.* 1611. [perh. back-formation f. CARLING², taken as a ppl. form.] To parch (peas); to bristle.

† **Ca·rlin.** Also **carline.** 1705. [–(O)Fr. *carlin* – It. *carlino*, f. *Carlo* King of Naples.] A silver coin current in Naples and Sicily, worth four-pence English, or, later, two-pence –1818.

Carline¹, **-ing** (kā·ɹlin). [ME. *kerling* – ON. *kerling*, fem. of *karl* CARL *sb.*¹ (*-ing* = -EN¹).] A woman, *esp.* an old one; particularly a witch.

Carline² (kā·ɹlin). 1578. [– Fr. *carline* = Sp., It. *carlina*, med.L. *carlina*, perh. alt. of *cardina* (f. L. *cardo* thistle) by assoc. with *Carolus* Magnus (Charlemagne) to whom it was revealed as a remedy for pestilence.] A genus of Composite plants, allied to the thistles, whence called Carline Thistle.

Carling¹, **carline** (kā·ɹliŋ, -lin). 1611. [– ON. *kerling*, CARLINE¹.] **1.** *Naut.* One of the pieces of timber about 5 inches square in section, lying fore and aft under the deck of a ship, with their ends let into the beams. **2. Carling-knee**: a piece of timber lying transversely from the ship's side to the hatchway, serving to support the deck between the two 1626.

Carling² (kā·ɹliŋ). 1562. [perh. f. *care* in CARE SUNDAY.] Peas parched, or otherwise prepared, for eating on C. or Care Sunday. *Carling Sunday*: = CARE SUNDAY.

Carlism (kā·ɹliz'm). 1830. [– Fr. *carlisme* – Sp. *carlismo*, f. name of Don *Carlos*, second son of Carlos IV, regarded as the legitimate successor of Fernando VII (d. 1833); see -ISM.] Attachment to Don Carlos, second son of Charles IV of Spain, and his heirs; Spanish legitimism. So **Carlist** *sb.* and *a.*

Carlock (kā·ɹlǫk). 1768. [– Russ. *karlúk* isinglass; cf. Fr. *carlock.*] Isinglass from the bladder of the sturgeon, imported from Russia. (Dicts.)

† **Ca·rlot.** [f. CARL *sb.*¹ + -OT¹.] A churl, peasant. *A.Y.L.* III. v. 108.

Carlovingian (kāɹlovi·ndʒiăn), *a.* 1781. [– Fr. *carlovingien*, f. *Karl* Charles, after *mérovingien* MEROVINGIAN; largely superseded by *Carolingian.*] Belonging to the dynasty of kings founded by Carl the Great (Charlemagne).

Carlylism (kaɹləi·liz'm). 1841. [f. Thomas *Carlyle* + -ISM.] The literary manner or teachings of Carlyle; a mannerism of Carlyle.

So **Carly·lean** *a.* and *sb.* **Carly·lese,** the style of Carlyle.

‖ **Carmagnole** (karmanʸo·l). 1796. [Fr., orig. jacket which became popular during the Revolution in France, prob. from name of *Carmagnola* in Piedmont.] **1.** A popular song and dance of the time of the French Revolution 1827. **2.** A nickname for a French soldier of that time; applied by Burns to Satan 1796. **3.** A bombastic report from the French revolutionary army 1860.

2. That curst c., auld Satan BURNS.

Carman¹ (kā·ɹmæ̆n). 1580. [f. CAR *sb.*] A man who drives a car; a carter, carrier.

† **Ca·rman**². OE. [– ON. *karmann*, var. of *karlmann*; see CARL *sb.*¹] A man, an adult male –ME.

Carmelite (kā·ɹmĕləit), *sb.* and *a.* 1500. [– Fr. *carmélite* or med.L. *carmelita*; cf. late L. *Carmelites* inhabitant of Mount *Carmel*.] **1.** A member of an order of mendicant friars founded on Mount Carmel in the 12th century; a *White Friar*. Also as *adj.* **2.** A fine woollen stuff; perh. = Fr. *carmeline* 'wool of the vicuña' (Littré) 1828. vars. † **Carme,** † **Ca·rmelin,** † **Ca·rmelitan.** Hence **Ca·rmeli:tess,** a female C.

† **Ca·rminate,** *v.* 1601. [– *carminat-*, pa. ppl. stem of L. *carminare* (cf. late L. *carmen, -min-* card for wool); see -ATE³.] Of medicines: To expel (wind) from the stomach or bowels –1655.

Carminative (kā·ɹmineⁱtiv). 1655. [–(O)Fr. *carminatif, -ive,* or med.L. *carminat-*, pa. ppl. stem of *carminare* heal by incantation; see CHARM, -ATIVE.] *adj.* Of medicines, etc.: Having the quality of expelling wind; *orig.*, of making 'grosse humors fine and thin' (Florio). *sb.* [sc. *medicine* or *agent.*] 1671.

Carmine (kā·ɹmin). 1712. [– (O)Fr. *carmin* or med.L. *carminium*, perh. conflation of *carmesinum* (see CRIMSON, KERMES, ALKERMES) and *minium* cinnobar.] **1.** A beautiful red or crimson pigment obtained from cochineal. *Chem.* = *Carminic acid.* **2.** *transf.* As the name of a colour 1799. Also as *adj.* Hence **Carmi·nic** (*Chem.*), in *C. acid*: the colouring matter of cochineal.

† **Carmot.** 1851. [Origin unkn.] *Alch.* The substance of which the philosopher's stone was supposed to consist. (Dicts.)

‖ **Carnac** (kā·ɹnæk). *rare.* 1704. [– Fr. *cornac*, Pg. *cornaca*, perh. – Sinhalese **kūrawanayaka* elephant tamer; cf. *cournakeas*, reported by a Du. traveller XVII.] The driver of an elephant, a mahout.

Carnage (kā·ɹnĕdʒ). 1600. [– Fr. *carnage* – It. *carnaggio* (cf. Pr. *carnatge* heap of slain) :– med.L. *carnaticum*, f. L. *caro, carn-* flesh; see -AGE.] **1.** Carcases collectively; *esp.* of men slain in battle. ? *Obs.* 1667. **2.** The slaughter of a great number, *esp.* of men; butchery, massacre 1600. Also personified.

1. The future c. of the fight GAY. **2.** Such as delight only in c. and bloudshed HOLLAND. Yea, c. is Thy daughter WORDSW.

† **Carnal,** *sb.* 1528. Perversion of *cardinal* –1598.

Carnal (kā·ɹnăl), *a.* ME. [– Chr.L. *carnalis* (Tertullian), f. *caro, carn-* flesh + *-alis* -AL¹.] † **1.** Bodily, corporeal –1847; related 'according to the flesh' –1598. **2.** Pertaining to the body; fleshly, sensual; sexual ME. **3.** Not spiritual (*arch.*) 1483. † **4.** Carnivorous; *fig.* bloody SHAKS. Also in *comb.*

1. C. interment SIR T. BROWNE. His c. mother 1509. **2.** Blynded with sensualite & carnall pleasure 1526. C. desire MILT. **3.** To minister vnto them in carnall things *Rom.* 15:27. Doubt And c. fear MILT. *P.L.* XI. 212. Hence † **Ca·rnal** *v.* (*rare*) to make c.; *intr.* to have c. intercourse *with*. **Ca·rnalism,** the practice of what is c. (*rare*). † **Ca·rnalist,** a fleshly-minded man; var. † **Ca·rnalite. Ca·rnally** *adv.* **Ca·rnalness.**

Carnality (kaɹnæ·lĭti). ME. [– Chr.L. *carnalitas* (Augustine); see prec., -ITY.] **1.** Fleshiness. **2.** Sensuality; carnal intercourse ME. **3.** Unspirituality; *concr.* a carnal thing, etc. 1483.

2. To give up oneself to lewd c. BAXTER. The carnalitie of the lawe UDALL.

Carnalize (kā·ɹnăləiz), *v.* 1685. [f. CARNAL *a.* + -IZE.] To make carnal; to rob of spirituality.

Ca·rnallite. 1876. [f. von *Carnall*, a German mining engineer + -ITE¹ 2 b.] *Min.* A hydrous chloride of potassium and magnesium, occurring in the salt mines in Prussia and Persia.

† **Carnary** (kā·ɹnări). 1538. [– med.L. *carnarium* charnel-house (in cl.L. larder. meat-safe), subst. use of L. *carnarius* pertaining to flesh, f. *caro, carn-* flesh; see -ARY¹.] A charnel-house.

Carnassial (kaɹnæ·siăl), *a.* (*sb.*) 1849. [f. Fr. *carnassier* carnivorous (– Pr. *carnasier*) + -AL¹.] *Anat. adj.* Relating to flesh eating: used of certain teeth. *sb.* A carnassial tooth.

† **Carna·tion**¹. ME. [– OFr. *carnacion, -tion* app. aphetic f. *incarnation*.] = Incarnation –1710.

Carnation² (kaɹnēⁱ·ʃən). 1535. [– Fr. *carnation* – It. *carnagione* – late L. *carnatio, -ōn-* fleshiness, corpulence, f. *caro, carn-* flesh; see -ATION.]

A. *sb.* **1.** † Flesh-colour; a light rosy pink, or occas. crimson. **2.** *pl.* 'Flesh tints' in a painting 1704. **3.** A variety of cherry 1664.

1. Her complexion of the most delicate c. LYTTON. Hence **Carna·tioned** *a.* † flesh-coloured; reddened.

B. *adj.* [The sb. used attrib.] Flesh-coloured; rose-pink 1565.

Carnation³ (kaɹnēⁱ·ʃən). 1538. [In XVI also *coronation incarnation*; the reason for these three forms is unexplained.] *Bot.* Name for the cultivated varieties of the Clove-pink (*Dianthus caryophyllus*).

Carnations, and streak'd Gilly-vors *Wint. T.* IV. iv. 82.

† **Ca·rnel.** ME. only. [– OFr. *carnel, quernel* (mod. *créneau*); see CRENEL.] Battlement, embrasure. Hence † **Carneled** *a.*

Carnelian (kaɹnī·liăn). 1695. [var. of CORNELIAN¹, after L. *caro, carn-* flesh.] CORNELIAN; a flesh-coloured, deep red, or reddish-white variety of Chalcedony. var. † **Ca·rneol.**

Carneous (kā·ɹnĭəs), *a.* 1578. [f. late L. *carneus* of flesh, carnal (f. L. *caro, carn-* flesh) + -OUS.] **1.** Consisting of flesh, fleshy. † **2.** Flesh-coloured, palə red 1673.

Carney, *sb.* ? *Obs.* 1678. [Origin unkn.] A disease in horses in which the mouth becomes furred so that they cannot eat.

‖ **Carnifex** (kā·ɹnifeks). Now *Hist.* 1521. [L.; in ancient L. 'executioner', but in med. L. often 'butcher'.] An executioner. Hence **Carnifi·cial** *a.* belonging to an executioner, or to a butcher.

Carnification (kā:ɹnifikēⁱ·ʃən). 1734. [f. CARNIFY; see -FICATION; cf. Fr. *carnification* (XVIII).] † **1.** The formation of flesh. **2.** The act or process of conversion into flesh 1758.

2. *C. of the lung* 1881. The miracle of c. 1827.

Carnify (kā·ɹnifəi), *v.* 1639. [f. L. *caro, carn-* flesh + -FY.] **1.** To convert into flesh; (*intr.*) to become like flesh 1643. † **2.** To generate flesh –1829.

Carnival (kā·ɹnivăl). 1549. [– It. *carne-, carnovale* (whence Fr. *carnaval*), with dial. vars. *carnelevare, karlevá* – med.L. *carnelevamen, -levarium* Shrovetide, f. L. *caro, carn-* flesh + *levare* lighten, raise; lit. 'cessation of flesh-eating'.] **1.** The week (*orig.* the day) before Lent, devoted in Italy and other Roman Catholic countries to revelry and riotous amusement, Shrove-tide; the festivity of this season. **2.** *fig.* Any season or course of feasting or riotous revelry 1598.

1. *attrib.* In their Carnoual time (which we call shroftide) 1549. BYRON *Beppo* vi. **2.** A c. of intellect without faith LOWELL. Hence **Ca:rnivale·sque** *a.* of the style of the c.

‖ **Carnivora** (kaɹni·vŏră), *sb. pl.* 1830. [mod.L. *carnivora* (sc. *animalia*); see CARNIVOROUS.] *Zool.* A large order of flesh-eating Mammalia, including the feline, canine, and ursine families. (For a sing., see CARNIVORE.) Also, occ. applied to other animals, as beetles, etc.

Ca:rnivora·city. [Humorous extension of *carnivorous* after *voracity*.] Appetite for flesh. POPE.

Carnivore (kā·ɹnivōəɹ). 1854. [– Fr. *carnivore* – L. *carnivorus*; see next.] One of the CARNIVORA. Also, a carnivorous plant.

Carnivorous (kaɹni·vŏrəs), *a.* 1646. [f. L. *carnivorus*, f. *caro, carn-* flesh; see -VOROUS.] Feeding on flesh; applied: (*Zool.*) to animals which naturally prey on other animals (*esp.* to the CARNIVORA); (*Bot.*) to plants which absorb animal substances as food; and (*Med.*) to caustics as destructive of flesh.

Carno·se, *a.* 1562. [– L. *carnosus* (f. *caro, carn-* flesh) see -OSE¹.] = CARNOUS.

Carnosity (kaɹnǫ·sĭti). 1533. [–(O)Fr. *carnosité* or med.L. *carnositas*, f. L. *carnosus*; see prec., -ITY.] † **1.** Fleshiness; pulpiness; flesh or pulp –1657. **2.** A morbid fleshy growth, a caruncle 1559. Also † *fig.*

1. The c. of an olive HOLLAND, of an apple 1657. **2.** A c. in the bladder 1618. *fig.* [Consciences] overgrown with a c. SPELMAN.

Carnoso- (kaɹnōᵘ·so), comb. form of L. *carnosus*, = 'carnose and..'.

Carnous (kā·ɹnəs), *a.* 1577. [– L. *carnosus*; see CARNOSE, -OUS.] **1.** Consisting of or abounding in flesh; fleshy. **2.** Of fruits, roots, etc.: Pulpy, fleshy 1601.

1. A fair and c. state of Body SIR T. BROWNE.

Carny, carney (kā·ɹni), *v. dial.* and *colloq.* 1811. [Origin unkn.] To act in a wheedling or coaxing manner. Also *trans.*

Carob (kæ·rǫ̆b). 1548. [– Fr. †*car(r)obe* (mod. *caroube*), superseding OFr. *carouge* :– med.L. *carrubia, -ium* – Arab. *ḵarrūba*.] The fruit of an evergreen leguminous tree (*Ceratonia siliqua*), Carob-tree, a native of the Levant: a long flat horn-like pod containing numerous hard seeds embedded in pulp. Also called *carob-bean, -pod.* Also, the tree 1548.

Supposed to be the husks of *Luke* 15:16; and the locusts eaten by the Baptist, whence called *Locust-pods* and *St. John's Bread.*

Caro·che, *sb. arch.* 1591. [– Fr. †*carroche* (XVI) – It. *carroccio, -ia,* augm. of *carro* chariot; see CAR, CAROSSE.] The 17th-c. name of a coach representing the modern carriage for town use. Now *Hist.* Hence † **Caro·che** *v.* to ride or convey in a c. **Caro·ched** *ppl. a.* seated in a c.

Caroigne, obs. f. CARRION.

Carol (kæ·rəl), *sb.* ME. [– OFr. *carole* (surviving dial. in senses '(round) dance', 'dance song', 'merrymaking') = Pr. *carola, corola* (whence It. *carola*), of doubtful origin.] **1.** A ring-dance with song. Hence **2.** A song; now usually one of a joyous strain ME. **3.** A song or hymn of joy; *esp.* A Christmas *carol* 1502. † **4.** A ring, *e.g.* of standing stones –1470. † **5.** An enclosure or study in a cloister (? hence *c.-window*) –1810.

1. Faire is carole of maide gent ME. **2.** The whiles the maydens doe theyr carroll sing SPENSER. The fife-like c. of the lark CAMPBELL. **3.** Holly carolles SURREY. MILT. *P.L.* XII. 367.

Carol (kæ·rŏl, -əl), *v.* ME. [– OFr. *caroler*; see prec.] † **1.** *intr.* To dance in a ring and sing –1530. Hence **2.** To sing; now usu.: To sing a lively or joyous song ME. **3.** *trans.* To sing; to celebrate in song 1575.

2. And c. lowd of love, and loves delight P. FLETCHER. Merrily merrily c. the gales TENNYSON. **3.** To carroll out this roundelay GREENE. The shepherds..C. her goodness loud in rustic lays MILT. *Comus* 849. Hence **Ca·roler, -oller.** † **Ca·rolet,** a little c.

‖ **Carolin** (kæ·rŏlin). 1821. [– G. *Karolin*, f. med.L. *Carolus* Charles.] A gold coin formerly current in Bavaria and Würtemberg, and worth about 20*s.* sterling.

Carolina (kærŏləi·nă). 1734. The name (after Charles II) of a N. American colony; hence used in **Carolina Pink,** *Spigelia marilandica,* also called Indian Pink Hence **Caroli·nian** *a.* belonging to North or South C.

Ca·roline, *sb.* 1555. [subst. use of the adj. (see next). Cf. CARLIN, CAROLIN, CAROLUS.] A name of various coins.

Caroline (kæ·rŏləin), *a.* 1652. [– med. or mod.L. *Carolinus*, f. med.L. *Carolus* Charles; see -INE¹.] Of or pertaining to Charles; *e.g.* to Charles the Great, or to Charles I and II of England and their period.

Caroli·ngian, *a.* [Re-formation of CARLOVINGIAN on *Carolus* Charles. Cf. Fr. *carolingien*.] = CARLOVINGIAN.

Caroli·tic, *a. Arch.* Erron. f. COROLLITIC.

Carolus (kæ·rŏlŏs). 1687. [f. *Carolus*, Latinized form of Karl, Charles.] A gold piece struck in the reign of Charles I; worth orig. 20*s.*, later 23*s.*

Carom, carrom (kæ·rəm). 1779. [Shortening of CARAMBOLE.] = CANNON *sb.*¹ 6.

Caromel, var. of CARAMEL.

† **Caroo·n, carroo·n, caroo·me.** 1720. [Origin unkn.] 'A licence by the Lord Mayor of London to keep a cart' (Wharton) –1832.

† **Caro·sse.** 1598. [– Fr. *carosse* (mod. *carrosse*) – It. *carrozza*, augm. of *carro* chariot, etc.; cf. CAROCHE.] A CAROCHE –1657.

‖ **Carotee·l, -e·l.** 1704. [perh. – Arab. *ḳirṭāl* – Gr. κάρταλλος kind of basket.] A tierce or cask for dried fruit, etc., averaging about 7 cwt.

Carotic (kărǫ·tik), *a.* 1656. [– Gr. καρωτικός stupefying; see next, -IC. Cf. Fr. *carotique.*] *Phys.* **1.** Having power to stupefy; of the nature of or pertaining to stupor or carus 1684. **2.** = CAROTID (*rare*).

1. C. sleep 1881. **2.** C. Arteries 1656, blood 1843.

Carotid (kărǫ·tid). 1667. [– Fr. *carotide* or mod.L. *carotides* – Gr. καρωτίδες, pl. of καρωτίς, f. καροῦν stupefy; so named because compression of these arteries produces stupor (Galen).]

A. *adj.* Epithet of the two great arteries of the neck, which supply blood to the head. **b.** Pertaining to or adjoining the carotid arteries 1842. var. † **Caro·tidal, Caroti·dian.**

B. *sb.* A carotid artery 1741.

Carou·ba. A var. of CAROB (tree).

Carousal (kărau·zăl). 1765. [f. CAROUSE *v.* + -AL 2.] A fit of carousing, a carouse; a drunken revel.

The swains were preparing for a c. STERNE.

† **Carou·se,** *adv.* 1567. [In phr. *drink* or *quaff carouse* (XVI) repr. G. *garaus trinken* drink completely (lit. 'quite out'; cf. ALL OUT *adv.*).] (*To drink, quaff,* etc.) to the bottom, a full bumper –1667.

Carouse (kărau·z), *sb.* 1559. [The prec. adv. taken for obj. of the vb.] † **1.** The act or fashion of 'drinking carouse' –1611. † **2.** A full bumper, a toast –1813. **3.** A drinking bout 1690.

2. Quaffe Carowses to our Mistresse health *Tam. Shr.* I. ii. 277. **3.** The early feast and late c. POPE.

Carouse (kărau·z), *v.* 1567. [f. CAROUSE *adv.*] *intr.* To drink 'all out', drink freely and often; to drink a bumper *to.* Also † *trans.*

Some..garoused of his wine till they were reasonable pleasant RALEGH. Hence **Carou·ser.**

Carousel (karuze·l). Also **carrousel.** 1650. [– Fr. *carrousel* – It. *carosello, ga-.*] A tournament in which knights, in companies, variously dressed, engaged in plays, exercises, chariot races, etc.

¶By many erron. identified with *carousal.*

Carp (kāɹp), *sb.* ME. [– (O)Fr. *carpe* – Pr. *carpa*, or the common source, late L. *carpa* (Cassiodorus) name of a fish of the Danube.] **1.** A freshwater fish, *Cyprinus carpio*, the type of the family *Cyprinidæ*; commonly bred in ponds. **2.** Applied to other species of the genus, as the Gold and Silver Fish, etc. 1786.

1. The C...a stately, a good, and a very subtle fish WALTON.

Carp (kāɹp), *v.* ME. [Senses 1–3 – ON. *karpa* brag; later senses (4–5) either infl. by, or a new formation on, L. *carpere* pluck, fig. slander, calumniate.] † **1.** To speak (*trans.* and *intr.*) –1605. † **2.** *intr.* To sing or recite –1802. † **3.** To prate, chatter –1557. **4.** *spec.* To talk querulously, censoriously, or captiously; to find fault, cavil. (The current sense.) 1548. Also with *at.* † **5.** To take exception to –1678. ¶Assoc. w. CARK.

4. The king..carpeth upon the marriage DIGGES. To c. at a great writer M. ARNOLD. Hence **Ca·rper.**

Carpal (kā·ɹpăl), *a.* 1743. [f. CARPUS + -AL¹.] *Anat.* Of or pertaining to the carpus or wrist. *sb. pl.* = Carpal bones 1855.

Carpel (kā·ɹpĕl). 1835. [– Fr. *carpelle* or mod.L. *carpellum* (Dunal, 1817), f. Gr. καρπός fruit; see -EL.] *Bot.* One of the cells of a compound pistil or fruit; or the single cell of a simple pistil or fruit. Hence **Ca·rpellary** *a.* pertaining to, or of the nature of, a c. var. **Ca·rpid.**

Carpent (kā·ɹpĕnt), *v. rare.* 1623. [– med. L. *carpentare*; see next.] To make as a carpenter; also *fig.* Hence † **Ca·rpentage,** carpentry.

Carpenter (ka·ɹpĕntəɹ), *sb.* ME. [– AFr. *carpenter*, OFr. *carpentier*, (also mod.) *charpentier* :– late L. *carpentarius* (sc. *artifex*) carriage-maker, f. L. *carpentum* two-wheeled carriage, of Gaulish origin (cf. *carrus* CAR); see -ER².] **1.** 'An artificer in wood' (J.); one who does the framework of houses, ships, etc., as opp. to a joiner, cabinet-maker, etc. **2.** = *c.-ant, -bee*, etc. 1883.

1. Is not this the c., the sonne of Mary *Mark* 6:3. *Comb.*, etc.: **c.-ant,** a species of tree-ant which bores into the trunk of a tree; **-bee,** a genus of solitary bees, *Xylocopa*, the females of which excavate cells in decaying wood in which to deposit their eggs; **carpenter's measure,** tonnage as measured by the cubic foot. Hence **Ca·rpentership,** the art of a c.

Ca·rpenter, *v.* 1815. [f. prec.] To do carpenter's work; to make by carpentry; to put together mechanically.

Carpentry (kā·ɹpĕntri). ME. [– AFr. *carpentrie* = (O)Fr. *charpenterie*, f. *charpentier* (cf. late L. *carpentaria* (sc. *fabrica*) carriage-maker's work-shop; see prec., -RY.] **1.** The trade or art of cutting, working, and joining timber into structures. **2.** Timberwork constructed by the carpenter; *e.g.* the pieces of a roof, floor, centre, etc. 1555. Also *attrib.*

Carpet (kā·ɹpėt), *sb.* [– OFr. *carpite* or med.L. *carpita* – It. † *carpita* woollen counterpane, corresp. to Fr. *charpie* lint, subst. use of pa. pple. of *charpir* :– Rom. **carpire*, for L. *carpere* pluck, pull to pieces.] † **1.** A thick fabric, commonly of wool, used to cover tables, beds, etc.; a table-cloth –1728. **2.** A similar fabric, generally worked in a pattern of divers colours, used to spread on a floor or the ground, or (now usually) to cover a floor or stair. Also the material. ME. **3.** *fig.* A covering resembling a carpet in smoothness, softness, or colouring 1593. **4.** = *c.-moth* 1856.

1. A C. for the Communion Table 1702. *On the c.*: under consideration. **2.** No Persian carpets spread th' imperial way DRYDEN. † *Knight of the c.*: one dubbed in time of peace upon the c., as opp. to one dubbed in the field; also = CARPET-KNIGHT. **3.** Vpon the Grassie C. of this Plaine *Rich. II.* III. iii. 50.

Comb., etc. **c.-dance,** an informal dance for which the c. is not taken up; **-moth,** a name for species of Geometer moths, from their variegated colouring; **-snake,** a large Australian snake (*Morelia variegata*); **-sweeper,** a mechanical apparatus for sweeping a carpet. Also CARPET-KNIGHT (q.v.), and the like, in which *carpet* implies haunting the boudoir, dilettantism, etc. Hence **Ca·rpetless** *a.*

Carpet (kā·ɹpėt), *v.* 1626. [f. the sb.] **1.** To cover or spread with or as with a carpet. **2.** *colloq.* To call into a room to be reprimanded 1840.

1. A fair Chamber..carpeted under Foot BACON. **2.** They had done nothing! Why were they carpeted? 1840.

Ca·rpet-ba·g. 1844. A travelling bag, properly one made of carpet. Also *attrib.*

Ca·rpet-bagger. orig. *U.S. slang.* 1868. [f. prec. + -ER¹.] A scornful appellation for Northerners who went south after the American Civil War of 1861–5, seeking private gain or political advancement; a political candidate in a locality with which he is unconnected. Hence **-bagging.**

Carpeting (kā·ɹpėtiŋ), *sb.* 1806. [f. CARPET *sb.* or *v.* + -ING¹.] **1.** The action of covering (as) with carpet. **2.** Material for carpets 1806. Also *transf.*

Ca·rpet-kni:ght. 1576. Orig. perh. = *Knight of the carpet*; but usually a contemptuous term for a stay-at-home soldier.

Brave C. Knights in Cupid's fights D'URFEY.

Carpholite (ka·ɹfŏləit). 1844. [– G. *karpholith* (Werner 1819), f. Gr. κάρφος straw; see -LITE.] *Min.* A hydrous silicate of alumina and manganese, occurring in silky fibres of a straw-yellow colour.

Carphology (kaɹfǫ·lŏdʒi). 1851. [– Gr. καρφολογία (Galen), f. κάρφος straw, etc., + λέγειν collect.] *Med.* The movements of delirious patients, as if searching for imaginary objects, or picking the bed-clothes; floccilation.

Carpo-¹, comb. f. Gr. καρπός CARPUS, wrist.

Carpo-², comb. f. Gr. καρπός fruit, as in: **Ca·rpolite, -lithe** [Gr. λίθος], a fossil fruit. **Carpo·logy** [Gr. -λογια], the part of botany which is concerned with the study of fruits; hence **Carpolo·gical** *a.*, **-lo·gically** *adv.*, **-logist.** **Carpo·phagous** [Gr. -φαγος] *a.*, (*Zool.*) fruit-eating. **Ca·rpophore** [Gr. -φορος], (*Bot.*) a prolongation of the axis of a flower, raising the pistil above the stamens, as in *Geraniaceæ* and *Umbelliferæ.* **Ca·rpophyll** [Gr. φύλλον], (*Bot.*) the modified leaf which by its folding produces a carpel. **Ca·rpospore** [Gr. σπόρος], (*Bot.*) in Thallophytes, the spore formed in a sporocarp; hence **Carpospo·rous** *a.*, applied to certain Algae.

Carpocra·tian. 1587. [See -IAN.] A follower of Carpocrates of Alexandria (A.D. 120), who asserted the mortality of Christ's body and the creation of the world by angels.

‖ **Carpus** (kā·ɹpŏs). 1679. [mod.L. – Gr. καρπός wrist.] *Anat.* The part of the skeleton which unites the hand to the fore-arm, consisting in the higher vertebrates of eight small bones. In man it forms the *wrist*; in the horse, the *knee.*

Carr¹ (kāɹ). *dial.* OE. [ONorthumb. *carr* rock.] A rock; now *esp.* used of insulated rocks off the Northumbrian and Scottish coasts.

Carr², **car** (kāɹ). *local.* ME. [– ON.; cf. OIcel. *kjarr-mýrr* marsh-ground covered with brush-wood, Da. *kær, kjær* pool, pond, Sw. *kær* fen, morass, marsh, moor, Norw. *kjær, kjerr* pool, marsh.] **1.** A pool; a fen; now usu., wet boggy ground; a meadow recovered from the bog. **2.** A fenny copse ME. Also *attrib.*

Carrack, carack (kæ·răk). Now *Hist.* ME. [– (O)Fr. *caraque*, prob. (like It. *caracca*) – Sp. *carraca* – Arab. *ḳarāķir.*] A large ship of burden, also fitted for warfare, formerly used by the Portuguese in trading with the East Indies; a galleon.

Here a vast Carrack flies, while none pursue DE FOE.

Carrageen, -gheen (kæ·răgīn). 1834. [f. *Carragheen* in Ireland.] A kind of seaweed (*Chrondus crispus*), also called *Irish moss*, of a cartilaginous texture and a purplish colour, becoming yellowish-white when dried. It yields a jelly, used for food and in medicine.

Carrat, Carraway; see CARAT, CARAWAY.

Carrefour; see CARFOUR.

Carrell, obs. f. CAROL.

Carriage (kæ·ridʒ). ME. [– ONFr. *cariage*, f. *carier* CARRY *v.*; see -AGE.]

I. 1. The action of carrying; conveyance (*esp.* of merchandise). † **2.** A toll on transport –1771. † **3.** An obsolete feudal service. Cf. AVERAGE *sb.*¹ –1835. **4.** The cost of carrying 1753. † **5.** Power or capacity for carrying –1740. **6.** Action of carrying out; conduct, administration 1601. **7.** The carrying (of a motion) 1879.

1. Mules or horses for c. DE FOE. **5.** *L.L.L.* I. ii. 74. **6.** C. of affaires 1601, of an Enterprise 1652, a sale 1876, an order 1884.

II. 1. Manner of carrying (one's body, or any part of it, oneself); mien; deportment; behaviour 1590. **2.** Habitual conduct (Referring to *morals.*) 1588. † **3.** Manner of conducting –1696.

1. A stately c. 1653. A graceful c. of the head DE QUINCEY. *Com. Err.* III. ii. 14. **3.** The present c. of matters at Court EVELYN.

III. 1. Something carried; a load 1458. † **2.** Baggage –1743. † **3.** Meaning (of words) –1607.

2. Dauid left his cariage in the hand of the keeper of the cariage 1 *Sam.* 17:32. † **3.** *Haml.* I. i. 94.

IV. 1. Means of conveyance; *esp.* a wheeled vehicle 1450. Often in *comb.* **2.** *spec.* A wheeled vehicle kept for private use for driving in 1771.

1. A cart, or other cariage 1611. Comb.: *Railway-, travelling-c.* **2.** A c. and pair 1879. *Techn. uses*: (*a*) A wheeled support; *e.g.* a gun-c., the c. of a coach, etc. (*b*) A mechanical contrivance which moves and carries some part of a machine 1688. (*c*) *Arch.* A supporting framework, *e.g.* the c. of a staircase 1823.

Comb.: **c.-company,** people who keep private carriages; **c. dog,** a Dalmatian dog; **-drive; -horse,** one that runs in a c.; **-way,** that part of roads, etc., intended for vehicular traffic. Hence **Ca·rriageable** *a.* portable (*rare*); practicable for wheeled carriages. **Ca·rriaged** *a.* † having a deportment; furnished with carriages.

Ca·rrick be·nd. 1819. [perh. f. *carrick*, var. of CARRACK, + BEND *sb.*¹ 3.] *Naut.* A kind of knot for splicing two ropes together.

Ca·rrick bi·tts. 1847. [Cf. prec., BITT.] *Naut.* The BITTS near the end of the windlass; windlass-bitts.

Carrier (kæ·riəɹ). ME. [f. CARRY *v.* + -ER[1].] **1.** One who or that which carries (see CARRY *v.*); a bearer. **2.** One whose occupation is to carry loads, a porter 1511. **3.** *spec.* One who undertakes for hire the conveyance of goods and parcels. (The familiar current sense.) 1471. **4.** = CARRIER-PIGEON 1641. **5.** A conduit for water, etc. 1797. **6.** A person or animal that carries and disseminates disease-germs 1906.

1. A carier of letters 1580. One of Cupid's Carriers *Merry W.* II. ii. 141. *Techn. uses.* Used of parts of instruments and machines which act as bearers and transmittors; in *Mech.* esp. a piece of iron in a lathe by which what is being turned is carried round in the machine. *Electr.* The wave, or current, or frequency transmitted in electrical communication. **3.** By the Cork c. BERKELEY. 'North Western Railway Company, carriers' 1888.

Comb.: **c.-bird,** the pelican, the carrier-pigeon; **-shell,** **-trochus,** a genus of molluscs, which attach pieces of stone, coral, etc., to their shells.

Ca·rrier-pi·geon. 1647. A breed of pigeons with strong homing instincts, used for carrying letters. Also *fig.*

Carriole (kæ·ri,oᵘl). 1808. [– Fr. *carriole* – It. *carriuola,* dim. of *carro* CAR.] **1. a.** A small open carriage with a seat for one 1834. **b.** A light covered cart 1860. **2.** A sledge used in Canada 1808.

Carrion (kæ·riən), *sb.* (and *a.*) [ME. *charoine, caroyne, -oigne* – AFr., ONFr. *caroine, -oigne,* OFr. *charoigne* (mod. *charogne*) :– Rom. **caronia,* f. L. *caro* flesh.]

A. *sb.* † **1.** A dead body –1763. **2.** Dead putrefying flesh of man or beast; flesh unfit for food ME. Also *fig.* † **3.** Used of a living human body, or living person –1661; also of animals (in sense 'vermin'; occ. merely 'worthless beast') –1639.

2. Whan a beast is tourned to careine LYDG. **3.** Old feeble Carrions *Jul. C.* II. i. 130. Hence †**Ca·rrionly** *a.* and *adv.*

B. *attrib.* **1.** Of, or pertaining to, corrupting flesh 1535. Also *transf.* **2.** †Carrion-like; rotten; loathsome 1565

2. Mounted..on lean c. Tits that were nothing but skin and bone 1653. *Comb.* **c.-flower,** the genus *Stapelia,* also *Smilax herbacea,* from the scent of their blossoms.

Carrion crow. 1528. A species of Crow (*Corvus corone*) which feeds on carrion, small animals, poultry, etc.

Carritch, -es (kɑ·ritʃ, -ĭz). *Sc.* 1761. [*Carritches* (XVIII) is a perversion of † CATECHISE (XVI) – Fr. *catéchèse,* and has been treated as a plural with sing. *carritch.* The Sc. *carritch* rests on a pronunc. (kɑ·titʃèz; cf. Fr. kateʃęz).] = CATECHISM.

Carriwi·tchet, carwi·tchet. 1614. [Origin unkn.] A pun, quibble; a hoaxing question.

Wounded with a quibble or a carwitchet at the Mermaid SCOTT.

Carrom, var. of CAROM, CARAMBOLE.

Carronade (kærŏnēⁱ·d). 1779. [f. *Carron,* near Falkirk in Scotland, where originally cast, + -ADE.] *Mil.* A short piece of ordnance, usually of large calibre, having a chamber for the powder like a mortar: chiefly used on shipboard.

Carron oil. 1884. [From *Carron* ironworks, where said to have been first used.] A liniment of linseed oil and lime water in equal parts.

Carrot (kæ·rət. 1533. [– (O)Fr. *carotte* – L. *carota* – Gr. καρωτόν.] **1.** An umbelliferous plant (*Daucus carota*) having a large tapering root, which in cultivation is bright red, fleshy, and edible 1538; usually the root itself 1533. **2.** *pl.* (*joc.*) Red hair, or a name for one who has such hair 1685. Hence **Ca·rroty** *a.* red; Of persons: red-haired.

† **Ca·rrow.** 1577. [Ir. *cerrbach* (mod. sp. *cearrbhach*) gambler.] An Irish itinerant gambler –1829.

Carry (kæ·ri), *v.* ME. [– AFr., ONFr. *carier,* var. of *charier* (mod. *charrier* cart, drag), corresp. to Pr. *carrejar,* f. *car* CAR + *-ier, -eier* (:– Rom. **-idiare*).] **I. 1.** *trans.* To convey, orig. by cart, hence in any vehicle, on horseback, etc. Also *absol.* and *fig.* **2.** To bear from one place to another; to go supporting ME. Also *fig.* **3.** To conduct, lead, take with one; to take *to.* Now *arch.* and *dial.* 1513. **4.** To transfer (a number, an entry, etc.) to another column, book, etc. 1745. **5.** To cause to go or come; to conduct, impel 1703. **6.** *fig.* To continue to have with one as one moves on 1777. **7.** To extend or continue (a line, a piece of work) ME.; also *fig.* 1711. **8.** To take as the result of effort, to win: also with *off* 1607. **9.** To take by assault 1601. Also *transf.* and *fig.* **10.** To gain victory for (a measure, one's candidate, etc.) 1619. **11.** To conduct, manage (an affair, etc.) Now *arch.* 1590. **12.** *Falconry.* To fly away with the quarry. [So Fr. *charrier.*] 1615.

1. C. corne *Gen.* 42:19. To c. 40*l.* in toys DE FOE, wheat 1801. *fig.* To c. (a person) through Virgil's Æneid CHATHAM. **2.** Wel coude she carie a morsel CHAUCER. He shall..carrie them [the lambes] in his bosome *Isa.* 40:11. *To c. coals* (fig.); see COAL. *To c. a hawk,* i.e. bear it on the fist 1826. To c. a letter 1591. *fig.* [Private judgment] carried into politics BUCKLE. **3.** To c. a ship to Lisbon DE FOE, a horse to water 1822, [a person] before a justice 1799. **5.** *To c. all before one.* The Canal..serves to c. the water..to this city 1750. As high as a crossbow can c. 1869. Where winds can c. POPE. **7.** To c. a wall from sea to sea 1878. *fig.* To c. Good-manners to an Excess ADDISON. **8.** *To c. it*: to win the contest. So *To c. the day.* **9.** To c. a position 1876.

II. 1. To bear, hold up, while marching, running, or moving about; to bear about with one; to bear ME. **2.** To bear (the body, head, etc.) in a certain way 1583. **3.** *refl.* To comport, behave, demean oneself 1593. † **4.** To wield –1651. **5.** *Mil.* To hold a weapon in position for saluting 1796. **6.** To support, sustain the weight or burden of, bear 1626.

1. *To c. weight* (in *Horse-racing*): i.e. such extra weight as equalizes the competitors. To c. a swerd WYCLIF, the Standard 1703, arms JOWETT. More rum than he could c. SMOLLETT. Mrs. Thrale.. fancies she carries a boy JOHNSON. To c. a distinction in our thoughts BERKELEY. To c. a grave face 1873, value 1693, weight 1691, authority BUTLER, a sense, as words HOBBES, a consequence 1877. A contract which carries interest BLACKSTONE. **2.** To carry one's head high 1723. **3.** Carrying themselves rudely 1719. **4.** † *To c. a* (*great*) *stroke*: to wield great influence. **6.** *To c. sail*: said of the ship or those who work it 1631. Arches carried by pillars RUSKIN. To c. a crop 1799, cattle 1884, an inference, etc. (*mod.*).

III. Combined with adverbs, in specialized combinations. (See also the preceding senses and the adverbs.)

Carry about. To drive hither and thither, *Ephes.* 4:14. **Carry away. a.** *trans.* = *carry off,* a. **b.** To move forcibly from the footing of reason and judgement. **c.** *trans.* To break off; to lose by breakage; and *intr.* Chiefly *Naut.* **d.** *To c. it away*: to gain the day. *Haml.* II. ii. 377. **Carry forward.** To transfer to another column, page, or book, or to the next account. **Carry off. a.** To remove from this life. **b.** To win. **c.** To make passable. **d.** To bear it out. **Carry on. a.** To advance (a proceeding). **b.** To keep up. **c.** To work at, prosecute. **d.** *intr.* (*Naut.*) To move on. **e.** (*colloq.*) To behave or 'go on'. **Carry out. a.** To conduct to conclusion; to carry into practice, etc. **b.** *To c. out one's bat* (in Cricket): to be 'not out' at the close of the innings or the game. **c.** To bear out for burial. **Carry over. a.** To take with one to the other side. **b.** To allow an account to remain open over the day when its settlement is due: also said of the debtors. **Carry through.** To conduct safely through difficulties; to prosecute to the natural end. **Carry up. a.** To continue (building, etc.). **b.** To trace back in time. † **c.** To hold up. **d.** = *Carry over* or *forward* in accounts.

Carry (kæ·ri), *sb.* 1605. [f. prec.] **1.** A vehicle; *spec.* a two-wheeled barrow. *Sc.* and *n. dial.* **2.** The position required by the command to 'carry arms'; cf. CARRY *v.* II. 5. 1833. **3.** Range (of a gun) 1858. **4.** A portage between navigable rivers or channels. *U.S.,* etc. 1860. **5.** The drift of the clouds. *Sc.* 1819.

Carry-all, carryall (kæ·ri,ǭl). *U.S.* 1837. [f. CARRY *v.* + ALL: altered by pop. etym. from CARRIOLE.] A light carriage for one horse, usually four-wheeled, with room for several persons. Also *transf.*

Carrying (kæ·ri,iŋ), *vbl. sb.* [f. CARRY *v.* + -ING[1].] **1.** The action of the vb. CARRY. **2.** *attrib.,* as in *carrying power,* etc.; **c.-place** = CARRY *sb.* 4; **c. trade,** the business of carrying goods, *esp.* by sea.

Carryke, obs. var. of CARRACK.

† **Ca·rry-tale.** 1577. A tale-bearer –1824.

Carse (kāɹs, Sc. kęrs). *Sc.* ME. [perh. f. pl. of CARR *sb.*[2]] The stretch of low alluvial land along the banks of some Scottish rivers.

Cart (kāɹt), *sb.* [ME. *carte*: (i) partly metathetic repr. of OE. *cræt* carriage, chariot, (once, late) *cert*; (ii) partly – cogn. ON. *kartr* cart; and prob. infl. by AFr., ONFr. *carete* (mod. *charette* cart) dim. of *car, char* CAR.] † **1.** A carriage of any kind; a chariot, car –1602. **2.** *spec.* A strong springless vehicle with two wheels, used in farming operations, for carrying heavy goods, etc. (see CART *v.* 2); specialized as *baggage-, harvest-, hay-,* etc. *cart* ME. **3.** A two-wheeled vehicle of lighter make, with springs; a *spring-cart, mail cart, village cart* 1823.

1. Phoebus C. *Haml.* III. ii. 165. **2.** Like thief and parson in a Tyburn-c. DRYDEN.

Phr. *In the c.* (slang), in an awkward or losing position. *To set* or *put the c. before the horse*: to reverse the natural or proper order.

Comb.: † **c.-bote, -boot** (*Feudal Syst.*), an allowance of wood to a tenant for making and repairing carts (see Boot *sb.*[1]); **-head** (cf. *cart's-tail*); **-horse,** a horse used to draw a cart; a horse used for heavy work; **-house,** a shed in which carts are kept; † a house on wheels; **-load,** the load which a c. can carry; *fig.* a heap; **-man,** a man who drives a c.; **-road** = *cart-way*; **cart's-tail,** *occ.* **cart-tail,** the hinder part of a c., to which offenders were tied to be whipped through the streets; **-way,** a way passable by carts; **-whip,** a long heavy horse-whip; also as *v.*

Cart (kāɹt), *v.* ME. [f. the sb.] **1.** To carry or convey in a cart; also *fig.* † **2.** *spec.* To carry in a cart through the streets, by way of punishment –1812. **3.** *intr.* or *absol.* To work with or use a cart ME.

2. To see Bawds carted BUTLER *Hud.* II. I. 81.

Ca·rtable, *a.* 1684. [f. CART *sb.* or *v.* + -ABLE.] That can be carted; passable by carts.

Ca·rtage (kā·ɹtėdʒ). ME. [f. as prec. + -AGE.] The process or cost of conveying by cart.

Carte[1] (kāɹt, kart). ME. [– Fr. *carte* :– L. *carta, charta* paper.] † **1.** A chart, plan –1683; a charter –1640. **2.** *Sc.* A playing-card; *pl.* cards 1497. ‖ **3.** A bill of fare. [mod. Fr.] 1818. ‖ **4.** = CARTE-DE-VISITE 1861.

Carte[2] (kāɹt). 1707. [var. sp. of QUARTE.] *Fencing.* One of the eight parries and two usual guards of the small-sword.

‖ **Carte-blanche** (kart blāñʃ). 1707. [Fr.; = blank paper.] **1.** A blank paper given to any one to fill up with his own terms. **2.** Hence *fig.* Full discretionary power 1766. **3.** *Piquet.* A hand without picture-cards 1820.

‖ **Carte-de-visite** (ka·rt,də,vizi·t). Pl. **cartes-de-visite.** 1861. [Fr.; = visiting card.] A small photographic portrait mounted on a card, 3½ by 2¼ inches.

Cartel (kā·ɹtĕl), *sb.* 1560. [– Fr. *cartel* – It. *cartello* placard, challenge, dim. of *carta* paper, letter; see CHART, -EL[2].] **1.** A written challenge; a letter of defiance. **2.** A written agreement as to the exchange or ransom of prisoners; such exchange itself 1692; also = *cartel-ship,* a ship employed in such exchange 1769. **3.** *gen.* A paper or card, with writing or printing 1693.

1. To send a c. of defiance 1560. **2.** To establish a c. of exchange WELLINGTON. **3.** A c. with some Greek verses H. WALPOLE. Hence † **Ca·rtel** *v. trans.* to serve with a challenge. **Ca·rtelling** *vbl. sb.* making of cartels, exchanging of prisoners.

Carter (kā·ɹtəɹ). ME. [f. CART *sb.* + -ER[1].] † **1.** A charioteer –1580. **2.** One who drives a cart ME.; *hence,* a boor 1509. **3.** Also **carter-fish:** the WHIFF 1884. Hence † **Ca·rterly** *a.* and *adv.*

Cartesian (kaɹtī·ziăn, -ʒ[i]ăn). 1656. [– mod. L. *Cartesianus,* f. *Cartesius,* latinized f. René *Descartes* (1596–1650); see -IAN.] **A.** *adj.* Pertaining to Descartes, his philosophy or mathematical methods. **B.** *sb.* A follower of Descartes 1660.

A. *Cogito*: *Ergo sum,* this famous enthymem of the C. philosophy HALLAM.

Cartesian devil, C. diver: a hollow figure, partly filled with water and partly with air, and made to float in a vessel nearly filled with water, having an air-tight elastic covering. By pressing down the covering, the air inside is compressed, and more water forced through an aperture into the figure, which sinks, to rise again when the pressure is removed. Hence **Carte·sianism,** the philosophy of Descartes.

‖ **Carthamus** (kā·ɹþămǿs). 1548. [mod.L. – Arab. *ḳirṭim, ḳurṭum* safflower; cf. Fr. *carthame* (XVI).] A genus of composite plants; esp. *C. tinctorius* (Safflower or Bastard Saffron), yielding red and yellow dyes. Hence **Cartha·mic** *a.* as in *Carthamic acid* = **Ca·rthamin,** the red colouring matter of safflower.

Carthusian (kaɹþiū·ziăn, -ʒⁱăn). ME. [– med.L. *Carthusianus*, f. *Cart(h)usia* Chartreuse, near Grenoble, France. See CHARTERHOUSE, CHARTREUSE.] **1.** *adj.* Of or belonging to an austere order of monks founded in Dauphiné, by St. Bruno, in the year 1086. *sb.* A monk of this order. **2.** *adj.* Of the Charterhouse School, founded on the site of a Carthusian monastery in London. *sb.* A scholar of this school. 1860.

Cartilage (kā·ɹtilėdʒ). 1541. [– Fr. *cartilage* – L. *cartilago, -agin-*.] A firm elastic tissue, of a translucent colour; gristle; a gristly part, as the *costal cartilages*.

Temporary c. is that which occurs in early life, and subsequently ossifies; *permanent c.*, e.g. the *articular c.* which coats the joints, always retains its character. Hence **Ca:rtilagi:nifica·tion** the formation of or conversion into c. **Ca:rtilagi·niform** *a.* resembling c. **Cartila·ginoid** *a.* of the form or nature of c.

Cartilaginous (kăɹtilæ·dʒinəs), *a.* 1541. [– OFr. *cartilaginous, -eus* (mod. *-eux*) or L. *cartilaginosus*; see prec., -OUS.] **1.** Of, or of the nature of, cartilage. **2.** *Bot.* Of the texture of cartilage 1677. var. † **Cartilagi·neous.**

1. *C. fishes*: an order of fishes having a c. skeleton.

Cartographer (kaɹtǫ·grăfəɹ). Also **charto-.** 1863. [f. next, or after Fr. *cartographe*; see -GRAPHER, -ER¹ 4.] One who makes charts or maps.

Cartography (kaɹtǫ·grăfi). Also **charto-.** 1859. [– Fr. *cartographie*, f. *carte* map; see CHART, -GRAPHY.] The drawing of charts or maps. Hence **Cartogra·phic, -al** *a.*

Cartomancy (kā·ɹtomæ:nsi). 1871. [– Fr. *cartomancie*, f. *carte* CARD *sb.*²; see -MANCY.] Divination by playing-cards.

Carton (kā·ɹtən). 1864. [– Fr. *carton* – It. *cartone*, augm. of *carta* paper; see CARD *sb.*², -OON.] **1.** A white disc within the bull's-eye of a target; a shot which hits this. **2.** A light pasteboard or cardboard box or case for holding goods; the material used for this 1891.

Cartoon (kaɹtū·n), *sb.* 1671. [In sense 1 – It. *cartone*; see prec. Sense 2 is an Eng. application.] **1.** A drawing on stout paper as a design for painting, tapestry, mosaic, etc. **2.** A (full-page) illustration in a (comic) paper or periodical 1863.

1. Cartoons and other drawings of Raphael EVELYN. Hence **Cartoo·n** *v.* to design, as a c. (sense 1); to caricature. **Cartoo·nist,** one who draws cartoons.

Cartouche (kaɹtū·ʃ). 1611. [– Fr. *cartouche* cornet of paper, cartridge – It. *cartoccio*, f. *carta* paper; see CARD *sb.*²] **1.** (= Fr. *cartouche* fem.) *Mil.* A roll or case of paper, etc., containing a charge for a firearm; a cartridge. ? *Obs.* † **b.** A case of wood, etc., containing iron balls to be shot from a cannon –1768. **c.** = *cartridge-box*. **2.** (= Fr. *cartouche* masc.) *Arch.* **a.** A corbel, mutule, or modillion; var. † **Cartouse** 1726. **b.** Any ornament in the form of a scroll 1611. **c.** A tablet for an inscription or for ornament, representing a sheet of paper with the ends rolled up; a drawing of this. Often *attrib.* 1776. **b.** *Archæol.* Name for the oval figures in Egyptian hieroglyphics, enclosing royal or divine names or titles 1830. *Comb.* **c.-box** = *cartridge-box*.

Cartridge (kā·ɹtridʒ). 1579. [alt. of prec., but actually recorded earlier.] **1.** *Mil.* The case in which the exact charge of powder for fire-arms is made up; of pasteboard, flannel, metal, etc. Also *transf.* and *fig.* † **2.** *Arch.* = CARTOUCHE 2 a, b, c. –1756.

Comb., etc.: **ball-c.,** a c. containing a bullet; **blank c.,** a c. containing no ball; **c.-bag,** a flannel bag, etc., containing the charge of powder for a cannon; **-belt,** a belt having pockets for cartridges; **-box,** a box for storing or carrying cartridges; **-case,** = *cartridge-box*; also, the paper which contains the powder of a c.; **-paper,** a strong kind of paper, used for making cartridges, and also for rough drawings, etc.

Cartulary (kā·ɹtiŭlări). Also **Chartu-,** q.v. 1541. [– med.L. *c(h)artularium*, f. *c(h)artula*, dim. of *c(h)arta* paper; see CARD *sb.*², CHART, -ARY¹.] 'A place where papers or records are kept' (J.); whence, the records (of a monastery, etc.); or the book containing them; a register. var. † **Ca·rtuary, Cha·rt-.**

† **Ca·rtware.** 1562. [See WARE *sb.*²] A team of horses –1577.

Ca·rt-wheel. ME. **1.** The wheel of a cart. **2.** *joc.* Any large coin, as a crown, etc. 1867.

To turn cart-wheels: to execute lateral somersaults, as if the hands and feet were spokes of a wheel.

Cartwright (kā·ɹtˌrəit). ME. [f. CART *sb.* + WRIGHT.] A carpenter who makes carts.

† **Ca·ruage.** *erron.* **carvage.** 1610. [– ONFr. *caruage*, f. *carue* (mod. *charrue*) plough + *-age* -AGE; cf. AL. *carruagium* (XII), and see next.] *Old Law.* **1.** Ploughing –1688. **2.** = CARUCAGE.

Carucage, carr- (kæ·riukėdʒ). 1577. [– med.L. *car(r)ucagium*; see prec., CARUCATE.] *Feudal Syst.* A tax levied on every carucate of land.

Carucate, carr- (kæ·riukeⁱt). 1577. [– med. L. *car(r)ucata*, f. *car(r)uca* orig. coach, chariot, in Gaul early applied to the wheel-plough, rel. to *carrus* CAR; see -ATE¹.] *Feudal Syst.* As much land as could be tilled with one plough (and 8 oxen) in a year; a ploughland. var. † **Carue,** *erron.* **carve.**

Caruncle (kărʊ·ŋk'l). 1615. [– Fr. †*caruncle* (mod. *caroncule*) – L. *caruncula*, dim. of *caro* flesh.] **1.** A small fleshy excrescence: applied in Anat. to the lachrymal and urethral caruncles, the wattles of the turkey-cock, etc. **2.** *Bot.* 'An excrescence at or about the hilum of certain seeds' (Gray). Hence **Ca·runcular** *a.* of the nature of or like a c. **Caru·nculate(d** *a.* having a c. or caruncles; var. **Caru·nculous.**

‖ **Carus** (kēᵊ·rǿs). 1678. [mod. alt. of late L. *caros* – Gr. κάρος, heavy sleep, torpor. Cf. Fr. *carus* (XVIII).] *Med.* Extreme insensibility; *esp.* the fourth degree of insensibility, the others being sopor, coma, and lethargy.

Carvage, erron. sp. of CARUAGE.

Carve (kāɹv), *v.* [OE. *ċeorfan* = OFris. *kerva*, (M)Du. *kerven*, MHG. *kerben* :– WGmc. **kerfan*.] † **1.** To CUT –1560. **2.** To hew, cut, or sculpture (*out of* stone, *in* ivory, etc.) OE.; to shape by cutting 1535. **3.** To cut or engrave *on* (*in, into*) a surface; to cover with cut figures ME. Also *intr.* or *absol.* **4.** To cut up meat at table ME. Also *trans.* **5.** *fig.* To do or † take one's pleasure 1602. **6.** To cut up or subdivide 1711.

1. Quen corne is coruen ME. *To c. in two, in* or *to pieces.* To c. a way 1490. Also *fig.* **2.** An angel.. carved in stone TENNYSON. To c. mount Athos into a statue of Alexander BENTLEY. **3.** We carved not a line and we raised not a stone WOLFE. Wrinkles carved his Skin TENNYSON. We c. and paint EMERSON. **4.** A man who..cannot c. CHESTERF. *To c. a fowl*, etc. **5.** *Haml.* I. iii. 20. **6.** To c. the whole fee in particular estates CRUISE. **To c. out:** (in *Legal lang.*) To cut a smaller estate out of a larger one. Also *transf.* (*Macb.* I. ii. 19), and † *fig.* (*L.L.L.* V. ii. 323). Hence **Carve** *sb.* a stroke of carving. **Carved** *ppl. a.*; also **carven** (*poet.* and *rhet.*).

Carvel (kā·ɹvel). 1462. [– OFr. *carvelle* (XV) – Pg. *caravela* (whence also Fr. *caravelle*), dim. of Pg. *caravo* :– late L. *carabus* (Isidore) – Gr. κάραβος horned beetle, crayfish, light ship. See CARAVEL.] *Naut.* The Eng. form of the name for a small, light, and fast ship, chiefly of Spain and Portugal. (Since 1650 only *Hist.*, and written *caravel.*) † **2. a.** The Paper Nautilus. **b.** The floating mollusc *Ianthina*. **c.** A jellyfish (*Medusa*).

Comb. **c.-built,** (*Naut.*) having the planks all flush and smooth, instead of clinker-built, i.e. overlapping, So **c.-planked** *a.*

Carvene (kā·ɹvīn). 1876. [f. med.L., Fr. etc. *carvi* CARAWAY + -ENE.] *Chem.* A hydrocarbon $C_{10}H_{16}$, found in oil of Caraway.

Carver (kā·ɹvəɹ). ME. [f. CARVE *v.* + -ER¹.] **1.** *gen.* One who cuts or carves. **2.** *spec.* One who carves wood, ivory, stone, etc.; a sculptor ME. **3.** One who carves at table ME. **b.** A carving knife 1840.

2. The carver's chissel DODSLEY. **3.** An expert c. 1888. *A pair of carvers*: a carving knife and fork.

Carving (kā·ɹviŋ), *vbl. sb.* ME. [f. as prec. + -ING¹.] **1.** The action of the vb. CARVE. **2.** Carved work; a carved figure or design ME.

2. The c. on the reading-desk SCOTT.

† **Carvist.** 1677. [Origin unkn.] *Falconry.* A hawk in its first year, of proper age to be carried on the fist –1800.

Carvy, Sc. f. CARAWAY.

Caryatid (kæriˌæ·tid). Pl. usu. **-ides;** also **-ids.** 1563. [– Fr. *caryatide* – It. *cariatide*, or their source, L. *caryatides* (Vitruvius) – Gr. καρυάτιδες (pl.) priestesses of Artemis at Καρύαι (Caryæ) in Laconia.] *Arch.* A female figure used as a column to support an entablature. Also *attrib.*

Caryophyllaceous (kæ:riofilēⁱ·ʃⁱəs), *a.* 1835. [f. mod.L. *caryophyllus* – Gr. καρυόφυλλον clove-pink; see -ACEOUS.] *Bot.* **a.** Belonging to the order *Caryophyllaceæ*. **b.** Used of a corolla having five petals with long claws, as in the clove-pink. var. **Ca:ryophy·lleous.**

‖ **Caryopsis** (kæriǫ·psis). Pl. **-ides** (-idīz). 1830. [mod.L., f. Gr. κάρυον nut + ὄψις appearance.] *Bot.* A small one-seeded dry indehiscent fruit, whose pericarp adheres to the seed throughout so as to form one body with it, as in wheat, barley, etc.

Ca. sa. (kā sā). 1796. Short for *capias ad satisfaciendum* (see CAPIAS).

Casal (kēⁱ·săl), *a.* 1834. [f. CASE *sb.*¹ + -AL¹.] Of or belonging to grammatical case.

‖ **Casal, casale.** 1506. [It. *casale*, f. *casa* house.] A hamlet (in Italy, Malta).

Cascabel (ka·skăbel). 1639. [– Sp. *cascabel* – Cat. (Pr.) *cascavel* :– med.L. *cascabellus* little bell.] **1.** *Gunnery.* Formerly the knob at the rear end of a cannon; now all behind the base ring. ‖ **2.** A rattlesnake; also its rattle. [Sp.] 1760.

Cascade (kæskēⁱ·d), *sb.* 1641. [– Fr. *cascade* – It. *cascata*, f. *cascare* fall :– Rom. **casicare*, f. L. *casus* fall; see CASE *sb.*¹, -ADE.] A waterfall; usually, a small fall; *esp.* one of a series. Also *transf.* and *fig.*

An artificial c. MRS. PIOZZI. A c. of ice TYNDALL, of lace 1882.

Cascade (kæskēⁱ·d), *v.* 1702. [f. the sb.] To fall or pour in a cascade. Also *transf.* **b.** *vulgar.* To vomit 1805.

‖ **Cascara** (ka·skăra). 1882. [Sp., = bark.] A bark canoe (in Spanish America).

Cascarilla (kæskări·lă). 1686. [– Sp. *cascarilla*, dim. of *cascara* bark.] The bark of the plant *Croton eleuteria*, used as a tonic. Also called *c. bark*. Hence **Cascari·llin, a** bitter substance ($C_{12}H_{18}O_4$) obtained from c. bark.

† **Caschielawis.** *Sc. pl.* 1596. [Origin unkn.] An instrument of torture.

‖ **Caschrom** (ka·sχrom). 1806. [Gael. *cas* foot, *chrom* crooked.] An instrument of tillage, called also 'foot-plough'.

Case (kēⁱs), *sb.*¹ [ME. *cas, caas* – (O)Fr. *cas* – L. *casus* fall, chance, occasion, misfortune, (tr. Gr. πτῶσις lit. fall) grammatical case, f. base of *cadere* fall.] † **1.** A thing that befalls or happens; an event, occurrence, hap, or chance –1596. † **2.** Chance, hazard, hap –1560. **3.** An instance ME. **4.** *The case*: The actual state of matters; the fact ME. **5.** Condition (*esp.* physical condition), plight ME. **6.** *Law.* **a.** A cause or suit. **b.** A statement of the facts of a matter *sub judice*, for a higher court. **c.** A decided case. **d.** The case as put by one of the parties. 1523. **7.** *Med.* **a.** The condition of disease in a patient 1709. **b.** An instance of disease; 'a record of the progress of disease in an individual' (*Syd. Soc. Lex.*) 1732. **c.** *U.S. slang.* Of persons: an oddity 1848. **8.** *Grammar.* [L. *casus* used as tr. Gr. πτῶσις, restricted by the Stoics to nouns, and including the nominative.] **a.** One of the forms of a sb., adj., or pron., which express its relations to some other word, *e.g.* as subject, object etc. **b.** *loosely,* The relation itself. ME.

1. I you recount a ruefull cace SPENSER. **2.** By caase of fortune CAXTON. **3.** In manye Caasis 1449. **4.** The c. with me is the reverse MACAULAY. This is not the c. 1888. When a lady's in the c. GAY. † *All a c.*: all one. **5.** [They] came home ageyne in werse caas than they wente CAXTON. *In good case*: well off; also, in good physical condition (*arch.*). *In c. to* or *for*: prepared, ready. **6. c.** *A leading c.*: one frequently cited as having settled some point. **d.** 'That is our c., my lord' 1888. † *Action on the c.*: a form of procedure in common law, for remedy in cases not specifically provided for, so called from the words *in consimili casu* in the Statute of Westminster the Second. Called also *trespass on the c.*, or *c.* simply. *C. of conscience* (tr. L. *casus conscientiæ*): a question of conduct concerning which conscience may be in doubt, and requiring CASUISTRY to deal with it. **7. b.** A c. of small-pox 1851.

Phrases. *In case*: † **a.** in fact; **b.** if; **c.** lest; **d.** *In case of*: in the event of. † *If case*: if perchance. *To put* or *set* (*the*) *case*: to suppose. *In any case*: † by any means; at all events, anyhow. So *In no case*. *Comb.*: † **c.-divinity,** casuistry; **-law,** the law as made by decided cases; † **-putting,** stating of a legal c., the making of hypotheses.

Case (kēⁱs), *sb.*² [ME. *case, caas, cass* – OFr. *casse*, dial. var. of *chasse* (mod. *châsse* reliquary, frame) :– L. *capsa* box, bookcase, f. base of *capere* hold.] **1.** A thing fitted to contain something else; a box, chest, bag, sheath, etc. **2.** The covering part of anything ME. Also *fig.* **3.** The frame in which a door or window is set; cf. STAIR-CASE. 1663. **4.** The shell or carcass of a building 1677. **5.** A box with its proper contents 1540; hence, A set 1599. **6.** *Printing.* The frame in which the compositor has his types, divided into compartments. (Ordinarily there are two, the *upper case* for capitals, etc., and the *lower case* for the small letters, etc.) 1588. **7.** *Mil.* = *case-shot* 1667.

1. A c. for books WOTTON. *A candle-, card-, cigar-c.* **2.** The c. of a watch, of a firework, a sausage, a chrysalis, etc. *spec.* In *Bookbinding*: The boards and back of a book bound in cloth; also, a cover to hold pamphlets, etc., without binding 1868. *fig.* The c. of that huge Spirit now is cold *Ant. & Cl.* IV. xv. 89. **5.** A c. of arms, glass, etc. A c. of teeth SCOTT. *A c. of pistols*: a brace.

Case, *sb.*³ Also **case-char.** 1751. [Origin unkn.] One of the family *Salmonidæ*.

† **Case,** *v.*¹ 1647. [f. CASE *sb.*¹] To put as a supposition; *intr.* = *To put case* (see CASE *sb.*¹ Phrases).

Case (kēⁱs), *v.*² 1575. [f. CASE *sb.*²] **1.** *trans.* To enclose in or as in a case; to encase, surround *with.* **2.** To fit with cases 1884. † **3.** To strip off the case; to skin –1803.

1. Bones of seals..now cased in ice KANE. Men cased in iron 1863. To c. a brick wall with stone GWILT. **3.** *All's Well* III. vi. 111.

Caseation (kēⁱsi,ēⁱ·ʃən). 1866. [f. L. *caseatus* mixed with cheese; see -ATION.] The coagulation of milk; in *Pathol.* a degeneration of morbid products into a cheesy material.

Case-harden (kēⁱ·s,hā:ɹd'n), *v.* 1677. [f. CASE *sb.*² (in locative constr.).] **1.** To harden on the surface, as iron by partial cementation. **2.** *fig.* To harden in constitution or spirit 1713.

2. A case-hardened or weather-beaten tar FALCONER.

Caseic (keⁱsī·ik), *a.* 1840. [f. L. *caseus* + -IC.] *Chem.* In *C. acid* = *Lactic acid*.

Casein (kēⁱ·si,in). *Erron.* **-ine.** 1841. [f. as prec. + -IN¹.] *Chem.* A Proteid or Albuminoid, one of the chief constituents of milk; chemically identical with the Legumin (or *vegetable c.*) of the seeds of leguminous plants. It is coagulated by acids, and forms the basis of cheese.

Case-knife (kēⁱ·s,nəif). 1704. [f. CASE *sb.*²] **a.** A knife carried in a case or sheath. **b.** A large table knife.

Casemate (kēⁱ·s,mēⁱt). 1575. [orig. – It. *casamatta* or Sp. *casamata*; later assim. to Fr. *casemate* – It., earlier *camata*, perh. – Gr. χάσμα, pl. χάσματα gap, CHASM.] **1.** *Fortif.* A vaulted chamber built in the thickness of the ramparts of a fortress, with embrasures for the defence of the place; used as a barrack, a battery, or both. **2.** *Arch.* = CASEMENT 1. 1611. Hence **Ca·semated** *a.* provided with casemates; strongly fortified.

Casement (kēⁱ·smĕnt, kēⁱ·z-). ME. [– AL. *cassimentum* – AL. *cassimentum* casement of window (XV), f. *cassa* (repr. L. *capsa* CASE *sb.*²) as in *cassa fenestre* casement or moulding (XIV); see -MENT.] **1.** *Arch.* A hollow moulding, such as the *cavetto*. **2.** A frame forming a window or part of a window, opening on hinges attached to the upright side of the frame in which it is fixed. (The usual sense.) 1556. Also *fig.*

2. A c. of the great chamber window *Mids. N.* III. i. 57. *C. cloth*, cotton fabric such as is used for c. curtains. Hence **Ca·semented** *a.*

Caseous (kēⁱ·siəs), *a.* 1661. [f. L. *caseus* cheese + -OUS.] **1.** Of the nature of cheese, cheesy. **2.** *Pathol.* Cheese-like in appearance 1753.

1. (*joc.*) That c. and wrathful people [the Welsh] SYD. SMITH.

Casern, -e (kăzē·ɹn). 1696. [– Fr. *caserne* – Pr. *cazerna* :– Rom. **quaderna* for *quaterna* (hut) for four.] One of a series of small (temporary) buildings for soldiers between the ramparts and houses of a fortified town; also a barrack.

Case-shot (kēⁱ·s,ʃǫ:t). 1625. [f. CASE *sb.*²] *Mil.* A collection of small projectiles put up in cases to fire from a cannon; canister-shot. Also, a shrapnel-shell.

Ca·se-weed. 1578. [f. CASE *sb.*²] Shepherd's Purse.

Ca·se-worm. 1606. [f. as prec.] A caddis-worm; see CADDIS².

Cash (kæʃ), *sb.*¹ 1596. [– Fr. † *casse*, or its source It. *cassa* :– L. *capsa* CASE *sb.*²] † **1.** A box for money, a cash-box –1734; a sum of money –1752. **2.** Money; in the form of coin, ready money 1596. *Banking* and *Comm.*: Specie; also, more loosely, bank-notes which are at once convertible, as opp. to bills, etc.

1. This bank is properly a general c., where every man lodges his money TEMPLE. **2.** Those who have c., come here to spend 1810. So *Hard c.*, *ready c.*, *c. in hand*. He bets..freely when he is in c. THACKERAY. Also *Out of c.*

Comb., etc.: **c.-book,** in *Book-keeping*, a book in which is entered a record of c. paid and received; **-credit,** an overdrawn account; **-payment,** *spec.* the payment of c. for government paper, etc.; **-price,** the price for payment in ready money; **-register** (orig. *U.S.*), a till furnished with an apparatus which visibly records the amounts put into it; **-sale,** a sale for ready money.

Cash (kæʃ), *sb.*² 1598. [ult. – Pg. † *caxa*, *caixa* – Tamil *kāsu* :– Skr. *karsha*. The earlier Eng. form was *cass*.] One of various coins of low value in the East Indies and China: *esp.* The Chinese *le* and *tsien*, coins made of an alloy of copper and lead, with a square hole in the centre; of these 1000 made a tael or liang.

† **Cash,** *v.*¹ 1564. [var. of CASS *v.*] = CASHIER 1. –1829.

Cash (kæʃ), *v.*² 1811. [f. CASH *sb.*²] To give or get the cash for; to convert into cash, as 'to c. a cheque'.

‖ **Cashel** (kæ·shĕl). 1845. [= Ir. *caiseal* bulwark, wall, prob. – L. *castellum* fortlet.] *Ir. Antiq.* A circular wall enclosing a group of churches and their appurtenances.

Cashew (kăʃū·). 1703. [– Pg. *caju*, var. of *acaju* (whence Fr. *acajou* mahogany) – Tupi *caju, acaju*.] *C.-tree*, a large tree (*Anacardium occidentale*) cultivated in tropical countries, bearing a kidney-shaped fruit (*cashew-nut*) placed on the end of a fleshy pear-shaped receptacle (*c. apple*), popularly taken for the fruit. *Comb.* **c.-bird,** *Tanagra zena*.

Cashier (kæ̆ʃīᵊ·ɹ), *sb.* 1596. [– Du. *cassier*, or its source Fr. *caissier*, f. *caisse* CASH *sb.*¹; see -IER.] One who has charge of the cash of a bank or mercantile firm, paying and receiving money, and keeping the cash account. † **b.** A money-dealer –1687.

Cashier (kăʃīᵊ·ɹ), *v.* 1592. [Early forms *casseer, -ier* – early Flem. *kasseren* disband (soldiers), revoke (a will) – Fr. *casser* break, dismiss, rescind = It. *cassare* cancel :– L. *quassare* QUASH.] † **1.** To dismiss from service or fellowship; also generally –1791. **2.** To dismiss from a position of command or authority; to depose. Also *transf.* and *fig.* 1599. **3.** To discard, get rid of 1603; † to make void –1650. ¶ In *Merry W.* I. i. 184, app. = 'to ease of cash'.

2. *spec.* in the army and navy involving disgrace and disqualification from further government employment in any capacity (cf. DISMISS *v.* 3). *Oth.* II. iii. 381. To c. the King LD. SHEFFIELD. **3.** To casheere their Ruffianly Haire PRYNNE. To c. an election 1601. Hence **Cashie·rer. Cashie·rment.**

Cashmere (kæ·ʃmīᵊɹ, kæʃmīᵊ·ɹ). 1822. [– *Cashmere* (*Kashmīr*) name of a province in the W. Himalayas, India. Cf. CASSIMERE.] **a.** More fully *C. shawl*: A costly shawl made of fine wool obtained from the Cashmere goat and the wild goat of Tibet. **b.** The material of which these shawls are made. **c.** A woollen fabric made in imitation of the true cashmere.

Cashmerette (kæ:ʃmĭre·t). 1886. [f. prec. + -ETTE.] A dress fabric with a soft and glossy surface, made in imitation of cashmere.

Cashou, Cashu, obs. ff. CACHOU.

Ca·sing, *sb. n. dial.* Usu. in pl. 1516. [Origin unkn.] Dried dung of cattle used for fuel.

Casing (kēⁱ·siŋ), *vbl. sb.* 1575. [f. CASE *v.*² + -ING¹.] **1.** The action of the vb. **2.** *concr.* Something that encases, as the c. of a fly, a building, a well, etc. Also in techn. uses. 1791.

Casino (kăsī·no). 1789. [– It. *casino*, dim. of *casa* house.] ‖ **1.** A summer-house (in Italy) 1831. **2.** A public room used for social meetings; *esp.* a public music or dancing saloon, freq. also with facilities for gambling 1789. **3.** A game of Cards; see CASSINO.

Cask (kɑsk), *sb.* 1557. [– Fr. *casque* or Sp. *casco* helmet, CASQUE. Sense 1 appears only in Eng.] **1.** A wooden vessel of cylindrical form, made of curved staves bound together by hoops, with flat ends; a barrel. Cf. BARREL *sb.* 1. Also *fig.* **2.** A cask and its contents; hence as a measure of capacity 1727. † **3.** = CASKET. **b.** Case, shell. –1727. † **4.** = CASQUE –1696. Also *attrib.* and in *comb.*

Cask, *v.* 1562. [f. prec.] To put into a cask.

† **Caskanet.** 1607. [Made up of *casket* and *carkanet*, perh. orig. a misprint.] Used by some as = CARCANET, by others as = CASKET –1693.

A c. of Jewells 1621. A c. wᵗʰ red stones in it 1638.

Casket (kɑ·skĕt), *sb.*¹ 1467. [Of obscure origin; perh. – AFr. alt. of synon. (O)Fr. *cassette* – It. *cassetta*, dim. of *cassa*; – L. *capsa* (see CASE *sb.*², CASH *sb.*¹); see -ET.] **1.** A small box or chest for jewels, letters, or other things of value, itself often of value and richly ornamented. Also *fig.* **b.** Occ. the title of a book of selections 1850. **2.** A coffin. *U.S.* 1870.

1. A richly carved c. of ivory 1876. *fig.* They found him dead..An empty c. *John* V. i. 40.

Casket, *sb.*², var. of GASKET.

Ca·sket, *v.* 1601. [f. CASKET *sb.*¹] To enclose or put up in a casket.

I have..casketted my treasure *All's Well* II. v. 26.

Casque (kɑsk). 1580. [– Fr. *casque* – Sp. *casco*; cf. CASK.] A piece of armour to cover the head; a helmet. Used loosely of all military head-pieces, and now hist., poet., or foreign. Also *transf.* in *Bot.* and *Zool.*

My good blade carves the casques of men TENNYSON. Hence **Casqued** *ppl. a.* having a c. on.

Casquet (kɑ·skĕt, kaske). 1611. [– Fr. *casquet*, dim. of *casque*; see CASQUE, CASK, -ET.] A light and open helmet.

† **Cass,** *a.* 1549. [– L. *cassus* empty, void, vain.] Dismissed, cashiered; null –1651.

Cass, *v.* Still *Sc.* 1460. [– Fr. *casser*, f. L. *quassare* break in pieces, annexing in later times the senses of L. *cassare* to annul.] **1.** To make void, annul, quash. *Sc. Law.* † **2.** To dismiss; disband, cashier –1709.

Cassada, var. of CASSAVA.

‖ **Cassareep** (kæ·sărīp). 1832. [Carib.] 'The inspissated juice of the cassava, which is highly antiseptic, and forms the basis of the West Indian pepper-pot' (*Treas. Bot.*).

† **Ca·ssate,** *v.* 1512. [– *cassat-*, pa. ppl. stem of L. *cassare*; see CASS *v.*, -ATE³.] = CASS *v.* –1744.

Cassation (kæsēⁱ·ʃən). ME. [– (O)Fr. *cassation*, f. *casser* QUASH; see -ATION.] The action of making null and void.

Court of C. [Fr. *Cour de cassation*], in France, the supreme court of appeal, having power to quash (*casser*) decisions of the other courts.

Cassava (kæ̆sā·vă). 1555. [orig. *cas(s)avi*, etc. – Taino (Haiti) *casavi*; later alt. after Fr. *cassave* from same source.] **1.** A plant, *Manihot utilissima* (N.O. *Euphorbiaceæ*), called also Manioc, with fleshy tuberous roots, used as food in tropical America.

There are two varieties, Sweet C. (*M. aipi*), prepared as a vegetable, and Bitter C., containing a virulent but volatile poisonous juice, which is expelled by heat.

2. The nutritious starch obtained from the roots; the bread made from this 1577.

Casse paper, cassie-. 1688. [perh. repr. Fr. *papier cassé* 'broken paper'.] The paper of the two outside quires of a ream.

‖ **Casserole** (kæsěrōᵘ·l). 1706. [Fr., extension of *cassole*, dim. of *casse* – Pr. *casa* :– Rom. (late L.) *cattia* ladle, pan – Gr. *κυάθιον*, *-ειον*, dim. of *κύαθος* cup.] **1.** A kind of stew-pan 1725. **2.** The edging of certain dressed dishes 1706.

‖ **Cassette** (kase·t). 1793. [Fr., dim. of *casse*, *caisse* CASE *sb.*²] **1.** A casket. **2.** *Photogr.* A small flat box used as a container in transporting a plate or film 1875. **3.** *Ceramics.* = SAGGAR 1.

† **Casshe.** Also **Caxes.** 1548. [var. of KEX.] The wild chervil; used vaguely of other plants –1640.

Cassia (kæ·sia). OE. [– L. *cas(s)ia* – Gr. *κασία* – Heb. *ḳᵉṣī'āh* bark resembling cinnamon.] **1.** An inferior kind of Cinnamon, *esp.* the bark of *Cinnamomum cassia.* More fully *C.-bark.* **2.** The tree, *Cinnamomum cassia* 1553. **3.** *poet.* A fragrant shrub or plant. (Cf. *Ps.* 45:8.) 1594. **4.** *Bot.* A genus of trees, shrubs, or herbs (N.O. *Leguminosæ*) of many species, the leaflets of several of which are the *Senna leaves* of medicine. The name *Cassia fistula* was given early to one species, the Pudding Pipe tree, a native of India, but cultivated elsewhere, which produces the *cassia pods* containing a pulp used as a laxative. Thence the name has been extended to the genus. ME. **b.** Any medicinal product obtained from this 1543.

Comb., etc.: **c.-bark,** also called **c. lignea** (see above, 1); **-buds,** the unexpanded buds of several species of Cinnamon, esp. *Cinnamomum aromaticum*, used like cloves; **-oil,** common oil of cinnamon.

Cassi·deous, *a.* 1835. [f. L. *cassis, -id-* helmet + -EOUS.] *Bot.* Helmet-shaped. So **Cassi·diform** *a.*

† **Cassidoine, -done, -dony**¹. ME. [– OFr. *cassidoine*, pop. var. of *calcidoine* – L. *chalcedonius* (*lapis*).] = CHALCEDONY –1753.

Cassidony (kæ·sidəni). 1578. [Origin unkn.] *Bot.* **1.** The plant *Lavandula stæchas*, French lavender. **2.** *Mountain* or *Golden C.*: the Gnaphalium of books.

Cassie, -y (kæ·si). *dial.* 1693. [= O.Icel. *kass*, mod. *kassi* a case, creel, etc.] A kind of basket made of straw. (Orkney and Caithness.)

Cassimere (kæ·simiᵊɹ). 1774. [Early var. of CASHMERE. Cf. Fr. *casimir*, It. *casimirra*, Du. *kazjmier*, KERSEYMERE.] A thin fine twilled woollen cloth used for men's clothes. Cf. KERSEYMERE.

†‖ **Cassine.** 1708. [Fr. – It. *cassina* – med. L. *cas(s)ina* hut, small cottage, dim. of L. *casa* cottage.] *Mil.* A farm-house, where a number of soldiers have posted themselves, to make a stand –1753.

Cassinette (kæsine·t). 1846. [perh. a factitious name suggested by CASSIMERE.] A modification of cassimere, with the warp of cotton, and the weft of fine wool, or wool and silk.

Cassinian (kæsi·niăn), *a.* 1726. [f. proper name *Cassini.*] Of or pertaining to G. D. Cassini (1625–1712), or his descendants, French astronomers, or to their researches.

C. oval: = CASSINOID.

Cassino (kăsī·no). Also **casino.** 1792. [var. of CASINO.] A game at cards in which the ten of diamonds (*great cass*) counts two points, and the two of spades (*little cass*) one; eleven points constituting the game.

Cassinoid (kæ·sinoid). [– Fr. *cassinoïde*; see CASSINIAN, -OID.] *Geom.* An oval having two foci, such that the product of the focal radii of any point on the curve is constant: a curve which Cassini wished to substitute for the ellipse, in explaining planetary movements.

Cassioberry (kæ·sio,be:ri). 1753. [Origin unkn.] The fruit of *Viburnum lævigatum*, the *C.-bush.*

Cassiope·ian, *a.* 1630. [See -AN.] Of Cassiopeia, a northern constellation. (In 1572 a brilliant new star appeared in this constellation, only to disappear again.)

Cassique, obs. f. CACIQUE. Also, the Mocking Bird of Guiana 1825.

Cassiterite (kăsi·těrəit). 1858. [f. Gr. *κασσίτερος* tin + -ITE¹ 2 b.] *Min.* Native stannic dioxide, the most common ore of tin, called also tin stone. **Cassi:terota·ntalite,** a tantalite which contains much stannic acid.

Cassius (kæ·siɒs). 1865. Name of a German physician of 17th c.; whence *Purple of C.*, a purple pigment produced by the action of chloride of tin on a solution of chloride of gold.

Cassock (kæ·sək), *sb.* 1550. [– Fr. *casaque* – It. *casacca*, prob. – Turkic *quzzāk* vagabond, nomad; see COSSACK.] † **1.** A cloak or long coat worn by some soldiers; also that of a horseman –1699. † **2.** A long loose coat or gown, orig. worn by both sexes –1628. **3.** A close-fitting garment with sleeves, fastened up to the neck and reaching to the heels, worn under surplice, alb, or gown by clerics, choristers, etc., at church services; or as ordinary clerical costume 1663. **4.** = Clerical office; wearer of a c. 1628.

4. During the war, he laid aside the cassoc ROBERTSON. He had a suspicion of all cassocks THACKERAY. Hence **Ca·ssock** *v.* to dress in a c.

Cassolette (kæsole·t). 1657. [– Fr. *cassolette* – Pr. *casoleta*, dim. of *casola*; see CASSEROLE.] **1.** A vessel in which perfumes are burned. **2.** A box with a perforated cover to diffuse perfumes 1851.

† **Cassonade.** 1657. [– Fr. *cassonade*, f. *casson* broken sugar, f. *casser* break (QUASH *v.*); see -ADE.] Unrefined cane sugar imported in casks –1810.

Cassoon (kăsū·n). 1799. Occ. var. of CAISSON, q.v.

Cassowary (kæ·sŏwěri). 1611. [– Malay *kasuārī*, *kasavārī*.] **1.** A genus of large cursorial birds, related to the Ostrich, inhabiting New Guinea, etc. They stand about five feet high; the wings are useless for flight, but are furnished with quills, like spines, which serve for combat or defence. **2.** *New Holland C.*: the EMU. 1842.

‖ **Cassumu·nar.** 1693 [app. Eastern.] *Med.* The tuberous root of an East Indian plant; it is warm, bitter, aromatic, and smells like ginger. (Cf. ZEDOARY.) var. **Casumuniar.**

Cast (kɑst), *sb.* ME. [f. the vb.] **I. 1.** The act of casting or throwing (simply); a throw; the distance thrown. **2.** *spec.* A throw of dice 1509. Also *fig.* **3.** A throw or stroke of fortune; *hence*, fortune; fate. *Obs.* or *dial.* ME. **4.** A throw of a sounding-lead, fishing-line, net, dredge, etc. 1616; *spec.* in *Angling*, that which is so cast 1556; a spot suitable for casting 1823. **5.** A throwing of the eye in any direction; a glance, a look, expression. ?*Obs.* ME. **6.** A lift in a conveyance. Also *fig.* 1630. **7.** *fig.* 'A stroke, a touch' (J.), specimen, taste 1553.

1. The disputed c. was a drawn one SCOTT. *A measuring c.*: one in which the results require measurement. About a stones c. *Luke* 22:41. **2.** 'Tis no winning c. MILT. *To set, stake upon a c.* **3.** Black be their c. 1722. † *At the last c.*, i.e. the last shift. **4.** The right to a c. of the net BURTON. A c. suited to the state of the water 1883. **5.** With a sad, leaden, downward c. MILT. *Pens.* 43. **7.** A c. of one's office 1575, cunning 1589, politics 1676.

II. A throw in wrestling; an overthrow (*arch.*) ME.

III. A throwing; the quantity thrown 1450.

A c. of scatter'd dust DRYDEN. A c. (= a couple) of hawks, etc. 1470. † A c. (= a batch) of bread B. JONS. A c. (= the number in one throw, viz. three or four, a warp) of herrings 1577.

IV. That which is thrown off or out.

A c. (= a second swarm) of bees FULLER. The c. (= what is thrown up from the crop) of a hawk TENNYSON. The c. of an earthworm G. WHITE.

V. Calculation; *techn.* the addition of the columns of an account 1575.

† **VI.** Device, design; trick –1609.

VII. Form into which a thing is thrown; disposition, arrangement 1579. **2.** *Theat.* The assignment of the parts in a play to the several actors; † the part assigned to any actor; the set of actors collectively 1631.

1. The c. of draperies (in *Painting*) 1784, of a sentence M. ARNOLD. **2.** A powerful c. (*mod.*).

VIII. † **1.** Casting or founding 1602. **2.** A model made in a mould; *occ.*, the negative impression taken from the original, a mould 1502. Also *transf.* and *fig.*

1. C. of Brazon Cannon *Haml.* I. i. 73. **2.** Books, pictures, castes EVELYN. A c. of my head JOHNSON. *Renal casts*: the urinary tubules found in kidney disease.

IX. A twist or turn, *esp.* to one side; a bearing 1505.

C. of the eye: a slight squint.

X. 1. Dash or shade of colour; tinge, hue; shade 1602. Also *fig.* **2.** A dash 1662.

1. The pale C. of Thought SHAKS. A deeper c. of dejection 1820. **2.** A c. of ironical humour SCOTT.

XI. Kind, sort, style, quality, stamp, type 1653.

A sinister c. of countenance MARRYAT. This C. of mind ADDISON. A C. (= bent) towards Devotion 1711. A c. of talk JOHNSON. Heroines of such a c. GIBBON.

XII. *Hunting.* The spreading out of the hounds in search of a lost scent 1830. Also *fig.*

Cast (kɑst), *v.* Pa. t. and pa. pple. **cast.** [ME. *casten* – ON. *kasta* to cast; replacing OE. *weorpan* (see WARP), and now itself replaced in the literal sense by THROW, q.v.] **I. 1.** *trans.* To project with a force of the nature of a jerk; to THROW; to fling, hurl, pitch, toss. Also *fig.* Occ. *absol.* **2.** *refl.* To throw oneself (not colloq.) ME. **3.** To throw forth ME. † **4.** To emit –1742. **5.** To cause to fall *on, over*, etc. ME. † **6.** To toss (the head) –1792.

1. Certayn men . . keste water vpon him CAXTON. † *To c. seed.* Now usu. *fig.* C. thy bread vpon the waters *Eccles.* 11:1. To c. dice 1565, votes 1871. *To c. lots*: see LOT. † To c. an arrow WYCLIF. *C. ashore, away*, etc. **2.** Low on her knees herself she cast TENNYSON. **3.** To c. a net 1526, an angle B. JONS., a flye 1651, an anchor 1798, a lure 1682. *To c. an eye, glance, look*, etc. † *To c. a reflection upon.* **5.** *To c. light, a shadow* (*on*). *To c. into the shade.*

II. 1. To throw down, overthrow, defeat 1481. † **2.** To find guilty, convict –1849. † **3.** To condemn. Const. *for* (the penalty). –1816. Also *fig.* and *transf.*

1. The king was cast from the throne 1755. To c. a horse 1577, a sheep 1882. To c. in wrestling *Macb.* II. iii. 46. Now *arch.* Cast in damages 1854. **3.** Cast for transportation 1772.

III. 1. To throw off, out, away ME. **2.** *esp.* To shed, or drop, out of due season 1477. **3.** To vomit. Now only of hawks, etc. (exc. *dial.*) ME. Also *absol.* **4.** To dismiss, reject; *esp.* as disqualified or unfit ME.

1. To c. a shoe SCOTT, a rider SPENSER. Cast not a clout till May be out *Old Maxim.* To c. the skin, as reptiles, caterpillars 1626; so, to c. hair, horns, teeth, leaves (now *arch.*). To c. spawn WALTON, eggs ADDISON, young 1769. To c. a swarm (of bees) 1523. **2.** As a figge tree casteth her vntimely figs *Rev.* 6:13. To c. a calf, a lamb 1523. **3.** *To c. the gorge*: to retch. *Temp.* II. i. 251. To c. a sigh CAXTON, a shout POPE. **4.** The State. Cannot with safetie c. him *Oth.* I. i. 150. Horses cast from the cavalry 1817. C. in an examination 1854.

IV. To throw up with a spade or shovel; *hence*, † to clear out (a ditch, etc.) –1614; † to raise (a mound, etc.) –1667.

To c. sods, turf, peat (north.). To c. a rampart MILT.

V. 1. To put with force, decisiveness, or haste. (Now usu. *throw.*) ME. Also *fig.* **2.** To put *into* ME. † **3.** To set *to* (*upon*) some action –1662. **4.** To confer, allot (*arch.*) 1612.

1. Cast thy mantle aboute the COVERDALE *Acts* 12:8. To c. cares 1751, blame 1842, an imputation 1883, upon a person. **2.** To c. into prison ME., into hell JOWETT. **4.** To c. an estate upon the heir TOMLINS.

VI. To reckon, calculate (orig. by means of counters) ME.

(*intr.*) † *To c. at accounts.* To c. and balance at a desk TENNYSON. (*trans.*) The books were cast 1805. *To c. accounts*: orig. to sum up accounts: now to perform the operations of arithmetic. To c. the tides 1642. *To c. a horoscope, nativity*, etc. Also *absol.* † *To c. water*: to diagnose by the inspection of (urine). *To c. beyond the moon*: to conjecture wildly. † (trans.) *To c. danger, peril, the worst.*

VII. To resolve in one's mind, deliberate ME.; to contrive ME.; † to design (*to do*) –1808.

They caste..how they myght breng hym out of prison CAXTON. Cast to have the wind on your back WALTON.

VIII. 1. To dispose, arrange ME. **2.** *Theat.* To allot (the parts) *to* the actors; to appoint (actors) *for* the parts 1711.

1. To c. streets in comely fashion BIBLE *Pref.* 8. To c. (facts) under heads 1710, into a series of letters H. MILLER. † To c. a drapery (in *Painting*) 1706. **2.** Our parts in the other world will be new cast ADDISON. They..cast me for the part 1809.

IX. To form (metal, etc.) *into* a shape, by pouring it when melted into a mould; to found. (Now a frequent literal sense.) ME. Also *fig.*

To c. into candlesticks 1814. A figure cast in soft wax HOGARTH. *fig.* To c. inventions in a new mould 1606.

X. To turn, twist. [Parallel to *warp*.] **1.** Of timber, etc.: To warp 1544. **2.** *Naut.* To veer 1671. Also *trans.* **3.** To turn (the scale or balance) (*arch.*) (Cf. *casting-vote*.) 1597.

1. Oake..will shrink, cast, drawe a nayle 1641. **2.** To c. to port 1882. **3.** To c. the balance J. H. NEWMAN.

† **XI.** To cover by casting (mortar, etc.) on. (Cf. ROUGH-CAST.) –1663.

XII. Unplaced senses. † **1.** To tie (a knot) –1825. **2.** *Hunting. intr.* To spread out and search for a lost scent 1704. Also *transf.* and *fig.* 1823. (*trans.*) To put on the scent 1781.

2. Cast forward first..Cast far and near, cast all around R. E. WARBURTON. *fig.* To c. for excuses BROWNING.

Phrases and Combs. **1. To c. loose:** to unfasten with force, set adrift. **To c. anchor, a damper, lots:** see those words. **2.** (See also simple senses and advbs.) **To c. about: a.** *intr.* to turn about; *Naut.* to change the course; **b.** to go searching this way and that, *orig.* a hunting locution; **c.** to devise means. **To c. aside:** to throw aside from use. **To c. away: a.** to put from one; **b.** to throw away, i.e. in waste or loss; **c.** to wreck; to strand. **To c. back:** to go back over the same course, revert. † **To c. by:** to throw aside from use. **To c. down: a.** to demolish; **b.** to bend and turn downward (the eyes, etc.); **c.** to deject in spirits. **To c. forth: a.** to expel, eject; † **b.** to throw out (branches, etc.). **To c. in:** to throw in (as something extra); in *To c. in one's lot among* or *with*: to become a partner with. **To c. off: a.** to throw off (clothes, etc.); also *fig.*; **b.** *fig.* to put from one, abandon; **c.** to slip (dogs); to let fly (hawks); **d.** *Naut.* to loosen and throw off (a rope, etc.); **e.** to estimate space taken in print by MS. copy; **f.** *Knitting*, to close loops and make selvedge. **To c. out: a.** to expel, make an outcast (*lit.* and *fig.*); **b.** to thrust out of doors, society, etc.; **c.** to vomit; also *transf.* and *absol.*; **d.** *intr.* to quarrel (*Sc.* and *n. dial.*). **To c. up:** † **a.** to vomit; said also of the sea; **b.** to raise suddenly (the eyes, the head); **c.** to throw up (with a shovel); **d.** to rake up and throw in one's teeth (*Sc.* and *n. dial.*); **e.** to add up, calculate; **f.** *intr.* to turn up, appear (*Sc.* and *north.*).

Ca·stable, *sb. rare.* 1821. [f. prec. + -ABLE.] The projection of waste metal on cast articles.

Castalia (kæstēⁱ·liă), **Castalie, -y** (kæ·stăli). 1591. [– L. *Castalia* – Gr. Κασταλία; *castalie, -ly* is the regular adoptive form in Eng.] A spring on Mount Parnassus, sacred to the Muses; often used allusively. Hence **Casta·lian** *a.* of Castalia or the Muses.

† **Castane, -anie, -ayne.** ME. [– ONFr. *castanie, castaine* (mod. *châtaigne*) :– L. *castanea*.] A chestnut –1567.

Castaneous (kæstēⁱ·niŏs), *a.* 1688. [f. L. *castanea* chestnut + -OUS; see -EOUS.] Chestnut-coloured. So **Casta·nean.**

Castanet (ka·stănĕt, -ane·t). 1647. [– Sp. *castañeta* (with later assim. to Fr. *castagnette*), dim. of *castaña* :– L. *castanea* CHESTNUT; see -ET.] A small concave shell of ivory or hard wood, used by the Spaniards, Moors, and others, to produce a rattling sound or rhythmic tapped accompaniment to dancing; a pair of them, fastened to the thumb, are held in the palm of the hand, and struck with the middle finger. Usu. in *pl.*

Castinettas, knackers, of the form of chesnuts.., used by the Spaniards in their dances 1647.

Castaway (ka·stăweⁱ). 1526. [f. CAST *v.*] **A.** *adj.* Rejected; reprobate; useless; stranded 1542.

C. bones of the deer, bear, and wild-ox PAGE.

B. *sb.* One who or that which is cast away or rejected; a reprobate 1526; a shipwrecked man 1799. Also *fig.*

Reprobates and castawaies 1563. Wreck and stray and c. SWINBURNE. The castaways of Society 1869.

Caste (kast). 1555. [– Sp. and Pg. *casta*, subst. use (sc. *raza, raça* race) of fem. of *casto* pure, unmixed (see CHASTE).] † **1.** A race, stock, or breed –1774. **2.** *spec.* One of the hereditary classes into which society in India has long been divided. Also *transf.* 1613.

The members of each caste are socially equal, have the same religious rites, and generally follow the same occupation or profession; they have no social intercourse with those of another caste. The original castes were four: 1st, the *Brahmans* or priestly caste; 2nd, the *Kshatriyas* or military caste; 3rd, the *Vaisyas* or merchants; 4th, the *Sudras*, or artisans and labourers. Now almost every variety of occupation has its caste.

3. *fig.* A class who keep themselves socially distinct, or inherit exclusive privileges 1807. **4.** This system among the Hindus; also the position it confers, as in *To lose*, or *renounce c.* 1811. Also *gen.* and *fig.*

3. That repose Which stamps the c. of Vere de Vere TENNYSON. **4.** *fig.* Loss of c. in society 1816.

† **Ca·sted,** *ppl. a.* Earlier f. CAST. SHAKS.

Castellan (ka·stĕlăn). [ME. *castelain* – ONFr. *castelain* (mod. *châtelain*) :– med. L. *castellanus* governor of a castle, in cl. L. adj. pertaining to a *castellum* fortified place; see CASTLE, -AN. Current sp. refash. after L.] The governor or constable of a castle. Hence **Ca·stellany,** the lordship of a castle, or its district.

Castellar (kæste·lăɹ), *a.* 1789. [f. L. *castellum* castle + -AR¹.] Pertaining to, or of the nature of, a castle.

Castellated (kæ·stĕleⁱtĕd), *ppl. a.* 1679. [f. med. L. *castellatus*, f. L. *castellum* CASTLE; see -ATE², -ED¹.] **1.** Built like a castle; having battlements. Also *transf.* † **2.** 'Enclosed within a building, as a fountain or cistern' –1766. **3.** Dotted with castles 1808. **4.** Lodged in a castle (*rare*) 1837.

1. *transf.* C. mountains H. WALPOLE. **3.** The c. Rhine BYRON. So **Ca·stellate** *a.* (*rare*). Hence **Ca·stellate** *v.* to build with battlements.

Castellation (kæstĕlēⁱ·ʃən). 1818. [f. *castellat-*, pa. ppl. stem of med.L. *castellare* build castles, f. L. *castellum* CASTLE; cf. prec., see -ION.] The building of castles; the furnishing of a house with battlements; *concr.* a castellated structure; a battlement.

Ca·stellet, -elet. ME. [– ONFr. *castelet* (mod. *châtelet*), dim. of *castel*; see CASTLE, -ET, CHATELET.] A small castle. var. † **Ca·stlet.**

Casten, *ppl. a.* By-form of CAST pa. pple. Now *dial.*

Caster (ka·stəɹ). ME. [f. CAST *v.* + -ER¹.] One who casts (see CAST *v.*). **2.** See CASTOR².

1. A c. of accounts 1598, of nativities 1611, of the evil eye 1887. *spec.* A c. in brass 1662, of cannon 1884.

Castigate (kæ·stigeⁱt), *v.* 1607. [– *castigat-*, pa. ppl. stem of L. *castigare* correct, reprove, f. *castus* pure; see -ATE³. Cf. CHASTISE, CHASTEN.] **1.** To chastise, correct; to subdue by punishment or discipline; now usu., to punish or rebuke severely. Also † *transf.* **2.** To correct, revise, and emend 1666. Hence **Ca·stigator,** one who castigates. **Ca·stigatory,** *a.* corrective, punitive; † *sb.* an instrument of chastisement.

Castigation (kæstigēⁱ·ʃən). ME. [– L. *castigatio*, f. as prec.; see -ION.] **1.** † Corrective punishment or discipline –1677; now, severe punishment or rebuke, flagellation 1640. **2.** Correction, emendation 1611.

1. A well-merited c. 1831.

Castile soap (kăsti·l sōᵘ·p). Formerly **castle-soap.** 1616. [f. *Castile*, in Spain, where orig. made.] A fine hard soap, white or mottled, made with olive oil and soda.

Casti·lian, *sb.*¹ 1570. [var. of CASTELLAN.] One living in a castle; one of the garrison of a castle. Now *Hist.*

Castilian (kĕsti·liăn), *a.* and *sb.*² 1526. [In sense 1 – Sp. *Castellano* pertaining to Castile (*Castella*, so called from the forts erected by Alfonso I for its defence).] **1.** Of or pertaining to Castile; a native of Castile; the language of that province, *hence*, standard Spanish 1796. **2.** A Spanish gold coin worth about 5*s.* *Hist.* 1526.

Casting (ka·stiŋ), *vbl. sb.* ME. [f. CAST *v.* + -ING¹.] **1.** The action of the vb. **2.** *concr.* **a.** Any product of casting in a mould. **b.** The earth cast up by worms. **c.** Vomit; *esp.* what is cast up by hawks and the like. late ME.

1. A c. of the skin BACON, of a story M. ARNOLD, of a nativity 1825. Reasoning is..c. about LOCKE. C. or warping 1823.

Comb., etc.: **c.-box,** † a dice-box; also, a box used for taking a cast in stereotyping; † **-counters** *pl.*, counters used in calculation; **-bottle,** a vinaigrette.

Casting (ka·stiŋ), *ppl. a.* ME. [f. as prec. + -ING².] **1.** That casts (see CAST *v.*). **2.** That turns the scale, deciding, as in *c. voice, vote, weight* 1622.

Cast iron, cast-i·ron. 1664. [See CAST *v.* IX.] **1.** Iron run in a molten state into moulds where it has cooled and hardened. Also *attrib.* (*commonly hyphened.*) **2.** *fig.* Hard, insensible to fatigue; rigid, stern; wanting in pliancy. (*hyphened.*) 1830.

2. A cast-iron Statesman 1830, rule 1876.

Castle (ka·s'l), *sb.* [– AFr., ONFr. *castel*, var. of *chastel* (mod. *château*) :– L. *castellum*, dim. of *castrum* fortified place. In late OE. and ME. biblical use rendering L. *castellum* in the sense 'village' (Gr. κώμη) and as tr. of L. *castra* camp. See CHESTER.] **I.** From Latin. † **1.** As tr. L. *castellum* of the Vulgate, village –1564. † **2.** *pl.* As tr. L. *castra* camp –1483.

II. From French. **1.** A large building or set of buildings fortified for defence; a fortress. Retained as a name for large mansions which were formerly feudal castles. OE. Also *fig.* (or *allegorical*). **2.** *poet.* or *rhet.* for: A large ship 1642. **3.** A tower borne on the back of an elephant ME. **4.** *Naut.* A tower on the deck of a ship. Cf. FORECASTLE. ME. **5.** Applied (in proper names) to ancient earthworks, as *Round C.* near Oxford, etc. **6.** *Chess.* One of the pieces, made to represent a castle; a ROOK 1649.

1. A castel al of lime and ston CHAUCER. The mill buys out the c. EMERSON. *The Castle*, in reference to Ireland, means specifically *Dublin Castle*, as the seat of the vice-regal court and administration; hence, in politics, the authority centred there, the officials who administered the government of Ireland. Also *attrib.* Phr. *An (English)man's house is his c.* **2.** The floating Castles dance upon the Tide 1695.

Phrase. **Castle in the air,** visionary project, day-dream, idle fancy. Occ. *castle in Spain* [= Fr. *château en Espagne*] is found; also *castle* alone.

Comb.: † **c.-bote,** the keeping of a c. in repair, a contribution levied for this purpose; **-town,** a town defended by a c.; also (*Sc.*) a collection of houses lying under or near a c. Hence **Ca·stle-like** *a.* and *adv.*

Castle (ka·s'l), *v.* ME. [f. prec.] **1.** To enclose in, or as in, a castle 1587. † **2.** To ornament with battlements. CHAUCER. **3.** *Chess.* To move the king laterally towards the castle (rook), which is then moved to the square next to him on the other side 1656.

Ca·stle-bui:lder. 1711. One who builds castles in the air, a day-dreamer, a visionary schemer. So **Ca·stle-bui:lding** *vbl. sb.* and *ppl. a.*

Castled (ka·s'ld), *ppl. a.* 1662. [f. CASTLE *sb.* + -ED².] **1.** Furnished with a castle or castles. **2.** Castellated 1789.

1. Norham's c. steep SCOTT. **2.** In the c. house.. Which sheltered their childhood M. ARNOLD.

Castle-guard. 1. The guard of a castle. **2.** *Feudal Syst.* A kind of knight-service, whereby a tenant was bound, when required, to defend the lord's castle; the tenure of such service 1576. **3.** A tax orig. in commutation of this service; also the land chargeable therewith 1576.

† **Ca·stlery, castelry.** 1679. [f. *castel*, CASTLE *sb.* + -(E)RY; or – OFr. *castelerie* territory belonging to a castle, med. L. *castellaria* in same sense.] The jurisdiction of a castle; the territory subject to it. var. † **Ca·stleship.**

Castle-soap, see CASTILE SOAP.

Ca·stleward. ME. [See WARD *sb.*] † **1.** The warden of a castle. **2.** = CASTLEGUARD 2, 3. 1576.

† **Castling** (kɑ·stliŋ), *sb.* 1580. [f. CAST *ppl. a.* or *sb.* + -LING[1].] **1.** The offspring of an untimely birth; an abortion –1704. **2.** The second (or third) swarm from one hive in the season –1662.

1. C. Foles of Bal'am's Ass BUTLER *Hud.* II. ii. 539.

Ca·stling, *vbl. sb.* [f. CASTLE *v.* + -ING[1].] See CASTLE *v.*

† **Cast-me-down.** A popular perversion f. CASSIDONY.

Ca·st-off, *ppl. a.* and *sb.*[1] 1741. [f. CAST *ppl. a.*] *ppl. a.* Thrown off, discarded: as clothes, a lover, etc. 1746. *sb.* [sc. *person* or *thing.*] (*Cast-offs* is the better pl.)

Cast-off, *sb.*[2] 1881. [f. CAST *sb.* + OFF.] The twist of a gun-stock.

Castor[1] (kɑ·stəɹ). 1547. [– (O)Fr. or L. *castor* – Gr. κάστωρ beaver.] **1.** The beaver. (Now *rare.*) **2.** A reddish-brown unctuous substance, having a strong smell and nauseous bitter taste, obtained from two sacs in the inguinal region of the beaver; used in medicine and in perfumery; castoreum 1601. **3.** A hat, orig. of beaver's fur; later of rabbit's fur and spelt *caster.* Now *colloq.* or *slang.* Cf. BEAVER. 1640. **4.** 'A heavy quality of broadcloth used for overcoats' (Webster).

3. A Beaver [and] a new Caster 1688.

Castor[2] (kɑ·stəɹ). Also **caster.** 1676. [var. of CASTER; the sp. *-or* for *-er* (still current) may have been favoured as being more appropriate to an instrument; cf. words in *-ator*, and see -OR 2 d.] **1.** A small vessel with a perforated top, from which to cast ground pepper, etc.; extended to other vessels used to contain condiments at table, as in 'a set of castors'. **2.** A small wheel and swivel attached to furniture, so that it may be moved without lifting; see CAST *v.* X. 1748.

1. *C. sugar*: powdered sugar, so called as being suitable for use in a c.

Ca·stor[3]. 1526. **1.** The first star in the constellation Gemini or the Twins, the second being Pollux; the two representing the twin sons of Tyndarus and Leda. **2.** CORPOSANT or St. Elmo's fire 1708.

Castor[4] (kɑ·stəɹ). 1888. [Origin unkn.] The piece of horn inside the hock of the horse. Cf. CHESTNUT.

Castor[5]. *Min.* See CASTORITE.

‖ **Castoreum** (kæstō̆ᵊ·riə̆m). ME. [L., f. *castor* beaver.] = CASTOR[1] 2. var. † **Ca·story.**

Casto·rial, *a.* [f. CASTOR[1] 3 + -IAL.] (*joc.*) Pertaining to a hat. LOWELL.

Ca·storin. 1831. [f. CASTOR[1] + -IN[1].] *Chem.* A crystalline substance obtained from castoreum.

Ca·storite. 1868. [This mineral and another were at first named *Castor* and *Pollux*, see -ITE[1] 2 b.] *Min.* A variety of Petalite.

Castor oil (kɑ·stəɹ oi·l). 1746. [History of present use is obscure; it is supposed that this oil took the place in medical use of the drug castoreum (called *huile de castor* by Paré XVI).] A pale yellow oil obtained from the seeds of *Ricinus communis* or Palma Christi; used as a purgative, and, locally, in lamps. Also *attrib.*

Castral (kæ·străl), *a.* 1844. [f. L. *castra* camp + -AL[1].] Belonging to the camp.

Castrametation (kæ:strămĭtēⁱ·ʃən). 1679. [– Fr. *castramétation*, f. L. *castra metari* measure or mark out a camp (*meta* boundary, prop. pillar, post).] The art or science of laying out a camp.

Ca·strate, *a.* (sb). 1639. [– L. *castratus*, pa. pple. of *castrare*; see next, -ATE[2], [1].] *adj.* Castrated. *Obs.* exc. in *Bot.* 1704. † *sb.* [sc. *man.*] –1691.

Castrate (kæ·streⁱt), *v.* 1613. [– *castrat-*, pa. ppl. stem of L. *castrare*, perh. f. **castrum* knife; see -ATE[3].] **1.** To remove the testicles of; to geld. Also *transf.* and *fig.* **2.** To mutilate (a book, etc.) by removing parts of it; *esp.* to remove obscene or objectionable passages from; to expurgate 1627.

2. The following letter, which I have castrated in some places ADDISON. Hence **Castra·tion.**

‖ **Castrato** (kastrā·to). Pl. **castrati.** 1763. [It.; pa. pple. of *castrare* used subst.] A male singer castrated in boyhood so as to retain a soprano or alto voice.

Castrensian (kæstre·nsiăn), *a.* 1657. [f. L. *castrensis* pertaining to a camp (*castra*) + -AN; see -IAN.] Of or pertaining to a camp; camp-. So † **Castre·nsial.**

Casual (kæ·ʒⁱuăl, kæ·ziuăl), *a.* (*sb.*) ME. [Late ME. *casuel, -all* – (O)Fr. *casuel* and L. *casualis* (in its late and med. uses), f. *casus* CASE *sb.*[1]; see -AL[1].] **1.** Subject to or produced by chance; accidental, fortuitous. **2.** Coming at uncertain times; not to be calculated on, unsettled 1460. **3.** Occurring without design 1667. † **4.** Liable to happen –1645. † **5.** Subject to chance or accident –1729. **6.** Of persons, etc.: Not to be depended on, uncertain, happy-go-lucky (*colloq.*) 1883. † **7.** Casuistic (*rare*) –1753. ¶ **8.** = CAUSAL 1578.

1. That which seemeth most c. and subject to fortune RALEIGH. **2.** Both the known and c. Revenue CLARENDON. **3.** To talk of c. things DE FOE. **6.** A c. man 1883. Hence c. (= occasional) *labourer, poor, ward*, etc. A *c. ejector* (*Law*) was a fictitious ejector in an action formerly allowed to determine the title to land. Hence **Ca·sual-ly** *adv.*, **-ness** (*rare*).

B. *sb.* † **1.** A chance. (Chiefly in *pl.*) –1652. **2.** [sc. *revenue*] 1825. **3.** *colloq.* = c. workman, visitor, pauper, ward, etc. 1860.

Ca·sualism. 1873. [f. prec. + -ISM.] The doctrine that all things exist or happen by chance; a state of things in which chance reigns. So **Ca·sualist,** one who holds the doctrine of c.

† **Casua·lity.** 1540. [– Fr. *casualité* – med.L. *casualitas*; see CASUAL, -ITY. Superseded by (earlier form) CASUALTY.] **1.** Chance; a chance; *esp.* an unfortunate accident –1792. **2.** A casual source of income –1649.

Casualty (kæ·ʒⁱu₁ălti, kæ·ziu₁ălti). ME. [– med.L. *casualitas* (see prec.), on the model of forms like *royalty, penalty*; thus *speciality specialty*; see -TY[1].] **1.** Chance (as a state of things). ? *Obs.* **2.** A chance occurrence, an accident; now generally a fatal or serious accident. **b.** *Mil.* Used of losses by death, desertion, etc. 1494. † **3.** Liability to accident –1812. **4.** A casual charge or payment 1529. ¶ Erron. for CAUSALITY 1635.

1. Combinations of genius with happy c. JOHNSON. **2.** Casualties of the service 1810, on our coast 1861. *attrib.* in *c. ward*, the ward in a hospital where accidents are treated.

‖ **Casuarina** (kæ:siu₁ărəi·nă). 1806. [f. mod. L. *casuarius* cassowary, from the likeness of the branches to the feathers of the bird.] *Bot.* A genus of trees, with jointed leafless branches, resembling gigantic horse-tails (*Equiseta*), natives of Australia, etc. The Australian species is known as *Beef-wood*, and Oak.

Casuist (kæ·ziu₁ist, kæ·ʒⁱu₁ist). 1609. [– Fr. *casuiste* – Sp. (mod. L.) *casuista*, f. L. *casus* CASE *sb.*[1]; see -IST.] One who studies and resolves cases of conscience. (Often used in a sinister sense; see CASUISTRY.)

Casuists willing and competent to soothe his conscience with Sophisms MACAULAY. Hence † **Ca·suist** *v.* to play the c. **Ca·suistess,** a female c. **Casui·stic, -al,** *a.* pertaining to casuists or casuistry. **Casuis·tically** *adv.*

Casuistry (kæ·ziu₁istri, kæ·ʒⁱu-). 1725. [f. CASUIST + -RY. At first contemptuous; cf. *sophistry*, etc.] The science, art, or reasoning of the casuist; that part of Ethics which resolves cases of conscience, applying the general rules of religion and morality to particular instances which disclose special circumstances, or conflicting duties. Often applied to a quibbling or evasive way of dealing with difficult cases of duty; sophistry. **2.** A register of (medical) cases 1883.

1. C. destroys, by distinctions and exceptions, all morality BOLINGBROKE.

† **Ca·sule.** [In XVI – OFr. *casule* or its source, late L. *casula* hooded cloak, (later) chasuble. In late OE. direct – late L. See CHASUBLE.] = CHASUBLE –1824.

†‖ **Ca·sus.** 1571. [L., = fall, falling.] Each of the segments of the base of a triangle cut off by a perpendicular falling from the vertex.

Cat (kæt), *sb.*[1] [OE. *catt* m. (= ON. *kǫttr*), *catte* fem. (= OFris., MDu. *katte*, Du. *kat*, OHG. *kazza*, G. *katze*); reinforced in ME. by *cat, kat* – AFr., ONFr. *cat*, var. of (O)Fr. *chat* = Pr., Cat. *gat*, Sp. *gato*, It. *gatto* :– late L. *cattus* (Palladius), also *catta* fem., which superseded the older *feles* on the introduction of the domestic cat into Rome.] **I. 1.** A carnivorous quadruped, *Felis domesticus*, which has long been domesticated. The Wild c., *Felis sylvestris*, native and still found in Great Britain, is larger than the domestic cat. Also *fig.* **2.** *Zool.* (usu. in *pl.*) A member of the genus *Felis* or *Panthera*, including the lion, tiger, etc. 1607. **3.** Used of animals of similar appearance, as *civet-, pole-c.*, etc.; also in **flying-c.,** an owl (cf. F. *chat-huant*); **sea-c.,** the Wolf-fish 1553. † **4.** Cat-skin, cat's fur –1677.

1. The mouse hounter or catte is an onclene beste 1520. *fig.* His mother called me an old c. MARRYAT. **3.** *A.Y.L.* III. ii. 70.

II. Transf. **1.** A movable pent-house, used in sieges, also called *cat-house* 1489. † Also = CAVALIER A. 4. –1652. **2.** *Naut.* Applied to different parts of the tackle used to raise an anchor out of the water to the deck of the ship, or suspend it outside clear of the bows; chiefly = CAT-HEAD 1626. **3.** = CAT-O'-NINE-TAILS 1788. **4.** A double tripod with six legs, so placed that it always rests on three legs 1806. **5.** A term used in games: *esp.* A piece of wood tapering at each end, used in tip-cat; also, the game itself 1598.

3. This Cat's a cousin-german to the Knout WOLCOTT. Phrases. *To turn c. in pan*: to change sides, from motives of interest, etc. *To see (watch) which way the c. jumps*: i.e. which direction events are taking. *To let the c. out of the bag*: see BAG. *To grin like a Cheshire c.* (see N. & Q. 1852 V. 402).

Comb., etc.: **c.-block** (*Naut.*), a two- or three-fold block forming part of the c.-tackle; **-fall** (*Naut.*), the rope between the c.-block and the sheaves in the c.-head; **-gold, cat's-gold** (Ger. *katzengold*), a yellowish variety of mica (cf. *cat-silver*); **-ha·mmed,** having hams like those of a c.; **-hook** (*Naut.*), a strong hook on the c.-block; **-house** (see 1 above); **-ice, cat's ice,** thin ice of a milky white appearance in shallow places; **-ladder,** a kind of ladder used on sloping roofs; **-nap,** a short nap while sitting; **-purchase** (*Naut.*) = *cat-tackle*; **-rope** (*Naut.*), a line for hauling the c.-hook about; **-salt,** a kind of common salt, finely granulated, formed out of the bittern or leach brine; **-silver,** mica with a silvery appearance; **-sleep** = *cat-nap*; **-tackle** (*Naut.*), the tackle to raise the anchor to the c.-head.

† **Cat,** *sb.*[2] Also **catt.** 1699. [perh. the same wd. as prec. Cf. med.L. *catta* kind of ship, OFr. *chat*, etc., merchant ship.] A strong vessel with a narrow stern, projecting quarters, and a deep waist; formerly used in the coal and timber trade on the north-east coast –1825. ? Hence **c.-boat,** a sailing-boat having the mast placed very forward and rigged with one sail; **c.-rig,** a rig of one fore-and-aft mainsail.

Cat (kæt), *v.* 1769. [Goes with CAT *sb.*[1] II 2, and CAT-HEAD.] **1.** *Naut.* To raise (the anchor) from the surface of the water to the cat-head. **2.** To flog with the cat-o'-nine-tails 1856. **3.** *slang.* To vomit 1877.

Cata- (kata-), cat-, cath-. [Gr. κατα-, κατ-, καθ-, used in comp.] **a.** Down (locally); **b.** down, away, entirely; **c.** implying disparagement (= *mis-*); **d.** inferior; **e.** down upon; **f.** against and reflected back, *hence*, answering to; **g.** intensive, downright, completely; **h.** *hence*, like Eng. *be-*, making a vb. transitive.

† **Cataba·ptist.** 1561. [– med.Gr. καταβαπτιστής (Gregory of Nazianzen) administrator of irregular or schismatic baptism, f. καταβαπτίζειν; see CATA-, BAPTIST.] One who opposes baptism –1864.

‖ **Cataba·sion.** 1753. [Gr. καταβάσιον.] A place for relics under the altar of a Greek church.

Catabatic (-bæ·tik), *a.* 1881. [– Gr. καταβατικός affording an easy descent, f. καταβαίνειν go down; see -IC.] *Med.* Of a fever: Declining by degrees.

Catacaustic (kætăkǭ·stik), *a.* and *sb.* 1708. [f. CATA- + CAUSTIC 3. Cf. Fr. *catacaustique.*] *C.* (*curve*): a caustic curve formed by reflection.

‖ **Catachresis** (kætăkrī·sis). 1589. [L. – Gr. κατάχρησις misuse (of a word), f. καταχρῆσθαι misuse.] Improper use of words; application of a term to a thing which it does not properly denote; abuse of a trope or metaphor.

Lakes..by the figure c. called seas 1605. Hence **Catachre·stic, -al** *a.* of the nature of c.; **-ly** *adv.*

Catachthonian, -thonic, *a.* 1884. [– Gr. καταχθόνιος, f. κατά under + χθόνιος of the ground, + -IAN.] Subterranean.

Cataclasm (kæ·täklæz'm). 1829. [– Gr. κατάκλασμα breakage, f. κατακλᾶν break down.] A break or disruption. Hence **Cataclas·mic** *a.*

Cataclysm (kæ·täkliz'm). 1637. [– Fr. *cataclysme* – L. *cataclysmos* – Gr. κατακλυσμός deluge, f. κατά down + κλύζειν wash.] A great and general flood of water; *esp.* the Flood. (In *Geol.* used vaguely for a sudden convulsion or alteration of physical conditions.) Also *fig.*

fig. That the Indian army surgeons will be swept away in the general c. 1861. Hence **Catacly·smal, Catacly·smic** *adjs.* of, pertaining to, or like a c.

Cataclysmist (kætäkli·zmist). 1887. [f. prec. + -IST.] One who adopts the hypothesis of cataclysms in Geology; a catastrophist. var. **Catacly·smatist** (*rare*).

Catacomb (kæ·täkōᵘm). OE. [– Fr. *catacombes* – late L. *catacumbas*, specific name from c. 400 of the cemetery of St. Sebastian on the Appian Way, (*Cœmeterium*) *Catacumbas.* Ult. origin unkn.] **1.** A subterranean place for the burial of the dead, consisting of galleries with recesses in their sides for tombs.

a. Used in the 5th c. in connection with the cemetery under the Basilica of St. Sebastian, on the Appian Way, near Rome. **b.** Applied later (in the pl.) to all the subterranean cemeteries lying around Rome. In the sing. applied to a single crypt or gallery. 1662. **c.** Extended to similar works elsewhere, as in Egypt, etc. 1705.

2. Any subterranean receptacle of dead bodies, as the catacombs of Paris, which are worked-out stone quarries; also *fig.* **3.** *transf.* A compartment with recesses in a wine-cellar 1795.

2. *fig.* A perfect c. for monsters of extinct races DARWIN.

Catacoustics (kætăkau·stiks). 1683. [f. CATA- f. + ACOUSTICS. Cf. CATOPTRICS.] The science of reflected sounds.

Catadioptric, -al (kæ:tă,dəi,ǫ·ptrik, -ăl), *a.* 1723. [f. CATA- in CATOPTRIC + DIOPTRIC.] Pertaining to or involving both the reflection and the refraction of light. So **Catadio·ptrics,** the science of c. phenomena.

Catadrome (kæ·tădrōᵘm). 1623. [– L. *catadromus* – Gr. κατάδρομος lists for exercising.] † **1.** A course for tilting. (Dicts.) **2.** A machine for lifting or lowering heavy weights 1656.

Catadromous (katæ·drŏməs), *a.* 1881. [f. CATA- + -δρομος running + -OUS, after ANADROMOUS.] **1.** *Zool.* Of freshwater fishes: Descending to or towards the sea to spawn; as the Eel 1883. **2.** *Bot.* Of ferns: Having the lowest secondary branches originating on the posterior side of the pinnæ 1881.

† **Ca·tadupe.** 1596. [– Fr. *catadoupe*, also *-dupe* (XVI) – L. *catadupa* (pl.) – Gr. κατάδουποι (pl.) the cataracts of the Nile, f. κατά down + δοῦπος thud.] A cataract or waterfall, *orig.* those of the Nile –1755.

Catafalque (kæ·tăfælk). 1641. [– Fr. *catafalque* – It. *catafalco* (also used), of unkn. origin. See SCAFFOLD.] **1.** A temporary structure of carpentry, representing a tomb or cenotaph, and used in funeral ceremonies. **2.** An open hearse 1855. Also *transf.*

Catagma·tic, *a.* 1657. [– Fr. † *catagmatique* (Cotgrave):– Gr. καταγματικός of or for fracture, f. κάταγμα (*Med.*) fracture; see -IC.] *Med.* Of or belonging to fractures or their treatment 1684. quasi-*sb.* A medicine of use in healing fractures.

† **Catai·an,** *a.* 1598. Var. of *Cathaian*, a man of Cathay or China; ? a thief, scoundrel, blackguard (*Twel. N.* II. iii. 80) –1649.

Catalan (kæ·tălĕn), *a.* 1480. [– Fr. *catalan* – Pr., Sp. *catalan*, adj. of Sp. *Cataluña*, Cat. *Catalunya.*] Of or belonging to Catalonia. As *sb.* A native of Catalonia; the language of Catalonia.

C. forge, a blast-furnace for reducing iron ores, much used in Catalonia and the neighbouring districts.

Catalectic (kætăle·ktik), *a.* 1589. [– late L. *catalecticus* – Gr. καταληκτικός, f. καταλήγειν leave off.] *Pros.* Of a verse: Wanting a syllable in the last foot.

† **Ca·talects,** *sb. pl. rare.* 1610. [– late L. *catalecta* – Gr. κατάλεκτα, n. pl. of ppl. a. of καταλέγειν reckon in the list of; cf. Fr. *catalectes.*] In sense of L., a collection of short poems ascribed to Vergil; also, detached pieces.

Catalepsy (kæ·tălepsi). ME. [– Fr. *catalepsie* or late L. *catalepsia*, f. Gr. κατάληψις, f. καταλαμβάνειν seize upon; see -Y³.] **1.** *Med.* A disease characterized by a seizure or trance, with suspension of sensation and consciousness. **2.** *Philos.* Comprehension, apprehension 1656. var. (in L. form) **Catalepsis.**

Cataleptic (kætăle·ptik), *a.* 1684. [– late L. *catalepticus* – Gr. καταληπτικός; see prec., -IC.] **1.** *Med.* Of, pertaining to, or affected by, catalepsy. **2.** *Philos.* Pertaining to apprehension 1847. As *sb.* One affected by catalepsy. Hence (in *Med.*) **Catale·ptiform, Catale·ptoid** *adjs.* resembling catalepsy.

Catallactic (kætălæ·ktik), *a.* 1831. [– Gr. καταλλακτικός (not recorded in this sense), f. καταλλάσσειν change, exchange.] *adj.* Pertaining to exchange 1862. As *sb. pl.* Political Economy as the 'Science of Exchanges'. Hence **Catalla·ctically** *adv.* by way of exchange.

† **Catalogize** (kæ·tălǫdʒəi:z, -gəi:z). 1602. [f. Gr. καταλογίζεσθαι reckon up; influenced by CATALOGUE. Cf. *cataloguize.*] **1.** To reckon up. **2.** To insert in a catalogue –1665.

Catalogue (kæ·tălǫg), *sb.* 1460. [– (O)Fr. *catalogue* – late L. *catalogus* – Gr. κατάλογος, f. καταλέγειν pick out, enlist, enrol.] **1.** A list, register, or complete enumeration; in this sense now *arch.* Also *fig.* **2.** Now, a list or enumeration systematically arranged in alphabetical or other order, often with the addition of brief particulars 1667.

1. The C. of the Slain ADDISON. **2.** Finished my C. of books PEPYS. Hence **Catalo·gic, -al** *a.* of the nature of, or pertaining to, a c.

Catalogue (kæ·tălǫg), *v.* 1598. [f. prec.] **1.** *trans.* To make a catalogue or list of. **2.** To insert in a catalogue. Also *fig.* 1635.

1. To c. a woman's features 1863, a library 1886. **2.** To c. innocent acts with sins H. WALPOLE. Hence **Ca·talo:guer,** one who catalogues; also **Ca·talo:guist,** var. **Catalogist. Ca·talogui:ze** *v.* (*trans.*) to CATALOGUE.

‖ **Catalpa** (kătæ·lpă). [Indian of Carolina, where Catesby discovered *C. bignonioides* in 1726.] *Bot.* A genus of trees (N.O. *Bignoniaceæ*), natives of N. America, W. Indies, Japan, and China, having large simple leaves, and terminal panicles of trumpet-shaped flowers.

Catalysis (kătæ·lisis). 1655. [– mod.L. – Gr. κατάλυσις, f. καταλύειν dissolve.] † **1.** Dissolution, destruction, ruin (*rare*) –1660. **2.** *Chem.* Berzelius' name for the effect produced in facilitating a chemical reaction, by the presence of a substance, which itself undergoes no permanent change. Also called *contact action.* 1836.

1. This sad c. and declension of piety EVELYN. Hence **Cataly·tic** *a.* of the nature of, or pertaining to, c.; having the power of acting by c. **Cataly·tically** *adv.*

Catamaran (kæ:tămăræ·n, kătæ·mărăn). 1697. [– Tamil *kaṭṭumaram* 'tied wood'.] **1.** A kind of raft or float, consisting of two or more logs tied together side by side, the middle one being longer than the others; used, *esp.* on the Coromandel coast, for communication with the shore. Also applied to similar craft used in the West Indies, off the coast of S. America, and on the St. Lawrence and its tributaries. Also *attrib.* † **2.** A kind of fire-ship or torpedo –1832. **3.** A cross-grained person, *esp.* a woman. *colloq.* [? Assoc. w. *cat.*] 1833.

2. He experimented with Fulton's 'catamarans'—the prototypes of the modern fish torpedoes—against the Boulogne flotilla ALLARDYCE.

‖ **Catamenia** (kætămī·niă), *sb. pl.* 1754. [Gr., neut. pl. of καταμήνιος monthly.] The menstrual discharge. Hence **Catame·nial** *a.*

Catamite (kæ·tămait). 1593. [– L. *catamitus* – (through Etruscan *catmite*) Gr. Γανυμήδης GANYMEDE.] A boy kept for unnatural purposes.

Catamount (kæ·tămaunt). 1664. [Short f. CATAMOUNTAIN.] † **1.** = CATAMOUNTAIN –1736. **2.** In U.S. the puma or cougar 1794.

Catamountain, cat o' mountain (kætămau·ntĕn, -o,mau·ntĕn). ME. [Earlier *cat of the mountain* (XV–XVI), which was first used to render L. *pardus*, Gr. πάρδος PARD¹.] **1.** *Orig.*, the leopard or panther; also the Ocelot (*Felis pardalis*), or other Tiger-cat. **2.** *transf.* A wild man from the mountain 1616.

2. *attrib.* Cat-a-Mountaine lookes *Merry W.* II. ii. 27.

† **Catana·dromous,** *a.* 1753. [f. mod. L. *catanadromi*, f. Gr. κατά down + ἀνά up + -δρομος running.] *Zool.* = ANADROMOUS.

Cat and dog, cat-and-dog. 1579. **1.** *attrib.* Full of strife; inharmonious. **2.** A game played with a piece of wood called a cat (cf. CAT *sb.*¹) and a club called a dog 1808.

Phr. *To rain cats and dogs*: to rain very heavily.

Catapan (kæ·tăpæn). 1727. [– med. L. *catapanus, cate-*; f. Gr. κατεπάνω τῶν ἀξιωμάτων (he who is) placed over the dignities (Littré).] The officer who governed Calabria and Apulia under the Byzantine emperors.

† **Ca·tapasm.** 1657. [– Gr. κατάπασμα, f. καταπάσσειν besprinkle.] *Med.* An old name for 'any dry medicine in powder, which was sprinkled on ulcers'.

Catapetalous (kætăpe·tăləs), *a.* 1847. [f. Gr. κατά each to each + πέταλον PETAL + -OUS.] *Bot.* Having the petals united only by cohesion with united stamens, as in Mallow.

Catapho·nic, *a.* [f. Gr. κατά CATA- + φωνή voice, sound + -IC.] Pertaining to cataphonics (Dicts.).

Cataphonics (kætăfǫ·niks), *sb. pl.* 1683. [f. as prec.; see -IC 2.] = CATACOUSTICS.

Cataphract (kæ·tăfrækt). 1581. [– L. *cataphractes* (in sense 2 *cataphractus*) – Gr.; f. καταφράσσειν clothe in mail.] **1.** An ancient coat of mail. *Hist.* Also *transf.* in *Zool.* **2.** A soldier in full armour 1671. ¶ *Catachr.* for CATARACT 1581.

2. Archers and slingers, cataphracts and spears MILT. *Sams.* 1619. Hence **Ca·taphracted** *a.*, *Zool.* covered with a scaly armour. **Cataphra·ctic** *a.* pertaining to or resembling a c.

Cataphrygian (kætăfri·dʒ¹ăn), *a.* and *sb.* 1585. [f. late L. *Cataphrygæ* (pl.), repr. Gr. ἡ κατὰ φρύγας αἵρεσις + -IAN.] *Ch.Hist.* A Montanist; so called because the sect originated in Phrygia.

† **Cataphy·sic, -al,** *a.* 1654. [f. Gr. κατά CATA- + φύσις nature + -IC, -AL¹.] Contrary to nature. So **Cataphysics** *sb. pl.* (*nonce-wd.*)

Cataplasm (kæ·tăplæz'm). 1563. [– (O)Fr. *cataplasme* or late L. *cataplasma* – Gr. κατάπλασμα, f. καταπλάσσειν plaster over.] *Med.* A poultice; † a plaster. Also *fig.* Hence **Catapla·smic, -al** *a.* of the nature of a c.

Cataplexy (kæ·tapleksi). 1883. [– Gr. κατάπληξις stupefaction, f. καταπλήσσειν strike down with terror; cf. Fr. *cataplexie.*] The hypnotic state in animals when 'shamming dead'. Hence **Catawple·ctic** *a.* of or pertaining to c.

† **Catapuce.** ME. [– (O)Fr. *catapuce* = It. *catapuzza*, med.L. *cataputia.*] *Herb.* Lesser Spurge –1794.

Catapult (kæ·tăpɒlt). 1577. [– (O)Fr. *catapulte* or L. *catapulta* = Gr. καταπέλτης, f. κατά CATA- + **pel-*, var. of base of πάλλειν hurl.] **1.** An ancient military engine worked by a lever and ropes for discharging darts, stones, etc. **2.** A boy's shooting contrivance consisting of a forked stick and elastic band 1871. **3.** Applied to mechanical contrivances by which objects are shot out at a great speed. **Catapu·ltic** *a.* **Catapultie·r** [-IER (2)].

Catapult, *v.* 1848. [f. prec.] To hurl as from a catapult; to shoot (at) with a catapult. *intr.* To discharge a catapult.

Cataract (kæ·tărækt), *sb.* ME. [– L. *cataracta* – Gr. καταρ(ρ)άκτης down-rush, waterfall, subst. use of adj., down-rushing.] † **1.** *pl.* The 'flood-gates' of heaven (see *Gen.* 7:11, 8:2) –1684. Used also of waterspouts; and *transf.* **2.** A waterfall; prop. a large one, falling over a precipice, as opp. to CASCADE 1594. Also *transf.* and *fig.* † **3.** A portcullis. [Early in Gr. but rare in Eng.] –1853. **4.** *Pathol.* An opacity of the crystalline lens of the eye, or of its capsule, or of both, producing impairment of sight, but never complete blindness. [App. a fig. use of 3.] 1547. Also *fig.* **5.** *Mech.* A form of governor for single-acting steam-engines, in which the stroke is regulated by the flow of water through an opening 1832.

1. MILT. *P.L.* xi. 824. **2.** *fig.* Cataracts of declamation COWPER. Hence **Ca·taracted** *ppl. a.* having cataracts. † **Catara·ctic** *a.* of the nature of a c. **Catara·ctous** *a.*, *Pathol.* affected with c.

Cataract, *v.* 1796. [f. prec.] *trans.* To pour like a cataract (*nonce-use*). *intr.* To fall in a cataract.

Catarrh (kătā·ɹ). 1533. [– Fr. *catarrhe* – late L. *catarrhus* – Gr. κατάρρους rheum, f. καταρρεῖν run down.] † **1.** The profuse discharge from nose and eyes which generally accompanies a cold, formerly supposed to run down from the brain; a running at the nose –1796. † **2.** Cerebral effusion or hæmorrhage; apoplexy –1708. **3.** Inflammation of a mucous membrane, causing increased flow of mucus, and often attended with sneezing, cough, and fever 1588.

3. *Epidemic c.*, influenza. *Summer c.*, hay-fever. Hence **Cata·rrhal** *a.* **Cata·rrhous** *a.* ? *Obs.*

Catarrhine, catarhine (kæ·tărəin), *a.* 1862. [f. Gr. κατά CATA- + ῥίς, ῥιν- nose.] *Zool.* A division of the order *Quadrumana*, including apes or monkeys having the nostrils close together, oblique, and directed downwards.

Cataspilite (kătæ·spiləit). 1868. [f. Gr. κατάσπιλος spotted + -ITE[1] 2 b.] *Min.* A hydrous silicate of alumina, with some iron, manganese, etc.

‖ **Catasta.** 1650. [L., = scaffold, stage.] *Hist.* **a.** A block on which slaves stood for sale. **b.** A bed of torture.

Catastaltic, *a.* 1851. [– late L. *catastalticus* – Gr. καταςταλτικός, f. καταστέλλειν repress, check.] *Med.* Restraining, checking: used of astringent and styptic substances.

‖ **Catastasis** (kătæ·stăsis). 1656. [Gr., = settling, appointment.] **1.** The third part of the ancient drama, in which the action is heightened for the catastrophe. **2.** *Rhet.* The narrative part of a speech, usu. the exordium, in which is set forth the subject to be discussed (Dicts.). **3.** *Med.* The state or condition of anything; constitution; habit of body (Dicts.).

1. No catastrophe, rather a c. or heightening CARLYLE.

Catasterism (kătæ·stĕriz'm). 1803. [– Gr. καταστερισμός 'placing among the stars', f. κατά CATA- and ἀστήρ star. Cf. ASTERISM.] **a.** *pl.* A treatise attributed to Eratosthenes giving the legends of the different constellations. **b.** A constellation.

Catastrophe (kătæ·strŏfi). 1579. [– L. *catastropha* – Gr. καταστροφή overturning, sudden turn, f. καταστρέφειν overturn.] **1.** The change which produces the final event of a dramatic piece; the dénouement. **2.** 'A final event; a conclusion generally unhappy' (J.); overthrow, ruin 1601. **3.** An event producing a subversion of the order or system of things 1696. *esp.* in *Geol.* A sudden and violent physical change, such as an upheaval, depression, etc. (See CATACLYSM, CATASTROPHISM.) 1832. **4.** A sudden disaster. (Used very loosely.) 1748.

2. The late war, and its horrid c. MARVELL. Used *joc.* in 2 *Hen. IV*, II. i. 66. Hence **Catastro·phic, -al** *a.* of the nature of, or belonging to, a c.; **-ly,** *adv.*

Catastrophism (kătæ·strŏfiz'm). 1869. [f. CATASTROPHE 3 + -ISM.] The theory that certain geological and biological phenomena were caused by catastrophes, or sudden and violent disturbances of nature. So **Cata·strophist,** one who holds this theory.

Catawba (kătǭ·bă). 1857. [f. the river in S. Carolina, U.S. (named from the *Katahba* Indians), where the grape was found.] **a.** An American species of grape (*Vitis labrusca*). **b.** The light sparkling wine made from this grape.

Catbird (kæ·tbɔ̄ɹd). 1713. [From its cry of alarm.] An American thrush (*Mimus carolinensis*).

Catcall (kæ·tkǭl), *sb.* 1659. [From the cry of the cat.] **1.** A squeaking instrument, used *esp.* in play-houses to express disapprobation, etc. **2.** The sound, a shrill screaming whistle, made with this or with the voice 1749.

1. I was very much surprised with the great Consort of Cat-calls..a kind of Catterwawling ADDISON. Hence **Ca·tcall** *v.* to sound a c.; *trans.* to assail with catcalls.

Catch (kætʃ), *sb.*[1] ME. [f. the vb.] **1.** The act or fact of catching (see CATCH *v.*) 1580. **2.** The catching of fish; the number caught at one time 1465. † **3.** *Sc.* Tennis –1599. † **4.** A catching question –1693. **5.** Something intended to catch the attention, etc. 1781. † **6.** A glimpse –1796. **7.** *concr.* That by which anything is caught and held 1496. **8.** That which is caught or is worth catching 1596. † **9.** A fragment or scrap of anything caught up; a snatch –1830. **10.** *Mus.* Orig. a ROUND; subseq. a round in which one singer catches at the words of another, producing ludicrous effects 1601.

1. † *To lie (be) at (upon) the c.*, to be on the watch for an opportunity of catching or seizing something: On the c. for a husband JANE AUSTEN. To miss a c. (*Cricket*) 1770. Also *transf.*: H. J. Ford; a safe c. 1884. **5.** This is a ha'penny c. 1871. **7.** For a katch for my gate *jd.* 1520. **8.** The Gentleman had got a great C. of her, as they say DRYDEN. **9.** It has been writ by catches, with many intervals LOCKE (J.). We retain a c. of these pretty stories GLANVILL.

† **Catch,** *sb.*[2] [ME. *catche*, prob. f. CATCH *v.* or *sb.*[1] See KETCH *sb.*[1]] = KETCH –1693.

Catch, *a.*; see CATCH-.

Catch (kætʃ), *v.* Pa. t. and pple. **caught** (kǭt), though *catched, cotched* are still in dial. and vulgar use. [ME. *cac(c)he* – AFr., ONFr. *cachier*, var. of OFr. *chacier* (mod. *chasser*) :– Rom. **captiare*, repl. L. *captare* try to catch, lie in wait for, (hence) hunt; see CHASE. *Catch* took over the sense 'seize' and its conjugational forms from the native LATCH *v.*[1]]

I. † To chase. *trans.* and *intr.* –1526.

II. 1. To capture, *esp.* that which tries or would try to escape. (The main sense.) ME. **2.** *fig.* To ensnare; to deceive ME. † **3.** *fig.* To attain –1605. **4.** To overtake (an agent in motion). Now usu. *to c. up.* 1610. *Hence*, To reach in time 1826. **5.** To come upon suddenly or unexpectedly; to surprise (*in, at,* or *doing* something) 1610. **6.** To reach with a blow. Said also of the missile, etc. To hit. 1583.

1. To c. a Butterfly *Cor.* I. iii. 6, a Bird 1672. **2.** To c. him in his words *Mark* 12:13. **4.** To c. a horse near the winning post 1791. Caught in a shower ADDISON. To c. a train 1872, the post, 1889. **5.** Caught napping 1734, in the act DICKENS.

III. 1. To seize and keep hold of ME. Also *fig.* (*Obs.* exc. of fire.) **2.** *intr.* (for *refl.*) To become entangled or fixed 1787.

1. The fire caught many houses CARLYLE. *intr.* The flame hath caught SOUTHEY. *Oth.* III. iii. 90. **2.** The bolt would not c. 1889.

IV. To take ME. Also *fig.*

Catching cat-naps as I could KANE.

V. To snatch, *esp.* with *away, up, at* 1525.

He..hastily caught His bundle..and went his way TENNYSON.

VI. To intercept and lay hold of (anything) in its course 1548.

To c. a ball (in *Cricket*) 1849. Hence *To c. out* or *c. (a person)*: to put him out by catching the ball from his bat. To c. an opportunity SIR T. BROWNE. *To c. one's breath*: see BREATH. His robe being catched by a bramble 1734.

VII. To get or take a thing passively; *esp.* to take, incur, or contract by exposure, infection, sympathy, or imitation ME.

To c. one's death of cold, a mischief, it (colloq.). To c. the breeze ADDISON. Used also *ellipt.* with reference to fire, frost, the wind. To c. the plague *Twel. N.* I. v. 314. She 'caught the trick of grief, and sighed' MRS. GASKELL.

VIII. To seize by the senses or intellect; to apprehend 1560.

To c. a sound GOLDSM., what a man says HAZLITT, the meaning 1837, an attitude from life 1883.

IX. To arrest the attention, mind, fancy, etc.; to captivate ME.

To c. the fair DRYDEN, the eye *Tr. & Cr.* III. iii. 183.

Phrases. *C. me (at it)!* (see II. 5). *To c. it*: to get a thrashing or a scolding (*colloq.*). *To c. the eye of* another: to arrest the glance of the other. *To c. fire*: *fig.* to become inflamed or inspired. *To c. a* CRAB, *a* TARTAR: see these wds.

Comb. (with advs.) **C. away:** to snatch away. **C. on: a.** *intr.* to join on (*colloq.*); **b.** *U.S.* to apprehend; **c.** to 'take' (*colloq.*). **C. up: a.** to carry suddenly aloft; **b.** to lift suddenly; **c.** to adopt quickly; **d.** to interrupt, pull up; **e.** *U.S.* to prepare the horses and mules for the march. *trans.* and *absol.*

Hence **Ca·tchable** *a.* that can be caught. **Ca·tcher,** one who or that which catches. **Ca·tching** *ppl. a.* that catches; (*spec.*) infectious; uncertain; (*fig.*) deceptive, catchy; taking. **Ca·tchingness.**

Catch-, in *comb.* and *attrib.* Mainly the vb. in phraseological combination: **a.** with sbs., in sense 'one who or that which catches' (the object), as *c.-all*, etc.; also in sense 'to catch, the catching of (the object)', as *c.-ball, -cold*, etc.; **b.** in attrib. relation to a sb., in sense 'that catches or for catching', as **c.-basin,** the receptacle placed beneath the grating of a sewer, etc., to catch the dirt that is washed in; **-drain, -water, -work,** a drain to catch the surface water; **-meadow,** ? a meadow irrigated by c.-drains.

Catchfly (kæ·tʃfləi). 1597. [f. CATCH *v.* + FLY *sb.*] A name orig. for *Silene armeria*; now for *Lychnis viscaria* and the various species of *Silene*.

Catchment (kæ·tʃmĕnt). 1847. [f. CATCH *v.* + -MENT.] = CATCHING; appropriated to the catching of the rainfall over a natural drainage area, in *c. basin, area.*

Catchpenny (kæ·tʃpeni), *a.* (*sb.*) 1759. [f. CATCH- + PENNY.] **1.** Got up merely to sell. **2.** *sb.* Any catchpenny production.

Catchpole, -poll (kæ·tʃpōᵘl). OE. [Late OE. *kæćepol* – AFr., OFr. **cachepol*, var. of OFr. *chacepol*, or – AL. *cacepollus* (X), f. Rom. **captiare* CHASE, CATCH + L. *pullus* fowl.] † **1.** A tax-gatherer; a Roman publican –1652. **2.** A sheriff's officer, *esp.* a bum-bailiff ME. Also *attrib.* Hence **Ca·tchpolery, -pollery. Ca·tchpolled** *ppl. a.* arrested by a c.

Ca·tchup, ca·tsup. 1690. = KETCHUP, q.v.

Ca·tchweed. 1776. [f. CATCH *v.*] *Herb.* CLEAVERS, q.v.

Catchword (kæ·tʃwɔ̄ɹd). 1730. [f. CATCH- b.] **1.** *Printing.* The first word of the following page inserted at the right-hand lower corner of each page of a book, below the last line. (Now rarely used.) **2.** A word so placed as to catch the eye; *spec.* the last word in an actor's speech, serving as a guide to the next speaker; a cue 1780. **3.** A word caught up and repeated, *esp.* in connection with a party 1795.

3. The catchwords of party politics LOWELL.

Catchy (kæ·tʃi), *a. colloq.* 1831. [f. CATCH *v.* + -Y[1].] **1.** Attractive, taking. **2.** That entraps 1885. **3.** Readily caught up 1881. **4.** Spasmodic, fitful 1872.

Cate, usu. in *pl.* **cates** (kēᵢts). 1461. [aphet. f. ACATE: orig. = purchase.] † **1.** *pl.* Provisions bought (as opp. to home-made); later, = victuals, food –1866. Hence **2.** Choice viands; dainties, delicacies 1578. Also *fig.*

2. These curious cates are gracious in mine eye GREENE. *Tam. Shr.* II. i. 190. Taste of every c. HEYWOOD. Hence † **Cate** *v.* to dress (food).

‖ **Catechesis** (kætĭkī·sis). 1753. [eccl. L. (Jerome) – Gr. κατήχησις instruction by word of mouth, f. κατηχεῖν; see CATECHIZE.] **1.** Oral instruction given to catechumens; catechizing. **2.** A book for such instruction 1753. var. † **Catechese.**

Catechetic (kætĭke·tik). 1661. [– eccl. Gr. κατηχητικός, f. κατηχητής catechist, f. κατηχεῖν; see CATECHIZE, -IC.] *adj.* Of or pertaining to catechesis; according to the manner of a catechism. See next. *sb.* mostly *pl.* **catechetics.** That part of Christian theology which treats of catechesis.

Catechetical (kætĭke·tikăl), *a.* 1618. [f. as prec; see -ICAL.] **1.** Of, pertaining to, or connected with catechetics or catechesis 1624. **2.** Of, pertaining to, or in accordance with the catechism of a church 1618. **3.** 'Consisting of questions and answers' (J.) 1691.

3. Socrates introduced a c. Method of Arguing ADDISON. Hence **Cateche·tically** *adv.*

Ca·techin. 1853. [f. CATECHU + -IN[1].] *Chem.* A substance obtained from catechu, etc., after the removal of the tannin; a white powder composed of small silky needles.

Catechise (kæ·tĭkiz). Now *dial.* 1552. [app. – Fr. *catéchèse* CATECHESIS, confounded with the verb CATECHIZE, in Fr. *catéchiser.* See CARRITCH, -ES.] = CATECHESIS, CATECHISM.

Catechism (kæ·tĭkiz'm). 1502. [– eccl. L. *catechismus* (Augustine) – eccl. Gr. *κατηχισμός, f. κατηχίζειν; see CATECHIZE, -ISM.] † **1.** Catechetical instruction; catechesis –1600. **2.** A treatise for instruction in the elements of the Christian religion, in the form of question and answer, as the (*Church*) *C.*, the *Longer* and *Shorter Catechisms*, etc. 1509. Also *transf.* **3.** *fig.* A course of question and answer 1596.

1. *A.Y.L.* III. ii. 241. **2.** We can never see Christianity from the c. EMERSON. *transf.* The Freethinker's C. 1754. Hence **Catechi·smal** *a.* of the nature of, or pertaining to, a c.

Catechist (kæ·tĭkist). 1563. [– eccl. L. *catechista* (Jerome) – eccl. Gr. κατηχιστής, f. κατηχίζειν; see CATECHIZE.] A teacher who gives oral instruction according to a catechism, or by question and answer; a native teacher in a mission church. Hence **Catechi·stic, -al** *a.* of or pertaining to a c., or to a catechism; consisting of question and answer. **Catechi·stically** *adv.*

Catechize (kæ·tĭkəiz), *v.* ME. [– Chr.L. *catechizare* (Tertullian) – eccl. Gr. κατηχίζειν, f. κατηχεῖν sound through, instruct orally, spec. in N.T. in the elements of religion, f. κατά CATA- + ἠχεῖν sound; see ECHO, -IZE.] **1.** To instruct orally; to give systematic oral instruction, *esp.* in the elements of religion, by repeating it until it is learnt by heart, or by question and answer; in the Ch. of England, to teach the catechism. **2.** To examine with or as with a catechism 1684. **3.** To question or interrogate; *esp.* with a view to reproof or condemnation 1604.

3. Catechising him where he had been SWIFT. Hence **Ca·techizer,** one who catechizes.

Catechu (kæ·tĭʃu, -tʃu). 1683. [– mod. L. *catechu*, defined as 'terra japonica' (Japanese earth) on account of its appearance, unexpl. deriv. of Malay *kachu*; see CACHOU.] A name given to several astringent substances, containing from 40 to 55 per cent. of tannin, which are obtained from *Acacia catechu* and other Eastern trees and shrubs. Used in medicine, and in the arts. Called also GAMBIER, *Terra Japonica*, CUTCH, etc. Hence **Catechu·ic** *a.* of or pertaining to c., as in *catechuic acid* = CATECHIN.

Catechumen (kætĭkiū·mĕn). ME. [– (O)Fr. *catéchumène* or eccl. L. *catechumenus* – Gr. κατηχούμενος being instructed, pres. pple. pass. of κατεχεῖν; see CATECHIZE.] A new convert under instruction before baptism. Used in reference to the ancient church and to modern missions. Occ. applied to young Christians generally, *esp.* those preparing for confirmation. Also *transf.* var. † **Catechu·menist.** Hence **Catechu·menate,** condition or position of a c., var. **Catechu·menism;** also, a house for catechumens. **Catechu·menical** *a.* of or pertaining to catechumens. † **Catechu·menize** *v.* to instruct as a c.

Categorem (kæ·tĭgŏre:m, kăte·gŏrem). 1588. [– Gr. κατηγόρημα, -ματ- accusation, (in logic) predicate, f. κατηγορεῖν accuse, etc.] *Logic.* † PREDICATE; a categorematic word.

Categorematic (kæ:tĭgǫrĭmæ·tik), *a.* 1827. [f. as prec. + -IC.] Of a word: Capable of being used by itself as a term.

† **Categorema·tical,** *a.* [f. as prec.; see -ICAL.] = CATEGORICAL. JER. TAYLOR.

Categoric (kætĭgǫ·rik). ? *Obs.* 1677. [– Fr. *catégorique* or late L. *categoricus* – Gr. κατηγορικός accusatory, affirmative, (later) categorical; see CATEGORY, -IC.] *adj.* = CATEGORICAL. *sb.* [sc. *proposition*.]

Categorical (kætĭgǫ·rikăl), *a.* (*sb.*) 1598. [f. as prec.; see -ICAL.] *adj.* **1.** *Logic.* Of a proposition: Asserting absolutely; unqualified. *gen.* Direct, explicit, unconditional 1619. **2.** *Logic.* Of or belonging to the categories 1817. **3.** *sb.* A categorical proposition or syllogism 1619.

1. *C. syllogism*: one consisting of c. propositions. I could never persuade her to be c. MME. D'ARBLAY. Hence **Catego·ricalness. Catego·rically** *adv.*

Categorist (kæ·tĭgŏrist). *rare.* 1847. [f. next; see -IST.] One who classifies; one who deals with the categories.

Categorize (kæ·tĭgŏrəiz), *v.* 1705. [f. CATEGORY + -IZE.] To place in a category or categories; to classify.

Category (kæ·tĭgŏri). 1588. [– Fr. *catégorie* or its source, late L. *categoria* – Gr. κατηγορία accusation, predication, f. κατήγορος, f. κατηγορεῖν accuse, etc.] **1.** *Logic* and *Metaph.* A term (meaning literally 'predication' or 'assertion') originally used by Aristotle, whose ten categories or predicaments are 'a classification of all the manners in which assertions may be made of the subject' (L. and S.). Kant applied the term to: The pure *a priori* conceptions of the understanding, in which (as forms) the mind envisages matter. **2.** A predicament; a class to which a predication applies 1678. **b.** A class, or division, in a scheme of classification 1660.

2. Any offender who was not in any of the categories of proscription MACAULAY. **b.** With him there are but two moral categories, riches and poverty HAZLITT.

Catel, obs. f. CATTLE.

Catelectrode (kætĭle·ktroᵘd). [f. CATA- + ELECTRODE; cf. ANELECTRODE.] The negative pole of a galvanic battery.

Catelectrotonus (kæ:tĭlectrǫ·tŏnŏs). 1866. [f. κατά + ἤλεκτρον (see ELECTRIC) + τόνος tension; cf. ANELECTROTONUS.] *Phys.* A state of increased irritability produced in a nerve near the negative pole of an electric current which traverses it. Hence **Ca:telectroto·nic** *a.*

‖ **Catena** (kătī·nă). 1644. [Short for eccl. L. *catena patrum* 'chain of the Fathers' (viz. of the Church).] A chain, a connected series. Also *transf.*

A c. of opinions MAURICE, of platitudes 1883.

Catenary (kătī·nări). 1788. [– mod.L. *catenaria*, subst. use of fem. of L. *catenarius*; see prec., -ARY[1].] **A.** *sb. Math.* The curve formed by a chain or rope of uniform density hanging freely from two fixed points not in the same vertical line. **B.** *adj. C. curve* = CATENARY. **2.** Relating to a catena or series 1855. var. **Catena·rian** *a.* (*sb.*)

Catenate (kæ·tĭneⁱt), *v.* 1623. [– *catenat-*, pa. ppl. stem of L. *catenare*, f. *catena* chain; see -ATE[3].] To form into a catena. *fig.* To chain. Hence **Catena·tion,** a linking into a chain; connected succession.

Catenulate (kătī·niŭlĕt), *a.* 1880. [f. L. *catena* chain; see -ULE, -ATE[2].] *Bot.* Formed of parts united end to end like the links of a chain. *Zool.* Having on the surface a chain-like series of oblong tubercles.

† **Ca·ter,** *sb.*[1] [ME. *catour*, aphet. of *acatour*; see ACATER. Superseded before 1700 by CATERER.] A CATERER –1621. *transf.* and *fig.* = Purveyor –1665.

Cater (kēⁱ·təɹ, kæ·təɹ), *sb.*[2] 1519. [– (O)Fr. *quatre*; see QUATRE.] † **1.** Four (*rare*) 1553. † **2.** Four at dice or cards; also *cater-point.* (Dicts.) **3.** *pl. Change-ringing.* A name for the changes on nine bells 1872.

Cater (kēⁱ·təɹ), *v.*[1] 1600. [f. CATER *sb.*[1]] **1.** *intr.* To act as caterer *for.* Also *absol.* and *trans.* **2.** *transf.* and *fig.* To provide (requisites, things desired, etc.) *for* 1650. Occas. with *to* 1840.

1. He that ..prouidently caters for the Sparrow *A.Y.L.* II. iii. 44.

Cater (kēⁱ·təɹ), *v.*[2] *dial.* 1577. [f. CATER *sb.*[2] or Fr. *quatre* four.] To set rhomboidally; to cut, go, etc. diagonally. So **Ca·ter** *adv. dial.*, diagonally. **Ca·ter-cornered** *a.*

Cateran (kæ·tĕrăn). ME. [– med.L. *cateranus*, *kethernus*, and its source Gael. *ceathairne* peasantry, corresp. to Ir. *ceithern* KERN.] **1.** *prop.* † Common people of the Highlands in a band. Hence, One of such a band; a Highland reiver. **2.** Freebooter 1870.

† **Ca·terbrawl.** 1565. [f. CATER *sb.*[2] four + BRAWL *sb.*[2]] A kind of dance or 'brawl' –1618.

† **Ca·tercap.** 1588. [f. as prec.] The square cap worn by academics. Hence *transf.* A university man. –1691.

Cater-cousin (kēⁱ·təɹ,kʊ:z'n). 1547. [Of unkn. origin; perh. f. CATER *sb.*[1] + COUSIN, as if the orig. notion was of persons being catered for or boarded together; cf. *foster-brother*, etc.] A name for persons on terms of cousinship or familiarity with each other, who were not cousins by blood (cf. to CALL *cousins*).

To be cater-cousins: to be good friends.

Caterer (kēⁱ·tərəɹ). 1592. [f. CATER *v.*[1] + -ER[1].] One who caters; *spec.* one who purveys provisions for a household, club, etc., one who supplies the viands at an entertainment, public dinner, etc. So **Ca·teress.**

Caterpillar (kæ·təɹpiləɹ). 1440. [Earliest *catyrpel*, prob. – AFr. var. (cf. Norman-Picard *katplöz*, *ka(r)plüz*, *-plöz*) of OFr. *chatepelose* 'hairy cat' (pop. L. **catta pilosa*); assoc. in XVI with †*piller* ravager, plunderer.] **1.** The larva of a butterfly or moth; occ. those of other insects, as saw-flies. **2.** *fig.* A rapacious person; an extortioner; one who preys upon society 1541. **3.** *Herb.* A name for plants of the genus *Scorpiurus* from the shape of their pods 1597. **4.** Trade name for either of two endless metal belts or treads, one on each side of a vehicle, which facilitate travelling over very rough ground; chiefly *attrib.*, in *c. lorry, track, tractor, wheel*, etc. 1914.

2. The Augustine friers in London..those Caterpillers and blouddy beastes BARNES.

Comb.: **c.-catcher, -eater,** a sub-family of shrikes which feed on caterpillars; **-plant** = sense 3 above.

Caterwaul (kæ·təɹwǭl), *v.* ME. [f. CAT *sb.*[1] + *-wawe*, *-wrawe*, *-wall*, etc., of imit. origin; the relation between the many forms is not clear.] **1.** *intr.* To make the noise proper to cats at rutting time. Also *transf.* **2.** To be in heat; to behave lasciviously; to woo (*contemptuous*) 1599.

2. Always together, always caterwauling FIELDING. Hence **Ca·terwaul** *sb.* **Ca·terwauler.**

† **Ca·tery.** 1455. [aphet. f. † *acatery*, – OFr. *acaterie*; see CATER *sb*[1], -Y[3].] The office concerned with the catering for the royal household –1779.

Cates; see CATE *sb.*[1]

Cat-fish. 1620. **1.** A name given to: **a.** The *Anarrhicas* or Wolf-fish. **b.** Species of *Pimelodus*, esp. *P. catus*, the common cat-fish. **2.** The cuttle-fish or other cephalopod 1678.

Catgut (kæ·tgɒt). 1599. [f. CAT *sb.*[1] + GUT; cf. synon. CATLING; the reason for the use of *cat* is unkn., but cf. synon. Du. *kattedarm.*] **1.** The dried and twisted intestines of sheep, also of the horse and ass; used for strings of musical instruments, etc. **2.** A violin; stringed instruments 1709. **3.** A coarse cloth of thick cord, formerly used as stiffening 1731. Also *attrib.*

† **Ca·tharan.** 1574. [– late L. *Cathari* 'the pure' (– Gr. καθαροί) + -AN; cf. Fr. *Cathare.*] One who professes superior purity, as a Novatian, Paulician, etc., also an English Puritan –1657.

Ca·tharist. 1600. [– late L. *Catharistæ* = Gr. καθαρισταί; so Fr. *Cathariste.*] A Paulician, Manichæan, etc.; cf. CATHARAN. Hence **Ca·tharism,** the doctrine of the Catharists.

Catharize (kæ·þărəiz), *v.* 1832. [– Gr. καθαρίζειν purify, f. καθαρός pure.] To purify.

Cat-harpings; see HARPINGS.

‖ **Catharsis** (kăþā·ɹsis). 1803. [mod.L. – Gr. κάθαρσις purification.] **1.** Purgation. **2.** Purification of the emotions by vicarious experience, as through the drama (in ref. to Aristotle's *Poetics* 6) 1904.

Cathartic (kăþā·ɹtik). 1612. [– late L. *catharticus* – Gr. καθαρτικός, f. καθαίρειν cleanse; see -IC.] **A.** *adj. Med.* Cleansing (the bowels), purgative. Also *gen.* (and *fig.*). Hence **Catha·rtical-ly** *adv.*, **-ness. B.** *sb.* A purgative. More strictly: 'a medicine.. producing the second grade of purgation, of which laxative is the first and drastic the third' (*Syd. Soc. Lex.*) 1651.

Catha·rtin. 1830. [f. *cathart-* (see prec.) + -IN[1].] A bitter substance extracted from senna, a purgative.

Cat-head (kæ·t,hed). 1626. [See CAT *sb.*[1] II 2, CAT *v.*] **1.** *Naut.* A beam projecting at each side of the bows of a ship, for raising the anchor, or carrying it suspended. See also CAT *sb.* **2.** *Mining.* A small capstan; also, a broad-bully hammer 1858.

‖ **Cathedra** (kăþī·dră, -e·dră, kæ·þĕdră). 1829. [L. – Gr. καθέδρα chair.] The chair of a bishop in his church; hence, the episcopal see.

Ex cathedrâ L.: 'from the chair', *i.e.* in the manner of one speaking officially, with authority; also *attrib.* = officially uttered.

Cathedral (kăþī·drăl), *a.* ME. [– (O)Fr. *cathédral* – late L. *cathedralis*, f. L. *cathedra*; see prec., -AL¹.] **1.** Of or pertaining to the bishop's throne or see; *esp.* in *c. church* = CATHEDRAL *sb.* **2.** Of or pertaining to the chair of office or authority; *ex cathedrâ* 1603.

2. The c. utterances of Leo XIII 1886. The Schoolmens..C. Decisions HALES.

Cathedral (kăþī·drăl), *sb.* 1587. [Short for *cathedral church*; see prec., and cf. med.L. *cathedralis* (sc. *ecclesia*), (O)Fr. *cathédrale*.] **1.** The principal church of a diocese, containing the bishop's cathedra or throne. **2.** *fig.* Chief centre of teaching 1643. Also *attrib.*, as *c. glass, music, walk* (= resembling an aisle in a c.). Hence **Cathe·draled** *a.* like or having a c. **Cathedra·lic** *a.* like a c. † **Cathe·dralist,** a supporter of the c. system; one of the c. clergy.

† **Cathedrated,** *ppl. a.* 1626. [– *cathedrat-*, pa. ppl. stem of med.L. *cathedrare* enthrone; see -ATE³, -ED¹.] Installed in a cathedra –1654.

Cathedra·tic, *a.* 1661. [– med.L. *cathedraticus*, f. as prec.; see -IC.] **1.** *Law.* Pertaining to the bishop's seat or see, as *c. payment, right*, etc. Also as quasi-*sb.* = *c. payment.* **2.** Pronounced *ex cathedrâ a*1850.

Catheretic (kæþĕre·tik), *a.* 1634. [– Gr. καθαιρετικός (Galen) destructive, f. καθαιρεῖν. Cf. Fr. *cathérétique*.] *Med.* Having power to destroy, reduce, or consume; corrosive. As *sb.* Any mild caustic used to consume superfluous flesh 1887.

Catherine (kæ·þĕrin). Also **Catharine, Kath-.** 1861. [mod.L. *Catharina*, earlier *Katerina*, repr. Gr. Αἰκατερίνα, assim. to καθαρός pure.] Name of a legendary Saint and Martyr of Alexandria; whence a female Christian name.

C. wheel. 1. The figure of a wheel with spikes projecting from its circumference (in reference to St. Catherine's martyrdom). *esp.* in Her. **2.** *Arch.* = *Catherine-wheel window*, a circular window with radiating spokes. **3.** A firework which rotates in the manner of a wheel. Also *transf.* and *fig.*

Ca·thern. 1596. [Syncopated form of CATHERINE.] A festival on St. Catherine's day (Nov. 25.)

Catheter (kæ·þitəɹ). 1601. [– late L. *catheter* – Gr. καθετήρ, f. *καθε-, καθιέναι send or let down.] *Med.* A tubular instrument, more or less curved at the end, for passing into the bladder to draw off urine, etc.; a similar tube for use with other canals (*e.g.* the Eustachian c.). Hence **Ca·theterize** *v.* to employ a c. **Ca·theterism, Ca·theteriza·tion,** the employment of a c.

Cathetometer (kæþitǫ·mītəɹ). 1864. [f. next + -METER.] An instrument for measuring vertical distances, *esp.* small differences of level of liquid columns in tubes.

‖ **Cathetus** (kæ·þitŏs). Also **kath-.** 1571. [L. – Gr. κάθετος (sc. γραμμή) perpendicular line, f. καθιέναι let down.] A straight line falling perpendicularly on another straight line or surface.

Cathodal (kæ·þodăl), *a.* Also **kath-,** 1882. [f. CATHODE + -AL¹.] *Electr.* Belonging to the cathode.

Cathode (kæ·þōᵘd). Also **kath-.** 1834. [– Gr. κάθοδος going down, way down, f. κατά CATA- + ὁδός way.] *Electr.* The path by which an electric current leaves the electrolyte and passes into the negative pole; the point or surface in contact with the negative pole. **b.** The negative pole. Opp. to *anode.*

Cathodic (kăþǫ·dik), *a.* Also **kath-.** 1852. [f. as prec. + -IC.] *Phys.* Of nerve force: Efferent.

Cat-hole, *sb.* OE. † **1.** The den of the wild cat. OE. only. **2.** A hole large enough to let a cat through 1625. **3.** *Naut.* One of the two holes at the stern of the ship, through which a cable or hawser can be passed 1642.

Catholic (kæ·þŏlik). ME. [– (O)Fr. *catholique* or its source Chr.L. *catholicus* – Gr. καθολικός general, universal, f. καθόλου (i.e. καθ' ὅλου) in general, generally, f. κατά in respect of, ὅλος whole.]

A. *adj.* **I. 1.** *gen.* Universal 1551. † **2.** Universally prevalent or applicable –1752; entire –1671. **3.** Embracing all 1566.

1. Science is truly c. 1885. **2.** Just reasoning is the only C. remedy HUME. In C. Health DRYDEN. **3.** A taste so c., so unexcluding LAMB.

C. Epistle: a name for the 'general' epistles of James, Peter, and Jude, and the first of John, as not being addressed to particular churches or persons.

II. In eccl. use. **1.** Of or belonging to the church universal, universal Christian 1579. **2.** Of or belonging to the church universal as organized on an accepted basis of faith and order; of the true apostolic Church, orthodox 1500. **3.** As applied (since the Reformation) to the Church of Rome = ROMAN CATHOLIC, q.v. 1554. **4.** Recognizing all Christians 1658.

1. *C. Church*: the whole body of Christians, the Church universal. **2.** And the Catholike faithe is this: that we worship one God in trinitie [etc.] *Bk. Com. Prayer.* The C. fathers 1593. The Anglo-C. Church HOOK. **3.** She [Q. Eliz.] hath abolished the C. religion 1588. † *C. seat*: = APOSTOLIC *See. C. King*, etc.: a title of the kings of Spain. **4.** The Lord Protector is..a man of a c. spirit, desirous of the unity and peace of all the servants of Christ BAXTER. *C. (and) Apostolic Church*: the Irvingites.

B. *sb.* **1.** A member of a church recognized or claiming to be 'Catholic' in sense A. II. 2; *esp.* of the Western or Latin Church ME. **2.** *spec.* A member of the Roman Church 1570. † **3.** = CATHOLICOS –1735.

2. The Catholicks (meaning Popish Romanists) A.V. *Pref. German C., Old C.*: names taken by religious parties who separated from the R.C. communion in Germany, the former under Ronge in 1845, the latter after the Vatican Council in 1870–71. *attrib.* in *C. Emancipation*, etc. Hence † **Catho·lical** *a.* = CATHOLIC *a.* I. **Catho·lically** *adv.*

Catho·licate. 1878. [– med.L. *catholicatus* f. *catholicus* CATHOLIC; see -ATE¹, and cf. CATHOLICOS.] The jurisdiction of an Armenian *Catholicos.*

Catholicism (kăþǫ·lisiz'm, kæ·þŏlisiz'm). 1609. [f. CATHOLIC + -ISM. So mod.L. *catholicismus.*] **1.** The system, faith, and practice of the Catholic Church, or adherence thereto 1656; usu. of the Roman Catholic Church 1613. **b.** A note or act of a good Catholic 1609. † **2.** = CATHOLICITY 3. JER. TAYLOR. **3.** = CATHOLICITY 1 (*rare*) 1796.

Catholicity (kæþŏli·sĭti). 1830. [f. as prec. + -ITY; cf. Fr. *catholicité*.] **1.** The quality of being catholic in feeling, etc. 1841. **2.** Universality 1843. **3.** The character of belonging to, or being in accordance with, the Catholic Church 1830. **b.** *spec.* of the Church of Rome: The doctrine or faith of that Church, Catholicism 1847.

1. The lessons of c. and toleration 1882. **3.** A sincere..trust in the C. of the Church of England 1868.

Catholicize (kăþǫ·lisəiz, kæ·þŏlisəiz), *v.* 1611. [f. as prec. + -IZE.] To make, or become, catholic or a Catholic.

Ca·tholicly, *adv.* 1542. [f. as prec. + -LY².] **1.** Universally. ? *Obs.* 1631. **2.** In a Catholic manner 1542.

† **Ca·tholicness.** 1605. [f. as prec. + -NESS.] Catholic quality, catholicity –1674.

Catho·lico-. Comb. f. CATHOLIC.

Catholicon (kăþǫ·likǫ̆n). 1483. [– Fr. *catholicon, -cum* (Paré XVI), – mod.L. *catholicum* (sc. *remedium*), subst. use of *catholicus* universal; see CATHOLIC. In sense 2 cf. med.L *-con* dictionary XIV.] **1.** A universal remedy; panacea. Also *fig.* **2.** A comprehensive † formula 1647, treatise 1483.

‖ **Catholicos** (kăþǫ·likǫ̆s). 1625. [med.Gr. καθολικός Patriarch of Armenia; earlier = supervisor of accounts (= L. *procurator*); see CATHOLIC.] The Patriarch of Armenia.

Ca'-thro'. *Sc.* [f. *ca'* (see CALL *v.* III) + THROUGH.] A great disturbance. SCOTT.

Ca·tiline. 1592. [– L. *Catilina.*] A Roman who conspired against his country B.C. 63: taken as a type. Hence **Catilina·rian** *a.*

Cation (kæ·tiǫ̆n). 1834. [– Gr. κατιόν, subst. use of n. of κατιών, pr. pple. of κατιέναι, f. κατά CATA- + ἰέναι go.] *Electr.* Faraday's name for an ion carrying a positive charge of electricity by virtue of which it is attracted, on electrolysis, to the cathode. Cf. ANION.

Catkin (kæ·tkin). 1578. [– Du. † *katteken* lit. kitten, dim. of *katte* CAT *sb.*¹] *Bot.* A unisexual inflorescence, consisting of rows of apetalous flowers ranged in circles along a slender stalk; the whole forming a cylindrical, downy-looking, usu. pendant, spike; an amentum.

Cat-lap (kæ·tlæp). *dial.* or *slang.* 1785. [See LAP *sb.*²] Stuff fit for a cat to lap; tea or other weak drink.

Ca·t-like, *a.* (*adv.*) 1600. Like a cat, or that of a cat; *esp.* stealthy, noiseless.

Catling (kæ·tliŋ). 1606. [f. CAT *sb.*¹ + -LING¹.] **1.** A little cat; a kitten 1630. **2.** Catgut; a small-sized lute-string 1606. **3.** *Surg.* A double-edged, sharp-pointed, straight knife for amputations 1612. † **4.** ? Misprint for CATKIN –1704.

Catlinite. 1858. [f. Geo. *Catlin*, the delineator of the American Indians + ITE¹ 2 b.] *Min.* The sacred pipe-stone of the American Indians, a red clay from the Upper Missouri region.

Catmint (kæ·tmint). ME. [f. CAT *sb.*¹ + MINT *sb.*², after med.L. *herba catti, h. cattaria*; so Fr. *herbe du chat*, G. *katzenmünze*, Du. *kattekruid.*] *Bot.* A labiate plant, *Nepeta cataria.* Also the Eng. name of the genus. Called in U.S. **Cat-nip.**

‖ **Catoblepas.** ME. [L. – Gr. κατωβλεψ 'looking down', f. κάτω downwards + βλέπειν look.] *Zool.* In ancient authors, some African animal, perh. the gnu. Now the name of a genus including the GNU.

Catocathartic (kæ:tokăþā·ɹtik). 1704. [f. Gr. κάτω downwards + καθαρτικός CATHARTIC; cf. ANOCATHARTIC.] *adj.* Purgative. *sb.* [sc. *medicine.*]

‖ **Catochus** (kæ·tǫ̆kǫ̆s). 1656. [Gr. κάτοχος (Galen) = κατοχή catalepsy, f. κατέχειν hold down, seize.] *Med.* Catalepsy; a similar affection, but with rigidity of the limbs; also, coma vigil. var. †‖ **Catoche.**

Cat o'mountain; see CATAMOUNTAIN.

Catonian (kătōᵘ·niăn). 1534. [– L. *Catonianus*, f. *Cato*, esp. Cato the Censor, and Cato of Utica; see -IAN.] *adj.* Pertaining to or resembling Cato; severe 1676. *sb.* A follower of Cato. So **Cato·nic** *a.*, **Ca·tonism**; also **Ca·toism.**

Cat-o'-ni·ne-tails, *sb.* 1695. [See CAT *sb.*¹] **1.** A whip with nine knotted lashes; an instrument of punishment formerly used in the British army and navy. **2.** A bulrush. *U.S.* 1858.

Catoptric (kætǫ·ptrik). 1570. [– Gr. κατοπτρικός, f. κάτοπτρον mirror; see -IC.] **A.** *adj.* Relating to a mirror, or to reflection 1774. Hence **Cato·ptrical** *a.*, **-ly** *adv.* **B.** *sb.* **1.** *pl.* **Catoptrics:** That part of Optics which treats of reflection 1570. † **2.** An instrument for producing effects by reflection –1644.

Catoptromancy (kætǫ·ptrǒmænsi). 1613. [f. Gr. κάτοπτρον mirror + -MANCY.] Divination by means of a mirror. Hence **Catoptroma·ntic** *a.*

Cat's-cradle. 1768. [prob. fanciful.] A children's game in which two players alternately take from each other's fingers an interwined cord so as to produce a symmetrical figure.

Cat's-eye. 1555. **1.** The eye of a cat; a cat-like eye. **2.** A variety of chalcedonic quartz, displaying, when held to the light, a lustre resembling the contracted pupil of a cat's eye 1599. **3.** The Germander Speedwell, *Veronica chamædrys*; also the Forget-me-not, etc. 1817.

3. The glow Of the wild cat's eyes KEATS.

Cat's foot. 1597. **1.** The foot of a cat; † used *lit.* in reference to the tale of a monkey using the foot or paw of a cat to rake roasted chestnuts out of the fire 1661. † **2.** Hence *fig.* = CAT'S-PAW 2. –1699. **3. a.** Ground-ivy, *Nepeta glechoma.* **b.** Mountain Cudweed, *Antennaria dioica* 1597.

Cat's-head. 1617. **1.** 'A kind of apple' (J.). **2.** An ornament in Norman architecture 1848. **3.** Var. of CAT-HEAD.

† **Ca·tso.** *slang.* 1602. [– It. *cazzo* membrum virile; also exclam. See CARGO[2], GADSO.] In 17th c. in the It. senses; also = Rogue, scamp –1708.

Cat's pa·w, ca·t's-paw. 1769. **1.** The paw of a cat; also *fig.* 1821. **2.** A person used as a tool by another; see CAT'S-FOOT 1785. **3.** *Naut.* A slight and local breeze, perceived by ripples on the surface of the sea 1769. **4.** *Naut.* A twisting hitch in the bight of a rope, so as to form two bights, to hook a tackle on 1794. Hence **Cat's-pawed** *ppl. a.* (in senses 3, 4).

Cat's tail, ca·t's-tail. Also **cat-tail.** 1450. **1.** The tail of a cat; name of a fur for the neck 1550. **2.** A name given to plants from the resemblance of parts; *esp.* the Reed-Mace *Typha latifolia*, from its long cylindrical furry spikes; also the Horse-tail, *Equisetum* 1450. **3.** = *Cat's-tail grass*: the genus *Phleum*; esp. *P. pratense*, Timothy grass 1597. **4.** A catkin 1611. **5.** *Naut.* The inner end of the CAT-HEAD.

Ca·t-stick. 1626. [See CAT *sb.*[1] II. 5.] A stick used in tip-cat and trap-ball.

Catsup = CATCHUP and KETCHUP.

† **Ca·tting,** *vbl. sb.* 1681. [As if f. CAT *v.* + -ING[1].] Caterwauling; going after the opposite sex –1725.

Cattish (kæ·tiʃ), *a.* 1598. [f. CAT *sb.*[1] + -ISH[1].] Of or like a cat. **b.** *fig.* Sly and spiteful 1883.

Cattle (kæ·t'l), *sb.* [ME. *catel* – AFr., ONFr. *catel*, var. of *chatel*, whence CHATTEL; see CAPITAL *a.*]

† **I.** (*catel, cattel(l).* † **1.** Property; strictly personal property –1495. *fig.* Rubbish. MILT. † **2.** = CHATTEL, with *collect. pl.* (From law-Latin.) –1720.

1. By loue of worldly catall W. DE WORDE. 2. *Goods and cattell*: see CHATTEL.

II. Live stock. (*Catel, cattel(l, cattle.*) **1.** A collective name for the bovine genus, but formerly, and still locally, for live animals held as property, or reared to serve as food, or for their milk, skin, wool, etc. ME. **2.** Extended to vermin, insects, etc. 1616; also to men and women (*arch.*) 1579. Also *attrib.*

1. Hors, asse, mule, ox, camell . all þair catell ME. In breeding of Cattell, as Pigs, Hens, and Chickens, and the like 1622. *Neat c., horned c.*: oxen. *Black c.*: 'oxen, bulls, and cows' (J.); prob. at first used only of black Highland cattle. 2. Nelly, concubines, and cattell of that sort EVELYN. Astrologers, and such like c. H. WALPOLE.

Comb.: **c.-gate,** a 'walk' or pasture for one's c., beast-gate; **-leader,** a nose-ring for c.; **-lifter,** a marauder who steals c.; so *cattle-lifting*; **-piece** a painting of c.; **-post, -ranch, -range, -run, -station,** a district, tract of country, etc., occupied for the pasturing of c.

Ca·ttle-guard. 1843. A trench on each side of a level crossing, to prevent cattle from straying along the line. (in U.S.)

Ca·ttle-plague. 1866. A highly contagious disease affecting cattle, called also *rinderpest*.

Catty (kæ·ti), *sb.* 1598. [– Malay-Javanese *kātī, katī*; cf. CADDY[1].] A weight = 16 taels or 1⅓lb. avoird., used in China and the Eastern Archipelago.

Ca·tty, *a.* 1886. [-Y[1].] = CATTISH.

†‖ **Catur.** 1653. [Origin unkn.] A light rowing vessel formerly used on the coast of Malabar –1686.

Ca·t-witted, *a.* 1673. Small-minded, obstinate, and spiteful.

‖ **Caubee·n.** 1831. [Ir. *caipín* dim. of *cap*, or f. Ir. *cába* cap + dim. *-een*.] An Irish hat.

Caucasian (kǫkē[i]·ʃiăn), *a.* 1807. [f. *Caucasus* or *Caucasia* + -IAN.] Of or belonging to the region of the Caucasus; Blumenbach's name for the 'white' race of mankind, which he derived from this region. Hence *sb.* A member of this family; an Indo-European.

Caucus (kǭ·kəs). 1763. [perh. f. Algonquin *cau'-cau-as'u* 'one who advises, urges, encourages' (Dr. J. H. Trumbull).] **1.** In *U.S.* A private or preliminary meeting of members of a political party, to select candidates for office, or to concert measures for furthering party interests; a meeting of wire-pullers. **2.** In England; a committee popularly elected for the purpose of securing concerted political action in a constituency; as a term of abuse, an organization seeking to manage the election and dictate to the constituencies 1878. Also *attrib.*

1. A c. rather than a general gathering MOTLEY. 2. 'Government by Caucus' 1882. Hence **Cau·cus** *v.* to hold a c.; to control by caucuses.

Caudal (kǭ·dăl), *a.* 1661. [– mod.L. *caudalis*, f. L. *cauda* tail; see -AL[1].] *Zool.* Of, belonging to, or of the nature of, a tail; situated in or near the tail. As quasi-*sb.* (= *c. fin, vertebra*, etc.) 1834.

The male . . bird, remarkable for his c. plumes DARWIN. Hence **Cau·dally** *adv.*

Caudate (kǭ·de[i]t), *a.* 1600. [– med.L. *caudatus*, f. as prec.; see -ATE[2].] Having a tail; *Zool.* and *Bot.* having an appendage resembling a tail 1830. var. **Cau·dated.**

† **Caudebeck.** 1680. [f. *Caudebec* in Normandy.] A kind of woollen hat.

‖ **Caudex** (kǭ·deks). Pl. **caudices** (kǭ·disīz). 1830. [L., earlier form of CODEX.] *Bot.* The axis of a plant, consisting of stem and root; *esp.* of palms, ferns, etc.

Caudicle (kǭ·dik'l). 1830. [f. L. *caudex, caudic-* (see prec.), after *caulicle*, etc.; see -CULE.] *Bot.* The small stalk-like appendage to the *pollinia* or pollen-masses of orchids. var. **Caudi·cula.**

Caudiform (kǭ·difǭɹm), *a.* 1839. [f. L. *cauda* tail + -FORM.] Tail-shaped.

Caudle (kǭ·d'l), *sb.* ME. [– ONFr. *caudel*, var. of *chaudel* (mod. *chaudeau*) :– med.L. **caldellum*, dim. of L. *caldum* hot drink, subst. use of n. of *cal(i)dus* hot.] A warm drink; thin gruel, mixed with wine or ale, sweetened and spiced, given to sick people; also to their visitors.

Hempen c.: = hanging 2 *Hen. VI*, IV. vii. 95.

Caudle (kǭ·d'l), *v.* 1607. [f. prec.] **1.** To administer a caudle to. **2.** To mix, as in a caudle 1790.

1. Cawdled like a Haberdashers Wife 1672.

Cauf, Sc. f. CALF[1], CHAFF *sb.*[1]; dial. f. CORF.

Caufle, var. of COFFLE.

Caught (kǭt), pa. t. and pple. of CATCH *v.*

Cauk (kǭk), *sb.* ME. [perh. north. var. of *chalk*, or – MDu. *calc* (Du. *kalk*); see CHALK.] **1.** = CHALK (*dial.*). † **2.** Lime. **3.** Barytes, or heavy spar; 1653.

† **Cauk,** *v.* ME. [– ONFr. *caukier, cauquer* (mod. *côcher* tread, as birds) :– L. *calcare* tread; cf. CALK *v.*[3], CAULK *v.*] *intr.* To tread, as birds –1704.

Cauking (kǭ·kiŋ), *vbl. sb.* See CAULK *v.*

Caul (kǭl), *sb.*[1] [ME. *calle*, perh. – (O)Fr. *cale* head-covering, f. *calotte* (see CALOTTE) by back-formation; but the Eng. word is recorded earlier. Cf. KELL.] **1.** A netted cap, worn by women; a net for the hair (*Hist.*); the back part of a woman's cap 1740. † **2.** *gen.* A net –1681. † **3.** A spider's web –1631. † **4.** *Anat.* Any investing membrane –1684. **5.** *spec.* **a.** The epiploön or omentum ME. **b.** The amnion or inner membrane enclosing the fœtus before birth; *esp.* this or a portion of it sometimes enveloping the head of the child at birth, regarded as lucky, and supposed to be a preservative against drowning 1547. Also *attrib.*

1. The peculiar net cap, with its high c. and neat little border 1862. 4. *C. of the heart*: app. the pericardium; also *fig.* (*Hosea* 13:8). 5. b. Yo' were borne with a caule o' your head B. JONS.

† **Caul,** *sb.*[2] OE. [– L. *caulis*; see also COLE[1], KALE.] **1.** A cabbage –1727. **2.** Stem, stalk. ME. only.

Cauldrife (kǭ·ldrif), *a.* *Sc.* 1768. [f. *cauld* cold + RIFE, q.v.] Causing, or susceptible to, cold. Also fig.

Cauldron, caldron (kǭ·ldren). [ME. *caudroun* – AFr., ONFr. *caudron* (mod. *chaudron*), augm. of Rom. **caldario*, L. *caldarium* hot bath, f. *cal(i)dus* hot. The etymologizing sp. with *l* appeared XV and subseq. infl. the pronunc., as in *fault*.] A large kettle or boiler. Also *transf.*

Fire burne and Cauldron bubble *Macb.* IV. i. 11. Vesuvio's horrid cauldrons roar SHENSTONE. Hence **Cau·ldron** *v.* to put in, or as in, a c. (*rare*).

Caulescent (kǭle·sĕnt), *a.* 1794. [f. L. *caulis*, perh. after Fr. *caulescent*; see -ESCENT.] *Bot.* Having an obvious stem.

Caulicle (kǭ·lik'l). 1657. [– L. *cauliculus*, dim. of *caulis* stalk; see -CULE; cf. Fr. *caulicule* (XVI) in same sense.] *Bot.* A little stalk or stem; *spec.* the radicle in an embryo.

Caulicole (kǭ·liko[u]l). 1816. [– Fr. *caulicole* or its source It. *colicolo* – L. *caulicolus* (Vitruvius) in same sense; see prec.] *Arch. pl.* 'The eight lesser branches or stalks in the Corinthian capital springing out from the four greater or principal caules or stalks' (Gwilt).

Caulicule (kǭ·likiul). 1835. [– Fr. *caulicule* – L. *cauliculus*; see next.] *Bot.* The point of union of the base of the plumule with the radicle and cotyledons.

‖ **Cauliculus** (kǭli·kiŭlɒs). 1830. [L., dim. of *caulis* stalk; see -CULE.] In *Bot.* = CAULICLE, CAULICULE; in *Archit.* = CAULICOLE.

Cauliflower (kǫ·liflau[ə]ɹ), *sb.* 1597. [Earliest *cole flory, colliflory*, alt. (by assim. to COLE) of Fr. † *chou fleuri* (*flori*), prob. – It. *cavolfiore*, pl. *cavoli fiori* or mod.L. *cauliflora* 'flowered cabbage'. Assim. to FLOWER XVII, as in Fr. *chou-fleur*.] A cultivated variety of the cabbage (*Brassica oleracea botrytis cauliflora*), the young inflorescence of which forms an edible head. Also *attrib.* Hence **Cau·liflower** *v.* ? to powder (a wig) (*rare*).

Cau·liform, *a.* 1847. [f. L. *caulis* stem + -FORM.] Stem-shaped.

Cauline (kǭ·ləin), *a.* 1756. [f. as prec. + -INE[1].] *Bot.* Of or belonging to the stem. var. **Cau·linar, -ary.**

‖ **Caulis** (kǭ·lis). Pl. **caules** (kǭ·līz). 1563. [L., in Gr. καυλός.] **1.** *Arch.* Each of the four principal stalks in the Corinthian capital. **2.** *Bot.* The stalk or stem of a (herbaceous) plant 1870.

Caulk (kǭk), *sb.* 1833. [perh. f. CAULK *v.*] *Naut. slang.* A dram.

Caulk, calk (kǭk), *v.* 1500. [– OFr. *cauquer, caukier*, north. var. of OFr. *cauchier* tread, press with force (mod. *côcher*, see CAUK *v.*) :– L. *calcare* tread, press, f. *calx, calc-* heel.] **1.** To stop up the seams of (a ship, etc.) by driving in oakum, or the like, melted pitch being afterwards poured on, to prevent leaking. **2.** To stop up the crevices of (windows, etc.) 1609. **3.** *Naut. slang. trans.* To 'shut up'; *intr.* to sleep 1836.

1. Shyppes calked with towgh 1552. 2. The windores close shut, and calk'd B. JONSON.

Caulker (kǭ·kəɹ). 1495. [f. prec. + -ER[1].] **1.** One who caulks ships. † **2.** ? A caulking-iron –1779. **3.** *slang.* A dram 1808. **4.** *slang.* Anything incredible, etc.; cf. *crammer*.

Caulo- (kǭ·lo), comb. f. Gr. καυλός (or L. *caulis*) stem of a plant, as in **Cauloca·rpic, Cauloca·rpous** *a.* producing flowers and fruit on its stem year after year, as ordinary shrubs.

Caulome (kǭ·lō[u]m). 1875. [– mod.L. *cauloma*, f. Gr. καυλός stem + *-oma*; see -OMA, -OME.] *Bot.* The leaf-bearing axis of a plant; a stem or branch, or the like. var. **Cau·loma** Hence **Caulo·mic** *a.*

‖ **Cauma** (kǭ·ma). 1811. [Late L. – Gr. καῦμα burning heat.] *Med.* The burning heat of a fever. Hence **Cauma·tic** *a.* relating to c.

Caunter. *dial.* 1810. [app. f. CANT *sb.*[1] or *v.*[2], with -ER unexpl.] *Mining.* A cross-vein. Also *attrib.*

† **Cau·ponate,** *v.* 1653. [– *cauponat-*, pa. ppl. stem of L. *cauponari* traffic or trade in, f. *caupo, -ōn-* huckster, innkeeper; see -ATE[3].] **1.** To sell liquor or victuals (Dicts.). **2.** To deal like a huckster with –1715. Hence † **Caupona·tion,** petty dealing; adulteration.

† **Cau·ponize,** *v.* 1652. [f. L. *caupo, -ōn-* (see prec.) + -IZE.] **1.** To act as victualler 1765. **2.** To mix and adulterate for gain –1771.

‖ **Cau·sa.** ME. The L. word for CAUSE, occas. used in Eng.

Causable (kǭ·zăb'l), *a.* *rare.* 1646. [f. CAUSE *v.* + -ABLE.] That can be caused.

Causal (kǭ·zăl), *a.* (*sb.*) 1530. [– late L. *causalis*, f. *causa* CAUSE *sb.*; see -AL[1].] **1.** Of or relating to a cause or causes 1570. **2.** Of the nature of, or acting as, a cause 1642. **3.** Of the nature of cause and effect 1656. **4.** *Gram.* and *Logic.* Expressing a cause 1530.

4. C. propositions are, where two propositions are joined by c. particles WATTS.

B. *sb.* A causal conjunction or particle 1530.

Causality (kǭzæ·lĭti). 1603. [– Fr. *causalité* or med.L. *causalitas*; see prec., -ITY.] **1.**

Causal quality, or agency. **2.** The operation or relation of cause and effect 1642. **3.** *Phren.* The faculty of tracing effects to causes 1874.

1. To ascribe a real C. to free-will HARTLEY. **2.** The necessary laws of C. and Time BOWEN.

Causally (kǭ·zăli), *adv.* 1638. [f. CAUSAL + -LY².] In the manner of, or as being the cause; by way of cause and effect.

C. guilty of Calamities 1640.

Causation (kǭzēⁱ·ʃən). 1646. [– (O)Fr. *causation* or L. *causatio*, *-ōn-* in med.L. sense 'action of causing'.] The action of causing; the operation of causal energy; the relation of cause and effect.

The c. of a movement STUBBS. Some latent chain of c. W. IRVING. Hence **Causa·tionism,** the theory of universal c. **Causa·tionist,** one who adopts this.

Causative (kǭ·zătiv), *a.* ME. [– (O)Fr. *causatif, -ive* or late L. (in med.L. sense) *causativus*; see CAUSE *v.*, -ATIVE.] **1.** Effective as a cause; productive *of.* **2.** *Gram.* = CAUSAL 4. As *sb.*, a causative word. 1600.

1. A superhuman c. agency MORLEY. Hence **Cau·satively** *adv.* **Causati·vity,** c. quality.

†‖ **Causa·tor.** [med.L., f. *causare*; see CAUSE *v.*, -OR 2.] A causer. SIR T. BROWNE. So †‖ **Causa·trix.** ‖ **Causa·tum,** the product of causation.

Cause (kǭz), *sb.* ME. [– (O)Fr. *cause* – L. *causa* reason, motive, lawsuit.] **I.** General. **1.** That which produces an effect. (*Cause* and *effect* are correlative terms.) **2.** A person or other agent who occasions something, with or without intention ME. **3.** That which moves a person to action; ground of action; reason, motive; *esp.* adequate ground of action. ME. **4.** The object of action; purpose, end. (*Obs.* exc. in *Final cause.*) ME.

1. The occasion, not the c., of joy 1827. The c. of a phenomenon, . . the antecedent or concurrence of antecedents, on which it is invariably and unconditionally consequent MILL. **2.** Howe much mischiefe such women bee c. of 1540. **3.** Just c. of suspicion CUDWORTH. A c. of action 1883. *To show c.*, esp. in Eng. Law, to argue against the confirmation of a 'rule nisi', etc. **4.** *Final c.*: the purpose or end of the thing caused. (The other three of Aristotle's *four causes* were the *efficient c.*, the producing agency; the *formal c.*, the form or essence; and the *material c.*, the matter.) *Occasional causes*: see OCCASIONAL.

Phr. †*For my* (*his*, etc.) *c.*: for my (his, etc.) sake.

II. Legal, etc. **1.** *Law.* The case of one party in a suit ME. Also *fig.* **2.** *Law.* A matter in litigation; an action, process, suit; = CASE *sb.*¹ 6. ME. Also *fig.* † **3.** A matter of concern –1660. **4.** That side of a question espoused, advocated, and upheld by a person or party 1581. † **5.** Disease –1607.

1. *To plead a c.* **4.** The c. of the Poles BURKE. Phr. *To make common c.* (*with*). **5.** *All's Well* II. i. 114. Hence **Cau·seful** *a.* having (good) c.; that is a c. of (*rare*).

Cause (kǭz), *v.* ME. [– (O)Fr. *causer* or med.L. *causari, causare*.] **1.** *trans.* To be the cause of; to effect, bring about, produce, induce, make. † **2.** To give excuses [= L. *causari*] SPENSER. Hence **Cau·ser.**

1. A Drench of Wine . . the Patient's Death did c. DRYDEN. I will c. the Sunne to go downe at noone *Amos* 8:9. This caus'd, that many died . . in the streets suddenly DE FOE.

Cause, 'cause, *conj.* 1513. *dial.* = BECAUSE.

‖ **Cause célèbre** (kōz selębr). 1858. [Fr.] A notorious legal case.

Causeless (kǭ·zlės), *a.* ME. [f. CAUSE *sb.* + -LESS.] **1.** Having no antecedent cause. **2.** Without (good) cause; groundless ME.

1. His c. power, the cause of all things known 1712. **2.** A c. pain KEN. Hence **Cau·seless-ly** *adv.*, **-ness.**

‖ **Causerie** (kōᵘ·zəri, kozri). 1827. [Fr., f. *causer* to talk.] Informal talk; a chatty article.

‖ **Causeuse** (kozö·z). 1883. [Fr., f. as prec.] A small sofa for two persons.

Causeway (kǭ·zwēⁱ), *sb.* [In XV *caucéwey*, f. *caucé* CAUSEY + WAY; largely superseding *causey*.] **1.** = CAUSEY 2. **2.** = CAUSEY 3. 1611. Also *fig.* Hence **Cau·sewayed** *ppl. a.*, **Cau·sewaying** *vbl. sb.* (Mostly for *causeyed, -ing.*)

Causey (kǭ·zeⁱ, kǭ·seⁱ), *sb.* [Early forms *cauce, cauci* – AFr. **caucé(e* = ONFr. *caucíée* (mod. *chaussée*) :– Rom. **calciata* (sc. *via* way, road), fem. pa. pple. f. L. *calx, calc-* lime, CHALK.] † **1.** A mound, embankment, or dam –1774. **2.** A raised way formed on a mound, *esp.* across low wet ground, a bog, marsh, etc. Now CAUSEWAY. ME. **3.** Hence, A highway; *esp.* a paved way; the paved part of a way (still *dial.*) ME. (*Sc.*) A small area paved with cobbles 1481.

2. A Stone-Causey thorow a Bogg 1643. **3.** The c., called Via Appia HEARNE. Hence **Cau·sey** *v.* to pave with small stones. (Chiefly *Sc.* and *dial.*)

Causidical (kǭzi·dikăl), *a.* 1797. [f. L. *causidicus* pleader + -AL¹.] Of or pertaining to a pleader of legal causes.

† **Cau·son.** ME. [– late L. *causon* fever – Gr. καύσων burning heat.] ? Inflammation, ? heartburn –1661.

Caustic (kǭ·stik). 1555. [– L. *causticus* – Gr. καυστικός capable of burning, f. καυστός combustible, f. καίειν burn.] **A.** *adj.* **1.** Burning, corrosive, destructive of organic tissue. **2.** *fig.* Sharp, biting, sarcastic 1771. **3.** *Math.* Epithet of a curved surface formed by the ultimate intersection of luminous rays proceeding from a single point and reflected or refracted from a curved surface. A caustic by reflection is called a *catacaustic*, that by refraction a *diacaustic*. So *c. line, surface.* 1727.

1. *C. alkali* (*Chem.*): a name of the hydrates of potassium and sodium, called *c. potash* (KHO) and *c. soda* (NaHO) respectively; *c. lime*, quicklime (CaO). **2.** His shrewd, c. . . remarks SCOTT. Hence † **Cau·stical** *a.*, **-ly** *adv.*; var. **Cau·sticly** (*rare*).

B. *sb.* **1.** *Med.* A substance which burns and destroys living tissue when in contact with it 1582. Also *fig.* **2.** *Math.* = *C. curve* or *surface*; cf. A. 3.

1. *Common* or *Lunar c.*: nitrate of silver.

Causticity (kǭsti·sĭti). 1772. [f. prec. + -ITY; cf. Fr. *causticité*.] **1.** Caustic quality; corrosiveness. **2.** *fig.* Of speech or humour 1785.

2. I . . endeavoured to repair my c. H. WALPOLE. So **Cau·sticness** (*rare*).

Cau·tel, *sb.* ME. [– (O)Fr. *cautèle* or L. *cautela*, f. *caut-* pa. ppl. stem of *cavēre* take heed.] **1.** A crafty device –1611. **2.** Craftiness, trickery –1580. **3.** Heedfulness –1664. **4.** A precaution; in *Law*, etc. an exception by way of precaution 1541. Hence † **Cau·telous** *a.* full of cautels; crafty; cautious. † **Cau·telously** *adv.* † **Cau·telousness.**

Cauter (kǭ·təɹ). 1534. [– (O)Fr. *cautère*, – L. *cauterium*; see CAUTERY.] = CAUTERY 1.

Cau·terant. 1846. [f. prec. + -ANT¹.] A cauterizing substance.

† **Cau·terism.** 1640. [f. after CAUTERIZE; see -ISM.] The application of cautery –1688.

Cauterize (kǭ·tĕrəiz), *v.* Also **-ise.** 1541. [– (O)Fr. *cautériser* – late L. *cauterizare*, alt. – Gr. καυτηριάζειν, f. καυτήριον; see CAUTERY. -IZE.] **1.** *Med.* To burn or sear with a hot iron or a caustic. Also *absol.* **2.** *fig.* To sear (the conscience, etc.). See 1 *Tim.* 4:2. 1586.

1. To c. a wound 1865. *fig.* To c. unsoundness of doctrine LANDOR. Hence **Cau:teriza·tion.**

Cautery (kǭ·tĕri). 1543. [– L. *cauterium* – Gr. καυτήριον branding-iron, f. καίειν burn.] **1.** A hot iron or the like used for burning or searing organic tissue; also a caustic drug or medicine. The former is called an *actual*, the latter a *potential*, c. **2.** The operation of cauterizing, the application of a caustic 1575. Also *fig.* † **3.** An eschar thus made. [So Gr.] 1651.

Caution (kǭ·ʃən), *sb.* ME. [– (O)Fr. *caution* – L. *cautio*, f. *caut-*, pa. ppl. stem of *cavēre* take heed. A re-adoption from L. took place *c.* 1600; see -TION.] **1.** Security given for performance of an engagement; bail; a guarantee. Still in Sc. law, and in U.S. † **2.** A proviso –1667. **3.** A caveat, monition 1605. **b.** *slang.* (orig. U.S.) An extraordinary thing or person 1835. **4.** The taking of heed; 'provident care, wariness against evil' (J.); cautiousness, circumspectness 1651. † **5.** (with *pl.*) A precaution –1801.

1. To give c. of his future obedience HOBBES. Hostages, as cautions for . . 1586. On the payment of c. (= caution-money) 1830. **3.** For thy good c. thanks *Macb.* IV. i. 73. **4.** Godfrey . . had learned c. MILMAN. **5.** *Macb.* III. vi. 44.

C.-money, money deposited as security for good conduct, *esp.* by a student on entering a college. Hence † **Cau·tionate** *v.* to take precautions; to guard with provisos. **Cau·tioner,** a surety (*Sc. Law*); one who cautions. (Dicts.) **Cau·tionless** *a.* **Cau·tionary** = CAUTION *sb.* 1. (*Sc. Law.*)

Caution (kǭ·ʃən), *v.* 1641. [f. the sb.] † **1.** *intr.* To give a warning –1678. † **2.** To guard with a saving clause –1681. **3.** To advise or charge to take heed. Usu. with *against* or *to* with *inf.* 1683.

3. To c. any one to be moderate in his food 1845.

Cautionary (kǭ·ʃənări), *a.* 1597. [f. med.L. *cautionarius* (XIV), f. L. *cautio*; see CAUTION *sb.*, -ARY².] **1.** Of, pertaining to, of the nature of a pledge or security; held as a pledge or security. Now *Hist.* or *Sc.* † **2.** Cautious –1831. **3.** Warning, admonitory 1638. † **4.** Precautionary –1826. Also as *sb.*

1. C. towns 1597. **3.** C. precepts STEELE. Hence † **Cau·tionarily** *adv.*

Cautious (kǭ·ʃəs), *a.* 1640. [f. CAUTION + -OUS, on the model of *ambition, ambitious*, etc.; see -TIOUS.] Distinguished by caution; heedful, wary, careful, circumspect. Const. † *of, how, lest, to* (formerly in sense *not to*) with *inf.*

'C. speed SOUTHEY. A c. policy 1842. Be c. how you trump out 1820. Hence, **Cau·tious-ly** *adv.*, **-ness.**

‖ **Cava.** 1809. *Phys.* Short f. *vena cava.*

Cavalcade (kævălkēⁱ·d), *sb.* 1591. [– Fr. *cavalcade*, earlier *-ate* – It. *cavalcata*, f. *cavalcare* :– Rom. **caballicare* ride, f. L. *caballus* pack-horse, nag.] † **1.** A march or raid on horseback –1647. **2.** A procession on horseback, *esp.* on a festive or solemn occasion. ? *Obs.* 1644. Also *concr.* **3.** *transf.* and *fig.* Procession 1670.

2. The c. of the new Pope EVELYN. **3.** He made a C. of his Devils . . through the Town *Rabelais*. Hence **Cavalca·de** *v.* to ride in a c.

Cavalier (kævălīᵊ·ɹ). 1560. [– Fr. *cavalier* or its source It. *cavaliere*, deriv. of L. (Rom.) *caballus* horse; see prec., -IER. Cf. late L. *caballarius* rider, ostler.]

A. *sb.* **1.** A horseman, *esp.* a horse-soldier; a knight 1600. **2.** 'A gay sprightly military man' (J.); *gen.* a courtly gentleman, a gallant 1589. **3.** A name (orig. reproachful) for those who fought for Charles I against the Roundheads; a 17th c. Royalist 1641. **4.** *Fortif.* 'A work generally raised . . higher than the rest of the works . . to command all the adjacent works and the country round' (Stocqueler) 1560.

C.-servant, or in It. form *cavaliere-servente*: a man who devotes himself wholly to attendance on a lady as her professed slave. Hence **Cavalier** *v.* to play the c.; to escort (a lady). **Cavalie·r-ish** *a.*, **-ism.**

B. *attrib.* or *adj.* † **1.** Gallant 1641. **2.** Offhand in manner, free and easy 1657. **b.** Haughty, disdainful, supercilious 1751. **3.** Royalist; see A 3. 1844.

1. Not valiant, and not much c. SUCKLING. **2.** This c. tone from an unknown person . . did not please me CARLYLE. **3.** An old C. family DISRAELI. Hence **Cavalie·rly** *a.* and *adv.*

Cavally (kăvæ·li). 1634. [– Sp. *caballo*, for *caballa*; forms in *-ally* perh. depend on It. *cavalli*, pl. of *cavallo* mackerel.] A name of 17th c. navigators for species of horse-mackerel.

Cavalry (kæ·vălri). 1591. [– Fr. *cavallerie* – It. *cavalleria*, f. *cavallo*; see CAVALIER, -ERY, -RY.] † **1.** Horsemanship –1670. † **2.** Knighthood; an order of chivalry –1632. **3.** That part of a military force which consists of mounted troops. Opp. to *infantry*. (Usu. w. pl. vb.) 1591. *transf.* Horses, horsemen, etc., collectively 1684. Also *attrib.*

‖ **Cavatina** (kavătī·nă). 1836. [It.] *Mus.* A short song of simple character, prop. one without a second strain and repeat; occ. 'a smooth melodious air, forming part of a grand scena or movement' (Grove).

Cave (kēⁱv), *sb.* ME. [– (O)Fr. *cave* – L. *cava*, subst. use of fem. sing. or n.pl. of *cavus* hollow.] **1.** A hollow place opening under the ground; a cavern, den, habitation in the earth. † **2.** *gen.* Any hollow place, a cavity –1626. **3.** *Political slang.* The secession of a small body of politicians from their party on some special question; the body so seceding; see ADULLAMITE 1866.

2. So is the Eare a sinuous Caue BACON.

Comb., etc.: **c.-breccia** (*Geol.*), breccia deposited in caves; **-deposit** (*Geol.*); **-dweller,** one of the prehistoric men who dwelt in caves; **-fish,** a (blind) fish inhabiting subterraneous streams or lakes in caves; **-man** = *cave-dweller*. Also in names of extinct animals whose remains are found in caves, as *c.-bear*, etc.

† **Cave,** *a.* 1540. [- Fr. *cave* - L. *cavus* hollow; see prec.] Hollow, concave. Of the moon: Waning (L. *luna cava* Plin.). -1677.

Cave (kēiv), *v.*[1] 1541. [f. CAVE *sb.*] **1.** *trans.* To hollow, hollow out. **2.** *intr.* To lodge in a cave 1611.

1. Where the mouldred earth had cav'd the banke 1596. **2.** Such as wee Caue heere, hunt heere SHAKS.

Cave (kēiv), *v.*[2] 1796. [prob. of East Anglian origin and a var. of dial. (esp. eastern) *calve* (XVIII), *cauve*, perh. of LG. origin; cf. WFlem. *inkalven* fall in, Du. *afkalven* fall away, *uitkalven* fall out.] **1.** *To cave in*: to fall in over a hollow, as earth on the side of a pit or cutting; to fall in in a concave form. Chiefly *colloq.* **2.** *fig. colloq.* To yield to pressure; to break down, give way, submit 1837. Hence **Cave-in** *sb.*

Cave (kēiv), *v.*[3] ME. Dial. f. CHAVE.

‖ **Cave** (kēi·vi), *int.* 1868. [L., imper. sing. of *cavēre* beware.] Beware!

Caveat (kēi·vi,æt), *sb.* 1557. [L., 3rd sing. pres. subj. of *cavēre* beware.] **1.** *Law.* A notice given by some party to the proper officer not to take a certain step until the party has been heard in opposition 1654. **2.** *transf.* A warning, admonition, caution 1557. † **3.** = CAUTION *sb.* 2, 5. -1648. **4.** *U.S. Patent Laws.* A description of some invention, designed to be patented, lodged in the office before the patent right is taken out, operating as a bar to other applications respecting the same invention 1879.

1. Phr. *To enter* or *put in a c.*: also *fig.* **2.** A caueat, to be ware of to moche confidence RECORDE. She enters a silent c. by a blush FULLER. Hence **Ca·veat** *v.* † to enter a c. against; † to serve with a c.; *Fencing*, to shift one's sword to the other side of one's adversary's sword, to disengage. **Ca·vea:tor.**

Ca·vel, *sb. n. dial.* ME. [Identical with Du. *kavel* lot, parcel (*kavelen* cast lots, etc.), MDu. *cavele* lot; cf. MLG. *kavele* 'little stick (inscribed with runes) for casting lots'.] **1.** A lot (that is cast). Also *fig.* **2.** A division made by lot; an allotment 1652. Hence **Ca·vel** *v.* to cast lots; to allot. (Now *dial.*)

Cavendish (kæ·vĕndiʃ). 1839. [Said to be named after an American manufacturer.] Tobacco softened and pressed into solid cakes.

Cavern (kæ·vəɹn), *sb.* ME. [- (O)Fr. *caverne* or L. *caverna*, f. *cavus* hollow; cf. CAVE.] A hollow place underground; a cave. (More rhet. than *cave*.) Also † *transf.*

transf. The cauerne of the Eare BACON, of the forehead BUCHAN. Hence **Ca·vern** *v.* to enclose as in a cavern; to hollow out into caverns.

Cavernous (kæ·vəɹnəs), *a.* 1447. [- (O)Fr. *caverneux* or L. *cavernosus*; see prec., -OUS.] **1.** Abounding in caverns. **2.** Full of cavities and interstices 1597. **3.** Of the nature of or resembling a cavern 1830. **4.** Of or pertaining to a cavern 1833.

2. It [cancer] is hard, unequall, and c. or hollow 1597. **3.** C. eyes 1865. var. **Cave·rnal** (in sense 4).

Cavernulous (kăvə·ɹniŭləs), *a.* 1757. [f. L. *cavernula*, dim. of *caverna* (see -ULE), + -OUS.] Full of minute cavities; porous.

Copper . . is c. and weak BLACK. var. **Cave·rnulated** *a.*

Cavesson (kæ·vĕsən). 1598. [- Fr. *caveçon* - It. *cavezzone*, augm. of *cavezza* halter :- Rom. **capitia*, f. med.L. *capitium* head-covering, f. L. *caput*, *capit-* head.] A kind of nose-band, used to curb unmanageable horses. Earlier *cavezan*, *-zon*.

‖ **Cavetto** (kave·tto). 1677. [It., dim. of *cavo* hollow, f. L. *cavus*; see CAVE *sb.*] *Arch.* A hollowed moulding, whose profile is the quadrant of a circle.

Caviar, caviare (kavi,ā·ɹ, kav,yā·ɹ, also kavi,ēə·ɹ). 1591. [Early forms repr. It. *caviale* (whence Fr. † *cavial*), Sp. *cabial*, Pg. *caviar*, † *cavial*, Fr. *caviar*, all based on Turk. *hāvyar*.] The roe of the sturgeon, etc., pressed and salted, and eaten as a relish; *esp.* in the east of Europe.

And for our home-bred British Cheer, Botargo, Catsup, and Caveer SWIFT. *Cauiarie to the Generall*: a phrase from *Haml.* II. ii. 457, referring to the circumstance that *caviar* is generally unpalatable to those who have not acquired a taste for it.

Cavicorn (kæ·vikǭɹn). [f. L. *cavus* hollow + *cornu* horn.] *Zool.* One of a family (*Cavicornia*) of Ruminants having hollow horns.

Cavie (kēi·vi). *Sc.* 1756. [app. - MDu. *kēvie*, Du. or Flem. *kevie*, XVI c. Flem. also *kavie* cage, coop, ult. - L. *cavea*; see CAGE.] A hen-coop.

Cavil (kæ·vil), *sb.* 1570. [f. the vb.] **1.** A captious, quibbling, or frivolous objection. **2.** Cavilling 1600. † **3.** Gibe 1615.

1. That's but a c. SHAKS. **2.** Liable to c. 1729.

Cavil (kæ·vil), *v.* 1548. [- (O)Fr. *caviller* - L. *cavillari*, f. *cavilla* scoffing, mockery.] **1.** *intr.* 'To raise captious and frivolous objections' (J.); to find fault unfairly or without good reason. Const. *at*, *about*. **2.** *trans.* To object to captiously 1581.

1. But in the way of Bargaine . . Ile cauill on the ninth part of a hayre SHAKS. Hence **Ca·viller.**

Cavillation (kævilēi·ʃən). ME. [- (O)Fr. *cavillation* - L. *cavillatio*, *-ōn-*; see prec., -ATION.] † In early use, *esp.* The use of legal quibbles, so as to overreach or defraud; hence, chicanery, overreaching sophistry. Subseq. = Cavilling 1540; CAVIL *sb.* 1 (*arch.*) 1532.

† **Ca·villato:ry,** *a. rare.* 1641. [- late L. *cavillatorius*, f. L. *cavillator*; see prec. and -ORY[2].] Of the nature of cavilling -1643.

† **Ca·villous,** *a.* 1572. [- OFr. *cavilleus* or late L. *cavillosus*; see CAVIL, -OUS.] Full of cavils or cavilling; apt to cavil -1851. Hence † **Ca·villous-ly** *adv.*, † **-ness.**

Cavin (kæ·vin). 1708. [- Fr. *cavin* sunken road.] *Mil.* A hollow way, capacious enough to cover troops, and facilitate their approach to a fortress. (Dicts.)

Cavitary (kæ·vitări), *a.* (*sb.*) 1835. [- Fr. *cavitaire*, f. *cavité*; see CAVITY, -ARY[1].] † **1.** Having a cavity, as *c. worms.* (Adaptation of Cuvier's term, *vers cavitaires*, used of intestinal worms having a distinct mouth and anus.) Also as *sb.* -1847. **2.** Of the nature of, or belonging to, a cavity 1861.

Cavity (kæ·vĭti). 1541. [- Fr. *cavité* (OFr. *caveté*) or late L. *cavitas*, f. *cavus* hollow; see -ITY.] † **1.** Hollowness (*rare*) 1679. **2.** A hollow place; a void space within a solid body 1541. **3.** *Naval Arch.* Displacement 1850.

2. The cavities as well of the mouth as of the stomache HOLLAND. Little cavities, or vesicles, in this scoria HUXLEY.

‖ **Cavo-rilie·vo.** [It. (kā·vo rilyē·vo) = hollow relief.] A style of relief in which the highest portions of the figures are on a level with the general surface.

Cavort (kăvǭ·ɹt), *v. U.S. vulgar.* 1848. [perh. perversion of CURVET suggested by *vault.*] *intr.* To curvet, caper about, frisk.

Cavy (kēi·vi), *sb.* 1796. [- mod.L. *cavia*, f. Galibi (French Guiana) CABIAI. Cf. Fr. *cavié*.] A rodent of the genus *Cavia* or family *Cavidæ*, natives of America, as the Guinea-pig or the Capybara.

Caw (kǭ). 1666. [Echoic.] The cry or call of a rook, crow, raven, etc. Also as *int.*

Caw (kǭ), *v.* 1589. [Echoic.] *intr.* Of rooks, crows, etc.: To utter their natural cry 1590. Also *transf.* Of persons 1589.

Choughes . . (Rising and cawing at the guns report) *Mids. N.* III. ii. 22.

Cawk, *sb.*[1] var. of CAUK, q.v. Hence **Caw·ky** *a.* barytous.

Cawk (kǭk), *sb.*[2] 1856. [Echoic.] The cry of rooks, divers, etc. Hence **Cawk** *v.*

Cawker, var. of CAULKER; also of CALKER[2].

Cawl (kǭl). Now *dial.* [OE. *cawl*, *ceawl.*] A basket; in Cornwall, a creel.

† **Caxon**[1] (kæ·ksen). 1756. [perh. f. the surname.] A kind of wig -1834.

‖ **Caxon**[2]. ? *Obs.* 1669. [OSp., now *cajon* (kaχo·n), augm. of *caxa*, now *caja* CASE *sb.*[2]; cf. Fr. *caisson.*] A chest of ores for refining.

Caxton (kæ·kstən). 1811. [f. the surname.] **1.** *ellipt.* A book printed by William Caxton (died 1492). **2.** A variety of type, imitating that of Caxton.

Cay (kēi, kī). Also KEY[2], *q.v.* 1707. [- Sp. *cayo* shoal, sandbank, barrier-reef - Fr. *quai*, † *cay* QUAY.] A low insular bank of sand, mud, rock, etc.; a range of low lying reefs or rocks.

Cayenne (kēi,e·n, kai,e·n). 1756. [Early forms *kayan*, *kian*; orig. - Tupi *kyynha*, *quiynha*, later assim. to *Cayenne*, chief town of French Guiana.] (Also *Cayenne pepper.*) A very pungent powder obtained from the dried and ground seeds and pods of species of *Capsicum*, esp. *C. annuum* and *C. frutescens*, of S. America; used as a condiment; formerly called Guinea pepper. Also *fig.* Hence **Caye·nned** *ppl. a.* seasoned with c.

Cayleyan (kēi·li,ăn). 1852. [f. Prof. *Cayley* of Cambridge + -AN.] *Math.* A certain curve of the third order.

Cayman, caiman (kēi·măn). 1577. [- Sp., Pg. *caiman* - Carib *acayuman*, *cay(e)man.*] A name applied to some large saurians, *esp.* the S. American ALLIGATOR; and, *loosely*, to all large American saurians, including crocodiles.

† **Cay·nard.** ME. only. [- AFr. **cainard*, **caynard*, perh. repr. by Fr. *cagnard* sluggard (XVII), f. *cagne* bitch; see -ARD.] A sluggard.

Cayuse (ka,yū·s). *U.S. local.* 1882. [Chinook Indian.] An Indian pony.

‖ **Ca·zimi.** 1614. [prob. - Arab. *kaṣamīm* in the phr. *kaṣamīm-aš-šams* middle of the sun.] *Astrol.* The centre of the sun. *In cazimi*: said of a planet when distant not more than 17 minutes from the sun.

Cazique, var. of CACIQUE.

Ce (sī), name of the letter C. Cf. CEE.

Cease (sīs), *v.* [ME. *cesse*, *cese* - (O)Fr. *cesser* :- L. *cessare* stop, f. *cess-*, pa. ppl. stem of *cedere* yield; see CEDE.]

I. *intr.* **1.** To stop, give over, discontinue, desist. † **2.** To rest -1660. **3.** Of actions, feelings, etc.: To come to or be at an end ME. † **4.** To fail, become extinct, pass away -1710.

1. To c. from wanderings TENNYSON, to fyght CAXTON. **3.** Miracles are ceast SHAKS. **4.** The poore shall neuer c. out of the land *Deut.* 15:11.

II. *trans.* **1.** To stop ME. † **2.** To cause to leave off (*of* an action); to quiet -1585.

1. He, her fears to c., Sent down the meek-eyed Peace MILT. Fond Nature, c. thy strife POPE. The snow never ceased falling TYNDALL. Hence † **Ceased** *ppl. a.* that has come to an end. † **Cea·ser.**

Cease (sīs), *sb.* ME. [- OFr. *ces*, f. *cesser*; see prec.] = *ceasing*, CESSATION. *Obs.* exc. in *Without cease.* (Cf. Fr. *sans cesse.*) Hence **Cea·seless** *a.* without ceasing. **Cea·selessly** *adv.* **Cea·selessness.**

‖ **Cebus** (sī·bŏs). 1863. [mod.L. - Gr. κῆβος.] A genus of long-tailed monkeys of S. America, including the Sapajous. Hence **Ce·bine** *a.*

Cecity (sī·sĭti). *arch.* 1528. [- L. *cæcitas*, f. *cæcus* blind; cf. (O)Fr. *cécité*; see -ITY.] Blindness. (Usu. *fig.*)

After life's term, a term of c. M. ARNOLD.

Cecum, var. of CÆCUM, the blind-gut.

Cecutiency (sĭkiū·fiĕnsi). [f. *cæcutient-*, pres. ppl. stem of *cæcutire* be blind, f. *cæcus* blind; see -ENCY.] A tendency to blindness; partial blindness. SIR T. BROWNE.

Cedar (sī·dəɹ). OE. [ME. *cedre* - OFr. *cedre* (mod. *cèdre*) - L. *cedrus* - Gr. κέδρος juniper, cedar. OE. *ceder* from L.] **1.** An evergreen conifer, the *Pinus cedrus* of Linnæus, *Abies cedrus*, *Cedrus libani* of other botanists, called Cedar of Lebanon from its most famous early locality. The wood of this tree ME. **2.** Applied to the genus *Cedrus*, or subgenus of *Abies*, including the Mount Atlas or Silvery Cedar and the Deodar or Indian Cedar. Also to various trees more or less resembling the true cedar: including species of *Cedrela*, *Juniperus*, *Thuja*, *Cupressus*, *Pinus*, etc. 1703. Also *attrib.*

1. The beames of our house are cedars *Song of Solomon* 1:17. *Comb.* **c.-bird,** the American Waxwing, *Ampelis carolinensis*, a species of Chatterer haunting cedar trees. Hence **Ce·dared** *ppl. a.* furnished with cedars (*rare*). **Ce·darn** *a. poet.* of cedar-trees or -wood. † **Ce·dary, Ce·dry** *a.* having the properties of c. **Ce·drine** *a.* of or pertaining to c.

Cede (sīd), *v.* 1633. [- Fr. *céder* or L. *cedere* go, go away, retire, yield.] † **1.** *intr.* To give way, yield *to* -1756. **2.** *trans.* To give up, grant; to yield, surrender 1754.

2. This copy has been ceded to me as a favor T. JEFFERSON. To c. provinces to the Company WELLINGTON. Hence **Ce·der.** So **Ce·dent,** one who assigns property to another. *Sc. Law.*

Cedilla (sĭdi·lă). 1599. [– Sp. *cedilla,* now *zedilla,* dim. of *zeda* letter Z.] The mark ¸ written under *c* when it precedes *a, o, u,* and has the sound (s). Also var. † **Cerilla** 1591, – Sp. *cerilla*; cf. Fr. † *cérille.*

Cedr-, repr. L. *cedrus,* cedar, forming terms of chemistry, etc.:

Ce·drene, a liquid hydrocarbon ($C_{32}H_{24}$) found in the resin of the cedar of Lebanon. **Cedriret,** a product obtained from the tar of beechwood, crystallizing in fine needles.

Cedrat, -ate (sī·drĕt). 1781. [– Fr. *cédrat* – It. *cedrato,* f. *cedro* citron :– L. *citrus.*] A variety of the citron or lemon. var. ‖ **Ce·dre** [Fr.].

‖ **Cedrela** (sĭdrī·lă). 1836. [mod.L. – Sp. *cedrela,* dim. of *cedro, cedra* CEDAR.] A genus of large trees, species of which are called *Cedar* or *Bastard Cedar.* Hence **Cedrela·ceous** *a.* (*Bot.*) of or pertaining to the *Cedrelaceæ,* or Cedrela order.

Ce·dron. 1859. A small tree of New Granada (*Simaba cedron,* N.O. *Simarubaceæ*); also its fruit. Also *attrib.*

‖ **Ce·dula.** 1724. [Sp. *cédula* (þe·dula) SCHEDULE, q.v.] A permit or order issued by the Spanish government; also a name of some S. American securities.

Cedule, early f. SCHEDULE.

† **Ce·duous,** *a. rare.* [f. L. *cæduus,* f. *cædere* fell; see -UOUS.] Ready for felling. EVELYN.

Cee (sī). 1542. [OE. *cē* (Ælfric); cf. Fr. *cé,* L. *cē.*] Name of the letter C. Formerly, a term for a certain quantity of beer. Hence **Cee spring, C-spring,** in *Coach-building.*

‖ **Ceiba** (səi·bă). 1812. [Sp. (þei·ba); perh. W. Indian.] The Silk Cotton-tree of the W. Indies, *Eriodendron anfractuosum* (*Bombax ceiba*). (Miller.)

Ceil (sīl), *sb. poet. rare.* 1840. [f. next.] = CEILING.

Ceil, ciel (sīl), *v.* ME. [In XV–XVII *cele, sele, ceal, seal,* corresp. in form to L. *celare* hide, cover up, and Fr. *céler*; but the ult. origin, and its relations with CEILING, CELURE are unexplained.] † **1.** ? To furnish with a canopy, hangings, or a screen. ME. only. † **2.** To line (the roof or walls of a room, etc.) with woodwork, plaster, etc.; to wainscot –1615. **3.** *esp.* To line the roof of, construct an inner roof for; *usually,* to plaster the roof 1519.

2. The greate house syled he with Pyne tre COVERDALE 2 *Chron.* 3:5. Hence **Ceiled, cieled** *ppl. a.* † wainscoted; provided with a ceiling; also *fig.*

Ceiling, cieling (sī·liŋ), *vbl. sb.* [Late ME. *celynge, sil-, syling,* early mod.Eng. *syll-, seel-, ciel-, seyl-,* contemp. with *celure, selure, sil(l)our,* later *seller* canopy, hangings, tapestry (XIV–XVI), and somewhat earlier than *cele* CEIL *v.* (XV–XVII); these forms correspond in use to med.L. *celum* (XII), *celatura* (XIII), *celura* (XIV), and vb. *celare*; but it remains doubtful whether L. *cælum* heaven is the ult. base, and how far L. *cælare* engrave, *cælatura* engraving, carving, are concerned.] **1.** The action of the vb. CEIL 1497. † **2.** *concr.* A screen of tapestry, a curtain –1632. **3.** † Panelling; wainscoting –1634; *Naut.* = FOOT-*waling* 1633. **4.** *esp.* The undercovering of a roof or floor, concealing the timbers; the plaster at the top of a room 1535. **b.** Maximum height of an aircraft 1917. **c.** An upper limit (to quantity, expenditure, etc.) 1936. Hence **Cei·linged** *ppl. a.*

† **Ceinte.** ME. [– OFr. *ceint* :– L. *cinctus* girdle, f. *cingere* gird.] A girdle –1530.

‖ **Ceintu·re.** *rare.* 1856. [Fr. :– L. *cinctura.*] = CINCTURE.

Celadon (se·lădǫn). 1768. [– Fr. *céladon,* name of a languorous gallant in the 'Astrée' of d'Urfé (1610).] A pale willow green colour. Also as *adj.* Hence **Ce·ladonite,** *Min.* green earth of Verona.

Celandine (se·lăndəin). [ME. *celidoine* – OFr. *celidoine* – med.L. *celidonia,* for L. *chelidonia* (sc. *herba* plant), *-onium* – Gr. χελιδόνιον, f. χελιδών swallow; for the intrusive *n* (XV) cf. *messenger.*] **a.** Common or Greater Celandine, *Chelidonium majus* (N.O. *Papaveraceæ*); called by Lyte *swallow-wort.* Its thick yellow juice was supposed to benefit weak sight. **b.** Small or Lesser Celandine, the Pilewort, *Ranunculus ficaria* 1578. var. † **Ce·lidony.**

Celarent (sĭlēᵊ·rĕnt). 1551. [L.] A mnemonic word designating the second mood of the first syllogistic figure, in which a universal negative major premiss and a universal affirmative minor give a universal negative conclusion.

Ce·lation. 1567. [– late L. *celatio* (Boethius), f. *celat-,* pa. ppl. stem of *celare* conceal; see -ION.] Concealment; *esp.* of birth or pregnancy.

Celature (sī·lătiŭɹ). ME. [– L. *cælatura,* f. *cælare* emboss, engrave.] Embossing; *concr.* that which is embossed.

† **Cele,** *sb.* 1708. [mod.L. – Gr. κήλη swelling.] *Med.* A tumour caused by the protrusion of any soft part –1881.

Celebrant (se·lĭbrănt). 1839. [– Fr. *célébrant,* or *celebrant-,* pres. ppl. stem of L. *celebrare*; see next, -ANT.] One who celebrates; *esp.* the priest who officiates at the Eucharist.

† **Ce·lebrate,** *ppl. a.* 1471. [– L. *celebratus,* pa. pple. of *celebrare,* f. *celeber, -br-* frequented, renowned; see -ATE².] **1.** Performed with due rites: solemnly held –1564. **2.** Celebrated –1680. **3.** Consecrated 1632.

Celebrate (se·lĭbreⁱt), *v.* 1534. [f. L. *celebrat-*; see prec., -ATE³.] **1.** To perform publicly and in due form (any religious ceremony); to hold (a church council); to solemnize 1564. Also *absol.* (with the Eucharist as implied obj.) 1534. Also † *transf.* **2.** To observe with solemn rites; to honour with ceremonies, festivities, etc. 1560. **3.** To make publicly known, proclaim 1597. **4.** To extol, publish the fame of 1611.

1. To c. the holy communion 1574, nuptials 1772, (*transf.*) a contract 1592. **2.** To c. the Sabbath 1560. **3.** Whose name..we c. with due honour HOOKER. **4.** Death cannot c. thee *Isa.* 38:18. Hence **Cele·brative** *a.* pertaining to celebration (*rare*). **Ce·lebrator,** † **-er,** one who CELEBRATES. var. † **Ce·lebre, -er.** CAXTON.

Celebration (selĭbrēⁱ·ʃən). 1529. [– (O)Fr. *célébration* or L. *celebratio, -ōn-,* f. *celebrat-*; see prec., -ION.] **1.** The action of celebrating. † **2.** = CELEBRITY –1779.

1. To go to early c. 1889. C. of Easter LINGARD. His memory deserving a particular c. CLARENDON.

Celebrious (sĭle·briəs), *a.* 1555. [f. L. *celebris* + -OUS; cf. ALACRIOUS.] † **1.** Frequented; attended by throngs; festive –1680. **2.** Renowned (*arch.* or *dial.*) 1608. var. † **Ce·lebrous** (sense 2).

Celebrity (sĭle·brĭti). 1600. [– (O)Fr. *célébrité* or L. *celebritas,* f. as prec.; see -ITY.] † **1.** Solemnity –1631. † **2.** A solemn ceremony, a celebration –1774. **3.** The condition of being much talked about; famousness, notoriety 1600. **4.** A person of celebrity 1839.

1. To hold a synod with great c. 1612. **3.** They had c., Spinoza has fame M. ARNOLD. **4.** One of the celebrities of wealth and fashion EMERSON.

Celeriac (sĭle·riæ̆k). 1743. [f. CELERY, with arbitrary use of suffix -AC.] A turnip-rooted variety of the garden celery.

Celerity (sĭle·rĭti). 1483. [– (O)Fr. *célérité* – L. *celeritas,* f. *celer* swift; see -ITY.] **1.** Swiftness, speed. Now *esp.* of living beings. † **2.** A rate of speed. (Repl. in science by *velocity.*) –1794.

Celery (se·lĕri). 1664. [– Fr. *céleri* – dial. It. (Lombard) *selleri* :– L. *selinon, -selinum* – Gr. σέλινον.] An umbelliferous plant (*Apium graveolens*); its blanched stalks are used as a salad and vegetable.

Celeste (sĭle·st). 1880. [– Fr. *céleste* – L. *cælestis*; see next.] **1.** A colour, sky-blue [Fr. *bleu céleste*] 1881. **2.** (= *voix céleste*): A stop on the organ or harmonium. Also, a form of the soft pedal on a piano.

Celestial (sĭle·stiăl). ME. [– OFr. *celestial, -el* – med.L. *cælestialis,* f. L. *cælestis,* f. *cælum* heaven; see -AL¹, -IAL.] **A.** *adj.* **1.** Of or pertaining to the material heavens. **2.** Of or pertaining to heaven, as the abode of God, angels, spirits, etc. ME. **3.** Divine, heavenly ME. Also as quasi-*sb.*

1. The altitude of the sonne or of othre c. bodies CHAUCER. **2.** The lorde that is Celestyall FABYAN. **3.** C. food NEALE, beauties 1704. Hence **Cele:stia·lity. Cele·stially** *adv.*

The C. Empire: tr. native name for China. So *C. Emperor*; and (*joc.*) *celestial* = Chinese.

B. *sb.* **1.** An inhabitant of heaven 1573. **2.** A Chinese 1863.

† **Cele·stify,** *v. rare.* 1646. [f. L. *celestis* + -FY; cf. OFr. *celestifier.*] To make heavenly –1768.

† **Ce·lestine,** *a.* and *sb.*¹ ME. [– OFr. *celestin, -ien* – late L. *cælestinus,* f. *cælestis* heavenly; see -INE¹.] ? = CELESTIAL *a.* and *sb.* –1509.

Celestine (se·lĕstəin, -tin, sĭle·stin), *sb.*² 1530. [– late and med.L. *Cælestinus,* f. the proper names *Cælestius* and *Cælestinus.*] **a.** One of a sect named after Cælestius, an associate of Pelagius, in 5th c. **b.** One of a reformed branch of the Benedictines, founded by Celestine V in 13th c.

Celestine (se·lĕstin), *sb.*³ 1798. [– Fr. *célestine,* perh. – It. *celestino* sky-blue; see -INE⁵.] *Min.* = CELESTITE. Formerly also a blue alabaster.

Celestite (se·lĕstəit, sĭle·stəit). 1854. [Dana's var. of CELESTINE; see -ITE¹ 2 b, -INE⁵.] *Min.* Native sulphate of strontia, $SrO.SO_3$, so called from the sky-blue colour it occ. presents.

Cele·stitude. 1824. [f. L. *cælestis* heavenly, + *-tude,* after *altitude,* etc.] *joc.* A Celestial (Chinese) dignitary. var. **Cele:stia·lity.** LANDOR.

‖ **Celeu·sma.** *rare.* 1680. [L. *celeu(s)ma* – Gr. κέλευ(σ)μα.] A watchword, battle-cry, etc.

Celiac, var. of CŒLIAC.

Celibacy (se·libăsi). 1663. [f. L. *cælibatus,* f. *cælebs, -ib-* unmarried, bachelor; see -ACY.] The state of living unmarried.

St. Paul's advice for cœlebacy 1663.

Celibatarian (se:libătēᵊ·riăn), *a.* 1839. [f. Fr. *célibataire* (f. *célibat* CELIBATE *sb.*¹ + *-aire* = -ARY¹, -AR¹) + -IAN; see -ARIAN.] Characterized by, or characteristic of, celibacy; favouring celibacy. As *sb.* One who lives in or advocates celibacy 1863.

The Queen's c. prejudices 1839.

Celibate (se·libeⁱt), *sb.*¹ *arch.* 1614. [– Fr. *célibat* or its source L. *cælibatus* celibacy; see -ATE¹.] State of celibacy; order of celibates. Hence **Celiba·tic** *a.* **Ce·libatist,** an advocate of celibacy.

Celibate (se·libeⁱt), *a.* and *sb.*² 1829. [f. CELIBACY, after such pairs as *magistracy, magistrate*; see -ATE¹,².] *adj.* Unmarried, single; bound not to marry. *sb.* [sc. *man* or *woman.*] 1869. var. **Ce:libatai·r(e** (*rare*). Hence **Ce·libate** *v.* to compel to celibacy.

Celido·graphy. 1775. [f. Gr. κηλίς spot + -GRAPHY; cf. Fr. *célidographie.*] A description of the spots in the sun or planets. (Dicts.)

Cell (sel). [– OFr. *celle,* or its source L. *cella* store-room, chamber, small apartment, 'chapel' in a temple.]

I. † **1.** A store-closet –1583. **2.** A monastery or nunnery dependent on some larger house OE. **3.** A dwelling consisting of a single chamber, inhabited by a solitary ME. **4.** One of a number of small apartments, as in a monastery, a nunnery, a prison, occupied by a single person ME. **5.** *Arch.* = CELLA.

2. The house was once a c. to the Abby PENNANT. **3.** The c. of an anchorite H. E. MANNING. *poet.* Poore shepheards' cels QUARLES. Hunted stag, in mountain c. SCOTT. Nor dreaming of the narrow c. NEALE. **4.** *Condemned c.*: a c. occupied by one who is condemned to death.

II. 1. *gen.* A compartment, *e.g.* of a cabinet, a honeycomb, etc. 1577. **2.** *spec.* **a.** in *Archit.* The space between the ribs of a vaulted roof 1850. **b.** *Entom.* The space between the nerves of the wings of insects 1881. **c.** *Electr.* Orig., a compartment of a wooden trough; now, a vessel containing one pair of plates immersed in fluid; or a voltaic apparatus containing one pair of metallic elements. Several *cells* united form a battery. 1828.

III. 1. An enclosed space, cavity, or sac, in organized bodies, or (*transf.*) in mineral products ME. **2.** *Biol.* The ultimate element in organic structures; a minute portion of protoplasm, enclosed usu. in a membrane 1672.

1. *Cells of the brain*: the imaginary cavities in that organ, supposed to be the seats of particular mental faculties, or pigeon-holes for knowledge. Now only *fig.* The cells of lava DARWIN. **2.** Hepatic cells 1845, nerve cells BAIN.

IV. Any hollow receptacle or containing cavity 1704. Also *attrib.* Hence † **Cell** *v.* to shut up, or dwell, in a c. (*rare*).

‖ **Cella** (se·lă). 1676. [L.] *Arch.* The body of the temple, as dist. from the portico, etc.

Cellar (se·lǝɹ), *sb.* [ME. *celer* – AFr. *celer* = OFr. *celier* (mod. *cellier*) :– late L. *cellarium* set of cells, storehouse for food, f. *cella* CELL; see -ARY¹.] **1.** A store-house or store-room, above or below ground, for provisions. *Obs.* exc. in *fish-c.* **2.** An underground chamber ME. **3.** = *wine-c.*; hence *transf.* a person's stock of wines 1541. † **4.** A case; *esp.* of bottles –1667. Also *attrib.*

3. *Temp.* II. ii. 137. **4.** A c. of waters of her own distilling PEPYS. Hence **Ce·llar** *v.* to store up in or as in a c. **Ce·llarer,** the officer in a monastery, etc., who had charge of the c. So **Ce·llaress. Ce·llaring** *sb.* = CELLARAGE 1. **Ce·llerman. Ce·llarous** *a.* (*joc.*) of or pertaining to a c. DICKENS.

Cellarage (se·lǝrėdʒ). 1512. [f. prec. + -AGE; cf. AL. *celleragium* (XIII), *-ar-* (XIV) cellarage, (payment for) storage in cellar.] **1.** Cellar accommodation; cellars 1602. Also *transf.* **2.** † A feudal duty upon wine when placed in the cellar; charge for the use of a cellar.

Cellaret (selǝre·t). 1806. [f. as prec. + -ET.] A case of cabinet-work, or a sideboard with compartments, made to hold wine-bottles, etc.

Celled (seld), *ppl. a.* 1650. [f. CELL + -ED².] **1.** Furnished with cells; made or arranged in the form of cells 1776. So **Ce·llate** *a.*, **Ce·llated. 2.** Enclosed in a cell 1650.

Cellepore (se·lĭpōᵊɹ). 1811. [f. *cella* CELL, after MADREPORE.] A genus of *Polyzoa*, consisting of a group of vase-like chambers with a beak on one or both sides. Also *attrib.*

Celliferous (seli·fĕrǝs), *a. rare.* [f. *celli-*, comb. f. L. *cella* + -FEROUS.] Bearing or producing cells. So **Ce·lliform** *a.* cell-shaped.

'Cello (tʃe·lo). 1881. Short f. VIOLONCELLO. So **'Ce·llist, 'Ce·lloist,** a VIOLONCELLIST.

Celloid (se·loid), *a.* 1849. [f. CELL + -OID.] Cell-like.

Cellular (se·liŭlăɹ), *a.* 1753. [– Fr. *cellulaire* – mod.L. *cellularis*, f. L. *cellula*; see next, -AR¹.] **1.** Of, pertaining to, or characterized by cells 1823. **2.** Containing cells; porous 1816. **3.** *Phys.* Consisting of cells. As used of vegetable tissues, opp. to *vascular.* As *sb. pl.* Cellular plants (in L. form *Cellulares*); those without distinct stem or leaves, as Cryptogams 1879.

1. C. discipline LAMB. **2.** C. basalt DARWIN. **3.** *C. tissue*, † *membrane*, in Animal Physiology, a synonym of *areolar* or *connective tissue*. *C. pathology*: the study of morbid changes in the cells. Hence **Cellula·rity,** c. quality or condition. var. **Ce·llulate, Ce·llulated** *ppl. a.* (in senses 2, 3). **Cellula·tion,** development of cells.

Cellule (se·liul). 1652. [– Fr. *cellule* or L. *cellula*, dim. of *cella* CELL; see -ULE.] † **1.** A pigeon-hole –1819. **2.** A minute cell, cavity, or pore 1830. Hence **Cellu·lic** *a.* of or pertaining to cellules or cells. **Celluli·ferous** *a.* bearing or producing cellules. **Ce·llulin** (*Chem.*) = CELLULOSE. **Ce·lluloid** *a.*

Cellulitis (seliulǝi·tis). 1861. [f. L. *cellula* + -ITIS.] Inflammation of the cellular tissue.

Cellulo-, comb. f. CELLULE, L. *cellula*, forming adjs., with sense CELLULAR: e.g. *c.-adipose*, (tissue) partly cellular partly adipose.

Celluloid (se·liŭloid), *sb.* 1871. [f. CELLULOSE + arbitrary use of -OID.] A substance consisting essentially of soluble cellulose nitrate and camphor, used in the manufacture esp. of photographic film.

Cellulose (se·liŭlōᵘs). 1753. [As adj. – mod.L. *cellulosus*; as sb. – Fr. *cellulose* (Payen, 1863); see CELLULE, -OSE¹, ².] **A.** *adj.* Consisting of cells; full of minute cavities. var. **Ce·llulous.**

B. *sb.* [– Fr.] One of the AMYLOSES. A substance also called *lignin*, which constitutes the essential part of the solid framework of plants, and occurs in the animal body. It is amorphous, tasteless, inodorous, insoluble in water, alcohol, ether, dilute acids, and alkalis. 1835. **b.** In popular use, designating compounds of cellulose, esp. c. acetate and c. nitrate, solutions of which give the 'cellulose' finish used in varnishing metal, woodwork, etc. 1898.

C. . in fine linen and cotton, which are almost entirely composed of it WATTS. Hence **Celluło·sity,** the condition of being c.; also *concr.*

Celo·tomy. Also **ke-.** 1847. [– Gr. κηλοτομία, f. κήλη rupture + -τομία -TOMY.] *Surg.* The operation for strangulated hernia by cutting down and dividing the stricture. So **Ce·lotome,** the knife used in c.

Ce·lsitude. 1450. [– L. *celsitudo*, f. *celsus* lofty; see -TUDE.] † **1.** Loftiness –1680. **2.** Height. (Now *joc.*) 1678.

Celt¹ (selt). Also **Kelt.** 1607. [In earliest use – L. *Celtæ* pl. – Gr. Κελτοί (later Κέλται, perh. f. L.); in mod. use – Fr. *Celte* (Pezron, 1703), applied first to the Bretons as representatives of the ancient Gauls.] **1.** *Hist.* Applied to the ancient peoples of Western Europe; the Gauls and their (continental) kin. **2.** A general name for peoples speaking languages akin to those of the ancient Galli, including the Bretons, Cornish, Welsh, Irish, Manx, and Gaelic. See also CELTIC. 1773.

Celt² (selt). 1715. [– (reputed) L. *celtes* stone-chisel.] A prehistoric edged implement of bronze or stone (occ. of iron).

Celtic (se·ltik), *a.* Also **Keltic.** 1656. [– L. *Celticus* and Fr. *celtique*; see CELT¹, -IC.] **1.** *Hist.*, etc. Of or belonging to the ancient Celtae. **2.** Epithet of the languages and peoples akin to the ancient Celtic; *esp.* of the great branch of the Aryan family of languages which includes Breton, Welsh, Irish, Manx, Gaelic, Cornish, and the ancient languages which they represent. Also absol. = *Celtic tongue*. 1707. Hence **Ce·ltically** *adv.* **Ce·lticism,** a C. custom or expression; devotion to C. customs. **Ce·lticize** *v.* to render C.; *intr.* to adopt C. fashions, etc.

Celto-, comb. f. CELT¹, as in **Ce·ltophil,** a friend of the Celts and Celtic studies.

† **Ce·lure.** [ME. *celure, selure*; see CEILING.] A canopy. Also the hangings of a bed, etc. –1553.

Ce·mbalist. *rare.* 1871. [f. It. *cembalo*, abbr. from *clavicembalo* (for the harpsichord or pianoforte part); see -IST.] *Mus.* One who plays the pianoforte in an orchestra.

Cement (sĭme·nt, † se·mĕnt), *sb.* [ME. *si·ment* – (O)Fr. *ciment* :– L. *cæmentum* quarry stone, pl. chips of stone, f. *cædere* hew; see -MENT.] **1.** Any powdered substance that, made plastic with water, is used in a soft and pasty state (which hardens on drying) to bind together bricks, stones, etc., in building, to cover floors, walls, etc., or (with a suitable aggregate) to form concrete. (See HYDRAULIC c., PORTLAND c., ROMAN c.) **2.** *gen.* Any substance applied to the surface of solid bodies to make them cohere firmly 1562; *fig.* a principle of union (*rare*) 1604. **3.** *transf.* **a.** A cement-like substance used for stopping up small cavities (e.g. in teeth) 1489. **b.** *Physiol.* The bony tissue forming the outer crust of the fang of the tooth 1849. **c.** *Metall.* A finely divided metal obtained by precipitation, esp. in *c.-copper, -gold, -silver* 1874.

1. The name was also formerly, and is still loosely, applied to *mortar*. *In c.* adj. phr. applied to brick-work, etc., built with mortar composed of c. and sand (*c. mortar*). Hence **Ceme·ntal** *a.*

Cement (sĭme·nt), *v.* ME. [– (O)Fr. *cimenter*, f. *ciment*; see prec.] **1.** To unite with or as with cement. Also *fig.* **2.** To apply cement to 1886. **3.** *intr.* (for *refl.*) To cohere firmly by the application of cement; to stick 1677. Also *fig.*

Hence **Ceme·nter. Ceme·nting** *vbl. sb.*

Cementation (sĭmĕntēⁱ·ʃǝn). 1594. [f. prec. + -ATION.] **1.** The action or process of cementing; the state thus produced. Also *fig.* 1660. **2.** The process by which one solid is made to combine with another at a high temperature so as to change the properties of one of them, without liquefaction taking place 1594. **3.** Encasing or lining with cement 1886.

Cementi·tious, *a. rare.* 1828. [f. L. *cæmenticius*, f. *cæmentum* (but in sense from CEMENT) + -OUS; see -ITIOUS¹.] Of the nature of cement.

Cemetery (se·mĭtĕri). 1460. [– late L. *cœmeterium* – Gr. κοιμητήριον dormitory, (in Christian writers) burial-ground, f. κοιμᾶν put to sleep.] A place, usually a ground, set apart for the burial of the dead; † a church-yard; any burial-ground.

fig. It is with libraries as with other cœmeteries SWIFT. Hence **Cemete·rial** *a.* relating to a c.

Cenacle (se·năk'l). ME. [– (O)Fr. *cénacle* – L. *cenaculum* dining-room, f. *cena* dinner; see -CULE.] A supping room; an upper chamber; *esp.* that in which the Last Supper was held.

Cenanthy (sĭnæ·nþi). 1881. [f. Gr. κενός empty + ἄνθος flower + -Y³.] *Bot.* The absence of stamens and pistils in a flower.

† **Cena·tion.** 1599. [– L. *cenatio* dining-room; in mod.L. use '(act of) dining'.] Dining, supping –1646. So † **Ce·natory** *a.* pertaining to c. (*rare*).

‖ **Cendre.** 1805. [Fr. 'cinder, ash'.] Ash-.

† **Cene.** ME. [– (O)Fr. *cène* :– late and med.L. *cena* Lord's supper, in cl. L. dinner.] The Last Supper; also = *Cene Thursday*, Maundy Thursday –1491.

Cenobite, -itic, cenobium; see CŒ-.

Cenogamy; see CŒ-.

Cenotaph (se·nŏtɑf). 1603. [– Fr. *cénotaphe* – late L. *cenotaphium* – Gr. κενός empty + τάφος tomb.] An empty tomb; a sepulchral monument erected in honour of a person whose body is elsewhere.

The C., erected in Whitehall, London, as a memorial to the British who fell in the war of 1914–18.

Cenozoic, var. sp. of CÆNO-, CAINO-.

† **Cense,** *sb.*¹ ME. Aphetic f. INCENSE –1540.

† **Cense,** *sb.*² 1524. [– OFr. *cense* – med.L. *censa*, for L. *census* (whence mod.Fr. *cens*), f. *censēre* rate, assess.] **1.** = CENSUS 1, 2, 3. –1763. **2.** Rating; income –1650.

Cense (sens), *v.*¹ ME. [aphetic – (O)Fr. *encenser*, or † *encense*, var. of INCENSE *v.*] **1.** To perfume with odours from burning incense; to offer incense to. † **2.** *intr.* To burn or offer incense –1732. var. † **Censer** (*rare*).

1. In the temple. . hem to scence bothe clene and pure ME.

† **Cense,** *v.*² 1606. [– L. *censēre* assess. Cf. CENSE *sb*².] **1.** To estimate, reckon –1697. **2.** To take a census of. ADDISON.

Censer (se·nsǝɹ), *sb.* ME. [– AFr. *censer, senser*, OFr. *censier*, aphet. of *encensier*, f. *encens* INCENSE *sb.*] **1.** A vessel in which incense is burnt; a thurible. **b.** = CASSOLETTE. *Tam. Shr.* IV. iii. 91. **2.** One who perfumes with incense 1670.

1. Another aungel. . hauynge a golden c. WYCLIF.

Censor (se·nsǝɹ), *sb.* 1533. [– L. *censor*, f. *censēre* pronounce as an opinion, rate, assess; see -OR 2.] **1.** One of two magistrates in ancient Rome, who drew up the census of the citizens, etc., and had the supervision of public morals. **b.** *transf.* One who has the supervision of the conduct of a body of people, as in some colleges 1592. **2.** *spec.* An official whose duty it is to inspect books, journals, plays, etc., before publication, to secure that they shall contain nothing immoral, heretical, or offensive or injurious to the State 1644. **b.** One who censors private correspondence (as in time of war) 1914. **3.** † A critic; a fault-finder 1599. **4.** *Psycho-analysis.* A mental power or force which represses certain elements in the unconscious 1912. [Mistranslation of Freud's *Zensur* censorship.]

1. b. Punch is a censor but not censorious 1871. C. of Non-collegiate Students *Oxf. Univ. Cal.* **2.** The censors of the press W. IRVING. **3.** Eulogists or censors MACAULAY. Hence **Ce·nsor** *v. trans.* to examine (books, plays, news, correspondence) as c. **Ce·nsorship,** the office or function of a c.; official supervision 1591.

Censorial (sensōᵊ·riăl), *a.* 1592. [f. L. *censorius* + -AL¹; see -ORIAL. Cf. Fr. *censorial.*] **1.** Of, pertaining to, or characteristic of a censor 1772. † **2.** Censorious –1596.

1. The c. inspection of the publick eye BURKE. So **Censo·rian.**

Censorious (sensōᵊ·riǝs), *a.* 1536. [f. as prec. + -OUS; cf. OFr. *censorieux.*] **1.**

Addicted to censure; severely critical; fault-finding. Const. *of*; † *on*, † *upon*. † **2.** Befitting a censor; grave, severe –1660.

1. To read with a c. eye CAMDEN. **2.** His [Bacon's] language. . was nobly c. B. JONS. Hence **Censo·rious-ly** *adv.*, **-ness.**

Censual (se·nsiuăl), *a.* 1613. [– late L. *censualis*, f. CENSUS; see -AL¹; cf. (O)Fr. *censuel.*] Of or relating to a census, as a *c. roll.*

Censure (se·nsiŭɹ, se·nʃ¹ŭɹ), *sb.* ME. [– (O)Fr. *censure* – L. *censura*; see CENSUS, -URE.] † **1.** A judicial (*esp.* ecclesiastical) sentence; a condemnatory judgement –1727. † **2.** A formal opinion (of an expert, etc.) –1625. **3.** *gen.* Judgement; opinion; criticism (*arch.*) 1576. **4.** *spec.* An unfavourable opinion, hostile criticism; blaming, finding fault with, or condemning as wrong; expression of condemnation. (The usual sense.) 1603. **5.** Censorship 1534. **6.** Correction; *esp.* critical recension (*rare*) 1613.

1. He was brought to. . the House of Lords to receive his C. MAY. The censures of holy churche 1494. **4.** No might nor greatnesse in mortality can c. scape SHAKS. **6.** The c. of the Vulgate text HALLAM.

Censure (se·nsiŭɹ, se·nʃ¹ŭɹ), *v.* 1589. [– Fr. *censurer*, f. *censure* CENSURE *sb.*] † **1.** To form or give a censure or opinion of; to estimate, criticize, judge –1729. Also † *intr.* with *of* or (occ.) *on*; and † *absol.* † **2.** To pronounce judicial sentence on; to sentence *to* –1682. **3.** To pronounce an adverse judgement on, critcize unfavourably; to find fault with, blame, condemn. (The current sense.) 1596. Also *absol.* † **4.** To exercise censorship over. BACON.

1. *Jul. C.* III. ii. 16. Content to be censured idle SIR R. CECIL. C. better of me 1618. **3.** Would not C., or Speake ill of a Man BACON. Hence **Ce·nsurer. Ce·nsureship** = CENSORSHIP.

Census (se·nsŏs), *sb.* 1613. [– L. *census*, f. *censēre* assess, etc.] **1.** The registration of citizens and their property in ancient Rome for taxation 1634. † **2.** A poll-tax –1864. **3.** An official enumeration of the population of a country, etc., with statistics relating to them. Also *attrib.* 1769.

A census of the population has been taken every tenth year since 1801 in Great Britain.

Cent[1] (sent). ME. [– Fr. *cent*, It. *cento*, L. *centum* hundred.] † **1.** ? A hundred. [– Fr. *cent.*] ME. only. **2.** *Per cent*: for (in, to) every hundred; used in stating a proportion. [? At first in It. form *per cento*; or due to Fr. *pour cent.*] 1568. **3.** A hundredth 1685. Hence, **4.** In U.S.: The hundredth part of a dollar; a coin of this value 1782; in France, etc.: A centime 1810.

2. Th' interest of xij. per cent by the yeare GRESHAM. *Three* (etc.) *per cents* = three (etc.) per cent stocks, *i.e.* stocks bearing that rate of interest. C. per c. 1677. Hence **Ce·ntage**, now PERCENTAGE.

† **Cent**[2]. 1532. **1.** An old game at cards, said to have resembled piquet, with 100 as the point that won the game –1636. **2.** A counter used in playing Ombre –1878.

Cental (se·ntăl). [f. L. *centum* 100, perh. after *quintal.*] A weight of one hundred pounds avoirdupois, introduced into the Liverpool cornmarket in 1859, and since legalized.

Centaur (se·ntǭɹ). ME. [– L. *centaurus* – Gr. κένταυρος of unkn. origin.] **1.** *Mythol.* A fabulous creature, with the head, trunk, and arms of a man, joined to the body and legs of a horse. Also *fig.* **2.** One of the southern constellations 1667. † **3.** A kind of ship 1622. Hence various *nonce-wds.*, as **Ce·ntaurdom,** etc.

Centaury (se·ntǭri, -əri). ME. [– late L. *centauria, -ea*, for L. *centaurion, -eum* – Gr. κενταύρειον, -ταύριον, f. κένταυρος CENTAUR.] *Bot.* **1.** A plant, said to have been discovered by Chiron the centaur; its two species, *Centaurion majus* and *C. minus*, have been identified (prob. correctly) with *Chlora perfoliata* and *Erythræa centaureum.* **2.** In 16th c. *Great C.* was applied to a composite plant or plants; and to the genus containing these Linnæus gave the name *Centaurea.* 'Centaury' has since been extended as a book-name to all the species. 1551.

American C.: a name for *Sabbatia*, a genus of N. American herbs of the Gentian family.

Centenarian (sentĭnēᵊ·riăn). 1846. [f. as next + -AN.] **A.** *adj.* **1.** A hundred years old 1849. **2.** Of or belonging to a centenary celebration 1864. **B.** *sb.* A person a hundred years old 1846.

Centenary (se·ntĭnări, also sentī·nări; *erron.* sente·nări). 1598. [– L. *centenarius* containing a hundred, f. *centeni* hundred each, f. *centum* 100; see -ARY¹; cf. (O)Fr. *centenaire.*] **A.** *adj.* **1.** Of or pertaining to the space of a hundred years 1647. **2.** *gen.* Of or belonging to a hundred 1768.

1. C. years returned but seldom FULLER.

B. *sb.* † **1.** A weight of a hundred pounds –1788. **2.** A centennium or century 1607. **3.** A centennial anniversary; the celebration of the accomplishment of a centennium 1788.

1. Thirty-four centenaries of gold GIBBON. **2.** To complete one's c. 1884. **3.** The second c. of Handel's birth 1885.

Centenier (se·ntĕniᵊɹ). [ME. *centener* – AFr. *centener*, (O)Fr. *centenier* :– late L. *centenarius* (Vegetius) for L. *centurio* CENTURION; see prec., -IER.] † **1.** A centurion –1603. **2.** A police-officer in Jersey 1862.

Centennial (sente·niăl), *a.* (*sb.*) 1797. [f. L. *centum* 100, after *biennial.*] **1.** Of a hundred years' standing; a hundred years old; completing a hundred years; of or relating to the hundredth anniversary. **2.** *sb.* A hundredth anniversary or its celebration; a centenary 1876.

Centennial State (U.S.): appellation of Colorado, admitted as a state in the c. year of the existence of the United States (1876).

Cente·nnium. [f. as prec., after *biennium, millenium.*] A period of a hundred years.

Center; see CENTRE.

Centering, centreing (se·ntəriŋ), *vbl. sb.* Also **centring.** 1766. [f. *center*, CENTRE *v.* + -ING¹; *centering* is the usual spelling.] **1.** The action of the vb. CENTRE. **2.** *spec.* The setting of lenses so that their axes are in the same straight line 1768. **3.** *Arch.* The temporary framing, whereon any vaulted work is constructed 1766. Also *attrib.*

Centesimal (sente·simăl), *a.* (*sb.*) 1682. [f. L. *centesimus* hundredth (f. *centum* 100) + AL¹.] † **1.** Hundred-fold. **2.** Hundredth 1809. **3.** *sb.* A hundredth part 1698.

3. The Height. . in Inches and Centesimals 1698. Hence **Cente·simally** *adv.* **Cente·simate** *v.* to select every hundredth for punishment. So **Cente·simation,** execution of every hundredth man.

† **Ce·ntesm.** 1483. [– OFr. *centiesme, -isme, -esme* (mod. *centième*) :– L. *centesimus*; see prec.] A hundredth part –1827.

† **Ce·ntgrave.** 1649. [– G. *cent-, zentgraf*, MHG. *zentgrave*, f. *zent, cent* – med.L. *centa* district of 100 hamlets.] Used as tr. OE. *hundreds ealdor*; also as tr. Ger. *centgraf* –1762.

Centi-, comb. f. L. *centum* hundred, used in the Metric System for the hundredth part of a unit, as *centiare*, $\frac{1}{100}$ of an are, etc.

Centigrade (se·ntigreᶦd), *a.* 1812. [– Fr. *centigrade* (in *thermomètre centigrade*), f. CENTI- + L. *gradus* step, GRADE.] Having a hundred degrees; usually applied to Celsius's thermometer, in which the space between the freezing and boiling points of water is divided into 100 degrees. (Symbolized by C., as 40° C.)

Centigramme (se·ntigræm, Fr. saṅtigram). 1801. [Fr.; see CENTI- and GRAMME.] A weight = $\frac{1}{100}$ of a gramme, or ·1543248 of a grain troy. So **Ce·ntilitre** (se·ntilītəɹ, Fr. saṅtilītr), a measure of capacity = $\frac{1}{100}$ of a litre, or ·61028 of a cubic inch.

Centi·loquy. 1588. [– med.L. *centiloquium*, also *-logium*; see CENTI- and SOLILOQUY.] A work attributed to Ptolemy, consisting of a hundred aphorisms of astrology.

‖ **Centime** (saṅti·m). 1801. [Fr.; see CENTESM.] A French coin = $\frac{1}{100}$ of a franc.

Centimetre (se·ntimītəɹ, Fr. saṅtimẹ·tr). 1801. [Fr.; see CENTI- and METRE.] A measure of length = $\frac{1}{100}$ of a metre, or ·3937 (nearly $\frac{2}{5}$) of an inch.

Centinel, obs. f. SENTINEL.

† **Centinody.** 1611. [– med.L. *centinodium*, subst. use of late L. *centinodius* 'having 100 knots' (in *centinodia herba*) f. *centi-* + *nodus* knot; cf. Fr. *centinode.*] *Bot.* The plant Knotgrass (*Polygonum aviculare*).

Centipedal (senti·pĭdăl), *a.* 1879. [f. L. *centum* 100 + *pes, ped-* foot + -AL¹.] Of one hundred (metrical) feet.

Centipede (se·ntipīd). 1601. [– Fr. *centipède* or L. *centipeda*, f. *centi-* + *pes, ped-* foot.] A name for wingless vermiform articulated animals having many feet, constituting the order *Cheilopoda* of the class *Myriapoda.* Those in tropical countries are venomous. Also *transf.* and *fig.* var. **Centiped** (in Dicts.).

Centner (se·ntnəɹ). 1683. [– G. *centner* (now *zentner*) – L. *centenarius*; see CENTENARY.] **1.** A measure of weight used in Germany, varying from 100 to 120 English lb. **2.** *Metall.* A weight divisible first into a hundred parts, and then into many smaller parts. The centner of the metallurgists is 100 lb., of the assayers 1 dram. 1753.

Cento (se·nto). Pl. (now usu.) **centos.** 1605. [– L. *cento* patch-work garment, poem made up of verses from other sources.] † **1.** A piece of patchwork –1643. **2.** 'A composition formed by joining scraps from other authors' (J.) 1605. Also *transf.*

1. His apparel is a c. SHIRLEY. **2.** Quilted. . out of sherds of diuers Poets, such as Schollers do call a C. CAMDEN. Hence **Ce·ntoism** (also **Ce·ntonism**).

Central (se·ntrăl), *a.* 1647. [– Fr. *central* or L. *centralis*, f. *centrum* CENTRE; see -AL¹.] **1.** Of or pertaining to the centre or middle; situated in, proceeding from, containing or constituting the centre. **2.** *fig.* Chief, leading, dominant; controlling the branches (opp. to *local*) 1647. **3.** *Phys.* Of or pertaining to a nerve-centre; in *Pathol.* used of local affections caused by lesions of the brain or spinal cord, as opp. to local causes 1865.

1. A good c. position 1889. **2.** The c. figure of a poem JOWETT. The approbation of the C. Junta WELLINGTON. **3.** On C. Paralysis (*title*) 1865.

Phr. *C. force* (*Math.*): a force attracting to or repelling from a centre. *C. fire*: applied *attrib.* to a cap or cartridge having the fulminate in a central position. Hence **Ce·ntralism,** a centralizing system, centralization. **Ce·ntralist,** an upholder of centralization. **Ce·ntrally** *adv.* **Ce·ntralness.**

‖ **Centrale** (sentrēᶦ·li). 1872. [L.] *Anat.* Short for *os centrale*, a bone of the carpus.

Centrality (sentræ·lĭti). 1647. [f. CENTRAL + ITY.] The quality or fact of being central; central nature or position. Also *fig.*

fig. Clear grasp of ideas, c. of purpose 1862.

Centralization (se:ntrăləizēᶦ·ʃən, -izēᶦ·ʃən). 1801. [f. next + -ATION, or – Fr. *centralisation.*] **1.** The action of centralizing; being centralized; gathering to a centre. **2.** *esp.* The concentration of administrative power in a central authority 1801.

2. To combine. . local self-government and c. 1863.

Centralize (se·ntrăləiz), *v.* Also **-ise.** 1800. [f. CENTRAL + -IZE, or Fr. *centraliser.*] **1.** *intr.* To come together at a centre; to concentrate. **2.** *trans.* To bring to a centre, make central; *esp.* to concentrate (administrative powers) in a single head or centre 1801.

2. Business always tends to c. itself HELPS. Hence **Ce·ntralizer,** one who centralizes or promotes centralization.

† **Centra·tion.** *rare.* 1647. [– mod.L. *centratio*, f. late L. *centratus* in the centre, on the anal. of similar pairs; see -ATE², -ATION.] placing in the centre –1736.

Centre, center (se·ntər), *sb.* and *a.* ME. [– (O)Fr. *centre* or its source L. *centrum* – Gr. κέντρον goad, peg, stationary point of a pair of compasses, f. base of κεντεῖν prick. In XVI-XVII spelt *center* (as still in U.S.); *centre* from XVIII.]

I. 1. The middle point of a circle or sphere, equally distant from all points on the circumference. Also *fig.* **2.** *ellipt.* The centre of the earth ME.; the earth, as the centre of the universe 1606. **3.** The point, pivot, axis, or line round which a body turns or revolves ME. **4.** A form of bearing adjustable in the direction of its length and having a conical point entering into a corresponding depression in the end of the revolving object which it supports, as in the lathe 1797. **5.** *fig.* (See quots.) 1626. **6.** =*nerve-centre* 1847. **7.** A leader of the Fenians 1865. **8.** The part of a target between the bull's-eye and the outer; also (*ellipt.*) the hitting of this 1887.

2. *Haml.* II. ii. 159. As from the Center thrice to th' utmost pole MILT. *P.L.* I. 74. 3. As a c., firm *P.R.* IV. 534. 5. The Center of Business STEELE. The c. of a world's desire TENNYSON. Centres of nutrition 1872.

II. 1. The middle point or part, the middle or midst of anything. Also *fig.* 1591. **2.** The point or position of equilibrium of a body. Also *fig.* ME. **3.** *Archit.* A temporary framework upon which an arch or dome is supported while building; also *gen.* 1611. **4.** *Politics.* In the French Chamber (which is in the form of an amphitheatre), the deputies of moderate opinions who occupy the central benches in front of the president, between the extreme parties who sit to the right and left. Also used *transf.* of the political opinions so indicated; and of the politics of other countries. 1837.

1. The c. of a deep but narrow bay SCOTT. *C. of a higher curve* (*Geom.*): the point in which two diameters meet. *fig.* The very Center and life of Logicke 1628. 2. If the man is off his c., the eyes show it EMERSON. *C. of gravity*, etc. 3. *Wint.T.* II. i. 102.

Phrases. *C. of an army*: the main body of troops occupying the space between the two wings. *C. of attraction*: the point to which bodies tend by gravity, etc.; also *fig.* *C. of curvature*: see CURVATURE. *C. of a fleet*: the division between the van and the rear, or between the weather and lee divisions. *C. of gravity* orig. = *c. of attraction*; subseq. = *c. of mass*: the point of a body or system of bodies about which all the parts exactly balance each other, and which being supported, the body or system will remain at rest in any position. *C. of gyration*: the point at which if the whole mass of a revolving body were collected, the rotatory motion would remain the same. *C. of inertia*: = *c. of gravity* or *mass*. *C. of mass*: that point in relation to a body or system of bodies so situated that any plane whatever that passes through it divides the body or system into two parts of which the masses are exactly equal. *C. of motion*: the point which remains at rest while all the other parts move round it. *C. of oscillation*: the point of a body suspended by an axis at which, if all the matter were concentrated, the oscillations would be performed in the time actually taken. *C. of percussion*: in a moving body, that point where the percussion is greatest, in which the whole percutient force of the body is supposed to be collected. *C. of pressure*: the point at which the whole amount of pressure may be applied with the same effect as when distributed.

Combs. etc.: **c.-bit,** an instrument turning on a projecting c.-point, for boring holes; **-board,** in a sailing-boat, a board or plate that can be lowered through the keel 1849; **-fire** = *central fire* (see CENTRAL); **-piece,** *spec.* a piece of plate or glass for the c. of a table; **-second(s,** a seconds hand on a clock or watch mounted on the centre arbor.

Centre, center (se·ntəɹ), *v.* 1610. [f. CENTRE *sb.* In XVII–XVIII spelt *center*, as still in U.S.]

I. *intr.* † **1.** To rest as on a centre, to repose –1719. **2.** To find or have their (its) centre; to be concentrated; 'to be collected to a point' (J.), to gather as round a centre; to be placed as at a centre; to move round as a centre. Often with a mixture of notions. 1691.

2. That bliss which only centres in the mind GOLDSM. The supreme authority centered at last in a single person W. ROBERTSON.

II. *trans.* **1.** To place or fix in the centre; to provide with a centre 1610. † **2.** To fix *to*, repose *upon*, as a centre –1721. **3.** To collect, bring, as to a centre; to concentrate *in*, *on* 1702.

3. In reverie centred GOLDSM. To c. one's hopes in 1844. Hence **Ce·ntred, Ce·ntered** *ppl. a.*

Ce·ntremost, *a. rare.* 1866. [f. CENTRE *sb.* + -MOST.] Most central, mid-most. Cf. *middlemost.*

Centric (se·ntrik), *a.* 1590. [– Gr. κεντρικός, f. κέντρον; see CENTRE *sb.*, -IC.] **1.** That is in or at the centre, central. **2.** Of, pertaining to, or characterized by a centre; *spec.* (in *Phys.*) a nerve centre 1712. **3.** quasi-*sb.* A circle with the earth in its centre 1667.

1. This c. earth MARLOWE. 2. C. forces E. B. BROWNING, tetanus 1871. So **Ce·ntrical** *a.* Hence **Centrica·lity** (*rare*). **Centrically** *adv.* **Ce·ntricalness** (*rare*). **Centri·city,** c. quality or position; relation to a centre.

Centrifugal (sentri·fiŭgăl), *a.* 1721. [f. mod.L. *centrifugus* (Newton, f. *centrum* + *-fugus*) + -AL[1]. Cf. CENTRIPETAL.] **1.** Flying or tending to fly off from the centre. Also *fig.* **2.** *Bot.* **a.** Of inflorescence, in which the terminal flower opens first and the lateral ones successively after. **b.** Of an embryo: Having the radicle turned towards the sides of the fruit. 1830. **3.** *Phys.* Of nerve fibres: Conveying impulses from a centre (see CENTRE *sb.* I. 6); efferent 1855.

C. force, tendency: the force with which a body moving round a centre tends to fly off from that centre; the tendency of a revolving body to do this. ('Centrifugal force' is really Inertia.) **C. machine,** *gen.* any machine in which c. force is employed; *spec.* a machine for drying yarn, cloth, sugar, etc., these being placed in a rapidly revolving cage, whence the moisture is thrown off by c. force, a *hydro-extractor*. **C. pump,** a rotary pump in which the fluid is driven outward and upward from a centre. Hence **Centri·fugally** *adv.* **Centri·fugence.** EMERSON.

Ce·ntrifuge. 1801. [– Fr. *centrifuge*; see prec.] *adj.* = prec. *sb.* A centrifugal machine; *spec.* for separating cream from milk by rotary motion.

Centring, -reing, *vbl. sb.* and *ppl. a.* See CENTRE *v.*, and CENTERING.

Centripetal (sentri·pĭtăl), *a.* 1709. [f. mod. L. *centripetus* (Newton) centre-seeking + -AL[1].] **1.** Tending towards the centre; opp. to *centrifugal.* Also *fig.* and *transf.* **2.** *Bot.* Tending or developing from without toward the centre 1870. **3.** *Biol.* **a.** Proceeding from the exterior to the interior or centre. **b.** Of nerves: Conveying an impulse from the periphery to the centre; afferent. 1836.

1. *C. force*: a force which draws or impels a body toward some point as a centre; also called *c. tendency*. 2. *C. inflorescence*: that in which the lowest or outermost flowers blossom first, as in spikes or umbels. Hence **Centri·petally** *adv.*

Centri·petence. 1847. [f. CENTRIPET(AL + -ENCE. Cf. mod.L. *centripetentia* (Newton).] Centripetal motion or action. So **Centri·petency.**

Centrist (se·ntrist). 1872. [– Fr. *centriste*, f. *centre* CENTRE *sb.* + *-iste* -IST.] A member of the (French) Centre.

Centro- (sentro). Stem of L. *centrum* and Gr. κέντρον, used as a comb. form, with senses 'centre, central, centrally'.

Centrocli·nal *a.* (*Geol.*), applied to strata dipping to a common centre. **Centroli·nead** (*Geom.*), an instrument for drawing lines to inaccessible vanishing points in perspective. **Centroli·neal** *a.*, applied to a series of lines converging to a centre. **Centrosta·ltic** *a.* (*Med.*), applied by Hall to the action of the *vis nervosa* in the spinal centre.

Centrobaric (sentrobæ·rik), *a.* 1727. [f. CENTRO- + Gr. βάρος weight + -IC, after τὰ κεντροβαρικά title of treatise by Archimedes on centre of gravity. Cf. Fr. *centrobarique.*] Of or relating to the centre of gravity, or to the process of finding it.

C. method (*Math.*): a method of determining the area, or the volume, generated by the revolution of a line or surface respectively about a fixed axis, on the principle that the superficies or solid so formed is equal to the product of the generating line or surface and the length of the path of its centre of gravity; sometimes called the *theorem of Pappus.*

Centrode (se·ntrōᵘd). 1878. [f. L. *centrum* centre + Gr. ὁδός path, as in *anode, cathode*, etc.] *Math.* A locus traced out by the successive positions of an instantaneous centre of pure rotation. (See next.)

Centroid (se·ntroid). 1876. [f. CENTRE + -OID.] *Math.* **1.** = CENTRODE. (Now abandoned.) **2.** Centre of mass, or of gravity 1882.

Centronote (se·ntronōᵘt). 1836. [– Fr. *centronote*, f. Gr. κέντρον sharp point + νῶτος back.] A genus of fishes (*Centronotus*) having a spur-like prickle pointing forwards on the back.

‖ **Centrum** (se·ntrŏm). 1854. [L.; see CENTRE *sb.*] The L. wd. for centre, used techn. in *Animal Phys.*: The body of a vertebra.

† **Centry,** *sb.* 1583. [f. CENTRE *sb.*; the *-y* is unexpl. Cf. AL. *centrie*, *-ii* (pl.) mid parts (XIII).] **1.** Centre, midst –1594. **2.** The centre or centering of a bridge –1834.

† **Centry,** *a.* 1486. Also **sentry.** [– Fr. *centré* centred; see -Y[5].] In *Her.*

‖ **Centum.** [L.] A hundred; see CENT.

‖ **Centu·mvir.** pl. **Centu·mviri.** 1601. [L. *centum* hundred, *viri* men.] *Rom. Antiq.* (In *pl.*) A body of judges appointed by the prætor, called for conciseness 'the Hundred Men', but numbering 105, and, later, 180. Hence **Centu·mviral** *a.* of or pertaining to the centumviri. **Centu·mvirate,** the office of the Roman centumviri; the centumviri collectively; a body of 100 men.

Centuple (se·ntiup'l), *a.* 1609. [– Fr. *centuple* or eccl. L. *centuplus*, var. of *centuplex*, f. *centum* hundred.] A hundred-fold. Hence **Ce·ntuple** *v.* to multiply a hundred-fold; var. **Centu·plicate** *v.*, whence **Centu·plicate** *a.* and *sb.* hundred-fold; **Centu:plica·tion.**

† **Ce·nture, ce·nter.** 1595. [– (O)Fr. *ceinture* :– L. *cinctura* CINCTURE.] A CINCTURE.

Centurial (sentiŭᵊ·riăl), *a.* 1610. [– L. *centurialis*, f. *centuria*; see CENTURY, -AL[1].] Of or pertaining to a CENTURY.

C. Assemblys 1656. Legionary or c. tablets 1851. C. associations LOWELL.

† **Centu·riate,** *a.* 1600. [– L. *centuriatus*, pa. pple. of *centuriare*; see next, and -ATE[2].] In *c. assemblies*, tr. L. *comitia centuriata*, in which all the Roman people voted by centuries (see CENTURY 2).

† **Centu·riate,** *v. rare.* [– *centuriat-*, pa. ppl. stem of L. *centuriare* divide into centuries, f. *centuria*; see CENTURY, -ATE[3].] 'To divide into bands of hundreds' (Bailey 1721).

Centuriator (sentiŭᵊ·rieⁱtəɹ). 1660. [mod. L., f. as prec.; see -OR 2.] *pl.* (usu. *Centuriators of Magdeburg*): A number of 16th c. Protestant divines who compiled a Church History in thirteen volumes, each volume embracing a century. Formerly called CENTURISTS.

Centurion (sentiŭᵊ·riən). ME. [– L. *centurio, -ōn-*, f. *centuria* CENTURY.] The commander of a century in the Roman army. Also *transf.*

† **Centurist.** = CENTURIATOR.

Century (se·ntiŭri). 1533. [– L. *centuria*, assembly of 100 things, etc., f. *centum* hundred; see -Y[3].] **1.** *Rom. Hist.* A division of the Roman army, constituting half a maniple, and prob. consisting orig. of 100 men. *transf.* Any body of 100 men 1612. **2.** *Hist.* One of the 193 divisions by which the Roman people voted in the *Comitia centuriata* 1604. **3.** A group of a hundred things; a hundred (*arch.*) 1598. **4.** A period of 100 years; orig. 'a c. of years' 1626. **5.** Each of the successive periods of 100 years, reckoning from a received chronological epoch, *esp.* from the birth of Christ. **6.** *pl.* The Church History of the CENTURIATORS, divided into centuries 1606.

1. *Cor.* I. vii. 3. 3. A c. of prayers *Cymb.* IV. ii. 391, of sonnets BROWNING. To score a c. in an innings 1883. 5. The rebellion in the last c. 1771. *The first c.* (A.D. 1–100 inclusive). *The nineteenth c.* (A.D. 1801–1900). *Comb.*: **c.-plant,** the AGAVE or American Aloe; **-writer** = CENTURIATOR. Hence **Ce·nturied** *a.* centuries old.

Century, obs. var. of SENTRY.

Ceorl (kʸeᵊrl, tʃeᵊrl). OE. = CHURL, q.v.

† **Cepa·ceous, cæ-,** *a.* 1657. [f. L. *cæpa*, *cepa* onion + -ACEOUS.] Of the nature of an onion.

Cephalalgy (se·fălældʒi). 1547. [– L. *cephalalgia* – Gr. κεφαλαλγία, f. κεφαλή head + ἄλγος pain; see -Y[3]; cf. (O)Fr. *céphalalgie.*] Headache. Hence **Cephala·lgic** *a.* of, pertaining to, or affected with c.; *sb.* a medicine for c. (Dicts.)

‖ **Cephala·nthium.** 1880. [mod.L., f. Gr. κεφαλή head + ἄνθος flower.] *Bot.* = ANTHODIUM.

‖ **Cephala·spis.** 1842. [mod.L., f. Gr. κεφαλή head + ἀσπίς shield.] *Palæont.* A genus of fossil ganoid fishes found in the Old Red Sandstone, having a large buckler-shaped plate attached to the head: also called *buckler-heads.*

Cephalate (se·fălĕt). 1862. [f. Gr. κεφαλή head + -ATE[2].] A mollusc having a distinct head, or belonging to the Encephalous division (*Cephalata*).

Cephalic (sĭfæ·lik), *a.* (*sb.*) 1599. [– (O)Fr. *céphalique* – L. *cephalicus* – Gr. κεφαλικός, f. κεφαλή head; see -IC.] **1.** Of or pertaining to the head; of the nature of a head. **2.** Relieving disorders of the head 1656. As *sb.* A cephalic remedy 1656.

1. *C. index*: a number indicating the ratio of the transverse to the longitudinal diameter of the skull. *C. vein*: the principal vein of the arm, which anciently was opened to relieve disorders of the head. Hence **cepha·lically** *adv.* in relation to the head.

‖ **Cephalitis** (sefăləi·tis). 1811. [mod.L., f. Gr. κεφαλή + -ITIS.] *Med.* Inflammation of the brain and its membranes.

Cephalization (se:fălәizēⁱ·ʃən). 1864. [f. Gr. κεφαλή head + -IZE + -ATION.] *Biol.* Dana's term to express the degree to which the head is developed and dominates over the rest of the body. So **Ce·phalized** *a.* having the head developed.

Cephalo- (se·fălo), comb. f. Gr. κεφαλή head, used:

a. in combs., such as **c.-catha·rtic** *a.* purging the head; **-extra·ctor,** an instrument for extracting a fœtus by the head.

b. in derivative formations, as **Ce·phalocele** [see CELE], a tumour in the head. **Cephalo·logy,** a treatise on the head. † **Ce·phaloma:ncy** [Gr. μαντεία], divination by means of a head. **Cephalo·meter** [Gr. μέτρον], an instrument formerly used for measuring the size of the fœtal head during parturition; also *gen.* **Cephalo·phorous** *a.* [Gr. -φορος], epithet of the Cephalates. **Cephalo·pterous** [Gr. πτέρον] *a.*, having a winged or feathered head. **Ce·phalosta:t** [Gr. στατός], a head-rest. **Ce·phaloto:me** [Gr. -τομος adj., cutting], an instrument for cutting the head of the fœtus in embryotomy. **Cephalo·tomy** [Gr. -τομία sb.], the dissection of the head; also, as under *cephalotome.* **Ce·phalotri:be** [Gr. τρίβειν], an instrument used in cephalotripsy. **Ce·phalotri:psy** [Gr. τρῖψις], the operation of crushing the head of the fœtus with a cephalotribe, in cases of difficult delivery.

Cephaloid (se·făloid), *a.* 1847. [– Gr. κεφαλή head + -OID.] Shaped like a head.

Cephalopod (se·fălŏpǫd). 1826. [– mod.L. *cephalopoda*; see next.] *Zool.* One of the *Cephalopoda.*

‖ **Cephalopoda** (sefălǫ·pŏdă), *sb. pl. Sing.* **-pod** or **-podan.** 1802. [mod.L., f. CEPHALO- + Gr. πούς, ποδ- foot; see -A 4.] *Zool.* The most highly organized class of *Mollusca*, characterized by a distinct head with arms or tentacles attached to it; comprising Cuttle-fishes, the Nautilus, etc., and many fossil species. Hence **Cephalo·podal, Ce:phalopo·dic, Cephalo·podous** *adjs.* belonging to the *Cephalopoda*; pertaining to a cephalopod. **Cephalo·podan** *a.*; as *sb.* = CEPHALOPOD.

Cephalothorax (se:fălopō͘ə·ræks). 1835. [f. CEPHALO- + THORAX.] *Zool.* The anterior division of the body, consisting of the coalesced head and thorax, in certain *Arachnida* and *Crustacea* (as spiders and crabs). Hence **Ce:phalothora·cic** *a.*

Cephalous (se·făləs), *a.* [f. Gr. κεφαλή head + -OUS.] *C. mollusc* = CEPHALATE.

† **Ce·phen.** 1609. [– Gr. κηφήν.] A drone-bee –1657.

† **Ce·pous,** *a.* 1657. [f. L. *cæpa, cepa* onion + -OUS.] Like an onion; bulbous.

Ceraceous (sĭrēⁱ·ʃəs), *a.* 1768. [f. L. *cera* wax + -ACEOUS.] Of the nature of wax, waxy.

Cerago (sĭrēⁱ·go). 1839. [app. mod.L., f. L. *cera* wax. The regular AL. term was *ceragium* (XII).] Bee-bread.

Ceral (siə·răl). *a.* 1874. [(In sense 1) f. CERE *sb.* 3; (in sense 2) f. L. *cera* wax + -AL[1].] **1.** Pertaining to the CERE of a bird's bill. **2.** Relating to wax 1883.

Ceramic (sĭræ·mik), *a.* (*sb.*) Also **ker-.** 1850. [– Gr. κεραμικός, f. κέραμος potter's earth, pottery; see -IC.] **1.** Of or pertaining to pottery, *esp.* as an art. **2.** As *sb.* in *pl.* The ceramic art. So **Ce·ramist,** a c. artist.

Cerargyrite (sĭrā·ɹdʒirəit). 1868. [Improperly f. Gr. κέρας, -ατ- horn + ἄργυρος silver, + -ITE[1] 2 b.] *Min.* Native chloride of silver, horn silver.

Cerasin (se·răsin). 1838. [f. L. *cerasus* cherry + -IN[1]; cf. Fr. *cérasine.*] *Chem.* The insoluble portion of the gum of the cherry, and other trees.

‖ **Cerastes** (sĭræ·stīz). ME. [L. – Gr. κεράστης, f. κέρας horn.] *Zool.* A genus of venomous serpents found in Africa, etc., having a horny scale above each eye; the horned viper.

C. hornd MILT. *P.L.* X. 525. var. † **Cerast(e.**

Cerate (siə·rĕt). 1543. [– L. *ceratum* (also *cerotum* – Gr.; see CEROTE) = Gr. κηρωτόν, n. of adj. κηρωτός covered with wax. Cf. Fr. *cérat.*] *Med.* A stiff ointment composed of wax, lard or oil, and other ingredients. Hence **Ce·rated** *a.* covered with wax.

Ceratinous (sĭræ·tinəs), *a.* 1881. [f. Gr. κεράτινος (f. κέρας, -ατ- horn: see -INE[2]) + -OUS.] Of horny structure or nature.

† **Ceration.** 1610. [– med.L. *ceratio, -ōn-*, f. *cerat-* pa. ppl. stem of *cerare*, f. *cera* wax; see -ION.] *Alchem.* The action of covering anything with wax, or of softening a hard substance; also, the fixation of mercury –1751.

‖ **Ceratium** (sĭrēⁱ·ʃiŏm). 1880. [L. = *siliqua* – Gr. κεράτιον carob-bean, dim. of κέρας horn.] *Bot.* A siliquiform capsule. GRAY.

Cerato- (se·răto), comb. f. Gr. κέρας, κερατ- horn, used chiefly to denote relation to a cornu or horn, or to the cornea.

Cerato-bra·nchial [Gr. βράγχια gills] *a.*, *Anat.* epithet of one of the main portions of permanent branchial cartilage in fishes and Amphibia. **Ceratocele** (-sīl) [Gr. κήλη tumour], *Pathol.* a hernia of the cornea of the eye. **Cerato-hy·al** [see HYOID], *a.*, the part of the hyoid arch in mammals below the styloid process. **Ce·ratoplasty** [Gr. πλάσσειν], *Med.* the artificial restoration of the cornea.

Ceraunics (sĭrǭ·niks), *sb. pl. rare.* [f. Gr. κεραυνός thunderbolt + -ICS; see -IC.] That branch of physics which treats of heat and electricity. (Dicts.)

† **Ceraunite** (sĭrǭ·nəit). 1814. [f. Gr. κεραυνός thunderbolt + -ITE[1] 2 b. Cf. Fr. *céraunite.*] Thunder-stone; used of meteorites, or meteoric iron; also of belemnites, and of flint arrow-heads.

Ceraunoscope (sĭrǭ·nŏskōᵘp). 1827. [– Gr. κεραυνοσκοπεῖον.] A machine used by the ancients in their mysteries to imitate thunder and lightning.

Cerberus (sɔ̄·ɹbĕrŏs). ME. [L. – Gr. Κέρβερος.] *Gr. and L. Mythol.* The watch-dog which guarded the entrance of the infernal regions, represented as having three heads. Used allusively.

I must give the C. a sop, I suppose. (Cf. *Æneid* vi. 417.) FOOTE. Hence **Cerbe·rean** *a.* (*improp.* **-ian**). **Cerbe·ric** *a.*

‖ **Cercaria** (sərkēə·riă). 1841. [mod.L. *cercaria* (whence Fr. *cercaire* XVIII), irreg. f. Gr. κέρκος tail + *-aria* (see -ARY[1] 3.] *Zool.* A kind of trematode worm in its second larval stage, shaped like a tadpole. Hence **Cerca·rial, -ian, -iform** *adjs.*

‖ **Cercopithecus** (sɔ̄:ɹkopiþī·kŏs). 1572. [L. – Gr. κερκοπίθηκος, f. κέρκος tail + πίθηκος ape.] *Zool.* A genus of long-tailed African monkeys, having cheek-pouches, and callosities on the buttocks. Hence **Cercopithe·coid** *a.*

Cere (sīəɹ), *sb.* 1486. [– med.L. use of L. *cera* wax.] *Ornith.* The naked wax-like membrane at the base of the beak in certain birds, in which the nostrils are pierced. var. **Sear.**

Cere (sīəɹ), *v.* 1465. [ME. *cere* (rarely *cire*, – (O)Fr. *cirer*), usu. as pa. pple. *cered*, – L. *cerare* to wax, pa. pple. *ceratus.*] † **1.** To cover with wax, to wax –1601. **2. a.** To wrap in a cerecloth. † **b.** To anoint with spices, etc. 1465. † **c.** To seal up (in lead, etc.) 1525. Also *fig.*

Cereal (sīə·ri,ăl), *a.* (*sb.*) 1818. [– L. *cerealis* pertaining to the cultivation of grain, f. *Ceres* goddess of agriculture; see -AL[1].] *adj.* Of or pertaining to corn or edible grain 1818. *sb.* (usu. in *pl.*; also in L. form *cerealia.*) Any grasses which are cultivated for their seed as human food; commonly comprised under the name of *corn* or *grain* 1832.

Cerealin (sīə·riălin). 1861. [f. prec. + -IN[1].] *Chem.* A nitrogenous substance found in bran, closely resembling diastase.

‖ **Cerebellum** (serĭbe·lŏm). Also † **ce·rebel.** 1565. [L., dim. of *cerebrum*; see next.] *Phys.* The little or hinder brain, situated behind and below the cerebrum, and above the medulla oblongata. Hence **Cerebe·llar, Cerebe·llic** *adjs.* of or pertaining to the c.

Cerebral (se·rĭbrăl), *a.* (*sb.*) 1805. [f. L. *cerebrum* brain + AL[1]; cf. Fr. *cérébral.*] **1.** Pertaining or relating to the brain; analogous to a brain 1816. **2.** *Cerebral letters*: name for a class of consonants in Sanskrit, etc., developed from the dentals by retracting the tongue and applying its tip to the palate. Also as *sb.*

1. A c. ganglion 1889. Hence **Ce·rebralism,** the theory that mental operations arise from the action of the brain. **Ce·rebralist,** one who holds this.

Cerebrate (se·rĭbreⁱt), *sb.* 1872. [f. CEREBRIC; see -ATE[4].] *Chem.* A salt of cerebric acid.

Cerebration (serĭbrēⁱ·ʃən). 1853. [f. L. *cerebrum* brain + -ATION.] Brain-action (*esp.* unconscious). Hence **Ce·rebrate** *v.* to perform by c. (*rare*).

Cerebric (sĕre·brik), *a.* 1839. [f. L. *cerebrum* brain + -IC.] Pertaining to the brain. *C. acid (Chem.)*, a fatty acid obtained from the brain.

Cerebriform (sĕre·brifǭɹm), *a.* 1834. [f. as prec. + -FORM.] Resembling the brain in form or texture; encephaloid.

Cerebri·fugal, *a.* [f. as prec. + L. *-fugus* (see -FUGE) + -AL[1].] Epithet of nerve-fibres which run from the brain to the spinal cord, and convey cerebral impulses outward. So **Cerebri·petal** *a.* epithet of nerve-fibres which run in the opposite direction, and convey sensations to the brain.

Cerebrin (se·rĭbrin). Also **-ine.** 1830. [f. as prec. + -IN[1].] *Chem.* A name used for several substances obtained from the brain; *esp.* a light white hygroscopic powder, obtained by the action of baryta and heat on brain-tissue.

‖ **Cerebritis** (serĭbrəi·tis). 1866. [f. as prec. + -ITIS.] *Path.* Inflammation of the substance of the brain.

Cerebro- (se·rĭbro), comb. f. L. *cerebrum* brain; used:

a. as in **cerebro-ca·rdiac** *a.*, relating to the brain and heart. **b.** in forming hybrid derivatives, as **Cerebro·logy** [see -LOGY], the science or discussion of brains. **Cerebro·meter** [see -METER], an instrument for recording cerebral pulsations. **Cerebro·pathy** [Gr. -πάθεια], the series of hypochondriacal symptoms accompanying overwork of the brain. **Cerebro·scopy** [Gr. -σκοπια, f. σκοπεῖν], the use of the ophthalmoscope to determine the state of the retina and deduce the condition of the brain.

Cerebroid (se·rĭbroid), *a.* 1854. [f. L. *cerebrum* brain + -OID.] Resembling or akin to brain; brainlike.

Cerebro·se, *a. rare.* [– L. *cerebrosus*, f. *cerebrum* brain; see -OSE[1].] 'Brain-sick, mad-brained, wilful, stubborn' (Bailey 1727). Hence † **Cerebro·sity** 1586.

Cerebro-spinal (se:rĭbro,spəi·năl), *a.* 1826. [f. CEREBRO- + SPINAL.] Relating to the brain and spinal cord.

Cerebro-spinal axis: the brain and spinal cord as together constituting the central or main part of the *cerebro-spinal system*, the chief of the two great nerve systems of vertebrates. *Cerebro-spinal fluid*: a serous fluid occupying the space between the arachnoid membrane and *pia mater.*

‖ **Cerebrum** (se·rĭbrŏm). 1615. [L.] The brain proper; the anterior, and, in the higher vertebrates, largest part of the brain; in man it fills nearly the whole cavity of the skull.

Cerecloth (sīə·ɹklǫþ), *sb.* 1540. [orig. *cered cloth*; see CERED.] Cloth smeared or impregnated with wax or some glutinous matter: used **a.** as a winding-sheet 1553; † **b.** as a plaster in surgery –1818; **c.** as a waterproof material 1540.

b. To bed, & there had a c. laid to my foot PEPYS. Hence † **Ce·recloth** *v.* to apply a c. to; to wrap in a c.

Cered (sīəɹd), *ppl. a.* ME. [See CERE *v.*, -ED[1].] Smeared, anointed, or saturated with wax, *esp.* in *Cered cloth* = CERECLOTH.

Cerement (sīə·ɹmĕnt, also *erron.* se·rĭ-). 1602. [Substituted by Shakespeare for the usual *cerecloth.*] Usu. in *pl.* Waxed wrappings for the dead; *loosely*, grave-clothes. Rarely in *sing.* = cerecloth; shroud. Also *fig.*

Tell Why thy Canoniz'd bones Hearsed in death Haue burst their cerments *Haml.* I. iv. 48.

Ceremonial (se·rĭmōᵘ·niăl), *a.* and *sb.* ME. [– late L. *cærimonialis*, f. *cærimonia* CEREMONY; see -AL[1]; cf. (O)Fr. *cérémonial.*]

A. *adj.* 1. Relating to, or consisting of, ceremonies or rites; ritual; formal. † 2. Addicted to ceremony or ritual; formal, ceremonious –1653.

1. The ceremoniall rites of marriage *Tam. Shr.* III. ii. 6. C. manners 1851.

B. *sb.* † **1.** A ceremonial commandment or ordinance –1621. **2.** A prescribed system of ceremonies; a ritual. *rarely*, A rite or ceremony. 1672. **3.** = CEREMONY 2, 3. 1749. † **4.** A ceremonial robe; = CEREMONY 4. 1610. **5.** *R.C.Ch.* The order for rites and ceremonies, or a book containing this 1612.

2. The c. prescribed in the Anglican service D'ISRAELI. Hence **Ceremo·nialism,** addiction to external ceremonies in religion; ritualism. **Ceremo·nialist,** a ritualist. **Ceremo·nially** *adv.*

† **Ceremo·niary.** [f. CEREMONY + -ARY[1] B 2, after *breviary*, etc.] A directory or rule of ceremony. JEWEL.

Ceremonious (serĭmōᵘ·niəs), *a.* 1555. [– Fr. *cérémonieux* or late L. *cærimoniosus*, f. *cærimonia*; see next, -OUS.] **1.** Pertaining to, or consisting of, ceremonies; = CEREMONIAL. **2.** Full of ceremony; accompanied with rites 1611. **3.** According to customary formalities or punctilios 1593. **4.** Addicted to ceremony; punctilious in observance of formalities 1553.

1. The c. lawe of Moises 1555. 2. *Wint. T.* III. i. 7. 3. His..somewhat c. politeness 1863. Hence **Ceremo·nious-ly** *adv.*, **-ness.**

Ceremony (se·rĭməni). [– (perh. through (O)Fr. *cérémonie*) L. *cærimonia* religious worship, (pl.) ritual observances; see -MONY.] **1.** An outward rite or observance, religious or held sacred; the performance of some solemn act according to prescribed form; a solemnity; *disparagingly*, An empty form 1533; *loosely*, A stately formality 1802. **2.** A usage of courtesy, politeness, or civility ME. **3.** (without *a* or *pl.*) **a.** Performance of (religious) rites, ceremonial observance 1759. **b.** Precise observance of conventional forms of deference or respect 1603. **c.** Pomp, state (*arch.*) 1599. † **4.** *concr.* An external accessory or symbolical attribute of worship, state, or pomp –1709. † **5.** A portent, omen 1601.

1. The ceremonyes of the Masse 1535. Old antiquated Ceremonies 1710. A mere c. THIRLWALL. The c. of dinner 1802. **2.** The c. of waiting for answers MISS BURNEY. **3. a.** A..christian, in substance, not in c. 'JUNIUS'. **b.** *Without c.* *To stand upon c.* **4.** *Jul. C.* I. i. 70. **5.** *Jul. C.* II. i. 197. *Master of 'the' ceremonies*: the person who superintends the ceremonies observed in a place of state or on some public occasion. Hence † **Ce·remony** *v.* to sanctify or treat with c. QUARLES.

Cereous (sīᵊ·rĭ,əs), *a.* 1601. [– L. *cereus* waxen + -OUS.] Of the nature of wax, waxen, waxy.

Cererite, Cererium; see CERITE, CERIUM.

‖ **Cereus** (sīᵊ·rĭ,ŏs). 1730. [L.; see CEREOUS.] *Bot.* A large genus of cactuses, natives of tropical America; the Torch-thistle.

† **Ce·rfoil.** *rare.* ME. [– OFr. *cerfoil* (mod. *cerfeuil*) – L. *cærefolium* – Gr. χαιρέφυλλον; see CHERVIL.] = CHERVIL –1567.

Ceric (sīᵊ·rik), *a.*[1] 1863. [f. CERIUM + -IC.] *Chem.* Of or belonging to cerium; as in *c. salts.*

Ce·ric, *a.*[2] 1838. [f. L. *cera* wax + -IC.] *Chem.* Chemically related to wax; as in *C. acid*, obtained by treating cerin with nitric acid.

† **Ceri·lla.** 1591. [Sp., var. of *cedilla.*] = CEDILLA –1863.

Cerin (sīᵊ·rin). 1850. [f. L. *cera* + -IN[1].] *Chem.* **1.** A waxy substance extracted by alcohol or ether from grated cork. † **2.** A name applied to the portion of bees-wax which is readily soluble in alcohol –1865.

Cerine (sīᵊ·rəin). 1814. [f. CERIUM + -INE[5].] *Min.* A variety of ALLANITE or cerium-epidote.

Cerinthian (sĭri·nþiăn), *a.* 1576. [f. *Cerinthus* + -IAN.] Of or pertaining to the teaching of Cerinthus (c A.D. 88), who attempted to unite Christianity with a mixture of Gnosticism and Judaism. As *sb.* A follower of Cerinthus.

Ceriph (se·rif). 1830. [See SERIF.] One of the fine lines of a letter, *esp.* the fine hair-line at the top or bottom of capitals, as of I.

‖ **Cerise** (səri·z), *a.* and *sb.* 1858. [Fr.] A light bright clear red, resembling that of some cherries.

Cerite (sīᵊ·rəit). 1804. [f. as CERIUM + -ITE[1] 2 b.] The rare mineral hydrated silicate of Cerium.

C. metals: cerium, didymium, and lanthanum.

Ce·rite[2]. 1811. [– Fr. *cérite* – mod.L. *cerithium*, name of the genus, inexactly – Gr. κηρύκιον trumpet-shell. Cf. -ITE[1] 2 a.] *Palæont.* A genus of fossil brachiopod molluscs. Also *attrib.*

Cerium (sīᵊ·riŏm). 1804. [– mod.L. (Hisinger and Berzelius, 1804), named, along with its source *cerite*, after the planet *Ceres*, discovered 1801; see -IUM.] *Chem.* A rare metallic element, discovered in the mineral called CERITE; it has the colour and lustre of iron, and takes a high polish, but tarnishes in moist air; it is malleable and ductile, of specific gravity 6·63 to 6·73. Atomic weight 138; symbol Ce. Also *attrib.* = CERIC *a.*[1]

† **Cern,** *v.* For CONCERN. *Tam. Shr.* V. i. 77.

Cernuous (sɔ̄·ɹniu,əs), *a.* 1653. [f. L. *cernuus* + -OUS.] Bowing downwards; in *Bot.* drooping, nodding: said of a flower.

Cero-, comb. f. L. *cera* or Gr. κηρός wax; also the first element in many derivatives.

Cerography (sĭrǫ·grăfi). 1593. [– Gr. κηρογραφία; see CERO-, -GRAPHY.] Writing or painting on wax, as the encaustic painting of the ancients. **b.** Applied also to a method of taking stereotype plates from superposed sheets of engraved wax. So **Ce·rograph,** a writing on wax. **Cerogra·phic, -al** *a.* pertaining to c. **Cero·graphist.**

Cerolite (sīᵊ·rŏləit). Also **ker-.** 1868. [f. Gr κηρός wax; see -LITE.] *Min.* A hydrous silicate of aluminum, having a waxy lustre and greasy feel.

‖ **Ceroma** (sĭrōᵘ·mă). 1842. [L. – Gr. κήρωμα, ointment for wrestlers, anything made of wax.] 'An apartment in the Gymnasium and baths of the ancients, where the bathers and wrestlers were anointed' (Gwilt).

Ceromancy (sīᵊ·rŏmænsi). 1652. [– Fr. *céromancie*, med.L. *ceromantia*; see CERO-, -MANCY.] Divination by dropping melted wax into water.

Ceromel (sīᵊ·rŏmel). [– Fr. *céromel*, f. L. *cera* wax + *mel* honey.] A mixture of wax and honey, used as an ointment in hot climates.

Ceroo·n. U.S. var. of SEROON.

Ceroplastic (sīᵊroplæ·stik), *a.* 1801. [– Gr. κηροπλαστικός; see CERO-, PLASTIC.] **1.** Relating to modelling in wax. **2. Ceroplastics** *sb.* the art of modelling in wax; *concr.* waxworks. 1882. So **Ce·roplasty,** modelling in wax.

Cerosin (sīᵊ·rŏsin). 1865. [– Fr. *cérosine*, f. L. *cerosus*; see -IN[1], -INE[5].] *Chem.* A wax-like substance obtained by scraping the surface of some kinds of sugar-cane.

Ceroso-. *Chem.* Comb. f. CEROUS *a.*

† **Cerote.** 1562. [– L. *cerotum* – Gr. κηρωτόν; see CERATE.] = CERATE –1669.

Cerotic (sĭrǫ·tik). 1850. [f. as prec. + -IC.] *Chem.* In *C. acid*, $C_{27}H_{54}O_2$, the essential constituent of cerin (see CERIN 2). Its salts are called **Ce·rotates.** So **Ce·rotene,** an olefine ($C_{27}H_{54}$) obtained by the dry distillation of Chinese wax. **Ce·rotin,** hydrate of ceryl, $C_{27}H_{56}O$. **Ce·rotyl** = CERYL.

Cerous (sīᵊ·rəs), *a.* 1863. [f. CERIUM + -OUS.] *Chem.* Applied to compounds in which cerium combines as a triad, as in *c. salts*, etc.

† **Cerre-tree.** *rare.* 1577. [– L. *cerrus.*] The Turkey Oak or the Holm Oak. So † **Ce·rrial,** *a.* ME. [– OIt. *cereale*, f. *cerro*, L. *cerrus*], of or pertaining to evergreen oak –1500.

Cert (sɔ̄ɹt). 1889. [abbrev. of CERTAIN(TY).] *slang* (orig. *Racing*). A horse that is certain to win; a 'sure thing'.

Certain (sɔ·ɹtĕn, -t'n), *a.*, *sb.*, and *adv.* ME. [– (O)Fr. *certain* :– Rom. **certanus*, extension of L. *certus* settled, sure.]

I. 1. Determined, fixed; not variable. (Occ. put after its sb. in this sense.) **b.** Definite, exact (*arch.*) ME. **2.** Sure, reliable ME.; inevitable ME.; unfailing 1636. **3.** Not to be doubted; established as a truth or fact ME. **4.** Having no doubt; assured; sure (= 'subjectively certain'). Const. *of*, *that* with *cl.* ME. † **5.** Self-determined, resolved; steadfast –1690.

1. Payment of money on a day c. 1845. **2.** To repose upon..c. experience JOHNSON. The certeine perill he stood in SPENSER *F.Q.* I. i. 24. A c. remedy for a distemper 1754. **3.** A fact as c. as it appears incredible HUME. **4.** *Ant. & Cl.* II. ii. 57. *Morally c.*: so sure that one is justified in acting upon the conviction. **5.** I with thee have fixt my Lot, C. to undergoe like doom MILT. *P.L.* IX. 953.

II. Used to indicate things which the mind particularizes, but which are not further identified in speech: in *sing.* = a particular, in *pl.* = some particular, some definite ME.

Till some c. shot be paid *Two Gent.* II. v. 6. *A c. age.* (Mostly said of women.) *Spec. uses.* **a.** = some at least: He kept up a c. degree of intercourse S. AUSTIN. **b.** = unknown except by name: A c. lord Archibald Hamilton COWPER.

B. quasi-*sb.* or *ellipt.* † **1.** What is certain; certainty –1631. † **2.** A definite quantity or amount (*of*) –1621.

1. *For c.*: as a certainty, assuredly. [= Fr. *pour certain.*] ME. † *In c.*: in truth, truly –1493. *Of a c.* (arch.), formerly *of c.*: as a matter of certainty, assuredly 1485.

C. *adv.* **1.** Certainly ME. **2.** Emphasizing *sooth, true, sure.* (Now *dial.*) 1500.

Hence **Ce·rtainly** *adv.* with certainty; fixedly; without doubt; unquestionably. † **Ce·rtainness.**

† **Certain,** *v. rare.* ME. [f. prec., or OFr. *certainer*, f. *certain.*] To make certain; to certify –1523.

Certainty (sɔ̄·ɹtĕnti). ME. [– AFr. *certainté*, OFr. *certaineté*; see CERTAIN, -TY[1].] **1.** That which is certain, the fact, the truth. ? *Obs.* **2.** A fact or thing certain or sure (with *pl.*) 1611. † **3.** Surety. ME. only. **4.** The quality of being certain ME. † **5.** A definite number or quantity –1603.

2. Small certainties are the bane of men of talents 1775. **4.** The c. of Geometry 1738. To affirm with c. ADDISON. *Moral c.*; see CERTAIN. *For*, († *in*, † *at*), *of*, *to* (*a*) *c.*: as a matter of c., beyond doubt, assuredly.

Certes (sɔ̄·ɹtĕz), *adv. arch.* ME. [–(O)Fr. *certes*, prob. :– Rom. *(*ad*) *certas* (sc. *res*) for a certainty, used in the sense of late L. *ad certum, ex certo*, etc.] Of a truth, assuredly.

This, certs, I know FULLER. And c. not in vain WORDSW. ? Hence **Certie, certy** (*Sc.*) (taken as sing. of *certes*).

Certi·ficate, *ppl. a.* 1547. [– *certificatus*, pa. pple. of med.L. *certificare*; see next, and -ATE[2].] Certified.

Certificate (səɹti·fikĕt), *sb.* 1472. [– Fr. *certificat* or med.L. *certificatum*, subst. use of pa. pple. of *certificare*; see CERTIFY -ATE[1].] † **1.** Certification –1661. **2.** A document wherein a fact is formally certified 1489; occ. = *licence* 1549; also *gen.*, a certification 1718. **3.** *Law.* A writing made in one court, by which notice of its proceedings is given to another 1607. Also *attrib.*

2. A c. of health DE FOE, of character 1790, of baptism SCOTT. The suspension of Captain Stone's c. 1863. **3.** *Trial by c.*: a form of trial in which the testimony of facts as certified by any proper authority decides the point at issue.

Certificate (səɹti·fikeⁱt), *v.* 1768. [f. the sb.] **1.** To attest by a certificate. **2.** To furnish with a certificate 1818.

2. To c. midwives 1870, teachers 1864.

Certification (sɔ̄ɹtifikēⁱ·ʃən). 1440. [– (O)Fr. *certification* or med.L. *certificatio*, -*ōn*-; see CERTIFY, -FICATION.] The action of certifying or fact of being certified; the form in which this is embodied.

The c. of elementary teachers 1889.

Certificatory (səɹti·fikătəri), *a.* 1520. [– med.L. *certificatorius*, f. *certificare* CERTIFY; see -OR 2, -ORY[1].] Of the nature of a certificate, as *Letter c.*: a written testimonial.

Certify (sɔ̄·ɹtifəi), *v.* ME. [– (O)Fr. *certifier* – late and med. L. *certificare*, f. *certus*; see CERTAIN, -FY.] **1.** To make (a thing) certain; to guarantee as certain; to give certain information of. **2.** To declare or attest by a formal or legal certificate 1461. **3.** To make (a person) certain (*of*); to assure; to give (a person) legal or formal attestation (*of*) ME. **4.** *intr.* To testify *to*, vouch *for* 1625.

1. To certefye this thinge, sende for the damoysell LD. BERNERS. **2.** Cause sertified and allowed by the Captain 1651. **3.** These are to Certifye all whom it may concerne 1675. To c. a person that [etc.] TINDALE. **4.** To c. to a person's insanity 1874. Hence **Ce·rtifi:able** *a.* **Ce·rtifier.**

Certiorari (sɔ̄ɹʃi,orēᵊ·rəi). 1523. [pass. of late legal L. *certiorare* inform, f. *certior*, compar. of *certus* CERTAIN.] *Law.* A writ, issuing from a superior court, upon the complaint of a party that he has not received justice in an inferior court, or cannot have an impartial trial, by which the records are called up for trial in the superior court.

Certiorate (sɜ̄·ɹʃioreⁱt), *v.* 1637. [f. *certiorat-*, pa. ppl. stem of late L. *certiorare*; see prec., -ATE[3].] To inform authoritatively.

Certitude (sɜ̄·ɹtitiūd). ME. [– late and med.L. *certitudo*, f. *certus*; see CERTAIN, -TUDE; cf. Fr. *certitude* (XVI).] **1.** Subjective certainty. (The prevailing sense.) With *a* and *pl.* 1611. **2.** Objective certainty. ? *Obs.* 1538.

Cerulean (sĭrū·lĭăn), *a.* Also **cæ-.** 1667. [f. L. *cæruleus* sky-blue, sea-blue (or -green), f. *cælum* sky, heaven; see -EAN.] Of the colour of the cloudless sky, blue, azure. Chiefly *poet.* As quasi-*sb.* Cerulean hue 1756; (*joc.*) a blue-stocking 1821.

He spread the pure C. Fields on high BLACKMORE. vars. **Ce·rule** (*poet.*), † **Ceru·leous** *adjs.*

Cerulein (sĭrū·lĭ,in), **Cerulin** (sīᵊ·rŭlin). Also **cæ-.** 1810. [f. as prec. + -IN[1].] A deep blue substance in many essential oils; azulene.

Ceru·leo-, comb. f. L. *cæruleus.*

† **Ceruli·fic,** *a. rare.* 1701. [f. L. *cæruleus* cerulean + -FIC.] 'Having the power to produce a blue colour' (J.).

Cerumen (sĭrū·men). 1741. [– mod.L. *cerumen*, f. L. *cera* wax; cf. Fr. *cérumen.*] The yellow wax-like secretion in the external canal of the ear. Hence **Cerumini·ferous** *a.* producing c. **Ceru·minous** *a.* of, of the nature of, or secreting, c., as *c. glands.*

Ceruse (sīᵊ·rus, sĭrū·s). ME. [– (O)Fr. *céruse* – L. *cerussa*, perh. – Gr. *κηρόεσσα, f. κηρός wax.] **1.** = WHITE LEAD; used as a white paint, or a cosmetic: often vague. **2.** = CERUSSITE.

1. Eye-sight..too weak to distinguish c. from natural bloom MACAULAY. Hence † **Ceruse** *v.* to paint (the face) with c.

Cerussite, cerusite (sīᵊ·rŏsəit). 1850. [f. L. *cerussa* CERUSE + -ITE[1] 2 b.] *Min.* Native carbonate of lead, white lead ore.

Cervantic (sɜ̄ɹvæ·ntik), *a.* 1759. Pertaining to Miguel de *Cervantes* Saavedra (1547–1616), Sp. novelist and dramatist. So **Cerva·ntist.**

Cervantite (sərvæ·ntəit). 1856. [f. *Cervantes* (in Galicia, Spain) + -ITE[1] 2 b.] *Min.* A native tetroxide of antimony (Sb_2O_4), called also *antimony ochre.*

‖ **Cervelat** (sɛ̨rvəla). 1864. [Fr. † *cervelat* (mod. *cervelas*) XVI – It. *cervellata* Milanese sausage.] A short reed musical instrument, resembling the bassoon in tone. var. **Cervalet.**

Cervical (sɜ̄·ɹvikăl, sɜ̄ɹvəi·kăl), *a.* 1681. [– Fr. *cervical* or mod.L. *cervicalis* (cf. L. *cervical* pillow, bolster), f. *cervix, -ic-* neck; see -AL[1].] *Phys.* Of or belonging to the CERVIX. As *sb.* = c. nerve, vertebra, etc.

Ce·rvicide. *rare.* 1864. [– med.L. *cervicida*, f. *cervus* deer; see -CIDE.] The killing of a deer.

Cervico- (səɹvəi·ko), comb. f. L. *cervix, -īcis* neck, as in **cervi:co-bra·chial** *a.* belonging to the neck and arm, etc.

Cervine (sɜ̄·ɹvəin), *a.* 1832. [– L. *cervinus*, f. *cervus* deer; see -INE[1].] Of or belonging to deer, or to the family *Cervidæ.* Also as *sb.*

Cervi·sial, *a. joc.* 17... [f. L. *cervisia* beer + -AL[1].] Of or pertaining to beer.

‖ **Cervix** (sɜ̄·ɹviks). 1741. [L.] *Phys.* The neck. Also applied to analogous parts of the womb, the bladder, etc.

Ceryl (sīᵊ·ril). 1873. [f. Gr. κηρός wax + -YL.] *Chem.* The hypothetic radical ($C_{27}H_{55}$) of *Ceryl* or *Cerotyl alcohol* or cerotin, $C_{27}H_{56}O$, a waxy substance obtained from Chinese wax.

Cesar, -ean, etc.; see CÆ-.

Cesare (sĭ·zări). 1588. *Logic.* A mnemonic word representing the first mood of the second syllogistic figure, in which a universal negative major premiss and a universal affirmative minor yield a universal negative conclusion.

Cespititious (sespiti·ʃəs), *a.* 17... [– late L. *cæspiticius* made of turf (f. *cæspes, -it-* turf), + -OUS; see -ITIOUS[1].] Made of turf, turfen.

Cespitose (se:spitōᵘ·s), *a.* 1793. [– mod.L. *cespitosus*, f. as prec.; see -OSE[1]. Cf. L. *cæsposus.*] Also CÆSPITOSE, q.v. Turfy, growing in tufts or clumps.

Cess (ses), *sb.*[1] Also SESS(E. 1531. [var. of *sess*, aphet. f. ASSESS *sb.*] **1.** An assessment, tax, or levy. In Eng. use replaced by *rate*, exc. *dial.*; in Ireland still the official term. **2.** *Ireland.* The obligation to supply the soldiers and the lord deputy's household with provisions at prices 'assessed'; hence *loosely*, military exactions. Now *Hist.* 1571. † **3.** Assessment, estimation –1596.

3. The poore Iade is wrung in the withers, out of all cesse SHAKS.

† **Cess,** *sb.*[2] 1689. [var. of CEASE; cf. CESS *v.*[2]] **1.** Cessation 1703. **2.** = CESSER 3. 1869.

Cess (ses), *sb.*[3] *Anglo-Irish.* 1859. [perh. w. ref. to CESS *sb.*[1] 2.] In *bad cess to* = 'evil befall'.

Cess (ses), *v.*[1] 1494. [prop. SESS *v.*, aphet. f. ASSESS *v.*; cf. CESS *sb.*[1]] † **1.** = ASSESS *v.* 1. –1764. † **2.** = ASSESS *v.* 2. –1612. **3.** *Ireland.* To impose (soldiers) upon a community, to be supported at a fixed rate. Now *Hist.* 1612. † **4.** = ASSESS *v.* 3. –1738. † **5.** = ASSESS *v.* 4. STOW.

† **Cess,** *v.*[2] 1555. [var. of CEASE *v.*] *intr.* To cease to perform a legal duty –1741.

† **Ce·ssant,** *a. rare.* 1648. [– *cessant-*, pres. ppl. stem of L. *cessare* CEASE; see -ANT.] That ceases to act –1746. Hence **Ce·ssantly** *adv.* intermittently.

Cessation (sesēⁱ·ʃən). ME. [– L. *cessatio, -ōn-*, f. *cessat-*, pa. ppl. stem of *cessare* cease; see -ION.] **1.** Ceasing, discontinuance, stoppage. † **b.** ellipt. = *Cessation of* or *from arms*: armistice, truce –1755. † **2.** Inactivity –1697.

1. The C. of the Oracles SIR T. NORTH. **2.** The spent Earth may..better'd by C., bear the Grain DRYDEN.

‖ **Cessavit** (sesēⁱ·vit). 1555. [L., 3rd sing. pret. of *cessare* CEASE.] A writ to recover lands, which lay when a tenant ceased to pay rent, or perform legal duties, for the space of two years.

Cesser (se·səɹ). 1531. [subst. use of AFr., (O)Fr. *cesser* cease; see -ER[4].] **1.** *Law.* Ceasing (of a tenant) to pay rent, or perform legal duties, for the space of two years. **2.** Cessation, termination 1809. † **3.** = CESSION 2. –1689.

† **Ce·ssible,** *a. rare.* 1645. [– med.L. *cessibilis* yielding, f. *cess-*, pa. ppl. stem of L. *cedere* yield; see -IBLE; cf. Fr. *cessible* (XVI) 'that may be given up'.] Yielding; ready to give way. Hence † **Cessibi·lity,** yieldingness.

‖ **Cessio bonorum** (L. 'cession of goods') = CESSION 3 b.

Cession (se·ʃən). ME. [– (O)Fr. *cession* or its source L. *cessio, -ōn-*, f. *cess-*, pa. ppl. stem of *cedere* CEDE; see -ION.] † **1.** The action of giving way or yielding –1693. † **2.** The vacating of an office either by retirement or death –1738. **b.** *Eccl. Law.* The vacating of a benefice by taking another without dispensation 1641. **3.** The action of ceding to another rights, property, etc.; concession ME. **b.** *Civil Law.* The voluntary surrender by a debtor of all his effects to his creditors 1622.

3. The c. of Maestricht TEMPLE.

Cessionary (se·ʃənări). 1611. [– med.L. *cessionarius* sb., f. CESSIO BONORUM; see -ARY[1].] † **1.** A bankrupt who makes *cessio bonorum* –1694. **2.** An assignee 1754.

† **Ce·ssment.** 1540. [var. of *sessment*, aphet. f. ASSESSMENT.] = ASSESSMENT –1733.

† **Ce·ssor**[1]. Also † **-er.** 1565. [f. CESS *v.*[1] + -ER[1], -OR 2.] = ASSESSOR, q.v. –1596.

Cessor[2] (se·sǫɹ, -əɹ). 1727. [f. CESS *v.*[2] + -OR 2.] *Law.* One who cesses; see CESS *v.*[2]

Cesspipe (se·s,pəip). [f. *cess* in CESSPOOL.] A pipe for carrying off the overflow from cesspools, sinks, or drains. So **Cesspit,** a pit for the reception of night-soil and refuse; a midden.

Cesspool (se·s,pūl). 1671. [perh. alt., with assim. to POOL *sb.*[1], of *cesperalle, susprall, suspirel* settling tank, cesspool (XVI), vars. of † *suspiral* vent, esp. of a conduit, waterpipe – OFr. *souspirail* (mod. *soupirail*) air-hole, f. *sou(s)pirer* SUSPIRE + L. *spiraculum* air-hole.] **1.** A well made in the bottom of a drain, under a grating, to collect sand or gravel carried by the stream. **2.** A well sunk to receive the soil from a water-closet, kitchen sink, etc. Also *fig.* 1782.

2. *fig.* The c. of agio CARLYLE.

Cest(e. 1577. [– Fr. *ceste* or L. *cestus.*] = CESTUS[1].

Cestoid (se·stoid). Also **cestode.** 1836. [f. L. *cestus* CESTUS[1] + -OID.] **A.** *adj.* Ribbon-like, as the tape-worm. **B.** *sb.* A worm of this kind. Also *attrib.* 1837.

† **Ce·ston.** 1583. [– Fr. † *ceston*, deriv. of *ceste* CESTUS[1].] = CESTUS[1].

‖ **Cestracion** (sestrēⁱ·siǫn). 1876. [Cf. Gr. κέστρα a kind of fish, also κέστρος sharpness, and ἀκή point.] A kind of shark now peculiar to Australia; the Port Jackson shark. It has sharp teeth in front, and flat pavement-like teeth behind. Hence **Cestra·ciont,** belonging to the C. family of fishes.

Cestrian (se·striăn), *a.* 1703. [f. *Cester*, OE. form of *Chester.*] Of or pertaining to Chester or to Cheshire.

‖ **Cestui** (se·stwi, se·twi). Also **cestuy,** pl. **cestuis.** 1555. [– AFr., OFr. *cestui*:– Rom. **eccistui*, f. L. *ecce* lo! + *iste* that (one), with element *-ui* as in *cui*, dat. of *quis* who.] The person (who), he (who).

Cestui que (qui) trust, cestui que use, more fully *cestui a que use* (= *al use de qui*) *le trust est créé*: the person for whose benefit anything is given in trust to another. *Cestui (a) que vie*: he on or for whose life land is held or granted.

‖ **Cestus**[1] (se·stŏs). 1577. [– L. *cestus* – Gr. κεστός, subst. use of ppl. a., 'stitched'.] A belt or girdle for the waist; *esp.* that of Aphrodite or Venus. Also *fig.*

‖ **Cestus**[2] (se·stŏs). 1734. [– L. *cæstus*, f. *cædere* strike.] A covering for the hand made of thongs of bull-hide, loaded with strips of iron and lead. Used by boxers of ancient Rome.

Cesure; see CÆSURA.

Cet-, f. L. *cetus*, Gr. κῆτος whale, comb. f. signifying 'derived from spermaceti'.

Cetane (sī·tēⁱn), the paraffin of the hexdecyl or cetyl series, $C_{16}H_{34}$. **Cetene** (sī·tīn), the olefine of the same series, $C_{16}H_{32}$. **Ce·tic** *a.*, of the whale, or of spermaceti. **Cetin** (sī·tin), a white crystalline fatty substance ($C_{32}H_{64}O$), forming the essential part of spermaceti. **Ce·tyl,** the hydrocarbon radical ($C_{16}H_{33}$) assumed to exist in Cetic acid, and the other members of the *Cetyl* or *Cetylic* series, including *Cetyl* or *Cetylic Alcohol*, or *ethal* ($C_{16}H_{33}$.OH). **Cety·lic** *a.* of cetyl, as in *Cetylic alcohol.*

‖ **Cetacea** (sĭtēⁱ·ʃ'ă), *sb. pl.* 1830. [mod.L., f. L. *cetus* – Gr. κῆτος whale; see -ACEA.] *Zool.* The order of marine Mammalia containing the whales and their congeners. Hence **Ceta·cean** *a.* of or pertaining to the *C.*; *sb.* [sc. *animal*]. **Ceta·ceous** *a.* belonging to the *C.*; of the whale kind or nature.

Cete[1] (sīt). ME. [– OFr. *cete* fem. – L. *cete* pl. neut. – Gr. κήτη (sg. κῆτος) whales.] A whale, a sea-monster.

† **Cete**[2]. 1486. [perh. – L. *cœtus.*] A 'company' of badgers.

Ceteosaur, -us (sī·ti,osōᵊɹ, -sōᵊ·rŏs). 1872. [f. Gr. κῆτος whale (gen. κήτεος) + σαῦρος lizard.] *Palæont.* A gigantic fossil saurian, found in the oolite and chalk.

Ceterach (se·tĕræk). 1551. [– med.L. *ceterach* – Pers. *šaytarak* – Arab. *šaytaraj.*] *Bot.* A genus of ferns, including *C. officinarum*, Scale-fern.

Cetology (sitǫ·lŏdʒi). *rare.* 1851. [f. Gr. κῆτος whale + -LOGY.] That part of zoology which treats of the whales. Hence **Ceto·lo·gical** *a.* **Ceto·logist.**

Cetrarin (se·trărin, sī-). 1861. [f. mod.L. *cetraria*, generic name of Iceland moss, f. L. *cetra* targe; see -IN[1].] *Chem.* A white crystalline substance ($C_{18}H_{16}O_8$) forming the bitter principle of Iceland moss (*Cetraria islandica*). Also called **Cetra·ric acid.**

Ceylonite, ceylanite (sī·lənəit). 1802. [– Fr. *ceylanite*, f. *Ceylan*, Fr. form of Ceylon; see -ITE[1] 2 b.] *Min.* Iron-Magnesia Spinel from Ceylon.

Ch, a consonantal digraph, has the sound of (tʃ) in all native words; of (k) in words taken from Greek (or Hebrew through Greek); of *sh* (ʃ) in words from modern French; and of (χ) only in Scotch, Welsh, and foreign words. OE. *c(e)-, c(i)-* has regularly become *ch-*;

and other CH- words in mod. Eng. are supplied by the Old French words in *ch-* from L. *ca-*. For the history of the digraph see O.E.D.

† **Ch, 'ch,** *pron. dial.* ME. Aphet. f. *ich, utch* = I, occurring before verbal forms beginning with a vowel, *h*, or *w*; as in *cham* (tʃɑm), (earlier *icham*) I am, *chave, chad*, etc.

‖ **Cha.** 1616. [Chinese (Mandarin) *ch'a* tea.] A Chinese name of TEA occas. used in Eng. at its first introduction.

Chabazite, chabasite (kæ·băzəit). Also **chabasie, -zie.** 1804. [– Fr. *chabazie* (1780), from Gr. χαβάζιε, erron. reading for χαλάζιε, voc. of χαλάζιος, f. χάλαζα hail; see -ITE[1] 2 b.] *Min.* A colourless, or flesh-coloured, mineral occurring in glassy rhombohedral crystals, composed chiefly of silica, alumina and lime.

‖ **Chablis** (ʃablī). 1668. [Fr.] A white French wine made at *Chablis* (Yonne), in central France.

Cha·bot. 1610. [– (O)Fr. *chabot*, also OFr. *cabot*; cf. CABOT.] *Her.* The fish called Miller's Thumb.

‖ **Chabouk, -buk** (tʃā·buk). 1815. [– Urdu *chābuk*.] A (Persian) horsewhip. See also CHAWBUCK.

Chace, obs. f. CHASE.

Chack (tʃæk), *v.* 1513. [In sense 1, echoic; cf. *clack*.] **1.** *Sc.* To snap with the teeth; to crush with a snap of the jaws, or by the sudden shutting of a door, window, etc.; to clack. **2.** A sudden toss of a horse's head, to avoid the subjection of the bridle. ? *Obs.* 1731.

Chack (tʃæk), *sb. Sc.* 1804. [f. prec., or of parallel formation.] **1.** The act of chacking (in sense 1). **2.** A snack 1818. **3.** Name of the Wheat-ear (from its note) 1804.

‖ **Chacma** (tʃæ·kmă). 1835. [Native name.] A kind of baboon (*Cynocephalus porcarius*) found in S. Africa.

Chaco (ʃæ·ko). Also **chako,** and usu. SHAKO, q.v. 1826. [– Magyar *csákó*; see SHAKO.] A military cap having the form of a truncated cone with a peak in front.

‖ **Chaconne** (ʃako·n, tʃăkǫ·n). 1685. [Fr. – Sp. *chacona*.] An obsolete dance; the music to which it was danced, moderately slow, and usu. in 3–4 time.

Chad, var. of SHAD.

‖ **Chætodon** (kī·todǫn). 1750. [f. Gr. χαίτη hair + ὀδούς (ὀδοντ-) tooth.] *Zool.* A Linnæan genus of spiny-finned fishes (modern family *Chætodontidæ*) having bristle-like teeth and bright colours.

Chætophorous (kītǫ·fŏrəs), *a.* 1877. [f. Gr. χαίτη hair, mane + -PHOROUS.] *Zool.* Bristle-bearing; applied to certain Annelids.

Chætopod (kī·topǫd). 1864. [f. as prec. + πούς (ποδ-) foot.] *Zool.* Belonging to the order *Chætopoda* of Annelids, with bristle-bearing feet.

Chafe (tʃēⁱf), *v.* [Late ME. *chaufe* – OFr. *chaufer* (mod. *chauffer*) :– Rom. **calefare*, for L. *cal(e)facere* make warm.]

I. *trans.* † **1.** To heat (*lit.* and *fig.*) –1716. **2.** To rub with the hand; *esp.* in order to restore warmth or sensation ME. **3.** To rub so as to abrade; to fret, gall. Also *fig.* ME.

2. He took his arms..and chafed and rubbed them with his hands DE FOE. *absol.* Keep chafing, for she moans BROWNING. **3.** All the boats were badly chafed KANE. *fig.* I c. you if I tarrie. Let me go SHAKS.

II. *intr.* † **1.** To become warm or hot –1581. **2.** To rub; to press or strike with friction (*on, upon, against*) 1605. **3.** *fig.* To wax warm; to be angry, to rage; now usu., to display irritation by fretting and fuming 1525.

2. Seamen say, a Rope chafes 1704. If the currents c. upon it MAURY. **3.** Let the loser c. COWPER. To c. under an affront PRESCOTT. The great sea chafes PROCTER. Hence **Cha·fant** *a.* (*Her.*) applied to a boar when enraged.

Chafe (tʃēⁱf), *sb.* 1551. [f. the vb.] **1.** Heat; rage, passion, fury; temper (*arch.*). **2.** Rubbing, fretting, friction 1848. **3.** A chafing against restraints 1869.

1. The pope is in a wonderful c. ASCHAM. **2.** The c. of the sail 1882.

Chafer[1], **chaffer** (tʃēⁱ·fəɹ, tʃæ·fəɹ). [OE. *ċeafor* :– Gmc. **kabraz, -uz*, parallel to *ċefer* = OS., (M)Du. *kever*, OHG. *chevar, -iro* :– Gmc. **kebraz*; rel. to CHAFF *sb.*[1], CHAVEL, JOWL.] The COCKCHAFER; used also of the ROSE-CHAFER.

Chafer[2] (tʃēⁱ·fəɹ). ? *Obs.* [ME. *chaufour* (see -OUR), later *chaufer*, f. CHAFE *v.* + -ER[1]; with sense 1 cf. OFr. *chaufoire*.] † **1.** A vessel for heating water, var. † **Cha·fern, cha·ffern;** also, a chafing-dish –1825. † **2.** = CHAFE-WAX –1805. **3.** One who chafes or fumes. ? *Obs.* 1625.

Chafery (tʃēⁱ·fəri). 1663. [prob. repr. earlier **chauferie* – (O)Fr. *chaufferie*, f. *chauffer*; see CHAFE *v.*, -ERY.] *Metall.* A forge in which iron is reheated.

† **Cha·fe-wax.** Also **chaff-.** 1607. [f. CHAFE *v.* (sense 1) + WAX *sb.*, after (O)Fr. † *chauffe-cire*.] An officer in Chancery who prepared the wax for sealing documents.

Cha·feweed, † **cha·ffweed.** 1548. [f. CHAFE *v.* (sense I 3) + WEED.] *Herb.* A name for species of *Gnaphalium* and the allied *Filago*.

Chaff (tʃɑf), *sb.*[1] [OE. *ċæf, ċeaf* = MLG., (M)Du., MHG. *kaf* (G. dial. *kaff*), corresp. to OHG. *keva* husk; prob. f. Gmc. base **kaf-* **kef-* gnaw, chew; cf. CHAFER[1].] **1.** *collect.* The husks of corn or other grain separated by threshing or winnowing. Also *fig.* and † *transf.* **2.** Cut hay and straw used for feeding cattle OE. **3.** *Bot.* **a.** The bracts of the flower of grasses, *esp.* the inner pair. **b.** The bracts at the base of the florets in Compositæ. 1776. **4.** *transf.* and *fig.* Refuse ME.

1. The light c., before the breezes borne POPE. *fig. Merch. V.* I. i. 117. *An old bird is not caught with c.* Provb. **4.** The chaffe and ruine of the times *Merch. V.* II. ix. 48. *Comb.* **c.-cutter,** a machine for cutting hay and straw for fodder.

Chaff (tʃɑf), *sb.*[2] *colloq.* ? 1648. [perh. a var. of *chafe* (sense II 3).] Banter, ridicule; badinage. (Somewhat vulgar.)

Chaff, *v.*[1] 1552. [f. CHAFF *sb.*[1]] **1.** = CHAVE *v.* **2.** To cut (hay, etc.) for fodder 1883.

Chaff (tʃɑf), *v.*[2] *colloq.* 1827. [See CHAFF *sb.*[2]] *trans.* To banter, rail at, or rally, in a light manner. Also *absol.* (Considered slangy.)

Palmerston..pleasantly 'chaffing' militia colonels MCCARTHY. Hence **Cha·ffingly** *adv.*

Chaffer (tʃæ·fəɹ), *sb.*[1] [ME. *chaffare*, etc., :– OE. **ċēapfaru*, f. *ċēap* bargain, sale + *faru* going, journey, proceedings (prob. after ON. *kaupfǫr* trading journey); see CHEAP sb., FARE *sb.*[1]] † **1.** Trade; dealing –1662. **b.** In mod. use: Chaffering, haggling as to price 1851. † **2.** Wares –1693. Also † *fig.* Hence † **Cha·ffery** (*rare*), wares; traffic. **Cha·ffless** *a.* (*rare*).

Chaffer (tʃɑ·fəɹ), *sb.*[2] *colloq.* 1851. [f. CHAFF *v.*[2] + -ER[1].] One who chaffs.

Chaffer (tʃæ·fəɹ), *v.*[1] ME. [f. CHAFFER *sb.*[1]] † **1.** *intr.* To trade, deal in merchandise –1640. **2.** Now: To bargain, haggle about terms or price 1725. **3.** *transf.* and *fig.* To haggle, bandy words ME. † **4.** *trans.* To buy and sell; to traffic in; to barter –1680. Also † *fig.* ¶ **5.** 'To talk much and idly'. TRENCH.

1. (passing into 2) To c. for preferment with his gold DRYDEN. **2.** They will c. half a day about a penny W. PALGRAVE. **3.** To stand chaffering with Fate CARLYLE. **4.** He chaffred Chayres in which Churchmen were set SPENSER. Hence **Cha·fferer.**

Chaffinch (tʃæ·finʃ). [OE. *ċeaffinċ*, f. CHAFF *sb.*[1] + FINCH; cf. its late L. name *furfurio*, f. *furfur* bran.] A very common British bird, *Fringilla cælebs*, with pretty plumage and pleasant short song.

Cha·ffron, var. of CHAMFRAIN.

Chaff-weed (tʃɑ·f,wīd). 1776. [app. orig. CHAFEWEED.] † **1.** = CHAFEWEED. **2.** *Centunculus* or Bastard Pimpernel.

Chaffy (tʃɑ·fi), *a.* 1552. [f. CHAFF *sb.*[1] + -Y[1].] **1.** Full of or covered with chaff. **2.** Consisting, or of the nature, of chaff; *spec.* in *Bot.* paleaceous 1597. **3.** Resembling chaff 1583. **4.** *fig.* Light, empty, and worthless as chaff 1594.

1. Like..c. grain COLERIDGE. **3.** The c. snow 1791. **4.** Chaffye thoughtes 1594. A c. lord, Not worth the name of villain 1612.

Chafing (tʃēⁱ·fiŋ), *vbl. sb.* ME. [f. CHAFE *v.* + -ING[1].] The action of the vb.

Comb.: **c.-dish,** a vessel to hold burning fuel, for heating anything placed upon it; a portable grate; **-gear** (*Naut.*), 'the stuff put upon the rigging and spars to prevent their being chafed' (Smyth); **-pan** = *chafing-dish*.

Chaft (tʃɑft). Now *n. dial.* ME. [– ON. **kjǫft-* jaw, rel. to CHAVEL.] The jaw, chap; usu. in *pl.*

‖ **Chagan** (kagā·n). *Hist.* 1776. [– med.L. *chaganus, caganus*, in Byz. Gr. χαγᾶνος – OTurk. *khāqān* king, sovereign; see CHAM, KHAN.] Var. of KHAN; applied to the sovereign of the Avars in the 6th and 7th centuries.

Chagrin (ʃăgrī·n, -gri·n), *sb.* 1656. [Sense 1 – Fr. *chagrin* (XVII) rough skin, SHAGREEN; senses 2 and 3 – Fr. *chagrin* vexation (implied in *chagrineux* XIV).] † **1.** A species of skin or leather with a rough surface: now usu. spelt SHAGREEN, q.v. –1842. † **2.** That which frets or worries the mind –1847. **3.** *esp.* Mortification arising from disappointment, thwarting, or failure 1716. In *pl.* Vexations 1744.

2. Hear me, and touch Belinda with c. POPE. **3.** The c. of an unfortunate wretch who had not obtained what he wanted LANGHORNE. To have one's own petty chagrins MISS FERRIER.

† **Chagrin,** *a.* 1666. [– Fr. *chagrin* adj., f. the sb.; see prec.] **1.** Troubled –1722. **2.** Chagrined –1711.

Chagrin (ʃagrī·n, -gri·n), *v.* 1733. [– Fr. *chagriner*, f. the sb.] *trans.* To worry, vex; *esp.* to mortify 1748.

Chagrined at his disappointment MORSE.

Chain (tʃēⁱn), *sb.* ME. [– OFr. *chaine*, for earlier *chaeine* (mod. *chaîne*) :– L. *catena*.]

I. 1. A connected series of links (usually of metal) passing through each other, or otherwise jointed together, so as to form a strong but flexible ligament or string. **2.** As employed to restrain or fetter; hence a bond or fetter; *esp.* in *pl.*; *abstr.* imprisonment, captivity. Also *fig.* ME. **3.** As a personal ornament; occ. an ensign of office ME. **4.** *fig.* A connected series; a sequence 1651.

1. Gold, iron, cable, draught, watch chains (*mod.*) **2.** To dwell In Adamantine Chains and penal Fire MILT. *P.L.* I. 48. *fig.* The c. of habit HAZLITT. **3.** The Mayor wearing his c. of office 1889. **4.** The c. of Discourse HOBBES, of Thought STEELE, of proofs BENTHAM, of events FREEMAN, of nerve ganglia ROLLESTON, of lakes 1867. The c. (= *mountain-chain*) called Olympus GROTE.

II. Spec. uses.

1. A chain used as a barrier; a boom ME. **2.** A chain fixed to a door-post, to secure the door when slightly opened 1839. **3.** A measuring line, used in land-surveying, formed of one hundred iron rods called links. (The one now adopted is Gunter's chain, measuring 66 feet or 4 poles, divided into 100 links.) 1610. **b.** A chain's length = 66 feet or 4 poles 1661. **4.** *Arch.* A bar of iron, etc., built into walls to increase cohesion 1764. **5.** *Mil.* = CHAIN-SHOT 1804. **6.** *Weaving.* The warp 1721. **7.** *Naut.* A contrivance, consisting of c.-wale, c.-plates, dead-eyes, etc., used to carry the lower shrouds of a mast outside the ship's side 1627.

III. *attrib.* Of chains; chain-like; of the nature of chain-mail ME.

Combs.: **c.-armour** = *chain-mail*; **-belt,** a c. adapted as a belt for transmitting power; **-boat,** a boat fitted with windlasses, etc., for raising mooring-chains, anchors, etc.; **-bolt,** (*a*) *Naut.* one of the bolts by which c.-plates are fastened to the ship's side; (*b*) the knob at the end of a door c. (see II. 2); **-bond** (*Arch.*), a c. or tier of timber built in a brick wall to increase its cohesion (see II. 4); **-cable,** a ship's cable formed of a c.; also *attrib.*; **-coupling,** a secondary coupling, consisting of chains and hooks, between railway carriages or trucks; **-gang,** a gang of convicts chained together while at work, etc.; **-hook,** *Naut.* an iron rod with a hook at one end, for hauling the c.-cables about; **c. letter,** a letter, copies of which are designed to pass from one to another of a series of recipients; **-mail,** mail made of interlaced links or rings; **-moulding,** a moulding imitating chains; **-pier,** a pier supported by chains like a c.-bridge; **-plate** (*Naut.*), one of the iron plates by which the shrouds are secured to the ship's side; **-pulley,** a pulley having depressions in its periphery to fit the links of a chain with which it is worked; **-rule,** a rule of arithmetic, by which is found the relation of equivalence between two numbers for which a c. of intervening equivalents is given; **-saw** (*Surg.*), a vertebrated saw forming a c.; **-timber** = *chain-bond*; **-wale,** *Naut.* = CHANNEL *sb.*[2]; **-wheel,** (*a*) a wheel used with a c. for the transmission of power; (*b*) a machine which is an inversion of the c.-pump, the descending water pressing upon the plates or buckets and so driving the machinery. Hence **Chai·nless** *a.* (*poet.*). **Chai·nlet,** a little c.

Chain (tʃēⁱn), *v.* ME. [f. the sb.] **1.** *trans.* To bind, fasten, secure, with a chain. Also *transf.* and *fig.* **2.** To fetter or confine with a chain or chains; to put in chains ME. Also *fig.* **3.** To obstruct or close with a chain 1603. † **4.** To surround like a chain 1606. **5.** To measure with a (surveyor's) chain 1610.

1. The rampant Beare chain'd to the ragged staffe 2 *Hen. VI*, v. i. 203. *fig. Two Gent.* I. i. 3. **2.** *fig.* Horror chained My parting footsteps 1870. **3.** To c. or obstruct a street 1674. **4.** *Ant. & Cl.* IV. viii. 14.

Chai·n-bri:dge. 1818. A suspension-bridge supported by chains.

Chained (tʃēⁱnd), *ppl. a.* 1552. **1.** From the vb.: In the senses of the vb. 1613. **2.** From the sb.: Fitted, provided, or adorned with a chain or chains 1552. **3.** Of lightning: Having the form of a long zigzag line 1859.

Chai·n-pump. 1618. A machine for raising water by means of an endless chain; most commonly the chain, passing upwards through a tube, raises the water by means of discs or valves which fit the tube.

Chai·n-shot. 1581. Two balls, or half-balls, connected by a chain, chiefly used in naval warfare to destroy masts, rigging, and sails; a discharge of this. Also *fig.*

Chai·n-stitch. 1598. **1.** In needle-work: An ornamental stitch resembling the links of a chain; chain-work. **2.** In a sewing-machine: A stitch produced by looping the upper thread into itself on the under side of the work, or by using a second thread to engage the loop of the upper thread; opp. to the lock-stitch. Also *attrib.* 1867.

Chai·n-work, chain work. 1551. **1.** Ornament resembling chains. **2.** Work consisting of metal links or rings intertwined 1864. **3.** A texture formed by knitting or looping with a single thread, as in hosiery 1833.

Chair (tʃēᵊɹ), *sb.* [– AFr. *chaere*, OFr. *chaiere* (mod. *chaire* bishop's throne, see, pulpit, professorial chair, the ordinary word for 'chair' being *chaise*) :– L. *cathedra* – Gr. καθέδρα; see CATHEDRAL.] **1.** A seat for one person; now usu. the movable four-legged seat with a rest for the back. Also *fig.* **2.** A seat of authority, state, or dignity; a throne, bench, judgement-seat, etc. ME. Also *fig.* **3.** The seat of a bishop in his church; hence *fig.* episcopal dignity or authority (*arch.*) 1480. **4.** A pulpit (*arch.*) 1648. **5.** The seat, and hence the office, of a professor 1449, of a mayor 1682, of chairman of a meeting, or of the Speaker of the House of Commons 1647. † **6.** A vehicle for one person; a sedan carried on poles –1836; a light chaise drawn by one horse –1821. **7.** *Railways.* An iron or steel socket with a deep notch, to receive the rail and secure it to the sleeper 1816.

1. *To take a c.*: to be seated. *fig.* The scorner's C. WESLEY. [Thy Father's] drooping Chaire 1 *Hen. VI*, III. ii. 51. **2.** At the Soldans c. Defi'd the best of Panim chivalry MILT. *P.L.* I. 764. **3.** His first C., namely that of Antioch BREVINT. **5.** The C. of Poetry at Oxford M. ARNOLD. *Past, above,* or *below the C.* (of aldermen of the City of London): having served or not served as Lord Mayor. *To take the c.*: to assume the position of chairman. *To put in the c. In the c. To leave or vacate the c. To address, support, the c.* (*i.e.* the chairman). Cries of 'Chair' [*i.e.* appeals to the chairman] DICKENS. **6.** She..lik'd three footmen to her c. SWIFT. A one-horse c. 1753. *Comb.* **c.-days,** old age; **c. organ**: see CHOIR ORGAN.

† **Chair,** *sb.*[2] ME. [var. of CHAR *sb.*[2], assim. to prec.] A chariot or car –1814.

Chair (tʃēᵊr), *v.* 1552. [f. CHAIR *sb.*[1]] **1.** *trans.* To place in a chair. **b.** To place in a chair or seat, and carry aloft in triumph 1761. **2.** To provide with a chair or chairs 1844.

Chairman (tʃēᵊ·ɹmǣn). 1654. **1.** The occupier of a chair of authority; the person chosen to preside over a meeting, a company, a corporate body, etc. **2.** One whose occupation it is to carry persons in chairs, or to wheel a Bath-chair 1682. Hence **Chai·rmanship,** the office of c.; the action of presiding as c. **Chai·rwoman,** a woman who occupies the chair.

Chaise (ʃēⁱz). 1701. [– Fr. *chaise* (XV, Villon), var. of *chaire* CHAIR, the substitution of z for r being specially characteristic of Parisian speech in XV–XVII. Treated as pl. with sing. CHAY, SHAY.] A pleasure or travelling carriage; *esp.* a light open carriage for one or two persons, with a top or calash, orig. drawn by one horse; *loosely*, any pleasure cart or light carriage. Also, = POST-CHAISE, q.v. Hence **Chai·seless** *a.*

‖ **Chaise-longue** (ʃēz,loṅg). 1825. [Fr., 'long chair'.] A kind of sofa with a rest for the back at one end only.

†‖ **Chaise-marine** (ʃēz,marī·n). 1739. [Fr.] ? A kind of chaise, the body of which rests on suspension-straps between cee-springs –1823.

‖ **Chal.** 1865. The Gipsy word for 'person, man, fellow', with fem. *chai.*

Chalastic (kălæ·stik), *a.* 1621. [– late L. *c(h)alasticus* – Gr. χαλαστικός laxative; also as CALASTIC. Cf. Fr. *chalastique.*] *Med.* Having power to remove rigidity or stiffness; relaxing. Also as *sb.*

‖ **Chalaza** (kălēⁱ·ză). Pl. **-æ.** 1704. [mod.L. – Gr. χάλαζα hail; cf. Fr. *chalaze.*] **1.** *Zool.* Each of the two membranous twisted strings by which the yolk-bag of an egg is kept in position; the tread or treadle. **2.** *Bot.* A spot on the seed where the nucleus joins the integuments 1830. Hence **Chala·zal** *a.* **Chalazi·ferous** *a.* bearing the c. or chalazæ.

‖ **Chalazion** (kălēⁱ·ziǫn). Occas. as L. *chalazium.* 1708. [– Gr., dim. of χάλαζα; see prec.] A small pimple or tubercle; *esp.* a stye.

† **Cha·lcanth, chalca·nthum.** 1678. [– L. *chalcanthum* – Gr. χάλκανθον, f. χαλκός copper + ἄνθος flower.] Blue vitriol (sulphate of copper); also, an ink made from it –1718. Hence **Chalca·nthite,** *Min.* native blue vitriol. † **Chalca·nthous** *a.* of the nature of ink or blacking (*rare*).

Chalcedonic (kælsīdǫ·nik), *a.* 1828. [f. CHALCEDONY; see -IC.] Of or belonging to chalcedony.

Chalcedony, cal- (kælse·dəni, kæ·lsīdəni). See also CASSIDOINE, -DONY. ME. [– L. *c(h)alcedonius*, used in the Vulgate as tr. Gr. χαλκηδών, in *Rev.* 21:19, found nowhere else. The supposed connection with Chalcedon in Asia Minor is very doubtful.] *Min.* A precious stone; a crypto-crystalline sub-species of quartz (a true quartz, with some disseminated opal-quartz), having the lustre nearly of wax, and being either transparent or translucent. In mod. lapidary work called variously *agate, cornelian, cat's eye, chrysoprase, onyx, sard,* etc., according to colour and structure.

Chalchuite (tʃæ·ltʃu,əit). 1843. [f. the Mexican name *chalchihuitl* + -ITE[1] 2 b.] *Min.* A green variety of turquoise from Mexico.

Chalcidian (kælsi·diăn). [f. mod.L. *chalcidæ* (f. L. *chalcis* = Gr. χαλκίς a kind of lizard); see -ID[3], -IAN.] *Zool.* Of or pertaining to the family of Chalcidæ or Snake Lizards.

‖ **Chalci·tes.** [L. – Gr. χαλκῖτις copper-ore.] Green vitriol (sulphate of copper). BACON.

Chalco- (kæ·lko). Occas. **chalko-.** Stem and comb. form of Gr. χαλκός copper, brass, used in the names of minerals, as in **Cha·lcocite,** native sulphide of copper, copper glance; **Cha:lcopy·rite** [+ PYRITE], an ore of copper, called yellow or copper pyrites, native sulphide of copper and iron.

Chalcographer (kælkǫ·grăfəɹ). 1662. [f. Gr. χαλκός copper + -GRAPHER; cf. Fr. *chalcographe.*] One who engraves on copper. So **Chalcogra·phic, -al** *a.* of, pertaining to, or of the nature of, chalcography. **Chalco·graphist,** = CHALCOGRAPHER. **Chalco·graphy,** the art of engraving on copper.

Chaldaic (kældē·ik). 1662. [– L. *Chaldaicus* – Gr. χαλδαϊκός, f. χαλδαία (sc. γῆ), subst. use of fem. of χαλδαῖος; see CHALDEE, -IC.] *adj.* Of or pertaining to Chaldæa. *sb.* The language of the Chaldeans. So **Chalda·ical** *a.* **Cha·ldaism,** a C. idiom or mode of speech. † **Cha·ldic** *a.* = CHALDEE.

Chaldean (kældī·ăn). 1581. [f. L. *Chaldæus* (see next) + -AN; see -EAN.] *adj.* Of or pertaining to Chaldæa or the Chaldeans; hence, to occult science 1732. *sb.* A native of Chaldæa, *esp.* (as at Babylon) one skilled in occult learning, astrology, etc.; hence *gen.* a soothsayer, astrologer. (So in Gr. and L.) 1581.

Chaldee (kæ·ldī, kældī·). ME. [repr. L. *Chaldæi* (pl. of *Chaldæus* – Gr. Χαλδαῖος, f. Assyr. *Kaldū*), freq. used for the name of the country *Chaldæa* – Gr. Χαλδαία (sc. γῆ); see CHALDAIC.] *adj.* = CHALDEAN, CHALDAIC. *sb.* **1.** A native of Chaldæa. **2.** The language of the Chaldeans; also the biblical Syriac or Aramaic.

Chalder[1] (tʃǭ·ldəɹ). *Sc.* ME. [– (O)Fr. *chaudière* – late L. *caldaria*, f. *cal(i)dus* hot; superseded by CHALDRON. *Chalder* was a northern word brought to London with the coal trade.] **1.** An obsolete dry measure of capacity; in Scotland 16 bolls or 64 firlots of corn; for lime and coal 32 to 64 imperial bushels. † **2.** In England = CHALDRON, but for coal and lime varying from 32 to 40 bushels –1778.

Chalder[2] (tʃǭ·ldəɹ). [Origin unkn.] *Naut.* A rudder-brace or gudgeon.

† **Chalde·se,** *v.* Also **caldese.** 1664. [perh. f. *Chaldee* or *Chaldees*, with the notion of 'cheat as an astrologer'.] To cheat, trick, take in –1697.

Chaldron (tʃǭ·ldrən, tʃă·drən). 1555. [Earlier forms *chauderne, chaudron*, – OFr. *chauderon* (mod. *chaudron*), augm. of *chaudère, -ière*; see CHALDER[1], -OON. The etymologizing sp. with *l* dates from XVII. See also CAULDRON.] † **1.** = CAULDRON –1750. **2.** A dry measure of 4 quarters or 32 bushels; now only used for coals (36 bushels) 1615.

Chaldron, obs. f. CHAWDRON.

‖ **Chalet** (ʃale). 1817. [– (Swiss) Fr. *chalet*, dim. of OFr. *chasel* farm-stead, dairy :– Rom. **casale*, f. L. *casa* hut, cottage.] **1.** A herdsman's hut on the Swiss mountains; hence, the small wooden cottage of the Swiss peasant; *gen.* a villa built in the style of a Swiss cottage. **2.** = Fr. *chalet de nécessité*, a street lavatory, etc. 1882.

1. On the slopes were innumerable châlets TYNDALL.

Chalice (tʃæ·lis). [– OFr. *chalice* – L. *calix, -ic-* cup, rel. to Gr. κάλυξ CALYX, κύλιξ CYLIX.] **1.** A drinking cup or goblet. (Now only in poetic or elevated language.) Also *fig.* **2.** *spec.* The cup used in the celebration of the Eucharist OE. *transf.* A flower-cup 1650. Hence **Cha·liced** *a.* having a cup-like blossom; contained in a cup.

‖ **Chalicosis** (kælikōᵘ·sis). [– Gr. χάλιξ small stone + -OSIS.] *Med.* Disease of the lungs caused by the inhalation of fine siliceous particles.

Chalk (tʃǭk), *sb.* [OE. **cælc, ċealc* = OS. *calc* (Du. *kalk*), OHG. *kalk* (G. *kalk*), WGmc. – L. *calx, calc-* CALX, lime.] † **1.** ? Lime –1572. **2.** An opaque soft white earthy limestone, consisting chemically of carbonate of lime with some impurities OE. **3.** Applied to other earths resembling chalk 1601. *spec.* Applied to preparations used in the form of crayons for drawing. With *pl.* Also *attrib.* drawn with chalk. 1481. **4.** A score at an ale-house, etc. (formerly written up with chalk); credit, 'tick' 1529. **5.** A mark, line, or score made with chalk, as in various games 1680.

3. *Fuller's c.*: ? fuller's earth. *Brown c.*: umber. *French c.*: a kind of steatite. *Red c.*: a bed of chalk of a red colour in Norfolk; also, ruddle. Two heads in chalks 1832. *attrib.* A c. head of a dog 1883.

Phrases. (*By*) *a long c.*, also *by long chalks, by chalks* (colloq.): in a great degree, by far (see senses 4, 5). *To walk one's chalks* (slang): to be off.

Comb., etc.: **c.-bed,** a stratum of c.; **-drawing,** one executed in c.; **-flint, -fossil,** etc., one found in c.; **-line,** a line rubbed with c., used for laying down straight lines, as a guide in cutting; **-marl,** an argillaceous stratum just beneath the Lower White C.; **-pit, -quarry,** one from which c. is dug; **-white** *a.*

Chalk (tʃǭk), *v.* 1575. [f. prec. sb.] **1.** To manure (land) with chalk. **2.** To rub, mark, or write with chalk 1592. *fig.* To make white or pale as by rubbing with chalk; to blanch 1633.

2. One chalks down nine figures 1823. † *To c. it*: to run up a score. *fig.* Fear..chalk'd her face TENNYSON.

Phr. **Chalk out.** *fig.* † **a.** To mark *out*, as with chalk. **b.** To sketch *out*, adumbrate. **c.** *fig.* To trace *out*, as a course to be followed.

Chalk-stone (tʃǭ·kˌstōᵘn). ME. † **1.** Lime, limestone. † **2.** ? A piece of chalk –1611. **3.** A chalk-like concretion, chiefly of sodium urate, occurring in the tissues and joints, *esp.* of the hands and feet, in severe gout.

Chalky (tʃǭ·ki), *a.* ME. [f. CHALK *sb.* + -Y[1].] **1.** Consisting of, or abounding in, chalk; resembling chalk 1611. **2.** *Pathol.* Of the nature of chalk, or of a CHALK-STONE (sense 3), or containing chalk-stones 1782.

1. The c. cliffs salute their longing eyes FALCONER. C. white flowers 1882. Hence **Cha·lkiness.**

Challenge (tʃæ·lėndʒ), *sb.* [ME. *calenge, chalenge, -ange* :– OFr. *ca-, chalenge* :– L. *calumnia* false accusation; see CALUMNY.] † **1.** An accusation, reproach, objection –1692. **2.** The act of calling to account; *esp.* the act of a sentry in demanding the countersign ME.; in *Hunting*, the opening and crying of hounds at finding the scent. **3.** *Law.* An exception taken, against persons or things; *spec.* an objection made to jurymen in a trial. Also, an exception taken to a vote, etc. 1530. **4.** A calling in question; the being called in question 1820. † **5.** A claim –1750. **6.** An invitation to a trial or contest of any kind; a defiance ME. **7.** *spec.* A summons to fight, *esp.* to single combat or duel 1530. Also *attrib.*

3. *Principal challenge*, mostly in civil actions, a cause of exception allowed at once if found true. *Peremptory c.*, in criminal actions, an exception allowed without cause alleged. *C. to the array*, an exception to the whole panel. *C. to the polls*, an exception to particular jurors. *C. to the favour*, an exception on probable circumstances of suspicion, as acquaintance, and the like. **4.** To bring her title into c. SCOTT. **6.** A c. to scrutiny L. HUNT. **7.** Heere's the C., reade it *Twel. N.* III. iv. 157.

Challenge (tʃæ·lėndʒ), *v.* [– OFr. *ca-, chalengier* :– L. *calumniari* accuse falsely; see CALUMNIATE.] † **1.** *trans.* To accuse, bring a charge against –1693. Also *absol.* To accuse one of –1485. **2.** To reprehend; to call to account. Also *absol.*, in *Hunting*, = OPEN *v.* II. 6. Now only *dial.* exc. of a sentinel. ME. **3.** *Law.* To object to (a juryman, evidence, etc.). Also *absol.* ME. **4.** To call in question ME. **5.** To lay claim to, demand as a right, claim *for* (*arch.* or *Obs.*) ME. Also *fig.* **6.** To summon to a contest of any kind; to defy, dare. (Often *to do*, or *to* an *action.*) 1513. **b.** To invite (hostile or critical action of any kind) 1614. **7.** *spec.* To call upon to answer an imputation by combat 1588. *intr.* or *absol.* ME.

2. On any one approaching his post, he must c. them by the words '*Who comes there?*' 1833. When a hound challenges P. BECKFORD. **4.** To c. the wisdom of a measure HUXLEY. **5.** A Gentleman that challenges the Title of Honourable BENTLEY. To c. place among the [chief] cities of Europe 1673. To c. the admiration of all ages 1787. **6.** I..c. Dagon to the test MILT. *Samson* 1151. **b.** To c. controversy 1882. **7.** *absol.* They c., and encounter breast to breast DRYDEN. Hence **Cha·llengeable** *a.* open to challenge. **Cha:llengee·**, one who is challenged (*rare*). **Cha·llenger,** one who challenges.

Challis (tʃæ·lis, ‖ʃa·li). 1849. [perh. f. Eng. surname *Challis*; in Fr. *challis, chaly(s)*.] A fine silk and worsted fabric, very pliable and without gloss, used for ladies' dresses. Also *attrib.*

† **Chalon.** ME. [app. f. *Châlons-sur-Marne* in France; see SHALLOON.] A blanket for a bed –1616. Hence † **Cha·loner,** a maker of chalons.

‖ **Chaloupe** (ʃalu·p). 1699. [Fr. – Du. *sloep* SLOOP.] A kind of French boat; = SHALLOP.

‖ **Chalumeau** (ʃalümō). 1713. [Fr. :– late L. *calamellus*, dim. of L. *calamus* reed.] **a.** A reed, pipe. **b.** The lowest register of the clarinet.

Chalybean (kælibī·ăn), *a.* [f. L. *chalybeius* of steel + -AN; see next.] Pertaining to the Chalybes, an ancient nation of Asia Minor famous for their skill in working iron. MILT.

Chalybeate (kăli·biĕt), *a.* 1634. [– mod.L. *chalybeatus*, f. L. *chalybs* – Gr. χάλυψ steel; see -ATE[2].] Impregnated or flavoured with iron. As *sb.* A chalybeate medicine or spring 1667. Hence † **Chaly·beate** *v.* to impregnate with iron.

Chalybite (kæ·libəit). 1847. [f. Gr. χάλυψ -υβ- steel + -ITE[1] 2 b.] *Min.* = SIDERITE.

Cham (kæm), *sb.* 1553. [Earlier *Cane, Chane* – Fr. *cham, chan* – Turki *khān* lord, prince; see CHAGAN, KHAN.] An obs. form of KHAN, q.v. Also *transf.* and *fig.* That great C. of literature, Samuel Johnson SMOLLETT.

Cham, chamm (tʃæm), *v.* Still *dial.* ME. [See CHAMP *v.*] **1.** To bite, chew. **2.** To pound, mash. *Sc.*

‖ **Chama** (kē̆ⁱ·mă). 1753. [L. *chama* or *chema* – Gr. χήμη cockle.] *Zool.* A genus of bivalve molluscs, including *C. ˈgigas*, the largest known.

‖ **Chamade** (ʃama·d). 1684. [Fr. – Pg. *chamada*, f. *chamar* :– L. *clamare* to call; see CLAIM.] *Mil.* A signal by beat of drum or sound of trumpet inviting to a parley.

‖ **Chamærops** (kămīᵊ·rǫps). 1852. [L. – Gr. χαμαίρωψ, f. χαμαί on the ground + ῥώψ shrub, bush.] *Bot.* A northern genus of palms, including *C. humilis*, the smallest of the order, and *C. Fortuni.*

‖ **Cha·mbellan.** 1710. The French form of CHAMBERLAIN, used as a foreign title.

Chamber (tʃē̆ⁱ·mbəɹ), *sb.* ME. [– (O)Fr. *chambre* :– L. *camera, camara* – Gr. καμάρα vault; see CAMERA.] **I.** A room (in a house). **1.** An apartment; a private room; now *esp.* a bedroom. (In colloq. use repl. by *room.*) Also *fig.* **2.** *pl.* Sets of rooms occupied by single persons; *esp.* rooms in the Inns of Court by lawyers. **b.** The room in which a judge sits to transact minor business. 1641. **3.** A hall in which a deliberative, legislative, or judicial body meet 1543. **b.** A judicial or deliberative body; now *esp.* one of the divisions of a legislative body, as 'the popular c.', i.e. the House of Commons ME. **4.** The place where the funds of a government, corporation, etc., are (or were) kept; chamberlain's office; treasury. [Cf. med.L. *camera.*] 1632. † **5.** [= med.L. *camera*, Fr. *chambre.*] A province, city, etc., directly subject, and yielding revenue to the king; more loosely: Metropolis; ? royal port –1699. **6.** The hangings and furniture of a chamber. ? *Obs.* 1612. **b.** *euphem.* for *chamber-pot.*

1. They laid her in an vpper c. *Acts* 9:37. *Presence-, audience-c.*: the reception room in a palace. **2.** I have chambers in the Temple STEELE. **3.** *C. of Commerce*, a board organized to protect the interests of commerce. **5.** London..the kings of England's c. HOLLAND.

II. An enclosed space, cavity, etc. **1.** An enclosed space in the body of an animal or plant ME. **2.** An artificial space, cavity, or room for various purposes 1769. **3.** † **a.** A detached charge piece put into the breech of a gun –1627. † **b.** A small piece of ordnance without a carriage, standing on its breech, used to fire salutes –1727. **c.** That part of the bore of a gun in which the charge is placed 1627. **d.** The cavity in a mine for the reception of the powder 1730.

1. The chambers of the brain ME., of a shell 1889. **2.** The c. of a pump (*i.e.* the part in which the piston works) 1769, of a canal lock (*i.e.* the space enclosed between the gates) 1837. **3. b.** 2 *Hen. IV*, II. iv. 57.

Phr. **C. of Dais.** *Sc.* Also **c. of deas.** A parlour; also a best bedroom. (Jam.)

Comb.: **c.-concert,** a concert where c.-music is performed; **-counsel,** private counsel *Wint. T.* I. ii. 237; opinion given by a lawyer in private chambers (see I. 2); a lawyer who gives opinions in private, not in court, so **-counsellor**; **-fellow** (*arch.*), one who shares a room or rooms with another; **-lye,** urine, *esp.* as used for washing; **-milliner,** one who carries on business in a private house, not in a shop; **-music,** music specially fitted for performance in a private room or small audience hall; **-orchestra, -organ,** a small orchestra or organ; **-pot,** a vessel used in a bedroom for urine and slops (often euphemized as *chamber*); **-practice** (*Law*), practice in chambers; **-utensil, -vessel** = *chamber-pot.*

Chamber (tʃē̆ⁱ·mbəɹ), *v.* ME. [f. the sb.] **1.** To place in, or as in, a chamber; to shut *up* (*arch.*) 1575. Also † *fig.* **2.** To form into a chamber or chambers 1674. **3.** To provide (a gun) with a chamber 1708. † **4.** To lodge in, or as in, a chamber 1611. ¶ **5.** To indulge in lewdness 1607.

1. The best blood chamber'd in his bosome SHAKS. Hence **Cha·mbered** *ppl. a.* in senses of sb. and vb.; † also = cambered (see CAMBER *v.*). **Cha·mbering** *vbl. sb.* † the furnishing of a room; † *concr.* hangings –1480; † sexual indulgence –1613; also *attrib.*; the providing (a gun) with a chamber.

Chamber-deacon, -deakin, -deken, etc. ME. [app. f. CHAMBER + DEACON.] **1.** One of the poor clerks, chiefly from Ireland, who frequented the English Universities in the 15th c., and did not belong to any college or hall. Now *Hist.* † **2.** An attendant who kept the chambers of noblemen and others attending court –1483.

Chamberer (tʃē̆ⁱ·mbərəɹ). *arch.* ME. [– AFr. *chamb(e)rer(e* = OFr. *-ier, -iere* (mod. *chambrier, -ière* chamber-maid), f. *chambre* CHAMBER *sb.*; see -ER[2], and cf. late L. *camerarius* chamberlain.] † **1.** A chambermaid –1733. † **2.** A chamberlain, valet –1640. **3.** One who frequents ladies' chambers; a gallant (*arch.*) 1604.

Chamberlain (tʃē̆ⁱ·mbəɹlin). ME. [– OFr. *chamberlain, -lenc* (mod. *chambellan*) – Frank. **kamerling* (whence med.L. *camerlingus*), f. OS. *kamera*; see CHAMBER, -LING[1].] **1. a.** A chamber attendant of a lord or king (*arch.*); also = CHAMBERER 1 (*obs. rare*). **b.** An officer having charge of the private chambers of a sovereign or nobleman. **2.** A steward; an officer who receives the rents and revenues of a corporation or public office (see CHAMBER *sb.* I. 4) ME. † **3.** An attendant at an inn, in charge of the bedchambers –1829.

1. *Lord Great Chamberlain of England*: a hereditary officer, whose duty it is to attend upon and attire the sovereign at his coronation, to furnish Westminster Hall and the Houses of Parliament on state occasions, to attend upon peers and bishops at their doing of homage, etc. *Lord Chamberlain of the Household*: a chief officer, who shares the oversight of all officers of the Royal Household. He appoints the royal tradesmen, etc., has control of the actors at the royal theatres and is the licenser of plays. Hence **Cha·mberlainship,** the office of c.

Chambermaid (tʃē̆ⁱ·mbəɹmēⁱd). 1587. **1.** A female servant in a house or inn, who attends to the bedrooms. † **2.** A lady's maid –1719.

Cha·mber-master. 1851. *Shoemaking.* A shoemaker who works in his own house.

‖ **Chambertin** (ʃaṅbęrtęṅ). 1755. [Fr.; place-name.] A wine, a superior kind of Burgundy.

‖ **Chambranle** (ʃaṅbrā·ṅl'). 1704. [Fr.] *Arch.* 'An ornamental bordering on the sides and tops of doors, windows, and fireplaces' (Gwilt).

Chambrel, var. of CAMBREL (sense 2).

Chameleon (kămī·liən). ME. [– L. *chamæleon* – Gr. χαμαιλέων, f. χαμαί on the ground + λέων lion.] **1.** A saurian reptile of the genus *Chamæleo*, distinguished by a prehensile tail, long tongue, eyes moving independently, but esp. by their power of changing the colour of the skin, varying through different shades of yellow, red, grey, brown, and dull inky blue. Formerly supposed to live on air (*Haml.* III. ii. 98). Also *fig.* (= variable person.) 1586. **2.** One of the southern circumpolar constellations 1835. Also *attrib.*

Comb.: **c. fly,** *Stratiomys chamæleon*; **-like** *a.* and *adv.*

White C. (*Bot.*), *Carlina gummifera*; **Black C.,** *Cardopatium corymbosum*. *Mineral c.*, or *c. mineral* (*Chem.*), manganate of potassium (K_2MnO_4), the solution of which in water changes colour, on exposure to the air, from deep green to deep purple, owing to the formation of the permanganate ($KMnO_4$). Hence **Chame:leo·nic** *a.* given to change. **Chame·leonize** *v.* to change colour like a c. (*rare*).

Chamfer (tʃæ·mfəɹ), *sb.* 1601. [f. CHAMFER *v.*] † **1.** A small groove, channel, etc. –1708. **2.** The surface produced by bevelling off a square edge or corner equally on both sides; if made concave, it is called a *hollow c.* 1842.

Chamfer (tʃæ·mfəɹ), *v.* 1565. [Back-formation from *chamfering* – (with assim. to -ING[1]) Fr. *chamfrain*, f. *chant* edge (see CANT *sb.*[1]) + *fraint*, pa. pple. of OFr. *fraindre* :– L. *frangere* break.] **1.** To channel, flute, furrow. **2.** To make a chamfer on; to bevel *away, off*; var. † **Cha·mfret** *v.* 1688. Hence **Cha·mfering** *vbl. sb.* (? the earliest word, and directly – Fr. *chamfrein, -frin*).

Cha·mfrain, -fron. *arch.* 1465. [– (O)Fr. *chamfrein*, perh. for **chafrein*, f. OFr. *chafresner* (= Pr. *capfrenar*) put on a bridle, f. *chef* head (see CHIEF) + *frein* :- L. *frenum* bridle, bit.] The frontlet of a barded horse.

Chamlet(t, -lot, -lyt, obs. ff. of CAMLET.

Chamois (ʃæ·moi, ʃæ·mi, ‖ ʃamwā). 1560. [-(O)Fr. *chamois,* prob. ult. from Swiss Romanic. Cf. Gallo-L. *camox* (Polemius Silvius, V).] **1.** A capriform antelope (*A. rupicapra* or *Rupicapra tragus*), inhabiting the loftiest parts of the Alps, Pyrenees, Taurus, etc. Its agility and keen scent make its chase most difficult. Also *attrib.* **2.** A soft leather, orig. prepared from the skin of the chamois, now also from the skins of sheep, goats, deer, etc. More fully *chamois- (shamoy-, shammy-) leather.* See SHAMMY. 1575. *attrib.* as a material 1603. **3.** Of the colour of this leather, fawn-coloured 1882. Hence **Chamois** *v.* [Fr. *chamoiser*] to prepare leather in imitation of c.-leather.

Chamoisite (ʃæ·mwăzəit). 1832. [f. *Chamoison,* in Switzerland, + -ITE[1] 2 b.] *Min.* A hydrous silicate of iron often occurring in grains.

Chamomile, -mel, vars. of CAMOMILE.

† **Champ,** *sb.*[1] ME. [-(O)Fr. *champ* in same senses :- L. *campus* field; cf. CAMP *sb.*] **1.** A field -1816. **2.** *Her.* The field of a shield -ME. **3.** The ground, as in embroidery, painting, etc. 1573.

1. *Champ clos, c. of battle*: the ground enclosed for a judicial duel, or tourney; also a battle-field.

Champ (tʃæmp), *sb.*[2] 1604. [f. CHAMP *v.*] **1.** The action of champing. *dial.* Appetite. **2.** *dial.* Anything champed or mashed 1825.

Champ (tʃæmp), *sb.*[3] 1830. [- Hindi *champa* = CHAMPAC.] The timber of the Champac tree. Also *champ-wood.*

Champ (tʃæmp), *v.* 1530. [prob. imit.] **1.** To chew by vigorous and noisy action of the jaws; to munch. Also *fig.* **2.** To bite upon (anything hard) 1577. *intr.* and *absol.* 1558. † **3.** To gnash (the teeth), close the jaws with violence and noise -1791. **4.** *Sc.* To crash, mash, pound; to trample underfoot 1788.

1. Champing golden grain the horses stood TENNYSON. **2.** To c. the bit GODWIN, a bullet 1655. *absol.* The war-horse..Champs SCOTT.

Champac (tʃæ·mpæ̆k, tʃɒ·mpɒk). 1770. [- Hind. *champak* (Skr. *champaka*).] A species of Magnolia (*Michelia champaca*), an Indian tree, bearing orange-coloured highly fragrant flowers.

The Champak odours fail SHELLEY.

Champagne (ʃæmpē[i]·n). 1664. [See CHAMPAIGN, CAMPAIGN.] A province of eastern France; hence, a well-known wine, white and red, and still or sparkling, made in this district. Also *attrib.*

French kick-shaws, cellery, and Champain 1688.

Champaign (tʃæ·mpē[i]n; occas., XIX only, tʃæmpē[i]·n). ME. [- OFr. *champagne* :- late L. *campania,* fem. sg. and n. pl., subst. uses of adj., f. L. *campus* level field. See CAMPAIGN.]

A. *sb.* **1.** An expanse of level, open country. † **2.** Unenclosed or common land -1649. † **3.** The field of military operations -1665. **4.** *transf.* and *fig.* 1596.

1. Looking round the c. wide KEATS. (Without *pl.* or *article*): Fair Champain with less rivers intervein'd MILT. *P.R.* III. 257. (With *the*; without *pl.*): Where the mountains sink down upon the c. SCOTT. **4.** Through Heav'ns wide champain MILT. *P.L.* VI. 2.

B. *adj.* (or *sb.* used *attrib.*) **1.** Of the nature of a champaign; level and open 1523. **3.** Field-; of champaign land 1599.

† **Champain.** 1562. [Cf. Fr. *champagne* 'the lower third of the shield'.] *Her.* A broken or deflected line in an ordinary -1708.

‖ **Champart** (ʃaṅpar). 1651. [(O)Fr. *champart* :- legal L. *campi pars* (*part-*). See CHAMPERTY.] A form of tenure, in which the landlord receives a fixed share of the produce. Still in use in the Channel Islands.

Champed, *ppl. a.*[1] In senses of CHAMP *v.*

† **Champed,** *ppl. a.*[2] *Sc.* **champit.** 1501. [perh. f. CHAMP *sb.*[1] + -ED[2].] Having raised figures; embossed, diapered. (Jam.)

Champer (tʃæ·mpəɹ). 1599. [f. CHAMP *v.* + -ER[1]. One who or that which champs, chews, or mashes.

† **Cha·mpertor.** 1500. [- AFr. *champartour,* OFr. *-tëor,* f. *champarter,* f. (O)Fr. *champart* CHAMPART.] One guilty of champerty -1668.

Cha·mpertous *a.* 1641. [f. next + -OUS.] Of the nature of champerty.

Champerty (tʃæ·mpəɹti). ME. [- AFr. *champartie,* f. (O)Fr. *champart*; see CHAMPART.] † **1.** Division of lordship -1532. **2.** *Law.* The illegal proceeding, whereby a party not naturally concerned in a suit engages to help one of the litigants to prosecute it, on condition that, in the event of success, he is to receive a share of the property in dispute ME.; an act or case of champerty 1450. Also *fig.*

1. Thus may ye seen þat wysdom ne richesse.. Ne may with Venus holde champartie CHAUCER. ¶ Lydgate, followed by others, took this phrase to mean 'To hold contest *against,* resist'.

† **Champian, -ion,** *a.* and *sb.* 1523. A var. of CHAMPAIGN, -PAIN, in all senses and constructions -1751.

Champignon, -pinion (tʃæ̆mpi·niən, ʃæm-). 1578. [- Fr. *champignon,* in OFr. *champaignon, -ol,* f. *champagne* with dim. suff.; see CHAMPAIGN.] orig. Fungi or mushrooms generally; in 18th c. edible mushrooms, esp. *Agaricus campestris*; subseq. only the Fairy Ring Agaric.

Champine, var. of CHAMPAIGN, etc.

Champion (tʃæ·mpiən), *sb.*[1] ME. [- (O)Fr. *champion* :- med.L. *campio, -ōn-* ('*campiones* gladiatores, pugnatores', Isidore), f. *campus* field; cf. CAMP *sb.*[1]] **1.** A fighting man; a stout fighter. Also *fig.* **2.** One who fights on behalf of another, or of any cause ME.; one who fights in 'wager of battle' in his own cause 1593. *fig.* and *transf.* ME. **3.** One who has defeated all opponents in any trial of strength or skill, and is open to contend with any new competitor 1825; used *transf.* of animals, plants, etc. 1880. Also *attrib.*

1. A stouter C. neuer handled Sword 1 *Hen. VI,* III. iv. 19. **2.** God will raise me up a c. SCOTT. To heauen, the widdowes C. *Rich. II,* I. ii. 43. The c. of vaccination 1806. **3.** Five tons of Scotch Champions 1880. *attrib.* C. fighting-cock 1860, pugilist 1887. Hence **Cha·mpioness,** a female c. **Cha·mpionless** *a.*

Champion, *sb.*[2] and *a.*; see CHAMPIAN.

Champion (tʃæ·mpiən), *v.* 1605. [f. CHAMPION *sb.*[1]] † **1.** To challenge to a contest (*rare*) -1821. **2.** To fight for; to defend or protect as champion 1820. Also *fig.*

1. *Macb.* III. i. 72. **2.** Championed or unchampioned, thou diest by the stake and fagot SCOTT. *fig.* To c. a cause 1844, an idea DICKENS.

Championize (tʃæ·mpiənəiz), *v. rare.* 1598. [See -IZE.] † *intr.* To play the champion -1637; *trans.* to act as champion of 1840.

Championship (tʃæ·mpiənʃip). 1825. [See -SHIP.] **1.** The position or office of a champion; advocacy, defence 1840. **2.** The position of champion in any contest or trial 1825. Also *attrib.*

Chance (tʃɑns), *sb.* [ME. *chea(u)nce, chaunce* - AFr. *ch(e)aunce,* OFr. *chëance* (mod. *chance*), f. *chëoir* fall, befall :- Rom. **cadēre* for L. *cadere* fall. Cf. CADENCE.] **1.** The happening of events; the way in which things fall out; fortune; case; a fortuitous circumstance; = ACCIDENT 1. **2.** (with *pl.*) A fortuitous event or occurrence; often a mischance (*arch.*) ME. † **3.** (One's) hap, luck, lot -1674. **4.** An opportunity ME. **5.** A possibility or probability: as distinct from a certainty. *Math.* = PROBABILITY; so also *theory* or *doctrine of chances.* 1778. **6.** Absence of design or assignable cause, fortuity; often spoken of as a cause of events; = ACCIDENT 2. 1526.

1. The c. of war Is equal, and the slayer oft is slain BRYANT. It was a c. that happened to vs *Sam.* 6:9. **2.** All the changes and chances of this mortal life *Bk. Com. Prayer.* **3.** *Twel. N.* III. iv. 177. **4.** A change of climate is his only c. BURKE. **5.** The chances are a hundred to one that [etc.] EMERSON.

Phrases. *By chance*: As it falls or fell out; without design. *On the c.*: acting on the possibility (*of* or *that*..); see sense 5. *To take one's c.* to take what may befall one, to risk it; to seize one's opportunity (see sense 4). *The main c.*: † **a.** the paramount issue; **b.** that which is of chief importance; now *esp.* the chance of gain, one's own interests. (A cant phrase; see further under MAIN.) *To stand a (good, fair) c.*: see STAND.

B. *attrib.* or *adj.* That occurs or is by chance; casual, incidental 1676.

C. as *adv.* By chance, haply 1595.

Comb. (cf. B), = by chance, casual, -ly; as *c.-comer*; also **-child,** an illegitimate child; **-wise** *adv.*

Chance (tʃɑns), *v.* ME. [f. prec. sb.] **1.** *intr.* To come about by chance. Often with *it* preceding the vb. and the subject cl. following it. *arch.* **2.** To happen to come (*on* or *upon*). Somewhat *arch.* 1536. † **3.** To speed, have luck -1553. **4.** *trans.* To risk, take one's chance of (*colloq.*) 1859. ¶ In *How chance* = 'how chances it that', *chance* takes no inflection, and is almost an adv. *Merry W.* V. v. 230.

1. Bare graine, it may c. of wheat 1 *Cor.* 15:37. **2.** Wee chanced on a..shippe..bound for Callis 1630. **4.** We'll c. it 1870.

Chanceable (tʃɑ·nsăb'l), *a. arch.* 1549. [f. CHANCE *v.* + -ABLE.] Fortuitous. Hence **Cha·nceableness. Cha·nceably** *adv.*

Chanceful (tʃɑ·nsful), *a* 1591. [f. CHANCE *sb.* + -FUL.] Dependent on chance (*arch.*) 1594; †risky -1610; eventful 1849. Hence **Cha·ncefully** *adv.*

Chancel (tʃɑ·nsĕl). ME. [- OFr. *chancel* (now latinized as *cancel*) :- L. *cancelli* (pl.) lattice, grating, dim. of *cancer* lattice, perh. dissim. form of *carcer* barrier, prison.] The eastern part of a church, appropriated to the use of the officiating clergy, and separated from the other parts by a screen, railing, etc. Also † *transf.* of the temple at Jerusalem, heathen temples, etc. *Comb.* **c.-table,** a communion-table. Hence **Cha·ncelled** *pa. pple.* and *ppl. a.* placed in, or having, a c.

Chancellery, -ory (tʃɑ·nsĕləri). ME. [- (O)Fr. *chancellerie,* f. *chancelier*; see CHANCELLOR, -ERY.] **1.** The position or dignity of a chancellor. **2.** A chancellor's court or office, with its officials 1803. **3.** The office of a court secretary or notary 1683. **4.** The office attached to an embassy or consulate 1869. **5.** The building or room occupied by the chancellor's office 1831.

4. The Chancelleries of the Great Powers 1881.

Chancellor (tʃɑ·nsĕləɹ). late OE. [Earliest forms *canceler, cancheler,* later *chanceler, -our, -or* - AFr. *canceler, chanceler,* OFr. *cancelier,* (also mod.) *chancelier,* semi-learned - late L. *cancellarius* porter, secretary, f. *cancelli* (see CHANCEL) + *-arius* -ER[2]; the L. word was orig. applied to an officer whose position was *ad cancellos* at the bars.]

[In the Eastern Empire this officer had risen to be a secretary or notary, and, later, had judicial functions. Edward the Confessor introduced the office into England, and its importance increased under the Norman Kings. From the Roman Empire the office also passed into the Church.]

I. *gen.* Secretary, official secretary: † **a.** of the King of England -1500; **b.** of ancient potentates ME.; **c.** of great lords SHAKS. **d.** Occas. used as repr. Fr. *chancelier,* the chief secretary of an embassy 1788.

II. Mod. uses.

1. *Chancellor of England,* also called *Lord C.,* and *Lord High C.*: orig. the *King's C.,* or official Secretary (see I). He is the highest judicial functionary in England, and ranks after princes of the blood and the archbishop of Canterbury; he is keeper of the Great Seal, is styled 'Keeper of the King's conscience', and is prolocutor of the House of Lords; he presides in the Chancery Division of the Supreme Court; appoints all justices of the peace; is the general guardian of infants, lunatics, and idiots; etc. late OE.

2. *C. of the Exchequer*: the highest finance minister of the British government: historically, he is the under-treasurer of the Exchequer ME.

3. *C. of the Duchy of Lancaster*: a minister of the crown, who presides in the Duchy Court of Lancaster, deciding on all matters of equity connected with lands held of the crown in that Duchy 1553.

4. *C. of a chapter*: **a.** *of a cathedral*: one of the four chief dignitaries in the cathedrals of old foundation. He applies the seal, writes letters, etc. 1578; **b.** *of an order of Knighthood*: the officer who seals the commissions and mandates of the chapter and assembly of the knights, keeps the register, and delivers their acts under the seal of their order 1577.

5. The titular head of a university. The actual duties are performed in the English Universities by a *Vice-C.* ME. **6.** In *Scotland,* the foreman of a jury 1762.

III. In foreign countries.

1. Most of the European countries have or formerly had a chief minister with this title; it was abolished in France at the Revolution; it was retained in Austro-Hungary from the Holy

Roman Empire, and used in the new German Empire, as title of the President of the Federal Council, who had the general conduct of the imperial administration.
2. *U.S.* The title of certain judges of courts of chancery or equity, established by the statutes of separate states.
Hence **Cha·ncellorate, Cha·ncellorshi:p,** the office of c.

Chance-medley (tʃɑ:ns,me·dli). 1494. [– AFr. *chance medlee*, i.e. CHANCE *sb.* + *medlee* fem. pa. pple. of *medler* mix; see MEDDLE.] **1.** *Law.* Casualty not *purely* accidental, but of a mixed character. Also *fig.* **2.** Haphazard action into which chance largely enters. (*Erron.* put for 'pure chance', and for 'a fortuitous medley'.) 1583. Also *attrib.*
1. *Manslaughter by chance-medley* (called later *Chance-medley*): homicide by misadventure. **2.** Left to the guidance of unreason and chance medley JOWETT.

Chancery (tʃɑ·nsĕri). ME. [A reduced form of late ME. *cha(u)ncel(e)rie* CHANCELLERY.] † **1.** Chancellorship –1658. **2.** The court of the Lord Chancellor of England, the highest court of judicature next to the House of Lords; but, since 1873, a division of the High Court of Justice ME. **b.** Applied to similar courts elsewhere; in U.S. 'a court of Equity' (Webster) 1555. **c.** An office in the General Register House, Edinburgh (formerly called *chancellary*), in which is kept a record of writs, crown charters, etc. 1807. Also *fig.* **3.** A court of record; archives; also *fig.* 1523. **4.** = CHANCELLERY 2. 1561. **5.** = CHANCELLERY 5. 1578. **6.** *Pugilism.* (From the control of the Court of Chancery, and the certainty of cost and loss to property 'in chancery'.) The position of the head when held under the opponent's left arm to be pommelled; hence *fig.* an awkward predicament. 1832.
2. The heiress is a ward in C. 1889. **6.** He'll not 'put his head in chancery', that's clear MARRYAT.

Chancre (ʃæ·nkəɹ). 1605. [– Fr. *chancre*, semi-learned – L. *cancer, cancr-* crab; see CANCER, CANKER.] A venereal ulcer. Hence **Cha·ncriform** *a.* of the form or nature of a c. **Cha·ncrous** *a.*

Chancroid (ʃæ·ŋkroid). 1861. [f. prec. + -OID.] A synonym of *soft chancre.* Also *attrib.*

Chancy (tʃɑ·nsi), *a.* 1513. [f. CHANCE *sb.* + -Y[1].] **1.** *Sc.* Lucky. **2.** *Sc.* Lucky to meddle with; 'canny' 1774. **3.** Uncertain, risky, untrustworthy (*colloq.*) 1860. Hence **Cha·nciness,** casual quality.

Chandelier (ʃændĕlīᵊ·ɹ). 1663. [– Fr. *chandelier*, f. *chandelle*; see CANDLE, -IER.] **1.** An ornamental branched support to hold a number of lights (originally candles), usu. hung from the ceiling 1736. **2.** *Mil.* 'A wooden frame, which was filled with fascines, to form a traverse in sapping' (Stocqueler) 1663. Also *attrib.*

Chandler (tʃɑ·ndləɹ). [– AFr. *chaundeler*, OFr. *chandelier* candle-maker or -seller, f. *chandele* CANDLE; see -ER[2].] † **1.** A candlestick; a chandelier. (Chiefly *north.*) –1733. **2.** One who makes or sells candles ME. **3.** Hence, A retailer of provisions, groceries, etc.: often contemptuous. In *comb.* = dealer, as in *corn-chandler*, SHIP-CHANDLER. 1583.
3. Another steps into the chandler's shop, to purchase a pound of butter SCOTT. Hence † **Cha·ndlerly** *a.* c.-like, pertaining to a c. MILT. † **Cha·ndling** *vbl. sb.* the business of a c. (*rare*).

Chandlery (tʃɑ·ndləri). 1601. [f. CHANDLER + -Y[3]; see -ERY.] **1.** A place where candles, etc., are kept. **2.** The commodities sold by a chandler (also in pl. *chandleries*) 1601.

‖ **Chandoo, -du** (tʃændū·). 1847. [Hindi.] A preparation of opium used in China for smoking.

† **Cha·ndry.** 1478. [contr. f. *chandlery*; cf. *chancery.*] **1.** = CHANDLERY 1. –1668. **2.** = CHANDLERY 2. 1651. **3.** Candlemas 1478.

‖ **Chanfrin** (ʃæ̃·nfrĕn). 1730. [– Fr. *chanfrein*; see CHAMFRAIN.] The fore-part of a horse's head. (Dicts.)

Change (tʃēⁱndʒ), *sb.* ME. [– AFr. *chaunge*, (O)Fr. *change*, f. *changer* :– late L. (Rom.) *cambiare*, f. L. *cambire* exchange, barter, prob. of Celtic origin.] **1.** The act or fact of changing (see CHANGE *v.* 1, 2); substitution or succession of one thing in place of another; substitution of other conditions, variety. † **2.** Exchange, *esp.* of merchandise –1606. **3.** A place where merchants meet for the transaction of business, an exchange. (Since 1800, erron. written *'Change*, as if for *Exchange.*) ME. **4.** Alteration in the state or quality of anything; variation, mutation ME. **5.** That which is or may be substituted for another of the same kind. (In this sense occas. with pl. *change.*) 1592. **6.** Money given in exchange for coins, notes, etc., of another kind; hence generally, small money. Hence the balance returned when anything is paid for by a piece of money greater than its price. 1622. *slang.* Something given or taken in return, as in *take your c. out of that!* 1830. **7.** *spec.* in *pl.* † **a.** *Math.* Permutations –1751. **b.** *Bell-ringing.* The different orders in which a peal of bells may be rung 1669. **8.** *Sc.* An ale-house; = CHANGE-HOUSE 1730.
1. C. of Consuls COWLEY. Our fathers did, for c., to France repair DRYDEN. I waite, till my c. come *Job* 14: 14. † *To put the c. upon*: to deceive, mislead (a person). **2.** *Much Ado* IV. i. 185. **4.** C. is the law of organic life 1858. *Lear* I. i. 291. *C. of life*: the period in the life of a woman when menstruation is about to cease. The changes of the Moone *Oth.* III. iii. 178. **5.** Thirtie sheetes, and thirtie c. of garments *Judg.* 14:12. **6.** C. for a guinea SHERIDAN. No c. given 1889. **7.** Four bells admit twenty-four changes in ringing 1669.
Phr. *To ring the changes* (sense 7): *fig.* to go through all the possible variations of any process, set of words, argument, etc. (Constr. *on, upon*; now usu. contemptuous.) (*b*) *slang.* To substitute bad money for good. *Comp.* **c.-wheel,** one of a set having varying numbers of cogs of the same pitch, used to connect the main arbor of the lathe with the feed-screw.

Change (tʃēⁱndʒ), *v.* [ME. – (O)Fr. *changer*; see prec.] **1.** *trans.* To put or take another (or others) instead of; *spec.* to give or procure money of another kind in exchange for. *intr.* To change one's clothes (*colloq.*) 1634. **2.** With pl. obj.: To quit one and take another, as *to change carriages* 1670. Also *intr.* or *ellipt.* **3.** *trans.* To give and receive reciprocally, interchange. (Now repl. by *exchange*, exc. *dial., arch.*, and *poet.*, and in 'change places', etc.) **4.** *intr.* To make an exchange 1567. **5.** *trans.* To render different, alter, transmute. Also with *into* or *to.* ME. **6.** *intr.* (for *refl.*) To become different, alter. Also with *into* or *to.* ME. Of the moon: (*a*) To pass through her phases. (*b*) To pass through the phase of new moon; occas. of full moon. ME. † *spec.* To change countenance. SHAKS. **7.** *intr.* To be shifted or transferred (*rare*; occas. with *about, over*, etc.) ME.
1. To c. one's things 1805, a Rauen for a Doue *Mids. N.* II. ii. 114, a guinea SCOTT, English gold 1876. *intr.* After dinner I..washed and changed COLERIDGE. **3.** Wilt thou c. Fathers? *A.Y.L.* I. iii. 93. I scorn to c. my state † *with kings* (*i.e.* with that of kings) SHAKS. **4.** But might I of Jove's nectar sip I would not c. for thine B. JONS. **5.** To c. one's purpose PALEY. To c. (or *turn*) milk (*colloq.*). **6.** I am the Lord, I c. not *Malachi* 3: 6. And every winter c. to spring TENNYSON.
Phrases. *To c. arms*: (*Mil.*) to shift the rifle from one shoulder to the other. *To c. front*: (orig. *Mil.*) to face in another direction; usu. *fig.* *To c. hands* (see sense 2): to pass from one person's possession to another's. *To c. hand* or *c. a horse*: (*Horsemanship*) to turn the horse's head from right to left or *vice versa.* *To c. one's note* or *tune*: to alter one's manner of speaking, to speak more respectfully (*colloq.*). *To c. sides*: see sense 2. *To chop and c.*: see CHOP *v.*[2]

Changeable (tʃēⁱ·ndʒăb'l), *a.* ME. [– (O)Fr *changeable*; see CHANGE *v.*, -ABLE.] **1.** That may change or be changed (by others); subject to change; mutable, variable, inconstant. **2.** Showing different colours in different aspects; shot, changing-coloured (*arch.*) 1480. Also as *sb.* [sc. *person* or *thing.*] (*rare.*)
1. C. weather 1885, places of meeting D'ISRAELI. **2.** C. sylke 1550. Hence **Changeabi·lity, Cha·ngeableness,** the quality of being c. **Cha·ngeably** *adv.* in a c. or changing manner.

Changeful (tʃēⁱ·ndʒful), *a.* 1606. [f. CHANGE *sb.* + -FUL.] Full of change; variable, inconstant. (Chiefly *poet.*)
The c. year KEBLE. **Cha·ngeful-ly** *adv.*, **-ness.**

Cha·nge-house. *Sc.* 1620. [f. the sbs.] A small inn or alehouse. (Perh. a wayside inn at which horses were changed.)

Changeless (tʃēⁱ·ndʒlĕs), *a.* 1580. [f. CHANGE *sb.* + -LESS.] Without change, unchanging, immutable.
Changelesse fate HEALEY. **Cha·ngeless-ly** *adv.*, **-ness.**

Changeling (tʃēⁱ·ndʒliŋ), *sb.* (*a.*) 1555. [f. CHANGE *v.* + -LING[1].] **1.** One given to change; a waverer, turncoat (*arch.*). **2.** A person (*esp.* a child) or thing (surreptitiously) put in exchange for another 1561. Also *attrib.* **3.** A half-witted person (*arch.*) 1642. † **4.** *adj.* Variable –1702.
1. That c. the Moon HOWELL. **2.** *Haml.* V. ii. 53. Such, men do chaungelings call, so chaung'd by Faeries theft SPENSER. *attrib.* A little c. boy *Mids. N.* II. i. 120. **3.** Just like a fool or c. PEPYS.

Cha·ngement. *rare.* 1584. [– (O)Fr. *changement*; see CHANGE *v.*, -MENT.] Change.

Changer (tʃēⁱ·ndʒəɹ). [ME. *changeour* – AFr. *changëour*, OFr. *changëor* (mod. *changeur*), in med.L. *cambiator*; see CHANGE *v.*, -ER[2]; also immed. f. CHANGE *v.* + -ER[1].] **1.** One who or that which changes anything; see CHANGE *v.* 1, 5. † **2.** A money-changer –1611. **3.** An inconstant person (*rare*) 1605.

Chank (tʃæŋk). 1698. [– Hindi *çankh*, partly through Pg. *chanco, chanquo.*] A large kind of shell (*Turbinella rapa*) used by the Hindus for offering libations, etc., and for cutting into ornaments. Also *attrib.*

Channel (tʃæ·nĕl), *sb.*[1] [– OFr. *chanel*, partly latinized var. of *chenel* :– L. *canalis* pipe, groove, channel, f. *canna* pipe, CANE; see -EL[2], CANAL.]
I. 1. The hollow bed of running waters; also, the bed of the sea, etc. † **2.** A stream –1705. **3.** A gutter. (Still common locally.) ME. **4.** *Geog.* A piece of water, somewhat wider than a strait, connecting two larger pieces, usually seas 1553. *The Channel*: *spec.* the English Channel (Fr. *La Manche*). † **5.** = CANAL –1683. **6.** A tube or tubular passage, usually for liquids or fluids ME.
1. Flye from thy chanell Thames 1563. **3.** Overturned in the c. as we were going to the playhouse VANBRUGH.
II. *fig.* from I. **1.** Course in which anything moves outward; line of action, thought, etc. 1631. **2.** That through which information, news, trade, etc., passes; means, agency 1537.
1. The world went on in the old c. SWIFT. **2.** The great Channels of Trade 1719.
III. *transf.* **1.** A groove or furrow; *spec.* in *Arch.* a fluting of a column 1682. † **2.** The neck; the throat. (Cf. CANNEL-BONE.) –1590. **3.** *Sc.* Gravel 1743.
Comb.: **c.-bill,** an Australian bird, *Scythrops novæ hollandiæ*; † **-bone** = CANAL-BONE; **-stone,** a stone used in paving gutters.

Cha·nnel, *sb.*[2] 1769. [alt. of CHAIN-*wale* (WALE *sb.*[1]); cf. *gunnel* for GUNWALE.] *Naut.* One of the broad thick planks projecting horizontally from the ship's side, nearly abreast of the masts.
Comb.: **c.-plate** = *chain-plate*; **-wale,** one of the strakes worked between the gun-deck and the upper deck ports of large ships.

Channel (tʃæ·nĕl), *v.* 1596. [f. CHANNEL *sb.*[1]] **1.** *trans.* To form channels in; to wear or cut into channels; to furrow, groove. **2.** To cut out as a channel 1816. **3.** To convey through or as through a channel 1648. † **4.** *intr.* To pass by (or as by) a channel –1664.
1. No more shall trenching Warre channell her fields 1 *Hen. IV*, I. i. 7.

Channelled, -eled (tʃæ·nĕld), *ppl. a.* 1567. [f. CHANNEL *sb.*[1] and *v.*] **1.** Having channels or grooves; having a gutter; in *Bot.* = CANALICULATE. **2.** Conveyed along a channel; formed with a channel 1796.

Cha·nnelling, -eling, *vbl. sb.* 1580. [f. as prec. + -ING[1].] **1.** Channelled work; grooving. **2.** Making of channels; providing with a gutter 1885.

Cha·nnelly, -ely, *a.* *Obs.* exc. *Sc.* 1615. [f. CHANNEL *sb.*[1] III. 3 + -Y[1].] Gravelly.

Cha·nnelure. = CANNELURE.

‖ **Chanson** (ʃā̃nsoṅ). [(O)Fr. :– L. *cantio, -ōn-*; see CHANT *sb.*] A song (French, or of France). *Haml.* II. ii. 438.

‖ **Chansonette** (ʃansone·t). 1813. [Fr.; dim. of prec.] A little song.
The Miller's maid Colette Sung, while he supped, her c. S. ROGERS.

Chant (tʃɑnt), *sb.* Also **chaunt.** 1671. [f. CHANT *v.*; cf. (O)Fr. *chant* :– L. *cantus* song.] **1.** A song, a melody; singing. *poet.* (and in rogues' cant). **2.** *Mus.* A short melody or phrase to which the Psalms, Canticles, etc., are sung in public worship 1789; a psalm, etc., so chanted 1856. **3.** A measured monotonous song; the musical recitation of words 1815; a distinctive intonation 1848.

1. C. of tuneful birds MILT. *P.R.* II. 290. **3.** The low monotonous c. of an Arab party 1882.

The *Anglican c.* (derived from the old Gregorian) is either single or double. A *single c.* is sung to one verse of a psalm, and consists of two strains, of 3 and 4 bars respectively, each beginning with a reciting-note. A *double c.* has twice the length of a single one, and is sung to two verses.

Chant (tʃɑnt), *v.* ME. [– (O)Fr. *chanter* :– L. *cantare*, frequent. of *canere* sing.] **1.** *intr.* To sing, warble (*arch.* or *poet.*). Also *transf.* **2.** *trans.* To utter musically. Chiefly *poet.* 1588. **3.** To celebrate in song. *poet.* 1583. **4.** *Mus.* To recite musically, intone; to sing to a CHANT (sense 2). *intr.* ME.; *trans.* 1526. **5.** *fig.* To talk monotonously 1572. **6.** *slang* (*trans.*) To cry up (a horse) fraudulently 1816.

1. To c. to the sound of the viol *Amos* 6:5. **2.** [The wild swan] chanted a melody loud and sweet TENNYSON. **5.** To c. of prerogatives MILT. To c. the praises of the Darwinian system 1885. Hence **Cha·ntable** *a.*

‖ **Chantage** (ʃɑ̃nta·ʒ, tʃɑ·ntėdʒ). 1874. [Fr.] A mode of extorting money by threatening to make scandalous revelations.

‖ **Chantant** (ʃɑ̃ntaṅ, tʃɑ·ntănt), *a.* 1789. [Fr., pres. pple. of *chanter* CHANT *v.*; see -ANT.] Of a singing style, melodious, tuneful.

†‖ **Chantepleure.** ME. only. [Fr., f. *chanter* sing + *pleurer* weep.] Name of a French poem addressed to those who sing in this world and shall weep in the next; hence, a mixture of joy and sorrow.

Chanter (tʃɑ·ntəɹ). [– AFr. *chauntour*, OFr. *chantëor* (mod. *chanteur*) :– L. *cantator* singer; see CHANT *v.*, -ER[2]; in sense 1, aphet. f. AFr. *enchauntour* ENCHANTER.] † **1.** A magician. ME. only. **2.** One who chants or sings; a chorister; a precentor ME. **3.** The finger-pipe of a bagpipe, on which the melody is played 1631. **4.** The Hedge-sparrow (*Accentor modularis*) 1865. **6.** One who sells horses fraudulently 1836. Hence **Cha·ntership,** the office of a c.

‖ **Chanterelle**[1]. 1601. [Fr.] † **1.** A decoy bird. **2.** The highest string of a musical instrument 1878.

Chanterelle[2] (tʃɑ·ntĕre:l). 1775. [– Fr. *chanterelle* – mod.L. *cantharellus*, dim. of *cantharus* – Gr. χάνθαρος drinking-vessel; see -EL[2].] The edible fungus *Cantharellus cibarius.*

Chant(e)y, var. ff. of SHANTY[2].

Chanticleer (tʃɑ·ntiklīᵊɹ). ME. [– OFr. *chantecler* (mod. *chanteclair*), name of the cock in *Reynard the Fox.*] A proper name applied to a cock; but now mostly written without a capital. (Cf. *Bruin*, etc.)

Sche had a cok hight Chaunticlere CHAUCER.

‖ **Chantier.** 1880. [Canadian Fr.] SHANTY[1].

Chantress (tʃɑ·ntrės). ME. [Sense 1: aphet. f. ENCHANTRESS; sense 2: – OFr. *chanteresse*; see CHANTER, -ESS[1].] † **1.** A female magician. ME. only. **2.** A female chanter or singer; also of birds, etc. (*arch.* or *poet.*) 1450.

Chantry (tʃɑ·ntri). ME. [– AFr. *chaunterie*, OFr. *chanterie*, f. *chanter* sing; see CHANT *v.*, -ERY, -RY.] † **1.** Chanting (of the mass.) ME. only. † **2.** Incantation –1460. **3.** An endowment for the maintenance of priests to sing masses, usually for the soul of the founder. Also, the body of priests so endowed. ME. **b.** A chapel or altar so endowed ME.

Chaos (kē·ǫs). ME. [– Fr. *chaos* or L. *chaos* – Gr. χάος vast chasm, void.] † **1.** A gaping void, yawning gulf, chasm, or abyss –1667. **2.** The 'formless void' of primordial matter 1531. **b.** *personified.* 1651. **3.** *transf.* and *fig.* A state of utter confusion and disorder 1606; a confused mass 1579. † **4.** An amorphous lump –1593. † **5.** ? Element –1753.

1. Betweene us and you there is fixed a great chaos N.T. (*Rhem.*) *Luke* 16:26. **2.** In the Beginning how the Heav'ns and Earth Rose out of C. MILT. *P.L.* I. 10. **4.** 3 *Hen. VI*, III. ii.161.

Chaotic, -al (ke,ǫ·tik, -ăl), *a.* 1713. [f. CHAOS, after *erotic, hypnotic.*] Of, pertaining to, or resembling chaos; utterly confused or disordered. Hence **Chao·tically** *adv.*

Chap (tʃæp), *sb.*[1] ME. [rel. to CHAP *v.*[1]] **1.** An open fissure or crack; *esp.* a crack in the skin, descending to the flesh. Also *fig.* **2.** A stroke, knock, rap. *Sc.* and *n. dial.* 1785.

Chap (tʃæp), *sb.*[2] 1555. [Origin unkn. Cf. synon. CHOP *sb.*[2]] **1.** Either of the two bones (with its covering of flesh, etc.) which form the jaw; in *pl.* the jaws as forming the mouth; used of animals, and colloq. of human beings. **2.** The cheek 1708. **3.** The lower jaw 1846. † **4.** *pl. Mech.* The jaws of a vice, etc. –1831.

1. Open your chaps againe *Temp.* II. ii. 89. **2.** She threatned to slap my chaps 1708. *Chaps of the Channel*: see CHOP *sb.*[2] 3. Hence **Cha·pless** *a.* without the lower jaw.

Chap (tʃæp), *sb.*[3] 1577. [abbrev. f. CHAPMAN.] **1.** A buyer, customer. Still *dial.* **2.** *colloq.* 'Customer', fellow, lad. (Now chiefly of young men.) 1716.

1. Perhaps Mrs. Mead would buy..but she would be a hard c. WILKES.

Chap (tʃæp), *v.*[1] ME. [Similar in meaning to (M)LG., (M)Du. *kappen* chop off, but no connection can be made out.] † **1.** (with *off*). To chop off. ME. only. **2.** To crack or cause to crack in fissures ME. **3.** To strike, to rap at a door. *n. dial.* 1565. **4.** *Sc.* To choose 1720.

2. Chapped with the winters blast LYLY. **3.** *To c. hands*: to strike hands in concluding a bargain. Till the hour c. 1652.

Chap, *v.*[2] *dial.* [In ME. app. a var. of OE. *ćeapian* CHEAP *v.*; in mod. dial. perh. f. CHAPMAN; cf. CHEAP *v.*, CHOP *v.*[2] in the same sense.] To buy; to buy and sell; to truck.

‖ **Chaparejos** (tʃæpărēⁱ·hōᵘs). 1861. [Mex Sp.] Trousers worn by cowboys as a protection against thorny bushes (cf. next). Abbrev. **Chaps.**

‖ **Chaparral** (tʃæ:păræ·l). *U.S.* 1850. [– Sp., f. *chaparra, -arro* evergreen oak.] *prop.* A thicket of low evergreen oaks; hence *gen.* Dense tangled brushwood, as in Mexico and Texas.

C. cock: a species of cuckoo (*Geococcyx californianus*) in the west of North America.

Chap-book (tʃæ·p,buk). 1824. [f. *chap* in CHAPMAN.] A small pamphlet of popular tales, ballads, tracts, etc., as hawked by chapmen.

Chape (tʃēⁱp), *sb.* ME. [– (O)Fr. *chape* cope, hood (whence Sp., Pg. *chapa*) in techn. uses; see CAPE *sb.*[2]] † **1.** A plate of metal with which anything is overlaid. ME. only. **2.** The metal plate of a scabbard; *esp.* that which covers the point ME. (See also O.E.D.) **3.** The tip of a fox's tail 1677. **4.** The part of a buckle by which it is fastened to a strap. [So in Fr.] 1679. Hence **Cha·peless** *a.* wanting a sheath. SHAKS.

Chape, *v.* ME. [f. prec.] To furnish a scabbard, etc., with a chape. CHAUCER.

‖ **Chapeau** (ʃapō). 1523. [Fr., in OFr. *capel*, *chapel* :– L. *cappellum*, dim. of *cappa* CAP *sb.*[1]] A covering for the head. Now chiefly in *Her.*

Chapeau-bras (ʃapō brā): a small three-cornered flat silk hat which could be carried under the arm: worn by gentlemen at court or in full dress in 18th c.

Chapel (tʃæ·pĕl), *sb.* [ME. *chapele* – OFr. *chapele* :– med.L. *capella*, dim. of *cappa*, cloak, cape, cope (see CAP *sb.*[1]). From the *capella* or cloak of St. Martin, the name was applied to the sanctuary in which this was kept under the care of its *cappellani* or chaplains, and thence generally to a sanctuary, and ult. to a building for worship, not being a church. The earlier name for a church was *Oratorium*, ORATORY.] **1.** *gen.* A place of Christian worship, not being a parish or cathedral church; an oratory. **2.** *spec.* A private place of worship ME. **3.** A place of public worship of the Established Church, subordinate to, or dependent upon, the church of the parish (see quots.) 1491. **4.** Used of places of Christian worship other than those of the established church of the country 1662. (Now 'church' is used for 'chapel' by Roman Catholics, Scotch Episcopalians, and many Nonconformists.) **5.** A chapel service 1662. **6.** *gen.* A lesser temple, fane, or sanctuary, having an altar to a deity ME. **7.** A body of singers attached to a chapel (usu. of a king or prince) ME. **8.** The sacred vessels etc., used in a church or chapel. Now *Hist.* **9.** A printing-office; an association of the journeymen in a printing-office. Hence *to hold a c.*, to have a meeting of the association. 1688.

2. The c. of the Castle WALPOLE, of New College EVELYN. *Mortuary c.*: an oratory in a mausoleum, burial vault or aisle, etc., having an altar for masses for the soul of the deceased (*chantry c.*). Hence, a compartment of a cathedral, etc. (usu. in the aisle), separately dedicated and having its own altar. *Lady-c.*: see LADY. **3.** *C. of ease*: one built for the use of parishioners who live far from the parish church. *Parochial c.*: that of an ancient division of a parish attached to it by custom and repute; now usually called CHURCH. *Free c.*: one founded by the king, and not subject to the jurisdiction of the ordinary. **5.** *To keep a c.*: to attend chapel once. So to *miss, lose a c.*

Comb.: **c.-master,** occas. tr. of Fr. *maître de chapelle* or Ger. *Kapellmeister*, director of the music of a royal (or other) c. (sense 7). Hence **Cha·pel** *v.*[1] *nonce-wd.* To put (bury, etc.) in a c. **Cha·pel** *v.*[2] *Naut.* To turn a ship round in a light breeze when close-hauled, so as to make her lie as she did before. **Cha·pelwa:rden,** now 'churchwarden'.

† **Cha·pelet**[1]. 1587. [f. prec. + -ET.] A little CHAPEL –1675.

Chapelet[2] (tʃæ·pĕlėt). 1753. [– Fr. *chapelet* CHAPLET.] **1.** A pair of stirrup leathers, with stirrups, buckled together, and fastened to the pommel of the saddle. **2.** A chain pump with buckets attached to an endless chain passing over two axles. So called in French from its likeness to a rosary. 1874.

† **Cha·pelize,** *v.* [See -IZE.] To make into a chapel. FULLER.

Cha·pellage. [See -AGE.] *rare.* = CHAPELRY 2. SCOTT.

Cha·pellany. ? *Obs. rare.* 1726. [– Fr. *chapellenie* benefice of a chaplain.] = CHAPELRY.

Chapelry (tʃæ·pĕlri). 1591. [– OFr. *chapelerie*, in med.L. *cappellaria* XII; see CHAPEL, -ERY.] **1.** The district attached to a chapel. **2.** A chapel with its precinct, etc.; a chapelstead 1817.

Chaperon (ʃæ·pĕrǫn, -ōᵘn). ME. [– (O)Fr. *chaperon*, f. *chape* cope, CAPE *sb.*[2]] **1.** A hood or cap. Now *Hist.* † **2.** A small escutcheon placed (*esp.*) on the forehead of a horse drawing a hearse –1783. **3.** *fig.* A person, *esp.* a married woman, who, for the sake of propriety, accompanies a young unmarried lady in public, as guide and protector 1720. Also *transf.*

1. *C.*, the Hood anciently worn by the Knights of the Garter PHILLIPS. Hence **Cha·peronage,** attendance as c.

Chaperon (ʃæ·pĕrǫn, -ōᵘn), *v.* 1796. [f. prec.] *trans.* To act as chaperon to; to escort.

I shall be very happy to c. you JANE AUSTEN.

Chap-fallen (tʃæ·p,fǭ:lĕn), *a.* Also **chop-.** 1598. [f. CHAP *sb.*[2]] **1.** With the chap or lower jaw hanging down, as an effect of exhaustion, a wound, or *esp.* of death. **2.** *fig.* Dispirited; crest-fallen 1608.

1. Trooping from their mouldy dens The chapfallen circle spreads TENNYSON.

Chapiter (tʃæ·pitəɹ). ME. [– (O)Fr. *chapitre*, earlier *chapitle* – L. *capitulum*, dim. of *caput* head. Cf. CAPITLE.] † **1.** *gen.* Earlier sp. of CHAPTER. † **2.** *spec.* A summary –1670. **3.** *Arch.* The capital of a column –1878.

† **Cha·pitle.** ME. only. [– OFr. *chapitle*; see prec. and cf. CAPITLE.] = CHAPTER 1, 4.

Chaplain (tʃæ·plėn). [Early ME. *capelein*, superseding OE. *capellān* and superseded by *chapelein*, – AFr., OFr. *capelain*, *chapelain* :– med.L. *cappellanus*, orig. custodian of the cloak of St. Martin, f. *capella*; see CHAPEL, -AN.] **1.** *gen.* The priest, clergyman, or minister of a CHAPEL; in ME. a chantry priest. **2.** *spec.* A clergyman who conducts religious services in the private chapel of a sovereign, lord, or high official, of a public institution, or in the household of a person of quality, in a legislative chamber, regiment, ship, etc. OE. Used of a nun who officiates in a nunnery ME. Also *transf.* Hence **Cha·plaincy, Cha·plainry** = *chaplainship.* **Cha·plainship,** the office of a c.

Chaplet (tʃæ·plet) late ME. [– (O)Fr. *chapelet*, orig. a crown of roses, dim. of *chapel* (mod. *chapeau* hat) :– Rom. *cappellus, dim of *cappa* hood, CAPE *sb.*[2]; see -ET.] **1.** A wreath for the head; a circlet, coronal. *Her.* A bearing representing a garland of leaves with four flowers at equal distances 1688. **2.** A string of beads; *esp.* one used for counting prayers, one third of the length of a rosary. Also, the prayers themselves. 1653. Also *transf.* **3.** A moulding of the astragal species 1623. **4.** *Founding.* One of the metal supports of the core of a hollow moulding, e.g. of a cylindrical pipe 1885. **5.** See CHAPELET[2].

1. A c. of precieuse stones 1450, of flowers GREENE, of Roses STEELE. Hence **Cha·pleted** *a.*

Chapman (tʃæ·pmæ̆n). [OE. *ćēapman*, f. *ćēap* barter, dealing + MAN; see CHEAP *sb.* and *v.*] **1.** A man who buys and sells; a merchant, trader, dealer (*arch.*). **2.** An itinerant dealer; a hawker, pedlar 1592. †**3.** A broker –1659. †**4.** A customer –1807. Hence †**Cha·pmanhood, -head** = *chapmanship.* **Cha·pmanship,** the employment of a c.

Cha·p-money. *dial.* 1881. [See CHAP *sb.*[3]] A small sum returned by the vendor to the purchaser on receiving payment.

†**Chapourn.** 1688. [Said to be – (O)Fr. *chaperon* hood; see CHAPERON *sb.*] *Her.* = next.

Chapournet. 1562. [dim. of prec.; see -ET.] *Her.* In a coat of arms, a chief divided by a bow-shaped line, said to represent a hood.

‖ **Chappe.** 1825. [Fr. *chappe*, XVI var. of *chape*; see CHAPE *sb.*] A cape or cloak.

Chapped (tʃæpt), *ppl. a.*[1] 1460. [f. CHAP *sb.*[1] and *v.*[1]] **1.** Fissured; cracked; as the ground in summer, or the hands with frost. *slang.* Thirsty. **2.** Chopped small 1730.

Chapped (tʃæpt), *ppl. a.*[2] 1678. [f. CHAP *sb.*[2] + -ED[2].] Having a chap or jaw; chiefly in *comb.*

Chappie, -y (tʃæ·pi). *colloq.* 1821. [f. CHAP *sb.*[3] + -IE, -Y[6].] Little chap or fellow. Orig. *Sc.*

‖ **Chappow** (tʃapau·). *Anglo-Ind.* 1860. [– Pushtu.] A plundering expedition; a raid.

Chappy (tʃæ·pi), *a.* 1611. [f. CHAP *sb.*[1] + -Y[1].] Full of chaps or clefts.

Chapter (tʃæ·ptəɹ), *sb.* ME. in *Sc.* [– (O)Fr. *chapitre*, earlier *chapitle* – L. *capitulum*, dim. of *caput* head; see CAPITLE, CHAPITER, CHAPITLE.] **1.** A main division of a book, or of the Acts of Parliament of a single session. **2.** *fig.* Heading, subject, category. (Usu. preceded by *on, upon.*) (*arch.*) ME. **3.** A short lesson read in some services of the Latin Church 1450. **4.** A general meeting or assembly of the canons of a collegiate or cathedral church, of the members of any monastic or religious order, or of an order of knights. (The name *chapter* was thus transferred to the *meeting* at which a chapter (sense 3) was read, and thence to those who met.) ME. **5.** The members of such an assembly as a body: *esp.* The body of canons of a collegiate or cathedral church, presided over by the dean 1491. **6.** A decretal epistle 1726. †**7.** *Arch.* The capital of a column: cf. CHAPITER 3.

1. Unable to read a c. in the bible JOHNSON. *fig. Twel. N.* I. v. 242. A curious c. in modern history EMERSON. **2.** And more particularly on the c. of women CARLYLE.

Phrases. *C. and verse*: (*fig.*) exact authority *for. To the end of the c.*: (*fig.*) throughout. *The c. of accidents*: the unforeseen course of events.

Comb.: **c.-house,** a building attached to a cathedral, etc., where a c. meets; **-lands,** lands belonging to a c. (sense 5).

Chapter (tʃæ·ptəɹ), *v.* 1485. [f. prec.] **1.** To divide into chapters. **2.** To reprove, take to task. [Cf. Fr. *chapitrer.*] 1693.

1. Langton's chaptering the Bible FULLER.

Chaptrel (tʃæ·ptrĕl). 1677. [dim. of CHAPTER (in sense 7).] *Arch.* An impost.

†**Cha·pwoman.** 1624. [After CHAPMAN.] A female dealer or hawker –1823.

†**Char,** *sb.*[1] See CHARE *sb.*[1]

†**Char,** *sb.*[2] ME. [– (O)Fr. *char* :– L. *carrum, carrus,* or ONFr. *charre* :– Rom. **carra*; of Celtic origin. See CAR.] **1.** A chariot; a cart, wagon –1677. **2.** ? A cart-load –1721.

2. *Char of lead*: thirty pigs, each pig containing 70 pounds. [*Charge of lead,* due to Bailey, and copied into mod. Dicts., is non-existent.]

Char (tʃāɹ), *sb.*[3] 1662. [Of unkn., perh. Celtic origin.] *Zool.* **1.** A small fish (*Salmo salvelinus*) of the trout kind, found in the lakes of mountainous districts. **2.** The Brook Trout (*Salmo fontinalis*) of U.S.

Char, *sb.*[4] 1879. [f. CHAR *v.*[2]] A charred substance.

Char, *v.*[1] See CHARE *v.*

Char (tʃāɹ), *v.*[2] Pples. **charred, charring.** 1679. [app. f. *char-* in CHARCOAL; cf. synon. CHARK *v.*[2]] **1.** To reduce by burning to charcoal or carbon; to burn slightly or partially, scorch. **2.** *intr.* To become reduced to charcoal 1727.

Char, *v.*[3] 1846. [Origin unkn.] To hew (stone).

Char-, see CHARE *sb.*[1], and CHARWOMAN.

‖ **Chara** (kē^ə·rā). 1753. [L. name of an unkn. plant.] *Bot.* A genus of aquatic acrogenous plants, type of the N.O. *Characeæ*, which become encrusted with calcareous matter. Hence **Chara·ceous** *a.* **Cha·racin,** (*Chem.*) a camphorous substance found in *Characeæ*, etc.

‖ **Char-à-banc** (ʃaraban̈). 1832. [– Fr. *char-à-bancs* lit. 'carriage with seats'.] A long and light vehicle with transverse seats looking forward.

Charact (kæ·ræ̆kt). *arch.* ME. [– OFr. *charact, characte*; see CARACT.] †**1.** An engraved or impressed mark; a stamp; a letter, figure, etc. –1603. **2.** A cabbalistic sign or emblem 1560.

2. Inscribed with talismans and characts BURTON.

Charact, obs. f. CARAT.

Character (kæ·ræ̆ktəɹ), *sb.* [ME. *caracter* – (O)Fr. *caractère* – (mostly late) L. *character* – Gr. χαρακτήρ instrument for marking, f. χαράσσειν engrave; assim. to L. sp. XVI.]

I. Literal senses. **1.** A distinctive mark; a brand, stamp. Also *fig.* **2.** *esp.* A graphic symbol standing for a sound, syllable, or notion, used in writing or printing 1490. **3.** *collect.* Writing, printing 1600; handwriting 1603; style of type 1641. **4.** = CHARACT 2. 1590. †**5.** *gen.* A symbol; an expression –1702. **6.** A cipher for secret correspondence 1659.

1. *fig.* Stamped with the c. of sublimity 1794. **2.** [The] caracters *y* and *v* PALSGR. Runic characters 1851. **3.** SHAKS. *Sonn.* lix. Imitation of printed Roman c. LYTTON. **6.** I..interpreted my Lord's letter by his c. PEPYS.

II. Fig. senses. **1.** A feature, trait, characteristic. Now *esp.* in *Nat. Hist.* 1502. **2.** Essential peculiarity; nature; sort 1659. †**3.** Personal appearance. *Twel. N.* I. ii. 51. **4.** Mental or moral constitution 1647. **5.** Distinct or distinguished character 1735. **6.** Good repute 1712. **7.** A detailed report of a person's qualities 1645; *esp.* one given to a servant by an employer 1693. Also †*transf.* of things. **8.** Recognized official rank; status; position 1645. **9.** A personage 1749. **10.** A personality in a novel or a play 1749. **11.** *colloq.* An odd or eccentric person 1773. Also *attrib.*

1. Tell me, what one c. of liberty the Americans have BURKE. **2.** To give to the war the c. of a crusade MACAULAY. **4.** Thorough selfishness formed the basis of Henry's c. 1839. **5.** Most Women have no Characters at all POPE. Men of c. WHISTON. **6.** Shops of established c. MCCULLOCH. **7.** [I] took the rascal upon his word without a c. 1785. **9.** Eminent characters have.. played the fool FIELDING. **10.** The comic c. of Sir Trusty J. WARTON. *In* (or *out of*) *c.*: in (or at variance with) the part assumed; hence *gen.* in (or out of) harmony. **11.** The old man..was a bit of a c. 1832.

Character (kæ·ræ̆ktəɹ), *v.* 1591. [f. prec. In Shaks. and XVII often *chara·cter.*] **1.** To engrave; to inscribe. Also *fig.* **2.** To represent (*arch.*) 1594. **3.** = CHARACTERIZE *v.* 3. 1618. **4.** = CHARACTERIZE *v.* 4. 1647. **5.** = CHARACTERIZE *v.* 5. 1654.

1. What's in the braine that Inck may c. SHAKS. *Sonn.* cviii. *fig. Haml.* I. iii. 59.

†**Characte·rical,** *a.* 1634. [f. Gr. χαρακτηρικός + -AL[1]; see -ICAL.] **1.** Of or pertaining to symbolic characters, magical symbols, or charms –1691. **2.** Characteristic –1766.

†**Characterism** (kæ·ræ̆ktĕri:z'm). 1614. [– late L. *characterismus* – Gr. χαρακτηρισμός.] **1.** = CHARACTERIZATION –1825. **2.** A CHARACTERISTIC –1871.

Characterist (kæ·ræ̆ktĕrist). 1691. [f. CHARACTER *sb.* + -IST.] †**a.** One who employs magical symbols. **b.** One who depicts character.

Characteristic (kæ:ræ̆ktĕri·stik). 1664. [– Fr. *caractéristique* or med.L. *characteristicus* – late Gr. χαρακτηριστικός.] **A.** *adj.* That serves to indicate character; distinctive; typical 1665.

The c. letter, and the termination of verbs GIBBON.

B. *sb.* **1.** A distinctive mark; a distinguishing peculiarity or quality 1664. **2.** *Math.* The whole number in a logarithm 1727.

1. Superstition is..not the c. of this age 'JUNIUS'.

Cha:racteri·stical. *arch.* 1621. [f. as prec. + -AL[1]; see -ICAL.] *adj.* = CHARACTERISTIC *a.* *sb.* = CHARACTERISTIC *sb.* 1. 1660. Hence **Cha:racteri·stically** *adv.* in cipher; in a c. manner. **Cha:racteri·sticalness.**

Characterization (kæ:ræ̆ktĕrəizē^i·ʃən). 1570. [f. next + -ATION.] The action or result of characterizing; portrayal in words; creation of fictitious characters.

Characterize (kæ·ræ̆ktĕrəiz), *v.* 1591. [– Fr. *caractériser* or med.L. *characterizare* – Gr. χαρακτηρίζειν; see CHARACTER, -IZE.] †**1.** = CHARACTER *v.* 1. –1811. †**2.** = CHARACTER *v.* 2. –1710. **3.** To describe the peculiar qualities of 1626. **4.** To be a characteristic of 1744. **5.** To impart character to; also *absol.* 1807.

3. I do not choose to use the expression which alone could c. it RUSKIN. **4.** The excellent taste which characterises her writings SCOTT. **5.** To leave out..all that characterises OPIE. Hence **Cha·racteri:zer.**

Cha·racterless, *a.* 1606. [f. CHARACTER *sb.* + -LESS.] Without distinctive feature; without individuality; without (testimony to) personal character. Hence **Cha·racterlessne:ss.**

Charactery, rarely **-try** (kæ·ræ̆ktĕri; in Shaks. kăræ·ktĕri). 1588. [f. CHARACTER *sb.*; see -ERY.] **1.** Expression of thought by symbols or characters; the characters or symbols collectively 1598; † *spec.* shorthand 1588. †**2.** Delineation of character 1614.

1. I will construe to thee All the Charractery of my sad browes *Jul. C.* II. i. 308. Nor mark'd with any sign or c. KEATS.

Charade (ʃărā·d). 1776. [– Fr. *charade* – mod.Pr. *charrado* conversation, f. *charra* chatter, perh. of imit. origin.] A kind of riddle, in which each syllable of a word to be guessed, and sometimes the word itself, is enigmatically described, or acted. Also *attrib.*

Charbocle, obs. f. CARBUNCLE.

‖ **Charbon** (ʃarbon̈). 1753. [Fr., = charcoal, carbon; also in sense 2.] **1.** A small black spot or mark remaining in the cavity of the corner tooth of a horse after the large spot or mark has become obliterated. ? *Obs.* **2.** = ANTHRAX 2. 1869.

Charcoal (tʃā·ɹkō^u l), *sb.* ME. [The second element, COAL, orig. meant 'charcoal'; the first element is obscure; see CHAR *v.*[2], CHARK *sb.*[1]] **1.** The black porous residue, consisting (when pure) wholly of carbon, obtained from partly burnt wood, bones, etc. Hence specified as *wood, vegetable, animal c.* †**2.** *collect. pl.* in sense of 1. –1719. **3.** A charcoal crayon 1688. **4.** A charcoal drawing 1884.

1. Sea-coal last longer than Char-coal BACON.

Comb.: **c.-black,** a pigment obtained from c.; **-iron,** iron containing a percentage of carbon; **-point** (*Electr.*) = *carbon-point* (see CARBON). Hence **Cha·rcoal** *v.* to mark with c.; to suffocate with the fumes of c.

†**Chard**[1], **charde.** 1570. [Fusion of CARD and CHART.] Card, map, chart –1655.

Chard[2] (tʃāɹd). 1658. [– Fr. *carde* (see CARD *sb.*[3]), or alt. of this by assoc. with *chardon* thistle :– late L. *cardo, -ōn-*, for L. *carduus.*] = CARD *sb.*[3]

Chare, char (tʃē^ə ɹ, tʃāɹ), *sb.*[1] [OE. *ćerr*, WS. *ćierr*, (late) *ćyrr*, rel. to *ćierran* turn away or aside; see CHARE *v.*, CHAR *v.* In mod. Eng. usu. *char*, exc. in sense 2; in U.S. also CHORE.] †**1.** The returning of a time –ME.; a turn –1680. **2.** *esp.* An odd job, *esp.* of household work; in *pl.* the housework of a domestic servant ME. Also in *comb.*, as *char-parson*, etc. 1662.

Chare (tʃēᵊɹ), *sb.*² ME. [perh. the same as CHARE turning; cf. Sc. *wynd.*] A narrow lane, or wynd. *local.*

Chare, *sb.*³, chariot, car; see CHAR *sb.*²

† **Chare,** *a.* 1564. [app. shortened from CHARY.] = CHARY –1587. Hence † **Cha·rely** *adv.*

Chare, char (tʃēᵊɹ, tʃāɹ), *v.* [OE. *ćierran* turn away or aside, see CHARE, CHAR *sb.*¹ Now usu. *chare.*] † **1.** To turn; *esp.* to turn away or aside. *trans., intr.,* and *refl.* –1674. **2.** *trans.* To do (a turn of work) (*arch.*) 1570. **3.** *intr.* To do odd jobs, *esp.* of housework by the day; hence *colloq.* to do the cleaning work of (a house) 1732.

† **Charet, charette.** ME. [– (O)Fr. *charrette* two-wheeled carriage, dim. of *charre*; see CHAR *sb.*², CAR, -ET, -ETTE. Concurrent in use w. CHARIOT XV–XVII.] **1.** A wheeled conveyance (for persons or goods) –1654; a war-chariot –1676. Hence † **Cha·reter,** a charioteer.

Charge (tʃāɹdʒ), *sb.* ME. [– (O)Fr. *charge* :– Rom. **carrica*, f. late L. *car(ri)care* load; see CHARGE *v.*]

I. † **1.** A (material) load, burden, weight –1704. [¶ *Charge of Lead*: see CHAR *sb.*² 2.] **2.** The quantity of anything, as powder, coal, ore, etc., which any receptacle, piece of mechanism, etc., *e.g.* a fire-arm, gas-retort, furnace, is constructed to bear, take in, or receive at one time 1653. **3.** *Her.* A BEARING 1599. **4.** *Farriery.* A thick adhesive plaster 1607.

II. 1. *fig.* A load (of trouble, inconvenience, etc.). *Obs. concr.* Anything burdensome. ME. † **2.** *fig.* Importance, moment –1598. **3.** Pecuniary burden; cost 1460; the price demanded for services or goods 1848. *pl.* Expenses: in much the same sense as the sing. (*arch.*) 1514. *Comm.* Incidental expenses 1546. **4.** A liability to pay money laid upon a person or estate 1570. **5.** Commission, trust, responsibility ME. **6.** Care, custody, superintendence ME. **7.** A thing or person entrusted to the care of any one. *spec.* The people or district committed to the care of a clergyman. 1530. **8.** A precept, injunction, mandate, order ME. *spec.* An official instruction or admonition given by a judge to a jury, by a bishop to his clergy, etc. 1690. **9.** Accusation 1477. *spec.* The accusation upon which a prisoner is brought up for trial; hence *colloq.*: A prisoner so brought up 1859.

2. The Letter was..full of c., Of deare import *Rom. & Jul.* v. ii. 18. **3.** Thou hast lytle money & much c. MORE. *pl.* At his own charges THACKERAY. **5.** Pastors have a dreadfull c., not performed by a formal preachment twice a week MILT. **6.** He shall geue his angels c. ouer the COVERDALE *Ps.* 90[91]: 11. Children in c. of a nurse, a nurse in c. of children 1888. So, *Officer, clerk, curate in c. To give* (a person) *in c.*: to hand over to the custody of the police. **9.** *To lay to one's c.*: to charge one with.

III. An impetuous attack, etc. † **1.** The position of a weapon ready for action –1650. **2.** *Mil.* An impetuous attack or onset; the act of bearing down impetuously upon the adversary. Also said of a bull, an elephant, a player at football, etc. 1568. Also *fig.* **3.** *Mil.* A signal for the attack sounded upon a trumpet, etc. 1650.

1. 2 *Hen. IV*, IV. i. 120. **2.** The two armies rushed with equal fury to the c. GIBBON. **3.** The pipers on both sides blew their c. SCOTT.

Comb.: **bursting c.**: see BURST *v.*; **c.-inspector,** an officer who inspects the charges in a c.-sheet; **-sheet,** the paper kept at a police-station on which are entered all names of persons arrested, with the charge against them, etc. Hence † **Cha·rgeful** *a.* burdensome; responsible. **Cha·rgeless** *a.* free from cost; without a (clerical) c. † **Cha·rgeous** *a.* heavy; burdensome.

Charge (tʃāɹdʒ), *v.* ME. [– (O)Fr. *charger* – late L. *car(ri)care* to load, f. L. *carrus* wagon, CAR; cf. CARRY, CARK.]

I. To cause to bear. † **1.** *trans.* To load –1854. † **2.** To place as a load *upon* –1601. **3.** To put in or on (a thing) or cause it to receive what it can bear or is adapted to receive ME.; *spec.* to load (a fire-arm) 1541. Also *fig.* **4.** *Her.* To place a bearing on 1572. Also *transf.* **5.** To fill (any substance) *with* other matter (*e.g.* the air *with* vapour, etc.) Usu. in pa. pple. 1756.

1. A tre, That charged was with fruyt CHAUCER. **3.** To c. a rocket 1799, an accumulator 1888, a pipe BROWNING. Canon charged to the mouthes *John* II. i. 382. *fig.* A face charged with memories GEO. ELIOT. *fig. L.L.L.* v. ii. 88. **5.** Clouds charged with electricity PHILLIPS.

II. To load heavily. † **1.** To overload –1784. † **2.** To press hard –1568. † **3.** *fig.* To burden *with* sin, care, sickness, etc. –1633. † **4.** To put to expense –1647. **5.** To burden, entrust, commission *with*, † *of* ME. Also *refl.* **6.** To lay a command or injunction upon; to exhort authoritatively. Const. with *inf.*, or with cl.; also *simply.* ME. Also *absol.* to deliver a charge. Cf. CHARGE *sb.* II. 8. 1618. **7.** To censure; to accuse ME. **8.** *To c.* (a fault, etc.): see quots. **9.** To subject (a person, estate, etc.) to a pecuniary liability. Const. *with*, † *to.* 1626. **10.** *To c.* (a sum or price): see quots. **11.** *To c.* (a thing sold or offered for sale): see quots.

1. To c. childrens memories with rules LOCKE. **4.** Let not the church be charged 1 *Tim.* 5:16. **5.** What you haue charg'd me with, that haue I done *Lear* V. iii. 163. **6.** On thy life I c. thee, hold *Twel. N.* IV. i. 49. To c. a jury 1618, the clergy of a diocese 1870. **7.** To c. me with offence 1559. **8.** To impute as a fault: C. the crime, On native sloth DRYDEN. † To impute *to*: It [a poem] is charged to me SWIFT. To state in an indictment: We ought..not to c. what we are unable to prove BURKE. **10.** To impose as a liability *on*: Debts.. charged upon the real estate CRUISE. To state as the price due *for*: [The price] she charged for eggs 1787. Also *absol.* **11.** To put as a charge *to* or *against*: C. these to (or against) me 1888. To rate: He charges coal at 8*d*. a cwt. 1888.

† **III.** To attach weight or importance to; to regard –1587.

IV. To attack impetuously, etc. **1.** To place (a weapon) in position for action; to level 1509. **2.** To bear down upon with impetuosity. *Esp.* in military use. Cf. also CHARGE *sb.* III. 2. 1583. Also *intr.* and *absol.*

1. *C. bayonets!*: advance on the enemy with bayonets fixed. **2.** The bull charged one of the horses 1888. *absol.* 'C., Chester, c.! On, Stanley, on!' SCOTT. Hence **Charged** *ppl. a.* filled, etc.; now *esp.* = 'Charged with electricity'.

‖ **Chargé,** in full **Chargé d'affaires** (ʃa·rʒe dafẹ̄·r). 1850. [Fr.; = (one) in charge of affairs.] **1.** A minister who transacts diplomatic business during the temporary absence of the ambassador; also, the representative of a country at a minor foreign court 1876. **2.** *gen.* Man or officer in charge (for the time).

Chargeable (tʃā·ɹdʒăb'l), *a.* 1480. [– OFr. *chargeable* in same senses; see CHARGE, -ABLE.] † **1.** Of the nature of a charge or burden; responsible; burdensome; costly –1796. **2.** Capable of being, or liable to be, charged (see CHARGE *v.*) 1546.

1. A c. office FRITH. C. apparell 1568. 2 *Sam.* 13:25. **2.** Writing signed by the party c. 1845. C. with guilt JOHNSON, with money 1641, to a Parish ADDISON, upon the Rector 1654, to general average BOWEN. Hence **Chargeabi·lity,** the condition of being c. **Char·geableness.** † **Cha·rgeably** *adv.*

† **Cha·rgeant,** *a.* ME. only. [– AFr. *chargeaunt*, (O)Fr. *chargeant*, f. *charger* CHARGE *v.*; see -ANT¹.] Burdensome.

Cha·rgeant, *sb.* 1887. [See CHARGE *sb.* II. 4, *v.* II. 9, and -ANT.] = CHARGEE.

Chargee (tʃāɹdʒī·). 1884. [f. CHARGE *v.* or *sb.* + -EE¹.] The holder of a charge upon property, or of a security over a contract.

Cha·rge-house. † **1.** A house for the charge of youth *L.L.L.* v. i. 87. **2.** A building in which cartridges are charged.

Charger¹ (tʃā·ɹdʒəɹ). [ME. *chargeour* – AFr. *chargeour*; see CHARGE *v.*, -OUR. Cf. OFr. *chargeoir* basket strapped on the back, *chargeoire* device for loading guns.] A large plate or flat dish.

Giue me heere Iohn Baptists head in a c. *Matt.* 14:8.

Cha·rger². 1483. [f. CHARGE *v.* + -ER¹.] **1.** One who or that which charges. **2.** One who has a charge on an estate, etc. 1869. **3.** A horse ridden by an officer in the field or in action 1762.

3. Furious every c. neighed CAMPBELL.

Charily (tʃēᵊ·rili), *adv.* 1579. [f. CHARY + -LY².] In a CHARY manner; carefully; cautiously; sparingly.

Chariness (tʃēᵊ·rinės). 1571. [f. as prec. + -NESS.] **1.** The quality of being CHARY. † **2.** Scrupulous integrity –1794.

2. The charinesse of our honesty *Merry W.* II. i. 102.

Chariot (tʃæ·riət). ME. [– (O)Fr. *chariot* waggon, augm. of *char* CAR. See CHARET.] **1.** A wheeled vehicle; †a cart –1693; a carriage of state ME.; also *fig.*; a car used in ancient warfare 1581. *spec.* A light four-wheeled carriage with only back seats 1661. † **2.** *fig.* Vehicle –1678.

1. *fig.* Like the sun's c. at mid-day 1883. He burneth the c. in the fire *Ps.* 46: 9.

Chariot (tʃæ·riət), *v.* 1627. [f. prec.] To carry or convey in a chariot 1659. Also *absol.* Bright-charioted Aurora COWPER.

Chariotee (tʃæ:riŏtī·). 1864. [f. CHARIOT *sb.* + -EE² (vaguely, as in *settee*).] A light covered pleasure chariot, with four wheels and two seats. (Webster.)

Charioteer (tʃæ:riŏtīᵊ·ɹ), *sb.* [f. CHARIOT + -EER, superseding ME. *charietere*, etc. – OFr. *charieter, charioteur.*] The driver of a chariot. Hence **Charioteership,** performance as a c.

Charioteer, *v.* 1802. [f. prec.] **1.** *intr.* To act as charioteer; to drive. **2.** *trans.* To drive (a chariot, a person in a chariot) 1849.

Chariotry (tʃæ·riətri). 1828. [f. as prec. + -RY.] The body of soldiers who fought from chariots. Cf. *cavalry*, etc.

Charism (kæ·riz'm). Pl. **-ata** and **-s.** 1641. [– eccl.L. *charisma* – Gr. χάρισμα f. χάρις favour, grace.] A favour specially vouchsafed by God; a grace, a talent. Hence **Charisma·tic** *a.* of or pertaining to a c.

Charitable (tʃæ·rităb'l), *a.* ME. [– (O)Fr. *charitable*, f. *charité*; see CHARITY, -ABLE.] † **1.** Showing Christian charity or the love of God and man –1641. † **2.** Tender-hearted; well-disposed –1634. **3.** Full of active charity; *esp.* liberal in almsgiving to the poor ME. **4.** Connected with an object of charity, *esp.* as defined in statutes; of the nature of a charity 1597. **5.** Inclined to judge favourably of men, their actions, etc. 1626.

3. With your charatable almes the poore man to comforte ME. **4.** The great statute of c. uses is st. 43 El. c. 4. POWELL. To aid some c. object 1872. **5.** A c. construction 1626, hope 1846. Hence **Cha·ritableness,** the quality of being c. **Cha·ritably** *adv.*

† **Cha·ritative,** *a.* 1582. [– OFr. *charitatif* – med.L. *caritativus*; see CHARITY, -IVE.] Of the nature of charity or a charitable gift –1751.

Charity (tʃæ·rĭti). OE. [– (O)Fr. *charité* :– L. *caritas, -tat-*, f. *carus* dear; see -ITY, and cf. CHERTE.] **1.** Christian love; *esp.* the Christian love of our fellow men. Often personified. ME. **2.** Love, natural affection; spontaneous goodness ME. *pl.* Affections 1667. **3.** A disposition to judge hopefully of men and their actions, and to make allowance for their shortcomings 1483; † fairness, equity –1647. **4.** Benevolence, *esp.* to the poor; charitableness; alms-giving OE. *pl.* Acts of charity done to the poor 1607. **5.** Alms ME. **6.** A bequest, foundation, institution, etc., for the benefit of others, *esp.* of the poor or helpless 1697.

1. The charite [A.V. love] of God, that is in Jhesu Crist oure Lord *Rom.* 8: 39. The c. of the Gospel should extend to men of every Religion 1796. *In, out of, c.*: in or out of the Christian state of c. **2.** *pl.* MILT. *P.L.* IV. 756. **3.** C. bids hope for the best DRYDEN. **4.** C., or tenderness for the poor JOHNSON. *pl.* Deferre not Charities till Death BACON. **5.** To beg a c. DRYDEN. **6.** Christ's Hospital..a..noble, pious and admirable c. EVELYN.

Phrases. *C. begins at home*: used to express the prior claims of ties of family, friendship, etc. (cf. 1 *Tim.* 5: 8). *Brother or Sister of C.*: a member of a religious organization devoted to c.

attrib., etc. (see senses 4–6), as *c. land, money*; *c.-boy, -girl*, etc.; **c.-school,** one supported by charitable bequests or gifts, for the education of the poor.

Charivari (ʃa:ri,va·ri). 1735. [– Fr. *charivari* (earlier *chalivali, -vari*), of unkn. origin.] A serenade of rough music, made with kettles, pans, tea-trays, etc., used in France, in derision of incongruous marriages, etc.; hence a babel of noise.

Chark (tʃāɹk), *sb.*¹ 1708. [app. subst. use of CHARK *v.*²] Wood or coal charred; charcoal; coke.

‖ **Chark** (tʃāɹk), *sb.*[2] 1591. [– Russ. *charka.*] A small (Russian) glass.

Chark, *v.*[1] Now *dial.* [OE. *ćearcian* creak, whence also ME. var. *cherk, chirk;* see CHIRK *v.*] † **1.** To creak –ME. **2.** To be querulous. *Sc.* 1825.

Chark (tʃāɹk), *v.*[2] 1655. [From the analysis of CHARCOAL as †*chark coal* (XV); see CHAR *v.*[2]] To char; to coke (coals).

Charlatan (ʃā·ɹlătăn, -tæn). 1618. [– Fr. *charlatan* – It. *ciarlatano*, f. *ciarlare* babble, patter, f. imit. base **char-* as in Pr. *charra*; see CHARADE.] † **1.** A mountebank who descants volubly in the street; *esp.* an itinerant vendor of drugs, etc. –1771. **2.** An empiric who pretends to wonderful knowledge or secrets, *esp.* in the healing art; an impostor, a quack 1680. Also as *adj.*

2. A c. in religion is sure to like other sorts of charlatans GEO. ELIOT. Hence **Charlata·nic, -al** *a.* **Cha·rlatanish** *a.* **Cha·rlatani:sm,** the practice of a c.; the being a c. **Cha·rlatanry,** quackery.

Charles's Wain. [OE. *Carles wæġn* the wain of Carl (Charlemagne). Orig. the wain of *Arcturus*, verbally assoc. with *Arturus.* Arthur and Charlemagne are associated in legend.] The asterism comprising the seven bright stars in Ursa Major; known also as The Plough.

Charley, Charlie (tʃā·ɹli). *colloq.* 1812. [dim. of *Charles*; see -IE, -Y[6].] **1.** A night-watchman. **2.** A small triangular beard, as worn by Charles I. 1834. **3.** A proper name for the fox 1857.

Charlock (tʃā·ɹlǫk). [OE. *ćerlic, ćyrlic,* of unkn. origin.] *Bot. Sinapis arvensis* or Field Mustard; also used of other field-weeds. **Joint-podded c.:** *Raphanus raphanistrum.*

Charlotte (ʃā·ɹlət). 1855. [Fr.] Apple marmalade covered with bread-crumbs. Hence **C. Russe,** custard enclosed in sponge-cake.

Charm (tʃāɹm), *sb.*[1] ME. [– (O)Fr. *charme* :– L. *carmen* song, verse, oracular response, incantation.] **1.** *orig.* The chanting of a verse having magic power; incantation; hence, a magic spell; a talisman; an amulet, etc. Also *fig.* (cf. *spell.*) **2.** *fig.* That which fascinates or attracts, exciting love and admiration. In *pl.*, esp. of female beauty. 1697. **b.** (without *pl.*) Attractiveness 1830. **c.** *Charms* (*U.S. slang*): Money. **3.** A small trinket worn fastened to a watch-chain or girdle 1865.

1. To..woundes..Somme hadden salues and somme hadden charmes CHAUCER. *fig.* The c. of the Roman name STUBBS. **2.** Scornful virgins who their charms survive POPE. **3.** A bunch of charms 1870. Hence **Cha·rmless** *a.* **Cha·rmlike** *a.*

Charm (tʃāɹm), *sb.*[2] 1548. [Later var. of *cherme* (XV), see CHIRM; repr. OE. *ćirm, ćyrm, ćerm* clamour, cry.] **1.** A blended noise, as of birds, school-children, etc. † **2.** Song –1633.

1. [Morn's] rising sweet With c. of earliest Birds MILT. *P.L.* IV. 642.

Charm (tʃāɹm), *v.*[1] ME. [– (O)Fr. *charmer,* f. *charme* CHARM *sb.*[1]] **1.** *trans.* To act upon with or as with a charm or magic; to put a spell upon; to bewitch, enchant. **2.** To endow with supernatural powers by means of charms; *esp.* to fortify against dangers 1564. **3.** *intr.* To work charms, use spells, practise magic ME. **4.** To subdue, as if by magic power; to soothe, allay 1540. **5.** *fig.* To powerfully attract (the mind, senses, etc.); to fascinate ME. Also *absol.* † **6.** To conjure, entreat –1734. † **7.** To tune, play –1609. Also *intr.* (of an instrument).

1. They wanted me to c. or cure him KANE. **2.** I, in mine owne woe charm'd, Could not finde death *Cymb.* V. iii. 68. **3.** That she shulde not heare the voyce of the charmer, charme he neuer so wysely *Ps.* 57[58]: 5. **4.** Music the fiercest grief can c. POPE. **5.** There's something charms me mightily about London SWIFT. Hence **Cha·rmedly** *adv.*

Charm, *v.*[2], var. of CHIRM *v.*; see CHARM *sb.*[2]

Charmer (tʃā·ɹməɹ). ME. [f. CHARM *v.* + -ER[1].] **1.** One who uses magic powers; an enchanter. **2.** One who fascinates; usually applied to a woman 1676. † **Cha·rmeress,** a female c.

Cha·rmful, *a.* 1656. [f. CHARM *sb.*[1] + -FUL.] Full of spells or charms.

His c. lyre COWLEY. Hence **Cha·rmfulness.**

Charming (tʃā·ɹmiŋ), *vbl. sb.* ME. [f. CHARM *v.*[1] + -ING[1].] **1.** The operation or using of charms. **2.** Fascination (*obs.*); now, fascinating 1720. Also *attrib.*

2. She has lost none of her power of c. 1888. Hence **Cha·rming-ly** *adv.*, **-ness.**

† **Cha·rneco.** 1593. [Said to be from the name of a village near Lisbon.] A kind of wine –1631.

Charnel (tʃā·ɹnĕl), *sb.*[1] (and *a.*). ME. [– OFr. *charnel* :– med.L. *carnale* (glossed by OE. *flæsć-hūs* 'flesh-house'), subst. use of n. of late L. *carnalis* CARNAL.] A cemetery (*obs.*); a charnel house. Also *attrib.*

The commune charnell of the city 1526.

B. *adj.* Of, pertaining to, or fit for a charnel, or the remains there preserved; sepulchral; ghastly 1824.

C. house: a house or vault for the bones of the dead.

† **Charnel** (tʃā·ɹnĕl), *sb.*[2] ME. [– OFr. *charnel*, prob. :– L. *cardinale*, n. of *cardinalis* pertaining to a hinge, f. *cardo, -in-* hinge; see -AL[1].] A hinge –1741.

Charon (kēə·rǫn). 1513. [– L. *Charon* – Gr. Χάρων.] **1.** *Gr.* and *Rom. Mythol.* The ferryman who conveyed the shades across the Styx. **2.** Ferryman (*joc.*) 1861.

‖ **Charpie** (ʃā·ɹpī, ʃarpī). 1797. [Fr.; subst. use of pa. pple. fem. of *charpir* shred; see CARPET.] Old linen unravelled into short ends of thread for surgical dressings.

‖ **Charpoy** (tʃā·ɹpoi). *Anglo-Ind.* 1845. [– Hind. *chārpāī.*] The common Indian bedstead.

‖ **Charqui** (tʃā·ɹki). 1760. [– Quechua *echarqui.*] Beef cut into thin slices and dried in the sun and wind; 'jerked' beef (see JERK *v.*[2]).

Charry (tʃā·ri), *a.* 1786. [f. CHAR *v.*[2] or CHARCOAL + -Y[1].] Of the nature of charcoal.

Chart (tʃāɹt), *sb.* 1571. [– (O)Fr. *charte* – L. *charta* – Gr. χάρτης papyrus leaf. See CARD *sb.*[2]] **1.** A map or chart; *spec.* a map for the use of navigators; a delineation of a portion of the sea, indicating the outline of the coasts, the position of rocks, sandbanks, channels, anchorages, etc. Also *fig.* 1696. **2.** A sheet bearing information of any kind arranged in a graphical or tabular form. Also *transf.* and *fig.* 1792. † **3.** = CARD *sb.*[2]: An ordinary card; a playing-card; the compass-card –1796. † **4.** A charter; a deed or document of any kind –1775.

1. Our navigation is safer for the c. EMERSON. A magnetic c. 1872. A c. of temperature 1888. A military c. 1580. **2.** A barometric c. 1888. Gentone's C. of Inheritance (*title*) 1840. Hence **Cha·rtless** *a.*

Chart (tʃāɹt), *v.* 1842. [f. prec.] To make a chart of; to map. Also *fig.*

‖ **Charta** (kā·ɹtă). OE. [L. – Gr. χάρτης a leaf of papyrus or paper.] † **1.** In OE. form *carta*: Paper, letter. **2.** A CHARTER; *esp.* in MAGNA CHARTA. Also used *fig.* 1698.

Chartaceous, cart- (kaɹtēi·ʃəs), *a.* 1655. [f. late L. *chartaceus* (f. *charta* paper) + -OUS; see -ACEOUS.] Of the nature of paper; papery.

Charter (tʃā·ɹtəɹ), *sb.* [– OFr. *chartre* :– L. *chartula*, dim. of *charta* CHART. For the phonology cf. CHAPTER.] *lit.* A leaf of paper (in OE. called *bóc* BOOK). **1.** A written document delivered by the sovereign or legislature: **a.** granting privileges or recognizing rights; **b.** creating a borough, university, company, or other corporation 1474. **2.** A written evidence, instrument, or contract executed between man and man; *esp.* a conveyance ME. *spec.* A CHARTER-PARTY, q.v. Also the contract thereby made. 1794. **3.** Privilege, exemption, publicly conceded right 1565.

1. a. *Great C.*: see MAGNA CHARTA. Charters are donations of the sovereign; and not laws, but exemptions from law HOBBES. **b.** The renewal of the Company's c. 1844. *People's C.*: the document (published 8 May, 1838) embodying the principles and demands of the Chartists. **3.** Ye haue a C. to speake what ye list JEWEL.

Comb.: **c.-bond** = CHARTER-PARTY; **-land,** land held by c.; freehold land (in OE. *bócland*). Hence **Cha·rterless** *a.*

Charter (tʃā·ɹtəɹ), *v.* ME. [f. prec.] **1.** To establish by charter. **2.** To privilege 1542. **3.** To hire (a ship) by charter-party. Hence *colloq.* to hire (a vehicle, etc.) 1806.

1. The different Chartered Companies 1800. **2.** The Ayre, a charter'd Libertine *Hen. V*, I. i. 48.

Cha·rterer. 1598. [f. CHARTER *sb.* and *v.*] **1.** A freeholder; a freeman of a chartered borough. **2.** One who charters a ship 1833.

Charterhouse (tʃā·ɹtəɹhaus). 1534. [ME. *chart(h)ous* Carthusian (XIV) – OFr. *Charteuse* (see CARTHUSIAN), later (and mod.) *Chartreuse* which, as AFr. *Chartrous,* was adopted in later ME. and assim. to HOUSE *sb.*[1], resulting in the present form.] **1.** A Carthusian monastery (*arch.*). **2.** Hence: Name of a hospital founded in London, in 1611, upon the site of the Carthusian monastery, which has since become a public school 1655. As *attrib.* Carthusian 1577.

† **Cha·rterism, -ist,** early ff. CHARTISM, -IST.

Charter-party (tʃā·ɹtəɹ,pā:ɹti). 1539. [In XVI *chart parte, chartipartie* – Fr. *charte partie* – med.L. *charta partita* 'divided charter', indenture. The assim. *charter-* dates from XVI.] † **1.** *gen.* An INDENTURE, q.v. **2.** Now only: The charter or deed made between owners and merchants for hire of a ship, and safe delivery of the cargo 1539.

Cha·rter School. One of the schools established in Ireland by the Charter Society founded in 1733, to provide Protestant education for the Catholic poor.

Chartism (tʃā·ɹtiz'm). [f. as next + -ISM.] *Eng. Hist.* The democratic movement and principles of the Chartists, 1838–48.

Chartist (tʃā·ɹtist). 1838. [f. L. *charta*, used in the sense of 'charter', + -IST.] One of the body of political reformers (chiefly operatives), whose principles were embodied in the 'People's Charter' (CHARTER *sb.* 1 quots.). Also *attrib.*

Chartographer (kaɹtǫ·grăfəɹ). 1864. [var. sp. of CARTOGRAPHER, after L. *charta.*] = CARTOGRAPHER. So **Chartogra·phic, -al** *a.* **Charto·graphist. Charto·graphy.**

‖ **Chartreuse** (ʃartrö·z). 1866. [Fr., fem. of *Chartreux*; see next, and CHARTERHOUSE.] **1.** A liqueur made by the monks of La Grande Chartreuse, near Grenoble, with aromatic herbs and brandy. **2.** A colour; pale apple-green 1884.

‖ **Chartreux** (ʃa·rtrō). ME. [Fr., alt. f. OFr. *Charteus* :– med.L. *Carthusius*; see CARTHUSIAN.] **1.** A Carthusian; also *attrib.* **2.** The Charterhouse (School) 1779.

Chartulary[1] (ka·ɹtiŭlări). 1571. [– med.L. *c(h)artularium*; see CARTULARY.] A collection or set of charters; = CARTULARY, q.v.

Cha·rtulary[2]. 1678. [– med.L. *c(h)artularius*; see prec. and -ARY[2].] A keeper of the archives.

Charwoman (tʃā·ɹwu:măn). 1596. [f. CHARE, CHAR *sb.*[1] and *v.*[1]] A woman hired by the day to do odd jobs in a house. So **-lady** *joc.* 1895.

Chary (tʃēə·ri), *a.* [OE. *ćeariġ, *cæriġ* = OS. *carag*, OHG. *karag* :– WGmc. **karaʒ-*, f. **karō* CARE *sb.*; see -Y[1].] † **1.** Sorrowful –ME. † **2.** Dear; cherished –1820. **3.** Careful, cautious, shy, frugal, sparing (*of*) 1542. **4.** quasi-*adv.* Carefully 1590.

2. Fill the stirrup cup..from a butt yet charier SCOTT. **3.** 'Faith, I am very c. of my health COWPER. *Haml.* I. iii. 36.

Charybdis (kări·bdis). 1597. [L. – Gr. χάρυβδις.] A dangerous whirlpool on the coast of Sicily (now Calofaro), opposite the Italian rock Scylla. Used allusively, *esp.* in combination with Scylla, of the danger, in avoiding one peril, of running into its opposite.

Chase, chace (tʃēⁱs), *sb.*[1] [ME. *chace* – OFr. *chace* (mod. *chasse*) :– Rom. **captia*, f. **captiare*; see CHASE *v.*[1]] **1.** The action of chasing (see CHASE *v.* 1). **2.** The right of hunting over a tract of country; also, that of keeping beasts of the chase therein 1460. **3.** A tract of unenclosed land reserved for breeding and hunting wild animals ME. **4.** That which is hunted ME. **5.** Those who hunt 1811. **6.** The chase-guns of a ship; the part of the ship where the chase-ports are 1622. **7.** *Tennis.* Applied to the second impact on the floor (or in a gallery) of a ball which the opponent has not returned. (See O.E.D.) ME.

1. *The c.*: Ardently fond of the c. LANE. To give c. to (= pursue) a ship 1634. *Stern c.*: a c. in which the chaser follows the chased astern. **3.** Their wide enclosed parks, and unenclosed chaces STUBBS. **6.** *Stern c.*: the guns in the stern.

attrib. and *Comb.*: **c.-gun,** a gun removed to the c.-ports ahead or astern; **-ports,** the ports at the bows or through the stern of the ship.

Chase (tʃēⁱs), *sb.*[2] 1580. [– Fr. *châsse* shrine of relics, setting of gems, casing, case :– L. *capsa* box, repository, f. *capere* take, receive. Cf. CASE *sb.*[2]] **1.** The setting of a gem. **2.** *Printing.* The quadrangular iron frame in which pages or slips of type are locked up 1612.

Chase (tʃēⁱs), *sb.*[3] 1611. [– Fr. *chas*, orig. enclosure, enclosed place, mod. eye of a needle, perforated sinker, – Pr. *cas, caus* – med.L. *capsum* thorax, nave of church.] *gen.* A groove or furrow. **1.** The cavity of a gun barrel; the part of a gun in front of the trunnions 1647. **2.** A groove cut in the face of a wall, to receive a pipe, etc.; a trench for drain tiles 1871. **3.** *Shipbuilding.* A kind of joint by which the overlapping joint of clinker-built boats passes at the stem and stern into a flush joint as in carvel-built boats.

Chase, chace (tʃēⁱs), *v.*[1] [– OFr. *chacier* (mod. *chasser*) :– Rom. **captiare*, for L. *captare*, frequent. of *capere* take. See CATCH.] **1.** To pursue with a view to catching (see quots.). Also *intr.* (*absol.*) and *fig.* **2.** *trans.* To run after in play 1830. **3.** *intr.* To run with speed. Still *dial.* ME. **4.** To drive precipitately *from, out of, to, into,* etc.; to drive *away, forth,* etc. ME.; to put to flight (*arch.*) ME. † **5.** To drive (cattle, etc.) –1670.

1. To c. the hart TENNYSON, a process-server 1886, a ship SWIFT. *intr.* To c. in the woods LD. BERNERS, with the squadron 1748. *fig.* To c. riches BURNS. **2.** Chasing each other merrily TENNYSON. Hence **Cha·seable, Cha·sable** *a.* fit to be hunted.

Chase (tʃēⁱs), *v.*[2] ME. [app. short for ENCHASE.] **1.** To adorn (metal, etc.) with work embossed or engraved in relief. **2.** To set (a gem, etc.) *in.* Also *fig.* (*rare*) 1859.

Chase, *v.*[3] 1823. [f. CHASE *sb.*[3]] To groove, indent.

Chaser[1] (tʃēⁱ·səɹ). ME. [– OFr. *chacëour, chacëur* (mod. *chasseur*), f. *chasser*; see CHASE *v.*[1], -ER[2].] **1.** One who chases or hunts. **2.** One who or that which pursues ME. **3.** *Naut.* A *chase-gun*; see BOW-*chaser*, STERN-CHASER 1794.

Chaser[2] (tʃēⁱ·səɹ). 1707. [f. CHASE *v.*[2] + -ER[1].] **1.** One who chases or engraves metal. **2.** A tool used for cutting the threads of screws 1881.

Chasing (tʃēⁱ·siŋ), *vbl. sb.* 1835. [f. CHASE *v.*[2] + -ING[1].] **1.** The act or art of embossing or engraving in relief; also *attrib.* **b.** *concr.* The figures or design so produced 1862. **2.** The cutting of a screw 1881.

Chasm (kæ·z'm). 1596. [– L. *chasma* – Gr. χάσμα yawning hollow.] **1.** A deep yawning rent in the surface of the earth or other cosmical body; later, a fissure or gap 1636. **2.** A wide crack, break, void, hiatus. Also *fig.* 1641.

1. Volcanic chasms CARLYLE. **2.** Chasms in a rampart SCOTT. The c. of Seven Centuries CARLYLE. The c. Tom's departure has made MACAULAY. Hence **Cha·smal** *a.* **Cha·smed** *ppl. a.* having chasms. **Cha·smy** *a.* abounding with chasms; of the nature of or like a c.

‖ **Chasse**[1] (ʃās). 1670. [Fr. *châsse*; see CHASE *sb.*[2]] A case for the relics of a saint.

‖ **Chasse**[2] (ʃas). 1800. [Fr., f. *chasser*; see CHASE *v.*[1], -OR 2.] A small glass of some liqueur, taken to remove the taste of coffee, etc. So ‖ **Chassé** *pa. pple.* treated with a chasse.

‖ **Chassé** (ʃase), *sb.* 1867. [Fr.; lit. 'chasing, chase'.] *Dancing.* A gliding step, executed by bringing one foot behind the other while this is at the same time advanced; also, a figured step containing two of these, the direction for which is *chassez croisez.*

‖ **Chassé,** *v.* Also **chassez.** 1803. [– Fr. *chasser.*] **1.** *Dancing.* To execute the step or movement called a *chassé.* **2.** *trans.* To dismiss. (*Society slang.*) 1847.

2. He was *chasséd* on the spot THACKERAY.

‖ **Chasselas** (ʃasəlā). 1664. [Fr.] A white grape named from *Chasselas*, near Mâcon.

‖ **Chasse-marée** (ʃas,marē). 1801. [Fr. = chase-tide.] A coasting-vessel, used on the French side of the Channel.

‖ **Chassepot** (ʃa·spo). 1869. [f. *Chassepot*, the inventor.] A breech-loading, centre-fire needle-gun adopted for the French army in 1866.

‖ **Chasseur** (ʃasör). 1796. [Fr., f. *chasser*; see CHASE *v.*[1]] **1.** A huntsman; a hunter. **2.** A soldier equipped and trained for rapid movement 1796. **3.** An attendant upon a person of rank and wealth, dressed in a military style 18 . . .

1. Chasseurs..beat its woods OUIDA. **3.** A servant in chasseur's livery entered GEO. ELIOT.

‖ **Chassis** (ʃa·si). 1664. [– Fr. *châssis* :– Rom. **capsicium*, f. L. *capsa* CASE *sb.*[2]] † **1.** A SASH –1711. **2.** The base-frame, off which the carriage of a barbette or casemate gun slides backward and forward 1869. **3.** The base-frame of a motor car 1903.

Chaste (tʃēⁱst), *a.* ME. [– (O)Fr. *chaste* – L. *castus.*] **1.** Pure from unlawful sexual intercourse; continent, virtuous. Also *transf.* † **2.** Celibate, single –1596. † **3.** Morally pure, innocent –1535. Also *fig.* **4.** Decent; free from indecency or offensiveness 1621. **5.** *fig.* Chastened; restrained from all excess 1774.

1. *transf.* Chast and honest eyes 1565. **2.** *Rom. & Jul.* I. i. 223. **3.** *fig.* Let me not name it to you, you c. Starres *Oth.* V. ii. 2. **4.** C. deportment STERNE. **5.** A. c. interpretation of nature REID. c. tastes 1825. A c. and correct writer J. WARTON. *C. tree*: the tree AGNUS CASTUS. Hence **Cha·stely** *adv.* **Cha·steness,** the quality or state of being c.

† **Chaste,** *v.* [– OFr. *chastier* (mod. *châtier*) :– L. *castigare* CASTIGATE. Repl. by CHASTEN.] To CHASTEN –1621.

Chastelain (tʃa·stēleⁱn). Now *Hist.* ME. [– OFr. *chastelain* (mod. *châtelain*) :– L. *castellanus* (in med.L. sense); see CASTELLAN, CHATELAIN, -AINE.] = CASTELLAN.

Chasten (tʃēⁱ·s'n), *v.* 1526. [f. CHASTE *v.* + -EN[5].] **1.** To correct or discipline by punishment; to chastise. (Usu. of Divine chastisement.) **2.** To render pure in character or style; to refine 1715. **3.** *fig.* To restrain from excess; to moderate 1856.

1. Whom the Lorde loveth, him he chasteneth *Hebr.* 12 : 6. **3.** Time and experience have chastened me KANE. Hence **Cha·stenedly** *adv.* (*rare*). **Cha·stener.**

† **Cha·stiment.** ME. [– OFr. *chastiement* (mod. *châtiment*), f. *chastier*; see CHASTE *v.*, -MENT.] Chastisement; rebuke –1500.

Chastise (tʃæstəi·z), *v.* ME. [Of doubtful origin; prob. (like CHASTEN) a new formation on earlier CHASTE *v.*, CHASTY.] † **1.** To correct (authoritatively) the faults of; to reform –1579. † **2.** To censure –1699. **3.** To punish, with a view to amendment; also simply, to inflict (*esp.* corporal) punishment on ME. **4.** = CHASTEN 2 (*arch.*) 1620. **5.** = CHASTEN 3 (*arch.*) 1704.

2. He chastises me for saying [etc.] BENTLEY. **3.** My father hath chastised you with whippes, but I will c. you with scorpions 1 *Kings* 12 : 11. A plan to c. the intruder ELPHINSTONE. **5.** With Pity to c. Delight STEELE. Hence **Chasti·ser.**

Chastisement (tʃæ·stizmĕnt). ME. [f. prec. + -MENT.] † **1.** Discipline, training –1601. **2.** Disciplinary punishment; also simply punishment ME. **3.** Restraint; refining (*arch.*) 1849.

1. Experyence is a good c. EARL RIVERS. **2.** The chasticement..of our peace was vpon him T. NORTON.

Chastity (tʃæ·stĭti). [ME. *chastete* – (O)Fr. *chasteté* – L. *castitas*; see -ITY. Later assim. to L. spelling.] The quality or state of being chaste (see CHASTE *a.* 1–3, 5).

[Una]..the flowre of faith and c. SPENSER *F.Q.* I. iii. 23. The law wych byndyth prestys to chastyte T. STARKEY. C. of dress SHENSTONE, of Style HALLAM, of Renown STEELE.

Chastize, var. of CHASTISE.

† **Chasty,** *v.* ME. [– OFr. *chastier* (mod. *châtier*) :– L. *castigare* CASTIGATE. Repl. by CHASTISE.] To correct, amend –1500; to reprove (ME. only); to inflict disciplinary punishment on –1549.

Chasuble (tʃæ·siŭb'l). [ME. *chesible* – OFr. *chesible* (cf. AL. *cassibula* XIII); from XVII superseded by *chasuble* – (O)Fr. *chasuble* :– late L. *casubla*, obscure alt. of L. *casula* little cottage, hut, hooded cloak (Augustine, Isidore), dim. of *casa* house.] **1.** An ecclesiastical vestment, a sleeveless mantle covering the body and shoulders, worn over the alb and stole by the celebrant at Mass or the Eucharist. † **2.** Used also of the Jewish ephod, etc. ME. only. var. **Chasule.** FULLER.

Chat (tʃæt), *sb.*[1] 1530. [f. CHAT *v.*] † **1.** Chatter –1768. **2.** Familiar and easy talk or conversation 1573. **3.** *dial.* Impudence.

2. A c. about old times 1870.

Chat (tʃæt), *sb.*[2] 1697. [prob. imit. of their note.] A name applied to several birds, chiefly *Sylviadæ* or Warblers; as the Furze-c., Stone-c., and Wheat-ear; in N. America, to the Yellow-breasted C. (*Icteria polyglotta*) and Long-tailed C. (*I. longicauda*).

Chat (tʃæt), *sb.*[3] ME. [– Fr. *chats* lit. 'cats', barren (downy) flowers of walnut, hazel willows, etc.; cf. Fr. *chatons*, Eng. CATKINS.] **1.** A name given to the catkin, † inflorescence, or † seed of various plants. *Obs.* or *dial.* **2.** A small branch or twig 1670. Also **Chat-wood** (*dial.*).

Chat, *sb.*[4] *dial.* 1840. [Origin unkn.] A small poor potato.

Chat, *sb.*[5] 1876. [Origin unkn.] *Mining.* Ore with rock adhering to it.

Chat (tʃæt), *v.* ME. [short. f. CHATTER.] **1.** † *intr.* To chatter –1617. Also † *trans.* **2.** *intr.* To talk in a light and informal manner; to converse familiarly 1556. † *trans.* To talk of –1607.

1. *Tam. Shr.* III. ii. 123. **2.** The shepherds on the lawn..Sat simply chatting in a rustic row MILT.

‖ **Château** (ʃātō). Pl. **châteaux.** 1789. [Fr. :– OFr. *chastel*; see CASTLE.] A castle; a large mansion or country-house: now used only in reference to the Continent.

The c. of a German nobleman H. WALPOLE.

‖ **Chatelain** (ʃātəlæ̃, ʃa·tĕleⁱn). 1523. [Fr. *châtelain*; see CHASTELAIN.] = CHASTELAIN, CASTELLAN. (*Obs.* as an Eng. title.)

‖ **Chatelaine** (ʃa·tĕleⁱn). 1851. [Fr. *châtelaine*, fem. of prec.] **1.** A female castellan; the mistress of a country house 1855. **2.** An ornamental appendage worn by ladies at their waist, having short chains attached for keys, scissors, penknife, thimble-case, etc. Also *attrib.*

Cha·telet. Now *Hist.* 1494. [– OFr. *chastelet* (mod. *châtelet*), dim. of *castel* CASTLE; see -ET, and cf. CASTELLET.] A little castle; the name of an ancient prison in Paris.

Chatellany (ʃa·tĕlăni). 1668. [– Fr. *châtellenie.*] = CASTELLANY.

† **Chateus, -eux.** ME. only. [– OFr., pl. of *chatel*; see CHATTEL.] = CHATTELS.

† **Chatoyant** (ʃatwayaṅ, ʃătoi·ănt). 1798. [Fr., pres. pple. of *chatoyer.*] **A.** *adj.* Having a changeable, undulating lustre, like that of a cat's eye in the dark –1860. **B.** *sb.* **1.** Chatoyant quality 1798. **2.** A chatoyant stone, as the Cat's eye. So ‖ **Chatoy·ement,** changing or undulating lustre (*rare*).

‖ **Chatta** (tʃæ·tă, tʃā·tā). 1796. [Hindi *chhātā.*] *Anglo-Ind.* An umbrella (in India).

Chattel (tʃæ·t'l). ME. [– OFr. *chatel* (var. *catel* CATTLE) = Pr. *captal* :– med.L. *capitale*; see CAPITAL *sb.*[2]] † **1.** Property; goods; money ME. only; live stock (*rare*) –1696. **2.** With *pl.* A movable possession; any piece of property other than real estate or a freehold. (Usu. in *pl.*) 1549. Also *transf.* and *fig.*

2. *Goods and chattels*: all kinds of personal property. *Chattels personal*: all movable goods, as money, plate, cattle. *Chattels real*: such as concern the realty, as leases, etc. *Comb.* **c.-interest,** an interest in leasehold property. Hence **Cha·ttelism,** the system of holding human beings as chattels.

Chatter (tʃæ·təɹ), *v.* ME. [imit., of frequent. formation; see -ER[5]. Cf. CHITTER.] **1.** Of birds: To utter short vocal sounds in rapid succession; now applied to sounds approaching those of the human voice. **2.** Of human beings: To talk rapidly, incessantly, and with more sound than sense. *intr.* and *trans.* ME. **3.** To make a noise by rapidly repeated collisions. Also *causally.* ME.

1. The jay makes answer as the magpie chatters WORDSW. **2.** To c. about marriage 1549, like Apes *Temp.* II. ii. 9. **3.** My teeth c. BOYLE. The vibration causes the work and the tool to c. upon each other HOLTZAPFEL. Hence **Chattera·tion** (*joc.*), systematic chattering. **Cha·tterbox,** an habitual chatterer. **Cha·tteringly** *adv.*

Chatter (tʃæ·təɹ), *sb.* ME. [f. prec.] **1.** The chattering of birds, apes, etc. **2.** Incessant trivial talk; prate, tattle 1851.
2. Your words are but idle and empty c. LONGF.
Chatterer (tʃæ·tərəɹ). 1540. [f. as prec. + -ER¹.] **1.** One who chatters; a tattler. var. † **Cha·tter.** **2.** Any bird of the family *Ampelidæ*; *esp.* the Bohemian C. or Waxwing (*Ampelis garrula*); in N. Amer. the Cedar-bird or C. of Carolina (*A. carolinensis* or *cedrorum*) 1730.
† **Cha·ttery,** *sb.* [f. CHAT *v.* + -ERY.] Chatter. MME. D'ARBLAY.
Cha·ttery, *a.* [f. CHATTER *sb.* + -Y¹.] Given to chatter (*rare*).
‖ **Chatty** (tʃa·ti), *sb.* 1781. [Hindī *chāṭī.*] *Anglo-Ind.* An East Indian pot for water.
Chatty (tʃæ·ti), *a.* 1762. [f. CHAT *sb.*¹ + -Y¹.] Given to chat. Hence **Cha·ttiness,** the quality of being c.
Chaucerian (tʃǭsiə·riăn), *a.* (*sb.*) 1660. [f. the proper name + -IAN.] **1.** Of, pertaining to, or characteristic of Chaucer or his writings. **2.** *sb.* A student of Chaucer 1868. So **Chau·cerism,** an expression used by, or imitated from, Chaucer.
Chaud-mellé, -mella. ME. [– OFr. *chaude, mellee* 'heated affray'; see MÊLÉE. (Erron. identified with *chance medley.*)] *Sc. Law.* A sudden affray arising from the heat of passion; hence, the wounding or killing of a man in such an affray, without premeditation.
‖ **Chaudron** (ʃōdroṅ). 1883. [Fr., = cauldron; see CHALDRON.] A reddish colour, resembling copper. Also *attrib.*
Chaudron, obs. f. CHALDRON.
Chauffer (tʃǭ·fəɹ). 1833. [var. of CHAFER¹, perh. infl. by Fr. *chauffoir*, f. *chauffer*, heat, CHAFE *v.*] A metal basket containing fire, formerly used in lighthouses; a small portable furnace, usually of iron, with air-holes and a a grate.
Chauffeur (ʃō·fəɹ, *colloq.* ʃo·vəɹ, Fr. ʃofǫ̈r). 1899. [– Fr. *chauffeur* stoker, fireman, f. *chauffer* heat up. The first motor-cars were steam-driven.] A professional driver of a motor car.
Chauldron, obs. f. CHALDRON.
Chaum, *sb.* and *v. dial.* = CHAWM.
‖ **Chaumontel** (ʃōmōṅtęl). 1755. [Name of a village in France.] A large variety of pear.
Chaun-, obs. sp. of CHAN-.
Chau·noprockt. [– Gr. χαυνόπρωκτος 'wide-breeched' (L. & S.).] A 'wide-breeched' person. BROWNING.
‖ **Chaussée** (ʃose). 1817. [Fr.; see CAUSEY.] A causeway; a high road (in France, Belgium, etc.).
‖ **Chausses.** *pl. Hist.* 1484. [Fr., = clothing for the legs. Formerly naturalized (tʃau·sėz).] Pantaloons or tight coverings for the legs and feet; *esp.* of mail (in OFr. *chauces de fer*).
‖ **Chaussure** (ʃosü·r). [ME. *chawcer* – AFr. *chaucer* = OFr. *chaucier*, Pr. *causier* shoe; mod.Fr. *chaussure* (whence mod.Eng. form) is alt. with suffix -URE, but cf. med.L. *calceatura* (XII).] Anything worn on the feet; shoes, boots, etc.
‖ **Chauvin** (ʃōvęṅ). [Fr.; from Nicolas *Chauvin* of Rochefort, a veteran soldier of the First Republic and Empire, whose demonstrative patriotism was ultimately ridiculed by his comrades.] Popularized as name of a character in Cogniard's vaudeville, *La Cocarde Tricolore.* 1831.
Chauvinism (ʃōᵘ·viniz'm). 1870. [– Fr. *chauvinisme* (1843), f. prec.; see -ISM.] Exaggerated and bellicose patriotism. So **Chau·vinist. Chauvini·stic** *a.*
† **Chave,** *v.* ME. [f. CHAFF; cf. *half, halve.*] **1.** To mix or strew with chaff. ME. only. **2.** To separate the chaff from –1726.
Chavel, ME. form of JOWL, *sb.*¹ Hence † **Cha·vel** *v.* to wag the jaws, chatter; *trans.* to mumble (food).
Cha·vender. 1475. [rel. to CHEVIN.] = CHEVIN, the chub (fish).
† **Chaw, chawe,** *sb.*¹ 1530. [var. of JAW *sb.* (XVI–XVII), perh. by blending with CHEW *v.*] *pl.* Jaws –1626. Rarely in *sing.* A jaw –1601.
Chaw, *sb.*² (now *vulgar*). 1772. [f. CHAW *v.*] An act of chewing; also, that which is chewed.

Chaw (tʃǭ), *v.* (now *vulgar*). 1530. [var. of CHEW *v.*] **1.** To chew; now *esp.* to chew without swallowing; to champ. Also *intr.* † **2.** *fig.* To mumble (words) –1649; to ruminate upon, brood over 1558. **3.** *U.S. slang. To c. up*: to 'do for' 1844.
1. Chawe your meat well 1562. As venemous as a chaw'd bullet 1683. **2.** To c. one's malice 1600. Hence **Chaw·er** (*rare*).
Chaw·-bacon. 1822. [f. prec.] A country bumpkin.
† **Chaw·buck,** *sb.* 1698. [– Urdu *chābuk* horse-whip.] A whip; flogging with a whip –1784. Hence † **Chaw·buck** *v.* to whip.
Chaw·dron. [ME. *chaudoun* – OFr. *chaudun* offal, pettitoes – med.L. *calduna* (whence also MLG. *kaldūne*, G. *kaldaunen*), app. – L. *cal(i)dus* hot. Present sp. (XVII) assim. to CHALDRON.] † **1.** A sauce, consisting of chopped entrails, spice, etc. –1615. **2.** Entrails, *esp.* as used for food (*arch.*) 1578.
† **Chawn,** *sb.* 1601. [Identical in meaning with CHINE *sb.*¹, and perh. a deriv. of CHINE *v.*¹ (pa. t. *chane, chone* in ME.).] A gap, cleft, fissure; a chine –1799. Hence † **Chawn** *v.* to gape or cause to gape open.
Chaw·-stick. 1756. [f. CHAW *v.* + STICK *sb.*] A species of Gouania (*G. domingensis*, N.O. *Rhamnaceæ*), so called in Jamaica because its stems are chewed as a stomachic.
‖ **Chay, choy** (tʃēⁱ, tʃai, tʃoi), **chaya** (tʃai·a). 1598. [– Tamil *saya*, in other Indian vernaculars *shaya, chaya.*] The root of the Indian plant *Oldenlandia umbellata* (N.O. *Cinconaceæ*), which yields a deep red dye.
Chay. [f. CHAISE, mistaken for a pl. form; cf. SHAY.]
† **Che** (tʃə), *pron.* An expanded form of CH, for *ich* I.
† **Cheap,** *sb.* [ME. *chēp*, OE. *ćēap* barter, bargain, price, market = OFris. *kāp*, OS. *kōp* (Du. *koop*), OHG. *kouf* (G. *kauf*), ON. *kaup* n. :– Gmc. **kaupaz, -am*, rel. to OE. *ćiepan* (see CHEAP *v.*); all based on an early Gmc. adoption of L. *caupo* small tradesman, innkeeper. OE. *ćēap* survives in the proper names *Cheapside, East Cheap, Chepstow*; *Chapman.* Cf. CHAP *sb.*³] **1.** A bargain; bargaining –ME. **2.** Market; a market-place. (Hence in place-names, as *Cheapside*, etc.) –1596. **3.** Price –1440. **4.** Goods, *esp.* (live) cattle (OE. only).
2. *Good cheap*: a cheap market. (Hence *cheap* alone: Plenty; opp. to *dearth.*) quasi-*adj.* That is a good bargain; cheap. quasi-*adv.* Cheaply.
Cheap (tʃīp). 1509. [ellipt. for † *good cheap* (XIV–XVII), earlier † *at good cheape* (XIV–XV) 'as a good bargain', phr. formed, after (O)Fr. *à bon marché* 'at good market', on ME. *chēp*; see prec.]
A. *adj.* **1.** Low in price; inexpensive. Opp. to *dear.* Also *transf.* (of the price, the market, etc.) 1598. **2.** Well worth the price 1611. **3.** *fig.* Costing little labour, trouble, etc. 1603. **4.** Hence, Worthless 1571. **5.** Lightly esteemed, common 1591.
1. Cheapest, say the prudent, is the dearest labour EMERSON. **2.** Goods may be low-priced, and not c. DE FOE. **4.** His c. Latin 1872. **5.** Making the king c. PEPYS. Phr. *Dirt c.*: as c. as dirt. So *Dog c.* (colloq.). Hence **Chea·p-ish** *a.*, **-ly** *adv.*, **-ness.**
B. *advb.* At a low price, cheaply; easily 1568.
C. *subst.* in *On the c.*: on the cheap scale, cheaply 1888.
Comb.: **C. Jack** or **C. John,** a travelling hawker who offers bargains; **c. trip**: see TRIP; hence **cheap-tripper.**
† **Cheap,** *v.* [OE. *ćiepan* (:– **kaupjan*) and *ćēapian* trade, bargain, = OS. *kopian, kopon*, OHG. *koufen, koufōn*, ON. *kaupa*, Goth. *kaupōn* – L. *caupo*; see CHEAP *sb.*] **1.** *orig.* (*intr.*) To barter; to trade –ME. **2.** *trans.* To buy –ME.; to offer to buy, price –1614; to offer for sale –1580.
Cheapen (tʃī·p'n), *v.* 1574. [f. CHEAP *a.* and *v.* + -EN⁵.] **1.** To ask the price of, bid for. Also *fig.* (*arch.*). **2.** To make cheap, lower the price of 1833. Also *fig.* **3.** *intr.* To become cheap (*lit.* and *fig.*) 1805.
1. I cheapened a pig and was asked only eighteen sols WILKES. **2.** To c. production MILL. Hence **Chea·pener,** † a bidder, var. † **Chea·per;** one who makes a thing cheap.
† **Chea·ping,** *vbl. sb.* OE. [f. CHEAP *v.* + -ING¹.] **1.** Bargaining; buying and selling –1580. **2.** Market, a market-place. (Hence in place-names, as *Chipping Norton*, etc.) –1587.

Cheare, obs. f. CHAIR, CHEER.
Cheat (tʃīt), *sb.*¹ [In sense 1 ME. *chet(e*, aphet. f. *achet*, var. of *eschet* ESCHEAT. Sense 3 is of doubtful origin; senses 4–6 are from the vb.] † **1.** An ESCHEAT –1649. † **2.** Booty, spoil –1610. † **3.** *Thieves' Cant.* 'Thing, article', usually with a descriptive word –1826. **4.** † The action of cheating; fraud –1696; a fraud, an imposition 1648. **5.** One who or that which cheats 1532. **6.** Local name for grasses, which resemble the grain among which they grow.
3. *The c.* (= *nubbing-, topping-, treyning-c.*): the gallows. **4.** Those who live by cheats and quirks 1690. **5.** Extortioners and cheats FARRAR. Callinge . . the dice Chetes 1532.
† **Cheat,** *sb.*² 1450. [Origin unkn.; cf. MANCHET.] Wheaten bread of the second quality; see MANCHET –1655.
Cheat (tʃīt), *v.* 1440. [ME. *chete*, aphet. f. *achete* (ACHEAT), phon. var. of *eschete* ESCHEAT; see A- *pref.* 9.] † **1.** *trans.* To escheat. ME. only. **2.** To deprive *of* by deceit 1590; to impose upon 1634. **3.** *intr.* To practise deceit 1647. **4.** To beguile (weariness, etc.) 1712. † **5.** To obtain by cheating –1737.
2. The Scaffold of its prey to c. 1821. To c. the eye with blear illusion MILT. **3.** To c. in an examination 1889. **4.** To c. the time SCOTT. Hence **Chea·table** *a.* that may be cheated. **Cheatee·,** one who is cheated (*colloq.*). **Chea·ter,** † an escheator; one who cheats. (An habitual *cheater* is now called a CHEAT.) **Chea·tery,** the practice of cheating.
Che·bacco. 1837. [app. – Pg. *xabeco* (ʃabe·ko); cf. next and XEBEC.] *C.-boat*: A kind of vessel employed in the Newfoundland fisheries; called also *pinkstern.*
Chebec, -ck (ʃībe·k). Now usu. **Xebec.** 1762. [– Fr. *chebec* – It. *sciabecco* – Arab. *šabāk*; see XEBEC.] A small three-masted Mediterranean vessel, a XEBEC.
‖ **Chebule** (kĕbū·l). 1599. [– Fr. *chébule*; perh. – Urdu *Kābulī* of Cabul.] The dried prune-like astringent fruit of *Terminalia Chebula*, imported under the name of myrobalan. Also *attrib.* Hence **Chebu·lic** *a.*
Check (tʃek), *int.* and *sb.*¹ [Aphetic – OFr. *eschec* (mod. *échec*), alt. of **eschac* (pl. *-as*) = Pr. *escac*, It. *scacco* :– Rom. (med.L.) *scaccus* – Arab. – Pers. *šāh* king, SHAH; cf. CHECKMATE, CHESS, EXCHEQUER.]
A. *int.* A call at chess by which an opponent is notified that his King is exposed. Also *fig.*
fig. Therewith Fortune said Checke here CHAUCER.
B. *sb.* **1.** *Chess.* The act of threatening the King; the position of the King when he is exposed to the attack of one of the opponent's men ME. Also *fig.* and *transf.* † **2.** A taunt –1635; a rebuke, censure –1751. **3.** A sudden arrest given to the onward course of anything; a rebuff, repulse, reverse 1515. **4.** *Hawking.* A false stoop, when a hawk forsakes her quarry for baser game. *Hist.* ME. Also, the baser game itself 1575. **5.** A sudden stoppage or pause 1532. † **6.** A stoppage of wages or a fine; the amount stopped –1708. **7.** Restraint upon action or conduct by a controlling power 1579. **8.** Any person or thing that checks 1647. **9.** Control by which accuracy, etc., is secured 1786. **10.** A mark made against an item in an account, list, etc., to show that it has been checked. **11.** A counterfoil, token, ticket, or other means to secure accuracy, security from fraud, etc. 1706. **12.** A counter used in games at cards. *U.S.* 1870. † **13.** Short for CHECK-ROLL –1611.
3. A c. to industry MCCULLOCH. Our c. in Holland 1799. The hounds ran him without a c. WHYTE-MELVILLE. **4.** *To fly at c.* Of dogs: *To run at c.* **5.** † *To take c.*: to pull up, take offence. **7.** *In c.*: under control. **8.** Of the checks to population MALTHUS. **12.** *To hand in one's checks*: to die (*colloq.*).
Clerk of the c.: an officer in the royal household keeping the c.-roll and having control of the yeomen of the guard, etc.; † formerly, an officer of control in the dockyards, etc.
Check (tʃek), *sb.*² ME. [prob. short for *checker*, CHEQUER *sb.*¹] **1.** *Her. and gen.* A pattern of cross lines forming small squares, as in a chess-board. **2.** A fabric with such a pattern 1614. Also *attrib.*
Check, *sb.*³, var. of CHEQUE.

Check (tʃek), *v.*[1] [Aphetic – OFr. *eschequier* play chess, give check to, f. *eschec* CHECK *sb.*[1]] **I. 1.** *Chess.* To give check to an opponent's King (see CHECK *sb.*[1] 1) 1614. Also *fig.* † **2.** To strike, hit –1608; *intr.* to clash –1632.

2. If it [Loue] checke once with businesse BACON.

II. 1. To stop or retard the motion or course of ME. † **2.** *intr.* (for *refl.*) To stop short; to stand *at*; to wince (*at*) –1724. *Hawking.* To forsake the quarry and fly at baser game (cf. CHECK *sb.*[1] 4) 1522. † **3.** To stop (a person) from receiving part of his wages; to fine, mulct –1803.

1. *To c. a brace* (Naut.): to ease it off when too stiffly extended. *C. her* (a ship): stop her way. (Adm. Smyth.) **2.** That which you c. at is the immortality of the soul JER. TAYLOR. *To c. at the fist* (Hawking): to shy at, recoil from, the fist.

III. † **1.** To taunt, revile –1592. **2.** To rebuke 1514.

2. † *To c. at* (intr.): to aim reproof at.

IV. 1. *fig.* To stop (action, growth, etc.); to repress, restrain 1581. **2.** To curb, control; to act as a check on 1630. **3.** To control (a statement, account, etc.) by some method of comparison. Also *to c. a person* (in his account, etc.) 1695.

1. If I can checke my erring loue, I will *Two Gent.* II. iv. 213. To c. a laugh JANE AUSTEN. **2.** In England, the strong classes c. the weaker EMERSON. **3.** *To c. off*: to tick off as found correct. *To c. up*: to examine or count up in detail.

V. *intr.* To draw a cheque (*upon* a person, *for* an amount). *U.S.* 1843.

Hence **Checked** *ppl. a.*[1] stopped in progress; repressed; restrained. **Checker** *sb.*[1] one who checks.

Check (tʃek), *v.*[2] ME. [Goes with earlier CHECK *sb.*[2]; short for *checker*, CHEQUER *v.*] To mark with a pattern of † squares, or crossing lines. Also *transf.* and † *fig.* Hence **Checked** *ppl. a.*[2] **Che·cker** *sb.*[2] = CHEQUER, q.v.; *spec.* in *pl.* Draughts.

Check-, in *comb.* [from the stem of CHECK *v.*[1]]:

check-book, a book in which items of control are entered (but see also CHEQUE); **-clerk**; **-key,** a latch-key; **-lock,** a small lock for securing a lock, bar, bolt, etc.; **-man,** one who checks fares, tickets, etc.; **-nut,** a nut screwed over another one to keep it from loosening; **-rein,** (*a*) a coupling-rein; (*b*) a strap which prevents a horse from lowering his head; **-strap,** the strap of a helmet, etc., running under the chin; **-taker**; **-till,** a till with a contrivance to check the receipts; **-weigher, -weighman,** at collieries, a man acting for the workmen who checks the weight of the coal sent up.

Checker, *v.*; see CHEQUER.

Che·cker-berry. 1823. [Cf. CHEQUER *sb.*[2]] The fruit of *Gaultheria procumbens*; hence the plant itself; the winter-green. ¶ The Partridge-berry, *Michella repens* (Webster).

† **Che·cker-roll, che·quer-roll.** 1461. [f. *checker*, CHEQUER *sb.*[1]] A roll of persons chargeable to the royal exchequer; CHECK-ROLL. *transf.* A roll of persons. –1589.

Che·ckery. ME. [aphet. f. AFr. *eschekeré*, OFr. *eschequeré* a. and sb., pa. ppl. formation on *eschequier* (see EXCHEQUER); cf. the parallel formation CHEQUERED. See -Y[5].] † Checked cloth –1472; chequed pattern (*rare*) 1837.

† **Checklaton,** var. of CICLATON. Spenser.

† **Che·ckle,** *v.* 1627. [= north. KECKLE *v.*[1]; cf. CHUCKLE.] *intr.* To laugh giddily –1684.

Che·ckless, *a. rare.* 1604. [f. CHECK *sb.*[1] + -LESS.] Unchecked.

Checkmate (tʃe·kmē̆i·t), *int.* and *sb.* [aphet. – OFr. *eschec mat* = Pr. *escac mat* – Pers. *šāh māt* the king is dead; see CHECK *sb.*[1], MATE *a.*]

A. *int.* Exclam. at chess by a player on putting the opponent's King into inextricable check, whereby the game is won; orig. meaning '(your) King is dead'. (Now MATE.) Also *transf.*

B. *sb.* **1.** This exclam. as a name for itself, and for the conclusive move which it announces. *To give c. to*: to make this move. (Also MATE.) ME. Also *fig.* and *transf.* † **2.** (*erron.*) An equal in a contest, a match; as if 'a mate that checks' –1651.

1. *fig.* Loue they him called, that gaue me c. SPENSER.

Checkmate (tʃe·kmē̆i·t), *v.* ME. [f. the sb.] **1.** *Chess.* To give checkmate to; see the sb. sense 1. (Now to MATE.) 1789. **2.** *transf.* To arrest or defeat utterly. Now, often: To defeat the 'game' of, by a counter-move. ME.

2. To c. the ingenuity of the local taxmasters 1884.

† **Check-roll.** 1450. [Later var. of CHECKER-ROLL, influenced by CHECK *v.*] **1.** = CHECKER-ROLL –1769. **2.** A list of servants –1636. **3.** *fig.* A muster-roll –1653.

Che·ck-stone. 1587. [Origin unkn.; cf. Sc. *chuckie-stones*.] A small smooth round pebble; a game played with these. Also *fig.* Still *dial.*

Che·ck-string. 1774. A string by which the occupant of a carriage may signal to the driver to stop.

Che·cky, chequee, *a.* 1486. [orig. aphet. – OFr. *eschequié, eschequé* (see -Y[5]); later assim. to Eng. adjs. in -Y[1].] *Her.* and *gen.* Checked, chequered.

Che·ddar. 1666. Name of a village in Somerset. Hence *Cheddar cheese* (or *Cheddar*).

† ‖ **Chedreux.** 1678. [Proper name.] A kind of peruke –1745.

‖ **Chee-chee.** 1781. [perh. – Hindi *chhī-chhī* fie! (lit. filth).] *Anglo-Ind.* The minced English of half-breeds or Eurasians; the class of half-breeds.

Cheek (tʃīk), *sb.* [OE. *ċēoce* = OFris. *ziāke* :– WGmc. *keuka; varying with OE. *ċēace, ċēce* = (M)LG. *kāke, kēke*, MDu. *kāke* (Du. *kaak*) :– WGmc. *kæka.] **I.** *lit.* † **1.** The jaw, jaw-bone –ME.; *pl.* (also *sing.*) the fauces –1450. **2.** The side of the face below the eye OE. Also *fig.* **3.** *colloq.* Insolence in speaking to anyone 1840; cool confidence, effrontery 1852.

2. *fig.* Ocean's c. BYRON. **3.** *To give c.*: = CHEEK *v.* *To have the c.* (to do anything). *To one's own c.* (vulgar): to oneself. Phr. **C. by jowl**: side by side; in the closest intimacy.

II. Transf. and techn. Mostly in *pl.* **1.** *gen.* Side 1555. **2.** The side-posts of a door, gate, etc. ME. **3.** *Harness.* The ring or other part at each end of the bit 1617. **4.** *Mech.*, etc. Those parts of machines, etc., which are arranged in lateral pairs: *e.g.* the side-pieces of a piece of ordnance; the jaws of a vice; in *Founding*, one of the parts of a flask consisting of more than two parts 1650. **5.** *Naut.*: **a.** the projections on each side of a mast on which the trestle-trees rest; **b.** the outside wooden part of a block, etc. 1627.

1. By the cheeks of a red fire STEVENSON. **2.** To name sic a word at my door c. SCOTT.

Comb.: **c.-bone,** † the bone of the lower jaw; the bone above the c. forming the lower boundary of the orbits of the eyes; **-pouch,** a pouch-like enlargement of the c., *esp.* in some monkeys; **-tooth,** a molar.

Cheek (tʃīk), *v.* 1538. [f. prec.] **1.** *trans.* To form a cheek or side to. **2.** *colloq.* To address cheekily; to face with effrontery 1840.

Cheeked (tʃīkt), *a.* 1552. [See -ED[2].] Having a cheek or cheeks; in *comb.* as *red-c.*, etc.

Cheeky (tʃī·ki), *a. colloq.* 1859. [f. CHEEK *sb.* I. 3 + -Y[1].] Characterized by cheek. Hence **Chee·kiness** (*colloq.*).

Cheep (tʃīp), *sb.* Chiefly *Sc.* 1774. [f. next.] A faint shrill sound, such as the voice of a young bird or a mouse.

Cheep (tʃīp), *v.* Chiefly *Sc.* 1513. [Of imit. origin; cf. PEEP *v.*[1]] *intr.* To utter cheeps, like young birds, mice, bats, etc. Also *trans.*

trans. 'Hold hard now', cheeps little Conchy M. SCOTT. Hence **Chee·per**; *esp.* of the chicks of partridge and grouse. **Chee·py** *a.* given to cheeping.

Cheer (tʃīᵊɹ), *sb.* [ME. *chere* – AFr. *chere*, OFr. *chiere* face :– late L. *cara* face – Gr. κάρα head.] † **1.** The face –1590; the expression of the face; countenance (*arch.*) –1830. **2.** Disposition, mood; usu. qualified as 'good', 'glad', etc. ME. **3.** Gladness, mirth, gaiety ME. † **4.** Hospitable reception or entertainment –1666. **5.** *concr.* Fare, viands, food ME. **6.** Solace; encouragement 1549. **7.** A shout of encouragement, welcome, approbation, or congratulation; *esp.* in *pl.* 1720.

1. To dreden the chere of them WYCLIF *Jer.* 1:17. **2.** So I piped with merry c. BLAKE. *To be of good c.* *What c.?*: 'how are you?' **5.** To fede on simple cheare 1567. *The fewer the better c.*, i.e. the more for each to eat. **7.** The result was received with cheers and counter-cheers 1889. Hence **Chee·rless** *a.* devoid of c. **Chee·rless-ly** *adv.*, **-ness.**

Cheer (tʃīᵊɹ), *v.* ME. [f. the sb.] † **1.** *refl.* and *intr.* To assume a disposition or state of mind –1725. **2.** To make of good cheer ME.; *refl.* to take heart (mostly in imper.) ME. **3.** To make cheerful ME.; also † *intr.* **4.** *trans.* † To feast –1697; to solace as food does 1548. **5.** To brighten up (the face, etc.) 1611. **6.** To encourage, inspirit, animate, or incite; now *esp.* by cries or shouts ME. **7.** To salute with cheers 1798. Also *intr.*

1. How c. you gentlemen GREENE. **2.** So cheard he his fair Spouse MILT. *P.L.* v. 129. **4.** The cups, That c. but not inebriate COWPER. **6.** He cheer'd the dogs to follow her who fled DRYDEN. **7.** The ship was cheer'd COLERIDGE.

Cheer up, to raise the spirits of by cheering words; *intr.* (for *refl.*) to take courage. Hence **Chee·rer,** he who or that which cheers; *Sc.* a cheering cup. **Chee·ringly** *adv.*

Cheered (tʃīᵊɹd), *a.* ME. [f. CHEER *sb.* and *vb.* + -ED.] **1.** Having a (certain) cheer or countenance. **2.** *ppl. a.* Made cheerful.

Cheerful (tʃīᵊ·ɹful), *a.* ME. [f. CHEER *sb.* + -FUL.] **1.** Full of cheer; of good cheer; blithe, lively and in good spirits. **2.** Cheering, animating; bright, enlivening 1460.

1. God loveth a c. giver 2 *Cor.* 9:7. **2.** C. Chambers BACON, colours BURKE. **Chee·rfulize** *v.* to make c. **Chee·rful-ly** *adv.*, **-ness.**

Cheerio (tʃīᵊ·riōᵘ·), *int.* Also **cheero.** 1910. [f. CHEER(Y + O *int.*] A parting exclamation of encouragement.

Cheerly (tʃīᵊ·ɹli). 1558. [f. CHEER *sb.* + -LY[1] and [2].] **A.** *adj.* Cheerful (*arch.*) 1571. **B.** *adv.* **1.** Cheerily (*arch.*) 1558. *spec.* Heartily, with a will. *Temp.* I. i. 6. **2.** Cheeringly 1794. Hence † **Chee·rliness.**

Cheer-up, var. CHIRRUP.

Cheery (tʃīᵊ·ri), *a.* 1611. [f. CHEER *sb.* + -Y[1].] **1.** Abounding in cheerfulness; lively. **2.** Such as to cheer; cheering 1720.

1. The Corporal, with c. eye STERNE. **2.** A c. bowl GAY. Hence **Chee·rily** *adv.* **Chee·riness.**

Cheese (tʃīz), *sb.*[1] [OE. *ċēse*, *ċīese, *ċӯse* = OS. *kāsi, k(i)ēsi* (Du. *kaas*), OHG. *chāsi, kāsi* (G. *käse*) :– WGmc. *kāsi – L. *cāseus*.] **1.** The curd of milk (coagulated by rennet) separated from the whey and pressed into a solid mass; (with *pl.*) a shaped mass of this. **2.** *transf.* (in *Cider-making*) A mass of pomace pressed together in the form of a cheese 1796. **3.** The fruit of the common Mallow (*Malva silvestris*), of a flattened cheese-like shape 1527.

1. See also GREEN C. **2. b.** A conserve of fruit pressed into the consistency of cheese (cf. DAMSON-*cheese*).

Phr. *To make cheeses* [Fr. *faire des fromages*]: a school-girls' amusement, consisting in turning rapidly round and then suddenly sinking down, so that the petticoats take something of the form of a cheese. Hence occas., a deep curtsying.

Comb.: **c.-cake,** a tart, orig. containing c.; now filled with a mixture of milk-curds, sugar, and butter, or whipped egg and sugar; **-fly,** a small black fly (*Piophila casei*) bred in c.; **-hopper,** the maggot of the c.-fly; also the fly; **-maggot** = *cheese-hopper*; **-mite,** the minute arachnid (*Acarus domesticus*) which infests old c.; **-press,** an apparatus for pressing the curds in cheese-making; **-rennet, -running,** *Galium verum*, Lady's Bedstraw, occas. used to coagulate milk; **-vat,** † **-fat,** the mould in which the curds are pressed and the c. shaped.

Cheese (tʃīz), *sb.*[2] *slang.* 1818. [– Hind. – Pers. *chīz* thing.] The correct thing.

Cheese, *v.* 1812. [Origin unkn.] *Thieves' slang.* To stop, leave off. *C. it!* = have done! run away!

Chee·selip, -lep[1]. Now *dial.* [OE. *ċēse-lyb(b*; f. CHEESE + a word = ON. *lyf* herb, mod. G. dial. *lüpp* rennet.] **1.** Rennet, for use in cheese-making. **2.** The dried stomach of a calf, etc., similarly used OE.

† **Chee·selip, -lep**[2]. 1530. [Origin unkn.] The common wood-louse; also, the allied Armadillo wood-louse (? *dial.*).

Chee·semonger. 1510. One who deals in cheese.

Chee·se-pa:ring. 1597. *sb.* A paring of the rind of cheese. Also *fig.* *vbl. sb.* The paring of cheese. *fig.* Parsimonious saving 1871. *ppl. a.* Parsimonious 1867.

Cheesy (tʃī·zi), *a.* ME. [f. CHEESE *sb.*[1] + -Y[1].] **1.** Of or belonging to, abounding in, or resembling, cheese. ¶ **2.** [prob. f. CHEESE *sb.*[2]] Fine, showy 1858. Hence **Chee·siness.**

Cheetah (tʃī·tă). 1781. [– Hind. *chītā*.] The Hunting Leopard, *Acinonyx jubatus* (*Felis jubata*), used for hunting deer in India.

Cheewink, che-, (tʃī͵wi·ŋk). 1796. [From its note; also *towhee.*] A N. Amer. bird (*Pipilo erythrophthalmus*), also called Ground-robin.

‖ **Chef** (ʃef). 1842. [Fr.; = 'head'.] A head cook in the kitchen of a large household.

‖ **Chef d'œuvre** (ʃędö·vr). Pl. **chefs-d'œuvre.** 1762. [Fr.; *lit.* 'chief (piece) of work'.] A masterpiece.

Chego, obs. f. CHIGOE.

Cheil-, cheilo-, repr. Gr. χειλο-, comb. f. χεῖλος lip, used more commonly in the Latinized spelling *chil-*, CHILO-.

Cheir-, cheiro-, repr. Gr. χειρο-, comb. f. χείρ hand; also written *chir-*, CHIRO-, q.v.

Chei·ropod, -ped. 1837. [f. CHEIRO- + Gr. πούς, ποδ- foot.] *Zool.* A name applied to mammals possessed of hands, including the Bimana and Quadrumana.

‖ **Cheiroptera** (kəirǫ·ptĕră), *sb. pl.* Occas. **chir-.** 1835. [mod.L. (Cuvier) f. CHEIRO- + Gr. πτερόν wing; see -A *suff.* 4.] *Zool.* An order of Mammalia, having elongated finger-bones supporting a membrane attached to the posterior limbs and the side of the body, and adapted for flight; the Bats. Hence **Cheiro·pteran** *a.* and *sb.* **Cheiro·pterous** *a.*

‖ **Cheirotherium** (kəiᵊrop̄īᵊ·riŏm). 1855. [f. CHEIRO- + Gr. θηρίον beast.] *Palæont.* A large extinct four-footed animal, whose footprints resemble a human hand. Hence **Cheirothe·rian** *a.*

Cheka, see **Tcheka.**

‖ **Chela**[1] (kī·lă). Pl. **chelæ** (kī·lī). 1646. [mod.L. alt. of L. *chele* or its source Gr. χηλή.] The prehensile claw of crabs and lobsters; also, of scorpions. Hence **Che·late, Cheli·ferous, Che·liform** *adjs.*

‖ **Chela**[2] (tʃēⁱ·lă). 1883. [Hindi; = 'slave, servant'.] In esoteric Buddhism, a novice. Hence **Che·laship.**

Chele·rythrine. [f. L. *chel(idonia* celandine + Gr. ἐρυθρός red + -INE[5].] *Chem.* An alkaloid forming orange-red salts, obtained from *Chelidonium.*

Chelicer, -cere (ke·lisəɹ, -sīᵊɹ). 1835. [– Fr. *chélicère*, mod.L. *chelicera*, f. Gr. χηλή (see CHELA[1]) + κέρας horn.] One of the prehensile claws which arm the proboscis of scorpions and spiders. Hence **Cheli·ceral** *a.*

Chelidonic (kelidǫ·nik), *a.* 1863. [f. L. *chelidonia* celandine + -IC.] *Chem.* In *C. acid*, $C_7H_4O_6$, obtained from the juice of the Greater Celandine.

‖ **Chelifer** (ke·lifəɹ, kī·li-). 1865. [f. CHELA[1] + L. *-fer* bearing; cf. Fr. *chélifère.*] *Zool.* A genus of Spiders having the appearance of small tailless scorpions, called also *Book-scorpion.*

Cheloid (kī·loid). 1876. [– Fr. *chéloïde*, f. Gr. χηλή; see CHELA[1], -OID.] *Med.* A disease of the skin, having claw-like processes radiating from its extremities. Also *attrib.*

Chelonian (kĭlōᵘ·niăn), *a.* 1826. [f. mod.L. *Chelonia* (cf. Gr. χελώνη tortoise) + -AN; see -IA[2], -A *suff.* 4.] Of or belonging to the order of reptiles called *Chelonia*, distinguished by having the body enclosed in a double shell, and comprising tortoises and turtles. *sb.* [sc. *animal.*]

† **Chelydre.** ME. [– OFr. *chelydre* – L. *chelydrus* – Gr. χέλυδρος, f. χέλυς tortoise + ὕδρος water-serpent.] A kind of fetid amphibious serpent –1607.

Chemiatric (kemi͵æ·trik), *a.* 1837. [– mod.L. *chemiatria*, Paracelsian term (f. Gr. χημία alchemy, chemistry + ἰατρεία medical treatment) + -IC.] Relating to a (Paracelsian) theory of medicine, according to which diseases are referred to disturbances of fermentations in the body, and are treated accordingly. As *sb.* One who held this theory.

Chemic (ke·mik). 1576. [– Fr. *chimique*, or mod.L. *chim-*, *chymicus*, for med.L. *alchymicus*; see ALCHEMIC.] **A.** *adj.* **1.** Alchemic. † **2.** = CHEMIATRIC *a.* –1763. **3.** Of or belonging to chemistry. (*poet.* for CHEMICAL.) 1634.

1. Chimick Gold DRYDEN. **3.** The c. labour of the blood TENNYSON.

B. *sb.* † **1.** An ALCHEMIST –1673. † **2.** = CHEMIATRIC *sb.* –1660. † **3.** A chemist –1651. **4.** *Bleaching.* Chloride of lime 1875.

Che·mic, *v.* 1614. [f. prec.] † **1.** To transmute by or as by alchemy –1720. **2.** *Bleaching.* To treat with solution of chloride of lime 1875.

Chemical (ke·mikăl), *a.* 1576. [f. CHEMIC *a.* and *sb.* + -AL[1].] † **1.** Alchemical –1747. † **2.** = CHEMIATRIC, as opp. to 'Galenical' –1747. † **2.** = CHEMIATRIC, as opp. to 'Galenical' –1782. **3.** Relating or belonging to chemistry; obtained by chemistry 1576. **4.** Versed in chemistry 1615. **5.** as *sb.* (*esp.* in *pl.*) A substance obtained or used in chemical operations 1747.

3. *C. attraction*, etc.: see ATTRACTION, etc. The c. composition of plants SIR H. DAVY, of the atmosphere HUXLEY. **Che·mically** *adv.*

Chemico- (ke·miko), comb. f. CHEMIC *a.*, in sense 'chemically', 'relating to chemistry in connection with . . .'; as in *c.-agricultural.*

Chemise (ʃĭmī·z). ME. [– (O)Fr. *chemise* :– late L. *camisia* shirt, nightgown (Jerome).] **1.** A body garment: formerly variously used, later *spec.* a woman's undergarment (= SHIFT *sb.* III. 3), now largely superseded (see CAMISOLE). Cf. SHIMMY[1]. **2.** *Fortif.* A wall with which a bastion, etc., is lined 1704.

Chemisette (ʃemize·t). 1807. [– Fr. *chemisette*, dim. of *chemise* (prec.); see -ETTE.] **1.** A bodice, more or less like the upper part of a chemise. **2.** An article, usually of lace or muslin, made to fill in the open front of a woman's dress 1844.

Chemism (ke·miz'm). *rare.* 1851. [– Fr. *chimisme*, parallel to *chimiste* CHEMIST; see -ISM.] Chemical action, activity, or force.

Chemist (ke·mist, ki·mist). 1562. [Earlier *chymist* – Fr. *chimiste*, † *chymiste* – mod.L. *chimysta*, *chimista*, for *alchimista* ALCHEMIST. See ALCHEMY.] † **1.** = ALCHEMIST –1732. † **2.** = CHEMIATRIC *sb.* –1616. **3.** One versed in chemistry; one who makes chemical investigations 1626. **4.** One who deals in or retails medicinal drugs 1683. var. (now *rare*) **Chy·mist.** Hence † **Che·mistic (-al),** *adjs.* (*rare*).

Chemistry (ke·mistri). 1605. [In XVII *chymistrie*, f. *chymist*; see CHEMIST, -RY.] † **1.** ALCHEMY –1788. † **2.** The 'Chemical' or 'Paracelsian' practice of medicine –1711. **3.** That branch of science which deals with the several elementary substances, or forms of matter, of which all bodies are composed, the laws that regulate the combination of these elements in the formation of compound bodies, and the phenomena that accompany their exposure to diverse physical conditions. (The reference in early writers and dictionaries is to chemistry as an art only, i.e. *practical* or *applied* c.) 1646. Also *fig.*

3. *Chymistry*, is the Anatomy of natural Bodies by fire BAILEY. *Inorganic c.*: that which deals with inorganic bodies. *Organic c.*: that treating of the substances found only in organic structures. *Agricultural c.*: that bearing upon agriculture. *fig.* The world has a sure c., by which it extracts what is excellent in its children EMERSON.

Chemitype (ke·mitəip). 1851. [f. *chemi-* in CHEMIC, etc. + TYPE.] A stereotype, obtained in relief from an engraved plate by a chemical process; hence *c. process*, **Che·mitypy.**

Chemolysis (kĭmǫ·lisis). *rare.* 1872. [f. *chem-* in CHEMIC + -LYSIS, after *electrolysis.*] The decomposition of organic compounds into more simple substances by merely chemical agents. So **Chemoly·tic** *a.* relating to c.

‖ **Chemosis** (kimōᵘ·sis). 1708. [Gr. χήμωσις (Galen), f. χήμη cockle-shell; see -OSIS.] *Med.* An affection of the conjunctiva of the eye, which causes it to be elevated and projected over the edge of the cornea. Hence **Chemo·sed** *ppl. a.*

‖ **Chemosmosis** (kemǫzmōᵘ·sis). [mod.L., f. *chem-* in CHEMIC, etc. + OSMOSIS.] Chemical action taking place through an intervening membrane (Dicts.).

‖ **Chenar** (tʃīnāɹ). 1634. [Pers. *chinār.*] Name of the Oriental Plane-tree.

Chenille (ʃĭnī·l). 1738. [– Fr. *chenille* hairy caterpillar :– L. *canicula*, dim. of *canis* dog.] Velvety cord, having fibres of silk and wool standing out round a core of thread or wire; used in trimming and bordering dresses, etc.

Chenopod (ke·nopǫd). 1555. [– mod.L. *chenopodium*, f. Gr. χηνόπους goose-foot.] *Bot.* The plant genus *Chenopodium* or Goose-foot.

Cheque, check (tʃek). 1706. [See CHECK *sb.*[1] 10 and CHECK *v.*[1] IV. 3. *Cheque* is a var. of *check* (also used, *esp.* in U.S.).] † **1.** The counterfoil of a bank bill, draft, etc. –1782. **2.** A draft form having a counterfoil 1717. **3.** A written order to a banker directing him to pay money as stated therein 1774. Also *fig.*

3. *Blank c.*: a cheque signed by the drawer but with the amount left blank to be filled up by the donee. *Comb.*: **c.-book,** *formerly*, a book in which the Bank kept a register of cheques issued; *now*, a book containing cheque forms with their counterfoils.

Chequeen, chequin (tʃĭkī·n). *arch.* 1583. [– It. *zecchino* (tsekkī·no), f. *zecca* the mint at Venice.] = SEQUIN, q.v.

Chequer, checker (tʃe·kəɹ), *sb.*[1] [ME. *cheker*, aphet. f. ME. and AFr. *escheker*; see EXCHEQUER.]

I. † **1.** A chess-board –1828. † **2.** The game of chess. ME. only. **3.** *pl.* The game of draughts (*dial.* and *U.S.*) 1838. **4.** A chess-board as the sign of an inn; a name for a public-house ME.

II. † **1.** The Court of EXCHEQUER –1691. † **2.** Treasury (*lit.* and *fig.*) –1692.

III. 1. *pl.* Squares or spots like those of a chess-board 1629. **2.** Chequer-work 1779. **3.** *Arch.* in *pl.* 'In masonry, stones in the facing of walls which have all their thin joints continued in straight lines, without interruption or breaking joints' (Gwilt).

Che·quer, *sb.*[2] *dial.* 1649. [app. from the appearance of the fruit; cf. CHECKER-BERRY.] In *pl.* The berries of the Wild Service tree, *Pyrus torminalis.* In *sing.* also the tree.

Chequer, checker (tʃe·kəɹ), *v.* ME. [f. CHEQUER *sb.*] **1.** *trans.* To divide or mark like a chess-board in sections (with or without reference to colour) 1486. **2.** To diversify with or as with a different colour or shade; to interrupt the uniformity of ME. **3.** To arrange chequer-wise 1677. † **4.** To deposit in an exchequer –1734.

2. *Rom. & Jul.* II. iii. 2. His sleep was checkered with starts and moans DICKENS. The good and ill that c. life COWPER.

† **Chequer-chamber.** 1494. **1.** Treasury-room –1011. **2.** A court of appellate jurisdiction; = EXCHEQUER-CHAMBER –1714.

Chequered, checkered (tʃe·kəɹd), *ppl. a.* 1486. [f. CHEQUER *sb.* and *v.*] **1.** Marked like a chess-board; hence, having a pattern of various crossing colours. **2.** Diversified in colour, light and shade, character; full of alternation 1656.

1. His chequer'd plaid SCOTT. **2.** Dancing in the Chequer'd shade MILT. Weather. .chequered, a fair and a rainy day SWIFT.

Che·quer-wise, *adv.* ME. Like a CHEQUER or chess-board. (Orig. *in chequer wise.*)

Che·quer-work, che·cker-work. 1519. **1.** Work chequered in pattern. Also *attrib.* **2.** *transf.* and *fig.* Anything chequered with contrasting characters 1618.

1. The checkerworke pavements HOLLAND. **2.** Now joy with sorrow, checkerworke T. ADAMS.

Chequin, var. of CHEQUEEN.

† **Chere,** *a.* ME. [– (O)Fr. *cher*, *chère* (orig. *chier(e)* :– L. *carus* dear. In sense 2 confused w. *chary.*] **1.** Dear: precious –1450. **2.** Careful (*over*). Cf. CHARY. –1496. Hence † **Che·rely** *adv.*

‖ **Cherimoya** (tʃerimoi·ă). Also **chiri-, -moyer.** 1736. [– mod.L. *cherimolia* – native name; cf. Fr. *chérimolier.*] **1.** A small tree (*Anona cherimolia*), a native of Peru. **2.** The pulpy fruit of this tree 1760.

Cherish (tʃe·riʃ), *v.* [– (O)Fr. *chériss-*, extended stem of *chérir*, f. *cher* dear :– L. *carus* (see CHERE); see -ISH[2].] † **1.** *trans.* To hold dear, tenderly care for –1745; to fondle –1814. **2.** To foster. Also *transf.* and *fig.* ME. † **3.** To entertain kindly (a guest) –1738; to cheer –1734. **4.** To keep warm; to give ease to (*arch.*) ME. **5.** To entertain in the mind, harbour fondly, cling to (a hope, etc.). (The usual current sense.) ME.

2. As a nurse cherisheth her children *Thess.* 2:7. **3.** 1 *Hen. IV*, III. iii. 194. **4.** To c. Our Limbs benumm'd MILT. *P.L.* X. 1068. **5.** To c. Rebellion SHAKS., fancies MARVELL, errors 1798, resentment 1866. Hence **Che·risher. Che·rishingly** *adv.*

Cherishment (tʃe·riʃmĕnt). 1561. [f. CHERISH *v.* + -MENT, perh. through OFr. *chérissement.*] The process or fact of cherishing; † *concr.* nourishment –1689.

Chermes, obs. f. KERMES.

‖ **Cherni·tes.** 1731. [Gr. χερνίτης.] An ivory-like marble.

† **Che·rogril, chœ·rogryl.** ME. [– eccl.L. *chyrogryllius* (Jerome) – Gr. χοιρογρύλλιος, f. χοῖρος young pig + γρύλλος pig.] The CONEY of the A.V.

Cheroot (ʃĭrū·t, tʃ-). 1669. [– Fr. *cheroute* – Tamil *shuruṭṭu* roll of tobacco.] A cigar made in Southern India or Manila. Hence, any cigar truncated at both ends.

Cherry (tʃe·ri), *sb.* (*a.*) [ME. *cheri(e), chiri(e)* – ONFr. *cherise* (which was apprehended as pl.), mod. *cerise* :– med.L. *ceresia*, for **cerasia*, perh. orig. n.pl. of adj. *ceraseus*, f. L. *cerasus* – Gr. κέρασος.] **1.** A well-known stone-fruit; the pulpy drupe of certain species of *Prunus* (N.O. *Rosaceæ*). When unqualified it usually means the fruit of the cultivated tree (*Prunus cerasus* or *Cerasus vulgaris*); the common Wild Cherry or Gean, a form of this, is sometimes considered a distinct species (*P. avium*). **2.** Short for **C.-tree** 1626; **C.-wood** 1793. **3.** With qualifying words, applied **a.** to many species of the genus *Prunus*, including BIRD-*c.*, CHOKE-*c.*, GROUND-*c.*, etc.; q.v.; **Black C.,** a name of the Wild Cherry (*P. avium*), **American Wild Black C.** (*P. serotina*), etc. **b.** Also to trees resembling the cherry-tree in fruit, wood, etc. See BARBADOES-*c.*, WINTER *c.*, etc. Also used *fig.* **4.** *Mech.* A spherical bur or reaming-tool 1874. **5.** *adj.* Cherry-coloured 1447.

Comb.: **c.-bay** = *cherry-laurel*; **-bird,** the American Wax-wing or Cedar-bird; **-blossom; -bounce** = *cherry-brandy* (*colloq.*); also, brandy and sugar; **-brandy,** brandy in which cherries have been steeped, sweetened with sugar; **-chopper, snipe, -sucker,** the Spotted Fly-catcher; **-laurel,** the common Laurel (*Cerasus laurocerasus*); **-pepper,** a species of Capsicum (*C. cerasiforme*); **-pit,** a child's game, in which cherry-stones are thrown into a small hole; a c.-stone *U.S. dial.*; **-plum,** a species of plum (*Prunus cerasifera*) bearing cherry-like fruits; **-red** *a.*; **-ripe** *a.*; **-rum,** rum in which cherries have been steeped; **-stone; -tree,** the tree which bears cherries; **-wine,** wine made from cherries, *esp.* MARASCHINO; **-wood,** the wood of the c.-tree; the Wild Guelder-rose (*Viburnum opulus*).

† **Che·rry,** *v.* [– Fr. *chérir* (pa. pple. *chéri*) cherish.] To cheer. SPENSER.

Cherry-me·rry, *a. colloq.* 1775. [perh. f. *cheery* + *merry.*] Merry: *esp.* from conviviality.

Chersonese (kəɹsŏnī·s). 1601. [– L. *Chersonesus* – Gr. Χερσόνησος, f. χέρσος dry + νῆσος island.] A peninsula; spec. the Thracian peninsula west of the Hellespont. (Now usu. *poet.* or *rhet.*)

Chert (tʃɔ̄ɹt). 1679. [Local (n. midl.) name of unkn. orig.] A flint-like quartz, occurring in strata; *hornstone.* Also applied to various impure siliceous rocks, including the jaspers. Also *attrib.* Hence **Che·rty** *a.*

† **Che·rte, -tee.** ME. [– OFr. *chierté*, later and AFr. *cherté* :– L. *caritas, -tat-*; see CHARITY.] **1.** Dearness –1613. **2.** Cheerfulness –1505.

Cherub (tʃe·rŏb). Pl. **cherubs, cherubim** (tʃe·rⁱubim). [OE. and ME. *cherubin*, ME. and mod. *cherub*; repr. OTest. Heb. *kᵉrūb, kᵉrūḇîm*. The form *cherub* was introduced by WYCLIF. The early pl. '*cherubins*' became successively *cherubims, cherubim.*] † **1.** In early use: (*Cherubin, -yn, -m,* treated as sing. or collect.) † **a.** The seat of the Deity –1568. † **b.** The proper name of an angel; *esp.* of *Uriel* –1537. † **c.** An order of angels –1613. **2.** In extant use: **a.** One of the 'living creatures' mentioned in the O.T., and figured in the Jewish Temple. **b.** One of the second order of angels, excelling specially in knowledge; a conventional representation of such a being. (In early Christian art they were app. coloured red. In mod. art, a cherub is represented as a beautiful winged child, or child's head.) ME. **3.** *transf. esp.* A beautiful and innocent child (*cherub*) 1705. Also *attrib.*

1. a. That sittest vpon cherubyn WYCLIF *Ps.* 79[80]:2. ¶ In the *Te Deum*, in 15th c., *cherubin* and *seraphin* may have been taken as singular. They are now taken as plural. **3.** *Oth.* IV. ii. 63. The..rosy cherub before him SCOTT. Hence **Cheru·bic, -al** *a.*, **Cherubi·mic, -al** *a.*, † **Cherubi·nical** *a.*

Cherubim, -in, *sb.*; see CHERUB.

Cherup, obs. f. CHIRRUP.

Chervil (tʃɔ̄ɹvil). [OE. *ċerfille, -felle*, corresp. to (M)LG., (M)Du. *kervel*, OHG. *kervela* (G. *kerbel*) – L. *chærephylla, -phyllum* – Gr. χαιρέφυλλον.] *Bot.* A garden pot-herb (*Anthriscus cerefolium*), the aromatic leaves of which are used to flavour soups, etc.

† **Che·sboll.** ME. [The second element is presumably BOLL *sb.*[1] (sense 3), the first is unexpl.] A poppy –1688; = CHIBOL, an onion –1500.

Chese, obs. f. CHEESE, CHOOSE.

Cheselip, -lope, obs. ff. CHEESELIP[1] and [2].

Cheshire (tʃe·ʃəɹ). The name of an English county. Hence **C. cheese** (a well-known kind). Phr. *To grin like a C. cat.* [unexplained.]

Chesil[1], **chisel** (tʃe·zil, tʃi·zĕl). [OE. *ċiosol, ċisel, ċysel* = MDu. *kezel*, LG. *kesel*, OHG. *kisil* (G. *kiesel*) f. WGmc. base **kis-*, whence MHG. *kis*, G. *kies* gravel.] Gravel, shingle. (Earlier, also = a siliceous stone, with *pl.*)

Chesil[2], **chissal.** 1664. [Origin unkn.] A small, smooth green variety of Pear.

Cheslep(e, -lip, -lop(e, obs. ff. CHEESELIP.

† **Che·soun,** *sb.* ME. Aphet. f. ACHESOUN, ENCHESOUN, q.v. –1560.

Chess (tʃes), *sb.*[1] [Aphetic – OFr. *esches* (mod. *échecs*), pl. of *eschec* CHECK *sb.*[1]] **1.** A game of skill, played by two persons, on a board divided into sixty-four squares; each player having a set of sixteen men, viz. king, queen, two bishops, two knights, two castles or rooks, and eight pawns; the object of the game is to place the adversary's king in checkmate. Also *fig.* † **2.** = The CHESSMEN –1618. **3.** Used as tr. Gr. ἀστράγαλοι, L. *tesseræ*, etc. Hence **Che·ss-board**

Chess, *sb.*[2] Now *dial.* 1460. [Origin unkn.] **1.** A tier or layer; a storey; a row. **2.** *Mil.* in *pl.* The parallel planks of a pontoon bridge 1803.

Chess, *sb.*[3] 1736. [Origin unkn.] A kind of grass (*Bromus secalinus*), which grows as a weed among wheat; now chiefly in *U.S.* Cf. *cheat, cheats.*

† **Chess-apple.** 1640. [Cf. CHEQUER *sb.*[2]] The fruit of the WHITEBEAM, *Pyrus aria.*

Chessel. 1721. [app. f. CHEESE *sb.*[1] + WELL *sb.*] A cheese-vat.

Chess-men (tʃe·smen). Rarely in sing. **-man.** 1474. [Partly alt. of *chessemeyn* 'chess company' (see MEINIE sense 4); partly f. CHESS *sb.*[1] + *pl.* of MAN (used for a piece *c.* 1400).] The pieces with which chess is played.

† **Che·ssom,** *a.* 1626. [Origin unkn.] Loose, friable, and free from grit –1675. ¶ Taken erron. by Johnson for a sb.

Che·ss-tree. 1627. [f. unidentified element + *tree* 'wood'.] A piece of wood bolted perpendicularly on a ship's side, used to confine the clew of the mainsail.

Chest (tʃest), *sb.*[1] [OE. *ċest,* **ċiest, ċyst*, corresp. to OFris., MDu. *kiste* (Du. *kist*), OHG. *kista* (G. *kiste*), ON. *kista* :– Gmc. **kistō, -ōn* – L. *cista* – Gr. κίστη box, chest.] **1.** A box, a coffer; now mostly a large box of strong construction, used for the safe custody of the contents. (Often including the contents.) Also *fig.* **2.** A coffin. Still *dial.* OE. **3.** *Comm.* A case in which certain commodities, as tea, sugar, etc., are packed for transport; hence, a measure of quantity 1708. **4.** That part of the body enclosed by the ribs and breast-bone; the thorax 1530. Also † *fig.* –1647.

1. *A seaman's c.*; *a carpenter's, surgeon's c*; *a medicine c.* A pittance from the University C. 1883. **2.** He is now..nayled in his c. CHAUCER.

Phr. *C. of drawers*: see DRAWER[2] b. *C. of viols*: a chest containing a set of viols: the set of viols itself; also a party of players so equipped. *Comb.*: **c.-founder, -foundering:** see FOUNDER *sb.*[4] 2.

† **Chest,** *sb.*[2] [OE. *ċēast*, refash. of earlier *ċēas*, corresp. to OHG. *cōsa* point of dispute :– WGmc. **kausa* – L. *causa* CAUSE.] Strife, contention –1450.

Chest (tʃest), *v.* 1473. [f. CHEST *sb.*[1]] **1.** *trans.* To put into a chest or coffin. **2.** To meet or strike with the chest 1843.

1. He dieth and is chested *Gen.* 50. (*headnote*).

Chested (tʃe·stĕd), *ppl. a.* 1601. **1.** [f. prec.] Enclosed in a chest or coffin. **2.** [f. CHEST *sb.*[1]] Having a chest; chiefly in comb., as *deep-c.*, etc. 1662

† **Chesteine, chesten.** [ME. *chesteine, chasteine* – OFr. *chastaine* (mod. *châtaigne*) :– L. *castanea* – Gr. καστανέα chestnut, also καστάνειον, short for καστάνειον κάρυον nut of Castanæa (Pontus) or Castana (Thessaly).] A chestnut-tree –1601; a chestnut –1674.

Che·ster. [OE. *ċeaster* :– prehist. OE. **cæstra* – L. *castra.* Still existing in place-names; also in the forms *-caster, -cester.*] A walled town; orig. one that had been a Roman station in Britain.

Chesterfield (tʃe·stəɹfīld). [f. an Earl of *Chesterfield.*] A kind of overcoat 1889, also a kind of large overstuffed sofa 1900. **Chesterfie·ldian** *a.* relating to or characteristic of the fourth Earl (1694–1773), a writer on manners and etiquette.

Chesterlite (tʃe·stəɹləit). 1850. [f. *Chester* Co., Penn., U.S. + -LITE.] *Min.* A variety of orthoclase.

Chestnut, chesnut (tʃe·snʊt). 1519. [orig. *chesten nut* (XVI), f. *chesten*, later form of CHESTEINE, + NUT. *Chesnut* was till 1820, *chestnut* is, the current form.] **A. 1.** The edible nut of the chestnut-tree (*Castanea vesca*), said to have been introduced from Asia Minor. Two or more of the nuts are enclosed in a prickly burr. **2.** The tree itself; also its wood 1578. **3.** Applied to the HORSE-CHESTNUT, or its seed 1832. **4.** The hard knob in the skin of the horse at the inner side of the fore-legs 1859. **5.** *slang.* A venerable joke or story 1886. **B.** as *adj.* **1.** Of the colour of a chestnut; deep reddish brown 1656. **2.** Short for *c. horse.* (*colloq.*) 1840.

Chetah, var. of CHEETAH.

† **Chevachee.** ME. [– OFr. *chevauchiee*, pa. ppl. formation on *chevauchier* (mod. *chevaucher*) :– late L. *caballicare* ride, f. *caballus* horse.] An expedition on horseback; a raid, campaign –1592.

Che·vage. Now *Hist.* 1461. [– OFr. *chevage* capitation, f. *chef* head; see CHIEF, -AGE.] Capitation or poll-money.

‖ **Cheval** (ʃeva·l). 1609. Fr. for 'horse', used in comb., as in CHEVAL-GLASS, and in the Fr. phrase *à c.* 'on horseback', 'with one foot on each side'; *Mil.* 'in command of two roads or lines of communication'.

‖ **Cheval de frise**; usu. pl. **Chevaux de frise** (ʃəvō· də frī·z). 1688. [Fr.; lit. 'horse of Friesland'; because first employed there.] *Mil.* A large joist, with six sides, traversed with iron-pointed spikes above six feet long, and crossing one another; used to check cavalry charges and stop breaches. Also *transf.*

The Danes..had planted themselves..behind their Chevaux de Frize 1710.

‖ **Chevalet** (ʃəvale). 1810. [Fr., dim. of *cheval.*] A trestle for a bridge.

Cheval-glass (ʃəva·lglas). 1855. [f. Fr. *cheval* + GLASS.] A mirror swung on a frame, and large enough to reflect the whole figure.

Chevalier (ʃevălīᵊɹ). [ME. *chevaler* – AFr. *chevaler*, (O)Fr. *chevalier* :– med.L. *caballarius*, f. L. *caballus* horse; refash. after Fr. in XVI. Cf. CAVALIER.] **1.** A horseman; *esp.* a mounted soldier, a knight (*arch.*). **2.** A member of certain orders of knighthood, etc. 1728. **3.** A chivalrous man; a gallant 1630.

The C. or *C. de St. George*: James Stuart, son of James II, the Old Pretender. *The Young C.*: Charles Edward Stuart, the Young Pretender. *C. of industry* (F. *chevalier d'industrie*) also *C. of fortune*: one who lives by his wits, a sharper.

Chevaline (ʃe·vălin), *a.* 1550. [– Fr. *chevalin, -ine*, f. *cheval* horse; see -INE[1].] Of or pertaining to horses, horse-. Also *subst.* horse-flesh.

† **Che·vance, chie·vance.** ME. [ME. *chevaunce* – (O)Fr. *chevance* wealth acquired, f. (O)Fr. *chevir* achieve, f. *chef* head; cf. ACHIEVE. Cf. CHEVISANCE.] **1.** Acquisition of wealth; *concr.* estate –1603. **2.** Raising of money –1645. **3.** Achievement –1600.

† **Cheve, chieve,** *v.* ME. [ME. *cheve, chieve* – OFr. *chever* come to an end (of), f. *chef* head; in sense 6 aphet. f. ACHIEVE q.v.] **1.** *intr.* To fare (*well, ill,* etc.) –1674. **2.** *intr.* To get (*to* a place). ME. only. **3.** To acquire. ME. only. **4.** *intr.* To happen. ME. only. **5.** To do homage *to*. ME. only. **6.** To achieve –1530.

‖ **Chevelure** (ʃəvĕlü·r). 1470. [– OFr. *chevelëure* (mod. *-elure*) :– L. *capillatura*, f. *capillatus* haired, f. *capillus* hair; see -URE. In XVII – mod.Fr.] **1.** A head of hair; † a wig. **2.** *transf.* The luminous appearance surrounding the nucleus of comets; the diffused light round certain nebulous stars. [So in Fr.] 1672.

Cheven, obs. f. CHEVIN.

Cheventayn, -eyn, etc.; see CHEVETAINE.

† **Che·verel.** [ME. *chev(e)rell(e)* – OFr. *chevrele*, dim. of *chèvre* goat.] *lit.* Kid; used in the sense of kid-leather –1609. Also *attrib. fig.* Flexible, elastic –1705.

fig. The lawiers have such chauerell consciences 1583. Hence † **Che·verelize** *v.* to make capable of stretching, like c.-leather (*rare*).

† **Che·vesaile.** ME. [– OFr. *cheveçaille*, f. *chevece* collar :– L. *capitia*, pl. of *capitium* opening for the head in a tunic, etc.] The collar of a coat, gown, etc.; in the 14th c. often ornamented.

‖ **Chevet** (ʃəvę). 1809. [Fr., = pillow.] The apsidal termination of the east end of a church.

† **Che·vetaine.** [ME. – OFr. *chevetaine*, semi-pop. – late L. *capitaneus*; see CAPTAIN, CHIEFTAIN.] = CHIEFTAIN –1586.

‖ **Cheville** (ʃĕvī·l). 1883. [Fr., = pin, plug, etc.] A word or phrase inserted solely to round off a sentence or complete a verse.

Chevin (tʃe·vin). 1450. [– OFr. *chevenne, chevesne* (mod. *chevanne*) :– Rom. **capitine*, f. L. *capito* orig. big-head, f. *caput, -it-* head. Cf. CHAVENDER.] The CHUB.

Cheviot (tʃi·viət, tʃe·v-). 1815. [Name of a range of hills on the Sc. border.] **1.** *C. sheep*, in pl. *Cheviots*: a breed of short-wooled sheep, thriving on the C. hills, and valued for their wool. **2.** A cloth made from this wool 1883.

† **Che·visance.** ME. [– OFr. *chevisance*, f. as next + *-ance* -ANCE. Cf. CHEVANCE.] **1.** Achievement; furtherance (ME. only); resource –1650; provision, supply (also *concr.*) –1611; booty –1658. **2.** *spec.* Borrowing; a loan; gain (in a bad sense) –1626. **3.** The lending of money, goods, etc., for profit; dealing for profit –1602. ¶ Confused by Spenser and others with *chivalry, chevauchee*, etc.: Enterprise; chivalry; prowess, etc.

† **Che·vise,** *v.* [– *cheviss-*, extended stem of (O)Fr. *chevir* achieve, f. *chef* head; cf. ACHIEVE.] **1.** *trans.* To achieve; *intr.* to succeed. ME. only. **2.** *intr.* (*refl.*) To get on *with* –1491. **3.** *refl.* To help, take care of (*oneself*) –1500. **4.** To provide, obtain; to borrow –1487.

‖ **Chevrette** (ʃəvre·t). 1731. [Fr., dim. of *chèvre* goat.] † **1.** A machine for raising guns or mortars into their carriages –1772. **2.** A thin goatskin leather for gloves 1884.

Chevron (ʃe·vrən), *sb.*[1] ME. [– (O)Fr. *chevron* :– Rom. **caprione*, f. L. *caper* goat.] **1.** A beam or rafter; *esp.* in *pl.* the couples of the roof which meet at the ridge 1580. **2.** *Her.* A charge on the escutcheon, consisting of a bar bent like two meeting rafters, thus, ∧. ME. **3.** The same shape used in decorative art, etc. 1608. **4.** *esp.* A distinguishing mark on the sleeve of non-commissioned officers, policemen, etc. 1813.

Comb.: **c.-bone,** the V-shaped bone branching from the vertebral column of some animals; **-moulding,** a moulding of a zigzag pattern; **-work.** Also **-wise** (**-ways**) *adv.*, in the manner of a c. Hence † **Che·vron** *v.* to fit with chevrons or chevronwise (*rare*).

† **Che·vron,** *sb.*[2] 1754. [app. an error for CHEVEREL.] A glove.

Chevronel (ʃe·vrŏnel). 1572. [dim. of CHEVRON *sb.*[1]; see -EL[2].] *Her.* A bent bar on the escutcheon half the breadth of the chevron.

Chevrotain, -in (ʃe·vroteⁱn, -tin). 1774. [– Fr. *chevrotain, -tin*, dim. of OFr. *chevrot*, dim. of *chèvre* goat.] The smaller species of Musk Deer, found in SE. Asia.

Chevy, chivy (tʃe·vi, tʃi·-), *sb.* Also **chivvy.** 1785. [This and the vb. probably arise out of CHEVY CHASE.] **1.** A hunting cry. **2.** A chase 1824.

Chevy Chase: the scene of a Border skirmish; hence, *transf.* a running pursuit; a bustle.

Chevy, chivy (tʃe·vi, tʃi·-), *v.* 1830. [See the sb.] To chase; *intr.* to scamper.

Chew (tʃⁱū), *v.* [OE. *ċēowan* = MLG. *keuwen* (Du. *kauwen*), OHG. *kiuwan* (G. *kauen*) :– WGmc. **kewwan.*] **1.** To crush, bruise, and grind by the action of the molar teeth; *esp.* to masticate (food). **2.** *fig.* and *transf.* To examine or plan deliberately; to meditate on ME. **3.** *intr.* To perform the action described in sense 1; to bite, champ (*on, upon*) ME. **4.** *fig.* To meditate, ruminate *upon, on*, occas. *at* 1580.

Phr. *To c. the cud*: to bring food back into the mouth and c. it over again, as a cow does; *fig.* to ruminate. Hence **Chew·er. Chew·ing** *vbl. sb.*, *attrib.* **c.-gum** (*U.S.*), a flavoured preparation of the gum-like substance (*chicle*) obtained from the bully tree and the sapodilla, used as a masticatory.

Chew (tʃⁱū), *sb.* ME. [f. prec.] **1.** The action of the vb. **2.** That which is chewed or for chewing; *spec.* a quid 1725.

† **Chew·et**[1]. ME. [Origin unkn.] A dish of various kinds of meat and fish, minced and seasoned –1688.

† **Chew·et**[2]. *rare.* [– Fr. *chouette* in obs. sense chough, jackdaw (Cotgr.).] A chough; applied to a chatterer. 1 *Hen. IV*, v. i. 29.

Chewink, var. of CHEEWINK.

† **Chey·ney.** 1668. [var. of CHINA.] A worsted or woollen stuff –1757.

‖ **Chia.** 1601. = CHA, q.v.

Chian (kəi·ăn), *a.* 1631. [f. L. *Chius* (– Gr. Χῖος adj., of Χίος) + -AN.] Of or pertaining to Chios (now Scio) in the Ægean Sea. *absol.* An inhabitant of Chios; also = *C. wine.*

C. earth (*Chia terra*): an earth obtained from Chios, formerly used as an astringent and a cosmetic.

Chianti (kiæ·nti). 1833. A dry red wine produced in the *Chianti* Mountains, Tuscany.

‖ **Chiaroscuro** (kyā:roskū·ro). 1686. [It., f. *chiaro* CLEAR + *oscuro* dark, OBSCURE.] † **1.** The style of pictorial art in which only the light and shade are represented; black (or sepia) and white –1830. **2.** The disposition of the brighter and darker masses in a picture 1686. Also *transf.* and *fig.* Also *attrib.* var. **Chiaro-oscuro.** Hence **Chiaroscu·rist,** a painter distinguished for his c.

‖ **Chiasma** (kəiæ·zmă). Also **chiasm.** 1839. [mod.L. – Gr. χίασμα cross-piece of wood, cross-bandage, decussation, f. χιάζειν; see next.] *Anat.* Intercrossing or decussation.

Optic c.: the optic commissure or decussation of the fibres of the optic nerves. Hence **Chia·smal** *a.* of the nature of c.

‖ **Chiasmus** (kəiæ·zmŏs). 1871. [– mod.L. – Gr. χιασμός diagonal arrangement (*Gram.*), f. χιάζειν mark with the letter *X* (χῖ, χεῖ).] *Gram.* A figure by which the order of words in one clause is inverted in a second clause. Hence **Chia·stic** *a.* marked by c.

Chiastolite (kəiæ·stŏləit). 1800. [f. Gr. χιαστός arranged crosswise (see CHIASMA) + -LITE.] *Min.* A variety of Andalusite, a transverse section of which often exhibits the figure of a cross.

‖ **Chiaus** (tʃaus, tʃauʃ). 1599. [– Turk. *çavuş* messenger, herald, sergeant. Cf. Fr. *chiaoux.*] A Turkish messenger, lictor, or sergeant.

Chibol (tʃi·bəl). Still *dial.* [ME. *chibol(l)e* – **chibole*, north. var. of OFr. *cibole* (mod. *ciboule*) – late L. *cæpulla* (cl. *cæpina*) onion-bed, f. *cepa, cæpa* onion.] **1.** A species of Allium (*A. fistulosum*), known also as Welsh Onion. **2.** A spring onion with the green stalk attached 1848.

‖ **Chibouk, chibouque** (tʃibu·k). 1813. [– Turk. *çubuk* (tube of) pipe, partly through Fr. *chibouque.*] The long pipe smoked by the Turks.

‖ **Chic** (ʃik), *sb. slang.* 1856. [Fr.] Artistic skill and dexterity; style. As *adj.* [Not so used in Fr.] Stylish.

‖ **Chica**[1] (tʃī·kă). 1830. [Native name.] A red pigment obtained from the *Bignonia chica*, a native of Guiana and Columbia, used by some tribes for painting the skin.

Chica[2]; see CHICHA.

Chicane (ʃikēⁱ·n), *sb.* 1676. [– Fr. *chicane* f. *chicaner*; see next.] **1.** = CHICANERY 1. 1692. † **2.** (with *pl.*) An instance of chicanery; a subterfuge, quibble –1752. **3.** *Bridge.* The condition of holding no trumps 1886.

1. C. in furs, and Casuistry in lawn POPE. **2.** One who takes advantage of such chicanes, is not commonly regarded as an honest man HUME.

Chicane (ʃikēⁱ·n), *v.* 1672. [– Fr. *chicaner* pursue at law (XV), quibble, wrangle, of unkn. origin.] **1.** To employ chicanery; to quibble, cavil. **2.** *trans.* To quibble over; to overreach by chicanery. Hence **Chica·ner.**

Chicanery (ʃikēⁱ·nəri). 1613. [– Fr. *chicanerie*, f. *chicaner*; see prec., -ERY.] **1.** Legal trickery, pettifogging; the use of subterfuge and trickery in debate or action; quibbling, sophistry. **2.** (with *pl.*) A dishonest artifice of law; a sophistry, quibble, trick 1688.

1. The c. of the lawyers RICHARDSON. **2.** Impatient of such chicaneries BOSW. SMITH.

Chich (tʃitʃ), *sb.* ? *Obs.* [ME. *chiche* – Fr. *chiche* (also OFr. *ciche*, whence the form *ciches* XVI–XVIII) – L. *cicer* chick-pea.] *Bot.* The CHICK-PEA; occas. used of the Lentil (*Ervum lens*).

‖ **Chicha** (tʃī·tʃă). Also *erron.* **chica.** 1760. [Amer. Sp. – Haytian name.] A fermented liquor made from maize by the natives of S. America.

Chich(e)ling, obs. f. CHICKLING.

† **Chi·chevache.** ME. [A perversion of Fr. *chicheface*, lit. 'thin face', found only in Eng.] A fabulous cow that fed only on patient wives, and was therefore always lean and hungry.

Chick (tʃik), *sb.*[1] ME. [Short for CHICKEN. Treated as a dim. of CHICKEN; but in s.w. dial., *chick* is sing., *chicken* pl.] **1.** A chicken; occas., the young of any bird. **2.** *transf.* A child; a term of endearment ME.

‖ **Chick, cheek,** *sb.*[2] 1698. [Hindi *chik.*] A screen-blind made of finely split bamboo, laced with twine; used in doorways or windows.

Chick, *sb.*[3] *Sc.* 1791. [Echoic.] A tick (of a clock, etc.).

Chick, *v.* Now *dial.* ME. [Echoic; cf. CHIP.] *intr.* To sprout; to crack as a seed does in sprouting; to chap. Also *trans.*

Chickabiddy. 1785. [f. CHICK[1] + BIDDY[2].] A term of endearment to a child.

Chickadee (tʃikădī·). *U.S.* 1854. [From its note.] The Black-cap Titmouse (*Parus atricapillus*) of N. America.

Chickaree (tʃikărī·). *U.S.* 1854. [From its cry.] The larger American Red Squirrel.

Chicken (tʃi·kėn). [OE. *ċicen, ċȳcen,* **ċiecen* :– Gmc. **kiukīnam*, f. **keuk-*, gradation-var. of **kuk-* COCK. Cf. (M)Du. *kieken*, (M)LG. *küken*, MHG. *küchelīn* (G. *küchlein*), ON. *kjúklingr.*] **1.** The young of the domestic fowl; its flesh. Occas. used as *pl.* or *collect.*; esp. *dial.* **2.** *transf.* A child ME. **3.** *fig.* One young and inexperienced 1711; one who is CHICKEN-HEARTED 1611.

2. *Macb.* IV. iii. 218. **3.** Your hints that Stella is no c. SWIFT. Chikins, to be afraid of every cloud 1633.

Phr. *Mother Cary's* (or *Carey's*) *c.*: a sailors' name for the Stormy Petrel; also (in *pl.*) for falling snow. *Comb.*: **c.-breast,** a malformed projection of the breast-bone; hence **-breasted** *a.*; **-cholera,** an infectious disease of chickens; **-heart,** a heart as timorous as a chicken's; a cowardly person; hence **-hearted** *a.*; **-pox,** a mild eruptive disease, which chiefly attacks children; Varicella; **chickenwort,** = CHICKWEED. Hence **Chi·ckenhood.**

Chi·cken-ha·zard. 1845. [f. CHICKEN in the sense of 'small', or f. *chickeen*, var. of CHEQUEEN, as if a hazard or stake not exceeding that amount.] A form of hazard (HAZARD *sb.*[1]).

Chi·cken-meat, chicken's meat, chick-meat. [OE. *ċicena mete* chickens' food.] Food for chickens. Hence, a name for various plants, including endive; now *dial.* for CHICKWEED.

Chi·ckling[1]. [See -LING[1].] A tiny chick. (Dicts.)

Chickling[2], **chichling** (tʃi·kliŋ, tʃi·tʃliŋ). 1548. [In XVI *cicheling, chicheling*, dim. of *ciche* CHICH, repr. L. *cicercula* as dim. of *cicera*. The sp. with *-ck-* was app. at first a misprint.] *Bot.* The Common cultivated Vetch (*Lathyrus* *sativus*), grown in England for fodder. Now **Chickling Vetch.**

Chick-pea (tʃi·k pī·). 1548. [orig. *ciche pease*, later (to XVIII) *chich peas* – Fr. (*pois*) *chiche* (earlier † *ciche*); see CHICH. The form *chick-pea* (XVIII) perh. originated in a misprint.] *Bot.* A dwarf species of pea (*Cicer arietinum*), widely used for food. Called earlier *cich*, CHICH.

Chickweed (tʃi·kwīd), occas. **chicken-weed.** ME. [f. CHICKEN *sb.* + WEED, as eaten by chickens.] *Bot.* A name applied *esp.* to *Stellaria media* (N.O. *Caryophyllaceæ*), and to many allied or merely similar plants.

Chicory (tʃi·kŏri). 1450. [Late ME. *cicoree* – Fr. † *cicoree*, mod. *chicorée* endive – med.L. *cic(h)orea*, for L. *cichoreum*, *-ium* – Gr. κιχόρεια, κίχορα n. pl., κιχόριον. Cf. SUCCORY.] The plant *Cichorium intybus* (N.O. *Compositæ*); also its root, ground and roasted as an addition to or substitute for coffee.

Chide (tʃəid), *v.* Pa. t. **chid** (tʃid); pa. pple. **chid, chidden** (tʃi·d'n). [OE. *ċīdan*, of unkn. origin.] **1.** *intr.* † **a.** To contend with loud and angry altercation, brawl, wrangle –1693; † **b.** to scold –17..; **c.** to utter rebuke ME. Also *fig. Const.* with preps., esp. † *at*, † *with* (later, *against*). **2.** *trans.* To scold, rebuke, find fault with. (The main mod. use, but now chiefly *lit.* and *arch.*) ME. Also *fig.* and *transf.* **3.** With *adv.*, etc.: To drive, impel, or compel by chiding 1590.

1. c. To..present My true account, lest he, returning, c. MILT. *Sonn.* xiv. *fig.* The silver snarling trumpets 'gan to c. KEATS. 2. Having chidden her for undutifulness JOHNSON. *fig.* The Sea That chides the Bankes of England 1 *Hen. IV*, III. i. 45. 3. He hath chid me hence *Mids. N.* III. ii. 312. Hence **Chi·der,** one who chides; so † **Chi·deress,** † **Chi·dester,** a female chider. **Chi·dingly** *adv.*

Chide, *sb.* ME. [f. prec.] † **1.** Wrangling; an angry rebuke –1666. **2.** *transf.* Brawling (of streams) (*rare*).

2. The c. of streams and hum of bees THOMSON.

Chief (tʃīf), *sb.* [– (O)Fr. *chef*, †*chief* :– Rom. **capum*, for L. *caput* head.]

I. † **1.** *lit.* The head (of the body) (*rare*) –1535. † **2.** The head, top, upper end –1579. **3.** *Her.* The upper third of the field 1440.

3. *In c.*: borne on the upper part of the shield.

II. Transf. and fig. **1.** The head of a body of men, of an organization, state, town, party, office, etc.; foremost authority, leader, ruler ME.; *spec.* the head man of a clan, tribe, etc. 1587. † **2.** The head town or city; the CAPITAL –ME. † **3.** The best part; the height –1607. † **4.** Chief position, excellency –1602. **5.** = *chief-rent* 1601.

1. The c. of the Kitchen THACKERAY, of Glengarry SCOTT. Chiefs out of war, and Statesmen out of place POPE. 3. In the c. of summer 1607. 4. *Haml.* I. iii. 74.

Phr. *In chief.* **a.** *Feudal Law.* [med.L. *in capite.*] Applied to a tenant holding, or tenure held, immediately from the Lord Paramount. Hence extended to tenancy by a perpetual ground-rent. **b.** In the chief place or position. Often in titles, as *Commander-in-C.*, etc. **c.** Chiefly. *Comb.*: **c.-rent,** a rent paid under a tenure in c.; now = quit-rent. Hence **Chie·fdom,** the estate, position, or dominion of a c. **Chie·fery, chie·fry,** (*Ir.*) the office and territory of an Irish c.; the dues belonging to the chief of a clan or district; the analogous payments of rent or tribute. **Chie·fess,** a female (ethnic) c. **Chie·fless** *a.* **Chie·fly** *a.* pertaining to a c. **Chie·fship,** the office and function of c.

Chief (tʃīf), *a.* and quasi-*adv.* ME. [f. prec.] **1.** = HEAD-; as *C. Baron, Constable, Justice, Rabbi, Secretary*, etc. **2.** At the head in importance; principal, foremost, greatest ME. **3.** 'Of the first order' (J.); prominent, leading. (In this use, formerly compared *chiefer*, *chiefest.*) ME. † **4.** Best, finest; choice –1660. **5.** *Sc.* Intimate (see *Prov.* 16:28) 1530. **6.** *absol.* or *ellipt.* **a.** *pl.* Chief people 1568. **b.** The most; the bulk 1833. **7.** *adv.* Chiefly, principally (*arch.*) 1553. So *chiefest*.

2. His c. intimate HAWTHORNE. My cheif design BOYLE. 3. The cheiffe peeres of the realme 1536. A c. object of the expedition MACAULAY. 4. His c. companion was ever some c. book FULLER. Phr. *Chief good*: used as tr. L. *summum bonum.*

Chiefage, var. of CHEVAGE.

Chiefly (tʃī·fli), *adv.* ME. [f. CHIEF *a.* + -LY².] **1.** In particular; pre-eminently; especially; most of all. **2.** Mainly, for the most part ME.

1. Not life, but a good life, is to be c. valued JOWETT. 2. Cæsar's character is c. made up of Good-nature ADDISON.

Chieftain (tʃī·ftĕn). [Late ME. *cheftain*, alt., by assim. to CHIEF, of earlier CHEVETAINE.] † **1.** = CHIEF *sb.* II. 1. –1837. **2.** A captain (*arch.* and *poet.*) ME. **3.** The CHIEF of a clan or tribe 1587. † **4.** One who takes a leading part –1600.

3. Chieftains, which in the Highland acceptation, signifies the head of a particular branch of a tribe,..Chief,..the leader and commander of the whole name SCOTT. Hence **Chie·ftaincy** [after *lieutenancy*, etc.], the position of a c.; government by a c. **Chie·ftainess,** a female chief or c. **Chie·ftainry,** the rank, rule, or territory of a c.; a body of chieftains collectively. **Chie·ftainship,** the position of a c.

† **Chie·fty.** 1552. [f. CHIEF *sb.* + -TY¹.] Headship; chief place or degree –1644.

Chield (tʃīld). *Sc.* 1758. [var. of CHILD.] Fellow, chap.

Chierete, chierte(e, obs. ff. CHERTE.

Chieve; see CHEVE.

Chiff-chaff (tʃi·fˌtʃaf). 1780. [From its note.] A bird, one of the *Sylviinæ* or Warblers, also called Lesser Pettychaps (*Phylloscopus rufus*).

‖ **Chiffon** (ʃifoṅ). 1876. [Fr., f. *chiffe* rag.] **1.** *pl.* Ornamental adjuncts to a lady's dress, 'fal-lals'; feminine dress. **2.** (ʃi·fǫn). A diaphanous silky muslin used in dressmaking 1890.

Chiffonier (ʃifŏnīᵊ·ɹ). Also **-onnier(e, cheffonier.** 1806. [Formerly *chiffon(n)iere* – Fr. *chiffonnier, -ière* rag-picker; *transf.* a piece of furniture with drawers for odds and ends.] **1.** A small cupboard with a top forming a sideboard. ‖ **2.** A rag-picker; a collector of scraps. [Fr.] 1856.

‖ **Chignon** (ʃinʸoṅ). 1783. [– Fr. *chignon* orig. nape of the neck, earlier *chaaignon* :– Rom. **catenione*, f. L. *catena* CHAIN; cf. -OON.] A large coil or hump of hair, worn by women at various times on the back of the head.

These girls..are all alike—from c. to ankle 1817.

Chigoe (tʃi·go). Also JIGGER. 1691. [Earliest in Fr. form *chique*; later *chego(e)*, *chig(g)er, jigger*; presumably a native name.] A small species of flea (*Pulex* or *Sarcopsylla penetrans*), found in the West Indies and South America. The female burrows beneath the skin of the human feet (and hands), and causes itching and painful sores.

Chilblain (tʃi·lbleⁱn). 1547. [f. CHILL *sb.* + BLAIN, or reduction of **chilled blain.*] An inflammatory swelling produced by exposure to cold, affecting the hands and feet, accompanied with heat, itching, and occasionally ulceration. Hence **Chi·lblained** *a.* affected with chilblains. **Chi·lblainy** *a.*

Child (tʃəild), *sb.* Pl. **children** (tʃi·ldrĕn). [OE. *ċild* :– **kilþam*, rel. to Goth. *kilþei* womb, *inkilþo* pregnant, quasi 'fruit of the womb'. Peculiar to English. The ME. pl. *childre, childer* became *childeren, children* in the south, and this is now the standard form.]

I. 1. Fœtus, infant. *spec.* A female infant (*dial.*) 1611. **2.** A boy or girl OE. In the Bible, used, as tr. Heb., of youths entering upon manhood (see *Dan.* 1:17). **3.** *transf.* One who is as a child in character, manners, attainments, and *esp.* in experience or judgement ME. **4.** A pupil at school ME.; a chorister 1510. **5.** A youth of gentle birth: used as a kind of title (*arch.* and now spelt *chylde* or *childe*). OE. † **6.** A lad in service; a page, etc. –1610.

1. If she beare a maid c. *Lev.* 12:5. A boy, or a Childe I wonder? *Wint. T.* III. iii. 71. 3. Men are but children of a larger growth DRYDEN. 4. *spec.* Campaspe, played..by..the children of Paules LYLY. 5. Childe Rowland *Lear* III. iv. 187.

II. As correlative to parent. **1.** The offspring, male or female, of human parents ME. Also *fig.* and *transf.* **2.** *pl.* In Biblical and derived uses: Descendants; members of the tribe or clan ME. **3.** Applied (chiefly in *pl.*) to disciples *of* a teacher. (Chiefly Biblical.) ME. **4.** *fig.* Expressing origin, extraction, dependence, attachment, or natural relation to a place, time, circumstance of birth, ruling quality. Orig. a Hebraism. ME.

1. *fig.* Thou c. of the devil *Acts* 13:10. Dreames: Which are the children of an idle braine *Rom. & Jul.* I. iv. 97. 2. *Judg.* 4:6. *C. of God* (Theol.): *i.e.* by creation or by regeneration and adoption. 3. 1 *John* 2:1. 4. Children of the East *Judg.* 6:3, of nature WORDSW.; of light ME., yre ME., death 2 *Kings* 6:32; of fancy MILT.; of the Renascence 1876.

Phrases. **a.** *With c.*: *lit.* pregnant; † *fig.* teeming; eager (*to* do a thing). **b.** *Child's play*: *lit.* childish sport; *fig.* a piece of work easily done, trifle. *Comb.*: **c.-crowing,** spasmodic croup; **-rites** *sb. pl.*, the rites connected with the baptism of children.

Hence **Chi·lded** *ppl. a.* provided with a c. or children. † **Chi·lder,** dial. pl. of CHILD, whence † **Chi·lderless. Childie,** dim. of CHILD (*rare*). † **Chi·lding** *vbl. sb.* child-bearing; also *ppl. a.* **Chi·ldless** *a.* **Chi·ldlessness. Chi·ldling** (*rare*). **Chi·ldly** *a.* childish or childlike; also as *adv.* **Chi·ldliness. Chi·ldness,** † childish humour *Wint. T.* I. ii. 170; quality of being a c. **Chi·ldship** (St. Paul's υἱοθεσία), the relation of child to parent; filiation, adoption.

† **Child** (tʃəild), *v.* ME. [f. prec.] **1.** *intr.* To be delivered –1808. **2.** *trans.* To bring forth (a child) –1611. Also *fig.*

1. Within ii dayes they chylded both LATIMER.

Chi·ld-bearing, *vbl. sb.* ME. Parturition; gestation (*rare*).

Childbed (tʃəi·ldbed). ME. [f. CHILD *sb.* + BED *sb.*] **1.** The bed in which a child is born 1594. **2.** The state of a woman in labour ME. **3.** The womb. Now *dial.* 1535. Also *attrib.*

Child-birth (tʃəi·ldbɔ̄ɹþ). 1549. [f. as prec. + BIRTH.] The bearing or birth of a child.

Childe; see CHILD *sb.* I. 5.

Childermas (tʃi·ldəɹmæ̆s). *arch.* [repr. OE. *ċildramæsse*, f. *ċildra* gen. pl. of *ċild* CHILD + *mæsse* MASS *sb.*¹] The festival of the Holy Innocents (the 28th of December), commemorating the slaughter of the children by Herod (*Matt.* 2:16). Usually *c.-day, -tide.*

Childhood (tʃəi·ldhud). [OE. *ċildhād*; see CHILD *sb.*, -HOOD.] **1.** The state or stage of life of a child; the time during which one is a child; the time from birth to puberty. Also *fig.* **2.** *concr.* This state or age personified 1605. † **3.** Childishness –ME. † **4.** = *childship* –1626. Also *attrib.*

1. *fig.* The C. of our ioy *Rom. & Jul.* III. iii. 95. 2. The well-governed c. of this realm SCOTT. 4. *Lear* II. iv. 181. Phr. *Second c.*: the state of childishness incident to extreme old age.

Childish (tʃəi·ldiʃ), *a.* [OE. *ċildisċ*; see -ISH¹.] **1.** Of, belonging to, or proper to a child or to childhood. **2.** Not befitting mature age; puerile, silly ME.

1. C. trebble *A.Y.L.* II. vii. 162. 2. What cannot be auoided, 'Twere c. weaknesse to lament 3 *Hen. VI*, V. iv. 38. Hence **Chi·ldish-ly** *adv.*, **-ness.**

Childlike, child-like (tʃəi·ldləik), *a.* 1586. [See -LIKE.] **1.** Belonging to or becoming a child; filial. **2.** Like a child; (of qualities, etc.) like those of a child. (Usu. in a good sense, as opp. to *childish.*) 1738. Also as *adv.*

1. Her child-like dutie *Two Gent.* III. i. 75. 2. The c. heart WESLEY. Hence **Chi·ldlikeness.**

† **Childrè, children,** pl. of CHILD.

Childwife, child-wife. † **1.** (tʃəi·ldˌwəif), A woman in, or just out of, childbed –1636. **2.** (tʃəi·ldˌwəi·f), A wife who is a child. (Always with hyphen.) 1852.

† **Childwite** (tʃəi·ldwəit). ME. [See WITE *sb.*] *Old Law.* A fine paid to the lord for getting his bondwoman with child –1607.

Chile, chili, vars. of CHILLI.

Chiliad (ki·liăd). 1598. [– late L. *chilias*, *-ad-* – Gr. χιλιάς, -αδ-, f. χίλιοι 1000.] **1.** A group of 1,000 (things); a thousand. **2.** A period of 1,000 years 1653; *esp.* the millennium (*Rev.* 20:1–5) 1702.

2. After some..Centuries, or even Chiliads HARTLEY.

Chiliagon (ki·liăgŏn). 1692. [mod.L. – Gr. χιλιάγωνος, f. χίλιοι 1,000 + γωνία angle.] A plane figure with a thousand angles.

Chiliahedron (ki:liăhī·drŏn). *rare.* 1690. [f. Gr. χίλιοι 1,000 + ἕδρα seat, side, after *hexahedron*, etc.] A plane figure having a thousand sides.

Chiliarch (ki·liˌaɹk). 1656. [– late L. *chiliarches, -us* – Gr. χιλιάρχης, -ος, f. χίλιοι 1,000 + ἀρχός ruler.] The commander of a thousand men. So **Chi·liarchy,** † a body of a thousand men; the post of c.

Chiliasm (ki·liˌæz'm). 1610. [– Gr. χιλιασμός, f. χιλιάς CHILIAD.] The doctrine of the millennium; the opinion that Christ will reign in bodily presence on earth for a thousand years. So **Chi·liast,** an adherent of c. **Chilia·stic,** † **-al** *a.*, **-ally** *adv.*

† **Chili·ndre.** ME. [– med.L. *chilindrus*, for L. *cylindrus* – Gr. κύλινδρος CYLINDER.] A portable sun-dial of cylindrical form used in early times –1530.

Chilio-; see KILO-.

Chill (tʃil), *sb.* [OE. *ćele, ćiele* cold, coldness (:– **kaliz*, f. **kalan* be cold). Obs. by c1400, but revived XVII from the vb.]

† **I.** In OE. and ME. (*chile, chele, cheele.*) Replaced by mod. COLD.

II. [f. the vb. or adj.] (*chill.*) **1.** An unnaturally lowered bodily temperature marked by shivering, etc.; the cold fit of an ague; now *esp.* a sudden affection of physical cold, which is often a first stage or symptom of illness 1601. **2.** A coldness of the air, water, etc., which makes one shiver; a cold which has a depressing effect on the body 1788. Also in *pl.* **3.** *fig.* A depressing influence upon the feelings; depressing coldness of manner 1821. **4.** *techn.* An iron mould, or a piece of iron in a sand mould, for making chilled castings; cf. CHILL *v.* 1874.

1. *To catch, give one, a c.* **2.** *To take the c. off* (a liquid): to raise it to a temperate heat. The chills of night 1833. **3.** A c. Comes o'er my heart BYRON. *To cast* or *throw a c. over.*

Chill (tʃil), *a.* 1513. [Possibly alt. f. † *child* (see next) on the anal. of *cool, cold.*] **1.** Cold; now always depressingly or injuriously cold; that chills, or causes to shiver. **2.** Depressingly affected by cold 1608. **3.** *fig.* That tends to repress warmth of feeling, etc. 1750; repressed, deadened, in feeling 1633.

1. A c. easterly wind SCOTT. **2.** My veins are c. *Per.* II. i. 77. **3.** C. Penury repress'd their noble rage GRAY. Hence **Chi·llish** *a.* (*rare*). **Chi·llness,** c. quality or condition.

Chill (tʃil), *v.* ME. [First found in XIV, of obscure orig.; in the pa. pple. † *child* (Piers Plowman) it may repr. an OE. **ćieldan*, **ćildan* (:– Gmc. **kalþjan*, f. **kalþaz* COLD). See CHILL *sb.*]

I. *intr.* **1.** To become cold. **2.** To take a chill 1830.

II. *trans.* **1.** To make cold; to affect injuriously with cold ME. **2.** *fig.* To affect as with cold; to check (warmth, etc.); to damp, dispirit 1597. **3.** *techn.* To cool and harden the surface of cast iron by contact with cold iron, or by casting in an iron mould. Also *gen.* 1831. **4.** *Painting.* To deaden (a varnished surface) by cold, etc. 1859. **5.** *colloq.* To take the chill off 1825.

1. Ev'ry Lady's Blood with Fear was chill'd DRYDEN. **2.** Nothing chills the heart like..distrust 1849. Hence **Chi·ller. Chi·llingly** *adv.* *Comb.* **c.-room,** a room for chilling meat.

Chilli, chilly (tʃi·li). 1662. [– Sp. *chile, chili* – Aztec *chilli.*] The dried pod of species of Capsicum or Red Pepper; also, the shrub which bears chillies.

‖ **Chi·llum.** 1781. [Hindi *chilam.*] The part of the hookah containing the tobacco, etc.; *loosely*, the hookah, the act of smoking, the 'fill' of tobacco.

‖ **Chillumchee.** 1715. [Hindi *chilamchī.*] A wash-hand basin of brass or tinned copper.

Chilly (tʃi·li), *a.* 1570. [f. CHILL *sb.* + -Y[1].] **1.** That chills; disagreeably cold. **2.** Affected by a chill; sensitive to cold 1611. **3.** *fig.* Adverse to warmth of feeling 1841.

3. *fig.* C. to general theories MORLEY. Hence **Chi·llily** *adv.*; also **Chi·lly. Chi·lliness.**

Chilo-; see CHEIL(O)-.

‖ **Chilognathan** (kəilǫ·gnăþăn), *a.*, *sb.* 1835. [f. mod.L. *Chilognatha* sb. pl., name of the order, f. Gr. χεῖλος lip + γνάθος jaw + -AN.] *Zool.* Belonging to, or one of, an order of Myriapoda or Centipedes, with segmented bodies and heads furnished with two pairs of maxillæ, of which the second pair are united to form a lower lip.

‖ **Chiloma** (kəilōᵘ·mă). [mod.L. – Gr. χείλωμα rim, edge, f. χεῖλος lip; see -OMA.] *Zool.* The upper lip of a mammal when tumid and continued without interruption from the nose.

Chilopod (kəi·lopǫd). 1837. [f. mod.L. *Chilopoda* sb. pl., name of the order, f. Gr. χεῖλος lip + πούς, ποδ- foot.] *Zool.* One of the *Chilopoda*, an order of Myriapoda, having segmented bodies, and two anterior pairs of legs converted into foot-jaws. The order contains the Centipedes proper. Hence **Chilo·podan** *a.* and *sb.* **Chilo·podous** *a.* of the nature of the Chilopoda.

Chilostomatous (kəilostǫ·mătəs), *a.* 1881. [f. Gr. χεῖλος lip + στόμα, -ματ- mouth + -OUS.] *Zool.* Having the cell-mouth closed with a movable lip.

Chiltern (tʃi·ltəɹn). [In OE. Chron. anno 1009 *Ciltern*: unexplained.] **1.** Proper name of a range of hills which extend from Oxfordshire, across Buckinghamshire, into Bedfordshire and Hertfordshire. **2.** *a.* and *sb.* Applied to a kind of soil, and to districts having this soil 1523.

Chiltern Hundreds: a tract of Crown lands which contain the Chiltern Hills. The *Stewardship of the Chiltern Hundreds* is by a legal figment held to be an office of profit under the Crown, and is conferred on any member of parliament desiring to resign his seat, which by law he cannot do, so long as he is duly qualified. A member who accepts an office of profit under the Crown must vacate his seat, subject to re-election.

Chilver (tʃi·lvəɹ). [OE. *ćilfer-, ćilfor-lomb* ewe-lamb, corresp. to OHG. *kilbur(ra), -irra* (G. Bav. dial. *kilbare, -bere*); rel. to CALF.] A ewe-lamb: commonly **c.-lamb** (*dial.*).

Chimæra, var. of CHIMERA.

Chimæroid (kəimīᵊ·roid), *a.* 1854. [f. CHIMERA + -OID.] *Zool.* Related to the genus of fishes *Chimæra*, having the tail ending in a thread, the head pointed, and only one spiracle.

Chimbe, var. of CHIME.

Chimbley, dial. var. of CHIMNEY.

Chime (tʃəim), *sb.*[1] ME. [ME. *chimbe, chymbe, chim(e* prob. arose from *chym(b)e bell* (XIII–XV), which may have been an analysis of a ME. **chimbel* :– OE. *ćimbal* – L. *cymbalum* CYMBAL.] † **1.** A cymbal. ME. only. **2.** An apparatus for striking a set of bells so as to make them chime 1463. **3.** Hence, A set of bells, so attuned as to chime when thus struck, or when slightly swung 1562. **4.** The series of musical sounds thus produced 1530. **5.** The rhythm of verse; jingle 1649. **6.** *transf.* and *fig.* A system of which all the parts are in harmony 1630; harmony, accord 1847.

3. Noise Of clocks and chimes TENNYSON. **4.** Wee haue heard the Chymes at mid-night 2 *Hen. IV*, III. ii. 228. **5.** Now the C. of Poetry is done DRYDEN. **6.** Nature's c. MILT.

Chime, chimb (tʃəim), *sb.*[2] [prob. identical with the sb. occurring in OE. *ćimstān* base, pedestal, *ćimīren* clamp-iron, *ćimbing* joint, corresp. to MDu. *kimme* (Du. *kim*) edge of a cask, MLG. *kimme, kimm* (whence G. *kimme*).] **1.** The rim at the ends of a cask, formed by the ends of the staves. **2.** *Naut.* That part of the water-way which is left the thickest, and above the deck-plank 1833.

Chime (tʃəim), *v.*[1] [ME. *chimbe, chyme*, the rel. of which to the sb. is not clear.] **1.** *intr.* To resound when struck, give forth a musical sound. Also *trans.* (*arch.*) 1613. **2.** *intr.* To produce a musical sound from a bell by striking it ME.; *trans.* to strike (a bell, etc.) so that a musical sound is given forth 1697. **3.** To ring chimes. *intr.* (and *trans.*, with the bells as obj.) 1530. **4.** Said of a set of bells. *trans.* and *intr.* 1562. Also *fig.* **5.** To recite or repeat in cadence or mechanically. *trans.* and *intr.* ME. **6.** To rime or jingle 1667; *fig.* (*intr.*) to harmonize, agree 1690.

2. They..c. their sounding Hammers in a Row DRYDEN. **4.** Those great bells Began to c. TENNYSON. *fig.* My guts c. twelve 1693. **5.** To c. verse BYRON. **6.** The intention and expectation c. or go together 1832. To c. with one's mood DICKENS.

Phr. **Chime in.** To join in harmoniously (in music, conversation, etc.). So *To c. in with*: to be in complete (but subordinate) accord *with.*

Chime (tʃəim), *v.*[2] 1880. [f. CHIME *sb.*[2]] To groove or chamfer cask-staves for the chime.

Chimer[1], **chimere** (tʃi·məɹ, tʃimīᵊ·ɹ). ME. [Obscurely rel. to Sp. *zamarra* sheepskin cloak, It. *zimarra, cimarra* long robe (whence Fr. *simarre*, † *chimarre* loose gown XVII). See SIMAR.] A loose upper robe; *esp.* that worn by a bishop, to which the lawn sleeves are attached.

Chimer[2] (tʃəi·məɹ). 1611. [f. CHIME *v.*[1] + -ER[1].] One who chimes bells.

Chimera, chimæra (kimīᵊ·ră, kəi-). [– L. *chimæra* – Gr. χίμαιρα she-goat, monster, f. χίμαρος he-goat. Preceded XIV–XVI by an anglicized form † *chimere* (cf. Fr. *chimère*).] **1.** *Gr. Myth.* A fire-breathing monster, with a lion's head, a goat's body, and a serpent's tail, killed by Bellerophon. **2.** In *Arch., Painting*, etc. A grotesque monster 1634. **3.** *fig.* A mere wild fancy; an unfounded conception. (The ordinary mod. use.) 1587. Also *attrib.*

2. An excellent Hand at a Chimera ADDISON. **3.** Exploded chimera's, the..philosopher's stone, etc. 1712. Hence **Chime·ric, -al** *a.* imaginary, fanciful, visionary; prone to entertain chimeras. **Chime·rically** *adv.* † **Chi·merize** *v.* to indulge in chimeras.

† **Chi·min.** 1613. [– (O)Fr. *chemin* road, in AL. *cheminus, chim-*.] *Old Law.* A way –1670.

Chi·minage. 1594. [– OFr. *cheminage*; see prec., -AGE; in AL. *chem-, chiminagium.*] *Feudal Law.* A toll for liberty of passage through a forest.

Chimney (tʃi·mni). [– (O)Fr. *cheminée* fireplace, chimney – late L. *caminata*, perh. orig. for *camera caminata* room with a fire-place, f. L. *caminus* forge, furnace – Gr. κάμινος oven, furnace.] **1.** A fireplace or hearth. Now *dial.* † **2.** As tr. Gr. κάμινος furnace –1611. † **3.** A (portable) stove –1616. **4.** The passage or flue by which the smoke from a fire, etc., ascends ME.; the part which rises above the roof ME. **5.** The funnel of a steamboat, etc.; the tube of glass placed over the wick of a lamp 1816. Also *transf.* **6.** A cleft in a vertical cliff by which it may be scaled 1871. **7.** *Mining.* An ore-shoot. Also *attrib.*

1. Stretch'd out all the chimney's length MILT. *L'Alleg.* 111. **2.** 2 *Esdras* 6:4. **4.** Our Chimneys were blowne downe *Macb.* II. iii. 60. **5.** *transf.* The chemineys of Veseuus CHAUCER.

Comb.: **c.-board,** a board used to close up a fireplace in summer; **-breast,** the projecting part of the wall between the c.-flue and the room; **-corner,** the corner or side of the old-fashioned open fire-place or hearth; hence, the seat of the old, infirm, or idle; also *attrib.*; **-hook,** a hook on which to suspend pots and pans over a fire, etc.; † **-money,** a tax on fire-hearths in England and Wales; † **-man,** the collector of this tax; **-pot,** a cylindrical pipe of earthenware, sheet-metal, etc., fitted on the top of a c.-shaft; hence, *c.-pot hat*, from its shape; **-shaft** = *chimney-stalk*; **-stack,** a group of c.-stalks; **-stalk,** (*a*) the part of a c. which rises from a house-top; (*b*) a tall mill- or factory-c.; **-swallow,** the common swallow, *Hirundo rustica*; **-tax** = *chimney-money*; **-sweep, -sweeper,** one who sweeps chimneys and clears them of soot; **-top,** the part of a c. which rises above the roof, *esp.* its flat upper surface.

Hence **Chi·mney** *v.* (*nonce-wd.*) to furnish with chimneys LAMB. **Chi·mneyless** *a.*

Chi·mney-piece. 1611. [PIECE in the artistic sense.] † **1.** A picture, etc., placed as an ornament over a fire-place –1672. **2.** The ornamental structure over and around the open recess of a fireplace; now often used for the MANTEL-SHELF 1680.

1. The Chimney-peece Chaste Dian, bathing SHAKS.

Chimpanzee (tʃimpæ̆nzī·, tʃimpæ·nzi). 1738. [– Fr. *chimpanzé* – native name in Angola, W. Africa.] A genus of African apes (*Anthropopithecus*), resembling man more closely than any of the anthropoids. *A. troglodytes* (formerly *T. niger*) was long the only species recognized.

Chin (tʃin), *sb.* [OE. *ćin(n)*, corresp. to OFris. *kin*, OS. *kinni* (Du. *kin*), OHG. *kinni* (G. *kinn*), ON. *kinn* chin, lower jaw, Goth. *kinnus* cheek; :– Gmc. **kinn-* :– **kenw-*, cogn. w. L. *gena* cheek, Gr. γένυς jaw.] The part of the face below the under-lip formed by the prominent extremity of the lower jaw. Also *fig.*

Phr. *Up to the c.*: reaching to the c.; deeply immersed *in.* *Comb.*: **c.-music** (*U.S.*), talk, chatter; **-mute,** a mute applied to the violin by the action of the c.; **-wag** (*slang*), chat, talk; **-welk,** a disease affecting the c. Hence **Chin** *v.* to bring (a fiddle) up to the c.; to chat, chatter (*U.S.*). **Chi·nless** *a.* without a c.; also *fig.* **Chinned** *a.* having a c.

China[1] (tʃəi·nă), *sb.* and *a.* 1555. [Not a native Chinese name, but found in Skr. as *Chīna* about the beginning of the Christian era, and in various modified forms employed by other Asiatic peoples. The origin is still in dispute.]

I. a. The country so called, in Asia. † **b.** A Chinaman –1634. Also *attrib.*, but now mostly repl. by CHINESE *a.*

Comb.: **C.-aster** (see ASTER); **-crape,** a kind of silk crape; **-grass,** *Bœhmeria (Urtica) nivea*; also its strong fibre, used in the making of grass-cloth; **-ink** = INDIAN-INK; **-orange,** the sweet orange of commerce, orginally brought from China; **-pink,** *Dianthus chinensis*; **-root** (see CHINA[2]); **-rose,** (*a*) the Monthly Rose (*Rosa indica*) and the Red Rose (*R. semperflorens*) with their varieties; (*b*) *Hibiscus rosa-sinensis* (N.O. *Malvaceæ*), a tree 20 to 30 feet high; **-tree** (*U.S.*) the AZEDARAC; **-ware,** ware from China (see below); **-wax,** a white crystalline wax, the product of *Coccus sinensis.*

II. China Porcelain, China-ware, china. [The Pers. name, widely diffused as *chīnī*, was prob. introduced in the 17th c. into England, whence the former pronunc. tʃēⁱ·ni, also tʃī·ni, tʃi·ni, which still survive in the dialects.] A fine, semi-transparent earthenware, brought from China into Europe in the 16th c. by the Portuguese, who named it *porcelain.* (*China-ware* meant orig. 'ware from China'. This, shortened to *China*, became the name also of the material, so that 'china-ware' is now 'ware made of china or porcelain'.) Also *fig.* and *attrib.*

[A] collection of China-ware MRS. PIOZZI. Women, like Cheney, shou'd be kept with care 1685.

Comb.: **C.-clay,** a fine white potter's clay, called also kaolin; also *attrib.*; **-glaze,** a preparation for painting blue fret, composed of glass, lead, and blue calx; † **-metal,** porcelain or majolica; **-ware.**

III. = CHEYNEY, q.v.

China[2] (tʃəi·nă). 1582. [From *China* in Asia.] The thick fleshy root-stock of a plant (*Smilax china*, L.) akin to Sarsaparilla; called also *China root.* Hence **C.-ale,** ale flavoured with china root; **-broth,** etc.

China[3] (kəi·na, kī·na). 1866. [var. of *kina* or *quina* (see QUININE), Peruv. for 'bark'.] A name of Cinchona bark. Also, a homœopathic medicine prepared from cinchona. In comb. *chin-* = QUIN-.

Chinaman (tʃəi·nămæ̆n). 1772. [f. CHINA[1].] **1.** A dealer in porcelain. **2.** A native of China 1854. Hence **Chinaman's hat,** a gastropod shell, also called *Cup-and-Saucer.*

China-mania, chinama·nia. 1875. [See CHINA[1] II.] A mania for collecting (old) china. Hence **China-ma·niac.**

† **Chin-bone.** OE. [Late OE. *ćinbān.*] The jaw-bone –1592.

‖ **Chincapin, chinquapin** (tʃi·nkăpin). 1676. [Corruption of North Amer. native name.] The Dwarf Chestnut (*Castanea pumila*), a native of Virginia, etc., a shrubby tree, from 6 to 20 ft. high, with a small, very sweet nut.

Chinch (tʃintʃ), *sb.*[1] 1625. [– Sp. *chinche* = It. *cimice* – L. *cimex, -ic-.*] **1.** The bed- or house-bug. (Now only *U.S.*) **2.** An insect resembling the bed-bug in its disgusting odour, which is very destructive to wheat and other grasses; called also *chinch-, chink-bug.* (Webster.)

† **Chinch,** *a.* and *sb.*[2] [ME. *chiche, chinche* – (O)Fr. *chiche*, later also *chinche*, whence the Eng. † *chinche* (XIV–XVI).] *adj.* Niggardly. *sb.* A niggard, miser; a wretch –1570.

Chinchilla (tʃintʃi·lă). 1604. [– Sp. *chinchilla*, dim. of *chinche* CHINCH *sb.*[1]] **1.** A genus of small rodents peculiar to S. America; also, short for *c. fur* 1824. **2.** A cloth with a long nap gathered in little tufts. **3.** A variety of rabbit bred for its fur 1904.

‖ **Chin-chin** (tʃin tʃin), *sb.* 1795. [Chinese *ts'ing ts'ing.*] An Anglo-Chinese phrase of salutation. Hence **Chin-chin** *v.* to salute.

Chinchona; see CINCHONA.

Chincough (tʃi·nˌkǫf). Now *dial.* 1519. [For *chink-cough*, in n. dial. KINKCOUGH, f. CHINK *v.*[1], KINK *v.*[1] + COUGH. See also KINKHOST, HOAST. With KINKHOST cf. MLG. *kinkhōste*, LG. *kinkhost*, Du. *kinkhoest, kik-, kickhoest*, f. Gmc. base **kik-* (in WGmc. **kink-*) gasp.] Now called WHOOPING-COUGH.

Chine (tʃəin), *sb.*[1] [OE. *ćinu* = MDu. *kēne* (Du. *keen*), f. Gmc. base **kī-* burst open, repr. also by OE. *ćīnan* = OS., OHG. *kīnan*, Goth. *keinan* sprout, shoot forth; see CHINE *v.*[1], CHIT *sb.*[3]] † A fissure or crack –1582. *spec.* A deep and narrow ravine cut in soft rock by water, as *Shanklin C.* in the I. of Wight.

Chine (tʃəin), *sb.*[2] ME. [aphet. – OFr. *eschine* (mod. *échine*) :– Rom. **skīna*, blending of Gmc. **skin-* (see SHIN) and L. *spina* SPINE.] **1.** The spine, or backbone; 'the part of the back in which the spine is found' (J.) (*arch.* and *techn.*). † **2.** The back –1775. **3.** *Cookery.* The whole or part of the backbone of an animal, with the adjoining flesh ME. **4.** *transf.* A ridge, crest, arête 1855.

3. A c. or saddle of mutton MRS. GLASSE. Hence **Chined** *a.* having a c.

Chine (tʃəin), *sb.*[3] 1460. = CHIME *sb.*[2], q.v.

† **Chine,** *v.*[1] [OE. *ćīnan*; see CHINE *sb.*[1]] To burst asunder; to crack, chink, etc. –1530.

Chine, *v.*[2] 1513. [f. CHINE *sb.*[2]; cf. Fr. *échiner* break the back of.] **1.** To cut along or across the chine; to cut the chine-piece. **2.** To break the back of 1596. **3.** *intr.* and *trans.* To ridge. (In Blackmore only.)

1. And the Pigge you shal c. MARKHAM. You c. the Salmon 1651. **2.** Ill c. the villain OTWAY.

† **Chine·nses,** *sb. pl.* 1621. [f. *China*, on anal. of L. *Sinensis*, pl. *-es.*] Chinese –1649.

Chinese (tʃəinī·z). 1577. [f. CHINA[1] (Indian name) + -ESE.]

A. *adj.* Of or pertaining to China.

C. compliment: a pretended deference to the opinions of others, when one's mind is already made up.

B. *sb.* **1.** A native of China 1606. [pl. † *Chineses* (17th c.), *Chinese.* The sing. *Chinee* is U.S. colloq.] **2.** The Chinese language 1727.

1. Where Chineses drive With Sails and Wind MILT. *P.L.* III. 438. var. † **Chi·nian, -ean** *a.* and *sb.*

Chink (tʃiŋk), *sb.*[1] 1767. [f. CHINK *v.*[1]; = north. KINK *sb.*[2]] A convulsive fit of coughing or laughing.

Chink (tʃiŋk), *sb.*[2] 1535. [rel. in some way to CHINE *sb.*[1]] **1.** = CHINE *sb.*[1] Also *fig.* **2.** A long and narrow aperture through an object; a slit, etc. 1552. var. † **Chi·nker.** Hence **Chi·nky** *a.*

Chink (tʃiŋk), *sb.*[3] 1581. [Echoic; cf. CHINK *v.*[3]] **1.** The short, sharp sound produced by pieces of metal or glass striking one another; any similar sound. † **2.** *pl.* Coins –1611. **3.** *colloq.* Ready cash 1573. **4.** [from its note.] The Chaffinch (*dial.*) 1797.

1. The c. of their money FULLER. **2.** *Rom. & Jul.* I. v. 119. **3.** A man of c. SWIFT.

Chink, *sb.*[4] 1901. orig. *U.S.* A Chinaman.

Chink (tʃiŋk), *v.*[1] *dial.* Also KINK[1]. [Origin unkn. Cf. LG., Du. *kinken* cough, repr. WGmc. base **kink-*; see CHINCOUGH.] *intr.* To gasp convulsively for breath in coughing or laughing.

Chink (tʃiŋk), *v.*[2] 1552. [Goes with CHINK *sb.*[2]] † **1.** *intr.* To open in cracks –1693. † **2.** *trans.* To crack or chap –1656. **3.** To fill (*up*) chinks 1822.

3. The women c. the cracks 1881.

Chink (tʃiŋk), *v.*[3] 1589. [Echoic; cf. CHINK *sb.*[3] and Du. *kinken.*] **1.** *intr.* To emit a short, sharp, ringing sound, as coins or glasses do in striking each other. **2.** *trans.* To cause (things) to make this sound by striking them together; *esp.* coins 1728. Hence **Chi·nkle** *v.* to c. continuously.

Chink, *v.*[4] *dial.* 1825. [Origin unkn.; cf. KINK *sb.*[1], *v.*[2]] To give a twist to; to sprain.

† **Chino,** *sb.* Also **Chinao.** 1588. [– OSp.] **1.** A Chinese –1641. **2. Chino-** in comb., as in *Chino-Japanese*, etc. (*mod.*).

Chinoidine (kinoi·dəin). 1875. [f. CHINA[3] + -OID + -INE[5].] A resinous substance, contained in the refuse of quinine.

† **Chinois.** 1613. [– Fr. *chinois.*] = CHINESE –1684. Hence ‖ **Chinoiserie** [mod.Fr.], Chinese conduct, art, notion, etc.

Chinoline (ki·nŏləin). 1853. [f. CHINA[3] + L. *oleum* oil + -INE[5].] A tertiary amine, C_9H_7N (belonging to the series $C_nH_{2n-11}N$), an oily fluid, obtained by the distillation of quinine with potassium hydroxide; and also by the dry distillation of coal.

Chino·logist. = SINOLOGIST, q.v.

Chinook (tʃinū·k). *U.S.* and *Canada.* 1840. [Native name of an Indian tribe on the Columbia river, N. America.] A jargon which originated in the intercourse of the Hudson Bay Company's servants with the Indians of Oregon and Columbia, and is used as a means of intercourse between different tribes and with the white man.

C. wind: a warm moist wind from the Pacific, blowing across the Rocky Mountains.

Chinquapin, var. of CHINCAPIN.

Chinse (tʃins), *v.* 1513. [app. the typical form is *chinch*, dial. var. of CHINK *v.*[2] Of this *chinse* and *chintze* are corruptions.] **1.** *dial.* = CHINK *v.*[2] 3. **2.** To caulk; now *Naut.* to caulk slightly or temporarily. Hence **Chinsing-iron,** a caulker's tool.

Chintz (tʃints). *pl.* **chintzes.** 1614. [Fanciful sp. of *chints*, orig. pl. of *chint* – Hindi *chīṇt.*] *orig.* The painted calicoes imported from India; *now*, a name for cotton cloths fast-printed with designs of flowers, etc., in a number of colours, and usually glazed. Also *attrib.*

Chiolite (kəi·ŏləit). [Named 1846, irreg. f. Gr. χιών snow + -LITE.] *Min.* A fluoride of aluminium and sodium occurring in the Ilmen mountains.

Chiopin(e, obs. f. CHOPINE.

Chip (tʃip), *sb.*[1] ME. [repr. OE. *ćipp, ćyp* beam, corresp. to OS. *kip* post, *kipa* stave (Du. *kip* beam of a plough), OHG. *kipfa* (G. dial. *kipf, kipfe*) axle, stave, ON. *keppr* stick, staff.] **1.** A small, and *esp.* thin, piece of wood, or other (specified) material, separated by hewing, cutting, or breaking; a thin fragment chopped or broken off. Also *fig.* **2.** *spec. Naut.* A small quadrant-shaped piece of wood at the end of a log-line 1874. **3.** *spec.* A counter used in games of chance; hence, (*slang*) a sovereign 1873. **4.** A name for the keys of a spinet (SHAKS. *Sonn.* cxxviii). **5.** Wood (or woody fibre) split into thin strips for making hats and bonnets 1771. **6.** Anything worthless, without flavour, innutritious, or dried up 1639. **7.** A slight fracture caused by chipping; also *dial.* an act of chipping 1888. Also *attrib.* and *Comb.*, as *c.-bonnet, -hat* (see 5); also **c.-shot** (*Golf*), a short lofting stroke, played with back-spin.

1. Lyke sawdust or drye chyppes SKELTON. To make Orange Chips MRS. RAFFALD. *fig. C. of the old block*: one that resembles his father; also applied to things. **6.** To roast things to a c. A. YOUNG. **7.** The cup has a c. on the edge 1888.

Chip (tʃip), *sb.*[2] 1830. [f. CHIP *v.*[2]] *Wrestling.* **1.** A trip, a trick, a special mode of throwing one's opponent. **2.** A tiff (*dial.*) 1877.

Chip (tʃip), *v.*[1] 1461. [Cf. OE **ćippian* (in *forćypped* 'præcisus') = (M)LG., (M)Du. *kippen* hatch out by chipping the shell.] † **1.** *To c. bread*: to pare away the crust –1727. **2.** *gen.* To hew or cut with an axe, adze, etc. 1606. **3.** To break off small fragments from wood, stone, etc. (*esp.* from an edge); to shape by so doing. (A kind of dim. of *chop.*) 1859. Also *intr.* (for *refl.*) † **4.** *trans.* To chap –1508. † **5.** *intr.* To break open, burst –1734. **6.** To crack and break (the shell) 1606. **7.** *Australia.* To harrow (ground) 1798.

3. Statues were chipped..into decency GREEN. **5.** When..trees did c. [*note*, blossom] COLVIL. **6.** Thou isle!..That saw'st the unfledged eaglet c. his shell BYRON.

Phr. *To c. in* (colloq.): to interpose smartly, cut in.

Comb. **c.-axe,** a small axe used in chipping. Hence **Chi·pper,** one who or that which chips.

Chip (tʃip), *v.*[2] Chiefly *north.* 1788. [Cf. ON. *kippa* 'to scratch, pull', *refl.* 'to struggle'; also Du. *kippen* to seize.] *trans.* To trip up. *intr.* To trip along; to fall *out.*

Chipmunk, -muck (tʃi·pmɒŋk, -mɒk). Also **-minck, -monk, -muk.** 1842. [Of Algonquian origin.] A species of ground-squirrel, the Striped Squirrel, Hackee, or Chipping Squirrel, of N. America.

Chippendale (tʃi·pĕndeⁱl), *a.* 1876. [f. name of Thomas *Chippendale*, *c*1718–79, cabinet-maker.] Applied to a style of light and elegant drawing-room furniture; also to a style of book-plates.

Chipper (tʃi·pəɹ), *a.* *U.S.* 1837. [app. = north. *kipper* lively, nimble, frisky; now prob. infl. by next.] Lively, cheerful; chirpy.

Chipper (tʃi·pəɹ), *v. dial.* and *U.S.* 18... [Partly a metathesis of *chirrup*; partly echoic.] **1.** *intr.* To twitter; to babble, chatter. **2.** *trans.* To make chipper, cheer *up* (*U.S.*) 1873.

Chipping (tʃi·piŋ), *vbl. sb.* ME. [f. CHIP *v.*[1] + -ING[1].] **1.** The action of the verb CHIP 1611. **2.** *concr.* † A paring of the crust of a loaf. (Usu. in *pl.*) –1727. Also *gen.* ME.

Comb.: **c.-bird,** a small species of sparrow (*Zonotrichia socialis*); **-squirrel** = CHIPMUCK.

Chippy (tʃi·pi), *a.* 1729. [f. CHIP *sb.*[1] and *v.*[1] + -Y[1].] **1.** Of, or composed of, chips. **2.** Resembling a chip; as dry as a chip 1866. Hence **Chi·ppiness** (*joc.*).

† **Chira·grical,** *a.* 1644. [f. L. *chiragricus* (– Gr. χειραγρικός, f. χειράγρα gout in the hand) + -AL[1].] Pertaining to, or having, gout in the hand –1646.

‖ **Chirayta** (tʃirai·tă), **chiretta** (tʃire·tă). 1831. [Hindi *chirāitā*.] A plant, *Ophelia* (or *Agathotes*) *chirayta*, N.O. *Gentianaceæ*; also the bitter tonic obtained from it.

Chi-rho (kəi·rōᵘ). 1868. First two letters of XPICTOC CHRIST, used to symbolize the name.

Chirk (tʃɜ̄ɹk), *v.* OE. [Expressive var. of CHARK *v.*[1]] **1.** *intr.* To make a strident noise; to grate, creak, croak. Now *Sc. dial.* **2.** To chirp; to squeak (*arch.* and *dial.*) ME. **3.** To cheer *up* (*U.S. colloq.*) 1860.

Chirk (tʃɜ̄ɹk), *a.* *U.S. colloq.* 1828. [perh. f. prec., but prob. assoc. with *cheer*.] Lively, in good spirits.

Chirl (tʃɜ̄ɹl), *v.* *Sc.* 1818. [Echoic; cf. CHIRR.] To warble. Hence **Chirl** *sb.*

Chirm (tʃɜ̄ɹm), *sb.* *arch.* and *dial.* [OE. *ćearm, ćierm* noise, crying out, = OS. *karm*, see next.] **1.** Din, chatter, vocal noise; *esp.* the mingled noise of many birds or voices. † **2.** A flock (of finches) –1688.

Chirm (tʃɜ̄rm), *v.* *arch.* and *dial.* [OE. *ćirman* cry out, make a noise, corresp. to MDu. *kermen, carmen* mourn, lament (Du. *kermen*), MHG. *karmen*.] *intr.* To cry out, roar; now only, to chatter or warble, as birds. Also *trans.*

Chiro-, chir-, = Gr. χειρο-, comb. form of χείρ hand.

Chiro·gnomy, cheir- [Gr. γνώμη], the art or science of estimating character by the inspection of the hand; hence, **Chiro·gnomist. Chirogy·mnast** [Gr. γυμναστής], an apparatus for exercising the fingers for pianoforte playing. **Chiro·logy** [– Fr. *chirologie*], † the art of speaking by signs made with the hands or fingers; the study of the hand, whence **Chiro·logist, Chirolo·gical** *a.*, **-ally** *adv.* **Chi·romancy, cheir-** [Gr. μαντεία] divination by the hand, palmistry; hence, **Chi·romancer, Chi·romant, Chiroma·ntic** *a.* and † *sb.*, **Chiroma·ntical** *a.* **Chi·romys, cheir-** [Gr. μῦς], the AYE-AYE of Madagascar. **Chiro·nomy, cheir-** [Gr. -νομος], the art or science of gesticulation in oratory, pantomime, etc.; hence, † **Chiro·nomer, Chirono·mic** *a.*, † **Chironoma·tic** *a.* **Chi·roplast** [Gr. πλάστης], an apparatus for keeping the hands in a correct position in pianoforte playing; hence, **Chi·roplastic** *a.* **Chi·ropod**; see CHEIROPOD. **Chiro·podist** [Gr. πούς, ποδ-], one who treats diseases of the hands and feet; now usu. one who treats corns and bunions; so **Chiropo·dical** *a.* pertaining to chiropody; **Chiro·podism, Chiro·podistry** = *Chiropody*; **Chiropodo·logy,** a treatise on corns, warts, etc.; **Chiro·pody,** the art of treating corns, warts, defective nails, etc., on feet or hands. **Chiro·sophist, cheir-** [Gr. σοφός], † one who practises sleight of hand; = *Chiromancer*; so **Chiro·sophy. Chiro·tony** [– Gr. χειροτονία], election by vote (*rare*).

Chirograph (kəi³·rograf). 1483. [– Fr. *chirographe* – L. *chirographum* – Gr. χειρόγραφον; see CHEIRO-, -GRAPH.] **1.** One of various documents formally written, engrossed, or signed. **a.** = CHARTER-PARTY 1. Now *Hist.* 1727. **b.** The indenture of a fine; one of the counterparts of such indenture 1671. **c.** A bond given in one's own handwriting 1483. **d.** A form of Papal expression in writing 1528. **2.** *gen.* Any formal written document; handwriting (*rare*) 1613. Hence **Chiro·graphal** *a.*, **Chiro·graphary** *a.* related to or given in one's own handwriting; **Chiro·graphate,** to set one's hand to; **Chirogra·phic, -al** *a.* of, pertaining to, or in handwriting; **Chiro·graphist** (used by Pope for *chirognomist*).

Chirographer (kəirǫ·grăfəɹ). ME. [orig. – med.L. *chirographarius* sb. (in late L., adj.), and AFr. *cirographer*; in later use f. prec. + -ER[1] 4.] **1.** *Law.* The officer appointed to engross fines (chirographs), in the Court of Common Pleas. (Abolished in 1833.) **2.** A writing-master; a copying clerk 1755.

Chirography (kəirǫ·grăfi). 1654. [f. CHIRO- + -GRAPHY.] Handwriting; † autograph.

Chiropractic (kəi³ropræ·ktik). 1908. [See CHIRO- and PRACTIC *sb.*[1] and *a.*] **a.** *sb.* Manipulation of the joints, esp. of the spine, as a method of curing disease; also, a practitioner of this. **b.** *adj.* That practices or is concerned with this method. Hence **Chi·ropractor.**

Chirp (tʃɜ̄ɹp), *v.* ME. [Symbolical modification of earlier CHIRK *v.* or CHIRT *v.*] **1.** *intr.* To utter a short sharp thin sound, as of a bird or insect. Also *trans.* **2.** To make a sound more or less like the chirp of a bird; to cheep, talk cheerfully, CHIRRUP 1575. Hence **Chirp** *sb.* **Chi·rper. Chi·rpiness. Chi·rpingly** *adv.* **Chi·rpy** *a. colloq.* given to chirping; lively, merry.

Chirr (tʃɜ̄ɹ, tʃərr), *v.* 1639. [Echoic.] *intr.* To trill, as a grasshopper. (Expressing a more continuous and monotonous sound than CHIRP.)

Rustles the lizard, and the cushats chirre BROWNING. Hence **Chirr** *sb.* the sound itself.

Chirrup (tʃi·rŏp), *v.* 1579. [Modification of CHIRP *v.* by trilling the *r*.] **1.** *intr.* To chirp, *esp.* with a sustained and lively effect. Also *trans.* **2.** To make a sharp thin sound (by suction) with the lips compressed by way of encouragement (to a horse, etc.) 1726. Also *trans.* **3.** To speak in sprightly tones 1775.

1. Whit, whit, whit,..chirrupt the nightingale TENNYSON. Hence **Chi·rrup** *sb.* **Chi·rruper. Chi·rrupy** *a. colloq.* given to c.; lively, cheery.

Chirt (tʃɜ̄ɹt), *v.* Now *Sc.* ME. [A parallel form to CHIRK, CHIRR.] † **1.** *intr.* To chirp. ME. only. **2.** *intr.* To spirt 1513. **3.** *trans.* To squeeze, press out 1805. Hence **Chirt** *sb.*

Chirurgeon (kəirɔ̄·ɹdʒən, tʃi-). *arch.* [ME. *cirurgian*, etc. – OFr. *cirurgien* (mod. *chir-*); see SURGEON. Assim. to L. *chir-* XVI.] A SURGEON. † **Chiru·rgeonly** *adv.* SHAKS.

Chirurgery (kəirɔ̄·ɹdʒeri). *arch.* [ME. *syrurgerie, cir-,* – OFr. *cirurgerie*, f. stem of *cirurgien* (see prec.) + *-erie* -ERY; see SURGERY.] = SURGERY.

† **Chiru·rgy.** *rare.* [ME. *cirurgie, syr-,* – OFr. *cir-, sirurgie* (mod. *chirurgie*) – *cirurgia*, med.L. sp. of L. *chirurgia* – Gr. χειρουργία; see SURGERY.] = Surgery, CHIRURGERY. Hence **Chiru·rgic, -al** *a.* (arch.).

Chisel (tʃi·zĕl), *sb.*[1] ME. [– ONFr. *chisel* (mod. *ciseau*, in pl. scissors) :– Rom. **cisellum*, for **cæsellum* after late L. *cisorium*, f. *cis-*, var. of *cæs-*, stem of *cædere* cut. See SCISSORS.] A cutting tool of iron or steel with the cutting face transverse to the axis, and more or less bevelled on one or both sides; used for cutting wood, metal, stone, bone, etc., and worked by pressure or by the blows of a mallet or hammer. Also *attrib.*

What fine Chizzell Could euer yet cut breath SHAKS.

Chisel, chissel (tʃi·z'l, tʃi·s'l), *sb.*[2] 1607. [The same word as CHESIL[1].] Bran; occas. 'whole meal'.

Chisel (tʃi·zĕl), *v.* 1509. [f. CHISEL *sb.*[1] Cf. Fr. *ciseler*.] **1.** To cut, grave, pare, shape, etc., with a chisel. Often with *out*. Also *transf.* and *fig.* **2.** *colloq.* To cheat 1808. Hence **Chi·selled, -eled** *ppl. a.* shaped with or like a chisel; also *fig.* **Chi·seller, -eler.**

Chiselly (tʃi·z'li), *a.* and *adv. dial.* 1649. [f. CHESIL[1], CHISEL *sb.*[2] + -Y[1].] Gravelly; grittily.

Chit (tʃit), *sb.*[1] ME. [app. the same word as CHIT *sb.*[3]] † **1.** The young of a beast; whelp; kitten –1713. **2.** A (very young) child (cf. *kid*); *contemptuous*, a girl or young woman 1624.

2. A little c. of a miller's daughter of eighteen DICKENS.

† **Chit,** *sb.*[2] 1533. [f. CHICH, corrupted to *chits*, and taken as plural.] **1.** = CHICH –1610. **2.** A freckle or wart –1755.

Chit (tʃit), *sb.*[3] Now *dial.* 1601. [perh. repr. obscurely OE. *ćíþ*, ME. *chithe* shoot, sprout, seed, mote (in the eye), corresp. to OS. *kīth* sprout, shoot, MDu. *kijt*, OHG. *-kīdi* sprout, f. Gmc. **kī̆-* split; see CHINE *sb.*[1], CHITHE.] A shoot, sprout.

† **Chit,** *sb.*[4] 1610. [From its feeble note.] A bird; the Titlark –1668.

Chit (tʃit), *sb.*[5] *Anglo-Ind.* 1785. Short for CHITTY *sb.*

Chit, *sb.*[6] 1874. [Origin unkn.] A small cooper's cleaving tool.

Chit (tʃit), *v.* Now *dial.* 1601. [conn. w. CHIT *sb.*[3]] To sprout.

Chit-chat (tʃi·t,tʃæt). 1710. [f. CHAT *sb.*[1] by reduplication.] **1.** Light familiar chat. **2.** Matter of current gossip 1710. Also *attrib.*

† **Chithe.** [OE. *ćíþ*, f. (ult.) root **kī̆-* to split; see CHINE *sb.*[1], *v.*[1], CHIT *sb.*[3]] A tiny shoot or sprout; a mote –ME.

Chitin (kəi·tin). Also **-ine.** 1836. [– Fr. *chitine*, irreg. f. Gr. χιτών tunic; see -IN[1], -INE[5].] *Zool.* and *Chem.* The organic substance which forms the elytra and integuments of insects and the carapaces of crustacea. Hence **Chi·tinize** *v.* to convert into c. **Chi·tiniza·tion. Chi·tinous** *a.* like, or consisting of, c.

Chitling (tʃi·tliŋ). Also **chitlin.** 1848. [Contracted (dial.) form of CHITTERLING.] **1.** = CHITTERLING (*dial.* and *U.S.*) 1886. **2.** *fig.* (in *pl.*) Rags, tatters (*U.S.*).

Chiton (kəi·tǫn). 1816. [Gr. χιτών.] ‖ **1.** The Greek tunic 1850. **2.** A genus of Molluscs having a shell composed of eight plates overlapping each other.

Chitter (tʃi·təɹ), *v.* ME. [A parallel form to CHATTER; cf. *jabber, jibber*, etc.] **1.** Of birds: To utter a series of sharp thin sounds (? *dial.*). **2.** To shiver or chatter with cold (*dial.* and *Sc.*) 1526. Hence **Chi·tter** *sb.* twitter.

Chitterling (tʃi·təɹliŋ). Mostly in *pl.* ME. [orig. form uncertain; perh. OE. **ćieter-*, f. Gmc. **keut-* **kut-*, whence synon. MHG. *kutel* (G. *kutteln*); see -LING[1].] **1.** The smaller intestines of the pig, etc., *esp.* as fried for food. Also *fig.* † **2.** The frill down the breast of a shirt; also *gen.* (The mesentery is called by butchers the 'frill'.) –1849. **3.** [as dim. of CHIT *sb.*[1]] A little chit 1675.

Chitty, *sb.* *Anglo-Ind.* 1698. [Hindi *chiṭṭhī* :– Skr. *chitra* spot, mark.] A letter or note; also, a certificate or pass.

† **Chitty,** *a.*[1] *rare.* 1552. [f. CHIT *sb.*[2] + -Y[1].] Freckled or warty –1729.

Chitty, *a.*[2] 1616. [app. deduced from CHITTY-FACE, but later assoc. w. CHIT *sb.*[1]] Pinched in face; baby-like, puny.

† **Chitty-face.** 1601. [poss. orig. f. Fr. *chicheface* (see CHICHEVACHE), perverted by assoc. w. CHICH, CHIT *sb.*[1] or [2], or CHITTY[1].] **1.** A term of reproach: pinched-face; later, baby-face –1725. Hence **Chitty-faced** *a.* (*dial.*)

Chiule. *Hist.* [– *chiula, cyula*, the Latinized form (Nennius IX, Gildas VI) of OE. *ćíol, ćéol*; see KEEL *sb.*[2]] An old English or Norse war-ship.

Chivachee, -ie, obs. var. of CHEVACHEE.

Chivalresque (ʃivălre·sk), *a.* Also **chev-.** 1800. [– Fr. *chevaleresque*; see CHEVALIER, -ESQUE.] Wearing the garb, manners, or spirit of chivalry.

Chivalric (ʃivæ·lrik, ʃi·vălrik, tʃ-), *a.* 1797. [f. CHIVALRY + -IC.] Chivalrous.

Some extant spirit of c. kind CAMPBELL.

Chivalrous (ʃi·vălrəs, tʃi·v-), *a.* [Late ME. *chevalrous, chiv-* – OFr. *chevalerous*, f. *chevalier*; see CHEVALIER, -OUS.] † **1.** Like a (mediæval) knight or man-at-arms; *esp.* doughty –1596. **2.** Of or pertaining to the Age of CHIVALRY, or to its knights 1774. **3.** Of, belonging to, or characteristic of, the ideal knight; gallant, courteous, magnanimous. Occas. = 'quixotic'. 1818.

1. In brave poursuitt of chevalrous emprize SPENSER *F.Q.* I. ix. 1. Hence **Chi·valrous-ly** *adv.*, **-ness.**

Chivalry (ʃi·vălri, tʃi·-). [– (O)Fr. *chevalerie*, † *chiv-*, – med.L. *caballerius*, for *caballarius* CAVALIER; see -Y[3], -ERY.] **1.** *collect.* Knights or horsemen equipped for battle; *esp.* the mediæval 'men-at-arms'; more widely, gallant gentlemen. **2.** The position and character of a knight, knighthood ME. † **3.** A knightly feat –1823. **4.** The knightly system of feudal times with its religious, moral, and social code and practices 1765. **5.** The character of the ideal knight; disinterested bravery, honour, and courtesy 1790.

6. *Old Law.* Tenure by knight's service (abolished in 1662). Now *Hist.* 1574. ¶ **7.** *improp.* Team of horses. 1863.
1. Busiris and his Memphian Chivalrie MILT. *P.L.* I. 307. Belgium's. .Beauty and her C. BYRON. **2.** *Rich. II,* II. i. 54. Orders of C. BACON. The feats of Chivalry BOLTON. **4.** The age of c. is gone BURKE. *Flower of C.*: fairest type of knighthood; pick of a force of armed knights.
† *Court of C.* (*curia militaris*): a court formerly held before the Lord High Constable and the Earl Marshal of England, having cognizance of matters relating to deeds of arms done out of the realm.

Chive[1] (tʃəiv), also **cive** (səiv). ME. [– dial. var. **chive* (cf. Picard *chivot* green onion) of (O)Fr. *cive* (whence the Eng. form *cive*) :– L. *cēpa* onion.] **1.** A cultivated species of *Allium* (*A. schœnoprasum*). Its leaves are used in soups and stews. **2.** A small bulb or bulbil; *esp.* one of the cloves of a bulb of garlic 1551. Also *attrib.*

† **Chive**[2]. (Mostly in *pl.*) 1530. [app. orig. *chithe*, partly affected by CHIVE *sb.*[1]] **1.** *Bot.* The filament of the stamen, or the stamen as a whole –1807. **2.** = CHITHE 1610. **3.** One of the lamellæ of an agaric 1721.

Chive[3] (tʃiv). *Thieves' Cant.* 1673. [Origin unkn.] A knife. Hence **Chive** *v.* to 'knife'.

Chivvy (tʃi·vi), *v.* Later var. of CHEVY *v.*, esp. in the sense 'harass persistently'.

Chlamydate (klæ·mideᶦt), *a.* [f. Gr. χλαμύς, -υδ- mantle + -ATE[2].] *Zool.* Having a mantle.

Chlamydeous (klămi·diəs), *a.* [f. mod.L. *Chlamydeæ* (f. as prec.) + -OUS.] *Bot.* Having one or more floral envelopes.

Chlamydophore (klæ·midofōᵊːɹ). Also **chla·myphore.** 1836. [– mod.L. *chlamydophorus*, f. as prec.; see -PHORE.] A South American edentate mammal allied to the Armadillo, having the upper surface covered with a cuirass of leathery plates.

‖ **Chlamys** (klæ·mis). 1748. [Gr. χλαμύς.] **1.** *Gr. Antiq.* A short mantle worn by men in ancient Greece. **2.** *Bot.* The floral envelope.

‖ **Chloasma** (klo,æ·zmă). *Pl.* **-mata.** 1876. [f. Gr. χλοάζειν become green.] *Med.* An affection of the skin, characterized by yellowish-brown or blackish patches. *pl.* These patches.

Chlor-[1], comb. f. Gr. χλωρός green, used bef. a vowel; cf. CHLORO-[1].

Chlor-[2]. *Chem.* Comb. f. *chlorine* (*chloric, chloride*, and *chlorous*) used (chiefly bef. a vowel) in forming names of chlorine compounds: *e.g.* **a. Chlorace·tic,** name of acids derived from Acetic acid, by substitution of 1, 2, or 3 atoms of chlorine for hydrogen. Similarly *chlo·ramide, chlora·nil, -anila·mic*, etc. **b.** Also **Chlora·lum,** a disinfecting agent, consisting of aluminium chloride and sulphide, with some impurities; **Chlorau·rate;** see CHLORO-AURATE in CHLORO-[2]; **Chlorhy·drate,** a salt of **Chlorhy·dric** acid = Hydrochloric acid (HCl); **Chlorhy·drin,** a chlorhydric ether of glycerin, analogous to bromhydrin; **Chlorio·dic,** combining chlorine and iodine. **c.** *Min.* **Chloralu·minite,** 'a hydrous chloride of aluminium' (Dana); **Chlora·patite,** a variety of APATITE, containing chlorine.

Chloral (klōᵊ·răl). [– Fr. *chloral* (Liebig, 1831), f. CHLOR(INE + AL(COHOL, after ETHAL.] *Chem.* A thin colourless oily liquid with a pungent odour, obtained by the action of chlorine upon alcohol; = *trichloraldehyde* ($CCl_3.CHO$). Pop. and comm. = *chloral hydrate* ($CCl_3.CH._2OH$), a white crystalline substance resulting from the combination of water and chloral, and much used as a hypnotic and anæsthetic. Hence **Chlo·ralism** (*Med.*), a morbid condition produced by the long-continued use of chloral hydrate. **Chlo·ralize** *v.* to bring under the influence of c.

Chloranthus (kloræ·nþəs), *a.* 1871. [f. CHLOR-[1] + Gr. ἄνθος flower.] *Bot.* Having green flowers. Hence **Chlora·nthy,** a condition in which the coloured floral organs of a plant return to leaves.

Chlorate (klōᵊ·rĕt). 1823. [f. CHLOR(IC + -ATE[4].] *Chem.* A salt of chloric acid, e.g. *c. of potash.*

Chloric (klōᵊ·rik), *a.* 1810. [f. CHLOR(INE + -IC.] *Chem.* Of or pertaining to chlorine; containing chlorine in smaller proportion, relatively to oxygen, than *chlorous* compounds; as in *chloric acid*, HO_3Cl.
Chloric ether, = *ethyl chloride*, C_2H_5Cl; in *Med.* occas. applied to a solution of chloroform in alcohol.

Chloridate (klōᵊ·rideᶦt), *v.* [f. next + -ATE[3].] *Photography.* To treat with a chloride; *e.g.* to treat (a plate) with chloride of silver, so as to render it sensitive.

Chloride (klōᵊ·rid, -əid). Rarely **chlorid.** 1812. [f. CHLOR(INE + -IDE.] **1.** *Chem.* A simple compound of chlorine with a metal or an organic radical. **2.** Applied to various bleaching and disinfecting compounds, such as 'c. of lime', 'c. of potash', 'c. of soda', which are not simple chlorides 1826. **3.** A name for ores containing c. of silver. *U.S.* Hence **Chlo·ridize** *v.* = CHLORIDATE; *Mining*, to convert into c.

Chlorimeter, -try; see CHLOROMETER, -TRY.

Chlorinate (klōᵊ·rineᶦt), *v.* (Chiefly in *pass.*) 1856. [f. CHLORINE + -ATE[3].] To act upon or impregnate with chlorine.

Chlorination (klōᵊrinēᶦ·ʃən). 1854. [f. as prec. + -ATION.] *Chem.* Treatment with chlorine; *Mining*, the process of extracting gold and silver from certain ores by means of chlorine.

Chlorine (klōᵊ·rin, -əin), *sb.* 1810. [Named by Sir H. Davy from its colour; f. Gr. χλωρός yellowish or pale green + -INE[5]. In Fr. *chlore*, G. *chlor.*] *Chem.* One of the non-metallic elements; a yellowish-green heavy gas, having a peculiar irritating smell, and very active chemical properties. It is a powerful bleaching and disinfecting agent. Symbol Cl; atomic weight 35·5. As *attrib.* = *chloric, chlorous, of chlorine.* Hence **Chlorini·ferous** *a.* **Chlo·rinize** *v.* to treat with c. **Chlo·rinous** *a.*

Chlo·rine, *a. rare.* 1849. [f. as prec.] Light-green.

Chlorite[1] (klōᵊ·rəit). 1794. [– L. *chloritis* – Gr. χλωρῖτις precious stone of a grass-green colour.] *Min.* A name applied to certain green hydrous silicates of magnesia and alumina occurring in ancient rock-formations; orig. specific, but now a vague popular term. Also *attrib.* as in **c. schist, slate,** a green slaty rock, consisting largely of c. in foliated plates. Hence **Chlori·tic** *a.*, **Chloritous** (klorəi·təs) *a.* consisting of, or containing, c.

Chlo·rite[2]. 1853. [f. CHLOR(INE + -ITE[1] 4 b.] *Chem.* A salt of chlorous acid; *e.g.* c. of silver.

Chloritoid (klōᵊ·ritoid). 1837. [f. CHLORITE[1] + -OID.] *Min.* A foliated hydrous silicate of alumina and iron, varying in colour from greenish-black to grey; *chlorite spar.*

Chloro-[1] (klōᵊ·ro), bef. a vowel usually CHLOR-. [– Gr. χλωρο-, comb. f. χλωρός green, pale-green.] Hence:
Chlorocru·orin [+ CRUORIN], a green substance supposed to be the cause of the green colour in some species of Sabella; **Chloro·melan, -ite** [Gr. χλωρομέλαν-], *Min.* CRONSTEDTITE; **Chloropha·ite** [Gr. φαιός brown], *Min.* a hydrated silicate of iron, of a dark green colour, changing on exposure to brown or black; **Chlo·rophane** [Gr. -φανης, -φανος showing], *Min.* a variety of fluor spar showing a green phosphorescence when heated; **Chlo·rophyte** [Gr. φυτόν], *Bot.* any plant having a successive evolution and green parts or expansions.

Chloro-[2]. *Chem.* Comb. f. *chlorine, chloride, chloric, chlorous*, used chiefly bef. a consonant; see CHLOR-[2]. Hence: **a. Chlorobe·nzene,** formed from benzene by the substitution of one or more chlorine atoms for hydrogen atoms; and the like. **b. Chloro-aurate,** a compound of chloride of gold with a basic chloride or a hydrochlorate; **chlorobromide,** a compound containing chlorine and bromine in union with a metal or organic radical, as 'c. of silver'; **chlorocarbonic acid,** a synonym of Carbonyl chloride or Phosgene gas ($COCl_2$); **chlorocyanic acid,** early name of **cyanogen chloride,** CNCl; **chloropi·crin,** a colourless oily liquid formed by distilling picric acid with chloride of lime; **chloropla·tinate,** a compound of tetrachloride of platinum; so **chloropla·tinous** *a.*; and the like.

Chlorodyne (klōᵊ·rŏdəin). 1863. [A factitious formation from *chloroform* and *anodyne.*] A popular anodyne composed of chloroform, morphia, Indian hemp, prussic acid, etc.

Chloroform (klōᵊ·rŏfǭɹm), *sb.* [– Fr. *chloroforme* (J. Dumas, 1834), f. CHLORO- + *form(yl)*, as being a chloride of *formyl* (in its obsolete sense of methenyl, CH). See FORMYL.] A thin colourless liquid, Cl_3CH, having an ethereal odour and a sweetish taste, the vapour of which when inhaled produces insensibility; hence used as an anæsthetic in surgical and obstetrical operations. Hence **Chlo·roformic** *a.* relating to c. **Chlo·roformist,** one who administers c. **Chlo·roformi:ze** *v.* = CHLOROFORM *v.*; whence **Chlo:roformiza·tion,** the occurrence or the induction of anæsthesia due to c.

Chloroform (klǭᵊ·rŏfǭɹm), *v.* 1848. [f. prec. sb.] To administer or apply chloroform to. Also *transf.* and *fig.*

Chloroid (klōᵊ·roid), *a.* [f. CHLOR(INE + -OID.] *Chem.* and *Electr.* Akin to or resembling chlorine.

Chlorometer (klorǫ·mĭtəɹ). Also **chlori-.** 1826. [f. CHLORO-[2] + -METRE. Cf. Fr. *chloromètre.*] An instrument for measuring the bleaching power, etc., of chlorine in chlorinated lime, soda, potash. Hence **Chlorome·tric** *a.*; **Chloro·metry** (also *chlori-*).

Chloropal (klorōᵘ·păl). 1826. [f. CHLOR-[1] + OPAL.] *Min.* A greenish opal-like hydrated silicate of iron.

Chlorophyll (klōᵊ·rŏfil). (Also **-phyl(e, -phylle.**) 1819. [– Fr. *chlorophylle*, f. CHLORO-[1] + Gr. φύλλον leaf.] *Bot.* and *Chem.* The colouring matter of the leaves, etc., of plants; found usually in the cells as minute granules. It occurs also in various green water-animalcules, *e.g. Hydra viridis.* Hence **Chlorophy·llous** *a.* characterized by, or of the nature of c.

Chlorosis (klorōᵘ·sis). 1681. [f. Gr. χλωρός green; see -OSIS.] **1.** *Path.* Green sickness; a disease of young women, marked by anæmia, irregularity of the menses, and a pale or greenish complexion. **2.** *Bot.* A disease of plants, in which the green parts lose their colour, or parts normally of another colour turn green 1807. Hence **Chloro·tic** *a.* affected with c.

Chlorous (klōᵊ·rəs), *a.* 1845. [f. CHLORINE + -OUS.] *Chem.* and *Electr.* **1.** Abounding in chlorine; *spec.* containing chlorine in greater proportion relatively to oxygen than chloric compounds, as in **c. acid,** $HClO_2$, the salts of which are *chlorites.* **2.** Of the quality of chlorine: applied to elements or radicals which unite with hydrogen to form an acid, and are relatively electro-negative 1881.

Choak, obs. f. CHOKE *sb.* and *v.*

Choanite (kōᵘ·,ănəit). 1846. [f. Gr. χοάνη funnel + -ITE[1] 2 a.] *Palæont.* A fossil Zoophyte, characterized by a funnel-shaped skeleton.

Choanoid (kōᵘ·,ănoid), *a.* 1839. [f. as prec. + -OID.] *Phys.* Funnel-shaped; applied to one of the muscles of the eye in many vertebrata.

‖ **Chobdar** (tʃōᵘ·bdāɹ). 1701. [Pers. and Urdu.] *Anglo-Ind.* In India, an usher bearing a staff, who attends on persons of consequence.

Chock (tʃǫk), *sb.* Also **choak** and CHUCK, q.v. 1674. [With its var. CHUCK *sb.*[4] prob. – ONFr. **choque*, **chouque* (mod. Picard *choke* big log, Norman *chouque*), var. of OFr. *çoche, çouche* (mod. *souche*) log, block of wood, of unkn. origin.] **1.** A log, *esp.* for burning. **2.** *Turning.* = CHUCK. Also *attrib.* 1703. **3.** A block of wood (usually wedge-shaped), or stone, used to stop a cask, wheel, etc., from moving, or to add weight and steadiness to a machine 1769.

Chock (tʃǫk), *v.*[1] 1662. [f. prec. sb.] † **1.** *intr. To c. in*: to wedge in –1786. **2.** *trans.* To fit or make fast with a chock or chocks; to wedge (a wheel, cask, etc.); also with *up* 1854.

Chock, *v.*[2], obs. f. SHOCK.

Chock, *adv.* Also **choke.** 1799. [prob. f. *chock-full*; see next.] As close or tight as can be. Also with adverbs, as *c.-aft, -home,* etc. **b. Chock-a-block** (*Naut.*), said of two blocks run close together in a tackle; *transf.* crammed (*with*), chock-full (*of*) 1840.

Chock-full, choke- (tʃǫ·kful, tʃōᵘ·kful), *a.* ME. [The isolated ME. *chokkefulle, chekeful* (XIV) are of doubtful form and origin; mod. *choke-full* dates from XVII, *chock-full* from XVIII, with a var. *chuck-full.*] Filled so as to leave no vacant space; cram-full.

Chocolate (tʃǫ·kŏlĕt), *sb.* (*a.*). 1604. [– Fr. *chocolat*, or its source Sp. *chocolate* – Aztec *chocolatl* article of food made from cacao seeds; this seems to have been confounded with unrelated *cacaua-atl*, drink made from cacao.] **1.** A beverage made from the seeds of the cacao-tree; now, that made by dissolving chocolate cake in boiling water or milk. **2.** A paste or cake composed of the seeds of the cacao-fruit roasted and ground, sweetened and flavoured with vanilla, etc. 1659. **b.** *esp.* (in full *eating c.*) A sweetmeat made with this in the form of cakes, bars, etc. † **3.** *erron.* The cacao-tree or its fruit –1794. **4.** Chocolate colour 1776; as *adj.* 1771.

Comb.: **c.-house,** a house for the supply of c., as a beverage; **-nut,** the cacao-fruit or its seed (not a *nut*); **-tree,** the cacao-tree, *Theobroma cacao.*

Choctaw (tʃǫ·ktǭ). 1892. [Name of an Amer. Indian tribe, perh. alt. of Sp. *chato* flat, the tribe being so named from their custom of flattening their heads.] *Skating.* A step from either edge on one foot to the opposite edge on the other foot, in an opposite direction.

‖ **Chœnix** (kī·niks). 1603. [Late L. – Gr. χοῖνιξ.] A dry measure, = 1 quart or 1½ pints imperial.

Chogset (tʃǫ·gset). *U.S.* 1848. [Indian name.] A small salt-water fish; the Burgall.

Choice (tʃois), *sb.* [ME. *chois* – OFr. *chois* (mod. *choix*), f. *choisir* choose :– Gallo-Rom. **causire* = Gmc. **kausjan*, f. **kaus-* **keus-*; see CHOOSE.] **1.** The act of choosing; preferential determination between things proposed; selection, election. **2.** The power, right, or faculty of choosing; option ME. **3.** That which is chosen or to be chosen, the preferable part of anything, the pick, flower, *élite* 1494. Also *concr.* **4.** Scope or field for choice 1586; a well-chosen supply 1591. † **5.** Care in choosing, judgement, discrimination –1765. † **6.** Estimation 1601. **7.** An ALTERNATIVE 1794. Also *attrib.*

1. Grace to gyde my choyce MORE. *To take one's c.*: to choose what one will have. *For c.*: by preference. **2.** *To have one's c. Hobson's c.*: the option of taking the thing offered or nothing. See *Spect.* 1712, No. 509. **3.** The flower and c. of many Provinces MILT. *P.R.* III. 313. For me, the Wilds and Desarts are my C. DRYDEN. **4.** Faith..there's small choise in rotten apples *Tam. Shr.* I. i. 138. Repleate with c. of all delights 1 *Hen. VI*, V. v. 16. **5.** Collected with Iudgement, and C. BACON. **6.** *All's Well* III. vii. 26. Hence **Choi·ceful** *a.* fickle in choosing; offering choices. **Choi·celess** *a.* (*rare*).

Choice (tʃois), *a.* ME. [f. prec. sb.] **1.** Worthy of being chosen, select, of special excellence. **2.** Well-chosen 1588. † **3.** Nice in choosing –1656.

Hence **Choi·ce-ly** *adv.*, **-ness.**

Choil. 1888. [Origin unkn.] *Cutlery.* The indentation in a pocket-knife where the edge of the blade adjoins the 'tang' or thick part by which it is hafted. Hence **Choil** *v.* to make this; **Choi·ler,** an instrument for making it.

Choir, quire (kwəiᵊɹ), *sb.* [ME. *quer(e)* – OFr. *quer* (mod. *chœur*) – L. *chorus*; see CHORUS. The development of *quere* to *quire* is paralleled by *briar, friar, umpire*; the sp. *choir*, w. assim. to Fr. and L., was established XVII.] **1.** The organized body of singers in cathedral or church service. **2.** That part of a church appropriated to the singers; the chancel ME. **3.** *gen.* A company of singers; a choral society or institution 1553. **b.** A chorus or subdivision of a chorus. **4.** = CHORUS *sb.* 1. 1656. **5.** *gen.* An organized company or collection ME. **6.** *Mus.* A group of instruments of the same class in an orchestra, or of players on them: cf. BAND *sb.*³ 4. **b.** = CHOIR ORGAN.

Comb.: **c.-boy,** a boy who sings in a c.; so **-man; -master,** an instructor of a c.; **-office,** a service appointed to be recited in choir (the canonical hours, Anglican matins and evensong); *attrib.* or as *adj.* belonging to that class in a religious order which is bound to recitation of the choir offices (contrasted with *lay*), as *c. brother, monk, nun, sister.*

Choir, quire (kwəiᵊɹ), *v. poet.* 1596. [f. prec. sb.] To sing, as a choir, *trans.* and *intr.*

Choired (kwəiᵊɹd, kwəiᵊ·red), *ppl. a. rare.* 1796. [f. CHOIR *sb.* or *v.*] Assembled in a choir.

Choir organ. 1776. Also **chair organ** 1606–1796. [A perversion of *chair organ* (XVII), which may have been so called because it often formed the back of the organist's seat.] One of the aggregated organs which go to make up a large organ, having stops of a light and soft character and used principally for accompaniments.

Choise, *v.* Now *Sc.* 1505. = To CHOOSE.

† **Chok, chokke,** *v.* ME. only. [– OFr. *choquier* collide, thrust; mod. *choquer* collide, surprise, whence SHOCK (XVI).] ? To thrust, push, or drive with force.

Choke (tʃōᵘk), *sb.*¹ 1562. [f. CHOKE *v.*] **1.** What chokes. **2.** The action and noise of choking 1839. † **3.** A dead-lock –1729. **4.** A constriction; *e.g.* in the case of a rocket, etc. Cf. CHOKE-BORE. 1786. **5.** The mass of immature florets in the centre of an artichoke head. Cf. ARTI-CHOKE, pop. taken as 'choke in the heart'. 1736. Hence **Cho·kage,** a choked up state.

Choke, *sb.*² Now *dial.* ME. [prob. var. of CHEEK, but Sc. *chowk* suggests ON. *kjálki* jaw-bone.] The chops.

Choke (tʃōᵘk), *v.* Pa. t. and pple. **choked.** [ME. *cheke, choke*, aphetic f. *acheke, achoke* (Chaucer) :– late OE. *āćēocian* (once), f. *ā-* A- pref. 1 + *ćēoce, ćēce* jaw, CHEEK; cf. late ME. *athrote* throttle, f. *throte* THROAT.] **1.** To stop the aperture of the throat so as to prevent breathing; to suffocate completely or partially. **2.** *intr.* (for *refl.*) To suffer suffocation ME. Also *transf.* **3.** *transf.* To smother, stifle 1526; also *fig.*; † to silence in argument –1649. Also *intr.* (for *refl.*) **4.** To close or greatly narrow (a tube, etc.) 1635; to block up a channel; to congest 1612. Also *intr.* (for *refl.*) **5.** To fill chock-full (*lit.* and *fig.*) 1712. **6.** To stop the movement of by clogging, etc. 1712. **7.** To fit *in* tightly, jam *in* 1747.

1. Choked with bones FULLER, dust BUNYAN, Spleen and Rage SWIFT, smoke JOHNSON, contending emotions LYTTON. **2.** I must say—or c. in silence BROWNING. **3.** To c. the *breath, tongue, utterance*, etc. Field choked with briars 1874. All pity choak'd *Jul. C.* III. i. 269. *Macb.* I. ii. 9. **4.** To c. a rocket 1635, the neck of a bottle BOYLE, the avenues of the capital MACAULAY. **5.** Partylies..the press is chok'd with them ADDISON. Hence **Cho·kingly** *adv.*

Choke-, in *comb.* [the stem of the vb.] **1.** = 'choking, that chokes': as **c.-coil,** a coil of low resistance inserted in an alternating-current circuit to impede or modify the current; **-damp,** the carbonic acid gas which accumulates in the lower parts of coal-mines, wells, etc.; after an explosion it rises and contributes to constitute the *after-damp*; **-strap,** a strap which connects the collar with the belly-band and keeps the collar in place when a horse backs; **b.** *esp.* with fruit- and plant-names, as **c.-apple,** the Crab-apple; **-berry,** the astringent fruit of *Pyrus arbutifolia*; **-cherry,** *U.S.*, two N. Amer. species of cherries with astringent properties; also the trees, *Prunus borealis* and *P. hyemalis*; **-pear,** name for harsh and unpalatable varieties of the pear, used for perry; *fig.* a difficulty, something hard to 'swallow'; **-weed,** species of Broomrape, *Orobanche rapum.* **2.** = 'what chokes': as **c.-dog,** a name for hard Dorset cheese, etc.

Choke-bore (tʃōᵘ·kˌbōᵊɹ). 1875. The bore of a fowling-piece which narrows towards the muzzle and thus keeps the shot together. Also a fowling-piece with such a bore. So **Choke-bored** *ppl. a.*

Choke-full, *a.*; see CHOCK-FULL.

Choker (tʃōᵘ·kəɹ). 1552. [f. CHOKE *v.* + -ER¹.] **1.** One who or that which chokes. **2.** *slang.* A large neckerchief worn high round the throat; as a *white c.*, worn *esp.* by clergymen 1848. Hence **Cho·kered** *ppl. a.* attired in a c.

Chokidar (tʃōᵘ·kidāɹ). *Anglo-Ind.* 1696. [Urdu *chaukīdār*, f. Hindi *chaukī* watching.] A watchman, in India.

Choky (tʃōᵘki), *sb. Anglo-Ind.* 1608. [– Hindi *chaukī* shed, watch-house, station, lock-up.] **1.** A custom or toll station, in India; a station for horses, etc.; a police-station. **2.** A lock-up (in India) 1866. (Similarly in Eng. *slang*, by assoc. w. *choke.*)

Choky (tʃōᵘ·ki), *a.* Now *colloq.* 1579. [f. CHOKE *v.* + -Y¹.] **1.** Apt to choke; harsh, dry, and gritty. Of fruit, and *transf.* **2.** Having tendency to choking 1857.

2. To feel rather chokey HUGHES.

Chol-, var. of CHOLE-, Gr. χολή bile, used bef. a vowel: **Cholæ·mia** (also *cholehæ·mia*), bile in the blood, as in jaundice; hence **Cholæ·mic** *a.* **Cho·late,** a salt of cholic acid.

Cholagogue (kǫ·lagǫg). 1671. [– Fr. *cholagogue* (*a.* and *sb.*) or late L. *cholagogus* adj. – Gr. χολαγωγός, f. χολή bile + ἀγωγός leading.] *Med.* A medicine that carries off bile.

Chole- (kǫli), repr. Gr. χολή gall, bile; **Cho·leate,** a salt of choleic acid. **Chole·ic** *a.* = taurocholic (acid). **Cho·lelith,** a gall-stone.

Cholecyst (kǫ·lĭsist). *rare.* 1881. [– mod. L. *colecystis*, f. Gr. χολή bile + κύστις bladder, cyst.] The gall-bladder. Hence **Cholecysti·tis,** ulceration of the c. **Cholecyste·ctomy** [Gr. ἐκτομία], cutting out of the c. **Cholecysto·tomy** [Gr. τομία], the opening of the c. in order to remove gall-stones.

Choledoch (kǫ·lĭdǫk), *a.* 1681. [– Fr. *cholédoque* – mod.L. *choledochus* – Gr. χοληδόχος containing bile, f. χολή bile + δοχός containing, receiving.] *Med.* Containing or receiving bile; as *c. duct, canal.* As *sb.* The c. duct.

† **Choledo·graphy, choledo·logy.** Barbarous forms of CHOLOGRAPHY, CHOLOLOGY.

Choler (kǫ·ləɹ), *sb.* [ME. *coler(e)* – (O)Fr. *colère* – L. *cholera* (see next). In late L. *cholera* took over the meanings of Gr. χολή bile, anger, and became the techn. name of one of the four 'humours' of the old physiologists (cf. MELANCHOLY).] **1.** Bile; formerly as one of the four humours, supposed to cause irascibility of temper. **2.** Anger, heat of temper, wrath; irascibility. Cf. *bile.* 1530.

1. I conseille yow..That bothe of Colere and of Malancolye Ye purge yow CHAUCER. **2.** Hollis, in c., pulled him by the Nose CLARENDON.

C. adust, also **Black c.** = *black bile*, ATRABILE, q.v. Hence † **Cho·lerous** *a.*

Cholera (kǫ·lĕrǎ). ME. [– L. *cholera* – Gr. χολέρα. The L. word was orig. applied, like the Gr., only to the disease, but later took over the sense 'bile', 'anger' from Gr. χολή (see GALL *sb.*¹). See prec.] † **1.** = CHOLER 1. –1561. **2.** A disorder, attended with bilious diarrhœa, vomiting, stomach-ache, and cramps. (Called also *C. morbus, C. nostras, Summer C.*, etc.) It is rarely fatal to adults. 1601. **3.** A malignant disease (not bilious), endemic in India and occas. epidemic elsewhere. It is characterized by violent vomiting, purging with watery rice-coloured evacuations, severe cramps, and collapse, death often occurring in a few hours. (Called also *Asiatic, Epidemic, Malignant*, etc., *C.*, and vulgarly *C. morbus.*) 1819.

Comb.: **Chicken C.**: an infectious disease of chickens; so called from its prevalence during a c. epidemic, but not akin to CHOLERA 2, 3; **c.-fungus,** a name for certain fungi, etc., occurring in the dejections of those suffering from malignant c.; **-typhoid,** the secondary fever of malignant c. Hence **Cholera·ic** *a.* **Cholera:iza·tion,** the artificial communication of c. to the lower animals. **Cho·lerifo:rm** *a.* **Cho·leroid** *a.*

Choleric (kǫ·lĕrik), *a.* ME. [– (O)Fr. *cholérique* – L. *cholericus* bilious – Gr. χολερικός of or like cholera.] **1.** Having CHOLER as the predominant humour; bilious. Now *Hist.* † **2.** Subject to or causing biliousness –1634. **3.** Irascible, passionate 1583. **4.** In a passion, angry 1590. **5.** Choleraic 1834.

1. The Reue was a sclendre colerik man CHAUCER. 4. A chollericke word *Meas. for M.* II. ii. 130. So † **Chole·rical.** Hence † **Cho·leric-ly** *adv.*, † **-ness.**

Cholerine (kǫ·lĕrəin, -īn). 1847. [– Fr. *cholérine*, dim. of *choléra* CHOLERA.] **1.** British or Summer Cholera. **2.** A mild diarrhœa; the early stage of cholera 1850. **3.** The zymotic cause of malignant cholera 1852.

Cholesterin (kǒle·stĕrin). 1827. [f. Gr. χολή bile + στερεός stiff + -IN[1].] *Chem.* A tasteless, inodorous, fatty-looking substance ($C_{26}H_{44}O$), found in most animal liquids and solids, and in the fruit and seed of many plants. In a crystallized form it is the chief constituent of gall-stones. (Now superseded by **Chole·sterol.**) Hence **Choleste·ric** *a.* pertaining to or produced from c.

Choliamb (kǭu·liæmb). 1844. [– late L. *choliambus* – Gr. χωλίαμβος 'limping iambus', f. χωλός lame, halting + ἴαμβος IAMBUS.] *Pros.* An iambic verse with a spondee or trochee instead of an iambus in the last (sixth) foot. Hence **Cholia·mbic** *a.* and *sb.* (in *pl.*). **Cholia·mbist.**

Cholic (kǫ·lik), *a.* 1846. [– Gr. χολικός, f. χολή bile; see -IC.] Of or pertaining to bile. **C. acid,** an acid ($C_{24}H_{40}O_5$), which is produced from the nitrogenized acids of bile during its putrefaction. Formerly a name for *Glycocholic acid.*

Choline (kǫ·ləin). 1869. [f. Gr. χολή + -INE[5].] *Chem.* An organic base, identical with or akin to neurine. Hence **Choli·nic** *a.*

Cholo-, Gr. χολο-, comb. f. χολή bile: **Cho·lochrome** [Gr. χρῶμα], general name for the colouring matters of bile, including **Cholophæ·in,** the brown pigment, etc. **Cholo·graphy,** a treatise on the bile. **Cho·lolith,** a gall-stone. **Cholo·logy,** the part of physiology and pathology which deals with the bile.

Cho·loid, *a.* [f. Gr. χολή bile + -OID.] Resembling bile.

Choltry, var. of CHOULTRY.

‖ **Cho·lum.** 1858. [Tamil.] A grass, the Indian Millet, grown for food in India.

Chomp, var. (*U.S.* and *dial.*) of CHAMP *v.*

Chondre. *rare.* 1882. [– Gr. χόνδρος granule or lump of salt, groats.] One of the small rounded grains which occur in some stony meteorites.

Chondrify (kǫ·ndrifəi), *v.* 1872. [f. Gr. χόνδρος cartilage + -FY.] To turn into cartilage. Hence **Chondrifica·tion.**

Cho·ndrigen = CHONDRO-.

Chondri·genous, *a.* 1882. [f. Gr. χόνδρος cartilage + *-gen* producing + -OUS.] Furnishing cartilage.

Chondrin (kǫ·ndrin). (Formerly **-ine.**) 1838. [f. as prec. + -IN[1]. Cf. Fr. *chondrine.*] *Chem.* A substance resembling gelatin, obtained from the cellular cartilages by boiling them in water.

Cho·ndrite. [– mod.L. *chondrus,* name of a genus of sea-weeds (– Gr. χόνδρος cartilage) + -ITE[1] 2 a.] *Palæont.* A fossil marine plant of the chalk and other formations.

‖ **Chondritis** (kǫndrəi·tis). 1836. [mod.L., f. Gr. χόνδρος cartilage + -ITIS.] *Med.* Inflammation of cartilage.

Chondro- (kǫ·ndro), comb. f. Gr. χόνδρος, a grain, cartilage: **Cho·ndrogen** = Chondrin, or 'the tissues which yield chondrin'. **Chondroge·nesis,** the development of cartilage. **Chondro·logy** [Gr. -λογία], a discourse or treatise on cartilages. **Chondro·meter** [Gr. μέτρον], a steelyard for weighing grain. **Cho·ndropteryg·gian,** *sb.* a member of the order *Chondropterygii,* fishes having a cartilaginous endoskeleton, as the shark, ray, and sturgeon; *adj.* = **Cho:ndroptery·gious** *a.,* belonging to the *Chondropterygii.* **Chondro·stean** *a.,* belonging to the *Chondrostea,* a sub-order of ganoid fishes, in which the vertebral column consists of a simple soft *chorda; sb.,* a member of this sub-order. **Chondro·tomy** [Gr. -τομία], dissection or cutting of cartilage.

Chondrodite (kǫ·ndrŏdəit). 1822. [f. Gr. χονδρώδης granular (f. χόνδρος groat, grain, granule) + -ITE[1] 2 b.] *Min.* A yellowish or brownish-red silicate of magnesium containing a little fluorine. It often occurs in imbedded grains.

Chondroid (kǫ·ndroid), *a.* 1847. [f. Gr. χόνδρος cartilage + -OID.] Resembling cartilage.

‖ **Chondrosis** (kǫndrǭu·sis). [f. as prec. + -OSIS] *Phys.* The formation of cartilage.

Chonicrite (kǫ·nikrəit). Also **-krite.** 1834. [f. Gr. χωνεία fusion + κριτός separated.] *Min.* A native fusible silicate of aluminium and magnesium.

Choose (tʃūz), *v.* Pa. t. **chose** (tʃǭuz), pa. ppl. **chosen** (tʃǭu·z'n). [OE. *ćēosan* = OFris. *kiāsa, ziāsa,* OS. *kiosan* (Du. *kiezen*), OHG. *kiosan,* ON. *kjósa,* Goth. *kiusan* :– Gmc. **kiusan,* cogn. w. L. *gustare* taste. The normal ME. repr. of OE. *ćēosan* was *chēse* (XII–XVI). This was superseded by *chōse* (from the treatment of *ćeósan* as with a rising diphthong), whence mod. *choose.*] **1.** To take by preference out of all that are available; to select. Also with *infinitive obj.* ME. **2.** To will, to wish; to desire to have (*vulgar*) 1619. **3.** *intr.* or *absol.* To exercise choice ME. † **4.** To gather at pleasure –ME. † **5.** To pick out by sight –ME.

1. Chuse thee what armes thou likest SIDNEY. To c. a man Pope 2 *Hen. VI,* I. iii. 65. Some chose to go by the worlde 1526. 2. To c. to remain concealed GOLDSM. The landlady returned to know if we did not c. a more genteel apartment GOLDSM. 3. Here doe I c., and thriue I as I may *Merch. V.* II. vii. 60. *Cannot c.*: = have no alternative. (*Obs.* exc. with *but.*) He cannot c. but hear COLERIDGE. Phr. *To pick and c.*: to select with careful scrutiny. Hence **Choo·seable, choosable** *a.* (*rare*). **Choo·ser,** one who chooses. **Choo·singly** *adv.* by choice.

† **Choose,** *sb.* ME. [var. of CHOICE treated as vbl. sb. from CHOOSE.] The act, power, right, or privilege of choosing –1620.

Chop (tʃǫp), *sb.*[1] ME. [f. CHOP *v.*[1]] **1.** An act of chopping; a cutting blow. **2.** A piece chopped off; a slice (*esp.* of mutton or pork), a cutlet. Also *fig.* 1461. † **3.** A fissure, cleft, crack; a CHAP in the skin –1767. **4.** A short broken motion (of waves) 1858.

Phr. † *At the first c.*: at the first stroke (Fr. *du premier coup*); immediately (Fr. *tout à coup*).

Chop (tʃǫp), *sb.*[2] 1505. [var. of CHAP *sb.*[2]] **1.** A jaw; usu. *pl.* jaws; sides of the face. **2.** *pl.* The jaws as forming the mouth, fauces, parts about the mouth. (Usu. contemptuous or humorous.) 1589. **3.** *transf.* The entrance of an abyss, cannon, valley, channel, etc. 1636.

3. Cruising in the chops of the Channel 1748.

Chop (tʃǫp), *sb.*[3] 1670. [f. CHOP *v.*[2]] An exchange, barter.

C. and change: a change; cf. CHOP *v.*[2]

Chop, *sb.*[4] 1653. [f. CHOP *v.*[3]] A snap with the jaws.

Chop (tʃǫp), *sb.*[5] 1614. [– Hindi *chhāp* stamp, brand.] **1.** In *India, China.* A seal; an official impress or stamp. **2.** A licence or permit duly authenticated 1699. **3.** *China trade.* A trade-mark; hence, a brand of goods. Also *attrib.* 1828.

3. *First* (*second*) *c.*: first (or other) rank, quality, etc.; also *attrib.*: A sort of second-c. dandies THACKERAY.

Comb.: **c.-boat,** a licensed lighter for transporting goods; **-house,** a custom-house where transit duties are levied.

Chop (tʃǫp), *v.*[1] ME. [A form of CHAP *v.*[1]] **1.** To cut with a quick and heavy blow, *e.g.* with an axe or cleaver; to cut into pieces; to mince. Often with *up.* Also *fig.* **2.** *intr.* To aim a hacking or hewing blow *at* ME. † **3.** To thrust, to go or come, with suddenness or force (*esp.* with *in, into*) –1816. **4.** = CHAP *v.*[1] 2. –1759. Also *trans.* † **5.** = CHAP *v.*[1] 3. *Sc.* –1657.

1. They breake their bones, and c. them in pieces *Micah* 3:3. *fig.* She was nervous..and chopped her words 1882. 3. You c. in the word *offer* SIR E. DERING. [They] c. in with their nimble tongues DE FOE. *To c. to an anchor* (Naut.): to come to an anchor hastily.

Chop (tʃǫp), *v.*[2] [First evidenced in CHOP-CHURCH; perh. var. of ME. *chappe,* which appears to have been evolved from OE. *ćēapian* (*ćeápian*) with influence from *chapman* (see CHEAP).] **1.** To barter. *trans.* and † *intr.* Also *fig.* 1485. **2.** *intr.* To change; esp. *Naut.* Of the wind: To veer or shift its direction suddenly 1642. Also *transf.* and *fig.* **3.** To bandy words 1525. Also † *intr.*

1. To c. horses in Smithfield SHADWELL. **To c. and change:** to buy and sell (*trans.* and *intr.*); to make frequent changes; to make different. 2. The wind..soon chopped about FIELDING. 3. *To c. logic.* (Also referred *erron.* to CHOP *v.*[1] 1, as if 'to mince'.) 1525. *intr.* Let not the Counsell at the Barre, c. with the Iudge..after the Iudge hath Declared his Sentence BACON.

Chop (tʃǫp), *v.*[3] 1581. [app. f. CHOP *sb.*[2]] † **1.** To take into the jaws and eat; to snap *up* –1701. Also † *fig.* † **2.** *intr.* To snap, to bite *at* –1694. **3.** *Hunting.* To seize (prey) before it is fairly away from cover 1624.

† **Chop-cherry.** 1561. [f. prec.] A game; = BOB-CHERRY –1684.

† **Cho·p-church.** ME. [See CHOP *v.*[2]] A trafficker in ecclesiastical benefices –1695.

Cho·p-fa:llen, *a.* 1602. [f. CHOP *sb.*[2]] = CHAP-FALLEN.

Chop-house. 1690. [f. CHOP *sb.*[1] 2.] An eating-house where mutton-chops and the like are supplied.

Chopin (tʃǫ·pin). *sb.* ME. [–(O)Fr. *chopine* – LG. *schopen* an old measure = half a pint (whence G. *schoppen*).] A liquid measure containing, in France, half an Old French *pinte,* in Scotland a Scotch half-pint = about an English quart. Also *attrib.* Hence † **Chopin** *v.* to tipple.

Chopine, chopin (tʃopī·n, tʃǫ·pin), *sb. arch.* 1577. [app. orig. – Sp. *chapin* = Pg. *chapim,* OFr. *chapin.*] A kind of shoe raised above the ground by means of a cork sole or the like. Spelt *c.* 1600 *cioppino,* pl. *cioppini,* as if Italian.

Neerer Heauen..by the altitude of a Choppine *Haml.* II. ii. 445.

† **Cho·p-lo:gic.** 1533. [f. CHOP *v.*[2] 3.] **1.** Disputatious argument –1688. **2.** One who chops logic; a sophistical arguer –1592. So † **Chop-logic.** Hence **Chop-logical** *a.*

Chopper[1] (tʃǫ·pəɹ). 1552. [f. CHOP *v.*[1] + -ER[1].] **1.** One who chops. **2.** An instrument for chopping; *spec.* a butcher's cleaver 1818.

Chopper[2]. 1581. [f. CHOP *v.*[2] + -ER[1].] One who barters; *esp.* a trafficker in ecclesiastical benefices.

Chopper[3] (tʃǫ·pəɹ). *Anglo-Ind.* 1780. [– Hindī *chhappar.*] A thatched roof. Also *attrib.* Hence **Choppered** *a.* thatched.

Chopping (tʃǫ·piŋ), *a.* 1566. [f. CHOP *v.*[1] + -ING[2].] Big and vigorous; strapping.

Choppy (tʃǫ̆·pi), *a.*[1] 1605. [f. CHOP *sb.*[1] + -Y[1].] **1.** = CHAPPY *a.*[1] **2.** Of the sea: Breaking in short abrupt waves 1867.

Choppy, *a.*[2] 1865. [f. CHOP *v.*[2] + -Y[1].] Given to change like the winds; unstable, as 'c. markets'.

Chop-stick (tʃǫ·pstik). 1699. [f. Chinese and Pidgin English *chop* quick + STICK *sb.*[1]; tr. Chinese *k'wâi-tsze* nimble boys, nimble ones.] *pl.* The two small sticks of bone, wood, etc., held between the thumb and fingers of one hand by the Chinese in place of a fork.

Chop-suey (tʃǫ:psū·i). 1904. [Chinese, 'mixed bits'.] A Chinese dish, consisting of meat, rice, etc., fried in sesame oil.

Choragic (koræ·dʒik, -ēi·dʒik), *a.* 1763. [– Gr. χορηγικός; see CHORAGUS, -IC.] Pertaining to a choragus.

The c. monument of Lysicrates 1820.

‖ **Choragium.** 1682. [L. – Gr. χορηγεῖον, -ιον place where a chorus was trained.] Dancing-ground.

‖ **Choragus** (korēi·gǒs). Also **choregus.** Pl. **-agi, -egi.** 1626. [L. *choragus* – Gr. χοραγός, var. of χορηγός, f. χορός CHORUS + ἄγειν lead.] **1.** *Gr. Antiq.* The leader of a CHORUS; *spec.* at Athens, one who defrayed the cost of bringing out a chorus 1820. **2.** The title of a functionary in the University of Oxford, originally appointed to superintend the practice of music 1626. Also *transf.* and *fig.*

Choral (kǭə·răl), *a.* 1587. [– med.L. *choralis*; see CHORUS, -AL[1].] Of or belonging to, sung by a choir or in chorus; containing a chorus or choruses.

C. service: a church service in which the canticles, anthem, etc., are sung by the choir; in a *full c. service* the versicles, responses, etc., are also chanted. *Vicar c.*: a cathedral officer whose duty it is to sing that part of the music of the services which can be performed by laymen or men in minor orders. **Cho·ralist,** one who sings in a chorus. **Cho·rally** *adv.*

Choral, chorale (korā·l). 1841. [– G. *choral,* from *choralgesang,* tr. med.L. *cantus choralis.*] *Mus.* A metrical hymn set to a simple devotional tune, and usually sung in unison; as Luther's '*Ein feste Burg*'.

Chord (kǭɹd), *sb.*[1] 1570. [refash. of CORD, after L. *chorda*.] **1.** A string or small rope. Now CORD. 1645. **2.** *spec.* A string of a musical instrument. (Now only *poet.*) 1667. Also *fig.* of the emotions, feelings, etc. 1784. **3.** *Phys.* Applied to structures in an animal body resembling strings 1541. **4.** The straight line joining the extremities of an arc 1570.
3. *Vocal, spermatic, spinal*, etc., *c.* (see VOCAL, etc.).

Chord (kǭɹd), *sb.*[2] ? 1475. [orig. *cord*, aphet. f. ACCORD *sb.*, q.v.; confused with prec.] † **1.** = ACCORD *sb.* 4. –1636. † **2.** *Mus.* A CONCORD *pl.* The notes added to a bass to make up a 'chord' in the mod. sense (see 3) –1753. **3.** *Mus.* A combination, rarely of two, usually of three or more, simultaneous notes 1752. Also *transf.* of colours 1856.
3. *Common* (also *perfect*) *c.*: the combination of any note with its third (major or minor), perfect fifth, and octave. The c. of C inverted BURNEY.

Chord, *v.*[1] *rare.* [f. CHORD *sb.*[2]; perh. a survival of CORD *v.*[2] short for *accord*.] *intr.* To form a chord (with); to harmonize; to sound together in harmony. **b.** *trans.* To cause to accord or harmonize.

Chord, *v.*[2]; var. CORD *v.*[1]

Chordal (kǭ·ɹdăl), *a.* 1619. [f. CHORD *sb.*[1] and [2] + -AL[1].] Relating to, consisting, or of the nature, of a chord or chords. So **Cho·rded** *a.* having chords; combined in chords, in harmony.

Chordee (kǭ·ɹdī). 1708. [– Fr. *cordée* in *chaudepisse cordée*.] *Path.* A painful inflammatory downward curving of the penis.

† **Chore, chor** (kōᵊɹ), *sb.*[1] OE. [– L. *chorus* (see CHORUS), at different times, app. independently, in OE., ME., and XVI.] = CHOIR (exc. in sense 1) –1680.

Chore (tʃōᵊɹ), *sb.*[2] *dial.* and *U.S.* 1746. [unexpl. var. of CHARE *sb.*[1]] = CHARE *sb.*[1] 2. Hence **Chore** *v.* (*intr.*) to do chores.

‖ **Chorea** (korī·ă). 1686. [Short for L. *chorea Sancti Viti*; L. *chorea* – Gr. χορεία, f. χορός; see CHORUS.] *Path.* St. Vitus's dance; a convulsive disorder, characterized by irregular involuntary contractions of the muscles; also affecting horses. Hence **Chor·e·al, Chore·ic** *adjs.* pertaining to or affected with c.

Choree (korī·). 1586. [– L. *choreus* – Gr. χορεῖος pertaining to a dance. Cf. DICHOREE.] *Pros.* The foot more commonly called TROCHEE, q.v. Hence **Chore·ic** *a.* characterized by trochees.

Choregy (korī·dʒi, kǫ·rėdʒi). 1847. [– Gr. χορηγία office of a χορηγός; see CHORAGUS, -Y[3].] *Gr. Antiq.* The function of a choragus in ancient Athens.

Choreic; see CHOREA and CHOREE.

Choreograph (kǫ·riŏgrɑf). 1876. [f. Gr. χορεία choral dance with music; see -GRAPH.] A designer or arranger of a ballet. So **Choreo·grapher. Cho:reogra·phic** *a.* pertaining to (ballet-) dancing. **Choreo·graphy,** † the written notation of dancing; the choreographer's art.

† **Chorepiscope.** *rare.* 1660. [– late L. *chorepiscopus* (the form now used) – Gr. χωρεπίσκοπος, f. χώρα or χῶρος country + ἐπίσκοπος BISHOP.] A country or suffragan bishop of the early church –1844. Hence **Chorepi·scopal** *a.* belonging to a c.

Chori- (kōᵊri), bef. a vowel **choris-** (kōᵊris), – Gr. χωρι, χωρίς asunder, apart: as in **Chori·pe·talous** *a.*, having separate petals, etc.

Choriamb (kōᵊ·riæmb, kǫ·r-). 1844. [– late L. *choriambus* (also used) – Gr., f. χορεῖος CHOREE + ἴαμβος IAMB.] *Pros.* A foot composed of a choree followed by an iamb (–⏑⏑–). Hence **Choria·mbic** *a.* consisting of or containing choriambs; also as *sb.* [sc. *verse, foot.*]

Choric (kǫ·rik, kōᵊ·rik), *a.* 1819. [– late L. *choricus* – Gr. χορικός, f. χορός CHORUS; see -IC.] Of, pertaining to, or in the style of, a chorus. Hence **Chorics** *sb. pl.* (*nonce-wd.*; cf. *heroics*, etc.) the verses of a chorus. So **Cho·rical** *a.* (*rare*).

‖ **Chorion** (kōᵊ·riǫn). 1545. [Gr. χόριον.] **1.** *Anat.* The outermost membrane enveloping the fœtus before birth. **2.** *Bot.* The pulpy substance of the nucleus of the seed 1816. **3.** *Anat.* The *cutis vera* or true skin; = CORIUM 1831. Hence **Cho·rial** *a.* of or pertaining to the c.

Chorisis (kōᵊ·risis). 1835. [mod.L. – Gr. χώρισις separation.] *Bot.* The splitting of an organ into parts, each of which is a perfect organ. So **Cho·rism, Choriza·tion. Cho·ristate** *a.* formed by c.

Chorist (kǫ·rist, kōᵊ·rist). 1538. [– (O)Fr. *choriste* – med.L. *chorista*; see CHORUS, -IST.] † **1.** A member of a choir –1766. **2.** *Gr. Antiq.* A member of the chorus 1762. **3.** One who sings in a chorus 1835.

Chorister (kǫ·ristəɹ). [ME. *queristre* – AFr. **cueristre*, var. of OFr. *cueriste*, f. *quer* CHOIR; refash. (XVI) after † CHORIST.] **1.** A member of a choir; *spec.* a choir-boy. † **2.** A singer –1640. † **3.** *Gr. Antiq.* A member of the chorus 1603. Hence **Cho·ristership.**

Chori·stic, -al, *a. rare.* 1660. [f. as prec. + -IC, -ICAL.] Choric, choral.

‖ **Chorizontes** (kōᵊrizǫ·ntīz), *sb. pl.* 1887. [Gr. χωρίζοντες, pl. of pres. pple. of χωρίζειν separate.] A name for those grammarians who ascribed the Iliad and Odyssey to different authors. So **Chorizo·ntal, -ic,** *adjs.*; **Chorizo·ntist.**

Chorograph (kōᵊ·rogrɑf). 1839. [f. Gr. χώρα or χῶρος place, spot + -γραφος -GRAPH; see next.] An instrument to determine the position of a station, given the angles made by it to three points in the same plane whose positions are known.

Chorography[1] (korǫ·grăfi). 1559. [– Fr. *chorographie* or L. *chorographia* – Gr. χωρογραφία, f. χώρα, χῶρος country; see -GRAPHY.] The art of describing, or of delineating on a map, particular regions or districts; opp. to *geography* and *topography*. Also *concr.* and *transf.*
transf. I have . . beheld . . the C. of their provinces SIR T. BROWNE. Hence **Choro·grapher. Chorogra·phic, -al** *a.* **Chorogra·phically** *adv.*

Chorography[2] (korǫ·grăfi). ? *Obs.* 1710. [f. Gr. χορός dance; see -GRAPHY.] Dance notation.

Choroid (kōᵊ·roid), *a.* (*sb.*) 1741. [– Gr. χοροειδής, for χοριοειδής (χοριοειδὴς χιτών, choroid coat of the eye, Galen); see CHORION, -OID. Cf. Fr. *choroïde*.] *Anat.* Applied to structures resembling the chorion in form and vascularity; as the *c. coat* (or *tunic*) of the eye-ball, and the *c. plexus*, a plexus of blood-vessels connected by a thin membrane derived from the *pia mater*, in each lateral ventricle of the brain, etc. Also as *sb.* [sc. *coat.*] Hence **Choroi·dal** *a.* **Choroi·dean** *a.* **Choroidi·tis,** *Path.* inflammation of the c. coat.

Chorology (korǫ·lŏdʒi). 1879. [f. Gr. χώρα, χῶρος country, region, + -LOGY.] The scientific study of the geographical extent or limits of anything.
Its *Distribution* or *C.* HUXLEY. Hence **Choro·lo·gical** *a.*

Chorometry (korǫ·mėtri). 1823. [– Gr. χωρομετρία, see prec., -METRY.] The art of surveying a country.

Chortle (tʃǭ·ɹt'l), *v. intr.* 1872. A word coined by the author of *Through the Looking-Glass*; app. a fusion of *chuckle* and *snort*.

Chorus (kōᵊ·rɒs), *sb.* Pl. **choruses.** 1561. [– L. *chorus* – Gr. χορός; cf. CHOIR.] **1.** *Gr. Antiq.* An organized band of singers and dancers in the religious festivals, etc.; also, their song. (In the Attic tragedy, the chorus gave expression, between the acts, to the moral and religious sentiments evoked by the action of the play.) **b.** In English drama, reduced by Shakespeare and others to a single personage, who speaks the prologue, and explains or comments on the course of events 1561. Also *fig.* **2.** An organized band of singers, a choir; *spec.* those who sing the choral parts in an opera, oratorio, etc. 1656. **3.** The simultaneous utterance of song by many; anything sung by many at once 1711. Also *transf.* of speech, laughter, the cry of hounds, etc. 1735. **4.** *Mus.* A vocal composition, written in any number of parts, each part being sung by a number of voices 1744. **5.** The burden of a song, which the audience join the performer in singing 1599. Also *transf.*
1. b. Y'are as good as a C., my Lord *Haml.* III. ii. 255. **3.** One c. let all Being raise POPE. *transf.* A c. of loud laughter 1862.

Chorus (kōᵊ·rɒs), *v.* Pa. t. and pple. **chorused** (-ɒst). 1703. [f. prec. sb.] **1.** To sing or speak in chorus. *trans.* and *intr.* 1748. **2.** *trans.* To furnish with a chorus. Also *fig.* 1703.

‖ **Chose** (ʃoz), *sb.* ME. [(O)Fr. *chose* :– L. *causa* matter, affair, thing.] **1.** *Law.* A thing, chattel, piece of property 1670. † **2.** Thing (as a vague general term). ME. only.
1. *C. in action*, is a thing incorporeal and onely a right, as an annuity, . .—and generally all Causes of Suit for any Debt or Duty, Trespass or Wrong BLOUNT. Choses in possession (movables) 1875. **2.** CHAUCER *Wife's Prol.* 447.

Chose, pa. t. and † pple. of CHOOSE *v.*

Chosen (tʃōᵘ·z'n), *ppl. a.* ME. [See CHOOSE *v.*] **1.** Selected, picked out. **2.** *Theol.* Chosen of God; *absol.* (mostly *pl.*) elect ME.
1. A c. array 1871. **2.** The c. people ADDISON. He . . inspireth Light, into the Face of his C. BACON.

‖ **Chouan** (ʃu,aṅ), *sb.*[1] 1794. [Fr.; perh. f. the name Jean *Chouan*.] A name given to irregular bands who maintained in the west of France a partisan war against the Republic and the first Empire, after 1793; hence, a partisan of the Bourbons. Also *attrib.* Hence **Chouanize** *v.* to play the C.

†‖ **Chouan,** *sb.*[2] 1712. [Fr.] The seed of *Anabasis tamariscifolia* –1819.

Chough (tʃɒf). [The type *chough* remains unexplained. ME. *choȝe, choghe, chouȝe, chow(e)* do not repr. directly synon. OE. *ćēo, ćīo*. Some ME. forms, e.g. *co, cowe, chowe* may be – OFr. *cauwe, choue*. No doubt orig. imit.] **1.** A bird of the crow family; applied to any of the smaller chattering species. **2.** Now, the Red-legged Crow (*Fregillus graculus*), which frequents the sea-cliffs in many parts of Britain, *esp.* in Cornwall; the *Cornish Chough* 1566.
2. The Crowes and Choughes, that wing the midway ayre *Lear* IV. vi. 13.

Choule, obs. f. JOWL.

‖ **Choultry** (tʃɑu·ltri). Also **choltry.** *Anglo-Ind.* 1698. [Corruption of Telugu *chāwaḍi*.] **1.** A caravanserai. **2.** The colonnade of a temple 1772.

Chouse (tʃaus), *sb.* 1610. [Earlier *chiause*, later *chowse, chouse*; the forms suggest identity with CHIAUS, but connection of meaning has not been made out.] † **1.** = CHIAUS, q.v. –1639. † **2.** A cheat, a swindler –1658. † **3.** A dupe, tool –1755. **4.** *slang.* [f. the vb.] A swindle, sham, 'sell' 1708.

Chouse (tʃaus), *v. colloq.* 1659. [Earliest forms *chiause, chiauze*; f. prec. sb.] To dupe, cheat, trick; to defraud *of* or *out of*.
[He] only wants to c. you MISS BURNEY. Hence **Chou·ser.**

‖ **Chout** (tʃaut). 1674. [Marathi *chauth* 'a fourth part'.] The blackmail of one-fourth of the revenue formerly exacted by the Marathas. Also similar exactions.

Chow (tʃau). 1889. Short for next, 3.

‖ **Chow-chow** (tʃau·tʃau). 1845. [perh. Pidgin English, of unkn. origin.] **1.** *sb.* A medley; *e.g.* mixed pickles 1850. **2.** *adj.* Miscellaneous, mixed, assorted; of water, 'broken'. *Chow-chow chop*: the last lighter containing the sundry small packages to fill up a ship. 1845. **3.** A domestic dog of a Chinese breed 1886.

Chowder (tʃau·dəɹ), *sb.* 1762. [perh. – Fr. *chaudière* pot, CAULDRON, in phr. *faire la chaudière*.] **1.** A dish made of fresh fish (*esp.* cod) or clams, stewed with slices of pork or bacon, onions, and biscuit. **2.** *C. beer*: 'a liquor made by boiling the black spruce in water and mixing molasses with the decoction'. Hence **Chow·der** *v.* to make a c.

‖ **Chowry** (tʃau·ri). 1777. [– Hindi *chaunrī*.] A whisk or fly-flapper (prop. the bushy tail of the Tibetan Yak).

Choy, var. of CHAY.

Chrematist (krī·mătist). *rare.* 1845. [– Gr. χρηματιστής trafficker, money-maker; see next, -IST.] One who studies the science of wealth; a political economist.

Chrematistic (krīmăti·stik). 1752. [– Gr. χρηματιστικός, f. χρηματίζειν make money, f. χρῆμα, -ματ- money; see -IC.] **1.** *adj.* Of, pertaining to, or engaged in the acquisition of wealth. **2.** *sb.* usually **Chrematistics,** the science of the wealth of nations; political economy, or a branch thereof. [Gr. ἡ χρηματιστική.]

Chreotechnics (krīote·kniks). *rare.* [f. Gr. χρεία use + τέχνη art; see -IC.] The useful arts, *esp.* agriculture, manufactures, and commerce.

Chrestomathy (krestǫ·măþi). 1832. [- Fr. *chrestomathie*, or its source Gr. χρηστομάθεια, f. χρηστός useful + -μαθεια learning.] A collection of choice passages, *esp.* one intended to be used in the acquirement of a language.

C. of the Pushtu or Afghan Language 1847. Hence **Chrestoma·thic** *a.* teaching useful matters.

Chrism (kriz'm). [OE. *crisma* - med.L. *crisma*, eccl.L. *chrisma* - Gr. χρῖσμα, f. χρίειν anoint; refash. (like Fr. *chrême*) in XVI after L. *chrisma*. See CREAM.] **1.** Oil mingled with balm, consecrated for use as an unguent in the administration of certain sacraments; an unguent 1833. Also *fig.* **2.** A sacramental anointing; unction ME.; *spec.* Confirmation 1597. Also *transf.* and *fig.* **3.** = CHRISOM OE. Also *attrib.* Hence † **Chrismed** *ppl. a.* anointed with c. **Chri·smal** *a.* of or pertaining to c.

† **Chrisma·tion.** 1537. [- med.L. *chrismatio*, f. *chrismat-*, pa. ppl. stem of late L. *chrismare* anoint; see -ION.] Application of the chrism; sacramental unction -1753.

C., or consigning with ointment, was us'd in baptism JER. TAYLOR.

Chrismatory (kri·zmătəri). 1450. [- med. L. *chrismatorium*, f. *chrisma, -mat-* CHRISM; see -ORY[1].] **1.** The vessel containing the chrism. **2.** Sacramental anointing; unction 1563.

Chrisom (kri·səm). ME. [Differentiated form of CHRISM (cf. *alarm, alarum*) first appearing in XIII (*crisum*).] **1.** (In full *c.-cloth, -robe*, etc.): A white robe, put on a child at baptism as a token of innocence. If the child died within a month from baptism, it was used as a shroud. **2.** (In full *c.-child, -babe*, etc.): orig. A child in its chrisom-cloth; an innocent babe. (In obituaries, etc., applied to a child that died during the first month, or ? that died unbaptized.) ME. Also *gen.* Infant, innocent 1596. Also *attrib.* var. † **Chriso·mer** (in sense 2).

Christ (krəist). [OE. *Crīst* = OS., OHG. *Crīst, Krist* - L. *Christus* - Gr. χριστός subst. use of χριστός anointed, f. χρίειν anoint; tr. Heb. *māšîaḥ* MESSIAH.] **1.** The Messiah or 'Lord's Anointed'. (In the Geneva and 1611 versions of the N.T. often preceded by *the*.) **2.** The title given to Jesus of Nazareth, as fulfilling Messianic prophecy; treated as a proper name OE. Also *fig.* † **3.** In versions of the O.T. = 'a king by divine right' (see ANOINTED) -1609. ¶ Exc. CHRISTEN *v.*, the derivs. of *Christ* are now always written with a capital.

1. If thou be the Christe, tel vs plainly BIBLE (Genev.) *John* 10:24.

Comb. **Christ's thorn,** a name given to several shrubs, fabled to have formed Christ's crown of thorns.

Christ-cross, criss-cross (kri·s,krǫs). ME. [lit. *Christ's cross*; treated in sense 2 as a reduplication of *cross*.] **1.** † The figure of a cross (✠) in front of the alphabet in horn-books, etc. -1659; hence, the alphabet (now *dial.*) 1553. Also *fig.* **2.** The mark of a cross 1607.

1. *fig.* Christ's cross in the chriss-cross of all our happiness QUARLES.

Christ-cross-row, criss-cross-row (kri·s,krǫs,rōᵘ). 1563. [f. prec.] **1.** The alphabet; so called from the figure of a cross prefixed to it in horn-books. Also CROSS-ROW, q.v. (*arch.* and *dial.*) † **2.** *fig.* The whole series -1652.

Christdom (kri·stdəm). *rare.* 1463. [f. CHRIST + -DOM.] Short for CHRISTENDOM, the Christian domain. (*Obs.*).

Christed, *pa. pple.* 1641. Made one with Christ. (A 'Familist' wd.)

† **Christen,** *a.* (*sb.*) [OE. *crīsten* = OS., OHG. *kristīn* - L. *christianus*; see CHRISTIAN.] **1.** = CHRISTIAN -1640. **2.** *absol.* A Christian (with pl. *-s* after 1500) -1530. Hence † **Chri·stenly** *adv.* † **Chri·stenman, cri-.** † **Chri·stenmas** = CHRISTMAS.

Christen (kri·s'n), *v.* [OE. *crīstnian* f. *crīsten* Christian; see prec.] **1.** To christianize (*arch.*). **2.** To administer baptism to ME. Also *absol.* **3.** To give a name to at baptism; usu. *pass.* 1450; † to stand sponsor to at baptism -1667. Also *transf.* **4.** *gen.* To name; call by the name of (*colloq.*) 1642.

3. *transf.* To c. bells 1533, ships CLARENDON. **4.** Chambermaids c. this worm a deathwatch SWIFT.

Christendom (kri·s'ndəm). [OE. *cristendōm*, f. *crīsten* (CHRISTEN *a.*); see -DOM.] † **1.** = CHRISTIANITY 3. -1681. † **2.** = CHRISTIANITY 2. -1649. **3.** Christians collectively; the church ME.; the Christian domain ME. † **4.** Baptism; christening -1680.

3. The creed of C. 1866. The king of Kirsendom MIDDLETON. **4.** A world Of pretty fond adoptious christendomes *All's Well* I. i. 188.

† **Christenhead, -hood.** *rare.* 1449. [f. CHRISTEN *a.*; see -HOOD, -HEAD.] Christianity; christening; a Christian domain -1762.

Christhood (krəi·st,hud). ME. [f. CHRIST + -HOOD.] Messiahship.

Christian (kri·styăn). 1526. [- L. *Christianus* (Tacitus), f. *Christus*; see -IAN. Superseded CHRISTEN *a.*; cf. OFr. *chrestiien, -tien* (mod. *chrétien*).]

A. *adj.* **1.** Believing, or professing, the religion of Christ 1553. **2.** Pertaining to Christ or Christianity 1553. **3.** Following the precepts and example of Christ; Christ-like 1597. **4.** Of or belonging to a Christian or Christians 1596. **5.** Human; civilized, decent, respectable (*colloq.* or *slang*) 1577.

1. The Rulers of this C. land KEBLE. *Most C.*: a title of the kings of France. **2.** To be buried in C. burial *Haml.* V. i. 2. *Court C.*: an ecclesiastical court. Now *Hist.* **3.** The mutual exercise of C. Charity HOOKER. **4.** *Merch. V.* IV. i. 310.

Phrases. *C. name*: the name given at christening; the personal name, as opp. to the family name or *surname*. *C. era*: the era reckoned from the accepted date of the birth of Christ. Hence † **Chri·stian** *v.* to christen. **Chri·stian-ly** *adv.*, **-ness** (*rare*).

B. *sb.* **1.** One who believes or professes the religion of Christ 1526. **2.** One who follows the precepts and example of Christ 1529. **3.** A human being; a decent, respectable, or presentable person (*colloq.*) 1591. **4.** Used as a sectarian name, as in 'Bible Christians', etc. 1818. † **5.** A variety of pear or plum -1655.

1. So that the disciples were at Antioche first named CHRISTIANS N.T. (Rhem.) *Acts* 11:26. † *Even C.*: FELLOW-C. **3.** A fitter food for a horse than a C. FIELDING. Hence † **Chri·stiandom** = CHRISTENDOM. **Chri·stianlike** *a.* and *adv.* **Chri·stianly** *a.*

Christianism (kri·styăniz'm). 1576. [- Fr. *christianisme* or eccl.L. *christianismus* - Gr. χριστιανισμός; see CHRISTIAN, -ISM.] **1.** The Christian religious system. (*Obs.* exc. as an *-ism.*) **2.** Christianity of a sort or form (*disparaging*) 1674.

Christianity (kristi,æ·nĭti). ME. [ME. *cristianite*, superseding, by assim. to L., earlier *cristiente, cristente* (- OFr. *chrestienté* (mod. *chrétienté*), f. *crestien*), after late L. *christianitas*; see -ITY.] † **1.** The whole body of Christians, CHRISTENDOM -1650. **2.** The Christian faith; the system of doctrines and precepts taught by Christ ME. **3.** State or fact of being a Christian; Christian spirit or character ME. † **4.** *Eccl.* Ecclesiastical jurisdiction -1878.

1. To Walys fledde the Cristyanytee Of olde Britons, dwellynge in this Ile CHAUCER. **4.** *Dean of C.*, orig. = Rural Dean.

Christianize (kri·styănəiz), *v.* 1593. [f. CHRISTIAN *a.* + -IZE; orig. perh. - late L. *christianizare*.] **1.** To make Christian, convert to Christianity. **2.** To give a Christian character or form to 1693. **3.** *intr.* To adopt Christianity 1598.

1. He was Christianized and baptiz'd 1676. Hence **Chri:stianiza·tion** (in senses 1, 2). **Christiani·zer.**

Christia·no-, comb. f. L. *Christianus* CHRISTIAN, as in *C.-Platonical a.*; † **-ma·stic,** a scourge of Christians.

Christian Science. 1866. A theory, founded on principles formulated by Mrs. Eddy of U.S.A., according to which disease, etc., is an error of the mind and may be cured without medical treatment by mental effect of patient's Christian faith. So **C. Scientist.**

Christless (krəi·stlės), *a.* 1652. [f. CHRIST + -LESS.] Without Christ; unchristian. Hence **Christlessness.**

Christ-like (krəi·stləik), *a.* 1680. [f. CHRIST + LIKE *a.*; not continuous with OE. *cristlīć*.] Like Christ or that of Christ. Hence **Christlikeness.** So **Chri·stly** *a.*

Christmas (kri·smăs), *sb.* [Late OE. *Crīstes mæsse*, the mass of Christ.] **1.** The festival of the nativity of Christ, kept on the 25th of December; Christmas-time. **2.** *dial. and nursery lang.* Holly, etc., used for decorations at Christmas 1825. Also *attrib.*

1. Christmasse cometh but once a yeare CAMDEN *Proverbs*. *Comb.*: **C.-box,** † a box in which gratuities were collected at Christmas, by apprentices, etc., and afterwards shared; a present or gratuity given at Christmas; **-day,** the 25th of December; **-eve,** the day preceding Christmas-day; **-flower,** (*a*) the Christmas Rose, *Helleborus niger*; (*b*) the Winter Aconite, *Eranthis hyemalis*; **-tide,** the season of Christmas; **-tree,** a small (fir-) tree, set up in a room, illuminated, decorated, and hung with Christmas presents; borrowed from Germany. Hence **Chri·stmas(s)y** *a. colloq.* characteristic of C.

Christmas (kri·smăs), *v. colloq.* 1594. [f. prec.] To adorn with Christmas decorations; *intr.* to celebrate Christmas.

Christo- (kri:sto), comb. f. Gr. Χριστός or L. *Christus* CHRIST, as in **C.-centric** *a.* having Christ as its centre, etc.

Christology (kristǫ·lŏdʒi). 1673. [f. CHRISTO- + -LOGY.] That part of theology which relates to Christ; a doctrine or theory concerning Christ. Hence **Christolo·gical** *a.* **Christo·logist,** one who treats of C.; one who holds a theory about Christ.

Christo·phany. 1846. [f. CHRISTO- + -PHANY.] An appearance of Christ.

Christopher (kri·stŏfəɹ). ME. [- (ult.) Gr. Χριστοφόρος Christ-bearing.] † **1.** A figure of St. Christopher -1488. † **2.** A bearer 1563. **3.** *Herb C.*: the Bane-berry (*Actæa spicata*); also formerly *Osmunda regalis* 1578.

† **Christ-tide.** 1589. [See TIDE *sb.* 1.] Christmas -1656.

Christward. 1645. [See -WARD.] Towards Christ.

Christy minstrel. 1873. One of a troupe of minstrels imitating negroes, such as that originated by George *Christy* of New York.

Chromascope (krōᵘ·mă,skoᵘp). 1810. [irreg. f. Gr. χρῶμα colour + -SCOPE.] *Optics.* Lüdicke's instrument for showing the optical effects of colour.

Chromate (krōᵘ·meⁱt). 1819. [f. CHROMIUM + -ATE[4].] *Chem.* A salt of chromic acid.

Chromatic (krōᵘmæ·tik), *a.* (and *sb.*) 1603. [- Fr. *chromatique* or L. *chromaticus* - Gr. χρωματικός, f. χρῶμα, -ματ- colour; see -IC.] **A.** *adj.* **1.** Of or belonging to colour or colours; consisting of or produced by colour 1841. **2.** Highly coloured 1864. **3.** *Mus.* Pertaining to or including notes which do not belong to the diatonic scale 1603. **b.** Of, pertaining to, or giving all tones of the c. scale. **c.** *transf.* of persons 1711.

1. C. memory, or the memory of colours 1869. *C. aberration*: see ABERRATION. *C. printing*: printing from blocks or types inked with various colours. **3.** *C. scale*: a scale which proceeds by semitones. Hence † **Chroma·tical** *a.*, **-ally** *adv.*

B. quasi-*sb.* † **1.** The art of colouring -1761. **2.** *Chromatics.* The science of colour 1790. **3.** *pl.* Chromatic notes, harmonies, etc. 1708. **4.** = ACCIDENTAL B. b.

Chromatin (krōᵘ·mătin). 1882. [f. Gr. χρῶμα, -ματ- colour + -IN[1].] *Biol.* Tissue which can be stained by immersion in colouring matter.

Chromatism (krōᵘ·mătiz'm). ? *Obs.* 1721. [- Gr. χρωματισμός colouring; see prec., -ISM.] **1.** Natural colouring. **2.** *Optics.* Chromatic aberration 1854. **3.** = CHROMISM.

Chromato- (krōᵘ·măto), bef. a vowel **chromat-,** comb. f. Gr. χρῶμα -ματ- colour:

Chromato·genous *a.*, *Path.* generating colour. **Chromato·graphy** [+ -GRAPHY], description of colours. **Chromato·logy** [+ -LOGY], the science of colours. **Chromato·meter** [+ -METER], a measure or scale of colours. **Chro·matophore,** also **-phor** [+ Gr. -φορος], *Phys.* a pigment-cell, possessing contractile processes, contained in the skin of Cephalopoda, and other animals; hence

Chromato·phorous *a.* **Chromato·scopy,** the examination of the colour of bodies. **Chro·matosphere** [+ SPHERE] = CHROMOSPHERE.

Chromatrope (krō^u·mătro^up). 1860. [irreg. f. Gr. χρῶμα + -τροπος turning.] A magic-lantern slide consisting of two superposed circular glasses, brilliantly coloured, one of which rotates in front of the other.

Chromatype; [irreg. var. of CHROMOTYPE.] see CHROMOTYPE.

Chrome (krō^um). 1800. [– Fr. *chrome* (Vauquelin, 1797) – Gr. χρῶμα colour; so named from the brilliant colours of its compounds.] *Chem.* **1.** The metal CHROMIUM. **2.** The yellow pigment and colour obtained from chromate of lead; as *orange, lemon, c. attrib.* and *Comb.*: **c. alum,** a double sulphate of chromium and an alkali-metal, isomorphous with common alum; **c. green,** (*a*) the sesquioxide of chromium (Cr_2O_3), used as a pigment; (*b*) a pigment made by mixing chrome yellow with Prussian blue; **c. orange, c. red,** pigments prepared from the dibasic chromate of lead ($2PbO, CrO_3$); **c. yellow,** the neutral chromate of lead ($PbCrO_4$), used as a pigment; also *attrib.*

Chromic (krō^u·mik), *a.* 1800. [f. prec. + -IC, cf. Fr. *chromique.*] *Chem.* Of or belonging to chromium; containing chromium in chemical combination. Applied to compounds in which chromium combines as a triad, as *c. acid* or *c. anhydride*, CrO_3, etc.

Chro·mism. 1881. [f. Gr. χρῶμα colour + -ISM.] *Bot.* Abnormal excess of coloration in plants.

Chromite (krō^u·məit). 1840. [f. CHROME or CHROMIUM + -ITE[1] 4 b.] *Chem.* A compound of sesquioxide of chromium (Cr_2O_3) with the protoxide of another metal. Hence *Min.* Name for **chrome iron ore,** consisting chiefly of chromic oxide (Cr_2O_3) and ferrous oxide (FeO).

Chromium (krō^u·miŏm). 1807. [f. CHROME + -IUM.] *Chem.* A metallic element, symbol Cr, not found free, discovered by Vauquelin in 1797. It is remarkable for the brilliant colours of its compounds.

Chromo- (krō^u·mo).
1. *Chem.* Comb. f. CHROMIUM, as in *c.-carbon.* **2.** Short for CHROMATO-, q.v. Hence.
Chro·moblast [Gr. βλαστός], a variety of connective tissue corpuscles containing a black pigment. **Chro·mogen** [+ -GEN], (*a*) a supposed vegetable colouring matter which is acted upon by acids and alkalis in producing red, yellow, or green tints; (*b*) the compound which requires only the presence of a salt-forming group to convert it into a dye-stuff. Hence **Chromoge·nic** *a.* **Chro·mograph** [+ -GRAPH], an apparatus for multiplying copies of written matter; hence, **Chro·mograph** *v.* **Chromo·meter** [+ -METER], an instrument for determining by means of colour the presence of minerals in ores. **Chro·mophane** [Gr. -φανής], the colouring matters present in the inner segments of the cones of the retina where they are held in solution by a fat. **Chro·mophore** [Gr. -φορος], the body whose presence, in conjunction with a salt-forming group, determines the possession of tinctorial power (cf. *Chromogen*). **Chromophoto·graphy,** the production of photographs in colour. **Chromopho·tolithograph,** a photolithograph produced in colours. **Chro·mophyll** [Gr. φύλλον], the colouring principles of plants other than chlorophyll. **Chro:moxylo·graphy,** printing in colours from wooden blocks.

Chromo (krō^u·mo). *colloq.* 1868. Short for CHROMOLITHOGRAPH. Also in comb.

Chromoli·thograph, *sb.* 1860. [f. CHROMO- 2.] A picture printed in colours from stone. Also *attrib.* So **Chromoli·thograph** *v.* to print thus. **Chromolitho·grapher. Chromolithogra·phic** *a.* **Chro:molitho·graphy.**

Chromosome (krō^u·mŏsō^um). 1890. [– G. *chromosom* (Waldeyer, 1888), f. CHROMO- 2 + Gr. σῶμα body.] *Biol.* Each of the rods or threads into which the chromatin of the cell-nucleus is transformed previous to the mitotic division of the cell.

Chromosphere (krō^u·mŏ,sfi^əɹ). 1868. [f. CHROMO- 2 + SPHERE.] *Astron.* The red gaseous envelope round the sun, outside the photosphere. Hence **Chromosphe·ric** *a.*

Chromotype (krō^u·mŏtəip). Also **chroma-.** 1843. [f. CHROMO- 1.] *Photogr.* A process for obtaining photographs by means of paper sensitized by a salt of chromium; a picture thus produced. Also *attrib.* Hence **Chro:motypo·graphy, -typy,** printing in colours.

Chromous (krō^u·məs), *a.* 1840. [f. CHROME + -OUS.] *Chem.* Of or pertaining to chromium; applied to compounds in which it combines as a dyad.

† **Chromule.** 1835. [f. Gr. χρῶμα colour + ὕλη matter; see -YL.] = *chromophyll* (see CHROMO- 2) –1870.

Chronal (krō^u·năl), *a. rare.* 1875. [f. Gr. χρόνος time + -AL[1].] Of or relating to time.

Chronic, -al (krǫ·nik, -ăl), *a.* 1601. [– Fr. *chronique* – L. *chronicus* (in late L. of disease) – Gr. χρονικός, f. χρόνος time; see -IC, -ICAL.] † **1.** Of or relating to time; chronological 1605. **2.** [= Gr. χρόνιος.] Lasting a long time, lingering, inveterate; opp. to *acute* 1601. *transf.* Constant; also, bad 1860.
2. C. pains, which surely kill, though slow H. VAUGHAN. A c. invalid 1842. *transf.* C. doubts 1871. Hence **Chro·nically** *adv.* **Chroni·city,** c. quality or condition (of disease).

Chronicle (krǫ·nik'l) *sb.* [ME. *cronikle* – AFr. *cronicle*, var. of OFr. *cronique* (mod. *chronique*) – L. *chronica* – Gr. χρονικά annals. For the parasitic *l* cf. *participle, principle.*] **1.** A detailed and continuous register of events in order of time. Also *fig.* **2.** spec. *Chronicles*: name of two historical books of the O.T. 1535. **3.** *gen.* A record, narrative ME.
1. Broþer Ranulf. . compiled and made þis present cronicle TREVISA. *fig. Tr. & Cr.* IV. v. 202.

Chronicle (krǫ·nik'l), *v.* ME. [f. prec.] To enter or record in a chronicle; *gen.* to put on record, register.
To. . c. small Beere *Oth.* II. i. 161. Hence **Chro·nicler,** a writer of a chronicle, a recorder of events.

† **Chro·nique.** ME. [– OFr. *cronique* – med.L. *cronica, chronica*, from L. *chronica* pl. 'matters of time' – Gr., f. χρόνος, time.] A CHRONICLE –1671.

†‖ **Chrono·crator.** 1647. [Gr.] *Astrol.* A ruler of time –1862.

Chronogram (krǫ·nŏgræm). 1621. [f. Gr. χρόνος time + -GRAM.] A phrase, sentence, or inscription, in which certain letters (distinguished from the rest) express by their numerical values a date or epoch.
Thus a pamphlet published in 1666, when an engagement between the English and Dutch navies was expected, had in place of the imprint of the year this sentence: 'LorD haVe MerCIe Vpon Vs.' The sum of the numerical values of the capital letters is 1666. (See *Athenæum*, No. 2868.) Hence **Chro:nogramma·tic, -al** *a.,* **-ally** *adv.* **Chronogra·mmatist,** a maker of chronograms.

Chronograph (krǫ·nŏgrɑf). 1662. [f. as prec. + -GRAPH.] † **1.** = CHRONOGRAM. **2.** An instrument, *esp.* a watch or clock, for recording time with exactness 1868. Also *attrib.* Hence **Chronogra·phic, -al** *a.* (in both senses). **Chronogra·phically** *adv.*

Chronographer (kronǫ·grăfəɹ). 1548. [f. late L. *chronographus* – Gr. χρονογράφος annalist (f. χρόνος time; see -GRAPH) + -ER[1] 4; see -GRAPHER. Cf. obs. Fr. *chronographe.*] A writer of chronography, a chronicler, chronologist.

Chronography (kronǫ·grăfi). Also † **crono-.** 1548. [– late L. *chronographia* – Gr. χρονογραφία, f. χρόνος time; see -GRAPHY.] The chronological arrangement of past events; † chronology.

Chronologer (kronǫ·lŏdʒəɹ). 1572. [f. CHRONOLOGY + -ER[1] 4.] One who studies chronology; a chronologist.

Chronology (kronǫ·lŏdʒi). 1593. [– mod.L. *chronologia*, f. Gr. χρόνος time; see -LOGY.] **1.** The science of computing time or periods of time, and of assigning events to their true dates. **2.** A chronological table, list, or treatise 1614.
1. If C. had not contradicted it, it would have been concluded, that he had been an Auditour of Pythagoras himself CUDWORTH. Hence **Chronolo·gic, -al** *a.* of, belonging to, or in accordance with c.; arranged in order of time; relating to or dealing with c. **Chronolo·gically** *adv.* **Chrono·logist,** a CHRONOLOGER. **Chrono·logize** *v.* † to chronicle; to apply c. to, to arrange chronologically.

† **Chronoma·stix.** *rare.* 1628. [f. Gr. χρόνος time + μάστιξ scourge.] A scourge of the time.

Chronometer (kronǫ·mîtəɹ, krǫ-). 1735. [f. Gr. χρόνος time + -METER; cf. Fr. *chronomètre.*] **1.** An instrument for measuring time; spec. applied to time-keepers having a special escapement and a compensation balance, used for determining longitude at sea, and for other exact observation. Also *fig.* † **2.** *Mus.* A METRONOME 1837.
Phr. *To rate a c.*: to compare its daily loss or gain with the true time. *Comb.* **c.-escapement,** one in which the movement of the balance is opposed by the wheels at only one point in a complete oscillation.

Chronometry (kronǫ·mĕtri). 1833. [f. as prec. + -METRY.] The art or science of accurately measuring time; measurement of time. Hence **Chronome·tric, -al** *a.* of or pertaining to c.; relating to the measurement of time. **Chronome·trically** *adv.*

Chronopher (krǫ·nŏfəɹ). 1867. [irreg. f. Gr. χρόνος time + L. *-fer* bearing, carrying; cf. -FEROUS.] An apparatus for the distribution of electric time-signals.

Chronoscope (krǫ·no,skō^up). 1704. [f. Gr. χρόνος time + -SCOPE.] An instrument for observing and measuring very short intervals of time; *esp.* one invented by Wheatstone, used chiefly in determining the velocity of projectiles. Hence **Chronosco·pic,** *a.* So **Chrono·scopy,** observation and exact estimation of time.

Chrys- (kris), comb. f., bef. a vowel, of Gr. χρυσός gold; properly denoting compounds of a golden-yellow colour: as
Chrysa·niline, a brilliant golden-yellow dye ($C_{20}H_{17}N_3$), obtained as a secondary product in the manufacture of rosaniline. **Chrysa·robin,** the medullary matter of the stem and branches of *Andira araroba* dried and powdered, Goa Powder. **Chry·sene,** a crystalline hydrocarbon ($C_{18}H_{12}$), of the Anthracene group, obtained in bright yellow glistening scales, etc.

Chrysalid (kri·sălid). 1777. [f. L. *chrysal-(l)id-*, Gr. χρυσαλλιδ-, stem of χρυσαλλίς CHRYSALIS; cf. Fr. *chrysalide.*] **1.** = CHRYSALIS. Also *fig.* **2.** *attrib.* Of or pertaining to a chrysalis (*lit.* and *fig.*) 1802.

Chrysalis (kri·sălis). Pl. **chrysalides** (krisæ·lidīz) or **chrysalises** (kri·sălisėz); also *chrysalids*; cf. *orchids.*] 1658. [– L. *chrysal-(l)is* – Gr. χρυσαλλίς gold-coloured sheath of butterflies, f. χρυσός gold.] The state into which the larva of most insects passes before becoming an imago. In this state it is wrapped in a hard sheath. Also *fig.* Also *attrib.* Hence **Chry·saline** *a.* [irreg. as if f. *chrysal-*] of, or of the nature of, a c. So **Chry·salize** *v. nonce-wd.* **Chry·saloid** *a.* c.-like.

Chrysanthemum (krisæ·nþǐmŏm). 1578. [– L. *chrysanthemum* – Gr. χρυσάνθεμον, f. χρυσός gold + ἄνθεμον flower.] **1.** The Corn Marigold (now *C. segetum*), a composite plant with brilliant yellow flowers: hence the name of the genus, having species with flowers of many colours, *e.g.* the Ox-eye Daisy. **2.** *Hort.* Usually applied to a number of cultivated late-blooming species of this genus, esp. *C. sinense* 1798. Also *attrib.*

Chryselephantine (kris,elĭfæ·ntin), *a.* 1827. [– Gr. χρυσελεφάντινος, f. χρυσός gold + ἐλέφας, -αντ-, elephant, ivory; see -INE[1].] Of gold and ivory: applied to statues overlaid with gold and ivory, such as the Olympian Zeus, etc. Also *fig.*

Chryso- (kriso), bef. a vowel CHRYS-, comb. f. Gr. χρυσός gold.
1. **Chry·sobull,** a golden bull or *bulla aurea*, **Chry·sochlore** [Gr. χλωρός green], the Cape Mole, whose fur has a gold-green lustre. **Chryso·cracy** [after *aristocracy*], plutocracy. **Chryso·graphy** [Gr. χρυσογραφία], writing in letters of gold. So **Chry·sograph** *v.* **Chryso·logy** [Gr. -λογια] the science of gold or wealth. **Chryso·philist, -philite** [Gr. χρυσόφιλος], a lover of gold. **Chrysopoe·tic** [Gr. ποιητικός] *a.,* goldmaking; also quasi-*sb.* in *pl.* † **Chry·sosperm** [Gr. σπέρμα], *Alch.* a substance that is the 'seed of gold'. **Chry·sotype** [see -TYPE], *Photogr.* a process in which chloride of gold is used to develop the negative; a picture thus produced.
2. *esp.* in *Chem.* and *Min.* **Chry·sogen** [see -GEN], an orange-coloured hydrocarbon contained in crude anthracene. **Chry·sophan(e** [Gr. *φαν-, φαίνειν], *Chem.* a name for an orange-red bitter substance contained in the alcoholic extract of rhubarb; also for *chrysophanic acid.* **Chry·sophyll** [Gr. φύλλον], the yellow colouring matter of plants. **Chry·sotile** [Gr. τίλος fibre], a fibrous variety of serpentine.

Chrysoberyl (kri·sobe:ril). 1661. [– L. *chrysoberyllus*, f. Gr. χρυσός gold + βήρυλλος BERYL.] *Min.* † **1.** A variety of beryl, with a tinge of yellow. **2.** A yellowish green gem, in composition an aluminate of glucinum. A variety is cymophane or *c. cat's-eye*.

Chrysocolla (krisokǫ·lă). 1600. [– L. *chrysocolla* – Gr. χρυσόκολλα.] **1.** A name meaning 'gold-solder', anciently given to borax, malachite, or other minerals. Now *Hist.* var. † **Chry·socoll.** **2.** *Min.* A hydrous silicate of copper, green, with a shining lustre 1794.

Chrysoidine (krisō·idəin, -oi·dəin). 1878. [f. Gr. χρυσοειδής gold-like (see -OID) + -INE[5].] *Chem.* A colouring base ($C_{12}H_{12}N_4$), intermediate between aniline yellow and phenylene brown. The chrysoidine of commerce is the hydrochloride.

Chrysolite (kri·sŏləit). [ME. *crisolite* – OFr. *crisolite* (mod. *ch-*) – med.L. *crisolitus*, for L. *chrysolithus* – Gr. χρυσόλιθος; see CHRYSO-, -LITE.] A name formerly given to various gems of a green colour, such as zircon, tourmaline, topaz, and apatite. Now restricted to a yellow variety of olivine, a species which includes the green mineral peridot as another of its varieties. It is a silicate of magnesia and iron found in lava. Also *attrib.*

One entyre and perfect C. *Oth.* v. ii. 144.

Chrysoprase (kri·sŏpre[i]z). In *Rev.* 21:20 **chrysoprasus** (krisǫ·prăsŏs). [ME. *crisopace, -pase* – OFr. *crisopace* – L. *chrysopassus* var. of *chrysoprasus* – Gr. χρυσόπρασος, f. χρυσός gold + πράσον leek.] **1.** The ancient name of a golden-green precious stone, perh. a variety of the beryl. **2.** *Min.* An apple-green variety of chalcedony ME.; also, its colour 1835.

1. Crisopassus is..hyd in lyghte and seen in derknesse TREVISA.

Chrysosto·mic *a. rare.* 1816. [f. Gr. χρυσόστομος (f. χρυσός gold + στόμα mouth) + -IC.] Golden-mouthed, an epithet applied to orators.

Chthonian (kþō[u]·niăn), *a.* 1850. [f. Gr. χθόνιος (f. χθών earth) + -AN.] Dwelling in or beneath the earth. So **Chthonic** *a.*

Chub (tʃɒb). 1496. [Of unkn. origin. Cf. CHEVIN, CHAVENDER.] **1.** A river fish (*Cyprinus* or *Leuciscus cephalus*) of the Carp family (*Cyprinidæ*), also called the Chevin. In U.S., the Black Bass (*Perca huro*); also the Black-fish (*Tautoga americana*). † *transf.* A dolt –1745. **2.** *dial.* A wood-log 1796. **3.** *attrib.* C.-like 1681. Hence † **Chubbed** *a.* = CHUBBY 1, 2; of or belonging to a dolt. † **Chu·bbish** *a.*

Chubb (tʃɒb). 1833. [Inventor's name.] Short for *Chubb-lock*: a patent lock with tumblers, that cannot be picked.

Chubby (tʃɒ·bi), *a.* 1611. [f. CHUB + -Y[1].] † **1.** Short and thick like a chub. **2.** Round-faced; plump 1722. Also *transf.*

2. A sow and her c. pigs 1859. **Chu·bbiness.**

Chuck (tʃɒk), *sb.*[1] ME. [Echoic. Cf. CHUCK *v.*[1], CHUCKLE.] A species of cluck; *e.g.* that of a hen calling chickens.

Chuck (tʃŏk), *sb.*[2] 1588. [alt. of CHICK, infl. by prec.] **1.** A term of endearment. **2.** Chick, chicken, fowl, *n. dial.* Also *fig.* 1675.

1. Vse lenitie sweet C. *Hen. V*, III. ii. 26.

Chuck (tʃɒk), *sb.*[3] 1611. [Goes with CHUCK *v.*[2]] **1.** A slight tap under the chin. **2.** A toss, a jerk 1843; a throw. *colloq.* **3.** Short for *chuck-farthing* 1711. **4.** *Sc.* A small rounded quartz pebble used in the game of 'chuckie-stanes'; hence *chucks*, a name of this game. Also *chuckstone*, 1822.

1. There's a double c. at a double chin HOOD.

Chuck (tʃɒk), *sb.*[4] 1674. [var. of CHOCK *sb.* Cf. CHUNK.] **1.** A CHOCK; a CHUNK. Chiefly *dial.* **2.** A cut of beef extending from the horns to the ribs, including the shoulder-piece (*dial.*) 1881. **3.** A boat-chock 1789. **4.** *Turning.* A contrivance for fixing the material to be turned to the mandril of the lathe. Formerly CHOCK. 1703.

Chuck, *v.*[1] ME. [Echoic; cf. CHUCK *sb.*[1]] **1.** *intr.* To make a clucking noise like a fowl. † **2.** *intr.* To chuckle –1599.

Chuck, *v.*[2] 1583. [perh. – OFr. *chuquer*, earlier form of *choquer* knock, bump, of unkn. origin.] **1.** To give a gentle blow under the chin. **2.** To throw with the hand with little action of the arm; to toss; prob. at first said of tossing light things only; by workmen used for *throw* in all senses 1593. **3.** *intr.* To play chuck-farthing 1735.

2. They'll..c. us into the sea 1825.

Comb.: **c.-farthing,** a game in which coins were pitched at a mark, and then chucked at a hole; **-halfpenny,** = *chuck-farthing*; **-hole,** (*a*) = *chuck-farthing*; (*b*) 'a deep hole in a waggon-rut' (Webster).

Chuck, *v.*[3] 1869. [f. CHUCK *sb.*[4]] To fix on the lathe by means of a CHUCK, q.v.

Chuck, *adv.* 1751. = CHOCK *adv.*; with direct impact.

Chucker (tʃɒ·kəɹ). 1760. [f. CHUCK *v.*[2] + -ER.[1]] **1.** A small pebble. (Cf. CHECKER *sb.*[2]) **2.** One who chucks or throws 1884.

Chucker-out (*vulgar colloq.*), a bully who ejects fleeced victims from a gambling-hell, tavern, or brothel; a rough hired to expel opponents from a political or other meeting.

Chuckie. *Sc.* 1793. [dim. of CHUCK *sb.*[3], sense 4.] Quartz pebble: also *c. stone* or *stane*. *C.-stanes*: = *Chucks*.

Chuckie; see CHUCKY.

Chuckle (tʃɒ·k'l), *v.* 1598. [f. CHUCK *v.*[1] + -LE.] † **1.** *intr.* To laugh vehemently or convulsively –1823. **2.** To laugh in a suppressed manner; to make or show inarticulate signs of exultation 1803. **3.** To cluck as a hen 1700.

Chuckle (tʃɒ·k'l), *sb.*[1] 1754. [f. CHUCKLE *v.*] **1.** An act or state of chuckling (see CHUCKLE *v.* 1, 2). **2.** The call of some birds to their young; the cackle of a hen 1773.

Chuckle (tʃɒ·k'l), *a.* and *sb.*[2] 1721. [prob. rel. to CHUCK *sb.*[4]; now repr. mainly by *chuckle-head(ed)*.] *adj.* Big and clumsy, blockish: used *esp.* of the head. *sb.* A big hulking fellow, a chuckle-head 1731. Hence **c.-head,** a blockhead; a stupid lout; **-headed** *a.*; **-headedness.**

‖ **Chuckler** (tʃɒ·kləɹ). 1759. [Corruption of Tamil *shakkili*.] One of a very low caste in Southern India, the members of which are tanners or cobblers; *colloq.* a native shoemaker.

Chuck-will's-widow. 1828. [From its cry.] *U.S.* A species of Goat-sucker (*Caprimulgus carolinensis*).

Chucky (tʃɒ·ki). Also *Sc.* **chuckie.** 1727. [dim. of CHUCK *sb.*[2]; see -Y[6].] **1.** Little or dear chuck. **2.** A chicken; a fowl 1789.

‖ **Chuddar** (tʃɒ·dăɹ). *Anglo-Ind.* 1614. [Hindi *chadar*.] A large sheet worn as a shawl by women in northern India.

Chuet, obs. var. of CHEWET.

Chufa (tʃū·fă). *U.S.* 1860. [– Sp. *chufa*.] The Earth Almond (*Cyperus esculentus*), a plant producing small tubers about the size of a bean. (In Fr. *souchet comestible*.)

Chuff (tʃɒf), *sb.*[1] ME. [Origin unkn.] A rustic, boor, clown, churl.

A Rich Penurious C. 1668. Hence **Chu·ffy** *a.*[1] **Chu·ffily** *adv.* **Chu·ffiness.**

† **Chuff,** *sb.*[2] 1530. [Origin unkn.] A cheek swollen with fat –1611. Hence **Chu·ffy** *a.*[2]

Chuff (tʃɒf), *a.*[1] Now *dial.* 1609. [See prec.] **1.** Puffed out with fat; chubby. **2.** Pleased, happy 1860.

Chuff, *a.*[2] Now *dial.* 1832. [See CHUFF *sb.*[1]] Churlish; gruff, morose.

Chukker (tʃɒ·kəɹ). 1900. Also **chucker.** [Hind. *chak(k)ar* = Skr. *cakra* WHEEL.] *Polo.* Each of the 'periods' of play.

Chum (tʃŏm), *sb.* Now *colloq.* 1684. [prob. short for *chamber-fellow* (XVI), orig. a word of Oxford univ. sl. corresp. to the Cambridge *crony*.] One who shares apartments with another or others; also, an associate, an intimate friend. In colloq. use with schoolboys, students, criminals, etc. Hence **Chu·mmy** *a.* **Chu·mship.**

Chum (tʃɒm), *v. colloq.* 1730. [f. prec.] **1.** To share chambers, to live together. **2.** *trans.* To put as a chum 1837.

2. You'll be chummed on somebody DICKENS. Hence **Chu·mmage,** the system of chumming one person on another; also, garnish, footing.

Chu·mmy, *sb.*[1] *low colloq.* 1836. [f. *chumley* = CHIMNEY.] A chimney-sweeper's boy.

Chummy, *sb.*[2] *colloq.* 1864. [dim. of CHUM *sb.*; *see* -Y[6].] = CHUM.

Chump (tʃɒmp). 1703. [perh. blending of CHUNK with LUMP or STUMP.] **1.** A short thick lump of wood; an end-piece. **2.** The blunt end of anything; also *c.-end*. **3.** *fig.* A block, blockhead 1883.

2. *Off his c.* (joc.): off his head. *Comb.* **c.-chop,** a chop from the c.-end of a loin of mutton.

‖ **Chunam** (tʃuna·m). 1687. [Tamil *chuṇṇam* lime.] Cement or plaster made of shell-lime and sea-sand. Used in India. Also *attrib.* Hence **Chuna·m** *v.* to cover with c.

Chunk (tʃɒŋk). *colloq.* and *dial.* 1691. [app. modified f. CHUCK *sb.*[4]] A thick solid lump cut off anything. Also *fig.* Hence **Chu·nky** *a.*

‖ **Chupatty** (tʃŏpɑ·ti). *Anglo-Ind.* 1810. [Hindi *chapātī*.] A small cake of unleavened bread, of coarse wheaten meal, flattened, and baked on a griddle.

‖ **Chuprassy** (tʃŏprɑ·si). 1828. [Hindi *chaprāsī*, f. *chaprās* official badge.] A wearer of an official badge; an attendant, messenger, or henchman.

Church (tʃɔ̄ɹtʃ), *sb.* [OE. *ċiriċe, ċirċe, ċyr(i)ċe* = OFris. *szereke, szurka, tzierka*, OS. *kirika, kerika* (Du *kerk*), OHG. *chirihha, kiricha* (G. *kirche*):– WGmc. **kirika* (ON. *kirkja* KIRK is – OE) – med.Gr. κυρικόν, for κυριακόν, subst. use (sc. δῶμα house) of n. of κυριακός pertaining to the Lord, f. κύριος master, lord.]

I. 1. A building for public Christian worship. (Cf. CHAPEL, ORATORY.) **2.** Applied to public places of worship of any religion, as Moslem mosques, etc.

II. 1. The Christian community collectively. (More fully the *C. Universal* or *Catholic*.) OE. **2.** A particular organized Christian society, separated by peculiarities of doctrine, worship, or organization, or confined to limits territorial or historical OE. **3.** The ecclesiastical organization of Christianity, or of a great Christian society; *esp.* The clergy, etc., of this society as a corporation having continuous existence, and as an estate of the realm. (In this sense opp. to 'State'.) OE.

1. *C. militant*: the C. on earth as warring against the powers of evil. *C. triumphant*: the portion of the church which has overcome the world and entered into glory. **2.** *C. of England, English or Anglican C.*: the English branch of the Western Church, which at the Reformation asserted the supremacy of the Sovereign over all persons and in all causes in his dominions. *Established C.*: the Church as by law established in any country, as the state-recognized form of religion. So *State C.* **3.** *Holy C.*: the Church Catholic, as divinely instituted and guided; also, in early times = the clergy. *High, Low, Broad C.*: see these words.

III. A congregation of Christians locally organized ME.

IV. 1. a. Used as tr. of L. *ecclesia*, Gr. ἐκκλησία, of the Vulgate and the LXX, in its pre-Christian sense 'congregation'. **b.** Later, a retrospective application of the Christian sense to the Israelites, and the 'Old Testament saints'. **2.** Applied to various societies, religious and other (*e.g.* the *C. of Humanity*, the Comtists) 1528.

1. a. Why have you brought forth the C. of our Lord into the wildernesse BIBLE (Douay) *Numb.* 20:4. Also *Acts* 7:38. **b.** History of the Jewish C. (*title*) STANLEY.

V. *attrib.* 'Church' is used (often hyphened) with the function of an adjective, signifying 'of the church, of a church, of churches, ecclesiastical', and in England *spec.* 'of the Church of England'.

Comb.: **c.-ale,** a periodic festive gathering held in connection with a c.; **-bell; -book,** one belonging to, or used in, connection with, a c.; **-flag,** a flag hoisted on board a ship during divine service; **-folk,** people at c.; adherents of the established c., as opp. to 'chapel-folk'; **-goer,** one who regularly goes to c.; so **-going** *vbl. sb.* and *a.*; † **-hawe, -hay,** a churchyard; **-house,** one belonging to a or the c., or used for c. purposes; **-land,** land belonging to a or the c.; **-lease,** a lease of c. property; **-living,** a living in an established c.; *esp.* in the C. of England; **-me·mber,** a member of the or a c.; so **-me·mbership; -mode,** a mode in mediæval c.-music; **-office,** an office in the c.: the form prescribed for the conduct of a c.-service; **-officer; -owl,** the BARN-OWL; **-rate,** a rate levied on parishioners for the maintenance of the c. and its services; † **-reeve,** a churchwarden; **-service,** the public worship of a c.; *pop.* a service-book; *esp.* the Book of Common Prayer, with the lessons, psalms, etc., added; † **-soken,** the territory of a c.; inhabitants of this district; **-text,** the Old English or Black-letter; **-way,** the public way leading to a c.; **-woman; -work,** work at the edifice of a c. (= work that proceeds slowly); work for, or in connection with, a c.; so **-worker.**

Hence **Chu·rchdom,** ecclesiastical status; the system of a c. **Churchia·nity** [after *Christianity*], devotion to the C. rather than to Christianity. **Chu·rchiness. Chu·rchish** *a.* (*rare*) = CHURCHY. **Chu·rchism,** ecclesiasticism; c.-partisanship; often short for *English Churchism.* **Chu·rchless** *a.* not having or belonging to a c.; not blessed by the c. **Chu·rchlet,** a little c. **Chu·rchlike** *a.* like a c.; befitting a c. **Chu·rchly** *a.* ecclesiastical. † **Churchship,** the being a c. **Chu·rchward** *a.* and *adv.*, **-wards** *adv.* **Chu·rch-wise** *a.* and *adv.*

Church (tʃɒ̄ɹtʃ), *v.* ME. [f. prec. sb.] To bring, take, or conduct to church, in order to receive its rites or ministrations. Said *esp.* of a woman after childbirth, when thanks are publicly offered for her safe delivery.

† **Church-chopper.** 1631. [See CHOP *v.*²] A trafficker in ecclesiastical benefices –1656.

Church-door. OE. The outer door of a church, where marriages, etc., were ordained to be performed.

Housbondes at chirche dore she hadde fyue CHAUCER.

† **Church-gang.** ME. only. [See GANG *sb*] Going to church; churching of a woman after childbirth.

Church-garth. *dial.* 1570. [See GARTH.] A churchyard.

Church-government. 1594. The government of the affairs of a church; the form of polity, as Episcopal, Presbyterian, etc., upon which a church is organized. So **Church-governor.**

Churchman (tʃɒ̄·ɹtʃmæ̆n). ME. **1.** 'An ecclesiastic; a clergyman' (J.). † **2.** A church-warden –1598. **3.** A member of the Anglican or other established church 1677. Hence **Chu·rchmanly** *a.* **Chu·rchmanship,** the position, quality, or action of a c.

† **Church-papist.** 1601. In 17th c., a Roman Catholic who conformed outwardly to the Church of England –1682.

Church-scot, -shot. [orig. OE. *ċiriċ-sċeatt*, f. *sċeatt* property, wealth, piece of money; later assim. to SCOT², SHOT *sb.*¹] lit. = *Church-tribute*: in OE. times a custom of corn collected on St. Martin's day; extended to other similar contributions.

Church-ward, *sb.* Now *Hist.* (= OE. *ċiriċ-weard*). The custodian of a church (building).

Churchwarden (tʃɒ̄:ɹtʃwǭ·ɹd'n). 1494. [See WARDEN.] **1.** One of the lay officers (usually two) elected annually to assist the incumbent of a parish or district church, to manage various parochial offices, and generally to act as the lay representative of the parish in matters of church-organization. **2.** *colloq.* A clay pipe with a very long stem 1863. Hence **Chu:rchwa·rdenship.**

Churchy (tʃɒ̄·ɹtʃi), *a. colloq.* 1864. [See -Y¹.] Strongly smacking of the Church; obtrusive in conformity to the Church.

Churchyard (tʃɒ̄·ɹtʃyaɹd). ME. [See YARD *sb.*¹] **1.** The enclosure in which a church stands; a burial-ground. † **2.** The precincts of a church (*rare*) –1577. Also *attrib.*

1. Like Graues i'th holy C. *Cor.* III. iii. 51. **2.** In Powles churche yarde 1577.

Churl (tʃɒ̄ɹl). [OE. *ċeorl* = OFris. *tzerl, tzirl*, MLG. *kerle* (whence G. *kerl* fellow), (M)Du. *kerel*:– WGmc. **kerl-*, rel. to **karl-* CARL.] **1.** A man; *esp.* as correlative to 'wife'. (In ME. mixed with other senses.) **2.** In OE. times: A man; a member of the lowest rank of freemen. Now *Hist.* † **3.** A serf –1607. **4.** A rustic, boor ME. **5.** A rude low-bred fellow ME. **6.** *spec.* A niggard; a miser 1535.

2. The Saxons..made three degrees of freemen; to wit—an earl, a thane, and a c. RISDON. Gentleman or C. SHELTON. **6.** The c. [shall be no more] said to be bountiful *Isa.* 32:5. Hence † **Chu·rldom,** the state of being a c. **Chu·rlhood,** † the quality of a c.; the order of the churls.

Churlish (tʃɒ̄·ɹliʃ), *a.* [OE. *ċeorlisċ, ċierlisċ*, f. prec. + -ISH¹.] **1.** Of or relating to a churl; pertaining to churls (*arch.*). **2.** Brutal, surly, ungracious ME. Also *transf.* and *fig.* **3.** Sordid, niggardly, grudging 1566. **4.** Difficult to work, intractable 1577. Also *fig.*

1. C. birth FREEMAN. **2.** The reply C. *A.Y.L.* v. iv. 98. C. Blasts CUDWORTH. **3.** Thy c. courtesy.. Reserve SCOTT. **4.** C. ground 1577, metal FULLER. Hence **Chu·rlish-ly** *adv.*, **-ness. Chu·rly** *a.* (*rare*).

Churn (tʃɒ̄ɹn), *sb. N. dial.* KIRN, q.v. [Late OE. *ċyrin*, var. of **ċirn*, **ċiern* = MLG. *kerne, kirne*, MDu. *kerne*, ON. *kirna*:– Gmc. **kernjōn*, of unkn. origin.] **1.** A vessel or machine for making butter, in which cream or milk is shaken, beaten, or broken, so as to separate the oily globules from the serous parts. Used also of vessels or instruments resembling this, as a pump, a milkcan, etc. **2.** [from the vb.] Churning (of water, etc.) 1882. Also *attrib.*

Churn (tʃɒ̄ɹn), *v.* ME. [f. prec. sb.] **1.** To agitate *milk* or *cream* in a churn so as to make butter; to produce *butter* thus. Also *intr.* **2.** To agitate, stir, and intermix; to produce (froth, etc.) thus 1697. Also *intr.*

2. Winds churn'd white the waves CAMPBELL. Hence **Chu·rning** *vbl. sb.* the quantity of butter produced at a churning. **Chu·rner.**

Comb.: **c.-milk,** butter-milk; **-owl,** the Night-Jar (*dial.*); **-staff,** a staff for agitating the milk in the c.

Churr (tʃɒ̄ɹ), *v.* 1555. [Echoic; cf. CHIRR.] To make a deep trilled or whirring sound, as some birds. Hence **Churr** *sb.* this sound; also, any bird which makes this sound, *esp.* the Partridge (*local*).

‖ **Chu·rrus.** 1860. [Hindi *charas.*] The resinous exudation of the hemp-plant (*Cannabis indica*), used in India as an intoxicant.

Chu·rr-worm. 1668. [From the sound it makes; see CHURR.] The Mole-cricket. *local.*

Chuse, var. of CHOOSE *v.*, q.v.

Chusite (tʃiū·zəit). 1811. [perh. f. Gr. χύσις fusion + -ITE¹ 2 b.] *Min.* A variety of Olivine.

Chut (tʃɒt), *int.* 1825. [Cf. Fr. *chut.*] An exclam. of impatience.

Chute (ʃut). Also **shute.** 1847. [– Fr. *chute* fall; often extended to senses which originated with *shoot* or are still commonly so spelt.] **1.** A fall of water; a steep channel by which water descends in force. **2.** A sloping channel or passage for the conveyance of water, or things floating on water, to a lower level 1878. **3.** A steep channel or enclosed passage down which ore, coal, grain, or the like is shot. In England, usually *shoot.* 1881. **4.** A steep slope or cutting 1847.

Chutney, chutnee (tʃɒ·tni). 1813. [Hindi *chaṭnī.*] A relish compounded of sweet fruits with acid flavouring from lemons, etc., and sour herbs, and hot seasoning from chillies and spices.

† **Chyazic** (kəiæ·zik), *a.* 1819. [f. *c*(*arbon* + *hy*(*drogen* + *az*(*ote* + -IC.] *Chem.* Now called *Prussic* (*Acid*).

Chylaqueous (kəilē^i·kwi,əs), *a.* 1859. [f. CHYLE + AQUEOUS.] Of the nature of chyle mixed with water.

C. fluid: a transparent colourless fluid circulating in some invertebrata.

Chyle (kəil). 1541. [– late L. *chylus* – Gr. χυλός animal or plant juice; cf. Fr. *chyle.*] The white milky fluid formed by the action of the pancreatic juice and the bile on the chyme, and contained in the *lacteals.* Also *attrib.* Hence **Chyla·ceous** *a.* (*rare*). **Chy·loid** *a.* (*rare*).

Chyli·ferous, *a.* 1669. [f. CHYLE + -FEROUS.] Bearing or containing chyle.

Chylific (kəili·fik), *a.* 1836. [f. as prec. + -FIC.] Chyle-producing. So **Chylifa·cient** *a.* (*rare*). **Chylifa·ctive** *a.* (*rare*). **Chylifa·ctory** *a.*

Chylify (kəi·lifi), *v.* 1663. [f. as prec. + -FY.] To turn into or produce chyle. Hence **Chy:lifica·tion,** † **Chylifa·ction,** chyle-making.

Chylo- (kəilo), comb. f. Gr. χυλός CHYLE, as in *c.-serous*, etc.

Chylopoietic, -poetic (kəi:lopoie·tik, -po,e·tik), *a.* 1735. [f. CHYLO-; see POIETIC.] Of or relating to the formation of chyle; chyle-producing.

Chylous (kəi·ləs), *a.* 1666. [– med.L. *chylosus*; see CHYLE, -OUS.] Of, pertaining to, like, or full of chyle.

‖ **Chyluria** (kəilū^ə·riă). 1860. [mod.L.; see *chylo-*, -URIA.] *Path.* The disorder of chylous urine.

Chym-; see CHIM-.

Chyme (kəim). 1607. [– late L. *chymus* – Gr. χυμός animal or plant juice. Cf. Fr. *chyme.*] **1.** The semi-fluid pulpy acid matter into which food is converted in the stomach by the action of the gastric secretion. From the stomach it passes into the small intestine, where it is converted into chyle. **2.** The sap of plants. Hence **Chymi·ferous** *a.* **Chy:mifica·tion. Chy·mify** *v.* to turn into c. **Chy·mous** *a.*

Chymic, Chymist, etc.; see CHEMIC, etc.

Chymo- (kəi·mo), bef. a vowel CHYM-, comb. f. L. *chymus* CHYME, as in **Chy·mosin** = pepsin, etc.

Chyometer (kəiǫ·mĭtəɹ). 1880. [f. Gr. χυ-, stem of χέειν pour + -METER.] An instrument, consisting of a tube with a graduated piston-rod moving in it, used for measuring liquids.

Ci-. In words beginning with *ci-* and *cy-*, which (exc. CINDER) are all non-Teutonic, *c* has normally the sound of *s*.

† **Ci·baries,** *sb. pl.* 1599. [– L. *cibaria* subst. use of n.plur. of adj. *cibarius*, f. *cibus* food; see -ARY¹.] Things used for food, victuals –1657.

Cibarious (sibē^ə·riəs), *a. rare.* 1656. [f. L. *cibarius* (see prec.) + -OUS.] Relating to or useful for food.

† **Ciba·tion** 1471. [– late L. *cibatio, -ōn-*, f. *cibat-*, pa. ppl. stem of L. *cibare* feed, f. *cibus* food; see -ION.] **1.** *Alchem.* Name of a process, 'feeding the matter' –1662. **2.** *gen.* Taking food 1651.

Cibol, ciboule (si·bǒl). 1632. [– OFr. *cibole* (mod. *ciboule*), with north. Fr. var. **chibole*; see CHIBOL.] Var. of CHIBOL.

‖ **Ciborium** (sibō^ə·riŏm). 1651. [med.L., – Gr. κιβώριον cup-shaped seed-vessel of the Egyptian water-lily, drinking-cup made from this. In sense 2 prob. assoc. w. L. *cibus* food.] **1.** *Arch.* A canopy raised over the high altar 1787. **2.** A receptacle for the reservation of the Eucharist.

Cicada (sikē^i·dă). ME. [– L. *cicada*, also *cicala.*] A homopterous insect with large transparent wings, living on trees or shrubs. The male makes a shrill chirping sound.

‖ **Cicala** (sikā·lă). 1821. [It. – L. *cicala*; see prec.] = CICADA.

The shrill cicalas, people of the pine BYRON.

Cicatrice (si·kătris). ME. [– (O)Fr. *cicatrice* or L. *cicatrix, -tric-* (also used in Eng. from XVII).] The scar of a healed wound; a scar-like mark. Also *transf.* Hence **Cicatri·cial** *a.* of, pertaining to, or of the nature of, a c.

Cicatricula (sikătri·kiŭlă). Also **Cicatricle** (sikæ·trik'l), **Cicatricule** (sikæ·trikiul). 1664. [– L. *cicatricula*, dim. of *cicatrix*; see prec., -ULE.] **1.** *Biol.* A round white spot on the surface of the yolk-bag of a bird's egg, consisting of the germinal vesicle. **2.** *Bot.* Applied to the hilum of grains, etc. 1828. **3.** *Med.* A small scar 1783. Hence **Cicatri·cular** *a.*

Cicatrisive (sikătrəi·siv), *a.* 1730. [irreg. f. CICATRIZE, *-ise* vb.; see -IVE.] Tending to promote the formation of a cicatrice. (Dicts.)

‖ **Cicatrix** (sikē^i·triks, si·kătriks). 1641. Pl. **-trices** (trəi·sīz). [– L. The word in scientific use.] **1.** *Pathol.* The scar or seam of a healed wound, sore, or ulcer. Also *fig.* **2.** *Bot.* The scar left by the fall of a leaf, etc.; the hilum of seeds 1826.

Cicatrizant (sikătrəi·zănt.) 1661. [f. next + -ANT, after Fr. *cicatrisant.*] *adj.* That heals by forming a cicatrice. *sb.* [sc. *medicine*, or *application.*]

Cicatrize (si·kătrəiz), *v.* 1563. [– (O)Fr. *cicatriser*, † *-icer*, f. *cicatrice* CICATRIX; in Eng. assim. to verbs in -IZE.] **1.** To heal by inducing a cicatrice; to skin over. Also *intr.* **2.** To mark with scars. Also *fig.* 1708. Hence **Ci:catriza·tion,** the formation of a cicatrice. **Ci·catrizer,** one who or that which cicatrizes.

Cicely (si·sĭli, səi·sli). 1597. [app. – L. *seselis* – Gr. σέσελις, w. subseq. assim. to the female name *Cicely.*] A popular name of several umbelliferous plants, almost coextensive with CHERVIL; as Sweet C. (*Myrrhis odorata*), etc.

†‖ **Cicer** (si·səɹ). ME. [L.] A chick-pea –1764.

‖ **Cicerone** (tʃitʃerō·ne, sisĕrō^u·nĭ). Pl. **-o·ni,** rarely **-o·nes.** 1726. [It.:– L. *Cicero, -ōn-*, cognomen of the Roman orator Marcus Tullius *Cicero.*] A guide who shows the antiquities or curiosities of a place to strangers. Also *transf.*

An army of virtuosi, medalists, ciceroni POPE. Hence **Cicero·ne** (tʃitʃerō·n, sisĕrōᵘ·n) *v.* to act as c. to.

Ciceronian (sisĕrōᵘ·niăn). 1581. [– L. *Ciceronianus*, f. *Cicero*; see prec., -IAN.] *adj.* Pertaining to, or after the manner of, Cicero 1661. *sb.* An admirer or imitator of Cicero's style.

The superstitious avoidance of new or post-Augustan words which the Ciceronians affected M. PATTISON. Hence **Cicero·nianism**, imitation of Cicero in Latin style and diction; *concr.* a Ciceronian expression.

†‖ **Cichar.** [Heb. *kikkār.*] A talent. HOOKER.

Cichoraceous (sikŏrēⁱ·ʃəs), *a.* 1729. [f. mod.L. *Cicoraceæ* (f. *cichorium* CHICORY) + -OUS; see -ACEOUS.] *Bot.* Of or belonging to the sub-order *Cichoraceæ*, comprising Chicory, Dandelion, etc.

Cich-pea, obs. f. CHICK-PEA.

‖ **Cicisbeo** (tʃiₗtʃizbē·o). *Pl.* **-bei,** also **-beos.** 1718. [It., of unkn. origin.] **1.** In Italy: The recognized gallant or *cavalier servente* of a married woman. **2.** A knot of ribbon fastened to a sword-hilt, walking-stick, etc. 1771. Hence **Cicisbe·ism** (tʃitʃisbī·iz'm), the practice of a c.

† **Ciclatoun.** ME. [– OFr. *ciclaton*, *-un*, etc., f. (ult.) Pers. *saklāṭūn* name of the town in Asia Minor where the rich tissue was woven.] Cloth of gold or other rich material, much esteemed in the Middle Ages –1400.

† **Cicone, ciconie.** ME. [– L. *ciconia.*] A stork –1549.

† **Ci·curate,** *v.* 1606. [– *cicurat-*, pa. ppl. stem of L. *cicurare*, f. *cicur* tame; see -ATE³.] To tame; to render mild –1710. var. † **Cicure** *v.* (*rare*). Hence † **Cicura·tion.**

‖ **Cicuta** (sikiū·tă). ME. [L. *cicuta* the hemlock given as poison.] A genus of poisonous umbelliferous plants, including the Water Hemlock, *C. virosa*. Formerly a name of the Common Hemlock. Hence **Cicutene, Cicutine, Cicutoxin,** chemical principles or compounds obtained from *C.*

‖ **Cid** (sid, Sp. þid). 1687. [Sp. *cid* chief, commander – Arab. *sayyid* master, chief, lord.] A title given in Spanish literature to Ruy Diaz, Count of Bivar, a champion of Christianity against the Moors in the 11th century; and to the epic celebrating his exploits.

‖ **Ci·daris.** 1658. [L. – Gr. κίδαρις, κίταρις; = Heb. *keṯer* (Persian) crown, diadem.] The royal tiara of the ancient Persians.

-cide (səid), *suffix.* **1.** – Fr. *-cide*, L. *-cida*, f. *cædere*, in comp. *-cidere*, cut, kill, as in *homicide*, *lapicide*, *regicide*, etc. **2.** – Fr. *-cide*, L. *-cidium*, cutting, killing, of same deriv. as 1. The two imply each other, as in 'the homicide is he who commits homicide', etc.

Cider (səi·dəɹ). [ME. *sither(e)*, *cidre* – OFr. *sidre*, earlier *cisdre* (mod. *cidre*) :- eccl.L. *sicera* (med.L. *cisera*) – eccl. Gr. σικέρα – Heb. *šēkār* 'strong drink'. See SICER.] A beverage made from the juice of apples expressed and fermented. Formerly including drinks made from other fruits.

Comb.: **c.-brandy,** a brandy distilled from c.; **cellar,** a cellar in which c. is stored; name of a drinking-shop in Maiden-lane, London; **-mill,** a mill in which apples are crushed for making c.; **-press,** a press in which the juice of the crushed apples is expressed. Hence **Ci·derish** *a.* (*rare*). **Ci·derist,** one who makes or affects c. **Ci·dery** *a.* (*rare*).

Ciderkin (səi·dəɹkin). 1676. [f. prec. + -KIN.] A kind of weak cider made by watering the cider-pressings and subjecting them to a second pressure; *water-cider.*

‖ **Ci-devant** (siₗdəvaṅ), *a.* 1790. [Fr.; = heretofore.] Former, late; that was formerly. A *ci-devant* friend of mine BURNS.

Cierge (sīᵊ·ɹdʒ, or as Fr. sięˑrʒ). [ME. *cerge, cierge* – OFr. *cerge*, (also mod.) *cierge* :- L. *cereus* wax taper, f. *cera* wax.] A wax candle, *esp.* as used in religious ceremonies.

‖ **Ciga·la, ciga·le.** [It. *cigala*, Fr. *cigale* – L. *cicala*; see CICADA.] = CICADA, CICALA.

Cigar, segar (sigā·ɹ). 1735. [– Fr. *cigare* or its source Sp. *cigarro*, supposed, but without direct evidence, to be f. *cigarra* cicada, the roll of tobacco-leaf being compared to the insect.] A compact roll of tobacco-leaves for smoking. Hence **Cigare·sque** *a.* having a c. (or cigars) as a prominent feature (*joc.*). **Ciga·rless** *a.*

Cigarette (sigăre·t). 1842. [– Fr. *cigarette*; see prec., -ETTE.] A roll of finely-cut tobacco in a cylindrical case, usu. of thin paper, open at both ends. Earlier **Cigar(r)i·to** (Sp.-Amer.) 1838.

‖ **Cilia** (si·liă), *sb. pl.* Sing. *cilium* (rare). 1715. [L., pl. of *cilium* eye-lid, eye-lash.] **1.** The eyelids, the outer edges of the eyelids; the eye-lashes 1838. **2.** Delicate hairs resembling eye-lashes, *e.g.* on the margins of leaves, the wings of some insects, etc. 1794. **3.** *Phys.* Minute hair-like appendages found on the tissues of most animals, and in some vegetable organisms. They are in incessant vibratile movement, and in some of the lower animal forms that live in water serve as organs of locomotion. 1835. Hence **Ci·lii-form, -liform** *a.* **Ci·liolate** *a. Bot.* fringed with minute c.

Ciliary (si·liări). Also † **ci·liar.** 1691. [f. L. *cilium* (see prec.) + -ARY¹; cf. Fr. *ciliaire.*] **1.** Of or pertaining to the eyelids or eyelashes. **2.** Pertaining to or caused by, CILIA (sense 3) 1835.

1. *C. muscle* or *circle*: unstriped muscular fibres situated beneath the sclero-corneal junction behind the iris and around the margin of the lens. *C. processes*: the plaits into which the anterior part of the choroid membrane is gathered around the crystalline lens. **2.** *C. motion*: the vibratile motion of the cilia, also locomotion by means of this.

Ciliate (si·lieⁱt), *a.* 1794. [f. as prec. + -ATE².] **1.** Fringed or surrounded with cilia. **2.** Furnished with vibratile cilia (see CILIA 3) 1868. var. **Ci·liated** *a.* Hence **Cilia·tion,** ciliated condition.

Cilice (si·lis). 1599. [– Fr. *cilice* – L. *cilicium* – Gr. κιλίκιον, f. Κιλικία Cilicia. Not continuous w. OE. *ċilic* – L.] Hair-cloth; a rough garment of this.

Monks..with their shaven crowns, hair-cilices, and vows of poverty CARLYLE. Hence **Cili·cious** *a.*

Cilicism (si·lisiz'm). 1848. [f. *Cilicia*, in Asia Minor, + -ISM.] A form of speech characteristic of Cilicia.

Ciliograde (si·liₗogreⁱd). 1835. [f. *cilio-*, comb. form of L. *cilium* (see CILIA) + *-gradus* walking, proceeding. Cf. Fr. *ciliograde.*] *adj.* Moving by means of vibratile cilia. *sb.* One of the *Ciliograda*, a tribe of Acalephans which swim by means of cilia 1835.

Cilio-spi·nal, *a.* 1881. [f. as prec. + SPINAL.] In *C. centre*, the direct centre in the spinal chord, where the nerve-fibres that cause contraction, etc., of the pupil of the eye take their origin.

Cill, var. of SILL, still occas. used.

‖ **Cillosis** (silōᵘ·sis). 1811. [irreg. f. L. *cillere* move, agitate + -OSIS.] A spasmodic trembling of the eyelids.

Cima, var. of CYMA.

† ‖ **Cimelia,** *sb. pl. rare.* 1664. [plur. of late L. *cimelium* (church) treasure – Gr. κειμήλιον anything stored up as valuable.] Treasures laid up in store –1736. So † **Cime·liarch,** treasurer; store-house.

Cimeter, -itar, -iter, obs. ff. SCIMITAR.

‖ **Cimex** (səi·meks). Pl. **cimices.** 1585. [L.] A bed-bug. Now only as the name of the genus. Hence **Cimi·cic** *a. Chem.*, in *Cimicic Acid*: a yellow crystallizable acid, of rancid odour, obtained from the liquid secreted by a bug. vars. **Cimise, cimisse.**

Cimmerian (simīᵊ·riăn), *a.* 1598. [f. L. *Cimmerius* (– Gr. Κιμμέριος, 'Odyssey' XI. 14) + -AN; see -IAN.] Of or belonging to the Cimmerii, a people fabled by the ancients to live in perpetual darkness. Hence, an epithet of dense darkness.

In dark C. desert MILT. *L'Allegro* 10.

Cimnel, obs. f. SIMNEL.

Cimolite (si·moləit). 1801. [f. L. *Cimolia* (also used), Gr. Κιμωλία (γῆ) a soft earth found in Cimolus, now Argentiera. See -ITE¹ 2 b.] *Min.* A soft hydrous silicate of alumina, allied to fuller's earth.

Cinch (sintʃ, sinʃ), *sb. U.S.* 1872. [– Sp. *cincha* cingle.] **1.** The saddle-girth used in Mexico, etc., usually made of separate twisted strands of horse-hair. **2.** *fig.* A firm hold; a certain thing, dead certainty. *U.S.* 1888. **Cinch** *v.* to girth tightly; *fig.* to 'put the screw on'.

Cinchona (siŋkōᵘ·nă). Also **chinchona.** 1742. [Named by Linnæus after the Countess of *Chinchón*, who, when vice-queen of Peru, was cured of a fever by Peruvian bark, and afterwards brought a supply of it into Spain.] **1.** A genus of evergreen trees or shrubs growing in the tropical valleys of the Andes, and now extensively cultivated in India and Java for the sake of the bark. **2.** The bark of species of Cinchona, Peruvian bark; also the drug prepared from it 1800. Also *attrib.*

Comb.: **c.-bark,** the bark of species of c., of value as a tonic and febrifuge. Called also *Jesuit's bark*, *Peruvian bark*, *Quinquina.*

Hence **Cinchona·ceous** *a.* belonging to the natural order of *Cinchonaceæ* of which C. is the typical genus. **Cincho·nal** *a. Bot.* related to the *Cinchonaceæ*. **Cincho·nia,** *Chem.* = *Cinchonine.* **Cincho·nic** *a.* of or pertaining to c., as in *Cinchonic Acid*, $C_{11}H_{14}O_9$. **Cincho·nicine, Cincho·nidine,** two of the cinchona bases, isomeric with cinchonine. **Ci·nchonine,** *Chem.* an organic alkaloid, $C_{20}H_{24}N_2O$, with febrifuge qualities, commonly associated with quinine, in various cinchona barks. **Ci·nchonism,** the condition produced by the excessive use of quinine. **Ci·nchonize** *v.* to act upon with quinine.

Cinct (siŋkt), *ppl. a. rare.* ME. [– L. *cinctus*, pa. pple. of *cingere* gird.] Girt, encircled. (Cf. *compact.*)

Cincture (si·ŋktiŭɹ), *sb.* 1587. [– L. *cinctura*, f. *cinct-* (see prec.) + *-ura* -URE.] **1.** A girding, encompassing, or encircling; enclosure, girdle. **2.** *concr.* That which encircles or encompasses 1667; in *Arch.* 'the ring, list, or fillet at the top or bottom of a column which divides the shaft from the capital and base' (Gwilt) 1696.

2. Her dress A vest with woollen c. tied WORDSW.

Cincture (si·ŋktiŭɹ), *v.* 1791. [f. prec.] To gird; to encompass, surround.

Cinder (si·ndəɹ), *sb.* [OE. *sinder* = MLG. *sinder*, OHG. *sintar* (G. *sinter*), ON. *sindr*; respelt with *c* from XVI after unrelated Fr. *cendre* (L. *cinis, ciner-* ashes).] **1.** Scoria, slag. (Usu. in *sing.*) Now *techn.* **2.** The residue of a combustible substance, *esp.* coal, after it has ceased to flame, and so also, after it has ceased to burn 1530. **b.** *pl.* Vaguely used for: Residue of combustion, ashes. Also *fig.* ME. **3.** *slang.* Brandy, whisky, etc., taken in tea, or other drink 1873.

1. Smiths cinders 1646. The volcano ejected cinders GOLDSM. **2.** A red-hot c. 1889. Sifting cinders STEELE. **b.** *Tit. A.* II. iv. 37.

Comb.: **c.-bed,** a stratum of cinders; in *Geol.* a stratum in the Middle Purbeck series, consisting chiefly of oyster-shells; **-notch,** the hole through which cinder is tapped from a furnace; **-path,** a running-path laid with cinders.

Hence **Ci·nderous** *a.* (*rare*). **Ci·ndery** *a.* of the nature of a c.; full of cinders.

Cinder (si·ndəɹ), *v.* ME. [f. prec.] To reduce to cinders. Also *fig.*

Cinderella (sindəre·lă). [f. CINDER + fem. ending *-ella*, after Fr. *Cendrillon*, f. *cendre* cinders, ashes + dim. ending *-illon.*] Name of the heroine of a familiar fairy-tale; *allus.* a drudge; a despised partner, etc. Also short for *c. dance*, a dance stopping at midnight.

Cine- (si·nĭ), abbrev. of next in comb. 1897.

Cinema (si·nĭmă). 1910. [– Fr. *cinéma*, abbrev. of *cinématographe*, f. Gr. κίνημα movement: see -GRAPH.] Short for **Cinematograph** (sinĭmæ·tŏgraf) 1896. A device by which a series of instantaneous photographs of moving objects is projected on a screen so as to produce the effect of a single motion scene; also, short for *cinema hall, theatre.* So **Ci:nemato·grapher,** one who takes **Ci:nematogra·phic** pictures, or practises **Cinemato·graphy** 1897.

Cinenchym(a (sine·ŋkim(ă). 1835. [f. Gr. κινεῖν move + ἔγκυμα infusion, after *parenchyma*, etc.] *Bot.* Laticiferous tissue.

‖ **Cineraria** (sinĕrēᵊ·riă). Pl. **-as.** 1597. [mod.L., fem. (sc. *herba* plant) of L. *cinerarius* (see CINERARY); so called from the ash-coloured down on the leaves.] *Bot.* A genus of composite plants, mostly natives of S. Africa, with bright-coloured flowers.

‖ **Cinerarium** (sinĕrēᵊ·riŏm). 1880. [late L., subst. use of n. sing. of L. *cinerarius*; see next and -ARIUM.] A place for depositing the ashes of the dead after cremation.

Cinerary (si·nĕrări), *a.* 1750. [– L. *cinerarius*, f. *cinis, ciner-* ashes; see -ARY [1].] Of or pertaining to ashes.

C. urn, vase: a sepulchral urn used in ancient times to preserve the ashes of the dead after cremation.

Cinereous (sinīᵊ·rĭəs), *a.* 1661. [f. L. *cinereus* + -OUS.] Of the nature of ashes; ash-coloured, as *c. crow*.

Cineritious (sinĕri·ʃəs), *a.* 1686. [f. L. *cinericius* + -OUS; see -ITIOUS[1].] **1.** Ash-coloured, ashen-gray, as the 'gray or c. matter' of the brain. **2.** Of the nature of ashes or cinders 1732.

Cingalese (siŋgălī·z). 1613. [– Fr. *Cing(h)alais*, Pg. *Singhalez*, f. Skr. *Sinhalam*. See SINHALESE.] *adj.* Of Ceylon. *sb.* A native of Ceylon; the language of Ceylon.

Cingle (si·ŋg'l). ME. [– OFr. *cengle* (mod. *sangle*) :– L. *cingulum, -la* girdle, f. *cingere* gird.] A girdle; a girth, a belt. Hence † **Cingling** *vbl. sb.* (*rare*).

‖ **Cingulum** (si·ŋgiulŏm). 1847. [L., see prec.; = 'girdle, belt'.] Occas. used techn. for **a.** The girdle of a priest's alb. **b.** A surgical cincture; also, the waist. **c.** A band surrounding the base of the crown of the tooth. **d.** The *clitellum* of earth-worms.

†‖ **Ciniphes**, *sb. pl.* 1571. [repr. Vulg. *sciniphes* – Gr. σκνίφες (LXX), pl. of σκνίψ.] The insects which constituted the third plague of Egypt (*Exod.* 8:17); ? gnats, lice, fleas –1662.

Cinnabar (si·năbaɹ). ME. [– L. *cinnabaris* (also used) – Gr. κιννάβαρι, of Oriental origin; cf. (O)Fr. *cinabre*.] **1.** The red or crystalline form of mercuric sulphide (Hg″S). Originally applied to native cinnabar, a rhombohedral mineral, the most important ore of mercury 1599. **2.** The same used as a pigment; VERMILION ME. † **3.** DRAGON'S-BLOOD, q.v. –1607. **4.** *attrib.* Vermilion-coloured 1807.

1. *Hepatic c.*: a variety of native c. of a liver-brown colour. Hence **Cinnaba·ric, Ci·nnabarine** *adjs.* consisting of, containing, or pertaining to, c.

Ci·nnamate. [f. L. *cinnamum* + -ATE[4].] A salt of cinnamic acid. So **Cinna·mein** = benzyl cinnamate $C_9H_7O_2 \cdot C_7H_7$. **Ci·nnamene,** an aromatic hydro carbon C_8H_8, or C_6H_5—C_2H_3; also called **Cinnamol** and *Styrol*. **Cinna·mic** *a.* of or pertaining to cinnamon, as in *Cinnamic acid* $C_9H_8O_2$, or C_6H_5—$C_2H_2O.OH$. **Ci·nnamyl,** the aromatic monatomic radical, C_9H_7O, of cinnamic acid, etc.

Cinnamo·mic, *a.* 1837. [f. L. *cinnamomum* (see next) + -IC.] Of cinnamon; in *Chem.* = *Cinnamic*. var. **Cinnamo·nic** *a.*

Cinnamon (si·nămən). [Late ME. *sinamome* – (O)Fr. *cinnamome* – L. *cinnamomum* – Gr. κιννάμωμον; later refash. after L. *cinnamon, -mum* – Gr. κίνναμον, of Semitic origin (cf. Heb. *ḳinnāmôn*).] **1.** The inner bark of an E. Indian tree (*Cinnamomum zeylanicum*, N.O. *Lauraceæ*), dried in the sun, and used as a spice. It is yellowish-brown in colour, brittle, fragrant, and aromatic, and acts as a carminative and restorative. **2.** The tree itself ME. **3.** *attrib.* Cinnamon-coloured 1685.

1. White C.: the inner bark of *Canella alba*; see CANELLA. **2. Wild C.,** *Canella alba* and *Myrcia acris*. *Comb.*: **c.-oil,** or *oil of c.*, a sweet aromatic yellow oil obtained from c.-bark, cassia-bark, etc., consisting chiefly of cinnamic aldehyde; **-stone,** a name for brown and yellow varieties of garnet.

† **Cinquanter.** 1611. [app. f. Fr. *cinquante*.] A man of fifty; an old stager –1675.

Cinque, cinq (siŋk). ME. [– OFr. *cinc, cink* (mod. *cinq*) :– pop. L. *cinque* for L. *quinque* five.] **1.** The number five, as marked on dice; a throw which turns up five. **2.** *pl. Change-ringing.* A name for the changes on eleven bells 1872. Hence † **Ci·nquangle, cinkangle,** a pentagon; **cinquangled** *a.*

Comb. **c.-spotted** *a.* having five spots *Cymb.* II. ii. 38.

‖ **Cinquecento** (tʃiŋkwe,tʃe·nto). 1760. [It. = five hundred.] The 16th century (15—), and that style of art which arose in Italy about 1500. Also *attrib.* Hence **Cinquece·ntist,** an artist or writer of that period.

Cinquefoil, cinqfoil (si·ŋkfoil). ME. [repr. L. *quinquefolium*, f. *quinque* five + *folium* leaf.] **1.** The plant *Potentilla reptans* (N.O. *Rosaceæ*), with compound leaves each of five leaflets. Also used of other species, and of the genus. 1545. **2.** An ornamental design resembling the leaf of cinquefoil; in *Arch.* an ornament used in the Pointed style, inscribed in an arch or in a circular ring ME. As *adj.* = **Ci·nquefoiled** *a.* furnished with cinquefoils, cinquefoil-shaped.

1. *Marsh c.*: = *Comarum palustre*.

† **Cinquepace** (si·ŋkəpēⁱs). 1570. [– Fr. † *cinq pas* five paces.] A lively dance, identified with the *galliard*; 'the steps were regulated by the number five' (Nares) –1647.

Cinque Ports. [In XIII *sink pors* – OFr. *cink porz*, repr. L. *quinque portus*.] A group of English sea-ports (orig. five, viz. Hastings, Sandwich, Dover, Romney, Hythe, and later also Rye and Winchelsea with the privileges of ports), which in ancient times furnished the chief part of the navy, and in return had many important privileges and franchises. **b.** = 'Barons of the Cinque Ports' SHAKS. Also *attrib.*

Cintre (si·ntəɹ). *rare.* ME. [– (O)Fr. *cintre* in same sense, f. *ceintrer* vault over.] The centre or centering of a bridge or arch.

‖ **Cion** (səi·ən). 1811. [Gr. κίων.] **a.** The uvula. **b.** The septum between the nostrils. Hence **Cio·notome,** an instrument for excision of the uvula. **Ciono·tomy.**

Cion, obs. f. SCION.

Cipher, cypher (səi·fəɹ). [Late ME. *siphre, sipher* – OFr. *cif(f)re* (mod. *chiffre*) – med.L. *cif(e)ra*, partly through It. *cifra*, † *cifera*, f. Arab. *ṣifr*; see ZERO.] **1.** An arithmetical symbol (0) of no value by itself, but which when placed after a figure or figures in whole numbers increases their value tenfold. **2.** *fig.* He who or that which fills a place but is of no importance, a nonentity 1579. **3.** A figure or number 1530. † **4.** *gen.* A symbolic character –1614. **5.** A secret manner of writing by any of various methods intelligible only to those possessing the key. Also anything written in cipher, and the key to such a system. 1528. Also *fig.* **6.** An intertexture of letters, *esp.* the initials of a name; a literal device, monogram 1631. **7.** The continuous sounding of any note upon an organ, owing to the imperfect closing of the valve 1779. Also *attrib.*

1. You are..like cyphers, which supply a place but signifie nothing 1593. **2.** The Raja was a cypher: the Dewan usurped the whole power H. H. WILSON. **5.** Cypher letter..which I cannot decypher, for Colonel Stewart took the cypher with him GEN. GORDON. *Comb.* **c.-key,** the key to writings in c.

Cipher (səi·fəɹ), *v.* 1530. [f. prec. sb.] **1.** *intr.* To use the Arabic numerals in the processes of arithmetic; to work the elementary rules of arithmetic; to think *out* (*U.S. colloq.*) 1837. **2.** To express by (occult) characters 1563. † **3.** *gen.* To express, delineate. Const. *forth, out.* –1640. † **4.** To decipher SHAKS. † **5.** To express by a monogram, etc. –1688. **6.** *intr.* Of an organ: To sound any note continuously without pressure on the corresponding key 1779. **7.** *Naval Arch.* To bevel *away* 1674.

1. To read, write and c. M. PATTISON. **2.** His notes he cyphered with greeke characters 1630. **3.** To c. me how fondlie I did dote SHAKS. Hence **Ci·pherable** *a.* **Ci·phered** *ppl. a.* (senses 2, 7). **Ci·pherer.**

Cipolin (si·pŏlin). Occas. **cipollino** (tʃipolli·no). 1798. [– Fr. *cipolin* or its source It. *cipollino*, f. *cipolla* onion (L. *cepa*); so called from the resemblance of its foliated structure to the coats of an onion.] An Italian marble interfoliated with veins of talc, mica, quartz, etc., showing alternations of (*esp.* white and green) colourings.

‖ **Cippus** (si·pŏs). 1621. [L. *cippus*, pale, stake.] **1.** (as in late L.) The stocks. **2.** *Arch.* A small low column, sometimes without a base or capital, and usually bearing an inscription, used by the ancients as a landmark, a sepulchral monument, etc. 1708.

Circ, var. of CIRQUE.

Circa (sɔ̄·ɹkă), L. *prep.* and *adv.* Around, round about, about, as *circa* 1400 (*c* 1400), *circa-continental* adj., etc.

‖ **Circar** (sɔ̄·ɹkăɹ). 1782. [– Pers. *sarkār* 'administrator; province'.] A province or division of Hindustan under the Moguls. See also SIRKAR.

‖ **Circa·ssian.** 1853. [An ethnic name, from *Circassia*.] A thin worsted fabric.

Circe (sɔ̄·ɹsi). ME. [L.; Gr. Κίρκη.] **1.** *Mythol.* The name of an enchantress who dwelt in the island of Æa, and transformed all who drank of her cup into swine; often used allusively. **2.** *Astr.* One of the asteroids 1855.

1. *Com. Err.* v. i. 270. Hence **Circe·an** *a.*

Circensian (səɹse·nsiăn), *a.* 1598. [f. L. *circensis* + -AN; see -IAN.] Of, pertaining to, or celebrated in the Roman Circus (see CIRCUS). Var. † **Circe·nsial.** SIR T. BROWNE.

Circinal (sɔ̄·ɹsinăl), *a. rare.* [f. L. *circinus* pair of compasses (– Gr. κίρκινος) + -AL [1].] *Bot.* = CIRCINATE.

Circinate (sɔ̄·ɹsinĕt), *a.* 1830. [– *circinat-*, pa. ppl. stem of L. *circinare* make round, f. *circinus* (see prec.); see -ATE[2].] *Bot.* Rounded, made circular; spec. of that mode of vernation in which the leaf is rolled up on its axis from the apex to the base, as in ferns.

Circination (sɔ̄ɹsinēⁱ·ʃən). 1592. [f. L. *circinatio*; see prec., -ION.] † **1.** *gen.* A circling or turning round –1681. Also † *concr.* **2.** *Bot.* Circinate vernation 1857.

1. *concr.* The circinations and sphærical rounds of Onyons SIR T. BROWNE.

‖ **Circinus** (sɔ̄·ɹsinŏs). 1837. [L.; see CIRCINAL.] *Astr.* The Compasses, a southern constellation.

Circle (sɔ̄·ɹk'l), *sb.* [ME. *cercle* – (O)Fr. *cercle* :– L. *circulus*, dim. of *circus* circle (see CIRCUS); later respelt after L.]

I. A figure or appearance. **1.** A perfectly round plane figure. In *Geom.* a plane figure bounded by a single line, called the circumference, which is everywhere equidistant from a point within it called the centre. Also, the circumference alone. Often used vaguely. ME. **2.** *Astr.* (See quots.) OE. **3.** *formerly*, The sphere or heaven in which a heavenly body was supposed to revolve; *now*, The orbit of a planet or other body ME. **4.** The orb of a heavenly body (?) 1667. **5.** A luminous ring in the sky, a halo OE.

1. *To square the c.*: see SQUARE. Fairie circles 1596. Love..in the c. of his arms Enwound us both TENNYSON. **2.** *C. of altitude*: a small c. parallel to the horizon, having its pole in the zenith; an almacantar. *C. of curvature*: see CURVATURE. *C. of declination*: a great c. passing through the poles of the celestial equator. *C. of latitude*: a great c. perpendicular to the plane of the ecliptic; also used = *parallel of latitude*. *C. of longitude*: a small c. parallel to the ecliptic. *C. of perpetual apparition*: that c. around the elevated celestial pole at any place, within which the stars never set. *C. of perpetual occultation*: that c. around the depressed pole, within which the stars never rise. *C. of position*: see POSITION. *Diurnal c.*: the c. described by a heavenly body in its apparent diurnal rotation round the earth. *Great c.* (*of a sphere*): a c. on the surface of a sphere, whose plane passes through the centre; if not through the centre, the c. is a *small c.* *Horary circles*: the lines marking the hours on a sun-dial. *Vertical c.*: a great c. perpendicular to the horizon. **3.** Hee thought the Sunne, would soner have fallen from his c. 1568.

II. 1. Any material object that is circular, as a ring, crown, coronet; one of the tiers of seats in a theatre ME. **2.** *Archæol.* A series of stones set up in a ring, as at Stonehenge, etc. 1772. **3.** *Astr.* An instrument of observation, the graduated limb of which consists of an entire circle, as *mural, reflecting, repeating, transit c.* (see MURAL, etc.).

1. *Dress c.*: the lowest gallery in a theatre; *upper* or *family c.*: that above.

III. Transf. and fig. **1.** The circuit or compass of a place ME. **2.** A cycle, period; 'any series ending as it begins, and perpetually repeated' (J.) ME. **3.** A completed series of parts forming a system 1531. **4.** *Logic.* A fallacious mode of reasoning, wherein a premiss is used to prove a conclusion, and the conclusion is used to prove the premiss. Hence *to reason* or *argue in a c.* 1646. **5.** A group of persons surrounding a centre of interest 1714. **6.** A set or coterie; a class or division of society 1646. **7.** A territorial division; *esp.* in Germany under the Holy Roman Empire 1675. **8.** The area over which anything exerts influence 1664.

1. Within the cercle of the Cité ME. **2.** The Wheele is come full c. *Lear* v. iii. 174. **3.** Orr's C. of Sciences (*title*) 1854. **5.** A c. of lookers on JOWETT. **6.** Political, social, and literary circles 1885. **8.** Within the c. of possibilities 1664.

Phr. † *To give the lie in c.*: i.e. circuitously, indirectly B. JONS.

Circle (sɔ̄·ɹk'l), *v.* [ME. *cercle*, later *circle*, f. CIRCLE *sb.*] **1.** = ENCIRCLE 1. (Now *poet.*) **2.** To move round 1583. **3.** *intr.* To move in a circle (*round, about*, etc.) ME. **4.** *intr.* To stand or extend in a circle (*rare*) 1613.

1. Th' Imperiall mettall, circling now thy head SHAKS. **2.** Other planets c. other suns POPE. **3.** While the bowl circles POPE. Hence **Ci·rcled** *ppl. a.* surrounded with, or as with, a circle; marked with a circle or circles; circular. **Ci·rcler,** one who encircles; one who or that which moves in a circle; cyclic poet (as tr. L. *scriptor cyclicus*) B. JONS.

Circlet (sɔ̄·ɹklėt). 1481. [f. CIRCLE *sb.* + -ET; perh. partly through Fr. †*cerclet.*] **1.** A small CIRCLE (in various senses) 1528. **2.** A ring or band (*e.g.* of gold or jewels) worn as an ornament, *esp.* on the head 1481. Also *gen.* † **3.** A round piece of wood, etc., put under a dish at table –1878.

1. Sure pledge of day, that crownst the smiling Morn With thy bright C. MILT. **2.** A plain c. of gold was the substitute for the crown STUBBS.

Ci·rcle-wise, *adv.* 1542. [See -WISE.] In the form of a circle.

Circocele, var. of CIRSOCELE.

† **Ci·rcue,** *v.* 1450. [– OFr. *circuir* – L. *circuire*, var. of *circumire*; see next.] To go or travel round –1494.

Circuit (sɔ̄·ɹkit), *sb.* ME. [– (O)Fr. *circuit* – L. *circuitus*, f. *circuit-*, pa. ppl. stem of *circuire*, var. of *circumire*, f. *circum* around + *ire* go.] **1.** The line described in going round any area; the distance round; the circumference. † *concr.* = CIRCLET. Shaks. **2.** The space enclosed by a containing line; area, extent 1483. Also *fig.* **3.** The action of going or moving round or about; a roundabout course; *fig.* revolution, round ME. **4.** *spec.* The journey of judges (and others) through various places in succession, for the purpose of holding courts, etc. 1494; *concr.* those making the circuit; now *esp.* the barristers 1714. **5.** The district through which the judge makes his circuit 1574. **6.** A district of Methodist churches supplied by a series of itinerant preachers 1766. **7.** *Electr.* The course traversed by an electric current between the two poles of a battery; the path of a voltaic current 1800. † **8.** Roundabout process or mode of speech or of reasoning –1836; *Law* = CIRCUITY –1751. **9.** *Path.* The period of a disease.

1. Java . . is nyghe 2000 Myle in circuyt MANDEV. **2.** A great c. of ground in a very good soyle ESSEX. **3.** I devoted many hours . . to the c. of Paris GIBBON. *fig.* The daies cercuit 1601. *To make a c*: to make a detour. **8.** To avoid c. of speech BACON.

Comb.: **c.-breaker,** an instrument which at regular intervals interrupts an electric current; **-court,** in Scotland, a court held periodically in the principal towns; in U.S. (*a*) Federal Courts intermediate in authority between the District Courts and the Supreme Court; (*b*) various State Courts. Hence **Circuitee·r,** a judge or barrister on c.; *gen.* one who makes a c.; var. **Ci·rcuiter.** † **Circuitee·r** *v.* to go on c.

Circuit (sɔ̄·ɹkit), *v.* 1549. [f. prec. sb.] **1.** To go or travel round. **2.** *intr.* To go or move in a circuit 1611.

1. The Phenicians circuited the greatest part of the habitable world GALE.

Circuition (səɹkiŭ,i·ʃən). *arch.* 1533. [– L. *circuitio*, f. *circuit-*; see CIRCUIT *sb.*, -ION; cf. OFr. *circuition.*] A going round or about; *fig.* circumlocution.

‖ **Circuitor** (sɔ̄ɹkiŭ·itəɹ). 1811. [L.] One who goes his rounds, a travelling inspector, etc.

Circuitous (səɹkiū·itəs), *a.* 1664. [– med.L. *circuitosus*, f. *circuitus* CIRCUIT; see -OUS.] Of the nature of a circuit, roundabout, indirect. Hence **Circu·itous-ly** *adv.*, **-ness.**

Circuity (səɹkiū·ĭti). 1542. [– OFr. *circuité* circuit, ambit, etc., f. L. *circuitus* app. after *gratuité, vacuité*, etc.] † **1.** Ambit –1580. **2.** Circuitous quality or process 1626.

2. *C. of action* (Law): an action rightfully brought, but unnecessarily roundabout.

Circulable (sɔ̄·ɹkiŭlăb'l), *a.* 1793. [f. CIRCULATE, on the analogy of pairs like *separate, separable*; *venerate, venerable.*] That can be circulated.

Circular (sɔ̄·ɹkiŭlăɹ). [– AFr. *circuler*, OFr. *circulier* (mod. *-aire*), learned alt. of *cerclier* :– late L. *circularis*, f. *circulus* CIRCLE; see -AR [1].]

A. *adj.* **1.** Of the form of a circle; round in superficies ME. † **2.** *transf.* Perfect, full –1659. **3.** Moving in or passing over a circle, as *c. tour* 1450. Also *fig.* **4.** Of the nature of arguing in a circle 1646. **5.** Circuitous 1617. † **6.** = CYCLIC (*rare*). J. DENNIS. **7.** Affecting or relating to a number of persons 1659. **8.** Of or pertaining to the circle or its properties 1599.

2. In this, sister, Your wisdom is not c. MASSINGER. **4.** To praise the Work from the Vertue of the Worker, is a c. proof HOBBES. **7.** *C. letter*, 'a letter addressed in identical terms to several persons'. *C. note* (*a*) = *Circular letter*; (*b*) a letter of credit addressed by a banker to several other bankers, in favour of a person named therein. **8.** *C. arc, cubic*, etc. *C. line*, (*a*) one of such straight lines as are divided by means of an arc of a circle, as Sines, Tangents, etc.; (*b*) the imaginary straight line joining the centre of any circle to either of the two circular points, and forming a tangent to the circle. *C. points*, the two imaginary points at infinity through which all circles pass, also called *focoids*. *C. instruments*, instruments for measuring angles, graduated round the whole circumference of a circle, *i.e.* 360°. *C. number*, a number whose powers terminate in the same digit as the number itself. *C. sailing* (Naut.): navigation by the arc of a great circle (see CIRCLE *sb.*).

Hence **Ci·rcularism,** a theory that space is c. **Ci·rcularly** *adv.* **Ci·rcularness.** var. † **Ci·rcularly** *a.*

B. *sb.* † **1.** A circular figure or space (*rare*) –1815. **2.** Short for *circular letter* or *circular note*: now *esp.* a business notice, reproduced in large numbers for circulation 1818.

Circularity (sɔ̄ːɹkiŭlæ·rĭti). 1582. [– med. L. *circularitas*, f. *circularis*; see prec., -ITY.] Circular quality, form, or position.

Circularize (sɔ̄·ɹkiŭlărəiz), *v.* 1799. [f. CIRCULAR + -IZE.] **1.** To make circular. **2.** To send circulars to 1848.

Circulate (sɔ̄·ɹkiŭleˈt), *v.* 1471. [– *circulat-*, pa. ppl. stem of L. *circulare, -ari*, f. *circulus*; see CIRCLE, -ATE [3].] † **1.** *Old Chem.* To subject to continuous distillation in a circulatory (see CIRCULATORY *sb.*) –1696. **2.** *intr.* To move round, revolve; now round a circuit, circuitous course, system of pipes, etc. 1672. Also †*trans.* **3.** *intr.* To pass from place to place, from hand to hand, or from mouth to mouth; to pass into the hands of readers, as a newspaper 1664. **4.** *trans.* To put into circulation 1777. **5.** *Math.* Of decimal fractions: To recur in periods of several figures 1768.

2. Blood is blood which circulates EMERSON. **3.** Air EVELYN, money, trade LOCKE, circulates. **4.** To c. a report SHERIDAN, the Bible 1815, the loving cup 1884. **Circulating library,** a library of which the books circulate among subscribers 1742.

Circulation (səɹkiŭlēˈ·ʃən). 1535. [– (O)Fr. *circulation* or L. *circulatio*, f. as prec.; see -ION.] † **1.** Movement in a circle, or in a course or round which returns into itself –1795. † **2.** A continuous repetition of a series of actions, events, etc.; a round –1731; alternation –1647. † **3.** *Old Chem.* Continuous distillation in a CIRCULATORY –1641. **4.** The circuit of the blood from the heart through the arteries and veins, and back to the heart; often called 'the c.' Hence, of sap through the vessels of plants. 1656. **5.** Transmission or passage from hand to hand, or from person to person; dissemination, publication 1684; the extent to which a newspaper, etc., is circulated 1847. † **6.** A statement circulated BURKE. **7.** *concr.* A circulating medium, a currency 1790.

1. The waters of the earth are in a state of constant c. HUXLEY. **4.** Stoppage of the C. ARBUTHNOT. **5.** The free c. of information MCCULLOCH. A limited c. DE QUINCEY. **7.** A paper c. BURKE.

Circulative (sɔ̄·ɹkiŭleˈtiv), *a.* 1635. [f. CIRCULATE + -IVE.] Circulating; producing circulation.

Circulator (sɔ̄·ɹkiŭleˈtəɹ). 1607. [– L. *circulator* peddler, mountebank (whence Fr. † *circulateur*), f. as prec. + -OR 2.] He who or that which circulates; *spec.* † a travelling mountebank –1659; † a traveller –1734; a scandal-monger, etc. 1792; a circulating decimal. Hence † **Circulato·rious** *a.* (*rare*).

† **Ci·rculatory,** *sb.* 1559. [– med.L. *circulatorium*; see next, -ORY [1].] An alembic or retort having the neck or necks bent back so as to re-enter the lower part of the retort, a 'pelican'; used in the old chemical process of distillation –1751.

Circulatory (sɔ̄·ɹkiulătəri), *a.* 1605. [f. CIRCULATE + -ORY [2]; cf. Fr. *circulatoire*; in sense 2 – L. *circulatorius* of a mountebank, quackish.] **1.** Of the nature of, or pertaining to, CIRCULATION (senses 3, 4). † **2.** Of or pertaining to a mountebank –1774. † **3.** *C. letter*: = Circular letter –1735.

† **Ci·rcule,** *v.* [– (O)Fr. *circuler* – L. *circulare*; see CIRCULATE.]

Circulet, obs. f. CIRCLET.

‖ **Circulus** (sɔ̄·ɹkiŭlŏs). L. for 'circle, ring'; name for various instruments in Surgery, etc.; also, a tool for cutting circular portions of glass, also for cutting off the necks of glass-ware.

Circum- (sɔ̄ɹkŏm). **1.** A Latin adv. and prep. meaning 'around, round about', much used in composition with vbs., and the sbs. and adjs. formed from them, such as:

† **Circumcursa·tion** [f. L. *circumcursare*], running round or about; rambling. **Circumdenuda·tion** *Geol.* denudation all around. † **Circu·mflant** [L. *circumflant-*] *a.*, blowing around. † **Circumfu·lgent** [L. *circumfulgent-*] *a.*, shining around. **Circumu·ndulate** *v.*, to flow round in undulations; so **Ci:rcumundula·tion.** † **Circumve·ct** [f. L. *circumvehere*] *v.*, to carry about; so † **Circumve·ction.**

2. A rarer use, after L., in which *circum* (= around, surrounding) prepositionally governs a sb. implied in the second part of the compound, gives *circumpolar, circumlittoral*, etc.

† **Circuma·ction.** 1578. [– L. *circumactio* turning round, revolving; see CIRCUM-, ACTION.] Communication of circular motion –1667.

Circumadja·cent, *a.* 1762. [CIRCUM- 1.] Lying immediately around.

† **Circuma·gitate,** *v.* 1655. [f. CIRCUM- 1.] *trans.* To move round or about –1667. So † **Circumagita·tion.**

Circuma·mbages. *rare.* 1650. [f. CIRCUM- 1.] Roundabout methods or modes of speech.

Circumambient (sɔ̄ɹkŏm,æ·mbiĕnt), *a.* 1641. [f. CIRCUM- 1 + AMBIENT; cf. late L. *circumambire.*] Going or extending round; encompassing, environing, as *c. gloom, air*, etc. Also *fig.* and *absol.* Hence **Circuma·mbience,** the act or fact of going round or surrounding. **Circuma·mbiency** = prec.; also, c. quality or condition; environment.

Circumambulate (sɔ̄ɹkŏm,æ·mbiuleˈt), *v.* 1656. [f. CIRCUM- 1 + AMBULATE; cf. late L. *circumambulare.*] To walk round about. Also *intr. fig.* To beat about the bush. 1837. Hence **Ci:rcumambula·tion. Circuma·mbulator.**

Circumbendibus (sɔ̄ɹkŏmbe·ndibŏs). 1681. [joc. f. CIRCUM- + BEND, as a L. ablative pl.] A roundabout process or method; a twist; circumlocution.

Circumcellion (sɔ̄ɹkŏmse·liən). 1564. [– eccl. L. *circumcelliones* (pl.), f. *circum* around + *cella* CELL.] **1.** *pl. Eccl. Hist.* Donatist fanatics in Africa in the 4th c., who used to rove from house to house. **b.** Vagabond monks. † **2.** *transf.* A vagrant –1631.

Circumcise (sɔ̄·ɹkŏmsəiz), *v.* ME. [– OFr. *circonciser*, or *circoncis-*, pa. ppl. stem of *circoncire* – L. *circumcīdere* (tr. Gr. περιτέμνειν), f. *circum* CIRCUM- + *cædere* cut.] **1.** To cut off the foreskin or prepuce of (males), or the internal labia of (females). *fig.* To purify spiritually ME. † **2.** To cut round –1672; *fig.* to cut short; to cut off –1672. var. † **Circumcide** *v.* Hence **Ci·rcumcised** *ppl. a.* (Allusively used for 'Jewish' or 'Moslem'.) **Ci·rcumciser.**

Circumcision (sɔ̄ɹkŏmsi·ʒən). ME. [– (O)Fr. *circoncision* – late L. *circumcisio* (tr. Gr. περιτομή), f. *circumcīs-* pa. ppl. stem of *circumcīdere*; see prec., -ION.] **1.** The action of circumcising; practised as a religious rite by Jews and Moslems; also as a surgical operation. *fig.* Spiritual purification.

2. *transf.* The circumcised people, the Jews; *fig.* 'the Israel of God' ME. **3.** *Eccl.* The festival of the Circumcision of Christ, observed on the 1st of January ME. † **4.** Cutting round –1761.

Circumclu·de, *v. rare.* 1677. [– L. *circumcludere*, f. *circum* CIRCUM- 1 + *cludere* shut, close.] To shut in on all sides. So **Circumclu·sion.**

† **Ci·rcumdate,** *v.* 1578. [– *circumdat-*, pa. ppl. stem of L. *circumdare* surround; f. as prec. + *dare* give, place.] To surround –1657.

Circumduce (sɔ̄ɹkɒ̆mdiū·s), *v.* 1578. [– L. *circumducere*, f. as prec. + *ducere* lead.] † **1.** To carry or move round (an axis) –1657. **2.** *Sc. Law.* To declare (the term) elapsed for leading a proof 1609.

Circumduct (sɔ̄ɹkɒ̆mdɒ·kt), *v.* 1599. [– *circumduct-*, pa. ppl. stem of L. *circumducere*; see prec.] **1.** = CIRCUMDUCE 1. **2.** *Law.* To cancel, annul 1726.

Circumduction (sɔ̄ɹkɒ̆mdɒ·kʃən). 1578. [– L. *circumductio* leading round; f. as prec; see -ION.] **1.** A leading round or about 1602. **2.** *Phys.* The rotatory movement by which a limb is made to describe a cone having its apex at the joint 1578. **3.** *Law.* Annulling; cancellation 1609.

† **Circumfe·r,** *v.* 1605. [– L. *circumferre*, f. as prec. + *ferre* carry.] To carry or bear round –1648.

Circumference (səɹkɒ·mfĕrĕns), *sb.* ME. [– (O)Fr. *circonférence* – L. *circumferentia*, tr. Gr. περιφέρεια PERIPHERY; cf. prec., -ENCE.] **1.** The line that forms the encompassing boundary, *esp.* of anything rounded in form; *spec.* in *Geom.* periphery. † **2.** The surface of anything circular or rounded –1794; the whole circle 1667. **3.** *gen.* Compass, bound 1598. **4.** Environment (*rare*) 1643. † **5.** A circuit –1700. Also *fig.*

2. MILT. *P.L.* I. 286. Hence **Circu·mference** *v.* to form the c. of (*rare*). So † **Circu·mferent** *a.* forming the c. of; travelling around. **Circu:mfere·ntial** *a.* of, pertaining to, or of the nature of the c.; † circuitous, indirect. **Circu:mfere·ntially** *adv.*

Circumferentor (səɹkɒ·mfĕrentəɹ). 1610. [f. *circumferent*; see prec., -OR 2.] **1.** *Surveying.* An instrument consisting of a flat brass bar with sights at the ends and a circular brass box in the middle, containing a magnetic needle, which plays over a graduated circle; the whole being supported on a tripod. (Now mostly superseded by a THEODOLITE.) **2.** An instrument for measuring the circumference of a wheel; a tyre-circle 1874.

Circumflect (sɔ̄ɹkɒ̆mfle·kt), *v.* 1643. [– L. *circumflectere* bend round, f. *circum* CIRCUM- + *flectere* bend.] **1.** *Gram.* To mark with a circumflex accent. **2.** To bend round (Dicts.).

Circumflex (sɔ̄·ɹkɒ̆mfleks), *a.* and *sb.* 1577. [– L. *circumflexus* (pa. pple. of *circumflectere*; see prec.), tr. Gr. περισπώμενος drawn around, in ref. to its shape.]

A. *adj.* **1.** *Gram.* An accent-mark ˆ, ˆ, or ˜, placed, originally in Greek, over long vowels having a particular accent (see ACCENT 1); and in Latin, etc., indicating a contraction, or a particular variety of long vowel. Occas. applied to the tone, quantity, or quality thus indicated. **2.** Bent or bending round; † circuitous 1707. **3.** *Anat.* Applied to structures of curved form, or which bend round others; as the *c. arteries* of the arm, thigh, and knee; the *c. nerve* of the arm; the *c. muscle* of the palate 1831.

B. *sb.* **1.** *Gram.* A circumflex accent (sign); see A. 1. † **2.** Bending round, winding, curve –1773. **3.** A curved line, (or {, bracketing two or more lines of writing. ? *Obs.* 1801.

Circumflex, *v.* 1565. [– L. *circumflex-* (see prec.); in sense 2 from prec.] **1.** *trans.* To bend or wind round 1644. Also † *intr.* **2.** *trans.* To write or pronounce with a circumflex 1565. Hence **Circumfle·xion, -fle·ction.**

Circumfluence (səɹkɒ·mfluĕns). *rare.* 1881. [f. next: see -ENCE.] A flowing round.

Circumfluent (səɹkɒ·mfluĕnt). 1577. [– *circumfluent-*, pres. ppl. stem of L. *circumfluere* flow round.] Flowing round; ambient as a fluid.

Whose bounds the deep c. waves embrace POPE.

Circumfluous (səɹkɒ·mfluəs), *a.* 1615. [f. L. *circumfluus* flowing round + -OUS.] **1.** = CIRCUMFLUENT 1638. **2.** Flowed round, surrounded by water.

Circumforaneous (sɔ:ɹkɒ̆mforē·niəs), *a.* Now *rare.* 1650. [f. L. *circumforaneus* (f. *circum* + *forum*) + -OUS.] Strolling from market to market; vagrant; quack.

The c. Emperick 1654. vars. † **Circumfora·neal,** † **-nean** *adjs.*

Circumfuse (sɔ̄ɹkɒ̆mfiū·z), *v.* 1596. [– *circumfus-*, pa. ppl. stem of L. *circumfundere* pour around; cf. FUSE *v.*] **1.** To pour or spread (a fluid) *around* or *about* (anything) 1648. **2.** To surround *with* or *in*; to bathe.

2. A face, all circumfused with light B. JONS. Hence **Circumfu·sion.**

Circumfu·sile, *a. rare.* [f. as prec. + -ILE.] Poured or spread around. POPE.

Ci:rcumgesta·tion. ? *Obs.* 1564. [– mod. L. *circumgestatio*, f. L. *circumgestare* carry around; cf. GESTATION.] A carrying about (ceremonially or in procession).

C. of the Eucharist to be adored JER. TAYLOR.

Circumgyrate (sɔ̄ɹkɒ̆mdʒəi·rē^i^t), *v.* 1647. [f. CIRCUM- + GYRATE; cf. late L. *circumgirare* go round.] **1.** *trans.* To cause to turn or wheel round. ? *Obs.* **2.** *intr.* To turn or roll round; to travel round 1683. Hence **Ci:rcumgyra·tion,** the act of turning, rolling, or wheeling round; also *fig.* **Circumgy·ratory** *a.* marked by circumgyration. var. † **Circumgy·re** *v.*

Circumincession (sɔ̄:ɹkɒ̆m,inse·ʃən). 1644. [– med.L. *circumincessio*, f. *circum* CIRCUM- + *incessio*, f. *incēdere* move, proceed, tr. Gr. περιχώρησις going round, circuition (John Damascene, see *John* 14 : 10). Often altered to *circuminsession*, for 'reciprocal indwelling', because of the difficulty of connecting the required sense with the proper form.] *Theol.* The reciprocal existence of the persons of the Trinity in one another.

Circumjacence (sɔ̄ɹkɒ̆mdʒē^i^·sĕns). 1884. [f. CIRCUMJACENT; see -ENCE.] The fact or condition of being circumjacent.

Circumjacency (sɔ̄rkɒ̆mdʒē^i^·sĕnsi). 1748. [f. as prec.; see -ENCY.] The quality of being circumjacent; *concr.* (in *pl.*) circumjacent parts.

Circumjacent (sɔ̄ɹkɒ̆mdʒē^i^·sĕnt), *a.* 1490. [– *circumjacent-*, pres. ppl. stem of L. *circumjacēre* lie around; cf. JACENT.] Lying around, adjacent on all sides.

Circumjovial (sɔ̄ɹkɒ̆mdʒō^u^·viăl), *a.* (*sb.*) 1696. [– mod.L. *circumjovialis* (Newton); see CIRCUM- 2, JOVIAL 2.] *Astr.* Revolving round Jupiter. † *sb.* A satellite of Jupiter.

Circumli·ttoral, *a.* [f. CIRCUM- + LITTORAL[1].] Bordering the shore

Circumlocution (sɔ̄:ɹkɒ̆mlokiū·ʃən). 1510. [– Fr. *circumlocution* or L. *circumlocutio*, tr. Gr. περίφρασις PERIPHRASIS; see CIRCUM-, LOCUTION.] Roundabout speaking; the use of several words instead of one, or many instead of few; a roundabout expression.

Circumloqution..as when we say: The Prince of Peripateticks, for Aristotle 1595. *C. Office*: a satirical name applied, by Dickens, to Government Offices, on account of the multiplication of formalities in which they excel. Hence **Circumlocu·tional, -ary, -ory** *adjs.* pertaining to, given to, or marked by c.

Circum-meri·dian, *a.* 1852. [CIRCUM- 2.] *Astr.* Situated about or near the meridian.

Circummure (sɔ̄ɹkɒ̆mmiū^ə^·ɹ), *v.* 1603. [f. CIRCUM- 1 + MURE *v.*] To wall round.

Circumna·vigable, *a.* 1691. [f. as next; see -ABLE.] That can be circumnavigated.

Circumnavigate (sɔ̄ɹkɒ̆mnæ·vigē^i^t), *v.* 1634. [– L. *circumnavigare*; see CIRCUM- 1, NAVIGATE.] To sail round.

With a design of circum-navigating the island COOK. Hence **Ci:rcumnaviga·tion. Circumna·vigator. Circumna·vigatory** *a.*

Circumnutate (sɔ̄ɹkɒ̆mniū·tē^i^t), *v.* 1880. [f. CIRCUM- 1 + NUTATE.] *Bot.* To move in CIRCUMNUTATION.

Circumnutation (sɔ̄:ɹkɒ̆mniutē^i^·ʃən). 1880. [f. CIRCUM- 1 + NUTATION 3.] *Bot.* A movement of growing plants, in which the growing part (*e.g.* the apex of a stem) describes a sort of circular spiral path. So **Circumnuta·tory** *a.*

Circumo·ral, *a.* 1847. [f. CIRCUM- 2 + ORAL 3.] *Phys.* Situated round the mouth.

† **Circumple·ct,** *v.* 1578. [– L. *circumplectere* clasp round.] To clasp around. Also † **Circumple·x** *v.*, † **Circumple·xion.** –1660.

Circumpolar (sɔ̄ɹkɒ̆mpō^u^·lăɹ), *a.* 1686. [f. CIRCUM- 2 + POLAR.] Round or about the pole; in *Astr.* applied to stars which describe the whole of their diurnal circles above the horizon.

Circumpose (sɔ̄ɹkɒ̆mpō^u^·z), *v.* ? *Obs.* 1578. [repr. L. *circumponere*, after *compose*, etc.] To place around; † to place within any encircling space; to pot (a plant). So **Ci:rcumposi·tion.**

†‖ **Circumqua·que.** 1556. [L., = on every side, all round.] A CIRCUMBENDIBUS, q.v. –1591.

Circumrotation (sɔ̄:ɹkɒ̆mrotē^i^·ʃən). 1610. [f. CIRCUM- 1 + ROTATION. Cf. med.L. *circumrotatio*, perh. the source.] **1.** Turning round as a wheel; revolution on an axis; a complete rotation 1656. † **2.** A changing about in rotation –1767. So **Circumro·tatory** *a.*

† **Circumsatu·rnian,** *a.* (*sb.*) 1664. [– mod.L. *circumsaturnius* (Newton); see CIRCUM- 2, SATURNIAN.] *Astr.* Round Saturn; a satellite of Saturn –1714.

Circumsciss (sɔ̄·ɹkɒ̆msis), *a.* 1870. [f. L. *circumscissus*, pa. ppl. of *circumscindere* cleave or tear around.] *Bot.* Opening by circumscissile dehiscence.

Circumscissile (sɔ̄ɹkɒ̆msi·sil), *a.* 1835. [f. as prec. + -ILE; see SCISSILE.] *Bot.* Dehiscing or opening by a transverse circular line, said of the seed-vessel (*pyxidium*).

Circumscribe (sɔ̄ɹkɒ̆mskrəi·b), *v.* 1529. [– L. *circumscribere*, f. *circum*, CIRCUM- 1 + *scribere* draw lines, write.] **1.** To draw a line round; to encompass, bound; to encircle 1578. **2.** To mark out the limits of; to confine (usually *fig.*); *esp.* to hem in, restrain, abridge 1529. **3.** *Geom.* To describe (a figure) about another figure so as to touch it at certain points without cutting; also with the figure as subject of the verb 1570. † **4.** To write or inscribe around (*esp.* a coin, etc., *with* an inscription, or an inscription *on* or *about* a coin, etc.) –1692.

1. I was alone, circumscribed by the ocean DE FOE. **2.** Therefore must his choyce be circumscrib'd *Haml.* I. iii. 22. Hence **Circumscri·bable** *a.* that may be circumscribed; var. † **Circumscri·ptible. Circumscri·ber,** one who or that which circumscribes; *esp.* one who signs a round robin. **Ci·rcumscript** *a.* circumscribed. (Now *rare.*) **Ci·rcumscri·ptly** *adv.* (*rare*).

Circumscription (sɔ̄ɹkɒ̆mskri·pʃən). 1531. [– L. *circumscriptio*, f. *circumscript-*, pa. ppl. stem of *circumscribere*; see prec., -ION.] **1.** The action of circumscribing or fact of being circumscribed; limitation, restriction; the having defined limits 1604. **2.** *concr.* Boundary, outline, periphery 1578. **3.** A material surrounding 1578. **4.** A circumscribed space or place 1831. **5.** *fig.* Definition 1531. **6.** *Geom.* The act of circumscribing one figure about another (see CIRCUMSCRIBE 3) 1570. **7.** An inscription around something, *e.g.* a coin, etc. 1569.

1. *Oth.* I. ii. 27. **4.** The diocese or ecclesiastical c. MORLEY. **5.** Drunkennesse..hath its c. 1654.

Circumscriptive (sɔ̄ɹkɒ̆mskri·ptiv), *a.* 1565. [f. med.L. *circumscriptivus*, f. as prec.; see -IVE.] Pertaining to, or having the attribute of, limitation in space. Hence **Circumscri·ptively** *adv.* with limitation in space. ? *Obs.*

† **Circumscrive,** *v.* late ME. [– (O)Fr. *circonscrire.*] = CIRCUMSCRIBE.

Circumsession (sɔ̄ɹkɒ̆mse·ʃən). ? *Obs. rare.* 1652. [– L. *circumsessio* siege; see CIRCUM- 1, SESSION.] **1.** Besetting. **2.** *Theol.* Erron. for CIRCUMINCESSION 1667.

Circumso·lar, *a.* 1846. [f. CIRCUM- 2 + SOLAR. Cf. mod.L. *circumsolaris* (Newton).] Revolving round, or situated about, the sun.

Circumspect (sɔ̄·ɹkɒ̆mspekt), *a.* ME. [– L. *circumspectus*, pa. pple. of *circumspicere* look round.] **1.** Marked by circumspection, well-considered, cautious. **2.** Attentive to all circumstances that may affect action or decision, cautious 1430.

1. C. Remedy 1562. **2.** High-reaching Buckingham growes c. *Rich. III*, IV. ii. 31. Hence

Circumspe·ction, vigilant and cautious observation of circumstances or events; circumspect action or conduct; caution, circumspectness. So **Circumspe·ctive** *a.* scanning on all sides; given to circumspection. **Circumspe·ctively, Ci·rcumspectly** *advs.* **Ci·rcumspectness,** the quality of being c.

Circumstance (sɜ̄·ɹkǒmstǎns), *sb.* ME. [– (O)Fr. *circonstance* or L. *circumstantia*, f. *circumstant-*, pres. ppl. stem of *circumstare* stand around, surround; see -ANCE.] **I.** † **1.** That which stands around or surrounds; surroundings –1562. **2.** *pl.* The adjuncts of an action or fact; in *sing.* any one of these ME. **3.** The state of (*esp.* pecuniary) affairs surrounding and affecting an agent ME. (Mere situation is expressed by '*in* the circumstances', action takes place '*under* the circumstances'.)

2. Neither in time, manner, or other c. *Meas. for M.* IV. ii. 109. 3. The web of c. 1887. Easy in their circumstances ADDISON.

II. Words or ado made *about* anything; circumlocution; ceremony ME.

Pompe and C. of glorious warre *Oth.* III. iii. 354.

III. 1. That which is non-essential, accessary, or subordinate; a detail, a particular ME. **2.** An incident; a matter or fact 1586.

1. Tell us the sum, the c. defer MILT. *Sams.* 1557.

Circumstance (sɜ̄·ɹkǒmstǎns), *v.* ME. [f. prec.] † **1.** To condition –1736. **2.** To place in particular circumstances or relations. Chiefly in pa. pple. 1644. † **3.** To supply with attendant circumstances –1774.

3. The Poet took the matters of Fact as they came down to him, and circumstanced them after his own manner ADDISON. Hence **Ci·rcumstanced** *ppl. a.* placed in certain circumstances or relations; † subject to circumstances *Oth.* III. iv. 201; circumstantiated.

† **Ci·rcumstant.** 1494. [– L. *circumstant-*; see CIRCUMSTANCE, -ANT.] *adj.* Standing around, circumjacent –1666; incidental –1656. *sb. pl.* Bystanders –1675.

The c. cold ayre 1545, causes 1656.

Circumstantial (sɜɹkǒmstæ·nʃǎl). 1600. [f. L. *circumstantia* CIRCUMSTANCE + -AL¹.] **A.** *adj.* **1.** Of, relating to, or dependent on circumstances; *esp.* adventitious, accidental 1608. **2.** Full of circumstances, details, or minutiæ, particular 1611.

1. *C. evidence*: indirect evidence founded on circumstances which limit the number of admissible hypotheses. *The lie c.* (Shaks.): a contradiction given indirectly by circumstances. The c. part and pomp of life POPE. C. prosperity COLERIDGE. 2. C. detail H. WALPOLE.

B. *sb.* (*pl*). Circumstantial matters; particulars; non-essentials 1647.

Ye fools and blind! to fix your whole attention on the circumstantials of religion WESLEY.

Hence **Ci:rcumstantia·lity,** c. quality, particularity; a detail. **Circumsta·ntially** *adv.* in a c. manner; incidentally; in every particular, minutely. † **Circumsta·ntialness,** circumstantiality.

Circumstantiate (sɜɹkǒmstæ·nʃiᵉit), *v.* 1638. [f. CIRCUMSTANCE + -ATE³, after *substance, substantiate*; cf. Fr. *circonstancier*.] † **1.** 'To place in particular circumstances' (J.), to define or limit by imposed conditions –1711. **2.** To set forth, or support, with circumstances 1658.

1. A Committee to consider how that title [Lord Protector] may be bounded, limited, and circumstantiated 1657. 2. To c. false historical records DE QUINCEY. Hence **Circumstantia·tion,** circumstantiating. **Circumsta·ntiator.**

† **Circumterra·neous,** *a.* 1678. [f. CIRCUM- 2 + TERRANEOUS.] Situated, dwelling, etc., round the earth, as *c. demons.* So † **Circumterre·strial** *a.*

Circumvallate (sɜɹkǒmvæ·lět), *a.* 1661. [– L. *circumvallatus*, pa. pple. of *circumvallare* surround with a rampart (*vallum*); see -ATE².] Surrounded as with a rampart or trench.

Circumvallate (sɜɹkǒmvæ·leⁱt), *v.* 1823. [f. as prec. + -ATE³.] To surround with or as with a rampart or trench.

Five circumvallating walls were not uncommon 1884.

Circumvallation (sɜ:ɹkǒmvǎleⁱ·ʃən). 1641. [– late L. *circumvallatio*, f. as prec.; see -ATION.] **1.** The making of a rampart, etc., round a place. **2.** A rampart or entrenchment constructed round any place by way of investment or defence 1645. Also *transf.* and *fig.*

1. At night we rode about the lines of c. EVELYN.

Circumvent (sɜ̄ɹkǒmve·nt), *v.* 1553. [– *circumvent-*, pa. ppl. stem of L. *circumvenire* surround, beset, deceive (*venire* come).] **1.** To surround by hostile stratagem. **2.** To encompass with evils, or malice; to try to entrap in conduct or speech 1581. **3.** To get the better of by craft or fraud; to overreach 1564. Also *absol.* **4.** To encompass (*literally*) 1824. **5.** To go round 1840.

3. Should Man. . Fall circumvented thus by fraud MILT. *P.L.* III. 152. Hence **Circumve·ntor, -er,** one who circumvents; also = CIRCUMFERENTOR. var. **Circumve·ne.** (Chiefly *Sc.*)

Circumvention (sɜ̄ɹkǒmve·nʃən). 1534. [– late L. *circumventio*, f. as prec.; see -ION.] The action of circumventing; overreaching. ¶ *ellipt.* = the *means of* circumvention *Cor.* I. ii. 16.

The. . circumuention of the false wilye diuel MORE.

† **Circumve·st,** *v.* 1599. [– L. *circumvestire* clothe around.] To enwrap as with a garment –1657.

† **Circumvoisin,** *a.* 1548. [– Fr. *circonvoisin*. Cf. med.L. *circumvicinus* (XIII).] Neighbouring on all sides –1641.

Circu·mvolant, *a.* 1623. [– *circumvolant-*, pres. ppl. stem of L. *circumvolare* fly around; see -ANT.] Flying around. So **Circumvola·tion.**

Circumvolute (sɜɹkɒ·mvolⁱūt), *v.* 1599. [– *circumvolut-*, pa. ppl. stem of L. *circumvolvere* roll round (or – frequent. L. *circumvolutare*).] **1.** *trans.* To roll round. Also *fig.* **2.** To enwrap by twisting or winding something round 1599.

Circumvolution (sɜ̄:ɹkǒmvolⁱū·ʃən). 1447. [f. as prec., after *revolution*; see -ION.] **1.** Rolling round an axis or centre; revolution; a revolution. Also *fig.* **2.** The rolling of a thing round something else; a fold or turn 1599. **3.** A winding or moving in a sinuous course; *concr.* a sinuosity 1633. Also *fig.*

1. To behold the c. of the stars HEALEY. 3. Neither time nor temper for sentimental circumvolutions DISRAELI. The circumuolutions. . in the brayne 1578.

Circumvolve (sɜ̄ɹkǒmvǫ·lv), *v.* Now *rare.* 1599. [– L. *circumvolvere* (trans.) roll round.] **1.** *trans.* To turn, move, or roll round 1647; to move round in a circular path (*rare*) 1610. Also *intr.* † **2.** To wind, fold, or twist round –1704. Also *fig.*

Circus (sɜ̄·ɹkɒ̆s). 1546. [– L. *circus* circle, circus = Gr. κίρκος, κρίκος ring, circle.] **1.** *Rom. Antiq.* A large building, generally oblong or oval, surrounded with rising tiers of seats, for the exhibition of public spectacles, races, and the like. **2.** *Mod.* A circular arena surrounded by tiers of seats, for the exhibition of equestrian, acrobatic, and other performances. Also, the troupe of performers and their equipage. 1791. **3.** A natural amphitheatre; a rounded hollow or plain encircled by heights 1836. † **4.** A circle or ring –1748. **5.** *vaguely.* Compass (*rare*) 1817. **6.** A circular range of houses. Often in proper names as *Oxford C.*, etc. 1771. Also *attrib.*

5. The narrow c. of my dungeon wall BYRON.

‖ **Cire perdue** (sīr pęrdü). 1876. [Fr. 'lost wax'.] A method of casting bronze in which the wax covering the model is melted out.

Cirl (sɜ̄ɹl), in **Cirl bunting.** 1783. [It. *cirlo*, prob. f. *zirlare* to whistle as a thrush.] A species of Bunting, *Emberiza cirlus*.

Cirque (sɜ̄ɹk). 1601. [– Fr. *cirque* – L. *circus*.] = CIRCUS 1–4.

The grassy c. SHENSTONE. A dismal c. Of Druid stones, upon a forlorn moor KEATS. *Comb.* **c.-couchant,** lying coiled up in circles KEATS.

Cirrated (si·reⁱtėd), *a. rare.* 1854. [f. L. *cirratus* (see CIRRUS, -ATE²) + -ED¹.] Fringed with cirri.

Cirrh-, bad spelling of *cirr-*, in CIRRUS and its derivs., as if a –. (non-existent) Gr. κιρρός = *cirrhus*; for other words see below.

Cirrhopod (si·ropǫd). 1843. [– Fr. *cirrhopode* (Cuvier) – mod. L. *Cirrhopoda*, f. CIRRH- + Gr. πούς, ποδ- foot.] *Zool.* = CIRRIPED.

Cirrhosis (sirōᵘ·sis). Occas. **cirrho·se.** 1839. [mod.L. (Laennec) – Gr. κιρρός orange-tawny + -OSIS.] *Path.* A disease of the liver, consisting in chronic interstitial hepatitis, with atrophy of the cells and increase of connective tissue. Subseq. extended to similar conditions of the kidneys, lungs, etc. Hence **Cirrho·sed, Cirrho·tic** *adjs.* affected with c.

Cirriferous (siri·fĕrəs), *a.* Erron. **cirrh-.** 1819. [f. L. *cirrus* CIRRUS + -FEROUS.] Cirrus-bearing.

Cirriform (si·rifǫɹm), *a.* 1815. [f. as prec. + -FORM.] *Meteor.* and *Zool.* Cirrus-shaped.

Cirrigerous (siri·dʒĕrəs), *a.* 1736. [f. as prec. + -GEROUS.] Bearing cirri.

Cirrigrade (si·rigreⁱd), *a.* 1837. [f. as prec. + L. *-gradus* going, proceeding.] *Zool.* Moving by means of cirri.

Cirriped, -pede (si·riped, -pīd). Erron. **cirrhi-.** 1828. [– mod.L. *Cirripeda*, *-ia* (also used in Eng.), f. L. *cirrus* curl + *pes, ped-* foot. See CIRRH-, CIRRHOPOD.] *Zool.* A member of the *Cirripedia* or *Cirripeda*, a class of marine animals of the sub-kingdom Annulosa, closely related to the Crustacea; including the barnacles and acorn-shells. The legs can be protruded like a curled lock of hair from between the valves of the shell; hence the name.

Cirro- (si·ro), comb. f. CIRRUS, as in: **Ci·rrostome** *a.*, having the mouth cirrose or bearded; also *subst.* **Cirro-cu·mulus,** *Meteor.* a form of cloud combining the shapes of the cirrus and cumulus, and consisting mainly of a series of roundish and fleecy cloudlets in contact; hence **-cumular, -cumulated, -cumulative, -cumulous** *adjs.* **Cirro-stra·tus,** a form of cloud combining the shapes of the cirrus and stratus, consisting of horizontal or inclined sheets attenuated upwards into light cirri; hence **-strative, -stratous** *adjs.*

Cirrose (sirōᵘ·s), *a.* Erron. **cirrh-.** 1814. [f. L. *cirrus* CIRRUS + -OSE¹.] **1.** *Bot.* and *Zool.* Bearing a cirrus or cirri 1819. **2.** *Meteor.* Of the nature of cirrus-clouds.

Cirrous (si·rəs), *a.* Erron. **cirrh-.** 1658. [f. as prec. + -OUS.] **1.** *Bot.* and *Zool.* Of the nature of a cirrus or cirri; bearing cirri. **2.** Of or pertaining to cirrus-clouds 1815.

‖ **Cirrus** (si·rɒ̆s). Erron. **cirrh-.** 1708. [L., = curl, fringe.] **1.** *lit.* A curl-like tuft, fringe, or filament. **2.** *Bot.* A tendril 1708. **3.** *Zool.* A filamentary process or appendage, as the beard of some fishes, the feet of *Cirripedes*, etc. 1753. **4.** *Meteor.* A form of cloud, generally at a high elevation, presenting the appearance of diverging filaments or wisps, often resembling a curl or lock of hair or wool 1803. Also *attrib.*

Comb. **c.-bag,** 'the sheath containing the cirrus of trematode and other worms'.

Cirrus, ? misprint of CERUSE *sb.* BACON.

Cirsocele (sɜ̄·ɹsosīl). Erron. **circo-.** 1708. [– Gr. κιρσοκήλη, f. κιρσός enlargement of a vein + κήλη tumour. Cf. Fr. *cirsocèle*.] *Path.* A varicose enlargement of the spermatic vein.

Cirsoid (sɜ̄·ɹsoid), *a.* 1860. [– Gr. κιρσοειδής see prec., -OID.] *Path.* Varix-like, varicose.

Cirsotome (sɜ̄·ɹsotoᵘm). [f. as prec. + -TOME¹.] *Surg.* An instrument used for extirpating varix. So **Cirso·tomy.**

Cis-, prefix, repr. L. *cis* prep. 'on this side of'; opp. to *trans* or *ultra*, across, beyond; also used in comb. as in *cis-alpinus*, etc.

In mod. use, either as – L., as **Cis-alpine,** on this (the Roman) side of the Alps, *i.e.* south; **Cis-padane,** on this side the Po, etc., or formed on the adjs. belonging to modern names, as **Cis-atlantic; Cis-leithan,** on this side the Leitha which separates Austria and Hungary, etc. Also *transf.* to *time* = Since, as *cis-Elizabethan*, etc.

‖ **Cisco** (si·sko). *U.S.* 1848. [Origin unkn.] A fish of the herring kind which abounds in Lake Ontario.

Cismontane (sismǫ·ntēⁱn), *a.* 1792. [– L. *cismontanus*, f. *mons, mont-* mountain; see CIS-, -ANE.] On this side of the mountains, *esp.* of the Alps: opp. to *ultramontane*; spec. of the Gallican Church movement. Also *sb. pl.*

Cissoid (si·soid). 1656. [– Gr. κισσοειδής, f. κισσός ivy; see -OID.] *Math.* A curve of the second order invented by Diocles. Hence **Cissoi·dal** *a.* pertaining to a c.

Cissy (si·si). 1915. Variant of *sissy* (SISS *sb.*¹).

Cist (sist). Erron. **cyst.** 1804. [– L. *cista* – Gr. κίστη box, chest; see CHEST, KIST *sb.*¹ In sense 1 from Welsh *cist*; see KISTVAEN.] **1.** *Archæol.* A sepulchral chest or chamber excavated in rock, etc.; *esp.* a stone-coffin formed of slabs placed on edge, and covered on the top by one or more horizontal slabs. **2.** *Gr. Antiq.* A small receptacle for sacred utensils carried in procession on the occasion of mystic festivals 1847. Hence **Ci·sted** *a.* containing a c. or cists. **Ci·stula,** a little c.

Cist, obs. f. CYST bladder, confused w. prec.

Cistaceous (sistēⁱ·ʃəs), *a.* [f. mod.L. *Cistaceæ* (f. CISTUS) + -OUS; see -ACEOUS.] *Bot.* Of or pertaining to the genus *Cistus* or Rock Rose and its congeners, of the N.O. *Cistaceæ*. Hence **Ci·stal** *a.*

Cistercian (sistə̄·ɹʃⁱăn), *a.* 1602. [– Fr. *cistercien*, f. L. *Cistercium* Cîteaux, near Dijon (cf. med.L. *Cisterciensis*); see -IAN.] Of or belonging to the monastic order founded at Cîteaux in 1098 by Robert, abbot of Molesme. It was an offshoot of the Benedictines. As *sb.* A monk of this order 1616.

Cistern (si·stəɹn). ME. [– OFr. *cisterne* (mod. *citerne*) :– L. *cisterna*, f. *cista* CHEST *sb.*[1]] **1.** An artificial reservoir for water, or other liquid; *esp.* a water-tight tank. **2.** A natural reservoir or depression containing water, *e.g.* a pond 1606. **3.** Applied to a cavity, or vessel in an organism 1615. Also *fig.* and *attrib.*

1. Broken cisternes *Jer.* 2:13. A copper c. for the table PEPYS *Diary* 7 Sept. 1667. A c. of punch 1815. **2.** Lakes..are real reservoirs, or cisterns of water 1796. Hence **Ci·stern,** *v.* to enclose in, or fit with, a c.

Cistus (si·stŏs). 1551. [mod.L. – Gr. κίστος, κίσθος.] *Bot.* A genus of shrubs (N.O. *Cistaceæ*) known as Rock Rose and Gum Cistus. *Ladanum* or *Labdanun* is obtained from several species, esp. *C. creticus* and *C. ladaniferus*.

Cistvaen; see KISTVAEN.

Cit (sit). *arch.* 1644. [Shortening of CITIZEN. Cf. FAN *sb.*[2], MOB *sb.*[1]] Short for *citizen*; usually applied, more or less contemptuously, to a townsman or to a shopkeeper.

The cits of London and the boors of Middlesex JOHNSON.

Ci·table, *a.* 1820. [f. CITE *v.* + -ABLE.] That can be cited.

Citadel (si·tădĕl). 1586. [– Fr. *citadelle* or its source It. *citadella*, dim. of *cittade*, obs. var. of *città* :– L. *civitas*, *-at-* CITY.] **1.** The fortress commanding a city, which it serves both to protect and to dominate. (Used as tr. Gr. ἀκρόπολις and L. *arx*.) **2.** *gen.* A stronghold 1796. Also *transf.* and *fig.* **3.** The heavily plated erection containing the guns in an ironclad 1884.

2. *fig.* Within these citadels of superstition SCOTT.

† **Cital** (səi·tăl). *rare.* 1596. [f. CITE *v.* + -AL[1].] **1.** *Law.* Citation, summons 1760. **2.** *fig.* 'Impeachment' (Johnson); 'mention' (Schmidt). See 1 *Hen. IV*, v. ii. 62.

Citation (səitēⁱ·ʃən). ME. [– (O)Fr. *citation* – L. *citatio*, f. *citat-*, pa. ppl. stem of *citare* CITE; see -ION.] **1.** *Law.* A citing to a court of justice, a summons; the form of summons, or the document containing it. † **2.** Recital (*rare*) 1666. **3.** The action of citing any words or written passage, quotation; in *Law*, a reference to cases or authorities 1651. **4.** *concr.* A quotation 1548.

1. Ecclesiastical causes commence by *c.* of the defendant COX.

Citatory (səi·tătəri), *a.* 1611. [– med.L. *citatorius* adj. (implied in late L. *citatorium* summons), f. L. *citat-*; see prec., -ORY[2].] Having the faculty of citing; concerned with citation; *esp.* in *Letters c.* vars. **Ci·tative** *a.* (*rare*), † **Citato·rial** *a.*

Cite (səit), *v.* 1483. [– (O)Fr. *citer* – L. *citare*, frequent. of *ciēre*, *cīre* set in motion, call.] **1.** To summon officially to appear in court of (usu. eccles.) law. Also *fig.* **2.** *gen.* To summon; arouse 1534. **3.** To quote (a passage, book, or author) 1535. **4.** To adduce by way of example, proof, precedent, etc. 1663. **5.** To call to mind; mention; refer to *as*; † evidence 1588.

1. Fee but the Sumner, and he shall not c. thee 1616. **2.** In a storm cited by the finger of God he died DE QUINCEY. **3.** The diuell can c. Scripture for his purpose *Merch. V.* I. iii. 99. **5.** We cited vp a thousand heauy times *Rich. III*, I. iv. 14. *All's Well* I. iii. 216. Hence **Citee·**, one who is cited (Dicts.). **Ci·ter.**

Citess. 1685. [f. CIT + -ESS[1].] **1.** A female cit. † **2.** A citizeness. (Used in U.S. as tr. Fr. *citoyenne*.)

‖ **Cithara** (si·pără). 1789. [L. *cithara* – Gr. κιθάρα.] *Mus.* An ancient instrument of triangular shape with from seven to eleven strings; a sort of lyre. Hence **Ci·tharist,** a player on the c. **Citharœ·dic** *a.* pertaining to a citharist or c. (*rare*).

Cither (si·pəɹ). 1606. [– (O)Fr. *cithare* or G. *zither* (cf. ZITHER) – L. *cithara* – Gr. κιθάρα, lyre-like instrument.] An anglicized form of CITHARA, applied also to the CITHERN, ZITHER, etc.

Cithern, cittern (si·pəɹn, si·təɹn). *arch.* 1566. [– L. *cithara* (see prec.) crossed with GITTERN.] *Mus.* A sort of guitar, strung with wire, and played with a plectrum. (The ZITHER is the Tyrolese form of this.)

Comb. † **cittern-head,** a term of contempt, referring to the grotesquely carved head of a c. SHAKS.

Citicism; see CITYCISM.

Citied (si·tid), *a.* 1612. [f. CITY + -ED[2].] Made into or like a city; occupied by a city or cities.

Kinsfolk on the c. earth KEATS.

Citigrade (si·tigreⁱd), *a.* 1845. [– mod.L. *Citigrada*, f. *citus* swift + *-gradus* walking, stepping.] *lit.* Moving swiftly; applied to a tribe of spiders, *Citigrada*, and *subst.* one of these.

Citizen (si·tizĕn). [ME. *citisein*, *-zein* – AFr. *citesein*, *-zein*, alt. of OFr. *citeain* (mod. *citoyen*) :– Rom. **civitatanus*, f. L. *civitas* CITY. The *s*, *z* in the AFr. form was prob. due to assoc. w. *deinsein* DENIZEN.] **1.** An inhabitant of a city or (often) of a town; *esp.* a freeman of a city; a townsman 1514; a civilian 1607. **2.** A member of a state, an enfranchised inhabitant of a country, as opp. to an alien; in U.S. a person, native or naturalized, who has the privilege of voting for public offices, and is entitled to protection in the exercise of private rights ME. **3.** *transf.* Inhabitant, denizen ME. **4.** *adj.* City-bred (*nonce-use*). *Cymb.* IV. ii. 8. Also *attrib.*, as *c.-king*.

1. I am a man..of Tarsus..a citeseyn or burgeys, of a citee not unknown WYCLIF *Acts* 21:39. Both citizens and peasants S. AUSTIN. **2.** *Citizen of the World*: one who is at home, and claims his rights, everywhere. Hence **Ci·tizen** *v.* to address as 'citizen'. **Ci·tizeness,** a female c. **Ci·tizenhood,** the state of being a c.; the body of citizens. **Ci·tizenish** *a.* of the nature of or relating to citizens. **Ci·tizenism,** the principle of citizenship; CIVISM. **Ci·tizenize** *v.* † to make citizen-like; to make a c. **Ci·tizenry,** citizens collectively; *a citizenry*, a body of citizens. **Ci·tizenship,** the position or status of a c.

Citole. Now *Hist.* ME. [– OFr. *citole* (= Pr. *citola*), obscurely derived from L. *cithara* w. dim. suffix.] *Mus.* A stringed instrument of 13–15th c.; perh. a special form of the *cithara*. Hence † **Citoler.**

Citr-, citro-, f. L. *citrus* citron, used as comb. f. *citric* and its derivs.; as **Citraco·nic** [see ACONIC] *a.*, in *Citraconic acid*, $C_5H_6O_4$, obtained in a crystalline form in the distillation of citric acid. Its salts are **Citraconates.**

Citra- (sitră), *prefix* [L. *citra* adv. and prep., on this side (of), prop. abl. fem. of *citer* adj., 'hither'], as in **Citramo·ntane** *a.* = CISMONTANE.

Citrate (si·treⁱt). 1794. [f. CITRIC + -ATE[4].] *Chem.* A salt of citric acid.

Citrean (si·tri‚ăn), *a.* 1616. [f. L. *citreus* of the citrus tree + -AN.] **1.** Made of citrus-wood (CITRUS 2). † **2.** Citron-coloured 1656.

Citric (si·trik), *a.* 1800. [– Fr. *citrique* (de Morveau, 1787), f. L. *citrus*; see CITRON and -IC.] *Chem.* Derived from the citron; as in *C. acid*: a colourless inodorous acid, $C_6H_8O_7$, of a very sharp taste, found in the juice of oranges, lemons, limes, citrons, etc.

Ci·tril. 1688. [app. shortened f. It. *citrinella*, dim. of *citrina* citrine-coloured (bird).] In **c.-finch:** *Fringilla citrinella.*

† **Citrination** (sitrinēⁱ·ʃən). ME. [– med.L. *citrinatio*, f. pa. ppl. stem of *citrinare*, f. late L. *citrinus* adj. lemon-coloured (implied in *citrinitas*); see CITRUS, -INE, -ION.] *Alch.* The turning of a substance yellow, looked upon as indicating the state of perfection or complete digestion –1645.

Citrine (si·trin). ME. [– (O)Fr. *citrin*, *-ine* lemon-coloured – late L. *citrinus* (see prec.), f. *citrus* CITRUS + *-inus* -INE[1].] **A.** *adj.* Greenish-yellow; lemon-coloured; var. **Ci·trinous. B.** *sb.* **1.** Citrine colour 1879. **2.** *Min.* A glassy wine-yellow variety of quartz; *false topaz* 1748.

C. ointment: the ointment of nitrate of mercury. So † **Citrinize** *v.*, *Alch.* to render c.

Citron (si·trən). 1530. [– (O)Fr. *citron*, f. (after *limon* lemon) L. *citrus* (i) thuya, (ii) citron-tree.] **1.** An ovate acid juicy tree-fruit, larger, less acid, and thicker in the rind than the lemon. Formerly the name included the LEMON, and perhaps the LIME. **2.** The tree *Citrus medica*, which bears this fruit 1530. **3.** = CITRINE B. 1. 1610. † **4.** = CITRUS 2. Also *attrib.* –1740. † **5.** = *Citron-water* –1735. Also *attrib.*

5. Now drinking c. with his Grace and Chartres POPE. *Comb.* † **c.-water,** a drink made from brandy flavoured with c.- or lemon-peel.

† **Citronize,** *v.* *Alch.* [var. of *citrinize*; see CITRINATION, -IZE.] To become of a citron colour. B. JONS.

† **Citrul.** ME. [– OFr. *citrule* (mod. *citrouille*), ult. f. L. *citrus* (see next) w. dim. suffix.] The Water-Melon; also the Pumpkin –1755.

‖ **Citrus** (si·trŏs). 1865. [L., = (i) thuya, (ii) citron-tree, prob., like Gr. κέδρος CEDAR, an adoption from a non-IE. language.] *Bot.* **1.** The name now used for the genus which includes the citron, lemon, lime, orange, shaddock, and their varieties 1882. **2.** Roman name of an African tree, prob. *Callitris quadrivalvis*, the fragrant wood of which was prized for making furniture.

Cittern; see CITHERN.

City (si·ti). [ME. *cite* – (O)Fr. *cité* :– L. *civitas*, *-tat-* condition (see -TY[1]) of a citizen, etc., f. *civis* citizen.] † **1.** *orig.* A town or other inhabited place –1611. **2.** *spec.* A title ranking above that of 'town'. **a.** used vaguely ME. **b.** in Great Britain and Ireland: Associated with episcopal seats, and ancient royal burghs, and in recent times conferred by royal authority on important boroughs, as Birmingham, etc. ME. **c.** in *U.S.*: 'A town or collective body of inhabitants incorporated and governed by a mayor and aldermen' (Webster); also, in the newer States, used loosely 1843. Also *transf.* and *fig.* **3.** The community of the inhabitants of a city ME. **4.** *The City*: short for *the City of London*, that part of London situated within the ancient boundaries 1556; *esp.* the business part, or the business community, in the neighbourhood of the Exchange and Bank of England 1751. **5.** As tr. Gr. πόλις, L. *civitas*, a self-governing city or state 1540. **6.** *attrib.* Of or pertaining to a city or the City. (Often hyphened.) ME.

1. A citie called Nain *Luke* 7:11. **2. b.** My Lord Coke's Observation, that every C. is, or was, a Bishop's See, is not very exact 1714. *Holy C.*, Jerusalem. *Eternal C.*, *C. of the Seven Hills*, Rome. **5.** SHAKS. *Cor.* III. i. 199.

Comb.: **C.-article,** the summary of financial and commercial news in a newspaper; **C. Company:** see COMPANY; **C.-editor,** the editor of the C.-article, etc.; **c.-father,** a civic ruler; **-ward:** see WARD.

Hence **Ci·tycism,** c. manners, etc. **Ci·tyful,** as many as a c. will contain. **Ci·tyish** *a.* smacking of the c. **Ci·tyless** *a.* without a c. or cities; † that is no c. (*nonce-use*). **Ci·tyward(s** *adv.*

Cive (səiv). Now CHIVE, q.v.

Civet (si·vĕt), *sb.*[1] 1532. [– Fr. *civette* – It. *zibetto* – med.L. *zibethum* – Arab. (*qaṭṭ*) *azzabād* 'cat producing the secretion *zabād*'.] **1.** A genus of carnivorous quadrupeds, yielding the secretion called by the same name. Spec., the central African species, *Viverra civetta*; called also *Civet Cat.* The allied Asiatic species *V. zibetha* is often called ZIBET. The Javanese species is the Rasse. 1532. **2.** A yellowish or brownish unctuous substance, having a strong musky smell, obtained from glands in the anal pouch of the Civet. It is used in perfumery. 1553. Also *attrib.*

† **Civet,** *sb.*[2] 1531. [– Fr. *civette*, dim. of (O)Fr. *cive*; see CHIVE, -ET.] = CIVE or CHIVE –1712.

† **Civet,** *sb.*[3] 1708. [– Fr. *civet* (OFr. *civé*) kind of jugged hare, etc., f. *cive* CHIVE. Cf.

CIVY.] A way of dressing chickens, hares, etc., first frying them brown, and then stewing them in broth –1727.

Civet, *v.* 1601. [f. CIVET *sb.*[1]] To perfume with civet.

Civet-cat. 1607. = CIVET 1. (Also, a person perfumed with civet.)

Civic (si·vik), *a.* 1542. [– Fr. *civique* or L. *civicus*, f. *civis* citizen; see -IC.] Of or pertaining to citizens, to a city 1656, or to citizenship 1789.

C. crown [L. *corona civica*]: a garland of oak-leaves and acorns, bestowed upon one that saved the life of a fellow-citizen in war. *C. oath* [F. *serment civique*]: an oath of allegiance to the new order of things, demanded from citizens in the French Revolution. So † **Ci·vical** *a.*, whence **Ci·vically** *adv.* **Civics,** *pl.* used *subst.*, the theory of the rights and duties of citizenship.

Civicism (si·visiz'm). 1874. [f. prec. + -ISM.] Civic system; the principle that all citizens have equal rights and duties.

Civil (si·vil), *a.* ME. [– (O)Fr. *civil* – L. *civilis*, f. *civis* citizen; see -IL, -ILE.] **1.** Of or belonging to citizens; † of the nature of a citizen 1592. **2.** Of or pertaining to the community of citizens ME. † **3.** Civic –1713. **4.** Of, pertaining to, or befitting a citizen 1526. † **5.** Orderly, well-governed –1685. **6.** Civilized 1553. † **7.** Educated; refined –1716. † **8.** Sober, decent, grave –1691. † **9.** Humane, gentle –1684. **10.** Polite; in recent use, 'decently polite', 'not (actually) rude' 1606. Also *transf.* **11.** Pertaining to the *ordinary* life and affairs of a citizen; as distinguished from *military, ecclesiastical*, etc. 1592. **12.** *Law.* Pertaining to the *private* rights and remedies of a citizen; as distinguished from *criminal, political*, etc. 1611. **13.** *Legal* as distinguished from *natural* 1656. **14.** Of divisions of time: Legally recognized 1601. **15.** Of or according to the Roman CIVIL LAW. See also CIVIL LIST, CIVIL SERVICE, *Civil Servant* (see CIVIL SERVICE), *Civil Engineer* (see ENGINEER).

1. Where c. blood makes c. hands unclean *Rom. & Jul.* Prol. **2.** C. dominion HOOKER, war 1550. **4.** Slaves have no c. liberty LANE. C. knowledge H. WALPOLE. **5.** Ciuill streets SHAKS. **7.** C. and well bred men LOCKE. **10.** 'Well, he was c., which is something' 1889. **11.** *C. righteousness*: goodness as a citizen, but not as a saint. **13.** *C. death* (*i.e.* in all that respects legal rights or standing).

† **B.** as *sb.* **1.** = CIVILIAN 1. ME. only. **2.** *pl.* Civil matters; τὰ πολιτικά –1717.

† **C.** as *adv.* = CIVILLY –1767.

Civilian (sivi·liăn). ME. [– OFr. *civilien* in *droit civilien* civil law, f. *civil*; see CIVIL, -IAN. Later uses in Eng. start from other senses of CIVIL.] **1.** One who studies or has studied the Civil Law. † **2.** *Theol.* One who followed after civil righteousness (see CIVIL 11, quot.) –1645. **3.** A non-military man or official 1766. Also *attrib.*

1. Both the Canonists and the Civilians BAXTER. **3.** Civilians and Indian officers returning from sick furlough 1829.

Civilisation, -ise; see CIVILIZATION, -IZE.

† **Civilist.** 1549. [– med.L. *civilista*, f. *civilis* CIVIL + *-ista* -IST.] = CIVILIAN 1, 2. –1725.

Civility (sivi·lĭti). ME. [– (O)Fr. *civilité* – L. *civilitas*; see CIVIL, -ITY.]

I. Obs. senses, connected with citizenship, etc. † **1.** Citizenship –1568. † **2.** A civil capacity. LATIMER. † **3.** Polity –1670. † **4.** Social order –1611. † **5.** Good citizenship –1758. † **6.** Secular quality –1649. † **7.** Civil righteousness; see CIVIL 11, quot. –1640.

4. To inbreed and cherish in a great people the seeds of vertu, and publick civility MILTON.

II. Senses connected with civilization. **1.** The state of being civilized (*arch.*) 1549. **2.** Polite or liberal education (*arch.*) 1533. **3.** Behaviour proper to the intercourse of civilized people; politeness; an act of politeness 1561. † **4.** Seemliness; see CIVIL 8. –1672.

1. The progress of arts and c. JOHNSON. **2.** Bring c. and learning into France J. WARTON. **3.** The common forms of c. MACAULAY. † *C.-money*: money given in consideration or anticipation of good offices.

Civilizable (si·viləizăb'l), *a.* 1840. [See -ABLE.] Capable of being civilized.

Civiliza·de. *nonce-wd.* [Cf. *Crusade*, etc.] A crusade on behalf of civilization. MILL.

Civilization (sivilizē̆i·ʃən, -əizē̆i·ʃən). Also **-isation.** 1704. [f. CIVILIZE + -ATION. Cf. Fr. *civilisation.*] † **1.** *Law.* The assimilation of the Common Law to the Civil Law –1812. **2.** The action or process of civilizing or of being civilized 1775. **3.** (More usually) Civilized condition or state 1772. Also *transf.*

3. The more advanced the c., the less powerful is the individual HELPS. Hence **Ci:viliza·tional** *a.*

Civilize (si·viləiz), *v.* 1601. [– Fr. *civilizer* (XVI; now *-iser*); see CIVIL, -IZE.] To make CIVIL; to bring out of a state of barbarism, to instruct in the arts of life; to enlighten and refine. Also *transf.* † **2.** To make proper in a civil community (*rare*) 1643. **3.** *intr.* To become civilized or elevated 1868.

1. To c. the rude unpolish'd world ADDISON. **2.** With an ignominious note of civilizing Adultery MILT. Hence **Civilizee·**, a person civilized. **Ci·vilizer.**

Civil law, † **right.** ME. [L. *jus civile*, Fr. *droit civil.*] The law of Roman citizens; thence, the Roman law as a whole. (See LAW.) Also, the law of any city or state regulating the private rights and duties of the inhabitants.

Civil List. 1712. *orig.* A list of the charges for the civil administration of the state; the establishment supported by the moneys voted on this list (*obs.*); *now*, the amount voted by parliament for the household and personal expenses of the monarch, and for the *Civil List pensions, i.e.* pensions granted by the royal bounty.

Civilly (si·vili), *adv.* 1552. [f. CIVIL *a.* + -LY[2].] In a civil manner (see CIVIL 4, 6, 7, 8, 11, 15). **Ci·vilness,** civility (*rare*).

Civil Service. 1785. *orig.* That part of the service of the East India Company carried on by the covenanted servants who did not belong to the Army or Navy (cf. SERVICE); *now*, all the non-warlike departments of the public administrative service of the state. Also the body of servants of the state employed in this service. **Civil Servant,** a member of the Civil Service.

Civism (si·viz'm). 1791. [– Fr. *civisme*, f. L. *civis* citizen; see -ISM.] Principles of good citizenship. (A term of the French Revolution.) Also *fig.*

† **Civy, civey.** [ME. *cive* – OFr. *civé* (XIII), mod. *civet*; see CIVET *sb.*[3], -Y[5].] A broth or sauce for a hare. (Cf. CIVET[3].) –1460.

Cizar, -zer, obs. ff. SCISSOR, SIZAR.

Cize, obs. f. SIZE.

Clabber (klæ·bəɹ). 1634. [– Ir. and Gael. *clabar* mud.] **1.** *dial.* Mud 1824. **2.** = BONNY-CLABBER, q.v. Hence **Clabber** *v. intr.* to curdle, as milk.

Clachan (kla·χăn). *Sc.* and *north-Ir.* ME. [Gael., app. f. *clach* stone.] A small village in the Highlands of Scotland.

The c. yill had made me canty BURNS.

Clack (klæk), *sb.* ME. [f. CLACK *v.*[1]; cf. ON. *klak* chirping of birds, Du. *klak*, MHG. *klac.*] **1.** A sudden, sharp, dry sound as of two flat pieces of wood striking each other 1598. **2.** Anything which makes this noise, as † the clapper of a mill, a clack-valve, a rattle to scare away birds, etc. ME. **3.** Clatter of human tongues; senseless or continuous chatter ME. **4.** *contemptuously*, The tongue. (Cf. 2.) 1598.

1. The great wheel's measured c. MORRIS. **3.** Whose chief intent is to vaunt his spiritual c. SOUTH.

Comb.: **c.-box,** the box or chamber containing the c.-valve of a pump; **-dish,** a wooden dish with a lid clacked by beggars to attract notice; **-door,** an opening into the c.-box; **-valve,** a form of valve in pumps, hinged at one side, which is raised by the upward motion of the fluid, and falls back with a c.

Clack (klæk), *v.*[1] ME. [prob. – ON. *klaka* twitter, (of birds) chatter, of imit. origin; cf. Du. *klakken* crack, Fr. *claquer.*] **A. 1.** *intr.* To chatter, prate, talk loquaciously. **b.** *trans.* To blab 1590. **2.** To cluck, or cackle, as a hen 1712. **3.** *intr.* To make a sound intermediate between a clap and a crack as one flat piece of wood does in striking another 1530; *trans.* to cause to make such a sound 1542.

1. 'Tis not euer true, that what the hart thinketh the tongue clacketh GREENE. **3.** He clackt his whip HOBBES. Hence **Cla·cker,** † **Cla·cket,** that which clacks; the clapper of a mill, etc.

† **B.** Used advb.: At once, pat, 'slick' 1734.

† **Clack,** *v.*[2] ME. [orig. Flemish *klacken.*] *trans.* To remove the dirty clots, etc., from (a fleece of wool) –1726.

Clad (klæd), *ppl. a.* [ME. *clad(d*, f. OE. *claþod, -ed*; see CLOTHE *v.* Also *yclad* with prefix *y-*, revived by the archaists.] Covered with or as with clothing; arrayed, decked.

Clad, *v. arch.* 1579. [app. educed from prec.] To CLOTHE. Also *transf.* and *fig.*

† **Clade.** ME. [– L. *clades* disaster.] A disaster, plague –1604.

Clado- (klædo, klē̆ido), bef. a vowel **clad-,** comb. f. Gr. κλάδος young shoot or branch, as in **Clada·nthous** *a.*, bearing the fructification on short lateral branchlets, as some Mosses; so **Cladoca·rpous** *a.*; **Cla·dophyll,** also **-phyllon,** pl. **-a,** a branch assuming the form of foliage.

‖ **Cladodium** (klădōᵘ·diŏm). Also **cla·dode.** 1870. [mod.L., f. late Gr. κλαδώδης with many shoots, f. κλάδος shoot, slip; cf. *phyllodium*, etc.] *Bot.* An axis flattened and more or less leaf-like.

Claes (klēz). 1549. *Sc.* and *n. dial.* form of CLOTHES.

Clag, *sb. n. dial.* 1641. [f. the vb.] **1.** The process or product of clagging. **2.** An encumbrance. *Sc.* 1697. Hence **Cla·ggy** *a.* adhesive.

Clag (klæg), *v. n. dial.* 1470. [perh. of Scand. orig.; cf. Da. *klag, klagge* sticky mud, clay, *klæg, klæget* viscous, rel. to OE. *clǣg* CLAY; perh. infl. by *clog.*] **1.** *trans.* To bedaub, to clot *with* anything sticky; to clog by so doing 1526. **2.** *intr.* To stick tenaciously; also *transf.* 1563. **3.** *dial* = CLACK *v.*[2] 1863. Hence **Cla·ggum,** treacle-toffee.

Claik (klē̆ik), *sb. Sc.* 1455. [f. CLAIK *v.*] **1.** The call of geese, etc. 1549. **2.** The Barnacle-goose (prob. from its call).

Claik, *v. Sc.* 1513. [prob. – ON. *klaka* chatter; cf. CLACK *v.*[1]] *intr.* To cry as geese, etc.; to chatter.

Claim (klē̆im), *sb.* ME. [– OFr. *claime*, f. *clamer*; see next.] **1.** A demand for something as due; an assertion of a right to something. (Const. as in 2.) **2.** Right of claiming; right or title (*to* something or *to* with *inf. phrase*; also *on, upon* a person, etc.) ME. **3.** That which is claimed; *spec.* in *U.S.* and *Australia*, a piece of land allotted and taken, *esp.* for mining purposes 1863. † **4.** A call, shout. SPENSER *F.Q.* IV. x. 11.

1. *To lay c. to*: to claim. **2.** A c. to kindness JOHNSON, to call itself owner PENNANT. Hence **Clai·mless** *a.* (*rare*).

Claim (klē̆im), *v.* ME. [– OFr. *claim-*, tonic stem of *clamer* cry, call, appeal:– L. *clamare* cry, call, proclaim.] **1.** To demand as one's own or one's due; to seek or ask for on the ground of right. **2.** To assert and demand recognition of (an alleged right, title, or the like); to assert as one's own ME. In *U.S., loosely*, To assert. **3.** Of things: To call for; to be entitled to 1606. † **4.** To proclaim (with *complement*) –1596. **5.** *intr.* To put forward a claim. (Later, app. an absolute use of 1 or 2.) ME.

1. To c. Precedence MILT. *P.L.* II. 32, to be exempt ME., that his word should be law MERIVALE. **2.** That claymethe gentyle for to be CHAUCER. **4.** † *To claim quit, also to quit claim* (a person or thing); to proclaim quit or released. **5.** Say from what scepter'd ancestry ye claim POPE. Hence **Clai·mable** *a.* **Clai·mance,** the action of claiming. **Clai·mant,** one who makes or enters a claim; one who has a claim *upon* anything. **Clai·mer,** a claimant.

Clairaudience (kleᵊr,ǭ·diĕns). 1864. [f. Fr. *clair* + AUDIENCE, after CLAIRVOYANCE.] The faculty of mentally perceiving sounds beyond the range of hearing, alleged to be induced under certain mesmeric conditions. So **Clairaudient** *a.* and *sb.*

Clair-obscure. 1717. [– Fr. *clair-obscur*, tr. of It. *chiaroscuro.*] = CHIAROSCURO, q.v.

‖ **Clairschach** (klā·ɹʃăχ). 1490. [Ir. and Gael. *clairseach.*] The old Celtic harp strung with wire. Hence ‖ **Clai·rschacher,** a player on the c.

Clairvoyance (kleᵊrvoi·ăns, or as Fr. klęrvoyāñs). 1847. [– Fr., f. *clair-voyant*, f. *clair* clear + *voyant*, pres. pple. of *voir* see.] **1.** The faculty of mentally perceiving objects at a distance or concealed from sight, attributed to certain persons, or to persons under certain mesmeric conditions. **2.** Keenness of mental perception, insight 1861. So **Clairvoy·ant(e** *a.* and *sb.* (in both senses). **Clairvoy·antly** *adv.*

Clake, clakke, obs. ff. CLAIK, CLACK *v.*

Clam (klæm), *sb.*¹ [OE. *clam* bond, fetter, corresp. to OHG. *klamma* (G. dial. *klamm*), and MHG., G. *klemme*, Du. *klemme, klem*, f. Gmc. **klam-* press or squeeze together.] † **1.** Anything that holds tight; bond, chain; *pl.* bondage. (In OE.) **2.** An instrument for clasping rigidly or holding fast; a clamp, vice, pair of pincers, etc.; also, a lining for the jaws of a vice ME. † **3.** *pl.* Clutches, claws –1574.

Clam (klæm), *sb.*² 1500. [orig. *clam-shell*; app. from prec.] **1.** A name applied to various bivalve shell-fish; *esp.* **a.** in Scotland, to the genus *Pecten*; **b.** to the Giant C. or Clamp (*Tridacna gigas*) of the East Indies; **c.** in U.S., to the Hard or Round C. (*Venus mercenaria*), and the Soft or Long C. (*Mya arenaria*): whence *c.-bake* and *c.-chowder*. Also applied to freshwater mussels. **2.** *U.S.* A term of contempt; one who is 'as close as a c.' 1871. **3.** *U.S. slang.* The mouth 1825.

Comb.: **c.-bake,** a baking, Indian-fashion, upon hot stones, of a mass of clams, a favourite feature of seaside picnics in U.S.; hence, the picnic party; **-chowder,** one made with clams.

Clam (klæm), *sb.*³ 1554. [perh. a back-formation from CLAMMY.] † **1.** A soft mass. (Cf. CLOAM.) **2.** Clamminess 1694.

Clam (klæm), *sb.*⁴ 1702. [Echoic, with more notion of crash than *clang*.] The crash of two or more bells of a peal rung together.

Clam (klæm), *a.*¹ Now *dial.* ME. [Cf. CLAM *v.*¹] Sticky; cold and damp; clammy.

Clam, *a.*² 1829. [perh. – L. *clam* secretly.] *Sc.* Base, mean; a school term. ?*Obs.*

Clam (klæm), *v.*¹ Now *dial.* [ME. *clamme*, var. of *cleme*, OE. *clǣman*; see CLEAM, CLEME *v.* Perh. infl. by CLAM *a.*¹, CLAMMY.] **1.** To smear, or spread unctuous matter *on*; to daub *with*. **2.** To bedaub (a thing) so that it sticks 1598. **3.** To clog or choke up 1527. **4.** *intr.* To be moist and sticky; to stick, adhere 1610.

Clam (klæm), *v.*² 1674. [See CLAM *sb.*⁴] **1.** Of bells: To crash together (*trans.* and *intr.*) 1702. **2.** *fig.* To silence 1674.

Clamant (klēⁱ·mănt, klæ·m-), *a.* 1639. [– *clamant-*, pres. ppl. stem of L. *clamare* cry out; see CLAIM, -ANT¹.] **1.** *lit.* Clamorous. **2.** *fig.* Crying, urgent 1723.

1. C. for food 1806. **2.** C. abuses 1858. Hence **Cla·mantly** *adv.*

† **Clama·tion.** 1502. [– OFr. *clamation* or late L. *clamatio*, f. *clamat-*, pa. ppl. stem of L. *clamare* cry out; see -ION.] A crying out, invocation. SIR T. BROWNE.

Clamber (klæ·mbəɹ), *v.* ME. [Of frequent. form, prob. f. *clamb*, obs. pa. t. of *climb*; see -ER⁵. Cf. the equiv. dial. *climber*.] *intr.* To climb by catching hold with hands and feet; to climb with difficulty. Also *trans.* Of plants: To climb by means of tendrils, etc. 1601. Also *transf.* and *fig.*

The Kitchen Malkin..Clambring the Walls to eye him *Cor.* II. i. 225. The narrow street that clamber'd toward the mill TENNYSON. Hence **Cla·mber** *sb.* an act of clambering. **Cla·mberer,** he who or that which clambers; *esp.* a climbing plant.

Clamjamphrie (klæmdʒæ·mfri). *Sc.* and *n. dial.* 1816. [Of unkn. origin.] Trumpery; spoken rubbish, 'rot'; rabble, canaille.

Clammy (klæ·mi), *a.* [ME., f. *clamme* (see CLAM *v.*¹) + -Y¹.] **1.** Soft, moist, and sticky; viscous, adhesive. † **2.** *fig.* Sluggish 1613.

The c. water [of the Dead Sea] FULLER. C. fogs 1697, sweat 1703, hands 1626. Hence **Cla·mmily** *adv.* **Cla·mminess.** † **Cla·mmish** *a.* somewhat c.

Clamor, var. of CLAMOUR.

Clamorous (klæ·mŏrəs), *a.* 1526. [f. late L. *clamorosus* + -OUS. Cf. OFr. *clamoreus*.] **1.** Of the nature of clamour; uttered with, or accompanied by, shouting; noisy. **2.** Vociferous; loudly urgent. Said of persons and other agents; also *transf.* of places where they are. 1540. Also *fig.*

1. The c. nonsense of the hour EMERSON. **2.** C. War-pipes SCOTT, river-banks CORY. *fig.* C. debts ARBUTHNOT. Hence **Cla·morous-ly** *adv.*, **-ness.**

Clamour, -or (klæ·məɹ), *sb.* ME. [– AFr. *clamur*, OFr. *clamour* – L. *clamor*, rel. to *clamare*; see CLAIM, -OUR.] **1.** Loud shouting or outcry, vociferation: commonly implying a mingling of voices. Also with *a*, and *pl.* ME. **2.** *fig.* General vehement expression of feeling, *esp.* of discontent or disapprobation; popular outcry ME. **3.** Any loud noise, as of beasts, birds, a storm, etc. 1592.

2. The c. for war continued D'ISRAELI. Hence **Cla·mourist** (*rare*), one who belongs to a party of c. **Cla·moursome** *a.* (*n. dial.*).

Clamour, -or (klæ·məɹ), *v.*¹ ME. [f. prec. sb.] **1.** *intr.* To make a clamour; to raise an outcry, make a noise or din of speech. **2.** *intr.* To raise an outcry *for*; to demand importunately *to do* a thing 1651. **3.** *trans.* † To disturb with clamour, din –1671; also with *out of, into, down*, etc. **4.** To utter clamorously 1856.

1. The obscure Bird clamor'd the liue-long Night *Macb.* II. iii. 65. **2.** Men were eagerly clamouring to go home FREEMAN. **3.** Clamouring thir God with praise, Who had made thir dreadful enemy thir thrall MILT. *Sams.* 1621. **4.** Hungry crows.. Clamoured their piteous prayer incessantly LONGF. Hence **Cla·mourer.**

Cla·mour, -or, *v.*² Also **clamber.** 1611. [f. CLAM *v.*², or conn. w. prec.] **1.** *Bell-ringing.* To repeat the strokes more quickly, when they are at the height, in order to cease them 1747. **2.** To silence 1611.

2. Clamor your tongues, and not a word more *Wint. T.* IV. iii. 250.

Clamp (klæmp), *sb.*¹ ME. [prob. of LG. orig.; cf. Du., LG. *klamp*, † *klampe* (whence G. *klampe*), f. **klamp-*, by-form of **klamb-* (cf. CLIMB), **klamm-* (cf. CLAM *sb.*¹).] **1.** A brace, clasp, or band, usually of rigid material, used for strengthening or fastening things together: *e.g.* a piece of wood inserted into another to prevent warping, etc. Also *fig.* **2.** A name of appliances with opposite parts which may be brought together, so as to seize, hold, compress, or pinch anything: *e.g.* with *Joiners*, an appliance for holding articles together while being formed; a check for a vice, etc. 1688. **3.** *Naut.* One of the thick planks in a ship's side below the shelf-piece which support the ends of the deck-beams 1626. Also *attrib.*

Comb.: **c.-nail,** a large-headed nail for fastening iron clamps; **-plate** (*Ship-building*), an iron plate serving to unite two bodies.

Clamp, *sb.*² 1624. [perh. f. prec.; cf. CLAM *sb.*¹, ².] † **1.** *U.S.* Earlier name of CLAMS. **2.** Usu. *C.-shell*: the large bivalve shell of the molluscs *Chama* and *Tridacna* (Family *Chamaceæ*) 1835.

Clamp (klæmp), *sb.*³ 1596. [prob. as a brick-making term – (M)Du. *klamp* heap, rel. to CLUMP.] A heap or pile of bricks for burning, of earth to cover potatoes, etc., of ore for roasting, of coal for coking, etc.

Clamp, *sb.*⁴ Chiefly *dial.* 1879. [f. CLAMP *v.*³] A heavy, solid tread, or stamp with the feet.

Clamp (klæmp), *v.*¹ 1677. [f. CLAMP *sb.*¹] *trans.* To make fast with a clamp or clamps. Hence **Cla·mper,** that which clamps; clams, pincers, an ice-creeper, etc.

Clamp, *v.*² 1834. [f. CLAMP *sb.*³] To pile *up* (bricks, earth, etc.) in a heap; to store (potatoes, etc.) in a clamp. Hence **Cla·mper** *v.*¹ to botch, patch up.

Clamp, *v.*³ Chiefly *dial.* 1808. [Goes with CLAMP *sb.*⁴; cf. CLOMP *v.*, CLUMP *v.* 1.] To tread or stamp heavily; to clump. So **Cla·mper** *v.*²

Clan (klæn), *sb.* ME. [– Gaelic *clann* offspring, family, stock, race, corresp. to OIr. *cland*, (mod.) *clann* – L. *planta* sprout, scion, PLANT.] **1.** A number of persons claiming descent from a common ancestor, and associated together; a tribe. **2.** *contemptuously*, A collection of people having common attributes; a fraternity, party, set, lot 1536. Also *transf.* and *fig.* Also *attrib.*

1. 'The Gathering of the Clans' 1889. Another c. of the Arabs MAUNDRELL. **2.** The whole c. of the enlightened among us BURKE. A c. o' roosty craws STEVENSON. Hence **Clan** *v.* (*rare*) to combine as members of a c. **Cla·nless** *a.* (*rare*).

† **Cla·ncular,** *a.* 1621. [– L. *clancularius*, f. *clanculum* adv., dim. of *clam* in secret; see -AR².] Secret; clandestine –1735. So † **Cla·nculary.** Hence † **Cla·ncularly** *adv.*

Clandestine (klæ̆nde·stin), *a.* 1566. [– Fr. *clandestin* or L. *clandestinus*, f. *clam* secretly.] Secret, concealed; usually in a bad sense; underhand, surreptitious.

A certain c. Hostility cover'd over with the name of Peace MILT. Hence **Clande·stinely** *adv.* **Clandesti·nity,** secrecy; usually in bad sense.

Clang (klæŋ), *sb.* 1596. [imit. formation parallel to OHG. *klanc, klang-* (G. *klang*). See next.] **1.** A loud resonant ringing sound; orig., as in L., that of a trumpet; now that of metal when struck. Also *fig.* (Cf. Ger. *klang* 'sound'.) **2.** The loud harsh scream of certain birds. (As in L. and Gr.) 1667. **3.** *Acoust.* = Ger. *klang*: A composite musical sound 1867.

1. Trumpetts clangue *Tam. Shr.* I. ii. 207. *fig.* A c. of turgid extravagances MERIVALE. **2.** Their [cranes'] loud c. SOMERVILLE. So † **Clange.** CHAPMAN.

Clang (klæŋ), *v.* 1576. [Goes with CLANG *sb.*; perh. partly – L. *clangere* resound (as a trumpet).] **1.** *intr.* To emit a CLANG. **2.** *trans.* To strike together with clanging sound 1720. **3.** *intr.* Of some birds: To utter their loud harsh cry 1832.

1. Armes clatter and c. FLORIO. **2.** They [eagles] wheel on high, And c. their wings POPE.

Clangor, -our (klæ·ŋgəɹ, klæ·ŋəɹ), *sb.* 1593. [– L. *clangor*, f. *clangere* resound; see CLANG *v.*] Loud resonant ringing sound; a CLANG. Occas. with *a* and *pl.* Hence **Cla·ngor, -our** *v. intr.* to clang. **Cla·ngorous** *a.* full of c.; so † **Cla·ngous** *a.* (*rare*) SIR T. BROWNE. **Cla·ngorously** *adv.*

Clanjamfray, -phrey; see CLAMJAMPHRIE.

Clank (klæŋk), *sb.* 1656. [imit. formation parallel to MLG., M(Du.) *klank*, OHG. *klanc, klank-*. Cf. CLANG, CLINK.] A sharp abrupt sound, as of *e.g.* links of a heavy chain struck together; differing from *clang* in ending abruptly like a *clink*.

The c. of machinery 1845. Hence **Cla·nkless** *a.* (*rare*).

Clank (klæŋk), *v.* 1614. [Goes with prec. sb.] **1.** *intr.* To make, or move with, a clanking sound. **2.** *trans.* To cause to emit, or to utter with, a clanking sound 1743.

1. The old dinner-bell will clang, or rather c., in a few minutes SCOTT.

Clannish (klæ·niʃ), *a.* 1776. [f. CLAN + -ISH¹.] Of or pertaining to a clan; having the sympathies, prejudices, etc., of a clan; attached to one's own clan. Hence **Cla·nnish-ly** *adv.*, **-ness.**

Clanship (klæ·nʃip). 1772. [f. CLAN *sb.* + -SHIP.] **1.** The system of clans; union of persons in, or as in, a clan. **2.** Clannishness 1809.

Clansman (klæ·nzmæ̆n). 1810. [f. *clan's* + MAN.] A man belonging to a clan.

Clap (klæp), *sb.*¹ [f. CLAP *v.*¹] **1.** An abrupt explosive noise, as of two hard flat surfaces struck on one another. **2.** = CLACK. Now *dial.* ME. **3.** The noise made by striking the hands together; the act of so doing; applause 1599. **4.** A sounding blow; in *Sc. esp.* a pat ME. † **5.** A sudden stroke (*lit.* and *fig.*). (Cf. AFTERCLAP.) –1768. **6.** *Falconry.* The lower mandible of a hawk 1486. † **7.** A poster –1735. **8.** = CLAPPER *sb.*¹ (in various senses) ME. **9.** *Farriery.* A disease of horses. ? *Obs.* 1684.

1. A terrible c. of thunder HAKLUYT. **3.** Applause..with c. of hands, and thump of sticks HAWTHORNE. **5.** *In a c.*: at once. (Cf. Fr. *coup.*) **7.** Plaster'd posts, with claps in capitals POPE.

Comb.: **c.-bill** = sense 7; **-bread, -cake,** oatmeal cake, beaten thin, and baked hard; **-dish** = CLACK-*dish*; **-net,** a net used by fowlers, entomologists, etc., which can be suddenly closed by pulling a string.

Clap (klæp), *sb.*² Now *vulgar.* 1587. [Shortened f. OFr. *clapoir* venereal bubo (whence obs. Du. *klapoore*), also *clapoire* bubo, brothel, venereal disease.] Gonorrhœa. Also with *a* and *pl.*

Clap (klæp), *v.*¹ [OE. *clappian* throb, beat = OFris. *klappia*, MLG. *klappen*, OHG. *klapfōn*, ON. *klappa*, beside OE. *clæppan* = OFris. *kleppa*, MLG. *kleppen*, OHG. *klepfen*; of imit. origin.] **1.** *intr.* To make the noise described under CLAP *sb.*¹ (Now *dial.*) 1509. † **2.** = CLACK *v.*¹ 1. –1562. **3.** *intr.* To make this noise by † rapping, shutting (*to*), etc. ME. **4.** *trans.* To strike the palms of *the hands* together with noise ME.; also *ellipt.* to clap the hands at 1555; *intr.* (without 'hands') to applaud by clapping hands 1613. **5.** *trans.* To strike with sounding blows (*arch.*) ME. †**6.** To strike (hands) reciprocally, in token of a bargain –1614. **7.** Of a bird: To flap (the wings) ME. **8.** To slap with the palm of the hand, in token of approval; in *n. dial.* to pat 1530. **9.** To put, place, set, or stick, with promptness and effect; *esp.* to put *in* prison. Also simply *to clap up*. 1515. **10.** *fig.* To impose as with authority *upon, on*, etc. 1609. †**11.** To stick *together*, put *up*, hastily –1711. †**12.** *intr.* (for *refl.*): To throw oneself, strike *in* –1750. Also †*fig.* to strike *into* SHAKS. Also *absol.* (colloq.).

1. Doors creak and windows c. BLAIR. **3.** [Sche] clapt the wyndow to CHAUCER. **4.** Clappyn hondys togedyr for ioy ME. **6.** And so c. hands, and a bargaine *Hen. V*, v. ii. 133. Cf. *Wint. T.* I. ii. 104. **9.** C. on more sailes *Merry W.* II. ii. 142. The uncivil Lord..clapt irons on my heels 1605. To c. spurs to a horse 1710. *To c. eyes on* (colloq.). Let them be clapt vp close SHAKS. **10.** To c. a writ upon his back 1690. **11.** Was euer match clapt vp so sodainly *Tam. Shr.* II. i. 327. **12.** *Meas. for M.* IV. iii. 43.

Clap (klæp), *v.*² Now *vulgar*. 1658. [f. CLAP *sb.*²] To infect with clap.

Clapboard (klæ·pˌbōᵊɹd, klæ·boɹd), *sb.* 1520. [Partial tr. of †CLAPHOLT, with *board* for LG. *holt*.] **1.** A small size of split oak, for barrel-staves, and wainscoting. **2.** In *U.S.* A board, thinner at one edge, used to weather-board the sides or roofs of houses 1641. †**3.** Used without *a* or *pl.* –1745. Hence **Cla·pboard** *v.* to cover or line with clapboards (*U.S.*).

Clape (klēⁱp). 1860. [perh. f. CLEPE *v.*] A bird; the FLICKER.

†**Clapholt.** 1477. [– LG. *klappholt* = Du. *klaphout*, f. *klappen* crack + *holt* wood. See CLAPBOARD.] = CLAPBOARD *sb.* 3. –1721.

Cla·pmatch. 1743. [– Du. *klapmuts(rob)* hooded seal, f. *klapmuts* cap with flaps; so called from the cartilaginous hood which covers its eyes.] A kind of seal.

Clapped, clapt, pa. pple. of CLAP *v.*

Clapped, *ppl. a.* [f. CLAP *sb.*¹ 9 + -ED².] *Farriery.* Affected with clap. STERNE.

Clapper (klæ·pəɹ), *sb.*¹ ME. [f. CLAP *v.*¹ + -ER¹.] **1.** That which claps or makes a noise, as the CLACK of a mill, the tongue of a bell, etc.; also *fig.* the human tongue. **2.** One who claps; a claquer 1824.

†**Clapper,** *sb.*² ME. [– AFr. *claper* = OFr. *clapier* – Pr. *clapier* rabbit-warren, orig. heap of stones; cf. med.L. *clapus, clapa* (in both senses), of Gaulish origin, also *claperius*.] A rabbit-burrow –1725.

Clapper (klæ·pəɹ), *v.* 1872. [f. CLAPPER *sb.*¹] **1.** To sound (a bell) by pulling the clapper. **2.** *intr.* To make a noise like a clapper 1884.

Clapperclaw (klæ·pəɹklǭ), *v. arch.* 1590. [Obscurely f. CLAPPER *sb.*¹ + CLAW *v.*] **1.** *trans.* To claw with the open hand and nails; to drub. **2.** *fig.* To revile 1692. Hence **Cla·pperclawer.**

Clapperdudgeon. *arch.* 1567. [app. f. CLAPPER *sb.* + DUDGEON hilt of a dagger.] *Cant.* A beggar born; also, as a term of insult.

Claps(e, obs. and dial. f. CLASP.

Claptrap (klæ·pˌtræp), 1727. [f. CLAP *sb.*¹ 3 + TRAP *sb.*] **1.** A trick, device, or language designed to catch applause. (Also without *a* or *pl.*) Also *attrib.* †**2.** A contrivance for making a clapping noise in theatres, etc. –1866. Hence **Cla·ptrappy** *a.* (*nonce-wd.*).

‖**Claque** (klɑk). 1864. [Fr.; f. *claquer* to clap.] A band of hired applauders in a theatre; also *transf.* of political followers.

Claquer (klæ·kəɹ), ‖**claqueur** (klakör). 1837. [– Fr. *claqueur*, f. as prec.] A hired applauder.

Clarabella (klārabe·lă). Also **clari-**. 1840. [f. L. *clarus, -a* clear + *bellus, -a* beautiful.] An organ-stop of a powerful fluty tone, invented by Bishop.

Clare. 1818. A nun of the order of St. Clare.

Clarence (klæ·rĕns). 1837. [f. the Duke of *Clarence*, afterwards William IV.] A close four-wheeled carriage with seats for four inside; also *attrib.*

Clarenceux, -cieux (klæ·rĕnsiū). ME. [– AFr. *Clarenceux* (in AL. *Clarencius*), f. *Clarence*, an English dukedom named from *Clare* in Suffolk.] The second King-of-Arms in England, who officiates south of the river Trent.

Clarendon (klæ·rĕndən). 1848. [Named after the *Clarendon* Press, Oxford.] *Printing.* A thick-faced condensed type, in capital and small letters, made in many sizes.

Clare-obscure, = CLAIR-OBSCURE.

†**Claret,** *sb.*¹ ME. [– med.L. *claretum, claratum* spiced, honeyed wine; see CLARY *sb.*¹] = CLARY *sb.*¹ –1559.

Claret (klæ·rĕt), *sb.*² ME. [orig. qualifying *wine*, after OFr. *vin claret* (mod. *clairet*), superseding OFr. *claré* (see CLARY *sb.*¹), and being later applied to light red wines.] **1.** *orig.* A name of yellowish or light red wines, as distinguished from 'red' and 'white' wines; used, about 1600, for red wines generally. Now applied to the red wines imported from Bordeaux. Also as †*adj.* **2.** *slang.* Blood 1604. **3.** The colour of claret 1648; also as *adj.* claret-coloured 1547. Hence **Claretee·r,** a drinker of c. **Cla·rety** *a.*

Claribella, var. of CLARABELLA.

Cla·richord. *Hist.* 1502. [A perversion of CLAVICHORD, assoc. w. L. *clarus*.] = CLAVICHORD, q.v. So †**Claricy·mbal** = CLAVICYMBAL.

Clarification (klæ:rifikēⁱ·ʃən). 1612. [In sense 1 f. CLARIFY (senses 1, 3), partly – Fr. *clarification*; see -FICATION. In sense 2 – eccl. L. *clarificatio* glorification, f. *clarificare*; see CLARIFY, -ATION.] **1.** The action or process of clarifying, *esp.* liquids. †**2.** Glorifying; transfiguration –1683.

2. Elevation and c. of his veri mortal Bodie 1683.

Clarify (klæ·rifəi), *v.* ME. [– (O)Fr. *clarifier* – late L. *clarificare*, f. L. *clarus* CLEAR *a.*; see -FY.] †**1.** *trans.* To CLEAR, in various senses –1696. Also *intr.* (for *refl.*). Also *fig.* †**2.** *fig.* To make illustrious; to glorify –1649. **3.** To make pure, or clean (*physically*, also *morally*); to free from all impurities, defecate ME. Also *fig.*

1. To c. the day LYDG., the sight 1525, the voice 1585; (*fig.*) to c. a subject 1841. **2.** Fadir, clarifie thi name WYCLIF *John* 12:27. **3.** To c. butter 1769, the atmosphere 1879; (*fig.*) to c. the intellect 1851, the popular creed 1869. Hence **Cla·rifier,** one who or that which clarifies; *spec.* a vessel used in clarifying sugar.

†**Cla·rigate,** *v. rare.* 1601. [– *clarigat-*, pa. ppl. stem of L. *clarigare*; see -ATE³.] To make through heralds a solemn demand for redress, prior to declaration of war. Hence †**Clariga·tion** (*rare*).

†**Cla·rine.** ME. [– OFr. *clarin*, by-form of *claron* CLARION.] –1620.

Clarinet (klæ·rinet, -ne·t). 1796. [– Fr. *clarinette*, dim. of *clarine*; see -ETTE.] A wooden single-reed instrument, having a cylindrical tube with bell-shaped orifice, and played by means of holes and keys. Hence **Clarine·ttist.**

‖**Clarino** (klărī·no). [It.] = CLARION 1, 3.

Clarion (klæ·riən), *sb.* ME. [– med.L. *clario, -on-*, f. L. *clarus* CLEAR; cf. OFr. *claron* (mod. *clairon*).] **1.** A shrill-sounding trumpet with a narrow tube. (Now chiefly *poet.* or *Hist.*) **2.** *poet.* The sound of a trumpet, or any similar rousing sound 1667. **3.** An organ-stop of like quality of tone 1670. **4.** *attrib.* Of or pertaining to, or sounding like, a clarion ME.

1. The warlike sound Of..Clarions MILT. *P.L.* I. 532. **2.** The cock's shrill c. GRAY. **4.** The c. couplets of Pope 1879. Hence **Cla·rion** *v.* (*rare*) to blow the c.; also *trans.* †**Cla·rioner,** †**Cla·rionist.**

Clarionet (klæ·riŏnet, -e·t). 1784. [f. prec + -ET; partly alt. of CLARINET.] = CLARINET. Also *fig.*

†‖**Clari·ssimo.** 1605. [It.; a learned adoption of L. *clarissimus* 'most illustrious', a title of honour.] A Venetian grandee –1630.

†**Cla·ritude.** 1560. [– L. *claritudo*, f. *clarus* CLEAR; see -TUDE.] Clearness, brightness; a thing of brightness –1670.

Clarity (klæ·rĭti). ME. [– L. *claritas*, f. *clarus* CLEAR; see -ITY. Superseded ME. *clarte* – OFr. *clarté* :– L.] †**1.** Brightness –1698. †**2.** Glory –1675. **3.** Clearness: in various senses 1616.

3. C. of understanding SIR T. BROWNE, of style FULLER, heaven BROWNING, a gem 1871.

Clarkia (klā·ɹkiă). 1864. [mod.L., f. name of W. *Clarke*, U.S. explorer, see -IA¹.] A plant of the genus of this name, consisting of annuals bearing white, rose, lake, and purple flowers.

†**Claro obscuro.** 1706. = CHIAROSCURO.

Clarre, -y, obs. ff. CLARY.

Clart (klāɹt), *sb.* *Sc.* and *n. dial.* 1808. [See next.] Sticky or claggy dirt; (with *pl.*), a daub of sticky dirt. Hence **Cla·rty** *a.* dirty, sticky.

Clart (klāɹt), *v. trans.* 1681. [Of unkn. origin.] To smear or daub with, or † as with, dirt.

†**Cla·ry,** *sb.*¹ [ME. *claré* – OFr. *claré* :– med.L. *claratum* (sc. *vinum*) 'clarified wine', subst. use of n. pa. pple. of *clarare*, f. L. *clarus* clear; see -Y⁵; cf. CLARET.] A liquor consisting of a mixture of wine, clarified honey, pepper, ginger, etc. Occas. *c. wine.* –1700.

Clary (klēᵊ·ri), *sb.*² [– Fr. †*clarie*, repr. med.L. *sclarea*; the loss of initial *s* is unexpl.] A labiate plant, *Salvia sclarea*; also other plants, app. as considered good for the eyes, *e.g.* Celandine, and species of Fennel. Also *attrib.*

Comb. **c.-water,** cordial made from c. flowers.

†**Cla·ry,** *v.* 1440. [app. f. CLARION.] To clarion –1587.

Clash (klæʃ), *sb.* 1513. [imit.] **1.** A loud but broken sound resulting from collision. **2.** Collision, conflict; *esp.* of arguments or opinions 1646. **3.** Chatter; the country talk; an item of gossip (usu. malicious). *Sc.* and *n. dial.* 1685.

1. The c. of hail SHELLEY, of Swords STEELE, cymbals MACAULAY, rain COLERIDGE. **2.** The c. of arguments and jar of words COWPER.

Clash (klæʃ), *v.* 1500. [Goes with prec.] **1.** *intr.* To make the sound described under CLASH *sb.* 1; also *trans.* with object of result 1667. **2.** *trans.* To strike (things) together with this noise 1686. **3.** *intr.* To come into violent collision, or conflict (*with, against*) 1618; also *fig.* to conflict; to be incompatible; to disagree (*with*). (The chief current use.) 1646. **4.** To strike in conflict (*trans.* and *intr.*) 1650. **5.** = *dash.* Often with *down. Sc.* 1805. **6.** To slam (a door, etc.). Now *dial.* 1637. **7.** *intr.* To talk maliciously; to gossip. *Sc.* 1697.

1. Arms on Armour clashing bray'd Horrible discord MILT. *P.L.* VI. 209. **3.** His Lordship's statement..may seem to c. with Lord Eldon's J. POWELL. Hence **Cla·sher. Cla·shingly** *adv.*

‖**Clashy, -ee,** *sb. Anglo-Ind.* 1785. [Urdu *khalāṣī*.] A tent-pitcher; a native sailor.

Clasp (klɑsp), *sb.* ME. [Also *clapse* (XV–XVII). See next.] **1.** A fastening, generally of metal, consisting of two interlocking parts; used for holding together parts or ends of anything, *e.g.* parts of garments, the ends of a belt, the covers of a book, etc. Also *fig.* **2.** The act of surrounding or comprehending and holding; embrace (*lit.* and *fig.*) 1604. **3.** A military decoration; a bar of silver bearing the name of a battle, etc., fixed transversely upon the ribbon by which a medal is suspended 1813.

Comb.: **c.-hook,** a pair of hooks, etc., with overlapping jaws; **-knife,** a large knife the blade of which folds or shuts into the handle; **-nail,** a nail with a flat head to clasp the wood.

Clasp (klɑsp), *v.* ME. [Also *clapse* (XIV–XVII). Perh. f. CLIP *v.*¹ after the pair *grasp, grip*; for the terminal sounds cf. HASP and MLG., MDu. *gaspe, gespe* (Du. *gesp* clasp, buckle).] **1.** *trans.* To fasten with or as with a clasp. Also with †*to*, †*together*. **2.** To furnish with a clasp 1460. **3.** To take hold of by means of encircling parts; *loosely* and *poet.* to surround, enfold ME.; to embrace (*lit.* and *fig.*) 1549. **4.** To hold with close pressure of the curved hand 1583. †**5.** *intr.* To lay hold by clasping –1730. **6.** *causal.* To bend or fold tightly *round* or *over* 1798.

3. Thy suppliant I beg, and c. thy knees MILT. *P.L.* X. 918. **4.** We'll c. hands *Per.* II. iv. 57. Hence **Clasped** *ppl. a.* held by or in a clasp; also [f. *sb.*], having a clasp or clasps.

Clasper (klɑ·spəɹ), 1551. [f. prec. + -ER¹.] **1.** One who or that which clasps: *Bot.* a tendril 1577; *Zool.* (in *pl.*) appendages of the male of certain fishes and insects, serving to hold the female 1839. **2.** One who makes clasps 1885.

1. The clasperes of the fyshe called polypus 1551.

Class (klɑs), *sb.* 1656. [prob. first in gen. use in sense 3; – L. CLASSIS. Cf. (O)Fr. *classe.*] **1.** *Rom. Hist.* Each of the six orders into which Servius Tullius divided the Roman people for purposes of taxation. **2.** A division of society according to status 1772; rank (*esp.* high rank), caste 1845. **3.** A division of scholars or students receiving the same instruction or ranked together as of the same standing 1656. **4.** A division of candidates according to merit. Also *attrib.*; and *ellipt.* a class degree 1807. **5.** A division of things according to grade or quality, as *high* or *low, first, second*, etc. 1694. **6.** *gen.* A number of individuals (persons or things) possessing common attributes, and grouped together under a general or 'class' name; a kind, sort, division. (Now the leading sense.) 1664. **b.** *Nat. Hist.* A group intermediate between a *kingdom* and an *order* 1753. **7.** In the Methodist societies: A subdivision of a congregation or society, meeting under a class-leader for religious purposes 1742. Also *attrib.*

2. Higher (Upper), Middle, Lower Classes 1889. **4.** *To take a c. at Oxford*: to take an honours degree. *Comb.*: **c.-list,** a list of the members of a c. (sense 3); also *spec.* a list of names of candidates arranged in classes according to merit, as a result of examination; **-man,** one whose name appears in a class-list; **-name,** a general name.

Class (klɑs), *v.* 1705. [f. prec. sb.] † **1.** To CLASSIFY –1794. **2.** To place in a class, or class-list 1776. **3.** *intr.* (for *refl.*) To rank; to be classed 1748.

2. You c. injustice with wisdom and virtue JOWETT. Tom was not classed at all THACKERAY. Hence **Cla·ssable** *a.*; also (badly) **Cla·ssible. Cla·sser.**

Classic (klæ·sik). 1613. [– Fr. *classique* or L. *classicus*, f. *classis* CLASS; see -IC.]

A. *adj.* **1.** Of the first rank or authority; standard, leading. **2.** Of the standard Greek and Latin writers; belonging to the literature or art of Greek and Roman antiquity 1628. **3.** Belonging to Greek and Latin antiquity 1701. **4.** = CLASSICAL 6. 1744. **5.** *transf.* Of literary or historical note 1787. **6.** *joc.* Recognized, standard 1648. † **7.** = CLASSICAL 7. –1648.

1. But in Latin we have none of c. authority extant MILT. **2.** The Classick Authors STEELE. The C. Renaissance SIR G. SCOTT. **3.** In c. lands COLERIDGE. **4.** A c. purity of design 1889. **5.** C. ground BURNS. **6.** *C. races*: the Two Thousand Guineas, One Thousand Guineas, Derby, Oaks, and St. Leger.

B. *sb.* **1.** A writer, or work, of the first rank and of acknowledged excellence; *esp.* (as originally used) in Greek or Latin literature; in *pl.* the general body of Greek and Latin literature 1711. **2.** A classical scholar 1805. **3.** One who adheres to classical rules and models. (Opp. to *romantic.*) 1885. **4.** Short for *c. style, art*, etc. (see A. 4) 1864.

1. The study of the classics GODWIN. Dante was the c. of his country D'ISRAELI. **2.** A fine c., and a youth of promise LAMB.

Classical (klæ·sikăl), *a.* 1599. [f. L. *classicus* (see prec.) + -AL[1]; see -ICAL.] **1.** = CLASSIC *a.* 1. **2.** = CLASSIC *a.* 2. 1607. **3.** Learned in the classics (CLASSIC *sb.* 1) 1711. **4.** Relating to the classics (CLASSIC *sb.* 1) 1839. **5.** = CLASSIC *a.* 5. 1820. **1.** Of literature: Conforming to the rules or models of Greek and Latin antiquity; hence *transf.* of art; opp. to *romantic* 1820. **1.** *Hist.* Of or pertaining to a classis in a Presbyterian Church (see CLASSIS 3) 1586. † **1.** Class-. –1819.

6. The problem is to present new and profound ideas in a perfectly sound and c. style M. ARNOLD. **7.** C., provincial, and national synods MACAULAY. Hence **Cla·ssicalism** = CLASSICISM. **Cla·ssicalist. Classica·lity,** c. quality or character; c. scholarship; an instance of c. learning, etc. **Cla·ssicalize** *v.* = CLASSICIZE. **Cla·ssically** *adv.*

Classicism (klæ·sisiz'm). 1837. [f. CLASSIC + -ISM.] **1.** The principles of classic literature or art; adherence to classical style. **2.** A classical (*i.e.* Latin or Greek) idiom or form 1873.

Classicist (klæ·sisist). 1839. [f. as prec. + -IST.] An upholder of classic style or form; also, one who advocates the teaching of the Greek and Latin classics in schools.

Classicize (klæ·sisəiz), *v.* 1854. [f. as prec. + -IZE.] To make classic; *intr.* to affect classic style or form.

Classico-, comb. f. L. *classicus* CLASSIC.

Classifiable (klæ·sifəiăb'l), *a.* 1846. [f. CLASSIFY + -ABLE.] Capable of being classified.

Classific (klæ̆si·fik), *a.* *rare.* 1809. [f. *classify*, after pairs like *pacify, pacific*, etc.; see -FIC.] That constitutes a class or classes; pertaining to classification.

Classification (klæ:sifikē̆ⁱ·ʃən). 1790. [– Fr. *classification* (1787); see CLASS *v.*, -FICATION.] **1.** The action of classifying. **2.** The result of classifying; a systematic distribution or arrangement in a class or classes 1794. Hence **Cla:ssifica·tional** *a.* of or pertaining to c.

Classificatory (klæ·sifikēⁱ:təri), *a.* 1837. [f. CLASSIFICATION, after *pacification, pacificatory*; see -ORY[2].] Tending or relating to classification, as the *c. sciences.*

Classify (klæ·sifəi), *v.* 1799. [Back-formation from CLASSIFICATION.] To arrange or distribute in classes according to a method or system. Hence **Cla·ssifier,** one who classifies.

‖ **Classis** (klæ·sis). Pl. **classes.** 1593. [L., see CLASS *sb.*] **1.** = CLASS *sb.* 1. 1601. † **2.** A division according to rank; a CLASS –1714. **3.** *Eccl.* In certain churches: an inferior judicatory consisting of the elders or pastors of the parishes or churches of a district; a presbytery 1593; the district thus united 1653. † **4.** In a library: The compartment formed by the book-shelves in the adjacent sides of two stalls, together with those under the window between them –1710.

Cla·ssmate, -mate. 1862. A fellow student in the same class.

Classy (klɑ·si), *a.* *slang* or *colloq.* 1891. [f. CLASS *sb.* + -Y[1].] Superior, high-class.

Clastic (klæ·stik), *a.* 1875. [– Fr. *clastique* in same senses, f. Gr. κλαστός broken in pieces + *-ique* -IC.] **1.** *Geol.* Consisting of broken pieces of older rocks 1877. **2.** *Anat.* (Of a model) Composed of separable pieces; pertaining to such a model 1875.

Clathrate (klæ·þreⁱt), *a.* 1858. [– L. *clathratus, clathrare*, f. *clathri* (pl.) lattice (Gr. κλῆθρα bars); see -ATE[2].] *Bot.* Resembling lattice-work; cancellate. So **Cla·throid** *a.*

Clatter (klæ·təɹ), *sb.* 1460. [In XV *clater*, but possibly coeval with the verb; corresp. to MDu. *klatere*, Du. *klater* rattle.] **1.** A rattling noise made by the rapidly repeated collision of sonorous bodies that do not ring 1578. **2.** Noisy talk; gabble 1460; in *mod. Sc.*, gossip, tittle-tattle 1596.

1. The c. of the hoes among the pebbles KINGSLEY. **2.** Hold stille thi clattur 1460. Such a c. of tongues in empty heads LONGF. Hence **Cla·ttery** *a.* (*colloq.*).

Clatter (klæ·təɹ), *v.* [OE. *_clatrian_, implied in *clatrung*, corresp. to (M)Du. *klateren* rattle, chatter.] **1.** *intr.* To make the noise described under CLATTER *sb.*; to rattle. Said of the instruments or the agent. Also with *along, down, over*, etc. **2.** *trans.* To cause to rattle 1537. **3.** *intr.* To chatter, babble; in *mod. Sc.*, to tattle ME. † **4.** To utter in a chattering way; prate about –1735. Also *absol.*

1. They fall a-clattering with . . drums and kettles DE FOE. **2.** The servants c. the plates and glasses TUCKER. **3.** The Load-starre of Reformation as some men c. MILT. Hence **Cla·tterer.**

Claucht; see CLEEK *v.*

Claude Lorraine glass. Also **Claude-glass.** 1789. [Named from *Claude* (of) *Lorraine* (1600–1682).] A somewhat convex dark or coloured hand-mirror, used to reduce the proportions of a landscape.

† **Clau·dicant,** *a.* 1624. [– *claudicant-*, pres. ppl. stem of L. *claudicare* limp, f. *claudus* lame; see -ANT[1].] Lame, halting (*lit.* and *fig.*) –1708. So † **Claudica·tion** the action of limping.

Claught, pa. t. of CLEEK *v.*, to snatch, clutch. Also as *sb.* and *v.* *Sc.* 1800.

Clause (klǭz). ME. [– (O)Fr. *clause* = Pr. *clauza* = Gallo-Rom. *_clausa_, for L. *clausula* close of a rhetorical period, (later) conclusion of a legal formula, section of law, fem. dim. f. *claus-*, pa. ppl. stem of *claudere* CLOSE *v.*] **1.** A short sentence; a single passage of a discourse or writing; a distinct member of a sentence, *esp.* in *Gram.* one containing a subject and predicate. **2.** A particular and separate article, stipulation, or proviso, in any formal or legal document ME. † **3.** Close; *esp.* the close of a sentence –1724.

2. The passing of a statute of twenty clauses STUBBS. *Penal C., Saving C.* **3.** The sweet falling of the clauses BACON. *Comb.* **C.-rolls,** = CLOSE-*rolls*.

† **Clau·ster, -re.** [OE. *clauster* – L. *claustrum*; see CLOISTER. In ME. prob. formed anew from L.] A cloister, cell, or monastery –1726.

Claustral (klǭ·străl), *a.* ME. [– late L. *claustralis*, f. *claustrum* CLOISTER; see -AL[1].] **1.** Pertaining to a cloister. **2.** Cloister-like 1862.

Claustrophobia (klǭstrŏfōᵘ·biă). 1879. [mod.L., f. *claustrum* CLOISTER + -PHOBIA.] *Path.* A morbid dread of confined places.

† **Clau·sure.** ME. [– late L. *clausura*; see CLOSURE.] The action of closing or enclosing –1670; closed condition –1815; that which encloses –1669.

Claut (klǭt), *sb.* *Sc.* and *n. dial.* 1697. [perh. conn. w. *claw* or *claught.*] A handful, a rakeful, a scraping. So **Claut** *v.* to scratch, claw, rake, scrape out, etc.

Clavate (klē̆ⁱ·veⁱt), *a.* 1661. [– mod.L. *clavatus*, f. *clava* club; see -ATE[2].] † **1.** Knobbed. **2.** *Zool.* and *Bot.* Club-shaped; thickened towards the apex like a club 1813. So **Cla·vated** *a.*

Clave, pa. t. of CLEAVE *v.*

‖ **Clavecin** (klæ·vĭsin). 1819. [Fr. – med.L. *clavicymbalum*; see CLAVICYMBAL.] The French name of the Harpsichord. Hence **Cla·vecinist,** a player on the c.

Clavel (klæ·vĕl). Now *dial.* 1602. [– OFr. *clavel* (mod. *claveau*) :– med.L. *clavellus* dim. of L. *clavis* key; see -EL.] The lintel over a fire-place. Also in *comb.*, as **c.-piece,** mantel-piece. var. **Clavy.**

† **Cla·vellated,** *a.* 1660. [– med.L. *clavellatus* (*cineres clavellati, clavati*), f. *clavellus*, dim. of L. *clavus* nail, + *-atus* -ATE[2]. So OFr. *cendre clavelée* (mod. *gravelée*).] In *Clavellated Ashes*: Potash obtained from the dried and calcined lees of wine, for the use of dyers –1735.

Claver (klē̆ⁱ·vəɹ), *sb.* *Sc.* and *n. dial.* 1689. [Goes with CLAVER *v.*[2]] Idle garrulous talk; a piece of idle gossip.

Ane Knox deaving us a' wi' his clavers ?1689.

Claver (klæ·vəɹ), *v.*[1] Now *dial.* ME. [Cf. Da. *klavre*, and mod.Du. *klaveren*, in same sense.] To climb, clamber.

Claver (klē̆ⁱ·vəɹ), *v.*[2] *Sc.* and *n. dial.* 1605. [Origin unkn.] To talk idly; to gossip, prate.

Clavichord (klæ·vikǭɹd). Now *Hist.* 1483. [– med.L. *clavichordium*, f. L. *clavis* key + *chorda* string, CHORD.] A musical instrument with strings and keys, in its developed form resembling a square pianoforte.

Clavicle (klæ·vik'l), 1615. [– L. *clavicula* small key, door-bolt, applied in mod.L. to the bone because of its shape, dim. of *clavis* key; see -CULE.] **1.** *Anat.* The collar-bone, which extends from the breast-bone to the shoulder-blade, forming part of the pectoral arch. In birds the two clavicles are united into the furculum or merrythought. † **2.** *Bot.* A tendril –1750. † **3.** *Conch.* The head of a spiral shell –1774.

Clavicorn (klæ·vikǭɹn). [– mod.L. *clavicornis*, f. L. *clava* club + *cornu* horn. Cf. Fr. *clavicorne* adj.] *Ent.* Club-horned: applied to the *Clavicornes*, a subsection of pentamerous beetles having club-shaped antennæ.

Clavicular (klævi·kiŭlăɹ), *a.* 1824. [f. L. *clavicula* + -AR[1].] Of or pertaining to the CLAVICLE. Hence **Clavi·cularly** *adv.*

Clavicymbal (klævisi·mbăl). Now *Hist.* 1492. [– med.L. *clavicymbalum*, f. *clavis* key + *cymbalum* CYMBAL. See also CLAVECIN.] An old name of the Harpsichord.

‖ **Clavicytherium** (klæ:visiþīᵊ·riŏm). [Better *clavicitherium*, f. L. *clavis* + CITHER.] An early musical instrument; in effect, an upright spinet. var. **Clavici·thern.** BROWNING.

‖ **Cla·vier.** 1708. [– Fr. *clavier*, or its deriv. G. *klavier* – med.L. *claviarius*, orig. 'key-bearer', f. L. *clavis* key.] **1.** The keyboard or set of keys of a musical instrument. **2.** (klăvīᵊ·r). A German name of all keyboard instruments with strings; now *esp.* the pianoforte 1845. **3.** A dummy keyboard for practice.

Claviform (klæ·vifǭɹm), *a.* 1817. [f. L. *clava* club + -FORM.] Club-shaped.

† **Claviger** (klæ·vidʒəɹ). 1606. [– L. *claviger*, f. *clavis* key or *clava* club + *-ger*; see -GEROUS.] One who carries a key or a club –1712. So **Clavi·gerous** *a.* (Dicts.)

‖ **Clavis** (klēⁱ·vis). 1649. [L.] A key.

‖ **Clavus** (klēⁱ·vɒ̆s). [L. *clavus* nail.] **1.** = CORN *sb.*² **2.** The disease ERGOT.

Claw (klǭ), *sb.* [OE. *clawu* (new f. the obl. cases, the orig. nom. being repr. by *clēa* CLEE) = OFris. *klē*, *klāwe*, OS. *clāuua* (Du. *klauw*), OHG. *klāwa* (G. *klaue*) :– WGmc. **klāwa*.] **1.** The sharp horny nail arming the feet of birds and some beasts; also *transf.*; *loosely*, the foot thus armed OE. † **2.** A hoof, or one of the parts of a (cloven) hoof –1661. **3.** *fig.* ME. **4.** *transf.* Any contrivance resembling a claw OE. **5.** *Bot.* The narrow sharpened base of the petal, in some flowers, by which it is attached 1794.

3. *In one's claws*: in one's possession or power. **4.** The C. of a Hammer 1677.

attrib. and *Comb.*: **c.-hammer,** a hammer with a c. for extracting nails; **-hammer coat** (*colloq.*), a tail coat for evening dress; † **-poll,** a toady (cf. *claw-back*).

Hence **Clawed** *a.* having claws. **Claw·less** *a.*

Claw (klǭ), *v.* Pa. t. and pple. **clawed.** [OE. *clawian*, deriv. of *clawu* CLAW.] **1.** *trans.* To scratch or tear with or as with claws. **2.** To seize, grip, clutch, or pull with claws 1557; *intr.* to grasp or clutch (*at*, etc.); to scratch *at* ME. **3.** *trans.* To scratch gently, so as to relieve itching or to soothe ME. Also † *fig.* **4.** Hence: To flatter, cajole, fawn upon. Now *dial.* ME. Also † *intr.* **5.** *Naut.* (*intr.*) To beat to windward from a lee-shore. Also *to c. off* or *from* (the shore). 1642. † **6.** To strike as with claws; to beat. Now *dial.* 1584.

2. But Age..hath clawed me in his clutch *Haml.* v. i. 80. **3.** If eny wight wold c. us on the galle CHAUCER.

Phrases. † *To c. the back of* (see sense 3); hence † **Claw·-back,** a toady. *C. me and I'll c. thee* (see sense 4). † *To c. away, off*: to rate soundly, scold; † to get rid of.

Clay (klēⁱ), *sb.* [OE. *clǣġ* = OFris. *klāy*, (M)LG., (M)Du. *klei* :– WGmc. **klaija*, f. **klai-* **klei-* **kli-*; see CLAM *v.*¹, CLEAM, CLEAVE *v.*²] **1.** A stiff viscous earth, consisting mainly of aluminium silicate, and derived mostly from the decomposition of felspathic rocks. It is found in beds or other deposits at various depths, and forms with water a tenacious paste which may be moulded into any shape, and hardens when dried. † **2.** Used *transf.* of *bitumen*, etc. –1584. **3.** Used loosely for: Earth, moist earth, mire, mud ME. **4.** Earth as the material of the human body (cf. Gen. 2:7); hence, the human body; the material part of man ME. **5.** Short for *clay-pipe* (colloq.) 1863. **6.** *attrib.* Of or made of clay 1523.

1. *Boulder, Kimmeridge, London, Oxford, Purbeck C.*, etc. *Brick, fire, plastic, porcelain, potter's c.*; *pipe-c.*, etc. **2.** The toughe cleye of Babilon called Bitumen EDEN. C. and C., differs in dignity *Cymb.* IV. ii. 4. *To moisten* or *wet one's c.* (joc.): to drink.

Comb.: **c.-band,** a thin stratum of c.; hence *c.-band ironstone*, a variety of Chalybite; **-brained** *a.*, dull, clod-pated; **-cold** *a.*, as cold as c.: usually of a dead body; **c. iron-ore, c. ironstone,** any iron-ore containing much c., *esp.* argillaceous hæmatite; **-mill,** a mill for mixing and tempering c.; **-pipe,** a tobacco-pipe made of baked c. (pipe-c.); **-pit,** a pit from which c. is dug; **-puddle** (see PUDDLE); **-slate,** an argillaceous sedimentary rock, of bluish or greenish colour, having a cleavage which crosses the original stratification at all angles; **-stone,** *Min.* a felspathic rock which emits an odour of damp c. when breathed upon.

Hence **Cla·yen** *a.* (*arch.*) of c.; clay-. **Clay·ey** *a.* full of c.; of the nature of c.; soiled with c.; c.-like; also *fig.* of 'mortal clay'. **Clay·ish** *a.* ? *Obs.*

Clay (klēⁱ), *v.* 1523. [f. prec. sb.] **1.** To cover or dress with clay. **2.** To treat (sugar) with clay in refining 1703.

Claye (klēⁱ). 1708. [– Fr. *claie* :– med.L. *clāta, clēta*, of Gaulish orig.; cf. Ir. *cliath* hurdle.] A hurdle.

Claymore (klēⁱ·mōᵊɹ). 1772. *Hist.* [f. Gaelic *claidheamh* klai·əv sword + *mór* great.] The two-edged (rarely *two-handed*) broadsword of the ancient Scottish Highlanders. Also *ellipt.* a man armed with this.

Cleach, cleech (klītʃ), *v.* Now *dial.* [ME. *cleche*, repr. OE. **clǣċan* (**clǣhte*) clutch, of unkn. orig. See CLEEK *v.*, CLICK *v.*²] **1.** To clutch (*trans.* and *intr.*). **2.** To lift (water, etc.) in the hollow of the hand, or with a shallow vessel. ME.

Clead, cleed, *v.* [ME. (north.) *cleþe*, pa. t. *cledde* – ON. *clæða*, pa. t. *klædda* :– Gmc. **klaiþjan*, f. **klaiþa-* cloth.] = CLOTHE *v.* Hence **Clea·ding** *vbl. sb.* clothing (*Sc.* and *n. Eng.*); *Mech.* a casing (as of felt or wood), to prevent radiation of heat, etc.

Cleam, cleme, *v.* Now *dial.* [OE. *clǣman* smear, anoint, daub = MDu. *klēmen*, OHG. *kleimen*, ON. *kleima* daub, plaster :– Gmc. **klaimjan*, f. **klaimaz* clay, f. base repr. by CLAY.] To smear, bedaub, plaster; to cause to stick.

Clean (klīn), *a.* [OE. *clǣne* = OFris. *klēne*, *kleine*, OS. *klēni* (Du. *kleen*, *klein* small), OHG. *kleini* clear, delicate, neat, small (G. *klein* small) :– WGmc. **klaini*. The historical orig. sense 'clear, pure' is most nearly preserved by Eng.] † **1.** Clear; undimmed –1708. **2.** Pure; free from foreign matter OE. **3.** Free from dirt or filth. Now the ordinary sense. OE. **4.** Free from spiritual or moral pollution. Const. † *of*, *from*. OE. **5.** Free from ceremonial or sanitary defilement OE. **6.** Clean in habit 1568. **7.** Of style or language: Free from faults, correct, pure (*arch.*) ME. **8.** Proper; well-built, shapely; clever, smart, dexterous ME. **9.** Clear of obstructions, inequalities, or unevennesses ME. **10.** With nouns of action, etc.; Entire, complete, perfect, sheer. (Cf. *To sweep clean.*) ME. Also in *comb.*; see after the adv.

1. All of Diamond perfect pure and cleene SPENSER *F.Q.* I. vii. 33. **2.** C. water ME., coal 1872, land (*mod.*). **3.** Cleane linnen *Mids. N.* IV. ii. 41. A c. ship DE FOE. A c. copy 1889. *C. Bill of Health* (fig.): see BILL *sb.*³ *To make a c. breast* (fig.): see BREAST. **4.** Create in mee a cleane heart, O God *Ps.* 51:10. **7.** A clene and elegant stile ELYOT. **8.** The hocks and legs..'clean' 1836. A..c. field *Cricket Annual.* **9.** C. coast, harbour SMYTH, oak 1884. A c. wound 1807. **10.** To make cleane work COTGR. Hence **Clea·nish** *a.* pretty c.

Clean (klīn), *adv.* [OE. *clǣne*, *clēne*, f. the adj.] **1.** In a clean manner (see CLEAN *a.* 1, 2, 8, 10). **2.** Without anything omitted or left; wholly, quite, absolutely OE.

1. The room must be c. swept 1889. **2.** C. off his head 1883. C. dismay'd SPENSER, bowled 1888.

Clean-, *adj.* and *adv.* in *comb.*

1. With pples., as *c.-built, -complexioned, -going*, etc. **2. c.-cut,** sharply defined; **-fingered,** with nimble fingers; scrupulous, honest; **-handed,** having clean hands, free from wrong-doing; **-limbed,** shapely of limb; **-timbered,** well-built, clean-limbed.

Clean (klīn), *v.* 1450. [In XV *clene*, f. the adj.; in current use more literal than *to cleanse.*] To make CLEAN (see CLEAN *a.*). Also *absol.* and *intr.* 1708.

To c. shoes 1714, a portrait TYNDALL, a ship's bottom DAMPIER, fish LANE, land 1886.

Phrases. *To c. out*: to c. by emptying; *transf.* to exhaust, leave bare. Also *fig. slang.* To rook. Hence **Clea·nable** *a.* **Clea·ner,** one who or that which cleans.

Clean, *sb.* 1872. [f. the verb.] An act of cleaning: chiefly in comb., as *a clean up, out*, etc. *spec.* (in *U.S. Mining*) *clean-up*: the collecting of all the product of a given period or operation.

Cleanly (kle·nli), *a.* [OE. *clǣnlić*; see -LY¹.] † **1.** Morally or spiritually clean –1683. † **2.** Clean: as clothes, etc. –1590. **3.** Habitually clean; habitually kept clean 1500. **4.** Conducing to cleanness 1611. † **5.** Neat; dexterous, elegant –1712.

1. A man of c. behaviour 1683. **3.** Some plain but c. country maid DRYDEN. An honest c. Alehouse WALTON. **4.** A c. diet BURTON. Hence **Clea·nlily** *adv.* **Clea·nliness,** c. quality or state.

Cleanly (klī·nli), *adv.* [OE. *clǣnlīće*; see -LY².] In a clean manner (see CLEAN *a.*); † completely –1655; † ably, adroitly –1642.

Ile purge..and liue c. 1 *Hen. IV*, v. iv. 169.

Cleanness (klī·nˌnes). [OE. *clǣnnes*; see -NESS.] The quality or state of being CLEAN (*lit.* and *fig.*).

† *C. of teeth*: scarcity of food. (*Amos* 4:6.)

Cleansable (kle·nzăb'l), *a.* 1483. [f. CLEANSE *v.* + -ABLE.] That can be cleansed.

Cleanse (klenz), *v.* [OE. *clǣnsian*; the mod. sp. follows the adj.] **1.** To make clean; to purify, to free from dirt, infection, guilt, pollution, ℞ charge, etc. Also *absol.* In the literal senses now usually *clean.* **2.** To clear, to rid *of*, *from* ME. **3.** To purge; also *absol.* OE.

1. You cannot c. your heart with tears TRENCH. What God hath cleansed, that call not thou common *Acts* 10:15. Hence **Clea·nser.**

Clear (klīᵊɹ), *a.*, *adv.*, and *sb.* [ME. *clēr* – OFr. *cler* (mod. *clair*) :– L. *clarus* bright, clear, etc.]

A. *adj.* **I. 1.** Of light: † *orig.* Brightly shining –1667; *now*, pure, unclouded. Of a fire: Without flame or smoke. 1611. **2.** Fully light, bright, serene (*arch.*); free from cloud, mists, and haze; *fig.* serene ME. **3.** Transparent, translucent ME. **4.** Shining; lustrous ME.; † of women: Beauteous –1578. † **5.** *fig.* Illustrious. [So L. *clarus.*] –1605.

1. Cleare as the sun *S. of S.* 6:10. **2.** Almost cleere dawn *Meas. for M.* IV. ii. 226. A c. frosty evening 1872. *fig.* His brow grew c. LYTTON.

II. 1. Clearly seen, distinct 1835. **2.** Easy to understand, perspicuous ME. **3.** Distinct, free from confusion ME. **4.** Evident, plain ME. **5.** Of the eyes, etc.: Having keen perception 1576. **6.** That discerns without confusion of ideas ME. **7.** Of persons: Subjectively free from doubt; certain, positive, determined 1604.

2. The words are cleare and plaine 1615. To make oneself c. JOWETT. **3.** C. notions of law and government MACAULAY. **4.** Quoth Hudibras, The case is c. BUTLER. **6.** C. thinkers always have a c. style BUCKLE. **7.** I am not c. on the point HT. MARTINEAU.

III. Of sound: Ringing, pure and well-defined; distinctly audible ME.

IV. 1. *fig.* from I. 3: Pure, unsophisticated ME. **2.** Unspotted; innocent ME.

1. Fame is the spur that the c. spirit doth raise *Lycidas* 70. **2.** Duncane..hath bin So cleere in his great Office *Macb.* I. vii. 18.

V. 1. Unencumbered; net 1500. **2.** Unqualified; absolute, complete; sheer 1529. **3.** Free from contact; quite free; quit, rid 1658. **4.** Unobstructed; unoccupied; open 1568. **5.** Emptied of contents, load, or cargo 1607. **6.** Free from legal or other complications 1635. **7.** *U.S. slang.* Unadulterated, pure, real 1837.

1. A c. thousand a year for doing..nothing COBBETT. **2.** Three feet c. 1889. **3.** Let me be cleere of thee *Twel. N.* IV. i. 4. **4.** Seeing the coast cleere GREENE. **6.** I was now a c. man DE FOE.

B. *adv.* [Partly the adj. used predicatively; partly after native Eng. advs., *esp.* CLEAN *adv.*] **1.** Brightly ME. † **2.** = CLEARLY –1782. † **3.** = CLEAN *adv.* 2. –1690.

C. *sb.* **I.** Ellipt. † **1.** A fair lady (in ME.). † **2.** Brightness, clearness –1611. **3.** Clear space 1715.

2. Thy cleere with cloudy darkes is scar'd LODGE. **3.** *In the c.*: in interior measurement.

II. Verbal sb. f. CLEAR *v.* A clearing of the sky, weather, etc. 1694.

Comb.: **c.-cut** *a.* sharply chiselled, sharply defined; **-eyed** *a.* having clear eyes (*lit.* and *fig.*); **-headed,** having, or characteristic of, a clear head; **-hea·dedness; -si·ghted** *a.* having clear sight; **-ness.**

Hence **Clea·rish** *a.* **Clea·rly** *adv.* **Clea·rness.**

Clear (klīᵊɹ), *v.* ME. [f. CLEAR *a.*] **1.** To make or become CLEAR or bright. Also with *up.* **2.** To make pure from stain; to purify, clarify; to prove innocent; to acquit ME. **3.** To make (a person) clear as to a matter ME.; to elucidate ME.; † to prove –1770. **4.** To make clear of things or persons that obstruct or cumber a space 1530. **5.** Hence, *gen.* To free or rid *of.* Now a leading sense. 1535. **6.** To remove, so as to leave the place or way clear. Also with *away, off, out.* 1672. **7.** *intr.* To depart, so as to leave the place clear. Also with *off, out.* 1832. **8.** To make or become clear of contents or burden; to exhaust 1699. **9.** To get (a thing or oneself) clear *of* or *from* 1599; to pass clear of, get clear through or away from 1634; to leap clear over, pass over 1791. **10.** To settle, discharge a *debt*, *bill*, etc. Also with *off*. 1596. † *intr.* To settle *with* –1796. **11.** To set free from debt, etc. 1704. Also *absol.* **12.** To free (a ship or cargo) by satisfying the customs, harbour dues, etc. 1703; also *absol.*; *hence*, to leave a port under such conditions 1807. **13.** To make in clear profit 1719. **14.** To pass through the Clearing-House 1868.

1. *To c. the air*: *orig.* to free from mists, etc.; *now*, from sultry conditions which precede a storm. To c. the sight SHAKS., the brain DISRAELI, the Voice DE FOE. **2.** How! would'st thou c. rebellion ADDISON. To c. oneself of an imputation LOCKE. **3.** To c. one's meaning 1857. The evidence of time doth c. this assertion BACON. **4.** Police to c. the way SALA. To c. the coasts 1530, the decks 1870, a ship for action 1889, land (for cultivation) 1705. **5.** To c. the house of people 1860, cotton †*from* dirt URE. **6.** To c. a wreck 1823. **8.** *To c. a ship*: to discharge it of its cargo. **9.** With one brave bound the copse he cleared SCOTT. **11.** To c. an encumbered estate W. PENN. **12.** The steamer..cleared at Christiania..bound for New York 1889.

With adverbs: **To c. out: a.** To 'clean out' of cash. **b.** To clear on leaving port. **To c. up:** To make or become clear, orderly, or perspicuous.

Hence **Clea·rage**, the action of clearing; † a clearing. **Clea·rer**, one who or that which CLEARS; also used *techn.*

Clearance (klīᵊ·răns). 1563. [f. CLEAR *v.* + -ANCE.] **1.** The action of clearing, or making clear. **2.** *Comm.* The clearing of a ship at the Custom-House. Cf. CLEAR *v.* 12. 1731. **3.** A clear space. *spec.* In the steam-engine: the distance between the cylinder-cover and the piston when at the end of its stroke. 1788. **4.** A CLEARING (sense 2) 1839. **5.** A certificate that a ship has been cleared on leaving port 1727. **6.** Clear or net profit (*rare*) 1864.

1. The c. of a property from encumbrances 1884, of a storm FROUDE. The Highland clearances 1883.

Clear-cole (klīᵊ·ɹkoᵘl). 1823. [– Fr. *claire colle* clear glue or size.] A preparation of size mixed with whiting or white-lead used as a first coating in house-painting; a coating of size in gilding.

Clearing (klīᵊ·riŋ), *vbl. sb.* ME. [f. CLEAR *v.* + -ING¹.] **1.** The action of the vb. CLEAR, in various senses. **2.** A piece of land cleared for cultivation 1823. † **3.** *Comm.* = CLEARANCE 2. –1769. **4.** The passing of cheques, bills, etc., through a clearing-house 1883. Also *attrib.*

1. Upon his said Justification, and C. 1604. **2.** A tiny c. pared from the edge of the wood LOWELL.

Clearing House, clearing-house. 1832. An institution in London established by the bankers for the adjustment of their mutual claims for cheques and bills, by exchanging them and settling the balances. Extended to similar institutions, as the *Railway Clearing House*, etc. Also *attrib.*

Clear-obscure. [After Fr. *clair-obscur.*] 1778. = CHIAROSCURO.

Clear-starch, *v.* 1709. To stiffen and dress linen with clear or colourless starch.

Clear-story, var. of CLERESTORY.

Cleat (klīt), *sb.* [OE. **clēat* = MLG. **klōt* (Du. *kloot*) ball, sphere, OHG. *klōz* clod, lump, wedge (G. *kloss* clod, dumpling):– WGmc. **klaut-*, rel. to **klūt-* CLOT, CLOUT *sb.*¹] **1.** A wedge ME. **2.** *Naut.* Orig. a small wedge of wood bolted on its side to a spar, etc., to stop anything from slipping (*stop-c.*), afford a footing (*step-c.*), or serve as a point of attachment or resistance ME. Extended to pieces of wood (or iron) of various shapes, bolted on to parts of a ship for various purposes, as a *belaying c.*, a *launching c.*, etc. 1769. **3.** A wedge-shaped or other piece fastened on, or left projecting, for any purpose; *e.g.* as a handle 1611.

Cleat (klīt), *v.* 1794. [f. prec. sb.] To fasten to, or with, a cleat; to strengthen with thin plates of metal (*dial.*).

Cleavable (klī·văb'l), *a.* 1846. [f. CLEAVE *v.*¹ + -ABLE.] That can be cloven, cleft, or split.

Cleavage (klī·vĕdʒ). 1816. [f. as prec. + -AGE.] **1.** The action or faculty of cleaving or splitting asunder; the state of being cleft; division (*lit.* and *fig.*) 1867. **2.** *spec.* (*Min.*) Arrangement in laminæ which can be split asunder, and along the planes of which the substance naturally splits; the property of splitting along such planes 1830. **3.** (*Geol.*) *Slaty c.*: the fissile structure in clay slate and similar rocks, whereby these split into the thin laminæ or slates used in roofing, etc. This structure is quite distinct from, and in origin posterior to, the stratification and jointing. 1839. (with *pl.*) The plane in which a crystal or rock may be split 1817.

Cleave, *sb. Ir.* 1586. [– Ir. *cliabh* basket, cage, chest.] A basket.

Cleave (klīv), *v.*¹ Pa. t. **clove, clave, cleaved, cleft**; Pa. pple. **cloven, clove, cleaved, cleft.** [OE. *clēofan* = OS. *klioban* (Du. *klieven*), OHG. *kliuban* (G. *klieben*), ON. *kljúfa*:– Gmc. **kleuƀan.*] **1.** *trans.* To part or divide by a cutting blow; to hew asunder; to split; to pierce and penetrate 1558. **2.** To separate or sever by dividing or splitting ME. **3.** *intr.* (for *refl.*) To split or fall asunder ME. **4.** *intr.* To cleave one's way 1655.

1. Abraham..claue the wood for the burnt offering *Gen.* 22:3. To cleaue a heart in twaine *Meas. for M.* III. i. 63. To c. the flood MILT. *P.R.* III. 433. **3.** The ground claue asunder *Numb.* 16:31.

Cleave (klīv), *v.*² Pa. t. **cleaved, clave.** Pa. pple. **cleaved.** [The pres. form repr. OE. *cleofian, clifian* = OS. *clibon* (Du. *kleven*), OHG. *klebēn* (G. *kleben*) :– WGmc. wk. vb. **kliƀōjan, -æjan*, f. **kliƀ-*, the strong form of which is repr. by OE. *clīfan*, ME. *clive*, pa. t. *claf*, later *clave* (A.V.) = O.S. *bikliƀan* (Du. *beklijven*), OHG. *klīban*, ON. *klīfa*; f. **klī-* stick, adhere (cf. CLAY, CLIMB).] **1.** To stick fast or adhere, as by a glutinous surface, *to*. Also *fig.* **2.** In wider sense: To cling or hold fast *to*; to attach oneself *to* ME. **3.** To adhere or cling *to* (a person, party, principle, etc.); to remain attached *to* ME. † **4.** To remain steadfast –1594.

1. Their tongue cleaued to the roof of their mouth *Job* 29:10. *fig.* A..phrase cleaving as it were to the memory PALEY. **3.** He schal clyue to his wyf WYCLIF *Ephes.* 5:31. The mercenary soldiers..clave to King Henry FREEMAN.

Cleavelandite (klī·vlăndəit). 1823. [f. *Cleaveland* the mineralogist + -ITE¹ 2 b.] *Min.* A variety of albite from Chesterfield, Mass.

Cleaver (klī·vəɹ). 1483. [f. CLEAVE *v.*¹ + -ER¹.] One who or that which cleaves; *spec.* a butcher's chopper for cutting up carcasses.

Cleavers (klī·vəɹz), **cli-** (kli-). [Earliest forms *cliure, clyure*, superseding OE. *clīfe* = OS. *klība*, OHG. *klība*, f. base of CLEAVE *v.*² Apprehended as an agent-noun of *clive*, CLEAVE.] *Bot.* The climbing plant *Galium aparine* or Goose-grass, which adheres by its hooked prickles to clothes, etc.

‖ **Cleché, -ée** (kle·tʃi, ‖ kleʃe), *a.* 1688. [Fr. *cléché* key-holed.] *Her.* **a.** Voided or hollowed throughout, as a cross showing only a narrow border. **b.** Of a cross: Having the extremities shaped like the handle of an ancient key.

Cleck (klek), *v.* Chiefly *Sc.* ME. [– ON. *klekja* hatch. Cf. CLETCH.] *trans.* Of birds: To hatch. Also *transf.* and *fig.* Hence **Cle·cking** *vbl. sb.* hatching.

Cledge (kledʒ). 1723. [prob. conn. w. CLAG.] In Kent, etc., clay or clayey soil; in Bedfordshire, the upper of the two beds of Fuller's Earth. Hence **Cle·dgy** *a.* clayey; sticky.

Clee. Now *dial.* OE. [var. of CLAW, repr. OE. *clēa* (*clēo*). See CLAW.] = CLAW *sb.* 1, 2.

Cleek (klīk), *sb.* Chiefly *Sc.* ME. [f. CLEEK *v.*; cf. CLICK *sb.*²] **1.** A large hook or crook for catching hold of something. **2.** *Golf.* An iron-headed club with a straight narrow face and a long shaft 1829.

Cleek (klīk), *v. n. dial.* Pa. t. **claucht, claught.** ME. [north. var. of *cleach, cleech*, repr. OE. **clǣćan* clutch; cf. CLICK *v.*²] **1.** *trans.* To seize with the clutch or hand; to clutch firmly, suddenly, or eagerly. **2.** To snatch ME. **3.** To lay hold of with a cleek 1857.

Clef¹ (klef). 1579. [– Fr. *clef* :– L. *clavis* key.] *Mus.* A character placed on a particular line of a stave, to indicate the name and pitch of the notes standing on that line, and hence of the other notes. Occas. loosely = *stave*. Also *fig.*

There are three clefs in use, the C, tenor, or alto clef, the G or treble clef, and the F or bass clef, which denote respectively the middle C on a piano, the G above, and the F below. They are written respectively as here shown. In modern music the C clef is called the soprano, alto, or tenor clef, as it is placed upon the first, third, or fourth line of the stave.

† **Clef**². *rare.* 1494. [app. AFr. **clef* :– L. *clavus* nail.] The pin of a weighing beam –1568.

Cleft, clift, *sb.* [Earliest form *clift*; the present form, due to assim. to *cleft*, pa. pple. of CLEAVE *v.*¹, dates from XVI. In XVI–XVIII confounded w. CLIFF.] **1.** A space or division made by cleaving; a split, fissure, crack, crevice. **2.** *spec.* **a.** The parting of the thighs, the fork. Now *dial.* ME. **b.** A crack of the skin; a disease of the feet of horses 1576. **3.** Split wood, *esp.* for fuel. Now *dial.* ME.

Comb. **c.-graft** *v.* to graft in a c. or slit made for the purpose.

Cleft (kleft), *ppl. a.* ME. [f. CLEAVE *v.*¹; cf. CLOVEN.] Split asunder; partly split; bifurcate. Also *fig.*

C. palate: a malformation in which a longitudinal gap exists in the middle or on either side of the roof of the mouth. *A c. stick*: a position in which advance and retreat are alike impossible, a fix. *C. foot, hoof*: = *cloven foot*, etc.

Cleft, pa. t. and pple. of CLEAVE *v.*¹; occas. of CLEAVE *v.*²

Cleg (kleg). Now *Sc.* and *dial.* 1449. [– ON. *kleggi*, mod. Norw. *klegg.*] A gadfly, horse-fly, or breeze.

Cleido-mastoid (kləido,mæ·stoid), *a.* [f. Gr. κλείς, κλειδ- key, clavicle + MASTOID.] *Anat.* Pertaining to the clavicle and mastoid process.

Cleistogamic (kləistogæ·mik), *a.* 1877. [f. Gr. κλειστός closed + γάμος marriage + -IC; cf. *phanerogamic.*] *Bot.* Applied to certain small inconspicuous permanently closed flowers, adapted for self-fertilization, occurring in various plants on the same individuals as the normal flowers, which in such cases are either cross-fertilized or barren. So **Cleisto·gamous** *a.* **Cleisto·gamy,** th occurrence of cleistogamous flowers.

Cleithral (kləi·þrăl), *a.* 1850. [f. Gr. κλεῖθρον bar for closing a door + -AL¹.] *Gr. Arch.* Of a temple: Covered in: opp. to HYPÆTHRAL.

Clem (klem), **clam** (klæm), *v. dial.* 1540. [repr. OE. *beclemman* confine, shut in, OS. *klemmian* pinch, constrain :– WGmc. **klammjan*, f. Gmc. **klam-* press or squeeze together; see CLAM *sb.*¹] *trans.* To pinch; to waste with hunger, starve. Also *intr.*

Clematis (kle·mătis). 1551. [– L. *clematis* – Gr. κληματίς, f. κλῆμα vine-branch.] *Bot.* A genus of twining shrubs (N.O. *Ranunculaceæ*), having flowers with a showy calyx and no corolla, and seed-vessels adorned with long feathery appendages. The only British species is *C. vitalba*, also called Virgin's Bower, Traveller's Joy, and Old Man's Beard. † **2.** The Periwinkle –1607.

† **Cle·mence.** [– Fr. *clémence* – L. *clementia*; see next.] = next.

Clemency (kle·mĕnsi). 1553. [– L. *clementia*; see -ENCY.] **1.** Mildness or gentleness of temper in the exercise of authority or power; mercy, leniency. **2.** Mildness of weather or climate 1667.

1. A prince..famous for his c. FULLER. C...is the standing policy of constitutional governments HALLAM.

Clement (kle·mĕnt), *a.* 1483. [– L. *clemens, -ent*; see -ENT. Cf. Fr. *clément.*] **1.** Mild and humane in the exercise of power or authority; merciful, lenient, kindly. **2.** Of weather, etc.: Mild; opp. to *inclement* (*rare*) 1622. Hence **Cle·mently** *adv.* var. † **Cleme·ntious, -ly.**

Clementine (kle·mĕntəin), *a.* ME. [– med.L. *Clementinus*, f. *Clemens*, the adj. used as a proper name.] Of or pertaining to Clement: *esp.* to Clement of Rome and writings ascribed to him; also, to Pope Clement V and his Constitutions. Also as *sb.* (in both applications).

Clench (klenʃ), *sb.* 1598. [f. CLENCH *v.*] **1.** = CLINCH *sb.* q.v. **2.** The action of clenching (the fists, etc.); *fig.* conclusive confirmation, etc. Formerly also CLINCH. 1779.

Clench (klenʃ), *v.* [OE. *-clenćan* = OHG. *klenken* :- Gmc. **klaŋkjan*, f. **klaŋk-* **kleŋk-* **kluŋk-*, parallel to **klaŋg-*, etc. (see CLING *v.*); see CLINCH *v.*] **1.** = CLINCH. **2.** To set firmly together, close tightly (the fingers, fist, teeth). Formerly also CLINCH. 1747. Also *fig.*

Clenched (klenʃt, *poet.* kle·nʃèd), *ppl. a.* ME. [f. prec. + -ED¹.] Firmly fastened, tightly closed.

Clencher (kle·nʃəɹ). 1559. [f. as prec. + -ER¹.] He who or that which clenches; a conclusive statement, argument, etc. (more commonly *clincher*).

Clencher-built: see CLINKER *sb.*²

† **Clepe**, *v.* [OE. *clipian* :- Gmc. **klipōjan*, also **klippjan* repr. by OFris. *klippa, kleppa* ring, LG. *klippen* sound, resound.] **1.** *intr.* To cry, call –1563. **2.** *trans.* To call (a person) –1567; to address –1513. **3.** To call by the name of, call, name. Still used as *arch.*, esp. in the pa. pple. *ycleped, yclept* (ikle·pt). OE. **4.** *ellipt.* To speak of. CHAUCER. Hence † **Clepe** *sb.* a call (*rare*).

‖ **Clepsydra** (kle·psidrǎ). Pl. **-as**, and **-æ.** 1646. [L. – Gr. κλεψύδρα, f. κλεψ-, comb. form of κλέπτειν steal + ὕδωρ water.] A water-clock used by the ancients to measure time by the discharge of water.

Cleptomania, var. of KLEPTOMANIA.

Clerestory (kliᵊ·ɹstōᵊri). ME. [f. *clere* CLEAR *a.* ('light, lighted') + STOREY. Cf. AL. *historia* (= storey) *clara* XV.] The upper part of the nave, choir, and transepts of any large church, containing a series of windows, clear of the roofs of the aisles, admitting light to the central parts of the building. Also *transf.*

attrib. Clerestory window: a window having no cross piece to divide the light.

† **Cle·rete.** [ME. *clerte*, var. of *clarte* – (O)Fr. *clarté* :- L. *claritas*. The var. *clerte* was due to assim. to the adj. *cler* CLEAR. Superseded by CLARITY.] Clearness, brightness, lustre; glory, renown –1520.

Clergess. *Hist.* ME. [– OFr. *clergesse*, fem. of *clerc*; see CLERK, -ESS¹.] A female scholar; a member of a female religious order.

† **Cle·rgion.** Also **-eon.** ME. [– OFr. *clerjon* (mod. *clergeon*), dim. of *clerc* CLERK.] A young clerk or chorister; also *fig.* –1540.

Clergy (klɔ̄·ɹdʒi). ME. [repr. two Fr. words: (O)Fr. *clergé* :- eccl.L. *clericatus*, f. *clericus* (see CLERK, -ATE¹), and (O)Fr. *clergie*, f. *clerc* + *-ie* -Y³, with *-g-* after *clergé*.] † **1.** The clerical office –1561. **2.** *concr.* The clerical order; the body of men set apart by ordination for religious service in the Christian church; opp. to *laity*. (Orig. a term of the Catholic church.) ME. † *transf.* of the priestly order in non-Christian religions –1727. **3.** As tr. Gr. κλῆρος, and κλήρων in 1 *Pet.* 5:3 ME. **4.** Clerkly skill; learning (mod. Fr. *clergie*). *Obs.* exc. in provb. ME. **5.** Old Law. *Benefit of (his) clergy*, also simply (*his*) *clergy*: orig. the privilege allowed to clergymen of exemption from trial by a secular court; modified and extended later to every one who could read. (Thus 'benefit of the clerical office' became = 'benefit of scholarship'.) Abolished in 1827. Cf. NECK-VERSE. ME. Also *attrib.*

2. The c. and laity BLACKSTONE. A married c. WHATELEY. **4.** An Ounce of Mother-Wit is worth a Pound of C., or Book-learning 1690. **5.** By the Laws of this Realm the Benefit of C. is not allowed to Women convicted of Felony 1623. Hence **Cle·rgiable** *a.* admitting benefit of c. † **Cle·rgial** *a.* clerkly.

Clergyman (klɔ̄·ɹdʒimǎn). 1577. A man of the clerical order; an ordained minister of the Christian church. (In England, commonly meaning a minister of the Church of England.) † *transf.* (see CLERGY 2) –1693. So **Cle·rgy-woman,** † a nun; † a priestess; a clergyman's wife, etc. (*joc.*)

Cleric (kle·rik). 1621. [– eccl.L. *clericus* (Jerome) – Gr. κληρικός (eccl.) belonging to the Christian ministerial order, f. κλῆρος lot, heritage, as used (e.g.) in Acts 1:17 'the lot (κλῆρος) of this ministry'.] **A.** *adj.* Of or pertaining to the clergy, CLERICAL. **B.** *sb.* A clergyman. Often used instead of CLERK (sense 1), as less ambiguous. 1621.

Clerical (kle·rikǎl), *a.* (*sb.*) 1592. [– eccl.L. *clericalis*, f. *clericus*; see CLERIC, -AL¹.] **1.** Of, pertaining to, or characteristic of, the clergy or a clergyman. **2.** Of or pertaining to a CLERK or penman, of clerks 1798. **3.** *sb.* A cleric 1837.

1. C. garb LYTTON. **2.** A c. error GURWOOD. Hence **Cle·ricalism,** c. principles; c. rule; c. partisanship. **Clerica·lity,** a c. trait; c. quality or condition. **Cle·rically** *adv.*

Cle·ricate. [– eccl.L. *clericatus*; see CLERGY, -ATE¹.] Clerical office. BROWNING.

Clericity (klĭri·sĭti). [f. CLERIC; see -ICITY.] Clerical quality or status.

Clerico- (kle·riko), comb. f. L. *clericus*, = clerically-, clerical and.., as in *c.-liberal*, etc.

Clerisy (kle·rĭsi). 1818. [app. after G. *klerisei*.] **1.** Learned men as a body, scholars. **2.** = CLERICITY 1858.

1. A learned body, or c., as such COLERIDGE.

Clerk (klāɹk, klɔ̄ɹk), *sb.* [Late OE. *cleric*, *clerc* – eccl.L. *clericus* CLERIC; this merged with ME. *clerc* – (O)Fr. *clerc* of the same origin.] **1.** A churchman, clergyman, or ecclesiastic. (Now often repl. by CLERIC.) **2.** Before the Reformation, *esp.* a member of the five 'minor orders', as distinct from 'holy orders'. Hence, applied to laymen who perform such of these offices as survive. 1549. **3.** A man (or woman) of book learning, one able to read and write; a scholar. (Now *arch.*) ME. † **4.** In early times, *Clerks* (in sense 1, identical with 3) transacted all business involving writing –1555. **5.** Hence, in current use: **a.** An officer who has charge of the records, correspondence, etc., and conducts the business, of any department, court, corporation, or society 1526. **b.** A subordinate employed to make written entries, keep accounts, etc. 1512.

1. The placing of one c. in two churches HOOKER. **2.** *The Parish C.*, the lay officer of a parish church who assists the clergyman by leading the people in responses, assisting at marriages, baptisms, etc. *Bible C.*, a scholar who reads the lessons in some college chapels. **3.** That noble poete and grete clerke vyrgyle CAXTON. **5. a.** *C. to the School-board, Town-c.*, etc. **b.** The telegraph c. 1865.

Hence **Clerk** *v.* (*colloq.*) to act as c. **Cle·rkage,** clerk's work. **Cle·rkdom,** the status or function of a c.; clerks collectively. **Cle·rkhood,** the status of a clergyman (*arch.*), or of an office c. **Cle·rkish** *a.* **Cle·rkless** *a.* **Clerk-like** *a.* and *adv.* **Cle·rkling,** a young or petty c. **Cle·rkship,** the position or function of a c.; book-learning.

Clerkly (klā·ɹkli), *a.* 1528. [f. CLERK *sb.* + -LY¹, modelled on *clerkly* adv., which is after late L. *clericaliter*.] **1.** Clerical 1565. **2.** Book-learned (*arch.*) 1528. **3.** Skilled in penmanship 1808. **4.** Of or belonging to an office clerk 1845. So **Cle·rkly** *adv.* Hence **Cle·rkliness,** c. quality.

Clero- (klīᵊ·ro), comb. f. late L. *clerus*, Gr. κλῆρος, in the sense of 'clergy', as † **Clerola·ical** *a.*, composed of clergy and laity.

Cle·romancy. ? *Obs.* 1620. [f. Gr. κλῆρος lot + -MANCY.] Divination by lots.

Clerstory, obs. f. CLERESTORY.

Cleruch (klīᵊ·rŏk, -ŭk). 1847. [– Gr. κληροῦχος allottee, f. κλῆρος lot + ἔχειν have, hold.] *Gr. Antiq.* At Athens, a citizen who received an allotment of land in a foreign state, but retained his rights as a citizen at home. Hence **Cleruchy** (klīᵊ·rŭki) [Gr. κληρουχία], allotment of land among cleruchs; a body of cleruchs.

‖ **Cle·rum.** 1655. [Short for *concio ad clerum*, discourse to the clergy.] A Latin sermon preached on certain occasions at the English Universities.

Cletch, *sb. dial.* Also **clatch.** 1691. [f. CLECK *v.*; cf. *bake, batch*, etc. Cf. CLUTCH *sb.*²] A hatching (of chickens); *contempt.* a family.

Cleuch, cleugh (kliuχ, klŭχ). *Sc.* ME. [Sc. form of CLOUGH, q.v.] **1.** A ravine with steep sides, usually that of a stream or torrent. (Freq. in place-names, as *Buccleuch*, etc.) **2.** The precipitous side of a gorge 1533.

Cleve, cleeve (klīv). Now *local.* [ME. *cleof, cleove*, var. of *clif* CLIFF, founded on OE. *cleofu, cleofum*. (Occas. erron. *cleave*, as if conn. w. *cleave* to split.) Freq. in local names, as *Clevedon, Cleveland*, etc.] **1.** = CLIFF (*dial.*). † **2.** The shore of the sea. ME. only. **3.** = Sc. *brae* ME.

Clever (kle·vəɹ), *a.* Also **cliver, cleaver.** ME. [perh. rel. to CLIVER *sb.* in the sense of 'nimble of claws, sharp to seize'. Cf. rare Sc. *cleverous* apt to seize, similarly assoc. w. *cluik* claw. Corresp. in form and sense to LG. *klöver, klever*, MDu. *klever* sprightly, brisk, smart, suggests that the word may belong to the LG. area.] **1.** Nimble-handed; adroit, dexterous in the use of the limbs, etc. **2.** Possessing skill or talent; dexterous; adroit. (The current sense.) 1716. Of things: Done with adroitness or skill, ingenious 1704. **3.** Nimble, active (*dial.*) 1694. **4.** Clean-limbed, well-made; handsome. Now *dial.* and *U.S.* 1674. **5.** Handy 1715; 'nice'; convenient; agreeable, amiable 1738. Also as quasi-*adv.* (*dial.*).

1. The old mare is as c. as a cat 1888. **2.** C. drawings MME. D'ARBLAY. **4.** The girl was a tight c. wench as any was ARBUTHNOT (J.). **5.** A c. boat STEVENSON. Then come, put the jorum about, And let us be merry and c. GOLDSM. Hence **Cle·verish** *a.* somewhat c. **Cle·verly** *adv.* in a c. manner (in all senses); *dial.* and *U.S.* completely; quite, 'clean'. **Cle·verness,** the quality of being c.

Clevis (kle·vis). 1592. [perh. repr. OE. **clyfes* :- **klubisī*, f. **klub-* wk. grade of **kleub-*; see CLEAVE *v.*¹, the thing being perh. orig. a forked or cloven piece.] A U-shaped piece of iron, with a pin or bolt passing through holes in the two ends, for bolting on to the end of a beam or the like so as to form a loop to which tackle may be attached.

Clew (kliu), *sb.* See also CLUE. [OE. *cliwen*, *cleowen* = MLG., Du. *kluwen*, f. base of OHG. *kliuwa, kliuwi* ball, sphere, prob. ult. rel. to CLAW. For loss of final *n* cf. *eve, game, maid*.] † **1.** A globular body; a ball –1796. **2.** *esp.* A ball of thread or yarn. (The regular term in Sc. and n. Eng.) OE. Also *fig.* **3.** Hence, that which guides or threads a way through a maze, perplexity, difficulty, intricate investigation, etc. ME.; hence, an indication to follow, a key. See CLUE. 1724. **4.** A thread or cord (in a series) 1700; the series of cords by which a hammock is suspended 1834. **5.** *Naut.* A lower corner of a square sail, or the aftmost corner of a fore-and-aft sail 1627.

2. *fig.* You haue wound a goodly clewe *All's Well* I. iii. 188. **3.** With clews like these they tread the maze of state CRABBE. The c. to the great puzzle FREEMAN. *Comb.*: **c.-bottom,** a reel to wind a c. on; **-garnet, clue-garnet,** *Naut.* a tackle to clew up the courses or lower square-sails in furling; **-line, clue-line,** a tackle connecting the c. of a sail to the upper yard or the mast; occas. = *c.-garnets.*

Clew, clue (klū), *v.* ME. [f. prec.] **1.** *trans.* To coil *up* into a ball. **2.** To point *out* as by a clew 1625. **3.** To track as by a clew 1663. **4.** *Naut. To c. up*: to draw the clews (of sails) up to the yard in preparation for furling. *To c. down*: to let down (sails) by the clews in unfurling them. Also *absol.*

2. A woman might..clew me out the way to happinesse BEAUM. & FL.

‖ **Cliché** (kliʃe). 1832. [Fr., subst. use of pa. pple. of *clicher* stereotype, said to be imit. of the sound produced by dropping the matrix on the molten metal (cf. G. *klitsch* slap, clash, perh. the immed. source).] A stereotype block; a cast or 'dab'; *esp.* a metal stereotype of a wood-engraving used to print from. **b.** *fig.* A stereotyped expression, a commonplace phrase 1892.

Click (klik), *sb.*¹ 1611. [imit.; cf. OFr. *clique* tick of a clock, *cliquer* click (whence mod. Fr. *cliqueter, cliquetis*), Du. *klik* tick, MDu. *klikken*. Cf. CLIQUE.] **1.** A slight, sharp, hard, non-ringing sound of concussion, thinner than a *clack*, such as is made by the cocking of a gun, etc. **2.** *Mech.* A piece of mechanism which makes this noise; *e.g.* the catch or detent which falls into the notches of a ratchet-wheel; the catch for a lock or bolt, a latch, etc. **3.** A defect in a horse's action, causing the toe of the hind hoof to strike the shoe in front 1886. **4.** *Zool.* A name for beetles of the family *Elateridæ*, from the clicking sound with which they spring upward when they have fallen on their backs. Also *c.-beetle*. 1848. **5.** A class of articulations occurring in certain languages of S. Africa, consisting of sharp non-vocal sounds formed by suction, with the sudden withdrawal of the tongue from the part of the mouth with which it is in contact. Also CLUCK. 1857. *Comb.* **c.-beetle** (see sense 4). Hence **Cli·cky** *a.* full of clicks (sense 5). **Click-clack** *sb.* and *v.*, also **Click-click,** expressions for recurring or successive sounds of the c. type, also for chattering.

Click, *sb.*[2] 1872. [var. of CLEEK; also CLICK *v.*[2] used as *sb.*] **1.** = CLEEK 1883. **2.** A jerk with a cleek or hook 1886. **3.** *Wrestling.* A trick, whereby the adversary's foot is sharply knocked off the ground 1872.

Click (klik), *v.*[1] 1581. [imit.; see CLICK *sb.*[1]] **1.** *intr.* To make the sound described under CLICK *sb.*[1] 1. 1611. **2.** *trans.* To strike with this noise; to cause to make such a noise 1581.

1. The solemn death-watch click'd GAY. **2.** They..clicked their glasses together MARRYAT. Merry milkmaids c. the latch TENNYSON.

Click (klik), *v.*[2] Chiefly *dial.* 1674. [var. of CLEEK *v.* with shortened vowel, as in *sick* = ME. *sēke.*] = CLEEK. Also with *up.*

Cli·cker. 1690. [f. CLICK *v.*[1] or [2].] **1.** *slang.* A shop-keeper's tout. **2.** A foreman shoemaker who cuts out the leather and gives out work. (App. the orig. sense.) 1680. **3.** *Printing.* The foreman of a companionship of compositors who distributes the copy, etc. 1808.

Clicket (kli·kėt), *sb.* Now *dial.* ME. [– (O)Fr. *cliquet*, f. OFr. *clique* door-latch; see -ET. Cf. AL. *clikettum* XIII.] **1.** The latch of a door or gate. Still *dial.* †**2.** A latch-key –1579. †**3.** A contrivance for making a clicking sound; as a clapper, bones, etc. –1737. *Comb.* **c.-gate,** a gate with a latch. Hence **Cli·cket** *v.* to chatter; of a fox, to be in heat.

Cliency (klǝi·ĕnsi). *rare.* 1660. [– med.L. *clientia* (Du Cange); see next, -ENCY.] The state of being a client.

Client (klǝi·ĕnt). ME. [– L. *cliens, -ent-*, earlier *cluens*, subst. use of pr. pple. of *cluere, cluēre* hear, listen; lit. one who is at another's call.] **1.** *Rom. Antiq.* A plebeian under the protection of a patrician, in this relation called a patron (*patronus*). **2.** *gen.* One who is under the protection or patronage of another, a dependant ME. **3.** *spec.* One who employs the services of a legal adviser; he whose cause an advocate pleads ME.; also *trans.* a customer 1608.

2. We are very Curious to observe the Behaviour of great Men and their Clients STEELE. **3.** Good Counsellors lacke no Clients *Meas. for M.* I. ii. 109. Hence **Cli·entage,** a body of clients; the relation of c. to patron. **Clie·ntal** *a. rare,* of or pertaining to a c. or clients. † **Cli·ented** *ppl. a.* furnished with clients. **Cliente·lage,** = *Clientage.* **Cli·entless** *a.* **Cli·entry,** the relation of clients; a body of clients. **Cli·entship,** state or relation of a c.: cf. *patronage.*

Clientele (klǝiĕntī·l, -te·l). Also **-el, -elle,** and in Fr. form **clientèle.** 1563. [orig. (XVI) – L. *clientela*, but obs. in XVII and re-adopted from Fr. *clientèle* c1850.] †**1.** The relation or status of a client; clientship –1654; patronage –1692. **2.** A body of clients or dependants; a body of adherents; a following 1563. **3.** The whole professional connection of a lawyer, physician, etc.; a body of supporters or customers generally 1865.

Cliff (klif). [OE. *clif* = OS. (Du.) *klif*, OHG. *klep*, ON. *klif* :- Gmc. **klibam*; beside MDu. *klippe* (whence G. *klippe*) :- **klibn-*, and ON. *kleif*; of unkn. origin.] **1.** A high steep face of rock; *esp.* (now) a steep face of rock on the seashore. †**2.** Hence, Shore, coast, strand –1600. **3.** = CLEVE 3. ME. **4.** The strata of rock lying above or between coal seams 1676.

1. There the Eagle and the Stork On Cliffs and Cedar tops thir Eyries build MILT. *P.L.* VII. 424. Hence **Cliffed** *ppl. a.* having cliffs. **Cli·ffy** *a.* having cliffs, precipitous, craggy.

Clift, *sb.*[1] Now usually CLEFT, q.v. Hence **Cli·fted** *a.*

Clift (klift), *sb.*[2] = CLIFF, q.v. Hence **Cli·fty** *a.*

† **Climacter.** 1609. [– Gr. κλιμακτήρ, f. κλῖμαξ ladder.] A CLIMACTERIC year or epoch –1656.

Climacteric (klǝimæ̆kte·rik, -æ·ktĕrik). 1601. [– Fr. *climatérique* or L. *climactericus* – Gr. κλιμακτηρικός, f. κλιμακτήρ critical period – κλῖμαξ, -μακ- ladder; see CLIMAX, -IC.]

A. *adj.* **1.** Pertaining to or constituting a climacter or critical period in human life; *transf.* critical, fatal. **2.** = CLIMACTIC 1791.

1. *C. year* = *climacteric*, also = *grand climacteric*: see B. *C. disease*: an unexplained disease of advanced life, characterized by loss of strength, sleeplessness, etc.

B. *sb.* **1.** A critical stage in human life; a period supposed to be specially liable to change in health or fortune. Some held all the years denoted by multiples of 7 (7, 14, 21, etc.), others only the odd multiples of 7 (7, 21, 35, etc.) to be climacterics; some included the multiples of 9. 1634. **2.** *transf.* A critical point or period 1630.

1. *Grand* († *great*) *c.* (occas. *the c.*): the 63rd year of life (63 = 7 × 9), supposed to be specially critical. (According to some, also the 81st year.) **2.** At her advanced age, every day is a c. POPE. var. **Climacte·rical** *a.* and *sb.*

† **Clima·ctery.** 1654. [– Fr. † *climacterie* (Cotgr.), f. Gr. κλιμακτήρ + *-ie*; see CLIMACTER, -Y[3].] **1.** = CLIMACTERIC B. 1. 1658. **2.** Progress by successive steps –1734.

Climactic (klǝimæ·ktik), *a.* 1872. [irreg. f. CLIMAX, prob. infl. by *climacteric.*] Pertaining to or forming a climax or ascending series. Hence **Clima·ctically** *adv.*

Climatal (klǝi·mătăl), *a.* 1830. [f. CLIMATE + -AL[1].] Of or pertaining to climate.

† **Climata·rchic,** *a. rare.* 1794. [f. Gr. κλιμάταρχος, in Byzantine Gr. governor of a province, f. κλίματ- region + -αρχος ruling; see -IC.] Presiding over a climate.

Climate (klǝi·mĕt), *sb.* ME. [– (O)Fr. *climat* or late L. *clima, -mat-* – Gr. κλίμα, -ματ-, in the sense 'zone or region of the earth occupying a particular elevation on the supposed slope of the earth and sky from the equator to the poles', which had developed from the gen. sense 'slope of ground'; f. **klī-*, as in κλίνειν slope, LEAN *v.*[1] Cf. CLIMAX.] †**1.** A belt of the earth's surface contained between two given parallels of latitude –1796. †**b.** *vaguely*: A region of the earth, a clime –1794. **2.** A region considered with reference to its atmospheric conditions, or to its weather 1601. **3.** Condition (of a region or country) in relation to prevailing atmospheric phenomena, as temperature, humidity, etc., *esp.* as these affect animal or vegetable life 1611. †**4.** = CLIMACTER –1586.

1. There are 24 climates between the equator and each of the polar circles MORSE. **3.** The Clymat's delicate, the Ayre most sweet *Wint. T.* III. i. 1. Hence † **Cli·mate** *v.* to sojourn in a particular c. **Clima·tic, -al** *a.* relating to c. **Clima·tically** *adv.* **Cli·matize** *v. rare* = ACCLIMATIZE.

Climato·graphy. 1864. [f. CLIMATE + -GRAPHY.] The description of a climate or climates (Dicts.).

Climatology (klǝimătǫ·lŏdʒi). 1843. [f. as prec. + -LOGY; cf. Fr. *climatologie.*] That branch of science which deals with climate, and investigates climatic conditions. (Occas. used for the conditions themselves as a subject of science.) Hence **Cli:matolo·gic, -al** *a.*, **-ally** *adv.* **Climato·logist.**

† **Cli·mature.** 1604. [f. CLIMATE + -URE.] **1.** ?A region. *Haml.* I. i. 126. **2.** Meteorological condition resulting from latitude; = CLIMATE 3. –1806.

Climax (klǝi·mæks), *sb.* 1589. [– late L. *climax* – Gr. κλῖμαξ ladder, f. **klī-*. See LEAN *v.*[1]] **1.** *Rhet.* A figure in which a number of propositions or ideas are set forth in a series in which each rises above the preceding in force; gradation. †**2.** *gen.* An ascending series –1793. **3.** [A misuse of the term.] The last term of a rhetorical climax 1856; also *gen.* the highest point, culmination, acme 1789.

2. The top of the c. of their wickedness BURKE. **3.** Jerusalem is the c. of the long ascent STANLEY. Hence **Cli·max** *v. prop.* to ascend, or arrange, in a c.; *pop.* to come, or bring to, a culmination.

Climb (klǝim), *v. Pa. t.* and *pple.* **climbed** (klǝimd); *arch.* **clomb** (klōᵘm). [OE. *climban* = (M)LG., (M)Du. *klimmen*, OHG. *klimban* (G. *klimmen*) :- WGmc. **klimban*, nasalized var. of **klīban* (see CLEAVE *v.*[2]), the orig. sense being 'hold fast'.] **1.** *intr.* To raise oneself by grasping or clinging, or by the aid of hands and feet; to ascend a steep place. Often with *up.* **2.** *trans.* To ascend by hands and feet; to mount, scale ME.; to attain (a point) by climbing 1580. **3.** To mount slowly upwards. *trans.* and *intr.* ME. **4.** Of plants: To creep up by the aid of tendrils or by twining. *trans.* and *intr.* 1796. **5.** *transf.* To rise, force its way upward. *trans.* and *intr.* Also *fig.* OE.

1. *To c. down*: *fig.* to retreat from a position taken up. **2.** They shall clime the wall like men of warre *Joel* 2:7. I must climbe her window *Two Gent.* II. iv. 181. **3.** Where entrance up from Eden easiest climbes MILT. *P.L.* XI. 119. The slow moon climbs TENNYSON. **5.** Let the labouring Barke climbe hills of Seas *Oth.* II. i. 189. *fig.* To clym to kyngs astate ME. Hence **Climb** *sb.* the act of climbing; an ascent. **Cli·mbable** *a.* that can be climbed. **Cli·mber,** one who or that which climbs; *spec.* (*Bot.*) a plant which climbs; (*Ornith.*) in *pl.* an order of birds (L. *Scansores*), which climb. **Cli·mbing** *vbl. sb.* and *ppl. a.*; whence **climbing-perch,** a fish (*Anabas scandens*): see ANABAS.

Clime (klǝim). Now chiefly *poet.* 1542. [– late L. *clima*; see CLIMATE.] †**1.** = CLIMATE 1. –1697. **2.** = CLIMATE 1 b. 1542. *fig.* = Region, realm 1667. **3.** = CLIMATE 3. Also *fig.* = Atmosphere. *poet.* 1598.

2. Every man of every c. BLAKE. *fig.* The Climes of bliss MILT. *P.L.* XI. 708.

‖ **Clinamen** (klǝinēⁱ·men). 1704. [L.] An inclination, bias.

‖ **Clina·ndrium.** 1864. [mod.L., f. Gr. κλίνη couch + ανδρ- male, taken for 'stamen'.] *Bot.* The cavity at the apex of the gynostemium in Orchids, in which the anther is embedded.

‖ **Clina·nthium, clina·nthus.** 1881. [mod. L., f. as prec. + ἄνθος flower.] *Bot.* The receptacle or torus of a Composite flower.

Clinch (klinʃ), *sb.* 1627. [var. of CLENCH *sb.*; cf. CLINCH *v.*] **1.** A fastening in which the end of a nail or bolt is beaten back or flattened after passing through anything; the clinched point of a nail; a clinched nail or bolt. Occas. CLENCH. 1659. **2.** *Naut.* 'A method of fastening large ropes by a half-hitch, with the end stopped back to its own part by seizings' (Adm. Smyth): that part of a rope which is clinched 1627. **3.** A thing which clutches, grips, or fixes fast 1822. **4.** A clinching or riveting together 1855. **5.** A word-play, a pun 1630. **6.** *U.S.* A struggle at close grips 1860. **b.** *Boxing.* Grappling at close quarters 1899.

4. Give my conviction a c. BROWNING. *Comb.* **c.-work,** lap-jointed work.

Clinch (klinʃ), *v.* 1570. [Later var. of CLENCH *v.*; prob. by assimilation to CLINK.] **1.** *trans.* To fix (a nail or bolt) securely, *esp.* by beating back or flattening the end which has been driven through anything; to make fast thus. Also *absol.* Occas. CLENCH. †**2.** To close tightly (the hand or fist). Now always CLENCH. –1802. Also † *intr.* (for *refl.*). **3.** *trans. Naut.* To make fast the end of a rope in the way described under CLINCH *sb.* 2. 1769. **4.** *intr.* To fix oneself *on* 1793. **5.** *trans.* To make firm and sure (an argument, bargain, etc.); to drive home; to make conclusive, confirm, establish. Also CLENCH. 1716. †**6.** To secure (*rare*). (Cf. *nail.*) 1803. †**7.** To make clinches or puns –1688. **8.** *Boxing,* etc. (Cf. CLINCH *sb.* 6) 1860.

5. The council of Trent..clincheth the business SOUTH. Hence **Cli·ncher,** one who or that which clinches; *esp.* a conclusive statement, argument, etc.; † a *clinker-built* vessel; see CLINKER.

† **Clinchpoop, clenchpoop.** 1568. [Origin unkn.] A term of contempt; = lout –1589.

† **Cline,** *v.* ME. [– OFr. *cliner* – L. *clinare.*] To bow, incline –1538.

Cling (kliŋ), *v. Pa. t.* and *pple.* **clung** (klɒŋ). [OE. *clingan*, corresp. to MDu. *klingen* stick, adhere, MHG. *klingen* climb :- Gmc. **kliŋg-* **klaŋg-* **kluŋg-*, parallel to **kliŋk-*, etc.; see CLENCH *v.*] †**1.** *intr.* To adhere together in a stiff mass –1577. **2.** To become 'drawn', to shrink up, wither. Now *dial.* OE. **3.** *trans.* To cause to adhere, stick *together* (*dial.*) 1627; to cause to shrink or draw together 1540. **4.** *intr.* To adhere, stick *to* ME. **5.** *intr.* To adhere, attach oneself firmly *to.* (Now the leading sense.) ME. Also *transf.* **6.** *fig.* To cleave *to* 1583. †**7.** To cause to cling, make fast. (Perh. a by-form of CLINCH or CLINK.) –1774.

3. Vpon the next Tree shalt thou hang aliue Till Famine c. thee *Macb.* V. v. 40. **4.** His Armes clung to his Ribs MILT. *P.L.* X. 512. **5.** The broken ice clung to the rocks KANE. My maids clung round me JOHNSON. *transf.* Some heavy clouds..clung to the mountains TYNDALL. **6.** To c. to a doctrine MACAULAY. **7.** I clung my legs as close to his sides as I could SWIFT. Hence **Cling** *sb.* the act of clinging; adhesion; *spec.* a disease of cattle, which makes them hidebound. **Cli·nger. Cli·ngy** *a.* sticky, tenacious.

Cli·ngstone, *a.* and *sb.* 1840. A variety of the peach in which the flesh clings to the stone.

Clinic (kli·nik), *sb.*[1] and *a.* 1626. [- L. *clinicus* - Gr. κλινικός, f. κλίνη bed (see LEAN *v.*); see -IC; cf. Fr. *clinique*.] **A.** *sb.* **1.** One who is confined to bed by sickness or infirmity. **2.** *Ch. Hist.* One who deferred baptism until the death-bed 1666. **B.** *adj.* **1.** Of or pertaining to the sick-bed 1626. **2.** = CLINICAL 1. 1751.

1. *C. baptism*: private baptism administered on the sick bed.

Clinic, *sb.*[2], **clinique.** 1843. [= F. *clinique*, - Gr. κλινική the clinic art.] **1.** The teaching of medicine or surgery at the bedside of a sick person. **2. a.** A private hospital, etc., to which patients are recommended by individual doctors. **b.** An institution attached to a hospital, etc., at which patients receive treatment free of cost or at reduced fees 1892.

Clinical (kli·nikăl), *a.* 1780. [f. as CLINIC *sb.*[1] and *a.* + -AL[1]; see -ICAL.] **1.** *Med.* Of or pertaining to the sick-bed, *spec.* to that of indoor hospital patients. **2.** *Eccl.* Administered on the sick-bed 1844.

1. *C. lecture*, a lecture at the bedside of the patient upon his case. *C. medicine, surgery*, medicine or surgery as taught at the bedside, *esp.* in hospital practice. Hence **Cli·nically** *adv.* **Clini·cian,** a c. investigator.

Clink (kliŋk), *sb.*[1] ME. [f. CLINK *v.*[1]] **1.** A sharp abrupt ringing sound, clearer and thinner than a *clank*, as of glasses struck together. **2.** Mere assonance of rhyme 1716. **3.** *dial.* A smart sharp blow 1722. **4.** *colloq. Sc.* COIN; = CHINK 1729.

1. The clinke and fall of Swords *Oth.* II. iii. 234.

Clink, *sb.*[2] 1515. [Origin unkn.] The name of a prison in Southwark; also (*esp.* in Devon and Cornwall) a small prison-cell; a lock-up.

Clink (kliŋk), *v.*[1] [prob. - (M)Du. *klinken* sound, ring, tinkle, rel. to MLG., (M)Du. *klank* sound (cf. CLANK); cf. CLANG.] **1.** *intr.* To make the sound described under CLINK *sb.*[1] 1. **2.** To cause to sound in this way ME. **3.** *intr.* To rhyme 1729. Also *trans.* **4.** *intr.* To move with a clinking sound 1818.

1. As the fool thinketh, so the bell clinketh 1684. **2.** And let me the Cannakin clinke, clinke *Oth.* II. iii. 71.

Clink (kliŋk), *v.*[2] *n. Eng.* and *Sc.* ME. [Northern form; = CLINCH, CLENCH.] *trans.* To clench, rivet.

Clinkant, obs. f. CLINQUANT.

Clink-clank. 1790. A succession or alternation of clinking sounds; *fig.* a senseless jingle of words.

Clinker (kli·ŋkəɹ), *sb.*[1] 1641. [Earlier *klincard, clincart* – early mod.Du. *klinckaerd* (now *klinker*), f. *klinken* to ring; see CLINK.] **1.** A very hard brick of a pale colour, made in Holland, and used for paving. **2.** A brick whose surface has been vitrified by intense heat; a mass of bricks fused by excessive heat, and adhering together 1659. **3.** A hard mass formed by the fusion of the earthy impurities of coal, limestone, iron ore, or the like, in a furnace or forge; a mass of slag 1769. **4.** A mass of hardened volcanic lava 1850. **5.** A scale of oxide of iron formed in forging.

Cli·nker, *sb.*[2] 1690. [f. CLINK *v.*[1] + -ER[1].] He who or that which clinks; *spec.* in *pl.* fetters (*slang*).

Cli·nker, *sb.*[3] 1656. [f. CLINK *v.*[2] + -ER[1]; prob. infl. by LG., Du. *klinken* rivet. *Clincher-built* has varied with clinker-built from XVIII.] He who or that which clinches (*lit.* and *fig.*). *Comb.* **c.-built** *a.*: applied to ships and boats, the external planks of which overlap each other below, and are fastened with clinched copper nails; cf. CLINCHER.

Cli·nkstone. 1811. [After Ger. *klingstein*: so called from its clinking when struck.] *Min.* A compact greyish-blue felspathic rock, of lower specific gravity than grey basalt.

Clino- (kləi·no). Comb. f. Gr. stem κλιν- in the sense of 'sloping, inclining'; used in connection with the monoclinic system of crystals, characterized by one plane of symmetry.

Clinoba·sic *a.* = *clinorhombic*. **Clinodia·gonal** *sb.*, the inclined axis in the monoclinic system of crystals; *adj.* pertaining to, or in the line of, this axis. **Clinopi·nacoid** [Gr. πίναξ, πίνακος a board], one of the three principal planes in the monoclinic system, running parallel to the vertical and inclined axes. **Clinorho·mbic, -rho·mboid** *adjs.*, crystallizing in an oblique form, monoclinic.

Clinographic (kləinogræ·fik), *a.* [f. CLINO- + -GRAPHIC.] Pertaining to that mode of projection in drawing, in which the rays are assumed to fall obliquely on the plane of projection (Dicts.).

Clinoid (kləi·noid), *a.* 1741. [f. Gr. κλίνη bed; see -OID.] *Anat.* Resembling a bed: applied to the four apophyses of the sphenoid bone.

Clinometer (kləinǫ·mǐtəɹ). 1811. [f. CLINO- + -METER.] A measurer of slopes and elevations; *esp.* an instrument for measuring the dip of mineral strata, or the slope of cuttings, embankments, etc.; also for taking altitudes. Hence **Clinome·tric, -al** *a.* pertaining to or determined by the c.; *Min.* pertaining to the measurement of oblique crystalline forms. **Clino·metry** (Dicts.).

Clinquant (kli·ŋkănt). 1591. [- Fr. pres. pple. of † *clinquer* ring, glitter (*clinquant d'or* XVI) - LG. *klinken* CLINK *v.*[1]] *adj.* Glittering with real or mock gold or silver; tinselled, 'dressed in spangles' (J.). Also *fig.* *sb.* Tinsel, Dutch gold. Also *fig.* 1691.

Clint (klint), *sb.* Chiefly *Sc.* ME. [- Da. and Sw. *klint* :- OSwed. *klinter* rock.] A hard or flinty rock. Hence **Cli·nty** *a.* consisting of or characterized by clints.

Clio (kləi·o). 1835. [Gr. Κλειώ (f. κλείειν celebrate), the Muse of epic poetry and history; also a sea-nymph.] **1.** *Zool.* A genus of pteropods found in the Arctic seas. **2.** *Astron.* The 84th asteroid 1867.

Clip (klip), *v.*[1] [OE. *clyppan* = OFris. *kleppa* :- WGmc. **kluppjan*.] **1.** *trans.* To clasp with the arms, embrace, hug (*arch.* and *dial.*). Also *fig.* Also *absol.* and *intr.* **2.** *trans.* To surround closely, encompass, hug. Also with *about, in*. OE. **3.** To grip tightly OE.

1. He kisseth hire and clippeth hire ful ofte CHAUCER. **2.** Yon fair sea that clips thy shores COWPER.

Clip (klip), *v.*[2] [- ON. *klippa*, prob. imit.; cf. LG., Fris. *klippen*.] **1.** To cut with scissors or shears. Also with *away, off, out, from*. **2.** *fig.* To cut short 1588. Also *absol.* and *intr.* **3.** *intr.* To move the wings rapidly (*arch.*) 1613. **4.** *intr.* (*colloq.*) To move or run rapidly. Cf. *cut*. 1833.

1. I'll c. his wings MARLOWE. To c. the heads of the peasant-girls 1859, sheep WYCLIF, coin GRAFTON. **2.** To c. the Queen's English 1755. **3.** Some falcon..flies at check and clips it down the wind DRYDEN. Hence **Clipped, clipt** *ppl. a.*

Clip (klip), *sb.*[1] 1470. [f. CLIP *v.*[1]] † **1.** An embrace –1683. **2.** That which clips or clasps, *e.g.* in *Carriages*, the embracing-strap which connects the spring and axle; in *Farriery*, a projecting flange on the upper surface of the toe of a horseshoe, which clasps the front of the hoof; a spring-holder for letters, etc. 1470. Also *transf.* and *fig.* **3.** *attrib.* That has, or acts as, a clip 1861.

Clip (klip), *sb.*[2] 1681. [f. CLIP *v.*[2]] **1.** *pl.* Shears. **2.** That which is clipped; a clipping (*esp.* a season's clipping of wool) 1825. **3.** An act of clipping or shearing 1825. **4.** A smart blow, stroke, or cut 1830. Also *attrib.*

Clipper (kli·pəɹ). ME. [f. as prec. + -ER[1].] **1.** One who clips; *spec.* one who clips coin. Also *fig.* **2.** That which clips; *e.g.* a pruning-hook, and in *pl.* scissors, etc. 1578. **3.** One who or that which moves swiftly, or scuds along (cf. CLIP *v.*[2] 4); *e.g.* a vessel with sharp forward-raking bows and masts raking aft 1830. **4.** *slang.* Anything first-rate of its kind 1848.

1. Fals money makers and clepars of money ARNOLDE. **4.** Wasn't Reynolds a c. THACKERAY. *Comb.* **c.-built** *a.*

Clipping (kli·piŋ), *vbl. sb.* ME. [f. CLIP *v.*[2] + -ING[1].] **1.** The action of cutting with (or as with) shears or scissors. **2.** That which is clipped off, a cutting, paring, shaving, shred, etc. 1461.

1. The Jews..were also accused of c. of money 1460. **2.** Clippings from popular writers 1866.

Clipping (kli·piŋ), *ppl. a.* 1635. [f. CLIP *v.*[2] + -ING[2].] **1.** That cuts with shears; that flies or moves fast. **2.** *slang.* First-rate 1861.

† **Clips(e,** *sb.* and *v.* ME. Aphetic f. ECLIPSE *sb.* and *v.* –1612.

Clique (klīk). 1711. [- (O)Fr. *clique*, f. OFr. *cliquer* make a noise - MDu. *klikken* (see CLICK *v.*[1]); for the sense-development cf. CLAQUE.] A small and exclusive party or set, a narrow coterie or circle: a term of reproach or contempt. Hence **Clique** *v. colloq.* to combine in, or act as, a c. **Cli·quish** *a.* savouring of a c. or cliques. **Cli·quishness. Cli·quism, cliqueism,** the spirit, principles, and methods of a c.; party exclusiveness. **Cli·quy, -ey** *a.* of the nature of, or characterized by, cliques.

Clish-ma-claver (kliʃmăklēⁱ·vəɹ), *sb. Sc.* 1728. [Cf. *clish-clash* idle gossip and CLAVER *sb.*] Gossip, foolish talk. Also as vb.

Clitch (klitʃ), *v.* Now *dial.* [ME. *clicche*, varying with *clucche* :- OE. *clyććan*; see CLUTCH *v.*[1]] † **1.** *trans.* To crook or bend; to close (the hand) clench (the fist) –1574. **2.** To grasp tightly ME. **3.** To make fast; in mod. dial. to stick (things) *to* or together ME.

Clite (kləit). 1597. [Parallel form to *clete*, CLOTE; cf. OE. *clīte* colt's-foot.] **1.** The burdock. ? *Obs.* **2.** The Cleavers or Goose-grass 1847.

‖ **Clitellum** (kləite·lŏm). 1839. [mod.L., f. L. *clitellæ* (pl.) pack-saddle.] *Zool.* The raised band encircling the body of earth-worms towards the middle.

‖ **Clitoris** (kləi·tǫris). 1615. [mod.L. - Gr. κλειτορίς.] *Phys.* A homologue of the male penis, present in the females of many of the higher vertebrata.

† **Cli·ver,** *sb.* OE. [app. rel. to OE. *clifian* (:- **klib*-) *clīfan* (:- **klīb*-) cling, cleave, f. Gmc. **klī*-; see CLEAVE *v.*[2] and CLEAVERS.] A claw, talon –ME.

Clivers, var. of CLEAVERS, q.v.

‖ **Cloaca** (klo,ēⁱ·kă). Pl. **-æ.** 1656. [L. *cloaca, cluaca*, rel. to *cluere* cleanse.] **1.** An underground conduit for drainage, a sewer; a privy. Also *fig.* and *transf.* **2.** *Phys.* The common excretory cavity at the end of the intestinal canal in birds, reptiles, most fishes, and the monotreme animals 1834. Hence **Cloa·cal** *a.*

Cloak (klōᵘk), *sb.* ME. [- OFr. *cloke, cloque*, dial. var. of *cloche* (i) bell, (ii) cloak :- med.L. *clocca* (VII), perh. of Ir. origin; cf. CLOCK *sb.*[1]] **1.** A loose outer garment worn by both sexes over their other clothes. † **2.** A clerical gown; *esp.* the Geneva gown –1727. **3.** *fig.* That which covers over and conceals; a pretext, pretence, outward show 1526.

1. My Russett ryding clok 1612. **3.** I haue nights cloake to hide me from their eyes *Rom. & Jul.* II. ii. 75. *Comb.* † **c.-bag,** a bag in which to carry a c. or other clothes; a valise; also *fig.* Hence **Cloa·kless** *a.* without a c.

Cloak (klōᵘk), *v.* 1509. [f. prec.] **1.** To cover with or wrap in a cloak 1514. **2.** *fig.* † To cover, protect –1590; to cover over, conceal, disguise 1509.

2. To cloke her guile with sorrow SPENSER *F.Q.* II. i. 21. Hence **Cloaked** *ppl. a.* (*lit.* and *fig.*); † **Cloa·kedly** *adv.* apparently; disguisedly. **Cloa·king** *vbl. sb.* concealment; material for cloaks.

Cloa·k-room. 1852. A room in which cloaks, coats, hats, etc., may be left; also, an office at railway-stations, etc., where luggage is temporarily taken charge of.

Cloam (klōᵘm), *sb.* Now *s. w. dial.* [OE. *clām* mud, clay, corresp. to MDu. *cleem* potter's clay :- WGmc. **klaim*-, deriv. of Gmc. **klī*- daub, smear; see CLAM *v.*[1], CLAY *sb.*] In OE. Mud, clay. Hence, now: Earthenware, clay. Also *attrib.*

Clobber (klǫ·bəɹ). [Origin unkn.] A black paste used by cobblers to fill up and conceal cracks in leather. DICKENS.

‖ **Cloche.** 1882. [Fr., = bell.] **1.** = BELL-*glass*. **2.** = BELL *sb.*[1] 5. **3.** A close-fitting bell-shaped hat for women 1907.

Clocher (klōᵘ·ʃəɹ), *sb.* ME. [- AFr. *clocher*, OFr. *clochier*, (also mod.) *clocher*, f. *cloche* bell (see CLOCK *sb.*[1]) + *-er* -ER[2]; in med.L. *cloccarium*.] A bell-tower; a belfry.

Clock, *sb.*¹ [– MLG., MDu. *klocke* (LG., Du. *klok*), corresp. to OE. *clucge*, OFris. *klokke*, OHG. *glocka* (G. *glocke* bell), ON. *klokka*, *klukka*; Gmc. – med.L. *clocca* bell (whence Fr. *cloche*, etc.; cf. CLOAK *sb.*).] † **1.** A bell. *Later*, the gong of a striking watch. –1664. **2.** An instrument for the measurement of time; properly, one which strikes. The mechanism consists of a train of wheels set in motion by weights or a spring, actuating and regulated by a pendulum or balance-wheel; the passage of hours, minutes, etc., is indicated by hands on a dial-plate. ME. Also *transf.* and *fig.* † **3.** The hour as struck by the clock *Cymb.* III. iv. 44. **4.** A watch. *Obs.* exc. in mod. slang. 1559. **5.** The pappus of the dandelion, etc. 1847.

2. Like damag'd clocks, whose hand and bell dissent YOUNG. *O'clock* is short for *of the clock*; other variants were † *of clock*, † *a clock* (see A *prep.*²).

Phr. *To know (find) what o'clock it is*: to know (discover) the real state of things.

Comb.: **c.-face,** the dial-plate of a c., *techn.* the time shown by it; **-like** *a.* regular, monotonous; **-quarters,** the bells in a large c. on which the quarter-hours are struck; **-tower,** one built for a large c.; **-watch,** one that strikes; **-wise,** in the direction in which the hands of a clock move.

Clock (klǫk), *sb.*² 1530. [Origin unkn.] An ornamental pattern in silk worked on the side of a stocking. Hence **Clocked** *a.* embroidered with clocks.

Clock (klǫk), *sb.*³ 1550. [Origin unkn.] A name for any kind of beetle; esp. *Geotrupes stercorarius*.

Clock, *v.*¹ 1872. [f. CLOCK *sb.*¹] **1.** *trans.* To time by a clock or stop-watch 1883. **b.** with *in, off, on, out*: To register one's entry or exit by means of an automatic clock 1924. **2.** = CLAPPER *v.* 1.

Clock (klǫk), *v.*² Now *Sc.* and *n. dial.* [OE. *cloccian*, cf. MDu. *clocken* (Du. *klocken*), Sw. dial. *klokka*; see CLUCK.] **1.** *intr.* and † *trans.* To cluck. **2.** *intr.* and *trans.* To sit on eggs. (The current use in n. dial.) 1721. Hence **Clo·cker,** a sitting hen.

Clock-work (klǫ·kwɒɹk). 1662. The mechanism of a clock, or mechanism similar to that of a clock; *esp.* with reference to its automatic action, or its unvarying regularity. Also *fig.* **2.** *attrib.* Of or like clock-work 1764.

Clod (klǫd), *sb.* [ME. var. of CLOT; now differentiated, as shown in *clod of earth*, and *clot of blood*.] † **1.** = CLOT –1758. **2.** A mass or lump *of* any solid matter, *e.g.* earth, loam, etc. (Formerly CLOT.) ME. **3.** Without *pl.* The soil or dust of the ground in its lumpy character. (Often *depreciatory*.) 1573. **4.** *fig.* That which is of 'clay', or 'of the earth, earthly', as the body of man, etc. 1595. **5.** *fig.* A clod-pate; a clod-hopper 1605. **6.** The coarse part of the neck of an ox, nearest the shoulder 1601. **7.** *Coal-Mining.* Soft shale or slate 1867.

1. Clods of bloud FAIRFAX, of a slimy substance CAREW (J.). **2.** Two massie clods of Iron and Bras MILT. *P.L.* XI. 565. The crumbling Clods DRYDEN. **5.** This fleamy clodd of an Antagonist MILT. Hence **Clo·ddish** *a.* somewhat c.-like; boorishly stolid, awkward. **Clo·ddishness.**

Clod (klǫd), *v.* ME. [f. CLOD *sb.*; cf. CLOT *v.*] † **1.** *trans.* To free (land) from clods –1743. **2.** To form or turn into clods or (formerly) clots. *trans.* and *intr.* 1530. **3.** *trans.* To pelt with clods 1755. **4.** *gen.* To heave or throw heavily. *n. dial.* 1815.

Hence **Clo·dded** *ppl. a.* stuck together in clods; also formerly = Clotted.

† **Clo·dder,** *v.* 1499. [var. of CLOTTER *v.*] See CLOTTER *v.* –1876.

Cloddy (klǫ·di), *a.* 1545. [CLOD *sb.* + -Y¹.] † Clotted –1658; characterized by, or full of, clods 1545; clod-like 1712. Hence **Clo·ddiness.**

Clo·d-hopper. 1690. [f. CLOD *sb.* + HOPPER¹.] One who walks over ploughed land; a ploughman; hence, a clumsy awkward boor. So **Clo·d-hopping** *a.* following the plough; boorish.

Clo·d-pate. 1636. [See PATE.] A thick-head. Hence **Clo·d-pated** *a.*

Clo·d-poll, clod-pole. 1601. [See POLL *sb.*¹] = CLOD-PATE.

Clof, cloff, *Sc.* and *n. dial.* 1538. [– ON. *klof* space between the legs, fork, also *klofi* cleft, rift in a hill, cleft stick; cf. OS. *fugal/klovo* cleft stick for catching birds, OHG. *klobo*; f. weak grade of **kleub-* CLEAVE *v.*¹] A cleft, fissure.

Cloff (klǫf). Also *erron.* **clough.** 1502. [Origin unkn.] *Commerce.* An allowance (now of 2 lbs. in 3 cwt.), given with certain commodities, to make the weight hold good when they are sold by retail.

Clog (klǫg), *sb.* ME. [Origin unkn.] **1.** A thick piece of wood; a block, clump. Still in *Sc.* **2.** A block of wood, or the like, attached to a man or beast, to impede motion 1450. **3.** *fig.* Anything that impedes; an impediment, encumbrance, hindrance 1526. † **4.** The cone of the fir tree –1727. **5.** A wooden-soled shoe, or overshoe, worn to protect the feet from wet and dirt ME. † **6.** A kind of calendar notched upon a square block of wood, etc. –1843.

1. *Yule c.*: a Christmas log. **2.** With a clogge upon myn hele 1461. **5.** I remember at the playhouse, they used to call on Mrs. Oldfield's chair, Mrs. Barry's clogs, and Mrs. Bracegirdle's pattens H. WALPOLE. *Comb.*: **c.-almanac** = sense 6; **-dance,** a dance performed in clogs, or wooden-soled shoes; hence, **-dancer.** Hence **Clo·ggy** *a.* knotty, lumpy; apt to clog; full of clogging matter. **Clo·gginess.**

Clog (klǫg), *v.* ME. [f. the sb.] **1.** To fasten a clog or block of wood to; to fetter by this means. **2.** *fig.* To load so as to encumber; to hamper, impede 1583. **3.** To encumber by adhesion 1526. **4.** To fill up so as to impede action or function; to choke *up*, obstruct 1586. † **5.** *fig.* To cloy –1704. **6.** *intr.* (for *refl.*) To become obstructed, to stick (*lit.* and *fig.*) 1633. **7.** To put wooden soles on (shoes, etc.) 1640.

1. Chained, locked, and clogged, to staie his running awaie 1587. **2.** Fingers clogged with rings 1583. Clogging it [an Estate] with Legacies COWPER. To c. enterprise 1876. **3.** *Twel. N.* III. ii. 66. **4.** When the Eustachian tube is clogged up with mucus DUFTON. **6.** Move it sometimes.. that the seeds c. not together EVELYN. Hence **Clo·gger,** one who makes clogs, or wooden soles for shoes.

‖ **Cloison** (kloi·z'n, klwazoṅ). 1693. [Fr. = partition.] A partition, division.

‖ **Cloisonné** (klwazone), *a.* (*sb.*) 1863. [Fr., pa. pple. of *cloisonner*, f. prec.] Divided into compartments: applied to enamels. Also = *cloisonné enamel*.

In cloisonné enamels the compartments are made with thin plates set on edge upon a foundation plaque, and into these the variously coloured enamels are put in the state of powder, and then melted in the furnace. In *champlevé*, i.e. field-raised, enamel the compartments are excavated in the substance of the foundation plaque itself.

Cloister (kloi·stəɹ), *sb.* [– OFr. *cloistre* (mod. *cloître*), earlier *clostre* :– L. *claustrum*, *clostrum* lock, bar, enclosed place, f. *claud-*, stem of *claudere* CLOSE *v.* + *-trum*, instr. suffix.] **1.** An enclosed place, enclosure (*arch.*). **2.** A place of religious seclusion; a monastery or nunnery ME. Also *fig.* **3.** A covered walk or arcade connected with a monastery, college, or other building, serving sometimes as a place of exercise or study; often running round the open court of a quadrangle ME.

2. Fitter for a Cloyster than a Crowne DANIEL. *The c.*: monastic life. **3.** To walk the studious cloister's pale MILT. *Pens.* 156. *Comb.*: **c.-garth,** the open court enclosed by a c.; **-wise** *adv.* Hence **Cloi·steral,** var. of CLOISTRAL. **Cloi·sterer,** one who dwells in a c.; whence † **Cloi·stress,** a nun. **Cloi·sterless** *a.* **Cloi·sterly** *a.* proper to, or of the nature of, a c.

Cloister (kloi·stəɹ), *v.* 1581. [f. the sb.] **1.** To shut *up* in a CLOISTER (sense 2) 1591. **2.** To shut up in any seclusion 1581. **3.** *fig.* To confine, restrain 1627. **4.** To furnish with a CLOISTER (sense 3) 1625.

1. High thee to France, And Cloyster thee in some Religious House *Rich. II*, V. i. 23. **4.** Where, cloister'd round, the garden lay SCOTT.

Cloistral (kloi·străl), *a.* 1605. [f. CLOISTER *sb.* + -AL¹; cf. med.L. *claustralis*, (O)Fr. *claustral*.] Pertaining to, or dwelling in, a cloister; cloister-like.

A C. Exercise DANIEL. C. glades 1844.

Cloke, var. of CLOAK.

Clomp, *v.*, dial. f. CLAMP or CLUMP.

Clong, obs. f. CLUNG.

Clonic (klǫ·nik), *a.* 1849. [f. Gr. κλόνος violent confused motion + -IC.] *Path.* Of spasms in which violent muscular convulsions take place; opp. to *tonic*. So ‖ **Clonus** (klǭ·nǫs) [mod.L. – Gr.], a series of muscular contractions in which the individual contractions are visible 1899.

Cloop (klūp), *sb.* 1848. [Echoic.] The sound made by drawing a cork from a bottle, or any similar sound.

He can imitate any..c. of a cork wrenched from a bottle THACKERAY. So **Cloop** *v.* to make this sound.

Cloot (klut, *Sc.* klüt). *Sc.* and *n. dial.* 1725. [prob. – ON. *kló* CLAW.] **1.** The hoof, or one of its divisions, in the ox, sheep, swine, etc. **2.** pl. *Cloots*: the Devil 1787. Hence **Cloo·tie,** dim. of CLOOT (in both senses).

Close (klǭs). ME. [– (O)Fr. *clos* :– L. *clausus*; see next. The final *e* is a graphic expedient to mark the long vowel.]

A. *adj.* **I. 1.** *gen.* Closed, shut. Of vowel-sounds: Pronounced with lips partly closed, or with contraction of the oral cavity. Opp. to *open*. 1760. **2.** Enclosed or shut in; confined, narrow. Const. *in, from*. 1489. **3.** Strictly confined; also applied to the confinement ME. **4.** Shut up from observation; hidden; secluded ME. **5.** Of the atmosphere or weather: Confined, stifling, without free circulation; opp. to *fresh* 1591. **6.** Practising secrecy; reserved, uncommunicative; not open ME. **7.** Close-fisted 1654. **8.** Not open to public access or competition 1812. **9.** Of a season: Closed for the purposes of sport 1814. † **10.** Strict, severe –1770.

1. A c. mouth catcheth no flies 1712. A c. carriage 1867. **2.** To c. prison *Two Gent.* III. i. 235. C. alleys SCOTT. A c. landscape 1845. **3.** Kept c. in a Castell GRAFTON. In c. arrest WELLINGTON. **4.** My hid and c. sins 1554. In a c. Parloure 1581. *To keep c., lie c.*, etc. **5.** Keepe them [silkworms] not in roomes too hot and c. 1599. C. and sultry weather ANSON. **6.** For secrecie, No Lady closer 1 *Hen. IV*, II. iii. 113. **7.** A c., griping fellow SWIFT. **8.** *C. borough*: see BOROUGH. **10.** Devowt and clos conversation 1464. *C. mourning*: deep mourning.

II. Of proximity. The primary notion is that of having intervening space or spaces *closed* up. **1.** Having the component parts near together; dense or compact in consistency or arrangement, *e.g.* of *thickets*, close-planted; *fig.* of *reasoning*, concise 1500. **2.** In immediate proximity, very near 1489; hence, with nouns of condition, e.g. *close order*, or of action, as *close fight*, etc. 1625. Also *fig.* **3.** Close-fitting 1488. **4.** Closely attached, intimate, confidential 1577. **5.** Of attention, etc.: Strict, minute, searching 1662. **6.** Said of a contest in which the two sides are very nearly equal 1855.

1. The water made itself way through the pores of that very c. metal LOCKE. *fig.* A c. reasoner COLERIDGE. **2.** But in c. fight a champion grim SCOTT. In c. proximity 1886. C. shaving as the cause of collisions at sea 1888. *fig.* A c. translation 1718. Naut. *Close to (by, on, upon) a wind.* **3.** Her simple c. cap SCOTT. **4.** A c. Intimacy STEELE, alliance 1815, friendship MACAULAY. **5.** Under a c. cross-questioning 1857. **6.** Vehement debates and c. divisions MACAULAY.

B. *adv.* (For the adverbial use of the adj. *closely* is now preferred.) **1.** As near as can be, very near ME. † **2.** Secretly, covertly –1650. **3.** Tightly 1596. **4.** = CLOSELY 1642.

1. Where all the guests sit c. G. HERBERT. **3.** C. plastered HARINGTON. **4.** It is good to follow the light c. FULLER.

Comb.: † **c.-guard,** a guard in fence; **-harbour,** one enclosed by breakwaters or excavated in the shore; **-rolls,** the rolls in which c.-writs, etc., are recorded; **-up,** part of a cinema film taken at short range in order to magnify detail; also *fig.*; **-writs,** writs closed and sealed under the great seal.

Close (klǭs), *sb.*¹ ME. [- (O)Fr. *clos*. :– L. *clausum*, closed place, enclosure, subst. use of n. of pa. pple. of *claudere* shut, close.] **1.** *gen.* An enclosed place. **2.** An enclosure about or beside a building; *e.g.* † a quadrangle –1646; a farm-yard ME.; the precinct of a cathedral ME. **3.** An entry or passage. Now, in Scotland, *esp.* one leading from the street to dwelling-houses, etc., at the back, or to a common stair. † **4.** An enclosing line, circuit –1645.

1. † *In c.*: in a closed place; shut up. *Breaking one's c.* (law L. *clausum frangere*): i.e. the visible or invisible boundary which encloses the land of every owner or occupier. **2.** Alle the hennes in the clos CHAUCER. Closes surrounded by the venerable abodes of deans and canons MACAULAY.

Close (klōᵘz), *sb.*² ME. [f. CLOSE *v.*] **1.** The act of closing; conclusion, end. **2.** *Mus.* The conclusion of a musical phrase, theme, or movement; a CADENCE 1597. **3.** A closing or uniting together; union, junction 1591. **4.** A closing in fight; a grapple 1596. † **5.** The closing in (of night, etc.). DRYDEN.

1. When he shall come to his last c. [death] BP. HALL. **2.** The air..prolongs each heavenly c. MILT. **3.** The holy c. of lippes *Twel. N.* v. i. 161. **4.** In eager c. With Death PROCTER.

Close (klōᵘz), *v.* [f. *clos-*, pa. ppl. stem of (O)Fr. *clore* :– L. *claudere.* See CLOSE *sb.*¹] **I. 1.** *trans.* To stop up (an opening); to shut, cover in. (*Close* is more general than *shut*, and hence is more used when the notion is that of the resulting state.) **2.** *intr.* (for *refl.*) To shut itself, become shut ME. **3.** *trans.* To ENCLOSE, confine, shut up *in*, *within*. *Obs.* or *arch.* ME. Also *fig.* **4.** To fill up; to bound, shut in 1697. **5.** To cover from a blow or aim, or from sight ME.

1. To c. a dore LD. BERNERS, weary lips GRAY. Sleep..clos'd mine eyes MILT. *P.L.* VIII. 459. **2.** The grave had closed over all he loved 1891. **3.** *fig.* I clung to all the present for the promise that it closed TENNYSON. **4.** Lebanon closes the Land of Promise on the north STANLEY.

II. 1. To bring to a close; to finish, complete ME. **2.** *intr.* To come to an end 1821.

1. To c. one's days ME., a bargain DICKENS. *To c. an account*: see ACCOUNT *sb.* **2.** The sweet summer closes TENNYSON.

III. † **1.** To bring close together so as to leave no gap; to conjoin, unite, bind together, etc. –1655. Also *techn.* (see quots.). **2.** *intr.* To come close together; to join, coalesce, meet in a common centre 1551. **3.** *intr.* To draw near, approach close; also with *about*, *on*, *round*, *upon* 1523. *trans.*, chiefly *Naut.* 1673. **4.** To come to grips; to grapple *with* 1950. **5.** To come to terms (*with* a person) 1603; *to close with* an offer, etc.: to accede to, accept 1745; *to close upon*, to agree upon 1698.

1. To c. files 1649, ranks 1796. *Shoemaking. To c. a shoe:* to join together the uppers. *Electr. To c. a circuit:* to unite its parts so as to make it complete. **2.** Many Lynes c. in the Dials centre *Hen. V.* I. ii. 210. **3.** The men closed round him 1891. *To c. the wind*: to come near to it, to luff. **4.** Achilles closes with his hated foe POPE. **5.** C. with him, giue him Gold *Wint. T.* IV. iv. 830.

Clo·se-bodied, *a.* 1677. [See -ED².] **1.** Of a coat, etc.: Fitting closely. **2.** Of close grain 1726.

Closed (klōᵘzd). 1481. [CLOSE *v.*, -ED¹.] Shut up; † enclosed; limited to certain persons, etc. *C. shop*, an establishment in which only trade-union members are employed 1923.

† **Clo·se-fights,** *pl.* 1602. *Naut.* Barriers of wood fitted with loopholes, stretching across a vessel in several places; used as a place of retreat when a ship is boarded.

Clo·se-fi:sted, *a.* 1608. [See -ED².] That keeps the hand tightly shut; usu. *fig.* loath to give, niggardly, penurious. Opp. to *open-handed.*

Clo·se-grained, *a.* 1754. [See -ED².] Having the structural elements fine and closely arranged; of close texture.

Clo·se-ha:nded, *a.* 1585. **1.** = CLOSE-FISTED (*arch.*). **2.** Hand-to-hand.

Close-hauled, *ppl. a.* 1769. [See -ED¹.] *Naut.* With the sail-tacks hauled close, for sailing as near the wind as possible.

Closely (klōᵘ·sli), *adv.* 1552. [f. CLOSE *a.* + -LY².] **1.** In a CLOSE manner; usually opp. to *openly*. † **2.** Secretly, covertly, privately –1643.

1. C. confined 1891. Hair c. cut PAYN. Molecules c. packed TYNDALL. C. connected with the Sanskrit BORROW. To look at a case c. LINDLEY. **2.** We have c. sent for Hamlet hither *Haml.* III. i. 29.

Closeness (klōᵘ·snės). 1450. [f. as prec. + -NESS.] CLOSE quality or condition.

Small diffrens betweene cloosnes and consealyng 1562. Almost stifled by the c. of the room SWIFT. C. of texture 1692. C. of an imitation H. D. TRAILL. An Affectation of C. and Covetousness ADDISON.

Close quarters, *pl.* 1753. **1.** *Naut.* = earlier CLOSE-FIGHTS. **2.** *fig.* Immediate contact with the foe 1809.

† **Clo·ser**¹. ME. [– AFr. *closer*, *-ere* = OFr. *closier*, *-iere* garden, close = med.L. *closaria*, *-arius* in same sense; see CLOSE *sb.*¹, -ER².] **1.** An enclosed place; a closet –1530. **2.** That which encloses. [app. = CLOSURE in this sense.] –1605.

Closer² (klōᵘ·zəɹ). 1611. [f. CLOSE *v.* + -ER¹.] **1.** One who or that which closes (in various senses); *spec.* the workman that closes the uppers of boots. **2.** *Building.* A small stone or brick, used to end a wall, or course of brickwork 1703.

Close-reef (klōᵘ·s,rīf), *v.* 1758. [See REEF *v.*¹] To take in all the reefs of (a sail or ship); *orig.* in pa. pple. **Clo·se-reefed.**

Close-stool (klōᵘ·s,stūl). ME. [See STOOL *sb.* 3.] A chamber utensil enclosed in a stool or box. Also *attrib.*

Closet (klǫ·zet), *sb.* ME. [– OFr. *closet*, dim of *clos*; see CLOSE *sb.*¹, -ET.] **1.** A room for retirement; a private room; in later use always a small room. Also *transf.* and *fig.* **2.** The private apartment of a monarch or potentate. Now *Hist.* ME. **3.** A cabinet 1601; a side-room or recess for storing utensils, provisions, etc. **4.** Short for 'Water-closet' 1662. **5.** *attrib.* 1612.

4. In eager c. With Death PROCTER.

1. When thou prayest, enter into thy c. *Matt.* 6:6. A play for the c. 1880. † *C. of the heart*: the pericardium; also *fig.* **3.** I haue lock'd the Letter in my Closset *Lear* III. iii. 12. **5.** † **C.-sins:** secret sins.

Closet (klǫ·zėt), *v.* 1595. [f. prec. sb.] To shut up in a closet, as for private conference, or secret treaty; also *fig.*

Our Constitution was overthrown..by closetting and corrupting Members of Parliament 1690. *fig.* Oh why doth Neptune c. vp my deere 1595.

† **Closh,** *sb.*¹ 1477. [– Flem. and Du. *klos* bowl (for playing).] A game, supposed by Cowell to be ninepins, prohibited by many statutes in 15th–16th c. –1861.

Closh, *sb.*² 1572. [Origin unkn.] Swollen neck, a distemper in cattle –1727. *erron.* = FOUNDER 1726.

Closure (klōᵘ·ʒ¹ŭɹ). ME. [– OFr. *closure* :– late L. *clausura*, f. *claus-*; see CLOSE *sb.*¹, -URE.] † **1.** That which encloses, shuts in, or confines –1871. † **2.** An enclosed place –1609. † **3.** The act of enclosing, etc.; being enclosed; enclosure –1711. **4.** The act of shutting 1600; closed condition 1845. † **5.** An agreeing upon terms; agreement, union –1668. † **6.** That by which anything is fastened; a fastening –1744; *spec.* = CLOSER² 2. 1703. **7.** A bringing to a conclusion; end 1588. **8.** *spec.* The closing of a debate in a legislative assembly by vote of the house or by other authority. See also CLOTURE, the French term, occasionally used at first. 1882.

1. Within the guiltie C. of thy Walls *Rich. III*, III. iii. 11. **4.** Before Augustus's second c. thereof [i.e. of the temple of Janus] HOLLAND. **5.** So much do I desire a c. with you CROMWELL. **6.** Without a seal, wafer, or any c. whatever POPE. Hence **Clo·sure** *v.* to apply the c. to (a debate or speaker).

Clot (klǫt), *sb.* [OE. *clot(t)* = MHG. *kloz* (G. *klotz*) :– WGmc. **klutt-*, f. Gmc. **klut-* **kleut-* **klaut-*; cf. CLEAT, CLOUT.] **1.** A mass, lump, rounded mass; *esp.* a semi-solid lump formed of coagulated liquid. **2.** = CLOD 1. Still *dial.* ME. **3.** *fig.* A dull fellow. B. JONS.

1. Clots of gold STOW, of bloud 1676. The white of an egg, with spirit of wine, doth bake the egg into clots, as if it began to poch BACON (J.). *The c.*: that part of blood which turns solid, and separates from the *serum* or permanently liquid part.

Clot (klǫt), *v.* 1500. [f. prec.] **1.** *trans.* To free (lands) from clods; *absol.* to crush clods. Still *dial.* Cf. CLOD *v.* **2.** *intr.* To form into clots, lumps, etc. 1530. **3.** Of fluids: To coagulate, run into clots 1591. **4.** *trans.* To cause to cohere in clots; to cover with clots 1697.

† **Clot-bird,** 1544. [f. CLOT clod.] The wheat-ear (*Saxicola œnanthe*): so named as frequenting fallow-land. *local.* –1753.

Clot-bur (klǫ·t,bɒɹ). 1548. [f. CLOTE *sb.* + BUR; for the vocalism, cf. *bonfire*.] The Burdock.

Clote (klōᵘt). [OE. *clāte* (:– **klaitōn*), f. Gmc. **klai-* **klei-* **kli-* stick; cf. CLAY.] The Burdock; also its prickly burs. Also applied to Clivers, the Bur-weed, the Yellow Water Lily, etc. OE.

Cloth (klǫþ), *sb.* Pl. CLOTHES in the sense 'garments'; in other senses **cloths** (klǫþs, klǫðz). [OE. *clāþ* = OFris. *klāth*, *klēth*, MDu. *kleet* (Du. *kleed*), MHG. *kleit* (G. *kleid*); of unkn. origin.]

I. With *a* in *sing.* Pl. *cloths*, † *clothes.* **1.** A piece of woven or felted stuff, suitable for wrapping, spreading over, etc.; as, a TABLE-CLOTH; † a sail; a breadth of canvas in a sail; a CANVAS for painting on; etc. † **2.** A length of woven fabric; a piece –1721.

1. Having a c. round the waist LANE.

II. Without *a* in *sing.* A fabric woven, felted, or otherwise formed, of filaments, as of wool, hair, silk, the fibres of hemp, flax, cotton, asbestos, spun glass, wire. When used simply, usually a woollen fabric suitable for wearing apparel; also, more specifically, a *plain-wove* woollen fabric; as BROAD-CLOTH. ME.

C. of gold: a c. woven wholly or partly of threads of gold. *American c.*: an enamelled leather-like c. *To cut the coat according to the c.* (see CUT *v.*).

III. [See CLOTHES.] † **1.** *collect.* Clothing (no *pl.*) –1816. † **2.** A (single) garment –ME. † **3.** The distinctive dress worn by members of any calling or profession –1823. **4.** Hence: One's profession; *esp.* the clerical profession. Cf. COAT *sb.* 5. 1634.

1. Gentle folks..hae..meat and claith SCOTT. **3.** Unworthy of the king's c. 1740. **4.** *The c.*: the clergy; the office of a clergyman.

Comb.: **c.-measure,** the lineal measure used for c., in which the yard is divided into quarters and nails (sixteenths); **-paper,** a coarse paper used to lay between the folds in pressing and finishing woollen cloths; **-shearer,** one who shears off the superfluous nap on woollen clothing after teaseling; **-wo:rker,** a manufacturer of woollen c.; **-yard,** the yard by which c. was measured: chiefly in *Cloth-yard shaft.* Hence **Clo·th(e)less, clothesless,** *a.*

† **Cloth** (klǫþ), *v.* 1599. [f. prec.] To make into cloth –1641. See also CLOTHE.

Clothe (klōᵘð), *v.* Pa. t. and pple. **clothed** (klōᵘðd), **clad** (klæd). [ME. *clāþen*, pointing to OE. **clāþian*, f. *clāþ* (CLOTH *sb.*); also *clæþan*, whence ME. pa. t. *cladde*, pa. pple. *clad*, of which ON. *klæðda*, *klæddr* were partly the source.] **1.** *trans.* To cover or provide with clothing; to dress. Const. *with*, *in.* **2.** *intr.* (for *refl.*) To clothe oneself or be clothed ME. **3.** *trans.* † To put on (ME. only); to cover as with clothing ME. **4.** To cover with a cloth or cloths; *Naut.* to rig ME. **5.** *transf.* To cover as or as with clothing ME. **6.** *fig.* To cover, invest, or endow, as with a garment. Const. *with*, *in.* ME.

1. Drousinesse shall cloath a man with ragges *Prov.* 23:21. **2.** Care no more to cloath and eate *Cymb.* IV. ii. 266. **3.** In mighty armes he was yclad anon SPENSER *F.Q.* I. ii. 11. **5.** Winter when 'tis clad with snow COWLEY. Will..blossoms c. the hawthorn spray SCOTT. **6.** Hast thou clothed his necke with thunder *Job* 39:19. So shall I cloath me in a forc'd content *Oth.* III. iv. 120. Thoughts.. in sighs thus clad MILT. *P.R.* II. 65.

Clothes (klōᵘðz, *colloq.* klōᵘz), *sb. pl.* [OE. *clāþas*, ME. *clāþes*, *clōþes* (later † *cloaths*, † *close*, north. *clāþis*, Sc. *claes*).] **1.** Covering for the person; wearing apparel; dress, raiment, vesture. **b.** *spec.* Garments washed or to be washed ME. **2.** = BED-CLOTHES ME.

1. Freend, hou entridist thou hidir withut bride clothis WYCLIF *Matt.* 22:12. To wear fine cloaths FIELDING. Send the c. to the wash 1891. **2.** So a bad me lay more C. on his feet *Hen. V*, II. iii. 24.

Comb.: **c.-brush; -horse,** a wooden frame on which c. are hung out to dry; **-line, -rope,** a cord or wire on which to hang out washed c. to dry; **-moth,** a small moth, of the genus *Tinea*, the larva of which is destructive to c.; **-peg, -pin,** a forked peg used to fasten c. on a c.-line; **-press,** a receptacle for c.

Clothier (klōᵘ·ðiəɹ). ME. [Orig. *clother* (-ER¹); see -IER 1.] A maker of woollen cloth; one who sells cloth and men's clothes; a fuller and dresser of cloth (*U.S.*); etc.

Clothing (klōᵘ·ðiŋ), *vbl. sb.* ME. [f. CLOTHE *v.* + -ING¹.] **1.** The action of CLOTHE *v.*; also *fig.* **2.** Clothes collectively, apparel, dress ME.; † livery, a Livery Company –1610. Also *fig.* **3.** A covering or casing of cloth, or the like; *Mech.* = CLEADING 1789; *Naut.* sails 1798. † **4.** Clothmaking –1662. Also *attrib.*

2. The Scribes, which loue to goe in long c. *Mark* 12:38. *fig.* Words are the Cloathing of our Thoughts SWIFT. **4.** C. is plied in this city FULLER.

Clo·th-maker. ME. A maker of woollen cloth.

Clot-poll, -pole. 1606. = CLOD-POLL.

Clotted (klǫ·tėd), *ppl. a.* 1605. [f. CLOT *v.* + -ED[1].] **1.** Gathered into clots, or clods. **2.** Stuck together in or with clots; covered with clots 1725.

1. Clotted cream: = CLOUTED-cream. Wash off The c. blood MASSINGER. **2.** The c. scourge 1804.

† **Clo·tter,** *v.* ME. [frequent. of CLOT *v.*; see -ER[5]. Cf. CLUTTER *v.*] To run together in clots, to coagulate. *trans.* and *intr.* Also *fig.* –1700.

The gore congealed was clottered in his hair DRYDEN. Hence † **Clo·ttered** *ppl. a.* = CLOTTED.

Clotty (klǫ·ti), *a.* 1523. [f. CLOT *sb.* + -Y[1].] Full of clots, inclined to clot; † CLODDY.

‖ **Cloture** (klōtür). 1871. [Fr. *clôture.*] = CLOSURE 8. Hence **Cloture** *v. trans.* and *intr.* (*colloq.*)

Clo·tweed. *rare.* 1804. [f. CLOTE; cf. CLOT-BUR.] The Bur-weed.

‖ **Clou** (klū). 1883. [Fr., = nail, peg.] The point of greatest interest, the chief attraction.

Cloud (klaud), *sb.* [OE. *clūd*, prob. rel. to CLOD. In sense 3 it superseded OE. *wolcen* WELKIN and ME. *skie* SKY.] † **1.** A mass of rock, a hill –ME. † **2.** = CLOD 2, 3. –1460. **3.** A visible mass of condensed watery vapour floating at various heights in the upper air ME. *rhet.* in *pl.* The heavens ME. **4.** *transf.* A cloud-like mass of smoke or dust floating in the air ME. **5.** An appearance of dimness in a clear liquid or transparent body 1533; a patch of indeterminate outline on a surface of another colour 1606. **6.** A cloudlike body of insects, birds, etc.; hence, a multitude, a crowd ME. **7.** A loose-knitted woollen scarf worn by ladies 1877. **8.** *transf.* and *fig.* Anything that obscures or conceals 1509. **9.** *fig.* Anything that darkens or overshadows with gloom, trouble, suspicion; a state of gloom, etc.; a darkening of the countenance ME.

3. Euery C. engenders not a Storme 3 *Hen. VI*, V. iii. 10. She is aduan'st Aboue the Cloudes, as high as Heauen it selfe *Rom. & Jul.* IV. v. 74. *Magellanic Clouds*: the two large nebulæ near the south pole of the heavens so named. **4.** A thicke c. of incense went vp *Ezek.* 8:11. *To blow a c.*: to smoke tobacco (*slang*). **5.** A plain iron gray Nag, with a c. in his face 1675. **6.** So greet a c. of witnessis WYCLIF *Heb.* 12:1. A c. of gnattes SPENSER, Locusts MILT., arrows GIBBON. **8.** To go abroad under c. of night 1752. *In the clouds*: obscure; fanciful; above the range of common understanding. **9.** A c. of ignorance 1572, suspicion MERIVALE. *Under a c.*: in trouble or difficulties; out of favour; with a slur on one's character.

Comb.: **c.-assembler,** he who collects the clouds (tr. Gr. νεφεληγερέτα, epithet of Zeus in Homer); **-built** *a.* built of clouds; *fig.* built in the clouds; **-burst** [G. *Wolkenbruch*] (*U.S.*), a violent storm of rain, a waterspout; **-capt, -capped** *a.* having clouds about its summit; **-compeller,** = *cloud-assembler*; also *joc.* a smoker; **-drift,** a body of clouds drifting through the air; **-rack,** a collection of broken clouds drifting across the sky; **-ring,** *spec.* the cloudy zone of calms and variable winds at some distance on each side of the equator; **-wards** *adv.*; **-world,** = CLOUDLAND.

Hence **Clou·dage.** *rare.* [see -AGE.] **Clou·dless** *a.* unclouded; **Clou·dlessly** *adv.*; **Clou·dlessness. Clou·dlet,** a little c. **Clou·dscape** [after *landscape*], a scene composed of clouds (*rare*).

Cloud (klaud), *v.* 1513. [f. prec. sb.]

I. *trans.* To cover or darken with clouds; *fig.* to overshadow; to darken with trouble 1583. **2.** *transf.* and *fig.* To render obscure; to dim, darken 1513. † **3.** To veil –1711. **4.** To cast a slur upon, asperse, sully 1611. **5.** To diversify with patches of undefined outline 1710.

1. The moon being clouded presently is miss'd SHAKS. Your dislikes..Doth c. my ioyes with danger, and with sorrow 3 *Hen. VI*, IV. i. 74. **2.** Our moral judgement may..be clouded 1856. **4.** To heare My Soueraigne Mistresse clouded so *Wint. T.* I. ii. 280.

II. *intr.* **1.** To become cloudy or dim; to become overcast with clouds. Const. *over, up.* 1562. **2.** *fig.* To become gloomy 1588.

2. Worthies away, the Scene begins to c. SHAKS.

Cloudland (klau·dlænd). 1817. *poet.* and *rhet.* **1.** The region of clouds; a 'cloudscape'. **2.** *fig.* A region of fancy, myth, or unreality 1847.

Cloudy (klau·di), *a.* OE. [f. CLOUD *sb.* + -Y[1].] † **1.** Rocky; hilly –ME. **2.** Of cloud; of or pertaining to the clouds ME. **3.** Characterized by, or full of, clouds ME. **4.** Not clear; having cloud-like markings 1587. **5.** *fig.* Darkened by ignorance, etc.; dim, obscure, indistinct ME. **6.** Darkened by misfortune, grief, anger, forebodings, etc.; gloomy, sullen, frowning ME.

2. He spake unto them in the c. pillar *Ps.* 99:7. The cloudie region 1635. **3.** The c. north DRYDEN. **4.** C. Ale 1679. **5.** The c. knowledge of mankinde SIDNEY. **6.** The Scithians..have all c. foreheads 1650. Hence **Clou·dily** *adv.* **Clou·diness.**

Clough (klɒf, klau). [OE. *clōh* (in place-names) :- Gmc. **klaŋχ-*, rel. to OHG. *klinga* (G. dial. *klinge*) ravine.] **1.** A ravine or valley with steep sides ME. † **2.** *Occas.* = 'cliff' –ME.

Clough, erron. sp. of CLOFF, CLOW.

Clour (klūᵊɹ), *sb. Sc.* and *n. dial.* 1508. [Origin unkn.] A bump (on the head); a knock such as would raise a bump; a dint. Hence **Clour** *v.* to raise a lump on, etc.

Clout (klaut), *sb.*[1] *arch.* and *dial.* [OE. *clūt*, corresp. to (M)LG., MDu. *klūt(e)* (Du. *kluit* lump, clod), ON. *klútr* kerchief; rel. to CLEAT, CLOT.] **1.** A piece of cloth, leather, metal, etc.; a patch. **2.** A plate of iron; *esp.* one fixed on an axletree, to prevent wear. [Cf. CLEAT.] Now *dial.* OE. **3.** *spec.* A rag; a cloth (*esp.* one put to mean uses) ME. † **4.** *spec.* in *pl.* Swaddling clothes –1826. † **5.** *Archery.* The mark shot at; *ellipt.* a shot that hits the mark –1868. **6.** A heavy blow, *esp.* with the hand. Cf. CLOD *sb.* Now *dial.* ME.

1. Cloutes and patches pieced one by one 1563. **3.** Driven, like turkeys to market with a stick and a red c. STERNE. Till May be out Ne'er cast a c. *Provb.* **5.** Though the c. we do not always hit B. JONS. *Comb.* **c.-nail,** a flat-headed nail, used for fastening a c. on an axle, studding boots, etc.

Clout, *sb.*[2] Now *dial.* [ME. *clūte*, prob. same word as prec.] **1.** Clot of earth, clod. † **2.** Clouted cream –1648.

Clout (klaut), *v.* Now *arch.* or *dial.* ME. [f. CLOUT *sb.*[1]] **1.** *trans.* To mend with a CLOUT; to patch. Also *fig.* † **2.** To put *in, on,* or *to* by way of a patch. Also *absol.* To add patches. –1581. **3.** To protect with an iron plate; also, to stud shoes with clout-nails ME. † **4.** *fig.* To patch clumsily or botch *up* –1602. **5.** To cover with, or as with, a cloth (*arch.*) 1579. **6.** To cuff heavily. Now *dial.* ME.

1. *fig.* He clowteth the old broken holes with patches of papistry BALE. **5.** He..showed a leg clouted up 1709. **6.** The late Queen of Spain took off one of her chapines, and clowted Olivarez about the noddle with it HOWELL. Hence **Clou·ted** *ppl. a.*[1] **Clou·ter,** a cobbler or patcher; a botcher. † **Clou·terly** *a.* and *adv.*

Clou·ted, *ppl. a.*[2] 1542. [perh. f. **clout*, unrecorded var. of CLOT *sb.*[1] or CLOT *v.* + -ED[2], -ED[1].] Said of cream obtained by scalding, which makes it thick or clotted.

† **Clou·t-shoe.** Now (*arch.*) **Clouted shoe.** 1463. [f. CLOUT *sb.*[1]] **1.** A shoe studded with large-headed nails. (Or ? a patched shoe.) † **2.** One who wears clouted shoes; a boor. (Cf. *Colin Clout.*) –1704.

1. The dull swain..with his clouted shoon MILT. [Cf. 'clowted brogues' *Cymb.* IV. ii. 214.]

Clove (klōᵘv), *sb.*[1] [OE. *clufu*, corresp. to the first element in OS. *cluflōc* 'clove-leek', garlic, OHG. *klovolouh* (G. *knoblauch*), f. weak grade of Gmc. **kleub-*; see CLEAVE *v.*[1]] **1.** One of the small bulbs which make up the compound bulb of garlic, shallot, etc. **2.** A natural segment of a fruit 1634. Hence † **Cloved** *ppl. a.* divided into cloves.

Clove (klōᵘv), *sb.*[2] [orig. *clow (of) gilofer* – (O)Fr. *clou de girofle* (*gilofre*) 'nail of clove-tree'; see GILLYFLOWER.] **1.** The dried flower-bud of *Caryophyllus aromaticus*, much used as a pungent aromatic spice. (Usu. in *pl.*) **2.** The tree, *Caryophyllus aromaticus*, orig. a native of the Moluccas 1594. **3.** Short for *clove-pink*, or *clove-gillyflower* 1746. **4.** *Cloves.* A cordial flavoured with this spice 1852.

Comb.: **c.-bark,** the bark of *Cinnamomum culilawan*, which has a flavour of cloves; **-pink,** a c.-scented species of *Dianthus*: see CLOVE-GILLYFLOWER.

Clove, *sb.*[3] ME. [repr. AL. *clavus*, AFr. *clou.*] A weight formerly used for wool and cheese, equal to 7 or 8 lbs. avoirdupois.

Clove, *sb.*[4] *U.S.* 1779. [– Du. *klove*, also *kloof*, in MDu. *clove*, MLG. *klove* split, cleft. Rel. to CLEAVE *v.*[1]] A rocky cleft; a gap, ravine: used chiefly in place-names; as, *C. of Kaaterskill, Stony C.*

Clove (klōᵘv), *v.* 1863. [f. CLOVE *sb.*[2]] To spice with cloves; to stick (an onion, etc.) with cloves.

Clove, *pa. pple.* 1561. Short f. CLOVEN, still occas. in verse. Hence **c.-hitch,** a hitch round a spar, etc., formed by passing the rope twice round in such a way that both ends pass under the centre of the loop in front; **-hook,** an iron clasp in two overlapping parts, used for bending chain-sheets to clews of sails, etc.

Clove, pa. t. of CLEAVE *v.*

Clove-gillyflower (klōᵘ·v dʒi·liflauᵊɹ). ME. [orig. *clowe gilofre* (XIV–XV); see CLOVE *sb.*[2], GILLYFLOWER.] † **1.** The spice CLOVE *sb.*[2] 1. –1486. **2.** A clove-scented species of Pink (*Dianthus caryophyllus*), whence the carnation, etc. 1535.

Cloven (klōᵘ·v'n), *ppl. a.* ME. [pa. pple. of CLEAVE *v.*] Divided lengthwise; split.

C. hoof or *foot*, the divided hoof of ruminant quadrupeds; ascribed in pagan mythology to the god Pan, and thence to the Devil, and often used allusively as the indication of Satan, or Satanic agency. Hence **c.-hoofed, -foo·ted** *adjs.*

Clover (klōᵘ·vəɹ). [OE. *clāfre* = (M)LG., Du. *klāver* :- Gmc. **klaibrōn*, the first syll. corresp. to OS. *klē*, OHG. *klēo* (G. *klee*) :- WGmc. **klaiwaz, -am* clover.] The common name of the species of Trefoil (*Trifolium*, N.O. *Leguminosæ*), esp. *T. repens* and *T. pratense*, both cultivated largely for fodder. Applied also locally to many plants with similar characters.

Phr. *To live* (or *be*) *in c.*: to live luxuriously, as cattle do in a field of c.

Comb.: **c.-hay worm,** the larva of a moth, *Asopia costalis*, very destructive to clover-hay in N. America; **-weevil,** a small weevil, *Apion apricans*, which feeds on the seeds of c. Hence **Clo·very** *a.* (*rare*).

Clo·ver, *v.* 1649. [f. the sb.] To sow or lay down with clover. So **Clo·vered** *ppl. a.* sown or covered with clover.

† **Clover-grass.** = CLOVER.

Clow (klau), *sb.* ME. [A false singular f. *clowes, clowis*, in ME. *clowse, clowze*, OE. *clūse* – late L. *clusa*, var. of *clausa*, a closed place or way. Cf. CLOSE *sb.*[1] In XVIII erron. spelt *clough*, by engineers, etc.] **1.** A dam for water. ? *Obs.* **2.** A sluice 1483.

Clow(e)-gilofre, *etc.*, earlier f. CLOVE-GILLYFLOWER.

Clown (klaun), *sb.* 1563. [perh. of LG. origin; cf. NFris. *klönne, klünne* clumsy fellow, *klünj* clod, lump, and the like.] **1.** A countryman, or peasant; a boor. **2.** *transf.* An ignorant, uncouth, ill-bred man 1583. **3.** A fool or jester; in mod. use, one of the characters in a pantomime, a circus, etc. 1600. Also *attrib.*

1. The c., the child of nature, without guile COWPER. A clod-pated C. 1733. **2.** By blood a king, at heart a c. TENNYSON. **3.** The clowne shall make those laugh whose lungs are tickled a' th' sere *Haml.* II. ii. 336. Hence † **Clow·nage,** behaviour or function of a c. **Clow·nery,** clownishness; performance of a c.

Clown (klaun), *v. rare.* 1579. [f. the sb.] To perform as a (stage-)clown. *To c. it*: to play the clown.

Clownish (klau·niʃ), *a.* 1570. [f. CLOWN *sb.* + -ISH[1].] **1.** Of, belonging, or proper to a CLOWN. **2.** Clown-like, rude, boorish; ignorant; clumsy; coarse 1581.

1. In c. apparell 1581. **2.** C. or uncivill fashions 1586. Hence **Clow·nish-ly** *adv.*, **-ness.**

Clownship (klau·nʃip). 1606. [See -SHIP.] The condition or estate of a clown or clowns; also as a mock title.

Cloy (kloi), *v.*[1] ME. [Aphetic f. † *acloy*, – AFr. *acloyer* (see A- *pref.* 10), var. of OFr. *encloyer* (mod. *enclouer*) :- Rom. **inclavare*, f. L. *in* EN-[1] + *clavus* nail.] † **1.** To nail (ME. only). † **2.** To pierce with or as with a nail –1726. † **3.** To spike (a gun) –1768. † **4.** To stop up, block (a passage, etc.); to crowd or fill *up* –1636. † **5.** *fig.* To clog (movement, etc.); to weigh down –1665. **4.** To fill to loathing; to surfeit. *lit.* and *fig.* Also *absol.* 1530.

2. He never shod horse but he cloyed him BACON. [A wild boar] with his cruell tusk him deadly cloyd SPENSER *F.Q.* III. vi. 48. **4.** To c. a harbour by sinking ships laden with stones SPEED. **6.** Who can..c. the hungry edge of appetite By bare imagination of a Feast *Rich. II*, I. iii. 296. *fig.*

Often preaching cloyeth the people UDALL. † **Cloy·ment,** satiety (*rare*). **Cloy·some** *a. rare*, of cloying quality.

† **Cloy,** *v.*[2] *rare*. Explained as 'To claw' (Steevens); 'to strike the beak together' (Johnson). *Cymb*. v. iv. 118.

Cloy·less, *a.* 1606. [f. CLOY *v.*[1] + -LESS.] That does not CLOY (sense 6).

† **Cloyne, cloine,** *v.* 1538. [perh. – OFr. *cluignier* blink or wink the eyes (mod. *cligner*) as the expression of secret understanding, etc.] **1.** *intr.* To cheat, deceive –1569. **2.** *trans.* To take furtively or fraudulently; to grab –1566.

Club (klɒb), *sb.* [– ON. *clubba*, assim. form of *klumba* (cf. *klumbu-*, *klubbufótr* club-footed), rel. to CLUMP.]

I. 1. A heavy staff for use as a weapon, thin at one end for the hand, and thicker at the other; also = *Indian club*. **2.** A stick or bat used in various games of ball, as golf, hockey, etc. 1450. **3.** The butt-end of a gun 1724. **4.** Any club-shaped organ, structure, etc. 1707.

1. The geaunte bare a clubbe CAXTON. † *Clubs are trump(s*: physical force is to rule the day; a punning allusion to II. **4.** A nose which had a red c. to it MARRYAT. A c., otherwise a very thick pigtail 1850.

II. In cards. *pl.* The suit of cards distinguished by the representation of a trefoil leaf in black; in *sing.* a card of this suit.

[A tr. of Sp. *basto*, or It. *bastone* (see BASTO, BASTON), the 'club' figured on Spanish cards. The English figure is the French *trèfle* trefoil.]

III. A combination. [See the vb. The course of development is uncertain.] † **1.** Combination into one mass; aggregate –1674. † **2.** A combination of contributions to make up a total sum; one share of this –1792. † **3.** A social meeting the expenses of which are jointly defrayed –1801. † **4.** A clique; a secret society –1730. **5.** An association of persons meeting periodically (under certain regulations), at some house of entertainment, for social intercourse, etc. 1670. **6.** An association of persons interested in the promotion of some object; as *Alpine, Yacht C.*, etc.; *Benefit, Goose C.*, etc. 1755. **7.** An association of persons formed mainly for social purposes, and having buildings for the exclusive use of the members, and always open to them as a place of resort, or, in some cases, of temporary residence 1776; the buildings occupied by such a society 1837. Also *attrib.*

2. We dined merry: but my c. and the rest come to 7/6*d.*, which was too much PEPYS. **3.** This Tavern, where they held their C. DE FOE. **4.** The Jacobite clubb 1695. **5.** In my absence they had erected a C. and made me one SWIFT. **7.** They sent for me at my c. 1883.

Comb.: **c.-house,** the house occupied by a c.; **-land** (*colloq.*), the vicinity of St. James's, in London; **-money,** subscription to a benefit c. or provident society; **-root,** a disease of turnips, etc., anbury; **-wood,** CASUARINA. Hence **Clu·bbable, clubable** *a.* fit to be a member of a c. **Clu·bbish** *a.* clownish (*dial.*); addicted to clubs. **Clu·bless** *a.*

Club (klɒb), *v.* 1593. [f. CLUB *sb.* I.] **1.** To beat with or as with a club. **2.** To gather into a club-like mass 1625; hence, to gather together 1641. **3.** *intr.* To combine together 1649. **4.** To combine, or contribute, to a common end 1632. **5.** To combine, or contribute, to make up a total sum 1655. **6.** *Mil.* To throw into a confused mass 1806. **7.** *Naut.* To drift down a current with an anchor out (Dicts.) 1850.

1. *To c. a musket*: to use it as a club. **2.** Hair clubbed, atop, Chinese fashion FORREST. To c. quotations MILT. **4.** They clubbed their small means together CARLYLE. **5.** To find out a ninepence to c. with me for the coach PEPYS. **6.** To c. the battalion WINDHAM. Hence **Clu·bbing** *vbl. sb., spec.* a disease in cabbages, etc.

Clubbed (klɒbd), *ppl. a.* ME. [1 f. the *sb.* + -ED[2]; 2 f. the vb. + -ED[1].] **1.** Shaped like a club; thick-set. **2.** Used as a club 1724; thrown into a confused mass, as a *c. battalion* 1823.

Clubber (klɒ·bəɹ). 1633. [f. CLUB *v.* or *sb.* + -ER[1].] **1.** One who clubs or belongs to a club. **2.** One who wields a club 1887.

Clubbism (klɒ·biz'm). 1837. [f. CLUB *sb.* + -ISM.] The club system.

To passionate Constitutionalism..C. will..seem the root of all evil CARLYLE. So **Clu·bbist,** a member or supporter of the political clubs of the French Revolution, or of their principles, a member of a club.

† **Club-fist.** 1575. A large clenched fist; hence, a rough, brutal fellow –1589. So **Club-fisted** *a.*

Clu·b-foot. 1538. **1.** A name for various distortions, generally congenital, which give the foot a lumpy, club-like appearance. **2.** A foot of a stunted, lumpy appearance 1683. Also *attrib.* Hence **Clu·b-foo:ted** *a.*

Club-haul (klɒ·bˌhǭl), *v.* 1794. *Naut.* To tack a ship by letting the lee-anchor down as soon as the wind is out of the sails, by which her head is brought to wind; when she then pays off, the cable is cut, and the sails are trimmed to the other tack: a last resort in very perilous positions.

Club-law. 1612. The use of the club, or physical force, as contrasted with argument; law of the physically stronger.

Argumenta ad baculum, vulgarly termed club-law 1829.

Club-man (klɒ·bmǣn). 1597. **1.** A man armed with a club. **2.** A member of a club 1851.

Club-moss (klɒ·bˌmǫs). 1597. [tr. L. *Muscus clavatus*.] A name properly applied to *Lycopodium clavatum* from the club-like shape of its upright fertile spikes of spore-cases; thence extended to other, and occas. to all, *Lycopodiaceæ*.

Clu·b-:riser. 1645. [See RISER I. 2.] *Eng. Hist.* pl. Bodies of untrained and half-armed countrymen during the Civil War.

Clu·b-rush. 1677. Any plant of the genus *Scirpus* (N.O. *Cyperaceæ*).

Club-shaped (klɒ·bˌʃēⁱpt), *a.* 1776. Thickening towards one extremity which is blunt and rounded; in *Zool.* and *Bot.* = CLAVATE.

Clu·bster. 1727. [See -STER.] = CLUBMAN.

Cluck (klɒk), *sb.* 1703. [f. CLUCK *v.*] **1.** *interj.* An imitation of the abrupt hollow guttural sound made by a hen desiring to sit or calling her chickens 1829. **2.** A name for this, or any similar sound, *e.g.* the S. African click (see CLICK *sb.*[1] 5) 1703.

Cluck (klɒk), *v.* 1481. [Of imit. origin, corresp. to MHG. *klucken*, (also mod.) *glucken*, Da. *klukke*, Sw. *klucka*; see CLOCK *v.*[2]] **1.** *intr.* To make the sound described under CLUCK *sb.*, or any similar sound 1611. † **2.** *trans.* To call (chickens) as a hen does. Also *fig.* –1687.

2. *fig.* That he may c. sinners to himself 1658.

Clu·dder, *v.*, a var. of CLODDER, q.v.

Clue (klū, klⁱū). 1596. [Later form (XV) of CLEW.] = CLEW. Used in all senses, but *esp.* in the *fig.*

A c. of yarn 1834. And treads the maze of life without a c. POMFRET. A c. to the identity of one C. BRONTË. Research which has..joined the broken c. of history from contemporaneous monuments 1876. Hence **Clue·less** *a. Comb.* **c.-line:** see CLEW-LINE.

† **Clum,** *sb.* (*interj.*) ME. [Origin unkn.] **1.** Silence, quiet (ME. only). **2.** ? A note of silence; cf. *mum!* –1616.

Clumber (klɒ·mbəɹ). 1865. [f. *Clumber*, a seat of the Duke of Newcastle.] Name of a breed of spaniels.

Clump (klɒmp), *sb.* 1586. [– MLG. *klumpe* (LG. *klump*), rel. to MDu. *klompe* (Du. *klomp*) lump, mass, and OE. *clympre* (see CLUMPER), CLAMP *sb.*[3], CLUB *sb.*] **1.** A compact (shapeless) mass, a heap, a lump 1690. **2.** A cluster; a tuft; a patch 1586. **3.** *Clumps*: a parlour game of questions and answers 1883. **4.** A thick extra sole on a shoe 1879. **5.** *Mining.* = CLUNCH 1865. ¶ *Erron.* used for CLAMP 1825.

2. A c. of Scots Fir Trees 1759. New clumps of young plants VINES. *Comb.* **c.-boot, -shoe,** one with a **c.-sole,** or thick double sole for rough wear. Hence **Clu·mpish** *a.* heavy and clumsy. **Clu·mpy** *a.* clump-like; clumpish.

Clump (klɒmp), *v.* 1665. [Partly f. CLUMP *sb.*; cf. CLAMP *v.*[3]] **1.** To tread heavily and clumsily. **2.** *trans.* To put together into a clump; to plant in a clump 1824. **3.** To add an extra thick sole; to clog. Hence **Clumped** *ppl. a.* † clubbed, as in *clumped foot*; furnished with clumps of trees, or with clump-soles.

Clumper, *sb.* Now *dial.* [OE. *clympre*; see CLUMP *sb.*] = CLUMP *sb.* 1.

† **Clumper,** *v.* 1562. [f. prec.] To form into lumps or masses –1647.

Vapours..Clumper'd in balls of clouds HY. MORE.

Clumps, a game; see CLUMP *sb.* 3.

Clumse, *a.* (*sb.*) Now *dial.* 1611. [rel. to CLUMSE *v.*; kindred adjs. in mod. Scand. are Icel. *klumsa* lock-jawed, Sw. dial. *klumsen* benumbed, dazed, *klumsig* numb, clumsy.] Benumbed with cold; hence, stupid; unhandy, lazy; in mod. dial., also, surly.

† **Clumse,** *v.* [Earliest as *clumsed* (XIII), prob. of Scand. origin; cf. Norw. dial. *klumsen* strike dumb, clog, hamper, *klumst* clumsy.] **1.** To be or become numb with cold (ME. only). **2.** *trans.* To stupefy (ME. only). Hence † **Clumsed, clumst** *ppl. a.*

Clumsy (klɒ·msi), *a.* 1597. [f. CLUMSE *v.* + -Y[1]. Cf. Sw. *klumsig* (see CLUMSE *a.*).] † **1.** Benumbed with cold –1602. **2.** Acting or moving as if benumbed; heavy and awkward; ungainly, unhandy 1597. **3.** *fig.* Ill-contrived, awkward 1681. **4.** Rudely constructed; inelegant, unwieldy 1763.

1. Clumsie winter MARSTON. **2.** Clumsie fingers RAY. A c., aukward, and unhandy people SWIFT. **3.** In c. verse, unlick'd, unpointed DRYDEN. C. apologies SWIFT. **4.** The boots..are a trifle c. 1888. Hence **Clu·msily** *adv.* **Clu·msiness,** c. quality.

Clunch, *a.* Now *dial.* 1776. [prob. f. LG. *klunt*, Du. *klont* 'lump, clod, clown'.] Lumpy; stiff; thickset, 'chunky' in figure.

She is fat, and c., and heavy, and ugly MME. D'ARBLAY.

Clunch (klɒnʃ), *sb.* 1602. [prob. subst. use of prec. But the analogy of *bump, bunch, hump, hunch* suggests a similar relation of *clump, clunch*.] **1.** A lump (*dial.*). **2.** A lumpish fellow, a lout. Now *dial.* 1602. **3.** Any of various stiff clays 1679. **4.** A soft limestone forming one of the beds of the lower chalk 1823.

Clunch, *v. rare.* 1628. By-form of CLENCH. Hence † **Clunchfist,** a clenched fist (*lit.* and *fig.*); a miser.

Clung (klɒŋ), *ppl. a. arch.* and *dial.* ME. [f. CLING *v.*] Drawn together, shrunk; of soil: Clinging, stiff.

Clung, pa. t. and pple. of CLING *v.*, q.v.

† **Clung,** *v.* 1601. By-form of CLING *v.* –1715.

Cluniac (klū·niæk). 1631. [– med.L. *Cluniacus*, f. *Clun(i)æum* Cluny or Clugny, France; see -AC.] *adj.* Belonging to the monastery of Cluny, near Mâcon in France. *sb.* A monk of Cluny. So **Cluniace·nsian, Clunist.**

Clupeoid (klū·piˌoid). 1880. [f. L. *clupea* a kind of small river-fish, taken as the generic name of the herring, etc. + -OID.] A fish belonging to the herring family (*Clupeidæ*).

Cluster (klɒ·stəɹ), *sb.* Also **gluster** (*Spenser*). [OE. *clyster*, (rare) *cluster*, also *ġeclystre* bunch of grapes, prob. f. **klut-* (see CLOT). For the vocalism cf. BLUSH.] **1.** A collection of things of the same kind, growing closely together; a bunch. † **2.** A rounded mass; a clot –1548. **3.** A number of persons, animals, or things close together; a group, swarm, crowd ME. Also *fig.*

1. The glusters of ripe grapes SPENSER. A c. of nuttis 1483, egges EDEN, flowers GRAY. **3.** As bees..all in a c. PURCHAS. Clusters of islets SIR J. ROSS, stars 1854. *fig.* Ideas..in clusters TUCKER. *Comb.* **c.-candlestick,** a branched candlestick. Hence **Clu·stery** *a.* (Dicts.).

Cluster (klɒ·stəɹ), *v.* ME. [f. prec. sb.] **1.** *trans.* To gather or group in clusters; to cover with clusters ME. **2.** *intr.* To congregate in a cluster 1541; to grow or be situated in a cluster or clusters 1590.

1. Not less..would..The foxglove c. dappled bells TENNYSON. Ylion was..clustrit with towres ME. **2.** Woes c.; rare are solitary woes YOUNG. [Curls] clustered round her head WORDSW. Hence **Clu·stered** *ppl. a., spec.* in *clustered pillar*, etc.: 'several slender pillars or shafts attached to each other so as to form one' (Gwilt). **Clu·steringly** *adv.*

† **Clusterfist.** 1611. [f. CLUSTER in sense of lump; cf. *clunchfist*.] A clumsy- or close-fisted fellow; a lout, a niggard –1675.

Clutch (klɒtʃ), *sb.*[1] [f. CLUTCH *v.*[1]; earlier synon. forms are (dial.) *cloke*, † *cloch* (XIII), Sc. *cluk, cleuk* (XIV), † *clouch* (XV), † *clooch* (XVI). The interrelation and history of the series of forms is obscure.] **1.** The claw of a beast or bird of prey, or of a fiend: mostly in *pl.*; also *contempt.* the human hand. **2.** The hand, or in *pl.* 'hands in a sense of rapacity and cruelty' (J.). Now usu. *grasp.* 1526. **3.** Tight grip or grasp; clutching 1784. **4.** An act of grasping *at* 1831. **5.** *Mech.* A coupling for throwing the working parts into or out of action at will 1814. **6.** *Mech.* A contrivance with two hooked arms for clutching bodies to be lifted by a crane, etc. 1874.

2. But Age..hath caught me in his c. *Haml.* v. i. 80. The Clutches of the Hangman STEELE. **3.** The c. of poverty COWPER. **4.** An expiring c. at popularity CARLYLE. *Comb.* **c.-fist,** a miser, also as *adj.*

Clutch, *sb.*[2] 1721. [prob. of southern dial. origin like synon. north. *cletch* (cf. CLETCH *sb.*), rel. obscurely to *cleck* hatch (XV, chiefly Sc.); see CLECK *v.*] A var. of CLETCH.

Clutch (klɒtʃ), *v.*[1] [ME. *clucche*, varying with *cliche* (see CLITCH *v.*), repr. OE. *clyććan* crook, clench :– **klukjan*.] † **1.** = CLITCH 1, –1703. **2.** *trans.* To seize with claws or clutches; to seize eagerly ME. Also *absol.* **3.** To hold tightly in the closed hand 1602. Also *fig.* **4.** *intr.* To make a clutch *at* 1831.

1. Not that I haue the power to c. my hand, When his faire Angels would salute my palme SHAKS. **2.** I clutched up the cat HELPS. **3.** Is this a Dagger, which I see before me? Come, let me c. thee SHAKS. *fig.* To c. the globe in one intellectual grasp COLLIER. **4.** How we c. at shadows CARLYLE.

Clutch, *v.*[2] [f. CLUTCH *sb.*[2]] To hatch (chickens). GOLDSM.

Clutter (klɒ·təɹ), *sb.* 1580. [Goes with CLUTTER *v.*; has been assoc. to some extent with *cluster* and *clatter*.] † **1.** A clotted mass –1611. **2.** A confused collection 1666; crowded confusion, litter (*dial.* and *U.S.*) 1694. **3.** Bustle, stir (*arch.*) 1649; hubbub (*arch.*) 1656; mingled rattle (*arch.*) 1655.

2. A c. of Citations 1666. He saw what a C. there was with huge, over-grown Pots R. L'ESTRANGE **3.** I heard such a c. of small shot VANBRUGH.

Clu·tter, *v.* 1556. [var. of CLOTTER, CLODDER; see prec.] † **1.** *intr.* To clot. Also *trans.* –1676. **2.** To crowd together in heaps 1556. **3.** To run in bustling disorder or with a confused noise; to make a clatter 1602. **4.** To crowd *with* a litter of things 1674. **5.** To utter words confusedly 1654.

Hence **Clu·tterment,** confused bustle, crowd.

Cly, *sb. Thieves' cant.* 1690. [poss. of LG. origin; cf. LG. *kleien* scratch, claw.] Money; also, a pocket. So **Cly** *v.* to take; *esp.* to steal.

Clydesdale (kləi·dzdeⁱl). 1831. A breed of heavy draught horses orig. from the Clyde valley, Scotland.

Clypea·ster. 1836. [f. CLYPEUS + Gr. ἀστήρ star.] *Zool.* A genus of echinoid Echinoderms, allied to the common sea-urchin, but having mouth and vent both below. Hence **Clypea·stroid** *a.* and *sb.*

Clypeate (kli·pi,eⁱt), *a.* 1711. [f. as prec. + -ATE[2].] Shaped like a round shield. So **Cly·peiform** *a.*

Clypeo-, comb. f. CLYPEUS, as in *c.-frontal* (*Entom.*), common to the clypeus and front.

Clypeole (kli·piōᵘl). 1882. [– L. *clypeolum*, dim. of *clypeum*, *clypeus* shield.] A little shield; 'term applied to the lamina on the inner surface of which the sporangia are attached in Equisetum'. Hence **Cly·peolar** *a.* formed like a c. **Cly·peolate** *a.* furnished with clypeoles.

‖ **Clypeus** (kli·piɒ̆s). 1834. [var. of L. *clipeus*, *clupeus* round shield.] *Entom.* The broad shield-shaped part of the head of some insects. Hence **Cly·peal** *a.* of or pertaining to the c.

Clysmian (kli·zmiăn), *a. rare.* 1882. [f. as next + -IAN.] Epithet of soils produced by transport and mechanical deposit, of which water has been the agent.

Clysmic (kli·zmik), *a.* 1847. [f. Gr. κλυσμός liquid used for washing out + -IC.] Washing, cleansing.

Clyster (kli·stəɹ), *sb.* ME. [– (O)Fr. *clystère* or L. *clyster* – Gr. κλυστήρ syringe, f. κλύζειν wash out, drench.] **1.** A medicine injected into the rectum; an injection, enema; *occas.*, a suppository. † **2.** The pipe or syringe used in injection 1527. Hence **Cly·ster** *v.* to treat with clysters. † **Cly·sterize** *v.* to inject as a c. *Comb.* **c.-pipe** = CLYSTER 2.

Cn-, in OE. and early ME. See KN-.

Cnemial (knī·miăl), *a.* 1871. [f. Gr. κνήμη tibia + -IAL.] Relating to the tibia.

‖ **Cnida** (knəi·dă). Pl. **cnidæ.** 1876. [mod. L. – Gr. κνίδη nettle.] *Zool.* The nettle cell of the *Cœlenterata* (jelly-fish, etc.), in which their sting resides: usually called *nematocyst*. Hence **Cni·doblast** [Gr. βλαστός], the cell in which a nematocyst is developed. **Cni·docil** [L. *cilium*], the external irritable ciliary process of cnidoblasts. **Cnidophore** [Gr. -φορος], a process bearing a battery of cnidoblasts.

Co. 1759. **1.** (kōᵘ). An abbrev. of COMPANY; used *esp.* for: The partners of a firm whose names do not appear in the style or title. **2.** A written abbrev. of *county* 1866.

Co-, *prefix*, repr. L. *com-*, *con-*, *co-*, in the sense of 'together', 'in company', 'in common', 'joint, -ly', 'equal, -ly', 'reciprocally', 'mutually'. It combines with verbs, adjs., adverbs, and sbs. **2.** *Math.* (short for *complement*). Used in the sense '. . . of the complement', or 'complement of . . .'; see COSINE, CO-LATITUDE, etc.

† **Coacervate** (as next, or kōᵘ,ăsə̄·ɹvĕt), *a.* 1626. [– L. *coacervatus*, pa. pple. of *coacervare*; see next, -ATE[2].] Heaped together; gathered into one place –1677.

Coacervate (ko,æ·səɹveⁱt), *v.* ? *Obs.* 1623. [– *coacervat-*, pa. ppl. stem of L. *coacervare* heap together, f. *acervus* heap; see CO-, -ATE[3].] To heap together; accumulate; also *fig.* Hence **Coacerva·tion,** the action of heaping together, or fact of being heaped together; a mass heaped together ME.

Coach (kōᵘtʃ), *sb.* 1556. [– Fr. *coche*, ult. – Magyar *kocsi* (ko·tʃi) adj., f. *Kocs* name of a town near Raab in Hungary, the full form being *kocsi szeker* 'Kocs cart'.] **1.** A large kind of carriage: in 16th and 17th centuries, usually a state carriage; now, usually, a large close carriage with four wheels, with seats inside, and several outside, used for public conveyance of passengers (see STAGE-COACH). Applied by railway employes to a railway carriage: in U.S. *esp.* a sleeping-car 1866. **2.** *Naut.* An apartment near the stern of a man-of-war, usually occupied by the captain 1660. **3.** *Univ. colloq.* A private tutor, who 'coaches' a pupil 1848; also, *transf.*, one who trains others for an athletic contest 1885.

1. The roiall Dame..for her coche doth call SPENSER *F.Q.* I. iv. 16. **2.** The Commanders all came on board, and the council sat in the c. PEPYS. **3.** Kitcat, a Trinity c., has a party at Drumnadrochet CLOUGH.

Comb.: **c.-dog,** a spotted Dalmatian dog, kept to run in attendance on a carriage; † **fellow,** a horse yoked in the same carriage with another; *joc.* a companion, mate; **-horse; -house,** an out-house for a c., etc.; **-office,** a booking-office for a stage-coach; **-wagon,** tr. Ger. *kutsch-wagen*, coach.

Coach, *v.* 1612. [f. the sb.] † **1.** To convey in or provide with a coach –1849. **2.** *intr.* To ride or drive in a coach (*colloq.*) 1630. **3.** *Univ. colloq.* To prepare *for* an examination, or *in* special subjects; also, to train for an athletic contest 1849; *gen.* to prime with information. *intr.* To read with a coach 1849.

2. To c. it thro' the town 1797. **3.** *intr.* Do you mean to c. this term (*mod.*).

Coa·ch-box. 1651. [f. COACH *sb.* + BOX *sb.*[2], in the sense of 'seated compartment'.] The seat occupied by the driver of a coach.

Coachee, coachy (kōᵘ·tʃi). 1790. [Cf. *cabby* (-Y[6]), etc.] A coachman (*colloq.*). So **Coa·cher,** a coach-horse.

Coachful (kōᵘ·tʃful). 1654. [See -FUL.] As many as will fill a coach.

Coachman (kōᵘ·tʃmæ̆n). 1579. **1.** The man who drives a coach. **2.** *Angling.* A kind of artificial fly 1839. Hence **Coa·chmanship,** skill in driving a coach.

Coa·ch-whip. 1736. **1.** A whip used in driving a coach 1833. **2.** *fig.* A long thin strip; *pl.* shreds 1781. **3.** *Naut.* 'The pendant' (Adm. Smyth).

Coach-whip snake, a snake so called from its resemblance to the lash of a coach-whip.

† **Coact,** *ppl. a.* ME. [– L. *coactus*, pa. pple. of *cogere*; see next.] Compelled, forced –1635.

Coact (ko,æ·kt), *v.* ME. [– *coact-*, pa. ppl. stem of L. *cogere* compel, contr. f. *co-agere* (CO-, ACT *v.*).] † **1.** *trans.* To compel, force –1651. † **2.** To restrain (*rare*) –1529. † **3.** To contract; to concentrate –1657. **4.** *intr.* To act together (*rare*) 1606. (Cf. AL. *coagere* act together IX.)

4. If I tell how these two did c. SHAKS. Hence **Coa·ction,** coercion (now *rare*); action in concert.

Coactive (ko,æ·ktiv), *a.* 1596. [– (O)Fr. *coactif*, *-ive* or late L. *coactivus* compulsory, f. as prec.; see -IVE. In sense 2 f. CO- + ACTIVE, but AL. *coactivus* acting jointly (XIV) is partly the source.] **1.** Of the nature of force or compulsion. (Qualifying *power* or the like. Now *rare*.) 1605. † **b.** In passive sense: Compulsory –1661. **2.** Acting or taking place together 1611.

1. A c., or coercitive jurisdiction JER. TAYLOR. C. obedience ABP. USSHER. **2.** With what's vnreall thou c. art *Wint. T.* I. ii. 141. Hence **Coa·ctively** *adv.* by way of compulsion. † **Co-activity,** activity in concert; c. quality.

Co-adaptation (ko,ædæ̆ptēⁱ·ʃən). 1803. [See CO-.] Mutual adaptation.

Coadjacent (kōᵘ,ădʒēⁱ·sĕnt). 1842. [See CO-.] *adj.* Adjacent to each other, mutually contiguous. *sb.* Any object or idea so related to another. Hence **Co-adja·cence, -ency.**

Co-adjust (kōᵘ,ădʒɒ·st), *v.* 1864. [See CO-.] To adjust mutually. Hence **Coadjustment.**

Coadjutant (kōᵘ,ădʒⁱū·tănt, ko,æ·dʒⁱutănt). 1708. [f. CO- + ADJUTANT.] *adj.* Helping another or others; co-operating. *sb.* One who helps another or others 1728. So † **Coadju·te** *v.*; whence † **Coadju·ting** *ppl. a.* † **Coadju·tive** *a.*

Coadjutor (ko,ădʒⁱū·təɹ). ME. [– (O)Fr. *coadjuteur*, † *-tor* – late L. *coadjutor*, f. CO- + L. *adjutor* helper, f. *adjuvare* help.] **1.** One who works with and helps another; an assistant. **2.** *spec. Eccl.* One appointed to assist a bishop or other ecclesiastic. Cf. SUFFRAGAN. 1549.

1. Euery one a c. to the worke of all the other 1619. Hence **Coadju·torship,** the office of a c.; helping co-operation. **Coadju·tress,** † **Coa·djutrice, Coadju·trix,** a female c. var. **Coa·djutator** (*rare*).

Coadjuvant (ko,æ·dʒⁱuvănt). 1625. [As adj. :– *coadjuvant-*, pr. ppl. stem of med.L. *coadjuvare*; see CO-, ADJUVATE, -ANT; cf. Fr. *coadjuvant*; in *Med.* use f. CO- + ADJUVANT.] *adj.* Assisting, helpful. ? *Obs.* *sb. Med.* An ingredient that assists the main agent 1864. **Coa·djuvancy,** c. quality or action.

Coadnate, *a.* 1866. [f. CO- + ADNATE.] *Bot.* = CONNATE.

Coadunate (ko,æ·diunĕt), *a.* 1839. [– *coadunatus*, pa. pple. of late L. *coadunare* unite, join together. See -ATE[2].] *Phys.* and *Bot.* Joined together; congenitally united. var. **Coa·dunated.**

Coadunation (ko,æ:diunēⁱ·ʃən). 1558. [– late L. *coadunatio* intimate union; see CO-, ADUNATION.] The action of joining or state of being joined together in one.

A..c. of body, soul, and spirit MANNING. So † **Coadunition.**

Co-adve·nture, *v.* 1642. [See CO-.] To venture together (with). So **Coadve·nture** *sb.* a joint adventure; **Co-adve·nturer.**

Coæ-; see COE-.

† **Co-afforest,** *v.* [See CO-.] To afforest as an addition to an existing forest. HOWELL.

Co-agency (ko,ēⁱ·dʒĕnsi). 1611. [See CO-.] Joint or combined agency. So **Co-a·gent.**

† **Coagitate,** *v.* 1545. [– *coagitat-*, pa. ppl. stem of L. *coagitare* shake together; see CO-, AGITATE.] To shake or mix together –1741.

Coagment (ko,ægme·nt), *v.* ? *Obs.* 1603. [– L. *coagmentare* glue together, cement, f. *coagmentum* joining; see -MENT. Found only as pa. pple.] To cement or join together. var. † **Coa·gmentate** *v.*

† **Coagmenta·tion.** 1578. [– L. *coagmentatio*, f. as prec.; see -ATION.] **1.** The action of joining, or state of being joined, together; junction, concretion –1674. **2.** A mass formed by this action –1684.

Coagulable (ko,æ·giŭlăb'l), *a.* 1652. [– Fr. *coagulable* or med.L. *coagulabilis*; see CO-AGULE, -ABLE.] That can be coagulated; capable of coagulation. Hence **Coa:gulabi·lity,** c. quality; capacity of coagulating. So **Coagulant,** a coagulating agent, as rennet.

Coagulate (ko,æ·giŭlĕt), *ppl. a.* ME. [– L. *coagulatus*, pa. pple. of *coagulare*; see next, -ATE[2].] **1.** as *adj.* Coagulated; congealed. ? *Obs.* † **2.** as *ppl. a.* Concreted; combined in a mass 1610.

Coagulate (ko,æ·giŭleit), *v.* 1606. [– *coagulat-*, pa. ppl. stem of L. *coagulare*, f. *coagulum* rennet; see -ATE[3].] **1.** *trans.* To convert (certain fluids) into a soft solid mass, as by chemical action, heat, etc.; to curdle, clot, congeal 1611. **2.** To form into a mass. *lit.* and *fig.* ?*Obs.* 1610. **3.** *intr.* To become converted into a soft solid mass 1606; † to solidify by evaporation –1713.

1. Albumen. .is coagulated by heat, alcohol, etc. R. KNOX. **2.** Venus. .was. .coagulated of that foam HOWELL. **3.** The blood. .began to c. in the Vein 1667. Hence **Coa·gulative** *a.* having the property of producing or undergoing coagulation. **Coa·gulator,** that which coagulates. **Coa·gulatory** *a.* productive of coagulation (*rare*).

Coagulation (ko,ægiŭlēi·ʃən). 1477. [– (O)Fr. *coagulation* or L. *coagulatio*, f. as prec.; see -ION.] **1.** The action or process of coagulating; clotting, curdling, setting 1477; *concr.* a coagulated mass 1683. † **2.** Solidification by evaporation –1718. **3.** The forming or uniting into a mass; concretion, cohesion 1610. Also *fig.* *concr.* A concreted mass 1664.

1. A c., like that of whites of egges SIR T. BROWNE. The c. of the blood ABERNETHY. **3.** The casuall c. of atomes HEALEY.

† **Coa·gule,** *v.* ME. [– (O)Fr. *coaguler*, f. L. *coagulare*; see COAGULATE *v.*] Earlier f. COAGULATE *v.* –1549.

Coa·guline. 1868. A kind of cement.

‖ **Coagulum** (ko,æ·giŭlŏm). Pl. **coagula.** 1658. [L., = rennet, f. *cogere*, cause to run together.] † **1.** A substance that coagulates a liquid –1713. **2.** A mass of coagulated matter, a clot of blood 1658; that part of the blood which clots 1800. Also *fig.*

‖ **Coaita** (ko·aitā·). 1774. [Tupi; = Red-faced Spider-monkey.] *Zool.* The Red-faced Spider-monkey (*Ateles paniscus*) found in tropical S. America. Also other species of *Ateles*.

Coak (kōᵘk), *sb.* 1794. [perh. repr. ONFr. **coque* = (O)Fr. *coche*, It. *cocca* notch; cf. COCK *v.*[3]] **1.** A tabular projection left on the face of a scarfed timber, to fit into a recess in the face of another which is to be joined to it, so as to prevent slipping. ? *Obs.* † **2.** A pin of hard wood, a dowel, used for the same purpose as in sense 1. –1874. **3.** The bush of a block or sheave in which the pin revolves. Also called *cock*; see COCK *sb.*[1] 1862.

Coak (kōᵘk), *v.* 1794. [Cf. prec., and COCK *v.*[3]] To join by the aid of coaks. Also *intr.*

Coak, obs. f. COKE.

Coal (kōᵘl), *sb.* [OE. *col*, corresp. to OFris., MLG. *kole* (LG. *kale*), MDu. *cole* (Du. *kool*), OHG. *kol*, *kolo* (G. *kohle*), ON. *kol* :– Gmc. **kolam*, **kolon*.] **1.** A piece of carbon glowing without a flame. (Now *arch.*) Also *fig.* † **2.** A piece of burnt wood, etc., that is still capable of combustion without flame –1611; cinder, ashes –1665. Also *fig.* † **3.** = CHARCOAL. Used in *pl.*, or as a *collect. sing.* –1799. Also *attrib.* **4.** A mineral, solid, hard, opaque, black or blackish, found in seams in the earth, and largely used as fuel; it consists of carbonized vegetable matter. (According to the degree of carbonization it is *anthracite* or *glance* coal, *black* or *bituminous* coal, or *brown* coal or *lignite*.) In the ordinary sense, used without qualification, as *collect. sing.*, and (of coal in pieces for burning) in *pl.* ME. Used also with defining words, as *sea*, BROWN, CANNEL *c.*, etc.

1. Þair hertes sal bryn with-in als a cole HAMPOLE. *Coals of fire*; *hot, live, quick coal(s.* **2.** Phr. *Black as a c.* (now usu. assoc. with sense 4). Starres, Starres, And all eyes else, dead coales *Wint. T.* v. i. 68. *fig.* Affection is a coale that must be coold SHAKS.

Phrases. *To heap*, etc., *coals of fire on the head* (see Rom. 12:20): to produce remorse by requiting evil with good. *To haul, call*, etc., *over the coals*: to reprimand, call to task; orig. in reference to the treatment of heretics. *To carry coals to Newcastle*: to do what is absurdly superfluous.

Comb.: **c.-bearing** *a.* (*Geol.*), carboniferous; **-bed** (*Geol.*), a stratum of c.; **-black,** as black as a c., dead black; **-box; -breaker,** *techn.* a building containing the machinery for breaking, sizing, and cleaning c.; **-factor,** an agent between coal-owners and customers; **-field,** a series of strata containing c.; the tract of country occupied by them; **-flap,** a flap (on the pavement) covering the entrance to a c.-cellar; **-goose,** the cormorant (*local*); **-heaver,** a labourer employed in carrying c., **-master,** a c.-owner; **-oil,** an early name of petroleum; **-owner,** the owner of a colliery; **-plant,** a plant of the c.-measures; **-seam,** = *coal-bed*; **-yard.** Hence **Coa·lery;** now COLLIERY.

Coal (kōᵘl), *v.* 1602. [f. the sb.] **1.** To convert into charcoal; to char. † **2.** To write with charcoal. CAMDEN. **3.** To supply (a steamship, etc.) with coal for fuel 1864. **4.** *intr.* To take in a supply of coal 1858.

1. Buying the wood. .fetching the same, when it is coaled CAREW. Hence **Coa·ler,** one who or that which coals steam-vessels.

Coalesce (kōᵘ,ăle·s), *v.* 1541. [– L. *coalescere*, f. *com* Co- + *alescere* grow up, f. *alere* nourish.] † **1.** To cause to grow together, to unite –1790. **2.** *intr.* To grow or come together, so as to form one body or association 1656.

2. Carpels which have coalesced to form the ovary VINES. When two Vowels. .c. in one Syllable 1668. The Conquerors and Conquered coalesced into one and the same People 1692. Never to c. with Pitt MACAULAY.

Coalescence (kōᵘ,ăle·sĕns). 1541. [f. prec. + -ENCE; see -ESCENT.] **1.** The process or action of the vb. COALESCE; coalesced condition or group 1656. **2.** *Biol.* The growing together of separate parts 1541. So † **Coale·scency.**

Coalescent (kōᵘ,ăle·sĕnt), *a.* (*sb.*) 1655. [– *coalescent-* pres. ppl. stem of L. *coalescere*; see COALESCE, -ENT.] **1.** That coalesces; coalescing; growing together or combining. **2.** *sb.* One who or that which coalesces (*mod.*).

Coa·l-fish. 1603. [From the dusky pigment which tinges its skin.] A fish (*Merlangus* or *Pollachius carbonarius* or *Gadus virens*), allied to the Cod. (In U.S. called *pollock*.)

Coa·l-gas. 1809. The mixture of gases produced by the destructive distillation of coal, consisting mainly of carburetted hydrogen; when purified, it is the common lighting gas.

Coa·l-house. 1555. A covered-in place for storage of coal.

Bishop Bonner used his coal-house as a place of confinement during the Marian persecution (1553–58); hence many contemporary and historical allusions.

Coalier, obs. f. COLLIER.

Coalise, -ize (kōᵘ·ăləiz), *v.* 1794. [– Fr. *coaliser*, f. *coalition*, on the analogy of similar pairs.] To enter into, or form, a coalition. Hence **Co·aliser.**

† **Co·alite,** *v.* 1735. [– *coalit-*, pa. ppl. stem of L. *coalescere*; see COALESCE *v.*, -ITE[2].] *intr.* and *trans.* To form into a coalition; to unite –1791.

Let the friends of liberty. .c. BOLINGBROKE. Time has. .blended and coalited the conquered with the conquerors BURKE. So **Co·alite** *a.* grown together.

Coalition (kōᵘ,ăli·ʃən). 1612. [– med.L. *coalitio*, f. as prec.; see -ION.] † **1.** Coalescence –1767. **2.** Combination 1620. **3.** *esp. Polit.*: A temporary alliance of distinct parties for a limited purpose 1715. Also *attrib.*

1. The C. of several Corpuscles into one visible Body BOYLE. **2.** [A] c. of vowels WHEWELL, of interests JOHNSON. **3.** I am sick of coalitions, royal, military or ministerial LD. AUCKLAND. Hence **Coali·tioner,** one who forms or joins a c.; so **Coali·tionist.**

Co-ally·. 1828. [See Co-.] A joint ally. So **Co-allie·d** *ppl. a.* 1740.

Coa·l-man. 1582. A man who has to do with coal; also, a coal-ship or collier (*nonce-use*).

Coa·l-measure. 1665. **1.** A measure for measuring coal. **2.** † A stratum of coal. In *pl.* (*Geol.*) The whole of the series of rocks formed by the seams of coal and the intervening strata of clay, sandstone, etc., in a coal-field, constituting the upper division of the carboniferous formation. Also *attrib.* [The different seams of a coal-field have long been named by their measure or thickness.]

Coa·l-meter. 1648. [See METER *sb.*[1]] One who measures or weighs coal; formerly an official of the corporation of London.

Coalmouse, colemouse (kōᵘ·lmaus). [OE. *colmāse*, corresp. to MDu. *koolmēze* (Du. *koolmees*), MHG. *kolemeise* (G. *kohlmeise*), f. *col* COAL + *māse* (see TITMOUSE).] A bird, *Parus ater*; also called *Coal* (or *Cole*) *Titmouse*.

Coa·l-pit. OE. **1.** A place where charcoal is made. Still in *U.S.* **2.** A pit where coal is dug 1447.

Coa·l-sack. 1632. **1.** A sack to carry coal in. **2.** A name given to black patches in the Milky Way; *esp.* to one near the Southern Cross 1870.

Coa·l-scuttle. 1825. A coal-scoop. Hence *Coal-scuttle bonnet*: a woman's bonnet resembling an inverted coal-scuttle, usually projecting much beyond the face.

† **Coal-stone.** 1728. 'A sort of cannel-coal' (J.).

Coal-tar. 1785. A thick, black, viscid liquid, a product of the destructive distillation of bituminous coal. It is a compound of many substances, chiefly hydrocarbons, and is the source of paraffin, naphtha, benzene, creosote, the aniline or *coal-tar colours*, etc.

Coa·l-tit, coal-ti·tmouse. 1777. = COALMOUSE, q.v.

Coa·l-whipper. 1836. One who raises coal out of a ship's hold by means of a pulley.

Coa·l-works. 1665. A place where coal is worked; a colliery. (Cf. *ironworks*.) So **Coa·l-working,** in same sense.

Coaly (kōᵘ·li), *a.* 1565. [f. COAL *sb.* + -Y[1].] Abounding in coal; covered with coal or coal-dust; carbonaceous; coal-black.

Coaming (kōᵘ·miŋ). 1611. [Origin unkn.] In *pl.*: The raised borders about the edge of the hatches and scuttles of a ship, which prevent water on deck from running below. (*Erron.* identified with *combings*.)

Co-appea·r, *v. rare.* 1635. [See Co-.] To appear together or in conjunction. So **Co-appearance,** † **Co-appari·tion.**

Coapt (ko,æ·pt), *v.* 1586. [– late L. *coaptare* fit together; see Co-, APT *v.*] To fit together 1655; † to make fit 1586.

Coaptation (kōᵘ,æptēi·ʃən). 1561. [– late L. *coaptatio*, f. *coaptare*; see prec., -ATION.] Adaptation or adjustment of things, parts, etc., to each other; *e.g.* of the ends of a fractured bone.

Co-aration (kōᵘ,ărēi·ʃən). 1883. [See Co-.] Co-operative tillage.

‖ **Coarb** (kōᵘ·ɑɹb). 1656. [– Ir. *comharba*.] *Celt. Ch.* Successor in an ecclesiastical office, abbot, vicar; an order of old Irish monks.

† **Coa·rct,** *v.* ME. [– L. *coar(c)tare*, f. Co- + *artare*, f. *artus* confined. See ART *v.*[1]] **1.** *trans.* To press or draw together –1604. **2.** To restrict the action of (a person) –1819. **3.** To confine within narrow limits; also *fig.* –1628.

Coarctate (ko,ā·ɹkteit), *a.* ME. [– L. *coar(c)tatus*, pr. pple. of *coar(c)tare*; see prec., -ATE[2].] Pressed close together, contracted, confined; in *Entom.* applied to a pupa enclosed in a smooth horny case, which conceals its form.

† **Coa·rctate,** *v.* 1620. [– *coarctat-*, pa. ppl. stem of L. *coar(c)tare*; see prec., -ATE[3].] = COARCT –1669.

Coarctation (kōᵘ,aɹktēi·ʃən). 1545. [– L. *coar(c)tatio*, f. as prec.; see -ION.] **1.** The action of compressing tightly; compressed state. **2.** Confinement or restriction as to limits 1605.

1. A c. and straitness of the Urinary Duct 1684.

Coarse (kōᵊɹs), *a.* ME. [Earliest forms *cors(e)*, *course*; the pres. form appears XVII, but is anticipated by † *cowarce* (XVI); the earliest application is to cloth or clothes; of unkn. origin; that it should be based on the phr. *of course* customary, usual (XVI) seems to be chronologically impossible.] † **1.** Ordinary, common; of inferior quality or value –1695. **2.** Wanting in delicacy of texture, granulation, or structure; consisting of comparatively large parts or particles. Opp. to *fine*. 1582. **3.** Rough, harsh, or rude 1607. **4.** Wanting in refinement or delicacy, rough; rude, vulgar 1680; indecent 1711.

1. Too [two] cors bordcloþes ME. Now I feele Of what course Mettle ye are molded *Hen. VIII*, III. ii. 239. **2.** Course black canvas 1796. C. shingle TYNDALL, lips KINGSLEY, complexions

1883. **3.** C. fare 1607, travelling DE FOE, weather BADHAM, quality of tone STAINER. **4.** Appetites too c. to taste OTWAY. A c. age MILMAN, joke DORAN. *Comb.*: **c.-fibred, -grained** *a.* having c. fibres, or texture; also *fig.* having a c. nature. Hence **Coa·rsely** *adv.* **Coa·rsen** *v.* to make or become c. **Coa·rseness,** c. quality. **Coa·rsish** *a.* somewhat c.

Coarti·culate, *v.* 1578. [See CO-.] *Anat.* To unite to form a joint.

Coarticula·tion. ? *Obs.* 1615. [– mod.L. *coarticulatio*, tr. Gr. συνάρθρωσις; see CO-, ARTICULATION.] Jointing together of two bones.

Co-asse·ssor. 1644. [See CO-; cf. AL. *coassessor* XIII.] A joint assessor.

Co-assi·st, Co-assu·me; see CO-.

Coast (kōust), *sb.* [ME. *cost(e)* – OFr. *coste* (mod. *côte*):– L. *costa* rib, flank, side.] † **1.** The side of any body –1818; *transf.* the side (of anything) –1704. **2.** The side of the land next the sea, the seashore ME. † **3.** The border of a country; borderland. (Chiefly *pl.*) –1618. † **4.** A tract or region –1667. † **5.** SIDE, quarter, part –1513. **6.** [repr. Fr. *côte* hill-side.] A slope down which one slides on a sled; the act of so sliding down. (*U.S.* etc.) 1775. **7.** Hence, A run downhill on a bicycle, etc., without pedalling, etc. 1886.

1. Take a c. of lamb, and parboil 1676. **2.** Capernaum, which is vpon the Sea c. *Matt.* 4:13. *The coast*: a term applied to specific littoral districts, as the Coromandel c. *The c. is clear*: *i.e.* of enemies who would dispute an attempt to land or embark; hence, 'the danger is over, the enemies have marched off' (J.). See CLEAR *a.* V. 4. **3.** Judah tooke Gaza with the c. therof *Judg.* 1:18. **4.** The costes of the firmament CHAUCER.

Comb.: **c.-cocket,** a certificate for the carriage of goods by water along the c.; **-guard,** a body of men employed originally to prevent smuggling, but now, under the Admiralty, a general c.-police; hence **-guard-man** (also *coastguardsman*); **-line** [LINE *sb.*[2] II. 7], the contour of a coast 1860; **-rat,** the Sand-mole of S. Africa, a species of *Bathyergus*; **-waiter,** a custom-house officer who superintends the landing and shipping of goods coastwise; **-ward(s** *a.* and *adv.*; **-ways, -wise** *adv.* by way of, or along, the c.; **-wise** *a.* carried along the c.

Hence **Coa·stal** *a.* pertaining to the c. 1883.

Coast (kōust), *v.* [In early use *costay, -ey, -ie* – OFr. *costeier* (mod. *côtoyer*), f. *coste* (prec.); later assim. to the form of the sb.] † **1.** *trans.* To keep by the side of; *esp.* to march on the flank of –1670; *intr.* –1548. † **2.** *trans.* To go or move by the side of; to skirt –1742; *intr.* with *by, along*, etc. –1837. **3.** To proceed by the coast of (*arch.*) ME. **4.** *intr.* To sail *by* or *along* the coast; to sail from port to port of the same country 1555. † **5.** To explore, scour –1633; *intr.* with *about, through*, etc. –1643. † **6.** To border upon, adjoin, bound –1630; *intr.* with *on, upon*, etc. –1652. Also *fig.* † **7.** To accost (see ACCOST *v.*) –1713. † **8.** *trans.* To place with reference to the points of the compass –1715. **9.** in *U.S.* To slide down a slope in a sled. Hence, to run downhill on a bicycle, etc., without pedalling, etc. 1859.

2. [He] coasted aloofe lyke a Hawke that lykethe not her praye GRAFTON. **3.** To c. the lake WORDSW. To c. it along the lake COOK. **4.** C. along the Shore in sight of Land DRYDEN. **5.** To c. the seas HALL, the country MASSINGER. **7.** 3 *Hen. VI*, I. i. 268.

Coa·sted, *ppl. a.* ME. [f. COAST *v.* 6 + -ED[1].] Situated beside, or on the coast of –1611.

Coaster (kōu·stəɹ). 1574. [f. COAST *v.* + -ER[1].] **1.** One who or that which sails along the coast; a coasting-vessel, its master, or its pilot. **2.** One who dwells by the seacoast 1612. **3.** A low round stand for a decanter 1887. **4.** *U.S.* One engaged in the sport of coasting; also, a sledge for coasting 1881.

Coasting (kōu·stiŋ), *vbl. sb.* 1621. [f. COAST *v.* and *sb.*] **1.** Sailing along a coast or trading between the ports of a country 1679. **2.** The configuration of the coast; delineation of a coast-line 1621. **3.** *U.S.* The sport of sliding on a sled downhill, or shooting downhill on a bicycle, etc. 1855. Also *attrib.* and in *comb.*, as *c.-trade, -vessel*, etc.

Coat (kōut), *sb.* [ME. *cote* – OFr. *cote* (mod. *cotte* petticoat):– Rom. **cotta* – Frank. **kotta* of unkn. origin.] **1.** An outer garment, *esp.* one worn by men; usually of cloth, with sleeves. **2.** A petticoat. Usu. in pl. = *petticoats*. Now *dial.* ME. **3.** Used as tr. L. *tunica*, Gr. χιτών, Heb. *k'thōneth, kuttōneth* ME. **4.** *Her.* = COAT OF ARMS ME. † **5.** Garb as indicating profession (*e.g.* clerical); hence, profession, class, sort, party. Common in 17th c. (Cf. CLOTH.) –1774. **6.** *transf.* A natural covering or integument, as of an animal, an organ of an animal body, a plant, etc. (see quots.) ME. **7.** *Naut.* A piece of tarred canvas nailed round the mast, bowsprit, or pumps, where they enter the deck, to keep the water out 1626. **8.** A layer of any substance covering a surface; a coating 1663. **9.** *fig.* Anything that covers, invests, or conceals 1611. † **10.** = COAT-CARD –1630. † **11.** = COAT-MONEY –1721. Also *attrib.*

1. *C. of mail*: a linen or leathern jacket quilted with rings or plates of steel (see MAIL *sb.*[1]). Ther was kut mony a kote ME. Ladies' Long Cloth Coats 1889. **2.** A child in coats LOCKE (J.). **3.** A c. of many colours *Gen.* 37:3. **4.** They may giue the dozen white Luces in their Coate *Merry W.* I. i. 17. *fig.* She was sought by spirits of ritchest cote SHAKS. **5.** I know no man of his c. who would fall in so well with you BURKE. **6.** A Hawk of the first c. 1681. A mule's c. R. FORD. The *arachnoid c.* of the brain. The *choroid c.* of the eye. The Coats of the Bean 1671, of an Onion CHEYNE. **8.** A c. of rich mould SWIFT. **9.** A c. of darkness 1771.

Phrases. *To cut the c. according to the cloth*: see CUT *v.* † *To turn one's c.*: to desert one's party (cf. TURNCOAT). *To wear the king's c.*: to serve as a soldier. *Comb.* **c.-link,** a pair of buttons joined by a short link, or a button with a loop, for holding together the lappets of a c.

Coat (kōut), *v.* ME. [f. prec. sb.] **1.** To provide with a coat; to clothe. **2.** To cover with a coating or coatings of any substance; also predicated of the substance 1753.

2. To c. electrical jars with leaf tin FRANKLIN. Layers of ice..coating a white..central mass HUXLEY.

Coat-armour (kōut,ā·ɹməɹ). ME. [– OFr. **cotte d'armure* (cf. *coat-of-arms* XV – Fr. *cotte d'armes*).] † **1.** = COAT OF ARMS 1. –1639. † **2.** = COAT OF ARMS 2. –1625. **3.** (without *pl.*) Blazonry, arms 1486. Hence † **Coat-armoured** *a.*

† **Coat-card.** 1563. A playing card bearing a coated figure (king, queen, or knave); now corrupted into COURT-*card* –1690.

Coated (kōu·tėd), *ppl. a.* 1563. [f. COAT *sb.* and *v.* + -ED[1].] **1.** Furnished with or having a coat or coats. Often in *comb.* **2.** Covered with a coating of some substance 1766.

Coatee (kōutī·). 1775. [f. COAT *sb.* + -EE[2].] A close-fitting coat with short tails.

Coati (ko,ā·ti). 1676. [– Tupi *coati, coatim*, f. *cua* cincture + *tim* nose.] An American plantigrade carnivorous mammal of the genus *Nasua* (family *Ursidæ*), resembling the Racoon, with a remarkably elongated flexible snout. Also called **Coati-mondi.** [f. Braz. *mondi* solitary.]

Coating (kōu·tiŋ), *vbl. sb.* 1770. [f. COAT *v.* and *sb.*] **1.** = COAT *sb.* 8. **2.** Clothing of the nature of a coat 1798. **3.** [f. the sb.] Material for coats. (Cf. *shirting*, etc.) 1802.

1. A thin..c. of vegetation STANLEY.

Coatless (kōu·tlės), *a.* 1586. [See -LESS.] **1.** Without a coat of arms. **2.** Without a coat (garment) 1850.

Coa·t-money. 1557. *Hist.* Money to provide a coat for each man furnished for military service.

The new taxe of Coate and Conduct Mony, with undue meanes used to inforce the payment of it 1640.

Coat of arms. 1489. [tr. Fr. *cotte d'armes.*] *Her.* **1.** *Hist.* A coat or vest embroidered with heraldic arms; a tabard. **2.** The distinctive bearings of a gentleman (*armiger*) originally borne on a 'coat of arms'; a shield, escutcheon 1562. Also *fig.* † **3.** = *Coat of mail* –1844.

Co-atte·st, *v.* 1650. [See CO-.] *trans.* To attest together or in conjunction (*with*). So **Co-attesta·tion, Co-attesta·tor.**

Coax (kōuks), *v.* 1589. [orig. 'make a *cokes* [i.e. fool] of', of unkn. origin. See COKES.] † **1.** *trans.* To befool –1806. † **2.** To make a pet of; to fondle –1831. **3.** To persuade by caresses, flattery, etc.; to wheedle 1663. **4.** *intr.* To employ coaxing 1706.

3. It was Seneca's principle..to c., rather than drive, his pupil into virtue MERIVALE. Hence **Coax** (*colloq.*), **Coa·xer,** one who coaxes. **Coa·xingly** *adv.*

Coaxal (ko,æ·ksăl), *a.* 1879. [f. CO- + AXAL.] *Math.* = COAXIAL.

† **Coaxation** (kōu,æksēi·ʃən). 1642. [f. L. *coaxare* (f. Gr. κοάξ) + -ATION.] The croaking of frogs –1696.

Coaxial (ko,æ·ksiăl), *a.* 1881. [f. CO- + AXIAL.] *Math.* Having a common axis. Hence **Coa·xially** *adv.*

Cob (kǫb), *sb.*[1] ME. [Origin unkn.] **I.** With the notion 'big' or 'stout'. **1.** A great man, big man, leading man; † a wealthy man, a miser –1681. **2.** A male swan; also *cob-swan* 1570. † **3.** A fish, the Miller's Thumb –1804. **4.** A short-legged, stout variety of horse 1818.

1. The rich cobs of this worlde UDALL.

II. With the notion 'rounded', 'rounded mass' or 'lump'. **1.** Applied to: COB-NUTS 1589; the stone of a fruit 1825; a testicle (*dial.*) 1818. **2.** A small stack of hay (*dial.*) 1616; a chignon (*colloq.*) 1865; a small heap or lump *of* (anything), as coal, bread, etc. (*dial.*) 1606.

III. With the notion 'head', 'top'. † **1.** The head of a (red) herring. (The sense 'young herring' is prob. a mistake for this.) –1632. **2.** The seeding head of wheat, clover, etc. (*dial.*) 1847. **3.** The rachis on which the grains of maize grow 1702.

1. Lord high regent of rashers of the coles and red herring cobs NASHE.

Comb. **c.-coal,** also *cobbles*, large pit-coals; **-loaf,** a small loaf made with a round head.

Cob (kǫb), *sb.*[2] 1602. [Origin unkn.] Clay (marl or chalk) mixed with gravel and straw, used for building walls, etc.

The poor Cottager contenteth himself with C. for his Wals CAREW.

Cob, cobb (kǫb), *sb.*[3] 1580. [perh. of LG. origin; cf. Du. *kobbe, kobmeeuw*, EFris. *sêkobbe.*] A species of Gull, *esp.* the Greater Black-backed Gull (*Larus marinus*); also called *Sea-cob(b.*

† **Cob,** *sb.*[4] *rare.* 1657. [prob. extracted from COBWEB.] A spider.

Cob (kǫb), *sb.*[5] 1672. [perh. f. COB *sb.*[1] I, as the biggest silver coin.] A name formerly given in Ireland to the Spanish dollar or 'piece of eight'. *Comb.* **c.-money** (*U.S.*): old silver coins found at Fort Edward.

Cob, cobb (kǫb), *sb.*[6] *dial.* 1691. [Origin unkn.] A wicker basket to carry on the arm.

Cob, cobb (kǫb), *sb.*[7] *local.* 1605. [perh. as constructed of 'cobs' (short for *cobble*).] A mole or pier (? as constructed of cobblestones).

Cob, cobb, *sb.*[8] 1828. [f. COB *v.*[1]] A blow.

Cob (kǫb), *v.*[1] ME. [Origin unkn.; perh. echoic.] † **1.** *intr.* To give blows. ME. only. **2.** To crush (ore) 1778. **3.** To strike; esp. *Naut.* To strike on the buttocks with a flat instrument 1769. **4.** To thresh or beat out (seed). Also *intr.* of the seed. 1796. **5.** To throw (*dial.*) 1867.

Cob, *v.*[2] *dial.* Also **cop.** 1847. [f. COB *sb.*[1]] *trans.* To top, excel, beat.

Cobalt (kōu·bǫlt). 1728. [Earlier *cobolt* (XVII) – G. *kobalt, -old*, † *-olt*, † *-elt*, disparaging application of MHG. *kobolt* (mod. *kobold*) fairy or demon of the mine, from the miners' belief that cobalt ore was deleterious to the silver ores in which it occurred; for similar applications cf. *nickel, wolfram.*] **1.** A metal of a greyish colour inclining to red, brittle, slightly magnetic; in many respects resembling nickel; not found native, but extracted from various ores. Symbol Co. **2.** The blue pigment, also called **c.-blue,** prepared from this mineral. Also the colour of this. 1835. In this sense also as *adj.*

Comb.: in names of colours or pigments prepared from salts of c., as *cobalt-blue* (see sense 2), *green, ultramarine, yellow*; also **c.-bloom,** = ERYTHRITE; † **-crust,** the earthy variety of *cobalt-bloom*; **-glance** [G. *Kobalt-glanz*], = COBALTITE; **-vitriol,** = a native sulphate of c., also called *Bieberite*.

Hence **Coba·ltic** *a.* of, pertaining to, or of the nature of, c.; applied to the tri-compounds of the metal, as *Cobaltic oxide*, Co_2O_3. **Cobalti·ferous** *a.* containing or yielding c. **Coba·ltous** *a.* of the nature of c.; applied to the di-compounds of the metal, as *Cobaltous oxide*, CoO.

Coba·lti-. *Chem.* Comb. f. COBALT used in the names of tri-compounds, as in *c.-cyanide* of copper, etc.

Cobaltite (kōᵘ·bǫltəit). 1868. [f. COBALT + -ITE¹ 2 b.] *Min.* Native sulpharsenide of cobalt, of silver-white colour, with metallic lustre, also called *cobalt-glance,* and † *cobaltine.*

Coba·lto-. *Chem.* Comb. f. COBALT used in the names of di-compounds, as *c.-cyanide* of potassium, etc.

† **Co·bbing,** *a.* 1599. [f. COB *v.*² + -ING².] Playing the cob –1608.

Of them all c. countrey chuffes which make their bellies and their bagges theyr gods are called riche cobbes NASHE.

Cobble (kǫ·b'l), *sb.*¹ 1475. [f. COB *sb.*¹ II + -LE. Earliest in *cob(b)ylstone.*] **1.** A water-worn rounded stone, *esp.* of the size suitable for paving. Also *transf.* **2.** *pl.* Coal of the size of small cobble stones 1815.

1. Their slings held cobles round 1600.

Cobble, *sb.*² 1859. [f. COBBLE *v.*¹] A clumsy mending.

Cobble, *sb.*³, var. of COBLE.

Cobble (kǫ·b'l), *v.*¹ 1496. [Back-formation from COBBLER.] **1.** *trans.* To mend (*esp.* shoes); to mend roughly or clumsily; to patch. Also with *up.* Also *absol.* **2.** To put together roughly or clumsily. Also *intr.* or *absol.* 1589.

1. Men..c. up old houses PETTY. 2. To coble verse as well as shoes 1764.

Co·bble, *v.*² 1691. [f. COBBLE *sb.*¹] To pave with cobbles.

Cobbler (kǫ·blər). ME. [Origin unkn.] **1.** One who mends shoes. **2.** A botcher 1594. **3.** *colloq.* 'A drink made of wine, sugar, lemon, and pounded ice, and imbibed through a straw' 1809.

2. *Jul. C.* I. i. 11. *Comb.*: **c.-fish,** a W. Indian fish, *Blepharis crinitus,* having long rays likened to a cobbler's strings; **cobbler's punch,** a warm drink of ale with spirit, sugar, and spice added.

Cobble-stone. 1475. See COBBLE *sb.*¹

Cobby (kǫ·bi), *a.* 1691. [f. COB *sb.*¹ + -Y¹.] **1.** Stout, hearty (*dial.*). **2.** Headstrong 1785. **3.** Of the nature of or like a cob (horse) 1871.

Cobdenism (kǫ·bdəniz'm). 1887. [f. name Richard *Cobden* (1804–65).] A policy advocating free trade, peace, and international co-operation. So **Co·bdenite.**

Cob-iron. Now *dial.* 1485. [app. f. COB *sb.*¹ II + IRON *sb.*¹, referring to knobs at the ends.] *pl.* The irons which supported the spit. Also explained as = ANDIRON.

Co-bi·shop. *rare.* 1726. A coadjutor bishop.

Coble (kōᵘ·b'l). OE. [In AL. *cobellum* (XIII), *cobla* (XIV); poss. of Celtic origin (cf. W. *ceubal* ferry-boat, skiff, lighter, Breton *caubal,* AL. *caupallus* VII).] **1.** *Sc.* A short flat-bottomed rowing-boat for crossing rivers, etc. **2.** A sea fishing-boat with a flat bottom, square stern, lug-sail, and rudder extending 4 or 5 feet below the bottom; used chiefly on the NE. coast of England 1493. Also *attrib.*

Cob-nut (kǫ·bˌnʌt). 1532. [Earlier †*cobble-nut*; cf. COBBLE *sb.*¹] **1.** A large short ovate nut, borne by a cultivated variety of the hazel; also the tree. Also *transf.* 1580. **2.** A game played by children with nuts.

Cobra (kōᵘ·bră, kǫ·bră). 1817. Short for next. Also *attrib.*

‖ **Cobra de capello** (kōᵘ·bră di kăpe·lo). 1668. [Pg. *cobra* (:– L. *colubra*) snake, *de* with, *capello* hood (:– med.L. *cappellus,* dim. of *cappa*; see CAPE *sb.*²).] The Hooded or Spectacle snake (*Naja tripudians*), a venomous serpent found in India, having the power of dilating the head and neck when irritated, so as to produce the resemblance of a hood.

Co-bro·ther. 1589. [See CO-.] Brother in the same craft; = Fr. *confrère.*

Cob-swan; see COB *sb.*¹ I. 2.

Coburg (kōᵘ·bɒɹg). 1882. [f. name of Prince Albert of Saxe-*Coburg,* consort of Queen Victoria of England.] A thin fabric of worsted and cotton or worsted and silk for women's dresses.

Cobweb (kǫ·bˌweb). [ME. *cop(pe)web,* f. *coppe,* short for *attercop(pe)* :– OE. *ăt(t)ŏrcoppe,* f. *ăt(t)ŏr* poison + *coppe* head = MDu. *koppe,* prob. rel. to COB *sb.*¹; see WEB.] **1.** The fine network spun by a spider to catch its prey; also, the substance. **b.** A single thread spun by a spider 1837. † **2.** Threads similar to the spider's –1626. **3.** *fig.* See quots. **4.** Short for *Cobweb bird,* the Spotted Flycatcher, which uses spiders' webs in constructing its nest 1712. Also *attrib.*

1. b. The immoveable c., or zero of the scale [of the c. micrometer] 1837. 3. The sophist's rope of c. BEATTIE. The dust and cobwebbes of that vnciuil age SIDNEY. The cobwebs of petty inquisitiveness JOHNSON. C. Laws MILT.

Comb.: † **c. lawn,** a very fine transparent lawn; **c. micrometer,** one with c. threads instead of wires; **c. bird;** see sense 4.

Hence **Co·bwebbed** *ppl. a.* covered or hung with, or (*Bot.*) as with, cobwebs. **Co·bwe:bbery,** the spinning of cobwebs; a texture of cobwebs. **Co·bwebby** *a.* cobwebbed; resembling cobwebs.

Coca (kōᵘ·kă). 1616. [– Sp. *coca* – Quechua *cuca.*] The name in Bolivia of *Erythroxylon coca*; hence, applied to its dried leaves, which are chewed, with powdered lime, to appease hunger, and stimulate the nervous system. Also *attrib.*

Cocaigne; see COCKAIGNE.

Cocaine (kokēⁱ·n; prop. kōᵘ·keˌəin). 1874. [f. COCA + -INE⁵.] An alkaloid obtained from the leaves, etc., of the coca plant, valuable as a local anæsthetic.

Cocao, obs. f. CACAO.

Cocarde; see COCKADE.

Coccagee (kǫ:kăgī·). 1727. [– Ir. *cac a' ghéidh* 'dung of goose'; so called from its greenish-yellow colour.] A cider apple formerly in repute; also, the cider made from it.

Cocceian (kǫksī·iăn), *a.* 1685. [f. the prop. name + -AN.] Of, or pertaining to the opinion of, John Cocceius of Leyden, who taught that the Old Testament history was a foreshadowing of the history of Christ and his church.

‖ **Coccidium** (kǫksi·diŏm). 1867. [mod.L., as if f. dim. of Gr. κοκκίς, -ιδ-, dim. of κόκκος grain, berry.] *Bot.* A spherical or hemispherical conceptacle found in the rhodospermous algæ.

† **Cocci·ferous,** *a.* 1727. [f. L. *coccum* berry + -FEROUS.] Berry-bearing –1755. So † **Cocci·gerous** *a.* 1657.

Coccin (kǫ·ksin). 1836. [f. mod.L. *coccus* COCCUS + -IN¹.] *Chem.* A nitrogenous principle obtained from the cochineal and other insects.

† **Cocci·neous,** *a.* 1654. [f. L. *coccineus* scarlet (f. *coccum* berry) + -OUS.] Scarlet –1693.

‖ **Cocco.** Also **cocoa, coco,** pl. **cocoes.** 1756. The tuber of an Araceous plant, *Colocasia esculenta* or taro-plant, cultivated as an article of food in the W. Indies.

Coccolite (kǫ·kŏləit). 1801. [f. Gr. κόκκος berry + -LITE.] *Min.* A granular variety of pyroxene of green or greenish colour.

Coccolith (kǫ·kŏliþ). 1868. [f. as prec. + -LITH.] *Biol.* Huxley's name for minute round or oval disc-like organic bodies found in deep-sea dredging, etc. Now believed to be of algal nature.

Coccosphere (kǫ·koˌsfiᵊɹ). 1868. [f. as prec. + SPHERE *sb.*] *Biol.* A spheroidal aggregation of coccoliths.

Cocco·steid. 1862. [f. Gr. κόκκος grain, berry + ὀστέον bone + -ID³.] *Palæont.* A member of the family *Coccosteidæ* of ganoid fishes, which includes the fossil genus *Coccosteus,* so called from the berry-like tubercles with which the plates were studded.

Coccule (kǫ·kiul). 1835. [– mod.L. *cocculum,* dim. of L. *coccum* berry; see -ULE.] *Bot.* A small berry or coccus. Hence **Cocculi·ferous** *a.* c.-bearing.

‖ **Co·cculus i·ndicus.** 1591. [mod.L. (irreg. for prec.).] The dried berry of *Anamirta* (formerly *Menispermium*) *cocculus,* a climbing plant found in Malabar and Ceylon. It is a violent poison.

‖ **Coccus** (kǫ·kŏs). 1763. [mod.L. – Gr. κόκκος berry, seed.] **1.** The genus of Homopterous insects which includes the Cochineal (*C. cacti*), the Kermes (*C. ilicis*), the Lac insect (*C. lacca*), and others. **2.** One of the carpels of a dry fruit, which burst from the common axis 1800.

Coccy- (kǫ·ksi). Short for *coccygo-,* comb. f. COCCYX.

Coccygeal (kǫksi·dʒiăl), *a.* 1836. [f. mod.L. *coccygeus* + -AL¹.] Pertaining to the coccyx. So **Coccy·gean** *a.*

Coccygo- [Gr. κοκκυγο-], bef. a vowel **coccyg-,** comb. f. COCCYX.

Coccyx (kǫ·ksiks). 1615. [– L. *coccyx* – Gr. κόκκυξ, -υγ- cuckoo, also the *os coccygis,* so called in man as resembling the bill of the cuckoo.] *Anat.* The small triangular bone appended to the sacrum, and terminating the spinal column in man, formed by the coalescence of four rudimental vertebræ; also, an analogous part in other animals.

Cochin-China (kǫ·tʃin tʃəi·nă). 1853. Name of a country in the Eastern Peninsula; hence, short for *Cochin-China fowl,* a breed of poultry from Cochin-China.

Cochineal (kǫ·tʃinīl). 1586. [– Fr. *cochenille* or Sp. *cochinilla,* gen. referred to L. *coccinus* scarlet (Gr. κόκκος kermes), but its orig. application is doubtful.] **1.** A dye-stuff consisting of the dried bodies of the insect *Coccus cacti,* found on several species of cactus in Mexico and elsewhere. It is used for making carmine, and as a scarlet dye. **2.** The colour of this dye, scarlet 1632. **3.** The cochineal-insect (*Coccus cacti*) 1697. **4.** *C. Fig*: the cactus-plant, *Opuntia* (*Nopalea*) *cochinillifera,* on which the cochineal-insect feeds 1697.

‖ **Cochlea** (kǫ·kliˌă). 1538. [– L. *coc(h)lea* snail-shell, screw – Gr. κοχλίας, prob. rel. to κόγχη CONCH.] † **1.** A spiral staircase; a screw; the water-screw of Archimedes –1679. **2.** *Phys.* The spiral cavity of the internal ear 1688. **3.** *Conchol.* A snail-shell 1846. Hence **Co·chlean, Co·chlear** *adjs.* pertaining to a c.

‖ **Cochleare** (kǫkliˌēᵊ·ri). 1708. [L. *coc(h)leare* spoon.] *Med.* A spoon or spoonful (in prescriptions).

Cochleariform (kǫkliˌēᵊ·rifǭɹm), *a.* 1836. [f. prec. + -FORM.] Spoon-shaped.

† **Co·chleary,** *a.* 1646. [f. L. *coc(h)lea* (see above) + -ARY².] Resembling a snail-shell, spiral, winding –1664. So **Co·chleate(d** *a.* in same senses.

Co·chlite. 1698. [f. Gr. κόχλος spiral sea-shell + -ITE¹ 2 b.] *Palæont.* A fossil spiral shell.

Co·cin, co·cinin (Watts). 1865. [f. COCO + -IN¹.] *Chem.* A fat (glyceride of **Cocinic** acid, a fatty acid obtained from coco-nut oil).

Cock (kǫk), *sb.*¹ [OE. *cocc, kok* = ON. *kokkr,* prob. – med.L. *coccus* (Salic Laws), of imit. origin; reinforced in ME. by (O)Fr. *coq.*]

I. 1. The male of the common domestic fowl, *Gallus domesticus* OE.; also of various other birds ME. **b.** Short for WOODCOCK 1530. **2.** = Crow of cock; also as an imitation of the cluck of the bird CHAUCER. **3.** A weather-cock 1605.

1. *Fighting c.*: one bred and trained for cock-fighting. 2. We were carowsing till the second C. *Macb.* II. iii. 27. 3. You Cataracts, and Hyrricano's spout, Till you haue drench'd our Steeples, drown the Cockes *Lear* III. ii. 3.

II. 1. One who arouses slumberers: applied to ministers of religion 1614. **2.** Leader, head, chief man; formerly, also, victor 1542. **3.** *colloq.* One who fights with pluck. Hence, a vulgar term of appreciation. 1639.

2. At cuffs I was always the c. of the school SWIFT. *C. of the walk*: see WALK *sb.* II. 3. The Doctor being a shy c. SMOLLETT.

III. Techn. **1.** A spout with an appliance for controlling the flow of liquids through it; a tap 1481. **2.** In fire-arms, a lever, or spring hammer, part of the mechanism for discharging the piece. (So called from its original shape.) 1566. **3.** The pointer of a balance 1611; the gnomon of a sundial 1613. **4.** A bracket attached to the plate of a watch or clock to support the outer end of the pivot of a wheel or pendulum 1678. **5.** = COAK *sb.* 3. 1627. **6.** The mark at which curlers aim 1787. **7.** = PENIS (*vulgar*) 1730.

2. *At c., at (on) full c.*: with the c. drawn full back. *At (on) half-c.*: with the c. lifted to the first catch, at which position the trigger does not act.

Cock (kǫk), *sb.*² ME. [perh. Scand. (cf. Norw. *kok* heap, lump, Da. dial. *kok* haycock, Sw. *koka* clod), but an OE. *cocc hill has been assumed for the place-names *Cockhampstead, Cookham* (*Coccham* VIII),

Coughton (*Cocton* XIII).] A conical heap of produce or material; *esp.* of hay (rarely corn) in the field.

† **Cock,** *sb.*[3] ME. [*Cock* XV (in AL. *cocha, coqua, cocco*) – OFr. *coque*, dial. var. of *coche* = Pr. *coca*, OIt. *cocca* :– med.L. *caudica*, f. L. *caudex, codex* block of wood. See COCK-BOAT, COG *sb.*[1]] Now always COCK-BOAT –1631.

Cock (kǫk), *sb.*[4] 1711. [f. COCK *v.*[1]] **1.** An upward or significant turn 1717. **2.** An upward turn of the brim of a hat; the turned-up part 1711.

1. With a knowing c. of his eye to his next neighbour SCOTT. 2. The wind being high, he let down the cocks of his hat BOSWELL.

Cock, *sb.*[5] [f. COCK *v.*[2]] A cocked position of the hammer of a pistol or gun.

† **Cock,** *sb.*[6] ME. Perversion of the word GOD, used in oaths and exclams., as *by cock and pie, cock's body*, etc.

[**Cock,** *sb.*[7] 'The notch of an arrow' (J.). Prob. an etymological figment. See O.E.D.]

Cock (kǫk), *v.*[1] ME. [From the name of the fowl. But with sense 1 cf. Ir. *cog-aim* 'I war', stem in OIr. *coc-*.] † **1.** *intr.* To fight –1600. † **2.** To strut, brag, crow *over* –1713. **3.** To stick stiffly *up* or *out* 1600; *intr.* to stick conspicuously up 1629. **4.** To turn up the brim of (a hat) 1663. *intr.* 1672. **5.** *intr.* To train or use fighting cocks 1546. **6.** To shoot woodcocks 1696.

3. *To c. the ears*: to prick up the ears in attention, said humorously of persons. *To c. the nose*: to turn it up in contempt. *To c. the eye*: to turn the eye with a knowing look; to wink. *To c. the hat*: to stick it jauntily on one side of the head. 4. Mrs. Stewart.., with her hat cocked and a red plume PEPYS.

Cock, *v.*[2] 1598. [f. COCK *sb.*[1]] † **1.** To place (a match) in the cock of an old matchlock gun –1648. **2.** To draw the cock back 1649.

2. Cock'd—fired—and miss'd his man BYRON.

Cock, *v.*[3] Also **cauk, caulk, calk,** and recently **cog.** 1663. [See COAK *sb.*] **1.** To secure crossing beams by means of a dove-tail, a mortice and tenon, or the like. **2.** See COAK *v.*

Cock, *v.*[4] ME. [f. COCK *sb.*[2]] To put up in cocks.

† **Cock,** *v.*[5] 1573. [perh. short for COCKER *v.*, COCKLE *v.*[2], but relations are uncertain.] To pamper.

Cock, *v.*[6] *dial.* To rough-shoe; = CALK *v.*[2]

Cockabondy (kǫkəbǫ·ndi). 1852. [– W. *coch a bon ddu* 'red with black (*du*) trunk or stem (*pon*)'.] An angler's artificial fly.

Cockade (kǫkēi·d). Also † **cockard.** 1709. [– Fr. *cocarde*, orig. in phr. *bonnet à la coquarde* (Rabelais) cap worn assertively on one side; fem. of †*coquard* proud, saucy, as sb. coxcomb, f. *coq* COCK *sb.*[1]; see -ARD. The ending assim. to -ADE.] A ribbon, knot of ribbons, rosette, etc., worn in the hat as a badge of office or party, or as part of a livery dress.

He's ta'en the field wi' his white c. *Jacobite Song*. Hence **Cocka·ded** *ppl. a.* wearing a c.

Cockadoodledoo·. 1573. The crow of a cock.

Cock-a-hoop. ME. [Of obscure origin.] † **1.** Phr. *To set* (*the*) *cock on* (*the*) *hoop*: app. to turn on the tap and drink without stint –1658. **2.** as *pred. adj.* In a state of elation; crowing with exultation 1663. Also *attrib.* Exultant 1837.

Cockaigne, Cockayne (kǫkēi·n). [– OFr. *cocaigne*, as in *pais de cocaigne* fool's paradise (mod. *cocagne*), corresp. to Sp. *cucaña*, Pg. *cucanha*, It. *cuccagna* – MLG. *kokenje* small very sweet cake sold to children at fairs, dim. of *koke* CAKE.] **1.** An imaginary country, the abode of luxury and idleness. **2.** *joc.* London, as the country of Cockneys 1824.

Cockal (kǫ·kăl, kǫ·kǫ̆l). ? *Obs.* 1562. [app. orig. written as two words, *cock all*; of unkn. origin.] **1.** The knuckle-bone or astragalus. **2.** A game played with knuckle-bones; 'dibs'. Also, as tr. L. *ludus talaris*. 1586.

1. A little transverce bone; Which boyes and bruckel'd children call (Playing for points and pins) cockall HERRICK.

Cock-a-leekie, var. of COCKY-LEEKY.

Cockalo·rum. *colloq.* 1715. [An arbitrary deriv. of COCK *sb.*[1]] **1.** Applied to a person: = Little cock, bantam: self-important little man. **2.** Crowing 1884.

Hey (*hay, high*) *c.*: an exclam.; also a boys' game in which some make a chain of backs and others jump astride them.

Cock-and-bull. 1621. [orig. in phr. *talk of* (*a story of*) *a cock and a bull* (XVII); parallel to Fr. *coq-à-l'âne*, orig. in phr. *saillir du coq en l'âne* 'jump from the cock to the ass'.] **1.** *lit.* 1660. **2.** *A story of a cock and a bull*: a long, rambling, idle story 1621. **3.** *A cock and bull story*: an idle, concocted, incredible story; a canard 1796.

† **Cock and pie.** 1550. [f. COCK *sb.*[6] and PIE *sb.*[3], pre-Reformation manual of ecclesiastical rules.] Used as an asseveration –1854.

Cockatiel, -eel (kǫkătī·l). 1880. [– Du. *kaketielje* assim. to COCK *sb.*[1]] The Cockatoo Parrakeet, or Crested Grass Parrakeet of S. Australia (*Calopsitta* or *Nymphicus novæhollandiæ*).

Cockatoo (kǫkătū·). 1634. [– Du. *kaketoe* – Malay *kakatua*; infl. by COCK *sb.*[1]] The name of numerous birds of the parrot kind, *esp.* the genus *Cacatua*, inhabiting Australia and the E. Indian Islands, distinguished by a crest on the head, which can be raised or depressed at pleasure. **2.** *Australia.* (*colloq.*) A small farmer 1864.

Cockatrice (kǫ·kătrəis, -tris). ME. [– OFr. *cocatris* – med.L. *calcatrix, caucatrix* (fem. agent-noun f. L. *calcare* tread, (later) track, f. *calx* heel) used to render Gr. ἰχνεύμων ICHNEUMON.] **1.** A serpent, identified with the BASILISK, fabled to kill by its glance, and to be hatched from a cock's egg. (Used in Bible versions as tr. L. *basiliscus, regulus.*) † *Occas.* confounded with the CROCODILE –1583. In *Her.* figured with head, wings, and feet of a cock, terminating in a serpent with a barbed tail 1563. **2.** *fig.* Applied to persons 1500. † **3.** A whore –1747.

1. He shal put his hande in to the Cockatryce denne COVERDALE *Isa.* 11:8. The death-darting eye of C. *Rom. & Jul.* III. ii. 47. 2. This little C. of a King that was able to destroy those that did not espie him first BACON.

Co·ck-bill, *sb.* 1648. [In XVII *cock-bell*, of unkn. origin.] *Naut.* In *a-cock-bill*. See A-COCK-BILL. Hence **Co·ck-bill** *v.* to place a-cock-bill.

Cock-boat (kǫ·kbōᵘt). ME. [f. COCK *sb.*[3] + BOAT.] A small ship's boat, *esp.* one towed behind a vessel going up or down river.

But a c. compared with the Warrior 1861.

† **Cock-brain.** 1567. One having the brain of a cock; a light-headed, foolish person. Cf. *bird-witted*. –1675. Hence **Co·ck-brained** *a.* foolish and light-headed, silly.

Cockchafer (kǫ·kˌtʃēⁱ:fəɹ). 1712. [f. *Cock* + CHAFER[1] beetle.] A coleopterous insect or beetle (*Melolontha vulgaris*); it comes forth from the chrysalis late in May (hence called Maybug), and flies with a whirring sound.

Co·ck-crow. ME. = COCK-CROWING.

Co·ck-crowing. ME. The crowing of a cock; the time when cocks crow, early dawn.

Cocked (kǫkt), *ppl. a.* 1647. [f. COCK *v.*[1] + -ED[1].] Set erect; having a pronounced upward turn.

Cocked hat. 1. A (three-cornered) hat with the brim permanently turned up. Now, a triangular hat (without cocks) pointed before and behind and rising to a point at the crown. 1673. **2.** A game like ninepins, played with three pins, set up in a triangular position. *U.S.* Phr. *To knock into a cocked hat*: to damage beyond recognition.

Co·cker, *sb.*[1] Now *dial.* [OE. *cocor* = OFris. *koker*, OS. *cocār*(*i* (Du. *koker*), OHG. *kohhar*(*i* (G. *köcher*).] † **1.** A case for arrows –ME. **2.** A casing for the leg; a high laced boot, or a kind of legging ME.

Cocker (kǫ·kəɹ), *sb.*[2] ME. [f. COCK *v.*[1] + -ER[1]; with sense 3 cf. COCKING 3.] † **1.** A fighter –1460. **2.** A patron of cock-fighting; one who breeds and trains game-cocks 1689. **3.** A breed of spaniels trained to start woodcocks, etc. 1823.

Cocker, *sb.*[3], **coker.** ME. [f. COCK *v.*[4] + -ER[1].] Orig., one who puts hay in cocks, a hay-worker; later, a harvest-labourer.

Cocker (kǫ·kəɹ), *sb.*[4] 1825. [Name of an arithmetician (d. 1675).] *According to C.*: in accordance with strict rule or reckoning.

Cocker (kǫ·kəɹ), *v.* 1440. [rel. obscurely to COCK *v.*[5] and COCKLE *v.*[2] (both XVI); the status of Flem. *kokelen, keukelen* 'nutrire sive fovere culina' (Kilian) and Fr. *coqueliner* 'to dandle, cocker, pamper' (Cotgr.) is doubtful.] *trans.* To pamper; to treat with excessive tenderness or care. Also with *up*. Also *fig.*

C. thy childe, and hee shall make thee afraid *Ecclus.* 30:9. *fig.* To c. up an evil 1861.

Cockerel (kǫ·kĕrĕl). ME. [dim. of COCK *sb.*[1]; see -REL, -EREL.] A young cock (*arch.* or *dial.*). Also *fig.* of a young man 1571.

† **Cockerno·ny.** *Sc.* 1718. [Origin unkn.] The gathering up of a young woman's hair in a snood –1833.

Cocket (kǫ·kėt), *sb.*[1] ME. [In AFr. *cokete*, AL. *coketa, coketum*; poss. from the concluding words of the document, *quo quietus est* by which he is quit.] **1.** *Hist.* A seal belonging to the King's Custom House. **2.** A sealed document delivered to merchants as a certificate that their merchandise has been duly entered and has paid duty. (Now disused.) ME. **3.** The customs duty 1483.

Co·cket, *sb.*[2] ME. [Origin unkn. In AL. *coketus*, adj. and sb. cocket-loaf (XIII–XIV) in *panis coketus, panis de coketo*.] A second quality of bread; also, a loaf of this. Now *Hist.*

Co·cket, *a.* Now *dial.* 1537. [perh. – Fr. *coquet, -ette* gallant, recorded XVII. In Eng. infl. by COCK *sb.*[1], but cf. Fr. *coqueter* strut.] 'Stuck up'; pert; brisk; in *mod. dial.* merry.

Co·cket, *v.*[1] ME. [f. COCKET *sb.*[1]] *trans.* To furnish with a cocket.

Co·cket, *v.*[2] 1583. [Cf. COCK *v.*[3] and see COAK *sb.*] *Arch.* To mortise, joint.

Cock-eye. *colloq.* 1825. [app. f. COCK *v.*[1]] A squinting eye. Hence **Co·ck-eyed** *a.*, squinting, cross-eyed; *transf.* and *fig.* crooked, askew.

Cock-fight (kǫ·kˌfəit). 1494. A match or fight between cocks. Also *transf.*

Co·ckfighter. 1721. = COCKER *sb.*[2] 2.

Co·ck-fighting. 1450. The sport of making cocks fight each other; made illegal by Act 12 & 13 Vict. c. 92.

To beat c.: to surpass everything (*colloq.*).

Cock-horse (kǫ·kˌhǭ·ɹs). 1540. **1.** Anything a child rides astride upon, a hobby-horse, any one's knee, etc. *transf. A-cock-horse, on* (*a*) *cock-horse*: mounted; astride. 1564. † **2.** *fig.* An exalted position. Usu. with *on, a-*. –1829. **3.** *fig.* A high horse; a stallion 1599. Also as *adv.*, in sense 1.

1. 'Ride a cock-horse To Banbury Cross' *Nursery Rhyme*. Riding a cock-horse on a star COMBE. 2. A slave, whom vilany hath set a cock-horse 1658.

Cockie-leekie, var. of COCKY-LEEKY.

Co·cking, *vbl. sb.* ME. [f. COCK *v.*[1] + -ING[1].] † **1.** Fighting, strife –1542. **2.** = COCK-FIGHTING 1546; a cock-fight 1630. **3.** The shooting of woodcocks 1696. *Comb.*: **c.-dog, -spaniel,** one of a breed used in hunting woodcocks, etc.

Cockish (kǫ·kiʃ), *a.* 1546. [f. COCK *sb.*[1] + -ISH[1].] **1.** Cocklike (*joc.*) 1577. **2.** Strutting, self-assertive, cocky 1546. **3.** Lecherous. Now *dial.* 1570. Hence **Co·ckish-ly** *adv.*, **-ness.**

Cock-laird. *Sc.* 1721. A small landholder; a yeoman.

Cockle (kǫ·k'l), *sb.*[1] [OE. *coccul, -el*, perh. – med.L. **cocculus*, f. late L. *coccus*, earlier *coccum* kermes – Gr. κόκκος.] **1.** The name of a plant, *Lychnis* (or *Agrostemma*) *githago*, which grows in cornfields. Also called *Corn Cockle*. **2.** Used as tr. *zizania* (Matt. 13), or L. *lolium*. (The plant thus named was the grass *Lolium temulentum* or Darnel, not cockle.) OE. Also *fig.*

2. *fig.* The C. of Rebellion, Insolence, Sedition SHAKS.

Cockle (kǫ·k'l), *sb.*[2] ME. [– (O)Fr. *coquille* shell :– med.L. **cochilia* – med.Gr. κοχύλια, pl. of κοχύλιον, for Gr. κογχύλιον, f. κόγχη CONCH.] **1.** The English name of bivalve molluscs of the genus *Cardium*, esp. *C. edule*, much used for food. (Formerly applied more vaguely.) **2.** = COCKLE-SHELL 1507. **3.** *Cockles of the heart*: explained (1) by the likeness of a heart to a cockle-shell; (2) by the zool. name for the cockle, *Cardium* (Latham). 1671. Also *attrib. Comb.*: **c.-hat,** a hat with a c. or scallop-shell in it, worn by pilgrims; **-stairs,** winding stairs. Hence **Co·ckled** *a.* furnished with a shell. **Co·ckler,** one who gathers cockles.

Cockle, *sb.*[3] 1522. [Goes with COCKLE *v.*[1]] A pucker, or bulge on what ought to be a flat surface, as cloth, paper, etc.

Cockle, *sb.*[4] 1688. [poss. – Du. (XVI) *kākel, kaekel, kāchel,* esp. in *kacheloven* – G. *kachel* stove-tile, *kachelofen* stove made of these.] **1.** The fire-chamber of a hop or malt kiln. Also called **c. oast. 2.** A kind of heating stove, also called **c. stove.** Sometimes used of 'the fireplace of an air stove' or of 'the dome of a heating furnace'. 1774.

† **Cockle,** *sb.*[5] 1761. [Origin unkn.] A miner's name for Black Tourmaline –1788.

† **Cockle,** *a.* 1708. [perh. attrib. use of COCKLE *sb.*[2]] Whimsical. Hence *c.-brained, -headed* –1818.

Cockle (kǫ·k'l), *v.*[1] 1552. [– Fr. *coquiller* blister (bread) in cooking (cf. *recoquiller* turn or curl up, dog's ear), f. *coquille* shell, etc.; see COCKLE *sb.*[2]] **1.** *intr.* To go into rucks, to pucker, as cloth, paper, etc. **2.** *trans.* To cause to pucker, to wrinkle, crease 1691. **3.** *intr.* To rise into short tumbling waves.

† **Cockle,** *v.*[2] 1570. [See COCKER *v.*] = COCKER *v.* –1579.

Cockle-shell (kǫ·k'l,ʃel). ME. [f. COCKLE *sb.*[2] + SHELL *sb.*] **1.** The shell of the cockle; usu. one of its valves. Formerly applied more widely. **2.** A small frail boat 1829.

1. Wearers of the C., the emblems of a pilgrimage to Compostella BLADES.

† **Cockloche.** ? *slang.* 1611. [Origin unkn.] A silly coxcomb –1863.

Cock-loft. 1589. [prob. f. COCK *sb*[1] + LOFT *sb.*] A small upper loft, usually reached by a ladder; 'the room over the garret' (J.).

Co·ck-master. 1610. One who rears game-cocks.

† **Co·ck-match.** 1680. A cock-fighting match –1814.

Co·ck-nest. 1859. A nest built by a male bird, to roost in.

Cockney (kǫ·kni), *sb.* (*a*). [ME. *cokeney cokenay,* prob. f. *cocene,* gen. pl. of *cok* COCK *sb.*[1] + *ey, ay* (OE. *ǣġ*) egg; cf. the formation of G. *hahnenei* 'cocks' egg'. Sense 2 was assoc. w. COCKER *v.*]

A. *sb.* † **1.** An egg; or perh. one of the small or malformed eggs called popularly 'cocks' eggs', in Ger. *hahneneier* –1600. † **2.** 'A child that sucketh long'; a cockered child; hence, a milk-sop –1783. † **3.** *contempt.* A townsman –1826. **4.** *spec.* One born in the city of London. (Always contemptuous or bantering.) 1600.

1. I haue no salt Bacon, Ne no Cokeneyes, bi Crist, Colopus to maken LANGL. [Egs, as we say cockanegs FLORIO.] **2.** Brought up with great cockering, as Cockneys bee 1598. **4.** I scorne..To let a Bow-bell C. put me downe 1600.

B. *adj.* (*sb.* used *attrib.*) **1.** Cockered; squeamish 1573. **2.** Pertaining to or marking the London Cockney 1632.

Hence **Co·ckneydom,** the domain of cockneys; cockneys collectively. **Co·ckneyfy, -ify** *v.* to render or become c. **Co·ckneyish** *a.* savouring of the c. **Co·ckneyism,** c. quality; a c. characteristic (*e.g.* in idiom or pronunciation). **Co·ckneyize** *v.* to make c.; to play the c., use cockneyisms.

† **Cockney,** *v.* 1583. [f. COCKNEY *sb.* (sense 2).] To cocker –1625.

Cock-paddle. Also **-paidle.** *Sc.* 1672. [f. COCK *sb.*[1] + PADDLE *sb.*[2] (lump fish), perh. so named from the elevated dorsal ridge which resembles a cock's comb.] The Common Lump-fish. *Cyclopterus lumpus.*

† **Co·ck-pe·nny,** 1524. [f. COCK *sb.*[1]] A customary payment at Shrovetide, formerly made to the schoolmaster in certain schools in the north of England. (Originally applied to defray the expense of cock-fighting.) –1870.

Cockpit (kǫ·kpit). 1587. [f. COCK *sb.*[1] + PIT *sb.* 5.] **1.** A pit or enclosed area constructed for cock-fighting. † **b.** Applied to a theatre; and to the PIT of a theatre –1635. Also *fig.* **2.** *Naut.* The after part of the orlop deck of a man-of-war; in action appropriated to the wounded 1706.

1. A Circle dug in the Earth, like a C. DE FOE. † *The Cockpit*: (*a*) name of a theatre in London, in 17th c., on the site of a c. (*b*) The block of buildings on the site of the C. at Whitehall, London, used as government offices; hence = 'the Treasury'; 'the Privy Council'. *fig.* Belgium..the C. of Europe 1858.

Cockroach (kǫ·krōᵘtʃ). 1624. [Earlier *cacarootch, cockroche* – Sp. *cucaracha* unaccountably assim. to *cock* and *roach.*] The name of orthopterous insects of the genus *Blatta,* esp. *B. orientalis,* commonly called *black-beetle,* infesting kitchens in large numbers.

† **Co·ck-road, rood.** 1648. [COCK *sb.*[1] I b; see COCKSHOOT.] = COCKSHOOT –1751.

Cocks. Also *Fighting cocks.* 1847. *dial.* The Ribwort Plantain.

Cock's-comb, cockscomb (kǫ·kskōᵘm). Also, in fig. senses, COXCOMB, q.v. ME. **1.** The comb of a cock. **2.** A jester's cap, resembling a cock's-comb 1562. † **3.** *joc.* The head –1654. † **4.** A conceited fool. Now COXCOMB. –1706. **5.** A name given to plants; *esp.* the Yellow Rattle (*Rhinanthus crista-galli*), *Celosia cristata,* and in the W. Indies *Erythrina crista-galli.* **6.** A kind of oyster having both valves plaited 1776. Also *attrib.*

Co·ck's-foot, cocksfoot. 1697. A grass, *Dactylis glomerata.*

Cock's-head, cockshead. ME. Applied to some kinds of Trefoil; *esp.* a species of Sainfoin, *Onobrychis caput-galli*; also common Red Clover. Also Plantain, Knapweed, etc. (*local*).

† **Co·ckshoot.** 1530. [f. COCK *sb.*[1] I. 1 b + SHOOT.] A broad glade in a wood, through which woodcocks might dart or shoot, so as to be caught by nets stretched across the opening –1691. Hence in local names, as *Cockshott Wood, Farm,* etc. ¶ The statement that the net itself was the *cockshoot,* and the spelling *cock-shut,* are dictionary blunders.

Cock-shut (kǫ·k,ʃɒt). Now *dial.* 1594. [f. COCK *sb.*[1] + SHUT *sb.* 2: perh. the time when poultry are shut up.] **1.** *attrib.* in *c. light, time,* etc.: twilight. **2.** *sb.* Twilight 1598.

Cock-shy (kǫ·k,ʃəi:). *colloq.* 1836. [f. COCK *sb.*[1] + SHY *sb.*[2]] **1.** Applied to cock-throwing and the like 1851. **2.** A shy at an object set up for the purpose, as a form of amusement. Also *transf.* and *attrib.* 1836. **3.** The object at which the shy is made. Also *transf.* 1836. **4.** A pitch where sticks may be thrown at coco-nuts for payment 1879.

3. What a fine c. he would make 1836.

Co·ckspur. 1591. **1.** The spur of a cock. **2.** A kind of Caddis-worm 1653. **3.** Short for *c. burner, thorn* 1808.

Comb.: **c.-burner,** a gas-burner with three holes; **c. hawthorn, c. thorn,** *Cratægus crus-galli,* a native of N. America.

Cock-sure (kǫk,ʃūᵊ·ɹ), *a.* 1520. [Earliest (XVI) 'absolutely secure, safe', etc. (assoc. with COCK *sb.*[1] is much later), f. COCK *sb.*[6] (= God) + SURE; cf. *God-save* (for *-safe*) XV.] † **1.** Absolutely safe or certain –1742. **2.** Feeling perfectly certain. Const. *of, about.* 1672. **3.** Dogmatically self-confident 1755. Also as *adv.*

1. To make the Event cock sure NORTH. **2.** 'Are you sure?' said his mother. 'Cock sure!' said Andy S. LOVER. **3.** A conceited and c. style DARWIN. *adv.* We steale as in a Castle, c. 1 *Hen. IV.* II. i. 94.

Cockswain, earlier f. COXSWAIN.

Cocksy, coxy (kǫ·ksi), *a.* 1825. [f. COCK *sb*[1] + -SY.] Impudent, bumptious, cocky. Hence **Co·xiness.**

Cocktail (kǫ·ktēⁱl). Also **cock-tail.** 1808. [*lit.* 'a tail like that of a cock', or 'a tail that cocks up'.] **1.** A cocktailed horse (see COCKTAILED 1); any horse of racing qualities, but not thorough-bred. *transf.* of persons 1854. Also as *adj.* **2.** (more fully *C. Beetle*): A brachelytrous beetle which cocks up its tail when irritated; the Devil's Coach-horse 1880. **3.** A drink made of spirit, bitters, some sugar, etc. Chiefly *U.S.* 1809. Also as *adj.*

1. *transf.* Such a..coxcomb as that, such a c. THACKERAY.

Co·ck-tailed, *a.* 1769. **1.** Of horses: Having the tail docked. **2.** Having the tail (or hinder part) cocked up 1798.

Co·ck-up, cockup. 1693. [f. *cock up*; see COCK *v.*[1]] **1.** A distinct turn up at the end 1826. **2.** A hat or cap cocked up in front 1693. **3.** A freshwater fish of India (*Lates calcarifer*) 1845. **4.** As *adj.* 1832.

Cockweed (kǫ·kwīd). Now *dial.* 1585. † **1.** ? A species of *Lepidium* –1783. **2.** = Corn Cockle.

Co·cky, *sb.* 1687. [f. COCK *sb.*[1] + -Y[6].] (Formerly a term of endearment.)

Cocky (kǫ·ki), *a.* 1768. [f. COCK *sb.*[1] + Y[1].] Arrogantly pert (*colloq.*).

Cocky-leeky (kǫki,lī·ki). *Sc.* 1771. [f. COCK *sb.*[1] + LEEK, with suffix *-ie,* -Y[6].] Soup made of a cock boiled with leeks.

Cockyolly (kǫki,ǫ·li). 1837. In *c. bird*: = 'dear little bird'; cf. *Dicky-bird.*

Coco, cocoa (kōᵘ·ko). 1555. [– Pg. and Sp. *coco* 'grinning face'; the name referring to the face-like appearance of the base of the shell. The spelling *Cocoa* was originated (app. by accident) in Dr. Johnson's Dictionary. See next.] † **1.** = COCO-NUT below –1740. **2.** The palm-tree *Cocos nucifera,* which produces the coconut 1555. Also *attrib. Comb.*: **Coco-nut, cocoa-nut, coker-nut. a.** The nut or seed of the coco-palm. **b.** = *Coco-nut palm.* **c.** In pugilistic slang: The human head. **Double Coco-nut,** in Fr. *coco-de-mer, coco-des-Maldives*: the immense woody nut of a gigantic palm. *Lodoicea sechellarum,* found native only on two small islands of the Seychelles group.

Cocoa (kōᵘ·ko). 1707. [Alteration of CACAO, also † *cacoa* – Sp. *cacao* – Aztec *kakaua-,* comb. form of *kakaua-atl* (see CHOCOLATE).] † **1.** The seed of *Theobroma cacao*) more correctly called CACAO –1790. **2.** The Cacao-tree. (*rare* and *improper.*) 1876. **3.** A powder made from the seeds; also, a beverage made from this powder, or from the prepared seeds. (The ordinary sense.) 1788.

Comb. **c.-nib,** the cotyledon of the cacao seed; † **-nut,** a name for the cacao seed; now disused.

Cocoon (kokū·n). 1699. [– Fr. *cocon,* † *coucon* – mod. Pr. *coucoun* egg-shell, cocoon, dim. of *coca* shell.] The case of silky threads, in which the silkworm is enclosed in the chrysalis state; hence, analogous structures formed by any insects; also the silken case spun by spiders to receive their eggs. Also *fig.* and *attrib.* Hence **Cocoo·nery** (*U.S.*), a room for rearing silkworms and obtaining cocoons.

Coco-plum. 1676. The fruit of a W. Indian tree, *Chrysobalanus icaco*; also the tree.

† **Coct,** *v.* 1605. [– *coct-,* pa. ppl. stem of L. *coquere* cook.] *trans.* To boil –1624; to digest 1662; to bake (earthenware) –1678.

Coctile (kǫ·ktil, -təil), *a.* 1678. [– L. *coctilis* baked, burnt, f. as prec.; see -ILE.] Made by baking; formed of baked bricks.

Coction (kǫ·kʃən). Now *rare.* 1572. [– L. *coctio* digesting of food (Pliny), in late L. action of cooking; f. as prec.; see -ION.] **1.** Boiling; cooking 1605. † **2.** The action of heat in preparing any substance –1766. † **3.** *Old Med.* The ripening of morbific matter before elimination from the body –1738. **4.** *Phys.* Digestion. ? *Obs.* 1667.

Cocus (kōᵘ·kǒs). 1794. The wood of *Brya ebenus,* a W. Indian tree, used by turners. Also *c.-wood.*

Cod (kǫd), *sb.*[1] [OE. *cod(d)* bag, scrip, husk, corresp. to ON. *koddi,* O Da. *kodde,* Sw. *kudde* cushion, pillow, pad, Norw. *kodd* testicle, scrotum; f. Gmc. *kud- *keud- (whence OE. *ċēod* pouch).] **1.** A bag. **2.** A husk; a pod; cf. PEASCOD. Now *dial.* OE. **3.** The scrotum; improp. in *pl.* testicles. (Not in polite use.) ME. † **4.** A cocoon. (cf. 2.) –1802.

1. The bag or c. [of a net] to enclose the fish 1750.

Cod (kǫd), *sb.*[2] *North.* ME. [See prec.] **1.** A pillow, cushion. *Sc.* and *n. dial.* **2.** One of the bearings of an axle ME.

Cod (kǫd), *sb.*[3] ME. [Origin unkn.] **1.** A well-known sea-fish, *Gadus morrhua,* which inhabits the Atlantic and its connected seas. Sometimes extended (with qualifications, drawn from their habitats, colour, food, etc.) to other members of the *Gadidæ* or Cod-tribe. (Pl. now rare: *cod* being used instead.) More fully **cod-fish. 2.** Applied to other fishes which take the economic place of the true cod in other regions; *esp.* to the *Bastard, Blue, Buffalo, Cultus, Green cod* of the Pacific coast 1880. See also ROCK COD.

Comb.: **c.-bank,** a submarine bank (BANK[1]) on which c. are caught; **-fishery,** fishing for c., *esp.* as a branch of industry; **-line,** a line used in fishing for c.; **-oil** = COD-LIVER OIL.

Cod, *sb.*[4] *slang.* 1690. [Origin unkn.; synon. CODGER appears much later. See COD *v.*[3]] A fool, (old) fellow, CODGER.

† **Cod** (kǫd), *v.*[1] 1532. [f. COD *sb.*[1]] **1.** *intr.* To produce pods –1710. **2.** *trans.* To gather the pods of (peas) –1730. **3.** *intr.* with *out.* To shake out. Hence **Co·dder** (insense 2) (*dial.*).

Cod, *v.*[2] 1861. [f. COD *sb.*[3]] To fish for cod.

Cod, *v.*[3] *slang.* or *dial.* 1873. [perh. = 'make a cod of', f. COD *sb.*[4]; cf. the earlier KID *v.*[3]] *trans.* To hoax, 'stuff', fool.

‖ **Coda** (kō·da, kōᵘ·dă). 1753. [It. :– L. *cauda* tail.] *Mus.* A passage added after the natural completion of a movement, so as to form a more definite and satisfactory conclusion.

Cod-bait. 1626. = CAD-BAIT (see CAD [3]).

† **Co·dding,** *a.* [perh. f. COD *sb.*[1] 3.] ? Lecherous. *Tit. A.* v. i. 99.

Coddle (kǫ·d'l). *v.*[1] 1598. [Origin unkn.; see next.] To boil gently, parboil, stew (*esp.* fruit). Also *fig.*

We'll go said my father, whilst dinner is coddling STERNE. *fig.* Hee is tane from Grammar-schoole halfe codled OVERBURY.

Coddle (kǫ·d'l), *v.*[2] 1815. [prob. of dial. origin and a var. of CAUDLE *v.*; but perh. a fig. use of prec. Cf. MOLLY-CODDLE.] To treat as an invalid; to nurse overmuch, cocker. Often with *up.*

Let womankind alone for coddling each other SCOTT. Hence **Coddle** *sb. colloq.* one who coddles himself or is coddled.

Coddle, *v.*[3]; dial. f. CUDDLE.

Coddy-moddy. *dial.* 1676. [Origin unkn.] The Blackheaded Gull.

Code (kōᵘd), *sb.* ME. [–(O)Fr. *code* – L. *codex*; see CODEX.] **1.** *Rom. Law.* One of the systematic collections of statutes made by the later emperors; *spec.* the *code of Justinian.* Hence, **2.** A digest of the laws of a country, or of those relating to any subject 1735. **3.** *transf.* A system of rules or regulations on any subject 1809. **4.** A system of signals 1808; (*Telegr.*) a system of words arbitrarily used for other words or phrases, to secure brevity and secrecy; also *attrib.* 1880. † **5.** A collection of writings forming a book, or volume –1794.

3. In the legislative as in the religious c. COLERIDGE. **4.** A c. of signals for the army WELLINGTON. *attrib.* C. telegrams 1880.

Code (kōᵘd), *v. rare.* 1815. [f. CODE *sb.*] To enter in a code.

Co-defe·ndant. 1640. [See CO-.] Joint defendant.

Codeine (kōᵘ·di,əin). 1838. [f. Gr. κώδεια head, poppy-head, + -INE[5].] *Chem.* A white crystalline alkaloid ($C_{18}H_{21}NO_3$) contained in opium, and used as a hypnotic; called also *codeia.*

‖ **Codetta** (kode·tta). 1869. [It., dim. of CODA.] *Mus.* A short coda.

Codex (kōᵘ·deks). Pl. **codices** (kōᵘ·disīz). 1581. [L. *codex, codic-* block of wood, block split into leaves or tablets, book.] † **1.** = CODE *sb.* 1–3. –1753. **2.** A manuscript volume: *e.g.* the *Codex Sinaiticus, Vaticanus,* etc., of the Scriptures 1845. **3.** *Med.* 'A collection of receipts for the preparation of drugs'. Hence **Co·dical** *a.* (Webst.)

Cod-fish; see COD *sb.*[3]

Codger (kǫ·dʒəɹ). *dial.* and *colloq.* 1756. [perh. var. of CADGER.] **1.** *dial.* A mean or miserly (old) fellow; *occas.* a pedlar or tramp 1796. **2.** *low colloq.* A term applied irreverently to an elderly man, with a whimsical implication 1756; more generally = Fellow, chap. 1839.

2. A gouty old c. of an alderman W. IRVING.

Codicil (kǫ·disil). 1422. [– L. *codicillus* (chiefly in pl.), dim. of *codex* CODEX.] **1.** *Law.* A supplement to a will. **2.** *transf.* and *fig.* Supplement, appendix 1784.

2. A [bitter] c. to a most severe Winter H. WALPOLE. Hence **Codici·llary** *a.* of the nature of, or belonging to, a c.

Codify (kōᵘ·difəi, kǫ·d-), *v.* 1800. [f. CODE + -FY; cf. Fr. *codifier.*] **1.** To reduce (laws) to a code. **2.** *gen.* To systematize 1873. Hence **Co:difica·tion,** reduction to a code; systematization. **Co·difier,** one who codifies.

Codilla (kodi·lă). 1785. [app. dim. of It. *coda*:– L. *cauda* tail.] The coarse tow of flax or hemp.

Codille (ko·dil). 1712. [– Fr. *codille* – Sp. *codillo* 'elbow-joint', term at ombre, dim. of *codo* elbow.] A term used at ombre when the game is lost by the player who challenges to win it.

† **Codi·niac.** 1539. [– Fr. †*codignac*, etc. (mod. *cotignac*), f. (ult.) L. *cotoneum*; see QUINCE.] Quince-marmalade, quiddany –1668.

Codist (kōᵘ·dist). *rare.* 1853. [f. CODE *sb.* + -IST.] One learned in legal codes.

Codling[1] (kǫ·dliŋ). ME. [f. COD *sb.* + -LING[1].] **1.** A young or small cod. **2.** *U.S.* Applied to fishes and the genus *Phycis,* allied to the cod.

Codling[2], **-lin** (kǫ·dliŋ, -lin). late ME. [Early *querdling* is identical with the surname = AFr. *Quer de lion* (Fr. *Cœur de lion*) 'lion-heart'.] **1.** A variety of apple, elongated and tapering towards the eye. (Formerly, a hard kind of apple, not suitable to be eaten raw; hence, any half-grown apple.) **b.** A tree bearing codlings 1657. † **2.** *fig.* A raw youth –1663.

1. As a C. when tis almost an Apple *Twel. N.* I. v. 167. *Hot codlings*: roasted apples (formerly sold hot in London streets). *Comb.* **c.-moth,** a species of moth (*Carpocapsa pomenella*), the larva of which feeds on the apple.

Co·dling[3]. 1874. [Origin unkn.] A balk sawed into lengths for staves.

Co·d-liver oi·l. 1783. Oil expressed from the liver of the cod-fish, much used in medicine.

† **Cod-piece.** 1460. [f. COD *sb.*[1] 3.] A bagged appendage to the front of the breeches; often conspicuous –1761. Also *fig.* and *attrib.*

† **Cods, cod's.** 1569. A perversion of *God's,* in oaths, etc. –1698.

Coe, *sb. local.* Also Sc. **cow.** 1653. [Of LG. origin; cf. MDu., MLG. *kouwe,* MHG. *kouwe, kow* (G. *kaue*) in same sense :– WGmc. **kauja* – L. *cavea* (see CAGE).] *Mining.* A little hut built over a mine-shaft.

Cœcal, cœcum, etc.; see CÆCAL, etc.

Co-ed (koᵘe·d). *U.S. colloq.* 1889. [See next.] A female co-educational student.

Co-educa·tion. 1874. [See CO-: of U.S. origin.] Education of the two sexes together in school, etc. **Co-e·ducate** *v.*, **-educa·tional** *a.*

Co-effe·ct. 1768. [See CO-.] A joint effect.

Co-e·fficacy. *rare.* [See CO-.] Joint efficacy. BROWNE.

Coefficient (kōᵘ,éfi·ʃent). 1665. [– mod.L. *coefficiens*; see CO-, EFFICIENT. In senses A and B 1 often with a hyphen. Cf. Fr. *coefficient sb.*]

A. *adj.* Co-operating to produce a result.

B. *sb.* **1.** A coefficient cause 1708. So † **Co-effi·ciency** (*rare*). **2.** *Math.* A number or quantity placed (usually) before and multiplying another quantity known or unknown; thus in $4x^2 + 2ax$, 4 is the c. of x^2, 2 of ax, and $2a$ of x. 1708. **3.** *Physics.* A multiplier that measures some property of a particular substance, for which it is constant, while differing for different substances; e.g. *c. of friction, expansion,* etc. 1829.

Differential c.: the quantity which measures the rate of change of a function of any variable with respect to that variable.

Coehorn, cohorn (kōᵘ·hǭɹn). 1705. [f. Baron van Menno *Coehoorn* (1641–1704), a Dutch engineer.] *Mil.* A small mortar for throwing grenades. In full *c. mortar.* Also *attrib.*

Cœlacanth (sī·lăkænþ). 1864. [– mod.L. *Cœlacanthus,* name of the typical genus, f. Gr. κοῖλος hollow + ἄκανθα spine.] *adj.* Having a hollow spine; said of an extinct family of fishes. *sb.* A fish of the genus *Cœlacanthus* or the family *Cœlacanthidæ.* Hence **Cœlaca·nthid,** one of this family. **Cœlaca·nthine** *a.* pertaining to Cœlacanths. **Cœlaca·nthoid, Cœlaca·nthous** *adjs.*

Cœlelminth (sī·lelminþ). 1836. [– mod.L. *Cœlelmintha,* f. Gr. κοῖλος hollow + ἕλμινς, ἑλμινθ-, intestinal worm.] *Zool.* One of the *Cœlelmintha,* a cavitary intestinal worm.

‖ **Cœlenterata** (sīlentĕrēⁱ·tă), *sb. pl.* Also **cœlentera.** 1872. [mod.L., f. Gr. κοῖλος hollow + ἔντερον intestine + *-ata* -ATE[2].] *Zool.* **1.** The group of the Animal Kingdom comprising *Ctenophora, Actinozoa,* and *Hydrozoa,* distinguished by having a digestive cavity with which a peripheral system of canals frequently communicates, with prehensile organs round the mouth, and nearly all provided with nematocysts. **2.** In later classifications the lower subdivision of the Metazoa, having an intestinal canal but no cœlome. It includes also the *Porifera* or Sponges. So **Cœlenterate,** belonging to, or one of, the *Cœlenterata.*

Cœlestial, etc.; see CEL-.

Cœliac, † **-al** (sī·liæk, -ăl), *a.* 1662. [– L. *cœliacus* – Gr. κοιλιακός, f. κοιλία belly, bowels, f. κοῖλος hollow; see -AC, -ACAL; cf. Fr. † *cœliaque,* mod. *céliaque.*] Of or belonging to the cavity of the abdomen.

C. artery or *axis,* a short thick branch issuing from the aorta just below the diaphragm. † *C. passion* or *flux,* a kind of chronic flux of the intestines. *C. canal,* in crinoids, one which runs into the arms from the cœloma.

Cœlio- (sī·lio), bef. a vowel **cœli-,** comb. f. Gr. κοιλία belly.

Cœlo- [1] (sī·lo), bef. a vowel **cœl-,** comb. f. Gr. κοῖλος hollow:

Cœ·lodont [Gr. ὀδούς, ὀδοντ-], *a.* hollow-toothed (epithet of certain lizard-like reptiles.) **Cœlo-spe·rmous** [Gr. σπέρμα], *a.* hollow-seeded; having the seed excavated on the flat side, as in coriander; etc.

Cœlo- [2], prop. **cælo-,** comb. f. L. *cælum* heavens.

Cœloma; see CŒLOME.

‖ **Cœlomata** (sīlōᵘ·mătă), *sb. pl.* 1877. [mod.L., f. Gr. κοίλωμα, -ματ- hollow, cavity; see -A 4.] *Zool.* A name for the higher division of Enterozoa (= *Metazoa*); see CŒLENTERATA 2. It comprises all the more highly developed animals, together with *Vermes.* Hence **Cœlomate** *a.* having a cœlome: belonging to the *Cœlomata*; *sb.* [sc. *animal.*] So **Cœlo·matous** *a.*

Cœlome, cœlom (sī·lōᵘm, -ǫm). Also in L. form **cœlo·ma.** 1878. [– Gr. κοίλωμα; see CŒLOMATA.] *Zool.* The body-cavity of a cœlomate animal. Hence **Cœlomic** *a.* pertaining to, or of the nature of, a c.

Coemption (ko,e·mᵖʃən). ME. [f. L. *coemptio,* f. *coempt-,* pa. ppl. stem. of *coemere* buy up; see -ION.] **1.** The buying up of the whole supply of any commodity. **2.** *Rom. Law.* A form of civil marriage consisting in a mutual fictitious sale of the two parties 1677. Hence **Coe·mptive** *a.* of the nature of c.

‖ **Cœnæsthesis** (sīnesþī·sis). 1837. [f. Gr. κοινός common + αἴσθησις sensation, perception.] *Psychol.* The general sense of existence arising from the sum of bodily impressions; the vital sense.

Cœnenchym (sine·ŋkim). Also in L. form **cœne·nchyma.** 1875. [f. Gr. κοινός common + ἔγχυμα infusion.] *Zool.* **a.** The calcareous framework by which corallites are united into one corallum. **b.** The cœnosarc of a compound Anthozoan.

Cœno- (sī·no), bef. a vowel **cœn-,** comb. f. Gr. κοινός common:

‖ **Cœnœ·cium** [Gr. οἶκος], *Zool.* the common dermal system of a colony of Polyzoa. **Cœno·gamy** [Gr. -γαμια, γάμος], community of husbands or wives. **Cœ·nosarc** [Gr. σάρξ, σαρκ-], *Zool.* the common living basis or flesh which unites the individuals of a compound zoophyte. ‖ **Cœno·steum** [Gr. ὀστέον], *Zool.* the common calcareous skeleton of the Hydrocorallina, a division of the Hydrozoa.

Cœnobite, cenobite (sī·nobəit, se·nobəit). 1638. [– (O)Fr. *cénobite* or eccl.L. *cœnobita,* f. *cœnobium* – Gr. κοινόβιον community life, (eccl.) convent, f. κοινός common + βίος life; see -ITE[1].] A member of a religious order living in a community; opp. to an *anchoret.* Hence **Cœnobi·tic, -al, cen-,** *a.* pertaining to a c.; relating to, or of the nature of, a monastic community. **Cœ·nobiti:sm, ce·n-** the practice or system of cœnobites.

‖ **Cœnobium, cen-** (sinōᵘ·biŏm). Pl. **cœnobia.** 1817. [eccl.L.; see prec.] **1.** = CŒNOBY. **2.** *Bot.* **a.** The multilocular fruit of *Labiatæ,* etc. 1866. **b.** A structure formed by the union of a number of cells, as in certain Algæ 1882. **3.** *Zool.* A cluster of 'colonial' Protozoa 1888.

Cœnoby, cen- (sī·nobi, se·n-). 1475. [– prec.] A conventual establishment.

Cœnure (sī·niuɹ). 1847. [– mod.L. *cœnurus* (more commonly used), f. Gr. κοινός common + οὐρά tail.] *Zool.* The many-headed bladder-worm; the hydatid which produces staggers in sheep; it is the cystic stage of *Tænia cœnurus*, one of the tape-worms of the dog.

Coequal (ko,ī·kwǫl), *a.* 1460. [– L. *coæqualis* of the same age; in *Theol.* use – eccl.L., of the Trinity, etc. See Co-, EQUAL.] **1.** Equal *with* († *to, unto*) one another or others in rank, power, etc. **2.** Co-extensive *with* 1853. As *sb.* One who is the equal of another 1577.

1. If once he come to be a Cardinall, Hee'l make his cap coequall with the Crowne 1 *Hen. VI*, v. i. 33. Hence † **Coe·qual** *v.* to be or become c. with; to make equal with. **Coequa·lity,** c. state or condition. **Coe·qually** *adv.*

† **Co·equate, Coequa·ted,** *ppl. a.* 1592. [– *coæquat-*, pa. ppl. stem of L. *coæquare*, f. *æquare* make equal; see EQUATE.] Made equal with something else. In *c. anomaly*, the true anomaly of a planet; see ANOMALY. –1769.

Coerce (ko,ɜ̄·ɹs), *v.* 1475. [– L. *coercēre*, f. *com* Co- + *arcēre* restrain.] **1.** To constrain or restrain by force, or by authority resting on force. Also *absol.* 1659. † **2.** To subject to restraint in the matter of (*rare*) 1780. **3.** To effect by compulsion. (*U.S.*) 1850.

1. The Punishments..sufficient to c. this profligate sort of Men AYLIFFE. **2.** The debtor is ordered..to be coerced his liberty until he makes payment BURKE. **3.** To c. obedience WEBSTER. Hence **Coe·rcer. Coe·rcible** *a.* that can be coerced.

Coercion (ko,ɜ̄·ɹʃən). 1495. [Earlier *cohercion* – OFr. *cohercion*, *-tion* – L. *coer(c)tio* (med.L. *coercio*), var. of *coercitio*, f. *coercit-*, pa. pple. stem of *coercēre*; see prec., -ION.] **1.** The action of coercing; constraint, restraint, compulsion. **2.** Government by force; the employment of force to suppress political disaffection and disorder. Also *attrib.* 1798. **3.** Physical pressure; compression 1830. † **4.** Coercitive power or jurisdiction –1700. Also *fig.*

1. The moral c. of public opinion MILL. C. of outrage HALLAM. **2.** The cant which brands as 'coercion' that which is the duty of every Government DK. ARGYLL. Hence **Coe·rcionist,** one who supports government by c., *esp.* in Ireland.

Coercive (ko,ɜ̄·ɹsiv), *a.* 1600. [f. stem of COERCE + -IVE, as in *conduce, conducive.*] Of the nature of coercion; coercing. Also as quasi-*sb.*

In painful dungeons and c. chains POPE.
C. force: the hypothetical force in a magnetic substance which resists magnetization or demagnetization 1839.
var. **Coe·rcitive** *a.* (and *sb.*). ? *Obs.* Hence **Coe·rcively** *adv.* **Coe·rciveness,** c. quality.

Coessential (kōu,ėse·nʃăl), *a.* 1471. [– eccl. L. *coessentialis* (tr. Gr. ὁμοούσιος of the same substance), predicated attribute of the Trinity; see Co-, ESSENTIAL.] **1.** United in being. **2.** One in essence 1587.

2. Wee blesse and magnifie that Coessentiall Spirit eternally proceeding from both HOOKER. Hence **Coesse:ntia·lity,** c. quality or nature. (*Theol.*)

Co-esta·blishment. 1791. [See Co-.] Joint or concurrent establishment.

Co-esta·te. 1756. [See Co-.] An estate or state possessing co-ordinate authority or rank with another.

† **Coeta·nean.** 1616. [f. as next + -AN.] *adj.* = next –1641. *sb.* A contemporary, a coeval; var. † **Co·etan(e** (*rare*) –1694.

Coetaneous (kōu,itē·nīəs), *a.* Also **coæt-.** 1608. [f. L. *coætaneus* contemporaneous + -OUS.] = COEVAL *a.* in all senses. Hence **Coeta·neous- ly** *adv.*

Coeternal (kōu,itɜ̄·ɹnăl). *a.* ME. [f. eccl. L. *coæternus* (also *coæternalis*) + -AL¹. See Co-, ETERNAL.] Equally eternal. Also as *sb.*

Hail holy light, of spring of Heav'n first-born, Or of th' Eternal C. beam MILT. *P.L.* III. 2.
var. † **Coete·rn(e** *a.* Hence **Coete·rnally** *adv.*

Coeternity (kōu,itɜ̄·ɹnĭti). 1587. [– late L. *coæternitas*; see Co-, ETERNITY.] Coeternal existence or quality; eternal existence with another; equal eternity.

Aristotle's tenet of the c. of matter MILMAN.

Coeval (ko,ī·văl), *a.* and *sb.* 1605. [f. late L. *coævus*, f. *com* CO- + *ævum* age; see -AL¹.]

A. *adj.* Const. *with*, † *to*. **1.** Of contemporaneous origin 1622. **2.** Equally old 1700. **3.** Existing at the same time 1704. **4.** Of coincident duration 1742.

1. Ideas in the Understanding are c. with Sensation LOCKE. **4.** Were men to live c. with the sun YOUNG. vars. † **Coe·ve,** † **Coe·vous.** Hence **Coeva·lity,** var. † **Coe·vity,** c. quality. **Coe·vally** *adv.*

B. *sb.* **1.** One of the same age or standing 1656. **2.** A person (or thing) belonging to the same period 1605.

1. He is forlorn among his coevals; his juniors cannot be his friends LAMB.

Co-executor (kōu,ekse·kiŭtəɹ, -ŏɹ). ME. [– med.L. *coexecutor*; see Co-, EXECUTOR.] A joint executor. So **Co-exe·cutrix,** a joint executrix.

Co-exist (kōu,egzi·st), *v.* 1677. [– late L. *coexistere*; see Co-, EXIST; cf. (O)Fr. *coexister.*] To exist at the same time, in the same place, etc., *with* another.

They [Generations of Mankind] never c., but are successive HALE. No real greatness can c. with deceit COLERIDGE. Hence **Coexi·sting** *ppl. a.* existing together.

Coexistence (kōu,egzi·stĕns). 1646. [– med.L. *coexistentia*; see Co-, EXISTENCE; cf. Fr. *coexistence.*] Existence together or in conjunction.

In the relation to each other..of succession and not of c. 1822. var. † **Coexi·stency.**

Coexistent (kōu,egzi·stĕnt). 1662. [f. as COEXIST; see -ENT; cf. Fr. *coexistent.*] *adj.* Existing together or in conjunction. *sb.* That which coexists with something else 1846.

Coexte·nd, *v.* 1617. [See Co-; cf. med.L. *coextendere.*] To make or be coextensive.

The manhood is not coextended with the Godhead 1656. So **Coexte·nsion,** coincidence in extension.

Coextensive (kōu,ekste·nsiv), *a.* 1771. [See Co-.] Extending over the same space or time; coinciding in limits; in *Logic*, having the same logical extension. Also as *sb.*

C. to dominion is jurisdiction BENTHAM. So **Coexte·nsive-ly** *adv.*, **-ness.**

Co-feoffee (kōu·fefī). 1458. [f. Co- + FEOFFEE; in med.L. *cofeoffatus.*] A joint feoffee.

Coffee (kǫ·fi). 1598. [Ult. – *kahveh*, Turkish pronunc. of Arab. *kahwa*, through Du. *koffie.*] **1.** A drink made by infusion or decoction from the seeds of a shrub (see sense 3) roasted and ground or (in the East) pounded. **b.** A repast or course including or consisting of coffee. **2.** The berries (collectively), either whole or ground 1626. **3.** The shrub from which coffee is obtained; a species of *Coffea*, chiefly *C. arabica*, a native of Abyssinia and Africa, but now widely cultivated throughout the tropics. It bears fragrant white flowers, succeeded by red fleshy berries, each containing two seeds (*coffee-beans*). 1623.

1. There came in my time [i.e. 1636] to the College, one Nathaniel Conopios, out of Greece.. He was the first I ever saw drink c. EVELYN. *Black c.*: c. without milk.
Comb.: **c.-berry,** the fruit of the c.-plant, also, loosely, the seed; **-bug,** an insect (*Lecania coffeæ*) of the family *Coccidæ*, destructive to c.-plants; **-grounds** *sb. pl.*, the granular sediment remaining in coffee after infusion; † **-man,** a man keeping a c.-house; **-pot,** a pot in which c. is made or served; **-rat,** an insular variety of *Mus hirsutus*, found in Southern India; **-wit,** a wit who frequents c.-houses.

Co·ffee-house. 1615. A house of entertainment where coffee and other refreshments are provided. (Much frequented in 17th and 18th c. for the purpose of political and literary conversation, circulation of news, etc.) Also *attrib.*

The leaders of the legislative clubs and coffee-houses BURKE.

Co·ffee-room. 1712. A public room where coffee and similar refreshments are served; now, generally, the public dining-room in a hotel.

Coffer (kǫ·fəɹ), *sb.* [– (O)Fr. *coffre* :– L. *cophinus* basket; see COFFIN.] **1.** A box, chest: *esp.* a strong box in which money or valuables are kept. In *pl.*: often = Treasury, funds ME. † **2.** An ark –1711. † **3.** A coffin –1555. **4.** *Arch.* A sunk panel in a ceiling or soffit, of ornamental character 1664. **b.** A space within a wall, etc., filled up with concrete or rubble 1715. † **5.** *Fortif.* A trench dug athwart a dry moat, and furnished with a parapet and embrasures, for purposes of defence. **6.** *Hydraulics.* A caisson or COFFER-DAM, q.v.; 'the lock for a barge' 1822.

1. He gooth vn to his cofre And broghte gold CHAUCER. The coffers of the government had long been empty H. MARTINEAU. **3.** My body to be buryed in a cofer of tree 1488. *Comb.* **c.-fish,** a trunk-fish, a species of *Ostracion.*

Coffer (kǫ·fəɹ), *v.* ME. [f. the *sb.*] **1.** To enclose in, or as in, a coffer; to treasure *up* (*arch.*). **2.** *Arch.* To adorn with coffers (see COFFER *sb.* 4). **3.** *Mining.* 'To secure a shaft from leaking by ramming in clay behind the masonry or timbering' 1881.

Coffer-dam. 1736. [f. COFFER + DAM *sb.*¹] A water-tight enclosure, usually made of piles with clay packed between them, from which the water is pumped to obtain a dry foundation for bridges, piers, etc.

Cofferer (kǫ·fərəɹ). Now *Hist.* ME. [– AFr. *cofrere* treasurer, = AL. *cofferarius*; corresp. to OFr. *cofrier* box-maker (med.L. *cofferarius*); see COFFER, -ER².] **1.** A treasurer; *spec.* one of the treasurers of the royal household 1538. † **2.** One who makes coffers –1515.

† **Co·ffer-work.** 1708. [f. COFFER *sb.* 4 b.] *Arch.* Masonry having coffers fitted with rubble, etc. Formerly also, building in concrete. –1742.

Coffin (kǫ·fin), *sb.* [– OFr. *cof(f)in* little basket, case – L. *cophinus* – Gr. κόφινος basket. Cf. COFFER.] † **1.** A basket –1552. † **2.** A chest, case, casket, box –1677. **3.** *spec.* The box in which a corpse is enclosed for burial. (The current sense.) 1525. Applied (*Naut.*) to an unseaworthy vessel (*colloq.*) 1833. † **4.** *Cookery.* The crust of a pie –1750; a pie-dish –1662. **5.** A paper case; *spec.* a cornet for groceries, etc. 1577. **6.** *Farriery.* The whole of a horse's hoof below the coronet 1607. **7.** *Printing.* The carriage of a printing machine 1659. **8.** A case in which articles are baked or fired in a furnace; = Fr. *cassette* 1679. **9.** *Mining.* An old open working (*Cornwall*); also, the mode of open working by casting up ore, etc., from platform to platform 1778.

2. A c. for a book 1677. **3.** His coffers from the c. could not save SWIFT. **4.** Of the paste a coffen I will reare *Tit. A.* v. ii. 189.
Comb.: **c.-bone,** a small spongy bone in a horse's hoof, being the last phalangeal bone of the foot; **-joint,** the joint at the top of a horse's hoof; **-plate.** Hence **Co·ffinless** *a.*

Coffin (kǫ·fin), *v.* 1564. [f. the sb.] To enclose in, or as in, a coffin (see COFFIN *sb.* 3, 4).

Wouldst thou have laugh'd had I come coffin'd home *Cor.* II. i. 167. C. them alive In some kind clasping prison B. JONS.

Coffle (kǫ·f'l). 1799. [– Arab. *ḳāfila* caravan; see CAFILA.] A train of slaves or beasts driven along together.

Coffret (kǫ·frĕt), **cofferet** (kǫ·fĕrĕt). 1485. [– (O)Fr. *coffret*, dim. of *coffre*; see COFFER, -ET.] A small coffer.

Cog, *sb.*¹ Now *Hist.* [– MLG., MDu. *kogge* (Du. *kog*), whence also OFr. *cogue, koge.*] **1.** An early form of ship; broadly built, with roundish prow and stern. **2.** Also app. = COCK *sb.*³, COCK-BOAT ME.

Cog (kǫg), *sb.*² [ME. *cogge* (in AL. *cogga, coggus* XIII), of unascertained origin, but prob. Scand. (cf. synon. Sw. *kugge, kughjul* cog-wheel, Norw. *kug.*] **1.** One of a series of teeth, etc., on the circumference of a wheel, etc., which, by catching similar projections on another wheel, etc., transmit or receive motion. **2.** Short for: † **a.** The series of cogs round a wheel; **b.** a cog-wheel 1712. **3.** *Mining.* A block used in building up a support for the roof of a mine 1881.

Cog, *sb.*³ 1856. [See COG *v.*³] *Carpentry.* A tenon on the end of a beam, which is received into a corresponding mortice on the surface of another beam or support; in a scarf-joint, etc.

† **Cog**, *sb.*[4] 1532. [Goes w. COG *v.*[3]] **1.** The act of cogging at dice; a way of doing this –1658. **2.** A deception, trick –1630.

Cog (kǫg), *v.*[1] 1499. [f. COG *sb.*[2]] **1.** To furnish (a wheel, etc.) with cogs. **2.** To steady anything with a wedge. *n. dial.* 1635.

Cog, *v.*[2] 1823. [app. var. of COCK *v.*[3]] To connect timbers by means of a cog; cf. COCK *v.*[3]

Cog (kǫg), *v.*[3] 1532. [prob. a canting term, of unkn. origin] **1.** *intr.* (*Dicing.*) To practise certain tricks in throwing dice. **2.** *trans.* To *c. a die* or *the dice*: fraudulently to control their fall 1565. † **3.** *intr.* To cheat –1683. **4.** To jest, quibble (*arch.*) 1588. † **5.** To fawn, wheedle –1728. † **6.** *gen.* To produce cunningly and fraudulently –1651.

3. Out-facing. . boyes, That lye, and c., and flout *Much Ado* v. i. 95. **5.** *Merry W.* III. iii. 76. **6.** Every Cobler can cogge a Syllogisme 1588.

Cogency (kō^{u}·dʒĕnsi). 1690. [f. COGENT: see -ENCY.] † **1.** Compulsion 1702. **2.** The quality of being cogent; *esp.* power of compelling assent 1690. *concr.* (with *pl.*) A convincing argument 1851.

2. The c. of distress JOHNSON, of Axioms LOCKE. var. **Co·gence** (*rare*).

Cogenial, cogenite; see CONGENIAL, etc.

Cogent (kō^{u}·dʒĕnt). 1659. [– *cogent-*, pres. ppl. stem of L. *cogere* drive together, compel, f. *com* Co- + *agere* drive; see -ENT.] **1.** Constraining; powerful, forcible 1718. **2.** *esp.* Having power to compel assent; convincing 1659.

1. To insist in c. terms KINGLAKE. **2.** Undeniable c. demonstrations LOCKE. The testimony of a number is more c. than the testimony of two or three NEWMAN. Hence **Co·gently** *adv.* in a c. manner.

Cogged (kǫgd), *ppl. a.*[1] 1825. [f. COG *sb.*[2] or *v.*[1] + -ED.] Furnished with cogs: having cog-wheels.

C.-wheel breathing, rhythm (*Med.*): a jerky respiratory sound in chest-affections, as of a cogged wheel in motion.

Cogged (kǫgd), *ppl. a.*[2] 1589. [f. COG *v.*[3] + -ED[1].] **1.** Corruptly influenced 1781. † **2.** Feigned in order to cheat –1656 ¶ **3.** Of dice: Loaded. (A misuse.) 1806.

Cogger (kǫ·gəɹ). 1576. [f. as prec. + -ER[1].] A sharper; a false flatterer. So † **Co·ggery**, trickery; *concr.* a trick.

Coggle (kǫ·g'l), *sb.*[1] Now *dial.* ME. [perh. var. of COBBLE *sb.*[1]; cf. dial. *knoggly, knobbly* 'having rounded protuberances'.] A rounded water-worn stone; *esp.* a cobble. Hence **Co·ggly** *a.* shaky, unsteady when stepped on.

† **Coggle**, *sb.*[2] 1695. [app. an error.] A small boat.

Cogie, coggie (kō·gi). *Sc.* 1750. [f. COGUE + -IE, -Y[6].] A small wooden bowl or its contents.

Cogitable (kǫ·dʒităb'l), *a.* 1688. [– L. *cogitabilis*; see COGITATE, -ABLE.] That can be thought or conceived; thinkable, conceivable. Also as *sb.*

Something not perceivable by sense, but only c. GROTE. Hence **Cogitabi·lity**, c. quality (*rare*).

Cogitabund (kǫ·dʒităbʊnd), *a.* 1649. [– L. *cogitabundus* in deep meditation; see COGITATE.] Meditative, deep in thought.

Co·gitant, *a. rare.* 1681. [f. COGITATE; see -ANT.] Thinking.

Cogitate (kǫ·dʒitē^{i}t), *v.* 1563. [– *cogitat-*, pa. ppl. stem. of L. *cogitare* think, f. *com* Co- + *agitare* put in motion; see AGITATE, -ATE[3].] **1.** *intr.* To think; to exercise the thinking faculties 1631. **2.** *trans.* with object. Hence: To devise, plan 1563.

1. For he that calleth a thing into his mind, whether by impression or recordation, cogitateth and considereth, and he that employeth the faculty of his phansie also cogitateth, and he that reasoneth. tr. BACON. **2.** To c. objects a priori. tr. KANT. To c. mischief (*mod.*).

Cogitation (kǫdʒitē^{i}·ʃən). ME. [– OFr. *cogitacion* – L. *cogitatio*, f. *cogitat-*; see prec., -ION.] **1.** The action or faculty of thinking. **2.** (with *pl.*) A thought or reflection ME.; a design 1538.

1. What by c., wee find to be the cause of anything HOBBES. **2.** The cogitations and purposes of your adversaries FLEMING.

Cogitative (kǫ·dʒitē^{i}tiv), *a.* 1490. [– Fr. † *cogitatif, -ive* or late L. *cogitativus*, f. as prec.; see -IVE.] **1.** Having the faculty of thought; thinking. **2.** Given to cogitation 1651.

1. The cogitatiue or knowing soule 1594. Hence **Co:gitati·vity**, c. capacity (*rare*).

† **Co·gmen.** *rare.* ME. only. Men to whom the cloth called *cogware* was sold.

Cognac (ko·nyak). 1594. [Fr., place-name.] **1.** *C. wine*: wine produced at Cognac. **2.** A French brandy distilled from Cognac wine; any French brandy 1687.

Cognate (kǫ·gnē^{i}t). 1645. [– L. *cognatus*, f. *com* Co- + *gnatus* born; see -ATE[2].] **A.** *adj.* **1.** Descended from a common ancestor; of the same family, coming from the same stock or root 1827. **2.** *gen.* Akin in origin; allied in nature, and hence, akin in quality; having affinity. (Const. *with*, rarely *to*.) 1645.

1. C. tribes 1827. A c. language G. HIGGINS, word GLADSTONE. *C. accusative*: one of kindred sense or derivation; *spec.* one that may adverbially follow an intr. vb., as in 'to die the death'. **2.** Geometry and the c. sciences JOWETT.

B. *sb.* **1.** *Rom. Law.* One related by blood to another; a kinsman; *pl.* those descended from the same ancestor, whether through males or females. Hence, *Sc. Law.* A relative on the mother's side. 1754. **2.** A cognate word, term, or thing 1865.

Hence **Cogna·teness**, c. quality. **Cogna·tic** *a.* pertaining to or reckoned through cognates.

Cognation (kǫgnē^{i}·ʃən). ME. [– L. *cognatio*, f. *cognatus*; see prec., -ION.] **1.** Relationship by descent from a common ancestor. In *Sc. Law.* Relationship through females only. 1751. † **2.** *collect.* Kindred, relations –1542. **3.** *Philol.* Relationship by descent from a common source or a common root 1741. **4.** Affinity, connection, relation, likeness. (Now *rare* or *Obs.*) 1555.

1. The c. [of the Phenicians] with the Jews GALE. **3.** The difference between c. and derivation 1862.

Cognition (kǫgni·ʃən). 1447. [– L. *cognitio*, f. *cognit-*, pa. ppl. stem of *cognoscere* get to know, investigate, f. *com* Co- + (*g*)*noscere*; see -ION.] **1.** † The action or faculty of knowing; knowledge, consciousness –1796; a product of such an action 1819. **2.** *Law.* = COGNIZANCE 3. (Chiefly *Sc.*) 1523. † **3.** Recognition. EVELYN.

1. I will not be my selfe, nor haue c. Of what I feele *Tr. & Cr.* v. ii. 63. Hence **Cogni·tional** *a.*

Cognitive (kǫ·gnitiv), *a.* 1586. [– med.L. *cognitivus*, f. as prec.; see -IVE.] Of or pertaining to cognition; having the attribute of cognizing, as *c. powers*.

Cognizable, -isable (kǫ·gnizăb'l, kǫ·ni-), *a.* 1678. [f. COGNIZE + -ABLE. In sense 1 often (kǫgnəi·zăb'l).] **1.** Capable of being known, perceived, or apprehended; perceptible; recognizable. **2.** Capable of being, or liable to be, judicially tried; within the jurisdiction of a court of law, etc. 1681.

2. *Cognizable offence* (Anglo-Ind. Law): any offence for which a police-officer may arrest without warrant. Hence **Co:gnizabi·lity**, c. quality (*rare*). **Co·gnizably** *adv.* in a c. manner.

Cognizance, -sance (kǫ·gnizăns, kǫ·ni-). ME. [– OFr. *conis(s)aunce, conus-*, vars. of *conois(s)ance* (mod. *connaissance*) – Rom. **connoscentia*, f. *cognoscent-*, pres. ppl. stem of L. *cognoscere*, see COGNITION, -ANCE. Latinization of the sp. by insertion of *g* has infl. the pronunc., but in legal use the older pronunc. survives.] **1.** † Knowledge –1651; † recognition SPENSER; *esp.* knowledge as attained by observation or information; perception, notice, observation 1642. **2.** *Law.* **a.** The hearing and trying of a cause. **b.** The right of dealing with any matter judicially; jurisdiction. Also *fig.* 1523. **3.** Acknowledgement; admission of a fact alleged; *esp.* acknowledgement of a FINE. **b.** A plea in replevin that defendant holds the goods in the right of another as his bailiff. Cf. AVOWRY. 1570. **4.** A device by which a person, company, etc., is distinguished, as a crest, etc.; a badge; *spec.* in *Her.* a device borne for distinction by all the retainers of a noble house. Also *fig.* ME.

1. The tree of cognizance of Good and Evill HOBBES. SPENSER *F.Q.* II. i. 31. Phrases. *To have c. of; to come (fall, be, lie) under, within, beyond, out of the c.; to take c. of.* **4.** In the chief three mullets stood, The cognizance of Douglas Blood SCOTT. If generous honesty, valour, and plain dealing, be the c. of thy family SIR T. BROWNE.

Cognizant, -isant (kǫ·gnizănt, kǫ·ni-), *a.* 1820. [f. prec.; see -ANT.] Having cognizance (see COGNIZANCE 1, 2); aware (*of*); *Philos.* that cognizes 1837.

Cognize, -ise (kǫgnəi·z), *v.* 1658. [Extracted from COGNIZANCE, COGNIZOR.] † **1.** *Law* (*absol.*) To take cognizance. **2.** *trans.* To take cognizance of, notice, observe 1821. **3.** *Philos.* To make (anything) an object of cognition 1836.

3. They first know—they first cognise, the things and persons presented to them SIR W. HAMILTON.

Cognizee, -isee (kǫgnizī·, kǫni-). 1531. [Correl. to COGNIZOR, see -EE[1].] *Old Law.* The party in whose favour a fine of land was levied.

Cognizor, -isor (kǫ·gnizǭ·ɹ, kǫ·ni-). 1531. [– AFr. *coniso(u)r* = OFr. *conoisseor*, f. *conoistre* know; see CONNOISSEUR.] *Old Law.* The party who levies a fine of land.

‖ **Cognomen** (kǫgnō^{u}·men). 1809. [L.] **1.** The third or family name of a Roman citizen, as Caius Julius *Cæsar*; also, an agnomen 1879. Hence, **2.** A nickname 1811. **3.** An (English) surname 1809. **4.** *loosely.* Name, appellation. [So in L.] 1852. Hence **Cogno·minal** *a.* having the same c., of or pertaining to a c.; † *sb.* namesake. **Cogno·minally** *adv.*

Cognominate (kǫgnǫ·minē^{i}t), *v.* 1609. [– *cognominat-*, pa. ppl. stem of L. *cognominare* to give a 'cognomen' to; see -ATE *v.*[3]] To give a surname or nickname to; to name. Hence **Cognomina·tion**, the action of cognominating; *concr.* = COGNOMEN.

Cognosce (kǫgnǫ·s), *v.* Chiefly *Sc. Law.* 1583. [– L. *cognoscere*; see COGNITION.] **1.** *intr.* To make inquiry; to take cognizance of a cause, etc. **2.** *trans.* To take judicial cognizance of; to investigate, try 1607. **3.** Judicially to examine and pronounce to be of a certain status; *esp.* (*ellipt.*) to pronounce to be an idiot or lunatic 1670. **4.** = COGNIZE 1874.

3. 'If he gangs daft, we'll hae him cognosced' SCOTT. Hence **Cogno·scence**, = COGNIZANCE 1. **Cogno·scent** *a.* (*rare*), cognitive; cognizant. **Cognoscibi·lity**, knowableness. **Cogno·scible** *a.* capable of being known; *sb.* that which can be known. **Cogno·scitive** *a.* [non-etymological var. of COGNITIVE], apprehensive; **Cogno·scitively** *adv.*

‖ **Cognoscente** (konʸoʃe·nte). Pl. **-ti** (-*ti*). 1778. [It., latinized form of *conoscente* :– L. *cognoscent-*, pres. ppl. stem of *cognoscere*; see prec., -ENT.] One who knows a subject thoroughly; a connoisseur.

‖ **Cognovit** (kǫgnō^{u}·vit). 1762. [Short for L. formula *cognovit actionem* he has acknowledged the charge; 3rd. sing. pa. t. of *cognoscere*; see prec.] *Law.* An acknowledgement by a defendant that the plaintiff's cause is just; whereupon judgement is entered without trial.

Co-gua·rdian. 1643. [Co-.] Joint guardian.

Cogue, cog (kō^{u}g, *Sc.* kōg, kǭg). Chiefly *Sc.* 1568. [Origin unkn.] **1.** (*Sc.*) A wooden pail. **2.** A small cup, of wood; also † a cogueful 1690. Hence **Cogueful, cogful**, as much as a c. will hold.

† **Co·gware.** ME. [Origin unkn. Cf. COGMEN.] A coarse cloth, resembling frieze, made of the poorest wool –1483.

Cog-wheel. ME. [See COG *sb.*[2]] A wheel with cogs or teeth; a gear-wheel.

Cog-wood. 1725. [f. COG *sb.*[2]] A timber-tree of Jamaica, *Laurus chloroxylon*.

Cohabit (kohæ·bit), *v.* 1530. [– late L. *cohabitare*; see Co-, HABIT *v.*; cf. (O)Fr. *cohabiter.*] **1.** To dwell or live together (*with*) (*arch.*) 1601; *fig.* of things 1653. **2.** To live together as husband and wife: often used *spec.* of persons not legally married 1530.

1. They were not able to c. with that Holy Thing [the Ark] SOUTH. *fig.* Peace, and patience, and a calm content did c. in the cheerful heart of Sir Henry Wotton WALTON. So **Coha·bitancy**, the state or fact of being a cohabitant (*rare*). **Coha·bitant**, one who dwells together with another or others. **Coha·biter** (*rare*) = *Cohabitant.*

Cohabitation (kohæbitē^{i}·ʃən). 1450. [– late L. *cohabitatio*; see Co-, HABITATION; cf. (O)Fr. *cohabitation.*] **1.** Dwelling or living together; community of life (*arch.*) (or hyphened). Also *transf.* and *fig.* **2.** Living together as husband and wife 1548.

2. For..holding correspondence and c. with one not his wife LUTTRELL.

Coheir (ko,ēə·ɹ). 1532. [– L. *coheres*; see CO-, HEIR; cf. OFr. *cohoir.*] One who participates in an inheritance; a joint heir. Also *fig.* (See *Romans* 8:17.)

Wint. T. II. i. 148. **Coheiʹrship.** So **Coheiʹress.**

Cohere (kohīə·ɹ), *v.* Also † **cohære.** 1598. [– L. *cohærēre*, f. *com* CO- + *hærēre* stick.] **1.** *intr.* To cleave or stick together; said of parts, and of the mass 1616; *transf.* of non-material things, etc. 1603. **2.** To unite or remain united in action 1651. **3.** To be congruous or consistent 1598; † to agree –1634.

1. The grains simply c. 1879. The hard mass became fluid. It still cohered KINGLAKE. The moral principles by which society coheres LECKY. **3.** *Twel. N.* V. i. 259. Hence **Coheʹrer,** *spec.* a detector of electric waves consisting of a glass cylinder containing metal filings which cohere when struck by a wave. **Coheʹring** *ppl. a.*; in *Bot.* united externally to each other, as anthers, etc.

Coherence (kohīə·rĕns). Also † **cohærence.** 1580. [– L. *cohærentia*, f. as next; see -ENCE; cf. Fr. *cohérence.*] **1.** *lit.* The action or fact of sticking together; cohesion 1613. Also *transf.* and *fig.* **2.** Logical connection; congruity, consistency 1588; † agreement –1680. **3.** Harmonious connection of the several parts of a discourse, system, etc., so that the whole hangs together 1623. † **4.** Context –1737.

1. *transf.* They have not enough of c. among themselves, nor of estimation with the publick BURKE. **3.** The c. in dreams 1856. So **Coheʹrency,** the quality of being coherent.

Coherent (kohīə·rĕnt), *a.* (*sb.*) 1555. [– *cohærent-*, pres. ppl. stem of L. *cohærēre*; see COHERE, -ENT; cf. Fr. *cohérent.*] **1.** That sticks or clings firmly together. Const. *to*, *with*. Said of parts and of the mass. 1578. Also *transf.* † **2.** Accordant logically or in sense; congruent –1601. **3.** Of thought, speech, etc.: Of which all the parts are consistent, and hang together 1580. Also said of persons 1724. † **4.** *sb.* One who or that which coheres –1657.

1. *transf.* C. with this is a Third property of.. love BARROW. **2.** *All's Well* III. vii. 39. **3.** Good C. Sense CUDWORTH. A c. story BURNET, thinker WATTS. Hence **Coheʹrently** *adv.*

Coheʹritor. 1550. [f. Co- + HERITOR.] = COHEIR.

† **Coheʹrt,** *v.* 1475. [app. – *coert-*, a form of the pa. ppl. stem of L. *coercēre* COERCE.] = COERCE –1543.

Cohesion (kohī·ʒən). Also † **cohæsion.** 1678. [f. *cohæs-*, pa. ppl. stem of L. *cohærēre* COHERE, after *adhæsio* adhesion, *inhæsio* inhesion (**cohæsio* is not extant). See -ION.] **1.** The action or condition of cohering; *spec.* the force with which the molecules of a body cleave together; cf. ATTRACTION *of Cohesion.* **2.** *Bot.* The superficial union of like organs 1835. **3.** *transf.* Of non-material union 1690.

1. Water..loosens the c. of a steep bank GEIKIE. **3.** Ideas that have no natural c. LOCKE.

Cohesive (kohī·siv), *a.* 1727. [f. as prec. + -IVE.] Having the property of cohering; characterized by cohesion.

Tracts of c. soil 1799. A soft c. mass SIR H. DAVY. To show how little c. force the league possessed S. AUSTIN. Hence **Coheʹsive-ly** *adv.*, **-ness.**

Cohibit (kohi·bit), *v.* Now *rare.* 1544. [– *cohibit-*, pa. ppl. stem of L. *cohibēre* restrain, f. *com* CO- + *habēre* have; cf. *prohibit.*] To restrain, check; to restrict. So **Cohibiʹtion,** restriction; stoppage.

†‖ **Cohob.** [perh. root of next, or contr. of *cohobation.*] *Med.* A Paracelsian term meaning repetition.

Cohobate (kōu·hobeit), *v.* 1641. [– mod.L. *cohobare*, = Fr. *cohober*; see -ATE[3]; see prec.] *Old Chem.* To subject to repeated distillation, by pouring a liquid back again and again upon the matter from which it has been distilled. Hence † **Cohobaʹtion,** this operation.

Cohorn; see COEHORN.

Cohort (kōu·hǫɹt), *sb.* 1489. [– (O)Fr. *cohorte* or L. *cohors, -hort-* enclosure, company, crowd, f. *com* CO- + **hort-*, as in *hortus* garden.] **1.** *Rom. Antiq.* A body of from 300 to 600 infantry; the tenth part of a legion. **2.** *transf.* A band of warriors 1500. **3.** *fig.* A company, band 1719. **4.** *Zool.* and *Bot.* A large group superior to a natural order; in *Bot.* = ALLIANCE 1845.

2. The C. bright Of watchfull Cherubim MILT. *P.L.* XI. 127. **3.** The c. of the Fathers Who kept the Faith below NEALE.

Cohortation (kōuhǫɹtēi·ʃən). *arch.* 1642. [– L. *cohortatio*; see CO-, HORTATION.] Exhortation. So **Cohoʹrtative** *a.* (*sb.*) pertaining to c.: in *Heb. Grammar*, the future paragogic.

Cohosh (kohǫ·ʃ). 1796. [The Indian name.] Name of N. American plants which have been used medicinally. **Black c.,** *Cimicifuga racemosa.* **Blue c.,** *Caulophyllum thalictroides.* **Red c.,** *Actæa spicata.* **White c.,** *Actæa alba.*

Cohow, cahow, cohoo (kəhū·). 1615. [From its cry.] A bird of the Bermudas, a species of Shearwater, now nearly exterminated.

‖ **Cohune** (kohū·n). 1805. A species of palm (*Attalea cohune*) found in Honduras.

Coif (koif), *sb.* [– OFr. *coife* (mod. *coiffe*) head-dress :– late L. *cofia* helmet.] **1.** A close-fitting cap covering the top, back, and sides of the head, worn by both sexes. † **2.** An ecclesiastical head-dress –1574. **3.** A white cap formerly worn by lawyers; *esp.* that worn by a serjeant-at-law as part of his official dress ME. Hence, The position or order of serjeant-at-law 1522. **4.** The skull-cap of a helmet. Now *Hist.* ME. **5.** The calyptra of mosses 1882.

1. The c.—the apron—the blue-checked gown, were all those of old Ailie SCOTT. **3.** A linnen Coife..an ornament which onely Sergeants at Law doe weare HOOKER. A Brother of the C. ADDISON.

Coif (koif), *v.* Pa. t. and pple. **coifed.** 1530. [orig. – Fr. *coiffer*, f. *coiffe* (prec.); in later use f. prec. sb.] **1.** To cover with, or as with, a coif; to invest with the serjeant's coif. **2.** To dress (the hair). Cf. *coiffure.* 1862.

1. There be in these times that are coif'd with such Opinions, that to shew Scripture to be Reason, is to make it lose weight with them J. HARRINGTON.

‖ **Coiffeur, -euse** (kwa-). 1858. [Fr.: see prec.] A male, female hairdresser.

‖ **Coiffure** (kwafü·r). 1631. [f. as prec.; see -URE.] A fashion of dressing the hair; head-dress.

Coign (koin), *sb.* Also **coigne.** 1605. [obs. sp. of COIN *sb.*, retained chiefly in connection w. the phr. *coign of vantage.*] **1.** A projecting corner. **2.** *Occas.* **a.** A corner-stone 1843. **b.** A wedge (in *Printing*, etc.) 1755.

Coign of vantage: a position affording facility for observation or action. *Macb.* I. vi. 7.

Coigne, coigny (*Irish Hist.*); see COYNYE.

† **Coil,** *v.*[1] ME. [An earlier form of CULL *v.*[1]] = CULL *v.*[1] –1800.

† **Coil,** *v.*[2] Also **coyle.** 1530. [Origin unkn.] To beat, thrash –1590.

Coil (koil), *v.*[3] 1611. [– OFr. *coillir* (mod. *cueillir* gather) = Pr. *colhir*, Sp. *coger*, Pg. *colher* (also) furl, coil (rope) :– L. *colligere* (see COLLECT).] **1.** To lay up (a cable, etc.) in concentric rings. Const. with *up*. **2.** To enwrap within coils 1616. **3.** To twist in or into a circular, spiral, or winding shape; to wind round. Also *refl.* 1664. **4.** *intr.* (for *refl.*) To throw oneself into a spiral or winding form; often with *round* 1798. **5.** To move in a spiral or winding course 1816.

3. Quoil'd in Dust like Snake or Adder 1711. **4.** Convolvuluses That coil'd around the stems TENNYSON.

Coil (koil), *sb.*[1] *arch.* or *dial.* 1567. [Of unkn. origin; now familiar mainly in *mortal c.* (from Shaks. 'Hamlet' III i. 67).] **1.** Noisy disturbance, row. **2.** Clutter, rattle 1582. **3.** Fuss, ado; a 'business' 1593.

3. *To keep a c.*: to make or keep up a disturbance. *Mortal c.*: the bustle of this mortal life SHAKS.

Coil (koil), *sb.*[2] 1627. [Goes with COIL *v.*[3], cf. *roll, twist, tie, fold.*] **1.** *orig.* (*Naut.*) A length of cable, rope, etc., when coiled; hence, the whole quantity coiled. **2.** A series of concentric rings in which a body has been disposed 1661. **3.** A single complete turn of any coiled body 1805. **4.** An arrangement of a wire, sheet metal, etc., in windings 1826. **5.** In gun-making: A bar of wrought iron coiled and welded into a tube 1859.

2. A Snake..lying round in a C. 1723. High-looped coils on the top of the head 1888. **4.** The induction-c...a primary c. of thick wire and few convolutions 1881. Coils of hot-water pipes 1869.

Coil (koil), *sb.*[3] *n.* and *midl.* 1800. [Goes with COIL *v.*[1]] A cock of hay.

Coillen, -on, obs. ff. CULLION.

Coin (koin), *sb.* ME. [– (O)Fr. *coin*, †*coing*, wedge, corner, †stamping-die :– L. *cuneus* wedge. See COIGN, QUOIN.] **1.** A corner-stone; also, a wedge-shaped stone of an arch. Now usu. QUOIN. † **2.** *gen.* A corner, angle –1658. † **3.** A wedge –1779. † **4.** A die (? wedge-shaped), for stamping money; the device stamped upon money –1682. **5.** A piece of metal of definite weight and value, stamped with an officially authorized device; a piece of money ME. **6.** (without *pl.*) Coined money; specie, money ME. Also *fig.*

1. *Cor.* V. iv. 1. **5.** A coyne that beares the figure of an Angell *Merch. V.* II. vii. 56. **6.** A faire tongue with a foule heart is false quoyne 1569. To pay a slanderer in his own c. 1713. *Comb.* **c.-balance,** a delicate balance for weighing gold coins.

Coin (koin), *v.*[1] ME. [– OFr. *coignier* mint, f. *coin*; see prec.] **1.** To make (money) by stamping metal. Also *transf.* and *fig.* **2.** To make (metal) into money by stamping pieces of definite weight and value with authorized marks ME. *intr.* (for *refl.*) 1700. Also *fig.* **3.** *fig.* (from 1.) To make, devise, produce; *esp.* in a bad sense 1561.

1. The kynge caused, in siluer, the halfe-peny to be coygned FABYAN. *To c. money* (mod. colloq.): to gain it rapidly and with ease. **2.** Tin was coined by Charles II, in 1684 CRUMP. **3.** Let them coyne his Nose 1 *Hen. IV*, III. iii. 90. To c. a smile GREENE, a lie 1780, a word DRYDEN. Hence **Coiʹnable** *a.* that may be coined (*lit.* and *fig.*). **Coiʹner,** one who coins (*esp.* false) money; *fig.* a fabricator.

Coin (koin), *v.*[2] 1488. [f. as prec. Now usually COIGN.] To furnish with quoins, wedges, or corner-stones.

Coinage (koi·nėdʒ). ME. [– OFr. *coigniage*, f. *coignier*; see COIN *v.*[1], -AGE.] **1.** The action or process of coining money. **2.** *concr.* Coins collectively; a system of coins in use; the currency 1467. **3.** *fig.* The formation or fabrication of something new or specious 1693. **4.** *concr.* That which is formed or fabricated. (Often disparaging.) 1602.

2. The bronze c. (*mod.*). **3.** The right of c. of Political Lyes SWIFT. Words of modern c. FREEMAN. **4.** This is the very coynage of your Braine SHAKS.

Coincide (kōu,insəid), *v.* 1715. [– med.L. *coincidere* (in astrol.), f. *com* CO- + *incidere* fall upon or into; cf. (O)Fr. *coïncider.* In XVII the L. inf. was used in Eng. contexts.] **1.** *intr.* To occupy the same portion of space (as *e.g.* the superposed triangles in Euclid I. 8); to be identical in position and area. **2.** To occur at the same time; to occupy the same space of time 1809. **3.** To be identical; to agree exactly *with* 1722. **4.** To concur (in opinion, etc.) 1734.

1. If the equator and ecliptick had coincided CHEYNE. **2.** The chief feast of the year..coincides with the Festival of the vintage STANLEY. **3.** His interest happily coincided with his duty FREEMAN. **4.** To c. in a doctrine LYELL. Hence **Co,inciʹder** (*rare*).

Coincidence (ko,i·nsidĕns). 1605. [– med.L. *coincidentia*, f. *coincidere*; see prec., -ENCE; cf. Fr. *coïncidence.*] **1.** The fact or condition of being coincident 1626. Also *fig.* and *transf.* (with *pl.*) A case of coincidence 1837. **2.** Occurrence or existence at the same time 1650. **3.** Exact correspondence in substance, nature, character, etc. 1605. (with *pl.*) An instance of this 1661. **4.** Concurrence (in opinion or sentiment) 1795. † **5.** Blending 1645.

1. The c. of planes CHEYNE, points 1870. **2.** There might be a casuall c. of this feast and his presence at Jerusalem FULLER. A 'strange c.' BYRON. **3.** Evidence arising from various coincidences BUTLER. So † **Co,iʹncidency,** c. quality or state.

Coincident (ko,i·nsidĕnt), *a.* 1563. [f. *coincident-*, pr. ppl. stem of med.L. *coincidere*; cf. prec., -ENT.] Occupying the same place 1656; exactly contemporaneous 1598; in exact agreement, wholly consonant *with* 1563. Also as † *sb.*

Duty and interest are perfectly c. BUTLER. Hence **Co,incideʹntal** *a.*; **-ly** *adv.* **Co,iʹncidently** *adv.*

† **Co,i·ndicate,** *v.* 1623. [f. Co- + INDICATE.] To indicate conjointly; *spec.* in *Med.* to furnish coindicant symptoms. So † **Co,i·ndicant** *a.* (*sb.*).

Co,indica·tion. 1623. [f. Co- + INDICATION.] Conjoint or concurrent indication; a concurrent sign.

Co-i·nfinite, *a.* 1654. [See Co-.] Equally infinite with another or others; conjointly infinite.

† **Co-inha·bit,** *v.* 1624. [See Co-.] *intr.* To dwell together. So **Co-inhabitant;** † **Co-inhabitor.**

Co-inhere (kōᵘ,inhiᵊ·ɹ), *v.* 1836. [See Co-.] *intr.* To inhere together. So **Co-inhe·rence.**

Co-inhe·ritor. 1526. [See Co-.] A joint heir. So **Co-inhe·ritance.**

† **Co,i·nquinate,** *v.* 1528. [f. *coinquinat-*, pa. ppl. stem of L. *coinquinare* pollute utterly; see Co-, INQUINATE *v.*] To soil all over, pollute, defile (*lit.* and *fig.*) –1652. So † **Co,inquina·tion.**

Coinstantaneous (ko,instăntēⁱ·niəs), *a.* 1768. [See Co-.] Occurring or existing at the same instant. var. † **Co,instanta·nean.**

Cointense (ko,inte·ns), *a.* 1855. [See Co-.] Conjoined or equal in intensity. Hence **Co-inte·nsion.**

Coir (koiᵊɹ). 1582. [– Malayalam *kāyar* cord, f. *kāyaru* be twisted.] The prepared fibre of the husk of the coco-nut, used for making ropes, cordage, matting, etc. Orig. the cordage made of this fibre. Also *attrib.*

Coistrel. ? *Obs.* 1577. [var. of CUSTREL, q.v.] **1.** A groom or servant in charge of the horses of a knight. **2.** A term of reproach or contempt: Knave, base fellow, low varlet 1581.

Coit, coite, obs. ff. QUOIT.

Coition (ko,i·ʃən). 1541. [– L. *coitio, -ōn-*, f. *coit-*, pa. ppl. stem of *coïre* go together, f. *com* Co- + *ire* go.] † **1.** Going or coming together; conjunction –1761. **2.** Sexual conjunction, copulation 1615. Also *transf.* and *fig.* vars. † **Co·it,** ‖ **Co·itus** (in sense 2).

† **Cojoin,** obs. var. of CONJOIN *v.*

Cojuror. 1735. [See Co-.] One who takes an oath along with, or in confirmation of, another.

Coke (kōᵘk), *sb.* 1669. [orig. north. (formerly often pl.); prob. identical with north. dial. COLK (XIV) core, of unkn. origin.] Mineral coal deprived by dry distillation of its volatile constituents.

Coke (kōᵘk), *v.* 1804. [f. prec. sb.] To convert into coke. Also *intr.* (for *refl.*).

Coker, obs. f. COCO.

† **Cokes.** 1567. [Of unkn. origin; see COAX.] A silly fellow, ninny, simpleton –1690.

Cokewold, Cokil(le, obs. ff. CUCKOLD, COCKLE.

‖ **Col** (kol). 1853. [Fr. :– L. *collum* neck.] A depression in the summit-line of a mountain chain, generally forming a pass.

Col-, form of the prefix COM- bef. *l.* See COM-.

Cola (kōᵘ·lă). 1795. [*Kola*, etc., in Negro langs. of W. Africa.] A genus of trees, N.O. *Sterculiaceæ*, natives of western tropical Africa; esp. *C. acuminata.*

Comb. **c.-nut, -seed,** the seed, brownish and bitter, of *C. acuminata*, largely used for chewing.

Cola, pl. of COLON² 1.

Co-la·bourer. 1859. [See Co-.] Fellow-labourer.

† **Co·lament.** [med.L. *colamentum* (XIII), f. L. *colare* strain, filter; see -MENT.] Product of straining. SIR T. BROWNE.

Colander, cullender (kʊ·lĕndəɹ). 1450. [perh. alt. of Pr. **colador* (whence mod.Pr. *couladou*) = Sp. *colador* :– Rom- **colator*, f. L. *colare* strain; cf. med.L. *colatorium*, Fr. *couloir, -oire.*] A vessel, usually of metal, closely perforated at the bottom with small holes, and used as a drainer in cookery. Also *transf.* and *fig.* **2.** A similar vessel used in the casting of shot 1875. Hence as *vb.*, to strain, to perforate with holes.

† **Co·laphize,** *v.* 1450. [– OFr. *colafisier, colaphiser* or eccl.L. *colaphizare* – (N.T.) Gr. κολαφίζειν buffet, cuff.] To buffet –1656.

Cola·tion. 1612. [– med.L. *colatio*, f. L. *colare*; see COLATURE, -ION.] The action of passing through a strainer. ? *Obs.*

Co-la·titude. 1790. [See Co-.] *Astron.* The complement of the latitude, *i.e.* the difference between it and 90 degrees.

Co·lature. ? *Obs.* 1548. [– (O)Fr. *colature* or late and med.L. *colatura*, f. *colat-*, pa. ppl. stem of L. *colare* filter, strain; see -URE.] **1.** Colation 1657. **2.** The product of straining 1601. **3.** A strainer (also *colatory*) 1548.

† **Colbertine.** Also **-een.** 1685. [f. *Colbert*, French proper name; see -INE⁴.] 'A kind of open lace with a square ground' –1851.

[She] Scarce knows what difference is between Rich Flanders lace and Colberteen SWIFT.

Colchicine (kǫ·lkisəin), also **Colchicia** (kǫlki·ʃia). 1853. [f. COLCHICUM + -INE⁵.] *Chem.* An organic alkaloid, $C_{17}H_{19}NO_5$, found in all parts of the *Colchicum autumnale.*

‖ **Colchicum** (kǫ·lkikǒm, *vulg.* kǫ·ltʃikǒm). 1597. [L. (Pliny) – Gr. κολχικόν, subst. use of n. of Κολχικός pertaining to Colchis. The name has reference to the poisonous arts of Medea.] **1.** *Bot.* A genus of liliaceous plants, the best-known species of which is *C. autumnale*, the Meadow-saffron. **2.** A medicine containing the active principle of this plant, used in gout and rheumatic affections 1791.

Colcothar (kǫ·lkoþaɹ). 1605. [– Arab. *ḳulḳuṭār.*] A brownish red peroxide of iron obtained from iron sulphate. Called also *rouge*, and *Crocus martis.*

Cold (kōᵘld), *a.* [OE. *cald* (WS. *ċeald*) = OFris., OS. *cald* (Du. *koud*), OHG. *kalt* (G. *kalt*), ON. *kaldr*, Goth. *kalds* :– Gmc. **kaldaz*, rel. to L. *gelu* frost.] **I.** *lit.* **1.** Of a temperature sensibly lower than that of the living human body. Comp. *colder, coldest.* **2.** Of a relatively low temperature; not heated ME. **3.** Feeling cold. (Usu. in predicate.) 1570. **4.** Of soil: Slow to absorb heat ME.

1. I'th c. wind *All's Well* I. i. 115. A thrust of c. iron SMOLLETT. I would Thy toung were coold J. HEYWOOD. **2.** *C. bath, bathing*: a bath in unheated water. C. chicken 1883. **3.** When I am c., he heates me with beating *Com. Err.* IV. iv. 33. **4.** Clay soils are c. 1877.

II. *fig.* † **1.** In ME. physiology applied (with *hot, dry, moist*) to the 'complexion' of things –1732; the opposite of pungent –1614. **2.** Void of warmth, or intensity of feeling; indifferent, apathetic ME.; † free from passion, cool 1794; cold-blooded 1849. **3.** Not cordial or friendly 1557. **4.** Gloomy, dispiriting ME. **5.** Felt as cold, chilling ME. **6.** Without power to move; stale 1705. **7.** *Hunting.* Of scent: Not strong, faint; weak 1592. **8.** *Painting.* Applied to blue and grey, and tints akin to these 1706.

2. The c. charities of man to man CRABBE. A c. forgery PALEY. C. chastity SHAKS. The too c. calculation of our powers RUSKIN. **3.** A c. welcome 1703. C. looks 1833. **4.** A c. misgiving and a killing dread COWPER. **5.** C. comfort J. H. NEWMAN. **6.** The jest grows c. . . when it comes on in a second scene ADDISON. **7.** At a c. sent *Twel. N.* II. v. 134.

Comb.: **c. abscess** [Fr. *abscès froid*], an abscess formed without the first three of the Celsian symptoms of inflammation (pain, redness, heat, and swelling); **c. bed** *Gardening*, opp. to HOT-BED; so *c. frame*; **c. blast,** air forced into a furnace unheated; **c. chisel,** a strong chisel of iron or steel highly tempered, so as to cut cold iron; **c. feet** *slang*, fear, funk; **c. war,** a state of hostility consisting in threats, obstruction, propaganda, etc., without physical violence; **c. without** (*colloq.*), spirits and cold water without sugar. Hence **Co·ldly** *adv.* **Co·ldness.**

Cold (kōᵘld), *sb.* [OE. *cald, ċeald* neut., the adj. used subst.] **1.** The opposite or the absence of heat; coldness. (Usually spoken of as a positive agent.) ME. **2.** The sensation produced by loss of heat from the body, or by exposure to a lower temperature ME. Also *fig.* **3.** An indisposition of the body caused by exposure to cold; *esp.* catarrh ME.

1. Heat and C. are Natures two hands, whereby she chiefly worketh BACON. 15 *degrees of c.* = 15 degrees below the freezing-point of water (32° Fahr.). Phr. *To be left out in the c.*, i.e. neglected. **3.** I haue taken colde. . .This wounde on your heed hath caught ouermoche colde MALORY.

† **Cold,** *v.* [OE. *caldian* (in *acaldian* ACOLD), *ċealdian*, f. *ċeald, cald* COLD *a.*] To make or become cold; also *fig.* –1598.

Cold blood. 1608. [See COLD *a.* II. 2.] In *in c. blood*: Without excitement; with cool deliberation.

A resolution framed in c. blood SIR F. VERE. Killing in c. blood ADDISON.

Cold-blooded, *a.* 1595. [f. prec. + -ED².] **1.** Having the blood (physically) cold, or not warmer than the external air or water: said *esp.* of fishes and reptiles 1602. **2.** Without excitement or sensibility, callous; deliberately cruel 1595.

2. Cold-blooded malice MACAULAY, crime 1882.

Cold-finch. 1676. *Ornith.* The Pied Flycatcher.

Co·ld-hea:rted, *a.* 1606. [f. *cold heart* + -ED².] Wanting in sensibility or natural affection; unkind. Hence **Cold-hea·rtedness.**

Co·ld-short, *a.* 1601. [Earlier *colsar, col(e)shire, coldshare, -shore, -shire* (XVII), later *coldshort* (XVIII) – Sw. *kallskör* (= Norw., Da. *koldskjør*), n. *kallskört* (sc. *jern* iron), f. *kallr* cold + *skör* (pron. ʃȫr) brittle. The development of the form in *-short* was assisted by the prevalence of *short* in the sense of 'brittle'. Cf. RED-SHORT.] Of iron: Brittle when cold.

Cold shoulder. 1816. Used *fig.*, chiefly in *to show the cold shoulder*, 'to appear cold and reserved'. Hence **Cold-shoulder** *v.* to treat with coldness or contemptuous neglect.

Cole¹ (kōᵘl). Now *rare.* [Late ME. *cōl, coole* – ON. *kál* (see KALE, KAIL), corresp. to OE. *cāwel, cāul*, MDu. *cōle* (Du. *kool*), OHG. *chōl(i), chōlo, -a* (G. *kohl*) – L. *caulis* (later *caulus, -a*) stem, stalk, cabbage.] **1.** A name for various species of *Brassica*; now *esp.* Rape (*B. napus*); also applied to Sea-kale. † **2.** Pottage; = KALE or *kail* –1674.

† **Cole**². ME. [Origin unkn.] **1.** ? Jugglery –1564. **2.** A sharper (at dice) 1532.

Cole³ (kōᵘl). *Cant.* 1673. [perh. slang use of *cole* = COAL.] Money.

To post the c.: to pay down the money.

Cole·ctomy. 1882. [f. Gr. κόλον colon + ἐκτομή excision.] *Surg.* Excision of part of the colon.

Cole-goose; see *coal-goose*, s.v. COAL.

Colemanite (kōᵘ·lmănəit). 1884. [f. W. T. *Coleman* + -ITE¹ 2 b.] *Min.* A hydrous borate of calcium, found in California.

Colemouse, var. of COALMOUSE.

Coleopter (kǫli,ǫ·ptəɹ). 1860. [f. next; cf. Fr. *coléoptère.*] One of the Coleoptera.

Coleoptera (kǫli,ǫ·ptĕră), *sb. pl.* In sing. **coleopteron** (*rare*); see also prec. 1763. [mod.L. n. pl. – Gr. κολεόπτερος sheath-winged, f. κολεόν sheath + πτερόν wing.] *Zool.* An order of insects having the anterior pair of wings converted into elytra or hard sheaths which cover the other pair when not in use; the Beetles. (See BEETLE *sb.*²) Formerly, the elytra of beetles. 1826. Hence **Coleopteral, Coleo·pterous** *adjs.* belonging or relating to the C. **Coleo·pteran** *sb.* one of the C. **Coleo·pterist,** one who studies the C. **Coleo·pteroid** *a.* like the C. var. **Coleo·ptra.**

‖ **Coleorhiza** (kǫ:liorəi·ză). 1866. [f. Gr. κολεόν sheath + ῥίζα root.] *Bot.* The root-sheath in the embryo of grasses, etc.

† **Cole-prophet.** Also, later, **cold(e prophet.** 1532. [app. f. COLE *sb.*² *Cold* is due to pop. etym.] A wizard, diviner, necromancer, fortune-teller –1614.

Colera, obs. f. CHOLERA (in sense *choler*).

Cole-rake, colrake. ME. [perh. orig. f. *col, cole* COAL (in its sense of *cinder*) + RAKE *sb.*¹] An instrument for raking ashes, etc., out of an oven or furnace.

Coleseed (kōᵘ·lsīd). 1670. [prob. – Du. *koolzaat*; see COLZA.] The seed of *Brassica campestris* or *napus*, var. *oleifera*; also the plant.

Cole-slaw (kōᵘ·l,slǭ). *U.S.* 1862. [– Du. *koolsla*, f. *kool* cabbage + *sla* salad; see SLAW.] Sliced cabbage dressed as a salad.

Co-lessee, co-lessor; see Co-.

Cole-staff, var. of COWL-STAFF.

† **Co·let.** ME. [Short f. ACOLYTE.] = ACOLYTE –1765.

Cole-tit, var. of COAL-TIT.

‖ **Coleus** (kōᵘ·liŏs). 1885. [mod.L., f. Gr. κολεός, var. of κολεόν, sheath, so called from the union of the filaments.] *Bot.* A genus of Labiate plants, allied to the Mints.

Colewort (kōᵘ·lwɒɹt). *arch.* ME. [See COLE *sb.*[1]] **1.** Orig., any plant of the cabbage kind, genus *Brassica*. **2.** Later, *esp.* kale, greens, etc., which do not heart, or cabbage-plants before they heart 1683.
Coleworts twice sodden: stale news.

† **Co·lfox, colefox.** ME. only. [f. *col* COAL + FOX = *coal-fox*, as in *cole-tit*, etc.] The BRANT-FOX, a variety with much black in its fur.

† **Colia·nder.** [ME. *coliaundre* – OFr. *coliandre* (mod. *coriandre*) – late L. *coliandrum*, dissim. form of L. *coriandrum*; see CORIANDER. OE. *cellendre* is direct – late L.] = CORIANDER, q.v. –1614.

‖ **Colibri** (kǫ·libri). 1740. [– Fr., Sp. *colibri*, of Carib origin.] A kind of humming-bird.

Colic (kǫ·lik). ME. [– (O)Fr. *colique* – late L. *colicus* (in med.L. as sb. fem. for *colica passio* colic), f. *colon*; see COLON[1], -IC.]
A. *sb.* A name for severe paroxysmal griping pains in the belly, due to affections of the bowel or other parts; also for the affections themselves.
The colike..ingendreth in a gutte named colon 1528. *Comb.* **c.-root,** a name for *Aletris farinosa*, *Dioscorea villosa*, and *Liatris squarrosa*.
B. *adj.* **1.** Of or pertaining to the colon, as in *c. arteries* 1615. **2.** Affecting the colon; of, or of the nature of, colic; in *c. passion* = COLIC A., *c. pains*, etc. 1586. Hence **Co·lical** *a.* of, pertaining to, or of the nature of, c.; subject to c. **Co·licky** *a.* colical; tending to produce c.

Colies (kōᵘ·liz), *sb. pl.* 1847. [f. mod.L. *colius* – Gr. κολιός a kind of woodpecker.] *Ornith.* The *Colidæ*, a family of African birds.

Colin (kǫ·lin). 1678. [erron. form of Mex. *çolin.*] The American quail; also called *bob-white*.

Coliseum, var. of COLOSSEUM.

‖ **Colitis** (koləi·tis). 1860. [mod.L., f. COLON + -ITIS.] *Med.* Inflammation of the colon.

Colk. Now *dial.* ME. [Of unkn. origin; see COKE *sb.*] The core of an apple, etc., of a horn, heart of wood, or the like.

† **Coll,** *v.*[1] ME. [Either aphet. f. *acole* ACCOLE or – OFr. *coler* = *accoler* put the arms round the neck; see ACCOLADE.] To embrace, hug.

Coll, *v.*[2] Now *Sc.* 1483. [perh. of Scand. origin; cf. Icel. *kollr* head, poll, shaven crown, *kolla* beast without horns, Norw. *kylla* poll, prune, cut.] To poll, cut off the hair of, clip, cut close.

Collaborate (kǒlæ·bŏreᶦt), *v.* 1871. [– *collaborat-*, pa. ppl. stem of late L. *collaborare*, f. *com* COL- + *laborare* LABOUR *v.*] To co-operate; *esp.* in literary, artistic, or scientific work. Hence **Colla:bora·tion. Colla·borator,** one who works in conjunction with another or others.

‖ **Collaborateur** (kolaboratör). 1801. [Fr.; see prec.] = *Collaborator.*

Collagen (kǫ·lădʒen). 1865. [– Fr. *collagène*, f. Gr. κόλλα glue + *-gène* = -GEN 'producing'.] *Biol.* That constituent of connective tissue which yields gelatin on boiling. Hence **Collage·nic, Colla·genous** *adjs.* of the nature of, or containing c.

Collapse (kǒlæ·ps), *sb.* 1808. [– medical L. *collapsus*; see next.] **1.** The action of collapsing (see COLLAPSE *v.*). Originally a term of physiology. 1833. **2.** *Med.* The sudden loss of vital properties and consequent general or local prostration under exhaustion or disease 1808. **3.** Failure, break-down (of an institution, enterprise, etc.) 1856.

Collapse (kǒlæ·ps), *v.* 1732. [Back-formation from pa. pple. *collapsed* (XVII), f. L. *collapsus*, pa. pple. of *collabi*, f. *com* COL- + *labi* fall; see LAPSE, -ED[1].] **1.** *intr.* To fall together, as the sides of a body, or the body itself, by external pressure or withdrawal of the contents; to break down, fall in; to shrink together suddenly, contract. **2.** *transf.* and *fig.* To break down, come to nothing, fail; to lose force suddenly 1801.
1. The sides of the canals c. ARBUTHNOT. The air suddenly collapsed to a fraction of its original dimensions TYNDALL. The extensive warehouse.. collapsed 1888. **2.** The present agitation would c. 1887. Hence **Colla·psed** *ppl. a.*; † *spec.* lapsed, fallen (used in 17th c. of 'perverts' to the Church of Rome). **Colla·psible, -able** *a.* capable of collapsing; made to fold together. † **Colla·psion,** the action of collapsing (*lit.* and *fig.*); a collapsed condition.

Collar (kǫ·lăɹ), *sb.* [ME. *coler* – AFr. *coler*, OFr. *colier* (mod. *collier*) :– L. *collare*, f. *collum* neck; see -AR[1].]
I. 1. Something worn or placed about the neck; now *esp.* the band of linen, muslin, lace, etc., worn as a finish to the upper part of the ordinary dress of men and women. **2.** *spec.* The ornamental chain which forms part of the insignia of orders of knighthood 1488. **3.** A leather-covered roll fitted round the neck of a draught animal, forming that part of the harness through which the power of drawing is directly exerted; in *breast collar*, applied to parts of the breast harness serving the same purpose ME.
1. The coler of his haubrek 1450. Collars of golde HULOET, of Pearl 1642. A grehownd colere 1475. Yeomen of the c. 1530. **2.** A c. of the garter 1577. *Collar of SS., S's*, or *Esses*: a chain consisting of a series of S's; originally a badge of the House of Lancaster. **3.** A tedious and stiff pull against the c. (*mod.*). Phr. † *To slip (the) c.*: to escape. *Out of* (or *in*) *c.*: out of (or in) regular employment.
II. Transf. and techn. **1.** An encompassing or restraining band or strap 1507. **2.** *Mech.* A ring, circle, flange, or perforated disc, surrounding a rod, shaft, pipe, etc., for restraining lateral motion; forming a steam-, or watertight joint, and the like; a short piece of pipe serving as a connection between two pipes, etc. 1703. **b.** *Coining.* A metal ring, which prevents the blank from spreading when stamped 1826. **3.** *Naut.* **a.** 'A rope formed into a wreath, with a dead-eye seized in the bight, to which the stay is confined at the lower part'. **b.** 'An eye in the end or bight of a shroud or stay to go over the masthead' (Smyth). 1626. **4.** *Mining.* The timbering round a shaft's mouth 1849. **5.** *Arch.* **a.** = COLLARINO 1727. **b.** Short for *collar-beam* 1856. **6.** *Zool.* A band of a distinct colour or texture round the neck of an animal 1664. In Molluscs: A thickened muscular and glandular border of the mantle 1847. **7.** *Bot.* **a.** 'The ring upon the stipe of an agaric'. **b.** 'The point of junction between the radicle and the plumule'. 1866. **8.** † **a.** The neck-piece (of brawn). **b.** A piece of meat, a fish, etc., tied up in a roll. 1610.
Comb: **c.-beam,** a horizontal beam connecting a pair of rafters, which prevents them from sagging; **-day,** a day on which Knights wear the c. of their Order, when taking part in any court ceremony; **-gall,** a wound produced (on a horse) by the rubbing of the c.; **-like** *a.*; **-proud** *a.* (*dial.*) restive when in harness; **-work,** work in which a horse strains hard against the c.; severe work.
Hence **Co·llarless** *a.* without a c.

Collar (kǫ·lăɹ), *v.* 1555. [f. prec. sb.] **1.** To put a collar on; to surround as with a collar 1601. **2.** To seize by the collar; loosely: To capture 1613. **3.** *slang.* To appropriate, master 1700. **4.** *Cookery.* To roll up (meat, etc.) and tie it with a string; also, to cut up and press into a roll 1670.

Co·llar-bone. 15.. *Anat.* The CLAVICLE.

Collard (kǫ·lăɹd). *dial.* and *U.S.* 1755. [Earlier *collart*, reduction of COLEWORT.] A variety of cabbage which does not heart; = COLEWORT 2.

Collared (kǫ·lăɹd), *ppl. a.* ME. [f. COLLAR *sb.* and *v.*] **1.** Wearing a collar (round the neck); in *Her.* 1681. **2.** Furnished or fitted with or as with a collar 1650. **3.** See COLLAR *v.* 4. 1681.
1. The c. knights E. B. BROWNING. **2.** A coat c. with velvet 1823. The c. turtle-dove 1865. **3.** *C. pork, head*, etc.

Collarette, -et (kǫlăre·t). 1690. [– Fr. *collerette* (also used), dim. of *collier* COLLAR.] A small collar; a collar of linen, lace, etc.

‖ **Collarino** (kǫlărī·no). 1688. [It., dim. of *collare* COLLAR.] *Arch.* **1.** The astragal of a column. **2.** The neck of a column 1715.

Collate (kǒlēᶦ·t), *v.* 1558. [– *collat-*, stem of the form used as pa. pple. of L. *conferre*; see CONFER, -ATE[3].] **1.** To put or bring together 1678. **2.** To compare 1612; *esp.* to compare critically (a copy of a text) *with* other copies or *with* the original, in order to correct and emend it 1658. **3.** *Printing* and *Bookbinding.* To examine the sheets of a printed book, so as to verify their number and order 1770. † **4.** To bestow *on, upon*; to give *to* –1717. **5.** *Eccl.* † To confer (a benefice) *on* –1670; to institute (a cleric) *to* a benefice (now said of an ordinary who has the benefice in his own gift) 1647. *absol.* To appoint to a benefice 1606.
2. I collated such copies as I could procure JOHNSON. **5.** *absol.* If the Bishop does not c. in half a year more, it [the Living] lapses to the Archbishop 1708. Hence **Colla·table** *a.* that may be collated. **Colla·ted** *ppl. a.* compared; conferred.

Collateral (kǒlæ·tĕrăl). ME. [– med.L. *collateralis*; see COL-, LATERAL.]
A. *adj.* **1.** Situated or running side by side, parallel 1450. Const. *to* 1833. **2.** *fig.* Attendant, concomitant ME.; † co-ordinate –1656; corresponding 1653. **3.** Lying aside from the main subject, action, issue, etc.; side-; subordinate, indirect ME. Const. *to* 1614. **4.** Descended from the same stock, but in a different line; pertaining to those so descended. Opp. to *lineal.* ME. Also *transf.* and *fig.* **5.** *Law.* (See quots.)
1. From his radiant seat he rose Of high c. glory MILT. *P.L.* x. 86. *C. circulation* (Phys.): 'circulation carried on through lateral or secondary channels after stoppage or obstruction in the main vessels' (*Syd. Soc. Lex.*). **2.** We mistake..a c. effect for a cause HUME. **4.** *C. ancestor*: a brother or sister of a lineal ancestor. **5.** *C. assurance*, assurance made over and above the principal deed; *c. security*, any property or right of action, given as additional to the obligation of a contract or the like; so *c. bond, surety. C. issue*, where a criminal convict pleads any matter allowed by law, in bar of execution, as pregnancy, etc.
B. *sb.* † **1.** A colleague, an assessor –1726. † **2.** An equal in rank –1660. **3.** An accompanying circumstance (*rare*) 1635. **4.** A collateral kinsman 1691. **5.** Anything given as collateral security 1887. Hence **Colla:tera·lity** (*rare*), c. quality or position. **Colla·terally** *adv.* in a c. manner or position (*lit.* and *fig.*).

Collation (kǒlēᶦ·ʃən), *sb.* ME. [– OFr. *collacion*, *-tion* – L. *collatio* contribution, collection, comparison, in med.L. conference, repast, f. *collat-*; see COLLATE *v.*, -ION.]
I. † **1.** A bringing together or collection, *esp.* of money; a contribution –1725. **b.** *Roman* and *Scotch Law.* The bringing together of the possessions of several persons, in order to an equal division of the whole; hotch-pot; L. *collatio bonorum* 1828. **2.** Comparison ME. **3.** *esp.* Textual or critical comparison of documents, manuscripts, or editions 1532; also, the recorded result of such comparison 1699. **4.** *Printing*, etc. The action of collating the sheets or quires of a book or MS. 1834.
1. '*C. of seals* (in ancient Deeds), when one Seal was set on the Back of another, upon the same Ribbon or Label' KERSEY.
II. † **1.** A (private or informal) conference –1666; a discourse; a treatise –1655. **2.** The title of Cassian's *Collationes Patrum* ME. **3.** The reading from the *Collationes* instituted by St. Benedict in his monasteries before compline ME. **4.** The light repast taken after this reading. **5.** Hence, A light repast (often 'a cold collation') 1525.
5. Come to the Hope about one and there..had a collacion of anchovies, gammon, etc. PEPYS.
III. † **1.** Conferring or bestowal –1775. **2.** *Eccles.* **a.** The bestowal *of* a benefice upon a clergyman. **b.** (more usually) The appointment of a clergyman to a benefice; now *techn.* Institution by the ordinary to a living which is in his own gift. ME. **c.** Right of institution 1480.
1. The indiscriminate c. of degrees JOHNSON.
Hence † **Colla·tion** *v.* to COLLATE; to partake of, or entertain with, a c. † **Colla·tioner,** a collator; one who partakes of a c.

Collatitious (kǫlĕti·ʃəs), *a.* 1656. [f. L. *collaticius* raised by contribution (*collatio*) + -OUS. See -ITIOUS[1].] Characterized by collation; done by way of general contribution –1670.

Collative (kǒlēᶦ·tiv), *a.* 1617. [In sense 1 – L. *collativus*, f. *collat-* (see COLLATE, -IVE). Senses 2–3 f. COLLATE *v.* 4–5 + -IVE, perh. through Fr. *collatif.*] † **1.** = COLLATITIOUS

–1813. **2.** That confers or can confer. Const. *of.* 1644. **3.** *Eccl.* Where the ordinary (being himself the patron) collates 1725.

Collator (kǫlēⁱ·təɹ). ME. [– L. *collator*, f. as prec.; see -OR 2. In senses 2–3 = med.L. *collator*, Fr. *collateur*.] † **1.** One who collects (*rare*) –1430. **2.** One who collates texts, documents, the sheets of a book, etc. 1601. **3.** One who bestows 1627. **4.** *Eccl.* One who collates to a benefice 1612.

† **Collaud** (kǫlǭ·d), *v.* 1512. [– L. *collaudare* praise highly, f. *com* COL- + *laudare* praise. Cf. OFr. *collauder*.] To praise highly, extol –1670. Hence **Collauda·tion** (*arch.*).

Colleague (kǫ·līg), *sb.* 1533. [– Fr. *collègue* – L. *collega* partner in office, f. *com* COL- + *lēg-* of *lex* law, *lēgare* depute.] One who is associated with another (or others) in office, or special employment. (Not applied to partners in trade or manufacture.) Also *fig.*

fig. Mercie collegue with Justice MILT. *P.L.* x. 59. Hence **Co·lleagueship,** position or relation of a c.

Colleague (kǫlī·g), *v.* 1534. [– OFr. *colliguer* later *colléguer* – L. *colligare* bind together, f. *com* COL- + *ligare* bind. Sp. after LEAGUE (as in Fr. *léguer*). Not rel. etymologically to prec.] *intr.* and † *trans.* To join in alliance; also (*intr.*), to conspire, cabal. Hence † **Collea·guer,** one who colleagues (*rare*).

Collect (kǫ·lekt), *sb.* ME. [– (O)Fr. *collecte* – L. *collecta* gathering, collection, (late) assembly, meeting, subst. use of fem. pa. pple. of *colligere*; see COLLECT *v.*] † **1.** Collection –1681. † **2.** Assembly, *esp.* for worship –1728. **3.** *Liturg.* A short prayer usu. concerned with one topic; *spec.* the prayer appointed to be used for a particular day (*c. of the day*) or season at the choir-offices and at the Eucharist (before the Epistle).

3. I learnt the collects and the catechism E. B. BROWNING.

Colle·ct, *ppl. a.* ME. [– L. *collectus*, pa. pple. of *colligere*; see next.] = COLLECTED as *pa. pple.* (obs.) or *adj.* (arch.).

Collect (kǫ̆le·kt), *v.* 1573. [– (O)Fr. *collecter* or med.L. *collectare*, f. *collect-*, pa. ppl. stem of L. *colligere*, f. *com* COL- + *legere* collect, assemble, choose, read.] **1.** To gather together into one place or group; to gather in (money, debts, etc.) 1643; to make a collection of (specimens, curiosities, etc.) 1749. **2.** *intr.* (for *refl.*) To assemble, accumulate 1794. **3.** *trans.* To regain control over (one's thoughts, feelings, or energies); to summon up (courage, etc.) 1602. **4.** To form a conclusion, draw an inference. Now usually *gather*. 1581.

1. To c. materials for a work RUSKIN. In Collecting of Customs PETTY. To c. Editions DIBDIN. **2.** A force was collecting at Bridport MACAULAY. **3.** Affrighted much, I did in time c. my selfe *Wint. T.* III. iii. 8. **4.** What the Judges collected to be the intention of the testator CRUISE. Hence **Colle·ctable** *a.* that may be collected.

‖ **Collectanea** (kǫlektēⁱ·niă), *sb. pl.* 1791. [L. n.pl. of adj. *collectaneus* as used in *dicta collectanea* of Cæsar, and *sb.* in *collectanea* of Solinus (III); see prec.] Passages, remarks, etc., collected from various sources; (as *collect. sing.*) a miscellany.

Collected (kǫ̆le·ktėd), *ppl. a.* 1610. [f. COLLECT *v.* + -ED¹.] **1.** *lit.* Gathered together 1670. **2.** *fig.* Composed, self-possessed. Opp. to *distracted*. 1610. Hence **Colle·cted-ly** *adv.*, **-ness**.

Collection (kǫ̆le·kʃən). ME. [– (O)Fr. *collection* – L. *collectio*; see COLLECT *v.*, -ION.] **1.** The action of collecting or gathering together. **2.** *spec.* The action of collecting money for a religious or charitable purpose, or to defray expenses; also *concr.* the money so collected 1535. **b.** The gathering in of money due, as taxes, etc. 1659. **3.** *concr.* A group of things collected or gathered together; *e.g.* of literary materials 1460; of specimens, works of art, etc. 1651; of waters 1697. † **4.** An abstract, summary –1703. † **5.** The action of inferring; an inference –1705. **6.** A collectorate 1786. **7.** *pl.* A college examination held at the end of each term in Oxford, Durham, and elsewhere 1799.

1. C. of himself B. JONS. Collections and Deliveries *P.O. Notice*. **2.** Collections for the poore STUBBES. **3.** A c. of proverbs TRENCH, of plants EVELYN, of floating vapours HERVEY.

Collective (kǫ̆le·ktiv), *a.* 1520. [– (O)Fr. *collectif, -ive* or L. *collectivus*; see COLLECT *v.*, -IVE.] **1.** Formed by collection; constituting a collection; aggregate, collected. (Opp. to *individual*, and to *distributive*: so in sense 2.) 1600. **2.** Of, pertaining to, or derived from, a number of individuals taken or acting together 1650. **3.** Denoting (in the singular) a collection of individuals; as a *collective noun, idea, notion,* etc. † **4.** That deduces or infers; inferential –1646. † **5.** Having the attribute of collecting (*rare*) 1742. As *sb.* (*ellipt.*) A collective noun, body, or whole.

1. A c. edition of his works 1819. *C. fruit* (*Bot.*): fruit formed by the aggregation of several flowers, as the mulberry, etc. **2.** *C. note*: in diplomacy, an official note signed by the representatives of several governments. **3.** C. ideas of substances, as a Troop, Army 1727. **4.** Controulable..by criticall and c. reason SIR T. BROWNE. Hence **Colle·ctively** *adv.* in a c. manner or capacity; in a body, in the aggregate. **Colle·ctiveness,** c. quality (*rare*).

Collectivism (kǫle·ktiviz'm). 1880. [f. prec. + -ISM, after Fr. *collectivisme*.] The theory that land and the means of production should be owned by the community for the benefit of the people as a whole. So **Colle·ctivist,** one who adheres to c.; also *attrib.*

Collectivity (kǫlekti·vīti). 1862. [f. as prec. + -ITY; in senses 2 and 3, after Fr. *collectivité*.] **1.** Collective state or quality; *concr.* the aggregate. **2.** Collective ownership 1872. **3.** The State 1881.

Collector (kǫ̆le·ktəɹ). [– AFr. *collectour* – med.L. *collector*; see COLLECT *v.*, -OR 2.] **1.** One who or that which collects or gathers together; *spec.* one who collects specimens, works of art, curiosities, etc.; also, a compiler (now *rare*) 1582. **2.** One who collects money; an officer who receives money due, as taxes, customs, etc. ME. **3.** In India, the chief administrative official of a district, whose special duty is the collection of revenue 1772.

1. Conductors or electric collectors of copper and lead FARADAY. A c. of butterflies GOLDSM., proverbs D'ISRAELI. **2.** A c. of poor rates 1885. **3.** Such a magnificent person was the C. of Boggleywallah THACKERAY. Hence **Colle·ctorate** (*Anglo-Ind.*), the district under the jurisdiction of a c. **Colle·ctorship,** the office of a c.; in India = *collectorate*; the practice of a c. of curiosities. **Colle·ctress** (*rare*).

‖ **Colleen** (kǫlī·n kǫ·līn). *Anglo-Ir.* 1828. [– Ir. *cailin*, dim. of *caile* countrywoman, girl.] A girl.

Collegatary (kǫ̆le·gătări). 1590. [– L. *collegatarius*, f. *com* COL- + *legatarius* LEGATARY.] A co-legatee.

College (kǫ·lėdʒ), *sb.* ME. [– (O)Fr. *collège* or its source L. *collegium* association, partnership, guild, corporation, f. *collega* COLLEAGUE *sb.*] **1.** An organized society of persons possessing certain common functions possessing special rights and privileges. **2.** *loosely.* Company, collective body, assemblage ME.; *occas.* repr. G. *collegium* 'reunion, club' 1703. **3.** A community of clergy living together on a foundation for religious service, etc. Now chiefly *Hist.* ME. **4.** A society of scholars incorporated within, or in connection with, a University, or otherwise formed for purposes of study and instruction ME. **5.** The building or set of buildings occupied by such society ME. Also *transf.* **6.** A course of lectures at a foreign university; a distinct course of study leading to a degree (*U.S.*) 1700. **7.** A charitable foundation of the collegiate type, as *Chelsea College* 1694. **8.** *slang.* A prison. (*fig.* from 7.) 1690. Also *attrib.* (chiefly in sense 4).

1. *Apostolic c.*: the body of Christ's Apostles (or their descendants). *Sacred c.*: the 70 cardinals. I would the Colledge of the Cardinalls Would chuse him Pope 2 *Hen. VI*, I. iii. 64. The Colledge of physitians BROME. *C. of Justice*: in Scotland, the supreme civil courts. **2.** Thick as the c. of the bees in May DRYDEN. **3.** A Colledge of a hundred priests MORE. **4.** New C.; Winchester C.; Gresham C.; Harvard C.; Owens C.; Royal Naval C.; Cheltenham C. **5.** The quere of Wynchestre C. at Oxenford 1448. *Comb.* **c.-living,** a benefice in the gift of a c.

Colleger (kǫ·lėdʒəɹ). 1560. [f. prec. + -ER¹.] † A member of the same college; *spec.* one of the 70 boys on the foundation of Eton College.

Collegial (kǫ̆lī·dʒiăl), *a.* 1530. [– (O)Fr. *collégial* or late L. *collegialis*; see COLLEGE, -IAL.] **1.** Of the nature of, or constituted as, a college. **2.** Of or belonging to a COLLEGE (senses 1, 4) 1603.

1. *C. church*: = collegiate church. Hence **Colle·gialism,** the theory that the (or a) church is a voluntary association (*collegium*), and stands in no other relation to the civil magistrate than any other voluntary association. **Colle:gia·lity,** colleagueship. **Colle·gially** *adv.* in a c. manner or capacity.

Collegian (kǫ̆lī·dʒⁱăn). 1462. [– med.L. *collegianus*; see prec., -IAL.] A member or inmate of a college; also *spec.* a 'colleger' 1462; (*slang*) an inmate of a prison 1837. As *adj.* = COLLEGIAL. So **Colle·gianer.** *Obs.* exc. *Sc.*

Collegiate (kǫ̆lī·dʒiĕt). 1514. [– late L. *collegiatus* member of a college (in med.L. as adj.), f. *collegium* COLLEGE; see -ATE-¹, ².]

A. *adj.* **1.** Of the nature of, or constituted as, a college 1581. **2.** Of or belonging to a college 1564. **3.** Corporate; combined 1625.

1. *C. church*: (*a*) one which is endowed for a chapter, but has no bishop's see; (*b*) in Scotland, one served by joint pastors; (*c*) in U.S. 'one united with others under the joint pastorate of several ministers'. **2.** A c. life did not suit me DE FOE. **3.** Mutuall Ayds and C. endeavours 1665.

B. *sb.* † **1.** = COLLEGIAN –1818. † **2.** *slang.* An inmate of an asylum, prison, or the like –1734. † **3.** A colleague –1696.

Hence **Colle·giate** *v.* to constitute as a college or c. church. **Colle·giately** *adv.* in a c. manner.

Collenchyma (kǫle·ŋkimă). 1835. [f. Gr. κόλλα glue + ἔγχυμα infusion.] *Bot.* † **1.** The cellular substance in which pollen is generated –1866. **2.** Tissue of cells with walls thickened at the angles, as in the leaf-stalks and young stems of many Dicotyledons 1857. Hence **Collenchy·matous** *a.* belonging to or of the nature of c.

Collery (kǫ·ləri). *Anglo-Ind.* 1763. [– Tamil *kallar* thieves.] The name of a Dravidian people inhabiting part of India east of Madura; hence **C.-horn** (corrupted into *cholera-horn*); **C.-stick,** a boomerang used by the Colleries.

Collet (kǫ·lėt), *sb.*¹ 1528. [– (O)Fr. *collet*, dim. of *col*:– L. *collum* neck. See -ET.] † **1.** The neckband of a garment; a necklet –1644. **2.** An encompassing ring or band; as, a ring, collar, or flange on a rod or spindle, a circular metal lining to a hole, a ferrule or socket, etc. Also *attrib.* 1530. **3.** *Jewelry.* The circle or flange in a ring in which the stone is set 1528. Also *fig.* Hence **Co·llet** *v.* to set in, or provide with, a c.

Collet (kǫ·lėt), *sb.*² 1675. [Earlier f. CULET², q.v.; cf. prec., sense 3.] The horizontal base of a diamond when cut as a brilliant.

‖ **Colleter** (kǫ̆lī·təɹ). 1875. [– Gr. *κολλητήρ, f. κολλᾶν to glue.] *Bot.* One of the glandular hairs found on leaf-buds, etc., which secrete the blastocolla or bud-glue.

‖ **Colleterium** (kǫlitīᵊ·riǒm). 1864. [See prec.] *Zool.* An organ in certain insects, secreting a substance for cementing the ova together. Hence **Collete·rial** *a.* of the nature of, or pertaining to, a c.

Colletic (kǫle·tik). ? *Obs.* 1715. [– late L. *colleticus* or its source Gr. κολλητικός, f. κολλᾶν to glue; see -IC.] *adj.* Agglutinant. *sb.* An agglutinant.

Colley; see COLLIE.

Collide (kǫ̆ləi·d), *v.* 1621. [– L. *collidere* clash together, f. *com* COL- + *lædere* hurt by striking.] **1.** To bring into collision, strike or dash together. Now *rare* or *Obs.* **2.** *intr.* To come into collision, strike or dash together; *fig.* to clash, conflict 1700.

2. The flints..thus toss'd in air, c. DRYDEN. The attraction urges them [atoms]. They c., they recoil TYNDALL. *fig.* Colliding passions 1865.

Collidine (kǫ·lidəin). 1855. [f. Gr. κόλλα glue + εἶδος form + -INE⁵.] *Chem.* An alkaloid, $C_8H_{11}N$, found among the products of the dry distillation of animal substances and of coal. It is a colourless, oily, aromatic liquid.

Collie, Colly (kǫ·li), *sb.* 1651. [perh. f. *coll* COAL (from its black colour) + -IE, -Y⁶; cf. COLLY *a.*] A Scotch sheep-dog with long hair, pointed nose, and bushy tail. Often *c. dog.*

Collier (kǫ·liəɹ). [ME. *colyer*, f. *col* COAL; see -IER.] † **1.** A maker of wood charcoal –1608. † **2.** One who carries coal (orig. charcoal) for sale –1719. **3.** A coal-miner 1594. **4.** *transf.* A ship engaged in the carriage of coal. Also *attrib.* 1625. **b.** One of its crew 1727.

Colliery (kǫ·liəri). 1635. [f. prec. + -Y³.] **1.** A place where coal is worked; a coal-mine. † **2.** The coal trade 1673. † **3.** The ships, or a ship, employed in the coal trade –1763. Also *attrib.*

Collieshangie (kǫli,ʃæ·ŋi). *Sc.* 1745. [Origin unkn.] Noisy quarrel; confused fight.

Colliflower, obs. f. CAULIFLOWER.

† **Colligance.** 1541. [– OFr. *colligance* or med.L. *colligantia*; see COLLEAGUE *v.*, -ANCE.] Attachment together, connection –1708. † **Colligate** *a.* bound together, attached (*lit.* and *fig.*).

Colligate (kǫ·ligeᶦt), *v.* 1545. [– *colligat-*, pa. ppl. stem of L. *colligare*, f. *com* COL- + *ligare* bind; see -ATE³.] † **1.** To bind together, connect –1773. Also *fig.* **2.** *Logic.* To connect together (isolated facts) by a general notion or hypothesis 1856.

1. Conbyndyng, colligatyng, or knittyng together the muskles 1545. **2.** The phenomena which we are attempting to c. MILL.

Colligation (kǫligēᶦ·ʃən). 1502. [– OFr. *colligation* or L. *colligatio*, f. as prec.; see -ION.] **1.** † Material binding together –1646; *fig.* conjunction 1651. **2.** *Logic.* The binding together of a number of isolated facts by a general notion or hypothesis 1837.

2. The C. of Facts WHEWELL. The c. of social phenomena MAINE.

Colligible (kǫ·lidʒib'l), *a.* ?*Obs.* 1650. [f. stem of L. *colligere* (see COLLECT *v.*) + -IBLE.] That may be collected.

Collimate (kǫ·limeᶦt), *v.* 1623. [f. *collimare* (used by astronomical writers, e.g. Kepler), erron. reading in some editions of Cicero for *collineare* aim; see COLLINEATE *v.*] *trans.* To adjust the line of sight of (a telescope); to place (two lenses, etc.) so that their optical axes are in the same line. Also, to make parallel, as a lens, the rays of light passing through it.

Collimation (kǫlimēᶦ·ʃən). 1686. [f. as prec.; see -ION.] The adjustment of the line of sight of a telescope, etc. Also *attrib.*

Line of c.: the line of sight or optical axis. *Error of c.*: the amount by which the line of sight deviates from its position of accurate adjustment.

Collimator (kǫ·limēᶦtəɹ). 1825. [f. as prec.; see -OR 2.] **1.** A small fixed telescope with cross-wires at its focus, used for adjusting the line of collimation of another instrument. **2.** The tube with a slit and lens (or the lens itself) used in the spectroscope to collect the light and throw it upon the prism in parallel rays 1865.

Collin (kǫ·lin). 1882. [f. Gr. κόλλα glue + -IN¹.] Gelatin of absolute purity. Hence **Colli·nic** *a.* (*Chem.*), as in *C. acid*, $C_8H_4O_2$, an aromatic acid, obtained from gelatin, etc.

† **Colline,** *sb.* 1630. [– Fr. *colline* hill.] A small hill –1697.

A..wooded, and watered park, full of fine collines and ponds EVELYN.

Collinear (kǫ̆li·niăɹ), *a.* 1863. [f. COL- + LINEAR.] *Geom.* Lying in the same straight line. Hence **Colli:nea·rity,** the quality or fact of being c. **Colli·nearly** *adv.* in the same line.

Collineate (kǫ̆li·nieᶦt), *v.* 1631. [– *collineat-*, pa. ppl. stem of L. *collineare* aim, f. *com* COL- + *lineare* make straight, f. *linea* LINE *sb.*²; see -ATE³.] † **1.** *intr.* To meet together or converge, as lines, to a point; also *fig.* –1651. **2.** = COLLIMATE, q.v. Hence **Collinea·tion,** the act of aiming anything in a straight line towards an object; also, = COLLIMATION.

Collingual (kǫ̆li·ŋgwăl), *a. rare.* 1847. [f. COL- + LINGUAL.] Agreeing together in language.

† **Colli·quable,** *a. rare.* 1666. [f. stem of med.L. *colliquare* COLLIQUATE + -ABLE. Cf. LIQUABLE (XV).] Capable of being liquefied or dissolved –1677.

† **Colli·quament.** *rare.* 1656. [f. as prec. + -MENT. Cf. late L. *liquamentum*.] Something melted or of a liquid consistence; hence, applied by Harvey to the earliest embryo –1657.

† **Co·lliquate,** *v.* 1603. [– *colliquat-*, pa. ppl. stem of med.L. *colliquare*, f. COL- intensive + L. *liquare* make liquid, melt; see -ATE³. Cf. LIQUATE (XVII).] **1.** *trans.* To fuse together –1680. **2.** To reduce to a liquid consistence –1684. **3.** *intr.* To melt 1646.

1. When Ashes and Sand are Colliquated into Glass BOYLE. **3.** Ice..will c. in water SIR T. BROWNE.

† **Colliquation** (kǫlikwēᶦ·ʃən). 1601. [– med. and mod.L. *colliquatio*, f. as prec.; see -ION. Cf. LIQUATION (XV), and obs. Fr. *colliquation*.] **1.** The action or process of melting together –1681. **2.** Melting, fusion. Also *fig.* –1744. **3.** *spec.* in *Old Phys.* and *Path.* **a.** The melting down of solid parts, as in an abscess; the excessive fluidification of the humours, *esp.* the blood –1710. **b.** The wasting away of the solid parts of the body; consumption –1756.

1. When Sand and Ashes are well melted together ..there is generated by the c. that sort of Concretion we call Glasse BOYLE.

Colliquative (kǫ̆li·kwătiv), *a.* 1666. [f. as prec.; see -IVE. Cf. obs. Fr. *colliquatif*.] *Med.* Having the power or effect of liquefying; as, *c. diarrhœa.*

† **Colli:quefa·ction.** *rare.* 1612. [f. as prec.; see -FACTION, LIQUEFACTION.] Melting together –1626.

Incorporation of metals by simple c. BACON

Collision (kǫ̆li·ʒən). ME. [– late L. *collisio*, f. *collis-*, pa. ppl. stem of *collidere*; see COLLIDE, -ION.] **1.** The action of colliding; violent encounter of a moving body with another; now *esp.* of railway trains or ships. **2.** *fig.* Clashing, hostile encounter 1662; coming into contact (without opposition) 1664. Also *attrib.*

1. C. of carriages on the..railway 1835. The c. of harsh consonants GRAY. **2.** The c. of contrary false principles WARBURTON. Constant c. with good company CHESTERF. *Lett.* So **Collisive** (kǫ̆ləi·siv) *a.* pertaining or tending to c. (*rare*).

Collocal (kǫ̆lōᵘ·kăl), *a. rare.* 1813. [See COL-.] Of, belonging to, or occupying the same place with another.

† **Co·llocate,** *ppl. a.* 1529. [– L. *collocatus*, pa. ppl. of *collocare*; see next, -ATE².] Set, placed; *fig.* laid out –1626.

Collocate (kǫ·lŏkeᶦt), *v.* 1513. [– *collocat-*, pa. ppl. stem of *collocare*, f. *com* COL- + *locare* place, LOCATE; see -ATE³.] To arrange; to set in a place or position.

To marshall and c. in order his battailes MORE. Original Sin (somewhat oddly collocated in the list) G. S. FABER. Hence **Co·llocative** *a.* of the nature of, or relating to, collocation.

Collocation (kǫlokēᶦ·ʃən). 1605. [– L. *collocatio*, f. as prec.; see -ION.] The action of setting in a place or position; disposition or arrangement with, or in relation to, others; the state of being so placed.

All languages use greater freedom of c. in poetry than in prose EARLE. Hence **Colloca·tional** *a.* of or belonging to c. (*rare*).

Collocution (kǫlokiū·ʃən). *rare.* 1460. [– L. *collocutio*, f. *collocut-*, pa. ppl. stem of *colloqui*; cf. LOCUTION.] Talking together, colloquy. So **Collocutor** (kǫ·lŏkiūtəɹ, kǫ̆lǫ·kiutəɹ), one who takes part in a dialogue or conversation. **Collo·cutory** *a.* of the nature of dialogue (*rare*).

Collodio- (kǫ̆lōᵘ·dio), comb. f. COLLODION, as in **c.-type,** a photograph obtained by the collodion process; also, the process itself.

Collodion (kǫ̆lōᵘ·diən). Also **collodium.** 1851. [f. Gr. κολλώδης glue-like, f. κόλλα glue, with Gr. termination.] A solution of guncotton in ether, forming a colourless gummy liquid, which dries rapidly; used in photography for covering plates with a thin film, and in surgery for coating wounds, burns, etc. Also *attrib.*, as *c. process* (in photography), etc. Hence **Collo·dionize** *v.* to treat with c.

Collogue (kǫ̆lōᵘ·g), *v.* 1602. [prob. alt., by assoc. w. L. *colloqui* converse, of COLLEAGUE *v.*] † **1.** *intr.* To gloze; to deal flatteringly or deceitfully *with* –1719. † **2.** *intr.* To feign agreement or belief –1649. † **3.** *trans.* To influence by blandishment –1755. **4.** *intr.* To have a private understanding *with*; to intrigue, conspire. Now *dial.* 1646. **5.** To confabulate (*colloq.* or *joc.*) 1811.

4. To bring this to effect, it was necessary for him to c. with England EARL MONM. **5.** They wagged their old heads sadly when they collogued in clubs THACKERAY. Hence **Collo·guer,** a glozer, intriguer.

Co·lloid. 1847. [f. Gr. κόλλα glue + -OID.]

A. *adj.* **1.** Of the nature or appearance of glue. **2.** *Chem.* Applied to a state of aggregation in which substances exist; opp. to *crystalloid*. So called because gelatin may be taken as the type of the class. 1861. **3.** *Min.* One of the forms in which minerals occur; distinguished from *crystalline, vitreous,* and *amorphous* 1879.

1. *C. degeneration*: transformation of tissue into a homogeneous or slightly granular glue-like substance, as in *c. cancer.*

B. *sb.* **1.** *Path.* The jelly-like substance formed in colloid degeneration 1849. **2.** *Chem.* A substance in which the particles vary from molecular size to that of coarse suspensions (see A. 2) 1861.

So **Colloi·dal** *a.* in the same senses; see -AL¹. Hence **Colloida·lity.**

Collop¹ (kǫ·ləp). [ME. *coloppe, colhoppe* – Scand. word repr. by OSw. *kolhuppadher* roasted on coals (f. *kol* COAL + *huppa* leap; cf. SAUTÉ), Sw. *kalops*, dial. *kollops* dish of stewed meat.] **1.** † An egg fried on bacon –1530; later, called *collops and eggs* by itself 1542. **2.** A slice of meat ME.; *locally*, meat cut into small pieces 1648. † **3.** *transf.* A piece of flesh –1666. **4.** A thick fold of fat on the body. Now *Sc.* and *dial.* 1560. **5.** *fig.* A slice; a cantle 1580.

2. *Scotch collops*: now, a steak with onions. **3.** To say this Boy were like me..Most dear'st, my C. *Wint. T.* I. ii. 137. Hence **Co·lloped** *ppl. a.* having thick folds of fat.

‖ **Collop**². *Anglo-Ir.* 1672. = Ir. *colpa*, 'A full-grown cow or horse'. Hence, a cow's grass for a year, or its equivalent.

Colloque, *sb. Obs.* (exc. as Fr.) 1482. [– Fr. *colloque* – L. *colloquium*; see COLLOQUY.] † **1.** A place for conversation (in a monastery). † **2.** A conference –1677. ‖ **3.** = COLLOQUY 3. 1846. So **Collo·que** *v.* to hold colloquy.

Colloquial (kǫ̆lōᵘ·kwi,ăl), *a.* 1751. [f. L. *colloquium* COLLOQUY + -AL¹.] **1.** Of or pertaining to colloquy; conversational. **2.** *spec.* Of words, phrases, etc.: Belonging to common speech or ordinary conversation. (The usual sense.) 1752.

1. His..c. judgments DE QUINCEY. **2.** To clear it [our language] from c. barbarisms JOHNSON. The c. language of real life J. R. GREEN. Hence **Collo·quialism,** c. quality or style; a c. expression. **Collo·quialist,** a (good) talker; one who uses colloquialisms. **Collo:quia·lity,** = *Colloquialism.* **Collo·quially** *adv.*

Colloquist (kǫ·lŏkwist). 1792. [f. as prec. + -IST.] One who takes part in a conversation; an interlocutor.

‖ **Colloquium** (kǫ̆lōᵘ·kwi,ǒm). 1609. [L.] † **1.** A colloquy –1765. **2.** An assembly for discussion; a conference, council. (Not in ordinary Eng. use.) 1844.

Colloquize (kǫ·lŏkwəiz), *v.* 1823. [f. prec. + -IZE.] *intr.* To engage in colloquy.

Colloquy (kǫ·lŏkwi), *sb.* 1581. [– L. *colloquium*, f. *com* COL- + *loqui* speak.] **1.** A talking together; a dialogue; converse. † **2.** A meeting for conference –1679. **3.** *Eccl.* = CLASSIS 3, PRESBYTERY 4. 1672.

1. Frantick men that boasted of..colloquies with God 1660. Shunning..All further c. BYRON. Hence **Co·lloquy** *v.* to hold c.

Collotype (kǫ·lŏtəip). 1883. [f. Gr. κόλλα glue + -TYPE.] A thin sheet of gelatin, the sensitized surface of which has been etched by the action of the actinic rays, so that it can be printed from; also the print, and the process. Hence *c. plate, process, printing,* etc.

Collow (kǫ·lōᵘ, -ǒ), *v.* Now *dial.* [ME. *colwen*, perh. :– OE. **colgian*, f. **coliġ* coaly, f. *col* COAL. See also COLLY *v.*¹ and *a.*] To blacken, smut, begrime. ? Hence **Co·llow** *sb.* (now *dial.*), soot; smut; coal-dust.

Colluctation (kǫlɒktēⁱ·ʃən). *arch.* 1611. [– L. *colluctatio*, f. *colluctat-*, pa. ppl. stem of *colluctari* struggle together, f. *com* COL- + *luctari* wrestle, strive. Cf. OFr. *colluctacion.*] A wrestling or struggling together; conflict, opposition.

Colluctations between the flesh and the Spirit DONNE. vars. † **Collu·ctance** (*rare*), † **Collu·ctancy** (*rare*).

Collude (kǫlⁱū·d), *v.* 1525. [– L. *colludere* have a secret agreement, f. *com* COL- + *ludere* play.] **1.** *intr.* To act in secret concert *with*; to play into one another's hands; to conspire; to play false; to act in play merely. † **2.** *trans.* To stir up by collusion –1834. † **3.** To elude by trickery –1679.

1. The French sought to weaken the King by colluding with his factious Enemies NORTH. Hence **Collu·der,** one who colludes.

Collusion (kǫlⁱū·ʒən). ME. [– (O)Fr. *collusion* or L. *collusio*, f. *collus-*, pa. ppl. stem of *colludere*; see prec., -ION.] **1.** Secret agreement or understanding for purposes of trickery or fraud; underhand scheming or working with another; deceit, fraud, trickery. **2.** *spec.* in *Law*. See quot. 1509. † **3.** A trick, or ambiguity, in words or reasoning –1659.

1. Yf he can by sume collucione Do his neyghtboure wronge CHAUCER. But for the c. of the false Templars and Hospitallers with the infidels FULLER. **2.** *C.* is a deceitful agreement or contract between two or more persons, for the one to bring an action against the other, to some evil purpose, as to defraud a third person of his right TOMLINS.

Collusive (kǫlⁱū·siv), *a.* 1671. [f. *collus-* (see prec.) + -IVE.] **1.** Characterized by collusion; fraudulently concerted or devised 1678. **2.** Given to collusion 1671.

1. C. ambiguity MARVELL. A c. treaty with the enemy 1747. **2.** C. ministers of justice 1671. Hence **Collu·sively** *adv.* in a c. manner.

† **Collu·sory,** *a.* 1706. [– late L. *collusorius*, f. *collus-* (see COLLUSION) + *-orius* -ORY².] Collusive –1755. Hence † **Collu·sorily** *adv.*

† **Collu·tion.** 1601. [– L. *collutio*, f. *collut-*, pa. ppl. stem of *colluere* rinse, f. *com* COL- + *luere* wash; see -ION.] A wash or rinse for the mouth; a lotion –1684.

‖ **Colluvies** (kǫlⁱū·vi,iz). 1647. [L., f. *colluere*; see prec.] **1.** Chiefly *Med.* A collection of foul matter; *spec.* foul discharge from an ulcer 1651. **2.** Conflux (of waters, etc.) 1665. **3.** Medley, rabble 1647. Hence **Collu·vial** *a.* of or pertaining to a c.; sink-like (*rare*).

Colly (kǫ·li). Now *dial.* 1708. [f. COLLY *a.*] **1.** Soot; smut. **2.** The Blackbird 1805.

Co·lly, *a.* Now *dial.* 1609. [In XVI *colie* COALY.] Dirtied with coal-dust or soot; grimy; coal-black.

Colly (kǫ·li), *v.*¹ *arch.* and *dial.* 1590. [app. a var. of COLLOW *v.*, q.v.] To blacken with coal-dust or soot; to begrime, blacken. Also *fig.*

An old hag Collied with chimney-smutch COWPER. Briefe as the lightning in the collied night SHAKS.

† **Co·lly,** *v.*² ME. [– OFr. *coleier, coloier* turn the neck, f. *col* neck; cf. *manier* handle.] To move the neck; to turn the head from side to side: said of birds –1783.

† **Co·llybist.** ME. [– late L. *collybista* – Gr. κολλυβιστής, f. κόλλυβος small coin.] A money-changer, usurer; miser –1615.

Collyridian (kǫliri·diăn). 1565. [– late L. *collyridianus*, f. late L. *collyrida* – Gr. κολλυρίς, -ιδ-, bread roll; see -IAN.] One of a sect of heretics in the 4th and 5th c. who worshipped the Virgin Mary and offered cakes to her as 'Queen of Heaven' (cf. Jer. 7:18). Also as *adj.*

Collyrite (kǫ·lirəit). 1826. [f. Gr. κολλύριον eye-salve, also 'Samian earth'; see -ITE¹ 2 b.] *Min.* A hydrous silicate of alumina, a white clay-like mineral, with a greasy feel.

‖ **Collyrium** (kǫli·riŏm). Pl. **collyria** (kǫli·riă). ME. [L. – Gr. κολλύριον poultice, eye-salve, f. κολλύρα roll of coarse bread.] **1.** An eye-salve or eye-wash. **2.** A suppository 1748. vars. † **Collyre,** † **Collyrie.**

Collywobbles (kǫ·liwǫb'lz). 1841. *colloq.* [Fancifully f. COLIC and WOBBLE.] Pain or looseness in the bowels.

Colmar (kǫ·lmăɹ). 1727. [A town in Alsace.] **1.** A kind of pear 1741. **2.** A kind of fan of Queen Anne's time.

‖ **Colobium** (kolōᵘ·biŏm). 1603. [late L. – Gr. κολόβιον, f. κολοβός curtailed.] A half-sleeved or sleeveless tunic worn by the early clergy, by monks, and by kings at their coronation. In later eccl. use repl. by the DALMATIC.

‖ **Coloboma** (kǫlobōᵘ·mă). 1843. [mod.L. – Gr. κολόβωμα, f. κολοβός curtailed; see -OMA.] *Path.* A malformation or mutilation of an organ; *spec.* a defect in the iris of the eye, due to imperfect closure of the choroidal fissure.

‖ **Colocolo, -la** (kǫlokōᵘ·lŏ, -lă). 1880. Native name for the wild cat of S. America (*Felix colocolo*).

Colocynth (kǫ·lŏsinþ). 1565. [– L. *colocynthis* – Gr. κολοκυνθίς, -ιδ- (Dioscorides).] The Bitter-apple (*Citrullus colocynthis*), a plant of the Gourd family, the fruit of which contains a light spongy and extremely bitter pulp, furnishing a purgative drug. Also the fruit, and the drug. Also *attrib.* Hence **Colocy·nthin** (*Chem.*), the bitter principle of c., a resin-like substance, readily soluble in alcohol.

Cologne (kolōᵘ·n). ME. [In Fr. *Cologne*, Ger. *Köln* :– L. *Colonia Agrippina.*] Name of a German city on the Rhine: used *attrib.* to designate things obtained from the city or district, as *C. brand, sword*, etc.

C. earth (umber, brown), a brown pigment obtained or prepared from lignite, orig. from a bed near C. **C. water** = EAU DE COLOGNE, a perfumed spirit, manufactured at C. since 1709; in U.S. often called simply *Cologne.*

Cololite (kǫ·lŏləit). 1837. [f. Gr. κόλον COLON¹ + -LITE.] *Geol.* An intestine-like mass or impression found in the oolitic rocks of Solenhofen, and regarded as worm-casts.

Colombier, etc.; see COLUM-.

Colombo, obs. f. CALUMBA.

Colon¹ (kōᵘ·lǫn). ME. [– (O)Fr. *côlon* or L. *colon* – Gr. κόλον food, meat, colon.] *Anat.* The greater portion of the large intestine, extending from the cæcum to the rectum. † Formerly, *pop.*, the belly or guts.

Colon² (kōᵘ·lǫn). 1589. [– L. *colon* – Gr. κῶλον limb, clause.] ‖ **1.** In *Gr. Rhetoric* and *Poetry*, a member of a sentence or rhythmical period; hence in *Palæography*, a clause or group of clauses written as a line, or taken as a standard of measure in ancient MSS. or texts. *pl.* **cola. 2.** A punctuation-mark [:] usually indicating a discontinuity of grammatical construction less than that marked by a period. *pl.* **colons.**

Co·lon³. *rare.* 1606. [– Fr. *colon* – L. *colonus*; see COLONY.] A husbandman.

Colonel (kɒ̄·ɹnĕl). 1548. [– Fr. †*coronel* (so also Sp.), later and mod. *colonnel* – (orig. with dissimilation of *l* . . . *l* to *r* . . . *l*) It. *colonnello*, f. *colonna* COLUMN, the officer being so named as leader of the first company of a regiment (*compagnia colonella*). In earliest use both *coronel* and *colonel*, but the first prevailed before mid-XVII. The present pronunc., which was established by the late XVIII, depends on the form †*coronel*; but (kɒ·lnəl) is the only pronunc. recorded by Johnson, 1775.] The superior officer of a regiment. He ranks above the *Lieutenant-Colonel*, and below the general officer, who is attached to no one regiment. Hence **Colonel** *v.* to make a c. of; *intr.* to play the c. **Colonelcy** (kɒ̄·ɹnĕlsi), the post, rank, or commission of c. **C. commandant:** see BRIGADIER.

† **Co·loner.** 1600. [f. Fr. *colon* or L. *colonus* + -ER¹.] = COLONIST –1610.

Colonial (kŏlōᵘ·niăl), *a.* (*sb.*) 1796. [f. COLONY + -AL¹, perh. after Fr. *colonial.*] **1.** Of, belonging to, or relating to a colony, or (*spec.*) the British colonies; in American history, of or belonging to the United States while they were still colonies. **2.** *Biol.* Forming a colony (see COLONY) 1885. **3.** *sb.* An inhabitant of a colony; a colonist 1865.

1. C. Councils BURKE, articles MᶜCULLOCH, mints JEVONS. Hence **Colo·nialism,** a c. practice, idiom, or manner; the c. system. **Colo·nially** *adv.* in a c. manner; in relation to the colonies.

† **Colo·nical,** *a.* [– L. *colonicus* (see COLON³) + -AL¹; see -ICAL.] Of or pertaining to husbandmen or tillage. SPELMAN.

Colonist (kǫ·lŏnist). 1701. [f. COLONIZE; see -IST.] **1.** One who settles in a new country; an inhabitant of a colony. **2.** *transf.* Of animals and plants 1878.

Colonitis (kǫlŏnəi·tis). 1834. [irreg. f. COLON¹ + -ITIS.] *Med.* Inflammation of the colon.

Colonization (kǫ:lŏnəizēⁱ·ʃən). 1770. [f. COLONIZE + -ATION.] The action of colonizing or fact of being colonized; establishment of a colony or colonies.

Our growth by c. and by conquest BURKE. Hence **Coloniza·tionist,** an advocate of c.; *spec.* in *U.S. Hist.* an advocate of the c. of Africa by Negroes from America.

Colonize (kǫ·lŏnəiz), *v.* 1622. [f. COLONY; see -IZE.] **1.** To settle (a country) with colonists; to plant or establish a colony in. **2.** To establish in a colony 1816. **3.** *intr.* To form or establish a colony or settlement; to settle. Also *transf.* of animals and plants. 1817.

1. They that would thus c. the stars with Inhabitants HOWELL. Hence **Co·lonizable** *a.* that can be colonized. **Co·lonizer.**

Colonnade (kǫlŏnēⁱ·d). 1718. [– Fr. *colonnade* (earlier † *-ate*), f. *colonne* COLUMN, after It. *colonnato* († *-ata*); see -ADE.] **1.** *Arch.* A series of columns placed at regular intervals, and supporting an entablature. **2.** *transf.* of trees, etc. 1784.

2. A length of C. . . These chestnuts rang'd in corresponding lines COWPER. Hence **Colonna·ded** *a.* having a c.

Colonne·tte. 1872. [– Fr. *colonnette*, dim. of *colonne* COLUMN; see -ETTE.] A small column.

Colony (kǫ·lŏni). ME. [– L. *colonia* farm, settlement, f. *colonus* tiller, settler, f. *colere* cultivate; see -Y³.]

I. After Roman use. † **1.** A farm, estate in the country –1656. **2.** Applied to a Roman *colonia, i.e.* a settlement of Roman citizens in a hostile or newly conquered country ME. **3.** Applied to a Greek ἀποικία, *i.e.* a settlement of 'people from home' as an independent self-governed πόλις or state 1580.

II. In mod. use. **1.** A settlement in a new country; a body of settlers, forming a community politically connected with their parent state; the community so formed, as long as the connection lasts 1548; the territory thus peopled 1612. **2.** *transf.* A number of people of one nationality residing in a foreign city or country; the quarter thus occupied 1711. **3.** *transf.* and *fig.* of animals, etc. 1658. **4.** *Biol.* An aggregate of individual animals or plants, forming a physiologically connected structure, as the coral-polyps, etc. 1872. Also *attrib.*

1. The British colonies are divided into three classes: CROWN colonies; colonies with representative governments, in which the crown partly controls the legislature and has the right of veto on local legislation; colonies with responsible governments, the crown having only the right of veto.

Coloph-, Colophon-, short for COLOPHONY, used as stems for names of related substances, as **Co·lophene** ($C_{20}H_{32}$), an oily colourless liquid obtained by distilling oil of turpentine with strong sulphuric acid.

Colophon (kǫ·lŏfǫn). 1621. [– late L. *colophon* – Gr. κολοφών summit, finishing touch.] † **1.** Finishing stroke –1635. **2.** *spec.* The inscription or device formerly placed at the end of a book, etc., and containing the title, the printer's name, date and place of printing, etc. 1774.

When the c., or final description, fell into disuse . . since the titlepage had become the principal direct means of identifying the book DE MORGAN.

Colophonite (kǫ·lŏfonəit). 1808. [f. COLOPHONY + -ITE¹ 2 b.] *Min.* A brown or reddish variety of garnet, resembling colophony.

Colophony (kǫ·lŏfoᵘni, kŏlǫ·fŏni). ME. [– L. *colophonia* for *Colophonia resina* resin of Colophon (a town of Lydia).] Rosin.

Coloquintida (kǫlŏkwi·ntidă). ME. [– med.L. *coloquintida*, f. stem of Gr. κολοκυνθίς; see COLOCYNTH.] The COLOCYNTH. Also *fig.*, referring to its bitterness.

Color, -ed, -ing, etc.; see COLOUR, etc.

Colorado (kǫlŏrā·do). One of the States of the American Union, named after its great river [Sp. *Rio Colorado* 'coloured river'].

Hence **Colorado (Potato) Beetle,** a yellow beetle (*Doryphora decemlineata*), first observed (*c* 1824) near the Upper Missouri. Its larva, the *potato-bug*, is destructive to the potato.

Coloradoite (kǫlŏrā·doˌəit). 1876. [See -ITE[1] 2 b.] *Min.* A native telluride of mercury, found in Colorado.

Colorant (kǫ·lŏ-, kɒ·lərănt). *rare.* 1884. [– Fr. *colorant*, pres. pple. of *colorer*; see COLOUR *v.*, -ANT.] A colouring matter, pigment.

† **Co·lorate,** *a.* 1678. [– L. *coloratus*, pa. pple. of *colorare* COLOUR *v.*; see -ATE[2].] Coloured –1691.

Coloration, colouration (kǫlŏrēⁱ·ʃən, kɒlə-). 1612. [– Fr. *coloration* or late L. *coloratio*, f. *colorat-*, pa. ppl. stem of L. *colorare* COLOUR *v.*; see -ION.] The action or mode of colouring; coloured condition; colouring.

‖ **Coloratura** (koloratū·ra). 1876. [It., f. as prec.; see -URE.] *Mus.* Florid ornaments in vocal music, such as runs, trills, etc. **b.** Music characterized by this style, or the ability to sing it; also, a singer of c. parts. Also *attrib.* or as *adj.*

Colorature (kǫ·lŏ-, kɒ·lərătiuɹ). 1753. [Anglicized f. prec.; cf. Fr. *colorature*, G. *koloratur*.] = prec.

Colorific (kǫlŏ-, kɒləri·fik), *a.* 1676. [– Fr. *colorifique*, or mod.L. *colorificus*; see COLOUR, -FIC.] Producing colour or colours; *loosely*, pertaining to colour. Also *fig.*

Colorimeter (kǫlŏ-, kɒləri·mītəɹ). 1863. [f. comb. form of L. *color* COLOUR + -METER; cf. Fr. *colorimètre*.] An instrument for measuring intensity of colour. Hence **Colorime·tric, -al** *a.* **Colori·metry.**

Colorize, colour- (kɒ·lərəiz), *v. rare.* 1611. [f. L. *color* or Eng. COLOUR + -IZE.] *trans.* To colour. Hence **Co:loriza·tion, co:lour-.**

Coloss, -osse (kolǫ·s). *arch.* 1561. [– Fr. *colosse* – L. *colossus*.] = COLOSSUS.

Colossal (kəlǫ·săl), *a.* 1712. [– Fr. *colossal*, f. *colosse*; see prec., -AL[1].] Like a colossus, of vast size, gigantic, huge.

Hence **Colo·ssally** *adv.* var. **Colosse·an** (*arch.*).

‖ **Colosseum, coliseum** (kǫlǫ̆sī·ŏm, kǫli-). 1708. [Earliest sp. *coliseum* – med.L. *coliseum* (whence Fr. *colisée*, It. *coliseo*), subst. use of n. of L. *colosseus* gigantic, colossal, f. *colossus* (see next). Mod. sp. *-oss-* assim. to L.] The amphitheatre of Vespasian at Rome. Also *transf.*

While stands the Coliseum, Rome shall stand BYRON. var. † **Colossee, colisee.**

Colossus (kolǫ·sŏs). Pl. **-i, -uses.** ME. [– L. *colossus* – Gr. κολοσσός applied by Herodotus to the statues of Egyptian temples.] **1.** A statue of very large dimensions; *esp.* the bronze statue of Apollo at Rhodes, reputed to have stood astride the entrance to the harbour. **2.** *transf.* and *fig.* Anything gigantic 1794.

He doth bestride the narrow world Like a C. SHAKS. **2.** Laud stood the c. of his own cast D'ISRAELI. The C. of the North [Russia] 1831. var. † **Colo·sso.**

‖ **Colostrum** (kǒlǫ·strŏm). 1577. [L. (also *colostra* fem. sing., and neut. pl.)] *Med.* The first milk secreted by a mammal after parturition; the 'beestings' or 'green milk'. Hence **Colostra·tion,** an indisposition of new-born children attributed to the c.

Colotomy (kolǫ·tŏmi). 1867. [f. Gr. κόλον COLON[1] + -TOMY.] *Surg.* The operation of opening the colon.

Colour, color (kɒ·ləɹ), *sb.* [ME. – OFr. *colur, colour* (mod. *couleur*) :– L. *color-*. *Color* has been used occas. in Eng. from XV, and is now the prevalent sp. in U.S.]

I. 1. The quality in virtue of which objects present different appearances to the eye, in respect of the kind of light reflected from their surfaces. **2.** A particular hue or tint; often spec. one distinct from the prevailing tone, as in *Bot.* any hue save green ME. **b.** *spec.* The hue of the darker varieties of mankind 1796. **3.** Complexion, hue; freshness of hue ME. **4.** *spec.* in *Art.* Colouring 1661. Also *fig.*

1. Would you say that whiteness is c. or a c. JOWETT. **2.** *Accidental colours, Complementary c.*: see these words. *Fundamental, Primary*, or *Simple colours*: formerly, the seven colours of the spectrum; now, red, green, and violet (or, with painters, red, yellow, and blue). *Secondary colours*: colours resulting from the mixture of primary colours. Al colours of the Rainebow 1577. **b.** She is a woman of c. STEVENSON. **3.** The duke a lytell chaunged c. LD. BERNERS. **4.** *Dead c.*: the first laying-in of a portrait. The dead c. of my wife is good above what I expected PEPYS.

II. 1. (in *pl.*) A coloured device, badge, or dress ME. Also *fig.* **2.** (usu. in *pl.*) A flag, ensign, or standard of a regiment or a ship 1590, Also *fig.* **3.** A colouring matter, pigment, paint 1580. **4.** *pl.* Coloured dresses 1716. **5.** *Mining.* 'A particle of metallic gold.' RAYMOND.

1. The servants . . wore the colours of the Prince's household SCOTT. To come out in one's true colours DICKENS. **2.** Sound Trumpets, let our bloody Colours waue SHAKS. A soldier deserting his colours MACAULAY. *A pair of colours*: an ensign's commission (*arch.*). To hang out false colours STEELE.

III. Fig. **1.** Outward appearance, show, aspect, semblance *of* (something) ME. **2.** A show of reason ME.; † *occas.*, excuse –1724. **3.** *esp.* in *Law.* An apparent or *prima facie* right, as in *C. of title.* Also *spec.* in Pleading, 'a probable but really false plea, the design of which was to draw the decision of the case from the jury to the judges'. 1531. **4.** *pl.* Rhetorical modes or figures; ornaments of style or diction ME. **5.** *Mus.* Timbre. Also, variety of expression (cf. next). 1597. **6.** (an extension of III. 1). General complexion or tone; kind 1600.

1. A Table of Coulers, or apparances of good and euill BACON. **2.** No man should have even a c. to assert that I received a compensation BURKE. Phrases. *Under c. of*; *without c.*; *to give c.*; † *to take c. with*, i.e. to side ostensibly with. **4.** I lerned neuere Rethorik. . Colours ne knowe I none CHAUCER. **6.** Boyes and women are for the most part, cattle of this c. *A.Y.L.* III. ii. 435. Words of an opposite c. 1822.

Comb.: **c.-blind,** *a.* blind to certain colours, unable to discriminate between colours; also *fig.* of racial colour, etc.; hence, **-bli:ndness;** † **-deroy,** orig. purple, later, bright tawny; **-man,** one who deals in colours; **-serjeant, -sergeant,** an army serjeant who performs the duty of attending the regimental colours on ceremonial occasions.

Colour, color (kɒ·ləɹ), *v.* ME. [– OFr. *colourer* (mod. *colorer*) – L. *colorare*, f. *color* (see prec.).] **1.** *trans.* To give colour to; to paint, stain, dye. Also with *over.* Also *fig.* **2.** To represent in fair colours; to gloss, cloak, disguise, excuse; to render specious or plausible. Const. *out, over.* ME. **b.** To misrepresent ME. † **3.** To lend one's name to; represent as one's own –1726. **4.** To imbue with its own character 1835. **5.** *intr.* To become coloured 1667. **6.** *spec.* To blush. Also with *up.* 1721.

1. Color hit with safroune ME. **2.** Whych thyng, though it be colowryd *per Jus Regale*, yet it is Tyrannye FORTESCUE. **b.** To suppress and c. evidence DICKENS. **5.** This meerschaum won't c. 1891. **6.** The poor woman coloured 1787. Hence **Co·lourer, co·lorer.**

Colourable, color- (kɒ·ləɹăb'l), *a.* ME. [– OFr. *colorable* having bright colours; in sense 2 from COLOUR III; see COLOUR, -ABLE.] † **1.** Possessed of colour –1705. **2.** *fig.* Having an appearance of truth or right; specious, plausible ME.; pretended ME.; deceptive, as ship's papers, etc. 1750.

2. C. error 1581, grounds of complaint DE QUINCEY. The conveyance was c. and collusive DALLAS. Hence † **Co·lourableness, co·lor-,** c. state or quality. **Co·lourably, co·lor-,** *adv.* in a c. manner.

Co·lour-box. 1858. **1.** A paint-box 1891. **2.** *Calico printing.* The box which supplies calico to the printing rollers 1858. **3.** An instrument for compounding the colours of the spectrum in any given proportion 1870.

Coloured, colored (kɒ·ləɹd), *ppl. a.* ME. [f. COLOUR *v.* or *sb.* + -ED.] **1.** Having a colour or colours. (Strictly, exclusive of black and white; also, exclusive of the prevailing hue, *e.g.* in *Bot.* of green.) Also *fig.* of style, etc., 1855. **2.** Of the complexion, as *fresh-c.*, etc.; *spec.* having a skin other than white 1611; of or belonging to the Negro race 1866. † **3.** Made to look well; specious –1576; glossed over –1557; pretended –1610.

1. White or c. shirts 1891. **2.** The . . Negro women, or the c. women as they are called here 1760. C. suffrage 1878. **3.** A false fained and c. frende GRAFTON.

Colouring, coloring (kɒ·ləriŋ), *vbl. sb.* ME. [f. COLOUR *v.* + -ING[1].] **1.** The action of the vb. COLOUR; esp. *fig.* the giving of a specious appearance to what is bad 1549. **2.** The effect of the application of colour, the style in which anything is coloured 1707; pervading character 1769. **3.** Colouring matter 1460.

1. Let them leaue their colourynge and cal them by their Christian name Brybes LATIMER.

Colourist, colorist (kɒ·lərist). 1686. [f. COLOUR + -IST after It. *colorista* (whence Fr. *coloriste*).] A painter skilful in colouring; a master of colour. Also *fig.* of writers.

Colourless colorless (kɒ·ləɹlės), *a.* ME. [f. COLOUR *sb.* + -LESS.] **1.** *gen.* Without colour. **2.** Without distinctive character, vividness, or picturesqueness 1861; neutral 1868.

1. A c. and transparent . . body HUXLEY. A c. face TENNYSON, landscape 1878. **2.** A c. religion MAX-MÜLLER. C. words 1883. Hence **Co·lourlessly** *adv.* **Co·lourlessness, color-,** c. quality or state.

Coloury, colory (kɒ·ləri), *a.* 1853. [f. as prec. + -Y[1].] *Comm.* Having a colour characteristic of good quality; as hops, coffee beans, etc.

Colp. Irish; see COLLOP[2].

‖ **Colportage** (kolporta·ʒ, kǫ·lpǫɹtėdʒ). 1846. [Fr., f. as next; see -AGE.] The work of a colporteur.

‖ **Colporteur** (kolportör, kǫ·lpǫɹtəɹ). 1796. [Fr., f. *colporter*, presumably alt. of *comporter* – L. *comportare* transport, f. *com* COL- + *portare* carry (cf. PORTER *sb.*[2]).] A hawker of books, newspapers, etc., *esp.* (in Eng. use) one employed by a religious society.

Colstaff, var. of COWL-STAFF.

Colt (kōᵘlt), *sb.*[1] [OE. *colt* young ass, young camel; of obscure origin, but cf. Sw. *kult, kulter, kulting*, applied to half-grown animals and boys.] **1.** The young of the horse, or of animals of the horse kind; also, in Scripture, of the camel. Cf. FOAL. **2.** *fig.* A young or inexperienced person ME.; *spec.* in *Cricket*, a professional cricketer during his first season 1873. **3.** *Legal slang.* The barrister that attended on a serjeant-at-law at his induction 1765. **4.** *Naut.* A piece of rope used as an instrument of chastisement 1769.

Comb.: **Colt's tooth:** *lit.* one of the first set of teeth of a horse (or ass); *fig.* youthful desires; inclination to wantonness; **c.-drift,** the drift of colts or ponies on Dartmoor (see DRIFT). Hence **Co·ltbood,** quality of being a c.

Colt (kōᵘlt), *sb.*[2] 1852. [In full *Colt's revolver*, invented by Samuel *Colt* (1814–62) of Connecticut, U.S.A.] A type of repeating pistol.

Colt (kōᵘlt), *v.* 1580. [f. COLT *sb.*[1]] † **1.** *intr.* To frisk or run wild as a colt (usually implying wantonness) (*rare*) –1746. † **2.** *trans.* To befool, take in –1618. † **3.** (See quot.) **4.** To beat with a colt (see COLT *sb.*[1] 4) 1732.

3. She hath bin colted by him *Cymb.* II. iv. 133. Hence **Co·lting** *vbl. sb.* (sense 4).

Colter, var. of COULTER.

Coltish (kōᵘ·ltiʃ), *a.* ME. [f. COLT *sb.*[1] + -ISH[1].] Of, pertaining to, or like a colt or colts; frisky, † salacious.

He was al coltissch, ful of ragerye CHAUCER. Hence **Co·ltish-ly** *adv.*, **-ness.**

Colt-pixie. 1542. [See PIXIE.] A mischievous sprite, in the form of a ragged colt.

Coltsfoot (kōᵘ·ltsfut). ME. [tr. med.L. *pes pulli* 'colt's foot', from the shape of the leaves.] A name of *Tussilago farfara* (N.O. *Compositæ*); its leaves used for smoking as a cure for asthma; an infusion of the leaves.

Colt's tail. 1735. **1.** A cloud with a ragged edge, portending rain. (Cf. *mare's tail.*) **2.** The Canadian Flea-bane, *Erigeron canadensis.*

‖ **Coluber** (kǫ·liŭbəɹ). 1763. [L., = snake.] *Zool.* A genus of harmless snakes. (The name was formerly not limited to harmless snakes.)

Colubriform (kǒlⁱū·brifǭɹm), *a.* 1847. [f. comb. form of prec. + -FORM.] Having the form of a coluber; applied to certain venomous snakes.

Colubrine (kǫ·liŭbrəin), *a.* (*sb.*) 1528. [– L. *colubrinus*, f. *coluber* snake; see -INE[1].] **1.** Of or belonging to a snake. **2.** *Zool.* Of the nature of the Coluber or snake: applied to serpents 1844. **3.** *sb.* A colubrine snake.

Columba; see CALUMBA.

Columbaceous (kǫlɒmbēⁱ·ʃəs), *a.* 1693. [f. L. *columba* dove + -ACEOUS.] Of the nature of a dove or a pigeon; pertaining to the sub-order Columbacei.

‖ **Columbarium** (kǫlɒmbēᵊ·riɒ̆m). Pl. **-ia.** 1846. [L., f. *columba* dove, pigeon; see -ARIUM.] **1.** A pigeon-house, dove-cote; a pigeon-hole 1881. **2.** *Rom. Antiq.* A subterranean sepulchre with niches in its walls for cinerary urns; one of these niches.

Columbary (kǫ·lɒmbări). 1549. [– prec.; see -ARY[1].] A pigeon-house or dove-cote.

Columbate (kǒlɒ·mbeⁱt). 1816. [f. COLUMBIUM + -ATE[4].] *Chem.* A salt of columbic acid.

Columbiad (kǒlɒ·mbi,æ̆d). 1798. [f. *Columbia* (see next) + -AD I b.] **1.** An epic of America. **2.** A kind of heavy cast-iron cannon formerly used in the U.S. army 1844.

Columbian (kǒlɒ·mbiăn), *a.* 1828. [f. mod. L. *Columbia*, poet. name for America (f. Columbus) + -AN.] Of or belonging to America or (*esp.*) the United States.

Columbic (kǒlɒ·mbik), *a.*[1] 1807. [f. COLUMBIUM + -IC.] *Chem.* Of or pertaining to columbium.

C. acid: the same as *niobic acid*; see NIOBIC.

Colu·mbic, *a.*[2], var. of *calumbic*; see CALUMBA.

Columbier (kǒlɒ·mbiəɹ). 1875. [– Fr. *colombier*, lit. 'dove-cote'.] A size of paper measuring about 34½ inches by 24.

Columbi·ferous, *a.* 1828. [f. COLUMBIUM + -FEROUS.] Yielding or containing columbium.

Columbin (kǒlɒ·mbin). 1882. [transf. use of Fr. *colombin.*] *Elect.* An insulating material (now made of a mixture of calcium and barium sulphates) used for connecting the sockets of the Jablochkoff candle.

Columbin(e, var. of *calumbin*; see CALUMBA.

Columbine (kǫ·lɒmbəin), *a.* and *sb.*[1] ME. [– (O)Fr. *colombin*, *-ine* – L. *columbinus*, f. *columba* dove; see -INE.] Of, belonging to, or of the nature of, a dove or pigeon 1656; dove-like, as *c. simplicity* ME.; dove-coloured ME. quasi-*sb.* Short for *columbine colour* 1606.

Columbine (kǫ·lɒmbəin), *sb.*[2] ME. [– OFr. *colombine* – med.L. *columbina* (sc. *herba*) 'dove's plant', so called from the resemblance of the inverted flower to five pigeons clustered together.] The English name for plants of the genus *Aquilegia*, esp. *A. vulgaris*; † also, a name for *Verbena officinalis* –1597. Also *attrib.*

Columbine (kǫ·lɒmbəin), *sb.*[3] 1727. [– Fr. *Colombine* – It. *Colombina*, subst. use of fem. of *colombino* dove-like in gentleness.] The mistress of Harlequin in Pantomime or Harlequinade.

Columbite (kǒlɒ·mbəit). 1805. [f. COLUMBIUM + -ITE[1] 2 b.] *Min.* The native ore of columbium, a black columbate of iron and manganese; niobite.

Columbium (kǒlɒ·mbiɒ̆m). 1801. [f. *Columbia* poet. name for America; see -IUM.] *Chem.* A metallic element, occurring in columbite and other minerals. Discovered in a specimen of columbite brought from Massachusetts. Symbol Cb. Now called *niobium.*

Columbo, var. of CALUMBA.

Columel (kǫ·liŭmel). 1610. [– L. *columella*, dim. of *columna*; see COLUMN, -EL.] A small column. Also *transf.* and *attrib.*

‖ **Columella** (kǫliume·lă). 1585. [L.; see prec.] **1.** *Anat.* Applied to the uvula, the axis of the cochlea of the ear (*c. cochleæ*), and other analogous structures. **2.** *Conch.* The axis of a spiral shell 1755. **3.** *Bot.* **a.** 'The long axis round which the parts of a (dehiscent) fruit are united'. **b.** The axis of the spore-case of an urn-moss. **c.** The axis over which the spore-cases of such ferns as *Trichomanes* are arranged. 1760. **4.** *Zool.* **a.** A part of the pterygoid bone in the skull of lizards (*c. cranii*). **b.** A delicate bone in the middle ear of birds, reptiles, and amphibians (*c. auris*). **c.** The central axis of the visceral chamber of many corals. 1848. Hence **Colume·llar** *a.* of or belonging to a c. **Colume·lliform** *a.* shaped like a little pillar.

Column (kǫ·lɒ̆m), *sb.* ME. [Partly – OFr. *columpne* (mod. *colonne*, after It. *colonna*), partly – its source L. *columna* pillar.] **1.** *Arch.* A cylindrical or slightly tapering body of considerably greater length than diameter, erected vertically as a support for some part of a building; *spec.* in the classic orders, a round pillar, with base, shaft, and capital supporting the entablature. Sometimes standing alone as a monument: *e.g.* Trajan's Column at Rome. 1481. **b.** Anything of columnar shape or appearance, as *a c. of water, air, mercury, smoke, the spinal c.*, etc. 1671. **c.** *fig.* Support or prop. (Cf. *pillar.*) 1619. **2.** A narrow division of a page, etc., formed by vertical lines or separating spaces; also, letterpress, letters, or figures arranged vertically. In *pl.* said *esp.* of the vertical divisions in a newspaper, etc. ME. **3.** *Bot.* The upright structure formed by the coalescence of the filaments, as in the mallow, or by the union of the stamens with the style, as in orchids 1807. **4.** *Mil.* A formation of troops narrow laterally and deep from front to rear 1677. **5.** *Naut.* A body or division of ships 1805.

1. Where the shatter'd columns lie, Showing Carthage once had been SCOTT. *Comb.* **c.-rule** (*Printing*), a thin piece of brass used to separate columns of type.

‖ **Columna** (kǒlɒ·mnă). Pl. **-æ.** 1758. [L.] A column or pillar; a name given to many parts of the body.

Columnar (kǒlɒ·mnăɹ), *a.* 1728. [– late L. *columnaris*, f. *columna* COLUMN; see -AR[1].] **1.** Of the nature or form of a column (or columns). Also *fig.* **2.** Written or printed in columns 1846. **3.** Characterized by, or raised on, columns 1849. vars. **Colu·mnal, Columna·rian** (*rare*), † **Colu·mnary.**

Columned (kǫ·lɒ̆md), *ppl. a.* 1791. [f. COLUMN *sb.* + -ED[2].] **1.** Furnished with columns. (Chiefly *poet.*) **2.** Columnar 1871. **3.** Divided into columns 1821.

1. Ilion's c. citadel TENNYSON. vars. (in sense 1) **Co·lumnated, Colu·mniated** *ppl. adjs.*

Columnia·tion. 1592. [alt. f. *columnation* (– L. *columnatio*) by assim. to *intercolumniation.*] **1.** *Arch.* 'The employment of columns in a design' (Gwilt). **2.** Division (of a page) into columns. LAMB.

Columni·ferous, *a.* 1730. [f. late L. *columnifer* (f. *columna* COLUMN) + -OUS; see -FEROUS.] Bearing a column or columns. In *Bot.* cf. COLUMN 3. So **Colu·mniform** *a.* column-shaped.

Colure (kolⁱū̆ᵊ·ɹ, kōᵘ·liuɹ). ME. [– late L. *coluri* pl. – Gr. κόλουραι (sc. γραμμαί lines), pl. of κόλουρος truncated, lit. dock-tailed, f. κόλος docked + οὐρά tail; so called because their lower part is permanently cut off from view.] *Astron.* Each of two great circles which intersect each other at right angles at the poles, and divide the equinoctial and the ecliptic into four equal parts. One passes through the equinoctial, the other through the solstitial, points of the ecliptic.

From Pole to Pole, traversing each C. MILT. *P.L.* IX. 66.

‖ **Colutea** (kolⁱū̆·ti,ă). 1664. [L. – Gr. κολουτέα.] *Bot.* Bladder-senna.

Coly; see COLIES.

Colza (kǫ·lză). Also **colsa.** 1712. [– Fr. (Walloon) *kolza*, earlier *kolzat* – LG. *kōlsāt*, Du. *koolzaad*; see COLE[1], SEED.] The French name of COLESEED. **C.-oil:** the oil expressed from the seeds, much used for burning in lamps.

Com-, *prefix*, the archaic form of cl. L. *cum*, meaning, 'together, together with, in combination or union', also 'altogether, completely', and hence *intensive*. The form *com-* is used before *b, p, m*, and before a few words beginning with vowels; the *m* was assimilated before *r, l*, and in later times *n*; dropped before vowels generally, *h* and *gn-*; before all other consonants *com-* became CON-, q.v. See also CO-.

Coma[1] (kōᵘ·mă). 1646. [– medical L. – Gr. κῶμα, -ματ-, rel. to κοίτη bed, κεῖσθαι lie down.] *Pathol.* A state of unnatural, heavy, prolonged sleep, with complete unconsciousness and slow, stertorous breathing, frequently ending in death.

Coma vigil: a state in which a typhus fever patient lies with wide open eyes, totally unconscious, but muttering in delirium.

Coma[2] (kōᵘ·mă). Pl. **-mæ** (-mī). 1669. [– L. *coma* – Gr. κόμη hair of the head.] **1.** *Bot.* **a.** A tuft of silky hairs at the end of some seeds. **b.** A tuft of bracts occurring beyond the inflorescence. **c.** The arrangement of branches forming the head of a tree. **2.** *Astron.* The nebulous envelope round the nucleus of a comet 1765. **Co·mal** *a.*

Co-ma·rt. See 1605 (Q°.) SHAKS. *Haml.* I. i. 93. The Folios have 'cou'nant'.

Co:-ma·rtyr, comma·rtyr. 1555. [– late L. *commartyr* (Tertullian); later f. CO- + MARTYR.] A fellow-martyr.

‖ **Comarum** (kǫ·mărɒ̆m). 1778. [Bot. L. – Gr. κόμαρον some plant.] *Bot.* A Linnæan genus of *Rosaceæ*, including the Purple Marsh Cinquefoil.

Co-mate (kōᵘ,mēⁱt: the stress varies). 1576. [See CO-.] Companion, fellow, mate.

† **Co·mate,** *a.* 1600. [– L. *comatus*, f. *coma* COMA[2].] Hairy.

Comatose (kōᵘ·mătōᵘ·s), *a.* 1755. [f. COMA[1] + -OSE[1].] **1.** Affected with coma; of the nature of coma 1761; drowsy, lethargic 1828. Var. † **Co·matous.**

‖ **Comatula** (komæ·tiulă). Pl. **-læ** (-lī). 1851. [subst. use of fem. of late L. *comatulus*, dim. of L. *comatus* COMATE.] *Zool.* A genus of free-swimming Crinoid Echinoderms, of a radiate shape with (usually) ten cirrous arms; the feather-star. So **Coma·tulid,** any of the *Comatulidæ*, the family containing the c.

Comb (kōᵘm), *sb.*[1] [OE. *camb, comb* = OS. *camb* (Du. *kam*), OHG. *kamb* (G. *kamm*), ON. *kambr* :– Gmc. **kambaz*. The sense 'honeycomb' is an exclusively Eng. use, the origin of which is doubtful.] **1.** A strip of wood, bone, horn, metal, etc., with teeth; used for disentangling, cleaning, and arranging the hair, or keeping it in place. Also *fig.* **2.** An instrument composed of a series of such strips, used for currying horses; a CURRY-COMB ME. **3.** *transf.* Anything resembling a comb in function, structure, or appearance; as (*a*) a toothed instrument used in dressing wool or flax; (*b*) a tool with teeth, used for cutting the thread of a screw or work in the lathe; (*c*) a toothed instrument used in graining or marbling; (*d*) the notched scale of a wire-micrometer; (*e*) *Electr.* a comb-like row of brass points for collecting the electricity from the plate of an electrical machine. ME. **4.** Any natural formation resembling a comb; *esp.* **a.** *Zool.* (*pl.*) the pair of abdominal appendages in Scorpions 1834; **b.** the red fleshy crest or caruncle on the head of the domestic fowl (cf. COCK'S-COMB) OE. **5.** Anything resembling a cock's comb in position or appearance (= crest); as, the crest of a helmet OE., of a wave 1886, the projection on the top of the cock of a gun-lock 1867, and the like. **6.** The flat cake or plate consisting of a double series of hexagonal cells of wax made by bees; a honeycomb [Eng. only] ME.

4. b. *To cut the c. of*: to take down, humiliate. All the Counts in Cumberland shall not cut my c. SCOTT. **6.** Wordis wel set togidere is a coomb of hony WYCLIF *Prov.* 16:24. Hence **Co·mbwise** *adv.* **Co·mby** *a.* having combs or a comb-like structure.

Comb (kŭm), *sb.*[2], var. of COOMB[1], a measure.

Comb (kŭm), *sb.*[3], var. of COOMB[2], a valley.

Comb (kōᵘm), *v.* ME. [f. COMB *sb.*[1], repl. *kemb*, OE. *cemban* (:– **kambjan*), which survives in UNKEMPT.] **1.** *trans.* To clean, disentangle, or arrange with a comb. **2.** To dress with a comb 1577; *transf.* to scrape or rake as with a comb 1654. **3.** *intr.* Of waves: To roll over and break with a foamy crest 1808. orig. *U.S.* **4.** *trans.* To search (as with a tooth-comb) 1904; to clean *out* 1916.

1. Combe downe his haire 2 *Hen. VI*, III. iii. 15. **2.** They don't..c. wool in the Monasteries DE FOE. Voters to be combed off by a Radical GEO. ELIOT. **3.** The waves combed over the vessel W. C. RUSSELL.

Comba·ron. ME. [– AFr. *combaron* (AL. *combaro* XIII); see COM-, BARON.] *Hist.* A fellow-baron (of the Cinque Ports).

Combat (kǫ·mbæ̆t, kɒ·mbæ̆t), *sb.* 1567. [– Fr. *combat*, f. *combattre* – late L. *combattere*, f. *com* COM- + **battere* for L. *batuere* fight; cf. ABATE.] **1.** An encounter or fight between two persons (parties, animals, etc.). Hence, *single combat.* 1622. **2.** *gen.* A fight between opposing forces; usually on a smaller scale than a *battle* 1583. Also *fig.*

1. *Trial by c.*: = BATTLE *sb.* 2. Where Champions bold..Defi'd the best of Panim chivalry To mortal c. MILT. *P.L.* I. 766. **2.** *fig.* The combate of wits HOBBES.

Combat (kǫ·mbæ̆t, kɒ·mbæ̆t), *v.* 1564. [– Fr. *combattre*; see prec.]

1. *intr.* To fight or do battle (orig. *esp.* in single combat). Const. *with, against.* Also *fig.* **2.** *trans.* To fight with, engage, oppose in battle 1590. Also *fig.* (Now most usual.)

1. I will not c. in my shirt *L.L.L.* v. ii. 711. *fig.* His face still combating with teares and smiles *Rich. II*, v. ii. 32. **2.** He hath no more Antagonists to combate 1652. *fig.* To c. reasons MILT. *Sams.* 864, truth WOLLASTON, prejudice BURKE. Hence **Co·mbatable** *a.* capable of being combated (*rare*). **Co·mbater** (*rare*). **Co·mbative** *a.* given to c., pugnacious. **Co·mbatively** *adv.* **Co·mbativeness,** propensity to fight. (Orig. a Phrenological term.)

Combatant (kǫ·m-, kɒ·mbătănt). 1489. [– OFr. *combatant*, pres. pple. of *combattre*; see prec., -ANT.] **A.** *adj.* Fighting, ready to fight 1632. **b.** *Her.* Rampant with the forepaws raised as if in fight; said of two lions, etc., rampant and facing each other (*affronté*). (Freq. spelt *combattant.*) 1500.

B. *sb.* One who combats, a fighter; in early use *esp.* one who fought in single combat 1489. Also *fig.*

So frownd the mighty Combatants MILT. *P.L.* II. 719.

Co·mb-brush. 1611. **1.** 'A brush to clean combs'. † **2.** A lady's maid –1749.

Combe, var. of COOMB[2]; obs. f. COOMB[1].

Comber[1] (kōᵘ·məɹ). 1646. [f. COMB *v.* + -ER[1].] **1.** One who or that which combs; *spec.* one who combs wool. **2.** A combing wave; see COMB *v.* 3, and cf. *beach-comber* 1840.

Comber[2] (kǫ·mbəɹ). 1769. [Origin unkn.] A fish: *Serranus cabrilla*; also, short for *Comber Wrasse.*

Combinable (kǫ̆mbəi·năb'l), *a.* 1749. [f. COMBINE *v.* + -ABLE.] Capable of combining or of being combined. Hence **Combi·nableness.**

Combinant (kǫ·mbinănt). 1628. [f. COMBINE + -ANT; in sense 1 = contemp. COMBINATOR, COMBINER (see COMBINATION 4, COMBINE 5.] † **1.** A confederate. **2.** *Math.* (See quot.) 1853.

2. An invariant of a system of quantics of the same degree is called a c. if it is unaltered (except by a constant multiplier) not only when the variables are lineally transformed, but also when for any of the quantics is substituted a linear function of the quantics SALMON. Hence **Co·mbinantive** *a.* pertaining to, or of the nature of, a c.

Combinate (kǫ·minĕt), *a. rare.* 1583. [– late L. *combinatus*, pa. pple. of *combinare* COMBINE; see -ATE[2].] Combined. In *Meas. for M.* III. i. 231 taken as 'Betrothed, promised, settled by contract' (J.).

Combination (kǫmbinēⁱ·ʃən). 1532. [– OFr. *combination* (mod. *combinaison*) or late L. *combinatio*, f. *combinat-*, pa. ppl. stem of *combinare*; see COMBINE, -ION.] **1.** The action of combining two or more separate things 1613. **2.** Combined state or condition; conjunction 1597. **3.** *concr.* A group of things combined into a whole 1532. **4.** The association of persons for a common object: usually in a bad sense 1593; *concr.* an association thus formed 1571. **5.** *Math.* (*pl.*) The different groups of a definite number which can be made of any number of given individuals without regard to the order of arrangement 1673. **6.** *Chem.* Chemical union, in which substances combine to form new compounds; *concr.* a compound so formed 1766. **7.** Short for *c.-room* 1749. **8.** *pl.* = *c.-garment* 1884. **9.** A motor-cycle with side-car attached 1914.

1. Combinations of letters CUDWORTH, of ideas LOCKE. **2.** The same images in the same c. JOHNSON. **4.** Either by c. or by any other sort of violence 1776. A solemne C. shall be made Of our deere soules SHAKS.

Comb.: **c. garment,** an under-garment consisting of combined chemise or undershirt and drawers, worn mostly by women; **c. laws,** laws directed against combinations of masters or workmen, repealed in 1824; **c. pedal** = COMPOSITION *pedal*; **c. -room (-chamber),** in the University of Cambridge (England) = COMMON-ROOM. Hence **Combina·tional** *a.* of or pertaining to c.

Co·mbinator. *rare.* 1611. [var., with L. suffix *-ator*, of COMBINER, COMBINANT; see prec.] = COMBINER.

Combinative (kǫ·mbineⁱtiv), *a.* 1855. [f. COMBINAT(ION + -IVE, on the analogy of *create/creation/creative*; see -ATIVE.] **1.** Having the faculty of combination. **2.** Of, pertaining to, or of the nature of combination; cumulative 1867. var. **Combina·tory.** So **Co:mbinato·rial** *a.* of or relating to (mathematical) combinations.

† **Combi·nd,** *v.* 1477. [Fusion of *combine* and *bind.*] *trans.* and *intr.* = COMBINE –1605.

Combine (kǫ̆mbəi·n), *v.* ME. [– (O)Fr. *combiner* or late L. *combinare* join two and two, f. *com* COM- + *bini* two together.] **1.** *trans.* To couple or join together; to join in action, condition, or feeling; to conjoin, associate, ally. **2** To cause to unite or coalesce into one body or substance; *esp.* in *Chem.* 1799. **3.** To unite (distinct qualities) 1827. **4.** *intr.* To come together into one body, coalesce; *esp.* in *Chem.* Cf. COMBINATION 6. 1712. **5.** To unite together for a common purpose; to form a union, *spec.* for some economic, social, or political purpose; to form a combination 1605. Also *fig.* of things. ¶ **6.** In *Meas. for M.* IV. iii. 149, perh. = To bind.

1. To c. a sinew cut asunder 1599. God..C. your hearts in one, your Realmes in one *Hen. V*, v. ii. 388. Phr. *To c. efforts, forces*, etc. **3.** Combining French clearness with old English depth CARLYLE. **5.** When bad men c., good men must associate BURKE. Hence † **Combi·nement,** combination. **Combi·ner,** one who or that which combines.

Combine (kǫ·mbəin, kǫ̆mbəi·n), *sb.* 1610. [f. prec.] † A conspiracy. **b.** *U.S. colloq.* A combination of persons for commercial, political, or fraudulent ends 1887.

Combined (kǫ̆mbəi·nd), *ppl. a.* ME. [f. COMBINE *v.* + -ED[1].] United; confederated; performed by agents acting in combination; produced by combination. Hence **Combi·nedly** *adv.* **Combi·nedness.**

Combing (kōᵘ·miŋ), *vbl. sb.* 1575. [f. COMB *v.* + -ING[1].] **1.** The action of COMB *v.* **2.** *concr.* (usu. *pl.*) The produce of combing; hairs combed off; borders, etc., made of these 1656.

2. The baldnesse, thinnesse, and..deformity of their haire, is usually supplyed by borders and combings 1656. *Comb.* **c.-machine,** one for combing wool.

Combing (kōᵘ·miŋ), *ppl. a.* 1857. [f. as prec. + -ING[2].] That combs; *esp.* of a wave (see COMB *v.* 3).

Combing, var. of COAMING.

Combless (kōᵘ·mlės), *a.* 1596. [See -LESS.] Without a comb (in various senses; see COMB *sb.*[1]).

Combre, obs. f. CUMBER.

Combretaceous (kǫmbritēⁱ·ʃəs), *a.* 1864. [f. L. *Combretaceæ* (f. generic name *Combretum* – L. *combretum* kind of rush) + -OUS; see -ACEOUS.] *Bot.* Of or belonging to the N.O. *Combretaceæ*, of which the typical genus *Combretum* consists of trailing or climbing tropical shrubs.

† **Combu·re,** *v.* 1570. [– OFr. *comburer* or L. *comburere* burn up.] To burn up. Also *intr.* (for *refl.*) –1613. So **Combu·rence,** comburent quality or action (*rare*). **Combu·rent** *a.* and *sb.* † burning, causing combustion (*rare*).

Comburgess (kǫmbɒ̄·ɹdʒės). 1517. [f. COM- + BURGESS, after med.L., AL. *comburgensis.*] *Hist.* **1.** A fellow-burgess, fellow-citizen or freeman of a borough. † **2.** One of the municipal magistrates formerly chosen by and from among their fellow-burgesses in certain English boroughs –1835.

Combust (kǫ̆mbɒ·st), *a.* ME. [– L. *combustus*, pa. pple. of *comburere* burn up; cf. OFr. *combust.*] † **1.** Burnt; *spec.* calcined –1678; adust –1607. **2.** *Astrol.* Of the planets: Burnt up (as it were) by the sun in or near conjunction; (app.) extinguished by the sun's light ME.

2. Planets that are oft Combust..untill the opposite motion of their orbs bring them..where they may be seen MILT. Hence **Combu·st** *v.* to burn up; to calcine. (Now joc. or affected.)

Combustible (kǫ̆mbɒ·stib'l), *a.* (*sb.*) 1529. [– (O)Fr. *combustible* or med.L. *combustibilis*, f. *combust-* (see next, -IBLE).] **1.** Capable of being consumed by fire, fit for burning, burnable. **2.** *fig.* Easily kindled to violence or passion; excitable; inflammable 1647. **3.** *sb.* [sc. substance or matter.] Also *fig.* 1688.

1. Stubble, and such like c. matter GOLDSM. **2.** The commons, aware of what c. materials the army was composed HUME. **3.** *sb.* Tar and other combustibles 1748. Hence **Combustibi·lity, Combu·stibleness,** c. quality.

Combustion (kǫmbɒ·stiən, -tʃən). 1477. [– (O)Fr. *combustion* or late L. *combustio*, f. *combust-*, pa. ppl. stem of L. *comburere* burn up.] **1.** The action or process of burning 1600; † a conflagration –1664. Also *fig.* and *transf.* **2.** The development of light and heat, chemical combination 1477. **b.** In the obs. sense of 'combination of a body with oxygen', applied to processes of oxidation unaccompanied by evolution of light, as *internal c.*, etc. 1800. † **3.** *Path.* A burn; also, inflammation –1656. † **4.** *Astrol.* Obscuration by proximity to the sun. See COMBUST *a.* 2. –1743.

1. The c. of incense 1867. *Spontaneous c.*: see SPONTANEOUS. In spiritual invisible c. [mounts up] one authority after another CARLYLE. The inn-yard was in a sort of c. SCOTT. Hence † **Combu·stious** *a.* burning; combustible; tumultuous. So **Combu·stive** *a.* having the quality of causing c.

Come (kɒm), *v.* Pa. t. **came** (kēⁱm); pa. pple. **come** (kɒm). [OE. *cuman* = OFris. *kuma*, OS. *cuman* (Du. *komen*), OHG. *queman*, *coman* (G. *kommen*), ON. *koma*, Goth. *qiman* :– Gmc. **kweman*, **kuman.*] *gen.* An elementary intrans. vb. of motion expressing movement towards the speaker or a point where he mentally places himself, towards the person spoken to, or towards the person spoken of; opp. to *go.*

I. 1. To move towards; *esp.* to reach by moving towards; hence, To arrive. Const. with *infin.* with *to*; *vbl. sb.* with *a*; *and*; pple. in *-ing*; *advb. accus.* **2.** To move or be brought hitherward or *to* a particular position. Const. as in 1. ME. **3.** To extend, reach, to or towards ME.

1. Here comyn our enmyes CAXTON. **2.** The winde came Easterly 1633. The..arrows came thick among them DE FOE. The horse..came on his head 1804. **3.** Does the railway c. near the town (*mod.*). Phr. *To c. to an end, a point*, etc.

II. 1. To fall to one ME. **2.** To happen *to*, befall OE. **3.** To flow, be derived, descend *from, of* ME. **4.** To enter *into* 1513. **5.** To come into existence, appear ME.

1. The Papacy came to Alexander the Third 1674. **2.** All things c. alike to all *Eccles.* 9:2. A knock came to his door 1849. Phr. *To c. into one's head, to one's knowledge.* **3.** Come of gentle kin C. BRONTË. Some Mischief will c. of it BUTLER *Hud.* I. i. 758. **4.** To c. into fashion 1825, existence 1850, contact 1850, play 1850. **5.** To churn milk till butter c. 1641.

III. 1. To arrive at in due order ME.; to be present in due course ME. **2.** To reach, attain *to*, as an end 1475. **3.** To come about; to arrive, take place ME. **4.** To be brought, attain *to* ME. **5.** To become, get to be ME.; to turn out to be 1862.

1. We now c. to the reign of Queen Mary 1781. The time must c. 1833. **2.** To c. to an understanding FIELDING, to abusive words SCOTT, to blows MACAULAY. **3.** How commeth this 1548. For March, There come Violets BACON. **4.** His Sonnes c. to honour *Job* 14:21. He comes to his full Growth in a Year 1758. **5.** To 'come untied' DICKENS. Law comes rather expensive (*mod.*).

† **IV.** To become, belong *to*, befit. [L. *convenire.*] –1670.

V. Quasi-*trans.* uses. **1.** To act, to perform one's part (*colloq.*) 1812; to play (a dodge or trick), *esp.* with *over* (*colloq.*) 1785; to act the part of (*slang* or *colloq.*) 1837. **2.** To attain to, reach, achieve (*dial.* and *colloq.*) 1888. **3.** *To come* or *be coming* (now *rising*) *six*, etc.: to be in one's sixth year 1675.

1. To c. it strong 1825. To c. the religious dodge THACKERAY. To c. the bully over 1850. **2.** To c. a cropper: see CROPPER³. **3.** She is in Fole, and cometh six 1682.

VI. Spec. uses of parts of the verb.

1. *To come*, the dative infinitive, is used: **a.** *attrib.* (after sb.) = That is to come ME.; **b.** *absol.* The future 1597. **2.** *Come*, the imperative, is used: **a.** as an invitation to action, usu. along with the speaker OE.; **b.** as a call or appeal implying impatience, remonstrance, or mild protest ME. **3.** *Come*, the present conj., is used: **a.** with a future date following as subject, as in 'come Easter' *i.e.* let Easter come (*arch.* and *dial.*) ME.; **b.** with an interval of time (week, month, etc.) following and qualifying a date, as in 'at Midsummer come a year'. Now *dial.* ME. **4.** *Coming*, pres. pple., used of age: see V. 3. **b.** = 'I am coming', 'directly!' 1701.

VII. With prepositions.

1. The preposition naturally following *come* is *to*; instead of which, however, any other may follow, in which the notion *to* is contained or involved, as *into, unto, towards, against, on, upon, about, around, beside, near, above, beneath, before, behind, over, under* the point of direction; *before* a person, a tribunal, etc. Relations of other kinds may also be considered, e.g. *from* the point left, *across, along, through, by, over, under, up, down* a route followed or things passed, *with* a companion, etc., *by, in* a conveyance, *for* a thing wanted, *after* a person or thing followed or sought.

2. In specialized senses. **To c. across —.** To meet, meet with; to fall in with by chance. **To c. at —** (= L. *accedere*). † **a.** To come so as to be present *at.* † **b.** To touch or know carnally. **c.** To get at, reach (with effort), obtain. **d.** To make for, attack. **To c. by —.** To come near, to get at; hence, to obtain. **To c. into —. a.** See II. 4. † **b.** To accede to. **c.** To come into possession of. **To c. of —. a.** See. II 3. **b.** = Become of. **To c. on —** = *Come upon* (see below). **To c. over —. a.** See VII. 1. † **b.** To surpass. **c.** To take possession of (*fig.*). So *Come over with* (Shaks.). **d.** To befall. **e.** To get the better of. **To c. round —.** = *Come over* e. **To c. to —. a.** See VII. 1. **b.** To succeed in due course to. **c.** To amount to. **d.** To cost. **e.** *fig.* To mean. **f.** To turn in the end to. **g.** *Come to oneself*, etc.: To recover consciousness; to come to one's right mind. **To c. under —. a.** To rank, fall, be classed under. **b.** To be subjected to. **To c. unto —. a.** See VII. 1. † **b.** = *Come to.* **To c. upon —. a.** See VII. 1. **b.** To attack, invade. **c.** To make a demand or claim upon. **d.** To become a burden on. **e.** To meet with as it were by chance. **To c. within —.** See WITHIN.

VIII. With adverbs in specialized senses.

To c. about. a. = *Come round* b, c, d. **b.** To come to pass. † **c.** To fulfil itself *Rom. & Jul.* I. iii. 45. **To c. abroad.** To come forth from house or seclusion; to appear (*arch.*). **To c. again.** To return. **To c. along.** To move onward (toward or with the speaker). **To c. away. a.** To come on one's way; see AWAY. **b.** To come from the place; see AWAY. **c.** To detach itself; see AWAY. **d.** To grow apace. **To c. back.** To return (hither), in space or time. **To c. by.** To come near; to pass. **To c. down. a.** To descend; see DOWN *adv.* **b.** To extend downward. **c.** To fall. **d.** To be lowered. **e.** *To come down upon* —: to descend with authority, severity, hostility, or suddenness upon. **f.** *To come down* (*with*) —: to bring or put down (*esp.* money) (*colloq.*) **To c. in. a.** To enter hither, *esp.* into a house, room, land, etc. † **b.** (in *Script.*) *To come in unto*: to have carnal intercourse with. **c.** To move or advance inwards; to arrive. † **d.** *Fencing.* To get within the opponent's guard. † **e.** To submit. **f.** To be successful in a candidature; to come into power. **g.** Of things: To be brought or given in. **h.** To begin to be in season, use, or fashion; to be opportune. **i.** To take its place. **j.** To begin, as a time or season. **k.** *To come in for*: to receive incidentally. **l.** *To come in upon, on*: to enter one's mind. **To c. near.** To approach in place, order, qualities, etc.; see NEAR *adv.*² So *come nigh.* **To c. off. a.** To come away from *e.g.* a ship, a coast, etc. **b.** To become detached. **c.** To retire or extricate oneself from any engagement; as *to c. off second best*, etc. † **d.** Of things: To turn out. **e.** To take place. † **f.** To pay. **To c. on. a.** To advance hitherward. **b.** To advance in growth or development. **c.** To supervene: said of bad weather, fits of illness, etc. **d.** To come in course to be dealt with. **e.** To come upon the scene of action. **f.** *Come on!* used *esp.* as a challenge or call of defiance. **To c. out. a.** *lit.* i.e. out of a place, a house, etc. **b.** *esp.* 'out into the field', *i.e.* to fight. **c.** To leave one's employment, *e.g.* on strike. **d.** To emerge from a contest, competition, etc. **e.** To appear, as the sun, etc. **f.** To protrude. **g.** To come into public view; to become public; to be played, as a card. **h.** To result. **i.** To develop; as flowers, diseases, etc. **j.** To become evident. **k.** To be published. **l.** To show or declare oneself. **m.** To make a *début.* **n.** To make a formal entry into society. **To c. out of. a.** *lit.* To issue from. **b.** To escape. **c.** To extend out of (a place); to project or grow out of. **To c. out with.** To bring out; to utter, give vent to. **To c. over. a.** *lit.* To come, passing over; to cross. **b.** To change sides, hitherward. **To c. round. a.** To come by a circuitous route; to come in an informal way. **b.** To come with the revolution of time or events. **c.** To veer round, as the wind, to a more favourable quarter; to turn favourably in opinion. **d.** To return to a normal state or to a better mood; to recover from a swoon, etc. **To c. to. a.** = OE. *tó-cuman* to arrive; L. *advenire.* **b.** *Naut.* To come to a standstill; also, to come close to the wind. **c.** To come round to accord, or a pleasant mood. Now *dial.* **d.** To recover (from a swoon, etc.). **To c. up. a.** *lit.* To ascend; to come to a place viewed as higher, or as a centre, *e.g.* the capital or a university. **b.** To come close forward (*to*). **c.** To come right forward from the rear; esp. *to c. up with*, to overtake. **d.** To spring up, as a plant. **e.** To originate, come into use. **f.** To turn up; to arise in the mind. **g.** To amount *to*; to equal. **h.** *Naut.* To come to a direction. **i.** To slacken (a rope, cable, etc.), as in *C. up Capstan*, i.e. 'slack the Cable which you heave by'. **j.** In the imperative, a call to a horse. **k.** *Marry c. up!* see MARRY *int.*

Phrases. **C. and go. a.** To come to a place and depart again; to pass to and fro. **b.** To be first present and then absent; to approach and recede; to arrive and pass, as time, etc. *C. your ways*: see WAY *sb.* IV.

For other phrases, as *c.* AMISS, HOME, SHORT, of AGE, to ANCHOR, to BLOWS, to CLOSE QUARTERS, to GRIEF, to HAND, to HEEL, to LIFE, to LIGHT, to the FRONT, to the POINT, to TERMS, up to the MARK, to the SCRATCH, etc., see under these words.

Come (kɒm), *sb.* [OE. *cyme* :– **kumiz*, f. **kuman* (see prec.); early ME. *kime* was assim. to the verb XIII.] Approach, arrival, coming. (*Obs.* exc. in comp., as *income*, etc.) *C. and go*: passage to and fro. Also *attrib.*

Come-at-able (kɒmˌæ·tăb'l), *a. colloq.* 1687. [f. phr. *come at* + -ABLE; prob. first in the neg. *uncomeatable.*] That may be come at or reached; accessible.

Co·me-back. 1. An act of retaliation; a retort (*U.S.*) 1889. **2.** A return 1922.

Co·me-by-chance. *colloq.* 1760. One who or that which comes by chance; a bastard.

Comedian (kŏmī·diăn). 1581. [– Fr. *comédien*, f. *comédie* COMEDY.] **1.** A player in comedies; *occas.*, an actor 1601. Also *fig.* **2.** A writer of comedies 1581. Also *attrib.*

1. Are you a C.? SHAKS. var. † **Come·diant.**

‖ **Comédienne** (komedie·n). [Fr., fem. of *comédien.*] A comedy actress.

Comedietta (kŏmīdiˌe·tă). 1836. [– It., dim. of *comedia.*] A short or slight comedy.

‖ **Comedo** (kǫ·mĭdo). Pl. **-o·nes, -os, -ons.** 1866. [L. *comedo* glutton, f. *comedere* eat up.] 'A small worm-like yellowish black-tipped pasty mass which can in some persons be made, by pressure, to exude from hair follicles. They are found on the cheeks, forehead, and nose.' Also, the skin disorder in which these are found.

Come-dow·n, *sb.* 1840. [f. phr. *to come down*; see COME *v.*] A downfall; a notable reverse.

Comedy (kǫ·mĭdi). ME. [– (O)Fr. *comédie* – L. *comœdia* – Gr. κωμῳδία, f. κωμῳδός comic actor, comic poet, f. κῶμος revel.] **1.** A light and amusing stage-play, with a happy conclusion to its plot. Applied also, formerly, to narrative poems, mystery plays, and interludes, with a happy ending. **2.** That branch of the drama which adopts a humorous or familiar style, and depicts laughable characters and incidents. (Occas. *personified.*) ME. *fig.* of incidents, etc. in real life 1570. Also *attrib.*

1. Mr. William Shakespeares Comedies, Histories, & Tragedies (*title*) 1623. **2.** Persons, such as c. would choose. When she would shew an image of the times, And sport with human follies, not with crimes B. JONS. *fig.* The great human c. MORLEY.

Comeliness (kɒ·mlinės). ME. [f. COMELY *a.* + -NESS.] The quality of being COMELY.

Hee hath no forme nor comelinesse *Isa.* 53:2. Things. .which a Man cannot, with any Face or Comelines, say or doe Himselfe BACON.

Comeling (kɒ·mliŋ). *arch.* and *dial.* [ME., repr. OE. **cumeling*, f. COME + -LING¹.] An immigrant, not a permanent resident; also † a novice.

These new comelings began to molest the homelings 1577.

Comely (kɒ·mli), *a.* [ME. *cumelich, cumli*, prob. aphet. of † *becumelich* (XII), f. BECOME + -LY¹; cf. MHG. *komlich* suitable (beside *bekōme* suitably; G. dial. *kommlich, kömmlich*), Du. † *komlick* fitting.] **1.** Fair, pretty, beautiful, nice. (As used of persons, it implies a homelier style of beauty, which pleases without exciting admiration.) **2.** Pleasing to the moral sense or æsthetic taste; becoming, proper, decorous ME.

1. Comly apparell 1535. Civil-suited Morn. . Cherchef't in a comly Cloud MILT. *Pens.* 125. No comlyar creatur of goddes creacyon 1485. Rather c. than beautiful GAY. **2.** Prayse is c. for the vpright *Ps.* 33:1. Marching home In c. order POPE. Hence **Co·melily** *adv.* ? *Obs.* † **Co·mely** *adv.*

Come-o·ff, *sb.* 1634. [f. phr. *to come off*; see COME *v.*] **1.** A finish-up, a conclusion. **2.** An evasion, excuse for non-performance 1849.

Comer (kɒ·məɹ). ME. [f. COME *v.* + -ER¹.] **1.** One who comes; a visitor, an arrival. Often qualified, as *first c.*, NEW-COMER, etc. † **2.** Of a plant: A grower. BACON.

1. *All comers*: everybody or anybody that comes.

‖ **Comes.** 1683. [L., = companion, comrade, f. *com* COM- + *ire, it-* go.] **a.** *Eccl. Antiq.* A book containing the epistles and gospels read at mass. **b.** *Mus.* The answer to the first subject (*dux*) in a fugue.

† **Comessation.** ME. [– L. *comessatio* (better, *comissatio*) Bacchanalian revel, whence also OFr. *comessacion.*] **1.** Feasting, 'riotous eating' –1642. **2.** Eating together –1686.

Comestible (kǫ̆me·stib'l). 1483. [– (O)Fr. *comestible* – med.L. *comestibilis* (Isidore), f. *comest-*, pa. ppl. stem of L. *comedere* eat up, f. *com* COM- + *edere* eat; see -IBLE.] † *adj.* Fit to eat, edible –1683. *sb.* Anything to eat; *pl.* eatables. (Usually *joc.*) 1837.

1. All the metes of therthe that ben c. CAXTON. So † **Come·stion,** eating; also *fig.* of fire.

Comet (kǫ·mėt). ME. [– (O)Fr. *comète* – L. *cometa* – Gr. κομήτης long-haired, sb. comet (for ἀστὴρ κομήτης 'long-haired star').] **1.** A celestial body moving about the sun in an elongated elliptical, or a parabolic orbit, and consisting (when near the sun) of a star-like nucleus surrounded with misty light, and a train of light or 'tail'. Also *fig.* † **2.** A card-game –1742. **3.** = *Cometes*, a genus of Humming-birds with long tails 1862.

1. *fig.* The grave of him who blazed The c. of a season BYRON. *Comb.*: **c.-finder, -seeker,** a telescope of low power and large field, used in searching for comets; **-wine,** wine made in a c.-year, reputed to have superior flavour; **-year,** one in which a notable c. has appeared.

Hence **Cometa·rium,** a contrivance for illustrating motion in an eccentric orbit. **Co·metary** *a.* pertaining to a c. or comets; c.-like. **Come·tic, -al,** *a.* cometary; *fig.* blazing, portentous, erratic. **Cometo·grapher,** one who describes comets. **Cometo·graphy,** that part of astronomy which treats of comets. **Cometo·logy.** (Dicts.)

Comfit (kɒ·mfit), *sb.* [ME. *confyt* – OFr. *confit, confite* :– L. *confectum, confecta,* subst. uses of n. and fem. of *confectus*, pa. pple. of *conficere* prepare; see CONFECTION.] A sweetmeat made of some fruit, root, etc., preserved with sugar; a sugar-plum. Hence † **Co·mfit** *v.* to preserve, to pickle; *esp.* to make into a c.

Comfiture (kɒ·mfitiŭɹ). ? *Obs.* ME. [– (O)Fr. *confiture*, f. *confit* (see COMFIT) + *-ure* -URE.] † **1.** A preparation of drugs. CHAUCER. **2.** A preserve, confection 1558.

Comfort (kɒ·mfəɹt), *v.* ME. [– OFr. *conforter* – late L. *confortare* strengthen, f. *com* COM- + *fortis* strong.] † **1.** To strengthen; to encourage; to support; to invigorate –1674. † **2.** To aid, abet, countenance. (Formerly common in legal use.) –1726. † **3.** To cheer –1612; to relieve –1798. **4.** To soothe in grief or trouble; to console. (The current sense.) ME. *pass.*, also † *intr.* (for *refl.*) To take comfort ME. **5.** To make comfortable (*mod.*).

1. Wynges, to c. the bataylles, if nede requyred LD. BERNERS. To c. the memory LYTE, the braine 1637, the stomach 1671. **2.** Guilty of comforting and assisting the Rebels AYLIFFE. **3.** A mynstral. .alle peuple to comfortye LANGL. To c. the poor 1529. **4.** To c. the afflicted state of Christians 1641. *intr.* Liue a little, c. a little, cheere thy selfe a little *A.Y.L.* II. vi. 5. **5.** A comforting beverage (*mod.*).

Comfort (kɒ·mfəɹt), *sb.* ME. [– OFr. *confort* – Rom. sb. f. late L. *confortare*; see prec.] † 1. Strengthening; encouragement; aid, support, countenance. (*Obs.* exc. in legal phr. *aid and c.*) –1769. † *concr.* A support –1577. † 2. Pleasure, delight –1568; relief or aid in want, etc. –1647. 3. Consolation, solace ME.; the production of content and restfulness (*mod.*); a source or means of comfort ME.; a comforting fact or reflection 1553. 4. The condition or quality of being COMFORTABLE 1814. 5. A thing that ministers to enjoyment and content. (Usu. *pl.*; opp. to *necessaries*, and *luxuries*.) 1659. 6. A quilted coverlet 1863. † 7. As an interjection; = Take comfort. SHAKS.

1. That we may receiue the fruites of the yearth to our comforte *Bk. Com. Prayer. concr.* Oure confort and Defender 1455. 3. None else there is gives c. to my griefe DRAYTON. When other helpers fail and comforts flee 1847. Nobody..can lose a penny by me—that is one c. SCOTT. 4. In peace and c. WORDSW. 5. *Creature comforts*: food, etc. So *home comforts*. 7. *Wint. T.* IV. iv. 848. Hence **Co·mfortful** *a.* full of c. **Co·mfortless** *a.*, **-ly** *adv.*, **-ness.**

Comfortable (kɒ·mfəɹtăb'l), *a.* (*sb.*) ME. [– AFr. *confortable* (mod.Fr. is – Eng.), f. *conforter*; see COMFORT *v.*, -ABLE.]

A. *adj.* I. 1. Strengthening or supporting (*arch.*) ME.; † helpful –1725. † 2. Affording pleasure or delight –1748; satisfactory; tolerable (*colloq.*) –1728. 3. Consolatory: of persons (*obs.*) or things (*arch.*) ME. 4. Affording or fitted to give tranquil enjoyment and content. (This and II. 2 are the current senses.) 1769. Also *absol.*

1. The c. expectation of Immortality BERKELEY. This c. cordial 1744. 2. The c. Sense of his [God's] Presence HARTLEY. His [the boy's] Skull seems to be of a c. thickness 1728. 3. For heauens sake speake c. words SHAKS. 4. In c. circumstances (*mod.*).

II. With pass. or neut. sense. † 1. In a state of consolation; cheerful –1755. 2. Free from pain and trouble; at ease 1770; *colloq.* of persons, placidly self-satisfied 1856.

1. His c. temper forsook him *Timon* III. iv. 71. 2. Let it freeze without, we are c. within SCOTT. A motherly c. woman 1878.

B. *sb.* † 1. That which gives comfort; *pl.* comforts –1675. 2. a. A worsted covering for the wrist. b. A COMFORTER for the neck. c. (*U.S.*) = COMFORT *sb.* 6. 1835.

Hence **Co·mfortableness**, the state of being c. **Co·mfortably** *adv.* in a c. manner.

† **Comforta·tion.** Also **con-**. ME. [– OFr. *confortacion* (mod. *-tion*) – late L. *confortatio* strengthening; see COMFORT *v.*, -ATION.] Comforting; delight –1485; strengthening –1626.

† **Comfortative,** *a.* and *sb.* [ME. *con-*, – OFr. *confortatif, -ive* in same sense, – late L. *confortativus*; see COMFORT *v.*, -ATIVE.] *adj.* Having the quality of comforting –1683. *sb.* A cordial. Also *fig.* –1742. var. † **Co·mfortive.**

Comforter (kɒ·mfəɹtəɹ). ME. [– AFr. *confortour* = OFr. *conforteör*; see COMFORT *v.*, -OUR, -ER[2]. As a title of the Holy Ghost tr. eccl.L. *consolator* (Jerome, Augustine), rendering Gr. παράκλητος (in Vulg. *paraclitus*) PARACLETE.] 1. One who or that which comforts or consoles. In *Theol.* the Holy Spirit. † 2. A small kind of spaniel –1790. † 3. One who aids, countenances, or abets. (Chiefly legal.) –1570. 4. A long woollen scarf worn round the throat 1833. b. = COMFORT *sb.* 6. (*U.S.*) 5. A baby's dummy teat 1898.

1. The doctor is the best of comforters FIELDING. WYCLIF *John* 14:16. See also JOB *sb.*[3]

Co·mfortress. *rare.* ME. [– OFr. *conforteresse*, fem. of *conforteère* comforter; see -ESS[1].] A female comforter.

Comfrey (kɒ·mfri, kǫ·m-). ME. [– AFr. *cumfirie*, OFr. *confire, confiere* (mod. dial. *confier*, etc.), with var. *confierge* :– med.L. **confervia*, for L. *conferva*, f. *confervēre* intr. heal, prop. boil together.] The Eng. name of *Symphytum officinale* (N.O. *Boraginaceæ*), a tall plant, with rough leaves; formerly esteemed as a vulnerary. Also applied to other plants.

Comfy (kɒ·mfi), *a.* 1829. *colloq.* (orig. infantile or feminine). = COMFORTABLE.

Comic (kǫ·mik). 1576. [– L. *comicus* – Gr. κωμικός, f. κῶμος; see COMEDY, -IC.]

A. *adj.* 1. Of, proper, or belonging to comedy, as dist. from tragedy. 2. Burlesque, funny 1839. 3. = COMICAL 4. 1751.

1. C. opera is the opera of comedy, not 'comic' in the vulgar English sense 1878.

B. *sb.* † 1. = COMEDIAN 1, 2. –1738. 2. *colloq.* = *c. paper* 1889. 3. quasi-*sb.* *The c.*: that which is c. 1842.

Comical (kǫ·mikăl), *a.* 1557. [f. as prec. + -AL[1]; see -ICAL.] † 1. = COMIC 1. –1725. † 2. Trivial, low; opp. to *tragical*, or *elevated* –1687. † 3. Like the ending of a comedy; fortunate. (Opp. to *tragical.*) –1677. 4. Mirth - provoking, humorous; ludicrous, laughable. (The ordinary sense.) 1685. 5. Queer (*colloq.* and *dial.*) 1793.

1. One Plautus, a comicall poet 1577. 3. But Comicall was the end of Job FULLER. 4. But the dog [S. Foote] was so very c., that I was obliged to..laugh it out JOHNSON. Hence **Comica·lity,** c. or comic quality. **Co·mical-ly** *adv.*, **-ness.**

‖ **Comices,** *sb. pl. rare.* 1533. [Fr. – L. *comitia* (cf. *notice*, etc.).] = COMITIA 1.

Comico- (kǫ·miko), comb. f. L. *comicus*, Gr. κωμικός.

Co·micry. *rare.* 1850. [f. COMIC + -RY.] Comic action or practice.

Coming (kɒ·miŋ), *vbl. sb.* ME. [f. COME *v.* -ING[1].] 1. The action of the vb. COME: drawing near; arrival, advent. † 2. Access –1715. **Coming in.** a. Entrance, commencement, etc. 1586. † b. A means of entrance –1719. c. *pl.* Revenues, receipts; income 1599.

Co·ming, *ppl. a.* 1460. [f. as prec. + -ING[2].] 1. Approaching in space or time. 2. Inclined to make or meet advances; forward 1600.

1. The comming morne *Mids. N.* V. i. 372. Indications of a c. storm MACAULAY. 2. Sometimes c., sometimes coy SEDLEY.

Comintern (kǫ·mintəɹn). 1925. [Russ.] The international organization, 1919–1943, of the Communist Party.

Comitadji (kǫmitæ·dʒi). 1903. [– Fr. *comitadji* – Common Balkan f. Turk. *komita* – Fr. *comité* COMMITTEE + *-ji*.] A band of irregular soldiers.

‖ **Comitatus** (kǫmitē̆i·tɒ̆s). 1875. [L., collective deriv. of *comes, comit-*, companion.] 1. A body of *comites*; a retinue of warriors or nobles attached to the person of a king or chieftain. 2. An (English) county, as in *posse comitatus*, q.v.

‖ **Comitia** (kǫ̆mi·ʃiă), *sb. pl.* 1625. [L., pl. of *comitium*, f. *com* COM- + *-itium*, noun of action f. *it-, ire* go.] 1. *Rom. Antiq.* An assembly of the Roman people for electing magistrates and passing laws. Formerly COMICES. 2. An assembly (*rare*) 1625. 3. A name formerly given to the Encænia at Oxford 1714.

Comitial (kǫmi·fiăl), *a.* 1533. [– L. *comitialis*, f. prec.; see -AL[1].] Of or pertaining to the Roman comitia, or to some modern assemblies.

Comity (kǫ·miti). 1543. [– L. *comitas*, f. *comis* courteous; see -ITY.] Courtesy, civility, urbanity; kindly and considerate behaviour towards others, as *c. of manner*, etc.

Comity of nations: a. The courteous and friendly understanding by which each nation respects the laws and usages of every other, so far as may be without prejudice to its own rights and interests. b. *erron.* The company of nations mutually practising this.

Comma (kǫ·mă). Pl. **commas** (formerly **-aes**); as L. or Gr. **commata** (kǫ·mătă). 1586. [– L. *comma* – Gr. κόμμα piece cut off, short clause.] 1. In *Gr. Rhet.* and *Pros.*: A group of words less than a colon (q.v.). Hence † A short member of a period. 2. A punctuation-mark [now,] used to separate the smallest members of a sentence. (Often erron. said to be the mark of a short pause.) 1589. *fig.* = Break, pause 1602. 3. *Mus.* A minute interval or difference of pitch 1597. 4. One of the quotation-marks now called *inverted* commas 1705.

C. (*butterfly*): a butterfly (*Grapta comma album*) with a white c.-shaped mark on the underside of the wing. *C.* (*bacillus*): a bacillus of curved shape, said to be present in cholera.

Command (kǫ̆ma·nd), *v.* [– AFr. *com(m)a(u)nde* – AFr. *comaunder* (mod. *comm-*) :– late L. *commandare*, f. *com* COM- + *mandare* commit, enjoin.] 1. To order, enjoin, bid with authority or influence. (For const. see quots.). Also *fig.* of things. *absol.* ME. 2. To order to come or go *to, from, into, upon, away, here, home*, etc. ME. *fig.* To cause to come 1611. † 3. To demand with authority; occas. with *of* or *from* –1786. 4. *trans.* To have authority over; to be master of; to sway, rule ME. Also *fig. absol.* To have the command 1601. 5. To have at one's call or disposal 1561. 6. To exact, compel (respect, etc.) 1591. 7. To dominate; to control; *spec.* said of the artillery of a fortified eminence 1603; to overlook 1697. † 8. = COMMEND –1530.

1. C. mee any seruice to the world's end *Much Ado* II. i. 271. The Scriptures we are commanded to search A.V. *Transl. Pref.* If you can c. these Elements to silence *Temp.* I. i. 23. Iacob had made an end of commanding his sonnes *Gen.* 49:33. The rule of life which religion commands FROUDE. He..commanded Paul to be brought *Acts* 25:6. *absol.* Man to c., and woman to obey TENNYSON. 2. To c. them off DE FOE. *fig.* I will c. my blessing vpon you *Lev.* 25:21. 3. *Cymb.* I. v. 9. 4. The haughty Dane commands the narrow Seas MARLOWE. *absol.* Born to c. 1799. To c. his old soldiers 1848. To c. oneself 1706. 5. 'Tis not in mortals to c. success ADDISON. It is not every day I can c. that sum BURKE. C. me while I liue *Two Gent.* III. i. 23. Phr. *Yours to c.* 6. She..must..c. your sympathy 1802. 7. The vantage ground of Truth: a hill not to be commanded BACON. A Window commanding a very lovely view RUSKIN. Phr. *To c. a suit of cards* (mod.). 8. Phr. *To c. to God.*

Command (kǫ̆ma·nd), *sb.* 1552. [f. prec.] 1. The act of commanding; bidding 1591. 2. A COMMANDMENT 1552. 3. The faculty of commanding; rule, control, sway. Also *fig.* 1593. 4. Power of control; mastery; possession with full power to use 1642. 5. Coercion 1692. 6. The power of dominating surrounding country 1628; range of vision 1697. 7. A position in which one commands; *e.g.* a naval commander's post. 8. The body of troops or district under a commander 1592.

1. Doeth the Eagle mount vp at thy commaund *Job* 39:27. 3. High c. Spake in his eyes BYRON. [To] have the c. of a ship PEPYS. 4. Phr. *C. of language, words*, etc. *At c.*: ready to receive or obey orders; available to use, spend, etc. 6. His c. of the passes of the Alps FREEMAN. 7. District Commands (Home) Aldershot 1886. 8. Colonel Dodge ordered the c. to halt 1841. The city of Paris is to be divided into four commands 1871.

Comb.: **c.-in-chief,** supreme military c.; **-night,** the nights on which something is performed by (royal) c.

Comma·ndable, *a.* 1646. [f. COMMAND *v.* + -ABLE.] Capable of being commanded.

Commandant (kǫmănda·nt), *sb.* 1687. [– Fr. *commandant*, or It., Sp. *-ante*; see -ANT.] A commanding officer: irrespective of rank. Applied often as a foreign title, as *the c. from Seville.* Hence **Commanda·ntship.**

† **Comma·ndatory,** *a.* 1659. [f. *commandat-*, pa. ppl. stem of late L. *commandare* COMMAND + -ORY[2].] Mandatory –1670.

‖ **Commandee·r,** *v.* 1881. [– S.Afr.Du. *kommanderen* – Fr. *commander.*] To command for (or as for) military service. Also *fig.* and *gen.*

Commander (kǫ̆ma·ndəɹ). ME. [– OFr. *comandere, -eör*, AFr. *-dour* (mod. *-deur*) :– Rom. **commandator, -ato·r-*; see -ER[2].] 1. One who commands, or has the disposal *of*; one who exercises authority, a leader. 2. *spec.* The officer in command of a military force 1598. b. In the *Navy*: An officer who ranks above a first lieutenant 1450. 3. The administrator of a COMMANDERY, a COMMENDATORY 1611. 4. Hence, a member of a higher class in certain Orders of Knighthood 1846. 5. A large wooden mallet or beetle 1573. † 6. *Surg.* = AMBE –1783.

1. King and C. of our Common-weale *Tit. A.* I. ii. 247. *C. of the Faithful* (cf. ADMIRAL): a title of the caliphs, first assumed (*c* 640) by Omar I. 2. **Commander-in-chief.** The supreme commander of all the military land forces of a State. b. In U.S. vested in the President. c. In the *Navy*: The senior officer in any port or station holding command over all other vessels within assigned limits. Hence **Comma·ndership,** the office or position of c.

Commandery, -dry (kǫ̆ma·ndəri, -a·ndri). 1534. [– Fr. *commanderie*, f. *commander*; see COMMAND *v.*, -ERY.] † 1. A benefice held *in commendam* –1807. 2. *esp.* in *Hist.* An estate or a manor belonging to an Order of Knights, and placed under the charge of one of them (with title of *commendator*, COMMANDER 3).

1534. **b.** *Occas.* applied to the buildings 1712. **3.** The rank of a Commander in an order of Knighthood 1611. † **4.** The office of a commander –1630. † **5.** A district under a commander –1813.

2 b. The C. here..is a fine old House of Timber, in the Form of a Court DE FOE.

Commanding (kǫ̆ma·ndiŋ), *ppl. a.* 1483. [f. COMMAND *v.* + -ING².] **1.** *gen.* Possessing or exercising command, ruling, controlling. **2.** Indicating or expressing command 1591. **3.** Dominating by height or position; having a wide outlook 1634.

1. C. ship 1758, officer 1796. **2.** The majesty of c. beauty MASSINGER. **3.** A high and c. turret 1634. C. views in literature EMERSON. Hence **Comma·nding-ly** *adv.*, **-ness** (*rare*).

‖ **Commandite** (komãndi·t). 1844. [Fr., f. *commander* in sense to entrust.] 'A company to which persons advance capital without assuming the functions of partner, or incurring any responsibility' (Littré).

Commandment (kǫ̆ma·ndmĕnt). [ME. *com(m)a(u)ndement* (4 syll.) – OFr. *comandement* (mod. *comm-*), f. *comander* COMMAND; see -MENT.] **1.** An authoritative order or injunction; a precept (*arch.*). **2.** *esp.* A divine command ME. *spec.* (*pl.*) The *Ten Commandments* of the Mosaic Decalogue ME. Also used allusively 1577. **3.** slang. *The ten commandments*: the ten finger-nails (*esp.* of a woman) 1540. † **4.** The action or fact of commanding; bidding –1676. † **5.** Authority, control; military command –1641. † **6.** *Old Law.* 'The offence of inducing another to transgress the law' –1641.

1. To the contrary I haue expresse c. *Wint. T.* II. ii. 8. **2.** A newe commaundement geve I vnto you TINDALE *John* 13:34. 2 *Hen. VI*, I. iii. 145. **5.** Haue I commandement on the pulse of life *John* IV. ii. 92.

‖ **Commando** (kǫ̆ma·ndo). *S. Afr.* 1834. [– Pg. *commando*, f. *commandar* COMMAND *v.*] A party called out for military purposes; a (quasi-military) expedition (*esp.* of the Boers) against the natives.

Commandress (kǫ̆ma·ndrĕs). 1592. [f. COMMANDER + -ESS¹.] A female commander. Also *fig.*

Commandrie, -ry, vars. of COMMANDERY.

† **Commark.** *rare.* 1612. [– Sp. *comarca* – med.L. *commarca, -cia, -cha*, f. *com* COM- + *marca* MARCH *sb.*³] Border-country –1654.

Commata, L. and Gr. pl. of COMMA.

† **Commate·rial,** *a.* [See COM-.] Identical in material. BACON.

Commatic (kǫ̆mæ·tik), *a. rare.* 1844. [– late L. *commaticus* – Gr. κομματικός consisting of short clauses, f. κόμμα, -ματ- comma; see -IC.] Consisting of short clauses or lyric measures. So **Co·mmatism,** c. character.

Commea·surable, *a.* = COMMENSURABLE.

Commeasure (kǫ̆me·ʒ'ŭɹ), *v.* 1614. [See COM-.] To equal in measure or extent.

Until..the full-grown will, Circled thro' all experiences..C. perfect freedom TENNYSON.

Commeate (kǫ·mi,eⁱt), *v.* ? *Obs.* 1655. [– *commeat-*, pa. ppl. stem of L. *commeare* go, pass to and fro, f. *com* COM- + *meare* go; see -ATE³.] *intr.* To pass to and fro, penetrate in all directions.

‖ **Comme il faut** (kǫm il fǭᵘ), *adj. phr.* 1756. [Fr.] As it should be, proper.

Commemorate (kǫ̆me·mŏreⁱt), *v.* 1599. [– *commemorat-*, pa. ppl. stem of L. *commemorare*, f. *com* COM- + *memorare* relate, f. *memor* (see MEMORY).] **1.** *trans.* † **a.** To make mention of or rehearse. **b.** To mention as worthy of remembrance; to celebrate in speech or writing. **2.** To call to remembrance by some solemnity or celebration 1638. **3.** Of things: To be a memorial of 1766.

1. The..Tempter did c. unto her..the Prohibition 1693. **2.** We are called upon to c. a revolution ..happy in its consequences ATTERBURY. **3.** Dates, which c. events D'ISRAELI. Hence **Comme·morative** *a.* having the attribute of commemorating; also as *sb.* **Comme·morator** (*rare*), one who commemorates. **Comme·morato·ry** *a.* (*rare*), commemorative.

Commemoration (kǫ̆me:mŏrēⁱ·ʃən). ME. [– (O)Fr. *commemoration* or L. *commemoratio*; see prec., -ION.] **1.** † **a.** Recital, mention –1631. **b.** Eulogistic mention 1823. **2.** A calling to remembrance by some solemnity or celebration ME. **b.** A service, or a prayer, in memory of a saint or of a sacred event ME. **c.** At Oxford, an annual celebration in memory of the Founders and Benefactors 1750.

1. b. Yet there were several [names] worth c. BYRON. **2.** To celebrate the c. of the most glorious death of thy Son *Bk. Com. Prayer*. The c. of the Martyrdom of King Charles Ist 1779.

Commence (kǫ̆me·ns), *v.* [ME. *comence* – OFr. *com(m)encier* (mod. *commencer*) :– Rom. **cominitiare*, f. *com* COM- + L. *initiare* INITIATE.] **1.** *trans.* To begin, enter upon. **2.** *intr.* with *infin.* To begin *to do* ME. **3.** *intr.* To make a start ME.; to begin to be; to start as (*arch.*) 1642. **4.** [tr. med.L. *incipere.*] To take a full degree *in* any faculty at a university ME. Also *transf.* and *fig.*

1. Commencing with the Sun his Toil 1696. Phr. *To c. an action, a suit, proceedings*, etc. **2.** And comenced to loue hir anonright ME. **3.** Here the anthem doth c. SHAKS. The time..when pig is to c. bacon SOUTHEY. **4.** He..that hath comensid in art WYCLIF. This is mi year to commens master of art G. HARVEY. Hence **Comme·nceable** *a.* that can commence (sense 4) or be commenced. **Comme·ncer,** one who commences. (*Obs.* in sense 4 of the verb.)

Commencement (kǫ̆me·nsmĕnt). Earlier **com-.** ME. [– (O)Fr. *commencement*; see prec., -MENT.] **1.** The action or process of commencing; beginning; time of beginning. **2.** The action of taking a full degree; *esp.* at Cambridge, Dublin, etc., the great ceremony when these are conferred ME. Also *transf.* and *fig.*

1. The Origin and Commencement of this greefe *Haml.* III. i. 185.

Commend (kǫ̆me·nd), *v.* ME. [– L. *commendare*, f. *com* COM- + *mandare* commit, entrust; cf. COMMAND *v.*, MANDATE.] **1.** To give in trust or charge; to commit. **2.** To present as worthy of acceptance or regard; to direct attention to, as worthy of notice; to RECOMMEND ME. **3.** *gen.* To praise ME. Also *absol.* † **4.** To set off; to adorn or grace –1644. **5.** To recommend to kindly remembrance (now *arch.*) 1463. **6.** *Eccl.* To bestow *in commendam.* Also *absol.* 1616. **7.** *Hist.* To place under the protection of a feudal lord 1867.

1. To her white hand see thou do c. This seal'd vp counsaile *L.L.L.* III. i. 169. I comende you my wyfe..& my children CAXTON. **2.** Harts-ease..is commended for a rupture COGAN. I c. vnto you Phebe our sister *Rom.* 16:1. **3.** C. it, or come and mend it 1634. **4.** What..more commendeth a woman than constancie LYLY. Phr. *C. me (us) to*: = 'give me by choice'. Orig. of a person. Hence **Comme·nder.** † **Comme·ndment.**

† **Comme·nd,** *sb.* 1470. [– Fr. *commende* (in sense 1), and from prec.] **1.** *Eccl.* = COMMENDAM 1. *Sc.* –1513. **2.** Commendation –1608. **3.** A greeting, remembrance –1645.

2. Speak in his just c. *Per.* II. ii. 49. **3.** Tell her I send to her my kind commends *Rich. II*, III. i. 38.

Commendable (kǫ̆me·ndăb'l), *a.* ME. [– (O)Fr. *commendable* – L. *commendabilis*; see COMMEND *v.*, -ABLE.] **1.** Proper to be commended, laudable. † **2.** Commendatory 1576. Hence **Comme·ndableness. Comme·ndably** *adv.*

‖ **Commendado·r.** 1580. [Sp. *comendador.*] A commander.

Commendam (kǫ̆me·ndæm). 1563. [acc. sing. of eccl. L. *commenda* – L. *commendare* COMMEND *v.*, in phr. *dare in commendam*, to give (*sc.* a benefice) in charge or trust.] **1.** In the phrase *in commendam*: used of the tenure of a benefice 'commended' or given in charge to a clerk or layman to hold with enjoyment of the revenues until an incumbent was provided or for life. (Abolished in England in 1836.) Also *transf.* 1658. **2.** As English *sb.* (with *pl.*) The tenure of a benefice held as above 1563; the benefice or office so held 1607.

Comme·ndatary. 1539. [– med.L. *commendatarius* (in same senses), f. *commendat-*, pa. ppl. stem of L. *commendare*; see COMMEND *v.*, -ARY¹.] **1.** *adj.* = COMMENDATORY 2. **2.** *sb.* **a.** *Eccl.* A commendator. **b.** *gen.* A commissioner.

Commendation (kǫmĕndēⁱ·ʃən). ME. [Earliest in liturgical use, – (O)Fr. *commendation* – L. *commendatio*, f. as prec. + *-io* -ION.] **1.** The action of COMMENDING; † giving in charge 1583; approval, recommendation ME. **2.** (gen. in *pl.*) Remembrances sent to those at a distance; respects, greetings (*arch.*) 1529. † **3.** A thing that recommends –1697. **4.** *Liturg.* (gen. in *pl.*) An office commending the souls of the dead to God ME. **5.** *Feudal Law.* The cession by a freeman of himself and his lands to the protection of a feudal lord 1818. **6.** *Eccl.* The giving of benefices *in commendam* 1883.

1. You haue deseru'd High c. *A.Y.L.* I. ii. 275. This letter of owre c. EDEN. **2.** Aftyr my moste herty commendacions WOLSEY. **3.** Good-nature is the most godlike c. of a man DRYDEN.

Commendator (kǫ̆·mĕndēⁱtəɹ). 1561. [– L. *commendator* one who commends, in med.L. as in senses 1 and 2; f. as prec.; see -OR 2.] **1.** One who holds a benefice *in commendam* 1561. † **2.** The president of a COMMANDERY –1688. **3.** = COMMENDADOR 1583.

Commendatory (kǫ̆me·ndătəri). 1555. [– late L. *commendatorius*, f. L. *commendator*; see prec., -ORY².]

A. *adj.* **1.** Having the attribute of commending or recommending. **2.** Holding a benefice *in commendam* 1682. **3.** Pertaining to feudal commendation 1867.

1. *C. letters* 1555. *C. prayer*: one commending a dying person to God's mercy. **2.** C. abbots BURKE.

B. *sb.* † **1.** A commendatory fact or word –1716. † **2.** A knight-commander –1762. † **3.** One who holds a benefice *in commendam* –1726. † **4.** = COMMANDERY –1762.

1. A sufficient evidence and c. of his own piety MILT.

†‖ **Comme·ndum.** = COMMENDAM 2.

Commensal (kǫ̆me·nsăl). ME. [– Fr. *commensal* or its source med.L. *commensalis*, f. *com-* COM- + *mensa* table; see -AL¹.]

A. *adj.* **1.** Eating at the same table. **2.** *Biol.* Applied to animals or plants which live as tenants of others and share their food (dist. from *parasitic*) 1877.

B. *sb.* **1.** A messmate 1460. **2.** *Biol.* A commensal animal or plant 1872. Hence **Comme·nsalism,** a c. condition. **Commensa·lity,** c. state. So † **Commensa·tion,** eating at the same table. SIR T. BROWNE.

Commensurable (kǫ̆me·nsiŭrăb'l, -ʃŭr-), *a.* (*sb.*) 1557. [– late L. *commensurabilis* (Boethius), f. *com* COM- + *mensurabilis* MEASURABLE; cf. Fr. *commensurable.*] **1.** Having, or reducible to, a common measure; measurable by the same standard. **2.** Proportionable in measure, etc.; proportionate *to* 1645. † **3.** Measurable (*by* something) –1660. Also as *sb.*

1. Mind is not c. with Space DOVE. Hence **Comme:nsurabi·lity,** c. quality. **Comme·nsurableness,** c. quality or state. **Comme·nsurably** *adv.*

Commensurate (kǫ̆me·nsiŭrĕt, -ʃŭr-), *a.* 1641. [– late L. *commensuratus* (Boethius), f. *com* COM- + *mensuratus* pa. pple. of *mensurare*; see MEASURE *v.*, -ATE².] **1.** Having the same measure; coextensive. Const. *with*, † *to.* **2.** Of corresponding extent or degree; proportionate, adequate. Const. *to*, *with.* 1649. † **3.** Corresponding in nature (*with, to*) –1678. **4.** = COMMENSURABLE 1 (*rare*) 1690.

1. Matter and gravity are always c. BENTLEY. **2.** You know how it can act when its power is c. to its will BURKE. Hence **Comme·nsurate-ly** *adv.*, **-ness.**

† **Commensurate** (kǫ̆me·nsiŭreⁱt, -ʃŭr-), *v.* 1643. [f. prec.; see -ATE³.] **1.** *intr.* To agree or square *with* (*rare*). **2.** *trans.* To make commensurate, to proportion –1711. **3.** To reduce to a measure or standard; to define the extent of –1660.

Commensuration (kǫ̆me:nsiŭrēⁱ·ʃən, -ʃŭr-). Now *rare.* 1526. [In sense 3 – late L. *commensuratio* (Boethius), f. as prec. + *-io* -ION; senses 1, 2 app. f. COM- + MENSURATION.] **1.** The measuring of things against each other. † **2.** Measurement –1682. **3.** The action of proportioning, or fact of being proportioned; proportion 1626.

3. A c. or proportion between the Body moved, and the force BACON.

Comment (kǫ·ment), *sb.* ME. [– L. *commentum* invention, contrivance, (in Isidore) interpretation, comment, f. *comment-*, pa. ppl. stem of *comminisci* devise, contrive; see next.] † **1.** An exposition; a commentary –1877. **2.** A remark or note in explanation or criticism of a literary passage; an annotation 1509. Also *collect.* and *fig.* 1589. **3.** The action of commenting; criticism 1847.

1. This tretys..this lytil coment 1475. 2. Some Comments clear not, but increase the doubt CLEVELAND. *fig.* Some adopted the c., others stuck to the text BURKE.

Comment (kǫ·ment, kǒme·nt), *v.* 1450. [f. prec., or Fr. *commenter*; in sense 1, – med.L. *commentare*, L. *-ari*, devise, invent, frequent. of L. *comminisci* (see prec.).] † **1.** *trans.* To devise, invent (*esp.* in a bad sense) –1596. **2.** *trans.* To furnish with comments; to annotate (*arch.*) 1599. **3.** *intr.* To write explanatory or critical notes (*on, upon*) 1611. **4.** To make (unfavourable) comments (*on, upon*) 1591. † **5.** To ponder –1602.

1. SPENSER *F.Q.* VII. vii. 53. 2. To c. an author JOHNSON. 4. Not an eye that sees you, but is a Physician to c. on your Malady *Two Gent.* II. i. 42. 5. *Rich. III*, IV. iii. 51.

Co·mmentaried, *ppl. a. rare.* [f. COMMENTARY *sb.* or *v.* + -ED.] Chronicled; annotated. G. DANIEL.

Commentary (kǫ·mĕntări). 1531. [– L. *commentarius, -arium* adj. used subst. (sc. *liber* book, *volumen* volume), f. *commentari*; see COMMENT *v.*] † **1.** A note-book (*rare*) –1538. **2.** A memoir; in *pl.* memoirs, historical records (less formal than a *history*). (Chiefly *Hist.*) 1538. **3.** A treatise consisting of a series of comments on a text 1538; also *transf.* and *fig.*

2. Cesars Commentaries 1547. 3. The commentaryes of Auicen and Aueroyes BALE. 3. *fig.* A just Pronunciation is a good C. 1748.

Commentate (kǫ·mĕnteᶦt), *v. rare.* 1794. [app. back-formation from COMMENTATOR.] **1.** *trans.* = COMMENT *v.* 2. **2.** *intr.* = COMMENT *v.* 3–5. 1859.

Commentation (kǫmĕntē·ʃən). 1579. [– L. *commentatio*, f. *commentat-*, pa. ppl. stem of *commentari*; see COMMENT *v.*, -ION. For sense cf. *comment, commentary*, etc.] † **1.** A comment; a commentary –1712. † **2.** Invention, concoction –1734. **3.** The making of comments 1833.

2. By subtile commentations, and wild inferences NORTH.

Co·mmentator. 1641. [– L. *commentator*, f. as prec.; see -OR 2.] **1.** The writer of a COMMENTARY (sense 3). **2.** An eyewitness whose description of a ceremony, sporting event, etc., is broadcast.

1. Cornelius à Lapide, a..great Commentatour upon holy Scripture 1641. Hence **Commentato·rial** *a.* pertaining to a c. or commentators. **Co·mmenta:torship,** the office or performance of a c.

Commenter, -or (kǫ·mĕntəɹ, kǒme·ntəɹ). ME. [f. COMMENT *v.* + -ER¹, -OR 2.] One who comments. (*Obs.* in spec. sense.)

† **Commentitious** (kǫmenti·ʃəs), *a.* 1614. [f. L. *commenticius, -tius* (f. *comment-*, see COMMENT *sb.*) + -OUS; see -ITIOUS¹.] Feigned, fictitious, lying –1849.

Commerce (kǫ·məɹs), *sb.* 1537. [– Fr. *commerce* or L. *commercium* trading, merchandise, (earlier in actual evidence) intercourse, f. *com* COM- + *merx, merc-* merchandise. Orig. stressed on second syll.] **1.** Exchange between men of the products of nature and art; buying and selling together; exchange of merchandise, *esp.* on a large scale between different countries or districts 1587. **2.** Intercourse in the affairs of life; dealings 1537. **3.** Intercourse of the sexes; *esp.* in a bad sense 1624. † **4.** Interchange (*esp.* of letters, ideas, etc.) –1741. † **5.** Communication –1757. **6.** *Cards.* A game in which barter is the chief feature 1732.

1. There c. plenty brings from foreign coasts GAY. *Chamber of Commerce*: see CHAMBER *sb.* 2. He is now in some c. with my Ladie *Twel. N.* III. iv. 191. For..c. be had between God and us HOOKER. †*Of good c.*: pleasant to meet.

Commerce (kǒmɜ̄·ɹs), *v.* 1587. [f. prec.; in sense 1 perh. through Fr. *commercer*. Cf. late L. *commercari, -iari.*] † **1.** *intr.* To trade, traffic –1660. **2.** To hold intercourse or communication, associate *with* (*arch.*) 1596.

1. To c. and exchange with one another 1660. 2. With..looks commercing with the skies MILT. *Pens.* 39. Hence † **Comme·rcer,** a trader; a person that one has to do with.

Commercial (kǒmɜ̄·ɹʃăl), *a.* (*sb.*) 1687. [f. COMMERCE + -IAL.] **1.** Engaged in commerce; trading. **2.** Of or relating to commerce or trade 1744. **3.** Such as passes current in the transactions of commerce 1752. **4.** Viewed as a matter of profit and loss 1882. **5.** *sb.* = *Commercial traveller* 1855.

1. A rich c. city BURKE. 2. The c. History of..Japan 1744. C. Laws 1765. C. freedom McCULLOCH. A c. crisis MILL. 3. C. morality 1879. The c. acid is generally not quite pure 1865. 4. A c. success 1882.

Phrases. *C. letter, note*: sizes of writing paper in U.S. *C. traveller*: an agent for a manufacturer, etc., who travels over a district, soliciting orders. Hence **Comme·rcialism,** the c. spirit and practice. **Comme·rcialist,** one engaged in commerce; an adherent of commercialism. **Commer:cia·lity,** c. quality or nature. **Comme·rcialize** *v.* to make a matter of trade; to subject to commercialism. **Comme·rcially** *adv.*

† **Commigra·tion.** 1627. [– L. *commigratio*, f. *commigrat-*, pa. ppl. stem of *commigrare*; see COM-, MIGRATE.] Migration; *esp.* on a large scale –1755.

† **Commi·litant.** 1577. [– *commilitant-*, pres. ppl. stem of L. *commilitare* soldier with; see COM-, MILITATE, -ANT.] A fellow-soldier –1728. So †‖ **Commilito.**

Comminate (kǫ·mineᶦt), *v.* 1611. [– *comminat-*; see next, and -ATE³.] *trans.* To anathematize. Also *intr.* Hence **Co·mminative** *a.* conveying a commination (*rare*). **Co·mminator. Co·mminatory** *a.* denunciatory.

Commination (kǫminēᶦ·ʃən). 1460. [– L. *comminatio*, f. *comminat-*, pa. ppl. stem of *comminari* menace; see -ION.] **1.** Denunciation of punishment or vengeance; *loosely*, denunciation (*mod.*). **2.** *Liturgy.* A recital of Divine threatenings against sinners; part of an office appointed to be read in the Church of England on Ash-Wednesday and at other times. Also, the whole office. 1552. Also *attrib.*

1. The terrible comminacion and threate..in the Apocalyps vnto the byshoppe of Ephesy MORE. Their orthodox c. of all taxation 1865.

Commingle (kǒmi·ŋg'l), *v.* 1626. [See COM-.] To mingle or mix together; to blend.

Comminute (kǫ·miniūt), *v.* 1626. [– *comminut-*, pa. ppl. stem of L. *comminuere*, f. *com* COM- + *minuere* lessen.] **1.** *trans.* To reduce to minute particles; to pulverize, triturate. **2.** *transf.* To divide minutely or into small portions 1667.

1. To c. hard bones 1880. 2. To c. Bloud 1667. patronage SIR H. TAYLOR. Hence **Co·mminuted** *ppl. a.* reduced to minute particles; *Surg.* broken into several pieces, as in *c. fracture.*

Comminution (kǫminiū·ʃən). 1578. [– late L. *comminutio*, f. as prec. + *-io* -ION.] **1.** Reduction into small fragments; pulverization, trituration. *Surg.* Cf. *Comminuted.* 1820. **2.** *transf.* 1751.

2. This natural and necessary c. of our lives JOHNSON.

† **Commis.** 1573. [– Fr. *commis.*] A deputy, delegate, clerk –1779.

† **Commi·se,** *v.* [– Fr. *commis, -ise*, pa. pple. of *commettre*; see COMMIT. Cf. DEMISE *v.*, DEMIT *v.*²] Earlier f. COMMIT *v.*

Commiserable (kǒmi·zĕrăb'l), *a.* 1609. [f. COMMISER(ATE + -ABLE. Cf. *abdicate, abdicable*; *predicate, predicable*.] Deserving commiseration.

Commiserate (kǒmi·zĕreᶦt), *v.* 1606. [– *commiserat-*, pa. ppl. stem of L. *commiserari, -are*, f. *com* COM- + *miserari* lament, pity, f. *miser* wretched; see -ATE³.] **1.** *trans.* To feel or express pity for; to compassionate. **2.** To condole with 1655.

1. This great victory..did move the Britains more to c. than to fear 1706. 2. The aptitude..to c. and comfort 1767. Hence **Commi·seratingly** *adv.* † **Commi·serator,** one who commiserates.

Commiseration (kǒmi:zĕrē·ʃən). 1585. [– L. *commiseratio*, f. as prec.; see -ION.] The action of commiserating; sorrow for the affliction or distress of another; pity, compassion.

Let no man help him, nor take c. vpon his infants 1604.

Commissar (kǫmisā·ɹ). 1918. [Russ. – Fr. *commissaire* – med.L. *commissarius* COMMISSARY.] The head of a government department of the U.S.S.R. So **Commissa·riat** 1918.

Commissarial (kǫmisēᵊ·riăl), *a.* 1702. [f. med.L. *commissarius* COMMISSARY + -AL¹.] Of or pertaining to a commissary.

Commissariat (kǫmisēᵊ·riăt). Also **-ot.** 1609. [partly – med.L. *commissariatus*; partly – Fr. *commissariat*; see -ATE¹.] **1.** *Sc. Law.* A commissary court; the office, jurisdiction, or district of a commissary. **2.** *Mil.* That department charged with the duty of providing food and supplies for the army 1779. **3.** *transf.* 1812. **4.** Food-supply 1861. Also *attrib.*

3. There is no c. for supplying London SOUTHEY.

Commissary (kǫ·misări). ME. [– med.L. *commissarius* officer in charge, f. *commiss-*; see next, -ARY¹.] **1.** One to whom a special duty or charge is committed by a superior power; a commissioner; a delegate. **2.** *Eccl.* An officer exercising jurisdiction as the representative of the bishop in parts of his diocese ME. **3.** *Eng. Univ.* † **a.** At Oxford, the Vice-Chancellor. **b.** At Cambridge, an assistant or assessor to the vice-chancellor in his court 1797. **4.** *Mil.* An officer or official who has charge of the supply of food, stores, and transport; † also, formerly, one who inspected musters 1489. **5.** A superior officer of police (in France) 1855.

1. *fig.* Great Destiny, the C. of God DONNE. 4. The Commissaries for victuall 1623. Commissaries of the Musters 1633.

Phrases. **C. court. a.** The court of a bishop's c. **b.** *Sc. Law.* A sheriff or county court which appoints and confirms executors of deceased persons leaving personal property in Scotland. **C. general.** A chief or head c.; *spec.* (*Mil.*) the chief of a commissariat service. Hence **Co·mmissaryshi:p,** the office of a c.

Commission (kǒmi·ʃən), *sb.* ME. [– (O)Fr. *commission* – L. *commissio, -ōn-*, f. *commiss-*, pa. ppl. stem of *committere* COMMIT; see -ION.] **1.** Authoritative charge to act in a prescribed manner. **2.** Authority committed to any one 1480; *spec.* that of an officer in the army or navy 1672. **3.** An instrument conferring such authority ME.; *spec.* the warrant by which an officer in the army or navy is appointed to the rank and command he holds 1643. **4.** An office conferred by such a warrant 1708. **5.** The condition of being authoritatively entrusted or given in charge 1573. **6.** A body of persons charged with some specified function 1494. **7.** The entrusting *of* (authority, etc., *to*) 1883. **8.** A charge or matter entrusted to any one to perform 1570. **9.** Authority given to act as agent for another in business 1622. **10.** A *pro rata* remuneration for work done as agent 1725. **11.** The committing (of crime, etc.) 1597.

1. I have it in c., to comfort the feeble minded BUNYAN. 2. Act within your C. SELDEN. *spec.* Cowards must lay their bought Commissions down 1705. *C. of the peace*: the authority given under the Great Seal empowering certain persons to act as Justices of the Peace. 3. Whil'st our C. from Rome is read *Hen. VIII*, II. iv. 1. My c. [as lieutenant] had been made out MARRYAT. Phrases (combining senses 2 and 3, and sometimes 6): *C. of array* (see ARRAY); † *c. of bankruptcy*, a c. issued by the Lord Chancellor, appointing commissioners to administer a bankrupt's estate on behalf of the creditors; *c. of lunacy*, a c. issued to investigate whether a person is a lunatic or not. 5. *In commission.* Of an office: Placed by warrant in the charge of a body of persons, instead of the ordinary constitutional administrator. Of a ship of war: Manned, armed, and ready for sea; said also of the officer in command. So *Out of c.* 6. The Parnell C. (*mod.*). 8. If I can execute any little c. for you DICKENS. 9. Sold by c. from the makers DE FOE. 11. Sinnes of omission and c. HOWSON.

Comb.: **c.-agent, -merchant,** an agent, etc., who transacts business for others on the principle of percentage; so *c.-business*; **-broker,** an agent for the sale or purchase of commissions in the army or navy.

Commission (kǒmi·ʃən), *v.* 1661. [f. prec. sb.] **1.** *trans.* To furnish with a commission or legal warrant. **2.** To empower; to entrust with an office or duty 1683. **3.** To send on a mission 1697. **4.** To give a commission or order to or for 1790.

1. Commissioned to ride the circuit FULLER, for the 'Adamant' of fifty guns BENTINCK. The new ships we c. BURKE. 3. A chosen band He first commissions to the Latian land, In threat'ning embassy DRYDEN. var. † **Commi·ssionate** (in senses 1–3).

Commissionaire (komi:sionē·r). 1765. [– Fr.] ‖ **1.** One entrusted with small commissions; a messenger or light porter. **2.** *spec.* One of the *Corps of Commissionaires*, an association of pensioned soldiers, started in London in 1859, organized to act as porters, messengers, etc.

Commissional (kǒmi·ʃənăl), *a.* 1540. [– med.L. (AL.) *commissionalis*; see COMMISSION, -AL[1].] Of or pertaining to a commission.

† **Commi·ssionary,** *a.* 1600. [– med.L. *commissionarius* adj.; see COMMISSION, -ARY[1].] Appointed by warrant; delegated –1649.
Our judges..are either ordinary or c. HOOKER.

Commissioner (kǒmi·ʃənəɹ). 1448. [– med.L. *commissionarius* sb.; see COMMISSION, -ARY[1], -ER[1,2].] **1.** One appointed by commission to carry out some specified work; a delegate; a member of a commission. **b.** A member of a permanently constituted government board 1532. **c.** The representative of the supreme authority in a district, governmental department, etc. 1535. **2.** A book-maker (*slang*) 1860. **3.** Occas. = COMMISSIONAIRE (*mod.*).
1. One of the..commysioners to make inquisicion of these thre pointes 1557. **b.** Charity Commissioners for England and Wales 1886. **c.** Special C. in Bechuanaland 1884.
Lord High C.: the representative of the Crown at the annual General Assembly of the Church of Scotland. Hence **Commi·ssionership.**

Commissive (kǒmi·siv), *a.* 1816. [f. COMMISSION (sense 11) + -IVE, after *omission, omissive*.] Characterized by commission. **Commi·ssively** *adv.*

Commissure (kǫ·misiŭɹ). ME. [– L. *commissura*, f. *commiss-*; see COMMISSION, -URE.] **1.** A joining together; the place where two bodies touch or unite; a joining, juncture, seam. **2.** The line of junction or angles of the two lips, eyelids, etc. 1755. **3.** Various bands of nerve-substance, which connect parts of the brain, the two sides of the spinal cord, etc. 1809. **4.** *Bot.* The line of the cohering faces of two carpels, moss-cells, etc. 1830. Hence **Commissu·ral** *a.* of, pertaining to, or of the nature of a c.

† **Commi·stion.** ME. [– med.L. *commistio*, var. of *commixtio* COMMIXTION.] = COMMIXTION, COMMIXTURE –1667.

Commit (kǒmi·t), *v.* ME. [– L. *committere* join, practise, entrust, (med.L.) consign to custody, f. *com* COM- + *mittere* put, send (see MISSION).] **1.** To give in charge or trust, entrust, consign *to*. **2.** *spec.* To consign officially to custody or confinement 1467. **3.** To refer or entrust (a bill) to committee 1621. † **4.** To charge with a duty or office –1549. **5.** To perpetrate or perform (in a bad sense); as, a crime, a folly, etc. 1490. Also †*absol.* –1660. **6.** To put together 1545; to engage (parties) as opponents, to match (*with*) 1612; to embroil 1855. **7.** To involve, compromise 1770; to pledge by implication *to* 1839.
1. Committe alle thy causes to god EARL RIVERS. Phr. *To c. to writing* (*to paper*, etc.), † *history, memory, the earth, the flames*, etc. **2.** Commytted to prison for felony 1467. Committed for cheating at play FIELDING. **5.** *absol.* C. not with any mans sworne Spouse *Lear* III. iv. 83. (*joc.*) 'Committing' puns DISRAELI. **6.** I apprehend everything from his committing the army with Buonaparte 1815. *fig.* Committing short and long [quantities] MILT. **7.** Without committing the honor of your sovereign 'JUNIUS'. Committed to the slave trade cause 1839. To c. oneself to an evil line of conduct J. H. NEWMAN. Hence **Commi·ttable, -ible** *a.* that may be committed. **Commi·tter.**

Commitment (kǒmi·tmĕnt). 1611. [f. prec. + -MENT.] **1.** The action of entrusting, giving in charge, or commending 1677. **2.** The action of committing to custody, or the state of being so committed 1621; a warrant or order for imprisonment 1755. **3.** *Legisl.* The action of referring or entrusting (a bill, etc.) to a committee 1640. † **4.** = COMMISSION 11. –1738. † **5.** Hostile engagement (*rare*) –1793. **6.** Committing oneself or being committed (*to*) 1793; an engagement 1864.
2. This dubious interval between the c. and trial BLACKSTONE. **3.** Deferring the motion till the day of the c. H. WALPOLE. **6.** The commitments of this country are too great DISRAELI.

Committal (kǒmi·tăl). 1625. [f. as prec. + -AL[1].] The action of committing; COMMITMENT.

Committee (see below). 1495. [f. COMMIT + -EE[1].]
I. (kǫmitī·). **1.** A person to whom some charge, trust, or function is committed. *Obs.* exc. in *Court of Committees* (of Guy's Hospital). **2.** *Law.* A person to whom the charge of a lunatic or idiot is committed 1765.
1. To the..Four and Twenty Committees of the Honorable the East-India Company 1681. **2.** She was the c. of the lunatic 1884.
II. *Now* (kǒmi·ti). A body of persons appointed or elected for some special business or function. (Each member was originally called *a committee* in sense I. 1.) 1621. Also, † a meeting of such a body –1742. Also *attrib.*
In the usage of Parliament, etc.: *C. of the whole House*: the whole of the members sitting as a Committee to consider the details of a measure which has been committed, or for kindred purposes, as in the *C. of Ways and Means*, etc. *Standing C.*: a permanent committee to deal with all matters within a particular sphere, during the existence of the body appointing them. Hence **Committee·ship,** the office or function of a c. (now in sense I. 2).

Committor (kǒmi·tǭɹ). [f. COMMIT *v.* + -OR 2.] *Law.* A judge (usu. the Lord Chancellor) who commits a lunatic or idiot to the custody of a *committee* (see COMMITTEE I. 2).

Commix (kǒmi·ks), *v.* ME. [f. L. *commixtus*, first adopted as *commixt* pa. pple., whence *commix*. See s. v. MIX.] To mix or mingle together; to blend. Now *arch.* or *poet.* Also *intr.*
Profit must with honour be commix'd 1596. *intr.* These elements..c. together daily 1519. Hence **Commi·xed, -mi·xt** *ppl. a.* var. † **Commi·xt** *v.* (*rare*).

Commi·xtion, -xion. ME. [– late L. *commixtio*, f. *commixt-*, pa. ppl. stem of L. *commiscēre*; see COM-, MIXTION.] = COMMIXTURE (now only in sense 5).

Commixture (kǒmi·kstiŭɹ). 1588. [– L. (late L.) *commixtura*; f. as prec. + -URE.] **1.** The action of mixing or mingling together 1592. **2.** The condition or product resulting from this; a mixture, a compound 1593. † **3.** Complexion 1588. † **4.** Sexual union 1682. **5.** The putting of a small piece of the host into the chalice, typifying the reunion of body and soul at the resurrection 1850.
1. By a c. of good and euil Actes BACON. **2.** Demetrius was a C. of vertues, and vices CORNWALLIS. **3.** *L.L.L.* v. i. 296.

Commodate (kǫ·mŏdĕt). 1727. [– L. *commodatum* loan, subst. use of n. of *commodatus*, pa. ppl. of *commodare* accommodate, lend; cf. Fr. *commodat*.] *Rom. Law.* A free loan, for use, of anything not perishable.

† **Commo·de,** *a.* 1637. [– Fr. *commode* adj. in same senses; see next.] **1.** Convenient, suitable –1740. **2.** Accommodating; usu. in a bad sense –1760. Hence † **Commo·dely** *adv.*

Commode (kǒmōᵘ·d), *sb.* 1688. [– Fr. *commode*, subst. use of *commode* adj. (prec.) – L. *commodus*; see COMMODIOUS.] **1.** A tall head-dress formerly worn by women, consisting of a wire frame-work variously covered with silk or lace. † **2.** A procuress –1753. **3.** A piece of furniture with drawers and shelves; a chest of drawers; a chiffonier 1786. **4.** An article of furniture enclosing a chamber utensil; a close-stool 1851.
1. Wir'd Comode..Cock'd Three Stories high D'URFEY.

† **Commo·derate,** *a. rare.* 1647. [– late L. *commoderatus* brought into the right measure, exact; see COM-, MODERATE *a.*] Brought into due measure; commensurate *to*. So † **Commodera·tion.**

Commodious (kǒmōᵘ·diəs), *a.* ME. [– Fr. *commodieux* or med.L. *commodiosus*, f. L. *commodus* of due measure, convenient, f. *com* COM- + *modus* measure. See -OUS.] † **1.** Profitable, of use –1751. **2.** Convenient (*arch.*) 1549; † opportune –1750. † Of persons: Accommodating. SHAKS. **3.** Convenient for accommodation, shelter, etc. (*arch.*) 1568; *absol.* roomy, spacious (the current sense) 1553. † **4.** Of *life, living*: Endowed with conveniences –1663.
1. Nothing..c.., except fyshe BOORDE. **2.** A work c. in form DIBDIN. A c. drab *Tr. & Cr.* v. ii. 197. **3.** C. to winter in *Acts* 27:12. C. dwellings BEWICK. Hence **Commo·dious-ly** *adv.*, **-ness.**

Commodity (kǒmǫ·dĭti). ME. [– (O)Fr. *commodité* or L. *commoditas*, f. as prec.; see -ITY.] † **1.** The quality of being commodious; commodiousness –1682. **2.** Convenience (*arch.*) 1488; †expediency –1788; †advantage, profit, (selfish) interest –1836. † **3.** Opportunity, occasion –1632. **4.** *concr.* A thing of use or advantage to mankind; *spec.* in *Comm.* a kind of thing produced for use or sale; in *pl.* goods, merchandise, produce ME. Also *fig.* and *transf.* † **6.** A parcel. SHAKS.
2. Doubled in two..For more c. of carriage BROWNING. *John* II. i. 573. **4.** Cattle, Corne, and all Commodities will thrive 1657. Some offer me Commodities to buy SHAKS. *Staple c.*: leading article of trade. **6.** Now Ioue in his next c. of hayre, send thee a beard *Twel. N.* III. i. 50. (See also D'Israeli *Cur. Lit.*, *Usury*, and cf. *Meas. for M.* IV. iii. 5.)

Commodore (kǫ·mədōᵊɹ). 1694. [orig. *commadore* (temp. William III), prob. – Du. *komandeur* – Fr. *commandeur* COMMANDER; but the form suggests Sp. or Pg. influence.] **1.** *Naval.* An officer in command, ranking above captain and below rear-admiral. (In the British Navy, a temporary rank, given to senior officers in command of detached squadrons.) 1695. **2.** A courtesy-title given to: **a.** the senior captain when ships of war are cruising in company; **b.** the senior captain in a fleet of merchantmen; **c.** a captain of pilots; **d.** the president of a yacht-club. 1832. **3.** The commodore's ship 1694; also, the leading vessel in a fleet of merchantmen 1769.

† **Commoi·gne.** ME. [– OFr. *commoi(g)ne*, f. *com* COM- + *moine* monk; cf. med.L. *commonachus*.] Brother-monk –1670.

† **Commoli·tion.** *rare.* [– *commolit-*, pa. ppl. stem of L. *commolere* grind up, f. *molere* grind; see -ION.] Grinding together. SIR T. BROWNE.

Common (kǫ·mən), *a.* [ME. *comun* – OFr. *comun* (mod. *commun*) :– L. *communis*.]
I. 1. 'Belonging equally to more than one' (J.); belonging to all mankind alike. **2.** Joint, united ME. **3.** General ME. **4.** Of or belonging to the community, or to a corporation; public ME. **5.** Free to be used by every one; public ME. **6.** Generally known 1568. † **7.** [L. *communis*.] Generally accessible –1609.
1. A C. enemy MILT. *Sams.* 1416. Longing the c. Light again to share DRYDEN. **2.** This was the comyn voys of every man CHAUCER. *To make c. cause* (*with*). **3.** C. notions ABP. THOMSON. **4.** *C. crier*, public or town crier. *C. seal*, the official seal of a corporation. So *C. Council, Hall, Serjeant, C. hangman*. The cok, commune astrologer CHAUCER. *C. right*: the right of every citizen. **5.** A theeuish liuing on the c. rode *A.Y.L.* II. iii. 33. *C. woman, prostitute. C. alehouse, lodging-house*, etc. **6.** *C. bruit, fame*, etc. *C. scold, nuisance*, etc.
II. 1. In general use; ordinary, prevalent, frequent ME. **2.** Undistinguished; ordinary ME. **3.** Belonging to the commonalty. (Occas. *contemptuous*.) ME. **4.** Familiar, not specific ME. **5.** Of inferior quality or value, mean ME.; vulgar, as persons 1866. **6.** Not ceremonially clean. (In N.T.: = Hellenistic Gr. κοινός.) ME.
1. The word is not c. among us 1586. **2.** The c. Run of Mankind ADDISON. C. manners SWIFT, honesty JOWETT. Dayes, whether c. or sacred BP. HALL. **3.** The c. herd JOWETT. *C. soldier*: one without rank or distinction. **4.** C. fire..as well as electrical fire FRANKLIN. **5.** He is but the commonest clay BYRON. She has rather a c. look (*mod.*). **6.** *Acts* 10:14.
III. Technical uses.
1. *Math.* Said of a number or quantity which belongs equally to two or more quantities; as in *c. divisor, measure, multiple*, etc. 1594. **2.** *Gram. & Logic.* Applicable to each individual of a class or group, as *c. noun, name, term*, etc. **b.** In L. and Gr., etc.: Of either gender. In mod. Eng. Grammar: Applicable to individuals of either sex, as *parent*, etc. **c.** *Pros.* Of syllables: Optionally short or long. (Marked thus: ⏓ or ⏒). **d.** *Anat.* Said of the trunk from which two or more arteries, veins, or nerves are given off, as the *c. carotid arteries*.
Phrases (*mostly from* I.):
C. assurances: legal evidences of the translation of property. *C. bench*: see BENCH *sb.* *C. field, land*: = COMMON *sb.* *C. jury*: cf. JURY I. *C. metre*: an iambic stanza of 4 lines containing 8 and 6 syllables alternately. *C. recovery*: see RECOVERY. *C. school* (U.S.): one publicly maintained for primary education.
† **B.** quasi-*adv.* = COMMONLY –1784.

Common (kǫ·mən), *sb.* ME. [Partly repr. Fr. *commune* = med.L. *communa, communia* (see COMMUNE *sb.*[1]); partly L. *commune*, or the Eng. adj. as sb.] † **1.** The community or commonalty; *occas.*, the commonwealth. (L. *commune*, Gr. τὸ κοινόν.) –1646. † **2.** The common people. Often = the COMMONS, q.v. –1663. **3.** A common land or estate; the undivided land held in joint-occupation by a community. Now often applied to unenclosed or waste land. 1479. Also *fig.* **4.** *Law* (Also *right of c., c. right.*) The profit which a man has in the land or waters of another; as *c. of* PASTURE, PISCARY, TURBARY, ESTOVERS (see these sbs.); = COMMONAGE, COMMONTY ME. **5.** *Eccl.* [L. *commune*, Fr. *commun.*] A service common to a class of festivals. (Opp. to *proper.*) ME.

2. The c. is deuided into marchauntes and manuaries 1581. Touching the Weale a' th' C. *Cor.* I. i. 154. **3.** They enclose oure commens 1550.

Phrases. **The c.** (quasi-*sb.*): (*a*) that which is ordinary; (*b*) the vulgar tongue *A.Y.L.* v. i. 54. **In c.,** † in general; ordinarily; in joint use or possession; holding by several titles, but by unity of possession, as *tenants in c.*, etc.; in communion; in participation. **In the c. of** (*Sc.*): in the debt of.

† **Common** (kǫ·mən), *v.* [ME. *comune*, orig. form of COMMUNE *v.*, with stress shifted to the first syll.] **I. 1.** *trans.* To communicate –1548. **2.** *intr.* To participate, share *with*, *in* –1602. **3.** To have intercourse –1555. **II.** (cf. COMMUNE.) **1.** *intr.* To confer, converse –1596. **2.** *trans.* To confer about; talk of –1607. **3.** To administer the Communion to; *refl.* and *pass.* to communicate –1500. **III.** (f. COMMON, (-S,) *sb.* or *adj.*) **1.** *intr.* To exercise a right of common –1697. **2.** To eat at a common table –1766.

Commonable (kǫ·mənăb'l), *a.* 1620. [f. COMMON *v.* III. 1. + -ABLE.] **1.** That may be pastured on common lands. **2.** That is or may be held in common; pertaining to commoning 1649.

1. C. beasts are either beasts of the plough, or such as manure the ground BLACKSTONE. **2.** C. land 1832, rights ROGERS.

Commonage (kǫ·mənědʒ). 1610. [f. COMMON *sb.* (or *v.*) + -AGE.] **1.** The practice of commoning; right of common (usu. 'of pasture'); the condition of land held in common 1808; *concr.* common land, a common 1771. **2.** The estate of the commons 1649.

1. Open fields..shackled with the rights of c. A. YOUNG. **2.** The whole baronetage, peerage, c. of England THACKERAY.

Commonalty (kǫ·mənălti). ME. [– OFr. *comunalté* (mod. *communauté*) – med.L. *communalitas*; see COMMON *a.*, -AL[1], -ITY.] † **1.** A community, commonwealth –1631; a self-governing community –1660. **2.** A body corporate 1425. **3.** The common people, as dist. from 'the upper classes'; the commons ME. † **4.** The Commons as an estate of the realm –1648. **5.** *transf.* The general body 1594.

2. The Maire and cominaltie of the Citie of New Sarum 1520. **3.** Plebs in englishe, is called the comunaltee ELYOT. **5.** The c. of mankind GALT. var. **Commona·lity.**

† **Commo:nefa·ction.** 1619. [f. pa. ppl. stem (*-fact-*) of L. *commonefacere* admonish + -ION.] An admonition –1679.

Commoner, compar. of COMMON *a.*

Commoner (kǫ·mənəɹ), *sb.* ME. [– med.L. *communarius*, f. *communa* COMMON *sb.*; see -ER[2] 2.] † **1.** A burgess –1643. **2.** One of the common people. (Now used of all below the rank of a *peer.*) ME. **3.** A member of the House of Commons. Now *rare.* 1648. † **4.** One who shares in anything –1661. **5.** At Oxford: An undergraduate who is not on the foundation of a college, but pays for his commons (called at Cambridge a *pensioner*) 1613. **6.** One who enjoys a right of common 1540. Also *fig.* † **7.** A common harlot –1695.

2. He dyned at a knyghtes bridale, and woulde not eate at the bridale of a communer LD. BERNERS. **6.** *fig.* The Birds, great Nature's happy Commoners ROWE.

Co·mmonish, *a. rare.* 1792. [f. COMMON *a.* + -ISH[1].] Rather common.

Commonition (kǫmǒni·ʃən). *rare.* 1730. [– L. *commonitio* admonition, f. pa. ppl. stem of *commonēre* remind forcibly; see -ION.] Admonition; a formal reminder. So † **Commo·nitive** *a.* serving as a c. † **Commo·nitory** *a.* serving to admonish; *sb.* a commonitory writing.

Common law. ME. [tr. med.L. *jus commune* (Du Cange, where the expression is used also of France and the Empire); cf. also Fr. *droit commun* in sense 1.] † **1.** The general law of a community, as opp. to local or personal customs –1551. **2.** The unwritten law of England, administered by the King's courts, based on ancient and universal usage, and embodied in commentaries and reported cases. (Opp. to *statute law.*) ME. **b.** The law administered by the King's ordinary judges. (Opp. to *equity*, *eccl.* and *admiralty* law, etc.) 1848. Also *attrib.* Hence **Common lawyer,** one versed in, or practising, this.

Commonly (kǫ·mənli), *adv.* ME. [f. COMMON *a.* + -LY[2].] † **1.** Generally, universally –1656. † **2.** Unitedly –1563. † **3.** Familiarly –1590. † **4.** Publicly –1611. **5.** Usually, ordinarily ME. **6.** Meanly, cheaply 1891.

3. SPENSER *F.Q.* I. x. 56. **5.** In this Land the shining Ones c. walked BUNYAN. Hardly c. civil 1706.

Commonness (kǫ·mən,nės). 1530. [f. COMMON *a.* + -NESS.] **1.** The state or quality of being common or usual. **2.** Meanness; want of distinction. (Less offensive than *vulgarity.*) 1872.

1. Communion is a c...between God and a man 1657. C. of use 1876.

Co·mmonplace. 1549. [tr. L. *locus communis*, tr. Gr. κοινὸς τόπος (in Aristotle simply τόπος).]

A. *sb.* **As two words.* † **1.** A passage of general application –1581. **2.** A notable passage, entered, for use, in a COMMONPLACE-BOOK 1561. † **3.** A commonplace-book –1749. **As one word.* **4.** A statement generally accepted; a stock theme; a platitude 1560. **5.** Anything common and trite 1802; *collect.* 1732. **6.** Commonplace quality 1842.

2. Whatever in my small Reading occurs, concerning this our Fellow-Creature [Ass], I do never fail to set it down by way of Common Place SWIFT. **4.** The paradoxes of one age often become the commonplaces of the next JOWETT. **6.** The c. of his [Addison's] ideas M. ARNOLD.

Comb. **c.-book,** a book in which one records passages to be remembered or referred to.

B. *adj.* [attrib. use of A.; now written as one word.] Of the nature of a commonplace; trite, trivial, hackneyed 1609.

A Common-Place Talker STEELE. C. virtues MORLEY. *The c.*: that which is c., commonplaceness.

Hence **Co:mmonpla·ceness,** c. quality. **Co·mmonpla:cer,** † a c. book; a person who keeps one.

Co·mmonplace. *v.* 1609. [f.prec.] **1.** *trans.* To arrange under general heads; to enter in a commonplace-book 1656. **2.** *intr.* To cite, repeat, or utter commonplaces 1609.

Common Pleas. ME. [repr. AFr. *communs pletz*, pl. of *plait* :– L. *placitum*; see PLEA.] Civil actions at law brought by one subject against another. (Opp. to *pleas of the crown*; see Blackstone *Comm.* III. 40.) Used chiefly as a contr. of *Court of Common Pleas*, now merged in the King's Bench Division of the High Court of Justice.

Common prayer. 1526. Prayer in which worshippers publicly unite; *esp.* the liturgy of the Church of England, set forth in the *Book of Common Prayer* of Edward VI (1549). Also, = *Common Prayer Book* 1712.

Co·mmon-room. 1670. At Oxford, the college-room to which the fellows and others retire after dinner. Also *transf.* Hence, the members of this room, as a body.

Commons (kǫ·mənz), *sb. pl.* ME. [Pl. of COMMON *sb.*]

I. 1. The commonalty; the lower order, as dist. from those of noble or knightly or gentle rank. **2.** The third estate in the English (or other similar) constitution. (In early use excluding the clergy.) Hence, the representatives of the third estate in Parliament; the Lower House. ME.

1. Rude Comouns MAUNDEV. Your Highnes pore commons 1546. **2.** The commons included the whole people, not lords 1817. An assembly called the house of commons..to represent the wisdom of the whole nation SWIFT.

II. 1. Provisions for a community or company in common; the common expense of such provisions; also the share due to each member ME. **b.** Used as *sing.* A common table; cf. *Doctors' Commons. spec.* At Oxford, a definite portion of victuals supplied from the college buttery or kitchen, at a fixed price. 1641. **2.** Rations; daily fare 1540.

1. A C. of Bread and Water DRYDEN. **2.** *Short c.*: scant fare.

Common sense, -sense. 1535. [repr. Gr. κοινὴ αἴσθησις, L. *sensus communis.*] † **1.** An internal sense which was regarded as the common bond or centre of the five senses 1543. **2.** Ordinary, normal, or average understanding. (Without this a man is foolish or insane.) 1535. **b.** Good sound practical sense; general sagacity 1726. **c.** A thing approved by common sense 1803. **3.** The general sense of mankind, or of a community 1596. **4.** *Philos.* The faculty of primary truths 1758. Also *attrib.* (hyphened).

2. Common sense will not teach us metaphysics any more than mathematics JOWETT. **b.** Rich in saving common-sense TENNYSON. **c.** Is this common sense? MACKINTOSH. **4.** *Philosophy of Common Sense*: the theory which accepts as the criterion of truth the primary cognitions of mankind. Hence **Common-se·nsible** *a.* possessing, or marked by, common sense; **-bly** *adv.*

Commonty (kǫ·mənti). ME. [ME. *comunete* – OFr. *comuneté* (mod. *communité*) :– L. *communitas, -tat-*; see COMMUNITY.] † **1.** The commonalty –1600. † **2.** A community –1523. **3.** Commonage. *Sc.* 1540. **4.** Land held in common; 'a common'. *Sc.* 1600. ¶ **5.** *joc.* for *comedy. Tam. Shr.* Induct. ii. 140.

Common weal, commonweal (kǫ·mənwi·l). *arch.* ME. [COMMON *a.* + WEAL *sb.*[1]] **1.** (Prop. two wds.) Common well-being 1469. **2.** = COMMONWEALTH 2.

Commonwealth (kǫ·mənwelþ). 1470. [See COMMON *a.* and WEALTH.] **1.** Public welfare; general good. *Obs.* in ordinary use. **2.** The body politic; a state, *esp.* viewed as a body in which the whole people have a voice or an interest 1513. **3.** A republic 1618. **4.** The republican government in England between 1649 and 1660. **5.** *transf.* and *fig.* 1551.

3. Better things were done..under a C. than under a King PEPYS. **b.** Since 1891 the title of the federated states of Australia. **5.** The Common-wealth of Learning 1664, of nations BURKE. Hence **Co·mmonwealth's-man,** † one devoted to the c.; an adherent of the English C. (*Hist.*); † *gen.* a republican.

Commorancy (kǫ·mŏrănsi). 1586. [f. COMMORANT; see -ANCY.] *Law.* Abiding; sojourning; tarrying. var. † **Co·mmorance.**

Commorant (kǫ·mŏrănt). 1556. [– *commorant-*, pres. ppl. stem of L. *commorari* sojourn, f. *com* COM- + *morari* delay, tarry; see -ANT.] *adj.* Abiding, dwelling, resident. *sb.* A dweller, sojourner, resident 1670. So † **Commora·tion.**

Commorient (kǫmǒ[a]·riĕnt), *a.* 1646. [– *commorient-*, pres. ppl. stem of L. *commori* die with, f. *com* COM- + *mori* die.] Dying together or simultaneously. Also as *sb.*

† **Commo·rse.** [– *commors-*, pa. ppl. stem of L. *commordēre*, after *remorse.*] Compassion. DANIEL.

‖ **Commot** (kɒ·mət). 1495. [– W. *cymwd*, *kymwt*, mod.W. *cwmmwd* neighbourhood, locality.] *Welsh Hist.* A division subordinate to a *cantred*; occas., a seigniory or manor.

Commote (kŏmǭ[u]·t), *v. rare.* 1852. [– *commot-*; see next.] To put into commotion, disturb.

Commotion (kŏmǭ[u]·ʃən). 1471. [– (O)Fr. *commotion* or L. *commotio*, f. *commot-*; see COM-, MOTION.] † **1.** *lit.* Continuous or recurring motion –1650. **2.** Physical disturbance, more or less violent 1592. **3.** Bustle, stir 1616. **4.** Public disturbance; tumult, sedition 1471. † **5.** Mental perturbation; agitation –1768.

2. The billows' c. SOUTHEY. **4.** The open c. of your people FULLER. The punishment of the Leaders..in a C. HOBBES. **5.** Achilles in c. rages *Tr. & Cr.* II. iii. 185. Hence † **Commo·tioner,** one who excites or takes part in a c.

Commove (kŏmū·v), *v.* Chiefly in pa. pple. ME. [orig. – OFr. *commovoir*; see COM-, MOVE; later f. on MOVE, with reminiscence of L. *commovēre.*] **1.** *trans.* (*lit.*) To move violently, set in commotion; to disturb. **2.** To move in mind or feeling; to excite ME.

1. From its depths commoved, Infuriate ocean raves SOUTHEY.

Communal (kǫ·miunăl), *a.* 1811. [– Fr. *communal*, in OFr. *-el*, – late L. *communalis*; see COMMUNE *sb.*[1], -AL[1].] **1.** Of or belonging to a COMMUNE 1811; of or pertaining to the Paris Commune 1871. **2.** Of or pertaining to a (or the) community 1843; esp., in India, of any of the racial or religious communities. Hence **Co·mmunalism,** a theory of government which advocates the widest extension of local autonomy for each locally definable community. **Co·mmunalist,** a supporter of a communal system. **Co:mmunali·stic** *a.* of or pertaining to this theory. **Co:mmunaliza·tion,** the renderingof anything (*e.g.* land, gas, etc.) c. **Commu·nalize** *v.* to render c. **Co·mmunally** *adv.*

Communard (kǫ·miunaɹd). 1874. [– Fr. *communard*, f. *commune* COMMUNE *sb.*¹ + *-ard* (depreciatory) -ARD.] An adherent of the Commune of Paris of 1871. Also *attrib.*

Commune (kǫ·miūn), *sb.*¹ 1792. [– Fr. *commune* – med.L. *communia*, n.pl. of L. *communis* COMMON, taken as fem. sing. in sense 'group of people having a common life'.] **1.** *Hist.* As tr. med.L. *communa*, etc.: **a.** the commonalty; **b.** a municipal corporation; **c.** a community 1818. **2.** In France, a small territorial division governed by a maire and municipal council 1792; any similar division elsewhere 1832.

2. The average of France is nearly fifteen communes to a canton 1837. *The C.* (*of Paris*): (*a*) a body which usurped the government of Paris, and played a leading part during the Reign of Terror, till suppressed in 1794; (*b*) the government on communalistic principles established in Paris in 1871; (*c*) the principles and practices embodied in the latter.

Commune (kǫ·miūn), *sb.*² 1814. [f. COMMUNE *v.*; cf. *converse*.] The action of communing (see COMMUNE *v.*).

Commune (kǫ̆miū·n, kǫ·miūn), *v.* ME. [– OFr. *comuner* share, f. *comun* COMMON *a.*; see COMMON *v.*]

† **I.** Var. of COMMON *v.* I. 1–3. –1827.

II. Current senses, now always *commune.* † **1.** *intr.* To talk together, converse; to confer –1611. **2.** *intr.* To hold intimate (mental or spiritual) intercourse (*with*). (Now only literary, devotional, and poetic.) 1671. **3.** *intr.* To receive the Holy Communion, to communicate. (Common in U.S.) 1550.

1. *Acts* 24:26. **2.** As thus he communed with his soul apart POPE.

Communicable (kǫ̆miū·nikăb'l), *a.* ME. [– (O)Fr. *communicable* or late L. *communicabilis*; see COMMUNICATE *v.*, -ABLE.] † **1.** Communicating –1677. **2.** That may be communicated or imparted 1534. † **3.** Suitable for communication (*rare*) –1643. **4.** Affable 1534.

2. Lost bliss, to thee no more c. MILT. *P.R.* I. 419. **4.** Be..c. with your inferiours LD. BERNERS. Hence **Commu:nicabi·lity, Commu·nicableness,** the quality or faculty of being c. **Commu·nicably** *adv.* in the way of communication.

Communicant (kǫ̆miū·nikănt). 1552. [– *communicant-*, pres. ppl. stem of L. *communicare*; see COMMUNICATE *v.*, -ANT.]

A. *sb.* **1.** One who partakes of the Holy Communion. **2.** One who, or that which, communicates, in various senses 1597.

1. There are..1500 Communicants in that Parish HALE. **2.** An anonymous c. 1881.

B. *adj.* (*rare.*) **1.** Having a part in common 1557. **2.** Furnishing communication 1703. **3.** Being a communicant (see A. 1) 1834.

1. Two c. or overlapping Genera BOWEN.

Communicate (kǫ̆miū·nikeᶦt), *v.* 1526. [– *communicat-*, pa. ppl. stem of L. *communicare* impart, share, etc., f. *communis* COMMON *a.* + *-ic-*, formative of factitive verbs; see -ATE³.] **1.** *trans.* To give to another as a partaker; to impart, confer, transmit. Const. *to.* 1538. **2.** *spec.* To impart (information, etc.); to inform a person of. Const. *to*, † *with*, or *absol.* 1529. **3.** To give, bestow. ? *Obs.* 1582. **4.** To share in; to use, or enjoy, in common *with*; to share *with* (*arch.*) 1526. † **5.** *intr.* To participate, share –1709. **6.** To partake of the Holy Communion 1549; † *trans.* –1709. **7.** To administer the Communion to 1539. **8.** *intr.* To hold intercourse or converse; to make a communication. Const. *with.* 1598. † *refl.* –1781. **9.** To open into each other; to have communication or continuity of passage 1731.

1. To receive or c. pleasure JOHNSON. To c. the pestilence to 1769. **2.** To c. a secreate to 1555, information (*mod.*). **4.** Thousands, that c. our loss B. JONS. **5.** Ye did c. with my affliction *Phil.* 4:14. **6.** Every one who was baptized communicated daily WESLEY. **7.** Whether children ought to be communicated 1616. **8.** No means of communicating with others but by signs 1865. **9.** A system of such canals, which all c. with one another ARBUTHNOT. A dressing-room communicating with this bedroom 1891.

Communication (kǫ̆miūnikēᶦ·ʃən). ME. [f. as prec.; see -ION.] **1.** The action of communicating. Now rare of material things. **2.** *spec.* The imparting, conveying, or exchange of ideas, knowledge, etc. (whether by speech, writing, or signs) 1690. **3.** *concr.* That which is communicated, as a letter, or its contents 1490. † **4.** Interchange of speech –1605. **5.** Converse, intercourse 1580. **6.** Access or means of access between two or more persons or places; passage 1684. † **7.** Common participation –1771. **8.** The Holy Communion; its observance (*rare*) 1610. **9.** *Rhet.* A figure, in which a speaker assumes his hearer as a partner in his sentiments, and says We, instead of I or Ye 1553.

1. C. of commodities 1623, of a disease 1806, of motion (*mod.*). **2.** To make Words serviceable to the end of C. LOCKE. **4.** Euil communications corrupt good manners 1 *Cor.* 15:33. **6.** Two vessels at different temperatures in c. with each other B. STEWART. Lee's communications through South-Western Virginia 1864.

Communicative (kǫ̆miū·nikĕtiv), *a.* ME. [– late L. *communicativus* (Boethius), f. as prec.; see -IVE; cf. (O)Fr. *communicatif, -ive.*] **1.** That has the quality or habit of communicating ME.; ready to communicate information, etc.; open, talkative 1654. † **2.** Communicable –1742. **3.** Of or pertaining to communication 1670.

1. That no less C. then Judicious Antiquary FULLER. **2.** C. Distempers RICHARDSON. **3.** A c. or social Principle 1710. Hence **Commu·nicative-ly** *adv.*, **-ness.**

Communicator (kǫ̆miū·nikeᶦtəɹ). 1662. [f. COMMUNICATE *v.* + -OR 2.] One who or that which communicates. **Commu·nicatory** *a.* tending to the communication or imparting of anything, as † *C. letters* (*Eccl. Hist.*).

Communion (kǫ̆miū·niən, -yən). ME. [– (O)Fr. *communion* or L. *communio*, f. *communis* COMMON *a.*; see -ION. The religious uses depend on Chr.L. *communio ecclesiæ catholicæ, c. sanctorum, c. carnis Christi, c. sancti altaris*, etc., and similar uses of Gr. *κοινωνία*.] **1.** Sharing or holding in common; participation; community. **2.** Fellowship 1553; spiritual intercourse 1600; communing (*poet.*) 1800; † common action –1796. **3.** The fellowship between members or branches of the same church ME. **4.** An organic union of persons united by common religious faith and rites 1565. **5.** Community of functions 1538. **6.** Intercourse 1614. **7.** Participation in the sacrament of the Lord's Supper; also, the sacrament itself, the Eucharist ME. † **b.** = *C. Service* (cf. SERVICE¹ III. 4, 5) –1575.

1. Having no c. of nature with other things GROTE. **2.** What c. hath light with darknesse 2 *Cor.* 6:14. A close c. with Nature FORD. **3.** The c. of saints, their c. not with one another merely, but [etc.] TRENCH. (Note. The phrase *c. of saints* has been used also in sense 4.) **4.** Some of the Romish C. 1642. **5.** To dissever the soul from the c. of the body JOWETT. **7.** Phrases. *C. in one kind, in both kinds, half c.*, etc.: terms of the dispute whether the laity should receive one or both elements in the c. *Close* or *strict, free* or *open c.*: among Baptists, a division as to admitting to the Lord's Table persons not baptized by immersion. Hence **Commu·nionist,** (*a*) † a communicant; an adherent of a communion 1644; † (*b*) a communist 1827.

Communion table. 1566. [COMMUNION 7.] The table used in celebrating the Communion of the Lord's Supper. See under ALTAR.

‖ **Communiqué** (kǫ̆miū·nikēᶦ, ‖ komünike). 1852. [Fr., pa. pple. of *communiquer* communicate, used subst.] An official intimation or report.

Communism (kǫ·miuniz'm). 1843. [– Fr. *communisme* (1840, Estienne Cabet), f. *commun* COMMON *a.*; see -ISM.] **1.** A theory of society according to which all property should be vested in the community and labour organized for the common benefit. **2.** Any practice which carries out this theory; also *transf.* 1857.

2. In these curious creatures c. prevails to its fullest extent, one for all and all for one J. G. WOOD.

Communist (kǫ·miunist). 1841. [– Fr. *communiste*, f. as prec.; see -IST.] An adherent of the theory of communism.

attrib. The C. doctrine of not paying a man in proportion to his work 1848. Hence **Communi·stic** *a.*

Communitarian (kǫ̆miū:nitēᵊ·riăn). 1841. [f. COMMUNITY + -ARIAN, after *unitarian*, etc.] A member of a community practising communistic theories. So **Communito·rium,** the home of such a community.

Community (kǫ̆miū·nĭti). [Late ME. *comunete*, see COMMONTY; later assim. to L. *communitas, -tat-*, f. *communis*; see COMMON *a.*, -ITY.]

I. 1. The quality of appertaining to all in common; common ownership, liability, etc. 1561. **2.** Common character; agreement, identity 1587. **3.** Social intercourse; communion 1570. **4.** Society, the social state 1652. † **5.** Commonness –1646.

1. Anabaptists, that hold c. of goods USSHER. **2.** The points of c. in their nature WORDSW. **3.** Men have a certain c. with God in this world 1570. **4.** [Marriage] is the foundation of c. STEELE. **5.** 1 *Hen. IV*, III. ii. 77.

II. † **1.** The commonalty –1700. **2.** A body of people organized into a political, municipal, or social unity ME. **3.** *spec.* A body of persons living together, and practising community of goods 1727. **4.** *transf.* and *fig.* 1746.

2. Those little Communities..[called] Neighbourhoods 1711. The Jewish c. 1888. *The c.*: the people of a country (or district); the public. **3.** The Abbot and C. of St. Mary's SCOTT. The Mormon c. 1890. **4.** Creatures that in communities exist WORDSW.

Commutable (kǫ̆miū·tăb'l), *a.* 1649. [– L. *commutabilis*; see COMMUTE, -ABLE.] That may be commuted or exchanged.

Offences not c. by fine 1880. Hence **Commu:tabi·lity,** the quality of being c.

Commutation (kǫmiutēᶦ·ʃən). 1496. [– (O)Fr. *commutation* or L. *commutatio*, f. *commutat-*, pa. ppl. stem of *commutare*; see COMMUTE *v.*, -ION.] **1.** The action or process of changing or altering; change, mutation. ? *Obs.* 1509. † **2.** Exchange, barter –1744. **3.** Substitution, interchange 1597. **4.** *spec.* **a.** The substitution of one kind of payment for another; also *fig.* 1597. **b.** *Law.* The substitution of a lesser punishment for a greater. (See COMMUTE *v.*) 1824. **c.** *concr.* The price paid by way of commutation 1707. **5.** *Electr.* The altering of the course of an electric current. (See COMMUTATOR.) 1876. **6.** *Angle of c*: (*Astron.*) the distance between the sun's true place seen from the earth, and the place of a planet reduced to the ecliptic 1751.

1. Such a scene of revolution and c. SYD. SMITH. **2.** The use of money..is that of saving the c. of more bulky commodities ARBUTHNOT. **4.** The c. of Penance 1640. A c. of his own sentence from death to the galleys W. IRVING. The C. of Tithes SYD. SMITH.

Comb.: **C. Act,** an act for the c. of tithes in England, passed in 1836; **-ticket** (*U.S.*), a ticket issued by a railway company, etc., entitling the holder to travel, etc., during its currency at a reduced rate; a season-ticket.

Commutative (kǫ̆miū·tĕtiv, kǫ·miuteᶦtiv), *a.* 1531. [–(O)Fr. *commutatif, -ive* or med.L. *commutativus*, f. as prec.; see -IVE.] **1.** Pertaining to exchange. **2.** Relating to or involving substitution or interchange 1836.

1. C. Justice, is..a Performance of Covenant HOBBES. **2.** Every..crime had its c. fine MILMAN. Hence **Commutatively** *adv.* in a c. manner. var. **Commu:tato·rial** (in sense 1).

Commutator (kǫ·miuteᶦtəɹ). 1839. [mod., f. as prec. + -OR 2.] He who or that which commutes; *Electr.* a contrivance for altering the course of an electric current.

Commute (kǫ̆miū·t), *v.* 1633. [– L. *commutare* change altogether, exchange, f. *com* COM- + *mutare* change.] **1.** *trans.* To change (*for* or *into*); to exchange 1633; to interchange 1667. **2.** To change an obligation, etc., into something lighter or more agreeable. Const. *for, into*, occ. *with.* 1633. **3.** To change (a punishment, or a sentence) *for* (*to, into*) a lighter one, or a fine 1642. **4.** To change (one kind of payment) *into* or *for* another 1795. *absol. spec.* (*U.S.*) To purchase and use a commutation-ticket. **5.** *intr.* To make up, compound *for*; to serve as a substitute *for* 1645.

1. May..exchange and c...Moneys currant of England, into Moneys of..Ireland 1633. **2.** To c. a penance 1633, one Duty for another 1723. **3.** To c. whipping into money FULLER, punishments for fines LD. BROUGHAM. **4.** To c. average receipts into a fixed charge MILL. To c. an annuity into a capital sum LD. SELBORNE. **5.** Perhaps the shame and misery of this life may c. for hell 1663. Hence **Commu·ter**, one who commutes; one who holds a commutation-ticket (orig. *U.S.*).

Commutual (kǫmiū·tiuăl), *a.* 1602. [f. Co-, COM- + MUTUAL.] Mutual, reciprocal. (Chiefly *poet.*)

Since.. Hymen did our hands Vnite comutuall *Haml.* III. ii. 170.

Comose (kōᵘmōᵘ·s), *a.* 1793. [– L. *comosus*; see COMA², -OSE¹.] Furnished with a COMA; of seeds: Downy or hairy. var. **Co·mous.**

Compact (kǫ·mpækt), *sb.*¹ 1590. [– L. *compactum*, subst. use of n. of pa. pple. of *compacisci* make an agreement; see COM-, PACT. Cf. OFr. *compact.*] A covenant or contract between two or more. Used without *a* in phrases, as *by c.*, etc. 1591. † **b.** In a bad sense: Plot, conspiracy –1652.

Family c., social c.: see FAMILY, SOCIAL.

† **Compact,** *sb.*² 1601. [subst. use of COMPACT *ppl. a.*¹] A structure; a composition; build; compaction –1817.

Compact (kǫmpæ·kt), *ppl. a.*¹ ME. [– L. *compactus*, pa. pple. of *compingere* put closely together, f. *com* COM- + *pangere* fasten. Cf. (O)Fr. *compact* adj.]

I. *pa. pple. arch.* **1.** Compacted, firmly put together. **2.** Composed *of* 1531.

1. A farre greater Empire..and better c. 1636. **2.** If he c. of iarres, grow Musicall *A.Y.L.* II. vii. 5.

II. *adj.* **1.** Closely packed or knit together; dense, firm ME.; not scattered or diffuse 1642. **2.** *transf.* and *fig.* 1576.

1. The c. tissue [of bones] 1831. Paris is c.; ..[her] strength is collected and condensed within a narrow compass BURKE. **2.** A man..c., instant, selfish, prudent EMERSON. In verse well-disciplined, complete, c. COWPER. Hence **Compa·ct-ly** *adv.*, **-ness.**

† **Compa·ct,** *ppl. a.*² 1597. [As *compacted* (XVI–XVII), f. L. *compactus*, pa. pple. of *compacisci* (see COMPACT *sb.*¹) + -ED¹; see COMPACT *v.*²] Joined in compact. *Meas. for M.* V. i. 242.

Compact (kǫmpæ·kt), *v.*¹ 1530. [f. *compact-*, pa. ppl. stem of L. *compingere*; see COMPACT *ppl. a.*¹] **1.** *trans.* To join or knit (things) firmly and tightly together, or *to* each other; to consolidate 1530; to condense, solidify 1633. Also *transf.* and *fig.* **2.** To make up or compose 1570. Also *fig.*

1. The Ligaments, that should c. and keep them [Limbs] in their Functions 1709. Now the bright sun compacts the precious stone 1712. **2.** Who out of nothing all things did c. 1652. Hence **Compa·cted-ly** *adv.* (*rare*), **-ness. Compa·cter, -or.**

† **Compa·ct,** *v.*² 1535. [In earliest use *compacted*, f. COMPACT *ppl. a.*² + -ED¹; hence as finite verb; cf. OFr. *compacter*, med.L. *compactare*, f. *compactum* COMPACT *sb.*¹] **1.** *intr.* To make a compact –1690. **2.** To plan by compact 1667.

1. Slaves could never have a Right to c. or consent LOCKE.

† **Compa·ctile,** *a. rare.* [– L. *compactilis*, f. *compact-*; see COMPACT *ppl. a.*¹, -ILE.] Made up by being joined or put together. SIR T. BROWNE.

Compaction¹ (kǫmpæ·kʃən). ME. [– L. *compactio*, f. as prec.; see -ION. Cf. OFr. *compaction* in same sense.] The action or process of making or becoming compact; the state of being so compacted.

† **Compa·ction².** 1528. [– OFr. *compaction* or med.L. *compactio* (*compacter, compactare*); see COMPACT *v.*², -ION.] The making of an agreement; an agreement made –1539.

† **Compa·cture.** 1590. [– L. *compactura*, f. *compact-*; see COMPACT *ppl. a.*¹, -URE.] Manner of putting closely together; compact structure –1641

With comely compasse and c. strong SPENSER.

Compages (kǫmpē̆i·dʒīz). 1638. [– L. *compages*, f. *com* COM- + *pag-*, as in *pangere* fasten, fix.] **1.** A whole formed by the compaction of parts; a complex structure. Also *fig.* and *transf.* **2.** Solid structure, consistency (as a quality) 1660.

1. The structure and c. of the human frame 1819. *fig.* The whole c., or fabrick of the Christian faith WATERLAND. var. † **Compage** (cf. *jointage*, etc.).

Compaginate (kǫmpæ·dʒineⁱt), *v.* 1648. [– *compaginat-*, pa. ppl. stem of late L. *compaginare*, f. *compago, -agin-*, syn. of prec.] To join firmly together; to connect, unite (*lit.* and *fig.*).

The side-pieces which..c. the whole frame 1648. So **Compa:gina·tion.**

† **Companable,** *a.* ME. [var. in ME. (with *n* instead of the normal *ny* for OFr. *gn* '*n* mouillé') of COMPANIABLE.] Sociable, companionable –1611.

† **Co·mpanage.** ME. [– OFr. *companage*, *-penage* (whence med.L. *companagium*) :– med.L. *companaticum*, f. *com* COM- + *panis* bread; see -AGE. Cf. COMPANION *sb.*²] Anything eaten as a relish with bread, *e.g.* butter, cheese, meat, etc. –1679.

† **Compa·niable,** *a.* ME. [– OFr. *compaignable*, f. *compaigner* accompany; see COMPANY *v.*, -ABLE; see also the var. COMPANABLE.] Var. of COMPANABLE –1822.

Companion (kǫmpæ·nyən), *sb.*¹ ME. [– OFr. *compaignon* :– Rom. **companio, -ōn-*, f. L. *com* COM- + *panis* bread.] **1.** One who associates with or accompanies another; a mate, a fellow. † **2.** An associate in some specific or legal relation; a colleague, partner, etc. –1769. **3.** *fig.* of things 1577. **4.** As a term of contempt. Cf. 'fellow'. –1764. **5.** A knight, formerly of any, now of the lowest, grade in certain orders 1568. **6.** A person employed to live with another in need of society. (Now usu. of women.) 1766. **7.** A thing which matches another 1762. Also *attrib.* and quasi-*adj.*

1. Companions in sin QUARLES. *Boon c.*: see BOON *a.* **2.** Thyne owne companyon and maried wife COVERDALE *Mal.* 2:14. **3.** With no c. but a pocket compass 1882. **4.** 2 *Hen. IV*, II. iv. 132. **5.** *C. of the Bath* (C.B.). Hence **Compa·nionage**, companionship (*rare*); the body of (Knight) Companions. **Compa·nionhood** = COMPANIONSHIP. **Compa·nionless** *a.* without a c.

Companion (kǫmpæ·nyən), *sb.*² 1762. [alt., by assoc. w. prec., of Du. †*kompanje* (now *kam-*) – OFr. *compagne* – It. *compagna* (for *camera della compagna* store-room for provisions, including esp. the *companatico* = COMPANAGE).] A skylight or window-frame to admit light to a lower deck or cabin; a wooden hood over the entrance of the master's cabin in small ships. *Occas.* = *c.-ladder, -way.*

Comb.: **c.-hatch, -head**, a wooden covering over the staircase to a cabin; **-ladder**, a ladder leading from the deck to a cabin; also, the ladder by which officers ascend to, and descend from, the quarterdeck; **-way**, the staircase or porch of the ladderway to the cabin.

Companion (kǫmpæ·nyən), *v.* 1606. [f. COMPANION *sb.*¹] † **1.** *trans.* To make companion or fellow –1803. **2.** To go or be with as a companion 1622. **3.** *intr.* To keep company 1845.

1. *Ant. & Cl.* I. ii. 30. **2.** His statue..still companions the winged lion on the opposing pillar of the piazzetta RUSKIN.

Compa·nionable, *a.* 1627. [alt., after COMPANION *sb.*¹, of earlier COMPANABLE, COMPANIABLE.] **1.** Fitted for companionship; sociable. **2.** Fitted to match (*rare*) 1823.

A C. life FELTHAM, wit CLARENDON. Hence **Compa·nionableness. Compa·nionably** *adv.*

Companionate (kǫmpæ·nyoneⁱt), *a.* 1927. [f. COMPANION *sb.*¹ + ATE².] *C. marriage*, marriage with legalized birth-control and provision for divorce by mutual consent.

Compa·nioned, *ppl. a.* 1820. [f. COMPANION *sb.*¹ and *v.* + -ED.] Having, or accompanied by, a companion or companions.

Companionship (kǫmpæ·nyənʃip). 1548. [f. COMPANION *sb.*¹ + -SHIP.] **1.** The relation of being a companion; association of persons as companions; fellowship. (Also said of things.) **2.** A body of companions; *spec.* in *Printing*, a company of compositors working together under a clicker 1824. **3.** The dignity of a Companion in an order of knighthood 1870.

Company (kɒ·mpăni), *sb.* ME. [– AFr. *compainie*, OFr. *compa(i)gnie* :– Rom. **compania*, f. **companio*; see COMPANION, -Y³. In the commercial sense orig. dependent on It. *compagnia*; in the spec. mil. sense on Fr. *compagnie.*] **1.** Companionship, fellowship, society; † also *transf.* of things. † **2.** Sexual connection –1616. **3.** A number of individuals assembled or associated together ME. **4.** *collect.* Persons casually or temporarily brought into association. More loosely, 'People such as prevent privacy'. ME. **b.** The person or persons with whom one habitually associates 1601. Also *fig.* **5.** A gathering of people for social intercourse; a circle; †an assembly 1653; society (*arch.*) 1576. **6.** A body of persons combined or incorporated for some common object; *esp.* to carry on some commercial or industrial undertaking ME. **b.** The partner or partners in a firm whose names are not included in the style or title; generally written Co., Comp. 1569. **7.** *Mil.* A body of soldiers ME.; *spec.* a subdivision of an infantry regiment commanded by a captain 1590. **8.** *Naut.* (in full *ship's c.*) 'The whole crew of any ship, including her officers, men, and boys' 1610.

1. My sone..be wele ware of womans companye 1440. *For c.*: for company's sake. *To keep c.* (*with*): to associate *with*; *esp.* (*vulgar* and *dial.*) to court. **3.** A compagnie Of sondry folk CHAUCER. A c. of horses *S. of S.* 1:9. **4.** C. coming in, they made off 1693. **b.** Phr. *To know a man by his c.* **5.** Another of the c. that shall be nameless WALTON. To let them see C. FORDYCE. **6.** Companies or guilds 1839. A c. of players DENNIS (J.). *Joint Stock C.*: see JOINT STOCK. *Chartered C.*: see CHARTER *v.* *John C.*: see JOHN.

Company (kɒ·mpăni), *v.* ME. [– OFr. *compaignier*, f. *compaing*, nom. of (the acc. form) *compaignon* COMPANION *sb.*¹] **1.** *trans.* To accompany; to keep company with (*arch.*). † **2.** To associate in companionship –1590. **3.** *intr.* To keep company, consort ME.; † to cohabit (*with*) –1680. Also *absol.* † **4.** *intr.* 'To be a gay companion' (J.). SPENSER.

1. Best companied when most I am alone DRUMM. OF HAWTH. **2.** To c. my heart with sad laments MARLOWE.

Comparable (kǫ·mpărăb'l), *a.* ME. [– (O)Fr. *comparable* – L. *comparabilis*; see COMPARE *v.*¹, -ABLE.] **1.** Able to be compared (*with*). **2.** Worthy of comparison; to be compared (*to*) 1483.

2. None c. to hyr in wytte and wysdom CAXTON. **Co·mparableness. Co·mparably** *adv.*

† **Co·mparate.** 1650. [– L. *comparatus* pa. pple. of *comparare*; see COMPARE *v.*¹, -ATE².] *adj.* Of comparison, comparative –1668. *sb. Logic.* A thing compared with another –1680. So † **Compara·tion,** COMPARISON.

Comparative (kǫmpæ·rătiv). ME. [– L. *comparativus*, f. *comparat-*, pa. ppl. stem of *comparare*; see COMPARE *v.*¹, -IVE, -ATIVE.]

A. *adj.* **1.** Of or pertaining to comparison 1602; *spec.* involving comparison as a method, as *c. anatomy, philology*, etc. 1675. **2.** *Gram.* Expressing a higher degree of the quality or attribute denoted by the simple adjective or adverb, as *tru-er, more often.* Cf. COMPARISON, POSITIVE. ME. **3.** Estimated by comparison 1597; relative 1774. † **4.** Comparable –1819.

1. An Act of Choice or Preference is a c. Act 1754. The C. method of investigation MAINE. **3.** The c. claims of pleasure and wisdom JOWETT. A matter of c. indifference JEVONS.

B. *sb.* **1.** *Gram.* The comparative degree (see A. 2); an adjective or adverb in the comparative degree 1530. † **2.** A compeer, rival –1611. † **3.** ? One ready to make comparisons –1823.

1. *Older* and *oldest* are the ordinary comparatives now in use 1873. **2.** Gerrard ever was His full c. BEAUM. & FL. **3.** The push of euery Beardlesse vaine Comparatiue 1 *Hen. IV*, III. ii. 67.

Hence **Compa·ratively** *adv.* by way of comparison; somewhat, rather. **Compa·rativist,** one who employs the c. method.

Comparator (kǫ·mpăreⁱtəɹ). 1883. [f. as prec. + -OR 2.] An instrument for comparing, *e.g.* the lengths of nearly equal bars.

† **Compa·rcioner.** ME. [– AFr., = OFr. *comparçonnier, -sionier*; see COM-, PARCENER. Cf. COPARCENER.] = COPARCENER –1537.

Compare (kǫmpēᵊ·ɹ), *sb.*¹ 1536. [In XVI *compair*, var. of COMPEER; later assim. to COMPARE *v.*¹; see next.] † **1.** An equal, rival, COMPEER –1617. **2.** *Without c.*: = 'without compeer'. (Referred later to COMPARE *v.*; see next.) 1621. Hence † **Compa·reless,** peerless, incomparable.

Compare (kǫ̆mpēᵊ·ɹ), *sb.*[2] 1589. [f. COMPARE *v.*[1]; perh. arising from a false analysis of such phrases as 'without compare' (see prec.).] Comparison. Chiefly in *beyond (past) c.*

Wit beyond c. 1621. Nor are its churches anything considerable in c. to Oxford EVELYN.

Compare (kǫ̆mpēᵊ·ɹ), *v.*[1] ME. [– (O)Fr. *comparer* – L. *comparare* pair, match, f. *compar* like, equal, f. *com* COM- + *par* equal; see PEER *sb.*] **1.** *trans.* To represent as similar; to liken. Const. *to*. **2.** To mark the similarities and differences of; to bring together for the purpose of noting these. Const. *with, to*; *together*. 1509. **3.** *Gram.* To form the comparative and superlative degrees of (an adjective or adverb) 1612. **4.** *intr.* (for *refl.*) To be compared; to bear comparison; to vie *with*, rival 1450.

1. All the things thou canst desire, are not to be compared vnto her *Prov.* 3:15. He compares it to a Sloe, in shape and taste DAMPIER. **2.** To c. Great things with small MILT. *P.L.* II. 921. *To c. notes* (often *fig.*): to exchange views, confer, discuss. **3.** Words of one syllable are usually compared by *er* and *est* W. WARD. Some adverbs are compared, thus; 'Soon, sooner, soonest'. .Those ending in *ly* . .by *more* and *most* L. MURRAY. **4.** Art, stryving to compayre With Nature SPENSER *F.Q.* II. v. 29. Hence **Compa·rer. Compa·ringly** *adv.*

† **Compare,** *v.*[2] *rare.* 1532. [– L. *comparare*, f. *com* COM- + *parare* get ready, provide, etc.; cf. OFr. *comparer*.] **1.** *trans.* To get, acquire –1590. **2.** ? To allege 1536.

1. To fill his bags, and richesse to c. SPENSER.

Comparison (kǫ̆mpæ·risən), *sb.* ME. [– OFr. *comparesoun* (mod. *-aison*) :– L. *comparatio, -iōn-*; see COMPARE *v.*[1], -ISON.] **1.** The action, or an act, of comparing or likening. **2.** Capacity of being compared; comparable condition or character. (Always with negative expressed or implied.) ME. **3.** 'A simile in writing or speaking; an illustration by similitude' (J.) ME. **4.** The action, or an act, of noting similarities and differences; see COMPARE *v.*[1] 2. ME. **5.** *Gram.* The action of comparing an adj. or adv. 1530.

1. The c. of philosophy to a yelping she-dog JOWETT. **2.** A Pallace without c. to any other 1662. Phr. *Without c., out of all c., beyond all c.* **3.** Comparisons may sometimes illustrate, but prove nothing 'JUNIUS'. A man. .Full of comparisons, and wounding floutes *L.L.L.* v. ii. 854. **4.** The Words Great and Little. .do import a C. to something else 1640. The Sculptor's art is limited in c. of others SIR J. REYNOLDS. A sterre in clerenes [is] nothinge in comparyson to the sonne WYCLIF. In c. with other things 1646. Penrith. . seems here, by c., like a metropolis SOUTHEY. **5.** *Degrees of c.*: the positive, comparative, and superlative degrees of an adjective or adverb.

† **Compa·rison,** *v.* ME. [f. prec. sb.] **1.** = COMPARE *v.*[1] 1, 2. –1626. ¶ **2.** In Wyclif as tr. L. *comparare*.

Compart (kǫmpā·ɹt), *v.* 1575. [– OFr. *compartir* or late L. *compartiri* share with another, f. *com* COM- + *partiri* divide, share.] † **1.** To divide –1605. **2.** To partition into smaller parts 1785.

2. The interior was comparted by willow screens 1876.

Compartition (kǫmpaɹti·ʃən). 1624. [– med.L. *compartitio*, f. *compartit-*, pa. ppl. stem of *compartiri*; see prec., -ION.] The action of comparting; one of the parts so marked out and divided.

Save in their Temples. .which needed no Compartitions WOTTON.

Compartment (kǫ̆mpā·ɹtmĕnt). 1564. [– Fr. *compartiment* – It. *compartimento*, f. *compartire* share; see COMPART, -MENT.] **1.** A division separated by partitions; a part partitioned off; *e.g.* one of the divisions of a railway-carriage, a large ship, etc. † **2.** The proper disposition and distribution of the parts of any design –1736.

1. The ceiling was divided into thirty-nine compartments 1873. *Comb.* **c.-bulkhead,** one of the partitions which divide the hold of a ship into watertight compartments.

† **Compa·rtner.** 1563. A CO-PARTNER –1701.

Compass (kɒ·mpăs), *sb.*[1] (*a.* and *adv.*) ME. [– (O)Fr. *compas* † measure, rule, pair of compasses, f. *compasser*, see COMPASS *v.*[1]] **1.** † Measure, proper proportion –1612; due limits (now *dial.*) 1579. † **2.** Artifice, ingenuity; craft, cunning –1597; an artifice –1559. **3.** An instrument for taking measurements and describing circles, consisting (in its simplest form) of two straight and equal legs connected at one end by a movable joint. Now usu. in *pl.*; also *pair of compasses.* ME. † **4.** A circumference, a circle –1655; anything circular in shape –1681. † **5.** A circular arc, sweep, curve –1697. **6.** A circumference, boundary, enclosing line or limit ME.; circuit, girth 1526. **7.** Circumscribed area; space, area, extent ME. Also *transf.* and *fig.* **8.** *fig.* Bounds, limits; range, reach, scope 1555. **9.** *Mus.* The full range of tones which a voice or instrument can produce 1597. **10.** Circuit, round; a roundabout course or journey (*arch.*) ME.; a circuit of time 1601. **11.** An instrument for determining the magnetic meridian or one's direction with respect to it, consisting of a magnetized needle turning on a pivot; used *esp.* at sea (the *Mariner's* or *Seaman's c.*) 1515. Also *fig.*

1. Phr. *By c.*, with measure and order, regularly. *Within* or *out of c.* **2.** Things that proceede from our owne care, and compasse BACON. Fetches and. .far compasses to bring things to their purposes LATIMER. **3.** BOW-COMPASSES, *beam-, calliper-, hair-compasses*, etc.: see these sbs. **5.** The shaft. .flyeth a round compace ASCHAM *Toxoph.* **6.** To touch the c. of a wide subject RUSKIN. The Duke's chase, thirty miles in c. SHORTHOUSE. **7.** Of the tryne compas lord and gyde CHAUCER. In the C. of a Crown piece 1710, (*fig.*) of one verse 1734. **8.** Within the compasse of mans Wit *Oth.* III. iv. 21, of our belief FULLER. **9.** *Haml.* III. ii. 383. **10.** They wenten in compas, Daunsinge aboute this flour CHAUCER. Where I did begin, there shall I end: My life is run his compasse *Jul. C.* v. iii. 25. Phr. *To cast, fetch, go, set, take a c.* **11.** *C. box*: see BOX *sb.*[2] *C. card*: see CARD *sb.*[2] *Points of the c.*; see POINT *sb.*[1] *To box the c.*: see BOX *v.*[2] *Azimuth c.*: see AZIMUTH. (*Note.* The *dip, surveying, variation compasses*, etc., are varieties of the Mariner's compass specially constructed for particular purposes.) *fig.* Profit is the Compasse by which Factious men steer their course 1649.

B. *adj.* Round, circular, curved. (Still techn.) 1523.

A c. ring, set round with little diamonds CHESTERF.

C. *adv.* [Cf. *in c.*] † **1.** In compass –1587. † **2.** In a circular arc, curvedly –1655. † **b.** Archery. *To shoot c.*: to shoot high, so as to allow for the curve of the projectile –1630.

Comb.: (sense 11) *c.-bowl, -needle*, etc.; † **c.-dial,** a portable sun-dial adjustable by an attached c.-needle; **-flower, -plant,** a N. Amer. composite (*Silphium laciniatum*) with large much-divided leaves, of which the lower 'are said to present their faces uniformly north and south' (Asa Gray); **-saw,** a saw with a narrow blade for cutting out curves of moderate size; **-timber,** curved timber, *esp.* as used for ship-building; **-window,** a semicircular bay-window.

† **Co·mpass,** *sb.*[2] 1573. Corrupt f. COMPOST *sb.*[1] –1700.

Compass (kɒ·mpăs), *v.*[1] ME. [– (O)Fr. *compasser* (now only) measure as with compasses, repr. Rom. *compassare measure, f. L. *com* COM- + *passus* step, PACE.] † **1.** To design (a work of art). ME. only. **2.** To contrive, devise, machinate (a purpose). Usually in a bad sense. ME. **3.** To pass or move round; to make the circuit of ME. Also *absol.* **4.** To close round, as a multitude; to surround, with friendly or hostile intent; to hem in; occas. *spec.* 'to besiege, block' (J.) ME. Also *fig.* **5.** To encircle, environ, lie round and enclose. Also with *round, about, in* ME. **6.** To surround *with* ME. **7.** To grasp with the mind 1576. **8.** To accomplish 1549; to attain 1591. † **9.** To circumvent –1642. **10.** To curve or be curved 1542.

2. To compass or imagine the imprisonment of the King 1681. **3.** The Bisquayn Ship. .wherein Magellan compassed the World H. COGAN. **4.** Myne enemies. .compassed me rounde aboute COVERDALE *Ps.* 26[27]:6. *fig.* All the blessings Of a glad father, c. thee about *Temp.* v. i. 180. **5.** Like the Sea they c. all the land POPE. **8.** That were hard to compasse *Twel. N.* I. ii. 45. To compasse such a bondlesse happinesse *Per.* I. ii. 24. **10.** *Merry W.* III. v. 112. Hence **Co·mpassable** *a.* attainable. **Co·mpassed** *ppl. a.* † contrived; encircled; circumscribed; † curved, † circular, † arched. **Co·mpasser.**

† **Co·mpass,** *v.*[2] 1557. [See COMPASS *sb.*[2]] To COMPOST –1632.

Compassion (kǫ̆mpæ·ʃən), *sb.* ME. [– (O)Fr. *compassion* – eccl.L. *compassio*, f. *compass-*, pa. ppl. stem. of *compati* suffer with, feel pity; see COM-, PASSION.] † **1.** Suffering together with another; fellow-feeling, sympathy –1625. **2.** Pity that inclines one to spare or to succour ME. † **3.** Grief –1590.

2. Every claim to c. that can arise from misery and distress 'JUNIUS'. Phr. *To have* († *take*) *c.* (*upon*, † *of*).

Compa·ssion, *v. rare.* 1588. [f. prec., or – Fr. † *compassionner* feel pity (for), f. the sb.; see prec.] To have compassion on, to pity. *Tit. A.* IV. i. 124. Hence **Compa·ssionable** *a.* † pitiful; pitiable (*rare*).

Compassionate (kǫ̆mpæ·ʃənĕt), *a.* 1587. [– Fr. † *compassionné*, pa. pple. of *compassionner* (see prec.) + -ATE[2]; cf. *affectionate.*] **1.** Affected with, or expressing compassion; pitiful, sympathetic. † **2.** Fitted to excite compassion; pitiable, piteous –1767.

1. It is a fault. .to bee too c. of an Heretique DONNE. Hence **Compa·ssionate-ly** *adv.*, **-ness.**

Compassionate (kǫ̆mpæ·ʃəneⁱt), *v.* 1598. [f. prec., or Fr. † *compassionner*; see -ATE[3], and cf. *affectionate* v. (XVI–XVII).] To regard or treat with compassion; to commiserate (a person, or his distress, etc.).

Men. .naturally c. all. .whom they see in distress BUTLER.

Compassive (kǫ̆mpæ·siv), *a.* 1612. [– AFr., OFr. *compassif, -ive* or late L. *compassivus*, f. *compass-*; see COMPASSION, -IVE.] Compassionate, pitiful.

Co·mpassless, *a.* 1864. [f. COMPASS + -LESS.] Without a compass.

† **Co·mpassment.** ME. [– AFr., OFr. *compassement* machination, f. *compasser*; see COMPASS *v.*[1], -MENT.] Compassing; contrivance, machination –1593.

Compaternity (kǫ̆mpătə̄·ɹnĭti). ME. [– med.L. *compaternitas*, f. *compater* godfather, f. *com* COM- + *pater* father; see -ITY.] The relationship existing between godparents mutually, or between them and the actual parents of a child.

Compatibility (kǫ̆mpæ:tĭbi·lĭti). 1611. [– Fr. *compatibilité*; see next, -ITY.] The quality of being compatible; mutual tolerance, consistency, congruity.

The c. of such properties in one thing BARROW.

Compatible (kǫ̆mpæ·tib'l), *a.* 1490. [– Fr. *compatible* – med.L. *compatibilis*, f. late L. *compati* suffer with; see COMPASSION *sb.*, -IBLE.] † **1.** Sympathetic –1618. **2.** Mutually tolerant; capable of existing together in the same subject; accordant, consistent, congruous. Const. *with*. 1532.

2. Wedlocke and priesthod be not repugnant but c. of their nature MORE. Heat is c. with Moisture 1688. Hence **Compa·tibleness. Compa·tibly** *adv.*

† **Compa·tient,** *a.* ME. [– OFr. *compacient* or *compatient-*, pres. ppl. stem of late L. *compati*; see prec., -ENT.] Suffering along with, sympathetic, compassionate –1646. So † **Compa·tience.**

Compatriot (kǫ̆mpēⁱ·triət, -pæ·t-). 1611. [– (O)Fr. *compatriote* – late L. *compatriota* (tr. Gr. συμπατριώτης); see COM-, PATRIOT.] A fellow-countryman. *attrib.* and *adj.* Of the same country 1744.

They. .are ready to think a c. braver. .and more deserving than any foreigner TUCKER. And Wolfe's great name c. with his own COWPER. Hence **Compatrio·tic** *a.* of or pertaining to compatriots; belonging to the same country. **Compa·triotism,** the position of being compatriots; c. feeling or sympathy.

Compear (kǫ̆mpīᵊ·ɹ), *v. Sc.* 1450. [ME. *compere* – *comper-*, tonic stem of OFr. *compareir* :– L. *comparēre*, f. *com* COM- + *parēre* come into view. Cf. APPEAR.] † **1.** To appear –1661. **2.** *Sc. Law.* To appear in a court, either in person or by counsel 1450. So **Compea·rance.**

Compeer (kǫ̆mpīᵊ·ɹ), *sb.* [ME. *comper* – OFr. *comper*; see COM-, PEER *sb.*] **1.** One of equal rank or standing; an equal, peer. **2.** A companion, comrade, fellow ME. Also *transf.* and *fig.*

1. Brian Boroimhe. .a c. of King Alfred and of Washington 1886. **2.** He axed lodgynge. .for hym and his Comperys FABYAN. Dryden and several of his compeers MACAULAY. Hence † **Compee·r** *v. rare*, to equal, rival, be the c. of.

Compel (kǫmpe·l), *v.* ME. [– L. *compellere*, f. *com* COM- + *pellere* drive.] **1.** *trans.* To urge irresistibly, to constrain, oblige, force. **2.** † To take or get by force, to extort –1601; to constrain (an action); to bring about by force, or moral necessity; to command 1671. **3.** To force to come, go, or proceed; to force. Also (as in L.): To gather into a company by force. Cf. *cloud-compeller*. (Now *rare* and *poet*). 1447. **4.** force by pressure, compress. *Obs.* exc. *fig.* 1657. † **5.** To overpower, constrain (*rare*) 1697.

1. C. them to come in *Luke* 14 : 23. C. the idle into occupation RUSKIN. **2.** We give expresse charge, that..there be nothing compell'd from the Villages *Hen. V*, III. vi. 116. He compell'd the Devil's assent FLAVEL. **3.** Compelling here and there the Stragglers to the Flock SWIFT. † **5.** Easy sleep their weary limbs compell'd DRYDEN. Hence **Compe·llable** *a.* that may be compelled. (Const. *to do, to,* or *absol.*) (Chiefly in legal use.) **Compe·llent, -ant** *a.* compelling. **Compe·ller,** one who compels or constrains; one who drives.

Compellation (kǫmpĕlēi·ʃən). Now *arch.* 1603. [– L. *compellatio*, f. *compellat-*, pa. ppl. stem of *compellare* accost, address, f. *compell-* in *compellere* (prec.); see -ION; cf. APPELLATION.] **1.** Addressing or calling upon any one; an address (*arch.*). **2.** Addressing by a name or title; style of address; an appellation 1637.

1. His c., Incline thine eare, hearken unto me 1642. **2.** The..c. of him by his Christian Name 1691. That name and c. of little Flocke 1643. Abraham..agreed with her..to go by the C. of his sister 1654.

Compellative (kǫ̆mpe·lătiv). *rare.* 1656. [f. † *compellate*, or its source L. *compellare* (see prec.) + -IVE, after APPELLATIVE.] A word used as a name, title, or appellation.

Compend (kǫ·mpĕnd). 1596. [– L. COMPENDIUM; cf. STIPEND.] = COMPENDIUM.

The C. of Aldrich SIR W. HAMILTON.

† **Compe·ndiary.** 1589. [– L. *compendiarius* short, and *-arium* subst. use of n. sing.; see COMPENDIUM, -ARY[1].] *sb.* A compendium –1631. *adj.* Compendious, expeditious, brief –1815.

† **Compe·ndiate,** *v.* 1614. [– *compendiat-*, pa. ppl. stem of late L. *compendiare* shorten, abridge; see COMPENDIUM, -ATE[3].] *trans.* To sum up concisely –1639.

Compendious (kǫ̆mpe·ndiəs), *a.* ME. [– (O)Fr. *compendieux* – L. *compendiosus* abridged, brief, see next, -OUS.] **1.** Containing the substance within small compass, concise, summary. † **2.** Of a way, method, etc.: That saves time or space, expeditious, direct; summary –1774.

1. Man..an extract or c. image of the world BACON. **2.** A way not so safe as c., when the tyde is out CAREW. Hence **Compe·ndious-ly** *adv.*, **-ness.**

Compendium (kǫ̆mpe·ndiə̆m). Pl. **-ums, -a.** 1581. [L., lit. 'that which is weighed together', saving, abbreviation, f. *compendere*, f. *com* COM- + *pendere* weigh.] † **1.** A short cut. **2.** An abridgement of a larger work or treatise, giving the sense and substance, within smaller compass; an epitome, a summary, a brief 1589. **3.** *transf.* and *fig.* An embodiment in miniature; an abstract 1602. † **4.** Economy –1812.

2. Compendiums of mathematics and natural philosophy 1793.

Compenetrate (kǫ̆mpe·nĭtreit), *v.* 1686. [f. COM- + PENETRATE.] To penetrate in every part, pervade. Hence **Compenetra·-tion.**

Compensate (kǫ·mpĕnseit, kǫ̆mpe·nseit), *v.* 1646. [– *compensat-*, pa. ppl. stem of L. *compensare* weigh (one) against another, counterbalance, f. *com* COM- + *pensare*, frequent. of *pendere* weigh; see -ATE[3].] **1.** *trans.* To counterbalance, make up for, make amends for 1646. Also *absol.* **2.** *intr.* To be an equivalent, to make up *for* 1648. **3.** *trans.* To make equal return to, to recompense or remunerate (a person) *for* 1814. **4.** *Mech.* To provide with mechanical compensation; to make up for (the variations of a pendulum). *trans.* and *intr.* 1819.

1. To c. their neglect HY. MORE. Compensating good with good 1672. To c. to us..what we have lost BURKE. **2.** Skill might c. for defective numbers FROUDE. **3.** To c. yourself for your rent and services CRUISE. Hence **Compensatingly** *adv.*

Compensation (kǫmpĕnsēi·ʃən). ME. [– (O)Fr. *compensation* – L. *compensatio*, f. as prec.; see -ION.] **1.** The action of compensating, or condition of being compensated; counterbalance, requital, recompense. **b.** *Mech.* The balance or neutralization of opposing forces 1789. **2.** Recompense, remuneration, amends 1610. **b.** Recompense *for* loss or damage 1804. **c.** *Civil Law.* (See quot.) 1848.

1. The Spartan idea of human life was one of strict c...you must fight for the State if [it] is to keep you MOZLEY. **2.** The c. which the borrower pays to the lender ADAM SMITH. **c.** *Compensation*..a sort of right by set-off, whereby a person who has been sued for a debt demands that the debt may be compensated with what is owing to him by the creditor WHARTON.

Comb. **c.-balance, -pendulum,** in a chronometer, a balance-wheel or a pendulum having arrangements which neutralize the effect of the expansion or contraction of the metal under variations of temperature.

Hence **Compensa·tional** *a.* of or relating to c. **Compe·nsative** *a.* = *Compensatory.*

Compensator (kǫ·mpĕnseitəɹ). 1837. [f. COMPENSATE + -OR 2.] One who or that which compensates; *spec.* a contrivance for producing mechanical compensation, as the *magnetic c.* Hence **Compe·nsatory** *a.* compensating.

† **Compe·nse,** *v.* ME. [– (O)Fr. *compenser* – L. *compensare*; see COMPENSATE.] = COMPENSATE *v.* 1, 2. –1825.

‖ **Compère** (koṅpɛr, kǫ·mpēəɹ). 1928. [Fr. 'godfather', 'accomplice', 'announcer' – Rom. *compater, f. *com* COM- + *pater* father.] The organizer or general director of a musical or vaudeville entertainment. So **Co·mpère** *v.*

† **Compert.** 1534. [– L. *compertum*, n. of pa. pple. of *comperire* ascertain, perh. from the opening words of a judical report (in med. L. *compertorium*) *compertum est* 'it was found' (by the court) XIII–XIV.] A thing found out by judicial inquiry –1539.

Compesce (kǫ̆mpe·s), *v. arch.* ME. [– L. *compescere* restrain.] To restrain, repress, curb.

† **Compester,** *v.* 1628. [– OFr. *compester*, var. of *composter* manure; see COMPOST *v.*] To manure –1696.

† **Compete,** *v.*[1] *rare.* 1541. [– (O)Fr. *compéter* – L. *competere* in its earlier sense 'fall together, coincide, be convenient or fitting, be due'; see next.] To be suitable, applicable, or competent.

Compete (kǫ̆mpī·t), *v.*[2] 1620. [– L. *competere*, in its late sense of 'strive for (something) together with another', f. *com* COM- + *petere* aim at, seek; cf. prec.] **1.** *intr.* To enter into or be put in rivalry *with.* **2.** To strive *with* another, *for*, or *in doing*, something 1795.

1. The sages of antiquity will not dare to c. with the inspired authors 1800. **2.** And man competes with man, like foe with foe CAMPBELL.

Competence (kǫ·mpĭtĕns). 1594. [f. COMPETENT; see -ENCE; cf. COMPETE *v.*[1] and (for sense 1) *v.*[2]] † **1.** Rivalry. † **2.** A sufficiency *of* –1740. **3.** = COMPETENCY 3. 1632. **4.** Sufficiency of qualification, capacity 1790; *esp.* (*Law*), legal capacity 1708; adequacy 1851.

2. A c. of land freely allotted MASSINGER. **3.** A c. is vital to content YOUNG. Robbed of c., And her obsequious shadow, peace of mind WORDSW. **4.** To make men act zealously is not in the c. of law BURKE.

Competency (kǫ·mpĭtĕnsi), 1594. [f. as prec.; see -ENCY.] † **1.** Rivalry –1638. † **2.** = COMPETENCE 2. –1734. **3.** A sufficiency, without superfluity, of the means of life 1598; the condition of having a sufficient income 1596. **4.** = COMPETENCE 4. 1597.

2. A c. of discretion and foresight CLARENDON. **3.** To retire upon a c. SMILES. **4.** References as to character and c. C. BRONTË.

Competent (kǫ·mpĭtĕnt), *a.* ME. [– (O)Fr. *compétent* or *competent-*, pres. ppl. stem of L. *competere* in the sense 'be fit, proper, or qualified'; see COMPETE *v.*[1], -ENT.] † **1.** *gen.* Suitable, fit, proper –1791. **2.** Answering the requirements of the case (*arch.*) ME.; sufficient in amount, quality, or degree ME. **3.** Properly qualified 1647. **4.** *Law.* Legally qualified or sufficient 1483. **5.** Of things, etc.: Belonging *to*; within one's rights; legitimate 1614.

2. A c. annuite for lyff ME., liuing TUSSER. A c. while before Christmas EVELYN. A c. reason 1597. **3.** A matter..allowed by all c. Judges BENTLEY. **4.** Any competente courte 1536. C. witnesses BLACKSTONE. **5.** Though it is c. for Parliament to legislate for the colonies STEPHEN. Hence **Co·mpetently** *adv.*

Co·mpetent, *sb.* Pl. also **-entes.** 1655. [– eccl.L. *competens, -ent-* candidate for baptism, usually in pl. *competentes*, pres. ppl. of L. *competere* in later sense; see COMPETE *v.*[2], -ENT.] *Eccl. Hist.* A candidate for baptism.

† **Competible,** *a.* 1586. [f. COMPETE *v.*[1] and COMPET(ENT) + -IBLE.] Appropriate, suitable, befitting; competent –1660. Also with *to, with.*

Competition (kǫmpĭti·ʃən). 1605. [– late L. *competitio* agreement, judicial demand, rivalry, f. *competit-*, pa. ppl. stem of L. *competere*; see COMPETE *v.*[2], -ION.] **1.** 'The action of endeavouring to gain what another endeavours to gain at the same time' (J.); the striving of two or more for the same object; rivalry 1605; in *Commerce*, rivalry in the market 1793. Const. *for*, † *to.* **2.** (with *a* and *pl.*) A contest for the acquisition of something; a match; a trial of ability 1618.

1. The place will be filled by open c. (*mod.*). From c. among traders [comes] reduction of prices BENTHAM. C. to the crown there is none nor can be BACON (J.). The Priest-hood, which ever hath been in some c. with Empire BACON. **2.** For the next lot..there was a keen c. 1891. *Comb.* **c.-wallah** [Urdu *-wala* = L. *-arius*, Eng. *-er*] = *Competitioner*; applied in 1856 to members of the I.C.S., then first admitted on the competitive system. Hence **Competi·tioner,** a competitor; one who enters a service, etc., by c.

Competitive (kǫ̆mpe·titiv), *a.* 1829. [f. as prec. + -IVE.] Of, pertaining to, or characterized by competition; as a *c. examination.*

Competitor (kǫ̆mpe·titəɹ). 1534. [– Fr. *compétiteur* or L. *competitor*, f. as prec.; see -OR 2.] **1.** One who competes; one who seeks an object which others also seek; a rival. † **2.** An associate –1681.

1. They..cannot brooke Competitors in loue *Tit. A.* II. i. 77. **2.** *Two Gent.* II. vi. 35. Hence **Compe·titorship,** the office or action of a c. **Compe·titory** *a.* belonging to competitors or competition; competitive. So **Compe·titress,** † **-trice,** † **-trix,** a female c.

Compilation (kǫmpilēi·ʃən). ME. [– (O)Fr. *compilation* – L. *compilatio*, f. *compilat-*, pa. ppl. stem of *compilare*; see next, -ION.] **1.** The action of compiling; see COMPILE *v.* **2.** *concr.* That which is compiled; a literary work or the like formed by compilation ME. † **3.** Accumulation –1728.

2. That all compilations are useless I do not assert JOHNSON. So **Co·mpilator,** a compiler. **Compi·latory** *a.* belonging to a compiler or a c.

Compile (kǫ̆mpəi·l), *v.* ME. [– (O)Fr. *compiler* put together, collect, or its presumed source L. *compilare* plunder, (contextually) plagiarize.]

I. 1. To collect and put together (materials), so as to form a treatise. **2.** To construct (a written or printed work) out of materials collected from various sources ME. † **3.** To compose (*e.g.* a sonnet) –1598.

1. Compiling notes to the Iliad from Eustathius STEPHEN. **2.** To c. a Dictionary 1748. **3.** *L.L.L.* IV. iii. 134.

II. † **1.** To heap together, pile up –1812. † **2.** To construct by putting together materials –1682. **3.** *Cricket slang.* To 'pile up' (a large number of runs) 1884.

3. New South Wales 'compiled'..412. 1884. Hence † **Compi·lement,** compilation; *concr.* that which is compiled. **Compi·ler,** one who compiles, † composes, or † builds.

† **Compi·nge,** *v.* [– L. *compingere* fix together, confine, f. *com* COM- + *pangere* fix.] To compress. BURTON.

Compital (kǫ·mpităl), *a.* 1656. [– L. *compitalis*, f. *compitum* place where roads cross; see -AL[1].] *Rom. Antiq.* Of or pertaining to the cross-ways, as a *c. shrine*; also to the *compitalia*, an annual festival in honour of the Lares. Also as *sb.*

Complacence (kǫ̆mplēi·sĕns). Now *rare.* ME. [– med.L. *complacentia*; see COMPLACENT, -ENCE.] **1.** Self-satisfaction. † **2.** Pleasure, delight, satisfaction –1754; *concr.* An object of pleasure and satisfaction 1667. † **3.** Disposition to please; complaisance –1749.

1. This c. is vayn glorye CAXTON. **2.** A Man unable to take C. in wicked Persons or Things 1754. *concr.* O Thou My sole c. MILT. *P.L.* III. 276. **3.** All people were so full of c. S. BUTLER.

Complacency (kǫmplē̆ⁱ·sĕnsi). 1643. [f. as prec.; see -ENCY.] **1.** The fact or state of being pleased with a thing or person; tranquil satisfaction. **2.** *spec.* Self-satisfaction 1650. **3.** Pleasure, delight (*arch.*) 1652. † **4.** Contented acquiescence –1709. **5.** = COMPLACENCE 3. 1651.

1. He regards the enemies of pleasure with c. JOWETT. **2.** The c. of such women BULWER. **5.** The c. of a few courtiers FROUDE. Hence † **Complace·ntial** *a.* complaisant; **-ly** *adv.*

Complacent (kǫmplē̆ⁱ·sĕnt), *a.* 1660. [– *complacent-*, pres. ppl. stem of L. *complacēre*, f. *com* COM- + *placēre* please; see -ENT.] † **1.** Pleasant –1772. **2.** *spec.* Self-satisfied 1767. **3.** Obliging in manner, complaisant 1790.

1. In the c. moneth of May 1660. **2.** With c. smile 1767. **3.** The..c. flattery of Leicester SCOTT. Hence **Compla·cently** *adv.*

Complain (kǫmplē̆ⁱ·n), *v.* [ME. *compleigne* – (O)Fr. *complaign-*, pres. stem of *complaindre* :– Rom. (med.L.) *complangere*, f. *com* COM- + *plangere* lament; cf. PLAIN *v.*] † **1.** *trans.* To bewail, lament –1700. Also † *refl.* † **2.** *intr.* To give expression to sorrow; to make moan, lament –1647. **3.** *intr.* To suffer, be ailing. (Now *dial.*) 1607. **4.** *intr.* To express discontent; to murmur, grumble ME. With *of*. (Now the leading use.) 1584. **5.** *intr.* (orig. *refl.*) To make a formal complaint *to* or *before*; to bring a charge 1449. **6.** *transf.* and *fig.* To emit a mournful sound 1697; to groan or creak, as a mast 1722.

1. To complayne the dethe of the kyng LD. BERNERS. **3.** *To c. of*: to let it be known that one is suffering from (any pain, etc.). **4.** The Heat they c. of cannot be in the Weather ADDISON. Others..c. that Fate Free Vertue should enthrall to Force or Chance MILT. *P.L.* II. 550. **5.** Domitius Corbulo..complained before the Lords of the Senate..that [etc.] 1598. Hence **Complai·n** *sb.* complaining (*Obs.* exc. *poet.*). **Complai·nable** *a.* to be complained of. **Complai·ner,** one who complains; in *Law* = COMPLAINANT. **Complai·ning-ly** *adv.*, **-ness.**

Complainant (kǫmplē̆ⁱ·nănt). 1495. [– Fr. *complaignant*, pres. pple. of *complaindre*; see prec., -ANT.] **1.** *Law.* One who enters a legal complaint; a plaintiff or prosecutor. **2.** *gen.* One who complains 1525. Also as † *adj.*

1. The same compleynaunt, not provyng the mater of his seid bill to be true 1495. **2.** No want of complaint, nor of complainants CARLYLE.

Complaint (kǫmplē̆ⁱ·nt). ME. [– (O)Fr. *complainte*, subst. use of fem. of pa. pple. *complaint* of *complaindre* COMPLAIN.] **1.** The action of complaining; grieving. **2.** An expression of grief; a plaint ME. **3.** Utterance of grievance ME.; a statement of injustice suffered ME. **4.** *Law.* A statement of injury or grievance laid before a court (prop. a Court of Equity) for purposes of prosecution and redress; an accusation or charge; in *U.S.* the plaintiff's case in a civil action ME. **5.** The subject of complaint 1745. **6.** *spec.* A bodily ailment or disorder (*esp.* of chronic nature) 1705.

1. For whom was maked moch compleynt CHAUCER. **2.** Compleynte of Pité CHAUCER (*title*). **3.** Tho was compleinte on every side GOWER. **5.** The poverty of the clergy of England hath been the c. of all who wish well to the church SWIFT. **6.** This..was mistaken for a bowel c. 1809. Hence † **Complai·ntful** *a.* full of c.

Complaisance (kǫ·mplezɑ·ns, kǫ:mplezɑ·ns). 1651. [– (O)Fr. *complaisance*, f. as next; see -ANCE.] The action or habit of making oneself agreeable; desire and care to please; deference to the wishes of others; obligingness, courtesy, politeness; (with *pl.*) an act of complaisance.

Compleasance; that is to say, That every man strive to accommodate himselfe to the rest HOBBES. For c., and breeding sake I'll do it SHADWELL. How the complaisances we use.. shame us now EMERSON. var. † **Co·mplaisancy** (*rare*).

Complaisant (kǫ·mplezɑ:nt, kǫ:mplezɑ·nt), *a.* 1647. [– Fr. *complaisant* obliging, pres. pple. of *complaire* acquiesce in order to please, repr. L. *complacēre*; see COMPLACENT.] Disposed to please; obliging, courteous; accommodating.

That's very c...Mr. Bayes, to be of another Man's Opinion, before he knows what it is VILLIERS *Rehearsal*. The French..are..c., cordial, and well-bred SMILES. Hence **Complaisantly** *adv.*

† **Co·mplanate,** *v.* 1643. [– *complanat-* pa. ppl. stem of L. *complanare* make level, f. *com* COM- + *planare*, f. *planus* flat, level; see -ATE³.] To make plane, to flatten –1713. So **Co·mplanate** *a.* made plane, lying in one plane, flattened. **Complana·tion,** making plane or level, flattening out.

Complect (kǫmple·kt), *v.* 1523. [– L. *complecti, complectere* embrace, encircle, f. *com* COM- + *plectere* plait, twine.] † **1.** To embrace (*lit.* and *fig.*) –1657. **2.** To connect together; to interweave 1578. Hence **Comple·cted** *ppl. a.*¹

Comple·cted, *ppl. a.*² 1860. *U.S. dial.* or *colloq.* [app. f. COMPLEXION.] = COMPLEXIONED.

Complement (kǫ·mplĭmĕnt), *sb.* ME. [– L. *complementum*, f. *complēre*; see COMPLETE *a.*; -MENT. In II latterly supplanted by COMPLIMENT.]

I. † **1.** The action of fulfilling or completing –1721. † **2.** Completeness, fullness –1677. *Her.* Fullness (of the moon) 1610. **3.** That which completes or makes perfect; the completion, consummation ME. **4.** The quantity or amount that completes or fills; complete set; totality 1589. **5.** That which, when added, completes a whole; each of two parts which mutually complete each other. (See quots.) 1570.

3. Love is the c. of the law and the supplement of the Gospel TRAPP. **4.** Matter sufficient to make a full periode or c. of sence PUTTENHAM. Brains that want their c. of Wits WOLCOT. *The c. of a ship*: the full number required to man it. **5.** *Math. Arithmetical c.*: the sum which, added to a given number, makes up unity, ten, or the next higher multiple of ten. *Complements of a parallelogram*: the two lesser parallelograms not on the diagonal, made by drawing lines parallel to the sides of a given parallelogram, through the same point in its diagonal. *C. of an arc or angle*: the amount which, added to the arc or angle, makes up 90 degrees. *Mus. C. of an interval*: the interval wanting to make up a complete octave.

II. † **1.** A completing accessory –1693. † **2.** A personal accomplishment or quality –1636. † **3.** A ceremony, a formality –1646.

Complement (kǫmplĭme·nt), *v.* 1612. [f. prec.] **1.** To make complete or perfect; to form the complement to 1641. † **2.** = COMPLIMENT *v.* 1, 2, 4. Hence **Compleme·nter, -or,** one who, or that which, complements; † formerly = *Complimenter.*

Complemental (kǫmplĭme·ntăl), *a.* 1602. [f. COMPLEMENT *sb.* + -AL¹.] **1.** Of the nature of a complement; complementary (*to*). † **2.** Accessory –1655; ceremonious –1695; accomplished –1636. † **3.** = COMPLIMENTARY –1703.

1. *C. air*: the 100 cubic inches of air which can be added after an ordinary inspiration [230 cubic inches]. *C. male* (in *Zool.*): Darwin's name for a minute rudimentary male parasitic on the hermaphrodite in certain cirripeds, etc. Hence **Compleme·ntally** *adv.*

Complementary (kǫmplĭme·ntări). 1599. [f. COMPLEMENT *sb.* + -ARY¹.]

A. *adj.* **1.** Forming a complement, completing 1836. † **2.** Ceremonious –1657.

1. *C. angles*: two angles which together make up a right angle. *C. colours*: colours which, when mixed, produce white light.

B. *sb.* † **1.** A master of accomplishments B. JONS. **2.** Short for 'c. colour' 1865.

Complete (kǫmplī·t), *a.* ME. [– (O)Fr. *complet* or L. *completus*, pa. pple. of *complēre* fill up, finish, fulfil, f. *com* COM- + **plē-*, base of *plenus* full.] **1.** Having all its parts or elements; entire, full. **2.** Whole; finished, ended, concluded ME. **3.** Entire 1645. **4.** Without defect ME. **5.** Consummate. ? *Obs.* 1526. **6.** quasi-*adv.* = COMPLETELY.

1. Shoulders broad for c. armour fit MARLOWE. C. intelligence JOHNSON. **2.** The space of v. yeres c. FABYAN. **3.** C. inability to obtain drink KANE. C. combustion 1854. **5.** The Compleat Angler WALTON.

Phr. *C. flower*: † (*a*) one which possesses stamens and pistils; (*b*) one which also possesses the floral envelopes. Hence **Comple·te-ly** *adv.*, **-ness.**

Complete (kǫmplī·t), *v.* 1530. [f. the adj., cf. Fr. *compléter*.] **1.** *trans.* To bring to an end, finish. **2.** To make whole or entire 1726. **3.** To make perfect 1667. **4.** To accomplish (a vow, etc.) (*rare*) 1680.

1. To c. a work 1751. **2.** To c. the sense 1795. **3.** That fair femal Troop..completed to the taste Of lustful appetence MILT. *P.L.* XI. 618. Hence † **Comple·tement. Comple·ter. Comple·tive** *a.* completing.

Completion (kǫmplī·ʃən). 1657. [– L. *completio*, f. *complet-*; see COMPLETE *a.*, -ION.] The action of making complete; the condition of being completed; accomplishment (of a wish, etc.).

They may tend to the c. of the business CROMWELL. The apparent completions of prophecy BUTLER.

Completory (kǫmplī·tŏri). 1450. [– late and med.(eccl.)L. *completorius*, as sb. *-ium*, f. as prec.; see -ORY¹,².] *adj.* Having the function of completing 1659. *sb.* **1.** A completory thing 1659. **2.** = COMPLINE 1450.

adj. C. of ancient..predictions BARROW.

Complex (kǫ·mpleks), *sb.* 1652. [– L. *complexus, -ūs*, f. pa. ppl. stem of *complectere* (see next); later apprehended as subst. use of *complex* adj.] **a.** A complex whole. **b.** Jung's term for a group of ideas associated with a particular subject; hence, pop., a mental tendency or obsession, as *inferiority c.* 1910.

Government, taken in the whole c. of it, cannot.. provide against all Emergencies 1695.

Complex (kǫ·mpleks), *a.* 1652. [– Fr. *complexe* or its source L. *complexus*, pa. pple. of *complectere, complecti*, encompass, embrace, comprehend, comprise; but sometimes analysed as COM- + *plexus* woven.] **1.** Comprehending various parts connected together; composite, compound. **2.** *esp.* Consisting of parts involved in various degrees of subordination; involved, intricate 1715.

1. Ideas thus made up of several simple ones put together I call C.; such as are Beauty, Gratitude, a Man, an Army LOCKE. *C. fraction* in *Arith.*: one that has a fraction for its numerator, or denominator, or both. (Cf. COMPOUND.) *C. number* in *Math.*: a number of which part is real and part imaginary. Hence **Co·mplexly** *adv.* † collectively; in a c. manner. **Co·mplexness.**

Complex (kǫmple·ks), *v. rare.* 1470. [– *complex-*, stem of L. *complexus*; see prec.; in sense 2 prob. f. the adj.] † **1.** To attach. **2.** To combine into a complex whole; to complicate 1658. Hence † **Complexed, complext** *ppl. a.* **Comple·xedness.** ? *Obs.*

Complexion (kǫmple·kʃən), *sb.* ME. [– (O)Fr. *complexion* – L. *complexio* combination, association, (late) bodily habit, f. *complex-*; see prec., -ION.]

I. From Rom. and med.L. **1.** The combination of qualities (*cold* or *hot*, and *moist* or *dry*), or of 'humours', in a certain proportion; 'temperament'. *Obs.* exc. *Hist.* † **b.** Also = 'humour', or 'collection of humours' –1689. † **2.** Bodily or mental habit; nature –1856. **3.** The colour and texture of the skin, *esp.* of the face; *orig.* as showing the 'temperament'. (Now the ordinary sense.) 1580. † **b.** Face. *Oth.* IV. ii. 62. **4.** *transf.* and *fig.* 1589.

2. Mee thinkes it is very soultry, and hot for my C. *Haml.* V. ii. 102. A very amorous c. HUME. **3.** Mislike me not for my c. *Merch. V.* II. i. 1. **4.** The c. of the Skie *Rich. II*, III. ii. 194, of the times FULLER.

II. From old L. senses. † **1.** Embrace (*rare*) 1493. † **2.** Complication, combination –1725. Also quasi-*concr.* † **3.** = COMPLEX *sb.* a. –1741.

Hence **Comple·xional** *a.* † of or pertaining to the (physical or mental) constitution; pertaining to the c. (of the skin). **Comple·xionally** *adv.* † **Comple·xionary** *a.* pertaining to the c. **Comple·xionless** *a.* pale, colourless.

Complexion (kǫmple·kʃən), *v.* ME. [f. prec. sb.] † **1.** To constitute by combination of various elements –1658. **2.** To give a colour or tinge to 1612.

Complexioned (kǫmple·kʃənd), *ppl. a.* ME. [f. prec. sb. and v. + -ED.] † **1.** Having a (specified) temperament –1795. **2.** Having a (specified) colour and texture of skin 1615. Also *transf.*

1. A wel complexyoned body LYDG., Soul NORRIS. **2.** The people..are all fair-c. 1859.

Complexity (kǫmple·ksĭti). 1721. [f. COMPLEX *a.* + -ITY; cf. Fr. *complexité*.] **1.** The quality or condition of being complex; intricacy. **2.** quasi-*concr.* A complicated condition; a complication 1794.

1. C. of organisation DARWIN. 2. The..many-corridor'd complexities Of Arthur's palace TENNYSON.

† **Comple·xive,** *a.* 1654. [– L. *complexivus* connective, in late L. comprehensive (Boethius); see COMPLEX, -IVE.] Comprehensive –1672.

‖ **Complexus** (kǭmple·ksǒs). 1871. [f. COM- + PLEXUS.] An interwoven structure; a complex, 'tissue'.

Compliable (kǭmpləi·ăb'l), *a.* 1635. [f. COMPLY *v.*¹ + -ABLE.] **1.** Apt or inclined to comply; compliant. ? *Obs.* † **2.** Reconcilable –1746.

1. The uniting of another c. mind MILT. 2. The Jews..had made their religion c. and accommodated to their passions JORTIN.

Compliance (kǭmpləi·ăns). 1641. [f. COMPLY *v.*¹ + -ANCE. Cf. APPLIANCE.] † **1.** Complaisance –1754; accord –1722. **2.** The acting in accordance *with* a desire, condition, etc.; an acceding *to*; practical assent. Often *absol.*; also in bad sense. 1647.

1. All her words and actions mixed with love And sweet c. MILT. *P.L.* VIII. 603. 2. All politics necessitates questionable compliances 1863. In c. with your wishes 1866. var. **Compli·ancy.**

Compliant (kǭmpləi·ănt), *a.* 1642. [f. COMPLY + -ANT; in sense 2 prob. after *pliant*.] **1.** Complying, disposed to comply; complaisant. † **2.** Pliant –1793. Also as *sb. Obs.*

1. C. with the royal will J. R. GREEN. Hence **Compli·antly** *adv.*

Complicacy (kǫ·mplikăsi). 1827. [f. COMPLICATE + -ACY 3. Cf. *intricacy, advocacy*.] **1.** Complicated quality. **2.** A complicated structure, matter or condition 1849.

2. Difficulties, complicacies, very many CARLYLE.

Complicate (kǫ·mplikĕt), *ppl. a.* 1626. [– L. *complicatus*, pa. pple. of *complicare*; see next, -ATE².] **1.** Interwoven (*arch.*). **2.** Compound, complex (*arch.*) 1638; intricate 1672. **3.** *Bot.* = CONDUPLICATE 1866. Hence † **Co·mplicate-ly** *adv.*, † **-ness.**

Complicate (kǫ·mplikeⁱt), *v.* 1621. [– *complicat-*, pa. ppl. stem of L. *complicare*, f. *com* COM- + *plicare* fold; see -ATE³.] † **1.** To fold, wrap, or twist together –1691. † **2.** To combine intimately –1691. **3.** To mix up *with* in an involved way 1673. † **4.** To compound –1707. **5.** To make complex or intricate 1832.

3. A disease complicated with other diseases ARBUTHNOT. 4. Ideas..complicated of various simple Ideas LOCKE. Hence **Co·mplicated-ly** *adv.*, **-ness.**

Complication (kǫmplikēⁱ·ʃən). 1611. [–(O)Fr. *complication* or late L. *complicatio*, f. as prec.; see -ION.] † **1.** The action of folding together; the condition of being folded together –1691. † **2.** Combination, conjunction –1699. **3.** An involved condition or structure 1666. **4.** Complicated condition, structure, or nature; involved relation 1793; quasi-*concr.* a complicated mass or structure 1647.

3. That c. of probabilities by which the Christian history is attested PALEY. 4. Amid tumult and c. J. H. NEWMAN. The coexistence of a dislocation with a fracture, is a serious c. 1883.

† **Co·mplicative,** *a.* (*sb*). [f. as (or directly from) COMPLICATE *v.* + -IVE.] **1.** Tending to complicate. **2.** *sb.* 1654.

Complice (kǫ·mplis). 1475. [–(O)Fr. *complice* – late L. *complex, complic-* adj. confederate, f. *com* COM- + *plic-* (cf. *complicare* COMPLICATE and *simplex* SIMPLE).] † **1.** *gen.* An associate –1734. **2.** *spec.* An associate in crime (*arch.*). Now ACCOMPLICE. 1581.

1. 2 *Hen. IV*, I. i. 163. 2. To quell these Traitors and their compleases 1594.

Complicity (kǭmpli·sĭti). 1656. [Sense 1, f. COMPLICE + -ITY; so Fr. *complicité*. Sense 2 f. COMPLIC(ATE + -ITY; cf. COMPLICACY.] **1.** The being an accomplice. **2.** = COMPLEXITY 1847.

1. The charge..of c. in the designs of his patron HALLAM.

Complier (kǭmpləi·əɹ). 1612. [f. COMPLY *v.*¹ + -ER¹.] † **1.** An accomplice –1649. **2.** One who complies *with* (any humour, fashion, etc.); † *spec.* a conformist in politics or religion 1644.

2. In the changes of religion he was a c. STRYPE.

Compliment (kǫ·mplimĕnt), *sb.* 1654. [– Fr. *compliment* – It. *complimento*, repr. Rom. **complimentum* for L. *complementum* COMPLEMENT. The earlier sp. was *complement*, the orig. sense of 'filling up, fulfilment, accomplishment' becoming specified as 'fulfilment or observance of the requirements of courtesy'.] **1.** A ceremonial act or expression as a tribute of courtesy, 'usually understood to mean less than it declares'(J.); now, *esp.* a neatly-turned remark addressed to any one, implying praise; complimentary language. **2.** usually in *pl.* Formal respects 1733. **3.** A complimentary gift (*arch.* or *dial.*) 1722. Also *fig.*

1. C.—a thing often paid by people who pay nothing else HOR. SMITH. In a style of c. POPE. 2. Make my compliments to your mamma CHESTERF. Hence **Complime·ntal** *a.* † formal; of the nature of a c.; † given to paying compliments; **-ly** *adv.*

Compliment (kǫ·mpliment), *v.* 1663. [– Fr. *complimenter*, f. *compliment*; see prec.] **1.** *intr.* To employ formal courtesy in act or expression. **2.** *trans.* To address with formal expressions of civility, etc.; to pay a compliment to; to flatter with delicate praise 1735. Also *fig.* **3.** To congratulate formally (*up*)*on* 1717. **4.** *spec.* To present *with* as a mark of courtesy 1717.

1. Believe me, I never c. JANE AUSTEN. 3. To c. a boy on his progress 1884.

Complimentary (kǫmplime·ntări), *a.* 1716. [f. prec. + -ARY¹.] Expressive of, conveying, or of the nature of a compliment.

Compline, complin (kǫ·mplin). ME. [alt., prob. after *matines, matins*, of (O)Fr. *complie* (now *complies*), subst. use of fem. pa. pple. of †*complir* complete. See next.] In Catholic ritual: The last service of the day, completing the services of the canonical hours; also, the hour of that service. Also *attrib.*

At complyn hyt was y-bore To the beryynge, That noble corps of Jhesu Cryst, ME.

† **Co·mplish,** *v.* ME. [– *compliss-*, extended stem of OFr. *complir* complete :– Rom. **complire*, for L. *complēre* fill up, COMPLETE. Later perh. aphet. for *accomplish*.] **1.** To fill up 1450. **2.** To fulfill –1596. Hence † **Co·mplishment.**

Complot (kǫ·mplǫt), *sb.* Now *rare.* 1577. [–(O)Fr. *complot* †dense crowd, secret project, of unkn. origin, by assoc. with PLOT *sb.* II scheme, outline. Superseded by PLOT *sb.* III.] A covert design planned in concert; a conspiracy, a PLOT.

To lay a c. to betray thy Foes *Tit. A.* V. ii. 147.

Complot (kǭmplǫ·t), *v.* Now *rare.* 1579. [– Fr. *comploter*, f. *complot*; see prec.] **1.** *intr.* To combine in a plot. **2.** *trans.* To combine in plotting (some act, usually criminal) 1593.

2. To plot, contriue, or c. any ill *Rich. II*, I. iii. 189. Hence † **Complo·tment,** conspiracy; secret plan. **Complo·tter,** a conspirator.

Complutensian (kǫmplute·nsiăn), *a.* 1660. [f. L. *Complutensis* + -IAN.] Of or belonging to *Complutum*, a town in Spain, now *Alcalá de Henares*; as the *C. Polyglot*, published at Alcalá.

‖ **Compluvium** (kǭmplū·viǒm). 1832. [L.] *Rom. Antiq.* A square opening in the roof of the atrium, through which fell the rain-water collected from the roof.

Comply (kǭmpləi·), *v.*¹ 1602. [– It. *complire* – Cat. *complir*, Sp. *cumplir* – L. *complēre*; see COMPLETE *a.*] † **1.** *trans.* To fulfil (*rare*) –1634. † **2.** To observe the formalities of civility (*with* any one) –1639. † **3.** To be complaisant *with, to*, in conduct or action –1683. **4.** To accede, or consent to 1650. Also *absol.* † **5.** To accord *with* or *together* –1655. † **6.** *trans.* To conform *to* –1683. † **7.** To ally oneself *with* –1651. † **8.** Of a thing: To fit. Const. *with* (*to*). –1704.

3. Willing to flatter and c. with the Rich ETHEREDGE. † *To c. with* (intr.): to accommodate oneself to (circumstances, etc.); to conform to (opinions, customs, etc.); also *absol.* 4. How reddy we are to c. with his desire 1650. He that complies against his will Is of his own opinion still BUTLER *Hud.* III. iii. 547. 6. To my sad tears c. these notes of yours DRUMM. OF HAWTH. 8. To make the Jewish Year c. with the Solar Year HEARNE.

† **Comply·,** *v.*² *rare.* 1611. [In meaning app. repr. COMPLICATE *v.* (in senses 1 and 2); in form infl. by APPLY, PLY *v.*¹ (from L. *plicare*).] **1.** *trans.* To compose by intertexture. **2.** To enfold. HERRICK.

Compo (kǫ·mpo). 1823. [Short for *composition, composite.*] **1.** Stucco, cement. Also *attrib.* **2.** A metallic or other composition 1879. **3.** A composition paid by a debtor. **4.** *attrib.* = COMPOSITE 4. 1878.

† **Compo·ne.** *v.* [ME. *compoun(e)* – OFr. *compo(u)n-*, pres. stem of *compondre*; see COMPOUND *v.*] **1.** *trans.* To compose –1848. **2.** *intr.* To compound –1645.

Compo·né, compony, *a.* 1572. [–(O)Fr. *componé* in same sense; see -Y⁵.] *Her.* Composed of a row of squares of two alternate tinctures. var. † **Compo·ned** *ppl. a.*

Component (kǭmpōᵘ·nĕnt), 1645. [– *component-*, pres. ppl. stem of L. *componere*; see COMPOUND *v.*, -ENT.] *adj.* Composing, making up, constituent 1664. *sb.* A constituent part or element.

adj. Thy c. dust SOUTHEY. Hence **Compo·nency,** composition (*rare*).

Comport (kǭmpōᵊ·ɹt), *v.* 1565. [– L. *comportare*, f. *com* COM- + *portare* carry, bear; cf. (O)Fr. *comporter.*] † **1.** *trans.* To bear –1818. **2.** *refl.* To conduct or behave oneself; to behave 1616. Also † *intr.* (for *refl.*) –1734. † **3.** *lit.* To collect (*rare*) –1660.

1. *To c. with* (intr.): to bear with. 2. He comported himself with extraordinary courage WOODHEAD. *To c. with* (intr.): to accord with; to befit. Phr. † *To c. the pike*: to carry it grasped near the middle and pressed to the right side of the body, with the point raised. Hence † **Compo·rtable** *a.* † **Compo·rtance,** bearing, behaviour; accordance. † **Comporta·tion,** collecting; a collection.

† **Comport** (kǭmpōᵊ·ɹt), *sb.*¹ 1635. [Sense 1 from prec.; sense 2 – OFr. *comport*, f. *comporter* (see prec.).] **1.** The action or position of comporting a pike –1690. **2.** Comportment –1700.

2. I..mark'd their rude c. DRYDEN.

Co·mport, *sb.*² 1771. [app. abbrev. of *comportier* (1764), var. of COMPOTIER, infl. by COMPOTE.] A dessert dish raised upon a stem.

Comportment (kǭmpōᵊ·ɹtmĕnt). Now *rare.* 1599. [– Fr. *comportement*, f. *comporter*; see COMPORT *v.*, -MENT.] Personal bearing, carriage; behaviour.

Ceremoniall in his outward c. SANDYS.

† **Compo·sal.** 1630. [f. COMPOSE + -AL¹.] The action of composing –1700.

Co·mposant, comozant, corrupt ff. CORPOSANT. q.v.

Compose (kǭmpōᵘ·z), *v.* 1481. [–(O)Fr. *composer*, based on L. *componere*; see COMPOUND *v.*, POSE *v.*¹]

I. † **1.** *trans.* To make by putting together parts or elements; to make up, frame, fashion, produce –1788. **2.** To constitute 1665; *pass.* 1541. **3.** *spec.* To make or produce in literary form, to write as author (poetry, essays, or the like) 1483. Also *absol.* **4.** *Mus.* To invent and put into proper form 1597; to set to music 1691. Also *absol.* **5.** *Print.* To set up (type); to set up (an article, etc.) in type 1637. Also *absol.* **6.** To put together so as to make a whole; *spec.* in artistic use 1655; *intr.* (for *refl.*) to admit of artistic grouping 1828.

1. So well compos'd a man D'URFEY. 2. He is compos'd and fram'd of treacherie *Much Ado* V. i. 257. 3. To c. a philosophical poem WORDSW. Easier to criticize than to c. PARR. 6. Symmetry without proportion is not composition. To c. is to arrange unequal things RUSKIN.

II. *trans.* To settle, adjust, arrange 1563. Also *absol.*

To c. a difference HUME, the country FROUDE.

III. 1. *trans.* To adjust to any attitude, to 'make up' 1606; † to dispose, to order –1674. **2.** To arrange, adjust; to lay out (a dead body) 1677. **3.** To make calm or tranquil 1607.

1. To c. oneself to write 1716, to sleep 1709. 2. To c. one's countenance THACKERAY. 3. To c. this midnight noise PRIOR. For Heaven's sake, Amanda, c. yourself MRS. OLIPHANT. Hence **Compo·sed** *ppl. a.* † made up of parts; † elaborately put together; made calm or tranquil; calm and self-possessed (opp. to *excited*); *Her.* = COMPONÉ. **Compo·sedly** *adv.* **Compo·sedness,** c. state or quality.

Composer (kǭmpōᵘ·zəɹ). 1561. [f. COMPOSE *v.* + -ER¹.] **1.** One who or that which composes (see COMPOSE *v.*). **2.** One who composes music. (The usual sense, when used without defining words.) 1597.

1. Composers of green Arbours 1693, of Tragedies HOLLAND. A Printer's C. 1708. Composers of the soul HAMMOND. 2. The well studied chords of some choice c. MILTON.

Composing (kǫmpōᵘ·ziŋ), *vbl. sb.* 1574. [f. COMPOSE *v.* + -ING[1].] The action of the verb COMPOSE.

Comb. (in sense I. 5 of the verb): **c.-frame,** the frame at which a compositor stands; **-rule,** a brass or steel rule against which the type is set in a c.-stick, a setting-rule; **-stand** = *composing-frame*; **-stick,** an instrument, now of metal, of adjustable width, in which the type is set before being put on a galley.

Composite (kǫ·mpǒzit, †kǒmpǫ·zit) *a.* and *sb.* 1500. [– Fr. *composite* or L. *compositus*, pa. pple. of *componere*; see COMPOUND *v.* and -ITE[2].] **1.** Made up of various parts or elements; compound 1678. **2.** *Arch.* The name of the fifth of the classical orders, being 'composed of the Ionic grafted upon the Corinthian'. At first *Composita* (sc. *columna*). 1563. **3.** *Bot.* Belonging to the N.O. *Compositæ*, in which the head is made up of many florets sessile on a common receptacle, and surrounded by a common involucre of bracts; as the daisy, etc. Also *sb.* A plant of this order. 1832. **4.** In various techn. uses (see quots.) 1845.

1. We cannot decompose what is not already c. SIR W. HAMILTON. *C. number* (Math.): one which is the product of two or more factors, greater than unity. **2.** *C. arch*: 'the pointed or lancet arch' (Gwilt). **4.** *A c. vessel*: one built of both wood and iron. *C. carriage*: a railway carriage with compartments of different classes. *C. candle*: one made of stearic acid and the stearin of coco-nut oil. *C. sailing* (*Naut.*): a combination of great-circle and parallel sailing.

B. *sb.* † **1.** A component part (*rare*) 1657. **2.** A compound 1656. **3.** *Gram.* A compound word or term (*rare*) 1708.

Hence **Co·mposite-ly** *adv.*, **-ness.**

Composition (kǫmpǒzi·ʃən). ME. [–(O)Fr. *composition* – L. *compositio*, f. *componere*; see COM-, POSITION.]

I. 1. The action of combining; the fact of being combined; combination (of parts or elements of a whole). **2.** The forming (*of* anything) by combination of parts, etc.; formation, construction 1555. **3.** Orderly arrangement; ordering (*arch.*) 1598. **4.** Specifically: **a.** = SYNTHESIS 1570. **b.** Combination of factors, ratios, forces, or elements, so as to produce a compound resultant 1557. **c.** *Gram.* The combination of two (or more) words to form one compound word 1530. **d.** The art of constructing sentences and of writing prose or verse 1553. **e.** The practice or art of literary production 1577. **f.** The action or art of disposing the parts of a work of art, so as to form a harmonious whole 1695. **g.** The action or art of composing music 1597. **h.** *Printing.* The setting up of type; the composing of matter for printing 1832. **i.** The settling of a debt, liability, etc., by some mutual arrangement; compounding 1557.

1. The C. of Atomes in Bodies GREW. **2.** The c. of a pudding GOLDSM. **4. a.** As in Mathematicks, so in Natural Philosophy, the investigation..by the method of analysis, ought ever to precede the method of c. NEWTON. *Fallacy of c.* (Logic): the fallacy of arguing that what is true of each of several things is true of all taken together. **b.** *C. of forces*: the uniting of two or more forces into one, which shall have the same effect. **d.** All candidates must pass in Latin prose c. (*mod.*). **e.** [Dryden's] haste of c. JOHNSON. **i.** To come to c., and lose one half of the Debt to save the rest 1707.

II. 1. The manner in which a thing is composed; constitution, make, with reference to ingredients ME. **2.** The state or quality of being composite 1541. **3.** Mental or †bodily constitution 1593. **4.** Artistic manner, style 1532. † **5.** Consistency. *Oth.* I. iii. 1.

1. The c. of white light BREWSTER. **3.** *Rich. II*, II. i. 73. Whatever there is of the man of business in my c. LAMB. **4.** The c. of a speech STANHOPE, of a natural landscape POE.

III. The product. **1.** *quasi-concr.* A combination, aggregate, mixture *of* 1551. **2.** *concr.* A substance formed by combination of various ingredients (in techn. uses often shortened to COMPO) 1555. **3.** A literary, artistic, or other intellectual production 1601. **4.** An agreement (*arch.*); a contract, a treaty (*arch.*); a compromise ME. **5.** A compounding for some claim or liability; *spec.* an agreement by which a creditor accepts part of a debt, in satisfaction, from an insolvent debtor 1570; the sum paid 1581. Also *attrib.*

1. Every soil is a c. of different earths 1765. **3.** Aldhelm's Latin compositions 1774. Handel's compositions 1789. **5.** The Irish admitted the c. or fine for murder HALLAM.

Comb.: **c.-cloth,** a waterproof material made from long flax, used for trunk-covers, etc.; **-deed,** a deed for effecting a composition (see III. 5) between a debtor and creditors; **-face** (*Crystallogr.*) = *composition-plane*; **-metal,** a kind of brass composed of copper, zinc, etc., used for the sheathing of ships; **c. pedal,** an organ pedal which acts on a number of stops at once; **-plane** (*Crystallogr.*), the common plane or base between the two parts of a twin crystal.

Compositive (kǒmpǫ·zitiv), *a.* 1601. [f. COMPOSITE and COMPOSIT(ION + -IVE.] † **1.** Of composite nature or character –1687. **2.** Synthetic 1652.

Compositor (kǒmpǫ·zitəɹ). ME. [– AFr. *compositour* = (O)Fr. *-eur* – L. *compositor*, f. *composit-*, pa. ppl. stem of *componere*; see -OUR, -OR 2.] † **1.** One who composes –1533. **2.** *Printing.* A type-setter 1569. Hence **Compositorial** *a.* of or pertaining to composers or compositors.

Compo·sitous, *a. rare.* 1859. [f. Bot. L. *Compositæ.* + -OUS.] = COMPOSITE *a.* 3.

‖ **Compos mentis** (kǫ·mpǫs me·ntis), *adj. phr.* 1679. [L.] Having control of one's mind, in one's right mind. Also simply *compos.*

Compo·ssible, *a.* 1638. [– OFr. *compossible* – med.L. *compossibilis*; see COM-, POSSIBLE.] Possible in coexistence with something else.

Compost (kǫ·mpǫst), *sb.*[1] ME. [– OFr. *composte* and *compot* :– L. *composta*, *-tum*, subst. uses of fem. and n. pa. pple. of *componere* COMPOUND *v.*] **1.** A composition, combination, compound 1640. † **2.** *Cookery.* = COMPOTE –1601. **3.** A prepared manure or mould 1587. Also *fig.* Also *attrib.*

3. *fig.* Martyrs ashes are the best c. to manure the church FULLER.

† **Co·mpost,** *sb.*[2] 1535. [– OFr. *compost*, erron. form of *compot* (nom. *compoz*, *compos*) :– L. *computus*; see COMPUTE.] = COMPUTUS; *esp.* a calendar –1656.

Compost (kǫ·mpǫ̆st), *v.* 1499. [– OFr. *composter* (cf. med.L. *compostare*), f. *compos(e) sb.*; see COMPOST *sb.*[1]] **1.** To treat with compost, to manure. **2.** To make into compost 1829.

Composture (kǒmpǫ·stiŭɹ). Now *dial.* 1607. [– OFr. *composture* composition, manure (cf. med.L. *compostura* manure), f. as prec.; see -URE.] **1.** Composition, composure 1614. **2.** Compost, manure 1607.

Composure (kǒmpōᵘ·ʒⁱŭɹ). 1599. [f. COMPOSE *v.* + -URE; cf. *exposure.*] † **1.** = COMPOSITION, in nearly all senses. **2.** Composed condition of mind, feelings, etc.; calmness 1667.

2. To whom the Virgin Majestie of Eve..With sweet austeer c. thus reply'd MILT. *P.L.* IX. 272.

Compotation (kǫmpotēⁱ·ʃən). 1593. [– L. *compotatio* (in Cicero tr. Gr. συμπόσιον); see COM-, POTATION.] A drinking together, drinking-bout, symposium. So **Co·mpotator,** a fellow-drinker. **Compo·tatory** *a.*

Compote (kǫ·mpoᵘt). 1693. [– Fr. *compote*, later form of OFr. *composte* stew, dish containing fruit :– **compos(i)ta*, subst. use of fem. of L. *compos(i)tus*, pa. pple. of *componere*; cf. COMPOST *sb.*[1]] **1.** Fruit preserved in syrup. **b.** A dish of fruit salad or (mixed) stewed fruit 1863. ‖ **2.** A manner of preparing pigeons 1769.

‖ **Compotier** (kǫmpǫtīᵊ·ɹ, ‖ koṅpotye) 1755. [Fr., f. *compote* (see prec.).] = COMPORT *sb.*[2]

Compound (kǒmpaund), *v.* [ME. *compoun(e)* (XIV–XVII), superseded (XVI) by the present form, on the model of EXPOUND. See COMPONE *v.*]

I. † **1.** *trans.* To put together; to apply –1660. **2.** To combine, mix (elements, etc.) ME. Also † *intr.* (for *refl.*). **3.** To make up by the combination of elements ME. **4.** To compose; to form ME.; † to constitute, as elements –1691.

2. Thus saugh I fals and sothe compouned CHAUCER. SHAKS. *Sonn.* lxxi. **3.** I..did c. for her A certaine stuffe *Cymb.* V. v. 254. **4.** To c. a riddle JOWETT, an army of great strength RALEGH.

II. † **1.** *trans.* To settle (disturbance, strife, etc.) –1757. **2.** To compromise (a matter) 1659. **3.** To settle or discharge a debt, or other liability, by an agreement for the payment of a sum of money, or the like 1665. † **4.** *intr.* To agree, make terms (*with*, *for*) ME. **5.** To come to terms by mutual concession 1528; to come to terms and pay *for*; to compromise; to pay 1555. **6.** To settle with creditors and pay a percentage in discharge of their full claims 1654. **7.** To accept a composition in lieu of one's full claims, etc. 1611; hence, to accept terms of settlement in lieu of prosecution 1576.

1. To c. a quarrell *Tam. Shr.* I. ii. 28. **2.** To c. a suit CRUISE. **3.** Pitkin..has compounded his debts for 8*s.* 6*d.* in the pound LUTTRELL. *To c. a felony*: to forbear prosecution for a consideration. So *To c. an information.* **5.** C., and share the prize QUARLES. Their purses c. for their follies SIR T. BROWNE. C. for Sins they are inclin'd to By damning those they have no mind to BUTLER *Hud.* I. i. 215. **6.** He failed..compounded, and went to America FRANKLIN.

Hence **Compou·ndable** *a.* capable of being combined or commuted for money. **Compou·nder,** one who compounds, in the various senses of the vb.; *Hist.* One of those who wished for a restoration of James II on conditions. **Co·mpoundness.**

Compound (kǫ·mpaund), *a.* ME. [orig. pa. pple. of *compoun(e)*; see COMPONE *v.*, and prec.] Made up by the combination of elements or parts; composite ME; combined, collective 1711.

The Gryphons, those c. animals 1798.

Phrases. **a.** *Surg.* and *Med.* in *c. fracture*, usually fracture of a bone, with a coexisting skin wound with which it communicates. **b.** *Arith.* and *Alg.* (*a*) Made up by combination of several elements, as in *c. fraction*, a fraction of a fraction; *c. number*, a composite number; *c. quantity* (in *Alg.*), a quantity consisting of more than one term; (in *Arith.*) a quantity expressed in terms of various denominations, as pounds, shillings, and pence; *c. ratio*, the ratio formed by multiplying together the antecedents, and also the consequents, of two or more ratios. (*b*) Dealing with numbers of various denominations, as in *c. addition, subtraction, multiplication, division.* (*c*) Proceeding by other than simple process, as *c. interest, proportion.* **c.** *Archit. C. order*; COMPOSITE order. **d.** *Zool.* and *Bot.* Consisting of a combination of individual organisms, as *c. animal, zoophyte, coral*, etc., or of simple parts, as *c. eye, stomach, flower, fruit, leaf, umbel*, etc. **e.** *Mech.* and *Physics*, as in *c. engine*, a condensing engine in which the mechanical action of the steam is begun in one cylinder and ended in a larger cylinder; *c. microscope*, one in which not less than two lenses are employed; *c. motion*, that which is produced by two or more forces, acting in different directions, on the same body, at the same time; *c. screw.* **f.** *Mus.* in *c. interval*, one exceeding an octave; *c. time*, time or rhythm, usu. in multiples of three, in which each bar is made up of more than one bar of simple time. **g.** *C. householder*: a householder whose rates are included in his rent, and paid by the landlord.

Compound (kǫ·mpaund), *sb.*[1] 1530. [The adj. used subst.] **1.** *quasi-concr.* A combination *of* elements 1621. **2.** *concr.* A compound substance 1611, word 1530, thing 1890. † **3.** A thing made up –1773. **4.** Compounding 1671.

1. A c. of Two very different Liquors ADDISON. **2.** These most poysonous Compounds (i.e. compounded drugs) *Cymb.* I. v. 9.

Compound (kǫ·mpaund), *sb.*[2] *Anglo-Ind.* 1679. [– Pg. *campon* or Du. *kampoeng* – Malay *kampong*, *-ung* enclosure, fenced-in space.] The enclosure within which a residence or factory (of Europeans) stands, in the East; also, any similar enclosure round native houses.

Comprador (kǫmprădōᵊ·ɹ). 1615. [– Pg. *comprador* buyer :– late L. *comparator*, f. L. *comparare* purchase.] **1.** Formerly, a native house-steward. *Obs.* in India. **2.** In China, a native servant, employed as head of the native staff, and as agent, by European houses.

Comprecation (kǫmprĭkēⁱ·ʃən). 1635. [– L. *comprecatio*, f. *comprecat-*, pa. ppl. stem of *comprecari*, f. *com* COM- + *precari* pray; cf. OFr. *comprecation.*] A praying together, joint supplication.

Comprehend (kǫmprĭhe·nd), *v.* ME. [– OFr. *comprehender* or L. *comprehendere*, f. *com* COM- + *prehendere* seize.] † **1.** To lay hold of –1650; † to overtake, or attain to; † to accomplish –1607. **2.** To grasp with the mind, take in ME. **3.** To apprehend with the senses, *esp.* sight. [L. *comprehendere visu.*] ME. † **4.** To embrace or describe summarily –1612. **5.** To take in, include, comprise, contain ME. Also *transf.* and *fig.*

2. To c. is to know a thing as well as that thing can be known DONNE. **4.** All precepts concernyng kinges, are in effect comprehended, in those two Remembrances BACON. **5.** In this boke, I cannot comprehende..yᵉ sege of Rone 1530. A single term to c. both divisions of the..period LYELL. As able to c. the sea in a cockle-shell 1662. *fig* As muche ioye as herte may comprehende CHAUCER. Vnder lesse then three lines, can no figure be comprehended 1570. The Air, comprehending the Earth STURMY. Hence **Comprehe·nder** (*rare*). **Comprehe·ndible** *a. rare*, comprehensible. **Comprehe·ndingly** *adv.*

Comprehensible (kǫmprǐhe·nsǐb'l), *a.* 1529. [– Fr. *compréhensible* or L. *comprehensibilis*, f. *comprehens-*, pa. ppl. stem of *comprehendere*; see prec., -IBLE.] **1.** That may be comprised or contained. **2.** That may be grasped: † palpable –1579; intelligible 1598.

1. He is not comprehensyble nor circumscribed no where MORE. **2.** C. to the meanest capacity 1815. Hence **Comprehensibi·lity**, quality of being c. So **Comprehe·nsibleness. Comprehe·nsibly** *adv.*

Comprehension (kǫmprǐhe·nʃən). 1541. [– Fr. *compréhension* or L. *comprehensio*, f. as prec.; see -ION.] **1.** The action of comprehending, comprising, or including; the fact of being so comprehended or comprised; *spec.* in *Rhet.* (see quots.). **2.** The faculty of comprehending; comprehensiveness 1614. † **3.** A summation *of* any matter –1684. **4.** *Logic.* The sum of the attributes comprehended in a concept 1725. **5.** The action, condition, or faculty of comprehending with the mind; understanding 15... † **6.** Physical grasping –1768.

1. In the Old Testament there is a close c. of the New, in the New an open discovery of the Old HOOKER. *Comprehension*, a..figure, whereby the name of a whole is put for a part; or that of a part for a whole E. CHAMBERS. An Act of C... for admitting of all persuasions in religion to the public observation of their particular worship PEPYS. **5.** The c. which she hath of God HOOKER. A..constitution, beyond our c. BUTLER. Hence † **Comprehe·nsional** *a. rare*, comprehensive.

Comprehensive (kǫmprǐhe·nsiv), *a.* 1614. [– Fr. *compréhensif, -ive* or late L. *comprehensivus*, f. as prec.; see -IVE.] **1.** *gen* Characterized by comprehension; comprising much; of large content or scope; *occas.*, compendious. **2.** Characterized by mental comprehension 1628. **3.** *Logic.* Intensive 1725.

1. His Aim is more C. STANLEY. **2.** C. knowledge 1641. He [Chaucer] must have been a man of a most wonderful c. nature DRYDEN. Hence **Comprehe·nsive-ly** *adv.*, **-ness.**

† **Comprehe·nsor.** 1653. [mod.L., f. as prec. + -OR 2.] One who has attained to full comprehension. (In 17th c. Divinity, with reference to *Phil.* 3:12, 13.)

Thou art yet a traveller, they [Saints] comprehensors BP. HALL.

† **Compre·nd,** *v.* ME. [- (O)Fr. *comprendre* or L. *comprendere*, contr. f. *comprehendere* COMPREHEND.] = COMPREHEND –1594.

† **Compre·sbyter.** 1600. [– eccl.L. *compresbyter* (Cyprian); see COM-, PRESBYTER.] A fellow-presbyter –1650.

Compress (kǫ̆mpre·s), *v.* ME. [– OFr. *compresser* or late L. *compressare*, frequent. of L. *comprimere*, or – pa. ppl. stem (*compress-*) of *comprimere*; see COM-, PRESS *v.*[1]] **1.** To press together, to squeeze; *Surg.* to close by compression. **2.** To squeeze together, so as to make more firm and solid ME.; to reduce in volume by, or as by, pressure; to condense, concentrate 1677. † **3.** *fig.* To keep under restraint –1847. † **4.** To embrace sexually –1725.

1. To c. an artery MARRYAT. **2.** To c. a sponge 1789, air HALE, water TYNDALL, thoughts BURKE. To collect and c. feeble rays of light 1851. Hence **Compre·ssingly** *adv.*

Compress (kǫ·mpres), *sb.* 1599. [– Fr. *compresse* (Paré), f. *compresser*; see prec.] **1.** *Surg.* A soft pad of linen, lint, etc., used with a bandage, to maintain due pressure on any part. In hydropathic use, a piece of cloth, wetted with water, and tightly covered with an impervious bandage, applied to the body for the relief of inflammation. **2.** A machine for pressing cotton-bales, etc. 1874.

Compressed (kǫ̆mpre·st), *ppl. a.* ME. [f. COMPRESS *v.* + -ED[1].] **1.** Pressed together closely, so as to occupy small space; pressed into a smaller volume; condensed; also *fig.* **2.** Having the two opposite sides nearly plane or flat 1668.

Compressed air engine: an engine operated by compressed air, as an elastic substitute for steam. Hence **Compre·ssedly** *adv.*

Compressibility (kǫ̆mpresǐbi·lǐti). 1691. [f. next + -ITY; cf. Fr. *compressibilité*.] The quality of being compressible; *esp.* in *Physics*, the quality in virtue of which the volume of a gas, etc., may be diminished without decrease of its mass.

Compressible (kǫ̆mpre·sǐb'l), *a.* 1691. [f. COMPRESS *v.* + -IBLE. Cf. Fr. *compressible*.] That may be compressed; capable of compression; applied to a feverish pulse, which seems to vanish under pressure.

Compression (kǫ̆mpre·ʃən). ME. [– (O)Fr. *compression* – L. *compressio*, f. *compress-*; see COMPRESS *v.*, -ION.] **1.** The action of compressing; also *fig.* **2.** A state of being compressed; also *fig.* 1603. **3.** *Surg.* Short for 'compression of the brain' 1847.

2. C. of thought JOHNSON, of heart FARRAR. Hence **Compre·ssional** *a.*

Compressive (kǫ̆mpre·siv), *a.* 1572. [– (O)Fr. *compressif, -ive* or med.L. *compressivus*, f. as prec.; see -IVE.] Having the attribute of compressing; tending to compress. Hence **Compre·ssively** *adv.*

Compressor (kǫ̆mpre·səɹ). 1839. [f. COMPRESS *v.* + -OR 2.] One who or that which compresses. *Spec.* **a.** *Anat.* A muscle which compresses a part. **b.** *Surg.* An instrument for compressing a nerve, artery, duct, or other part; also a tourniquet. **c.** An instrument for compressing objects in microscopical investigations; called also *compressorium*. **d.** *Naut.* An iron lever for checking or stopping the chain-cable as it runs out. **e.** *Gun.* A mechanism for pressing a gun-carriage to its platform during the recoil. **f.** A machine for compressing air; an *air-compressor*.

Compressure (kǫ̆mpre·ʃ'ŭɹ, -əɹ). 1644. [– med.L. *compressura*, f. as prec.; see -URE.] Compressing; pressure together; † repression.

† **Compriest.** [f. COM- + PRIEST, perh. after COMPRESBYTER. Cf. OFr. *comprestre*.] A fellow-priest. MILT.

† **Comprint,** *v. rare.* 1634. [See COM-.] To share in printing; as the Universities of Oxford and Cambridge shared with the King's Printer and the Company of Stationers the right to print privileged books –1684.

¶ The meaning 'to print surreptitiously another's copy' and **Comprint** *sb.* are mod. dict. figments.

Comprisal (kǫ̆mprəi·zăl). ? *Obs.* 1643. [f. COMPRISE *v.* + -AL[1].] The action of comprising; a compendium.

Comprise (kǫ̆mprəi·z), *v.* Also † **comprize.** ME. [– Fr. *compris, comprise*, pa. pple. of *comprendre* COMPREHEND; cf. APPRISE.] † **1.** To lay hold on, seize; *Sc.* to 'attach' –1637. † **2.** To take in (mentally), comprehend –1680. **3.** To include, embrace; to comprehend compendiously ME. **4.** To contain, consist of 1481; to extend to, cover 1541. † **5.** To put together (a treatise) –1628. † **6.** To constitute (*rare*) –1794.

3. Behold a Nation in a Man comprised DRYDEN. **4.** The house comprises box-room, nine bedrooms, etc. (*Mod. Advt.*). Hence **Compri·sable** *a.*

† **Co·mprobate,** *v.* 1531. [– *comprobat-*, pa. ppl. stem of L. *comprobare* approve, prove; see COM-, PROBATE.] *trans.* To prove, confirm; to approve –1660. So † **Co·mprobate** *pa. pple.* † **Comproba·tion.**

† **Comprodu·ce,** *v. rare.* 1630. [See COM-.] *trans.* To produce together (*with*) –1674. So † **Comprodu·ction,** production in combination, joint product.

Compromise (kǫ·mprŏməiz), *sb.* ME. [– (O)Fr. *compromis* – juridical L. *compromissum*, subst. use of n. of pa. pple. of *compromittere* consent to arbitration, f. *com* COM- + *promittere* promise. Cf. COMPROMIT.] † **1.** A joint promise or agreement made by contending parties to abide by the decision of an arbiter. ME. only. **2.** Arbitration 1479. **3.** Arrangement of a dispute by concessions on both sides; partial surrender of one's position, for the sake of coming to terms; the terms offered by either side 1516. **4.** *fig.* Adjustment for practical purposes of rival courses of action, systems, theories, etc., by the surrender of a part of each 1711; anything that results from or embodies such an arrangement 1797. **5.** A putting in peril, exposure to risk or suspicion; see COMPROMISE *v.* 4. 1603.

3. War'd he hath not, But basely yeelded vpon comprimize, That which his Ancestors atchieu'd with blowes *Rich. II*, II. i. 253. **4.** Logic admits of no c.; the essence of politics is c. MACAULAY. All virtue is a c. between opposite motives and inducements GODWIN.

Compromise (kǫ·mprŏməiz), *v.* 1596. [f. the sb.; in some uses replacing COMPROMIT.] † **1.** To adjust or settle (differences, etc.) between parties. Also *fig.* –1798. **2.** Of the parties: To settle by mutual concession 1679. **3.** *intr.* To come to terms by mutual concession 1656. **4.** To expose (oneself, one's own or another's reputation, credit, etc.) to risk or danger, to imperil; to involve in a hazardous course, to commit (oneself) 1696.

1. † *To be compromised*: to be agreed by compromise (*Merch. V*, I. iii 79). **2.** With much difficulty, the dispute was compromised MACAULAY. **3.** To induce him to c. on those terms RICHARDSON. **4.** It behov'd him not to C. his Honour and his Reputation 1696. Hence **Co·mpromiser,** † one who acts as arbiter; one who compromises or advocates compromise. **Co·mpromisingly** *adv.*

† **Compromi·ssion.** ME. [– (O)Fr. *compromission* or med.L. *compromissio*, f. *compromiss-*, pa. ppl. stem of L. *compromittere*; see next, -ION.] **1.** Submission to an arbitrator for decision –1524. **2.** Election by compromise, *i.e.* by agreement of the electing body to entrust the election to one or more of its members. *Hist.* ME. **3.** A compromising –1624.

Compromit (kǫmprŏmi·t), *v.* ME. [– L. *compromittere* (in sense 1), f. *com* COM- + *promittere* PROMISE; cf. COMPROMISE *sb.*] † **1.** *refl.* (and *pass.*) To bind themselves mutually (see COMPROMISE *sb.* 2) –1565. † **2.** *trans.* To refer to arbitration –1606. Also *fig.* † **3.** To settle by arbitration –1693. Also *fig.* † **4.** To delegate to another or others one's right of voting in an election –1573. **5.** *U.S.* (*Obsolescent.*) = COMPROMISE *v.* 4. 1787.

Comprovi·ncial, *a.* 1590. [– late L. *comprovincialis* (of bishops) belonging to the same province; see COM-, PROVINCIAL.] Of or belonging to the same province. As *sb.* A bishop of the same province 1642.

‖ **Compsognathus** (kǫmpsǫ·gnăþǫs). 1878. [mod. L., f. Gr. κομψός elegant + γνάθος jaw.] *Palæont.* A genus of reptiles, remarkable for their bird-like affinities. Hence **Compso·gnathous** *a.*; **Compso·gnathid** *a.* and *sb.* (a member) of the family *Compsognathidæ* (order *Deinosauria*) to which these creatures belonged.

† **Compt,** *a.* ME. [– L. *comptus*, pa. pple. of *comere* comb, dress (the hair).] Dressed, as to the hair; *more gen.*, trim, spruce, polished. Also *transf.* –1693. Hence † **Co·mptly** *adv.* † **Co·mptness.**

Compt, Comptable, etc.; see COUNT, etc.

Compter (kau·ntəɹ). ME. Old spelling of COUNTER *sb.*, formerly used in all senses, and from 17th c. as: The name of certain city prisons for debtors, etc., in London, Exeter, etc.

‖ **Comptoir** (kŏ̃ntwar). 1722. [Fr.] A commercial agency or factory (in a foreign country).

Comptonite (kǫ·mptənəit). 1822. [f. Earl *Compton*, who brought it from Vesuvius, + -ITE[1] 2 b.] *Min.* = THOMSONITE.

Comptrol, etc.; see CONTROL, etc.

Comptroller (kǫ̆ntrōᵘ·ləɹ). Spelling of CONTROLLER, due to assoc. of *cont-* with COUNT *sb.*[1] (L. *computus*), used in certain official designations. Hence **Comptrollership.**

Compulsative (kǫ̆mpʊ·lsătiv), *a.* [f. *compulsat-*, pa. ppl. stem of *compulsare*, frequent. of *compellere* COMPEL + -IVE.] Of the nature of compulsion, compulsory. *Haml.* I. i. 103. Hence **Compu·lsatively** *adv.*

† **Compulsatory** (kǫ̆mpʊ·lsătəri), *a.* 1603. [f. as prec. + -ORY[2].] Of the nature of or subject to compulsion; compulsory –1827. Hence **Compu·lsatorily** *adv.*

Compulse (kǫ̆mpʊ·ls), *v.* ? *Obs.* ME. [– OFr. *compulser* compel – L. *compulsare*, frequent. of *compellere* (in late L.) COMPEL.] † **1.** *trans.* To compel, force –1632. **2.** To force to move. (Cf. *repulse.*) CARLYLE.

Compulsion (kǒmpɒ·lʃən). 1462. [– (O)Fr. *compulsion* – late L. *compulsio*, f. *compuls-*, pa. ppl. stem of L. *compellere* (in late L.) COMPEL; see -ION.] The action, or an act, of compelling, or the condition of being compelled; constraint, obligation, coercion.

Wherefore was there such **c.** us'd..about conforming to a Liturgy MILT. The tribute..would not be forthcoming except on c. 1859.

Compulsitor (kǒmpɒ·lsitəɹ). 1816. [app. erron. f. *compulsator*, Sc. for COMPULSATORY; see -OR 2, -ORY[2].] *Sc. Law.* A compulsatory instrument, act, or proceeding.

Compulsive (kǒmpɒ·lsiv), *a.* 1602. [– med. L. *compulsivus*, f. *compuls-*; see COMPULSION, -IVE.] **1.** = COMPULSORY *a.* 2. †**2.** = COMPULSORY *a.* 1. –1836.

1. The power of the magistrate is c. 1873. **2.** Freed..from all c. tributes and taxes MILT. Hence **Compu·lsively** *adv.*

Compulsory (kǒmpɒ·lsəri). 1516. [f. med. L. *compulsorius*, f. as prec.; see -ORY[2].]

A. *adj.* **1.** Produced by or acting under compulsion; forced 1581. **2.** Coercive 1631.

1. Of compulsary single life 1581. **2.** C. process for obtaining witnesses 1789.

B. *sb.* A compulsory agency or means; a legal mandate compelling obedience 1516.

Hence **Compu·lsorily** *adv.* **Compu·lsoriness.**

† **Compu·nct,** *ppl. a.* ME. [– *compunctus*, in eccl.L. stung by remorse, pa. pple. of L. *compungere* prick severely, sting, f. *com* COM- + *pungere* prick.] Affected with compunction. (Usually construed as a pple.) –1659. var. † **Compu·ncted.**

Compunction (kǒmpɒ·ŋkʃən). ME. [– (O)Fr. *componction* – eccl.L. *compunctio*, f. *compunct-*; see prec., -ION.] **1.** Pricking or stinging of the conscience or heart; uneasiness of mind consequent on wrong-doing; remorse, contrition. **2.** In mod. use: A slight or passing regret for wrong-doing, or a feeling of regret for some slight offence (sometimes including pity for the person wronged) 1712. †**3.** In physical sense: The action of pricking –1656.

1. A remorse, and c. for former sins DONNE. **2.** They quitted it [the Reformed Communion] without c. BUCKLE. Hence **Compu·nctionless** *a.*

Compunctious (kǒmpɒ·ŋkʃəs), *a.* 1605. [f. stem of *compunction* + -OUS; cf. *factious.*] **1.** Of the nature of compunction. **2.** Having compunction 1816.

1. Stop vp th' accesse, and passage to Remorse, That no c. visitings of Nature Shake my fell purpose *Macb.* I. v. 46. Hence **Compu·nctiously** *adv.* So † **Compu·nctive** *a. rare*, tending to compunction.

† **Compu·pil.** A fellow-pupil. [See COM-.] WALTON.

Compurgation (kǫmpɒ̆ɹgēⁱ·ʃən). 1658. [– med.L. *compurgatio*, f. *compurgat-*, pa. ppl. stem of L. *compurgare* purge completely; see COM-, PURGATION.] **1.** The action of clearing a man from a charge by the oaths of a number of others; also, generally, vindication; evidence to this effect. **2.** *esp.* The Old English mode of trial and purgation by means of the *consacramentales*; known to the Common Law as WAGER OF LAW. See COMPURGATOR 1. 1658.

1. [He] was privileged..from suspicion of Incontinency and needed no c. HACKET.

Compurgator (kǫ·mpɒɹgēⁱtəɹ, kǒmpɒ̆·ɹgătəɹ). 1533. [– med.L. *compurgator* (XIII), f. *com* COM- + *purgator* purger; see prec., -OR 2. Cf. OFr. *compurgateur.*] **1.** A witness to character who swore along with the person accused, in order to the acquittal of the latter. (Originally a term of the Canon Law; applied by modern historians to the 'oath-helpers' (in Ger. *Eideshülfe*) of the Old English mode of trial and purgation, and sometimes used by modern legal writers with reference to WAGER OF LAW.) **2.** *gen.* One who vouches for, or clears from any charge. Also *fig.* 1613.

1. The compurgators of our oldest law were not a jury in the modern sense, but they were one of the elements out of which the jury rose FREEMAN. **2.** He calleth God to be his c. SANDERSON. Hence **Compurgato·rial** *a.* of or pertaining to compurgators; so **Compu·rgatory** *a.*

Compu·rsion. [joc. f. COM-, PURSE *v.*] A pursing together. STERNE.

Computable (kǒmpiū·tăb'l, kǫ·mpiutăb'l), *a.* 1646. [– L. *computabilis*, f. *computare*; see COMPUTE *v.*, -ABLE.] Capable of being computed.

† **Co·mputate,** *v.* 1602. [f. as next; see -ATE[3].] *trans.* = COMPUTE –1619.

Computation (kǫmpiutēⁱ·ʃən). ME. [– L. *computatio*, f. *computat-*, pa. ppl. stem of *computare*; see COMPUTE *v.*, -ION. Cf. Fr. *computation* (XVI).] **1.** The action or process of computing; a method of reckoning. **2.** A computed result 1713. † **3.** Ratiocination –1656.

1. The Gregorian C..being eleven days before the Julian STEELE. Hence **Computa·tional** *a. rare*, of or pertaining to c. So **Compu·tative, co·mp-** *a.* given to c. † **Co·mputator,** a calculator.

Compute (kǒmpiū·t), *sb.* Now *rare.* ME. [– Fr. *comput* COMPUTUS (in sense 1), and f. the vb.] † **1.** (*co·mpute*) = COMPUTUS 2. –1533. **2.** Computation; now chiefly in *beyond c.* 1588. †**3.** Judgement –1682.

Compute (kǒmpiū·t), *v.* 1631. [– Fr. *computer* or L. *computare*, f. *com* COM- + *putare* clear or settle (an account), reckon, think.] **1.** *trans.* To determine by calculation; to reckon, count; to take account of 1647. **2.** *intr.* To make computation 1634.

1. The radii of curvature for these lenses, as computed by Mr. Herschel BREWSTER. What's done we partly may c., But know not what's resisted BURNS. **2.** To c. by weight 1872. Hence **Compu·ter,** one who computes; *spec.* one employed to make calculations in an observatory, etc. **Co·mputist,** one skilled in the computus or calendar; † an accountant; a computer.

‖ **Computus** (kǫ·mpiutɒ̆s). *Hist.* Also **compotus.** [Late L., 'computation', in med.L. as in sense 2; see prec.] **1.** A reckoning; an account 1848. **2.** A set of mediæval tables for astronomical and calendarial calculations 1832.

Comrade (kǫ·mrĕd). 1591. [Earlier *camerade, camarade* – Fr. *camerade, camarade* (orig. fem.) – Sp. *camarada* (i) barrack-room, (ii) chamber-fellow, mate, f. *camara* CHAMBER; see -ADE.] *orig.* One who shares the same room, tent, etc., a 'chum'; *esp.* a fellow-soldier (also *Comrade-in-arms*); hence *gen.* an associate in friendship, occupation, fortunes, etc., mate. Also *transf.* and *fig.*

His comrade's face each warrior saw SCOTT. To be a C. with the Wolfe and Owle *Lear* II. iv. 213. Hence **Co·mrade** *v.* to associate *with*, as a c.; **Co·mradely** *a.* like a c. **Co·mradery** (*rare*), **Co·mradeship,** the position of being a c., camaraderie.

† **Comra·do.** 1598. [– Sp. *camarada*, also † *-ado*; see prec., -ADO.] = COMRADE –1636.

Co·mrogue. *arch.* 1621. [See COM-.] A fellow-rogue.

‖ **Comte** (kǒṅt). 1611. [Fr.] A French title: COUNT.

Comtian (kǫ·mtiăn, ko·ṅtiăn). Also **Comtean.** 1855. [f. Auguste *Comte* (d. 1857), a French philosopher, the founder of POSITIVISM; see -IAN.] *adj.* Of or originating with Comte. *sb.* A Comtist. So **Co·mtism,** positivism. **Co·mtist,** a positivist; also *attrib.* or as *adj.*

‖ **Comus** (kōᵘ·mɒ̆s). 1634. [L. – Gr. κῶμος revel.] A revel; revelry personified as a deity.

Con (kǫn), *v.*[1] [Mainly repr. ME. *cunn-* or *conn-* from OE. *cunn-* (= kun); but in part ME. *con*, from OE. *con*, for *can* (= kǫn). See further under CAN *v.*[1]]

†**I. 1.** To know: repl. by CAN *v.* –1674. **2.** To know how; hence, to be able; repl. by CAN *v.* –1489.

II. 1. To get to know; to study or learn; hence, to pore over, commit to memory; to inspect, examine ME. **2.** *To cun* or *con thank(s* (OE. *þanc cunnan*): to acknowledge one's gratitude; to thank OE. So †*To* (*cun*) *con gree* or *malgre*: to express one's satisfaction or displeasure [Fr. *savoir gré*].

1. An Oration which..Lysander should have conned without book NORTH. Conning old topics like a parrot SWIFT.

Con, conne, cun (kɒn, kǫn), *v.*[2] 1626. [Reduced form of COND, CUND.] *trans.* To direct the steering of (a ship). Also *absol.* and *fig.*

Con, conn (kɒn, kǫn), *sb.*[1] 1825. [f. CON *v.*[2]] The action or post of conning a ship, steerage.

Con (kǫn), *sb.*[2] 1620. [Also †*con* vb.; perh. – Fr. *cogner* strike, thump.] A rap with the knuckles, a knock.

Con (kǫn), *sb.*[3] *n. dial.* 1600. [poss. short for *cony, coney*, spec. applied to the squirrel, as *puss* to the hare.] A squirrel.

Con (kǫn), *adv.* (*sb.*) 1470. Short for L. *contra* 'against', in PRO and CON (q.v.) 'for and against'. As *sb.* A reason, argument, or arguer against, *esp.* in *pros and cons.*

‖ **Con,** *prep.* It. :– L. *cum* with, as in CON AMORE, q.v., *con affetto, con brio*, etc.

Con-, *prefix*, of L. origin. The form assumed by L. *com-* bef. all consonants exc. *b, m, h, r*, and *l*. For meaning see COM-.

† **Co·nable,** *a.* ME. Phonetic reduction of COVENABLE.

Conacre (kǫ·nēⁱkəɹ), *sb.* Also **corn-acre.** 1824. [orig. *corn-acre*, i.e. CORN *sb.*[1], ACRE.] The letting by a tenant, for the season, of small portions of land ready prepared for a crop (*Ireland*). Hence **Co·nacre** *v.* to sublet in c. **Co·nacrer,** one who uses a piece of land on this system.

Conama·rin. 1882. [f. L. *conium* hemlock + *amarus* bitter + -IN[1].] A bitter principle said to exist in *Conium maculatum.*

‖ **Con amore** (kǫn ămōᵊ·ri). 1826. [It.; = 'with love'.] With love, zeal, or delight. Also as quasi-*adj.*

Conario- (konēᵊ·rio). 1881. Comb. form of CONARIUM, as in *c.-hypophy·sial canal*, a passage connecting the infundibulum with the pineal gland; so *c.-h. tract.*

‖ **Conarium** (konēᵊ·riɒ̆m). 1656. [mod.L. – Gr. κωνάριον, dim. of κῶνος pine-cone.] The pineal gland of the brain.

Conation (konēⁱ·ʃən). 1615. [– L. *conatio*, f. *conat-*, pa. ppl. stem of *conari* endeavour; see -ION.] † **1.** Endeavour. **2.** *Philos.* The faculty of volition and desire; also (with *a* and *pl.*) the product of this faculty 1836. So **Co·native** *a.* pertaining to, or of the nature of, c.

‖ **Conatus** (konēⁱ·tɒ̆s). 1665. [L., f. *conari*; see prec.] **1.** An effort, endeavour 1722. **2.** *transf.* A force, impulse, or tendency simulating a human effort; a nisus.

2. What blind c. of nature should produce it in birds PALEY.

Conaxial (kǫnæ·ksiăl), *a.* = COAXIAL.

Concamerate (kǫnkæ·mĕreⁱt), *v.* 1611. [– *concamerat-*, pa. ppl. stem of L. *concamerare* vault; see CAMERA, -ATE[3].] **1.** To vault or arch. ? *Obs.* **2.** To divide into chambers or cells 1746.

2. The nautilus..is a concamerated shell 1754. Hence **Concamera·tion,** vaulting, vaulted roof, etc.; division into chambers or cells; a chambered formation; one of the chambers of a series.

† **Concarnation** (kǫnkaɹnēⁱ·ʃən). *rare.* 1638. [– med.L. **concarnatio*, f. CON- + L. *caro, carn-* flesh + *-atio* -ATION.] Union of flesh with flesh, or of a bone with another bone by means of muscles –1685.

Concatenate (kǫnkæ·tĭneⁱt), *v.* 1598. [– *concatenat-*, pa. ppl. stem of late L. *concatenare*, f. *com* CON- + *catena* CHAIN; see -ATE[3].] To chain together (*obs.*); to connect like the links of a chain, to link together. *fig.*

The world concatenated together vnder a Crowne Imperiall MALYNES. So **Conca·tenate** *ppl. a.* Hence **Conca·tenator,** one who concatenates.

Concatenation (kǫnkætĭnēⁱ·ʃən). 1603. [– Fr. *concaténation* or late L. *concatenatio*, f. as prec.; see -ION.] **1.** Union by linking together; concatenated condition. **2.** *esp.* Union in a series or chain 1614. **3.** quasi-*concr.* A concatenated series or system, an unbroken sequence, a chain 1622.

2. The necessary c. of ideas which should reproduce the c. of objects LEWES. **3.** This vile c. of straight lines RUSKIN.

Concate·rvate, *ppl. a.* 1882. [– late L. *concatervatus*, f. *com* CON- + *caterva* crowd + *-atus* -ATE[2].] Heaped up together.

Concaule·scence. *rare.* 1882. [f. CON- + CAULESCENT; see -ENCE.] *Bot.* The coalescence of separate axes, *e.g.* of the leaf-stalk and stem.

Concause (kǫ·nkǭz). 1619. [– med.L. *concausa*; see CON-, CAUSE.] A co-operating cause. Hence **Concausal** *a.* (and *sb.*).

Concave (kǫ·nkēⁱv), *sb.* 1541. [– OFr. *concave* – the adj. (see next); cf. L. *concava* hollows; later, absol. use of the adj.] **1.** † A hollow –1814; a concave part of a machine 1874. **2.** A concave surface 1552; *spec.* the vault of heaven 1635. †**3.** A concave lens, speculum, etc. –1797.

2. On high within the c., as are the..starres 1635.

Concave (kǫ·nkēⁱv), *a.* 1571. [– L. *concavus* (perh. through (O)Fr. *concave*), f. *com* CON- + *cavus* hollow.] †**1.** Hollow –1659. **2.** Having the outline or surface curved like the interior of a circle or sphere; the reverse of convex; incurvated 1571.

1. As concaue as..a Worme-eaten nut *A.Y.L.* III. iv. 26. **2.** The c. mirror is the staple instrument of the magician's cabinet BREWSTER. Hence **Co·ncavely** *adv.*, **-ness.** var. † **Co·ncavous.**

Concave (kǫ·nkēⁱv), *v.* 1652. [– OFr. *concaver* or L. *concavare*, f. *concavus*; see prec.] *trans.* To make concave; † to vault. Hence † **Concava·tion** (Dicts.).

Concavity (kǫ̆nkæ·vĭti). 1483. [– (O)Fr. *concavité* or late L. *concavitas*; see CONCAVE *a.*, -ITY.] **1.** The condition of being concave 1578. **2.** A concave surface or side 1483. **3.** A hollow; a cavity 1513.

Concavo- (kǫ̆nkēⁱ·vo), in comb. = Concavely, concave and —, as in **C.-co·ncave,** concave on both sides; **C.-co·nvex,** concave on one side and convex on the other, and thinnest in the centre.

Conceal (kǫ̆nsī·l), *v.* ME. [– OFr. *conceler* – L. *concelare*, f. *com* CON- + *celare* hide.] **1.** *trans.* To keep from the knowledge or observation of others. **2.** *trans.* To put or keep out of sight or notice, to hide 1595.

1. Thy praise hee..Conceales not from us MILT. *P.L.* IX. 751. To dissemble or concele that Fidelity..they ow'd CLARENDON. **2.** The Army, that lies conceal'd for him in Knightsbridge 1671. Hence **Concea·lable** *a.* (*rare*). **Concea·led-ly** *adv.*, **-ness.**

Concealer (kǫ̆nsī·ləɹ). 1514. [– AFr. *concelour*, f. *conceler* (see prec.); see *-our*, -ER².] **a.** One who conceals. †**b.** *Law.* In 17th c., applied to persons who sought by surreptitious means to disturb possessors of 'concealed land', *i.e.* land privily held from the king without a proper title. See CONCEALMENT 1 b.

Concealment (kǫ̆nsī·lmĕnt). ME. [– OFr. *concelement*; see CONCEAL, -MENT.] **1.** The concealing (of any information). In *Law*, The intentional suppression of truth or fact known, to the injury or prejudice of another. **b.** *esp.* The holding of land against the king's rights, without a proper title 1623. **2.** *gen.* The action of concealing 1600. †**3.** A secret, a mystery –1622. **4.** The condition of being concealed 1605; the capacity of concealing; in *pl.* conditions that conceal 1728.

2. Let c. like a worme i'th budde Feede on her damaske cheeke SHAKS. **4.** Some dear cause Will in c. wrap me up a while SHAKS. The clefted tree Offers its kind c. to a few (birds) THOMSON.

Concede (kǫ̆nsī·d), *v.* 1632. [– Fr. *concéder* or L. *concedere* withdraw, yield; see CON-, CEDE.] **1.** *trans.* To admit, allow, grant (a proposition, claim, etc.); *occas.*, To allow formally for the sake of argument 1646. **2.** To grant, yield, or surrender (*e.g.* a right, a privilege) 1632. **3.** *intr.* or *absol.* To make a concession 1780.

1. Conceding, for a moment, that there is any analogy between a bee and a man DICKENS. **3.** When..I wished you to c. to America, at a time when she prayed concession at our feet BURKE. Hence † **Conce·dence.** RICHARDSON. **Conce·der.**

Conceit (kǫ̆nsī·t), *sb.* ME. [f. CONCEIVE on the anal. of the pairs *deceive, deceit, receive, receit.*] †**1.** That which is conceived in the mind, a conception, notion, idea, thought; device –1823. †**2.** The faculty or action of conceiving; conception; apprehension –1805. †**3.** Personal opinion or judgement, usually 'in a neutral sense' (J.). –1759. **4.** Favourable opinion, esteem. Now *dial.*, exc. in *out of c. with.* 1462. **5.** Short for SELF-CONCEIT 1605. **6.** A fanciful notion; a whim 1530; fancy 1578. **7.** A fanciful, ingenious, or witty notion or expression; an affectation of thought or style; = CONCETTO 1513; a trick 1520; sentiment 1589; wit 1597. †**8.** *concr.* A fancy article –1823. †**9.** A (morbid) seizure of the body or mind; see CONCEIVE *v.* –1622.

1. Fluent in language to express their conceits FULLER. A glimmering c. of some such thing LAMB. **2.** A Gentleman of good c. *A.Y.L.* V. ii. 48. Wise in C., in Act a very sot DRAYTON. **3.** That good self-conceit and opinion of his owne HOLLAND. **4.** To be out of c. with our lot in life NEWMAN. **5.** It takes the c. out of a man R. FORD. **6.** In c. build castles in the sky GREENE. **7.** How..our toung may be framed to pretie conceiptes 1581. Some to c. alone their taste confine POPE. 2 *Hen. IV*, II. iv. 263. **9.** The Conceipt of the stone..hath ..so stopped my urine FLORIO. Hence † **Concei·tful** *a.* witty; imaginative. **Concei·tless** *a.* **Concei·ty** *a.* (*Sc.*) abounding in conceits, or in self-conceit.

Conceit (kǫ̆nsī·t), *v.* 1557. [f. CONCEIT *sb.*] †**1.** To form a conception of; to conceive –1602. † *intr.* To conceive –1828. **2.** To imagine 1600. **3.** *trans.* To inspire with a fancy 1587. Also *refl.* **4.** To take a fancy to. Now *dial.* 1589. †**5.** To conceive as a design –1638.

1. *Jul. C.* I. iii. 162. *intr.* One that so imperfectly conceits *Oth.* III. iii. 149. **2.** I did c. a most delicious feast G. HERBERT. **3.** *refl.* We..c. ourselves that we contemplate absolute existence SIR W. HAMILTON.

Conceited (kǫ̆nsī·tĕd), *ppl. a.* 1542. [f. CONCEIT *sb.* and *v.* + -ED.]

I. †**1.** Having a conceit (of such a kind); ingenious; witty –1681. **2.** Having an opinion, opinioned. Now *dial.* 1587. † Possessed with a good opinion *of* –1734. **3.** Vain. Orig. *self-c.* (The principal existing sense.) 1608. Also with *of* 1618. **4.** Full of notions, fastidious. Now *dial.* 1609.

3. The c. are rarely shy DARWIN. The less a man knows, the more c. he is of his proficiency NEWMAN.

II. From the *vb.* **1.** Conceived (*arch.*) 1598; † imagined; imaginary –1703. **2.** † Ingeniously devised 1594; 'fancy' 1615.

2. A conceyted chayre to sleep in with the legs stretcht out EVELYN. Hence **Concei·tedly** *adv.* in a c. manner. **Concei·tedness,** † cleverness; † imagination; self-conceit.

Conceivable (kǫ̆nsī·văb'l), *a.* 1646. [f. CONCEIVE *v.* + -ABLE. Cf. Fr. *concevable.*] That can be imagined, or thought of; *occas.*, = just credible. Also as *sb.* [sc. *thing.*]

A particle..minuter than all..c. dimension PALEY. Hence **Conceivabi·lity,** c. quality or condition. **Concei·vableness. Concei·vably** *adv.*

Conceive (kǫ̆nsī·v), ME. [– *conceiv-*, tonic stem of (O)Fr. *concevoir*, repr. L. *concipere*, f. *com* CON- + *capere* take.] **1.** *trans.* To receive (seed) in the womb; to become pregnant with (young); *pass.* to be created in the womb. **2.** *intr.* To become pregnant ME. †**3.** *pass.* To become or be pregnant –1646. †**4.** *transf.* To take on (any state: e.g. *fire, moisture*, etc.) –1756. **5.** To take or admit into the mind; to become affected with ME. **6.** To form in the mind, devise ME. **7.** To form or have a conception of ME. Also *absol.* or *intr.* **8.** To grasp with the mind; to apprehend; cf. CATCH *v.* ME. **9.** To be of opinion; to fancy; also used as a modest way of expressing one's opinion ME. †**10.** (after L.) To take in, comprise –1571. †**11.** To institute (an action at law). [L. *concipere actionem.*] –1574. **12.** To formulate. [Cf. L. *concipere aliquid verbis.*] 1560.

1. Through faith also Sara her selfe receiued strength to conceiue seede *Heb.* 11:11. **2.** And the flockes conceiued before the rods *Gen.* 30:38. **4.** To c. a siknesse GOWER. **5.** To c. prejudices SHERLOCK, a dislike 1802, a good opinion HOBBES. **6.** He first conceives, then perfects his design COWPER. **7.** I cold not conceve wherefore the same was spooken THYNNE. *To c. of* a better course 1623. **8.** I conceyve youre entent ME. I doe now conceave you SPENSER. **12.** To c. an answer in the tone of insult GIBBON. Hence **Concei·vement** (*rare*), conception. **Concei·ver.**

Concelebrate (kǫnse·lĭbrēⁱt), *v.* 1572. [– *concelebrat-*, pa. ppl. stem of L. *concelebrare*; see CON-, CELEBRATE.] †**1.** *trans.* To celebrate together –1610. **2.** *R.C. Ch.* Said of newly ordained priests: To celebrate mass along *with* the ordaining bishop. Hence **Concelebra·tion.**

Concent (kǫ̆nse·nt), *sb.* Also 6–7 (confused with) **consent.** 1585. [– L. *concentus* harmony, f. *concinere* sing together, harmonize, f. *con* CON- + *canere* sing. Cf. CONCINNATE *v.*] **1.** Harmony (of sounds); concord of voices or parts. Also with *a* and *pl.* ? *Obs.* 1589. **2.** *transf.* and *fig.* Harmony; accord 1588.

2. So their affections, set in keys alike, In true c. meet, as their humours strike DRAYTON. Hence † **Conce·nt** *v.* to make to accord.

Concenter; see CONCENTRE.

Concentrate (kǫ·nsĕntrēⁱt, kǫ̆nse·ntrēⁱt), *v.* 1640. [Latinized form of CONCENTRE, or analogical formation on Fr. *concentrer*; see -ATE³.] **1.** *trans.* To bring to or towards a common centre, or focus; to collect as at a centre 1646. Also *fig.* **2.** *Chem.* To increase the strength of (a solution) by contraction of its volume 1689. **3.** *Mining.* To separate metal or ore from the gangue 1872. **4.** To bring the parts of into closer union; to condense 1758. Also *intr.* and *absol.* (usually for *refl.*) 1640. *Mil.* of troops: To collect in one quarter 1813.

1. The different rays concentrated by the lens BREWSTER. To c. attention 1879. **2.** To c. spirit of vinegar 1731. **4.** The obstinacy of my whole sex..was concentrated in me C. BRONTË. *intr.* The news..obliged him to c. on the Elbe 1813. Hence **Conce·ntrate** *a.* concentrated; *sb.* the product of concentration.

Concentration (kǫnsĕntrēⁱ·ʃən). 1634. [f. prec. + -ATION.] **1.** The action of concentrating; the state of being concentrated. Also *fig.* **2.** *Chem.* The strengthening of a solution by contraction of its volume (*e.g.* by evaporation); the condition thus produced 1790. **3.** *Mining.* The removal by mechanical means of the less valuable parts of ore 1873. **4.** Condensation 1865.

1. The c. of your force in one position WELLINGTON. The power of intellectual c. 1846. **4.** My affected c. of language RUSKIN. *C. camp*, a camp where non-combatants of a district are accommodated.

Concentrative (kǫ̆nse·ntrătiv), *a.* 1822. [f. CONCENTRATE *v.* + -IVE.] Concentrating; characterized by concentration.

Your nature is c., rather than diffuse 1881. Hence **Conce·ntrativeness,** c. quality. (Orig. *Phren.*)

Concentrator (kǫ·nsĕntrēⁱtəɹ). 1853. [f. as prec. + -OR 2.] One who or that which concentrates. **1.** An apparatus for concentrating solutions, etc. 1853. **2.** *Fire-arms.* A ring of hard paper or wire fitted inside the cartridge case, to keep the shot together after discharge 1875. **3.** An apparatus for the mechanical concentration of ores 1873.

Concentre, -center (kǫ̆nse·ntəɹ), *v.* 1591. [– Fr. *concentrer*, f. *con-* CON- + *centre* CENTRE; cf. It. *concentrare*, Sp. *concentrar.* See CONCENTRATE.] **1.** *trans.* To bring or direct to a common centre 1633; *occas.*, to attract to itself as a centre 1795. Also *fig.* **2.** To pack closely as round a centre; *hence*, to increase the vigour or intensity of 1598. **3.** *intr.* (for *refl.*) To move towards, or meet in, a common centre (*lit* and *fig.*) 1630. †**4.** To agree, coincide –1755.

1. *fig.* To c. the mind on one sole object BURKE. **3.** This jealousy of control from without concentred in the subject of taxation BANCROFT.

Concentric, -al (kǫ̆nse·ntrik, -ăl), *a.* (and *sb.*) ME. [– (O)Fr. *concentrique* or med.L. *concentricus* (adj. and sb.), f. *com* CON- + *centrum* CENTRE; see -IC.] *adj.* Having a common centre. *sb.* A concentric circle, etc. 1551. *Mil. C. fire*: firing concentrated on one point. Hence **Conce·ntrically** *adv.* **Concentri·city.**

† **Conce·ntricate,** *v.* 1641. [f. prec. + -ATE³.] = CONCENTRATE –1787.

Conce·ntual, *a. rare.* 1785. [f. L. *concentus* CONCENT + -AL¹.] Harmonious, accordant.

‖ **Conce·ntus.** 1609. [L.: in med.L. applied to that part of the choral service of the Church in which the whole choir joined. Cf. CONCENT.] A singing or sounding together in accord; harmony.

Concept (kǫ·nsept), *sb.* 1556. [– late L. *conceptus*, f. pa. ppl. stem of *concipere*, f. *com* CON- + *capere* take; cf. CONCEIVE.] †**1.** = CONCEIT, in various senses –1591. **2.** *Logic* and *Philos.* The product of the faculty of conception; an idea of a class of objects, a general notion 1663.

2. Concepts are merely the results, rendered permanent by language, of a previous process of comparison SIR W. HAMILTON.

Conceptacle (kǫnse·ptăk'l). 1611. [– Fr. *conceptacle* or L. *conceptaculum*; see CON-, RECEPTACLE.] † **1.** A receptacle –1855. **2.** † **a.** *Anat.* Any cavity of the body –1668. † **b.** *Bot.* = FOLLICLE 1823. **c.** *Biol.* A cavity-like organ containing the reproductive cells in some plants and animals of low organization 1835. Hence **Concepta·cular** *a.* of or pertaining to conceptacles.

† **Conce·ptible,** *a.* 1650. [– med.L. *conceptibilis*, f. as next; see -IBLE. Cf. Fr. *conceptible.*] = CONCEIVABLE –1695. Hence † **Conceptibi·lity,** c. quality. CUDWORTH.

Conception (kǫnse·pʃən). ME. [– (O)Fr. *conception* – L. *conceptio*, f. *concept-*, pa. ppl. stem of *concipere*; see CONCEIVE, -ION.] **1.** The action of conceiving, or fact of being conceived, in the womb. Also *fig.* and † *transf.* **2.** *concr.* That which is conceived; embryo, † child ME. **3.** The action or faculty of conceiving in the mind; apprehension, imagination ME. **4.** *Philos.* **a.** In a general sense = prec.; † **b.** reproductive imagination (STEWART); **c.** the action or faculty of forming a CONCEPT 1830. **5.** That which is conceived in the mind; an idea, notion 1526; †a mere fancy (SHAKS.). **6.** *Philos.* **a.** In a general sense = 5. 1640. **b.** A general notion, a CONCEPT 1785. **7.** Origination in the mind 1822; an original idea; a design, plan 1606. † **8.** A conceit. DRYDEN.

1. *fig.* Ioy had the like c. in our eies, And at that instant, like a babe sprung up *Timon* I. ii. 115. **3.** Lovely beyond c. TYNDALL. *In my c.*: to my apprehension. **4. a.** All evidence is c., and all c. is imagination, and proceedeth from sense HOBBES. **5.** I can give you no c. of my welcome here DICKENS. **6. a.** The mind..can never attain a full and adequate c. of infinity HUME. **b.** The object of a c. is universal, of a perception, individual 1889. **7.** I haue a young c. in my braine *Tr. & Cr.* I. iii. 312. Hence **Conce·ptional** *a.* pertaining to, or of the nature of, a c. † **Conce·ptionalist,** erron. f. *Conceptualist.* So **Conce·ptionist.** † **Conce·ptious,** apt to conceive.

Conceptive (kǫnse·ptiv), *a.* 1640. [– L. *conceptivus*, f. as prec.; see -IVE. Cf. Fr. *conceptif.*] Having the faculty or attribute of conceiving. (Rare in the physical sense.)

Conceptual (kǫnse·ptiuăl), *a.* 1834. [– med.L. *conceptualis*, f. *conceptus* conceiving, f. as prec.; see -AL[1].] Of, pertaining to, or relating to, mental conceptions or concepts.

Conceptualism (kǫnse·ptiuăli:z'm). 1837. [f. prec. + -ISM; cf. Fr. *conceptualisme.*] **1.** The scholastic doctrine that universals exist as mental concepts (only): opp. to Realism and Nominalism. **2.** The psychological doctrine that the mind is capable of forming an idea (*i.e.* mental image) corresponding to the general term 1837. So **Conce·ptualist,** an adherent of C. Also *attrib.*

Concern (kǫnsɔ̄·ɹn), *v.* 1450. [– (O)Fr. *concerner* or late L. *concernere* sift, distinguish, in med.L. have respect or reference to, f. *com* CON- + *cernere* sift.] † **1.** To distinguish, perceive –1589. **2.** *trans.* To have relation or reference to 1526. **3.** To affect; to involve 1586. **4.** To be of importance to 1603. Also † *absol.* or *intr.* † **5.** To engage the attention of –1749. † **6.** To cause to have a part *in*; to engage –1679. **7.** In the imperative = 'Confound!' *dial.* 1877. **8.** Passive, *To be concerned.*

This occurs in senses 5, 6, which are obsolete in the active; in other senses it is more used than the active.

2. Prudence concerns the present time EMERSON. *As concerns* (= *as it concerns*): with regard to. **3.** Such things as..concerne the honour of the Scotish nation THYNNE. **4.** *Meas. for M.* I. i. 78. *Two Gent.* II. ii. 77. **5.** Which to deny, concernes more than auailes *Wint. T.* III. ii. 87. **6.** *To c. oneself*: to interest oneself *with, in, about, to do a thing.* **8.** I..am Concerned to see the time goe away and nothing done 1693. (Cf. sense 5.) To be concern'd in a Patent BENTLEY, riot 1802. (Cf. sense 6.)

Concern (kǫnsɔ̄·ɹn), *sb.* 1589. [f. prec. vb.; cf. *regard, respect.*]

I. † **1.** Regard; concernment –1694. **2.** (Usu. in *pl.*) A business or practical relation 1699. **3.** Interest, share *in* 1720. **4.** Solicitous regard, anxiety 1697.

2. *To have no c.* (formerly *concerns*) *with*: to have nothing to do with. **3.** How many gentlemen.. took a c. in the..undertaking of 1745 SCOTT: **4.** Without c. he hears..Of..distant war DRYDEN.

II. 1. A matter that relates to some person or thing 1707. *pl.* Affairs 1675. **2.** A matter that affects or touches one 1700. † **3.** *pl.* Belongings 1693. **4.** A business; a firm 1681. **5.** *familiarly.* Any contrivance or object; usu. depreciatory 1834.

1. † *General* or *public c.*: the commonwealth. Of ..every-day concerns SOUTHEY. **2.** It is no c. of mine (*mod.*). **4.** The bank..became a flourishing c. CRUMP. **5.** A tin c., like a chimney-cowl S. LOVER.

† **Conce·rnancy.** *rare.* [f. CONCERN *v.* + -ANCY. Cf. Fr. † *concernance.*]? = CONCERNMENT. *Haml.* V. ii. 128. (Qq.).

Concerned (kǫnsɔ̄·ɹnd), *ppl. a.* 1656. [f. CONCERN *v.* + -ED[1].] **1.** Interested, involved; troubled, anxious; showing concern. **2.** *U.S. slang.* Confounded. **3.** *adv.* 1848.

Phr. *C. with (in) drink*: the worse for liquor; also simply *concerned.* Now *low* or *dial.* Hence **Conce·rned-ly** *adv.*, **-ness.**

† **Conce·rning,** *vbl. sb.* 1594. [f. as prec. + -ING[1].] The taking of concern; concernment; a concern –1642.

Conce·rning, *ppl. a.* 1649. [f. as prec. + -ING[2].] That is of concern; important (*arch.*). So c. a truth MORE. Soul-c. doctrines 1869. Hence † **Conce·rningly** *adv.* in a c. manner. **Conce·rningness,** importance; bearing.

Concerning (kǫnsɔ̄·ɹniŋ), *prep.* 1535. [f. prec., prob. modelled on a similar use of Fr. *concernant.*] **1.** Regarding, touching, in reference or relation to; about. † **2.** = 'As to'. (Now usually *as concerns.*) –1656.

1. I spake it not to you c. bread *Matt.* 16 : 11.

Concernment (kǫnsɔ̄·ɹnmĕnt). 1610. [f. CONCERN *v.* + -MENT.] † **1.** A matter concerning any person or thing –1654. **2.** An interest (*arch.*) 1627. **3.** An affair, business, concern 1621. **4.** Relation. Commonly after *of.* 1622. **5.** Importance 1642. † **6.** Interest –1691. **7.** Interference, participation 1647. **8.** Solicitude, anxiety, etc. 1652.

2. The concernments of the poor FULLER. **3.** Our civil concernments WATTS. **4.** Matters of private c. LD. BROUGHAM. **5.** Matter of vital c. MORLEY. **8.** A sensible c. at what had passed 1693.

Concert (kǫ·nsəɹt). *sb.* 1665. [– Fr. *concert* – It. *concerto*, f. *concertare*; see next.] **1.** Agreement in a plan, or design; union formed by such agreement; accordance, harmony. † **2.** Accordance of voices or instruments –1770. Also *transf.* and *fig.* † **3.** A choir –1743. **4.** A musical performance in which several performers take part 1689.

1. By c. and agreement DE FOE. To work in c. TYNDALL. **2.** A rare c. of four Trumpets Marine 1674. **4.** Going..to Martini's c. at Milan STERNE. *Dutch c.*, 'where each performer plays a different tune'. *Slang Dict. Comb.* **c.-pitch,** 'a pitch slightly higher than the ordinary pitch, used at concerts for brilliancy and effect' (Grove); also *fig.*

Concert (kǫnsɔ̄·ɹt), *v.* 1598. [– Fr. *concerter* – It. *concertare* bring into agreement or harmony, of obscure origin.] † **1.** *trans.* To bring to unity –1696. **2.** To arrange by mutual agreement 1694; to plan 1712; *intr.* to form plans (? *Obs.*) 1707. † **3.** [L. *concertare.*] To dispute 1689.

2. To c. an insurrection THIRLWALL. I must now c. matters about y[t] Affair HEARNE. *intr.* We concerted on the most proper methods NELSON. Hence **Conce·rted** *ppl. a.* agreed upon; planned, contrived; done in concert; *Mus.* arranged in parts for several voices or instruments. **Conce·rter.**

‖ **Concertante** (kontʃerta·nte), *sb.* and *a.* 1730. [It. ppl. a. f. *concertare.*] *Mus.* A piece of music for orchestra in which there were parts for solo instruments; also, a composition for several solo instruments without orchestra. Now usu. *attrib.*

† **Concerta·tion.** 1509. [– L. *concertatio*, f. pa. ppl. stem. of *concertare* contend together, f. *com* CON- + *certare* contend; see -ATION.] Contention; disputation –1677.

Concertina (kǫnsəɹtī·nă). 1837. [f. CONCERT *sb.* + *-ina*, after *seraphina*; see SERAPHINE.] A portable musical instrument, consisting of a pair of bellows, usually polygonal in form, with a set of keys at each end, which on being pressed admit wind to free metallic reeds. Hence **Concerti·nist.**

‖ **Concertino** (kǫntʃertī·no). 1880. [It. dim. of *concerto.*] *Mus.* **1.** A shorter concerto. **2.** The group of solo instruments in a concerto.

‖ **Concerto** (kontʃe·rto, kǫnsɔ̄·ɹto). 1730. [It., f. *concertare*; see CONCERT *v.*] *Mus.* A composition for one, or sometimes more, solo instruments accompanied by orchestra; now usually in three movements. (Formerly applied to various compositions for a number of instruments.)

Concessible (kǫnse·sib'l), *a.* 1767. [f. *concess-* in CONCESSION + -IBLE. Cf. med.L. *concessibilis.*] That can be conceded.

Concession (kǫnse·ʃən). 1611. [– (O)Fr. *concession* or L. *concessio*, f. *concess-* pa. ppl. stem of *concēdere*; see CONCEDE, -ION.] **1.** The action of conceding (anything asked or required) 1647; a grant 1611. **2.** Admission of a point claimed in argument 1628. **3.** A grant by government of a right or privilege, or of land 1656; land so allotted 1846.

1. The c. of these charters was in a parliamentary way HALE. **2.** The atheists of the age have been described as triumphing in my concessions PRIESTLEY. **3.** The execution of the [Suez] canal ..A Frenchman has obtained the c. 1856. In Canada..Between the concessions there are roads, called c. roads 1846. So ‖ **Concessionaire, -onnaire,** a person who has obtained a c. Hence **Conce·ssionary** *a.* pertaining to, or of the nature of, c.; *sb.* = *Concessionaire.* **Conce·ssionist,** one who advocates c.

Concessive (kǫnse·siv), *a.* (and *sb.*) 1711. [– late L. *concessivus*, f. as prec.; see -IVE.] **1.** Of the nature of or tending to concession 1876. **2.** *Gram.* Expressive of concession. **3.** *sb. Gram.* A concessive particle, clause, etc. 1765. Hence **Conce·ssive·ly** *adv.*, **-ness.**

Concessor (kǫnse·səɹ). *rare.* 1660. [– late L. *concessor*, f. as prec.; see -OR 2.] One who concedes. Hence † **Conce·ssory** *a. rare* = CONCESSIVE 1.

‖ **Concetto** (kontʃe·tto). Pl. **-tti.** 1737. [It. :– L. *conceptus* (in late L.) thought, purpose. See CONCEPT.] = CONCEIT *sb.* 7. Hence **Conce·ttism,** use of *concetti* in literature.

Conch (kǫŋk). 1520. [– L. *concha* bivalve, shell of snail, etc. – Gr. κόγχη.] **1.** A shell-fish; orig. a bivalve; later, a large gastropod, esp. *Strombus gigas.* **2.** The shell of a mollusc 1774. **3.** Such a shell used as an instrument of call. *esp.* That used by Tritons as a trumpet. 1764. **4.** A Roman vessel [L. *concha*], used for oil, salt, etc. Also *fig.* 1839. **5.** *Archit.* The domed roof of a semicircular apse; also the apse 1849. **6.** *Anat.* The external ear; = CONCHA 4. 1836. **7.** (Also *conk.*) A nickname for the lower class of inhabitants of the Bahamas, the Florida Keys, etc., from their use of conchs as food. Hence **Conched** *ppl. a.* having a c.

‖ **Concha** (kǫ·ŋkă). Also (in sense 2) **conca.** 1613. [L.; see prec.] † **1.** *Zool.* = CONCH 1, 2. –1776. **2.** *Archit.* = CONCH 5; also, a coved ceiling 1613. **3.** = CONCH 4. **4.** *Anat.* The central concavity of the external ear; *occas.*, the whole external ear 1683. Hence **Co·nchate** *a.* = *Conched.* **Conchi·fera** *sb. pl.*, *Zool.* a division of Molluscs: the *Lamellibranchiata* or ordinary bivalves, as the Oyster, etc.; *sing.* **Co·nchifer,** one of these. **Conchi·ferous** *a.* shell-bearing; *occas.*, bivalve; *Geol.* containing shells.

Co·nchinine. [Transposition of *cinchonine.*] *Chem.* = QUINIDINE.

Conchiolin (kǫŋkəi·ǒlin). 1870. [L. *concha* + *-ol-* dim. + -IN[1].] *Chem.* The organic constituent of the shells of molluscs.

† **Conchite** (kǫ·ŋkəit). 1677. [– Gr. κογχίτης (λίθος) 'shelly stone'; see -ITE[1] 2 b.] A stone resembling a shell, a fossil shell –1758. Hence **Conchi·tic** *a.*, *Geol.* abounding in (fossil) shells.

Conchoid (kǫ·ŋkoid). 1797. [f. CONCH + -OID; cf. Fr. *conchoïde.*] *sb. Geom.* A plane curve of the fourth order invented by Nicomedes 1798. As *adj.* = CONCHOIDAL.

Conchoidal (kǫŋkoi·dăl), *a.* 1666. [f. as prec. + -AL[1].] **1.** *Geom.* Pertaining to, or resembling, a conchoid. **2.** *Min.* etc. Applied to a fracture presenting smooth shell-like convexities and concavities 1802.

Conchologist (kǫŋkǫ·lŏdʒist). 1784. [f. next + -IST.] A student of conchology; a collector of shells; a carrier-shell mollusc.

Conchology (kǫŋkǫ·lŏdʒi). 1776. [f. Gr. κογχο-, comb. f. Gr. κόγχη; see -LOGY.] The science or study of shells and shell-fish. Hence **Concholo·gical** *a.* of or relating to c. **Concholo·gically** *adv.*

Conchometer (kǫŋkǫ·mĭtəɹ). 1828. [f. as prec. + -METER.] An instrument for measuring shells and the angles of their spires. So **Concho·metry.**

Conchospi·ral. 1864. [f. as prec. + SPIRAL *a.*] A kind of spiral curve exemplified in shells.

† **Conchyle.** 1610. [– L. *conchylium*; see next, and cf. COCKLE *sb.*[2]] A shell-fish; a conch –1706. Hence † **Conchyla·ceous** *a.* shelly 1799.

‖ **Conchy·lia,** *sb. pl.* 1619. [L. pl. of *conchylium* – Gr. κογχύλιον, dim. of κογχύλη = κόγχη; see CONCH.] Shell-fish, *Conchifera.* Hence **Conchylia·ceous** *a.* of the nature of molluscous shells; shelly. **Conchy·liated** *a.* embodied in or derived from shells. **Conchy·li·ferous** *a.* conchiferous. **Conchylio·logist, -o·logy** = CONCHOLOGIST, -OLOGY. **Conchylio·meter, -o·metry** = CONCHOMETER, etc. **Conchyliomo·rphite,** the fossil impression of a shell. **Conchy·lious** *a.* of or belonging to the CONCHYLIA.

† **Conciator.** [– It. *conciatore* mender.] A workman who assorts and allots the proportion of salt required in glass-making. (Never in Eng. use.)

‖ **Concierge** (konsyęrʒ). 1646. [Fr., in OFr. *cumcerges* :– Rom. *conservius* fellow slave.] **1.** The custodian of a house, castle, prison, etc. Now *Hist.* **2.** In France, etc.: The person who has charge of the entrance of a building; a janitor, porter. Hence ‖ **Concie·rgerie,** the office, lodge, or residence of a c.; also, name of a person belonging to the Palace of Justice in Paris.

† **Conci·le,** *v.* ME. [– L. *conciliare*; see CONCILIATE.] To reconcile; to conciliate –1744. Hence † **Conci·liable** *a.*

† **Conci·liable,** *sb.* 1521. [– L. *conciliabulum* place of assembly, f. *concilium* assembly; in med.L. used depreciatively.] A small or secret assembly; a conventicle –1642. var. **Conci·liabule.** (Also in mod.Fr.)

Conciliar (kǫ̆nsi·liăɹ), *a.* 1677. [– med.L. *consiliarius* counsellor (XIII); see -AR[2].] Of or pertaining to a council. var. † **Conciliary.**

Conciliate (kǫ̆nsi·li,eᶦt), *v.* 1545. [– *conciliat-*, pa. ppl. stem of L. *conciliare* combine, unite, procure, gain, win, f. *concilium* COUNCIL; see -ATE[3].] † **1.** *trans.* To procure as an addition –1794. **2.** To gain (goodwill, etc.) by acts which induce friendly feeling. Const. *to, for.* 1545. **3.** To reconcile, make accordant 1573. † **4.** *intr.* To make friends *with* –1775. **5.** To soothe, placate. Also *absol.* 1782.

2. The arts which c. popularity MACAULAY. **3.** To c. the qualities of a soldier with those of a philosopher GIBBON. Hence **Conci·liative** *a.* conciliatory. **Conci·liator. Conci·liatoriness. Conci·liatory** *a.* tending, or calculated, to c.

Conciliation (kǫ̆nsi:li,eᶦ·ʃən). 1543. [– L. *conciliatio*, f. as prec.; see -ION. Cf. (O)Fr. *conciliation.*] The action of conciliating, or state of being conciliated.

A policy of studied c. FROUDE. The c. of human libertie with Divine predetermination of the wil GALE. *Court of c.*: a court for composing disputes by offering to the parties a voluntary settlement.

‖ **Conci·lium.** 1834. The Latin equiv. of COUNCIL; occas. used in techn. language.

Concinnate (kǫ̆nsi·nět), *ppl. a. rare.* 1548. [– L. *concinnatus*, pa. pple. of *concinnare*; see next, -ATE[2].] † **1.** As *pa. pple.* Made fit –1613. **2.** *adj.* Of language: Of studied beauty 1548.

Concinnate (kǫ̆nsi·neᶦt), *v.* Now *rare.* 1601. [– *concinnat-*, pa. ppl. stem of L. *concinnare* join fitly together, etc.; see -ATE[3].] To put together fitly; to set right; to trim, adjust. So † **Conci·nne** *a.*

Concinnity (kǫ̆nsi·nĭti). 1531. [– L. *concinnitas*, f. *concinnus* skilfully put together, etc.; see prec., -ITY.] **1.** Skilful fitting together of parts; harmony; a harmony. **2.** Studied elegance of style 1577.

2. The graceful c. of Livy 1881.

Concinnous (kǫ̆nsi·nəs), *a.* 1654. [f. L. *concinnus* (see prec.) + -OUS.] **1.** Fitly put together, harmonious (*rare*) 1662. **2.** Characterized by studied elegance of style 1831.

2. That most c...of professors, Mr. Heyne DE QUINCEY.

† **Co·ncion.** 1533. [– L. *contio* (later *concio*), contr. from *conventio* CONVENTION; cf. OFr. *concion.*] **1.** An assembly –1587. **2.** An oration before an assembly; a public speech –1644. Hence † **Co·ncional** *a.*; var. † **Co·ncionary.** † **Co·ncionate** *v.* to deliver an oration; to preach. † **Co·nciona:tor,** a preacher. † **Co·ncionato:ry** *a.* belonging to a concionator.

Conci·pient, *a. rare.* 1812. [– *concipient-*, pres. ppl. stem of L. *concipere* CONCEIVE; see -ENT.] That conceives, conceiving.

Concise (kǫ̆nsəi·s), *a.* 1590. [– Fr. *concis, -ise* or L. *concisus* divided, broken up, brief, pa. pple. of *concidere*, f. *com* CON- + *cædere* cut.] Brief and comprehensive in statement; not diffuse: used of speech or writing; also of persons. Also *transf.*

The c. style, which expresseth not enough, but leaves somewhat to be understood B. JONS. No wonder he was c. JANE AUSTEN. *transf.* His c. repast COWPER. Hence **Conci·se-ly** *adv.*, **-ness.**

† **Concise** (kǫ̆nsəi·z), *v. rare.* 1659. [– *concis-*, pa. ppl. stem of L. *concidere*; see prec.] To cut off, mutilate –1660.

Concision (kǫ̆nsi·ʒən). ME. [– L. *concisio*, f. as prec.; see -ION. Cf. Fr. *concision* (sense 3).] **1.** A cutting to pieces or cutting away. **2.** In *Phil.* 3:2, as tr. Gr. κατατομή 'cutting up', applied to the Judaizing Christians 1557; hence, †a schism –1716. **3.** = CONCISENESS 1774.

1. Peplis in the valley of concisioun or sleaynge to gydre WYCLIF *Joel* 3:14.

† **Conci·te,** *v. rare.* 1554. [– OFr. *conciter* or L. *concitare* stir up, frequent. of *conciēre*; see CON-, CITE.] To stir up, excite –1642. So † **Concita·tion.**

† **Conci·tizen.** ME. [app. f. CON- + CITIZEN; cf. Fr. *concitoyen.*] Fellow-citizen –1604.

Concla·mant, *a. rare.* 1890. [– *conclamant-*, pres. ppl. stem of L. *conclamare*; see next and -ANT.] Calling out together.

Conclamation (kǫŋklămēᶦ·ʃən). 1627. [– L. *conclamatio*, f. *conclamat-*, pa. ppl. stem of *conclamare*, f. *com* CON- + *clamare* shout; see -ION.] A loud calling out of many together.

Before his funerall c. MAY. Applauses and conclamations HOWELL.

Conclave (kǫ·nklēᶦv). ME. [– Fr. *conclave* – L. *conclave*, f. *com* CON- + *clavis* key.] † **1.** A private room, closet –1753. Also *fig.* **2.** *spec.* The place in which the Cardinals meet in private for the election of a Pope ME. **3.** The assembly of cardinals met for this purpose 1625; *loosely*, the body of cardinals 1613. Also *attrib.* **4.** Any close assembly 1568.

2. He..takes care to have the C. built with Timber 1691. **3.** Allotting it to the Conclaue of Cardinals HEYLIN. **4.** The three..who composed the secret c. or cabinet MOTLEY. Hence **Co·nclavist,** †one of the cardinals in c.; one who attends on a cardinal in c.

Conclude (kǫ̆nklū·d), *v.* ME. [– L. *concludere*, f. *com* CON- + *claudere* shut.]

I. 1. To shut up, enclose, include (*arch.*). † **2.** To comprehend, comprise –1828; to restrict –1679. † **3.** To shut up *from*; to estop –1705. **b.** To shut up *to*; to bind (still in legal use) ME. † **4.** To overcome in argument; to confute; to convince –1704.

1. *fig.* God hath concluded them all in vnbeliefe *Rom.* 11:32. **2.** Schortly to concluden al his wo CHAUCER. **3. b.** In settling the value of a copyhold fine the tenant is not concluded by the amount of rent..reserved on the premises 1883.

II. 1. To bring to an end; to finish ME. **2.** *absol.* To end, finish, close (*with* or *by*) 1514. **3.** *intr.* To come to an end; to close 1592.

1. This concluded the proceedings (*mod.*). **2.** And to c., The Victorie fell on vs *Macb.* I. ii. 57. **3.** Her heavy anthem still concludes in woe SHAKS.

III. 1. To come to a conclusion, infer, deduce ME. † **2.** *trans.* To lead to the conclusion; to prove –1797. † **3.** *intr.* To be conclusive –1714.

1. Therefore wee c., that a man is justified by faith *Rom.* 3:28. **3.** Thy reason in this case concludeth not 1526.

IV. 1. *trans.* To bring to a decision; to settle 1523. **2.** To decide (*to do* a thing), determine, resolve ME. † **3.** *intr.* To come to a decision *of, on, upon* –1796; to come to terms *with* –1680. † **4.** *trans.* To decide upon –1603.

1. To c. a truce GRAFTON, peace SHAKS. **2.** It was concluded to bring him to trial HALLAM. **3.** To c. on another maner of peace LD. BERNERS.

Hence † **Conclu·dence, -dency,** concludent quality. † **Conclu·dent** *a.* conclusive, convincing. † **Conclu·dently** *adv.* **Conclu·der. Conclu·dingly** *adv.*

† **Conclu·sible,** *a.* 1654. [f. *conclus-* (see next) + -IBLE.] That may be concluded or inferred.

Conclusion (kǫ̆nklū·ʒən). ME. [– (O)Fr. *conclusion* or L. *conclusio*, f. *conclus-*, pa. ppl. stem of *concludere*; see CONCLUDE, -ION.] **1.** The end, close, finish, wind up (*e.g.* of a speech). **2.** An issue, outcome ME. **3.** *Logic.* A judgement arrived at by reasoning; an inference, deduction, induction ME.; *spec.* the third proposition of a syllogism, deduced from the two premisses 1474; the action of inferring (*rare*) 1532. † **4.** A proposition, dogma –1687; a problem –1663; an experiment –1670. † **5.** Purpose, end. ME. only. **6.** Final determination; final agreement ME. **7.** The concluding (*of* a peace, etc.) 1568. **8.** *Law.* A binding act; an estoppel 1531. **9.** *Sc. Law.* The concluding clause of a Summons 1826.

1. To drawe to a conclusyoun Of thys long tale 1447. The c. is a clarkely gatherynge of the matter spoken before 1553. **2.** What will be the c. of all this 1635. Phr. *In c.*: †at last; to conclude; also (formerly) in short. **3.** The sober conclusions of science TYNDALL. He granted him both the major and the minor; but denied him the c. ADDISON. Your Wife Octauia, with her modest eyes, and still C. *Ant. & Cl.* IV. xv. 28. **4.** Certayn..conclusions towchyng women CAXTON. She hath persu'de Conclusions infinite Of easie wayes to dye *Ant. & Cl.* V. ii. 358. Phr. *To try conclusions*: to experiment; *transf.* to engage in a trial of skill, etc. (Now assoc. with sense 2, as if = 'to try the issue.') **6.** He has come to the c. not to prosecute (*mod.*). **7.** By the c. of treaties SEELEY.

Conclusive (kǫ̆nklū·siv), *a.* 1590. [– late L. *conclusivus*, f. as prec.; see -IVE.] † **1.** Summing up. **2.** Occurring at or forming the end; final. (Now *rare.*) 1612. **3.** That closes the question; decisive 1649. † **4.** *Law.* Binding 1649.

2. A c. revolt from Rome FROUDE. **3.** Whether these Arguments be c. or no LOCKE. Hence † **Conclu·sive-ly** *adv.*, **-ness.** var. **Conclu·sory.**

‖ **Conclusum** (kǫ̆nklū·sǫ̆m). 1798. [L., n. pa. pple. of *concludere* CONCLUDE.] *Diplomacy.* A *résumé* of the demands of a government; dist. from an *ultimatum*, as being open to discussion.

Concoct (kǫ̆nkǫ·kt), *v.* 1533. [– *concoct-*, pa. ppl. stem of *concoquere* digest, mature, consider, f. *com* CON- + *coquere* cook.] † **1.** *trans.* To make ready, or mature, by heat (*lit.* and *fig.*) –1673. † *intr.* (for *refl.*) –1830. † **2.** To digest –1825. Also † *fig.* † **3.** To digest in the mind, ruminate on –1654; to brook –1679. † **4.** To secrete –1741. **5.** To make up by mixing a variety of ingredients 1675. **6.** To make up, plan by concert; to make up (a story, project, etc.) 1792.

5. The most potent ale, concocted with spices and a little white sugar SCOTT. **6.** A fraud which he had either concocted or condoned W. BLACK. Hence † **Conco·ct** *pa. pple.* and *ppl. a.* **Conco·cter, -or.**

Concoction (kǫ̆nkǫ·kʃən). 1531. [– L. *concoctio*, f. as prec.; see -ION.] † **1.** Digestion (of food) –1788. Also † *fig.* † **2.** Ripening, maturation –1706. **3.** The act of concocting or preparing from a variety of ingredients; a broth, drink, etc., so concocted 1851. **4.** The making up (of a story, plot, or scheme) to suit a purpose 1823; a statement fictitiously made up 1885.

4. His affidavit was a c. from beginning to end 1885.

Concoctive (kǫ̆nkǫ·ktiv), *a.* 1578. [f. CONCOCT + -IVE.] Of or pertaining to concoction; digestive.

Concolorous (kǫ̆nkɒ·lǒrəs), *a.* 1840. [f. L. *concolor* of the same colour + -OUS.] *Nat. Hist.* Of uniform colour, vars. **Conco·lorate,** † **Co·ncolour.**

Concomitance (kǫ̆nkǫ·mităns). 1535. [– med.L. *concomitantia*; see next and -ANCE. Cf. (O)Fr. *concomitance.*] **1.** The fact of being concomitant; subsistence together; quasi-*concr.* an instance of this 1652. **2.** *Theol.* The coexistence of the body and blood of Christ in each of the eucharistic elements (*esp.* in the bread) 1535. **3.** *Math.* Exact correspondence of functional transformation between two sets of variables. var. **Conco·mitancy.**

Concomitant (kǫnkǫ·mitănt). 1607. [– *concomitant-*, pres. ppl. stem of late L. *concomitari* accompany; see -ANT. Cf. Fr. *concomitant.*]

A. *adj.* Going together, accompanying, concurrent, attending. Const. *with.*

Either c., assisting, or sole causes. .of melancholy BURTON. Hence **Conco·mitantly** *adv.*

B. *sb.* **1.** An attendant state, quality, circumstance, or thing 1621. † **2.** A companion –1794. **3.** *Math.* Sylvester's name for 'all functions whose relations to the quantic are unaltered by linear transformation' 1853.

1. Death is not so terrible in it selfe, as the concomitants of it BURTON.

† **Conco·mitate,** *v.* 1604. [– *concomitat-*, pa. ppl. stem of late L. *concomitari*; see prec., -ATE[3].] To go with, accompany –1666. Hence † **Concomita·tion.**

Concord (kǫ·nkǫɹd, kǫ·ŋkǫɹd), *sb.* ME. [– (O)Fr. *concorde* – L. *concordia*, f. *concors, concord-* of one mind, f. *com* CON- + *cor, cord-* heart.] **1.** Agreement between persons. **2.** A state of peace and amity between nations; a treaty establishing such relations ME. **3.** *Law.* An agreement made in court respecting the conveyance of a fine of lands 1531. **4.** Agreement or harmony between things ME. **5.** *Mus.* A combination of notes which is in itself satisfactory to the ear; opp. to *discord* 1589. **6.** *Gram.* Agreement between words in case, number, gender, and person 1530.

1. Devil with Devil damn'd Firm C. holds MILT. *P.L.* II. 497. **2.** Abiding by the c. of Salamanca PRESCOTT. **4.** C. of sweet sounds *Merch. V.* V. i. 84. If Nature's c. broke MILT. *P.L.* VI. 311. Hence **Concoʼrdal** *a.* of or relating to c. (in *Gram.*).

Concord (kǫnkǫ·ɹd), *v.* Now *rare.* ME. [– (O)Fr. *concorder* – L. *concordare*; see prec.] **1.** *intr.* To agree. † **2.** *trans.* To arrange by agreement –1670; to bring into concord –1670. Hence † **Conco·rdable** *a.* † **Conco·rdably** *adv.*

Concordance (kǫnkǫ·ɹdăns), *sb.* ME. [– (O)Fr. *concordance* – med.L. *concordantia*, f. *concordant-*; see CONCORDANT, -ANCE.] **1.** Agreement, harmony 1450. † **2.** *Gram.* = CONCORD *sb.* 6. 1570. **3.** † A citation of parallel passages in a book, *esp.* in the Bible –1714. **b.** An alphabetical arrangement of the principal words contained in a book (*orig.* in the Bible), with citations of the passages in which they occur. Orig. in *pl.*, each group of parallel passages being properly a *concordantia.* ME.

1. Contrasts, and yet concordances CARLYLE. **3.** With a true Concordaunce in the margent COVERDALE. I had not a Bible or C. at hand BOYLE. Hence **Conco·rdance** *v.* to make a c. to. **Conco·rdancer. Concorda·ntial** *a.* of or pertaining to a c.

† **Conco·rdancy.** 1586. [f. prec.; see -ANCY.] Agreement –1793.

Concordant (kǫnkǫ·ɹdănt), *a.* 1477. [– (O)Fr. *concordant* – *concordant-*, pres. ppl. stem of L. *concordare*, f. *concors*; see CONCORD *sb.*, -ANT.] Agreeing; harmonious; consistent; correspondent.

The c. Voice of all the curious Judges 1691. On four c. lines E. DARWIN. Hence **Conco·rdantly** *adv.*

Concordat (kǫnkǫ·ɹdæt). 1616. [– Fr. *concordat* or L. *concordatum*, subst. use of n. pa. pple. of *concordare*; see prec., -ATE[1].] An agreement, a compact; now, an agreement between church and state, *esp.* between the Roman See and a secular government relative to matters that concern both.

The Agreement settled between Pope Leo X. and Francis I. by an Instrument called the C. 1688.

‖ **Concorda·tum.** 1625. [L.; see prec.] In *Irish Hist.*, An order in Council relative to the disposal of money set apart for particular purposes of state; a payment under such an order; *loosely*, the *c.-fund*, whence such payments were made.

Concorporate (kǫnkǫ·ɹpŏreˈt), *v.* 1552. [– *concorporat-*, pa. ppl. stem of L. *concorporare* incorporate, f. *com* CON- + *corpus, corpor-* body; see -ATE[3].] To unite or coalesce into one body or mass. So **Conco·rporate** *a.* united into one body or mass. † **Concorpora·tion.**

Concourse (kǫ·nkoᵊɹs, kǫ·ŋ-). ME. [– (O)Fr. *concours* – L. *concursus*, f. *concurs-*, pa. ppl. stem of *concurrere* run together.] **1.** A running, flowing together, or meeting; † hostile encounter –1667. **2.** An assemblage of people or things; a crowd, throng ME. † **3.** The place of meeting of lines, surfaces, or bodies –1811. † **4.** Concurrence in action, co-operation –1837. † **5.** Course (of time) –1657.

1. Riga, a citty of great c. 1601. The coalition of the good frame of the Universe was not the product of chance, or fortuitous c. of particles of matter HALE. **2.** The whole admiring c. gazed on him COWPER. Under some c. of shades MILT. *P.R.* IV. 404. **4.** Gods c. working this or that 1617.

Concreate (kǫ·nkri,ēˈ·t), *v.* Now *rare.* 1625. [– *concreat-*, pa. ppl. stem of eccl.L. *concreare* create together; see CON-, CREATE.] *trans.* To create together.

To create a Soul, is to c. the qualities. .of it MORE. So † **Concreate** *a.* coeval in creation.

† **Concre·dit,** *v.* 1593. [– *concredit-*, pa. ppl. stem of L. *concredere* entrust; see CON-, CREDIT *v.*] **1.** To entrust –1689. **2.** To accredit 1659.

Concremation (kǫnkrimēˈ·ʃən). *rare.* 1730. [f. CON- + CREMATION.] **1.** Cremation together. **2.** Consumption by fire 1860.

Co·ncrement. 1656. [f. CON- + *-crement* in *decrement, increment, excrement*; cf. next.] A growing together; growth by assimilation; a concretion.

Concrescence (kǫnkre·sĕns). 1610. [f. CON- + *-crescence* in *accrescence, decrescence, increscence, excrescence.* See prec., -ENCE.] † **1.** Growth by assimilation 1614. **b.** *Biol.* Growing together of cells, organs, etc.; the coalescence of two individual organisms of low type in generation 1878. **2.** A concretion. ? *Obs.* 1610. So **Concre·scible** *a.* capable of solidifying; capable of growing together. † **Concre·ssion,** erron. f. CONCRETION.

Concrete (kǫ·nkrīt, -krī·t). 1471. [– Fr. *concret* or L. *concretus*, pa. ppl. of *concrescere* grow together, f. *com* CON- + *crescere* grow.]

A. *adj.* † **1.** Grown together –1650. **2.** Made up *of* various elements; composite, compound. ? *Obs.* 1536. **3.** Formed by union or cohesion of particles into a mass; solid (as opp. to *fluid*) 1533. **4.** *Logic* and *Gram.* Applied to a quality viewed *concreted* or adherent to a substance, viz. the adjective; thus *white* (paper, etc.) is the concrete quality, as dist. from *whiteness*, the abstract quality 1528. **5.** Hence, *gen.* Embodied in matter, actual practice, or a particular example. Opp. to *abstract.* (The ordinary current sense) 1656. **6.** Made of concrete.

3. Even to the c. bloud That makes the liver CHAPMAN. **4.** The reader should carefully observe that adjectives are c., not abstract JEVONS. **5.** It is with man in the c. . .you are to be concerned BURKE. Hence **Concrete-ly** *adv.*, **-ness.**

B. *sb.* **1.** quasi-*sb.* *A c., the c.*; see A. 4, 5. 1528. **2.** *gen.* A concreted mass; a concrete substance. Also *fig.* (*Obs.* in *lit.* sense, exc. as in next.) 1656. **3.** *spec.* A composition of stone chippings, sand, gravel, pebbles, etc., formed into a mass with cement (or lime); used for building under water, for foundations, pavements, etc. Often *attrib.* 1834.

2. That. .c. of truth and error. .the Roman Catholic Church 1831.

Concrete (kǫnkrī·t), *v.* 1635. [f. CONCRETE *a.*] **1.** *trans.* To form by cohesion or coalescence of particles, to form into a mass; †to combine (attributes, etc.) –1829. **2.** *intr.* To run into a mass, form a concretion 1677. **3.** To render concrete (*rare*) 1654. **4.** *co·ncrete.* [f. the *sb.* 3.] To treat with concrete; *intr.* to use concrete in building 1875.

1. Sensations combined, blended, or (if one may so speak) concreted together BERKELEY. **3.** Without being concreted into an earthly deed HAWTHORNE. Hence **Concre·ter, -or,** one who or that which concretes.

Concretion (kǫnkrī·ʃən). 1541. [– Fr. *concrétion* – L. *concretio*, f. *concret-*, pa. ppl. stem of *concrescere*; see CONCRETE *sb.*, -ION.] **1.** The action or process of concreting; concrescence, coalescence 1603. **2.** Congelation or coagulation of a liquid 1612. † **3.** Union with something material or actual –1741. **4.** quasi-*concr.* A concrete mass *of* 1626. Also *fig.* **5.** *concr.* A solid mass formed by aggregation and cohesion of particles; a lump, nodule, clot; *esp.* (*Path.*). a calculus; (*Geol.*) a mass formed by aggregation of solid particles, usually round a nucleus 1646.

3. The soul. .because of her c. with this mortal body 1652. **4.** Salt is a C. of Sea Water 1697. **5.** He cut a stony C. out of the Liver 1702. Hence **Concre·tional** *a.* of or pertaining to concretions. **Concre·tionary** *a.* (*Geol.*) of the nature of a c.; consisting of, containing, or characterized by, concretions.

Concretism (kǫ·nkrītiz'm). *rare.* 1865. [f. CONCRETE *a.* + -ISM.] The practice of regarding what is abstract as concrete.

Concretive (kǫnkrī·tiv), *a. rare.* 1646. [– med.L. *concretivus*, f. *concret-*; see CONCRETION, -IVE.] † **1.** Apt to produce concretions. SIR T. BROWNE. † **2.** = CONCRETE *a.* 5. 1656. **3.** Mentally constructive. Hence **Concre·tively** *adv.*

† **Concrew·**, *v.* [f. CON- + *-crewe* in *accrewe* (see ACCRUE), perh. after OFr. *concrëu*, pa. pple. of *concroistre* grow together.] *intr.* To grow into a mass. SPENSER *F.Q.* IV. vii. 40.

Concubinage (kǫnkiū·binėdʒ). ME. [– Fr. *concubinage*, f. *concubin*; see CONCUBINE, -AGE.] The cohabiting of a man and a woman who are not legally married; the practice of having a concubine; the state of being a concubine. **b.** *Rom. Law.* 'A kind of inferior marriage of which the issue were natural children, not bastards' (Milman). vars. † **Concu·binacy, Concu·binate.**

Concubinary (kǫnkiū·binări). 1563. [– med.L. *concubinarius*, f. L. *concubina*; see next, -ARY[1]. Cf. Fr. *concubinaire.*] *adj.* Relating to concubinage; living in, or sprung from, concubinage. *sb.* One who lives in concubinage 15. . . var. **Concubina·rian** *a.*

Concubine (kǫ·ŋkiubəin), *sb.* ME. [– (O)Fr. *concubine* – L. *concubina*, f. *com* CON- + *cub-* lie down.] **1.** A woman who cohabits with a man without being his wife; a kept mistress. Among polygamous peoples: A 'secondary wife', having a legal status inferior to that of a wife. † **2.** A male paramour –1540.

Co·ncubine, *v. rare.* 1596. [f. prec.] † **1.** To take as a concubine. **2.** To furnish with a concubine or concubines 1800.

† **Concu·lcate,** *v.* 1555. [– *conculcat-*, pa. ppl. stem of L. *conculcare* tread under foot, f. *com* CON- + *calcare* tread; see INCULCATE.] To tread under foot –1708. Also *fig.* Hence † **Conculca·tion.**

† **Concu·mbency.** [f. L. *concumbere* lie together + -ENCY.] A lying together. JER. TAYLOR.

Concupiscence (kǫnkiū·pisĕns). ME. [– (O)Fr. *concupiscence* – late L. *concupiscentia*, f. *concupiscent-*, pres. ppl. stem of L. *concupiscere*, inceptive of *concupere*, f. *com* CON- + *cupere* desire.] **1.** Vehement desire; in *Theol.* use, desire for the 'things of the world'. **2.** *esp.* Libidinous desire, sexual appetite, lust ME.

1. Such is the fire of c., raging within, that. .no houses or fields content these PUSEY. var. † **Concu·piscency** (*rare*). So **Concu·piscent** *a.* eagerly desirous; lustful; **-ly** *adv.* Hence † **Concupisce·ntial** *a.* relating to, or of the nature of, c. So † **Concupisce·ntious** *a.*

Concupiscible (kǫnkiū·pisib'l), *a.* ME. [– late L. *concupiscibilis*, f. *concupiscere*; see prec., -IBLE. Cf. (O)Fr. *concupiscible.*] † **1.** Vehemently to be desired –1762. **2.** Vehemently desirous; of the nature of concupiscence ME.

2. The irascible or the c. principle is ever insurgent against reason NEWMAN.

† **Co·ncupy.** ? Abbrev. of *concubine*; or ? =*concupiscence.* *Tr. & Cr.* V. ii. 177.

Concur (kǫnkɔ̄·ɹ), *v.* 1470. [– L. *concurrere*, f. *com* CON- + *currere* run.] **1.** *intr.* To run together; to meet; to converge and meet, as lines, etc.; to coincide. *Eccl.* Of two feasts: To fall on two consecutive days, so that the second vespers of the one coincide with the first of the other 1883. **2.** To combine in action, to co-operate 1549. **3.** To agree in opinion (*with*) 1590. † **4.** To agree in quality, character, etc. –1788. **5.** *Law.* Of rights, etc. : To cover the same ground ; hence, to conflict 1613.

1. Anon, they fierce encountring both concur'd, With griesly looks 1587. The..humours do concurre together unto the offended part 1643. Right and victory do not always c. SELDEN. **2.** All things concurre to give it a perfection G. HERBERT. **3.** For the censure I doe concurre with Mr Chancellor 1631. **4.** It was now twilight concurring with the disorder of his mind H. WALPOLE. Hence **Concu·rringly** *adv.*

Concurbit, obs. f. CUCURBIT. CHAUCER.

Concurrence (kǫnkɒ·rěns). 1525. [f. next; see -ENCE; or – med.L. *concurrentia.*] **1.** A running together in time or place; meeting, combination. *Eccl.* (see CONCUR *v.* 1) 1863. **2.** Co-operation of agents or causes 1525. **3.** Agreement; assent, consent 1669. ‖ **4.** Competition. (Now a Gallicism.) 1603. **5.** Joint right or authority 1809.

1. A c. of three strong tides BRERETON. A c. of all nations LITHGOW. The c. of the optic axes BERKELEY. Our Behaviour in every C. of Affairs ADDISON. **2.** Their mutual C. in doing good ADDISON. **4.** To reduce, by increased c., the wages of the remainder LECKY. var. **Concu·rrency.**

Concurrent (kǫnkɒ·rěnt). 1495. [– *concurrent-*, pres. ppl. stem of L. *concurrere*; see CONCUR, -ENT. Cf. med.L. *concurrens*, (O)Fr. *concurrent.*]

A. *adj.* **1.** Running together in space; going on side by side; existing or arising together; conjoint, associated. **2.** *Geom.* Meeting in or tending to the same point. **3.** Acting in conjunction; co-operating 1532. **4.** Agreeing; expressing concurrence 1542. **5.** *Law.* Covering the same ground (hence = conflicting, as titles); co-ordinate 1531.

1. The c. existence of two distinct systems of jurisprudence WILLIAMS. **4.** A c. consent of all Histories R. COKE. **5.** The chancery has a c. jurisdiction with them BLACKSTONE. **Concu·rrently** *adv.*, **-ness.**

B. *sb.* **1.** A concurrent circumstance, a contributory cause 1667. **2.** A competitor. Now *rare* (exc. as a Gallicism). 1581. † **3.** A contemporary person or thing –1668. **4.** 'One of the supernumerary days of the year over fifty-two complete weeks;—so called because they concur with the solar cycle, the course of which they follow' (Webster).

1. Each of these three concurrents must be considered as a partial cause, for, abstract one, and the effect is not produced SIR W. HAMILTON.

Concu·rsion. ? *Obs.* 1533. [– L. *concursio*, f. *concurs-*, pa. ppl. stem of *concurrere*; see CONCUR, -ION.] Rushing together; concourse.

Concuss (kǫnkɒ·s), *v.* 1597. [– *concuss-*, pa. ppl. stem of L. *concutere* dash together, shake violently, f. *com* CON- + *quatere* shake.] **1.** *trans.* To shake violently. Chiefly *fig.* **2.** To injure by concussion 1689. **3.** To force by threats (*into, to do*); also *absol.* 1839. Hence † **Concussa·tion,** violent shaking.

Concussion (kǫnkɒ·ʃən). 1490. [– L. *concussio*, f. *concuss-*; see prec., -ION.] **1.** The action of violently shaking; particularly, the shock of impact. Also *transf.* and *fig.* **2.** *Surg.* Injury caused to the brain, spine, etc., by the shock of a heavy blow, fall, etc. 1541. **3.** Extortion by threats or violence. Orig. in *Rom. Law.* 1597.

1. A c. of the Heavens HOBBES. **3.** C., rapine, pillories, Their catalogue of accusations fill DANIEL. *Comb.* **c.-fuse,** a fuse (in a shell) ignited by c. or impact. Hence † **Concu·ssionary,** one who practises c. (sense 3). So **Concu·ssive** *a.* of the nature of or pertaining to c. **Concu·tient** *a.* meeting with c. THACKERAY.

Concyclic (kǫnsi·klik), *a.* 1871. [See CON-.] *Geom.* **a.** Lying (as a series of points) on the circumference of one circle. **b.** Of two or more conicoids: Giving circular sections when cut by the same system of parallel planes. Also *absol.*

Cond, cund (kɒnd, kǫnd), *v.* ? *Obs.* ME. [†*cond*, †*cund* (XVII), shortening of †*condie*, *condue* (XIV) – (O)Fr. *conduire* :– L. *conducere* CONDUCT *v.*] = CON *v.*[2]

Condemn (kǫnde·m), *v.* ME. [– OFr. *condem(p)ner* (mod. *condamner*) – L. *condem(p)nare*, f. *com* CON- + *damnare* DAMN.] **1.** To pronounce an adverse judgement on; to censure, blame. **2.** To give judicial sentence against; to convict. Opp. to *acquit, absolve.* ME. **3.** To pronounce guilty *of* 1535. **4.** *fig.* to doom 1653. **5.** To adjudge or pronounce forfeited, as a prize of war, etc. 1705. **6.** To adjudge or pronounce to be unfit for use or consumption 1745. **7.** Of a door or window: To close or block up 1565.

1. A fault in reasoning which Aristotle condemns REID. Their looks c. them (*mod.*). **2.** The Iudges ..shall justifie the righteous, and condemne the wicked *Deut.* 25:1. Condemned in as much as they are worth 1642, to do penance in the streets of London GREEN. **3.** Condempned of highe treason 1535. **4.** Condemn'd in bus'ness or in arts to drudge POPE. Hence **Conde·mnable** *a.*; **-bly** *adv.* **Conde·mned** *ppl. a.* in the senses of the vb.; *spec.* appropriated to condemned persons, or things rejected. **Conde·mner. Conde·mningly** *adv.*

Condemnation (kǫndemnēi·ʃən). ME. [– late L. *condemnatio*, f. *condemnat-*, pa. ppl. stem of L. *condemnare*; see prec., -ION.] **1.** The action of condemning; judicial conviction; expression of disapprobation. **2.** The fact or condition of being condemned 1557. **3.** The ground or reason for condemning 1534. **4.** A sentence of forfeiture. Cf. CONDEMN 5. 1885.

1. A manifest c. of the Innocent HOBBES. His illiberal c. of a medicine 1803. **2.** To whom belongs But c., ignominy and shame MILT. *P.R.* III. 136. **3.** Speake, or thy silence on the instant, is Thy c. and thy death *Cymb.* III. v. 98.

Condemnatory (kǫnde·mnătəri), *a.* 1563. [orig. – med.L. *condemnatorius*, f. as prec.; see -ORY[2]. Cf. Fr. †*condemnatoire.*] Having the character of condemning; expressing condemnation.

After the c. sentence SPEED.

Condensable (kǫnde·nsăb'l), *a.* Also *erron.* **-ible.** 1644. [f. CONDENSE + -ABLE.] That may be condensed, as *c. vapour.* Hence **Condensabi·lity.**

Condensate (kǫnde·nseit), *v.* Now *rare* or *Obs.* 1555. [– *condensat-*, pa. ppl. stem of L. *condensare*; see CONDENSE, -ATE[3].] To condense (*trans.* and *intr.*). So † **Conde·nsate** *ppl. a.* **Conde·nsate** *sb.* a product of condensation. Hence **Conde·nsator** (*rare*), a condenser.

Condensation (kǫndensēi·ʃən). 1603. [– late L. *condensatio*, f. as prec.; see -ION. Cf. (O)Fr. *condensation.*] **1.** The action of making or becoming more dense. **2.** *spec.* The conversion of a substance from the state of gas or vapour to the liquid, or (rarely) to the solid, condition 1614. **3.** Condensed condition 1626; a condensed mass *of* anything 1665. **4.** *fig.* Compression of thought into few words 1794.

1. The c. of air in the receiver LARDNER. C. (of light) by means of a lens 1832. **2.** The c. of milk into a viscous mass (*mod.*). **4.** A want of arrangement and c. in his memoirs LYELL.

† **Condense,** *a.* 1610. [– L. *condensus*; see next.] Dense, condensed –1794.

Condense (kǫnde·ns), *v.* 1477. [– (O)Fr. *condenser* or L. *condensare*, f. *condensus* very dense; see CON-, DENSE.] **1.** To make dense, increase the density of; to reduce in volume; to compress, thicken, concentrate. **2.** To reduce from the form of gas or vapour to the liquid or (rarely) the solid condition 1662. Also *intr.* **3.** *transf.* and *fig.* To bring together closely or in small compass; to concentrate 1803. **4.** *intr.* (for *refl.*) To become dense; to become reduced in volume 1704.

1. Sweet Honey some c. DRYDEN. A lens..to collect and c. [the light] on the object 1787. To c. electricity 1870. **2.** The air was condensed into clouds 1662. **3.** Pope had the art of condensing a thought SHENSTONE. Hence **Conde·nsedness. Conde·nsedly** *adv.* **Conde·nsing** *vbl. sb.* and *ppl. a.* (= 'for condensing').

Condenser (kǫnde·nsəɹ). 1686. [f. prec. + -ER[1]. Cf. Fr. *condenseur.*]

I. One who or that which condenses.

Mountain ranges..serve as condensers for the aqueous vapour 1880. The c. of Bolingbroke LOWELL.

II. Specific and technical senses:

1. A vessel or apparatus in which vapour is reduced to the liquid (or solid) form; *esp.* **a.** *Steam Engine.* A chamber in which the steam is condensed into water on leaving the cylinder, either by injection of cold water, or by exposure to a chilled surface (*surface c.*) 1769. **b.** *Gas-works.* An apparatus in which the tar, ammonia, etc., mixed with the heated gas are condensed and separated by cooling 1809. **c.** The worm of a still 1874. **2.** *Pneumatics.* An apparatus for compressing air; a pneumatic force-pump 1727. **3.** *Electr.* An apparatus for accumulating or increasing the intensity of an electric charge 1782. **4.** *Optics.* A lens or system of lenses by which light is concentrated on one point or object 1798.

Condensible; see CONDENSABLE.

Condensity (kǫnde·nsĭti). 1611. [– Fr. † *condensité* or late L. *condensitas*, f. *condensus*; see CONDENSE, -ITY.] † **1.** Density –1814. **2.** Pithiness 1885.

† **Co·nder.** 1603. [f. COND *v.* + -ER[1].] **1.** One who conds or cons a ship –1751. **2.** A man stationed on a height overlooking the sea to direct fishing-boats after a shoal of herrings or pilchards; a balker –1867.

Condescend (kǫndĭse·nd), *v.* ME [– (O)Fr. *condescendre* – eccl.L. *condescendere* stoop (fig.), in med.L. accede, agree to, f. *com* CON- + *descendere* DESCEND.] † **1.** *lit.* To descend –1686. **2.** *fig.* To stoop, so far as a particular action is concerned, from one's position of dignity or pride; to deign ME. **3.** To be condescending in one's relations with others 1611. † **4.** To make concessions; to agree –1774. **5.** † To come definitely *to* (a point in narration) –1528; to particularize 1549.

2. The Cavaliers condescended to take a lesson in the art of taxation from the Roundheads MACAULAY. **3.** Like a true lout, he does not see that they have condescended to him 1863. **4.** He was resolved to c. no further to the whims of a person GODWIN. To which desire he condescended WHISTON. **5.** We are not going to c. upon particulars 1888. Hence † **Condescended** *ppl. a.* agreed. **Condesce·ndence,** condescension; compliance, concession; *Sc.* a specification of particulars. So † **Condesce·ndency. Condesce·ndent,** one who condescends. **Condesce·nder** (*rare*).

Condesce·nding, *ppl. a.* 1654. [f. prec. + -ING[2].] **1.** That condescends; characterized by condescension. Now usually, Patronizing 1707. † **2.** Consenting 1654. **3.** *Sc.* Going into details 1755. Hence **Condesce·ndingly** *adv.*

Condescension (kǫndĭse·nʃən). 1642. [– Fr. †*condescension* (mod. *condescendance*) – (orig.) eccl. L. *condescensio*, f. *condescens-*, pa. ppl. stem of L. *condescendere*; see CONDESCEND, -ION.] The action, habit, or quality of condescending. **1.** Affability to one's inferiors 1647. † **2.** The action of stooping to things unworthy –1797. **3.** Complaisance 1650. † **4.** Concession –1720.

1. Familiarity..in Superiors [is] C. STEELE. **2.** Every vice, every c. was imputed to the Duke H. WALPOLE. **3.** In..c. to the custom of their Country BENTLEY. So † **Condesce·nsive** *a.* characterized by or given to c. † **Condesce·nt,** condescension; act of condescending.

Condiction (kǫndi·kʃən). 1818. [– L. *condictio*, f. *condict-*, pa. ppl. stem of *condicere*, f. *com* CON- + *dicere* say; see -ION.] *Rom. Law.* A formal claim of restitution; reclaim of undue payment. So **Condicti·tious** *a.* pertaining to a c.

Condign (kǫndəi·n), *a.* ME. [– (O)Fr. *condigne* – L. *condignus* wholly worthy, f. *com* CON- + *dignus* worthy.] † **1.** Equal in worth or dignity (*to*) –1854. † **2.** Worthy, deserving –1632. † **3.** Worthily deserved, merited; adequate –1683. **b.** Since 1700 usually = 'merited by crimes'.

2. As most condigne to beare the principalite 1513. **3.** Euery man shall receaue condigne rewarde or punyshement EDEN. **b.** Brought to c. punishment as a traitor MACAULAY. **Condi·gn-ly** *adv.*, **-ness.**

Condignity (kǫndi·gnĭti). 1554. [– med.L. *condignitas*, f. *condignus*; see prec., -ITY. Cf. Fr. *condignité.*] † **1.** Worthiness, merit –1668. *spec.* in *Scholastic Theol.* That worthiness of eternal life which a man may possess through good works performed while in a state of grace 1554. † **2.** Desert –1654.

Condiment (kǫ·ndimĕnt), *sb.* ME. [– L. *condimentum*, f. *condire* preserve, pickle, embalm, by-form of *condere* preserve. See CONDITE, -MENT.] Anything of pronounced flavour used as a relish, or to stimulate the appetite.

As for Raddish, and Tarragon..they are for Condiments BACON. Hence † **Condiment** *v. rare*, to season or flavour with a c. **Condime·ntal** *a.* of or belonging to a c.; spicy.

Condisciple (kǫndisəi·p'l). 1554. [– L. *condiscipulus* fellow scholar; see CON-, DISCIPLE.] A fellow-disciple; a schoolfellow or fellow-student.

† **Condite,** *sb.* 1610. [– Fr. *condit* or its source *conditum*, n. of pa. pple. of *condire*; see next.] A preserve or pickle; an electuary –1657.

† **Condi·te,** *a.* ME. [– L. *conditus*, pa. pple. of *condire* pickle, etc.; see next, and CONDIMENT.] Preserved, pickled; seasoned –1639.

† **Condi·te,** *v.* ME. [– *condit-*, pa. ppl. stem of L. *condire* pickle, etc.; see prec., and CONDIMENT.] **1.** *trans.* To preserve; to pickle –1725. **2.** To embalm. Also *fig.* –1659. **3.** To season. Also *fig.* –1679.

Condition (kǒndi·ʃən), *sb.* [– OFr. *condicion* (mod. *condition*) – L. *condicio* agreement, situation, etc., rel. to *condicere* agree upon, promise, f. *com* CON- + *dicere* declare, say. See -ION.]

I. 1. Something demanded or required as a prerequisite to the granting or performance of something else; a provision, a stipulation. **2.** *Law.* In a legal instrument, a provision on which its legal force or effect is made to depend 1588. † **3.** Covenant, contract, treaty –1718. **4.** Something that must exist or be present if something else is to be or take place; a prerequisite ME. † **5.** A restriction or qualification –1841. **6.** A clause expressing a condition in sense 4; called in Logic the *antecedent*, in Grammar the *protasis*, of a conditional proposition 1864.

1. Wilt thou enjoy the good, Then cavil the conditions MILT. C. (= *on c. that*) I had gone barefoote to India SHAKS. **2.** *Conditions of sale*: the provisions under which sale by auction takes place. **3.** *Merch. V.* I. iii. 149. **4.** The air I breathe, is the c. of my life, not its cause COLERIDGE.

II. 1. Mode or state of being ME. **2.** State in regard to wealth; circumstances; hence, social position, estate, rank ME. † **3.** Mental disposition; character; temper –1611; † *pl.* personal qualities –1830. † **4.** Nature, character –1586. † **5.** A characteristic, attribute (of men or things) –1712.

1. His fall'n C. MILT. *P.L.* III. 181. Out of C. to keep the field 1719. *To change one's c.*: to get married (*arch.*). **2.** I am, in my c. A Prince *Temp.* III. i. 59. All sorts and conditions of men *Bk. Com. Prayer.* Dress'd like a Woman of C. STEELE. **3.** Ye have knavysche condycyouns SHELTON. **5.** Heere is the Cate-log of her Conditions *Two Gent.* III. i. 273. Hence † **Condi·tionly** *adv.* = *Conditionally.*

Condi·tion *v.* 1494. [– OFr. *condicionner* (mod. *-tionner*) or med.L. *condicionare* (*-tion-*); see CONDITION *sb.*] **1.** *intr.* To treat about conditions; to make conditions, bargain *with.* **2.** *trans.* To stipulate for; to make the condition 1549; to agree by stipulation *to do* something 1624. **3.** To make conditional *on, upon* 1530. **4.** To govern as a condition 1619. **5.** *Metaph.* To subject to the qualifying conditions of finite existence or cognition. Also *transf.* 1829. **6.** To charge (a bond) with clauses or conditions 1675. **7.** *Comm.* To test the condition or state and quality of goods; *esp.* the amount of moisture in silk 1858. **8.** *U.S. Colleges.* To admit under conditions; *i.e.* to admit (a student) to a class conditionally on his passing within a given time in any subject in which he failed at his entrance examination.

Dishonouring..to c. or make any tearmes with such Rascalls SPENSER. **2.** We c. with him to obey him 1629. **4.** Limits we did not set C. all we do M. ARNOLD. **5.** The natural human tendency to c. God by time KINGSLEY. **6.** Recognizances..to be Conditioned in the Form hereunder expressed 1675.

Conditional (kǒndi·ʃənăl). [– OFr. *condicionel* (mod. *-tionnel*) or late L. *condicionalis*; see CONDITION *sb.*, -AL[1].]

A. *adj.* **1.** *gen.* Subject to, depending on, or limited by, one or more conditions; not absolute; made or granted on certain terms ME. **2.** *Logic* and *Gram.* Expressing a condition 1530.

1. A Possessor of a Bill may protest against a limited and c. Acceptance 1682. **2.** *C. judgement* or *proposition*: one consisting of two categorical clauses, the former of which, expressing a condition, is called the *antecedent* (in Grammar *protasis*), the latter, stating the conclusion, is called the *consequent* (*apodosis*). *C. syllogism*: one having a c. proposition for its major premiss.

B. *sb.* (the adj. used ellipt.) A conditional word, clause, conjunction, mood, proposition, or syllogism 1533.

Disjunctives may be turned into Conditionals ATWATER. Hence **Conditiona·lity,** c. quality. **Condi·tionally** *adv.* in a c. manner; † on condition (that).

Conditionate (kǒndi·ʃənět), *a.* 1533. [– med.L. *condicionatus* (*-tion-*), pa. pple. of *condicionare*; see CONDITION *v.*, -ATE[2].] Conditioned; limited by conditions; formerly said of limited monarchs. Hence **Condi·tionately** *adv.* As *sb.* A thing conditioned; a contingency 1678.

Conditionate (kǒndi·ʃəneit), *v.* 1533. [– *condicionat-*, pa. ppl. stem of med.L. *condicionare* (*-tion-*); see prec., -ATE[3].] † **1.** To stipulate (*trans.* and *intr.*) –1642. **2.** *trans.* To limit as a condition; to be, or act as, a condition of 1646.

Conditioned (kǒndi·ʃənd), *ppl. a.* 1450. [f. CONDITION *sb.* and *v.* + -ED.] **1.** (from the *sb.*) Having a (specified) disposition or temperament; in a (specified) condition or state 1548; circumstanced, situated 1831. **2.** (from the *vb.*) Subjected to conditions or limitations 1841. † **3.** Used *absol.* = Provided, on the condition –1641.

1. An ill-c. woman 1860, planet HELPS. **2.** The ultimate purpose of all c. existence 1849. *The c.* (*Metaph.*): That which is subject to the conditions of finite existence and cognition; opp. to the *unconditioned, absolute*, or *infinite* 1829.

† **Co·nditory.** 1705. [– L. *conditorium*, f. *condere* lay up; see -ORY[1].] A repository; *spec.* for the dead.

Condivi·sion. 1837. [See CON-.] One of two or more co-existing logical divisions.

† **Condo·g,** *v.* 1592. [perh. joc. for *concur* (*cur* = dog).] *intr.* To concur –1678.

Condolatory (kǒndōu·lătəri), *a.* 1730. [f. CONDOLE, after *console, consolatory.*] Expressive of or intending condolence.

Condole (kǒndōu·l), *v.* 1460. [– Chr. L. *condolēre*, f. *com* CON- + *dolēre* suffer pain, grieve.] **1.** *intr.* † To sorrow greatly –1650; to grieve or express sympathy *with* 1603. Also *absol.* † **2.** *trans.* To grieve over, lament –1788; to grieve with (a sufferer) –1827. Also † *refl.*

1. I contented myself to sit by him, and c. with him in Silence STEELE. **2.** A person..whose sufferings I c. RICHARDSON. Let vs c. the Knight SHAKS. Hence **Condo·lement,** condolence; † lamentation. **Condo·ler. Condo·lingly** *adv.*

Condolence (kǒndōu·lĕns). 1603. [f. the vb.; in sense 2 orig. †*condoleance*, later †*condolance* – Fr. *condoléance*; hence stress on the second syllable.] † **1.** Sympathetic grief –1721. **2.** Outward (*esp.* formal) expression of sympathy with the grief of others 1619.

2. Compliments of C. H. WALPOLE. The condolences of his numerous friends 1817. vars. † **Condoleance, Condolance** (in sense 2); † **-ency.**

Condolent (kǒndōu·lĕnt), *a.* 1460. [– L. *condolens, -ent-*, pres. pple. of *condolēre*; see CONDOLE, -ENT.] † **1.** Sorrowing greatly –1490. **2.** Sorrowing for another; expressing sympathetic grief 1598.

‖ **Condominium** (kǫndomi·niǒm). 1714. [mod.L.: see CON-, DOMINIUM.] Joint control of a state's affairs vested in others.

Condonation (kǫndonēi·ʃən). 1625. [– L. *condonatio*, f. as next; see CON-, DONATION; adopted from casuistic use.] The pardoning or remission (now *esp.* by implication) of an offence or fault. **b.** *Law.* The action of a husband or wife in the forgiving, or implying forgiveness, of matrimonial infidelity 1788.

Mrs. Brander's easy c. of the sins of one who was 'so pleasant in society' 1885.

Condone (kǒndōu·n), *v.* 1857. [– L. *condonare* deliver up, surrender, refrain from punishing as a favour, f. *com* CON- + *donare* give.] **1.** *trans.* To forgive or overlook (an offence); *esp.* to forgive tacitly by not allowing the offence to make any difference in one's relations with the offender. **2.** Of actions, facts: To cause the condonation of 1871.

1. To c. the adultery 1858, his cowardice DE QUINCEY. **2.** That fact alone would c. many shortcomings 1871. Hence **Condo·ner.**

Condor (kǫ·ndǫɹ). 1604. [– Sp. *cóndor* – Peruv. *cuntur.*] **1.** A very large S. American bird of the vulture kind (*Sarcorhamphus gryphus*), inhabiting chiefly the high regions of the Andes. **b.** *California Condor*: the great vulture of California (*Cathartes californianus*). **2.** A S. American gold coin.

‖ **Condottiere** (kondǫttyē·re). Also (erron.) **-ero.** *Pl.* **condottieri** (-rī). 1794. [It., f. *condotto* leadership, CONDUCT.] A professional military captain, who raised a troop, and sold his service to states or princes at war. The system prevailed over Europe from the 14th to the 16th c.

Conduce (kǒndiū·s), *v.* 1475. [– L. *conducere* bring together, etc., f. *com* CON- + *ducere* lead.] † **1.** *trans.* To lead, conduct, bring (*lit.* and *fig.*). Const. *to.* –1658. † **2.** To bring about –1529. **3.** *intr. To c. to*: to lead or tend towards (a result); to contribute to, make for. (The current sense.) 1586.

1. To c. hither the most lovely and vertuous princesse 1651. **3.** How circumstances c. severally to the production of effects HOBBES. Virtues which c. to success in life MACAULAY. Hence † **Condu·ceful** *a.* conducive. † **Condu·cement,** the action of conducing, or conducing *to*; tendency. † **Condu·cent** *a.* that conduces; serviceable. † **Condu·cible** *a.* conducive; advantageous; *sb.* a conducible or conducive thing. † **Conducibi·lity.** † **Condu·cibleness. Condu·cingly** *adv.*

Conducive (kǒndiū·siv), *a.* 1646. [f. CONDUCE *v.* after *conduct, conductive*, etc.] **1.** Conducing or tending to (a specified end); fitted to promote or subserve. Const. *to, towards.* † **2.** Advantageous (*rare*) 1710.

1. Early rising is c. to health 1803. Hence **Condu·civeness.**

Conduct (kǫ·ndǒkt), *sb.*[1] ME. [– L. *conductus*, f. *conduct-*, pa. ppl. stem of *conducere* (see CONDUCE). In earliest use *conduit(e*, etc.; see CONDUIT.]

I. 1. The action of conducting; guidance, leading (*lit.* and *fig.*) 1534. **2.** Provision for guidance or conveyance; an escort, a convoy; a pass. *Obs.* exc. in SAFE-CONDUCT. ME. † **3.** A conductor, guide (*lit.* and *fig.*) –1684. † **4.** = CONDUCT-MONEY –1721.

1. By c. of some star SPENSER. Under the c. of chance JOHNSON. **2.** I desire of you A C. ouer Land, to Milford-Hauen *Cymb.* III. v. 8.

II. 1. Leadership, command 1470. **2.** Direction, management; handling 1475. † **3.** Skill in managing affairs; discretion –1815. **4.** Manner of conducting oneself or one's life; behaviour. (Now the leading sense.) 1673. (with *a*) † A proceeding; a course of conduct (*rare*) 1706.

1. The c. of the arrere-guard HOLLAND, of the vessel 1812. **2.** Conduycte of a mater PALSG. The nice c. of a clouded cane POPE. The c. of the background SIR J. REYNOLDS. **3.** Thus c. won the prize when courage fail'd DRYDEN. Owing to the Prudence and C. of the Lord Mayor DE FOE. **4.** I trusted to profession, when I ought to have attended to c. BURKE.

III. The leading (of water) by a channel 1847; † a CONDUIT, q.v.

Conduct, *pa. pple., a.*, and *sb.*[2] ME. [– L. *conductus* hired, pa. pple. of *conducere* in the sense of 'hire'.] † **A.** *pa. pple.* and *ppl. a.* **1.** Hired –1526. **2.** Conducted –1620. **B.** *sb.* † **1.** A hired workman –1647. **2.** † A salaried priest –1830. **b.** An Eton College chaplain.

B. 2. Standing over against a c. to be catechised H. WALPOLE.

Conduct (kǒndɒ·kt), *v.* ME. [orig. *conduite, -dyte* – (O)Fr. *conduite* (see CONDUIT); later assim. to L. *conductus*; cf. CONDUCT *sb.*] **1.** To lead, guide; to escort. Also *fig.* and *absol.* **2.** To lead, command 1450; to direct (an orchestra, a meeting, etc.) 1791; to manage 1632. **3.** *refl.* To comport or behave oneself (in a specified way) 1706. **4.** To convey; (*Physics*) to transmit, serve as a channel or vehicle for ME. † **5.** = CONDUCE –1685.

1. They that conducted Paul, brought him vnto Athens *Acts* 17:15. **2.** Hasten his Musters, and c. his powres *Lear* IV. ii. 16. Conducting the correspondence and accounts HT. MARTINEAU. **3.** The army never..conducted itself better WELLINGTON. **4.** They conducted water across hills and vallies 1808.

Conductance (kǒndɒ·ktăns). 1885. [f. CONDUCT *v.* + -ANCE.] *Electr.* Conducting power.

Conductible (kǒndɒ·ktĭb'l), *a.* 1847. [f. CONDUCT *v.* + -IBLE; cf. Fr. *conductible.*] Capable of conducting (heat, etc.) or being conducted. Hence **Conductibi·lity,** capacity for conducting (heat, etc.); capacity of being conducted (*rare*).

Conduction (kǫndʋ·kʃən). 1538. [– (O)Fr. *conduction* or L. *conductio*, f. *conduct-*; see CONDUCT *sb.*¹, -ION.] † **1.** = CONDUCT *sb.*¹ I. I. –1653. † **2.** = CONDUCT *sb.*¹ II. 1-3. –1644. **3.** The conducting of (liquid through a channel or pipe) 1612. **4.** *Physics.* The transmission of heat, etc., from particle to particle of a substance. (The chief current sense.) 1814. **5.** Hiring. *Obs.* exc. in *Rom. Law.* 1538.
4. We know of no other mode of employing a nerve thread than in C. BAIN.

Conducti·tious, *a.* 1607. [f. L. *conducticius, -tius* (f. *conduct-*; see CONDUCT pa. pple.) + -OUS; see -ITIOUS.] Hired; open to hire.

Conductive (kǫndʋ·ktiv), *a.* 1528. [f. CONDUCT *v.* + -IVE.] † **1.** Having the property of conducting or leading –1654. **2.** *Physics.* Conducting, or pertaining to the conduction of, some form of energy (as heat, etc.) 1840.
2. Bodies are c.; and their property is conductivity WHEWELL. Hence **Conducti·vity,** c. quality; var. **Conducti·lity** (*rare*). **Condu·ctively** *adv.* by means of conduction.

Co·nduct-money. 1512. [See CONDUCT *sb.*¹] **1.** *Hist.* Money paid for the travelling expenses of soldiers; also, an impost exacted under this head by Charles I. **2.** Money paid for the travelling expenses of seamen for the navy 1702, or of witnesses in a trial 1864.

Conductor (kǫndʋ·ktəɹ). 1450. [– (O)Fr. *conducteur* – L. *conductor*, f. *conduct-*; see CONDUCT *sb.*¹, -OR 2; earlier *conduitour, conditour* – OFr.] **1.** One who leads, guides, or escorts; a leader, guide (*lit.* and *fig.*) 1481. **2.** †A commander –1649; a director (esp. *Mus.* of an orchestra or chorus) 1784; a manager 1634. **3.** The official who has charge of the passengers, collects fares, etc., on an omnibus, tram-car, or (in U.S.) railroad train (= Fr. *conducteur*) 1837. **4.** One who hires. [Only as Latin.] 1652. **5.** Anything that conducts, leads, or guides; a channel 1796. † **6.** *Surg.* An instrument formerly used in lithotomy to guide the course of the forceps; a gorget –1847. **7.** *Physics.* A substance having the property of conducting heat, electricity, etc.; *spec.* the name of a certain part of a frictional electric machine, for collecting the electricity, the *prime c.*; also short for *lightning-c.* 1770.
1. Pray do you go along with us, I will be your C. BUNYAN. A Principal C. for the Artillery for draught Horses and Ammunition 1661. Hence **Condu·ctorship,** the office or function of a c. **Condu·ctress.**

†**Condue·, condye·,** *v.* (ME. only.) [– (O)Fr. *conduire* :– L. *conducere* CONDUCT *v.*] To conduct, guide.

Conduit (kʋ·ndit, kǫ·ndit). [ME. *condut, condit* – (O)Fr. *conduit* :– med.L. *conductus*, f. *conduct-*; see CONDUCT *sb.*¹] **1.** An artificial channel or pipe for conveying water, etc.; an aqueduct, a canal. Also *transf.* and *fig.* **b.** *Electr.* A tube or trough for protecting electric wires; also *attrib.*, as *c. system* 1884. **2.** A fountain (*arch.*) ME. **3.** *Archit.* A walled passage underground for secret communication 1875.
1. As water, whanne the conduyte broken ys CHAUCER. The pores and conduites of the skinne LYTE. *fig.* Language being the great C., whereby Men convey..Knowledge, from one to another LOCKE. **2.** The conduits round the garden sing ROSSETTI. *Comb.* **c.-pipe,** a c. of tubular form; also *fig.*

Conduplicate (kǫndiū·plikět), *a.* 1777. [– L. *conduplicatus*, pa. pple. of *conduplicare*, f. *com* CON- + *duplicare* DUPLICATE *v.*; see -ATE³.] *Bot.* Doubled or folded together: said of leaves folded down lengthwise along the middle. var. **Condu·plicated.** (Dicts.) So **Conduplica·tion,** a doubling, a repetition 1619.

Condurrite (kǫndʋ·rəit). 1827. [f. *Condurrow* + -ITE¹ 2 b.] *Min.* A soft black arsenical ore of copper, found in the Condurrow mine, Cornwall.

Condyle (kǫ·ndil). Also **condyl.** 1634. [– Fr. *condyle* (Paré, XVI) – L. *condylus* – Gr. κόνδυλος knuckle.] **1.** *Anat.* A rounded process at the end of a bone serving to form an articulation with another bone. **2.** Applied to the rounded ends of the tibia, and similar parts in arthropoda. Hence **Co·ndylar** *a.* pertaining to a c. **Co·ndyloid** *a.* resembling a c.; pertaining to a c.

‖ **Condyloma** (kǫndilōᵘ·mă). In 7 **-ome.** Pl. **-omata.** 1656. [– L. *condyloma* – Gr. κονδύλωμα callous knob or lump, f. κόνδυλος; see CONDYLE, -OMA.] *Pathol.* A conical or discoidal prominence of the skin, sometimes syphilitic, occuring near the external openings of the mucous passages, in the larynx, or elsewhere. Hence **Condylo·matous** *a.* of the nature of a c.

Condylopod (kǫndi·lǒpǫd). 1855. [f. mod. L. *Condylopoda* name of the class, f. Gr. κόνδυλος CONDYLE + πούς, ποδ- foot; see -A *suffix* 4.] *Zool.* One of the *Condylopoda*, now called ARTHROPODA. var. **Co·ndylope.**

‖ **Condylura** (kǫndiliūᵊ·ra). 1837. [mod.L. (Illiger), f. Gr. κόνδυλος CONDYLE + οὐρά tail.] *Zool.* Generic name of the Star-nosed Mole of N. America; so called from the knotty appearance of the tail in dried specimens.

Cone (kōᵘn), *sb.* 1562. [– Fr. *cône* – L. *conus* – Gr. κῶνος pine-cone, etc.] **1.** A solid figure or body, of which the base is a circle, and the summit a point, and every point in the intervening space is in a straight line between the vertex and the circumference of the base 1570. (Called a *right circular c.* when the vertex is on the perpendicular to the centre of the base; an *oblique c.*, when it lies without it.) **b.** In *mod. Geom.*, a solid generated by a straight line which always passes through a fixed point called the vertex, and describes any fixed curve (not necessarily a circle) 1865. **c.** A conical mass *of* any substance 1577. **2.** Any cone-shaped object; *esp.* a volcanic peak, formed by the accumulation of scoriæ round the crater 1830. **3.** *Bot.* The fruit of pines and firs; a dry scaly multiple fruit, formed by hard persistent imbricated scales covering naked seeds; a strobile 1562. **4.** *Conchol.* A marine shell of the genus *Conus*, or family *Conidæ*, of Gastropods 1770. **5.** *Meteorol.* A cone-shaped vessel, hoisted as a foul-weather-signal 1875. **6.** *Phys.* One of the minute cone-shaped bodies which form, with the rods, the bacillary layer of the retina 1867. **7.** Any conical apex or point; *e.g.* the apex of a helmet, †of the heart 1603. Also †*transf.*
C. of rays (in *Optics*): a pencil of rays of light diverging from an illuminating point and falling upon a surface. *C. of shade* (in *Astr.*): the conical shadow projected into space by a planet on the side turned from the sun. [Cf. L. *coni umbræ.*] MILT. *P.L.* IV. 776.
Comb.: **c.-bit,** a conical boring-bit; **-flower,** the genus *Rudbeckia*; **-gear,** a method of transmitting motion, by means of two cones rolling together; **c.-in-c.,** a peculiar geological structure, suggesting a number of cones packed one inside another; **-pulley,** a pulley shaped like a truncated c.; **-seat,** a piece of iron forming a seat for the c. or vent-plug in fire-arms; **-shell,** = CONE 4; **-wheel,** a wheel shaped like a truncated c., for transmitting a variable motion to another wheel. Hence **Cone** *v.* to shape like a c. or segment of a c.; *intr.* to bear cones.

Coneine; see CONIINE.

Conenchyma (koᵘne·ŋkimă). 1866. [f. Gr. κῶνος cone + ἔγχυμα infusion.] *Bot.* The tissue of the hairs of plants consisting of conical cells.

‖ **Conepatl** (kōᵘ·nīpɑt'l). 1774. [Mexican: lit. 'little fox'.] An American skunk (genus *Conepatus*, J. E. Gray, 1837).

Conessine (kone·səin). [f. *Conessi* + -INE⁵.] A bitter base from the bark of *Wrightia antidysenterica* (*Conessi cortex*). Also called *Wrightine.*

Coney, var. of CONY, q.v.

Confab (kǫnfæ·b), *sb.* 1701. [colloq. abbrev. of CONFABULATION.] A talk together; familiar talk. So **Confa·b** *v.*

Confabulate (kǫnfæ·biŭleⁱt), *v.* 1613. [– *confabulat-*, pa. ppl. stem of L. *confabulari* converse; see CON-, FABLE, and -ATE³.] *intr.* To talk familiarly together, converse, chat.
I shall not ask Jean Jacques Rousseau If birds c. or no COWPER. Hence **Confabula·tion,** familiar talk; a chat. **Confa·bulator. Confa·bulatory** *a.*

Confarreation (kǫnfæ:ri,ēⁱ·ʃən). 1598. [– L. *confarreatio*, f. *confarreat-*, pa. ppl. stem of *confarreare* unite in marriage (see below): f. *com* CON- + *farreum* spelt-cake; see -ATION.] *Rom. Antiq.* The most solemn form of marriage among the Romans, in which an offering of bread was made in the presence of the Pontifex Maximus and ten witnesses.

Confa·ted, *ppl. a.* 1768. [See CON-.] Fated together with (something else).

Confect (kǫ·nfekt), *sb.* 1587. [– med.L. *confectum, -ta*, subst. use of the pa. pple. of L. *conficere*; see next and cf. COMFIT.] A comfit.
Cacao..roasted, and made into Confects 1662.

Confect (kǫnfe·kt), *v.* 1545. [– *confect-*, pa. ppl. stem of L. *conficere* put together, prepare, etc., f. *com* CON- + *facere* make.] *trans.* † **1.** To put together; to compound –1651. **2.** To make into a confection. ? *Obs.* 1558. † **3.** To prepare (food) for digestion –1605. **4.** To make. [After Fr. *confectionner.*] 1677.
1. The Phisitions prescription confected by the Apothecary 1580. **4.** Patchwork quilts, confected by fingers of three or four years 1880. So † **Confe·ct** *ppl. a.* confected.

Confection (kǫnfe·kʃən), *sb.* ME. [– (O)Fr. *confection* – L. *confectio* preparation (abstr. and concr.), f. *confect-*; see prec. and -ION.] **1.** Making by mixture of ingredients; mixing, compounding 1477. **2.** A preparation of drugs; a conserve, an electuary ME.; a preparation of fruits, spices, sugar, or the like ME. ‖ **3.** *Dress-making.* The French word for any ready-made article of attire; *esp.* for mantles, cloaks, wraps, etc. 1885.
1. Pots of jam of her c. THACKERAY. **2.** Confections are medicinal substances beaten up with sugar into a pasty mass 1875. Delicat confections of spiceries STUBBES. Hence **Confe·ction** *v.* to make into a c.

Confectionary (kǫnfe·kʃənări). 1599. [f. CONFECTION + -ARY¹. With B. cf. med.L. *confectionarius* maker of confections, apothecary.]
A. *adj.* Of the nature of a confection; pertaining to confections or confectioners' work 1669.
The biscuit or c. plum COWPER. C. doings 1824.
B. *sb.* † **1.** A confectioner –1641. **2.** A place where confections are kept or prepared 1616. **3.** A sweetmeat 1599. **4.** *erron.* for CONFECTIONERY 1743.
1. And he will take your daughters to be confectionaries, and to be cookes 1 *Sam.* 8:13.

Confectioner (kǫnfe·kʃənəɹ). 1591. [f. CONFECTION *v.* + -ER¹.] † **1.** A compounder of medicines, poisons, etc. –1651. **2.** One who makes or sells confections 1591.

Confectionery (kǫnfe·kʃənəri). 1769. [f. prec. + -Y³; see -ERY.] **1.** Things made or sold by a confectioner; a collective name for sweetmeats and confections. **2.** The art and business of a confectioner 1872. **3.** A confectioner's shop (*mod.*).

† **Co·nfectory,** *a.* 1648. [f. CONFECT *sb.* + -ORY².] Pertaining to the making of confections.

† **Confe·cture.** ME. [– med.L. *confectura* confection, sweetmeat, (L. = preparation), f. as CONFECT *v.*; see -URE.] = CONFECTION, CONFITURE –1693.

† **Confe·der,** *v.* ME. [– (O)Fr. *confédérer* – L. *confœderare* league together.] The earlier equiv. of CONFEDERATE *v.* –1596.

Confederacy (kǫnfe·dĕrăsi). ME. [– AFr., OFr. *confederacie*, f. stem of *confederer*, *confederation*; see -ACY.] **1.** A union by league or contract between persons, bodies of men, or states, for mutual support or joint action; an alliance, compact. **b.** *Law* (and thence *gen.*); A league for an unlawful or evil purpose; a conspiracy ME. **2.** Condition or fact of being confederate; alliance; conspiracy 1594. **3.** quasi-*concr.* A body of confederates; now *esp.* a union of states, a confederation 1681.
1. A general c. against the Ottoman power 1769. **2.** In a perpetual state of c. and rebellion 1828. **3.** The stile of this c. shall be 'The United States of America' *U.S. Senate Manual* 1777. The literary world is made up of little confederacies W. IRVING. *Southern C.*: the Confederate States of America.

Confederal (kǫnfe·dĕrăl), *a.* 1866. [After *federal*; see CON-.] Pertaining to a confederation; *spec.* in *U.S. Hist.* pertaining to the organization of the United States under the Articles of Confederation of 1781. Hence **Confe·deralist,** a member of a confederation.

Confederate (kǫ̆nfe·dĕrĕt), *a.* and *sb.* ME. [– late (eccl.) L. *confœderatus*; see CON-, FEDERATE.]

A. *adj.* **1.** United in a confederacy; leagued, allied, confederated. Also *fig.* **2.** Of or belonging to the Confederate States of America 1861.

1. Syria is c. with Ephraim *Isa.* 7:2. My heart is not c. with my hand *Rich. II*, v. iii. 53. **2.** The C. flag 1861, army 1863.

Phr. *C. States* (*of America*), abbreviated *C.S.A.*: the name assumed by the eleven southern states which seceded from the American Union in 1860–61, and formed a confederacy of their own, which was finally overthrown in 1865.

B. *sb.* **1.** A person or state in league with another or others for mutual support or joint action; an ally 1548. **2.** *Law* (and thence *gen.*): An accomplice 1495. **3.** *U.S. Hist.* One belonging to or on the side of the Confederate States in the War of Secession, 1861–5.

1. The confederates of Cambray MACAULAY. **2.** Betrayers of their country, confederates with Wood SWIFT.

Confederate (kǫ̆nfe·dĕrēit), *v.* 1531. [prob. f. prec.] To unite in a league. *trans.* and *intr.* (for *refl.*)

To c. others in their design BURKE. The wits easily confederated against him JOHNSON.

Confederation (kǫ̆nfedĕrēi·ʃən). ME. [– OFr. *confederacion* (mod. *-tion*) or late L. *confederatio* (Jerome), f. *confederat-*, pa. ppl. stem of L. *confœderare*, f. *com* CON- + *fœderare* league together, f. *fœdus fœder-* league, treaty.] **1.** The action of confederating, or condition of being confederated; a league, an alliance (now only between states); † conspiracy. **2.** A number of states (or formerly of persons) united by a league (now usually on a more permanent basis than in the case of *confederacy*) 1622.

1. Articles of C. and perpetual union between the States of New Hampshire, Massachusetts Bay, Rhode Island, etc. 1777 (*title*). [A] scheme for the c. of the colonies 1885. *Articles of c.*: provisions (in clauses) in accordance with which parties confederate.

Confederative (kǫ̆nfe·derĕtiv), *a.* 1819. [– Fr. *confédératif, -ive*, f. stem of *confédération* + *-if* -IVE; see also -ATIVE.] Of or relating to confederates or confederating.

Confederator (kǫ̆nfe·dĕrēitəɹ). ? *Obs.* 1536. [– AFr. *confederatour*, f. as CONFEDERATE *v.* + -OUR, -OR 2.] A confederate, conspirator.

Confer (kǫ̆nfə̄·ɹ), *v.* 1528. [– L. *conferre*, f. *com* CON- + *ferre* bring.] † **1.** *trans.* To bring together, collect –1618. † **2.** To contribute. Const. *to.* –1677. Also † *absol.* **3.** To grant, bestow 1570. † **4.** To bring into comparison, compare, collate. Also *absol.* –1753. † **5.** *intr.* To conform (*with, to*) –1641. **6.** *intr.* To converse, talk together; to take counsel, consult 1545. † **7.** *trans.* To consult about –1689.

2. It confers somewhat to the need, convenience, or comfort of those..creatures BARROW. **3.** The stile and title..which the king is pleased to c. BLACKSTONE. The joy of heart which perfect health confers TYNDALL. **4.** C. future and times past with present BURTON. **6.** They sit conferring by the Parler fire *Tam. Shr.* v. ii. 102. Hence **Conferee·**, one who is conferred with (*U.S.*); one on whom something is conferred. **Confe·rment,** the action of conferring; † something conferred. **Confe·rrable** *a.* that may be conferred. **Confe·rrer.**

Conference (kǫ·nfĕrĕns), *sb.* 1538. [– Fr. *conférence* or med.L. *conferentia*; see CONFER, -ENCE.] † **1.** Collection; adding up –1651. † **2.** Comparison, *esp.* of texts; collation –1663. **3.** The action of conferring or taking counsel, now always on a serious matter; formerly: Conversation 1555. † **4.** Communication –1651. **5.** A formal meeting for consultation or discussion 1586. **6.** The annual assembly of ministers, etc., of the Wesleyan Methodist Connexion, constituting its central governing body; also the name of other religious bodies. (With capital C.) 1744.

3. Reading maketh a full man, c. a readye man, and writing an exacte man BACON. Moments of serious c. JANE AUSTEN. **5.** A message came.. from the Lords for present C. upon four bills sent up to them MARVELL. **6.** 'C. has forbid the women preaching' GEO. ELIOT. Hence **Co·nference** *v. rare*, to hold c. **Confere·ntial** *a.* of or relating to c., or to a c.

Conferruminate (kǫnferū·minĕt), *a.* 1855. [– L. *conferruminatus*, pa. pple. of *conferruminare* solder together; see CON-, FERRUMINATE *v.*] *Bot.* Of cotyledons: Consolidated into one body by the coalescence of the contiguous faces. var. **Conferru:mina·ted** *ppl. a.*

‖ **Conferva** (kǫ̆nfə̄·ɹvă). Pl. **-væ** (-vi). 1757. [L., perh. comfrey.] *Bot.* A genus of plants consisting of certain fresh-water Green Algæ (*Chlorophyllæ*), composed of unbranched many-celled filaments, and reproduced by zoospores. Formerly of more heterogeneous application. Hence **Conferva·ceous** *a.* of the nature of or allied to the genus *C.*; belonging to the N.O. *Confervaceæ*, comprising that genus and its allies. **Confe·rval** *a.* and *sb.* = *confervoid.* **Confe·rvite,** a fossil plant, allied to *C.*, found chiefly in the chalk. **Confe·rvoid** *a.* of the nature of or resembling a *C.*; *sb.* an alga of the genus *C.* or of any allied genus.

Confess (kǫ̆nfe·s), *v.* ME. [– (O)Fr. *confesser* :– Rom. **confessare*, f. L. *confessus*, pa. pple. of *confiteri* acknowledge, f. *com* CON- + *fateri* declare, avow.]

I. *gen.* **1.** *trans.* To declare or disclose (something previously kept secret as being prejudicial to oneself); to acknowledge, own, or admit (a crime, charge, fault, or the like). Also *absol.* **b.** Often introducing a statement of private feeling or opinion 1450. **2.** To acknowledge for oneself (an assertion or claim, that might be challenged) 1450. **3.** To avow formally *that*, esp. as an article of faith 1509. **4.** To declare belief in (a person or thing) as having a certain character or certain claims 1526. **5.** *fig.* To manifest, prove, attest (*poet.*) 1646.

1. And both confess'd..thir faults, and pardon beg'd MILT. *P.L.* x. 1100. **b.** The hazard I confesse is great 1632. **2.** You c. that parliaments are fallible 'JUNIUS'. **4.** Al they that do confesse thy holy name *Bk. Com. Prayer.* **5.** The voice divine confess'd the warlike maid POPE.

Phr. *C. to* (a thing): To plead guilty to (a charge), own to (a fault); to admit; also, short for *c. to have* (or *having*), as in *to c. to* [*having*] *a dread.*

II. *specifically.* **1.** *Law. intr.* To admit the truth of what is charged; *trans.* to admit as proved or legally valid 1586. **2.** *Eccl.* To acknowledge sins orally as a religious duty (*spec.* to a priest), with repentance and desire of absolution ME. **3.** *trans.* Of the priest: To hear the confession of, to shrive. Also *absol.* ME. *pass.* Of the penitent: To be shriven ME.

1. Phr. *To c. and avoid*: to admit a charge, but show it to be invalid in law. **2.** C. yourselves to Almighty God with full purpose of amendment of life *Bk. Com. Prayer.* **3.** I haue confes'd her, and I know her vertue *Meas. for M.* v. 533.

Hence **Confe·ssant,** one who confesses, *esp.* to a priest. **Confe·ssed** *ppl. a.* acknowledged as true; admitted; made manifest; shriven. **Confe·ssedly** *adv.* admittedly; avowedly. **Confessee·**, one who is confessed; one to whom confession is made (*rare*). **Confe·sser,** one who confesses or makes confession.

† **Confe·ssary.** 1608. [– med.L. *confessarius* (adj. and sb.), f. *confessare*; see CONFESS, -ARY[1].] **1.** A casuist who deals with confession –1649. **2.** A father confessor 1656. **3.** A confessant.

Confession (kǫ̆nfe·ʃən). ME. [– (O)Fr. *confession* – L. *confessio*, f. *confess-*, pa. ppl. stem of *confiteri*; see CONFESS *v.*, -ION.] **1.** A making known or acknowledging of one's fault, wrong, crime, weakness, etc. 1602. **b.** *Law.* Acknowledgement before the proper authority of the truth of a statement or charge 1574. **2.** The acknowledging of sin or sinfulness ME.; *spec.* the confessing of sins to a priest; more fully, *sacramental* or *auricular c.* ME. **3.** Acknowledgement of a statement, claim, etc.; admission ME. **4.** The acknowledging (of a person or thing) as having a certain character or certain claims ME. **5.** The matter confessed ME. **6.** A formulary containing a general acknowledgement of sinfulness 1535. **7.** (More fully *C. of Faith.*) A formulary in which a church or body of Christians sets forth the religious doctrines which it considers essential; a creed 1536. **8.** A tomb in which a martyr or confessor is buried; the structure erected over it; the crypt, shrine, etc., in which the relics are placed 1670.

1. When we would bring him on to some C. Of his true state *Haml.* III. i. 9. **b.** *C. and avoidance*: admission to the truth of an adverse allegation, with the allegation of matter tending to avoid its legal effect. **2.** Public c. they thought necessary by way of discipline HOOKER. **4.** *Haml.* IV. vii. 96. **5.** His c. is taken *All's Well* IV. iii. 130. **6.** A General C. for every sinner 1535.

Hence **Confe·ssionary** *a.* of or pertaining to c. **Confe·ssionary** *sb.* a confessional; also = CONFESSION 8. **Confe·ssionist,** an adherent of a religious c., *spec.* a Lutheran; a confessionalist. **Confe·ssionless** *a.* having no C. of Faith.

Confe·ssional, *sb.* 1727. [– Fr. *confessional* – It. *confessionale* – med.L. *confessionale*, subst. use of n. sing. of adj. *confessionalis*; see CONFESSION, -AL[1].] A stall or box in which a priest hears confessions.

Confessional (kǫ̆nfe·ʃənăl), *a.* 1817. [f. CONFESSION + -AL[1].] **1.** Of the nature of or pertaining to confession. **2.** Of or pertaining to Confessions of Faith or Creeds 1882. Hence **Confe·ssionalism,** the principle of formulating a Confession of Faith; adherence to a formulated theological system. **Confe·ssionalist,** one who makes confession.

Confessor (kǫ̆nfe·səɹ). ME. [AFr. *confessur*, OFr. *confessour* (mod. *-eur*) – eccl. L. *confessor*, f. *confess-*; see CONFESS *v.*, -OR 2.] **1.** *gen.* One who makes confession of anything. **2.** *Eccl.* One who avows and adheres to his faith under persecution and torture, but does not suffer martyrdom. (The earliest sense in English.) ME. **3.** (Often kǫ·nfĕsǫɹ) A priest who hears confessions, prescribes penance, and grants absolution ME.

2. Alle the seyntes of that cuntre [Ireland] be confessores, and noo martir tr. *Higden* (Rolls). *The C.*: = King Edward the C. (d. 1066), canonized in 1611. Hence **Confe·ssoress. Confe·ssorship.**

Confest, etc., var. CONFESSED, etc.

‖ **Confetti** (kǫ̆nfe·ti), *sb. pl.* 1860. [It., pl. of *confetto* COMFIT.] Bonbons, or imitations of these, thrown during carnival in Italy; in Eng., *esp.* little discs of coloured paper thrown at weddings, etc.

† **Confi·cient.** *rare.* 1614. [– L. *conficiens, -ent-*, pres. pple. of *conficere* accomplish; in late and med.L. with ref. to the Eucharist.] An officiating priest –1638.

Confidant (kǫ·nfidænt). 1714. [Superseding the earlier CONFIDENT *sb.*, presumably to repr. the pronunc. of Fr. *confidente* (a conventional character of the French stage).] 'A person trusted with private affairs, commonly with affairs of love' (J.). Now used more widely.

He was accustomed to make her his c. in his ecclesiastical proceedings J. H. NEWMAN. So **Co:nfida·nte,** a female c. (perh. formed before the masc.)

Confide (kǫ̆nfəi·d), *v.* 1455. [– L. *confidere*, f. *com* CON- + *fidere* trust.] **1.** *intr.* To trust or have faith; to put trust, repose confidence *in*, † *on*, † *to*. Also *absol.* **2.** *trans.* To impart in confidence (*to* a person) 1735; to entrust (an object, task, etc.) *to* a person with reliance on his fidelity or competence 1861.

1. Such a person..'as they could c. in' (an expression that grew from that time to be much used) CLARENDON. Judge before Friendship, then c. till Death YOUNG. **2.** The execution of the plan was confided to Aranda BUCKLE. Hence **Confi·der. Confi·ding-ly** *adv.*, **-ness.**

Confidence (kǫ·nfidĕns). ME. [– L. *confidentia*, f. *confident-*, pres. ppl. stem of *confidere* CONFIDE; see -ENCE. Cf. (O)Fr. *confidence*.] **1.** The mental attitude of trusting in or relying on; firm trust, reliance, faith. Const. *in* († *to, on, upon*). **2.** Assurance; assured expectation 1555. **3.** Assurance arising from reliance (on oneself, circumstances, etc.) 1526. **4.** Excess of assurance, hardihood, presumption, impudence 1594. **5.** That which gives confidence 1535. **6.** Confidential intimacy 1592. **7.** A confidential communication 1748. † **8.** Trustworthiness, as a personal quality –1800. † **9.** *Law.* = TRUST –1848.

1. C...in foraigne ayde 1649. **2.** A vain c. of his own abilities 1790. In c. thereof, the Duke left him 1654. **3.** Your wisedome is consum'd in c.: Do not go forth to day *Jul. C.* II. ii. 49. **5.** For the Lord shalbe thy c. *Prov.* 3:26. **6.** Speaking in c., for I should not like to have my words repeated JOWETT. **7.** He will..be well informed..by the confidences made him CHESTERF. **8.** A person of c. 1777.

Phr. *C. trick* (*game*, etc.): a method of swindling, in which the victim hands over valuables as a token of c. in the sharper. *C. man*: one who practices this trick. So **Co·nfidency** (*rare*).

Confident (kǫ·nfidĕnt). 1588. [In sense 1 – L. *confidens, -ent-* (see prec.); in later senses, and as *sb.*, – Fr. *confident* – It. *confidente*. See CONFIDANT.]

A. *adj.* † **1.** Trustful, confiding –1666. **2.** Having confidence; feeling certain, fully assured, sure 1601. **3.** Full of assurance, self-reliant, bold; having no fear of failure 1576. **4.** Overbold; forward, presumptuous, impudent. *Obsolescent.* 1597. **5.** Positive; dogmatical 1611. † **6.** Trusty –1714. **7.** Confidential 1608.

1. Rome, be as iust and gracious vnto.me, As I am c. and kinde to thee *Tit. A.* I. i. 61. **2.** Reasons they had to be c. of victory THIRLWALL. C. in thy defence WESLEY. **3.** His forces strong, his Souldiers c. *John* II. i. 61. **4.** A c. slut FIELDING. **5.** Your c. and positive way of talking BERKELEY. **6.** C. newes 1619. **7.** A. c. servant of my masters 1623. Hence **Co·nfidently** *adv.*

B. *sb.* **1.** A trusty adherent; a confidential friend 1619. **2.** *spec.* = CONFIDANT 1647.

Confidential (kǫnfide·nʃăl), *a.* 1759. [f. CONFIDENT + -IAL, infl. by CONFIDENCE.] **1.** Of the nature of confidence; spoken or written in confidence 1773. **2.** Betokening private intimacy 1759. **3.** Enjoying another's confidence; entrusted with secrets 1805.

1. *C. communication*: one made between parties who stand in a c. relation to each other, and therefore privileged in law. **2.** Talking the c. language of friendship in the public theatre BURKE. Hence **Confidentia·lity**, c. quality. **Confide·ntial-ly** *adv.*, **-ness.**

Configurate (kǫ̆nfi·giŭreᶦt), *v.* Now *rare.* 1566. [– *configurat-*, pa. ppl. stem of L. *configurare* fashion after a pattern; see CON-, FIGURE, -ATE [3].] **1.** *trans.* To frame; to give a configuration to. Also *fig.* † **2.** (?) *intr.* ? To show congruity of structure 1650.

2. Where pyramids to pyramids relate, And the whole fabrick doth c. 1650. So **Confi·gurative** *a.* of or pertaining to configuration. **Confi·gurature**, shape of countenance.

Configuration (kǫ̆nfigiŭrēᶦ·ʃən). 1559. [– late L. *configuratio*, f. as prec.; see -ION. Cf. (O)Fr. *configuration*.] **1.** Arrangement of parts in a form or figure; the form resulting from such arrangement; conformation; outline, contour (of geographical features, etc.) 1646. **2.** *Astron.* Relative position, apparent or actual, of celestial bodies; *esp.* the planetary 'aspects', recognized in Judicial Astrology 1559. † **3.** An image. HALE.

1. The remarkable c. of the Atlantic sea-bed HUXLEY. **2.** The Disease is found out..from the Configurations of the Planets SALMON.

Configure (kǫ̆nfi·giŭɹ), *v.* Now *rare.* ME. [– L. *configurare*, see CONFIGURATE *v.* Esp. allusive to Phil. 3:10 (Vulg. *configuratus*).] **1.** *trans.* To fashion according to a model. **2.** To put together in a form or figure 1652. Also *fig.*

Confinable (kǫ̆nfəi·năb'l), *a.* 1610. [f. CONFINE *v.* + -ABLE.] To be confined, capable of confinement.

Vertue..not c. to any limits BP. HALL.

† **Confine,** *a.* 1579. [– OFr. *confin, -fine* bordering :– L. *confinis*; see CONFINES.] Neighbouring, adjacent –1653.

† **Confine,** *sb.*[1] Always *pl.* **confines.** 1531. [– L. *confinis* neighbour, subst. use of *confinis* adj.; see prec.] *pl.* Neighbours –1598.

Confine (kǫ·nfəin), *sb.*[2] Mostly in *pl.* **confines.** ME. [– Fr. *confins*, † *confines* – L. *confinia*, pl. of *confine* and *confinium*, f. *confinis* bordering, f. *com* CON- + *finis* end, limit (pl. *fines* territory).] **1.** *pl.* Boundaries, borders 1548; † region –1670. Rarely in *sing.* Also *fig.* **2.** (kǫ̆nfəi·n). Confinement; limitation (*poet.*) 1597; † a place of confinement –1650.

1. Thextreme confines of Egypt EDEN. Heere in these Confines slily haue I lurkt SHAKS. *fig.* The.. confines between Virtue and Vice BENTLEY. **2.** Think on the dungeon's grim c. BURNS. Th' extrauagant, and erring Spirit, hyes To his c. *Haml.* I. i. 155. Hence **Confi·neless** *a.* unlimited *Macb.* IV. iii. 55.

Confine (kǫ̆nfəi·n), *v.* 1523. [– Fr. *confiner*, f. *confins* (see CONFINES), prob. after It. *confinare*.] **1.** *intr.* To have a common boundary *with*; to border *on*, be adjacent *to*. Now *rare.* † **2.** *trans.* To border on, bound –1694. † **3.** To relegate *to* certain limits; to banish –1653; to shut up, imprison 1602; to fasten, keep in place 1595. **4.** To keep indoors, or in bed. Usually in passive. Const. *to*. 1634. **5.** *fig.* To limit, restrict 1597. **6.** To constipate; to BIND 1870.

1. The princes which c. upon that sea 1577. **3.** And for the day confin'd to fast in Fiers *Haml.* I. v. 11. Now let not Natures hand Keepe the wilde Flood confin'd 2 *Hen. IV*, I. i. 154. **4.** To be confined by gout BERKELEY. Phr. *To be confined*: to be in childbed; to be delivered *of*. **5.** Cabin'd, crib'd, confin'd, bound in, To sawcy doubts, and feares *Macb.* III. iv. 24. Hence **Confi·ned-ly** *adv.*, **-ness.**

Confinement (kǫ̆nfəi·nmĕnt). 1646. [f. CONFINE *v.* + -MENT, or – Fr. *confinement* (in sense 1).] **1.** The action of confining; being confined; imprisonment. **2.** Restriction, limitation 1678. **3.** *spec.* The being in childbed; delivery, accouchment. (The ordinary term in colloq. use.) 1774.

1. The c. of his body within four walls 'JUNIUS'. **2.** C. to spare diet BENTHAM.

† **Co·nfiner**[1]. 1599. [f. CONFINE *sb.* or *v.* (1, 2) + -ER[1].] **1.** One who dwells on the confines; a borderer, neighbour –1682. **2.** One living within the confines; an inhabitant 1611.

2. Happie confiners you of other landes DANIEL.

Confi·ner[2]. *rare.* 1654. [f. CONFINE *v.* + -ER[1] 2.] One who or that which confines.

Confinity (kǫ̆nfi·nĭti). ? *Obs.* 1544. [– (O)Fr. *confinité* or med.L. *confinitas*, f. *confinis* (see CONFINE *a.*); see -ITY.] Neighbourhood, contiguity.

Confirm (kǫ̆nfə̄·ɹm), *v.* [ME. *conferme, -firme* – OFr. *confermer* (later *confirmer*) – L. *confirmare*, f. *com* CON- + *firmare* strengthen, f. *firmus* FIRM.] **1.** *trans.* To make firm or more firm, to add strength to, establish firmly. **2.** To make valid by formal authoritative assent; to ratify, sanction ME. **3.** *Eccl.* To administer CONFIRMATION to; formerly 'to bishop' ME. **4.** To strengthen (in an opinion, action, or purpose) 1485. **5.** To corroborate; to verify, put beyond doubt ME. † **6.** To affirm *that* –1668. † **7.** To assure, convince –1771.

1. His alliance will confirme our peace 1 *Hen. VI*, V. v. 42. Confirme the feeble knees *Isa.* 35 : 3. **2.** The charters were confirmed by *inspeximus* on the 12th [Oct. 1297] STUBBS. He was confirmed bishop of Couentrie HOLINSHED. Confirme the Crowne to me and to mine Heires 3 *Hen. VI*, I. i. 172. **3.** He ordeyned that a chylde sholde be confyrmed as soone as it myght, namely after it was crystened CAXTON. **4.** When Mackbeth is confirming himself in the horrid purpose JOHNSON. **5.** The News..has not yet been confirmed ADDISON. Hence **Confi·rmable** *a.* that may be confirmed. † **Confi·rmance**, confirmation. **Confi·rmative** *a.* having the property of confirming; **-ly** *adv.* † **Confirmator,** one who or that which confirms. **Confi·rmatory** *a.* corroborative; † *Eccl.* relating to confirmation. **Confirmee·**, *Law.* one to whom a confirmation is made; *Eccl.* one who is confirmed. **Confi·rmer,** one who or that which confirms. † **Confi·rmment,** confirmation. **Confi·rmor** (*Law*), a party who confirms a voidable estate, etc.

Confirmation (kǫ̆nfəɹmēᶦ·ʃən). ME. [– (O)Fr. *confirmation* – L. *confirmatio*, f. *confirmat-*, pa. ppl. stem of *confirmare*; see prec., -ION.] **1.** The action of making firm or sure; strengthening, settling, establishing 1480. **2.** The action of confirming or ratifying ME. **3.** The action of corroborating, or verifying; verification, proof ME.; a confirmatory statement or circumstance 1553. **4.** *Law.* See quots. Also as in 2. 1495. **5.** *Eccl.* A rite administered to baptized persons in various Christian churches; formerly called 'bishoping'. (It is held to convey special grace which strengthens the recipient for the practice of the Christian faith.) ME.

1. C. of our faith SANDYS, of a title FREEMAN. **2.** *C. of the Charters*: *spec.* the c. of Magna Charta and the Charter of the Forests by Edward I in 1297. C. of the Speaker 1886. **3.** *Oth.* III. iii. 323. **4.** A C. is a conueyance of an estate or right in esse, whereby a voidable estate is made sure and vnauoidable, or whereby a particular estate is encreased COKE.

Confirmed (kǫ̆nfə̄·ɹmd), *ppl. a.* ME. [f. CONFIRM *v.* + -ED[1].] **1.** In the senses of the vb. **2.** *spec.* Of a disease: Firmly established in the system; inveterate, chronic, as a *c. cancer* ME. **3.** Firmly established in the habit, etc., expressed by the appellative, as a *c. invalid* 1826.

Confiscate (see the vb.), *ppl. a.* 1533. [– L. *confiscatus*, pa. pple. of *confiscare*, f. *com* CON- + *fiscus* chest, treasury; see FISCAL, -ATE[2].] **1.** Appropriated to the use of the state, adjudged forfeited. **2.** Deprived of property as forfeited 1618.

1. And let it be c. all *Cymb.* V. v. 323.

Confiscate (kǫ·nfiskeᶦt, -fi·skeᶦt), *v.* 1533. [– *confiscat-*, pa. ppl. stem of L. *confiscare*; see prec., -ATE[3].] **1.** *trans.* To appropriate (private property) to the public treasury by way of penalty. † **2.** To deprive of property as forfeited to the state –1662. **3.** *loosely.* To seize as if by authority 1819.

2. The forenamed Lords..were condemned and confiscate RALEGH. **3.** The cargoes he confiscated BYRON. So **Confi·scable** *a.* liable to confiscation. **Confisca·table** *a.* **Co·nfiscator,** one who confiscates. **Confi·scatory** *a.* of the nature of, or tending to, confiscation; robbing under legal authority (*colloq.*).

Confiscation (kǫnfiskēᶦ·ʃən). 1543. [– L. *confiscatio*, f. as prec.; see -ION. Cf. (O)Fr. *confiscation*.] **1.** The action of confiscating. **2.** Robbery under legal authority 1832.

1. The C. of the Abbey lands FROUDE. Ruined by fines and confiscations GIBBON.

Confit, -fite, obs. f. COMFIT *sb.* and *v.*

Confitent (kǫ·nfitĕnt), 1606. [– *confitent-*, pres. ppl. stem of L. *confiteri* confess; see -ENT.] One who confesses; a penitent.

‖ **Confiteor** (kǫ̆nfi·tiˌǭɹ). ME. [L., 'I confess', the first word of the formula *Confiteor Deo Omnipotenti* I confess to Almighty God, etc.] A form of prayer or confession of sins, used in the Latin Church at the beginning of the mass, and elsewhere.

‖ **Confiture.** Obs. f. COMFITURE; also the mod.Fr. form (koṅfitü·r), occas. used for 'Confection'.

Cates and confitures DISRAELI.

Confix (kǫ̆nfi·ks), *v.* 1603. [f. CON- + FIX *v.*] To fix firmly, fasten. *Meas. for M.* V. i. 232. So **Confi·xative** *a.* (*rare*). † **Confi·xure,** firm fixing.

Conflagrate (kǫ·nflăgreᶦt), *v.* 1657. [– *conflagrat-*, pa. ppl. stem of L. *conflagrare* burn up, f. *com* CON- + *flagrare* blaze; see -ATE[3].] **1.** *intr.* To catch fire. Also *fig.* **2.** *trans.* To set ablaze; to burn up. Also *fig.* 1835. So **Confla·grant** *a.* in conflagration.

Conflagration (kǫnflăgrēᶦ·ʃən). 1555. [– L. *conflagratio*, f. as prec.; see -ION; cf. Fr. *conflagration*.] † **1.** The burning up *of* (anything) –1825. **2.** A great and destructive fire; the burning of a town, a forest, or the like 1656. Also *fig.* and † *transf.*

2. The Burning of London..that dreadful C. 1680. So **Co·nflagrative** *a.* productive of c. **Co·nflagrator,** an incendiary. **Confla·gratory** *a.* inflammatory.

Conflate (kǫ·nflēᶦt), *ppl. a.* 1541. [– L. *conflatus*; see next.] † **1.** Blown together; composed of various elements –1638. **2.** *spec.* Formed by fusion of two readings 1881.

Conflate (kǫ̆nflēᶦ·t), *v.* 1610. [– *conflat-*, pa. ppl. stem of L. *conflare* lit. 'blow together', kindle, effect, fuse, f. *com* CON- + *flare* blow.] **1.** *trans.* To blow or fuse together; to bring together; to compose; produce, bring about. Now *rare.* **2.** To combine two readings into a composite reading. (In *passive.*) 1885.

1. The States-General, created and conflated by the passionate effort of the whole Nation CARLYLE.

Conflation (kǫ̆nflēᶦ·ʃən). 1626. [– late L. *conflatio* fanning (of fire), fusion (of metals), f. as prec.; see -ION.] **1.** The action of blowing or fusing together. Also *concr.* the result of this action. **2.** The fusion of two readings into a composite reading. Also *concr.* the reading thus formed. 1881.

Conflict (kǫ·nflikt), *sb.* ME. [– L. *conflictus*, f. *conflict-*, pa. ppl. stem of *confligere*, f. *com* CON- + *fligere* strike.] **1.** An encounter with arms; a fight; *esp.* a prolonged struggle. Also *transf.* and *fig.* **2.** Dashing together of physical bodies 1555.

1. Fourty thousand were slaine in the c. 2 *Macc.* 5 : 14. *fig.* With c. of contending hopes and fears COWPER. **2.** The conflicts of the ice-masses in their rotation KANE.

Conflict (kǫ̆nfli·kt), *v.* ME. [f. L. *conflict-*; see prec.] **1.** *intr.* To fight, contend, do battle.

Also *transf.* and *fig.* **2.** *fig.* Of interests, etc.: To come into collision, to clash; to be incompatible. (Now the chief sense.) 1647.

1. These two with Hector and his host Conflicted COWPER. *transf.* A horrible thundering of fire and water conflicting together BACON. **2.** The perplexities of conscience..in which duties appear to c. with each other T. H. GREEN. Hence **Confli·ction,** the action of conflicting; conflicting condition. **Confli·ctive** *a. rare,* of conflicting nature.

† **Conflo·w,** *v.* 1606. [f. CON- + FLOW *v.*] To flow together, as rivers, crowds, etc. –1627.

Confluence (kǫ·nfluěns). ME. [– late L. *confluentia*, f. *confluent-*, pres. ppl. stem of L. *confluere*, f. *com* CON- + *fluere* flow; see -ENCE.] **1.** A flowing together; the junction and union of two or more streams, etc. 1538. Also *fig.* and *transf.* **2.** The place where two or more rivers, etc., unite 1538. **3.** A combined flood 1615. **4.** A flocking together; concourse ME. **5.** A numerous concourse or collection ME.

1. An island, formed by the c. of two rivers 1828. **2.** Built upon the c. of the rivers JEPHSON. **5.** You see this c., this great flood of visitors *Timon* I. i. 42. A c. of associations STANLEY.

Confluent (kǫ·nfluěnt), *a.* 1611. [– *confluent-*, pres. ppl. stem of L. *confluere*; see prec., -ENT.] **1.** Flowing or running together; uniting so as to form one 1612. Also *fig.* **2.** Flowing together in a body 1718. Also *fig.* **3.** Meeting or running into each other, so as to form one mass or surface; as the vesicles in smallpox, spots, markings, etc. 1722. † **4.** Affluent *in*. CHAPMAN.

1. C. floods DRAYTON, roads DE QUINCEY, valleys GEIKIE, leaves CRABB, bones OWEN. **3.** The c. variety of Small-pox CARPENTER.

Confluent (kǫ·nfluěnt), *sb.* 1600. [See prec.; in sense 1 – L. *confluens*, pl. *confluentes* (cf. Fr. *confluent* in same sense); in sense 2 subst. use of prec.] † **1.** A confluence of rivers; the place where they unite. Rarely in *pl.* –1611. **2.** A stream which unites and flows with another; *occas.* but *loosely*, used for *affluent* 1850.

Conflux (kǫ·nflǫks). 1606. [– late and med.L. *confluxus*, f. *com* CON- + *fluxus* FLUX *sb.*] **1.** Flowing together; flowing into a common body. **2.** = CONFLUENCE 2. 1712. **3.** = CONFLUENCE 4. 1614. **4.** = CONFLUENCE 5. 1654.

1. As knots by the c. of meeting sap, Infect the sound Pine *Tr. & Cr.* I. iii. 7. **4.** Such a c. of misery JOHNSON. So † **Confluxibi·lity,** tendency to flow together. † **Conflu·xible** *a.* † **Conflu·xion,** the action of flowing together.

Confocal (kǫ̆nfōᵘ·kal), *a.* 1867. [See CON-.] *Geom.* Having the same focus or foci, as *c. hyperbolas.*

Conform (kǫ̆nfǭ·ɹm), *a.* ? *Obs.* ME. [– Fr. *conforme* – late L. *conformis*, f. *com* CON- + *forma* shape, FORM.] **1.** = CONFORMABLE 1, 2. † **2.** Conforming religiously, conformist –1711.

1. Made conforme to the Image of the same God MARBECK. C. to usage 1805. † **Confo·rmly** *adv.*

Conform (kǫ̆nfǭ·ɹm), *v.* ME. [– (O)Fr. *conformer* – L. *conformare*; see CON-, FORM *v.*] **1.** *trans.* To form according to some model; to make like. **2.** To bring into harmony or conformity; to adapt. Also *refl.* = 3. ME. **3.** *intr.* (for *refl.*) To act conformably or in conformity *to* ME.; *spec.* to comply with the usages of the Church of England 1619. **4.** Of things: To follow in form or nature 1699.

1. In all thynge to conforme my wyll to thy blessed wyll 1526. **3.** To c. to the ways of the world LAW. When any dissenter conforms LOCKE. **4.** The path..conforms to the water DODSLEY. Hence **Confo·rmance,** the action of conforming. † **Confo·rmant** *a.* conforming. SIR T. BROWNE. **Confo·rmate** *a. rare,* conformed. **Confo·rmer.**

Conformability (kǫ̆nfǭɹmăbi·lĭti). 1864. [f. next + -ITY.] The quality or condition of being conformable; *spec.* in *Geol.*, the relation of strata, one of which rests on the other and lies parallel to it.

Conformable (kǫ̆nfǭ·ɹmăb'l), *a.* 1511. [– med.L. *conformabilis*; see CONFORM *v.*, -ABLE.] **1.** According in form of character *to*; like. Const. *to*. **2.** Corresponding so as to fit; consistent, harmonious; fitting 1555. **3.** Disposed or wont to conform; tractable; compliant *to* 1525; *spec.* conforming to the usages of the Church of England 1597. **4.** *Geol.* Having the same direction or plane of stratification: said of strata in contact 1813. Also as quasi-*adv.* Conformably *to* 1588.

1. True holinesse is c. to the first pattern of holinesse 1646. **2.** What is c., or disagreeable to Reason, in the actions of common life HOBBES. To make matters somewhat c. for the old Knight SCOTT. **3.** In the meantime be humble and c. OTWAY. Hence **Confo·rmableness. Confo·rmably** *adv.* in a c. manner; in conformity with; agreeably; compliantly; *Geol.* in c. order.

Conformation (kǫnfǫɹmēⁱ·ʃən). 1511. [– L. *conformatio*, f. *conformat-*, pa. ppl. stem of *conformare* CONFORM *v.*; see -ION.] **1.** The action of conforming or bringing into conformity (*to*). **2.** The forming or fashioning of a thing in all its parts 1615. **3.** Form depending upon arrangement of parts; structure, organization 1646.

1. I shall speak..Of C...Be not conform'd to this World COLET. **2.** Male children..haue their c. the thirtieth day 1615. **3.** Government wants amendment in its c. BURKE.

Conformist (kǫ̆nfǭ·ɹmist). 1634. [f. CONFORM *v.* + -IST.] One who conforms *to* any usage or practice; *spec.* in *Eng. Hist.* to the usages of the Church of England; opp. to *dissenter, non-conformist*. Also *attrib.*

Several pliant conformists with all changes HALLAM. vars. † **Confo·rmitan,** † **Confo·rmitant.**

Conformity (kǫ̆nfǭ·ɹmĭti). ME. [– (O)Fr. *conformité* or late L. *conformitas*; see CONFORM *v.*, -ITY.] **1.** Correspondence in form or manner; agreement in character; likeness; congruity. **2.** Action in accordance with some standard; compliance, acquiescence 1494. **3.** *spec.* Conformity in worship; in *Eng. Hist.* compliance with the usages of the Church of England 1622.

1. The C. of these Moons with our Moon 1665. With strict c. to nature JOHNSON. The c. between the testimony and the facts JAS. MILL. **2.** Their C. to the Roman Religion BRAMHALL. **3.** The Act for universal C. MARVELL.

Confort, earlier f. COMFORT *v.* and *sb.*, found also in all the ME. derivatives.

Confound (kǫ̆nfau·nd), *v.* ME. [– AFr. *confundre, -foundre,* (O)Fr. *confondre*:– L. *confundere* pour together, mix up, f. *com* CON- + *fundere* pour.] **1.** *trans.* To overthrow, defeat, or bring to nought; † to waste –1701. **2.** In curses or imprecations = 'to bring to perdition'. Since 1700 considered a milder curse. ME. **3.** To discomfit, abash, put to shame. (Usu. in *pass.*) Chiefly Scriptural. ME. **4.** To throw into confusion or disorder; to perplex ME. **5.** To mix up so that the elements become difficult to distinguish; to CONFUSE 1538. **6.** To mix up in idea, fail to distinguish 1581.

1. Lest He is wrath c. me SOUTHEY. C. their politicks CAREY. He did c. the best part of an hour 1 *Hen. IV*, I. iii. 100. **2.** Mahounde confounde the LD. BERNERS. C. her impudence J. PAYN. **3.** Silent, and in face Confounded long they sate, as struck'n mute MILT. *P.L.* IX. 1064. **4.** Pale and dumb he stood, like one confounded 1682. Confusion worse confounded MILT. **5.** *Rich. II*, IV. i. 141. **6.** To c. Puritanism with Presbyterianism J. R. GREEN.

Hence **Confou·ndable** *a.* (*rare*). **Confou·nded** *ppl. a.* discomfited, abashed; confused, etc.: used as a mild curse (sense 2); also as *adv.* **Confou·nded-ly** *adv.*, **-ness. Confou·nder.**

† **Confra·ct,** *a.* [– L. *confractus*, pa. pple. of *confringere* break in pieces, f. *com* CON- + *frangere* break.] Completely broken, crushed. H. MORE.

† **Confra·ction.** 1541. [– OFr. *confraction* or late L. *confractio*; see CON-, FRACTION.] Breaking into small fragments; smashing, smash; crushing –1646.

† **Confrago·se,** *a.* [– L. *confragosus*, f. *com* CON- + *frag-* stem of *frangere* break; see -OSE¹.] Rough with breaks; broken. EVELYN.

Confraternity (kǫnfrătə̄·ɹnĭti). 1475. [– (O)Fr. *confraternité* – med.L. *confraternitas*, f. *confrater*; see next, FRATERNITY.] **1.** A brotherhood; an association of men united for some purpose, or in some profession. var. † **Confrai·ry. 2.** Brotherly union or communion 1680.

1. The Lord Maior with his c. of Aldermen 1654. A c. of monks 1882.

Confrere (koñfrẹr, kǫ̆nfrēᵊ·ɹ). ME. [– (O)Fr. *confrère* – med.L. *confrater*; see CON-, FRIAR.] **1.** A fellow-member of a fraternity, a colleague in office –1688. vars. †‖ **Confra·ter,** † **Confrier.** ‖ **2.** A fellow-member of a learned profession, scientific body, etc. [From mod.Fr.] 1753.

† **Confrication** (kǫnfrikēⁱ·ʃən). ME. [– late L. *confricatio*, f. *confricat-*, pa. ppl. stem of L. *confricare*, f. *com* CON- + *fricare* rub.] Rubbing together, friction –1798. var. † **Confri·ction.**

Confront (kǫ̆nfrǫ·nt), *v.* 1568. [– Fr. *confronter* – med.L. *confrontare*, f. L. *com* CON- + *frons, front-* forehead, face, FRONT.] † **1.** *intr.* To border *upon, against* –1614. **2.** *trans.* To stand or meet facing; to face, *esp.* in hostility or defiance; to present a bold front to (*lit.* and *fig.*) 1568. **3.** *trans.* To bring together face to face; to bring face to face *with* 1627. **4.** To set face to face or side by side *with* for purposes of comparison, etc. 1613.

2. We foure indeed confronted were with foure In Russia habit *L.L.L.* V. ii. 367. He spoke, and then confronts the bull DRYDEN. To c. an accuser JAS. MILL. **3.** To c. a man with his accusers MACAULAY. **4.** The old order of things..when confronted with the new JOWETT. Hence † **Confro·nt** *sb.* frontier (*rare*); the act or position of facing; an affront. **Confronta·tion,** the action of confronting. **Confro·nter. Confro·ntment** opposition; confronting.

‖ **Confronté** (kǫnfrǫ·nte). 1823. [Fr., pa. pple. of *confronter* (see prec.).] *Her.* 'Facing one another, or full-faced'.

Confucian (kǫ̆nfiū·ʃian). 1837. [f. name *Confucius*, Latinized f. the Chinese *K'ung Fû tsze*, = 'K'ung the Master (or Philosopher)' + -IAN.] **A.** *adj.* Of or relating to the Chinese philosopher Confucius, or his teaching, or followers. **B.** *sb.* A follower of Confucius. Hence **Confu·cianism,** the doctrines or system of Confucius and his followers; **Confu·cianist,** an adherent of Confucianism; also *attrib.*

† **Confuse,** *a.* [– (O)Fr. *confus, -use* – L. *confusus*, pa. pple. of *confundere* CONFOUND.] = CONFUSED –1737. Hence † **Confu·sely** *adv.*

Confuse (kǫ̆nfiū·z), *v.* ME. [Inferred from *confused*, f. (O)Fr. *confus* or its source L. *confusus* + -ED¹; see prec.] [† **1.** *trans.* = CONFOUND 1. Only *passive.* ME.] **2.** To discomfit in mind or feelings; to abash; to bewilder. Till 19th c. only *passive.* ME. **3.** To throw into disorder or confusion. Till 19th c. only *passive.* 1635. [**4.** = CONFOUND 5. Only *passive.* 1550.] **5.** To mix up in the mind, fail to distinguish 1862. Also *intr.* (*rare*).

2. Or has the shock..Confused me TENNYSON. **3.** He has done more to c. and mystify the subject than to clear it up 1861. **4.** A thick nose, confused on either side with the projecting cheek 1819. **5.** We in reality c. wealth with money RUSKIN. Hence **Confusabi·lity** (*rare*). **Confu·singly** *adv.*

Confused (kǫ̆nfiū·zd), *ppl. a.* ME. [For the adj., see prec.; as pa. pple. f. CONFUSE *v.* + -ED¹.]

I. As *pa. pple.* this dates back to 14th c.

II. as *adj.* **1.** Amazed, bewildered, disconcerted, etc. **2.** Disordered, disorderly 1576. † **3.** Blended, mixed (*rare*) –1677. **4.** Obscure, indistinct 1611. Hence **Confu·sed-ly** *adv.*, **-ness.**

Confusion (kǫ̆nfiū·ʒən). ME. [– (O)Fr. *confusion* or L. *confusio*; see CON-, FUSION.] **1.** Discomfiture, ruin. ? *Obs.* **2.** Mental discomfiture ME. **3.** Embarrassment, perplexity 1596. **4.** The action of throwing into disorder ME. **5.** A disordered condition 1530. **6.** Tumult; civil commotion 1555. **7.** Mixture in which the distinction of the elements is lost ME. **8.** The quality of being confused 1729. **9.** Failure to distinguish 1771.

1. Ruin seize thee, ruthless King! C. on thy banners wait GRAY. **3.** You amaze me. How shall I conceal my c. GOLDSM. **4.** The c. of tongues BACON. **5.** The enemy..fled in the utmost c. WELLINGTON. **6.** The late unhappy confusions *Bk. Com. Prayer.* **7.** In the case of *c. of goods,* where those of two persons are so intermixed that the several portions can no longer be distinguished BLACKSTONE. **8.** C. in writing BUTLER. Hence **Confu·sional** *a.* characterized by (mental) c.

† **Confu·sive,** *a.* 1611. [f. CONFUSE *v.* + -IVE. Cf. med.L. *confusivus.*] That tends to confuse –1790. Hence † **Confu·sively** *adv.*

Confutation (kǫnfiutēⁱ·ʃən). 1526. [– Fr. *confutation* or L. *confutatio*, f. *confutat-*, pa.

ppl. stem of *confutare*; see next.] The action of confuting; disproof; the complete argument in which anything is confuted.

Confutations were published GIBBON.

Confute (kǫ̆nfiū·t), *v.* 1529. [– L. *confutare* check, restrain, answer conclusively, f. *cum* CON- + **fūt*-, as in *refutare* refute.] **1.** *trans.* To prove (a person) to be wrong; to convict of error by argument or proof 1533. Also *transf.* **2.** To prove (an argument or opinion) to be false, invalid, or defective; to refute 1529. **3.** To render futile 1589.

1. If you want to win a man's heart, allow him to c. you DISRAELI. *transf.* Goliath..shall be confuted with a pebble 1614. **2.** Macaulay himself ..presently confutes his own thesis M. ARNOLD. Hence **Confu·table** *a.* that can be confuted. So † **Confu·tant,** one who confutes. MILTON. **Confu·tative** *a.* tending to confutation. **Co·nfutator,** a confuter. † **Confu·te** *sb.* confutation. So **Confu·tement.** MILTON. **Confu·ter,** one that confutes.

‖ **Congé**; see CONGEE.

‖ **Congé.** 1703. [– Fr. *conge*, adopted earlier (XV) as *congie*; see CONGÉE.] *Arch.* APOPHYGE.

† **Congeable,** *a.* 1574. [– Fr. *congéable*, f. OFr. *congéer* (mod. *congédier*) + *-able* -ABLE.] Permissible, allowable –1654.

Congeal (kǫ̆ndʒī·l), *v.* [– (O)Fr. *congeler* – L. *congelare*, f. *com* CON- + *gelare* freeze.] **I.** *trans.* **1.** To convert, by cold, from a fluid or soft to a solid state; to freeze. † **2.** To solidify as by freezing –1678. **3.** To curdle, clot, coagulate ME. Also *fig.*

1. Whan ayre is congelyd it makyth snowe and hayle TREVISA. **2.** Salt, congealed by the sun 1727. **3.** Too much sadnesse hath congeal'd your blood *Tam. Shr.* Induct. ii. 134.

II. *intr.* **1.** To become solid and stiff by or as by freezing; to freeze, †to crystallize, †petrify ME. **2.** To coagulate, clot, or curdle ME. Also *fig.*

1. Wine of it owne nature will not congeale and freeze HOLLAND. **2.** My blood congeals MARLOWE. *fig.* Least zeale now melted..Coole and congeale againe to what it was *John* II. i. 479.

Hence **Congea·lable** *a.*; **-ness. Congea·led** (also †*co·ngeal'd*) *ppl. a.* **Congea·ler. Congea·lment,** the act of congealing and of being congealed; *concr.* a congealed mass.

Congee, ‖ **congé** (kǫ·ndʒi, kǫ̃ʒe), *sb.* [– OFr. *congié* (mod. *congé*) :– L. *commeatus* passage, leave to pass, furlough, f. *com* CON- + *meare* go, pass.] † **1.** Authoritative leave to depart; passport –1789. † **2.** Ceremonious dismissal and leave-taking –1830. **3.** A bow; orig. at taking one's leave (*arch.*) 1586. **4.** Dismissal without ceremony. [From mod.Fr., and often *joc.*] 1847. **5.** Permission (for any act) 1475.

2. Phr. †*To take congee*: to take leave (to go). Also †*to give c.*: to bid farewell. **3.** With coniayes all salute him DRAYTON. **4.** Should she pay off old Briggs, and give her her *congé* THACKERAY.

Congé d'élire [AFr. *conge de eslire*]: royal permission to a monastic body or cathedral chapter, to fill up a vacant see or abbacy by election.

Congee, *sb.* and *v.* *Anglo-Ind.*; see CONJEE.

Congee, congé, *v. arch.* ME. [– OFr. *congeer, congier*, f. *congié* sb.] † **1.** *trans.* To dismiss –1577. † **2.** To license –1532. **3.** *intr.* To pay one's respects at leaving 1601. **4.** To bow in courtesy or obeisance. Also *fig.* 1606.

Congelation (kǫ̆ndĕlē̆ⁱ·ʃən). ME. [– (O)Fr. *congelation* or L. *congelatio*, f. *congelat-*, pa. ppl. stem of *congelare*; see CONGEAL, -ION.] **1.** The action of congealing or freezing; the process or state of being congealed 1536; *concr.* a frozen mass 1686. **2.** *gen.* Conversion from a fluid to a solid state ME.; *concr.* a concretion, crystallization, petrifaction 1605. Also *transf.* and *fig.*

1. The solid obtained by the c. of water is termed ice HUXLEY. *concr.* A Multitude of Congelations in Jellies of various Colours ADDISON. So † **Co·ngelative** *a.* having the quality of congealing.

Congener (kǫ·ndʒĭnəɹ). 1730. [– L. *congener*, f. *com* CON- + *genus, gener-*; see GENUS.] A member of the same kind or class (rarely 'of the same genus') with another, or nearly allied to another in character.

This sort of fruit hath been by many people grafted upon the Lawrel, to which it is a c. 1751. Hence † **Conge·neracy,** community or affinity of origin, kind, or nature. **Conge·nerate** *v.* to beget together; to class as a c. (*rare*). **Conge·nerate** *a.* (*rare*). **Congene·ric, -al** *a.* of the same genus, kind, or race; allied in nature or origin.

Congenerous (kǫ̆ndʒe·nĕrəs), *a.* 1646. [f. L. *congener* (see prec.) + -OUS.] Of the same kind, akin in nature or character; congeneric. *C. muscles* (Phys.): muscles which concur in the same action. Hence **Conge·nerousness.** var. † **Conge·nious** *a.*

Congenial (kǫ̆ndʒī·niăl), *a.* 1625. [– mod. L. **congenialis*, f. L. *com* CON- + GENIUS, after GENIAL.] **1.** Partaking of the same disposition, or temperament; kindred, sympathetic. Const. *with* (occ. *to*). **2.** Suited to one's temperament or disposition 1770. Also *transf.* † **3.** CONGENITAL –1775; native –1774; congenerous –1804.

1. A soul c. to to his [Chaucer's] DRYDEN. C. tastes FREEMAN. **2.** To me more dear, c. to my heart GOLDSM. *transf.* C. to the liberal Arts SHAFTESB. Hence **Congenia·lity,** the quality of being c.; affinity of genius or disposition; agreeableness to one's nature. **Conge·nialize** *v.* to make c.; *intr.* to be or become c. *with* (*rare*). **Conge·nially** *adv.*

Congenital (kǫ̆ndʒe·nităl), *a.* 1796. [f. L. *congenitus* born along with, connate, f. *com* CON- + *genitus*, pa. pple. of *gignere* produce; see GENITAL.] Existing or dating from one's birth, born with one.

C. hernia S. COOPER, differences of character KINGSLEY. Hence **Conge·nitally** *adv.* from birth.

† **Conge·nite,** *a.* 1610. [– L. *congenitus*; see prec.] Born or produced along with, connate, congenital; natural. Of ideas, etc.: Innate. Const. *to, with.* –1716.

Sinful habits..congenit with our natures SOUTH.

† **Co·ngeon, co·njon.** [ME. *cangun*, etc., poss. repr. ONFr. **cangiun*, **cangeon* :– med.L. *cambio, cambion-*, f. L. *cambire*; see CHANGE.] A dwarf –1768; a half-wit; also as a term of contempt, abuse, or dislike (ME. only).

Conger[1] (kǫ·ŋgəɹ). ME. [– (O)Fr. *congre* :– L. *congrus*, also *conger*, – Gr. γόγγρος.] A species of eel living in salt water and attaining a length of from six to ten feet; the sea-eel.

Conger[2] (kǫ·ŋgəɹ). 1700. [Origin unkn.] A Society of Booksellers, who sold or printed books for their common advantage. Now *Hist.*

Conger-eel (kǫ·ŋgər,ī·l). 1602. [f. CONGER[1].] **1.** = CONGER[1]. **2.** In U.S. applied also to other species of eel.

Congeries (kǫ̆ndʒiᵊ·ri,īz). 1619. [– L. *congeries* heap, pile, f. *congerere*; see CONGEST *v.*] A collection of things merely heaped together; a mass, heap.

† **Congest,** *sb. rare.* 1630. [– L. *congestus* accumulation, heap, f. as next.] A collected mass –1657.

Congest (kǫ̆ndʒe·st), *v.* 1538. [– *congest-*, pa. ppl. stem of L. *congerere* carry together, heap up, f. *com* CON- + *gerere* carry.] † **1.** *trans.* To gather together; to heap up, to mass –1758. Also *refl.* and *intr.* **2.** *trans.* To affect with congestion 1758.

1. He had congested and amassed together such infinite monies 1619. So **Conge·stive** *a.* of the nature of, relating to, or produced by, congestion.

Congested (kǫ̆ndʒe·stĕd), *ppl. a.* 1578. [f. prec. + -ED[1].] † **1.** Heaped together –1651. **2.** *Med.* Overcharged with an unnatural accumulation of blood; affected with congestion 1758; hence, *transf.* Overcrowded 1862. **3.** *Bot.* 'Crowded very closely' 1866.

2. The c. state of the goods traffic 1891.

Congestion (kǫ̆ndʒe·styən). 1593. [– (O)Fr. *congestion* – L. *congestio*, f. *congest-*; see CONGEST *v.*, -ION.] † **1.** The action of heaping together in a mass; accumulation –1671; † *concr.* a heap –1834. † **2.** *Med.* The accumulation of blood or morbid matter in any part of the body –1811. **3.** *transf.* and *fig.* Overcrowded condition 1868.

1. The c. of dead bodies one upon another EVELYN. **2.** C. of the lungs 1875. **3.** That local c. of the population 1887.

Congiary (kǫ·ndʒiări). 1601. [– L. *congiarium*, f. *congius* (next); see -ARY[1].] *Rom. Antiq.* A gift divided among the people or the soldiers, orig. something measured in a congius, *e.g.* corn or wine.

‖ **Congius** (kǫ·ndʒiŏs). Pl. **-ii.** ME. [L.] **1.** *Rom. Antiq.* A measure for liquids, containing about 7 pints. **2.** *Pharm.* A gallon, often shortened to the letter C.

† **Congla·ciate** *v.* 1646. [– *conglaciat-*, pa. ppl. stem of L. *conglaciare* freeze up, f. *com* CON- + *glaciare* turn to ice, f. *glacies* ice. See -ATE[3].] **1.** *trans.* To make into or like ice –1686. **2.** *intr.* To become ice –1808. So † **Conglacia·tion.**

Conglobate (kǫ·nglobeⁱt), *v.* 1635. [– *conglobat-*, pa. ppl. stem of L. *conglobare*, f. *com* CON- + *globare* make into a ball, f. *globus* ball; see -ATE[3].] To gather or form into a ball or globe, or a rounded mass. *trans.* and *intr.* (for *refl.*)

Not conglobated into one bodie as the stars are 1635. Hence **Congloba·tion.**

Conglobate (kǫ·nglobeⁱt), *a.* 1649. [– L. *conglobatus*, pa. pple. of *conglobare*; see prec., -ATE[2].] Formed or gathered into a ball, rounded, globular.

The kidnies are c. HOME. Lymphatic glands, named also c. glands QUAIN. Hence **Co·nglobately** *adv.* in a rounded form or manner.

Conglobe (kǫ̆nglōᵘ·b), *v.* 1535. [– Fr. *conglober* or L. *conglobare*; see prec.] = CONGLOBATE *v.*

Conglo·bulate, *v. rare.* [f. L. *globulus*, dim. of *globus* ball, after CONGLOBATE *v.*] *intr.* To collect into a rounded or compact mass. JOHNSON.

Conglomerate (kǫ̆nglǫ·mĕrĕ̆t). 1572. [– L. *conglomeratus*, pa. pple. of *conglomerare*, f. *com* CON- + *glomus, glomer-* ball; see -ATE[2].]

A. *adj.* **1.** Gathered together into a more or less rounded mass, or consisting of parts so gathered; clustered. Also *fig.* **2.** *Geol.* Composed of the fragments of pre-existing rocks cemented together 1813.

1. The Beams of Light, when they are multiplied and c. BACON. *C. glands*, a synonym of Acinous glands *Syd. Soc. Lex.* C. tumours 1870.

B. *sb.* The adj. used *absol.* **1.** *Geol.* (= *c. rock.*) A composite rock of rounded and waterworn fragments of previously existing rocks, united by some kind of cement; often called *puddingstone*. (Cf. BRECCIA.) 1818. Also *transf.* **2.** *fig.* A mixture of various elements, clustered together without assimilation 1837.

1. Shell c. is largely burnt for lime 1880. **2.** That immense c. of useful and useless knowledge 1864. Hence **Conglomera·tic** *a.* of the nature or character of c. (*sb.* 1); var. **Conglomeri·tic.**

Conglomerate (kǫ̆nglǫ·mĕreⁱt), *v.* 1596. [– *conglomerat-*, pa. ppl. stem of L. *conglomerare*; see prec., -ATE[3].] To form into a ball or (more or less) rounded mass, or (*transf.*) into a compact body (*trans.* and *intr.*). Also *fig.*

Conglomeration (kǫ̆nglǫmĕrēⁱ·ʃən). 1626. [– late L. *conglomeratio*, f. as prec.; see -ION.] **1.** The action of conglomerating, or condition of being conglomerated. **2.** quasi-*concr.* † A coil or ball; a cluster, coherent mass 1659.

Conglutin (kǫ̆nglⁱū·tin). 1879. [f. CON- + GLUTIN.] *Chem.* The legumin of almonds and lupins.

† **Conglu·tinant,** *a.* 1828. [– *conglutinant-*, pres. ppl. stem of L. *conglutinare*; see CONGLUTINATE *v.*, -ANT.] Gluing, uniting; healing. As *sb.* A medicine that heals wounds. (Dicts.)

Conglu·tinate, *ppl. a.* 1531. [– L. *conglutinatus*, pres. pple. of *conglutinare*; see next, -ATE[2].] † **1.** Conglutinated –1610. **2.** *Bot.* Cohering as if glued together 1866.

Conglutinate (kǫ̆nglⁱū·tineⁱt), *v.* Now *rare.* 1546. [– *conglutinat-*, pa. ppl. stem of L. *conglutinare* glue together, f. *com* CON- + *glutinare* to glue, f. *gluten, glutin-* glue. See -ATE[3].] **1.** *trans.* To glue together, to cause to cohere. **2.** *Med.* To unite (wounded parts or broken bones); to heal –1797. Also *fig.* **3.** *intr.* To cohere (*lit.* and *fig.*) 1625.

1. This medicine..conglutinates ruptured vessels 1797. Hence **Conglu·tina·tion,** the action of conglutinating, or condition of being conglutinated. **Conglu·tinative** *a.* having the property of conglutinating or (*Med.*) uniting wounded parts. **Conglu·tinator** (*rare*), an agent that conglutinates. var. † **Conglu·tine** (*rare*).

Congo (kǫ·ŋgo). The name of a country on the west coast of Africa, south of the Equator. Hence, **1.** A Negro from Congo 1886. **2. C. monkey,** a black S. Amer. monkey, a species of the Howler, *Mycetes palliatus*; **C. snake,** a name of one or two blue-black amphibians, species of *Amphiuma* (U.S.).

Congou (kǫ·ŋgu, kǫ·ŋgǒ). Also **congo.** 1725. [– Chinese (Amoy) *kung hu tē*, for *kung fu ch'a* tea on which labour has been expended, f. *kung fu* work, workman, *ch'a* TEA.] A kind of black tea imported from China.

Congratulate (kǒngræ·tiǔlēit), *v.* 1548. [– *congratulat-*, pa. ppl. stem of L. *congratulari*, f. *com* CON- + *gratulari* manifest one's joy, f. *gratus* pleasing; see -ATE[3].] † **1.** *intr.* To rejoice along *with* another. Const. *with* the person, *for, on* the thing. –1824. † **2.** *trans.* To express sympathetic joy on the occasion of; to express pleasure at –1819; † to celebrate *with* (some act) –1661. † **3.** To rejoice at –1741. **4.** To compliment upon any happy event; to felicitate 1548. Const. *on, upon,* †*for,* or with *cl.* Also *absol.* † **5.** To salute –1611.

1. I c. with you, for losing your great acquaintance SWIFT. **2.** The obsequious assembly congratulated their own and the public felicity GIBBON. **4.** The king in person..Comforts the sick, congratulates the sound DRYDEN. A stranger's purpose in these lays Is to c. and not to praise COWPER. **5.** *L.L.L.* V. i. 93. So **Congra·tulable** *a.* calling for congratulation. **Congra·tulant** *a.* that congratulates; *sb.* a congratulator. Hence **Congra·tulatingly** *adv.* **Congra·tulator. Congra·tulatory** *a.* conveying congratulations: inclined to c.

Congratulation (kǒngræ:tiǔlēi·ʃən). 1591. [– L. *congratulatio*, f. as prec.; see -ION.] **1.** The action of congratulating; felicitation; (with *pl.*) an expression of such pleasure 1632. † **3.** Rejoicing on one's own behalf –1623.

1. I thank you for your kind congratulations on my marriage 1781.

† **Congree,** *v.* [f. CON- + GREE *v.*] *intr.* To accord. *Hen. V.* I. ii. 182 (Fo.).

† **Congree·t,** *v.* [f. CON- + GREET *v.*[1]] *intr.* To greet mutually *Hen. V.* V. ii. 31.

Congreganist (kǒŋgre·ganist), *a.* 1861. [– Fr. *congréganiste*, as *sb.* a member of a congregation of laymen directed by ecclesiastics, as *adj.* in *école c.*, opp. to *école laïque*.] Of French schools: Conducted by the Brethren of the Christian Schools, or by Sisters of various religious orders.

Co·ngregate, *ppl. a.* ME. [– L. *congregatus*, pa. pple. of *congregare*; see next, -ATE[2].] **1.** Congregated. **2.** Collective 1890.

Congregate (kǫ·ŋgrǐgēit), *v.* ME. [– *congregat-*, pa. ppl. stem of L. *congregare* collect together, f. *com* CON- + *gregare* collect into a flock, f. *grex, greg-* flock; see -ATE[3].] **1.** *trans.* To collect or gather together into a mass or crowd; to assemble. **2.** *refl.* and *intr.* To flock or assemble together; to meet in a large body 1538.

1. These waters were afterwards congregated and called the sea RALEGH. Bells..to c. the People EVELYN. **2.** Euen there where Merchants most doe c. *Merch. V.* I. iii. 50. Hence **Co·ngregated** *ppl. a.* in the senses of the vb.; (*Bot.*) aggregated; †organized on a Congregational basis. **Co·ngregative** *a.* tending to c.; **-ness. Co·ngregator,** one who congregates or assembles.

Congregation (kǫŋgrǐgēi·ʃən). ME. [– (O)Fr. *congrégation* or L. *congregatio*, f. as prec.; see -ION.] **1.** The action of congregating or collecting in one body or mass. **2.** A gathering, assemblage, or company ME. **3.** *Acad.* A general assembly of the members of a University, or of such of them as possess certain qualifications 1532. **4.** In the O.T.: The collective body, or an actual assembly, of the Israelites in the wilderness: so *c. of the Lord*, etc. Hence, in certain phrases = whole body. ME. † **5.** Used by Tindale as tr. ἐκκλησία in the N.T., and by the 16th c. Reformers instead of CHURCH 1526. **6.** A body of persons assembled for religious worship. (The most common modern use.) 1526. **b.** The body of persons who belong to a particular place of worship 1597. **7.** *Sc. Hist.* The party of Protestant Reformers during the reign of Mary 1557. **8.** *R.C.Ch.* A community or order bound together by a common rule, without (solemn) vows. **b.** A group of monasteries of some great order, united by closer ties of doctrine and discipline 1885. **c.** Any of the permanent committees of the Roman College of Cardinals; *spec.* the Congregation *de propaganda fide* 1670.

2. A squadron of men is..a c. of souldiers orderly ranged and set 1598. A foule and pestilent c. of vapours *Haml.* II. ii. 315. The anger of that terrible C. [the Long Parliament] CLARENDON. **4.** It is a sinne offering for the C. *Lev.* 4:21. The c. of hypocrites *Job* 15:34. **7.** *Lords of the C.*: the nobles and other chief men who subscribed the National Covenant. Hence † **Congrega·tioner,** a member of the association of Reformers formed in 1557 (see CONGREGATION 7); a Congregationalist. **Congrega·tionist,** † a Congregationalist; also = CONGREGANIST. **Congrega·tionless** *a.* having no c.

Congregational (kǒŋgrǐgēi·ʃənăl), *a.* 1639. [f. prec. + -AL[1].] **1.** Of or pertaining to a congregation; performed by a congregation. **2.** Of or pertaining to CONGREGATIONALISM; Independent 1642.

1. We heard..fine c. singing 1860. **2.** *Congregational* is a word used of such Christians as hold every congregation to be a separate and independent church JOHNSON. Hence **Congrega·tionally** *adv.*

Congregationalism (kǫŋgrǐgēi·ʃənăliz'm). 1716. [f. prec. + -ISM.] **1.** A form of church polity in which all legislative, disciplinary, and judicial functions are vested in the local Congregation of believers. Also called Independency. **2.** The congregational practice within the pale of a church territorially organized 1882. So **Congrega·tionalist,** an adherent of the Congregational church polity; a member of a Congregational church; an Independent. **Congrega·tionalize** *v.* to make congregational.

Congress (kǫ·ŋgres), *sb.* 1528. [– L. *congressus*, f. *congress-*, pa. ppl. stem of *congredi* go together, meet, f. *com* CON- + *gradi* step, walk.] **1.** The coming together (of persons): a meeting, interview. † **2.** A coming together, meeting (of things) –1759. † **3.** An encounter –1727. **4.** Sexual union 1589. **5.** Social intercourse, converse 1628. **6.** An assembly or conference for the discussion or settlement of some question; *spec.* (in politics) a formal meeting of envoys, deputies, or plenipotentiaries representing sovereign states, or of sovereigns themselves, for the settlement of international affairs. Also a periodical meeting or series of meetings of some association or society, or of specialists. 1678. **7.** The national legislative body of the United States of America (as a permanent institution, and as a body elected for two years; also the session of this body) 1775. **8.** The corresponding body in the republics of South and Central America 1837.

2. A fortuitous C. of Atoms WOODWARD. **3.** In divers hazardous congresses and battels 1646. **5.** *Bird of c.*: a gregarious bird; The crane..is also a bird of c. 1766. **6.** Deputies..had been sent to Vienna during the C. 1847. An architectural c. BERESF. HOPE. The haunters of Social Science Congresses M. ARNOLD. **7.** 'The *C. of the United States* (commonly referred to simply as "Congress"), which met for the first time on 4 March 1789, was preceded by the *C. of the Confederation*, representing the several states under the Articles of Confederation, from 1781 to 1789, and this again by the three so-called *Continental Congresses* of the revolting colonies, which met in 1774, 1775, and 1776 respectively. But these last were properly congresses in sense 6.' O.E.D. The *Indian National Congress* (usu. abbrev. *Congress*), founded in 1885 by A. O. Hume for the fusion of all elements and strengthening of union with England, became dominated in 1920 by Mahatma Gandhi and subsequently worked for the independence of India.

Comb.: **C. boot,** a high boot with elastic sides; **C. water,** a mineral water from Congress Springs, Saratoga, N.Y.

Congressional (kǒŋgre·ʃənăl), *a.* 1691. [f. CONGRESS with insertion of *-ion-* from L. *congressio(n-)* to avoid the awkwardness of immed. derivation; see -ION, -AL[1].] Of or pertaining to a congress; *esp.* to a legislative Congress, as of the United States, etc. Hence **Congre·ssionalist,** a supporter of a congress; a member of a c. party. So **Congre·ssionist. Co·ngressist** (*rare*).

Co·ngressman. 1834. A member of Congress (in U.S.).

Congreve (kǫ·ŋgrīv). 1809. [f. Sir. W. *Congreve* (1772–1828), the inventor of both.] **1.** Also *C. rocket*: A kind of rocket for use in war, invented in 1808. **2.** Also *C. match*: A kind of friction match.

Congrid (kǫ·ŋgrid). [f. mod.L. *Congridæ*, f. *congrus* CONGER; see -ID[3].] *Zool.* A fish belonging to the family *Congridæ*, or allied to the CONGER.

Congroid (kǫ·ŋgroid). [f. L. *congrus* CONGER + -OID.] *adj.* Allied to the conger and its family. *sb.* A fish allied to the conger.

† **Congrue,** *a.* ME. [– (O)Fr. *congru, congrue* – L. *congruus* agreeing, suitable, f. *congruere*; see CONGRUENT.] **1.** Fitting, suitable –1587. **2.** Grammatically correct –1569. Hence † **Congrue·ly, -gru·ly** *adv.* congruously. So **Congrue** *v. rare,* to agree, accord.

Congruence (kǫ·ŋgru͵ěns). ME. [– L. *congruentia* – *congruent-*; see CONGRUENT, -ENCE.] **1.** The fact or condition of according or agreeing; correspondence. Const. *with* 1533. **2.** = CONGRUITY 2, 3, † 4, 5. **3.** *Theory of Numbers.* The relation between two numbers which being divided by a third number, called the *modulus*, give the same remainder; also an expression exhibiting two congruous quantities in the form of an equation; thus $A \equiv B$ (mod. P). 1889.

Congruency (kǫ·ŋgru͵ěnsi). 1494. [f. as prec.; see -ENCY.] **1.** = CONGRUENCE 1. **2.** *Geom.* A system of lines in which the parameters have a two-fold relation, such as a system of lines each of which twice touches a given surface 1864.

Congruent (kǫ·ŋgru͵ěnt), *a.* ME. [– *congruent-*, pres. ppl. stem of L. *congruere* meet together, agree, correspond, f. *com* CON- + *gruere, *ruere* fall, rush; see -ENT.] **1.** = CONGRUOUS 1, 2. Hence **Co·ngruently** *adv.*

Congruism (kǫ·ŋgruiz'm). 1885. [– Fr. *congruisme*, f. *congru* (see CONGRUE *a.*) + *-isme* -ISM.] *Theol.* The doctrine which derives the efficacy of grace from its adaptation to the character and circumstances of the person called. So **Co·ngruist,** one who holds the doctrine of C. **Congrui·stic** *a.*

Congruity (kǒŋgrū·iti). ME. [– Fr. *congruité* or late L., med.L. *congruitas*, f. L. *congruus* agreeing, suitable; see -ITY.] **1.** The quality of being congruous; agreement in character or qualities; accordance, harmony. Const. *with,* occas. *to.* **2.** Self-accordance 1827. **3.** Accordance with the requirements of the case; fitness, propriety 1530. † **4.** *Gram.* Agreement or concord; hence, grammatical correctness –1736. **5.** *Theol.* **a.** (*Doctrine of Merit.*) With the Schoolmen, its being 'congruous' that God should confer the 'first grace' in response to the performance of good works by man. Opp. to CONDIGNITY. 1553. **b.** (*Doctrine of Grace.*) The suitability of divine grace to the character and circumstances of the person called, to which some theologians attribute its efficacy (see CONGRUISM) 1650. † **6.** *Geom.* Coincidence; exact agreement in superposition –1755.

1. There is, at least, moral c. between the outward goodness and the inner life TYNDALL. These..congruities [of poesy] with man's nature and pleasure BACON. **5. a.** Neither do thei [workes done before the grace of Christe]..deserue Grace of congruitie *Articles of Relig.* xii.

Congruous (kǫ·ŋgru͵əs), *a.* 1599. [f. L. *congruus* (see prec.) + -OUS.] **1.** Agreeing or corresponding in character or qualities; accordant, suitable, in harmony. Now usu. *with.* **2.** Having CONGRUITY (senses 2, 3, † 4, 5, † 6) 1631, or CONGRUENCE (sense 3) 1859.

1. All the parts of his bodie were in good proportion, and c. as a man could wish 1599. Hence **Co·ngruous-ly** *adv.*, **-ness.**

† **Congu·stable,** *a.* [f. CON- + GUSTABLE.] Having a like taste. HOWELL.

Conhydrine (kǒnhəi·drəin). 1863. [f. CON(INE + HYDR(ATE + -INE[5].] *Chem.* An alkaloid existing, together with conine, in the flowers and seeds of *Conium maculatum*, and crystallizing in iridescent laminæ; also **Conhy·dria.**

Conia (kōᵘ·niă). 1842. [f. L. *conium* hemlock; see -IA[1] (as in *ammonia*).] = CONINE.

Conic (kǫ·nik). 1570. [– mod.L. *conicus* – Gr. κωνικός; see CONE, -IC.]

A. *adj.* **1.** Having the form of a cone; cone-shaped, CONICAL 1614. **2.** Of or pertaining to a cone 1570.

1. A succession of c. hills COOK. **2.** *C. section*: a figure formed by the section of a right circular cone by a plane; a plane curve of the second degree. The section is an ELLIPSE, HYPERBOLA, or PARABOLA, as the inclination of the cutting plane to the axis is greater or less than that of the edge of the cone, or parallel to the edge. Hence **Coni·city.**

B. *sb.* **1.** pl. *Conics*: that branch of Geometry which treats of the cone and the figures formed by plane sections of it. (Now regarded as the *pl.* of 2). 1571. **2.** A conic section 1879.

Conical (kǫ·nikăl), *a.* 1570. [f. as prec. + -AL[1]; see -ICAL.] **1.** Shaped like a cone. **2.** Of, pertaining, or relating to a cone 1570.

1. Taproots are..C., when tapering regularly..as in carrots A. GRAY. **2.** *C. point*: a singular point on a surface at which the tangent lines form a cone. Hence **Co·nical-ly** *adv.*, **-ness.**

Conichalcite (kǫnikæ·lsəit). 1850. [f. Gr. κονία in sense 'powdered lime' + χαλκός copper + -ITE[1] 2 b.] *Min.* A green hydrous phosphate and arseniate of lime and copper.

Conico- (kǫ·niko), bef. a vowel occas. **conic-** [Gr. κωνικο-], comb. f. CONIC *a.*: = Conically, with a tendency to being conical; as **C.-cylindrical,** nearly cylindrical, but slightly tapered like a cone; **C.-hemispherical,** nearly hemispherical, but with a tendency towards the conical; *c.-elongate*, etc.

Conicoid (kǫ·nikoid). 1863. [f. CONIC + -OID, after *ellipsoid*, etc.] *Geom.* A surface of which every plane section is a conic (see CONIC B. 2); a surface of the second degree.

‖ **Conicopoly** (kǫnikǫ·pǒləi). *Anglo-Ind.* 1680. [– Tamil *kanokka-pillai* 'account-man'.] A native clerk or writer in the Madras Presidency.

‖ **Conidium** (koni·diǒm). Pl. **-dia.** 1870. [mod.L., f. Gr. κόνις dust, with dim. ending.] *Bot.* A unicellular asexual reproductive body occurring in certain fungi. Hence **Coni·dial** *a.* of, or pertaining to, of the nature of or relating to, a c. or conidia. **Conidii·ferous** *a.* [L. *-fer*], **Conidio·phorous** *a.* [Gr. -φορος], bearing conidia. **Coni·dioid** *a.* like a c. **Coni·diophore,** a stalk or branch of the mycelium bearing conidia.

Conifer (kōu·nifəɹ). 1851. [– L. *conifer* cone-bearing, f. *conus* CONE + *-fer* bearing. Cf. Fr. *conifère.*] *Bot.* A plant belonging to the *Coniferæ*, an order of gymnospermous exogens, comprising trees (mostly evergreen) bearing cones.

Coniferin (koni·fĕrin). 1867. [f. as prec. + -IN[1].] *Chem.* 'A glucoside occurring in the cambium of coniferous woods' (Watts).

Coniferous (koni·fĕrəs), *a.* 1664. [f. L. *conifer* (see above) + -OUS; see -FEROUS.] *Bot.* Bearing cones; belonging to the *Coniferæ* (see CONIFER); pertaining to or consisting of conifers.

Coniform (kōu·nifǫɹm), *a.* 1790. [f. L. *conus* cone + -FORM.] Cone-shaped.

Conine, coniine (kōu·nəin, kōu·ni,əin). 1831. [f. L. *conium* (– Gr. κώνειον hemlock) + -INE[5].] *Chem.* An alkaloid ($C_8H_{15}N$) which forms the poisonous principle of hemlock (*Conium maculatum*); it is an oily liquid, with a suffocating odour, and violently poisonous. Also *conia, conicine.*

‖ **Coniomycetes** (kǫ:nio,məisī·tīz), *sb. pl.* 1866. [mod.L., f. Gr. κονία, κόνις dust + μύκης (pl. μύκητες) mushroom.] *Bot.* A group of fungi, so named from their dusty spores. The division is no longer retained. Hence **Coniomycetous** *a.*

Coniospermous (kǫniospɔ̄·ɹməs), *a.* 1874. [f. as prec. + -σπερμος (from σπέρμα seed) + -OUS.] *Bot.* Of fungi: Having spores resembling dust.

Coniroster (kouniro·stəɹ). 1842. [– Fr. *conirostre* – mod.L. *conirostris*, f. L. *conus* CONE + *rostrum* beak, bill.] *Zool.* A member of the *Conirostres*, a group of insessorial birds having a conical bill. So **Coniro·stral** *a.* conical-billed.

Conisance, -sante, etc., obs. ff. COGNIZANCE, etc.

Conite (kōu·nəit). 1808. [perh. f. Gr. κόνις, κονία dust, ashes + -ITE[1] 2 b.] *Min.* A magnesian variety of DOLOMITE; in colour ash-gray or greenish gray.

‖ **Conium** (kounəi·ǒm). 1862. [L. – Gr. κώνειον hemlock.] **a.** *Bot.* The umbelliferous genus to which the common Hemlock belongs. **b.** *Med.* The hemlock or its extract as a drug.

† **Conject** (kǒndʒe·kt), *v.* ME. [– L. *conjectare*, frequent. of *conicere* throw together, put together in speech or thought, conclude; see CON-, ABJECT (etc.).] To conjecture –1734; to plot, plan –1552; to throw (*rare*) –1657. Hence † **Conje·ctor.**

Conjecturable (kǒndʒe·ktiūrăb'l), *a.* 1656. [f. CONJECTURE *v.* + -ABLE.] That may be conjectured. Hence **Conje·cturably** *adv.*

Conjectural (kǒndʒe·ktiūrăl), *a.* 1553. [– Fr. *conjectural* – L. *conjecturalis*; see CONJECTURE, -AL[1].] **1.** Of the nature of, depending on, or involving conjecture. **2.** Given to making conjectures 1642.

1. I doubt it is too Conjecturall to venture upon BACON. C. criticism JOHNSON, solutions PALEY, emendations 1883. **2.** Her touching, foolish lines We mused on with c. fantasy E. B. BROWNING. Hence † **Conjectura·list** (*rare*), one who deals in guesses. † **Conjectura·lity** (*rare*), c. quality; *pl.* c. matters or statements. SIR T. BROWNE. **Conje·cturally** *adv.*

Conjecture (kǒndʒe·ktiŭɹ, -tʃəɹ), *sb.* ME. [– (O)Fr. *conjecture* or L. *conjectura* conclusion, inference, f. *conject-*, pa. ppl. stem of *conicere*; see CONJECT *v.*, -URE.] † **1.** Divining; a prognostication –1697. † **2.** Supposition –1599. **3.** The action or habit of guessing or surmising 1535. **4.** (with *a* and *pl.*) An opinion offered on insufficient presumptive evidence; an unverified supposition 1527. † **5.** A contrivance; a plot –1494.

1. To cast Ominous c. on the whole success MILT. *P.L.* II. 123. **2.** *Hen. V*, IV. Prol. 1. **3.** But this is only c. BOYLE. **4.** Dreams, Conjectures, fancies, built on nothing firm MILT. *P.R.* IV. 292.

Conjecture (kǒndʒe·ktiŭɹ), *v.* ME. [– (O)Fr. *conjecturer* – late L. *conjecturare*, f. L. *conjectura* (see prec.); superseding CONJECT *v.*] † **1.** *trans.* and *intr.* To divine, prognosticate –1652. † **2.** *trans.* To infer from probabilities –1618. **3.** To form an opinion or supposition on grounds admittedly insufficient; to guess, surmise 1530. **4.** *intr.* To form a conjecture, guess. Const. *of* (arch.), † *at.* 1587.

3. As I c., it wyll be founde PALSGR. **4.** As a mother Conjectures of the features of her child Ere it is born TENNYSON. Hence **Conje·cturer,** one who † divines or conjectures.

Conjee, congee (kǫ·ndʒi). *Anglo-Ind.* 1698. [– Tamil *kānji.*] The water in which rice has been boiled. *Comb.* **c.-house:** a military 'lock-up'; so called because the inmates are fed on c.

Conjobble (kǒndʒǫ·b'l), *v.* 1694. [f. CON- and perh. JOB *sb.*[1] and *v.*[2], or JABBER, + -LE.] 'To concert, to settle, to discuss: a low cant word' (J.). Still in colloq. use.

Conjoin (kǒndʒoi·n), *v.* [Late ME. *conjoigne* – (O)Fr. *conjoign-*, pres. stem of *conjoindre* – L. *conjungere*, f. *com* CON- + *jungere* JOIN *v.*] **1.** *trans.* To join together; connect, unite. **2.** To combine, ally ME. **3.** *intr.* To become joined together; to unite 1578.

1. The knowledge of God and of ourselves, are things conjoyned 1561. Any inward impediment why you should not be conioyned *Much Ado* IV. i. 13. **2.** Whome a like punishment conioyned, a farre vnlike cause disioyned 1588. Hence **Conjoi·ned** *ppl.a.* joined together; allied; in *Her.* connected together, as two or more charges. **Conjoi·nedly** *adv.* **Conjoi·ner,** one who or that which conjoins.

Conjoint (kǒndʒoi·nt), *a.* ME. [– (O)Fr. *conjoint*, pa. pple. of *conjoindre*; see prec.] † **1.** As pa. pple. of CONJOIN *v.* –1694. **2.** as *adj.* United, combined, conjoined, as *c. causes* 1725.

C. degrees (Mus.): two notes which immediately follow each other in the order of the scale. Hence **Conjoi·ntly** *adv.*

Conjubilant (kǒndʒū·bilănt), *a. rare.* 1851. [– *conjubilant-*, pres. ppl. stem of med.L. *conjubilare* (Bernard of Cluny) rejoice exceedingly; see CON-, JUBILANT.] Jubilant together.

Conjugable (kǫ·ndʒŭgăb'l), *a. nonce-wd.* 1890. [f. CONJUG(ATE *v.* + -ABLE. Cf. Fr. *conjugable.*] That can be conjugated.

Conjugacy (kǫ·ndʒŭgăsi). 1659. [f. CONJUGATE *a.*; see -ACY.] † **1.** Married state (*rare*). **2.** Conjugate relation 1881.

Conjugal (kǫ·ndʒŭgăl), *a.* 1545. [– L. *conjugalis*, f. *conjug-*, *-ju(n)x* consort, spouse, f. *com* CON- + **jug-*, base of *jungere* join; see -AL[1]. Cf. (O)Fr. *conjugal.*] Of or pertaining to marriage or to husband and wife in their relation to each other, matrimonial.

To countenance the c. state of her clergy STRYPE. Phr. *C. rights*: the privilege which husband and wife have of each other's society, comfort, and affection. Hence **Conjuga·lity,** c. state or condition. **Co·njugally** *adv.*

Conjugate (kǫ·ndʒŭgeit), *v.* 1530. [– *conjugat-*, pa. ppl. stem of L. *conjugare*; see prec., -ATE[3].] **1.** *trans.* To yoke together, to couple; to unite (*rare*) 1570. **2.** *Gram.* To inflect (a verb) in its various forms of voice, mood, tense, number, and person 1530. **3.** *intr.* To unite sexually; *Biol.* to unite in CONJUGATION 1790.

Conjugate (kǫ·ndʒŭgĕt). 1471. [– L. *conjugatus*, pa. pple. of *conjugare*; see prec., -ATE[2].]

A. *adj.* **1.** Joined together, *esp.* in a pair, coupled; connected. **2.** *Gram.* Said of words directly derived from the same root or stem, and therefore usually of kindred meaning. [L. *conjugata verba.*] 1862. **3.** *Chem.* Of compounds, etc.: Formed by the direct union of two bodies, with elimination of water 1882. **4.** *Bot.* Said of leaves which grow in pairs 1794. **5.** *Path. C. deviation*: the forced and persistent turning of both eyes to one side while their relation to each other remains unaltered 1882. **6.** *Math.* and *Physics.* Joined in a reciprocal relation, as two points, lines, quantities, or things which are interchangeable with respect to the properties of each 1680.

(Math.) *C. axes* or *diameters* (of a conic): two axes, etc., such that each is parallel to the tangent at the extremity of the other. *C. axis* (or *diameter*) of an ellipse or hyperbola: that which is c. to the transverse axis, the minor axis. *C. hyperbolas*: those which have the same axes and asymptotes, but the principal axis of each is the second axis of the other. *C. point* (of a curve): an acnode. (Optics.) *C. mirrors*: two parabolic mirrors so placed face to face that rays of heat or light emanating from the focus of either are reflected in parallel lines to the second, and thence to its focus. var. **Co·njugated** *ppl. a.*

B. *sb.* **1.** One of a group of conjugate words (see CONJUGATE *a.* 2) 1586. † **2.** Anything connected in idea with another –1663. **3.** *Chem.* Short for *c. compound, acid,* or *radical.* **4.** *Math.* Short for *c. axis, diameter, point,* etc. 1726.

1. The word *utility*, and its conjugates, do not express our judgments in cases of moral conduct WHEWELL.

Conjugation (kǒndʒŭgēi·ʃən). 1528. [– L. *conjugatio* (in *Gram.* late L.), f. *conjugat-*; see prec., -ION. Cf. OFr. *conjugacion* (mod. †-*tion*, now *conjugaison*).] **1.** The action of joining together or combining; the being joined together; conjunction, union, combination 1605. † **2.** Relation; the relation of conjugate words –1656. **3.** *Gram.* **a.** A scheme of all the inflexional forms belonging to a verb; a division of verbs according to differences of inflexion 1528. **b.** The inflexion of a verb 1530. **c.** In the Semitic langs., the simple and each of the derivative forms which express a modification of meaning corresponding to the distinction of voice, etc., in Aryan languages 1593. † **4.** *Phys.* Each pair of the cerebral nerves –1713. **5.** *Biol.* The union or fusion of two (apparently) similar cells for reproduction, occurring in plants and animals of low organization 1843.

1. The doctrine of C. of men in Socyety BACON. The elements and their conjugations 1626. Hence **Conjuga·tional** *a.* of or pertaining to c.; *Phys.* Situated at the junction of two bones; **-ly** *adv.* So **Co·njugative** *a.* tending to c.

Conjuga·to-, comb. f. L. *conjugatus* CONJUGATE, in sense 'conjugately, conjugate and—'.

Conjugial (kǒndʒiū·dʒiăl), *a.* 1790. [– rare L. *conjugialis* connubial, f. *conjugium* wedlock, f. *conjug-*; see CONJUGAL, -AL[1], -IAL.] Used by Swedenborg instead of CONJUGAL.

Conjunct (kǒndʒɒ·ŋkt), *a.* (*sb.*) ME. [– L. *conjunctus*, pa. pple. of *conjungere*, f. *com* CON- + *jungere* join; cf. CONJOINT.] **A.** *adj.* Joined together, conjoined, united, combined in conjunction. **B.** *sb.* A person or thing conjoined or associated with another 1667.

Mus. C. degrees: see CONJOINT.

Conjunction (kǒndʒɒ·ŋkʃən). ME. [– (O)Fr. *conjonction* – L. *conjunctio*, f. *conjunct-*; see prec., -ION.] **1.** The action of conjoining; the fact or condition of being conjoined; union, connection, combination. † **2.** *spec.* Sexual union –1794. **3.** *Astrol.* and *Astron.* An apparent proximity of two planets or other heavenly bodies; the position of these when they are in the same longitude or right ascension ME. **4.** *Gram.* One of the Parts of Speech; an uninflected word used to connect words, clauses, or sentences ME.

1. We will vnite the White Rose, and the Red. Smile Heauen vpon this faire C. *Rich. III*, v. v. 20. The c. of so many and so great calamities 1684. **3.** The technical phrase 'conjunction' does not necessarily imply any very close proximity 1889. **4.** Conjunctions show the relation of one *thought* to another. Hence conjunctions for the most part join one sentence to another 1876. Hence **Conju·nctional** *a.* pertaining or relating to c. or to a c.; **-ly** *adv.*

‖ **Conjunctiva** (kǫndʒɒŋktəi·vă). 1543. [med.L.; short for *tunica c.* (XIII); see CONJUNCTIVE.] *Anat.* The mucous membrane which lines the inner surface of the eyelids and is reflected over the front of the eye-ball, thus conjoining this with the lids. Hence **Conjuncti·val** *a.* of or pertaining to the c.

Conjunctive (kǫ̆ndʒɒ·ŋktiv). 1581. [– late L. *conjunctivus*; see CONJUNCT, -IVE. Cf. (O)Fr. *conjonctif, -ive.*]

A. *adj.* **1.** Serving to conjoin or unite; connective. **2.** = CONJUNCT 1602. **3.** *Gram.* Connective; uniting the sense as well as the construction, as a *c. conjunction* 1667; which can be used only in conjunction with another verb, as the *c. mood* 1730. **4.** *Logic.* Conditional 1848. Hence **Conju·nctive-ly** *adv.*, **-ness.**

B. *sb.* **1.** *Gram.* A conjunction; a copulative conjunction; the conjunctive mood 1589. **2.** *Logic.* A conjunctive proposition or syllogism 1848. **3.** *Math.* A syzygetic function of a given set of functions 1853.

Conjunctivitis (kǫ̆ndʒɒ:ŋktivəi·tis). 1835. [f. CONJUNCTIVA + -ITIS.] *Path.* Inflammation of the conjunctiva.

Conjunctly (kǫ̆ndʒɒ·ŋktli), *adv.* 1514. [f. CONJUNCT *a.* + -LY².] In conjunction, in combination, conjointly, unitedly, together.

Conjuncture (kǫ̆ndʒɒ·ŋktiŭɹ). 1605. [var. of CONJUNCTION by suffix-substitution. In sense 2 prob. after Fr. †*conjuncture*, now *conjoncture* (XVI), – It. *congiuntura*; see CONJUNCT, -URE.] † **1.** The action of joining together; the fact or state of being joined together; a joining, conjunction, combination –1736. **2.** *spec.* A meeting of circumstances or events; a juncture, crisis. (The only current sense.) 1605.

1. By the c. of philosophy and divinity HOBBES. **2.** In certain conjunctures, ignorance and folly.. may have their advantages BUTLER. In this c. of tyme 1624, of affairs STERNE.

Conjuration (kǫndʒurēⁱ·ʃən). ME. [– OFr. *conjuracion*, (also mod.) *-tion*, – L. *conjuratio*, f. *conjurat-*, pa. ppl. stem of *conjurare* CONJURE; see -ION, and CONJURISON.] † **1.** A swearing together; a making of a league by a common oath; a conspiracy –1771. **2.** A solemn charging or calling upon by appeal to something sacred or binding; solemn entreaty, adjuration (*arch.*) 1450. **3.** The effecting of something supernatural by a spell or by the invocation of a sacred name ME. **4.** A magic spell, incantation, charm ME. **5.** *transf.* Conjuring 1734.

1. The coniuracion, that Catilina inuented agaynste his countreye 1533. **2.** We charge you in the name of God take heed..Vnder this Coniuration, speake my Lord SHAKS. **3.** A.. generall abuse of Scripture is the turning of Consecration into C. HOBBES.

Conjurator (kǫ·ndʒureⁱtəɹ). 1549. [– AFr. *conjuratour* or med.L. *conjurator*, f. as prec.; see -OR 2. Cf. Fr. *conjurateur*. See CONJURER, -OR.] One joined with others by an oath; a fellow-conspirator.

Conjure (kɒ·ndʒəɹ and kǫ̆ndʒū̆ᵊ·ɹ), *v.* ME. [– (O)Fr. *conjurer* plot, exorcise, adjure :– L. *conjurare* band together by an oath, conspire, in med.L. invoke, f. *com* CON- + *jurare* swear.] † **1.** *intr.* To swear together; to conspire –1656. **2.** *trans.* To call upon, constrain by oath, or by appealing to some sacred person or thing; to adjure –1797. Also *intr.* or *absol.* **3.** To appeal solemnly or earnestly to; to implore 1450. † **4.** *trans.* To affect by invocation or incantation; to charm, bewitch –1834. **5.** To affect, effect, bring *out*, convey *away*, by or as by magic or the arts of the conjurer 1535.

1. Art thou hee Who..Drew after him the third part of Heav'ns Sons Conjur'd against the highest MILT. *P.L.* II. 693. **2.** I c. the in the name of the fader, sone and holy goste that thow haue no power me to be-gyle 1450. The fiend himself they c. from his den G. FLETCHER. **3.** He conjured them to act like men S. TURNER. **5.** Christ took bread and left it bread: the priest taketh bread and conjureth it away GRINDAL. The very sight of the narrow old streets conjures up the scene MRS. OLIPHANT. Hence **Co·njured** *ppl. a.* † sworn as a member of a conspiracy; † exorcised. † **Conjurement**, the exorcising of spirits by invocation; adjuration, solemn appeal.

Conjurer, conjuror (see senses). ME. [Partly – prec., partly – AFr. *conjurour*, OFr. *conjurere, -eor* – med.L. *conjurator* (see prec.); see -ER¹ and ².] **1.** (kɒ·ndʒərəɹ). One who practises conjuration, a magician; a juggler 1727. Also *fig.* and *transf.* **2.** (kǫ̆ndʒū̆ᵊ·rəɹ). One who is bound with others by a solemn oath; one who solemnly entreats. (Dicts.)

1. *No c.*: one who is far from clever. A man without being a c., might guess BP. BERKELEY. So **Co·njuress,** a female c., a sorceress.

† **Conju·rison.** ME. [– OFr. *conjureison, -ison*, (later Central Fr.) *-oison* :– L. *conjuratio*; see CONJURATION, -ISON.] = CONJURATION 1, 3, 4. –1483.

Conk (kǫŋk). *slang.* 1812. [prob. an application of CONCH.] The nose. Hence **Co·nky,** nosey.

Conkers (kǫ·ŋkəɹz), *sb. pl.* 1877. [f. dial. *conker* snail-shell, presumably f. CONCH; assoc. w. *conquer*.] A boys' game, orig. played with snail-shells, now with horse-chestnuts through which a string is threaded, the object being to break that held by the opponent.

† **Conna·scency.** 1646. [f. *connascent-*, pres. ppl. stem of late L. *connasci*; see next, -ENCY.] **a.** A being born together; a monstrous birth in which two individuals are united, **b.** A growing together. –1676. So **Connascence** (J.). **Conna·scent** *a. rare*, born together; produced at the same time.

Connate (kǫ·nēⁱt), *a.* 1641. [– late L. *connatus*, pa. pple. of *connasci*, f. *com* CON- + *nasci* be born; see -ATE².] **1.** Born with a person; inborn, innate, congenital. (Usu. of ideas, etc.) 1652. var. † **Conna·tive.** **2.** Born together, as qualities, etc. 1819. **3.** Akin or agreeing in nature; allied; congenial 1641. **4.** *Bot.* and *Zool.* Congenitally united; used, *e.g.*, of leaves united at the base; of elytra (in insects), bones (in vertebrates), etc. 1794.

C.-perfoliate (in *Bot.*): used of opposite leaves united at the base so as apparently to form a single broad leaf through which the stem passes, as in *Chlora perfoliata*.

Connation (kǫ̆nēⁱ·ʃən). 1846. [f. as prec.; see -ION.] † **1.** Union by birth. **2.** Connate condition; see CONNATE 4. 1854.

Connatural (kǫ̆næ·tiŭrăl), *a.* 1592. [– late L. *connaturalis*, f. *com* CON- + *naturalis* NATURAL.] **1.** Belonging to or inherent by nature or from birth; congenital, innate, natural. **2.** Of the same or like nature, allied, cognate, congenerous 1601. † **3.** Congenial –1687. Also as *sb.* (sc. *person, thing.*)

1. Vice is congenit or connatural to beasts HY. MORE. Hence **Conna:tura·lity,** c. quality; likeness or agreement of nature. **Conna·turalize** *v.* to make c. (senses 2, 3). **Conna·tural-ly** *adv.*, **-ness.**

Connature (kǫ̆nēⁱ·tiŭɹ). 1872. [See CON-.] Likeness or sameness of kind or nature; connaturality.

C.; or to speak..more comprehensibly..sameness in kind H. SPENCER.

Connect (kǫ̆ne·kt), *v.* 1537. [– L. *connectere*, f. *com* CON- + *nectere* bind, fasten.] **1.** *trans.* To join, fasten, or link together. Const. *to, with.* Also *fig.* **2.** To associate in occurrence, action, or idea 1709. **3.** To unite (a person) *with* others. Chiefly *pass.* and *refl.* 1750. **4.** *intr.* (for *refl.*) To become united or joined; to join on 1744. Also *fig.*

1. He fills, he bounds, connects, and equals all POPE. The connexion of each intermediate idea with those it connects LOCKE. **3.** People connected with the Court MRS. CARLYLE. **4.** I connected much more with him than I am apt to do with new acquaintances H. WALPOLE. Hence **Conne·cted** *ppl. a.*; **-ly** *adv.*; **-ness.** **Conne·ctible** *a.* that can be connected.

Connecter, -or (kǫ̆ne·ktəɹ). 1795. [f. prec. + -ER¹; see -OR 2.] **1.** One who, or that which, connects 1815. **2.** *spec.* **a.** A small tube of india-rubber, etc., for connecting other tubes. **b.** *Electr.* A device for holding two parts of a conductor in contact. **c.** A railway-coupling.

Conne·cting, *ppl. a.* 1690. [f. CONNECT *v.* + -ING².] That connects, joining.

Phr. *C. link*: *fig.* that which connects or links one thing or member of a series with another; *techn.* a link with a movable section, used to connect two links of a broken chain. **C. rod.** *gen.* A rod serving to connect a crank with any other part of a machine. † **b.** The outside coupling rod which connects together the wheels of some locomotive engines.

Connection, connexion (kǫ̆ne·kʃən). 1609. [– L. *connexio*, f. *connex-*, pa. ppl. stem of *connectere*; see CONNECT, -ION. Cf. (O)Fr. *connexion*. The etym. sp. *connexion* is the orig. in Eng. The later sp. *-tion* is after *connect* (XVII–), and is now frequent, esp. in U.S.] **1.** The action of connecting; the condition of being connected. **2.** Relation between things one of which is bound up with, or involved in, another 1613. **3** Anything that conneets 1712. **4.** A personal or practical relation; a having to do *with*. Often with *pl.* 1768. **5.** Relationship by family ties, as marriage, etc. 1773; a person who is connected with others by ties of any kind; *esp.* a relative by marriage, etc. 1777. **6.** A body, or circle of persons connected together, or with whom one is connected by political, religious, or commercial ties. Hence, as used by Wesleyans, etc. = 'denomination'. 1753. **7.** The meeting of one means of communication by another at an appointed time and place 1862. **8.** The phr. *in c. with* occurs in most of the senses 1768.

1. The c. of Church and State BRYCE. Martin took the sentence out of its c. PORSON. **2.** Knowledge and Wisdom..Have ofttimes no c. COWPER. **4.** A criminal c. BOSWELL. My c. with glaciers TYNDALL. **5.** He was, by hereditary c., a Cavalier MACAULAY. **6.** The Dissenting c. THACKERAY. **7.** Phr. *To run in c., to make connections*, etc. Hence **Conne·ctional** *a.*, also **Conne·xional,** pertaining to, or of the nature of, c.; of or pertaining to the Methodist C. **Conne·ctionalism,** the system of the Methodist C. in theory and practice.

Connective (kǫ̆ne·ktiv). 1655. [f. CONNECT *v.* + -IVE, superseding † CONNEXIVE (XVI – L. *connexivus*).]

A. *adj.* Serving or tending to connect.

C. tissue (in *Phys.*): one of the tissues of the animal body, which serves to connect and support the various organs, and to form the framework in which their proper cells are sustained; it consists of fibres and corpuscles imbedded in a structureless substance. Also called *areolar* or *cellular tissue*. (Some physiologists make it include cartilaginous and osseous tissues.)

B. *sb.* [the adj. used ellipt.] **1.** *Gram.* A connective word or particle 1751. **2.** *Bot.* The portion of the filament which connects the lobes of the anther 1830. **3.** *Phys.* = *Connective tissue* 1883.

Hence **Connecti·val** *a.* of or belonging to the c. **Conne·ctively** *adv.*

Connector; see CONNECTER.

Conner¹ (kɒ·nəɹ, kǫ·nəɹ). *arch.* [OE *cunnere*; see CON *v.*¹, -ER¹.] One who tries tests, or examines; an inspector.

Conner² (kǫ·nəɹ). 1809. [f. CON *v.*¹ + -ER¹.] One who cons.

Conner³ (kǫ·nəɹ, kɒ·nəɹ). = CONDER (sense 2).

Conner⁴, var. of CUNNER, name of a fish.

Connex, *sb.* 1490. [– OFr. *connexe* (fem.) annexe, dependence, f. med.L. **connexa* (n. pl.), f. pa. pple. of L. *connectere*; see CONNECT *v.*] † **1.** A bond or tie (*rare*). † **2.** A connected incident –1676. † **3.** A connex proposition –1660. **4.** *Math.* The aggregate of an infinite number of points and an infinite number of lines represented by an equation which is simultaneously homogeneous in point- and line-coordinates 1874.

† **Connex,** *a.* 1589. [– (O)Fr. *connexe* or L. *con(n)exus*, pa. pple. of *connectere*; see CONNECT *v.*] **1.** Connected –1680. **2.** *Logic.* = CONNEXIVE 1. –1699.

† **Conne·x**, *v.* 1541. [– OFr. *connexer*, app. f. *connexe* adj.; see prec.] To CONNECT –1699.

Connexion; see CONNECTION.

Connexity (kǫne·ksĭti). 1603. [–(O)Fr. *connexité*, in med.L. *connexitas*, f. *connexe* adj.; see CONNEX *a.*, -ITY.] Connectedness.

† **Conne·xive**, *a.* 1584. [– L. *connexivus*, f. as prec.; see -IVE.] **1.** Conditional, hypothetical –1725. **2.** Conjunctive –1776. **3.** Connective, as *c. tissue* 1776. Hence † **Conne·xively** *adv.*

‖ **Connexi·vum.** 1882. [L.; see prec.] *Entom.* The expanded border of the sides of the abdominal segments in hemipterous insects (bugs).

† **Conne·xure.** 1615. [f. *connex-*, pa. ppl. stem of L. *con(n)ectere*; see CONNEX *a.*, -URE.] = CONNECTION –1669.

Co·nning, *vbl. sb.*[1] ME. [f. CON *v.*[1] + -ING[1].] **1.** Obs. f. CUNNING, q.v. **2.** Studying or learning, *esp.* by repetition; poring over. ME.

Conning, *vbl. sb.*[2] [f. CON *v.*[2] + -ING[1].] Directing the helm. Hence **Conning-tower**, the pilot-house of a war-ship.

Connivance, -ancy; see CONNIVENCE, -ENCY.

Connive (kǫnəi·v), *v.* 1602. [– Fr. *conniver* (*à*) – L. *con(n)ivēre* shut the eyes, f. *com* CON- + **nivēre*, rel. to *nictare* (see NICTITATE).] **1.** *intr.* To shut one's eyes to a thing that one dislikes but cannot help, to pretend ignorance. Const. *at* (*arch.*). **2.** To wink *at*, be secretly privy. (The ordinary sense.) 1632. † **3.** To remain dormant (*rare*). (So in L.) –1671. † **4.** *trans.* To wink at, tacitly permit, pass over –1643. † **5.** *intr.* To wink. ADDISON. **6.** *Nat. Hist.* To be CONNIVENT, q.v. (*rare*) 1830.

2. To c. at abuses while pretending to remove them MACAULAY. To c. at knaves and tolerate fools CHESTERF. **3.** MILT. *Sams.* 465. **4.** Divorces were not conniv'd only, but with open eye allow'd of old MILT. **5.** To teach them how..to c. with either Eye ADDISON. Hence **Conni·ver**, one who connives.

Connivence, -ance (kǫnəi·vĕns). 1596. [orig. sp. *-ence* – Fr. *connivence* or L. *conniventia*; the sp. *-ance* has prevailed since *c* 1700. See -ENCE, -ANCE.] **1.** The action of conniving; the action of winking at, overlooking, or ignoring; tacit sanction; encouragement by forbearing to condemn 1611. † **2.** *lit.* Winking –1614. **3.** *Nat. Hist.* The fact of being CONNIVENT, q.v. 1830. var. **Conni·vency** (*arch.*).

Connivent (kǫnəi·vĕnt), *a.* 1642. [– *connivent-*, pres. ppl. stem of L. *con(n)ivēre*; see CONNIVE, -ENT.] † **1.** Conniving; disposed to connive at –1648. † **2.** Dormant. MILT. **3.** *Nat. Hist.* Gradually convergent; approaching at the extremity: of the anthers, etc., in flowers, and the wings in certain insects 1757.

3. *C. valves* (*valvulæ conniventes*): circular folds in the mucous membrane of the small intestine.

Connixation. [f. L. *nix* snow, after *conflagration*.] H. WALPOLE.

‖ **Connoissa·nce.** 1730. [Fr., now *connaissance* knowledge, acquaintance.] See quot.

Being in search of a proper term for this science, Mr. Prior proposed to name it *connoissance*; but that word has not obtained possession as *connoisseur* has H. WALPOLE.

‖ **Connoisseur** (konesör, kǫnisiū^ə·ɹ). 1714. [Fr., earlier sp. (cf. prec.) of *connaisseur*, f. *connaiss-*, pr. ppl. stem of *connaître*, + *-eur* -OR 2; cf. *reconnoitre*.] † **1.** One who knows –1734. **2.** *spec.* A critical judge of art, *esp.* of one of the fine arts; also, a judge in other matters of taste (*e.g.* of wines, etc.) 1714.

1. No ordinary c. in the sciences NORTH. **2.** Painters and connoisseurs are the only competent judges 1753. Hence **Connoisseu·rship.**

† **Connotate**, *v.* 1596. [– *connotat-*; see next and -ATE[3].] = CONNOTE 1, 2. –1697.

Connotation (kǫnotē^i·ʃən). 1532. [– med.L. *connotatio*, f. *connotat-*, pa. ppl. stem of *connotare*; see CONNOTE *v.*, -ION.] **1.** The signifying in addition; inclusion of something in the meaning of a word besides what it primarily denotes; implication. **2.** *Logic.* The attribute or attributes connected by a term; *loosely*: Meaning 1662.

Connotative (kǫ̆nō^u·tătiv), *a.* 1614. [– med.L. *connotativus*, f. as prec.; see -IVE.] Having the quality of connoting; pertaining to connotation.

C. term: according to J. S. Mill, one which denotes a subject and connotes its attributes. Hence **Conno·tatively** *adv.*

Connote (kǫ̆nō^u·t), *v.* 1655. [– schol. L. *connotare* mark in addition, f. *com* CON- + *notare* NOTE *v.*[2]] **1.** *trans.* To signify secondarily or in addition; to include or imply along with the primary meaning 1664. **2.** Of things or facts: To imply or involve 1655. † **3.** To have a meaning only when conjoined –1805. **4.** *Logic.* With J. S. Mill: To imply attributes, while denoting a subject 1829; hence, loosely: To imply 1865.

1. Good..over and above the bare Being of a Thing, Connotes also a certain sutableness or agreeableness of it to some other thing SOUTH. **2.** But 'punishment always connotes 'guilt' WESLEY.

Connubial (kǫ̆niū·biăl), *a.* 1656. [– L. *connubialis*, f. *connubium* marriage, wedlock, f. *com* CON- + *nubere* marry; see -AL[1].] **1.** Of or pertaining to marriage or the married state; nuptial, matrimonial. **2.** *transf.* Married, wedded; also *fig.* 1808.

1. The Rites Mysterious of c. Love MILT. *P.L.* IV. 743. **2.** C. vines 1808. Hence **Connubia·lity**, c. state or condition; the practice or right of marrying; (with *pl.*) any action characteristic of the married state. **Connu·bialize** *v. intr.* (*joc.*) to marry. **Connu·bially** *adv.*

Connu·merate, *v. rare.* 1678. [– *connumerat-*, pa. ppl. stem of late L. *connumerare*; see CON-, NUMERATE. Cf. OFr. *connumerer*.] *trans.* To reckon or count together. Hence **Connumera·tion.**

Co·nnusable, -ance, -ant, -or, obs. ff. COGNIZABLE, etc.

Conny, n. Eng. dial. f. CANNY.

Conocarp (kō^u·nokāɹp). 1866. [= mod.L. *conocarpium*, f. Gr. κῶνος cone + καρπός fruit.] A fruit consisting of carpels arranged upon a conical centre, as the strawberry. So **Conoca·rpous** *a.* having conical fruit.

Conocuneus (kō^unoˌkiū·niˌŭs). 1662. [f. L. *conus* cone + *cuneus* wedge.] *Geom.* A figure with a circular base like a cone, but having instead of an apex a ridge or edge like a wedge.

Conodont (kō^u·nodǫnt). 1859. [f. Gr. κῶνος cone + ὀδούς, ὀδοντ- tooth.] *Palæont.* A small conical tooth-like body, at first supposed to be a tooth of a cyclostomous fish; now considered to be the remains of some invertebrate animal.

Conoid (kō^u·noid). 1664. [– Gr. κωνοειδής cone-shaped; see CONE, -OID.]

A. *adj.* Approaching a cone in shape 1668.

B. *sb.* **1.** *Geom.* **a.** A solid generated about its axis; a conicoid of revolution (*esp.* a paraboloid or hyperboloid). This is the κωνοειδές of Archimedes. 1664. **b.** A surface generated by a straight line which continues parallel to a given plane, and passes through a fixed straight line and a fixed curve 1862. **2.** *gen.* Any body of a shape more or less approaching a cone 1793. **3.** *Anat.* The pineal gland; called also *conoid body* 1828. So **Conoi·dal** *a.* pertaining to, or of the form of, a c.; approaching in shape to a c. **Conoi·do-**, comb. f. of CONOID.

Co-nominee; see Co- *prefix*.

Conormal (konǭ·ɹmăl), *a.* [See Co-.] *Math.* Having common normals.

‖ **Conoscente** (konoʃe·nte). Pl. **-ti** (-ti). 1766. [It.] = COGNOSCENTE, q.v.

† **Conquassate**, *v. rare.* 1656. [– *conquassat-*, pa. ppl. stem of L. *conquassare*, f. *com* CON- + *quassare*, frequent. of *quatere* shake; see -ATE[3].] To shake violently –1666. So **Conqua·ssant** *a.* shaking severely. † **Conquassa·tion.**

Conquer (kǫ·ŋkəɹ), *v.* ME. [– OFr. *conquerre* :– Rom. **conquerere*, for L. *conquirere* seek for, procure, gain, win, f. *com* CON- + *quærere* seek.] † **1.** *trans.* To acquire, get possession of (by effort); to win, gain, attain to –1552. **2.** To acquire by fighting, win in war; to subjugate ME. Also fig. **3.** To overcome (an adversary), vanquish, subdue ME. **4.** *transf.* and *fig.* To get the better of; to master, overcome 1654. **5.** *absol.* and *intr.* To be the conqueror, make conquests, be victorious ME.

2. By conquering this new world MILT. *P.L.* IV. 391. For to conquere a name in armes CAXTON. *fig.* C. his daily bread by the threats of his dragoman KINGLAKE. **3.** If we be conquered, let men c. vs, And not these bastard Britaines *Rich. III*, V. iii. 332. **4.** The ruling Passion conquers Reason still POPE. **5.** Hee went foorth conquering, and to conquere *Rev.* 6:2. Hence **Co·nquerable** *a.* capable of being conquered, or overcome. **Co·nquerableness.** **Co·nqueress**, a female conqueror. **Co·nqueringly** *adv.* **Co·nquerless** *a.* (*poet.*) invincible. † **Co·nquerous** *a.* victorious.

Conqueror (kǫ·ŋkərəɹ). ME. [– AFr. *conquerour*, OFr. *-eor*, nom. *-ere*, f. *conquerre*; see prec., -OR 2.] One who gains possession of a country, etc., by force of arms; one who conquers, subdues, or overcomes. Also *transf.* and *fig.* **b.** *colloq.* = Conquering game (1891.).

1. Both tugging to be victors, brest to brest: Yet neither C., nor Conquered 3 *Hen. VI*, II. v. 12. *The C.*: in *Eng. Hist.* surname of William I.

Conquest (kǫ·ŋkwest), *sb.* ME. [– OFr. *conquest*, *conqueste* (mod. *conquête*), repr. subst. uses of n. and fem. of Rom. **conquestus*, pa. pple. of **conquerere* CONQUER.] **1.** The action of gaining by force of arms; subjugation of a country, etc. [OFr. *conqueste*.] Also *transf.* and *fig.* **2.** The action of overcoming; gaining of victory. Also *fig.* ME. **3.** That which is acquired by force of arms: formerly including booty. [OFr. *conquest*.] ME. Also *transf.* and *fig.* **4.** *Sc. Law.* **a.** The personal acquisition of real property otherwise than by inheritance. **b.** Real estate so acquired, as opp. to *heritage*. ME.

1. C...is the Acquiring of the Right of Sovereignty by Victory HOBBES. **2.** 3 *Hen. VI*, V. ii. 10. **3.** Wherefore reioyce? What C. brings he home *Jul. C.* I. i. 37. *transf.* To resign Conquests is a Task as difficult in a Beauty as an Hero STEELE.

Phr. *The C.* or *Norman C.*: the acquisition of the Crown of England by William, Duke of Normandy, in 1066. So † **Conquest** *v.* to gain; to conquer; to vanquish. † **Conquest** *pa. pple.* gained (*Sc.*); conquered; vanquished. † **Conquestor** = CONQUEROR.

† **Conquisi·tion.** *rare.* [– L. *conquisitio* a bringing together, collecting, f. *conquisit-*, pa. ppl. stem of *conquirere*; see CONQUER, -ION.] A getting together, procuring with care. BP. HALL.

‖ **Conquistador** (kǫŋki:stadǭ·r). 1830. [Sp.] = CONQUEROR.

† **Conrey.** ME. only. [– OFr. *conrei*, *conroi*; see ARRAY *sb.* and *v.*, CURRY *sb.*[1] and *v.*[1], CORRODY.] **1.** Equipment. **2.** A company equipped for fight.

† **Consacre**, *v.* 1491. [– Fr. *consacrer* – pop.L. *consacrare* for cl. L. *consecrare* CONSECRATE.] To consecrate, dedicate –1618.

Consanguineous (kǫnsæŋgwi·niəs), *a.* 1601. [f. L. *consanguineus* of the same blood (f. *com* CON- + *sanguis*, *sanguin-* blood) + -OUS.] **1.** Of the same blood, related by blood, akin; of or pertaining to those so related. **2.** *Rom. Law.* Related as children of the same father: opp. to *uterine*; pertaining to those so related 1861. vars. **Consa·nguine, Consangui·nean.** Hence **Consangui·neously** *adv.*

Consanguinity (kǫnsæŋgwi·nĭti). ME. [– L. *consanguinitas*, f. *consanguineus*; see prec., -ITY.] **1.** Relationship by descent from a common ancestor; blood-relationship. (Opp. to *affinity*, *i.e.* relationship by marriage.) Also *transf.* and *fig.* † **2.** *collect.* Blood-relations (*rare*) –1705.

1. He inhibited the marriage as within the fourth degree of c. MILMAN.

† **Consa·rcinate**, *v.* 1610. [– *consarcinat-*, pa. ppl. stem of L. *consarcinare* patch together, f. *com* CON- + *sarcinare* patch; see -ATE[3].] *trans.* To patch together –1656. Hence **Consarcina·tion.** ? *Obs.*

Conscience (kǫ·nʃəns). ME. [–(O)Fr. *conscience* – L. *conscientia* privity of knowledge, consciousness, f. *conscire* know or be privy with (another or oneself); see CON-, SCIENCE. Superseded INWIT.] † **1.** Inward knowledge or consciousness; internal conviction –1745. † **2.** Inmost thought; mind, heart –1611. **3.** The internal recognition of the moral quality of one's motives and actions; the faculty or principle which pronounces upon the moral quality of one's actions or motives, approving the right and condemning the wrong ME. † **4.** Conscientious observance *of*, or regard *to* –1671. **5.** Conscientiousness (*arch.*) ME. † **6.** Tenderness of feeling. ME. only. † **7.** Scruple; also compunction –1608. **8.** *Mech.* = BREAST-PLATE 3a. 1874.

1. Without sense of good or c. of evil DE FOE. **2.** By my troth, I will speake my c. of the King *Hen. V*, IV. i. 123. **3.** And I will place within them as a guide My Umpire C. MILT. *P.L.* III. 195. I feele not This Deity in my bosome: Twentie consciences That stand twixt me and Millaine, candied be they, And melt, ere they mollest *Temp.* II. i. 278. **5.** I cannot with c. take it *Wint. T.* IV. iv. 660.

Phrases. *Upon, in (one's) c.*: by one's sense of right, truly. Also as a mere exclam. (*Sc.*). *In (all) c.*: in reason or fairness (*colloq.*). *A matter of c.*: a matter in which c. is concerned; hence *to make (a thing) a matter of c.*: to deal with it conscientiously. *To make (a) c.* (obs. or arch.): to make it a matter of c., to have scruples about.

Comb.: **c. clause,** a clause in an act or law to ensure respect for the consciences of those affected, *spec.* one relating to religious teaching in public schools; **c. money,** money sent to relieve the c., *esp.* in connection with previous evasions of the income-tax; **c.-wise** *adv.* in relation to the c.

Hence **Co·nscienced** *ppl. a.* having a c. (of such a kind). **Co·nscienceless** *a.*; **-ly** *adv.*; **-ness.**

Conscient (kǫ·nʃiĕnt), *a.* (*sb.*) Now *rare.* 1605. [– *conscient-*, pres. ppl. stem of L. *conscire*; see prec., -ENT.] Conscious. As *sb.* A conscious being 1768.

Conscientious (kǫnʃiˌe·nʃəs), *a.* 1611. [– Fr. *conciencieux* – med.L. *conscientiosus*, f. L. *conscientia*; see CONSCIENCE, -OUS.] **1.** Obedient to conscience; habitually governed by a sense of duty; scrupulous. **2.** Of or pertaining to conscience; done according to conscience; scrupulous 1631. † **3.** Conscious (*of*) –1656.

1. A c. tradesman DE FOE. **2.** To live in the c. practice of all that is good BUTLER. Hence **Conscie·ntiously** *adv.* **Conscie·ntiousness,** the quality of being c.; loyalty to conscience.

Conscionable (kǫ·nʃənăb'l), *a.* Now app. *Obs.* 1549. [f. †*conscions*, var. of *conscience* + -ABLE. Obs. exc. as in UNCONSCIONABLE.] **1.** Having a (good) conscience; conscientious –1708. **2.** Showing regard for, or conformable to, conscience; conscientious –1702.

2. Truly a very fair and c. Reckoning MARVELL. Hence **Co·nscionableness.** ? *Obs.* **Co·nscionably** *adv.* ? *Obs.*

Conscious (kǫ·nʃəs), *a.* 1601. [f. L. *conscius* knowing something with others, knowing in oneself + -OUS.] † **1.** Knowing together with another –1664. **2.** *fig.* Chiefly *poet.* 1601. **3.** Inwardly sensible or aware 1620; † having guilty knowledge (*of*); also *absol.* –1827. **4.** Having internal perception or consciousness; also *absol.* 1651. **5.** Characterized by the presence of consciousness 1725. **6.** Aware of what one is doing or intending to do 1860. **7.** = SELF-CONSCIOUS 1728. **8.** *transf.* Of things: **a.** Known to oneself, felt. **b.** Aware of itself. 1667.

2. The c. air SOUTHEY. **3.** If they say, That a man is always c. to himself of thinking LOCKE. **4.** Who, c. of the occasion, feared the event DRYDEN. Thought is c. of itself 1863. **5.** Man, as a c. being MOZLEY. And when at last he was c. LYTTON. **6.** Pope was..a c. and deliberate artist L. STEPHEN. **7.** The c. simper POPE. **8. b.** Knowledge is c. power HAZLITT. Hence **Co·nsciously** *adv.*

Consciousness (kǫ·nʃəsnės). 1632. [f. prec. + -NESS.] † **1.** Mutual knowledge (*rare*) 1681. **2.** Knowledge as to which one has the testimony within oneself; *esp.* of one's own innocence, etc. 1632. **3.** The state or fact of being conscious *of* 1746. **4.** *Philos.* The state or faculty of being conscious, as a concomitant of all thought, feeling, and volition 1678; (with *a* and *pl.*) state of consciousness 1805. **5.** The totality of the impressions, thoughts, and feelings, which make up a person's conscious being. Also limited by a qualifying epithet to a special field. In *pl.* = Conscious personalities. 1690.

2. Happy in the c. of a well-spent life JOWETT. **4.** C. is the perception of what passes in a Man's own mind LOCKE. Consciousnesses not to be subdued WORDSW. **5.** The commencement of a moral c. MARY HOWITT. Matters of so-called universal c. HT. MARTINEAU.

Phr. *Double c.*: a condition showing in some measure two independent trains of thought and two independent mental capabilities in the same individual.

Conscribe (kǫ̆nskrəi·b), *v.* 1548. [– L. *conscribere*; see next.] † **1.** *trans.* To enrol; to enlist –1660. † **2.** To circumscribe –1704. **3.** To enlist by CONSCRIPTION, q.v. 1820. Also *transf.*

Conscript (kǫ·nskript). 1533. [– L. *conscriptus*, pa. pple. of *conscribere* enrol, f. *com* CON- + *scribere* write.]

A. *adj.* **1.** Enrolled or elected a senator. **2.** Enrolled or formed by conscription, as a soldier, or an army 1823.

C. fathers [L. *patres conscripti*, orig. *patres et conscripti*]: a collective title of the Roman senators; also applied allusively to members of the administrative council of a nation, municipality, etc.; rarely in *sing.*

B. *sb.* [Fr. *conscrit.*] One compulsorily enlisted for military (or naval) service 1800.

Conscript (kǫ̆nskri·pt), *v.* 1813. [Back-formation from CONSCRIPTION. (Orig. U.S. 1813).] *trans.* To compel to military service by conscription.

Conscription (kǫ̆nskri·pʃən). ME. [After Fr. *conscription*, which was introduced in connection with the law of the French Republic, 5 Sept. 1798, which dealt with this; – late L. *conscriptio* levying of troops; see CONSCRIPT *a.*, -ION.] † **1.** Writing down together –1483. † **2.** Enrolment or enlistment (of soldiers) –1656. **3.** *spec.* The compulsory enlistment of men for military (or naval) service 1800; the conscripts collectively 1823.

3. The C. of 1813 has furnished 160,000 men 1813. Hence **Conscri·ptional** *a.*

Consecrate (kǫ·nsĭkrĕt), *ppl. a.* ME. [– L. *consecratus*, pa. pple. of *consecrare*, f. *com* CON- + *sacrare* dedicate, f. *sacer* SACRED; see -ATE[2].] = CONSECRATED.

Consecrate (kǫ·nsĭkreⁱt, *v.* ME. [– *consecrat-*, pa. ppl. stem of L. *consecrare*; see prec., -ATE[3].] **1.** *trans.* To set apart as sacred to the Deity; to dedicate solemnly to some sacred or religious purpose; to make sacred or holy. Const. *to, unto.* Also *fig.* **2.** *transf.* To devote or dedicate *to* some purpose 1555. **3.** To make an object of veneration; to hallow, sanctify; to sanction [= mod. Fr. *consacrer*] 1693. † **4.** To devote or doom. [A Latinism.] –1652. † **5.** To apotheosize. [A Latinism.] –1736.

1. To c. churches or chapels COKE, bread and wine *Bk. Com. Prayer*, a king TREVISA. **2.** To c. one's life to letters PRESCOTT. **3.** Writers, whose reputation consecrates their opinions LINGARD.

Hence **Co·nsecrated** *ppl. a.* dedicated to a sacred purpose; hallowed; set apart with religious forms for public worship, or the burial of the dead, and having the status this gives; *fig.* sanctioned by usage. **Co·nsecrator. Co·nsecra:tory** *a.* that consecrates.

Consecration (kǫnsĭkrēⁱ·ʃən). ME. [– (O)Fr. *consécration* or L. *consecratio*, f. as prec.; see -ION.] **1.** The action of consecrating (see CONSECRATE *v.*). **2.** *Rom. Antiq.* Apotheosis; also *transf.* 1490. **3.** Dedication or devotion to some purpose or pursuit; also, appropriation to a special purpose 1781. **4.** Sanction by law, custom, or usage. [mod.Fr.] 1861.

1. The c. of a church 1570, of the bread and wine 1659, of a bishop MORE.

Consectary (kǫ̆nse·ktări). 1588. [– L. *consectarius* (also subst. *-aria*, n. pl.), f. *consectari*, frequent. of *consequi*; see next, -ARY[1].]

† **A.** *adj.* Following logically; consequent –1650.

B. *sb.* A consequence; a deduction, conclusion, corollary. (Common in 17th c.) 1588.

To mind fundamentals more than consectaries BP. BERKELEY.

† **Co·nsecute,** *v. rare.* 1536. [f. *consecut-*; see next.] To follow with success, overtake, attain –1589.

Consecution (kǫnsĭkiū·ʃən). 1532. [– L. *consecutio*, f. *consecut-*, pa. ppl. stem of *consequi* follow closely; see -ION.] **1.** Logical sequence; inference; a train of reasoning. **2.** Succession, sequence 1651.

† *Month of c.* in *Astr.*: a lunar or synodic month, a lunation.

Consecutive (kǫ̆nse·kiŭtiv), *a.* 1611. [– Fr. *consécutif, -ive* – med.L. *consecutivus*, f. as prec.; see -IVE.] **1.** Following continuously; following each its predecessor in uninterrupted succession. **2.** Characterized by logical sequence 1755. † **3.** Following as a consequence or effect; consequent (*to*) –1705. **4.** *Gram.* Expressing consequence or result 1871. **5.** *Mus.* Applied to the immediate succession of intervals of the same kind (*esp.* fifths and octaves) occurring between two voices or parts in harmony 1819. (As *sb.* in *pl.* = C. fifths or octaves.) **6.** *Magnetism. C. points*; see CONSEQUENT *a.*

1. The actions of a Man c. to volition LOCKE. **2.** The ground of a c. reasoning SIR W. HAMILTON. Hence **Conse·cutive-ly** *adv.*, **-ness.**

Consenescence (kǫnsĭne·sĕns). 1692. [f. CON- (intensive) + SENESCENCE.] The growing old together; general decay.

† **Con-sense.** [f. CON- + SENSE, tr. Gr. συναίσθησις.] Joint-sense (= consciousness). CUDWORTH.

Consension (kǫ̆nse·nʃən). *rare.* 1563. [– L. *consensio*, f. as CONSENSUS; see -ION. Cf. OFr. *consencion, -sion.*] Agreement.

Consensual (kǫ̆nse·nsiuăl, -ʃuăl), *a.* 1754. [f. L. *consensus* (see next) + -AL[1].] **1.** Relating to or involving consent. **2.** Happening as if by consent, caused by sympathetic action independently of the will, as the *c. actions in man* 1800.

1. *C. contract* (in *Rom. Law*): a contract which requires only consent of the parties to make it obligatory: so *c. obligation.* Hence **Conse·nsually** *adv.*

‖ **Consensus** (kǫ̆nse·nsŏs). 1854. [L. = agreement; f. *consens-*, pa. ppl. stem of L. *consentire*; see CONSENT.] **1.** *Phys.* General concord of different organs of the body in effecting a given purpose; sympathy. Also *transf.* **2.** Agreement in opinion. Also *transf.* 1861.

2. The c. of the Protestant missionaries 1861. *C. of opinion, authority, testimony*, etc. 1891.

Consent (kǫ̆nse·nt), *v.* ME. [– (O)Fr. *consentir* – L. *consentire* agree, accord, f. *com* CON- + *sentire* feel.] **1.** *intr.* To agree together, or *with*, † *to*, † *unto* (*arch.*). † **2.** To act or be affected in sympathy –1756. **3.** Voluntarily to accede to or acquiesce in a proposal, request, etc.; to agree, comply, yield. Const. *to, to do*, or *that.* ME. † **4.** *trans.* To allow, agree to, consent to –1588.

1. All your Writers do c., that ipse is hee *A.Y.L.* V. i. 48. **3.** He wold haue consentyd to the deth of Huon LD. BERNERS. And whispering 'I will ne'er c.'—consented BYRON. † *To be consented*: to be agreed; to be a consenting party (*to*). **4.** Interpreters..will not c. it to be a true story MILT. Hence **Conse·nter. Conse·nting-ly** *adv.*, **-ness. Conse·ntive** *a.* = CONSENTIENT.

Consent (kǫ̆nse·nt), *sb.* Also 4–6 **concent(e.** [ME. *consente* – OFr. *consente*, f. *consentir*; see prec.] **1.** Voluntary agreement to or acquiescence in what another proposes or desires; compliance, concurrence, permission. **2.** Agreement as to a course of action; concert ME. **3.** Agreement of opinion, consensus (*arch.*) 1529. **4.** Agreement in feeling, sympathy; accord (*arch.*) ME. † **5.** *Phys.* Sympathy between one organ or part of the body and another. Cf. CONSENSUS 1. –1797. † **6.** Feeling, opinion –1599.

1. The C. of a Subject to Soveraign Power HOBBES. Silence gives c. RAY. *Age of c.*: the age fixed by law at which a person's c. to certain acts (*e.g.* marriage, sexual intercourse) is valid in law. **2.** Phr. *With one c., by common c.* **3.** The general c. of Antiquity HOOKER. **4.** Such is the World's great harmony, that springs From Order, Union, full C. of things POPE. **6.** 1 *Hen. VI*, I. ii. 44.

Consentable (kǫ̆nse·ntăb'l), *a.* 1853. [– OFr. *consentable* in agreement, f. *consentir*; see prec., -ABLE.] In the law of Pennsylvania: Agreed upon by consent of parties, as a *c. line* of boundary.

Consentaneous (kǫnsentē̆ⁱ·niəs), *a.* 1625. [f. L. *consentaneus* (f. *consentire* CONSENT v.) + -OUS.] **1.** Agreeing, accordant; suited. **2.** Done by common consent, unanimous, concurrent 1774.

1. Inducements..c. to our own feelings MILL. So **Consentane·ity,** c. quality. Hence **Consenta·neous-ly** *adv.*, **-ness.**

Consentant (kǫ̆nse·ntănt), a. ME. [– (O)Fr. *consentant*, pres. pple. of *consentir* CONSENT *v.*; see -ANT.] Consenting.

Consentience (kǫ̆nse·nʃⁱĕns). 1877. [f. next; see -ENCE.] **1.** Consentient quality or condition; agreement of opinion 1879. **2.** The sensuous equivalent, in unconscious, involuntary, or reflex action, of consciousness in conscious action.

Consentient (kǫ̆nse·nʃⁱĕnt), *a.* 1622. [– *consentient-*, pres. ppl. stem of L. *consentire*; see CONSENT *v.*, -ENT.] **1.** United in opinion; concurrent; having or exhibiting consentience (sense 2). **2.** Accordant in opinion, or consenting, *to* 1661.

1. The c. acknowledgement of mankind 1659. With great and c. labour RAMSAY. Hence **Consentiently** *adv.*

† **Conse·ntment.** ME. [– (O)Fr. *consentement*, f. *consentir*; see CONSENT *v.*, -MENT. Cf. med.L. *consentimentum.*] The action of consenting, consent –1660.

Consequence (kǫ·nsĭkwĕns), *sb.* ME. [– (O)Fr. *conséquence* – L. *consequentia*, f. *consequent-*, pr. ppl. stem of *consequi* follow closely; see CON-, SEQUENCE.] **1.** A thing or circumstance which follows as an effect or result from something preceding. **2.** The action, or condition, of so following; the relation of a result to its cause or antecedent 1656. **3.** A logical result or inference ME.; logical sequence 1571. **4.** Importance, moment, weight. (Originating in the phr. *of c.*: *i.e.* having results, and therefore important.) 1593. **5.** Importance in rank and position 1602. **6.** *Astr.* Motion from west to east; also a position more to the east 1683.

1. Death is the c. of Adam's sin BURNET. **2.** Such fatal c. unites us three MILT. *P.L.* x. 364. **3.** Phr. *In, of, by c.*: as a result or inference; consequently. **4.** As often as we do anything of note or c. A.V. *Transl. Pref.* **5.** A person of some c. SWIFT. No form of property gives its owners so much c. as land FROUDE. Hence † **Co·nsequence** *v.* to draw inferences. MILT.

† **Co·nsequency.** 1548. [– L. *consequentia*; see prec., -ENCY.] = CONSEQUENCE 1–3. –1718.

Consequent (kǫ·nsĭkwĕnt), *sb.* ME. [– (O)Fr. *conséquent*, f. as next, f. L. pr. pple. used subst.] † **1.** = CONSEQUENCE 1. –1756. **2.** † **a.** *Logic.* = CONSEQUENCE 3. –1838. **b.** The second part of a conditional proposition 1628. **3.** Anything which follows something else; *Math.* the second of two numbers, etc., in a ratio; the second and fourth in a compound ratio 1570. † **4.** A person who follows –1654.

2. The Antecedent is false. Therefore the C. falls of course WESLEY. **3.** Justification [is] a c. of believing, no effect issuing out of the virtue and merit of faith 1627.

Consequent (kǫ·nsĭkwĕnt), *a.* 1475. [– (O)Fr. *conséquent* – L. *consequent-*; see CONSEQUENCE, -ENT.] **1.** Following as an effect or result 1509. **2.** Following as a logical conclusion 1638. † **3.** Following in time or order (contrasted with *antecedent*) –1742. **4.** Logically consistent 1849. Also quasi-*adv.*

1. The very rapid increase of Trade, and the c. influx of Wealth 1800. **4.** To be c., they should have shewn that, etc. LEWES.

C. points (in Magnetism): successive points in the length of a magnetized bar, at which the direction of the magnetization is reversed. Also called *consecutive points*. Hence **Co·nsequently** *adv.* † subsequently; † in sequence; by consequence; consistently.

Consequential (kǫnsĭkwe·nʃăl), *a.* 1626. [f. L. *consequentia* CONSEQUENCE + -AL¹; cf. med.L. *consequentialis.*] **1.** Following, *esp.* as an effect, immediate or eventual, or as a logical inference. **2.** = CONSEQUENT *a.* 4. 1659. † **3.** Of consequence, important –1821. **4.** Having social consequence 1833. **b.** Self-important 1758. **5.** *sb. pl.* Consequential matters 1734.

1. Wars and their c. burthens 1829. *C. damages*: 'losses or injuries which follow an act, but are not direct and immediate upon it' (Wharton). These are c. to our former conclusions LD. PRESTON. **4. b.** Pampered and c. freedmen FARRAR. Hence **Conseque:ntia·lity,** logical consistency; air of importance. **Conseque·ntially** *adv.* † subsequently; † as a consequence; indirectly; with logical consistency; in a c. manner. **Conseque·ntialness** (*rare*).

Consertion; see CONCERTION.

Conservable (kǫ̆nsɔ̄·ɹvăb'l), *a.* 1623. [– late L. *conservabilis*; see CONSERVE *v.*, -ABLE.] Capable of being conserved; preservable.

† **Conse·rvacy.** 1558. [– AFr. *conservacie*; see next.] Repl. by CONSERVANCY –1758.

Conservancy (kǫ̆nsɔ̄·ɹvănsi). 1755. [alt., by assim. to -ANCY, of CONSERVACY – AFr. *conservacie* – AL. *conservatia* (see -ACY), by-form of L. *conservatio* CONSERVATION.] **a.** A commission or court to regulate the fisheries, navigation, etc., of a port or river. **b.** The official preservation of trees, forests 1859. Also *gen.*

† **Conse·rvant,** *a.* 1588. [– *conservant-*, pr. ppl. stem of L. *conservare*; see CONSERVE *v.*, -ANT.] That conserves, preserving, as in *c. cause* (med.L. *causa conservans*) –1679. So **Co·nservate** *v.* to CONSERVE, preserve (*rare*).

Conservation (kǫnsəɹvēⁱ·ʃən). ME. [– (O)Fr. *conservation* or L. *conservatio*, f. *conservat-*, pa. ppl. stem of *conservare*; see CONSERVE *v.*, -ION.] **1.** The action of conserving; preservation from destructive influences, decay, or waste; preservation in being, health, etc. **2.** Official charge and care of rivers, sewers, forests, etc.; conservancy 1490. **3.** The preserving of fruit or the like 1873.

1. Matter..cannot subsist without the divine c. BP. BERKELEY. C. of order 1538, of existing territorial limits 1864.

Phrases. *Psychol. Faculty of c.*: the power of retaining knowledge, as dist. from reminiscence the power of recalling it. *Nat. Phil. C. of energy, force*: the doctrine that 'the total energy of any body or system of bodies is a quantity which can neither be increased nor diminished by any mutual action of those bodies, though it may be transformed into any one of the forms of which energy is susceptible'; and that the universe is such a system. So *c. of mass*, etc. *Astron. C. of areas*: the describing of equal areas in equal times by the radius vector of a planet moving in its orbit. Hence **Conserva·tional** *a.*

Conservatism (kǫ̆nsɔ̄·ɹvătiz'm). 1835. [f. CONSERVATIVE + -ISM.] The doctrine and practice of Conservatives; = Toryism. Hence, generally, conservative principles in politics, theology, criticism, etc.

Conse·rvatist. *rare.* 1867. [f. CONSERVATIVE (A., B. 2); see -IST.] *sb.* One who would preserve (institutions, etc.) unchanged. *adj.* = CONSERVATIVE.

Conservative (kǫ̆nsɔ̄·ɹvătiv). ME. [– late L. *conservativus*, f. as CONSERVATION; see -IVE; in politics 1830 (J. W. Croker).]

A. *adj.* **1.** Characterized by a tendency to preserve or keep intact and unchanged; preservative. **2.** Designation of the English political party, the characteristic principle of which is the maintenance of existing institutions, political and ecclesiastical. (*With capital C.*) 1830. **b.** [from the *sb.*] Of, belonging to, or characteristic of Conservatives, or the Conservative party 1831. **3.** Applied to a similar spirit in general politics, theology, business, etc. 1845. **b.** orig. *U.S.* Of an estimate, etc.: Moderate, cautious, purposely low 1900.

1. The c. virtues of lock and key W. IRVING. *C. faculty* (Psychol.): the faculty of CONSERVATION, q.v. *C. system* (Physics): a system of bodies in which the doctrine of the Conservation of Energy is exemplified. **3.** The c. side of the Conqueror's policy FREEMAN. Hence **Conse·rvatively** *adv.* So **Conse·rvatize** *v.* to make or become c. (*rare*).

B. *sb.* [The adj. used absol.] **1.** A preserving agent or principle; a preservative ME. **2.** *Eng. Politics.* A member of the Conservative party, a Tory; in early use, a supporter of Sir Robert Peel 1831. **b.** In general politics, religion, criticism, etc. 1843.

1. Education, as a corrective and c. SOUTHEY. **2. b.** Bull is a born c. CARLYLE.

‖ **Conservatoire** (koṅsɛrvatwā·r). 1771. [Fr. – It. *conservatorio*; see CONSERVATORY.] A public establishment for special instruction in music and declamation.

Conservator (kǫ·nsəɹvēⁱtəɹ). ME. [– AFr. *conservatour*, (O)Fr. *conservateur* – L. *conservator* keeper, preserver, f. as CONSERVATION; see -OR 2.] **1.** One who preserves from injury; a preserver, guardian, keeper, custodian. **2.** In various titles official or descriptive ME.

1. The infinite C. of the World DERHAM. The c. of a museum 1835. **2.** *Conservators of the Peace* (*Custodes Pacis*): applied in a general sense, to the Sovereign, Lord Chancellor, the Justices of the King's Bench, etc. *Conservators of a river*: see CONSERVANCY a. So † **Conse·rvatrice, -a·trix,** a female c. Hence **Conserva·torship.**

Conservatory (kǫ̆nsɔ̄·ɹvătəri), *sb.* 1563. [– late L. *conservatorium*, subst. use of n. of adj. *-orius*, f. as CONSERVATION; see -ORY¹. In sense 4 rendering It. [*conservatorio*, Fr. *-toire.*] † **1.** That which preserves, a preservative –1660. **2.** A place where things are preserved; *esp.* a greenhouse for tender flowers or plants 1664. † **3.** A hospital for the rearing of foundlings and orphans –1693. **4.** A school or academy of music; a CONSERVATOIRE, q.v. (Freq. in U.S.) 1842.

The Italian *conservatorios* originated in hospitals for foundlings (see prec. sense), in which a musical education was given.

Conservatory (kǫ̆nsɔ̄·ɹvătəri), *a.* 1576. [– late L. *conservatorius*; see prec., -ORY².] **1.** Adapted to conserve. **2.** = CONSERVATIVE *a.* 1822. **3.** Of or pertaining to conservators 1881.

Conserve (kǫ̆nsɔ̄·ɹv), *sb.* ME. [– (O)Fr. *conserve*, = It., Sp., med.L. *conserva*, f. the verb; see next.] † **1.** A preservative –1590. † **2.** A greenhouse. EVELYN. † **3.** A store –1651. **4.** A medicinal or confectionary preparation of some part of a plant, preserved with sugar. *pl.* Preserves. 1530.

1. A conserue against such lawlesse concupiscence GREENE. **4.** *Tam. Shr.* Induct. ii. 3.

Conserve (kǫ̆nsɔ̄·ɹv), *v.* ME. [– (O)Fr. *conserver* – L. *conservare*; see CON-, SERVE.] **1.** To keep in safety, or from harm, decay, or loss; now usually, to preserve in its existing state from destruction or change. † **2.** To preserve in being; to keep alive –1698. † **3.** To make into a conserve; to preserve in sugar, etc. –1773.

1. One ancient lancet window has been carefully conserved 1861. Hence **Conse·rver.**

Consider (kǫ̆nsi·dəɹ), *v.* ME. [– (O)Fr. *considérer* – L. *considerare*, f. *com* CON- + base **sider-*, found also in *desiderare* DESIRE.] **1.** To view attentively, to survey, examine, inspect (*arch.*). **2.** *intr.* To look attentively ME. **3.** *trans.* To contemplate mentally; to think over, meditate on, give heed to, take note of. Also with *of* (*arch.*) ME. **4.** *intr.* To think deliberately, bethink oneself, reflect 1460. † **5.** *trans.* To judge of –1539. **6.** To take into practical consideration; to regard, make allowance for ME. † **7.** To recognize in a practical way; to requite, recompense; see CONSIDERATION –1698. **8.** To hold in consideration; to esteem, respect 1692. **9.** To look upon (*as*), take for 1533; with *obj. clause*: To think, suppose 1830.

1. She considreth a field and byeth it *Prov.* 31:16. **3.** Is man no more then this? C. him well *Lear* III. iv. 107. Thou must consyder thy seruantes be men as thou arte CAXTON. **4.** 'Twere to c. to curiously to c. so *Haml.* v. i. 227. The matter's weighty, pray c. twice POPE. **6.** Blessed is he that considereth the poor *Ps.* 41:1. **7.** *Meas. for M.* I. ii. 114. **8.** A pamphlet..which was..enough considered to be both seriously and ludicrously answered JOHNSON. **9.** He considers wealth of little importance 1784. I c. him to have acted disgracefully (*mod.*).

Hence **Consi·dered** *pa. pple.*; also used *absol.* = 'being taken into account'. **Consi·derer. Consi·dering** *vbl. sb.* and *ppl. a.*; also as *prep.* = 'taking into account'; *ellipt.* considering everything: used *advb.* (*colloq.*). **Consi·deringly** *adv.* thoughtfully; in a considering manner, tone, or attitude.

Considerable (kǫ̆nsi·dərăb'l), *a.* (and *sb.*) 1449. [– med.L. *considerabilis* worthy to be considered, f. L. *considerare*; see prec., -ABLE.] † **1.** That may be considered or viewed (*rare*) –1668. † **2.** That should be considered, taken into account, or noted; notable –1707. **3.** Worthy of consideration or regard, important; of consequence 1619. **4.** Worthy of consideration by reason of magnitude; pretty large; a good deal of. (The usual current sense.) 1651. **5.** As *adv.* = CONSIDERABLY. Now *dial.* 1657. † **6.** *sb.* A thing to be considered. Chiefly *pl.*; cf. *valuables*, etc. –1677.

3. The town is still a very c. place 1872. Some of the most c. citizens were banished HALLAM. **4.** A very c. part of the people HOBBES. A c. sum of money MAR. EDGEWORTH.

Hence **Consi:derabi·lity,** the quality of being c. **Consi·derableness,** importance. **Consi·derably** *adv.* † in a way or to a degree that ought to be noticed; much, a good deal.

† **Consi·derance.** ME. [– OFr. *considerance* – L. *considerantia*; see CONSIDER, -ANCE.] The action of considering; reflection –1597.

Considerate (kǫnsi·dərĕt), *a.* 1572. [– L. *consideratus*, pa. pple. of *considerare*; see CONSIDER, -ATE².] **1.** Marked by consideration; well-considered, deliberate. **2.** Of persons, etc.: Having or showing consideration; thoughtful, deliberate, prudent. *Obsolescent.* 1581. † **3.** Having regard, regardful *of* –1667. **4.** Thoughtful for others. Now the chief sense. 1700.

1. The national courage..c. and determined EMERSON. **2.** C. and careful parentes MULCASTER. **4.** Was I more c. of you and your comfort JANE AUSTEN. Hence **Consi·derate-ly** *adv.*, **-ness.**

Consideration (kǫnsi:dərēⁱ·ʃən). ME. [– (O)Fr. *considération* – L. *consideratio*, f. *considerat-*, pa. ppl. stem of *considerare*; see CONSIDER, -ION.] † **1.** The action of looking at; beholding, contemplation –1651. **2.** The keeping of a subject before the mind; attentive thought, reflection, meditation ME.; (with *pl.*) a reflection 1489. **3.** The action of taking into account; the being taken into account; regard 1540. **4.** The taking into account of anything as a reason or motive; a fact or circumstance taken, or to be taken, into account 1460. **5.** Something given in payment; a reward, remuneration; a compensation 1607. **6.** *Law.* Anything regarded as recompense or equivalent for what one does or undertakes for another's benefit; *esp.*, in the law of contracts, 'the thing given or done by the promisee in exchange for the promise' (Langdell 1880 § 45) 1530. **7.** Regard for the circumstances, feelings, etc., of another ME. **8.** Estimation; regard among men; consequence 1598.

2. C. like an Angell came, And whipt th'offending Adam out of him SHAKS. Phr. *To take into c., under c.* **3.** Wherefore, in c. of the premisses, be it enacted [etc.] 1540. **4.** Induced to adopt this course by considerations of state policy SMILES. **5.** They hoped that I would giue them some c. to be carryed in a chaire to the toppe CORYAT. **6.** C. is the materiall cause of a contract, without the which no contract can binde the partie *Termes de la Ley* 77. **8.** A man of the first c. 1859. There is nothing in this World that is of any C. in comparison with Eternity LOCKE.

† **Consi·derative,** *a.* 1449. [– OFr. *consideratif, -ive*, med.L. *considerativus* reflective, thoughtful; later f. CONSIDERATE + -IVE.] = CONSIDERATE 1, 2, 4. –1825.

† **Consi·derator.** 1658. [– L. *considerator*; see CONSIDERATION, -OR 2.] One who considers –1695.

Consign (kǫnsəi·n), *v.* ME. [– Fr. *consigner* – L. *consignare* attest with a seal, f. *com* CON- + *signare* SIGN *v.*¹]

I. † **1.** *trans.* To mark with the sign of the cross; *spec.* to confirm; with *to, unto*: To dedicate thus –1683. † **2.** To attest, confirm, ratify –1849. † **3.** To seal, sign, subscribe –1714. † **4.** *intr.* To set one's seal, subscribe, agree *to* –1611.

4. All Louers young, all Louers must Consigne to thee, and come to dust *Cymb.* IV. ii. 275.

II. To hand over formally. **1.** To make over as a possession, to deliver formally or commit, *to* a state, fate, etc. 1632. **2.** To hand over to another for custody 1528. **3.** To deposit (money) 1633. **4.** *Comm.* To deliver or transmit (goods) for sale or custody: usually implying their transit by ship, railway, etc. 1653.

1. When this vital breath Ceasing, consigns me o'er to rest and death M. PRIOR. To c. anything to a use DRYDEN, to writing ADDISON. **2.** Consigning our horses to the care of our grooms LYTTON. **3.** To c. money in a public bank 1861. **4.** A ship.. laden with goods and consigned to Robert Morris 1866. Hence **Consi·gnable** *a.* that can be consigned. **Consi·gnatary,** a consignee. ? *Obs.* **Consignee·**, a person to whom goods are consigned. **Consi·gner.**

Consignation (kǫnsignēⁱ·ʃən). 1537. [– med.L. senses of L. *consignatio* (see prec., -ATION); partly f. prec. + -ATION. Cf. (O)Fr. *consignation*.] † **1.** The action of marking with the sign of the cross –1642. Also *fig.* † **2.** Sealing; confirmation; attestation –1849. † **3.** A consigning *to* a state or condition –1684. † **4.** Formal delivery –1678. **5.** The action of formally paying over money, as into a bank, etc. 1588. **6.** = CONSIGNMENT 3. 1755.

6. *To the c. of*: = addressed to as consignee.

Consignatory, var. of CO-SIGNATORY.

‖ **Consigne** (koṅsi·nʸ). 1864. [Fr., f. *consigner* give instructions to a sentry.] Order given to a sentinel; watchword; countersign.

‖ **Consigné** (koṅsinʸe). [Fr.; pa. pple. of *consigner* (prec.).] A person commanded to keep his quarters, or to stay within certain bounds. (Dicts.)

Consignificant (kǫnsigni·fikănt), *a. rare.* 1612. [f. as CONSIGNIFY; see -ANT.] Conjointly significant; having a meaning in combination. So **Co:nsigni·ficative** *a.* (*rare*).

Consigni·ficate. [– med.L. *consignificatum*; see next, -ATE¹.] That which is consignified.

Consignification (kǫnsi:gnifikēⁱ·ʃən). *rare.* 1701. [– med.L. *consignificatio* (XII), – *consignificat-*, pa. ppl. stem of *consignificare*; see next, -ION.] Joint signification; connotation; conjoint signification.

Consignify (kǫnsi·gnifəi), *v. rare.* 1646. [– med.L. *consignificare* (Duns Scotus); see CON-, SIGNIFY.] To signify conjointly; to signify when combined with something.

The cypher, which has no value of itself, and only serves..to connote and c. HORNE TOOKE.

Consignment (kǫnsəi·nmĕnt). 1563. [f. CONSIGN *v.* + -MENT.] **1.** Sealing or dedicating with a sign. **2.** Delivering over; committal; allotment 1668. **3.** The consigning of goods or a cargo, *esp.* to an agent for sale or disposal 1709. **4.** *concr.* A quantity of goods consigned to an agent or factor 1722.

4. A large c. of pearls entrusted to the captain 1877.

Consignor (kǫnsəinǭ·ɹ). 1789. [f. as prec. + -OR 2 d.] One who dispatches goods to another; opp. to *consignee*. More techn. than *consigner*.

† **Consi·liary,** *a.* 1642. [– L. *consiliarius*, f. *consilium* COUNSEL *sb.*; see -ARY¹.] Of, pertaining to, or of the nature of, counsel; giving counsel –1662.

Consilient (kǫnsi·liĕnt), *a.* 1867. [– mod.L. **consiliens, -ent-* 'jumping together' (cf. RESILIENT), after *concurrent*.] 'Jumping together', concurrent, accordant. Hence **Consi·lience,** the fact of 'jumping together'; coincidence, concurrence: said of inductions.

Consimilar (kǫnsi·milăɹ), *a.* Now *rare.* 1548. [f. CON- + SIMILAR; cf. CONSIMILE.] † **1.** = CONSIMILE –1651. **2.** Entirely similar, like 1645. Hence **Consimila·rity** (*rare*).

† **Consi·milate,** *v.* 1731. [– *consimilat-*, pa. ppl. stem of late L. *consimilare* make like, compare; cf. ASSIMILATE.] To make or become like –1756.

† **Consi·mile,** *a.* ME. [– L. *consimilis* similar in all respects, f. *com* CON- + *similis* like.] Like throughout, homogeneous, as animal tissues, etc. –1577. So † **Consimi·litude,** † **Consimi·lity,** similarity, mutual likeness.

Consist (kǫnsi·st), *v.* 1526. [– L. *consistere* stand still, remain firm, exist, f. *com* CON- + *sistere* place, stand firm or still. Cf. Fr. *consister*.] **1.** *intr.* To have a settled existence, subsist, hold together, exist, be (*arch.*) 1551. † **2.** To exist together as compatible facts, to co-exist –1814; to be possible and so compatible *with* –1846. **3.** To be consistent; to be congruous; to harmonize (*with*) 1638.

1. And by him all things c. *Col.* 1: 17. **2.** Fayeth can not consiste wyth an euell conscience 1548. Health consists with temperance alone POPE. **3.** To c. and hang together BP. BERKELEY.

With preps. † **C. on** or **upon:** to stand on, rest upon; to insist *upon* 2 *Hen. IV*, IV. i. 187. So † **C. by. C. in:** to have its being in; to be comprised or contained in; to be constituted of (now the usual sense); to be composed of (*arch.*). So † **C. by. C. of:** to be made up or composed of. (*Of* was here orig. = *from, out of.*)

Consistence (kǫnsi·stĕns). 1598. [– Fr. *consistance*, †*-ence* or late L. *consistentia*, f. *consistent-*, pres. ppl. stem of *consistere*; see prec., -ENCE.] † **1.** Standing or remaining still, quiescence; state of rest –1751. † **2.** A settled condition –1702. **3.** Material coherence and permanence of form; solidity enough to retain its form 1626; †*concr.* matter dense enough to cohere (*poet.*) –1774. **4.** The degree of firmness with which the particles of a substance cohere; degree of density. (Usu. of more or less viscous liquids.) 1626. Also *fig.* † **5.** Combination –1702. † **6.** Coexistence as compatible facts 1659. **7.** = CONSISTENCY 4, 5. 1670.

3. Putrefaction; which ever dissolveth the C. of the Body BACON. *fig.* Reports..begin to acquire c. 1884. **4.** A due C. of the Blood is very necessary for Health ARBUTHNOT.

Consistency (kǫnsi·stĕnsi). 1594. [f. prec., or as prec.; see -ENCY.] † **1.** = CONSISTENCE 2. –1705. **2.** = CONSISTENCE 3. 1594. **3.** = CONSISTENCE 4. 1661. **4.** The quality, state, or fact of being consistent; agreement (*with* something, *of* things, etc.) 1658. **5.** The quality of being self-consistent; see CONSISTENT 7. 1716.

4. The c. of the two records PALEY. **5.** C. of behaviour ADDISON. The doubtful virtue of c. MAINE.

Consistent (kǫnsi·stĕnt). 1574. [– *consistent-*, pres. ppl. stem of L. *consistere*; see CONSIST, -ENT.]

A. *adj.* † **1.** Standing still or firm; not moving or giving way –1664. † **2.** Settled, persistent; durable –1684. † **3** Consisting *in* or *of*, composed *of* –1671. † **4.** Holding together as a coherent material body. (Now *rare.*) 1647. † **5.** Existing together or simultaneously *with* (*rare*) –1733. **6.** Agreeing or according in substance or form; congruous, compatible. (This and 7 are the current senses.) 1646. † **b.** Used *advb.* = Consistently –1842. **7.** Of persons or conduct: Marked by consistency; constantly adhering to the same principles of thought or action 1732.

2. † *C. age*: the age when growth has ceased and decay has not begun. **4.** A black c. peat-earth 1799. **6.** An habite..not c. with the words of our Saviour SIR T. BROWNE. A solid, regular, and c. Structure 1726. **7.** C. in our follies and our sins POPE.

† **B.** *sb. Eccl. Hist.* One of the fourth class of penitents (*consistentes*) in the Eastern Church, who took their station with the faithful, but were not admitted to communion.

Hence **Consi·stently** *adv.* in a c. manner.

† **Consi·stible,** *a.* Also **-able.** 1642. [f. CONSIST + -IBLE.] That may consist (*with* something); compatible –1660.

Consistorial (kǫnsistōᵊ·riăl), *a.* 1450. [– (O)Fr. *consistorial* or med.L. *consistorialis*, f. late L. *consistorium*; see next, -AL¹.] **1.** Of or pertaining to a consistory. **2.** Of or pertaining to church government by consistories; Genevan, presbyterian 1561.

1. The c. court of the archdeaconry of Wells 1805. **2.** The c. or presbyterian form of polity 1889. var. † **Consisto·rian** *a.*

Consistory (kǫ·nsistəri, kǫnsi·stəri). ME. [– AFr. *consistorie* = (O)Fr. *consistoire* – late L. *consistorium*; see CONSIST, -ORY¹.]

I. † **1.** A place where councillors meet, a council-chamber –1756. **2.** A meeting of councillors, a council. *Obs.* exc. *Hist.* or *poet.* ME. Also † *fig.* † **3.** A tribunal –1685. † **4.** A court, as in *heavenly c.* –1641.

2. In mid air To council summons all his mighty peers..A gloomy c. MILT. *P.R.* I. 40. **3.** This false Iuge..As he was wont sat in his Consistorie And yaf his doomes CHAUCER.

II. Eccl. senses. **1.** The senate in which the Pope, presiding over the Cardinals, deliberates upon the affairs of the church. Also, a meeting of this body. ME. **2.** The diocesan court, held by the chancellor of the diocese ME. Also *fig.* **3.** In the Lutheran Church, a board of clerical officers, usually appointed by the sovereign, to supervise ecclesiastical affairs 1698. **4.** In the Reformed, Genevan, or Presbyterian polity, a court of presbyters; corresponding, in Holland, etc., to the kirk-session in Scotland; in France, to a presbytery 1593. Also *attrib.*

1. His Holiness said that he would deliberate upon the appeal with the c. FROUDE.

† **Consi·tion.** *rare.* 1656. [– L. *consitio*, f. *conserere, -sit-* sow; see -ION.] A sowing –1692.

Conso·ciate. 1471. [– L. *consociatus*, pa. pple. of *consociare*; see next, -ATE².] *adj.* Associated together. In early use as *pa. pple.* = CONSOCIATED. *sb.* A partner, confederate 1579.

Consociate (kǫ̆nsōᵘ·ʃiˌeⁱt), *v.* 1566. [– *consociat-*, pa. ppl. stem of L. *consociare*, f. *com* CON- + *sociare* associate; see -ATE³.] **1.** *trans.* To bring into association, companionship, partnership; to conjoin in action, etc. **2.** *intr.* To enter into association; *spec.* in New England, to join in a consociation of churches 1638. **3.** To keep company *with* 1656.

1. Colly consociateth its waters with Axe RISDON. **2.** They c...to fight against his annoynted TRAPP.

Consociation (kǫ̆nsōᵘ:ʃiˌēⁱ·ʃən, -siˌēⁱ·ʃən). 1593. [– L. *consociatio*, f. as prec.; see -ION.] **1.** The action or fact of associating together; combination 1593. **2.** Fellowship, companionship 1609. †**3.** An alliance or confederation –1685. **4.** *Eccl.* A confederation of Christian churches or religious societies. In U.S. a body of the nature of a permanent Council, elected from and representing the Congregational churches of a district, and possessing a certain tacitly conceded ecclesiastical authority. 1644.

1. The c. of tribes for plunder or defence 1804. **2.** She glorifieth her nobilitie, having c. with God BIBLE (Douay) *Wisd.* 8:3. Hence **Consocia·tional** *a.* **Consocia·tionism,** the c. of churches.

Consol (kǫ̆nsǫ·l). Pl. **consols.** 1770. In *pl.* Short for *Consolidated Annuities*, i.e. the government securities of Great Britain; see CONSOLIDATED. (The sing. is used only *attrib.* and in *comb.*)

†**Consolate** (kǫ·nsŏlět), *ppl. a.* 1475. [– L. *consolatus*, pa. pple. of *consolari*; see CONSOLATION, -ATE².] **1.** Consoled, comforted –1818. **2.** *loosely.* Consolatory 1748.

†**Consolate** (kǫ·nsŏleⁱt), *v* 1475. [f. as prec.; see CONSOLATION, -ATE³.] = CONSOLE *v.* –1773.

Consolation (kǫnsŏlēⁱ·ʃən). ME. [– (O)Fr. *consolation* – L. *consolatio*, f. *consolat-*, pa. ppl. stem of *consolari*; see CONSOLE *v.*, -ION.] **1.** The action of consoling; the state of being consoled; alleviation of sorrow or mental distress. **2.** (with *pl.*) An act or instance of consolation; a person or thing that affords consolation ME.

1. Some source of c. from above MILT. *Sams.* 664. **2.** Pericles in the funeral oration is silent on the consolations of immortality JOWETT. Phr. *C. race, match*, etc.: one open only to those who have been defeated in the preceding 'events'. So *c. stakes.*

†**Consola·tor.** 1540. [– L. *consolator*, in eccl.L. (Jerome) equivalent of Vulg. *paraclitus* PARACLETE, f. as prec., see -OR 2.] Consoler.

Consolatory (kǫ̆nsǫ·lătəri). ME. [– L. *consolatorius*, f. *consolator*; see -ORY².] *adj.* Tending to console; bringing consolation. †*sb.* 'A speech or writing containing topicks of comfort' (J.). –1671. Hence **Conso·latorily** *adv.*

Consolatrix (kǫnsŏlēⁱ·triks). *rare.* 1632. [– late L. *consolatrix*; see CONSOLATOR, -TRIX.] A female consoler.

Console (kǫ·nsoᵘl), *sb.* Also **consol.** 1706. [– Fr. *console*, obscure deriv. of *consolider* CONSOLIDATE.] **1.** *Arch.* A variety of the bracket or corbel; 'an ornament in any material which projects about half its height or less, for the purpose of carrying anything'. **2.** Short for *c.-table* (see below) 1840. **3.** The desk from which an organ is played, containing keyboards, stop action, etc. 1881.

1. The drawing-room, in which, on consoles, are the twelve Caesars BP. POCOCKE. *Comb.* **c.-table,** a table supported by a fixed bracket against a wall; also, a movable side-table supported by consoles.

Console (kǫ̆nsōᵘ·l), *v.* 1693. [– Fr. *consoler* – L. *consolari* (see CONSOLATION). Repl. CONSOLATE *v.* (XV).] *trans.* To comfort in distress or depression; to alleviate the sorrow of; 'to free from the sense of misery' (J.).

What, thou think'st men speak in courtly chambers Words by which the wretched are consoled M. ARNOLD. Earth can c., Heaven can torment no more SHELLEY.

Hence **Conso·lable** *a.* that can be consoled. **Conso·ler,** one who consoles; repl. CONSOLATOR.

†**Conso·lidant.** 1661. [– Fr. *consolidant*, pres. pple. of *consolider*; see CONSOLIDATE, -ANT.] *adj.* That consolidates. Of medicines: Tending to unite or heal (wounds, fractures, etc.) 1755. *sb.* A c. medicine. (Now only in Dicts.)

Consolidate (kǫ̆nsǫ·lidět), *ppl. a.* 1531. [– L. *consolidatus*, pa. pple. of *consolidare*; see next, -ATE².] = CONSOLIDATED.

Consolidate (kǫ̆nsǫ·lideⁱt), *v.* 1511. [– *consolidat-*, pa. ppl. stem of L. *consolidare*, f. *com* CON- + *solidare*, f. *solidus* SOLID; see -ATE³.] **1.** *trans.* To make solid; to form into a compact mass; to solidify 1653. **2.** To make firm or strong; to strengthen (now chiefly power, etc.) 1540. **3.** To combine compactly into one mass, body, or connected whole 1511. †**4.** *spec.* To cause (the parts of a wound or fracture) to unite and so to heal –1788. Also *absol.* **5.** *intr.* (for *refl.*) To become solid or firm; to combine or unite solidly or compactly 1626.

2. To c. an empire THIRLWALL, the social order MORLEY. **3.** To c. two Churches PRIDEAUX, the Scottish Acts 1864, the customs duties MCCULLOCH. **5.** Hurts and ulcers of the head.. dryness maketh them more apt to c. BACON. Hence **Conso·lidative** *a.* serving to c. **Conso·lidator,** one who or that which consolidates.

Consolidated (kǫ̆nsǫ·lideⁱtěd), *ppl. a.* 1753. [f. prec. vb. + -ED¹.] Made solid, firm, or compact; combined, unified: said *esp.* of sources of revenue, funds, debts, etc.

C. Annuities: the Government securities of Great Britain, which were consolidated in 1751 (25 George II, c. 27) into a single stock bearing interest at 3 per cent. (Now reduced to 2½.) See also CONSOL(S. *C. Fund*: the united product of various branches of the revenue of Great Britain and Ireland, whence the interest of the national debt, the grants to the Royal Family, the Civil List, etc., are paid.

Consolidation (kǫ̆nsǫ:lidēⁱ·ʃən). ME. [– late L. *consolidatio*, f. *consolidat-*; see CONSOLIDATE *v.*, -ION. Cf. (O)Fr. *consolidation*.] **1.** The action of consolidating; solidification 1603. Also *fig.* **2.** Combination into a compact mass, single body, or coherent whole; combination, unification ME. **3.** *Bot.* = ADNATION 1851.

1. Formed..by the c. of fibrin CARPENTER. *fig.* The c. of our Union 1787. **2.** The first germs of social c. and growth MORLEY. The 'Companies' Clauses C. Act' 1846. The c. of the customs duties MCCULLOCH. *C. of actions*: the merging of two or more actions at law by a court or judge to save expense and delay. Hence **Consolida·tionist,** one who advocates c.

Consols, *sb. pl.*: see CONSOL.

‖**Consommé** (koṅsome). 1824. [Fr., subst. use of pa. pple. of *consommer* – L. *consummare* CONSUMMATE.] A strong broth or soup made from meat; now *esp.* clear soup.

Consonance (kǫ·nsŏnăns). ME. [– (O)Fr. *consonance* or L. *consonantia*; see CONSONANT, -ANCE.] **1.** = ASSONANCE 1. 1589. **2.** Pleasing combination of sounds 1594. **3.** *Mus.* The sounding together of two notes in harmony; the quality or fact of being CONSONANT. (Opp. to DISSONANCE.) 1694. **b.** A consonant 'interval', a concord 1624. **4.** *fig.* Agreement, harmony, concord ME.

2. Winds and Waters flow'd in C. THOMSON. **4.** The c. and agreement they have either with reputation or dignity 1592. Phr. *In c. with.* var. **Co·nsonancy** (in senses 1, 2, 4).

Consonant (kǫ·nsŏnănt), *a.* 1483. [– OFr. *consonant*, pres. pple. of *consoner* (mod. *conson(n)er*) – L. *consonare*; see next.] **1.** In agreement, accordance, or harmony; accordant (*to*); consistent (*with*) 1489. †**b.** *advb.* –1744. †**2.** Consistent –1744. **3.** Of sounds or music: Harmonious 1515; *Mus.* concordant, constituting a consonance 1609. **4.** Of words: Agreeing in sound 1645. †**5.** Of the nature of a consonant (*rare*) 1751.

1. With one c. heart and voice 1563. The opinion is c. to law COKE. C. with the doctrine of St. Paul 1857. **3.** An euphonius melody and consonent cadence K. WHITE. **4.** The four c. rhymes required in each [Spenserian] stanza PALGRAVE. Hence **Co·nsonantly** *adv.* Const. *to, with.*

Consonant (kǫ·nsŏnănt), *sb.* ME. [– OFr. *consonant* – *consonant-*, pres. ppl. stem of L. *consonare* (in *consonans littera* 'consonant letter') sound together; see CON-, SONANT.] **1.** An alphabetic or phonetic element other than a vowel; an elementary sound of speech which in the formation of a syllable is combined with a vowel. Applied both to sounds and letters.

Elementary sounds have been classed, according to the degree in which they may function as vowels, as (1) vowels, (2) semi-vowels (Eng. y and w), (3) liquids (l, lʸ, r), (4) nasals (m, n, nʸ, ŋ), (5) fricatives or spirants, *voice* (v, ð, z, ʒ, γ), and *breath* (f, þ, s, ʃ, χ), (6) mutes or stops, *voice* (b, d, g), and *breath* (p̀, t, k). Only class 6 have the consonantal function exclusively, *p, t, k*, being the most typical consonants. Consonants may also be classed, according to the part of the mouth where they are formed, into labials (p, b, f, v, m, w), dentals, palatals, gutturals, and other minor groups.

†**2.** *Mus.* = CONSONANCE 3 b. –1712. Also *attrib.* Hence **Consona·ntal** *a.* of the nature of a c.; characterized by consonants; var. **Consona·ntic** (*rare*). **Co·nsonanti:sm,** use of consonants; a consonant formation. **Co·nsonantize** *v.* to turn (a vowel) into a c. (e.g. *u* into *w*).

Co·nsonate, *v.* *rare.* 1882. [– *consonat-*, pa. ppl. stem of L. *consonare*, f. *com* CON- + *sonare* sound.] *intr.* To sound in sympathy.

Consonous (kǫ·nsŏnəs), *a. rare.* 1654. [f. L. *consonus* harmonious (f. *com* CON- + *sonus* sounding) + -OUS.] **1.** Harmonious. †**2.** = CONSONANT *a.* 1. 1660.

†**Co·nsopite,** *v.* (erron. in Dicts. **consopiate.**) 1647. [– *consopit-*, pa. ppl. stem of L. *consopire*, f. *com* CON- + *sopire* lull to sleep.] *trans.* To lay or lull to sleep; to compose; to stupefy. (Usu. *fig.*) –1685. So †**Co·nsopite** *ppl. a.* laid to sleep. †**Consopi·tion** (erron. *consopiation*), a laying or lulling to sleep.

Consort (kǫ·nsǭɹt), *sb.*¹ ME. [– Fr. *consort*, fem. *-sorte* – L. *consors, -sort-* sharing in common, partner, colleague, f. *com* CON- + *sors* portion, lot. Orig. stressed conso·rt.] †**1.** A partner, companion; a colleague –1755. Also *fig.* **2.** A ship sailing in company with another 1602. **3.** A husband or wife, a spouse 1634. Also, of animals 1796.

1. To seeke good consorts and companions GREENE. **2.** Our c., the Rescue KANE. **3.** The Queen, whether regnant or c. 1845. *Prince-c.*: the title of Prince Albert, husband of Queen Victoria.

†**Consort** (kǫ·nsǭɹt), *sb.*² 1584. [Partly deriv. of CONSORT *v.*, suggested by L. *consortium* partnership; partly (sense 3) early form of CONCERT *sb.*]

I. 1. A fellowship, partnership, company –1702. **2.** Accord; agreement –1793.

1. Wilt thou be of our c.? Say I, and be the captaine of vs all *Two Gent.* IV. i. 64. Five or six boates in a c. 1591. Experiments in C. BACON. **2.** To act in c. with me 1793.

II. CONCERT of music. **1.** The accord of instruments or voices –1711. Also *fig.* **2.** A company of musicians making music together –1704. **3.** = CONCERT *sb.* 4. –1774. Also *attrib.*

1. Visit by night your Ladies chamber-window With some sweet C. *Two Gent.* III. ii. 84. **2.** Lord place me in thy c.; give one strain To my poore reed G. HERBERT.

Consort (kǫ̆nsǭ·ɹt), *v.* 1588. [In senses 1–2 f. CONSORT *sb.*¹; in senses 3–7 prob. a reinforcement of SORT *v.* (II 4b).] †**1.** *trans.* To accompany; to escort, attend –1622. †**2.** To be a consort to –1618. **3.** To sort together. Const. *with.* 1588. †**4.** *refl.* To associate *oneself* (*with*) –1692. **5.** *intr.* To associate 1588. **6.** To accord. Const. *to, with.* 1599. †**7.** To play, sing, or sound together –1734.

1. Sweet health..c. your grace *L.L.L.* II. i. 178. **3.** C. me quickly with the dead 1596. **4.** When he begins to c. himself with men, and thinks himself one LOCKE. **5.** Men c. in camp and town EMERSON. To c. with Lutherans MACAULAY. **6.** It did not c. with his idea MILL.

Hence †**Conso·rtable** *a.* capable of consorting together or of being consorted. **Conso·rter.** So †**Conso·rtion,** intercourse; alliance. †**Conso·rtment,** association as partners.

Consortism (kǫ·nsǭɹtiz'm). 1880. [f. CONSORT *sb.*¹ + -ISM.] *Biol.* The association during life of two organisms, each of which is dependent on the other for its existence or well-being. Cf. SYMBIOSIS.

‖**Consortium** (kǫ̆nsǭ·ɹʃiǒm). 1881. [L. *consortium* partnership, f. *consors* CONSORT *sb.*¹] Partnership, association. So **Conso·rtial** *a.* pertaining to a c.

Consortship (kǫ·nsǭɹtˌʃip). Now *rare.* 1592. [f. CONSORT *sb.*¹ + -SHIP.] The state or position of a consort; association, partnership.

†**Consoude,** now **Consound** (kǫ̆nsau·nd), *sb.* OE. [– (O)Fr. *consoude* – late L. *consolida* (whence late OE. *consolde*) comfrey, black bryony, f. L. *consolidare* (see CONSOLIDATE *v.* 4). The form *consound* was assim. by

pop. etym. to SOUND *a.*] *Herb.* A herb to which healing virtues were attributed; probably the comfrey (*Symphytum officinale*) –1807. So † **Consoude, consou·nd** *v.* = CONSOLIDATE *v.* 4.

Consound; see CONSOUDE.

Conspe·cies. 1837. [See CON-.] In *pl.* Fellow species of a genus. Hence **Conspeci·fic** *a.* specifically identical.

† **Conspe·ction.** *rare.* 1611. [– OFr. *conspection* or late L. *conspectio*, f. *conspect-*, pa. ppl. stem of *conspicere* behold.] The action of beholding –1654.

† **Conspectu·ity.** [app. joc. f. L. *conspectus.*] Faculty of sight, vision. *Cor.* II. i. 70.

‖ **Conspectus** (kǫnspe·ktǒs). 1836. [L., f. *conspect-*, pa. ppl. stem of *conspicere* look at attentively, f. *com* CON- + *specere* look (at).] **1.** A comprehensive survey. **2.** More usually *concr.* A synopsis, digest 1838.

1. To get at a c. of the general current of affairs rather than to study minutely a single period 1879.

Consperse (kǫnspə̄·ɹs), *a.* [– L. *conspersus*, pa. pple. of *conspergere* besprinkle.] Sprinkled; *spec.* in *Entom.* thickly strewn with minute punctures or dots. So † **Conspe·rsion,** the action of sprinkling; *concr.* dough, paste. [Cf. Vulg. I Cor. 5: 7.]

Conspicuity (kǫnspikiū·Iti). Now *rare.* 1601. [f. late L. *conspicuitas* distinction, eminence; see next, -ITY.] = CONSPICUOUSNESS.

Conspicuous (kǫnspi·kiu,əs), *a.* 1545. [f. L. *conspicuus* (f. *conspicere* look at attentively) + -OUS.] **1.** Clearly visible, obvious or striking to the eye. **2.** Obvious to the mental eye, plainly evident; striking; hence, eminent, remarkable, noteworthy 1613.

1. A Rock Of Alablaster, pil'd up to the Clouds, C. farr MILT. *P.L.* IV. 545. **2.** Frankfurt—a city c. for its loyalty to the imperial house S. AUSTIN. Phr. *C. by its absence.* (Cf. Tacitus *Ann.* iii. 76.) Hence **Conspi·cuous-ly** *adv.*, **-ness.**

Conspiracy (kǫnspi·răsi). ME. [– AFr. *conspiracie*, alt. (cf. CONSERVANCY) of (O)Fr. *conspiration* – L. *conspiratio*, f. *conspirat-*, pa. ppl. stem of *conspirare*; see CONSPIRE, -ION.] **1.** The action of conspiring. **2.** (with *a* and *pl.*) A combination of persons for an evil or unlawful purpose; an agreement between two or more to do something criminal, illegal, or reprehensible; a plot ME.; † a body of conspirators –1600. **3.** *fig.* Union or combination for one end or purpose (*arch.*) 1538.

1. Combin'd In bold c. against Heav'ns King MILT. *P.L.* II. 751. **2.** In all conspiracies there must be great secrecy CLARENDON. **3.** So is the c. of her several graces, held best together to make one perfect figure of beauty SIDNEY.

Conspirant (kǫnspəiə·rănt). *rare.* 1603. [– Fr. *conspirant*, pr. pple. of *conspirer* CONSPIRE; see -ANT.] *adj.* Conspiring. *sb.* A conspirator.

Conspiration (kǫnspirē̆i·ʃən). *Obs.* exc. *fig.* ME. [– (O)Fr. *conspiration*; see CONSPIRACY.] = CONSPIRACY.

Conspirator (kǫnspi·rătəɹ). [ME. – AFr. *conspiratour* = (O)Fr. *-eur* – L. *conspirator*; see CONSPIRE, OR- 2.] One engaged in a conspiracy; one who conspires with others to commit treason. Hence **Conspi:rato·rial** *a.* pertaining to or characteristic of conspirators or conspiracy. **Conspi·ratress,** † **-trice,** a female c.

Conspire (kǫnspəiə·ɹ), *v.* ME. [– (O)Fr. *conspirer* – L. *conspirare* agree, combine, f. *com* CON- + *spirare* breathe.] **1.** *intr.* To combine privily to do something criminal, illegal, or reprehensible (*esp.* to commit treason or murder, excite sedition, etc.); to plot. **2.** *trans.* To plot, devise, contrive ME. **3.** *intr.* To combine in action or aim; to concur, co-operate as by intention 1538. †**4.** To agree –1737. † **5.** *trans.* To unite in producing –1669.

1. They conspired against him, to slay him *Gen.* 37:18. **2.** The Countree waxed wery of hym, & conspyrid his deth FABYAN. **3.** Therefore must your labour c. with my inventions 1657. Hence **Conspi·rer, Conspi·ringly** *adv.*

† **Conspissate,** *v.* 1647. [Back-formation from contemp. *conspissation*; cf. L. *conspissatus*, pa. pple. f. *com* CON- + *spissatus* thickened. See -ATE³, -ATION.] *trans.* To thicken, condense –1681. Hence † **Conspissa·tion.**

† **Conspurcate,** *v.* 1600. [– *conspurcat-*, pa. ppl. stem of L. *conspurcare*, f. *com* CON- + *spurcare*, f. *spurcus* unclean.] *trans.* To defile, pollute (*lit.* and *fig.*) –1669. Hence † **Conspurca·tion.**

Constable (kɒ·nstăb'l, kǫ·n-). [ME. – OFr. *cunestable, conestable* (mod. *connétable*), repr. late L. *comes stabuli* (V) lit. COUNT (i.e. head officer) of the STABLE. Cf. the sense-development of *marshal.*] **1.** *gen.* The chief officer of the household, court, administration, or military forces of a ruler. **2.** The governor or warden of a royal fortress or castle. (Still in Eng. use.) ME. **3.** A military officer ME. **4.** An officer of the peace 1597.

1. *C. of France*: the principal officer of the household of the early French kings, who ultimately rose to be commander-in-chief of the army in the absence of the monarch. He was the supreme judge of questions of chivalry. (Abolished in 1627.) *C. of England, Lord High C.*: one of the chief functionaries in the English royal household, with duties and powers similar to those of the same officer in France. The office was forfeited in 1521; since which time the title has been granted only for particular occasions, *esp.* the sovereign's coronation. **4.** *High C.*: an officer of a hundred or other like district, appointed to act as conservator of the peace within his district, and to perform various other duties. (Abolished in 1869.) *Petty* or *Parish C.*: a conservator of the peace, etc., within a parish or township. (Now incorporated in the County Police system.) *Chief C.*: the officer at the head of the police force of a county or equivalent district. *Special C.*: a person sworn in to act as c. on special occasions.

Phr. *To outrun the c.*: to go at too great a pace, to go too far; to spend more money than one has; to get into debt; also *to overrun the c.*

Hence † **Constablery,** the office of, or district under, a c. **Co·nstableship,** the office of c. **Co·nstablewick,** † the office of a c. (in the earlier sense); the district of a (petty) c. So **Co·nstabless,** a female c.; the wife of a c.; also a foreign title.

Constabulary (kǫnstæ·biŭlări), *sb.* 1587. [– med.L. *con(e)stabularia* (sc. *dignitas*), subst. use of fem. of *con(e)stabularius*; see next.] † **1.** Constableship –1747. **2.** A constablewick 1631. **3.** The organized body of constables of a country or specified district 1837.

Constabulary (kǫnstæ·biŭlări), *a.* 1824. [– med.L. *con(e)stabularius*, f. *con(e)stabulus* CONSTABLE; see -ARY¹.] **1.** Of or pertaining to petty constables or to police officers. **2.** Of the nature or function of constables 1856. var. **Consta·bulatory.**

Constancy (kǫ·nstănsi). 1526. [– L. *constantia*; see next, -ANCY.] **1.** The state or quality of being unmoved in mind; steadfastness, firmness, fortitude. **2.** Steadfastness of attachment to a person or cause; fidelity 1548. **3.** The quality of being invariable; uniformity, unchangingness, regularity 1600. **4.** (with *a*) A permanency 1710. † **5.** = CONSISTENCE 1794.

1. C... wherby man or woman holdeth hole, and is not broken by impacyency 1526. **2.** A fellow of plaine and vncoyned Constancie *Hen. V*, v. ii. 161. **3.** The polar wind blows with equal c. in both the frigid zones 1794. var. † **Constance** (in senses 1, 2).

Constant (kǫ·nstănt), *a.* (*sb.*) ME. [– (O)Fr. *constant* – *constant-*, pr. ppl. stem of L. *constare* stand firm, f. *com* CON- + *stare* stand.]

A. *adj.* **1.** Standing firm in mind; steadfast, resolute. **2.** Steadfast in attachment to a cause or person; faithful, true (*to*) ME. † **3.** Certain –1667. **4.** Of things: Invariable, fixed, unchanging, uniform 1549. **5.** *Math.* and *Physics.* Remaining the same in quantity or amount under uniform conditions. Opp. to *variable.* 1753. **6.** Of actions, conditions, etc.: Continuing without intermission; continually recurring 1653; also *transf.* of a person 1639. † **7.** Steady (physically) –1741. † **8.** Consistent 1580.

1. The c. suffrings of ancient martyrs BP. HALL. **2.** To one thing c. neuer *Much Ado* II. iii. 67. Tho' fortune change, his c. spouse remains POPE. **3.** † *It is c.* = L. *constat.* **4.** Time keeps his c. pace FELTHAM. † *C. age*: see CONSISTENT. **6.** By c. vigils worn SHENSTONE. A c. reader of St. Paul's Epistles MILT. **7.** *Temp.* II. ii. 119.

B. *sb. Math.* and *Physics.* A quantity which does not vary throughout an investigation: opp. to *variable.* Also *fig.* 1832.

The proportion between the circumference and diameter of a circle is a determinate c. 1837.

Hence **Co·nstant-ly** *adv.*, **-ness.**

Constantinian (kǫnstănti·niăn), *a.* 1641. [See -IAN.] Of or belonging to the Roman Emperor Constantine the Great, or his period (A.D. 306–337).

Constantinopolitan (kǫnstæ:ntino,pǫ·li-tăn), *a.* 1568. [– late L. *Constantinopolitanus.*] Of or pertaining to Constantinople (Gr. Κωνσταντίνου πόλις), or to the Eastern Empire or Church; Byzantine.

‖ **Constat** (kǫ·nstæt). 1570. [L., = 'it is certain'; see CONSTANT.] † **1.** *Law.* A certificate stating what appears (*constat*) upon record in the Court of Exchequer touching any matter. Also an exemplification of the enrolment of letters patent under the Great Seal. –1670. † **2.** *fig.* Certifying evidence –1661.

Constate (kǫnstē̆i·t), *v. rare.* 1773. [– Fr. *constater* (XVIII), f. *constat* (see prec.).] To establish, ascertain, state.

Constellate (kǫ·nstĕlĕt, kǫnste·lĕt), *ppl. a.* 1649. [– late L. *constellatus*, f. *com* CON- + *stella* star; see -ATE².] = Constellated (see CONSTELLATE *v.* 2).

Constellate (kǫ·nstĕleⁱt, kǫnste·leⁱt), *v.* 1621. [f. as prec. + -ATE³; infl. by CONSTELLATION.] † **1.** *trans. Astrol.* **a.** To fashion under a particular constellation. **b.** To cast the horoscope of. **c.** *pass.* To be predestined (*to*) by one's 'stars'. –1829. **2.** To form into, or set in, a constellation. Often *transf.* 1643. **3.** To stud 1691. **4.** *intr.* To cluster together, as stars in a constellation 1647.

2. To them that know how to C. those lights BOYLE. **4.** Flowers, that c. on earth E. B. BROWNING.

Constellation (kǫnstĕlē̆i·ʃən). ME. [– (O)Fr. *constellation* – late L. *constellatio*, f. *com* CON- + *stella* star; see -ATION.] † **1.** *Astrol.* The position of 'stars' (*i.e.* planets) in regard to one another; *esp.* their position at the time of a man's birth; disposition as influenced by one's 'stars' –1863. **2.** A number of fixed stars grouped together within the outline of an imaginary figure traced on the face of the sky 1551. Also *transf.* and *fig.*

1. Some men holde opinion That it is constellacion Which causeth al that a man dothe GOWER. **2.** The c. which the Greeks called the Argo, was a representation of the sacred ship of Osiris 1794. A c. of fair ladies BOYLE.

Constellatory (kǫnste·lătəri), *a. rare.* 1652. [f. CONSTELLATION + -ORY².] † **1.** Pertaining to constellations (sense 1) –1801. **2.** Relating to, or of the nature of, a group of 'stars' 1823.

Consternate (kǫ·nstəɹneⁱt), *v.* 1651. [– L. *consternat-*; see next and -ATE³.] To fill with amazement and terror.

Consternation (kǫnstəɹnē̆i·ʃən). 1611. [– Fr. *consternation* or L. *consternatio*, f. *consternat-*, pa. ppl. stem of *consternare* lay prostrate, terrify, f. *com* CON- + *sternere* lay low; see -ATION.] Amazement and terror such as to prostrate one's faculties; dismay.

It is a question of c., a question that should strike him that should answer it dumb DONNE.

† **Co·nstipate.** *ppl. a.* 1542. [– L. *constipatus*, pa. pple. of *constipare*; see next, -ATE².] = Constipated –1733.

Constipate (kǫ·nstipeⁱt), *v.* 1533. [– *constipat-*, pa. ppl. stem of L. *constipare*, f. *com* CON- + *stipare* press, cram; see -ATE³.] † **1.** *trans.* To crowd, pack, or press closely together; to condense, thicken (liquids) –1709. † **2.** *Med.* To bind together (the tissues); to close (the pores or vessels) –1763. **3.** *spec.* To confine the bowels; to render costive 1533.

1. Vapours.. constipated and condensed into clouds 1709.

Constipation (kǫnstipē̆i·ʃən). ME. [– (O)Fr. *constipation* or late L. *constipatio* crowding together (in med.L. costiveness), f. as prec.; see -ION.] † **1.** The action of pressing closely together; the state of being so compressed; condensation –1713. † **2.** *Med.* Contraction or constriction of organic tissues, the veins, etc. –1660. **3.** *spec.* A state of the bowels in which the evacuations are obstructed or stopped; costiveness 1549.

1. A pretty close C. and mutual Contact of its Particles BENTLEY.

Constituency (kǫ̆nsti·tiu,ĕnsi). 1831. [f. CONSTITUENT *sb.*; see -ENCY.] A body of constituents, the body of voters who elect a representative member of a public body; in looser use, the whole body of residents in a place so represented, the place itself. Also *transf.* = CLIENTELE 3.

Constituent (kǫ̆nsti·tiu,ĕnt). 1622. [– (partly through Fr. *constituant*) L. *constituent-*, pres. ppl. stem of *constituere*; see next, -ENT.]

A. *adj.* † **1.** That constitutes a thing what it is –1863. **2.** That jointly constitute or compose; component 1660. **3.** That constitutes, appoints, or elects a representative 1769. **4.** Having the power to frame or alter a (political) constitution, as in *c. assembly, power* 1801.

2. The c. parts of water PALEY. 3. A question of right arises between the c. and the representative body 'JUNIUS'. Hence **Consti·tuently** *adv.* as regards c. parts.

B. *sb.* **1.** One who constitutes another his agent or representative 1622. **2.** *spec.* One of those who elect another as their representative; an elector; loosely, any inhabitant of the place so represented 1714; † = CONSTITUENCY –1797. † **3.** One who constitutes or frames 1677. **4.** A constituent element or part 1756.

1. The factor is answerable personally to his c. DALLAS. 2. Twenty-four Members whose constituents are upwards of 200,000 in number BRIGHT. 4. What is the special and necessary c. of royalty MAURICE.

Constitute (kǫ·nstitiūt), *v.* 1477. [– *constitut-*, pa. ppl. stem of L. *constituere* establish, appoint, f. *com* CON- + *statuere* set up.] † **1.** *trans.* To set, place –1728. **2.** To set up, ordain, appoint 1477. **3.** To set up 1549; to give legal form to 1638. **4.** To frame, form; to make up, compose 1646. **5.** To set up as 1534. **6.** (with simple *obj.*) To make (a thing) what it is 1848.

2. Where one Man..is constituted Representative of the whole number HOBBES. Laws..constituted by lawful authority JER. TAYLOR. 3. To c. a tribunal MACAULAY, the House 1714. 4. Many.. whose Livers are weakely constituted SIR T. BROWNE. The things which c. wealth HT. MARTINEAU. 5. He had constituted himself her companion W. BLACK. Hence **Co·nstituter, -or,** one who or that which constitutes.

† **Co·nstitute,** *ppl. a.* (*sb.*) 1483. [– L. *constitutus*, pa. pple. of *constituere*; see prec.] **1.** Constituted; see the verb –1808. **2.** *sb.* An ordinance –1610.

Constitution (kǫnstitiū·ʃən). ME. [–(O)Fr. *constitution* or L. *constitutio*, f. as CONSTITUTE *v.*; see -ION.] **1.** The action of constituting; see the verb 1582. † **2.** The action of decreeing or ordaining –1661. **3.** A decree, ordinance, law, regulation; *spec.* in *Rom. Law*, an enactment made by the emperor. Also *fig.* (Now *Hist.*) ME. **4.** The way in which anything is constituted or made up; make, frame, composition 1601. **5.** *spec.* **a.** Physical nature or character of the body in regard to healthiness, strength, vitality, etc. 1553. **b.** Nature, character, or condition of mind; disposition, temperament 1589. **6.** The mode in which a state is constituted or organized 1610. **7.** The system or body of fundamental principles according to which a nation, state, or body politic is constituted and governed 1735. Also *attrib.*

1. Before c. of Soveraign Power all men had right to all things HOBBES. 3. *Apostolical Constitutions* (in *Eccl. Hist.*): a collection of ecclesiastical regulations, ascribed to the apostles, but known to be of much later date. The Constitutions of Clarendon..forbad the ordination of villains FREEMAN. 4. C. of Nature BUTLER, of society HT. MARTINEAU, the world EMERSON, the solar spectrum BREWSTER. 5. a. His c. was far from robust PRESCOTT. b. His failings..flowed from his c., not his will 1741. 6. The original c. of England was highly aristocratical HALLAM. 7. The Twelve eldest are sent solemnly to fetch the C. itself, the printed Book of the Law CARLYLE. By the English c. we understand a few great traditional principles of government, any fundamental breach of which would involve either tyranny or anarchy 1864. Hence **Constitu·tioned** *a.* having (such and such) a c.

Constitutional (kǫnstitiū·ʃənăl), *a.* (*sb.*) 1682. [f. prec. + -AL[1]; cf. Fr. *constitutionnel* (1785).]

A. *adj.* **1.** Of, belonging to, or inherent in a person's constitution. **2.** Beneficial to the (bodily) constitution 1750. **3.** Forming an essential part or element; essential 1750. **4.** In harmony with, authorized by, or supporting, the political constitution 1765. Of a sovereign: Ruling according to a constitution 1801. **5.** Of, pertaining to, or dealing with the political constitution 1841.

1. Pope's c. irritability STEPHEN. 2. C. walks 1860. 3. The difference..between things..c. and arbitrary WARBURTON. 4. A c. proceeding 1846. A c. king 1801, government 1841. 5. C. History of England STUBBS (*title*).

B. *sb.* **1.** A walk taken for the benefit of one's health (*colloq.*) 1829. **2.** = CONSTITUTIONALIST 2. 1793.

1. He taketh a c. of forty minutes every day 1836. Hence **Constitu·tionalize** *v.* to make c.; to take a c.

Constitutionalism (kǫnstitiū·ʃənăliz'm). 1832. [f. prec. + -ISM.] **1.** A constitutional system of government. **2.** Adherence to constitutional principles 1871.

Constitu·tionalist. 1766. [f. as prec. + -IST.] **1.** One who studies or writes on the (political) constitution. **2.** An adherent of constitutional principles, or of a particular constitution. In England, about 1870–80, = CONSERVATIVE. 1793. var. **Constitu·tionist** (*rare*).

Constitutionality (kǫnstitiū:ʃənæ·lĭti). 1801. [f. as prec. + -ITY.] The quality of being in accordance with the constitution; constitutional character.

The c. of the execution by electricity 1890.

Constitutionally (kǫnstitiū·ʃənăli), *adv.* 1742. [f. CONSTITUTIONAL + -LY[2].] **1.** In constitution or composition 1767. **2.** As to the (bodily) constitution 1796. **3.** By virtue of one's constitution; naturally 1742. **4.** In accordance with the (political) constitution 1756.

3. All you English are c. sullen FOOTE. 4. His wish seems to have been to govern c. MACAULAY.

Constitutive (kǫ·nstitiūtiv), *a.* 1592. [– late and med.L. *constitutivus* confirmatory, defining, constitutive, constructive, f. as CONSTITUTE *v.*; see -IVE.] **1.** Having the power of constituting; constructive. **2.** That makes a thing what it is; essential 1610. **3.** That goes to make up; constituent, component 1640. **4.** With *of*: That constitutes 1658.

1. These ideas, if not c. principles to extend our knowledge beyond the bounds of experience, are regulative principles to arrange experience J. H. STIRLING. 2. The c. essences of all individual created beings CUDWORTH. 3. The c. parts of the drama are six J. HARRIS. Hence **Co·nstitutive-ly** *adv.*, **-ness.**

Constrain (kǫ̆nstrēⁱ·n), *v.* ME. [– OFr. *constraindre*, pres. stem *constraign-* (mod. *contraindre*) :– L. *constringere* bind tightly together; see STRAIN *v.*[1]] **1.** *trans.* To force, compel, oblige; also *absol.* In *Dynamics*, to restrict the motion of (a body or particle) to a certain course 1834. † **2.** To force out: 'to produce in opposition to nature' (J.) –1725 † **3.** To take by force; to violate –1699. † **4.** To straiten; to oppress, afflict –1859. † **5.** To compress into small compass; to contract (*rare*) ME. **6.** To confine forcibly, keep in bonds, imprison ME. Also *fig.* † **7.** = CONSTRINGE, CONSTRICT –1697.

1. Constreynyd to lerne the Latyn tong 1538. String constrained by pulley 1856. To c. assent WATTS. 2. To c. a smile POPE. 3. *Tit. A.* v. ii. 178. 6. How the strait stays the slender waste c. GAY (J.). 7. When Winter Frosts c. the Field with Cold DRYDEN. Hence **Constrai·nable** *a.* (*rare*). **Constrai·ned** *ppl. a.* forced; not natural; embarrassed; cramped. **Constrai·ned-ly** *adv.*, **-ness. Constrai·ner** (*rare*). **Constrai·ningly** *adv.*

† **Constrai·nt,** *ppl. a.* ME. [– OFr. *constreint, -aint*, pa. pple. of *constraindre*; see prec.] = Constrained.

Constraint (kǫ̆nstrē·nt), *sb.* [ME. *constreint(e)* – OFr. *constreinte*, subst. use of fem. of pa. pple. of *constraindre*; see prec.] **1.** Coercion, compulsion 1534. **2.** Confinement; restriction of liberty 1590. † **3.** Oppression, affliction –1579. **4.** Compulsion put upon the expression of feelings or the behaviour: always implying unnaturalness or embarrassment 1706. **5.** *Dynamics.* See CONSTRAIN *v.* 1. 1856.

1. Not from c. but choice W. ROBERTSON. 2. Let the captain talk of boisterous war; The prisoner of immured dark c. 1596. 4. You see I write to you without any sort of c. or method, as things come into my head 1706. Hence † **Constrai·ntive** *a.* having tendency to constrain (*rare*).

Constrict (kǫ̆nstri·kt), *v.* 1732. [f. as next.] **1.** *trans.* To draw together as by tightening an encircling string; to make small or narrow (an orifice, etc.); to contract, compress 1759. **2.** To cause to contract or shrink 1732.

1. The neck should not be constricted by a tight collar 1871. 2. Such things as c. the Fibres ARBUTHNOT. Hence **Constri·cted** *ppl. a.* drawn together by constriction; *Nat. Hist.* narrowed at some part, as if by constriction. **Constri·ctive** *a.* that tend to c.

Constriction (kǫnstri·kʃən). ME. [– late L. *constrictio*, f. *constrict-*, pa. ppl. stem of *constringere* bind together, f. *com* CON- + *stringere* draw tight; see -ION.] **1.** Drawing together as by an encircling pressure; the condition of being so drawn together; compression, contraction. **2.** *concr.* A constricted part 1826. **3.** Something which constricts 1650.

1. The c. of the pores..of the body VENNER. 2. A c. of the vast channel narrows it to a mile PARKMAN.

Constrictor (kǫ̆nstri·ktəɹ). 1735. [mod.L., f. as prec.; see -OR 2.] **1.** *Anat.* A muscle which draws together a part. **2.** *Surg.* An instrument for producing constriction; a compressor 1882. **3.** A large snake which crushes its prey; a BOA-CONSTRICTOR

Constringe (kǫ̆nstri·ndʒ), *v.* 1604. [– L. *constringere*; see CONSTRICT.] **1.** *trans.* = CONSTRICT 1. ? *Obs.* 1606. **2.** *Phys.* = CONSTRICT 2. 1604. **3.** *intr.* To become close or dense. BROWNING.

1. The neck [of the Bladder] is constringed with a muscle BURTON. 2. Constringing such [parts] as are dilated 1785.

Constringent (kǫ̆nstri·ndʒĕnt). 1603. [– *constringent-*, pres. ppl. stem of L. *constringere*; see CONSTRICT, -ENT.] Causing constriction. Hence **Constri·ngency,** c. quality.

Construable (kǫ̆nstrū·ăb'l), *a.* 1657. [f. CONSTRUE *v.* + -ABLE.] That may be construed.

Construct (kǫ̆nstrɒ·kt), *ppl. a. arch.* ME. [– L. *constructus*, pa. pple. of *construere*; see next.] **1.** *pa. pple.* Constructed. **2.** *adj.* in *C. state, state c.*, in *Heb. Gram.*: the form of the substantive used when standing before another having an attributive (or genitive) relation to it.

Construct (kǫ̆nstrɒ·kt), *v.* 1610. [– *construct-*, pa. ppl. stem of L. *construere*, f. *com* CON- + *struere* lay, pile, build.] **1.** *trans.* To make or form by fitting the parts together; to frame, build, erect 1663. Also *absol.* **2.** *Gram.* To combine in grammatical construction. (Used chiefly of the manner.) 1864. † **3.** To CONSTRUE 4. *Sc.* –1676.

1. To c. a ship 1794, road 1863, system JOHNSON. Hence **Constru·cted** *ppl. a.* (Usu. qualified, as *well-c.*) **Constru·cter, -or,** one who constructs or designs the construction of (*esp.* of ships for the navy).

Construction (kǫ̆nstrɒ·kʃən). ME. [– (O)Fr. *construction* – L. *constructio* (in gram. sense in Priscian, tr. Gr. σύνταξις SYNTAX), f. as prec.; see -ION.]

I. 1. The action of framing, devising, or forming, by the putting together of parts; erection, building; the art or science of constructing. **2.** The manner in which a thing is constructed or formed; structure 1707; constructive faculty 1826. **3.** A thing constructed 1796.

1. [The] Director of Naval C. 1891. *Arch of c.*: an arch built in the body of a wall or other structure to relieve the part below it. *C. of equations*: the method of reducing a known equation into lines and figures, whereby its truth may be demonstrated geometrically. 2. The bad c. of the hospitals 1799.

II. 1. *Gram.* The action of syntactically arranging words in a sentence: syntactical connection 1530; in *Heb. Gram.*, the relation of a sb. in the construct state 1762. † **2.** The action of construing; translation –1643. **3.** The construing, explaining, or interpreting of a text, statement, action, words, etc.; sense 1483.

1. That stands in c. with all tenses 1640. 3. C. of the tenor of a letter WELLINGTON.
Comb. c.-way, -railway, a temporary railway for use in the c. of a permanent railway, canal, or the like.
Hence **Constru·ctional** *a.* of or pertaining to c. **Constru·ctionally** *adv.*

Constru·ctionism. 1924. [f. prec. + -ISM.] Artistic expression by means of mechanical structures.

Constructionist (kǫ̆nstrʋ·kʃənist). 1844. [f. as prec. + -IST.] **1.** One who practises or advocates construction. **2.** With *strict, loose,* etc.: One who puts a strict, loose, or other construction upon a law, etc. (Used chiefly in reference to the Constitution of the United States.) **3.** One who follows the principles of constructionism 1924.

Constructive (kǫ̆nstrʋ·ktiv), *a.* 1680. [– late L. *constructivus*, f. as CONSTRUCT *v.*; see -IVE; in later use f. the verb.] **1.** Having the quality of constructing 1841. **2.** Of or pertaining to construction 1817. **3.** Resulting from a certain interpretation; not directly expressed, but inferred 1680.
1. A clear-headed c. theologian J. H. NEWMAN. 2. C. and Engineering Staff 1889. Design should be based upon c. exigencies 1874. 3. Phr. *C. blasphemy, notice, possession, treason, trust,* etc. *C. total loss* (in Marine Insurance): the assumption of the loss of a ship or cargo as total under certain circumstances, as when arrival or recovery seems highly improbable, etc.
Hence **Constru·ctive-ly** *adv.*, **-ness.**

Constru·ctivism. 1924. [f. prec. + -ISM.] = CONSTRUCTIONISM. Hence **Constru·ctivist** *a.*

† **Constru·cture.** 1620. [– OFr. *constructure* or late L. *constructura*; see CONSTRUCT *v.*, -URE.] Construction –1840.

Construe (kǫ·nstru, kǫ̆nstrū·), *v.* ME. [– L. *construere* (gram. use late L. in Priscian).] †**1.** *trans.* To CONSTRUCT –1605. **2.** *Gram.* To combine (words, or parts of speech) grammatically 1530. **3.** *Gram.* To analyse the grammatical construction of a sentence, adding, if necessary, a word for word translation; hence loosely, to translate a passage orally ME. Also *intr.* (for *pass.*) **4.** *trans.* To give the sense or meaning of; to take in a specified way ME. **5.** *transf.* To interpret, put a construction on (actions, things, or persons) 1465. **6.** To deduce; to infer 1450. Also *absol.*
2. The verb *hearken* is construed with *to, unto* (mod.). 3. He cannot c. a Greek author MACAULAY. 4. One crabbed question more to c. or *vulgo* conster BROWNING. Authority is of very little use in construing an unskilfully drawn will 1885. 5. To c. silence as an affront 1833. Hence **Co·nstrue** *sb.* an act of construing; a verbal translation. **Construer. Construing** *vbl. sb.*

† **Co·nstuprate,** *v.* 1550. [– *constuprat-*, pa. ppl. stem of L. *constuprare*, f. *com* CON- + *stuprare* ravish, f. *stuprum* defilement. See -ATE³.] To violate, ravish. Hence † **Constupra·tion.**

Consubsi·st, *v.* [See CON-.] *intr.* To subsist together. TUCKER.

Consubstantial (kǫnsʋbstæ·nʃăl), *a.* 1483. [– eccl. L. *consubstantialis* (Tertullian), tr. Gr. ὁμοούσιος; see CON-, SUBSTANTIAL, and cf. HOMOOUSIAN.] Of one and the same substance or essence; the same in substance. Also as quasi-*sb.*
The sone. . is consubstancial, that is to saye, he is of one nature and substaunce with the father 1526. Hence **Consubsta·ntialism,** the doctrine of consubstantiation. **Consubsta·ntialist,** one who believes in the consubstantiality of the three Persons of the Godhead; one who holds the doctrine of consubstantiation. **Consubsta·ntially** *adv.*

Consubsta·ntia·lity. 1526. [– eccl. L. *consubstantialitas* (Cassiodorus), f. as prec.; see -ITY. Cf. (O)Fr. *consubstantialité*.] Identity of substance, *esp.* of the three Persons of the Trinity.
Our Lord's C. and Coeternity with the Father J. H. NEWMAN.

Consubstantiate (kǫnsʋbstæ·nʃi,ēᶦt), *v.* 1597. [Deduced from late L. *consubstantiatus ppl. a.*, tr. Gr. ὁμοούσιος (cf. med.L. *consubstantiare* XIII). See CONSUBSTANTIAL, -ATE³.] **1.** *trans.* To unite in one common substance. Also *intr.* † **2.** To believe in consubstantiation –1715.
1. It [Gold] is not easily consubstantiated with us 1651. 2. The consubstantiating Church and Priest Refuse communion to the Calvinist DRYDEN. So **Consubsta·ntiate** *ppl. a.* made one in substance.

Consubstantiation (kǫ:nsʋbstæ:nʃi,ēᶦ·ʃən). 1597. [– mod.L. *consubstantiatio*, a Reformation word, after *trans(s)ubstantiatio* TRANSUBSTANTIATION.] **1.** The doctrine of the real substantial presence of the body and blood of Christ together with the bread and wine in the Eucharist, as dist. from *transubstantiation*. (A term used controversially to designate the Lutheran view, but not accepted by Lutherans.) † **2.** A rendering consubstantial –1774. Hence **Consubstantia·tionist,** one who holds the doctrine of c.

† **Consue·te,** *a.* ME. [– L. *consuetus*, pa. pple. of *consuescere* accustom, use; see next.] Accustomed –1656.

Consuetude (kǫ·nswitiud). ME. [– OFr. *consuetude* or L. *consuetudo*, f. *consuetus*; see CONSUETE, -TUDE.] **1.** Custom, usage, habit. (Chiefly *Sc.*) **2.** Familiarity; social intercourse. [So in L.] 1803.
1. The lawis and consuetudes of the burgh 1575. Hence **Consuetu·dinal** *a.* and *sb.* = next.

Consuetudinary (kǫ̆nswitiū·dināri). 1494. [– med.L. *consuetudinarium*, subst. use of n. of late L. *consuetudinarius* adj.; see prec., -ARY¹.] *adj.* Customary 1590. *sb.* A manual of customs or usages, local or particular to some body. Cf. ORDINARY.

Consul (kǫ·nsǒl), *sb.* ME. [– L. *consul* 'nominatus qui consularet populum et senatum' (Varro), rel. to *consultare*; see CONSULT.] **1.** The title of the two annually elected magistrates who exercised conjointly supreme authority in the Roman Republic. **2.** Hence, a title for the three chief magistrates of the French Republic, from 1799 to 1804. **3.** Used by mediæval Latin writers as = *comes*, count, earl. *Obs.* exc. *Hist.* 1494. † **4.** A member of a council –1753. † **5.** English appellation of various foreign officials and magistrates, *e.g.* the *savii* of Venice –1757. **6.** Hence: An agent commissioned by a sovereign state to reside in a foreign town or port, to protect the interests of its subjects there, and to watch over its commercial rights and privileges. So *C.-general, Vice-C.* (The ordinary current sense.) 1599. Also *transf.*
2. The late discussion with the First Consul 1802. 3. The Sherife was deputy of the Consull or Earle COKE. 5. Many of the Consuls, rais'd and met, Are at the Dukes already *Oth.* I. ii. 43. The consuls of the district waited on her to offer her a guard 1787. Hence **Co·nsulage,** consular charge or dues. **Co·nsuless,** the wife of a c. **Co·nsulship,** the office, or term of office, of a c.

Consular (kǫ·nsiŭlăɹ), *a.* (*sb.*) ME. [– L. *consularis*, f. *consul*; see -AR¹.] **1.** Of, pertaining to, or of the nature of a consul 1533. var. **Co·nsulary.** **2.** *sb.* A man of consular rank.

Consulate (kǫ·nsiŭlět, -sǒlět). ME. [– L. *consulatus*, f. *consul*; see CONSUL, -ATE¹.] **1.** Consular government; the office, dignity, or position of the consuls. **2.** The consular government in France, and its period (1799–1804). **3.** The office or establishment of a consul 1702.

Consult (kǫ̆nsʋ·lt), *v.* 1540. [– (O)Fr. *consulter* – L. *consultare*, frequent. f. *consult-*, pa. ppl. stem of *consulere* take counsel.] **1.** *intr.* To take counsel together, deliberate, confer 1565. † **2.** *trans.* To confer about, deliberate upon, consider –1703. † **3.** To take counsel to bring about; to plan, devise, contrive –1658. **4.** To provide for by consultation; to have an eye to. [L. *consulere alicui*.] 1658. **5.** To ask advice of, seek counsel from; to have recourse to for instruction or professional advice 1635; *spec.* to refer to (a book or author) 1635.
1. Come Gentlemen, Let vs c. vpon to morrowes Businesse *Rich. III*, v. iii. 45. Phr. *C. with*: to take counsel *with* (a person, a book, etc.). 2. Many things were then consulted for the future CLARENDON. 3. Thou hast consulted shame to thy house *Hab.* 2:10. 4. Every man. . Consulted soberly his private good DRYDEN. 5. To c. a practitioner 1878, the writings of learned men BERKELEY. *fig.* To c. one's pillow: see PILLOW. Hence **Co:nsultee·**, a person consulted. **Consu·lter, -or,** one who consults.

Consult (kǫ̆nsʋ·lt, kǫ·nsʋlt), *sb. Obs.* exc. *Hist.* 1533. [– Fr. *consulte* = It., Sp., med.L. *consulta*, subst. use of fem. of L. *consultus*, pa. pple. of *consulere*; see prec. In sense 3 repr. L. *consultum*.] **1.** The action of consulting; consultation 1560. **2.** A meeting for consultation; in 17th c. often *spec.* a cabal 1634. **3.** *Rom. Hist.* A decree of the senate. [L. *senatus consultum*.] 1533.
1. Seen In close c. POPE. Their consults produced resolutions of violence CARTE. 2. At a c. of the Jesuits in London SCOTT.

‖ **Consulta** (konsu·ltă). 1768. [It. and Sp.; cf. prec.] A meeting of council (It., Sp., or Pg.); the minutes of such a meeting.

Consultant (kǫ̆nsʋ·ltănt). 1697. [prob. – Fr. *consultant*; see CONSULT *v.*, -ANT.] **1.** One who consults (an oracle). **2.** A consulting physician, engineer, etc. 1878.

Consultary, obs. f. CONSULTORY.

Consultation (kǫnsʋltēᶦ·ʃən). ME. [– (O)Fr. *consultation* or L. *consultatio*, f. *consultat-*, pa. ppl. stem of *consultare*; see CONSULT *v.*, -ION.] **1.** The action of consulting or taking counsel together; deliberation, conference 1548. **2.** A conference in which the parties, *e.g.* lawyers or medical practitioners, consult and deliberate 1425. **3.** The action of consulting (a book) 1751. **4.** *Law.* A writ by which a cause having been removed by prohibition out of the ecclesiastical court to another, is returned thither again 1548.
1. If bishops did often use. . the help of mutual c. HOOKER.

Consultative (kǫnsʋ·ltătiv), *a.* 1583. [f. CONSULT *v.* + -ATIVE.] Of or pertaining to consultation; deliberative, advisory.
To have a consultatiue. . voice onely 1583.

Consultatory (kǫ̆nsʋ·ltătəri), *a.* 1600. [– late L. *consultatorius*, f. *consultat-*; see CONSULTATION, -ORY².] Pertaining to or serving for consultation (*e.g.* of an oracle, etc.); consultative.

Consu·lting, *ppl. a.* 1796. [See -ING².] That consults or asks advice.
C. physician, engineer, etc.: one who makes a business of giving professional advice. [Fr. *médecin consultant*; from obs. sense of *consulter* to give (professional) counsel.]

† **Consu·ltive,** *a.* 1616. [– med.L. *consultivus* (XIV); see CONSULT *v.*, -IVE.] Having the function of counselling or consulting; consultative –1823; deliberate. JER. TAYLOR. Hence † **Consu·ltively** *adv.* (= L. *consulto*).

† **Consu·lto.** 1659. [– Sp., It. *consulta* CONSULTA; for the var. *-to*, cf. -ADO.] = CONSULTA –1670.

Consultory (kǫ̆nsʋ·ltəri), *a.* ? *Obs.* 1616. [f. CONSULT(ATION + -ORY².] Relating to consultation (*e.g.* of an oracle, etc.); advisory.

Consumable (kǫ̆nsiū·măb'l), *a.* 1641. [f. CONSUME *v.* + -ABLE.] Capable of being consumed by fire, etc.; suited for consumption as food, etc. As *sb. pl.* Articles of consumption 1802.

† **Consuma·tion.** 1551. [– OFr. *consumacion*, f. *consumer*; see next, -ATION.] **1.** Destruction –1632. **2.** The disease CONSUMPTION 1551.

Consume (kǫ̆nsiū·m), *v.*¹ ME. [– (partly through Fr. *consumer*) L. *consumere*, f. *com* CON- + *sumere* take.] **1.** *trans.* To make away with, destroy, as by fire, evaporation, † decomposition, † disease, or the like, Also *fig.* **2.** To waste, squander 1460. **3.** To use up 1527; *esp.* to eat up, drink up 1587. **4.** To take up, spend, waste (time) 1533. **5.** *intr.* To waste away 1526; to burn away 1591.
1. To c. the remains in the forum MERIVALE. As the cloud is consumed *Job* 7:9. The rest were consumed either by Poverty or Diseases MANLEY. *pass.* to be 'eaten up' *with* (envy, etc.). 2. Caste her a-way & c. her goodes 1530. 4. To c. the best years of one's life in custody HALLAM. 5. Their beauty shall c. in the graue *Ps.* 49:14.
Hence **Consu·med** *ppl. a.* used up; † wasted with disease; † = 'confounded', as a term of dislike. **Consu·medly** *adv.* excessively, hugely. (App. at first = *confoundedly.*) **Consu·ming-ly** *adv.*, **-ness.**

† **Consu·me,** *v.*² 1483. [– Fr. *consumer*, var. of *consummer, consommer* – L. *consummare*; see CONSUMMATE *v.*] *trans.* To accomplish, complete –1541.

Consumer (kǫ̆nsiū·məɹ). 1535. [f. CONSUME *v.*[1] + -ER[1].] He who or that which consumes; in *Pol. Econ.* opposed to *producer*.
Every man is a c. and ought to be a producer EMERSON.

Consummate (kǫ̆nsɒ·mě̆t, kǫ·nsɒmě̆t), *a.* 1471. [– L. *consummatus*, pa. pple. of *consummare*; see next, -ATE[2].] † **1.** as *pa. pple.* Completed, perfected –1832; of marriage: Consummated –1765. **2.** *adj.* Complete, perfect 1527; supremely qualified 1643; supreme; utmost 1526.
2. Last the bright c. floure MILT. *P.L.* v. 481. The c. hypocrite MACAULAY. C. happiness WORDSW. Hence **Consummately** *adv.*

Consummate (kǫ·nsǒmeⁱt, kǫ̆nsɒ·meⁱt), *v.* 1530. [– *consummat-*, pa. ppl. stem of L. *consummare*, f. *com* CON- + *summa* SUM, *summus* highest, utmost, supreme; see -ATE[3].] **1.** *trans.* To bring to completion; to accomplish, fulfil, complete, finish. **2.** To complete *marriage* by sexual intercourse 1540. Also *absol.* † **3.** To make perfect –1678. Also *intr.* (for *refl.*)
1. God also consummated the Universe in six days RAY. Hence **Co·nsummative, consu·mmative** *a.* tending to c.; completory, final. **Co·nsummator.**

Consummation (kǫnsǒmē̆ⁱ·ʃən). ME. [– (O)Fr. *consommation* or L. *consummatio*, f. as prec.; see -ION.] **1.** The action of consummating (see CONSUMMATE, *v.* 1, 2). **2.** Completion, conclusion, as an event or condition; end, death 1475. **3.** The action of perfecting; perfection, acme 1526.
1. Between the beginning and c. or finishing of it 1665. She would have the wedding before c. FARQUHAR. **2.** 'Tis a c. Deuoutly to be wish'd *Haml.* III. i. 63. Quiet consumation haue, And renowned be thy graue *Cymb.* IV. ii. 280. The general c. of all things PRIESTLEY.

† **Consu·mpt**, *ppl. a.* ME. only. [– L. *consumptus*, pa. pple. of *consumere* CONSUME.] Consumed; as *pple.* and *adj.*

Consumption (kǫ̆nsɒ·mᵖʃən). ME. [– (O)Fr. *consomption* – L. *consumptio*, f. *consumpt-* pa. ppl. stem of *consumere*; see CONSUME *v.*[1], -ION.] **1.** The action or fact of consuming by use, waste, etc. (see CONSUME *v.*). **2.** Decay, wasting away, or wearing out; waste 1513. **3.** Wasting of the body by disease; a wasting disease; now applied *spec.* to pulmonary consumption ME. Also *fig.* **4.** *Pol. Econ.* The destructive employment of industrial products; the amount of them consumed 1662.
1. Till the c. of the world FOXE. The c. of heat in mechanical work TYNDALL. **2.** The C. of a Man's Estate 1691. **4.** Increased price will cause a diminished c. 1832. This immense home c. MCCULLOCH. Hence † **Consu·mptioner**, consumer. † **Consu·mptionish**, phthisical.

Consumptive (kǫ̆nsɒ·mᵖtiv). 1647. [– med. L. *consumptivus*, f. as prec.; see -IVE. Cf. (O)Fr. *consomptif*.]
A. *adj.* **1.** Having a tendency to consume; destructive 1664. † **2.** Characterized by being consumed –1664. **3.** Affected by wasting disease; sickly, reduced 1655. **4.** *spec.* Relating or belonging to, or affected by, phthisis 1660. **5.** *Comm.* Of or for consumption of produce 1864.
1. Too c. of time EVELYN. **2.** C. offerings to Saints JER. TAYLOR. **4.** A c. Cough WESLEY, patient 1757. **5.** Phr. *A c. demand*: a demand for purposes of c., not a *speculative* demand.
B. *sb.* [the adj. used ellipt.] † **1.** A consumptive or corrosive agent –1758. **2.** A consumptive person 1666.
Hence **Consu·mptive-ly** *adv.*, **-ness.**

† **Co·nsy.** ME. only. [ME. *concy* prob. an alternate sp. of *consy*, a misreading of *confy*, var. of *confit* (M.E.D.). See COMFIT.] *Cookery.* An ancient mode of cooking capons cut into small pieces, stewed, seasoned, and coloured with saffron.

Contabescent (kǫntăbe·sě̆nt), *a.* 1868. [– *contabescent-*, pres. ppl. stem of L. *contabescere* waste away; see -ENT.] Wasting away, atrophied; in *Bot.* characterized by suppression of pollen in the anthers of flowers. Hence **Contabe·scence.**

Contact (kǫ·ntækt). 1626. [– L. *contactus*, f. *contact-*, pa. ppl. stem of *contingere* touch closely, border on, f. *com* CON- + *tangere* touch. Cf. Fr. *contact*.] **1.** The state or condition of touching. Also *transf.* and *fig.* **2.** *Math.* The meeting of two curves (or surfaces) at a point so as to have a common tangent (or tangent plane) at that point 1660. **3.** *Geol.* 'The plane between two adjacent bodies of dissimilar rock' (Raymond) 1881.
1. Phr. *To make* or *break c.*: to complete or interrupt an electric circuit. *To come in c. with*: to meet, come across. *Comb.*: **c.-level**, an instrument in which a form of spirit-level is used to determine minute differences of length; **-mine,** a mine which explodes by c. Hence **Co·ntact** *v.* to bring or come into, or be in, c. (*rare, techn.*). **Conta·ctual** *a.* of or relating to c. (*rare*).

Conta·ctile, *a. rare.* 1882. [f. CONTACT + -ILE.] Relating to contact and the sensation of contact.

† **Conta·ction.** 1612. [f. CON- (intensive) + TACTION.] The action of touching –1682.

‖ **Contadino** (kontadī·no). It. pl. **-ini.** 1630. [It., f. *contado* county; cf. -INE[1].] An Italian peasant. Hence ‖ **Contadi·na** fem.; pl. **-ine.**

Contagion (kǫ̆ntē̆ⁱ·dʒən). ME. [– L. *contagio*, f. *com* CON- + **tag-*, base of *tangere* touch. Cf. Fr. *contagion*.] **1.** The communication of disease from body to body by contact direct or mediate 1535; contagious influence 1596. **2.** A plague or pestilence ME. **3.** = CONTAGIUM 2. 1603; *concr.* a poison that infects the blood. *poet.* 1602. **4.** *fig.* Contagious influence ME.; moral corruption 1533.
1. The Jewish Nation. . to avoid c. or pollution, in time of pestilence, burnt the bodies of their friends SIR T. BROWNE. To dare the vile c. of the night *Jul. C.* II. i. 265. **2.** That terrible c. known as the Black Death 1856. **3.** *concr.* Ile touch my point With this c. [a poisonous ointment] *Haml.* IV. vii. 148. **4.** The c. of fanaticism GIBBON, of example FROUDE. A few eminent men. . were exempt from the general c. MACAULAY. Hence **Conta·gioned** *ppl. a.* affected by c. **Conta·gionist,** one who believes that certain diseases, as the plague, etc., are contagious.

Contagious (kǫ̆ntē̆ⁱ·dʒəs), *a.* ME. [– late L. *contagiosus*, f. as prec.; see -OUS.] **1.** Of the nature of or characterized by contagion. Also *fig.* **2.** Of diseases: Communicable by contact ME. **3.** Tainted with and communicating contagion 1586. **4.** *fig.* Apt to be communicated from one to another 1660. † **5** Apt to breed or infect with disease –1792. † **6.** Pernicious, noxious –1653.
1. The c. vices of the court SOUTHEY. **2.** The Contagious Diseases (Animals) Act, 1878. *Times.* **3.** The absorption of. . bile, milk, c. matters 1813. **4.** I see this Folly is c. SHADWELL. **5.** Noisom and c. Vapours RAY. **6.** C. weather HAKLUYT. A c. broode of Scismatickes WEEVER. Hence **Conta·gious-ly** *adv.*, **-ness.**

‖ **Contagium** (kǫ̆ntē̆ⁱ·dʒiǒm). Pl. **-ia.** 1654. [L. var. form of *contagio* CONTAGION.] † **1.** = CONTAGION. **2.** *spec.* The supposed substance by which a contagious disease is transmitted 1870.

Contain (kǫ̆ntē̆ⁱ·n), *v.* [ME. *conteine, -tene*, repr. tonic stem of (O)Fr. *contenir* :– L. *continēre*, f. *com* CON- + *tenēre* hold.] **1.** *trans.* To HOLD. **2.** To comprise; to have in it ME. **3.** † To measure –1703; to be equal to ME. † **4.** To take up, occupy –1736. **5.** To enclose. *Obs.* exc. *pass.* ME. † **6.** To hold together –1579. † **7.** To keep under control, restrain, restrict, confine; to retain –1831. Also *refl.* **8.** *refl.* or *intr.* To restrain oneself; † *spec.* to be continent, keep oneself in chastity ME.
1. This pot contayneth eyght quartes PALSGR. **2.** And Grandsires Grandsons the long List contains DRYDEN. The rock. . contains a good deal of iron TYNDALL. **3.** A pound avoirdupois contains 7000 grains 1893. **5.** That part conteined betweene the French Seas POWEL. **8.** But if they cannot conteine, let them marry 1 *Cor.* 7:9. Hence **Contai·nable** *a.* that can be contained. **Contai·ner. Contai·nment** (*rare*), the action or fact of containing; holding; restraint; CONTENEMENT.

Contaminate (kǫ̆ntæ·minĕ̆t), *ppl. a. arch.* 1552. [– L. *contaminatus*, pa. pple. of *contaminare*; see next, -ATE[2].] Contaminated, defiled.

Contaminate (kǫ̆ntæ·mineⁱt), *v.* 1526. [– *contaminat-*, pa. ppl. stem of L. *contaminare*, f. *contamen, -min-*, contact, pollution, f. **tag-*, base of *tangere* touch; cf. CONTAGION. See -ATE[3].] *trans.* To render impure by contact or mixture; to corrupt, defile, pollute, sully, taint, infect.
Shall we now C. our fingers with base bribes *Jul. C.* IV. iii. 24. Air that is contaminated by respiration SULLIVAN. Hence **Conta:mina·tion,** the action of contaminating or state of being contaminated; that which contaminates. **Conta·minative** *a.* causing contamination. **Conta·minator.** So † **Conta·minous** *a.* infectious.

Contango (kǫ̆ntæ·ŋgo). 1853. [perh. arbitrary formation on the anal. of L. 1st. pres. sing. in -ō, poss. with the notion '(I) make contingent'.] *Stock Exchange.* The percentage which the buyer of stock pays to the seller to postpone transfer to the next settling-day; opp. to BACKWARDATION. **Conta·ngo** *v.*, to pay c. on (stocks or shares).

† **Co·nteck,** *sb.* [ME. *contek* – AFr. *contek* of unc. origin.] Strife or debate at law; discord; contumely –1618.
Contek with bloody knyf, and scharp manace CHAUCER. So † **Conte·ck** *v.* to contend. † **Contecker,** one who contends.

† **Conte·ction.** [– late L. *contectio* (Augustine), f. *contect-*, pa. ppl. stem of *contegere* cover up; see -ION.] Covering up. SIR T. BROWNE.

Contemn (kǫ̆nte·m), *v.* 1450. [– OFr. *contemner* or L. *contemnere*, f. *com* CON- + *temnere* despise. Now chiefly a literary word.] *trans.* To treat as of small value, view with contempt; to slight, scorn, disdain, despise.
I haue done pennance for contemning Loue *Two Gent.* II. iv. 129. Mr. Cooper contemned my lords' order, and would not obey it MRS. HUTCHINSON. Hence **Conte·mner, -or. Conte·mningly** *adv.*

Conte·mper, *v.* ? *Obs.* 1579. [– Fr. †*contempérer* or L. *contemperare* temper by mixing; see CON-, TEMPER *v.*] **1.** To mingle together. **2.** To moderate, qualify 1605. **3.** To adjust (*to*) by tempering 1600.
3. He contempereth his phrases to our capacitie 1600. Hence † **Conte·mperament,** the action of contempering or condition of being contempered.

† **Conte·mperate,** *v.* 1605. [f. L. *contemperat-* ppl. stem; see prec.] **1.** *trans.* To blend together 1655. **2.** = CONTEMPER 2. –1766. **3.** = CONTEMPER 3. –1713.
2. To c. the Acrimony of the Blood 1711. Hence † **Contempera·tion,** a blending together; blended condition; the action of tempering or moderating; adjustment; compromise.

Conte·mperature. Now *rare.* 1567. [var. of † *contemperation*, after TEMPERATURE.] A blending together; the product of such blending; harmonious mixture.
Whether colour be a quality emergent from the different c. of the elements SOUTH.

‖ **Contempla·men.** *rare.* 1678. [mod.L. f. *contemplari*; cf. *certamen*, etc.] An object of contemplation.

Contemplant (kǫ̆nte·mplănt), *a.* 1794. [– *contemplant-*, pres. ppl. stem of L. *contemplari*; see next, -ANT.] That contemplates.

Contemplate (kǫ·ntěmpleⁱt, kǫ̆nte·mpleⁱt), *v.* 1592. [– *contemplat-*, pa. ppl. stem of L. *contemplari*, f. *com* CON- + *templum* open space for observation, temple; see -ATE[3].] **1.** *trans.* To look at with continued attention, gaze upon, observe, BEHOLD 1605. **2.** To view mentally; to meditate upon, ponder, study 1594. **3.** To consider in a certain aspect, regard 1799. **4.** To have in view; to expect, take into account as a contingency 1792; to purpose 1816. **5.** *intr.* To be occupied in contemplation; to meditate, muse 1592.
1. The day whereon God did rest and c. his own works BACON. **2.** C. all this work of Time TENNYSON. **3.** To c. a bill with satisfaction 1844. **4.** Their opinions, however, c. the employment of force 1807. **5.** So many Houres, must I C. 3 *Hen. VI*, II. v. 33.
Hence **Contemplatingly** *adv.*

Contemplation (kǫntěmplē̆ⁱ·ʃən). ME. [– (O)Fr. *contemplation* – L. *contemplatio*, f. as prec.; see -ION.] **1.** The action of beholding 1480. **2.** The action of mentally viewing; attentive consideration, study; meditation ME. **3.** *spec.* Religious musing ME. **4.** *ellipt.* Matter for contemplation 1725. **5.** The action of taking into account; consideration, regard; view 1450. **6.** Prospect, expectation; intention 1659.
2. The sundrie c. of my trauells *A.Y.L.* IV. i. 18. **3.** In contemplacion and prayer CAXTON. **5.** At the c. of our prayers 1536. In c. of law 1819. **6.** *In c.*: in view (as a contingency, or an end).

Conte·mplatist. *Obsol.* 1669. [f. CONTEMPLATE + -IST.] One given to contemplation.

Contemplative (kǫ̆nte·mplătiv). ME. [– (O)Fr. *contemplatif, -ive*, or L. *contemplativus*; see CONTEMPLATE, -IVE.]

A. *adj.* **1.** Given to contemplation; meditative; † speculative. **2.** Characterized by, or tending to, contemplation ME. **3.** Opp. to *active* ME.

1. This Letter wil make a contemplatiue Ideot of him *Twel. N.* II. v. 23. **2.** Fix'd and c. their looks, Still turning over Nature's books DENHAM. **3.** Wrangling..whether the contemplatiue, or the actiue life doe excell SIDNEY. Phr. *C. of*: contemplating. Hence **Conte·mplative-ly** *adv.*, **-ness.**

B. *sb.* A person devoted to religious meditation; one who leads the contemplative life ME.

Contemplator (kǫ·ntĕmpleⁱtəɹ). 1607. [– L. *contemplator* (see CONTEMPLATE, -OR 2); partly f. CONTEMPLATE.] One who contemplates.

† **Conte·mple,** *v.* 1502. [– (O)Fr. *contempler* – L. *contemplari*; see CONTEMPLATE.] To CONTEMPLATE –1605.

Contemporaneity (kǫ̆nte:mpŏrănī·ĭti). Also *erron.* **cot-.** [f. next + -ITY. Cf. Fr. *contemporanéité.*] 1772. = *Contemporaneousness.*

Contemporaneous (kǫ̆nte:mpŏrēⁱ·niəs), *a.* Also *erron.* **cot-.** 1656. [f. L. *contemporaneus* (f. *com* CON- + *tempus, tempor-* time) + -OUS.] **1.** Existing or occurring at the same time. **2.** Of the same historical or geological period 1833.

1. Strictly c. testimony J. H. NEWMAN. **2.** Tumuli of the stone period believed to be c. with the mounds LYELL. vars. † **Conte·mporane,** † **Contempora·nean.** Hence **Contempora·neous-ly** *adv.*, **-ness.**

Contemporary (kǫ̆nte·mpŏrări). Also **cot-** ('a downright barbarism' Bentley). 1631. [– med.L. *contemporarius*, f. *com* CON- + *tempus, tempor-* time, after L. *contemporaneus* (see prec.) and late L. *contemporalis* (see CON-, TEMPORAL¹); see -ARY¹.]

A. *adj.* **1.** Living, existing, or occurring together in time. **2.** Equal in age, coeval 1667. **3.** Occurring at the same moment of time, or during the same period; contemporaneous, simultaneous 1656.

1. Writers c. with the events they write of M. PATTISON. **2.** A neighbouring Wood born with himself he sees, And loves his old c. Trees COWLEY.

B. *sb.* One who lives at the same time with another or others 1646. Also *transf.* of journals, etc.

Contemporize (kǫ̆nte·mpŏrəiz), *v.* 1646. [f. late L. *contemporare* (whence †*contemporate* (XVII) synchronize) + -IZE.] To synchronize or cause to synchronize. So † **Conte·mporate** *v.* to synchronize.

Contempt (kǫ̆nte·mᵖt), *sb.* ME. [– L. *contemptus*, f. *contempt-*, pa. ppl. stem of *contemnere* CONTEMN.] **1.** The action of contemning or despising; the mental attitude in which a thing is considered as of little account, or as vile and worthless. **2.** The condition of being contemned or despised; dishonour, disgrace 1450. † **3.** = Object of contempt –1832. **4.** *Law.* Disobedience or open disrespect to the authority or lawful commands of the sovereign, the privileges of the Houses of Parliament or other legislative body; and *esp.* action of any kind that interferes with the proper administration of justice by the various courts of law; in this connection called *C. of Court* 1621.

1. An outward c. of what the public esteemeth sacred BERKELEY. All the contempts they could cast at him were their shame not his MRS. HUTCHINSON. **2.** He would like to bring military glory into c. JOWETT. **4.** Phr. *In c.*: in the position of having committed c., and not having purged himself. Hence † **Conte·mpt** *v.* to contemn. † **Conte·mptful** *a.* contemptuous, contemptible.

Contemptible (kǫ̆nte·mᵖtib'l), *a.* ME. [– (O)Fr. *contemptible* or late L. *contemptibilis*; see prec., -IBLE.] **1.** To be despised; worthy only of contempt; despicable. **2.** Exhibiting contempt; full of contempt. *Obs.* in educated use. 1594.

1. So small and c. an Animal [the Flea] 1664. **2.** 'Tis very possible hee'l scorne it, for the man.. hath a c. spirit *Much Ado* II. iii. 187. Hence **Conte·mptibi·lity,** the quality or fact of being c. **Conte·mptibleness. Conte·mptibly** *adv.*

Contemptuous (kǫ̆nte·mᵖtiu,əs), *a.* 1529. [– med.L. *contemptuosus*, f. L. *contemptus*; see CONTEMPT, -UOUS.] **1.** Showing contempt. disdainful, scornful, insolent 1595. † **2.** Contemptible –1796.

1. Satan with c. brow MILT. *P.L.* IV. 885. An air of c. indifference GEO. ELIOT. **2.** C. base-borne Callot as she is 2 *Hen. VI*, I. iii. 86. Hence **Conte·mptuous-ly** *adv.*, **-ness.**

Contend (kǫ̆nte·nd), *v.* Pa. t. **contended;** † **content.** 1514. [– OFr. *contendre* or L. *contendere*, f. *com* CON- + *tendere* stretch.] † **1.** *intr.* To strive earnestly; to endeavour, to struggle –1820. **2.** To strive in opposition; to engage in conflict or strife; to fight 1529. Also *transf.* and *fig.* **3.** To strive in argument or debate; to dispute keenly; to argue 1530. **4.** To compete, vie 1589. † **5.** *trans.* To contest, dispute (an object) 1697. ¶ **6.** To urge one's course 1600.

1. I have contended to bring in honest men 1659. **2.** In Ambitious strength, I did C. against thy Valour *Cor.* IV. v. 119. A cause for which they are ready to c. to their life's end JOWETT. *transf.* Mad as the Seas, and winde, when both c. Which is the Mightier *Haml.* IV. i. 7. **3.** Chymistry, about which name we do not c. 1671. This plasticity [of ice] has been contended for by M. Agassiz TYNDALL. **5.** When Carthage shall c. the world with Rome DRYDEN. Hence † **Conte·ndent,** one who contends. **Conte·nder,** one who contends or is given to contention. **Conte·ndress** (*rare*), a female contender; one who urges her way (Chapman).

† **Conte·nement.** 1502. [– OFr. *contenement* or med.L. *contenementum*; see CON-, TENEMENT.] As tr. *contenementum* in Magna Carta: ? Holding, freehold; or ? Property necessary to the freeman's position –1818.

Content (kǫ̆nte·nt, kǫ·ntent), *sb.*¹ 1481. [– med.L. *contentum*, pl. *contenta* things contained, subst. use of n. of L. *contentus*, pa. pple. of *continēre* CONTAIN.] **1.** Now only in *pl.* (with *of* or possessive); That which is contained (in a vessel or the like, a writing, a book, etc.). † **2.** Tenor, purport (of a document) –1667. **3.** That which is contained in a conception; the substance or matter (of cognition, of art, etc.): opp. to the *form* 1845. **4.** Containing power (of a vessel, etc.); capacity 1491. **5.** Extent, area (now *rare*) 1570; volume (now the usual sense) 1612.

1. The contents of a Letter *A.Y.L.* IV. iii. 21, of the kiln 1832. *Table of contents*: a summary of the matters contained in a book, in the order in which they occur. Also simply *contents* († *content*). **3.** The inner c. or meaning of words WHITNEY. **4.** Fifteen hundred strong ships of great C. BACON. **5.** The area or c. of the Rectangle BARROW. The solid c. and height of any Tree 1612.

Content (kǫ̆nte·nt), *sb.*² 1579. [immed. source obscure; perh. f. next as a shorter form equiv. to the earlier † *contentation* (XV) or *contentment* (XV), and corresp. to Sp., Pg., It. *contento.*] **1.** Satisfaction, pleasure; a contented condition. † **2.** Acceptance of conditions or circumstances, acquiescence –1752. † **3.** A satisfaction; *pl.* pleasures, delights –1716.

1. In Concord and C. the Commons live, By no Divisions rent DRYDEN. I wish your Ladiship all hearts c. *Merch. V.* III. iv. 42. **2.** Phr. *To take upon c.*: to accept without examination. The sense they humbly take upon c. POPE. Hence **Conte·ntful** (now *rare*), full of c. † **Conte·ntless** *a.* unsatisfied.

Content (kǫ̆nte·nt), *a.* (*sb.*) ME. [– (O)Fr. *content*:– L. *contentus* that is satisfied, pa. pple. of *continēre* fig. repress, restrain (cf. CONTAIN *v.* 7, 8).] **1.** Having one's desires bounded by what one has; desiring nothing more, or nothing different; satisfied, contented. **2.** Pleased, gratified (= Fr. *content*); now only in *well c.* (*arch.*) ME. † **3.** Consenting, willing, ready –1709. **b.** *ellipt.* as an exclam.: = I am content –1820. **c.** In the House of Lords *C.* and *Not C.* = AYE and No in the House of Commons 1621. Hence as *sb.* in *pl.* Those who vote 'Content' 17 . . .

1. I haue learned in whatsoeuer state I am, therewith to bee c. *Phil.* 4:11. *Be c.* (Shaks.): be satisfied in mind. **3. c.** The House then divided on the second reading..C. 84, Not C. 23.

Content (kǫ̆nte·nt), *v.* ME. [– (O)Fr. *contenter* – Rom. (med.L.) *contentare*, f. *contentus* (see prec.).] **1.** *trans.* 'To satisfy so as to stop complaint' (J.); to be enough for; † to please, gratify 1477. Also *refl.* and † *intr.* **2.** *refl.* To be satisfied *with*; to limit one's action 1538. † **3.** To satisfy, pay in full; to remunerate –1822.

1. Pylate willinge to c. the people, loused Barrabas TINDALE *Mark* 15:15. *Two Gent.* III. i. 93. **2.** [He] contents himself with reporting the results of other scholars MAX-MÜLLER. **3.** To c. a dette 1433, the workeman for his paynes USSHER. Hence **Conte·ntable** *a.* satisfactory; able to be contented. **Conte·nted** *ppl. a.* satisfied; willing to put up *with* something; † willing (*to do* something). **Conte·nted-ly** *adv.*, **-ness.** † **Conte·ntive** *a.* fitted to c.

Contenta·tion. 1494. [– med.L. *contentatio*, f. *contentat-*, pa. ppl. stem of *contentare*; see prec., -ION. Cf. OFr. *contentacion.*] † The action of satisfying; † the fact of being satisfied; satisfied condition (*arch.*).

Contention (kǫ̆nte·nʃən). ME. [– (O)Fr. *contention* or L. *contentio*, f. *content-*, pa. ppl. stem of *contendere*; see CONTEND, -ION.] **1.** The action of straining or striving earnestly; effort, endeavour (*arch.*) 1580. **2.** Strife, dispute, verbal controversy ME. **3.** Competition 1576; † the matter in competition 1712. **4.** That which is contended for in argument; the point or thesis which a person strives to make good 1635. ¶ † **5.** = CONTENTATION –1579.

2. A great matter in contencion & debate betwene them MORE. *Bone of c.*: see BONE. The lot causeth contentions to cease *Prov.* 18:18. **3.** A kinde c., and emulation of aymiable Vertue 1633. **4.** This then is your c.—that [etc.] W. BLACK. Hence **Conte·ntional** *a.* of the nature or character of c. † **Conte·ntioner,** one given to c.

Contentious (kǫ̆nte·nʃəs), *a.* ME. [–(O)Fr. *contentieux* – L. *contentiosus*; see CONTENTION, -OUS.] **1.** Given to contention; prone to strife or dispute; quarrelsome 1533. Also *transf.* **2.** Characterized by or involving contention ME. **3.** *Law.* Of or pertaining to differences between contending parties 1483.

1. To dwell..with a c. and angry woman *Prov.* 21:19. *transf.* This c. storme *Lear* III. iv. 6. **2.** Forbearing to raise c. issues GLADSTONE. **3.** Phr. *C. jurisdiction*: right of jurisdiction in causes between contending parties. **Conte·ntious-ly** *adv.*, **-ness.**

Contentment (kǫ̆nte·ntmĕnt). 1474. [– Fr. *contentement*, f. *contenter*; see CONTENT *v.*, -MENT. In Eng. chiefly a noun of quality, as if = *contentedness.*] **1.** The action of satisfying; the process of being satisfied; satisfaction (*arch.*). **2.** The fact, condition, or quality of being contented; contentedness. (The usual mod. sense.) 1597. † **3.** Pleasure, gratification –1795; a pleasure –1692.

1. The guests took their leave..to the c. of mine host SCOTT. **2.** Godlinesse with c. is great gaine 1 *Tim.* 6:6. **3.** As for reading, I am past that c. LADY RUSSELL.

Contents; see CONTENT *sb.*¹

† **Co·ntenu, co·ntinue.** 1477. [– Fr. *contenu, -ue*, subst. use of pa. pple. of *contenir* CONTAIN.] = CONTENT *sb.*¹ 2.

Conte·rminable, *a. rare.* [f. † *contermine* *v.* end together (– Fr. *conterminer*) + -ABLE.] Liable to end together. WOTTON.

Conterminal (kǫ̆ntɜ̄·ɹminăl), *a.* 1802. [var. of CONTERMINOUS with substitution of suffix -AL¹.] **1.** = CONTERMINOUS 1. **2.** *Entom.* Attached end to end.

Conterminant (kǫ̆ntɜ̄·ɹminănt), *a.* 1640. [f. † *contermine* v. + -ANT; cf. CONTERMINABLE.] † **1.** = CONTERMINOUS 1. **2.** Terminating together (in time). LAMB.

Conterminate (kǫ̆ntɜ̄·ɹminĕt), *a.* 1578. [– late L. *conterminatus*, pa. pple. of *conterminare*; see next, -ATE².] = CONTERMINOUS.

† **Conte·rminate,** *v.* 1637. [– *conterminat-*, pa. ppl. stem of late L. *conterminare*, f. *conterminus*; see CONTERMINOUS, -ATE³.] To end together –1709. Hence † **Contermina·tion.**

Conterminous (kǫ̆ntɜ̄·ɹminəs), *a.* 1631. [f. L. *conterminus* (f. *com* CON- + *terminus* boundary) + -OUS.] **1.** Having a common boundary, bordering upon. **2.** Meeting at their ends 1734. **3.** Exactly coextensive 1817.

1. The side of Germany c. to France 1878.

† **Conterra·neous,** *a.* 1644. [f. L. *conterraneus* (f. *com* CON- + *terra* land) + -OUS.] Of or belonging to the same country –1711. var. † **Conterra·nean.**

† **Contessera·tion.** 1620. [– late L. *contesseratio* (Tertullian), f. *contesserare*; see CON-, TESSERA, -ION.] **1.** Contraction of friendship by means of the divided tessera, etc. **2.** [L. *tessera* a chequer.] A mosaic 1671.

2. So unusual a c. of elegancies 1671.

† **Contest,** *sb.*¹ 1551. [– med.L. *contestis* fellow witness, f. L. *com* CON- + *testis* witness.] A joint witness –1602.

Contest (kǫ·ntest), *sb.*² 1643. [– CONTEST *v.*, or Fr. *conteste*, f. *contester* CONTEST *v.*] **1.** Strife in argument, keen controversy, debate. **2.** Struggle for victory, for an object, etc.; conflict, strife, contention 1647. **3.** Amicable conflict; competition 1647.

1. Between Nose and Eyes a strange c. arose COWPER. **2.** The assistance they could not hope to receive from Athens in their c. with the enemy THIRLWALL. **3.** Musical contests JOWETT.

Contest (kǫnte·st), *v.* 1579. [– L. *contestari* call to witness, introduce (a suit) by calling witnesses, set on foot (an action), f. *com* CON- + *testari* bear witness.]

I. † **1.** *trans.* To swear to (a fact or statement) –1613. † **2.** To attest (*rare*) –1649. † **3.** To call to witness, adjure, charge, etc. –1621; *intr.* to bear witness –1609.

II. [f. L. *contestari litem.*] **1.** *intr.* To contend (*with* or *against*) in argument; to dispute keenly 1603. **2.** *trans.* To argue (a point, etc.); to dispute, controvert, call in question 1663. **3.** *intr.* To contend (generally) 1618. **4.** *trans.* To fight for; to dispute with arms 1626. **5.** *intr.* To contend in rivalry, vie (*with*) 1607. **6.** *trans.* To contend for in emulation 1725.

1. Inexplicable Thy Justice seems; yet to say truth, too late I thus c. MILT. *P.L.* x. 756. **2.** To c. the right of the pope S. AUSTIN. **3.** For Forms of Government let Fools c. POPE. **4.** To c. the crown J. R. GREEN. **5.** Of man, who dares in pomp with Jove c. POPE. **6.** To c. a race 1832.

Hence **Conte·stable** *a.* that may be contested. **Conte·ster.**

Contestant (kǫnte·stănt). 1665. [– Fr. *contestant*, pres. pple. of *contester* CONTEST *v.*; see -ANT. Cf. *combatant.*] One who takes part in a contest.

† **Contestate,** *v.* *rare.* 1575. [– *contestat-*, pa. ppl. stem of L. *contestari*; see CONTEST *v.*, -ATE³.] = CONTEST *v.* –1656.

Contestation (kǫntestēⁱ·ʃən). 1548. [– L. *contestatio*, f. as prec., see -ION. Partly through Fr. *contestation.*] † **1.** The action of calling or taking to witness, adjuration –1703. † **2.** Solemn asseveration –1642. **3.** Disputation or controversy; contention, conflict, emulation (now *Sc.*) 1580. **4.** The contesting (of a point, claim, etc.) 1638; a contention 1880.

3. Weary with the contestations of certain Pleaders SIR T. NORTH. Fire and water cannot meet without a hissing c. T. ADAMS. A c. of honour and preferment HOBBES. **4.** Phr. *In c.*: in dispute.

† **Conte·x,** *v.* 1542. [– L. *contexere*; see next.] To weave or knit together –1684. var. † **Conte·xt** *v.* Hence † **Conte·xt** *ppl. a.* woven or knit together; var. † **Conte·xted.**

Context (kǫ·ntėkst), *sb.* ME. [– L. *contextus*, f. *context-*, pa. ppl. stem of *contexere* weave together, f. *com* CON- + *texere* weave.] † **1.** Construction of speech –1645. † **2.** *concr.* A continuous text or composition –1641. † **3.** The connection of the parts of a discourse –1641. **4.** *concr.* The parts which immediately precede or follow any particular passage or text and determine its meaning 1568. Also *transf.* and *fig.*

4. To this I answer plainly according to all the light that the contexts afford in this matter 1714. Hence **Conte·xtual** *a.* of or belonging to the c.; depending only on the c. **Conte·xtually** *adv.*

Contexture (kǫnte·kstiŭɹ). Now *rare.* 1603. [– Fr. *contexture*, prob. repr. med.L. **contextura*; see CON-, TEXTURE.] **1.** The action of weaving together; the being woven together; texture 1649. Also *transf.* and *fig.* **2.** A mass *of* things interwoven together 1603; a fabric 1603. **3.** The weaving together of words, sentences, etc., in connected composition; the structure of a literary composition; a connected passage 1603. **4.** = CONTEXT 4. 1608.

1. The profitable C. of the Silk-worm 1691. *transf.* He was not of any delicate c.; his limbs rather sturdy than dainty WOTTON (J.). **2.** The most ingenious c. of truth and lies CHESTERF. Hence **Conte·xtural** *a.* **Conte·xture** *v.* to weave (*rare*).

Conticent (kǫ·ntisĕnt), *a.* *rare.* 1859. [– *conticent-*, pres. ppl. stem of L. *conticēre*, f. *com* CON- + *tacēre* be silent.] Keeping silence, silent.

The servants have left the room; the guests sit c. THACKERAY.

† **Contignate,** *v.* *rare.* [– *contignat-*, pa. ppl. stem of L. *contignare*, f. *com* CON- + *tignum* building material, piece of timber. See -ATE³.] *trans.* To join together with beams. HOWELL.

Contignation (kǫntignēⁱ·ʃən). *arch.* 1592. [– L. *contignatio*, f. as prec.; see -ION.] **1.** The joining together of beams or boards; jointing together 1630. **2.** Any conjoined structure 1634. **3.** *spec.* A floor, storey, or stage 1592.

1. *fig.* Linked by a c. into the edifice of France BURKE.

† **Conti·guate,** *a.* ME. [– med.L. *contiguatus*, f. L. *contiguus*; see CONTIGUOUS, -ATE².] Contiguous *to*; in contact *with* –1632.

Contiguity (kǫntigiū·Iti). 1641. [– late L. *contiguitas*, f. L. *contiguus*; see next, -ITY. Cf. Fr. *contiguité.*] **1.** The condition of being in contact; proximity. Also *fig.* † **2.** A continuous mass 1784.

1. Communicating expansion to all bodies in c. with it W. GROVE. C. in time or place HUME. **2.** Some boundless c. of shade COWPER.

Contiguous (kǫnti·giu,əs), *a.* 1611. [f. L. *contiguus* touching together (f. *contingere*, see CONTINGENT) + -OUS.] **1.** Touching, in contact; adjoining. † **2.** Continuous –1725. **3.** *loosely.* Neighbouring 1710.

1. An heiress whose land lies c. to mine JOHNSON. Two c. Moments of Time HARTLEY. *C. angles* (Math.): = adjacent angles. var. † **Conti·gual.** Hence **Conti·guous-ly** *adv.*, **-ness.**

Continence (kǫ·ntinĕns). ME. [– (O)Fr. *continence* or L. *continentia*, f. *continent-*, pres. ppl. stem of *continēre* restrain; see CONTAIN, -ENCE.] **1.** Self-restraint. **2.** *spec.* Self-restraint in the matter of sexual appetite, in the sense either of due moderation or (more frequently) of entire abstinence ME. **3.** Continuity 1726.

1. He knows when to leave off, a c. which is practised by few writers DRYDEN. **2.** Chastity is either abstinence or c.: abstinence is that of virgins or widows; c. of married persons JER. TAYLOR. var. (in senses 1, 2) **Co·ntinency.** (Now *rare.*)

Continent (kǫ·ntinĕnt), *a.* ME. [– *continent-*; see prec., -ENT.] **1.** Self-restraining, *esp.* in relation to bodily passions, appetites, or indulgences; temperate. **2.** *spec.* Self-restraining in the matter of sexual indulgence; chaste ME. † **3.** Restrictive –1605. **4.** Containing; capacious (*rare*) 1856. † **5.** Continuous in space –1692. †**6.** Continuous in duration; not intermittent. (*Old Med.*) –1783.

1. Of such c. moderation was he in coveting 1635. **2.** The chore or quyer signefieth the continente. And the body signefyeth thordre of them that ben maryed CAXTON. **3.** *Macb.* IV. iii. 64. **5.** The mayne and c. land of the whole worlde GRAFTON. **6.** A C. Fever 1783. Hence **Co·ntinently** *adv.* chastely, temperately; † continuously.

Continent (kǫ·ntinĕnt), *sb.* 1541. [In senses 1 and 2, – subst. use of L. *continent-* (see CONTAIN); in sense 5 corresp. to Fr. *continent*, It. *continente*, and repr. an ellipt. use of L. *terra continens* continuous land.] **1.** That which contains; also *fig.* Now *rare.* 1541. † **2.** Containing capacity –1666. † **3.** Land; the earth –1677. **4.** *esp.* Mainland. *Obs.* exc. as in 5. 1576. **5.** One of the main continuous bodies of land on the earth's surface, as Europe, Asia, Africa, America, North and South, and ? Australia, and the supposed Antarctic C. 1614. Also *transf.* and *fig.* † **6.** *Amer. Hist.* The colonies or states collectively (during the War of Independence) –1784. **7.** *Eccl. Hist.* = ENCRATITE 1702.

1. Heart, once be stronger then thy C., Cracke thy fraile Case *Ant. & Cl.* IV. xiv. 40. **3.** *2 Hen. IV*, III. i. 47. **4.** It is not known whether that country be an island or the c. DE FOE. Phr. *The C.*: the mainland of Europe, as dist. from the British Isles.

Continental (kǫntine·ntăl). 1760. [f. prec. + -AL.¹]

A. *adj.* **1.** Belonging to, or characteristic of, a continent 1818. **2.** *spec.* Of, on, or belonging to 'the Continent', *i.e.* the mainland of Europe 1760. **3.** *Amer. Hist.* Of or belonging to the colonies or States collectively (during and immediately after the War of Independence), as in *C. Congress* (see CONGRESS) 1775.

1. At the north it [the climate] was c., and consequently dry 1865. **2.** The c. tour LYTTON. *The C. System* (Hist.): the plan of Napoleon Bonaparte for cutting off Great Britain from all connection with the continent of Europe; instituted by the Berlin Decree of 19th Nov., 1806, which declared the British Islands in a state of blockade. **3.** The C. debt MORSE. C. money H. PHILLIPS.

B. *sb.* **1.** An inhabitant of a continent; *spec.* of the continent of Europe 1828. **2.** *Amer. Hist.* **a.** A soldier of the C. army in the War of Independence 1847. **b.** A currency note issued by the C. Congress; whence the phrase *Not worth a c.* 1872.

Contine·ntalist. 1834. [f. prec. + -IST.] **1.** = CONTINENTAL *sb.* 1. **2.** *Amer. Hist.* An advocate of the federation of the States after the War of Independence.

Contingency (kǫnti·ndʒĕnsi). 1561. [f. earlier *contingence* – late L. *contingentia* in its med.L. sense circumstance, contingency; see next, -ENCY.] † **1.** Touching, contact –1677. **2.** Connection, affinity of nature 1612. **3.** The quality or condition of being contingent 1561. **4.** A chance occurrence; a juncture 1616. **5.** An event conceived as of possible occurrence in the future 1626. **6.** A thing or condition of things contingent upon an uncertain event 1818. **7.** A thing incident to something else 1626.

3. The c. of human actions BP. WATSON. **4.** Drawing from the starres the euents of future contingencies 1620. **5.** A future estate of freehold, to arise either upon a c., or at a period certain CRUISE. **7.** All the..contingencies of marriage, number of children, etc. COBBETT. So **Conti·ngence** (in senses 1–4).

Contingent (kǫnti·ndʒĕnt). ME. [– *contingent-*, pres. ppl. stem of L. *contingere* be contiguous, in connection or in contact, befall, f. *com* CON- + *tangere* touch.]

A. *adj.* † **1.** In contact; tangential –1703. **2.** Liable to happen or not ME. **3.** Happening or coming by chance; fortuitous 1613. † **4.** Not determined by necessity; free –1796. † **5.** Subject to accidents –1745. **6.** *Metaph.* True only under existing conditions 1588; that exists in dependence on something else 1785; non-essential 1628. **7.** Dependent *on* or *upon* something prior 1613. **8.** *Law.* Dependent on a probability; conditional; not absolute 1710.

2. If Death were only c., and not certain 1684. C. expenses 1747. **3.** By various local and c. events 1799. **4.** If human actions are not C., what think you of the morality of actions BP. WATSON. **5.** The c. nature of trade DE FOE. **6.** *C. matter* (in Logic): the subject-matter of a proposition which is not necessarily or universally true. **7.** Things.. altogether c. and dependent of mans will SALKELD. Hence **Continge·ntial** *a.* of c. nature, non-essential (*rare*). **Conti·ngently** *adv.* in a c. manner.

B. *sb.* **1.** An accident 1548. **2.** A thing that may or may not happen 1623. **3.** 'The proportion that falls to any one on a division' (J.); a quota, *esp.* of troops 1727. Also *transf.* and *fig.*

2. It [Humane providence] cannot ascertain future Contingents 1623. **3.** The Nizam's C. as this force was denominated WELLINGTON.

Continual (kǫnti·niuăl), *a.* ME. [– (O)Fr. *continuel*, f. *continuer*; see CONTINUE, -AL¹.] **1.** Always going on, incessant, perpetual ME.; regularly recurring (*arch.*) 1500. † **2.** *transf.* Of persons and things: Continually existing or acting; constant, perpetual –1864. † **3.** Of diseases: Chronic, not intermittent –1751. † **4.** Continuous; forming a continuous series –1753.

1. One almost c. eruption PHILLIPS. Continuall victory maketh leaders insolent 1630. **2.** Yore contynwel servaunt and bedeman 1462. **4.** *C. proportion* (Math.): = CONTINUED proportion. Hence **Conti·nually** *adv.* always; very frequently; continuously. **Conti·nualness** the quality of being c. (*rare*).

Continuance (kǫnti·niu,ăns). ME. [– OFr. *continuance*, f. *continuer*; see CONTINUE, -ANCE.] **1.** Keeping up, going on with, maintaining, or prolonging (an action, process, state, etc.). **2.** *Law.* The adjournment of a suit or trial till a future date or for a period ME. **3.** Perseverance, persistence (said of agents) (*arch.*) ME.; the going on (of an action), the lasting (of a state) 1530. (The most usual current sense.) **4.** Stay ME. **5.** Course or length of time (*Obs.* or *arch.*) ME. † **6.** Lasting quality –1664; antiquity –1699; continuity (*lit.* and *fig.*) –1756. **7.** *concr.* = CONTINUATION 1552. Also *attrib.*

1. His own preservation, or the c. of his species ADDISON. 3. By patient c. in well doing *Rom.* 2:7. The c. of disorder HOBBES, a quarrel FROUDE. 4. Cloy'd With long c. in a setled place SHAKS.

†‖ **Continua·ndo.** 1607. [L., = 'by continuing'.] *Law.* In an indictment for trespass: A continuance or repetition of the act alleged. Hence *transf.* –1734.

Continuant (kǫ̆nti·niu,ănt). 1610. [Partly – Fr. *continuant*, pres. pple. of *continuer*; partly – *continuant-*, pres. ppl. stem of L. *continuare*; see CONTINUE, -ANT.]

A. *adj.* † **1.** Continuing, persisting in time; remaining in force –1660. **2.** Capable of a continuous sound, as some consonants.

B. *sb.* **1.** A consonant of which the sound can be prolonged, as f, v, s, etc. 1861. **2.** *Math.* In *Theory of Equations*, 'A determinant in which all the constituents vanish except those in the principal diagonal and two bordering minor diagonals'. SALMON.

† **Conti·nuate,** *ppl. a.* 1471. [– L. *continuatus*, pa. pple. of *continuare*; see CONTINUE, -ATE[2].] **1.** *pa. pple.* CONTINUED. **2.** *adj.* Continued without break or interstices –1656. **3.** Long-continued, chronic –1635.

3. An vntyreable and c. goodness *Timon* I. i. 11.

† **Conti·nuate,** *v.* 1578. [– *continuat-*, pa. ppl. stem of L. *continuare*; see CONTINUE, -ATE[3].] To make continuous in space or time –1834.

Continuation (kǫ̆nti:niu,ēi·ʃən). ME. [– (O)Fr. *continuation* – L. *continuatio*, f. as prec.; see -ION.] † **1.** The action of continuing; perseverance –1483 † **2.** Continuity in space –1726. **3.** Continuous existence or operation 1469. **4.** The causing of anything to continue 1586. † **5.** *Math.* In Fluxions: = integration by parts –1786. **6.** *Stock Exchange.* The carrying over of an account till next settling-day; see CONTANGO 1813. **7.** *concr.* That by which anything is continued 1580. **8.** *pl.* Gaiters continuous with 'shorts'. Hence, in *mod. slang*, trousers, as a c. of the waistcoat 1825.

3. The c. of weakness T. BROWN. 4. A decree made for the c. of the league KNOLLES. 7. Where it is crossed by the c. of Mount Imaus ELPHINSTONE.

Continuative (kǫ̆nti·niu,ĕtiv). 1530. [– late L. *continuativus*, f. *continuat-* (as prec.); see -IVE.]

A. *adj.* **1.** Serving to continue or impart continuity 1684. **2.** Expressing continuance.

B. *sb.* (the adj. used *absol.*) Anything that serves to continue or impart continuity; *spec.* † **a.** a conjunction that introduces a subordinate clause –1870; † **b.** a proposition expressing continuance, as *Rome remains to this day* 1725.

Continuator (kǫ̆nti·niu,eⁱtəɹ). 1646. [f. as prec., see -OR 2; in sense 2 repr. Fr. *continuateur.*] **1.** One who continues. **2.** One who continues work (*esp.* a book) begun by another 1656.

Continue (kǫ̆nti·niu), *v.* ME. [– (O)Fr. *continuer*, – L. *continuare* make continuous, (less commonly) be continuous, f. *continuus* uninterrupted.]

I. *trans.* **1.** To carry on, keep up, persist in (an action, usage, etc.). **2.** To cause to last or endure; to prolong (something external to the agent) ME.; to keep on, retain (in a place, condition, etc.) 1460. † **3.** To attach *to* –1646. **4.** To take up (a narrative, etc.); to carry on in space, succession, or development ME. **5.** *Law* and *Stock Exch.* To adjourn, put off 1469.

1. To c. a resolve SHAKS., a metaphor FIELDING, struggle 1874. 2. A good Way to c. their Memories SIR T. BROWNE. To c. him at School WALTON. 4. To c. the Story (with Sir John in it) 2 *Hen. IV*, Epil. To c. lines MOXON.

II. *intr.* **1.** To remain in existence or in its present condition; to last, endure ME. **2.** To remain (*in* a place) ME.; to remain (in a specified state or capacity) 1503. **3.** To persevere; to keep on. (Now rare of persons.) ME. **4.** To proceed in one's discourse; to resume 1711.

1. But now thy kingdom shall not c. 1 *Sam.* 13:14. 2. They continued there not many days *John* 2:12. To c. unhappy 1884. 3. The breeze continued LADY BRASSEY. Phr. *To c. doing* or *to do.* 4. Lord Erskine continues thus: 'If' [etc.] 1885.

† **III.** = CONTAIN –1572.

Such blasfemyes ben foundun & contynnued in þes sectis WYCLIF.

Hence **Conti·nuable** *a.* **Conti·nuingly** *adv.*

Continue *sb.*, var. of CONTENU.

Continued (kǫ̆nti·niud), *ppl. a.* ME. [f. prec. + -ED[1].] **1.** Carried on without cessation; continual. **2.** Carried on in space, time, or series; continuous 1607.

1. Cold Weather, and continu'd Rain DRYDEN. Phr. *C. fever*: see CONTINUAL *a.* 3. **2.** *C. proportionals*: a series of quantities such that the ratio is the same between every two adjacent terms. Such quantities are in *C. proportion. C. fraction*: a fraction whose denominator is an integer *plus* a fraction, which latter fraction has a similar denominator, and so on. † *Continued bass* = BASSO *continuo.*

Continuer (kǫ̆nti·niu,əɹ). 1548. [f. as prec. + -ER[1].] **1.** = CONTINUATOR 2. **2.** One who continues, in various senses.

2. I would my horse had the speed of your tongue, and so good a c. *Much Ado* I. i. 143.

Continuity (kǫntiniū·Iti). 1543. [– (O)Fr. *continuité* – L. *continuitas*; see CONTINUE, -ITY.] **1.** The state of being continuous; uninterrupted connection or succession; coherence, unbrokenness. **2.** Uninterrupted duration (*rare*) 1646. **3.** quasi-*concr.* A continuous or connected whole 1601.

1. The c. of the frontier WELLINGTON. C. of attention W. GROVE. 2. Their stedfast c. of gaze 1840.

Phrases. *Law* or *principle of c.*: the principle that all change, sequence, or series in nature is continuous, and does not go *per saltum. Solution of c.*: the fact or condition of being or becoming discontinuous; fracture, rupture, breakage, break. Orig. used of wounds, etc. in an animal body.

‖ **Continuo** (kǫ̆nti·niu,o). *Mus.* 1876. [It.] = BASSO *continuo.*

Continuous (kǫ̆nti·niu,əs), *a.* 1673. [f. L. *continuus* uninterrupted + -OUS.] **1.** Characterized by continuity; extending in space without a break; having its parts in immediate connection; connected, unbroken. **2.** Uninterrupted in time, sequence, or essence; going on without interruption 1751.

1. In most cases the area inhabited by a species is c. DARWIN. Anciently c. with Malacca RAY. 2. The power of..c. thought is very rare JOWETT. Phrases. *C. brake*: a c. series of carriage brakes controlled from one point in a train. *C. consonant*: = CONTINUANT *sb.* 1. *C. function* (Math.): one that varies continuously. *C. stem* (Bot.), one without articulations. *C. voyage*: one which is regarded, in spite of stoppages, as a single voyage in ref. to the object with which it was undertaken 1806. Hence **Conti·nuous-ly** *adv.*, **-ness.**

‖ **Continuum** (kǫ̆nti·niu,ŏm). Pl. **-a** (-ă). 1650. [subst. use of n. sing. of L. *continuus* uninterrupted, f. *continēre* in intr. sense 'to hang together', etc.] A continuous thing, quantity, or substance; a continuous series of elements passing into each other.

To these animals [the wolf and dog] the external world seems a c. of scents LEWES.

Co·nt-line. 1848. [perh. for CANT-*line* (see CANT *sb.*[1]).] **1.** The spiral intervals between the strands on the outside of a rope. **2.** 'The space between the bilges of two casks stowed side by side'. SMYTH.

Conto (kǫ·nto). 1601. [Pg.:– L. *computus* COUNT *sb.*[1]] In Pg., a million; hence, short for a million reis, worth about £220.

Contorniate (kǫ̆ntǭ·ɹni,ĕt). 1692. [– Fr. *contorniate* or its source It. *contorniato*, f. *contorniare* surround, border, edge.] *adj.* Of a medal or coin: Having a deep furrow round the disc, within the edge. var. **Conto·rniated.** *sb.* A medal (or coin) so furrowed: applied to certain brass pieces of Nero and other Roman Emperors.

‖ **Contorno** (konto·rno). 1758. [It. = circuit, contour.] Contour, outline of a statue, etc.

Contorsion, obs. f. CONTORTION.

Contort (kǫ̆ntǭ·ɹt), *v.* 1622. [– *contort-*, pa. ppl. stem of L. *contorquere*, f. *com* CON- + *torquere* twist.] *trans.* To twist, twist together; to draw awry; to distort greatly by twisting. Also *fig.*

The features are violently contorted BAIN. *fig.* Contorted from their established signification 1836.

Contorted (kǫ̆ntǭ·ɹtĕd), *ppl. a.* 1622. [f. prec. + -ED[1].] **1.** Twisted, twisted together; twisted awry or out of shape. **2.** *Bot.* Of petals: Overlapping at one margin and overlapped at the other 1760.

1. I'll..hang thee In a c. chain of icicles MASSINGER.

Contortion (kǫ̆ntǭ·ɹʃən). 1611. [– L. *contortio*, f. as CONTORT; see -ION. Cf. Fr. *contorsion.*] **1.** The action of contorting; the fact of being contorted; distortion by twisting. **2.** A contorted condition, state, or form 1664.

1. We strive..to alter ourselves by ridiculous contorsions of body MRS. CHAPONE. 2. The curious contortions of the rocks W. BLACK. Hence **Conto·rtionist,** one who professes and practises c.

Contortive (kǫ̆ntǭ·ɹtiv), *a.* 1859. [f. as prec. + -IVE.] Characterized by contortion.

Contortuplicate (kǫntǭɹtiū·plikĕt), *a.* 1816. [– L. *contortuplicatus*, f. *contortus* twisted together + *-plicatus* folded; see -ATE[2].] *Bot.* Twisted back upon itself.

Contour (kǫ·ntūᵊɹ, kǫntūᵊ·ɹ), *sb.* 1662. [– Fr. *contour* – It. *contorno*, f. *contornare* draw in outline, f. *con-* CON- + *tornare* turn.] **1.** The outline of any figure; *spec.* the line separating the differently coloured parts of a design. **2.** *gen.* 1769.

1. The whole c. of her form..resembled that of Minerva SCOTT. 2. The undulating line indicates the general c. of the surface of the country HUXLEY.

Comb.: **c.-feathers, -hairs,** those which form the surface and c. of an animal. **C. line,** a line representing the horizontal c. of the earth's surface at a given elevation. The c. line of a mountain at a given height represents the edge of a horizontal plane cutting the mountain at that height.

Contour (kǫ̆ntūᵊ·ɹ), *v.* 1871. [f. prec.] **1.** *trans.* To mark with contour lines. **2.** To carry (a road, etc.) round the contour of a hill.

‖ **Contourné** (kontu·rne), *a.* 1727. [Fr.] *Her.* Turned about, *i.e.* towards the sinister or left.

‖ **Contra** (kǫ·ntră), *adv., prep.* (*sb.*) ME. [L. *contra* against (adv. and prep.), abl. fem. of a compar. f. *com, cum* with. For the sense cf. OE. *wiđ, wiđer*, as in *wiđer-seċġan* = *contradicere.*]

A. *prep.* Against. Chiefly in *pro and contra* (now *con*) 'for and against' (the motion, etc.) 1450.

B. *adv.* On or to the contrary, contrariwise ME.

C. *sb.* The contrary or opposite; in *Book-keeping*, the opposite (*esp.* the credit) side of an account. Also *transf.* 1648.

Contra-, *prefix.* The L. adv. and prep. *contra* (see prec.), signifying 'against, in opposition to, opposite, in the opposite direction', used in comb. in many English words derived from or formed after L. or It. In the names of musical instruments and of organ-stops it denotes a pitch of an octave below; as in CONTRABASS; **Contrafagotto,** the double bassoon; etc.

Contraband (kǫ·ntrăbænd). 1529. [– Sp. *contrabanda* – It. *contrabando* (now *contrabb-*), f. *contra* CONTRA- + *bando*; see BAN *sb.*[1]]

A. *sb.* **1.** Illegal or prohibited traffic. **2.** Anything prohibited to be imported or exported; smuggled goods 1599. **3.** (In full *C. of war.*) Anything (*esp.* arms, stores, etc., available for hostile purposes) forbidden to be supplied by neutrals to belligerents in time of war 1753. **4.** *U.S.* During the Civil War; A negro slave, *esp.* a fugitive or captured slave 1862; from a decision of Gen. Butler in 1861 that such slaves were contraband of war 1862.

1. This folly has thrown open folding-doors to c. BURKE. Hence **Co·ntraband** *v.* to smuggle; † to declare c. **Co·ntrabandism,** smuggling. **Co·ntrabandist,** a smuggler; var. ‖ **Co:ntrabandi·sta.**

B. *adj.* Prohibited by law, proclamation, or treaty, to be imported or exported 1656.

Plate..is not counterband in its metallic capacity H. WALPOLE. *fig.* A c. preacher SOUTHEY.

Contrabass (kǫ·ntrăbēⁱs). Now *rare.* 1598. [– It. **contrabasso,** Fr. **contrebasse** (also used); see CONTRA-, BASS *sb.*[5]] **1.** *Mus.* The DOUBLE-BASS, used to add the lower octave to the bass in the orchestra. **2.** Applied to other instruments taking a similar part; chiefly *attrib.*, as *c. posaune* a kind of trombone, *c. tuba*, the bombardon.

Contraception (kǫntrăse·pʃən). 1917. [irreg. f. CONTRA- + *-ception* in CONCEPTION.] Prevention of uterine conception. So

Contrace·ptive *a.* and *sb.* pertaining to a (means of) procuring this 1897.
Earlier names were *anticonception, -ive, contraceptics.*

Contract (kǫ·ntrækt), *sb.*[1] ME. [– OFr. *contract* (mod. *contrat*) – L. *contractus*, f. *contract-*, pa. ppl. stem of *contrahere*; see next.] **1.** A mutual agreement between two or more parties that something shall be done or forborne by one or both; also, 'a writing in which the terms of a bargain are included' (J.). **2.** *Law.* An agreement enforceable by law ME. Also used *gen.* **3.** *spec.* of marriage; also, †betrothal ME. † **4.** Mutual attraction –1654. **5.** *attrib.*, as *c. work*, etc. 1665.
1. *C. bridge*: see BRIDGE *sb.*[2] **3.** [Time] trots hard with a yong maid, between the c. of her marriage, and the day it is solemnizd *A.Y.L.* III. ii. 332.

Contract (kǫntræ·kt), *ppl. a.* (ar ˈ *sb.*[2]). ME. [– OFr. *contract*, var. of *contrait*, – L. *contractus*, pa. pple. of *contrahere*, f. *com* CON- + *trahere* draw.] = CONTRACTED. *sb.* A contracted form or word 1669.

Contract (kǫ̆ntræ·kt), *v.* 1530. [Based on prec. (much earlier) ppl. a. For some time *contract* continued to interchange with *contracted*, not only in the pa. pple., but also in the pa. t. Cf. (O)Fr. *contracter* (XIV).] **1.** *trans.* To agree upon, establish by agreement, to undertake mutually, or enter upon. Now *rare*, exc. as in 3. 1548. **2.** *intr.* To enter into an agreement or contract 1530. **3.** *spec.* as to marriage. *trans.* To constitute by contract 1530; to betroth or engage 1536; intr. 1660. **4.** *trans.* To enter into, incur, become involved in, acquire 1553. † **5.** To draw or bring together, collect, concentrate –1782. **6.** To draw the parts of together; to cause to shrink; to knit (the brow) 1602. **7.** To reduce to smaller compass as by drawing together; to narrow, shorten 1626. Also *fig. intr.* (for *refl.*) 1641.
1. We haue contracted an inviolable amitie, peace and league with the aforesaid queene HAKLUYT. **2.** To c. for a loan MCCULLOCH. **3.** Of unsound mind and incapable of contracting marriage 1885. We were contracted before my father's death SHERIDAN. **4.** Phr. *To c. friendship, acquaintance*, etc. To c. the displeasure of the world PEPYS, Colds 1691, guilt MOZLEY, a habit CHESTERF., a debt 1719. **6.** Aches c., and sterue your supple ioynts *Timon* I. i. 257. **7.** You c. your eye, when you would see sharply BACON. *fig.* To c. his expence PEPYS, a vowel 1884.
Hence **Contra·ctable** *a.* liable to be contracted or acquired. **Contra·ctant**, a contracting party (*rare*). **Contra·ctible** *a.* contractile. **Contractabi·lity, -ibi·lity. Contra·ctive** *a.* having the property of contracting; tending to produce contraction.

† **Contracta·tion.** 1555. [XVI–XVII *contratation* – Sp. *contratación* trade, business transaction; early assim. to *contract, -ation*. The Fr. *contractation*, med.L. *contractatio* (making) an agreement, are not involved.] Mutual dealing, exchange –1725.

Contracted (kǫ̆ntræ·ktėd), *ppl. a.* 1548. [See CONTRACT *v.*] **1.** Established by agreement. ? *Obs.* 1589. † **2.** Betrothed –1624. **3.** Acquired 1640. **4.** Narrowed, shortened, shrunken, etc. 1603; *fig.* concise 1595; restricted 1710.
1. Our old c. amitie GREENE. **2.** 1 *Hen. IV*, IV. ii. 17. **3.** A self-contracted wretchedness GLANVILL. **4.** Narrow c. vallies 1786. *fig.* In his Style. .he is C. and Fluent HEARNE. Petty c. ideas LD. BROUGHAM. Hence **Contra·cted-ly** *adv.*, **-ness.**

Contractile (kǫ̆ntræ·ktil, -təil), *a.* 1706. [f. CONTRACT *v.* + -ILE; cf. *distractile*, f. DISTRACT *v.*]
1. Having the property of contracting. **2.** Of, pertaining to, or of the nature of contraction; producing contraction 1725.
1. The substance of the heart is c. HUXLEY. **2.** The c. action takes place in every direction 1836. Hence **Contracti·lity**, c. quality.

Contraction (kǫ̆ntræ·kʃən). 1589. [– (O)Fr. *contraction* – L. *contractio*, f. *contract-*, pa. ppl. stem of *contrahere*; see CONTRACT *sb.*[1], -ION.] **1.** The action of contracting or establishing by contract; *spec.* the action of contracting marriage; †also, betrothal 1598. **2.** The action of contracting (a debt, disease, habit, etc.) 1683. **3.** The action of contracting (*trans.* and *intr.*), or state of being contracted; shrinking, shortening, narrowing. (The most usual sense.) 1589. Also *fig.* **4.** Abbreviation; condensation (*arch.*) 1655. **5.** *Gram.* etc. The action of shortening (a word, etc.) by omitting or combining some elements, or by reducing two vowels or syllables into one 1706. **6.** *concr.* A contracted form of a word, etc. 1755.
1. *Haml.* III. iv. 46. **2.** Anterior to the c. of the. . debt EARL SELBORNE. **3.** A c. of the heart 1594. The c. of Liquors by Cold 1665. C. of the brow SMOLLETT, of certain muscles 1876. *fig.* The c. of credit MILL. Free from any narrowness or c. MISS BURNEY. Hence **Contra·ctional** *a.* relating to or produced by c. **Contra·ctionist,** one who advocates c. of the currency; opp. to *expansionist.*

† **Contra·ctly,** *adv.* 1570. [f. CONTRACT *ppl. a.* + -LY[2].] By contraction –1675.

Contractor (kǫ̆ntræ·ktəɹ). Also 6–7 **-er.** 1548. [– late L. *contractor*, f. *contract-* (CONTRACT *sb.*[1]); see -OR 2. In later use, f. CONTRACT *v.* + -OR 2.] **1.** One who contracts; a contracting party. *Obs.* exc. as in 2. **2.** *spec.* One who contracts to furnish supplies, or to perform any work or service at a certain price or rate; one who undertakes work by contract 1724. **3.** One who or that which contracts, narrows, or shortens; used *esp.* of certain muscles 1682.

Contractual (kǫ̆ntræ·ktiuăl), *a.* 1861. [f. L. *contractus* CONTRACT *sb.*[1] + -AL[1]. Cf. Fr. *contractuel.*] Of the nature of, pertaining or relating to, a contract, as *c. obligations.*

Contracture (kǫ̆ntræ·ktiŭɹ). 1658. [– Fr. *contracture* or L. and med.L. *contractura*, f. *contract-* (see CONTRACT *sb.*[1]) + *-ura* -URE.] *Path.* A condition of persistent contraction and rigidity in the muscles or the joints. Hence **Contra·ctured** *ppl. a.* affected by c.

Co·ntra-dance, -danse, corrupt ff. COUNTRY-DANCE; see CONTRE-DANSE.

Contradict (kǫntrădi·kt), *v.* 1570. [– *contradict-*, pa. ppl. stem of L. *contradicere*, orig. *contra dicere* speak against.] † **1.** *trans.* To speak against; to oppose in speech; to forbid; to oppose –1754. † *intr.* 1616. **2.** *trans.* To affirm the contrary of; to declare untrue or erroneous; to deny 1582. Also *absol.* **3.** *transf.* To be contrary to; to go counter to, go against 1600.
1. Stand in his face to c. his claime *John* II. i. 280. **2.** The statement has been officially contradicted (*mod.*). Deare Duff, I prythee c. thy selfe, And say, it is not so *Macb.* II. iii. 94. **3.** Their liues. .c. their doctrine PRYNNE.
Hence **Contradi·ctable** *a.* † **Contradi·cter, -or.**

Contradiction (kǫntrădi·kʃən). ME. [– (O)Fr. *contradiction* – L. *contradictio*, f. as prec.; see -ION.] **1.** The action of contradicting or opposing; gainsaying. **2.** Declaring to be untrue or erroneous; affirming the contrary; denial 1526. **3.** A statement that contradicts another 1724. **4.** A state of opposition in things compared; variance; (logical) inconsistency 1576. **5.** A statement or phrase containing contradictory propositions or terms ME. **6.** A contradictory act, fact, or condition 1614. **7.** A person made up of contradictory qualities 1735.
1. Those who pursue their own Way out of a Sourness and Spirit of C. STEELE. **2.** Without c. I haue heard that *Ant. & Cl.* II. vii. 40. **3.** It contains an official c. of the rumour (*mod.*). **4.** The manifest c. between these two accounts PRIESTLEY. Phr. *The principle* (or *law*) *of c.*: the axiom that 'a thing cannot be and not be at the same time' or 'that nothing can have at the same time and at the same place contradictory and inconsistent qualities'. **5.** Both parts of a c. cannot possibly be true HOBBES. A virtuous tyrant is a c. in terms JOWETT. **7.** Woman's at best a c. still POPE. Hence **Contradi·ctional** *a.* contradictory (*rare*). **Contradi·ctious** *a.* † contradictory, contrary; self-contradictory (*arch.*); given to c.; disputatious. **Contradi·ctious-ly** *adv.*, **-ness.**

Contradictive (kǫntrădi·ktiv), *a.* 1627. [f. CONTRADICT + -IVE.] **1.** Of contradictory quality or tendency. † **2.** Contradictious –1673. Hence **Contradi·ctively** *adv.*

Contradictory (kǫntrădi·ktəri). ME. [– late L. *contradictorius*; see CONTRADICT, -ORY[2].]
A. *adj.* **1.** *Logic* and *gen.* Having the quality of contradicting; denying that a thing stated is completely true 1605; that contradict each other; mutually inconsistent 1534; inconsistent in itself 1868. **2.** Of opposite character; diametrically opposed, contrary 1736. **3.** Contradictious 1891.
1. *C. opposition* (in Logic): the opposition between two *C. propositions*, i.e. such as differ both in quantity and quality (e.g. *All A is B*: *Some A is not B*); of which one must be true and the other false. *C. terms*: such as 'A and not-A'.
B. *sb.* **1.** A contradictory proposition, assertion, or principle; *spec.* in *Logic*; see A. 1. ME. **2.** The opposite, the contrary 1840.
1. You shall never be good logician, that would set together two contradictories: for that, the schoolmen say, God cannot do CRANMER.
Hence **Contradi·ctorily** *adv.* in a way that contradicts; *Log.* with c. opposition. **Contradi·ctoriness.** var. † **Co:ntradicto·rious.**

Contradistinct (kǫ:ntrădisti·ŋkt), *a.* 1621. [See CONTRA-.] Contradistinguished; distinct and in contrast.

Contradistinction (kǫ:ntrădisti·ŋkʃən). 1647. [See CONTRA-.] The action of contradistinguishing; distinction by contrast or opposition.
An *actual* possession by the bankrupt, in c. to a *constructive* possession 1789.

Contradistinctive (kǫ:ntrădisti·ŋktiv), *a.* 1641. [See CONTRA-.] Serving to contradistinguish; marking contradistinction (*rare*). Also as *sb.*

Contradistinguish (kǫ:ntrădisti·ŋgwiʃ), *v.* 1622. [See CONTRA-.] *trans.* To distinguish by contrasting.
The development which contradistinguishes the Hellene from the barbarian M. ARNOLD.

Contrafago·tto; see CONTRA-.

† **Contrafi·ssure.** 1676. [See CONTRA-.] *Surg.* A fracture of the skull produced on the contrary side to that which received the blow –1783.

Contrafocal (kǫntrăfōᵘ·kăl), *a.* 1866. [See CONTRA-.] *Math.* Of two conics, etc.: Having the sums of the squares of two corresponding axes equal: opp. to CONFOCAL conics.

Contragre·dient, *a.* 1853. [f. CONTRA- + L. *-gredient-* pres. ppl. stem of *gradi* step, proceed; see -ENT.] *Math.* Of two systems of variables: Such that when one undergoes linear substitution, the other undergoes linear substitution simultaneously, but of a contrary kind. So **Contragre·dience,** the quality of being c.

Contrahent (kǫ·ntrăhěnt). 1524. [– *contrahent-*, pres. ppl. stem of *contrahere*; see CONTRACT *v.*, -ENT.] *adj.* Contracting. *sb.* A contracting party.

Contra-indicant (kǫ:ntrăˌi·ndikănt). 1623. [See CONTRA-. Cf. next.] *Med.* A symptom which makes against a particular diagnosis, and indicates contrary or other treatment.

Contra-indicate (kǫ:ntrăˌi·ndikeⁱt), *v.* 1666. [See CONTRA-.] *Med. trans.* To give indications contrary to; said *esp.* of symptoms which make against a particular treatment or remedy.
Other urgent or contraindicating symptoms must be observed 1666.

Co:ntra-indica·tion. 1623. [See CONTRA-.] *Med.* An indication which makes against a particular treatment.

Contrala·teral, *a.* 1882. [See CONTRA-.] *Med.* That is on the opposite side.

Contra-lode (in *Mining*); see COUNTERLODE.

Contralto (kǫ̆ntra·lto). Pl. **-ti, -tos.** 1730. [– It., f. CONTRA- + ALTO *sb.*[2]; 'a counter treble in musicke' (Florio). Cf. COUNTERTENOR.] *Mus.* **a.** The part sung by the highest male or the lowest female voice; **b.** a voice of this compass; **c.** a singer having a contralto voice. (Now usually restricted to the female voice.) Also *attrib.* or *adj.*

Contramure, obs. var. of COUNTERMURE *v.*

Contranatural (kǫ:ntrăˌnæ·tiŭrăl), *a.* 1633. [See CONTRA-.] Contrary to what is natural; opposed to nature.

Contraplex (kǫ·ntrăpleks), *a.* 1879. [f. CONTRA- + *-plex* -fold, as in *simplex, duplex*, etc.] *Telegr.* Having two currents passing in opposite directions at the same time.

Contrapo·se, *v.* 1617. [– L. *contraponere*, with substitution of *-pose* for *-pone*, as in *compose, repose.*] **1.** To set in opposition, or over against each other. **2.** *Logic.* To convert by contraposition.

Contraposition (kǫ:ntrăpŏzi·ʃən). 1551. [– late L. *contrapositio* (Boethius), f. *contraposit-*, pa. ppl. stem of L. *contraponere*; see CONTRAPOSE, -ITION.] **1.** A placing over against; antithesis, opposition 1581. **2.** *Logic.* A mode of conversion in which from a given proposition we infer another having the contradictory of the original predicate for its subject; thus 'All S is P' becomes 'No not-P is S'. (Also called Conversion by Negation.)

Contrapositive (kǫ:ntrăpǫ·zitiv). 1870. [f. *contraposit-*; see prec., -IVE.] *adj.* Of, belonging to, or produced by contraposition. *sb.* Anything characterized by contraposition 1870.

Co:ntraprove·ctant. [See CONTRA-.] *Math.* A covariant regarded as generated by operating on any covariant with a contraprovector. So **Co:ntraprove·ctor,** the operator obtained by replacing the facients by symbols of partial differentiation in any contravariant. CAYLEY.

Contraption (kǫ̆ntræ·pʃən). 1834. *colloq.* [Of western dial. and U.S. origin; perh. f. *contrive*, vaguely after *deceive/deception*, by assoc. w. TRAP *sb.*[1]] A device, contrivance.

Contrapuntal (kǫntrăpɒ·ntăl), *a.* 1845. [f. It. *contrappunto* COUNTERPOINT + -AL[1].] Of, pertaining to, or of the nature of counterpoint; according to the rules of counterpoint. Hence **Contrapu·ntally** *adv.* **Contrapu·ntist,** one skilled in counterpoint.

Co:ntra-rela·ted, *ppl. a.* 1866. [See CONTRA-.] *Dynamics.* Having as their kinematical exponents contrafocal ellipsoids.

Co:ntra-remo·nstrant. 1618. [See CONTRA-.] One who remonstrates in answer or opposition to a remonstrance. Also *attrib.* So **Co:ntra-remo·nstrance.**

Contrariant (kǫ̆ntrēə·riănt), *pple., a.* and *sb.* ME. [- (O)Fr. *contrariant*, pres. pple. of *contrarier* oppose, act in opposition to, etc., - late L. *contrariare*, f. L. *contrarius*; see CONTRARY, -ANT.] †*pple.* Opposing. *adj.* **1.** Opposed, contrary *to* 1530; †contrary -1649. **2.** Mutually antagonistic 1560. *sb.* One who or that which is opposed in purpose or nature 1657. Hence **Contra·riantly** *adv.*

Contrariety (kǫntrărəi·ěti). ME. [- (O)Fr. *contrariété* - late L. *contrarietas*, f. *contrarius*; see CONTRARY, -ITY.] **1.** The state or quality of being contrary; opposition, repugnance, disagreement; inconsistency; (with *a* and *pl.*) an instance of this. **2.** Opposition to one's purpose or advantage; hence (with *a* and *pl.*) an adversity, mishap, disadvantage ME. **3.** *Logic.* Contrary opposition 1553.

1. That in the words of our Saviour there can be no c. MILT. He will be here, and yet he is not here: How can these contrarieties agree 1 *Hen. VI*, II. iii. 59. **2.** To shelter them from C. of Seasons 1620. **Contrarily,** *adv.* 1485; = CONTRARIWISE. So **Contrariness** late ME.

Contrarious (kǫ̆ntrēə·riəs), *a.* Now *rare.* ME. [- OFr. *contrarious* - med.L. *contrariosus*; see CONTRARY, -OUS.] **1.** † Contrary or repugnant -1656; opposed ME.; perverse ME. **2.** Adverse, untoward; vexatious ME. Hence **-ly** *adv.*, **-ness.**

Contrariwise, *adv.* ME. [Earlier *on the contrary wise*; see CONTRARY. Pronunciation kǫ·ntrări,wəi:z (the most frequent); also kǫntræ·riwəiz, and kǫntrēə·riwəiz.] **1.** On the other hand, on the contrary. **2.** In the opposite way, order, or direction; *vice versâ* 1570.

1. Heaven is compared to an hill. .Hell c. to a Pit 1605. **2.** It hath seldome or neuer been seene, that the farre Southern People have inuaded the Northern, but c. BACON.

Co:ntra-rota·tion. 1729. [See CONTRA-.] Rotation in the opposite direction.

Contrary (kǫ·ntrări). ME. [- AFr. *contrarie*, (O)Fr. *contraire* - L. *contrarius*, f. *contra* against, opposite; see CONTRA, -ARY[1]. Originally stressed *contra·ry*, which is still *dial.*]

A. *adj.* **1.** Opposed in nature or tendency; mutually opposed; †different -1696. **2.** The opposite, the other (of two things) ME. **3.** Of persons and actions: †Hostile -1662; contrarious. (Only in popular use, and pronounced *contrā·ry.*) 1850. †**4.** Of things: Prejudicial, untoward -1737. **5.** Opposite in position or direction ME. **6.** *Logic.* See quots.

1. Other. .helde contrarye oppynyon CAXTON. C. diseases should have c. remedies HOOKER. **2.** All ignorant of her c. sex SPENSER. **3.** Mary, Mary, quite c. *Nursery Rhyme.* **4.** Wayes. .either crosse or c. BP. HALL. **6.** *C. propositions*: those most opposed to each other in quality, each denying every possible case of the other, as *All A is B*: *No A is B.* *C. terms*: those furthest apart within the same class, as *black* and *white*. *C. opposition*: that of c. propositions or terms. var. † **Co·ntrair.** [f. OFr. *contraire.*]

B. *sb.* [the adj. used *absol.*] †**1.** Opposite position or side *Wint. T.* I. ii. 372. **2.** An object, fact, or quality that is the very opposite of another; often in *pl.* ME. †**3.** Hostility; an act of hostility -1565. †**4.** A denial -1555. †**5.** An adversary, enemy -1622. **6.** *Logic.* A contrary term or proposition; see A. 6. 1655.

2. For good and wikkednesse ben tuo contraries CHAUCER. Phr. *By contraries*: by direct contrast; also, just in the opposite way. *The c.*: the exact opposite or reverse. *On the c.*: on the other hand, in contradistinction; by no means, far from it. *To the c.*: to the opposite effect.

C. *adv.* **1.** Contrarily, contrariwise (*to*) 1463. **2.** Adversely 1497. **3.** On the contrary (*arch.*) 1549. **4.** In an opposite way; in *Her.* = COUNTER 1596.

2. What storme is this that blowes so contrarie? *Rom. & Jul.* III. ii. 64.

Contrary, *v.* Now *dial.* ME. [- (O)Fr. *contrarier*; see CONTRARIANT.] **1.** *trans.* To oppose, thwart; to contradict; to do what is contrary to 1581. **2.** *intr.* To act, speak, or write in opposition ME.

1. The winds contrarying his course 1649.

Contrast (kǫ̆ntra·st), *v.* 1489. [I. *contrest* (Caxton) - OFr. *contrester* resist, oppose :- med.L. *contrastare* withstand, strive (L. *contra* CONTRA, *stare* stand); II. (XVII) - Fr. *contraster* (XVII) - It. *contrastare* (as I).]

† **I.** To resist, *trans.* and *intr.* -1688.

II. 1. *trans. Fine Arts.* To put in contrast differences of form, colour, etc., so as to heighten the total effect 1695. **2.** *gen.* To set (objects) in opposition in order to bring out their differences, and compare their superiorities or defects. (Usu. of mental comparison only.) 1799. **3.** Of things: To set off (each other) by contrast 1695; to form a contrast to 1767. **4.** *intr.* To form a contrast; to exhibit a difference on comparison (*with*) 1715. (Also *pass.* of 3 in same sense.)

1. Contrasted by contrary motions, the most noble parts foremost in sight DRYDEN. **3.** The figures of the groups. .must c. each other by their several positions DRYDEN. Hence **Contra·stive** *a.* forming a contrast; standing in contrast (*to*).

Contrast (kǫ·ntrɑst), *sb.* 1597. [- Fr. *contraste* - It. *contrasto* strife, opposition, f. *contrastare* withstand, strive :- med.L. *contrastare*; see prec.] †**1.** Contention, strife -1670. **2.** *Fine Arts.* The juxtaposition of forms, colours, etc., so as to heighten the effect of corresponding parts and of the whole 1711. **3.** Comparison of objects of like kind whereby the difference of their qualities is brought out; an instance of this 1731. **4.** A person or thing of most opposite qualities 1764.

2. C. increases the splendour of beauty, but it disturbs its influence RUSKIN. **3.** A lucky parallel or a striking c. JOHNSON. **4.** What a c. from such an intention was the event MME D'ARBLAY. var. † **Contra·sto** (in sense 1).

Contrastimulant (kǫ:ntră,sti·miŭlănt). 1831. [- It. *contrastimolante.*] *Med.* A medicine that acts in opposition to a stimulant, or that reduces the force of the vital actions.

Contrate (kǫ·ntrět), *a.* 1450. [- med.L., Rom. *contrata* adj.; see COUNTRY.] †**1.** ?Opposed. **2.** *C. wheel*: a wheel having teeth set at right angles to its plane, as in certain watches 1696.

† **Contratenor** (kǫntrăte·nəɹ). 1552. [- It. *contratenore*; see CONTRA-.] *Mus.* = COUNTERTENOR -1782.

Contravallation (kǫ:ntrăvălēi·ʃən). 1678. [- Fr. *contrevallation* or It. *contravallazione*, f. L. *contra* CONTRA + *vallatio* entrenchment, f. late L. *vallare* entrench, f. *vallum* rampart; see WALL, -ATION.] *Mil.* A chain of redoubts and breastworks, constructed by besiegers, to protect their camp against sorties of the garrison.

Contravariant (kǫntrăvēə·riănt). 1853. [See CONTRA-.] *Math.* 'A function which stands in the same relation to the primitive function from which it is derived as any of its linear transforms to an inversely derived transform of its primitive' (Sylvester).

Contravene (kǫntrăvī·n), *v.* 1567. [- late L. *contravenire* (Augustine), f. *contra* CONTRA + *venire* come. Cf. Fr. *contrevenir.*] **1.** *trans.* To go counter to; to transgress (a law, etc.); to come in conflict with. **2.** To oppose in argument; to contradict, dispute, deny 1722.

1. Either to conform to the tenour of the article, or to c. it BURKE. To. .warn them against acts which c. this duty 1793. **2.** Conclusions so firmly based that we may not c. them HUXLEY. Hence **Contrave·ner.**

Contravention (kǫntrăve·nʃən). 1579. [- (O)Fr. *contravention* - med.L. *contraventio*; see CONTRA-, CONVENTION.] The action of contravening; violation, transgression.

C. of the church catechism DICKENS, of the chronological order STANLEY.

Contrave·rsion. *rare.* [f. CONTRA- + *-version* as in DIVERSION, tr. Gr. ἀντιστροφή.] A turning in the opposite direction. CONGREVE.

Contrayerva (kǫntrăyɜ̄·ɹvă). 1656. [Sp.; = 'counter-herb', *i.e.* one used as an antidote, f. CONTRA- + *yerva* (now *yerba*) HERB.] The root-stock of species of *Dorstenia* (*D. contrayerva* and *D. braziliensis*, N.O. *Urticaceæ*) native to tropical America, used as a stimulant and tonic, and formerly against snake-bites.

Contre-, *prefix.* Fr. *contre* :- L. *contra* has regularly given in Eng. COUNTER, q.v. Frequent in heraldic terms, as *c.-barré*, etc.; = COUNTER-BARRY, etc., q.v.

‖ **Contrecoup** (koṅtrəku). 1830. [Fr. 'counter-blow', f. *contre* against + *coup* blow.] **1.** 'A repulse in the pursuit of any object' (Jamieson). **2.** *Surg.* The effect of a blow, as an injury, fracture, produced exactly opposite, or away from, the part actually struck.

Contrectation (kǫntrektēi·ʃən). 1602. [- L. *contrectatio*, f. *contrect-*, pa. ppl. stem of *contrectare*, f. *com* CON- + *tractare* touch, handle.] Handling, touching.

Contre-dance, ‖ **-danse, contra-dance.** 1803. [- Fr., alteration of COUNTRY-DANCE, by assoc. w. *contre* against, opposite.] A country-dance; esp. a French country-dance.

Contrefort; see COUNTER-.

‖ **Contretemps** (kǒṅtr'taṅ). 1684. [Fr., orig. motion out of time, f. CONTRE- + *temps* time.] †**1.** *Fencing.* A pass or thrust made at a wrong or inopportune moment -1725. **2.** An inopportune occurrence; an unexpected mishap or hitch 1802.

2. Grieved. .by a cruel c. MAR. EDGEWORTH.

Contributable (kǫ̆ntri·biutăb'l), *a.* 1611. [f. CONTRIBUTE + -ABLE.] **1.** Liable to contribute. [So Fr. *contribuable.*] **2.** Payable as contribution 1824.

† **Contributary** (kǫ̆ntri·biutări), *a.* (and *sb.*) ME. [f. as prec. + -ARY[1]; cf. late L. *contributarius* jointly taxed.] Contributing; tributary -1801. *sb.* One who contributes; one who pays tribute -1599.

Contribute (kǫ̆ntri·biut), *v.* 1530. [- *contribut-*, pa. ppl. stem of L. *contribuere* bring together, f. *com* CON- + *tribuere* bestow.] †**1.** *trans.* To levy tribute upon (*rare*) 1559. †**2.** *intr.* To pay tribute (*to*). MARLOWE. **3.** To give or pay jointly with others; to furnish to a common fund or purpose 1530; *intr.* or *absol.* to give or make contribution 1610. **4.** *transf.* and *fig.* To give or furnish along with others to a collective stock 1653. *intr.* or *absol.* 1864. **5.** *fig.* To lend (agency or assistance) to a common result or purpose. *trans.* and (more usually) *intr.* 1605.

3. Every hand is open to c. something JOHNSON. *intr.* A fund was raised. .to which all parties. . contributed SMILES. **4.** Essays, contributed to the Edinburgh Review MACAULAY. **5.** *intr.* He contributed greatly to improve the national music W. IRVING. Hence **Contri·butive** *a.* that has the quality or power of contributing; fitted to c. (*to*).

Contribution (kǫntribiū·ʃən). ME. [- (O)Fr. *contribution* or late L. *contributio*, f. as prec.; see -ION.] **1.** The action of contributing (see CONTRIBUTE *v.*) 1582. **2.** A sum or thing contributed; now, *esp.* An imposition levied upon a district for the support of an army in the field ME. *transf.* and *fig.* 1648. **3.** *Law.* The payment by each of the parties interested of his share in any common loss or liability 1641. Also *attrib.*

1. To make a certaine c. for the poore Saints which are at Hierusalem *Rom.* 15:26. Phr. *To lay under c.*: to force to contribute. **2.** The smallest c. thankfully received 1893. *transf.* A letter.. apparently..a c. from a fresh hand 1882. Hence **Contribu·tional** *a.* of or pertaining to a c.

Contributor (kǫ̆ntri·biutəɹ). 1530. [– AFr. *contributour* (mod.Fr. *-eur*), f. as prec.; see -OUR, -OR 2.] **1.** One that contributes; *spec.* one who contributes literary articles to a journal, magazine, etc. †**2.** One who pays tribute –1630.

Contributory (kǫ̆ntri·biutəri). 1467. [– med.L. *contributorius*, f. as prec.; see -ORY[2].] **A.** *adj.* **1.** That contributes; †tributary –1601. **2.** Of the nature of contribution 1836.

1. C. allies GROTE. C. to our own destruction CLARENDON. *C. negligence*: negligence on the part of a person injured, which has conduced to the injury.

B. *sb.* **1.** One who, or that which, contributes 1467. **2.** *Eng. Law.* One who is bound, on the winding up of a joint stock company, to contribute toward the payment of its debts.

† **Contri·st**, *v.* 1490. [– (O)Fr. *contrister* – L. *contristare* sadden, f. *com* CON- + *tristis* sad.] *trans.* To make sad –1818. var. † **Contri·state;** whence † **Constrista·tion.**

Contrite (kǫ·ntrəit), *a.* (and *sb.*) ME. [– (O)Fr. *contrit, -ite* – L. *contritus*, pa. pple. of *conterere*, f. *com* CON- + *terere* rub, grind (see TRITE).] †**1.** *lit.* Bruised, crushed (*rare*) –1755. **2.** *fig.* Crushed or broken in spirit by a sense of sin; reduced to contrition ME.

1. A c. reed JER. TAYLOR. **2.** A broken and a c. heart, O God, thou wilt not despise *Ps.* 51:17. In very c. and earnest words 1868. So † **Contri·ted** *ppl. a.* Hence **Co·ntrite-ly** *adv.*, **-ness** (*rare*).

Contrition (kǫ̆ntri·ʃən). ME. [– (O)Fr. *contrition* – late L. *contritio*, f. *contrit-* pa. ppl. stem of *conterere*; see prec., -ION.] †**1.** *lit.* The action of rubbing together; grinding, pounding, or bruising (so as to pulverize) –1684. **2.** *fig.* The condition of being bruised in heart; affliction of mind for some fault or injury done; *spec.* penitence for sin. Cf. ATTRITION. ME.

1. Triturable, and reduceable to powder, by c. SIR T. BROWNE. **2.** In the tyme of thy repentaunce and contrycyon 1530.

Contriturate (kǫ̆ntri·tiŭreⁱt), *v. rare.* 1822. [f. CON- + TRITURATE.] To triturate thoroughly, pulverize.

Contrivance (kǫ̆ntrəi·văns). 1627. [f. CONTRIVE *v.*[1] + -ANCE.] **1.** The action of contriving; inventing, plotting, or planning 1646. **2.** Adaptation of means to an end; design 1695. **3.** The faculty of contriving; inventive capacity 1659. †**4.** The way in which a thing has been contrived –1834. **5.** Something contrived for a purpose; a plan, an artifice 1627; a mechanical device 1667. Also *fig.*

1. The preparations..yet are..in c. and agitation MAY. **2.** Proofs of C. in the Structure of the Globe WOODWARD. **5.** The grand Scheme and C. for our Redemption 1754. *fig.* The contrivances by which Orchids are fertilized DARWIN. vars. † **Contri·val. Contri·vancy** (in sense 3).

Contrive (kǫ̆ntrəi·v), *v.*[1] [ME. *controve, contreve* – OFr. *controver* (with suffix stress), *contreuve* (with stem-stress), mod.Fr. *controuver* invent, † imagine – med.L. *contropare* compare, prob. f. *com* CON- + *tropus* TROPE. For the ME. *contreve* cf. †*meve*, MOVE, †*preve*, PROVE. The form *contrive* is unexplained.] **1.** *trans.* To invent, devise, excogitate with ingenuity and cleverness. †**2.** *intr.* To form devices; to plot, conspire –1641. **3.** *trans.* To devise, design ME. †**4.** To find out –1600. †**5.** To concoct, fabricate. [Cf. Fr. *controuver.*] –1468. **6.** To bring to pass 1530. †**7.** To bring by ingenuity or skill *into* a place, position, or form –1701.

1. I will..sodainely contriue the meanes of meeting betweene him, and my daughter *Haml.* II. ii. 216. **2.** The Fates with Traitors do c. *Jul. C.* II. iii. 16. **3.** To c. a tubular bridge 1856. **6.** Prophecies when once they get abroad..C. their own fulfilment SHELLEY.

Hence **Contri·vable** *a.* that can be contrived † **Contri·vement**, = CONTRIVANCE 1, 4, 5. **Contri·ver.**

† **Contri·ve**, *v.*[2] ME. [app. irreg. f. L. *contrivi*, pret. of *conterere*.] *trans.* To wear down; to pass (time) –1596. *Tam. Shr.* I. ii. 276.

Control (kǫ̆ntrōᵘ·l), *sb.* 1590. [– next, or Fr. *contrôle*, f. the verb.] **1.** The fact of controlling, or of checking and directing action; domination, command, sway. **2.** Restraint, check 1594. **3.** A method or means of restraint; a check 1752. **4.** A person who acts as a check; a controller 1786.

1. Quenching my familiar smile with an austere regard of controll *Twel. N.* II. v. 74. **2.** Speak what thou know'st, and speak without controul POPE. **3.** The..checks and controuls provided by the constitution HUME. *C.-experiment*: a test experiment devised to check the inferences deduced from an experiment, by application of the Method of Difference. **4. b.** The apparatus for controlling an aeroplane or motor vehicle 1908. **c.** A section of the road over which speed is controlled, or where contesting machines are allowed time to stop for overhauling, etc. 1900.

Control (kǫ̆ntrōᵘ·l), *v.* 1475. [– AFr. *contreroller*, Fr. † *conteroller* (now *contrôler*) – med.L. *contrarotulare*, f. *contrarotulus*, f. *contra* opposite + *rotulus* ROLL *sb.*[1]] **1.** *trans.* To check or verify, and hence to regulate (payments, etc.): *orig.* by comparison with a duplicate register. Also *transf.* †**2.** Hence: To call to account, reprove (a person) –1692; to reprehend, object to (a thing) –1738. **3.** To exercise restraint or direction upon the free action of; to dominate, command 1495. Also *refl.* **4.** †To overpower –1755; in *Law*, to overrule 1724.

1. To controlle the receytes & all the yssues of the Thesaurers office 1475. *transf.* To c. statements 1878. **3.** But (oh vaine boast) Who can control his Fate *Oth.* V. ii. 265. Hence **Contro·llable** *a.*

Controller (kǫ̆ntrōᵘ·ləɹ). [ME. *counterrollour, -er* – AFr. *contrerollour*, f. *contreroller*; see prec., -OUR, -ER[2]. See COMPTROLLER.] **1.** One who keeps a counter-roll so as to check a treasurer or person in charge of accounts. †**2.** A censorious critic –1614. **3.** One who or that which controls: *Naut.* an apparatus for regulating or checking the motion of a chain-cable as it runs towards the hawse-holes 1867.

1. Comptroller of the houshold SWIFT, of the Navy SIR J. ROSS. **3.** It makes the great controwler of the world, a bare spectator PRYNNE. **C.-general:** an officer entrusted with the supreme control. Hence **Contro·llership,** the office of c.

Controlment (kǫ̆ntrōᵘ·lmĕnt). *arch.* 1494. [f. CONTROL *v.* + -MENT.] †**1.** The controlling of accounts –1565. **2.** = CONTROL *sb.* 1. 1494. **3.** = CONTROL *sb.* 2. 1525. †**4.** Censure –1646.

3. Heere haue we war for war, & bloud for bloud, Controlement for controlement *John* I. i. 20.

† **Controve·rsal**, *a.* 1612. [– late L. *controversalis*, irreg. var. of *controversialis*; see CONTROVERSIAL.] **1.** Turned or looking in opposite directions 1644. **2.** = CONTROVERSIAL –1697.

1. The Temple of Janus with his two c. faces MILTON.

† **Co·ntroverse,** *sb.* 15.. [– (O)Fr. *controverse* – L. *controversia* CONTROVERSY.] = CONTROVERSY –1636.

The c. of beauties soveraine grace SPENSER.

† **Co·ntroverse,** *v.* 1601. [Deduced from CONTROVERSED.] **1.** *trans.* To discuss, debate –1755. **2.** *intr.* To dispute *with* 1699.

† **Co·ntroversed,** *ppl. a.* 1575. [– Fr. *controversé*, for earlier *controvers* – L. *controversus* disputed, questionable, f. *contro-*, var. of CONTRA- + *versus*, pa. pple. of *vertere* turn.] Made the subject of controversy; controverted –1663. So † **Co·ntroverser, -or.**

Controversial (kǫntrǒvɜ̄·ɹʃăl), *a.* 1583. [– late L. *controversialis*, f. *controversia*; see CONTROVERSY, -AL[1].] **1.** Subject to controversy; questionable; disputed. **2.** Of, pertaining to, or of the nature of controversy; polemical 1659. **3.** Disputatious 1659.

1. As c. a point as the authorship of Junius J. WILSON. **2.** Polemical or c. divinity BP. BULL. **3.** The c. pen CRABBE. var. † **Controve·rsary, -ory.** Hence **Controve·rsialist,** one who is skilful in controversy; a disputant. **Controve·rsially** *adv.*

Controversion (kǫntrǒvɜ̄·ɹʃən). 1677. [– OFr. *controversion* controversy – late L. *controversio*, f. L. *controversus*; see next, -ION.] †**1.** A controversy –1762. **2.** The action of controverting 1762. **3.** = CONTRAVERSION, q.v. 1684.

Controversy (kǫ·ntrǒvɜ̄ɹsi), *sb.* ME. [– L. *controversia*, f. *controversus* disputed; see -Y[3]. Cf. Fr. †*controversie* (mod. *controverse* = CONTROVERSE *sb.*).] **1.** Dispute, contention (*esp.* when carried on in writing); contention as to rights, claims, and the like, or on a matter of opinion. **2.** (with *a* and *pl.*) A dispute, contention; *esp.* a discussion of contrary opinions 1573.

1. He..made hym a Iudge in causes of controuersie EDEN. Tossed..with their unballasted wits in fathomless and unquiet deeps of c. MILTON. Phr. *Without, beyond c.* [L. *sine controversia*]: without or beyond question or doubt. **2.** The great c. respecting the 'Origin of Evil' 1852. Hence † **Co·ntroversy** *v.* = CONTROVERSE *v.*

Controvert (kǫ·ntrǒvɜ̄ɹt, kǫntrǒvɜ̄·ɹt), *v.* 1609. [As pa. pple. and ppl. a. replacing CONTROVERSED, on the formal analogy of *converse, convert*, etc.] †**1.** *trans.* To dispute or contest (a title, etc.) –1682. **2.** To make the subject of controversy; to dispute about 1612. **3.** To oppose in argument; to dispute, deny 1613. **4.** *intr.* To engage in a controversy 1616.

2. Why melancholy men are witty..is a problem much controverted BURTON. **3.** The existence hereof men do not c. SIR T. BROWNE.

Hence **Controverted** *ppl. a.* subjected to controversy. **Controverter,** one who controverts. **Controve·rtible** *a.* capable of being controverted; disputable. **Controvertist,** a controversialist.

† **Contru·de,** *v.* 1609. [– L. *contrudere*, f. *com* CON- + *trudere* thrust, shove.] *trans.* To thrust or crowd together –1651. Hence † **Contru·sion** (*rare*).

Contubernal (kǫ̆ntiū·bəɹnăl). 1842. [– L. *contubernalis* tent-companion, f. *com* CON- + *taberna* hut, tent; see -AL[1].] *sb.* One who occupies the same tent. *adj.* Of or relating to occupation of the same tent 1873. So † **Contube·rnial** *a.* sharing the same tent. CHAUCER.

Contumacious (kǫntiumēⁱ·ʃəs), *a.* 1600. [f. as next; see -ACIOUS.] **1.** Exhibiting contumacy; stubbornly perverse, insubordinate, rebellious 1603. **2.** *Law.* Wilfully disobedient to the summons or order of a court 1600.

1. To reduce the c. monks to obedience 1772. Hence **Contuma·cious-ly** *adv.*, **-ness.**

Contumacy (kǫ·ntiŭmăsi). ME. [– L. *contumacia*, f. *contumax, -ac-*, perh. f. *com* CON- + *tumēre* swell; see -Y[3].] **1.** Perverse and obstinate resistance to authority. †**2.** Of diseases, etc.: Reluctance to yield to treatment –1661. **3.** *Law.* Wilful disobedience to the summons or order of a court ME.

1. Such acts Of contumacie will provoke the highest MILT. *P.L.* X. 1027. var. **Contuma·city** (*rare*).

† **Co·ntumax,** *a.* ME. [– L. *contumax* insolent, obstinate; see prec.] = CONTUMACIOUS –1587.

Contumelious (kǫntiumī·liəs), *a.* 1483. [– OFr. *contumelieus* (mod. *-eux*) – L. *contumeliosus*, f. *contumelia*; see next, -OUS.] **1.** Exhibiting CONTUMELY; despiteful; superciliously insolent 1548. †**2.** Reproachful, disgraceful –1663.

1. With scoffes and scornes, and c. taunts SHAKS. Curving a c. lip TENNYSON. **2.** In so base and c. a condition COWLEY. Hence **Contume·lious-ly** *adv.*, **-ness.**

Contumely (kǫ·ntiumīli). ME. [– OFr. *contumelie* – L. *contumelia*, f. *com* CON- + *tumēre* swell.] **1.** Insolent reproach or abuse; insulting or contemptuous language or treatment; despite; scornful rudeness; now *esp.* such as tends to dishonour or humiliate. (Also with *a* and *pl.*) **2.** Disgrace, reproach 1555.

1. The Oppressors wrong, the poore mans C. *Haml.* III. i. 71. **2.** It..casteth a kind of c. upon the author of it PEARSON.

Contund (kǫ̆ntʌ·nd), *v. rare.* 1599. [– L. *contundere*, f. *com* CON- + *tundere* beat, thump, etc.] †**1.** *trans.* To pound, beat small –1656. **2.** To affect with contusions; to pound (adversaries). *joc.* or *affected.* 1654.

† **Contu·ne,** *v.* Var. of CONTINUE.

† **Conturba·tion.** 1470. [– L. *conturbatio*, f. *conturbat-*, pa. ppl. stem of *conturbare* disturb greatly, f. *com* CON- + *turbare* disturb; see -ION.] Disturbance (physical or mental) –1816.

Contuse (kǫ̆ntiū·z), *v.* 1541. [– *contus-*, pa. ppl. stem of *contundere*; see CONTUND; cf.

OFr. *contuser*.] **1.** *trans.* To injure as by a blow without breaking the skin; to bruise. †**2.** To pound, beat small, bray –1626.

2. Roots, Barks, and Seeds, contused together 1626.

Contusion (kǫ̆ntiū·ʒən). ME. [– Fr. *contusion* – L. *contusio*, f. as prec.; see -ION.] **1.** The action of bruising, or condition of being bruised. Also *transf.* **2.** An injury, as from a blow with a blunt instrument or heavy body, which does not break the skin; a bruise 1593. †**3.** Beating small, pounding, or braying –1764.

2. That Winter Lyon who in rage forgets Aged contusions 2 *Hen. VI*, v. iii. 3. So **Contu·sive** *a.* bruising; of or belonging to a c.

Conundrum (kǒnʊ·ndrǒm). 1596. [Origin lost.] †**1.** ? Crotchet-monger. NASHE. †**2.** A whim, crotchet, maggot –1719. †**3.** A pun or word-play depending on similarity of sound in words of different meaning –1794. **4.** A riddle the answer to which involves a pun; also, any puzzling question, problem, or statement 1790. **5.** A 'what-d'ye-call-it' (*rare*). SCOTT.

2. (Tipsy man says) I begin To have strange conundrums in my head MASSINGER. **4.** 'You speak in conundrums,' said Morley; 'I wish I could guess them' DISRAELI.

†**Co·nusable, -ance, -ant,** etc.; earlier forms of COGNIZABLE, etc.

Convalesce (kǫnvăle·s), *v.* 1483. [– L. *convalescere*, f. *com* CON- + *valescere* grow strong, f. *valēre* be strong or well.] **1.** *intr.* To recover from sickness, get better. **2.** *Rom. Law.* To become valid 1875.

1. That illness when one does not c. at all THACKERAY. Hence **Convale·scence,** gradual recovery of health after illness. So **Convale·scency** (*rare*). **Convale·scent** *a.* recovering health after illness; *sb.* one who is recovering from sickness; *attrib.* of or for convalescents. **Convale·scently** *adv.*

Convallamarin (kǫnvæ:lămēᵊ·rin). 1863. [f. Vulg. L. *convallium* (see next) + *amarus* bitter + -IN¹.] *Chem.* A bitter glucoside, $C_{23}H_{44}O_{12}$, obtained from the Lily of the Valley (*Convallaria majalis*). So **Convalla·rin,** an acrid purgative glucoside, $C_{34}H_{62}O_{11}$, obtained from the Lily of the Valley.

†**Convally.** Adapted form of *lilium convallium* 'lily of the valleys' (Vulg., *S. of S.* 2:1), used by herbalists. vars. **Conval, convaile.**

Convection (kǫ̆nve·kʃən). 1623. [– late L. *convectio*, f. *convect-*, pa. ppl. stem of *convehere*, f. *com* CON- + *vehere* carry; see -ION.] *Physics.* The action of carrying; conveyance; *spec.* the transportation of heat or electricity by the movement of a heated or electrified substance, as in the ascension of heated air or water. Also *attrib.*

The passage of electricity from one place to another by the motion of charged particles is called Electrical C. or Convective Discharge MAXWELL.

Convective (kǫ̆nve·ktiv), *a.* 1859. [f. L. *convect-*, ppl. stem of *convehere* carry, convey.] **1.** Having the property of conveying. **2.** Of the nature of or relating to convection 1862.

1. The c. force of a stream of water 1862. Hence **Conve·ctively** *adv.*

†**Conve·ll,** *v.* 1536. [– L. *convellere*, f. *com* CON- + *vellere* tear, pull, pluck.] **1.** *lit.* To tear, wrench –1694. **2.** *fig.* To overthrow completely –1724. So **Conve·llent** *a.* wrenching, pulling up.

†**Convenable** (kǫ·nvĭnăb'l), *a.*¹ ME. [– Fr. *convenable* (OFr. also *covenable*, whence COVENABLE, CONABLE), f. *convenir* be fitting; see CONVENE, -ABLE.] **1.** Suitable, meet –1815. **2.** Consistent –1579. **3.** Convenient –1641.

1. A conuenable mariage 1579. **2.** With his word his work is c. SPENSER. Hence †**Co·nvenably** *adv.*

Convenable (kǫ̆nvī·năb'l), *a.*² 1755. [f. CONVENE + -ABLE.] Capable of being convened.

‖**Convenance** (koṅvənāṅs). 1483. [Fr., f. *convenir* be fitting; see CONVENE, -ANCE. Earlier COVENANCE.] †**1.** A convention, covenant (*rare*). †**2.** Concurrence (*rare*) –1677. ‖**3.** Conventional usage; in *pl.* the conventionalities 1847.

3. Her utter ignorance of London *convenances* and proprieties 1881.

Convene (kǫ̆nvī·n), *v.* ME. [– L. *convenire* assemble, be fitting, agree, suit, f. *com* CON- + *venire* come.]

I. 1. *intr.* To come together; to meet, *esp.* for a common purpose; *transf.* of things: To occur together 1541; †to unite –1738. **2.** *trans.* To cause to come together; to convoke 1596. **3.** To summon before a tribunal ME.

1. The two princes convened . . in the suburbs of Calais BACON. If the rays c. before the retina 1738. **2.** The Senate was convened by the tribunes FROUDE. **3.** Knapwell was convened before the Archbishop HOOK.

II. †**1.** *intr.* Of persons: To agree –1652. †**2.** To be suitable or fitting –1627. **3.** *intr.* To harmonize 1855.

3. Articles which the marriage-mongers cannot make to c. at all, tempers . . tastes, etc. THACKERAY.

Convener (kǫ̆nvī·nəɹ). 1572. [f. prec. + -ER¹.] **1.** One who assembles with others –1641. **2.** One who convokes (a meeting, etc.); *spec.* one appointed to summon the meetings of a committee, etc. (*Sc.*) 1680.

Convenience (kǫ̆nvī·niĕns), *sb.* ME. [– L. *convenientia*, f. *convenient-*; see next, -ENCE.] †**1.** Agreement, accordance –1652. †**2.** Accordance of nature; fitness –1756. **3.** The quality of being convenient, generally; suitability, commodiousness 1601. **4.** The quality of being personally convenient; ease in use or action; material advantage; commodity, comfort 1703. **5.** (with *a* and *pl.*) That which is convenient 1606; *pl.* convenient material arrangements or appliances. (Rarely in *sing.*) 1672.

3. The great c. and pleasure of navigation HY. MORE. **4.** Phr. *At one's c., to await one's c., marriage of c.*, etc. A building for the c. of the drinkers 1756. **5.** Riches . . with divers other conveniences 1647. That he may buy Books the next c. HEARNE. A c. to spit in SMOLLETT. To make a c. of one 1893. All the conveniences of a palace LADY M. W. MONTAGU.

Hence **Conve·nience** *v.* to accommodate. var. **Conve·niency** (now little used).

Convenient (kǫ̆nvī·niĕnt), *a.* ME. [– *convenient-*, pres. ppl. stem of L. *convenire*; see CONVENE, -ENT.] †**1.** Agreeing (in opinion) 1485. †**2.** Accordant, congruous (*to*) –1654. †**3.** In keeping with; befitting, becoming (*to* or *for*); proportionate (*to*) –1677. †**4.** Suitable, appropriate (*to* or *for*) –1790. †**5.** Morally becoming; proper –1727. **6.** Personally suitable; favourable to one's comfort or ease; commodious. (The current sense.) 1477. **7.** *colloq.* and *dial.* Handy 1848.

2. Equitable and c. to reason 1654. **4.** *Prov.* 30:8. **5.** Neither filthinesse, nor foolish talking, nor iesting, which are not conuenient *Eph.* 5:4. **6.** And so by conveniente jorneys came to the towne of Edenborough HALL. **7.** Heretics used to be brought thither c. for burning hard by THACKERAY. Hence **Conve·niently** *adv.*, †**-ness,** c. quality.

Convent (kǫ·nvĕnt), *sb.* [ME. *covent* (surviving in the name *Covent* Garden, London) – AFr. *covent*, OFr. *convent* (regularly with latinized sp., which finally prevailed in Eng.), mod. *couvent* :– L. *conventus* assembly, company, f. *convent-*, pa. ppl. stem of *convenire* CONVENE.] †**1.** A gathering; a meeting –1661. †**2.** A company; *spec.* that of the twelve apostles –1548. **3.** A religious association; a body of monks, friars, or nuns forming one local community ME. **4.** The buildings occupied by such a community. (The restriction of the word to a convent of women is not historical.) 1528. Also *attrib.*

1. In the c. of other witches GAULE. **3.** Saynt Audry, than abbesse, toke her holy couent And mette the sayd kynge BRADSHAW. **4.** Out of his c. of gray stone . . Walked the Monk Felix LONGF. Hence **Conve·ntical** *a.* conventual (*rare*).

Convent (kǫ̆nve·nt), *v.* Now *Hist.* 1514. [– *convent-*, pres. ppl. stem of L. *convenire* CONVENE; cf. *prevent*.] **1.** = CONVENE *v.* I. 1–3. –1718. †**2.** ? To covenant to give 1587. ¶**3.** ? = CONVENE *v.* II. 2.

3. When that is knowne, and golden time conuents A solemne Combination shall be made Of our deere soules *Twel. N.* v. i. 391.

Conventicle (kǫ̆nve·ntik'l). ME. [– L. *conventiculum* assembly, place of assembly, in form dim. of *conventus* meeting (see CONVENT *sb.*), but not used with derogatory reference till mediæval times.] †**1.** An assembly –1650. **2.** A meeting (*esp.* a religious meeting), of a private, clandestine, or illegal kind, as of Nonconformists or Dissenters in England, or of Covenanters in Scotland, during the reigns of Charles II and James II. 1438. †**3.** *contempt.* A 'hole-and-corner' meeting –1682. **4.** A place of meeting 1596; *esp.* a nonconformist or dissenting meeting-house. (Now *rhet.* or *contempt.*) 1550. †**5.** A small convent –1603.

1. He [the Mayor] called a Conuenticle of his Brethren GREENE. **2.** My selfe had notice of your Conuenticles, And all to make away my guiltlesse Life 2 *Hen. VI*, III. i. 166. When some Men seeke Christ, in the Conuenticles of Heretikes BACON. A c. of gloomy sullen Saints DRYDEN.

Comb. **C. Acts,** the acts 16 Chas. II, c. 4 and 22 Chas. II, c. 1 'to prevent and suppress seditious Conventicles'.

Hence **Conve·nticle** *v.*, *intr.* to meet in a c.; to hold or frequent conventicles. **Conventiclee:r, Conve·nticler,** a frequenter of conventicles; a schismatic.

Convention (kǫ̆nve·nʃən). ME. [– (O)Fr. *convention* – L. *conventio* meeting, covenant, f. *convent-*; see CONVENT *v.*, -ION.]

I. †**1.** The action of coming together –1782. Also †*fig.* of things. **2.** The action of summoning an assembly 1647. †**3.** The action of summoning before a tribunal –1726. **4.** An assembly of persons for some common object; *esp.* a formal assembly, ecclesiastical, political, or social 1552. **5.** *Eng. Hist.* An assembly of the Houses of Parliament, without the summons of the Sovereign; as that of 1660, which restored Charles II, and that of 1688, which declared the throne abdicated by James II. Hence *c. parliament.* 1660.

1. In this place of c. of merchants from all parts of the world EVELYN. **2.** The c. of the parliament CLARENDON. **4.** If that suffice not, they may call a new c. of estates HOBBES. **5.** In 1689, the C. declared itself a Parliament J. R. GREEN.

II. 1. An agreement or covenant between parties ME. **2.** *spec.* **a.** In *Diplomacy*: An agreement between sovereigns or states: formerly = TREATY; now an agreement less formal than a treaty 1603. **b.** *Mil.* An agreement made between the commanders of armies in time of war 1780. **3.** General agreement or consent, as embodied in any accepted usage, standard, etc.; in a bad sense: Conventionalism 1778. **4.** A conventionalism 1790.

1. Fraudulent conventions oblige not BP. HALL. **2. a.** An International C. respecting the Liquor traffic in the North Sea 1888. **b.** The conventions for suspending hostilities agreed upon by me with Marshals Soult and Suchet WELLINGTON. **3.** This Gorgon of C. and Fashion EMERSON.

Comb. **c.-coin, -dollar,** coins struck according to monetary conventions between different German states.

Conventional (kǫ̆nve·nʃənăl), *a.* 1583. [– Fr. *conventionnel* or late L. *conventionalis*; see prec., -AL¹.] **1.** Of, pertaining to, or of the nature of a convention or assembly 1812. **2.** Relating to, of the nature of, or settled by a convention or compact. In *Law*: Founded on contract (opp. to *legal* or *judicial*). 1583. **3.** Relating to convention or general agreement; established by social convention; arbitrarily or artificially determined 1761. **4.** Characterized by convention; not natural, original, or spontaneous; in *Art*, consisting in, or resulting from, an artificial treatment of natural objects; following traditions 1851.

3. In matters merely c., examples are more powerful than principles GIBBON. **4.** The c. phraseology with which English preaching had been so long encumbered STANLEY. Specimens of c. or imaginary foliage SIR G. SCOTT. Phr. *The c.*: that which is c. Hence **Conve·ntionally** *adv.*

Conventionalism (kǫ̆nve·nʃənăliz'm). 1837. [f. prec. + -ISM.] **1.** Adherence to or regard for that which is conventional (in conduct, thought, or art). **2.** (with *a* and *pl.*) Anything that is merely conventional; a conventional principle, idea, usage, or practice.

1. The incubus of c. HT. MARTINEAU.

Conventionalist (kǫ̆nve·nʃənălist). 1801. [f. as prec. + -IST.] **1.** A member or supporter of a Convention. **2.** One who follows conventional usage 1846.

Conventionality (kǫ̆nvenʃənæ·lĭti). 1834. [f. as prec. + -ITY.] **1.** The quality or state of being conventional; conventional character or style; obedience to mere convention 1842. **2.** A conventional thing or practice.

Conventionalize (kǫnve·nʃənăləiz), *v.* 1854. [f. as prec. + -IZE.] *trans.* To make conventional; to bring under conventional rules; in *Art*, to treat conventionally, represent in a conventional manner. Hence **Conve:ntionaliza·tion.**

Conventionary (kǫnve·nʃənări), *a.* and *sb.* 1602. [– med.L. *conventionarius*; see CONVENTION, -ARY¹.] **1.** Applied to tenants and tenure on terms originally fixed by convention (see CONVENTION II. 1) as distinguished from custom. **2.** *sb.* A c. tenant or tenure 1828.

Conventionist (kǫnve·nʃənist). 1768. [See -IST.] **1.** A member of a convention 1823. †**2.** One who enters into a contract. STERNE.

Conventual (kǫnve·ntiuăl), *a.* and *sb.* ME. [– med.L. *conventualis*, f. *conventus*; see CONVENT, -AL¹. Cf. (O)Fr. *conventuel*.]

A. *adj.* Of or belonging to a religious convent; characteristic of a convent.

In c. garb PRESCOTT. The c. discipline of prose LOWELL. Hence **Conve·ntually** *adv.*

B. *sb.* **1.** A member of a convent 1611. **2.** A member of that branch of the Franciscan order which lives in large convents and follows a mitigated rule; dist. from the Observants 1533.

Converge (kǫnvɜ̄·ɹdʒ), *v.* 1691. [– late L. *convergere* incline together, f. *com* CON- + L. *vergere* bend, turn, incline.] **1.** *intr.* To tend to meet in a point; to approach nearer together. The opposite of *diverge*. Also *fig.* **2.** *Math.* To approximate in the sum of its terms toward a definite limit 1796. **3.** *trans.* To cause to come together 1768.

1. The sides of the Ship c. into an Angle 1691. *fig.* Every circumstance converges to the same effect on the mind HALLAM. **3.** Power of converging the optic axes 1863.

Convergence (kǫnvɜ̄·ɹdʒĕns). 1713. [f. CONVERGENT; see -ENCE.] **1.** The action or fact of converging; movement toward or terminating in the same point. Also *fig.* and *transf.* **2.** *Math.* Of convergent series or fractions 1858.

1. In the metropolis of commerce the point of c. was the Exchange MACAULAY. *fig.* C. of effort LEWES.

Conve·rgency. 1709. [f. as prec.; see -ENCY.] **1.** Convergent quality. **2.** = CONVERGENCE 1791.

Convergent (kǫnvɜ̄·ɹdʒĕnt), *a.* 1727. [– *convergent-*, pres. ppl. stem of late L. *convergere*; see CONVERGE, -ENT.] **1.** Inclining towards each other, or towards a common point of meeting; tending to meet in a point or focus. Also *fig.* and *transf.* **2.** *Math.* = CONVERGING 2. 1816.

1. Rays [of light] may be either divergent, parallel, or c. TYNDALL. A c. attack 1862.

Conve·rgine:rved, *a.* [irreg. f. *convergenti-*, comb. form of the pres. pple. of late L. *convergere* (see prec.) + NERVE + -ED².] *Bot.* 'When the ribs of a leaf describe a curve and meet at the point' (*Treas. Bot.* 1866).

Converging (kǫnvɜ̄·ɹdʒiŋ), *ppl. a.* 1727. [f. CONVERGE *v.* + -ING².] **1.** = CONVERGENT 1. 1776. **2.** *Math.* Applied to an infinite series of terms, the sum of which, beginning with the first, continually approximates towards a definite limit as more and more are taken 1727. **3.** Causing convergence 1833.

3. The gathering or c. power of any glass. Hence **Conve·rgingly** *adv.*

Conversable (kǫnvɜ̄·ɹsăb'l), *a.*, (erron. **-ible.**) 1598. [– Fr. †*conversable* affable, etc. – med.L. *conversabilis*, f. L. *conversari*; see CONVERSE *v.*, -ABLE.] **1.** That may be conversed with (see CONVERSE *v.*); pleasant in conversation; disposed to converse. **2.** Of or pertaining to social converse 1631.

2. The evening was quiet and c. JANE AUSTEN. Hence **Conve·rsableness,** c. quality. **Conve·rsably** *adv.*

Conversance (kǫ·nvəɹsăns). 1609. [f. CONVERSANT; see -ANCE.] The state or quality of being conversant. So **Co·nversancy.**

Conversant (kǫ·nvəɹsănt). ME. [– (O)Fr. *conversant*, pres. pple. of *converser*; see CONVERSE *v.*, -ANT.]

A. *adj.* (usu. predicative). †**1.** Dwelling habitually or frequently *in* a place. **2.** Having familiar intercourse *with*, †*in*, †*among*, †*about* ME. **3.** Occupied *in*, †*about*, †*upon*; having to do *with* ME. **4.** Versed *in*; familiar *with* 1573. †**5.** Frequently occurring; familiar –1651.

2. C. with women STEELE, with Heaven COWPER. Conuersant in princes courtes BARET. **3.** C. in studies BACON, with man or men's affairs MILT., about language WHATELEY. **4.** C. in the Scriptures BACON, with questions of finance 1878.

† **B.** *sb.* One who is intimate with another –1680.

Conversation (kǫnvəɹsēⁱ·ʃən). ME. [– (O)Fr. *conversation* – L. *conversatio* frequent use or abode, intercourse, f. *conversari* CONVERSE *v.*; see -ATION.] †**1.** The action of living or having one's being *in* or *among*. Also *fig.* –1705. †**2.** The action of consorting with others; living together; commerce, society, intimacy –1770. **3.** Sexual intimacy 1511. †**4.** *fig.* Occupation *with* things; intimacy with a matter –1721. †**5.** Circle of acquaintance, society –1712. **6.** Behaviour, manner of life (*arch.*) ME. **7.** Interchange of thought and words; familiar discourse or talk 1580; a talk 1694. †**8.** An 'At Home' –1787. **9.** (In full *c. piece*): A kind of *genre* painting representing a group of figures. H. WALPOLE. ¶ **10.** = CONVERSION ME.

1. For our conuersation is in heauen *Phil.* 3:20. **3.** *Criminal c.* (abbrev. to *crim. con.*): adultery. **4.** Out of..much c. in books 1626. C. with Antiquity 1702. **6.** To him that ordereth his conuersation aright *Ps.* 50:23. **7.** To lead the c. JOHNSON. **8.** Lady Pomfret has a charming c. once a week H. WALPOLE.

Hence **Conversa·tional** *a.* ready to converse; addicted to c.; of, belonging to, or proper to c. **Conversa·tionalist, Conversa·tionist,** one who excels in c. **Conversa·tionally** *adv.* † **Conversa·tioned** *ppl. a.* behaved. BEAUM. & FL.

Conversative (kǫnvɜ̄·ɹsătiv), *a. rare.* 1631. [f. CONVERSE + -ATIVE.] †Sociable; talkative.

‖ **Conversazione** (kǫ:nvəɹsætsiōᵘ·ni). Pl. **-oni** (-ōᵘ·ni), now usu. **-ones.** 1740. [It. = conversation.] ‖ **1.** In Italy, an evening assembly for conversation, and recreation. † **2.** In England, an 'At Home'. Cf. CONVERSATION 8. –1823. **3.** A *soirée* or other assembly of an intellectual character, in connection with literature, art, or science 1792.

1. A *c.*, a sort of assembly at the principal people's houses, full of I cannot tell what GRAY.

Converse (kǫnvɜ̄·ɹs), *v.* ME. [– (O)Fr. *converser* †pass one's life, exchange words :– L. *conversari* live, have intercourse, middle use of *conversare* turn round, f. *com* CON- + *versare*, frequent. of *vertere* turn.] † **1.** *intr.* To move about, live *in* (*on, upon*), *among* (*with*) –1727. †**2.** To consort, keep company; to be familiar *with* –1819. **3.** To be engaged *in*; to have to do *with*; to be conversant *with*. *Obs.* exc. as *fig.* 1586. †**4.** To interchange ideas *with*, by speech or writing or otherwise –1771. **5.** *spec.* 'To convey the thoughts reciprocally in talk' (J.); to talk *with*. The ordinary current sense. 1615.

1. Cetaceous Fishes which c. chiefly in the northern Sea RAY. **2.** MILT. *P.L.* II. 184. They may lawfully c. together as man and wife 1656. **3.** A man..who has conversed, not only with books, but with lawyers and merchants..statesmen and princes MACAULAY. **4.** Like ships at sea, they must c. by signals DE FOE. **5.** You are cheerful, and love to c. upon death SOUTHEY. Hence **Conve·rser.**

Converse (kǫ·nvəɹs), *sb.*¹ 1604. [f. prec.; orig. stressed like the verb.] **1.** = CONVERSATION 2, 3. *Obs.* exc. in certain expressions now referred to 3. 1610. †**2.** = CONVERSATION 4. –1727. **3.** = CONVERSATION 7. Now *poet.* or *rhet.* 1604. **4.** Spiritual or mental communion 1668. †**5.** Manner of life –1702.

1. C. with the world will do more for you DISRAELI. **3.** Sweet is thy c. to each Social ear POPE. **4.** With Nature here high c. hold SHENSTONE.

† **Converse,** *a.*¹ and *sb.*² ME. [– (O)Fr. *convers* – L. *conversus*, subst. use of pa. pple. of L. *convertere* CONVERT *v.*] *adj.* Converted in mind or feeling. ME. only. *sb.* A lay member of a convent –1691.

† **Converse,** (kǫ·nvəɹs), *a.*² and *sb.*³ 1570. [– L. *conversus* turned about, transformed; see prec.]

A. *adj.* Turned round; opposite or contrary in direction or action 1794.

The c. arts of destruction and defence BURTON. Hence **Conve·rsely** *adv.*

B. *sb.* **1.** *gen.* A form of words derived from another by the transposition of two antithetical members; a thing or action which is the exact opposite of another 1786. **2.** *Math.* (One proposition is the c. of another, when the datum and conclusion of the one are respectively taken as the conclusion and datum of the other.) 1570. **3.** *Logic.* A converted proposition: formerly applied to the CONVERTEND, but now usually to that which results from conversion 1827.

1. What we gain in power is lost in time; and the c. EMERSON. **2.** The 8 proposition being the conuerse of the fourth BILLINGSLEY. **3.** The absolute quantity of the C. must be exactly equal to that of the Convertend SIR W. HAMILTON.

Conversible (kǫnvɜ̄·ɹsib'l), *a.* 1660. [– late L. *conversibilis*, f. *convers-*; see next, -IBLE.] Capable of being converted or transposed. ¶ See also CONVERSABLE.

Conversion (kǫnvɜ̄·ɹʃən). ME. [– (O)Fr. *conversion* – L. *conversio*, f. *convers-*, pa. ppl. stem of *convertere*; see CONVERT *v.*, -ION.]

I. †**1.** The action of converting; rotation –1726; turning –1712; returning –1682. **2.** Transposition, inversion; *spec.* in *Logic*, the transposition of the subject and predicate of a proposition to form a new proposition 1551. **3.** *Math.* The substitution of the difference of antecedent and consequent for the consequent in each of the ratios forming a proportion. ? *Obs.* 1570. **4.** *Law.* The action of (wrongfully) converting something to one's own use 1615.

1. The c. of the needle to the north SIR T. BROWNE. **4.** There may be a trover and no c., if he keep and lay up the goods, for the Owner COKE.

II. 1. The action of converting, or fact of being converted, to a religion, a belief, or opinion; *spec.* to Christianity ME. **2.** *Theol.* The turning of sinners to God; a spiritual change from sinfulness to a religious life ME. **3.** Change of form or properties, condition, or function 1549. Hence in many techn. uses in *Manuf.* †**4.** *Mil.* A change of front to a flank –1863.

1. The conuersion of the gentyles EDEN. **2.** See how God wrought for my conuersion GREENE. **3.** Not by conuersion of the Godhead into flesh *Bk. Com. Prayer.* The c. of a muzzle-loader 1874.

III. † **1.** Translation; a translation, version –1653. **2.** *Math.* Change of a number or quantity into another denomination 1557. **3.** Substitution of or exchange for something else 1607. **b.** *spec.* in *Law.* The operation of converting property (see CONVERT III. 2) 1788.

3. The c. of the four per cents into three and a half per cents was facilitated 1826. **b.** The usual trusts for sale and c. 1893.

Conversive (kǫnvɜ̄·ɹsiv), *a.* 1607. [– Fr. †*conversif, -ive* = med.L. *conversivus*, f. as prec.; see -IVE.] **1.** Having the power or function of conversion 1655. **2.** Convertible 1864. Hence † **Conversively** *adv.* conversely.

Convert (kǫnvɜ̄·ɹt), *v.* ME. [– (O)Fr. *convertir* :– Rom. **convertire*, for L. *convertere* turn about, transform, f. *com* CON- + *vertere* turn.]

I. †**1.** *trans.* To turn about, direct. *refl.* = To turn (*intr.*) –1738. Also † *fig.* †**2.** *trans.* To turn back –1633. **3.** † To invert, transpose –1551. **b.** *Logic.* To transpose the terms of (a proposition) by CONVERSION 1638. †**4.** *fig.* To reverse the course of; *pa. pple.* = opposite, contrary –1703. **5.** To turn or apply *to* (another use), to divert; *spec.* in *Law*, wrongfully to appropriate and apply *to* (one's own use). (Cf. CONVERSION I. 4.) 1480.

1. Priests..who usually in their Sacrifices..C. themselves unto the East HEYLIN. **5.** Receiuours of his reuenues..conuerted the same to their owne singuler profit 1542.

II. †**1.** *trans.* To turn in mind, feeling, or conduct –1577; *intr.* to turn *from* a course of conduct, etc. –1600. **2.** *trans.* To cause to turn to a religion, belief, or opinion; *spec.* to bring to Christianity ME. Also †*intr.* **3.** *Theol.* To cause to turn from a sinful to a religious life ME. Also †*intr.* **4.** To turn *into* something different; to transform; to change in character or function; also †*intr.* ME.

1. Blessid be Love, that can thus folk c. CHAUCER. *intr.* When thou from youth conuertest SHAKS. *Sonn.* xi. **2.** þar was conuerted thusand fiue ME. **3.** Rather that he should be conuerted and liue *Bk. Com. Prayer.* **4.** That still lessens The sorrow, and converts it nigh to joy MILT. *Sams.* 1564. To c. the Enfield rifle into a breech-loader 1874. In Rugby football, to kick a goal from (a try) 1896.

III. 1. To change by substituting an equivalent; † *spec.* to translate –1651. **2.** *Law.* To change the quality of property, as from real to personal, joint to separate, or *vice versâ* 1793.

1. To c. goods into money SMILES.

Convert (kǫ·nvəɹt). 1561. [f. prec. v., superseding and perh. infl. by synon. CONVERSE *sb.*²]

† **A.** *adj.* **1.** Brought over to a religious faith. **2.** *C. brother, sister*: = CONVERSE *sb.*² –1693.

B. *sb.* A person brought over to any religious faith, or (*transf.*) to any opinion, party, etc. 1561.

Convertend (kǫ·nvəɹte:nd). 1837. [– L. *convertendus*, *-um* to be converted, gerundive of *convertere* CONVERT *v.*] *Logic.* The proposition as it stands before conversion; opp. to *converse*.

Converter (kǫ̈nvə̄·ɹtəɹ). Also *erron.* **-tor.** 1533. [f. CONVERT *v.* + -ER¹.] **1.** One who makes converts 1570. **2.** One who converts (see CONVERT *v.*) 1533. **3.** That which converts: in *Steel Manuf.*, a retort, made of iron and lined with some refractory material (usually *ganister*), in which pig-iron is converted into steel by the Bessemer process; see BESSEMER.

Convertible (kǫ̈nvə̄·ɹtib'l), *a.* (*sb.*) ME. [– (O)Fr. *convertible* – L. *convertibilis*, f. *convertere* CONVERT *v.*; see -IBLE.] **1.** That may be converted; interchangeable. **2.** Capable of being turned to a particular use or purpose 1818. **3.** Capable of being turned *into* something else; capable of being changed in form, condition, or qualities 1533. **4.** Capable of being converted by exchange into property of another kind 1834. **5.** As *sb. pl.* = C. things or terms 1615.

1. [Those who] put prelacy and popery together as terms c. SWIFT. **3.** A rogue alive to the ludicrous is still c. EMERSON. Heat is c. into electricity HUXLEY. **4.** By rendering paper money c. into metallic currency HT. MARTINEAU. Hence **Conve:rtibi·lity,** c. quality. **Conve·rtibly** *adv.*

Convertite (kǫ·nvəɹtəit). *arch.* 1565. [f. after Fr. *converti*, subst. use of pa. pple. of *convertir*; see -ITE¹ 1.] A (professed) convert to religion; *spec.* a reformed Magdalen. Also *transf.*

Convex (kǫ·nveks). 1571. [– L. *convexus* vaulted, arched. Cf. (O)Fr. *convexe*.]

A. *adj.* Having a curvature that bulges towards the point of observation; the reverse of *concave*.

The convexe or out-bowed side of a vessel BP. HALL. The light is made by a c. glass or lens to converge to one point or focus 1833.

B. *sb.* [the adj. used *ellipt.*] † **1.** A convex body or surface –1796. **2.** A convex glass or lens 1705.

1. In circuit to the uttermost c. Of this great round MILT. *P.L.* VII. 266.

Hence **Convex** *v. rare*, to make c.; *intr.* to bow or bend convexly. **Convexed** *ppl. a.* made in a c. form. † **Conve·xedly, Co·nvexly** *advs.* in a c. form or manner. **Convexness,** c. quality.

Convexity (kǫ̈nve·ksĭti). 1600. [– L. *convexitas*, f. *convexus*; see prec., -ITY. Cf. Fr. *convexité*.] **1.** The condition of being convex; outward bulging 1605. **2.** A convex curve, surface, side, or part.

1. The finiteness or c. of heaven BACON.

Convexo- (kǫ̈nve·kso). In comb. = Convexly, convex and —, as in **c.-concave,** convex on one side and concave on the other; of the form of a meniscus; **c.-convex,** convex on both sides; **c.-plane,** convex on one side and flat on the other = *plano-c.*

Convey (kǫ̈nvēⁱ·), *v.* ME. [– OFr. *conveier* (mod. *convoyer* CONVOY *v.*) :– med.L. *conviare*, f. *com* CON- + *via* way.] † **1.** *trans.* To CONVOY, escort –1710. † **2.** To lead, conduct; also *fig.* –1713. **3.** To transport, carry, take from one place to another ME. † **4.** To take *away*, remove, *esp.* clandestinely –1697; hence, *euphem.* to steal –1753. † *refl* –1697. **5.** To lead or conduct as a channel or medium 1601. **6.** † To transmit, or cause to pass –1741; *esp.* to communicate, impart (an idea, benefit, etc.) ME.; hence, to express in words 1576. **7.** To transfer, as property, to another; now only in *Law*, to transfer by deed or legal process; also *absol.* 1495. † **8.** To bring down, derive –1606. † **9.** To conduct (an affair); to manage with privacy or craft –1661.

3. Luggage conveyed by these coaches will be charged for 1891. **4.** *Merry W.* I. iii. 31. Iesus had conueyed himself away *John* 5:13. **5.** Thro' reeden Pipes c. the Golden Flood DRYDEN. To c. the impressions of sound 1854. **6.** To c. a lesson 1766, Thoughts to one another SOUTH. **7.** The cost of conveying a small estate 1863. **9.** *Lear* I. ii. 109.

Hence † **Convey** *sb.* conveyance; a CONVOY. **Convey·able** *a.* that may be conveyed. **Convey·al,** the act of conveying, conveyance.

Conveyance (kǫ̈nvēⁱ·ăns). 1503. [f. prec. + -ANCE.] † **1.** Convoying –1604. **2.** The action of conveying, or transporting; carriage 1520. **3.** Furtive carrying off; stealing 1526. **4.** The communicating (*of* a thing *to* any one) 1662. **5.** Transmission, transference 1646. **6.** *Law.* The transference of (*esp.* real) property from one person to another by deed or writing 1523; the instrument of transfer 1576. **7.** The conveying of anything by a channel or medium 1577. † **8.** The conveying of meaning by words; hence, style –1775. † **9.** Management; *esp.* skilful, or cunning, management –1704; an artifice –1641. **10.** A conducting way, passage, etc. 1542. **11.** A means of transport from place to place 1598. † **12.** *fig.* A 'vehicle' (of thought, etc.) –1841.

1. *Oth.* I. iii. 286. **2.** Arrangements for the c. of money 1870. **3.** The simile..is stolen from Cowley, however little worth the trouble of c. JOHNSON. **6.** Covenous and fraudulent..conveyaunces..as well of landes..as of goodes and catals 1571. *Haml.* V. i. 119. **7.** C. by Condit or pumpe 1577. **9.** A pretty slip-skin c. MILT. **10.** *Cor.* V. i. 54. **11.** The steam-packet is a beastly c. DISRAELI.

Conveyancer (kǫ̈nvēⁱ·ănsəɹ). 1623. [f. prec.; see -ER¹ 1.] One who or that which conveys; *esp.* a lawyer who practises conveyancing.

Conveyancing (kǫ̈nvēⁱ·ănsiŋ), *vbl. sb.* 1676. [f. as prec. + -ING¹.] † **1.** Deceitful contrivance –1690. **2.** The drawing of deeds and other instruments for the transference of property from one person to another; the branch of the law which deals with titles and their transference 1714.

Conveyer (kǫ̈nvēⁱ·əɹ). 1513. [f. CONVEY *v.* + -ER¹.] **1.** One that conveys, carries, or transmits. † **2.** A light-fingered thief. *Rich. II*, IV. i. 317. **3.** One who transfers property 1647. **4.** That which conveys, or transmits; *spec.* any mechanical contrivance for conveying grain in a mill, timber in a saw-mill, etc. 1880. var. **Convey·or** (in senses 3, 4).

† **Convi·ciate,** *v.* 1604. [– *conviciat-*, pa. ppl. stem of L. *conviciari* (*-vit-*) revile, f. *convicium* (*-vit-*) loud reproach; see -ATE³.] *trans.* To revile, slander, rail at –1646. So † **Convi·ciatory,** † **Convi·cious** *adjs.* railing; reproachful.

† **Convici·nity.** *nonce-wd.* [See CON-.] Vicinity to each other. WARTON.

Convict (kǫ̈nvi·kt), *ppl. a.* ME. [– L. *convictus*, pa. pple. of *convincere* CONVINCE.] *pa. pple.* and *adj.* **1.** Proved or pronounced guilty. **2.** Overcome ME.

1. C. of having four Wives at one and the same time COTTON.

Convict (kǫ·nvikt), *sb.* 1530. [f. prec.] **1.** One judicially convicted of a criminal offence (*arch.*). **2.** *spec.* A criminal serving a sentence of penal servitude 1786. Also *attrib.*

2. Escape of a c. from Dartmoor 1893.

Convict (kǫ̈nvi·kt), *v.* ME. [– *convict-*, pa. ppl. stem of L. *convincere* CONVINCE.] **1.** *trans.* To prove to be guilty, or in the wrong; *esp.* by judicial procedure. Also *absol.* 1841. † **2.** To demonstrate or prove –1656. **3.** To bring conviction home to (a person) 1526. **4.** To disprove, refute (*arch.*) 1594. † **5.** To overcome –1607.

1. No englishman should be conuicted except by English Judges POWEL. Convicted of want of sensibility MORLEY. **3.** They..being conuicted by their owne conscience, went out one by one *John* 8:9. **4.** Which conceit being already convicted, not only by Scaliger, etc. SIR T. BROWNE. **5.** *John* III. iv. 2. Hence **Convi·ctable, -ible** *a.* (*rare*).

Conviction (kǫ̈nvi·kʃən). 1491. [– L. *convictio*, f. as prec.; see -ION.] **1.** Legal proof or declaration of guilt; the fact or condition of being convicted. † **2.** Demonstration, proof –1647. † **3.** Confutation –1661. † **4.** Detection and exposure –1724. **5.** The act of convincing 1664. **6.** The condition of being convinced; settled persuasion 1699. **7.** A settled persuasion 1841. **8.** *Theol.* The fact or condition of being convicted or convinced of sin 1675.

1. Summary convictions, without the intervention of a jury W. BELL. **4.** Further reproof and c. of the Roman errors JER. TAYLOR. **5.** The C. of those who are either of a contrary opinion..or who are in doubt WHATELY. **6.** A painful c. of his defects JOHNSON. Phr. *To carry c.* **8.** My soul was at that very time groaning under deep convictions 1821.

Convictism (kǫ·nviktiz'm). 1864. [f. CONVICT *sb.* + -ISM.] The system of penal settlements for convicts. **b.** The convict class or body.

b. The invasion of c. from Swan River 1868.

Convictive (kǫ̈nvi·ktiv), *a.* 1612. [f. CONVICT *v.* + -IVE.] Having power to produce conviction.

The c. answer of Christ BP. HALL. Hence **Convi·ctive-ly** *adv.*, **-ness.**

Convictor (kǫ̈nvi·ktəɹ, -ǫɹ). 1647. [– L. *convictor* one who lives with another, f. *convict-*, pa. ppl. stem of *convivere*, f. *com* CON- + *vivere* live; see -OR 2.] A table companion; a commoner.

Convince (kǫ̈nvi·ns), *v.* 1530. [– L. *convincere* convict of error, refute, f. *com* CON- + *vincere* overcome.]

I. † **1.** To overcome, vanquish. Also *absol.* –1633. † **2.** To overcome in argument; to confute –1708. **3.** To bring to acknowledge the truth *of*; to satisfy by argument or evidence. In *pass.*, To be brought to a full conviction. (= CONVICT *v.* 3.) 1632.

1. *Macb.* I. vii. 64. **2.** There was none of you that conuinced Iob, or that answered his words *Job* 32:12. **3.** I am convinced..and have nothing more to object JOWETT. To c. of a mistake 1797, of sin 1648.

II. † **1.** = CONVICT *v.* 1. –1776. † **2.** = CONVICT *v.* 2. –1730. † **3.** = CONVICT *v.* 4. –1625.

1. Which of you conuinceth mee of sin *John* 8:46. **2.** This may be easily convinced as false SALKELD. **3.** God neuer wrought Miracle to conuince Atheisme, because his Ordinary Works conuince it BACON. Hence **Convi·nced** *ppl. a.* brought to a state of conviction. **Convi·ncement,** conviction. **Convi·ncer** (*rare*). **Convi·ncing-ly** *adv.*, **-ness,** c. quality. † **Convi·ncive** *a.* having the power of convincing (*rare*).

Convincible (kǫ̈nvi·nsib'l), *a.* 1643. [– late L. *convincibilis*, f. *convincere*; see prec., -IBLE.] **1.** Capable of being †convicted or convinced. † **2.** Of convincing power 1647.

† **Convi·val.** 1615. [– L. *convivalis*, varying with *convivialis*; see CONVIVIAL, -AL¹.] *adj.* = CONVIVIAL –1755. *sb.* A guest 1615.

‖ **Convive** (kǫ̈ṅvīv, kǫ·nvəiv), *sb.* 1648. [Fr. – L. *conviva* fellow-feaster.] One who feasts with others; a fellow-banqueter. Hence † **Co·nvive** *v.* to feast together (*rare*).

Convivial (kǫ̈nvi·viăl), *a.* 1668. [– L. *convivialis*, var. of *convivalis* (see CONVIVAL), f. *convivium* feast, f. *com* CON- + *vivere* live; see -IAL.] **1.** Of or belonging to a feast or banquet; festive. **2.** Fond of feasting and good company, jovial 1784.

1. Which feasts c. meetings we did name DENHAM. **2.** The plump c. parson COWPER. Hence **Convi·vialist,** a person of c. habits. **Convi·vially** *adv.*

Conviviality (kǫ̈nvi:vi,æ·lĭti). 1791. [f. prec. + -ITY.] Convivial quality; the enjoyment of festive society, festivity; convivial spirit.

His [Pope's] disqualifications for the coarsest forms of c. L. STEPHEN.

Co·nvocate, *ppl. a.* 1532. [– L. *convocatus*, pa. pple. of *convocare*; see CONVOKE, -ATE².] *pa. pple.* and *adj.* Convocated (*arch.* and *poet.*).

Convocate (kǫ·nvokeⁱt), *v.* 1540. [– *convocat-*, pa. ppl. stem of L. *convocare*; see CONVOKE, -ATE³.] *trans.* To call or summon together (*arch.*).

Convocation (kǫnvokēⁱ·ʃən). ME. [– L. *convocatio*, f. as prec.; see -ION.] **1.** The action of calling together or assembling by summons. **2.** An assembly of persons thus convo] d

ME. **3.** *Eng. Ch.* A provincial synod, constituted by statute and called together to deliberate on ecclesiastical matters ME. **4.** At Oxford: The great legislative assembly of the University, consisting of all qualified members of the degree of M.A.; a meeting of this body 1577.

1. The c. of the Army 1678. **2.** And in the first day there shalbe an holy conuocation *Exod.* 12:16. **3.** They [the Thirty-nine Articles] were made at three several Convocations SELDEN. *Comb.* **C.-house,** the place where a c. meets; the assembly itself. Hence **Convoca·tional** *a.* of, belonging to, or of the nature of, a c. **Convoca·tionist,** a supporter of C.

Convoke (kǫnvōᵘ·k), *v.* 1598. [– L. *convocare* call together, f. *com* CON- + *vocare* call. Cf. (O)Fr. *convoquer.*] *trans.* To call together; to bring together by summons. Also *fig.*

For five years afterwards the Queen did not c. Parliament HALLAM.

Convolute (kǫ·nvoliut), *a.* 1794. [– L. *convolutus*, pa. pple. of *convolvere* CONVOLVE.] **1.** *Bot.* Coiled laterally upon itself, as a leaf in the bud. **2.** *gen.* Rolled or folded together; having convolutions 1874. Also as *sb.* So **Co·nvolute** *v. rare*, to coil up; *intr.* to wind about. **Co·nvoluted** *ppl. a.* coiled, twisted, or sinuous; exhibiting convolutions.

Convolution (kǫnvŏliū·ʃən). 1545. [– med.L. *convolutio*, f. *convolut-*, pa. ppl. stem of *convolvere*; see next.] **1.** The action of coiling, twisting, or winding together; the condition of being convoluted 1597. **2.** A fold, twist, turn, winding, sinuosity (of anything rolled or coiled up) 1545. **3.** *Anat.* Each of the sinuous folds of the cerebrum 1615.

1. Toss'd wide around, O'er the calm sky, in c. swift THOMSON.

Convolve (kǫnvǫ·lv), *v.* 1599. [– L. *convolvere*, f. *com* CON- + *volvere* roll.] †**1.** *trans.* To enclose in folds –1794. **2.** To roll together, coil, twist 1650. **3.** *intr.* To revolve together 1808.

2. Then Satan first knew pain, And writh'd him to and fro convolved MILT. *P.L.* VI. 329.

Convolvulaceous (kǫnvǫlviŭlēⁱ·ʃəs). 1847. [f. mod.L. *Convolvulaceæ* + -OUS.] *Bot.* Of or belonging to the natural order *Convolvulaceæ*, of which *Convolvulus* is the typical genus.

Convo·lvulin. 1850. [f. L. *convolvul(us* + -IN¹.] *Chem.* A glucoside, $C_{31}H_{50}O_{16}$, obtained from the rhizome of *Convolvulus schiedanus*, the officinal jalap-root.

Hence **Convolvuli·nic** acid, also called **Convo·lvulic,** $C_{31}H_{54}O_{18}$, a product of the action of fixed alkalis upon c.

Convolvulus (kǫnvǫ·lviŭlŏs). Pl. **-luses,** rarely **-li.** 1551. [– L. *convolvulus* bindweed.] *Bot.* A large genus of plants, having slender twining stems and trumpet-shaped flowers, including the English BINDWEEDS.

The lustre of the long convolvuluses That coil'd around the stately stems TENNYSON.

Convoy (kǫnvoi·), *v. trans.* ME. [– (O)Fr. *convoyer*, var. and mod. form of *conveier* CONVEY.] **1.** To escort. **2.** To escort with, or as, an armed force, either by sea or land, for protection 1559. †**3.** To convey, carry (*lit.* and *fig.*) –1703. †**4.** To manage. *Sc.* –1662.

1. To c...Miss Bellenden home SCOTT. **2.** The squadron..which convoyed the homeward trade in the next autumn 1885. Hence † **Convoy·ance,** artful management; conveyance. **Convoy·er,** one that convoys; a guide; a convoy-ship.

Convoy (kǫ·nvoi), *sb.* 1500. [– (O)Fr. *convoi*, f. the verb; see prec.] †**1.** Conduct (of oneself or of affairs). *Sc.* –1599. **2.** The act of escorting, for honour, guidance, or protection 1557. **3.** An escort 1523. **4.** A protecting escort; *esp.* ships of war 1596. †**5.** A guide –1726. **6.** A thing that conducts, a channel, way, etc.; *spec.* a clog or brake for conducting a vehicle down an incline 1764. **7.** An individual or company under escort; a supply of ammunition or provisions, or a fleet of merchant ships, under escort 1577. Also *attrib.*

2. Your C. makes the dangerous Way secure DRYDEN. **3.** Heavie funerals and convoies of the dead P. HOLLAND. **4.** And with a c. send him safe away DRYDEN. **7.** A c. of bread 1710, of mules laden with merchandise 1827, of Merchant-ships 1743.

Convulse (kǫnvɒ·ls), *v.* 1643. [– *convuls-*, pa. ppl. stem of L. *convellere* pull violently, wrest, wrench, f. *com* CON- + *vellere* pluck, pull.] **1.** *trans.* To shake violently; to agitate or disturb. **2.** *Path.* To affect with violent involuntary contractions of the muscles, so as to agitate the limbs or the whole body; to throw into convulsions. (Chiefly in *pass.*) 1681. **3.** *intr.* To become convulsed 1684.

1. To..be convulst and tremble at the name of death SIR T. BROWNE. **2.** Convulsing them with irresistible laughter JOHNSON. Hence **Convulse** *sb.* convulsion (*rare*). **Convu·lsingly** *adv.*

Convulsion (kǫnvɒ·lʃən). 1585. [– Fr. *convulsion* or L. *convulsio*, f. as prec.; see -ION.] †**1.** The action of wrenching, or condition of being wrenched –1825. Also † *fig.* **2.** *Path.* † **a.** Cramp; tetanus –1772. **b.** (usually *pl.*) An affection marked by irregular contractions or spasms of the muscles, alternating with relaxation 1650. **3.** Violent social, political, or physical disturbance 1643.

1. These two massy pillars With horrible c. to and fro He tugged, he shook MILT. *Sams.* 1649. **3.** A c. of the whole kingdom 1769. Earthquakes, volcanos, and convulsions SULLIVAN. Hence **Convu·lsional** *a.* of, pertaining to, or of the nature of c. (*rare*).

Convulsionary (kǫnvɒ·lʃənări). 1741. [f. CONVULSION + -ARY¹, after Fr. *convulsionnaire.*]

A. *adj.* Pertaining to, affected with, or marked by convulsion (*lit.* and *fig.*) 1798. **b.** Pertaining to the Convulsionaries 1814.

C. struggles SCOTT. **b.** The C. delusion 1874.

B. *sb.* One of a number of Jansenist fanatics in France in the 18th century, who fell into convulsions, etc., at the tomb of Francois de Pâris at St.-Médard 1741.

Convu·lsionist. 1865. [f. CONVULSION + -IST.] **1.** = CONVULSIONARY B. **2.** *Geol.* = CATASTROPHIST 1880.

Convulsive (kǫnvɒ·lsiv), *a.* 1615. [f. CONVULSE *v.* + -IVE; cf. Fr. *convulsif.*] **1.** Of the nature of, or characterized by convulsion. Also *fig.* **2.** Affected with convulsion (*lit.* and *fig.*) 1686. **3.** Productive of convulsion 1700.

1. *fig.* C. and perilous reforms 1835. **3.** Nothing so..c. to society, as the strain to keep things fixed STANLEY. Hence **Convu·lsive-ly** *adv.*, **-ness.**

Cony, coney (kōᵘ·ni, kɒ·ni), *sb.* Pl. **conies (coneys).** ME. [Earliest forms *cunin, cuning* – AFr. *coning*, OFr. *conin* :– L. *cuniculus.*] **1.** A rabbit. Still used in the Statutes, and in *Heraldry*. **2.** The fur of the rabbit. Now *dial.* ME. **3.** In O.T. as tr. Heb. *šāpān*, a small pachyderm (*Hyrax syriacus*) ME. **4.** Applied locally to the Cape Hyrax or Das, the Pika or Calling Hare (*Lagomys princeps*), etc. 1555. †**5.** A dupe –1736. †**6.** Some kind of shell-fish; ? a cone 1782. **b.** The Nigger-fish (*Epinephelus punctatus*) of the West Indies.

3. The conies are but a feeble folk, yet they make their houses in the rocks *Prov.* 30:26.

Comb.: † **c.-catch,** *v.* to dupe, gull; † **-catcher**; † **-catching** *vbl. sb.* and *ppl. a.*; **-fish,** the Burbot; **-garth,** a rabbit-warren; **-wool,** the fur of the rabbit.

† **Co·nyger, co·nynger.** [ME. *conynger(e*, etc. – OFr. *con(n)iniere*, parallel form of *con(n)il(l)iere* :– med.L. *cunicularium*, pl. *-aria*, f. L. *cuniculus*; see prec., -ARY¹. Cf. also AL. *coni(n)gera*, etc.] A rabbit-warren –1701.

Conylene (kǫ·nilīn). 1876. [f. CONIA + -YL + -ENE.] *Chem.* A liquid non-poisonous hydrocarbon, C_8H_{14}, having a pungent odour.

‖ **Conyza** (konai·ză). ME. [L. – Gr. κόνυζα.] *Bot.* A genus of strong-smelling Composite plants, formerly including the Flea-banes.

Coo (kū), *v.* 1670. [imit.] **1.** *intr.* To make the soft murmuring note characteristic of doves and pigeons. Also *transf.* **2.** To converse caressingly or amorously; usu. in phr. *to bill and coo* 1816. **3.** To utter by cooing 1798; to send *to rest*, etc. by cooing 1814.

1. So, two kind turtles sit alone, and c. DRYDEN. *transf.* He [the Baby] coos like a pigeon-house EMERSON. Hence **Coo** *sb.* a note of or as of doves or pigeons. **Coo·er,** one that coos.

Co-o·bligant. 1818. [See Co-.] One under joint-obligation. So **Co-o·bligor,** one who binds himself together with others.

Co-occupant; see Co-.

Cooee, cooey (kū·ī, kū·i), *sb.* 1790. The call (kūūūū,ī·!) used as a signal by the Australian aborigines, and adopted by the colonists in the bush. Hence **Coo·ee, coo·ey** *v. intr.* to utter this cry.

Cook (kuk), *sb.* [OE. *cōc* – pop.L. *cōcus*, for L. *coquus*, which is directly repr., with short vowel, by OS. *kok* (Du. *kok*), OHG. *koch* (G. *koch*), Icel. *kokkr.*] One whose occupation is the preparation of food for the table; see COOK *v.*¹ Orig. always masculine.

Comb.: **c.-book,** a cookery-book (U.S.); **-fish, -wrasse,** the male of a species of Wrasse (*Labrus mixtus*); **-house,** *Naut.* a ship's galley; **-maid,** a maid who cooks, or assists the c.; **-room,** a kitchen, or ship's galley; **-shop** (*orig.* **cook's shop**), an eating-house.

Cook (kuk), *v.*¹ ME. [f. the sb.] **1.** *intr.* To act as cook. (Now taken as *absol.* use of 2.) **2.** *trans.* To prepare (food); to make fit for eating by application of heat, as by boiling, baking, roasting, broiling, etc. 1611. *intr.* (for *refl.*) 1857. **3.** *fig.* Also with *up* 1588. **b.** To concoct 1624. **c.** To manipulate, tamper with (*colloq.*) 1636. **4.** To 'do for' (*slang*) 1851.

2. I will tel you..how to c. him WALTON. *intr.* These pears do not c. well 1893. **3. b.** We cooked up a bill for that purpose CHESTERF. **c.** Some falsified printed accounts, artfully cooked up SMOLLETT. **4. b.** Phr. *To c. any one's goose*: to 'do for'; to ruin or kill (*slang*). Hence **Coo·kable** *a.* and *sb.*

† **Cook,** *v.*² 1599. [imit.] To utter the note of the cuckoo –1724.

Cooker (ku·kəɹ). 1884. [f. COOK *v.*¹ + -ER¹.] **1.** A stove for cooking; a vessel in which food is cooked. **2.** A fruit, etc., that cooks well 1887.

Cookery (ku·kəri). ME. [f. COOK *sb.* or *v.*¹ + -ERY 2.] **1.** The art or practice of cooking. †**2.** A product of the cook's art. NORTH. †**3.** A place for cooking; a kitchen, etc. –1837. *Comb.* **c.-book,** a book of receipts, etc., in c.

Cookie (ku·ki). *Sc.* and *U.S.* 1730. [– Du. *koekje*, dim. of *koek* cake.] In Scotland, a baker's plain bun; in U.S., a small flat cake, with, or (locally) without, sweetening.

Cooking-range: cf. RANGE *sb.*¹ III. 1.

Coo·kish, *a. rare.* 1611. [-ISH¹.] Like a cook.

Cool (kūl), *a.* [OE. *cōl* = MLG., MDu. *kōl* (Du. *koel*) :– Gmc. **kōluz*, f. **kōl-* **kal-* (see COLD).] **1.** Moderately cold; neither warm nor disagreeably cold; producing or maintaining coolness; cooling. Also *fig.* **2.** *transf.* Applied to analogous sensations; or to anything which produces them 1647. †**3.** *fig.* Chilled; chilling –ME. **4.** Not affected by passion or emotion; unexcited; deliberate; calm OE. **5.** Deficient in ardour, interest, or zeal; wanting in cordiality 1593. **6.** Calmly audacious or impudent in making a proposal or demand: said of persons and their actions 1825. **7.** *colloq.* Applied to a large sum of money, to give emphasis to the amount 1728.

1. Vnder the coole shade of a Siccamore *L.L.L.* V. ii. 89. A c. dress (*mod.*). *fig.* Coole patience *Haml.* III. iv. 124. **2.** A c. taste 1800, scent 1647, colour (*mod.*). **4.** Coole reason *Mids. N.* V. i. 6. A c. and steady fire 1798. Phr. *In c. blood.* **5.** A c. friend BLACKIE, reception 1706. **6.** Such a request was a trifle C. W. BLACK. **7.** He had lost a c. hundred FIELDING.

Comb.: **c.-headed** *a.*, having a c. head; not easily excited in mind; hence **-hea·dedness; c. tankard,** a cooling drink, made of wine, water, lemon-juice, spices, and borage.

Cool (kūl), *sb.*¹ ME. [f. COOL *a.*] **1.** That which is cool; the cool part, place, time, thing, etc. †**2.** A cool breeze –1573. **3.** Coolness; also *fig.* ME.

1. In the coole of the daye *Gen.* 3:8. **3.** MILT. *P.L.* IX. 1109.

Cool (kūl), *sb.*² 1858. [var. of COWL *sb.*²] *Comm.* A tub of butter, usually of 28 lb.

Cool (kūl), *v.* [OE. *cōlian* = OS. *cōlon* :– Gmc. **kōlōjan*, f. **kōluz* (COOL *a.*).] **1.** *intr.* To become cool or less hot. **2.** *fig.* To lose the heat of excitement or passion; to become less zealous or ardent OE. †**b.** Of things: To lose opportuneness. SHAKS. **3.** *trans.* To make cool; to cause to become less hot ME. Also *absol.* **4.** *fig.* To make less ardent or zealous ME.; to deprive (a thing) of its opportuneness 1716.

1. No fear lest Dinner coole MILT. *P.L.* V. 396. **2.** Thou hast describ'd A hot friend cooling *Jul. C.* IV. ii. 19. **b.** Aduantage, which doth euer coole Ith' absence of the needer *Cor.* IV. i. 43. **3.** To be throwne into the Thames, and coold..like a

Horse-shoo *Merry W.* III. v. 122. **4.** Which cools the resolutions of the zealousest Prince 1670.

Phr. *To c. one's heels* († *hoofs*): *i.e.* by rest, after walking; hence, *ironically*, to be kept standing or waiting.

Cooler (kū·ləɹ). 1575. [f. COOL *v.* + -ER[1].] **1.** Anything that cools or makes cool. **2.** A vessel in which anything is cooled; *esp.* one used for cooling the wort in brewing 1616. **3.** *U.S.* (*Thieves' slang.*) A prison 1884.

† **Cooley.** *rare.* = CULLIS[1]. MRS. GLASSE.

Coolie, cooly (kū·li). 1598. [Of unc. origin; Urdu *qulī*, Bengali, etc. *kūlī*, perh. to be identified with the name *Kulī, Kolī* of an aboriginal tribe of Gujerat, India.] † **1.** An aboriginal tribe of Gujerat –1885. **2.** A native hired labourer or burden-carrier in India and China and elsewhere 1638. Also *attrib.*, as *c. labour.* Hence **Coo·lieism,** the c. system, the importation of coolies as labourers.

Cooling (kū·liŋ), *vbl. sb.* ME. [f. COOL *v.* + -ING[1].] The action of the vb. COOL.

Comb.: **c.-cup,** a cup for cooling liquids, into which is plunged another containing a heat-absorbing substance, as a solution of ammonium nitrate; **-floor,** a large shallow tank in which wort is cooled.

Cooling-card. *arch.* 1577. [CARD *sb.*[2] 1.] Something that dashes one's expectations.

Coolish (kū·liʃ), *a.* 1759. [f. COOL *a.* + -ISH[1].] Somewhat cool.

Coolly (kū·l,li), *adv.* 1580. [f. COOL *a.* + -LY[2].] **1.** With coolness; without heat (*lit.* and *fig.*). **2.** Indifferently; without enthusiasm 1626. **3.** With calm assurance 1844.

2. To receive a proposition c. MACAULAY.

Coolness (kū·lnės). OE. [f. as prec. + -NESS.] **1.** *lit.* The condition of being or feeling cool. **2.** *fig.* Freedom from excitement 1651. **3.** Want of fervour; absence of friendly warmth 1674. **4.** Calm assurance 1751.

3. They parted with such c. towards each other, as if they scarce hoped to meet again CLARENDON (J.).

Coolth (kūlþ). Now chiefly *joc. colloq.* 1547. [f. COOL *a.* + -TH[1] b.] Coolness.

† **Coo·ly,** *a. rare.* 1594. [f. COOL *sb.* + -Y[1].] Cool –1710.

Coom (kūm), *sb.* 1587. [In senses 1–2 app. var. of CULM[1]; senses 3–4 prob. repr. a different word.] **1.** Soot. Now *Sc.* **2.** Coal dust or refuse 1611. † **3.** The grease and dust from axles or bearings –1786. **4.** Saw-dust, etc. (*dial.*) 1811.

Coomb[1], **comb** (kūm). *dial.* [OE. *cumb* cup, vessel, prob. identical w. older LG. *kumb*, HG. *kump, kumpf*, mod.LG., HG. *kumm*, mod.G. *kumme.*] † **1.** (OE. *cumb.*) A vessel, cup. † **2.** A brewing vat –1688. **3.** A dry measure, equal to four bushels ME.

Coomb[2], **combe, comb** (kūm). [OE. *cumb*, not found in OE. or ME. literature, but occurring from early times in charter place-names belonging to the south of England, many of which survive, e.g. Batcombe, Southcombe. Its present gen. use goes back to XVI.] A deep hollow or valley; *esp.* one on the flank of a hill (*local*) 1674.

Coon (kūn). 1839. [U.S. abbrev. of RACOON.] **1.** The RACOON (*Procyon lotor*). **2. a.** One of the old U.S. Whigs, who had the coon as an emblem 1848. **b.** A sly, knowing fellow 1860.

Phrases. (*U.S. slang.*) *A gone c.*: a person or thing that is in a hopeless case. *A coon's age*: emphatic for 'a long time'.

Coontah, coontie (ku·ntă, -ti). 1852. The name in U.S. of a species of cycad (*Zamia integrifolia*), found in the West Indies, Florida, etc.; also of the arrowroot yielded by it.

Coop (kūp), *sb.*[1] ME. [– MLG., MDu. *kūpe* (Du. *kuip* tub, vat), parallel with OS. *kōpa*, OHG. *kuofa* (G. *kufe*) cask – L. *cūpa*, also med.L. *cōpa* tun, barrel.] † **1.** (ME. *cupe, coupe*, pl. *-en.*) A basket. **2.** A cage or pen of basket-work or the like for confining poultry, etc. ME. Also *transf.* and *fig.* **3.** A wicker-work basket used in catching fish; a KIPE 1469.

2. *fig.* Sunnebright honour pend in shamefull coupe SPENSER.

Coop, *sb.*[2], var. of COUP, a dung-cart.

Coop (kūp), *sb.*[3] 1825. [Origin unkn.] A small heap, as of manure.

Coop (kūp), *v.*[1] 1563. [f. COOP *sb.*[1]] *trans.* To put or confine in a coop; hence, to confine within a small space; also *c. up, in* 1563.

What! c. whole armies in our walls again POPE. They imagine that their souls are cooped and cabined in BURKE.

† **Coop,** *v.*[2] *rare.* 17.. [Back-formation on COOPER *sb.*] = COOPER *v.*

Shaken tubs..be new cooped P. HOLLAND.

Co-op (ko,ǫ·p). 1873. Colloq. abbrev. of CO-OPERATIVE 2; often ellipt. for *c. store.*

Coopee, obs. f. COUPEE.

Cooper (kū·pəɹ), *sb.* ME. [– MDu., MLG. *kūper*, f. *kūpe* COOP *sb.*[1]; see -ER[1].] **1.** A craftsman who makes and repairs wooden vessels formed of staves and hoops, as casks, buckets, tubs. **2.** One engaged in the trade of sampling and bottling wine; a wine-cooper 1502. **3.** ? A six- (or twelve-) bottle basket, used in wine-cellars 1817. **4.** A drink composed half of stout and half of porter. (So called in London.) 1871.

3. Give me a roaring fire and a six bottle c. of claret T. L. PEACOCK.

Cooper (kū·pəɹ), *v.* 1746. [f. COOPER *sb.*] **1.** To make or repair (casks, etc.). **2.** To put or stow in casks 1746. **3.** *intr.* To work as a cooper (Dicts.). **4.** To 'do for' (*slang*) 1851.

1. Coopered with brass hoops weather-tight 1834. Hence **Coopering** *vbl. sb.* the occupation of a cooper.

Cooperage (kū·pərėdʒ). 1714. [f. COOPER *sb.* + -AGE.] **1.** A cooper's workshop. **2.** Cooper's work 1740. **3.** Money payable for cooper's work 1755.

Co-operant (ko,ǫ·pĕrănt), *a.* 1598. [– *cooperant-*, pres. ppl. stem of eccl. L. *cooperari*; see CO-OPERATE, -ANT.] Working together or to the same end. Also as *sb.*

C. factors of human progress A. M. FAIRBAIRN. Hence **Co-o·perancy,** c. condition; † co-operation.

Co-operate (ko,ǫ·pĕreⁱt), *v.* 1604. [– *cooperat-*, pa. ppl. stem of eccl.L. *cooperari*, f. *com* Co- + *operari* OPERATE.] **1.** *intr.* To work together, act in conjunction (*with* another person or thing, *to* an end, or *in* a work). **2.** *intr.* To practise economic co-operation 1830.

1. Man..cooperateth with man unto repentance USSHER. All things c. for the best QUARLES.

Co-operate (ko,ǫ·pĕrĕt), *a.* 1868. [Deduced from CO-OPERATION on the anal. of *corporation, corporate*, etc.] Caused to co-operate; brought into co-operation.

Co-operation (ko,ǫ·pĕrēⁱ·ʃən). ME. [– L. *cooperatio* (f. as CO-OPERATE *v.*; see -ION), partly, in later use, through Fr. *coopération.*] **1.** The action of co-operating; joint operation. **2.** *Pol. Econ.* The combination of a number of persons, or of a community, for purposes of economic production or distribution. (As orig. used by Owen, the name contemplated communism.)

1. Not Holpen by the C. of Angels or Spirits BACON. **2.** The essential characteristic of c. is a union of capital and labour FAWCETT. Hence **Co-opera·tionist,** one who practises or advocates c.

Co-operative (ko,ǫ·pĕrĕtiv), *a.* (*sb.*) 1603. [– late L. *cooperativus* (Boethius), f. as prec.; see -IVE; partly, in later use, through Fr. *coopératif.*] **1.** Working together or with others to the same end; pertaining to co-operation. **2.** *Pol. Econ.* Pertaining to industrial co-operation 1821. **3.** *sb.* A co-operationist; a member of a co-operative society 1829.

1. Four great principles..mutually c. MILMAN. **2.** *C. society*: a union of persons for the production or distribution of goods, in which the profits are shared by all the contributing members. *C. store*: a store or shop belonging to a c. society, where goods are sold at a moderate price, the profits, if any, being distributed among the members and customers.

Co-operator (ko,ǫ·pĕreⁱtəɹ). 1600. [– eccl.L. *cooperator* fellow-worker, f. as prec.; see -OR 2.] **1.** One who co-operates with another or others. **2.** A member of a co-operative society 1863.

1. They are..Co-operatours with God BARROW.

Cooper's-wood. 1866. An Australian name for the wood of Red Ash (*Alphitonia excelsa*), and Victorian Hazel (*Pomaderris apetala*).

Coopery (kū·pəri). 1558. [f. COOPER *sb.* + -Y[3]; see -ERY.] Cooper's work; a cooper's workshop; cooper's ware. Also *attrib.*

Basket, C., and Turnery Wares 1695.

Co-opt (ko,ǫ·pt), *v.* 1651. [– L. *cooptare*, f. *com* Co- + *optare* choose.] *trans.* To elect into a body by the votes of its existing members.

These eight co-opted two more STUBBS.

Co-optate (ko,ǫ·pteⁱt), *v. arch.* 1623. [– *cooptat-*, pa. ppl. stem of L. *cooptare*; see prec., -ATE[3].] Now = CO-OPT; formerly, less definitely = To choose or elect to an office, into a body, etc.

Co-optation (ko,ǫptēⁱ·ʃən). 1533. [– L. *cooptatio*, f. as prec.; see -ION.] Election into a body by the votes of its existing members; formerly, Election, choice, adoption.

The first election and c. of a friend HOWELL. var. **Co-o·ption.**

Co-ordain (ko,ǫɹdēⁱ·n), *v. rare.* 1679. [See Co-.] *trans.* To ordain together. So **Co-ordai·ner.**

Co-o·rder, *v. rare.* 1678. [See Co-.] To arrange co-ordinately.

Co-o·rdinal, *a.* 1875. [f. Co- + ORDINAL, with reference to *co-ordinate.*] *Geom.* Having (so many) co-ordinates. CAYLEY.

Co-ordinate (ko,ǭ·ɹdinĕt). 1641. [f. Co- + L. *ordinatus* (see ORDINATE *a.*), after the earlier SUBORDINATE.]

A. *adj.* **1.** Of the same order; equal in rank (*with*); opp. to *subordinate.* In *Gram.* used *esp.* of the clauses of a compound sentence. **2.** Involving co-ordination 1769.

1. All these Churches are but C., not among themselves Subordinate 1641. **2.** So complex and c. a movement 1876. Hence **Co-o·rdinately** *adv.*

B. *sb.* **1.** One who or that which is co-ordinate; an equal; a co-ordinate element 1850. **2.** *Math.* Each of a system of two or more magnitudes used to define the position of a point, line, or plane, by reference to a fixed system of lines, points, etc. (Usually in *pl.*) 1823. Also *attrib.*

In the original system of *Cartesian co-ordinates*, the co-ordinates of a point (in a plane) are its distances from two fixed intersecting straight lines (the *axes of co-ordinates*), the distance from each axis being measured in a direction parallel to the other axis. The co-ordinates are *rectangular* when the axes are at right angles; otherwise *oblique*.

Hence applied to other systems; as *Polar co-ordinates*, co-ordinates defining a point (in a plane) by reference to a fixed line (*initial line* or *axis*) and a fixed point (*origin* or *pole*) in that line; the co-ordinates of any point being the length of the straight line (*radius vector*) drawn to it from the pole, and the angle which this line makes with the axis.

Both systems have been applied by an extension to points *in space*.

Co-ordinate (ko,ǭ·ɹdineⁱt), *v.* 1655. [f. Co- + L. *ordinare* (see ORDINATE *v.*), after SUBORDINATE.] **1.** *trans.* To make co-ordinate; to place in the same order, rank, or division. **2.** To place (things) in proper position relatively to each other and to the system of which they form parts 1847. **3.** *intr.* (for *refl.*) To act in combined order for the production of a particular result 1863.

1. These two..are not opposed, but co-ordinated 1665. **2.** An omnipresent humanity co-ordinates all his [Shakespeare's] faculties EMERSON. So **Co-o·rdinative** *a.* † co-ordinate; having the function of co-ordinating. **Co-o·rdinator.**

Co-ordination (ko,ǭ:ɹdinēⁱ·ʃən). 1605. [– (O)Fr. *coordination* or late L. *coordinatio* (Boethius), f. *com* Co- + *ordinatio* ORDINATION.] **1.** The action of co-ordinating; the condition of being co-ordinated or co-ordinate; co-ordinate relation. **2.** Harmonious combination of agents or functions towards the production of a result; said *esp.* in *Phys.* of the combined action of a number of muscles in the production of certain complex movements 1855.

1. What consent and c. there is in the leaves and parts of flowers SIR T. BROWNE. **2.** In each of these acts, the c. of a large number of muscular movements is required CARPENTER.

Co-o·rganize, Co-ori·ginal, etc.; see Co-.

Co-ortho·gonal, *a. Geom.* [See Co-.] = next.

Co-orthotomic (koᵘ,ǭɹþǫtǫ·mik), *a.* 1884. [See Co-.] *Geom.* Cutting one another at right angles at each point of intersection, as circles.

Co-ossify (ko,ǫ·sifəi), *v.* 1877. [See Co-.] To unite into one bone (*trans.* and *intr.*). Hence **Co-o:ssifica·tion.**

Coot (kūt). [ME. *cote*, *coote* (first in *balled cote* 'bald coot'), prob. of LG. origin (cf. Du. *koet* :– **kōte*).] **1.** A name originally given vaguely to various swimming or diving birds; often to the Guillemot (*Uria troile*). **2.** Later the Bald Coot (*Fulica atra*, fam. *Rallidæ*), a web-footed bird, having the bill extended so as to form a broad white plate on the forehead (whence the epithet *bald*); in U.S., *F. Americana* 1440. **3.** Locally applied to the Water-rail and Water-hen 1547. **4.** *fig.* A silly person, simpleton (*colloq.*) 1848.

2. The Brain-bald C. DRAYTON. Phr. *As bald (bare, black) as a c.*; *as stupid as a c.*

Cooter (kū·təɹ). 1884. [f. *coot* v. copulate (of tortoises) + -ER[1].] A Southern U.S. name of two tortoises, the Carolina Box-turtle (*Cistudo carolina*), and the 'Florida Cooter' (*Chrysemys concinna*), family *Testudinidæ*.

Cooth (kūþ). 1793. [Origin unkn.] The Coal-fish. (*Orkney & Shetland.*)

Coo·tie, *sb. Sc.* [Origin unkn.] A small wooden bowl or basin. BURNS.

Coo·tie, cooty, *a. Sc.* [f. Sc. *coot* ankle-joint, fetlock + -Y[1].] Having feathered legs. BURNS.

Co-ow·ner. 1858. [See Co-.] A joint owner.

† **Cop**, *sb.*[1] [OE. (late Northumb.) *copp* cup, vessel, = MLG., Du. *kop* drinking-cup, OHG., MHG. *kopf* beaker, bowl (G. *kopf* head), ON. *koppr*. Cf. CUP.] A drinking-vessel, a cup –1520. *Comb.*: **c.-ambry**, a closet for cups, etc.; **-house**, a house or room for cups, etc.

Cop (kǫp), *sb.*[2] [OE. *cop*, *copp* summit, thought by some to be identical with prec., on the analogy of MDu. 'skull', and mod.G. 'head'; but neither of these senses is known in the OE. word.] **1.** The top of anything; *esp.* of a hill –1599; a crest on the head of a bird –1787. †**2.** A round piece of wood within the top of a beehive 1609. **3.** *Spinning.* The conical ball of thread wound upon a spindle or tube in a spinning machine 1795. **4.** ? A heap, mound (*dial.*) 1666. **5.** A hedge-bank (*dial.*) 1600. **6.** The central ridge of a butt of ploughed land (*dial.*) 1859.

1. Upon the c. right of his nose he hade A werte, and theron stood a tuft of heres CHAUCER.

Comb.: **c.-bone**, the knee-cap (*dial.*); **-spinner**, a machine combining the advantages of the throstle and the mule; **-tube** (see sense 3); **-waste**, the waste cotton from the cops; **-yarn**, cotton yarn in cops.

† **Cop** (kǫp), *sb.*[3] ME. only. [OE. *-coppe* fem., prob. identical with prec.; see ATTERCOP, COBWEB.] A spider.

Cop, *sb.*[4] *slang.* 1859. [f. COP *v.*[2]] A policeman.

Cop (kǫp), *v.*[1] Now *dial.* 1552. [f. COP *sb.*[2]] **1.** *trans.* To pile up in a heap or mound. **2.** To put up unbound hay or corn in cops 1581.

Cop (kǫp), *v.*[2] *n. dial.* and *slang.* 1704. [prob. var. of CAP *v.*[2]] *trans.* To capture, catch.

Copaiba, -aiva (kopai·bă, -ē̆·bă, -ai·vă). 1712. [– Sp., Pg. *copaiba* – Guarani *cupauba*.] A balsam of aromatic odour and acrid taste, obtained from S. American plants of the genus *Copaifera*; used in medicine and the arts. Also *attrib.* Hence **Copai·vic** *a.* of or pertaining to c.

Copal (kōᵘ·păl). 1577. [– Sp. *copal* – Aztec *copalli* incense.] A hard translucent odoriferous resin obtained from various tropical trees, and from which a fine transparent varnish is prepared. **b.** *Fossil c.*: = COPALITE. Also *attrib.* Hence **Co·paline** (*Min.*) = COPALITE.

‖ **Copalche, -chi** (kopæ·ltʃi). 1866. [Mexican native name.] A shrub of Mexico, *Croton pseudo-china* or *niveus*, N.O. *Euphorbiaceæ*, yielding the *C.-bark*, used as a febrifuge; also a Brazilian tree, *Strychnos pseudo-china*.

Copalite (kōᵘ·pălait). 1868. [f. COPAL + -ITE[1] 2 b.] *Min.* Dana's name for the fossil *Highgate resin*, found in the blue clay of Highgate Hill.

Co·palm. 1858. In *c. balsam*, a yellowish balsam, exuding from the Sweet Gum-tree of N. America.

Coparcenary, -ery (koᵘ,pā·ɹsĭnĕri), *sb.* 1503. [f. as next + -Y[3]; see PARCENARY.] *Law.* **1.** Joint share in an inheritance; joint heirship. **2.** Co-partnership; joint ownership. Also *fig.* 1593. Hence **Copa·rcenary** *a.* of or pertaining to coparceners. var. **Copa·rceny.**

Coparcener (koᵘ,pā·ɹsĭnəɹ). 1503. [f. Co- + PARCENER.] *Law.* One who shares equally with others in inheritance of the estate of a common ancestor.

† **Copa·rt**, *v.* 1613. [f. Co- + PART *v.*] *trans.* and *intr.* To share –1670.

Copartiment, copartment, obs. vars. of COMPARTMENT.

Copartner (koᵘ,pā·ɹtnəɹ) 1503. [See Co-.] One who shares or takes part with others in any business, office, enterprise, or common interest. (Formerly = COPARCENER.) Also *transf.* of things.

You that have been copartners in our wars HEYWOOD. Hence **Copa·rtnership**, the relation of copartners; a company of copartners. var. **Copa·rtnery.** † **Copa·rtning** *ppl. a.* being or acting as copartners. MILT.

† **Copataine.** *rare.* App. = COPINTANK, q.v. *Tam. Shr.* V. i. 69.

Co-patriot, var. of COMPATRIOT.

Cope (kōᵘp), *sb.*[1] [Early ME. *cāpe*, repr. OE. *cāp* (in *cantelcāp*) and **cāpe* = ON. *kápa* (Da. *kaabe*) – med.L. *cāpa*, var. of *cappa* whence Fr. *chape*. Cf. CAP *sb.*[1], CHAPEL.] **1.** † A long cloak or cape –1745; *spec.* a cape or tippet of ermine worn by doctors of divinity on special occasions at Cambridge 1798. **2.** *Eccl.* A vestment resembling a long cloak made of a semicircular piece of cloth, worn by ecclesiastics in processions, at Vespers, etc. ME. **3.** *fig.* Anything resembling a cloak, canopy, or vault ME. ¶ In later use, vaguely used for (*a*) vertex; (*b*) firmament, expanse 1603. **4.** *Founding.* The outer portion or case of a mould 1856. **5.** The COPING of a wall, etc. 1847.

2. After them came. . Friers in their rich Coapes singing, carrying many Pictures and Lights PURCHAS. **3.** Undyr the c. of heven that is above CHAUCER. The cheapest country under the c. *Per.* IV. vi. 132. Larks in heaven's c. sing TENNYSON.

† **Cope**, *sb.*[2] 1525. [Either – COPE *v.*[2], or – OFr. *cop*, *colp* (mod. *coup*); see COPE *v.*[2]] The shock of combat; encounter. Also *fig.* –1773.

Cope, *sb.*[3] Now *dial.* 1520. [f. COPE *v.*[3]] † **1.** A bargain –1590. **2.** *Derbyshire Mines.* A duty paid by the miner for permission to raise lead ore 1631.

Phr. † *God's c.*: a very large sum.

Cope (kōᵘp), *v.*[1] ME. [f. COPE *sb.*[1]] **1.** *trans.* To furnish with a cope. **2.** *Archit.* To cover with, as, or as with, a COPING 1842. **3.** To cover as with a vault 1704. **4.** *intr.* To slope downwards or hang *over* like a coping 1601. Hence **Coped** *ppl. a.* (in senses 1, 4).

Cope (kōᵘp), *v.*[2] ME. [– OFr. *coper*, var. of *colper* (mod. *couper*) strike, (now) cut, f. *cop*, *colp* (mod. *coup*) blow :– med.L. *colpus* :– L. *colaphus* – Gr. κόλαφος blow with the fist, box on the ear.] † **1.** *intr.* To strike; to come to blows, encounter, engage. (Often with *with*.) –1725. **2.** To be or prove oneself a match for, contend successfully with 1583. Also *fig.* **3.** To have to do with (*arch.*) 1593. † **4.** *trans.* To meet, come into contact (hostile or friendly) with –1603. † **5.** To match (a thing) *with* (an equivalent). *Merch. V.* IV. i. 412.

1. Swear to stand neutral, while we c. in fight POPE. He wolde nevyr c. whithe no man 1467. **2.** Not a matche to coape with Achilles STANYHURST. To c. with evil 1850. **3.** *Haml.* III. ii. 60. **4.** They all straine curt'sie who shall c. him first SHAKS.

Cope (kōᵘp), *v.*[3] Now *dial.* ME. [– MDu., (M)LG. *kōpen* (Du. *koopen*) = G. *kaufen*; see CHEAP.] † **1.** *trans.* To buy –1599. **2.** To exchange, barter 1570. † **3.** *intr.* To make an exchange, bargain –1614. **4.** *Derbyshire Mines.* 'To agree to get ore at a fixed sum per *dish* or measure.' 1802.

2. I've seen scores of nets coped away for brandy 1887.

Cope (kōᵘp), *v.*[4] 1575. [app. – OFr. *coper* cut; see COPE *v.*[2]] *Falconry.* To cut, pare the beak or talons of a hawk.

Cope, *v.*[5] *dial.* 1601. [Origin unkn.] To tie or sew up the mouth of (a ferret); also *fig.*

Your lips coaped like a ferret DEKKER.

Copeck (kōᵘ·pek). 1698. [– Russ. *kopeĭka*, dim. of *kop'ë* lance.] A Russian copper coin, the $\frac{1}{100}$ part of a rouble, now worth from $\frac{1}{4}$ to $\frac{1}{3}$ of a penny English.

Co·peman, † **copesman.** *arch.* 1566. [orig. *copesman*, f. COPE *sb.*[3] (in poss. *cope's*) + MAN.] A chapman, dealer.

He would have sold his part of Paradise For ready money, had he met a copeman B. JONS.

† **Co·pemate, copesmate.** 1565. [orig. *copemate*, f. COPE *v.*[2] + MATE; assim. later to *copesman* or the like.] **1.** A person with whom one copes; an adversary –1645. **2.** A partner or colleague; an associate. Also *fig.* –1686. **3.** = FELLOW, in the vague sense –1744.

2. *fig.* Mis-shapen Time, copesmate of ugly Night SHAKS.

Copepod (kōᵘ·pĭpǫd). 1836. [f. Gr. κώπη handle, oar-handle, oar + πούς, ποδ- foot.] *Zool.* **A.** *adj.* Belonging to the order *Copepoda* of minute entomostracous Crustaceans, having four or five pairs of oar-like feet. **B.** *sb.* A member of this order. Hence **Cope·podan, Cope·podous** *adjs.*

Coper[1] (kōᵘ·pəɹ). 1609. [f. COPE *v.*[3] + -ER[1].] One who copes (see COPE *v.*[3]); *spec.* (= *horse-c.*) a horse-dealer.

Coper[2], **cooper** (kōᵘ·pəɹ). 1881. [– Flem. and Du. *kooper*, f. *koopen* buy, deal, trade.] A vessel fitted out to supply spirits, etc., usually in exchange for fish, to the deep-sea fishers in the North Sea; a floating grog-shop. Hence **Co·pering, coopering** *vbl. sb.*

Copernican (kopɔ̄·ɹnikăn). 1667. [f. *Copernicus*, L. form of *Koppernik*, name of an astronomer, a native of Thorn in Prussian Poland (1473–1543); see -AN.] *adj.* Of or pertaining to Copernicus. *sb.* One who holds the C. theory 1677.

C. system, theory: the astronomical system or theory propounded by Copernicus (and still held) that the planets move in orbits round the sun as a centre, and not round the earth. Hence **Cope·rnicanism.**

Copesman, -mate; see COPEMAN, -MATE.

Cope-stone (kōᵘ·pstōᵘn). 1567. [f. COPE *sb.*[1] + STONE; infl. in sense by COP top, or perh. by *cap*.] The top stone of a building; usu. *fig.*

‖ **Cophosis** (kofōᵘ·sis). 1657. [mod.L. – Gr. κώφωσις, f. κωφός deaf.] Total deafness.

Cophouse; see COP *sb.*[1]

‖ **Copia** (kōᵘ·piă). 1713. [L.; = plenty.] Plenty, a plentiful supply; now chiefly in the L. phrase *c. verborum*, a copious vocabulary.

Copiable (ko·pi,ăb'l), *a. rare.* 1755. [f. COPY *v.* + ABLE.] Capable of being copied.

Copiapite (kōᵘ·piăpəit). 1850. [f. *Copiapo* in Chile + -ITE[1] 2 b.] *Min.* A yellow translucent hydrous silicate of iron; *yellow copperas* or *misy*.

Copier (kǫ·pi,əɹ). 1597. [f. COPY *v.* + -ER[1].] One who copies or makes a copy; a transcriber; an imitator.

Coping (kōᵘ·piŋ), *sb.* 1601. [f. COPE *v.*[1] sense 2 + -ING[1].] **1.** *Archit.* The uppermost course of masonry or brickwork in a wall, usually of a sloping form to throw off rain. **2.** An overhanging shelf to protect wall-fruit 1881. *Comb.* **c.-stone,** one of the stones forming the c. of a wall.

† **Copintank, copentank, coptank.** 1508. [Origin unkn. Cf. COPATAINE.] A sugar-loaf hat –1603.

With a high coptank Hat on his head, narrow in the top, as the Kings of the Medes. . do use to wear them SIR T. NORTH.

Copious (kōᵘ·piəs), *a.* ME. [– (O)Fr. *copieux* or L. *copiosus*, f. *copia* abundance; see -OUS.] † **1.** Furnished plentifully with anything –1838. **2.** Abounding in matter 1500, †language –1672, or words 1549. **3.** Existing in abundance; plentiful. *Obs.* or *arch.* with names of material substances. ME. **4.** *adv.* Copiously 1791.

1. C. sources of knowledge PRESCOTT. **2.** This c. subject 1716. She will waxe c. and chop logicke MORE. A c. language HOBBES. **3.** A c. display of flowers 1845. Hence **Co·pious-ly** *adv.*, **-ness.**

† **Co·pist.** 1682. [– Fr. *copiste* or its source med.L. *copista*, f. *copiare* COPY *v.*] Early f. COPYIST –1779.

Coplanar (kōᵘplēⁱ·năɹ), *a.* 1862. [f. Co- + PLANAR.] *Math.* Situated or acting in the same plane.

Coplanation, erron. f. COMPLANATION.

Copolar (kōᵘpōᵘ·lăɹ), *a.* 1852. [f. Co- + POLAR.] *Math.* Having the same pole.

Copo·poda, var. of *Copepoda*; see COPEPOD.

‖ **Copopsia** (kopǫ·psiă). 1882. [mod.L., f. Gr. κόπος fatigue + ὄψις sight + -IA[1].] *Path.* Fatigue of sight.

† **Copo·rtion.** [See CO-.] A joint portion. SPENSER.

Copped (kǫ·pėd, kǫpt), *ppl. a.* OE. [f. COP *sb.*[2] + -ED[2].] † **1.** Polled. (OE. only.) **2.** 'Rising to a top or head' (J.); peaked ME. **3.** Crested. Now *dial.* ME. Also *fig.*

Copper (kǫ·pəɹ), *sb.*[1] [OE. *copor, coper,* corresp. to MDu. *coper* (Du. *koper*), ON. *koparr* :- **kupar*, of which the var. **kuppar* gave MLG. *kopper*, OHG. *kupfar* (G. *kupfer*) – late L. *cuprum* (IV), for L. *cyprium*, in full *cyprium æs* 'metal of Cyprus', so named from its most noted ancient source.] **1.** A well-known metal of a peculiar red colour; it is malleable, ductile, and very tenacious, and is found native and in many ores. Chemically it is a dyad: symbol Cu. Used, with qualification, in the names of various compounds and ores of the metal. **2.** Copper money; a copper (or bronze) coin 1712. **3.** A vessel made of copper; in *pl.*, *esp.* the large cooking vessels on board ship 1667. **4.** A COPPER-PLATE, q.v. 1668. **5.** A copper implement like a cotton reel hollow and open at the ends; used in annealing 1828. **6.** The copper sheathing of a vessel (*rare*) 1836. **7.** *attrib.* Made of copper; pertaining to copper; worthless; copper-coloured 1597.

2. He has 'no more c.' about him HONE. **7.** A c. Kettell 1624, mine 1776, crowne SHAKS. A hot and c. sky COLERIDGE.

Phr. *Hot coppers*: a mouth and throat parched through excessive drinking.

Comb.: **a. c.-beech** (see BEECH 1); **-belly,** the c.-bellied Snake (*Coluber erythrogaster*); **-bo·t-tomed** *a.*, having the bottom sheathed with c.; **-ca·ptain,** a sham captain; **-co·loured** *a.*; **-faced** *a.*, 'brazenfaced'; of printing-type, faced with c.; **-fastened** *a.* (of a ship), fastened with c. bolts to prevent corrosion; **-finch,** the Chaffinch (*local*); **-head,** the head of a c. or boiler; see also COPPERHEAD; **-nose,** a red nose caused by disease, intemperance, etc.; **-powder,** a precipitate of metallic c. used for bronzing; **-work, works,** a place where c. is worked or manufactured; **-zinc,** *attrib.*, of c. and zinc.

b. In the names of chemical compounds and of minerals: **c.-blende,** a sulpharsenite of c., TENNANTITE; **-emerald** = *emerald c.*, DIOPTASE; **-glance,** native cuprous sulphide, CHALCOCITE; **-nickel** [G. *kupfer-nickel*] = NICCOLITE; etc.

Hence **Co·pperish** *a.* somewhat coppery (*rare*). **Co·ppery** *a.* resembling or containing c.

Copper (kǫ·pəɹ), *sb.*[2] *slang.* 1859. [f. COP *v.*[2] + -ER[1].] A policeman.

Copper (kǫ·pəɹ), *v.* 1530. [f. COPPER *sb.*[1]] *trans.* To cover with copper; to sheathe the bottom and sides of a ship with copper.

A cast-iron statue coppered by electricity 1862. Hence **Co·pperer** (*rare*). **Co·ppering** *sb.* the copper sheathing of a ship's bottom.

Copperas (kǫ·pərăs). [ME. *coperose* – (O)Fr. *couperose* – med.L. *cup(e)rosa*, perh. orig. **aqua cuprosa* 'copperwater', but later assoc. with *rosa* rose, after Gr. χάλκανθον vitriol, lit. 'flower of brass'. Cf. G. † *kupferrose* and *kupferwasser*.] **1.** A name given from early times to the sulphates of copper, iron, and zinc (distinguished as *blue, green,* and *white* copperas respectively); in Eng. use, now exclusively to *green* copperas or ferrous sulphate ($FeSO_4$), also called *green vitriol*, used in dyeing, tanning, and making ink. **2.** *Min.* Applied generically to a group comprising the ordinary vitriols 1868. Also *attrib.* *Comb.* † **c.-stone,** iron pyrites or Marcasite. Hence † **Coppero·se** *a.* of or belonging to c. or vitriol.

Copperhead (kǫ·pəɹhed). 1823. [orig. attrib. in *copperhead snake*.] **1.** A venomous N. American snake (*Trigonocephalus contortrix*); so called from the coppery red colour of the top of its head. (It strikes without warning, and has thus become a type of unexpected hostility.) **2.** *U.S.* A nickname, during the Civil War, for a northern sympathizer with the Secessionists 1862. Also *attrib.*

Co·pper-pla:te, co·pperplate. 1663. **1.** *gen.* (Better as two words.) A plate of copper; also *collect.* 1665. **2.** *spec.* A polished plate of copper on which a design is engraved or etched 1668. **3.** An impression from such a plate 1663. **4.** *collect.* Copperplate engraving or printing 1817. **5.** *attrib.* (Better as one word.) 1824. Hence **Co·pperplate** *v.* to engrave on and print from a c.

Co·pper-smith. ME. **1.** An artificer in copper. **2.** In India, the Crimson-breasted Barbet (*Xantholæma indica*).

1. Alexander the coppersmyth did me moche evyll TINDALE 2 *Tim.* 4:14.

† **Co·pper-worm.** 1755. **1.** The ship-worm, *Teredo navalis.* **2.** A clothes-moth. **3.** 'A worm breeding in one's hand' (J.).

Coppice (kǫ·pis), *sb.* 1538. [– OFr. *copeïz* :- Rom. **colpaticium* (for the suffix cf. CHASSIS, GLACIS), f. **colpat-*, pa. ppl. stem of **colpare* cut (Fr. *couper*), f. med.L. *colpus* blow; see COPE *v.*[2] Cf. COPSE.] A small wood or thicket of underwood grown for the purpose of periodical cutting; underwood. *Comb.* **c.-wood** (see COPSEWOOD). vars. **Copy, coppy** [f. Fr. *copys* pl.]. Hence **Co·ppice** *v.* = COPSE *v.* 1. **Co·ppiced** *ppl. a.* cut down periodically; furnished with a c. or coppices.

Co·pping, *vbl. sb.* 1793. [f. COP *sb.*[2] 3 + -ING[1].] The formation of cops of thread. Used *attrib.*, as *c.-beam*, etc.

† **Co·pple.** 15.. [dim. of COP *sb.*[2] 1; see -LE.] **1.** A crest on a bird's head –1600. **2.** A little summit or eminence; = Fr. *coupeau* 1600.

2. It is a low Cape, and vpon it is a c. not very high HAKLUYT. Hence † **Co·ppled** *ppl. a.* crested; rising conically to a point.

Co·pple-crown. Now *dial.* 1634. [See prec.] A tuft of feathers on a fowl's head; a crest.

Like the Copple-crowne The Lapwing has RANDOLPH. Hence † **Co·pple-crowned** *ppl. a.* crested, peaked.

† **Copple-stone.** 1728. [Cf. COPPLING *ppl. a.* 3.] A COBBLE-STONE.

† **Co·ppling, copling,** *ppl. a.* 1667. [Related to COPPLE *sb.* 2 but in senses 2 and 3 app. infl. by *cockling, toppling.*] **1.** Swelling upwards towards a summit –1745. **2.** Of the sea: Tumbling 1667. **3.** Of stones, etc.: Unsteady, toppling 1825.

Copps, obs. f. COPSE.

Coppy, obs. f. COPPICE.

‖ **Copra** (kǫ·pra). 1584. [– Pg. (and Sp.) *copra* – Malayalam *koppara* coco-nut.] The dried kernel of the coco-nut, from which coco-nut oil is expressed.

Co-pre·sence. 1817. [See CO-.] Presence together; the state or fact of being co-present. So **Co-pre·sent** *a.* present together.

Copro-, bef. a vowel **copr-,** comb. f. Gr. κόπρος dung: hence,

Copræ·mia [Gr. αἷμα], blood-poisoning from the fæces in cases of costiveness. **Copre·mesis** [Gr. ἔμεσις], stercoraceous vomiting. **Co·prolite** [Gr. λίθος], a stony roundish fossil, supposed to be the petrified excrement of an animal. Hence **Coproli·tic** *a.* **Co·prolith,** a ball formed of hardened fæces in the bowels; also = *coprolite.* Hence **Copro-, koproli·thic** *a.* **Copro·logy** [cf. Gr. κοπρολόγος], a gathering of ordure; also *fig.* **Copro·phagan,** a dung-eating beetle. **Copro·phagist,** a dung-eater. **Copro·phagous** *a.*, dung-eating. **Copro·philous** *a.*, fond of dung; feeding or growing upon dung. **Copro·stasis** [Gr. στάσις a stopping], constipation.

Cop-rose, copper-rose. 1776. [Origin unknown.] A local name of the Red Corn Poppy (*Papaver rhœas*).

Cops, copse (kǫps). [OE. *cops, cosp* = OS. *cosp* fetter.] † **1.** A shackle for any part of the body –ME. **2.** A hasp for a door or gate ME. **3.** = CLEVIS 1797.

Copse (kǫps), *sb.* 1578. [Syncopated f. *copys, coppis,* COPPICE.] = COPPICE. Also as *pl.*, whence an erron. sing. *cop.* Also *transf.* and *fig.*

The willows and the hazel copses green MILT. *Lycidas* 42. *fig.* So to cares cops I came G. HERBERT. Hence **Copse** *v.* to make a c. of; to clothe with a c. **Co·psy** *a.* planted with copses.

Co·psewood, co·ppice-wood. 1543. **1.** A COPSE. ? *Obs.* **2.** The underwood of a copse 1809. Also *attrib.*

Copsole, copsil. Now *dial.* 1562. [f. COPS 3; the second element is unexpl.] = COPS 3.

Copt (kǫpt). 1615. [– Fr. *Copte* or mod.L. *Coptus*, also *Cophtus* – Arab. *al-ḳibṭ, al-ḳubṭ* (coll.) Copts – Coptic *Gyptios* – Gr. Αἰγύπτιος EGYPTIAN.] A native Egyptian Christian, belonging to the Jacobite sect of Monophysites. Hence **Co·ptic** *a.* of or pertaining to the Copts; *sb.* the language of the Copts. So † **Co·ptite.**

Coptine (kǫ·ptəin). 1879. [See -INE[5].] *Chem.* A colourless alkaloid found in *Coptis trifolia*, a ranunculaceous plant of N. America.

Copula (kǫ·piulă). 1650. [– L. *copula* tie, connection, linking of words, f. *com* CO- + *apere* fasten; see APT, -ULE.] **1.** *Logic* and *Gram.* That part of a proposition which connects the subject and predicate; the present tense of the verb *to be* (with or without a negative). **2.** *gen.* A connection 1656. **3.** *Anat.* A part (*e.g.* a bone, cartilage, or ligament) connecting other parts 1681. **4.** = COUPLER 2a. 1852. **b.** *Mus.* A short transition passage 1880. **5.** Sexual union. [A term of Roman Law.] 1864. Hence **Co·pular** *a.* pertaining to or of the nature of a c.

† **Co·pulate,** *a.* (*sb.*) ME. [– L. *copulatus*, pa. pple. of *copulare*; see next, -ATE[2].] **1.** Coupled; conjoined –1645. **2.** Copulative; as *sb.* A copulative word –1672.

Copulate (kǫ·piuleⁱt), *v.* 1632. [– *copulat-*, pa. ppl. stem of L. *copulare*, f. *copula*; see COPULA, -ATE[3].] † **1.** *trans.* To couple, conjoin –1822. † **2.** *intr.* To become conjoined or united 1645. **3.** *intr.* To unite in sexual congress 1632.

Copulation (kǫpiulēⁱ·ʃən). ME. [– (O)Fr. *copulation* – L. *copulatio*, f. as prec.; see -ION.] † **1.** The action of coupling or condition of being coupled; connection, union –1752. **2.** The union of the sexes in the act of copulating 1483.

1. Wit..is the unexpected c. of ideas JOHNSON.

Copulative (kǫ·piulătiv, -eⁱtiv). ME. [– (O)Fr. *copulatif, -ive* or late L. *copulativus*, f. as prec.; see -IVE.]

A. *adj.* **1.** Serving to couple or connect. † **2.** Connective –1676. **3.** *Zool.* and *Anat.* Relating to or serving for copulation 1841.

1. These c. particles, *and, again* GOUGE. The c. judgment ('*S* is both *p* and *q* and *r*') 1884. Hence **Co·pulatively** *adv.*

B. *sb.* **1.** *Gram.* A copulative conjunction or particle 1530. † **2.** *pl.* (*joc.*) Persons about to be coupled in marriage *A.Y.L.* v. iv. 58.

Copulatory (kǫ·piulătəri), *a.* 1839. [– late L. *copulatorius*, f. as prec.; see -ORY[2].] *Zool.* Pertaining to or serving for copulation, as *c. organs.*

Copy (kǫ·pi), *sb.* (*a.*) ME. [– (O)Fr. *copie* – L. *copia* abundance, plenty. The sense 'transcript', which is med.L. and Rom., arose from such phr. as *copiam describendi facere* give permission to transcribe, whence the sense 'right of reproduction' and simply 'reproduction'.]

A. † **1.** Plenty, abundance, a copious quantity –1656. **2.** A transcript, reproduction, or imitation of an original, as a writing, a picture, or other work of art ME. Also *fig.* **3.** *Eng. Law.* The transcript of the manorial court-roll (see COPYHOLD) 1463; a COPYHOLD 1626. Also *fig.* **4.** An individual example of a manuscript or print 1538. **5.** That from which a copy is made ME.; † *fig.* pattern, example –1775. **6.** *Printing.* Manuscript (or printed) matter prepared for printing 1485; † property in 'copy' –1781. **7.** Name of a size of paper 1712.

1. To excel in..copie of words 1586. **2.** Never buy a c. of a picture RUSKIN. *fig.* Pompey, the Clown, is a c. from the life MRS. CLARKE. **3.** *fig. Macb.* III. ii. 38. **4.** Being printed from a foul c. 1689. Copies of the fourth..Vol. of Leland HEARNE. The acting c. of a play DICKENS. **5.** Conferring the translation with the Coppie 1586. Why the Scholar writeth not like his C. BAXTER. *fig. All's Well* I. ii. 46. **6.** When he carried his copie to the Presse NASHE. Steele..sold the c. for fifty guineas JOHNSON.

Phr. *A c. of verses*: a short composition in verse: now chiefly applied to a school or college exercise.

B. † *adj.* = COPYHOLD 3. –1639.

Comb.: **c.-book;** a book containing copies of documents, accounts, etc. (now *U.S.*); a book containing lines of writing for pupils to imitate; also an exercise book; **-holder,** a proof-reader's assistant who reads the copy aloud to the proof-reader; † **-money,** money paid to an author for his c. or copyright.

Copy (kǫpi), *v.* ME. [– (O)Fr. *copier* – med.L. *copiare*, f. *copia* (see prec.).] **1.** *trans.* To make a copy of (a writing, a picture, or other work of art); to transcribe; to reproduce or represent in a picture, etc. **2.** *fig.* To imitate, reproduce, follow 1647. **3.** *absol.* or *intr.* 1680.

1. I like the worke well. .I would haue it coppied *Oth.* III. iv. 190. [He] has copied it out in full 1881. **2.** A wish to c. what he must admire COWPER. **3.** No painter who is worth a straw will ever c. RUSKIN.

Copyhold (kǫ·pihōᵘld). 1483. [f. COPY *sb.* 3 + HOLD *sb.*[1] II. 1; cf. *freehold.*] **1.** Tenure of lands being parcel of a manor, 'at the will of the lord according to the custom of the manor', by copy of the manorial court-roll. Also *fig.* **2.** An estate thus held; a copyhold estate 1529. **3.** *attrib.* or *adj.* Held by, relating to, or of the nature of, copyhold 1511.

1. *C.*, a base tenure founded upon immemorial custom and usage. .No c. estate can. .be created at the present day WHARTON. Hence **Copyholder**, one who holds an estate in c.

Copying (ko·pi,iŋ), *vbl. sb.* 1580. [f. COPY *v.* + -ING[1].] The action of the verb COPY.

attrib. and *Comb.*, *esp.* of appliances for copying writing by some transfer process, as *c.-book*, *-ink*, *-paper*, *-pencil*, *-press*; also **c.-ribbon**, a ribbon used in a type-writing machine, when a duplicate copy is taken; **-telegraph**, a telegraphic apparatus by which a written message placed in the transmitter is reproduced in the receiver on the passage of the current.

Copyism (kǫ·pi,iz'm). 1814. [f. COPY *sb.* or *v.* + -ISM.] The practice of copying; an instance of this. (Usu. contemptuous.)

Copyist (kǫ·pi,ist). 1699. [f. COPY *v.* + -IST; see COPIST.] One who copies; *esp.* one who transcribes documents.

Copyright (kǫ·pirəit). 1767. [f. COPY *sb.* 6 + RIGHT *sb.*] **1.** The exclusive right given by law for a certain term of years to an author, composer, etc. (or his assignee) to print, publish, and sell copies of his original work. **2.** *attrib.* or *adj.* Protected by copyright 1881.

1. We have international copyrights JEVONS. Hence **Co·pyright** *v. trans.* to secure c. for.

‖ **Coque** (kǫk), *sb.* 1821. [Fr., = shell.] † **1.** *Bot.* A COCCUS. **2.** *Millinery.* A small loop of ribbon, used in trimming.

‖ **Coquelicot** (ko·kliko:). 1795. [Fr.; the name of the Red Poppy.] The colour of the common Red Poppy, a brilliant orange-red. Also *attrib.*

† **Coqueluche.** 1611. [– Fr. *coqueluche* (1) woman's hood; (2) kind of *grippe* or epidemic catarrh. Of uncertain origin.] In 16th c. an epidemic catarrh; later, hooping-cough –1749.

Coquet (koke·t). 1696. [– Fr., orig. sb., dim. of *coq* cock; as adj. 'forward, wanton, gallant'; cf. COCK *v.*[1], also COCKISH *a.*, COCKY *a.*, and COCKET *a.* The sb. was formerly masc. and fem.; later the fem. became *coquette*, and the masc. obsolete.]

A. *adj.* † **1.** = COCKY. † **2.** Amorously forward –1711. **3.** Coquettish 1697.

3. Not far from Paris I observed two very c. sphinxes H. WALPOLE.

† **B.** *sb.* **1.** A male flirt –1732. **2.** Earlier f. COQUETTE, q.v.

Coquet, coquette (koke·t), *v.* 1701. [– Fr. *coqueter*, f. *coquet*; see prec. The sp. *coquette* is modern.] **1.** *intr.* 'To act the lover' (J.); to practise coquetry, to flirt *with.* (Now only of a woman.) † **2.** *trans.* 'To treat with an appearance of amorous tenderness' (J.); to flirt with –1773. **3.** *intr.* To dally, trifle, or toy *with* 1780.

2. He caught me one morning coquetting his wife SWIFT. **3.** He coquetted with peace to retain a county member 1796.

Coquetoon (kǫkətūn). 1846. [Native name.] A small W. African antelope (*Cephalophus rufilatus*, Gray).

Coquetry (kōᵘ·kĕtri). 1656. [– Fr. *coquetterie*, f. *coqueter* COQUET *v.*; see -RY.] **1.** Attractive pertness in women; the use of arts intended to excite admiration or love, merely for the gratification of vanity; a coquettish act. **2.** *fig.* and *transf.* 1770.

1. Coquettry is one of the main ingredients in the natural composition of a woman VANBRUGH.

Coquette (koke·t), *sb.* 1611. [– Fr. *coquette*, fem. of *coquet*; see COQUET *a.* and *sb.*] **1.** A woman who uses arts to gain the admiration and affection of men without any intention of responding to the feelings aroused; a flirt. Also *transf.* and *fig.* **2.** A genus of crested humming-birds. [Fr. *coquet* masc.] 1866. **3.** *attrib.* = COQUET *a.* 3. 1743.

1. *Cocquet*. .also a wanton Girl that speaks fair to several Lovers at once PHILLIPS. Hence **Coque·ttish** *a.* like a c.; of or characterized by coquetry; **-ly** *adv.*

‖ **Coquilla** (koki·lʸă). 1851. [app. Sp. or Pg., dim. of *coca* shell; cf. Fr. *coquille.*] In *C.-nut*, the nut of the Brazilian palm-tree, *Attalea funifera*, the shell of which is much used by turners.

Coquimbite (koki·mbəit). 1844. [f. *Coquimbo*, Chile + -ITE[1] 2 b.] *Min.* A native ferric sulphate, found chiefly in parts of S. America; native White Copperas.

‖ **Coquina** (kokī·na). 1883. [Sp. *coquina* shell-fish, cockle – OSp. *coca* = Fr. *coque* :– med.L. *coca*, by-form of L. *concha* mussel, shell.] A soft whitish rock made up of fragments of marine shells united by a calcareous cement; found in the West Indies and Florida, where it is used as a building material.

‖ **Coquito** (kokī·to). 1866. [Sp.; dim. of *coco* coco-nut.] A Chilean palm-tree, *Jubæa spectabilis*, from the sap of which palm-honey is obtained.

‖ **Cor**[1] (kǭɹ). ME. [Heb. *kōr* a measure (usu. dry), = *ḥōmer.*] A Hebrew measure of capacity, called earlier a *homer.*

‖ **Cor**[2]. 1870. [Fr., = horn.] In **c. anglais** (kōr aṅglę̄), lit. 'English horn': the tenor oboe; also, an organ stop of similar tone.

Cor-[1], assim. f. COM- *prefix*, bef. *r.* For the sense see COM-.

Cor-[2], **coro- (core-).** Gr. κόρη girl, doll, pupil of the eye cf. (BABY), taken as the basis of mod. surgical terms relating to the pupil. Hence **Core·ctomy, Coro·tomy (core-),** excision and incision of the pupil, **Co·roplasty (core-),** an operation for forming an artificial pupil; etc.

Coracine (kǫ·răsəin). 1624. [– L. *coracinus*, – Gr., f. κόραξ raven; so called from its black colour.] A Nile fish, resembling a perch.

Coracle (kǫ·răk'l). 1547. [– W. *corwgl*, *cwrwgl*, f. *corwc* coracle, † carcass (= Ir., Gael. *curach* CURRACH).] A small boat made of wickerwork covered with some water-tight material, used by the ancient Britons, and still by fishermen in Wales and Ireland.

Coraco- (kǫ·răko-), now used in *Anat.* as comb. f. CORACOID, in sense 'relating to the coracoid process and ——', as **c.-acromial,** connecting the coracoid and the acromial, as the *c.-acromial ligament*; **-clavicular; -costal** = COSTO-CORACOID; **-humeral;** etc.

Coracoid (kǫ·răkoid). 1741. [– mod.L. *coracoides* – Gr. κορακοειδής raven-like, f. κόραξ raven, crow; see -OID. Cf. Fr. *coracoïde.*]

A. *adj.* **1.** Beaked like a crow. Applied to a process of bone (*c. process*), extending in man from the scapula toward the sternum; also to the bone (*c. bone*) homologous with this process, which, in birds and reptiles, extends from the scapula to the sternum, and forms the distal or ventral element of the scapular arch. **2.** Pertaining to, or connected with, the coracoid process 1836.

B. *sb.* = *C. process* or *bone*; see A. 1.

Coracomo·rphic, *a.* 1867. [f. mod.L. *Coracomorphæ* (f. Gr. κορακο- raven, crow + -μορφος, f. μορφή form) + -IC.] *Zool.* Of or belonging to the group *Coracomorphæ* or birds of the crow form, nearly corresp. to PASSERINE.

‖ **Coracosteon** (kǫrăkǫ·sti,ǭn). 1882. [mod. L., f. as prec. + ὀστέον bone.] *Zool.* An additional symmetrical osseous centre formed in the sternum in certain birds. Hence **Coraco·steal** *a.*

Co-ra·dicate, *a.* 1882. [f. CO- + L. *radicatus* rooted, f. *radix* root.] In *Etym.*: Having the same root.

Corage, obs. f. COURAGE.

‖ **Coraggio** (kora·dʒo), *int.* 1601. [It.] Courage! as a hortatory exclam.

Corah (kōᵊ·ră), *a.* 1833. [Urdu *kōrā* new, unbleached.] Plain, undyed: as *sb.* 'an Indian pattern silk handkerchief' (Simmonds).

Coral (kǫ·răl), *sb.* ME. [– OFr. *coral* (mod. *corail*) :– L. *corallum*, *-alium* – Gr. κοράλλιον, κουράλιον, prob. of Semitic origin.] **1.** A hard calcareous substance consisting of the continuous skeleton secreted by many tribes of marine cœlenterate polyps for their support and habitation. Found, according to the species, in single specimens growing plant-like on the sea-bottom, or in accumulations (*coral-islands*, *-reefs*). **a.** Historically the name belongs to the *Red Coral*, an arborescent species, found in the Red Sea and Mediterranean. *Pink c.*: a variety of this. **b.** Afterwards extended to other kinds, as **White c., Black c.** (*Antipathes*), **Blue c.** (*Heliospora*), **Yellow c.,** etc.; and more recently, with reference to the appearance of the aggregate skeleton, to **Brain c.** (*Meandrina*), **Cup c.** (family *Cyathophyllidæ*), **Mushroom c.** (*Fungia*), **Organ-pipe c.** (*Tubipora*), **Star c.** (*Astroides*), etc. See also MADREPORE, MILLEPORE. 1600. **2.** (with *a* and *pl.*) = CORALLUM 1579; also, a piece of (red) coral 1607. **3.** A toy of polished coral, given to teething infants 1613. **4.** *fig.* ME. **5.** *transf.* The roe of the lobster: so called from its colour when boiled 1768. **6.** *attrib.* Formed or made of coral; of the colour of red coral 1452.

3. Art thou not breeding teeth. .I'll. .get a c. for thee BEAUM. & FL. **4.** Where she stood, Blood's liquid c. sprang her feet beneath DRUMM. OF HAWTH. **6.** C. clasps and amber studs MARLOWE. India's c. strand HEBER. Coral lips SHAKS.

Comb.: **c.-berry,** an American shrub (*Symphoricarpus vulgaris*), having the berries deep red; **-fish,** a name for fishes of the families *Chætodontidæ* and *Pomacentridæ* which frequent c.-reefs; **-insect,** erron. name for a c.-polyp; **-mud,** mud formed by decomposed c.; **-polyp,** one of the individual animals of a c. polypidom; **-rag,** *Geol.* the upper member of the Middle Oolite series; **-root,** book-name of the orchideous plant *Corallorhiza*; **-sand** (cf. *coral-mud*); **-zoophyte** = *coral-polyp.* See also C.-PLANT, etc. Hence **Co·ral** *v. rare*, to make red like c. **Coralla·ceous** *a.* of the nature of c. (*rare*). **Co·ralled** *a.* furnished or covered with c. **Cora·llian** *a. arch.* = CORALLINE *a.* **Coralli·ferous** *a.* c.-bearing. **Cora·lliform** *a.* having the form of c. **Coralli·genous** *a.* c.-producing.

Corallin (kǫ·rălin). 1873. [– L. *corallinus* coral-red (see -INE[1]); see -IN[1].] *Chem.* A red colouring matter, called also *Pæonin*, obtained by treating phenol with sulphuric and oxalic acids. *Yellow c.* (= *Aurin*), a yellowish red dye, obtained by heating carbolic acid with the same substances; so called because it can be converted into the *red c.*

Coralline (kǫ·răləin), *sb.*[1] 1543. [– It. *corallina*, dim. of *corallo* CORAL.] A name given to organisms thought to be of the nature of coral, but of more minute size, etc.; as the calcareous sea-weeds, esp. *Corallina officinalis*, the Polyzoa or Bryozoa, etc. *C. zone*: the third of the zones of the sea-depths, being that in which Polyzoa abound.

Coralline (kǫ·rălin, -əin), *a.* and *sb.*[2] 1633. [– Fr. *corallin*, *-ine* or L. *corallinus*; see CORAL, -INE[1].]

A. *adj.* **1.** Of the colour of red coral. **2.** Of the nature of coral 1660. **3.** Coral-like 1860.

B. *sb.* (improper uses.) **1.** A coral zoophyte 1860. **2.** = CORAL (the calcareous substance) 1779.

Corallite (kǫ·răləit). 1815. [f. L. *corallum* + -ITE[1] 2 a.] **1.** A fossil coral. **2.** The coral skeleton of an individual polyp 1861. **3.** Corallitic or coralline marble 1883. So **Coralli·tic** *a.* of the nature of coral.

Coralloid (kǫ·răloid). 1604. [f. L. *corallum* CORAL + -OID.] *adj.* Resembling or akin to coral. *sb.* Any coralloid organism 1748. So **Coralloi·dal** *a.*

‖ **Corallum** (koræ·lŏm). 1846. [L.] A coral; the calcareous skeleton of a coral polypidom; also the horny tubular envelope of any zoophyte, whether colonial or simple.

Coral-plant. 1774. † **1.** A coral of plant-like form. **2.** The plant *Jatropha multifida* (N.O. *Euphorbiaceæ*) 1813.

Coral reef. 1745. A reef formed by the growth and deposit of coral. The reef-building corals are chiefly madrepores of the genera *Meandrina*, *Caryophyllia*, and *Astroides.*

Co·ral-snake. 1760. A local name for various snakes marked with red zones; *esp.* the species of the genus *Elaps* found in southern U.S. and Central America.

Coral-tree. 1635. † **1.** The red or other branched coral –1698. **2.** The popular name of the trees of the genus *Erythrina* 1756.

Co·ral-wood. 1693. A hard red cabinet-wood from Central and S. America.

Co·ralwort. 1597. [See WORT[1].] Name of the plant *Dentaria bulbifera*, in allusion to its curiously toothed white rhizomes.

‖ **Coram** (kō^ə·ræ̆m). 1607. A Latin preposition meaning 'before, in the presence of', used in *c. judice* before a judge, *c. populo* in public, etc.

Phr. *To bring under c., call to* or *in c.*: to call to account, bring to book.

Coran, var. KORAN.

Cor anglais. *Mus.* See ‖ COR[2].

Coranoch, etc., var. CORONACH.

Coranto[1] (kora·nto). Now *Hist.* 1564. [alt., by addition of an It. termination, of Fr. *courante* (sc. *danse* dance) 'running, dance', pres. pple. fem. of *courir* run.] = COURANTE 1, 2. Also *attrib.*

Lauolta's high, and swift Carranto's *Hen. V*, III. v. 33.

† **Cora·nto**[2]. 1621. [var. of COURANT *sb.*[2], modified in the same way as prec.] = COURANT *sb.*[2] –1635.

‖ **Corban** (kǭ·ɹbæ̆n). ME. [– Vulg.L. – N.T. Gr. κορβᾶν – Heb. *ḳorbān* offering.] **1.** *Heb. Antiq.* An offering given to God, *esp.* in performance of a vow. † **2.** The treasury of the temple at Jerusalem, where money offerings of this sort were placed; also *transf.* Church treasury –1610.

† **Corbe.** *rare.* Shortened f. CORBEL. Spenser.

‖ **Corbeau** (korbō). 1833. [Fr., = crow, raven.] A trade name for a dark green colour verging on black.

Corbed, var. of † COURBED, bent, curved.

Corbeil, ‖ **corbeille.** 1706. [– (O)Fr. *corbeille* basket :– late L. *corbicula*, dim. of *corbis* basket]. † **1.** *Fortif.* A basket filled with earth and placed on a parapet to cover the defending soldiers. **2.** *Archit.* Carved work in the form of a basket. (Occas. erron. **corbel.**) 1734. ‖ **3.** As Fr., used for an elegant fruit or flower basket 1800.

Corbel (kǭ·ɹbĕl), *sb.* ME. [– OFr. *corbel* (mod. *corbeau*) crow, raven; also *Archit.*, dim. of OFr. *corp* :– L. *corvus*; see -EL[2].] † **1.** A raven. (ME. only.) **2.** *Archit.* A projection jutting out from the face of a wall to support a superincumbent weight. (The word was associated with grotesque ornamentation by Sir W. Scott; a corbel is not technically ornamental.) ME. **b.** A short timber laid upon a bearer to give a better bearing upon the wall or pier; a *c.-block* 1703.

2. The corbels were carved grotesque and grim SCOTT. *Comb.*: **c.-piece** = CORBEL; **-step,** a conjectural substitute for *Corbie-step*; **-table,** a projecting course resting on a series of corbels. Hence **Co·rbel** *v.* to support or (*intr.*) project on or as on corbels. **Co·rbelled** *ppl. a.* furnished with corbels; fashioned as a c. **Co·rbelling** *sb.* work consisting of corbels; also *attrib.*

† **Corbet.** [– OFr. *corbet* crow, raven, dim. of OFr. *corp* :– L. *corvus*; see -ET.] = CORBEL *sb.* 2. CHAUCER.

‖ **Corbicula** (koɹbi·kiulă). Also erron. **corbiculum.** 1816. [L., dim. of *corbis* basket.] *Entom.* A part of the hinder leg of a bee adapted to carry pollen; cf. BASKET. Hence **Corbi·culate** *a.* having *corbiculæ*.

Corbie (kǭ·ɹbi). *Sc.* 1450. [– OFr. *corb*, var. of *corp* (see CORBEL, CORBET) + -Y[6].] A raven; also, the carrion-crow, called also **c.-crow.**

Comb.: **c.-gable,** a gable having c.-steps; **c.-steps,** projections in the form of steps on the sloping sides of a gable. var. † **Corbin.**

‖ **Corbula** (kǭ·ɹbiulă). 1861. [L., dim. of *corbis*.] *Zool.* **1.** A receptacle in which groups of gonangia are enclosed, in some of the Cœlenterata. **2.** (*With capital C.*) A genus of bivalve molluscs living in mud or sand, related to the clam. var. **Co·rbule.**

Co·rcass. 1796. [Corrupt. of Ir. *corcach* marsh.] Name of the salt marshes along the banks of the Shannon and Fergus.

‖ **Corchorus** (kǭ·ɹkŏrŏs). 1759. [– Gr. κόρχορος name of a plant.] *Bot.* **1.** A genus of *Tiliaceæ*, including some species which yield jute. **2.** A name of *Kerria japonica* (N.O. *Rosaceæ, Spiræidæ*), of which the double-flowered variety is often trained as a wall plant for its yellow blossoms.

Corcle (kǭ·ɹk'l), **corcule** (kǭ·ɹkiul). 1810. [– L. *corculum*, dim. of *cor* heart.] *Bot.* The embryo in the seed of a plant.

Cord (kǭɹd), *sb.* ME. [–(O)Fr. *corde* :– L. *chorda* – Gr. χορδή; see CHORD.] **1.** A string, or (small) rope, composed of several strands twisted together. Also *transf.* **2.** A structure in the animal body resembling a cord; as the *spermatic, spinal*, and *umbilical c.*, the *vocal cords*, etc. (Cf. NERVE.) ME. † **3.** *Mus.* = CHORD *sb.*[1] 2. –1830. † **4.** *Math.* = CHORD *sb.*[1] 4. 1551. **5.** *Farriery.* (Usu. *pl.*) String-halt. ? *Obs.* 1523. **6.** A raised cord-like rib on cloth; corduroy; in *pl.* corduroy breeches 1776. **7.** A measure of wood, stone, or rock (? originally measured with a cord); a pile of wood, usu. 8 feet by 4, and 4 high 1616. **8.** *fig.* Chiefly with reference to the binding power of a cord ME.

8. The wicked shall be held fast in the cords of his own sin HOOKER. The cords of discipline STEVENSON.

Comb.: **c.-drill,** a drill worked by a c. twisted round it and pulled backwards and forwards; **-wood,** wood stacked in cords; wood for fuel cut in lengths (usually) of 4 feet.

Cord (kǭɹd), *v.*[1] ME. [f. CORD *sb.*] **1.** *trans.* To furnish with a cord. **2.** To bind or fasten with a cord or cords 1610. **3.** To stack (wood) in cords 1762.

† **Cord,** *v.*[2] ME. [aphet. f. ACCORD *v.*] = ACCORD *v.* in most senses –1535.

Cordage (kǭ·ɹdėdʒ). 1490. [– (O)Fr. *cordage*, f. *corde*; see CORD *sb.*, -AGE.] Cords collectively; *esp.* the ropes in the rigging of a ship. Also *transf.* and *fig.*

Wee'l give our hair for C., and our finest Linnen for Sails 1643. *fig.* The c. of his life CARLYLE.

† **Cordal.** 1688. [– OFr. *cordal, cordail* cord, f. *corde*; see CORD, -AL[1].] *Her.* The string of the mantle or robe of estate –1828.

Cordate (kǭ·ɹdeⁱt), *a.* 1651. [In sense 1 – L. *cordatus* wise, f. *cor, cord-* heart, in sense of judgement; in sense 3 – mod.L. (Linnæus); see -ATE[2].] † **1.** Wise, prudent –1734. † **2.** Cordial (*rare*) –1671. **3.** Heart-shaped, as *c. leaves* 1769. Hence **Co·rdately** *adv.*

‖ **Cordax** (kǭ·ɹdæks). 1531. [Gr.] A dissolute dance of the Old Greek Comedy.

Co·rded, *ppl. a.* ME. [f. CORD *sb.* and *v.*[1] + -ED.] **1.** Bound with cords; *Her.* bound or wound about with cords 1486. **2.** Made of or furnished with cords ME. **3.** Having lines or stripes like cords 1760. **4.** Piled in cords (see CORD *sb.* 7) 1847.

2. A Corded-ladder SHAKS. **3.** C. stuffs 1760. The hand..was lean, c., and knuckly STEVENSON.

Cordelier (kǭɹdĕlīᵊ·ɹ). ME. [– (O)Fr. *Cordelier*, f. †*cordele*, dim. of *corde* CORD; so named from their rope girdle.] **1.** A Franciscan friar of the strict rule: so called from the knotted cord they wear round the waist. **2.** *pl.* One of the political clubs of the French Revolution (*club des Cordeliers*), which met in an old convent of the Cordeliers 1837.

Cordeliere. 1725. [– Fr. *cordelière*, the cord of the Franciscans, f. prec.] *Her.* A knotted cord, put round armorial bearings in token of devotion to St. Francis of Assisi.

Cordelle (kǭ·dĕl), *sb.* 1823. [–(O)Fr. *cordelle*, dim. of *corde* CORD; see -EL[2].] † **1.** A twisted cord. HALLIWELL. **2.** *Canada* and *U.S.* A towing line or rope. Hence **Co·rdelle** *v.* to tow (a boat) with a c.

Corder (kǭ·ɹdəɹ). ME. [f. CORD *v.*[1] + -ER[1].] One who or that which cords or fastens with a cord; *spec.* an appliance in a sewing-machine for stitching a piping-cord, or the like, between the folds of a fabric.

Cordial (kǭ·ɹdiăl). ME. [– med.L. *cordialis*, f. *cor, cord-* heart; see -IAL.]

A. *adj.* † **1.** Of or belonging to the heart –1646. **2.** Stimulating, comforting, or invigorating the heart; reviving, cheering 1471. Also *fig.* **3.** Hearty; heartfelt; sincere, genuine, warm 1477.

1. *C. spirits* (in Mediæval Physiology) = VITAL *spirits*, for 'the Vital Spirit resides in the heart, etc.' **2.** This c. julep here..With spirits of balm and fragrant syrups mixed MILT. *Comus* 672. **3.** He was a stout and valiant gentleman, a c. protestant FULLER. Hence **Co·rdial-ly** *adv.*, **-ness.**

B. *sb.* A medicine, food, or beverage which invigorates the heart and stimulates the circulation. *Comm.* Aromatized and sweetened spirit, used as a beverage. Also *transf.* and *fig.* ME.

For gold in Phisik is a c., Therfore he louede gold in special CHAUCER.

Cordiality (kǭɹdiæ·lĭti). 1611. [f. prec. + -ITY; cf. Fr. *cordialité*.] † **1.** The quality of relating to the heart. SIR T. BROWNE. **2.** Heartiness; warmth 1611.

2. Margaret of Parma hated the Cardinal with great c. MOTLEY. His c. towards progress MORLEY.

Cordialize (kǭ·ɹdiăləiz), *v.* 1774. [f. as prec. + -IZE.] **1.** *trans.* To make into a cordial. **2.** To make cordial 1817. **3.** *intr.* To become cordial; to fraternize (*with*). Chiefly *Sc.* 1834.

Cordierite (kǭ·ɹdiərəit). 1814. [f. *Cordier*, a French geologist + -ITE[1] 2 b.] *Min.* = IOLITE.

Cordiform (kǭ·ɹdifǭɹm), *a.* 1828. [f. L. *cor, cord-* heart + -FORM.] Heart-shaped, as *c. tendon*, the central tendon of the diaphragm.

‖ **Cordillera** (kǫrdilyē·ră). 1704. [Sp., f. *cordilla*, dim. of *cuerda* CORD, string, chain.] A mountain-chain or ridge, one of a series of parallel ridges; in *pl.* applied originally by the Spaniards to the parallel chains of the Andes in S. America.

Cordinar, -er, obs. f. CORDWAINER.

Cording (kǭ·ɹdiŋ), *vbl. sb.* 1571. [f. CORD *v.*[1] + -ING[1].] **1.** Hanging 1619. **b.** *Weaving.* The connection of the treadles of a loom with the leaves of heddles by cords, so as to produce the pattern required 1822. **2.** Cordage; corded work 1571.

Cordite (kǭ·ɹdəit). 1889. [f. CORD *sb.* + -ITE[1] 4 a.] A smokeless explosive, so called from its cord-like appearance.

Cordon (kǭ·ɹdən, -ǫ̃n), *sb.* 1578. [– It. *cordone*, augm. of *corda* CORD; superseded by Fr. *cordon* (dim.); see -OON.] **1.** *Fortif.* A course of stones forming the coping of the escarp 1598. **2.** *Archit.* A string-course, or projecting band of stone, usually flat, on the face of a wall 1706. **3.** *Mil.* A line of men placed at detached intervals, to prevent passage to or from the guarded area; a chain of military posts 1758; *transf.* and *fig.* 1792. Also *attrib.* **4.** A guarded line between affected and unaffected districts, to prevent intercommunication and spread of a disease or pestilence; a *sanitary c.* 1826. **5.** An ornamental cord or braid forming a part of costume, or used as a heraldic bearing. Also, the cord worn by Franciscans. 1578. ‖ **6.** A ribbon, usually worn scarfwise, as part of the insignia of a knightly order. [As Fr. (korḍoṅ) or a Gallicism.] 1727. **7.** *Hort.* A fruit-tree made by pruning to grow as a single stem 1878.

6. *Grand c.*: that distinguishing the highest grade of a knightly order. *Blue c.* (Fr. *cordon bleu*): the sky-blue ribbon worn by the Knights-grand-cross of the Holy Ghost. Also applied to the wearers, and by extension to other persons of distinction; *cordon bleu*, jocularly or familiarly, a first-class cook.

‖ **Cordonnet.** 1858. [Fr., dim. of *cordon* (see prec.).] A loosely spun thick silk thread or weak cord, made from waste silk, and used for fringes, outlines of lacework, etc.

Cordovan (kǭ·ɹdŏvæn). 1591. [– Sp. *cordován* (now *-bán*); see CORDWAIN.]

A. *adj.* Of or pertaining to Cordova; made of leather of Cordova.

B. *sb.* **1.** One who belongs to Cordova 1599. **2.** = CORDWAIN 1625. † **3.** A skin of this leather –1750.

Corduroy (kǭɹdəroi·), *sb.* 1787. [prob. f. CORD *sb.* 6 + †*duroy*, †*deroy* (XVII) coarse West-of-England woollen stuff, of unkn. origin.] **1.** A kind of coarse thick-ribbed cotton stuff 1795. **2.** *pl.* Corduroy trousers (*colloq.*). **3.** A corduroy road (see 4) 1836. **4.** *attrib.* Made of corduroy 1795; ribbed like corduroy 1865; in *U.S.* applied to a road made of logs laid together transversely across a swamp or miry ground 1830.

4. Picking our way along the swampy c. road HT. MARTINEAU. Hence **Corduroy·** *v.* to form a c. road; to cross (a swamp) by such a road.

Cordwain (kǭ·ɹdwe^i^n). *arch.* [ME. *cordu-, cordewan(e* – OFr. *cordewan, cordoan,* f. *Cordoue* – Sp. *Cordoba,* †*Cordova* :– L. *Corduba* town in Spain where a goatskin (later, horsehide) leather was made.] Spanish leather, made of goatskins tanned and dressed, or, later, of split horse-hides; = CORDOVAN. Much used for shoes, etc., by the wealthy during the Middle Ages.

His schoon of cordewane CHAUCER. Hence **Co·rdwainer** (*arch.*), a worker in c.; a shoemaker. (Still used as the name of the trade-guild of shoemakers.) **Co·rdwainery,** shoemaker's work.

† **Cordyl.** 1607. [– Gr. κορδύλος water-newt.] A book-name of the water-newt; now applied to a genus of lizards (*Cordylus*).

‖ **Cordyline** (kǭɹdiləi·ni). 1866. [f. Gr. κορδύλη club.] *Bot.* A liliaceous genus of trees, sometimes called palm-lilies.

Core (kō^ə^ɹ), *sb.*[1] [ME. *core, coore,* of unkn. origin; superseded earlier *colk* (see COKE).] **1.** The dry horny capsule embedded in the centre of the pulp and containing the seeds of the apple, pear, quince, etc. Also † *fig.* **2.** An unburnt part in the centre of a coal, piece of limestone, etc. ME. **3.** The hard centre of a boil; also † *fig.* 1532; a disease in sheep, caused by worms in the liver 1750. **4.** *transf.* A central portion that is cut out; *e.g.* of rock 1649; or left; *e.g.* of a hay-rick, and in *Archæol.* of a flint nodule, from which flint knives have been chipped 1800. **5.** *transf.* A central part of different character from that which surrounds it: chiefly technical 1784. **6.** *Hydraul. Engineering.* A wall impervious to water, placed in a dike of porous material 1884. **7.** *Founding.* An internal mould filling the space intended to be left hollow in a hollow casting 1727. **8.** *Electr.* The central cord of insulated conducting wires in a cable 1892. **9.** The innermost part or heart of anything, as of a superficial area 1556. **10.** Used for 'heart' 1611.

1. *fig.* The coare of Adams apple is still in their throat DONNE. **3.** *fig.* The Canker, or Coar, of the late Rebellion SIR T. NORTH. **9.** In the C. of the Square, she raised a Tower RALEGH. A solid c. of heat TENNYSON, of fact 1865. **10.** In my hearts C.: I, in my Heart of heart *Haml.* III. ii. 78.

Comb.: **c.-barrel** (*Gunnery*), a long cylindrical iron tube through which cold water is run, used in casting guns to cool them from the inside; **-box,** a box in which a c. is made in founding; **-print,** a projecting piece on a pattern to form a recess in the mould, into which the end of the c. is inserted.

Core (kō^ə^ɹ), *sb.*[2] 1622. [app. an anglicized sp. of CORPS.] **1.** A body of people, a company. (Chiefly *Sc.*) **2.** A gang of miners working together in one shift 1778. **3.** A turn of work in a (Cornish) mine; a shift 1778.

1. In a C. of People, whose affections he suspected BACON.

Core (kō^ə^ɹ), *v.* 1597. [f. CORE *sb.*[1]] **1.** *trans.* To take out the core of; also with *out.* **2.** To enclose in the centre, enshrine 1816. **3.** *Founding.* To mould with a core 1865.

1. He's like a corn upon my great toe..he must be cored out MARSTON.

Core, var. of COR, Hebrew measure.

Core-, in surgical terms relating to the pupil of the eye; see COR-[2].

Co-regent (kō^u^ˌrī·dʒĕnt). 1799. [See CO-.] A joint regent or ruler.

Co-rela·tion. 1839. [See CO-.] Joint or mutual relation; CORRELATION.

Coreless (kō^ə^·ɹlės), *a.* 1813. [f. CORE *sb.*[1] + -LESS.] Without a core; hollow; heartless.

Co-religionist (kō^u^ˌrili·dʒənist). 1842. [f. CO- + RELIGION + -IST.] An adherent of the same religion.

Corella (kŏre·lă). 1885. The parakeet *Calopsitta novæ-hollandiæ,* also called *Cockateel.*

‖ **Coreopsis** (kǫriˌǫ·psis). 1753. [mod.L., f. Gr. κόρις bug + ὄψις appearance, in reference to the bug-like shape of the seed.] *Bot.* An American genus of *Compositæ,* several species of which are cultivated for their flowers with yellow or parti-coloured rays.

Corer (kō^ə^·rəɹ). 1796. [f. CORE *v.* + -ER[1].] An instrument for coring fruit.

Co-respondent (kō^u^rĭspǫ·ndĕnt). 1857. [See CO-.] *Law.* In a divorce suit, a man charged with the adultery and proceeded against together with the respondent or wife.

Corf (kǭɹf). Pl. **corves** (kǭɹvz). 1483. [– (M)LG., (M)Du. *korf* = OHG. *chorp, korb* (G. *korb*) – L. *corbis* basket.] † **1.** A basket –1543. **2.** *Mining.* A large basket formerly used in carrying or hoisting ore or coal 1653; *transf.* the wooden or iron tub which has replaced the basket 1831. **3.** *Fishing.* A basket, or a box with holes in it, in which fish, etc., are kept alive in the water 1825.

Coriaceous (kǫriˌē^i^·ʃəs, kō^ə^ri-), *a.* 1674. [f. late L. *coriaceus,* f. *corium* skin, hide, leather; see -ACEOUS.] **1.** Resembling leather in texture, appearance, etc.; leathery. **2.** Made of leather (*affected*) 1824.

Coriander (kǫriˌæ·ndəɹ). ME. [– (O)Fr. *coriandre* – L. *coriandrum* – Gr. κορίαννον.] An annual plant, *Coriandrum sativum,* N.O. *Umbelliferæ,* the fruit of which is carminative and aromatic. Also *attrib.*

Corindon (kori·ndǫn). 1802. [– Fr. *corindon*; see CORUNDUM.] *Min.* An early name of CORUNDUM, q.v.

Corinth (kǫ·rinþ). ME. [– Fr. *Corinthe* – L. *Corinthus* – Gr. Κόρινθος.] **1.** A city of ancient Greece celebrated for its artistic elegance, luxury, and licentiousness. † **2.** *pl.* Corinthians –1642. **3.** = CURRANT, q.v.

† **Corinthiac** (kŏri·nþiæk), *a. rare.* 1677. [– L. *Corinthiacus* or Gr. Κορινθιακός; see -AC.] = next.

Corinthian (kŏri·nþiăn), *a.* (*sb.*) 1577. [f. L. *Corinthius* (– Gr. Κορίνθιος) + -AN.]

A. *adj.* **1.** Of or pertaining to Corinth. **b.** *Archit.* The lightest and most ornate of the three Grecian orders, having a bell-shaped capital adorned with rows of acanthus leaves giving rise to graceful volutes and helices 1656. **c.** *C. brass* (*bronze*) [L. *Corinthium æs*]: an alloy of gold, silver, and copper, produced at Corinth. Also *fig.* (from the *fig.* sense of BRASS) shamelessness. Hence also *Corinthian* = 'brazen'. 1594. **2.** After the style of Corinthian art 1860. **3.** Profligate; in 19th c. use: Given to elegant dissipation 1642. **4.** (*U.S.*) *Yachting.* Amateur 1885.

2. The C. grace of Gertrude's manners EMERSON. **3.** The sage and rheumatic old prelatess, with all her young C. laity MILTON.

B. *sb.* **1.** A native or inhabitant of Corinth 1526. **2.** † **a.** A wealthy man; a gay, licentious man; a brazen-faced fellow –1879. **b.** A man about town 1819. **c.** A wealthy amateur of sport; *esp.* in *U.S.* an amateur yachtsman 1823. Hence **Cori·nthianism. Cori:nthiane·sque** *a.* approximating to the C. style. **Cori·nthianize** *v. intr.* to live licentiously; to imitate the C. order of architecture.

‖ **Corium** (kō^ə^·riŏm). 1826. [L., = skin, hide, leather.] **1.** *Phys.* The true skin under the epidermis 1836. **2.** *Entom.* The horny basal portion of the wing of a heteropterous insect 1826. **3.** *Antiq.* A leathern body-armour formed of overlapping flaps 1834.

Co-rival (kō^u^ˌrəi·văl). 1678. [mod. f. *corival,* an old var. of CORRIVAL; see CO-.] A joint rival with others. Also as *adj.* Hence **Co-ri·valry. Co-ri·valship. Co-ri·val** *v.* var. of CORRIVAL *v.*

Cork (kǭɹk), *sb.*[1] 1463. [prob. – Du., LG. *kork* (whence G. *kork*) – Sp. *alcorque* cork sole or shoe, perh. of Arab. origin (see AL- *pref.*[2]).] **1.** The bark or periderm of the cork-oak 1570. **2.** Anything made of cork; *e.g.* † a slipper; † a sole or heel for a shoe; a float for an angler, or a swimmer; *esp.* a stopper for a bottle, cask, etc. 1463. **3.** The cork-tree or cork-oak (*Quercus suber*) 1601. **4.** *Bot.* A protective tissue in the higher plants, forming the inner division of the *bark.* It consists of closely-packed air-containing cells, nearly impervious to air and water 1875. **5.** *transf.* 1671. **6.** *attrib.* Of cork 1716.

1. *Virgin c.*: the outer casing of the bark formed during the first year's growth. **5.** *Fossil c., mountain-c., rock-c.*: names of a very light asbestos.

Comb.: **c.-fossil** = *fossil-c.*; **-jacket,** a jacket made partly of, or lined with c., to support a person in the water; **-oak,** the tree (*Quercus suber*) from which c. is obtained; **-tree** = *cork-oak*; **-wing,** a fish, *Crenilabrus melas* or *cornubicus.*

Cork (kǭɹk), *sb.*[2] 1483. [app. contr. of *corkir* – Gael., Ir. *corcur,* orig. 'purple' – L. *purpur.*] = CUDBEAR.

Cork, *sb.*[3], **Corlk,** erron. spellings of CAUK.

Cork (kǭɹk), *v.*[1] 1580. [f. CORK *sb.*[1]] **1.** To furnish with a cork (as a †cork heel, a float, etc.). **2.** To stop (a bottle, etc.) with, or as with, a cork; and so to shut *up* (the contents); also *transf.* 1650. **3.** To blacken with burnt cork 1836.

Cork, *v.*[2], erron. f. CAULK *v.*

Corkage (kǭ·ɹkėdʒ). 1838. [f. CORK *sb.*[1] or *v.*[1] + -AGE.] The corking or uncorking of bottles; hence (= *c.-money*) a charge made by hotel-keepers, waiters, etc., for every bottle of wine, etc., uncorked and served, orig. when not supplied by them.

Corked (kǭɹkt), *ppl. a.* 1519. [f. CORK *v.*[1] and *sb.*[1] + -ED.] † **1.** Furnished with a cork sole or heel –1615. **2.** Stopped with a cork; also *fig.* 1836. **3.** Blackened with burnt cork 1836. **4.** Of wine: Tasting of the cork 1830.

Corker (kǭ·ɹkəɹ). 1723. [f. CORK *v.*[1] + -ER[1].] † **1.** ? A cork-cutter. **2.** *slang.* Something that closes a discussion; a 'settler'. Hence, something astonishing, *e.g.* a monstrous lie. 1837.

† **Corking-pin.** 1690. [app. corrupt f. *cawking,* CALKIN.] 'A pin of the largest size' (J.). –1840.

Corkscrew (kǭ·ɹkskrū), *sb.* 1720. [f. CORK *sb.*[1] + SCREW.] **1.** An instrument for drawing corks from bottles, consisting of a steel screw or helix with a sharp point and a transverse handle. **2.** *attrib.* Resembling a corkscrew; spirally twisted, as *c. curls,* a *c. staircase* 1830.

Corkscrew (kǭ·ɹkskrū), *v. colloq.* 1837. [f. prec.] **1.** To move or cause to move in a spiral course. **2.** To draw *out* as with a corkscrew 1852.

1. Mr. Bantam corkscrewed his way through the crowd DICKENS.

Corkwood (kǭ·ɹkwud). 1756. [f. CORK *sb.*[1] + WOOD.] A name given to several light and porous woods, and the trees yielding them; *e.g.* in the W. Indies, to *Anona palustris, Ochroma lagopus,* etc.; in N. S. Wales to *Duboisia myoporoides.*

Corky (kǭ·ɹki), *a.* 1601. [f. CORK *sb.*[1] + -Y[1].] **1.** Like cork in nature or character 1756. † **2.** *fig.* Dry and stiff, withered –1605. **3.** *fig.* Light, frivolous; buoyant, lively; hence, restive (*colloq.*) 1601. **4.** = CORKED 4. (Dicts.)

2. Binde fast his c. armes *Lear* III. vii. 29. Hence **Co·rkiness,** c. quality.

† **Corm**[1], **corme.** 1578. [– Fr. *corme* fruit of the service-tree, rel. to late L. *curmus* service-tree (Marcellus of Bordeaux, IV), prob. of Gaulish origin.] **1.** The service-tree, *Pyrus domestica*; also its fruit, the sorb –1658. **2.** The cornel-tree 1676.

Corm[2] (kǭɹm). 1830. [– mod.L. *cormus* – Gr. κορμός trunk of a tree with the boughs lopped off.] *Bot.* A bulb-like subterraneous stem of a monocotyledonous plant; also called *solid bulb.*

Cormo-, comb. f. Gr. κορμός trunk of a tree, stem: as in

Cormo·geny [Gr. -γένεια descent], that branch of ontogeny which deals with the germ-history of races or social aggregates. **Cormo·phyly** [Gr. φυλή, φῦλον], that branch of phylogeny which deals with the tribal history of races.

Cormogen (kǭ·ɹmŏdʒen). 1846. [f. CORMO- + -GEN.] = CORMOPHYTE. So **Cormo·genous** *a.* belonging to or like a c.; also, corm-bearing.

Cormophyte (kǭ·ɹmofəit). 1852. [f. CORMO- + -PHYTE.] *Bot.* Endlicher's name (*Cormophyta*) for one of his two primary divisions of the Vegetable Kingdom, comprising all plants that have a proper stem or axis of growth. Hence **Cormophy·tic** *a.* of the nature of a c.

Cormorant (kǭ·ɹmŏrănt). ME. [– OFr. *cormaran* (mod. *cormoran*), earlier *cormareng,* for **corp mareng,* repr. (with assim. of adj. suffix to Gmc. *-ing*) med.L. *corvus marinus* (VIII) 'sea raven'. For the final parasitic *t* cf. *peasant, tyrant,* etc.] **1.** A large and voracious sea-bird (*Phalacrocorax carbo*), about 3 feet in length, and black in colour, widely diffused over the northern hemisphere. Also the name of the genu.s **2.** *fig.* An insatiably greedy person or thing 1531. **3.** *attrib.* 1568.

2. Light vanity, insatiate c. *Rich. II,* II. i. 38. **3.** The C. belly *Cor.* I. i. 125.

‖ **Cormus.** 1800. [mod.L.; see CORM[2].] **1.** = CORM[2], q.v. **2.** Haeckel's name for the common stock of a plant or 'colonial' animal, bearing a number of individuals which originate by gemmation.

Corn (kǭɹn), *sb.*[1] [OE. *corn* = OFris., OS., OHG., ON. *korn*, Goth. *kaurn* :- Gmc. **kurnam*, rel. to L. *granum* GRAIN.] **1.** *gen.* A small hard particle, a grain, as of sand, salt, gunpowder. OE. and *mod. dial.* **2.** *spec.* The small hard seed or fruit of a plant; now usually with qualification, as *barley-*, *pepper-c.*, etc. OE. **3.** *spec.* The seed of the cereal or farinaceous plants; grain. (Locally, the word is understood to denote the leading crop of the district; hence in England 'corn' is = *wheat*, in Scotland = *oats*; in U.S., as short for *Indian corn*, it is = *maize*.) OE. **4.** Applied to the cereal plants while growing, or while still containing the grain OE. † **b.** A corn-stalk (*rare*) –1590. **5.** *attrib.* ME.

2. Each [coffee] berry contains two corns 1876. **3.** An ancient churl..Went sweating underneath a sack of c. TENNYSON. **4.** Her Foes shake like a Field of beaten Corne *Hen. VIII*, v. v. 32. **b.** Playing on pipes of Corne *Mids. N.* II. i. 67.

Comb.: **c.-ball** (*U.S.*), a sweetmeat made of popped c. or maize; **-beef,** corned beef; **-beetle,** a very small beetle, *Cucujus testaceus*, the larva of which often ravages stores of grain; **-bells,** a species of fungus, *Cyathus vernicosus*, found in England in corn-fields, etc.; **-bind,** the wild Convolvulus; also Running Buckwheat, *Polygonum convolvulus*; **-cockle,** the common Cockle, *Lychnis githago*; **-crib,** a crib for corn; **-cutter; -fly,** any of the genera *Chloris* and *Oscinis* which do great injury to growing crops; **-fritter** (*U.S.*), a fritter made of batter mixed with grated green Indian c.; **-land; -ma·rigold,** *Chrysanthemum segetum*; **-meal,** meal made of grain; in Scotl., oatmeal; in U.S., meal of maize; **-mill; -mint,** a species of Calamint, *C. acinos*; also, the Field-mint, *Mentha arvensis*; **-moth,** a species of moth, *Tinea granella*, the larva of which is destructive to c.; **-oyster** (*U.S.*), a c.-fritter with a taste as of oysters; **-parsley,** a kind of wild parsley, *Petroselinum segetum*, found in cornfields; **-popper** (*U.S.*), a wire pan or covered tray used in popping Indian c.; **-popping** (*U.S.*), the making of popped Indian c. by roasting it till it splits and the white flour swells out; a social gathering for doing this; † **-powder,** gunpowder that has been granulated; † **-rate** = -RENT; **-rose,** the Corn Poppy; also, the Cockle; **-shuck,** *U.S.* = C. HUSK; **-thrips,** a small insect, *Thrips cerealium*, which deposits its eggs on wheat, oats, grasses, etc.; † **-tree** = CORNEL-TREE; † **-violet,** *Campanula speculum*; **-worm,** the larva of the Corn-moth or other insect, destructive to c.

Corn (kǭɹn), *sb.*[2] ME. [– AFr. *corn* = (O)Fr. *cor* :- L. *cornu* HORN.] A horny induration of the cuticle, with a hard centre, caused by undue pressure, chiefly on the toes and feet. Cf. AGNAIL.

Phr. *To tread on any one's corns*: to wound his susceptibilities.

Corn (kǭɹn), *v.* 1560. [f. CORN *sb.*[1]] **1.** *trans.* To form into grains, as gunpowder. † **2.** *intr.* To become granular –1679. **3.** *trans.* To sprinkle with salt in grains; to season, pickle, or preserve with salt 1565. **4.** To give (a horse) a feed of oats. *Sc.* 1753. **5.** = KERN *v.* 1632. **6.** *trans.* To crop (land) with corn 1649.

3. The beef was woundily corned RICHARDSON. **4.** To c. a horse before a journey SCOTT.

Cornaceous (kǫɹnēi·ʃəs), *a.* [f. mod.L. *Cornaceæ* + -OUS.] *Bot.* Belonging to the Order *Cornaceæ*, of which the genus *Cornus*, Cornel, is the type.

Cornage (kǭ·ɹnėdʒ). [– OFr. *cornage*, f. *corn*, *corne* horn; in med.L. *cornagium*.] A feudal service, being a form of rent fixed by the number of horned cattle; horngeld. ¶ An erroneous explanation given first by Littleton, as an 'it is said', makes cornage 'to wind a horn when the Scots or other enemies entered the land'.

Cornbrash (kǭ·ɹn,bræʃ). 1815. [f. CORN *sb.*[1] + BRASH *sb.*[2]] *Geol.* The coarse brashy calcareous sandstone which forms the upper division of the Lower Oolite in parts of England.

Corn-cob (kǭ·ɹn,kǫb). *U.S.* 1817. [See COB *sb.*[1] III. 3.] The receptacle to which the grains are attached in the ear of maize. Also *attrib.*

Corn-crake (kǭ·ɹn,krēik). 1455. [See CRAKE *sb.*] A bird, also called Landrail, *Crex pratensis*, which lives concealed among standing corn, etc. It has a harsh grating note.

Cornea (kǭ·ɹni,ă). 1527. [mod.L., short for med.L. *cornea tela* or *tunica* horny tissue or coating; fem. of L. *corneus* CORNEOUS.] *Anat.* The horny transparent convexo-concave portion of the anterior covering of the eye-ball. Hence **Co·rneal** *a.*

Corned (kǭɹnd), *a.*[1] 1577. [f. CORN *sb.*[1] and *v.* + -ED.] **1.** Granulated. **2.** Of meat: Cured with salt 1621. **3.** Bearing seeds or grains 1800. **4.** *slang.* Intoxicated [cf. CORNY *a.*[1]] 1785.

† **Corned,** *a.*[2] 1529. [f. Fr. *corné*, with -ED[2] for *-é*.] Horned, peaked, pointed –1841.

Co·rneine. Also **-ean, -een.** 1839. [f. L. *corneus* horny + -INE[5].] *Min.* = APHANITE.

‖ **Corneitis** (kǭɹni,əi·tis). 1854. [f. CORNEA + -ITIS.] *Path.* Inflammation of the cornea.

† **Cornel**[1]. ME. var. of CARNEL, KERNEL = battlement –1602.

Cornel[2]. Now *dial.* ME. [– OFr. *cornal* corner, var. of *cornée*, *cornier*; see CORNER.] Corner, angle (of a house, etc.).

Cornel[3] (kǭ·ɹnĕl). 1551. [orig. in *cornel berry*, *cornel tree*, semi-tr. of G. *kornelbeere*, *kornelbaum* (OHG. *kornulberi*, *-boum*, the source of which is some med.L. deriv. of L. *cornus* cornel-tree).] **1.** English name of the botanical genus *Cornus*, formerly distinguished into *C. mas*, and *C. femina*. *C. mas* was the *Cornel-tree* or Cornelian Cherry-tree; *C. femina* the *Cornel-bush*, *Wild* or *Common Cornel*, or Dogwood (*C. sanguinea*). **b.** The fruit of the Cornel Tree 1601. **2.** *attrib.* Of cornel-wood 1671.

Comb.: **c.-tree,** the Cornelian cherry-tree; **-berry, -fruit:** = 1 b; **-wood,** the wood of *Cornus mascula*, of which anciently javelins, arrows, etc., were made.

Cornelian[1] (kǫɹnī·liăn). ME. [– OFr. *corneline* (mod. *cornaline*); refash. after med.L. *cornelius*, var. of *carneolus*.] A variety of chalcedony, a semi-transparent quartz, of a deep dull red, flesh, or reddish white colour; used for seals, etc. var. † **Co·rneole.**

Cornelian[2] (kǫɹnī·liăn). 1625. [f. CORNEL[3]; see -IAN.] † **1.** The fruit of the cornel-tree; also the tree –1664. **2. C. cherry** = 1; † **c. tree,** cornel-tree –1796.

† **Cornemuse.** ME. [– (O)Fr. *cornemuse*, f. (O)Fr. *corne* horn + OFr. *muse* (mod. *musette*) bagpipe; in med.L. *musa*, *cornamusa*.] A hornpipe; an early form of bagpipe –1882.

Co·rneo-. **1.** Comb. f. L. *corneus*, meaning 'with a horny admixture', as in **c.-calca·reous; c.-sili·cious.** **2.** Comb. f. CORNEA, as in **c.-iritis,** inflammation of the eye affecting both cornea and iris; **c.-sclero·tic,** pertaining to the cornea and sclerotic coat.

Corneous (kǭ·ɹni,əs), *a.* 1646. [f. L. *corneus* (f. *cornu* horn) + -OUS.] Horny, horn-like, as *c. membrane*, etc. (Now only techn.)

Corner (kǭ·ɹnəɹ), *sb.* ME. [– AFr. *corner*, OFr. *cornier* :- Rom. **cornarium*, f. L. *cornum*, *cornu* point, end; see -ER[2] 2. In med.L. *cornerium*.] **1.** *gen.* The meeting-place of converging sides or edges, forming an angular projection. Also *fig.* **2.** A salient angle ME. **3.** The space included between sides and edges at their meeting-place ME. **4.** *transf.* An out-of-the-way, secluded place, that escapes notice ME. Also *fig.* **5.** An end of the earth; a region; † a direction or quarter 1535. **6.** *Bookbinding.* A triangular tool used in gold or blind tooling. **7.** *Association Football* and *Hockey* (= *c.-kick*, *-hit*), a free kick or hit from the corner of the field obtained by the opposite side when a player sends the ball over his own goal-line 1887. † **b.** *Whist.* A point in a rubber –1824. **8.** *Comm.* A speculative operation in which a combination buy up the whole, or the whole available supply, of any stock or commodity, so as to compel speculative sellers to buy of the corner-men at their own price 1857. **9.** *attrib.* 1535.

1. The..hed of the c. WYCLIF *Ps.* 117[118]: 22. **2.** Now is shee without, now in the streetes, and lieth in waite at euery c. *Prov.* 7:12. **3.** In a c. of the halle CHAUCER. Phr. *To drive into a c.*: to drive into straits. **4.** For this thing was not done in a c. *Acts* 26:26. Phr. *Hole and c.*: see HOLE-AND-CORNER. **5.** Sits the winde in that c. *Much Ado* II. iii. 103.

Comb.: † **c.-cap,** a cap with four (or three) corners, worn by divines, etc.; also *fig.*; † **-cree:per,** *fig.* one whose proceedings are underhand and stealthy; **-kick** (see sense 7); **-tooth,** one of the four outer incisors in the jaw of a horse, which shoot in its fifth year.

Corner (kǭ·ɹnəɹ), *v.* ME. [f. the sb.] **1.** *trans.* To furnish with corners. (Chiefly in *pa. pple.*) **2.** To place in a corner ME. **3.** To drive into a corner; to force into an awkward or desperate position; to bring to bay. Also *fig.* (*colloq.*) 1841. **4.** *Comm.* To operate against by means of a CORNER (sense 8); to bring under the control of a corner. (Of *U.S.* origin.) 1857. **5.** *intr.* To abut *on* at a corner; to meet at an angle (*U.S.*) 1863.

3. A rat will fight a man if cornered 1884. *fig.* Morally cornered YATES. **4.** Those gentlemen who attempt to 'corner' cotton 1883.

Cornered (kǭ·ɹnəɹd), *ppl. a.* ME. [f. CORNER *sb.* + -ED[2].] **1.** Having a corner or corners. **2.** See CORNER *v.* 2, 3.

† *C. cap*: = CORNER-CAP.

Co·rner-man. 1873. **1.** The end man of a row of Negro minstrels. **2.** A rough who lounges about street corners 1885. **3.** *Comm.* One who makes a CORNER (sense 8). 1881.

Co·rner-stone. ME. [after L. *lapis angularis* (Vulg., e.g. Job 38:6, Eph. 2:20.)] **1.** One of the stones forming the quoin or salient angle of a wall. Also *fig.* † **2.** The coving of a fire-place 1703.

1. See you yond Coin a' th' Capitol, yond corner stone *Cor.* v. iv. 2. *fig.* Why should we make an ambiguous word the c. of moral philosophy JOWETT.

Co·rnerwise, *adv.* 1474. [See -WISE.] So as to form a corner; diagonally.

Cornet (kǭ·ɹnėt), *sb.*[1] ME. [– (O)Fr. *cornet*, dim. of Rom. **corno*, L. *cornum*, *cornu* horn; see -ET.] **1.** A wind-instrument: † **a.** In early times a horn. **b.** Now a brass instrument, with valves or pistons for producing notes additional to the natural harmonics; also called *cornet à piston*, and CORNOPEAN. **c.** The name given to several organ-stops 1660. **2.** A piece of paper rolled in a conical form and twisted at the apex, used by grocers, etc. 1530. **b.** A small funnel-shaped pastry, usu. filled with cream; also, an ice-cream cone. † **3.** A farrier's instrument for blood-letting –1721. **4.** *Metall.* In gold assaying: The small flat coil into which the gold-and-silver alloy is rolled after cupelling, before being boiled in nitric acid to free it from silver; the small coil of purified gold finally remaining. Also *cornette*. 1800. **5.** *Dressmaking.* The cuff of a sleeve opening like the large end of a trumpet.

1. *Cornet à piston*, *à pistons*: = 1 b; also the player. *Comb.* **c.-stop** = 1 c. Hence † **Co·rneter,** one who plays the c. **Co·rnetist,** a solo c.-player.

Cornet (kǭ·ɹnėt), *sb.*[2] Also *erron.* **coronet(t.** [– (O)Fr. *cornette*, dim. of *corne* horn, orig. collect. :- Rom. **corna*, for L. *cornuo*, pl. of *cornu* horn; see -ET.] **1.** A kind of head-dress formerly worn by ladies. **2.** A scarf anciently worn by Doctors of Physic or Law 1658. † **3.** The standard of a troop of cavalry –1838. † **4.** A troop of cavalry, so called from carrying such a standard –1838. **5.** The fifth commissioned officer in a troop of cavalry, who carried the colours. (Not now in use.) 1579.

4. A certaine Captaine over a c. of horse-men P. HOLLAND. **5.** I had notice that Cornet Joyce.. had seized on the King's person LD. FAIRFAX. Hence **Co·rnetcy,** the position or rank of a c.

Cornette, var. of CORNET.

Corneule (kǭ·ɹni,iūl). 1839. [– Fr. *cornéule*, dim. of *cornée* CORNEA; see -ULE.] The outer transparent covering of the compound eyes of arthropods.

Co·rnfactor. 1699. A dealer in grain.

Co·rn-flag. 1578. [See FLAG *sb.*[1]] A plant of the genus *Gladiolus*, N.O. *Iridaceæ*.

Corn-flour. 1851. Meal of ground Indian corn; also of rice or other grain.

Co·rn-flower. 1578. Any of various plants growing amongst corn; *esp.* the common Bluebottle (*Centaurea cyanus*), or the common Wild Poppy.

Co·rn-husk. *U.S.* 1808. The husk of coarse leaves enclosing the ear of Indian corn.

So **Co·rn-husker,** one who or that which husks Indian corn. **Co·rn-husking.**

Cornic (kǭ·ɹnik), *a.* 1838. [f. L. *cornus* (see CORNEL) + -IC.] *Chem.* In *C. acid*, a synonym of CORNIN, q.v.

Cornice (kǭ·ɹnis), *sb.* Also **cornish,** etc. 1563. [– Fr. *corniche*, †*-ice*, †*-isse* – It. *cornice*, perh. – L. *cornix*, *-ic-* crow (cf. the origin of CORBEL), but with blending of a deriv. of Gr. κορωνίς coping-stone.] **1.** *Arch.* A horizontal moulded projection which crowns a building or some part of a building; *spec.* the uppermost member of an entablature. **2.** An ornamental moulding running round the wall of a room, etc.; a picture-moulding, or the like; also, the ornamental projection within which curtains are hung 1670. **3.** *Mountaineering.* An eave or shelf of snow or rock overhanging a precipice.

Comb. **c.-ring,** the ring or moulding on a cannon next behind the muzzle-ring; = ASTRAGAL.

Hence **Co·rniced** *ppl. a.* having a c. † **Co·rnicement, Co·rnicing,** work consisting of a c. or cornices.

Cornicle (kǭ·ɹnik'l). 1646. [– L. *corniculus*, dim. of *cornu* horn; see -CULE.] A little horn (*obs.*); a small horn-like process, as the horns of a snail, etc. Hence **Corni·culate** *a.* horned; having horn-like projections.

† **Corni·culer.** ME. [– L. *cornicularius* soldier presented with a *corniculus* (see prec.) or horn-shaped ornament worn on the helmet, and thereby promoted; see -ARY [1].] An assistant officer –1447.

Corniferous (kǭɹni·fĕrəs), *a.* 1650. [f. L. *cornifer* (f. *cornu* horn + *-fer* bearing) + -OUS; see -FEROUS.] † **1.** Producing or having horns. **2.** *Geol.* Producing or containing hornstone 1873.

Cornify (kǭ·ɹnifəi), *v.* 1611. [f. L. *cornu* horn + -FY.] † **1.** *trans.* To fit with horns; to cuckold. **2.** *Phys.* and *Zool.* To turn into horn or horny substance 1859. Hence **Cornifica·tion.**

Corni·gerous, *a.* 1646. [f. L. *cornigerus* (f. *cornu* horn + *-ger* bearing) + -OUS; see -GEROUS.] Bearing horns; producing horn.

Cornin (kǭ·ɹnin). 1831. [f. L. *cornus* (see CORNEL) + -IN [1].] *Chem.* A bitter crystalline substance obtained from the root of *Cornus florida*; also called *cornic acid*.

Corning (kǭ·ɹniŋ), *vbl. sb.* 1560. [f. CORN *v.* + -ING [1].] **1.** Granulation. **2.** Pickling with salt 1655.

Comb. **c.-house,** the part of a powder-mill where the granulating is done.

Cornish (kǭ·ɹniʃ), *a.* (*sb.*) 1547. [f. first element of *Cornwall*, OE. *Cornwēalas*, f. OCelt. **Kornovjos*, *-ja*, whence med.L. *Cornubia* Cornwall; see WELSH, -ISH [1].] **1.** Of or belonging to Cornwall; applied *esp.* to the people and language; hence **Cornishman. 2.** *sb.* The ancient language of Cornwall, a member of the Brythonic branch of the Celtic languages 1547.

C. boiler, the cylindrical flue-boiler invented by Smeaton; **C. chough** (see CHOUGH); **C. engine,** a form of single-acting condensing steam-engine, used for pumping up water, first used in Cornwall; **C. pump,** a pump worked by a C. engine.

Co·rn-law, Corn Law. 1766. A law regulating the trade in corn, *esp.* its import and export. In England used spec. of the laws restricting the importation of cereals which were repealed in 1846. (In this application usually spelt with capitals.)

† **Co·rn-master.** 1580. One who has corn to sell –1667.

Cornmuse, var. of CORNEMUSE.

‖ **Corno** (korno). Pl. **corni.** 1818. [It. :– L. *cornu.*] A HORN, *esp.* the French horn. *C. inglese* = COR ANGLAIS; *c. di bassetto*, the basset-horn; also name of an organ-stop.

Cornopean (kǭɹnō[u]·piăn). 1837. [Obscurely f. CORNET *sb.* [1]] *Mus.* **1.** A name for the *cornet à piston*; see CORNET *sb.* [1] **2.** An 8 ft. reed-stop on an organ 1840.

Co·rn-rent. 1809. A rent paid in corn, or one determined each year by the price of corn.

Co·rn-sa:lad. 1597. A plant, *Valeriana olitoria*, or Lamb's-Lettuce, found wild in cornfields; used for salad.

Co·rn-snake. 1676. A large harmless snake, *Coluber guttatus*, common in the southern U.S.

Co·rn-stalk. 1816. **1.** A stalk of (in *U.S.* Indian) corn. **2.** *fig.* A tall lithe person; hence, a nickname, *esp.* for persons of European descent born in N.S. Wales 1865.

Cornstone (kǭ·ɹnstō[u]n). 1822. [f. CORN *sb.* [1]] *Geol.* An earthy concretionary limestone bed found in the Old Red Sandstone formation in parts of Britain. Also *attrib.*

‖ **Cornu** (kǭ·ɹniu). Pl. **cornua.** 1691. [L.] A horn: applied in *Anat.* to processes likened to a horn, as the *cornua uteri*, into which the Fallopian tubes open, etc. Hence **Co·rnual** *a.* of or pertaining to cornua.

Cornucopia (kǭɹniu,kō[u]·piă). Also **-copiæ.** 1592. [– late L. *cornucopia*, earlier *cornu copiæ* 'horn of plenty', emblem of fruitfulness and abundance.] **1.** The horn of plenty; in art, a goat's horn overflowing with flowers, fruit, and corn; also, an ornamental receptacle of similar shape. **2.** *fig.* An overflowing store 1611.

2. Her common-place book..Of scandal..a c. SWIFT. Hence **Cornuco·pian** *a.* pertaining to a c.; overflowingly abundant.

† **Cornu·te.** 1605. [– L. *cornutus* horned, f. *cornu* horn.] **1.** A retort for distilling –1736. **2.** A forked pennon 1625. **3.** One who is 'horned'; a cuckold –1707. **4.** *Logic.* A 'horned' argument, dilemma; the sophism 'Cornutus' –1739.

4. To take for an example of this fallacy, the κεράτινος or Cornutus:—it is asked;—Have you cast your horns? [etc.] SIR W. HAMILTON. So **Cornu·te** *v.* to cuckold (*arch.*). **Cornu·ted** *ppl. a.* horned; horn-shaped; cuckolded. †‖ **Cornu·to,** a cuckold. † **Cornu·tor.**

Cornutus; see CORNUTE *sb.* 4.

Corny (kǭ·ɹni), *a.* [1] ME. [f. CORN *sb.* [1] + -Y [1].] **1.** Of or pertaining to corn 1580. **2.** Of ale: ? Tasting strong of the malt. Now *dial.* ME. **3.** Producing corn; abounding in grains of corn 1580. **4.** Tipsy; = CORNED (*dial.*) 1825.

1. Up stood the cornie Reed MILT. *P.L.* VII. 321. **2.** A draughte of c. ale CHAUCER. **3.** That rich c. country CARLYLE. The c. chaff 1826.

† **Co·rny,** *a.* [2] *rare.* 15... [app. f. L. *cornu* horn + -Y [1].] Hard as horn, horny –1755.

Corny (kǭ·ɹni), *a.* [3] 1707. [f. CORN *sb.* [2] + Y [1].] Having corns on the feet; pertaining to corns.

Coro-; see COR- [2].

Corody, etc.; see CORRODY, etc.

Corolla (korǫ·lă). Pl. **corollas.** 1671. [– L. *corolla*, used bot. by Linnæus, dim. of *corona* CROWN.] † **1.** A little crown, coronet. **2.** *Bot.* The whorl of leaves (petals) forming the inner envelope of the flower; usually 'coloured' (*i.e.* not green). Cf. CALYX. 1753. Also in *comb.* var. † **Co·rol.** Hence **Corolla·ceous** *a.* of the nature of a c. So **Coro·llar** *a.* **Co·rollate** *a.* having or resembling a c. So **Co·rollated** *a.* **Corolli·ferous** *a.* corollate. **Coro·lline** *a.* pertaining to the c. **Coro·llist,** one who classifies plants according to their corollas (*rare*). **Coro·llule** = COROLLET.

Corollary (korǫ·lări, kǫ·rǫ̆lări). ME. [– L. *corollarium* money paid for a garland, present, gratuity, deduction (Boethius), f. *corolla*; see prec., -ARY [1].] **1.** In *Geom.*, etc. A proposition appended to another which has been demonstrated, and following obviously from it; hence *gen.* an immediate inference, deduction, consequence. **2.** *transf.* A practical consequence, result 1674. † **3.** An appendix; a finishing or crowning part –1717. † **4.** Something additional; a surplus; a supernumerary –1681.

1. This is but a c. from what goes before WOLLASTON. **2.** The art of Writing, of which Printing is a..c. CARLYLE. **4.** Now come my Ariell, bring a Corolary, Rather then want a Spirit *Temp.* IV. i. 57.

Corollary, *a. rare.* 1449. [attrib. use of prec. Cf. med.L. *corrolarie* by way of corollary.] **1.** Of the nature of a corollary. **2.** *Bot.* Corolline 1882.

† **Coro·llet.** 1794. [f. COROLLA + -ET.] *Bot.* The floret in an aggregate flower –1823.

Corollifloral (korǫ:liflō[ə]·răl), *a.* 1845. [f. mod.L. *Corollifloræ* (f. *corolla* + *flos, flor-*) + -AL [1].] *Bot.* Of or belonging to the *Corollifloræ*, a sub-class of dicotyledonous plants having calyx and corolla, the petals being united and the stamens usually attached to the corolla. (See De Candolle.) So **Corolliflo·rous.**

Corollitic (kǫrǫli·tik), *a.* 1819. [– Fr. *corollitique*, f. L. *corolla* (Littré).] *Arch.* Of columns: Having foliated shafts. vars. **Carolitic, -ytic.**

‖ **Corona** (korō[u]·nă). Pl. **-næ** (-nī), rarely **-as.** 1563. [L.] **1.** A small circle or disc of light (usually prismatic) appearing round the sun or moon. Also applied to other similar phenomena. **2.** *Astron.* The halo of radiating white light seen around the disc of the moon in a total eclipse of the sun; now known to belong to the sun 1851. **3.** A circular chandelier suspended from the roof of a church; more fully *corona lucis* 1825. **4.** *Arch.* A member of the cornice, above the bed-moulding and below the cymatium, usually of considerable projection; also called *drip* or *larmier* 1563. **5.** *Anat.*, etc. Applied to parts resembling or likened to a crown; also to the upper portion of any part, as of a tooth; cf. CROWN 1712. **6.** *Bot.* **a.** A crown-like appendage on the inner side of the corolla in some flowers, as the daffodil and lychnis. **b.** The *medullary sheath* in the stems of Dicotyledons and Gymnosperms. **c.** The crown of the root. 1753. **7.** (*Astron.*) *C. australis*, *C. borealis*: the Southern and Northern Crown, consisting of elliptical rings of stars.

Coronach (kǫ·rənaχ). *Sc.* and *Ir.* 1500. [– Ir. *coranach*, Gael. *corranach*, f. *comh-* together + *rànach* outcry.] † **1.** *gen.* A shouting of many –1680. **2.** *spec.* A funeral song or dirge in the Highlands of Scotland and in Ireland 1530.

2. Eachan Macrimmon is playing a c. as it were for a chief W. C. SMITH.

Coronal (kǫ·rŏnăl), *sb.* ME. [app. – AFr. **coronal*, f. *corone* CROWN *sb.* In 4 prob. – med.L. *coronalis.*] **1.** A circlet for the head; a coronet. Also *transf.* and *fig.* **2.** A wreath for the head; a garland 1579. Also *transf.* † **3.** The head of a tilting lance, ending in three or four short spreading points. (Often *cronall, cronel, curnall.*) –1470. † **4.** *Anat.* The frontal bone; cf. next –1758.

1. On hir head a coronall all of greet pearles HOLINSHED. **2.** Of rosemary a simple c. T. MARTIN. Hence **Co·ronalled** *a.* adorned with a coronet.

Coronal (korō[u]·năl, kǫ·rŏnăl), *a.* 1543. [– Fr., or L. (and med.L.) *coronalis*, f. *corona* CROWN *sb.*] † **1.** Pertaining to a crown, or to coronation –1813. **2.** *Anat.*, etc. **a.** *C. suture*: the suture separating the frontal bone from the parietal bones. So *c. region* (of the forehead), etc. *C. bone*: the frontal bone. 1543. **b.** Of or pertaining to the crown of the head 1828. **c.** Pertaining to the corona (see CORONA) 1846. **3.** *Bot.* Pertaining or similar to a corona (see CORONA) 1870.

1. The Law and his C. Oath requires his undeniable assent to what Laws the Parlament agree upon MILT. **2. c.** So abundant is the c. light.. during totality 1871. Hence † **Coronally** *adv.* in the manner of a crown or coronet.

Coronary (kǫ·rŏnări), *a.* 1610. [– L. *coronarius*, f. as prec.; see -ARY [1].] † **1.** Of the nature of or resembling a crown; pertaining to or forming a crown –1659. † **2.** Suitable for garlands or wreaths –1682. **3.** *Anat.* Encircling like a crown, as the *c. arteries* and *veins* of the heart, etc. 1679. **4.** *absol.* as *sb.* = CORONET 4. 1847.

1. *C. gold* [tr. L. *coronarium aurum*]: 'a present of gold collected in the provinces for a victorious general; orig. expended for a golden crown' (Lewis and Short).

† **Co·ronate,** *pa. pple.* 1470. [– L. *coronatus*, pa. pple. of *coronare*, f. *corona* CROWN *sb.* See -ATE [2].] Crowned –1513.

Coronate (kǫ·rŏnĕt, -e[i]t), *a.* 1846. [f. CORONA + -ATE [2].] *Bot.* and *Zool.* = CORONATED.

Coronate (kǫ·rŏne[i]t), *v. rare.* 1623. [– *coronat-*, pa. ppl. stem of L. *coronare*, f. *corona* CROWN *sb.*; see -ATE [3].] To crown. (See also next.)

Coronated (kǫ·rŏne[i]tĕd), *ppl. a.* 1676. [f. as prec.; see -ATE [3], -ED [1] 2.] † **1.** Of flowers: Arranged in a whorl. **2.** *Bot.* and *Zool.* Furnished with a corona; *spec.* in *Conchol.* of spiral shells which have their whorls surmounted by a row of tubercles 1698. † **3.** = CORONETED 1767.

Coronation (kǫrŏnēⁱ·ʃən). ME. [– (O)Fr. *coronation* – med.L. *coronatio*, f. as prec.; see -ION.] **1.** The action of crowning; the ceremony of investing with a crown as an emblem of royal dignity. Also *transf.* **2.** *fig.* Crowning of a work; completion 1582. **3.** *attrib.* 1587.

3. *C. oath*, that taken by a sovereign at his c.

† **Corone.** Early f. CROWN, obs. by 1500.

Coronel(l, obs. f. COLONEL, CORONAL.

Coroner (kǫ·rŏnəɹ). ME. [– AFr. *cor(o)uner*, f. *coro(u)ne* CROWN *sb.*, after the title *custos placitorum coronæ* guardian of the pleas of the crown; latinized as *coronarius, coronator* (XIII). From XV freq. *crowner* (from *corou·ner*).] An officer of a county, district, or municipality (formerly also of the royal household), originally charged with maintaining the private property of the crown; in mod. times his chief function is to hold inquest on the bodies of those supposed to have died by violence or accident.

Coroner's inquest: the investigation as to the cause of death held by the *Coroner's Court*, consisting of the c. and twelve jurymen summoned for the inquest. Hence **Co·ronership,** the office of a c.

Coronet (kǫ·rŏnĕt), *sb.* 1494. [– OFr. *coronet(t)e*, dim. of *corone* CROWN *sb.*; see -ET.] **1.** A small or inferior crown; *spec.* a crown denoting a dignity inferior to that of the sovereign. **2.** A fillet or wreath for the head; *esp.* a decorative plate or band of metal, or the like, worn by women round the brow, as part of a head-dress 1590. **3.** = CORONA 6 a. 1657. **4.** *Farriery.* The lowest part of the pastern of a horse 1696. **5.** = CORONAL *sb.* 3. 1731.

1. I sawe Marke Antony offer him a Crowne, yet 'twas not a Crowne neyther, 'twas one of these Coronets *Jul. C.* I. ii. 239. **2.** And on her brow. . A c. of pearls S. ROGERS.

Hence **Co·ronet** *v.* to confer a c. upon; to adorn as with a c. (*rare*). **Co·roneted, -etted** *ppl. a.* **Coronetty, -ee** *a. Her.* ornamented on the upper side c.-wise.

Coro·niform, *a. rare.* 1776. [f. L. *corona*; see -FORM.] Crown-shaped.

‖ **Coronis** (korōᵘ·nis). 1670. [L. – Gr. κορωνίς flourish at the end of a book or chapter.] † **1.** The end. **2.** *Greek Gram.* A sign (ʼ), placed over a vowel as a mark of contraction or crasis; *e.g.* κἀγαθός for καὶ ἀγαθός 1833.

Coronium (korōᵘ·niŏm). 1890. [f. CORONA 2 + -IUM.] An element supposed to exist in a gaseous state in the sun's corona. (Cf. HELIUM.)

† **Co·ronize,** *v.* 1592. [f. L. *corona* + -IZE.] To crown, adorn with a coronet or coronal –1623.

Coro·nograph. 1885. [f. *corono-*, comb. f. CORONA + -GRAPH.] *Astron.* An instrument for photographing the sun's corona in full sunlight. Hence **Coronographic** *a.*

Coronoid (kǫ·rŏnoid, korōᵘ·noˌid), *a.* 1741. [f. Gr. κορώνη crow; see -OID.] Applied to processes that are curved like a crow's beak, and to parts in connection with these; as the *c. process* of the lower jaw, and that of the ulna, and the *c. fossa* of the humerus.

Coronule (korōᵘ·niul). 1806. [– late L. *coronula*, dim. of *corona* CROWN; see -ULE.] **1.** *Bot.* A small crown or coronet surmounting a seed, etc. **2.** *Zool.* A kind of barnacle of the genus *Coronula* of Cirripeds; parasitic on Cetacea.

Coroplasty, Corotomy; see COR-².

Corosif, obs. f. CORROSIVE.

Coroun(e, corowne, obs. ff. CROWN.

‖ **Corozo** (korōᵘ·so). 1760. [Sp. – native name.] A South American tree, *Phytelephas macrocarpa*, allied to the palms; the hardened albumen of its seed (the *C.-nut* or *ivory-nut*) furnishes the substance called vegetable ivory.

Corp, Sc. and n. Eng. dial. f. CORPSE.

Corporal (kǭ·ɹpŏrăl), *a.* ME. [– OFr. *corporal* (mod. *corporel*) – L. *corporalis*, f. *corpus, -or-* body; see -AL¹.] **1.** Of or belonging to the body; bodily. † **2.** Of the nature of matter; corporeal, physical –1726. † **3.** Large of body –1630. † **4.** Solid –1667.

1. The c. or bodelye sight CAXTON. Corporall liberty HOBBES. **2.** What seem'd corporall Melted, as breath into the Wind *Macb.* I. iii. 81. **3.** A sufficient corporall Burgher 1630. Phrases. *C. oath* [med. L. *corporale juramentum*; cf. BODILY *Oath*]: an oath ratified by corporally touching a sacred object, *esp.* the gospels, but sometimes the host, or relics; dist. from a verbal oath. (The view that the attributive 'corporal' refers to the host is not historically tenable.) *C. punishment*: punishment inflicted on the body (as opp. to a fine, etc.). Now usually confined to flogging. *C. works of mercy*: works of mercy to the bodies of men, as, to feed the hungry, etc. Hence **Co·rporally** *adv.*

Corporal (kǭ·ɹpŏrăl), *sb.*¹ OE. [– (O)Fr. *corporal* or med.L. *corporale*, subst. use (sc. *pallium* PALL *sb.*¹) of *corporalis* (see prec.).] *Eccl.* † **1.** An ancient eucharistic vestment –1660. **2.** A linen cloth upon which the consecrated elements are placed during celebration, and with which they are subseq. covered. Called also *c.-cloth.* ME.

Corporal (kǭ·ɹpŏrăl), *sb.*² 1579. [– Fr. †*corporal*, var. of *caporal* – It. *caporale*, of which there appears to have been a Venetian form †*corporale*, f. *corpus, corpor-* body (of troops), the standard form being assim. to *capo* head. Cf. CORPORAL *a.*] **1.** A non-commissioned military officer ranking under a sergeant. **2.** *Naut.* Formerly, a petty officer on board ship, who taught the sailors the use of small-arms; now, a superior petty officer, who attends solely to police matters under the master-at-arms 1626.

1. *Corporal's guard*: a small armed detachment under a c. Hence *fig.* a small body of supporters. † *C. of the field*: in the 16th and 17th c. a kind of aide-de-camp to the sergeant-major. Hence **Co·rporalship,** †a body of soldiers under a c.; the office of a c.

Corporality (kǭɹpŏræ·lĭti). ME. [– late L. *corporalitas* (Tertullian), f. L. *corporalis* CORPORAL *a.*; see -ITY.] **1.** The quality of being corporal (see CORPORAL *a.* 2); materiality. **2.** Embodied existence or condition 1642. † **3.** Corporate organization of a society, town, etc.; a CORPORATION –1603. **4.** *pl.* Corporal matters. Cf. *temporalities.* 1748.

Corporas (kǭ·ɹpŏræ̆s). [ME. *corporaus* – OFr. *corporaus* (earlier *-als*), nom. sing. of *corporal* CORPORAL *sb.*¹ 2.] = CORPORAL *sb.*¹ 2.

Corporate (kǭ·ɹpŏrĕt), *ppl. a.* ME. [– L. *corporatus*, pa. pple. of *corporare* fashion into or with a body, f. *corpus, -or-* body; see -ATE².]

A. as *pa. pple.* **1.** United into one body (*arch.*). † **2.** Embodied 1555.

B. *adj.* † **1.** Corpulent –1533. † **2.** Pertaining to the body –1613. † **3.** Embodied; material –1865. **4.** Forming a body politic, or corporation 1512. Also *transf.* **5.** Of or belonging to a body politic, or corporation, or to a body of persons 1607.

4. *C. body, body c.*: see BODY *sb. C. town*: a town possessing municipal rights, and acting by means of a corporation. **5.** *C. name*: the name by which a corporation engages in legal acts. Hence **Co·rporately** *adv.* †as regards the body; in a c. capacity. **Co·rporateness.**

Corporate (kǭ·ɹpŏreⁱt), *v. arch.* 1531. [– *corporat-*, pa. ppl. stem of L. *corporare*; see prec., -ATE³.] † **1.** *trans.* To incorporate –1631. **2.** To combine in one body 1545. **3.** *intr.* To unite in one body (*rare*) 1647.

Corporation (kǭɹpŏrēⁱ·ʃən). ME. [– late L. *corporatio*, f. as prec.; see -ION.] † **1.** The action of incorporating, the condition of being incorporated –1542. **2.** A body of persons 1534. **3.** *Law.* A body corporate legally authorized to act as a single individual; an artificial person created by royal charter, prescription, or legislative act, and having the capacity of perpetual succession 1611. **4.** A trade-guild, a city 'company'. (Now only legal or formal.) 1530. **5.** The body; the abdomen. *colloq.* and *vulgar.* 1753. Also *attrib.*

3. *C. aggregate*: one comprising many individuals, as the mayor and burgesses of a town, etc. *C. sole*: one consisting of only one person and his successors, as a king, bishop, etc. *Municipal c.*: the mayor, aldermen, and councillors of a borough or incorporated town or city.

Corporative (kǭ·ɹpŏrătiv), *a.* 1833. [f. CORPORATE *ppl. a.* (sense 5) + -IVE; cf. Fr. *corporatif.*] = CORPORATE *a.* 5.

Corporator (kǭ·ɹpŏreⁱtəɹ). 1784. [irreg. f. CORPORAT(ION + -OR 2.] A member of a (municipal) corporation.

† **Corporature.** 1555. [– L. *corporatura*, f. as CORPORATE *v.*; see -URE.] **1.** Physique –1696. **2.** = CORPORALITY 1. 1647.

Corporeal (kǫɹpōᵊ·rĭăl), *a.* (*sb.*) 1610. [– late L. *corporealis* bodily, f. L. *corporeus*; see -AL¹.] **1.** Of the nature of the animal body as opp. to the spirit; physical; bodily; mortal. **2.** Material 1619. **3.** *Law.* Tangible; consisting of material objects; *esp.* in *C. hereditament* 1670. † **4.** In sense of CORPORAL –1831.

1. To couple a spiritual grace with matters of c. repast FULLER. **2.** Are genera and species c. or incorporeal REID.

B. *sb. pl.* Things material; things pertaining to the human body (*rare*).

Hence † **Corpo·realism,** materialism. † **Corpo·realist,** a materialist. **Corporea·lity,** the quality or state of being c.; materiality. **Corpo·really** *adv.* in or as to the body; bodily. **Corpo·realness,** c. quality or state (*rare*).

Corpo·realize, *v.* 1797. [f. prec. + -IZE.] To render corporeal; to materialize. Hence **Corporealization.**

Corporeity (kǭɹpŏrī·ĭti). 1621. [– Fr. *corporéité* or med.L. *corporeitas*, f. *corporeus*; see -ITY.] **1.** The quality of being, or having, a material body; *concr.* bodily substance. † **2.** Carnality –1681. **3.** Material nature or state. †Occas. = Density. 1664.

1. The notion of a Spirit, or substance void of c. HALE. **3.** His [Newton's] views of colours were entirely independent of his belief in the c. of light 1880.

† **Corpo·rify,** *v.* 1644. [f. L. *corpus, -or-* body + -FY, perh. through Fr. *corporifier.*] **1.** To cause to assume a material form –1707. **2.** To incorporate –1707. Hence † **Corpo:rifica·tion.** So † **Co·rporize** *v.*

Corposant (kǭ·ɹpŏzænt). 1561. [– OSp., Pg., It. *corpo santo* 'holy body', see BODY V. 1.] The ball of light sometimes seen about the masts or yard-arms of a ship during a storm; St. Elmo's fire.

Corps (kōᵊɹ). Pl. **corps** (kōᵊɹz). ME. [– Fr. *corps.* See CORPSE.] † **1.** Earlier var. of CORPSE, q.v. **2.** *Mil.* A division of an army, forming a tactical unit; a body of troops regularly organized; a body of men assigned to a special service 1711. Also *fig.* **3.** *gen.* A body of persons associated in a common organization, or acting under a common direction 1730.

2. ‖ *Corps d'armée* (Fr.): a main division of an army in the field, an army-corps. **3.** The whole dramatic c. CARLYLE. ‖ *Corps diplomatique* (Fr.): the diplomatic c. or body accredited to a particular Court or Capital. ‖ *Corps de ballet* (Fr.): the company of dancers in a ballet.

‖ **Corps de garde.** 1587. [Fr.; often corrupted to *Court o' guard*, COURT OF GUARD.] **1.** The small body of soldiers stationed on guard or as sentinels. **2.** A guard-room or guard-house 1587.

Corpse (kǭɹps, kǭɹs), *sb.* [ME. *corps*, orig. graphic var. of *cors* (see CORSE) – OFr. *cors* (mod. *corps*) :– L. *corpus* body. The inserted *p* was at first mute, as in Fr., but infl. the pronunc. before 1500; the final *e* now differentiates the word from CORPS.] † **1.** (rarely *corpse.*) The body of a man or animal; a (living) body; a person –1707. **2.** *esp.* The dead body of a man (or formerly any animal) ME. † **3.** (rarely *corpse.*) Collective whole or mass; BODY (of law, science, etc.) *Corps of Law* = *Corpus juris.* –1651. **4.** (*corps*, rarely *corpse.*) The endowment of an office, †civil or ecclesiastical; *esp.* of a prebend. (med.L. *corpus prebendæ.*) 1580.

2. Then make a Ring about the Corpes of Cæsar *Jul. C.* III. ii. 162. On the same day his Corps (pl. = 'remains') were buried at Westminster FULLER. **4.** Other portions of the estates. . became the corpses of various prebends FREEMAN.

Comb.: **c.-gate** (*dial.* **-yat, -yett,** etc.) = LICH-GATE; **-light** = CORPSE-CANDLE 2.

Corpse (kǭɹps), *v. slang.* 1874. [f. prec. sb.] **1.** To kill (*vulgar*) 1884. **2.** *Actors' slang.* To confuse or put out (an actor), or spoil (a piece of acting), by some blunder.

Co·rpse-can:dle. 1694. [f. CORPSE *sb.*] † **1.** 'A thick candle formerly used at lake-wakes' (Halliwell). **2.** A lambent flame seen in a churchyard, and believed to portend a funeral 1694.

Corpulence (kǭ·ɹpiŭlĕns), **Corpulency** (kǭ·ɹpiŭlĕnsi). 1477. [–(O)Fr. *corpulence* or L. *corpulentia*, f. *corpulentus*; see next, -ENCE.] †**1.** Habit of body; size –1491. **2.** Bulk of body; obesity 1581. †**3.** Material quality or substance; density (*rare*) –1691.

3. The heaviness and c. of the water RAY.

Corpulent (kǭ·ɹpiŭlĕnt), *a.* ME. [– L. *corpulentus*, f. *corpus* body; see -ULENT.] † **1.** Solid, dense, gross –1650. **2.** Fleshy, fat ME. † **3.** Corporeal; material –1643.

2. A goodly portly man yfaith, and a c. 1 *Hen. IV*, II. iv. 464.

‖ **Corpus** (kǭ·ɹpŏs). Pl. **corpora** (kǭ·ɹpŏră). ME. [L.] **1.** The body of a man or animal. (Now joc. or grotesque.) **2.** *Phys.* A structure of a special character or function in the animal body, as *c. callosum*, the transverse commissure connecting the cerebral hemispheres; so also *corpora quadrigemina, striata*, etc., of the brain; *c. spongiosum* and *corpora cavernosa* of the penis, etc. **3.** A complete collection of writings or the like 1727. **4.** The body or material substance of anything; principal, as opp. to interest or income 1844.

Phrases. *C. delicti*: 'the sum or aggregate of the ingredients which make a given fact a breach of a given law' (Austin). *C. juris*: a body of law. † *By c. bones*: ? a confusion of *c. Domini* and *Goddes bones*.

‖ **Corpus Christi** (kǭ·ɹpŏs kri·stəi, -ti). ME. [L.; = Christ's body.] *R.C. Ch.* The feast of the Blessed Sacrament or Body of Christ, observed on the Thursday after Trinity Sunday.

Corpuscle (kǭ·ɹpŏs'l, kǫɹpɒ·s'l). 1660. [– L. *corpusculum*, dim. of *corpus* body; see -CULE.] **1.** A minute body or particle of matter. Occas. = *atom*, or *molecule*. **2.** *Phys.* Any minute body (usu. of microscopic size), forming a distinct part of the organism; *esp.* (*pl.*) minute rounded or discoidal bodies, constituting a large part of the blood in vertebrates 1741. **3.** *Bot.* = CORPUSCULUM 1 b.

2. Such corpuscles of protoplasm as are provided with a nucleus are called cells 1878.

Corpuscular (kǫɹpɒ·skiŭlăɹ), *a.* 1667. [f. L. *corpusculum*; see prec., -AR¹.] **1.** Pertaining to, of the nature of, or consisting of, corpuscles 1671. **2.** Concerned with atoms; atomic; *esp.* in *C. philosophy, theory* 1667.

2. *C. theory* of light = EMISSION theory: see CORPUSCLE. Hence **Corpu:scula·rian** *a.* = CORPUSCULAR 1; *sb.* an adherent of the c. or atomic philosophy, or of the c. theory of light.

Corpuscule (kǫɹpɒ·skiul). 1816. [– L. *corpusculum*; see CORPUSCLE, -ULE. So (O)Fr. *corpuscule*.] = CORPUSCLE.

According to the former [theory], light consists in 'Corpuscules', or excessively minute material particles darted out in all directions from the luminous body HERSCHEL.

Corpusculous (kǫɹpɒ·skiŭləs), *a.* 1871. [f. as prec. + -OUS.] Characterized by the presence of corpuscles.

‖ **Corpu·sculum.** Pl. **-ula.** 1650. [L.; dim. of *corpus*.] **1.** = CORPUSCLE 1. **b.** *Bot.* The central cells of the archegonia of Gymnosperms 1844. † **2.** A small body of men –1659.

† **Corra·de,** *v.* 1619. [– L. *corradere*, f. *com* COR-¹ + *radere* scrape.] **1.** *trans.* To scrape together (*lit.* and *fig.*) –1659. **2.** To scrape, wear down by scraping 1646. Hence † **Corra·sion.**

Corradial (kǫ̆rēⁱ·diăl), *a. rare.* 1825. [f. COR-¹ + RADIAL.] Radiating to or from the same centre.

Corradiate (kǫ̆rēⁱ·diˌeⁱt), *v. rare.* 1800. [See COR-¹.] *intr.* To radiate together; to unite their rays. So **Corradia·tion** (*rare*).

Corral (koræ·l), *sb.* 1582. [– Sp., OPg. *corral*, Pg. *curral* (of Hottentot origin), whence KRAAL.] **a.** An enclosure for horses, cattle, etc.; a fold; a stockade. Cf. KRAAL. Also *transf.* **b.** An enclosure formed of wagons in an encampment, for defence against attack 1847. **c.** An enclosure for capturing wild animals 1845.

Corral (koræ·l), *v.* Chiefly *U.S.* 1847. [f. prec.] **1.** *trans.* To form (wagons) into a corral 1851. **2.** To shut up in, or as in, a corral 1847. **3.** *U.S. slang.* To lay hold of, 'collar' 1868.

2. Here they coralled us [prisoners] to the number of seven or eight thousand 1890.

Corrasive; see CORROSIVE.

Correal (kǫ̆rī·ăl), *a.* 1875. [– late L. *correus* prop. joint criminal, f. *com* COR-¹ + *reus* one under obligation.] *Rom. Law.* Under joint obligation. So **Correa·lity,** c. quality or state.

Correct (kǫ̆re·kt), *v.* *Pa. pple.* **corrected,** also, 5–8 **correct.** ME. [– *correct-*, pa. ppl. stem of L. *corrigere*, f. *com* COR-¹ + *regere* lead straight, direct.] **1.** *trans.* To set right, amend. Occas., loosely, to point out or mark the errors or faults in. Also *absol.* **2.** To set right, rectify (an error or fault) ME. **3.** To set right, amend (a person); to admonish or rebuke, or to point out the errors or faults of, in order to amendment ME. **4.** To punish for faults of character or conduct (prop., in order to amendment); to chastise ME. **5.** To bring or reduce to order 1594. **6.** To counteract or neutralize; to remove or prevent the ill effect of 1578. **7.** *Math.* To bring (a result) into accordance with certain standard conditions 1774. **8.** *Optics.* To eliminate the aberration of a lens, etc. 1831.

1. To c. a drawing D'ISRAELI, proof-sheets MORLEY. **3.** If I speak incorrectly you can c. me LAMB. **4.** Vagrants..are oftener corrected than amended FULLER. To c. an abuse 'JUNIUS'. **5.** His pruning-hook corrects the vines POPE. **6.** The heart..corrects the folly of the head FROUDE. Hence **Corre·ctable** *a.* (*rare*). † **Corre·ctedly,** correctly.

Correct (kǫ̆re·kt), *pa. pple.* and *a.* 1460. [– Fr. *correct* – L. *correctus* amended, correct, pa. pple. of *corrigere*; see prec.]

† **A.** *pa. pple.* Corrected; punished, amended –1712.

B. *adj.* **1.** In accordance with an acknowledged standard, *esp.* of style or of behaviour; proper 1676. **2.** In accordance with fact, truth, or reason; right 1705. **3.** Of persons; Adhering exactly to a standard 1734.

1. The c. thing R. FORD. **2.** Always use the most c. editions 1711. Mr. Hunt is..quite c. in saying [etc.] MACAULAY. **3.** C. with spirit, eloquent with ease POPE. Hence **Corre·ct-ly** *adv.*, **-ness.**

Correction (kǫ̆re·kʃən). ME. [– (O)Fr. *correction* – L. *correctio*, f. as CORRECT *v.*; see -ION.] **1.** The action of correcting or setting right; amendment. Hence, loosely, pointing out or marking of errors. **2.** (with *a* and *pl.*) An act or instance of emendation 1528. † **3.** Reprehension, rebuke, reproof –1814. **4.** The correcting by disciplinary punishment; chastisement; flogging (*arch.*) ME. **5.** The counteracting of the ill effect of 1477. **6.** *Math.* and *Phys.* The addition or subtraction of some quantity to or from a result, to bring it into accordance with certain standard conditions; the quantity so added or subtracted 1743. **7.** *Optics.* The counteraction of the aberration in a lens, etc. 1856. † **8.** Correctness 1759.

1. The c. of the calendar WHEWELL. *C. of the press*: i.e. of printers' errors. *Under c.*: subject to c.; an expression of deference. **3.** All Scripture.. is profitable..for c. 2 *Tim.* 3:16. **4.** Their ordinary c. is to beate them with cudgels CAPT. SMITH. *House of c.*: a building for the detention and punishment of offenders; a bridewell. Hence **Corre·ctional** *a.* of or pertaining to c.; corrective. † **Corre·ctioner,** one who administers c. SHAKS.

Correctitude (kǫ̆re·ktitiūd). 1893. [f. CORRECT, after *rectitude*.] Correctness of conduct.

Corrective (kǫ̆re·ktiv). 1531. [– (O)Fr. *correctif, -ive* or late L. *correctivus*, f. L. *correct-*; see CORRECT *v.*, -IVE.]

A. *adj.* Having the property of correcting, counteracting something hurtful, or restoring to a healthy condition 1533.

The penalty..is..c., not penal 1853. *C. justice*, a tr. of Aristotle's διορθωτικὸν δίκαιον (see COMMUTATIVE); used by Hooker in sense 'punitive'.

B. *sb.* [The adj. used *ellipt.*] **1.** That which is corrective or counteractive. Also *fig.* 1610. **2.** Something that tends to set right what is wrong, to counteract an evil, etc. 1734. **3.** Something that acts so as to correct what is erroneous 1677.

1. We take..some varieties of fruit as a c. HOLLAND. **2.** Patriotism is a c. of superstition BUCKLE. **3.** A c. of error JOWETT.

Hence **Corre·ctive-ly** *adv.*, **-ness.**

Corrector (kǫ̆re·ktəɹ). ME. [– AFr. *cor(r)ectour* = (O)Fr. *correcteur* – L. *corrector*, f. as prec.; see -OR 2.] **1.** One who or that which corrects. **2.** An official title = director, controller ME.

1. The c. of the press, or *reader* URE. To giue them [children] maisters, or correcters SIR T. NORTH. The..proper c. of opium..is vineger TIMME. So **Corre·ctress,** † **-trice,** † **-trix,** a female c.

Correctory (kǫ̆re·ktŏri). ? *Obs.* 1607. [– late L. *correctorius*, f. as prec.; see -ORY².] *adj.* Of the nature of a corrector or correction 1620. † *sb.* A corrective –1620.

‖ **Corregido·r.** 1594. [Sp., agent-noun f. *corregir* – L. *corrigere* CORRECT *v.*] The chief magistrate of a Spanish town.

Correlate (kǫ·rĭleⁱt), *sb.* 1643. [In form, an extension of RELATE *sb.*; perh. suggested by the earlier CORRELATION and CORRELATIVE; there may have been a mod.L. **correlatum* in philosophical use.] Either of the terms of a relation, viewed in reference to the other 1644.

Correlate (kǫ·rĭlĕt), *a. rare.* 1842. [f. COR-¹ + L. *relatus*, pa. pple. of *referre* refer.] Mutually related; involving correlation.

Correlate (kǫrĭlēⁱ·t), *v.* 1742. [Back-formation from CORRELATION, CORRELATIVE.] **1.** *intr.* To have a mutual relation; to be correlative (*with* or *to* another). **2.** *trans.* To place in or bring into correlation 1849. **3.** *pass.* To have correlation (*with*, occ. *to*) 1862.

1. Ethical obligation correlates..with ethical right GROTE. **2.** To c. interglacial beds J. GEIKIE. Hence **Correla·table** *a.*

Correlation (kǫrĭlēⁱ·ʃən). 1561. [– med. and schol. L. *correlatio*; see COR-¹, RELATION.] **1.** The condition of being correlated; mutual relation of two or more things (implying intimate or necessary connection). **2.** *Biol.* Mutual relation of association between different structures, characteristics, etc., in an animal or plant 1859. **3.** *Geom.* The reciprocal relation between propositions, figures, etc., derivable from each other by interchanging the words *point* and *plane*, or *point* and *line*; cf. CORRELATIVE *a.* 2. **4.** The action of correlating 1879.

1. How in animall natures, even colours hold correspondencies, and mutual correlations SIR T. BROWNE.

Phr. *C. of forces* (in *Physics*): the mutual relation that exists between the various forms of force or energy, by virtue of which any one form is convertible into an equivalent amount of any other. (Cf. *conservation of energy*, s. v. CONSERVATION.)

Correlative (kǫ̆re·lătiv). 1530. [– schol.L. *correlativus*; see COR-¹, RELATIVE. Cf. Fr. *corrélatif, -ive*.]

A. *adj.* **1.** Having, or involving, a reciprocal relation. Const. *with*, rarely *to*. 1690. **2.** *Geom.* Said of propositions, figures, etc., reciprocally related so that to a *point* in either corresponds (in solid geometry) a *plane*, or (in plane geometry) a *straight line* in the other 1881.

1. Father and son, husband and wife, and other such c. terms LOCKE. Hence **Corre·lative-ly** *adv.*, **-ness. Correlati·vity.**

B. *sb.* Each of two things correlative to one another 1545.

The words used..are what are called correlatives, one implies the other J. H. NEWMAN.

Correligionist, = CO-RELIGIONIST.

Correption (kǫ̆re·pʃən). ME. [– L. *correptio*, f. *corrept-*, pa. ppl. stem of *corripere*, f. *com* COR-¹ + *rapere* snatch.] † **1.** Reproof –1737. † **2.** A seizure. (Cf. RAPTURE.) –1664. **3.** *Gram.* Shortening in pronunciation 1873.

1. Of charitable correpcion or reproving WYCLIF. **3.** Liable to c. of its accented syllable EARLE.

Correspond (kǫrĭspǫ·nd), *v.* 1529. [– (O)Fr. *correspondre* – med.L. *correspondēre*; see COR-¹, RESPOND.] **1.** *intr.* To answer to something else in the way of fitness; to agree *with*; be conformable *to*; be congruous or in harmony *with*. **2.** To answer *to* in character or function; to be similar *to* (rarely *with*) 1645. † **3.** To respond –1826. **4.** To hold communication or intercourse (*with*). *Obs.* exc. as in 5. 1605. **5.** *esp.* To communicate (*with* another) by interchange of letters 1645. † **6.** *trans.* To answer to –1675.

1. Our nature corresponds to our external condition BUTLER. **2.** A richsdach, an assembly that corresponds to our parliament HOWELL. The silver penny..was supposed to c. with a pennyweight JEVONS. **5.** Locke and Newton had corresponded on the prophecies of Daniel as early as 1691 BREWSTER.

Correspondence (kǫrĭspǫ·ndĕns). ME. [– (O)Fr. *correspondence* – med.L. *correspondentia*; see next, -ENCE.] **1.** The action or fact of corresponding; congruity, agreement. **2.** Similarity, analogy 1605. † **3.** Concordant response –1680. † **4.** Relation between persons or communities. (Common in 17th c.) –1835. **5.** Intercourse, communication. *Obs.* exc. as in 6. 1603. Also *fig.* **6.** Communication by letters 1644; the letters sent and received; also, letters contributed to a newspaper 1771.

1. The c. of actions to the nature of the agent BUTLER. **4.** Our ill c. with the French Protestants MARVELL. **6.** Letter for letter is the law of all c. COWPER. The c. of Pope and Swift EMERSON. var. **Correspo·ndency** (*esp.* in senses 1, 2). Now *arch.*

Correspondent (kǫrĭspǫ·ndĕnt). ME. [– (O)Fr. *correspondant* or med.L. *correspondent-*, pres. ppl. stem of *correspondēre* CORRESPOND; see -ENT.]

A. *adj.* [Now more freq. CORRESPONDING.] **1.** Answering to or agreeing with something else or with each other; congruous *with*; conformable, analogous *to*. † **2.** Responsive; submissive –1647. † **3.** Answerable –1658. Hence **Correspo·ndently** *adv.*

B. *sb.* **1.** A correlative 1650. † **2.** A confederate, accomplice –1771. **3.** A person who has regular business relations with another (*esp.* in a distant place) 1674. **4.** One who communicates with another by letters. (The ordinary mod. use.) 1630. **b.** One who contributes letters to a journal; *spec.* one employed by a journal to supply it with news from some particular place 1711.

3. I..had gotten..a c. in London, with whom I traded DE FOE. **4.** The lady was a voluminous c. 1872. So **Corresponde·ntial** *a.* pertaining to correspondence, or to a c.

Corresponding (kǫrĭspǫ·ndiŋ), *ppl. a.* 1579. [f. CORRESPOND *v.* + -ING².] **1.** That corresponds or answers to another; correspondent. **2.** That corresponds by letters 1760.

1. His reserve..was met by a c. caution J. R. GREEN. **2.** *C. member* of a society: one residing at a distance, who corresponds with it by letters, but has no deliberative voice in its affairs. Hence **Correspo·ndingly** *adv.*

Correspo·nsive, *a.* Now *arch.* 1606. [f. COR-¹ + RESPONSIVE.] Corresponding, answering. *Tr. & Cr.* Prol. 18.

Corridor (kǫ·ridǭɹ). 1591. [– Fr. *corridor* – It. *corridore*, alt., by assim. to *corridore* runner, of *corridojo* running place.] † **1.** A passage or covered way between two places –1814. † **2.** *Fortif.* The covered way that surrounds the fortifications of a place –1706. **3.** An outside gallery or passage round the quadrangle or court of a building 1644. **4.** A main passage in a large building, upon which many apartments open 1814. **b.** A strip of a State's territory running through that of another, and giving access to the sea, etc. 1919. *Comb.* **c.-train** 1892.

Corrie (kǫ·ri). *Sc.* Also **correi.** 1795. [– Gael. *coire* (pronounced ko·re) cauldron; hence, circular hollow.] A circular hollow on a mountain side, where the deer often lie.

† **Corrige,** *v.* ME. [– (O)Fr. *corriger* – L. *corrigere* CORRECT *v.*] To correct –1490. So ‖ **Corrige·ndum** (usu. in *pl.* **-da**), something to be corrected.

† **Co·rrigent,** *a.* 1860. [– *corrigent-*, pres. ppl. stem of L. *corrigere* CORRECT *v.*; see -ENT.] Corrective. Also as *sb.* –1882.

Corrigible (kǫ·ridʒĭb'l), *a.* 1483. [– Fr. *corrigible* (OFr. *corrigeable*) – med.L. *corrigibilis*, f. L. *corrigere* CORRECT *v.*; see -BLE.] **1.** Capable of being corrected. **2.** Capable of reformation 1673. **3.** Submissive to correction 1583. † **4.** Deserving chastisement –1649. † **5.** Corrective –1604.

2. The other abuses will be easily c. 1833. **3.** Bending downe His c. necke *Ant. & Cl.* IV. xiv. 74. **5.** *Oth.* I. iii. 329. Hence **Co:rrigibi·lity, Co·rrigibleness, Co·rrigibly** *adv.*

Corrival (kǭrəi·văl), *sb.* and *a. arch.* 1579. [– Fr. *corrival* or L. *corrivalis;* see COR-¹, RIVAL Cf. CO-RIVAL.] **1.** One of several rivals. † **2.** A compeer, partner –1596. **3.** *adj.* Rival 1646. Hence † **Corri·val** *v.* to rival; *intr.* to vie *with.* † **Corriva·lity,** † **Corri·valry,** competition. † **Corri·valship,** the position of a c.

† **Co·rrivate,** *v. rare.* 1621. [– *corrivat-*, pa. ppl. stem of L. *corrivare*, f. *com* COR-¹ + late L. *rivare* draw off (water).] To cause to run together into one. (Misused by Burton.) Hence † **Corriva·tion,** the confluence of streams.

† **Corri·ve,** *v.* 1586. [In form answering to L. *corrivare* (see prec.), but used in a sense derived from CORRIVAL.] = CORRIVAL *v.* –1608.

Corroborant (kǒrǫ·bŏrănt), *a.* and *sb.* 1626. [– Fr. *corroborant* or – pres. ppl. stem of L. *corroborare*; see CORROBORATE *v.*, -ANT.] **1.** *adj.* Strengthening, invigorating. **2.** *sb.* A strengthening agent; a tonic 1727. **3.** A corroboratory fact 1805.

2. The best corroborants which we know, are the Peruvian bark and wine 1789.

Corroborate (kǒrǫ·bŏrĕt), *ppl. a. arch.* [– L. *corroboratus*, pa. pple. of *corroborare*; see next, -ATE².] Strengthened, confirmed.

There is noe trusting to the force of Nature.. except it be c. by Custome BACON.

Corroborate (kǒrǫ·bŏreⁱt), *v.* 1530. [– *corroborat-*, pa. ppl. stem of L. *corroborare*, f. *com* COR-¹ + *roborare* strengthen, f. *robur* strength; see -ATE³.] **1.** To strengthen, make strong 1533. **2.** To support, confirm 1530. † **3.** To concur in testimony (*rare*) –1784.

1. Nothing that I know corroborates the stomach so much as tar-water BERKELEY. To c. their Faith HEARNE. **2.** To c. a conveyance CRUISE. This observation corroborates those of Professor Forbes TYNDALL. var. † **Corro·bore** (*rare*). Hence **Corro·borator,** one who or that which corroborates. **Corro·boratory** *a.* corroborative.

Corroboration (kǒrǫ:bŏrēⁱ·ʃən). 1529. [– Fr. *corroboration* or late L. *corroboratio*, f. as prec.; see -ION.] † **1.** Strengthening –1816. **2.** Confirmation 1552. **3.** That which corroborates 1542.

3. It has thus much of c. from history, that [etc.] FREEMAN.

Corroborative (kǒrǫ·bŏrătiv). 1583. [– Fr. *corroboratif, -ive*, f. as prec.; see -IVE.] **1.** *adj.* Having the quality of corroborating. † **2.** *sb.* A strengthening agent or measure; in *Med.* = CORROBORANT –1805.

Corroboree (kǒrǫ·bəri). 1793. [A word of Port Jackson dialect, N.S.W.] The native dance of the Australian aborigines; it is either festive or warlike.

Corrode (kǒrōᵘ·d), *v.* ME. [– L. *corrodere*, f. *com* COR-¹ + *rodere* gnaw.] † **1.** *trans.* To eat into; to eat or gnaw away –1747. **2.** *transf.* To wear away or destroy gradually, as if by eating or gnawing away the texture ME. Also *fig.* **3.** *absol.* and *intr.* (in prec. senses) 1610. **4.** *intr.* (for *refl.*) To become corroded. (*lit.* and *fig.*) 1820.

1. No moth can c. their texture HERVEY. **2.** *Dürer*..the first who corroded his plates with *aqua-fortis* URE. **3.** Gold and silver do not rust, c., or decay ROGERS. Hence **Corro·der,** one who or that which corrodes. **Corro·dible** *a.*

Corrodent (kǒrōᵘ·dĕnt). ? *Obs.* 1599. [– *corrodent-*, pres. ppl. stem of L. *corrodere*; see prec., -ENT.] *adj.* Corroding, corrosive. *sb.* [sc. *agent.*] 1614.

Corrodiary (kǒrōᵘ·diări). 1638. [– AL. *corrodiarius*, f. AL. *corrodium*; see CORRODY, -ARY¹.] The recipient of a corrody; a prebendary. var. **Corro·dier.**

Corrody, corody (kǫ·rŏdi). ME. [– AFr. *corodie*, AL. *corrodium*, varying with *-radium, -redium*, f. OFr. *conrei, -roi* (mod. *corroi*); see CONREY, CURRY *v.*¹] Provision for maintenance, aliment; pension.

Corrosible (kǒrōᵘ·zĭb'l), *a.* 1721. [f. *coros-*; see next and -IBLE.] = CORRODIBLE. Hence **Corro:sibi·lity.**

Corrosion (kǒrōᵘ·ʒən). ME. [– OFr. *corrosion* or late L. *corrosio*, f. *coros-*, pa. ppl. stem of L. *corrodere* CORRODE; see -ION.] **1.** The action or process of corroding; the fact or condition of being corroded. Also *fig.* **2.** *concr.* A product of corrosion, as rust (*rare*) 1779.

1. C. of the stomach 1882. *fig.* Peevishness.. wears out happiness by slow c. JOHNSON.

Corrosive (kǒrōᵘ·siv, † kǫ·rŏsiv). ME. [– OFr. *corosif* (mod. *corr-*) – med.L. *corrosivus*, f. as prec.; see -IVE.]

A. *adj.* **1.** Having the quality of eating away, consuming, or destroying. **2.** *fig.* **a.** Destructive 1581. **b.** Fretting, wearing 1600.

1. The corrosiue aire of London EVELYN. C. fires MILT. *P.L.* II. 401, Ulcers SALMON. **2. b.** A pensive and c. desire that we had done otherwise HOOKER. Hence **Corro·sive-ly** *adv.*, **-ness.**

B. *sb.* A substance that corrodes, an acid drug, remedy, etc. Also † *fig.*

fig. In things past cure, care is a corasiue GREENE. **C. sublimate:** mercuric chloride or bichloride of mercury ($HgCl_2$), a white crystalline substance which acts as an acrid poison.

Corrugant (kǫ·rⁱugănt), *a.* 1706. [– *corrugant-*, pres. ppl. stem of L. *corrugare*; see CORRUGATE *v.*, -ANT.] Corrugating, wrinkling.

Corrugate (kǫ·rⁱugĕt), *ppl. a.* 1742. [– L. *corrugatus*, pa. pple. of *corrugare*; see next, -ATE².] **1.** Wrinkled; contracted into folds or wrinkles. Also *fig.* **2.** *Med.* and *Zool.* Having a wrinkled appearance; marked with parallel ridges and furrows 1826.

Corrugate (kǫ·rⁱugeⁱt), *v.* 1620. [– *corrugat-*, pa. ppl. stem of L. *corrugare*, f. *com* COR-¹ + *rugare*, f. *ruga* wrinkle; see -ATE³.] *trans.* To wrinkle (the skin), contract into wrinkles; hence *gen.* to draw, contract, or bend into parallel folds or ridges. *intr.* (for *refl.*) = To become corrugated 1753.

It [the muscle] corrugates the skin of the nose transversely TODD. Hence **Co·rrugated** *ppl. a.* wrinkled, marked as with wrinkles; bent into regular curved folds or grooves, as *c. iron.* **Co·rrugative** *a.* characterized by corrugation (*rare*).

Corrugation (kǫrⁱugēⁱ·ʃən). 1528. [– (O)Fr. *corrugation* or med.L. *corrugatio*, f. as prec.; see -ION.] **1.** The act of corrugating or state of being corrugated. **2.** That which is corrugated; a wrinkle, fold, etc. 1829.

2. A succession of mountain chains folded in broad corrugations 1872.

Corrugator (kǫ·rⁱugeⁱtəɹ). 1782. [mod.L., f. as prec.; see -OR 2.] **1.** Anything which causes corrugation (*rare*) 1782. **2.** *Anat.* Each of the two small muscles which contract the brows 1839.

Corru·gent, *a.* 1727. Erron. f. CORRUGANT; in *c. muscle* = CORRUGATOR 2.

† **Corru·mp,** *v.* ME. [– OFr. *corompre* (mod. *corr-*) :– L. *corrumpere*; see next.] **1.** *trans.* To bring to naught –1489. **2.** To corrupt –1532. **3.** *intr.* To become corrupt –1470. Hence † **Corru·mpable** *a.* = CORRUPTIBLE.

Corrupt (kǒrʊ·pt), *ppl. a.* ME. [– OFr. *corrupt* or L. *corruptus*, pa. pple. of *corrumpere* destroy, ruin, falsify, f. *com* COR-¹ + *rumpere* break.]

† **A.** as *pa. pple.* Corrupted –1600.

B. as *adj.* **1.** Changed from the naturally sound condition; putrid, rotten or rotting; infected or defiled (*arch.*). † **2.** Adulterated; debased, as money –1683. **3.** Debased in character; depraved; perverted ME. **4.** Influenced by bribery or the like; venal ME. **5.** Of language, texts, etc.: Destroyed in purity, debased; vitiated by errors or alterations ME.

1. A c. and stagnant air GOOCH. No title can be deduced through the c. blood of the father BENTHAM. **3.** A c. form of Christianity 1877. **4.** The general laws against c. practices at elections H. COX. **5.** The emendation of c. passages THEOBALD. Hence **Corru·pt-ly** *adv.*, **-ness.**

Corrupt (kǒrʊ·pt), *v.* ME. [f. prec., superseding CORRUMP.] **1.** *trans.* To turn from a sound into an unsound impure condition; to make rotten; to putrefy (*arch.*). Also *fig.* **2.** To infect, taint 1548; †to adulterate –1697. **3.** To render morally unsound; to pervert (a good quality); to debase, defile ME. **4.** To induce to act dishonestly or unfaithfully; to make venal; to bribe 1548. **5.** To debase, destroy the purity of (a language, etc.); to vitiate (a text, etc.) by errors or alterations 1630. **6.** To spoil (anything) in quality 1526. **7.** *intr.* To become corrupt or putrid; to putrefy, rot, decay ME.

1. The infectious air, that corrupted the blood of strangers LITHGOW. *fig.* The attainder of the father only corrupts the lineal blood CRUISE. **3.** That their virgynite shulde be corrupted PALSGR. **4.** By corruptyng with money diverse Burgesses of the towne BP. HALL. **5.** The Hereticks corrupted the New Testament HEARNE. **7.** Gold never corrupteth by rust FULKE. Hence **Corru·pted-ly** *adv.*, **-ness. Corru·pter, -or,** one who or that which corrupts. **Corru·ptful** *a.* fraught with corruption. **Corru·ptless** *a.* **Corru·ptress,** a female corrupter; also *fig.*

Corruptible (kǒrɒ·ptĭb'l), *a.* ME. [– eccl. L. *corruptibilis*; see CORRUPT *ppl. a.*, -IBLE. Cf. (O)Fr. *corruptible.*] **1.** Liable to corruption; perishable, mortal. (Chiefly Scriptural.) † **2.** Corrupt –1620. **3.** Capable of moral corruption; venal 1677.

1. This c. must put on incorruption 1 *Cor.* 15:53. **3.** The House of Commons. . was itself c. H. COX. Hence **Corru:ptibi·lity. Corru·ptibleness. Corru·ptibly** *adv.*

Corruption (kǒrɒ·pʃən). ME. [– (O)Fr. *corruption* – L. *corruptio*, f. *corrupt-*, pa. ppl. stem of *corrumpere*; see CORRUPT *ppl. a.*, -ION.] † **1.** The destruction or spoiling of anything, *esp.* by disintegration or decomposition; putrefaction –1718. † **2.** Infection, infected condition; also *fig.* contagion, taint –1598. **3.** *concr.* Decomposed or putrid matter; pus. *Obs.* exc. *dial.* 1526. Also *fig.* **4.** A making or becoming morally corrupt; the fact or condition of being corrupt; moral deterioration; depravity ME. **5.** Evil nature, 'the old Adam'; temper. Now *colloq.* 1799. **6.** Perversion of integrity by bribery or favour; the use or existence of corrupt practices ME. **7.** The perversion of anything from an original state of purity ME.

1. If you provide against the causes of Putrefaction, matter maketh not that haste to c., that is conceived BACON. **2.** *Law. C. of blood*: the effect of an attainder, by which the blood of the person attainted was held to have become tainted or 'corrupted' by his crime, so that he could no longer hold land, nor leave it to heirs, nor could his descendants inherit from him. **3.** *fig.* That foule Sinne gathering head, Shall breake into C. 2 *Hen. IV*, III. i. 77. **4.** The general C. of Manners in Servants STEELE. **6.** Simoniacal c. HOOKER. **7.** The c. then of Monarchy is call'd Tyranny J. HARRINGTON. The continual C. of our English Tongue SWIFT. Hence **Corru·ptionist,** a supporter or practiser of c., *esp.* in public affairs.

† **Corru·ptious,** *a.* 1540. [f. as prec. + -IOUS.] Characterized by corruption –1604.

Corruptive (kǒrɒ·ptiv), *a.* 1593. [– (O)Fr. *corruptif, -ive* or eccl.L. *corruptivus,* f. as prec.; see -IVE.] † **1.** Liable to corruption –1691. **2.** That tends to corrupt 1609.

1. Some c. quality for so speedy a dissolution of the Meat RAY. Hence **Corru·ptively** *adv.*

‖ **Co·rsac, corsak.** 1838. [Turki.] *Zool.* The Tartar fox.

Corsage (kǭ·ɹsėdʒ, or, more freq. as Fr. korsā·ʒ). 1481. [– (O)Fr. *corsage*, f. *cors* body; see CORSE, -AGE.] † **1.** Size and shape of body –1658. † **2.** The bust –1600. **3.** The body of a woman's dress; a bodice 1857.

† **Corsaint.** ME. [– OFr. *cors* (mod. *corps*) *saint.*] The body of a saint; a sainted person, (departed) saint –1500.

Corsair (kǭ·ɹsēᵊɹ). 1549. [– Fr. *corsaire* :– Rom. (med.L.) *cursarius*, f. *cursa* and *cursus* hostile inroad, plunder, a spec. use of L. *cursus* COURSE. See COURSER².] **1.** A privateer; chiefly applied to the authorized cruisers of Barbary. In English often = *pirate*. **2.** A pirate-ship sanctioned by the country to which it belongs 1632. Also *attrib.*

2. Tuscan corsairs covered the Western Mediterranean RAWLINSON.

Corse (kǭɹs), *sb.* [ME. *cors* – OFr. *cors* (mod. *corps*) :– L. *corpus* body. See CORPSE.] † **1.** = CORPSE 1. –1586. **2.** = CORPSE 2. ME. † **3.** *transf.* Of things: The main bulk –1506. † **4.** A ribbon, serving as a ground for ornamentation, and used as a girdle, garter, etc. –1573. † **5.** *Archit.* (*cors*) A square shaft or slender pier supporting a terminal 1478.

1. Hire semly cors for to embrace LYDG. **2.** The sencelesse c. appointed for the grave SPENSER *F.Q.* I. xi. 48. *Comb.* † **c.-present,** a mortuary.

Corse, course, *v.* Now *dial.* ME. [prob. rel. to synon. Coss *v.*; cf. SCORSE.] To exchange; to barter; to deal in (horses). Hence † **Corser, courser,** a jobber; *esp.* a horse-coper.

Corselet, var. of CORSLET.

Corset (kǭ·ɹsėt). ME. [– (O)Fr. *corset*, dim. of *cors* body; see CORSE, -ET.] **1.** A close-fitting outer body-garment worn by women, and formerly also by men. **2.** A closely, fitting inner bodice stiffened with whalebone etc., and fastened by lacing; worn chiefly by women to give shape and support to the figure; stays 1795. Also *attrib.*

1. Her senesshal. .in a rich c. of grene LD. BERNERS. Hence **Co·rseted** *ppl. a.* enclosed in a c.

Co·rsie, *sb.* and *a.* Now *dial.* 1450. [Reduced from *corĕsive* CORROSIVE.] **1.** *sb.* = CORROSIVE *sb.*; *fig.* a grievance. **2.** *adj.* Corrosive 1598. Hence † **Co·rsie** *v. rare*, to treat with a c.; *fig.* to vex. var. † **Corsive** *a.* and *sb.*

Corslet, corselet (kǭ·ɹslėt), *sb.* 1500. [– (O)Fr. *corselet*, dim. of *cors* body; see CORSE, -LET.] **1.** A piece of defensive armour covering the body 1563; † a soldier armed with a corslet –1709. **2.** A (tight-fitting) garment covering the body as dist. from the limbs 1500. **3.** The thorax of an insect 1753.

1. Surely a c. is no canonicall coat for me FULLER. Hence **Co·rslet** *v.* to encircle with, or as with, a c. (*rare*). † **Corsletee·r,** a soldier armed with a c.

Corsned (kǭ·ɹsned). Now *Hist.* [OE. *corsnǣd*, f. *cor* choice, trial + *snǣd* bit, piece, f. *snīdan* cut.] In OE. law, the morsel of trial, a piece of bread consecrated by exorcism (*panis conjuratus*) which an accused person was required to swallow as a trial of his guilt or innocence.

† **Corsy,** *a.* ME. [– Fr. *corsé* (OFr. *corsu*) having body, corpulent, f. *cors* body; see CORSE, -Y⁵.] Corpulent –1607.

‖ **Cortège** (kǫɹtē·ʒ). 1679. [– Fr. *cortège* – It. *corteggio*, f. *corteggiare* attend court, f. *corte* COURT *sb.*¹] A train of attendants, a procession.

‖ **Cortes** (ko·rtes). 1668. [Sp. and Pg. pl. of *corte* COURT *sb.*¹] The two chambers, constituting the legislative assembly of Spain and Portugal.

‖ **Cortex** (kǭ·ɹteks). Pl. **cortices** (kǭ·ɹtisīz). 1660. [L.] † **1.** *fig.* The outer shell or husk –1665. † **2.** *Med.* The bark of various trees; *absol.* Peruvian bark –1803. **3.** Applied to various external structures in a plant, animal body, or organ. *spec.* **a.** *Anat.* The outer gray matter of the brain. **b.** *Bot.* The bark.

Cortian (kǭ·ɹtiăn), *a.* 1872. [f. *Corti* (1729–1813) an Italian anatomist + -AN.] *Anat.* In *C. fibres, membranes*, etc., parts of the internal ear.

Cortical (kǭ·ɹtikăl), *a.* 1671. [– med.L. *corticalis*, f. L. *cortex, cortic-* bark; see -AL¹.] **1.** Belonging to the cortex or external part of a plant or animal body, or organ. (Opp. to *medullary.*) † **2.** *fig.* External, superficial –1856.

1. The Nerves arise from the medullary, not the c. Part HARTLEY. **2.** The C. or literal sense HY. MORE.

Corticate (kǭ·ɹtikĕt), *a.* 1846. [– L. *corticatus*, f. as prec.; see -ATE².] Having bark; made of the nature of bark. So **Co·rticated** *ppl. a.*

Cortici·ferous, *a. rare.* 1828. [f. as prec. + -FEROUS.] Bearing bark or a cortex. So **Corti·ciform** *a.* bark-like (*rare*).

Corticin (kǭ·ɹtisin). 1863. [f. as prec. + -IN¹.] *Chem.* An amorphous yellowish substance, found in the bark of the aspen.

Corticine (kǭ·ɹtisin). 1880. [f. as prec. + -INE⁴.] Name of a floor-covering made of ground cork with India rubber or the like.

Corticolous (kǫɹti·kǒləs), *a.* 1856. [f. as prec. + L. *-cola* inhabitant + -OUS.] *Bot.* Growing or living in the bark of trees. var. **Co·rticole.**

Corticose (kǭɹtikōᵘ·s), *a. rare.* 1730. [– L. *corticosus*, f. as prec.; see -OSE¹.] Abounding in bark; barky. var. **Co·rticous** (*rare*).

‖ **Cortile** (kortī·le). 1841. [It., deriv. of *corte* COURT *sb.*¹] (In Italy.) An enclosed area or courtyard within or attached to a building: usu. roofless; occ. used as a court of entrance.

Corundum (korɒ·ndəm). 1728. [– Tamil *kurundam* = Telugu *kuruvindam* – Skr. *kuruvinda, -as* ruby.] **1.** A crystallized mineral belonging to the same species as the sapphire and ruby, but more or less opaque; called also *Adamantine Spar*. **2.** *Min.* A mineral species, comprising the transparent sapphire (including the ruby, the oriental amethyst, emerald, and topaz), the opaque adamantine spar (= prec. sense), and the granular emery. It consists of crystallized alumina (Al_2O_3) variously coloured. Also *attrib.*, as in *c. tool*, etc.

Coruscant (korɒ·skănt), *a.* 1485. [– *coruscant-*, pres. ppl. stem of L. *coruscare*; see next, -ANT.] Coruscating. Also *fig.*

Coruscate (kǫ·rǒskeⁱt), *v.* 1705. [– *coruscat-*, pa. ppl. stem of L. *coruscare* vibrate, glitter; see -ATE³.] *intr.* To give forth intermittent flashes of light; to sparkle, glitter.

Coruscation (kǫrǒskēⁱ·ʃən). 1490. [– L. *coruscatio*, f. as prec.; see -ION.] The action of coruscating; usually: A vibratory or quivering flash of light, or a series of such flashes. Also *fig.*

The coruscations of the Aurora borealis E. DARWIN. *fig.* Coruscations of epigrammatic wit TODHUNTER.

Corve, var. CORF; obs. pa. t. and pple. of CARVE.

† **Corved,** *ppl. a.* 1641. [In *corved herring*, perh. part-transl. of synon. MDu. *korfharinck* 'herring (packed in) baskets'.] In *c. herring* (corruptly *corred, cored*): ? Brought ashore in baskets, as dist. from barrelled.

‖ **Corvée** (korve·). ME. [– (O)Fr. *corvée* = Pr. *corroada* :– Rom. **corrogata* (sc. *opera*) requisitioned (work).] *Feudal Law.* A day's work of unpaid labour due by a vassal to his feudal lord; the whole forced labour thus exacted; in France, extended to the statute labour upon the public roads exacted before 1776.

Corven, obs. pa. t. (pl.) and pa. pple. of CARVE.

Corvette (kǭɹve·t). 1636. [– Fr. *corvette* (beside †*corvot*), dim. of MDu. *korf* kind of ship; see -ETTE.] A flush-decked war-vessel, ship-, bark-, or brig-rigged, having one tier of guns; now, a small naval escort vessel.

Corvetto; see CURVET.

Corvine (kǭ·ɹvəin), *a.* 1656. [– L. *corvinus*, f. *corvus* raven; see -INE¹.] Of or pertaining to a raven or crow; of the crow kind.

Corvorant, perverted f. CORMORANT, q.v.

Corybant (kǫ·ribænt). Pl. **Corybants,** or, in L. form, **Corybantes** (kǫribæ·ntīz). ME. [– L. *Corybas, -bant-* – Gr. Κορύβας.] A priest of the Phrygian worship of Cybele, which was performed with noisy and extravagant dances.

Those mad Corybants, who dance and glow On Dindymus high tops DRUMM. OF HAWTH.

Hence **Coryba·ntian** *a.* of or pertaining to the Corybantes or their worship. **Coryba·ntiasm,** *Path.*, a sort of frenzy, in which the patient has fantastic visions. † **Coryba·ntiate** *v.* to act like a C. **Coryba·ntic, Coryba·ntine** *a.*, Corybantian.

Corydaline (kǫ·ridăləin). 1838. [f. *Corydalis* + -INE⁵.] *Chem.* An alkaloid existing in the root of *Corydalis tuberosa* and some allied plants.

Corydon (kǫ·ridǒn). 1581. [L. *Corydon*, Gr. Κορύδων proper name, applied to a shepherd; cf. Verg. Ecl. ii. 56.] A generic proper name in pastoral poetry for a rustic.

Where C. and Thyrsis met, Are at their savoury dinner set. . Which the neat-handed Phillis dresses MILT. *L'Allegro* 83.

† **Co·rylet.** *rare.* 1610. [– L. *coryletum*, f. *corylus* hazel.] A hazel copse.

Corymb (kǫ·rimb). 1706. [– Fr. *corymbe* or L. *corymbus* – Gr. κόρυμβος summit, cluster of fruit or flowers.] **1.** *Bot.* A species of inflorescence; a raceme in which the flowers form a flat or slightly convex head. Before Linnæus, applied to the discoidal head of a composite flower. ¶ **2.** A cluster of ivy-berries or grapes. (Not an Eng. sense.) 1706.

1. Sea Aster. . The flower-heads are in a compact c. 1861. Hence **Co·rymbed** *ppl. a.* fashioned as a c. † **Cory·mbiate** *a.* set with clusters of ivy-berries. **Corymbi·ferous** *a.* bearing corymbs; *spec.* belonging to the *Corymbiferæ*, a sub-order of Composite plants. **Cory·mbiform** *a.* of the form of a c. **Corymbo·se** *a.* growing in corymbs; like a c. **Corymbo·sely** *adv.* in corymbs.

Corynid (kǫ·rinid). 1870. [f. mod.L. *Corynidæ*, f. *Coryne*, generic name of a Hydromedusa – Gr. κορύνη club.] *Zool.* A member of the family *Corynidæ*, of the order *Hydroidea* of Cœlenterates. So **Cory·niform** *a.* having the form of a c.

Corynite (kǫ·rinəit). 1868. [f. Gr. κορύνη club + -ITE¹ 2 b.] *Min.* A native sulpharsen-antimonide of nickel.

‖ **Coryphæus** (kǫrifī·ǒs). 1633. [L. – Gr. κορυφαῖος (in the Attic drama) leader of the chorus, f. κορυφή head, top.] **1.** The leader of a chorus 1678. **2.** *fig.* The leader of a party, sect, school, etc. 1633.

2. Strauss, the c. of modern scepticism 1871.

‖ **Coryphée** (korifē·). 1866. [Fr. – L. *coryphæus*; see prec.] A leader of the corps de ballet.

Corystoid (kori·stoid), *a.* 1852. [f. *Corystes* name of a genus of crabs (– Gr. κορυστής helmeted soldier, f. κόρυς helmet) + -OID.] *Zool.* Allied to the genus of crabs *Corystes*, or the family *Corystidæ*.

‖ **Coryza** (korəi·ză). 1634. [L. – Gr. κόρυζα running at the nose.] *Path.* The running at the nose which accompanies a cold in the head; catarrh.

Cos (kǫs). 1699. [Gr. Κῶς an island in the Ægean (now Stanchio).] In full *C. lettuce*: a variety of lettuce introduced from Cos.

Cos, abbrev. of COSINE.

Co·salite. 1868. [f. *Cosala* in Mexico + -ITE[1] 2 b.] *Min.* A native sulphide of lead and bismuth.

‖ **Cosaque** (kosa·k). 1858. [app. f. Fr. *Cosaque* Cossack; prob. with reference to their irregular firing.] A cracker bon-bon.

Coscinomancy (kǫ·sinomæ:nsi). 1603. [– med.L. *coscinomantia, f. Gr. κοσκινόμαντις, f. κόσκινον sieve; see -MANCY.] Divination by the turning of a sieve (held on a pair of shears, etc.).

Cosecant (kō"sī·kănt). 1706. [– mod.L. *cosecans, -ant-*, Fr. *cosécant* (XVI); see CO-, SECANT.] *Trig.* The secant of the complement of a given angle. (Abbrev. *cosec.*)

Coseismal (kō"səi·zmăl), *a.* 1851. [See CO-.] Relating to the points of simultaneous arrival of an earthquake wave on the earth's surface; in *c. line, curve, zone*, etc. As *sb.* = *c. line, curve.* So **Cosei·smic** *a.* (in same sense).

Cosen, -age, -er, obs. ff. COUSIN, COZEN, etc.

Co-sentient (kō"se·nʃ[i]ěnt), *a.* 1801. [See CO-.] Jointly sentient. So **Co-se·ntiency.**

Cosey; see COSY.

Cosh (kǫʃ), *a. Sc.* and *dial.* 1774. [Origin unkn.] Quiet; snug; trim.

Cosher (kǫ·ʃəɹ), *v.*[1] *Ireland.* 1634. [repr. Ir. *coisir* feast.] *intr.* To feast; to live at free quarters upon dependants or kinsmen. Hence **Co·sherer,** one who coshers. **Co·shering** *vbl. sb.* †feasting; *spec.* = the custom of COSHERY.

Cosher (kǫ·ʃəɹ), *v.*[2] 1861. *trans.* To pamper; to cocker *up*.

Co·sher, *v.*[3] *colloq.* 1833. *intr.* To chat familiarly.

Cosher, *a.* (in Jewish use); see KOSHER.

Coshery (kǫ·ʃəri). *Ireland.* 1583. [f. Ir. *coisir* (kōʃər) feast, feasting, with ending assim. to Eng. sbs. in -ERY.] Feasting; *spec.* entertainment for themselves and their followers exacted by Irish chiefs from their dependants.

C...is somewhat analogous to the royal prerogative of purveyance HALLAM.

Cosier, a cobbler; see COZIER.

Co-signatory (kō"si·gnătəri). 1865. [See CO-.] *adj.* Signing jointly with others 1891. *sb.* A joint signatory.

Cosignificative, -ficator; see CONSIG-.

Cosily (kō"·zili), *adv.* Also **cozily,** etc. 1721. [f. COSY *a.* + -LY[2].] In a cosy manner; snugly and comfortably.

Cosin, -age, obs. ff. COUSIN, COZEN, -AGE.

Cosine (kō"·səin). 1635. [– mod.L. *cosinus*; see CO-, SINE.] *Trig.* The sine of the compliment of a given angle. Abbrev. *cos* (no period).

Cosiness (kō"·zinės). Also **cozi-.** 1834. [f. COSY *a.* + -NESS.] The quality or state of being cosy.

† **Co·sins.** [f. the maker's name.] A kind of stays. POPE.

Cosmete (kǫ·zmīt). [– Gr. κοσμητής, f. κοσμεῖν to order.] A state officer in charge of the ephebi at Athens.

Cosmetic (kǫzme·tik). 1605. [– Fr. *cosmétique* – Gr. κοσμητικός, f. κοσμεῖν adorn, f. κόσμος; see COSMOS[1], -IC.]

A. *adj.* Having power to beautify (*esp.* the complexion); also, relating to cosmetics 1650. var. **Cosme·tical.**

B. *sb.* **1.** A preparation for beautifying the hair, skin, or complexion 1650. **2.** The art of adorning or beautifying the body. Also *pl.* [= Gr. ἡ κοσμητική.] 1605. **3.** One who practises the cosmetic art. *nonce-use.* 1713.

Cosmic (kǫ·zmik), *a.* 1649. [f. COSMOS[1] + -IC, after Fr. *cosmique*.] † **1.** Of this world. **2.** Of or belonging to the universe considered as an ordered system or totality 1846; relating to the cosmos 1874. **3.** Belonging to the material universe as distinguished from the earth; extra-terrestrial 1871; characteristic of the vast scale of the universe and its changes 1874. **4.** Orderly; not *chaotic* (*rare*) 1858.

2. The great c. law of gravitation 1875. *C. philosophy*: = COSMISM. **3.** C. dust CARPENTER. *C. rays*, any of a class of rays having peculiar properties, still largely unascertained, which pass (or are believed to pass) through space, chiefly outside the earth's atmosphere.

Cosmical (kǫ·zmikăl), *a.* 1583. [f. as prec. + -AL[1]; see -ICAL.] † **1.** Relating to the world, *i.e.* the earth –1819. **2.** = COSMIC 2. 1685. **3.** = COSMIC 3. 1842. **4.** *Astron.* Coincident with the rising of the sun; said of the rising or setting of a star 1594. Hence **Co·smically** *adv.* (*esp.* in sense 4).

Cosmism (kǭ·zmiz'm). 1861. [f. as prec. + -ISM.] The theory which explains the cosmos as a self-existent, self-acting whole, according to the methods of positive science. So **Co·smist,** a believer in c.; a Secularist.

Cosmo-, bef. a vowel **cosm-,** comb. f. Gr. κόσμος COSMOS: hence,

Co·smocrat, lord or ruler of the world (*rare*); so **Cosmocra·tic** *a.*; **Cosmo·crator** = *Cosmocrat*; **Cosm:ogene·tic** *a.* of or pertaining to cosmogeny; **Cosmo·geny,** origin or evolution of the universe; **Co·smolabe,** an ancient instrument resembling the astrolabe; **Cosmo·latry,** worship of the world; † **Cosmo·metry,** measurement of the universe; **Cosmopla·stic** *a.* †maintaining an inanimate plastic nature to be the highest principle of the universe; moulding the universe; **Cosmora·ma,** a peep-show containing views of all parts of the world; also *transf.* and *fig.*; **Cosmora·mic** *a.*; **Cosmo·sophy,** knowledge or science of the cosmos; **Co·smosphere,** a hollow glass globe representing the celestial sphere, having within it a terrestrial globe, for showing the position of the earth, at any given time, with respect to the fixed stars; **Cosmothe·ism** (*rare*), the doctrine that identifies God with the cosmos; pantheism; **Cosmothe·tic, -al** *a.* that posits an external world, as *C. Idealism*.

‖ **Cosmognosis** (kǫzmognō"·sis). [f. COSMO- + Gr. γνῶσις knowledge.] 'The instinct which teaches animals the right time for migration, and the fitting place to which to go' (*Syd. Soc. Lex.*).

Cosmogony (kǫzmǫ·gŏni). 1696. [– Gr. κοσμογονία creation of the world, f. κόσμος world + -γονια begetting. So Fr. *cosmogonie*.] **1.** The generation of the existing universe 1776. **2.** A theory, system, or account of the generation of the universe.

2. The vast and imaginative cosmogonies of the East MILMAN. Hence **Cosmo·gonal, Cosmogo·nic, -al** *adjs.* of or pertaining to c. **Cosmo·gonist,** one who studies c.; †one who holds that the world was created.

Cosmographer (kǫzmǫ·grăfəɹ). 1527. [f. late L. *cosmographus* – Gr. κοσμογράφος, f. as COSMO- + -GRAPH. See -ER[1] 4. Cf. (O)Fr. *cosmographe*.] One skilled in cosmography. Formerly often = *geographer*.

Cosmography (kǫzmǫ·grăfi). ME. [– Fr. *cosmographie* or late L. *cosmographia* – Gr. κοσμογραφία description of the world; see COSMO-, -GRAPHY.] **1.** The science which describes and maps the general features of the universe (both the heavens and the earth). Formerly often = *geography*. 1519. **2.** A description or representation of the universe or of the earth in its general features ME.

2. The Body [of Man]..being..a little C. or Map of the Universe SOUTH. Hence **Co:smogra·phic, -al** *a.* of or relating to c. **Co:smogra·phically** *adv.* **Cosmo·graphist** (*rare*), cosmographer.

Cosmoline (kǫ·zmŏlin). 1876. [f. as COSMETIC + -OL + -INE[5].] 'A name of purified solid paraffin' (*Syd. Soc. Lex.*).

Cosmology (kǫzmǫ·lŏdʒi). 1656. [– Fr. *cosmologie* or mod.L. *cosmologia*, f. as COSMO- + -LOGY.] The theory of the universe as an ordered whole, and of the general laws which govern it. Also, a particular system of the universe and its laws. **b.** *Philos.* That part of metaphysics which deals with the idea of the world as a totality of all phenomena in space and time 1753.

b. Metaphysics..are subdivided [by Wolff] into Ontology, C., Psychology, Natural Theology J. H. STIRLING. Hence **Cosmolo·gic, -al** *a.* of or pertaining to c. **Cosmolo·gically** *adv.* **Cosmo·logist,** one who studies or discourses on c.

Cosmopo·licy. = *Cosmopolitism.* SHELLEY.

Cosmopolitan (kǫzmopǫ·lităn). 1645. [f. COSMOPOLITE + -AN; cf. *metropolitan*.]

A. *adj.* **1.** Belonging to all parts of the world; not restricted to any one country or its inhabitants 1848. **2.** Free from national limitations or attachments 1844. **3.** *Nat. Hist.* Found in all or many countries 1860.

1. Capital is becoming more and more c. MILL. **2.** [A] c. indifference to constitutions and religions MACAULAY.

B. *sb.* = COSMOPOLITE 1645.

He was no c. He was an Englishman of the English 1868. Hence **Cosmopo·litanism,** c. character.

Cosmopolite (kǫzmǫ·pŏləit). 1614. [– Fr. *cosmopolite* – Gr. κοσμοπολίτης, f. κόσμος world + πολίτης citizen.] **1.** A citizen of the world; one who has no national attachments or prejudices. (Often contrasted with *patriot*.) 1618. **2.** *transf.* At home in all parts of the world, as a plant, etc. 1832. † **3.** A man of this world –1657. **4.** *attrib.* and *adj.* = COSMOPOLITAN *a.*

1. You..have merged the patriot in the c. MEDWIN. **4.** C. doctrines 1862. Hence **Cosmopo·litic** *a.* cosmopolitan; *sb.* (*pl.*) world-politics. **Cosmopoli·tical** *a.* belonging to universal polity. **Cosmo·politism,** cosmopolitanism.

‖ **Cosmos**[1] (kǫ·zmǫs). 1650. [Gr. κόσμος order, ornament, world or universe.] **1.** The world or universe as an ordered system. **2.** Order, harmony; a harmonious system 1858. **3.** A plant of the American genus *Cosmos*, characterized by showy flowers.

1. As the greater World is called Cosmus from the beauty thereof 1650.

† **Cosmos**[2]. 1598. Early f. KOUMISS –1630.

Co-so·vereign. 1793. [See CO-.] A joint sovereign.

† **Coss,** *sb.*[1] Also **cosse.** 1570. [– obs. Fr. *cosse* – It. *cosa*, tr. of Arab. *šay'* 'thing' = the unknown quantity (or *x*) of an equation, etc.] In *Rule of C.* = Algebra –1796.

‖ **Coss, cos** (kǫs), *sb.*[2] *Anglo-Ind.* (*Pl.* same as *sing.*) 1616. [– Hindi *kos*, Pali *koss* :– Skr. *krōças* measure of distance, orig. cry, shout, (hence) range of the voice in calling or hallooing.] A measure of length in India, varying from 2½ miles or more down to about 1¼.

Coss, *v.* Chiefly *Sc.* 1470. [See CORSE *v.*, SCORSE *v.*] *trans.* To barter, exchange.

Cossack (kǫ·sæ̆k). 1598. [– Fr. *Cosaque*, varying in early use with *Casaque* (cf. CASSOCK) – Russ. *kazák*, †*kozák* – Turki *quzzāq* vagabond, nomad, adventurer.] Name of a group of peoples of the southern U.S.S.R. noted as horsemen from early times, when they had the task of guarding the frontiers of south-east Europe and adjoining parts of Asia.

C. and Russian Reel'd from the sabre-stroke TENNYSON.

Cosset (kǫ·sėt), *sb.* 1579. [dial. *cosset*, transf. use of AFr. *coscet, cozet* (Domesday Book) – OE. *cotsǣta* cottager, f. *cot* COT *sb.*[1] + *sǣt-, var. of *set-, base of *sitjan SIT.] A lamb (colt, etc.) brought up by hand; hence, a pet of any kind; a spoilt child. Also *attrib.* Hence **Co·sset** *v.* to fondle, pet, pamper; also *absol.*

† **Co·ssic, -al,** *a.* 1557. [– It. *cossico*; see COSS *sb.*[1]] Pertaining to algebra –1839.

‖ **Cossid** (kǫ·sid). *Anglo-Ind.* 1682. [– Pers. *ḳāṣid* foot messenger, courier.] A running messenger.

Cossyrite (kǫ·sirəit). 1882. [f. *Cossyra*, now the island of Pantellaria + -ITE[1] 2 b.] *Min.* A silicate of iron found in lava.

† **Cost,** *sb.*[1] OE. [ONorthumb. – ON. *kostr* :– Gmc. *kus-tuz, f. wk. grade *kus-* of *keus- kaus-* to taste, prove; cf. L. *gustus, gustare*, Gr. γεύ(σ)ειν, to taste. See also

CUST.] **1.** Way, manner; available course. *Needes c.*: in the way of necessity, necessarily. Hence prob. the mod. *at any cost*. –1449. **2.** A quality, habit; nature, character. Often in *pl.* –1440.

Cost (kǭst), *sb.*[2] ME. [– AFr. *cost*, OFr. *coust* (mod. *coût*), f. *coûter*; see COST *v.*] **1.** That which must be given in order to acquire, produce, or effect something; the price paid for a thing. **2.** *Law.* (*pl.*) The expenses of any legal transaction; *esp.* those allowed by law or by the court against the losing party ME. **3.** *transf.* Expenditure of time, labour, etc. ME. † **4.** A costly thing (*rare*) –1600. Also *attrib.*

1. Which of you intending to build a tower, sitteth not down first, and counteth the c. *Luke* 14:28. *Prime c.*: the first cost of production, before distribution. **2.** Thus much for judgments; to which costs are a necessary appendage BLACKSTONE. **3.** After so much c. Of time and blood HOBBES. **4.** SHAKS. *Sonn.* lxiv.

Phrases. *At the c. of* (*something*): at the expense of sacrificing it. So *at little c.*, *at any c.*, etc. *To any one's c.*: to his loss or detriment. *Comb.* **c.-book** (*Mining*), a book containing an abstract of all costs incurred in working a mine, and all returns from sales, etc. Also *attrib.*

† **Cost,** *sb.*[3] [OE. – L. *costum* (*costos*) – Gr. κόστος = Arab. *ḳust*, Skr. *Kuṣṭha*.] The herb also called ALECOST or COSTMARY –1598.

Cost (kǫst), *sb.*[4] 1572. [– OFr. *coste* (mod. *côte*) rib :– L. *costa*.] *Her.* = COTISE.

Cost (kǭst), *v.* ME. [– OFr. *coster*, *couster* (mod. *coûter*) :– Rom. **costare*, for L. *constare* stand firm, be fixed, stand at a price, f. *com* CON- + *stare* stand. The L. idiom which is the source of present usage is repr. by *Hoc constat mihi tribus assibus* 'stands me in' at three asses.] **1.** To be acquired or acquirable at (so much); to be of the price of, be bought or maintained for, necessitate the expenditure of (so much, *much*, *little*, etc.). **b.** With personal object (indirect): To 'stand (a person) in' (so much) ME. **2.** *fig.* ME. † **3.** Of persons: To be at charges; quasi- *trans.* to spend –1490. **4.** *Comm.* To estimate the cost of production of an article, etc. 1884.

1. [He] thereby knows what everything costs at first hand DE FOE. **b.** His Breeches cost him but a Crowne *Oth.* II. iii. 93. **2.** I am for you, though it cost mee ten nights watchings *Much Ado* II. i. 387. Phr. *To c.* (one) *dear* (*dearly*): to entail great loss upon.

‖ **Costa** (kǫ·stă). Pl. **costæ** (kǫ·stī). 1866. The L. word for rib, applied in Nat. Hist. and Phys. to various rib-like parts, also (after Fr. *coste*, *côte*) to the edges of certain parts.

† **Co·stage.** ME. [– AFr. = OFr. *coustage*, f. *coster*, *couster* to COST; see -AGE.] Expense, cost –1670.

Costal (kǫ·stăl), *a.* (*sb.*) 1634. [– Fr. *costal* – mod.L. *costalis*, f. L. *costa* rib; see -AL[1].] **1.** *Phys.* Pertaining to or connected with the ribs, as *c. respiration*. **2.** *Nat. Hist.* Pertaining to, or like, a COSTA, q.v. 1839. **3.** *sb.* Short for *c. vein*, *muscle*, *plate*, etc. 1828. Hence **Co·stally** *adv.* in a c. manner, position, or direction.

Costard (kǫ·stăɹd). ME. [– AFr. *costard*, f. *coste* rib :– L. *costa*; see -ARD. So called from being prominently ribbed.] **1.** A kind of apple of large size. **2.** Applied derisively to the head (*arch.*) 1530.

2. Ice try whither your C., or my Ballow be the harder *Lear* IV. vi. 247.

Costard-monger, obs. f. COSTERMONGER.

Costate (kǫ·stĕt), *a.* 1819. [– L. *costatus* ribbed, f. *costa* rib; see -ATE[2].] *Nat. Hist.* Having a rib or ribs; see COSTA. var. **Co·stated.**

Costean, costeen (kǫstī·n), *v.* 1778. [f. Cornish *cothas* dropped + *stean* tin.] *Cornish Mining.* To sink pits down to the rock in order to ascertain the direction of a lode. Usually **Costea·ning** *vbl. sb.* Hence **c.-pit.**

Coste·llate, *a. rare.* 1864. [Expressive var. of COSTATE.] Finely ribbed.

† **Co·ster**[1]. ME. [– AFr. *coster* = OFr. *costier* side, also 'piece of stuff placed on the side (e.g. of an altar)', f. *coste* side.] A hanging for a bed, the walls of a room, etc. –1482.

Coster[2] (kǫ·stəɹ). *colloq.* 1851. Short for next. Also *attrib.*

Costermonger (kǫ·stəɹmɒŋgəɹ). 1514. [f. COSTARD + MONGER.] *orig.* An apple-seller. Now, in London, a man who sells fruit, vegetables, fish, etc., in the street from a barrow. Also used as a term of abuse. 2 *Hen. IV*, I. ii. 119.

Costiferous (kǫsti·fĕrəs), *a.* 1878. [f. L. *costa* rib + -FEROUS.] *Anat.* Bearing ribs. So **Co·stiform** *a.* having the form of a rib or COSTA.

† **Costious,** *a.* ME. [– AFr. *coustous* = OFr. *cousteus*, now *coûteux*, f. *cost* COST *sb.*[2]] Costly, expensive –1564.

Costive (kǫ·stiv), *a.* ME. [– AFr. **costif*, for OFr. *costivé* :– L. *constipatus*; see CONSTIPATE. For the loss of Fr. *-é* cf. ASSIGN *sb.*[2]] **1.** Suffering from hardness and retention of the fæces; constipated. **2.** *fig.* Slow or reluctant in action; †reticent; niggardly 1594. † **3.** Hard and impervious 1707.

2. Somewhat caustiue of beliefe Toward your stone B. JONSON. **3.** Clay in dry seasons is c. MORTIMER. Hence **Co·stively** *adv.* **Co·stiveness,** the state or condition of being c. (*lit.* and *fig.*).

Costless (kǭ·stlĕs), *a.* 1509. [f. COST *sb.*[2] + -LESS.] Without cost.

† **Co·stlew,** *a.* ME. [f. COST *v.* or *sb.*[2] + -LEWE.] Costly, expensive; extravagant –1502.

Ther is also c. furrynge in hir gownes CHAUCER.

Costly (kǭ·stli), *a.* ME. [f. COST *sb.*[2] + -LY[1].] **1.** That costs much; sumptuous; expensive, dear. **2.** Lavish in expenditure (*arch.*) 1632.

1. Rare, exotic, and c. shrubs EVELYN. His wars are c. and chargeable HOOKER. **2.** To curse the C. Sex DRYDEN. Hence **Co·stliness,** c. quality.

Costmary (kǫ·stmē^əri). ME. [f. COST *sb.*[3] + (St.) *Mary*.] An aromatic perennial plant, *Chrysanthemum balsamita*, N.O. *Compositæ*, cultivated in English gardens; formerly used in medicine and to give a flavour to ale; see ALECOST.

Costo- (kǫ·sto), taken as comb. f. *costa* a rib, mostly in sense 'pertaining to, or connecting, the ribs and . .', as in **c.-abdominal, -central, -chondral** [Gr. χόνδρος], pertaining to the ribs and their cartilages. Also **Co·stotome** [Gr. -τομος], an instrument for cutting through the ribs or costal cartilages in dissection.

Costrel (kǫ·strĕl). Now *dial.* ME. [– OFr. *costerel* flagon, in form dim. of *costier* 'that is by the side'; cf. COSTER[1].] A large bottle with an ear or ears by which it could be suspended from the waist; a 'pilgrim's bottle'; also a wooden keg similarly used.

And therwithalle a c. taketh he And seyde 'Hereof a draught, or two, or three' CHAUCER. var. † **Costret.**

Costume (kǫstiū·m, kǫ·stium), *sb.* 1715. [– Fr. *costume* – It. *costume* custom, fashion, habit :– L. *consuetudo*, *-din-*; see CUSTOM.] **1.** In historical art: The costume and fashion proper to the time and locality in which a scene is laid (*obs.*). Also *transf.* **2.** The mode of personal attire and dress belonging to a nation, class, or period 1802. **3.** Dress considered with regard to its fashion or style; garb 1818. Also *fig.* **4.** (with *a* and *pl.*) A complete set of outer garments; a woman's gown, as the chief piece of her costume 1839.

1. I was extremely delighted with the poetical beauty of some parts [of the Lay of the Last Minstrel]. . The c., too, is admirable SIR J. MACKINTOSH. **2.** The clergy had no canonical c. 1809. **3.** A Court c. BEACONSFIELD. Hence **Costu·me** *v.* to provide with a c.; to arrange the get-up of a theatrical piece. **Costu·mer,** a dealer in costumes. **Costu·mery** arrangement of costumes; costumes in the mass (*rare*). **Costu·mic** *a. nonce-wd.*, of or pertaining to c.; in c.

Costumier (kǫstiū·miəɹ). 1831. [– Fr. *costumier*, f. *costumer* COSTUME *v.*] A dealer in costumes; *esp.* one who sells or lets out on hire costumes and properties for actors, etc.

Co-subordinate, -suffer, etc.; see CO*pref.*

† **Co-supreme.** 1599. [See CO-.] One who is supreme jointly with another; a joint overruler –1619.

Cosy, cosey, cozy (kō^u·zi). 1709. [orig. Sc.: deriv. unkn.]

A. *adj.* Snug; comfortable; sheltered and thus warm; sheltering.

B. *sb.* **1.** A quilted covering for a tea-pot, etc., to retain the heat 1863. **2.** A cosy seat; *spec.* a canopied seat for two. [Fr. *causeuse*.]

Cot (kǫt), *sb.*[1] [OE. *cot* = MLG., MDu., ON. *kot* :– Gmc. **kutam* (cf. ON. *kytja* hovel), rel. to COTE *sb.*[1]] **1.** A small house, a cottage; now chiefly *poet.*, and connoting humbleness, rather than the rudeness of *hut*. **2.** A small erection for shelter or protection; a COTE. Also in comb., as *bell-*, *sheep-c.* 1450. **3.** A case or sheath; a finger-stall; the covering of a drawing-roller in a spinning frame, etc. Now *dial.* or *techn.* 1617.

1. A few humble fishermen's cots 1849.

Comb.: **c.-house, co·te-house,** a small cottage; a shed, outhouse, etc.; **-town,** a hamlet of c.-houses. Hence **Co·tted** *a.* having cots.

Cot (kǫt), *sb.*[2] *dial.* [ME. – AFr. *cot*, poss. identical with med.L. *cottum*, *cotum* bed-quilt, stuffed mattress (being made of 'cot'); cf. OFr. *coterel* wadded wool.] **1.** Wool matted together in the fleece. **2.** A tangle 1851.

Cot (kǫt), *sb.*[3] *Irish.* 1537. [– Ir. and Gael. *cot* small boat.] A small roughly-made boat; a 'dug-out'.

Cot (kǫt), *sb.*[4] Also 7–9 **cott.** 1634. [– Hindi *khāt* bedstead, couch, hammock.] **1.** *Anglo-Ind.* A light bedstead. **2.** *Naut.* A sort of swinging bed on board ship, made of canvas, stretched by a frame, and suspended from the beams 1769. **3.** A small bed for a child; prop. a swing-cot 1818; hence, a bed in a children's hospital 1884. Also *attrib.*

Cot, abbrev. of COTANGENT.

Cotabulate, var. of CONTABULATE.

Cotangent (kō^utæ·ndʒĕnt), *sb.* (*a.*) 1635. [See CO-.] *Trig.* The tangent of the complement of a given angle. (Abbrev. *cot*) So **Cotange·ntial** *a.* having the same tangent.

Cotarnine (kotā·ɹnəin). 1857. [– Fr., f. *narcotine* by transposition.] *Chem.* A non-volatile organic base, $C_{12}H_{13}NO_3 + H_2O$, obtained by the action of oxidizing agents on narcotine.

Cote (kō^ut), *sb.*[1] [OE. *cote*, corresp. to LG. *kote* (whence G. *kote*) :– Gmc. **kutōn*, rel. to COT *sb.*[1]] **1.** A cot or cottage. Now *dial.* **2.** A shed, stall, or the like, for shelter or storage; *spec.* a sheepcote. (Now chiefly in comb., as in *dove-*, *bell-c.*, etc.) ME.

2. Stalles for all maner of beasts, and cotes for flocks 2 *Chr.* 32:28.

Cote (kō^ut), *sb.*[2] 1575. [f. COTE *v.*[1]] *Coursing.* The action of COTE *v.*[1]

Cote (kō^ut), *v.*[1] ? *Obs.* 1555. [perh. – OFr. *coster* proceed by the side of, follow closely, f. *coste* side.] **1.** *trans.* (*Coursing.*) Of one of two dogs running together: To pass by (its fellow) so as to turn the hare, etc. **2.** *transf.*, etc. To pass by, outstrip 1566.

2. Wee coated them on the way *Haml.* II. ii. 330.

Cote (kō^ut), *v.*[2] 1630. [f. COTE *sb.*[1]] To put in a cote.

Cote, *v.*[3] ME. Obs. f. QUOTE, q.v.

Cotemporanean, etc.; see CONT-.

Co-te·nant. 1822. [See CO-.] A joint tenant. Hence **Co-te·nancy.**

Coterell (kǫ·tĕrĕl). ME. [– OFr. *coterel*, med.L. *coterellus*, dim. of OFr. *cotier* COTTIER.] *Feudal Antiq.* A cottar; also, *erron.*, a cot.

Coterie (kō^u·tĕri). 1738. [– Fr. *coterie* (in OFr. feudal tenure, tenants holding land together), f. **cote* hut (cf. †*cotin*) – MLG. *kote* COTE *sb.*[1]; see -ERY.] † **1.** A club –1774. **2.** A circle of persons associated together and distinguished from 'outsiders'; a set; a clique 1738; a meeting of such a circle 1805.

2. The Holland House c. 1828. Catiline, Clodius, and some of that c. DE QUINCEY.

Cotesian (kotī·ziăn, -ʒ^iăn), *a.* 1753. Pertaining to Roger Cotes or his mathematical discoveries, see -IAN.

Cotham (kǫ·təm), name of a village near Bristol, designating a dendritic argillaceous limestone 1822.

Cothe, coath (kō^uð), *sb.* Now *dial.* [OE. *coðu*, *coðe* disease, pestilence.] † **1.** Sickness; an attack of illness –1460. **2.** Now a disease of sheep, etc., 'coe', rot 1784. Hence **Cothe** *v. dial.*, to give (sheep) the 'coe'; *intr.* to faint.

Cothurn (kō^u·þɒɹn, koþɒ̄·ɹn). 1606. [– Fr. *cothurne* – L. *cothurnus*] = next.

‖ **Cothurnus** (koþɒ·ɹnɒs). 1727. [L. – Gr. κόθορνος.] A thick-soled boot reaching to the middle of the leg, worn anciently by tragic actors; a buskin; *fig.* tragedy, a tragic style.

fig. She too wears the mask and the c., and speaks to measure THACKERAY. Hence **Cothu·rnal** *a.* of or pertaining to the c.; of tragedy, tragic. **Cothu·rnate** *a.* shod with the c.; tragic. So † **Cothurnated, Cothurned** *ppl. a.*

† **Coti·cular,** *a. rare.* 1799. [f. L. *coticula*, dim. of *cos, cot-* whetstone + -AR[1].] Of the nature of a whetstone.

Co-tidal (kouˈtəi·dăl), *a.* 1833. [See Co-.] Of or pertaining to the coincidence in time of tidal phenomena, *esp.* that of high water.

C. line, a line on a map connecting all those places at which high water occurs at the same hour.

Cotillion, ‖ **cotillon** (koti·lyən, kotiˈyoṅ). 1766. [– Fr. *cotillon* petticoat, dance, dim. of *cotte* COAT.] **1.** The name of several dances, chiefly of French origin, consisting of a variety of steps and figures. (In Eng. usage now only as Fr.; but in U.S. a generic name for quadrilles.) **2.** A piece of music arranged for the dance 1828. **3.** A woollen material in black and white for ladies' skirts 1858.

Cotinga (koti·ŋgă). 1783. [– Fr. *cotinga*, orig. native name in S. America.] A S. Amer. bird, or family of passerine birds, of brilliant plumage. **Coti·ngine** *a.* pertaining or related to the c.

Cotise (kǫ·tis), *sb.* Also **cottise.** 1572. [– Fr. *cotice*, XVI *cotisse*, of unkn. origin.] *Her.* An ordinary, in breadth the fourth part of a bend, usually one of two; cf. COST *sb.*[4] Hence **Co·tise** *v.* to border (a bend, etc.) on both sides with cotises, barrulets, etc.

Co·tland. Also **coth-.** *Hist.* OE. [f. COT *sb.*[1]] The land (about 5 acres) held with his cot by the Old English cottar.

Co·tman. *Hist.* OE. [f. as prec.] The tenant of a cot.

Co·to. 1879. In *C.-bark*, an officinal bark, obtained from Bolivia. Hence **Co·toin** (*Chem.*), a substance, in yellowish white crystals, obtained from c.-bark.

Cotoneaster (kotōuːniˌæ·stəɹ). 1753. [mod.L., f. L. *cotonium* QUINCE; see -ASTER.] A genus of small trees or trailing shrubs, N.O. *Rosaceæ*, inhabiting northern Europe and the Himalayas.

† **Cotquean** (kǫ·tkwīn). 1547. [f. COT *sb.*[1] + QUEAN.] **1.** The housewife of a cot; hence, a vulgar beldam, scold (cf. *huzzy* from *housewife*) –1633. **2.** A man that acts the housewife, and meddles with women's matters –1825.

1. Scold like a cot-quean; that's your profession FORD. **2.** I cannot abide these aperne husbands; such cotqueanes DEKKER. Hence **Cotquea·nity.** B. JONSON.

Co-trustee, etc.; see Co-.

Co·tset. *Hist.* [OE. *cot-sǣta* lit. 'occupant of a cot'; see COSSET *sb.*] In *OE. Law*: A villein who held a cot with an attached plot of land by service of labour. (See COTTAR.) var. † **Cotsetla,** † **cotsetle.**

Cotswold (kǫ·tswǒld). 1537. [ME. *coteswold*, f. personal name *Cōd* (Ekwall); see WOLD.] Name of a range of hills in Gloucestershire, England, noted for their sheep-pastures, and for a breed of long-woolled sheep named after them. Hence *C. lion*, (*joc.*) a sheep.

‖ **Cotta** (kǫ·tă). 1848. [– It. *cotta*; see COAT.] *Eccl.* A surplice.

‖ **Cottabus** (kǫ·tăbɒs). 1823. [L. – Gr. κότταβος.] *Gr. Antiq.* An amusement in vogue at drinking parties in ancient Greece, consisting in throwing the wine left in a cup into some vessel, so as to strike it in a particular manner.

Cottage (kǫ·tėdʒ). ME. [– AFr. **cotage*, AL. *cotagium* (XII), f. COT *sb.*[1], COTE *sb.*[1]; see -AGE.] **1.** A small or humble dwelling-house. Also *transf.* and *fig.* (obs.). † **2.** A small erection for shelter; a cot, hut, shed, etc. –1796. **3.** A small country or suburban residence 1765; in U.S. *spec.* a summer residence (often large and sumptuous) at a watering-place 1882.

1. A poure wydwe. .Was whilom dwellyng in a narwe cotage CHAUCER. (*fig.*) *Clay* or *earthen c.*: the body. Phr.: **c. allotment** (see ALLOTMENT); **c. farming,** spade husbandry; **c. hospital,** a small hospital, in a c., or the like; also, a hospital arranged on the principle of having several detached cottages. Hence **Co·ttaged** *ppl. a.* furnished with cottages. † **Co·ttagely** *a.* proper to a c.; humble, mean, poor.

Cottager (kǫ·tėdʒəɹ). 1550. [f. COTTAGE + -ER[1].] One who lives in a cottage; used *esp.* of agricultural labourers.

The yeomanry, or middle people, of a condition between gentlemen and cottagers BACON.

Cottar, cotter (kǫ·təɹ). 1552. [f. COT *sb.*[1] + -ER[1] (Sc. *-ar*); cf. med.L. *cotarius* and COTTIER.] **1.** = COTSET, q.v. **2.** *Sc.* A peasant who occupies a cottage belonging to a farm as a sort of out-servant 1552. **3.** *Irish.* = COTTIER 2. 1791. Also *attrib.*

1. The cottar, the bordar, and the labourer were bound to aid in the work of the home-farm GREEN.

Cotted (kǫ·tėd), *ppl. a.* 1793. [f. COT *sb.*[2] and *v.*[2]] Matted, tangled; said *esp.* of a fleece.

Cotter, *sb.*[1]; see COTTAR.

Cotter (kǫ·təɹ), *sb.*[2] 1649. [See earlier COTTEREL.] A pin, key, wedge, or bolt which fits into a hole and fastens something in its place. Hence **Co·tter** *v. trans.* to fasten with a c.

Cotterel (kǫ·tərĕl), *sb. dial.* 1570. [Closely rel. to COTTER *sb.*[2], which may be a shortened form, or the primitive of which this is a dim.] **1.** = COTTER *sb.*[2] Chiefly *north.* **2.** A trammel, crane, or bar, to hang a pot over a fire. *s. dial.* 1674. **3.** A washer 1869. Hence **Co·tterel** *v. dial.* to cotter.

Cottier (kǫ·tiəɹ). ME. [– OFr. *cotier* (in med.L. *cotarius, -erius*), f. *cote*; see COTERIE, -IER.] **1.** A peasant who lives in a cottage; *orig.* a COTSET, q.v. **2.** *spec.* In Ireland, a peasant renting a small holding under the system of *c.-tenure*, under which the land is let annually in small plots directly to labourers, the rent being fixed by public competition 1832.

1. They had cottiers, day labourers established in cottages, on their estate MAR. EDGEWORTH. Hence **Co·ttierism,** the system of cottier-tenure.

Cottise, -ize; see COTISE.

Cottoid (kǫ·toid), *a.* (*sb.*) 1854. [f. mod.L. *Cottus* name of a genus of fishes + -OID.] *Zool.* Belonging to a family of fishes of which the type is *Cottus*, a genus related to the 'Miller's thumb'. As *sb.* A fish of this family.

Cotton (kǫ·t'n), *sb.*[1] [ME. *coto(u)n* – (O)Fr. *coton* – Arab. *ḳuṭn*, in Sp. Arab. *ḳuṭun*. See ACTON.] **1.** The white fibrous substance which clothes the seeds of the cotton plant (*Gossypium*); used for making cloth and thread, etc. **2.** The cotton plant; the genus *Gossypium*. Also, cotton plants collectively. ME. **3.** Thread spun from cotton yarn; in full *c. thread* 1848. **4.** Any fabric made of cotton; in *pl.* cotton fabrics, also cotton garments ME. **5.** *transf.* A cotton-like down growing on other plants 1551. **6.** *attrib.* (without hyphen.) Made of cotton 1552.

Comb.: **corkwood c.,** the silky down of *Ochroma lagopus* (cf. SILK-COTTON); **c.-bagging,** a coarse wrapping material used for baling cotton-wool; **-cake,** compressed c.-seed freed from the oil, used for feeding cattle; **-chopper,** a machine for cleaning c. by scutching, blowing, etc.; **c. famine,** the failure of the supply of c. to English mills during the American Civil War; **c. flannel,** a strong c. fabric with a long plush nap, also called *c. plush* and *Canton flannel*; **c. gin,** a machine for freeing cotton-wool from the seeds; **c.-grass,** a general name for the species *Eriophorum*; **-mill,** a factory where cotton is spun or woven by steam or water power; **-opener,** a machine for loosening and blowing c. after its transport in compressed bales; **-picker,** one who or that which picks c. from the bolls of the plant; a machine for cleaning c.; **c. plush** = *cotton flannel* (above); **c. powder,** an explosive made from gun-c.; **c.-press,** a machine (or warehouse) for pressing c. into bales; **c. print,** c. cloth printed with a design in colours; **c.-rat,** a rodent (*Sigmodon hispidus*) common in southern U.S.; **-rose,** the plant-genus *Filago*; **-seed, c. seed,** the seed of the c. plant; also *attrib.*; **-spinner,** a c.-manufacturer or worker; **-stainer,** a heteropterous insect, *Dysdercus suturellus*, which gives a reddish stain to c.; **-tail,** the common rabbit of the U.S., *Lepus sylvaticus*, which has a white fluffy tail; **-thistle,** a tall species of thistle, *Onopordum acanthium*, entirely covered with white cottony down; **-tree, c. tree,** (*a*) a name of species of *Bombax* and *Eriodendron*; (*b*) a name for *Viburnum lantana* and *Populus nigra*; also = COTTONWOOD; **c. velvet,** a c. fabric made with a pile like velvet; **c. waste,** refuse yarn from c.-mills, used for cleaning machinery, etc.; **-wool, c. wool,** raw c., as gathered from the bolls of the plant; **-worm,** the larva of an insect (*Aletia xylina*) very destructive to the c. crops of America; **c. yarn,** c. prepared for weaving into fabrics; **mineral c.,** a wool-like metallic fibre, made by sending a jet of steam through a stream of liquid slag; † **philosophic c.,** an old name for flowers of zinc.

Hence † **Co·ttonary** *a.* cottony (Sir T. Browne). † **Co·ttoned** *ppl. a.* having a nap, friezed. **Cottonee·,** a Turkish fabric of c. and silk satinet. **Cottonee·r** (*rare*), a c.-manufacturer or worker. **Co·ttonize** *v.* to reduce (flax, hemp, etc.) to a short c.-like staple. † **Co·ttonous** *a.* cottony. **Co·ttony** *a.* downy; nappy; like, or of the nature of, c.

† **Cotton,** *sb.*[2] 1503. [poss. same as prec., conn. w. the sense 'down, nap'.] A woollen fabric of the nature of frieze, formerly manufactured in Lancashire, Westmorland, and Wales (*Manchester, Kendal,* and *Welsh c.*) –1840.

Cotton (kǫ·t'n), *v.* 1488. [f. the sb. Cf. Fr. *cotonner.*]

I. *lit.* † **1.** *trans.* To form a down or nap on; to frieze –1598. **2.** *intr.* Of cloth, etc.: To rise with a nap. ? *Obs.* 1608. **3.** *trans.* To furnish, clothe, stop *up*, with cotton 1661.

II. *fig.* (*intr.*) **1.** To prosper, 'get on' well. Now *dial.* 1560. **2.** To 'get on' together 1567. **3.** To fraternize. Const. *together, with.* 1648. **4.** To take *to*; to become drawn *to* 1805.

2. John a Nokes and John a Style and I cannot c. 1605. **3.** I love to see 'em hug and cotten together, like Down upon a Thistle CONGREVE. Phr. *C. up*: to make up to. **4.** 'I don't object to Short,' she says, 'but I c. to Codlin' DICKENS. Hence **Co·ttoner,** one who puts a nap on cloth.

Cottonade (kǫ·t'nēⁱd). Also **cotonnade.** 1858. [– Fr. *cotonnade*; see -ADE.] A name for various coarse cotton fabrics; cotton check. Also *attrib.*

Cotton lord, cotton-lord. 1823. A magnate of the cotton trade.

Cottonocracy (kǫt'nǫ·krăsi). *colloq.* 1845. [f. COTTON *sb.*[1]; see -CRACY.] Cotton lords as a class.

Cottonopolis (kǫt'nǫ·pŏlis). 1886. [f. as prec.; see -POLIS.] 'Cotton City'; *i.e.* Manchester.

Cotton plant, cotton-plant. 1751. A plant that yields cotton; a plant of the genus *Gossypium* or of an allied genus.

Co·ttonweed. 1562. A name for the species of *Gnaphalium* and the allied genera.

Co·ttonwood, co·tton-wood. 1823. The name of several species of poplar (*Populus*) in U.S.; so called from the cotton-like covering of the seeds.

Cotunnite (kotɒ·nəit). 1834. [f. Dr. *Cotugna* of Naples; see -ITE[1] 2 b.] *Min.* Native lead chloride found in white acicular crystals in the crater of Vesuvius.

Cotwal, var. of KOTWAL, an Indian police-officer.

‖ **Cotyle** (kǫ·tilī). 1707. [Gr. κοτύλη (in L. form *cotyla*) small vessel.] **1.** *Gr. Antiq.* A deep cup, taken as a measure of capacity. (Not in Eng. use.) **2.** *Anat.*, etc. A cup-like cavity or organ; *spec.* the ACETABULUM 1882. Hence **Co·tyliform** *a.* cup-shaped. **Cotyli·gerous** *a.* bearing cotyles or cup-like organs.

Cotyledon (kǫtilī·dən). 1545. [– L. *cotyledon* navelwort, pennywort – Gr. κοτυληδών applied to various cup-shaped cavities, f. κοτύλη hollow, cup, socket.] **1.** *Phys.* One of the separate patches of villi on the fœtal chorion of Ruminants. **2.** *Bot.* A genus of plants of the N.O. *Crassulaceæ*; the British species is *C. umbilicus*, Navelwort or Pennywort 1601. **3.** *Bot.* The primary leaf in the embryo of Phanerogams; the seed-leaf 1776. Hence **Cotyle·donal** *a.* (*rare*). **Cotyle·donary** *a.*, *Bot.* of the nature of a c.; *Phys.* characterized by the presence of cotyledons (sense 1). **Cotyle·donoid,** *Bot.* a name for the germinating threads of mosses. **Cotyle·donous** *a.* characterized by the presence of cotyledons.

Cotyloid (kǫ·tiloid), *a.* 1760. [– Gr. κοτυλοειδής cup-shaped: see COTYLE, -OID.] *Anat.* Shaped like a cup: applied *esp.* to the socket of the hip-joint (*c. cavity*); also to the coxal cavity in insects.

Cotylophorous (kǫtilǫ·fŏrəs), *a.* [f. COTYLE + -PHOROUS.] *Zool.* Having a cotyledonary placenta; belonging to the *Cotylophora* or typical Ruminants of Huxley's classification.

Couch (kautʃ), *sb.*[1] ME. [– (O)Fr. *couche*, f. *coucher*; see COUCH *v.*] **1.** A frame, with what is spread over it, on which to lie down; a bed. Now, in literary use, vaguely, that on which one sleeps. Also *transf.* and *fig.* **2.** The lair or den of a wild beast ME. **3.** A lounge for reclining or sitting on 1450. **4.** A layer (*esp.* of paint), a stratum, bed 1661. **5.** *Malting.* A layer of grain laid on the floor to germinate; also the floor 1615. **6.** *Paper Manuf.* A board covered with felt or flannel on which the sheets of pulp are placed to be pressed 1886.

1. I bad men schulde me myn couche make CHAUCER. *fig.* A c. whereupon to rest a searching and restless spirit BACON. **2.** A dog-otter. .rushed from his c. among the roots MEDWIN. *Comb.* **c.-bed, -bedstead,** a c. used as a bed.

Couch (kautʃ, kūtʃ), *sb.*[2] 1578. [var. of QUITCH.] A species of grass, *Triticum repens*, with long creeping root-stalks; usu. **c.-grass.** Also applied to other creeping grasses. Hence **Cou·chy** *a.* full of c.-grass.

Couch (kautʃ), *v.* ME. [– (O)Fr. *coucher* :– L. *collocare* lay in its place, lodge; see COLLOCATE.]

I. *trans.* **1.** To cause to lie down, to lay down; to put to bed; also *refl.* *Obs.* exc. in *pa. pple.* = Laid on, or as on, a couch. Also *fig.* † **2.** To cause to lie close; in *pa. pple.* prostrated, cowering –1725. † **3.** To lay (things); to set, bed, overlay, etc. –1794. **4.** †To lay, overlay, inlay, spread, set *with* (*of*). Chiefly in *pa. pple.* –1611. **b.** To embroider with gold thread or the like laid flat. Also *absol.* ME. **5.** *Malting.* To spread (grain) on a floor to germinate 1562. **6.** *Paper Manuf.* To lay (a sheet of pulp) upon a felt to be pressed 1751. **7.** To lower (a spear, etc.) to the position of attack; to level as a gun 1470. **8.** To lay down, lower, depress (a part of the body, etc.) 1611. **9.** *Surg.* To remove (a cataract) by depressing the opaque crystalline lens with a needle, until it lies below the axis of vision. Also *to c. the eye* or *a person.* 1601. † **10.** To place in a lodging; *pass.* to be lodged or located –1690. † **11.** To hide, conceal –1814. † **12.** To collocate, comprise –1729. **13.** To put together (words, etc.); to put into words 1529; to express in an obscure or veiled way 1563. Also †*transf.*

1. Thou look'st sunk-eyed; go c. thy head MARSTON. The Hind. .Then couched her self securely by his side DRYDEN. **3.** I c. it. .with all. . humilitie at her Majesties. .feete 1589. **4. b.** A cloth of Tars, Cowched of perlys whyte CHAUCER. **7.** A brauer Souldier neuer couched Launce 1 *Hen. VI*, III. ii. 134. **8.** Some six or eight thorns, some erect, others couched 1753. **11.** C. thee midway on the wold SCOTT. **13.** The words wherein the question. .is couched HOBBES.

II. *intr.* (Now chiefly of beasts.) **1.** To lie; *esp.* to lie at rest or in sleep ME. **2.** To crouch, cower; †to stoop under a burden; † to bow in obeisance; *fig.* to submit, succumb ME. Also †*transf.* of plants, etc. **3.** To lie in ambush, to lurk 1583. **4.** Of leaves, etc.: To lie in a heap for decomposition, etc. 1770.

1. The deep that coucheth beneath *Deut.* 33:13. **2.** An aged Squire. .That seemd to c. under his shield SPENSER. **3.** Bertram couches in the brake and fern, Hiding his face SCOTT.

Hence **Cou·ching** *vbl. sb.* the action of the *vb.*; (*Embroidery*) couched work; also *attrib.*

Couchancy (kau·tʃănsi). 1695. [f. COUCHANT; see -ANCY.] *Law.* The fact of being *couchant*; see next. var. **Cou·chance.**

Couchant (kau·tʃănt), *a.* 1496. [– (O)Fr. *couchant*, pres. pple. of *coucher*; see COUCH *v.*, -ANT.] **1.** Lying down; couching; *esp.* of an animal. **2.** *Her.* Of an animal: 'Lying on his belly, but with his head lifted up' 1766. † **3.** Bending down, crouching (*rare*) –1706. † **4.** Lurking (*lit.* and *fig.*) –1720.

1. *C. and levant*: lying down and rising up; said of cattle in permanent occupation of pasture. **2.** His crest was covered with a c. Hownd SPENSER.

‖ **Couché** (kuʃe), *a.* 1727. [Fr.; pa. pple. of *coucher* COUCH *v.*] Of a shield: Suspended by the sinister corner so as to hang slanting. Of a chevron: Borne sideways.

‖ **Couchee** (ku·ʃe). Rarely **coucher.** 1676. [– Fr. *couché*, var. of *coucher* lying down, going to bed (subst. use of *coucher* infin.). Cf. LEVEE *sb.*[2]] An evening reception.

Royal Drawing-rooms, Levees, Couchees CARLYLE.

Coucher[1] (kau·tʃəɹ). ME. [app. – AFr. *coucheour, f. *couche*; see COUCH *sb.*[1], -OUR, -ER[2]; cf. Fr. *coucheur* 'a coucher' (Cotgr.).] **1.** One lying down; in *Sc.* a poltroon. **2.** One who couches or crouches. BROWNING. † **3.** A large book, *e.g.* a breviary such as lay permanently on a desk or table –1559. † **4.** A resident factor in a foreign place –1706.

Comb. † **c.-book,** a large cartulary.

Cou·cher[2]. 1751. [In mod.Fr. *coucheur*, (etymol. = prec.) and *couchart.*] *Paper Manuf.* One who or that which couches pulp to be pressed.

Couéism (kū·eˌiz'm). 1922. [f. name of Emile *Coué*, French psychologist + -ISM.] Systematic auto-suggestion, usu. of a sanguine kind.

Cougar (kū·găɹ). Also **couguar** (kū·gwaɹ). 1774. [– Fr. *cougar* (Buffon) – Marcgraf's name *cuguacu ara*, repr. Guarani *guaçu ara.*] A large feline quadruped (*Felis concolor*); also called *puma, catamount, red tiger, American lion, mountain lion*, etc.

Cough (kǫf), *sb.* ME. [f. COUGH *v.*; cf. *laugh.*] **1.** A diseased condition of the respiratory organs manifesting itself in fits of coughing. (Till 1600 usually called *the cough*; *a cough* is a specific attack.) **2.** A single act of coughing; a violent expulsion of air from the lungs with the characteristic noise 1742.

Cough (kǫf), *v.* [ME. *coȝe, cowhe*, f. imit. base *kox- repr. by OE. *cohettan* shout, (M)LG., (M)Du. *kuchen* cough, MHG. *kūchen* breathe, exhale (G. *keuchen* pant).] **1.** *intr.* To expel air from the lungs with a violent effort and characteristic noise; usually in order to remove something from the air-passages. **2.** *trans.* To express by coughing 1450.

Phr. *To c. out, up*: to eject by coughing; † *fig.* to disclose. *To c. down*: to put down or silence a speaker by coughing. Hence **Cou·gher.**

Could (kud), pa. t. of CAN *v.*, q.v.

Coulée (kule, kū·lī). Also (*U.S.*) **-ee, -ie, coolie, -ey.** 1807. [– Fr. *coulée* flow, lava flow :– L. *colare* filter, strain, in Rom. flow, f. *colum* strainer.] **1.** *Geol.* A stream of lava, whether molten or solidified; a lava-flow 1839. **2.** In Western U.S. and Canada: A deep ravine or gulch scooped out by heavy floods, but dry in summer.

‖ **Couleur** (kulör). 1783. The Fr. for COLOUR. Hence *c. de rose* rose-colour; used in Eng., **a.** as *adj.* 'rose-coloured', 'roseate'; **b.** as *adv.* 'in a (too) rosy light'.

‖ **Coulisse** (kuli·s). 1819. [– Fr. *coulisse*, subst. use of fem. of *coulis*, orig. adj. sliding, f. *couler* glide; see COULÉE, CULLIS *sb.*[2], PORTCULLIS.] **1.** A groove in which a sluice-gate or the like slides up and down 1864. **2.** One of the side scenes of the stage in a theatre; also the space between them, the wings.

‖ **Couloir** (kulwar). 1855. [– Fr. *couloir* colander, lobby, etc., f. *couler* glide, slide + *-oir* -ORY[1]; see COULISSE.] A steep gorge or gully on a mountain side.

Up this c. we proposed to try the ascent TYNDALL

Coulomb (kulǫ·m). 1881. [After the French physicist, C. A. de *Coulomb* (1736–1806).] The unit of electrical quantity; the quantity of electricity conveyed in one second by a current of one ampère. (Previously called *Weber.*)

Comb. **c.-meter,** a metre for measuring electricity in coulombs.

Coulter, colter (kōᵘ·ltəɹ). [OE. *culter* – L. *culter* knife, ploughshare. The sp. *colter* is preferred in U.S.] The iron blade fixed in front of the share in a plough; it cuts the soil vertically. Also *attrib.*

Cou·lterneb. 1678. [f. COULTER + NEB.] A local name for the Puffin, so called from the shape of its bill.

Coumarin (kū·mărin). 1830. [– Fr. *coumarine*, f. *coumarou* = *cumarú*, native name in Guiana of the Tonka bean + -IN[1].] *Chem.* A crystalline substance ($C_9H_6O_2$), found in the seeds of the *cumarú, coumarou*, or Tonka bean; also in melilot, woodruff, etc. Hence **Cou·maric** *a.*, in *c. acid*, an acid ($C_9H_8O_3$) obtained from coumarin; **Cou·marate,** a salt of coumaric acid.

Council (kau·nsĭl). OE. [– AFr. *cuncile, concilie* – L. *concilium* convocation, assembly, meeting, f. *com* CON- + *calare* call, summon. In Eng. confused with *conseil*, later COUNSEL, till XVI.]

I. f. L. *concilium.* † **1.** *gen.* An assembly called together for any purpose. (ME. only.) **2.** *spec.* An assembly of ecclesiastics (with or without laymen) convened to regulate doctrine or discipline in the church, or, earlier, to settle points in dispute between the ecclesiastical and civil powers, and variously qualified according to its sphere, as *œcumenical, general, national, patriarchal, primatial, provincial, diocesan* (this = synod). **3.** In the N.T., used as tr. Gr. συνέδριον, Vulg. *concilium* ME.

2. All synods and councils since the Apostles' times, whether general or particular, may err, and many have erred *Westm. Confess. Faith*, 1643.

II. f. L. *consilium*, Fr. *conseil.* An assembly or meeting for consultation or advice, as a *family c.*, a *c. of physicians* ME.

Great C. (in *Eng. Hist.*): occas. applied to a *Witenagemōt*; more often to the assemblies under the Norman kings of tenants-in-chief and great ecclesiastics, out of which the House of Lords originated. *Cabinet C.*: see CABINET. *C. of War*: **a.** an assembly of officers called to consult with the general or commanding officer, usually in an emergency; **b.** a permanent advisory committee on military affairs. *Common C.*: the administrative body of a corporate town or city. (In England, retained as a title only in the case of London.)

III. A body of counsellors (or councillors). **1.** A body of men chosen or designated as permanent advisers on matters of state ME. **2.** A deliberative and administrative committee, associated with the president (or directors) of a society or institution 1682.

Comb.: **c.-board,** the table at which the councillors sit; hence, the councillors in session; **-book,** the book in which the acts of a c. are registered; the register of privy-councillors; **-chamber, -hall, -room,** an apartment appropriated to c.-meetings; **-fire,** a fire kindled by North American Indians when in c.; **-general,** a general or common c.; **-house,** (*a*) a house in which a c. meets; in Scotland, a town-hall; (*b*) a house erected under the authority of a town or district council; **-table** = *council-board*; †the Privy Council.

† **Cou·ncilist.** [f. prec. + -IST.] One versed in the subject of COUNCILS (sense I. 2). MILTON.

† **Cou·ncillary,** *a.* 1651. [f. as prec. + -ARY[2].] CONSILIARY. Hobbes.

Councillor (kau·nsiləɹ). ME. [alt. of COUNSELLOR by assim. to COUNCIL.] An official member of a council. Hence **Cou·ncillorship,** the office of a c.

† **Co-u·ne,** *v. rare.* 1627. [– med.L. *counire, -are*; see CO-, UNITE *v.* Cf. L. *adunare* in this sense, and ADUNATION.] *trans.* To unite, combine –1677.

Co-uni·te, *v.* 1548. [f. CO- + UNITE *v.*] To unite together (*trans.* and *intr.*). So † **Co-uni·te** *pa. pple.* = co-united.

Counsel (kau·nsĕl), *sb.* [– OFr. *cun-, conseil* (mod. *conseil*) :– L. *consilium* consultation, plan, deliberating body, f. *com* CON- + *sal-; see CONSUL, CONSULT. See also COUNCIL.] **1.** Interchange of opinions; consultation, deliberation. **2.** Advice, direction, as the result of deliberation ME. **3.** The faculty of counselling; judgement; prudence; sagacity. (*arch.*) ME. **4.** That in which deliberation results; resolution, purpose; plan ME. † **5.** A secret purpose or opinion –1652; a secret; a confidence –1613. † **6.** A body of advisers. Now COUNCIL. –1549; a counsellor –1654. **7.** A body of legal advisers, engaged in the conduct of a cause. (Usually a collective pl.; formerly treated as collective sing.) ME. **b.** as *sing.*: A single legal adviser 1709.

1. Who is this that darkneth counsell by words without knowledge *Job* 38:2. **2.** Taak no conseil of a fool CHAUCER. *C. of perfection* (see *Matt.* 19:21. *Evangelical counsels* (Theol.): the obligations of poverty, chastity, and obedience to a religious superior. **3.** *Job* 12:13. **4.** Hii. .were alle at conseyl to worry Engelond R. GLOUC. **5.** † *In c.*: in private, in confidence. *To keep* (†*hold*) *c.*: to observe secrecy (*arch.* and *dial.*). *To keep one's* (*own*) *c.*: to be reticent about one's intentions, etc. **7.** The second of our three C. was the best PEPYS. *King's* (*Queen's*) *C.*: barristers appointed

(on the nomination of the lord-chancellor) c. to the crown; also a member of this body. (*Abbrev.* K.C., Q.C.)
Hence † **Cou·nselful** *a.* **Cou·nselless** *a.*

Counsel (kau·nsĕl), *v.* [– (O)Fr. *conseillier* :– L. *consiliari*, f. *consilium*; see prec.] **1.** To give or offer counsel or advice to; to advise. Also *absol.* **2.** To recommend (a plan, suggestion, etc.) ME. † **3.** To consult –1547. Also †*refl.* to consider; also = next. (ME. only.) † **4.** *intr.* To take counsel with others; to deliberate –1795.

1. Pray be counsail'd *Cor.* III. ii. 28. Consail me fader, how to liue ME. **2.** Thus Belial. .Counsel'd ignoble ease MILT. *P.L.* II. 227. **4.** Wives must c. with husbands LATIMER. Hence **Cou·nsellable, -elable** *a.* willing to be counselled; to be recommended. **Cou·nselled, -eled** *ppl. a.* determined; recommended. **Cou·nselling, -eling** *vbl. sb.* giving or taking of counsel.

Counsellor, -elor (kau·nsĕləɹ). [ME. *conseiler, conseilour* – (O)Fr. *conseiller* :– L. *consiliarius* (see -ARY[1]) and *conseillour, -eur*, repr. L. *consiliator* (see -OR 2).] **1.** One who counsels; an adviser. Also *fig.* **2.** An official counsellor. (In this sense now spelt COUNCILLOR, q.v.) **3.** (More fully *c.-at-law.*) One whose profession is to give legal advice to clients, and conduct their cases in court; a barrister or advocate. *arch.* in Eng. use. 1531.

1. Wyse conseylyrs and polytyke men STARKEY **3.** Good Counsellors lacke no Clients *Meas. for M* I. ii. 109. Hence **Cou·nsellorshi:p,** the office of c.; formerly = COUNCILLORSHIP.

Count (kaunt), *sb.*[1] ME. [– OFr. *conte, counte* (mod. *compte* reckoning, *conte* tale) :– late L. *computus* calculation, f. *computare* COUNT *v.*] **1.** The action of counting; a computation. **2.** The result of reckoning; the reckoning; the sum total 1483. **3.** A reckoning as to money or property; *fig.* reckoning (cf. ACCOUNT *sb.*) ME. **4.** Estimation; the act or way of estimating; regard, notice (cf. ACCOUNT *sb.*) 1475. **5.** *Law.* Each particular charge in a declaration or indictment; also, in a real action, the whole declaration 1588.

1. Infinite. .because. .out of all c. *Two Gent.* II. i. 62. Phr. *To Put one out of c. To keep (lose) c.* **2.** Very near double the c. SWIFT. **3.** Look, Steward, to your compt 1610. *fig.* When we shall meete at compt, This looke of thine will hurle my Soule from Heauen *Oth.* V. ii. 273. **4.** They make no counte of generall councels ASCHAM.

Count (kaunt), *sb.*[2] 1553. [– OFr. *conte* (mod. *comte*) :– L. *comes, comit-* companion, overseer, attendant, etc., (late L. occupant of a state office, as e.g. in *comes littoris Saxonici* Count of the Saxon shore); f. *com* COM- + pa. ppl. stem *it-* of *ire* go.] A foreign title of nobility, corresponding to the English EARL.

Count Palatine: orig. in the later Roman Empire a count (*comes*) attached to the imperial palace, and having supreme judicial authority in certain causes; thence, under the German Emperors, etc., a count having supreme jurisdiction in his fief; in Eng. Hist. = *Earl Palatine*, the proprietor of a county palatine, now applied to the Earl of Chester, and Duke of Lancaster, dignities which are attached to the crown. See PALATINE.

Comb. **C.-bishop**, a bishop holding also the temporal dignity of *count*; so **c.-cardinal.**

Count (kaunt), *v.* ME. [– OFr. *counter, cunter* reckon, relate (mod. *compter* reckon, *conter* relate) :– L. *computare* calculate; see COMPUTE.]

I. *trans.* **1.** To tell over one by one, so as to ascertain the number of individuals in a collection; to number; to reckon up; also, to repeat the numerals one, two, three, etc., as *to c. ten.* **2.** To include in the reckoning 1526. **3.** To esteem, reckon, hold (a thing) to be (so and so) ME. **4.** To reckon, esteem (at such a value); †to hold of account ME. † **5.** To reckon or impute *to* –1701. † **6.** To tell, relate –1778.

1. Then must I c. my gaines SHAKS. Phr. *To c. out*: to c. and take out (from a stock), to c. so as to exhaust the stock. *To c. out the House* (of Commons): to bring the sitting to an end by pointing out to the Speaker that the number of members present is less than forty, the number required to 'make a House'; also *to c. out a measure*, etc., i.e. to stop it by this means. **3.** Coumptynge all fyshe that cometh to the net 1546. I c. you for a fool TENNYSON. **5.** Abram beleued the Lorde, and y[t] was counted vnto him for righteousnes COVERDALE *Gen.* 15:6.

II. *intr.* **1.** To reckon, make reckoning. *Obs.* exc. in *To c. without one's host.* ME. Also with *on, upon* († *of*). † **2.** To make account *of*; think (much, lightly, etc.) *of* –1846. **3.** (*absol.* use of 1.) To 'do sums'; to reckon numerically 1588. † **4.** *Law.* To plead in a court of law. [AFr. *counter*, in Law-books from 13th c.] –1809. **5.** To admit of being counted 1845. **b.** To amount to, number 1819. **6.** To enter into the account (with *compl.* or *absol.*) 1857.

1. There is less wisdom, honesty, and mercy in men than is counted on FULLER. **2.** *Two Gent.* II. i. 65. **3.** To c. by tens 1865. **4.** The plaintiff was said to 'count' when he declared. .the nature of his complaint, while 'plead' and 'plea' were specifically used of the defendant's answer O.E.D. **5. b.** The carambole counts two 1820. **6.** Many doubt whether good play really counts much at Whist PROCTOR.

Hence **Cou·ntable** *a.* †responsible; †sensitive *to*; proper to be counted, numerable.

Countenance (kau·ntĭnăns), *sb.* ME. [– AFr. *c(o)untenaunce*, (O)Fr. *contenance* bearing, behaviour, mien, contents, f. *contenir* maintain (oneself); see CONTAIN, CONTINENCE. The extension from 'mien' to 'face' is Eng.] † **1.** Comportment, demeanour; conduct –1719. † **2.** Appearance, look; mere show –1837. † **3.** A sign, gesture –1568. **4.** The expression of a person's face ME. **5.** The face ME. **6.** Composure of face ME. † **7.** Demeanour as expressing good or ill will –1632. **8.** Appearance on any side; moral support 1576. † **9.** Repute in the world –1745; position –1784.

4. Their countenances speak a different language 'JUNIUS'. Phr. *To keep one's c.*: to refrain from expressing emotion. **5.** A youth, and ruddy, and of a faire c. 1 *Sam.* 17:42. **6.** I will not be put out of c. *L.L.L.* V. ii. 611. Phr. *To keep (put) in c.*: to keep from being abashed. **8.** A doctrine which has no c. in reason or revelation PRIESTLEY. **5.** Men of c. and authority 1617. Hence **Countenanced** *ppl. a.*[1] having a (specified) c.

Countenance (kau·ntĭnăns), *v.* 1486. [f. prec. sb. Cf. Fr. † *contenancer* (Cotgr.).] † **1.** *intr.* To behave, pretend, or make (as if. .) –1519. † **2.** *trans.* To pretend. SPENSER. † **3.** To set off, grace –1603. **4.** To give countenance to; to favour, patronize, support 1568. † **5.** To keep in countenance. SHAKS.

4. To c. Burnet at the Hague MACAULAY, the practice 1832. **5.** As from your Graues rise vp. . To c. this horror *Macb.* II. iii. 85. Hence **Cou·ntenanced** *ppl. a.*[2] favoured, supported. **Cou·ntenancer**, one who supports or encourages.

† **Counter** (kau·ntəɹ), *sb.*[1] ME. [aphet. f. *acuntre*, ACOUNTER.] ENCOUNTER, opposition –1591.

Counter (kau·ntəɹ), *sb.*[2] ME. [f. COUNT *v.* + -ER; for sense 2, see (earlier) COUNTOUR.] **1.** One who counts or calculates. † **2.** A serjeant-at-law, etc. **3.** An apparatus for keeping count of revolutions, strokes of a piston, etc. 1803.

Counter (kau·ntəɹ), *sb.*[3] ME. [– AFr. *count(e)our*, OFr. *conteoir*, *-eor* (mod. *comptoir*) :– med.L. *computatorium*, f. L. *computare* COMPUTE; see -ER[2].] **1.** Anything used in counting or keeping count; as a piece of metal, ivory, or the like, used now *esp.* in games of chance, etc. Also, applied to the 'pieces' or 'men' used in chess, draughts, etc. **2.** An imitation coin; a token; money generally (*contempt.*) 1526. † **3.** A table or desk for counting money –1587. **4.** A banker's table; also, the table in a shop on which the money paid by purchasers is counted out 1688. † **5.** A counting-house –1809. † **6.** The court or hall of justice of a mayor –1734. **7.** The prison attached to such a city court; the name of certain prisons for debtors (see COMPTER). *Obs.* exc. *Hist.* ME.

1. What comes the wooll too? . .I cannot do't without Compters *Wint. T.* IV. iii. 38. Counters. . at a card-table are used. .as signs substituted for money BP. BERKELEY. The noblest aims and lives were only counters on her board J. R. GREEN. **2.** Silver, not as now a c., but the body of the current coin BURKE. **4.** In fair days he would take some £40 over the c. 1889.

Counter (kau·ntəɹ), *sb.*[4] 1575. [– COUNTER *a.* or *adv.*; the origin of senses 3 and 4 is unkn.] **1.** *Hunting.* The opposite direction to that taken by the game; see COUNTER *adv.* **2.** The contrary 1871. **3.** That part of a horse's breast which lies between the shoulders and under the neck 1678. **4.** The curved part of a ship's stern 1626.

3. For he was barbed from c. to tail SCOTT. **4.** The torpedo exploded under her c. 1864.

Counter (kau·ntəɹ), *sb.*[5] 1809. [– Fr. *contre*, corresp. to It. *contro*, subst. use of the prep. (see prec.).] **1.** *Fencing.* A name applied to all circular parries. Called also *c.-parry*, †*-parade*, †*-caveating parade.* **2.** *Pugilism.* A blow delivered as the adversary leads off 1861.

Counter (kau·ntəɹ), *sb.*[6] 1841. [Short for COUNTERFORT.] *Shoemaking.* The piece of stiff leather forming the back part of a shoe or boot round the heel.

Counter (kau·ntəɹ), *sb.*[7] 1869. *Mus.* Short for COUNTER-TENOR; also any voice part set in contrast to a principal melody.

Counter, *sb.*[8] 1881. *Mining.* Short for COUNTER-LODE.

Counter (kau·ntəɹ), *a.* 1596. [Arising chiefly from COUNTER- *pref.*] Acting in opposition; lying or tending in the opposite direction; opposed, opposite; duplicate, serving as a check. Mostly *attrib.*

C. orders 1780. The c. doctrine SIR W. HAMILTON, side TENNYSON, sect DE QUINCEY. A c. episcopate BP. WILBERFORCE.

Counter (kau·ntəɹ), *v.*[1] ME. [In senses 1, 2, aphet. f. ACOUNTER, ENCOUNTER; in later senses, cf. COUNTER- *pref.*, and COUNTER *sb.*[5] 2.] † **1.** *trans.* To meet –1813. **2.** *trans.* To encounter ME.; *intr.* (constr. *with*) ME. **3.** *trans.* (*fig.*) To go counter to ME. † **4.** *intr.* (*fig.*) To engage in contest, dispute *against, with* –1589. **5.** *Boxing.* To strike with a counterblow (*trans.* and *intr.*). Also *fig.* 1857.

3. To all which Matters. .his Answer countered every Design of the Interrogations NORTH. **5.** Of course I countered him there with tremendous effect HUGHES.

† **Counter,** *v.*[2] ME. [f. Fr. *contre* against; cf. Fr. *contre-chanter* in same sense, and COUNTER *sb.*[7]] *Mus.* To sing an accompaniment to a melody or plain-song –1562.

Counter (kau·ntəɹ), *adv.* ME. [– OFr. *countre* :– L. *contra* adv. and prep. against, in return. Due mainly to analysis of verbs, etc., in COUNTER-.] **1.** In the opposite direction; back again. Also *fig.* † **2.** In full face –1654. **3.** *fig.* In opposition; contrary 1643. † **4.** In opposite directions to each other –1704.

1. Phr. *To hunt, run, go c.*: *i.e.* in a direction opposite to that taken by the game. *Haml.* IV. v. 110. **3.** Let us go c. to tradition rather than to Scripture J. H. NEWMAN.

Cou·nter-, *pref.* [– AFr. *countre-*, (O)Fr. *contre* :– L. *contra-* CONTRA-.] Often viewed as an independent element, written separately, and practically treated as an adjective; see COUNTER *a.*

I. *verbs*, as COUNTERACT, COUNTERMINE, -MURE, q.v. (Stress on the root-word.)

II. *sbs.* (and *adjs.*) **1.** With sense '(actor or action) against or in opposition', as in *c.-exercise, -latration* (barking against), etc. **2.** Done, directed, or acting against, in opposition to, as a rejoinder or reply to another thing of the same kind already made or in existence; as in *c.-address, -affirmation*, etc. (Stress on the prefix.) Also with agent-nouns, as *C.-appellant.* **3.** Acting in reversal of a former action; as in C.-REVOLUTION. **4.** Reciprocal; as in *c.-assurance*, etc. **5.** Opposite locally; as C.-SEA, -SLOPE, -FISSURE, q.v. **6.** Crossing, making an angle with; as in C.-LODE. **7.** Forming the opposite one of two, as C.-BALANCE, -FOIL, -POISE, etc.; or constituting a second thing of the same kind standing opposite, parallel to, or side by side with the original, as C.-EARTH, *c.-branch, -pillar*; or denoting the duplicate, substitute, or that which is the 'second' of another, = *rear-, sub-*; as in *c.-base*, etc., C.-DRAIN [cf. †*contre-master*, a boatswain.] **8.** Running counter (to something else); as in *c.-hypothesis, -interest, -tendency*, etc. (The stress is usually equal.) **9.** In prepositional combination with an object: **a.** Against, ANTI-; as C.-NATURAL *a.* contrary to nature. **b.** False, counterfeit, pseudo-, ANTI-[1], as *c.-apostle, -taste*, etc. **10.** Mutually opposed, reciprocal, as C.-CHANGE, reciprocal exchange; C.-BATTERY, etc.; also *c.-curses, -ferments*, etc. **11.** *Mus.* See CONTRA-. **12.** *Mil.* Applied to works erected to act against the works of the enemy; as in C.-APPROACH, etc. **13.** *Her.* (*adjs.*) **a.** Turned in the contrary direction or in contrary directions, as C.-PASSANT, -SALIENT. **b.** On the two opposite sides, as *c.-indented*, etc., C.-EMBATTLED, -FLEURY. **c.** Having the tinctures reversed, as C.-ERMINE. **d.** Having two ordinaries of the same nature opposite to each other, so that colour is opposed to metal, and metal to colour: cf. *counterchanged* (see COUNTERCHANGE *v.*), etc.

Counter-acquittance; see COUNTER- II. 4.

Counteract (kauntəræ·kt), *v.* 1678. [COUNTER- I.] † **1.** To act in opposition to; to oppose –1832. **2.** To hinder or defeat by contrary action 1678.

2. Neither knowledge nor philosophy is..sufficient to c. the effect of human frailty SIR B. BRODIE. Hence **Countera·ctant** *sb.* a counteracting agency or force. **Countera·cter, -or. Countera·ction,** action in opposition to action, resistance; a counteracting influence or force. **Countera·ctive** *a.* tending to c.; *sb.* a counteracting agent or force. **Countera·ctively** *adv.*

Counter-a·gency. 1838. [COUNTER- II. 1.] Agency in opposition *to*. So **Counter-a·gent,** a counteractant.

Cou·nter-approa:ch. Usu. in *pl.* 1678. [– Fr. *contre-approche*. See COUNTER- II. 12.] *Mil.* A work constructed by the besieged to check and command the works of the besiegers.

Cou·nter-arch, *sb.* 1726. [COUNTER- II. 7.] **a.** An inverted arch opposite to another arch. **b.** An arch connecting counterforts at the top. Hence **Counter-a·rch** *v.* to furnish with a c.

Cou·nter-attra:ction. 1763. [COUNTER- II. 2, 8.] Attraction of a contrary tendency. So **Counter-attractive** *a.* having counter-attractions.

Counterbalance (kau·ntəɹbæ:lăns), *sb.* Also with hyphen. 1580. [COUNTER- II. 7.] † **1.** The opposite scale of a balance –1581. **2.** A weight used to balance another weight; *spec.* that used to balance the weight of a rotating or ascending and descending part, so as to make it easily moved 1611. **3.** *fig.* A power which balances the effect of a contrary one 1640.

3. Freedom was in his eyes a c. to poverty, discord, and war 1876.

Counterbalance (kau:ntəɹbæ·lăns), *v.* 1603. [COUNTER- I.] **1.** To act as a counterbalance to; to counterpoise. **2.** *fig.* To neutralize the effect of, by a contrary power or influence 1636.

2. A meeting-place to counter-balance the alehouse GEO. ELIOT.

† **Cou·nterband.** *rare.* 1611. = COUNTERBOND –1678.

† **Counter-ba·rry,** *a.* 1611. [–(O)Fr. *contrebarré*; see COUNTER- II. 13 d, BARRY *a.*] *Her.* Barry per pale counterchanged –1751.

Cou·nter-ba:ttery. 1592. [COUNTER- II. 1, 2, 10.] † **1.** A counter-attack with artillery –1670. Also *fig.* **2.** A battery raised against another. Also *fig.* 1603.

Cou·nter-beam. 1874. *Printing.* A beam connected to the platen by rods, by which the reciprocating motion is communicated to the platen.

Cou·nter-bi:ll. 1598. [COUNTER- II. 2, 7.] † **a.** The counterpart or duplicate of a bill. **b.** A (parliamentary) bill forming a set-off to another.

Counterblast (kau·ntəɹblast). 1567. [COUNTER- II. 2.] **a.** A blast blown in opposition to another. **b.** A strong declaration against something.

b. A Counterblaste to Tobacco (*title*) JAS. I.

Counterblow (kau·ntəɹblōᵘ:), *sb.* 1655. (COUNTER- II. 2, 4.) A return blow; the back-stroke of a rebound.

Counterbond (kau·ntəɹbǫ:nd). 1594. [COUNTER- II. 4.] A bond to indemnify one who has entered into a bond for another.

Counter-bore, *v.*; see COUNTER- I.

Cou·nter-brace, *sb.* 1823. [COUNTER- II. 2, 5.] **a.** A brace which counteracts the strain of another brace. **b.** *Naut.* The lee-brace of the fore-topsail-yard, when in tacking it is counter-braced to help to bring the ship round.

Cou:nter-bra·ce, *v.* 1867. [COUNTER I.] *Naut.* To brace the head-yards one way, and the after-yards another, so that the sails' counteract each other.

† **Cou·nterbuff,** *sb.* 1575. [COUNTER- II. 2, 10.] **1.** A blow in return or in the contrary direction –1641. **2.** A rebuff –1678. **3.** An encounter –1656. Hence **Cou·nterbuff** *v. arch.*, to give a c. to.

Counter-carte [f. COUNTER *sb.*⁵ + CARTE².] (*Fencing*); see COUNTER *sb.*⁵

† **Cou·nter-cast.** [COUNTER- II. 1.] An antagonistic artifice. SPENSER.

† **Cou·nter-ca:ster.** [COUNTER *sb.*³ 1.] One who reckons with counters; 'a word of contempt for an arithmetician' (J.). *Oth.* I. i. 31.

† **Cou·nterchange,** *sb.* 1579. [– Fr. *contre-change* = It. *contracambio*; see COUNTER II. 2, 4, 10.] **1.** Exchange –1706; equivalent return –1661. **2.** Transposition –1622.

Counterchange (kau:ntəɹ,tʃē·ndʒ), *v.* 1598. [– Fr. *contrechanger*; see COUNTER- I.] † **1.** *trans.* To exchange –1646. **2.** To change to the opposite (position, state, quality); to transpose 1613. **3.** *Her.* To interchange or reverse the tinctures; *transf.* and *fig.* to chequer 1614.

2. When they are counterchanged the Ranter becomes an Hypocrite, and the Hypocrite an able Ranter S. BUTLER. **3.** Witch-elms that c. the floor Of this flat lawn with dusk and bright TENNYSON. So **Cou:ntercha·nged** *ppl. a. Her.* Of a charge: Having the tinctures reversed; transmuted; also *transf.*

Countercharge (kau·ntəɹ,tʃā:dʒ), *sb.* 1706. [COUNTER- II. 2.] A charge brought in opposition to another, or against the accuser. So **Cou:ntercha·rge** *v.* 1611. **a.** To bring a charge against. † **b.** To oppose with a contrary charge. **c.** To charge contrariwise.

Cou·ntercharm, cou·nter-cha:rm, *sb.* 1601. [COUNTER- II. 2, 9.] A counteracting charm. So **Cou:ntercha·rm** *v.* to neutralize the effect of a charm upon; to affect with an opposing charm.

Countercheck, counter-check (kau·ntəɹ,tʃek), *sb.* 1559. [COUNTER- II. 1, 2.] † **1.** A check in return for another –1706. **2.** A check that arrests the course of anything 1595. **3.** A check that controls a check 1832.

1. If againe, it was not well cut, he wold say, I lie: this is call'd the counter-checke quarrelsome SHAKS.

Countercheck (kau:ntəɹ,tʃe·k), *v.* 1587. [COUNTER- I.] † **1.** *trans.* To check in reply to a check or rebuke, or in opposition –1598. **2.** To arrest by counteraction 1590.

Counter-che·vroned, counter-che·vrony, *a.* 1727. [COUNTER- II. 13 d.] *Her.* Of a shield: Chevrony and divided pale-wise, the half chevrons being of alternate tinctures.

Cou·nter-clai:m, cou·nterclaim, *sb.* 1876. [COUNTER- II. 2.] A claim set up against another, or against the plaintiff. So **Cou:nter-clai·m, cou·nterclai:m** *v. trans.*, to claim as against a prior claim, or against the plaintiff; also *absol.*

Cou:nter-clo·ckwise, *a.* and *adv.* 1888. [†*Counter* prep.] In a direction counter to that of the movement of the hands of a clock.

Counter-co·loured, *ppl. a.* 1572. [COUNTER- II. 13 d.] *Her.* Having the opposite parts of different tinctures: counterchanged.

Counter-company (kau·ntəɹkǫ́mpōᵘ·ni), *a.* 1610. [COUNTER- II. 13 d, see COMPONÉ, COMPONY.] *Her.* Composed of two conjoined rows of squares of alternate tinctures. var. † **Counter-compo·ned** *ppl. a.*

Counter-cou·chant, -cou·rant (*Her.*); see COUNTER- II. 13 a, COUCHANT, COURANT *a.*

Cou·nter-cu:rrent, *sb.* 1684. [f. COUNTER- II. 2, 5.] An opposite current. So **Counter-cu·rrent** *a.* running counter.

Cou·nter-deed. 1727. [COUNTER- II. 2.] *Law.* A secret writing or a private act, which annuls or alters some more public act.

Cou:nter-disenga·ge, *v.* 1889. [f. COUNTER- I, after Fr. *contre-dégager.*] *Fencing.* To disengage at the same time as the adversary.

† **Cou:nterdisti·nct,** *a.* 1662. [app. after It. *contradistinto.*] = CONTRADISTINCT –1680. So † **Cou:nterdisti·nction,** † **Cou:nterdisti·nguish** *v.*

Cou·nter-drain. 1842. [COUNTER- II. 7.] A drain parallel to a canal or embanked watercourse, for collecting and passing on the soakage water.

† **Counter-draw·,** *v.* 1727. [COUNTER- I.] To copy a design, etc., by means of oiled paper or other transparent material.

Cou·nter-earth. 1857. [COUNTER- II. 7: a tr. of Gr. ἀντίχθων.] An opposite or secondary Earth, in the Pythagorean system; cf. ANTICHTHON.

Cou:nter-emba·ttled, *ppl. a.* 1863. [COUNTER- II. 13 b.] *Her.* Of an ordinary: Embattled on opposite sides.

Counter-embowed (*Her.*); see COUNTER- II. 13 b, EMBOW.

Cou·nter-e:rmine. 1727. [COUNTER- II. 13 c.] *Her.* The reverse of ermine; = ERMINES.

Cou·nter-e:vidence. 1665. [COUNTER- II. 2.] Evidence tending to rebut other evidence.

Cou·nter-exte:nsion. 1860. [COUNTER- II. 5.] *Surg.* The pulling or holding of the upper part of a limb, etc., towards the trunk, while extension is practised on the lower part. So **Cou:nter-exte·nd** *v.* 1656.

Counter-faced (*Her.*) = COUNTER-FESSED

Cou·nter-fa:ller. 1836. [COUNTER- II. 7.] *Spinning.* In a mule, a wire which passes beneath the yarns, when pressed down by the faller-wire, so as to keep the tension uniform. Also *attrib.*

† **Cou·nterfei:sance.** 1590. [– OFr. *contrefaisance*, f. *contrefaire* COUNTERFEIT *v.*; see -ANCE.] The action of counterfeiting; deceit, dissimulation, fraud, imposture –1656.

Counterfeit (kau·ntəɹfit, -fīt), *a.* (*pa. pple.*) and *sb.* ME. [– OFr. *countrefet*, *-fait* (mod. *contrefait*), pa. pple. of *contrefaire* – Rom. (med.L.) *contrafacere* (cf. late L. *contrafactio* contrast), f. *contra* COUNTER- + *facere* make.]

† **A.** as *pa. pple.* Forged –1631; made to a pattern –1547; disguised CAXTON.

B. *adj.* **1.** Made in imitation of something else, 'imitation'; spurious, sham, base (*esp.* of coin) 1449; of writings: Forged ME. **2.** Of things immaterial: Pretended, false ME.; †disguised SWIFT. **3.** Of persons: Sham 1530; †false, deceitful –1732. † **4.** Deformed –1575. † **5.** Represented in a picture (or *transf.* in writing); portrayed –1838.

1. A Bait, which..proves but a c. Fly BOYLE. **2.** These C. Terrours often grow..to be Real 1718. **3.** This counterfeight Herault HALL. Fabulous or c. writers BP. BERKELEY. **5.** *Haml.* III. iv. 54. Hence **Cou·nterfeit-ly** *adv.*, **-ness.**

C. *sb.* **1.** A false or spurious imitation ME; a forgery 1613. † **2.** One who pretends to be another; a pretender, an imposter –1768. **3.** † A representation in painting, sculpture, etc.; an image, portrait –1843; *fig.* a copy (*arch.*) 1587. † **4.** A misshapen person –1578.

1. Neuer call a true peece of Gold a C. 1 *Hen. IV*, II. iv. 540. Els Justice..were..a fals counterfet of that impartial and Godlike vertue MILT. **3.** What finde I here? Faire Portias c. *Merch. V.* III. ii. 115.

Counterfeit (kau·ntəɹfit, -fīt), *v.* ME. [– AFr. *countrefeter*, f. *countrefet* pa. pple.; see prec.] **1.** *trans.* To make an imitation of, imitate (with intent to deceive); to forge. † **2.** To disguise, falsify –1722. **3.** To put on (with intent to deceive) the appearance of; to feign, simulate ME. † **4.** To pretend to be (a person, etc.); to personate –1622. **5.** *intr.* To feign, practise deceit ME. **6.** *trans.* To take, receive, or have the appearance of; to imitate, resemble, be like. (Without implying deceit.) ME. † **7.** To copy, make a copy of –1621. † **8.** To depict, delineate, portray –1660.

1. To c. a seal THIRLWALL, coins JEVONS, Mans voice MILT., a Letter 1726, a certificate 1873. **2.** I counterfeited my voice DE FOE. **3.** To c. a smiling welcome BP. HALL, death CARLYLE. **5.** Are you not mad indeed, or do you but c. *Twel. N.* IV. ii. 122. **6.** Where glowing embers through the room Teach light to c. a gloom MILTON.

Hence **Cou·nterfeiter,** one who makes fraudulent imitations; *spec.* a coiner; a dissembler; an imitator (without deceit).

Cou:nter-fe·ssed, *ppl. a.* 1486. [COUNTER- II. 13 d.] *Her.* Barry and divided pale-wise, the half bars being of alternate tinctures. var. **Counter-fe·ssy** *a.*

Cou·nter-fi:ssure. 1656. [COUNTER- II. 5.] *Surg.* A fracture of the skull occurring opposite the place where a blow was received.

Counterfleury, -flory (kau:ntəɹ,fl·ōri, -flōᵊ·ri), *a.* 1572. [COUNTER- II. 13 b.] *Her.* Of an ordinary: Having flowers on each side set opposite each other in pairs. So **Counter-flow·ered** *ppl. a.*

Counterfoil (kau·ntəɹfoil). 1706. [COUNTER- II. 7.] **1.** A complementary part of a bank cheque, receipt, or the like, containing the particulars of the principal part, to be retained by the person who gives out that part. † **2.** = COUNTERSTOCK –1708.

Cou·nter-fo:rce, cou·nterforce. 1609. [COUNTER- II. 1, 2.] A force acting in opposition to another.

Counterfort (kau·ntəɹfōᵊɹt). 1590. [– Fr. *contrefort* (OFr. *-forz*), f. OFr. *contreforcier* prop, buttress.] **1.** *Arch.* and *Fortif.* A buttress to support and strengthen a wall or terrace. **2.** *transf.* A lateral spur of a mountain 1847. † **3.** A fort raised by the besiegers. *nonce-use.* 1640.

Cou·nter-gauge, *sb.* Also **-gage, -guage** (a mere blunder). 1727. [COUNTER- II. 7.] 'An adjustable, double-pointed gage for transferring the measurement of a mortise to the end of a stick where a tenon is to be made, or *vice versa*' (Knight).

Cou·nter-gea:r. [COUNTER- II. 7.] The driving gear whence power is communicated by a belt, etc., to the separate machine driven by it.

Cou·nter-gua:rd, cou·nterguard, *sb.* 1523. [– Fr. *contregarde*; see COUNTER- II. 7, 12.] † **1.** An extra guard to check another, or to be a reserve –1651. † **2.** *Fortif.* 'A narrow detached rampart, placed immediately in front of an important work, to protect it from being breached' (Stocqueler) 1591. **3.** Part of a sword-hilt 1874. So † **Cou·ntergua:rd** *v.* to guard against (danger); to safeguard.

Cou·nter-he:m, *sb.* 1882. [COUNTER- II. 7.] *Needlework.* A hem parallel and opposite to a first hem. So **Counter-hem** *v.*

Cou·nter-indica:tion = CONTRA-INDICATION.

Cou:nter-i:nfluence, *sb.* 1834. [COUNTER- II. 2.] An influence in the opposite direction. So † **Cou:nter-i·nfluence** *v.* to affect with a counter-influence –1681.

Cou:nter-interroga·tion. 1808. [COUNTER- II. 2.] Cross-examination.

Cou:nter-i·rritant. 1854. [COUNTER- II. 2.] *Med.* An appliance used to produce irritation of the surface of the body, in order to counteract disease of more deeply-seated or distant parts. So **Counter-i·rritate** *v.*; **-irrita·tion,** irritation artifically produced in order to counteract the action of disease.

Cou·nter-jumper. *colloq.* 1841. [f. COUNTER *sb.*[3]] *lit.* One who jumps over a counter; used contemptuously of a shopman.

Cou·nter-lath, *sb.* 1659. [COUNTER- II. 6, 7.] *Roofing.* A lath placed by eye between every two gauged ones.

† **Cou·nter-le:tter.** 1603. [COUNTER- II. 2.] **1.** A letter of reply. **2.** A letter countermanding a letter; a counter-deed –1818.

Cou·nter-lode. [COUNTER- II. 6; cf. CAUNTER.] *Mining.* A lode running across a main lode.

† **Cou·nterly,** *a.* and *adv.* 1486. [f. COUNTER *a.* or *adv.* + -LY.] *Her. adj.* Of the shield, etc.: Divided into two parts of different tinctures –1586. *adv.* In a way that is counter to another; counterwise –1688.

Counterman (kau·ntəɹmæ̆n). 1853. [f. COUNTER *sb.*[3]] A shopman who serves at the counter.

Countermand (kau:ntəɹma·nd), *v.* ME. [– OFr. *contremander* – med.L. *contramandare*, f. L. *contra* CONTRA- + *mandare* command.] **1.** To command the opposite of; to revoke, annul by a contrary command. Also *intr.* or *absol.* † **2.** To command in reversal of a previous command –1568. **3.** To order back 1464. **4.** To revoke an order for 1552. † **5.** To go counter to –1662; to forbid –1658; to counteract –1711; to control –1654.

1. To declare his will to day, and c. it to morrow 1677. **3.** Our regiment is countermanded GOLDSM. **4.** To c. a movement THIRLWALL. Hence **Counterma·ndable** *a.* that can be countermanded.

Countermand (kauntəɹma·nd), *sb.* 1548. [– OFr. *contremand*, f. *contremander*; see prec.] **1.** A contrary command revoking or annulling a previous one. **2.** *Law.* An act that makes void something previously executed 1628. † **3.** A prohibition –1689.

1. Haue you no c. for Claudio yet? But he must die to morrow? *Meas. for M.* IV. ii. 95.

Countermarch (kau·ntəɹmāːɹtʃ), *sb.* 1598. [COUNTER- II. 5.] **1.** A march back. Also *fig.* † **2.** *Mil.* An evolution by which the front and rear, or the right and left file, of a body of cavalry or infantry change places, the original order of the files being retained –1884.

Countermarch (kau·ntəɹmāːɹtʃ), *v.* 1625. [COUNTER- I.; cf. prec.] **1.** *intr.* To march back 1644. **2.** *Mil.* To execute a countermarch (sense 2) 1625. **3.** *trans.* To cause to countermarch 1658.

2. The Regiment in Line is required to c. on its centre 1832. Hence **Cou·ntermarcher.**

Countermark (kau·ntəɹmāɹk), *sb.* 1502. [– Fr. *contremarque*; cf. COUNTER- II. 7.] **1.** An additional mark put on something that has been marked before, for greater security, etc. † **2.** A mark, letter, etc., on a plan, corresponding to one in a description 1665. **3.** An artificial cavity made in the teeth of horses that have outgrown the natural mark, to disguise their age 1727.

1. In goldsmiths works, etc. the *counter-mark* is the mark, or punchion, of the hall, or company, to shew the metal is standard, added to that of the artificer 1727. So **Cou:nterma·rk** *v.* to furnish with a c.

† **Cou·nter-marque.** 1502. [COUNTER- II. 2.] Reprisals against *Letters of Marque* –1755. So † **Counter-mart** (in same sense).

Countermine (kau·ntəɹməin), *sb.* 1548. [COUNTER- II. 2, 12. Cf. Fr. *contremine* (XVI), It. *contramina* (XVI).] **1.** *Mil.* A mine or subterranean excavation made by the defenders of a fortress, to intercept a mine made by the besiegers. **b.** A submarine mine sunk where it may explode the enemy's mines by the concussion of its explosion 1880. **2.** *fig.* A plot designed to frustrate another 1570.

2. With secret countermines and open weapons of Law 1611.

Cou:ntermi·ne, *v.* 1580. [f. prec.; cf. Fr. *contreminer*, It. *contraminare*, Sp. *contraminar.*] **1.** *Mil.intr.* To make a countermine 1583; *trans.* to make a countermine against 1684; in naval war: To lay down countermines 1880. **2.** *fig.* To defeat by a counterplot 1580. ¶ Erron. for *countermure* 1592.

2. Gods countermining of Hamans plot 1649.

Cou·nter-mo:tion. 1606. [COUNTER- II. 2, 5.] **1.** Motion in the opposite direction. **2.** A motion or resolution contrary to one already proposed 1893.

Cou·nter-move. 1858. [COUNTER- II. 2.] A move in opposition to another. (Orig. a term of chess.) So **Cou·nter-mo:vement,** a movement in opposition.

Countermure (kau·ntəɹmiūᵊɹ), *sb.* 1524. [–(O)Fr. *contremur*, f. *contre* = COUNTER II. 7 + *mur* wall.] *Mil.* A wall raised within (or outside) another wall for additional defence or to assist the besiegers. Also *fig.* Hence **Cou:ntermu·re** *v.* to defend with a c.; *intr.* to raise a c.

Counter-naiant, *a. Her.*; see COUNTER- II. 13 a, NAIANT.

† **Counterna·tural,** *a.* 1666. *rare.* = CONTRANATURAL.

Counter-nebulé, *a. Her.*; see COUNTER- II. 13 b, NEBULE.

Cou·nter-o:pening. 1611. [COUNTER- II. 5.] An opening opposite another.

† **Cou·nterpace.** 1580. [COUNTER- II. 5.] **1.** A movement in a contrary direction. **2.** A step against something –1731.

Cou·nter-pa:led, *a.* 1727. [COUNTER- II. 13d.] *Her.* Of a shield: Parted into an even number of divisions pale-wise, and divided fess-wise, the tinctures of the upper and lower halves being counterchanged. var. **Cou·nter-pa:ly.**

† **Cou·nterpane**[1]. 1475. [app. – AFr. *countrepan*, f. *contre-* + OFr. *pan* piece, part; cf. COUNTER-PAWN.] **1.** *Law.* The counterpart of an indenture –1693. Also *fig.* **2.** = COUNTERPART 2–4. –1670.

1. Read, Scribe, gi' me the Counterpaine B. JONS.

Counterpane[2] (kau·ntəɹpĕn, -peⁱn). 1603. [alt., by assim. to PANE *sb.*[1], of COUNTERPOINT *sb.*[2]] The outer covering of a bed, generally woven in raised figures, quilted, or the like; a coverlet.

On which, a Tissue counterpoyne was cast DRAYTON.

Counter-parade, -parry [f. COUNTER *sb.*[5] + PARADE *sb.* 6, PARRY *sb.*] (*Fencing*); see COUNTER *sb.*[5]

Cou·nter-paro:le. 1823. [COUNTER- II. 7.] An extra parole or password given in time of alarm. Cf. COUNTERSIGN *sb.*

Counterpart (kau·ntəɹpāɹt). 1617. [f. COUNTER- II. 7 + PART, after (O)Fr. *contrepartie*; see next.] **1.** *Law.* The opposite part of an INDENTURE, q.v.; each of the indented parts in its relation to the other; *esp.* that which is not the original. † **2.** *gen.* A duplicate or exact copy –1712. **3.** *fig.* A person or thing appearing to be an exact copy of another 1680. **4.** One of two parts which fit and complete each other; a person or thing forming a natural complement to another 1634. **5.** *Mus.* A part written to accompany another. [COUNTER- II. 11.] 1706. Also *attrib.*

1. A c. of the lease is to be executed by the lessee 1858. **4.** Oh c. Of our soft sex; well are you made our lords DRYDEN.

† **Cou·nter-pa:rty.** 1557. [–(O)Fr. *contrepartie*; cf. prec.] An opposite party in a lawsuit or contest –1624.

Cou:nter-pa·ssant, *a.* 1610. [COUNTER- II. 13 a.] *Her.* Passant in opposite directions.

† **Cou·nter-pawn.** 1611. [f. COUNTER- II. 4 + *pawn* but poss. – AFr. *countre-pan*; see COUNTER-PANE[1].] = COUNTERPANE[1] 1. –1634.

Cou·nter-penalty. 1847. [COUNTER- II. 2; tr. Gr. ἀντιτίμησις.] *Gr. Antiq.* The penalty which an accused person who had been pronounced guilty suggested for himself in opposition to that called for by the accuser.

Cou·nterplea. 1565. [COUNTER- II. 2.] *Law.* A replication to a plea or request made, in which arguments are advanced why the same should not be admitted.

† **Counterplea·d,** *v.* ME. [– AFr. *contrepleder*, f. *contre* + *pleder* PLEAD.] **1.** *Law.* To plead in opposition to; to make a counterplea –1642. Also *fig.* **2.** *gen.* To oppose in argument; to contradict. (ME. only.)

Cou·nterplot, *sb.* 1611. [COUNTER- II. 2, 1.] **1.** A plot contrived to defeat another. † **2.** A plotting against. MORE.

1. Plot and counter-plot, egad! SHERIDAN.

Cou·nterplo:t, *v.* 1597. [COUNTER- I.] **1.** *intr.* To devise a counterplot *against.* **2.** *trans.* To plot against; to frustrate by a counterplot 1662.

2. To c. that infamous trickster 1887.

Counterpoint (kau·ntəɹpoint), *sb.*[1] 1530. [–(O)Fr. *contrepoint* – med.L. *contrapunctum, cantus contrapunctus* 'song pointed-against', the accompaniment being orig. noted by points or pricks set against those of the plainsong melody. In senses 3 and 4, f. COUNTER- II. 2, 5, 7.] **1.** *Mus.* The melody added as accompaniment to a given melody or plain-song. Also *fig.* **2.** The art of adding one or more melodies as accompaniment to a plain-song according to certain rules; this style of composition 1597. † **3.** A contrary point (in an argument) –1626. **4.** The opposite point; † the antithesis 1599.

1. A rainy wind from 'twixt the trees arose, And sang a mournful c. to those MORRIS.

† **Cou·nterpoint,** *sb.*[2] 1450. [– OFr. *contrepointe*, alt. of. **coutrepointe, cou(l)tepointe* :– med.L. *culcit(r)a puncta* 'quilted mattress', i.e. *culcit(r)a* cushion, mattress, and *puncta*, fem. pa. pple. of *pungere* prick, stab.] A quilted cover for a bed; a COUNTERPANE[2] –1694.

Counterpoi·nted, -poi·nté, *a.* 1727. [– Fr. *contrepointé*, f. *contre* against + *point* point.] *Her.* Said of two chevrons in one escutcheon when they meet in the points.

Counterpoise (kau·ntəɹpoiz), *sb.* ME. [– OFr. *countrepeis, -pois* (mod. *contrepoids*), f. *contre* (COUNTER- II. 7) + *peis, pois* weight; see POISE *sb.*] **1.** A weight which balances another weight, or establishes equilibrium against a force. **2.** *transf.* and *fig.* That which serves as a counterbalance or set-off ME. **3.** The state of being balanced; equilibrium 1591. Also *fig.*

1. These. . are of the same weight, and therefore a counterpoize to each other SMEATON. **2.** Their

Second Nobles..are a Counterpoize to the Higher Nobility, that they grow not too Potent BACON. **3.** The pendulous round Earth, with ballanc't Aire In c. MILT.

Counterpoise (kau·ntəɹpoiz), *v.* [ME. *countrepese, -peise* – tonic stem of OFr. *contrepeser*; see COUNTER- II. 7, POISE *v.* In XV–XVII assim. to the sb.] **1.** *trans.* To balance by a weight on the opposite side or acting in opposition; to counterbalance 1566. **2.** *transf.* and *fig.* To balance in power, quality, or effect ME. † **3.** *intr.* To be equiponderant (*to, with, against*) –1561. **4.** *trans.* To bring into equilibrium (*lit.* and *fig.*) ME. **5.** To weigh (a thing) *with, i.e.* against (another) 1685. Also *absol.*

1. One shilling of siluer in those daies did counterpeise our common ounce 1577. **2.** And passed wo with ioie [to] countrepese CHAUCER.

Counterpoi·son, cou·nter-poi:son. *arch.* 1548. [– Fr. *contre poison*; see COUNTER- II. 8, 9.] **1.** An antidote. Also *fig.* **2.** An opposite poison 1789.

Cou·nter-po:le. 1839. [COUNTER- II. 5.] The opposite pole.

Counterpo·se, *v. rare.* = CONTRAPOSE.

Counter-po·tent, *a.* (*sb.*) 1610. [See COUNTER- II. 13.] *Her.* Of a 'fur': Having the potents arranged as in COUNTERVAIR.

Cou·nter-pre:ssure. 1651. [COUNTER- II. 2, 5.] Contrary pressure.

† **Cou·nter-pri:ce.** 1671. [tr. Gr. ἀντίλυτρον in 1 Tim. 2:6.] A ransom –1714.

Cou·nter-proo:f, *sb.* 1610. [COUNTER- II. 7, 8.] † **1.** Proof to the contrary. **2.** *Printing.* 'A print taken off from another fresh printed; which, by being passed through the press, gives the figure of the former, but inverted' (Chambers). So **Counterpro·ve** *v.* †to bring proof contrary to; to take a counterproof of.

Counter-qua·rtered, *a.* 1562. [COUNTER- II. 13.] *Her.* **1.** Of a charge: Borne counter-changed upon a field quarterly. **2.** Of an escutcheon: Quarterly, with each quarter also quartered. var. **Counter-qua·rterly** (in sense 2).

Counter-raguled, -raguly, -rampant, *Her.*; see COUNTER- II. 13, RAGULY, RAMPANT.

Cou·nter-reforma:tion. 1840. [COUNTER- II. 3.] Applied in *Hist.* to the movement in the Church of Rome which followed on the Protestant Reformation.

Cou·nter-revolu:tion. 1793. [COUNTER- II. 3.] A revolution opposed to a previous revolution or reversing its results.

Counter-ripo·ste. 1889. [– Fr. *contre-riposte*; see COUNTER *sb.*[5]] *Fencing.* A riposte delivered, still on the lunge, after parrying the adversary's first riposte.

† **Cou·nter-ro:ll,** *sb.* 1613. [– obs. Fr. *contrerolle*; see CONTROL and COUNTER- II. 7.] A copy of a roll or document, kept for purposes of checking –1863. So † **Cou:nterro·lment,** the entering in a counter-roll.

Cou·nter-round. ? *Obs.* 1590. [– Fr. *contre-ronde*, f. *contre* against + *ronde* ROUND *sb.*[1] III. 4.] *Mil.* A patrol of officers to inspect or check the rounds; also *concr.* these officers as a body.

Counter-sa·lient, *a.* 1610. [COUNTER- II. 13 a.] *Her.* Said of two animals borne as charges: Salient in opposite directions.

Cou·nter-sca:le. 1645. [COUNTER- II. 7.] The opposite scale (of the balance); chiefly *fig.*

Counterscarp (kau·ntəɹskāɹp), *sb.* 1571. [– Fr. *contrescarpe* – It. *contrascarpa*; see SCARP.] *Fortif.* The outer wall or slope of the ditch which supports the covered way; sometimes the whole covered way with the glacis. Also *transf.* and *fig.* var. **Counterscarf(e).**

† **Cou·nter-scu:ffle.** 1628. [COUNTER- II. 10.] A scuffle between opposing parties or persons –1682.

† **Cou·nter-sea:.** 1599. [COUNTER- II. 2, 5.] A sea running against the course of a ship, or against another sea –1610.

Cou·nter-sea:l, *sb.* Now *Hist.* 1611. [– OFr. *contre-seel*; cf. COUNTER- II. 7.] A smaller seal impressed upon the reverse of a main seal for further security, or sanction. Also, the reverse side of a seal. Hence † **Cou:nter-sea·l** *v.* to seal with a c.

Cou:nter-secu·re, *v.* 1667. [COUNTER- I.] **1.** *trans.* To secure (any one) against the risk he incurs by becoming security for another. **2.** To give additional security to 1796.

2. You are giving that pledge from the throne, and engaging parliament to c. it BURKE. So **Cou:ntersecu·rity,** security given in return; security given to any one to cover his risk in becoming surety.

Cou·nterse:nse. 1645. [– Fr. *contresens*, f. *contre* against + *sens* sense.] A meaning opposed to the true sense.

Countershaft (kau·ntəɹʃaft). 1864. [COUNTER- II. 7.] *Mech.* An intermediate shaft driven from a main shaft for giving motion to a particular machine.

Countersign (kau·ntəɹsəin), *sb.* 1591. [– Fr. *contresigne* – It. *contrasegno*; cf. COUNTER- II. 4.] **1.** A sign or signal used in reply to another sign; *spec.* a private signal, usually a word, to be given to a soldier on guard by any one entitled to pass 1598. **2.** = COUNTERMARK.

Countersign (kau:ntəɹsəi·n), *v.* 1662. [– Fr. *contresigner*; cf. COUNTER- I.] **1.** *trans.* To sign opposite to, alongside of, or in addition to, another signature; to add one's signature to (a document already signed by another) for authentication or confirmation 1696. Also *fig.* † **2.** To mark with a particular sign for authentication, identification, or reference –1665.

1. Charters are signed by the king, and countersigned by a secretary of state or lord chancellor 1806. So **Cou:nter-si·gnature,** the action of countersigning.

Countersink (kau·ntəɹsiŋk), *sb.* 1816. [f. next.] **1.** A tool for countersinking. **2.** The conical enlargement of the upper part of a hole for receiving the head of a screw or bolt.

Countersink (kau:ntəɹsi·ŋk), *v.* Pa. t. and pple. **-sunk.** 1816. [Cf. COUNTER- II. 7.] **1.** *trans.* To enlarge the upper part of (a hole) to receive the head of a screw, bolt, etc.; to bevel the edge of a hole 1831. **2.** To sink the head of (a screw, bolt, etc.) in a depression made to receive it, so that it lies flush with the surface.

Cou·nterslope, *sb.* 1838. [COUNTER- II. 5.] **1.** The opposite slope of a hill, a ridge, etc.; a slope in the opposite direction 1853. **2.** An overhanging slope. So **Cou:nterslo·pe** *v.* to slope on the opposite side.

Cou·nter-spe:ll. 1725. [COUNTER- II. 2, 9.] A spell against something; a spell to dissolve another.

Cou·nterstand, *sb.* [after It. *contrasto.*] Standing against. LONGF.

Cou·nter-sta:tement; see COUNTER- II. 2.

Cou·nter-ste:p. 1720. [COUNTER- II. 2, 5.] A step in opposition, or in the opposite direction.

† **Cou·ntersto:ck.** 1706. [COUNTER- II. 7.] That part of a tally retained by the payee –1708.

Counterstroke (kau·ntəɹstrōᵘk). 1596. [COUNTER- II. 1, 2, 5.] **1.** A stroke given in return. **2.** = CONTRECOUP 2. 1786.

Cou·ntersu:bject. 1854. [COUNTER- II. 11.] *Mus.* A subordinate melody, part of a fugue, written *against*, or as accompaniment to, the subject and answer.

Countersunk (kau·ntəɹsɒ:ŋk). 1794. [pa. pple. of COUNTERSINK *v.*] *ppl. a.* Of a hole: Cut to receive the head of a bolt, screw, etc. Of a bolt, screw, etc.: Sunk so as to lie flush with the surface. As *sb.* = COUNTERSINK *sb.* 2. 1794.

† **Cou·ntersway,** *sb.* [COUNTER- II. 5.] An exertion of opposing force. MILT. So † **Cou:ntersway·** *v. trans.*, to move forcibly to the opposite side; to counterweigh.

† **Cou·ntertai:l.** ME. [– OFr. *contretaille*; see COUNTER- II. 7, TAIL *sb.*[2] III.] **1.** = COUNTERSTOCK –1617. var. † **Cou·nterta:lly.** **2.** A counter-stroke. (ME. only.)

Phr. **At the c.**: in reply.

Counter-taste; see COUNTER- II. 9.

Counter-tendency, -term; see COUNTER-.

Counter-te·nor. ME. [– OFr. *contreteneur* – It. †*contratenore*; cf. med.L. *contratenens*; see COUNTER- II. 11.] *Mus.* **1.** A part higher in pitch than the tenor, sung by a high male voice; the alto. Also *fig.* **2.** A counter-tenor voice 1771. **3.** A singer with such a voice 1623. Also *attrib.*

Cou·nter-ti:de. 1570. [COUNTER- II. 5.] A tide running counter to the main current.

Counter-tierce (*Fencing*); see COUNTER *sb.*[5]

† **Cou·nter-time.** 1599. [tr. Fr. *contretemps.*] **1.** *Fencing.* A pass or thrust made at a wrong moment. Also *fig.* –1676. **2.** *Horsemanship.* Interruption by a horse of the cadence of movement, owing to bad horsemanship or to unruly disposition –1736.

Counter-trench; see COUNTER- II. 12.

Cou:nter-tri·pping, *a.* 1610. [COUNTER- II. 13.] *Her.* Said of two stags, hinds, etc.: Walking in opposite directions on the same plane. So **Cou:nter-tri·ppant.**

Cou·nter-tu:rn. 1589. [In senses 1 and 2, tr. Gr. ἀντιστροφή; in 3 and 4, f. COUNTER- II. 5.] † **1.** = ANTISTROPHE 1. B. JONS. † **2.** *Prosody.* The continued repetition of the same word at the end of successive clauses; = L. *conversio.* PUTTENHAM. **3.** A turn in the contrary direction 1744. **4.** An unexpected development of the plot of a play at the climax 1651.

Cou·nterty:pe. 1624. [COUNTER- II. 2, 7.] † **1.** = ANTITYPE. **2.** A parallel 1855. **3.** An opposite type 1880.

Countervail (kauntəɹvē^i·l), *v.* ME. [– AFr. *countrevaloir*, repr. L. *contra valēre* be of worth against; see VAIL *v.*[1]] † **1.** *trans.* To be equivalent to in value –1655. **2.** To equal (*arch.*) 1530; †to reciprocate –1633. **3.** To counterbalance 1547. Also *fig.* **4.** To make up for ME. **5.** *intr.* To avail *against*, †*with*, †*for* ME.; †to vie *with* –1581.

3. *fig.* No certificate of a judge was allowed ..to c. the oath of the jury BLACKSTONE. **5.** What name ..could c. against the High Priest of Science BREWSTER. Hence **Cou·ntervail** *sb.* that which countervails. † **Countervai·lable** *a.* to be set against as equivalent.

Countervair (kau:ntəɹvēᵊ·ɹ), *sb.* (*a.*) 1766. [COUNTER- II. 13.] *Her.* A variety of vair (one of the 'furs'), in which the bells or cups of the same tincture are placed base to base. So **Countervai·ry** *a.*

Countervalla·tion = CONTRAVALLATION.

† **Counterva·lue,** *v.* 1581. [COUNTER- I.] **1.** = COUNTERVAIL 1. –1656. **2.** *intr.* Of an accused person: To give a counter-estimate 1832.

Cou·nterview. 1590. [COUNTER- II. 7, 8.] † **1.** View from opposite sides –1780. **2.** The opposite opinion. (Better as two words.) 1852.

Counter-vote, etc.; see COUNTER- II. 2.

† **Cou:nter-wai·t,** *v.* ME. [– AFr. *countrewaiter*, OFr. *contreguaitier*, f. *contre* + *guaitier* WAIT, watch.] *trans.* To lie in wait against; to watch against –1602.

Cou·nter-wall. 1836. [COUNTER- II. 12.] A line of wall raised against the enemy's wall.

Counterweigh (kau:ntəɹwē^i·), *v.* ME. [COUNTER- I; cf. COUNTERPOISE *v.*] **1.** *trans.* To weigh (things) against each other; to balance. (Usually *fig.*) **2.** *intr.* To act as a counterpoise (*with, against*). *lit.* and *fig.* 1523. **3.** *trans.* To counterbalance 1825.

Counter-weight, counterweight (kau·ntəɹwē^it). 1693. [COUNTER- II. 7; cf. prec.] A counterbalancing weight. Also *fig.*

Cou:nterwhee·l, *v. rare.* 1659. [COUNTER- I.] To wheel round in the contrary direction.

Cou·nterwo:rk, *sb.* 1598. [COUNTER- II. 2, 12.] Any opposing work or operation; *spec.* in *Mil.* a work raised in opposition to those of the enemy.

Counterwork (kau:ntəɹwɒ·ɹk), *v.* Pa. t. and pa. pple. **-wrought** or **-worked.** 1602. [COUNTER- I.] **1.** *intr.* To work in opposition. **2.** *trans.* To work against; to counteract; frustrate 1628. Hence **Cou·nterworker,** a counteracter, an opponent.

Countess (kau·ntės). OE. [– OFr. *cuntesse, contesse* (mod. *comtesse*) :– med.L. *comitissa*, fem. of *comes, comit-*; see COUNT *sb.*[2], -ESS[1].] **1.** The wife or widow of a COUNT; in the peerage, the wife or widow of an EARL; also, a lady holding a position in her own right equal to that of count or earl. **2.** A middle size of roofing slate 1803.

Cou·nting, *vbl. sb.* Also **compting.** ME. [f. COUNT *v.* + -ING[1].] The action of COUNT *v.* *Comb.* **c.-house,** an office; now *spec.* a building or office in a commercial establishment, in which the book-keeping, correspondence, etc., are carried on; called also (chiefly in U.S.) a **c.-room.**

Countless (kau·ntlės), *a.* 1588. [f. COUNT *sb.*[1] + -LESS.] That cannot be counted: of number, less often of quantity or value.

One sweet kisse shall pay this comptlesse debt SHAKS.

Cou·ntour, -or. ME. [– AFr. *countour* lawyer = OFr. *conteör* :– L. *computator* (see COMPUTE, -OR 2.). See COUNTER *sb.*[2]] **1.** *Eng. Hist.* An accountant. (ME. only.) **2.** *Law.* A legal pleader, or serjeant-at-law; cf. COUNT *v.* Now *Hist.* ME.

Countre-, obs. f. COUNTER-.

Countrified, countryfied (kʌ·ntrifəid), *ppl. a.* 1653. [f. next + -ED[1].] **1.** Affected by or smacking of the country and its life; rustic. **2.** Of scenery: Rural 1756.

1. Miss Bell's a little countryfied THACKERAY.

Countrify (kʌ·ntrifəi), *v.* [f. next + -FY.] To make rural or rustic.

Country (kʌ·ntri). ME. [– OFr. *cuntrée* (mod. *contrée*) :– med.L., Rom. *contrata* (Leges Siciliæ), subst. use (sc. *terra* land) of fem. of adj. meaning 'lying opposite or facing one'. The original stress was on the final syllable, as still in ballads.] **1.** An expanse of land; a region, district. **2.** A tract or district having limits in relation to human occupation, *e.g.* owned by the same lord, or inhabited by people of the same race, dialect, occupation, etc. ME. **3.** The territory or land of a nation ME. **4.** The land of a person's birth, citizenship, residence, etc. ME. **5.** The rural districts as distinct from the town or towns; *occas.*, all outside the capital 1526. **6.** The people of a district or state; the nation ME. **7.** *Law.* Applied to a jury ME. **8.** *Naut.* A region of the sea; also, a station 1748. **9.** *Mining.* (*Cornwall.*) The rock in which a lode of ore occurs 1674. **10.** *attrib.* Of a country, district, or part of the world; national, native. Usu. with a possessive or demonstrative. Now *dial.* ME. **11.** Of or belonging to the rural districts 1525.

1. Marie wente into monteyne contre WYCLIF. **2.** The c. of the Mac-Gregors SCOTT. **4.** To weepe Ouer his Countries Wrongs 1 *Hen. IV*, IV. iii. 82. **5.** God made the c., and man made the town COWPER. **6.** And all countreys came into Egypt to Ioseph, for to buy corne *Gen.* 41:57. Phr. *To appeal* or *go to the c.*: to appeal to the constituencies from a vote of the House of Commons: see APPEAL *v.* **7.** When the prisoner has..for his trial put himself 'upon the country' (which c. the jury are) H. COX. **11.** A plain C.-fellow TRAPP. **C. cousin,** a cousin or relative of countrified habits; also *gen.* 1770.

Comb.: **c.-box,** small c.-house; **-dance** [cf. CONTRE-DANCE], an English dance of rural or native origin; *spec.* applied to dances in which a number of couples stand up face to face in two long lines, as in the *Sir Roger de Coverley*; **-fo:lk,** † compatriots; rustics; **-hou·se,** a house in the c.; a c.-seat; **c. party** (*Politics*): a party which advocates the interests and claims of the c. against the court, etc., or later of c. against town; **c.-peo:ple** = *country-folk*; **-sea·t,** the residence of a c. gentleman or nobleman; a c.-house; **-si·de,** = COUNTRY 2; the inhabitants of a tract of c.; **c. town,** a small town which forms the centre of a rural district, as dist. from a manufacturing town, etc.

Countryman (kʌ·ntrimĕn). ME. **1.** A native or inhabitant of a country or district. Often in *comb.* **2.** A man of one's own country; usu. with *possessive* ME. **3.** One who lives in the country; a husbandman 1577.

1. A Disease which seiz'd no Countrymen but English 1708. **2.** I am Welch you know, good Countriman SHAKS. So **Cou·ntry-wo:man.**

Countship (kau·nt,ʃip). 1703. [f. COUNT *sb.*[2] + -SHIP.] The office, dignity, domain, or jurisdiction of a count.

How his C. sulks BROWNING.

County[1] (kau·nti). ME. [– AFr. *counté*, OFr. *cunté*, *conté* (mod. *comté*) :– L. *comitatus*, f. *comes, comit-*; see COUNT *sb.*[2], -Y[5].] † **1.** The domain of a (foreign) count –1665. **2.** One of the territorial divisions of Great Britain and Ireland, forming an important unit for administrative, judicial, and political purposes. Cf. SHIRE. ME. In the United States, the political and administrative division next below the state 1683. **3.** *Eng. Hist.* The shire-moot, shire-court, county-court ME. **4.** The people of a county collectively; the county gentry or county families collectively 1647. **5.** *attrib.* Of a (or the) county; belonging or pertaining to a county 1656.

1. County palatine: *orig.* the dominion of a count or earl palatine; in England, a c. of which the earl or lord had originally royal privileges, with exclusive civil and criminal jurisdiction. The counties palatine are now *Cheshire* and *Lancashire*. **2.** Of the Old-English kingdoms several still survive as counties FREEMAN. **3.** Shires which haue and vse their Counties to bee holden euery six weekes *Act* 2–3 *Edw. VI*, c. 25.

Comb.: **c. borough:** = *county corporate* (see CORPORATE *ppl. a.* 4); **c. commissioner,** (*a*) a justice of the peace on the commission of a c.; (*b*) in *U.S.*, an elected administrative officer in many counties; **c. council,** a council which conducts the affairs of a c.; **c. court,** *orig.* = COUNTY[1] 3; *now*, a local judicial court for civil actions; hence **cou:nty-cou·rt** *v. colloq.* to sue in the county court: **c. family,** a family belonging to the nobility or gentry, having estates and a seat in the c.; **c. sessions,** the quarter sessions for a c.; **c. town,** the town which is the seat of the administration of a county.

† **Cou·nty**[2]. 1550. [app. an adoption of AFr. *counte*, or OFr. and It. *conte*, with unusual retention of the final vowel, and confused in form with COUNTY[1].] = COUNT *sb.*[2] –1848.

Coup (kaup), *sb.*[1] Now only *Sc.* ME. [Sense 1 – (O)Fr. *coup* (see COUP *sb.*[3]); remaining senses from COUP *v.*[3] See COPE *sb.*[2]] † **1.** = COPE *sb.*[2] –1535. **2.** A fall, upset 1535. **3.** A fault by which a coal-seam is tilted up 1795. **4.** The act of tilting rubbish from a cart, etc.; also the right to do this 1887.

Coup, coop (kūp), *sb.*[2] Now *dial.* 1582. [perh. the same word as COOP *sb.*[1]] A cart or wagon with closed sides and ends, for carting dung, lime, etc.; the load of such a cart. *Comb.* **c.-cart** (in same sense); also a cart with a body which can be tilted.

‖ **Coup** (kū), *sb.*[3] [Fr. *coup* blow :– med.L. *colpus*. Naturalized in late ME. in a lit. sense (see COUP *sb.*[1]); reintroduced XVIII in a fig. sense as French. See COPPICE.] **1.** A blow (that one sustains) (*rare*) 1793. **2.** A stroke, a move (that one makes); a 'hit' 1791. **3.** *Billiards.* The act of holing a ball without its first striking another ball 1770. **4.** Among N. American Indians: A successful stroke; *esp.* one that captures the weapon or horse of an enemy 1876.

Phrases. *Coup d'état* (kudeta) [Fr. *état* state]: a sudden and decisive stroke of state policy; *spec.* a change in the government carried out violently or illegally by the ruling power. *Coup de grâce* (kudəgrās) [*lit.* stroke of grace]: a blow by which one condemned or mortally hurt is put out of his misery; hence *fig.* a finishing stroke. *Coup de main* (kudəmæñ) [*lit.* stroke of hand]: 'a sudden and vigorous attack, for the purpose of instantaneously capturing a position' (Stocqueler); also *transf.* *Coup d'œil* (kudö̆ly) [Fr. *œil* eye]: (*a*) A comprehensive glance; a view as it strikes the eye at a glance. (*b*) *Mil.* The action or faculty of rapidly taking a general view of a position, and estimating its advantages and disadvantages. † *Coup de soleil* (kudəsolę̄ly) [Fr. *soleil* sun]: a sunstroke. *Coup de théâtre* (kudəte,ātr): a theatrical hit; a sensational turn or action in a play; also *transf.*

Coup, cowp (kaup), *v.*[1] *Sc.* and *n. dial.* ME. [– ON. *kaupa* buy, barter; see CHEAP *v.* and COPE *v.*[3]] † **1.** To buy; also *fig.* (ME. only.) **2.** To exchange, barter 1610. Hence **Couper, cowper,** one who buys and sells.

Coup, coupe (kūp), *v.*[2] ME. [– Fr. *couper*; see COPE *v.*[2] and *v.*[4]] † **1.** *trans.* To cut, slash. (Only in pa. pple.) (ME. only.) **2.** *Her.* To cut off clean (opp. to *erased, slipped*): said *esp.* of the head or any member of an animal; also of an ordinary (*e.g.* a cross) having the extremities cut off.

Coup (kaup), *v.*[3] *Sc.* ME. [prob. same as COPE *v.*[2]] † **1.** *intr.* To strike; to come to blows. (ME. only.) **2.** *trans.* To overturn, upset, tilt 1572. **3.** *intr.* To tumble over; to capsize 1785.

‖ **Coupé** (kupe), *a.* 1572. [Fr., pa. pple. of *couper* cut, f. *coup* COUP *sb.*[3]] *Her.* = Couped (see COUP *v.*[2]).

‖ **Coupé** (kupe), *sb.* 1834. [Fr., for *carrosse coupé* 'cut carriage'. See prec.] **1.** A short four-wheeled close carriage with an inside seat for two, and an outside seat for the driver. **2.** The front or after compartment of a continental *diligence* 1834; also, an end compartment in a railway carriage, seated on one side only 1853. **b.** A closed motor car, usually a two-seater 1912. **3.** *Dancing.* = COUPEE, q.v.

Coupee (kupī·, ku·pi). *sb.* Also †*coupie*, †*coupé*. 1673. [– Fr. *coupé* in same sense; see prec. and -EE[1] 2.] A dance step, in which the dancer rests on one foot and passes the other forward or backward, making a sort of salutation; hence, *occas.*, a bow made while advancing.

Why shall a man practise coupees, who only means to walk 1757. Hence **Coupee** *v. intr.* to make this movement.

‖ **Coupe-gorge** (kupgorʒ). ME. [Fr., lit, 'cut-throat', in mod. use 'cut-throat place' (cf. sense 2).] † **1.** A cut-throat. (ME. only.) **2.** *Mil.* Any position so disadvantageous that troops occupying it must either surrender or be cut to pieces. Also *fig.* 1612.

Couple (kʌ·p'l), *sb.* ME. [– OFr. *cople. cuple* (mod. *couple*) :– L. *copula* tie, connection.] **1.** That which unites two; *esp.* a brace or leash for hounds, etc. † **2.** Coupling in matrimony; the bond of wedlock; sexual union –1611. **3.** Two of the same sort taken together; a pair, a brace; often loosely = *two*. (The pl. after a numeral is often *couple*.) ME. **4.** A pair of opposite sexes; *e.g.* a wedded or engaged pair ME.; two partners in a dance 1759. **5.** One of a pair of rafters, that meet at the top, and are fixed at the bottom by a tie; a principal rafter, a chevron ME. † **6.** = COUPLET 1 (*rare*) –1589. **7.** *Dynamics.* A pair of equal and parallel forces acting in opposite directions, tending to produce a motion of rotation 1855. **8.** *Electr.* A pair of connected plates of different metals, used for creating either a galvanic or a thermo-electric current 1863.

1. Another company of houndes..had their couples cast off 1602. *transf.* and *fig.* *To go, hunt, run in couples* (now often = *pairs, twos*). **3.** A c. of as arrant knaues as any in Messina *Much Ado* III. v. 34. Skilfull Forresters..Do use to say, a C. of Rabbets or Conies GUILLIM. **4.** A very loving C. STEELE. I stood two c. above her 1759.

Couple (kʌ·p'l), *v.* ME. [– OFr. *copler, cupler* (mod. *coupler*) :– L. *copulare* COPULATE.] **1.** *trans.* To fasten (dogs) together in pairs. **2.** *gen.* To fasten or link together (prop. in pairs); to join or connect in any way ME. † **3.** To join in wedlock or sexual union –1754. **4.** *intr.* (for *refl.*) To pair ME. **5.** To associate in pairs (*trans.* and *intr.*) ME.

1. C. Clowder with the deepe-mouth'd brach *Tam. Shr.* Ind. i. 18. **2.** Wo that ioynen hous to hous, and feeld to feeld coupleth WYCLIF *Isa.* 5:8. To c. rhimes POPE, trucks together 1864. **3.** The Vicar of the next village..hath promis'd to..c. vs *A.Y.L.* III. iii. 45. **4.** Begin these wood birds but to c. now *Mids. N.* IV. i. 145. Hence **Cou·pled** *ppl. a.* tied, linked, or associated together in pairs. as *c. columns, windows*; *Her.* = CONJOINED.

† **Cou·ple-be:ggar.** 1702. [f. COUPLE *v.* 3.] A disreputable priest who made it his business to couple beggars (see COUPLE *v.* 3) –1744.

Couple-close. 1572. [app. f. Fr. *couple* + *close* closed, shut.] **1.** *Her.* A diminutive of the chevron, having one-fourth of its breadth, borne in couples, and usually cotising a chevron. **2.** A pair of rafters or couples in a roof. (See COUPLE *sb.*) 1849.

† **Couplement** (kʌ·p'lmĕnt). 1548. [– OFr. *couplement*; see COUPLE *v.*, -MENT.] **1.** Union of pairs –1670. **2.** A couple –1816.

Coupler (kʌ·pləɹ). 1552. [f. COUPLE *v.* + -ER[1].] **1.** One that couples. **2.** A thing that couples. *spec.* **a.** In an organ: A contrivance for connecting two manuals, or a manual with the pedals, or two keys an octave apart on the same keyboard 1668. **b.** The ring which slips upon the handle of a pair of tongs or a nipping-tool 1874. So **Cou·pleress** (*rare*), a female c.; a bawd.

Couplet (kʌ·plėt). 1580. [– (O)Fr. *couplet*, dim. of *couple*; see COUPLE *sb.*, -ET.] **1.** A pair of successive lines of verse, *esp.* when rhyming with each other. **2.** *gen.* A pair or couple 1601. **3.** *Archit.* A window of two lights 1844. **4.** *Mus.* Two equal notes inserted in a passage of triple rhythm and made to occupy the time of three 1876. Also *attrib.*

1. He [Chaucer] introduces a new metre..now famous as 'the heroic c.' SKEAT. **2.** Weel whisper ore a c. or two of most sage sawes *Twel. N.* III. iv. 412.

Coupling (kʊ·pliŋ), *vbl. sb.* ME. [f. COUPLE *v.* + -ING¹.] **1.** Joining in couples; see the vb. **2.** Sexual union ME. **3.** *concr.* Anything that couples 1549. †**4.** = COUPLE *sb.* 1. –1695. †**5.** = COUPLE *sb.* 5. –1611. **6.** In *Machinery*, etc.: The name of various contrivances for connecting parts of constructions or machinery, *esp.* in order to transmit motion; e.g. *box c.*, *clutch c.*, etc. 1814. **7.** Of a dog, etc.: 'The space between the tops of the shoulder-blades and tops of the hip-joints or huckle-bones' (V. Shaw).

Comb.: **c.-box,** a metal box joining the ends of two shafts, so that they may revolve together; **-chain,** the chain which couples railway carriages, trucks, etc.; **-pin,** a pin used for coupling railway carriages, etc.; **-pole,** the pole connecting the fore and hind gear of a wagon; **-reins,** the reins that couple a pair of horses together; **-rod,** the rod that couples the wheels of some locomotive engines.

Coupon (kū·pɒn, ‖ kupoṅ). 1822. [– Fr. *coupon*, earlier *colpon* piece cut off, slice (whence CULPON), f. *colper*, *couper* cut; see COUP *v.*², -OON.] A separable certificate, of which a series are attached to, and form part of, certain principal certificates, in order that they may be severally detached and given up as required. **b.** A party leader's recommendation to a political candidate 1918.

The coupons for interest annexed to any debenture shall also pass by delivery *Act* 37–8 *Vict.* c. 3 § 5. The [railway] tickets are..in the shape of small books of coupons 1864.

‖ **Coupure** (kūpiū°·ɹ). 1710. [Fr., f. *couper* cut; see -URE.] *Mil.* A ditch or trench; *esp.* one dug by the besieged for purposes of defence. *Fortif.* A passage cut through the glacis in the re-entrant angle of the covered way.

Courage (kʊ·rėdʒ), *sb.* ME. [– OFr. *corage*, *curage* (mod. *courage*) :– Rom. **coraticum*, f. L. *cor* heart; see -AGE.] †**1.** Spirit, mind, disposition, nature –1659. † Applied to a person –1647. †**2.** What is in one's mind or thoughts; purpose; inclination –1626. †**3.** Spirit, lustiness, vigour; also *fig.* –1705. **b.** Wrath; **c.** Pride; **d.** Confidence. –1608. **4.** That quality of mind which shows itself in facing danger without fear; bravery, valour ME.

1. Smale fowles maken melodie..So priketh hem nature in here corages CHAUCER. **2.** I'de such a c. to do him good *Timon* III. iii. 24. **4.** What man, corage yet *Merch. V.* IV. i. 111. C. never to submit or yield MILT. *P.L.* I. 108. Phr. *Dutch c.*: bravery induced by drinking (*colloq.*). Hence **Cou·raged** *a.* having c. **Cou·rageless** *a.* without c.

† **Cou·rage,** *v.* 1470. [f. prec. sb.] = ENCOURAGE –1614.

Courageous (kǒrē¹·dʒəs), *a.* ME. [– AFr. *corageous*, OFr. *corageus* (mod. *courageux*); see COURAGE *sb.*, -OUS.] **1.** Having courage; brave, fearless, valiant. †**2.** Eager (*to do* something) –1450. †**3.** Lively, lusty, vigorous –1577.

1. Bee thou strong, and very c. *Josh.* 1:7. Hence **Coura·geous-ly** *adv.*, **-ness.**

Courant, *a.* and *sb.*¹ 1601. [– Fr. *courant*, pres. pple. of *courir* run; see -ANT.] *adj.* †Running; in *Her.* applied to figures of animals represented as running 1727. † *sb.* A running-string. P. HOLLAND.

Courant (kuræ·nt), *sb.*² 1621. [Fr. *courant*, subst. use of pres. pple.; see prec. Cf. CORANTO².] †**1.** ? An express –1727. **2.** A paper containing news. (Now only in names of newspapers.) 1621.

Courant, *sb.*³; see COURANTE.

Courante, courant (kurā·ṅt, kura·nt). 1586. [– Fr. *courante* in same sense, lit. 'running (dance)', subst. use of fem. of pres. pple. of *courir* run; cf. COURANT *sb.*², CORANTO¹.] **1.** A dance characterized by a running or gliding step. **2.** *Mus.* The tune used for accompanying this dance, or a similar tune 1597.

‖ **Courap** (kū°·ræ̆p). 1706. [– west. Ind. vernacular *khurup* a kind of herpes.] 'Name given in India to cutaneous diseases attended with itching and eruptions' (*Syd. Soc. Lex.*).

Courbaril (kū°·ɹbăril). 1753. [Fr. *courbaril*, f. native name.] The West Indian Locust-tree; also its resin (called also ANIMÉ).

Courbash; see KOURBASH.

† **Courbe,** *a.* ME. [– (O)Fr. *courbe* :– L. *curvus* bent.] Bent, crooked –1579.

Her necke is short her shulders c. GOWER. So † **Courbe** *sb.* (see CURB *sb.*).

† **Courbe, courb,** *v.* ME. [– (O)Fr. *courber* :– L. *curvare*; see CURVE *v.*, CURB *v.*¹] *intr.* To curve, bend, bow –1602. Also *trans.* –1814.

I courbed on my knees and cryed hir of grace LANGL.

‖ **Courbette** (kurbę·t). 1648. [Fr.] = CURVET.

Courche, Courchie, obs. ff. CURCH.

Courier (ku·riəɹ, kū°·riəɹ). ME. [– Fr. †*courier*, (also mod. *courrier*) – It. *corriere* (med.L. *currerius*), f. *corre* :– L. *currere* run. In sense 1 †*cur(r)our* (XIV–XVII) – OFr. *coreor* (mod. *coureur*) :– Rom. **curritor, -ōr-*.] **1.** A running messenger; one sent in haste. †**2.** *Mil.* A light horseman acting as scout or skirmisher. Cf. AVANT-COURIER. –1603. **3.** A travelling servant, having the duty of making all the arrangements connected with the journey 1770. **4.** A title of newspapers 1798.

1. He delyuerd his letter to a courrour CAXTON.

‖ **Courlan** (kurlaṅ). [Fr. – S. Amer. name.] A S. Amer. bird of the genus *Aramus*, related to the Rails. (Dicts.)

Course (kō°ɹs), *sb.* ME. [– (O)Fr. *cours* :– L. *cursus*, f. *curs-*, pa. ppl. stem of *currere* run; reinforced XV by (O)Fr. *course* :– Rom. **cursa*, subst. use of corresp. fem. form of pa. pple.] †**1.** The action of running; a run; a gallop –1687. **2.** Onward movement in a particular path ME. **3.** A race (*arch.*) 1489. †**4.** Violent motion; impetus. (ME. only.) **5.** The charge of combatants in battle or tournament; onset; encounter (*Hist.*) ME. †**6.** A raid –1678. **7.** The action or practice of coursing (see COURSE *v.* 1) ME. †**8.** Running (of liquids); flow, flux –1665. **9.** Faculty of running, flowing, passing current, etc. ME.; †currency (of money, etc.) –1512. **10.** The line, path, or way, along which anything runs or travels ME. **11.** (*Naut.*) The direction in which, or point of the compass towards which, a ship sails 1553; *pl.* points of the compass 1610. **12.** *fig.* The continuous process (of time), succession (of events); progress onward or through successive stages ME. **13.** Habitual or ordinary manner of procedure; way, custom, practice ME. **14.** A line of (personal) action, way of acting 1583. **15.** A planned series of actions or proceedings: as of diet, etc. 1605. **16.** Each of the successive parts or members of a series ME. **17.** *pl.* The menses 1563. **18.** A row, range, or layer; *spec.* in *Building*, a continuous layer of stones, brick, or timber, of the same height throughout, in a wall, the face of a building, etc.; also, a row of slates, tiles, or shingles 1624; in *Mining*, a layer or lode of ore, etc. 1778. **19.** † (One's) turn –1665; one of several sets of persons appointed to serve in their turn 1535. **20.** *Naut.* Each of the sails attached to the lower yards of a ship; now *esp.* the fore-sail (*fore-c.*) and main-sail (*main-c.*) 1515.

2. To slacken one's c. JOHNSON. **5.** We ran our c., my charger fell SCOTT. **9.** Pray for vs, that the word of the Lord may haue free c. 2 *Thess.* 3:1. **10.** The c. of a ship 1665, of the Adige 1757. The round c. at Newmarket 1766. **11.** We sette owre c. south and by East EDEN. Set her two courses off to Sea againe, lay her off *Temp.* I. i. 53. **12.** The yeare hath runne his c. 1576. **13.** Phr. *C. of nature*: the natural order. *C. of Exchange*: see EXCHANGE *sb.* The law must take its c. 'JUNIUS'. **14.** Our wisest c. DISRAELI. Legal and moderate courses MACAULAY. Evil courses 1684. **15.** A c. of study and exercise GIBBON. A long c. of centuries 1828. The four-field or Norfolk c. 1844. **16.** A dinner of many courses O. W. HOLMES. A severe c. of the gout H. WALPOLE. Beare-like I must fight the c. (*i.e.* the successive attacks of dogs, a certain number at a time) *Macb.* V. vii. 2. **19.** A certaine priest, named Zacharias, of the c. of Abia *Luke* 1:5.

Prepositional Phrases. **In course.** † **a.** In turn. **b.** In the regular order. **c.** Naturally; = *of c.* (Now vulgar.) **In course of:** in process of. **Of course. a.** *adjectival.* Customary; natural, to be expected. **b.** *advb.* In ordinary or due course. **c.** Hence: Naturally; obviously.

Course (kō°ɹs), *v.* 1466. [f. COURSE *sb.* in various senses.] **1.** To hunt (game) with hounds; *spec.* to hunt (hares) with greyhounds, by sight 1550. Also *absol.* **2.** *trans.* To chase, pursue 1586. †**3.** To persecute –1600. †**4.** To chase with blows; hence, to thrash –1611. **5.** *intr.* To run, to run as in a race, to career; also *transf.* of liquids, etc. 1533; †*fig.* –1734. Also *trans.* To run over or along 1789. **6.** *intr.* To steer or direct one's course 1555. †**7.** *intr.* To run a course (see COURSE *sb.* 5). SPENSER. **8.** *causal.* To exercise in running 1568.

2. The big round teares Cours'd one another downe his innocent nose In pitteous chase *A.Y.L.* II. i. 39. **5.** Coursing like a colt across its lawns W. IRVING. In thoughtless gaiety I coursed the plain WORDSW. **8.** The greyhound ye desired to c. WOLCOT.

Coursed (kō°ɹst), *ppl. a.* 1740. **1.** [f. prec. + -ED¹.] Chased, *spec.* as a hare by greyhounds. **2.** [f. the sb.] Of masonry: Laid in courses 1851.

Courser¹ (kō°·ɹsəɹ). 1600. [orig. repr. OFr. *courseur*: later, prob. f. COURSE *v.* or *sb.* + -ER¹.] **1.** One who or a dog which courses (see COURSE *v.*) 1600. †**2.** *Oxford Univ.* A disputant in the schools –1688. **3.** A building stone used in forming a course 1885.

Courser² (kō°·ɹsəɹ). ME. [– OFr. *corsier* (mod. *coursier*) :– Rom. **cursarius*, f. *cursus* COURSE *sb.*; see -ER².] **1.** *orig.* A charger (see COURSE *sb.* 5); since 17th c.: A racer. Now *poet.* or *rhet.* **2.** A stallion. Now *Sc.* 1483.

1. A thousand coursers fleeter than the wind YOUNG.

Courser³ (kō°·ɹsəɹ). 1766. [app. a mod. formation from late L. *cursorius* 'adapted for running' used subst. as a generic name.] *Zool.* A bird of the genus *Cursorius*, noted for swift running; esp *C. isabellinus.*

Coursey, -ie, var. of COURSY.

Coursing (kō°·ɹsiŋ), *vbl. sb.* 1538. [f. COURSE *v.* + -ING¹.] **1.** The action of COURSE *v.* 1568. **2.** *spec.* The sport of chasing hares, etc., with greyhounds, by sight 1538. †**3.** *Oxford Univ.* The opposing of a thesis in the schools –1683.

† **Cou·rsy, -sey.** Also **-sie.** 1611. [– Fr. †*coursie*, *corsie* (XVI; now *coursier*) – It. *corsia*, f. *corso* COURSE *sb.*] A raised passage from prow to poop of a galley over the rowing benches –1693.

Court (kō°ɹt), *sb.*¹ [ME. *curt, court* – AFr. *curt*, OFr. *cort* (mod. *cour*) :– Rom. **curte*, earlier **corte* (– L. *cohors, cohort-*) yard, enclosure, (enclosed) crowd, retinue; see COHORT.]

I. 1. A clear space enclosed by walls or surrounded by buildings; a yard, a court-yard. Also, a section of the area of a museum, or the like. At Cambridge, a college quadrangle. ME. †**2.** A large building or set of buildings standing in a court-yard; a large house or castle. In early times = BURY *sb.* –1887. **3.** In a town: A confined space opening off a street, and built around with houses 1687. **4.** An enclosed quadrangular area, uncovered or covered, with a smooth level floor, for playing tennis, rackets, or fives; the plot of ground marked out for lawn-tennis; also each subdivision of such a plot 1519.

1. Esther..stood in the inner c. of the kings house *Esther* 5:1. My soule..fainteth for the courts of the Lord (*i.e.* the enclosures constituting the temple area round the sanctuary on Mount Moriah) *Ps.* 84:2. **2.** This Nutwell C. (which signifies a Mansion-house in a Seigniory) RISDON.

II. 1. The place where a sovereign (or high dignitary) resides and holds state, attended by his retinue ME. **2.** The establishment and surroundings of a sovereign with his councillors and retinue ME. **b.** without article (*at c.*, *to c.*, etc.), including place, persons, and proceedings. Cf. *at church*, etc. ME. **3.** The body of courtiers collectively. (Construed as pl.) ME. **4.** The sovereign with his ministers and councillors. (Construed as sing.) ME.

1. In Courts and Palaces he also Reigns MILT. *P.L.* I. 497. **2.** When the C. lay at Windsor *Merry W.* II. ii. 62. The court's a school, indeed BEAUM. & FL. **4.** The affaires of the French c. 1651.

III. An assembly held by the sovereign at his residence OE.

Arthur. .Held c. at old Caerleon upon Usk TENNYSON.

IV. A court of judicature, of law, or of administration. **1.** Applied to Parliament. Cf. Sp. *Cortes*. 1450. **2.** An assembly of judges or others persons legally appointed and acting as a tribunal to hear and determine any cause, civil, ecclesiastical, military, or naval ME.

Justice was formerly administered by judges who followed the king as officers of his court; hence the title *King's Courts* (*curia regis*).

3. The place, hall, or chamber in which justice is administered ME. **b.** without article (*in, into, out of c.*, etc.), including place and proceedings ME. **4.** A session of a judicial assembly ME. **5.** An assembly of the qualified members of a company or corporation, or of the council thereof 1527. **6.** Homage such as is offered at court; attention or courtship to one whose favour is sought: in phr. *to make* or *pay (one's) c. to* = COURT *v.* 2, 3. 1590.

1. A Prayer for the High C. of Parliament *Bk. Com. Prayer*. **2.** *Supreme C.*: the highest c. of a country or state. *C. of record*: one 'where the acts and judicial proceedings are enrolled in parchment for a perpetual memorial' (Blackstone). *C. of* ADMIRALTY, ARCHES, CHANCERY, COMMON PLEAS, EQUITY, PROBATE, etc.: see those words. **C. of Claims:** a c. in which claims are adjudicated on; in U.S., a c. sitting at Washington for the investigation of claims against the government. **C. of Conscience** or **of Requests:** a small debt c.; *c. of conscience* (fig.), conscience as a moral tribunal. **3.** Go one and cal the Iew into the C. *Merch. V.* IV. i. 14. **b.** The case was settled out of c. (*mod.*). Phr. *Out of c.*: said of a plaintiff who has forfeited his claim to be heard; now mostly *fig.* **6.** Flatter me, make thy c., and say it did DRYDEN.

V. *attrib.* **a.** Of or belonging to a royal court 1598. **b.** Of or belonging to a court of law 1571.

Comb.: **c.-almanac,** an annual handbook of royal families and their courts; **-calendar** = *court-almanac*; **-card,** var. of COAT-CARD, q.v.; a picture-card; **c. circular,** a daily record of the doings of the C., published in the newspapers; **-craft,** the art required or practised at c.; **-day,** a day on which a c. (legal, royal, etc.) is held; **-fool, -jester,** a jester kept for the amusement of a prince and his c.; **-guide,** a directory containing the names and addresses of the nobility and gentry; **-hand,** the handwriting in use in the English law-courts from the 16th c. to 1731; **-lands,** 'domains or lands kept in the lord's hands to serve his family' (Wharton); **-man,** a courtier; **† c. marshal,** the marshal of a prince's household; **-newsman,** a person appointed to furnish news of the doings of the C.; **-party,** a party which advocates the interests of the C.; **-room,** a room in which a c. is regularly held; **-suit,** (*a*) a suit preferred at C.; (*b*) a suit worn at C., c.-dress; **-sword,** a light sword worn as part of a man's c.-dress.

Hence **Cou·rtless** *a.* without a c.; without courtliness. **Cou·rtlet. Cou·rtlike, cou·rt-like** *a.* **Cou·rtling.**

† Court, *sb.*[2] 1576. Some kind of cart –1703.

Court (kōᵊɹt), *v.* 1515. [After OIt. *corteare* (lator *corteggiare*), OFr. *courtoyer* (later *courtiser*), f. *cort* COURT *sb.*[1]] **† 1.** *intr.* To be or reside at court –1568. **2.** *trans.* To pay courteous attention to 1590. **3.** To pay amorous attention to, woo (with a view to marriage). (Now *homely*; also *poet.*) 1580. *absol.* 1591. Also *fig.* and *transf.* **4.** To entice *into, to, from, out of,* etc. 1602. **5.** To seek to win or attract, to affect (a thing) 1571.

2. To flatter kings, or c. the great GOLDSM. **3.** *absol.* See how they kisse and c. *Tam. Shr.* IV. ii. 27. *fig.* Their broad sheets c. the breeze MOTHERWELL. **5.** Sylla never courted popularity FROUDE. Hence **Cou·rter,** one who courts.

‖ **Courtage** (kurtāʒ, kōᵊ·ɹtėdʒ). 1835. [Fr.] = BROKERAGE. So †‖ **Courtagie,** 1682.

Cou·rt-ba·ron. 1542. [– AFr. *court baron*, earlier *court de baroun*; AL. *curia baronis.*] The assembly of the freehold tenants of a manor under the presidency of the lord or his steward.

Court Christian; see CHRISTIAN *a.*

† Cou·rt-cupboard. 1592. A movable cabinet used to display plate, etc. –1821.

Court-customary; = CUSTOMARY court.

Court-dress. 1797. The dress worn by those who attend at Court, and on other state occasions. So **† Court-dresser.**

Courteous (kōᵊ·ɹtyəs, kɒ̄·ɹtyəs), *a.* ME. [– OFr. *corteis, curteis* (mod. *courtois*) :– Rom. **cortensis*, f. **corte* COURT *sb.*[1] + *-ensis* -ESE. The suffix -EOUS replaced *-eis* XVI.] **a.** Having such manners as befit the court of a prince; graciously polite and respectful in dealing with others; kind and complaisant. **b.** As a formula of address; *orig.* to superiors = Gracious (*arch.*) ME. Also *transf.*

A good man, sage, curtois, and valyaunt CAXTON. *transf.* This is call'd the retort c. *A.Y.L.* V. iv. 75. Hence **Cou·rteous-ly** *adv.*, **-ness.**

† Cou·rtepy. ME. [– MDu. *korte pīe*, i.e. *korte* short + *pīe* (whence PEE *sb.*[1]) coat of coarse woollen stuff, now *pij*; cf. PEA-COAT, PEA-JACKET.] A short coat of coarse material –1483.

A gay yeman. .He hadde vp-on a c. of grene CHAUCER.

† Courtesan, -zan, *sb.*[1] and *a.* ME. [– Fr. *courtisan* – It. *cortigiano* courtier, f. *corte* court.] *sb.* One attached to the court of a prince –1669. *adj.* The court language (of Italy) –1601.

Courtesan, -zan (kōᵊ·ɹtizæn, kɒ̄·ɹt-), *sb.*[2] 1549. [– Fr. *courtisane* – It. †*cortigiana*, fem. of *cortigiano*; see prec.] A court-mistress; a prostitute. (Somewhat euphemistic.)

Your whore is for euery rascall, but your Curtizan is for your Courtier 1607.

Courtesy (kōᵊ·ɹtėsi, kɒ̄·ɹ-), *sb.* ME. [– OFr. *cur-, co(u)rtesie* (mod. *courtoisie*), f. *curteis*, etc. COURTEOUS; see -Y[3]. Cf. CURTSY.] **1.** Courteous behaviour; graceful politeness or considerateness in intercourse with others; courteous disposition. **2.** *Of, by* (†*at*) *c.*: by favour or indulgence 1587. **3.** *Law.* A tenure by which a husband, after his wife's death, holds certain kinds of property which she has inherited. More fully called *Courtesy (Curtesy) of England* or *of Scotland*. 1523. **4.** (with *pl.*) A courteous act or expression 1450. **† 5.** The customary expression of respect by action or gesture, *esp.* to a superior –1645. **6.** = CURTSY *sb.* 2. 1575. **† 7.** A moderate quantity –1627.

1. A Knyght ther was. .he loued chiualrie, Trouthe and honour fredom and curteisie CHAUCER. Courtesie grows in court; news in the citie G. HERBERT. **2.** *C. title*: a title of no legal validity given by social custom; *e.g.* the prefix of *Honourable* to the names of the children of Viscounts and Barons. **3.** No man shall be tenant by the curtesie of Land, without his wife have possession in deed 1531. **4.** That curt'sie with like kindnesse to repay SPENSER. **5.** The Elephant hath ioynts, but none for curtesie SHAKS.

Hence **Cou·rtesy** *v.* †to treat with c.; *intr.* to make a curtsy.

Cou·rt-house. 1483. **1.** A building in which courts of law are held. **2.** A manorial dwelling (*South of Eng.*) 1857. **3.** *U.S.* = *County seat* (see COUNTY[1]) 1856.

Courtier (kōᵊ·ɹtiəɹ). [ME. *courteour* – AFr. *courte(i)our*, for OFr. **cortoyeur*, f. *cortoyer* be at the court; suff. assim. to -IER, through *-e(y)er.*] **1.** One who frequents the court of a sovereign; an attendant at court. Also *transf.* **† 2.** A wooer –1766.

1. Reynard the foxe is now asquyer and a courtyer CAXTON. False is the cringing Courtier's plighted word GAY. **2.** Courtiers of beautious freedome *Ant. & Cl.* II. vi. 17. Hence **Cou·rtierism,** the practice or quality of a c. **Cou·rtierly** *a.* **Cou·rtiership. † Cou·rtiery,** the manners of a c., or ? courtiers as a body B. JONS.

Court leet. 1588. [See LEET *sb.*[1]] A court of record held periodically in a hundred, lordship, or manor, before the lord or his steward, and attended by the residents of the district. (Practically superseded.)

Courtly (kōᵊ·ɹtli), *a.* 1450. [f. COURT *sb.*[1] + -LY[1].] **† 1.** Of or pertaining to the Court –1786. **2.** Having the manners or breeding befitting the Court; polished, of a high-bred courtesy 1450. **3.** Of things: Elegant, refined 1535. **4.** Given to flattery; subservient to the Court 1607.

1. In C. company 2 *Hen. VI*, I. i. 27. **2.** The French are passing c. FORD. **3.** You haue too C. a wit, for me *A.Y.L.* III. ii. 72. **4.** Truth sometimes escapes from the most c. pens H. WALPOLE. Hence **Cou·rtliness.** So **Cou·rtly** *adv.*

† Court-mantle. ME. [f. OFr. *curt, cort*, now *court* short (see CURT) + MANTLE.] One who wears a short cloak. (Surname of Henry II.) –1677.

Court martial, *sb.* Pl. **courts martial.** 1571. [orig. *martial court*; see MARTIAL.] A judicial court, consisting of military or naval officers, for the trial of military or naval offences, or the administration of martial law.

Drumhead court martial: a court martial summoned round an upturned drum, for summary treatment of offenders during military operations. Hence **Court-ma·rtial** *v. colloq.* to try by court martial.

† Cou·rtnoll. 1568. [f. COURT *sb.*[1] + NOLL.] A courtier (*contempt.*) –1658.

† Court of guard. 1590. A perversion of CORPS DE GARDE, q.v. –1810.

Court-plaster. 1772. [So called from being used for the black patches formerly worn by ladies at Court.] Sticking-plaster made of silk coated with isinglass.

Court roll. 1461. *Law.* The roll kept in connection with a manorial court, a copy of which constitutes the tenant's title to his holding.

Courtship (kōᵊ·ɹt,ʃip). 1588. [f. COURT *sb.*[1] + -SHIP.] **† 1.** Courtliness of manners –1673; courtesy –1719. **† 2.** The state befitting a court or courtier –1630. **† 3.** Office or position at court –1659. **† 4.** Court-craft; flattery, etc. –1734. **† 5.** The paying of court or courteous attentions –1729. **6.** The paying of court to a woman with a view to marriage; courting 1596. Also *transf.* and *fig.* **7.** *fig.* Endeavour to win over 1727.

1. *L.L.L.* V. ii. 363. **2.** *Rom. & Jul.* III. iii. 34. **5.** His C. to the common people *Rich. II*, I. iv. 24. **6.** C., and such faire ostents of loue *Merch. V.* II. viii. 44. Hence **† Cou·rtshipment** = COURTSHIP 4. LOVELACE.

Cou·rt-ya·rd, cou·rtyard. 1552. An open area surrounded by walls or buildings within the precincts of a large house, castle, etc.

‖ **Couscous,**[1] **couscoussou** (ku·skus, -kusu). 1600. [– Fr. *couscous* – Arab. *kuskus, kuskusū* – *kaskasa* to pound.] An African dish made of flour granulated, and cooked by steaming over the vapour of broth or meat.

‖ **Couscous**[2] (ku·skus). 1839. [Fr. *couscous* – Du. *koeskoes* – native Moluccas name.] A marsupial quadruped, the Spotted Phalanger of the Moluccas (*Cuscus maculatus*).

Cousin (kɒ·z'n), *sb.* ME. [– OFr. *cosin, cusin* (mod. *cousin*) :– L. *consobrinus* mother's sister's child.] **† 1.** A collateral relative more distant than a brother or sister; a relative –1748. **† b.** In legal language formerly = the next of kin, or the person to whom one is next of kin. (Here = L. *consanguineus.*) –1642. **2.** *spec.* The son or daughter of an uncle or aunt: = *own, first,* or *full c.*, C.-GERMAN. (The strict modern sense.) ME. Also *fig.* **3.** Used as a term of address by a sovereign of another sovereign, or a nobleman of the same country (in royal writs, etc., of earls and peers of higher rank); also familiarly, *esp.* in Cornwall ME. **† 4.** *cant.* A trull. So *C. Betty*. –1863.

1. How now brother, where is my cosen your son *Much Ado* I. ii. 2. **2.** Phr. *First, second c.*, etc.: expressing the relationship of persons descended the same number of steps in distinct lines from a common ancestor; thus the children of *first cousins* are *second cousins* to each other; and so on. **3.** Our brother and c. the King of Scotts EDW. IV in Ellis. C. of Exeter 2 *Hen. VI*, IV. viii. 34. C. Jacky from Redruth 1880.

Phrases: *To call cousins*: to claim kinship (*with*). †*To make a c. of*: ? to beguile. (See COZEN *v.*)

Hence **† Cou·sin** *v. rare*, to call c., claim kinship with. **† Cou·sinage,** cousinhood. **Cou·siness,** a female c. **Cou·sinhood,** cousins or kinsfolk collectively; the relation of being a c. or cousins. **Cou·sinly** *a.* and *adv.* **Cou·sinred,** cousinship, relationship. SCOTT. **Cou·sinry,** a body of kinsfolk. **Cou·sinship,** cousinhood; the action proper to a c.

Cousin-german. Pl. **cousins-german, † cousin-germans,** orig. **-s -s.** ME. [– Fr. *cousin germain*; see GERMAN *a.*[1]] = COUSIN *sb.* 2. (Now legal or techn.) Also *fig.*

† *Cousin german (once) removed*: = 'first cousin once removed', *i.e.* first cousin's child or *vice versa*.

‖ **Coussinet** (ku·sinet, or as Fr. kusinę). 1876. [Fr. dim. of *coussin* cushion.] *Archit.* **a.** 'A stone placed upon the impost of a pier for receiving the first stone of an arch.' **b.** 'The part of the Ionic capital between the abacus and quarter round, which serves to form the volute.' GWILT.

‖ **Couteau** (kuto). 1677. [Fr. :– OFr. *coutel*; see next.] A large knife worn as a weapon. *Couteau de chasse* (Fr.): a hunting-knife.

† **Coute·l.** 1647. [– OFr. *cotel, coutel* (mod. *couteau*) :– L. *cultellus* knife.] 'A short knife or dagger in use during the Middle Ages' (Fairholt) –1654.

Couter, cooter (kū·təɹ). *slang.* 1846. [perh. f. Danubian-Gipsy *cuta* gold coin.] A sovereign.

Couth (kūþ). Now *Sc.* [OE. *cūð*, pa. pple. of the vb. *cunnan* CAN; see UNCOUTH.] † **1.** *pa. pple.* Known –1613. † **2.** *adj.* Known; well known, familiar –1557. † **3.** Acquainted (*with, of,* or dative) –1450. **4.** Kind, agreeable. *Sc.* ME. **5.** Snug, cosy. *Sc.* 1749. Hence † **Couth** *adv.* clearly; familiarly. **Cou·thie** *a. Sc.* (in senses 4, 5).

Couth(e, obs. f. *could*, pa. t. of CAN *v.*[1]

Coutil (kuti·l). Also **coutelle, -ille.** 1853. [– Fr. *coutil* (kuti) quilt.] A close-woven sort of canvas, used in stay-making, etc.

‖ **Couvade** (kuva·d). 1865. [Fr., f. *couver* hatch. See next.] Tylor's name for the 'man-childbed' attributed to some primitive races, and the customs according to which, on the birth of a child, the man is put to bed, and treated as if he were physically affected by the birth.

† **Couve, cove,** *v.* [– Fr. *couver* hatch :– L. *cubare* lie down.] To incubate, hatch. P. HOLLAND. vars. † **Cou·vey, covie** *v.*

Couvre-feu; see CURFEW.

Cove (kōᵘv), *sb.*[1] [OE. *cofa* chamber = MLG. *cove*, MHG. *kobe* (G. *koben*) stable, pigsty, ON. *kofi* hut, shed :– Gmc. **kuƀon*.] † **1.** In OE.: A small chamber, cell, etc. **2.** A hollow in a rock; a cave, cavern, den (*Sc.* and *n.*) OE. **3.** A recess in the steep flank of a mountain. In U.S. occas. = gap, pass. 1805. **4.** A small bay, creek, or inlet 1590. Also *transf.* **5.** *Archit.* A concave arch or vault; an arched moulding running along the projecting member of a structure; *esp.* the concave arch of a ceiling 1511.

3. It was a c., a huge recess That keeps till June, December's snow WORDSW. **4.** We run our vessel into a little c. DE FOE. *Comb.* **c.-plane,** a plane for cutting coved surfaces.

Cove (kōᵘv), *sb.*[2] *slang.* 1567. [orig. thieves' cant, perh. identical with Sc. *cofe* chapman, pedlar. Cf. the origin of CHAP *sb.*[3], CUSS.] A fellow, chap, customer; *occas.* = BOSS *sb.*[5]

There's a gentry c. here, Is the top of the shire B. JONS.

Cove (kōᵘv), *v.* 1631. [f. COVE *sb.*[1]] † **1.** *intr.* To shelter in a cove. **2.** *trans.* To arch or vault; *esp.* to arch (a ceiling) at its junction with the wall 1756; to incline inwards (the sides of a fireplace) 1838.

2. The mosques..are rounded into domes and coved roofs 1779.

Cove, var. of COUVE *v.*; obs. f. COVEY *sb.*[1]

Covelline, covellite (kove·lәin, -әit). 1850. [f. *Covelli*, an Italian mineralogist + -INE[5], -ITE[1] 2 b.] *Min.* A native indigo-blue sulphide of copper; often called *blue* or *indigo copper.* var. **Cove·llinite.**

Coven, covin (kɒ·vėn). *Sc.* 1500. [var. of *covent* CONVENT.] A gathering; *esp.* of witches; cf. CONVENT.

† **Co·venable,** *a.* ME. [– AFr., OFr. *covenable*, early var. of *convenable*, whence CONVENABLE *a.*[1]] **1.** Suitable –1628; consistent. ME. only. **2.** Of persons: Seemly, comely. Cf. *proper.* –1523.

1. Withouten c. cause 1400. Hence † **Co·venableness** (*rare*). † **Covena·blete,** fitness; an opportunity. † **Co·venably** *adv.*

† **Co·venance.** 1475. [– OFr. *covenance*, now *convenance*; see CONVENANCE.] Agreement, covenant, convention –1500.

Covenant (kɒ·vĭnănt), *sb.* ME. [– OFr. *covenant* (later and mod. *convenant*), subst. use of pres. pple. of *co(n)venir* agree; see CONVENE, -ANT.] **1.** A mutual agreement between two or more persons to do or refrain from doing certain acts; sometimes, the undertaking of one of the parties. (Now mainly *legal* or *theological.*) † **2.** A vow. CHAUCER. † **3.** Each of the terms of an agreement –1614. **4.** *Law.* A formal agreement; *esp.* in Eng. Law, a promise or contract under seal ME.; a particular clause of such a contract 1611. † **5.** The matter agreed upon, undertaken, or promised, as covenanted duty, wages, etc. –1596. † **6.** Security. MILTON. **7.** *Theol.* Applied to engagements entered into by and with the Divine Being, as revealed in the Sciptures, etc. ME.; hence *occas.* = Dispensation 1818. **8.** *Eccl. Hist.* The name given *esp.* to the *Solemn League and C.* entered into in 1643 by the Scottish Presbyterians for the defence and furtherance of their ecclesiastical polity. (See also COVENANTER 2.) 1638. Also *attrib.*

1. They made couenaunt that they sholde sle him CAXTON. **4.** Leases..declared void for non-fulfilment of covenants 1872. **7.** And makes a C. never to destroy The Earth again by flood MILT. *P.L.* XI. 892. *Books of the Old and the New C.*: the O. and N. Testament, belonging to the Mosaic and Christian dispensations respectively. *C. of Works, C. of Grace*: the two relations subsisting between God and man, before and since the Fall. Baptism implieth a c. or league between God and man HOOKER. **8.** *Church C.*: the agreement subscribed by the members of a Congregational Church in order to constitute themselves a distinct religious society.

Hence **Covena·ntal** *a.* of or pertaining to a c.

Covenant (kɒ·vĭnănt), *v.* ME. [f. the sb.] **1.** *intr.* To enter into a covenant; to contract. **2.** *trans.* To agree or subscribe to by covenant ME. **3.** To stipulate 1577.

1. They couenanted with him for thirtie pieces of siluer *Matt.* 26:15. **2.** Nothing is covenanted as to any remainder GROTE. Hence **Cov:enantee·**, the person to whom a promise by covenant is made. **Co·venanto:r,** the party by whom the obligation expressed in the covenant is to be performed.

Covenanted (kɒ·vĭnăntėd), *ppl. a.* [f. prec. + -ED[1].] 1646. **1.** Secured by covenant, as *c. grace, mercies* (Theol.) 1651. **2.** Bound by a covenant 1646. **3.** *Hist.* Having subscribed the Covenant; see COVENANT *sb.* 8. 1660. **4.** *I.C.S.* Applied to the regular members of the service who used to enter into a covenant with the East India Company, and do so now with the Secretary of State for India 1757.

Covenanter (kɒ·vĭnăntəɹ). 1638. [f. as prec. + -ER[1].] **1.** *gen.* One who enters into a covenant 1643. **2.** *Sc. Hist.* A subscriber or adherent of the National Covenant signed 28 Feb. 1638, or of the Solemn League and Covenant of 1643. (In Scotland pronounced *covena·nter.*)

† **Covent.** Early f. CONVENT, surviving in *Covent Garden*, etc.

Co·ven-tree, covin-tree. *Sc.* 1823. [f. COVEN.] A large tree in front of old Scottish mansion-houses, where the laird met his guests or assembled his retainers.

Coventry (kǫ·vĕntri, kɒ·v-). An ancient town in Warwickshire.

Phr. *To send (a person) to C.*: to refuse to associate or have intercourse with him. [See CLARENDON *Hist. Reb.* vi. § 83.]

Comb.: † **C. Bells** = *Campanula medium*; also called *C. Rapes*: cf. CANTERBURY BELL. † **C. blue,** a kind of blue thread made at C., and used for embroidery; also simply *Coventry*.

Cover (kɒ·vəɹ), *v.*[1] ME. [– OFr. *cuvrir, covrir* (mod. *couvrir*) :– L. *cooperire*, f. *co*- CON- + *operire* cover.]

I. 1. *trans.* To overlay, overspread *with* something so as to hide or protect. **2.** To put a covering on ME. **3.** To clothe; to put on head-covering; to wrap, wrap up, invest ME. Also *fig.* and *transf.* **4.** To serve as a covering to ME.; to strew, occupy ME. **5.** Of a stallion: To copulate with (the mare); rarely of other animals. Also *absol.* and *casually* 1535. † Of a bird: To sit upon (eggs) –1711.

2. To c. a saucepan SOYER, a roof 1872, a table GRAFTON, a surface with a design JEVONS. Phr. †*To c. his feet* (a Hebraism): to ease himself. **3.** For whan I was a cold thou couerdest me CAXTON. C. thy head..Nay prethee be couer'd *A.Y.L.* v. i. 18. **4.** Feldes..coueryd with deed men LD. BERNERS.

II. 1. To shield, protect, shelter. Also *fig.* ME. **2.** To screen from view; to conceal ME. **3.** *To c.* (*with a gun*, etc.): to present a gun at (something) so as to have it directly in the line of fire 1687. **4.** *Mil.* To stand in line with from a point of sight 1796. **5.** *Cricket.* To take up such a position behind (another man) as to be able to stop the balls missed by him 1840.

1. To c. a march 1684, a retreat 1758. That the flag should c. the merchandise ALISON. **2.** There is nothing couered that shall not be reueiled *Matt.* 10:26. Frank laughed to c. his anxiety 1883.

III. 1. To be extensive enough to include 1793. **2.** To extend over, be co-extensive with, occupy 1862. Also *fig.* **3.** To pass over (ground); to get over (a given distance) 1818. **4.** To be sufficient to defray (a charge), or to meet (a liability); to compensate (a loss or risk); to protect by insurance or the like 1828; *absol.* to provide cover; to insure oneself 1882.

2. This [remark] covers the ground 1887. The loan was covered many times over 1890. **4.** A small charge..to c. the trouble and risk JEVONS. Phr. *To c. short sales*, or *shorts* (Stock Exch.): to buy in shares sold short (*i.e.* without being held by the seller), in order to make delivery, or to guard against loss. *To c. into the Treasury* (U.S.): to transfer the amount into the Treasury.

† **Co·ver,** *v.*[2] ME. [Aphetic f. *acover* to recover; but influenced by OFr. *covrer, couvrer* to get, acquire; cf. Fr. *re-couvrer*, L. *recuperare.*] **1.** *trans.* To get, gain, attain –1477. **2.** *trans.* To recover. (ME. only.) Also *refl.* **3.** *intr.* (for *refl.*) To recover; to be relieved –1768.

Cover (kɒ·vəɹ), *sb.*[1] ME. [f. COVER *v.*[1], or partly variant of COVERT *sb.*] **1.** That which covers: anything that is put or laid over, or that overlies or overspreads an object, so as to hide, shelter, or enclose it; *spec.* a lid, the boards of a book, an envelope, a wrapper, etc. **2.** A shelter, a hiding-place ME.; *fig.* a cloak, screen, disguise, pretence 1599. **3.** *Hunting.* Woods, undergrowth, and bushes, that serve to shelter game, etc. 1719. **4.** *Comm.* Funds adequate to meet a liability or secure against loss 1883. **5.** [after Fr. *couvert.*] The utensils laid for each person's use at table; the plate, napkin, knife, fork, spoon, etc. 1612.

1. [Her Waggon] Couer *Rom. & Jul.* I. iv. 60. Bound up in Past-Board Covers HEARNE. Direct to me..under c. to Alice JANE AUSTEN. **2.** Wisedome..was vnto them for a couer by day *Wisd.* 10:17. Under c. of the woods 1794. **3.** A c. that is full of foxes P. BECKFORD. **5.** Covers were laid for four THACKERAY.

Comb.: **c.-cloth,** a cloth used as a covering; **-glass,** *spec.* a slip of glass used to cover a microscopical preparation; **-shooting,** shooting in a c.; **-side,** the side of a fox-c., where the hunters congregate.

‖ **Cover** (kɒ·vəɹ), *sb.*[2] 1709. [repr. Welsh *cyfair.*] The ordinary measure of land in S. Wales, being ⅜ of an imperial acre.

† **Co·verchief.** ME. [– OFr. *cuevre-chief*, mod. *couvre-chef*; see COVER *v.*[1], CHIEF *sb.*] Earlier f. KERCHIEF, q.v. –1603.

Covercle (kɒ·vəɹk'l), *sb.* ME. [– OFr. *covercle* (mod. *couvercle*) – L. *cooperculum*, f. *cooperire* cover.] † **1.** A cover, a lid –1488. **2.** *Nat. Hist.* An OPERCULUM (*rare*) 1682.

Covered (kɒ·vəɹd), *ppl. a.* 1463. [f. COVER *sb.*[1] and *v.*[1] + -ED.] **1.** Having a cover, covering, or lid. † **2.** Hidden; ambiguous –1581. **3.** Covered with undergrowth. Now only in comb., as *moss-c.*, etc. 1632. **4.** Closed in overhead 1667. **5.** Having one's hat on 1669. **6.** Sheltered, protected, screened; *spec.* in *Fortif. c.-way* (formerly *covert-way*; see COVERT *a.*); see quots. 1685.

4. They walked about in the c. court JOWETT. **6.** The *Covered way* is a space of about 30 feet broad, extending round the counterscarp of the ditch, being covered by a parapet..with a banquette A. GRIFFITHS.

Coverer (kɒ·vərəɹ). ME. [f. COVER *v.*[1] + -ER[1].] One who or that which covers.

Covering (kɒ·vəriŋ), *vbl. sb.* ME. [f. as prec. + -ING[1].] **1.** The action of COVER, *v.*[1] **2.** That which covers or serves to cover; a cover ME.

2. Thicke cloudes are a c. to him that he seeth not *Job* 22:14. The geologist..finds its solid c. composed of rocks 1854. *Comb.* **c.-board** = PLANESHEAR. So **Co·vering** *ppl. a.* (*c. letter*, one sent with another document and indicating its contents).

Coverlet (kɒ·vəɹlėt). [ME. *coverled, -lite* – AFr. *covrelet, -lit*, f. *covre-* pres. stem of OFr. *covrir* COVER + *lit* bed.] **1.** The uppermost covering of a bed; a counterpane. **2.** *transf.* A covering of any kind 1551. Also *fig.*

Bitwene hir shete and hir couerlyte of hir bede 1440. var. **Co·verlid.**

Co·ver-poi:nt. 1850. [f. COVER *v.*[1] + POINT *sb.*[1]] **1.** *Cricket.* A fielder who stands behind, and a little to the bowler's side of, point; also, his position in the field. **2.** *Lacrosse.* A player who stands just in front of point.

Co-versed (koᵘvə̄·ɹst), *a.* 1706. [See Co- *pref.*] *Trig.* In *Co-versed sine*: the versed sine of the complement of an angle (see VERSED).

Co·ver-shame. 1629. Something used to conceal shame. **b.** The shrub Savin, used to procure abortion.

Co·ver-slut. 1639. Something worn to cover sluttishness, an apron or pinafore.

Covert (kɒ·vəɹt), *a.* (*pa. pple.*) ME. [– OFr. *covert* (mod. *couvert*), pa. pple. of *couvrir* COVER *v.*[1]] **1.** *lit.* Covered, hidden; sheltered. Now *rare*. **2.** *fig.* Concealed, secret; disguised ME. † **3.** Secretive; sly –1673. **b.** Of words: Of hidden meaning. Now *rare*. ME. **4.** *Law.* Said of a married woman: Under the cover, authority, or protection of her husband 1483.

1. A c. nook WORDSW. *C. way* (Fortif.): = COVERED *way*. **2.** A c. threat 1874, glance DICKENS. **3.** Under c. and indifferent words BACON. Hence **Co·vert-ly** *adv.*, **-ness.**

Covert (kɒ·vəɹt), *sb.* ME. [– OFr. *covert* (mod. *couvert*), subst. use of masc. pa. pple. of *covrir* COVER *v.*[1]] **1.** *gen.* A covering. **2.** = COVER *sb.*[1] 2. ME. **3.** = COVER *sb.*[1] 3. 1494. **4.** *Ornith.* in *pl.* Feathers that cover the bases of the wing and tail feathers of a bird 1774.

1. What c. dare eclipse thy face G. HERBERT. **2.** Holes and Coverts RAY. **3.** Like a Deere..to the C. doth himselfe betake DRAYTON. Phr. †*Under c.* (Law) = *Under* COVERTURE.

Co·vert-ba·ron, *a.* (*sb.*) 1512. [– AFr. *couverte baroun*, orig. *coverte de barun*.] *adj.* = COVERT *a.* 4. *sb.* The condition of a *feme covert*. So † **Covert-feme** (*joc.*) DRYDEN.

Coverture (kɒ·vəɹtiŭɹ). ME. [– OFr. *coverture* (mod. *couverture*) :– Rom. **coopertura*; see -URE.] **1.** Anything used to cover; covering 1450. † **2.** A coverlet –1697. **3.** Shelter; refuge. Also *fig.* 1450. **4.** Disguise, veil. Also *fig.* ME. **5.** *Law.* The condition of a *feme covert* (see COVERT *a.* 4) 1542.

1. Couches..with their rich covertures RAWLINSON. The waggon's c. E. B. BROWNING. **4.** The specious Mantle, and couerture of Religion 1625.

Covet (kɒ·vėt), *v.* [ME. *cuveite, coveite* – OFr. *cu-, coveitier* (mod. *convoiter*) :– Rom. **cupiditare*, f. *cupiditas* CUPIDITY.] **1.** *trans.* To desire; *esp.* to desire eagerly, long for. Also *fig.* † **2.** To desire with concupiscence –1577. **3.** To desire culpably; to long for (what is another's). (The ordinary sense.) ME. Also *absol.* † **4.** *intr.* To lust; also with *for, after* –1611.

1. Though thou gold coveyte ME. Couet earnestly the best gifts 1 *Cor.* 12:31. **3.** Thou shalt not couet thy neighbours house *Exod.* 20:17. Hence **Co·vetable** *a.* greatly desirable. **Co·veter.**

Covetise. *arch.* ME. [– OFr. *coveitise* (mod. *convoitise*), alt., with suffix-change, from *coveitié, covoitié* :– L. *cupiditas, -tat-* CUPIDITY.] **1.** Inordinate desire; lust. † **2.** *spec.* Inordinate desire of wealth, or of what is another's –1652.

† **Co·vetiveness.** 1815. [f. COVET *v.* + -IVE + -NESS.] *Phrenol.* = ACQUISITIVENESS –1827.

Covetous (kɒ·vėtəs), *a.* ME. [– OFr. *coveitous* (mod. *convoiteux*) :– Gallo-Rom. **cupiditosus*; see CUPIDITY, -OUS.] **1.** Eagerly desirous *of*, †*for*, *to do*, *have*, or *be*. **2.** Culpably desirous of wealth or possessions; *esp.* of what is another's; of actions, etc.: Proceeding from cupidity ME. ¶ Occas. written for COVETISE.

1. C. only of a virtuous praise COWPER. **2.** Ryches encreaseth auaryce in a couetous man CAXTON. The covetouse flatery, Which many a worthy king deceiveth GOWER. Hence **Co·vetously** *adv.*

Covetousness (kɒ·vėtəsnės). 1486. [f. prec. + -NESS.] **1.** Inordinate desire (*of*) –1595. **2.** Culpable desire of that which is another's 1526.

1. When Workemen striue to do better then wel, They do confound their skill in couetousnesse *John* IV. ii. 29.

Covey (kɒ·vi), *sb.*[1] 1440. [– OFr. *covée* (mod. *couvée*) :– Rom. **cubata* hatching, f. L. *cubare* lie.] **1.** A brood or hatch of partridges; a family of partridges keeping together during the first season. (Occas. also of grouse, etc.) **2.** *fig.* and *transf.* A family, party, set 1590.

1. Sinne is..like the Partridges, which flye by Coueys 1614. **2.** A c. of fiddlers BEAUM. & FL., of new doctrines SANDERSON.

† **Covey,** *sb.*[2] 1593. [perh. f. COVE *sb.*[1] in its OE. sense of 'closet', etc.] A pantry.

† **Co·vey,** *v.*; see COUVE.

† **Covid** (kɒ·vid). *Anglo-Ind.* 1685. [– Pg. *covado* cubit.] A lineal measure formerly used in India: it varied from 36 to 14 inches –1802.

Covin (kɒ·vin), *sb.* ME. [– OFr. *covin, covine* :– med.L. *convenium*, pl. or fem. sing. *-ia*, f. *convenire* come together, agree. See CONVENE.] † **1.** A company –1513. **2.** A privy agreement between two or more to the prejudice of another ME. **3.** Fraud, deceit (*arch.*) ME. So † **Covin** *v.* to agree upon. Hence **Co·vinous** *a.*; **-ly** *adv.* collusively.

Coving (kōᵘ·viŋ), *sb.* 1703. [f. COVE *sb.*[1] + -ING[1].] **1.** An arched or vaulted piece of building; coved work. **2.** *pl.* The inclined sides of a fireplace 1796.

Cow (kau), *sb.*[1] [OE. *cū* = OFris *kū*, OS. *kō* (Du. *koe*), OHG. *kuo, chuo* (G. *kuh*), ON. *kýr* :– Gmc. **kōuz*, **kōz*, fem., rel. to L. *bōs*, Gr. βοῦς. The normal descendant of the mutated OE. pl. *cȳ* (cf. G. *kühe*) is north. *kye*; the form *kine* (now arch.) descends from a ME. (XIII) extension of this with *-n* from the weak declension, which was mainly due to late OE. gen. pl. *cȳna* (for *cūa*). *Cows* hardly appears before 1600.] **1.** The female of the domestic or of any bovine animal OE. Also *transf.* **2.** The female of some other large animals, *e.g.* elephant, whale, seal, etc., the male of which is called a *bull* 1725. **3.** *Mining.* A kind of self-acting brake with two prongs used in ascending an inclined line of rails. (Also called *bull*.) 1834. Also *attrib.*

Comb.: **a. c.-baby,** a timorous person; **-bird** (*U.S.*), a name for species of *Molothrus*, esp. *M. ater* or *M. pecoris* (called also *cow blackbird, cow bunting*); so called because associated with cattle; also, the Yellow-billed Cuckoo (*Coccyzus americanus*); **-blakes** (*dial.*), dried cow-dung used for fuel; **-calf,** a female calf; **-catcher** (*U.S.*), an apparatus fixed in front of a locomotive engine, to remove straying cattle or obstructions from the line; **-gate, -gait,** pasture for a c.; **-heart,** a pseudo-etym. var. of COWARD; so **-hearted** *ppl. a.*; **-hee·l, -heel,** the foot of a c. or ox stewed into a jelly; the dish so made; **-hocked** *ppl. a.*, having hocks that turn inwards like a cow's (said of horses and dogs); **-house,** a shed for cows; **-keeper,** a keeper of cows, a dairyman; **-keeping**; **-la:dy,** a LADY-COW, Lady-bird; a fly used by anglers; **-leech,** a c.-doctor; hence **-leeching; -lick,** a tuft of hair which looks as if it had been licked by a c.; **-man,** (*a*) a man who attends to cows; (*b*) a ranchman in the western U.S.; **-milker,** a mechanical contrivance for milking cows; **-paps,** a marine polyp, *Alcyonarium digitatum*; **-path,** a path made or used by cows; **-pen,** a pen for cows, also as *v.*; hence **cowpen-bird** (*U.S.*) = *cow-bird*; **-pilot,** a fish (*Pomacentrus saxatilis*) of the West Indies, etc.; **-puncher** (*U.S.*), a c.-driver in the western States; **-quakes** (*dial.*), Quaking-grass, *Briza media*; also, Common Spurry; **-run,** a common on which cows pasture; **-shark,** a shark of the family *Hexanchidæ* or *Notidanidæ*; **-troopial** = *cow-bird*; **-woman.**

b. In names of plants, in some of which *cow-* means 'eaten by' or 'fit for cows', or, like 'horse-', indicates a coarse or wild species: **c.-berry,** the shrub *Vaccinium vitis-idæa*, and its fruit, called also Red Whortleberry, Red Huckleberry; **-chervil** = *cow-parsley*; **-cress,** a name for *Lepidium campestre*; **-grass,** a wild species of Trefoil, *Trifolium medium*; also, a cultivated form of Red Clover; **cow's lungwort,** *Verbascum thapsus*; **-parsley,** an umbelliferous plant, *Anthriscus* (*Chærophyllum*) *sylvestris*, also called *Cow-weed, Wild Chervil*, or *Cicely*; **-pa·rsnip,** a coarse umbelliferous plant, *Heracleum sphondylium*, wild in Britain; **-pea,** a name for *Vigna sinensis*, grown for fodder in the southern U.S.; **c. plant,** a climbing plant of Ceylon, *Gymnema lactiferum*, N.O. *Asclepiadaceæ*, yielding a milky juice used for food; **-thistle** (*Herb.*), *Carduus lanceolatus* or *C. palustris*; **-tree,** one of various trees yielding a milky juice; *esp.* a South American tree, *Brosimum galactodendron*, N.O. *Artocarpaceæ*; also the Cow-tree of Para, *Mimusops elata*, N.O. *Sapotaceæ*; of British Guiana, *Tabernæmontana utilis*; **-weed,** wild chervil; **-wheat,** a plant, *Melampyrum arvense*, N.O. *Scrophulariaceæ*, which grows in cornfields; also a name of other species of *Melampyrum*.

Cow, kow (kau), *sb.*[2] *Sc.* 1500. [Origin unkn.] A hobgoblin; a scarecrow; cf. WORRICOW.

Cow (kau), *sb.*[3] *local.* 1736. Phonetic var. of COWL *sb.*[1]

Cow (kau), *v.* 1605. [prob. – ON. *kúga* oppress, tyrannize over (Norw. *kue*, MSw. *kufwa*, Sw. *kuva*).] *trans.* 'To depress with fear' (J.); to dispirit, overawe, intimidate.

We feel faint and heartless..In plain words, we are cowed BURKE. To be cowed into submission 1847.

Cowage, cowhage (kau·ėdʒ). Also **cow-itch.** 1640. [– Hindi *kiwā̆nch, kawā̆nh, kawā̆ch*.] The stinging hairs of the pod of a tropical plant, *Macuna pruriens*, N.O. *Leguminosæ*; formerly used as an anthelmintic; also the plant, or its pods.

Cowan (kōᵘ·ăn). 1598. [Origin unkn.] **1.** *Sc.* One who does the work of a mason, but has not been apprenticed to the trade. **2.** Hence, One uninitiated in the secrets of Freemasonry 1707. **3.** *slang.* A sneak, eavesdropper.

Coward (kau·əɹd), *sb.* and *a.* [ME. *cu(e)ard* – OFr. *cuard*, later *couard*, f. Rom. **coda*, L. *cauda* tail; see -ARD.]

A. *sb.* **1.** One who displays ignoble fear in the face of pain, danger, or difficulty; a pusillanimous person. **2.** Applied to animals 1486.

1. Cowards dye many times before their deaths SHAKS. **2.** Don Juan..ran a c. throughout 1880.

B. *adj.* **1.** Destitute of courage; fainthearted ME. **2.** Of actions, etc.; = COWARDLY *a.* 2. 1600. **3.** *Her.* Of a lion, etc., borne as a charge: Having the tail drawn in between the legs 1500. Also as quasi-*adv.*

1. Nor undertake the same for cowheard feare SPENSER *F.Q.* V. x. 15. **2.** Hence with those c. terms; or fight, or fly POPE.

Hence † **Cow·ard** *v.* to make cowardly; to call, or show to be a c. **Cow·ardize** *v.* to make a c. of; to daunt. **Cow·ard-like** *a.* and *adv.* **Cow·ardly** *adv.* † **Cow·ardness,** cowardice. † **Cow·ardous** *a.* cowardly. † **Cow·ardship,** † **Cow·ardy,** cowardice.

Cowardice (kau·əɹdis). ME. [– OFr. *couardise*, f. *couard*; see prec., -ISE[2], -ICE.] The quality of a coward; cowardliness; want of courage to face danger; pusillanimity.

It is no c. to fly from the rage of persecutors 1703.

Cowardly (kau·əɹdli), *a.* 1551. [f. COWARD + -LY[1].] **1.** Having the character or spirit of a coward; wanting in courage; pusillanimous. **2.** Befitting a coward; proceeding from a spirit of cowardice 1601.

2. At c. distance..secure thou hast stood COLERIDGE. Hence **Cow·ardliness,** cowardice.

Cow·-bane. 1776. [f. COW *sb.*[1] + BANE *sb.*] The Water Hemlock, *Cicuta virosa* mentioned by Linnæus as fatal to cows. *Spotted c.*: an American species, *C. maculata.*

Cow·-boy, cow·boy. 1725. **1.** A boy who tends cows. **2.** *U.S. Hist.* Applied to some of the tory partisans of Westchester Co., New York, during the Revolutionary war, who were barbarous in the treatment of opponents 1775. **3.** In the western U.S.: A man employed to take care of grazing cattle on a ranch 1882.

3. The rough-and-ready life of men who have cast in their lot among cow-boys 1887.

Cower (kauᵊɹ), *v.* ME. [– MLG. *kūren* lie in wait (whence G. *kauern*).] **1.** *intr.* To stand or squat in a bent position; to bend with the knees and back; to crouch. **b.** *pa. pple.* = Cowering (*rare*). 1855. **2.** *trans.* To lower, bend down (*rare*) 1790.

1. They coure so over the coles, theyr eyes be blear'd with smooke 1575. **2.** My muse her wing maun c. BURNS. Hence **Cow·eringly** *adv.*

Cow·-fish. 1634. [COW *sb.*[1]] **1.** The sea-cow or manatee. **2.** A grampus 1860. **3.** A fish, *Ostracion quadricorne*, having two strong spines like horns over the eyes 1885.

Cowhage, var. of COWAGE.

Cow·herd. OE. [See HERD[2].] One whose occupation is to tend cows at pasture. So **Cow·herdess** (*rare*), a female c.

Cow·-hi:de, cow·hide, *sb.* 1640. **1.** The hide of a cow, or leather made of it. **2.** *U.S.* A strong whip made of the raw or dressed hide of a cow 1839. **3.** *attrib.* (kau·həid). Made of cow-hide 1840. Hence **Cow·-hide, cowhide** *v.* to flog with a cow-hide.

Cowish (kau·iʃ), *sb.* 1838. [prob. Amer. Indian.] A plant with an edible root found in Oregon.

Cowish (kau·iʃ), *a.* 1570. [f. Cow *sb.*[1] + -ISH[1].] **1.** Like a cow. † **2.** Cowardly –1605. **2.** The C. terror of his spirit *Lear* IV. ii. 12.

Cow-itch; see COWAGE.

Cowl (kaul), *sb.*[1] [OE. *cug(e)le, cūle,* corresp. to MLG., MDu. *cōghel,* OHG. *cucula, cugula, chugela* (G. *kugel, kogel*) – eccl. L. *cuculla,* f. L. *cucullus* hood of a cloak. In ME. reinforced by *kuuele* :– OE. *cufle,* and prob. by (O)Fr. *coule.*] **1.** A garment with a hood (*vestis caputiata*) worn by monks; *occas.*, the hood alone. **b.** Sometimes = Monk 1653. Also *transf.* and *fig.* **2.** A cowl-shaped covering, usually turning with the wind, placed on the top of a chimney or ventilating shaft, to assist ventilation. Also, a wire cage at the top of the funnel of a locomotive, etc. 1812. **b.** = SCUTTLE *sb.*[2] 3. **c.** (Also **cow·ling.**) A removable cover round the engine of an aeroplane 1917.

1. b. Bluff Harry..turn'd the cowls adrift TENNYSON. *Comb.* **c.-muscle,** the *cucullaris* or trapezius muscle. Hence **Cowl** *v.* to make a monk of; to cover as with a c. **Cowled** *ppl. a.* wearing a c.; (*Bot.*) cucullate.

Cowl, coul (kaul), *sb.*[2] [ME. **cuvel(e, covelle,* app. – OFr. *cuvele* :– L. *cupella,* dim. of *cupa* tub, cask.] A tub or the like for water, etc.; *esp.* one with two ears borne by two men on a cowlstaff (*arch.* or *dial.*). *Comb.* **Cowl-staff, coul-staff,** a stout stick used to carry a c., being thrust through the two handles of it; a stang.

Cowle (kaul). *Anglo-Ind.* 1688. [– Arab. *ḳawl* word, utterance, declaration.] An engagement, lease, or grant in writing; a safe-conduct or amnesty.

Co-wo·rk, *v.* 1613. *intr.* To work together. **Co-wo·rker,** a co-operator.

Cowperian (kupīə·riăn), *a.* 1738. [f. William *Cowper,* the anatomist (1666–1709); see -IAN.] *Cowperian glands*: a pair of glands situated beneath, and with ducts opening into, the urethra in male Mammalia. Also *Cowper's glands.* **Cowperi·tis,** inflammation of Cowper's glands.

Cow·-po:x. 1798. [Cow *sb.*[1]] A vaccine disease which appears on the teats of cows in the form of vesicles (pocks). The communication of this to the human subject by VACCINATION gives immunity (whole or partial) from small-pox. Occas. called *kine-pox.* (The pl. *pocks* as the name of the disease is conventionally spelt *pox.*) Hence † **Cow·-pox** *v.* to vaccinate.

Cowrie, cowry (kauə·ri). 1662. [– Urdu, Hindi *kauṛī.*] Any gastropod (or its shell) of the genus *Cypræa* or family *Cypræidæ*; *esp.* the shell of *Cypræa moneta,* found abundantly in the Indian Ocean, and used as money in parts of Africa and Southern Asia. Also *attrib.*

Cowrie pine; see KAURI.

Cowslip (kau·slip). [OE. *cūslyppe,* f. *cū* Cow *sb.*[1] + *slyppe* viscous or slimy substance, i.e. 'cowslobber' or 'cow-dung'; cf. OXLIP.] **1.** The common name of *Primula veris,* a well-known wild plant in pastures and grassy banks. Also called *Paigle.* **2.** *U.S.* The Marsh Marigold 1856.

Beyond into the fields, gathering of cowslipps PEPYS. **American C.,** *Dodecatheon meadia* (N.O. *Primulaceæ*), with umbels of large rose-purple or white flowers, found in woods in N. America. **French** or **Mountain C.,** the Auricula (*Primula auricula*). **Virginian C.,** *Mertensia* or *Pulmonaria virginica.*

Cowslip'd, cowslipt (kau·slipt), *a.* 1794. [f. prec. + -ED[1].] Covered with cowslips.

Cox (kǫks), *sb. colloq.* Abbrev. of COXSWAIN. Hence **Cox** *v.* to act as c. to (a boat); also *intr.* **Co·xless** *a.*

Cox, var. of COKES *Obs.*, fool.

‖ **Coxa** (kǫ·ksă). Pl. **coxæ.** 1706. [L.; = hip.] **1.** *Anat.* The hip, or hip-joint; also the ischium, the coccyx. **2.** *Zool.* The joint by which the leg is articulated in insects, arachnida, and crustacea 1826. Hence **Co·xal** *a.*

Coxa·gra [Gr. ἄγρα trap, after *podagra*], *Pathol.* pain in the hip. **Coxa·lgia** [Gr. -αλγία], **Coxa·lgy** [Fr. *coxalgie*], pain in the hip-joint; hip-disease. **Coxa·lgic** *a.* pertaining to or affected with coxalgia. **Coxarthri·tis** [ARTHRITIS], gout in the hip; coxitis.

Coxcomb (kǫ·kskōᵘm). 1573. [= COCKSCOMB.] † **1.** A cap worn by a jester, like a cock's comb in shape and colour –1605. † **2.** (*joc.*) The head –1866. **3.** A simpleton (*obs.*); now, a foolish, conceited, showy person; a fop 1573. † **4.** *Bot.* See COCKSCOMB –1756. † **5.** ? A kind of lace with an edging like a cock's comb –1760. Also *attrib.*

1. What is your Crest, a Coxcombe *Tam. Shr.* II. i. 226. **2.** *Twel. N.* V. i. 193. **3.** *Oth.* V. ii. 234. Those shallow atheistical coxcombs MACKINTOSH. Hence **Coxco·mbic, -al** *a.* like a c.; of or pertaining to a c. **Coxcombica·lity,** coxcombical quality or act. **Coxco·mbically** *adv.* like a c. † **Coxco·mbly** *a.* like or characteristic of a c. **Coxco·mbry,** †foolishness; foppery, a piece of foppery (var. **Coxco·mbity** *rare*); coxcombs collectively.

‖ **Coxe·ndix.** Pl. **coxe·ndices.** 1615. [L., f. *coxa* hip.] The hip or hip-bone; also the ischium, the ilium.

Coxitis (kǫksəi·tis). 1878. [f. COXA + -ITIS.] *Pathol.* Inflammation of the hip-joint.

Coxocerite (kǫksǫ·sĕrəit), 1877. [f. L. *coxa* + Gr. κέρας + -ITE[1] 3.] *Zool.* 'The basal segment of the antenna in Crustacea' (*Syd. Soc. Lex.*). Hence **Coxoceri·tic** *a.*

Coxo-fe·moral, *a.* 1831. [f. comb. form of COXA + FEMORAL.] *Anat.* Pertaining to the coxa or ilium and the femur; ilio-femoral.

Coxopodite (kǫksǫ·podəit). 1870. [f. comb. form of COXA + Gr. ποδ- foot + -ITE[1] 3.] *Zool.* The basal joint which connects the limbs to the body in the Arthropoda. Hence **Coxopodi·tic** *a.*

Coxswain, cockswain (kǫ·kswe[i]n, kǫ·k·s'n). Also **coxon, coxen.** 1463. [f. COCK *sb.*[3] ship's boat + SWAIN. Formerly also †*coxon, coxen*; cf. *boatswain, bosun.*] The helmsman of a boat; a petty officer having permanent charge of a ship's boat and its crew. Hence **Co·xswainless** *a.* without a c. **Co·xswainship,** skill in steering.

Coy (koi), *sb.* Now *dial.* 1621. [– Du. *kooi,* †*koye,* in same sense, a parallel development to MDu. *kouwe* (Du. dial. *kouw* cage), MLG. *kaue* – L. *cavea* cage. See DECOY *sb.*[2]] **1.** A DECOY. **2.** A lobster-trap 1733. **3.** = *Coy-duck.* Also *fig.* 1629. *Comb.* **c.-duck** = DECOY-DUCK; also *transf.*

Coy (koi), *a.* ME. [– (O)Fr. *coi,* earlier *quei* :– Rom. **quētus,* for L. *quietus* QUIET.] † **1.** Quiet, still –1632. **2.** Not demonstrative; shyly reserved or retiring ME. Of a place or thing: Inaccessible, secluded 1670. Also *fig.* † **3.** Distant, disdainful –1665.

2. 'Tis but a kiss I beg: why art thou c. SHAKS. [Feining] c. lookes SPENSER *F.Q.* I. ii. 27. The Nile's c. source 1767. Hence **Coy·ish** *a.* somewhat c. **Coy·ly** *adv.* †quietly; in a c. manner; †disdainfully.

Coy (koi), *v.* ME. [f. COY *a.*, or perh. orig. an aphetic form of ACCOY *v.*] † **1.** *trans.* To calm, appease –1530. † **2.** To stroke soothingly, caress –1674. † **3.** To coax, gain over by caresses –1634. **4.** *intr.* To behave coyly; to affect shyness or reserve (*arch.*) 1583; †to disdain 1607. **5.** *fig.* To withdraw itself 1864.

2. While I thy amiable cheekes doe c. *Mids. N.* IV. i. 2. **3.** Phr. *To c. with*: to coax. PEPYS. **4.** What! you c. it, my nymph of the high-way SCOTT. If he..coy'd To heare Cominius speake, Ile keepe at home *Cor.* V. i. 6.

† **Coyn, coyne.** ME. [– OFr. *cooin,* later *coin* (mod. *coing*); see QUINCE.] A quince –1575.

Coyn(e, obs. f. COIN, QUEAN, QUOIN.

Coyness (koi·nės). 1575. [-NESS.] The quality of being coy; an instance of this.

I scorne men's coynesse, women's stoutnesse hate STIRLING.

Coynye, coignye (koi·nʸi). *sb.* Also *erron.* **coyn, coin.** 1449. [– Ir. *coinnemh* (keinʸev) billeting, one billeted.] *Irish Hist.* The billeting of military followers upon private persons; food and entertainment exacted, by the Irish chiefs, for their attendants; an impost levied for the same purpose.

The damnable custome..of Coigne and Livory FULLER. Hence † **Coy·nye, coi·gnye** *v. trans.* to billet *upon*; also to exact c. from; *refl.* and *intr.* to quarter oneself *upon.*

‖ **Coyote** (ko,yōᵘ·te, ko,yōᵘ·t). 1850. [– Mex. Sp. – Aztec *coyotl.*] *Zool.* The name, in Mexico and now in U.S., of the prairie- or barking-wolf (*Canis latrans*) of the Pacific slope of North America.

Comb. **c.-diggings,** small shafts sunk by miners in California, compared to c.-holes. Hence **Coyo·te** *v.* to mine in irregular openings.

Coypu, coypou (koi·pu). 1793. [Native name.] A S. American aquatic rodent (*Myopotamus coypus*), nearly as large as the beaver; called also *C. Rat.*

Coystrel; see COISTREL, CUSTREL.

Coz (kɒz). 1559. An abbrev. of COUSIN, used both to relatives and in the wider sense.

Coze (kōᵘz), *v.* 1828. [app. – Fr. *causer* chat.] To have a long familiar talk. Hence **Coze** *sb.* a cosy friendly chat.

Cozen, obs. f. COUSIN.

Cozen (kɒ·z'n), *v.* 1573. [prob. orig. vagrants' cant, and perh. to be assoc. with COUSIN, through OFr. *cousin* dupe, or *cousiner* 'to clayme kindred for advantage, or particular ends' (Cotgrave); but frequent sp. with *-on* has suggested deriv. from It. *cozzonare* 'to play the horse-breaker, to play the craftie knaue' (Florio), f. *cozzone* middleman, broker = Fr. *cosson* dealer.] **1.** *trans.* To cheat, defraud by deceit. **2.** To dupe, beguile, impose upon 1583. Also *absol.*

1. He that trusts to a Greek is sure to be couzened HEYLYN. **2.** By gar I am cozoned, I ha married oon Garsoon, a boy *Merry W.* V. v. 218. Hence **Co·zenage,** the practice of cozening; deception; a deception. **Co·zener,** a deceiver, cheat.

Cozie, Cozily, -ness, Cozy; see COSY, etc.

† **Co·zier.** 1532. [– OFr. *cousere,* f. *coudre* sew; for *-ier* see -IER (1).] A cobbler –1658.

Cr., abbrev. of *Creditor, Credit.*

Craal, var. of KRAAL.

Crab (kræb), *sb.*[1] [OE. *crabba* = (M)LG., (M)Du. *krabbe,* ON. *krabbi,* rel. to MLG. *krabben,* ON. *krafla* scratch; see CRAB *v.*[2]] **1.** Any decapod crustaceous animal of the tribe *Brachyura*; *esp.* the edible species found on or near the seacoast. Also applied with qualifications to other Crustacea and Arachnida.

The common edible crab of Europe is *Cancer pagurus*; the edible or *blue crab* of the United States is *Callinectes hastatus.* Crabs can move in any direction, and frequently walk sideways or backwards: cf. *Haml.* II. ii. 205.

2. *Astron.* = CANCER 2. OE. **3.** Short for crab-louse 1840. **4.** A machine (orig. with claws) for hoisting or hauling heavy weights. **a.** A kind of small capstan. **b.** A portable machine for raising weights, etc., consisting of a frame with a horizontal barrel on which a chain or rope is wound by means of handles and gearing; used in connection with pulleys, a gin, etc.; a portable winch. 1627. **5.** *pl. slang.* The lowest throw at hazard, two aces 1768. **6.** *Rowing. To catch a c.*: to get the oar jammed under water (as if the rower had caught a crab, which was holding the oar down). Also *improp.*, the action of missing the water with the stroke, etc. 1785. Also *attrib.*

Comb.: **c.-catcher,** any of several species of herons which feed on small crabs; **-claw,** a claw for grappling or fastening; **-eater,** occas. name for the Little Bittern, *Ardetta minuta*; a scombroid fish, *Elacate canada*; † **-face,** an ugly ill-tempered looking face; so **-faced, -favoured; -lobster,** the porcelain-c.; **-louse,** a parasitical insect, *Phthirus inguinalis,* which infests parts of the body; **-pot,** a trap of wickerwork for taking crabs; **crab's-eye, -eyes,** (usu. *pl.*) a round concretion found in the stomach of the crayfish, etc., consisting mainly of carbonate of lime; used formerly as an absorbent and antacid; (*pl.*) the scarlet seeds of *Abrus precatorius*; also the plant; **-spider,** the name of several species of spiders.

Crab (kræb), *sb.*[2] ME. [contemp. with north. *scrab* (prob. of Scand. origin; cf. Sw. dial. *skrabba* wild apple), of which it may be an alt. by assoc. with prec. or CRABBED.] **1.** Name of the wild apple, especially connoting its sour, harsh quality; applied also to cultivated varieties. **2.** The wild apple-tree of northern Europe, the original of the common apple ME. **3.** A crabstick 1740. **4.** Applied to persons [orig. as *fig.* of 1; later, with reference to CRABBED, or ? to CRAB *sb.*[1]] 1580. Also *attrib.*

1. She's as like this, as a Crabbe's like an Apple *Lear* I. v. 15. 4. That sowre c. 1605. That c. of a priest LYTTON.

Comb.: **c.-apple**: see senses 1 and 2; **-stick,** a stick made of the wood of the crab-tree; also *fig.*; **-stock,** a young crab-tree used as a stock to graft upon; also *fig.*; **-tree,** the wild apple-tree; also *attrib.*

Crab (kræb), *sb.*³ 1769. [Alteration of *carap*, the S. Amer. tree *Carapa guianensis.*] Used in comb.: as **c.-nut,** the nut or seed of this tree; **-oil** (*carap oil*), the oil obtained from C.-nuts, used for lighting and as an anthelmintic; so **-tree, -wood.**

† **Crab** (kræb), *v.*¹ ME. [f. CRABBED *a.* or its source.] **1.** *trans.* To go counter to, to cross; to irritate, anger. *Sc.* –1605. **2.** *trans.* To sour 1662.

Crab (kræb), *v.*² 1575. [– (M)LG. *krabben*; see CRAB *sb.*¹] **1.** *Falconry.* Of hawks: To scratch, claw, or fight with each other (*trans.* and *intr.*). **2.** *trans.* To criticize adversely, peck at, pull to pieces (*colloq.*) 1812.

2. Men who want to 'c. the new rifle' 1890.

Crab, *v.*³ 1619. [Nonce-uses; see CRAB *sb.*¹, ².] † **1.** To cudgel. **2.** *Naut.* Of a ship: to drift sideways to leeward 1867. **3.** *U.S. colloq.* (*fig.*) To back out; = CRAWFISH *v.* **4.** *Dyeing.* To subject to the operation of CRABBING (*vbl. sb.*²) 1892. **5.** See CRABBING *vbl. sb.*¹

Crabbed (kræ·bèd), *a.* ME. [f. CRAB *sb.*¹ + -ED¹; cf. DOGGED. Orig. with ref. to the gait and habits of the crab, which suggest cross-grained or fractious disposition; cf. LG. *krabbe* cantankerous man, *krabbig* contentious, cross-grained. There has been later assoc. with CRAB *sb.*²] **1.** Of persons: *orig.* Cross-grained, perverse; later: Cross-tempered, churlish 1535. Also *transf.* of things. † **2.** Proceeding from or expressing a harsh or sour disposition –1641. † **3.** Unpalatable, bitter –1622. † **4.** Of trees, sticks, etc.: Crooked; gnarled; cross-grained –1675. **5.** Perversely intricate; hard to make sense of; difficult to decipher 1612. **6.** Of the nature of the crab-tree or its fruit; also *fig.* 1565.

1. For women are c., þat comes þem of kinde 1440. A cancred c. carle SPENSER. *transf.* How charming is divine Philosophy! Not harsh and c. MILT. *Comus* 477. 2. A c. face 1641. 5. In c. Scholastick style BAXTER. A c. hand 1800. 6. *Wint. T.* I. ii. 102.

Hence **Cra·bbedly** *adv.* **Cra·bbedness,** c. quality; asperity or sourness of temper; rugged or perverse intricacy.

Crabber (kræ·bəɹ). 1848. [f. CRAB *sb.*¹ + -ER¹.] One who fishes for crabs, or the boat he uses.

Crabbery (kræ·bĕri). 1845. [f. as prec. + -ERY.] A place abounding in crabs.

Crabbing, *vbl. sb.*¹ 1657. [f. CRAB *sb.*¹, ² + -ING¹, implying verb *to crab.*] **1.** Crab-fishing. Also *attrib.* **2.** Gathering crab-apples; cf. *nutting*, etc. 1877.

Cra·bbing, *vbl. sb.*² 1874. *Dyeing.* The operation of passing a woollen fabric in a state of tension through boiling water, and at once wrapping it on a roller, where it is subjected to great pressure. The object is to prevent unequal contraction, and to give the cloth a certain finish.

† **Cra·bbish,** *a.* 1485. [f. CRAB *sb.*¹ + -ISH¹.] Cross, crabbed –1606.

Crabby (kræ·bi), *a.*¹ 1583. [f. as prec. + -Y¹.] **1.** Crab-like. **2.** Abounding in crabs 1622.

Crabby (kræ·bi), *a.*² 1550. [f. CRAB *sb.*² + -Y¹.] † **1.** = CRABBED 4, 5. –1599. **2.** = CRABBED 1, 6. 1776.

† **Cra·ber,** *rare.* [– Fr. *crabier* (*raton crabier*), f. *crabe* CRAB *sb.*¹] The water-rat. WALTON.

† **Cra·b-fish.** ME. = CRAB *sb.*¹ 1. –1753.

Cra·b-grass. 1597. [f. CRAB *sb.*¹] **1.** The Glasswort, *Salicornia herbacea.* ? *Obs.* **2.** The Knot-grass. **3.** In *U.S.* A species of grass, *Panicum sanguinale*, and allied species 1881.

Cra·b-harrow. 1796. [f. CRAB *sb.*¹] A harrow with bent teeth for tearing up the ground; its latest form is the *drag-harrow.* Hence **Crab-harrow** *v.*

‖ **Crabier.** 1825. [Fr.; see CRABER.] = *Crab-catcher* (see CRAB *sb.*¹).

Crabite (kræ·bəit). *rare.* 1847. [– Fr. *crabite*, f. *crabe* CRAB *sb.*¹; see -ITE¹ 2 a.] A fossil crab.

Crablet (kræ·blėt). 1841. [f. CRAB *sb.*¹ + -LET.] A small or young crab. So **Cra·bling.**

Cra·b-sidle, *v.* [f. CRAB *sb.*¹ + SIDLE *v.*] To shuffle sideways like a crab. SOUTHEY.

† **Crabut.** 1626. [Origin unkn.; cf. Fr. *crapaudeau, crapaudine*, f. *crapeau* toad.] A kind of fire-arm, used in 17th c. –1659.

Crab yaws. 1740. [f. CRAB *sb.*¹ + YAWS.] In the West Indies, a kind of yaws attacking the soles of the feet, forming ulcers with very hard edges.

Crack (kræk), *sb.* [ME. *crak*, corresp. to MDu. *crak*, (OH)G. *krach*. Cf. next.]

I. Of sound. **1.** A sudden sharp and loud noise; *e.g.* the c. of a rifle, a whip, of thunder, etc.; a sharp, sounding blow (*colloq.*) 1838. **2.** The time occupied by a crack or shot; an instant 1725. **3.** Loud talk, brag; *occas.*, exaggeration, lie (*arch.*) 1450. **4.** Brisk talk; *pl.* news (*Sc.* and *n. dial.*) 1725.

1. What will the Line stretch out to th' cracke (*i.e.* the thunder-peal) of Doome *Macb.* IV. i. 117. A c. on the head DICKENS. 3. That's a damned confounded—c. GOLDSM.

II. Breaking, etc. **1.** *Thieves' slang.* House-breaking 1812. **2.** A break in which the parts do or do not remain in contact; a fissure; a partial fracture 1530. **3.** A flaw, deficiency, unsoundness 1570. **4.** The breaking of the voice 1611.

3. I cannot Beleeve this C. to be in my dread Mistresse *Wint T.* I. ii. 322. 4. *Cymb.* IV. ii. 236.

III. Transf. † **1.** A lively lad; a rogue. [? short for *crack-hemp.*] –1673. † **2.** A braggart, liar –1681. **3.** One full of conversation. *Sc.* 1827. † **4.** [? from II. 3.] A prostitute –1785. † **5.** A crack-brain –1711. **6.** That which is 'cracked up'; anything of superior excellence; see CRACK *a.* 1637. **7.** = CRACKSMAN 1749. **8.** *slang.* Dry wood 1851.

1. When hee was a C., not thus high 2 *Hen. IV*, III. ii. 34. 5. The Parliament. .look upon me, forsooth, as a C. and a Projector ADDISON. var. **Crake** (in sense I. 3).

Crack (kræk), *v.* [OE. *cracian* sound, resound = (M)Du. *krāken*, OHG. *krahhōn* (G. *krachen*).] *orig.* To make a sharp dry sound in breaking.

I. 1. *intr.* To make a sharp or explosive noise OE. **2.** *trans.* To cause (anything, *e.g.* a whip) to make a sharp noise 1647. **3.** To slap, smack, box. Now *dial.* 1470. **4.** *trans.* To utter briskly or with *éclat*, as in *c. a joke* ME. **5.** *intr.* to talk big, brag. Now *dial.* 1460. **6.** *intr.* To chat, talk of the news (*Sc.* and *n. dial.*) 1450. **7.** *C. up*: to eulogize (*colloq.*) 1844.

1. Moist wood that cracketh in the fire FULKE. 5. Thou art always cracking and boasting ADDISON.

II. Referring mainly to the breaking. **1.** *trans.* To break (a skull, a nut, etc.) with a sudden sharp report ME. † **b.** (from *fig.* use of phr. *to c. a nut*) To puzzle out, discuss –1768. **2.** *transf.* To get at the contents of (a bottle, etc.); to empty, 'discuss' 15.. **3.** *Thieves' slang.* To break open 1725. † **4.** To snap or split asunder. Also *trans.* –1745. **5.** *fig.* To come to pieces, break down 1658. **6.** *intr.* To break without complete separation of parts ME. **7.** *trans.* To break (anything) so that the parts remain in contact but do not cohere; to break into fissures 1605. **8.** To break the clearness of (the voice); to render hoarse. Also *intr.* 1602. **9.** *fig.* To render of unsound mind 1614. **10.** To damage (credit, etc.) so that it is no longer sound 1567.

1. b. Logic you cannot c. without a tutor WESLEY. 3. Phr. *To c. a crib*: to break open a house. 4. *trans.* Blow windes, and c. your cheekes SHAKS. 6. Heat causes these soils to c. 1855. 7. Glasses that are once crackt, are soon broken 1605. 8. *Timon* IV. iii. 153.

III. To move with a stroke or jerk; to 'whip' *out* or *on* (*colloq.*) 1541; *intr.* to 'pelt' *along* (*colloq.*) 1541.

Crack (kræk), *a. colloq.* 1793. [CRACK *sb.* III. 6, used *attrib.*] Pre-eminent, first-class, as *c. regiments.*

Crack (kræk), *adv.*, *int.* 1767. [The vb. stem so used.] **1.** *adv.* with a cracking sound. **2.** *int.* 1698.

1. C. went his whip SOUTHEY. 2. C.! all is gone 1756.

Crack- in comb.:

a. with *crack-* as the vb. stem governing an object, as † **c.-halter,** † **-hemp,** a gallows-bird; **-jaw** *a.*, fit to crack the jaws; † **-rope** = *crack-halter*; **-tryst,** one who breaks tryst. **b.** with *crack-* for *cracked-*, as **c.-brain(ed,** a crazy fellow, crazy; **-headed** = *cracked-brained*; **-skull** = *crack-brain*; **-winded** = BROKEN-WINDED.

Cracked (krækt), *ppl. a.* 1503. [f. CRACK *v.* + -ED¹.] **1.** Broken by a sharp blow 1562. **2.** Full of cracks 1570. **3.** Fractured; partially broken so as to be no longer sound 1503. **4.** *fig.* Damaged, having flaws; †bankrupt 1527. **5.** Somewhat deranged, crazy. (Now *colloq.*) 1611. **6.** Of the voice: Broken 1739.

1. Bloodie Noses, and crack'd Crownes SHAKS.

Cracker (kræ·kəɹ). 1509. [f. CRACK *v.* + -ER¹.] **1.** *gen.* One who or that which cracks; *esp.* a boaster; a liar. **2.** *colloq.* A lie 1625. **3.** *U.S.* A name for the 'poor whites' in southern States [? short for *whip-cracker*] 1767. **4.** A local name for the Pin-tail Duck, and the Corn-crake 1678. **5.** A firework which explodes with a succession of sharp reports 1590; also, a *bon-bon*, containing a fulminant, which explodes when pulled at both ends 1841. **6.** A thin hard biscuit. (Chiefly in U.S.) 1739.

Crackle (kræ·k'l), *sb.* 1591. [f. the vb.] **1.** The act of crackling 1833. † **2.** A child's rattle 1591. **3.** A kind of china ware showing what appear to be minute cracks all over its surface. So *C.-glass*, glass of a similiar character.

1. The c. of the blazing faggots 1855. 3. A skin like yellow c.-ware 1881.

Crackle (kræ·k'l), *v.* 1500. [dim. and frequent. of CRACK *v.* See -LE.] **1.** *intr.* To emit a rapid succession of slight cracks; to crepitate 1560. **2.** *trans.* To crush with slight but rapidly continuous crackling 1611. † **3.** *intr.* To crack and break *off* in small pieces 1735.

1. Huge logs blazed and crackled 1872.

Crackled (kræ·k'ld), *ppl. a.* 1659. [f. prec. + -ED¹.] Marked with cracks upon the surface. **b.** Of roast pork: Having the skin crisp and hard.

Crackling (kræ·kliŋ), *vbl. sb.* 1599. [f. as prec. + -ING¹.] **1.** The action of the verb CRACKLE; crepitation. Also *fig.* **2.** The crisp skin or rind of roast pork 1709. **3.** The residue of tallow-melting, used for feeding dogs. (Usu. *pl.*) 1621. **4.** = CRACKLE *sb.* 3. 1876.

1. The c. of thornes vnder a pot *Eccles.* 7:6. 2. The crisp, well-watched, not over-roasted, c., as it is well called LAMB. var. **Cra·cklin** (in sense 4).

Cra·ckmans. 1610. [See CRACK *sb.* III. 8. Cf. *darkmans* = night.] *Thieves' slang.* A hedge.

Cracknel (kræ·knĕl). ME. [alt. of (O)Fr. *craquelin* (whence dial. *crackling* XVI) – MDu. *krākelinc*, f. *krāken* CRACK *v.*] **1.** A light crisp biscuit, of a curved or hollowed shape. **2.** *pl.* Small pieces of fat pork fried crisp. **3.** = CRACKLE *sb.* 3.

Cracksman (kræ·ksmæ̆n). *slang.* 1812. [f. CRACK *sb.* II. 1.] A housebreaker.

Cra·ck-wi·llow. 1670. [f. CRACK *v.*] A species of willow with brittle branches, *Salix fragilis.*

Cracky (kræ·ki), *a.* 1725. [f. CRACK *sb.* + -Y¹.] **1.** Having cracks; prone to crack. **2.** Crazy 1854. **3.** Full of conversation. *Sc.* 1801.

‖ **Cracovienne** (krăkōᵘvi,e·n). 1844. [Fr. fem. adj. = Cracovian.] A light and lively Polish dance.

-cracy, formerly also **-cratie, -crasie,** repr. Fr. *-cratie* (-krasi), med.L. *-cratia*, Gr. -κρατία power, rule (f. κράτος strength, authority). The *o* which usually precedes the suffix, as in *aristocracy*, etc., has come to be viewed as part of it, whence the form *-ocracy*, which has been added to many English words; as in COTTONOCRACY, etc.

Cradle (krēⁱ·d'l), *sb.* [OE. *cradol*, of which a var. **crædel* was prob. the source of dial. *craddle, creddle*; perh. f. the same base as OHG. *kratto*, MHG., G. *kratte* basket.] **1.** A little bed or cot for an infant: properly, one mounted on rockers; often a swing-cot. Also *fig.* **2.** = Infancy, or the first stage of existence 1555. **3.** *fig.* The place in which anything is nurtured in its earlier stage 1590. **4.** That which serves as a place of repose (*poet.*) 1590. **5.** *Naut.* A standing bedstead for a wounded seaman 1803. **6.** Any framework of bars, cords, rods, etc., united by lateral ties; a grating, or hurdle-like structure ME. **7.** *Husb.* A light frame of wood attached to a scythe, having a row of long curved teeth parallel to the blade, to lay the corn more evenly in the swathe 1573. **8.** *Surg.* A protecting framework of different kinds for an injured limb, etc. 1704. **9.** *Naut.* The framework on which a ship rests during construction, etc. Also, that in which a vessel lies in a way or slip, or in a canal-lift; and the like 1627. **10.** An appliance in which a person or thing is swung or carried 1839. **11.** *Building.* The ribbing for vaulting ceilings, etc., intended to be covered with plaster 1874. **12.** *Engraving.* A chisel-like tool with a serrated edge, which is rocked to and fro over the metal plate, to produce a mezzotint ground 1788. **13.** *Gold mining.* A trough on rockers in which auriferous earth or sand is shaken in water, in order to separate the gold 1849. **14.** See CAT'S-CRADLE.

1. Wakynge a nyghtes..to rocke þe cradel LANGL. **2.** In the Latine wee haue been exercised almost from our verie c. A.V. *Transl. Pref.* **3.** Wessex the c. of the royal house FREEMAN.

Comb.: **c.-holding,** land held in BOROUGH-ENGLISH; **-hole** (*U.S.*), a depression in a road; also a spot from which the frost is melting; **-roof,** a roof, in shape like a half-cylinder, divided into panels by wooden ribs; **-scythe,** a scythe fitted with a c. (sense 7).

Cradle (krē¹·d'l), *v.* ME. [f. prec. sb.] **1.** *trans.* To lay in, or as in, a cradle; to rock to sleep; to hold as a cradle 1872. † **2.** *intr.* (for *refl.*) To lie as in a cradle. SHAKS. **3.** To nurture or rear in infancy 1613. **4.** *Husb.* To mow (corn, etc.) with a cradle-scythe. Also *absol.* 1750. **5.** To support in or on a cradle; to raise a vessel to a higher level by a cradle 1775. **6.** To support the back of (a picture, etc.) by ribs and transverse slips 1880. **7.** To wash (auriferous gravel) in a miner's cradle. Also *absol.* and *fig.* 1852. **8.** *Coopering.* To cut a cask in two lengthwise 1874.

1. Convey'd to earth and cradled in a tomb DRYDEN. **2.** Huskes Wherein the Acorne cradled *Temp.* I. ii. 464. **3.** A commonwealth..cradled in war BURKE.

Cradling (krē¹·dliŋ), *vbl. sb.* 1818. [f. prec. + -ING¹.] **1.** The action of CRADLE *v.* (*lit.* and *fig.*). **2.** A framework of wood or iron, *esp.* in *Archit.* 1823.

Craft (krɑft), *sb.* [OE. *cræft* = OFris. *kraft*, OS. *kraft* (Du. *kracht*), (OH)G. *kraft*, ON. *kraptr.* The transference to 'skill, art, occupation' is English only.] † **1.** Strength, power, force –1526. **2.** Intellectual power; skill; art; ability in planning or constructing, ingenuity, dexterity (*arch.*) OE.; †*spec.* occult art, magic –1483. † **3.** A device, artifice, or expedient –1533. **4.** In a bad sense: Skill or art applied to deceive or overreach; guile, fraud, cunning. (The chief mod. sense.) ME. † **5.** The learning of the schools; a branch of learning, a science –1530. **6.** A calling requiring special skill and knowledge; *esp.* a manual art, a HANDICRAFT OE.; *spec.* the occupation of a hunter or sportsman 1486. Also *fig.* **7.** The members of a trade or handicraft collectively; a trade's union, guild, or company ME. **8.** *collect.* (constr. as *pl.*) Vessels or boats 1671. **9.** *collect.* Implements used in catching or killing fish; now *esp.* in whaling 1688.

2. The lyf so short, the c. so long to lerne CHAUCER. **4.** That Crooked Wisdome, which is called C. HOBBES. **5.** *The seven crafts*: the 'seven arts' of the mediæval Universities: see ART *sb.* **6.** And because hee was of the same c., he abode with them *Acts* 18:3. The crafts of the shoemaker, tinman, plumber, and potter JOHNSON. Phr. *The c. of the woods* = WOODCRAFT. *Gentle c.*: see GENTLE. **8.** There is good lying for small C. 1699. Hence † **Craft** *v. intr.* to use crafty devices; to make a job of it *Cor.* IV. vi. 118. **Craftless** *a.* without c.

Craftsman (krɑ·ftsmæ̆n). ME. [orig. two words.] **1.** A man who practises a handicraft; an artisan. Also *transf.* and *fig.* **2.** One who cultivates one of the Fine Arts 1876. Hence **Cra·ftsmanship.** So **Cra·ftswoman** (*rare*). vars. † **Cra·ftiman,** † **Craftman.**

Craftsmaster (krɑ·ftsmɑstəɹ). *arch.* 1513. [orig. *craftes master.*] **1.** One who is master of his craft; usu. *transf.* an adept. † **2.** A master of craft or cunning –1734.

Crafty (krɑ·fti), *a.* [OE. *cræftiġ* = OS. *kraftag, -ig*, OHG. *kreftig* (G. *kräftig*), ON. *krǫptugr*; see -Y¹.] Having or characterized by CRAFT. † **1.** Strong, mighty (*rare*) –ME. **2.** Skilful, dexterous, clever, ingenious OE. **3.** (The current use): Cunning, artful; of actions, etc.: Showing craft ME.

2. The c. Poesie of excellent virgyll 1509. **3.** I was c., and toke you with gile TINDALE 2 *Cor.* 12:16. Hence **Cra·ftily** *a.* skilfully; artfully. **Cra·ftiness.**

Crag (kræg), *sb.*¹ ME. [Of Celtic origin, prob. from an OBrit. **crag* (:– **krako-*).] **1.** A steep rugged rock. **2.** A detached or projecting rough piece of rock ME. **3.** *Geol.* A name for deposits of shelly sand belonging to the Pliocene and Miocene strata 1735.

1. Bleak Craggs, and naked Hills COTTON. **2.** Covered, like the steeps of Helvellin, with a continued pavement of craggs 1786.

Crag (kræg), *sb.*² ME. [Chiefly north., prob. – LDu.; cf. MLG. *krage*, MDu. *crāghe*, Du. *kraag.* Cf. SCRAG.] **1.** The neck. (Chiefly *Sc.*) † **2.** A neck of mutton or veal. (Cf. SCRAG *sb.*¹) –1767.

1. Like wailefull widdowes hangen their crags SPENSER.

Cragged (kræ·gėd), *a.*¹ ME. [f. CRAG *sb.*¹; see -ED².] Formed into, beset with, or abounding in crags; *fig.* rugged, rough.

Mountains..with snowy peaks and c. sides W. IRVING. Hence **Cra·ggedness.**

Cra·gged, *a.*² Also *Sc.* **craiged.** 1607. [f. CRAG *sb.*² + -ED².] Chiefly in combs.: Having a..neck, -necked; as in *narrow-c.*

Craggy (kræ·gi), *a.* 1447. [f. CRAG *sb.*¹ + -Y¹.] Abounding in crags; of the nature of a crag, steep and rugged. Also *transf.* and *fig.*

fig. Byron 'liked something c. to break his mind upon' EMERSON.

Cragsman (kræ·gsmæ̆n). Also *Sc.* **craigs-.** 1816. [For *crag's man*, f. CRAG¹.] One accustomed to, or skilled in, climbing crags.

Craie, Craier, obs. ff. CRAYE, CRAYER.

Craig, Sc. and north. f. CRAG *sb.*¹ and ².

Craik, Crail, var. of CRAKE, CREEL.

Crake (krē¹k), *sb.* ME. [– ON. *krāka*, *krákr*, of imit. origin; cf. CROAK.] **1.** A crow or raven (*n. dial.*). **2.** Any bird of the family *Rallidæ*, esp. the CORN-CRAKE 1455. **3.** The cry of the corn-crake 1876.

Comb.: **c.-berry** (*north.*), the CROWBERRY; **-needle,** the Shepherd's Needle or Venus's Comb.

Crake (krē¹k), *v.*¹ ME. [prob. echoic.] *intr.* To utter a harsh grating cry; †to grate harshly, creak –1657.

Crake, *v.*² Now *dial.* [var. of CRACK *v.*] To boast, brag.

Cra·ker. *dial.* 1698. [f. CRAKE *v.*¹ + -ER¹.] = CRAKE *sb.* 2.

Craker, obs. f. CRACKER, *esp.* a boaster.

Crakow (kræ·kau). Now *Hist.* ME. [f. *Crakow, Krakau*, or *Cracovie*, in Poland.] A boot or shoe with a very long pointed toe, worn in the 14th century.

Cram (kræm), *v.* [OE. (*ġe*)*crammiam* corresp. to MLG. *kremmen*, ON. *kremja* squeeze, pinch; Du. *krammen* cramp, clamp, MHG. *krammen* claw; f. **kram-* **krem-*; cf. OE. (*ġe*)*crimman* cram, stuff.] **1.** *trans.* To fill (a space, etc.) with more than it properly holds, by compression; to fill quite full or overfull, pack. Const. *with.* **2.** To feed with excess of food (*spec.* poultry, etc., to fatten them); to stuff ME.; *intr.* (for *refl.*) to stuff oneself 1609. Also *fig.* **3.** To thrust, force, stuff, crowd (anything) *into* a space, etc., which it overfills ME. Also *fig.* **4.** *slang.* To stuff with lies, etc. 1794. **5.** *colloq.* To prepare (a person), or get up (a subject), hastily for an occasion, by stuffing the memory with facts 1825. Also *absol.* or *intr.* **6.** *slang.* To urge on forcibly (a horse) 1830.

1. A room crammed with fine ladies PEPYS. **2.** *intr.* Such a bevy of beldames..cramming like so many Cormorants 1634. *fig.* Cram's with prayse *Wint. T.* I. ii. 91. **3.** *fig.* You c. these words into mine eares, against The stomacke of my sense *Temp.* II. i. 106.

Cram (kræm), *sb.* 1614. [f. prec. vb.] **1.** Any food used to fatten (*dial.*). **2.** A dense crowd, crush, squeeze (*colloq.*) 1858. **3.** *slang* A lie 1842. **4.** The action of cramming information for an occasion (see CRAM *v.* 5); the information itself 1853. **5.** *Weaving.* 'A warp having more than two threads passing through each dent or split of the reed' (Webster).

† **Crambe** (kræ·mbi). 1565. [– L. *crambe* – Gr. κράμβη kind of cabbage. See CRAMBO.] Cabbage: only *fig.*, and usually in reference to *crambe repetita* cabbage served up again (Juvenal VII. 154) –1713. Hence, (Distasteful) repetition –1757.

Cramble (kræ·mb'l), *v.* Now *dial.* 1570. [Of symbolic form; cf. SCRAMBLE.] † **1.** *intr.* To creep and twist about: said of roots, etc. –1597. **2.** To crawl, hobble 1617.

Crambo (kræ·mbo). 1660. [Modification, on an It. or Sp. model, of earlier CRAMBE.] **1.** A game in which one player gives a word to which each of the others has to find a rhyme. **2.** *transf.* Rhyme, rhyming (*contemptuous*) 1697. † **3.** = CRAMBE, repetition –1705.

1. From thence to the Hague again playing at C. in the waggon PEPYS. **2.** His similies in order set, And ev'ry c. he cou'd get SWIFT.

Dumb c.: a game in which one set of players have to guess a word agreed upon by the other set, after being told what word it rhymes with, by acting in dumb show one word after another till they find it. (Occas. = dumb show.)

Crammer (kræ·məɹ). 1655. [f. CRAM *v.* + -ER¹.] **1.** One who or that which crams poultry, etc. **2.** *colloq.* One who crams pupils for an examination, etc.; rarely, a student who crams a subject 1813. **3.** *slang.* A lie 1862.

Cramoisy, cramesy (kræ·moizi, -ĕzi). *arch.* ME. [– early It. *cremesi* and OFr. *crameisi* (mod. *cramoisi*); see CRIMSON.] *adj.* Crimson 1480. *sb.* Crimson cloth ME.

adj. A blustering figure..in..cramoisy velvet CARLYLE.

Cramp (kræmp), *sb.*¹ [– OFr. *crampe* – MLG., MDu. *krampe* = OHG. *krampfo*, rel. to OS. *kramp*, (OH)G. *krampf*, subst. uses of an adj. meaning 'bent' (OHG. *krampf*, ON. *krappr* narrow, and OE. *crampiht*); cf. CRAMP *sb.*², CRIMP *v.*] An involuntary, violent, and painful contraction of the muscles, usually the result of a slight strain, a sudden chill, etc. (Usually spoken of as *cramp*, colloq. *the cramp*; *a cramp* is a particular case or form of cramp.)

Ile racke thee with old Crampes *Temp.* I. ii. 369.

Comb.: **c.-bark** (*U.S.*), the bark of the American Cranberry Tree, having anti-spasmodic properties; also the tree; **-bone,** the patella of a sheep, believed to be a charm against c.; **-fish,** the electric ray or torpedo, called also *c.-ray*, and *numb-fish*; **-ring,** a ring held to be efficacious against c., falling sickness, and the like; *esp.* one of those formerly hallowed by the kings of England on Good Friday for this purpose. Hence **Cra·mper** (*rare*), a kind of fish; a preventative of c.; **Cra·mpy** *a.* liable to, or suffering from, c.; inducing c.; of the nature of c.

Cramp (kræmp), *sb.*² 1503. [– MDu. *krampe* (whence G. *krampe*, Fr. *crampe*) = OS. *krampo*, of same ult. origin as prec.] **1.** = CRAMP-IRON 1. Now *dial.* **2.** = CRAMP-IRON 2. 1594. **3.** A portable tool or press with a movable part which can be screwed up so as to hold things together. Cf. CLAMP *sb.*¹ 1669. **4.** *Shoemaking.* 'A piece of wood having a curve corresponding to that of the instep, on which the upper leather of a boot is stretched to give it the requisite shape' (Webster). **5.** 'A pillar of rock or mineral left for support' (Raymond). **6.** *fig.* That which constrains and confines; a cramping restraint 1719. **7.** A cramped condition 1864.

6. Crippling his pleasures with the c. of fear COWPER. Attempts to fasten down the progressive powers of the human mind by the cramps of association HALLAM.

Cramp (kræmp), *a.* 1674. [perh. f. CRAMP *sb.*¹ or *v.*; a similar adj. is old in Gmc. (see CRAMP *sb.*¹), but connection cannot be made out.] **1.** Difficult to make out; crabbed; cramped. **2.** Strait, narrow; cramping 1785.

1. Your Lawyer's..C. Law Terms 1708. Hence **Cra·mpness,** c. or cramped state or quality.

Cramp (kræmp), *v.* 1555. [f. CRAMP *sb.*¹,².] **I.** Conn. w. CRAMP *sb.*¹ † **1.** *trans.* To cause to be seized with cramp –1700. **2.** To affect with the painful contraction of the muscles which characterizes cramp. Usu. in *pass.* 1639.

1. I'll c. your joints 1610. **2.** We stood till we were cramp'd to death, not daring to move 1778.

II. Conn. mainly w. CRAMP *sb.*[2] † **1.** To compress with irons in punishment, etc. Opp. to *to rack.* –1639. Also *fig.* and *transf.* **2.** To confine narrowly, fetter. Also *fig.* 1625.

2. *fig.* The want of money cramps every effort JEFFERSON.

III. Conn. w. CRAMP *sb.*[2] alone. **1.** To fasten or secure with a cramp or cramps; *esp.* in *Building.* Also *fig.* 1654. **2.** *Shoemaking.* To form on a boot-cramp 1864.

1. *fig.* The..fabrick of universal justice, is well cramped and bolted together in all its parts BURKE.

Hence **Cra·mpedness.**

Crampet (kræ·mpet). 1489. [app. f. CRAMP *sb.*[2]] **1.** The chape of the scabbard of a sword; occas. used in *Her.* as a charge. **2.** = CRAMP-IRON 2. (? error.) 1766. **3.** *Sc.* = CRAMPON 3; *esp.* one formerly used by curlers 1638.

Cra·mp-iron. 1565. [f. CRAMP *sb.*[2]] † **1.** A piece of iron bent in the form of a hook; a grappling-iron –1774. **2.** A small metal bar with the ends bent so as to hold together two pieces of masonry, timber, etc. 1598.

† **Cra·mpish,** *v.* ME. only. [– *crampiss-*, lengthened stem of OFr. *crampir*, f. *crampe* CRAMP *sb.*[2]; see -ISH[2].] *intr.* To become cramped; *trans.* to cramp.

Crampon (kræ·mpən), *sb.* Also **crampoon** (kræmpū·n). 1490. [– (O)Fr. *crampon* – Frankish **krampo*; see CRAMP *sb.*[2]] **1.** = CRAMP-IRON 1, 2. † **2.** 'The border of metal which keeps a stone in a ring' (Halliwell). **3.** A small plate of iron set with spikes which is fastened to the foot for walking over ice or climbing 1789. **4.** *Bot.* Adventitious roots which serve as fulcra or supports, as in the ivy 1870. So † **Cra·mpon** *v.* to fix with crampons. ‖ **Crampo·nnee** *a. Her.* Said of a cross having a bend shaped thus, ⌈, at the end of each limb.

Cran[1] (kræn). *Sc.* 1797. [*Crann* is used in Gael. in same sense, perh. identical w. Gael. *crann* 'lot', applied orig. to the 'lot' or share of fish that fell to each man engaged.] A measure of fresh herrings; now fixed at 37½ gallons (about 750 fish).

Cran[2]. *Sc.* 1796. [Sc. form of CRANE *sb.*[1]] † **1.** Applied to the Crane and the Heron. **2.** In the South of Scotland, the Swift 1840. **3.** An iron instrument, laid across the fire, to support a pot or kettle.

3. *To coup the crans*: *fig.* to have an upset; see COUP *v.*[3] (So Jamieson; but perhaps belonging to CRAN[1].)

Cranage (krē^i·nėdʒ). 1481. [f. CRANE *sb.*[1] 2 + -AGE.] The use of a crane to hoist goods; dues paid for such use.

Cranberry (kræ·nbĕri). Also **craneberry.** 1672. [Adopted by the colonists of N. America (whence in Eng. use) from G. *kranbeere* or LG. *kranebere* 'crane-berry'. Cf. G. *kranichbeere.*] The fruit of a dwarf shrub, *Vaccinium oxycoccos*, growing in turfy bogs: a small, roundish, dark red, very acid berry. Also the similar but larger fruit of *V. macrocarpon* (*Large* or *American Cranberry*). Also the name of the shrubs themselves.

Bush C., High C., or **C. Tree,** *Viburnum oxycoccos* (N.O. *Caprifoliaceæ*).

Crance (krans). 1846. [poss. – Du. *krans* wreath, garland; cf. GARLAND *sb.* 8 a. Cf. CRANTS.] *Naut.* 'A kind of iron cap on the outer end of the bowsprit, through which the jib-boom traverses.' Also, any boom-iron.

Cranch, var. of CRAUNCH.

Crane (krē^i n), *sb.*[1] [OE. *cran*, corresp. to MLG. *krān, krōn* and MDu. *crāne* (Du. *kraan*), OHG. *krano* (G. *kran* machine), also (with *-k* suffix; cf. *hawk, lark*) OE. *cranoc, cornuc*, MLG. *krānek*, OHG. *chranuh, -ih* (G. *kranich* bird); rel. to L. *grus*, Gr. γέρανος.] **1.** A large grallatorial bird of the family *Gruidæ*, characterized by very long legs, neck, and bill. The name belongs to the common European crane, *Grus cinerea*, of an ashen-grey colour, formerly abundant in Great Britain, but now extinct. About 15 closely allied species are found in other lands. Also, locally, a name for herons and storks; also for the Shag. 1678. **b.** *Astron.* The constellation *Grus* 1868. **2.** A machine for raising and lowering heavy weights; in its usual form it consists of a vertical post capable of rotation on its axis, a projecting arm or jib over which passes the chain or rope from which the weight is suspended, and a barrel round which the chain or rope is wound. [So Fr. *grue*, G. *kran*, etc.] ME. **3.** A machine for weighing goods, constructed on the principle of the crane described under 2. **b.** An upright revolving axle with a horizontal arm fixed by a fireplace, for suspending a kettle, etc. **c.** *Naut.* (*pl.*) Projecting pieces of iron or timber on board a ship, to support a boat or spar. **4.** A bent tube for drawing liquor out of a bottle; a siphon. [So G. *kran.*] 1634. **5.** An overhanging tube for supplying water to the tender of a locomotive; a water-crane. **6.** *attrib.* or as *adj.* †Crane-coloured, ashen-gray; crane-like; pertaining to a c. or the cranes 1517.

Comb.: **a.** in sense 1, as **c.-fly,** a two-winged fly of the genus *Tipula*; a *daddy-long-legs*; **-colour,** ashy gray; also *attrib.*; hence, **-coloured** *a.*; **-necked** *a.* having a long neck like a crane's; **-vulture,** the Secretary-bird.

b. In sense 2 or 3, as **c.-barge,** a barge carrying a c.; **-post,** the vertical post or axis of a c.; so **-shaft; -wheel,** a tread-wheel by which a c. was formerly worked.

Crane (krē^i n), *sb.*[2] *arch.* 1541. [– Fr. *crâne* – med.L. *cranium*; see CRANIUM.] The skull; = CRANIUM.

Crane (krē^i n), *v.* 1570. [f. CRANE *sb.*[1]] **1.** *trans.* To hoist or lower with, or as with, a crane. **2.** To stretch (the neck) like a crane 1799. **3.** *intr.* To lean or bend forward with the neck stretched out 1849. **4.** *Hunting.* To pull up at an obstacle and look over before leaping; hence *fig.* to hesitate at a danger, difficulty, etc. (*colloq.*) 1823.

1. Being safely craned up to the top of the crag SCOTT. **3.** Those who sat above craned forward 1887. **4.** A very fat pony, who would have craned if he had attempted to leap over a straw 1844.

Craner (krē^i·nəɹ). 1869. [f. CRANE *sb.*[1] and *v.* + -ER[1].] **1.** An official in charge of a crane or public weighing machine 1871. **2.** One who cranes at a dangerous leap, etc.

Crane's-bill, cranesbill (krē^i·nzbil). 1548. [f. CRANE *sb.*[1]] **1.** *Bot.* Any (*esp.* the native British) species of *Geranium*; so called from the long slender beak of the fruit. **2.** *Surg.* A kind of forceps with long jaws 1668.

† **Cra·net.** 1548. [– OFr. *crignete, crinete*, dim. of *crigne*, in sense of mod.Fr. *crinière* mane, f. *crin*, L. *crinis* hair.] A piece of armour covering a horse's neck or mane; a crinière –1611.

Crang (kræŋ). 1821. [var. of *krang*; see KRENG.] The carcass of a whale after the blubber has been removed.

Cranial (krē^i·niăl), *a.* 1800. [f. CRANIUM + -AL[1].] Pertaining to the cranium.

‖ **Crania·ta, cranio·ta,** *sb. pl.* 1878. [f. med.L. *cranium* and Gr. κρανίον, with respective suffixes, as in *pinnata*, πτερωτά. Introduced in the latter form by Hæckel, but gen. used in the former by English naturalists.] *Zool.* A primary division of the VERTEBRATA (q.v.), including those which possess a brain and skull.

Cranio- (krē^i·nio), bef. a vowel **crani-,** comb. f. Gr. κρανίον CRANIUM.

a. In combs.; as **c.-fa·cial** *a.*, belonging to the cranium and the face; **-spi·nal** *a.*, belonging to the cranium and the spine; also **-tabes** (-tē^i·bīz) [L. *tabes* wasting away], 'a form of rickets in which the skull bones are softened' (*Syd. Soc. Lex.*). **b.** In derivs., as **Cranie·ctomy** [Gr. ἐκτομή], excision of a strip of bone from the cranium to allow the brain to develop. **Cra·nioce:le** [see CELE *sb.*], 'the protrusion of a part of the encephalon from the cranial cavity' (*Syd. Soc. Lex.*). **Cra·nioclas:m** [Gr. κλάσμα breaking], the breaking up of the fœtal head in *craniotomy*; **Cra·niocla:st** [Gr. -κλάστης], an instrument for doing this. **Cranio·gnomy** [Gr. γνώμη], 'the science of the form and characteristics of the skull' (*Syd. Soc. Lex.*); hence **Cra:niogno·mic** *a.* So **Cranio·gnosy** [Gr. γνῶσις]. **Cra:niogra:ph** [Gr. -γραφος], an instrument for taking drawings of the skull; **Cranio·grapher; Cranio·graphy,** description of skulls. **Cranio·meter** [Gr. μέτρον], an instrument for taking measurements of skulls; hence **Cra:niome·tric, -al** *a.*; **Cra:niome·trically** *adv.*; **Cranio·metrist; Cranio·metry. Cranio·pathy** [Gr. -πάθεια, f. πάθος], 'disease of the cranium' (*Syd. Soc. Lex.*). **Cra·niopho:re** [Gr. -φορος bearing], Topinard's instrument for measuring the dimensions of the skull. **Cra·niopla:sty** [Gr. -πλαστία, f. πλαστός moulded], an operation for supplying deficiencies in the cranial structures. **Cranio·scopy** [Gr. -σκοπία, f. -σκοπος that views], examination of the size and configuration of the skull; formerly = PHRENOLOGY; hence **Cra:nio-sco·pic, -al** *a.*; **Cranio·scopist. Cranio:tomy** [Gr. -τομία, f. -τομος cutting], in obstetric surgery, an operation in which the head of the fœtus is cut open and broken down when it presents an obstacle to delivery.

Cranioid (krē^i·ni,oid), *a.* 1849. [See -OID.] *Zool.* Allied to the genus *Crania* of Brachiopods.

Craniology (krē^i ni,ǫ·lŏdʒi). 1806. [f. CRANIO- + -LOGY.] † **1.** = PHRENOLOGY –1843. **2.** The study of the size, shape, and character of the skulls of various races, as a part of anthropology 1851. So **Cra:niolo·gical** *a.* of or pertaining to c. **Cranio·logist,** one versed in c.

Craniota; see CRANIATA.

‖ **Cranium** (krē^i·niŏm). Pl. **crania** (krē^i·niă). 1543. [med.L. – Gr. κρανίον.] **1.** *Anat.*, etc., *strictly*, The bones which enclose the brain, the brain-case; *more widely*, the bones of the whole head; the skull. **2.** Used joc. for 'head' 1647.

Crank (kræŋk), *sb.*[1] [OE. *cranc* in *crancstæf* weaver's implement (cf. *crencestre* female weaver), rel. to *crinċan*, parallel to *cringan* fall in battle. The primary notion is that of something bent or crooked. (M)HG., Du. *krank* sick is a fig. development.] **1.** A portion of an axis bent at right angles, used to communicate motion, or to change reciprocal into rotary motion, or the converse. **2.** An elbow-shaped device in bell-hanging, whereby the rectilineal motion communicated to a bell-wire is changed in its direction, usually at right angles 1759. **3.** An elbow-shaped support or bracket 1769. **4.** A revolving disc, to which a regulated pressure can be applied, which criminals sentenced to hard labour are required to turn a certain number of times each day 1847.

Comb.: **c.-axle,** (*a*) the driving axle of an engine or machine; (*b*) a carriage-axle with the ends bent twice at a right angle; **-hook,** the rod which connects the treadle and the c. in a foot-lathe; **-pin,** the pin by which the connecting-rod is attached to the c.; **-shaft,** the shaft driven by a c.; **-wheel,** a wheel which acts as a c.; *esp.* one having near its circumference a pin to which the end of a connecting-rod is attached as to a c.-pin; a disc-c.

Crank (kræŋk), *sb.*[2] 1562. [prob. ult. identical with prec. In sense 5, orig. U.S., back-formation from CRANKY *a.*[1]] † **1.** A crook, bend, winding; a crooked path, course, or channel –1630. Also †*fig.* † **2.** A tortuous hole or crevice; a cranny –1612. Also *fig.* **3.** A twist or fanciful turn of speech; a conceit 1594. **4.** An eccentric notion or action; a crotchet, whim 1848. **5.** *U.S. colloq.* A person with a mental twist; an eccentric; *esp.* a monomaniac. [Prob. f. CRANKY, q.v.] 1881. **6.** *dial.* A slight ailment 1847.

1. The turnings and cranks of the Labyrinth NORTH. **3.** Quips, and cranks, and wanton wiles MILT. **4.** Subject to sudden cranks CARLYLE.

† **Crank,** *sb.*[3] *Thieves' slang.* 1567. [– Du. or G. *krank* sick; see CRANK *sb.*[1]] (In full *counterfeit c.*) A rogue who feigned sickness in order to move compassion and get money –1622.

Crank (kræŋk), *a.*[1] ME. [Origin unkn.] † **1.** Rank, lusty, vigorous –1659. **2.** Lively, brisk; merry; aggressively high-spirited, 'cocky'. Now *dial.* and in U.S. 1499.

2. How came they to grow so..c. and confident SOUTH. Hence **Cra·nkly** *adv.*

Crank (kræŋk), *a.*[2] 1696. [perh. to be connected with *crank* adj. crabbed, awkward, infirm, shaky (see CRANK *a.*[3]), and CRANK *sb.*[1]] *Naut.* Liable to lean over or capsize: said of a ship when she is built too deep or narrow, or has too little ballast to carry full sail. Also *fig.*

That c. little boat with its top-heavy sails W. BLACK. Hence **Cra·nkness. Crank-sided** *a.* (in same sense).

Crank (kræŋk), *a.*[3] 1729. [Senses conn. w. CRANK *sb.*[1], [2] and CRANKY *a.*[1]] **1.** Crooked; angularly bent. *Sc.* 1825. **2.** Crabbed, difficult to pronounce, understand, or do. Now *Sc.* 1729. **3.** = CRANKY 1 (*dial.*) 1802. **4.** Of machinery: Shaky; out of order; CRANKY 1831.

2. Hard, tough, c., gutt'ral, harsh, stiff names SWIFT. Hence **Cra·nkous** *a.* (*Sc.*), irritable, fretful.

Crank (kræŋk), *v.*[1] 1592. [f. CRANK *sb.*[1], [2].] † **1.** *intr.* To twist and turn about, zigzag –1891. † **2.** *trans.* To crinkle 1661. **3.** *trans.* **a.** To make crank-shaped. **b.** To furnish with a crank. 1793. **4.** To fasten with a crank 1879. **5.** To draw *up* by means of a crank, operate by a crank 1883.

1. See, how this Riuer comes me cranking in, And cuts me from the best of all my Land..a monstrous Cantle out 1 *Hen. IV*, III. i. 98.

Crank, *v.*[2] 1827. [app. echoic; cf. CLANK *v.*, and n. dial. CRONK to croak.] To make a jarring or grating sound.

Cranked (kræŋkt), *ppl. a.* 1862. [f. CRANK *sb.*[1] and *v.*[1] + -ED.] Formed into or furnished with a crank.

Crankle (kræ·ŋk'l), *v.* 1594. [frequent. of CRANK *v.*[1] Cf. CRINKLE.] **1.** *intr.* To run zigzag 1598. † **2.** *trans.* To zigzag; to crinkle (a surface) –1708.

1. The river crankles round an alder grove SIR H. TAYLOR. Hence **Cra·nkle** *sb.* a bend, twist; an angular prominence.

Cranky (kræ·ŋki), *a.*[1] 1787. [perh. orig. f. cant †*crank* (see CRANK *sb.*[3]), but infl. later by assoc. with CRANK *sb.*[2]; see -Y[1].] **1.** Sickly (*dial.*). **2.** *Naut.* = CRANK *a.*[2] **3.** Out of gear; crazy 1862. **4.** Cross-tempered, awkward 1821. **5.** Crotchety; peculiar 1850. **6.** Crooked; full of crannies 1836. Hence **Cra·nkily** *adv.* **Cra·nkiness.**

Cra·nky, *a.*[2] *dial.* 1811. [f. CRANK *a.*[1] + -Y[1].] = CRANK *a.*[1]

† **Crannel.** 1533. [– OFr. **cranel*, var. with *carnel* CARNEL, *crenel* CRENEL, *quernel* KERNEL *sb.*[2], dim. of *cran* notch; see CRANNY *sb.*[1], -EL.] A cranny, crevice, chink –1640.

Crannied (kræ·nid), *a.* 1440. [f. CRANNY *sb.*[1] + -ED[2].] **1.** Having crannies or chinks. **2.** Formed like a cranny. SHAKS.

1. As a Raine doth drench The c. Earth 1639.

Crannog (kræ·nǫg). Also (*erron.*) **crannoge.** 1851. [– Ir. *crannog*, Gael. *crannag* timber structure, f. *crann* tree, beam.] An ancient lake-dwelling in Scotland or Ireland.

Cranny (kræ·ni), *sb.*[1] 1440. [XV *crany* – OFr. *crané* (see -Y[5]), pa. pple. of *craner* (implied by *craneüre* notch), f. (O)Fr. *cran* :– pop.L. *crena*; see CRENA, CRENATE *a.*] A small narrow opening or hole; a chink, crevice, crack, fissure. Also *fig.*

Cranny, *sb.*[2] 1662. [Origin unkn.] *Glass Manuf.* An iron rod used in forming the necks of glass bottles.

Cra·nny, *v.* 1440. [f. CRANNY *sb.*[1]] † **1.** *intr.* To open in crannies or chinks –1607. **2.** To penetrate into crannies (*rare*) 1816.

Cranreuch (kra·nrəχ). *Sc.* 1682. [f. Gael. *crann* tree + *reodhadh* freezing.] Hoar-frost.

† **Crants.** 1592. [– G. *kranz* wreath; cf. CRANCE.] A garland, chaplet, wreath –1706.

† **Cra·ny.** 1525. [Anglicized form of CRANIUM.] = CRANIUM –1730.

Crap (kræp), *sb.*[1] Now *dial.* ME. [= Du. *krappe*, conn. w. *krappen* pluck off, cut off. Cf. also OFr. *crappe* siftings, AL. *crappa* chaff (XIII).] † **1.** The husk of grain –1483. **2.** A name of Buckwheat; also, locally, of Darnel, Rye-grass, Charlock, etc. ME. **3.** Residues, as of fat. (Usu. in *pl.*) 1490. **4.** Dregs of ale 1879. **5.** Money (*slang* or *dial.*) 1700. **6.** A SCRAP 1550. **7.** *Coarse slang.* Excrement; defecation 1898. **b.** *transf.* Rubbish; something worthless, inferior, or disgusting 1898. Hence **Crap** *v.*[1] *intr.* to defecate.

† **Crap,** *sb.*[2] 1721. [– Du. *krap* madder.] Madder –1812.

Crap, *sb.*[3] *Thieves' cant.* 1812. [– Du. *krap* cramp, clamp, clasp.] The gallows. Hence **Crap** *v.*[2] *trans.* to hang.

† **Crapaud.** 1440. [Earliest forms *crapault*, *crapaut* – OFr. *crapault*, *crapaut* (mod. *crapaud*), in med.L. *crapaldus*.] **1.** A toad –1634. **2.** (In full *c.-stone.*) A TOAD STONE. Cf. SHAKS. *A.Y.L.* II. i. 13. –1580.

Crapaudine (krapodī·n). 1558. [– (O)Fr. *crapaudine*, med.L. *crapaudinus, -ina* (XIII); see prec., -INE[1].] † **1.** ? = TOADSTONE. † **2.** *Farriery.* An ulcer on the coronet of a horse –1823. **3.** A socket in which the pivot of a swing-door turns; whence *c.-door*, one which turns on pivots at top and bottom 1876.

Crape (krē[i]p), *sb.* 1633. [Earliest forms *crispe, crespe* – Fr. †*crespe, crêpe*, subst. use of OFr. *crespe* curled, frizzed; see CRISP.] **1.** A thin transparent gauze-like fabric, plain woven, of highly twisted raw silk, with a crisped surface. Now chiefly of black silk (or imitation silk), and used for ladies' mourning dresses, etc. **b.** In the 18th c., 'a sort of thin worsted stuff, of which the dress of the clergy is sometimes made' (Bailey); hence, occas. = the clergy, a clergyman 1699. **2.** A band of crape worn round a hat, etc.; a mask of crape 1763. Also *attrib.*

1. b. A Saint in c. is twice a Saint in lawn POPE. **2.** A white hat with a c. round it THACKERAY.

Comb.: **c.-myrtle,** a Chinese shrub, *Lagerstrœmia indica*, with bright rose-coloured crumpled petals, cultivated in England, and in Southern U.S. **Canton** or **China c.** = *crêpe de Chine* (see CRÊPE).

† **Crape,** *v.*[1] 1786. [f. prec.; cf. Fr. *crêper.*] To make (the hair) wavy and curly; to crimp, to frizzle –1822.

Crape (krē[i]p), *v.*[2] 1815. [f. CRAPE *sb.*] To cover, clothe, or drape with crape. Also *transf.*

Cra·pe-fish. 1856. [Cf. ON. *krappr* narrow.] Cod-fish salted and pressed.

Crappie (kræ·pi). *U.S.* 1861. A species of sunfish, *Pomoxys annularis*, found in the Mississippi.

Cra·ppit-head. *Sc.* 1815. [Cf. Du. *krappen* to cram.] The head of a haddock stuffed with the roe, oatmeal, suet, and spices (Jamieson).

Craps (kræps). *U.S.* 1843. [app. alt. from *crabs*; see CRAB *sb.*[1] 5. The Fr. *crabs, craps* is from Eng. (XVIII).] A gambling game with two dice.

‖ **Cra·pula.** 1727. [L. *crapula* inebriation – Gr. κραιπάλη drunken headache.] Sickness following upon excess in drinking or eating.

Crapulence (kræ·piulĕns). 1727. [f. CRAPULENT; see -ENCE.] **1.** = CRAPULA. **2.** Gross intemperance; debauchery 1825. var. † **Cra·pulency** (in sense 2).

Crapulent (kræ·piulĕnt), *a.* 1656. [– late L. *crapulentus* very much intoxicated, f. CRAPULA.] **1.** Of or pertaining to crapulence. **2.** Given to gross intemperance 1888.

Crapulous (kræ·piŭləs), *a.* 1536. [– late L. *crapulosus*, f. as prec.; see -OUS.] **1.** Intemperate, debauched. **2.** Suffering from crapulence; resulting from intemperance 1755. Hence **Cra·pulousness.**

Crapy (krē[i]·pi), *a.* 1853. [f. CRAPE *sb.*[1] + -Y[1].] **1.** Crape-like 1853. **2.** Of crape; clothed in crape 1855.

Crare, obs. var. of CRAYER.

Crash (kræʃ), *v.* late ME. [imit. formation, perh. partly suggested by *craze* and *dash.*] **1.** *trans.* To dash to pieces, smash (now *rare*); to cause to come or go with a crash. **2.** *intr.* To break or fall to pieces with noise 1535; to move or go with crashing 1694. † **3.** *trans.* To strike (the teeth) together with noise; to gnash –1646. **4.** To make the noise that a hard body does when smashed, or a noise as of many hard bodies dashing and breaking together 1563. **5.** *intr.* Of an aeroplane, etc.: To come down violently out of control; also in corresp. trans. sense 1915. Hence *gen.*

1. Crashing the branches as he went DICKENS. **3.** He shakt his head and crasht his teeth for ire FAIRFAX. **4.** O'erhead the rolling thunders c. SKEAT.

Crash (kræʃ), *sb.*[1] 1549. [f. prec. vb.] **1.** A loud and sudden sound, as of a hard body or bodies broken by violent percussion; also *transf.* 1580. **2.** *fig.* The action of falling to ruin suddenly and violently; *spec.* sudden collapse of a mercantile undertaking or of credit generally 1817. † **3.** A short spell, spurt –1767.

1. The whole forest in one c. descends POPE. **2.** A great c. is expected..everybody has been over-speculating 1890. **3.** A c. at cards BROME.

Crash (kræʃ), *sb.*[2] 1812. [– Russ. *krashenina* dyed coarse linen.] A coarse kind of linen, used for towels, etc. Also *attrib.*

‖ **Crasis** (krē[i]·sis). 1602. [Gr., = mixture, combination.] **1.** The combination of elements, 'humours', or qualities in the animal body, in herbs, etc.; †constitution –1759; condition. ? *Obs.* **2.** *Gr. Gram.* The combination of the vowels of two syllables, *esp.* at the end of one word and beginning of the next, into one long vowel or diphthong; as in κἀγώ for καὶ ἐγώ, etc.

‖ **Craspedon, -dum** (kræ·spidǫn, -dŏm). Pl. **craspeda** (-dă). 1869. [Gr. κράσπεδον edge: the form in *-um* is mod.L.] *Zool.* The convoluted filament, charged with thread-cells, forming the border of the mesentery in Actinozoa.

Craspedote (kræ·spīdō[u]t), *a.* 1888. [f. as prec. + *-ote* = -OT[2]. Hence mod.L. *Craspedota* pl.] *Zool.* Applied to those *Medusæ* which have a velum along the margin of the bell.

Crass (kræs), *a.* 1545. [– L. *crassus* solid, thick, fat.] **1.** Coarse, gross, dense, thick. Now *rare*. **2.** Grossly dull or stupid; dense; unrefined (*rare*) 1861.

1. A crasse and fumide exhalation SIR T. BROWNE. C. ignorance 1859, minds GEO. ELIOT. Hence **Cra·ss-ly** *adv.*, **-ness.**

† **Cra·ssament.** 1615. [– L. *crassamentum* thick sediment, dregs, f. *crassare* thicken, f. *crassus*; see prec., -MENT.] The thick part of a non-homogeneous liquid, which solidifies or settles; *esp.* the coagulum of blood –1666.

†‖ **Crassities.** 1659. [L.] Density, materiality –1678.

Crassitude (kræ·sitiūd). ME. [– L. *crassitudo*, f. *crassus*; see CRASS *a.*, -TUDE.] † **1.** Thickness; volume –1703. † **2.** Density; coarseness –1822. **3.** The state or quality of being CRASS 1679.

‖ **Cra·ssula.** ME. [med.L., dim. of *crassa* (sc. *herba*); see CRASS.] *Bot.* Formerly, some species of *Sedum*, esp. Orpine; now, limited to a genus of succulent plants, the type of the N.O. *Crassulaceæ*, which includes the Stonecrops, Houseleeks, Echeveria, etc. Hence **Crassula·ceous** *a.* of the N.O. *Crassulaceæ.*

-crat, -ocrat, *suffix*, formerly also *-crate*, after Fr. *-crate* in *aristocrate*, etc., with the sense 'partisan of an aristocracy', etc. At the French Revolution *aristocrate* came to be used for 'a member of the aristocracy', after which (-o)*crat* is now used, as in *plutocrat*, etc. Hence **-cratic, -al.**

Cratch (krætʃ), *sb.*[1] [ME. *crecche* (mod. dial. *cretch*) – OFr. *creche* (mod. CRÈCHE) :– Rom. **creppja* – Gmc. **krippja* (whence OE. *cribb* CRIB).] **1.** A rack or crib to hold fodder for cattle; in early use sometimes 'a manger' (now *dial.*). **2.** A wooden grating or hurdle; a sparred frame or rack ME.

1. A stable was his beste house, and a cratche his cradle KINGESMYLL.

Cratch, *sb.*[2] Now *dial.* ME. [f. CRATCH *v.*] **1.** Some form of itch. **2.** *pl.* A disease in the feet of horses and sheep; the SCRATCHES 1523.

† **Cratch,** *v.* ME. [Of obscure origin, but its meaning associates it with the similar MLG., MDu. *kratsen*, OHG. *krazzōn* (G. *kratzen*), OSw. *kratta* scratch. See SCRAT, SCRATCH, SCR-.] **1.** *trans.* To scratch –1552. Also *absol.* or *intr.* **2.** *trans.* To snatch with, or as with, claws; to grab –1581.

Crate (krē[i]t). 1526. [Earliest forms *creat* (XVII), *crade* (XVIII); poss. introduced with imports from Holland; cf. Du. *krat* tailboard of a wagon, skeleton case, †basket, †box of a coach (Kilian), of unkn. origin. Sense 1 appears in AL. as *crata* (XIII).] † **1.** A hurdle. **2.** A large basket or hamper of wickerwork, for carrying crockery, glass, etc.; any case or box of open bars or slats of wood, for carrying fruit, etc. 1688. **b.** A glazier's frame for carrying glass; also measure of glass 1823. Hence **Cra·teman,** a hawker of pottery.

Crater (krē[i]·təɹ). 1613. [– L. *crater* – Gr. κρατήρ bowl, lit. mixing-vessel.] ‖ **1.** *Gr. Antiq.* 'A large bowl in which the wine was mixed with water, and from which the cups were filled' (Liddell and Scott). Also *krater.* 1730. **2.** A bowl- or funnel-shaped hollow at the summit or on the side of a volcano, from which eruption takes place; the mouth of a volcano 1613. ‖ **3.** *Astron.* A southern constellation, situated between Hydra and Leo 1658. **4.** *Mil.* The cavity formed by the explosion of a mine or shell 1839. **5.** *Electr.* The cavity formed in the positive carbon of an arc light in the course of combustion 1892. Hence **Cra·teral** *a.* of, belonging to, or like, a c. **Cra·teriform, crate·riform** *a.* c.-shaped; in *Bot.* cup- or bowl-shaped. **Cra·terlet,** a small c., *e.g.* on the moon. **Cra·terous** *a.* of the nature of a c.

Cratometer (krătǫ·mītəɹ). 1876. [f. Gr. κράτος power + -METER.] An apparatus for measuring power. (Better *crateometer.*) Hence **Cratome·trical** *a.*

Craunch, cranch (kranʃ, krǭnʃ), *v.* 1631. [In early use varying with SCRANCH (see SCR-), both prob. of echoic origin.] = CRUNCH *v.*

Craunch, cranch, *sb.* 1747. [f. prec.] **1.** An act, or the action, of craunching 1806. **2.** (*cranch.*) *Mining.* A part of a stratum or vein left in excavating to support the roof.

Cravat (krăvæ·t), *sb.* 1656. [– Fr. *cravate*, appellative use of *Cravate* – G. *Krawat*, pop. f. *Kroat* – Serbo-Croatian *Hrvat* Croat.] *orig.* A piece of lace or linen, or of muslin edged with lace, worn round the neck, and tied in a bow. More recently, a linen or silk handkerchief, or a woollen comforter, worn round the neck, chiefly by men. Also *fig.*

fig. The Gallows comes next..a hempen C. 1685. Hence **Crava·tted** *a.* wearing a c.

Crave (krēⁱv), *v.* [OE. *crafian* (:– *krabōjan), rel. to ON. *krǫf* request, *krefja* (:– *krabjan).] † **1.** *trans.* To demand, to ask with authority, or by right –ME. **2.** To ask earnestly, to beg for, *esp.* as a gift or favour. Const. *of, from.* ME. **3.** To dun. *Sc.* 1812. **4.** *transf.* Of persons (their appetites, etc.): To long or yearn for; to call for, in order to gratify an appetite; to have a craving for ME. **5.** *fig.* Of things: To need greatly, to call for (something necessary) 1576. Also *intr.* and *absol.*

2. Salomon..craued wisdom from heaven CAREW. I c. leave to observe [etc.] SCOTT. **4.** The more you drink, the more you c. POPE. **5.** The time craves speed SCOTT. *intr.* Once one may c. for love SUCKLING (J.). Hence **Crave** *sb.* = CRAVING. (Not in general use.) **Cra·ver. Cra·ving-ly** *adv.*, **-ness.**

Craven (krēⁱ·v'n). [ME. *crauaunt*, later *crauaunde, cravand*, perh. – clipped AFr. form (cf. ASSIGN *sb.*²) of OFr. *cravanté* overcome, vanquished, pa. pple. of *cravanter* crush, overwhelm :– Rom. **crepantare*, f. *crepant-*, pres. ppl. stem of L. *crepare* rattle, burst; the ME. form was later assim. to pa. pples. in -EN.]

A. *adj.* † **1.** Vanquished. (ME. only.) **2.** That owns himself beaten or afraid; abjectly pusillanimous ME.

1. *To cry c.*: to give up the contest, surrender. Also *fig.* Neither King nor Duke was a man likely to cry c. FREEMAN. **2.** *Haml.* IV. iv. 40. Hence **Cra·venly** *adv.*

B. *sb.* **1.** A confessed coward 1581. **2.** A cock that is not game 1596.

1. Hee is a Crauen and a Villaine else *Hen. V*, IV. vii. 139. **2.** No Cocke of mine, you crow too like a crauen *Tam. Shr.* II. i. 228.

Cra·ven, *v.* 1611. [f. prec.] To make craven.

Craving (krēⁱ·viŋ), *vbl. sb.* ME. [See -ING¹.] † **1.** Accusation. (ME. only.) **2.** Earnest or urgent asking; begging ME. **3.** Urgent desire; yearning 16..

3. A c. after prophecies FROUDE.

Craw (krǭ), *sb.* [– or orig. cogn. with MLG. *krage* (whence Icel. *kragi*), MDu. *crāghe* (Du. *kraag*) neck, throat, gullet = MHG. *krage* (G. *kragen*), of unkn. origin. The limitation of sense is peculiar to Eng.] **1.** The CROP of birds or insects. **2.** *transf.* The stomach (of man or animals). *derisive.* 1573.

Craw, Sc. and north. f. CROW.

‖ **Craw-craw** (krǭ·krǭ:). 1863. [app. Du. Negro, from Du. *krauwen* scratch.] *Pathol.* A malignant species of pustulous itch, prevalent on the African coast.

Crawfish (krǭ·fiʃ), *sb.* 1860. = CRAYFISH, q.v. Cf. also CRAWFISH *v.*

Cra·wfish, *v. U.S. colloq.* 1860. [f. prec.] To move backward like a crawfish; hence, to back out of a position.

Crawl (krǭl), *sb.*¹ 1818. [f. CRAWL *v.*] The action of crawling. **b.** A swimming stroke.

Crawl (krǭl), *sb.*² 1660. [– Colonial Du. *kraal* – Sp. CORRAL.] † **1.** A pen or enclosure for keeping hogs (in the West Indies) –1707. **2.** A pen or enclosure in shallow water on the sea-coast, to contain fish, turtles, etc. 1769. **3.** = KRAAL, q.v.

Crawl (krǭl), *v.* [Late ME. *crawle* superseding earlier *creule, croule*, of unkn. origin (but cf. Sw. *kravla*, Da. *kravle*).] **1.** *intr.* To move slowly in a prone position, by dragging the body along close to the ground, as a child on hands and knees, a worm, etc.; † *trans.* to crawl upon or over (*rare*) –1796. **2.** *transf.* To walk or move with a slow and dragging motion 1460. Also *fig.* **3.** Of plants, etc.: To trail, creep (*rare*) 1634. **4.** *transf.* To be alive *with* crawling things 1576. **5.** To have a sensation as of things crawling over the skin; to feel creepy ME.

1. Slow crawl'd the snail GAY. **2.** I can no further crawle *Mids. N.* III. ii. 444. *fig.* Months and seasons crawled along KINGSLEY. Cranmer.. Hath crawl'd into the fauour of the King SHAKS. **4.** The whole ground seemed alive and crawling with [ants] GOLDSM. Hence **Craw·ler,** *colloq.* a cab crawling along the streets in search of a fare.

Crawly (krǭ·li), *a. colloq.* 1860. [f. CRAWL + -Y¹.] Like or having the sensation of insects crawling over the skin.

† **Cray.** ME. [– Fr. *craie* :– L. *creta* chalk.] **1.** Chalk. (ME. only.) **2.** A disease of hawks, in which the excrements become hard and are passed with difficulty –1618.

† **Craye.** 1541. Erron. f. CRAYER –1627.

Crayer, crare (krēᵊɹ). Now *Hist.* ME. [– OFr. *crayer*, etc., in med.L. *craiera, creiera.*] A small trading vessel.

Crayfish (krēⁱ·fiʃ), **crawfish** (krǭ·fiʃ). [ME. *crevis(se, -es(se* – OFr. *crevice, crevis* – Frankish **krabitja* = OHG. *krebiz* (G. *krebs*) CRAB *sb.*¹ In ME. the second syllable was confounded with *vish* fish. *Crawfish* is chiefly U.S.] † **1.** *gen.* Any of the larger edible crustacea –1656; *spec.* the crab –1783. † **2.** A name for large crustacea other than crabs –1624. **3.** Now: **a.** *gen.* A fresh-water crustacean, *Astacus fluviatilis*, resembling a small lobster. Also applied to other species of *Astacus* and of the allied genus *Cambarus*, *e.g.* the blind crawfish of the Mammoth Cave of Kentucky (*C. pellucidus*). 1460. **b.** In Great Britain: The Spiny Lobster, *Palinurus vulgaris*, the *Langouste* of the French 1748.

Crayon (krēⁱ·ǫn), *sb.* 1644. [– Fr. *crayon*, f. *craie* chalk :– L. *creta* chalk, clay; see -OON.] **1.** A pointed stick or pencil of coloured chalk or other material for drawing. **2.** *transf.* A drawing in crayons; † *fig.* a sketch 1662. **3.** A carbon point in an electric arc lamp. Also *attrib.*

1. Sir Thomas showed me his picture..in c. in little, done exceedingly well PEPYS. **2.** *fig.* It is a poor c., which yourself..must fill up T. JEFFERSON.

Cray·on, *v.* 1662. [– Fr. *crayonner*; see prec.] **1.** *trans.* To draw with a crayon; to cover with drawing in crayons. **2.** *fig.* To sketch, chalk *out* 1734.

2. The other [books] will soon follow; many of them are writ, or crayoned out BOLINGBROKE.

Craze (krēⁱz), *v.* ME. [perh. – ON. **krasa* (cf. Sw. *krasa* crunch, *kras* in phr. *gå i kras* fly into pieces, *slå i kras* dash to pieces).] † **1.** *trans.* To break in pieces or asunder; to shatter –1667; to bruise, crush, damage –1726. Also †*intr.* **2.** *Mining.* To crush (tin ore) in a mill 1610. **3.** *trans.* To crack ME.; *spec.* to produce minute cracks on the surface of (pottery) 1874. Also *intr.* **4.** *fig.* To destroy the soundness of, impair, ruin. (Usu. in *pass.*) *arch.* 1561. **5.** To break down in health; to render infirm. (Usu. in *pa. pple.*) *arch.* 1476. Also †*intr.* **6.** To impair in intellect; to render insane, distract. Usu. in *pa. pple.* (The ordinary sense.) 1496. Also *intr.*

1. God..will..c. thir Chariot wheels MILT. *P. L.* XII. 210. **3.** I am right siker þat þe pot was crased CHAUCER. **5.** Till length of years And sedentary numbness c. my limbs MILT. *Sams.* 570. **6.** The greefe hath craz'd my wits *Lear* III. iv. 175. *Comb.* † **c.-mill,** a mill for crushing tin ore. Hence † **Cra·zedness,** the state of being crazed.

Craze (krēⁱz), *sb.* 1534. [f. CRAZE *v.*] † **1.** A crack, breach, flaw –1645. Also *fig.* **2.** An irrational fancy; a mania 1813; craziness 1841. **3.** *Mining.* (See quots. and cf. CRAZE *v.* 2.) 1778.

1. *fig.* Would it not argue a c. in the brayne 1608. **2.** The miser's c. for gold E. R. CONDER. **3.** The tin..is sorted into 3 divisions..the middle..being named..the crease 1778.

Crazy (krēⁱ·zi), *a.* 1576. [f. CRAZE *v.* or *sb.* + -Y¹.] **1.** Full of cracks or flaws; impaired; liable to fall to pieces; shaky 1583. † **2.** Indisposed; broken down, frail, infirm –1847. Also *fig.* and *transf.* **3.** Of unsound mind; insane, mad. Often in sense: Mad with excitement, perplexity, etc. 1617. **b.** Of things, actions, etc.: Showing derangement of intellect 1859.

1. A c. ship 1748, house ADAM SMITH, coach DICKENS. **2.** The king somewhat crasie, and keeping his Chamber SPEED. *fig.* A crazie and diseased Monarchy MILT. **3.** 'Lord, child, are you c.?' FRANKLIN. **b.** C. theories 1859. By c. fancies led WHITTIER. **c.** Used to denote a garden walk or pavement of irregular pieces of flat stone or tile 1923.

Comb.: **c. bone** (*U.S.*), the funny-bone, 'so called on account of the intense pain produced when it receives a blow' (Webster); **c. quilt** (*U.S.*), a patchwork quilt made in fantastic patterns or without any plan.

Hence **Cra·zily** *adv.* **Cra·ziness.**

‖ **Creagh, creach** (krex), *sb.* 1814. [– Gael. and Ir. *creach* plunder.] **1.** A foray. **2.** Booty, prey 1818. Hence **Creagh** *v.* to raid, plunder.

‖ **Creaght** (krext, krēᵊt), *sb.* 1596. [– Ir. *caeraigheacht*, f. *caera* sheep.] *Ir. Hist.* A nomadic herd of cattle. (The word often includes the herdsmen.) Also *transf.* Hence **Creaght** *v.* to take cattle about to graze.

Creak (krīk), *v.* ME. [orig. synon. with †CRAKE *v.*¹, CROAK *v.*, and of similar imit. origin.] † **1.** *intr.* To utter a harsh cry; to CROAK –1669. **2.** *intr.* To make a CREAK 1583. Also *transf.* of the noise of crickets, etc. † **3.** *intr.* To speak in a strident or querulous tone –1661. **4.** *trans.* To cause to make a creak 1601.

1. The Henne, the Goose, the Ducke, Might cackle, creake, and quacke 1604. **2.** No swinging sign-board creaked from cottage elm WORDSW. Where crickets c. BROWNING. **4.** Creeking my shoes on the plaine Masonry *All's Well* II. i. 31.

Creak (krīk), *sb.* 1605. [f. CREAK *v.*] A strident noise, as of an ungreased hinge, new boots, etc.; a harsh squeak.

Creaky (krī·ki), *a.* 1834. [f. prec. sb. or v. + -Y¹.] Apt to creak; crazy.

Cream, creme *sb.*¹ *Hist.* [ME. *creme* – OFr. *cresme* (mod. *chrême*) :– eccl.L. *chrisma* unction; see CHRISM.] = CHRISM.

Cream (krīm), *sb.*² [ME. *creme* – OFr. *creme, craime, cresme* (mod. *crème* fem.), repr. blending of late L. *crāmum* (Venantius Fortunatus), *crāma*, which is perh. of Gaulish origin, with eccl. L. *chrisma* CHRISM (mod. Fr. *chrême* m.).] **1.** The oily or butyraceous part of milk, which gathers on the top when the milk is left undisturbed; by churning it is converted into butter. **2.** *transf.* A fancy dish or sweet made with cream, or so as to resemble cream ME. **b.** A head of scum, froth, etc. 1669. **c.** A cream-like preparation used cosmetically 1765. **3.** *fig.* The most excellent element or part; the quintessence 1581. **4.** *attrib.* Cream-coloured 1861; *ellipt.* cream colour; also, a cream-coloured horse, etc. 1788.

1. *Clotted* or *clouted c.*: see CLOUTED. **2. b.** The c. of your champagne BYRON. **c.** In vain she tries her paste and creams To smooth her face or hide its seams GOLDSM. **3.** The c. of the correspondence GOLDSM., of wild-fowl shooting 1890.

C. of tartar: the purified and crystallized bitartrate of potassium, used in medicine and for technical purposes. *C. of lime*: pure slaked lime.

Comb.: **c.-cake,** a cake filled with a custard made of c., eggs, etc.; **-cups,** a papaveraceous plant, *Platystemon californicus*, with c.-coloured flowers; **-faced** *a.*, having a face of the colour of c. (from fear); **-fruit,** the juicy c.-like fruit of a plant found in Sierra Leone; **-laid** *a.*, applied to laid paper of a c. colour; **-nut** = *Brazil nut*; **-separator,** a machine for separating the c. from milk; **-slice,** a knife-like instrument for skimming milk, or for serving frozen c.; **-ware,** c.-coloured pottery ware; **-wove,** wove paper of c. colour.

Cream (krīm), *v.* ME. [f. CREAM *sb.*²] **1.** *intr.* Of milk: To form cream 1596; *trans.* to cause to form cream 1883. **2.** *intr.* Of other liquids: To form a scum on the top; to mantle, foam, froth ME. **3.** *trans.* To skim the cream from 1727. **4.** To separate as cream; *fig.* to take the choicest part of. Const. *off.* 1615. **5.** To add cream to tea, etc. 1834.

2. A sort of men, whose visages Do creame and mantle like a standing pond *Merch. V*, I. i. 89. **4.** Such a man, truly wise, creams off nature leaving the sour and the dregs, for philosophy and reason to lap up SWIFT. Hence **Creamed** *ppl. a.* having the cream formed or separated; made or flavoured with cream. **Crea·mer,** a flat dish for skimming the cream off milk; a machine for separating cream.

Cream-cheese. 1583. A soft, rich kind of cheese, made of unskimmed milk with added cream; a cheese of this kind. Also *fig.*

Creamery (krī·měri). 1879. [f. CREAM *sb.*[2] + -ERY, through Fr. *crémerie.*] **1.** A butter-factory (often worked on the joint-stock principle). Also *attrib.* **2.** A shop where milk, cream, butter, and light refreshments are supplied.

Creamometer (krīmǫ·mītəɹ). 1876. [f. as prec. + -METER, after LACTOMETER.] An instrument for measuring the percentage of cream in a sample of milk.

Creamy (krī·mi), *a.* 1610. [f. CREAM *sb.*[2] + -Y[1].] **1.** Containing or abounding in cream 1618. **2.** Resembling cream; *fig.* soft and rich 1610.

1. The milk was c. 1861. **2.** The..tender curving lines of c. spray TENNYSON. The thickest and creamiest paper 'VERN. LEE'. *fig.* A woman with a c. voice O. W. HOLMES. Hence **Crea·miness.**

Creance (krī·ăns), *sb.* [ME. *creaunce* – (O)Fr. *créance* :– med.L. *credentia*, f. L. *credere* believe; see -ANCE. Cf. CREDENCE.] † **1.** Belief –1490; the thing believed; (one's) faith –1669. † **2.** *Comm.* Credit –1496. **3.** *Falconry.* A long fine cord attached to a hawk's leash, to keep it from flying away when being trained ME. † **b.** Occas. spelt *cranes*, as if pl. –1685.

† **Creance,** *v.* [– OFr. *creancer* promise, engage, etc., f. *creance*; see prec.] *intr.* To pledge oneself to pay; to take credit. CHAUCER. So † **Creancer,** a creditor; a guardian, tutor.

† **Creant,** *a.*[1] ME. [app. abbrev. form of OFr. *recreant*; see RECREANT.] In phrases *To yield oneself c., to cry* (or *say*) *c.*: To acknowledge oneself vanquished –1480.

Creant (krī·ănt), *a.*[2] *rare.* [– *creant-*, pres. ppl. stem of L. *creare* create; see -ANT.] Creating, creative. E. B. BROWNING.

† **Crease,** *sb.*[1] ME. [f. CREASE *v.*[1]] = INCREASE *sb.* –1575.

Crease (krīs), *sb.*[2] 1578. [XVI–XVII also *creast*, which was a frequent var. of CREST (cf. *beast*); orig. *crēst*, which was reduced to *crease* by assim. to the var. *cress* (XVI–XVII) of the vb., the mark of a fold being looked at as a ridge in the material. Cf. OFr. *cresté* wrinkled, furrowed.] **1.** The mark produced on the surface of anything by folding; a fold, wrinkle, ridge. **2.** *Cricket.* The name of certain lines marked on the ground to define the positions of the bowler and batsmen 1755. **3.** *Archit.* A curved or ridge tile (app. error for CREST, q.v.) 1703.

2. *Bowling-c.*: a line drawn in the line of each wicket, from behind which the bowler delivers the ball. *Return-c.*: a short line at each end of the bowling-c., and at right angles to it, beyond which the bowler must not go. *Popping-c.* a line in front of each wicket, parallel to the bowling-c., behind which the batsman stands to defend his wicket. Hence **Crea·sy** *a.* full of creases.

Crease, *sb.*[3]; see CREESE.

† **Crease,** *v.*[1] ME. [app. aphet. f. *acrese*, ACCREASE.] = INCREASE *v.* –1547.

Crease (krīs), *v.*[2] 1588. [Also *cress* (XVI–XVII); see CREASE *sb.*[2]] **1.** *trans.* To make a crease or creases in or on the surface of, as by folding, etc. **2.** *intr.* To become creased 1876. **3.** *trans.* To stun (a horse, etc.) by a shot in the crest or ridge of the neck (*U.S.*) 1807.

1. A leafe of paper..cressed in the middes 1588. **2.** A material that is apt to c. 1893.

Creaser (krī·səɹ). [f. prec. + -ER[1].] One who or that which creases; *spec.* any contrivance for making creases or furrows in iron or leather, for creasing the cloth in a sewing-machine, etc.

Creasote, var. of CREOSOTE.

†‖ **Cre·at.** 1730. [Fr. *créat* – It. *creato* alumnus :– L. *creatus*; see next.] An usher to a riding-master.

† **Crea·te,** *ppl. a.* ME. [– L. *creatus*, pa. pple. of *creare* CREATE *v.*; see -ATE[2].] Created –1590.

Statutez..That creat were eternally to dure CHAUCER.

Create (kri,ē[i]·t), *v.* ME. [– *creat-*, pa. ppl. stem of L. *creare* bring forth, produce; see -ATE[3]. Earliest as pa. pple. *created*, an extension (see -ED[1]) of CREATE *ppl. a.*] **1.** *trans.* Said of God: To bring into being, cause to exist; *esp.* 'to form out of nothing' (J.). Also *absol.* **2.** *gen.* To make, form, constitute, or bring into legal existence 1592. Also *absol.* **b.** Of an actor: To be the first to represent (a rôle) and so to shape it. [Fr. *créer un rôle.*] 1882. **3.** To invest with rank, title, etc. 1460. **4.** To constitute; cause, produce, give rise to (a condition, etc.) 1599.

1. In the beginning God created the heaven and the earth *Gen.* 1:1. C. in mee a cleane heart, O God *Ps.* 51:10. **2.** To c. a fee simple CRUISE, wealth MACAULAY. **3.** I c. you Companions to our person *Cymb.* V. v. 20. **4.** 'Tis only fit to c. Mirth HEARNE.

Creatic (kri,æ·tik), *a.* Also **kr-.** 1891. [irreg. f. Gr. κρέας, (stem κρεο-) flesh + -IC.] Of or pertaining to flesh.

Creatine (krī·ătəin). Also **kr-.** 1840. [f. as prec. + -INE[5].] *Chem.* An organic base, $C_4H_9N_3O_2$, discovered in 1835 by Chevreul in the juice of flesh.

Creatinine (kri,æ·tinəin). Also **kr-.** 1851. [f. prec. + -INE[5].] An alkaline crystallizable substance, $C_4H_7N_3O$, a normal constituent of urine and of the juice of muscular flesh.

Creation (kri,ē[i]·ʃən). ME. [– (O)Fr. *création* – L. *creatio*, f. *creat-*; see CREATE *v.*, -ION.] **1.** The action of creating (see CREATE *v.*); the fact of being created; *absol.* the calling into existence of the world; the beginning, as a date 1593. **2.** *gen.* The action of making, forming, producing, or bringing into existence 1602. **3.** The investing with a title, dignity, or function 1460. **4.** *concr.* That which God has created; the world; creatures collectively 1611. **5.** An original production of human intelligence or power 1605.

1. We can think of c. only as a change in the condition of that which already exists MANSEL. *absol.* From the c. to the general doom SHAKS. *Lucr.* 924. **2.** The c. of estates tail BLACKSTONE. **4.** *Lord of c.* = man: see LORD. For wee know that the whole c. groaneth *Rom.* 8:22. **5.** Or art thou but A Dagger of the Minde, a false C. *Macb.* II. i. 38. A c. of the ballad-muse 1888. Hence **Crea·tional** *a.* of or pertaining to c. (*rare*).

Creationism (kri,ē[i]·ʃəniz'm). 1847. [f. prec. + -ISM.] A system or theory of creation: *spec.* **a.** The theory that God immediately creates a soul for every human being born (opp. to *traducianism*); **b.** The theory which attributes the origin of matter, species, etc., to special creation (opp. to *evolutionism*). So **Crea·tionist, -ism.**

Creative (kri,ē[i]·tiv), *a.* 1678. [f. CREATE *v.* + -IVE; see -ATIVE. Cf. OFr. *creatif, -ive*, med.L. *creativus* (XIV).] **1.** Having the quality of creating; of or pertaining to creation; originative. **2.** Productive *of* 1803.

1. Heav'n's c. hand SHENSTONE. Hence **Crea·tive-ly** *adv.*, **-ness.**

Creator (kri,ē[i]·təɹ). [– OFr. *creatour, -ur* (mod. *créateur*) – L. *creator, -ōr-*; see CREATE *v.*, -OR 2.] **1.** The Supreme Being who creates all things. **2.** *gen.* One who, or that which, creates or gives origin to 1579.

1. The creatour of euery creature CHAUCER. **2.** Since it thus appears that custom was the c. of prelaty MILT. Hence **Crea·torship. Crea·tress,** a female c.; var. ‖ **Crea·trix.**

Creature (krī·tiūɹ, krī·tʃəɹ). ME. [– (O)Fr. *créature* – late L. *creatura*, f. as prec.; see -URE.] **1.** Anything created; a created being, animate or inanimate. † **b.** Creation –1611. **c.** Anything that ministers to man's comfort 1614. **d.** *joc.* Strong drink; *esp.* whisky 1638. **2.** An animal; often as distinct from 'man' ME. In *U.S.*, used *esp.* of cattle. **3.** A human being; often in reprobation; also with qualifications expressing admiration, affection, compassion, etc. ME. **4.** *fig.* A result, product, or offspring *of* anything 1651. **5.** One who owes his position to another; one who is actuated by the will of another; an instrument or puppet. [So Fr.] 1587.

1. These thy gyftes and creatures of bread and wyne *Bk. Com. Prayer.* **b.** *Rom.* 8:19. **c.** Waste of the good creatures of God (cf. 1 *Tim.* 4:4.) 1658. **2.** 'Go, from the creatures thy instructions take' POPE. **3.** There is no C. loues me *Rich. III*, V. iii. 200. The creatures who govern at Cadiz WELLINGTON. The world hath not a sweeter C. *Oth.* IV. i. 194. **4.** Creatures of the Fancy HOBBES. **5.** Sir Francis Windebank..was a c. of Laud's HUME. *Comb.* **c.-comforts,** material comforts (food, clothing, etc.).

Hence **Crea·tural** *a.* pertaining to creatures; of the nature of a c. **Crea·turehood,** the condition of a c. **Crea·tureless** *a.* (*rare*). **Crea·turely** *a.* of or belonging to creatures; of the nature of a c.; hence **Crea·tureliness. Crea·tureship,** the condition of a c. † **Crea·turize** *v.* to invest with creaturehood.

Creaze (*Mining*); see CRAZE *sb.* 3.

Crebri- (krī·bri), comb. f. L. *creber* closely-placed, as in **Crebrico·state** *a.* [L. *costa*], having closely-set ribs or ridges; **Crebrisu·lcate** *a.* [L. *sulcus*], having closely-set furrows.

Crebrity (krī·brĭti). *rare.* 1656. [– L. *crebritas*, f. *creber* frequent; see -ITY.] Frequency.

‖ **Crèche** (krē[i]ʃ), *sb.* 1882. [Fr.; see CRATCH *sb.*[1]] A public nursery for infants, where they are taken care of while their mothers are at work, etc.

Credence (krī·děns), *sb.* ME. [– (O)Fr. *crédence* – med.L. *credentia*, f. *credent-*, pres. ppl. stem of *credere* believe; see -ENCE.] **1.** The mental action of accepting as true; belief. † **2.** Faith, confidence *in*, reliance *on* (a person or authority) –1548. † **3.** Trustworthiness, credit, repute –1822. **4.** Credentials; *transf.* the message entrusted to a messenger or embassy. *Obs.* exc. in *letter of c.* ME. † **5.** The tasting or assaying of meats as a precaution against poisoning –1460. † **6.** A side table or sideboard on which dishes, etc., were placed ready to be served at table –1834. **7.** *Eccl.* In R.C. and Anglican churches: A small side table or shelf to hold the eucharistic elements before consecration 1841.

1. Instructions, to which it seems c. was to be given BURKE. **4.** *Letter of c.*: a letter of recommendation or introduction. Hence † **Cre·dence** *v.* to give c. to.

‖ **Credenda** (kride·ndă), *sb. pl.* 1638. [n. pl. of gerundive of L. *credere*, believe.] Things to be believed; matters of faith. (Opp. to *agenda.*)

Is the power of selecting the c. of the nation to be vested in the civil magistrate MIALL.

Credent (krī·děnt), *a. rare.* [– L. *credent-*; see CREDENCE, -ENT.] 1602. **1.** Believing, trustful. † **2.** Having credit or repute *Meas. for M.* IV. iv. 29; credible *Wint. T.* I. ii. 142. Hence **Cre·dently.**

Credential (kride·nʃăl). 1524. [– med.L. *credentialis*, f. *credentia* CREDENCE; see -AL[1], -IAL.]

A. *adj.* Recommending or entitling to credit or confidence, as in phr. †*c. letters.*

B. *sb.* (Usu. in *pl.*) Letters or written warrants recommending or entitling the bearer to credit or confidence; *esp.* a letter of recommendation or introduction given by a government to an ambassador or envoy 1674. Also *transf.* and *fig.*

We will not take a Footman without Credentials from his last Master STEELE. *fig.* There stands The legate of the skies! His theme divine, His office sacred, his credentials clear COWPER.

Credibility (kredĭbi·lĭti). 1594. [– med.L. *credibilitas*, f. *credibilis*; see next, -ITY.] The quality of being credible; a case of this.

Christianity..rests on the c. of the Gospel history FROUDE.

Credible (kre·dĭb'l), *a.* ME. [– L. *credibilis*, f. *credere* believe; see -BLE.] **1.** Capable of being believed. **2.** Worthy of belief or confidence; trustworthy ME. † **3.** Ready to believe –1675. † **4.** Reputable –1712.

1. Things are made c. either by the known condition and quality of the utterer, or by the manifest likelihood of truth which they have in themselves HOOKER. **2.** Nay tis most c. *All's Well* I. ii. 4. Observations from c. Authors 1671. Hence **Cre·dibleness. Cre·dibly** *adv.*

Credit (kre·dit), *sb.* 1542. [– Fr. *crédit* – It. *credito* or L. *creditum*, n. pa. pple. of *credere* put trust in.] **1.** Belief, confidence, faith, trust. † **2.** Trustworthiness, credibility –1847; authority –1757. † **3.** Something believed. *Twel. N.* IV. iii. 6. † **4.** Trust, charge –1651. **5.** The estimate in which the character of a person (or thing) is held; reputation, repute 1576. **6.** Influence based on the confidence of others 1549. **7.** The commendation bestowed on account of an action, quality, etc. 1607. **8.** A source of commendation. (Now only with *a* and *to.*) 1586. **9.** *Comm.* **a.** Confidence in a buyer's ability and intention to pay at some future time, for goods, etc., entrusted to him without present payment 1542. **b.** Reputation of solvency and probity in business, entitling a person or body to be trusted 1573. **10.** A sum placed at a person's disposal in the books of a bank, etc.; any note, bill, etc., on security of which a person may obtain funds 1662. **11.** *Parliament.* A sum on account, voted by Parliament in anticipation of the Annual Estimates. Hence *Vote of c.* 1854. **12.** *Book-keeping.* The acknowledgement of payment by entry in an account. (with *pl.*) A sum entered on the credit side of an account; this side itself (abbrev. *Cr.*) 1745.

1. Charges like these may seem to deserve some ..c. GIBBON. 2. On the c. of an excellent witness FULLER. †*Letter of c.* = *letter of credence.* 5. John Gilpin was a citizen of c. and renown COWPER. 6. Buckingham..resolved to employ all his c. in order to prevent the marriage HUME. 7. The c. of inventing coined money 1876. 8. He..may be a C. to the College HEARNE. 9. a. C. being ..the Expectation of Money within some limited Time LOCKE. Phr. *To give c.*; *on* (*upon*) *c.*; *long c.*, i.e. c. for a long time; *six months' c.*, etc. b. Try what my c. can in Venice doe *Merch. V.* I. i. 180. 10. A letter..with a c. for the money DE FOE. *Letter* (*bill*) *of c.*: a letter or document granted by a bank, etc., authorizing a person named therein to draw money to a specified amount from their correspondents in other places.

Credit (kre·dit), *v.* 1541. [f. prec., or – *credit-*, pa. ppl. stem of L. *credere*; see prec.] **1.** *trans.* To give credit to, put faith in, believe, trust 1548. † **2.** *trans.* To entrust –1748. † **3.** To trust (a person) with goods or money on credit –1754. † **4.** To accredit –1664. **5.** To bring into credit; to do credit to (*arch.*) 1596. **6.** *Book-keeping.* To enter on the credit side of an account 1682. **7.** *fig.* *To c.* (something) *to* a person, or a person *with* something: to ascribe it to him 1850.

1. Credite not those..that talke that and this 1567. 5. That my actions might c. my profession MABBE. 7. To c. him with a desire to reform the Church FROUDE.

Creditable (kre·dităb'l), *a.* 1526. [f. CREDIT *v.* and *sb.* + -ABLE.] † **1.** Worthy to be believed –1808; in *Comm.*, having good credit –1822. **2.** That brings credit or honour; reputable 1659; †respectable, decent –1860.

1. Persons, sufficiently c., and perfectly informed 1669. The c. traders of any country ADAM SMITH. 2. Clive made a c. use of his riches MACAULAY. Hence **Cre·ditableness. Cre·ditably** *adv.*

Creditor (kre·ditəɹ). ME. [– AFr. *crediteur*, (O)Fr. *créditeur* – L. *creditor*; see CREDIT, -OR 2.] **1.** One who gives credit for money or goods; one to whom a debt is owing; correl. to *debtor* 1447. Also *fig.* **2.** *Book-keeping.* *Creditor* (or *Cr.*): applied to the right-hand or credit side of any account, or to what is entered there 1543. Also *attrib.* † **3.** One who becomes surety for –1523. † **4.** One who believes 1597.

1. Now unthriftes..byd their creditors go whistle MORE. 2. *attrib.* Cast up the Dr. and Cr. Sides of your Balance 1806. 4. The easie creditours of novelties DANIEL. Hence **Cre·ditress,** † **-rice, -rix** (? *Obs.*), a female c.

‖ **Credo** (krī·do). ME. [L.; = I believe.] **1.** The first word of the Apostles' and Nicene creeds, in Latin; hence, either of these Creeds; now *esp.* the name of a musical setting of the Nicene Creed. **2.** *gen.* A creed 1587.

Credulity (krĭdiū·lĭti). ME. [– (O)Fr. *crédulité* – L. *credulitas*, f. *credulus*; see next, -ITY.] † **1.** Belief, faith, credence; readiness to believe –1794. **2.** Readiness to believe on weak or insufficient grounds 1547.

2. A humbug, living on the c. of the people DICKENS.

Credulous (kre·diŭləs), *a.* 1576. [f. L. *credulus* (f. *credere* believe) + -OUS; see -ULOUS.] **1.** Disposed to believe. (Now *rare* exc. as in 2.) 1579. **2.** Apt to believe on weak or insufficient grounds 1576. *transf.* Of things: Arising from credulity 1648; †believed too readily 1625.

2. Thus c. Fooles are caught *Oth.* IV. i. 46. Hence **Cre·dulously** *adv.* **Cre·dulousness,** credulity.

Cree (krī) *v.* Chiefly *dial.* 1620. [The orig. form was app. *creve* (XIV) – (O)Fr. *crever* burst, split :– L. *crepare* crackle, crack. For the reduction to *cree*, cf. Sc. *preve, pree, leve, lee*, etc.] **1.** To soften by boiling (*trans.* and *intr.*). **2.** *trans.* To pound into a soft mass 1822. Hence **Creed** *ppl. a.*

Creed (krīd), *sb.* [OE. *crēda* – L. *credo* I believe, the first word of the Apostles' and the Nicene creeds in the Latin versions.] **1.** A brief summary of Christian doctrine. (*The C.* usually = the Apostles' Creed.) More generally: A confession of faith 1676. **2.** A professed system of religious belief 1573; *transf.* a set of opinions on any subject 1613.

1. The thre credes the whyche our moder holy chirche singeth CAXTON. 2. Every man is better and worse than his c. KINGSLEY. *transf.* The cynical c...of the market EMERSON. So † **Creed** *v. trans.* (also *absol.*) to believe. Hence **Cree·dal, cre·dal** *a.* pertaining to a c. **Cree·dless** *a.* **Cree·dlessness. Cree·dsman,** an adherent of a c. or of the same c. (*rare*).

Creek (krīk), *sb.* [(i) ME. *crike* – ON. *kriki* chink, nook, whence also (O)Fr. *crique*, which may be partly a source of the Eng. word; (ii) ME. *crēke*, either – MDu. *krēke* (Du. *kreek* creek, bay), or by lengthening of *ĭ* in *crike*; cf. AL. *crica* and *creca*; ult. origin unkn.] **1.** A narrow recess or inlet in the coast-line of the sea, or the tidal estuary of a river; a small port or harbour; an inlet within the limits of a haven or port. Also *transf.* **2.** In U.S. and British colonies: A branch of a main river, a tributary river; a small stream, or run 1674. † **3.** A cleft in the face of a rock, etc. –1635. **4.** A narrow or winding passage; an out-of-the-way corner. Also *fig.* 1573. † **5.** A turn, a winding. Also *fig.* –1680.

1. He knew..euery cryke in Britaigne and in Spayne CHAUCER. *transf.* Certain Creeks or corners of Land running into the up-lands BLITH. 4. A Labyrinth is a place made full of turnings and creekes 1582. They explore, Each c. and cranny of his chamber GRAY. Hence **Cree·kward** *a.* towards a c. **Cree·ky** *a.* full of creeks.

† **Creek,** *v.* 1538. [f. prec. sb.] To run (*up*) as a creek; to bend, turn, wind –1610.

Creel (krīl), *sb.*[1] ME. [orig. Sc., of unkn. origin.] **1.** A large wicker basket; now *esp.* a basket used for the transport of fish, and borne upon the back. Hence, An angler's fishing-basket. 1842. **2.** A trap of wicker-work for catching fish, lobsters, etc. 1457.

Phr. *To coup the creels* (Sc.): to cause or sustain an upset; in various *fig.* applications. *In a c.* (Sc.): in a state of temporary aberration.

Creel (krīl), *sb.*[2] 1788. [perh. the same word as prec., but evidence is wanting.] **1.** A framework, varying in form and use. **2.** *Spinning.* A frame for holding the paying-off bobbins in the process of converting roving into yarn, etc. Hence **Cree·ler,** one who attends to a c.

Creep (krīp), *v.* Pa. t. and pple. **crept** (krept). [OE. *crēopan* = OFris. *kriapa*, OS. *criopan*, ON. *krjúpa* :– Gmc. **kreupan, *kraup, *krupun, *krupanaz.*] **1.** To move with the body prone and close to the ground, as a reptile, an insect, a quadruped moving stealthily, etc. (Cf. CRAWL *v.*) OE. **2.** To move softly, cautiously, timorously, or slowly; to move quietly and stealthily; to steal (*into, away*, etc.) ME. **3.** *fig.* (of persons and things). **a.** To come on slowly, stealthily, or by degrees; to steal insensibly *upon* or *over* ME. **b.** To move timidly or diffidently; to cringe; to move on a low level 1581. **4.** Of plants: To grow extending along the ground, a wall, etc., and throwing out roots or claspers at intervals 1530. Also *fig.* **5.** *trans.* = *c. along* or *over* (*rare*) 1667. **6.** *intr.* To have a sensation as of things creeping over the skin; to be affected with a shiver ME. **7.** *Naut.* To drag in deep water with a creeper 1813. **8.** Of metal rails, etc.: To move gradually forward under pressure or, as the result of expansion and contraction on a gradient 1885.

1. [There] the slow-worm creeps TENNYSON. Children must learne to créepe ere they can go 1562. 2. The whining Schoole-boy..creeping like snaile Vnwillingly to schoole *A.Y.L.* II. vii. 146. The mists crept upward 1867. 3. a. Despondency began to c. over their hearts W. IRVING. b. Where men of judgment c. and feel their way COWPER. 4. The Ivy green, That creepeth o'er ruins old DICKENS. 6. You make..my flesh c. DICKENS.

Creep (krīp), *sb.* 1486. [f. the vb.] **1.** The action of creeping (*lit.* and *fig.*). **2.** A sensation as of creeping things on one's body. Usu. in *pl.* (colloq.). 1862. **3.** *Coal-mining.* The slow rising up of the floor of a gallery owing to pressure upon the pillars. 'Also any slow movement of mining ground' (Raymond). **4.** A small arch or other opening for an animal to creep through 1875.

4. A c. for cattle, on the Wigtown Railway 1875. *Comb.* **c.-hole,** a hole by which one creeps in and out; 'a hole into which any animal may creep to escape danger' (J.). Also *fig.* (cf. *loop-hole*).

Creeper (krī·pəɹ). OE. [f. CREEP *v.* + -ER[1].] **1.** One who creeps. **2.** An animal that creeps; a creeping thing 1577. **3.** A name for many small birds; *esp.* the common Brown Creeper or Tree-creeper, *Certhia familiaris* 1661. **4.** A plant that creeps along the ground, or (more usually) one that climbs trees, walls, etc., as ivy and the Virginia Creeper (*Ampelopsis hederacea*) 1626. **b.** *pl. Archit.* Crockets (see CROCKET 2) 1864. **5.** A kind of grapnel used for dragging the bottom of the sea or other body of water ME. † **6.** A small iron dog, of which a pair were placed between the andirons –1833. **7.** *local.* **a.** A kind of patten or clog. **b.** A piece of iron with spikes, worn under the feet to prevent slipping on ice, etc. **8.** An apparatus for conveying grain in corn-mills. **b.** An endless moving feeding-apron, in a carding-machine. **9.** A small iron frying-pan with three legs; a *spider.* (*U.S. local.*) 1880.

4. The c., mellowing for an autumn blush KEATS.

Creepie (krī·pi). *Sc.* and *dial.* 1661. [f. CREEP *v.* + -IE, -Y[6].] **1.** A low stool. **2.** A small speckled fowl. (*U.S. local.*)

Creeping (krī·piŋ), *vbl. sb.* (and *ppl. a.*) OE. [See -ING[1], -ING[2].] **1.** The action of the verb CREEP. **2.** The sensation as of something creeping on the skin; cf. FORMICATION 1799. **3.** In Canada: Stalking the Moose-deer, etc. 1869. *Comb.*: **c.-hole** = *creep-hole*; **-sheet,** the feeding-apron of a carding-machine. Hence **Cree·pingly** *adv.*

Creepy (krī·pi), *a.* 1794. [f. CREEP + -Y[1].] **1.** Characterized by creeping. **2.** Having a creeping of the flesh, caused by horror or repugnance 1831; *transf.* tending to produce such sensations 1883. Also **C.-crawly** 1861.

2. *transf.* A..romance of the c. order 1892.

Creese, crease (krīs), **kris** (kris), *sb.* 1577. [ult. – Malay *kirīs, krīs, kris*, but immed. – such forms as Du. *kris* (so in G.), Sp., Pg. *cris*, Fr. *criss.*] A Malay dagger, with a blade of a wavy form.

Which dagger they [of Java] call a Crise, and is as sharpe as a razor 1586. Hence **Creese, crease, kris** *v.* to stab with a c.

Creesh, creish (krīʃ), *sb. Sc.* ME. [– OFr. *craisse* = *graisse* :– L. *crassa* thick, fat. Cf. GREASE.] **1.** Grease, fat. **2.** A 'lick', a stroke 1774. Hence **Creesh** *v.* to grease. **Cree·shy** *a.* greasy.

‖ **Crémaillère** (krema[l]yęr). 1828. [Fr., formerly *cramaillère*, f. synon. *cramail* pot-hanger, chimney-hook.] *Field-fortif.* An indented or zigzag form of the inside line of a parapet.

Cremaster (krĭmæ·stəɹ). Pl. **-ers,** also ‖ **-eres.** 1678. [– Gr. κρεμαστήρ, f. κρεμα- hang.] **1.** *Anat.* The muscle of the spermatic cord, by which the testicle is suspended. **2.** *Entom.* The dorsal process or tip of the abdomen of the pupa of any insect that undergoes complete transformation. Hence † **Crema·steral, cremaste·ric** *a.* of or pertaining to the c.

Cremate (krĭmē[i]·t), *v.* 1874. [– *cremat-*, pa. ppl. stem of L. *cremare* burn, or back-formation from CREMATION; see -ATE[3].] To

consume by fire, to burn; *spec.* to reduce (a corpse) to ashes.
Satî, or a woman who is cremated with her husband 1874.

Cremation (krimēⁱ·ʃən). 1623. [– L. *crematio*, f. as prec.; see -ION.] The action of cremating; *spec.* the reduction of a corpse to ashes in lieu of interment.
When c. was abandoned for inhumation D. WILSON. Hence **Crema·tionist.**

Cremator (krimēⁱ·təɹ). 1877. [f. CREMATE *v.* + -OR 2.] One who, or that which, cremates.

Crematory (kre·mătəri). 1876. [f. CREMATE *v.* + -ORY¹ and ².] *adj.* Of or pertaining to cremation 1844. *sb.* A place for cremation; *spec.* an erection for the incineration of corpses; var. **Cremato·rium.** Hence **Cremato·rial** *a.*

Cremocarp (kre·mokāɹp). 1866. [irreg. f. Gr. κρεμα- hang + καρπός fruit.] *Bot.* A species of fructification, in which the fruit breaks up into two indehiscent one-seeded mericarps, which hang by their summits from the central axis.

Cremona¹ (krimōᵘ·nă). 1762. *attrib.* Pertaining to or made at Cremona, a town in Lombardy, as in *C. fiddle, school*; *absol.* A violin made there. Hence **Cremone·se** *a.*
'A Cremona', or 'a Cremonese violin' is often incorrectly used for an old Italian instrument of any make GROVE.

Cremo·na². 1660. [Perversion of KRUMMHORN, CROMORNE.] An organ reed-stop of 8-foot tone.

‖ **Cremor.** 1657. [L.] A thick juice or decoction. **b.** By erron. association with Fr. *crème*, CREAM *sb.*², a scum gathering on the top of a liquid.

Cremosin, -oysin, etc., obs. ff. CRIMSON.

‖ **Crena** (krī·nă). [mod.L. *crena* incision, notch, corresp. to It. *crena* notch, OFr. *crene* (mod. *cran*) :– pop.L. *crena* (in late gloss), of unkn. origin.] **1.** An indentation, a notch; *spec.* in *Bot.* one of the notches on a crenated leaf; *Anat.* the groove between the buttocks. **2.** A crenated tooth, a scallop; *spec.* in *Bot.* = CRENATURE, CRENEL; *Anat.* each of the serrations on the cranial bones by which these fit together in the sutures.

Crenate (krī·neⁱt), *sb.* 1838. [f. CREN(IC + -ATE⁴.] *Chem.* A salt of crenic acid. So **Cre·nated** *a.*

Crenate (krī·nĕt), *a.* 1794. [– mod.L. *crenatus* f. pop.L. *crena*; see CRENA, -ATE².] *Bot., Zool.*, etc. Having the edge notched or toothed with rounded teeth; finely scalloped. Hence **Cre·nated** *ppl. a.* (in same sense). **Crena·tion,** a crenated formation; a crenature.

Crenato- (krinēⁱ·to), comb. f. mod.L. *crenatus* CRENATE; crenately, crenate-.

Crenature (kre·nătiŭɹ, krī·n-). 1816. [f. mod.L. *crenatus* (see CRENATE *a.*) + -URE.] *Bot.* and *Zool.* A rounded tooth or denticulation on the margin of a leaf, etc. Also occas. the notches between the teeth.

Crenel, crenelle (kre·nĕl, krine·l), *sb.* 1481. [– OFr. *crenel* (mod. *créneau*) :– Gallo-Rom. **crenellum, -us*, dim. of pop.L. *crena*; see CRANNEL.] **1.** One of the indentations of an embattled parapet; an embrasure; see BATTLEMENT. In *pl.* = Battlements, embattled parapet. **2.** *Bot.* = CRENATURE 1835. Hence **Cre·nel** *v.* to crenellate (*rare*). **Cre·nelet,** a small c. (*rare*).

Crenellate, -elate (kre·neleⁱt), *v.* 1823. [f. (O)Fr. *créneler*, f. OFr. *crenel* embrasure; see prec., -ATE³.] To furnish with battlements; to furnish with embrasures or loopholes. Hence **Crenella·tion, -elation,** the action of crenellating or condition of being crenellated; a battlement; a notch or indentation.

†‖ **Crenellé, -elee,** *a.* 1586. [– Fr. *crénelé*, pa. pple. of *créneler*; see prec.] *Her.* EMBATTLED –1610.

Crengle, obs. f. CRINGLE.

Crenic (krī·nik), *a.* 1838. [f. Gr. κρήνη spring + -IC.] *Chem.* In *C. acid*, an organic acid, existing in humus, and in deposits of ferruginous waters.

Crenulate (kre·niulĕt), *a.* 1794. [– mod.L. *crenulatus*, f. *crenula*, dim. of *crena* (see CRENA) + -ATE².] *Zool.* and *Bot.* Minutely crenate; finely notched or scalloped: said of a leaf, a shell, etc. Hence **Crenula·tion,** a minute crenation.

Creole (krī·oᵘl). 1604. [– Fr. *créole*, earlier *criole* – Sp. *criollo*, prob. – Pg. *crioulo* Negro born in Brazil, home-born slave, formerly of animals reared at home, f. *criar* nurse, breed :– L. *creare* CREATE.]
A. *sb.* In the West Indies and other parts of America, Mauritius, etc.: *orig.* A person born and naturalized in the country, but of European or of African Negro race: the name having no connotation of colour.
a. But now, usually, = *creole white* 1604. **b.** Now, less usually = *creole negro*, as dist. from one freshly imported from Africa 1748.
a. [She] was a c.—that is, born in the West Indies, of French parents MARRYAT. **b.** The term 'Creole' is confined to negroes born in the country 1863.
B. *attrib.* or *adj.* **1.** Of persons: Born and naturalized in the West Indies, etc., but of European (or negro) descent; see A. 1748. Of animals and plants: Born or grown in the West Indies, etc., but not indigenous 1760. **2.** Belonging to or characteristic of a Creole 1828.
1. Fruits..of the C. kind, being European fruits planted there, but which have undergone considerable alterations from the climate 1760.
Hence **Creo·lian,** †*sb.* = CREOLE A.; *adj.* = CREOLE B. ? *Obs.* † **Cre·olism,** Creole descent.

Creophagous (kri,ǫ·fagəs), *a.* Also **kreo-.** 1881. [– Gr. κρεοφάγος, f. κρέας flesh; see -PHAGOUS.] Flesh-eating; carnivorous.

Creosol (krī·ŏsǫl). Also **crea-.** 1863. [f. CREOS(OTE + -OL.] *Chem.* A colourless highly refracting liquid ($C_8H_{10}O_2$) with aromatic odour and burning taste, forming the chief constituent of creosote.

Creosote (krī·ŏsōᵘt), *sb.* Also **crea-, kreo-.** 1835. [– G. *kreosote* (1832, Reichenbach), f. Gr. κρεο-, comb. form of κρέας flesh, + σωτήρ saviour, σωτερία safety, intended to mean 'flesh-saving' with ref. to the antiseptic properties.] A colourless oily liquid, with odour like that of smoked meat, and burning taste, obtained from the distillation of wood-tar, and having powerful antiseptic properties. Also *attrib.* **b.** Occas. applied to Carbolic Acid, also known as *coal-tar c.* 1863. *Comb.* **c.-bush, -plant,** a Mexican shrub (*Larrea mexicana*, N.O. *Zygophyllaceæ*) having a strong smell of c. Hence **Cre·osote** *v.* to treat with c., as a preservative.

Crepance. ? *Obs.* 1610. [In XVIII *crepanches, crepances* – It. *crepacci* pl. :– (ult.) L. *crepare* to crack, chap.] *Farriery.* A wound or chap on a horse's foot. [Misprinted *Crepane* by Johnson and later Dicts.]

‖ **Crêpe** (krēp). 1825. [Fr.; see CRAPE.] The French word for CRAPE, often borrowed as a term for all crapy fabrics other than black mourning crape.
Crêpe de Chine, a white or coloured crape made of raw silk. *Crêpe lisse*, crape which is not *crêpé* or wrinkled. Also *attrib.* Hence **Crêpe** *v.* to frizz.

† **Crepine, crespin(e.** 1532. [– OFr. *crespine* (mod. *crépine*), f. *crespe* frizzy :– L. *crispus* curled; see CRISP *a.*] A net or caul for the hair, formerly worn by ladies; also, a part of a hood; a fringe of lace or network for a dais, bed, etc. –1721.

‖ **Crepita·culum.** [L.; = rattle.] *Zool.* The rattle of the rattlesnake. *U.S.*

Crepitant (kre·pitănt), *a.* 1826. [– *crepitant-*, pres. ppl. stem of L. *crepitare*, crackle, etc., frequent. of *crepare*; see -ANT.] **1.** Making a crackling noise; crepitating 1855. **2.** *Entom.* That crepitates (see CREPITATE 2).

Crepitate (kre·piteⁱt), *v.* 1623. [– *crepitat-*, pa. ppl. stem of L. *crepitare*; see prec., -ATE³.] † **1.** To break wind –1768. **2.** *Entom.* Of certain beetles: To eject a pungent fluid suddenly with a sharp report 1826. **3.** To make a crackling sound: *spec.* of the tissue of the lungs 1853. **4.** To rattle.

Crepitation (krepitēⁱ·ʃən). 1656. [– Fr. *crépitation* or late L. *crepitatio*, f. as prec.; see -ION.] **1.** A crackling noise; crackling. **2.** *Med.* and *Path.* The slight sound and accompanying sensation caused by pressure on cellular tissue containing air, or by the entrance of air into inflamed lungs; or observed in the grating together of the ends of fractured bones; the crackling noise sometimes observed in gangrenous parts when examined with the fingers; the cracking of a joint when pulled. **3.** The breaking of wind (*rare*) 1822.

‖ **Crepitus** (kre·pitŏs). 1807. [L., f. *crepare* rattle, etc.] **1.** *Med.* and *Path.* = CREPITATION 2. **2.** = CREPITATION 3. 1882. Hence **Cre·pitous** *a.* of the nature of, or such as to produce, c.

‖ **Crépon** (kre·poṅ, kre·pən). 1887. [Fr., f. CRÊPE; see -OON.] A stuff resembling crape, made of fine worsted, silk, or worsted and silk.

Crept (krept). 1628. Pa. pple. of CREEP *v.*; *spec.* in *Coal-mining*, that has been subjected to a creep.

Crepuscle (krĭpɒ·s'l, kre·pŏs'l). 1665. [– L. *crepusculum.*] Twilight. var. **Crepuscule** (now *rare*).

Crepuscular (krĭpɒ·skiulăɹ), *a.* 1668. [f. prec. + -AR¹; cf. Fr. *crépusculaire.*] **1.** Of or pertaining to twilight 1755; hence *fig.* dim, indistinct; imperfectly enlightened 1668. **2.** *Zool.* Appearing or active in the twilight 1826.
1. *fig.* That c. period when the historical sense was scarcely brought to a full state of activity 1852. **2.** C. insects 1826. So **Crepu·sculine** *a.* (*rare*), **Crepu·sculous** *a.* (in sense 1).

‖ **Crepusculum** (krĭpɒ·skiulŏm). ME. [L., rel. to *creper* dusky, dark.] Twilight, dusk.
The same time..That clerkes call C. at eue LYDG.

† **Crescence.** 1602. [– L. *crescentia*; see CRESCENT, -ENCE.] Growth, increase –1736.

‖ **Crescendo** (kreʃe·ndo). 1776. [It., pr. pple. of *crescere* increase; see next.] *Mus.* A direction: To be gradually increased in volume of sound (usu. indicated by the abbrev. *cresc.* or the sign <). As *sb.*: Such an increase; a passage of this description. Also *transf.* and *fig.* Also as vb. (Opp. to DIMINUENDO.)
fig. The intense c. of the catastrophe 1886.

Crescent (kre·sĕnt), *sb.* [ME. *cressa(u)nt* – AFr. *cressaunt*, OFr. *creissant* (mod. *croissant*) :– L. *crescens, -ent-*, pres. pple. of *crescere* grow. See -ENT. In XVII assim. to L. form.] **1.** The waxing moon, during the period between new moon and full. Also *fig.* 1530. **2.** The convexo-concave figure of the waxing or waning moon, during the first or last quarter 1578. **3.** A representation of this phase of the moon: **a.** as an ornament ME. **b.** *Her.* as a charge 1486. **c.** as a badge or emblem of the Turkish sultans; hence *fig.* the Turkish power, and used rhetorically to symbolize the Moslem religion as a political force 1589. (The attribution of the *crescent* to the Saracens of Crusading times and to the Moors of Spain is an error.) **d.** used as the badge of an order of knighthood or as a decorative order ME. **4.** Anything of this shape, as a row of houses, etc. 1672.
2. *Mids. N.* v. i. 246. **3. c.** The C. gave way to the Cross, the Turks were broken to pieces 1684.
Hence **Crescenta·de,** *prop.*, a religious war waged under the Turkish flag; *rhet.*, a jihad or holy war for Islam. **Cre·scented** *ppl. a.* formed as a c. or new moon; ornamented, or charged, with crescents. **Cresce·ntic** *a.* c.-shaped. **Cresce·ntiform** *a.* crescentic.

Crescent (kre·sĕnt), *a.* 1574. [– *crescent-*, pres. ppl. stem of L. *crescere* grow; see prec., -ENT.] **1.** Growing, increasing. (Often with allusion to the moon.) **2.** Shaped like the new or old moon 1603.
1. My powers are Cressent, and my Auguring hope Sayes it will come to th' full *Ant. & Cl.* II. i. 10. **2.** Astarte, Queen of Heav'n, with c. Horns MILT.

Crescive (kre·siv), *a.* 1566. [f. L. *crescere* grow + -IVE.] Growing.
Vnseene, yet cressiue in his facultie *Hen. V*, I. i. 66.

Cresol (kre·sǫl). Also **cressol.** 1869. [f. *cres-* for CREOS(OTE + -OL.] *Chem.* An aromatic alcohol of the Benzene group (C_7H_8O), occurring along with carbolic acid in coal-tar and creosote. Hence **Cre·solene,** $C_6H_5CH_3O$, a product of coal-tar, related to carbolic acid. **Creso·tic** *a.* in (*ortho-, para-, meta-*) *cresotic acid* ($C_8H_8O_3$), obtained from the corresponding cresols.

Cress (kres). [OE. *cressa, cresse, cærse, cerse* = MLG. *kerse*, MDu. *kersse, korsse* (Du. *kers*), OHG. *kresso, kressa* (G. *kresse*) :– WGmc. **krasjō*.] **1.** The name of various cruciferous plants, having mostly edible leaves of a pungent flavour. (Until 19th c. almost always in pl.; sometimes construed with a vb. in the sing.) **a.** *spec.* Garden C., *Lepidium sativum*, or WATERCRESS, *Nasturtium officinale*. **b.** With defining words, applied to other cruciferous plants, and occas. to plants merely resembling cress in flavour or appearance. † **2.** As the type of something of little worth. (Cf. *rush, straw*.) –ME.

1. To strip the brook with mantling cresses spread GOLDSM. **2.** Wisdome and witte now is nouȝt worth a carse LANGL. Hence **Cre·ssy** *a.*

Cresset (kre·sėt). ME. [– OFr. *cresset, craisset*, f. *craisse*, var. of *graisse* oil, GREASE; see -ET.] **1.** A vessel of iron or the like, made to hold grease or oil, or an iron basket to hold pitched rope, wood, or coal, to be burnt for light; usually mounted on the top of a pole or building, or suspended from a roof. Also *transf.* and *fig.* **2.** *Coopering.* A fire-basket used to char the inside of a cask 1874. † **c.-light,** a blazing c.; the light of a c.

‖ **Cresson** (kresoṅ). 1883. [Fr.] A shade of green used for ladies' dresses.

Crest (krest), *sb.* ME. [– OFr. *creste* (mod. *crête*) :– L. *crista* tuft, plume.] **1.** A comb, a tuft of feathers, or the like, upon an animal's head. Also *fig.* (Cf. CREST-FALLEN.) **2.** An erect plume of feathers, horse-hair, etc., fixed on the top of a helmet or head-dress; any ornament worn there as a cognizance ME. **3.** *Her.* A figure or device (orig. borne by a knight on his helmet) placed on a wreath, coronet, or chapeau, and borne above the shield and helmet in a coat of arms; also used separately, as a cognizance, upon seals, plate, note-paper, etc. (Thus it is a vulgar error to speak of the arms or shields of a college or city as *crests*.) ME. Also *fig.* **4.** The apex of a helmet; hence, a helmet ME. **5.** The head, summit, or top of anything ME. **6.** *Archit.* The finishing of stone, metal, etc., which surmounts a roof-ridge, wall, screen, etc.; occas. applied to the finial of a gable or pinnacle ME. **7.** An elevated ridge. **a.** The ridge of a mountain, *col*, bank or the like. **b.** *Fortif.* The top line of a parapet or slope. **c.** The curling foamy ridge of a wave. 1440. **8.** The ridge of the neck of a horse, dog, etc. 1592. **9.** A raised ridge on the surface of any object; *spec.* in *Anat.*, etc.

1. Oft he [the serpent] bowd His turret C. MILT. *P.L.* IX. 525. *fig.* Then began the Argives to let fall their crests and sue for peace RALEGH. **2.** Warchiefs with..crests of eagle wings 1874. **3.** What is your C., a Coxcombe *Tam. Shr.* II. i. 226. **4.** On his c. Sat horror plum'd MILT. *P.L.* IV. 988. **7.** First curls the ruffl'd sea With whit'ning crests 1864. **8.** Chuse a horse with a deep neck, large c. MARKHAM.

Comb.: **c.-tile,** a bent tile used to cover the c. or ridge of a roof; **-wreath** (in *Her.*), the wreath or fillet of twisted silk which bears the c.

Crest (krest), *v.* ME. [f. CREST *sb.*] **1.** *trans.* To furnish with a crest. **2.** To serve as a crest to; to surmount as a crest; to crown 1606. **b.** To mark with long streaks, like the streaming hair of a crest 1596. **3.** To reach the crest 1851. **4.** *intr.* To erect one's crest 1713; to form a crest, as a wave 1850.

2. His legges bestrid the Ocean, his rear'd arme Crested the world *Ant. & Cl.* V. ii. 83. **b.** Like as the shining skie in summers night..Is creasted all with lines of firie light SPENSER *F.Q.* IV. i. 13. **3.** To c. a hill, a wave, etc. (*mod.*).

Crested (kre·stėd), *ppl. a.* ME. [f. CREST *sb.* and *v.* + -ED.] **1.** Wearing or having a crest; *spec.* applied to animals and plants distinguished by a crest; = L. *cristatus, -a.* Also *fig.* **2.** *Her.* Having a crest of a different tincture from that of the body 1572. † **3.** Ribbed –1834. **4.** Having a raised ridge. (See CREST *sb.* 9.) 1857.

1. Fair dames and c. chiefs SCOTT. *fig.* The c. pride Of the first Edward GRAY. **4.** Double-c. skulls WALLACE.

Crest-fallen (kre·st fǭ:lěn), *ppl. a.* 1589. **1.** With drooping crest; *hence*, cast down; humbled, dispirited. **2.** Of a horse: Having the crest or ridge of the neck hanging to one side 1696.

1. Let it make thee Crestfalne, I, and alay this thy abortiue Pride 2 *Hen VI*, IV. i. 59.

Cresting (kre·stiŋ), *vbl. sb.* 1869. [f. CREST *sb.* (sense 6) + ING[1].] *Archit.* An ornamental ridging to a wall or roof.

Cre·stless. *a.* 1591. Not bearing a crest. Spring Crestlesse Yeomen from so deepe a Root SHAKS.

Cresyl (kre·sil). Also **cressyl.** 1863. [f. CRES(OL + -YL.] *Chem.* The radical C_7H_7 of cresol. **Cre·sylate,** a salt of cresylic acid. **Cresy·lic** *a.* of cresyl, in *Cresylic acid* = CRESOL.

Cretaceo- (kritēi·ʃio), comb. f. of CRETACEOUS, = 'cretaceous and ——'.

Cretaceous (kritēi·ʃəs), *a.* 1675. [f. L. *cretaceus*, f. *creta* chalk; see -ACEOUS.] **1.** Of the nature of chalk; chalky. **2.** *Geol.* Of or found in the Chalk formation. So *C. group, series, system. C. period*: the period during which these strata were deposited. Hence **Creta·ceously** *adv.*

Cretic (krī·tik). 1603. [– L. *creticus* – Gr. κρητικός Cretan, f. Κρήτη Crete; see -IC.] *adj.* Belonging to Crete, Cretan; applied in Gr. and L. prosody to a particular metrical foot, or to verse characterized by these. *sb.* (without capital.) A metrical foot consisting of one short syllable between two long; = AMPHIMACER.

† **Cre·ticism.** 1614. [f. prec. + -ISM.] Cretan behaviour, *i.e.* lying –1656.

Cretify (krī·tifəi), *v.* 1859. [f. L. *creta* chalk + -FY.] To impregnate (a tissue of the animal body) with salts of lime. Hence **Cre:tifica·tion,** calcareous degeneration.

Cretin (krī·tin). 1779. [– Fr. *crétin* – Swiss Fr. *creitin, crestin* :– L. *Christianus* CHRISTIAN.] One afflicted with cretinism. Hence **Cre·tinous** *a.* pertaining to a c.; of the nature of cretinism.

Cretinism (krī·tiniz'm). 1801. [f. prec. + -ISM.] The condition of a cretin; a combination of deformity (usually with goitre) and idiocy, endemic in certain Alpine valleys and elsewhere. So **Cre·tinize** *v.* to reduce to c.

Cretion (krī·ʃən). 1880. [– L. *cretio*, f. *cret-*, pa. ppl. stem of *cernere* decide; see -ION.] *Rom. Law.* Declaration of acceptance of an inheritance; *transf.* the term allowed for this.

Cretize (krī·təiz), *v. arch.* 1653. [– Gr. κρητίζειν, f. Κρήτη Crete. (Cf. *Titus* 1:12.)] **1.** *intr.* To play the Cretan, *i.e.* to lie. † **2.** To outdo by lying 1673. So † **Cre·tism** (Dicts.).

‖ **Cretonne** (krəto·n, kre·tǫn). 1870. [– Fr. *cretonne*, f. *Creton* village in Normandy.] The French name of a strong fabric of hempen warp and linen woof; applied in England to a stout unglazed cotton cloth printed with a pattern in colours, and used for chair covers, curtains, etc.

Creutzer, obs. f. KREUTZER.

Crevasse (krĭvæ·s). 1819. [– Fr. *crevasse* (OFr. *crevace*); see next.] **1.** A fissure or chasm in the ice of a glacier, usually of great depth. Also *transf.* 1823. **2.** *U.S.* A breach in the bank of a river, canal, etc.; used *esp.* of a breach in the *levée* or artificial bank of the lower Mississippi. So **Creva·sse** *v.* to fissure with crevasses. **Creva·ssing** *vbl. sb.* formation of crevasses.

Crevice (kre·vis), *sb.* [ME. *crevace, -isse*, later *creves(se, -ice* – OFr. *crevace* (mod. *crevasse*), f. *crever* burst, split :– L. *crepare* rattle, crack, break with a crash.] **1.** An opening produced by a crack; a cleft, rift, chink, fissure. **2.** *spec.* (*Mining.*) A fissure in which a deposit of ore or metal is found 1872.

1. A creuisse of an olde cragge ME. Hence † **Cre·vice** *v. trans.* to make crevices in. **Cre·viced** *ppl. a.* having crevices, chinks, or cracks.

Crevis(e, -ish(e, -isse, -ys(e, obs. ff. CRAYFISH, CREVICE.

Crew (krū). 1455. [Late ME. *crue* – OFr. *creüe* (mod. *crue*), increase, subst. use of fem. pa. pple. of *croistre* (mod. *croître*) :– L. *crescere* grow, increase.] † **1.** An augmentation or reinforcement of a military force; hence, a company of soldiers –1587. **2.** By extension: Any organized band of armed men 1570. **3.** Any body of men organized or associated for a purpose; as, a squad of workmen under a foreman 1699; (*Naut.*) a gang of men under a petty officer, or told off for a particular duty 1692; and *esp.* the whole of the men (inclusive or exclusive of the officers) belonging to and manning a ship, boat, or other vessel afloat (now the leading sense) 1694. **4.** A number of persons associated together; a company 1579. **5.** A number of persons classed together; a lot, set, gang, mob, herd 1570.

3. To order the cooper and his c. to trim the casks SHELVOCKE. Supposing the Captain and Crew would soon be with him DAMPIER. **4.** Mirth, admit me of thy c. MILT. *L'Alleg.* 38. **5.** All the ravenous c. Of jobbers and promoters 1884.

Crew, pa. t. of CROW *v.*

† **Crewe.** [– OFr. *crue.*] A pot. SPENSER.

Crewel (krū·ěl), *sb.* 1494. [orig. *crule, crewle, croole* (monosyllable); of unkn. origin.] **1.** A thin worsted yarn, used for tapestry and embroidery. **2.** Short for CREWEL-WORK (*mod.*). Also *attrib.*

Crewels (krū·ělz), *sb. pl. Sc.* 1660. [– Fr. *écrouelles* scrofula.] The king's evil, scrofula.

Crew·el-work. 1863. Embroidery in which a design is worked in worsted on a background of linen or cloth.

Crewet, -ette, obs. f. CRUET.

Crib (krib), *sb.* [OE. *crib(b* = OFris. *cribbe*, OS. *kribbia* (Du. *kribbe, krib*), OHG. *krippa* (G. *krippe*).] **1.** A barred receptacle for fodder; a CRATCH OE. **2.** 'The stall or cabin of an ox' (J.) ME. **3.** A cabin, hovel; a narrow room; also *fig.* 1597. **b.** *Thieves' slang.* A dwelling-house, shop, etc. 1812. **4.** *fig.* A berth (*slang*) 1865. **5.** A small bed for a child, with barred sides. (*Occas.* = cradle.) 1649. **6.** *fig.* † ? Provender. *Thieves' cant.* Also a miner's 'bait'. † **7.** A wicker-work basket, pannier, or the like –1676. **8.** *Salt-making.* An apparatus like a hay-rack for draining the salt after boiling 1682. **9.** A framework of bars or spars for strengthening, support, etc. Cf. CRADLE *sb.* 1693. **10.** *Mining.* A framework of timber, etc., lining a shaft, to prevent caving, percolation of water, etc. 1839. **11.** A frame of logs secured under water to form a pier, dam, etc. (*Canada & U.S.*) 1874. **12.** A small raft of boards (*Canada & U.S.*) 1813. **13.** A bin for storing Indian corn (= CORN-*crib*); also for salt, etc. (*U.S.*) 1823. **14.** *Cards.* The cards thrown out from each player's hand, and given to the dealer, in the game of cribbage. Also, = CRIBBAGE (*colloq.*). 1680. **15.** A petty theft. (See CRIB *v.*) (*rare*) 1855. **16.** Something cribbed; a plagiarism (*colloq.*) 1834. **17.** A translation of a classic, etc., for the illegitimate use of students (*colloq.*) 1827.

1. Layd..In a cribbe, bytwen an ox and an asse HAMPOLE. **2.** Where no Oxen are, the c. is cleane *Prov.* 14:4. **3.** Why rather (Sleepe) lyest thou in smoakie Cribs..Then in the perfum'd Chambers of the Great 2 *Hen. IV*, III. i. 9. *fig.* The world.. Whithersoever we turn, still is the same narrow c. CLOUGH.

Comb.: **c.-biter,** a horse addicted to c.-biting; also *fig.*; **-biting,** the morbid habit of seizing the manger (or other object) with the teeth and noisily drawing in the breath; **cribwork,** work consisting of cribs (sense 11); also *attrib.*

Crib (krib), *v.* 1460. [f. CRIB *sb.*] † **1.** *intr.* ? To feed at a crib (*rare*). **2.** *trans.* To shut up as in a crib; to confine within narrow limits; to hamper. (In mod. use as an echo of Shaks.) 1605. **3.** *intr.* To lie as in a crib 1661. **4.** *trans.* To furnish with a crib or cribs (CRIB *sb.* 1, 9–11) 1669. **5.** To make up into cribs (CRIB *sb.* 12) (*U.S.*) 1876. **6.** *colloq.* To pilfer, purloin, steal; to appropriate furtively. [Prob. orig. *thieves' slang.*] 1748. **7.** *colloq.* To take (a passage, etc.) without acknowledgement and use as one's own; to plagiarize 1778. **8.** *intr.* Of horses: To practise crib-biting 1864.

1. Cabin'd, crib'd, confin'd, bound in *Macb.* III. iv. 24. **6.** Bits of ground cribbed..at different times from the forest COBBETT. Hence **Cri·bber** (*rare*), one who cribs or uses a CRIB (1, 17) (*colloq.*)

Cribbage (kri·bėdʒ). 1630. [Origin unkn.] **1.** A game at cards, played by two, three, or four persons, with a complete pack of cards, and a board with holes and pegs for scoring; the characteristic feature is a CRIB (sense 14).

2. The action of cribbing, or that which is cribbed (*colloq. rare*) 1830.

1. He proposed a game of four-handed c. DICKENS.
Comb.: **c.-board**, the board used for marking at c.; **-faced** *a.* pock-marked, and so like a c.-board.

Cribbing (kri·biŋ), *vbl. sb.* 1641. [f. CRIB *v.* (and *sb.*) + -ING[1].] **1.** The action of CRIB *v.* 1791. **2.** = Crib-biting; see CRIB *v.* 8. 1864. **3.** That which is cribbed 1837. **4.** *Mining.* Timbering forming the lining of a shaft, etc.; cribwork 1841. † **5.** *Thieves' cant.* Provender 1641.

Cribble (kri·b'l), *sb.* ? *Obs.* 1552. [– (O)Fr. *crible* :– pop.L. **criblum* for L. *cribrum* sieve.] **1.** A sieve 1565. † **2.** That which is left in the sieve; bran or coarse meal –1691. Also *attrib.* Hence † **Cribble** *v.* to sift. var. † **Cribe** *sb.* and *v.*

Cribrate (krəi·brĕt), *a.* 1846. [f. L. *cribrum* sieve, after *caudate*, etc.; see -ATE[2].] *Nat. Hist.* Perforated like a sieve.

† **Cri·brate,** *v.* 1631. [– *cribrat-*, pa. ppl. stem of L. *cribrare* sift, f. *cribrum* sieve; see -ATE[3].] *trans.* To sift; also *fig.* –1669. Hence † **Cribra·tion,** sifting; also *fig.*

Cribriform (krəi·brifǫɹm, kri·b-), *a.* 1741. [f. L. *cribrum* sieve + -FORM.] Having the form or appearance of a sieve; perforated with small holes.

The c. part of the *Os Ethmoides* MONRO. C. or Sieve-cells, a sort of ducts the walls of which have open slits, through which they communicate with each other A. GRAY.

Cribrose (krəibrōᵘ·s), *a.* 1857. [f. L. *cribrum* sieve; see -OSE[1].] Sieve-like, perforated. var. † **Cri·brous.**

Crick (krik), *sb.*[1] 1440. [Of unkn. origin.] A painful spasmodic affection of the muscles of the neck, back, or other part, appearing as a sudden stiffness which makes it almost impossible to move the part.

† **Crick,** *sb.*[2] 1530. [app. same word as Fr. *cric* jack-screw, etc.] The instrument for bending a cross-bow. [1874. A small jack-screw. KNIGHT.]

Crick, *sb.*[3], var. of CREEK *sb.*

Crick (krik), *v.*[1] 1861. [f. CRICK *sb.*[1]] *trans.* To give a crick to (the neck, etc.).

Crick, *v.*[2] 1601. [imit.; cf. Fr. *criquer* (XVI), *cric* int. Cf. CRICKET *sb.*[1]] To make a sharp abrupt sound, as a grasshopper.

Crick-crack, *sb.*, *v.*, *adv.* 1565. [Frequentative reduplication of CRACK; cf. Fr. *cric crac*, Du. *krikkrakken* crackle.] A representation of a repeated sharp sound.

Cricket (kri·kĕt), *sb.*[1] ME. [–(O)Fr. *criquet* †grasshopper, cricket, f. *criquer* crackle, of imit. origin; cf. (M)Du. *krekel* cricket, f. imit. base **krick-*.] Any saltatorial orthopterous insect of the genus *Acheta* or of the same tribe; as, the common house-cricket, *A. domestica*, the field-cricket, *A. campestris*, and mole-cricket, *Gryllotalpa vulgaris*. **b.** Used for CICADA.

As cheerful and lively as a c. 1873.
Comb.: **c.-bird,** the grasshopper warbler (*Locustella nævia*); **-frog,** a small tree-frog of the genus *Hylodes*, which chirp like crickets; **-teal,** the garganey (*Querquedula circia*).

Cricket (kri·kĕt), *sb.*[2] 1598. [Of disputed but unascertained origin.] A well-known open-air game played with ball, bats, and wickets, by two sides of eleven players each. Also *attrib.* **b.** Used *allus.* for: Fair play 1902. Hence **Cri·cket** *v.* to play c. **Cri·cketer.**

Cricket (kri·kĕt), *sb.*[3] 1643. [Of unkn. origin; cf. synon. north. dial. *cracket*, CROCK *sb.*[4]] A low wooden stool; a footstool. Now *local.*

Crico- (krəi·ko), comb. f. Gr. κρίκος = κίρκος ring, used in *Anat.* in sense 'pertaining to the cricoid cartilage', as **c.-thy·roid** *a.* pertaining to the cricoid and thyroid cartilages; also *sb.* (*sc.* muscle). **Crico·tomy,** the operation of dividing the cricoid cartilage.

Cricoid (krəi·koid). 1746. [– mod.L. *cricoides* – Gr. κρικοειδής ring-shaped; see CRICO-, -OID.] *adj.* Ring-shaped; applied *spec.* to the cartilage which forms the lower and back part of the larynx. *sb.* (*sc.* cartilage) 1842.

Cried (krəid), *ppl. a.* 1642. [f. CRY *v.* + -ED[1].] Proclaimed by crying, announced.

Crier (krəi·əɹ). [ME. *criour*, *criere* – AFr. *criour*, OFr. *criere*, nom. of *crieur*, f. *crier*; see CRY, -OUR, -ER[2] 3.] **1.** *gen.* One who cries. **2.** *spec.* An officer in a court of justice who makes the public announcements, etc.; a COMMON or TOWN *crier* ME.; one who cries goods for sale 1553.

All common Cryers were excluded from the Temple 1726.

Crikey (krəi·ki), *int. colloq.* or *slang.* 1842. [euphem. alteration of CHRIST; cf. CRIMINE.] An exclam. of surprise.

Crim. con. 1770. Abbrev. of *criminal conversation*, *i.e.* adultery. (See CRIMINAL *a.*)

Crime (krəim), *sb.* ME. [– (O)Fr. *crime*, †*crimne* :– L. *crimen* judgement, accusation, offence, f. reduced base of *cernere* decide, give judgement.] **1.** An act punishable by law, as being forbidden by statute or injurious to the public welfare. (Commonly used only of grave offences.) **b.** *collect. sing.* Violation of law 1485. **2.** An evil or injurious act; a (grave) offence, a sin 1514. **b.** *collect. sing.* Wrong-doing, sin ME. † **3.** Charge, or accusation; matter of accusation –1667.

1. If by this C., he owes the Law his life *Timon* III. v. 83. Men steeped in c. FROUDE. 2. All yᵉ crymes of yᵉ tonge, as sclaunders..and prevy backbytynges 1526. 3. That errour now, which is become my c., And thou th' accuser MILT. *P.L.* IX. 1181.
Hence **Crime** *v.* to charge with a c. (*rare*). **Cri·meful** *a.* full of c.; criminal. **Cri·meless** *a.* void of c.

Criminal (kri·minăl). ME. [– late L. *criminalis*, f. L. *crimen*, *crimin-*; see prec., -AL[1].]

A. *adj.* **1.** Of the nature of or involving a crime, or a grave offence. **2.** Relating to crime or its punishment 1474. **3.** Guilty of crime or grave offence 1489.

1. *C. conversation* (CONVERSATION 3): adultery, regarded as a *trespass* against the husband at common law. 2. Good lawes, civil and criminall 1590. An experienced c. lawyer LOWELL. 3. The neglect..renders us c. in the sight of God ROGERS (J.).

B. *sb.* † **1.** A person accused of a crime –1681. **2.** A person guilty or convicted of a crime 1626.

1. Was ever c. forbid to plead DRYDEN.
Hence **Cri·minalism,** the condition or practice of a c. **Cri·minalist,** one versed in c. law. **Crimina·lity,** the quality or fact of being a c.; a c. act or practice. **Cri·minally** *adv.* according to c. law; so as to constitute crime. † **Cri·minalness,** criminality.

Criminate (kri·mineⁱt), *v.* 1645. [– *criminat-*, pa. ppl. stem of L. *criminare*, f. as prec.; see -ATE[3].] **1.** *trans.* To charge with crime; to represent as criminal. **2.** To prove guilty of crime; to incriminate 1665. **3.** To represent as criminal; to condemn 1677.

1. I suppose the public servants will be criminated 1793. 2. Determined not to c. himself by any allusion to the circumstance 1841.
So **Crimina·tion,** the action of criminating; severe accusation or censure. **Cri·minative** *a.* tending to or involving crimination. **Cri·minator,** one who charges with crime. **Cri·minatory** *a.* criminative.

Crimine, -iny (kri·mini), *int.* 1681. [Euphemistic alteration of CHRIST; cf. CRIKEY.] A vulgar exclam. of astonishment: now *arch.*

Criminology (krimino̩·lŏdʒi). 1890. [f. L. *crimen* (cf. *criminal*) + -LOGY.] The science of crime; 'criminal anthropology'. So **Criminolo·gical** *a.*, **Crimino·logist.**

Criminous (kri·minəs), *a.* 1483. [– AFr. *criminous*, OFr. *crimineux* – L. *criminosus*, f. as prec.; see -OUS.] † **1.** Of the nature of a crime; criminal. **2.** Of persons: Guilty of crime 1535. Now only in *c. clerk* (CLERK *sb.* 1). † **3.** Of or relating to crime; involving crimination –1650.

Hence **Cri·minously** *adv.* **Cri·minousness.**

Crimison, crimosin(e, etc., obs. ff. CRIMSON.

Crimp (krimp), *sb.*[1] 1638. [Origin unkn.] † **1.** ? A term of reproach or derision. **2.** An agent who procures seamen, soldiers, etc., *esp.* by decoying or impressing them 1758. Also *transf.* and *fig.* † **3.** A coal broker –1791.

1. Yes, c.; 'tis a gallant life to be an old lord's pimp-whiskin FORD. Phr. †*To play c.*: 'to lay or bet on one side, and (by foul play) to let t'other win, having a share of it' B. E. *Dict. Cant. Crew.* Hence **Cri·mpage,** money paid to a c. for his services.

Crimp, *sb.*[2] 1632. [prob. f. CRIMP *v.*[1]] An obsolete game at cards.

Crimp (krimp), *sb.*[3] 1883. [f. CRIMP *v.*[1]] *pl.* Crimped tresses; cf. 'curls'. *U.S.*

Crimp (krimp), *a.* 1587. [app. allied to CRIMP *v.*[1]; cf. however MHG. *krimpf* crooked, curved (Kluge). Cf. also CRUMP.] **1.** Friable, brittle; crisp. † **2.** *fig.* 'Not consistent, not forcible' (J.). (But see quot., the sole evidence for this sense.) 1712. **3.** Said of hair, feathers, etc.: Crimped 1764.

1. The grass was c. and white with the hoar frost MRS. CAMERON. 2. The evidence is crimp (v.l. *scrimp*); the witnesses swear backwards and forwards, and contradict themselves ARBUTHNOT.
Hence **Cri·mpness,** friability.

Crimp (krimp), *v.*[1] ME. [prob. – (M)LG., (M)Du. *krimpen* shrink, wrinkle, shrivel = OHG. *krimphan* (MHG. *krimpfen*).] **1.** *intr.* To be compressed, pinched or indented (as *e.g.* the body of insects). † **2.** *trans.* To curl –1736. **3.** To compress or pinch into minute parallel plaits or folds 1712; to crisp the surface of 1772; to make flutings in (a brass cartridge case). **4.** To cause (the flesh of fish) to contract and become firm by gashing it before *rigor mortis* sets in 1698. Also *transf.* **5.** *spec.* To bend or mould into shape (leather for uppers, etc.) 1874. **6.** 'To pinch and hold; to seize' (Webster).

3. To c. the little frill that bordered his shirt-collar DICKENS.

Crimp (krimp), *v.*[2] 1812. [f. CRIMP *sb.*[1]] To impress (seamen or soldiers); to entrap.

Plundering corn and crimping recruits WELLINGTON.

Crimper[1] (kri·mpəɹ). 1819. [f. CRIMP *v.*[1] + -ER[1].] **1.** One who crimps. **2.** That which crimps:

a. An apparatus consisting of a pair of fluted rollers, for crimping cloth or the like. **b.** A toilet instrument for crimping the hair. **c.** A machine for crimping leather for uppers. **d.** An apparatus for bending leather into various shapes for saddles and harness. **e.** A small machine for crimping brass cartridge-cases.

Crimper[2]. 1868. [f. CRIMP *v.*[2] + -ER[1].] = CRIMP *sb.*[1] 2.

Crimple, *v.* ME. [perh. a dim. and iterative of CRIMP *v.*[1]] † **1.** *intr.* To be or become incurved, or drawn together; hence to stand or walk lame from such a cause –1736. **2.** *intr.* and *trans.* To wrinkle, crinkle, curl. Now *dial.* Hence **Cri·mpled** *ppl. a.* (in sense 2).

Crimson (kri·mz'n). [ME. *cremesin*, *cremesin*, with variant forms in Rom.; ult. – Arab. *ḳirmizī* KERMES; cf. CRAMOISI. For the sp. with *-son* cf. DAMSON.]

A. *adj.* **1.** The name of a colour: of a deep red inclining towards purple (see KERMES). **2.** *fig.* Sanguinary 1681.

1. This cramoysen gowne 1549. 2. C. conquest 1777.

B. *sb.* (The *adj.* used *absol.*) **1.** The colour or pigment ME. † **2.** Crimson cloth –1611.

1. Ros'd ouer with the Virgin C. of Modestie SHAKS.

Crimson (kri·mz'n), *v.* 1601. [f. CRIMSON *a.*] **1.** *trans.* To make crimson. **2.** *intr.* To become crimson; *esp.* in blushing 1805.

1. Heere thy Hunters stand..Crimson'd in thy Lethee *Jul. C.* III. i. 206. 2. As the fresh bud a crimsoning beauty shows MRS. NORTON.

Crinal (krəi·năl), *a. rare.* 1656. [– L. *crinalis*, f. *crinis* hair; see -AL[1].] Pertaining to the hair.

Cri·nate, by-form of CRINITE haired. So **Crina·ted** *a.*

Cri·natory, var. of CRINITORY.

Crinc-; see CRINK-.

Crine (krəin), *sb. rare.* 1614. [– OFr. *crine* hair of the head, mane, or its source L. *crinis* hair.] **1.** Hair, head of hair. Also *attrib.* **2.** = CRINET 2. 1883. Hence **Crined** *a.* (*Her.*), having the hair tinctured differently from the body, as a charge.

Crine (krəin), *v. Sc.* 1501. [app. – Gael. *crìon* wither.] *intr.* To shrink, shrivel.

Crinel, error for CRINET 2.

† **Crinet.** 1486. [f. OFr. *crine* or mod.Fr. *crin* (f. L. *crinis*) + -ET.] **1.** A hair 1572. **2.** *Hawking.* (*pl.*) The small hair-like feathers

which grow about the cere of a hawk. (Also written *crinites*; now called *crines*.) –1792. **3.** = CRINIÈRE 1586.

Cringe (krindʒ), *v.* [ME. *crenǵe*, varying with *crenche*, corresp. to OE. *crinǵan*, *crinćan* fall in battle, OFris. *krenza*, Du. *krengen* heel over, and rel. to ON. *krangr* weak, frail, *kranga* creep along, and MLG., Du., MHG. *krenken* weaken, injure, OFris., (M)LG., (M)HG. *krank* sick, ill, slight. Cf. CRANK *sb.*[1]] † **1.** *trans.* To draw in or contract (any part of the body); to distort (the neck, face, etc.) –1630. **2.** *intr.* To draw in the muscles of the body involuntarily; to shrink; to cower ME. **3.** *intr.* To bend the body timorously or servilely. Const. *to* (a person). 1575. **4.** *fig.* To behave obsequiously; to show base or servile deference 1620. † **5.** *trans.* To bow deferentially to –1660.

1. *Ant. & Cl.* III. xiii. 100. **2.** The Boys that went before were glad to c. behind, for they were afraid of the Lions BUNYAN. **3.** An opinion that to bow or c. (as they profanely call it) before Almighty God is superstition BEVERIDGE. **4.** To teach the people to c. and the prince to domineer MACAULAY. Hence **Cri·ngeling** (*rare*), a cringing creature; also *attrib.* **Cri·nger. Cri·nging-ly** *adv.*, **-ness.**

Cringe (krindʒ), *sb.* 1597. [f. prec. vb.] A deferential, servile, or fawning obeisance. Often applied to a bow. Also *fig.*

Performing cringes and congees like a court-chamberlain THACKERAY.

Cringle (kri·ŋg'l). 1627. [– LG. *kringel*, dim. of *kring* circle, ring, f. **kriŋg-*, parallel to **kriŋk-*; cf. CRANK *sb.*[1], CRINKLE.] **1.** *Naut.* A ring or eye of rope, containing a thimble, worked into the bolt-rope of a sail, for the attachment of a rope. **b.** A withe for fastening a gate (*dial.*) 1787. **2.** = CRINKLE (*dial.*) 1807. Hence **Cri·ngle** *v. dial.* to fasten with a c.

Crini-, stem of L. *crinis* hair: used as comb. form:

Crinicu·ltural *a.* of or pertaining to the growth of the hair. **Cri·niger** (*Ornith.*), a genus of African and Asiatic birds allied to the Thrush, having stiff setæ on their bills. **Crini·gerous** *a.* bearing or wearing hair. **Crini·parous** *a.* hair-producing.

Crinid (kri·nid, krəi-). 1862. [f. Gr. κρίνον lily + -ID[3].] *Zool.* (*pl.*) A family of the *Crinoidea* containing the typical crinoids with branching arms.

‖ **Crinière** (kriniẹ·r). 1598. [Fr. = mane, f. *crin* (horse) hair. Cf. CRINE.] The part of the bards of a war-horse which covered the ridge or back of the neck and the mane.

† **Crini·tal**, *a. rare.* 1583. [f. next + -AL[1].] = CRINITE *a.*

He the star c. adoreth 1583.

Crinite (krəi·nəit), *a.* 1600. [– L. *crinitus*, pa. pple. of *crinire* cover or provide with hair, f. *crinis* hair; cf. OFr. *crinite*. See -ITE[2].] Hairy; having a hairy or hair-like appendage; *spec.* in *Bot.* and *Zool.* having hairy tufts on the surface.

How comate, c., caudate starres are fram'd I knew FAIRFAX.

Crinite (kri·nəit, krəi-), *sb.* [f. Gr. κρίνον lily + -ITE[1] 2 b.] A fossil crinoid.

Cri·nitory, *a. rare.* 1836. [f. L. *crinitus* (see CRINITE *a.*) + -ORY[2].] Hairy.

Crinkle (kri·ŋk'l), *sb.* 1596. [prob. f. CRINKLE *v.*] A twist, winding, or sinuosity; a wrinkle or corrugation.

The crinkles in this glass making objects appear double TUCKER. Hence **Cri·nkly** *a.* full of crinkles.

Crinkle (kri·ŋk'l), *v.* ME. [frequent. f. base of OE. *crinćan* yield, orig. weaken; see CRINGE, -LE.] **1.** *intr.* To form many short twists or turns; to wind or twist; to contract wrinkles or ripples; to shrink *up*. **2.** To cringe; *fig.* to recede from one's purpose. Now only *dial.* 1610. **3.** *trans.* To twist or bend to and fro, or in and out; to wrinkle, crumple; to crimp (the hair) 1825. **4.** *intr.* To emit sharp thin sounds 1856.

1. It [a stream] seemed to ripple and c. LOWELL. **2.** I like him the worse, he crinkles so much in the hams FORD. **3.** And for the hous is krynkeled two and fro And hath so queynte weyis for to go CHAUCER. Her face all bowsy Comely crynklyd Woundersly wrynkled 1529. **4.** All the rooms Were full of crinkling silks 1856.

Cri·nkle-cra·nkle. 1598. [frequent. reduplic. CRANKLE.] *sb.* A winding in and out, a zig-zag. *adj.* and *adv.* Zigzag 1840.

† **Crinkum, crincum.** Also **grincome.** 1618. *slang.* In *pl.* The venereal disease –1719.

Cri·nkum-cra·nkum, *sb.* (*a.*) Also **crincum-crancum.** 1761. [Formation with variation of vowel intended to symbolize intricacy.] Anything full of twists and turns, or intricately elaborated (*joc.*).

Crinoid (kri·noid, krəi-). 1836. [– Gr. κρινοειδής, f. κρίνον lily; see -OID.] *adj.* Lily-shaped; applied to an order (chiefly fossil) of echinoderms, having a calyx-like body, stalked and rooted. As *sb.* (with pl. *crinoidea*, *crinoida*). A member of this order.

Crinolette (krinole·t). 1881. [dim. f. CRINOLINE, see -ETTE.] A sort of bustle for distending the back of a woman's skirt.

Crinoline (kri·nolīn, -ǒlin). 1830. [– Fr. *crinoline*, irreg. f. L. *crinis* hair (Fr. *crin* horsehair) + *linum* thread (Fr. *lin* flax), the intention being to denote the woof of horsehair and the weft of thread.] **1.** A stiff fabric made of horsehair and cotton or linen thread, formerly used for skirts, and still for lining, etc. **2.** A petticoat made of this or any stiff material, worn under the skirt in order to support or distend it; *hence*, a hoop-petticoat 1851. **3.** *transf.* A netting fitted round warships as a defence against torpedoes. Chiefly *attrib.* 1874.

Crinosity (krəinǫ·sĭti). *rare.* 1656. [f. L. *crinis* hair; see -OSITY.] Hairiness.

Crio- = Gr. κριο-, comb. f. κριός ram:

Crioce·ratite, a fossil of the genus *Crioceras*, a ram's-horn ammonite. **Cri·osphinx**, a sphinx having a ram's head.

Cripple (kri·p'l). [OE. (Northumb.) *crypel*, also *eorþcrypel* 'paralyticus', ME. (s.w.) *crüpel*, corresp. to OLG. *krupil*, f. **krup-*; also OE. *crēopel*, ME. *crēpel*, corresp. to MLG., MDu. *krēpel*, rel. to forms cited s.v. CREEP.]

A. *sb.* **1.** One who is disabled (either from birth or by accident or injury) from the use of his limbs; a lame person. **2.** *techn.* = *Cripplegap* (see below), where *cripple* = 'creeping' 1648. **3.** *slang.* A sixpence 1785.

1. A creeple from his mothers wombe *Acts* 14:8. *Comb.* **c.-gap, -hole** (*dial.*), a hole left in walls for sheep to creep through; cf. sense 2. Hence **Cri·ppledom, -hood, -ness. Cri·pply** *a.*

B. *adj.* Disabled from the use of one's limbs, lame. (*Obs.* or *dial.*, exc. as attrib. of prec.) ME.

Cripple (kri·p'l), *v.* ME. [f. CRIPPLE *sb.*] **1.** *trans.* To deprive (wholly or partly) of the use of one's limbs; to make a cripple of. **2.** *transf.* and *fig.* To disable, impair: **a.** the action or effectiveness of material objects 1694; **b.** a person in his resources, efforts, etc., or immaterial things, as trade, schemes, strength, etc. 1702. **3.** *intr.* To hobble. (Chiefly *Sc.*) ME.

1. Thou cold Sciatica, C. our Senators *Timon* IV. i. 24. **2.** The lower masts, yards and bowsprit all crippled NELSON. The trade..is crippled by the want of transport L. OLIPHANT. Hence **Cri·ppler.**

Crisis (krəi·sis). Pl. **crises,** rarely **crisises.** 1543. [– medical L. *crisis* (Seneca) – Gr. κρίσις decision, judgement, event, issue, turning-point of a disease (Hippocrates, Galen), f. κρίνειν decide.] **1.** *Pathol.* The point in the progress of a disease when a change takes place which is decisive of recovery or death; also, any marked or sudden change of symptoms, etc. † **2.** *Astrol.* Said of a conjunction of the planets which determines the issues of a disease or critical point in the course of events –1663. **3.** *transf.* and *fig.* A turning-point in the progress of anything; also, a state of affairs in which a decisive change for better or worse is imminent 1627. † **4.** Judgement, decision –1715. † **5.** A criterion, sign –1657.

1. I had enjoyed a favourable c. SMOLLETT. **3.** The ordinary statesman is also apt to fail in extraordinary crises JOWETT.

Crisp (krisp), *a.* [OE. *crisp*, *crips* – L. *crispus* curled. The development of branch II may be due to symbolic interpretation of the sound of the word.]

I. 1. Of the hair: Curly; now *esp.* stiff, closely curling, or frizzy; †also, having such hair. **2.** Having a surface fretted into ripples, folds, or wrinkles ME. † **3.** App. = Smooth, shining, clear –1623.

1. His crispe heer lyk rynges was yronne CHAUCER. **2.** The c. white crest of the running waves BLACK. **3.** All th'abhorred births below crispe Heauen SHAKS.

II. Brittle or short; said *esp.* of hard things which have little cohesion and are easily crushed by the teeth, etc. 1530. Also *transf.* and *fig.*

The c...not over-roasted crackling LAMB. *transf.* The c. frosty air 1883. *fig.* A c. touch on the piano 1857. What he said was c. and decided 1873. Hence **Cri·sp-ly** *adv.*, **-ness.**

Crisp, *sb.* ME. [app. f. the adj.; cf. OFr. *crespe* curly, mod.Fr. *crêpe*.] † **1.** A crape-like material, used for veils, etc.; also a veil, etc. of this –1619. † **2.** A curl (of hair); *esp.* a short or close curl –1680. **3.** The crackling of roast pork. Now *dial.* 1675.

Crisp (krisp), *v.* ME. [f. CRISP *a.*; cf. L. *crispare* curl, crisp, crimp.] **1.** *trans.* To curl into short, stiff, wavy folds or crinkles; to crimp. **2.** *intr.* To curl in short stiff curls 1583. **3.** *trans.* To make crisp or brittle. Also *transf.* and *fig.* 1815. **4.** *intr.* To become crisp 1805.

1. A cooling breeze which crisps the broad clear river BYRON. **2.** The leaues..do somewhat curle or crispe GERARDE. **3.** The snow..crisped by ..a severe frost SCOTT. **4.** The air chilled at sunset, the ground crisped C. BRONTË. Hence **Cri·sper.**

Crispate (kri·spĕt), *a.* 1846. [– L. *crispatus*, pa. pple. of *crispare* curl; see -ATE[2].] Crisped; *spec.* in *Bot.* and *Zool.* having the margin curled or undulated.

Crispation (krispēⁱ·ʃən). 1626. [f. *crispat-*, pa. ppl. stem of L. *crispare* curl; see -ION.] **1.** Curling, curled condition; undulation. **2.** A slight contraction of any part, as that of the skin in goose-skin, etc. 1710.

2. Few can look down from a great height without creepings and crispations O. W. HOLMES.

Cri·spature. *rare.* 1745. [f. as prec.; see -URE.] Crisped condition; crispation.

Cri·spin. 1645. A shoemaker, so named in allusion to St. Crispin, the patron saint of shoemakers; also sometimes a member of a union or benefit society of shoemakers.

Crispy (kri·spi), *a.* ME. [f. CRISP *a.* + -Y[1].] **1.** Curly, wavy; undulated. **2.** = CRISP *a.* II. 1611. Hence **Cri·spiness,** crispness.

Cri·ssal, *a.* Chiefly *U.S.* 1872. [– mod.L. *crissalis*, f. CRISSUM; see -AL[1].] *Ornith.* **1.** Pertaining to the crissum, as the *c. region*. **2.** Characterized by the colouring of the under tail-coverts, as *C. thrush* or *thrasher*.

Criss-cross (kri·sˌkrǫs), *sb.* [A reduction of CHRIST('S)-CROSS: latterly treated as a redupl. of *cross*.] **1.** = CHRIST-CROSS, q.v. **2.** [f. CRISS-CROSS *v.*] A transverse crossing 1876. **3.** *U.S.* A children's game, played on a slate; Fox and Geese 1860. Hence **Criss-cross-row**; see CHRIST-CROSS-ROW.

Criss-cross (kri·sˌkrǫs), *a.* and *adv.* 1846. [See prec.] *adj.* Crossing, crossed; marked by crossings or intersections. *adv.* Crosswise; *fig.* in a contrary way, awry.

Criss-cross (kri·sˌkrǫs), *v.* 1818. [See prec.] *trans.* To mark or cover with crossing lines.

To c. the letter KEATS.

‖ **Crissum** (kri·sǒm). 1874. [mod.L., f. *crissare* move the haunches.] *Ornith.* The anal region of a bird under the tail; the vent-feathers or lower tail-coverts.

Cristate (kri·stĕt), *a.* 1661. [– L. *cristatus*, f. *crista* CREST; see -ATE[2].] *Nat. Hist.*, etc. Crested; in the form of a crest. So **Crista·ted** *a.*

Criterion (krəitiᵊ·riən). Pl. **criteria**; occas. **-ons.** 1613. [– Gr. κριτήριον means of judging, test, f. κριτής judge.] † **a.** An organ or faculty of judging –1678. **b.** A canon or standard by which anything is judged or estimated 1622. † **c.** A characteristic attaching to a thing, by which it can be judged or estimated –1678.

b. Regular uniformity and the straight line were the criterions of taste and beauty 1788. So ‖ **Crite·rium,** L. form of Gr. (occas. used).

Crith (kriþ). 1865. [f. Gr. κριθή barley-corn, the smallest weight.] *Physics.* The weight of 1 litre of hydrogen at standard pressure and temperature; proposed by Hoffmann as the unit of weight for gaseous substances.

Crithomancy (kri·þomænsi). 1652. [f. Gr. κριθή; see prec., -MANCY.] Divination by meal strewed over animals sacrificed.

Critic, *a.* 1544. [– Fr. *critique* – late L. *criticus*; see next.] † **1.** *Med.*, etc. = CRITICAL 4, 5. –1605. **2.** Judging captiously or severely, censorious, carping 1598. **3.** = CRITICAL 3. 1626.

3. Matters historic, c., analytic, and philologic 1834.

Critic (kri·tik), *sb.*¹ 1588. [– L. *criticus* – Gr. κριτικός, subst. use of adj. f. κριτής judge; see -IC.] **1.** One who pronounces judgement on any thing or person; *esp.* a censurer, caviller. **2.** One skilled in literary or artistic criticism; a professional reviewer; also one skilled in textual or biblical criticism 1605.

1. Take heed of criticks: they bite, like fish, at anything, especially at bookes DEKKER. **2.** The poet [Milton], we believe, understood the nature of his art better than the c. [Johnson] MACAULAY. You know who the Critics are? The men who have failed in Literature and Art DISRAELI.

† **Critic** *sb.*² 1656. [– Fr. *critique* – (ult.) Gr. κριτική (sc. τέχνη) the critical art, criticism. Now spelt and pronounced as Fr.; see CRITIQUE.] **1.** The art of criticizing; CRITICISM. Also in *pl.* –1773. **2.** A CRITIQUE –1766.

1. Grammar and Criticks HOBBES. **2.** Make each day a critick on the last POPE.

† **Critic,** *v.* 1607. [– Fr. *critiquer*, f. *critique*; see prec.] **1.** *intr.* To play the critic, pass judgement (*on*) –1698. **2.** *trans.* To criticize; *esp.* (in earlier use) unfavourably –1751.

2. As Helluo. . Critick'd your wine and analysed your meat POPE. Hence **Cri·ticable** *a.* (*rare*).

Critical (kri·tikăl), *a.* 1590. [f. L. *criticus* (see CRITIC *a.*) + -AL¹.] **1.** Given to judging; *esp.* fault-finding, censorious. † **2.** Involving or exercising careful judgement or observation; nice, exact, punctual –1716. **3.** Occupied with or skilful in criticism 1641; belonging to criticism 1741. **4.** *Med.*, etc. Relating to the crisis of a disease; determining the issue of a disease, etc. 1601. **5.** Of the nature of, or constituting, a crisis; involving suspense as to the issue 1664. **6.** Decisive, crucial 1841. **7.** *Math.* and *Physics.* Constituting or relating to a point at which some action, property or condition passes over into another; constituting an extreme or limiting case 1841. **8.** *Zool.* and *Bot.* Of species: Uncertain or difficult to determine 1854.

1. I am nothing, if not Criticall *Oth.* II. i. 120. **3.** A c. writer 1766. C. acumen FREEMAN. **4.** And so the Fever terminates in a c. Abscess CHEYNE. **5.** Mrs. H—'s throat was badly cut, and her condition is deemed c. 1883. **7.** *C. angle* in *Optics*: that angle of incidence beyond rays of light are no longer refracted but totally reflected. *C. point* or *temperature*: that temperature above which a substance remains in the gaseous state and cannot be liquefied by any amount of pressure. Hence **Critica·lity** (*rare*), c. quality; a criticism; a crisis. **Cri·ticalness.**

Critically (kri·tikăli), *adv.* 1654. [f. prec. + -LY².] **1.** Nicely, accurately. † **2.** Punctually, exactly –1853. † **3.** At or in relation to a crisis –1670; at a critical moment –1799. **4.** Dangerously 1815. **5.** *Physics.* In a critical state 1881.

1. To look c. into ourselves 1660. **4.** Thus c. circumstanced 1815.

Criticaster (kritikæ·stəɹ). 1684. [f. CRITIC *sb.*¹ + -ASTER.] A petty critic. (Used in contempt.)

I perceived that note to be added by some Jewish C. 1684.

Criticism (kri·tisiz'm). 1607. [f. CRITIC or L. *criticus* + -ISM.] **1.** The action of criticizing, or passing (*esp.* unfavourable) judgement upon the qualities of anything; fault-finding. **2.** The art of estimating the qualities and character of literary or artistic work 1674; *spec.* the critical science which deals with the text, character, composition, and origin of literary documents 1669. **b.** The critical philosophy of Kant 1867. **3.** (with *pl.*) A critical remark; a CRITIQUE 1608. † **4.** A nice point or distinction; a quibble –1683.

1. Therfore (reader) doe I. . stand at the marke of criticisme. . to bee shot at DEKKER. **2.** C., as it was first instituted by Aristotle, was meant a standard of judging well DRYDEN. C. and the gospel history FROUDE. *Textual c.*: that which seeks to ascertain the genuine text and meaning of an author. The Higher or Historical C. [of the sacred books] 1881.

Criticize (kri·tisəiz), *v.* Also **-ise.** 1649. [f. as prec. + -IZE.] **1.** *intr.* To play the critic; to pass (*esp.* unfavourable) judgement upon something with respect to its qualities. Also with †*on* or †*upon*. **2.** *trans.* To discuss critically; to animadvert upon 1665; *esp.* to censure, find fault with 1704.

1. We c. much upon the Beauty of Faces HARTLEY. **2.** To c. his gait, and ridicule his dress SWIFT. Hence **Cri·tici:zable** *a.* **Cri·ticizer.**

Critico-, comb. f. (after Gr. κριτικο-), = critically, critical and . . . : as in **c.-historical.**

Critique (kritī·k). 1702. [Later form of CRITIC *sb.*², altered after Fr. *critique*, the orig. source.] **1.** An essay or article in criticism of a literary (or more rarely, an artistic) work; a review. **2.** The action or art of criticizing; criticism 1815.

1. I should as soon expect to see a C. on the Posie of a Ring, as on the Inscription of a Medal ADDISON. **2.** The c. of nature in detail is quite beyond us J. MARTINEAU. Hence **Critique·** *v. trans.*, to write a c. upon.

† **Cri·tism.** *rare.* 1651. [f. Gr. κριτής judge + -ISM.] = CRITICISM. So † **Cri·tist,** † **Cri·tize** *v.* –1677.

Crizzle (kri·z'l), *v.* Now *dial.* 1624. [perh. dim. of CRAZE *v.*; see -LE.] **1.** *intr.* To become rough on the surface, as glass, etc., by scaling 1673. **2.** *trans.* To roughen or crumple the surface of 1624.

‖ **Cro** (krō). ME. [Ir. *cró* death, blood, blood-wite.] 'The compensation or satisfaction made for the slaughter of any man, according to his rank' (Jam.).

Croak (krōᵘk), *sb.* 1561. [f. the verb.] The deep hoarse sound made by a frog or raven. Also *transf.* and *fig.*

Croak (krōᵘk), *v.* 1460. [imit.; preceded by synon. †*crok* (XIII), with similar imit. formations, viz. OE. *crakettan*, *cræcettan*, ME. †*crake* (XIV) and †*creke* (see CREAK), †*crouk* (XIV), †*craik* (XV, Henryson).] **1.** *intr.* To utter a deep, hoarse, dismal cry, as a frog or a raven. **2.** *transf.* Of persons: To speak with a hoarse hollow utterance; *fig.* to talk dismally, forebode evil 1460. **3.** *trans.* To utter or proclaim by croaking 1605.

1. Th' vnpleasant quyre of frogs still croking SPENSER. **2.** They, who c. themselves hoarse about the decay of our trade BURKE. **3.** The raven himselfe is hoarse That croakes the fatall entrance of Duncan *Macb.* I. v. 40. Hence **Croa·kery,** croakings collectively. CARLYLE.

Croaker (krōᵘ·kəɹ). 1637. [f. prec. vb. + -ER¹.] **1.** An animal that croaks; applied *spec.* to several N. American fishes, also to the Mole Cricket 1651. **2.** *transf.* One who talks dismally, one who forebodes evil.

Croaky (krōᵘ·ki), *a.* 1851. [f. CROAK *sb.* or *v.* + -Y¹.] Characterized by, or given to croaking. Hence **Croa·kily** *adv.*

‖ **Croc,** † **crock** (krǫk). [(O)Fr. *croc* hook, – ON. *krókr*; see CROOK *sb.*] A hook: in *Harquebus à (of) c.*: see HARQUEBUS.

† **Croceous** (krōᵘ·siəs, -ʃiəs), *a.* 1657. [f. L. *croceus* saffron-coloured + -OUS.] Saffron-coloured; deep reddish-yellow –1688. vars. † **Cro·ceal,** † **Cro·cean, Cro·ceate,** *adjs.*

† **Croche,** *sb.*¹ ME. [– ONFr. *croche* – OFr. *croce*; see CROSE.] **1.** A pastoral staff, crook, crosier –1563. **2.** A CRUTCH, q.v. –1500.

Croche, *sb.*² 1575. [– Fr. *croche* (XVI), cogn. w. (O)Fr. *croc* (XII); see CROC.] One of the buds at the top of a stag's horn.

Crochet (kro·ʃe, krōᵘ·ʃi), *sb.* 1848. [– Fr. *crochet*, dim. of *croc*, with *-ch-* from *crochié*, *crochu* hooked; see prec., -ET.] A kind of knitting done with a hooked needle; work so knitted. Also *attrib.*

A shirt as of c. of women CLOUGH.

Crochet (kro·ʃe, krōᵘ·ʃi), *v.* Pa. t. and pple. **crocheted** (krōᵘ·ʃed). 1858. [f. the sb.] *intr.* To work with a crochet-needle; *trans.* to knit in crochet.

†‖ **Crocheteur.** 1579. [Fr., f. *crocheter* carry on (the porter's) hook (*crochet*).] A porter –1613.

Crociary (krōᵘ·ʃiări). [– med.L. *crociarius*, f. *crocia* crosier; see -ARY¹.] *Eccl.* 'The person who carried the crosier before the abbot or bishop' (Ash 1775).

Crocidolite (krosi·dŏləit). 1835. [f. Gr. κροκίς, -ιδ-, nap of woollen cloth + -LITE.] *Min.* A fibrous silicate of iron and sodium, called also *blue asbestos*; sometimes massive or earthy. Also, a yellow fibrous mineral produced by natural alteration from the blue crocidolite, and much used for ornament.

Crocin (krōᵘ·sin). 1863. [f. L. *crocus* saffron + -IN¹.] *Chem.* A red powder, the colouring matter of Chinese Yellow pods, the fruit of *Gardenia grandiflora.*

Crock (krǫk), *sb.*¹ [OE. *croc* and *crocca*, rel. to synon. Icel. *krukka*, and prob. further to OE. *crōg* (= OHG. *kruog*, G. *krug*), OE. *crūce* (= OS. *krūka*, Du. *kruik*, MHG. *kruche*).] **1.** An earthen pot, jar, etc. **2.** A metal pot. (*S.W. of Eng.*) 1475. **3.** A broken piece of earthenware 1850.

1. Like foolish flies about an hony-crocke SPENSER.

Crock (krǫk), *sb.*² Now *dial.* 1657. [Origin unkn.] Smut, soot, dirt.

Crock (krǫk), *sb.*³ Chiefly *Sc.* 1528. [In earliest use Sc.; perh. of Flem. origin, but appropriate words have a different vowel, as MDu. *kraecke* (Du. *krak*), Flem. *krake*; presumably rel. to CRACK *v.*] **1.** An old ewe, or one past bearing. **2.** An old broken-down horse 1879; also *transf.*

† **Crock,** *sb.*⁴ [Origin unkn.; prob. rel. to CRICKET *sb.*³] ? A low stool. ADDISON.

Crock, *v.*¹ Now *dial.* 1594. [f. CROCK *sb.*¹] To put up in a crock or pot.

Crock, *v.*² Now *dial.* 1642. [f. CROCK *sb.*²] *trans.* To smut with soot, etc.; to soil, defile.

Crock, *v.*³ 1893. [f. CROCK *sb.*³ 2.] *intr.* and *trans.* To (cause to) collapse; often with *up.* So **Cro·cky** *a.*, broken-down.

† **Crockard.** ME. [– AFr. – OFr. *crocard* kind of base money (XIII–XIV), of unkn. origin.] A foreign coin, decried as base under Edward I. –1769.

† **Crocker.** ME. [f. CROCK *sb.*¹ + -ER¹.] A potter –1703.

Crockery (krǫ·kəri). 1719. [f. CROCKER; see -ERY.] Crocks collectively; *esp.* earthenware vessels. *Comb.* **c.-ware** = CROCKERY.

Crocket (krǫ·kėt). ME. [ONFr. var. of (O)Fr. *crochet* CROTCHET.] † **1.** A curl formerly worn. (ME. only.) **2.** *Archit.* One of the small ornaments, usually in the form of buds or curled leaves, placed on the inclined sides of pinnacles, canopies, etc., in Gothic architecture 1673. **3.** = CROCHE *sb.*² 1870. **4.** *attrib.* Decorated with crockets 1703.

3. You will discourse. . of the antlers and the crockets BLACK. Hence **Cro·cketing,** c.-work.

Crocodile (krǫ·kŏdəil). [– OFr. *cocodrille* (mod. *crocodile*) :– med.L. *cocodrillus* for L. *crocodilus* – Gr. κροκόδιλος. Refash. after L. and Gr. XVI–XVII.] **1.** A large amphibious saurian reptile of the genus *Crocodilus* or allied genera. The name belongs properly to the crocodile of the Nile (*C. niloticus* or *vulgaris*); but is extended to other species, and sometimes to all *Crocodilia*, including the Alligator and the Gavial. **2.** *fig.* A person who weeps hypocritically or with a malicious purpose, as the crocodile was fabled to do 1595. **3.** *Logic.* = CROCODILITE 1727. **4.** *joc.* A girls' school walking two and two in a long file 1870; also *transf.* **5.** *attrib.* 1563.

1. Cokadrilles. . Theise Serpentes slen men, and thei eten hem wepynge MAUNDEV. **5.** Thence came the Prouerb, he shed C. teares, *viz.* fayned teares 1623.

Hence **Crocodi·lian,** *a.* † like a c.; pertaining to a c.; belonging to the c. family; *sb.* an animal of the c. family.

† **Cro·codilite.** 1624. [– Gr. κροκοδιλίτης (sc. λόγος) a sophistic fallacy (Chrysippus).] *Logic.* Name of an ancient sophism (see STANLEY *Hist. Philos.*) –1660.

Crocoite (krōᵘ·ko,əit). 1844. [orig. Fr. *crocoise* – Gr. κροκόεις saffron-coloured; alt. to *crocoisite*, then to *crocoite*, as if f. Gr. κρόκος + -ITE¹ 2 b.] *Min.* Native chromate of lead, a mineral of a red or orange colour.

Croconic (krokǫ·nik), *a.* 1838. [f. L. *crocus* + *-on-* (meaningless) + -IC.] In *c. acid* ($C_5H_2O_5$), an inodorous, strongly acid substance, obtained in the form of yellow crystals or powder. Hence **Cro·conate,** a salt of this acid.

Crocus (krōᵘ·kŏs). 1639. [– L. *crocus* crocus plant, saffron – Gr. κρόκος of Sem. origin (cf. Heb. *karkōm*; Arab. *kurkum* saffron, turmeric). OE. had *croh* saffron, from Latin.] **1.** A genus of hardy dwarf bulbous plants, N.O. *Iridaceæ*, with brilliant flowers, usually deep yellow or purple, which appear before the leaves in early spring, or in some species in autumn. The autumnal species, *C. sativus*, yields SAFFRON. † **2.** Saffron; the stigma of *C. sativus*. (In OE. *croh.*) –1710. **3.** *Chem.* A name given to various yellow or red powders obtained from metals by calcination, as *c. of copper* (*c. veneris*), cuprous oxide, etc.; now chiefly to the peroxide of iron obtained by calcination of sulphide of iron, and used as a polishing powder 1640. **4.** *slang.* A quack doctor 1785. Hence **Cro·cused** *ppl. a.* bedecked with crocuses.

Croft (krǫft), *sb.*[1] [OE. *croft*, of unkn. origin.] **1.** A piece of enclosed ground, used for tillage or pasture; in most parts a small piece of arable land attached to a house. Also *fig.* **2.** A small agricultural holding worked by a peasant tenant 1842. **3.** *attrib.* 1791.

1. To occupy her husband's cottage, and cultivate..a c. of land adjacent SCOTT.

Croft, *sb.*[2] *rare.* 1470. [– MDu. *crofte* (MLG. *kruft*) cave, hole – med.L. *crupta* for L. *crypta* CRYPT. Cf. CROWD *sb.*[2]] A crypt, vault, cavern.

Croft (krǫft), *v.* 1772. [f. CROFT *sb.*[1]] To bleach (linen, etc.) on the grass.

Crofter (krǫ·ftəɹ). 1799. [f. CROFT *sb.*[1] + -ER[1].] One who rents and cultivates a croft; *esp.* in the Highlands and Islands of Scotland, one of the joint tenants of a divided farm. Also *attrib.*

Crofting (krǫ·ftiŋ), *vbl. sb.* 1743. [f. CROFT *sb.*[1] + -ING[1].] **1.** The state of being successively cropped; the land so cropped. **2.** The system of croft-tenancy; the holding of a crofter 1851.

† **Croh.** [OE. *crōg*, *crohh*; see CROCK *sb.*[1]] A pitcher –ME.

Croh, OE., f. CROCUS, saffron.

Crois, early f. CROSS, q.v.

Croisad(e, -ada, -ado, early ff. CRUSADE.

† **Croisard**, a crusader.

† **Croise**, *v.* ME. [– OFr. *cruisier, croisier* :– eccl.L. *cruciare* crucify, cl.L. torment, torture, f. *crux, cruc-* CROSS *sb.*] **1.** *trans.* To mark with a cross; *esp.* by way of giving sanctity to a vow; *refl.* and *pass.* to take the cross in solemnization of a vow –1639. **2.** To crucify –1450. Hence † **Croised** *ppl. a.* having taken the cross.

Croise, *sb.*; see CROISES.

† **Croisee, -ie, -y.** 1482. [– OFr. *croisee* (= med.L. *cruciata*), f. *crois* CROSS; see -Y[5], CRUSADE.] A crusade –1615. So † **Croiserie, -ry**, crusading; a crusade.

† **Croi·ses, croi·sees**, *sb. pl.* 1656. [– Fr. *croisés*, pl. of *croisé* (OFr. *croisié*), subst. use of pa. pple. of *croiser* (OFr. *croisier*, see CROISE *v.*) mark with a cross. In med.L. *cruciatus.*] Those who have been croised, crusaders. (Occas. used as an archaism for *Crusades*; hence an erron. sing. *croise.*) –1846.

Croissant, earlier f. CRESCENT.

† **Cro·ker.** *rare.* 1577. [app. f. CROCUS + -ER[1].] A cultivator or seller of saffron.

Crome, cromb (krōᵘm, krūm), *sb.* Now *local.* ME. [repr. an OE. **cramb*, **cromb*, rel. to *crumb* bent = OFris., OS. *krumb*, OHG. *krump, krumb-* (G. *krumm*); f. WGmc. **kramb-*, var. of **kramp-* CRAMP *sb.*[1]; cf. CRUMP *a.*[1]] A hook, a crook. †In early use, also = claw, talon. Hence **Crome, cromb** *v.* to seize or draw with a c.

Cromlech (krǫ·mlek). ME. [– W. *cromlech*, f. *crom*, fem. of *crwm* bowed, arched + *llech* flat stone.] A structure of prehistoric age consisting of a large flat unhewn stone resting horizontally on three or more stones set upright; found *esp.* in Wales, Devonshire, Cornwall, and Ireland. Also applied to similar structures elsewhere.

This is the application of the word in Welsh. In Brittany these structures are called *dolmen* (= tablestones), while *cromlech* is the name of a circle of standing stones. var. (*erron.*) **Crommel.** LYTTON.

Cromorne (kromǭ·ɹn). 1694. [– Fr. *cromorne* – G. *krummhorn* cornet, lit. 'crooked horn'. Cf. CREMONA[2].] = KRUMMHORN, CREMONA[2].

Cromwellian (krǫmwe·liăn). 1725. **A.** *adj.* Of or pertaining to Oliver Cromwell. **B.** *sb.* An adherent of Cromwell; one of the settlers in Ireland at the Cromwellian Settlement of 1652, or of their descendants.

Crone (krōᵘn), *sb.* ME. [prob. – MDu. *croonje, caroonje* carcass (Kilian), old useless ewe – ONFr. *carogne* CARRION (also, cantankerous or mischievous woman), which may be the immed. source of sense 1.] **1.** A withered old woman; occas. applied to a man 1630. **2.** An old ewe 1552.

1. This olde Sowdones, þis cursed c. CHAUCER. A few old battered crones of office DISRAELI. Hence † **Crone** *v.* to pick out and reject (the old sheep). Also *transf.*

Cronel, obs. f. CORONAL.

† **Cronet, cronett.** 1519. [Syncopated f. CORONET.] **1.** = CORONET, q.v. –1602. **2.** Some part of the armour of a horse 1633.

Cronian (krōᵘ·niăn), *a.* [f. Gr. Κρόνιος belonging to Cronos (Saturn) + -AN.] *C. sea*: the northern frozen sea. MILT. *P.L.* x. 290.

† **Cronie, crony.** *rare.* Var. of (or ? error for) CRONE. Burton.

Cronk (krǫŋk). 1878. *dial.* [imit.; cf. Icel. *krúnk* the raven's cry.] The croak of a raven; in U.S., the cry of the wild-goose.

Cronstedtite (krǫ·nstĕtəit). 1823. [f. *Cronstedt*, a Swedish mineralogist; see -ITE[1] 2 b.] *Min.* A hydrous silicate of iron and manganese.

Crony (krōᵘ·ni), *sb.* 1663. [Earliest form *chrony* – Gr. χρόνιος long-lasting, long-continued, f. χρόνος time; orig. university slang word ('vox academica', Skinner 1671), the Gr. word being perverted to the sense 'contemporary'. Pepys, who uses the word, and Skinner were Cambridge men. The corresp. Oxford term was *chum.*] An intimate friend or associate; a chum. Also *attrib.*

Jack Cole, my old schoolfellow..who was a great chrony of mine PEPYS. Hence **Cro·ny** *v.* to associate (*with*) as a c.

Crood, croud *v. Sc.* 1513. [imit.] *intr.* To coo as a dove. Hence **Croo·dle** *v.*[1] *intr.* (in same sense).

Croodle (krū·d'l), *v.*[2] *dial.* 1788. [Origin unkn.] *intr.* To cower or crouch down; to draw oneself close together, as for warmth; to nestle close together, or cling close to a person.

'There,' said Lucia, as she clung croodling to him KINGSLEY.

Crook (kruk). [ME. *crōc, crōk*, north. *crūk* – ON. *krókr* hook, barb, peg, bend, curve, winding, corner (Sw. *krok*, Da. *krog*).]

A. *sb.* **1.** Any implement of hooked form; a hook. *spec.* **a.** A shepherd's staff, having one end hooked, for catching the hinder leg of a sheep ME. **b.** The pastoral staff of a bishop, etc., shaped like a shepherd's staff; a crosier ME. **2.** Any incurved appendage ME. **3.** An odd corner, nook ME. † **4.** (*pl.*) Brackets, parentheses –1762. **5.** *Mus.* A piece of curved tubing added to a horn, cornet, etc., to raise or lower the pitch 1842. **6.** The act of crooking ME. **7.** A bending or curve 1486. † **8.** *fig.* Crooked conduct; a trick, wile –1594. **9.** One whose conduct is crooked; a swindler, sharper; a professional criminal. orig. *U.S.* 1886.

1. b. Er the bishop hent hem with his c. CHAUCER. 2. The young fronds of the..Ferns uncurling their crooks 1850. 3. It was full of nooks and crooks W. IRVING. 6. With sacrifice of knees, of crooks, and cringes B. JONSON. 7. The crooks of Tweed STEVENSON.

Phr. *On the c.*: dishonestly (*slang*). *C. in one's lot*: an affliction, trial. *Sc. By hook or by c.*: see HOOK.

B. *adj.* [? shortened f. *crookt, crooked.*] = CROOKED 1508.

Comb.: **c.-back**, † a crooked back; one who has a crooked back; a hunchback; hence, **-backed** *a.*; **-neck** (*U.S.*), a name of varieties of squash (*Cucurbita maxima*) having the neck recurved.

Crook (kruk), *v.*[1] ME. [f. CROOK *sb.*] **1.** *trans.* To distort from a straight line; to bend; to curve. † **2.** *fig.* To turn out of the straight course; to pervert, twist –1646. **3.** *intr.* To be or become crooked; to bend, curve ME. **4.** *intr.* To bend the body; to bow (*arch.*) ME. † **5.** *intr.* To turn aside out of the straight course (*lit.* and *fig.* –1607.

1. And crooke the pregnant hindges of the knee SHAKS. 2. There is no one thinge yat crokes youth more than suche unlefull games. ASCHAM. Hee crooketh them to his owne endes BACON. 3. A riuer both large and deepe..goeth crooking on the left hand 1579.

† **Crook**, *v.*[2] ME. [imit.; cf. CROAK.] **1.** *intr.* To croak. Rarely *trans.* –1617. **2.** To crood, as a dove. –1611.

Crooked (kru·kĕd), *a.* ME. [f. CROOK *sb.* + -ED[2], prob. after ON. *krókóttr* crooked, winding, cunning, wily.] **1.** Bent from the straight form; curved, bent, awry. **2.** Of persons: Deformed, bent or bowed with age. Hence *transf.* of *age*. ME. **3.** *fig.* Deviating from rectitude; not straightforward; dishonest, perverse; awry ME.; *colloq.* dishonestly come by. (*U.S.* and *Australia.*) 1876. **4.** quasi-*adv.* Not straight 1545.

1. If the drinke..touch my Palat adversly, I make a c. face at it *Cor.* II. i. 62. 2. A Sybil old, bow-bent with c. age MILT. 3. A peruerse and c. generation *Deut.* 32:5. Of c. counsels POPE. A c. horse R. BOLDREWOOD. Hence **Croo·kedly** *adv.* **Croo·ked·ness**, the quality or state of being c. (*lit.* and *fig.*).

† **Croo·ken**, *v.* 1552. [irreg. f. CROOK *v.* + -EN[5].] To make, be, or become crooked; also *fig.* –1828.

Crool (krūl), *v. rare.* 1580. [imit.; cf. CROAK, CROOD, CROOK *v.*[2]] To make an inarticulate sound more liquid and prolonged than a croak.

Croon (krūn), *v.* Chiefly *Sc.* 1460. [north. Eng. and Sc. *croyne, crune* – MLG., MDu. *krōnen* lament, mourn, groan (Du. *kreunen* groan, whimper), of imit. origin.] **1.** *intr.* To utter a continued, loud, deep sound; to bellow as a bull, boom as a bell, etc. (*Sc.* or *n. dial.*) 1513. **2.** To sing (or speak) in a low murmuring tone 1460; to make moan (*Sc.* or *n. dial.*) 1823. **3.** *trans.* To sing (a song, etc.) in a low murmuring undertone; to hum 1790.

2. I hear a mother crooning to her baby 1877. 3. Whiles crooning o'er some auld Scots sonnet BURNS. Hence **Croon** *sb.* a loud deep sound, such as the bellow of a bull, etc.; a low murmuring or humming sound. **Croo·ner**, one who croons; *spec.* in *Sc.*, a fish, the Grey Gurnard, from the noise it makes when landed.

Crop (krǫp), *sb.* [OE. *crop(p*, corresp. to MLG., MDu. *kropp*, (O)HG. *kropf*, ON. *kroppr*; further relations uncertain.] **1.** A pouch-like enlargement of the œsophagus or gullet in many birds, in which the food is partially prepared for digestion; the craw. **2.** *transf.* and *fig.* The stomach or maw; also the throat. Now *Sc.* and *dial.* Cf. GIZZARD. ME. † **3.** The head of a herb, flower, tree, etc.; a cyme; also *fig.* –1785. **b.** *Archit.* A finial 1478. **4.** The upper part of a whip; hence the stock or handle of a whip; *esp.* a whipstock with a handle and a loop instead of the lash; more fully a *hunting-crop* 1562. **5.** [from 3] The annual produce of plants grown or gathered for food; the produce of the field, either while growing or when gathered; harvest ME. **6.** The produce of some particular plant in one season or locality ME. Also *transf.* **7.** The entire hide of an animal tanned 1457. **8.** *transf.* and *fig.* A supply of anything produced or appearing 1575. **9.** *Tin-mining.* The best quality of tin-ore obtained after dressing; more fully *c.-ore, -tin* 1778. **10.** [f. CROP *v.*] The act of cropping or its result; *e.g.* the cutting or wearing of the hair short; a closely cropped head of hair 1795; an ear-mark 1675. **11.** *Min.*, etc. An outcrop 1679. † **12.** *attrib.* –1825.

3. Take..the crops of Thyme, Savory, Lavender, etc. 1686. 5. The husbandman looks not for a c. in the wild desart BP. HALL. 6. *The crops*: the whole of the agricultural yield of a particular district or season. 8. The annual academical c. of beardless youths 1830. 10. Newgate c. 1878.

Phr. *Neck and c.*: see NECK. *sb.*[1] *Comb.* **c.-hide**, a hide, *esp.* a cow- or ox-hide, tanned whole and untrimmed.

Crop (krǫp), *v.* ME. [f. CROP *sb.*] **1.** *trans.* To cut off or remove the crop, head, or terminal parts of; to pluck off, cull, browse. Also *fig.* **2.** To reap. Also *fig.* 1601. **3.** *intr.* To bear a crop or crops 1606. **4.** *trans.* To cause to bear a crop; to sow or plant with a crop 1607. **5.** To cut off the top or extremity of 1607; *spec.* to clip short the ears, hair, etc. 1796. **6.** *intr. Min.*, etc. Of a stratum, vein, etc.: To come *up* or *out* 1665.

1. Hee cropt off the top of his yong twigs *Ezek.* 17:4. Sheep..that c. the springing grass QUARLES. **5.** Having their ears cropt for perjury BP. WATSON. Phr. *To c. up* (fig.): to turn up unexpectedly. *To c. out* (rarely *forth*): to disclose itself incidentally.

† **Cro·p-ear.** 1596. [Cf. CROP *v.* 5.] An ear that has been cropped; hence, a crop-eared animal or person –1702. Hence **Cro·p-ea:red** *a.* having the ears cropped; also, having the hair cut short, so that the ears are conspicuous, as the Roundheads.

Cro·p-fu:ll, *a.* 1632. [f. CROP *sb.* 1–2.] Having the crop or stomach filled.

Cropper[1] (krǫ·pəɹ). 1655. [f. CROP *sb.* 1 + -ER[1].] A breed of pigeons having the power of greatly puffing up their crops; a pouter.

Cro·pper[2]. 1483. [f. CROP *sb.* or *v.* + -ER[1].] **1.** One who or that which crops. **2.** One who shears the nap of cloth; also, a machine for doing this 1711. **3.** One who raises a crop 1573. **4.** A plant which yields a crop 1845.

Cro·pper[3]. 1858. [perh. f. phrase *neck and crop.*] *colloq.* A heavy fall; often *fig.*

Croppy (krǫ·pi). 1798. [f. CROP *v.* 5 + -Y[1].] One who has his hair cut short; applied *esp.* to the Irish rebels of 1798, who thus showed their sympathy with the French Revolution.

Cro·p-sick, *a.* Now *dial.* 1624. [f. CROP *sb.* 1–2.] Disordered in stomach, *esp.* by excess in eating and drinking. Often *fig.* Hence **Cro·p-sickness.**

Croquet (krōᵘ·ke, -ki), *sb.* 1858. [Supposed to be – north.Fr. var. of Fr. *crochet* hook; see CROCHET, CROTCHET.] **1.** A game played upon a lawn, in which wooden balls are driven by wooden mallets through hoops fixed in the ground in a particular order. **2.** The action of the verb (see CROQUET *v.*) 1874.

Croquet (krōᵘ·ke, -ki), *v.* Pa. t. and pple. **croqueted** (krōᵘ·ked); also **croqueed, -éd, -ed.** 1858. [f. prec. sb.] In the game of croquet: To drive away a ball, after hitting it with one's own, by placing the two in contact and striking one's own with the mallet (*trans.* and *absol.*).

‖ **Croquette** (kroke·t). 1706. [Fr., f. *croquer* crunch; see -ETTE.] A ball of rice, potato, or finely minced meat or fish, seasoned and fried crisp.

‖ **Crore** (krōᵊɹ). *Anglo-Ind.* 1609. [– Hindi *k(a)rōṛ* :– Prakrit *kroḍi*, Skr. *koṭi* end, top, highest point.] Ten millions, or one hundred lakhs (of rupees).

† **Crose, croce.** ME. [– OFr. *croce* (pron. krǫtsə); see next.] **1.** A crosier –1617. **2.** A staff ME.

Crosier, crozier (krōᵘ·ʒⁱəɹ). ME. [Two words are blended; (i) – OFr. *croisier* (med.L. *cruciarius*) cross-bearer, f. *crois* CROSS *sb.*; (ii) – OFr. *crocier, crossier* bearer of a bishop's *crosse* or crook (OFr. *croce* :– Rom. **croccia*, f. **croccus* CROOK).] **1.** One who bears a cross before an archbishop. (prop. **croiser.**) Now *Hist.* † **2.** The bearer of a bishop's crook or pastoral staff. (prop. **crocer, croser.**) –1558. † **b.** Hence, apparently, *Crosier's staff, crosier staff*, the episcopal staff or crook –1733. **3.** The pastoral staff or crook of a bishop or abbot. (= med.L. *crocea, crocia.*) 1500. ¶ **b.** (*erron.*) The cross of an archibishop. (Chiefly 19th c.) Also *transf.* † **4.** *Astron.* The Southern Cross; *pl.* its four stars –1751. Hence **Cro·siered** *a.* bearing a c.

Croslet, obs. f. CROSSLET.

Cross (krǫs), *sb.* [Late OE. *cros* – ON. *kross* – OIr. *cros* (corresp. to Gael. *crois*, W. *croes*) – L. *crux, cruc-*, whence also OFr. *croiz, crois* (mod. *croix*); OFr. *croiz, crois* was adopted in ME. as *cr(e)oiz*, later *crois, croice* (XIII–XV); this became obsolete in XV, leaving the northern form, ME. *cros, crosse* – ON., as the surviving type.] **1.** A kind of gibbet; a stake, generally with a transverse bar, on which anciently certain criminals were put to a cruel or ignominious death ME. **2.** *spec.* The particular structure on which Jesus Christ suffered death; the holy ROOD. (Often written with a capital C.) ME. **3.** The sign of the cross made with the right hand, as a religious act ME. **4.** A representation or delineation of a cross on any surface; used as a sacred mark, symbol, badge, or the like ME. **5.** A figure of a cross as a religious emblem, set up in the open air or within a building, worn round the neck etc. ME. **6.** A staff surmounted by a cross, borne *esp.* as an emblem of office before an archbishop ME. **7.** A monument in the form of a cross, or having a cross upon it, erected in places of resort, at cross-ways, etc. ME.; *spec.* a market-cross 1465; hence, a market (*local*) 1577. **8.** *fig.* Used as the ensign and symbol of Christianity; the Christian religion ME. **9.** *fig.* The atonement wrought on the cross ME. **10.** A trial or affliction, viewed as to be borne with Christian patience ME.; also *gen.* Anything that thwarts or crosses 1573. **11.** Any cross-shaped object, figure, or mark ME. **12.** A surveyor's instrument; a CROSS-STAFF 1669. **13.** *Her.*, etc. A conventional representation of a cross, or of some modification of it, or of two crossing bars, used as an ordinary or charge, as an ornamental figure in art, etc. 1486. **14.** A figure of a cross used as the ensign of an order of knights; also, a wearer of such a cross 1651. † **15.** The figure of a cross stamped upon one side of a coin; hence, a coin bearing a cross; a coin generally –1797. † **16.** A crossing or crossed position; hence *on cross, o cross, a cross*: see ACROSS, CROSS *adv.* –1659. **17.** An intermixture of breeds or races, *esp.* in cattle-breeding; an animal, etc. due to crossing 1760; also *fig.* of men and things 1796. **18.** *slang.* That which is not fair and 'square' 1812. **19.** *Irish Hist.* = CROSSLAND 1612.

1. The body of Cleomenes was flayed and hung on a c. THIRLWALL. **2.** Those blessed feete..nail'd on the bitter Crosse 1 *Hen. IV*, I. i. 26. Phr. *Stations, way of the C.*: see STATION, WAY. **3.** Then he shall make a crosse upon the childes forehead and breste *Bk. Com. Prayer* 1548–9. **4.** His [the Pope's] slipper of crimson velvet, with a gold c. embroidered on it 1700. **6.** Thomas Bourchier archebysshop of Caunterbury..wythe hys crosse before hym, went forthe..toward Londoun 1465. **7.** At the crose in Cheppe 1553. **8.** Streaming the Ensigne of the Christian Crosse, Against black Pagans, Turkes, and Saracens *Rich. II*, IV. i. 94. **9.** The preaching of the Crosse 1 *Cor.* 1:18. **10.** No C. no Crown PENN. After all his losses and crosses ARBUTHNOT. **11.** The Southern c.—the pole-star of the South LOCKYER. The body of the Church formes a Crosse EVELYN. In the margent..yee shall set a crosse + 1588. **13. Greek c.**, an upright c. with limbs of equal length; **Latin c.**, in which the lower limb is longer than the others; **St. Andrew's c.**, or **c. saltier**, an X-shaped c.; **c. of St. Anthony** or *Tau c.*, a T-shaped c.; **c. patée** or **formée**, in which the limbs are narrow where they meet, and gradually expand, the whole forming nearly a square; **Maltese c., c. of Malta** or **c. of eight points**, a modification of the preceding, in which the extremity of each limb is indented; **c. of Jerusalem**, a c. having each arm capped by a cross-bar; **c. of St. George**, the Greek c., red on a white ground; **c. of St. Patrick**, the saltier c. of Ireland, red on a white ground, etc. **15.** To come and take up an honest house, without c. or coin to bless yourself with GOLDSM. Phr. **C. and (or) pile** [Fr. *croix et (ou) pile*]. **a.** Head or tail; hence occas.: a coin, money (*arch.*). † **b.** *fig.* A thing and its opposite –1663. † **c.** 'Tossing up'; *fig.* a mere 'toss-up' –1798. † **d.** *advb. phr.* By mere chance –1712. **17.** *fig.* A c. between a military dandy and a squire 1852. **18.** Phr. *On the c.*: in a dishonest fraudulent manner.

Cross (krǫs), *v.* Pa. t. and pple. **crossed, crost** (krǫst). ME. [f. CROSS *sb.*] † **1.** *trans.* To crucify –1550. **2.** To make the sign of the cross upon or over ME. † **3.** = CROISE 1. –1610. **4.** To cancel by marking with a cross or by drawing lines across; to erase (*lit.* and *fig.*). Const. *off, out.* 1483. **5.** To lay across; to place crosswise 1489; *Naut.* to set in position across the mast; to hoist (a CROSS-SAIL) ME. **6.** To lie or pass across; to intersect ME.; also *intr.*; *colloq.* to bestride (a horse, etc.) 1760. **7.** To draw a line or lines across; to write across 1703. **8.** To pass over; to pass from one side to the other (*trans.* and *intr.*) 1486. *causal.* To carry across 1804. **9.** To extend across 1577. **10.** To pass in opposite directions; to meet in passing 1782. **11.** To meet (*esp.* adversely) in one's way (*arch.*) 1598; to come across (*rare*) 1684. **12.** *fig.* To thwart, oppose 1555; †to debar *from* (*rare*) –1650; †to contravene –1702. **13.** *trans.* To cause to interbreed; to modify by interbreeding *intr.* to interbreed 1754.

2. Crossing their hands with coin CLARE. **4.** The debt is paid, the score is crossed BP. HALL. **5.** Few men ventured to c. swords with him SCOTT. **7.** I have..crossed the t's and dotted the i's THACKERAY. Phr. *To c. a cheque.* **8.** How yong Leander crost the Hellespont *Two Gent.* I. i. 22. Phr. *To c. the path of*: to come in the way of, thwart. **10.** A letter from me would have crossed yours..on the road MRS. CARLYLE. **11.** Ile crosse it, though it blast me *Haml.* I. i. 127. **12.** He was crossed in Love STEELE. To crosse me from the Golden time I looke for SHAKS. Hence **Crossed, crost** *ppl. a.* **Cro·sser.**

Cross (krǫs), *a.* 1523. [Partly attrib. use of CROSS *sb.*, partly ellipt. use of CROSS *adv.*] **1.** Lying or passing athwart; transverse; crossing, intersecting 1602; contrary 1617. Also *fig.* **2.** Contrary, opposite, opposed *to.* (Now rarely predicative.) 1565. **3.** Adverse, thwarting; contrary to one's desire or liking; unfavourable, untoward 1565. **4.** †Given to opposition, contrarious –1770; ill-tempered; out of humour (*colloq.*) 1639. **5.** Involving interchange or reciprocal action 1581; *spec.* in *Book-keeping* 1893. **6.** Cross-bred 1886. **7.** Dishonest; dishonestly come by. (Opp. to *square* or *straight.*) 1892.

1. As crosse as a pair of tailors' legs MARSTON. C. winds DE FOE. *fig.* C. interests DISRAELI. A c. issue M. PATTISON. **2.** Answers so very c. to the purpose LOWTH. **3.** C. luck 1565, fortune DEKKER, Fate DRYDEN. **4.** I have never had a c. word from him in my life JANE AUSTEN. Phr. *As c. as two sticks* (with play on sense 1). **5.** For hapning both to Love each other Sisters, They have concluded it in a c. Marriage DRYDEN. C. payments on revenue accounts GLADSTONE. Hence **Cro·ssly** *adv.* †crosswise; unfavourably; ill-humouredly. **Cro·ssness.**

Cross (krǫs), *adv.* Now *rare.* 1577. [aphet. f. ACROSS, q.v.] † **1.** Across, transversely –1793. † **2.** In a contrary way *to* –1732. **3.** Awry, amiss. Now *colloq.* 1603.

Cross, *prep.* 1551. [aphet. f. ACROSS; the prep. survives in *cross-country* adj. (XVIII).] = ACROSS *prep.* Now *dial.*, or *poet.* (and often written *'cross*).

Hardly could one see crosse the streetes EVELYN. *C. lots*, more usu. *across lots* (U.S.): across the lots or fields as a short cut.

Cross- in *comb.* In some of these relations the use of the hyphen is almost optional.

A. General uses. **1.** From CROSS *sb.* **a.** *objective*: as *c.-adoring, -bearing*, C.-BEARER, etc. 1631. **b.** *instrumental* and *locative*: as C.-FIXED 1839. **c.** *attrib.*: as *c.-days*, C.-BOW, -BUN, etc. ME. **2.** From CROSS *a.*: as *c.-band*, C.-BAR, *c.-vein*, C.-BONES, *c.-current* 1590. **3.** From CROSS *adv.* **a.** with *verbs*: as C.-CUT, -BREED, -QUESTION, *c.-invite* 1590. **b.** with *pr. pples.*: as *c.-pulling*, etc. 1634. **c.** with *pa. pples.*: as C.-GARTERED, etc. 1577. **d.** with *vbl. sbs.* and nouns involving action: as *c.-planking, -entry*, etc. 1684. **4.** From CROSS *prep.* With *object sbs.*: as *c.-country*, C.-COURSE *a.* 1589. **5.** Parasynthetic derivs.: as C.-HEADED, *c.-armed*, C.-LEGGED, etc. 1601.

B. Special combs.: **c.-action** (*Law*), an action brought by the defendant against the plaintiff or a co-defendant in the same action: cf. CROSS-BILL; **-axle,** (1) a shaft, windlass, or roller worked by opposite levers, as the copper-plate printing-press, etc.; (2) a driving-axle with cranks set at an angle of 90° with each other; **-banded** (*Carpentry*), having a veneer laid upon its upper side, with the grain of the wood crossing that of the rail; said of hand-railing; **-bedding** (*Geol.*), apparent lines of stratification crossing the real ones; **-belt,** orig., a belt worn over both shoulders, and crossing in front of the breast; also later, a single belt passing obliquely across the breast; hence **-belted** *a.*; **-birth,** a birth in which the child lies transversely to the uterus; **-bit** = CROSS-PIECE; **-channel** *a.*, passing or situated across the (English or other) channel; **-chocks,** 'pieces of timber fayed across the dead-wood in midships, to make good the deficiency of the lower heels of the futtocks' (Crabbe); **-file,** a file with two convex faces of different curvatures, used in dressing out the arms or crosses of fine wheels; **-finger** *v. intr.*, on wood-wind instruments: to finger out of serial order; **-frog,** a frog adapted for tracks that cross at right angles; **-guard,** a sword-guard consisting of a short transverse bar; **-index** *v.*, to index under another heading as a c.-reference; **-loop,** a loophole in a fort in the form of a cross so as to give free range to an archer, etc.; so *cross-oylet*; **-quarters** (*Arch.*), an ornament of tracery in the form of a cruciform flower; **-sea,** said of the sea, when the waves run athwart the direction of the wind, or when two sets of waves cross each other; **-talk** (*Telephone*), the sputtering noises induced in the telephone line by currents passing through some neighbouring line; **-tining** (*dial.*), cross-harrowing; **-valve,** a valve placed where a pipe has two cross-branches; **-vine,** a climber of the southern U.S., in which a section of the stem shows a cross-like appearance; **-webbing,** webbing drawn over the saddle-tree to strengthen the seat of a saddle; **-wire,** a wire that crosses; spec. = *cross-hair*.

† **Cross-aisle,** transept; see AISLE.

Cross-bar (krǫ·sbāɹ), *sb.* 1557. [CROSS- 2.] **1.** A transverse bar 1562; † = *cross-bar shot* (see below) –1712. **2.** A transverse line or stripe 1599. † **3.** *Her.* The bar sinister –1732. † **4.** *fig.* An impediment; a misfortune –1616. *Comb.* **c.-bar shot:** orig. a ball with a bar projecting on each side of it; later, a projectile which expanded on leaving the gun into the form of a cross, with one quarter of the ball at each radial point: cf. *bar-shot* (see BAR *sb.*[1]). Hence **Cross-bar** *v.* to furnish with cross-bars; to mark with cross-bars.

Cro·ss-beak. = CROSSBILL.

Cross-beam (krǫ·sbīm). 1594. [CROSS- 2.] A beam placed across some part of a structure or mechanism; a transverse beam.

Cross-bearer (krǫ·sbēᵊ:rəɹ). 1540. [CROSS- 1.] **1.** One who bears, wears, or carries a cross; *spec.* one who carries an archbishop's cross before him. **2.** *Cro·ss-bea·rer.* The transverse bars supporting the grate-bars of a furnace 1874.

Cro·ss-bea·rings. 1809. [CROSS *a.* or *adv.*] *Naut.* The bearings of two or more points taken from a point of reference so as to plot the position of a ship on a chart, etc.

Cro·ss-be·nch. 1846. [CROSS *a.*, CROSS- 2.] A bench placed at right angles to other benches. *spec.* In the House of Lords certain benches so placed, on which independent or neutral members sometimes sit. Also *attrib.* *attrib.* It would be well for this House if a great majority of its members had the c.-bench mind ARGYLL.

Crossbill (krǫ·sbil). 1672. [CROSS *a.*] A bird of the genus *Loxia* (family *Fringillidæ*) having the mandibles of the bill curved so as to cross each other when the bill is closed. The Common Crossbill is *L. curvirostra*.

Cross-bill, cross bill. 1637. [CROSS *a.*, CROSS- 3 d.] *Law.* A bill filed in Chancery by a defendant against the plaintiff or other co-defendants in the same suit. **b.** A bill of exchange given in consideration of another bill.

† **Cro·ssbi:te,** *v.* 1532. [CROSS- 3 a.] **1.** *trans.* To bite the biter; to take in, gull, deceive –1823. **2.** To censure bitingly or bitterly –1697. Hence † **Cro·ssbite** *sb.* a cheat, trick, deception.

Cro·ss-bond. 1876. [CROSS *a.*] *Bricklaying.* A bond in which a course of stretchers alternates with one of alternate stretchers and headers so as to break joint with it and also with the next row of stretchers.

Cro·ss-bones, *sb. pl.* 1798. [CROSS- 2.] A figure of two thigh-bones laid across each other, usually placed under the figure of a skull, as an emblem of death. Coffins, 'scutcheons, death's heads and cross-bones CANNING.

Cross-bow (krǫ·sbōᵘ). ME. [CROSS- 1 c.] **1.** A missile weapon consisting of a bow fixed across a wooden stock, having a mechanism for holding and releasing the string; an ARBALEST. **2.** *transf.* (*pl.*) Men armed with crossbows 1511. Also *attrib.* Hence † **Cro·ss-bower, Cro·ssbowman,** a soldier armed with a crossbow.

Cro·ss-bred, *ppl. a.* 1856. [CROSS- 3 c.] Bred from parents of different species or varieties; hybrid, mongrel. (Also *absol.* as *sb.*)

Cro·ss-bree·d, *v.* 1675. [CROSS- 3 a.] To breed from individuals of different species.

Cross-breed (krǫ·sbrīd), *sb.* 1774. [Cf. prec. and CROSS *a.*] A breed produced by crossing; *transf.* an animal of such a breed. It seems to me a barren thing, this Conservatism, an unhappy cross-breed; the mule of politics that engenders nothing DISRAELI.

Cro·ss-bu·n. 1733. [CROSS- 1 c.] A bun indented with a cross, eaten on Good Friday.

Cro·ss-bu·ttock, *sb.* 1714. [app. f. CROSS *prep.* + BUTTOCK.] A peculiar throw over the hip made use of in wrestling and formerly in pugilism.

† **Cro·ss-cloth.** 1541. [CROSS- 1 c.] **1.** *Eccl.* A cloth or hanging before the rood –1566. **2.** A linen cloth worn across the forehead –1699.

Cro·ss-country, *a.* 1767. [CROSS- 4.] Across the country transversely to the great highways; across the fields, etc.

Cro·ss-course, *sb.* 1802. [CROSS- 2.] *Mining.* A vein (usually barren) intersecting the regular vein at an angle; also = CROSS-CUT 2.

Cro·ss-cro·sslet. 1486. [f. CROSS *sb.* + CROSSLET[2].] *Her.* A cross having the extremity of each arm in the form of a small cross.

Cro·ss-cut, *sb.* 1789. [CROSS- 2.] **1.** (Usually *cross cut.*) A cut across; a direct path, diagonal to the main way 1800. **2.** *Mining.* A cutting across the course of a vein, or the main direction of the workings 1789. **3. a.** A step in dancing. DICKENS. **b.** A figure in skating.

Cro·ss-cut, *a.* 1645. **1.** Adapted for cross-cutting, as a *cross-cut saw*. **2.** [CROSS- 3 c.] Cut across; *esp.* of a file, having two sets of teeth crossing each other diagonally 1833. So **Cro:ss-cu·t** *v.* to cut across.

† **Cro·ss-days,** *sb. pl.* 1501. [CROSS- 1 c.] The three days preceding Ascension Day –1641.

Cro·ss-divi·sion. 1828. [CROSS- 3 d.] The division of any group according to more than one principle at the same time, so that the sub-divisions intersect; an instance of this. A division..of men into Frenchmen, Asiatics, the unproductive classes, and barbarians, would be a c.-division FOWLER.

Crosse (krǫs). [– Fr. *crosse*, OFr. *croce*; see CROSE, CROSIER.] An implement consisting of a long shank curved round at the end, with a net from the curve to the shank; a *lacrosse-stick*.

‖ **Crossette** (krǫse·t). 1730. [Fr., dim. of *crosse*; see prec., -ETTE.] *Archit.* A projection in the architrave or casing round a door- or window-opening, at the junction of the jamb and head; also a ledged projection in the voussoir of a flat arch, which rests in a recess in the adjoining voussoir.

Cro:ss-exa·mine, *v.* 1664. [CROSS- 3 a.] **1.** *trans.* To examine by cross-questioning; to examine minutely and repeatedly. **2.** *spec.* To subject (a witness) to an examination with the purpose of shaking his testimony or eliciting facts not brought out in his direct examination. Hence **Cro:ss-examina·tion,** the action of cross-examining. **Cro:ss-exa·miner, -exa·mining.**

Cro·ss-eye. 1826. [CROSS- 2.] *pl.* Squinting eyes. **b.** Internal strabismus. Hence **Cro·ss-eyed** *a.* squinting.

Cro·ss-fe·rtilize, *v.* 1876. [CROSS- 3 a.] *Bot.* To fertilize by pollen from another flower or plant. Hence **Cro·ss-fertiliza·tion.**

Cro·ss-fi·re. 1860. [CROSS- 3 d.] *Mil.* Lines of fire from two or more positions crossing each other. Also *fig.*

Cro·ss-fish. 1805. [CROSS- 1 c.] A star-fish.

† **Cro·ss-fixed,** *pa. pple.* 1618. [CROSS- 1 b; after L. *crucifixus*.] Fixed on a cross, crucified –1849.

Cro·ss-flower. 1597. [CROSS- 1 c.] Milk-wort. Milke woort..doth specially flourish in the Crosse or..Rogation weeke..in English we may call it Crosse flower GERARDE.

Cro·ss-fox. 1830. [Cross- 1 c.] A variety of the fox, having dark markings along the back and across the shoulders, forming a cross.

Cro·ss-ga·rnet. 1659. [CROSS- 1 c.] A ⊢-shaped hinge, with the vertical part fastened to the jamb of the doorcase, etc., and the horizontal to the door, etc.

† **Cro·ss-ga·rtered,** *ppl. a.* 1601. [CROSS- 3 c.] Having the garters crossed on the legs. *Twel. N.* II. v. 167.

Cro·ss-grain. 1681. [CROSS- 2.] **1.** A grain running across the regular grain. **2.** The grain cut across 1880.

Cross-grained (krǫ·s,greⁱnd), *a.* 1647. [f. prec. + -ED[2].] **1.** Of wood: Having the grain or fibre arranged in crossing directions, or irregularly 1673. **2.** *fig.* Contrarious; perverse 1647. **3.** *advb.* Across the grain (*lit.* and *fig.*) 1703. **1.** Elm..is the most Cross-grain'd Timber: that is, cleaveth so unevenly GREW. **2.** So cross-grain'd to all Novelty 1647. Hence **Cross-grai·nedness.**

Cro·ss-ha·tch, *v.* 1822. [CROSS- 3 a.] To engrave or hatch a surface with crossing sets of parallel lines; *esp.* to shade by this method. Hence **Cro·ss-ha:tching** *vbl. sb.* the process of marking thus; the effect so produced.

Cro·ss-hea:d, *sb.* 1827. [CROSS- 2.] **1.** The bar at the end of the piston-rod of a steam-engine, which slides between straight guides, and communicates the motion to the connecting-rods, etc. **2.** A heading to a paragraph printed across the page or column in the body of an article 1888. So **Cro·ss-hea:ded** *a.* having the head in the form of a cross.

Crossing (krǫ·siŋ), *vbl. sb.* 1530. [f. CROSS *v.* + -ING[1].] **1.** The marking with or making the sign of the cross. **2.** The action of drawing lines across (see CROSS *v.* 4, 7) 1652. **3.** The action of passing across; intersecting; traversing 1575. **4.** The intersection of two lines, tracks, streets, roads, etc.; in *Eccl. Archit.* that part of a cruciform church where the transepts cross the nave 1695. **5.** A place at which a street, river, etc., is crossed 1632. **6.** A thwarting, opposing, or contravening 1580. **7.** Cross-breeding 1851. **3.** The c. of the great and wide sea 1891. **4.** Statues..in the c. of streets, or in the squares DRYDEN. **6.** Cousin: of many men I doe not beare these crossings 1 *Hen. IV*, III. i. 36. *Comb.* **c.-sweeper,** one who sweeps a (street-) c.

Cross-jack, cro'jack (krǫ·s,dʒæk, krǫ·dʒĕk). 1626. *Naut.* A square sail bent to the lower yard of the mizen-mast.

Cross keys, cross-keys. 1550. [CROSS- 2.] Keys borne crosswise, as in the Papal arms.

† **Cro·ss-land.** 1568. [CROSS *sb.* 19.] *Irish Hist.* Land belonging to the Church in the Irish counties palatine.

Cross-legged (krǫ·s,legd), *ppl. a.* 1530. [CROSS- 5.] Having the legs crossed.

† **Cro·sslet**[1]. [ME. *cros(se)let*, f. AFr. *crosel* (= OFr. *croisel*, later *croiset* (mod. *creuset* crucible) lamp, crucible) + -ET. The sense 'lamp' is not recorded in Eng.] A crucible –1610.

Crosslet[2] (krǫ·slėt). 1538. [f. CROSS + -LET after AFr. *croiselette*; cf. OFr. *croisete* small cross.] **1.** A small cross; *spec.* in *Her.* † **2.** = CROSS-CLOTH 2. –1688. Hence **Cro·ssleted** *ppl. a.* bearing a c.

Cro·ss-light. 1851. [CROSS- 2.] A light which crosses another and illuminates parts which it leaves in shade. Often *fig.*

Cro·ss-multiplica·tion. 1703. [CROSS- 3 d.] = DUODECIMALS.

Crossopterygian (krǫsǫptĕri·dʒⁱăn). 1861. [f. mod.L. *crossopterygii* or *-ia* (f. Gr. κροσσός tassel, *pl.* fringe + πτέρυξ, πτερύγιον fin) + -AN[1].] *adj.* Belonging to the sub-class *Crossopterygia* or sub-order *Crossopterygidæ* of Ganoid fishes, so called from the arrangement of the paired fins to form a fringe round a central lobe. var. **Crossoptery·gious** *a.* *sb.* A fish of this class.

Cross-over (krǫ·sōᵘ:vəɹ). 1795. [From phr. *to cross over.*] **1.** *Textiles.* A fabric having the design running across from selvedge to selvedge; in *Calico-printing*, a stripe of colour printed across another colour. **2.** A woman's wrap worn crossed upon the breast 1868. **3.** *U.S.* A connection between the up and down lines of a railway for shunting purposes 1884.

Cro·ss-patch. *colloq.* 1700. [CROSS- 2.] A cross ill-tempered person. (Usu. feminine.)

Cross-pawl; see CROSS-SPALL.

Cro·ss-piece. 1607. [CROSS- 2.] **1.** A piece of any material placed across anything else. **b.** *Ship-building.* A rail of timber from the knight-heads to the belfry; *pl.* the pieces of timber bolted athwartships to the bitt-pins; *pl.* the pieces placed across the keel, which is let into them 1706. **c.** *Anat.* The corpus callosum connecting the two hemispheres of the brain. † **2.** [CROSS *a.*] A CROSS-PATCH –1694.

Cro·ss-plou:gh, *v.* 1644. [CROSS- 3 a.] To plough (a field) across the former furrows.

Cro·ss-point. 1709. [CROSS- 2.] One of the points of the compass intermediate between two cardinal points.

Cro·ss-pollina·tion. 1882. [CROSS- 3 d.] *Bot.* = CROSS-FERTILIZATION of plants.

† **Cro·ss-post.** 1750. [CROSS- 2.] The post for letters on cross-country routes –1880.

Cro·ss-pu·rpose. 1666. [orig. f. CROSS *prep.* contrary to the purpose: but now f. CROSS *a.*, CROSS- 2.] **1.** Contrary or conflicting purpose; contradictoriness of intention 1681. **2.** *pl.* A parlour game; cf. CROSS-QUESTION *sb.* Often *fig.* 1666.
2. Then to cross purposes, mighty merry; and then to bed PEPYS. Phr. *To be at cross purposes*: (of persons) to act counter from a misconception by each of the other's purpose. (Perh. from the game.)

Cro·ss-que·stion, *sb.* 1694. [orig. two words; cf. CROSS *a.*, and CROSS- 3 d.] **a.** A question put by way of cross-examination. † **b.** A question in return. **c.** *Cross questions and crooked answers*: a game in which questions and answers are connected crosswise; as *e.g.* the question asked on one's right with the answer given to another question on one's left, with ludicrous effect.

Cro:ss-ques·tion, *v.* 1760. [CROSS- 3 a.] *trans.* To interrogate with questions which cross, or tend to check the results of, previous questions; to cross-examine.

Cro·ss-ra:tio. 1881. [CROSS- 3 d.] *Math.* = ANHARMONIC ratio.

Cro·ss-rea·ding. 1768. [CROSS- 3 d.] A reading across the page instead of down the column (of a newspaper, etc.), producing a ludicrous connection of subjects. Also *fig.*

Cro:ss-re·ference. 1834. [CROSS- 3 d.] A reference made from one part of a book, register, etc., to another part where the same word or subject is treated of. Hence as vb.

Cross-remainder (*Law*); see REMAINDER.

Cro·ss-road. 1719. [CROSS- 2, CROSS *a.* 1.] **1.** A road crossing another, or running across between two main roads. **2.** The place where two roads cross. Also called *the cross roads.* 1812. **3.** *attrib.* Passing by cross-roads; situated at the crossing of two roads 1720.

† **Cro·ss-row.** 1529. [CROSS- 1 c: from the figure (✠) formerly prefixed to it.] The alphabet; = CHRIST-CROSS-ROW.
And from the Crosse-row plucks the letter G *Rich. III*, I. i. 55.

Cro·ss-ruff. 1592. [CROSS- 3 d.] † **1.** A game at cards; see RUFF *sb.*[3] -1693. **2.** *Whist.* (See quot.)
2. A Cross-ruff (saw or see-saw) is the alternate trumping by partners of different suits, each leading the suit in which the other renounces 'CAVENDISH'.

† **Cro·ss-sail.** ME. [CROSS- 2.] *Naut.* A square-sail, *i.e.* one placed across the breadth of the ship (not *fore-and-aft*); also a vessel with square-sails -1627.

Cro·ss-spa:ll, cro·ss-spa:le. 1850. [CROSS- 2.] *Ship-building.* One of the deals nailed to the frames of a ship at a certain height, to keep the frames in position until the deck-knees are fastened.

Cro·ss-spri·nger. 1816. [CROSS- 2.] *Archit.* One of the ribs extending diagonally from one pier to another in groined vaulting.

Cro·ss-staff. 1460. **1.** *Eccl.* An archbishop's cross; also, by confusion, used for CROSE-staff. Now *Hist.* † **2.** An instrument for taking the altitude of the sun or a star -1669. **b.** A surveyor's cross, used in taking offsets 1874.

Cro·ss-sti:tch, *sb.* 1710. [CROSS- 1 c.] A stitch formed of two stitches crossing each other, thus ×; also a kind of needlework characterized by these. Hence **Cro·ss-sti:tch** *v.* to sew with these.

Cro·ss-stone. 1770. [CROSS- 1 c.] *Min.* A name given to CHIASTOLITE; also to STAUROLITE and HARMOTOME, from the cruciform arrangement of the crystals.

Cro·ss-tail. 1839. [CROSS- 2.] *Mech.* In a back-action marine steam-engine: A transverse bar which connects the side levers at the end opposite to the cross-head.

Cro·ss-tree. 1626. [CROSS- 2.] **1.** *Naut.* (*pl.*) Two horizontal cross-timbers at the head of the lower and top masts, to sustain the tops, and to spread the top-gallant rigging. † **2.** A gallows 1638; a cross. HERRICK. Also *attrib.*

Cro·ss-vault. 1850. [CROSS- 1 c.] *Archit.* A vault formed by the intersection of two or more simple vaults. Hence **Cro·ss-vau·lting.**

Cro·ss-way, *sb.* 1490. [CROSS- 2, CROSS *a.* 1.] = CROSS-ROAD.

Crosswise (krǫ·swəiz), *adv.* ME. [CROSS *sb.* + -WISE.] **1.** In the form of a cross. **2.** Across, transversely 1580. **3.** *fig.* Perversely 1594.
1. A church built c. JOHNSON. **2.** A frame of logs placed c. JOWETT. vars. **Cro·ssway, Cro·ssways.**

Cro·ssword, cro·ss-word. 1924. [CROSS- 2.] A puzzle based on a criss-cross pattern of words for which clues are provided.

Crosswort (krǫ·swɒɹt). 1578. [CROSS- 1 c.] **1.** A name of various plants having leaves in whorls of four; esp. *Galium cruciatum.* **2.** *pl.* A book-name for the N.O. *Cruciferæ* 1861.

‖ **Crostarie** (krǫstā·ri). *Sc.* 1685. [- Gael. *cros-tàraidh, cros-tàra* the cross or beam of gathering.] The FIRE-CROSS or FIERY CROSS, used in the Sc. Highlands to summon the clans.

Crotal (krō^u·tăl). 1790. [- Fr. *crotale* or L. *crotalum.*] **1.** = CROTALUM 1. 1850. **2.** *Irish Antiq.* Applied to a small globular or pear-shaped bell or rattle, the nature and use of which are obscure.

Cro·talid. [- mod.L. *Crotalidæ*; see CROTALUS, -ID[3].] *Zool.* A serpent of the *Crotalidæ* or rattlesnake family.

Cro·taliform, *a.* [f. CROTALUS + -FORM.] Structurally like or related to the rattlesnake.

Cro·talin. [f. CROTALUS + -IN[1].] *Chem.* An albuminoid substance found in the venom of the rattlesnake.

Cro·taline, *a.* 1865. [f. as prec. + -INE[1].] Of or belonging to the rattlesnake family.

‖ **Cro·talo.** 1682. [It.] = CROTALUM.

‖ **Crotalum** (krǫ·tălŏm). 1727. [L. - Gr. κρόταλον rattle.] *Antiq.* A sort of castanet used in ancient religious dances.

‖ **Crotalus** (krǫ·tălŏs). 1834. [mod.L. - Gr. κρόταλον rattle.] *Zool.* The genus of American serpents containing the typical rattlesnakes.

Crotaphic (krotæ·fik), *a.* 1653. [f. Gr. κρόταφος, *pl.* -οι the temples + -IC.] *Anat.* Of or pertaining to the temples. **Cro·taphite** *a.* [Fr. *crotaphite*], temporal; † *sb.* the temporal muscle. **Crotaphi·tic** *a.* temporal, as in *c. nerve.*

Crotch (krǫtʃ). Now chiefly *U.S.* or *dial.* 1539. [perh. identical with ME. *croche* hook, crosier - OFr. *croche* hook, etc., f. *crocher*, f. *croc* hook - ON. *krókr* CROOK; see CROCHE *sb.*[1]] † **1.** A fork -1573. **2.** A stake or pole having a forked top 1573; *Naut.* = CRUTCH 4. **3.** The fork of a tree or bough 1573. **4.** The fork of the human body 1592. † **5.** *fig.* A dilemma 1622. *Comb.* † **c.-tail,** old name of the kite. Hence **Crotched** *a.* forked. (Now *U.S.*)

Crotchet (krǫ·tʃĕt), *sb.*[1] ME. [- (O)Fr. *crochet*, dim. of *croc* hook; see CROC, CROOK, -ET.] **1.** = CROCHET 1, 2. **2.** A hook or hooked instrument; *spec.* (*Surg.*) an instrument used in obstetrical surgery 1754. **3.** A natural hook-like organ or process 1678. **4.** *Mus.* A symbol for a note of half the value of a minim, made in the form of a stem with a round black head; such a note. Also *attrib.* ME. † **5.** *Typogr.* A square bracket -1832. **6.** A whimsical fancy; a perverse conceit; a peculiar notion on some (unimportant) point 1573; a fanciful device 1611. **7.** *Fortif.* A passage formed by an indentation in the glacis opposite a traverse 1853. † **8.** 'The arrangement of a body of troops, either forward or rearward, so as to form a line nearly perpendicular to the general line of battle' (Webster 1864).
2. A C. of 122 Diamonds, set..in Silver STEELE. **6.** That castle in the ayr, that c., that whimsie BURTON. *Comb.* **c.-monger,** a crotcheteer. Hence **Crotchetee·r,** a person with a c.; *esp.* one who pushes his crotchets in politics, etc.

† **Cro·tchet,** *sb.*[2] 1631. [dim. of CROTCH; see -ET.] = CROTCH 2. -1764.

Cro·tchet, *v.* 1587. [f. CROTCHET *sb.*[1]] †To break a longer note up into crotchets. **b.** To ornament with crotchets or crockets.

Crotchety (krǫ·tʃĕti), *a.* 1825. [f. as prec. + -Y[1].] Given to crotchets; of the nature of a crotchet.
All sorts of c. people BRIGHT. Hence **Cro·tchetiness,** c. quality.

Croton (krō^u·tǫn). 1751. [- mod.L. - Gr. κρότων sheep-tick, castor-oil plant.] **1.** *Bot.* A large genus of euphorbiaceous plants, mostly natives of tropical regions. **2.** Applied to *Codiæum pictum*, allied to the Crotons 1881.
Comb.: **C. oil,** a fatty oil existing in the seeds of the East Indian species, *C. tiglium*; it is a drastic purgative; **c. chloral** or **c. chloral hydrate,** a name of *butyl chloral hydrate*, given in error.

Croton-bug. *U.S.* 1842. [f. the *Croton* river, Westchester County, N.Y.] A name given to the Cockroach, *Blatta orientalis*, and other species of the same genus.

Crotonic (krotǫ·nik), *a.* 1838. [f. CROTON + -IC.] Of or derived from croton oil; as in *c. acid*, $C_4H_6O_2$, the second member of the Acrylic series. So **Cro·tonate,** a salt of c. acid. **Cro·tonyle:ne,** a hydro-carbon C_4H_6 (liquid below 15° C.), homologous with allylene.

Crottels (krǫ·t'lz), *sb. pl.* 1598. [app. dim. of (O)Fr. *crotte*, pellet of sheep's or goat's dung. See -LE.] The globular excrement of hares, etc.

Crottle (krǫ·t'l). *Sc.* 1778. [- Gael. *crotal, crotan* a lichen.] A name for various species of lichen used in dyeing; cf. CUDBEAR.

† **Crouch,** *sb.*[1] [Early ME. *cruche*, repr. OE. *crūć* - L. *crux, cruc-* cross.] = CROSS, in its early senses -1463.

Crouch (krautʃ), *sb.*[2] 1597. [f. CROUCH *v.*[1]] An act of crouching.

Crouch (krautʃ), *v.*[1] [Late ME. *cruche, crouche*, poss. - OFr. *crochir* be bent, f. *croc* hook - ON. *krókr* CROOK; the vocalism would be paralleled in *pouch, vouch.*] **1.** *intr.* To stoop or bend low, as in stooping for shelter, in fear, or in submission; to cower with the limbs bent. (To *cower* concerns chiefly the head and shoulders; to *crouch*, the body as a whole.) **2.** To bow or bend humbly or servilely; to cringe fawningly. Chiefly *fig.* 1528. **3.** *trans.* To bow or bend low (the knee, etc.): often with implication of cringing 1705.
1. We sat crouching for the space of three whole days upon this rock 1653. **2.** The free spirit must c. to the slave in office 1779. **3.** She..crouched her head upon her breast COLERIDGE. Hence **Crou·chant** *a.* crouching. **Crou·cher.**

† **Crouch,** *v.*[2] ME. [f. CROUCH *sb.*[1]; cf. CROSS *v.*] To cross; to sign with the cross -1620.

Crou·chback. Now *Hist.* 1491. [f. stem of CROUCH *v.*; cf. *crook-back.*] **1.** A crooked or hunched back. **2.** A hunchback. Also *attrib.*
Sir Edmunde ye kynges other sone, surnamed Crowch Bak FABYAN.

Crouched, earlier f. CRUTCHED (Friars).

† **Crou·chmas.** ME. [f. CROUCH *sb.*[1] + MASS *sb.*[1]] The festival of the Invention of the Cross, observed on May 3. -1706.

Crou·ch-ware. 1817. [Origin unkn.] *Pottery.* A name of the early salt-glazed pottery of Staffordshire.

† **Crouke, crowke.** [OE. *crūce* pot; see CROCK *sb.*[1]] A pitcher, a jug -ME.

Croup, croupe (krūp), *sb.*[1] ME. [- (O)Fr. *croupe* :- Rom. **croppa* - Gmc. **kruppō*, rel. to CROP *sb.*] **1.** The rump or hind-quarters, *esp.* of a beast of burden. **2.** (*crup*). The hinder end of a saddle 1869.
So light to the croupe the fair lady he swung SCOTT.

Croup (krūp), *sb.*[2] 1765. [f. CROUP *v.*] **1.** An inflammatory disease of the larynx and trachea of children, marked by a peculiar sharp ringing cough. **2.** The local name of the Northumbrian 'burr' (*mod.*). Hence **Crou·pal, Crou·pous** *adjs.* relating to, or of the nature of, c.; affected with c. So **Crou·py** *a.*

Croup (krūp), *v.* Now *dial.* 1513. [imit.] **1.** *intr.* To cry hoarsely; to croak. **2.** To make the hoarse ringing cough of the disease called croup 1801. **3.** To pronounce a rough uvular *r* (*r grasseyé*); to have the Northumberland 'burr' (*mod.*).

Croupade (krupē^i·d). 1849. [- Fr. *croupade* - It. *groppata* w. assim. to *croupe* CROUP *sb.*[1]] *Horsemanship.* A high curvet, in which the hind legs are brought up under the belly of the horse.

Croupe (krūp). 1808. [- Fr. *croupe*; see CROUP *sb.*[1]] **1.** = CROUP *sb.*[1], q.v. ‖ **2.** = CROUPADE. Byron. ‖ **3.** The rounded top of a mountain. [So in Fr.]

Croupier (krū·pi,əɹ, krupīᵊ·ɹ). 1707. [– Fr. *croupier*, orig. one who rides behind on the croup, f. CROUPE *sb.*[1]] † **1.** One who stands behind a gamester to back him up and help him. **2.** He who rakes in the money at a gaming-table 1731. **3.** One who sits as assistant chairman at the lower end of the table at a public dinner 1785.

1. Since I have such a C. or Second to stand by me as Mr. Pope WYCHERLEY.

Crou·pon. Now *dial.* ME. [– (O)Fr. *croupon* (in OFr. = croup), f. *croupe*; see CROUP *sb.*[1], -OON.] The croup or rump; the buttocks; *transf.* the hinder part of a thing; the crupper of the harness.

Crouse (krūs), *a. Sc.* and *n. dial.* [north. ME. *crūs, crouse*, agreeing in form with MHG. (G. *kraus*), MLG., LG. *krus* crisp, in sense with Du. *kroes* (– LG.) cross, out of humour, G. *kraus* sullen, crabbed; prob. – LG. or OFris.] † **1.** Angry, cross. (ME. only.) † **2.** Bold, audacious, 'cocky' –1883. **3.** Vivacious; pert, brisk, lively, jolly ME. Also as *adv.*

3. Now they're c. and cantie baith BURNS. Hence **Crou·sely** *adv.*

Crout, *sb.*; see SOUR-CROUT.

Crow (krōᵘ), *sb.*[1] [OE. *crāwe*, corresp. to OS. *krāia* (Du. *kraai*), OHG. *krāwa, krāja, krā* (G. *krähe*), f. the vb.] **1.** A bird of the genus *Corvus*; in England usually the Carrion Crow (*Corvus corone*); in the north of England, Scotland, and Ireland the Rook, *C. frugilegus*; in U.S. *C. americanus*. Also *fig.* **2.** *Astron.* The southern constellation *Corvus* 1658. **3.** A bar of iron with one end slightly bent and sharpened to a beak, used as a lever or prise; a CROW-BAR ME. † **4.** A grappling-hook, a grapnel –1751. † **5.** A kind of door-knocker. [med.L. *cornix.*] –1846. **6.** *Thieves' slang.* One who keeps watch while another steals 1851. **7.** *Mining.* Used *attrib.* to denote a poor or impure bed of coal, etc. *n.* and *Sc.* 1789.

1. The C. Makes Wing toth' Rookie Wood *Macb.* III. ii. 51. **3.** Well, Ile breake in: go borrow me a c. *Com. Err.* III. i. 80. Phrases. *To have a c. to pluck* or *pull* (rarely *pick*) *with anyone*: to have something awkward to settle, or some fault to find, with him. *As the crow flies*, etc.: in a direct line.

Comb., etc.: CARRION CROW; **c.-blackbird** (*U.S.*), a name for the Purple Grackle (*Quiscalus purpureus*), and allied species; **-coal** (see sense 7 above); **-iron,** a crow-bar; † **-keeper,** one who guards corn-fields from rooks; also a scarecrow; **crow's-meat,** food for crows, carrion; **c.-sheaf** (*Cornwall*), 'the top sheaf on the end of a mow'; **-shrike,** a bird of the sub-family *Gymnorhininæ* or Piping Crows; **Red-legged C.,** *C. graculus.*

Crow (krōᵘ), *sb.*[2] ME. [f. CROW *v.*] Crowing (of a cock). Also *transf.* and *fig.*

Crow (krōᵘ), *sb.*[3] 1662. [rel. to MHG. *(ge)krœse, krœs* (G. *gekröse* mesentery, (calf's) pluck, (goose's) giblets), MDu. *croos*, Du. *kroost* entrails, giblets, and, ult., to CROUSE *a.*] The mesentery of an animal.

Crow (krōᵘ), *v.* Pa. t. **crew** (krū), **crowed.** Pa. pple. **crowed,** [**crown** (krōᵘn)]. [OE. *crāwan*, corresp. to OS. **krāian* (Du. *kraaien*), OHG. *krāen* (G. *krähen*); WGmc. verb of imit. origin.] **1.** *intr.* To utter the loud cry of a cock. Also quasi- *trans.* **2.** *transf.* Of persons. To utter an inarticulate sound of joy or exultation 1579. **3.** *fig.* To exult loudly, boast, swagger 1522.

1. While he yet spake, the cocke crew *Luke* 22:60. **2.** [The] baby..would..c. with delight THACKERAY. **3.** Phr. *To c. over*: to triumph over; I'm not going to be crowed over by you DICKENS.

Crow-bar (krōᵘ·bāɹ). 1825. [f. CROW *sb.*[1] 3.] An iron bar with a wedge-shaped end, used as a lever or prise. Also *attrib.*

Crowberry (krōᵘ·beri). 1597. [prob. tr. G. *krähenbeere.*] The fruit of a small evergreen heath-like shrub (*Empetrum nigrum*); the berry is black and insipid. Also the plant itself. Called also *crakeberry* (see CRAKE).

Crow·bill. (Also **Crow's bill.**) 1611. *Surg.* A forceps for extracting bullets, etc., from wounds.

Crowd (kraud), *sb.*[1] Now *Hist.* or *dial.* ME. [– W. *crwth* fiddle; cf. Gael. and Ir. *cruit* harp, violin, OIr. *crot* harp, cithara. See ROTE *sb.*[1]] An ancient Celtic musical instrument, having three, or, later, six strings; an early form of the fiddle. Hence, a fiddle. Still *dial.*

Harpes, lutes, and crouddes ryght delycyous HAWES.

† **Crowd,** *sb.*[2] ME. [– AFr. *crudde*, app. corresp. to OFr. *crute, crote, croute* – med.L. *crupta* for L. *crypta* CRYPT. Cf. CROFT *sb.*[2] The *d* is unexplained.] A crypt. (Also in *pl.*) –1658.

Crowd (kraud), *sb.*[3] 1567. [f. CROWD *v.*] **1.** A number of persons gathered so closely together as to press upon each other; a throng. (The earlier term was *press.*) **2.** *transf.* A large number (*of* persons) 1654; the masses 1683; *colloq.* a company; set, lot (*U.S.* and *Colonies.*) 1857. **3.** *transf.* and *fig.* A number of things crowded together; a multitude 1627.

1. They could not come nigh unto him for the c. *Mark* 2:4. **2.** Far from the madding crowd's ignoble strife GRAY. **3.** In the croude of their vnknowne sinnes SANDERSON. *C. of sail* (Naut.): an unusual number of sails hoisted for the sake of speed.

Crowd (kraud), *v.*[1] [OE. *crūdan*, orig. str. vb. corresp. to MLG., MDu. *kruden* (Du. *kruien* push in a wheelbarrow); cf. OE. *croda, crod* crowd, MLG. *kroden*, MHG. *kroten* oppress. Rare down to 1600; not in the Bible of 1611.] **1.** *intr.* To press, push, thrust shove. **2.** *trans.* To press (anything), to push, shove. (Also *absol.*) Now *dial.* ME. **3.** *intr.* To push, or force one's way; to press *forward, up*, etc. Now only *fig.* ME. **4.** *intr.* To congregate closely so as to press upon one another; to throng ME. **5.** *trans.* To press (things) *in* or *into* a confined space; also, to press (things) in numbers *on* a person 1599; to compress, pack closely together 1612. Also *fig.* **6.** To fill *with* a crowd 1695; to throng (a place) 1646; † to beset or crowd upon (a person or place) –1783; *U.S. colloq.* to press by solicitation; to dun 1828.

3. He crowded into a Dancing Room 1687. **4.** There croud into his mind the ideas which [etc.] BERKELEY. **5.** The experience of years is crowded into hours 1848. **6.** A port crowded with shipping 1848. The Men..c. the chearful Fire DRYDEN.

Phrases. *To c. out*: to force out by pressure of a crowd (*obs.*); to exclude by crowding. *To c. sail* (Naut.): to carry a press of sail for speed.

† **Crowd,** *v.*[2] 1589. [f. CROWD *sb.*[1]] To fiddle –1693.

† **Crowd,** *v.*[3] 1575. [imit.; cf. CROOD, CROUD.] **1.** *intr.* To crow –1752. **2.** Var. of *croud*, CROOD *Sc.*

Crow·der[1]. Now *dial.* 1450. [f. CROWD *sb.*[1] or *v.*[2] + -ER[1].] A fiddler.

Crowder[2] (krau·dəɹ). 1581. [f. CROWD *v.*[1] + -ER[1].] One who crowds (see CROWD *v.*).

Crowdie, crowdy (krau·di). *Sc.* and *n. Eng.* 1668. [Origin unkn.] Meal and water made into a thick gruel; hence, brose or porridge generally.

Crow·-flower. 1597. The buttercup. **b.** The Ragged Robin (Gerarde).

Crowfoot (krōᵘ·fut). Pl. **-feet,** in senses 1 and 2 **-foots.** ME. **1.** A name for species of *Ranunculus*; also for the genus. **2.** Any plant of which the leaves or other part resemble a crow's foot; as **C. cranesbill, C. plantain,** the wild hyacinth, etc. 1578. **3.** = CROW'S-FOOT 1. 1614. **4.** *Naut.* A number of small cords rove through a long block or EUPHROE, used to suspend an awning, etc. 1627. **5.** *Mil.* A caltrop 1678. **6.** *Mining.* A tool with a side-claw, for recovering broken rods in deep bore-holes (Raymond).

Crow·-garlic. ME. A wild species of garlic, *Allium vineale.*

† **Crowl,** *v.* 1519. [imit.; emphatic var. of *growl.*] *intr.* To rumble in the stomach and bowels –1717.

† **Crow-leek.** OE. The wild hyacinth (*Scilla nutans*) –1597.

Crown (kraun). [ME. *crune, corune* – AFr. *corune*, OFr. *corone* (mod. *couronne*) :– L. *corona* wreath, chaplet – Gr. κορώνη anything bent (κορωνίς crown).]

I. 1. A fillet, wreath, or other encircling ornament for the head, worn for adornment, or as a mark of honour or achievement ME. Also *fig.* **2.** *spec.* The cincture or covering for the head, worn by a monarch as a mark of sovereignty OE. **3.** *fig.* The rule, position, or empire of a monarch ME. **4.** *fig.* The wearer of a crown; the monarch in his official character 1579. **5.** *fig.* That which adorns like a crown; a chief ornament ME.

1. This aungel had of roses and of lilie Corounes tuo CHAUCER. *fig.* Be thou faithful unto death, and I will give thee a c. of life *Rev.* 2:10. The c. of martyrdom 1839. **2.** Vneasie lyes the Head that weares a Crowne 2 *Hen. IV*, III. i. 31. **3.** Saul from his Asses, and David from his sheepe were called to the crowne 1577. **4.** The pardon of the C. was granted 1844. **5.** A bisi womman a croune is to hir man WYCLIF *Prov.* 12:4.

II. 1. Anything having or bearing the figure or the representation of a crown ME. **2.** A name of various coins; originally one bearing the imprint of a crown; *esp.* a coin (now silver) of Great Britain of the value of five shillings; hence the sum of five shillings ME. **3.** A size of paper, orig. watermarked with a crown 1712.

III. Something having the form of an encircling wreath. † **1.** The tonsure of a cleric –1533. **2.** = CORONA 1. 1563. **3.** † A whorl of flowers. **b.** = CORONA 6 a. 1578. † **4.** A ring –1706. **5.** = CORONA 3. 1845. **6.** *Surg.* The circular serrated edge of a trepan 1758.

1. Crounne & cloþ maken no prest WYCLIF.

IV. 1. The top part of the skull; the vertex ME.; hence, the head 1594. **2.** The rounded summit of a mountain or other elevation 1583. **3.** The highest or central part of an arch or arched surface 1635. **4.** The top of a hat; *esp.* the flat circular top of the modern hat 1678. **5.** The flattened or rounded roof of a tent or building 1725. **6.** *Archit.* = CORONA 4. 1611. **7.** In plants: **a.** The leafy head of a tree or shrub; **b.** The flattened top of a seed, etc. **8.** *Farriery.* The CORONET of a horse's hoof 1611. **9.** *Anat.* The part of a tooth which appears beyond the gums 1804. **10.** The part of a cut gem above the girdle 1875. **11.** The part of the shank of an anchor from which the arms proceed 1875. **12.** *Mech.* Any terminal flat member of a structure; the face of an anvil. **13.** *fig.* That which crowns anything; the consummation, completion, or perfection 1611.

1. Crowne is..the top of a mans head, where the haire windes about PUTTENHAM. **2.** Vpon the crowne o' th' Cliffe *Lear* IV. vi. 67. **3.** *C. of the causeway, road*: the central and most prominent part of the pavement or street. **7.** *C. of the root*: the junction of the root and stem. **13.** Thou art of all thy gifts thyself the c. COWPER.

V. *attrib.* **a.** Of or pertaining to the Crown (senses I. 2–4): as *c. demesne, due, duty, rent, revenue, vassal*, etc. **b.** In titles of foreign (chiefly Polish) officials, as *c. chamberlain*, etc. **c.** Pertaining to the coin, as *c. cribbage*, etc. **d.** Used to designate a quality or brand, as *c. soap*, etc. **e.** Pertaining to the top of the head, corona of a plant, etc., as *c. bloom*; *c.-distempered* adj.

Comb.: **c.-agent,** agent for the C.; in Scotland, a solicitor who takes charge of criminal proceedings, under the Lord Advocate; **-antler,** the topmost antler of a stag's horn; **-cases reserved,** criminal cases reserved on points of law for the consideration of the judges; **-colony,** one in which the legislation and the administration are controlled by the home government; **-court,** the court in which the criminal business of an Assize is transacted; **-crane,** the *demoiselle*; **-debt,** a debt due to the C., which has preference over other debts; **-gate,** the upstream gate of the lock of a canal; **-graft,** a graft inserted between the inner bark and the alburnum; hence **-grafting; -jewels,** the jewels which form part of the regalia; **c. law,** the criminal law; **c. lawyer,** a criminal lawyer; **c. living,** a church living in the gift of the C.; **c.-pigeon** = *crowned pigeon*: see CROWNED 6; **-saw,** a kind of circular saw with the teeth on the edge of a hollow cylinder, as in a trepan saw, etc.; **-sheet,** the upper plate of the fire-box of a locomotive; **-shell,** a barnacle or acorn-shell; **-side,** the portion of the Court of Queen's Bench which deals with criminal matters, the c. office; **c. solicitor,** a solicitor who prepares criminal prosecutions for the C.; **c.-sparrow,** one of the American genus *Zonotrichia*, with a coloured c.; **-tax,** a tax paid to the C.; **-tile,** a tile of a rectangular form; **-tree,** a support for the roof in coal-mines; **-valve,** a dome-shaped valve which works over a box with slotted sides; **-witness,** a witness for the C. in a criminal prosecution.

Hence **Crow·nless** *a.* **Crow·nlet** *sb.* a tiny c. **Crow·nling,** a scion of the c. (*rare*).

Crown (kraun), *v.*[1] [ME. *corune*, etc. – AFr. *coruner*, OFr. *coroner* (mod. *couronner*) :– L. *coronare*, f. *corona* CROWN.] **1.** *trans.* To place a crown, wreath, or garland upon the head of. **2.** *spec.* To invest with the regal crown, and hence with royal dignity ME.; to enthrone 1596. Also *fig.* **3.** To surmount (something) *with* ME. **4.** To form a crown to 1746. **5.** To adorn the surface of *with* 1697. **6.** To fill to overflowing 1605. **7.** *fig.* To complete worthily 1606. **8.** To bless with a successful issue 1602. **9.** To endow with honour, dignity, plenty, etc. Now *poet.* 1535. † **10.** To mark (a person) with the tonsure. (ME. only.) **11.** *Draughts.* To make (a piece that reaches the opponent's crown-head) into a king by placing another piece upon it 1850. **12.** *Mil.* To effect a lodgement upon, as upon the crest of the glacis, etc. (Webster).

1. He was crowned..with a crown of thornes HOBBES. **2.** *fig.* Thou..hast crowned him with glory and honour *Ps.* 8:5. **4.** Perugia..crowning a mighty hill HAWTHORNE. **5.** Where..vales with Violets once were crown'd DRYDEN. **6.** The Bowls were crown'd..and Healths went round PRIOR. **7.** No day without a deed to Crowne it *Hen. VIII*, v. v. 59. **9.** He that resisteth pleasures, crowneth his life *Ecclus.* 19:5. Phr. *To c. a knot* (Naut.): to finish a knot by interweaving the strands so as to prevent untwisting.

Crown, *v.*[2] Now *dial.* 1602. [f. CROWNER[2].] To hold a coroner's inquest on.

Crow·nal, *sb. arch.* 1500. [Phonetic var. of CORONAL.] = CORONAL *sb.* 1, 2.

† **Crownation.** 1530. = CORONATION –1604.

Crowned (kraund), *ppl. a.* ME. [f. CROWN *v.*[1] and *sb.* + -ED.] **1.** Invested with a crown or with royal dignity. **2.** Surmounted by a crown 1565. † **3.** Consummate; sovereign –1651. **4.** Brimming, bounteous 1605. **5.** Having a CROWN (in various senses) 1665. **6.** Crested 1698.

1. C. and mitred tyranny CAMPBELL. **2.** The Harpe C. 1633. **3.** His corouned malice CHAUCER. **5.** An antick sort of hat which is high crown'd 1665.

Crowner[1] (krau·nəɹ). ME. [f. CROWN *v.* + -ER[1].] One who, or that which, crowns.

Crowner[2]. Now *dial.* ME. = CORONER.

† **Crow·net.** ME. [A by-form of CORONET.] = CORONET –1842.

Crow·n-gla:ss. 1706. Glass composed of silica, potash, and lime (without lead or iron), made in circular sheets by blowing and whirling.

Crow·n Impe·rial. 1542. **1.** The crown of an emperor. **2.** A species of Fritillary (*Fritillaria imperialis*) from Levantine regions, bearing a number of pendent flowers forming a whorl round a terminal leafy tuft 1611.

2. Bold Oxlips, and The Crowne Imperiall SHAKS.

Crowning (krau·niŋ), *vbl. sb.* ME. [f. CROWN *v.* + -ING[1].] **1.** Coronation. † **2.** Tonsure. (ME. only.) **3.** Consummation; completion 1598. **4.** *Naut.* The finishing part of a knot made on the end of a rope (see CROWN *v.*) 1769. **5.** That which forms the crown of anything 1704.

Crow·ning, *ppl. a.* 1611. [f. as prec. + -ING[2].] **1.** That bestows crowns. *Isa.* 23:8. **2.** That forms the crown or acme 1651. **3.** Arching 1761.

2. The dimensions of this mercy are above my thought. It is for aught I know a c. mercy CROMWELL.

Crown-land, crow·nland. 1625. **1.** (*crow·n-la·nd.*) Land belonging to the Crown. Mostly in *pl.* **2.** (*crow·nland* = G. *kronland.*) The name of the administrative provinces of the Austro-Hungarian monarchy.

† **Crow·nment.** ME. [– OFr. *coronement* (mod. *couronnement*); see CROWN *v.*[1], -MENT.] Coronation –1592.

Crown office. 1631. The office in which was transacted, at certain stages, the business of the Crown side of the King's Bench. Now a department of the Central Office of the High Court of Justice. **b.** In Chancery: The office in which the Great Seal is, for most purposes, affixed 1863.

Crown-paper. 1630. = CROWN *sb.* II. 3.

Crown-piece, crow·npiece. 1648. **1.** (*crown-piece.*) = CROWN II. 2. **2.** (*crow·npiece.*) A piece that forms the crown or top 1794.

Crow·n-post. 1703. = KING-POST.

Crown prince. 1791. [tr. Ger. *kronprinz*, etc.] The heir-apparent to a sovereign throne, *esp.* in Germany, etc. Hence **Crown pri·ncess,** the wife of a crown prince.

Crow·n-scab. 1609. [CROWN *sb.* IV. 8.] A cancerous sore in the coronet of a horse's foot.

Crow·n-wheel. 1647. The balance- or escape-wheel of a vertical watch, the pinion of which is driven by the contrate wheel; but now = a CONTRATE wheel.

Crown-work. Formerly **crowned work.** 1677. *Fortif.* A work consisting of a bastion between two curtains, terminated by half bastions, and joined to the body of the place by two long sides.

Crow·-quill. 1740. A quill from a crow's wing, used as a pen for fine writing. Also used for a fine steel pen for map-drawing, etc.

Crow's foot, crow·'s-foot. ME. **1.** One of the wrinkles round the outer corner of the eye. † **2.** *Naut.* = CROWFOOT 4. –1806. **3.** *Mil.* A caltrop 1772. **4.** A three-pointed figure in embroidery 1879. **5.** *Mech.* A bent hook to hold the shoulder of a drill-rod while a section above it is being attached or detached 1874.

Crow-silk. 1721. [CROW *sb.*[1]] A name for the *Conferva* and other delicate green-spored Algæ with silky filaments.

Crow·'s nest, crow's-nest. 1604. † **1.** *Mil.* ? A fort placed on a height. **2.** A barrel or box fixed to the mast-head of a whaling or other ship, as a shelter for the look-out man 1818.

Crow·-step. 1822. *Archit.* = CORBIE-STEP (see CORBIE).

Crow·-stone. 1677. **1.** The fossil shell *Gryphæa* of the Oolite and Lias. **2.** A kind of hard white flinty sandstone 1778. **3.** 'The top stone of the gable end of a house' (Halliwell).

Crow-toe. Also **crow-toes.** *Sc.* and *n. dial.* 1562. A name of the wild hyacinth (*Scilla nutans*); also of *Orchis mascula, Lotus corniculatus*, and the Buttercups.

The tufted crow-toe, and pale jessamine MILT.

† **Crow·-tread,** *v.* 1592. To tread (a fowl) as crows were supposed to do; hence *fig.* to abuse –1652.

A crauen henne that is crow trodden N. BRETON.

Croyl. Now *dial.* 1836. [Origin unkn.] *Geol.* Indurated clay with shells. Hence, perh., † **Croylstone,** native sulphate of barium; cawk.

Croze (krōᵘz), *sb.* 1611. [perh. – Fr. *creux, creuse*, OFr. *croz*, Pr. *cros* hollow, groove, etc.] *Coopering.* The groove at the ends of cask staves, etc.; also the tool for making it.

Croze, *v.*[1] 1880. [f. prec.] *Coopering.* To make the croze in (cask staves, etc.).

Croze, *v.*[2] [Origin unkn.] *Hat-making.* To refold (a hat-body) so as to present a different surface to the action of the felting-machine.

Crozier, -ed; see CROSIER, -ED.

Crub. Now *dial.* 1565. = CURB *sb.*

Cruche, obs. f. CROCHE[1], CROUCH, CRUTCH.

† **Cruche.** [perh. repr. Fr. *crochet* in same sense.] A small curl lying flat on the forehead. EVELYN.

Crucial (krū·ʃiăl, -ʃ'ăl), *a.* 1706. [– Fr. *crucial* (XVI in medical use), f. L. *crux, cruc-* CROSS *sb* + -AL[1]; see -IAL.] **1.** (Chiefly *Anat.*) Of the form of a cross, as *c. incision*; *spec.* the name of two ligaments in the knee-joint, which connect the femur and tibia. **2.** That finally decides between two hypotheses; relating to, or adapted to lead to, such decision; decisive, critical. [From Bacon's phrase *instantia crucis* (see *Nov. Org.* II. xxxvi); see also CRUX.] 1830. ¶ **3.** App. assoc. w. CRUCIBLE 1856.

2. C. experiments for the verification..of his theory J. MARTINEAU. **3.** The imagination's c. heat E. B. BROWNING. Hence **Cru·cially** *adv.* in a c. manner.

Crucian, crusian (krū·ʃăn). 1763. [f. LG. *karusse, karuse, karutze* (G. *karausche*) + -AN, with accommodated sp., f. (ult.) L. *coracinus* – Gr. κορακῖνος; see CORACINE.] A species of fish, a native of Central Europe, also called *Crucian Carp*, and (when lean) *German* or *Prussian Carp*; now placed in the genus *Carassius*, being *C. carassius*.

Cruciate (krū·ʃiĕt), *a.* (*sb.*) 1684. [– mod.L. *cruciatus*, f. L. *crux, cruc-* cross; see -ATE[2] 2.] *Zool.* and *Bot.* Cross-shaped; arranged in the form of a cross 1826. †*sb.* = CRUCIAL incision.

Cruciate (krū·ʃieˈt), *v.* 1532. [– *cruciat-*, pa. ppl. stem of L. *cruciare* torture, f. *crux, cruc-* cross; see -ATE[3]. Sense 2 is f. eccl.L. use.] **1.** *trans.* To torture, torment, to EXCRUCIATE (*arch.*). † **2.** To crucify (*rare*) –1658.

Cruciation. Now *rare.* 15.. [– OFr. *cruciation* or eccl.L. *crutiatio*, f. as prec.; see -ION.] Torture, torment.

Cruciato-, comb. f. mod.L. *cruciatus* CRUCIATE *a.*, as in **c.-complicate,** at the same time crossed and folded, as the wings of insects, *e.g.* of the *Pentatoma*; **-incumbent,** laid upon the abdomen, and crossed but not folded, as in the *Apis*.

Crucible (krū·sib'l), *sb.* 1460. [– med.L. *crucibulum* night-lamp, crucible, f. L. *crux, cruc-* CROSS *sb.*] **1.** A vessel, usually of earthenware, made to endure great heat, used for fusing metals, etc.; a melting-pot. **b.** A basin at the bottom of a furnace to collect the molten metal 1864. **2.** *fig.* Used of any severe test or trial 1645. Also *attrib.*

2. In this Limbec and Crusible of Affliction HOWELL.

Crucifer (krū·sifəɹ). 1574. [– Chr.L. (applied to Christ by Prudentius), f. L. *crux, cruc-*; see CROSS *sb.*, -FEROUS.] **1.** *Eccl.* A cross-bearer. **2.** *Bot.* A CRUCIFEROUS plant 1846.

Cruciferous (krūsi·fĕrəs), *a.* 1656. [f. as prec. + -OUS.] **1.** Bearing a cross. **2.** *Bot.* Belonging to the *Cruciferæ*; bearing flowers with four equal petals arranged crosswise. Also said of the flowers; = CRUCIATE *a.* 1851.

Crucifier (krū·sifəiəɹ). ME. [f. CRUCIFY + -ER[1].] One who crucifies; one who torments or worries.

†‖ **Crucifige.** ME. [L.; = crucify (him)!] The cry of the Jews to Pilate; formerly as sb.: Popular clamour for the death of a victim –1652.

Crucifix (krū·sifiks), *sb.* ME. [– (O)Fr. *crucifix* – eccl.L. *crucifixus*, i.e. *cruci fixus* fixed to a cross.] † **1.** The Crucified One; Christ on the cross –1660. **2.** An image (formerly also a pictorial representation) of Christ upon the cross ME.

1. He that sweares by the Crosse, sweares by the Holy C., that is, Jesus crucified thereon JER. TAYLOR. (The conjectured sense 'The Cross or religion of Christ' is merely Todd's misunderstanding of this passage.) So **Cru·cifix** *v.* to crucify (*rare*).

Crucifixion (krūsifi·kʃən). 1648. [– eccl.L. *crucifixio* – *crucifix-*, pa. ppl. stem of *crucifigere*; see CRUCIFY, -ION.] **1.** The action of crucifying, or of putting to death on a cross; *spec. The C.*: that of Jesus Christ on Calvary 1649. **2.** *fig.* †Torture; the action of crucifying (passions, sins, etc.) 1648. **3.** A representation of the Crucifixion of Christ 1841.

2. Do ye prove What crucifixions are in love HERRICK.

Cruciform (krū·sifǭɹm), *a.* 1661. [f. L. *crux, cruc-* cross + -FORM.] Of the form of a (right-angled) cross; cross-shaped: *spec.* in *Bot.* of the flowers of cruciferous plants; in *Anat.* = CRUCIAL 1.

Crucify (krū·sifəi), *v.* ME. [– (O)Fr. *crucifier* – Rom. **crucificare*, repl. eccl.L. *crucifigere*, i.e. *cruci figere* FIX to a CROSS.] **1.** *trans.* To put to death by nailing or otherwise fastening to a cross; an ancient mode of capital punishment, considered specially ignominious by the Greeks and Romans. **2.** *fig.* **a.** To mortify; *esp.* to destroy the power of (passions, sins, the flesh, etc.) ME. † **b.** To torture; to excruciate. **c.** To torment, to prove a crux to 1621.

1. Thei cryeden, seyinge, do awey, do awey, crucifie hym WYCLIF *John* 18:15. **2.** Oure olde man is crucified with him also, that the body of synne myght vtterly be destroyed TINDALE *Rom.* 6:6. Hence **Cru·cified** *ppl. a.* nailed to a cross; *absol.* a crucified person; *spec.* = Christ.

† **Cruci·gerous,** *a.* [f. L. *crux, cruc-* CROSS *sb.*; see -GEROUS.] Bearing or marked with a cross. SIR T. BROWNE.

Crud(de, Cruddle, obs. or dial. ff. CURD, CURDLE.

Crude (krūd), *a.* ME. [– L. *crudus* raw, rough, cruel.] **1.** In the natural or raw state; 'not changed by any process or preparation' (J.); not manufactured, refined, tempered, etc. **2.** Not, or not fully, digested or concocted 1533; †*transf.* lacking power to digest

–1671. **3.** Of fruit: Unripe; sour or harsh 1555. **4.** Of a disease, etc.: In an early stage; not developed 1651. **5.** Not completely thought out or worked up; ill-digested; rough, unpolished; coarse 1611. **6.** Of action or speech: Rough, rude, wanting in amenity 1650. **7.** Of persons: Characterized by crudeness of thought, feeling, action, or character 1722. **8.** *Gram.* In *c. form*: The uninflected form or stem of a word 1805.

1. C. Lead BOYLE, Antimony 1822. Any c. or raw thing, as fruits, herbs COGAN. **2.** A c. indigested mass of humours W. BUCHAN. **3.** I come to pluck your berries harsh and c. MILT. **5.** The *ex tempore* and c. Prayers of the Ministers 1646. C. opinions DISRAELI, efforts JOHNSON, prose LAMB. **6.** So c. an answer COTTON. **8.** The base or c.-form of an adjective as adverb WHITNEY. **Cru·de-ly** *adv.*, **-ness.**

† **Crude·lity.** 1483. [– OFr. *crudelite* or L. *crudelitas*, f. *crudelis*; see CRUEL, -ITY.] = CRUELTY –1707.

Crudity (krū·dĭti). 1533. [– (O)Fr. *crudité* or L. *cruditas*, f. *crudus* CRUDE; see -ITY.] **1.** The state or quality of being CRUDE 1638; *concr.* (in *pl.*) raw products 1626. **2.** *Phys.* Indigestion; undigested (or indigestible) matter in the stomach 1533.

2. *fig.* Coryats Crudities, hastily gobled vp in fiue Moneths travells in France, Italy [etc.] 1611 (title).

Crudle, obs. f. CURDLE.

Crudy, obs. f. CURDY.

Cruel (krū·ėl), *a.* ME. [– (O)Fr. *cruel* :– L. *crudelis*, rel. to *crudus* CRUDE.] **1.** Disposed to inflict suffering; indifferent to or taking pleasure in another's pain; merciless, pitiless, hard-hearted. † **2.** Fierce, savage –1600. † **3.** Severe, vigorous –1670. **4.** Painful; distressing; *colloq.* = hard ME. **5.** as *adv.* Distressingly; hence = exceedingly 1573.

1. As c. as a schoolboy TENNYSON. A c. and frowning universe MORLEY. The Puritans had given..c. provocation MACAULAY. **4.** Intollerable turmentes..and moost cruell & bytter deth 1526. Hence **Cru·elly** *adv.* in a c. manner; excessively. † **Cru·elness.**

Cruel(s, var. of CREWEL, -ELS.

Cruelty (krū·ėlti). ME. [– OFr. *crualté* (mod. *cruauté*) :– Rom. **crudalitas* for L. *crudelitas*; see CRUDELITY.] **1.** The quality of being cruel; disposition to inflict suffering; delight in or indifference to another's pain; mercilessness, hard-heartedness. Also, an instance of this. † **2.** Severity of pain –1634. † **3.** Severity; rigour –1634.

1. The vice called crueltie, which is contrary to mercye ELIOT. 'Tis a c., To load a falling man *Hen. VIII*, v. iii. 76.

† **Cruentate,** *a. rare.* [– L. *cruentatus*, pa. pple. of *cruentare* make bloody, f. *cruentus* bloody.] Blood-stained. GLANVILL.

Cruentation (krūentē̆ⁱ·ʃən). [– late L. *cruentatio*, f. *cruentat-*, pa. ppl. stem of L. *cruentare*; see prec., -ION.] 'A term applied to the oozing of blood which occurs sometimes when an incision is made into the dead body' (*Syd. Soc. Lex.*).

† **Crue·ntous,** *a. rare.* 1648. [f. L. *cruentus* bloody + -OUS.] Bloody. (*lit.* and *fig.*) –1675.

Cruet (krū·ėt). ME. [– AFr. **cruet*, **cruete*, dim. of OFr. *crue* – OS. *krūka* (Du. *kruik*) = OE. *crūce*, MHG. *krūche* (G. *krauche*), rel. to CROCK *sb.*¹] **1.** A small bottle or vial; now only applied to a small glass bottle with a stopper, to contain vinegar, oil, etc., for the table. **2.** *Eccl.* A small vessel to hold wine or water for use in the celebration of the Eucharist, etc. ME. *Comb.* **c.-stand,** a frame for holding cruets and castors at table.

Cruise (krūz), *v.* 1651. [prob. – Du. *kruisen* cross, f. *kruis* CROSS *sb.*] *intr.* To sail to and fro over some part of the sea, on the look out for ships, for the protection of commerce, for plunder, or for pleasure. Also *transf.* and *fig.* **b.** *trans. rare.* To sail to and fro over 1687.

transf. Blackbirds will c. along the whole length of a hedge before finding a bush to their liking JEFFERIES. Hence **Cruise** *sb.* the action of cruising; a voyage in which the ships sail to and fro.

Cruiser (krū·zəɹ). 1679. [– Du. *kruiser*, f. *kruisen* CRUISE.] A person or a ship that cruises. In 18th c. commonly applied to privateers. Now, a class of warships less heavily armed than a battleship (*battle-c.*).

Comb. **c.-weight** (*Boxing*) = light heavy-weight (*colloq.*).

Cruive (krūv). ME. [orig. *Sc.* (krōv, krūv). Cf. *corve*, CORF, etc.] **1.** A hovel (*Sc.*) 1450. **2.** A pigsty (*Sc.*) 1575. **3.** A coop or enclosure of wickerwork or spars placed in tide-ways, etc., to trap salmon ME.

† **Crull,** *a.* [ME. *crolle, crulle* – MDu. *krul* curly, prob. :– **krusl-*, and rel. to MLG. *krus* crisp, curly; see CURL.] Curly. ME. only.

Cruller (krɒ·ləɹ). *U.S.* 1818. [app. – Du. *cruller*, f. *crullen* to curl.] A cake cut from dough containing eggs, butter, sugar, etc., twisted or curled, and fried crisp in lard or oil.

Crumb, crum (krɒm), *sb.* [OE. *cruma*, corresp. w. var. of vowel to MDu. *crūme* (Du. *kruim*), MLG., MDu. *crōme*, (M)HG. *krume*, Icel. *krumr, kraumr*. The parasitic *b* appears XVI; cf. *dumb, thumb*.] **1.** A small particle; *esp.* a small particle of bread, such as breaks off by rubbing, etc. **2.** *fig.* A scrap (of something immaterial) ME. **3.** The soft part of bread; opp. to *crust* ME.

1. Every crumme we put in our mouthes SANDERSON. **2.** Crumbs of Comfort D'URFEY. **3.** *Lear* I. iv. 217.

Phr. † *To gather* (or *pick*) *up one's crumbs*: to pick up strength. *Comb.*: **c.-brush,** a brush for sweeping crumbs from a table; **-cloth,** a cloth laid under the table to catch the crumbs and keep the carpet clean.

Crumb, crum (krɒm), *v.* ME. [f. prec. sb.] **1.** *trans.* To reduce to crumbs or small fragments. Now *rare.* † **2.** *intr.* To crumble –18.. **3.** *trans.* To thicken or cover with crumbs 1579. Hence **Cru·mmable** *a.* (*rare*).

Crumble (krɒ·mb'l), *v.* ME. [Earlier forms †*kremele* (XV), †*crimble* (XVI) repr. an OE. type **crymelan* (:– **krumilōn*).] **1.** *trans.* To reduce to crumbs or small fragments; to strew as crumbs. **2.** *intr.* To fall asunder in small particles; to become pulverized 1577.

1. Moisture softens and crumbles the shale PHILLIPS. *fig.* To fritter and c. down the attention BURKE. **2.** Marbles with their deepest inscriptions c. away EVELYN. *fig.* His influence was crumbling away FREEMAN. Hence **Cru·mble** *sb. rare*, a small crumb or particle; crumbling substance. **Cru·mbly** *a.* apt to c.

Crumby, *a.*, var. of CRUMMY, q.v.

† **Cru·menal.** *rare.* 1579. [f. L. *crumena* purse + -AL¹.] A purse or pouch –1647.

Crummy (krɒ·mi), *a.* 1567. [f. *crum*, CRUMB *sb.* + -Y¹.] † **1.** Crumbly –1725. **2.** Like the crumb of bread 1579. **3.** *slang.* Plump; comely; rich 1718. † **4.** Full of crumbs; now CRUMBY.

† **Crump,** *a.*¹ and *sb.* [OE. *crump* (= OHG. *krumpf*), a by-form, prob. intensive, of OE. *crumb*; see CROME, CROMB.] *adj.* Crooked –1783. *sb.* A crooked person, a hunchback –1765.

Crump (krɒmp), *a.*² *Sc.* and *n.* 1787. [A parallel form of CRIMP *a.* 1.] Brittle or friable under the teeth.

† **Crump,** *v.*¹ ME. [f. CRUMP *a.* or its source; cf. CRIMP *v.*¹ and CRAMP *sb.*¹] *trans.* and *intr.* To bend into a curve, crook, curl up –1818. Hence † **Crumped, crumpt** *ppl. a.* curved, crooked.

Crump (krɒmp), *v.*² 1646. [imit.; cf. *crunch, crush.*] *trans.* and *intr.* **1.** To eat with an abrupt but somewhat dulled sound; applied *esp.* to horses and pigs. Also *transf.* **2.** To strike with a brisk or abrupt effect 1850.

2. We could slog to square-leg, or c. to the off 1892. Hence **Crumper** *sb.* a 'whacker'; a 'thumping' lie.

Crumpet (krɒ·mpet). 1694. [Of doubtful origin; perh. to be connected with †*crompid cake* (Wycl. Bible; tr. Vulg. *laganum*), lit. 'curled up cake', and so rel. to MDu. *cromp* = OE. *crumb*, etc.; see CROME, CROMB.] † **1.** A thin griddle cake –1830. **2.** A soft cake made of flour, beaten egg, milk, and barm, mixed into batter, and baked on an iron plate 1769. **3.** *slang.* The head 1891.

Crumple, *sb.* 1607. [Cf. CRUMPLE *v.* see -LE.] A crushed fold or wrinkle.

† **Crumple,** *a.* 1523. [f. next.] = Crumpled: chiefly in comb., as *c-horned* adj. –1851.

Crumple (krɒ·mp'l), *v.* 1528. [In form, a dim. and iterative of CRUMP *v.*¹] **1.** *intr.* To become incurved or crushed together; to become creased by being crushed together. **2.** *trans.* To crook, bend together, contort 1613. **3.** To crush into creases 1632. **4.** To crinkle 1858. **5.** To crush together. Also with *up.* 1577.

1. To crompull to gether like parchement cast in the fire 1528. **3.** Sir Roger..exposing his palm..they crumpled it into all shapes and diligently scanned every wrinkle ADDISON. Hence **Cru·mpler.**

Cru·mpy, *a. dial.* 1808. [f. CRUMP *a.*² + -Y¹.] = CRUMP *a.*²

† **Cru·mster, cromster.** 1596. [f. Du. *krom* crooked: cf. Du. *kromsteven* 'genus navis' (Kilian), f. *krom* + *steven*; cf. STEM *sb.*²] A kind of galley –1600.

Crunch (krɒnʃ), *v.* 1801. [var. of CRAUNCH, assim. to MUNCH.] **1.** *trans.* To crush with the teeth; to chew or bite with a crushing noise 1814. Also *intr.* or *absol.* **2.** *trans.* To crush under foot, wheels, etc., with the accompanying noise 1849. Also *intr.* or *absol.* **3.** *intr.* To advance, or make *one's way*, with crunching 1853.

1. A herd of swine crunching acorns KINGSLEY. **2.** A sound of heavy wheels crunching a stony road C. BRONTË. **3.** The sound of our vessel crunching her way through the ice KANE. Hence **Crunch** *sb.* an act, or the action, of crunching. **Cru·nchy** *a.*

† **Crunk,** *v.* 1565. [Cf. Icel. *krúnka* to croak.] *intr.* Of some birds: To utter a hoarse harsh cry –1617. Hence **Crunk** *sb.* a croak.

Crunkle (krɒ·ŋk'l), *v.*¹ Chiefly *n. dial.* ME. [Parallel to CRINKLE.] *trans.* and *intr.* To crinkle.

† **Crunkle,** *v.*² 1611. [dim. of CRUNK *v.*] To cry like a crane.

Crunode (krū·nōᵘd). 1873. [irreg. f. L. *crux* + NODE.] *Geom.* A point on a curve where it crosses itself; a node with two real tangents. Hence **Crunodal** *a.* having a c.

‖ **Cruor** (krū·ǭɹ). 1656. [L., blood (when out of the body).] *Phys.* and *Med.* Coagulated blood; gore.

Cruorin (krū·ŏrin). 1840. [f. prec. + -IN¹.] *Chem.* The red colouring matter of blood-corpuscles; *hæmoglobin.*

Crup, *a. dial.* 1736. [perh. var. of CRUMP *a.*²] Short, brittle; also *fig.*, as a *c. answer.*

Crup(e, var. of CROUP *sb.*¹, hind-quarters.

Crupper (krɒ·pəɹ), *sb.* ME. [– AFr. *cropere*, OFr. *cropiere* (mod. *croupière*) :– Rom. **cropparia, -eria*, f. **croppa*; see CROUP *sb.*¹, -ER².] **1.** A leathern strap buckled to the back of the saddle and passing under the horse's tail, to keep the saddle from slipping forwards. **2.** *transf.* The rump of a horse 1591. **3.** The buttocks (of a man). Usually *joc.* 1594. **4. a.** *Naut.* = *c.-chain.* **b.** 'The train tackle ring-bolt in a gun-carriage' (Adm. Smyth).

Comb. **c.-chain** (*Naut.*), a chain to secure the jib-boom down in its saddle. Hence **Cru·pper** *v.* to put a c. upon.

Crural (krūᵊ·răl), *a.* 1599. [– Fr. *crural* or L. *cruralis*, f. *crus, crur-* leg; see -AL¹.] **1.** Of or belonging to the leg; *spec.* in *Anat.*, as in *c. artery, arch, canal, ring*, etc. **2.** Of the nature or form of a leg 1842.

‖ **Crus** (krɒs). Pl. **crura** (krūᵊ·ră). 1687. [L.; see prec.] † **1.** *Geom.* A straight line forming one side of a triangle (*rare*). **2.** *Anat.* **a.** The leg or hind limb; *spec.* the part between the knee and the ankle, the shank. **b.** Applied to parts occurring in pairs and likened to legs, as *crura of the diaphragm*, a pair of muscles connecting the diaphragm with the lumbar vertebræ; *crura of the penis, of the clitoris*, bodies forming the attachments of those organs, one on each side of the pubic arch. 1727.

Crusade (krusē̆ⁱ·d). 1577. [Earlier CROISÉE, -IE, -Y (q.v.) were superseded in XVI by (i) *croisade* – Fr. *croisade*, alt. of earlier *croisée* (whence Eng. CROISEE, etc.), by assim. to the Sp. form (see -ADE); (ii) *crusada, -ado* (see -ADO) XVI – Sp. *cruzada*; (iii) *croisada, -ado* (XVII), which are blends of (i) and (ii).] **1.** *Hist.* A military expedition undertaken by the Christians of Europe in the 11th, 12th, and 13th centuries to recover the Holy Land from the Moslems. Also *transf.* of any 'holy war'. **2.** *fig.* An aggressive movement or enterprise against some public evil 1786.

† **3.** A papal bull authorizing a crusade –1771. † **4.** *Span. Hist.* A levy of money, originally for aggression or defence against the Moors –1772. † **5.** The symbol of the cross, the badge borne by crusaders –1700.

2. A c. against ignorance T. JEFFERSON. Hence **Crusa·de** *v.* to go on a c. **Crusa·der,** one who goes on a c.

‖ **Crusado** (krusēⁱ·do). 1544. [– Pg. *cruzado* 'bearing a cross' 'crossed'.] A Portuguese coin bearing the figure of the cross; now = about 2*s.* 4*d.* sterling.

†‖ **Crusa·do²**. 1575. [– Sp., Pg. *cruzado* 'a crossed man'.] A crusader –1625.

Crusado³, var. of *crusada* = CRUSADE.

Cruse (krūs, krūz). *arch.* [ME. *cruse, crewse* perh. – (M)LG. *krūs*; not continuous with OE. *crūse* = MHG. *krūse* (G. *krause*), Icel. *krús*. Ult. relations unkn.] A small earthen vessel for liquids; a pot, jar, or bottle; also a drinking vessel. Also *fig.*

Neither did the c. of oil fail 1 *Kings* 17:16.

† **Cru·set.** 1558. [– (O)Fr. *creuset* crucible.] A crucible –1755.

Crush (krʌʃ), *v.* ME. [– AFr. *crussir, corussier,* OFr. *croissir, cruissir* gnash (the teeth), crash, crack :– Rom. **cruscire,* of unkn. origin. For *sh* cf. BUSHEL, etc.] † **1.** To dash together with the sound of violent percussion, to clash, crash. (ME. only.) **2.** *trans.* To compress with violence, so as to destroy natural shape or condition ME. Also *intr.* (for *refl.*). **3.** To press or squeeze forcibly or violently. (The force, not the effect, being prominent.) 1592. Also *intr.* (for *refl.*). **4.** *fig.* **a.** To break down the power of; to overcome completely 1596. **b.** To oppress with harshness or rigour 1611. **5.** To bruise, bray, break down into small pieces; to comminute (ore, etc.) 1588. **6.** To press or squeeze *out.* Also *fig.* 1602.

2. The Ostrich..leaueth her egges in the earth.. And forgetteth that the foot may c. them *Job* 39:15. Some..are crusht to death SIR T. HERBERT. **3.** To c. our old limbes in vngentle Steele 1 *Hen. IV*, v. i. 13. **4.** His enemies were crushed by his valour GIBBON. Crush'd is thy pride GAY. **b.** Yea kine of Bashan..which c. the needy *Amos* 4:1.

Phr. *To c. a cup of wine,* etc.: to drink it: cf. CRACK *v.* Hence **Cru·sher,** one who or that which crushes; *spec.* an apparatus for recording the pressure exerted on a gun by a charge of powder. **Cru·shingly** *adv.*

Crush (krʌʃ), *sb.* ME. [f. prec. vb.] † **1.** The noise of violent percussion; clashing; a crash. (ME. only.) **2.** The act of crushing; destruction by crushing; also *fig.* 1599. † **3.** A bruise or injury caused by crushing –1702. **4.** The crowding together of things, or *esp.* persons, so that they press forcibly upon each other; the mass so crowded together 1806; a crowded social gathering (*colloq.*) 1832.

2. The wrecks of matter, and the c. of worlds ADDISON. **4.** I fell in with her at Lady Grey's great c. MACAULAY.

Comb. (? f. verb-stem): **c. hat,** a soft hat which can be crushed flat; *spec.* a hat constructed with a spring so as to collapse; an opera-hat; **-room,** a room or hall in a theatre, etc., in which the audience may promenade between the acts.

Crusily, -illy (krū·sĭli), *a.* 1572. [– OFr. *crusillé,* var. of *croisillé,* f. (O)Fr. *croisille,* dim. of *croix* cross; see -Y⁵.] *Her.* Strewn with small crosses, as a charge.

Crust (krʌst), *sb.* [ME. *crouste* – OFr. *crouste* (mod. *croûte*) :– L. *crusta* rind, shell, incrustation.] **1.** The hard and dry outer part of bread; a scrap of bread which is mainly crust or is hard and dry 1561. Also *fig.* **2.** The paste or cover of a pie 1598. **3.** A hard dry formation on the surface of the body, caused by a burn, an ulcer, etc.; a scab, an eschar ME. **4.** †The upper or surface layer of the ground (in reference to a supposed molten interior of the earth); hence, *Geol.* the outer portion of the earth 1555. **5.** A more or less hard coating or deposit on anything, as the *c. of wine*; an encrustation 1540. **6.** The hard external covering of an animal or plant; *spec.* the shell of Crustaceans 1615. **7.** *fig.* 1651.

1. You know there can't be c. without crumb 1871. Bring me a cup of beer, and c. of bread 1837. **4.** The whole earth, in the opinion of some philosophers, is but a kind of bridge, or c. to the great body of waters included in it 1747. **5.** The c. formed over the lava 1869. **7.** The c. of his selfishness 1853.

Crust (krʌst), *v.* ME. [f. prec. sb.] **1.** *trans.* To cover as with a crust, to encrust. Also *fig.* 1545. **2.** *intr.* To form, or become covered with, a crust. Also *fig.* ME. **3.** To make hard like a crust 1671.

1. Snowe..whyche was harde and crusted by reason of the frost ASCHAM. Truth..crusted over with fictions FROUDE. **2.** The place that was burnt..crusted and healed in very few days TEMPLE (J.). **3.** Dirt..crusted on the glass 1857.

‖ **Crustacea** (krʌstēⁱ·ʃⁱa), *sb. pl.* 1814. [mod.L., n. pl. of the adj. *crustaceus,* f. L. *crusta* CRUST; see -ACEOUS, -A 4.] A large class of Arthropodous animals, mostly aquatic, characterized by a hard, close-fitting, usually chitinous shell or crust which is shed periodically; comprising Crabs, Lobsters, Shrimps, and many others. Hence **Crusta·cean** *a.* belonging to the C.; *sb.* one of the C. **Crusta·ceoid** *a.* crustacean-like (*rare*).

Crustaceo·logy. 1828. [f. prec. + -LOGY.] The scientific study of Crustacea. Hence **Crustaceolo·gical** *a.* pertaining to c.; **Crustaceo·logist,** one versed in c.

Crusta:ceoru·brin. 1882. [f. as prec. + L. *ruber* red + -IN¹.] *Chem.* A red colouring matter found in the bodies of some Crustacea.

Crustaceous (krʌstēⁱ·ʃəs), *a.* 1646. [f. mod.L. *crustaceus* (see CRUSTACEA) + -OUS; see -ACEOUS.] **1.** Pertaining to, or of the nature of, a crust or hard integument 1656. **2.** Of animals: Having a hard integument 1659. **3.** *Zool.* Belonging to the Crustacea, crustacean 1646; crab-like 1842. Hence **Crusta·ceousness.** (Dicts.)

Crustal (krʌ·stăl), *a. rare.* 1860. [f. L. *crusta* + -AL¹.] Of or pertaining to a crust. Hence **Crusta·logy,** etc., proposed by Webster for CRUSTACEO·LOGY, etc.

Crustate (krʌ·stĕt), *a.* 1661. [– L. *crustatus*; see CRUST *sb.*, -ATE².] Applied by Pliny to crustacea.] Crusted; crustaceous. So **Cru·stated** *ppl. a.* (in same sense). **Crusta·tion,** the formation of a crust; an encrustation.

Crusted (krʌ·stėd), *ppl. a.* ME. [f. CRUST *sb.* and *v.* + -ED.] Having or covered with a crust; that has deposited a crust, as old port, etc.; *fig.* antiquated, venerable; with a covered crust of prejudice (*humorous*) 1831.

fig. A fine old c. abuse 1884.

Crusto·se, *a. rare.* 1882. [– L. *crustosus,* f. *crusta* CRUST; see -OSE¹.] Of the nature of a crust; thick-skinned, as mushrooms. var. † **Cru·stous.**

Crusty (krʌ·sti), *a.* ME. [f. CRUST *sb.* + -Y¹.] **1.** Of the nature of a crust; hard like a crust. *spec.* Scabby; crusted (of wine). **2.** *fig.* Short of temper; harshly curt; not suave 1570.

1. If þe skyn be c. ME. Good old c. port 1866. **2.** Thou c. batch of Nature, what's the newes *Tr. & Cr.* v. i. 5. Hence **Cru·stily** *adv.* **Cru·stiness.**

Crut. 1847. [Origin unkn.] The rough part of oak bark. (Dicts.)

Crutch (krʌtʃ), *sb.* [OE. *cryć*(*ć* = OS. *krukka* (Du. *kruk*), OHG. *krucka* (G. *krücke*), ON. *krykkja* :– Gmc. **krukjō*, **krukjōn*. See CROOK. For the vocalism cf. BLUSH.] **1.** A staff for a lame or infirm person to lean upon in walking; now one with a cross-piece at the top to fit under the armpit (usu. *a pair of crutches*). Also *transf.* and *fig.* **2.** A support or prop, with a forked or concave top, for various uses; cf. CROTCH 1645. **3.** A forked rest for the leg in a side-saddle 1874. **4.** *Naut.* A forked support for a boom, mast, spar, etc., when not in use (also called *crotch*) 1769; crooked timbers or iron bands bolted to the stern-post and the sides of a vessel to unite these parts 1769. **5.** The fork of the human body 1748; the angle between the two flukes of a whale's tail-fin 1842.

1. Time goes on crutches, till Loue haue all his rites *Much Ado* II. i. 373. From cradle to the c. 1592. *fig.* Hold him fast: He is thy c. *Tr. & Cr.* v. iii. 60.

Comb.: **c.-boots,** tall sea boots; **-handled** *a.,* having a transverse handle like the head of a c.; **-stick,** a c.-handled stick.

Crutch (krʌtʃ), *v.* 1642. [f. prec.] **1.** *trans.* To support as with a crutch or crutches, to prop. Also with *up.* 1681. **2.** *intr.* To go on crutches, to limp 1828.

1. Two fools that c. their feeble sense on verse DRYDEN.

Crutched (krʌ·tʃėd), *ppl. a.¹* 1570. [ME. *Crouched Friars* (later *Crutched F.*), f. CROUCH *sb.¹* and *v.²* + -ED.] Having or bearing a cross.

C. or *Crouched* (also *Crossed*) *Friars* (*Fratres Cruciferi* or *Sanctæ Crucis*): a minor order of friars so called from their bearing or wearing a cross. Hence, a name for their quarters, or the part of a town where their convent stood.

Crutched (krʌtʃt, -ėd), *ppl. a.²* 1707. [f. CRUTCH *sb.* or *v.* + -ED.] **1.** Furnished with a crutch; crutch-handled. **2.** Supported on a crutch or crutches.

Crux (krʌks). 1641. [L.; see CROSS.] ‖ **1.** *Her.*, etc. = CROSS, as *crux ansata,* etc. ‖ **2.** *Astron.* The Southern Cross 1837. **3.** A thing that it puzzles one to interpret or explain; *occas.*, a conundrum, riddle 1718.

3. The unity of opposites was the c. of ancient thinkers in the age of Plato JOWETT.

Crwd, crwth; vars. of CROWD *sb.¹*

Cry (krəi), *sb.* Pl. **cries.** ME. [– (O)Fr. *cri*; common Rom. f. the verb.] **1.** The loud and chiefly inarticulate utterance of emotion; *esp.* of grief, pain, or terror. **2.** † Shouting –1440; a shout ME.; the loud utterance of words; the words as shouted ME. **3.** An importunate call, a prayer, entreaty ME. † **4.** A formal authoritative summons –1483. **5.** † A proclamation –1837; the calling of wares for sale in the streets; the words in which wares are cried 1642. † **6.** Clamour, tumultuous noise, outcry –1440. **7.** Public report 1568; the public voice loudly uttered in approbation, denunciation, etc. 1628. **8.** An opinion generally expressed 1688. **9.** A watchword; a war-cry; a rallying-cry (*lit.* and *fig.*) 1548. **10.** A fit of weeping 1852. **11.** The vocal utterance of any animal; *e.g.* of wolves, of hounds in the chase, etc. ME. **12.** *transf.* A pack of hounds 1590. † **13.** A pack (*of* people). *contempt.* –1658. **14.** The noise emitted by tin, etc., when bent 1882.

1. 'Tis some mischance; the c. is very direful *Oth.* v. i. 38. A c. of triumph SHELLEY, of joy 1891. **2.** Natives..uttering loud cries 1839. The c. is still they come *Macb.* v. v. 2. **3.** Whoso stoppeth his ear at the c. of the poor *Prov.* 21:13. **5.** The six o'clock cries are not all over HT. MARTINEAU. *Hue and c.*: see HUE AND CRY. **7.** Why, the c. goes, that you marry her *Oth.* IV. i. 127. Vice will always have the C. of her side NORRIS. **9.** The C. of *Talbot* serues me for a Sword 1 *Hen. VI*, II. i. 79. The Tory election c...was 'the Church in danger' BREWSTER. **11.** *Full c.*: full pursuit; also *fig.* **12.** *Mids. N.* IV. i. 131. **13.** A crie of Players *Haml.* III. ii. 289.

Phrases. *Great* (or *much*) *c. and little wool*: the proverbial result of shearing hogs; hence, much noise about nothing. *A far c.*: a very long distance.

Cry (krəi), *v.* ME. [– (O)Fr. *crier* :– L. *quiritare* cry aloud, wail, orig., according to Varro, call upon the *Quirites*, or Roman citizens, for help.] **1.** *trans.* To entreat, beg, beseech, implore in a loud and excited voice. **2.** To call in supplication or reverential invocation (*on, upon, unto, to* a person) (*arch.*). Also *fig.* ME. **3.** *intr.* To utter the voice loudly and with effort; to call aloud *to*, shout, vociferate ME. **4.** *trans.* To utter or pronounce in a loud voice, to call out; *spec.* to shout (a war-cry, or the like) ME. **5.** To announce publicly; to proclaim; to appoint by proclamation ME.; to announce (a sale, things for sale); to sell by outcry ME.; to give public oral notice of (things lost or found) 1596; to proclaim the marriage banns of 1775. † **6.** To call for –1798. † **7.** To extol –1628. **8.** *intr.* To utter inarticulate exclamations; *esp.* to weep and wail ME. **9.** Hence, To shed tears 1532. **10.** Of an animal: To give forth a loud call or vocal sound ME.

1. To c. QUARTER, TRUCE; see these words. Þe Knyght..cryed iesu mercy LANGL. **2.** How he cride to mee for helpe *Wint. T.* III. iii. 97. *fig.* Sir, these Things c. loud for Reformation STEELE. **3.** The watermen do loudly c. and bawl 1684. **4.** What cryes the University CORBET. I..cried Mum, and she cride budget *Merry W.* v. v. 209. **5.** I will c. broom, or cat's-meat, in Palermo MASSINGER. *To c. stinking fish* Provb. [The strayes] to be..cryed in three markets adjoyning BACON. **8.** When the wounded crie *Ezek.* 26:15. An infant crying in the night: An infant crying for the light: And with no language but a cry

TENNYSON. **9.** And c. my selfe awake *Cymb.* III. iv. 46. **10.** Frogs crying..forewarne us of a tempest FULKE.

Phrases. *To c.* AIM, CRAVEN, HALVES, HAVOC, etc.: see these words. **C. against** —. To utter protests or reproofs against; also *fig.* of things. **C. for** —. To call for loudly, or with tears; *fig.* to be in pressing need of. **C. on, upon** —: see senses 2, 3. **C. back.** *intr. Hunting.* To hark back; *fig.* to revert to an ancestral type. **C. down. a.** *trans.* To proclaim as unlawful; to decry. **b.** To condemn loudly, vehemently, or publicly. **c.** To put down by louder or more vehement crying. **C. off.** *intr.* To announce one's withdrawal *from* a treaty, engagement, etc. **C. out.** To exclaim; (of things) to emit a creaking sound. **C. up.** *trans.* To extol; †*intr.* to shout.

C.-baby *colloq.*, one who cries childishly 1851.

†**Cryal.** 1565. [Origin unkn.] The Egret or Lesser White Heron –1755.

Cry·ing, *ppl. a.* ME. [f. CRY *v.* + -ING².] That cries; of evils: That calls loudly for redress; clamant.

A c. shame (1890). Hence **Cry·ingly** *adv.*

Cryogen (krəi·ŏdʒen). 1875. [f. Gr. κρύος frost + -GEN.] *Chem.* A freezing-mixture.

Cryohydrate (krəio,həi·drĕt). 1874. [f. as prec. + HYDRATE.] *Chem.* A solid hydrate formed by the combination of a crystalloid, as salt, with water (ice) at a temperature below freezing-point.

Cryolite (krəi·oləit). 1801. [f. as prec. + -LITE.] *Min.* A native fluoride of aluminium and sodium, found in white or brownish semi-transparent masses or crystals.

‖ **Cryophorus** (krəiǫ·fŏrŏs). 1826. [mod.L., f. as prec. + Gr. -φορος; see -PHORE, -PHOROUS.] An instrument for illustrating the freezing of water by evaporation; Wollaston's consists of a glass tube with a bulb at each end.

Crypt (kript), *sb.* ME. [– L. *crypta* – Gr. κρύπτη vault, subst. use of fem. of κρυπτός hidden.] † **1.** A grotto or cavern. (ME. only.) **2.** An underground cell, chamber, or vault; *esp.* one beneath the main floor of a church, used as a burial-place, chapel, or oratory 1789. **3.** *fig.* A hiding-place 1833. **4.** *Anat.* A small simple tubular or saccular gland; a secretory cavity; a follicle 1840.

2. The chancel..stood upon a large vault or c. BRAND. **3.** [The Ballot] is..the c. of political honesty A. FONBLANQUE.

‖ **Crypta** (kri·ptă). 1563. [L.; see prec.] † **1.** = CRYPT 1, 2. –1703. **2.** *Anat.* = CRYPT 4. 1860.

Cryptal (kri·ptăl), *a.* 1842. [f. L. *crypta* (see prec.) + -AL¹.] Of the nature of or pertaining to a crypt. So **Cry·ptous** (*rare*).

Crypted (kri·ptĕd), *a. rare.* 1885. [f. CRYPT + -ED².] Vaulted.

Cryptic (kri·ptik), *a.* (*sb.*) 1605. [– late L. *crypticus* – Gr. κρυπτικός, f. κρυπτός; see CRYPT, -IC.] **1.** Secret, occult, mystical 1638. **2.** Of the nature of a crypt (*rare*) 1878. † **3.** *sb.* An occult method. BACON.

1. [Nature's] silent processes and more cryptick methods 1663. So **Cry·ptical.** Hence **Cry·ptically** *adv.*

Crypto- (kri·pto, bef. a vowel **crypt-,** comb. f. Gr. κρυπτός hidden, secret.

1. In mod. scientific words: **Cry·ptobranch** (-bræŋk), an animal with concealed branchiæ or gills; **Cryptobra·nchiate** *a.*, having the gills concealed. **Cry·ptocarp** = CYSTOCARP; hence **Cryptoca·rpic, Cryptoca·rpous** *a.*, having the fruit or fruiting organs concealed. **Cryptoce·phalous** *a.*, having the head concealed. **Crypto·cerous** *a. Entom.*, having concealed antennæ. **Cryptocla·stic** *a. Min.*, having grains so minute as to conceal the fragmental character of the rock. **Cryptocry·stalline** *a. Min.*, having the crystalline structure concealed; so **Cryptocrystalliza·tion. Cryptodi·rous** *a.*, having a concealed or concealable neck, as some tortoises. **Cry·ptodont** *a.* or *sb.*, having the teeth concealed or suppressed, as certain palæozoic bivalve molluscs. **Cry·ptolite** *Min.*, native phosphate of cerium found enclosed in crystals of apatite. **Cryptoneu·rous** *a.*, having no discernible nervous system. **Cryptopenta·merous** *Entom.*, having one of the five joints of the tarsi minute or concealed. **Crypto·pia, Cryptopine** *Chem.*, an alkaloid found in opium. **Crypto·rchid** *Path.*, one whose scrotum contains no testicles; hence **-o·rchidism, -o·rchism. Crypto·zygous** *a.*, in Craniology, having the zygomatic arches not seen when the skull is viewed from above; hence **Cryptozygo·sity.**

2. Prefixed, **a.** to sbs. of any origin, as in **C.-Calvinist,** a name given in the 16th c. to Lutherans and Roman Catholics who secretly held Calvinistic tenets; hence **C.-Ca·lvinism, -Calvini·stic** *a.*; **b.** to adjs. = 'unavowedly', as in *c.-splenetic.*

Cryptogam (kri·ptogæm). 1847. [– Fr. *cryptogame* – mod.L. *cryptogamæ* (sc. *plantæ*), fem. pl. of *cryptogamus*, f. CRYPTO- + γάμος marriage; see -Æ.] *Bot.* A plant of the class Cryptogamia.

† **Cry·ptogame,** *a. rare.* [– Fr. *cryptogame*; see prec.] Breeding in secret. WHITE.

‖ **Cryptogamia** (kriptogæ·miă). 1753. [mod.L. (Linnæus), f. CRYPTO- + Gr. γάμος marriage + *-ia* -Y³.] *Bot.* A large division of the vegetable kingdom, being the last class in the Linnæan system, comprising those plants which have no stamens and pistils, and therefore no proper flowers; including Ferns, Mosses, Algæ, Lichens, and Fungi. ¶ Erron. treated as pl. = Cryptogams 1813. Hence **Cryptoga·mian** *a.*, **Cryptoga·mic** *a.* (also as *sb.*), **-ga·mical** *a.* of or pertaining to the class Cryptogamia or to cryptogams; **Crypto·gamist,** a botanist who studies cryptogams; **Crypto·gamous** *a.* of the nature of a cryptogam; **Crypto·gamy,** cryptogamic condition or relations.

Cryptogram (kri·ptŏgræm). 1880. [f. CRYPTO- + -GRAM.] Anything written in cipher.

Cryptograph (kri·ptograf). 1849. [f. as prec. + -GRAPH.] **1.** = CRYPTOGRAM. **2.** A kind of type-writer for writing in cipher 1889. Hence † **Cryptogra·phal** *a.*, **Cryptogra·phic** *a.* of, or of the nature of, cryptography; † **Cryptogra·phical** *a.* dealing or concerned with cryptography; **Crypto·grapher, Crypto·graphist,** one who writes in cipher.

Cryptography (kriptǫ·grăfi). 1658. [– mod.L. *cryptographia*; see CRYPTO-, -GRAPHY.] A secret manner of writing intelligible only to those possessing the key; anything written in this way.

Cryptology (kriptǫ·lŏdʒi). 1645. [– mod.L. *cryptologia*; see CRYPTO-, -LOGY.] 'Secret speech or communication' (Blount); enigmatical language.

Cryptonym (kri·ptonim). *rare.* 1876. [f. CRYPTO- after ANONYM.] A private or secret name. So **Crypto·nymous** *a.*

‖ **Cryptoporticus** (kriptopǭ·ɹtikŏs). 1681. [L., f. as CRYPTO- + *porticus* gallery.] *Ancient Arch.* An enclosed gallery having, at the side, walls with openings instead of columns; also a covered or subterranean passage.

Crystal (kri·stăl). OE. [– (O)Fr. *cristal* – L. *crystallum* – Gr. κρύσταλλος ice.]

A. *sb.* † **1.** Ice, clear ice –1535. **2.** A mineral, clear and transparent like ice; *esp.* a form of quartz, now distinguished as *Rock-crystal* OE. Also *transf.* **3.** A piece of rock-crystal or similar mineral; *esp.* one used in magic art ME. Also *fig.* of the eyes 1592. **4.** Short for *crystal-glass*: a quality of glass of high transparency; also often a synonym for fine cut glass. [Ger. *krystallglas.*] 1594. **5.** Anything made of this glass; *esp.* the glass of a watch-case. Also *fig.* 1613. **6.** *Chem.* and *Min.* A form in which molecules regularly aggregate by the operation of molecular affinity: it has a definite internal structure, with the external form of a solid enclosed by a number of symmetrically arranged plane faces 1626. **b.** *Crystals*: *pl.* A quality of refined crystallized sugar 1875. **7.** *Wireless.* A mineral used in 'rectifying' an oscillatory current. Comb. *c. receiver, set* 1913.

1. He sendis his kristall as morcels HAMPOLE. **2.** A sea of glasse like vnto Chrystall *Rev.* 4:6. *Iceland c.* = Iceland spar. **3.** *fig.* Her eye seene in the teares, teares in her eye, Both cristals *Ven. & Ad.* 963. **4.** Eyeing the plate and c. THACKERAY.

B. *attrib.* and *adj.* Composed of crystal; clear and transparent, like crystal ME.

2. Her crystall eyes full of lowlenes HAWES.

Hence **Cry·stal** *v.* to make into c.; to crystallize. **Crysta·llic** *a.* pertaining to crystals or their formation. **Crystalli·ferous** *a.* containing or yielding crystals. **Crysta·lliform** *a.* having the form of a c. **Crystalli·gerous** *a.* bearing a c. or crystals.

Crystallin (kri·stălin). 1847. [f. L. *crystallum* + -IN¹.] *Chem.* An albuminoid substance contained in the crystalline lens of the eye.

Crystalline (kri·stălin, -ləin). ME. [– (O)Fr. *cristallin* – L. *crystallinus* – Gr. κρυστάλλινος; see -INE¹. Milton and others use (kristæ·lin), after L.]

A. *adj.* **1.** Consisting, or made, of crystal 1509. **2.** Clear and transparent like crystal ME. Also *fig.* **3.** Of the nature or structure of a crystal 1612. **4.** Of or pertaining to crystals and their formation 1866.

1. Cristallyne cuppes EDEN. **2.** Nor did the dancing ruby..Allure thee from the cool c. stream MILT. **3.** The c. grains are scarcely discernible KIRWAN.

Phr. *C. heaven* (*sphere, circle*): in the Ptolemaic astronomical system, a sphere (later two spheres) supposed to exist between the primum mobile and the firmament, by means of which the precession of the equinox and the motion of libration were accounted for. *C. lens* (formerly *humour*): a transparent body enclosed in a membranous capsule, situated immediately behind the iris of the eye.

B. *sb.* [the adj. used ellipt.] **1.** The crystalline heaven; see above (*arch.*) ME. **2.** The crystalline lens or humour; see above 1657. **3.** A crystal. E. B. BROWNING. † **4.** = ANILINE 1838.

Crystallite (kri·stăləit). 1805. [f. CRYSTAL + -ITE¹ 2 b.] *Min.* † **1.** A name applied to the somewhat crystalline form and structure taken by igneous rocks, lavas, etc., upon fusion and slow cooling –1852. **2.** = MICROLITE 1878.

Crystallization (kri:stăləizē¹·ʃən). 1665. [f. CRYSTALLIZE + -ATION.] **1.** The action of forming crystals, or of assuming a crystalline structure. Also *fig.* **2.** *concr.* A crystallized formation or body 1695.

1. *fig.* All systems tend to a certain..c. HELPS.

Crystallize (kri·stăləiz), *v.* 1598. [f. CRYSTAL + -IZE.] † **1.** *trans.* To make into or like crystal –1798. **2.** To cause to assume a crystalline form, to form into crystals 1664. **3.** *fig.* To give a definite or concrete form to 1663. **4.** *intr.* To become crystalline in structure 1641. Also *fig.*

3. The forms of Action..as crystallized in the law 1875. Hence **Cry·stalli:zable** *a.* **Cry·stallizer.**

Crystallo-, comb. f. Gr. κρύσταλλος crystal: **C.-cera·mic** *a.* pertaining to a method of encrusting a medallion of clay with glass; **-engrav·ing,** a method of making intaglio designs upon glass by means of casting; **-magne·tic** *a.* pertaining to the magnetic properties of crystals and crystallized bodies.

Crystallod; see OD² b.

Crystalloge·nesis. 1879. [f. CRYSTALLO- + -GENESIS.] The natural formation of crystals (as a department of science). So **Crystalloge·nic** *a.* crystal-forming. **Crystalloge·nical** *a.* relating to the formation of crystals. **Crystallo·geny,** the formation of crystals (as a subject).

Crystallography (kristălǫ·grăfi). 1802. [f. as prec. + -GRAPHY; cf. mod.L. *crystallographia* (1723), Fr. *cristallographie* (1772).] The scientific treatment and classification of crystals; a treatise on this subject.

Dr. Wollaston..almost the originator of the science of c. 1861. Hence **Crystallo·grapher,** one who studies c. **Cry:stallograp·hic, -al** *a.* of or pertaining to c.: of or belonging to crystals (as scientifically treated). **Crystallogra·phically** *adv.*

† **Crysta·llogy.** *rare.* 1811. [irreg. f. CRYSTALLO- + -LOGY.] = prec. Hence † **Crysta·llogist.**

Crystalloid (kri·stăloid). 1861. [f. CRYSTAL + -OID.]

A. *adj.* Crystal-like; *esp.* as opp. to *colloid* 1862.

B. *sb.* **1.** A crystalloid or crystalline body or substance, as dist. from a COLLOID 1861. **2.** A protoplasmic body resembling a crystal in form, occurring in certain vegetable cells 1875. Hence **Crystalloi·dal** *a.*

Crystallology (kristălǫ·lŏdʒi). 1864. [f. CRYSTALLO- + -LOGY.] The scientific study of crystals and crystallization.

Crystallomancy (kri·stălomæ:nsi). 1613. [f. as prec. + -MANCY.] Divination by means of a crystal.

Crystallometry (kristălǫ·mĕtri). 1837. [f. as prec. + -METRY.] The measuring of the angles of crystals, as a part of crystallography.

‖ **Ctenidium** (tĭni·diŏm). 1883. [mod.L. – Gr. κτενίδιον, dim. of κτεν- (κτείς) a comb.]

Zool. Each of the respiratory organs or gills of *Mollusca*, consisting of an axis with comb-like processes on each side. Hence **Cteni·dial** *a.* of or pertaining to a c.

Cteno-, comb. f. Gr. κτείς, κτενός a comb: **Ctenobranch,** a ctenobranchiate animal; **Ctenobra·nchia, -branchia·ta,** a family of Mollusca, also called *Pectinibranchiata*; **Ctenobra·nchiate** *a.* having pectinate gills. **Cte·nodont** *a.* having ctenoid teeth.

Ctenocyst (tī·nosist). 1861. [f. *cteno-* (used as abbr. of CTENOPHORA) + CYST.] *Zool.* The vesicle which constitutes the organ of sense (probably of hearing) in the *Ctenophora*.

Ctenoid (tī·noid), *a.* 1847. [f. CTENO- + -OID.] **1.** Having marginal projections like the teeth of a comb; pectinate; as the scales and teeth of certain fishes 1872. **2.** Belonging to the *Ctenoidei*, an order of fishes in Agassiz's classification, containing those with ctenoid scales. Also as *sb.* A ctenoid fish. (Now disused.) Hence **Ctenoi·dean** *a.* and *sb.* = CTENOID 2.

‖ **Ctenophora** (tinǫ·fŏră), *sb. pl.* 1855. [mod.L., n. pl. (sc. *animalia*) of *ctenophorus*; see CTENO-, -PHORE, -A 4.] *Zool.* A division of animals, formerly considered as an order of *Acalepha*, and now made a class of CŒLENTERATA. Hence **Cteno·phoral** *a.* of or pertaining to the C. **Cteno·phoran** *a.* of or belonging to the class C.; *sb.* a member of this class. **Cte·nophore** (tī·nofoᵊɹ), **a.** each of the eight meridionally arranged bands, bearing comb-like fringes, which are the locomotive organs of the Ctenophora; **b.** a Ctenophoran. **Ctenopho·ric, Cteno·phorous** *a.*

Cub (kɒb), *sb.*[1] 1530. [Origin unkn.] **1.** *orig.* A young fox. **2.** Hence: The young of the bear, lion, etc.; also of the whale 1596. Also *transf.* **b.** A junior member of the Boy Scouts 1922. **3.** *fig.* An awkward, unformed youth 1601.

2. Plucke the yong sucking Cubs from the she Beare *Merch. V.* II. i. 29. **3.** Like a bashful, great, awkward c. as you were STEELE. *Comb.*: † **c.-drawn** *a.*, drawn (or ? sucked dry) by its cubs; **-hunting,** hunting young foxes at the beginning of the season. Hence **Cu·bbing** *vbl. sb.* cub-hunting. **Cu·bbish** *a.* **Cu·bhood,** the state or condition of a c.

Cub (kɒb), *sb.*[2] Chiefly *dial.* 1546. [prob. of LG. origin; cf. EFris. *kübbing, kübben* in same sense, LG. *kübbing, kübje* shed or lean-to for cattle; cf. COVE *sb.*[1]] A stall, pen, or shed for cattle; also, a coop or hutch. **b.** A crib for fodder.

Cub (kɒb), *v.*[1] 1755. [f. CUB *sb.*[1] Cf. *whelp* vb.] To bring forth cubs (*trans.* and *intr.*).

Cub (kɒb), *v.*[2] Now *dial.* 1621. [f. CUB *sb.*[2]] To coop *up*.

Cuba (kiū·bă). 1837. [An island in the W. Indies, also called Havana.] A cigar made of tobacco grown in Cuba.

Cubage (kiū·bėdʒ). 1840. [f. CUBE *sb.* or *v.* + -AGE; cf. Fr. *cubage*.] Cubature; cubic content.

Cubation (kiubēⁱ·ʃən). *rare.* 1727. [f. CUBE *v.* + -ATION.] = CUBATURE.

Cubature (kiū·bătiŭɹ). 1679. [f. CUBE *v.* after *quadrature*; cf. (later) Fr. *cubature* (XVIII).] The determination of the cubic content of a solid.

† **Cu·bbridge head.** 1622. [Origin unkn.] *Naut.* A bulkhead across the forecastle and the half-deck of a ship –1642.

Cubby (kɒ·bi). *local.* 1842. [Related to CUB *sb.*[2]] **1.** = *Cubby-hole, -house* 1887. **2.** In Orkney, etc.: A straw basket. Hence **c.-hole, -house,** a snug place; also a closet.

Cube (kiūb), *sb.* 1551. [–(O)Fr. *cube* or L. *cubus* (Vitruvius) – Gr. κύβος cube.] **1.** *Geom.* A solid figure contained by six equal squares; a regular hexahedron. **2.** *Arith.* and *Alg.* The third power *of* a quantity 1557. **3.** *attrib.* (= CUBIC *a.* 2), and in *comb.*, as **c.-ore** = PHARMACOSIDERITE; **-root,** that number of which the given number is the c.; **-spar** = ANHYDRITE. **b.** *Occas.* as in 6 *feet c.* = of cubical form, and measuring 6 ft. in each direction.

Cube (kiūb), *v.* 1588. [prob. – Fr. *cuber* or mod.L. *cubare*, f. *cubus* CUBE *sb.*] **1.** *Arith.* and *Alg.* To raise to the third power. **2.** *Mensuration.* To determine the cubic content of 1668.

Cubeb (kiū·beb). ME. [–(O)Fr. *cubèbe*, †*quibibe* (med.L. *cubeba, quibiba*):– Rom. **cubeba* – Arab. *kobāba, kubāba*.] The berry of a climbing shrub *Piper cubeba* or *Cubeba officinalis*, a native of Java; it resembles a grain of pepper, and has a pungent spicy flavour, and is used in medicine and cookery. (Usually in pl. *cubebs*.) Also *attrib.* Hence **Cube·bene,** the chief constituent of oil of cubebs; **Cube·bic acid,** a resinous acid obtained from cubebs; **Cube·bin,** a crystalline substance existing in cubebs.

Cubi- (kiū·bi), bef. a vowel **cub-** (kiūb), comb. f. L. *cubus* CUBE, now denoting 'of the third degree, cubic', as *c.-cone*, etc.

Cubic (kiū·bik). 1551. [–(O)Fr. *cubique* or L. *cubicus* – Gr. κυβικός; see CUBE, -IC.]

A. *adj.* **1.** Of the form of a cube; cubical. **b.** *Crystallography.* = ISOMETRIC, as the *c. system* 1878. **2.** *Mensuration.* Of three dimensions; solid; *esp.* used to express the content of a cube whose edge is a given unit, as a *c. foot* 1660. **3.** *Arith., Alg.*, etc. Relating to or involving the cube; of three dimensions, of the third degree, as †*c. number* = CUBE number; *c. equation*, an equation of the third degree; *c. curve*, a curve represented by a c. equation.

B. *sb.* (the adj. used ellipt.) *Math.* A cubic expression or equation; a cubic curve.

Cubica (kiū·bikă). 1835. [Sp.] A very fine unglazed shalloon.

Cubical (kiū·bikăl), *a.* 1571. [f. CUBIC + -AL[1]; see -ICAL.] **1.** Of or pertaining to a cube; cube-shaped. (Now more usual than *cubic*.) 1592. **2.** *Mensuration.* = CUBIC *a.* 2. (Now less common than *cubic*.) 1571. **3.** *Arith., Alg.*, etc. = CUBIC *a.* 3. *Obs.* exc. in *c. parabola, hyperbola*, etc. Hence **Cu·bically** *adv.* **Cu·bicalness** (*rare*).

Cubicle (kiū·bik'l). 1483. [– L. *cubiculum*, f. *cubare* recline, lie in bed. See -CULE.] A bedchamber; in mod. use, one of a series of small separate sleeping chambers, as dist. from an undivided dormitory. So † **Cubi·cular** *sb.* an attendant in a bedchamber. **Cubi·cular** *a.* of or belonging to a bedchamber.

‖ **Cubiculum** (kiubi·kiŭlɒ̆m). Pl. **-a.** 1832. [L.; see prec.] A sleeping-chamber. In *Archæol.*, a burial-chamber in the Catacombs; also, a chapel or oratory attached to a church. var. ‖ **Cubi·culo.** *Twel. N.* III. ii. 56.

Cubit (kiū·bit). ME. [– L. *cubitum* elbow, etc.] † **1.** The forearm. **b.** The ulna, one of the two bones of the forearm. –1847. **c.** *Entom.* One of the veins or ribs of an insect's wing 1774. **2.** An ancient measure of land derived from the forearm; usually about 18–22 inches. Now *Hist.* ME. Also *attrib.*

Cubital (kiū·bităl), *a.* ME. [– L. *cubitalis*, f. *cubitus* CUBIT; see -AL[1].] **1.** Of the length of a cubit. **2.** *Anat.* Pertaining to the CUBIT (sense 1) 1611.

Cubito- (kiū·bito), used as comb. f. L. *cubitus*, in sense 'relating to the ulna and ——', as *c.-carpal, -digital, -radial*, etc.

Cubo- (kiū·bo), bef. a vowel sometimes **cub-** (kiūb), comb. f. Gr. κύβος die, CUBE:

† **cubo-cube** [Gr. κυβόκυβος], the sixth power of a quantity; so † **-cu·bic**; † **-cubocube,** the ninth power; **-cu·neiform** (*Anat.*), relating to the cuboid and cuneiform bones; also in *Solid Geom.*, etc., denoting a solid which combines the forms of a cube and another solid, as **cubo-octahe·dron** (*cuboctahedron*), a solid of fourteen faces formed by cutting off the corners of a cube, so as to add eight triangular faces corresponding to those of an octahedron; so **cubo-octahe·dral** *a.*, **cubo-dodecahe·dron, -al.**

Cuboid (kiū·boid). 1829. [– mod.L. *cuboides* – Gr. κυβοειδής; see CUBO-, -OID.] *adj.* Resembling, or approximating to the form of, a cube, as the *c. bone* of the foot, between the calcaneum and the fourth and fifth metatarsal bones. *sb. Anat.* Short for *c. bone*; see prec. 1839. Hence **Cuboi·dal** *a.* cuboid; in *Anat.*, of or belonging to the c. bone.

Cuca, Cucaine, etc., vars. of COCA, etc.

† **Cuck,** *v.*[1] ME. [– ON. (mod.Icel.) **kúka*, rel. to *kúkr* excrement.] *intr.* To void excrement –1606.

† **Cuck,** *v.*[2] 1611. [Back-formation from next.] *trans.* To set in the cucking-stool –1648.

Cucking-stool (kɒ·kiŋ-stūl). *Hist.* ME. [f. CUCK *v.*[1] + STOOL.] A chair (sometimes in the form of a close-stool), formerly in use for scolds, disorderly women, fraudulent tradespeople, etc., in which the offender was fastened and exposed to the jeers of the bystanders, or conveyed to a pond or river and ducked.

She..shall..be placed in a certain engine of correction called the trebucket, castigatory, or cucking stool..now it is frequently corrupted into ducking stool BLACKSTONE.

Cuckold (kɒ·kəld), *sb.* [ME. *cukeweld, cokewold* (3 syllables) – AFr. **cucuald*, var. of OFr. *cucuault* (XV), f. *cucu* CUCKOO + pejorative suffix *-ald, -aud, -ault*.] **1.** The husband of an unfaithful wife. *derisory.* Also *attrib.* **2.** The American cow-bird, *Molothrus ater.* **3.** Short for *Cuckold-fish*.

Comb.: † **c.-fish,** a fish with horn-like projections, prob. the cow-fish (*Ostracion quadricorne*); **-maker; -knot, neck,** a knot or loop made in a rope by crossing it over itself and binding it together with a cord at the point of crossing.

Hence **Cu·ckold** *v.* to make a c. of; said of a paramour, and of a wife. † **Cu·ckoldize** *v. trans.* to make a c. (*rare*). † **Cu·ckoldly** *a.* having the qualities of a c.; often a mere term of abuse. **Cu·ckoldom,** the state or position of a c.; cuckoldry. **Cu·ckoldry,** the making a c. of a husband; †the position of a c. **Cu·ckoldy** *a. arch.* = *cuckoldly*.

Cuckoo (ku·kū), *sb.* ME. [– OFr. *cucu* (mod. *coucou*), of imit. origin; cf. L. *cuculus*, Gr. κόκκυξ. Superseded OE. *ġeac* (see GOWK).] **1.** A bird, *Cuculus canorus*, well known by the call of the male during mating time. It is a migratory bird, and does not hatch its own offspring, but deposits its eggs in the nests of other birds. **b.** The family name of the *Cuculidæ*, including various genera and species 1797. **2.** The note of the bird, or an imitation of it ME. **3.** = Fool, 'gowk' 1596. **4.** (Usu. in *pl.*) A local name of several spring flowers 1878. **5.** A species of fish; also called *c.-fish, -wrasse*, etc. (*local*) 1848. **6.** *attrib.* Of or pertaining to the cuckoo; resembling the cuckoo and its uniformly repeated call 1650.

1. The merry Cuckow, messenger of Spring SPENSER. **2.** Cuckow, Cuckow: O word of feare *L.L.L.* V. ii. 911. **3.** The c. I travel with..he also has his uses SCOTT. **6.** The c. note..of 'the Bill, the whole Bill, and nothing but the Bill' 1831.

Comb.: **c.-bee,** a genus of bees which deposit their eggs in the nests of other bees; **c.('s) bread,** the Wood-sorrel; also the Lady's Smock; **-dove,** a genus of doves of the East Indies and Australia; **-fish:** see sense 5; also the boar-fish; **c.('s) fool, maid(en, mate,** the Wryneck, which arrives with the c.; **-orchis,** *Orchis mascula*; **-point** = CUCKOO-PINT; **-ray,** a fish, a species of ray; **-wrasse:** see sense 5.

Cuckoo (ku·kū), *v.* 1620. [f. prec.] **1.** *intr.* To utter the call of the cuckoo. **2.** *trans.* To repeat incessantly 1648.

Cuckoo-bud. 1588. A name of some plant; in Shaks., the buttercup, marsh-marigold, or cowslip.

Cu·ckoo-flow:er. 1578. A name of various spring wild flowers; as the Lady's Smock (*Cardamine pratensis*), the Ragged Robin, etc.

Cu·ckoo-fly. 1868. A name of species of hymenopterous insects belonging to the *Ichneumonidæ* and *Chrysididæ*, which deposit their eggs in the larvæ or nests of other insects.

Cuckoo-pint (ku·kupi:nt). 1551. [Short f. next.] The wild Arum, *A. maculatum*.

† **Cu·ckoo-pi:ntle.** 1450. [See PINTLE. From the form of the spadix.] = prec. –1682.

Cuckoo's meat, cuckoo-meat. 1516. Wood-sorrel, *Oxalis acetosella*; also called *gowk's-meat*.

Cu·ckoo-spi:t. 1592. [f. SPIT *sb.*[2], expectoration.] **1.** A frothy secretion exuded by the Frog-hopper and other insects, in which their larvæ lie enveloped on the leaves, axils, etc., of plants. **2.** The Lady's Smock (*local*) 1876.

Cu·ckoo-spi:ttle. 1646. = prec. (sense 1).

† **Cu·ckquean,** *sb.* 1562. [f. stem of *cuckold* + QUEAN.] A female cuckold –1652. Hence † **Cu·ckquean** *v.* to make a c. of.

† **Cuck-stool.** ME. var. of CUCKING-STOOL –1794.

Cucu·liform, *a. rare.* [f. L. *cuculus* + -FORM.] Cuckoo-like in form or structure.

Cu·culine, *a.* [f. as prec. + -INE[1].] Pertaining or related to the cuckoo.

Cucullate (kiū·kɒlĕt, kiukɒ·lĕt), *a.* 1794. [– late L. *cucullatus*, f. *cucullus* hood; see -ATE[2].] Hooded; shaped like a hood or cowl. So **Cu·cullated** *ppl. a.* (in same sense).

† **Cucu·lle.** ME. [– Fr. *cuculle* or its source L. *cucullus.*] A hood or cowl of a monk –1677.

Cuculliform (kiukɒ·lifǭɹm), *a.* 1835. [f. as prec. + -FORM.] Cowl-shaped, hood-shaped.

Cucumber (kiū·kɒmbəɹ). [Late ME. *cucumer* (– L.) was superseded by *cucumber* (XV), †*cocomber* by assim. to OFr. *co(u)combre* (mod. *concombre*) – L. *cucumer, cucumis* (-*er*-). The pronunc. of the first syll. has been infl. by the sp.; the development *cowcumber* (XVI) is still preserved in illiterate speech.] **1.** A creeping plant, *Cucumis sativus* (N.O. *Cucurbitaceæ*), long cultivated for its fruit. **2.** The fruit of this plant, commonly eaten as a salad, or pickled when young (see GHERKIN) ME. **3.** Applied to other plants allied to or resembling the common cucumber: as **Bitter C.,** the Colocynth, *Citrullus colocynthis*; **Indian C.** = *c.-root* (see below); **One-seeded, single-seeded,** or **Star C.,** the genus *Sicyos*; **Serpent** or **Snake C.,** *Trichosanthes colubrina* and *T. anguina*, also *Cucumis flexuosus* (from the appearance of the fruit); **Spirting** or **Squirting C.,** *Ecbalium agreste* (formerly called *Momordica elaterium*), the fruit of which when ripe separates from the stalk, and expels the seeds and pulp with force. Also *attrib.*

1. The cowcumber loveth water 1584. **2.** Phr. *Cool* (†*cold*) *as a c.*: perfectly self-possessed; showing no excitement. *Comb.*: **c.-root,** (*a*) the root of the c.; (*b*) the plant *Medeola virginica* (N.O. *Trilliaceæ*), from the taste of its rhizomes; **-tree,** (*a*) *Magnolia acuminata* and other American species, the fruits of which resemble small cucumbers; (*b*) *Averrhoa bilimbi*, an East Indian tree with an acid fruit resembling a small c.

†‖ **Cu·cupha.** 1656. [med.L.; a deriv. or reduplicated form of *cufa, cufia* COIF.] A cap with spices quilted in it, worn for certain nervous disorders in the head –1665.

† **Cucurbit**[1] (kiukɒ̄·ɹbit). ME. [– (O)Fr. *cucurbite* – L. *cucurbita* gourd, cupping-glass (whence sense 2).] **1.** A vessel or retort, originally gourd-shaped; forming the lower part of an alembic –1823. **2.** A cupping-glass 1541.

Cucurbit[2]. 1866. [– L. *cucurbita* gourd.] A cucurbitaceous plant; a gourd.

Cucurbitaceous (kiukɒ̄ɹbitē[i]·ʃəs), *a.* 1853. [f. mod.L. *Cucurbitaceæ*, f. *cucurbita* gourd; see -ACEOUS.] *Bot.* Belonging to the N.O. *Cucurbitaceæ*, comprising trailing or climbing plants with fleshy fruits, as the Gourd, Cucumber, Melon, etc.

Cucurbital (kiukɒ̄·ɹbităl), *a.* [f. L. *cucurbita* gourd + -AL[1].] *Bot.* Epithet of Lindley's alliance, including the *Cucurbitaceæ* and allied orders.

Cucurbitine (kiukɒ̄·ɹbitəin, -in), *a.* 1843. [f. as prec. + -INE[1].] Gourd-like: applied to a tapeworm, from the resemblance of each segment to the seed of a gourd. var. (erron.) † **Cucurbitive.**

‖ **Cucuy, cucuyo** (kukū·i, kukū·yo). Also erron. **cucullo.** 1591. [Sp. *cucuyo* – Haitian.] The West Indian firefly (*Pyrophorus noctilucus*).

Cud (kɒd), *sb.* [OE. *cudu*, earlier *cwudu, cwidu* what is chewed, mastic, corresp. to OHG. *quiti, kuti* glue (G. *kitt* cement, putty).] **1.** The food which a ruminating animal brings back into its mouth from its first stomach, and chews at leisure. **2.** Any substance used by men to keep in the mouth and chew. Now a dial. form of QUID *sb.*[3] OE.

1. Phr. *To chew the c.* (fig.): to recall and reflect on things past; to ruminate.

Cudbear (kɒ·dbē[ə]ɹ). 1766. [f. var. *Cudber(t)* of the Christian name of Dr. *Cuthbert* Gordon, who patented the powder. Cf. CUDDY[3].] **1.** A purple or violet powder, used for dyeing, prepared from various species of lichens, esp. *Lecanora tartarea* 1771. **2.** The lichen *Lecanora tartarea.*

Cudden (kɒ·d'n). 1673. † **1.** A born fool –1719. **2.** *local.* The coal-fish [Gael. *cudainn*] 1836.

1. The slavering c., propped upon his staff DRYDEN.

Cuddle (kɒ·d'l), *v.* 1520. [perh. f. dial. COUTH 5 + -LE; cf. *fondle* (f. *fond*). But cf. CULL *v.*[2], dial. var. of COLL *v.*[1]] **1.** *trans.* To hug affectionately, to fondle; also *absol.* **2.** *intr.* To lie close and snug 1711; to curl oneself up in going to sleep 1822. Also *fig.*

2. She [a partridge] cuddles low behind the brake M. PRIOR. **Cu·ddle** *sb.* **Cu·ddlesome, Cu·ddly** *adjs.*

Cuddy[1], **cudeigh.** 1450. [Corruption of Irish *cuid oidhche*, lit. 'evening portion'.] *Irel.* and *Scotl.* **1.** *orig.* A supper and night's entertainment due to the lord from his tenant (*Hist.*). **2.** Hence, a rent or present in lieu of this; a douceur, a bribe (*Hist.*) 15...

Cuddy[2] (kɒ·di). 1660. [prob. – early mod. Du. *kajute, kaiuyte* (now *kajuit*, whence Fr. *cajute*) – (O)Fr. *cahute* shanty, of unkn. origin.] **1.** *Naut.* A room or cabin in a large ship abaft and under the round-house. **2.** A small room, closet, or cupboard 1793. Also *attrib.*

Cuddy[3] (kɒ·di). Chiefly *Sc.* 1714. [perh. a use of *Cuddy* (XVI), pet form of *Cuthbert* (cf. CUDBEAR); cf. *dicky, neddy.*] **1.** A donkey. Also *fig.* **2.** = CUDDEN 2. 1775. **3.** *local.* The hedge-sparrow; also the moor-hen 1802. **4.** *Mech.* A lever mounted on a tripod for lifting stones, etc. 1852.

Cudgel (kɒ·dʒĕl), *sb.* [OE. *cyćgel*, of unkn. origin; for the phonetic development cf. BLUSH.] A short thick stick used as a weapon; a club. **b.** in *pl.* = CUDGEL-PLAY 1630. Also *fig.*

This deponent had a lytell cogell 1566. Phr. *To take up the cudgels* (fig.): to engage in a vigorous contest or debate (*for, in behalf of*, etc.). † *To cross the cudgels* (fig.): to forbear the contest. *Comb.*: **c.-play,** the art of combat with cudgels; a contest with cudgels; hence **-pla:yer, -play:ing.**

Cu·dgel, *v.* 1596. [f. prec.] **1.** To beat with a cudgel. **2.** *intr.* To play cudgels *for* 1840.

1. *fig.* Cudgell thy brains no more about it *Haml.* V. i. 63. Hence **Cu·dgelled** *ppl. a.* **Cu·dgeller.**

† **Cuds.** 1599. = CODS –1711.

Cudweed (kɒ·dwīd). 1548. [f. CUD *sb.*: the plant being administered to cattle that had lost their cud.] The genus *Gnaphalium* of composite plants, having chaffy scales surrounding the flower-heads: originally proper to *G. sylvaticum*; extended to allied or similar plants.

† **Cu·dwort.** 1548. = prec. –1725.

Cue (kiū), *sb.*[1] ME. **1.** The name of the letter Q, q.v. 1755. † **2.** The sum of half a farthing, formerly denoted in College accounts by the letter *q* (orig. for *quadrans*); hence *transf.* a small quantity of bread, or of beer –1831.

2. Hast thou worn Gowns in the university..ate cues, drunk cees? 1605.

Cue (kiū), *sb.*[2] 1553. [XVI (*q, qu, quew, kew, cue*). Of unkn. origin; the supposition that it is a use of Fr. *queue* tail, is not based on evidence.] **1.** *Theatr.* The concluding word or words of a speech in a play, serving as a signal to another actor to enter, or begin his speech. **b.** *Mus.* A few notes of some other part immediately preceding his own, printed as a guide to a singer or player to come in at the right time after a long rest 1880. **2.** *fig.* A sign or intimation when to speak or act; a hint 1565. **3.** The part assigned one to play; the proper course to take 1581. **4.** Humour, frame of mind, etc. (proper to any action) 1565.

1. Curst be thy stones for thus deceiuing mee.. *Deceiuing me* is Thisbies c.; she is to enter *Mids. N.* V. i. 186. **3.** Pat: he comes..my C. is villanous Melancholly *Lear* I. ii. 147. Hence **Cue** *v.*[1] *trans.* (*a*) to give a cue to as in performing a play; to prompt; (*b*) *Mus.* to insert notes as a cue; usu. with *in.*

Cue (kiū), *sb.*[3] 1731. [var. of QUEUE.] **1.** = QUEUE *sb.* 2. **2.** The straight tapering rod with which the balls are struck in billiards 1749. **Cue** *v.*[2] *trans.* to form into a c.; to furnish with a c. **Cue·ist,** a billiard-player. **Cue·less** *a.* without a pigtail.

Cue·-owl. 1855. [– It. *chiù, ciù*, from the sound of its cry.] The Scops-owl (*Scops giu*).

The Cue-owls speak the name we call them by BROWNING.

†‖ **Cuerpo.** 1625. [Sp. :– L. *corpus.*] Only in *in c.*: without the cloak, so as to show the shape of the body; also *fig.* –1748.

Boy: my Cloake and Rapier; it fits not a Gentleman of my ranck to walk the streets in *Querpo* FLETCHER.

Cuff (kɒf), *sb.*[1] [Of unkn. origin.] † **1.** A mitten or glove –1467. **2.** An ornamental part at the bottom of a sleeve, as a fold of the sleeve itself turned back, a band of linen, lace, etc., sewed on, or the like; also, the corresponding part of a shirt-sleeve, or a separate band of linen, etc., worn round the wrist and under the sleeve 1522. **3.** A HANDCUFF 1663.

2. She laid her hand upon the c. of my coat STERNE.

Cuff (kɒf), *sb.*[2] 1570. [f. CUFF *v.*[1]] A blow; *esp.* a blow with the open hand.

This mad-brain'd bridegroome tooke him suche a cuffe, That downe fell Priest and booke *Tam. Shr.* III. ii. 165. Phr. *At cuffs*: at blows, fighting.

Cuff, *sb.*[3] 1740. Var. (orig. Sc.) of SCUFF, SCRUFF, in *C. of the neck.*

Cuff (kɒf), *v.*[1] 1530. [perh. imit. of the sound; cf. G. slang *kuffen* thrash, Sw. *kuffa* thrust, push.] **1.** *trans.* To strike with the open hand; to strike, buffet. **2.** *absol.* or *intr.* To deal blows; to scuffle 1611.

1. Prieste..I meane..to cuffe you soundly 1 *Hen. VI*, I. iii. 48. Their opposites with beake and tallons rend; Cuffe with their wings G. SANDYS. Hence **Cu·ffer,** a boxer; †the fist (*joc.*).

Cuff (kɒf), *v.*[2] *rare.* 1693. [f. CUFF *sb.*[1]] To put cuffs on; to handcuff.

Cuffin (kɒ·fin). *Thieves' cant.* 1567. [Also *cuff* (XVII–XVIII); cf. CHUFF *sb.*[1]] = COVE *sb.*[2]

Cufic (kiū·fik), *a.* Also **Cuphic, Kufic.** 1706. [f. *Kūfa*, a city in Irak founded in 638 A.D. + -IC.] Of or pertaining to Cufa; applied to a variety of Arabic writing.

‖ **Cui bono** (kəi bō[u]·no). 1604. A Latin phrase, meaning 'To whom for a benefit', *i.e.* 'Who profits by it?' erron. taken in English to mean 'To what good purpose'; hence, occas. *subst.* Practical utility as a principle. As *adj.* or *attrib.* Relating to the question *cui bono?*; *occas.* = utilitarian.

Cuinage, cuynage, obs. ff. COINAGE. As applied to tin it means the official stamping of the blocks.

Cuirass (kwiræ·s, kiuræ·s), *sb.* 1464. [Late ME. *quyras, curas, curace* – OFr. *cuirace* (XIII), later †*curas*, †-*ace* (mod. *cuirasse*), for **coirace* – Rom. **coriacea* (subst. use of fem. of L. *coriaceus*, f. *corium* leather: see -ACEOUS), infl. by *cuir.*] **1.** A piece of armour for the body (originally of leather); *spec.* a piece reaching down to the waist, and consisting of a breast-plate and a back-plate, buckled or otherwise fastened together. (The breast-plate alone was sometimes called a cuirass, and the two pieces (*a pair of*) *cuirasses.*) Also *transf.* **2.** *fig.* and *transf.* The buckler of an animal; the armour-plating of a ship, etc. 1863.

1. The Man at Armes..with his cuyrasses of proofe 1598. *transf.* A dark brown [dress] with a c. of gold lace 1883. var. † **Curats, cuirats, curat,** etc. Hence **Cuira·ss** *v.* to cover with, or as with a c. **Cuira·ssed** *ppl. a.* furnished with a c.; of ships, etc.: armour-plated.

Cuirassier (kwirăsī[ə]·ɹ, kiū[ə]-). 1625. [– Fr. *cuirassier*; see prec., -IER.] A horse soldier wearing a cuirass.

‖ **Cuir-bouilli.** ME. [Fr. (kwir bu[l]yi) *lit.* 'boiled leather'.] Leather boiled or soaked in hot water, and, when soft, moulded or pressed into any required form, which it retains on becoming dry and hard.

Cuirie, var. of *quiry*, obs. aphet. f. EQUERRY, royal stables, stud.

‖ **Cuisine** (kwizī·n). 1786. [Fr. :– L. *coquina, cocina*, f. *coquere* to cook.] Kitchen; culinary department; manner or style of cooking. Hence **Cuisi·nier** [Fr.] a (French) cook.

Cuisse, cuish (kwis, kwiʃ). ME. [pl. *cus(c)hes, cushies, cuisses*, later forms of ME. *cussues, quyssewes* (XIV) – OFr. *cuisseaux*, pl. of *cuissel* :– late L. *coxale*, f. *coxa* hip.] *pl.* Armour for protecting the front part of the thigh; in *sing.* a thigh-piece.

† **Cuit, cute.** 1460. [– Fr. *cuit* (:– L. *coctus*), pa. pple. of *cuire* :– L. *coquere* cook, boil.] Orig. *adj.* in *wine cuit*, subseq. used *absol.*: New wine boiled down and sweetened –1756.

Cuittle (kū·t'l), *v. trans. Sc.* 1565. [Origin unkn.] **1.** To wheedle, coax. **2.** To tickle. (? for *kittle*.) 1790.

‖ **Cul** (kü, often kül). [Fr. = bottom, anus :– L. *culus*.]

‖ **Cul-de-four** (kü-d'fūr, often kül də fū·r). Pl. **culs-de-four.** 1727. [Fr.] *Archit.* 'A low vault spherically formed on a circular or oval plan' (Gwilt).

‖ **Cul-de-lampe** (kü-d'lāṅp, often kül də lāṅp). Pl. **culs-de-lampe.** 1727. [Fr.] **1.** *Archit.* An ornamental support of inverted conical form; a pendant of the same form. **2.** *Printing.* An ornament used to fill up a blank space in a page, as at the end of a chapter.

‖ **Cul-de-sac** (kü-d'sak, often kül də sæk). Pl. **culs-de-sac.** 1738. [Fr.] **1.** *Anat.* A vessel, tube, sac, etc., open only at one end; the closed end of such a vessel, etc. **2.** A passage closed at one end, a blind alley; a place having no outlet except by the entrance; in *Milit.* use, said of the position of an army hemmed in on all sides except behind 1819. Also *fig.*

-cula; see -CULUS.

Culbut, *v. rare.* 1693. [– Fr. *culbuter*; see CUL, BUTT *v.*[1]] To overturn backwards; to drive back in disorder.

Culch, cultch (kɒltʃ). 1667. [Origin unkn.] Rubbish, refuse; *spec.* the mass of hard material of which an oyster-bed is formed (*local*).

Culdee (kɒ·ldī). [– med.L. *Culdeus* (Hector Boece, 1526), alt. (after L. *cultor Dei* worshipper of God) of *Kel(e)deus* – OIr. *céle dé* (Ir. *ceilede*) anchorite, lit. associate or servant of God (*dé*, gen. of *dia*) God.]

A. *sb.* A member of an ancient Scoto-Irish religious order, found from the eighth century onwards. (Orig. a name given to solitary recluses.) ME.

The Culdees thus united in themselves the distinction of monks and of secular clergy PINKERTON.

B. *adj.* Of or belonging to the Culdees 1880. So **Culde·an** *a.*

-cule, *suffix,* corresp. to Fr. *-cule* – L. *-culus, -cula, -culum* dim. suffix; see -CULUS. In English, both Fr. endings *-cle* and *-cule* are found, and the L. endings *-culus, -culum* are sometimes retained.

Culerage; see CULRAGE.

Culet[1]. 1550. [– OFr. *cueillete* – med.L. *collecta* sum collected.] A sum collected from a number of persons chargeable; an assessment. *Hist.*

Culet[2] (kiū·lėt). 1678. [– Fr. *culet*, dim. of *cul*; see CUL, -ET.] **1.** The horizontal face forming the bottom of a diamond when cut as a brilliant. **2.** A piece of armour for protecting the hinder part of the body below the waist 1834.

‖ **Culex** (kiu·leks). 1483. [L.; = gnat.] A gnat; in *Entom.* the genus containing gnats and mosquitoes.

‖ **Culgee** (kɒlgī·). *Anglo-Ind.* 1688. [– Urdu *kalḡī* a jewelled plume surmounting the *sirpeš* or aigrette.] † **1.** A rich figured silk, worn as a turban, or otherwise –17... **2.** A jewelled plume surmounting the aigrette upon the turban 1715.

Culinary (kiū·linări), *a.* 1638. [– L. *culinarius*, f. *culina* kitchen; see -ARY[1].] **1.** Of or pertaining to a kitchen; kitchen-. **2.** Of or pertaining to cookery 1651; of vegetables: Fit for cooking 1796.

1. A very c. goddess 1856. **2.** The palate undepraved By c. arts COWPER. C. roots and plants MORSE. Hence **Cu·linarily** *adv.* (*rare*).

Cull, *sb.*[1] *dial.* 1490. [Origin unkn.] A fish, the Miller's Thumb.

Cull, *sb.*[2] *slang.* 1698. [perh. abbr. of CULLY.] = CULLY.

Cull (kɒl), *sb.*[3] 1618. [f. CULL *v.*[1]] † **1.** The act or product of culling. **2.** *Farming.* An animal drafted from the flock as being inferior or too old for breeding. (Usu. in *pl.*) 1791. **3.** *U.S.* (*pl.*) Any refuse stuff, as timber, etc. 1873.

Cull (kɒl), *v.*[1] ME. [– OFr. *coillier*, etc., (also mod.) *cueillir*, repr. L. *colligere* (see COLLECT), Rom. **colgere*.] **1.** *trans.* To choose; to select. **2.** To gather, pick, pluck (flowers, etc.) 1634. **3.** *transf.* To subject to the process of selection 1713.

1. Words aptly culled, and meanings well exprest CRABBE. **2.** The Sirens three Culling their potent herbs MILT. *Comus* 255. Hence **Culled** *ppl. a.* chosen; plucked; *spec.* of sheep: Draught (cf. CULL *sb.*[3] 2). **Cu·ller,** one who culls. **Cu·lling,** *vbl. sb.* the action of culling; *concr.* a selection; *pl.* portions drafted out.

Cull, *v.*[2] Now *dial.* 1564. [var. of COLL *v.*[1]] To hug.

Cullender; see COLANDER.

Cullet (kɒ·lėt). 1817. [var. COLLET[1].] *Glass-blowing.* Broken or refuse glass for remelting.

† **Cu·llible,** *a.* 1822. [Cf. CULL *sb.*[2], CULLY *v.* No verb *cull* is recorded.] Easily made a cull of; gullible. Hence † **Cullibi·lity,** gullibility.

Cullion (kɒ·lyən). ME. [– OFr. *coillon* (mod. *couillon*) :– Rom. **coleone*, f. L. *coleus, culleus* bag, testicle – Gr. κολεός sheath.] † **1.** A testicle –1737. † **2.** A despicable fellow; a rascal –1843. **3.** *pl.* A name of plants of the genus *Orchis*, from the form of the tubers 1611. Hence † **Cu·llionly** *a.* like a c.; rascally, despicable.

Cullis (kɒ·lis), *sb.*[1] Now *rare.* ME. [– OFr. *coleïz* (mod. *coulis*), subst. use of adj. :– Rom. **colaticius*, f. *colare* strain, flow, whence Fr. *couler*.] A strong broth of meat, fowl, etc., boiled and strained. Also †*transf.* and *fig.*

Use for a c., a leg of veal and a ham MRS. GLASSE.

Cullis (kɒ·lis), *sb.*[2] 1838. [– Fr. *coulisse*, subst. use of fem. of *coulis*; see prec.] *Archit.* A gutter, groove, or channel.

Cullisance, -sen, -son, -zan, obs. corruptions of COGNIZANCE, a badge, etc.

Cully (kɒ·li), *sb. slang.* 1664. [Origin unkn.] **1.** One who is cheated or imposed upon; a dupe, gull; a simpleton. **2.** A man; a mate 1676.

1. The whimper of a cheated c. SWINBURNE. Hence † **Cully** *v.* to make a fool of, cheat, take in. † **Cu·llyism,** the condition of a c.

Culm[1] (kɒlm). ME. [repr. earlier in *colmie* (XIII), *culmy* (XIV) sooty, now Sc. *coomy*; of unkn. origin, but presumably based on *col* COAL.] **1.** Soot, smut. Now *Sc.* **2.** Coal-dust, slack 1603; *spec.* the slack of anthracite coal, from the Welsh collieries 1736; hence = anthracite, or the slaty glance coal, one of its varieties 1742. **3.** *Geol.* (= *Culm measures* or *series*.) A name given by some geologists to a series of shales, sandstones, etc., containing, in places, beds of impure anthracite, which represent the Carboniferous series in North Devon. It includes the *calp* of Ireland. 1836.

Culm[2] (kɒlm). 1657. [– L. *culmus* stalk.] *Bot.* The stem of a plant; *esp.* the jointed stalk of grasses. Hence **Culm** *v. intr.* to form a c.

† **Culm**[3]. *rare.* 1587. [Short for CULMEN.] The summit, culminating point –1821.

‖ **Culmen** (kɒ·lmen). 1647. [L., contr. f. *columen* top, etc.] † **1.** *gen.* The top or summit; *fig.* the culminating point –1856. **2.** *Ornith.* The upper ridge of a bird's bill 1833. **3.** *Anat.* 'The superior vermiform process of the cerebellum' (*Syd. Soc. Lex.*).

Culmiferous (kɒlmi·fĕrəs), *a.*[1] 1837. [f. CULM[1] + -FEROUS.] *Geol.* Containing or producing culm.

Culmi·ferous, *a.*[2] 1704. [f. L. *culmus* CULM[2] + -FEROUS.] *Bot.* Of grasses: Having a jointed stalk.

Cu·lminal, *a. rare.* 1889. [f. L. *culmen, -min-* summit + -AL[1].] Of or pertaining to the summit; apical.

Culminant (kɒ·lminănt), *a.* 1605. [– *culminant-*, pres. ppl. stem of late L. *culminare*; see next, -ANT[1].] **1.** Of a heavenly body: That has reached its greatest altitude, that is on the meridian; hence *fig.* at its greatest height. **2.** Forming the highest point, topmost 1849.

Culminate (kɒ·lmineˈt), *v.* 1647. [– *culminat-*, pa. ppl. stem of late L. *culminare* exalt, extol, f. *culmen, -min-* summit; see -ATE[3].] **1.** *intr. Astron.* Of a heavenly body: To reach its greatest altitude, to be on the meridian 1647. Hence *fig.* **2.** *gen.* To reach its highest point; to rise to an apex. Const. *in.* 1665. **3.** *trans.* To bring (a thing) to its highest point; to crown (*rare*) 1659.

1. All Sun-shine, as when his Beams at Noon C. from th' Æquator MILT. *P.L.* III. 617. *fig.* Thus D'Aiguillon rose again and culminated CARLYLE. **2.** The mountain system culminates in Ararat 1869.

Cu·lminate, *a.* 1864. [– late L. *culminatus*, pa. pple. of *culminare*; see prec., -ATE[2].] 'Growing upwards, as distinguished from a lateral growth; applied to the growth of corals' (Dana).

Culmination (kɒlminēˈ·ʃən). 1633. [f. CULMINATE *v.* + -ION. Cf. Fr. *culmination*.] **1.** The attainment by a heavenly body of its greatest altitude; the act of reaching the meridian. **2.** *fig.* The attainment of the highest point; *concr.* that in which anything culminates 1657.

Cu·lmy. ME. [f. CULM[1] + -Y[1].] † **1.** Begrimed with soot. (ME. only.) **2.** Of the nature of culm, as *c. beds*, etc.

‖ **Culot** (külo). 1683. [Fr., dim. of *cul*; see CUL, -OT[1].] A little cup of sheet-iron inserted into the base of the Minié and other projectiles, so as to be driven into and enlarge the diameter of the ball when fired.

Culottic (kiulǫ·tik), *a.* [f. Fr. *culotte* breeches + -IC.] Wearing breeches, respectable; opp. to *sansculottic*. CARLYLE. So **Culo·ttism.**

† **Culp(e.** [ME. *cope, coupe*, later *coulpe* – OFr. *cope, coupe* (also mod.) *coulpe* – L. *culpa* fault.] Guilt, sin, fault, blame –1601.

Culpable (kɒ·lpăb'l, *a.* (*sb.*) [ME. *coupable* – (O)Fr. *coupable* :– L. *culpabilis*, f. *culpare*, f. *culpa* blame; see -ABLE.] **1.** Guilty, criminal; deserving punishment. ? *Obs.* **2.** Blameworthy 1613. † **3.** *sb.* A culprit –1734.

1. Phr. *C. of* (*punishment, death*, etc.): deserving, liable to. **2.** What circumstances make an action laudable or c. HOBBES. Hence **Culpabi·lity, Cu·lpableness,** c. quality. **Cu·lpably** *adv.*

Cu·lpatory, *a. rare.* 1762. [f. *culpat-*, pa. ppl. stem of L. *culpare* (see prec.) + -ORY[2].] Tending to or expressing blame.

† **Cu·lpon,** *sb.* ME. [– OFr. *colpon*, etc. (mod. *coupon*), f. *colper* (mod. *couper*) cut. Cf. COUPON.] A piece cut off; a portion, strip, slice, bit, shred –1825. Hence † **Cu·lpon** *v.* to cut up; to ornament with strips of a different-coloured material.

Culpose (kɒlpōᵘ·s), *a.* 1832. [f. L. *culpa* + -OSE[1], after *dolose*.] *Rom. Law.* Characterized by *culpa* or (criminal) negligence.

Culprit (kɒ·lprit). 1678. [According to legal tradition, compounded of *cul*, short for AFr. *culpable* guilty, and *pri(s)t* (= OFr. *prest*, Fr. *prêt*) ready; it is supposed that, when the prisoner had pleaded Not Guilty, the Clerk of the Crown replied with '*Culpable*; *prest daverrer notre bille*', i.e. 'Guilty: ready to aver our indictment', and that this was noted in the form *cul. prist*, which was later mistaken for a formula addressed to the accused.] **1.** *Law.* Used only in the formula 'Culprit, How will you be tried?' formerly said to a prisoner indicted for high treason or felony, on his pleading 'Not guilty'. **2.** Hence assumed to mean, Prisoner at the bar; the accused 1700. **3.** An offender [as if f. L. *culpa*] 1769.

2. An author is in the condition of a c.: the public are his judges M. PRIOR. **3.** The fled Hungarian, Who seems the c. BYRON.

† **Cu·lrage, culerage.** ME. [– OFr. *culrage*, (also mod.) *curage*, f. *cul* anus + *rage* rage, rabies.] The plant Water-pepper (*Polygonum hydropiper*) –1611.

Cult (kɒlt), *sb.* 1617. [– Fr. *culte* or L. *cultus* worship, f. *colere* inhabit, cultivate, protect, honour with worship.] † **1.** Worship –1683. **2.** A particular form of religious worship; *esp.* in reference to its external rites and ceremonies 1679. **3.** *transf.* Devotion to a particular person or thing, now *esp.* as paid by a body of professed adherents 1711.

2. The c. of Aphrodite MAHAFFY. **3.** The decay of the Wordsworth c. 1889.

Cultch, var. of CULCH.

Culter, obs. and dial. f. COULTER.

Cultism (kɒ·ltiz'm). 1887. [– Sp. *cultismo*, f. *culto* polished (:– L. *cultus*).] A kind of affected elegance of style which prevailed in Spanish literature in 16–17th c.; also called *Góngorism* after the poet Góngora. So **Cu·ltist,** a writer affecting c.

Cultivable (kɒ·ltivăb'l), *a.* 1682. [– (O)Fr. *cultivable*, f. *cultiver* CULTIVATE; see next, -ABLE.] Capable of being cultivated.

Cultivate (kʊ·ltivēᶦt), *v.* 1620. [– *cultivat-*, pa. ppl. stem of med.L. *cultivare* (cf. (O)Fr. *cultiver*), f. med.L. *cultivus* in *cultiva terra* arable land (cf. OFr. *terres cultives*), f. *cult-*, pa. ppl. stem of L. *colere* cultivate; see CULT, -IVE, -ATE [3].] **1.** *trans.* To bestow labour and attention upon (land) in order to the raising of crops; to till. **2.** To produce or raise by tillage. Also *transf.* 1697. **3.** *fig.* To improve and develop by education and training; to refine 1681. **4.** To promote the growth of; to foster 1662. **5.** To devote one's attention to, practise, cherish 1749.

1. A Country..miserably cultivated DE FOE. **2.** To c. pot-herbs DRYDEN. **3.** To c. the wild licentious savage ADDISON. **4.** To c. the Sciences EVELYN, friendship MILT., inward religion BUTLER. **5.** To c. bluntness 1863, [a man's] acquaintance BOSWELL. Phr. *To c. a person* (ellipt.): to court his acquaintance. Hence **Cu·ltiva:table** *a.* cultivable.

Cultivation (kʊltivēᶦ·ʃən). 1700. [– Fr. *cultivation*, f. *cultiver*; see prec., -ATION.] **1.** The tilling of land; husbandry 1725. **2.** The improvement of a plant by labour and care; the raising of (a crop) by tillage. Also *transf.* 1719. **3.** *fig.* The devoting of attention or study to the development of, or to progress in 1700. **4.** The condition of being cultivated; culture, refinement 1716.

3. Use and c. of reason SOUTH. **4.** Increased cultivation..produces..fastidiousness 1869.

Cultivator (kʊ·ltivēᶦtəɹ). 1665. [f. CULTIVATE + -OR 2, prob. after Fr. *cultivateur.*] **1.** One who cultivates (*lit.* and *fig.*) **2.** An agricultural implement for loosening the ground, and uprooting weeds between the drills of crops 1759.

† **Cu·ltive,** *v.* 1483. [– (O)Fr. *cultiver*; see CULTIVATE *v.*] = CULTIVATE –1635.

Cultrate (kʊ·ltrĕt), *a.* 1856. [– L. *cultratus*, f. *culter* knife; see -ATE [2].] Formed like a knife or coulter; sharp-edged. So **Cu·ltrated** *ppl. a.* **Cu·ltriform** *a.*

Culturable (kʊ·ltiŭrăb'l), *a.* 1796. [f. CULTURE *v.* + -ABLE.] Capable of culture or cultivation; cultivable. (*lit.* and *fig.*)

Cultural (kʊ·ltiŭrăl), *a.* 1868. [f. L. *cultura* tillage + -AL [1].] Relating to culture. Hence **Cu·lturally** *adv.*

Culture (kʊ·ltiŭɹ), *sb.* ME. [– Fr. *culture* or its source L. *cultura*, f. *cult-*; see CULTIVATE, -URE.] † **1.** Worship 1483. **2.** = CULTIVATION 1. ME. **3.** = CULTIVATION 2. 1626; *spec.* the artificial development of microscopic organisms, *esp.* bacteria, in prepared media; *concr.* the product of such culture 1884. **4.** *fig.* Improvement or refinement by education and training 1510. **5.** *absol.* The training and refinement of mind, tastes, and manners; the condition of being thus trained and refined; the intellectual side of civilization 1805. **6.** = CULTIVATION 3 (*rare*) 1876.

2. The soil is clay, and difficult of c. 1806. **3.** The c. of the vine 1856, of silk MORSE, oysters 1862. A c.-fluid..that contains..various species of organisms KLEIN. **4.** The education of Children [is called] a C. of their mindes HOBBES. **5.** C., the acquainting ourselves with the best that has been known and said in the world M. ARNOLD. Hence **Cu·ltureless** *a. rare*, uncultivated (*lit.* and *fig.*). **Cu·lturist**, one engaged in the c. of plants, fish, etc.; an advocate of c.

Culture (kʊ·ltiŭɹ), *v.* Now *rare*. 1510. [– Fr. †*culturer* or med.L. *culturare*; see prec.] To subject to culture, cultivate. *lit.* (usu. *poet.*) and *fig.*

Cultured (kʊ·ltiŭɹd), *ppl. a.* 1743. [f. CULTURE *v.* + -ED.] **1.** *lit.* Cultivated. (Chiefly *poet.*) **2.** *fig.* Improved by education and training; refined 1777.

1. Our cultur'd vales SHENSTONE. **2.** A c. man of science TYNDALL.

‖ **Cultus** (kʊ·ltŏs). 1640. [L., f. pa. ppl. stem of *colere*; see CULT.] = CULT *sb.* †1, 2, 3.

Cultus-cod (kʊ·ltŏs,kǫ:d). 1884. [Chinook *cultus* 'of little worth', G. B. Goode.] A chiroid fish (*Ophiodon elongatus*) of the Pacific coast of North America.

-culus, -cula, -culum, a L. dim. suffix of all three genders. See -CULE.

Culver [1] (kʊ·lvəɹ). [OE. *culfre, culufre, -efre, culfer* – **columbra*, for L. *columbula*, dim. of *columba* dove, pigeon.] A dove; now a local name of the wood-pigeon.

The Culuer on the bared bough Sits mourning SPENSER. *Comb.*: † **c.-foot,** Dove's-foot, a species of wild Geranium; † **-house,** a dove-cote; † **-tail** = DOVETAIL; hence **-tailed** *ppl. a.*

† **Cu·lver** [2]. *rare*. Used for CULVERIN (? confused with prec.). SCOTT *Last Minstr.* IV. xx.

Culverin (kʊ·lvĕrin). 1489. [– (O)Fr. *coulevrine* (cf. med.L. *colu-, colobrina*, It. *colubrina*), f. *couleuvre* snake :– Rom. **colobra*, for L. *colubra*, beside *coluber* snake; see -INE [1].] *orig.* A kind of hand-gun; later, a large cannon, very long in proportion to its bore.

He found the gate of Say's Court defended by men with culverins SCOTT. He..crouched beneath the carriage of a c. H. AINSWORTH. Hence **Cu:lverinee·r**, a soldier armed with, or in charge of, a c.

Cu·lverkeys. 1613. [f. CULVER [1] + KEY.] **1.** A popular name of plants, the flowers of which suggest a bunch of keys, *e.g.* the wild Hyacinth, *Scilla nutans*, the Cowslip, etc. **2.** The seed-pods of the ash, ash-keys (*dial.*) 1790.

1. I could..see..there a Girle cropping Culverkeys and Cowslips WALTON.

Culvert (kʊ·lvəɹt), *sb.* 1773. [Origin unkn.] A conduit or tunnelled drain of masonry conveying water across beneath a canal, railway embankment, or road. Hence **Cu·lvert** *v.* to provide with culverts.

Cu·lvertage. 1613. [– OFr. *culvertage*, f. *culvert* :– med.L. *collibertus* freed serf, in cl.L. fellow freedman, f. *col* COM- + *libertus* freedman. See -AGE.] *Feudal Law.* Villainage; forfeiture and degradation to the position of a *culvert* or serf.

‖ **Cum** (kʊm). 1589. L. prep., meaning 'with, together with', used in Eng. in local names, as *Chorlton-cum-Hardy*, etc. Also in several L. phrases, e.g. *cum grano salis* (or *cum grano*), lit. 'with a grain of salt', *i.e.* with some reserve; and in expressions imitating these, as *cum dividend* (*cum div.*) including the dividend announced on stock or shares purchased.

Cumbent (kʊ·mbĕnt), *a.* 1644. [repr. *-cumbent-*, pres. ppl. stem of L. *-cumbere* (only in comp., as *ac-, recumbere*) lie down; see -ENT.] Lying down; *esp.* of figures in statuary.

Cumber (kʊ·mbəɹ), *sb.* ME. [Either f. CUMBER *v.* or aphetic f. ENCUMBER *sb.*] † **1.** Overthrow (ME. only). **2.** Trouble, distress (*arch.*) 1500. **3.** That which cumbers. (*lit.* and *fig.*) ME. **4.** The action or quality of encumbering, or fact of being encumbered 1618. † **5.** Pressure of business –1849.

2. What Gains Shall answer all this C., all these pains 1682. **3.** A cloke is but a comber in faire weather COTGR. Hence **Cu·mberless** *a.* without c.

Cumber (kʊ·mbəɹ), *v.* ME. [prob. aphetic f. ACCUMBER, ENCUMBER, but there are difficulties of chronology.] † **1.** *trans.* To overthrow –15... † **2.** To harass, distress, trouble –1666; † to perplex –1616. **3.** To hamper, hinder ME. **4.** To occupy obstructively, or inconveniently ME. **5.** *fig.* (of prec. senses) ME. † **6.** To benumb. Cf. CUMBLE *v.* –1483.

2. Cumbred about much seruing *Luke* 10 : 40. **3.** The press was thik, and cummerit thaim full fast 1470. **4.** Why cumbereth it the ground *Luke* 13 : 7. **5.** Cares, that c. royal sway SCOTT.

Comb.: **c.-ground**, a thing or person that uselessly occupies the ground; so † **-world.**

Hence **Cu·mberer. Cu·mberment,** †distress; †perplexity; hindrance; that which cumbers. (Now *rare*.)

Cumbersome (kʊ·mbəɹsəm), *a.* ME. [f. prec. vb. + -SOME [1].] † **1.** Of places or ways: Presenting obstruction; difficult of passage –1681. **2.** Full of trouble; wearisome, oppressive. Now *dial.* 1535. **3.** Troublesome from bulk or weight; unwieldy, clumsy 1594. Also *fig.*

3. That c. Luggage of war MILT. *fig.* Useless and c. Ceremonies HY. MORE. **Cu·mbersome-ly** *adv.*, **-ness.**

† **Cu·mble.** [– (O)Fr. *comble*, f. *combler*; see next.] Apex, culmination. HOWELL.

Cu·mble, *v.* Now *dial.* ME. [– (O)Fr. *combler* load, etc. :– L. *cumulare*; see CUMULATE. The Eng. sense is app. not repr. in (O)Fr. Cf. ACUMBLE.] *trans.* To deprive of power; *esp.* to benumb with cold. Also *intr.*

‖ **Cumbly, cumly** (ka·mli). 1673. [Hind. *kamli* :– Skr. *kambala.*] A blanket, a coarse woollen cloth.

† **Cu·mbrance.** ME. [f. CUMBER *v.* + -ANCE.] The action of cumbering, harassing, hindering; an encumbrance –1671.

Extol not Riches then..The wise man's c. if not snare MILT. *P.R.* II. 454.

Cumbrous (kʊ·mbrəs), *a.* ME. [f. CUMBER *sb.* + -OUS.] † **1.** = CUMBERSOME 1. –1861. † **2.** = CUMBERSOME 2. –1667. **3.** = CUMBERSOME 3. ME. Also *fig.*

2. A cloud of c. gnattes doe him molest SPENSER. **3.** Armour..C. of size, uncouth to sight SCOTT. *fig.* To correct the style where it is c. or incorrect ARNOLD. Hence **Cu·mbrous-ly** *adv.*, **-ness.**

Cumene (kiū·mīn). 1863. [f. L. *cuminum* CUMIN + -ENE.] *Chem.* A hydrocarbon, C_9H_{12}, found in Roman cumin oil: it is a colourless strongly refracting oil, allied to Benzene; var. **Cumole.** So **Cumic** (kiū·mik) *a.* of or derived from cumin, as in *Cumic acid*, $C_{10}H_{12}O_2$, etc. **Cu·midine,** a base homologous with toluidine, formed by the action of ammonium sulphide on nitrocumene. **Cumi·nic** *a.* = *cumic.* **Cu·myl,** the acid organic radical, $C_{10}H_{11}O$, of Cumic acid, homologous with Benzoyl.

Cumin, cummin (kʊ·min). ME. [– OFr. *cumin, comin* :– L. *cuminum* – Gr. κύμινον, prob. of Semitic origin; cf. Heb. *kammōn*, Arab. *kammūn*. Superseded OE. *cymen* – L.] An umbelliferous plant (*Cummin cyminum*) resembling fennel: cultivated for its fruit or seed, which is aromatic and carminative; also called *Common, Garden*, or *Roman c.* Also *fig.* (see *Matt.* 23 : 23).

Rue, myrrh, and cummin for the Sphinx—Her muddy eyes to clear EMERSON.

Black C., a ranunculaceous plant, *Nigella sativa*, with black, acrid, and aromatic seeds; **Sweet C.,** the Anise, *Pimpinella anisum*; **Wild C.,** an umbelliferous plant, *Lagœcia cuminoides*. *Comb.* **c.-splitting** *a.* skinflint [cf. L. *cuminisector*].

Cummer, kimmer (kʊ·məɹ, kiməɹ,). *Sc.* ME. [– (O)Fr. *commère* :– eccl.L. *commater*, *-tr-*, f. *com* COM- + *mater* mother.] **1.** A godmother; a co-mother. **2.** A female intimate; a gossip 1500. **3.** A woman, a female; applied like 'fellow' to a man, and *spec.* to a witch, wise-woman, midwife, etc. 17...

‖ **Cummerbund** (kʊ·məɹbʊnd). *Anglo-Ind.* 1616. [– Hind. – Pers. *kamar-band* 'loin-band'.] A sash or girdle worn round the waist.

Cummin; see CUMIN.

‖ **Cumquat** (kʊ·m,kwǫt). 1699. [Cantonese dial. f. *kin kü* 'gold orange'.] A small orange (*Citrus aurantium*, var. *Japonica*), having a sweet rind and acid pulp; used in preserves, etc.

‖ **Cumshaw** (kʊ·mʃǭ). Also **kum-.** 1839. [repr. Chinese *kan* be grateful, *hsieh* thanks = 'grateful thanks'.] In the Chinese ports: A gratuity; a baksheesh. Hence **Cu·mshaw** *v.* to make a present to.

Cumulant (kiū·miŭlănt). 1853. [– *cumulant-*, pres. ppl. stem of L. *cumulare*; see next, -ANT.] *Math.* 'The denominator of the simple algebraical fraction which expresses the value of an improper continued fraction' (Sylvester).

Cumulate (kiū·miŭlĕt), *a.* 1535. [– L. *cumulatus*, pa. pple. of *cumulare*; see next, -ATE [2].] Formed or gathered into a heap.

Cumulate (kiū·miŭlēᶦt), *v.* 1534. [– *cumulat-*, pa. ppl. stem of L. *cumulare*, f. *cumulus* heap; see -ATE [3].] **1.** *trans.* To gather in a heap; to heap up; to accumulate. **2.** *trans.* To add over and above 1640. **3.** To put the crown or summit to (*arch.*) 1660.

1. Sholes of Shells..cumulated..Heap upon Heap WOODWARD. Hence **Cu·mulated** *ppl. a.* heaped up; of clouds: Formed into cumuli. **Cu·mulately** *adv.*

Cumulation (kiūmiŭlēᶦ·ʃən). 1616. [– late L. *cumulatio*, f. as prec.; see -ION.] **1.** The action of heaping up; a heap; accumulation. Chiefly *fig.* **2.** *Civil Law.* The joining of two or more actions or defences in a single proceeding 1645.

Cumulative (kiū·miŭlĕtiv), *a.* 1605. [f. as prec. + -IVE; cf. Fr. *cumulatif, -ive.*] † **1.** Such as is formed by heaping on (as opp. to organic growth). **2.** Constituted by accumulation; acquiring or increasing in force by successive additions, as *c. argument, evidence*, etc. 1668. **3.** *Sc. Law.* Concurrent 1746. **4.** That tends to accumulate. H. SPENCER.

1. As for knowledge which man receiveth by teaching, it is c., and not original BACON. 2. The force of character is c. EMERSON. Phr. *C. vote*, or *system of voting*: a system of voting in which each voter has as many votes as there are places to be filled, and may accumulate them upon one candidate or distribute them as he pleases. **Cu·mulative-ly** *adv.*, **-ness.**

Cumulato- (kiū·miulēⁱ·to), comb. f. L. *cumulatus*, in sense 'cumulately-', 'cumulate and —'.

Cu·mulo-, comb. f. CUMULUS, used in naming cloud-forms which combine the cumulus with other types: *e.g.* **Cu:mulo-stra·tus, -cirro-stra·tus,** etc.

‖ **Cumulus** (kiū·miŭlŏs). Pl. **cumuli.** 1659. [L.] **1.** A heap, pile; an accumulation; the conical top of a heap. **2.** *Meteorol.* A form of cloud, consisting of rounded masses heaped upon each other and resting on a nearly horizontal base 1803. **3.** *Anat.* The *Discus proligerus* (*Syd. Soc. Lex.*).

2. In the lower cumuli..the groups are..like towers or mountains RUSKIN.

Cun, cunne, *v. Obs.* (or ? *dial.*) [OE. *cunnian, -ode* wk. vb.:– WGmc. **kunnōjan*, deriv. of **kunnan* know; see CAN *v.*[1]] In OE.; To learn to know; whence **a.** To prove, test, try. **b.** To study; see CON *v.*[1] –1688.

Cun; see CAN *v.*[1] and [2], CON *v.*[1] and [2].

‖ **Cunabula** (kiunæ·biŭlă), *sb. pl.* 1789. [L. (neut. pl.). Cf. INCUNABULA.] **1.** A cradle; *fig.* the earliest abode. **2.** = INCUNABULA 1846.

Cunctation (kɒŋktēⁱ·ʃən). 1585. [– L. *cunctatio*, f. *cunctat-*, pa. ppl. stem of *cunctari* delay; see -ION.] The action of delaying; tardy action. Hence **Cuncta·tious** *a. rare*, prone to delay. So **Cu·nctative** *a.* (*rare*).

‖ **Cunctator** (kɒŋktēⁱ·təɹ). 1654. [L.; f. as prec. + *-or* -OR 2.] One who acts tardily, a delayer. Hence **Cu·nctatory** *a.* disposed to delay (*rare*).

Cunctipotent (kɒŋkti·pŏtĕnt), *a. rare.* 1485. [– late L. *cunctipotens, -ent-* (Prudentius), after *omnipotens* OMNIPOTENT, f. *cunctus* all.] Omnipotent.

Cund, var. of COND *v.*, to direct a ship.

‖ **Cundurango** (kɒndurae·ŋgo). Also **con-**. 1871. [Peruvian, f. *cundur, cuntur* eagle, condor + *ango* vine.] A Peruvian climbing shrub, *Gonolobus cundurango*, the bark of which was introduced into therapeutic use in 1871.

Cuneal (kiū·ni,ăl), *a.* ? *Obs.* 1578. [– med. or mod.L. *cunealis*, f. L. *cuneus* wedge; see -AL[1].] Wedge-shaped, cuneiform.

Cuneate (kiū·ni,ĕt), *a.* 1810. [f. L. *cuneus* wedge + -ATE[2]. Cf. *caudate*, etc.] Wedge-shaped, as *c. leaf*, a leaf with a truncated end, tapering gradually to the stipule. So **Cu·neated** *ppl. a.*, **Cunea·tic** *a.*

Cuneator (kiū·ni,ēⁱtəɹ). [med.L. equivalent of OFr. *coigneur* 'coiner', f. *cuneat-*, pa. ppl. stem of med.L. *cuneare* coin (= OFr. *coignier*), f. *cuneus* die. See COIN *v.*[1]] An official formerly in sole charge of all the dies used in the various English mints.

Cuneiform (kiunī·ifǫɹm, kiū·ni,i-). Also **cuniform** (kiū·nifǫɹm). 1677. [– Fr. *cunéiforme* or mod.L. *cuneiformis*, f. *cuneus* wedge; see -FORM.]

A. *adj.* **1.** Wedge-shaped. **2.** *spec.* Applied to the wedge-shaped or arrow-headed characters of the ancient inscriptions of Persia, Assyria, etc.; also, to the inscriptions 1818. Also *transf.*

1. *C. bone* (in *Anat.*): (*a*) one of the bones of the carpus; (*b*) each of three bones of the second row of the tarsus, called *internal, middle,* and *external*; (*c*) the sphenoid bone of the skull. 2. *transf.* C. scholars 1862, studies DEUTSCH.

B. *sb.* **1.** *Anat.* = *C. bone* in A. 1. 1854. **2.** The cuneiform character 1862.

Cuneo- (kiū·nio), comb. f. L. *cuneus*, used in *Anat.*, as **c.-sca·phoid** *a.*, relating to the cuneiform and scaphoid bones, etc.

‖ **Cunette** (kiune·t). 1688. [– Fr. *cunette* – It. *cunetta*, aphetic f. *lacunetta*, dim. of *lacuna* lagoon, ditch, etc.] *Fortif.* A trench sunk in a ditch or moat, serving as a drain, etc.

‖ **Cuniculus** (kiuni·kiŭlŏs). Pl. **-uli.** 1670. [L., = rabbit, burrow.] A burrow, underground passage, or mine; in *Roman Archæol.* applied to the ancient drains of Latium and Southern Etruria. Hence **Cuni·cular** *a.* of or pertaining to cuniculi. **Cuni·culate** *a.*, *Bot.* 'traversed by a long passage, open at one end, as the peduncle of *Tropæolum*' (*Treas. Bot.*). † **Cuni·culous** *a.* full of holes and windings; also, full of rabbits.

Cunner (kɒ·nəɹ). Also **conner.** 1602. [perh. = CONNER[3], CONDER (sense 2).] The name of two fishes of the family *Labridæ* or Wrasses: **a.** The Gilt-head (*Crenilabrus melops*). **b.** The Blue Perch or Burgall (*Ctenolabrus adspersus*), found on the Atlantic coast of N. America.

Cunning (kɒ·niŋ), *sb.* ME. [perh. – ON. *kunnandi* knowledge, accomplishments, f. *kunna* know; see CAN *v.*[1]] † **1.** Knowledge; erudition –1670. † **2.** Intelligence –1532. **3.** Knowledge how to do a thing; ability, skill. (Now *arch.*) ME. † **4.** A science or art, a craft. In early times often = occult art. –1592. **5.** Now usually: Skilful deceit, craft; craftiness 1583.

3. Let my right hand forget her c. *Ps.* 137:5. More by Chance, than C. 1743. 5. We take C. for a sinister or crooked Wisedome BACON. C. borders very near upon Knavery W. PENN.

Cunning (kɒ·niŋ), *a.* ME. [– ON. *kunnandi* knowing, pres. pple. of *kunna*; see prec.] † **1.** Learned –1667. Also *transf.* of things. **2.** Skilful, clever. (Now *arch.*) ME. Also *transf.* of things. † **3.** *spec.* Possessing magical knowledge or skill, in *c. man, c. woman* –1807. **4.** Knowing, clever 1671. **5.** In bad sense: Clever in circumventing; crafty, artful, sly. (Now the prevailing sense.) 1599. Also *transf.* of things. **6.** *U.S. colloq.* Quaintly interesting or taking. (Cf. CANNY.) 1854.

1. C. Latin books 1519. 2. C. in Fence *Twel. N.* III. iv. 312. *transf.* He made the brestplate of c. worke *Exod.* 39:8. 3. A c. man did calculate my birth 2 *Hen. VI*, IV. i. 34. 5. The c. will have recourse to stratagem JOHNSON. *transf.* By the sleight of men, and c. craftinesse, whereby they lye in waite to deceiue *Eph.* 4:14. Hence **Cu·nningly** *adv.* in a c. manner; craftily, artfully. **Cu·nningness.**

Cunningaire, var. CONYGER, rabbit-warren.

Cunt (kɒnt). *Coarse slang.* [ME. *cunte, count(e*, corresp. to ON. *kunta* (Norw., Sw. dial. *kunta*, Da. dial. *kunte*), OFris., MLG., MDu. *kunte*:– Gmc. **kuntōn* wk. fem.; ulterior relations unc.] **1.** The female external genital organs. **2.** Applied to persons, esp. women, as a term of vulgar abuse 1929.

Cup (kɒp), *sb.* [OE. *cuppe* – med.L. *cuppa*, presumably a differentiated var. of L. *cupa* tub, vat.] **1.** A small open vessel for liquids, usually hemispherical or hemi-spheroidal, with or without a handle; a drinking-vessel. In forms (*e.g.* a wine-cup, etc.) having a stem and foot, sometimes limited to the concave part that receives the liquid. **2.** *spec.* **a.** The CHALICE in which the wine is administered at the Communion 1449. **b.** An ornamental vessel offered as a prize for an athletic contest 1640. **3.** *Surg.* A vessel used for cupping; a cupping-glass. **b.** A vessel (holding usually four ounces), used to receive the blood in blood-letting. 1617. **4.** Anything having the form of a cup 1545. **5.** *Astron.* The constellation CRATER 1551.

1. Monkes haf grete kuppes WYCLIF. 4. Acorne cups *Mids. N.* II. i. 31. The cowslips golden c. 1743.

II. Transf. and fig. uses. **1.** A cup with its contents; a cupful ME.; *spec.* the wine taken at the Communion 1597. **2.** *fig.* Something to be partaken of; an experience, portion, lot (usually painful). Cf. CHALICE. ME. **3.** *pl.* The drinking of intoxicating liquor; potations, drunken revelry ME. **4.** A beverage consisting of wine sweetened and flavoured and usually iced; as *claret-c.*, etc. 1773.

1. I did send for a c. of tee (a China drink) PEPYS. 2. Are ye able to drink of the c. that I shall drink of *Matt.* 20:22. All Foes [shall taste] The c. of their deseruings *Lear* V. iii. 304. 3. Thence from Cups to civil Broiles MILT. *P.L.* xi. 718.
In one's cups: †(*a*) while drinking; (*b*) drunk.
Comb.: † **c. and can,** constant associates (the cup being filled from the can); **c.-and-cone** (*Mining*), an iron hopper with a large central opening, closed by a cone; **-coral** (see CORAL *sb.*); **-gall,** a cup-shaped gall found on oak-leaves; **-lichen,** *Cladonia pyxidata*; = CUP-MOSS; **-man,** a man addicted to drinking; **-mushroom,** a name for species of *Peziza*; **-plant,** *Silphium perfoliatum* of N. America.

Cup (kɒp), *v.* 1482. [f. CUP *sb.*] **1.** *Surg.* To apply a cupping-glass to; to bleed by means of a cupping-glass. Also *absol.* † **2.** To supply with cups, *i.e.* with liquor (*rare*) –1630; *intr.* to indulge in cups 1625. **3.** To receive as in a cup 1838. **4.** *intr.* To form a cup 1830.

2. C. vs till the world go round *Ant. & Cl.* II. vii. 124.

Cup and ball, cup-and-ball. 1760. **1.** = BILBOQUET 2. **2.** *attrib.* Of a joint or bones: = *Ball and socket*; see BALL *sb.*[1]

Cup-bearer (kɒ·pbēᵊ:rəɹ). 1483. One who carries a cup; an officer of a great household who served his master with wine.

For I was the king's cupbearer *Neh.* 1:11.

Cupboard (kɒ·bəɹd), *sb.* ME. [f. CUP *sb.* + BOARD.] † **1.** A board or table to place cups and plate on; a sideboard –1708. **2.** A closet or a cabinet with shelves, for keeping cups, dishes, provisions, etc. 1530. **3.** *transf.* Food, provisions 1665.

1. A Candlestick on a Cubbert 1663. 2. Lockers to put any thing in, as in little Cupberts 1627. Phr. *Skeleton in the c.*: see SKELETON. 3. Phr. *To cry c.*, to crave for food. ? *Obs.* *Comb.* **c.-love,** love displayed for the sake of what one can get by it. Hence **Cu·pboard** *v.* to keep in or as in a c.

Cupel (kiū·pĕl), *sb.* Also **coppel.** 1605. [orig. – Fr. *coupelle* – late L. *cupella*, dim of L. *cupa* (see CUP *sb.*); ult. assim. to the L. form.] A small shallow porous cup, usually made of bone-ash, and used in assaying gold or silver with lead. Also, a similarly-shaped movable hearth. Also *fig.* *Comb.* † **c.-ashes,** ashes used in purifying metals. Hence **Cu·pel** *v.* to assay or refine in a c. So **Cu·pellate** *v.* (*rare*).

Cupellation (kiūpĕlēⁱ·ʃən). 1691. [f. CUPEL *v.* + -ATION, after Fr. *coupellation.*] The process of assaying or refining the precious metals in a cupel; the separation of silver from argentiferous lead, on a large scale, on a cupel.

Cupful (kɒ·pful). Pl. **cupfuls.** ME. [f. CUP *sb.* + -FUL.] As much as fills a cup.

Cupid (kiū·pid). ME. [– L. *Cupido* personification of *cupido*, f. *cupere* to desire.] *Rom. Mythol.* The god of love, son of Mercury and Venus, identified with the Greek Eros. Also in *pl.* Hence, a representation of the god; a beautiful young boy.

Hir dowves and dan Cupido, Hir blinde sone CHAUCER.

Cupidity (kiupi·dĭti). ME. [– Fr. *cupidité* or L. *cupiditas*, f. *cupidus* eagerly desirous, f. *cupere* desire; see -ID[1], -ITY.] **1.** *gen.* Inordinate longing or lust; covetousness; (with *pl.*) an inordinate desire (*arch.*) 1542. **2.** *spec.* Inordinate desire to appropriate wealth or possessions ME.

2. No property is secure when it becomes large enough to tempt the c. of indigent power BURKE.

‖ **Cupidon.** [Fr. = CUPID.] An Adonis. BYRON.

Cupidone (kiū·pidōᵘn). 1866. [= prec.] Florist's name of a herbaceous border-plant, *Catananche cærulea.*

Cu·p-moss. 1597. A lichen, *Cladonia pyxidata.* **b.** Locally, the CUDBEAR.

Cupola (kiū·pŏlă), *sb.* 1549. [– It. *cupola* – late L. *cupula* little cask, small burying-vault, dim. of *cupa* (see CUP).] **1.** *Arch.* A rounded vault or dome forming the roof of a building or part of a building. Often *spec.*: A diminutive dome rising above a roof; also, the ceiling of a dome. Also *transf.* **2.** *Mech.* (= *c.-furnace.*) A furnace for melting metals for casting. Also, a furnace for heating shot. 1716. **3.** An armour-plated revolving turret to protect mounted guns on an iron-clad ship. Hence *c.-ship.* 1862. **4.** In *Anat.*, etc.: A dome-like organ or process; *esp.* the arched summit of the cochlea of the ear 1829. Hence **Cu·polaed, cu·pola'd** *ppl. a.* having a c.

Cupped (kɒpt), *a.* 1796. [f. CUP *sb.* or *v.* + -ED.] Formed like a cup, cup-shaped.

Cupper (kɒ·pəɹ). ? ME. [f. as prec. + -ER[1].] †**1.** = CUP-BEARER –1652. **2.** One who performs the operation of cupping 1812.

Cupping (kɒ·piŋ), *vbl. sb.* 1519. [f. CUP *v.* + -ING[1].] **1.** *Surg.* The operation of drawing blood by scarifying the skin and applying a CUP (sense 3), the air in which is rarefied by heat or otherwise. (Called distinctively *wet cupping.*) **2.** Drinking; a drinking-bout (*arch.*) 1625. **3.** The formation of a concavity; a concavity thus formed.

1. *Dry c.*: the application of a cupping-glass without scarification, as a counter-irritant. *Comb.* **c.-glass,** a glass cup with an open mouth to be applied to the skin in the operation of cupping.

Cuppy (kɒ·pi), *a.* 1882. [-Y[1].] Concave like a cup; *esp.* in *Golf*, full of small cavities.

Cu·prate. 1854. [f. CUPR(IC + -ATE[4].] A salt of cupric acid.

Cupreo-, comb. f. CUPREOUS 2.

Cupreous (kiū·pri,əs), *a.* 1666. [f. late L. *cupreus* (f. *cuprum* COPPER) + -OUS.] **1.** Of, of the nature of, or containing copper. **2.** Copper-coloured 1804.

Cupric (kiū·prik), *a.* 1799. [f. late L. *cuprum* COPPER + -IC.] *Chem.* Containing copper in chemical combination; applied to compounds in which copper is divalent, as *c. chloride*, $CuCl_2$.

Cupri·ferous, *a.* 1784. [f. as prec. + -FEROUS.] Yielding copper.

Cuprite (kiū·prəit). 1850. [f. as prec. + -ITE[1] 2 b.] *Min.* Native red oxide of copper.

Cupro- (kiūpro), bef. a vowel **cupr-,** used as comb. f. L. *cuprum* COPPER, in *Chem.* and *Min.*, as *cupro-sulphate*; **cuproma·gnesite,** a hydrous sulphate of copper and magnesium; **cupro-nickel,** an alloy comprising 75% copper and 25% nickel established for the so-called silver coinage of Great Britain by the Coinage Act of 1946.

Cuproso- (kiuprō[u]·so), *Chem.*, comb. f. mod.L. *cuprosus* CUPROUS.

Cuprous (kiū·prəs), *a.* 1669. [orig. f. late L. *cuprum* + -OUS; in mod. use, f. CUPR(IC; see -OUS c.] = CUPREOUS. In *Chem.* applied to compounds in which copper is univalent, e.g. *cuprous chloride*, Cu_2Cl_2.

Cu·p-shake. 1793. An opening between two of the concentric layers of timber. So **Cu·p-shaken, -shaky** *a.*

† **Cup-shot, -shotten,** *a.* ME. [f. CUP + SHOT *pa. pple.*] Intoxicated –1700.

Cupule (kiū·piul). 1826. [– late L. *cupula* (also used); see CUPOLA. Cf. Fr. *cupule*.] **1.** *Bot.* A cup-shaped involucre, as in the fruit of the oak, beech, hazel. Also, a cup-like receptacle found in *Peziza* and other fungi. 1830. **2.** A small cup-shaped depression on a surface 1883. **3.** *Zool.* A cup-shaped organ, as a sucker. Hence **Cu·pular** *a.*, *Bot.* c.-shaped. **Cu·pulate** *a.* cupular; having a c.

Cupuliferous (kiūpiuli·fĕrəs), *a.* 1847. [f. CUPULE + -FEROUS; cf. Fr. *cupulifère* adj.] *Bot.* Bearing a cupule or cupules; belonging to the N.O. *Cupuliferæ*, including the oak, beech, hazel, etc.

Cur (kɒɹ). ME. [prob. orig. in *cur-dog*; perh. – ON. *kurr* grumbling, *kurra* murmur, grumble, as if 'growling dog'.] **1.** A dog: now always depreciative; a low-bred, or snappish dog. **2.** *fig.* A surly, ill-bred, or cowardly fellow 1590. † **3.** A fish; the Red Gurnard, *Trigla cuculus* –1753. **4.** The Golden-eye duck, *Clangula glaucion*. (*dial.*) 1621.

1. The Mastiues, and such like curres MANWOOD. The beggarly curs of cities W. IRVING. **2.** What would you have, you Curres, That like nor Peace, nor Warre *Cor.* I. i. 172. *Comb.* **c.-dog** (in senses 1, 2).

Curable (kiū[ə]·răb'l), *a.* ME. [– (O)Fr. *curable* or late L. *curabilis*, f. *curare* CURE; see -BLE.] **1.** Capable of being cured; *fig.* remediable. † **2.** Able to cure –1615.

1. C. disorders HAZLITT. Hence **Curabi·lity,** † **Cu·rableness.**

‖ **Curaçao,** (*erron.*) **curaçoa** (kiū[ə]răsō[u]·). 1813. [– Fr. name of one of the Antilles that produces the oranges so used.] A liqueur consisting of spirits flavoured with the peel of bitter oranges, and sweetened.

Curacy (kiū[ə]·răsi). 1682. [f. CURATE; see -ACY.] The office of a curate; †or of a curator 1734.

‖ **Curare** (kiurā·ri). Also **curara, -ri.** 1777. [Also *woorara* (XVIII), OORALI, *urali, urari*, WOORALI, WOURALI (all XIX); language of the Macuchi Indians of Guiana.] A blackish-brown resinous bitter substance, extracted from *Strychnos toxifera*, and other plants; used by Indians to poison their arrows.

When introduced into the blood it is a powerful poison, arresting the action of the motor nerves; used largely in physiological experiments.

Hence **Cu·rarine,** *Chem.* a bitter poisonous alkaloid, $C_{10}H_{15}N$, obtained from c. **Cu·rarize** *v.* to administer c. to.

Curassow (kiū[ə]·răsō[u]). 1685. [Anglicized sp. of CURAÇAO.] One of a family of gallinaceous birds found in Central and South America; they resemble the turkey.

The most common species is the Crested C., *Crax alector*, of a greenish-black colour with a white crest; the Galeated C. or Cushew-bird, *Pauxis galeata*, has a large bony protuberance on the upper part of the bill.

Curat, -e, obs. ff. CUIRASS.

Curate (kiū[ə]·rĕt). ME. [– med.L. *curatus* one who has a cure or charge (of a parish), f. *cura* CURE *sb.*[1] 3; see -ATE[1].] **1.** One entrusted with the cure of souls; orig., any ecclesiastical or spiritual pastor, but now usu. limited to an assistant of a beneficed clergyman. † **2.** A curator, overseer –1660.

1. *Perpetual c.*: the incumbent of the chapel or church of an ecclesiastical district, forming part of an ancient parish, appointed by the patron and licensed by the bishop; he now ranks as a vicar.

Hence † **Cu·rateship,** the office or position of a c.; a curacy.

Curatel (kiū[ə]·rătel). 1875. [– med.L. *curatela* guardianship, f. *curator* overseer, guardian (cf. *tutor, tutela*). Cf. Fr. *curatelle* (XV).] *Rom. Law.* The position of being under the guardianship of a curator.

† **Cura·tion.** ME. [– OFr. *curacion* – L. *curatio*, f. *curat-*, pa. ppl. stem of *curare* CURE *v.*; see -ION.] **1.** Healing, cure –1677. **2.** Curatorship –1774.

Curative (kiū[ə]·rătiv), *a.* (*sb.*) 1533. [– Fr. *curatif, -ive* – med.L. *curativus*, f. as prec.; see -IVE, -ATIVE.] **1.** Of or relating to the curing of disease. **2.** Having the tendency or power to cure disease 1644; *fig.* remedial 1661. Also as *sb.* [sc. *agent.*] Hence **Cu·rative-ly** *adv.*, **-ness.**

Curator (kiurē[i]·təɹ, kiū[ə]·rătəɹ). ME. [– AFr. *curatour* = (O)Fr. *curateur*, or the source L. *curator*, f. *curare*; see CURE *sb.*[1], -OR 2.]

I. (*cu·rator.*) **1.** One appointed as guardian of a minor, lunatic, etc. † **2.** One who has a cure of souls –1450.

II. (*cura·tor.*) **1.** *gen.* One who has charge; a manager, steward 1632. **2.** *spec.* in *Universities.* A member of a board (or an individual) having general or specific charge and powers 1691. **3.** The officer in charge of a museum, library, etc.; a keeper, custodian 1661. **4.** A designation of officials under the Roman Empire 1728. Hence **Curato·rial** *a.* **Cura·torship,** the office or position of a c. **Cu·ratory** *sb.* curatorship; a college of curators.

Cu·ratory, *a.* 1644. [– late L. *curatorius*, f. *curator* (see prec.); see -ORY[2]. In mod. use referred to *curare* CURE *v.*] Curative.

Curatrix (kiurē[i]·triks). [Late L., fem. of *curator*; see -TRIX.] † **1.** A female curer. CUDWORTH. **2.** A female curator 1846.

Curb (kɒ̈ɹb), *sb.* 1477. [Early forms *courbe, corbe*, prob. from the vb.; see COURBE *v.*, CURB *v.*[1]]

I. 1. A chain or strap passing under the lower jaw of a horse, and fastened to the upper ends of the branches of the bit; used for checking an unruly horse. **2.** *fig.* Anything that curbs or restrains; a check, restraint 1613.

1. That trot became a gallop soon In spite of c. and rein COWPER. **2.** Service is to the Lofty minde A C., a Spur to th' abiect Hinde 1613.

II. Corresp. to Fr. *courbe* sb. **1.** A hard swelling on the hock or other part of a horse's leg 1523. † **2.** A curve, an arc (*rare*) –1759. **3.** A mould or template for marking out curved work. (Occas. spelt *kerb.*) 1792.

III. An enclosing framework, orig. of something round. **1.** A frame or 'coaming' round the top of a well 1511. **2.** A curvilinear plate or ring of timber, iron, etc., round the edge of any circular structure, or forming a base for the brickwork of a shaft or well 1733. **3.** A raised margin round an oast, a bed in a garden, a hearth, etc. 1731. **4.** The stone margin of a side-walk. Usu. spelt *kerb.* 1836. *attrib.* and *Comb.*: **c.-bit, bridle,** a bit (or bridle) with a c.; **-chain,** a chain acting as a c.; **-pins** (*Horology*), the pins on the lever of a watch-regulator, which control the balance.

† **Curb,** *v.*[1] *rare.* ME. [Early forms †*courbe*, † *corbe* (see COURBE *v.*) – (O)Fr. *courber* :– L. *curvare* CURVE *v.*] **1.** *trans.* To bend, bow, curve –1662. **2.** *intr.* To bend, bow, cringe –1808.

Curb (kɒ̈ɹb), *v.*[2] 1530. [f. CURB *sb.*] **1.** *trans.* To put a curb on; to restrain with a curb. **2.** *fig.* To restrain, keep in check 1588. **3.** To furnish or defend with a curb or curb-stone. (In the latter case usu. *kerb.*) 1861.

1. Part wield their Arms, part courb the foaming Steed MILT. *P.L.* XI. 643. **2.** To curbe our naturall appetites DONNE. To c...our own Subjects from their natural Rights 1719.

Cu·rbless, *a.* *rare.* 1813. [f. CURB *sb.* + -LESS.] Without restraint.

Cu·rb-plate. 1819. [CURB *sb.* III. 2.] = CURB III. 2.

Cu·rb-roof. 1733. [CURB *sb.*] A roof of which each face has two slopes, the lower one steeper than the other; a mansard-roof.

Cu·rb-, kerb-stone. 1806. One of the stones forming a curb; the stone edge of a side-path.

Curby (kɒ̈·ɹbi), *a.* 1841. [f. CURB *sb.* + -Y[1].] Liable to be affected with curb, as *c. hocks*.

Curch (kɒ̈ɹtʃ). *Sc.* 1447. [erron. sing. of *curches*, repr. OFr. *couvrechés*, pl. of *couvrechef*; see COVERCHIEF, KERCHIEF.] A covering for the head; a kerchief; formerly worn instead of a cap or mutch.

‖ **Curculio** (kɒɹkiū·lio). 1756. [L., = corn-weevil.] *Entom.* A Linnæan genus of Beetles, containing the Weevils. Now applied *esp.* to the common fruit-weevils, which are very destructive to plums. Hence **Curcu:lioni·deous** *a.* belonging to the *Curculionidæ* or weevil-family. **Curcu·lionist,** one who studies the *Curculionidæ*.

‖ **Curcuma** (kɒ̈·ɹkiumă). 1617. [– med.L. or mod.L. – Arab. *kurkum* (Pers. *karkam*) – Skr. *kuṅkuma*[m] saffron.] **a.** *Bot.* A genus of *Zingiberaceæ* consisting of plants with perennial tuberous roots. **b.** The substance called Turmeric, prepared from the tubers of *C. longa*. *Attrib.* as **c. paper,** turmeric paper used as a chemical test. Hence **Cu·rcumin,** *Chem.* the colouring matter of turmeric.

Curd (kɒ̈ɹd), *sb.* ME. [Earliest forms *crud(de, crod(de*; the present form dates from XV; of unkn. origin.] **1.** The coagulated substance formed from milk by the action of acids; made into cheese or eaten as food. (Often in *pl.*) **2.** *transf.* Any similar substance 1811.

1. The Queene of Curds and Creame *Wint. T.* IV. iv. 161. Hence **Cu·rdiness,** curdy state or quality. **Cu·rdless** *a.* **Cu·rdy** *a.* full of c.; c.-like.

Curd (kɒ̈ɹd), *v.* ME. [f. prec.] **1.** *trans.* = CURDLE *v.* 1. **2.** *intr.* = CURDLE *v.* 2. ME.

1. It doth posset And c., like Aygre droppings into Milke, The thin and wholsome blood *Haml.* I. v. 69.

Curdle (kɒ̈·ɹd'l), *v.* 1590. [frequent. of CURD *v.*; see -LE.] **1.** *trans.* To form into curd; to coagulate, clot, congeal. Also *transf.* and *fig.* **2.** *intr.* To become or form curd; to coagulate 1601. Also *transf.* and *fig.*

1. It wil cruddle milk as wel as rennet HOLLAND. An holy horror curdled all my blood 1760. **2.** *fig.* The blood thrills and curdles at the thought COWPER. Hence **Cu·rdly** *a.* apt to c.; of a curdled appearance.

Cure (kiū[ə]ɹ), *sb.*[1] ME. [– (O)Fr. *cure* :– L. *cura* care.] † **1.** Care, heed, concern –1605. † **2.** Care, charge; a duty, office –1641. **3.** *Eccl.* The spiritual charge of parishioners; the office or function of a CURATE. Usu. in *c. of souls*. Hence, A parish; a 'charge'. ME. **4.** † Medical treatment –1725; a particular method or course of treatment, as in *water-c.*, etc. 1842. **5.** Successful medical treatment; the action or process of healing; restoration to health. Also *fig.* ME. **6.** A means of healing; a remedy. Often *fig.* 1613. † **7.** The curing or preserving of fish, pork, etc. –1757.

1. I make of yt no c. CHAUCER. **2.** The c. of tyllage of the grounde EDEN. **3.** The people committed to your c. and charge *Bk. Com. Prayer.* A small c. was offered me GOLDSM. **5.** Past care, is still past c. *L.L.L.* V. ii. 28. I cast out deuils, and I doe cures *Luke* 13:32. **6.** Let the water and the blood..Be of sin the double c. 1766.

Cure (kiūᵊɹ), *sb.*² *slang.* 1856. [Shortening of *curiosity* (1862). Cf. CURIO.] An odd person; a funny fellow.

Cure (kiūᵊɹ), *v.* ME. [– (O)Fr. *curer* take care of, clean :– L. *curare* care for, cure.] † **1.** To take care of; to care for; *intr.* to take trouble; to take care –1623. † **2.** *trans.* (and *absol.*) To take charge of the spiritual interests of (a parish, etc.) –1581. † **3.** To treat surgically or medically –1592. **4.** To heal, restore to health (a sick person). Also *fig.* ME. **5.** To heal (a disease or wound); *fig.* to remedy, remove (an evil) ME. † **6.** *intr.* (for *refl.*) To get well again (*rare*) –1791. **7.** To prepare for keeping, by salting, etc.; to preserve (meat, etc.) 1665. Also *intr.* (for *refl.*).

4. Hee cured many of their infirmities *Luke* 7: 21. *fig.* Time cured him of his grief W. IRVING. **5.** Your tale, Sir, would c. deafenesse *Temp.* I. ii. 106. **6.** One desparate greefe cures with anothers languish *Rom. & Jul.* I. ii. 49. **7.** To c. Sponges 1665, hops 1711, grapes DE FOE, beef 1788, fish 1832.

‖ **Curé** (küre). 1655. [Fr. – med.L. *curatus*; see CURATE.] A parish priest in a French-speaking land.

Cu·re-a·ll. 1870. A universal remedy, panacea. Also *fig.*

Cu·reless, *a.* 1541. [f. CURE *sb.*¹ + -LESS.] Without cure; irremediable.

Curer (kiūᵊ·rəɹ). 1581. [f. CURE *v.* + -ER¹.] **1.** One who or that which cures or heals. **2.** One who cures fish, etc. 1791.

Curette (kiūᵊre·t). 1753. [– Fr. *curette*, f. *curer* (see CURE *v.*); see -ETTE.] *Surg.* A small instrument like a scoop, used in removing morbid matter from the eye, ear, throat, uterine cavity, etc. Hence **Cure·tte** *v.* to scrape with a c. So **Cure·ttage.**

Curfew (kɔ̄·ɹfiu). ME. [– AFr. *coeverfu*, OFr. *cuevrefeu* (mod. *couvrefeu*), f. tonic stem of *couvrir* COVER *v.*¹ + *feu* fire.] **1. a.** A regulation by which, at a fixed hour in the evening, a bell was rung, as a signal that fires were to be extinguished; also, the hour of ringing, and the bell. (The statement that the curfew was introduced into England by William the Conqueror as a measure of political repression is without early historical support.) **b.** Hence, the practice of ringing an evening (and †morning) bell, in many towns. **2.** A cover for a fire; a fire-plate 1626. Also *attrib.* *Comb.* **c.-bell** (see sense 1). Also *fig.*

1. Well, 'tis nine o'clock, 'tis time to ring c. 1608. **b.** *Rom. & Jul.* IV. iv. 4.

‖ **Curia** (kiūᵊ·riă). 1600. [L.] **1.** *Antiq.* **a.** One of the ten divisions of each of the three ancient Roman tribes; also *transf.* **b.** The building belonging to a Roman curia. **c.** The senate-house at Rome. **d.** A name for the senate of ancient Italian towns. **2.** A court of justice, counsel, or administration 1706. **3.** *spec. The C.*: The Papal court, including all its authorities and functionaries 1840. Hence **Cu·rial** *a.* †courtly; of or pertaining to a c.; *sb.* †a courtier; a member of an ancient Roman or an Italian c.; †a treatise on the Court. **Cu·rialism,** a curial or courtly system: *esp.* Vaticanism. **Cu·rialist,** a member of the Papal c.; a supporter of its policy. **Curiali·stic** *a.* of or pertaining to curialists or curialism. † **Curia·lity,** what pertains to a court, courtliness; = COURTESY 3.

Curiet, obs. f. CUIRASS.

Curing (kiūᵊ·riŋ), *vbl. sb.* ME. [f. CURE *v.* + -ING¹.] The action of the verb CURE. *Comb.* **c.-house,** a building where curing is carried on; *spec.* in the West Indies, one in which newly potted sugar is placed to harden and drain.

Curio (kiūᵊ·rio). 1851. [Short f. *curiosity*; cf. CURE *sb.*²] An object of art valued as a curiosity or rarity; a curiosity. Also in *Comb.*

Curiolo·gic *a.* 1669. [Better *cyriologic* – Gr. κυριολογικός, 'speaking literally', opp. to συμβολικός symbolic.] Pertaining to that form of hieroglyphic writing in which objects are represented by pictures. Also as *sb.* So **Curiolo·gical** *a.*

Curiosity (kiūᵊriǫ·sĭti). ME. [– OFr. *curiouseté* (mod. *curiosité*) – L. *curiositas*; see CURIOUS, -ITY.] † **1.** Carefulness –1747; scrupulousness, accuracy –1694; ingenuity –1772; undue niceness or subtlety –1766. **2.** Desire to know or learn; inquisitiveness ME.; inquisitiveness about trifles or other people's affairs 1577. † **3.** Scientific or artistic interest; connoisseurship –1781. † **4.** A hobby –1661. † **5.** A fancy, a whim –1718. † **6.** Careful or elaborate workmanship; nicety of construction –1807. **7.** Curiousness 1597. † **8.** A curious matter of investigation –1700. † **9.** A vanity, refinement –1705. † **10.** A curious detail or feature –1747. **11.** Anything curious, rare, or strange 1645.

2. A noble and solid c. of knowing things in their beginnings 1632. Curiositie, which I take to be a desire to know the faults and imperfections in other men P. HOLLAND. **7.** Rotterdam, where the c. of the place detained us three days 1686. **11.** Japanese goods, lacker-ware and curiosities 1869.

‖ **Curioso** (kiūᵊri,ōᵘ·so). *arch.* Pl. **-i, -os.** 1658. [It.] In 17th c., one curious in matters of science and art; later, a connoisseur, virtuoso.

Curious (kiūᵊ·riəs), *a.* ME. [– OFr. *curios* (mod. *curieux*) :– L. *curiosus* careful, assiduous, inquisitive, f. *cura* care; see CURE *sb.*¹, -OUS.]

I. † **1.** Careful –1781; solicitous –1697; nice –1821; accurate –1816; skilful –1771. **2.** Desirous of seeing or knowing; inquisitive. Often in bad sense: Prying. (The current subjective sense.) ME. † **3.** Skilled as a connoisseur or virtuoso –1792. Also *absol.* in pl.

2. He was a man very c., and much inclined to hear of novelties, and rare things H. COGAN. Crowded with c. idlers 1873. She stole a c. look at my face DICKENS.

II. As an objective quality of things, etc. † **1.** Made with care or art –1772. † **2.** Elaborate –1674. **3.** Of investigations, etc.: Careful, accurate, minute 1526. † **4.** Inquisitive –1742; abstruse –1664; occult –1619. † **5.** Exact, precise –1825. † **6.** Skilled, skilful –1776. **7.** Exquisite, choice, fine (in beauty, flavour, etc.). Now *dial.* ME. † **8.** Noteworthy –1816. **9.** Deserving or exciting curiosity; strange, singular; queer. (The current objective sense.) 1715. † **10.** Such as interests the curioso –1768.

3. A subject, which demands the most c. investigation DISRAELI. **9.** A most c. reason, truly! BURKE. No c. shell, rare plant, or brilliant spar, Inticed our traveller CRABBE.

Hence **Cu·rious-ly** *adv.*, **-ness.**

Curl (kɔ̄ɹl), *sb.* 1602. [f. CURL *v.*] **1.** A ringlet of hair. **2.** Anything of a spiral or incurved shape 1615. **3.** The action of curling, or state of being curled 1665. **4.** A disease of potatoes, and other plants, in which the shoots, or leaves, are curled up and imperfectly developed 1790.

2. [An oar] which breakes The waues in curles CHAPMAN. Curls of smoke 1832. **3.** The lip's least c. BYRON. To keep the hair in c. (*mod.*).

Curl (kɒɹl), *v.* ME. [First recorded (XIV) in pa. pple. *crolled, crulled*, extended form with -ED¹ of ME. *crolle, crulle*; see CRULL.] **1.** *trans.* To bend round, wind, or twist into ringlets, as the hair. † **2.** To furnish or adorn with curls; also *fig.* –1667. **3.** To twist or coil up into a spiral or incurved shape; to ripple (water) 1562. **4.** *intr.* Of hair: To form curls 1530. **4.** *intr.* Of hair: To form curls 1530. **5.** To take a spiral or incurved form. Often with *up.* 1694. **b.** To become affected with CURL (*sb.* 4) 1793. **6.** To move in spiral convolutions or undulations 1791. **7.** *Sc.* To play at CURLING 1715.

1. They curle their haire and are proud of it SIR T. HERBERT. **2.** The snakie locks That curld Megæra MILT. *P.L.* x. 560. **3.** Jack [the dog].. curled himself up on the sofa HUGHES. To c. the lip 1816. **5.** In stormy Weather little Waves c. on the top of the great ones 1694. **b.** A.. Potatoe that never curls 1793. Phr. *To c. up* (*Sporting*): to collapse. **6.** The damp vapours curled round him MRS. RADCLIFFE.

Curler (kɔ̄·ɹləɹ). 1638. [f. CURL *v.* + -ER¹.] **1.** One who or that which curls (hair, etc.) 1748. **2.** A player at the game of curling.

Curlew (kɔ̄·ɹlⁱū). [ME. *cor-, curlu(e)* – (O)Fr. *courlieu*, var. of *courlis*, orig. imit. of the bird's cry, but prob. assim. to OFr. *courliu* courier, messenger, f. *courre* run + *lieu* place.] **1.** A grallatorial bird of the genus *Numenius* (family *Scolopacidæ*), with a long slender curved bill; *esp.* the common European species *N. arquatus* (Sc. *whaup*). † **2.** Used (*esp.* in the Bible) as tr. L. *coturnix*, Gr. ὄρτυξ, a quail –1508.

Comb., etc.: **c.-jack, c. knot,** the Whimbrel, *N. phæops*; **c. sandpiper, pigmy c.,** *Tringa subarquata*; **stone c.,** the Norfolk plover (*Œdicnemus scolopax*); also, the whimbrel.

Curlicue (kɔ̄·ɹlikiū). Also **curlycue.** 1858. [f. CURLY + CUE, either = Fr. *queue*, or the letter Q (*Q*).] A fantastic curl or twist; a caper (*U.S.*).

Curlie-wurlie, curly-wurly (kɔ̄·ɹliwɔ̄·ɹli). 1772. [redupl. f. CURLY.] A fantastically curled ornament.

Curling (kɔ̄·ɹliŋ), *vbl. sb.* ME. [f. CURL *v.* + -ING¹.] **1.** The action of the verb CURL, q.v. **2.** A game played on the ice in which large rounded stones are hurled along a defined space called the *rink* towards a mark called the *tee* 1620.

Comb.: **c.-iron,** an instrument which is heated and then used for curling the hair; **-stone,** a cheese-shaped stone having an iron handle on the upper surface, with which the game of curling is played.

Curly (kɔ̄·ɹli), *a.* 1772. [f. CURL *sb.* + -Y¹.] **1.** Curling or disposed to curl. **2.** Having curled hair 1827. **3.** Of a curled form; wavy 1795. **4.** Of potatoes: Affected with CURL 1791. *Comb.*: **c.-pate,** a curly-headed person; **-pated** *a.* Hence **Cu·rliness.**

Curmudgeon (kɒɹmɒ·dʒən). 1577. [Origin unkn.] 'An avaricious churlish fellow; a miser, a niggard' (J.).

A rich uncle.. a penurious accumulating c. W. IRVING. Hence **Curmu·dgeonly** *a.* miserly, niggardly, churlish. Also as *adv.* (*rare*).

Curmurring (kɒɹmɒ·riŋ), *vbl. sb. Sc.* 1785. [imit.] A low rumbling, growling, or murmuring sound.

Some c. in his guts BURNS.

Curn. *north* and *Sc.* ME. [perh. rel. to KERN *sb.*² and *v.*¹] † **1.** *pl.* Grain. (ME. only.) **2.** *Sc.* A grain 1474; *transf.* a few 1785. Hence **Cu·rney** *sb. Sc.* a company, lot. **Cu·rny** *a.* granular.

Cu·rple. *Sc.* 1498. [Phonetic perversion of *curper* CRUPPER.] **1.** A crupper. **2.** *transf.* The posteriors 1787.

Curr (kɔ̄ɹ, kɒrr), *v.* 1677. [imit.] To make a low murmuring sound; to coo, purr.

‖ **Currach, -agh** (kɒ·ră, ku·răχ). 1450. [– Ir., Gael. *currach* boat; cf. CORACLE.] A boat made of wickerwork covered with hides; a coracle.

Currant (kɒ·rănt). ME. [orig. in pl. phr. *raysons of coraunce* – AFr. *raisins de corauntz*, for (O)Fr. *raisins de Corinthe* 'grapes of Corinth' (their orig. place of export).] **1.** The raisin prepared from a seedless grape, grown in the Levant: used in cookery. **2.** The small round berry of certain species of *Ribes* (*R. nigrum, R. rubrum*) called Black and Red Currants. (The White Currant is a variety of the Red.) 1578. **b.** The shrubs producing this fruit, and other shrubs of the same genus 1665. Also *transf.*

2. b. Corinthes or currans, as they are vulgarly called, are plants well known RAY.

Comb.: **c.-borer, -clearwing,** the clearwing moth *Ægeria tipuliformis* and its larva; **-gall,** a small round gall, formed on the male flowers and leaves of the oak by the insect *Spathegaster baccarum*; **-moth,** the Magpie-moth; **-worm,** a larva that infests currant-bushes.

Currency (kɒ·rĕnsi). 1657. [f. next; see -ENCY.] † **1.** The fact or condition of flowing, flow; course; *concr.* a current, stream (*rare*) –1758. **2.** The course (of time); the time during which anything is current 1726. **3.** Of money: The fact or quality of being current as a medium of exchange; circulation. Also *fig.* 1699. **4.** The circulating medium; the money of a country in actual use 1729. **b.** *spec.* Applied to a current medium of exchange when differing in value from the money of account; *e.g.* the former currency and banco of Hamburg (see BANCO *a.*) 1755. **5.** The fact or quality of being current; prevalence, vogue; *esp.* of ideas, reports, etc. 1722. Also *attrib.*

2. During the entire c. of the lease MCCULLOCH. **3.** The c. of Bills 1722, of Wood's copper coin in Ireland POPE. **4.** The paper currencies of North America ADAM SMITH. **5.** The story.. seems to have gained c. 1798. var. † **Cu·rrence** (*rare*).

Current (kɒ·rĕnt), *a.* [ME. *cora(u)nt* – OFr. *corant* (mod. *courant*), pres. pple. of *courre* :–

L. *currere* run; see -ENT.] **1.** Running; flowing. Also *fig.* (Now *rare.*) **2.** Running in time; in progress; belonging to the week, month, etc., now running 1608. **3.** Of money: Passing from hand to hand; in general use as a medium of exchange 1481. † **4.** Sterling, genuine: opp. to *counterfeit* –1744. **5.** Generally reported or known; in general circulation 1563. **6.** Generally accepted; in vogue 1593.

1. The c. streame MILT. *P.L.* VII. 67. **2.** The c. year 1734. C. services BURKE, expenses RUSKIN. **3.** Currant money amonge marchauntes COVERDALE *Gen.* 23:16. **4.** To put your love unto the touch, to try If it be currant, or but counterfeit 1599. **5.** The stories which were c. about..the Speaker MACAULAY. **6.** A word which is not c. English DRYDEN.

Phr. *To pass c.* (†*for c.*): to be generally related or accepted. *The 10th c.* (abbreviated *curt.*): the 10th day of the c. month.

Hence **Cu·rrently** *adv.* in a c. manner; flowingly; popularly. **Cu·rrentness.**

Current (kɒ·rěnt), *sb.* ME. [– OFr. *corant* (mod. *courant*), subst. use of the pres. pple.; see prec., -ENT.] **1.** That which runs or flows, a stream; *spec.* a portion of a body of water, or of air, etc. moving in a definite direction. **2.** The action or condition of flowing 1555. **3.** The inclination given to a gutter, roof, etc., to let the water run off 1582. **4.** *fig.* The course of time or of events 1586. **5.** Tendency, tenor, drift 1595. **6.** *Electr.* The apparent flow of electric force through a conducting body 1747. Also *attrib.*

1. Great ocean currents such as the Gulf Stream 1863. **2.** There is no great C. in the Bay Bp. BURNET. **4.** The c. of my speach MARSTON, of our story FREEMAN. **5.** The whole c. of modern feeling BRYCE.

Comb.: **c.-bedding,** the bedding of geological strata in a sloping direction caused by deposition in a c. of water; **-gauge, -meter,** an apparatus for measuring the flow of liquids through a channel; **-mill,** a mill driven by a c.-wheel; **-wheel,** a wheel driven by a natural c. of water. **b.** Of or pertaining to an electrical c.; as *c.-breaker, -meter*, etc.

Hence **Cu·rrentless** *a.* having no c.

Curricle (kɒ·rik'l). 1682. [– L. *curriculum* racing-chariot, dim. f. *currere* run.] † **1.** A course, running –1710. **2.** A light two-wheeled carriage, usu. drawn by two horses abreast 1756.

1. Upon a c. in this world depends a long course of the next SIR T. BROWNE.

‖ **Curriculum** (kŏri·kiŭlŏm). Pl. **-ula.** 1633. [L.; see prec.] A course; *spec.* a regular course of study as at a school or (Scottish) University.

Cu·rried, *ppl. a.* 1855. [f. CURRY *sb.*[2] and *v.*[3] + -ED.] Prepared with curry or curry-powder.

Currier[1] (kɒ·riəɹ). [ME. *corier* – OFr. *corier* :– L. *coriarius*, f. *corium* leather; see -ER [2].] **1.** One who dresses and colours leather after it is tanned. **2.** One who curries horses, etc. 1562.

† **Cu·rrier**[2]. 1557. [Origin unkn.] **1.** A fire-arm, of the same calibre and strength as the arquebus, but with a longer barrel –1659. **2.** A man armed with a currier –1581.

Currish (kŏ·riʃ), *a.* 1460. [f. CUR + -ISH[1].] **1.** Of, relating to, or resembling a cur 1565. **2.** *fig.* Like a cur in nature; snappish, quarrelsome, snarling; mean-spirited, base.

2. This c. Iew *Merch. V.* IV. i. 292. Quarrelsome and c. People that bark and snarl at one another 1705. Hence **Cu·rrish-ly** *adv.*, **-ness.**

† **Cu·rry,** *sb.*[1] *rare.* ME. only. [– (O)Fr. *corroi*; see CONREY, CURRY *v.*[1]] The currying of leather.

Curry (kɒ·ri), *sb.*[2] 1598. [– Tamil *kari* relish with rice, Canarese *karil.*] A preparation of meat, fish, fruit, or vegetables, cooked with bruised spices and turmeric, and used as a relish. Hence, *a curry* = a dish or stew flavoured with this.

† **Cu·rry, currie,** *sb.*[3] 1500. [– Fr. *curée* (XV), earlier OFr. *cuirée* (XII); generally referred to *cuir* leather; see -Y[5], QUARRY *sb.*[1]] The portions of an animal slain that were given to the hounds; the cutting up and disembowelling of the game; also *transf.* –1830.

Curry (kɒ·ri), *v.*[1] ME. [– OFr. *correier* (mod. *courroyer*) arrange, equip, curry (a horse) :– Rom. **conredare*, modelled on Gmc. **ʒaræðjan*, f. **ʒa-* Y- + **raiðjō* READY. Cf. CONREY, CORRODY.] **1.** *trans.* To rub down or dress (a horse, ass, etc.) with a comb. Also *transf.* and *fig.* **2.** To dress (tanned leather) by soaking, scraping, paring, beating, colouring, etc. ME. **3.** *transf.* To thrash one's hide for him, drub. Also *fig.* 1526. † **4.** *fig.* To employ flattery, etc., so as to cajole or win favour –1830.

3. He hath well curried thy cote BARET. **4.** I would currie with Maister Shallow 2 *Hen. IV*, V. i. 81.

Phr. *To c. favour* (orig. †*to c. favel* = OFr. *estriller fauvel* to c. the chestnut horse: cf. FAVEL): to solicit favour by flattery or complaisance.

† **Curry,** *v.*[2] 1608. [perh. f. *currier*, common XVI–XVIII form of *courier*, as if to ride post.] *intr.* To scurry –1676.

Curry (kɒ·ri), *v.*[3] 1839. [f. CURRY *sb.*[2]] *trans.* To flavour with curry.

Cu·rry-comb, *sb.* 1573. [f. CURRY *v.*[1]] A comb or instrument of metal for currying horses, etc. Hence **Cu·rrycomb, cu·rry-comb** *v.* to curry; also *transf.* and *fig.*

† **Cu·rry-favel(l.** 1515. [See CURRY *v.*[1], FAVEL B. 2.] One who solicits favour by flattery or complaisance –1589. So † **Cu·rry-favour.**

Curse (kŏɹs), *sb.* [Late OE. *curs*, of unkn. origin.] **1.** An utterance consigning (a person or thing) to evil; *spec.* a formal ecclesiastical anathema. **2.** A profane oath, an imprecation OE. **3.** An object of cursing ME. **4.** The evil inflicted in response to an imprecation, or in the way of retribution ME.; a thing which blights or blasts; a bane 1591.

1. God's c. can cast away ten thousand sail COWPER. A cursse was sent from the pope, which cursed both the king and the realme HOLINSHED. **2.** I giue him curses, yet he giues me loue *Mids. N.* I. i. 196. Phr. *Not worth a c.*: see CRESS. (But *damn* occurs as early as *curse.*) **3.** I..will make this city a c. to all the nations *Jer.* 26:6. **4.** C. on the stripling! how he apes his sire ADDISON. Phr. *C. of Scotland*: the nine of diamonds in a pack of cards. The origin of the name is doubtful. See O.E.D. Hence **Cu·rseful** *a.* fraught with curses (*rare*).

Curse (kŏɹs), *v.* [OE. *cursian*, f. prec.] **1.** *trans.* To utter against (persons or things) words which consign them to evil; to damn ME.; *spec.* to anathematize, excommunicate OE. **2.** Hence, To denounce with adjuration of the divine name; to pour maledictions upon; to swear at ME. **3.** To speak impiously against; to blaspheme OE. **4.** *absol.* or *intr.* To utter curses ME. **5.** *trans.* To afflict with such evils as indicate divine wrath or a malignant fate; to blast ME.

1. How shall I c., whom God hath not cursed *Num.* 23:8. **2.** I heard my brother damn the coachman, and c. the maids DE FOE. **3.** They shall ..c. their King, and their God *Isa.* 8:21. **4.** Then began he to c. and to swear *Matt.* 26:74. **5.** To be cursed with a bad temper (*mod.*). Hence **Cu·rser.**

Cursed, curst (kŏ·ɹsěd, kŏɹst), *ppl. a.* ME. [f. prec. + -ED[1].] **1.** Under a curse. **2.** Deserving a curse; execrable ME. **3.** (Usually spelt *curst.*) Malignant; perversely cross (*arch.*) ME.; † savage, vicious –1727.

1. The spot is c. WORDSW. **2.** To haue done suilk a curced dede ME. **3.** Curster than she, why 'tis impossible *Tam. Shr.* III. ii. 156. God sends a c. Cow short hornes *Much Ado* II. i. 25. Hence **Cu·rsed-ly** *adv.*, **-ness, curstness.**

† **Cu·rsement.** *rare.* ME. only. [f. CURSE *v.* + -MENT.] Cursing.

Cu·rsen, -son, dial. f. CHRISTEN *a.* and *v.*

Curship (kŏ·ɹʃip). 1663. [f. CUR + -SHIP.] The estate or personality of a cur: a mock title.

Cursitate (kŏ·ɹsite[i]t), *v. rare.* 1867. [– *cursitat-*, pa. ppl. stem of L. *cursitare*, frequent. of *currere* run; see -ATE[3].] *intr.* To run hither and thither. So † **Cursita·tion,** a running hither and thither 1630.

Cursitor (kŏ·ɹsitəɹ). Now *Hist.* 1523. [– legal AFr. *coursetour* – med.L. *cursitor*, f. *cursus* COURSE.] **1.** One of twenty-four clerks of the Court of Chancery, who made out all writs *de cursu*, i.e. of common course or routine. † **2.** A courier –1661. † **3.** A tramp –1725.

C. baron: the puisne baron of the Exchequer, who attended to matters 'of course' on the revenue side. Abolished in 1856.

Cursive (kŏ·ɹsiv), *a.* 1784. [– med.L. *cursivus* (in *scriptura cursiva*), f. *curs-*, pa. ppl. stem of L. *currere* run; see -IVE.] Of writing: Written with a running hand, so that the characters are rapidly formed without raising the pen. In ancient manuscripts distinguished from *uncial*. As *sb.* A cursive character or manuscript. Hence **Cu·rsively** *adv.* in c. characters (*rare*). **Cu·rsiveness,** c. quality (*rare*).

Cursor (kŏ·ɹsǫɹ). 1566. [– L. *cursor* runner, f. as prec.; see -OR 2.] † **1.** A running messenger –1632. **2.** A part of a mathematical instrument, which slides backwards and forwards 1594. ‖ **3.** In mediæval universities, a bachelor of theology who gave the preliminary courses of lectures on the Bible.

† **Cu·rsorary,** obs. *rare* = CURSORY. Shaks.

‖ **Cursores** (kɒɹsǒ·rīz), *sb. pl.* 1828. [L. pl. of *cursor*; see above.] *Ornith.* An order of birds, containing the ostrich and its allies, which are mostly swift runners; the *Ratitæ.* So **Curso·rial** *a.* adapted for running; *spec.* applied to the *Cursores*, orthopterous insects (*Cursoria*), and crustaceans. **Curso·rious** *a.*

Cursory (kŏ·ɹsŏri), *a.* 1601. [– L. *cursorius*, f. *cursor*; see CURSOR, -ORY[2].] **1.** Passing rapidly over a thing or subject; hasty, hurried. † **2.** Travelling (*rare*) –1650. **3.** *Entom.* Cursorious.

1. I had only a c. view of it, and that by chance 1661. Hence **Cu·rsori-ly** *adv.*, **-ness.**

Curst, *a.*; see CURSED.

Curstly, -ness; see CURSED-LY, -NESS.

‖ **Cursus** (kŏ·ɹsŏs). 1838. [L., f. *currere* run.] The Latin word for COURSE; occas. used for **a.** A running-ground or drive; **b.** A stated order of daily prayer; **c.** A curriculum.

Curt (kŏɹt), *a.* 1630. [– L. *curtus* cut short, mutilated, abridged.] **1.** Short; shortened 1664. **2.** Of words, style, etc.: Concise; terse to a fault; rudely brief 1630.

2. The dry and c. language of a petition in parliament ROGERS. He might have been a little less defiant and c. GEO. ELIOT. Hence **Cu·rt-ly** *adv.*, **-ness.**

† **Curt,** *v.* 1568. [– L. *curtare* shorten, f. *curtus* (see prec.).] *trans.* To shorten –1618. Hence † **Cu·rted** *ppl. a.*

Curt., curt. An abbrev. of CURRENT *a.*, q.v.

Curtail (kɒɹtē[i]·l), *v.* 1553. [orig. f. CURTAL (q.v.), from XVI assoc. w. *tail*, and perh. by some in XVII and XVIII w. Fr. *tailler* to cut.] † **1.** To make a curtal of; to dock –1611. **2.** To shorten in length, duration, extent, or amount; to abbreviate, abridge, or reduce 1553.

2. I, that am curtail'd of this faire Proportion *Rich. III*, I. i. 18. To c. salaries 1781, slumbers MRS. CARLYLE, jurisdiction FROUDE. Hence **Curtai·ler. Curtai·lment,** the action of curtailing; abridgement.

Curtail, obs. f. CURTAL *sb.* and *a.*

Curtail-step. Also **curtal-.** 1736. [Origin unkn.] The lowest step (or steps) of a stair, having the outer end carried round in the form of a scroll.

Curtain (kŏ·ɹtěn, -t'n) *sb.* [ME. *cortine, curtine* – OFr. *cortine* (mod. *courtine*) :– late L. *cortina*, used in the Vulgate (Exodus 26:1) to render Gr. αὐλαία curtain (f. αὐλή court).] **1.** A hanging screen of cloth, etc., admitting of being withdrawn sideways, and serving for purposes of use or ornament; *e.g.* to enclose a bed (the earliest English use), to divide a room, to prevent draughts, etc. Also *transf.* **2.** In a theatre, etc.: The screen separating the stage from the auditorium, which is drawn up at the beginning and dropped at the end of an act. Also *fig.* 1599. **3.** *transf.* and *fig.* Anything that covers or hides ME. **4.** *Fortif.* The part of the wall which connects two bastions, towers, gates, etc. 1569; *Archit.* a plain enclosing wall not supporting a roof 1633. Also *attrib.*

1. The Veile or Courtaine of the Temple did rend a sunder GOLDING. Phr. *To draw the c.*: (*a*) to draw it back, so as to disclose an object; (*b*) to draw it forward, so as to cover an object. *C. of mail*: = CAMAIL 1. **2.** Phr. *To drop* or *raise the c.*, to end or begin an action. *Behind the c.*: away from the public view.

Comb.: (in sense 2) as *c.-call, -fall, -tune*; **c.-angle,** the angle formed at a bastion, etc., where the c. begins; **-lecture,** 'a reproof given by a wife to her husband in bed' (J.); so † **-sermon; -raiser** [Fr. *lever de rideau*], a short piece played before the principal play.

Cu·rtain, *v.* ME. [f. prec.] To furnish, surround, adorn, with a curtain or curtains;

transf. and *fig.* to cover, conceal, protect, shut *off*, as with a curtain.
fig. Wicked Dreames abuse The Curtain'd sleepe *Macb.* II. i. 51.

Curtal (kō̆·ɹtăl). Now *Hist.* 1509. [XVI also *courtault* – Fr. *courtault*, *-auld* (mod. *courtaud*), f. *court* short (see CURT) + pejorative suffix *-ault* (mod. *-aud*). See CURTAIL.]
A. *sb.* **1.** A horse with its tail docked 1530. **2.** *transf.* and *fig.* Anything cut short 1607. **3.** *Cant.* A rogue who wears a short cloak 1561. **4.** A kind of cannon with a short barrel, formerly used 1509. **5.** A kind of bassoon; also, an organ-stop of similar tone 1582.
B. *adj.* **1.** Having the tail docked 1576. **2.** Shortened 1590; abridged; scant, curt 1579. **3.** *C. friar*: app. a friar with a short frock; cf. A. 3. 1610. Hence † **Cu·rtalize** *v.* = CURTAIL.

Cu·rtal-axe, -ax. Now *Hist.* or *arch.* 1579. [alt., by assim. to AXE *sb.*[1], of †*curtelace* (XVI), itself alt. (by assim. to *court* short) of *coutelace* CUTLASS.] A CUTLASS; any heavy slashing sword.

‖ **Curtana** (kɒɹtā·nă, -ē[i]·nă). Also **curtan.** ME. [– AL. *curtana*, fem. (sc. *spatha* sword) – AFr. *curtain*, OFr. *cortain* name of Roland's sword, so called because it had broken at the point when thrust into a block of steel, f. *cort*, *curt* short (see CURT).] The pointless sword borne before the kings of England at their coronation; emblematically considered the sword of mercy; also called the sword of King Edward the Confessor.

Curtate (kō̆·ɹtĕt), *a.* 1676. [– L. *curtatus*, pa. pple. of *curtare*; see CURT *v.*, -ATE[2].] *Geom.*, etc.: Shortened, reduced: applied to a line projected orthographically upon a plane.
C. distance: the distance of a planet or comet from the sun or earth, projected upon the plane of the ecliptic. *C. cycloid*: see CYCLOID *sb.*

Curta·tion. 1584. [– med. or mod.L. *curtatio*, f. *curtat-*, pa. ppl. stem of L. *curtare*; see prec., -ION.] † **1.** *Alchem.* The shorter process for transmuting metals into gold –1699. **2.** *Astron.* The difference between the true and the curtate distance of a planet from the sun 1706.

Curtays(e, -eis(e, obs. ff. COURTEOUS.
Curtein, -teyn; = CURTANA.
† **Curtelace,** obs. f. CUTLASS.
Curteous, etc.; see COURTEOUS, etc.

Curt-hose (kō̆·ɹt,hōᵘz). ME. [– OFr. *curte-hose* short boot, f. *hose*, *huese* boot, in med.L. *hosa*; see HOSE.] Short-boot; a surname of Robert, eldest son of William the Conqueror; = med.L. *Curta ocrea*.

Curtilage (kō̆·ɹtilĕdʒ). ME. [– AFr. *curtilage*, OFr. *co(u)rtillage*, f. *co(u)rtil* small court, f. *cort* COURT; see -AGE.] A small court, yard, or piece of ground attached to a dwelling-house, and forming one enclosure with it.

Curtsy, curtsey (kō̆·ɹtsi), *sb.* 1528. [var. of COURTESY, formerly used in various senses of this, but restricted since *c* 1700.] **1.** = COURTESY in various senses. **2.** An obeisance; now, a feminine movement of respect, etc., made by bending the knees and lowering the body 1575.

Curtsy, curtsey (kō̆·ɹtsi), *v.* 1553. [f. prec. sb.] *intr.* To make a curtsy; now said only of women. Also *transf.* and *fig.*
Emma curtsied, the gentleman bowed JANE AUSTEN.

‖ **Curucui** (kūᵊrukū·i). 1678. [Native name; imit.] A bird (*Trogon curucui*) found in Brazil and elsewhere.

Curule (kiūᵊ·r[i]ul), *a.* 1600. [– L. *curulis*, f. *currus* chariot, f. *currere* run.] **1.** *Rom. Antiq.* *C. chair*: a chair or seat inlaid with ivory and shaped like a camp-stool with curved legs, used by the highest magistrates of Rome 1695. **2.** Privileged to sit in a curule chair, as *c. magistrate*, etc. 1600. Also *transf.* of any high civic dignity.

Cu·rval, *a.* *Her.* = next.

Cu·rvant, *a.* 1830. [– *curvant-*, f. L. *curvare* curve; see -ANT.] *Her.* Curving.

Curvated (kō̆·ɹvĕtĕd), *a.* *rare.* 1727. [– L. *curvatus* (pa. pple. of *curvare* curve) + -ED[1].] Curved; of a curved form.

Curvation (kōɹvē[i]·ʃən). 1656. [– L. *curvatio*, f. *curvat-*, pa. ppl. stem of *curvare*; see CURVE *v.*, -ION. Cf. OFr. *curvacion*, mod. *curvation*.] Curving, bending.

Curvative (kō̆·ɹvătiv), *a.* *rare.* 1856. [f. as prec. + -IVE; cf. Fr. *curvatif* in same sense.] *Bot.* Of leaves: Having the margins slightly curved.

Curvature (kō̆·ɹvătiŭɹ). 1603. [– OFr. *curvature* – L. *curvatura*, f. as prec.; see -URE.] **1.** The action of curving or bending; the fact, or manner of being curved; curved form 1665. **2.** *Geom.* The amount or rate of deviation (of a curve) from a straight line, or (of a curved surface) from a plane 1710. **3.** *concr.* A curved portion of anything; a curve 1603.
1. A line..of that peculiar c. HOGARTH. *C. of the spine* (Path.): an abnormal curving of the spinal column, of which there are two sorts, *angular* or *Pott's c.*, and *lateral c.* **2.** *Circle of c.*: the circle which osculates a curve at any point, and serves to measure the c. of the curve at that point. *Centre of c.*, *radius of c.*: the centre and radius of the circle of c. *Double c.*: that of a curve which twists so as not to lie in one plane, *e.g.* the curve of a screw.

Curve (kōɹv). 1571. [– L. *curvus* bent.]
A. *adj.* Curved. Now *rare*.
The Tail is c. 1665.
B. *sb.* (Short for *c.-line*, etc.). **1.** *Geom.* A curved line: a locus traced by a point, moving in a direction which continuously deviates from a straight line. (In *Higher Geometry*, extended to include the straight line.) 1696. **2.** A curved form, outline, etc.; a curved thing or part 1728.

Curve (kōɹv), *v.* 1594. [– L. *curvare*, f. *curvus*; see prec.] **1.** *trans.* To bend so as to form a curve; to cause to take a curved form; to inflect 1669. **2.** *intr.* To have or take a curved form.
1. Curving a contumelious lip TENNYSON. **2.** The tentacles c. inwards DARWIN. Hence **Curved** *ppl. a.* (partly replacing CURVE *a.*). **Cu·rvedness.**

Curvet (kō̆·ɹvĕt, kōɹve·t), *sb.* 1575. [– It. *corvetta*, dim. of *corva*, early form of *curva* curve :– L. *curva*, fem. of *curvus*; see CURVE, -ET.] In the *manège*: A leap of a horse in which the fore-legs are raised together and equally advanced, and the hind-legs raised with a spring before the fore-legs reach the ground. (Also, any frisking motion; cf. CARACOL.)

Curvet (kōɹve·t, kō̆·ɹvĕt), *v.* 1592. [f. prec. sb.] **1.** *intr.* To execute a curvet, leap in a curvet; *trans.* to cause to curvet. **2.** *transf.* To leap about, frisk; also *fig.* 1600.
2. Cry holla to the tongue, I prethee: it curuettes vnseasonably *A.Y.L.* III. ii. 258. Hence **Cu·rveting, curve·tting** *vbl. sb.* and *ppl. a.*

Curvi- (kō̆·ɹvi), comb. f. L. *curvus* curved; chiefly in adjs. used in *Nat. Hist.*, as:
Curvicau·date [L. *cauda*], having a curved tail. **Curvico·state** [L. *costa*], having bent ribs. **Curvide·ntate** [L. *dens*, *dent-*], having curved teeth. **Curvifo·liate** [L. *folium*], having leaves bent back. **Cu·rviform,** of a curved shape. **Curvine·rvate, Curvine·rved** *Bot.*, having veins diverging from the midrib and converging towards the margin; also called *curve-veined*. **Curviro·stral** [L. *rostrum*], having a curved beak. **Curvise·rial,** forming a series disposed in a curve (of leaves on a stem).

Curvili·nead. 1826. [f. CURVI- + L. *linea* line, with fanciful application of *-ad*.] An instrument for drawing curved lines.

Curvilineal (kōɹvili·nĭăl), *a.* 1656. [f. CURVI-, after RECTILINEAL.] = next.

Curvilinear (kōɹvili·nĭăɹ), *a.* (*sb.*) 1710. [f. CURVI-, after RECTILINEAR.] Consisting of, or contained by, a curved line or lines. (Opp. to *rectilinear*, and in Gothic Archit. to *perpendicular*.) Hence **Curvilinea·rity. Curvili·nearly** *adv.*

† **Cu·rvity.** 1547. [– Fr. *curvité* or late L. *curvitas*, f. L. *curvus*; see CURVE, -ITY.] **1.** Curved or bent state; curvature; a curve –1831. **2.** *fig.* Moral obliquity –1678.

Cu·rvograph. 1817. [f. CURVE + -GRAPH.] An instrument for describing curves.

† **Cu·ry.** ME. [– OFr. *queuerie* kitchen, cookery, f. *queu* cook :– L. *coquus* cook; see -ERY.] Cookery; also, cooked food, a dish –1513.

Cusco-bark. Also **Cuzco-.** A kind of cinchona bark, obtained from Cuzco in Lower Peru. Also called **Cusco-china.**

‖ **Cuscus**[1] (ku·skus). 1625. [Arab. *kuskus*, *kuskusū*, of Berber origin.] The grain of the African Millet, *Holcus spicatus* Linn.

‖ **Cuscus**[2] (kɒ·skɒs). 1810. [– Pers. *kaškāš* poppy.] The aromatic root of an Indian grass, *Andropogon muricatus*, used for making fans, screens, etc. Hence *c.-grass*, *c.-root*.

‖ **Cuscus**[3] (kɒ·skɒs). 1662. [See COUSCOUS[2].] A genus of marsupial quadrupeds found in New Guinea.

Cushat (kɒ·ʃăt). Chiefly *Sc.* and *n. dial.* [OE. *cūsćute*, *-sć(e)ote*, of unkn. origin.] The wood-pigeon or ring-dove. So *C.-dove*.

Cu·shew-bird. Also **cashew-bird.** 1758. [From the blue knot on its forehead, which is like the *cashew-nut*.] The Galeated Curassow (*Pauxis galeata*).

Cushion (ku·ʃən), *sb.* [ME. (i) *quisshon*, (ii) *cushin* :– OFr. (i) *coissin*, *cuissin*, (ii) *cossin*, *cussin*, (also mod.) *coussin* :– a Gallo-Rom. form based on L. *culcita* mattress, cushion. For the phonology cf. *ambush*, *bushel*, *crush*, *usher*.] **1.** A case of cloth, silk, etc., stuffed with some soft elastic material, used to sit, recline, or kneel upon. **b.** The seat of a judge or ruler 1659. Also *fig.* **2.** Anything resembling or acting as a cushion 1813; †a swelling simulating pregnancy –1694. **3.** In various specific and technical applications: as, the elastic leathern pad on which gold-leaf is cut 1837; a pad worn by women under the hair 1774; the elastic rim of a billiard-table 1778; *Mech.* a body of steam left in the cylinder of a steam-engine to act as an elastic buffer to the piston 1848. **4.** In a horse, pig, etc.: The fleshy part of the buttock 1710. **5.** *Entom.* A pulvillus 1828; *Bot.* a pulvinus 1870. **6.** *Archit.* = COUSSINET, q.v.
1. They set them downe on cosshyns of sylke LD. BERNERS. *fig.* Idlenesse..the Devils C., as the Fathers call it 1652.
Attrib. and *comb.*: **c. capital** *Archit.*, a capital used in Romanesque architecture, resembling a c. pressed down by a weight; also, a cap consisting of a cube rounded off at its lower angles, used in the Norman period; † **cloth,** a c. case or covering; **-dance,** a round dance, formerly danced at weddings, in which the women and men alternately knelt on a c. to be kissed; **-star,** a fossil star-fish of the genus *Goniaster*; **-stitch,** a flat embroidery stitch used to fill in backgrounds in old needlework; etc.

Cushion (ku·ʃən), *v.* 1735. [f. prec. sb.] **1.** *trans.* To furnish with a cushion or cushions 1820. Also *fig.* **2.** To rest, seat, or set upon a cushion; to prop *up* with cushions 1735. **3.** *fig.* To suppress (anything) quietly 1818. **4.** *Billiards.* To leave a ball close to, or touching, the cushion. **b.** *intr.* (in U.S.) To make the ball hit the cushion before cannoning or after contact with one of the balls. **5.** To deaden the stroke of (the piston) by a cushion of steam; to form into a cushion of steam 1850.
2. Instead of inhabiting palaces, and being cushioned up in thrones BOLINGBROKE. **3.** The way in which complaints are cushioned in official quarters 1887.

† **Cu·shionet.** 1542. [– Fr. *coussinet*, dim. of *coussin*; see prec., -ET.] A little cushion; a pin-cushion –1721.

Cushiony (ku·ʃəni), *a.* 1839. [f. CUSHION *sb.* + -Y[1].] Resembling a cushion in shape, softness, etc., as *a soft c. feel*.

Cushy (ku·ʃi), *a.* *slang.* 1915. [Anglo-Ind.] Of a job, etc.: Easy. Of a wound: Not serious.

Cusk (kɒsk). 1624. [Origin unkn.] A name for two fishes of the cod tribe: **a.** In Great Britain, the Torsk, *Brosmius vulgaris*. **b.** In U.S., the Burbot, *Lota maculosa*.

Cusp (kɒsp). 1585. [– L. *cuspis*, *-id-* point, apex.] **1.** *Astrol.* The beginning or entrance of a 'house'. **2.** *gen.* A point, pointed end, peak 1647. **3.** *Astron.* Each of the horns of the crescent moon (or of Mercury and Venus) 1676. **4.** *Geom.* A point at which two branches of a curve meet, and stop, with a common tangent 1758. **5.** *Archit.* Each of the projecting points between the small arcs in Gothic tracery, arches, etc. 1813. **6.** *Anat.* A projection or point, *e.g.* on the crown of a tooth 1849. **7.** *Bot.* A sharp rigid point, *e.g.* of a leaf 1870. Hence (*erron.*) **Cu·spated** *a.* *Arch.*, furnished with a c. or cusps. **Cusped** *a.* cuspated. **Cu·sping** *sb.* *Arch.*, cusp-work.

‖ **Cuspa·ria.** 1852. [f. native name *Cuspare*.] *Bot.* A genus of trees, now usually called *Galipea*, species of which yield *Angus-*

tura bark; also = **Cu·sparin** (*Chem.*), a crystalline substance obtained from Angustura bark 1824.

Cuspid (kʊ·spid). 1743. [– L. *cuspis, cuspid-* point.] *sb.* † **1.** *Geom.* = CUSP 4. **2.** A cuspidated tooth 1878. *adj.* = CUSPIDATE 1882.

Cuspidal (kʊ·spidăl), *a.* 1647. [f. as prec. + -AL[1].] † **1.** Belonging to the apex. **2.** *Geom.* Having, related to, or of the nature of, a CUSP 1874. **3.** Of teeth, cuspidate 1867.

Cuspidate (kʊ·spidĕt), *a.* 1692. [– mod.L. *cuspidatus*, f. as prec.; see -ATE[2].] Having a cusp or sharp point. *spec.* **a.** Of leaves: Ending in a rigid point. **b.** Applied to the canine teeth. So **Cu·spidated** *a.* **Cuspida·tion,** cusping.

Cuspidine (kʊ·spidəin). 1882. [f. as prec. + -INE[5].] *Min.* A fluo-silicate of calcium from Vesuvius occurring in pale rosy spear-shaped crystals.

Cu·spidor, -ore. *U.S.* 1779. [– Pg. *cuspidor* spitter, f. *cuspir* spit.] A spittoon.

‖ **Cuspis** (kʊ·spis). Pl. **cuspides** (-idīz). 1646. [L.] = CUSP, q.v., in various senses.

Cuss (kʊs), *sb.* *U.S. colloq.* 1775. [Sense 1: vulgar disguising of CURSE; cf. *bust* for *burst*; sense 2: prob. orig. identical with sense 1, but later regarded as short for *customer* (cf. CHAP *sb.*[3]).] **1.** An execration, etc. 1848. **2.** Applied contemptuously or humorously to persons; also to animals. *Comb.* **c.-word,** an oath. So **Cuss** *v.* = CURSE. **Cu·ssed** *a.* cursed. **Cu·ssedness,** malignity, cantankerousness, contrariness.

Cusser, var. COURSER[2], a stallion. SCOTT.

† **Cust.** [repr. OE. *cyst* choice, excellence, etc., in the S.W. and w.midl. dialect.] **1.** Choice. OE. only. **2.** = COST *sb.*[1] –ME.

Custard (kʊ·stăɹd). 1450. [In early recipes varying with †*crustade*, also †*crustarde* – AFr. **crustade*, f. *cruste*, OFr. *crouste*; see CRUST, -ADE.] † **a.** = DARIOLE. **b.** In modern use, a mixture of milk and eggs beaten up and sweetened, and baked; also a similar mixture served up in a liquid form.

Comb.: **c.-apple,** the fruit of *Anona reticulata*; it has a dark-brown rind, and a yellowish pulp resembling c.; also called *bullock's heart*; † **-coffin,** the coffin or crust of a c.

Custode. ME. [orig. – (O)Fr. *custode* – L. *custos, -ōd-*. In mod. use – It. *custode* (kustō·de), pl. *-odi*.] One who has the custody of anything; a guardian, custodian.

Custodial (kʊstōᵘ·diăl). 1772. [f. L. *custodia* + -AL[1].] *adj.* Relating to custody or guardianship. *sb.* A vessel for preserving sacred objects, as the host, relics, etc. 1860.

Custo·diam. 1662. [L. *custodiam* (acc. sing.) custody, from the wording of the grant.] *Irish Law.* A grant by the Exchequer (for three years) of lands, etc., in possession of the Crown.

Custodian (kʊstōᵘ·diăn). 1781. [f. CUSTODY + -AN, after *guardian*.] One who has custody; a guardian, keeper. So **Custo·dier.** (Now *esp.* Sc.) **Custo·dianship.**

Custody (kʊ·stŏdi). 1491 [– L. *custodia*, f. *custos, -ōd-* guardian; see -Y[3].] **1.** Safe keeping, protection; charge, care, guardianship. **2.** The keeping of an officer of justice; confinement, imprisonment, durance 1590. † **3.** Guardianship –1613.

1. Ships for the c. of the narrow seas BACON (J.). **2.** Iaylor, take him to thy custodie *Com. Err.* I. i. 156.

Custom (kʊ·stəm), *sb.* ME. [– OFr. *custume, co(u)stume* (mod. *coutume*) :– **costumne*, for **costudne* :– L. *consuetudo, -in-*, f. *consuescere* accustom, accustom oneself, f. *com* CON- + *suescere* become accustomed.] **1.** A habitual or usual practice; common way of acting; usage, fashion, habit; the being or becoming accustomed 1526. **2.** *Law.* A usage which by continuance has acquired the force of a law or right, *esp.* the special usage of a locality, trade, society, or the like ME. † **3.** Any customary service, rent, or due paid to a lord or ruler –1730. **4.** Duty levied by the lord or local authority upon commodities on their way to market; *esp.* that levied in the name of the king upon exports or imports ME. **5.** The practice of habitually resorting to a particular shop, hotel, etc., to make purchases or give orders 1596.

1. A Custome More honour'd in the breach, then the obseruance *Haml.* I. iv. 15. C. makes all things easy 1867. † *C. of women*: menstruation. **4.** *The Customs*: the duties levied upon imports as a branch of the public revenue; the department of the Civil Service that levies these duties. (Now rarely in sing., and never with *a.*) Not to pay c. SWIFT. **5.** A tailor, whom I have presented my c. PEPYS.

Comb.: **c.-mill,** (*a*) a mill belonging to a feudal proprietor at which his tenants are obliged to grind their corn, paying c. for so doing; (*b*) a mill that grinds for customers; **-office** = CUSTOM-HOUSE.

Hence † **Cu·stomed** *ppl. a. arch.*, accustomed; charged with duty; patronized.

† **Custom** (kʊ·stəm), *v.* ME. [– OFr. *costumer*, f. *costume*; see prec. Cf. med.L. *custumare*.] **1.** *trans.* = ACCUSTOM 1. –1626. **2.** To accustom, habituate (oneself or another) –1855; *pass.* to be used (*to do* something) –1674. **3.** *trans.* To pay duty or toll on –1720. **4.** To bestow one's custom on; to frequent as a customer –1681.

2. Yf he be custommed to doo euylle CAXTON.

Customable (kʊ·stəmăb'l), *a.* ME. [– OFr. *customable*; see CUSTOM *sb.* and *v.*, -ABLE. Cf. med.L. *custumabilis*.] † **1.** Customary, usual –1663. † **2.** Of persons: Accustomed (*to*), wont (*to do*); habitual –1575. **3.** Dutiable (*rare*) 1529.

2. C. Swearers COVERDALE. Hence † **Cu·stomableness.** † **Cu·stomably** *adv.*

† **Cu·stomance, cu·stumance.** ME. [– OFr. *cost-, coustumance*, f. *costumer*; see CUSTOM *v.*, -ANCE.] Custom, habit –1528.

Customary (kʊ·stəmări), *a.* 1523. [– med.L. *custumarius*, f. *custuma* – AFr. *custume*, superseding CUSTOMABLE. See -ARY[1].] **1.** According to custom; commonly used or practised; usual, habitual 1607. **2.** Established by or depending on custom 1660. **3.** *Law.* Subject to customs or dues, as *c. tenants, tenure, lands*, etc. But now taken as: Holding or held by custom (*e.g.* of the manor) 1523.

1. His c. self-possession LYTTON. **2.** The family was a religious and c. institution JOWETT. **3.** *C. mill* = Custom mill (*a*): see CUSTOM. *C. court*: formerly a court which exercised jurisdiction over copyholders, and administered the custom of the manor. *C. holder*, a c. tenant. Hence **Cu·stomari-ly** *adv.*, **-ness.**

Customary (kʊ·stəmări), **custumary** (kʊ·stiumări), *sb.* 1604. [– med.L. *custumarius*, subst. use of the adj.; see prec.] **1.** *Law.* A collection of customs (see CUSTOM *sb.* 2); *esp.* one reduced to writing. **2.** *Eccl.* = CONSUETUDINARY *sb.* 1882.

1. The earliest written c. in France is that of Bearn HALLAM.

Customer (kʊ·stəməɹ), *sb.* ME. [orig. – AFr. *custumer*, med.L. *custumarius*; in some senses newly f. *custom*; see -ER[1].] † **1.** A customary tenant 1440. † **2.** One who collects customs; a custom-house officer –1748. **3.** One who customarily purchases anywhere; a buyer, purchaser. (The chief current sense.) 1480. † **4.** A person with whom one has dealings –1621; a prostitute (SHAKS.). **5.** *colloq.* A person to have to do with; chap, fellow 1589.

3. No Milliner can so fit his customers with Gloues *Wint. T.* IV. iv. 192. **5.** Queer customers those monks DICKENS. Hence † **Cu·stomership,** the office of a collector of customs.

Custom-house (kʊ·stəmhaus). 1490. [CUSTOM 4.] A house or office at which custom is collected; *esp.* a government office, at which customs are levied on imports or exports. Also, the office of the department which manages the customs. Also *attrib.*

‖ **Custos** (kʊ·stǫs). 1465. [L. Formerly treated as Eng.: now Latin, with pl. *custodes*.] A keeper, guardian, custodian.

C. rotulorum: the principal Justice of the Peace in a county, who has custody of the rolls and records of the sessions of the peace.

Custrel (kʊ·strĕl). Now *Hist.* 1492. [corresp. in meaning to OFr. *coustillier, -illeur*, soldier armed with a *coustille*, double-edged sword, but the Eng. form is unexpl.; sense 2 (not in Fr.) is app. infl. by CUSTRON; cf. COISTREL.] **1.** An attendant on a knight. **2.** A term of reproach: Knave. See COISTREL. 1581.

† **Cu·stron.** ME. [– OFr. *coistron*, nom. *cuistre* scullion :– pop.L. *coquistro, -ōn-* 'tabernarius' (Papias).] **1.** A kitchen-knave; hence a base-born fellow, cad, vagabond –1605. **2.** = CUSTREL 1. 1494.

Custumal (kʊ·stiumăl), **customal** (kʊ·stəmăl), *sb.* 1570. [– med.L. *costumale* customs-book, n. of *costumalis*, f. *costuma* – OFr. *costume* CUSTOM; see -AL[1].] *Law.* = CUSTOMARY *sb.*

Cu·stumal, *a.* 1889. [– med.L. *cos-, custumalis*, corresp. to OFr. *costumal, -el* adj.; see prec.] Having to do with the customs of a city, etc.

Cut (kʊt), *sb.*[1] Also **cutt, -e.** ME. [Taken usually as a special use of CUT *sb.*[2], but this is not certain.] **1.** = LOT: in the phr. *draw cuts*, orig. *draw cut*. (See O.E.D.). † **2.** (One's) lot; fate or fortune as a ruler of events –1635.

Cut (kʊt), *sb.*[2] ME. [Mostly f. CUT *v.*]

I. 1. The act of cutting 1808; a stroke or blow with a sharp-edged instrument 1601; a sharp stroke with a whip, cane, etc. 1725. **2.** *fig.* An act whereby the feelings are deeply wounded, as a sarcasm, etc.; a severe disaster; a shock 1568. **3.** An excision or omission of a part 1604. **4.** The act of cutting down rates, prices, salaries, etc.; a reduction of this kind (orig. *U.S.*) 1881. **5.** *Card-playing.* The act of cutting a pack; the card so obtained 1598. **6.** A step in dancing 1676. **7.** A particular stroke in *Cricket, Lawn-tennis*, etc. 1855. **8.** *colloq.* The act of cutting an acquaintance 1798.

1. The speech is all whet and no c. COBBETT. *C.-and-thrust* adj., adapted for both cutting and thrusting; also *fig.* **4.** A further c. of two cents 1881. **8.** The c. direct THACKERAY.

II. A way straight across. Also *concr.* and *fig.* 1577.

Phr. *Short c.*: a crossing that shortens the distance (*lit.* and *fig.*).

III. The style in which a thing is cut; fashion, shape 1579. Also *fig.*

Attyre of the new c. LYLY. Phr. *The c. of one's jib*: one's general appearance (*slang*) 1823. *A c. above*: a degree or stage above (*colloq.*) 1818.

IV. 1. An opening made by a sharp-edged instrument, an incision; a wound made by cutting, a gash 1530. **2.** A slash in the edge of a garment 1563. **3.** A passage or channel cut or dug out; a cutting 1548; †a strait –1678. **4.** An engraved block or plate; the impression from this; an engraving (see WOODCUT) 1646.

2. Cloth a gold and cuts, and lac'd with siluer *Much Ado* III. iv. 19. **3.** Through these Fens run great Cuts or Dreyns 1696. **4.** Bibles, with cuts and comments CRABBE.

V. 1. A piece cut off, *e.g.* of meat, cloth, yarn, etc. 1591. **2.** The quantity cut (*esp.* of timber). Chiefly *U.S.* 1805.

VI. The pa. ppl. used subst. † **1.** A cut-tail horse, or ? a gelding –1612. **2.** A term of abuse. (Perh. from prec. sense.) *Obs.* or *dial.* 1490.

2. If thou hast her not i' the end, call me C. *Twel. N.* II. iii. 203. Phr. † *To keep one's c., keep c.*: ? to keep one's distance, be reserved.

Cut (kʊt), *v.* ME. [The early dial. vars. *cutte, kitte, kette* point to an OE. **cyttan*, f. **kut-* (cf. Norw. *kutte*, Icel. *kuta* cut with a little knife, *kuti* sb. little blunt knife).]

I. 1. To penetrate so as to sever the continuity of with an edged instrument; to make incision in; to gash, slash. Said also of the instrument; also *transf.* **2.** *absol.* or *intr.* To make incision ME. **3.** To strike sharply as with a whip, etc. Also said of the whip, etc. Also *absol.* 1607. **4.** *fig.* (*trans.*) To wound deeply the feelings of 1582.

1. Kyt it wyth a knyf ARNOLDE. **2.** C. close to the Stem EVELYN. *fig.* The tongue is not steel, yet it cuts G. HERBERT. **4.** Every word in it will c. them to the heart BEVERIDGE.

II. 1. To divide into parts with a sharp-edged instrument; to sever ME. Also *fig.* **2.** *spec.* To carve; also *absol.* 1601. **3.** To make a narrow opening through, intersect 1590. **4.** To break up the viscidity of 1578. **5.** To sever for the purpose of taking the part detached; to reap, mow, hew, etc. ME. **6.** *intr.* (in *pass.* sense.) To suffer incision; to admit of being cut; to yield when cut 1560.

1. To c. a thread WYATT, asparagus MACAULAY. *fig.* [Friendship] cutteth Griefes in Halfes BACON. Phr. *To c. to* (or *in*) *pieces*: (*fig.*) to rout with great slaughter. **3.** To c. a Canal 1677, sea-dykes

PALMERSTON, a vein of ore 1778. **5.** Thy servants can skill to c. timber in Lebanon 2 *Chr.* 2:8. **6.** The trout. . cut red MEDWIN.

III. To separate or remove by cutting; to lop off. Also with *away, off, out.* ME.

Phr. †*To c. a purse*: to steal it by cutting it from the girdle.

IV. 1. *trans.* To pass through as in cutting; to intersect, to cross. Also *intr.* with *through*, etc. ME. **2.** *colloq.* To run away; to move sharply. Orig. with *away, off.* 1590.

1. The old part of the path which the line had cut across 1885.

V. To reduce by cutting; to trim, shear; to prune. Also *fig.* ME.

For cutting my haire, 6*d.* WOOD. *fig.* To c. rates 1888.

VI. 1. To shape, fashion, form, or make by or as by cutting 1511. **2.** To hollow out, excavate 1634. **3.** To perform or execute, as in *to c.* a CAPER, a DASH, a FIGURE, etc. (see these words) 1601.

1. Why should a man. . Sit like his Grandsire, cut in Alablaster *Merch. V.* I. i. 84. He knows. . when a Coat is well cut STEELE. His features were finely cut 1883. **2.** We do not see how the canals are to be cut 1887. Phr. *To c. one's way*, etc.: to advance by cutting through obstructions 1599.

VII. Special senses. **1.** *Surg.* **a.** To castrate 1465. **b.** To make an incision in the bladder for extraction of stone; also *absol.* 1566. **2.** Of horses: *intr.* To bruise the inside of the fetlock with the opposite foot; to interfere 1660. **3.** *Naut.* (*absol.*) To cut the cable 1707. **4.** *Card-playing.* To divide (a pack of cards) 1532. **5.** *Dancing.* (*intr.*) To spring and twiddle the feet one in front of the other alternately 1603. **6.** To execute a particular stroke in *Cricket, Lawn-tennis, Croquet,* etc. 1857. **7.** *colloq.* (*trans.*) To break off acquaintance with, affect not to know (a person); to give up (a thing) 1634. Also †*intr.* **8.** *Irish Hist.* (*trans.*) To levy (a tax, etc.). Also *absol.* [Cf. Fr. *tailler.*] –1612.

Phrases. *To c. a tooth, one's teeth*: to have them appear through the gums; also *fig.* to become knowing; so *to c. one's eye-teeth. To c. and carve*: an intensive phr. *To c. and run* (Naut.): to c. the cable and make sail without waiting to weigh anchor; *colloq.* to hurry off. *To c. short*: *trans.* to curtail; to break off or interrupt abruptly; *intr.* to be brief. *To c. one's stick* (slang): to be off. Also *to c. one's lucky. To c. the coat according to the cloth*: to adapt oneself to circumstances, to keep within the limit of one's means. *To c. to pieces*: see II. 1 (quots.). *To c. the grass under*, or *ground from under, a person's feet*: see GRASS, GROUND. *To c. the knot*: see KNOT *sb.*[1] II, 1.

Comb. (with adverbs): **C. down. a.** *trans.* To c. and bring down or let fall. **b.** To lay low with the sword. **c.** To take the lead of in a race, etc. **d.** To retrench, curtail. **C. in. a.** To carve or engrave in intaglio. **b.** To penetrate sharply or abruptly. **c.** To strike in. **d.** *Card-playing.* To join in a game by taking the place of a player *cutting out*, q.v. **C. off. a.** *trans.* To c. so as to take off, to sever. **b.** To put a stop to; to break off. **c.** To bring to an untimely end. **d.** To intercept. **e.** To interrupt, stop (communication, passage, etc.). **f.** To shut out; to debar. **g.** To disinherit. **C. out. a.** *trans.* To c. so as to take out. **b.** To excise, omit. **c.** To carry off (a ship) from a harbour, etc., by getting between her and the shore. **d.** *U.S.*, etc. To detach (an animal) from the herd. **e.** To get in front of a rival so as to take the first place from him. **f.** To excavate, carve out. **g.** To shape by cutting (out of a piece); also *fig.* **h.** To plan; to prepare (*work* to be done). See also WORK *sb.* (Phrases). **i.** To form by nature (*for* a purpose). **j.** *intr.* To admit of being cut into shape. **k.** *intr.* (orig. *pass.*) *Card-playing.* To be excluded from a game by cutting an unfavourable card: cf. *c. in.* **C. under.** To c. out by underselling (*colloq.*). **C. up. a.** *trans.* To root up by cutting; also *fig.* **b.** To c. in pieces; also *fig.* **c.** To c. to pieces: see II. 1 (quots.). **d.** To damage by or as by cutting; also *fig.* **e.** To wound deeply the feelings of. (Usu. in *pass.*) **f.** *intr.* To admit of being cut up, to turn out as to amount of fortune (*slang*). **g.** *To c. up rough*, etc.: (*intr.*) to become quarrelsome (*colloq.*). **h.** To behave (*badly*, etc.) in a race (*slang*).

Phraseological combs. **C.-and-come-again.** The act or faculty of helping oneself as often as one likes; hence, abundance; also *fig.* Also *attrib.* **C.-and-cover.** *Engineering.* A method of constructing a tunnel by making a cutting in which the brickwork lining is built and then covered in.

Cut (kɒt), *ppl. a.* ME. [f. CUT *v.*] **1.** Gashed or wounded with an edged instrument 1665; slashed, as clothes, etc. 1480. **2.** Affected by cutting 1588. **3.** Shaped or fashioned by cutting; having the surface shaped by grinding and polishing, as *c. glass* 1677. **4.** Divided into pieces by cutting ME. **5.** Detached by cutting, as *c. flowers* ME. **6.** Reduced by, or as by cutting; cut down 1646. **7.** Castrated 1624. **8.** *slang.* Drunk 1673.

Phr. *C. and dried* (also *c. and dry*): orig. of herbs in the herbalists' shops; hence *fig.* ready-made; also, ready shaped on *a priori* notions.

Cutaneous (kiutēⁱ·niəs), *a.* 1578. [f. mod. L. *cutaneus* (f. L. *cutis* skin) + -OUS.] Of, pertaining to, or affecting the skin, as *c. diseases, eruptions,* etc. Also *fig.* var. † **Cuta·nean.**

Cu·t-away, *a.* (*sb.*) 1841. [f. CUT *pa. pple.*] Of a coat: Having the skirt cut back from the waist in a slope or curve. As *sb.* (*ellipt.*) A cut-away coat.

Cutch[1] (kɒtʃ). 1759. [– Malay *kachu.*] = CATECHU.

Cutch[2] (kɒtʃ). 1879. [app. – Fr. *caucher* in same sense, f. OFr. *cauchier* tread, press down :– L. *calcare* tread under foot.] A pile of vellum leaves, between which laminæ of gold-leaf are placed to be beaten.

Cutch, var. of COUCH *sb.*[2] (*Triticum repens*).

‖ **Cutcha** (kɒ·tʃă), *a. Anglo-Ind.* Also **kutcha.** 1834. [– Hindi *kachchā* raw, crude, uncooked.] Slight, makeshift (opp. to *pucka* solid). As *sb.* Sun-dried brick.

Cutcher (in *Paper-making*) = COUCHER[2].

‖ **Cutcherry** (kŏtʃe·ri), **cutchery** (kɒ·tʃĕri). *Anglo-Ind.* 1610. [– Hindi *kachahrī, kachĕrī.*] **1.** A court-house. Also, a business office. † **2.** A brigade of infantry 1799.

Cute (kiūt), *a. colloq.* Also **'cute.** 1731. [aphet. f. ACUTE.] **1.** Acute, clever, sharp, shrewd. **2.** (*U.S. colloq.*, etc.) = CUNNING *a.* 6. 1868. Hence **Cu·teness.**

Cut-grass. 1840. [f. CUT *v.*: *lit.* 'grass that cuts'.] A genus of grasses, *Leersia*, esp. *L. oryzoides.*

Cuticle (kiū·tik'l). 1615. [– L. *cuticula*, dim. of *cutis* skin. See -CULE.] **1.** The EPIDERMIS or scarf-skin of the body; also *transf.* of other superficial integuments. **2.** *Bot.* Formerly, the primary integumentary tissue; now, a superficial film formed of the outer layers of the epidermal cells 1671. † **3.** A film or thin coating –1704. var. ‖ **Cuti·cula** [L.]. Hence **Cuti:cular** *a.* of, pertaining to, or resembling a c. **Cut:iculariza·tion,** the action or process of forming into c. **Cuti·cularize** *v. trans.*, to form into c.

Cutify (kiū·tifəi), *v.* 1890. [f. L. *cutis* skin; see -FY.] *intr.* To form skin. Hence **Cutifica·tion,** formation of cutis.

Cutikin (kü·tikin). *Sc.* 1816. [f. Sc. *coot*, earlier *cute* ankle, of LDu. origin; cf. MLG. *kote*, LG. *kote, köte*; see -KIN.] A gaiter, a spatterdash.

Cutin (kiū·tin). 1863. [f. CUTIS + -IN[1].] *Bot.* The cellulose body forming the cuticle of plants, CUTOSE. Hence **Cu·tinize** *v.* = *cuticularize.* **Cutiniza·tion.**

‖ **Cutis** (kiū·tis). 1603. [L.] **1.** *Anat.* The true skin or derma of the body. **2.** *Bot.* The peridium of certain fungi. Hence **Cuti·tis** *Path.*, inflammation of the skin.

Cutlass (kɒ·tlăs). 1594. [– Fr. *coutelas*, repr. Rom. **cultellaceum*, f. L. *cultellus*, dim. of *culter* COULTER, + augment. suffix *-aceum.* See CURTAL-AXE.] A short sword with a flat, wide, slightly curved blade; now *esp.* that with which sailors are armed.

Comb.: **c.-fish,** a species of fish, the Silvery Hair-tail, so named from its shape.

Cutler (kɒ·tləɹ). ME. [– AFr. *cotillere*, (O)Fr. *coutelier*, f. *coutel* (mod. *couteau*) knife :– L. *cultellus*, dim. of *culter* COULTER; see -ER[2].] One who makes, deals in, or repairs knives, etc.

Cutlery (kɒ·tləri). 1449. [– (O)Fr. *coutellerie*, f. *coutelier*; see prec., -ERY.] **a.** The art or trade of the cutler. **b.** *collect.* Articles made or sold by cutlers, as knives, scissors, etc.; also, implements for eating or serving food at table 1624.

Cutlet (kɒ·tlėt). 1706. [– Fr. *côtelette*, OFr. *costelete*, dim. of *coste* (mod. *côte*) rib :– L. *costa*; assim. to CUT *sb.*[2] and -LET. See COST *sb.*[4]] A small piece of meat, usually mutton cut off the ribs, or veal, used for broiling, frying, etc.

Cutling (kɒ·tliŋ), *vbl. sb. dial.* 1645. [f. as if from a verb *to cutle.*] The making of cutlery. Also *attrib.*

That the men of Toledo . . were excellent at c. MILT.

Cut-off (kɒ·tˌǫ·f, *attrib.* kɒ·tˌǫf), *sb.* 1741. [CUT *v.* (*comb.*).] **1.** An act of cutting off or portion cut off. **2.** A new and shorter passage cut by a river through a bend. *Western U.S.* 1830. **3.** A stopping of a continuance or flow 1881. **b.** *spec.* (*Steam-engine.*) An arrangement by which the admission of steam to the cylinder is cut off when the piston has travelled part of the stroke, so that the steam during the remainder of the stroke works expansively; a contrivance for effecting this. Also *attrib.* 1849. **c.** Any contrivance for stopping the flow of a liquid, cutting off a connection, and the like 1874.

Cutose (kiūtōᵘ·s). 1881. [f. CUTIS + -OSE[2].] *Chem.* One of the cellulose bodies; the hyaline substance which forms the cuticle of plants. Also called CUTIN.

Cut-out (kɒtˌau·t, kɒ·tˌaut), *sb.* 1874. [CUT *v.* (*comb.*).] *Electr. Engin.* A device for automatically cutting lamps, motors, etc., out of circuit when the current attains a point at which it is undesirable to work. **b.** In motor-vehicles, an appliance that gives a free opening to the exhaust gases 1905.

Cutpurse, cut-purse (kɒ·tpɒ̄ɹs). ME. [CUT *v.* III.] One who steals a purse by cutting it from the girdle, from which formerly it was suspended; hence, a pickpocket, thief; also *fig.*

How often hast thou seene the C. hanged with the purse about his necke GOLDING.

Cu·ttanee. 1622. [Urdu *kattānī*, f. Arab. *kattān* flax.] Fine linen from the East Indies.

Cutter (kɒ·təɹ), *sb.*[1] ME. [f. CUT *v.* + -ER[1].] **1.** One who cuts; one who shapes things by cutting; as *fustian-, stone-, wood-c.* 1483. **2.** *spec.* †A hair-cutter –1624; a carver, sculptor, engraver 1572; † a tailor; the person in a tailoring establishment who takes the measures and cuts out the cloth 1599; one who castrates animals 1562. †**3.** One over-ready to resort to weapons; a bully; also, a cutthroat –1826. **4.** That which cuts; an implement or tool for cutting; the cutting part of a machine, etc. 1631; †an incisor tooth –1691. **5.** *Mining.* A crack intersecting the lines of stratification; the cleavage of slate (usu. in *pl.*); a crack in a crystal (*dial.*) 1756. **6.** A superior quality of brick, which can be cut and rubbed 1842.

Comb.: **c.-bar,** (*a*) a bar in which cutting-tools are so fastened as to serve for circular cutting; (*b*) the bar in a mowing or reaping machine that bears the knives; **-grinder,** an instrument for sharpening the cutters of reaping machines, etc.; **-head,** the revolving head of a tool with cutters; **-wheel,** one serving for cutting.

Cutter (kɒ·təɹ), *sb.*[2] 1745. [perh. f. CUT *v.* + -ER[1]; but deriv. from Indo-Pg. *catur* (XVI) narrow vessel, cannot be excluded.] *Naut.* **1.** A boat, belonging to a ship of war, shorter and in proportion broader than the barge or pinnace, fitted for rowing or sailing, and used for carrying light stores, passengers, etc. **2.** A small, single-masted vessel, clinker- or carvel-built, furnished with a straight running bowsprit, and rigged much like a sloop, as a *revenue c.* 1762. **3.** *transf.* A small sleigh or sledge for one or two persons. *Canada* and *U.S.* 1836.

Comb. **c.-brig,** 'a vessel with square sails, a fore-and-aft main-sail, and a jigger-mast with a smaller one' (Smyth).

Cutthroat, cut-throat (kɒ·tˌþroᵘt). 1535. [See CUT *v.*] **1.** One who cuts throats; a ruffian who murders or does deeds of violence. Also *transf.* and *fig.* † **2.** A dark lantern –1825. **3.** The Mustang grape of Texas, having an acrid taste. **4.** A West African bird, *Amadina fasciata*, the male of which has a red mark round the throat 1872. **5.** *attrib.* Murderous, ruffianly 1567. **b.** Three-handed, as *c. bridge, euchre* 1904.

1. I am a soldier, sir, and not a cut-throat FROUDE.

Cutting (kɒ·tiŋ), *vbl. sb.* ME. [-ING[1].] **1.** The action of CUT *v.*, in various senses. † **2.** An intersection; also a section –1726. **3.** *concr.* A piece cut off; *esp.* a shred made in trimming an object for use ME. **4.** *spec.* A small shoot bearing leaf-buds cut off a plant, and used for propagation 1664; a piece cut out of a newspaper, etc. 1856. **5.** *Irish Hist.* Tallage 1596. **6.** A carving, etc. 1787. **7.** *Mining.* 'A poor quality of ore mixed with that which is better' (Knight) 1874. **8.** An excavation through ground that rises above the level of a canal, railway, or road which has to cross it 1836.

Comb.: **c.-box,** † (*a*) ? a chaff- or straw-cutter; (*b*) a receptacle for the diamond dust in diamond-cutting; **-shoe,** a special shoe for horses which cut or interfere (see CUT *v.* VII. 2).

Cu·tting, *ppl. a.* ME. [-ING².] **1.** That cuts, in various senses, as a *c. blade, wind, employer*, etc. **2.** That acutely wounds the feelings 1583. † **3.** That is a 'cutter' or swaggering blade –1592.

2. He can say the . . most c. things in the quietest of tones C. BRONTË. Hence **Cu·ttingly** *adv.*

Cuttle (kɒ·t'l), *sb.*¹ [Late OE. *cudele*, ME. (XV) *codel*, corresp. to OLFrank. *cudele*, Norw. dial. *kaule* (:– **kodle*), f. base of COD *sb.*¹, with allusion to its ink-bag.] A cephalopod of the genus *Sepia* or family *Sepiidæ*, esp. the common cuttlefish, *Sepia officinalis*, also called *ink-fish* from its power of ejecting a black fluid from a bag or sac, so as to darken the water and conceal itself. Thence extended to other decapods, and occas. to octopods, cephalopods. Now usually called **Cuttle-fish.** Also *attrib.*

† **Cuttle,** *sb.*² 1546. [app. – OFr. *coutel* (mod. *couteau*). See CUTLER.] A knife. Also *fig.* –1661. **b.** *transf.* 2 *Hen. IV*, II. iv. 139.

† **Cu·ttle,** *v. rare.* [Origin unkn.] To whisper; to talk privately and confidentially. H. WALPOLE.

Cu·ttle-bone. 1547. The internal calcareous shell of the cuttle-fish; used for pounce, as a polishing material, etc.

Cuttle-fish; see CUTTLE *sb.*¹

Cuttoe (kɒ·to). *Obs.* exc. *U.S.* 1678. [– Fr. *couteau*.] = COUTEAU.

Cu·ttoo. 1794. [Origin unkn.] *Carriage-building.* One of the projections covering the top of the wheels which shelter the axle-tree arms from the dirt.

Cutty (kɒ·ti). *Sc.* and *n. dial.* 17. . [f. *cut*, pa. pple. of CUT *v.* + -Y⁶.]

A. *adj.* Cut short, curtailed, as *c. knife, pipe, sark*, etc.

B. *sb.* **1.** Short for *c. spoon* (*Sc.*) 17. . **2.** Short for *c. pipe* 1776. **3.** A term for a testy or naughty girl or woman; often playful 1816. **4.** A local name for: **a.** The wren. **b.** The Black Guillemot. **c.** The hare. 1776.

Cutty-stool. *Sc.* 1774. [CUTTY *a.*] **1.** A low stool 1820. **2.** Formerly, in Scotland, a seat in a church, where offenders against chastity had to sit, and receive a public rebuke from the minister. Also *fig.*

Cutwal, -waul; see KOTWAL.

Cutwater, cut-water (kɒ·tˌwǭːtəɹ). 1644. **1.** The knee of the head of a ship, etc., which divides the water before it reaches the bow; also, the forward edge of the prow. **2.** The wedge-shaped end of the pier of a bridge, which serves to divide the current, break up ice, etc. 1776. **3.** An American sea-fowl, the Skimmer, *Rhynchops nigra* 1732.

Cu·t-work, cu·twork. 1470. **1.** *gen.* Work produced by cutting or carving 1662. **2.** Embroidery with cut-out edges, also a kind of openwork embroidery or lace, formerly worn. **b.** Appliqué work. 1470. † **3.** Flower-beds cut into patterns –1727.

Cu·tworm. 1808. A caterpillar which cuts off by the surface of the ground the young plants of cabbage, maize, melons, etc.; *esp.* in *U.S.* the larvæ of species of *Agrotis*, a genus of moths.

†‖ **Cuve.** ME. [– (O)Fr. cask, vat :– L. *cupa*.] A cask, vat –1673.

‖ **Cuvette** (küve·t). 1678. [Fr., dim of *cuve* (see prec.).] **1.** *Fortif.* = CUNETTE. **2.** An ornamental shallow dish for holding water, etc. 1706. **3.** *Glass-making.* A large clay basin or crucible used in making plate-glass 1832.

Cwt., abbrev. of HUNDREDWEIGHT. [f. *c* = L. *centum* + *wt.* = *weight.*]

-cy, suffix of sbs., originating in L. *-cia, -tia*, Gr. *-κια, -κεια, -τια, -τεια.* Occurring chiefly in the combined forms -ACY, -ANCY, -ENCY, -CRACY, -MANCY, q.v.

Cya-, shortened f. CYANO-, in names of chemical compounds, as **Cya·melide,** a white crystalline substance polymeric with cyanic acid; etc.

Cy·amid. [– mod.L. *Cyamidæ*, f. L. *cyamus* – Gr. *κύαμος* bean; see -ID³.] *Zool.* A crustacean of the family *Cyamidæ*; a whale-louse.

Cyamoid (səi·ǎmoid), *a. rare.* 1882. [See prec., -OID.] Resembling a small bean.

Cyan-. 1. Comb. f. Gr. *κύανος* and *κυάνεος* 'dark-blue' bef. a vowel. **2.** *Chem.* = CYANO- 2, used as comb. f. CYANOGEN bef. a vowel, as in **Cy·anamide,** the amide of cyanogen, CN_2H_2, a white crystalline body. **Cyanhy·dric** *a.* = hydrocyanic. **Cyanu·rate,** a salt of **Cyanu·ric** [URIC], or **Cyanure·nic** acid, an acid polymeric with cyanic acid, obtained by heating dry urea in a flask.

Cyanate (səi·ăneⁱt). 1845. [f. CYAN- 2 + -ATE⁴.] *Chem.* A salt of cyanic acid.

Cyan-blue. 1879. [f. Gr. *κύανος* or *κυάνεος*, cf. CYAN-] A greenish-blue colour, lying between green and blue in the spectrum.

‖ **Cyanea** (səiē̆ⁱ·niǎ). 1883. [fem. of L. *cyaneus*, Gr. *κυάνεος* dark blue; see -A 4.] A genus of jelly-fishes. Hence **Cya·neid,** one of these.

Cyaneous (səiē̆ⁱ·niəs), *a. rare.* 1688. [f. L. *cyaneus* (see prec.) + -OUS.] Deep blue, azure. var. **Cya·nean** (*rare*).

Cyanhydric; see CYAN- 2.

Cyanic (səiæ·nik), *a.* 1832. [f. CYAN- 2 + -IC.] **1.** *Chem.* Of or containing cyanogen. **2.** Blue, azure; *spec.* in *Bot.*, one of the two series into which Candolle divided the colours of flowers (the other being *xanthic* = yellow) 1849.

1. *C. acid*, a colourless, pungent, volatile, unstable liquid (CNHO).

Cyanide (səi·ǎnəid). 1826. [f. CYAN- 2 + -IDE.] *Chem.* A simple compound of cyanogen with a metal or organic radical, as *potassium c.* (KCy).

Cyanin (səi·ǎnin). 1863. [f. CYAN- 1 + -IN¹.] The blue colouring matter of some flowers, as the violet, etc.

Cyanine (səi·ǎnəin). 1872. [f. as prec. + -INE⁵.] *Chem.* A blue dye-stuff prepared from chinoline with amyl iodide, used in calico-printing.

Cyanite (səi·ǎnəit). 1794. [f. as prec. + -ITE¹ 2 b.] *Min.* **1.** A native silicate of aluminium, usually blue. **2.** A fire-proof priming for paint, etc. 1884.

Cyano- (bef. a vowel or *h* usually **cyan-**). **1.** Used as comb. f. Gr. *κυάνεος* a dark-blue mineral, *κυάνεος* adj. dark-blue, in scientific terms, as:

Cyano·chroite *Min.* [Gr. *χροιά*], a blue hydrous sulphate of copper and potassium. **Cyano·pathy** *Path.* [Gr. *-πάθεια*, f. *πάθος*.] = CYANOSIS. **Cyano·trichite** *Min.* [Gr. *θρίξ τριχ-*], a blue fibrous sulphate of copper and aluminium.

2. *Chem.* (= CYAN- 2): Of or containing cyanogen; in the names of cyanogen compounds.

Cyanogen (səiæ·nǒdʒen). 1826. [– Fr. *cyanogène* (Gay-Lussac, 1815), f. Gr. *κύανος* a dark-blue mineral + -GEN, named from its entering into the composition of Prussian blue.] *Chem.* A compound radical consisting of one atom of nitrogen and one of carbon (symbol CN or Cy). In the form of *dicyanogen* (C_2N_2), it is a colourless gas, highly poisonous, with an odour like that of prussic acid. It exists in many compounds, the cyanides, cyanates, cyanurets, etc.

Cyanometer (səiǎnǫ·mĭtəɹ). 1829. [f. CYANO- 1 + -METER.] An instrument for measuring the intensity of the blue of the sky. Hence **Cyanome·tric** *a.* **Cyano·metry.**

Cyanose (səi·ǎnōᵘs). 1834. [– Fr. *cyanose*, f. as next.] *Path.* = CYANOSIS. Hence **Cy·anosed** *ppl. a.* afflicted with cyanosis.

‖ **Cyanosis** (səiǎnōᵘ·sis). 1834. [mod.L. – Gr. *κυάνωσις* dark-blue colour; see CYAN-, -OSIS.] *Path.* Lividness of the skin owing to the circulation of imperfectly oxygenated blood; blue jaundice. Hence **Cyano·tic** *a.* pertaining to, or affected with, c.

Cyanotype (səiæ·nǒtəip). 1842. [f. CYANO- 2 + -TYPE.] A photographic process in which paper sensitized by a cyanide is employed; a print obtained by this process. Also *attrib.*

Cyanu·rate, -uric, etc.; see CYAN- 2.

Cyanuret (səiæ·niŭret). 1827. [f. CYAN- 2 + -URET.] *Chem.* = CYANIDE.

Cyanurin (səiǎniūᵊ·rin). 1845. [f. CYAN- 1 + URINE.] *Path.* A blue deposit occas. found in urine.

† **Cy·ath.** 1544. [– L. *cyathus*.] = CYATHUS 1. –1631.

Cyathiform (səi·ǎþifǫɹm), *a.* 1776. [f. CYATHUS + -FORM.] *Bot.*, etc. Shaped like a cup a little widened at the top.

Cyatholith (səiæ·þǒliþ). 1875. [f. CYATHUS + -LITH.] *Biol.* A kind of coccolith resembling two cups placed base to base.

Cyathophylloid (səiːǎþofi·loid). 1862. [f. mod.L. *Cyathophyllum* (f. Gr. *κύαθος* cup + *φύλλον* leaf) + -OID.] *adj.* Akin to the fossil cup-corals of the genus *Cyathophyllum*. *sb.* A coral of this family 1872.

Cyathozooid (səiˌǎþozōᵘ·oid). 1877. [f. Gr. *κύαθος* CYATHUS + ZOOID.] *Zool.* An abortive first stage of the embryo of certain compound ascidians, which becomes by gemmation the foundation of a colony.

‖ **Cyathus** (səi·ǎþɒ̆s). Pl. **cyathi** (-þəi). ME. [L. – Gr. *κύαθος* wine-cup, measure.] **1.** *Gr. and Rom. Antiq.* A cup or ladle used for drawing wine out of the CRATER or mixing-bowl; also a measure = about $\frac{1}{12}$ of a pint. **2.** *Bot.* The cup-like body which contains the reproductive bodies of *Marchantia* 1866.

Cycad (səi·kǎd). 1845. [– mod.L. generic name *Cycas, -adis* – supposed Gr. *κύκας*, scribal error for *κόϊκας*, acc. pl. of *κόϊξ*, the Egyptian doum-palm.] *Bot.* A plant of the genus *Cycas* which gives its name to the *Cycadaceæ*, a natural order of Gymnosperms, related to the Conifers. Hence **Cycada·ceous** *a.* of or belonging to the N.O. *Cycadaceæ* or Cycads; var. **Cyca·deous. Cyca·diform** *a.* resembling the cycads in form. **Cy·cadite,** a fossil c.

Cyclamen (si·klǎmen). 1550. [– med.L. *cyclamen*, for L. *cyclaminos, -on* – Gr. *κυκλάμινος*, perh. f. *κύκλος* circle, CYCLE, with ref. to its bulbous roots.] A genus of *Primulaceæ*, cultivated for their handsome early-blooming flowers; the fleshy root-stocks are sought after by swine, whence the name SOWBREAD. Also, a plant of this genus.

Cyclamin (si·klǎmin). 1842. [f. prec. + -IN¹.] *Chem.* A poisonous principle extracted from the tubers of Cyclamen; it is a non-azotized glucoside.

‖ **Cyclarthrosis** (siklǎɹþrōᵘ·sis). [mod.L., f. Gr. *κύκλος* circle + *ἄρθρωσις* articulation.] *Anat.* A circular or rotatory articulation, as that of the radius with the ulna. So **Cyclarthro·dial** *a.* of, or of the nature of, a c.

‖ **Cyclas** (si·klǎs). *Hist.* [L. – Gr. *κυκλάς* a woman's garment with a border all round it.] A tightly-fitting tunic anciently worn by women, and occas. by men, *esp.* the tunic or surcoat made shorter in front than behind, worn by knights over their armour in the 14th century. Also confused with CICLATOUN.

Cycle (səi·k'l), *sb.* ME. [– Fr. *cycle* or late L. *cyclus* – Gr. *κύκλος* circle.] **1.** *Astron.* A circle or orbit in the heavens 1631. **2.** A recurrent period of a definite number of years ME.; a period in which a certain round of events or phenomena is completed, recurring in the same order in equal succeeding periods 1662; a long indefinite period; an age 1842. **3.** A recurrent round or course (of successive events, phenomena, etc.) 1664. **4.** *gen.* A round, course, or period through which anything runs to its completion 1821. **5.** A complete set; a round 1662. **6.** *spec.* A series of poems or prose romances collected round a central event or epoch of mythic history and forming a continuous narrative; as *the Arthurian c.*, (*Mus.*) *c. of songs* 1835. **7.** *Bot.* A complete turn of the spire in leaf-arrangement 1857. **8.** *Med.* A course of remedies, continued during a fixed series of days 1882. **9.** *Zool.* In corals, a set of septa of like age 1877. **10.** *Geom.* A closed path in a cyclic region 1881. **b.** *Thermodynamics.* A series of operations at the end of which the working substance is brought back to its original state 1929. **c.** *Electr.* A full period of an alternating current. **11.** Short for *bicycle, tricycle*, or the like 1881. Also *attrib.*

2. *C. of Indiction*: see INDICTION. *Metonic* or *lunar c.*: a c. of 19 years, established by the Greek astronomer Meton, and used for determining Easter. *Solar c.*: a period of 28 years, at the end of which the days of the week recur on the same days of the month. The c. within which dearths and plenties make their revolution PETTY. A c. of Cathay TENNYSON. **4.** Doctrines which have run their c. 1869. Hence **Cy·cled** *ppl. a.* consisting of cycles, as *cycled times.*

Cycle (səi·k'l), *v.* 1842. [f. prec. sb.] **1.** *intr.* To move in cycles; to pass through cycles. **2.** To ride a cycle, to travel by cycle 1883. Hence **Cy·cler** = CYCLIST 1. **Cy·cling** *vbl. sb.*

Cy·clian, *a. rare.* 1699. [f. Gr. κύκλιος circular, cyclic + -AN.] = CYCLIC 2, CYCLIC *chorus.*

Cyclic (si·klik), *a.* 1794. [– Fr. *cyclique* or L. *cyclicus* or Gr. κυκλικός; see CYCLE, -IC.] **1.** Of, pertaining to, or of the nature of, a cycle; moving in cycles. **2.** Of or belonging to a cycle of mythic and heroic story; see CYCLE *sb.* 6. 1822. Also *transf.* **3.** *Bot.* Of a flower: Having its parts arranged in whorls 1875. **4.** *Math.* Of or pertaining to a circle or cycle 1852. **5.** *Gr. Prosody.* Of a dactyl or anapæst: Occupying in scansion three instead of four 'times' 1844.

1. Twenty c. years, of ten months each ARNOLD. **2.** *C. poet.*: one of the writers of the Epic cycle. **3.** *C. region* (*Math.*): a region within which a closed line can be drawn in such a manner that it cannot shrink indefinitely without passing out of the region.

Phr. *C. chorus* [Gr. κύκλιος χορός] in *Gr. Antiq.*: the dithyrambic chorus, which was danced in a ring round the altar of Dionysus.

Cyclical (si·klikăl), *a.* 1817. [f. as prec. + -AL[1]; see -ICAL.] **1.** Of a line: Returning into itself so as to form a closed curve (*rare*). **2.** = CYCLIC 1, 2, 3 (also *transf.* in *Zool.*).

Phr. *C. number*: a number in which the sum of the divisors equals the whole.

Cyclide (səi·klid, si·kləid). 1874. [– Fr. *cyclide.*] *Geom.* 'The envelope of a sphere whose centre moves on a fixed quadric, and which cuts a fixed sphere orthogonally' (Salmon).

Cyclist (səi·klist). 1882. [f. CYCLE *sb.* + -IST.] **1.** One who rides a cycle. **2.** One who reckons by a cycle or cycles; one who recognizes cycles in the course of phenomena.

‖ **Cyclitis** (sikləi·tis). 1861. [f. Gr. κύκλος circle + -ITIS.] *Path.* Inflammation of the ciliary body.

Cyclo- (səiklo, siklo), comb. f. Gr. κύκλος circle (see CYCLE), as in:

Cyclobra·nchiate *a.* [Gr. βράγχια gills], having gills circularly arranged; applied to a sub-order of gastropodous molluscs (*Cyclobranchia, -branchiata*); also said of the gills. **Cycloce·phalus** [Gr. κεφαλή], a monster having two contiguous eyes, or a double eye in the median line. **Cyclocli·nal** *a. Geol.* = QUAQUAVERSAL. **Cyclocœ·lic** *a.* [Gr. κοιλία], having the intestines coiled: said of birds. **Cy·clogen** [Gr. -γενης], *Bot.* = EXOGEN; so **Cyclo·genous** *a.* **Cy·clograph** [Gr. -γραφος], an instrument for tracing circular arcs. **Cyclo·grapher,** a writer of a cycle (of legends, etc.). **Cy·clolith** [Gr. λίθος], a name for a prehistoric stone circle. **Cycloneu·rous, -ose** *a. Zool.*, having the nervous axis circularly arranged, as in the *Radiata.* **Cyclo·pterous** *a.* [Gr. πτερόν], round-winged, round-finned. **Cy·closcope** [Gr. -σκοπος], (*a*) an apparatus for measuring velocity of revolution; (*b*) an instrument for setting out railway curves. **Cyclospe·rmous** *a.* [Gr. σπέρμα] *Bot.*, having the embryo coiled about the central albumen. **Cyclo·stomate, -sto·matous, -stomous** *a.* [Gr. στόμα], having a round sucking mouth, or a circular aperture of the shell; also belonging to a certain division of the Polyzoa (*Cyclostomata*). **Cy·clostome** *a.* = *Cyclostomous*; *sb.* a cyclostomous fish, as the lamprey; a cyclostomous gastropod. **Cyclosy·stem,** the circular arrangement of the pores in some *Hydrocorallina* (Millepores, etc.).

Cyclode (səi·klōud, si·k-). 1869. [f. Gr. κύκλος circle + ὁδός path.] *Math.* The INVOLUTE (B. 2) of any order to a circle. Sylvester.

Cycloid (səi·kloud, si·k-), *sb.* 1661. [subst. use of Gr. adj. κυκλοειδής; see CYCLE, -OID. Cf. Fr. *cycloïde.*] **1.** *Math.* The curve traced in space by a point in the circumference (or on a radius) of a circle as the circle rolls along a straight line. **2.** *Zool.* A cycloid fish; see next 1847.

1. The *common c.* is that traced by a point in the circumference of the circle, and has cusps where this point meets the straight line; that traced by a point within the circle is a *prolate c.* (with inflexions); by a point without the circle a *curtate c.* (with loops).

Cy·cloid, *a.* 1847. [See prec.] *Zool.* **a.** Said of the scales of certain fishes: Of a somewhat circular form, with concentric striations. **b.** Belonging to the *Cycloidei*, or order of fishes with cycloid scales.

Cycloidal (səikloi·dăl, sik-), *a.* 1704. [f. CYCLOID *sb.* + -AL[1]. Cf. Fr. *cycloïdal.*] **1.** *Geom.* Of, pertaining to, or of the form of a cycloid. **2.** *Zool.* = CYCLOID *a.* **a.** 1872.

Cycloi·dean. Also **-ian.** 1837. [f. CYCLOID + -EAN.] *adj.* Belonging to the cycloid fishes. *sb.* A cycloid fish.

Cyclometer (səiklǫ·mĭtəɹ). 1815. [f. Gr. κύκλος circle + -METER; in sense 2, f. CYCLE 11 + -METER.] **1.** An instrument for measuring circular arcs. **2.** An apparatus attached to a wheel, *esp.* of a cycle, for registering its revolutions 1880. So **Cyclo·metry,** measurement of circles 1656.

Cyclone (səi·klōun). 1848. [prob. intended to repr. Gr. κύκλωμα wheel, coil of a snake, f. κύκλος cycle. *Cyclome* occurs as an early variant.] *gen.* A term for all atmospheric disturbances in which the wind has a circular or whirling course. **b.** *spec.* A hurricane of limited diameter and destructive violence 1856. **c.** *Meteorol.* A system of winds rotating around a centre of minimum barometric pressure, the centre and whole system having itself also a motion of translation, which is sometimes arrested, when the cyclone becomes for a time stationary. (Cf. ANTICYCLONE.) Also *transf.* Hence **Cyclo·nal** *a.* of or pertaining to a c. So **Cyclo·nic, -al** *a.* cyclonal; of the nature of a c. **Cyclo·nically** *adv.*

Cyclop; see CYCLOPS.

Cyclopædia, -pedia (səiklopī·diă). 1636. [abbrev. of ENCYCLOPÆDIA, q.v.] † **1.** = ENCYCLOPÆDIA 1. –1676. **2.** = ENCYCLOPÆDIA 2, 3. 1728. Hence **Cyclopæ·dic, -pedic** *a.* pertaining to or of the nature of a c. **Cyclopæ·dically** *adv.* in a cyclopædic manner.

Cyclopean, -ian (səiklopī·ăn, səiklōu·piăn), *a.* 1641. [– L. *Cyclopeus, Cyclopius* – Gr. Κυκλώπιος (see CYCLOPS) + -AN; see -EAN, -IAN.] **1.** Belonging to or resembling the Cyclopes; monstrous, huge; single, or large and round, like the one eye of a Cyclops. **2.** Applied to an ancient style of masonry in which the stones are immense and irregular in shape; fabled to be the work of a gigantic Thracian race called Cyclopes. Also *transf.* 1835.

Cyclopia (səiklōu·piă). 1839. [mod.L. f. CYCLOPS + -IA[1], perh. infl. by *myopia*, etc.] *Zool.*, etc. The fusion of two eyes into one place in the middle of the forehead, as in a Cyclops.

Cyclopic, † **-al** (səiklǫ·pik, -ăl), *a.*[1] 1633. [– Gr. κυκλωπικός; see CYCLOPS, -IC, -ICAL.] Belonging to or resembling a Cyclops; monstrous; Cyclopean.

Cyclo·pic, *a.*[2] 1879. [f. botanical name *Cyclopia* + -IC.] *Chem.* In *c. acid*: an acid obtained from *Cyclopia vogelii*, a plant used in Africa for the preparation of tea.

Cyclopoid (si·klopoid, səi·-). 1852. [f. mod. L. *Cyclops* (in Zool.) + -OID.] *adj.* Belonging to, or resembling the family *Cyclopidæ* of Copepods, of which the genus Cyclops is the type. *sb.* One of the *Cyclopidæ.*

‖ **Cyclops** (səi·klǫps). Also **Cyclop.** Pl. **Cyclopes** (səiklōu·pīz); also **Cyclops, Cyclopses.** 1513. [– L. *Cyclops* – Gr. Κύκλωψ 'round-eyed', f. κύκλος circle + ὤψ eye.] **1.** *Gr. Mythol.* One of a race of one-eyed giants who forged thunderbolts for Zeus. **2.** *Zool.* A genus of small fresh-water copepods, having an eye (really double) situated in the middle of the front of the head 1849. Also *attrib.*

1. Such an obdurat C., to have but one eye for this text MILT. The Cyclop from his den replies POPE.

Cyclorama (səiklora·mă). 1840. [f. Gr. κύκλος circle + ὅραμα spectacle; cf. PANORAMA.] A picture of a landscape, etc., arranged on the inside of a cylindrical surface, the spectator standing in the middle. Hence **Cyclora·mic** *a.*

Cyclosis (səiklōu·sis). 1835. [– Gr. κύκλωσις encircling; see -OSIS.] **1.** *Biol.* A term for the circulation of latex in the vessels of plants; also for the circulation of protoplasm in certain cells. **2.** *Math.* The occurrence of cycles (see CYCLE 10) 1881.

Cyclostylar (səiklostəi·lăɹ), *a.* 1850. [f. CYCLO- + Gr. στῦλος pillar + -AR[1].] *Archit.* Relating to a structure composed of a circular range of columns without a core.

Cyclostyle (səi·klostəil). 1883. [f. CYCLO- + STYLE.] An apparatus for printing copies of writing. It consists of a pen with a small toothed wheel at the point which cuts minute holes in specially prepared paper; this paper is then used as a stencil-plate from which copies are printed.

Cyclo·tomy. 1879. [f. CYCLO- + -TOMY.] **1.** *Math.* The problem of the division of the circle into a number of equal parts. **2.** *Surg.* Division of the ciliary muscle 1889.

‖ **Cyclus** (si·klǒs, səi·klǒs). 1810. [L.] = CYCLE 6.

Cyder, var. of CIDER.

‖ **Cydippe** (səidi·pī). 1835. [mod.L. – Gr. Κυδίππη, one of the Nereids.] *Zool.* A typical genus of Ctenophora, including *C. pilosa.* Hence **Cydi·ppian** *a.* **Cydi·ppid,** a ctenophoran of the family of C.

† **Cydon.** *rare.* 1643. [– L. *cydonium* (sc. *malum*) apple of *Cydonia*, Κυδωνία town of Crete; see QUINCE.] Quince. **Cy·donin,** mucilage of quince seeds.

Cyesiology (səiᵢīsiǫ·lŏdʒi). 1846. [f. Gr. κύησις pregnancy + -LOGY.] That branch of physiology which treats of pregnancy.

Cygneous (si·gniᵢəs), *a.* 1880. [f. *cygneus*, var. of L. *cycneus* swan-like, + -OUS. See next.] Swan-like; in *Bryology*, curved like a swan's neck.

Cygnet (si·gnėt). ME. [– AFr. *cignet*, dim. of OFr. *cigne* (mod. *cygne*) :– med.L. (Rom.) *cicinus*, for L. *cycnus* (in late MSS. *cygnus*) – Gr. κύκνος; see -ET.] A young swan; *Her.* a swan borne in coat-armour.

So doth the Swan her downie Signets saue SHAKS.

Cylinder (si·lindəɹ). 1570. [– L. *cylindrus* – Gr. κύλινδρος roller, f. κυλίνδειν roll.] **1.** *Geom.* A solid figure of which the two ends are equal and parallel circles or ellipses, and the intervening curved surface is such as would be traced by a line with its ends in the circumferences of these figures, moving parallel to a fixed line which is the axis of the cylinder. **2.** Any body or object of cylindrical form 1641. **3.** *Mechanics.* Applied to many cylindrical parts of machines, etc.; *e.g.* the bore of a gun barrel, the part of a revolver which contains the chambers for the cartridges; the barrel of a pump, in which the piston works; the cylindrical chamber in which the steam (etc.) acts upon the piston; in *Printing*, the roller used in letterpress printing for inking the type (now *inking-roller*), pressing the paper against the type, or carrying the type or printing surface; etc. 1571.

Comb.: **c.-axis** = axis-cylinder (see AXIS[1]); **-bore,** (*a*) *sb.* a gun of which the bore is of uniform diameter; (*b*) *vb.* to make with a cylindrical bore; **-cock,** a cock at the end of the c. in a steam-engine to allow water of condensation to escape; **-cover,** the steam-tight lid at the end of a steam-c.; **-escapement,** a form of watch escapement (also called *horizontal escapement*); **-press** (U.S.), **-printing-machine,** a machine in which a c. is used either for carrying the type or giving the impression; **-watch,** one with a c. escapement.

Cylindra·ceous, *a.* 1676. [f. prec.; see -ACEOUS.] Like a cylinder in shape, cylindrical.

‖ **Cylindrenchyma** (silindre·ŋkimă). 1835. [f. Gr. κύλινδρος cylinder + ἔγχυμα instillation, infusion.] *Bot.* Tissue consisting of cylindrical cells.

Cylindric (sili·ndrik), *a.* 1688. [– mod.L. *cylindricus* – Gr. κυλινδρικός; see CYLINDER, -IC. Cf. Fr. *cylindrique.*] Having the form of a cylinder, cylindrical.

Cylindrical (sili·ndrikăl), *a.* 1646. [f. as prec. + -AL[1]; see -ICAL.] **1.** Of the form of a cylinder. **2.** Of, pertaining, or relating to a cylinder 1656.

1. *C. lens*: a lens of which one or both surfaces are portions of c. surfaces. *C. vault*: 'one in the shape of the segment of a cylinder' (Gwilt). **2.** *C. projection*: a form of projection in which part of a spherical surface is projected upon the surface of a cylinder, which is then unrolled into a plane. Hence **Cyli·ndrically** *adv.*

Cylindriform (sili·ndrifǭɹm), *a.* 1870. [f. L. *cylindrus* + -FORM.] Of the form of a cylinder.

Cylindro- (sili·ndro), comb. f. Gr. κύλινδρος CYLINDER, as in **Cylindrome·tric** *a.*, relating to the measurement of cylinders; etc.

Cylindroid (sili·ndroid, si·-). 1663. [f. CYLINDER + -OID.] *adj.* Resembling a cylinder; somewhat cylindrical in form 1839. *sb.* A figure resembling a cylinder; *spec.* an elliptic cylinder. So **Cylindroi·dal** *a.*

‖ **Cylix** (si·liks). 1850. [Gr. κύλιξ.] *Gr. Antiq.* A shallow cup with a tall stem; a tazza.

‖ **Cyma** (səi·mă). 1563. [– mod.L. *cyma* – Gr. κῦμα billow, wave, waved moulding.] **1.** *Archit.* A moulding of a cornice, the outline of which consists of a concave and a convex line; an ogee. **2.** *Bot.* = CYME¹ 1, 2. 1706.

1. *C. recta*: a moulding concave in its upper part, and convex below. *C. reversa* (rarely *inversa*): a moulding convex in its upper part, and concave below.

Cymagraph (səi·măgrɑf). 1837. [irreg. f. prec. + -GRAPH.] An instrument for copying mouldings.

‖ **Cymaise** (simē̆ⁱ·z). 1656. [Fr. *cimaise, cymaise* – L. CYMATIUM.] = CYMA 1, CYMATIUM.

Cymar (simā·ɹ). Also † **simar, symar.** 1697. [var. of SIMAR; see also CHIMER¹.] **1.** A loose light garment for women, *esp.* a chemise. **2.** = CHIMER¹ 1673.

1. Disrobed of all clothing saving a c. of white silk SCOTT.

Cymatium (simæ·tiǒm, -ēⁱ·ʃⁱǒm). 1563. [– L. *cymatium* ogee, Ionic volute – Gr. κυμάτιον, dim. of κῦμα CYMA.] *Archit.* = CYMA 1.

Cymbal (si·mbəl). OE. [ME. *cymbal, symbal* – L. *cymbalum* – Gr. κύμβαλον, f. κύμβη cup, hollow vessel. The sp. *symbal* reflects med.L. *simbalum* (also *cim-*) bell. OE. *cimbal, cymbal* from (med.)L.] **1.** One of a pair of concave plates of brass or bronze, which are struck together to produce a sharp ringing sound. Also *transf.* Also *fig.* (with ref. to 1 *Cor.* 13:1). **2.** A kind of stop on an organ 1852.

1. In vain with cymbals' ring They call the grisly king MILT. Hence **Cy·mbaled** *ppl. a.*, (*a*) furnished with cymbals; (*b*) produced or accompanied by cymbals. **Cy·mbalist, Cy·mballer,** a player on the cymbals.

‖ **Cymbalo** (si·mbălo). 1879. [– It. *cembalo, cimbalo*, repr. L. *cymbalum*, but applied to the dulcimer.] The DULCIMER, q.v.

Cy·mbiform, *a.* 1836. [f. L. *cymba* boat + -FORM.] *Bot.*, etc. Boat-shaped.

Cyme¹ (səim). Also † **cime.** 1725. [– Fr. *cyme*, var. of *cime* summit, top :- **cima*, pop. form of L. *cyma* – Gr. κῦμα (see CYMA) in the special sense of young cabbage-sprout.] † **1.** (*cime.*) A head (of unexpanded leaves, etc.) (*rare*). **2.** *Bot.* (*cyme.*) A centrifugal or definite inflorescence wherein the primary axis bears a single terminal flower which develops first: opp. to RACEME. Applied *esp.* to inflorescences of this type forming a more or less flat head. 1794. **3.** *Archit.* = CYMA 1 1877. Hence **Cy·mule,** a small c.

Cyme² (*Macb.* v. iii. 55, 1st Fo.), ? erron. for *cynne*, SENNA.

Cymene (səi·mīn). 1863. [f. Gr. κύμινον CUMIN + -ENE.] *Chem.* A hydrocarbon, $C_{10}H_{14}$, discovered in 1840 in oil of cumin, and in other plants. So **Cy·midine,** a base, $C_{10}H_{15}N$. **Cy·mol** = *Cymene.*

Cy·mling. 1796. [var. of *simlin*, var. of SIMNEL kind of squash (U.S.).] A variety of squash.

Cy:mobotryo·se, *a.* 1882. [f. L. *cyma* + BOTRYOSE.] Used of cymes arranged in a racemose manner.

Cymogene (səi·modʒīn). 1882. [f. *cymo-*, quasi comb. form of CYMENE, + *-gene*; see -GEN 1.] A gaseous substance, consisting chiefly of butane, given off during the distillation of crude paraffin, used condensed as a freezing-mixture.

Cy·moid, *a.* 1815. [f. CYMA + -OID.] Resembling a cyma.

Cymophane (səi·mofeⁱn). 1804. [f. Gr. κυμο- comb. f. κῦμα billow, + -φανης showing.] = CHRYSOBERYL. Hence **Cymo·phanous** *a.* having a wavy, floating light; chatoyant.

Cymose (səimōᵘ·s), *a.* 1807. [f. CYME¹ + -OSE¹.] *Bot.* Bearing cymes; of the nature of a cyme; arranged in a cyme. (Of an inflorescence = *centrifugal* or *definite*; opp. to *racemose.*) Hence **Cymo·sely** *adv.* in a c. manner. var. **Cy·mous** (Dicts.).

Cymric (ki·mrik), *a.* 1839. [f. W. *Cymru* Wales, *Cymry* the Welsh (:- **kombrogi* fellow-countrymen, f. COM-; cf. *Allobroges* men of another country); see -IC.] Of or pertaining to the Welsh people or language.

‖ **Cynanche** (sinæ·ŋki). 1706. [Late L. – Gr. κυνάγχη dog-quinsy, sore throat, f. κυν- dog + ἄγχειν throttle. See QUINSY.] *Path.* A name for diseases of the throat, marked by inflammation, swelling, and difficulty of breathing, etc.; *esp.* QUINSY.

Cynanthropy (sinæ·nþrŏpi). 1594. [– Fr. †*cynanthropie*, after *lycanthropie* (see LYCANTHROPY); cf. Gr. κυνάνθρωπος adj. of a dog-man.] A species of madness in which a man imagines himself to be a dog.

Cynarctomachy (sinaɹktǫ·măki). [f. Gr. κυν- dog + ἄρκτος bear + -MACHY.] Bear-baiting. BUTLER *Hud.* I. i. 752.

Cynareous (sinēᵊ·rĭəs), *a.* 1846. [f. mod.L. *Cynareæ* (f. Gr. κυνάρα, var. of κινάρα artichoke) + -OUS.] *Bot.* Belonging to the order *Cynaraceæ* proposed by Lindley of Composite plants, including the thistles, artichoke, burdock, etc. So **Cy·naroid** *a.* allied to the artichoke.

† **Cyne-** (künə-, kinə-), in OE. = royal; occurring in many compounds, as **cynebót** (see BOOT *sb.*¹), the king's boot, compensation paid to the people for the murder of the king; etc.

Cynegetic (sinidʒe·tik). *rare.* 1646. [– Gr. κυνηγετικός, f. κυνηγέτης hunter, f. κύων, κυν- dog + ἡγέτης leader; see -IC.] *adj.* Relating to the chase 1716. *sb. pl.* **Cynegetics**: the chase.

Cynic (si·nik). 1547. [– L. *cynicus* – Gr. κυνικός dog-like, currish, churlish, Cynic, f. κύων, κυν- dog; see -IC.]

A. *adj.* **1.** Belonging to or characteristic of the sect of philosophers called Cynics; see B. 1. 1634. **2.** Having the qualities of a cynic (see B. 2); pertaining to a cynic; cynical 1597.

2. The c. smile..the signal of a contempt which he was too haughty to express DISRAELI.

Phr. *C. year* or *period*: the canicular cycle of the ancient Egyptians; see CANICULAR. *C. spasm*: a convulsive contraction of the facial muscles of one side, so that the teeth are shown in the manner of an angry dog (*Syd. Soc. Lex.*).

B. *sb.* **1.** One of a sect of philosophers in ancient Greece, founded by Antisthenes, a pupil of Socrates, who contemned ease, wealth, and the enjoyments of life. The most famous was Diogenes, who carried the principles of the sect to an extreme. 1547. **2.** A person disposed to rail or find fault; now usually: One disposed to deny and sneer at the sincerity or goodness of human motives and actions 1596.

1. Like the Cynique shut up alwaye in a Tub HOWELL. 2. The c., who admires and enjoys nothing, despises and censures everything 1866.

Hence **Cy·nical** *a.* resembling the C. philosophers; surly, currish, misanthropic, captious; now *esp.* disposed to deny human sincerity and goodness; dog-like. **Cy·nically** *adv.*

Cynicism (si·nisiz'm). 1672. [f. CYNIC + -ISM.] **1.** (*with capital C.*) The philosophy of the Cynics; see CYNIC B. 1. **2.** Cynical disposition, character, or quality 1672; an instance of cynicism 1891.

2. The c. of his measured vice LYTTON. var. **Cy·nism** (*rare*).

‖ **Cynips** (si·nips). 1777. [Formed by Linnæus from Gr. κυν- dog + ἴψ a kind of cynips (Darmsteter).] *Entom.* The typical genus of the gall-flies, hymenopterous insects which puncture plants in order to deposit their eggs, and thus produce galls or gall-nuts. Hence **Cy·nipid,** an insect of the *Cynipidæ*, or family allied to *Cynips*. **Cyni·pidean, -deous, Cyni·pidous** *adjs.* of or pertaining to the *Cynipidæ*.

Cyno-, – Gr. κυνο-, comb. f. κύων (κυν-) dog; occurring in many compounds, technical terms, and nonce-words; as **Cy·noclept** [Gr. κλέπτης], a dog-stealer; etc.

‖ **Cynocephalus** (sino-, səinose·fălǒs). Pl. **-i.** ME. [L. – Gr. κυνοκέφαλος dog-headed, f. κυνο- CYNO- + κεφαλή head.] **1.** One of a fabled race of men with dogs' heads. **2.** The Dog-faced Baboon. In *Zool.* taken as the name of the genus. 1601. Hence **Cynoce·phalous** *a.* pertaining to or of the nature of a c.; dog-headed.

Cynoid (si·noid), *a.* [– Gr. κυνοειδής dog-like; see CYNO-, -OID.] Dog-like; belonging to the *Cynoidea* or canine division of the *Carnivora.*

Cynomorphic (sino-, səinomǫ·ɹfik), *a.* 1892. [ult. f. Gr. κυνόμορφος dog-shaped, f. κυνο- CYNO- + μορφή shape; see -IC.] **1.** *Zool.* Belonging to the division *Cynomorpha* of catarrhine monkeys. **2.** (after *anthropomorphic.*) Relating to a dog's ways of looking at things. So **Cynomo·rphism.**

Cynosure (si·no-, səi·nosiuɹ). 1596. [– Fr. *cynosure* or L. *cynosura* – Gr. κυνόσουρα, f. κυνός, gen. sing. of κύων dog + οὐρά tail.] **1.** The constellation Ursa Minor, which contains in its tail the Pole-star. **2.** *fig.* **a.** Something that serves to direct 1596. **b.** Something that is a centre of attraction 1601.

2. Some beauty..The C. of neighbouring eyes MILT. Hence **Cynosu·ral** *a.* relating to or like a c.

Cynthia (si·nþiă). 1632. [L. *Cynthia* (*dea*), the Cynthian goddess, *i.e.* Artemis or Diana, born on Mount Cynthus; hence the Moon.] A name for the Moon personified as a goddess. Hence **Cy·nthian** *a.*

While C. checks her dragon yoke MILT. *Pens.* 59.

Cyperaceous (sipĕrēⁱ·ʃəs), *a.* 1852. [f. Bot. L. *Cyperaceæ*, f. *Cyperus*; see -ACEOUS.] *Bot.* Belonging to the *Cyperaceæ* or Sedges.

‖ **Cyperus** (səipīᵊ·rǒs, səi·pĕrǒs). 1597. [L. – Gr. κύπειρος, κύπερος (Herod.), an aromatic marsh-plant.] *Bot.* A large genus of endogenous plants, giving its name to the N.O. *Cyperaceæ*. *C. longus* is the Sweet Cyperus, or English Galingale.

‖ **Cyphella** (səife·lă). Pl. **-æ.** 1857. [mod. L. – Gr. κύφελλα (pl.) the hollows of the ears.] *Bot.* A cup-like depression on the under surface of the thallus of some lichens.

Cypher, var. of CIPHER.

Cyphonism (səi·fŏniz'm). 1727. [– Gr. κυφωνισμός, punishment by the κύφων, crooked piece of wood, f. κυφός bent.] *Gr. Antiq.* Punishment by the κύφων, a pillory in which slaves or criminals were fastened by the neck.

‖ **Cypho·sis.** Also **ky-.** 1847. [mod.L. – Gr. κύφωσις, f. κυφός bent; see -OSIS.] *Path.* Backward curvature of the spine; hump-back. Hence **Cypho·tic** *a.* hump-backed.

‖ **Cypræa** (səiprī·ă). [mod.L., f. *Cypria* a name of Venus.] *Zool.* The genus of gastropods containing the cowries. Hence **Cypræ·id,** a gastropod of the cowrie family, *Cypræidæ*. **Cypræ·oid** *a.*

† **Cy·pre.** ME. [– L. *cyprus* (also used) – Gr. (from Κύπρος Cyprus).] **1.** The henna-shrub (*Lawsonia alba* or *inermis*) –1558. ¶ **2.** Confused with CYPRESS¹. –1632.

‖ **Cy pres** (sī prē̦). 1481. [Law-Fr. sp. (XV) of Fr. *si près* 'as near'.] *Law.* As near as practicable: applied to a process in equity by which effect is given to the general intention of a trust or charity, when a literal execution of the testator's intention becomes impossible. (Used as *adv.*, *sb.*, and *adj.*)

Cypress¹ (səi·prĕs). [ME. *cipres* (assim. later to L.) – OFr. *cipres* (mod. *cyprès*) – late L. *cypressus* – Gr. κυπάρισσος, of alien origin.] **1.** A well-known coniferous tree, *Cupressus sempervirens*, with hard durable wood and dense dark foliage. Hence, the English name of the genus. **b.** The wood of this tree. ME. **c.** The branches or sprigs of the tree, used at funerals, or as a symbol of mourning. Also *fig.* 1590. **2.** Applied to various trees and shrubs allied to the true cypress, as **Bald, Black,** or **Deciduous C.,**

Taxodium distichum; etc. Also, to plants taken to resemble the cypress-tree, as **Field C.**, *Ajuga chamæpitys*; **Summer C.**, *Kochia scoparia*; etc. **3.** *attrib.* Of cypress; cypress-like; dark, gloomy, funereal 1596.

1. c. But that remorseless iron hour Made c. of her orange-flower TENNYSON. *Comb.* **c.-vine**, a name of several American species of *Ipomæa*, convolvulaceous climbing plants.

† **Cy·press²**. ME. [Corrupt f. L. *cyperus* app. confused with prec.] The Sweet Cyperus or Galingale –1799.

† **Cy·press³**. ME. [– AFr. *cipres, cypres*, a use of OFr. *Cipre, Cypre* (now *Chypre*) the island of Cyprus.] **1.** A name of textile fabrics originally brought from Cyprus. **a.** A cloth of gold or the like. **b.** A valuable satin, called also *satin of Cypres, satin Cypres*. –1603. **c.** *esp.* (= *C. lawn*) A light transparent material resembling cobweb lawn or crape –1722. **2.** A piece of cypress, used in sign of mourning, and the like –1717. **3.** *attrib.* Of cypress –1678; like cypress in texture or colour –1713.

Cyprian (si·priăn). 1598. [f. L. *Cyprius* of Cyprus + -AN; see -IAN.] **A.** *adj.* **1.** Belonging to Cyprus, an island once famous for the worship of Aphrodite 1627. **2.** *transf.* Licentious, lewd 1599.

B. *sb.* An inhabitant or native of Cyprus, a Cypriote; hence *transf.* A licentious person; in later use *spec.* a prostitute 1598.

Cyprine (si·prəin, -in), *a.* 1828. [– L. *cyprinus* – Gr. κυπρῖνος carp.] *Ichth.* Belonging to the carp genus *Cyprinus*, or the carp family, *Cyprinidæ*.

Cyprinid (siprəi·nid). [f. mod.L. *Cyprinidæ*; see prec., -ID³.] *Ichth.* A fish of the carp family. So **Cypri·niform** *a.* carp-shaped.

Cyprinodont (siprəi·nodǫnt). 1857. [f. L. *cyprinus* – Gr. κυπρῖνος carp + Gr. ὀδοντ- tooth.] *sb.* A malacopterygious fish of the family *Cyprinodontidæ*, of which the typical genus is *Cyprinodon*. *adj.* Of or belonging to this family. Hence **Cyprinodo·ntid, -do·ntoid** *a.* of or allied to the Cyprinodonts.

Cyprinoid (siprəi·noid). 1849. [f. as prec. + -OID.] *Ichth. adj.* Resembling or allied to the carp; belonging to the *Cyprinoidea* 1859. *sb.* A fish belonging to the *Cyprinoidea*.

‖ **Cypripe·din.** 1863. [f. Fr. *cypripède* = Bot. L. *Cypripedium* Lady's slipper (Linn.) app. a corruption of *Cypripodium*, f. Gr. Κύπρις Aphrodite + ποδίς shoe + -IN¹.] *Med.* A brown powder prepared from the roots of *Cypripedium pubescens*; used as an anti-spasmodic.

‖ **Cypris** (səi·pris). 1832. [mod.L. – Gr. Κύπρις Aphrodite.] *Zool.* A genus of minute fresh-water crustacea, having the body enclosed in a delicate bivalve shell. Hence **Cy·proid**, a crustacean allied to the C.

Cyprus, cyprus-lawn; see CYPRESS³.

Cyprus (*Bot.*); see CYPRE.

‖ **Cypsela** (si·psĭlă). 1870. [mod.L. – Gr. κυψέλη hollow vessel, chest, etc.] *Bot.* A kind of dry one-seeded fruit; an achene with an adnate calyx, as in the *Compositæ*. Hence **Cy·pselous** *a.* of the nature of a C.

Cypseline (si·psĭləin), *a.* 1874. [f. L. *cypselus* – Gr. κύψελος the swift + -INE¹.] *Zool.* Of the family *Cypselidæ* or genus *Cypselus* of birds, comprising the Swifts. So **Cy·pseliform, Cy·pseloid** *adjs.* having the form of a Swift.

Cyrenaic (səirĭnē·ik). 1586. [– L. *Cyrenaicus* – Gr. Κυρηναϊκός, f. Κυρήνη Cyrene, a Greek colony in Africa.] *adj.* Belonging to the school of Aristippus of Cyrene, whose doctrine was one of practical hedonism 1641. *sb.* A Cyrenaic philosopher. Hence **Cyrena·icism**, the C. doctrine. So **Cyrene·an, Cyre·nian** *adjs.*

Cyrillic (siri·lik), *a.* 1881. [f. the proper name *Cyril* + -IC.] Applied to the alphabet employed by the Slavs of the Eastern Church, and ascribed to St. Cyril. The Cyrillic alphabet is distinguished from the Glagolitic (see Addenda).

Cyriologic, -al (siriolǫ·dʒik, -ăl), *a.* 1655. The analogical form of CURIOLOGIC, -AL.

Cyrto- (sɜ̄ɹto-), repr. Gr. κυρτο- from κυρτός curved. Hence **Cyrtoce·ratite** *Palæont.*, a fossil cephalopod of the genus *Cyrtoceras*, having the shell incurved. So **Cyrtocerati·tic, Cyrto·ceran** *adjs.*; **Cyrtoce·ratid. Cy·rtoid** *a.*, resembling a hump on the back. **Cy·rtolite** *Min.*, a variety of zircon with the pyramidal planes convex (Dana). **Cyrto·meter**, an instrument for measuring and recording curves; **Cyrtome·tric** *a.*, **Cyrto·metry. Cy·rtostyle**, a circular portico projecting from a building.

Cyst (sist). 1720. [– late L. *cystis*; see CYSTIS.] **1.** *Biol.* A thin-walled hollow organ or cavity in an animal body (or plant) containing a liquid secretion; a bladder, sac, vesicle. **2.** *Path.* A closed cavity or sac of an abnormal character, usually containing morbid matter 1731. **3.** *Biol.*, etc. A cell or cavity containing reproductive bodies, embryos, etc.; *e.g.* the spore-case of certain fungi 1857.

Cyst-, comb. f. Gr. κύστις CYST bef. vowels (cf. CYSTI-, CYSTO-): as **Cysta·lgia** [Gr. ἄλγος] *Path.*, pain in the bladder, *esp.* of a spasmodic character. **Cyste·ctasy** [Gr. ἔκτασις], dilatation of the bladder.

Cysted (si·stėd), *a. rare.* [f. CYST + -ED².] Encysted. (Dicts.)

Cysti- (sisti), comb. f. Gr. κύστις CYST; in many modern technical words: as **Cysti·colous** *a.* [L. *-colus*], inhabiting a cyst. **Cy·stiform** *a.*, of the form of a cyst. **Cysti·gerous** *a.* [L. *-ger*], bearing or containing cysts.

Cystic (si·stik), *a.* 1634. [– Fr. *cystique* or mod.L. *cysticus*; see CYSTIS, -IC.] **1.** *Anat.* Pertaining to or connected with the gall-bladder: as *c. artery, duct.* **2.** Pertaining to the urinary bladder 1881. **3.** *Path.* Of the nature of a cyst; characterized by formation of cysts, containing cysts (CYST 2) 1713. **4.** Enclosed in a cyst, as a hydatid 1859.

2. *C. oxide* = CYSTINE. *C. calculus*, a urinary calculus containing cystine; so *c. urine.* **4.** In this condition the animal is . . a C. worm, or bladder-worm HUXLEY.

‖ **Cysticercus** (sistisɜ̄·ɹkɒs) Pl. **-ci** (-səi). 1841. [mod.L., f. Gr. κύστις bladder + κέρκος tail.] *Zool.* The scolex or larva of a tape-worm in its encysted state; a hydatid. Hence **Cystice·rcoid** *a.* and *sb.*

Cysticle (si·stik'l). 1855. [dim. of CYST; see -CULE.] A small cyst: applied to an organ, supposed to be that of hearing, in some *Acalephæ*.

Cystid (si·stid). 1862. [f. CYSTIS + -ID³.] **1.** *Geol.* A member of the order *Cystidea* or *Cystoidea* of fossil echinoderms. **2.** *Zool.* 'The sac-like ciliated embryo of some of the *Polyzoa*' 1877. var. (sense 1) **Cysti·dean.**

‖ **Cysti·dium.** Pl. **-ia.** 1858. [mod.L., f. Gr. κύστις, -ιδ- bladder: occas. **Cystide.**] *Bot.* One of the projecting cells originating among the basidia of hymenomycetous fungi, and supposed to be sterile basidia.

Cystine (si·stəin). Also **-in.** 1843. [f. Gr. κύστις bladder + -INE⁵.] *Chem.* An organic base, $C_3NHO_2SO_2$, a yellowish crystalline substance, found in a rare kind of urinary calculus.

‖ **Cystis** (si·stis). 1543. [late L. – Gr. κύστις bladder.] = CYST.

‖ **Cystitis** (sistəi·tis). 1776. [f. prec. + -ITIS.] *Path.* Inflammation of the bladder.

Cysto- (sisto), comb. f. Gr. κύστη = κύστις bladder, cyst; as in:

Cy·stocarp (*Bot.*) [Gr. καρπός], the sexual fruit of the *Florideæ*, a group of *Algæ*; hence **Cysto·ca·rpic** *a.* **Cy·stocele** [Gr. κήλη tumour, CELE], hernia of the bladder. **Cy·stoplast** (*Biol.*) [Gr. πλαστός], a cell having a cell-wall. **Cystorrhœ·a** [Gr. ῥοία flux], vesical catarrh. **Cy·stoscope** [Gr. -σκοπος], *sb.* an instrument for examining the bladder; *v.* to examine (the bladder) with this instrument; hence **Cystosco·pic** *a.* **Cy·stotome** [Gr. -τομος], an instrument for the operation of cystotomy. **Cysto·tomy** [Gr. -τομια], cutting into the bladder for extraction of a stone, etc.

Cystoid (si·stoid). 1871. [f. Gr. κύστις bladder + -OID.]

A. *adj.* **1.** *Path.* Of the nature of a cyst. **2.** *Geol.* = CYSTID 1. 1876.

B. *sb. Path.* = CYST 2. 1872.

Cystolith (si·stolip). 1846. [f. CYSTO- + -LITH.] **1.** *Bot.* A club-shaped stratified out-growth of the walls of some cells, containing minute crystals 1857. **2.** *Path.* Calculus of the bladder. Hence **Cystoli·thic** *a.*

‖ **Cystoma** (sistōᵘ·mă). Pl. **-mata.** 1872. [f. CYST- + -OMA.] *Path.* A tumour containing cysts. **b.** A cyst which is a new formation.

-cyte (səit). [– Gr. κύτος receptacle.] Frequent in composition with the sense 'cell', as in *cystocyte*, etc.

Cytherean (siþĕrī·an). 1751. [f. L. *Cytherea* a name of Venus, from *Cythera* + -AN.] *adj.* Pertaining to Venus 1866. *sb.* A votaress of Venus; *spec.* a prostitute attached to an Indian temple.

Cytisine (si·tisəin). 1830. [f. next + -INE⁵.] *Chem.* A poisonous alkaloid, $C_{20}H_{23}N_3O$, extracted from the seeds of the Laburnum, *Cytisus laburnum*.

‖ **Cytisus** (si·tisɒs). 1548. [L. – Gr. κύτισος.] *Bot.* **a.** A shrubby plant mentioned by Greek and Roman writers; now identified with the Shrubby Medic, *Medicago arborea*. **b.** Adopted by Linnæus as the name of a genus of *Leguminosæ*, including the common Broom, the Laburnum, etc. *C. racemosus* is the *Cytisus* of florists.

Cyto-, comb. f. Gr. κύτος receptacle, etc., taken as = 'cell': as

Cy·toblast (*Biol.*) [+ -BLAST], the protoplasmic nucleus of a cell, regarded as the germinal spot from which development proceeds. **Cytoblaste·ma** (*Biol.*) [+ BLASTEMA], the protoplasm from which the cell is produced; hence **Cytoblaste·mal, -te·mic, -te·mous** *adjs.* **Cytoco·ccus** [Gr. κόκκος berry], the nucleus of a *Cytula* or impregnated ovum (Haeckel). **Cy·tode** (*Biol.*) [+ -ODE], a non-nucleated unicellular mass of protoplasm, the lowest form in which life is exhibited (Haeckel). **Cytoge·nesis**, the generation or production of cells; **Cytogene·tic** *a.*, pertaining to cytogenesis. **Cyto·genic, Cyto·genous** *adjs.*, producing cells. **Cyto·geny** = *cytogenesis.* **Cy·toid** *a.*, cell-like; also *sb.* **Cyto·logy**, the study of cells and their formation. **Cy·toplasm**, protoplasm; *spec.* the protoplasm of a cell as dist. from the nucleus; **Cytopla·smic** *a.*, pertaining to or consisting of cytoplasm; **Cy·toplast**, the unit of protoplasm contained in a cell. **Cytozo·a** *sb. pl.* (*Zool.*) [Gr. ζῷον], same as *Sporozoa* or *Gregarinida*.

‖ **Cytula** (si·tiŭla). 1879. [mod.L., f. Gr. κύτος hollow, receptacle + L. dim. suffix *-ula*; see -ULE.] *Biol.* The parent cell of an organism; an impregnated ovum. Hence **Cy·tuloplasm**, the protoplasmic substance of a c.

Cyul, cyule. Mod. adaptations of *cyula*, latinized f. OE. *cēol, ciol* :– *ciul* KEEL *sb.*², boat, etc.

Czar, tzar, tsar (tsāɹ, zāɹ). 1555. [– Russ. *tsar'* :– **tsisarĭ* :– O Russ. *tsĕsarĭ*, ult. repr. L. CÆSAR through the medium of Gmc. The sp. *cz-* is non-Slavonic.] The title of the autocrat or emperor of Russia, borne also formerly by Servian rulers. Hence **Cza·rate, Cza·rship, ts-**, the office or position of c. or tsar. **Cza·rdom, ts-**, the dominion, office, or power of a c. or tsar. **Cza·rian, Cza·ric, Cza·rish, ts-** *adjs.* of or pertaining to a or the c. or tsar. **Cza·rism, ts-**, the czar's or tsar's system of government.

‖ **Czarevitch, -wich, tsar-** (tsā·rĕvitʃ, Russ. tsarē·vitʃ). 1710. [– Russ. *tsarévich* = 'son of a tsar'.] A son of a czar or tsar. (The hereditary prince had the differentiated title *Cesare·vitch, -witch.*)

‖ **Czarevna, ts-** (tsare·vna). 1880. [Russ.] A daughter of a czar or tsar. (The title of the wife of the *Cesarevitch* was *Cesare·vna.*)

‖ **Czarina, ts-** (tsarī·nă, za-). 1717. [– It., Sp. *czarina, zarina* (= Fr. *czarine*) – G. (*c*)*zarin*, f. (*c*)*zar* + fem. suffix *-in*; the Russ. title was *tsari·tsa.*] The wife of a or the czar or tsar. Also ‖ **Czaritza, ts-** (tsarī·tsă). 1698.

Czech (tʃek). 1841. [Polish sp. of the native name *Čech* of the people of Bohemia (Czech *Čechy*, adj. *Česk*). Cf. Fr. *tchèque*, G. *Tschech, tschechisch.*] Bohemian. **Cze·chian, Cze·chic, Cze·chish** *adjs.*

Czechoslovak (tʃekoslōᵘ·væk). 1917. A native of the state including Bohemia, Moravia, and the northern Slavs of the extinct Austrian Empire. Also as adj.; so **-a·kian.**

D

D (dī), the fourth letter of the Roman alphabet, corresponding to the Phœnician and Hebrew *Daleth*, and Greek *Delta*, Δ, whence also its form. It represents the sonant dental mute, or point-voice stop consonant. Its phonetic value in English is constant, except in pa. pples., where *-ed* after a breath-consonant is pronounced *t*. *pl.* D's, Ds, de's.

II. 1. Used to denote serial order, with the value of *fourth*. **2.** *Mus.* The second note of the natural major scale. Also the scale or key which has that note for its tonic 1596. **3.** In *Algebra*: see A, II.

III. *Abbreviations*, etc. **1.** *d.* stands for L. *denarius*, and so for 'penny', 'pence'; as 1*d*. = one penny. †Formerly also, *d.* = one half (L. *dimidium*). **2.** D, the sign for 500 in Roman numerals. [Understood to be the half of CIↃ, earlier form of M = 1000.] **3.** D. = various proper names, as David, etc.; *d.* (usu. before a date) = died. D. = Distinguished, as D.C.M. (conduct medal), etc. In *Academical degrees* D. = Doctor, as D.D. (*Divinitatis Doctor*), D.Sc., Doctor of Science. D.B.E., Dame (Commander of Order of) British Empire. D.C. (*Mus.*) = *Da Capo* (q.v.). D.C., or d.c. (*Electr.*), direct current. D.G. = *Dei gratia* (q.v.). D.T., vulgar abbrev. of *delirium tremens*. D.V. = L. *Deo volente*, God willing.

'd, clipped form of *had, would*.

Dab (dæb), *sb.*[1] ME. [f. DAB *v.*[1]] **1.** A sharp and abrupt blow; a peck; an aimed blow. Also *fig.* **2.** A gentle blow or tap with a soft substance 1755. **3.** A flattish mass of some soft or moist substance dabbed on anything 1749. Also *fig.* **4.** A wet or dirty clout 1714.

1. Giving us several dabs with its beak SMOLLETT. **3.** How can two or three dabs of paint ever be worth such a sum as that MME. D'ARBLAY. *fig.* Several little dabs of money HERVEY.

Dab (dæb), *sb.*[2] 1577. [Origin unkn.] A species of small flat-fish, *Pleuronectes limanda*, resembling the flounder, common on the British coast; also a street term for any small flat fish.

Dab (dæb), *sb.*[3] 1691. [Origin unkn.] One skilful *at*, †*of*, *in* anything; an expert, an adept. Also *attrib.*

A third [writer] is a d. at an index GOLDSM.

Dab (dæb), *v.* ME. [Of imit. origin, but cf. DABBLE.] **1.** *trans.* To strike somewhat sharply and abruptly; to stick or thrust; to strike with a slight blow. *intr.* Of a bird: To peck with the bill 1805. **2.** To strike or cause to strike (usually with something soft) and then withdraw quickly 1562; *spec.* to strike or pat with a dabber 1759. **3.** A var. of DAUB *v.* to plaster 1577.

1. To dabbe him in the necke MORE. **2.** To d. a brush against paper TYNDALL. To d. glue on his gauzy wings READE. To d. a sore with fine lint 1739.

Dab, *adv.* 1608. [The vb.-stem used ellipt.] With a dab.

Dabber (dæ·bəɹ). 1790. [f. DAB *v.* + -ER.[1]] One who or that which dabs; *spec.* a rounded pad of some elastic material, used by printers, etc., for applying ink, colour, etc., evenly to a surface; in *Printing* = BALL *sb.*[1] 12. Also, a brush used in stereotyping for pressing the damp paper into the interstices of the type, etc.

Dabble (dæ·b'l), *v.* 1557. [– Du. †*dabbelen*, or f. DAB *v.* + -LE.] **1.** *trans.* To wet by splashing; to bespatter, besprinkle, bedabble. Also *causal.* **2.** *intr.* To move (with feet or hands, or the bill) in shallow water, mud, etc., so as to cause splashing; to paddle 1611. **3.** *fig.* To employ oneself in a dilettante way *in*; to work off and on *at*. Const. *in* (*with*, *at*, etc.). 1625. †**b.** To tamper *with*, interfere *in* –1794.

1. With bright hayre Dabbel'd in blood *Rich. III*, I. iv. 54. **2.** The long wet pasture grass she dabbles through CLARE. **3.** To d. in poetry B. JONS., with the text ATTERBURY. Hence **Da·bbler,** one who dabbles.

Dabby (dæ·bi), *a.* 1581. [f. DAB *sb.*[1] 4 + -Y[1].] Damp, moist: (of clothes) wet and clinging.

Dabchick (dæ·bˌtʃik). 1557. [Early forms *dap-*, *dopchick* and (later) *dipchick* suggest connection with OE. *dufe|doppa* 'pelicanus', ME. *doue|doppe*, *dyve|dap* (later *divedopper*, *-dapper*), OE. *dop|ened*, *dop|fugol* moorhen, and hence with the base **deup-* **dup-* (see DOP *v.*, DEEP *a.*, DIP *v.*).] The Little Grebe, *Podiceps minor*, a small water-bird, noted for its diving. In U.S., applied to *Podilymbus podiceps*. *fig.* Of a girl. B. JONS. var. **Dap-, dop-, dip-chick.**

‖**Daboya** (dăboi·ă, dɑ·boyā). Also **daboia.** 1872. [– Hindi *daboyā* 'lurker', f. *dabnā* lurk.] The large viper of the East Indies.

Dabster (dæ·bstəɹ). 1708. [f. DAB *sb.*[3]; see -STER.] **1.** One skilled at anything; an expert or dab. Chiefly *dial.* **2.** Used depreciatively; cf. DAUBSTER 1871.

‖**Dabuh.** 1600. [Arab.] The Striped Hyæna.

‖**Da capo** (da kā·po). 1724. [It. = 'from the beginning'.] *Mus.* A direction: Repeat from the beginning. (The end of the repeat is usually marked with a pause or the word *Fine.*) Abbrev. *D.C.* Also *fig.*

Dace (dēˈs). [– OFr. *dars*, nom. of *dart* dace (identical with DART *sb.*), whence also †*dare* (XIV–XVII). For the loss of *r* cf. BASS *sb.*[1]] A small fresh-water cyprinoid fish, *Leuciscus vulgaris*. *U.S.* Applied locally to fishes resembling or allied to this: as the genus *Rhinichthys*, and the redfin, *Minnilus cornutus*.

‖**Dachshund** (da·ksˌhund). 1881. [G. = badger-dog.] One of a German breed of short-legged long-bodied dogs, used to draw badgers.

‖**Dacoit** (dăkoi·t), *sb.* 1810. [Hindi *ḍakait*, orig. *ḍākait*, f. *ḍākā* gang-robbery.] One of a class of robbers in India and Burmah, who plunder in gangs. Hence **Dacoi·t** *v.* to plunder as a d.

‖**Dacoity** (dăkoi·ti). 1818. [– Hindi *ḍakaitī*, abstr. sb. fem. f. *ḍākait.*] Robbery with violence committed by a gang.

Dacryd (dæ·krid). 1846. [f. mod.L. *Dacrydium*, – Gr., dim. of δάκρυ tear, in allusion to resinous drops exuded by these trees.] *Bot.* A tree or shrub of genus *Dacrydium*.

Dacryolin (dæ·kriolin). 1875. [f. Gr. δάκρυ + -OL + -IN[1].] *Chem.* The form of albumin found in the tears.

Dacryolith, -lite (dæ·kriˌoliþ, -ləit). 1847. [f. as prec. + -LITH, -LITE.] *Path.* A calculus occurring in the lachrymal passages.

‖**Dacryo·ma.** 1830. [f. as prec. + -OMA.] *Path.* An impervious state of the puncta lachrymalia.

‖**Da·cryops.** 1857. [f. as prec. + Gr. ὤψ eye, face.] A clear cyst due to the distension of one of the lachrymal ducts. **b.** A watery eye.

Dactyl (dæ·ktil), *sb.* ME. [– L. *dactylus*, – Gr. δάκτυλος a finger, a date, a dactyl (from its 3 joints).] †**1.** A date –1656. **2.** *Prosody.* A metrical foot consisting of a long syllable and two short (or of an accented syllable and two unaccented) ME. **3.** A mollusc, the piddock (*Pholas dactylus*) 1802. Hence †**Da·ctylar** *a.* (*rare*). †**Dactyle·t** (*nonce-wd.*), a little d. †**Da·ctylist,** a writer of dactylic verse (*rare*).

Dactylic (dækti·lik), *a.* 1589. [– L. *dactylicus* – Gr. δακτυλικός; see prec., -IC.] Of, pertaining to, or of the nature of, a dactyl; consisting of or characterized by dactyls. *sb.* [*sc.* verse].

Dactylio-, comb. f. Gr. δακτύλιος finger-ring [see DACTYL], as in:

Dacty·lioglyph [Gr. δακτυλιογλύφος], an engraver of gems for finger-rings; also, 'the inscription of the name of the artist on a gem' (Brande); hence **Dacty:liogly·phic** *a.*; **Dactylio·glyphist** = *Dactylioglyph*; **Dactylio·glyphy,** the art of engraving gems. **Dactylio·grapher,** one who describes finger-rings, engraved seals, etc.; hence **Dacty:liogra·phic** *a.*; **Dactylio·graphy,** the description of finger-rings, 'the science of gem-engraving' (Brande). **Dactylio·logy,** the study of finger-rings.

Dactyliomancy (dækti·liomæ:nsi). *erron.* **dactylo-.** 1613. [f. Gr. δακτύλιος finger-ring + -MANCY.] Divination by means of a finger-ring.

‖**Dactylitis** (dæktiləi·tis). 1861. [-ITIS.] *Path.* Inflammation of a finger or toe.

Dactylo- (dæ·ktilo, dæktilǫ·), comb. f. Gr. δάκτυλος finger, as in:

Dactylo·logy, the art of speaking by signs made with the fingers. **Dactylo·nomy,** the art of counting on the fingers. **Dactylo·podite** (*Zool.*) [Gr. ποδ-], the terminal joint of a limb in Crustacea. **Da·ctylopo:re,** one of the pores in the corallum of Hydrocorallinæ, from which the dactylozoids protrude; hence **Dactylopo·ric** *a.* **Dactylo·pterous** *a.*, having the characters of the genus *Dactylopterus* of fishes, in which the pectoral fins are greatly enlarged and wing-like; so **Dactylo·pteroid** *a.* **Da:ctylozo·oid, -zo·id,** a mouthless cylindrical zooid in some Hydrozoa.

Dactyloid (dæ·ktiloid), *a. rare.* 1882. [– Gr. δακτυλοειδής; see -OID.] Resembling a finger.

Dactylose (dæktilōᵘ·s), *a. rare.* 1882. [f. Gr. δάκτυλος finger + -OSE[1].] 'Having fingers, or finger-shaped' (*Syd. Soc. Lex.*).

Dad (dæd). *colloq.* 1500. [In early Sc. *dade, daid, dadie* (XVI). Cf. *bab, babby, baby, baba* and *mam, mammy, mam(m)a*; perh. of infantile origin.] A childish word for father. So **Da·da, Dadda.**

Daddle (dæ·d'l), *sb. dial.* 1785. [Origin unkn.] The fist.

Da·ddle, *v. dial.* 1787. [f. *dad-* as in dial. *dadder* quake, tremble (cf. DADE, DIDDER, DODDER), + -LE.] *intr.* To walk totteringly or unsteadily; to dawdle.

Daddock (dæ·dək). *dial.* 1624. [First element unexpl.; cf. -OCK.] Rotten or decayed wood. Hence **Da·ddocky** *a.*

Daddy (dæ·di). *colloq.* 1500. [f. DAD + -Y[6].] An endearing form of DAD, father. Hence **Da·ddyism** *U.S.*, respect for ancestry.

Da:ddy-lo·ng-legs. 1814. [From its very long legs.] The CRANE-FLY. (Called also *father-* and *Harry-long-legs.*) **b.** A name for Arachnids of similar appearance, such as those of the genus *Phalangium*.

Dade (dēˈd), *v.* Now *dial.* 1598. [Cf. *dad-* in DADDLE *v.*] **1.** *intr.* To move slowly or totteringly, to toddle 1612. **2.** *trans.* To lead and support (one who totters). Also *fig.*

1. Which . . No sooner taught to d., but from their mother trip DRAYTON. **2.** The little children . . By painefull Mothers daded to and fro DRAYTON.

Dado (dēˈ·do). 1664. [– It. *dado* die, cube :– L. *datum*; see DIE *sb.*] *Archit.* **1.** The cubical portion of a pedestal, between the base and the cornice; the die. **2.** The finishing of wood running along the lower part of the walls of a room, made to represent a continuous pedestal. Hence, any lining, painting, or papering of the lower part of an interior wall different from that of the upper part. Also *attrib.* Hence **Da·doed** *ppl. a.* having a d.

†**Dæ·dal,** *sb.* Also **de-.** 1630. [– L. DÆDALUS.] **1.** Short for Dædalus; a skilful artificer like Dædalus. **2.** A labyrinth. EVELYN.

Dædal (dī·dăl), *a.* Also **de-.** Chiefly *poet.* 1590. [– L. *dædalus* – Gr. δαίδαλος skilful, variegated; see DÆDALUS.] **1.** Cunning to invent or fashion. **2.** = DÆDALIAN 1. 1630. **3.** Of the earth, etc.: 'Manifold in works'; hence, varied, variously adorned 1596.

1. The d. hand of . . Nature 1872. **2.** The d. dance LANDOR. **3.** What d. landscapes smile 1745.

Dæda·leous, *a.* 1835. [f. as next + -OUS.] *Bot.* Having a point of large circuit, but truncated and rugged.

Dædalian, -ean (dīdē·liăn), *a.* Also **De-.** 1598. [f. L. *Dædaleus*, Gr. δαιδάλεος + -AN; see -EAN, -IAN.] **1.** Of or after the style of Dædalus; formed with art; maze-like 1607. †**2.** = DÆDAL *a.* 3.

Dæ·dalist. [See -IST.] An imitator of Dædalus. ADDISON.

Dædalous (dī·dăləs), *a.* Also **de-.** 1828. [f. L. *dædalus* (see DÆDAL *a.*) + -OUS.] *Bot.* Of leaves: Having a margin with various windings.

‖**Dædalus** (dī·dălŏs). 1630. [L. – Gr. Δαίδαλος 'the cunning one', name of the workman who constructed the Cretan labyrinth, and made wings for himself and Icarus.] A cunning artificer (like Dædalus).

Dæmon, Dæmonic, etc.; see DEMON, etc.

Daer-stock (dā·ˌer-stǫk). 1875. [f. MIr. *dáer* servile + STOCK *sb.*[1] VII.] *Ir. Antiq.* Stock belonging to the landlord of which the tenant has the use; used *attrib.* in *d. tenant*, etc.

Daff (daf), *sb.* Now *n. dial.* ME. [Cf. DAFT.] One deficient in sense or in spirit; a simpleton; a coward.

Daff (daf), *v.*[1] Chiefly *Sc.* 1535. [f. prec.] **1.** To play the fool; to talk or behave sportively. †**2.** To daunt (*n. dial.*) 1674. Hence **Da·ffing** *vbl. sb.* fooling.

Daff (daf), *v.*[2] 1596. [var. of DOFF.] †**1.** *trans.* To put off (as clothes); to throw off –1606. **2.** To put or turn aside, to thrust aside 1596; †to put off (with an excuse, etc.) *Oth.* IV. ii. 176.

1. Till we do please To daft [= daff't] for our Repose SHAKS. **2.** The .. Mad-Cap, Prince of Wales .. that daft the World aside 1 *Hen. IV*, IV. i. 96.

Daffadowndilly, daffydowndilly. 1573. **1.** = *Daffodilly.* **2.** A shrub: prob. the Mezereon 1591.

Daffodil (dæ·fŏdil). 1548. [alt. f. AFFODILL. The initial *d* is unexpl.] †**1.** = AFFODILL; the genus *Asphodelus* –1607. †**2.** The genus *Narcissus* –1629. **3.** Now restricted to *Narcissus pseudo-Narcissus* (also called Lent Lily) 1592. **4.** The colour of the daffodil; a pale yellow. Also *attrib.* 1855.

3. Faire Daffadills, we weep to see You haste away so soone HERRICK. *Chequered D.*: the Fritillary, *Fritillaria meleagris.* var. **Da·ffodilly, daffadilly,** *poet.* (and *dial.*).

Daft (daft), *a.* Now *Sc.* and *north.* [ME. *daffte*, repr. OE. *ġedæfte* mild, gentle, meek :– Gmc. **ʒaðaftjaz*, f. **ʒaðafti*, f. stem **dab-* of Goth. *gadaban* become, be fitting; for the sense-development cf. SILLY. Cf. DEFT.] †**1.** Mild, meek, humble. (ME only.) **2.** Silly; wanting in intelligence, stupid ME. **3.** Of unsound mind, crazy 1536. **4.** Giddy in one's mirth; madly gay 1575.

3. The woman would drive any reasonable being d. SCOTT. Hence **Da·ftlike** *a.* **Da·ft-ly** *adv.*, **-ness.**

Dag (dæg), *sb.*[1] In 4–5 **dagge.** ME. [Of unkn. origin; the same senses are partly expressed by TAG *sb.*[1]] †**1.** A pendant pointed portion of anything; one of the pointed or laciniated divisions of the lower margin of a garment –1617. †**2.** = AGLET 1, 2. –1616. **3.** One of the locks of wool clotted with dirt about the hinder parts of a sheep 1731. Hence **Da·g-tailed** *a.* having the wool about the tail clotted with dirt.

†**Dag,** *sb.*[2] 1561. [Of unkn. origin; in earliest use Sc. – Gaelic.] A kind of heavy pistol or hand-gun formerly in use –1881.

[The sense 'dagger' (Johnson) is app. a mistake, due to misapprehension of 'dag and dagger'. The sense 'dagger-thrust' is a blunder.]

Dag (dæg), *sb.*[3] 1727. [– (O)Fr. *dague* long dagger, also = sense 1; see DAGGER.] **1.** The simple straight pointed horn of a young stag 1859. **2.** A pin or bolt.

Dag (dæg), *sb.*[4] *dial.* 1674. [– ON. *dǫgg* (gen. *dǫggvar*) dew, Sw. *dagg.* See DEW *sb.*] **1.** Dew. **2.** A drizzle; a mist 1808.

Dag, *v.*[1] ME. [conn. w. DAG *sb.*[1]] †**1.** *trans.* To cut the edge of (a garment) into jags; to slash –1523. **2.** To clog with dirt, bemire. Now *dial.* 1484. **3.** *Farming.* To cut the dags from (sheep) 1706.

†**Dag,** *v.*[2] ME. [Related to (O)Fr. *dague*; see DAG *sb.*[3]] To pierce or stab with or as with a pointed weapon –1794.

†**Dag,** *v.*[3] 1572. [f. DAG *sb.*[2]] *trans.* and *intr.* To shoot with a dag –1580.

Dag (dæg), *v.*[4] *dial.* 1825. [Goes with DAG *sb.*[4]; cf. ON. *dǫggva* (Sw. *dagga*) bedew. Cf. dial. var. *deg*, in same sense.] **1.** *trans.* To sprinkle, wet with sprinkling 1855. **2.** *intr.* To drizzle.

‖**Dagesh, daghesh** (dā·geʃ), *sb.* 1591. [Heb. *dāġeš*, letter sharpener or hardener.] *Heb. Gram.* A point or dot placed within a Hebrew letter, denoting either that it is doubled (*d. forte*), or that it is not aspirated (*d. lene*).

Dagger (dæ·gəɹ), *sb.* ME. [perh. f. DAG *v.*[2] + -ER[1], but infl. by (O)Fr. *dague* (see DAG *sb.*[3]) – Pr. or It. *daga.*] **1.** A short stout edged and pointed weapon, used for thrusting and stabbing. **2.** *fig.* Something that wounds grievously 1596. **3.** *Naut.* A piece of timber that faces on to the poppets of the bilge-ways, and crosses them diagonally 1850. †**4.** = DAG *sb.*[3] 1. 1616. **5.** *Printing.* A mark resembling a dagger (†), used for marginal references, etc.; also called *obelisk.* **6.** A name of moths of the genus *Acronycta* having a black dagger-like mark on the fore wing 1832. **7.** *pl.* A name of plants, as Sword-grass (*Poa aquatica*), etc. 1847. †**8.** Name of a tavern in Holborn *c*1600; hence *d.-ale*, etc. –1610.

1. The Honourable men, Whose Daggers haue stabb'd Cæsar *Jul. C.* III. ii. 157. †*D. of lath*; the weapon worn by the Vice in the old Moralities. Phr. *At daggers drawn*: in a state of open hostility. **2.** Phr. *To speak* or *look daggers*: to speak so as to wound. **5.** *Double d.*: a mark having each end hilted like a d. (‡), used for references, etc.

Hence **Da·gger** *v.* to stab, or (*Printing*) mark, with a d.

Daggle (dæ·g'l), *v.* 1530. [freq. of DAG *v.*[1] sense 2; see -LE; see also DAG *v.*[4]] **1.** *trans.* To trail, so as to clog with wet mud; in later use, To wet by splashing or sprinkling. **2.** *trans.* and *intr.* To drag or trail about (through the mire) 1681.

1. The .. plume .. Was daggled by the dashing spray SCOTT. **2.** You may d. about with your mother, and sell paint VANBRUGH.

Daggle-tail (dæ·g'lˌtēil), *sb.* 1577. Now *dial.* A person (*esp.* a woman) whose garments are bemired by being trailed over wet ground; a slut, slattern. Now DRAGGLE-TAIL. So **Da·ggle-tailed** *a.* (now *dial.*), having the skirts splashed in this way; slatternly.

Dag-lock. 1623. [f. DAG *sb.*[1] 3 + LOCK *sb.*[1]] *pl.* Locks of wool clotted with dirt about the hinder parts of a sheep.

Dago (dēi·go). *U.S.* 1888. [Earlier *dego*; alt. f. *Diego*, Sp. equivalent of the name JAMES.] A name originally given as a generic name to Spaniards; now used of the Latin races generally.

‖**Dagoba** (dā·gobă). 1806. [– Sinhalese *dāgaba.*] In Buddhist countries, a *tope* or dome-shaped structure containing relics of Buddha or some Buddhist saint.

†**Da·gon**[1]. ME. [perh. rel. to DAG *sb.*[1]] A piece (of cloth) –1486.

‖**Dagon**[2] (dēi·gǫn). ME. [– L. (Vulg.) *Dagon* – Gr. (LXX) Δαγών – Heb. *dāgôn* derived by folk etymology from *dāg* fish.] The national deity of the ancient Philistines; represented with the head, chest, and arms of a man, and the tail of a fish. Also *transf.* An idol.

†**Da·gswain.** ME. [With the first element cf. DAG *sb.*[1]; second element unexpl.] A coarse coverlet of rough shaggy material –1577.

Daguerreotype (dăge·rotəip), *sb.* 1839. [– Fr. *daguerréotype*, f. Louis-Jacques-Mandé *Daguerre* (1789–1851), the inventor; see -O-, -TYPE.] An early photographic process, in which the image was taken upon a silver plate sensitized by iodine, and then developed by vapour of mercury. Also, a portrait produced by this process. Also †*fig.* and *attrib.* Hence **Dague·rreotype** *v.* to photograph by the d. process; also †*fig.* So **Dague·rreotyper, -ist,** a photographer who uses the d. process. **Daguerreoty·pic, -al** *a.* relating to the d. process. **Dague·rreotypy** (-təipi), the d. process.

‖**Dahabeeyah, -biah** (dāhăbī·yă). 1877. [– Arab. *dahabīya* 'the golden' (sc. boat), name of the gilded state barge of the Moslem rulers of Egypt.] A large sailing-boat, used by travellers on the Nile.

Dahlia (dēi·liă, prop. dā·liă). 1804. [f. Andreas *Dahl*, a Swedish botanist; see -IA[1].] **1.** A genus of Composite plants, natives of Mexico, introduced into Europe in 1789. **2.** Name for a particular shade of red 1846.

1. *Blue d.*: *fig.* something impossible.

Dahlin (dā·lin). 1826. [f. prec. + -IN[1].] *Chem.* A name for INULIN from dahlia tubers.

‖**Dail Eireann** (dǭil ē·rən). 1919. [Ir., = assembly of Ireland.] Lower house of Parliament in Irish Free State. Abbrev. **Dail.**

Daily (dēi·li), *a.* [f. DAY *sb.* + -LY[1]; cf. OE. *-dæġlić.*] Of or belonging to each day; occurring every day; issued every (week-)day 1470. As *sb.* (*ellipt.*) A daily newspaper.

D. waiter, etc.: one who waits, etc., daily.

Daily (dēi·li), *adv.* ME. [f. DAY + -LY[2].] Every day, day by day; constantly.

With bended knees I dayly beseech God 1635.

‖**Daimio** (dai·mˌyo). 1839. [Jap., f. Chin. *dai* great + *mio, myo* name.] The title of the feudal nobles of Japan; now abolished.

‖**Daimon** (dai·mōun), a transliteration of Gr. δαίμων, one's genius or DEMON.

Dain, *sb.* ME. [syncop. f. *dedain* DISDAIN *sb.*] †**1.** Disdain –1591. **2.** Stink. Still *dial.* So †**Dain** *a.* haughty; stinking. †**Dain** *v.* to disdain. †**Dai·nful** *a.* disdainful.

†**Daint,** *a.* and *sb.* 1563. Short. f. DAINTY –1633.

†**Dai·nteous,** *a.* ME. [app. orig. *dayntivous*, f. †*daintive* + -OUS; subseq. alt. so as to appear f. *daynte* DAINTY *sb.* + -OUS. Cf. BOUNTEOUS, PLENTEOUS.] = DAINTY *a.* –1556.

Dai·nteth, -ith, *sb.* and *a. Sc.* [– OFr. *deintiet*, older form of *deintié*; see DAINTY *sb.*] = DAINTY.

Dai·ntify, *v.* [See -FY.] To make dainty. MME. D'ARBLAY.

Dai·ntihood. *rare.* 1780. [-HOOD.] Daintiness.

Daintily (dēi·ntili), *adv.* ME. [f. DAINTY *a.* + -LY[2].] †**1.** Handsomely –1640. **2.** In a dainty manner ME. **3.** Delicately, nicely, etc.; elegantly, neatly 1561. †**4.** Rarely –1581.

4. The Auncients .. neuer, or very d., match Hornpypes and Funeralls SIDNEY.

Daintiness (dēi·ntinės). 1530. [f. DAINTY *a.* + -NESS.] The quality of being dainty: †choiceness –1627; elegance; neatness 1580; niceness (of taste, sensibility, etc.) 1579; fastidiousness; softness 1530.

More notorious for the d. of the provision .. than for the massiness of the dish HAKEWILL. D. of expression in a lyric 1878. Daintinesse of eare *Rich. II*, V. v. 45. The People .. learnt .. of the Flemish d. and softness MILT.

†**Dai·ntrel.** 1575. [Obscurely f. DAINTY *sb.* + -REL, -EREL; cf. the clipped form DAINT *a.* and *sb.*] A dainty –1640.

Dainty (dēi·nti), *sb.* ME. [– AFr. *dainté*, OFr. *daintié, deintié* :– L. *dignitas, -tat-* worthiness, worth, beauty.] †**1.** Estimation; regard; affection –1513. †**2.** Liking *to do* or *see* anything; delight –1529. †**3.** Choice quality –1440. †**4.** Fastidiousness –1597. †**5.** *concr.* Anything which is dainty –1798. **6.** *esp.* A choice viand, a delicacy ME.

5. Plenty is no d. HEYWOOD. **6.** Let mee not eate of their dainties *Ps.* 141:4. Phr. †*To make d. of (anything)*: to set great store by; hence, to be chary of.

Dainty (dēi·nti), *a.* ME. [f. prec. sb.] **1.** Handsome; choice; delightful. Now *dial.* †**2.** Precious; hence, rare, scarce –1677. **3.** Pleasing to the palate ME. **4.** Of delicate beauty or taste ME. **5.** Of persons, etc.: Nice, fastidious, particular; sometimes, over-nice 1576. Also quasi-*adv.* (*rare*).

1. Full many a deynte hors hadde he in stable CHAUCER. **3.** D. bits Make rich the ribs *L. L. L.* I. i. 26. **4.** The grassye ground with daintye Daysies dight SPENSER. **5.** The hand of little Imployment hath the daintier sense *Haml.* V. i. 78. Let vs not be daintie of leaue-taking, But shift away *Macb.* II. iii. 150. Born with a d. tooth STEVENSON.

‖**Dairi** (dai·ri). 1662. [Jap., f. Chin. *dai* great + *ri* within.] In Japan, prop. the palace or court of the Mikado; also used for the Mikado. Hence **Dairi-sama,** *lit.* lord of the d., an appellation of the Mikado.

Dairy (dēᵊ·ri), *sb.* [ME. *deierie, dayerie,* f. *deie, daye,* female servant + -ERY, -RY; see DEY[1].] **1.** A room or building in which milk and cream are kept, and made into butter and cheese. Occas., in towns, a shop in which these are sold. **2.** That department of farming, or of a farm, which is concerned with the production of milk, butter, and cheese. Hence, occas., the milch cows on a farm collectively. ME. **3.** A dairy-farm 1562.

2. Grounds were turned much in England from breeding either to feeding or dairy TEMPLE. D. of 12 or 16 cows to be let 1882.

Comb.: **d.-farm,** a farm chiefly producing milk, butter, and cheese; **-farmer, -farming; -school,** a technical school for teaching d.-work or d.-farming; **-woman,** a woman who manages a d.

Dai·ry, *v. rare.* 1780. [f. DAIRY *sb.*] To keep or feed (cows) for the dairy. Hence **Dai·rying** *vbl. sb.* the business of a dairy.

Dairymaid (dēᵊ·rimēⁱd). 1599. A female servant employed in a dairy.

Dai·ryman. 1784. A man who keeps, or works in, a dairy, or sells dairy produce.

Dais (dēⁱs, dēⁱ·is). [ME. *deis* – OFr. *deis* (mod. *dais*) :– L. *discus* quoit, DISH, DISC, in med.L. table.] †**1.** A raised table in a hall, at which distinguished persons sat at feasts, etc.; the high table –1575. **2.** The raised platform in a hall for the high table, or for seats of honour, etc. ME. Also *transf.* **3.** A seat, bench (*n. dial.*) ME. **4.** [after mod.Fr.] The canopy over a throne, etc. 1863.

2. Like the d. or upper part of our old castle and college halls ARNOLD.

Daisied (dēⁱ·zid), *a.* 1611. [f. DAISY + -ED[2].] Adorned with or abounding in daisies, as *d. lawns.* (Chiefly *poet.*)

Daisy (dēⁱ·zi). [OE. *dæġes ēaġe* 'day's eye', so named from its covering the yellow disk in the evening and disclosing it in the morning.] **1.** The common name of *Bellis perennis,* N.O. *Compositæ,* having small flat flower-heads with yellow disk and white ray, which close in the evening. **2.** Applied to similar plants; as, in N. America, the Ox-eye D., *Chrysanthemum Leucanthemum*; in Australia, various *Compositæ*; **Michaelmas D.,** various cultivated species of *Aster* which blossom about Michaelmas; etc. **3.** *slang.* (chiefly *U.S.*) A first-rate thing or person; also as *adj.* **4.** *attrib.* 1605.

1. The dayeseye, or ellis the eye of day CHAUCER. Hence **Dai·sy** *v.* to cover or adorn with daisies (*rare*).

Dai·sy-cutter. 1791. [*lit.* 'cutter of daisies'.] **1.** A horse that in trotting steps low. **2.** *Cricket,* etc. A ball that skims along the ground without rising 1889.

Dak; see DAWK.

Daker. Also **daiker, dakir.** [– OFr. *dacre, dakere,* med.L. *dacra,* unexpl. var. of *dicra*; see DICKER *sb.*[1]] = DICKER *sb.*[1].

Daker-hen. *dial.* 1552. [Origin unkn.] The Corn-crake or Land-rail.

Dakoit, etc.; see DACOIT, etc.

‖**Dal** (dāl). *Anglo-Ind.* 1698. [Hindi.] Split-pulse, *esp.* that of *Cajanus Indicus,* used for food in the East Indies.

‖**Dalai, Dalai-lama;** see LAMA.

Dale[1] (dēⁱl). [OE. *dæl,* nom. pl. *dalu,* corresp. to OFris. *del,* OS. (Du.) *dal,* OHG. *tal* (G. *tal*), ON. *dalr,* Goth. *dals* or *dal* :– Gmc. **dalam,* **dalaz.*] **1.** A valley. In literary Eng. chiefly *poet.* Also *fig.* †**2.** A hollow, pit, gulf, etc. –1489.

1. By d. and eek by doune CHAUCER. That part of these dales which runs up far into the mountains WORDSW. *Comb.* **d.-land,** the lower ground of a district; so **-lander, -man.**

Dale[2] (dēⁱl). ME. [Northern var. of DOLE *sb.*[1], q. v.] A portion of land; *spec.* a portion of an undivided field indicated by landmarks only.

Dale[3] (dēⁱl). 1611. [prob. of LDu. origin; cf. LG., Du. *daal* (whence Fr. *dalle* conduit tube, etc.), in same sense; the same word as DALE[1].] A wooden tube or trough for carrying off water, as from a ship's pump.

Dalesman (dēⁱ·lzmæ̆n). 1769. [f. DALE[1].] A native or inhabitant of a dale; *esp.* of the dales in Cumberland, Westmorland, etc.

Dalf(e, obs. pa. t. of DELVE.

‖**Dalle** (dal). 1855. [Fr.; in sense 1 – LDu., see DEAL *sb.*[3]; for sense 2, see DALE *sb.*[3]] **1.** A flat slab of stone, marble, or terra-cotta, used for flooring. **2.** *pl.* In Western U.S.: Rapids where the rivers are compressed into long narrow trough-like channels 1884.

Dalliance (dæ·liăns). ME. [f. DALLY *v.* + -ANCE.] †**1.** Talk, confabulation, chat –1496. **2.** Sport, play; *esp.* amorous or wanton toying ME. **3.** Trifling; playing *with* a matter 1548. †**4.** Idle delay –1590.

2. The Primrose path of d. SHAKS. The lewd d. of the queen of love POPE. **3.** Vain d. with the misery Even of the dead WORDSW. **4.** *Com. Err.* IV. i. 59.

Dallop, var. of DOLLOP.

Dally (dæ·li), *v.* ME. [– OFr. *dalier* to converse, chat (frequent in AFr.), of unkn. origin.] †**1.** To talk lightly or idly, chat –1440. **2.** To make sport; to toy, sport *with, esp.* in the way of amorous caresses; to wanton ME.; to play *with* (temptation, etc.) 1548. **3.** To trifle *with* a person or thing 1548. **4.** *intr.* To spend time idly; to loiter 1538. †**5.** *trans.* To defer by trifling –1821. †**6.** To move by dalliance –1677.

2. Our Ayerie buildeth in the Cedars top, And dallies with the winde *Rich. III,* I. iii. 265. D. not with her, as Eve with the serpent 1642. **3.** Why will you d. with my pain ADDISON. **4.** We dallied not, but made all haste we could HEYWOOD. Hence **Da·llier,** one who dallies.

Dalmatian (dælmēⁱ·ʃən), *a.* 1824. [See -AN.] Of Dalmatia, the Austrian province on the Adriatic; whence *D. dog,* the spotted coach-dog. Hence *sb.,* A native of Dalmatia; a Dalmatian dog.

Dalmatic (dælmæ·tik), *a.* and *sb.* ME. [– (O)Fr. *dalmatique* or late L. *dalmatica,* subst. use (sc. *vestis* robe, prop. made of Dalmatian wool) of *Dalmaticus,* of Dalmatia; see -IC.]

A. *adj.* Belonging to Dalmatia 1604.

B. *sb.* An ecclesiastical vestment, with wide sleeves, and marked with two stripes, worn in the Western Church by deacons and bishops on certain occasions. **b.** A similar robe worn by kings at coronation.

Cf. ISIDORE *Orig.* XIX. xxii. 9 Dalmatica vestis primum in Dalmatia provincia Græciæ texta est, tunica sacerdotalis candida cum clavis ex purpura.

Dalt (dǫlt). *Sc.* 1775. [– Gael. *dalta.*] A foster-child.

Daltonian (dǫltōᵘ·niăn). 1841. [f. the chemist John *Dalton* (1766–1844), who was colour-blind.] *adj.* Relating to John Dalton, or the atomic theory first enunciated by him 1850. *sb.* A person who is colour blind.

Daltonism (dǫ·ltəniz'm). 1841. [– Fr. *daltonisme,* f. as prec.; see -ISM.] A name for colour-blindness, *esp.* as to red. Hence **Da·ltonist** = DALTONIAN *sb.*

Dam (dæm), *sb.*[1] ME. [– (M)LG., (M)Du. *dam* = OFris. *dam, dom,* MHG. *tam* (G. *damm* from LG.), from a base repr. also in OE. *fordemman* (ME. *demme*), OFris. *demmen,* Goth. *faurdammjan* dam up, close up; of doubtful origin.] **1.** A bank or barrier of earth, masonry, etc., built across a stream to obstruct its flow and raise its level; any similar work to confine water. Also *fig.* **2.** The body of water confined by a dam. (Now *local.*) ME. **3. a.** *Mining.* A partition of boards, masonry, etc. in a mine to keep out water, fire, or gas. **b.** *Smelting.* 'The wall of refractory material, forming the front of the fore-hearth of a blast furnace' (Raymond). **c.** *Dentistry.* A soft rubber guard to keep a tooth dry during an operation (*U.S.*) 1872.

Comb.: **d.-plate,** the plate upon the d.-stone or front stone of the bottom of a blast furnace RAYMOND.

Dam (dæm), *sb.*[2] ME. [var., due to lack of stress, of DAME.] †**1.** = DAME. (ME. only.) **2.** A female parent (now usually of quadrupeds). Correl. to *sire.* ME. **3.** = Mother (human): usually in contempt 1547. Also *fig.*

2. So Kids and Whelps their Sires and Dams express DRYDEN. Phr. *The Devil's dam,* applied opprobriously to a woman. **3.** *fig.* That high Priest of Rome, the d. of that..superstitious breed BURTON.

Dam, *sb.*[3] Chiefly *Sc.* 1580. [– Fr. *dame* lady (DAM[2], DAME), the name of each piece in the *jeu de dames* or draughts; cf. DAM-BROD.] Each of the pieces in the game of draughts (*obs.*); *pl.* the game itself.

†**Dam,** *sb.*[4], **damp.** ME. [– OFr. *dam* :– L. *dominus*; see DAN[1], and cf. DOM[1], DON *sb.*[1]] Lord; as a prefix = Sir, Master –1506.

Dam (dæm), *v.* 1553. [f. DAM *sb.*[1], replacing *dem,* OE. *demman.*] **1.** *trans.* To furnish with a dam; to obstruct or confine by means of a dam. Usu. with *up.* 1563. **2.** *transf.* and *fig.* To stop up, block, obstruct; to confine.

1. Now d. the Ditches and the Floods restrain DRYDEN. **2.** He doth also dambe vp the mercy of God by its contempt SANDERSON.

Damage (dæ·mėdʒ), *sb.* ME. [– OFr. *damage* (mod. *dommage*), f. *dam, damme* loss, damage, prejudice :– L. *damnum* loss, hurt; see DAMN *v.,* -AGE.] **1.** Loss or detriment caused by hurt or injury affecting estate, condition, or circumstances (*arch.*). **2.** Injury, harm ME. †**3.** A disadvantage –1721; a misfortune, a pity –1612. **4.** *Law.* (Now always in *pl.*) The value estimated in money of something lost or withheld; the sum claimed or awarded in compensation for loss or injury sustained 1542. **5.** *slang.* Cost, expense 1755.

1. As moche to oure d. as to oure profit CHAUCER. **2.** The d. done to the monastery HOOK. The damages which the kingdom has sustained by war GOLDSM. **3.** And of his deth it was ful gret d. CHAUCER. **4.** Damages for breach of contract 1858. Hence †**Da·mageful** *a.* hurtful.

Da·mage, *v.* ME. [– OFr. *damagier,* f. *damage*; see prec.] **1.** *trans.* To do or cause damage to; to hurt, harm, injure; now commonly to injure (a thing) so as to lessen its value. **2.** *intr.* To suffer damage (*rare*) 1821.

1. To stop all hopes, whose growth may dammage me *Rich. III,* IV. ii. 60. **2.** Her..clothes might d. with the dew CLARE. So **Da·mageable** *a.* †injurious; liable to be damaged.

Damage-feasant. 1621. [– OFr. *damage fesant,* Fr. *dommage faisant.*] *Law.* Said of a stranger's cattle, etc., found trespassing, and doing damage, as by feeding, etc. (Prop. *adj. phr.*; also as *sb.*)

†**Damageous,** *a.* ME. [– OFr. *damageus*; see DAMAGE *sb.,* -OUS.] Fraught with damage; causing loss or disadvantage –1637.

Damalic (dămæ·lik), **damolic** (dămǫ·lik), *a*1863. [f. Gr. δάμαλις, δαμάλη heifer + -IC. The second form is perh. short for *damalolic.*] *Chem.* In *d. acid,* an acid (C_7H_8O) existing in cows' urine. Hence **Damalu·ric** [URIC] *acid,* an acid ($C_8H_{10}O_2$) of the same origin.

‖**Daman** (dæ·măn). 1738. [From Arab. *damān 'isrā'īl* sheep of Israel.] The Syrian rock-badger or 'cony' of Scripture (*Hyrax syriacus*); also *H. capensis.*

Damascene (dæmăsī·n). ME. [– L. *Damascenus* – Gr. Δαμασκηνός, f. Δαμασκός – Semitic name (Heb. *dammešeḳ,* Arab. *dimišḳ, dimašḳ.*]

A. *adj.* Of or pertaining to Damascus 1543. **2.** Of or pertaining to damask (fabrics), or to the art of damascening metal 1541.

1. *D. plum*: see DAMSON.

B. *sb.* **1.** A native of Damascus ME. **2.** Damascene work; †damask 1481. **3.** See DAMSON.

Damascene (dæmăsī·n), *v.* 1585. [f. prec. adj.] To ornament (metal-work) with inlaid designs in gold or silver, or with a watered pattern. Also *transf.* and *fig.* Hence **Damascener.**

Damascus (dămæ·skŏs). Formerly also **Damasco.** 1625. [– L. *Damascus* – Gr. Δαμασκός; see DAMASCENE.] An ancient city, the capital of Cœle-Syria. Often used *attrib.,* as *D. blade*; also *absol.* = Damask steel, etc.

D. iron: a combination of pieces of iron and steel welded together and rolled out, in imitation of Damask steel. *D.-twist*: a kind of gun-barrel made of a ribbon of D. iron coiled around a mandrel and welded.

Damask (dæ·măsk). ME. [orig. attrib. uses of the name, in ME. *Damaske,* prob. – AFr. **Damasc* – L. *Damascus.* Cf. Fr. *damas.*]

I. †**1.** The city of Damascus –1539. **2.** *attrib.* = Made at or brought from Damascus.

2. †**D. plum, prune** = DAMSON. **D. rose,** a variety of rose, app. originally the *Rosa gallica* var. *damascena*, with semi-double pink or light-red (rarely white) flowers, cultivated in the East for attar of roses. †**D. water,** rose-water distilled from D. roses.

II. Substances orig. produced at Damascus. **1.** A rich silk fabric woven with elaborate designs and figures. (Also applied to fabrics of wool, linen, or cotton.) ME. **b.** A twilled linen fabric with designs which show up by opposite reflections of light from the surface; used chiefly for table-linen 1542. **2.** Steel manufactured at Damascus; also steel or a combination of iron and steel exhibiting a similar pattern on the surface: more fully *d. steel* 1603. **b.** The wavy pattern exhibited by these 1818. **3.** The colour of the damask rose 1600.

1. A quantity of China damasks, and other wrought silks DE FOE. **3.** She..Blush'd a live d. KEATS.

III. *attrib.* and *adj.* **1.** Made of damask (silk or cloth); furnished with damask 1489. **2.** Made of or resembling damask steel 1611. **3.** Of the colour of the damask rose 1588.

Comb.: **d. steel** (see above); **d.-stitch,** a name given to satin-stitch on a linen foundation; **-work,** damascening; incised patterns inlaid with gold or silver.

Damask (dæ·măsk), *v.* 1585. [f. prec. sb. Also *dama·sk* (Milton, etc.).] **1.** *trans.* To weave with richly-figured designs 1706. **2.** = DAMASCENE *v.* 1585. **3.** To ornament with or as with a variegated pattern; to diaper 1610. **4.** To deface or destroy, by stamping or marking with figures and lines 1673. †**5.** To warm (wine) (*slang*) –1778.

2. A faire basen of Copper damasked 1585. **3.** As they sat recline On the soft downie Bank damaskt with flowers MILT. *P. L.* IV. 334.

Damasked (dæ·măskt), *ppl. a.* 1599. [f. prec. + -ED¹.] **1.** In senses of DAMASK *v.* 1–3. **2.** Having the hue of the damask rose 1600. **3.** Furnished with damask 1861.

2. I haue seene Roses damaskt, red and white, But no such Roses see I in her cheekes SHAKS.

†**Damaskee·n, -kin.** 1551. [– Fr. *damasquin, -ine* – It. *damaschino*, f. *Damasco* Damascus.] *adj.* = DAMASCENE *a.* –1585. *sb.* A damask-work sword –1645.

Damaskee·n, *v.* 1585. [– Fr. *damasquiner*; see prec.] = DAMASCENE *v.*

‖**Damassé** (dăma·se). 1864. [Fr., pa. pple. of (O)Fr. *damasser*, f. *damas* DAMASK.] A kind of linen made in Flanders, woven with flowers and figures like damask.

Damassin (dæ·măsin). 1839. [Eng. f. Fr. *damas* DAMASK; cf. -INE⁴.] 'A species of woven damask with gold and silver flowers' (Brande).

Dambonite (dæ·mbŏnəit). 1879. [f. *dambo* native name + -ITE¹ 4.] *Chem.* A white crystalline substance ($C_4H_8O_3$) found in a kind of caoutchouc obtained from Western Africa.

Dambose (dæ·mbōᵘs). 1879. [f. prec. + -OSE².] *Chem.* A crystallizable sugar ($C_3H_6O_3$) obtained from dambonite.

Dam-brod, dam-board. *Sc.* 1779. [f. DAM *sb.*³ + *brod* (Sc.), BOARD.] A draught-board. *attrib.* Chequered.

Dame (dē¹m). ME. [– (O)Fr. *dame*, earlier †*damme* :– L. *domina*, fem. corresp. to *dominus* lord. Cf. DAM *sb.*², DAN¹, DOM¹, DON *sb.*¹] **1.** A female ruler or head: = 'lady', as fem. of *lord*. Also *fig.* (See also below.) **2.** The mistress of a household. Now *arch.* or *dial.*, or used of an aged housewife. ME. Also *transf.* **3.** The mistress of a children's school. ? *Obs.* 1649. **4.** At Eton: A matron (also a man) who keeps a boarding-house 1737. **5.** A form of address; = My lady, Madam: now left to women of lower rank ME. **6.** A title given to a woman of rank; = Lady, Mistress, Miss; *spec.* the legal title of the wife of a knight or baronet. Also *fig.*, as in *Dame Nature*, etc. ME. **7.** A woman of rank, a lady. Now *Hist.* or *poet.* 1530. **b.** *spec.* The wife of a knight, squire, citizen, yeoman (*arch.* or *dial.*) 1574. †**8.** = DAM *sb.*² –1709.

1. The title given to Benedictine nuns who have made their solemn profession; also, any fully professed nun. **7.** *D. Commander, D. Grand Cross,* the title, corresponding to *Knight*, of some women members of the Order of the British Empire, the Royal Victorian Order, etc., *Dame* being placed, like *Sir*, before the Christian name.

Dame's-violet. 1578. [tr. mod. L. *viola matronalis*. Hence by corruption *damas* or *damask v.*] The Garden Rocket, *Hesperis matronalis*.

‖**Dammar** (dæ·măɹ). 1698. [– Malay *damar* resin, whence the genus *Dammara* (N.O. *Coniferæ*), a species of which, *D. orientalis*, yields the resin in Amboyna and the Moluccas.] The name of various resins; *esp.* the cat's-eye resin (*E. India D.*) from *Dammara orientalis*, and the Kauri-gum from *D. australis* of New Zealand; both used for making varnish.

‖**Da·mmara.** 1863. [See prec.] *Bot.* A genus of trees yielding resin.

†**Da·mmaret.** 1635. [– Fr. *dameret*, f. *dame* lady.] A ladies' man –1649.

Damme (dæ·mi). 1618. **1.** *int.* Short f. *Damn me!* 1645. **2.** as *sb.* The oath itself 1775; †*transf.* one who uses this oath; a profane swearer –1674.

Damn (dæm), *v.* [ME. *dam(p)ne* – OFr. *dampner*, (also mod.) *damner* – L. *dam(p)nare* orig. inflict loss upon, f. *damnum* loss, damage, expenditure.] †**1.** *trans.* To affirm to be guilty; to sentence; to CONDEMN (*to*) –1734. **2.** To adjudge and pronounce to be bad; to denounce ME.; *spec.* to condemn (a play, etc.) as a failure; to condemn by public expression of disapproval 1654. **3.** *transf.* To be the ruin of 1477. **4.** *Theol.* To condemn to hell; *transf.* to cause or occasion the eternal damnation of ME. **5.** Used profanely (in optative, and with no subject expressed) in imprecations and exclamations. (Now often printed 'd—n', or 'd—'.) 1589. **6.** To imprecate damnation upon; to curse (using the word 'damn'). Also *absol.* 1624.

1. See Cromwell damned to everlasting fame POPE. **2.** And with faint praises one another d. WYCHERLEY. A comedy..which..in the playhouse phrase, was damned BOSWELL. **6.** Their proper business is to d. the Dutch DRYDEN.

Damn (dæm), *sb.* 1619 [f. prec. vb.] The utterance of the word 'damn' as an imprecation.

Damns have had their day SHERIDAN. *Not worth a d., not to care a d.*: phrases used vaguely.

Damnable (dæ·mnăb'l), *a.* (*adv.*) ME. [– OFr. *dampnable*, (also mod.) *damnable* – late L. *dam(p)nabilis*, f. *dam(p)nare*; see DAMN *v.*, -ABLE.] †**1.** Worthy of condemnation; reprehensible –1841. **2.** Liable to or worthy of damnation ME. †**3.** Pernicious (*rare*) –1659. **4.** = 'Confounded'. (Now vulgar or profane.) 1594. **5.** *adv.* Damnably –1735.

1. A d. game 1509, offence PRYNNE. **2.** O what must poore lamentable d. I doe to be saved 1614. Hence **Damnabi·lity. Da·mnableness. Da·mnably** *adv.*

Damnation (dæmnē¹·ʃən). ME. [– OFr. *dampnation*, (also mod.) *damnation* – L. *dam(p)natio*, f. pa. ppl. stem of *dam(p)nare*; see DAMN *v.*, -ION.] **1.** The action of condemning, or fact of being condemned; condemnation. **2.** *Theol.* Condemnation to eternal punishment in the world to come; perdition (opp. to *salvation*); sin incurring or deserving condemnation ME. **3.** In profane use: **a.** as an imprecation or exclamation 1604. **b.** as *adj.* or *adv.* = 'Damned' 1757.

1. Nethir thou dredist God, that thou art in the same dampnacion WYCLIF *Luke* 23:40. The d. of a play FIELDING. **2.** 'Twere d. To thinke so base a thought *Merch. V*, II. vii. 49. **3. a.** *Oth.* III. iii. 396.

Damnatory (dæ·mnătəri), *a.* 1682. [– L. *damnatorius*, f. as prec.; see -ORY².] **1.** Conveying or occasioning condemnation. **2.** *Theol.* Containing or uttering a sentence of damnation 1738.

2. I do not believe the d. clauses in the Athanasian Creed under any qualification given of them ARNOLD.

Damned (dæmd, *poet.* dæ·mnėd), *ppl. a.* ME. [f. DAMN *v.* + -ED¹.] †**1.** Condemned –1710. **2.** *Theol.* Condemned or consigned to hell ME.; *absol.* as *sb. pl.* The souls in hell 1507. **3.** Lying under, or worthy of, a curse; accursed, execrable 1563. **4.** (usually printed 'd—d'.) Used profanely to express reprehension, or as a mere intensive 1596. **b.** *adv.* Damnably 1607.

2. It was a torment To lay upon the damn'd *Temp.* I. ii. **3.** Out d. spot: out I say *Macb.* V. i. 39.

Damnify (dæ·mnifəi), *v.* 1512. [– OFr. *damnefier, dam(p)nifier* – late L. *damnificare* injure, condemn, f. L. *damnificus* hurtful; see DAMN *v.*, -FY.] **1.** *trans.* To cause injury, loss, or inconvenience to; to injure; to wrong. (Now *rare.*). †**2.** To bring to destruction –1693.

1. That the King might not be damnified by the loss of the tributes WHISTON. Hence †**Da·mnifiable** *a.* detrimental (*rare*). **Da:mnifica·tion,** the action of damnifying. (Now only in legal use.)

Damning (dæ·miŋ, dæ·mniŋ), *ppl. a.* 1599. [-ING².] **1.** That damns. **2.** That leads to condemnation or ruin 1798. **3.** Addicted to profane swearing. PEPYS.

2. The d. consciousness of being charlatans DISRAELI. Hence **Da·mning-ly** *adv.*, **-ness.**

Damnous (dæ·mnəs). 1870. [– L. *damnosus* hurtful; see DAMN *v.*, -OUS.] *Law.* Of the nature of a *damnum*, *i.e.* causing loss or damage of any kind.

Damocles (dæ·moklīz). 1747. [L. from Gr.] Name of a flatterer who, having extolled the happiness of Dionysius tyrant of Syracuse, was placed by him at a banquet with a sword suspended over his head by a hair, to impress upon him how precarious that happiness was.

Sword of D., Damocles' sword, used of an imminent danger, which may at any moment descend upon one. Hence **Damocle·an** *a.* of or as of D.

‖**Damoiseau** (dæ·mizō). *arch.* 1477. [Fr. *damoiseau*, OFr. *damoisel* m., corresp. to fem. *damoisele* (mod. *demoiselle*); see DAMSEL.] A young man of gentle birth, not yet made a knight.

Damoisel, -elle, etc., obs. ff. DAMSEL.

Damolic; see DAMALIC.

Damourite (dămūᵊ·rəit). 1846. [f. the Fr. chemist *Damour* + -ITE¹ 2b.] *Min.* A hydrous potash mica, with pearly lustre, occurring in small yellowish scales.

Damp (dæmp), *sb.* 1480. [– (M)LG. *damp* vapour, steam, smoke (so in mod. Du.) = (O)HG. *dampf* steam; – WGmc. **pamp-*.] **1.** A noxious exhalation; *spec.* in coal mines: (*a*) = CHOKE-DAMP, also called *black d., suffocating d.*; (*b*) = FIRE-DAMP, formerly *fulminating d.* 1626. †**2.** Visible vapour; fog, mist –1827. **3.** Moisture; dampness, humidity. (The ordinary current sense.) 1706; *slang.* a drink. DICKENS. †**4.** A dazed condition; stupor –1712. **5.** Depression of spirits 1606. **6.** A check 1587.

3. The morning mist and the evening d. JOHNSON. **4.** I felt a general D. and a Faintness all over me ADDISON. **5.** He found a great d. upon the spirit of the Governour CLARENDON. *Comb.* **d.-course,** *prop.* **d.-proof course,** a course of some damp-proof material laid slightly above the level of the outside soil, to prevent the damp from rising up a wall.

Damp (dæmp), *a.* 1590. [f. DAMP *sb.*] †**1.** Of the nature of, or belonging to, a damp; see DAMP *sb.* **1.** –1733. **2.** Affected with or showing stupefaction or depression of spirits (*arch.*) 1590. **3.** Slightly wet; holding water in suspension or absorption; moist, humid. (The ordinary current sense.) 1706.

1. MILT. *Sams.* 8. **2.** With looks Down cast and d. — *P. L.* I. 523. **3.** A d. bed 1894. Hence **Da·mp-ly** *adv.*, **-ness.**

Damp (dæmp), *v.* 1548. [f. DAMP *sb.*] **1.** *trans.* To affect with damp, to stifle; to dull, deaden (fire, sound, etc.). Also *fig.* 1564. †**2.** To stupefy, benumb, daze –1726. **3.** To depress, discourage, check 1548. **4.** To make moist or humid, to wet as steam, etc., does; to moisten 1671. **5.** *Gardening. To d. off* (intr.): Of plants: To rot from damp; to fog off 1846.

1. All shutting in of Air..dampeth the Sound BACON. *To d. down* (a fire, etc.): to cover it with small coal, etc., so as to check combustion and prevent its going out. Also *fig.* **3.** Sorrow damps my lays CLARE. To d. and spoyl our Trade C. MATHER. **4.** They [winds from South] d. linen and paper 1671.

Dampen (dæ·mp'n), *v.* Now chiefly *U.S.* 1630. [f. DAMP *a.* + -EN⁵, or DAMP *v.*] **1.** *trans.* = DAMP *v.* 1, 3, 4. **2.** *intr.* To become dull or damp 1686.

Damper (dæ·mpəɹ). 1748. [f. DAMP *v.* + -ER¹.] **1.** That which damps (see DAMP *v.*). **2.** A contrivance in a pianoforte for damping or stopping the vibrations of the strings; the mute of a horn, etc. 1783. **3.** A metal plate in a flue or chimney, used to control the combustion by regulating the draught 1788. **4.** *Australia.* A kind of cake or bread made, for the occasion, of flour and water and baked in hot ashes 1833. **5.** *Electr.* A device for diminishing or destroying the oscillation of a suspended magnetic needle or freely moving coil 1906.

1. Sussex is a great d. of curiosity H. WALPOLE. *Comb.* **d.-pedal,** that pedal in a pianoforte which raises all the dampers, etc., the 'loud pedal'.

Dampish (dæ·mpiʃ), *a.* 1577. [orig. f. DAMP *sb.* + -ISH[1]; subseq. treated as f. DAMP *a.*] †**1.** Vaporous –1649. **2.** Somewhat damp or moist 1641. Hence **Da·mpish-ly** *adv.*, **-ness.**

Dampne, etc., obs. ff. DAMN, etc.

Da·mpy, *a.* 1600. [f. DAMP *sb.* + -Y[1].] **1.** †Full of vapour or mist –1729; infested with damps, as a mine (*mod.*). **2.** Somewhat damp 1691.

Damsel (dæ·mzĕl), **damosel** (dæ·mozel). [ME. *dameisele, damisel* – OFr. *dameisele, damisele* (mod. *demoiselle*), alt. (after *dame*) of *danzele, donsele* :– Gallo-Rom. **dominicella*, dim. of L. *domina* lady; see DAME, DAMOISEAU.] **1.** A young unmarried lady; orig. one of noble or gentle birth. The 16–17th c. *damosel, damozel* is now used by poets, etc., as more stately than *damsel.* **2.** A young unmarried woman (sometimes slightingly); a girl, a country lass. (Not now in spoken use.) ME. **3.** A maid in waiting (*arch.*) ME. **4.** A hot iron for warming a bed. (Cf. 1 Kings 1:1–4.) 1727. **5.** A projection on the spindle of a mill-stone for shaking the shoot 1880.

1. Th' adventure of the errant damozell SPENSER *F. Q.* II. i. 19. **2.** The damosell is not dead, but sleepeth *Mark* 5:39, 41. *Comb.* **d.-fly,** the slender dragon-fly, *Agrion virgo*, called in Fr. *demoiselle.*

Damson (dæ·mz'n). [ME. *dama(s)cene, damesene* – L. *damascenum* (sc. *prunum*) plum of Damascus; cf. DAMASCENE.] **1.** A small plum, black or dark purple, the fruit of *Prunus communis* or *domestica*, variety *damascena.* **2.** The tree which bears this ME. **3.** *attrib.* Of the colour of the damson 1661.

Comb. **d.-cheese,** an inspissated conserve of damsons and sugar.

†**Dan**[1]. ME. [– OFr. *dan*, also *dam* (mod. *dom*) :– L. *dominus* master, lord; cf. DAM *sb.*[4], DOM[1], DON *sb.*[1]] = Master, Sir –1832.

The monke of Bury..Dane Johnn Lydgate SKELTON. D. Chaucer SPENSER.

Dan[2] (dæn). 1687. [Origin unkn.] A small buoy, supporting a pole which bears a flag by day and a lamp by night, used as a mark in deep-sea fishing.

Dan[3]. *local.* 1852. [Origin unkn.] *Coal-mining.* A small truck or sledge on which coal is drawn in mines.

Danaid (dæ·neˌid). [In Fr. *Danaïde* – Gr. Δαναΐς, pl. Δαναΐδες, the daughters of Danaus king of Argos, who murdered their husbands on the wedding-night, and were condemned eternally to fill sieve-like vessels with water.] A daughter of Danaus; used *attrib.* in reference to the labour of the Danaides: endless and futile. So **Danaide·an** *a.*

Danaide (dæ·neˌəid). 1825. [– mod.Fr. *danaïde* (see prec.): so named from analogy to the vessels of the Danaides.] A horizontal water wheel consisting of a vertical axis to which is attached a conical drum and case, with radial spiral floats: also called 'tub-wheel'.

Danaite (dē·năˌəit). 1833. [f. J. F. *Dana*, U.S. chemist + -ITE[1] 2b.] *Min.* A variety of arsenopyrite or mispickel, containing cobalt.

Danalite (dēⁱ·năləit). 1866. [f. J. D. *Dana*, U.S. mineralogist + -LITE.] *Min.* A silicate of iron, glucinum, etc. with sulphide of zinc, occurring in reddish octahedrons in granite.

Danburite (dæ·nbŏrəit.) 1839. [f. *Danbury*, Ct., U.S., where it occurs; see -ITE[1] 2b.] *Min.* A boro-silicate of lime, brittle, translucent, and yellowish or whitish in colour.

Dance (dɑns), *sb.* ME. [– (O)Fr. *dance*, (also mod.) *danse*, f. *danser*; see next.] **1.** A rhythmical skipping and stepping, with regular turnings and movements of the limbs and body, usually to the accompaniment of music; the action or an act or round of dancing. Also *transf.* and *fig.* **2.** A tune for regulating the movements of a dance, or composed in a dance rhythm 1509. **3.** A dancing party ME. †**4.** *fig.* Course of action; play, game –1733.

4. Of remedies of loue she knew per chaunce For she koude of that Art the olde daunce CHAUCER.

Phr. *To lead*, occas. *give* (*a person*) *a d.*; *fig.* to cause him to undergo exertion or worry with little result. *D. of death*: an allegorical representation of Death leading men of all conditions in the d. to the grave. Also called *d. of Macabre*, Fr. *danse macabre. St. Vitus's d.* = CHOREA, q.v.; also *fig.*

Dance (dɑns), *v.* ME. [– OFr. *dancer*, (also mod.) *danser* :– Rom. **dansare*, of unkn. origin.] **1.** *intr.* To leap, skip, hop, or glide with measured steps and rhythmical movements of the body, usually to a musical accompaniment. Also *transf.* and *fig.* **2.** To leap, skip, spring, or move up and down from excitement or strong emotion. Also *transf.* and *fig.* ME. **3.** Of things inanimate: To bob up and down 1563. **4.** *trans.* with cognate object ME. **5.** *causal.* **a.** To cause to dance 1665. **b.** To toss up and down with a jerky motion; to dandle ME.

1. Many a youth and many a maid Dancing in the chequer'd shade MILT. *L'Alleg.* 96. †*To d. barefoot*: said of an elder sister when a younger one was married before her. *To d. to* (*a person's*) *pipe, whistle*, etc.: *fig.* to follow his lead. **2.** I haue *Tremor Cordis* on me: my heart daunces, But not for ioy *Wint. T.* I. ii. 110. **3.** The mote that daunceth in the beam 1812. *To d. upon nothing*, to be hanged. **4.** A minuet, danced by two persons GOLDSM. †*To d. the Tyburn jig*: to be hanged. **5. a.** To d. a bear GOLDSM. **b.** I that danced her on my knee TENNYSON.

Phr. *To d. attendance*: to wait (upon a person) assiduously and obsequiously. See also ATTENDANCE.

Dancer (dɑ·nsəɹ). ME. [f. prec. vb. + -ER[1].] **1.** One who dances; *spec.* one who dances professionally in public. **2.** (*pl.*) A sect of enthusiasts who arose in 1374 in Flanders, and were noted for their wild dancing 1764. **3.** *pl.* Stairs (*slang*) 1671. **4.** *pl.* The aurora borealis. Also *Merry Dancers.* (Chiefly *Sc.*) 1717. †**Danceress,** a female d.

Dancette (dɑnse·t), *sb.* 1838. [Inferred from next.] **1.** *Her.* A fesse with three indentations 1864. **2.** *Archit.* A zigzag moulding.

Dancetté, -ee (dɑ·nsĕte, -ti), *a.* 1610. [alt. f. Fr. *danché, denché*, earlier †*dansié* :– late L. **denticatus*, f. L. *dens, dent-* tooth.] *Her.* = DANCY.

Dancing (dɑ·nsiŋ), *vbl. sb.* ME. [-ING[1].] The action of DANCE *v.*

Comb.: **d.-malady, -mania, -plague** = CHOREA; **-master; -mistress; -school.**

Da·ncing, *ppl. a.* 1563. [-ING[2].] That dances.

Comb. †**D.-goats** [L. *capræ saltantes*], a species of aurora.

Da·ncing-girl. 1760. [DANCING *ppl. a.*] **1.** A female professional dancer; *esp.* in India, a nautch-girl (in Pg. *bailadeira*, BAYADÈRE). **2.** *Dancing-girls*: a plant, *Mantisia saltatoria*, having purple and yellow flowers which somewhat resemble a ballet-dancer.

†**Dancy,** *a. rare.* 1611. [– Fr. †*dansié*; see DANCETTÉ.] *Her.* Toothed, indented –1706.

Dandelion (dæ·ndĭləiən). 1513. [– Fr. *dent-de-lion*, rendering med.L. *dens leonis* 'lion's tooth'; so called from the toothed leaves.] A well-known Composite plant (*Taraxacum dens-leonis* or *Leontodon taraxacum*), with widely toothed leaves, and a bright yellow flower; the leaves, stalk, and root contain a bitter milky juice. Also *attrib.*

Da·nder, *sb.*[1] *Sc.* 1791. [Origin unkn.] A calcined cinder.

Da·nder, *sb.*[2] = DANDRUFF, q. v.

Dander (dæ·ndəɹ), *sb.*[3] *U.S. colloq.* 1837. [perh. fig. use of *dander* ferment in working molasses, var. of DUNDER.] Ruffled or angry temper.

Da·nder, *sb.*[4] 1821. [f. DANDER *v.*] **1.** *Sc.* A saunter. **2.** *dial.* A fit of shivering 1877.

Dander (dæ·ndəɹ), *v.* 1600. [A frequent. form like *blunder, wander*; cf. DADDLE *v.*] **1.** *intr.* To stroll, saunter (*Sc.* and *n. dial.*). **2.** *dial.* To wander in talk; also, to vibrate 1724.

Dandiacal (dændəi·ăkăl), *a.* 1831. [f. DANDY, after *hypochondriacal*, etc.; see -ACAL.] Of the nature of, or characteristic of, a dandy; dandified.

Arrayed in the most d. manner SALA.

Da·ndie Di·nmont. Also **Dandy.** [From *Dandie Dinmont* in Scott's *Guy Mannering.*] One of a breed of terriers with long bodies, short strong legs, somewhat almond-shaped ears, and a slightly feathered tail carried gaily.

Dandify (dæ·ndifəi), *v. colloq.* 1823. [See -FY.] *trans.* To give the character or style of a dandy to; to trim like a dandy. Hence **Da:ndifica·tion** (*colloq.*), the act of dandifying; the being dandified; a dandified ornament. **Da·ndified** *ppl. a.* foppish.

Dandiprat (dæ·ndipræt). *arch.* 1520. [Origin unkn.] †**1.** A small 16th-c. coin, worth three halfpence –1641. **2.** A small, insignificant, or contemptible fellow. Also *attrib.* 1556.

Dandize·tte. 1821. [f. DANDY; after Fr. *grisette*, etc.] A female dandy.

Dandle (dæ·nd'l), *v.* 1530. [Origin unkn.] **1.** To move (a child, etc.) lightly up and down in the arms or on the knee. Also *fig.* and *transf.* **2.** *fig.* To make much of, pet, fondle, pamper 1575. †**3.** To trifle or toy with –1646. **4.** *intr.* To play or toy (*with*) (*rare*) 1829. †**5.** = DANGLE (? erron.) –1687.

1. He sits dandling his child upon his knee 1847. **2.** No man or nation was ever dandled into greatness GOLDWIN SMITH. **3.** They doe soe d. theyr doinges..as yf they would not have the Enemye subdued SPENSER. Hence **Da·ndler.** †**Da·ndling** *sb.* a dandled child; a pet.

Dandruff, dandriff (dæ·ndrŏf, -if). 1545. [The first element is obscure; the second, *-ruff*, may be identical with late ME. *rove*, later *rofe, roufe* scurfiness, scab – ON. *hrufa* or MLG., MDu. *rōve* (Du. *roof*).] Dead scarf-skin separating in small scales and entangled in the hair; scurf.

Dandy (dæ·ndi), *sb.*[1] (and *a.*) 1780. [perh. a shortening of JACK-A-DANDY, the last element of which may be identical with *Dandy*, pet-form of *Andrew.*]

A. 1. One who studies ostentatiously to dress elegantly and fashionably; a fop, an exquisite. Also *transf.* **2.** *slang* or *colloq.* In phr. *the d.*, 'the correct thing', 'the ticket' 1784. **3.** *Naut.* 'A sloop or cutter with a jigger-mast abaft, on which a mizen-lug-sail is set' (Smyth). **4.** *dial.* A bantam fowl. (*D. cock, d. hen.*) 1828. **5.** Short for DANDY-ROLLER 1851.

1. A D. is a Clothes-wearing Man CARLYLE. *transf.* The barque looked a real d. 1885.

B. *attrib.* and *adj.* Of, belonging to, or characteristic of a dandy or dandies; affectedly neat, trim, or smart 1813.

A d. little hand in a kid glove THACKERAY.

Hence **Da·ndily** *adv.* **Da·ndyish** *a.* foppish. **Da·ndyism.**

Dandy, *sb.*[2] Also **dandy-fever.** [var. in the West Indies of DENGUE.] 1828. See DENGUE.

‖**Dandy, dandi** (dæ·ndi), *sb.*[3] *Anglo-Ind.* 1685. [Hindi *ḍanḍī*, f. *ḍanḍ* staff, oar.] **1.** A boatman on the Ganges. **2.** (*Dandi.*) A S'aiva mendicant who carries a small wand 1832. **3.** 'A kind of vehicle consisting of a strong cloth slung like a hammock to a bamboo staff, and carried by two (or more) men' (Yule).

Da·ndy-brush. 1841. [f. DANDY *sb.*[1]] A stiff brush made of split whalebone, used in cleaning horses.

Dandy-cock, -hen; see DANDY[1] A. 4.

Da·ndy-horse. 1819. [DANDY *sb.*[1]] A kind of velocipede.

Da·ndy-line. 1882. A kind of line used in herring fishing, carrying at short intervals transverse pieces of whalebone or cane, having unbaited hooks at either end.

Da·ndy-roller. Also **-roll.** 1839. *Paper-making.* A perforated roller for solidifying the partly-formed web of paper, and for impressing the watermark.

Dane (dēⁱn). OE. [– ON. *Danir* pl. (late L. *Dani*); superseding OE. *Dene*, which is repr. in *Denmark* (OE. *Denemearc*).] **1.** A native or subject of Denmark; in older usage including Northmen generally. **2.** Applied to a breed or breeds of dogs 1774. **3.** *attrib.* = DANISH.

2. *Great D.* (also simply *D.*): a large, powerful, short-haired breed of dog, between the mastiff and the greyhound types. *Lesser D.*: the Dalmatian.

Danebrog; see DANNEBROG.

Danegeld, -gelt (dēⁱ·ngeld, -gelt). OE. [– ON. **Danagjald* (ODa. *Danegjeld*), f. gen. of *Danir* pl., Danes + *gjald* payment, tribute; cf. GELD *sb.*] *Eng. Hist.* An annual tax, imposed originally (as is supposed) to provide funds for the protection of England against the Danes, and continued subsequently as a land-tax.

Dane-law (dēⁱ·nlǭ). [Late OE. *Dena lagu* 'Danes' law'.] **1.** The Danish law anciently in force over that part of England occupied by the Danes. **2.** Hence, The district north-east of Watling Street, where this law prevailed 1837.

Da·nes'-blood. 1607. [f. as DANEWORT, q. v.] The Danewort. **b.** *Campanula glomerata* 1861. **c.** *Anemone pulsatilla.*

Daneweed (dēⁱ·nwīd). 1748. [See next.] †A local name for *Eryngium campestre.* **b.** = DANEWORT.

Danewort (dēⁱ·nwɒɹt). 1491. [f. DANE + WORT, the plants being supposed to spring up in places where Danish blood was spilt in battle.] The Dwarf Elder, *Sambucus ebulus.*

Dang, *v.* 1793. A euphemism for DAMN.

Dang, pa. t. of DING *v.*, to drive, push, knock, or dash.

Danger (dēⁱ·ndʒəɹ), *sb.* ME. [– AFr. *da(u)nger*, OFr. *dangier*, (mod. *danger*) :– Rom. **domniarium*, f. *domnus, dominus* lord, master; see -ER².] **1.** Power of a lord, jurisdiction, dominion; power to dispose of, or to harm (*arch.*). †**b.** Liability (to loss, punishment, etc.) –1689. †**2.** Difficulty (made or raised); chariness; coyness –1526. **3.** Liability or exposure to harm or injury; risk, peril. (From sense 1. Now the main sense.) Also with *a* and *pl.* 1489. †**4.** Mischief, harm –1601. †**5.** The lordship over a forest; the rent paid in acknowledgement of this (so OFr. *dangier*) 1693.

1. In dawngere had he..The ȝonge girles of þe diocise CHAUCER. Phr. *In (a person's) d.*: within his power. **b.** Phr. *Out of debt out of d.* (now taken in sense 3). **2.** Phr. †*To make d.* [OFr. *faire dangier (de)*]: to make a difficulty (about doing anything). **3.** Delay breeds D. SHELTON. In d. of their lives, of deth CAXTON, to die NORTH. Blind to the dangers of their country HELPS. **4.** *Jul. C.* II. i. 17. *Comb.* **d.-signal,** a signal indicating d.; *e.g.* on *Railways*, indicating an obstruction, etc. ahead. Hence †**Da·ngerful** *a.* **Da·ngerless** *a.* (and *adv.*). Now *rare.* **Da·ngersome** *a.* (*dial.*).

†**Da·nger,** *v.* ME. [– OFr. *dangerer*, f. *dangier*; see prec.] **1.** To render liable –1633. **2.** To endanger –1663. **3.** ? To damage. (Cf. DANGER *sb.* 4.) –1614.

Dangerous (dēⁱ·ndʒərəs), *a.* ME. [– AFr. *da(u)ngerous*, OFr. *dangereus* (mod. *-eux*); see DANGER *sb.*, -OUS.] †**1.** Difficult to deal with; not affable (ME. only); difficult to please –1577; chary *of* –1598. **2.** Fraught with danger or risk; perilous, hazardous, unsafe. (The current sense.) 1490. **3.** In danger; dangerously ill. Now *dial.* and *U.S. colloq.* 1616. †**4.** Injurious. (Cf. DANGER *sb.* 4.) –1576.

1. So fiers & daungerous was he, That he nolde graunte hir askyng CHAUCER. **2.** Delay herein is daungerous B. GOOGE. In most of the European nations there are d. classes HELPS. **3.** He's d.; they don't think he'll live 1884. **4.** Two vices, very daungerous and noysome among men FLEMING. Hence **Da·ngerous-ly** *adv.*, **-ness.**

Dangle (dæ·ŋg'l), *v.* 1590. [Of symbolic formation; cf. NFris. *dangeln*, Sw. *dangla*, Da. *dangle*, parallel to Icel., Sw. *dingla*, Da. *dingle*; see -LE.] **1.** *intr.* To hang loosely swaying to and fro 1590; to be hanged 1678. **2.** *trans.* To make (a thing) hang and sway to and fro; to hold or carry (it) suspended loosely 1612. Also *fig.* **3.** *fig.* (*intr.*) To hang *after* or about any one, *esp.* as a loosely attached follower 1607.

1. Our thinne nets dangling in the winde P. FLETCHER. And men [have] as often dangled for't, And yet will never leave the sport BUTLER *Hud.* **3.** Heirs of noble houses..dangling after actresses MACAULAY. *Comb.* **d.-berry,** Blue Tangle, *Gaylussacia frondosa*, an American shrub, N.O. *Vacciniaceæ.*

Hence **Da·ngle** *sb.* act of dangling; that which dangles (*rare*). **Da·ngle** *a.* dangling (*rare*). **Da·nglement,** dangling. **Da·ngler.**

†**Da·nic,** *a.* 1613. [– med.L. *Danicus*, f. *Dania* Denmark; see -IC.] = DANISH –1692. Hence **Da·nicism,** a Danish idiom.

Danish (dēⁱ·niʃ). OE. [ME. *danais, danis* :– AFr. *danes*, OFr. *daneis* (mod. *danois*) :– med.L. *Danensis*; later assim. to adjs. in -ISH¹; superseded the native †*densh* :– OE. *Denisć* = ON. *Danskr* :– Gmc. **daniskaz.*] *adj.* Of or belonging to the Danes and to Denmark. *sb.* The language of Denmark.

D. axe: a kind of battle-axe with a very long blade. *D. dog*: see DANE. Hence **Da·nishry** [cf. *Irishry*, etc.], the people of Danish race (in Britain). *Hist.*

Danism¹ (dēⁱ·niz'm). 1886. [f. DANE + -ISM.] Danicism.

†**Da·nism**². 1623. [– Gr. δανεισμός.] Money-lending on usury. (Dicts.)

†**Dank,** *sb.* ME. [app. f. DANK *a.*] Wetness –1602; a wet place –1667.

Dank (dæŋk), *a.* late ME. [Implied earlier in the deriv. DANK *v.* (XIII); prob. of Scand. origin; cf. Sw. *dank* marshy spot, Icel. *dökkr* pit, pool (:– **daŋku-*).] **1.** Wet, watery, wetting. **2.** Damp: as an injurious or disagreeable quality 1573. **3.** Said of weeds, etc. growing in damp places 1820.

1. The d. moisture of the ayre 1601. O'er the d. marsh SOMERVILLE. **2.** Vapours, d. and clammy COWPER. The d. and sable earth SCOTT. Hence **Da·nkish** *a.* dank; somewhat moist. **Da·nkishness. Da·nkly** *adv.* **Da·nkness.**

Dank (dæŋk), *v.* Now *dial.* ME. [See prec.] †**1.** To wet, damp, moisten –1634. Also *fig.* **2.** *intr.* To drizzle 1866.

‖**Dannebrog** (dæ·nĕbrǫg). Also **Dane-.** 1708. [Da., f. *Danne-, Dane-* + *brog* breech, cloth.] The Danish national flag; hence, a Danish order of knighthood.

‖**Danseuse** (dāṅsǒz). 1845. [Fr.] A female dancer, a ballet-dancer.

†**Dansk,** *a.* Also **Danisk.** 1569. [– Da., Sw., Icel. *Dansk.*] = DANISH –1610.

‖**Da·nsker.** [Da., f. prec.] A Dane. SHAKS.

Dante. 1600. [– Sp. *ante, dante* elk, buffalo, *danta* tapir; It. *dante*; ult. – Arab. *lamṭ* African antelope.] †**1.** (Also *dant.*) Some animal of the antelope or buffalo kind. **2.** (Also *danta.*) The American tapir 1601.

Dantean (dæ·ntiˌăn), *a.* 1850. [See -AN, -EAN.] Of, relating to, or resembling Dante or his writings. Also *sb.* A student of Dante. So **Dante·sque** *a.* **Da·ntist,** a Dante scholar. **Danto·philist,** an admirer of Dante.

Dap (dæp), *sb.* Now *dial.* 1583. [Sense 2 goes with DAP *v.*; sense 1 unexpl.] **1.** *pl.* Ways, modes of action; hence *dial.* likeness, image. **2.** A bounce of a ball, etc. 1835.

Dap (dæp), *v.* Also **dape.** 1653. [app. parallel to DAB, the final *p* expressing a lighter touch. Cf. also DOP.] **1.** *intr.* (rarely *trans.*) To fish by letting the bait dip and bob lightly on the water; to dib. Also *gen.* **2.** To rebound, bounce 1851.

1. How to catch a Chub with daping a Grashopper WALTON.

Daphnad (dæ·fnăd). 1847. [See next, -AD I. d.] *Bot.* Lindley's name for plants of the order *Thymelaceæ*, including *Daphne.*

Daphne (dæ·fni). ME. [Gr. δάφνη the laurel or bay-tree: in *Mythol.* a nymph who was changed into a laurel.] **1.** The Laurel. **b.** in *Bot.* The name of a genus of shrubs containing the Spurge Laurel and Mezereon. **2.** *Astron.* The 41st of the Asteroids. Hence **Da·phnean** *a.*

‖**Daphnia** (dæ·fniă). 1847. [See prec., -IA¹.] *Zool.* A genus of minute fresh-water entomostracans; a water-flea. Hence **Daphnia·ceous** *a.* **Da·phniad,** a member of the order containing the water-fleas. **Da·phnioid** *a.* allied in structure to Daphnia; *sb.* a daphniad.

Daphnin (dæ·fnin). 1819. [f. as prec. + -IN¹.] *Chem.* A bitter glucoside obtained from two species of Daphne. So **Da·phnetin,** a product of the decomposition of daphnin.

‖**Dapifer** (dæ·pifəɹ). 1636. [Late L., f. *daps, dap-* food, feast, + *-fer*; see -FEROUS.] One who brings meat to table; hence, the official title of the steward of a king's or nobleman's household.

Dapper (dæ·pəɹ), *a.* 1440. [– MLG., MDu. *dapper* heavy, powerful, strong, stout (Du. *dapper* bold, valiant) = OHG. *tapfar* heavy, weighty, firm (late MHG., G. *tapfer* brave), ON. *dapr* sad, dreary.] **1.** Neat, trim, smart, spruce in dress or appearance. (Formerly, but not now, appreciative.) **b.** *esp.* 'Little and active, lively without bulk' (J.) 1606. **2.** *transf.* Of animals and things 1579. †**3.** as *sb.* A dapper fellow –1747.

1. The spruce and d. importance of his ordinary appearance SCOTT. The d. elves MILT. *Comus* 118. **2.** My d. nagg, Pegasus WOOD. Hence **Da·pperling,** a d. little fellow. **Da·pper-ly** *adv.*, **-ness.**

Dapple (dæ·p'l), *sb.* 1580. [See DAPPLED.] †**1.** One of many spots of colouring on a surface –1611. **2.** Spotting, clouding; dappled condition, dappling 1591. **3.** An animal with a mottled coat 1635.

1. As many eyes upon his body, as my gray mare hath dapples SIDNEY.

Dapple (dæ·p'l), *a.* 1551. [See DAPPLED.] = DAPPLED.

A third sheykh, with a d. mule LANE.

Dapple (dæ·p'l), *v.* 1599. [See DAPPLED.] **1.** *trans.* To variegate with spots of different colour or shade. Also *fig.* **2.** *intr.* To become dappled 1678.

1. Day..Dapples the drowsie east with spots of grey *Much Ado* V. iii. 27. **2.** To d. into day BYRON.

Da·pple-bay, *sb.* 1835. [After *dapple-grey.*] A dappled bay (horse).

Dappled (dæ·pl'd), *a.* [Late ME. *dappled, dappeld*, whence DAPPLE *sb.*, *a.*, *v.* (all XVI); of unkn. origin.] Marked with spots of a different colour or shade; speckled. *Comb.* **d.-grey** = DAPPLE-GREY (horse).

Dapple-grey (dæ·p'lˌgrēⁱ), *a.* (sb.) ME. [Contemporary (Chaucer) with DAPPLED, which varies in Maundeville with *pomelee* (– OFr. *pomelé* 'appled'; cf. *pomely grey* in Chaucer – Fr. *gris pommelé*); cf. ON. *apalgrár*, OHG. *aphelgrāo* (G. *apfelgrau*), Du. *appelgrauw.*] Grey variegated with spots or patches of a darker shade: said of horses. *absol.* A horse of this colour 1639.

His steede was al dappull gray CHAUCER.

Darapti (dăræ·pti). 1551. *Logic.* A mnemonic term for the first valid mood of the third syllogistic figure, in which two universal affirmative premisses (*a, a*) yield a particular affirmative conclusion (*i*).

Darby (dā·ɹbi). 1575. A southern (not the local) pronunciation of *Derby*, the English town and shire. Hence an English surname. **1.** *Father Derby's* or *Darby's bands*: app. Some rigid form of usurer's bond 1576. **2.** *pl.* Handcuffs; *occas.*, fetters (*slang*) 1673. †**3.** Ready money (*slang*) –1785. **4.** Short for Derby ale 1704. **5.** *Plastering.* A plasterer's float with two handles, used in levelling surfaces, etc. 1819. **6. Darby and Joan:** an attached couple, *esp.* when old and in humble life. Hence *dial.* a pair of china figures for the chimney-piece. 1773.

Darbyism (dā·ɹbiˌis'm). 1876. [f. Rev. John N. *Darby*, their first leader + -ISM.] The principles of the Plymouth Brethren, or of a branch of these called Exclusive Brethren. So **Da·rbyite,** one who holds these principles.

Dardan (dā·ɹdăn). 1606. [– L. *Dardanus* Trojan.] *adj.* Trojan, of Troy. *sb.* A Trojan. So **Darda·nian** *a.* and *sb.*; ‖**Darda·nium,** a golden bracelet.

About thy wrist the rich Dardanium HERRICK.

Dare (dēᵊɹ), *v.*¹ Pa. t. **durst** (dǒɹst), **dared** (dēᵊrd); pa. pple. **dared.** [A pret.-pres. vb., OE. *durran*, pres. *dearr, durron*, pa. *dorste*, corresp. to OFris. *dūra*, OS. *gidurran*, OHG. *giturran*, Goth. *gadaursan*, f. the Gmc. series **ders-* **dars-* **durs-* (not ON.) :– IE. **dhers-* **dhors-* **dhr̥s-*, whence Skr. *dhr̥sh*, perf. *dadārsha* be bold, Gr. θαρσεῖν be bold. The 3rd sing. pres. *he dares* and pa. t. *dared* appeared in the south in the 16th c., and are always used in the transitive senses, and now also in the intrans. sense when followed by *to.* When followed by the infinitive without *to*, *dare* and *durst* are still in common use.]

I. *intr.* (Inflected *dare, durst*, also *dares, dared.*) **1.** To have boldness or courage (*to do* something); to be so bold as OE. **2.** *ellipt.* To dare to go, venture ME.

1. None of the disciples durst aske him, Who art

thou *John* 21:12. A Spanish Notary dared to appear publickly in the Rota 1619. No one durst to breathe otherwise GALE.

II. *trans.* (Inflected *dares, dared.*) **1.** To dare to undertake or do; to venture upon, have courage for 1631. **2.** To venture to meet; to challenge; to defy 1580.

1. To d. all things, but nothing too much 1631. **2.** I d. Damnation..onely Ile be reueng'd *Haml.* IV. v. 133. An English man..[cannot] suffer..to be dared by any LYLY. You..d. me to it MARRYAT.

Dare (dēəɹ), *v.*[2] Now *dial.* [OE. *darian*, f. stem of MDu. and LG. *bedaren* appease, calm, Flemish *verdaren* amaze.] †**1.** *intr.* To gaze fixedly or stupidly –1549; also *fig.* †**2.** To crouch. Also *fig.* –1500. †**3.** To lurk –1440. †**4.** *trans.* To daze; to fascinate –1671. **5.** To daunt, terrify. Now *dial.* 1611.

4. *To d. larks*, to fascinate and daze them in order to catch them.

Dare (dēəɹ), *sb.*[1] 1594. [f. DARE *v.*[1]] **1.** An act of defying; a challenge. Now *colloq.* †**2.** Boldness –1596.

1. Sin is the d. of God's justice BUNYAN. **2.** It lends..A larger D. to your great Enterprize SHAKS.

Dare (dēəɹ), *sb.*[2] 1860. [f. DARE *v.*[2]] A contrivance for fascinating larks.

†**Dare,** *sb.*[3] 1475. [A sing. f. *dars* – OFr. *dars*; see DACE.] = DACE –1740.

Dare-devil (dēəɹ,de:vil). 1794. [f. DARE *v.*[1] + DEVIL; cf. *cutthroat.*] *sb.* One ready to dare the devil. *adj.* Recklessly daring 1832.

Robert Clive..an idle dare-devil of a boy GREEN. *adj.* Dare-devil skippers MOTLEY. Hence **Da·re-de:vilry.**

Darer (dēə·rəɹ). 1614. [f. DARE *v.*[1] + -ER[1].] One who ventures; one who challenges.

Darg (dāɹg). *Sc.* and *n. dial.* ME. [Syncopated f. *daywerk*, or *daywark*, DAYWORK.] A day's work; also, a definite quantity of work. Hence **Da·rger, Da·rgsman,** day-labourer.

Daric (dæ·rik). 1566. [– Gr. Δαρεικός (sc. στατήρ stater); see -IC.] A gold coin of ancient Persia, named from the first Darius. Also a Persian silver coin of the same design.

Darii (dēə·riəi). 1551. *Logic.* A mnemonic term for the third valid mood of the first syllogistic figure, in which a universal major premiss (*a*) and a particular affirmative minor (*i*) yield a particular affirmative conclusion (*i*).

Daring (dēə·riŋ), *vbl. sb.* 1611. [-ING[1].] Adventurous courage, hardihood.

Da·ring, *ppl. a.* 1582. [-ING[2].] Bold, adventurous; hardy. Also *transf.* and *fig.*

The most d. of financiers MACAULAY. This d. legal fiction FREEMAN. Hence **Da·ring-ly** *adv.*, **-ness.**

Dariole (dæ·riōul). ME. [– (O)Fr. *dariole.*] Various sweet or savoury dishes; now, a savoury dish cooked and served in a small mould; also, the mould for this.

Dark (dāɹk), *a.* [OE. *deorc*, prob. f. Gmc. base *derk- *dark-, perh. rel. to OHG. *tarnjan* (G. *tarnen*) conceal.]

I. *literal.* **1.** Devoid of or deficient in light; unilluminated. **2.** Reflecting or transmitting little light; gloomy, sombre OE. **3.** Approaching black in hue; deep in shade (opp. to *light*); of the complexion: the opposite of fair ME.

1. A very darke night HALL. A d. house 1861. Phr. †*To keep* (*a person*) *dark*: to keep him confined in a dark room (as madmen were kept formerly). *D. moon* = *d. of the moon.* **2.** Cloudy and d. weather 1658. D. hills 1870. **3.** D. hair SOUTHEY. On the d. green grass THOMSON.

II. *fig.* **1.** Devoid of moral or spiritual light; evil, wicked; foul, iniquitous, atrocious OE. **2.** Gloomy, dismal, sad OE.; of the countenance: clouded, frowning 1599. **3.** Obscure in meaning ME.; indistinct, indiscernible 1592. **4.** Concealed, secret, as in *to keep d.* 1605; of a person: reticent, not open 1675. **5.** Of whom or which little is known 1831. **6.** Not able to see; blind. Now *dial.* ME. **7.** Void of intellectual light; ignorant ME.

1. To darke dishonours vse *Rich. II*, I. i. 169. This darke Conspiracy *Ibid.* V. ii. 96. The darkest and meanest vices MACAULAY. **2.** The d. side of things 1849. Men of d. tempers ADDISON. A smile amid d. frowns SHELLEY. **3.** The Cause is d., and hath not been rendred by any BACON. In d. obscurity SHAKS. D. oblivion COWPER. **4.** And Lyttelton a d., designing knave POPE. **5.** *D. horse* (*Racing slang*), a horse about whose 'form' little is known; hence *fig.* of a candidate or competitor. **7.** What in me is d. Illumine MILT. *P. L.* I. 26.

Combs., etc.: **D. Ages,** in its earliest use, the Middle Ages; later, the earlier period to *c.* 1100; **d.-house** = *dark-room* (*a*); **-room,** †(*a*) a room in which madmen were confined; (*b*) *Photogr.* a room from which all actinic rays of light are excluded, used by photographers when dealing with sensitized plates; †**d. tent,** a camera obscura.

Hence **Da·rkful** *a.* full of darkness (*rare*). **Da·rkish** *a.* somewhat d. **Da·rkly** *adv.* in a d. manner.

Dark (dāɹk), *sb.* ME. [f. DARK *a.*; cf. *light* sb. and adj.] **1.** Absence of light; darkness; the dark time; night, nightfall; a dark place. Also *fig.* **2.** Dark colour or shade; *spec.* in *Art*, a part of a picture in shadow, as opp. to *light* 1675. Also *fig.* **3.** Obscurity 1628. **4.** *In the d.*: in a state of ignorance 1677.

1. Nights darke approcht apace 1598. One evening after d. 1771. *D. of the moon*: the time near new moon when there is no moonlight. **4.** I am entirely in the d. about the designs..of [etc.] BURKE.

Dark (dāɹk), *v. arch.* or *dial.* ME. [f. DARK *a.*] †**1.** To make or become dark, darken –1715. Also *fig.* †**2.** *intr.* To lie in the dark, to lie hid –1447.

1. When the nyght darkes SKELTON. My somers day in lusty may is derked before the none 1500.

Darken (dā·ɹk'n), *v.* ME. [f. DARK *a.*, superseding DARK *v.*; see -EN *suffix*[5].] **1.** *intr.* To grow or become dark. (Occas. with *down.*) **2.** To grow clouded, gloomy, sad 1742. **3.** *trans.* To make dark, to deprive of light. Also *fig.* ME. **4.** To deprive of sight, to make blind (*lit.* and *fig.*) 1548. **5.** *fig.* To make dark in meaning 1548. **6.** *fig.* To cloud; to cast a gloom or shadow over 1553.

1. The Heaven darkens above SHELLEY. **2.** His face darkened with some powerful emotion HAWTHORNE. **3.** When Night darkens the Streets MILT. *P. L.* I. 501. *To d.* (*a person's*) *door or doors*: emphatic for to appear on the threshold (as a visitor). **4.** Let their eyes be darkened, that they see not *Ps.* 69:23. **5.** Who is this that darkeneth counsel by words without knowledge *Job* 38:2 **6.** To d. The Mirth o' th' Feast *Wint. T.* IV. iv. 41. Hence **Da·rkener.**

Da·rk-la·ntern. 1650. A lantern with an arrangement by which the light can be concealed.

Darkle (dā·ɹk'l), *v.* 1800. [Back-formation f. next.] **1.** *intr.* To show itself darkly 1819. **2.** To grow dark 1800. **3.** *trans.* To obscure 1884.

Darkling (dā·ɹkliŋ), *adv.* and *a.* [ME. *darkeling*, f. DARK *a.* + -LING[2].]

A. *adv.* In the dark; in darkness (*lit.* and *fig.*) 1450.

The wakeful Bird Sings d. MILT. *P. L.* III. 39. var. **Da·rklings** (*rare*).

B. *adj.* (taken also as *pres. pple.*) **1.** Being, proceeding, etc. in the dark 1763. **2.** Showing itself darkly; darksome, obscure 1739.

1. Ye writers..O spare your d. labours SHENSTONE. **2.** By the d. forest paths M. ARNOLD. D. was the sense SCOTT.

Da·rkmans. *Thieves' cant.* 1567. [f. DARK *a.*; cf. *lightmans* the day, etc.] The night.

Darkness (dā·ɹknės). [OE. *deorcnes*, -*nys*, f. *deorc* DARK *a.*; see -NESS.] **1.** Absence of light (total or partial). **2.** The quality of being dark in shade or colour ME. **3.** Blindness ME. **4.** *fig.* **a.** Want of spiritual or intellectual sight ME.; **b.** Death ME. **5.** Gloom of sorrow or distress 1645. **6.** Obscurity, concealment, secrecy ME. **7.** Obscurity of meaning 1553.

1. No light, But rather d. visible MILT. *P.L.* I. 63. **3.** His eyes..Were shrivell'd into d. in his head TENNYSON. **4. a.** The prynce of derknes..our goostly ennemy the deuyll 1526. The D. and Superstition of later Ages ADDISON. **5.** The d. of deepest dismay SHELLEY. **6.** What I tell you in d., that speak ye in light *Matt.* 10:27.

Darksome (dā·ɹksŏm), *a.* 1530. [f. DARK *sb.* + -SOME[1]; cf. *toilsome.*] **1.** Somewhat dark or gloomy. Now chiefly poetic for *dark.* Also *fig.* **2.** Sombre in shade or colour 1615.

1. The d. night STERNHOLD & H. *fig.* D. sense BP. HALL, fears HOOD, vices MCCARTHY. **2.** A darksom Cloud of Locusts MILT. *P. L.* XII. 185.

Darky, darkey (dā·ɹki). 1789. [f. DARK *a.* + -Y[6].] **1.** The night (*slang*). **2.** A dark-lantern (*slang*) 1812. **3.** A negro (*colloq.*). Also *attrib.* 1840.

Darling (dā·ɹliŋ). [OE. *dēorling*; see DEAR *a.*[1] and *sb.*[2], -LING[1].]

A. *sb.* **1.** The object of a person's love; a favourite; a pet. Also *transf.* and *fig.* †**2.** A variety of apple 1586.

1. The idol of my youth, The d. of my manhood TENNYSON. *fig.* The d. of the people STUBBS.

B. *adj.* [attrib. use of sb.] Dearly loved; best-loved, favourite 1596.

His [the devil's] d. sin Is pride that apes humility COLERIDGE.

Darn (dāɹn), *v.* 1600. [perh. a use of *darn*, later form of †DERN *v.*; cf. MDu. *dernen* stop holes in (a dike).] To mend (stockings, etc.) by filling-in a hole or rent with yarn or thread interwoven. (This is done with a *darning-needle.*) Also *fig.*

Four Pair of Silk-Stockings curiously derned STEELE.

Darn, *sb.* 1720. [f. prec.] The act or result of darning. Hence **Da·rner,** one who darns; a darning-needle.

Darn, Darnation, etc., colloq. f. DAMN, etc. (Chiefly *U.S.*)

Darnel (dā·ɹnĕl). ME. [Cf. Walloon dial. '*darnelle*, *ivraie*, *lolium temulentum*'; history unkn.] **1.** A deleterious grass, *Lolium temulentum*, which grows as a weed among corn. Also, a book-name of the genus *Lolium.* **2.** 'Applied to *Papaver Rhœas*' (Britten and Holland) 1612. **3.** *fig.* Cf. COCKLE, TARES 1444. Also *attrib.*

1. *Red d.*: Rye-grass, *L. perenne.* **3.** [Satan] sowing his d. of errors and tares of discord 1590.

Darning (dā·ɹniŋ), *vbl. sb.* 1611. [-ING[1].] **1.** The action of DARN *v.*, or its result. Also *fig.* **2.** Articles darned or to be darned 1894.

Comb.: **d.-ball, -last,** an egg-shaped or spherical piece of wood, etc., over which a fabric is stretched while being darned; **-needle,** a long and stout needle used in darning; **-stitch,** a stitch used in darning.

Darnix, darnock, obs. ff. DORNICK.

Daroga, darogha (dărōu·gă). *Anglo-Ind.* 1634. [– Pers. and Hind. *dārūġā.*] A governor, superintendent, chief officer, head of police or excise. Under the Mongols, the Governor of a province or city.

Darraign, -rain(e, etc., var. of DERAIGN *Obs.*

†**Darrei·n,** *a.* 1555. [– AFr., OFr. *derrein*, *darrein*, whence OFr. *derrenier*, (also mod.) *dernier* last.] *Old Law.* Last, ultimate, final; = DERNIER. *D. ressort*: = *dernier ressort.*

Dart (dāɹt), *sb.* ME. [– OFr. *dart* (mod. *dard*), acc. of *darz*, *dars* – Frankish **darođ* spear, lance, repr. by OE. *darop*, OHG. *tart*, ON. *darraðr.*] **1.** A pointed missile thrown by the hand; a light spear or javelin; any pointed missile, as an arrow, etc. Also *fig.* and *transf.* **2.** Anything resembling a dart: *spec.* in *Zool.*, the sting of a venomous insect, a dart-like organ in some gastropods (see *d.-sac* below), etc. 1665. **3.** *Dress-making.* A seam joining the two edges left by cutting a gore in any stuff 1884. **4.** = *d.-serpent*, *-snake* (see below) 1591. †**5.** The fish called also DACE or DARE 1655. **6.** [f. the vb.] The act of darting, or of casting a dart 1721.

1. As one shuteth deadly arowes and dartes COVERDALE *Prov.* 26:18. **b.** A light pointed missile thrown at a target in the indoor game of *darts.* 1901.

Comb.: **d.-moth,** a moth of the genus *Agrotis*, so called from a mark on the fore-wing; **-sac,** a sac connected with the generative organs of some gastropods, from which the darts are ejected; **-serpent, -snake,** a snake-like lizard of the genus *Acontias*, which dart upon their prey.

Dart (dāɹt), *v.* ME. [f. DART *sb.*; cf. Fr. *darder.*] †**1.** *trans.* To pierce with or as with a dart –1752. **2.** To throw, cast, shoot (a dart or other missile) 1580. **3.** *transf.* and *fig.* To send forth, or emit, suddenly and sharply; to shoot out 1592. **4.** *intr.* To throw a dart or other missile 1530. **5.** To move like a dart; to spring or start suddenly and rapidly; to shoot. Also *fig.* 1619.

1. To d. a whale 1752. **2.** Near enough to d. the harpoon 1839. **3.** Her eyes..darted flashes of anger as she spoke THACKERAY. **5.** A deer darts out of the copse 1885. Hence **Da·rtingly** *adv.*

†**Dartars.** 1580. [Earlier form of DARTRE.] A kind of scab on the chin of lambs –1741.

Darter (dā·ɹtəɹ). 1565. [f. DART *v.* + -ER[1].] **1.** One who or that which darts; one who throws or shoots darts. †**2.** Dart-snake –1820. **3.** A name for various birds; *esp.* the web-footed birds of the genus *Plotus*; so called from their way of darting on their prey 1825. **4.** A name for various fishes; *esp.* the fresh-water fishes of the N. American subfamily *Etheostominæ*, which dart from their retreats when disturbed 1884.

Dartle (dā·ɹt'l), *v. rare.* 1855. [dim. and iterative of DART *v.*; see -LE.] To dart or shoot forth repeatedly (*trans.* and *intr.*).
Chestnut logs which spit and d. 1893.

Da·rtman. 1605. A soldier armed with a dart.

Dartoid (dā·ɹtoid), *a.* 1872. [f. Gr. δαρτός + -OID; see next.] *Anat.* Like or of the nature of the dartos.

‖**Dartos** (dā·ɹtǫs). 1634. [– Gr. δαρτός flayed.] *Anat.* The layer of contractile tissue immediately beneath the skin of the scrotum.

Dartre (dā·ɹtəɹ). 1829. [– Fr. *dartre* :– med.L. *derbita*, of Gaulish origin (cf. Breton *dervoed*).] A vague generic name for various skin diseases, *esp.* herpes. Hence **Da·rtrous** *a.* pertaining to or of the nature of d.: applied to a certain diathesis.

Darwinian (daɹwi·niăn), *a.* (*sb.*) 1804. [f. proper name *Darwin*; see -IAN.] †**1.** Of or pertaining to Erasmus Darwin (1731–1802) –1842. **2.** Of or pertaining to the naturalist Charles Darwin (1809–1882), and to his views, *esp.* his theory of the evolution of species; see DARWINISM 2. 1867. **3.** *sb.* A follower of Charles Darwin 1871. Hence **Darwi·nianism** = DARWINISM 2; also, a D. idiom or phrase.

Darwinism (dā·ɹwiniz'm). 1856. [-ISM.] †**1.** The doctrine of Erasmus Darwin (*nonce-use*). **2.** The biological theory of Charles Darwin concerning the evolution of species, etc., set forth *esp.* in 'The Origin of Species by means of Natural Selection, or the preservation of favoured races in the struggle for life' (1859), and 'The Descent of Man and Selection in relation to Sex' (1871). So **Da·rwinist**, a Darwinian. **Da·rwinize** *v.* to speculate after the manner of (Erasmus or Charles) Darwin.

‖**Das** (das). 1481. [Du. = G. *dachs*; cf. DASSY.] †**1.** A badger. CAXTON. **2.** The daman or rock-badger of the Cape 1786.

Dase, obs. f. DACE, DAZE.

†**Dasewe**; see DASWEN *v.*

Dash (dæʃ), *v.* [ME. *dasche, dasse*, prob. of imit. origin; an appropriate base **dask-* is repr. by Sw. *daska*, Da. *daske* beat, but no older Scand. forms are recorded.]

I. *trans.* **1.** To strike with violence so as to shatter; to strike violently against 1611. **2.** To knock, drive, throw, or thrust (*away, down, out*, etc.) with violence ME. **3.** To throw or impel into violent contact with 1530. Also *fig.* **4.** To splash; to mark as with splashes 1530. **5.** To qualify *with* some (usually inferior) admixture. Also *fig.* 1546. **6.** *fig.* To destroy, frustrate. Now *Obs.* exc. in *to d.* (*any one's*) *hopes*. 1528. **7.** To depress; to daunt 1550; to confound, abash 1563. **8.** To write or sketch rapidly without premeditation 1726. **9.** To draw a dash through. Now *rare.* 1549. **10.** To underline 1836. **11.** *colloq.* = 'Damn' 1812.
1. A braue vessell..Dash'd all to peeces *Temp.* I. ii. 8. To d. on the lips COTGR. **2.** *Rom. & Jul.* IV. iii. 54. **3.** Dashing the salt water in our faces 1839. **4.** Floures..'poudered or dashte with small spottes LYTE. **5.** Vinegar..dashed with water 1684. To d. the Truth with Fiction ADDISON. **7.** This hath a little dash'd your Spirits *Oth.* III. iii. 214. **8.** Impressions..dashed off with a careless but graceful pen KINGSLEY.

II. *intr.* **1.** To move, fall, or throw itself with violence ME. **2.** Of persons: To throw oneself with violence; to rush with impetuosity, or with brilliant action. Also *fig.* ME. **3.** *colloq.* To 'cut a dash' 1786.
1. The full force of the Atlantic is dashing on the cliffs 1891. **2.** Doeg..dashed through thick and thin, Through sense and nonsense DRYDEN.
Comb.: **d.-pot**, a contrivance for producing gradual descent in a piece of mechanism; a hydraulic buffer; **-wheel** (*Bleaching*), a wheel with compartments, revolving partly in water, to wash and rinse calico in the piece, by dipping it and then dashing it about.

Dash (dæʃ), *sb.*[1] ME. [f. DASH *v.*] **1.** A violent blow, stroke, impact, or collision. †**2.** A sudden blow; an affliction, discouragement –1730. **3.** A splash; †*concr.* a portion of water splashed up 1677; the sound of dashing 1784. **4.** A small portion (of something) thrown upon or into something else. Often *fig.* 1611. **5.** A hasty stroke of the pen 1615. **6.** A stroke or line (usually short and straight) made with or as with a pen or the like, drawn through writing for erasure, forming part of a letter, etc., used as a flourish in writing, marking a break in a sentence, a parenthetic clause, an omission, to separate distinct portions of matter, or for other purposes. **b.** *Mus.* A short vertical mark (ˈ) placed above or beneath a note to indicate that it is to be performed *staccato*. 1552. (See also below.) **7.** A sudden impetuous movement, a rush; a sudden onset. Also *fig.* 1809. **8.** Spirited vigour of action; capacity for such action 1796. **9.** A showy appearance, display: usu. in phr. *to cut a d.* 1715. **10.** *Sporting.* A race run in one heat (*U.S.*) 1881. **11.** = DASH-BOARD 1. 1874.
1. The d. of oars LYTTON. *fig.* She takes vpon her brauely at first d. 1 *Hen. VI*, I. ii. 71. **4.** White relieved by a d. of yellow 1884. **6. c.** A stroke drawn through a figure in thoroughbass to indicate that the interval must be raised one semitone. **d.** The line between notes in old harpsichord music indicating a slur.
Comb.: **d.-guard**, the dash-board which protects the platform of a tram-car; **-lamp**, a carriage-lamp fixed on the dash-board; **-rule** (*Printing*), a strip of metal for printing a d.

‖**Dash**, *sb.*[2] 1788. [prob. alt. of *dashee*, *dasje* (XVIII), *dache* (Purchas), by taking the pl. *dashees* as *dashes*; native word of Guinea.] A gift, present, gratuity.

Dash, *adv.* 1672. [Stem of DASH *v.* used advb.] With a dash.

Da·sh-board. 1859. [f. DASH *v.* and *sb.*] **1.** A board or leathern apron in the front of a vehicle, to catch the mud thrown up by the heels of the horses. Also in motor vehicles, the partition between the engine and front seat. **2.** The spray-board of a paddle-wheel. **3.** *Archit.* A sloping board to carry off rain-water from the face of a wall 1881.

Dasher (dæ·ʃəɹ). 1790. [-ER[1].] **1.** A person who 'cuts a dash' (*colloq.*). **2.** That which dashes or agitates the cream in a churn 1853. **3.** = DASH-BOARD 1 (*U.S.*) 1858.

Dashing (dæ·ʃiŋ), *ppl. a.* ME. [-ING[2].] **1.** That dashes. **2.** Spirited, lively, impetuous 1796. **3.** Given to 'cutting a dash' 1801. Also *transf.* of things.
Hence **Da·shingly** *adv.*

Da·shy, *a.* 1822. [f. DASH *v.* + -Y[1].] = DASHING 3 (*colloq.*).

‖**Da·ssy.** 1882. [– Du. *dasje*, dim. of *das* DAS.] = DAS 2.

Dastard (da·stăɹd). 1440. [prob. to be referred ult. to ME. *dase* DAZE, but perh. immed. based on ME. †*dasart* (XIV) dullard (cf. MDu. *dasaert* fool) and †*dasiberd* (XIV), f. *dasi* inert, dull + *berd* BEARD (cf. LG. *dösbārt*), with influence from DOTARD.]

A. *sb.* †**1.** A dullard; a sot –1552. **2.** One who meanly shrinks from danger; *esp.* one who does malicious acts in a skulking way 1526.
2. He was, though a dwarf, no d. FULLER.

B. *adj.* Meanly shrinking from danger; showing base cowardice; dastardly 1489.
To waile thy haps, argues a d. minde 1602.
Hence †**Da·stard** *v.* to make a d. of; to cow. †**Da·stardice, -ise,** mean cowardice. **Da·stardize** *v.* = DASTARD *v.* **Da·stardliness,** the quality of being dastardly. **Da·stardly** *a.* †dull; showing despicable cowardice. †**Da·stardness, Da·stardy** (*arch.*), the quality of a d.

†**Daswen,** *v.* Also **dasewe(n.** ME. [conn. w. *dasen* DAZE *v.*] *intr.* Of the eyes or sight: To be or become dim –1496.

Dasymeter (dæsi·mĭtəɹ). 1872. [f. Gr. δασύς dense + -METER.] An instrument for measuring the density of gases.

Dasyphyllous (dæsifi·ləs), *a.* [f. Gr. δασύς rough + φύλλον leaf + -OUS.] *Bot.* Hairy- or woolly-leaved.

Dasypod (dæ·sipǫd). [f. generic name *Dasypus* – Gr. δασύπους, -ποδ-, hairy-footed.] *Zool.* Of or pertaining to *Dasypus*, a genus of armadillos; an animal of this genus. Hence **Dasy·podid** *sb.* **Dasy·podine** *a.*

‖**Dasyprocta** (dæsiprǫ·ktă). 1875. [mod.L., f. Gr. δασύπρωκτος having hairy buttocks.] *Zool.* A genus of rodents, the agoutis. Hence **Dasypro·ctid** *a.* (*sb.*). **Dasypro·ctine** *a.*

Dasypygal (dæsipəi·găl), *a.* 1875. [f. Gr. δασύπυγος + -AL[1].] *Zool.* Having hairy buttocks.

Dasyure (dæ·siˌiūəɹ). 1839. [– Fr. *dasyure* (H. E. Geoffroy St-Hilaire) – mod.L. *dasyurus*, f. Gr. δασύς rough, hairy + οὐρά tail.] *Zool.* An animal of the genus *Dasyurus* or subfamily *Dasyurinæ*, comprising the small carnivorous marsupials of Australia and Tasmania, also called 'brush-tailed opossums' or 'native cats'. Hence **Dasyu·rine** *a.* belonging to the subfamily *Dasyurinæ*.

Data (dēⁱ·ta), pl. of DATUM, q.v.

Datary[1] (dēⁱ·tări). 1527. [– med.L. *datarius*, f. *datum* DATE *sb.*[2]; see -ARY[1].] **1.** An officer of the Papal Court at Rome, charged with the duty of registering and dating all documents issued by the Pope, and of representing the Pope in matters relating to grants, dispensations, etc. †**2.** A chronologer (*rare*) –1661.

Da·tary[2]. 1645. [– med.L. *dataria*; see prec.] The office or function of dating Papal documents; a branch of the Apostolic Chancery at Rome. Also *attrib.*

Date (dēⁱt), *sb.*[1] ME. [– (O)Fr. *date* (mod. *datte*) :– L. *dactylus* – Gr. δάκτυλος finger, toe, date (see DACTYL). The application to the date-palm has reference to the finger-like shape of its leaves.] **1.** The fruit of the date-palm, an oblong single-seeded berry, growing in clusters, with sweet pulp. **2.** The tree which bears dates (*Phœnix dactylifera*) ME.
1. Dates..serve for the Subsistence of more than an hundred Millions of Souls 1712.
Comb.: **d.-palm** = sense 2; **-plum**, the fruit of species of *Diospyros* (N.O. *Ebenaceæ*); also the tree itself; **-shell**, a mollusc of the genus *Lithodomus*; so called from its shape; **-sugar**, sugar from the sap of the wild date-tree of India (*P. sylvestris*); **-wine**, wine made by fermenting the sap of the date-palm.

Date (dēⁱt), *sb.*[2] ME. [– (O)Fr. *date* – med.L. *data*, subst. use of fem. of *datus*, pa. pple. of *dare* give. Derived from the L. formula used in dating letters, e.g. *Data* (sc. *epistola*) *Romæ*, '(letter) given at Rome'.] **1.** The specification of the time (and often the place) of execution of a writing or inscription, affixed to it. **2.** The precise time at which anything takes place or is to take place; more vaguely, season, period ME. **b.** *U.S. colloq.* An engagement or appointment 1885. **3.** The period to which something ancient belongs ME. **4.** Duration; term of life or existence (*arch.*) ME. **5.** Limit, end ME.
1. A long Letter bearing D. the fourth Instant STEELE. **2.** The d. at which he received notice 1893. Not far remov'd the d., When commerce proudly flourish'd through the state GOLDSM. **3.** Antiquities of Roman d. FREEMAN. **4.** To lengthen out his D. A day DRYDEN. **5.** All has its d. below COWPER.
Phr. *Out of d.*: out of season; see also OUT-OF-DATE. Also UP TO DATE.
Comb.: **d.-line,** a line relating to dates; *spec.* the line (theoretically coincident with the meridian of 180° from Greenwich) at which the calendar day is reckoned to begin and end, so that at places east and west of it the d. differs by one day; **-mark,** a mark showing the d.

Date (dēⁱt), *v.* ME. [f. DATE *sb.*[2]] **1.** *trans.* To mark with a date. **2.** To fix the date or time of; to reckon as beginning *from* ME.; *absol.* to reckon 1742. †**3.** To put a period to –1618. **4.** *intr.* (for *refl.*) To be dated; to be written *from* 1850. **5.** To assign itself to, or have its origin *from*, a particular time 1828.
1. A Bill dated the 30th of January 1682. A Letter dated from York 1712. **b.** *pass.* To have its date fixed by some circumstance; *intr.* to bear evidence of or betray one's or its date 1895. **2.** I d. from this æra the corrupt method, etc. SWIFT. **4.** The letter dates from London 1894. **5.** The house dated as far back as the days of Matthew Stach KANE. Hence **Da·t(e)able** *a.* **Da·ter.**

Dateless (dēⁱ·tlės), *a.* 1593. [-LESS.] **1.** Undated 1644. **2.** Having no term; endless 1593. **3.** Immemorial 1794.
2. Thy datelesse fame 1624. **3.** The d. hills RUSKIN. Hence **Da·telessness.**

Dation (dēⁱ·ʃən). 1656. [– (O)Fr. *dation* and L. *datio*, f. *dat-*, pa. ppl. stem of *dare* give; see -ION.] The action of giving. †**a.**

Med. A dose. **b.** *Civil Law.* The act of giving or conferring.

‖**Datisca** (dăti·skă). 1863. [mod.L. (Linnæus gives no source).] *Bot.* The name of a genus of monochlamydeous exogens (N.O. *Datiscaceæ*). Hence **Dati·scin,** a glucoside, $C_{21}H_{22}O_{12}$, obtained from D.

Datisi (dătəi·səi). 1551. *Logic.* A mnemonic term for a valid mood of the third syllogistic figure, in which a universal affirmative major premiss (*a*) and a particular affirmative minor (*i*) yield a particular affirmative conclusion (*i*).

Dative (dēⁱ·tiv). ME. [– L. *dativus* of giving; in grammar (sc. *casus*) rendering Gr. (πτῶσις) δοτική (see CASE *sb.*¹); f. *dat-*, pa. ppl. stem of *dare* give; see -IVE.]

A. *adj.* **1.** *Gram.* The name of that case of nouns which denotes the indirect object, expressed in English by *to* or *for* with the objective. †**2.** Of the nature of a gift –1661. **3.** *Law.* **a.** In one's gift. **b.** Of an officer: Removable: opp. to *perpetual.* **c.** *Sc. Law.* Given by a magistrate, not by disposition of law: as in *executor d.*, one appointed by decree of the commissary, an administrator.

B. *sb.* (the adj. used ellipt.) *Gram.* Short for *d. case*; see A. 1520.

Hence **Da·tively** *adv.* in the d. case; as a d.

Datolite (dæ·toləit). *erron.* **datholite.** 1808. [irreg. f. the initial part of Gr. δατεῖσθαι divide + -LITE.] *Min.* A borosilicate of calcium, occurring in glassy crystals of various colours or in masses.

‖**Da·ttock.** 1884. [Native name.] The hard mahogany-like wood of a W. African tree, *Detarium senegalense*, N.O. *Leguminosæ*; the tree itself.

‖**Datum** (dēⁱ·tŏm). Pl. **data** (dēⁱ·tă). 1646. [L., neut. pa. pple. of *dare* give.] A thing given or granted; something known or assumed as fact, and made the basis of reasoning or calculation. Also in *comb.*, as *d.-line, -plane.*

Out of what Data arises the knowledge 1691.

‖**Datura** (dătiū̆ə·ră). 1662. [mod.L. – Hindi *dhatura.*] *Bot.* A genus of poisonous plants (N.O. *Solanaceæ*), of which *D. Stramonium* is the Strammony or Thorn-apple; it is a powerful narcotic. Hence **Datu·rine** (also **Datu·ria**), = ATROPINE.

Daub (dǭb), *v.* ME. [– OFr. *dauber* :– L. *dealbare* whiten, whitewash, plaster, f. *de* DE- + *albus* white.] **1.** *trans.* To coat or cover *with* plaster, mortar, clay, or the like. **2.** To plaster *with* some sticky or greasy substance, smear 1597. **3.** To soil, bedaub. Also *fig.* 1450. **4.** To paint coarsely and inartistically 1630. †**5.** To bedizen –1760. †**6.** *fig.* To cover with a specious exterior; to whitewash, cloak, gloss –1785. †**b.** *absol.* or *intr.* To put on a false show –1716.

1. Of his shepecote dawbe the walles round about 1515. **2.** Whose wrinkled furrows..Are daubed full of Venice chalk BP. HALL. **3.** Dawbing eche other with dirte and myer 1535. **4.** A trovell will serve as well as a pencill to d. on such thick course colours FULLER. **6.** So smooth he dawb'd his Vice with shew of Vertue *Rich. III*, III. v. 29. **b.** Poore Tom's a cold. I cannot d. it further *Lear* IV. i. 53.

Daub (dǭb), *sb.* ME. [f. DAUB *v.*] **1.** Material for daubing. Also *fig.* **2.** An act of daubing 1669. **3.** A patch or smear of some moist substance 1731. **4.** A coarsely executed painting 1761.

4. The diffrence of a Guido from a d. COWPER.

Dauber (dǭ·bəɹ). ME. [f. DAUB *v.* + -ER¹.] **1.** One who or that which daubs. **2.** A coarse or unskilful painter 1655. **3.** *U.S.* The mud-wasp 1844. **4.** Anything used to daub with.

2. Rather Dawbers then Drawers FULLER. Hence **Dau·bery, daubry,** the practice of daubing; the work of a d. **Dau·bster,** a clumsy painter.

Daubing (dǭ·biŋ), *vbl. sb.* ME. [-ING¹.] **1.** The action of the vb. DAUB. **2.** Material (*esp.* mortar or clay) used in daubing; roughcast ME. **3.** (*U.S.*) = DUBBING (Knight).

Daubreelite (dǫ·brīləit). 1892. [f. as next + -LITE.] *Min.* A black sulphide of chromium, found in meteoric iron.

Daubreite (dǫ·brīˌəit). 1876. [f. M. *Daubrée*, a French mineralogist; see -ITE¹ 2 b.] *Min.* A native oxychloride of bismuth.

Dauby (dǭ·bi), *a.* 1697. [f. DAUB *sb.* + -Y¹.] **1.** Sticky. **2.** Given to daubing; dirty, etc. (*dial.*) 1855. **3.** Of the nature of a daub 1829.

Daughter (dǭ·təɹ). [OE. *dohtor* = OFris. *dochter*, OS. *dohtar* (Du. *dochter*), OHG. *tohter* (G. *tochter*), ON. *dóttir*, Goth. *dauhtar* :– Gmc. **doxtēr*, earlier **dhuktēr* :– IE. **dhughətēr*, whence also Skr. *duhitā́*, Gr. θυγάτηρ; of unkn. origin.] **1.** *prop.* Female child or offspring. **2.** *transf.* A female descendant; a woman in relation to her native country or place OE. Also *fig.* **3.** A term of affectionate address used by a senior (*arch.*) OE. **4.** A girl, maiden, young woman (*arch.*) ME. **5.** *fig.* Anything (personified as female) viewed in relation to its origin or source ME.

1. Soch a mother, soch a doughter COVERDALE *Ezek.* 16:44. **2.** Daughters of Jerusalem, weep not for me *Luke* 23:28. *fig.* The daughters of musick *Eccl.* 12:4, of affliction WESLEY. **3.** D., be of good comfort *Matt.* 9:22. **4.** Many daughters haue done virtuously *Prov.* 31:39. **5.** Dulness..D. of Chaos and eternal Night POPE.

Comb. **d.-cell** (*Biol.*), one of the cells produced by the fission of a mother-cell.

Hence **Dau·ghterhood,** the condition of being a d.; daughters collectively. **Dau·ghterless** *a.* **Dau·ghterling** (*nonce-wd.*), little d.

Dau·ghter-in-law. ME. [See BROTHER-IN-LAW, -IN-LAW.] **1.** The wife of one's son. **2.** = STEPDAUGHTER. (Now considered incorrect.) 1841.

Daughterly (dǭ·təɹli), *a.* 1535. [-LY¹.] Such as becomes a daughter; filial.

Youre very d. dealing MORE. Hence **Dau·ghterliness.**

Dauk (dǭk). 1795. [Also *daugh*; of unkn. origin.] *Mining.* A bed or band of stiff sandy clay.

Dauk; see DAWK.

†**Dauke.** *rare.* 1450. [– L. *daucus, daucum* carrot.] The wild carrot, *Daucus carota* –1688.

Daun, obs. f. DAN¹.

Daunt (dǭnt), *v.* ME. [– AFr. *daunter*, OFr. *danter*, var. of *donter* (mod. *dompter*) :– L. *domitare*, frequent. of *domare* to tame.] †**1.** *trans.* To overcome, subdue –1610. †**2.** To tame –1569. Also *fig.* **3.** To abate the courage of, dispirit; to abash; to intimidate. (The current sense.) 1475. **4.** To daze. Now *dial.* 1581. †**5.** To dandle –1483. **6.** *Herring Fishery.* To press down salted herrings with a daunt 1733.

3. Thinke you a little dinne can d. mine eares *Tam. Shr.* I. ii. 200. Hence **Daunt** *sb.* †the act of daunting; a check; *spec.* a disc of wood used to press down salted herrings in the barrels. **Dau·nter.**

Dauntless (dǭ·ntlės), *a.* 1593. [f. DAUNT *v.* + -LESS.] Not to be daunted; bold, intrepid.

Browes Of d. courage MILT. *P.L.* I. 603. Hence **Dau·ntless-ly** *adv.*, **-ness.**

Dauphin (dǭ·fin). 1485. [– Fr. *dauphin*, earlier †*daulphin* – Pr. *dalfin* :– med.L. *dalphinus* (VIII), for L. *delphinus* – Gr. δελφίς, δελφιν-; see DOLPHIN.] The title of the eldest son of the King of France, from 1349 to 1830.

According to Littré, the name Dauphin, borne by the lords of the Viennois, was a proper name *Delphinus* (the same word as the name of the fish), whence their province was called *Dauphiné*. The province was ceded to Philip of Valois in 1349, subject to the condition that the title should be borne in perpetuity by the eldest son of the French king.

Hence **Dau·phinate,** the rule or jurisdiction of a d. (of Viennois). **Dau·phiness,** the wife of the d.

‖**Dauw** (dāu). 1802. [S. Afr. Du., f. native name.] A species of zebra, *Equus Burchellii.*

Davenport (dæ·v'npōəɹt). Also **devonport.** 1853. [From the maker's name.] A kind of small ornamental writing-table filled with drawers, etc.

Da·vidist. 1657. [f. the name *David* + -IST.] **1.** One of a sect founded by David George or Jores, a Dutch Anabaptist of the 16th c. **2.** A follower of David of Dinant.

Davit (dæ·vit, dēⁱ·vit). 1622. [– AFr., OFr. *daviot*, later *daviet* (now *davier*), dim. of *Davi* David.] *Naut.* **a.** A curved piece of timber or iron with a roller or sheave at the end, projecting from a ship's bow, and used to fish the anchor; a *fish-d.* **b.** One of a pair of cranes on the side or stern of a ship, fitted with tackle for suspending or lowering a boat.

Davy¹ (dēⁱ·vi). In full **D. lamp, Davy's lamp.** 1871. [f. Sir Humphry *Davy* (1778–1829).] The miners' safety-lamp invented by Davy, in which the flame is surrounded with wire-gauze, so as to prevent contact with explosive gases outside the lamp.

Da·vy². *slang.* 1764. Short for AFFIDAVIT.

Davy Jones (dēⁱ·vi dʒōᵘ·nz). 1751. In nautical slang: The spirit of the sea; the sailors' devil. *Davy Jones's* (or *Davy's*) *locker*: the ocean, *esp.* as the grave of those who perish at sea.

Davyne (dēⁱ·vin). 1826. [– It. *davina*, named after Sir H. Davy; see -INE⁵.] *Min.* A variety of nephelite, from Vesuvius.

Davyum (dēⁱ·viŏm). 1879. [Named as prec. + *-um* as in *platinum*, etc.] *Chem.* A supposed metal of the platinum group, said by Kern to have been found in Russian platinum ore.

Daw (dǭ), *sb.* ME. [prob. to be referred to an OE. **dāwe*, rel. to OHG. *tāha* (G. dial. *tach*), beside MHG. *dāhele, tāle* (G. *dahle, dohle*). See CADDOW¹.] **1.** A bird of the crow kind (*Corvus monedula*); a JACKDAW. **2.** *fig.* †A simpleton –1608; a sluggard, a slut (*Sc.*) 1460. Hence **Daw·ish** *a.* silly, sluttish.

Daw (dǭ), *v.*¹ Now *Sc.* [OE. *dagian*, corresp. to MDu. *daghen*, Du., LG. *dagen*, OHG. *tagēn* (G. *tagen*); f. WGmc. **daʒa* DAY. Cf. ADAW *v.*¹] **1.** *intr.* To dawn. Also *fig.* †**2.** = ADAW *v.*¹ 1, 2. –1612.

†**Daw,** *v.*² *rare.* 1616. [aphet. f. ADAW *v.*²] To daunt –1664.

Dawdle (dǭ·d'l), *v.* Also **daudle.** 1656. [prob. of dial. origin; cf. DADDLE, DODDLE.] *intr.* To idle, waste time; to be sluggish; to loiter. Also quasi-*trans.* (usu. with *away*).

To d. over a dish of tea JOHNSON. I..dawdled and fretted the time away until Tuesday evening MME. D'ARBLAY. Hence **Daw·dle** *sb.* one who dawdles; the act of dawdling. **Daw·dler.**

Dawe, obs. f. DAY.

Dawk (dǭk), *sb.*¹ *dial.* 1703. [Also *dalk, delk*; of unkn. origin.] A depression, furrow, incision. Hence **Dawk** *v.* to make a d. in.

‖**Dawk,** *sb.*², **dak** (dǭk, dāk). *Anglo-Ind.* 1727. [Hindi, Marathi *ḍāk*.] Post or transport by relays; a relay of men or horses for carrying mails, etc., or passengers in palanquins.

Phr. *To travel d.*: to travel in this way. *Comb.* **dak bungalow** (rarely **house**), an inn for travellers on a dak route.

Dawn (dǭn), *sb.* 1599. [f. the vb.] **1.** The first appearance of light before sunrise; the beginning of daylight; daybreak. **2.** *fig.* The beginning, rise, first appearance; an incipient gleam 1633. Also *attrib.*

1. Come away, it is almost cleere dawne SHAKS. *High d.*, d. appearing above a bank of clouds; *low d.*, d. appearing on the horizon. **2.** The d. of manhood 1752, of an idea LAMB, of history 1878.

Dawn (dǭn), *v.* 1499. [Back-formation from next; repl. ME. DAY *v.*¹, DAW *v.*¹] **1.** *intr.* To begin to grow daylight; also *transf.* **2.** *fig.* To begin to develop, expand, or brighten 1717. **3.** To begin to appear, become visible or evident 1744.

1. Until the day d. 2 *Pet.* 1:19. As soon as ever the Morning dawned 1726. **2.** In..1685 his fame..was only dawning MACAULAY. **3.** Underneath the dawning hills TENNYSON. The idea that [etc.] had never dawned upon her 1852.

Dawning (dǭ·niŋ), *vbl. sb.* [ME. *dai(ʒ)ening da(i)ning* (XIII), *dawening* (XIV), alt. of *daiing, dawing* (see DAW v.¹), after Scand. (OSw. *daghning*, Sw., Da. *dagning*); see DAY *sb.*, -ING¹.] **1.** The beginning of daylight; dawn; *transf.* the east. **2.** *fig.* The first gleam, appearance, beginning 1612.

1. The Bird of D. *Haml.* I. i. 160. **2.** The dawnings of a literary culture PRESCOTT.

Dawsonite (dǭ·sənəit). 1875. [f. Sir J. W. *Dawson* of Montreal; see -ITE¹ 2 b.] *Min.* A hydrous carbonate of aluminium and sodium, in white crystals.

Day (dēⁱ), *sb.* [OE. *dæġ* = OFris. *dei*, OS. (Du.) *dag*, OHG. *tac* (G. *tag*), ON. *dagr*, Goth. *dags* :– Gmc. **daʒaz.*] **I. 1.** 'The time between the rising and the setting of the sun' (J.); the interval of light between one night and the next; in ordinary usage including the lighter part of morning and evening twilight. **2.** Daylight ME. Also *fig.* †**3.** One of the 'lights' of a mullioned window. [Fr. *jour.*]

–1859. **4.** *Mining.* The surface of the ground over a mine. Hence *d.-coal*, etc. 1665.

1. *Break of d.*: dawn: see BREAK. It was then nyne of the d. LD. BERNERS. *Before d.*: before dawn. **2.** It was broad d. DE FOE. *fig.* I can not yet see d. in the businesse MARVELL.

II. As a unit of time. **1.** The time occupied by the earth in one revolution on its axis, in which the same terrestrial meridian returns to the sun; the space of twenty-four hours OE. **2.** The same space of time treated as a unit of time, on which anything happens, or which fixes a date OE.

1. *Solar* or *astronomical d.*: a period reckoned from noon to noon, and adjusted to its mean length, which is the *mean solar d. Civil d.*: the period from midnight to midnight, similarly adjusted. *Sidereal d.*: the time between the successive meridional transits of a star, or spec. of the first point of Aries, which is about four minutes shorter than the solar day. **2.** The first D. of the Week called the Lord's D. 1704. Phr. *One d.*: on a certain d. in the past; on some future d. So of future time, *some d., one of these days.*

III. A specified or appointed day OE.

New Year's d., settling-d., D. of Judgement, Wrath, etc. Or if my debtors do not keep their d. (*sc.* for payment) DRYDEN. We..went on her 'day' (*sc.* for receptions) MRS. H. WARD. Phr. *To carry, win, lose the d.* (= *day of battle* or *contest*).

IV. A space of time, a period ME.

†*A month's day* (*Sc.*), the space of a month. I'll give no d. (= credit)..I must have present money QUARLES. In the days (= time) of Josephus. The men of our d. JOWETT. Phr. *To this d., at the present d., at some future d. The d.*: time (now or then) present. Abbots honour'd in their d. (= lifetime) SOUTHEY. *To end one's days*: to die. Diplomacy has had its d. (= period of power) MIALL.

Phrases. *This d. week, twelve months*, etc.: the same day a week or a year after or before. **D. about,** on alternate days. **D. by d.,** daily, every day in its turn; also *attrib.* **D. after d.,** each day as a sequel to the preceding. **(From) d. to d.,** continuously without interruption; so *d. in (and) d. out.*

Comb.: **d.-boarder,** see BOARDER; **-boy,** a school-boy (at a boarding-school) who attends the daily classes without boarding there; **-coal** (see I. 4); **-drift, -hole** (*Coal-mining*), galleries driven from the surface so that men can walk underground to and from their work; **-eye,** a working open to daylight; **-hours** (*pl.*), those offices for the Canonical Hours which are said in the daytime; **-house** (*Astrol.*), a house in which a planet is said to be stronger by day than by night; **dayman,** one employed for the day, or for duty on a special day; **-room,** a room occupied by day only; **-scholar** = *day-boy*; **-school,** a week-day school; one carried on in the day (opp. to *night* school); one at which pupils are not boarded; **-shine,** day-light; **-student,** a student who comes to a college, etc., during the day for lectures or study, but does not reside there; **-ticket,** a railway or other ticket covering return on the same day; **-wages,** wages paid by the day; **-water,** surface-water.

†Day, *v.*[1] ME. [ME. *dæʒen*, alt. f. *dawen* (see DAW *v.*[1]) after the sb. *deʒ, dai, day.*] To dawn –1483.

†Day, *v.*[2] 1523. [f. DAY *sb.*] **1.** To submit to or decide by arbitration –1580. **2.** To give (a person) time for payment –1573. **3.** To measure by the day; to furnish with days –1839. **4.** *To year and d.*: to subject to the statutory period of a year and a day –1626.

Day·-bed. 1594. A bed to rest on by day; a lounge, sofa, couch.

Day·-blindness. 1834. A visual defect, in which the eyes see badly, or not at all, by daylight, but well by artificial light.

Day·book, day-book. 1580. A diary, journal; *Naut.* a log-book (*obs.*). **b.** *Book-keeping.* Orig., a book in which the transactions of the day, as sales, purchases, etc., are entered at once in the order in which they occur; now usually *Purchases D., Sales D.*, etc.

Day·break. 1530. [Cf. BREAK *v.* VII. 2 and *sb.*[1]] The first appearance of light in the morning; dawn.

Day·-dawn. *poet.* 1813. The dawn of day, daybreak.

Day·-dream. 1685. A dream indulged in while awake; a reverie, castle in the air.

A lover's day-dream SCOTT. So **Day·-dreamer.**

†Day·-fever. 1601. A fever lasting a day or coming on in the day-time; the sweating-sickness –1610.

Day·-flower. 1688. A flower that opens by day; *spec.* in *U.S.*, the genus *Commelyna* or Spiderwort.

Day·-fly. 1601. An ephemerid, which in the perfect state lives only a day or so.

†Day·ing, *vbl. sb.* 1484. [-ING[1].] The action of DAY *v.*[2], *esp.* arbitration –1611.

Day labour, day·-la:bour. 1449. Labour done by the day or for daily wages.

'Doth God exact day labour, light denied?' MILT. So **Day:-la·bourer,** one who works for daily wages.

Dayless (dē[i]·lės), *a.* ME. [f. DAY *sb.* + -LESS.] †**1.** Without result –1519. **2.** Dark 1816.

Daylight (dē[i]·ləit). ME. **1.** The light of day; *fig.* the light of knowledge; publicity 1690. **2.** The day-time; *spec.* daybreak ME. **3.** A clear visible interval, as between boats in a race, the rim of a wine-glass and the liquor, etc. 1820. **4.** *pl.* The eyes (*slang*) 1752. Also *attrib.*

1. The day-light fades POPE. Phr. *To let daylight into*: to make a hole in; to stab or shoot (*slang*). **3.** A toast!..No heel-taps—darken daylights SHELLEY.

Comb. **d.-saving** (cf. SUMMER-TIME 2).

Day·-lily. 1597. A lily, the flower of which lasts only for a day; a genus of liliaceous plants, *Hemerocallis*, with large yellow or orange flowers.

Daylong (dē[i]·lǫŋ). 1855. [f. DAY *sb.*] *adj.* Lasting all day. *adv.* All through the day.

Day·-mare. 1737. [After *nightmare.*] A condition similar to nightmare occurring during wakefulness. Also *attrib.*

†Day·ment. 1519. [f. DAY *v.*[2] + -MENT.] Arbitration –1580.

†Day·-net. 1608. A clap-net for catching small birds –1766.

Day·peep. 1606. Peep of day; earliest dawn.

†Day·-rawe. ME. [f. DAY + *rawe* ROW *sb.*[1]] The first streak of day.

†Day·-rule. 1750. A rule or order of court, permitting a prisoner to go without the bounds of his prison for one day –1813.

Day·-sight. 1834. A visual defect in which the eyes see clearly only in the day.

Daysman (dē[i]·zmæ̆n). 1489. [For sense 1, cf. DAY *v.*[2], DAYMENT.] **1.** An arbitrator (*arch.*). **2.** A day-labourer 1639.

1. Neither is there any d. betwixt us *Job.* 9:33.

Day·-spring. ME. [SPRING *sb.*[1] II. 1 a.] Daybreak. Now mainly *poet.* or *fig.*

The day-spring from on high hath visited us *Luke* 1:78.

Day·-star. OE. **1.** The morning star. **2.** The sun, as the orb of day (*poet.*) 1598. Also *fig.*

1. Early in the morning, so soone as the day starre appeared 1576. **2.** So sinks the day-star in his ocean bed MILT. *Lycidas* 168. *fig.* We lift our Hearts to Thee, O Day-Star from on High WESLEY.

Day's-work (dē[i]·z₁wɒ̄·ɹk). (Also as two words.) 1594. The work of a day. Also = DAYWORK 2 (*obs.*).

The log-board, the contents of which are termed 'the log',—the working it off, 'the day's work' *Rudim. Navig.* (Weale).

Day-tale, daytal, datal (dē[i]·tē[i]l, -tĕl, -t'l). 1530. [f. DAY + TALE reckoning, etc.] †**1.** Day-time. **2.** The reckoning (of work, wages, etc.) by the day. Chiefly *attrib.*, reckoned, paid, or engaged by the day, as in *day-tale labour, wages*, etc. Hence **Day-taler, dataller** (dē[i]·tĕləɹ) a day-labourer (*local*).

Day·-time. 1535. The time of daylight.

I cry in the day-time..and in the night season *Ps.* 22:2.

Day-woman, dairy-woman: see DEY *sb.*[1]

Day·work, day-work. [Cf. DARG.] OE. **1.** = DAY'S-WORK. Now *n. dial.* †**2.** The amount of land that could be worked in a day –1641. **3.** Day labour 1580.

†Day·-writ. 1809. = DAY-RULE.

Daze (dē[i]z), *v.* ME. [First in pa. pple. *dased* – ON. pa. pple. *dasaðr* weary or exhausted from cold or exertion (cf. Icel. *dasask* refl. become exhausted, *dasi* lazy fellow, Sw. *dasa* lie idle).] **1.** *trans.* To stupefy as by a blow on the head, cold, drink, excess of light, etc.; to stun; to benumb; to confuse; to dazzle. †**2.** *intr.* To be or become stupefied –1529. †**3.** Of the eyes, etc.: To become dazzled –1635. **4.** To become dazed (see DAZED 3) 1769.

1. The sudden light Dazed me half-blind TENNYSON. Dazed..by such a calamity MRS. OLIPHANT. **3.** Whose more than Eagle-eyes Can.. gaze On glitt'ring beams of honour, and not d. QUARLES.

Daze (dē[i]z), *sb.* 1671. [f. prec.] **1.** A dazed condition 1825. **2.** *Min.* Mica (from its glitter).

Dazed (dē[i]zd), *ppl. a.* ME. [f. DAZE *v.* + -ED[1].] **1.** Stupefied, bewildered; dazzled. **2.** Benumbed with cold (*north.*) 1513. **3.** Spoiled, as bread, etc.; rotten, as wood 1674. Hence **Da·zed-ly** *adv.*, **-ness.**

Dazy (dē[i]·zi), *a. rare.* 1825. [f. DAZE *v.* or *sb.* + -Y[1].] In a dazed condition. **b.** Chill, chilling (*dial.*).

Dazzle (dæ·z'l), *v.* [Late ME. *dasele*, f. *dase* DAZE *v.* + -LE.] †**1.** *intr.* Of the eyes: To lose the faculty of steady vision, *esp.* from too bright light (*lit.* and *fig.*) –1672. **2.** *trans.* To overpower or confuse (the vision), *esp.* with excess of brightness. (Also *fig.*) 1536. **3.** *fig.* To overpower or confound, *esp.* with brilliant or showy qualities; 'to strike or surprise with splendour' (J.) 1561. Also *absol.* **4.** To outshine, eclipse, dim (*rare*) 1643.

1. Perauenture his eyen daselyd as he loked from aboue doun CAXTON. **3.** Rhetorick may dazle simple men 1643. *absol.* Charms that d. and endear GOLDSM.

Hence **Da·zzle** *sb.* an act of dazzling; a brightness or glitter that dazzles; paint put on as camouflage (hence as *v. trans.*, and in *Comb.*, as *d.-painted, -painting*). **Da·zzlement,** the act of dazzling; a cause of dazzling; dazzled condition. **Da·zzler,** one who or that which dazzles. **Da·zzlingly** *adv.*

‖**De. 1.** (dī) A Latin prep., meaning 'down from, from, off, concerning', occurring in some Latin phrases used in English, as:

a. *de bene esse* (Law), as of 'well-being', as being good, of conditional allowance for the present.

b. *de facto*, in fact, in reality, in actual existence, force, or possession, as a matter of fact. As *adj.* = 'actual'.

c. *de jure*, of right, by right, according to law. As *adj.* = 'legal'. Usu. opp. to *de facto.*

d. *de novo*, anew, afresh, over again. Rarely as *adj.* = 'new, fresh'.

e. *de profundis*, the first words of the L. version of *Ps.* 130 = 'Out of the depths (have I cried)'; hence subst. (*a*) the name of this psalm; (*b*) a psalm of penitence; (*c*) a cry from the depths of sorrow, misery, etc.

2. The French prep. *de, d'* (də), meaning 'of, from', occurring in place-names, in territorial titles, and in personal surnames; also, in French phrases more or less in English use, as *coup d'état, c. de main*, etc. (see COUP); *de trop*, too much, (one) too many, in the way; etc.

De-, *prefix.* The Latin adv. and prep., used in comb. with vbs., and their derivs.

I. As an etymological element. In the senses:

1. Down, down from, down to, as in DEPRESS, etc. **2.** Off, away, aside, as in DECLINE, etc. **b.** Away from oneself, as in DEPRECATE, etc. **3.** Down to the bottom, completely; hence, thoroughly, on and on; as in DECLAIM, DENUDE, DERELICT, etc. **b.** To the dregs, as in DECOCT, etc. **4.** In a bad sense, so as to subject to some indignity, as in DECEIVE, etc. **5.** In late L., *decompositus* = 'formed or derived from a compound (word)', 'compounded over again'; hence its sense in DECOMPOSITE, DECOMPLEX, etc. **6.** In English, early words taken from OFr. with *des-* retained this form (refash. *dis-*), as in *disarm*, etc.; but later words have *de-* (Fr. *dé-* :– OFr. *des-* :– L. *dis*), treated as identical with L. *de-*; e.g. *debauch*, etc. In some words both forms are found, as *disfrock, defrock*, etc. Hence:

II. As a living prefix with privative force.

1. Forming compound vbs. (with their derivs.) having the sense of undoing the action of the simple vb., or of depriving (anything) of the thing or character therein expressed, e.g. *de-acidify, decephalize* (where no simple vb. is in use), etc.

2. Occas., vbs. (and their derivs.) are formed by prefixing *de-* to a noun, with the sense: **a.** To rid of the thing in question, as DEBOWEL, *depetticoated*, etc. **b.** To turn out of, as *decart*, DEHUSK, etc. **3.** In DEBARE, etc., *de-* is prefixed to adjs.

Deacon (dī·kən, -k'n), *sb.* [OE. *diacon* – eccl.L. *diaconus* – Gr. διάκονος servant, messenger, in eccl.Gr. Christian minister.] **1.** *Eccl.* The name of an order of ministers or officers in the Christian church. **a.** In Apostolic times (see Acts 6:1–6) OE. **b.** In

Episcopal churches, a member of the third order of the ministry, ranking below bishops and priests, and having the functions of assisting the priest, of visiting the sick, etc. OE. **c.** In the Presbyterian system, one of an order of officers appointed to attend to the secular affairs of the congregation (cf. ELDER *sb.*[2] 4) 1560. **d.** In Congregational churches, one of a body of officers elected to advise and assist the pastor and attend to the secular affairs of the church 1647. **e.** The cleric who acts as principal assistant at a solemn celebration of the Eucharist; the 'gospeller'. late ME. †**2.** Applied to the Levites –1449. **3.** In Scotland, the president of an incorporated craft or trade in any town ME.; *fig.* a master of his craft 1814. Hence **Dea·conhood,** the office of a d.; deacons collectively. **Dea·conry,** deaconship; deacons collectively; *R.C.Ch.* the chapel in charge of a cardinal d. **Dea·conship,** the office or position of a d.

Dea·con, *v.* *U.S. colloq.* 1845. [f. prec. sb.] **1.** *trans.* (usually *to d. off*). To read aloud (a hymn) one line at a time, the congregation singing the lines as read. Hence *fig.* **2.** To pack (fruit, etc.) with the finest on the top; also used of other forms of dishonest dealing 1860.

2. *To d. land,* to filch it from the highway, etc. FARMER. *To d. wine,* to doctor it (*slang*).

Deaconess (dī·kənės). 1536. [f. prec., after L. *diaconissa.*] **1.** *Eccl.* A female deacon: **a.** in the early church, with diaconal duties in relation to her sex; **b.** in some modern churches, with functions parallel to those of deacons in the same. **2.** The name taken by certain Protestant orders of women with aims similar to those of Sisters of Mercy 1867. **3.** A deacon's wife. O. W. HOLMES.

Dead (ded), *a.* (*sb., adv.*) [OE. *dēad* = OFris. *dād*, OS. *dōd* (Du. *dood*), OHG. *tōt* (G. *tot*), ON. *dauðr*, Goth. *dauþs* :– Gmc. **dauðaz* :– *dhautós*, pa. pple. of base **dhau-*, repr. also in OS. *dōian*, OHG. *touwen*, ON. *deyja* DIE *v.*[1]]

A. *adj.* **I.** Literally, etc. **1.** That has ceased to live; in that state in which the vital functions and powers have come to an end, and cannot be restored. **2.** Bereft of sensation or vitality ME. **3.** As good as dead *to*, or in some respect or capacity; *spec.* in *Law*, cut off from civil rights ME. **4.** Destitute of spiritual life or energy ME. **5.** *fig.* Of things: No longer in existence, or in use; *esp.* of languages 1591. **6.** Inanimate ME. **7.** *transf.* Composed of dead plants, or of dead wood, as *a d. hedge*, etc. 1563. **8.** Of or pertaining to a dead person, animal, plant, etc., or to some one's death 1580. †**9.** Causing death, mortal –1611. **10.** Devoid of life; hence, barren 1577.

1. The maid is not d., but sleepeth *Matt.* 9:24. D. fleshe EDEN, leaves SHELLEY. My wife is d. (= has died) to night *Rom. & Jul.* V. iii. 210. **2.** D. fingers 1893. In a d. faint 1894. **5.** My doubts are d. TENNYSON. **6.** D. matter H. MILLER. **8.** You breath these d. newes in as d. an eare *John* V. vii. 65. **10.** A bottom of d. sand 1806.

II. 1. Wanting some vital quality (see quots.) ME. **2.** Of sound: Without resonance 1530. **3.** Not fulfilling the normal purpose 1806.

1. D. Cider EVELYN. D. (= exhausted) steam 1874. The d. colour of her face DRYDEN. *Electr.* Carrying or transmitting no current, as *d. circuit* 1903. **2.** A dull d. sound 1783. **3.** *Dead.* .False; as of imitation doors or windows KNIGHT.

III. 1. Without animation OE. **2.** Inoperative ME. **3.** Profoundly quiet or still 1548. **4.** Without activity, dull; unproductive; unsaleable 1570. **5.** Of a ball: Out of play 1658.

1. A bare d. description 1665. **2.** A d. ordinance J. H. NEWMAN. **3.** The d. hours of the night KINGLAKE. **4.** In the deadest Vacation 1615. D. stock 1622, goods DRYDEN. **5.** *Golf.* So near the hole that it can be holed with certainty at the next stroke 1881.

IV. 1. Without motion OE. **2.** Characterized by abrupt cessation of motion, action, or speech.

1. D. still water WALTON. The wind had fallen d. HUGHES. The d. spindle of a lathe KNIGHT. **2.** At a d. stand 1647. D.-stroke hammer KNIGHT.

V. 1. Unrelieved, unbroken, absolute; complete; utmost 1561. **2.** Said of outlay: Unproductive 1715. **3.** Absolute 1660; sure, unerring 1592; direct 1881.

1. A d. wall DRYDEN, level POPE. A d. calm 1673, secret SCOTT. D. low water 1626. A d. pull 1812, strain BAIN. **2.** *D. rent*: a fixed rent which remains as a constant charge on a mining concession. **3.** A d. bargain GOLDSM., certainty 1878; d. earnest 1883; a d. shot 1776; a d. headwind 1881.

Phrases. *D. as a door-nail, d. as a herring*: completely or certainly dead. *D. horse*: see HORSE. *To wait for d. men's shoes*: see SHOE.

¶The compar. *deader* and superl. *deadest* are in use where the sense permits.

B. *sb.*[1] (or *absol.*) **1.** *sing.* A dead person. **b.** *pl. The dead.* ME. **c.** *From the dead* [orig. tr. L. *a mortuis*, Gr. ἐκ νεκρῶν]: from among the dead; hence nearly = from death OE. **2.** = Dead period, season, stage 1548. †**3.** = DEAD HEAT. Quarles. **4.** *Mining. Deads*: earth or rock containing no ore 1653. **5.** *attrib.*, as in *d. list*, list of the dead, etc. 1476.

2. D. of night SHAKS., of winter 1613.

C. *adv.* **1.** To a degree suggesting death; utterly, profoundly (as *d. asleep, calm, drunk*); 'to death' (as *d. run, tired, sick*) 1596. **2.** Hence: Utterly, absolutely, quite 1589. **3.** Directly, straight, as *d. against, d. on end*; also *fig.* 1800.

Combs. (of the *adj.* or *sb.*). **1.** With other adjs. or pples. = 'so as to be or seem dead, as if dead, to death, etc.' as in *d.-alive, -set*, etc.

2. Special combs.: **d. angle** (*Fortif.*), 'any angle of a fortification, the ground before which is unseen, and therefore undefended from the parapet' (Stocqueler); **-cart,** one in which d. bodies are carried away; **-clothes,** those in which the the d. are dressed; **d. dipping,** a process by which a d. surface is given to brass-work; **-end,** a closed end of a water-pipe, passage, etc.; also *attrib.*; **d. fin,** the second dorsal fin of a salmon; **-fire,** St. Elmo's Fire, believed to presage death; **-flat** (*Naut.*), the widest timber or frame in a ship; the midship bend; **-house,** a mortuary; **-latch,** a latch whose bolt may be so locked by a detent that it cannot be opened from the inside by the handle or from the outside by the key; **d. march,** a piece of solemn music played at a funeral procession; a funeral march; **-office,** the service for the burial of the d.; **d. oil,** a name for those products of the distillation of coal-tar which are heavier than water; *heavy oil*; **-plate,** an ungrated iron plate at the mouth of a furnace, on which coal is coked before being pushed upon the grate; †**-pledge** = MORTGAGE; **-rising** (*Naut.*), 'those parts of a ship's floor or bottom, throughout her whole length, where the floor-timber is terminated upon the lower futtock' (Falconer); **d. rope,** one that does not run in a block or pulley; **d. sheave,** a score in the heel of a top-mast, through which a second top-tackle pendant can be rove; **-shore,** a piece of timber worked up in brickwork to support a superincumbent mass until the brickwork to carry it is set; †**-slayer,** one guilty of manslaughter; **-smooth** *a.*, said of the finest quality of file; †**-sweat** = *death-sweat.*

Dead, *sb.*[2] The northern form of the word DEATH, still dial. in Sc.

Dead (ded), *v.* Now *local.* [OE. *dēadian* become dead, f. *dēad* DEAD. Repl. by DEADEN.] **1.** *intr.* To die. *fig.* To lose vitality or force; to lose heat ME. **2.** *trans.* To make dead (*lit.* and *fig.*) ME. **3.** *fig.* To deaden; to deprive of some form of vitality ME.

1. Iron, as soon as it is out of the Fire, deadeth straight-ways BACON. **2.** Endless griefe, which deads my life, yet knowes not how to kill 1586.

Dead beat, dea·d-bea·t, *sb.*[1] (*a.*) 1768. [DEAD *a.*] *Watch-making*, etc. A beat or stroke which stops dead without recoil. Usu. *attrib.* or *adj.*, as in *dead-beat escapement.*

Dead beat, dea·d-bea·t, *ppl. a.* (*sb.*[2]) 1821. [DEAD *adv.*, BEAT *ppl. a.*] *adj.* (or *pa. pple.*) Completely beat (*colloq.*). *sb. slang* (U.S.). A worthless sponging idler 1877.

Dea·d-born, *ppl. a.* ME. Born dead, still-born. Also *fig.*

Dea·d-ce:ntre. 1874. *Mech.* **1.** = DEAD-POINT. **2.** In a lathe, the centre which does not revolve 1879.

Dea·d co:lour. 1658. [DEAD *a.* II. 1.] The first or preparatory layer of colour in a painting. So. **Dea·d-co:lour** *v.* to paint in dead colour; **Dea·d-co:louring** *vbl. sb.*

†**Dea·d-do·ing,** *ppl. a.* 1590. Doing to death, murderous –1778.

Deaden (de·d'n), *v.* 1665. [f. DEAD *a.* + -EN[5], repl. DEAD *v.*] **1.** *intr.* To become dead (*lit.* and *fig.*); to lose vitality, force, etc. 1723. **2.** *trans.* To kill; *spec.* (*U.S.*) to kill (trees) by girdling 1775. **3.** To deprive of vitality, force, or sensibility 1684. **4.** To deprive of some effective physical quality, as lustre, flavour, etc.; to make (sound) dull; etc. 1666. **5.** To destroy or reduce the energy of (motion).

1. The dash Of the out-breakers deaden'd SOUTHEY. **3.** To benumb and d. worship MOZLEY. **4.** To d. the whiteness of a tissue OWEN, beer WEBSTER, a piercing sound SCOTT. **5.** To d. a ship's way SMYTH. Hence **Dea·dener.**

Dead-eye (de·dᵢəi). 1748. [DEAD *a.*] *Naut.* A round laterally flattened wooden block, pierced with three holes through which a lanyard is reeved, used for extending the shrouds.

Deadfall, dead-fall (de·dfǭl). Chiefly *U.S.* 1611. **1.** A kind of trap used *esp.* for large game, in which a weighted board or the like is arranged to fall upon and kill or disable the prey. **2.** A tangled mass of fallen trees 1883. **b.** A dumping-platform at the mouth of a mine 1874. **c.** A low drinking- or gaming-place. (*Western U.S.*)

Dea·d-hand. 1612. = MORTMAIN.

Dea·dhead, dead-head, dead head. 1576. †**1.** *Old Chem.* = CAPUT MORTUUM 2. –1707. **2.** *Founding.* The extra head or length of metal at the muzzle end of a gun-casting, which is cut off when cool. **b.** *Mech.* The tail-stock of a lathe, containing the dead spindle. **c.** *Naut.* A rough block of wood used as an anchor-buoy. 1867. **3.** *colloq.* (orig. *U.S.*) A person admitted without payment to a theatre, a public conveyance, etc. 1853.

Dea·d-hea·rted, *a.* 1642. Dead in feeling, callous, insensible. Hence **Dead-hea·rtedness.**

Dead heat. 1840. [Cf. DEAD *a.* V. 3.] *Racing*, etc. A race in which two or more competitors reach the goal at the same instant.

Deadish (de·diʃ), *a.* Now *rare.* 1450. [f. DEAD *a.* + -ISH[1].] Somewhat dead (in various senses), as *a d. paleness, sound*; *d. beer*, etc.

Dead letter. 1579. **1.** *orig.* A writing taken in a bare literal sense (cf. Rom. 7:6, 2 Cor. 3:6). **b.** A writ, statute, ordinance, etc., which is inoperative, though not repealed 1663. **2.** A letter which lies unclaimed for a certain time at a post office, or which cannot be delivered through any cause 1771.

2. *Dead-letter office*: a department of the Post Office in which dead letters are examined and dealt with; now styled *Returned Letter Office.*

Dead lift. 1551. [DEAD *a.* V. 1.] **1.** The pull of a horse, etc., exerting his utmost strength at a dead weight beyond his power to move. **2.** *fig.* An extremity, 'a hopeless exigence' (J.). (Now *arch.* or *dial.*) 1567.

2. You must helpe vs at that dead lift J. UDALL.

Dea·d-light. 1726. [DEAD *a.* and *sb.*] **1.** *Naut.* A strong shutter fixed inside or outside a porthole, etc., to keep out water in a storm. **2.** A corpse-light or corpse-candle (*Sc.*) 1813.

†**Dea·dlihead.** *rare.* 1612. [f. DEADLY *a.* + -HEAD.] The state of the dead –1642.

Dea·d-line. 1860. [DEAD *a.* IV.] **1.** A line that does not move or run. **2.** *Mil.* A line drawn round a military prison, beyond which a prisoner may be shot down 1868.

Dead lock, dea·d-lock. 1779. [Cf. DEAD *a.* V. 1.] **1.** A position in which it is impossible to proceed or act; a complete standstill. **2.** An ordinary lock which opens and shuts only with a key; occas., locally, a padlock. [DEAD *a.* IV. 2.] 1866. Hence **Dea·d-lo:ck** *v.* to bring to a dead-lock or standstill.

Deadly (de·dli), *a.* [OE. *dēadlić*; see DEAD *a.*, -LY[1].] †**1.** Subject to death –1839; *absol.* a mortal; usu. as *pl.* –1685. †**2.** In danger of death –1616; of or belonging to death –1483. †**3.** = DEAD *a.* I. 6 (*rare*) –1440. **4.** Causing or having the capacity of causing death; mortal, fatal OE. **5.** *Theol.* Of sin: Entailing spiritual death; mortal (opp. to *venial*) ME. **6.** Aiming, or involving an aim, to kill or destroy; implacable, mortal ME. **7.** Death-like ME. **8.** Excessive, 'awful' (*colloq.*) 1660.

4. A d. blow KNOLLES, poison 1866. *D. Nightshade*, the *Atropa belladonna* (N.O. *Solanaceæ*). **5.** *The seven d. sins*: see SIN. **6.** D. imprecations

1703. **7.** D. paleness SOUTHEY, faintness LYTTON. Dark and d. SHAKS. **8.** A d. drinker PEPYS. Hence **Dea·dlily** *adv.* (*rare*). **Dea·dliness.**

Deadly (de·dli), *adv.* [OE. *dēadlīće*; see DEAD *a.*, -LY².] †**1.** In a way that causes death; mortally –1816; *spec.* in *Theol.* –1579. †**2.** Implacably; to the death –1650. **3.** In a manner resembling or suggesting death; as if dead ME. **4.** Extremely, excessively (*colloq.*) 1589.

1. So d. cruel 1679. **3.** They..look'd d. pale SHAKS. **4.** D. slow 1688, dear 1703, dull 1865.

Dea·dman. ME. = *Dead man. Obs.* exc. as in *Deadman's Walk*, etc.

Dead man. 1700. **1.** pl. (*dead men*). Empty bottles (at a carouse, etc.) (*slang*). **2.** *Cards.* A dummy at whist 1786. **3.** *Naut.* (*pl.*) Reef- or gasket-ends left dangling when a sail is furled.

Dead men's bells, the Foxglove, *Digitalis purpurea* (*Sc.*). **Dead man's (men's) finger(s: 1.** in Shaks. prob. the Early Purple Orchis, *O. mascula*; also other species of *Orchis*, prop. those with palmate tubers. **2.** The zoophyte *Alcyonium digitatum*. **Dead man's hand: 1.** *Alcyonium digitatum*. **2.** *Orchis maculata*, *O. mascula*; *Nephrodium Filixmas*, and other ferns; also the seaweed Tangle. **Dead man's thumb:** *Orchis mascula*.

Deadness (de·dnės). 1607. **1.** The condition or quality of being dead (see DEAD *a.*). **2.** Want of some characteristic physical quality, as lustre, colour, taste, etc. 1707.

1. *fig.* The d. of trade 1642. Inward deadnesses 1749. D. to God 1858. **2.** D. in cyder 1707, in complexions 1785.

Dead-nettle (de·d,ne:t'l). ME. A name for plants of the genus *Lamium* (N.O. *Labiatæ*), having leaves like those of a nettle, but stingless.

†**Dead palsy, dea·d-pa:lsy.** 1592. [DEAD *a.* I. 2.] Palsy producing complete local insensibility or immobility –1761.

†**Dead pay.** 1565. [Cf. Fr. *morte-paye*.] **1.** Pay continued to a soldier, etc. no longer in active service; a soldier receiving such pay –1686. **2.** Pay dishonestly drawn in the name of a soldier, etc. actually dead or discharged; a person in whose name such pay is drawn –1663.

2. Like a covetous Captain will needs indent for a dead pay 1565.

Dea·d-point, dead point. 1830. [DEAD *a.* IV.] *Mech.* That position of a crank at which it is in a direct line with the connecting rod, and at which therefore the force exerted does not turn the crank.

Dead reckoning. 1613. [DEAD *a.* V.] The estimation of a ship's position from the distance run by the log and the courses steered by the compass, with corrections for current, leeway, etc., but without astronomical observations. Hence *dead* LATITUDE (q.v.), that computed by dead reckoning.

Dead Sea. ME. [tr. L. *mare mortuum*, Gr. ἡ νεκρὰ θάλασσα (Aristotle).] The inland sea in the south of Palestine, into which the Jordan flows; it has no outlet, and its waters are salt and bitter. Also *attrib.*, as in **Dead Sea apple, fruit** = *Apple of Sodom*; see APPLE.

Dea·d-tongue. 1688. The umbelliferous plant *Œnanthe crocata*, from its paralysing effect on the organs of speech.

Dead water, dead-water. 1561. [DEAD *a.* IV.] **1.** Still water 1601. **2.** *Naut.* The eddy water just behind the stern of a ship under way 1627. **3.** The neap tide 1561.

Dead weight, dea·d-weight. 1660. [DEAD *a.* V.] **1.** The heavy unrelieved weight of an inert body (*lit.* and *fig.*). **2.** *techn.* A vessel's lading when it consists of heavy goods; the weight of a vehicle, as dist. from the load; etc. 1858. **3.** *fig.* A heavy unrelieved weight or burden 1721. †**4.** An advance formerly made by the Bank of England to Government for the payment of pensions, etc. –1827.

Dead well, dea·d-we·ll. 1852. [DEAD *a.* II. 3, IV.] An absorbing well, to carry off refuse waters.

Dead wood, dea·d-wood. 1727. **1.** Wood dead upon the tree; hence *fig.* **2.** *Naut.* Solid blocks of timber fastened just above the keel at each end of the ship, to strengthen those parts.

Dea·d-work, dead work. 1653. †**1.** *Naut.* That part of a ship which is above water when she is laded –1769. **2.** *Mining.* Work not directly productive, but only preparatory 1869. **3.** Work in hand 1888.

Dea·dy. *slang.* 1819. [Distiller's name.] Gin.

De-aerate; see DE- II. 1 and AERATE.

Deaf (def), *a.* [OE. *dēaf* = OFris. *dāf*, OS. *dōf* (Du. *doof*), OHG. *toup* (G. *taub*), ON. *daufr*, Goth. *daufs* (-*b*-) :– Gmc. **daubaz*, f. IE. base **dhoubh-* **dheubh-* **dhubh-* repr. also in Gr. τυφλός blind. Cf. DUMB.] **1.** Lacking, or defective in, the sense of hearing OE. Also *fig.* **2.** *fig.* Unwilling to hear or heed, inattentive ME. †**3.** Of sounds: Dull and indistinctly heard; muffled –1700. **4.** Lacking its essential character; hollow, empty, unproductive; insipid. Now chiefly *dial.* OE.

1. But she was somdel deef CHAUCER. Then..the eares of the deafe shalbe vnstopped *Isa.* 35:5. Phr. *D. and dumb*: also used *absol.* (= DEAF-MUTE) and thence *attrib.* D. to harmony COWPER. **2.** Eares..To Counsell deafe, but not to Flatterie *Timon* I. ii. 257. **3.** A d. murmur through the squadron went DRYDEN. **4.** *D. nut*: one with no kernel; *fig.* something hollow or worthless.

Comb., etc.: **d.-adder,** the blind-worm; in U.S. a name for certain snakes; **-dumbness,** aphonia arising from deafness; **-nettle** = DEAD-NETTLE.

Deaf (def), *v. arch.* or *dial.* 1460. [f. DEAF *a.*] †**1.** *intr.* To become deaf 1530. **2.** *trans.* To make deaf. Also *fig.* and *transf.* 1460. **3.** To drown (a sound) *with* a louder sound 1640.

Deafen (de·f'n), *v.* 1597. [f. DEAF *a.* + -EN⁵, superseding DEAF *v.*] **1.** *trans.* To make deaf; to stun with noise. Also *fig.* **2.** To render (a sound) inaudible 1823. **3.** To make (a floor or partition) impervious to sound by means of pugging. Hence **Dea·fening** *vbl. sb.* material used for this purpose. 1814. †**4.** *intr.* To become deaf (*rare*) 1680.

1. Hunting horns..that almost d. the company 1717. Hence **Dea·feningly** *adv.*

De-afforest (dī,ăfǫ·rėst), *v.* 1640. [– med.L. *deafforestare*; see DE- *pref.* II. 1 and AFFOREST.] = DISAFFOREST. Hence **De-affo:resta·tion.**

Deafly (de·fli), *adv.* ME. [f. DEAF *a.* + -LY².] Without hearing (*lit.* and *fig.*). **b.** Dully, indistinctly.

Deaf-mute, *a.*, *sb.* 1837. [After Fr. *sourd-muet*.] Deaf and dumb. **b.** One who is deaf and dumb. Hence **Dea·f-mu·tism,** the condition of a deaf-mute.

Deafness (de·fnės). ME. [See -NESS.] The state or condition of being deaf.

Your tale, Sir, would cure deafenesse *Temp.* I. ii. 106.

Deal (dīl), *sb.*¹ [OE. *dǣl* = OFris., OS. *dēl* (Du. *deel*), OHG., G. *teil*, Goth. *dails* :– Gmc. **dailiz*, f. **dail-*; see DOLE *sb.*¹, DALE².] †**1.** A part or division of a whole; a portion –1737. **2.** A part allowed to any one; a share, dole. Now *dial.* OE. **3.** A quantity, an amount; qualified as *good*, *great*, *vast*, †*poor*, †*small*, etc. OE. Also *absol.* (the thing referred to being implied) 1450. **4.** *A deal*: an undefined but large quantity (*rarely* number); a lot (*colloq.*) 15..

1. A meate offering of three tenth deales of flowre *Numb.* 15:9. Suche godelyhede In speche and neuer a dele of trouthe CHAUCER. †*By a thousand d.*: a thousandfold. **3.** To make such a Tragical d. ado about it 1685. **4.** Talking a d. of nonsense 1875.

Adverbial phrases. †*Any d.*, any whit. †*Never a d.*, not a whit. *A great, good, vast d.*, considerably, vastly. *A d.*, much (*colloq.*).

Deal (dīl), *sb.*² 1588. [f. DEAL *v.*] **1.** An act or the act of dealing. **2.** *Cards.* The distribution of cards to the players for a round in a game 1607. **3.** A business transaction or bargain 1837; *spec.* a secret arrangement in commerce or politics entered into by parties for their mutual benefit; a job (*U.S.*) 1881.

Deal (dīl), *sb.*³ ME. [– MLG., M.Du. *dele* plank, floor (Du. *deel* plank), corresp. to OHG. *dil*, *dilo*, *dillo*, *dilla* (G. *diele* deal board, dial. floor), ON. *þilja*, OE. *þille* :– Gmc. **þelaz*, **þeliz*, **þeljōn*; see THILL¹.] **1.** A slice sawn from a log of timber, in Great Britain 9 inches wide, not more than 3 thick, and at least 6 feet long. If shorter, it is a *d.-end*; if not more than 7 inches wide, a BATTEN. **2.** The wood of fir or pine, such as deals (sense 1) are made of 1601.

2. *White d.*, the produce of the Norway Spruce (*Abies excelsa*); *red d.*, that of the Scotch Pine (*Pinus sylvestris*); *yellow d.*, that of the Yellow Pine (*P. mitis*), etc.

Comb.: **d.-end** (see sense 1); **-fish,** a genus of fishes of the ribbon-fish family; **-frame,** a gang-saw for cutting deals; **-tree** (*dial.*), a fir-tree.

Deal (dīl), *v.* Pa. t. and pple. **dealt** (delt). [OE. *dǣlan* = OFris. *dēla*, OS. *dēljan* (Du. *deelen*), OHG., G. *teilen*, ON. *deila*, Goth. *dailjan* :– Gmc. **dailjan*. Cf. DEAL *sb.*¹]

I. Mainly *trans.* †**1.** *trans.* To divide –1570. †**2.** To separate –ME. †**3.** To distribute in shares; to portion out –1535. **4.** To distribute or bestow. Now mostly *fig.* or with *out.* OE. Also †*intr.* **5.** To apportion (*to* a person). Also with *out.* ME. **6.** To bestow, render, deliver ME. **7.** *Cards.* To distribute (the cards) to the players; to give a player (such or so many cards) in distributing. Also *absol.* 1529.

4. The provident hand deals out its scanty dole SOUTHEY. **5.** To me..it deals eternal woe MILT. *P.L.* IV. 70. **6.** To d. blows DRYDEN, an ill turn FULLER. By fits he deals his fiery bolts about DRYDEN.

II. Mainly *intr.* †**1.** To take part *in.* Also with *with* or *of.* –1481. †**2.** To engage *with*; to contend –1667. **3.** *intr.* To have to do *with* (a person); to have dealings *with*; to associate *with* ME. **4.** To treat *with*; sometimes implying secret or sinister dealings ME. **5.** To do business (*with* a person, *in* an article) 1627. **6.** To have to do *with* (a thing) in any way ME. **7.** To act towards people generally (in some specified way) ME. †**8.** To act, proceed (usu. *in* a matter) –1599.

2. Brutish that contest..When Reason hath to d. with force MILT. *P.L.* VI. 125. **3.** [The charge] of dealing with a familiar spirit FREEMAN. **4.** It is generally better to deale by speech, then by letter BACON. **5.** I d. in dog's leather MIDDLETON. **6.** The first question with which I propose to d. HUXLEY. **7.** Let us d. justly *Lear* III. vi. 42. **8.** Do not you meddle, let me deale in this *Much Ado* V. i. 101.

Phr. *To d. in*: to occupy or exercise oneself in (a thing); to make use of. *To d. on, upon*: to set to work upon (*arch.*). *To d. with*: to act in regard to, handle, dispose of (a thing); **b.** to handle effectively; to grapple with; **c.** to treat (in some specified way). Also with *by* (= in regard to) in same sense.

Dea·lable, *a.* 1667. [f. prec. + -ABLE.] Capable of being dealt *with*; suitable for dealing.

Dealbate (di,æ·lbĕt), *a.* 1866. [– *dealbatus*, pa. pple. of L. *dealbare*; see next, -ATE².] Whitened; *Bot.* covered with an opaque white powder.

†**Dea·lbate,** *v.* 1623. [– *dealbat-*, pa. ppl. stem of L. *dealbare*, f. *albus* white; see DAUB *v.* and -ATE³.] *trans.* To whiten. Hence **Dealba·tion,** blanching, bleaching.

Dea·l-boa·rd. 1568. [f. DEAL *sb.*³] = DEAL *sb.*³ 1.

Dealer (dī·lǝɹ). OE. [f. DEAL *v.* + -ER¹.] **1.** One who deals (see DEAL *v.*); *spec.* the player who deals the cards. **2.** One who deals in merchandise, a trader; *spec.* one who sells articles in the same condition in which he bought them; often in comb., as *corn-*, *horse-*, *money-d.* 1611. **3.** A dealer on the Stock Exchange 1837.

Dealing (dī·liŋ), *vbl. sb.* ME. [f. as prec. + -ING¹.] **1.** Distribution (of gifts, blows, cards, etc.); sharing. **2.** Friendly or business communication. Now usually *pl.* 1538. **3.** Buying and selling 1664. **4.** Way of acting, conduct, behaviour 1483. Also with *with*.

†**Dea·mbulate,** *v.* 1623. [– *deambulat-*, pa. ppl. stem of L. *deambulare*, f. *de* DE- I. 3 + *ambulare* go about, walk; see -ATE³.] To walk abroad. Hence **Dea:mbula·tion.** †**Dea·mbula:tor,** one who walks abroad.

Dea·mbulatory. ME. [(A) – med.L. *deambulatorius*; see prec., -ORY²; (B) – late and med.L. *deambulatorium*, subst. use of n. sing. of the adj.; see -ORY¹. Cf. AMBULATORY *a.* and *sb.*] **A.** *adj.* Moving about from place to place; shifting 1607. **B.** *sb.* A place to walk in for exercise; *esp.* a covered walk or cloister.

Dean¹ (dīn). [ME. *deen*, *den*(*e*) – AFr. *deen*, *den*, OFr. *deien*, *dien* (mod. *doyen*) :– late L. *decanus*, f. L. *decem* ten, after *primanus*, perh. infl. by Gr. δέκα ten.]

†**1.** Repr. late L. *decanus*: A head, chief, or commander of a division of ten –1483. †**2.** As tr. med.L. *decanus*, applied to the *teoðing-ealdor*, the headman of a *tenmannetale*. (See Stubbs, *Const. Hist.* I. v. 87.) –1695. **3.** As tr. eccl.L. *decanus*, head of ten monks in a monastery 1641. **4.** Hence, The head of the chapter in a collegiate or cathedral church ME. **5.** A presbyter invested with jurisdiction or precedence (under the bishop or archdeacon) over a division of an archdeaconry; more fully called a *rural d.*; formerly, *d. of* CHRISTIANITY ME. **6.** In other eccl. uses 1647. **7.** The officer or officers in the colleges of Oxford and Cambridge appointed to supervise the conduct and discipline of the junior members 1577. **8.** The president of a faculty or department of study in a University; in U.S. the registrar or secretary of the faculty 1524. **9.** The president, chief, or senior member of any body. [= Fr. *doyen*.] 1687.

6. *D. of peculiars*: one invested with the charge of a peculiar, *i.e.* a parish or church exempt from the jurisdiction of the ordinary or bishop in whose diocese it lies, *e.g.* the Dean of Battle in Sussex. *D. of the Arches*: the lay judge of the Court of Arches. *D. of the Province of Canterbury*: the Bishop of London. **8.** *D. of Faculty*: the president of the Faculty of Advocates in Scotland. **9.** *D. of guild*: in Scotland, the head of the guild or merchant-company of a royal burgh, who is a magistrate charged with the supervision of all buildings within the burgh. *D. of the Sacred College*: the chief of the Sacred College, usually the oldest of the Cardinal Bishops, who presides in the consistory in the absence of the Pope.

Dean[2], **dene** (dīn). [OE. *denu* (:– **dani-*), rel. to DEN *sb.*[1]] A vale; now, usually, the deep, narrow, and wooded vale of a rivulet.

Tauntons fruitfull Deane DRAYTON. *Denes* which débouche upon the coast 1873.

Dean[3]. 1874. [Origin unkn.] *Cornish Mining.* The end of a level.

Deanery (dī·nəri). ME. [f. DEAN[1] + -ERY, after AFr. *denrie*.] **1.** The office of a dean. **2.** The group of parishes over which a rural dean presides; formerly, also, the jurisdiction of a dean ME. **3.** The official residence of a dean 1598.

Dea·-nettle. Now *dial.* 1523. [perh. reduced f. *dead-nettle*.] A name for the species of *Lamium* (DEAD-NETTLE) and other Labiates having nettle-like leaves; *esp.* applied to the Hemp-nettle, *Galeopsis tetrahit*.

Deanship (dī·nʃip). 1588. [f. DEAN[1] + -SHIP.] **1.** The office or rank of a dean 1611. **2.** Used humorously as a title.

2. I then shall not value his D. a straw SWIFT.

†**Dear,** *sb.*[1] ME. only. [app. repr. an OE. **dīeru*, **dēoru* = OHG. *tiurī*, *diurī* glory. See next.] Dearness, dearth.

Dear (dīᵊɹ), *a.*[1] and *sb.*[2] [OE. *dēore* (WS. *dīere*) = OFris. *diore*, OS. *diuri* (Du. *dier* beloved, *duur* high-priced), OHG. *tiuri* distinguished, worthy, costly (G. *teuer*), ON. *dýrr* :– Gmc. **deurjaz*, of unkn. origin.]

I. Of persons. †**1.** Glorious, honourable, worthy –1606. **2.** Regarded with esteem and affection; loved OE. **b.** Often used *absol.* = 'dear one' ME. †**3.** Affectionate, fond –1653.

1. *Tr. & Cr.* v. iii. 27. **2.** D. to God, and famous to all ages MILT. Deare Sir ABP. USSHER. Right dere and welbeloved 1450. **b.** Shall I go mourne for that (my deere) *Wint. T.* IV. iii. 15. **3.** Sir Henry Wotton, a d. lover of this Art WALTON.

II. Of things. †**1.** Of high estimation; precious, valuable –1600. **2.** Hence, Precious in one's regard, of which one is fond ME.; affectionate (*rare*) 1591. **3.** High-priced; costly, expensive: opp. to *cheap* OE.; said of *prices*, *rates*: = High ME. Also *fig.* †**4.** 'Heartfelt; hearty; hence earnest' (Schmidt) –1606.

1. My d. time's waste SHAKS. So dangerous and deare a trust 1 *Hen. IV*, IV. i. 34. **2.** This Land of such deere soules, this deere-deere Land *Rich. II*, II. i. 57. With d. Love..I salute thee 1683. Phr. *To ride for d. life.* **3.** Sell your face for fiue pence and 'tis deere *John* I. i. 153. *D. year*, a year in which prices are high. **4.** *L.L.L.* II. i. 1.

B. *sb.* = Dear one, darling ME.

C. Used interjectionally 1694.

Dear!, *Oh dear!*, *Dear, dear!*, *Dear me!*: exclams. of surprise, anxiety, regret, sympathy, etc. *Dear* (? repr. *dear Lord*) *knows!* goodness knows (*I* do not).

Dear, †**dere,** *a.*[2] *poet.* [OE. *dēor*, of unkn. origin; not in cogn. langs.] †**1.** Brave, strenuous, hardy. (OE. only.) **2.** Hard, heavy, grievous; fell, dire (*arch.*) OE. †**3.** Difficult ME.

2. Fortunes dearest spight SHAKS. *Sonn.* xxxvii. My dearest foe *Haml.* I. ii. 180. Sad occasion d. MILT. *Lycidas* 6.

Dear (dīᵊɹ), *adv.* [OE. *dīore*, *dēore* = OHG. *tiuro* (G. *teuer*).] **1.** At a high price. **2.** = DEARLY *adv.* 2. ME.

1. The people there [Holland]..eat d. YARRANTON.

Dear (dīᵊɹ), *v.* ME. [f. DEAR *a.*[1]] †**1.** *trans.* To make dear. *Sc.* (*rare*) –1462. †**2.** To endear (*rare*) 1603. **3.** To address (a person) as 'dear' 1829.

Dea·rborn. *U.S.* 1841. [The inventor's name.] A kind of light four-wheeled wagon.

Dea·r-bou·ght, *a.* ME. [DEAR *adv.*] Obtained at great cost, as *dear-bought experience*.

Deare, obs. f. DEAR, DEER, DERE.

†**Dear joy.** 1688. Familiar name for an Irishman –1710.

Dearling, obs. f. DARLING.

Dearly (dīᵊ·ɹli), *adv.* [OE. *dēorlīċe* = OS. *diurlīco*, OHG. *tiurlīhho*; see DEAR *a.*[1], -LY[2].] †**1.** In a precious, worthy, or excellent manner –1606. **2.** As one who is held dear; fondly. (Now only with the vb. *love*, or its equivs.) ME. †**3.** Heartily, earnestly –1606; keenly –1602. **4.** = DEAR *adv.* 1. 1489.

2. His dearly-loved mate MILT. **3.** My father hated his father d.*A.Y.L.* I. iii. 35. **4.** He shal derely abye it LD. BERNERS.

Dearn(e, -ful, -ly; see DERN, etc.

Dearn, obs. f. DARN *v.*

Dearness (dīᵊ·ɹnės). ME. [f. DEAR *a.*[1] + -NESS.] **1.** The quality of being held dear: hence **b.** Intimacy; **c.** Affection. **2.** Expensiveness, costliness 1530.

1. The d. that was between them, was now turned..to a most violent enmity BP. BURNET.

Dearth (dəɹþ), *sb.* [ME. *derþ*, f. *dēr* DEAR *a.*[1] + -TH[1]. Cf. OS. *diur(i)ða*, OHG. *tiurida*, *diurida*, ON. *dýrð*.] †**1.** Glory (*rare*). [= ON. *dýrð*.] (ME. only.) †**2.** Dearness –1602. **3.** A condition in which food is scarce and dear; earlier, a famine ME. Also *transf.* and *fig.*

2. The dearthe of the pryce thairof 1632. **3.** In the tyme of d. and famine *Bk. Com. Prayer.* Ther is no grete derthe..of women CAXTON. Hence †**Dearth** *v.* to make dear; to cause a d. of or in anything.

†**De-arti·culate,** *a.* 1650. [Cf. next and ARTICULATE *a.*] Divided by joints; freely articulated –1651. Also **De-arti·culated** *a.*

De:-articula·tion. 1615. [– Fr. †*déarticulation* or med.L. *dearticulatio*, tr. Gr. διάρθρωσις in Aristotle and Galen.] Division by joints; **b.** = DIARTHROSIS; **c.** Distinct articulation (of the voice).

†**Dea·rworth, derworth,** *a.* [OE. *dēor-*, *dȳrwurþe*, app. f. *dīeru*, *dēoru* DEAR *sb.*[1] + *wyrþe* worthy.] **1.** Precious –ME. **2.** = DEAR *a.* I. 1. –ME. **3.** Of persons: Dear –1557. var. †**Dea·rworthy, der-,** *a.*; whence †**Dea·rworthily** *adv.* †**Dea·rworthiness.**

Deary, -rie (dīᵊ·ri). 1681. [dim. of *dear*; see DEAR *a.*[1], -IE, -Y[6].] A little dear, a darling.

Deas(e, obs. f. DAIS.

‖**Deasil, deiseal** (dye·ʃəl, de·səl), *adv.*, *sb.* 1771. [Gael. *deiseil* (*deiseal*, *deasal*).] Right-handwise, towards the right; motion as in the apparent course of the sun (a practice held auspicious by the Celts).

Death (deþ). [OE. *dēath* = OFris. *dāth*, OS. *dōð* (Du. *dood*), OHG. *tōd* (G. *tod*), ON. *dauðr*, Goth. *dauþus* :– Gmc. **dauþuz*, f. **dau-* (cf. ON. *deyja* DIE *v.*[1]) + *-*þuz* :– *-*tus* -TH[1].] **1.** The act or fact of dying; the final cessation of the vital functions of an animal or plant. Often personified. **2.** The state of being dead OE. **3.** The loss or cessation of life in a part 1800. †**4.** State of unconsciousness, swoon (*rare*) 1596. **5.** *fig.* Loss of spiritual life OE.; deprivation of civil life (usually *civil d.*) 1622; end, extinction, destruction ME. **6.** Bloodshed, murder 1626. **7.** Cause or occasion of death; *poet.* a deadly weapon, poison, etc. OE. †**8.** A pestilence –1587. †**9.** *Hunting.* = MORT *sb.*[1] 2. 1741. **10.** As an exclam. 1604.

1. The d. of a deare friend *Mids. N.* V. i. 293. Deth is callyd mors for it is bitter TREVISA. Over them triumphant D. his Dart Shook; but delaid to strike MILT. *P.L.* XI. 490. **2.** His eyes were closed in d. 1894. **5.** *The second d.*: the punishment of lost souls after physical death. (Cf. *Rev.* 21:8.) This banishment is a kind of civil d. 1622. **6.** Not to suffer a man of d. to live BACON (J.). **7.** The clam'rous lapwings feel the leaden d. POPE. A school would be his d. GOLDSM. **8.** **Black d.,** the name given to the Great Pestilence or visitation of the Oriental Plague, which devastated Europe, and caused great mortality in England, in the 14th c.

Phrases. *To death* (Sc. *to deid*): **a.** *lit.* as *to beat*, *stone*, etc. *to d.*; hence *to do to d.* (arch.), to kill; *to put to d.*, to kill, to execute. **b.** with vbs. of feeling as *hate*, etc., or adjs., as *sick*, *wearied*: to the last extremity. *To catch one's d.*: see CATCH *v.* *To be the d. of*: see sense 7. *To be* (or *make it*) *d.*: *i.e.* to be (or make it) a matter of capital punishment. *Death's door*, *the gates* or *jaws of d.* (fig.): a near approach to, or great danger of, d. *To be in at the d.* (in *Fox-hunting*): to be present when the game is killed. *To be d. on* (slang): to be a good hand at dealing with; to be very fond of.

Comb.: **d.-adder,** a name for the genus *Acanthophis* of venomous serpents, esp. *A. antarctica* of Australia; also erron. f. *deaf-adder*: see DEAF *a.*; **-bill** (*Eccl.*), a list of dead for whom prayers were to be said; **-dance,** a dance at or in connection with d.; the Dance of Death; **-doing** *a.*, doing to d., murderous; **-duty,** a duty levied on the devolution of property in consequence of a d.; legacy, and probate and succession duties; **-feud,** a feud prosecuted to the d.; **-flame** = DEATH-FIRE 1; †**-head** = DEATH'S-HEAD; **-mask,** a cast taken from a person's face after d.; **-moth,** the Death's-head Moth; **-penalty,** capital punishment; **-pile,** a funeral pile; **-rate,** the proportion of deaths to the population; **-rattle,** a rattling sound in the throat of a dying person, caused by the partial stoppage of the air-passage by mucus; so **-ruckle, -ruttle** (*Sc.*); **-tick** = DEATH-WATCH 1; **-trance,** a trance in which reduced action of the heart, lungs, etc. produces the semblance of d.; **-trap,** any place or structure which is unhealthy or dangerous without its being suspected; **-weight,** a small weight placed on the eyelids of a corpse to keep them closed.

Death-bed (de·þbed). OE. The bed on which a person dies. (In OE. the grave.) Also *attrib.*

Death-bell (de·þbel). Also **dead-bell.** 1740. A bell tolled at the death of a person; a passing-bell.

Dea·th-bird. 1821. A carrion-feeding bird; a bird supposed to bode death; a name of a small N. American owl, *Nyctala richardsoni*.

Dea·th-blow. 1795. A blow that causes death.

fig. The death-blow of my hope BYRON.

Dea·th-day. OE. The day on which a person dies, or its anniversary.

The death-day of the founder..is still kept THACKERAY.

Dea·th-fire. 1796. **1.** = DEAD-LIGHT 2. **2.** A fire for burning a person to death 1857.

Deathful (de·þfŭl), *a.* ME. [See -FUL.] **1.** Fraught with death; deadly. **2.** Subject to death, mortal (*arch.*, *rare*) 1616. **3.** Having the appearance of death, deathly 1656.

1. Amidst the d. field COLLINS. **2.** That with a deathless goddess lay A d. man CHAPMAN. Hence **Dea·thful-ly** *adv.*, **-ness.**

Deathless (de·þlės), *a.* 1598. [See -LESS.] Not subject to death; immortal. Also *fig.* of things.

D. souls BOYLE, pain MILTON. Hence **Dea·thless-ly** *adv.*, **-ness.**

Deathlike (de·þləik), *a.* 1548. [f. DEATH + -LIKE.] †**1.** = DEATHLY 2. –1621. **2.** Resembling death 1605.

1. D. dragons SHAKS. **2.** The d. silence 1856.

Deathling (de·þliŋ). *rare.* 1598. [See -LING[1].] **1.** One subject to death, a mortal. Also *attrib.* **2.** *pl.* Young Deaths. SWIFT.

Deathly (de·þli), *a.* [OE. *dēaþlić* (= OHG. *tōdlīh*), f. DEATH + -LY[1]. Cf. DEADLY *a.*] †**1.** Subject to death, mortal –ME. **2.** Causing death, deadly ME. **3.** Resembling death, deathlike 1568. **4.** Of or pertaining to death (*poet.*) 1850. Hence **Dea·thliness.** So **Dea·thly** *adv.* to a degree resembling death.

†**Dea·th's-face.** = DEATH'S-HEAD 1. *L.L.L.* V. ii. 616.

Death's-head (de·þsˌhed). 1596. [See DEATH 1.] **1.** The head of Death figured as a skeleton; a human skull, *esp.* as an emblem of mortality. **2.** A South American monkey, *Chrysothrix sciureus*, from the appearance of its face and features.

1. Doe not speake like a Deaths-head: doe not bid me remember mine end 2 *Hen. IV*, II. iv. 255. **Death's-head Moth,** a large species of hawk-moth (*Acherontia atropos*), having markings on the back of the thorax resembling a human skull.

†**Dea·th's-herb.** 1607. Deadly Nightshade.

Dea·th-sick, *a.* 1628. Mortally sick.

Deathsman (de·þsmæn). *arch.* 1589. An executioner.

Dea·th-struck, *a.* Also **-stricken.** 1622. Smitten with a mortal wound or disease.

Death-throe. ME. The agony of death. Also *fig.*

Dea·thward, *adv.* ME. [See -WARD.] In the direction of death. var. **Dea·thwards** *adv.* (*adj.*).

Dea·th-wa:rrant. Also 7–8 **dead-.** 1692. A warrant for the execution of the sentence of death. Also *fig.*

Death-watch (de·þ,wǫtʃ). Also 8 **dead-.** 1688. **1.** Any of various insects which make a noise like the ticking of a watch, supposed by the superstitious to portend death; *esp.* the small beetles of the genus *Anobium*, and a minute insect, *Atropos pulsatorius*, known as destructive to botanical and other collections. **2.** A vigil by the dead or dying.

1. I listened for death-watches in the wainscot GOLDSM.

Dea·th-worm. 1773. †**1.** = DEATH-WATCH 1. **2.** *poet.* A worm of death 1821.

2. How like death-worms the wingless moments crawl SHELLEY.

Dea·th-wound. ME. A mortal wound.

Deathy (de·þi). 1796. [f. DEATH + Y¹.] *adj.* and *adv.* = DEATHLY *a.* 3, 4, *adv.*

†**Deau·rate,** *a.* ME. [– *deauratus*, pa. pple. of late L. *deaurare* gild (for cl.L. *inaurare*, see INAURATE *a.* and *v.*), f. *aurum* gold. Cf. DEALBATE *a.*] Gilded, golden –1616. So **Deaurate** (di,ǭ·re¹t), *v.* ? *Obs.*, to gild over (1562). Hence **Deaura·tion** (1658).

Deave (dīv), *v.* Now *Sc.* and *n. dial.* [OE. *dēafian* wax deaf.] †**1.** *intr.* To become deaf (*rare*) –ME. **2.** *trans.* To deafen; to stun with din ME.

Deb (deb). 1926. Colloq. abbrev. (orig. *U.S.*) of DÉBUTANTE. Hence **De·bby** *a.*

†**Deba·cchate,** *v. rare.* 1623. [– *debacchat-*, pa. ppl. stem of L. *debacchari*, f. *de* (see DE- I. 3) + *bacchari*, f. *Bacchus* god of wine.] To rage or rave as a bacchanal –1751. Hence †**Debaccha·tion.**

Debacle (dĭbā·k'l). Also **débâcle.** 1802. [– Fr. *débâcle*, f. *débâcler* unbar, f. *dé-* DE- I. 6 + *bâcler* to bar.] **1.** A breaking up of ice in a river; in *Geol.* a sudden deluge or violent rush of water, which carries before it blocks of stone and other debris. **2.** *transf.* and *fig.* A sudden breaking up; a confused rout, a stampede 1848.

1. They could have been transported by no other force than that of a tremendous deluge or d. of water W. BUCKLAND.

Debar (dĭbā·ɹ), *v.* ME. [– Fr. *débarrer*, OFr. *desbarrer*, f. *des-* DE- I. 6 + *barrer* to bar.] **1.** *trans.* To exclude *from* a place or condition; †to shut out, exclude. Also with *of* (*arch.*). **2.** To prohibit, prevent, stop 1526.

1. Debarred from voting JOHNSON. 2. Its Egress [would have been] utterly debarr'd WOODWARD. Hence **Deba·rment.**

Deba·rbarize, *v.* See DE- II. 1.

Debark (dĭbā·ɹk), *v.*¹ 1654. [– Fr. *débarquer*, f. *dé-* = *des-* (see DE- I. 6) + *barque* BARK *sb.*²] = DISEMBARK (*trans.* and *intr.*). Hence **Debarka·tion, debarcation,** the action of landing from a ship.

Debark (dĭbā·ɹk), *v.*² *rare.* 1744. [f. DE- II. 2 + BARK *sb.*¹] To strip of its bark. Also *fig.*

Debarrass (dĭbæ·răs), *v.* 1789. [– Fr. *débarrasser*, f. *dé-* = *des-* (see DE- I. 6) + *-barrasser* in *embarrasser* EMBARRASS.] *trans.* To disembarrass.

Debase (dĭbē¹·s), *v.* 1565. [f. DE- I. 1, 3 + BASE *v.*¹; cf. ABASE.] †**1.** *trans.* To lower in position, rank, or dignity; to abase –1827. †**2.** To decry, depreciate –1746. **3.** To lower in quality, or character; to degrade; *spec.* to depreciate (coin) 1591.

1. God sent her to d. me MILT. *Sams.* 999. 3. To d. commodities 1606, words JOHNSON. Hence **Deba·sed** *ppl. a.*, *Her.* reversed. **Deba·sement,** the act of debasing or state of being debased; degradation; †abasement. **Deba·ser. Deba·singly** *adv.*

Debatable (dĭbē¹·tăb'l), *a.* Also **debateable.** 1492. [– OFr. *debatable* (f. *debatre*) or AL. *debatabilis*; see DEBATE *v.*¹, -ABLE.] Admitting of debate or controversy; subject to dispute; questionable 1581.

The d. Elections 1685, opinions FROUDE. **The D. Land:** a tract between the Esk and Sark, claimed (before the Union) by both England and Scotland. Also used *fig.* of regions of thought, etc.

Debate (dĭbē¹·t), *sb.* [ME. *debat* – OFr. *debat* (mod. *débat*), f. *debatre*; see next.] **1.** Strife, dissension, quarrelling; a quarrel (*arch.*). **2.** Contention in argument; dispute, controversy; discussion; *esp.* discussion in Parliament; a discussion ME.

1. To seal the truce and end the dire d. POPE. Their d. was so cruell, that there was slaine v. capitaynes LD. BERNERS. 2. After much d., they concluded unanimously that [etc.] SWIFT. A full D. upon Public Affairs in the Senate STEELE.

Debate (dĭbē¹·t), *v.*¹ ME. [– OFr. *debatre* (mod. *débattre*) :– Rom. **desbattere* f. *battere* fight; see DE- I. 6, ABATE *v.*¹] †**1.** *intr.* To fight, strive, quarrel, wrangle –1665. Also *fig.* **2.** *trans.* To contest, dispute; to contend for; to carry on (a fight) (*arch.*) 1489. **3.** To dispute about, argue, discuss ME.; *intr.* to engage in discussion; *esp.* in a public assembly 1530. **4.** To consider (*trans.* and *intr.*) ME.

1. His cote-armour. .in which he wold d. CHAUCER. 2. [To] d. The martial prizes DRYDEN. In many a well debated field SCOTT. 3. The question has been debated among many great Clerks WALTON. Commission to d. of Religion FULLER. 4. I and my Bosome must d. awhile *Hen. V*, IV. i. 31.

Hence †**Deba·teful** *a.* contentious; pertaining to contention. †**Deba·tement,** the action of debating; strife. **Deba·ter,** †one who contends or strives; a controversialist. †**Deba·tive,** relating to, or of the nature of debate or discussion (*rare*). †**Deba·tous** *a.* contentious.

†**Debate,** *v.*² ME. [f. DE- I. 1, 3 + BATE *v.*², or by prefix-substitution f. ABATE *v.*¹] To abate (*trans.* and *intr.*) –1658. Hence †**Deba·tement²** = ABATEMENT¹.

Debauch (dĭbǭ·tʃ), *v.* 1595. [– Fr. *débaucher*, OFr. *desbaucher*, f. *des-* DE- I. 6 + an element of unkn. origin.] †**1.** *trans.* To turn or lead away *from* one to whom service, etc. is due –1765. **2.** To seduce from virtue or morality; to corrupt 1603. **3.** To vitiate (the taste, judgement, etc.) 1664. †**4.** To vilify; to disparage –1659. †**5.** To spend prodigally –1649. **6.** *intr.* To indulge to excess; to riot, revel. ? *Obs.* 1644.

1. He debauched Prince John from his allegiance HUME. 2. To d. one's conscience 1665, a country girl 1843. 3. A mind not yet debauched by learning BERKELEY. 6. Such as can drink and d. EVELYN. Hence **Debau·cher.** †**Debau·chment,** seduction from duty or virtue; debauched condition; a debauch.

Debauch (dĭbǭ·tʃ), *sb.* 1603. [– Fr. *débauche*, f. the verb.] **1.** Excessive indulgence in eating and drinking, or other sensual pleasures. **2.** The practice or habit of such indulgence 1673. **3.** *transf.* and *fig.* 1672. †**4.** = DEBAUCHEE –1719.

1. My head akeing all day from last night's d. PEPYS. 2. The first physicians by d. were made DRYDEN.

Debauched (dĭbǭ·tʃt), *ppl. a.* 1598. [f. DEBAUCH *v.* + -ED¹.] Seduced from duty or virtue; dissolute, licentious.

An vnthriftie, careles, debaucht or mislead man FLORIO. Hence **Debau·chedly** *adv.* **Debau·chedness;** †**Debau·chness.**

Debauchee (debǫʃī·). 1661. [– Fr. *débauché*, pa. pple. of *débaucher* DEBAUCH *v.*; see -EE¹ 2.] One given to excessive indulgence in sensual pleasures.

Debauchery (dĭbǭ·tʃəri). 1642. [f. DEBAUCH *v.* + -ERY.] **1.** Vicious indulgence in sensual pleasures. †**2.** Seduction from duty or virtue; corruption –1790.

1. Youth's deboichery 1647. 2. The republick of Paris will endeavour to compleat the d. of the army BURKE.

†**Debe·l, -ell,** *v.* 1555. [– L. *debellare*; see next. Cf. (O)Fr. *débeller.*] To vanquish; to expel by force of arms –1825.

†**Debe·llate,** *v.* 1611. [– *debellat-*, pa. pple. stem of L. *debellare*, subdue in fight, f. *de* DE- I. 1 + *bellare* wage war, f. *bellum* war; see -ATE³.] = DEBEL –1626. Hence †**Debella·tion,** conquest, subjugation. †**Debella·tor.** SWIFT.

De bene esse; see DE 1.

Debenture (dĭbe·ntiŭɹ). 1455. [– mod. use of L. *debentur* are owing or due, 3rd. pers. pl. pres. indic. pass. of *dcbēre* owe, occurring as the first word of a certificate of indebtedness; cf. legal Fr. *bille de debentour* (XV); final syll. assim. to -URE.] **1.** A voucher certifying that a sum of money is owing to the person designated in it. **b.** *spec.* At the Custom-house: A certificate given to an exporter of imported goods on which a drawback is allowed, certifying that the holder is entitled to an amount therein stated. 1662. Also †*transf.* and †*fig.* †**2.** A certificate of a loan made to the government for public purposes –1813. **3.** A bond issued by a corporation or company (under seal), acknowledging that it is indebted to the holder in a specified sum of money, bearing interest until repayment of the principal 1847.

1. Certeyn debentur conteynyng the seyd sommes 1455. 3. *Mortgage d.*: a d. the principal of which is secured by the pledging of the whole or a part of the property of the issuing company.

Comb.: **d.-bond** = DEBENTURE 3; **-stock,** debentures in the form of a stock, the nominal capital of which represents a debt of which only the interest is secured by a perpetual annuity.

Hence **Debe·ntured** *a.* furnished with or secured by a d., as *debentured goods, i.e.* goods on which a custom-house d. for a drawback is given.

Debile (de·bil), *a. arch.* 1536. [– Fr. *débile* or L. *debilis* weak.] Weak.

Debi·litant. 1857. [– Fr. *débilitant*, pres. pple. of *débiliter*; see DEBILITATE, -ANT.]

A. *adj.* Debilitating.

B. *sb. Med.* Debilitating remedies, *e.g.* low diet, etc.

Debilitate (dĭbi·lite¹t), *v.* 1533. [– *debilitat-*, pa. ppl. stem of L. *debilitare* weaken, f. *debilitas*; see next, -ATE³.] To render weak, enfeeble.

A feeble constitution, which he further debilitated by a dissipated life 1871. Hence **Debilita·tion,** the action of debilitating; enfeebled condition. **Debi·litative** *a.* tending to d.

Debility (dĭbi·lĭti). 1474. [– (O)Fr. *débilité* – L. *debilitas*, f. *debilis* weak; see -ITY.] **1.** The condition of being weak or feeble; weakness 1484. †**2.** An instance of weakness –1825.

1. D. of body 1563, of mind H. WALPOLE, of the realme of Englande LD. BERNERS.

†**Debi·nd,** *v.* [DE- I. 1.] To bind down. SCOTT.

Debit (de·bit), *sb.* 1450. [Sense 1, – L. *debitum* DEBT; sense 2, – Fr. *débit.*] †**1.** *gen.* A debt –1614. **2.** *Book-keeping.* An entry in an account of a sum of money owing; an item so entered. **b.** These items collectively; the left-hand side of an account on which debits are entered. (Opp. to CREDIT *sb.*) 1776. Also *attrib.*

Debit (de·bit), *v.* 1682. [f. DEBIT *sb.*] **1.** *trans.* To charge with a debt. **2.** To charge as a debt 1865.

1. He must and may d. the Principal for the said Value 1682. 2. To whom is it to be debited? 1894.

†**Debite,** *sb.* 1482. [var. of contemp. †*debity*, which is a perversion of DEPUTY.] A deputy –1549. So †**Debity.**

†**De·bitor.** 1484. A by-form of DEBTOR 15–17th c.)

Debitumenize, -ation; see DE- II. 1.

‖**Déblai** (de·blę). 1853. [Fr., vbl. sb. f. *déblayer* free from rubbish, clear (away).] *Fortif.* The hollow space formed by the removal of earth for parapets, etc.

†**Deboi·se,** *v.* 1632. [A by-form of *debosh* DEBAUCH.] = DEBAUCH *v.* 2, 5. –1662. So †**Deboise** *a.*, †**Deboi·st** *ppl. a.* debauched.

Debonair, -bonnaire (de:bŏnē³·ɹ), *a.* (*sb.*) ME. [– OFr. *debonaire* (mod. *débonnaire*), prop. phr. *de bon aire* of good disposition. Cf. BONAIR(E.)]

A. *adj.* Of gentle disposition, meek; gracious; courteous (*obs.*); pleasant and affable in address; now often connoting gaiety of heart.

Was neuer Prince so meeke and debonaire SPENSER.

B. *sb.* †**1.** [the adj. used *absol.*] Gracious being or person. (ME. only.) †**2.** = DEBONAIRTY –1748.

Hence **Debonai·r-ly** *adv.*, **-ness.**

†**Debonai·rty, debona·rity.** [ME. – (O)Fr. *debonaireté*, f. *debonaire*; see prec., -TY[1]; *debonarity* shows assim. to the type of *similarity*.] Debonair character or disposition –1688.

Debo·rd, *v.* ? *Obs.* 1620. [– Fr. *déborder*, f. *dé-* (DE- I. 6) + *bord* edge, border.] Of a body of water: To pass beyond its borders, to overflow. Also †*fig.* Hence †**Debo·rdment,** going beyond bounds, excess.

Debosh, -bosche, obs. or arch. f. DEBAUCH.

Debo·shed, *ppl. a.* 1599. Early var. of DEBAUCHED, repr. the pronunc. of Fr. *débauché*. Revived by Scott, and now frequent in literary English, with vaguer sense than *debauched*.

Deboshment, obs. f. DEBAUCHMENT.

Debouch (dĭbau·tʃ, dĭbū·ʃ), *v.* Also **debouche.** 1760. [– Fr. *déboucher*, f. *dé-* (DE- I. 6) + *bouche* mouth, after synon. It. *sboccare*.] *Milit.* (*intr.*) To issue from a confined place, as a defile or a wood, into open country; hence *gen.* to emerge. Also *transf.* of a ravine, river, etc.

We saw the column of infantry debouching into Minden plain 1760. Hence **Debou·ch(e)ment,** the action or fact of debouching.

‖**Débouché** (debuʃe). 1760. [Fr., f. *déboucher* (see prec.).] *Milit.* An opening where troops may debouch: *gen.* an outlet; *fig.* a market for goods.

One gate, as an additional *débouché* for the crowd 1857. var. **Debou·ch** (*rare*).

Debouchure (debuʃū·r). 1844. [alt. of EMBOUCHURE, after DEBOUCH. The sense is not Fr.] The mouth or outlet of a river, a pass, etc.

†**Debou·t,** *v.* 1619. [– Fr. *débouter*, f. *dé-* (DE- I. 6) + *bouter* to push; see BUTT *v.*[1]] To expel, oust –1644.

‖**Debris, débris** (dēⁱ·brī, de·brī). 1708. [Fr. *débris*, f. †*débriser* break down or up; see next.] The remains of anything broken down or destroyed; ruins, wreck: in *Geol.* any accumulation arising from the waste of rocks, etc.; hence, any similar rubbish formed by destructive operations.

The *débris* of the ancient rocks MURCHISON.

Debruise (dĭbrū·z), *v.* ME. [– OFr. *debruisier, debrisier*, f. *dé-* (DE- I. 6) + *bruisier, brisier* (mod. *briser*) to break.] †**1.** *trans.* To break down, break in pieces, crush, smash –1618. **2.** *Her.* (*trans.*) To cross (a charge, *esp.* an animal) with an ordinary so as apparently to press it down; usu. in *pa. pple.* **Debruised** 1572.

2. He..exhibited on his escutcheon the lions of England and the lilies of France without the baton sinister under which..they were debruised in token of his illegitimate birth MACAULAY.

Debt (det), *sb.* [ME. *det, dette* – (O)Fr. *dette* :– Rom. **debita*, feminized pl. of L. *debitum*, pa. pple. n. of *debēre* owe. From XIII to XVI spelt *debte* in Fr., whence *debt* in Eng. from XVI onwards.] **1.** That which is owed or due; anything (as money, goods, or service) which one person is under obligation to pay or render to another. **2.** A liability to pay or render something; the being under such liability ME. **3.** *fig.* As the type of an offence requiring expiation, a sin ME.

1. To paye large vsury besides the due det 1559. Love the gift is love the d. TENNYSON. **2.** A d. of speciall remembrance and thankefulnesse A.V. *Transl. Pref.* 5. **3.** And forgeue vs our debtes euen as we forgiue our debters *N.T.* (Geneva).

Phrases. *D. of honour*: a d. which depends for its validity solely on the honour of the debtor, *e.g.* a gambling d. *D. of* (or *to*) *nature* the necessity of dying, death. [L. *debitum naturæ*.] *National D.*: a d. owing by a sovereign state to private individuals for money advanced.

†**Debt,** *ppl. a.* ME. [prob. from *dette*, debt, esp. as in the phr. *it is dette* it is a duty.] Owed, owing –1602. *Haml.* III. ii. 203.

†**De·bted,** *ppl. a.* ME. [perh. aphet. f. *an-, en-, indebted* (XIII).] Owed; of persons, indebted –1590. *Com. Err.* IV. i. 31.

Debtee (de:tī·). 1531. [f. DEBTOR; see -EE[1].] One to whom a debt is due: a creditor.

Debtless (de·tlės), *a.* ME. [See -LESS.] Free from debt.

Debtor (de·təɹ). [ME. *det(t)ur, -our* – OFr. *det(t)or, -our* :– L. *debitorem*, nom. *debitor*; see -OR 2.] **1.** One who is indebted to another: correlative to *creditor*. **2.** *Book-keeping.* The left hand or debit side of an account, or what is entered there 1714. Also *attrib.* Hence **De·btorship.**

Debunk (dĭbʊ·ŋk), *v.* orig. *U.S.* 1927. [f. DE- II. 2 a + BUNK *sb.*[2]] *trans.* To remove the 'nonsense' or false sentiment from; hence, to remove (a person) from his 'pedestal'.

†**Debu·rse,** *v. Sc.* 1529. [– Fr. *débourser*.] To DISBURSE –1705.

Debus (dībʊ·s), *v.* *Army slang.* 1915. [f. DE- I. 1 + BUS *sb.*, after DETRAIN.] *trans.* and *intr.* To set down, or get down, from a motor vehicle.

‖**Début** (debü). 1751. [Fr., f. *débuter* lead off at billiards, etc.] Entry into society; first appearance in public of an actor or other performer. So **Début(e** *v.* to make one's d.

Débutant (debütaṅ). 1824. [– Fr. *débutant*, pres. pple. of *débuter*; see prec., -ANT.] A male performer or speaker making his first appearance before the public. So **Débutante** (-täṅt), a girl coming out or presented at court 1837.

Dec. Abbrev. of DECEMBER; in *Mus.* of DECRESCENDO; in *Med.* of L. *decoctum* (= decoction).

Deca-, dec-, Gr. δεκα- ten, an initial element in many technical words:

1. Decaca·rbon *a. Chem.* in *decacarbon series*, the series of hydrocarbon compounds containing C_{10}, as *decane, decene*, etc. ‖**Deca·cera** *sb. pl.* [Gr. κέρας, κερατ-], *Zool.* a name for the ten-armed cephalopods, called also *Decapoda*. **Decadi·anome** [Gr. διανομή], *Math.* a quartic surface (dianome) having ten conical points. **Dec·a·ngular** *a.* [L. *angulus*], having ten angles. **Decaphy·llous** *a.* [Gr. φύλλον], *Bot.* having ten leaves.

2. *esp.* in the French metric system, the initial element in names of measures and weights, composed of ten times a standard unit. Hence, **De·cagramme, -gram** (Fr. *décagramme*), the weight of 10 grammes (= 154·32349 troy grains, or ·353 oz. avoird.). **Decalitre** (de·kălītəɹ), [Fr. *déca-*], a measure of capacity, containing 10 litres (= 610·28 cubic inches, or a little over 2⅕ gallons). **Decametre** (de·kămītəɹ), [Fr. *déca-*], a lineal measure of 10 metres (= 32 ft. 9·7079 inches Eng.). **Decastere** (de·kăstīᵊɪ), [Fr. *décastère*], a solid measure = 10 steres or cubic metres.

Decachord (de·kăkǫɹd). 1526. [– late L. *decachordus* adj., *decachordus, -um* sb., – Gr. δεκάχορδος ten-stringed, f. δεκα- DECA- + χορδή CHORD *sb.*[1]]

A. *adj.* Ten-stringed.

B. *sb. Mus.* A ten-stringed instrument; var. †**Decacho·rdon.**

Decad (de·kăd). 1616. [– late L. *decas, -ad-* – Gr. δεκάς, f. δέκα ten; see -AD.] **1.** The number ten (the perfect number of the Pythagoreans). **2.** Earlier f. DECADE, q.v.

Decadal (de·kădăl), *a.* 1753. [f. as prec. + -AL[1].] Of or relating to the number 10; belonging to a decade.

De·cadarchy, deka-. 1849. [– Gr. δεκαδαρχία, f. δεκάδαρχος decurion, f. as prec. + ἀρχός chief.] *Gr. Hist.* A ruling body of ten.

Decadary (de·kădĕri), *a.* 1801. [Anglicization of Fr. *décadaire*; see next, -ARY[1].] Relating to a DECADE (1 b).

Decade (de·kėd). Also †**decad.** 1475. [– (O)Fr. *décade* – late L. *decas, decad-*; see DECAD.] **1.** A group or series of ten; *spec.* a period of ten years 1594. **b.** A period of ten days, substituted for the week in the French Republican calendar of 1793. **2.** A division of a literary work, containing ten books or parts 1475.

1. So many tens or decads of yeares 1605. **2.** The second d. of Livy MACAULAY.

Decadence (de·kădĕns, dĭkēⁱ·dĕns). 1549. [– Fr. *décadence* – med.L. *decadentia*, f. *decadent-*, pres. ppl. stem of Rom. **decadere*; see DECAY *v.*, -ENCE.] The process of falling away or declining; decay; impaired condition; *spec.* applied to a particular period of decline in art, literature, etc.

The men of the d., not less than the men of the renaissance, were giants of learning STUBBS.

Decadency (de·kădĕnsi, dĭkēⁱ·dĕnsi). 1632. [f. as prec.; see -ENCY.] Decaying condition; also = prec.

Decadent (de·kădĕnt, dĭkēⁱ·dĕnt), *a.* 1837. [– Fr. *décadent*; see DECADENCE, -ENT.] **1.** That is in a state of decay or decline. ‖**2.** Belonging to an age of decadence in literature and art: said of certain French writers, etc. 1888.

‖**Décadi.** 1795. [Fr.; f. Gr. δέκα + *-di* day in *Lundi*, etc.] The tenth day of the DECADE (1 b), superseding Sunday.

Decadic (dĭkæ·dik), *a.* 1838. [– Gr. δεκαδικός, f. δεκάς, δεκαδ-; see DECAD, -IC.] Reckoning by tens; denary.

Decagon (de·kăgǫn). 1613. [– med.L. *decagonum* – Gr. δεκάγωνον, f. δεκα- DECA- + γωνία angle.] *Geom.* A plane figure having ten sides and ten angles. Also *attrib.* Hence **Deca·gonal** *a.* of or pertaining to a d.; ten-sided.

Decagram; see DECA- 2.

Decagynous (dĭkæ·dʒinəs), *a.* [f. mod.L. *decagynus* + -OUS; see DECA-, -GYNOUS.] *Bot.* Having ten pistils. So **Decagy·nia,** a Linnæan order of plants having ten pistils.

Decahedron (dekăˌhī·drǫn). 1828. [f. DECA- + *-hedron*, after *hexahedron, tetrahedron*, etc. Cf. Fr. *décaèdre* (Haüy, 1801).] *Geom.* A solid figure having ten faces. Hence **Decahe·dral** *a.* having the form of a d.

Decalcify (dĭkæ·lsifəi), *v.* 1847. [f. DE- II. 1 + CALCIFY.] To deprive (*e.g.* bone) of its calcareous matter. Hence **Decalcifica·tion.**

Decalcoma·nia. Also, as Fr., **-manie.** 1864. [– Fr. *décalcomanie*, f. *décalquer* transfer a tracing + *-manie* -MANIA.] A process of transferring pictures from prepared paper to surfaces of glass, porcelain, etc., in vogue about 1862–4. Also *attrib.*

Decalitre; see DECA- 2.

Decalogue (de·kălǫg). ME. [– Fr. *décalogue* or eccl.L. *decalogus* – Gr. δεκάλογος, orig. fem. adj. (sc. βίβλος book); after οἱ δέκα λόγοι the ten commandments (LXX), f. δέκα ten + λόγος saying.] The Ten Commandments collectively as a body of law. Hence **Deca·logist,** one who expounds the d. (*rare*).

Decameron (dĭkæ·mĕrǫn). 1609. [– It. *Decamerone*, f. Gr. δέκα ten + ἡμέρα day, after late L. *hexameron* for *hexaēmeron*.] The title of a work by Boccaccio containing a hundred tales which are supposed to be related in ten days.

Decametre; see DECA- 2.

Decamp (dĭkæ·mp), *v.* 1676. [– Fr. *décamper*, f. *dé-* (DE- I. 6) + *camp* camp. Cf. DISCAMP.] **1.** *intr.* (*Mil.*) To break up a camp; to remove from a camping-place. Hence *gen.* **2.** To go away promptly; to take oneself off 1751. Also *fig.* ¶**3.** *catachr.* To camp 1698.

2. Probably the rascal is decamped; and where is your remedy? 1792.

Deca·mpment. 1706. [– Fr. *décampement*; see prec., -MENT.] The raising of a camp; a prompt departure.

Decan (de·kăn). ME. [– late L. *decanus*; see DEAN[1].] †**1.** A ruler of ten 1569. **2.** *Astrol.* The ruler of ten parts, or ten degrees, of a zodiacal sign; also this division itself 1588. †**3.** = DEAN[1]. –1538.

Decanal (dĭkēⁱ·năl), *a.* 1707. [f. med.L. *decanalis*; see prec., -AL[1].] **1.** Of or pertaining to a dean or deanery. **2.** Applied to the south side of the choir, on which the dean usually sits 1792.

2. On the D. or Southern side 1877.

†**De·canate.** 1647. [f. med.L. *decanatus*; see DECAN, -ATE[1].] *Astrol.* One third part, or ten degrees, of each zodiacal sign; = FACE, q.v. –1696.

‖**Deca·ndria.** 1775. [mod. Bot. L. (Linnæus), f. Gr. δέκα ten + ἀνδρ- man (= male organ).] *Bot.* A Linnæan class of plants having ten stamens. Hence **Deca·ndrous** *a.* having ten stamens.

Decane (de·kēⁱn). 1875. [f. Gr. δέκα + -ANE 2.] *Chem.* The saturated hydrocarbon $C_{10}H_{22}$; one of the paraffins found in coal-tar.

†**Deca·nery, -ary.** 1538. [f. L. *decanus* + -ERY.] = DEANERY –1647.

Decangular; see DECA- 1.

‖**Decani** (dĭkēⁱ·nəi). 1760. [L., genitive of *decanus* DEAN[1].] Dean's; in phrases *d. side, stall* (of a choir): = DECANAL 2. In *Mus.*, correlative to *cantoris* in antiphonal singing.

Decant (dĭkæ·nt), *v.*[1] 1633. [– med.L. *decanthare* (whence also Fr. *décanter*), f. L.

de- DE- 1 + *canthus* angular lip of a jug – Gr. κανθός corner of the eye.] To pour off (the clear liquid of a solution) gently, so as not to disturb the sediment. **b.** To pour (wine, etc.) from the bottle into a decanter; also, *loosely*, to pour out into a drinking vessel 1730. Also *transf.*

†**Deca·nt**, *v.*[2] 1674. [– L. *decantare*; see next.] = DECANTATE *v.* –1711.

†**Deca·ntate**, *v.* 1542. [– *decantat-*, pa. ppl. stem of L. *decantare* to sing over and over again, f. *de-* DE- I. 3 + *cantare* sing. See -ATE[3].] To sing or say over and over again –1659. So †**Deca·ntate** *pa. pple.* decantated.

Decantation (dīkæntēⁱ·ʃən). 1641. [– Fr. *décantation* or med.L. *decanthatio*, f. as prec.; see -ION.] The action of decanting; *esp.* of pouring off a liquid clear from a deposit.

Decanter (dĭkæ·ntəɹ). 1712. [f. DECANT *v.*[1] + -ER[1].] **1.** One who decants. (Dicts.) 1758. **2.** A vessel used for decanting or receiving decanted liquors: *spec.* a bottle of clear flint or cut glass, with a stopper, in which wine is brought to table, and from which the glasses are filled.

Decaphyllous; see DECA- 1.

Decapitate (dĭkæ·pitēⁱt), *v.* 1611. [– *decapitat-*, pa. ppl. stem of late L. *decapitare*, f. *de-* DE- I. 6 + *caput, capit-* head; see -ATE[3]. Cf. (O)Fr. *décapiter.*] **1.** To cut off the head of; to behead. **2.** *U.S. politics.* To dismiss summarily from office 1872. Hence **Deca·pitator**, one who or that which decapitates.

Decapitation (dĭkæpitēⁱ·ʃən). 1650. [– Fr. *décapitation* or med.L. *decapitatio* (f. as prec.; see -ION), or f. prec. on the analogy of similar pairs.] **1.** The action of decapitating; the being decapitated. **2.** *U.S. politics.* Summary dismissal from office 1869.

Decapod (de·kăpǫd). 1835. [– Fr. *décapode* – mod.L. *Decapoda*; see next.] *Zool.* **A.** *sb.* One of the *Decapoda*; in pl. = next. **B.** *adj.* Belonging to the *Decapoda*.

‖**Decapoda** (dĭkæ·pŏdă), *sb. pl.* [mod.L. (Latreille, 1806), prop. adj. pl. neut. (sc. *animalia*), f. DECA- + Gr. πούς, ποδ- foot.] *Zool.* **1.** The highest order of *Crustacea*, having ten feet or legs; it includes the lobster, crab, cray-fish, shrimp, etc. 1878. **2.** The ten-armed *Cephalopoda* (order *Dibranchiata*), distinguished from the *Octopoda*. Called also *Decacera*. 1851. Hence **Deca·podal** *a.* **Deca·podan** *a.* and *sb.* **Deca·podous** *a.* **Decapo·diform** *a.* having the form of a decapod crustacean.

Deca·rbonate, *v. rare.* 1831. [f. DE- II. 1 + CARBON + -ATE[3]. Cf. Fr. *décarbonater.*] = next.

Decarbonize (dīkā·ɹbŏnəiz), *v.* 1825. [f. DE- II. 1 + CARBON + -IZE.] To deprive of its carbon or carbonic acid. Hence **Decarboniza·tion.**

Deca·rburize, *v.* 1856. [f. DE- II. 1 + †*carbure* + -IZE, after Fr. *décarburer.*] = prec. Hence **Decarburiza·tion.**

Decarch, dek- (de·kaɹk), *sb.* 1656. [– Gr. δεκάρχης (-ος) decurion, f. δέκα ten + ἀρχός leader.] *Gr. Hist.* One of a ruling body of ten.

Decarch, dek- (de·kaɹk), *a.* 1884. [f. Gr. δέκα ten + ἀρχή, beginning, origin.] *Bot.* Proceeding from ten points of origin: said of the primary xylem of the root.

Decarchy, dek- (de·kaɹki). 1638. [– Gr. δεκαρχία; see DECARCH *sb.*, -Y[3].] *Gr. Hist.* = DECADARCHY.

†**Deca·rd**, *v.* 1550. [– Fr. †*décarter*; see DISCARD *v.*] = DISCARD *v.* –1621.

Decastere; see DECA- 2.

Decastich (de·kăstik). *rare.* 1645. [f. Gr. δέκα ten + στίχος verse.] A poem of ten lines.

Decastyle (de·kăstəil), *a.* 1727. [– Gr. δεκάστυλος having ten columns, f. δέκα ten + στῦλος column. Cf. Fr. *décastyle.*] *Archit.* Of a building: Having ten columns in front. Also *sb.* A portico or colonnade of ten columns.

Decasualize (dīkæ·ziuălәiz), *v.* 1907. [f. DE- + CASUAL *a.* + -IZE.] *trans.* To remove the casual element from (labour). So **Deca:sualiza·tion** (1892).

Decasyllabic (dekăsilæ·bik), *a.* (*sb.*) 1771. [f. DECA- + SYLLABIC. Cf. Fr. *décasyllabique.*] Consisting of ten syllables. As *sb.* A line of ten syllables. So **Decasy·llable** *sb.* and *a.*

Decatyl (de·kătil). 1869. [f. Gr. δέκατος tenth + -YL.] *Chem.* = DECYL.

Decay (dĭkēⁱ·), *sb.* 1460. [f. DECAY *v.*] **1.** The process of falling off from a thriving condition; progressive decline; decayed condition. †**b.** *Occas.* = Downfall; *poet.* fall, death –1724. †**2.** Falling off; decrease –1816. **3.** Wasting or wearing away; dilapidation 1523; †*pl.* ruins, debris –1777. **4.** Decline of the vital energy or faculties; †(with *pl.*) effect or mark of decay; †*spec.* phthisis –1818. **5.** The wasting of organic tissue; rotting 1594. †**6.** A cause of decay –1690. †**7.** Arrears. [med.L. *decasus redditus.*] –1546.

1. The d. of a town FROUDE. **3.** Who lets so fair a house fall to d. SHAKS. *Sonn.* xiii. 9. *fig.* Contraction and d. . of a language SAYCE. **6.** My loue was my d. SHAKS. *Sonn.* lxxx.

Decay (dĭkēⁱ·), *v.* 1483. [– (O)Fr. *decair*, byform of *decaoir*, var. of *dechaoir*, *decheoir* (mod. *déchoir*) :– Rom. **decadere*, **decadēre*, for L. *decidere*, f. *de-* DE- 1 + *cadere* to fall.] **I.** *intr.* **1.** To fall off; to deteriorate; †to decrease, dwindle away –1790. **2.** To fall into physical ruin 1494; to rot 1580. **3.** To fall off in vital energy, health, or beauty 1583.

1. Whereby learning. . decaieth STUBBES. Whan the vngodly haue the rule, if [the cite] decayeth COVERDALE *Prov.* 11:11. **2.** As winter fruits grow mild ere they d. POPE.

II. *trans.* †**1.** To cause to fall off, deteriorate, or dwindle –1691. **2.** †To waste or ruin physically –1703; to rot 1616. **3.** To cause to fail in vital energy, health, or beauty 1540.

1. A High Interest decays trade LOCKE. **3.** A. . face more decayed by sorrow than time 1718.

Hence **Decay·able** *a.* **Decay·edness.** **Decay·er**, one who, or that which, causes decay.

Decease (dĭsī·s), *sb.* [ME. *deces*, etc., – (O)Fr. *décès* – L. *decessus* departure, death, f. pa. ppl. stem of *decedere* go away, depart, f. *de-* DE- 2 + *cedere* go.] Departure from life; death. (The common term where the mere legal or civil incidence of death is in question.)

The decesse of one Pope. .and entrance of another 1654.

Decease (dĭsī·s), *v.* ME. [f. prec.] *intr.* To depart from life; to die; *fig.* to CEASE.

If he discesse without heires 1439.

Deceased (dĭsī·st, *poet.* dĭsī·sėd), *ppl. a.* 1489. [f. DECEASE *v.* + -ED[1].] **1.** Dead, 'departed'; *esp.* lately dead, 'late'. **2.** *absol.* †**a.** *pl.* *The d.*: the dead. **b.** The person (lately) dead or whose death is in question. 1625.

†**Dece·de**, *v.* 1655. [– L. *decedere* depart; see DECEASE *sb.*] *intr.* To depart; to secede; to give place, yield –1697.

Decedent (dĭsī·dĕnt). 1599. [– *decedent-*, pres. ppl. stem of L. *decedere* to die; see prec., -ENT.] A deceased person. *U.S.*, chiefly in *Law*.

Deceit (dĭsī·t). ME. [– (O)Fr. *deceit*, f. pa. pple. *deceit* (:– L. *deceptus*) of *deceveir* DECEIVE.] **1.** The action or practice of deceiving; concealment of the truth in order to mislead; deception, fraud, cheating. Used *spec.* in *Law*. **2.** An instance of deception; a device intended to deceive; a trick, stratagem, wile ME. **3.** Deceitfulness ME.

1. By violence? no. . But by d. and lies MILT. *P. L.* v. 243. Accion of desseyte ffor brekynge off promyse 1495. **2.** Venus thought on a d. SWIFT. **3.** Ulexes. . was. .full of desseit ME. Hence **Decei·tless** *a.* free from d. (*rare*).

Deceitful (dĭsī·tfŭl), *a.* 1483. [f. prec. + -FUL.] Full of deceit; given to deceiving; misleading, false. (As said of things often = DECEPTIVE.)

Appearances are d. LYTTON. Hence **Decei·tful-ly** *adv.*, **-ness**.

Deceivable (dĭsī·văb'l), *a.* ME. [– (O)Fr. *décevable*, f. *décevoir*; see DECEIVE, -ABLE.] **1.** *actively.* Having the quality of deceiving. *Obs.* (or *arch.*) **2.** *passively.* Capable of being deceived; fallible. Now *rare.* 1646.

1. D. speech BUNYAN. **2.** An ignorant and d. majority 1841. Hence **Decei:vabi·lity** (*rare*). **Decei·vableness** (now *rare*). †**Decei·vably** *adv.* deceitfully.

†**Deceivance.** ME. [– (O)Fr. *decevance*, f. *deceveir*; see next, -ANCE.] Deceit, deception –1486.

Deceive (dĭsī·v), *v.* ME. [– (O)Fr. *deceivre*, *deçoivre* :– L. *decipere*, f. *de-* DE- 4 + *capere* take, seize; or – *deceiv-*, tonic stem of *deceveir* (mod. *décevoir*) :– Rom. **decipēre.*] **1.** *trans.* To ensnare; to catch by craft; to overreach; to mislead. *Obs.* (or *arch.*) **2.** To cause to believe what is false; to lead into error, delude ME. Also *absol.* **b.** In *pass.* occas. = To be in error ME. †**3.** To be or prove false to; to betray –1658. Also *fig.* †**4.** To overreach; defraud; also with *of* –1761. †**5.** To beguile, wile away (time, etc.) –1841.

1. Giftes the wysest will deceave 1594. **2.** Who [can] d. his mind, whose eye Views all things at one view MILT. *P. L.* II. 189. He was not deceaued in his opinion EDEN. **3.** *fig.* Nor are my hopes deceiv'd 1700. **4.** [He] deceived me of a good sum of money which he owed me 1761. **5.** This while I sung, my sorrows I deceiv'd DRYDEN.

Hence **Decei·ver.** **Decei·vingly** *adv.*

Decelerate (dīse·lĕrēⁱt), *v.* 1899. [f. DE- II. 1, after ACCELERATE.] To diminish the speed (of). **Decelera·tion.** **Dece·lerator.**

Decem-, L. *decem* ten, used in comb., as: **Decemco·state** *a.* [COSTA], having ten ribs. **Decemde·ntate** *a.* [L. *dens*], having ten teeth or points. **Dece·mfid** *a.* [L. *-fidus*], cleft into ten parts. **Decemfo·liate, -fo·liolate** *a.* [L. *folium*, *foliolus*], having ten leaves or leaflets. **De:cemnovena·rian**, a man of the Nineteenth Century. **Dece·mpedal** *a.* [L. *pes, ped-*], (*a*) ten feet in length (*obs.*); (*b*) having ten feet.

December (dĭse·mbəɹ). Abbrev. **Dec.** ME. [– (O)Fr. *décembre* – L. *December*, f. *decem* ten; orig. the tenth month of the Roman year. The meaning of *-ber* is unkn.] The twelfth and last month of the year as now reckoned; that in which the winter solstice occurs in the northern hemisphere. Also *attrib.*

December's snow or July's pride SCOTT.

‖**Decemvir** (dĭse·mvəɹ). 1600. [L., sing. of *decemviri*, orig. *decem viri* ten men.] **1.** *Rom. Antiq.* (*pl.*) A body of ten men acting as a commission; *esp.* the two bodies of magistrates appointed in 451 and 450 B.C. to draw up a code of laws (the laws of the Twelve Tables) who were, during the time, invested with the supreme government of Rome. **b.** *transf.* Any council or ruling body of ten 1615. **c.** *sing.* A member of such a body 1703. Hence **Dece·mviral** *a.* of or pertaining to the decemvirs. **Dece·mvirate**, the office or government of decemvirs; a body of decemvirs.

Dece·nary, *improp.* **dece·nnary.** 1647. [– med.L. *decen(n)arius*, f. *decen(n)a* tithing; see DECENER, -ARY[1].]

A. *adj.* Of or pertaining to a *decena* 1752.

B. *sb.* = med.L. *decena* a tithing.

†**De·cence.** 1678. [– (O)Fr. *décence* – L. *decentia*; see next, -ENCE.] = next –1697.

Decency (dī·sĕnsi). 1567. [– L. *decentia*, f. *decent-* + *-ia*; see DECENT, -Y[3], -ENCY.] †**1.** Appropriateness to the circumstances of the case; fitness, seemliness, propriety; what is appropriate –1762. †**2.** Orderly condition of civil or social life –1705. **3.** Propriety of demeanour; due regard to what is becoming; *esp.* freedom from impropriety 1639; respectability 1751. **4.** *pl.* The observances of decorum; proprieties 1667; the outward requirements of a decent life 1798.

1. His discourse on the scaffold was full of d. and courage HUME. **3.** Immodest words admit of no defence; For want of d. is want of sense ROSCOMMON. To support oneself with d. JOHNSON. **4.** Content to dwell in decencies for ever POPE. Able to command the decencies of life MALTHUS.

Decene (dī·sīn). 1877. [f. Gr. δέκα + -ENE.] *Chem.* The olefine of the decacarbon or DECYL series, $C_{10}H_{20}$. Also called *Decylene*.

†**De·cener.** 1555. [– AFr. *decener*, (O)Fr. *decenier* (mod. *dizenier*), in med.L. *decen(n)arius*; see DECENARY, -ER[2].] **1.** One in command of ten soldiers –1627. **2.** The head of a *decena* or tithing; a borsholder; **b.** A member of a tithing –1752.

Decennary (dĭse·nări). 1822. [f. as DECENNIAL; see -ARY[1].] *adj.* DECENNIAL 1855. *sb.* A decennium.

Decennary; see DECENARY.

Decennial (dĭse·niăl). 1656. [f. L. *decennium* decade, f. *decennis*, f. *decem* ten + *annus* year; see -AL[1], -IAL.]

A. *adj.* Of or pertaining to a period of ten years; (of persons) holding office for ten years; var. †**Dece·nnal.** Hence **Dece·nnially** *adv.*

B. *sb.* A decennial anniversary. *U.S.*

‖**Decennium** (dĭse·niŏm). Pl. **-ia.** 1685. [L., f. *decennis* of ten years; see prec.] A decade (of years). Also **Dece·nniad** [-AD 1]. In the last decennia of the last century PUSEY.

†**Decennoval** (dĭse·nŏvăl), *a.* 1681. [– late L. *decennovalis*, f. *decemnovem* nineteen; see -AL[1].] Of or pertaining to nineteen (years) –1694. So †**Dece·nnovary,** †**Decennove·n(n)al.**

Decent (dī·sĕnt), *a.* 1539. [– Fr. *décent* or *decent-*, pres. ppl. stem of L. *decēre* be fitting; see -ENT.] **1.** Becoming, suitable, or proper to the circumstances of the case; seemly (*Obs.* or *arch.*). †**2.** Comely, handsome –1725. **3.** In accordance with propriety or good taste; *esp.* free from immodesty or obscenity 1545. **4.** Respectable 1696. **5.** Tolerable, passable; good enough in its way 1711. **6.** quasi-*adv.* Decently 1715.

1. A d. solemnity EVELYN. **2.** D. and Beautifull Arches BACON. **3.** To Praise a Mans selfe, cannot be D. BACON. Men of d. and honourable lives CHATHAM. **4.** A d. well-behaved man 1771. A d. suit of clothes 1843. **5.** Ability to write d. Latin prose 1894. Hence **De·cent-ly** *adv.*, †**-ness.**

Decentralization (dĭse:ntrăləizēⁱ·ʃən). 1846. [f. next + -ATION.] The action or fact of decentralizing; decentralized condition.

Decentralize (dĭse·ntrăləiz), *v.* 1851. [See DE- II. 1.] *trans.* To undo the centralization of; to distribute administrative powers, etc., which have been concentrated in a single centre.

What you want is to d. your Government BRIGHT.

Decephalize (dĭse·făləiz), *v.* 1861. [Back-formation from *decephalization*; see DE- II. 1,-IZE. Cf. CEPHALIZATION.] *Biol.* To reverse the cephalization of; to reduce, degrade, or simplify the parts of the head of (an animal). **Decephaliza·tion.**

†**Dece·ptible,** *a.* 1646. [– Fr. †*déceptible* or med.L. *deceptibilis*, f. *decept-*; see next, -IBLE.] Apt to be deceived. Hence **Decepti·bi·lity.**

Deception (dĭse·pʃən). ME. [– (O)Fr. *déception* or late L. *deceptio*, f. *decept-*, pa. ppl. stem of L. *decipere*; see DECEIVE, -ION.] **1.** The action of deceiving or cheating; deceived condition. **2.** That which deceives; a piece of trickery; a cheat, sham 1794.

1. D.—a principal ingredient in happiness HOR. SMITH. **2.** There is some d., some trick 1794.

Deceptious (dĭse·pʃəs), *a.* Now *rare.* 1606. [– OFr. *deceptieus* or late L. *deceptiosus*, f. as prec.; see -IOUS.] That tends to deceive, cheat, or mislead.

D. terms. 1. In the war department,—*honour* and *glory* BENTHAM. Hence †**Dece·ptiously** *adv.* So **Decepti·tious** *a.* (Bentham.)

Deceptive (dĭse·ptiv), *a.* 1611. [– OFr. *deceptif, -ive* or late L. *deceptivus*, f. as prec.; see -IVE.] Apt or tending to deceive, having the character of deceiving.

A mere shallow and d. nonentity CARLYLE.

Phr. *D. cadence* (Mus.): false or interrupted cadence: see FALSE *a.* Hence **Dece·ptive-ly** *adv.*, **-ness,** d. quality. **Decepti·vity,** deceptiveness; *concr.* a sham.

†**Dece·ptory,** *a.* ME. [– late L. *deceptorius*, f. as prec.; see -ORY[2].] Apt to deceive. (Dicts.)

Decern (dĭsɔ̄·ɹn), *v.* ME. [– (O)Fr. *décerner* – L. *decernere* decide, pronounce a decision, f. *de-* DE- I. 2 + *cernere* separate, sift. See DISCERN.] †**1.** *trans.* To decide, determine –1619. **2.** *trans.* To decree by judicial sentence. Now techn. in *Sc. Law.* 1460. Also *intr.* **3.** *trans.* To distinguish; to discern 1535. Hence †**Dece·rnment.**

Decerniture (dĭsɔ̄·ɹnitiuɹ). 1632. [irreg. f. prec., after such pairs as *invest, investiture.*] *Sc. Law.* The action of decerning; a DECREE of a (Scotch) court.

†**Dece·rp,** *v.* Pa. pple. **decerped, decerpt.** 1531. [– L. *decerpere* pluck off, f. *de-* DE- I. 2 + *carpere* pluck. Cf. DISCERP.] To pluck off or out; to excerpt –1678. var. †**Dece·rpt** *v.* So †**Dece·rption** (*rare*), a cropping off, that which is cropped off.

†**Decerta·tion.** 1635. [– L. *decertatio*, f. *decertat-*, pa. ppl. stem of *decertare*; f. *de-* DE- I. 3 + *certare* contend; see -ION.] Contention, strife, contest; dispute –1661.

Decession (dĭse·ʃən). Now *rare.* 1606. [– L. *decessio*, f. *decess-*, pa. ppl. stem of *decedere* depart, f. *de-* DE- I. 2 + *cedere* go; see -ION. Cf. (O)Fr. *decession.*] Departure, secession; diminution (opp. to *accession*).

†**Dece·ssor.** [– L. *decessor* a retiring officer, in late L. 'predecessor', f. as prec.; see -OR 2.] = PREDECESSOR. Jer. Taylor.

†**Decha·rm,** *v.* 16.. [– Fr. †*décharmer*, f. *dé-* DE- I. 6 + *charmer* CHARM *v.*[1]] To undo the effect of (a charm); to disenchant.

De-chri·stianize, *v.* 1834. [DE- II. 1.] To deprive or divest of its Christian character.

Deci- (desi), short f. L. *decimus* tenth, an initial element in names of measures and weights in the French metric system which are one-tenth of the standard unit. (Cf. DECA-.) Thus **Décigramme, -gram, Décilitre, Décimètre, Décistère,** the tenth part of the *gramme, litre, mètre,* and *stère* respectively. (The accents are usually omitted in Eng.)

Decide (dĭsəi·d), *v.* ME. [– Fr. *décider* or L. *decidere* cut off, determine, f. *de-* DE- I. 2 + *cædere* cut.] **1.** *trans.* To determine (a question, controversy, or cause) by giving the victory to one side or the other; to settle, resolve. **2.** To bring to a decision 1710. **3.** *absol.* or *intr.* To settle a question in dispute; to pronounce a final judgement 1732. **4.** *intr.* To come to a conclusion; determine, resolve 1830. †**5.** *trans.* To cut off. FULLER.

1. To the place of difference call the Swords Which must d. it 2 *Hen. IV*, IV. i. 182. Advocates plead causes, and judges d. them BARROW. **3.** Who shall d., when Doctors disagree POPE. **4.** To d. on a course 1894. Hence **Deci·dingly** *adv.*

Decided (dĭsəi·dĕd), *ppl. a.* 1790. [f. prec. + -ED[1].] **1.** Settled; definite; unquestionable. **2.** Resolute, determined 1790.

1. A most d. and complete success DICKENS. **2.** He found them vacillating, he left them d. ALISON. Hence **Deci·ded-ly** *adv.*, **-ness.**

†**Deci·dement.** *rare.* [f. as prec. + -MENT.] = DECISION. Fletcher.

†**Decidence** (de·sidĕns). 1646. [– med.L. *decidentia* diminution, loss, f. as next; see -ENCE.] Falling off –1684.

†**De·cident,** *a.* 1674. [– *decident-*, pres. ppl. stem of L. *decidere*, f. *de-* DE- I. 1, 2 + *cadere* to fall; see -ENT.] Falling.

‖**Decidua** (dĭsi·diu̦ă). 1785. [mod.L. *decidua* (sc. *membrana*), subst. use of fem. sing. of L. *deciduus* DECIDUOUS.] *Phys.* The lining membrane of the impregnated uterus in certain Mammalia; it forms the external envelope of the ovum, and is cast off at parturition (whence the name). Also *transf.* Hence **Deci·dual** *a.* of or pertaining to the d.

Deci·duary, *a. rare.* [f. as DECIDUOUS + -ARY[1].] Deciduous. DARWIN.

‖**Deciduata** (dĭsi:diu̦ēⁱ·tă), *sb. pl.* 1879. [mod.L., subst. use of n. pl. of adj. *deciduatus*, f. DECIDUA; see -ATE[2].] *Zool.* A term comprising all placental Mammalia which possess a decidua.

Deciduate (dĭsi·diu̦ĕt), *a.* 1868. [– mod.L. *deciduatus*; see prec., -ATE[2].] *Zool.* Possessing a decidua; of the nature of a decidua.

Decidu·ity. *rare.* 1846. [f. as next + -ITY.] Deciduousness.

Deciduous (dĭsi·diu̦əs), *a.* 1656. [f. L. *deciduus* (f. *decidere* fall down or off, f. *de-* DE- 2 + *cadere* fall) + -OUS; see -UOUS.] †**1.** Falling down or off; declining (*rare*). **2.** *Bot., Zool.*, etc. Of leaves, petals, teeth, horns, etc.: Falling off or shed at a particular time, season, or stage of growth. Opp. to *persistent* or *permanent.* 1688. Of a tree or shrub: That sheds its leaves every year; opp. to *evergreen* 1778. Of insects: That shed their wings after copulation, as the females of ants, etc. *Phys.* = Decidual 1829. **3.** *fig.* Transitory 1811. Hence **Deci·duous-ly** *adv.*, **-ness.**

Decigram, -gramme; see DECI-.

De·cil, decile. 1674. [corresp. to Fr. †*décile*, prob. – med.L. **decilis* f. L. *decem* ten; cf. Fr. *sextil* SEXTILE.] *Astrol.* The aspect of two planets when distant from each other a tenth part of the zodiac or 36 degrees.

Decilitre; see DECI-.

Decillion (dĭsi·lyən). 1845. [f. DECI-, after *million.*] The tenth power of a million; = 1 followed by 60 ciphers. Hence **Deci·llionth** *a.* and *sb.*

‖**Decima** (de·simă). 1630. [L., for *decima pars.*] **1.** A tenth part; a tax of one-tenth. **2.** *Mus.* The interval of a tenth (*rare*). var. †**De·cim** (in sense 1).

Decimal (de·simăl). 1608. [– mod.L. *decimalis*, f. L. *decimus* tenth, f. *decem* ten; see -AL[1].]

A. *adj.* **1.** Relating to tenth parts, or to the number ten; proceeding by tens. †**2.** Relating to tithes –1662.

1. *D. fraction* (†*number*): a fraction whose denominator is some power of ten (10, 100, 1000, etc.); *spec.* a fraction expressed by figures written to the right of the units figure after a dot (the *d. point*), and denoting respectively so many tenths, hundredths, thousandths, etc. The number of *d. places* is the number of figures after the d. point. *D. coinage* or *currency*: a monetary system in which each successive denomination is ten times the value of that next below it; so *d. system* of weights and measures.

B. *sb.* †**1.** A tenth part –1669. **2.** A decimal fraction (see above); in *pl.* often = the arithmetic of decimal fractions, decimal arithmetic 1651. Also *fig.*

2. *Recurring d.*: one in which one or more decimal figures are continually repeated; called *repeating* when one figure recurs as ·111 etc., written $\dot{1}$ (= $\frac{1}{9}$), and *circulating* when two or more recur as $\dot{1}4285\dot{7}$ (= $\frac{1}{7}$).

Hence **De·cimalism,** a d. system or theory. **De·cimalist,** an advocate of decimalism (in coinage, or weights and measures). **De·cimalize** *v.* to reduce to a d. system; whence **De·cimalization. De·cimally** *adv.* by tens or tenths; into tenths; in the form of a d. fraction.

Decimate (de·simeⁱt), *v.* 1600. [– *decimat-*, pa. ppl. stem of L. *decimare*, f. *decimus* tenth; see prec., -ATE[3].] †**1.** To exact a tenth or a tithe from –1845. **2.** *Milit.* To select by lot and put to death one in every ten of. 1600. **3.** *loosely.* To destroy a large proportion of 1663.

2. To d. a large body of mutineers MACAULAY. **3.** Typhus fever decimated the school C. BRONTË.

Decimation (desimēⁱ·ʃən). 1549. [– late L. *decimatio*, f. as prec.; see -ION.] **1.** The exaction of tithes, or of a tax of one-tenth; the tax itself. **2.** *Milit.* The selection by lot of one man in every ten as for punishment in cases of mutiny, etc. 1580. **3.** Destruction of a large proportion 1682.

3. The d. which their riot brought upon them 1856.

Decimator, -er (de·simeⁱtəɹ). 1862. [f. DECIMATE *v.* + -OR 2, -ER[1].] One who decimates.

†**De·cime**[1]. 1611. [– med.L. *decima* tenth, tithe, tithing.] A tithing as a division of the *hundred* in the English counties –1630.

‖**Décime**[2] (desī·m). 1810. [Fr., f. L. *decimus* tenth.] A French coin, one-tenth of a franc.

Decimestrial (desime·striăl), *a. rare.* 1842. [f. *decimestris*, var. of late L. *decemmestris*, + -AL[1].] Consisting of ten months, as the *d. year.*

Decimeter, -metre; see DECI-.

De·cimo-se·xto. ? *Obs.* 1599. [For L. *sexto-decimo* sixteenth (orig. with *in*).] The size of a book, or of the page of a book, in which each leaf is one-sixteenth of a full sheet; prop. SEXTO-DECIMO (abbrev. 16mo). Also *fig.*

Decine. 1875. [f. DECYL by substitution of *-ine* in ETHINE.] *Chem.* See DECYL.

Decipher (dĭsəi·fəɹ), *v.* 1528. [f. DE- I. 6 + CIPHER *v.*, after Fr. *déchiffrer.*] **1.** To convert (cipher) into ordinary writing; to interpret by means of the key 1545. **2.** *transf.* To make out the meaning of (anything obscure) 1605. †**3.** To find out, detect –1599. †**4.** To reveal, make known; to give the key to –1793. †**5.** To represent verbally, pictorially, or by some kind of cipher –1753.

2. To d. bad hand-writing BAIN, hieroglyphics PRESCOTT, an allusion SPURGEON. **3.** You are both decipherd..For villaines *Tit. A.* IV. ii. 8.

Hence **Deci·pher** *sb.* the translation of a cipher. **Deci·pherable** *a.* **Deci·pherer,** one who deciphers (formerly the title of a government official). **Deci·pherment,** deciphering; *esp.* interpretation of hieroglyphics or of obscure inscriptions.

Decipium (dĭsi·piŏm). [mod. irreg. f. L. *decipere*, with ending of *sodium*, etc.] *Chem.* A supposed rare metallic element of the cerium earth group. WATTS.

†**Deci·se**, *v.* 1538. [– *decis-*, pa. ppl. stem of L. *decidere* DECIDE; cf. *excise, incise*.] = DECIDE *v.* –1662. So †**Deci·sor, -er.**

Decision (dĭsi·ʒən). 1490. [–(O)Fr. *décision* or L. *decisio*, f. as prec.; see -ION.] **1.** The action of deciding (a contest, question, etc.); settlement, determination; (with *a* and *pl.*) a conclusion, judgement: *esp.* one formally pronounced in a court of law 1552. **2.** The making up of one's mind; a resolution 1886. **3.** As a quality: Determination, firmness, decidedness of character 1781. †**4.** Cutting off, separation –1659.

1. The decisions of the clergy were more satisfactory to themselves than to the laity FROUDE. **3.** We want courage and d. of mind BURKE. Hence **Deci·sional** *a.* of, or of the nature of, a d. (*rare*).

Decisive (dĭsəi·siv), *a.* 1611. [– Fr. *décisif, -ive* – med.L. *decisivus*, f. as prec.; see -IVE.] **1.** Having the quality of deciding or determining; conclusive, determinative. **2.** = DECIDED 2. 1736. **3.** = DECIDED 1. 1794.

1. That sure d. dart CRASHAW. D. experiments 1794. **2.** Not an age of d. thought or d. action MAX-MÜLLER. **3.** A d. leaning towards what is most simple I. TAYLOR. Hence **Deci·sive-ly** *adv.*, **-ness.**

Decistere; see DECI-.

Decitizenize; see DE- II. 1 and *citizenize*.

Decivilize (dĭsi·viləiz), *v.* 1859. [DE- II. 1.] To degrade from a civilized condition.

The decivilizing effect of the wars 1889.

Deck (dek), *sb.* 1466. [– MDu. *dec* roof, covering, cloak :– Gmc. **þakjam* THATCH *sb.* The nautical sense (1495, Sandahl) appears to be an Eng. development.] †**1.** A covering –1712. **2.** *Naut.* A platform extending from side to side of a ship or part of a ship, covering in the space below, and also serving as a floor 1513. **3.** In U.S. 'A passenger-car roof' (*Standard Dict.*). **b.** The floor of a tramcar or omnibus 1903; also, of a pier, landing-stage, or jetty 1872. **4.** A pack of cards. Now *dial.* and *U.S.* 1593. †**5.** A pile of things laid flat upon each other –1673.

2. The largest ships of the line had *main-d.*, *middle* and *lower d.*; also the *upper* or *spar-d.*, extending from stem to stern over the main-d., and the *orlop d.* (which carried no guns) below the lower d.; they had also a *poop-d.*, or short d. in the after part of the ship above the spar-d., and sometimes a *forecastle d.*, or similar short d. in the fore-part of the ship, sometimes retained in merchant ships and called the *top-gallant forecastle*. See also HALF-DECK, HURRICANE-*deck*, QUARTER-DECK, etc. (O.E.D.). Phr. BETWEEN-DECKS, *on d.*, *under deck(s; to clear, sweep the decks* (see CLEAR *v.*, SWEEP *v.*). **4.** 3 *Hen. VI*, v. i. 44.

Comb. (from sense 2): **d.-beam,** one of the strong transverse beams supporting the d.; **-bridge,** (*a*) a narrow platform above and across the d. of a steamer amidships; (*b*) a bridge in which the roadway is laid on the top of the truss (opp. to *through bridge*); **-chair,** a folding cane-panelled chair, usu. with adjustable leg rest, used in passenger steamers; also, a hammock chair; **-flats** (see FLAT *sb.*); **-hand,** a 'hand' employed on the d. of a vessel; **-house,** a room erected on the d. of a ship; **-plate,** a plate around the chimney of a marine-engine furnace to prevent contact with the wood of the d.; **-tennis,** a game played on the deck of a ship by tossing a ring or quoit of rubber, rope, etc. back and forth over a net.

Deck (dek), *v.* 1513. [– (M)Du. *dekken* cover = OE. *þeccan* cover, roof over, THATCH.] †**1.** *trans.* To cover; *esp.* to clothe –1600. **2.** To cover or clothe with what beautifies; to array, attire, adorn 1514. †**3.** To fit out, equip –1548. **4.** *Naut.* To furnish with a deck 1624.

2. Thou deckest thyself with light as with a garment COVERDALE *Ps.* 103:2. Daisies d. the green CLARE. **4.** Phr. *To d. in, over*: to cover in with the deck, in ship-building. Hence **Decked** *ppl. a.* adorned, set out; having a deck or decks. **De·cker**[1], one who decks or adorns. **De·cking** *vbl. sb.* the action of the vb.; adornment; planking or flooring forming a deck.

Decker[2] (de·kəɹ). 1781. [f. DECK *sb.* + -ER[1] 1.] **1.** A vessel having (so many) decks, as in *two-decker*, etc. Also *transf.* of an oven. **2.** A deck-hand; also a deck-passenger (*colloq.*) 1800.

Deckle (dek'l). Also **deckel.** 1810. [– G. *deckel*, dim. of *decke* covering; cf. -LE.] *Paper-making.* A thin rectangular frame of wood fitting close upon a hand mould, or a continuous band or strap on either side of the apron in a paper-machine, which confines the pulp and determines the size or width of the sheet.

Comb.: **d. edge,** the rough uncut edge of a sheet of paper, formed by the d.; also *attrib.* = next; **-edged** *a.*

Declaim (dĭklēⁱ·m), *v.* late ME. [– Fr. *déclamer* or L. *declamare*; see DE- I. 3, CLAIM *v.*] **1.** *intr.* To speak aloud with rhetorical expression; to make a speech on a set subject as an exercise in elocution. **b.** To recite with elocutionary effect (chiefly U.S.). 1552. **2.** To speak aloud in an impassioned manner; to harangue 1735. †**3.** *trans.* To discuss aloud. CHAUCER. **4.** To utter aloud or repeat rhetorically 1577.

1. Like a schoolboy declaiming EMERSON. **2.** Instead of giving a reason you d. BERKELEY. To d. against the growth of luxury STEPHEN. **4.** To d. a passage with too much emphasis SCOTT. Hence **Declai·mant** (*rare*), **Declai·mer,** one who declaims; one who harangues.

Declamation (deklămēⁱ·ʃən). 1523. [– Fr. *déclamation* or L. *declamatio*, f. *declamat-*, pa. ppl. stem of *declamare*; see prec., -ION.] **1.** The action or art of declaiming (see DECLAIM *v.* 1) 1552. **2.** A set speech in rhetorical elocution 1523. **3.** Speaking in an impassioned oratorical manner; *spec.* in singing 1614. **4.** A harangue 1594.

1. He publicly professed the arts of rhetoric and d. GIBBON. **2.** Theams more fit for schollars declamations 1573. **3.** In the heat of d. JOHNSON. **4.** An insolent d...full of fury and indecent invectives 1715.

De·clamator. ME. [– L. *declamator*, f. as prec.; see -OR 2.] A declaimer –1710.

Declamatory (dĭklæ·mătəri), *a.* 1581. [– L. *declamatorius*, f. as prec.; see -ORY[2].] Of or pertaining to rhetorical declaiming; of the nature of, or characterized by, declamation; †denunciatory 1589.

A d. theme WOTTON, style 1807, passage STEPHEN.

†**Decla·rable,** *a.* 1646. [f. DECLARE + -ABLE.] Capable of being declared –1678.

Declarant (dĭklēᵊ·rănt). 1681. [– Fr. *déclarant*, pres. pple. of *déclarer* DECLARE; see -ANT[1].] One who makes a declaration; *esp.* in *Law*.

Declaration (deklărēⁱ·ʃən). ME. [– L. *declaratio*, f. *declarat-*, pa. ppl. stem of *declarare* DECLARE; see -ION.] †**1.** The action of making clear; elucidation –1656. †**2.** The setting forth of a topic; exposition –1642. **3.** The action of setting forth or announcing openly, explicitly, or formally; positive statement or assertion ME. **4.** The action of declaring *for* or *against* 1736. **5.** A proclamation as embodied in a document, instrument, or public act 1659. **6.** *Law.* **a.** The plaintiff's statement of claim in an action; the writing in which this is made 1483. **b.** A simple affirmation (as opp. to an *oath*) 1834. **c.** The creation or acknowledgement of a *trust* or *use* in some form of writing; any writing containing a trust 1626. **7.** *Bezique.* The act of declaring a score by placing certain cards on the table 1870. **b.** *Bridge.* (Cf. DECLARE *v.* 8 b.) 1905.

3. Crosses to be sett vpon mens dores for the declaracion of the plage 1547. Phr. *D. of war, peace, the poll.* **5.** *D. of Indulgence*: see INDULGENCE. *D. of Rights*: see RIGHT. *D. of Independence*: the public act by which the American Continental Congress, on July 4th, 1776, declared the North American colonies to be free and independent of Great Britain; the document embodying this.

Declarative (dĭklæ·rătiv), *a.* 1536. [– (O)Fr. *déclaratif, -ive* or L. *declarativus*, f. as prec.; see -IVE.] Characterized by declaring (in the various senses of the vb.).

D. promises 1646, acts, statutes 1661. The times were too tender to endure them to be d. on either part N. BACON. Hence **Decla·ratively** *adv.*

Declarator (dĭklæ·rătəɹ). *Sc.* 1567. [repr. Fr. *déclaratoire* (*acte, sentence déclaratoire*); see DECLARATORY.] (*Action of*) *d.* (Sc. Law): a form of action in which something is prayed to be declared judicially, the legal consequences being left to follow as of course.

Declaratory (dĭklæ·rătəri). 1571. [– med.L. *declaratorius*, f. L. *declarator*, f. *declarat-*, pa. ppl. stem of *declarare* DECLARE; see -ORY[2].] Having the nature or form of a declaration; affirmatory. †*sb.* A declaration –1691.

D. act or *statute*: one which declares or explains what the existing law is. *D. action* (Sc. Law) = Action of DECLARATOR. Hence **Decla·ratorily** *adv.*

Declare (dĭklēᵊ·ɹ), *v.* ME. [– L. *declarare* make clear, f. *de-* DE- I. 3 + *clarare*, f. *clarus* clear. Cf. Fr. *déclarer*.] †**1.** *trans.* To make clear or plain –1691. †**2.** To make known; to state in detail; to recount, relate –1703. †**3.** *intr.* To make relation *of* –1533. **4.** *trans.* Of things: To manifest, prove ME. **5.** To make known or state publicly, formally, or in explicit terms ME. **b.** *Cricket.* To close an innings before the usual ten wickets have fallen 1897. **6.** To state emphatically, to aver 1709. **7.** *Law. intr.* To make a statement of claim as plaintiff in an action 1512. **b.** *trans.* To make a statement constituting or acknowledging a trust or use 1677. **c.** To make a full statement of or as to goods liable to duty 1714. **8.** *Bezique.* To declare a score by laying down certain cards on the table 1870. **b.** *Bridge.* To name the trump suit or call 'no trumps' 1905.

4. The heavens d. the glory of God *Ps.* 19:1. **5.** To d. an intention 1827, oneself a member of the Church of Rome MACAULAY. *To d. war* 1552, *a dividend* 1894.

Phrases. *To d. oneself*: to avow one's opinions or intentions; to reveal one's true character, etc.; also *fig.* of things. *To d. for* (*in favour of*) or *against*: to avow one's opinion, or resolution to act, for or against. *To d. off*: to withdraw, back out (*colloq.*).

Hence **Decla·red-ly** *adv.*, **-ness.** †**Decla·rement,** declaration. **Decla·rer,** one who or that which declares; one who makes or signs a declaration.

‖**Déclassé** (deklase). 1887. [Fr., pa. pple.] Degraded from one's social class.

Declension (dĭkle·nʃən). 1565. [repr. (O)Fr. *déclinaison*, f. *décliner* DECLINE *v.* after L. *declinatio* DECLINATION; retraction of the stress to the second syllable (cf. COMPARISON) produced *declynsone* (XV) and *declenson* (XV–XVI), the termination being subseq. assim. to *-sion*.] **1.** The action or state of declining; slope, inclination; the dip of the magnetic needle (= DECLINATION). ? *Obs.* 1640. **2.** *fig.* Declining from a standard; falling away, apostacy 1594. **3.** Declining into a lower condition 1602; sunken condition 1642. **4.** *Gram.* **a.** Inflexion of a noun, adjective, or pronoun, constituting its different cases (see CASE *sb.*[1]). **b.** Each of the classes into which nouns are grouped according to their inflexions. **c.** The action of declining, *i.e.* setting forth in order the different cases of a noun, etc. 1565. **5.** Courteous refusal (*rare*) 1817.

1. The d. of the land from that place to the sea T. BURNET. **2.** A d. from his own rules of life CLARENDON. **3.** Symptoms of d. or decay MAURICE. Hence **Decle·nsional** *a.* of or belonging to (grammatical) d.

Declinable (dĭkləi·năb'l), *a.* 1530. [–(O)Fr. *déclinable* or late L. *declinabilis*, f. *declinare* to DECLINE; see -ABLE.] *Gram.* Capable of being declined; having case-inflexions.

D. adjectives of number ROBY. var. †**Decli·nal** *a.* (*rare*).

Declinate (de·klinĕt), *a.* 1810. [– L. *declinatus*, pa. pple. of *declinare* DECLINE *v.*; see -ATE[2].] *Bot.* Inclined downwards or to one side. So †**De·clinated** *a.*

Declination (deklinēⁱ·ʃən). ME. [– L. *declinatio* – *declinat-*, pa. ppl. stem of *declinare* DECLINE *v.*; see -ION.] †**1.** = DECLENSION 2. –1814. †**2.** A leaning (away *from* or *towards*); a mental bias –1622. **3.** A leaning downwards; inclination from the vertical or horizontal position 1594. †**4.** A sinking into a lower position; descent towards setting –1630. †**5.** The gradual falling off from a condition of prosperity or vigour; decline; decay –1799. **6.** Non-acceptance; courteous refusal. ? *Obs.* 1612. **7.** *Astron.* The angular distance of a heavenly body (north or south) from the celestial equator: corresp. to terrestrial *latitude*. (The most usual sense.) ME. **8.** Of the magnetic needle: †**a.** The DIP; **b.** The deviation from the true north and south line, *esp.* the angular measure of this; also called VARIATION 1635. **9.** *Dialling.* Of a vertical plane: The angular measure of its deviation from the prime vertical (if reckoned from east to west), or from the meridian (if reckoned from north to south) 1593. †**10.** *Gram.* = DECLENSION 4. –1751.

1. The declinations from Religion BACON. **2.** The queen's d. from marriage STOW. **3.** A d. of the Antiquary's stiff backbone SCOTT. **5.** The d. of antient Learning 1673. Hence **Declina·tional** *a.*

Declinator (de·klinēⁱtəɹ). 1606. [f. as prec. + -OR 2; cf. Fr. *déclinateur* in sense 2.] †**1.** One who declines; a dissentient –1670. **2.** *Dialling.* An instrument for determining the declination of planes 1727.

Declinatory (dĭkləi·nătəri). 1673. [– med.L. *declinatorius* (f. as prec.; see -ORY²) in the legal expression *exceptio declinatoria*; cf. (O)Fr. *déclinatoire.*]

A. *adj.* That declines (sense II. 3); expressing refusal.

D. plea (Law): a plea of sanctuary, also pleading benefit of clergy before trial or conviction; abolished in 1826.

B. *sb.* **1.** *Law.* A declinatory plea 1693. †**2.** = DECLINATOR 2. –1751.

Declinature (dĭkləi·nătiŭɹ). 1637. [f. as prec. + -URE; in sense 1 perh. a 'rectification' of †*declinator* (*Sc. Law*) in same sense.] **1.** *Sc. Law.* A formal plea declining to admit the jurisdiction of a court or tribunal. **2.** *gen.* The action of declining; courteous refusal 1842.

Decline (dĭkləi·n), *sb.* ME. [f. the vb.; cf. (O)Fr. *déclin.*] **1.** The process of declining or sinking to a weaker or inferior condition; falling off, decay, diminution, deterioration. **b.** A gradual failure of the physical powers 1770. **c.** Any wasting disease; *esp.* tubercular phthisis 1783. **2.** Of the sun or day: The action of sinking towards its setting or close ME. **3.** A downward incline, a slope (*rare*) 1538.

1. The d. of my daughter's health GOLDSM. The d. of life STEELE. A d. in prices (*mod.*). The D. and Fall of the Roman Empire GIBBON. **c.** He fell into a rapid d., and died prematurely S. AUSTIN.

Decline (dĭkləi·n), *v.* ME. [–(O)Fr. *décliner* – L. *declinare*, f. *de-* DE- I. 2 + *clinare* to bend.]

I. *intr.* †**1.** To turn or bend aside; to deviate; to turn away –1839. †**2.** To have DECLINATION (senses 7–9) –1726. †**3.** *fig.* To turn aside in conduct; *esp.* to swerve (from rectitude, etc.) –1749. †**4.** *fig.* To lean *to* –1671. **5.** To slant or slope downward ME. **6.** To bend down ME. †**7.** To descend, fall –1602. **8.** Of the sun, etc.: To sink towards setting ME. Also *transf.* of the day, etc., and *fig.* of one's life. **9.** *fig.* To fall morally or in dignity, to sink. (Now only *lit.* and after *Haml.* I. v. 50.) ME. **10.** *fig.* To fall off in vigour or vitality; to decay, diminish, decrease; to deteriorate 1530.

3. Yet doe I not d. from thy testimonies *Ps.* 119:157. **5.** The ground on each side declining gently SIR T. HERBERT. **7.** *Haml.* II. ii. 500. **8.** The Sun declines, day ancient grows 1607. **10.** Who's like to rise, Who thriues, and who declines SHAKS.

II. *trans.* †**1.** To turn aside (*lit.* and *fig.*) –1750. †**2.** To turn aside from. (Merged in 3.) –1761. **3.** Not to consent or engage in, practise, or do 1631. **b.** Not to consent or agree to *doing*, or *to do*; hence practically = REFUSE: but a milder expression. (Constr. *vbl. sb.*, *inf.*; also *absol.* or *intr.*) 1691. **c.** Not to accept (something offered); implying polite refusal 1712. **4.** *Sc. Law.* To refuse or object to the jurisdiction of (a judge or court) 1450. †**5.** To abandon (a practice) –1749. **6.** To bend down, bow ME. †**7.** To depress (*lit.* and *fig.*) –1790. **8.** To cause to slant or slope 1578. †**9.** To undervalue –1649. **10.** *Gram.* To inflect or recite in order the cases (or forms) of (nouns, adjectives, pronouns, or, loosely, verbs) ME.; †*transf.* to recite in definite order –1627.

1. Counterfeiting a woman, thereby to d. suspicion HOLLAND. **2.** Despairing to d. their Fate KEN. **3.** To d. newspaper controversy T. JEFFERSON. **b.** I declined satisfying his curiosity CARLYLE. Shall we accept or d. 1894. **c.** The squire said they could not decently d. his visit SMOLLETT. **10.** *transf.* SHAKS. *Tr. & Cr.* II. iii. 55.

Hence **Decli·ned** *ppl. a.* **Decli·ner**, one who, or that which, declines.

Declinograph (dĭkləi·nograf). 1883. [irreg. f. L. *declinare* (as etymon of *declination*) + -GRAPH.] *Astr.* An instrument for automatically recording the declination of stars with a filar micrometer.

Declinometer (deklinǫ·mĭtəɹ). 1858. [irreg. f. as prec. + -METER.] **1.** *Magn.* An instrument for measuring the variation of the magnetic needle. **2.** *Astr.* An instrument for observing and registering declination 1883.

†**Declive** (dĭkləi·v), *a.* 1635. [– Fr. *déclive* – L. *declivis* sloping downward, f. *de-* DE- I. 1 + *clivus* slope.] Sloping downwards –1669.

Declivitous (dĭkli·vĭtəs), *a.* 1799. [f. DECLIVITY + -OUS.] Having a (considerable) declivity; steep.

Declivity (dĭkli·vĭti). 1612. [– L. *declivitas*, f. *declivis* sloping down; see DECLIVE, -ITY.] Downward slope (of a hill, etc.). Also *concr.*

I could see the stones..jumping down the declivities TYNDALL.

Declivous (dĭkləi·vəs), *a.* 1684. [f. L. *declivus*, rare var. of *declivis* (see DECLIVE) + -OUS. Cf. ACCLIVOUS.] Sloping downwards; slanting.

Declu·tch, *v.* 1905. [DE- II.] *intr.* To disengage the clutch of a motor vehicle.

†**Deco·ct**, *ppl. a.* ME. [– L. *decoctus*, pa. pple. of *decoquere*; see DECOCTION.] **1.** Decocted –1671. **2.** Bankrupt 1529.

Decoct (dĭkǫ·kt), *v.* ME. [– *decoct-*, pa. ppl. stem of L. *decoquere*; see next.] †**1.** To boil down or away –1620. Also *fig.* †**2.** To prepare as food by the agency of fire; to boil, cook –1657; †*transf.* to warm up, as in cooking 1599. †**3.** To digest in the stomach. (Regarded as a kind of cooking.) Also *fig.* –1608. †**4.** To prepare or mature (metals, etc.) by heat. (Cf. CONCOCT *v.* 2.) –1653. **5.** To boil so as to extract the soluble parts or principles of 1545.

Decoction (dĭkǫ·kʃən). ME. [– (O)Fr. *décoction* or late L. *decoctio*, f. *decoct-*, pa. ppl. stem of *decoquere* boil down, f. *de* DE- I. 3 + *coquere* COOK *v.*; see -ION.] **1.** The action of decocting; *esp.* boiling so as to extract the soluble parts or principles of a substance. †**2.** Maturing or perfecting by heat; *esp.* of metals, etc. –1671. †**3.** Boiling down; also *fig.* –1655. **4.** A liquor in which a substance has been decocted (see DECOCT *v.* 5) ME.

Decode (dĭkōᵘ·d), *v.* 1896. [f. DE- II. 2 b + CODE *v.*] To convert from code into ordinary language.

Decohere (dĭkohīᵊ·ɹ), *v.* 1899. [f. DE- + COHERE.] *Electr.* To restore (a coherer) to its normal condition of sensitiveness. Also *intr.* Hence **Decohe·rence, -cohe·sion. Decohe·rer**, a device for doing this.

†**Deco·ll**, *v.* 1648. [–(O)Fr. *décoller* or late L. *decollare*; see DECOLLATE *v.*] *trans.* = DECOLLATE –1653.

†**Decollate**, *ppl. a.* 1470. [– late L. *decollatus*, pa. pple. of L. *decollare*; see next, -ATE².] Beheaded –1868.

Decollate (dĭkǫ·leⁱt, de·kǫleⁱt), *v.* 1599. [– *decollat-*, pa. ppl. stem of L. *decollare* behead, f. *de-* DE- I. 6 + *collum* neck; see -ATE³.] **1.** To behead. **2.** *Conch.* To break off the apex of (a shell) 1847. Hence **Decollated** *ppl. a.* **De·collator** *spec.* in *Obstetric Surg.*

Decollation (dĭkǫlēⁱ·ʃən). ME. [– (O)Fr. *décollation* or late L. *decollatio*, f. *decollat-*; see prec., -ION.] **1.** The action of beheading; the state of being beheaded; *spec.* in *Obstetric Surg.*, severance of the head from the body of a fœtus. **2.** *Conch.* The truncating or truncated condition of a spiral shell 1866.

1. *Feast of the D. of St. John the Baptist*: a festival in commemoration of the beheading of St. John the Baptist, observed on the 29th of August.

‖**Décolleté** (deko lte), *ppl. a.*; fem. **-ée.** 1831. [Fr., f. *décolleter*, f. *de-*, *des-* (DE- I. 6) + *collet* collar of a dress, etc.] Of a dress, etc.: Cut low round the neck; low-necked. **b.** Wearing a low-necked dress. So ‖**Décolletage** (dekoltāʒ) [Fr.], (exposure of neck and shoulders by) low-cut neck of bodice.

Decolorant (dĭkɒ·lərănt). 1864. [– Fr. *décolorant*, f. *décolorer*; see DECOLOUR, -ANT¹.] *adj.* Decolorizing 1886. *sb.* A decolorizing agent.

Decolorate (dĭkɒ·lərĕt), *a.* 1882. [– L. *decoloratus*, pa. pple. of *decolorare* DECOLOUR; see -ATE².] Having lost its colour.

Decolorate (dĭkɒ·lereⁱt), *v.* 1623. [– *decolorat-*, pa. ppl. stem of L. *decolorare* DECOLOUR; see -ATE³.] †**a.** = DISCOLOUR. **b.** = DECOLOUR 2. Hence **Decolora·tion.**

Decolorize, -ourize (dĭkɒ·lərəiz), *v.* 1836. [f. DE- II. 1 + COLORIZE.] To deprive of colour. Hence **Decoloriza·tion, -izing, -izer.**

Decolour, -or (dĭkɒ·ləɹ), *v.* 1618. [– Fr. *décolorer* or L. *decolorare*, f. *de-* DE- I. 6 + *colorare* to colour. Cf. DISCOLOUR.] †**1.** To discolour; *fig.* to stain –1630. **2.** To deprive of colour 1832.

Decomplex (dī·kǫmple:ks), *a.* 1748. [f. DE- I. 5 + COMPLEX *a.*, after *decomposite*, *decompound.*] Repeatedly complex; made up of complex parts.

Decomponent (dĭkǫ̆mpōᵘ·nĕnt). ? *Obs.* 1797. [Inferred from *decompose*; see DE- I. 6, -ENT.] A decomposing agent. So **Decompo·nible** *a.* capable of being decomposed (*rare*).

Decomposable (dĭkǫ̆mpōᵘ·zăb'l), *a.* Also **-ible.** 1784. [f. next + -ABLE.] Capable of being separated into its constituent elements. Hence **Decomposabi·lity**, d. quality.

Decompose (dĭkǫ̆mpōᵘ·z), *v.* 1751. [– Fr. *décomposer*, f. *dé-* DE- I. 6 + *composer* COMPOSE.] **1.** *trans.* To separate into its constituent parts or elements; to disintegrate; to rot; also *fig.* **2.** *intr.* (for *refl.*) To suffer decomposition; to break up; to decay, rot 1793.

1. To d. green light BREWSTER, marble FARADAY, mental operations MILL. Hence **Decompo·sed** *ppl. a.* decayed, rotten. **Decompo·ser**, a decomposing agent. **Decompo·sing** *ppl. a.* that decomposes; usu. *intr.* in process of organic decay.

Decomposite (dĭkǫ·mpŏzit). 1622. [– late L. *decompositus* for Gr. παρασύνθετος (Priscian); see DE- I. 5.] *adj.* Further compounded; formed by adding an element to something already composite 1665. *sb.* A decomposite thing, word, etc. 1622.

Decomposition (dĭkǫmpŏzi·ʃən). 1659. [f. DECOMPOUND and DECOMPOSE.] †**1.** with DE- I. 5. Further composition; compounding of things already composite –1690. **2.** with DE- I. 6. The action or process of decomposing, separation or resolution (of anything) into its constituent elements; disintegration; putrescence. Also *fig.* 1672.

2. *D. of forces*, in Dynamics = RESOLUTION of forces. The d. of white light BREWSTER, of organic particles DARWIN. *fig.* The d. of society BURKE.

Decompound (dī·kǫmpau:nd). 1614. [f. DE- I. 5 + COMPOUND *a.*; cf. DECOMPOSITE.]

A. *adj.* Repeatedly compound; compounded of parts which are themselves compound; *spec.* in *Bot.* of compound leaves or inflorescences whose divisions are further divided (L. *decompositus*, Linnæus) 1691.

B. *sb.* A decompound thing, word, etc. 1614.

De:compou·nd, *v.* 1673. [DE- I. 5, II. 1.] †**1.** *trans.* To compound further; to form by adding an element to something already compound –1747. **2.** To DECOMPOSE 1751.

2. To d. names BOLINGBROKE, the solution of chalk 1766, States 1793. Hence **Decompou·ndable** *a.*

Decompress (dī:kǫ̆mpre·s), *v.* 1911. [DE- II. 1.] *trans.* To relieve the air pressure on (a worker in compressed air) by means of an air-lock. So **Decompre·ssion** (also in *Surg.*). **Decompre·ssive** *a.* **Decompre·ssor** (in a motor engine).

Deco·nsecrate, *v.* 1867. [DE- II. 1.] To deprive of sacredness. **Deconsecra·tion.**

Deconsi·der, *v. rare.* 1881. [– Fr. *déconsidérer*; see DE- II. 1 and CONSIDER.] To treat with too little consideration.

Decontrol (dĭkǫ̆ntrōᵘ·l), *sb.* 1919. [DE- II. 1 and 2.] The removal of control, *spec.* the removal of government control. Hence as vb.

‖**Décor** (dekǭr), **de·cor.** 1656. [Fr.; in sense 1, – L. *decor* DECORE *sb.*; in 2, f. *décorer* DECORATE.] **1.** Beauty, ornament –1681. **2.** The scenery and furnishings of a theatre stage; also, the layout of an exhibition, etc. 1927.

Decorament (de·kŏrămĕnt). *rare.* 1727. [– late L. *decoramentum* (Tertullian), f. *decorare* DECORATE *v.*; see -MENT.] Ornament.

Decorate (de·kŏrĕt), *ppl. a. arch.* 1460. [– L. *decoratus*, pa. pple. of *decorare* DECORATE *v.*; see -ATE².] Adorned, decorated; ornate.

Decorate (de·kŏreˈt), *v.* 1530. [f. prec., or *decorat-*, pa. ppl. stem of L. *decorare* beautify, f. *decus, decor-* embellishment; see -ATE³.] **1.** *trans.* To adorn, embellish; to honour (*arch.*). **2.** To furnish with anything ornamental 1782. **3.** To invest with a military or other decoration 1816.

1. War and plunder were decorated by poetry as the honourable occupation of heroic natures FROUDE. **2.** To d. churches with flowers PARKER. The old armour which decorated its walls 1870.

Decorated (de·kŏreˈtėd), *ppl. a.* 1727. [f. prec. + -ED¹.] Adorned; furnished with anything ornamental; invested with a decoration. **b.** *Archit.* Applied to the second or Middle style of English Pointed architecture, wherein decoration was increasingly employed 1812.

Decoration (dekŏrēˈ·ʃən). 1585. [– (O)Fr. *décoration* or late L. *decoratio*, f. *decorat-*, pa. ppl. stem of *decorare* DECORATE; see -ION.] **1.** The action of decorating (see the vb.); the fact or condition of being decorated. **2.** That which adorns; an ornament, embellishment 1678. **3.** A star, cross, medal, or other badge conferred and worn as a mark of honour 1816.

1. *D. day* (U.S.): the day (now May 30th) on which the graves of those who fell in the civil war of 1861–65 are decorated with flowers. She.. applied all her care to the d. of her person JOHNSON. **2.** The Decorations of the Stage 1706.

Decorative (de·kŏrĕtiv), *a.* 1791. [f. DECORATE *v.* + -IVE; cf. Fr. *décoratif, -ive.*] Pertaining to, or of the nature of, decoration. Hence **De·corative-ly** *adv.*, **-ness.**

Decorator (de·kŏreˈtəɹ). 1755. [f. DECORATE *v.* + -OR 2; cf. Fr. *décorateur.*] One who decorates; *spec.* one who professionally decorates houses, etc., with plaster-work, gilding, and the like. Hence **De·coratory** *a.* (*rare*).

†**Deco·re**, *sb.* 1513. [– Fr. †*décore* decorum (XVI), f. L. *decor* seemliness, grace, beauty.] Grace, honour, glory, beauty, adornment –1616.

†**Deco·re**, *v.* 1490. [– (O)Fr. *décorer* – L. *decorare* DECORATE.] To decorate, adorn, embellish –1818. So †**Deco·rement,** ornamentation (*rare*); an ornament.

Decorous (dĕkōᵊ·rəs, de·kŏrəs), *a.* 1664. [f. L. *decorus* seemly, etc., + -OUS.] †**1.** Seemly, appropriate –1691. **2.** Characterized by decorum or propriety of manners, behaviour, etc. 1792.

2. A d. character 1792, personage HAWTHORNE. D. language BURKE, silence BYRON. Hence **Decorous-ly** *adv.*, **-ness.**

Decorticate (dĭkǭ·ɹtikeˈt), *v.* 1611. [– *decorticat-*, pa. ppl. stem of L. *decorticare*, f. *de-* DE- I. 6 + *cortex, cortic-* bark; see -ATE³.] To remove the bark, rind, or husk from; to strip of its bark; also *fig.* **b.** *intr.* To come *off* as a skin 1805. Hence **Deco:rtica·tion,** the action of decorticating. **Deco·rticator,** a machine, tool, or instrument for decorticating.

Decorum (dĭkōᵊ·rŏm). 1568. [– L. *decorum*, subst. use of n. sing. of *decorus* seemly.] **1.** That which is proper, suitable, or seemly; fitness, propriety, congruity. **2.** Hence: †**a.** Beauty arising from fitness; comeliness –1729. †**b.** Orderliness –1684. **3.** Propriety of behaviour 1572. **4.** (with *a* and *pl.*) †**a.** An appropriate act –1717. **b.** An act of polite behaviour; chiefly in *pl.* proprieties 1601.

1. If that D. of time and place..be observed BURTON. Maiesty to keepe d., must No lesse begge then a Kingdome *Ant. & Cl.* V. ii. 17. **3.** She resolved to keep within the D. of her sex F. GREVILLE.

†**Decou·rse.** 1585. [– L. *decursus* downward course (f. pa. ppl. stem of *decurrere* run down), whence also the synon. var. *decurse* (XVI–XVII). The sp. has been assim. to COURSE.] Downward course. Also *fig.* –1597.

†**Decourt,** *v.* 1610. [See DE- II. 2.] To banish from court –1676.

†**Deco·y,** *sb.*¹ 1550. [Origin unkn.] An obsolete game of cards –1609.

Decoy (dĭkoi·), *sb.*² 1618. [perh. – Du. *de kooi* 'the decoy' (see COY *sb.*), prob. infl. by prec.] **1.** A pond or pool with arms covered with network or the like into which wild fowl, *esp.* ducks, are allured and there caught 1625. Also *fig.* **2.** A bird (or other animal) trained to lure others into a trap 1661. **3.** Applied to a person: †**a.** A sharper –1631. **b.** = DECOY-DUCK 2. **4.** Anything employed to allure, *esp.* into a trap; an enticement, bait, trap 1655.

1. The d. has superseded all those ancient methods of taking water fowl STONEHOUSE. *Comb.* **d.-man, decoyman,** one who attends to a d. for wildfowl.

Decoy (dĭkoi·), *v.* 1566. [f. DECOY *sb.*², but recorded earlier in *Sc.*] **1.** To allure or entice (animals) into a snare or place of capture 1671. **2.** To entice or allure (persons) by the use of cunning and deceitful attractions *into, away, out, from, to do.*

1. The Wild Elephants are by the tame females of the same kind as 'twere duckoy'd into a lodge with trap-doors 1671. **2.** Two of whom the mariners decoyed on ship-board GOLDSM. Hence **Decoy·er.**

Decoy-duck (dĭkoi·dɒ:k). 1625. [tr. Du. *kooieend* in same sense, whence also †*coy-duck* (see COY *sb.*).] **1.** A duck trained to decoy others 1651. **2.** *fig.* A person who entices another into danger or mischief.

Decra·ssify, *v. rare.* 1855. [f. DE- II. 1 + L. *crassus*, thick, gross + -FY.] To divest of what is gross or material.

Decrease (dĭkrī·s, dī·krīs), *sb.* ME. [– OFr. *de(s)creis*, f. stem of *de(s)creistre*; see next.] **1.** The process of growing less; diminution; diminished condition. †**2.** *spec.* The wane of the moon –1746.

While man is growing, life is in d. YOUNG.

Decrease (dĭkrī·s), *v.* ME. [– OFr. *de(s)creiss-*, pres. stem of *de(s)creistre* (mod. *décroître*), – Rom. **discrescere*, for L. *decrescere*, f. *de-* DE- I. 6 + *crescere* grow.] **1.** *intr.* To grow less; to diminish, fall off, shrink, abate. (Opp. to INCREASE *v.*) **2.** *trans.* To cause to grow less; to diminish 1470.

1. Now ebbe, now flowe, nowe increase, nowe dyscrease SKELTON. He must increace, but I must d. *John* 3:30. Tyrants fears D. not *Per.* I. ii. 85. **2.** Age decreaseth strength 1651. **Decrea·singly** *adv.*

†**Decreation** (dīkri,ēˈ·ʃən). 1647. [See DE- I. 6.] The undoing of creation; annihilation –1678. So †**Decrea·tor.**

Decree (dĭkrī·), *sb.* ME. [– OFr. *decré*, var. of *decret* – L. *decretum*, subst. use of n. of *decretus*, pa. pple. of *decernere* DECERN.] **1.** An ordinance or edict set forth by the civil or other authority; an authoritative decision having the force of law. Also *fig.* **2.** *Eccl.* An edict or law of an ecclesiastical council, settling some disputed point of doctrine or discipline, etc.; in *pl.* = DECRETALS ME. **3.** *Theol.* One of God's appointments whereby events are foreordained 1570. **4.** *Law.* A judicial decision; *spec.* in *Eng. Law*, the judgement of a court of equity (before the Judicature Act of 1873–5), or of the Court of Admiralty, Probate, and Divorce 1622.

1. The decrees of Venice *Merch. V.* IV. i. 102, of the Starre-Chamber 1637. *fig.* Fate's d. DRYDEN. **3.** Her Conscience tells her God's D. Full option gave, and made her free KEN.

Decree (dĭkrī·), *v.* ME. [f. DECREE *sb.*] **1.** *trans.* To command by decree; to order, appoint, or assign authoritatively, ordain. **b.** *fig.* To ordain by Divine appointment or by fate 1580. **2.** *Law.* To †decide (a cause), order, or determine judicially; to adjudge; *absol.* to give judgement 1530. **3.** To pronounce by decree 1571. **4.** To determine (*to do* something) (*arch.*) 1526. **5.** *absol.* or *intr.* To ordain 1591.

1. The stately triumph we decreed MARLOWE. *fig.* What is decreed, must be: and be this so *Twel. N.* I. v. 330. **4.** Here we decreed to rest and dine FIELDING. **5.** As the destinies d. *A. Y. L.* I. ii. 111. Hence **Decree·able** *a.* (*rare*). †**Decree·ment,** a decreeing, a decree. **Decre·er,** one who decrees.

Decreet (dĭkrī·t), *sb. Obs.* or *arch.* ME. [– (O)Fr. *décret* or L. *decretum*; see DECREE *sb.*] **1.** Earlier form of DECREE. (Now *Obs.* in Eng., and *arch.* in *Sc. Law.*) †**2.** A decision, determination (*rare*) –1470.

†**Decreet** (dĭkrī·t), *v.* ME. [f. the sb., or Fr. *décréter*, f. *décret*; see prec. Only *Sc.* after XV.] **1.** *trans.* To decree –1633. **2.** *intr.* To pronounce a decision or judgement –1609.

Decrement (de·krĭmĕnt). 1610. [– L. *decrementum*, f. *decre-*, stem of *decrescere* DECREASE *v.*; see -MENT.] **1.** The process or fact of growing gradually less, or (with *pl.*) an instance of this; decrease, diminution, waste, loss. (Opp. to *increment.*) **b.** *Crystall.* 'A successive diminution of the layers of molecules, applied to the faces of the primitive form, by which the secondary forms are supposed to be produced' (Webster) 1805. **2.** The quantity lost by diminution or waste; *spec.* in *Math.* a small quantity by which a variable diminishes 1666.

1. Rocks..suffer a continual D., and grow lower and lower WOODWARD. [The moon's] d. in her waning GUILLIM. *D. of life*: in the doctrine of annuities, etc.: The (annual) decrease of a given number of persons by death. **2.** The decrements of heat in each second PLAYFAIR.

Decrepit (dĭkre·pit), *a.* 1450. [– (partly through Fr. *décrépit* XVI) L. *decrepitus*, f. *de-* DE- I. 3 + *crepitus*, pa. pple. of *crepare* to rattle, creak.] Worn out with old age, enfeebled with infirmities; old and feeble. Also *fig.* of things.

To sustayne theyr parents decrepet age 1550. Decrepite superstitions 1646. var. †**Decrepid** (assim. to adjs. in *-id*). Hence **Decre·pit-ly** *adv.*, †**-ness.**

Decrepitate (dĭkre·piteˈt), *v.* 1646. [prob. – mod.L. **decrepitare* (pa. ppl. stem **decrepitat-*), f. *de-* DE- II. 1 + L. *crepitare* to crackle. Cf. Fr. *décrépiter* (XVII) in same sense.] **1.** *trans.* To calcine or roast (a salt or mineral) until it no longer crackles. **2.** *intr.* Of salts and minerals: To crackle and disintegrate when suddenly heated 1677. Hence **Decrepita·tion** (in both senses).

Decrepitude (dĭkre·pitiud). 1603. [–(O)Fr. *décrépitude*, f. L. *decrepitus* (see prec.) after *valetudo*, etc.; see -TUDE; superseded †DECREPITY (XVI–XVII).] The state of being decrepit; a state of feebleness and decay, *esp.* that due to old age (*lit.* and *fig.*). var. **Decre·pity.**

‖**Decrescendo** (dēkreʃe·ndo). [It. = decreasing.] *Mus.* A direction: With gradual diminution of force; = DIMINUENDO. Also as *sb.*

Decrescent (dĭkre·sĕnt). 1610. [– *decrescent-*, pres. ppl. stem of L. *decrescere* DECREASE *v.*; see -ENT.]

A. *adj.* Decreasing, growing gradually less. Between the increscent and d. moon TENNYSON.

B. *sb.* The moon in her decrement; in *Her.* represented with the horns towards the sinister side 1616.

Decretal (dĭkrī·tăl). ME. [Earliest as sb., – late and med.L. *decretale* (whence also (O)Fr. *décrétale*), subst. use of n. sing. of late L. *decretalis* adj., whence the Eng. adj. (med.L. *epistola decretalis, -æ -es*); f. *decret-*, pa. ppl. stem of L. *decernere* DECERN; see -AL¹.]

A. *adj.* **1.** Pertaining to, of the nature of, or containing, a decree or decrees 1489. †**2.** Imperative –1679. †**3.** Definitive (*rare*) –1697.

1. The canon laws, or d. epistles of the popes BLACKSTONE. A. D. Order made in the High Court of Chancery 1714

B. *sb.* **1.** *Eccl.* A papal decree or decretal epistle; a document issued by a Pope determining some point of doctrine or ecclesiastical law ME. **b.** *pl.* The collection of such decrees, forming part of the canon law ME. **2.** *transf.* A decree, ordinance 1588.

1. The false decretals of Isidore 1860.

Hence †**Decretaliarch** [Fr. *décrétaliarche*], the lord of decretals, the Pope. (A word of Rabelais.) †**Decre·taline** *a.* **Decre·talist,** one versed in the Decretals. **Decre·tally** *adv.* in a d. way.

Decre·te. 1832. **1.** Austin's adaptation of L. *decretum.* **2.** Obs. var. of DECREET.

†**Decre·tion.** 1635. [f. *decret-*, pa. ppl. stem of L. *decrescere* DECREASE *v.*; see -ION. Cf. ACCRETION.] Decrease –1659.

Decretist (dĭkrī·tist). ME. [– med.L. *decretista*, f. *decretum* DECREE *sb.* + *-ista* -IST. Cf. Fr. †*décrétiste*.] A decretalist.

Decretive (dĭkrī·tiv), *a.* 1609. [f. *decret-*, pa. ppl. stem of L. *decernere* DECERN + -IVE.] Having the attribute of decreeing; decretory.

†**Decreto·rial,** *a. rare.* 1588. [f. L. *decretorius* DECRETORY + -AL[1].] = DECRETORY 3. –1646.

†**Decreto·rian,** *a.* 1679. [f. as prec. + -AN.] = DECRETORY 2, 3. –1716.

Decretory (dĭkrī·təri), *a.* Now *rare* or *Obs.* 1577. [– L. *decretorius*, f. *decret-*, pa. ppl. stem of *decernere* determine; see DECERN, DECREE *sb.*, -ORY[2].] **1.** Of the nature of, involving, or relating to a decree 1631; †(of persons) positive, decided –1680. †**2.** Decisive –1737. **3.** *Old Med.* and *Astrol.* CRITICAL, 4. (*Obs.* or *arch.*) 1577. Hence **Decre·torily** *adv.* positively, decisively.

†**Decrew·**, *v. rare.* [– OFr. *decreü* (mod. *décru*), pa. pple. of *de(s)creistre*; see DECREASE *v.*] To decrease, wane. SPENSER.

Decrial (dĭkrəi·ăl). *rare.* 1711. [f. DECRY *v.* + -AL[1].] The act of decrying; open disparagement. So **Decri·er,** one who decries.

Decrown (dĭkrau·n), *v.* ? *Obs.* 1609. [f. DE- II. 2 + CROWN *sb.* Cf. *dethrone.*] To deprive of the crown, to discrown.

Decry (dĭkrəi·), *v.* Pa. t. and pple. **decried.** 1617. [f. DE- I. 4 + CRY *v.*, after Fr. *décrier*, in the senses of *cry down.*] **1.** *trans.* To denounce, suppress, or depreciate by proclamation, as coins, etc.; = *cry down* (see CRY *v.*) 1617. **2.** To cry out against; to disparage openly; to attack the credit of 1641.

1. The king may. . d., or cry down any coin of the kingdom, and make it no longer current BLACKSTONE. **2.** The goldsmiths do d. the new Act PEPYS. To d. usury 1872. Hence †**Decry·** *sb. rare*, the decrying (of money).

Decrystallization (dĭkri:stălǝizē[i]·ʃən). 1860. [f. DE- II. 1.] Deprivation of crystalline structure.

†**Decuba·tion.** *rare.* [f. L. *decubare* lie down; see -ATION.] The action of lying down. EVELYN.

‖**Decubitus** (dĭkiū·bitŏs). 1866. [mod.L., f. L. *decumbere* lie down, after *accubitus*, etc. So in Fr. (XVIII).] *Med.* The manner or posture of lying in bed, as the *dorsal d.* Hence **Decu·bital** *a.* pertaining to or resulting from d.

Decuman (de·kiumăn), *a.* 1659. [– L. *decumanus*, var. of *decimanus* of or belonging to the tenth part, or the tenth cohort, f. *decimus*: also, by metonymy, large.] **1.** Very large, immense: usu. of waves. **2.** *Rom. Antiq.* Belonging to the tenth cohort, as the *d. gate* (*porta decumana*) 1852.

1. That decumane Wave that took us fore and aft MOTTEUX. (See Sir T. Browne *Pseud. Ep.* VII. xvii. 2, on the vulgar error connected with the d. wave.) var. †**Decumanal** *a.* (in sense 1) (*rare*).

Decumbency (dĭkɒ·mbĕnsi). 1646. [f. DECUMBENT; see -ENCY.] **1.** Decumbent condition or posture. **2.** = DECUMBITURE 2. 1651.

1. The ancient manner of d. SIR T. BROWNE. So **Decu·mbence.**

Decumbent (dĭkɒ·mbĕnt), *a.* (*sb.*) 1641. [– *decumbent-*, pres. ppl. stem of L. *decumbere* lie down, f. *de-* DE- I. 1 + *cumbere* lie. See -ENT.] **1.** Lying down (now *rare*); †lying ill in bed –1732. **2. a.** *Bot.* Lying or trailing on the ground, but with the extremity ascending; as stems, etc. 1791. **b.** *Nat. Hist.* Of hairs or bristles: Lying flat on the surface 1826. †**3.** *sb.* One lying in bed –1699.

1. The d. portraiture of a woman ASHMOLE.

Decumbiture (dĭkɒ·mbitiŭɹ). ? *Obs.* 1647. [irreg. f. L. *decumbere* (see prec.) + -URE.] **1.** Lying down; *spec.* as an invalid in bed 1670. **2.** The act or time of taking to one's bed in an illness. **b.** *Astrol.* A figure erected for the time at which this happens, affording prognostics of recovery or death.

Decuple (de·kiup'l). ME. [– late L. *decuplus* adj., *decuplum* sb. Cf. Fr. *décuple* adj.] *adj.* Tenfold 1613. *sb.* A number ten times another; a tenfold amount ME.

Decuple (de·kiup'l), *v.* 1674. [– late L. *decuplare*, f. *decuplus*; see prec.] *trans.* To increase or multiply tenfold. var. **De·cuplate.**

Decurion (dĭkiū[ə]·riǫn). ME. [– L. *decurio*, *-ōn-*, f. *decem* ten, after *centurio* CENTURION. Cf. DECURY.] **1.** *Rom. Antiq.* An officer in command of a *decuria* or company of ten horse. Also *gen.* A captain of ten. **2.** *Rom. Hist.* A member of the senate of a colony or municipal town ME. **3.** A member of the Great Council in modern Italian cities and towns 1666. Hence **Decu·rionate, Decu·rionship,** the office of a d.

Decurrence (dĭkɒ·rĕns). 1659. [f. next; see -ENCE.] †**1.** The state or act of running down; lapse –1677. **2.** *Bot.* The condition of being DECURRENT, q.v. 1835. So **Decu·rrency.**

Decurrent (dĭkɒ·rĕnt), *a.* ME. [– *decurrent-*, pres. ppl. stem of L. *decurrere* run down, f. *de-* DE- I. 1 + *currere* run; see -ENT.] †**1.** Running down –1450. **2.** *Bot.* Of leaves, etc.: Extending down the stem below the point of insertion 1753. Hence **Decu·rrently** *adv.*

†**Decursion** (dĭkɒ̄·ɹʃən). 1630. [– L. *decursio*, f. *decurs-*, pa. ppl. stem of *decurrere*; see prec., -ION.] **1.** Downward course, lapse –1680. **2.** *Antiq.* A military evolution, performed under arms –1702.

Decu·rsive, *a.* 1828. [– mod.L. *decursivus*, f. as prec.; see -IVE.] = DECURRENT. Hence **Decu·rsively** *adv.*

†**Decu·rt,** *v.* 1550. [– L. *decurtare* to curtail, f. *de-* DE- I. 2 + *curtare* to shorten.] To cut down, shorten, curtail –1648.

†**Decu·rtate,** *v.* 1599. [– *decurtat-*, pa. ppl. stem of L. *decurtare*; see prec., -ATE[3].] = prec. –1676. So †**Decurta·tion,** shortening, abridging, cutting down.

Decurve (dĭkɒ̄·ɹv), *v. rare.* 1835. [f. DE- I. 1 + CURVE *v.*] To curve or bend down. Hence **Decurva·tion, Decu·rvature,** the action of decurving; the condition of being bent downwards.

Decury (de·kiŭri). 1533. [– L. *decuria*, f. *decem*, after *centuria* CENTURY.] *Rom. Hist.*, etc. A division, company, or body of ten.

5000 of these citizens were arranged in ten pannels or decuries of 500 each GROTE.

Decus (dī·kŏs). *slang.* 1688. [From the L. motto *decus et tutamen* on the rim.] A crown-piece.

Decuss (dĭkɒ·s), *v. rare.* 1782. [– L. *decussare* DECUSSATE *v.*] = DECUSSATE *v.*

Decussate (dĭkɒ·sĕt), *a.* 1825. [– *decussat-*; see next, -ATE[2].] **1.** Having the form of an X. **2.** *Bot.* Of leaves, etc.: Arranged in successive pairs, which cross each other at right angles 1846. Hence **Decu·ssately** *adv.*

Decussate (de·kŏse[i]t, dĭkɒ·se[i]t), *v.* 1658. [– *decussat-*, pa. ppl. stem of L. *decussare* divide cross-wise, f. *decussis* the number 10, 10-as piece, intersection of lines cross-wise (X), f. *decem* ten + AS *sb.*; see -ATE[3].] To cross, intersect, so as to form a figure like an X. Also *intr.*

The inner [fibres] always d. or cross the outer 1737. Hence †**Decu·ssative** *a.* crossing (*rare*). †**Decu·ssatively** *adv.*

Decussated (see prec.), *ppl. a.* 1658. [f. prec. + -ED[1].] Formed with crossing lines like an X; crossed, intersected; having decussations. **b.** *Rhet.* Consisting of two pairs of clauses or words, in which the terms correspond, but in reverse order; chiastic 1828.

Decussation (dekɒsē[i]·ʃən). 1656. [– L. *decussatio*, f. *decussat-*; see DECUSSATE *v.*, -ION.] Crossing (of lines, rays, fibres, etc.) so as to form a figure like an X. **b.** *Rhet.* An arrangement of clauses, etc. in which corresponding terms occur in reverse order 1841.

Single and masterly strokes, without decussations EVELYN.

†**Decu·ssion.** *rare.* [– late L. *decussio*, f. *decuss-*, pa. ppl. stem of L. *decutere* shake down, etc., f. *de-* DE- I. 1 + *quatere* shake; see -ION.] A shaking down or off. EVELYN.

Decyl (de·sil). 1868. [f. Gr. δέκα ten + -YL.] *Chem.* The univalent hydrocarbon radical $C_{10}H_{21}$; also called *Decatyl.* Also *attrib.* Hence **Decy·lic** *a.* of or pertaining to d., as in *decylic alcohol*, etc. So **De·cine,** the liquid hydrocarbon $C_{10}H_{18}$, the ethine or acetylene member of the d. series.

Dedal, Dedalian, etc.; see DÆDAL, etc.

‖**Dedans** (dədaṅ·). 1706. [Fr. *dedans* inside, *spec.* gallery of a tennis court.] *Tennis.* The open gallery at the end of the service-side of a tennis-court.

Dedd(e, dede, obs. ff. DEAD, DEATH, DEED.

Dedecorate (dĭde·kŏre[i]t), *v.* 1609. [In sense 1, – *dedecorat-*, pa. ppl. stem of L. *dedecorare* to dishonour, f. *dedecus*, *-cor* disgrace; see -ATE[3]. In sense 2, f. DE- II. 1 + DECORATE *v.*] †**1.** To dishonour –1623. **2.** To disfigure 1804.

Dedentition (dīdenti·ʃən). 1646. [f. DE- II. 1.] *Phys.* The shedding of the teeth.

De·dicate, *pa. pple.* and *ppl. a.* ME. [– L. *dedicatus*, pa. pple. of L. *dedicare* proclaim, devote, consecrate, f. *de-* DE- I. 2 + *dic-*, weak var. of *dīc-* say; see -ATE[2].] Dedicated.

Every true Christian. . is a person d. to joy and peace MILT.

Dedicate (de·dike[i]t), *v.* 1530. [– *dedicat-* pa. ppl. stem of L. *dedicare*, after prec. or DEDICATION; see -ATE[3].] **1.** *trans.* To devote (*to* the Deity or to sacred uses) with solemn rites; to surrender, set apart, and consecrate. (The leading sense.) Also *fig.* **2.** *transf.* To give up earnestly, or wholly, *to* a person or purpose; to appropriate; to devote 1553. **3.** To inscribe or address (a book, etc.) *to* a patron or friend 1542. **4.** *Law.* To devote to the use of the public (a highway, etc.) 1843.

1. To whom he buylded and dedicate a chapell and an altare EDEN. **2.** To her my thoughts I daily d. SPENSER. Hence **De:dicatee·**, one to whom anything is dedicated. **De·dicative** *a.* having the attribute of dedicating. **De·dicator,** one who dedicates; *esp.* one who inscribes a book to a friend or patron.

Dedication (dedikē[i]·ʃən). ME. [– (O)Fr. *dédication* or L. *dedicatio*, f. as prec.; see -ION.] **1.** The action of setting apart and devoting to the Deity or to a sacred purpose with solemn rites; the fact of being so dedicated. **b.** The day or feast of dedication (of a church) ME. **2.** *fig.* A devoting (of oneself, one's time, etc.) to a purpose 1601. **3.** The dedicating of a book, etc.; the form of words in which this is done 1598. **4.** *Law.* The action of dedicating (a highway, etc.) to the public use 1809.

1. The founder prepared to celebrate the d. of his city GIBBON. **2.** A wild d. of your selues To vnpath'd Waters *Wint. T.* IV. iv. 577.

Dedicatory (de·dike[i]təri, -kĕtəri). 1565. [f. late L. *dedicator*, f. as prec.; see -OR 2, -ORY[2]. Cf. Fr. *dédicatoire* (XVI).]

A. *adj.* Relating to, or of the nature of, dedication; serving to dedicate.

The epistle Dedicatorie *Bible.* var. **De:dicato·rial.** Hence **De·dicatorily** *adv.*

†**B.** *sb.* A dedicatory inscription or address –1674.

†**Dedigna·tion.** ME. [– OFr. *dedignation* – L. *dedignatio*, f. *dedignat-*, pa. ppl. stem of *dedignari* to DISDAIN; see -ION.] **1.** Disdain –1716. **2.** Indignation; *pass.*, state of being under a person's displeasure 1538.

‖**Dedimus** (de·dimŏs). 1489. [From the words of the writ, *dedimus potestatem*, L. 'we have given the power'.] *Law.* A writ empowering one who is not a judge to do some act in place of a judge.

Dedition (dĭdi·ʃən). ? *Obs.* 1523. [– OFr. *dedicion* or L. *deditio* surrender, f. *dedit-*, pa. ppl. stem of *dedere* give up, f. *de-* DE- I. 3 + *dare* give; see -ION.] Giving up, yielding, surrender.

†**De·dolent,** *a.* 1633. [– *dedolent-*, pres. ppl. stem of L. *dedolēre*, f. *de-* DE- II. 1 + *dolēre* grieve; see -ENT.] That feels sorrow no more; insensible, callous –1698. Hence †**De·dolence.**

Deduce (dĭdiū·s), *v.* 1528. [– L. *deducere*, f. *de-* DE- I. 2 + *ducere* to lead.] **1.** To bring, convey; *spec.* (after L.) to lead forth (a colony) (*arch.*). Also *fig.* **2.** To derive *from* (*trans.* and *intr.*). (Now *rare.*) 1565. **3.** *trans.* To trace the course of. †Formerly, also, To conduct (a process), deal with (a matter). 1528. **4.** To show or hold (a thing) to be derived *from* 1536. **5.** To draw as a conclusion *from* something known or assumed;

to derive by reasoning; to infer. (The chief current sense.) 1529. †6. To deduct –1662. †7. To reduce (to another form) –1749.

1. Advising him he should hither d. a colony SELDEN. 2. A ceremony deduced from the Romans SIR T. HERBERT. 4. He cannot d. his descent wholly by heirs male BLACKSTONE. 5. The knowledge of Causes is deduced from their effects 1696. Hence †**Dedu·cement,** a deduction, inference. **Dedu·cible** *a.* that may be deduced; *sb.* a deducible inference. **Deducibi·lity. Dedu·cibleness.**

†**Deduct,** *ppl. a.* ME. [– L. *deductus*, pa. pple. of *deducere* DEDUCE.] Deducted –1532.

Deduct (dǐdɒ·kt), *v.* 1524. [– *deduct-*, pa. ppl. stem of *deducere* DEDUCE, prob. after prec.] **1.** *trans.* To take away or subtract from a sum or amount. (The current sense.) †**2.** = DEDUCE 1–5. –1600. †**3.** To reduce. MASSINGER.

1. When we have deducted all that is absorbed in sleep JOHNSON. 2. A people deducted oute of the citie of Philippos COVERDALE. Which by Logicall consequence is not Necessarily deducted out of the Premisses 1609. Hence **Deduc·tible** *a.* (*rare*).

Deduction (dǐdɒ·kʃən). 1483. [– (O)Fr. *déduction* or L. *deductio*, f. as prec.; see -ION.] **1.** The action of deducting or taking away; subtraction; that which is deducted. **2.** A leading forth or away (*spec.* of a colony). ?*Obs.* 1615. †**3.** The action or result of tracing out; a detailed account –1826. †**4.** Derivation –1755. **5.** The process of deducing from something known or assumed; *spec.* in *Logic*, inference by reasoning from generals to particulars 1594; *transf.* that which is deduced 1532.

1. The interest given to them was exclusive of, and with a d. of, that sum 1827. 3. A clear d. of the affairs of Europe from the treaty of Munster to this time CHESTERF. 4. The d. of one word from another JOHNSON. 5. D. the process of deriving facts from laws, and effects from their causes ABP. THOMSON.

Deductive (dǐdɒ·ktiv), *a.* 1646. [– med.L. *deductivus*, *-ive*, (in sense 1); see DEDUCT *v.*, -IVE.] **1.** Of or pertaining to deduction; *spec.* in *Logic*, reasoning from generals to particulars (opp. to *inductive*); (of persons) reasoning deductively 1665. †**2.** Derivative. SIR T. BROWNE.

1. All knowledge of causes is d. GLANVILL. Women naturally prefer the d. method to the inductive BUCKLE. **Deduc·tively** *adv.* var. **Dedu·ctory** *a.* (*rare*).

†**Deduit,** *sb.* ME. [– (O)Fr. *déduit* entertainment, – pa. pple. of *déduire* :– L. *deducere* DEDUCE.] Diversion, pleasure –1483.

Deduplication (dǐdiūplikēi·ʃən). 1835. [– Fr. *déduplication*, latinized deriv. of *dédoubler* separate what is double, divide into two halves, f. *dé-* DE- I. 6 + *doubler* double.] *Bot.* Congenital division of one organ into two (or more); = CHORISIS.

Dee (dī), *sb.* 1794. Name of the letter D; applied to a D-shaped ring or loop used for connecting parts of harness, etc.

Dee (dī), *v.* 1845. Pronunc. of d——, for *damn*; whence *deed* (also *deedeed*) = d——d, damned.

Deed (dīd), *sb.* [OE. *dēd*, WS. *dǣd* = OFris. *dēd(e)*, OS. *dād* (Du. *daad*), OHG. *tāt* (G. *tat*), ON. *dað*, Goth. *-dēþs* :– Gmc. **dǣdiz* :– *dhētis*, f. IE. **dhē-* **dho-* DO *v.*] **1.** That which is done, acted, or performed by an intelligent agent; an act; a feat OE. **2.** Action generally. (Often opp. to *word.*) OE. †**3.** Thing to be done; task or duty –1580. **4.** *Law.* An instrument in writing (or other legible representation of words on parchment or paper), purporting to effect some legal disposition, and sealed and delivered by the disposing party or parties ME.

1. They that haue done this Deede, are honourable SHAKS. Their deeds did not agree with their words 1875. Deedes of Armes 1568. †*Deeds of the Apostles*: the Acts of the Apostles. 2. In som cas the good wylle of a man is accepted for the dede 1500.

Phr. *In d.*: in practice. *In d., in very d.*: in fact, in reality, in truth: hence INDEED.

Deed (dīd), *v.* *U.S.* 1816. [f. prec. sb.] *trans.* To convey or transfer by deed. Also *fig.*

Deed, *adv.* 1547. Aphet. f. *i'deed*, INDEED; now chiefly Sc.

†**Dee·dbote.** [OE. *dǣd* deed + *bōt* BOOT *sb.*[1]] Amends-deed, penance, repentance –ME.

Deedful (dī·dfŭl), *a.* 1834. [f. DEED *sb.* + -FUL.] Full of deeds, active, effective, as *a d. life.*

Dee·dless, *a.* 1598. [f. DEED *sb.* + -LESS.] Without action or deeds; (of persons) performing no deeds, inactive. *Tr. & Cr.* IV. v. 98.

Dee·d poll, deed-poll. 1588. [See POLL *a.*] *Law.* A deed made and executed by one party only; so called because the paper or parchment is 'polled' or cut even, not indented.

Deedy (dī·di), *a.* *dial.* 1615. [f. DEED *sb.* + -Y[1].] **1.** Full of deeds; active. †**2.** Real (*rare*) –1788. Hence **Dee·dily** *adv.*

Deem (dīm), *v.* [OE. *dēman* = OFris. *dēma*, OS. *dōmian* (Du. *doemen*), OHG. *tuomen*, ON. *dœma*, Goth. *domjan*, f. **dōmaz* DOOM.] †**1.** *intr.* To pronounce judgement –1579. **2.** *trans.* †To judge –1609; to administer (law) (*arch.*) ME. †**3.** To sentence –1602. Also *fig.* †**4.** To decree; to decide; to award –1605. †**5.** To judge of, estimate –1569; *intr.* to judge *of* –1586. **6.** To form the opinion, be of opinion; to conclude, consider, hold. (The ordinary current sense.) OE. **7.** *intr.* To judge or think (in a specified way) *of* ME. †**8.** To hope –1819. †**9.** *trans.* To think of as existent; to surmise –1599; *intr.* to think *of* 1814. †**10.** To pronounce; to tell, say, declare. [Only poetic, prob. derived from sense 4.] –1547.

2. That..the 24 Keys may be called..to d. the law truly 1718. 6. Wee may boldly deeme there is neither, where both are not HOOKER. 7. Let vs see how the Greekes..deemed of it [Poetry] SIDNEY. Hence †**Deem** *sb.* judgement, opinion, surmise. **Dee·mer,** one who deems.

Deemster (dī·mstəɹ). 1611. [f. prec. + -STER. Cf. DEMPSTER.] **1.** A judge. (*Obs.* or *arch.*) 1748. **2.** The title of each of the two judges of the Isle of Man 1611.

Deep (dīp), *a.* [OE. *dēop* = OFris. *diāp*, OS. *diop*, *diap* (Du. *diep*), OHG. *tiuf* (G. *tief*), ON. *djúpr*, Goth. *diups* :– Gmc. **deupaz*, f. **deup-* **dup-* (see DIP *v.*).]

I. Literal senses. **1.** Having great extension downward OE.; extending far inward from the outer surface or backward from the front OE. **2.** Having a (specified) dimension downward OE.; having a (specified) dimension inward from the surface, outer part, or front 1646. **3.** Placed far (or a specified distance) down; of a ship, low in the water. **b.** Far back. OE. **4.** Extending to or coming from a depth 1483. †**5.** Covered with a depth of mud, etc. –1828.

1. The greate deep valleis 1559. Phr. *To go (in) off the deep end*, etc.: to let oneself go. 2. A ditch.. eight feet d. 1832. The pleasure is but skin deepe 1646. The Thebans.. stood five-and-twenty d. THIRLWALL. 3. The frozen Earth..seven Cubits d. in Snow DRYDEN. The d. veins..of the body 1842. 4. A d. sigh ADDISON, plunge COWPER. 5. We..incountred with such d. sandy ground LITHGOW. [We now say 'd. in sand, mud, etc.'].

II. Fig. senses. **1.** Hard to fathom; not superficial; profound OE. **2.** Solemn; grave; serious OE. **3.** Deep-rooted; that affects one profoundly ME. **4.** In which the mind is profoundly absorbed 1586. **5.** Expensive; heavy 1577. **6.** Intense, profound; of actions, powerfully affecting, strong 1547. **7.** Of colour, etc.: Intense; highly chromatic. (Opp. to *faint* or *thin.*) 1555. **8.** Of sound, etc.: Low in pitch, grave; full-toned, resonant 1591. **9.** Penetrating, profound ME. **10.** Profound in craft; in *mod. slang*. artful, sly 1513. **11.** Of an agent: Who does (what is expressed) deeply 1526. **12.** Much immersed *in* 1567.

1. Thy thoughts are very d. *Ps.* 92:5. 2. In d. disgrace 1894. 3. A d. Sorrow STEELE, fear SOUTHEY. 4. In d. study LANE. 5. D. taxes FULLER, gaming SWIFT. 6. The d. influence of an anæsthetic 1889. D. silence WORDSW., night HAWTHORNE. 7. All manner of Blues, from the faintest to the deepest 1665. The deepest mourning GOLDSM. 8. And let the bass of heaven's d. organ blow MILT. 9. A deepe clerke, and one that read much HOLINSHED. 10. Deepe, hollow, treacherous, and full of guile SHAKS. 11. Two deepe enemies, Foes to my rest SHAKS. 12. Deepe..in debt 1587.

Deep (dīp), *sb.* [OE. *dēop*, neut. of *dēop* adj.; see prec.] †**1.** Depth (*rare*) –1635. **2.** That which is deep; the deep part of the sea, etc. (opp. to *shallow*); deep water OE.; a deep place; an abyss ME. Also *fig.* **3.** The remote central part (*rare*) ME. †**4.** The middle (of night, etc.) when the silence, or darkness, is most intense –1682. **5.** *Naut.* A term for the fathoms intermediate to those marked on the 20-fathom sounding-line 1769.

2. The Frenchmen..passed by and tooke the deepe of the Sea 1568. And in the lowest d. a lower d. Still..opens wide MILT. 4. *Merry W.* IV. iv. 40.

Phr. *The d.*: **a.** The deep sea, the main (*poet.* and *rhet.*). **b.** The abyss or depth of space. **c.** *Cricket.* (= *the deep field*), the part of the field near the boundary, esp. behind the bowler; also, a fieldsman or his position there.

Deep (dīp), *adv.* [OE. *dīope*, *dēope*.] **1.** *lit.* Deeply; far down, in, on, etc. **2.** *fig.* Profoundly, intensely, earnestly, heavily, etc. OE.

1. Waters do ebbe as deepe as they flow 1601. 2. That Fooles should be so deepe contemplatiue *A. Y. L.* II. vii. 31.

Comb. Freq. in comb. with pres. and pa. pples., as *d.-thinking*; *d.-cut*, *-drawn*, *-felt*, *-set*, etc. Also formerly, and still sometimes, used with adjs., as *d.-sore*, *-green*, etc.; **d.-dyed,** *fig.* 'steeped' in guilt.

Deep (dīp), *v.* *rare.* [OE. *dīepan*, *dȳpan* trans. = OFris. *diūpa* (Du. *diepen*), MHG. *tiefen*, *tiufen*, Goth. *gadiupjan*; f. *dēop* DEEP *a.* Cf. next.] †**1.** To deepen (*trans.* and *intr.*) –1616. †**2.** To plunge deeply (*lit.* and *fig.*) –1578.

Deepen (dī·p'n), *v.* 1605. [f. DEEP *a.* + -EN[5], superseding prec.] To make or become deep or deeper (in various senses).

To d. trenches STOW, colours 1612, convictions RUSKIN. The shades d. GOLDSM. The combat deepens CAMPBELL. The evening had deepened into..starlight GEO. ELIOT. Hence **Dee·pener.**

Deep-fetched, †**-fet** (dī·pˌfeːtʃt, -feːt), *ppl. a.* 1562. [DEEP *adv.*] Fetched from deep in the bosom, etc., as *deepe-fet groanes* (SHAKS.).

Deep-laid (dī·pˌlēi·d), *ppl. a.* 1768. [DEEP *adv.*] Deeply laid; planned with profound cunning, as a *deep-laid scheme* (TUCKER).

Deeply (dī·pli), *adv.* [OE. *dīoplīće* adv., f. *dēoplīć* adj.; see DEEP *a.*, -LY[2].] **1.** To a great depth; far downwards, inwards, etc. ME. **2.** *fig.* Profoundly, thoroughly OE.; with profound craft 1596. †**3.** Solemnly –1671. **4.** Gravely ME. **5.** With deep feeling, etc.; intensely ME. **6.** Profoundly; with deep colour; with a deep voice 1632.

1. I..sink in deep affliction, d. down PARNELL. D. he drank SCOTT. 2. Consider it not so d. *Macb.* II. ii. 30. D. you dissemble FLETCHER. 3. 'Tis deepely sworne *Haml.* III. ii. 234. 4. To commit oneself d. FROUDE. 5. They curst him d. 1634. 6. Some d. Red 1695. A pack of hounds..baying d. 1883.

Comb. Deeply qualifying a pple. is now usually hyphened when the pple. is used attrib., preceding its sb., as 'a deeply-serrated leaf'.

Dee·pmost, *a.* (*superl.*) *rare.* 1810. [f. DEEP *a.* + -MOST.] Deepest.

Deep-mouthed (dī·pˌmauðd, -mauþt), *a.* 1595. [f. *deep mouth* + -ED[2].] Having a deep or sonorous voice: *esp.* of dogs.

Deepness (dī·pnės). Now *rare*; displ. by DEPTH. [OE. *dīopnes*, *dēopnes*; see DEEP *a.*, -NESS.] **1.** The quality of being DEEP (in various senses); depth, profundity. †**2.** *concr.* A deep place, an abyss; a deep part of the sea, etc. –1502.

1. The d. of his obeisance SCOTT, of the way 1603, of the Sea 1665, thought 1720, Satan 1646.

Deep-read (dī·pˌre·d), *ppl. a.* 1639. [DEEP *adv.*] Deeply read; skilled by profound reading.

Sir Robert, deep-read in old wines BURNS.

Deep-rooted (dī·pˌrū:tėd), *a.* 1669. [DEEP *adv.*] Deeply implanted; chiefly *fig.* of feelings, etc.

Deep sea, deep-sea. 1626. The deeper part of the sea at a distance from the shore. Used *attrib.*: Of or belonging to the deep sea.

Deep-sea lead, line, a lead and line used for soundings in deep water. *Deep-sea fisheries*, fisheries prosecuted at a distance from land.

Deep-seated (dī·pˌsī:tėd), *a.* 1741. [DEEP *adv.*] Having its seat far beneath the surface, as *a deep-seated* abscess.

Deepsome (dī·psɒ̆m), *a.* *poetic. rare.* 1615. [f. DEEP *a.* or *sb.* + -SOME[1].] Having deepness or depths; more or less deep.

Deer (dī^{ə}ɹ), *pl.* **deer.** [OE. *dēor* = OFris. *diār*, OS. *dior* (Du. *dier*), OHG. *tior* (G. *tier*), ON. *dýr*, Goth. **dius* (in dat. pl. *diuzam*) :- Gmc. **deuzam* :- IE. **dheusóm*, orig. 'breathing creature'.] †**1.** A beast; usually a quadruped –1481. **2.** The general name of a family (*Cervidæ*) of ruminant quadrupeds, distinguished by the possession of deciduous branching horns or antlers, and by the presence of spots on the young: the genera and species being distinguished as *reindeer*, *moose-deer*, *red deer*, and *fallow deer* OE. Also *attrib.*

1. Se camal þæt micla dear OE. **2.** He chaced at the reed dere MALORY.

Phr. *Small d.*: orig. used in sense 1, but now associated with sense 2. Mice, and Rats, and such small Deare SHAKS.

Comb.: **d.-dog** = DEER-HOUND; **-fence,** a high railing such as deer cannot leap over; **-forest,** a forest or extensive tract of unenclosed wild land reserved for deer; **-neck,** a thin neck (of a horse), like a deer's; **deer's eye** = BUCK-EYE (the tree); **d.-tiger,** the puma or cougar; **-tongue, deer's tongue,** a N. Amer. Cichoraceous plant, *Liatris adoratissima*.

Deerberry (dī^{ə}·ɹbeːri). 1862. A name given to the berry of *Gualtheria procumbens* (N.O. *Ericaceæ*); also to *Vaccinium stamineum* (Squaw Huckleberry); also to the plants.

Dee·r-coloured, *a.* 1611. Tawny red.

Dee·r-hair, deer's hair. 1494. **1.** The hair of deer. **2.** A small moorland species of club-rush, *Scirpus cæspitosus* 1772.

Dee·r-hound. 1818. A dog used for hunting red-deer; *esp.* a large variety of the rough greyhound, standing 28 inches or more.

Dee·r-lick. 1876. A small spring or spot of damp ground, impregnated with salt, alum, or the like, where deer come to lick.

Dee·r-mouse. 1884. The popular name of certain American mice; *esp.* the white-footed mouse (*Hesperomys leucopus*).

Dee·rskin. ME. The skin of a deer, *esp.* as used for clothing. Also *attrib.*

Dee·r-sta:lker. 1875. [See STALK *v.*] **1.** One who stalks deer. **2.** A low-crowned close-fitting hat worn by deer-stalkers 1881.

Dee·r-stea:ler. 1640. A poacher who kills and steals deer.

†**De·ess, deesse.** 1549. [– (O)Fr. *déesse*, var., infl. by L. *dea*, of OFr. *dieuesse*, f. *dieu* god + *-esse* -ESS[1].] A goddess –1698.

Dees(se, obs. ff. DAIS, DICE.

De-e·thicize, *v.* 1887. [DE- II. 1.] To deprive of its ethical character; to separate from ethics.

Deface (dĭfē^{i}·s), *v.* ME. [– Fr. †*défacer*, earlier *deffacer*, for OFr. *desfacier*, f. *des-* DE- I. 6 + *face* FACE *sb.*] **1.** *trans.* To mar the face or appearance of; to spoil the form or beauty of; to disfigure. Also *fig.* †**2.** To destroy, lay waste –1632. **3.** To efface ME. Also *fig.* †**4.** To defame –1641. †**5.** To cast in the shade –1796.

1. Ancient statues..defaced by modern additions LADY M. W. MONTAGU. **2.** Now cleane defaste the goodly buildings fayre 1575. **3.** Characters that can never be defaced BENTLEY. *fig.* By false learning is good sense defaced POPE.

Hence †**Deface** *sb.* defacement. **Defa·cement,** the action of defacing; the state of being defaced; *concr.* a disfigurement. **Defa·cer.**

De facto; see DE 1 b.

Defæcate, -cation; see DEFECATE, etc.

†**Defai·l,** *v.* ME. [– (O)Fr. *défaillir* :- Rom. **defallire*; see DE- I. 3, FAIL *v.*] **1.** *intr.* To FAIL (in various senses) –1556. **2.** *trans.* To cause to fail: to defeat 1608. So †**Defai·llance, -faillance,** †**Defai·llancy,** †**Defai·lment,** †**Defai·lure,** failure.

Defaisance, obs. f. DEFEASANCE.

†**Defa·lcate,** *ppl. a.* 1531. [– med.L. *defalcatus*, pa. pple. of *defalcare*; see next.] Curtailed.

Defalcate (dĭfæ·lke^{i}t), *v.* 1540. [– *defalcat-*, pa. ppl. stem of med.L. *defalcare*, f. *de-* DE- I. 2 + L. *falx, falc-* sickle, scythe. Cf. (O)Fr. *défalquer*. See -ATE[3].] †**1.** *trans.* To cut or lop off (a portion from a whole); to retrench, deduct –1817. †**2.** To curtail, reduce –1817. **3.** *intr.* To commit defalcations; to misappropriate property in one's charge 1864.

1. To d. a substantiall part 1624. **3.** Head clerks have defalcated 1888. Hence **De·falcator,** one guilty of defalcation.

Defalcation (dĭfælkē^{i}·ʃən). 1476. [– med.L. *defalcatio*, f. as prec.; see -ION.] **1.** †Diminution by taking away a part –1712; *spec.* reduction of a claim by the amount of a set-off 1622. **2.** The action of cutting or lopping off; deduction (*arch.*) 1624; a deduction 1621. **3.** Diminution suffered; falling off (*arch.*) 1649. **4.** Defection; shortcoming, failure 1750. **5.** A fraudulent deficiency in money matters; also *concr.* (in *pl.*), the amount misappropriated 1846.

Defalk (dĭfǭ·lk), *v.* ? *Obs.* 1475. [– (O)Fr. *défalquer* or med.L. *defalcare*; see DEFALCATE *v.*] †**1.** *trans.* To reduce by deductions –1747. **2.** To lop off; to abate. *Obs.* exc. locally in U.S. legal use. 1524. †**3.** To allow (any one) a deduction; to mulct *of* (anything due) –1565.

Defamation (dĭfămē^{i}·ʃən, def-). ME. [– (O)Fr. *diffamation* – late L. *diffamatio*, – *diffamat-*, pa. ppl. stem of L. *diffamare*; see DEFAME, -ION.] †**1.** The bringing of ill fame upon any one; disgrace –1711. **2.** The action of defaming; the fact of being defamed; also, an act of defaming ME.

2. Diffamation, or D...is the uttering of reproachful Speeches, or contumelious Language of any one, with an Intent of raising an ill Fame of the Party thus reproached; and this extends to Writing..and to Deeds AYLIFFE.

Defamatory (dĭfæ·mătəri), *a.* 1592. [– med.L. *diffamatorius*, f. as prec.; see -ORY[2]. Cf. (O)Fr. *diffamatoire.*] **1.** Of the nature of, or characterized by, defamation; having the property of defaming. **2.** Addicted to defamation 1769.

1. D. writings CLARENDON. **2.** D. writers 'JUNIUS'.

Defame (dĭfē^{i}·m), *v.* [ME. *diffame, defame* – OFr. *diffamer*, also *desf-*, *def(f)-* – L. *diffamare* spread about as an evil report, f. *dis-* DIF-, DE- I. 6 + *fama* FAME *sb.*[1].]. **1.** *trans.* To bring ill fame upon, to dishonour or disgrace in fact; to render infamous. **2.** To attack the good name of; to dishonour by report ME. †**3.** To raise an imputation *of* (some offence) against (any one). Const. also with *with*, *by*, or clause. –1820. †**4.** To spread abroad. ME. only.

1. Ioseph, loth to d. her TINDALE *Matt.* 1:19. **2.** I am now in certayne she is vntruly defamed MALORY. **3.** Rebecca..is, by many..suspicious circumstances, defamed of sorcery SCOTT.

So †**Defa·me** *sb.* ill fame; infamy; defamation. **Defa·mer.**

†**Defamous,** *a.* ME. [f. †*defame* sb. (– OFr. *def(f)ame* dishonour) + -OUS.] Infamous. **b.** Defamatory. –1587. So †**De·famy** = DEFAMATION 1, 2.

†**Defa·tigable,** *a.* 1656. [Emphatic extension (see DE- I. 3), of earlier FATIGABLE.] Apt to be wearied; capable of being wearied –1662.

†**Defa·tigate,** *v.* 1552. [– *defatigat-*, pa. ppl. stem of L. *defatigare*, f. *de-* DE- I. 3 + *fatigare*; see FATIGATE *v.*, FATIGUE *v.*] To weary out –1666.

†**Defatiga·tion.** 1508. [– L. *defatigatio*, f. as prec.; see -ION. Cf. contemporary FATIGATION.] The action of wearying out or condition of being wearied out –1654.

Default (dĭfǭ·lt), *sb.* [ME. *defaut(e)* – (i) OFr. *defaute*, f. *defaillir* (see DEFAIL), on the model of *faute* FAULT, *faillir* FAIL; (ii) (O)Fr. *défaut*, back-formation from *défaute.*] **1.** = FAULT *sb.* 1. *Obs.* or *arch.* **2.** An imperfection, defect, blemish. *Obs.* or *arch.* ME. **3.** Failure to act; neglect; *spec.* in *Law*, failure to perform some legal requirement or obligation; *esp.* to attend court on the proper day ME. †**4.** Culpable neglect of some duty or obligation –1742. Also †*transf.* of things. †**5.** (with *pl.*) A failure in duty; a fault, misdeed, offence –1822. **6.** Failure; *esp.* to meet financial engagements ME.

1. Defalt of mete ME. **2.** Grave defaults all the while lay hidden under the surface KINGLAKE. **3.** Where a defendant makes d., judgment shall be had against him by d. CROKER. **4.** Phr. *To be in d.*: to fail in one's duty. **6.** Convicted of fraud or d. JEVONS. Hence †**Defau·ltive** *a.* faulty, remiss.

Default (dĭfǭ·lt), *v.* ME. [f. prec.; partly suggested by (O)Fr. *défaut*, 3rd. pres. indic. of *defaillir* DEFAIL.] **1.** *intr.* To be wanting; to fail. *Obs.* or *arch.* †**2.** To fail in strength, faint; to suffer failure –1617. **3.** To make DEFAULT (sense 3) 1596. **4.** *trans.* To put in default; in *Law*, to declare (a party) in default and enter judgement against him ME. †**5.** To omit –1656. **6.** To fail to pay 1889.

2. And can your..king D., ye lords, except yourselves do fail GREENE. **3.** The Dissenters..in the Weekly Schools..are grievously defaulting 1845. Last year..44 companies..defaulted 1886.

Defaulter (dĭfǭ·ltəɹ). 1666. [f. DEFAULT *v.* + -ER[1].] One who is guilty of default; *esp.* one who fails to perform some duty or obligation legally required of him. **b.** *Mil.* A soldier guilty of a military offence. Also *attrib.* 1823. **c.** One who fails properly to account for money or property entrusted to his care 1823. **d.** One who becomes bankrupt 1858. So **Defau·ltress** (*rare*), a female d.

Defeasance (dĭfī·zăns). ME. [– OFr. *defesance*, f. *defesant*, pres. pple. of *de(s)faire* (mod. *défaire*) undo, f. *des-* *dé-* DE- I. 6 + *faire* make; see -ANCE.] **1.** Undoing; ruin, defeat, overthrow. (Now coloured by 2.) 1590. **2.** *Law.* The rendering null and void (of an act, condition, right, etc.) 1592. **3.** *Law.* A condition upon the performance of which a deed is defeated or made void; a collateral deed or writing expressing such condition ME.

1. Where that champion stout After his foes defesaunce did remaine SPENSER *F. Q.* I. xii. 12. Hence **Defea·sanced** *ppl. a.* liable to d.

Defease, *v.* 1621. [Back-formation from prec. and next.] To undo, bring to nought, destroy (*rare*).

Defeasible (dĭfī·zĭb'l), *a.* 1586. [– AFr. *defeasible*, f. stem of OFr. *defesant*; see DEFEASANCE, -IBLE, FEASIBLE.] Capable of being undone, defeated, or made void, as a *d. estate*. Hence **Defea·sibleness, Defeasibi·lity.**

Defeat (dĭfī·t), *sb.* 1599. [f. next; cf. Fr. *défaite* sb.] †**1.** Undoing; ruin; act of destruction –1636. **2.** Frustration (of schemes, expectations, etc.). Now usu. *fig.* of 3. 1599. **3.** The act of overthrowing in a contest, the fact of being so overthrown 1600. **4.** *Law.* The action of rendering null and void.

1. Vpon whose property, and most deere life, A damn'd defeate was made SHAKS. **3.** The D. of the Armada GREEN, of the first Reform Bill 1884.

Defeat (dĭfī·t), *v.* [ME. *def(f)ete* – AFr. *defeter*, f. *defet*, OFr. *deffait, desfait*, pa. pple. of *desfairé* (mod. *défaire*) :- med.L. *disfacere* undo, L. *dis-* DE- I. 6 + *facere* make.] †**1.** *trans.* To unmake, undo; to destroy –1632. †**2.** To cause to waste or languish –1483. †**3.** To disfigure, deface, spoil –1604. **4.** To frustrate 1474. **5.** *Law.* To render null and void 1525. **6.** To do (a person) out *of*; to disappoint, cheat 1538; †to deprive *of* –1677. **7.** To vanquish, beat 1562. Also *transf.* and *fig.*

1. His vnkindnesse may d. my life *Oth.* IV. ii. 160. **4.** To thwart its influence, and its end d. COWPER. **5.** A condition that defeats an estate CRUISE. **6.** Death..Defeated of his seisure MILT. *P. L.* XI. 254. **7.** After this, he defeited Scipio and Ivba P. HOLLAND. Hence **Defea·ter. Defea·tment** = DEFEAT *sb.* 2, 3.

Defeatism (dĭfī·tiz'm). 1918. [– Fr. *défaitisme.*] Conduct tending to bring about acceptance of defeat, esp. by action on civilian opinion. So **Defea·tist** [Fr. *défaitiste*] *sb.* and *a.*

Defeature (dĭfī·tiŭɹ), *sb.* ? *Obs.* 1590. [– OFr. *deffaiture, desfaiture* destruction, disguise, f. *desfaire*: see DEFEAT *v.*, -URE; cf. also OFr. *desfaiturer* disfigure, deform. Assim. in sp. to *defeat*, and in sense 2 assoc. w. *feature.*] †**1.** = DEFEAT *sb.* 1, 2, 3. –1834. **2.** Disfigurement; marring of features.

1. For their first loves d. SPENSER. **2.** Carefull houres..Haue written strange defeatures in my face *Com. Err.* V. i. 299. **Defea·ture** *v.* to disfigure.

†**De·fecate,** *ppl. a.* Also †**defæcate.** 1450. [– L. *defæcatus*, pa. pple. of *defæcare*, f. *de-* DE- I. 6 + *fæx*, pl. *fæces* dregs; see FÆCES, -ATE[2].] Purified from dregs, clarified, clear and pure. Also *fig.* –1742.

A pure and d. Ætherial Spirit MORE.

Defecate (dĭ·fĭke^{i}t), *v.* Also **defæcate.** 1575. [f. prec.] **1.** *trans.* To clear from dregs or impurities; to purify, clarify, refine. **2.** *fig.* To purify from pollution or extraneous admixture (of things immaterial) 1621. **3.** To purge away (dregs or fæces); to void as excrement 1774; *absol.* to void the fæces 1864.

1. The gum, which they d. in water by boiling and purging 1707. **2.** To d. life of its misery 1870. Hence **Defeca·tion,** also **defæcation,** the action or process of defecating; cleansing from impurities; the discharging of the fæces. **De·fecator,** *spec.* in *Sugar Manuf.*, an apparatus for removing the feculent matters from a saccharine liquid.

Defect (dĭfe·kt), *sb.* ME. [– L. *defectus* defect, want, f. *defect-*, pa. ppl. stem of *deficere* leave, desert, fail, f. *de-* DE- I. 2 + *facere* make, do. Partly through OFr. *defect* deficiency.] **1.** The fact of falling short; lack or absence of something necessary to completeness (opp. to *excess*); deficiency 1589. **2.** A shortcoming; a fault, flaw, imperfection ME. †**3.** Defectiveness –1776. **4.** That by which anything falls short 1660. †**5.** Failure (of the sun, etc.) to shine –1692.

1. Holding on a meane path betweene excesse and d. 1632. Phr. *In d.*: wanting. **2.** Ill breeding.. is not a single d., it is the result of many FIELDING. **3.** When all my best doth worship thy d. SHAKS.

†**Defe·ct,** *a.* 1600. [– L. *defectus*, pa. pple. of *deficere*; see prec.] Defective, deficient, wanting –1664.

Defe·ct, *v.* 1579. [– *defect-*, pa. ppl. stem of L. *deficere*; see DEFECT *sb.*] †**1.** *intr.* To fail, fall short, become deficient –1677. **2.** To fall away *from* (a person or party). 1596. †**3.** *trans.* To cause to desert –1685. †**4.** To make defective; to dishonour –1639.

2. He defected, and fled to the contrary part GAULE.

Defe·ctible, *a.* 1617. [– late L. *defectibilis* (Augustine), f. as prec.; see -IBLE.] Liable to fail or fall short. Hence **Defe:ctibi·lity,** liability to become defective.

Defection (dĭfe·kʃən). 1544. [– L. *defectio*, f. *defect-*; see DEFECT *sb.*, -ION, and cf. (O)Fr. *défection*.] **1.** The action or fact of failing, or falling short; failure (*of* anything); †defectiveness; †a defect. **2.** The action of falling away from a leader, party, or cause; desertion 1552. **3.** A falling away from faith, or duty; backsliding; apostasy 1546.

1. Miserable defections of hope C. BRONTË. **2.** The d. of Iudas the traitour 1583. **3.** The d. and disobedience of the first Man HALE. Hence †**Defe·ctious** *a.* having defects; of the nature of d.

Defective (dĭfe·ktiv). ME. [– (O)Fr. *défectif, -ive* or late L. *defectivus*, f. as prec.; see -IVE.]

A. *adj.* **1.** Having a defect or defects; imperfect, incomplete 1472. †**2.** At fault –1677. **3.** Lacking (to completeness) 1603. **4.** *Gram.* Wanting one or more of the usual forms of declension, conjugation, etc. 1530.

1. D. weights and measures 1495, buildings 1663, sight COWPER. **3.** I wish you had a Fortunatus hat; it is the only thing d. in your outfit CARLYLE. Hence **Defe·ctive-ly** *adv.*, **-ness.**

B. *sb.* †**1.** *gen.* One who is defective 1592; *spec.* in *U.S.*, one who is deficient in one or more of the physical senses or powers 1881. **2.** *Gram.* A defective part of speech. 1612.

Defector (dĭfe·ktəɹ). 1662. [– L. *defector*, f. as prec.; see -OR 2.] One who falls away; a seceder or deserter.

†**Defe·ctuous,** *a.* 1553. [– med.L. *defectuosus*, f. *defectus* DEFECT *sb.*; see -UOUS. Cf. (O)Fr. *défectueux*.] Having defects; defective, faulty –1726. So †**Defectuo·sity,** defectiveness, faultiness.

†**Defedation** (dīːfidēⁱ·ʃən). Also **defœd-.** 1634. [– Fr. †*défédation* (XV–XVI) or med.L. *defoedatio*, f. *defoedat* , pa. ppl. stem of late L. *defoedare* to defile, f. *de-* DE- I. 3 + *foedare*, f. *foedus* foul.] The action of making impure; pollution. Also *fig.* –1793.

†**Defei·t, defe·t,** *a.* ME. [– OFr. *defeit, desfeit, -fait*, pa. pple. of *desfaire, defaire* undo; see DEFEAT *v.*] Marred, disfigured –1605.

Defence, defense (dĭfe·ns), *sb.* [ME. *defens, defense* – OFr. *defens(e)* (mod. *défense*) – L. (Rom.) *defensum, defensa*, subst. uses of n. and fem. pa. pple. of *defendere*; see next.] The action of defending (see DEFEND *v.*).

I. †**1.** The action of warding off –1588. †**2.** Prohibition –1698.

1. For yᵉ defence of his enemyes FABYAN. **2.** Phr. *In d.*: (of fish, or waters) prohibited from being taken or fished in.

II. 1. Protecting from attack; resistance against attack; warding off of injury; protection. (The chief current sense.) ME. †**b.** Capacity of defending –1654. **2.** The art or science of defending oneself (with weapons or the fists); self-defence 1602. **3.** Something that defends; *spec.* (*pl.*) fortifications ME. **4.** The defending by argument ME.; a speech or argument in self-vindication 1557.

1. His d. coude not auayle him LD. BERNERS. **b.** The Citie being but of small d. 3 *Hen. VI*, v. i. 64. **3.** The Lord is my d. *Ps.* 94:22. The defences of the Austrians on the right bank 1853.

III. *Law.* [Orig. allied to I, but now influenced by II.] The opposing or denial of the truth or validity of the prosecutor's complaint; the defendant's (written) pleading in answer to the statement of claim; the proceedings taken by an accused party or his legal agents, for defending himself 1595.

Hence †**Defence, defense** *v.* to provide with defences; to defend, protect (*lit.* and *fig.*). **Defe·nceless, defenseless** *a.* without d.; unprotected; †affording no d. (*rare*). **Defe·nceless-ly** *adv.*, **-ness.**

Defend (dĭfe·nd), *v.* ME. [– (O)Fr. *défendre* :– L. *defendere* ward off, protect, f. *de-* DE- I. 2 + *-fendere* (as in *offendere* OFFEND).]

I. †**1.** To ward off, keep off; to avert. (*Obs.* exc. as in III.) –1808. †**2.** To keep (*from* doing something), to prevent –1660. Also *refl.* **3.** To prohibit, forbid. Now *dial.* ME. ¶ In *God defend* = 'God forbid', senses 3 and 1 seem to unite.

II. 1. *trans.* To ward off attack from; to fight for the safety of; to protect, guard ME. Also *absol.* **2.** To support or uphold by speech or argument ME.; †to contend –1620.

1. From Turke and Pope d. vs Lord STERNHOLD. **2.** Erronyously defendyng and maynteynyng his seid obstynate opynyons *Act* 4 *Hen. VIII*, c. 19 Preamble. To d. general principles MORLEY.

III. *Law.* (Orig. belonging to I, but also with uses from II.) **a.** Of the defendant: To deny, repel, oppose the plaintiff's plea, the action raised against him; *absol.* to make defence. **b.** To vindicate (himself, his cause). **c.** Of a legal agent: To take legal measures to vindicate; to appear, address the court, etc. in defence of. ME.

So **Defe·ndable** *a. rare*, capable of being protected from assault or injury; capable of being vindicated. **Defe·nder,** one who defends, or wards off an attack; one who upholds or maintains by argument; the party sued in an action at law; = DEFENDANT *sb.* 3. **Defe·nderism** (*Irish Hist.*), the principles or policy of a society of Roman Catholics, formed in the 18th c. to resist the Orangemen.

Defendant (dĭfe·ndănt). ME. [– (O)Fr. *défendant*, pres. pple. of *défendre*; see prec., -ANT¹.]

A. *adj.* †**1.** Used as *pr. pple.* Defending. (ME. only.) **2.** Defending oneself, or an opinion, cause, etc., against attack. ? *Obs.* 1596. †**3.** Affording defence. *Hen. V*, II. iv. 8.

1. *Him self defendaunt* = in his own defence.

B. *sb.* †**1.** A defender against attack; opp. to *assailant* –1787. †**2.** The party who denies the charge and accepts the challenge of the *appellant* in wager of battle –1828. **3.** *Law.* A person sued in a court of law; the party in a suit who defends (orig. = *denies*); opp. to *plaintiff* ME.

Phr. *In my, his* (etc.) *d.*: in one's defence. [app. a corruption of *me, him, d.* in A. 1.]

Defendress (dĭfe·ndrĕs). Now *rare.* 1509. [– Fr. *défenderesse*; see -ESS¹.] A female defender or defendant. var. †**Defe·ndrix** (*rare*).

Defenestration (dīfenĕstrēⁱ·ʃən). 1620. [– mod.L. *defenestratio*, f. *de-* DE- I. 1 + *fenestra* window; see -ATION. So in Fr.] The action of throwing out of a window.

†**Defe·nsative.** Also **-itive.** 1576. [Extended form of DEFENSIVE (cf. *preventive, -ative*); see -ATIVE.]

A. *adj.* Having the property of protecting; defensive –1668.

B. *sb.* = DEFENSIVE *sb.* 1. –1783.

A good d. against all venemous humours 1612.

Defense, -fenser, var. ff. DEFENCE, DEFENSOR.

Defensible (dĭfe·nsĭb'l), *a.* [Late ME. *defensible* – late L. *defensibilis* (Cassiodorus), f. *defens-*, pa. ppl. stem of *defendere* DEFEND; see -IBLE.] †**1.** Defensive –1828. **2.** Capable of being defended; safe 1600. **3.** *fig.* Capable of being defended in argument. (The chief current sense.) ME.

1. D. men 1549, posts GIBBON, harness ME. **3.** A more d., or a juster claim FAWCETT. Hence **Defensibi·lity,** the quality of being d. **Defe·nsibleness. Defe·nsibly** *adv.*

†**Defension** (dĭfe·nʃən). ME. [– L. *defensio*, f. as prec.; see -ION. Cf. OFr. *defension*.] = DEFENCE –1555.

Defensive (dĭfe·nsiv). ME. [– (O)Fr. *défensif, -ive* – med.L. *defensivus*, f. as prec.; see -IVE.]

A. *adj.* **1.** Having the quality of defending; protective. **2.** Made, or carried on for the purpose of defence: opp. to *offensive* 1580. **3.** Of or belonging to defence 1643. **4.** Of the nature of a defence 1604.

1. As a Moate d. to a house SHAKS. **2.** D. war 1631. **3.** A d. position S. AUSTIN. **4.** A d. allegation BLACKSTONE. Hence **Defe·nsive-ly** *adv.*, **-ness.**

B. *sb.* **1.** Something that serves to defend or protect ME. **2.** A position or attitude of defence: usu. in phr. *on the d.* (see A. 3) 1601.

1. Wars preventive, upon just fears, are defensives BACON (J.).

Defensor (dĭfe·nsəɹ, -ǭɹ). [ME. *defensour* – AFr. *defensour* = OFr. *defensëor* (mod. *-eur*) :– L. *defensor*, f. as prec.; see -OR 2.] †**1.** A defender –1670. **2.** *Rom. Law.* One who took up the defence and assumed the liability of a defendant in an action 1875.

1. *Chief D. of the Christian Church*, a title formerly bestowed by the Pope, as upon Henry VII.

Defensory (dĭfe·nsŏri). ? *Obs.* 1552. [– late L. *defensorius*, f. *defensor*; see prec., -ORY¹,².]

A. *adj.* That serves to defend; defensive.

†**B.** *sb.* Something defensive; a defence –1677.

Defer (dĭfǭ·ɹ), *v.*¹ Inflexions **deferred, deferring.** [ME. *differre, deferre* – (O)Fr. *différer* defer, differ – L. *differre* carry apart, delay, etc. Orig. same word as DIFFER.] †**1.** *trans.* To put on one side. (ME. only.) **2.** To put off to some later time; to delay; postpone ME. Also *absol.* or *intr.* †**3.** To put off (time) –1633. To protract; *intr.* to linger –1561.

2. Deferre the spoile of the Citie vntill night 2 *Hen. VI*, IV. vii. 141. Be wise to-day; 'tis madness to d. YOUNG. **3.** Deferre no tyme, delayes haue dangerous ends 1 *Hen. VI*, III. ii. 33. Hence **Defe·rment,** a putting off; postponement. **Defe·rrer.**

Defer (dĭfǭ·ɹ), *v.*² Inflexions **deferred, deferring.** 1479. [–(O)Fr. *déférer* – L. *deferre* carry away, refer (a matter), f. *de-* DE- I. 2 + *ferre* bear, carry.] †**1.** *trans.* To carry down or away; to convey (*rare*) –1654. †**2.** To offer; in *Law*, to offer for acceptance. Const. *to*, rarely *on.* –1832. †**3.** To refer –1691. **4.** *intr.* To pay deference *to* 1686.

2. To deferre to them any obedience, or honour HOBBES. **4.** To d. to the judgment of others BURKE.

Deference (de·fĕrĕns). 1647. [– Fr. *déférence*, f. *déférer* DEFER *v.*²; see -ENCE.] †**1.** The action of offering (*rare*) 1660. **2.** Submission to the acknowledged superior claims, skill, judgement, etc., of another 1647. **3.** Courteous regard, as to one to whom respect is due 1660.

2. Charles often paid a strange d. to minds inferior to his own D'ISRAELI. **3.** Their age and learning..entitle them to all d. CHATHAM.

Phr. *In d. to*: out of practical respect or regard to.

Deferent (de·fĕrĕnt), *a.*¹ and *sb.* ME. [– Fr. *déférent*; in *Astron.*, – med.L. *deferens, -ent-*, subst. use of pres. pple. of L. *deferre*; see DEFER *v.*², -ENT.]

A. *adj.* Carrying or conducting 1626.

The..testes end in a pair of d. ducts HUXLEY.

B. *sb.* **1.** A carrying or conducting agent; *spec.* in *Phys.*, a duct for conveying fluids 1626. **2.** *Ptolemaic Astron.* The circular orbit of the centre of the epicycle in which a planet was conceived to move; corresp. (roughly) to the actual orbit of the planet ME. **3.** One who reports a matter 1670.

1. Though Aire be the most favourable D. of Sounds BACON.

Deferent (de·fĕrĕnt), *a.*² 1822. [f. DEFER *v.*², and DEFERENCE; see -ENT.] Showing deference, deferential.

His opposition..was always modest, d. 1822.

Deferential (defĕre·nʃăl), *a.*[1] 1822. [f. DEFERENCE + -IAL, after *prudence, prudential*, etc.] Characterized by deference; respectful. Hence **Deferentia·lity** *sb.* deference. **Defere·ntially** *adv.*

Defere·ntial, *a.*[2] 1877. [– Fr. *déférentiel*, f. *déférent* DEFERENT *a.*[1]] *Phys.* Serving to convey; pertaining to the deferent duct.

Defervescence (dīfəɹve·sĕns). 1721. [f. *defervescent-*, pres. ppl. stem of L. *defervescere* cease boiling, etc., f. *de-* DE- II. 1 + *fervescere*, incipient verb f. *fervēre* be hot; see -ENCE.] **1.** Cooling down. (Dicts.) **2.** *Path.* The decrease of bodily temperature which accompanies the abatement of fever; the period of this decrease 1866. var. †**Deferve·scency.** So **Deferve·scent** *a.* and *sb.*

Defeudalize; see DE- II. 1 and *feudalize*.

Defial (dĭfəi·ăl). *rare.* 1470. [– OFr. *defiaille*, f. *defier* defy (see -AL[1] 2); in mod. use f. DEFY + -AL[1].] = DEFIANCE.

Defiance (dĭfəi·ăns). ME. [– (O)Fr. *défiance* (now only distrust), f. *défier* DEFY; see -ANCE.] †**1.** Renunciation of faith, allegiance, or amity; declaration of hostilities –1649. **2.** A challenge; a summons to a combat or contest ME. **3.** The act of setting at nought 1710. †**4.** Declaration of aversion or contempt (*rare*) 1603. †**5.** Distrust [= mod.Fr. *défiance*.] PEPYS.

1. †*At d.*: at enmity or hostility; The Prouinces at d. with vs 1598. **2.** Shall we..send D. to the Traytor SHAKS. **4.** *Meas. for M.* III. i. 143.

Phr. *To bid d. to*: to defy; to brave, set at nought; so *to set at d. In d. of*: setting at nought.

Defiant (dĭfəi·ănt), *a.* 1837. [f. prec.; see -ANT[1].] **1.** Showing a disposition to defy. ‖**2.** Feeling distrust. [= mod.Fr. *défiant*.] 1872.

1. The man's heart that dare rise d...against Hell itself CARLYLE. **Defi·ant-ly** *adv.*, **-ness** (*rare*).

†**Defi·atory,** *a. rare.* 1635. [f. DEFY *v.*[1]; cf. *commendatory*.] Bearing defiance.

Defibrinate (dĭfəi·brineᶦt), *v.* 1845. [f. DE- II. 1 + FIBRIN + -ATE[3].] To deprive of fibrin. Hence **Defibrina·tion,** the process of depriving of fibrin. So **Defi·brinize** *v.* = DEFIBRINATE.

Deficiency (dĭfi·ʃĕnsi). Also †**deficience.** 1634. [f. next; see -ENCY.] The quality or state of being deficient; failure; lack; insufficiency. Also *attrib.*

In excess as well as in d. GROTE. Where art has to supply the deficiencies of nature NEWMAN.

D. of a curve (Math.): the number by which its double points fall short of the highest number possible in a curve of the same order.

Deficient (dĭfi·ʃĕnt). 1581. [– *deficient-*, pres. ppl. stem of L. *deficere* undo, leave, fail, f. *de-* DE- I. 2 + *facere* make, do.]

A. *adj.* **1.** Wanting something necessary to completeness; falling short *in* something; defective 1604. **2.** Insufficient; inadequate 1632. †**3.** Failing, fainting –1632.

1. Being not d., blind, or lame of sense *Oth.* I. iii. 63. D. memory JOHNSON. D. in knowledge about health 1861. *D. number*: a number the sum of whose factors is less than the number itself. **3.** *Lear* IV. vi. 23.

Phr. †*D. cause*: that failure to act, or absence of anything, which becomes the cause or negative condition of some result. Hence **Defi·ciently** *adv.*

†**B.** *sb.* **1.** Something that is wanting; the want of something; a deficiency –1686. **2.** A defaulter –1719.

Deficit (de·fisit, dĭ·fisit). 1782. [– Fr. *déficit* – L. *deficit* there is wanting, 3rd. pers. sing. pres. ind. of *deficere* (see DEFECT *v.*), formerly placed against an item in an account.] A falling short; deficiency in amount; the excess of expenditure or liabilities over income or assets.

There was a *surplus*..instead of a *d.* BENTHAM.

‖**De fide** (dī fəi·di), *predic.* or *attrib. phr.* [L.] That is 'of faith', to be accepted as an article of faith.

Defier (dĭfəi·əɹ). 1585. [f. DEFY *v.*[1] + -ER[1].] One who defies, as a *d. of the Gods*.

†**Defiguration** (dĭfigiŭrēᶦ·ʃən). 1585. [f. *defigure* v. + -ATION; cf. Fr. *défiguration*.] Disfigurement –1830.

So †**Defi·gure** *v.*[1] ME. only.

†**Defigure** (dĭfi·giŭɹ), *v.*[2] 1599. [f. DE- I. 3 + FIGURE *v.*] To figure, delineate. Also *fig.* –1631. *fig.* By this defigured they the perplexed life of man 1615.

Defilade (defilēᶦ·d), *sb.* 1851. [f. DEFILE *v.*[3] + -ADE.] = DEFILEMENT[2].

Defilade (defilēᶦ·d), *v.* 1828. [f. prec.] To arrange the plan and profile of fortifications, so that their lines shall be protected from enfilading fire, and the interior of the works from plunging or reverse fire.

Defile (dī·fəil, dĭfəi·l), *sb.* 1685. [orig. *defilé, defilee* – Fr. *défilé*, subst. use of pa. pple. of *défiler* DEFILE *v.*[2] For loss of final -*é* cf. ASSIGN *sb.*[2]] **1.** *Mil.* A narrow way along which troops can march only by files or with a narrow front; *esp.* a narrow mountain gorge or pass. **2.** The act of defiling, a march by files 1835.

Defile (dĭfəi·l), *v.*[1] ME. [alt. of DEFOUL, DEFOIL, by association with synon. BEFILE.] †**1.** To bruise. (ME. only.) **2.** To render foul; to dirty 1530. **3.** To render morally foul; to corrupt, taint, sully ME. †**4.** To violate the chastity of; to debauch –1769. **5.** To render ceremonially unclean 1500. †**6.** To sully the honour of –1708. †**7.** *absol.* To cause defilement; to drop excrement –1596.

2. An evyll birde that defiles hys own nest LATIMER. **3.** Defyled with syne 1450. **4.** The husband murder'd, and the wife defil'd PRIOR. **5.** They have defiled the priesthood *Neh.* 13:29. **6.** *Mids. N.* III. ii. 410. **7.** 1 *Hen. IV*, II. iv. 456. Hence **Defi·ler.**

Defile (dĭfəi·l), *v.*[2] 1705. [– Fr. *défiler*, f. *dé-* DE- I. 2 + *file* FILE *sb.*[2]] *Mil.* **1.** *intr.* To march in a line or by files; to file off. Also *transf.* **2.** *trans.* To traverse by files. ? *Obs.* 1762.

Defile, *v.*[3] *rare.* 1864. [– Fr. *défiler*, opp. of *enfiler*, ENFILADE *v.*] = DEFILADE *v.*

Defilement[1] (dĭfəi·lmĕnt). 1571. [f. DEFILE *v.*[1] + -MENT.] The act of defiling, the being defiled; *concr.* anything that defiles.

When Lust..Lets in D. to the inward parts MILT. *Comus* 466. Defilements in water 1871.

Defi·lement[2]. 1816. [– Fr. *défilement*, f. *défiler* DEFILE *v.*[3]; see -MENT.] *Fortif.* The act or operation of defilading.

Defilia·tion. [DE- II. 1.] Deprivation of a son. LAMB.

Definable (dĭfəi·năb'l), *a.* 1660. [f. DEFINE *v.* + -ABLE.] Capable of being defined.

As if infinite were d. DRYDEN. A d. interest GEO. ELIOT. Hence **Defi:nabi·lity. Defi·nably** *adv.*

Define (dĭfəi·n), *v.* ME. [– OFr. *definer* – Rom. **definare*, for L. *definire* (whence Fr. *définir*), f. *de-* DE- I. 3 + *finire* FINISH.] †**1.** *trans.* To bring to an end. Also *intr.* –1677. **2.** To determine the boundary or limits of. Also *fig.* ME. **b.** To make definite in outline or form 1815. †**3.** To limit, confine –1643. **4.** To lay down definitely, †to fix upon 1535; †*intr.* to decide –1612. †**5.** To state precisely –1669. †Also *intr.* **6.** To set forth the essential nature of. (In early use: To describe.) ME. **b.** To set forth what (a word, etc.) means. [Not in J.] 1532. Also *intr.* **7.** *transf.* To make (a thing) what it is; to characterize 1633. **8.** To separate by definition (*from*) (*rare*) 1807.

1. A more ready way to d. controversies BARROW. **2.** In nature everything is distinct, yet nothing defined WORDSW. **4.** He 'defined his position'.. very clearly 1867. **6.** I wyl descryue and dyffyne it [the courte] to the CAXTON. A lady once asked him how he came to d. *Pastern* 'the *knee* of a horse' BOSWELL. Hence **Defi·nement,** description, definition; †limitation (*rare*). **Defi·ner.**

†**Defi·nish,** *v. rare.* [– Fr. *définiss-*, lengthened stem of *définir*; see prec., -ISH[2].] *trans.* To define. CHAUCER.

Definite (de·finit), *a.* (*sb.*) 1530. [– L. *definitus*, pa. pple. of *definire*; see DEFINE *v.*] **1.** Having fixed limits; determinate; exact, precise 1553. Also *transf.* of persons, in reference to their actions 1611. **2.** *Gram.* **a.** Applied in German and Early English to those forms of the adjective which are used when preceded by the definite article or an equivalent. **b.** Of verbs: = Finite (*rare*). **c.** *D. article*: the article *the*, as indicating a defined or particularized individual. 1727. **3.** *Bot.* Said of inflorescence having the central axis terminated in a flower-bud which opens first: also called *centrifugal* or *determinate* 1876.

1. In a d. compass 1586. A d. understanding 1691, time 1726, answer DICKENS. Be more d. in your statements 1894. Hence **De·finite-ly** *adv.*, **-ness.**

B. *sb.* **1.** Something that is definite 1530. †**2.** 'Thing explained or defined' (J.) 1726.

Definition (defini·ʃən). ME. [– (O)Fr. *définition* (Eng. before XVI chiefly *diff-*, from OFr. *diff-*), – L. *definitio*, f. *definit-*, pa. ppl. stem of *definire*; see DEFINE *v.*] †**1.** The setting of bounds; limitation (*rare*) –1483. **2.** The action of determining a question at issue; *spec.* an ecclesiastical pronouncement ME. **3.** *Logic*, etc. The action of defining (see DEFINE *v.* 6) 1645. **4.** A precise statement of the essential nature of a thing ME. **b.** A declaration of the signification of a word or phrase. [Not in J.] 1500. **5.** The action of making definite; the condition of being made, or of being definite, in form or outline; *spec.* the defining power of an optical instrument 1859.

2. This challenge of infallibility..discrediteth their [councils'] definitions BRAMHALL. **3.** *D.* (with *Logicians*), an unfolding of the essence or being of a thing by its kind and difference BAILEY. **4.** The old d. of force was, that which caused change in motion W. GROVE. **5.** A d. of a word is any maner of declaration of a word 1551. Hence **Defini·tional** *a.* of or pertaining to a d. (*rare*).

Definitive (dĭfi·nĭtiv). ME. [– (O)Fr. *définitif* (Eng. before XVI *diff-*, after OFr. *diff-*: cf. prec.), – L. *definitivus*, f. as prec.; see -IVE.]

A. *adj.* **1.** Having the function of finally deciding; determinative, final. **2.** Having the character of finality; determinate. In *Biol.* opp. to *formative* or *primitive*, as *d. organs*. 1639. †**3.** *Metaph.* Having a definite position, but not occupying space: opp. to *circumscriptive* –1665. **4.** That specifies the individual referred to; *esp.* in *Gram.* 1731.

1. A d. answer RICHARDSON, treaty WILKES, verdict MACAULAY, †judge 1741. **2.** A d. system 1821, result 1865. **4.** *D. Article* BAILEY. D. verb W. WARD.

B. *sb.* (the *adj.* used *ellipt.*) †**1.** A definitive sentence, judgement, or pronouncement –1804. **2.** *Gram.* A definitive word 1751.

Hence **Defi·nitive-ly** *adv.*, **-ness.**

Definitor (definəi·tŏɹ). 1648. [med.L. sense of late L. *definitor* (Tertullian) one who determines, f. as prec.; see -OR 2.] **1.** An officer of the chapter in certain monastic orders, who decided points of discipline. †**2.** A kind of surveying instrument –1793.

Definitude (dĭfi·nitiud). 1836. [f. DEFINITE, after *infinite, infinitude*; see -TUDE.] The quality of being definite; precision.

Results of remarkable precision and d. LATHAM.

†**Defix** (dĭfi·x), *v.* ME. [– *defix-*, pa. ppl. stem of L. *defigere* fasten down, f. *de-* DE- I. 1 + *figere*; see FIX *v.*] To fasten down; to fix firmly or intently (*lit.* and *fig.*) –1679.

In intent and defixed thoughts upon some.. object GLANVILL.

Deflagrable (de·flăgrăb'l), *a. rare.* 1691. [f. L. *deflagrare* (see next) + -ABLE.] Capable of deflagration. Hence **Deflagrabi·lity,** d. quality, readiness to deflagrate (*rare*). BOYLE.

Deflagrate (de·flăgreᶦt), *v.* 1727. [– *deflagrat-*, pa. ppl. stem of L. *deflagrare* burn up, f. *de-* DE- I. 3 + *flagrare* burn; see -ATE[3].] **1.** *trans.* To cause to burn away with sudden bursting into flame and rapid combustion. **2.** *intr.* To burst into flame and burn away rapidly 1750.

1. When coal is deflagrated with nitre 1794. **2.** Such a degree of burning heat as would cause the nitre to d. G. ADAMS.

Deflagration (deflăgrēᶦ·ʃən). 1607. [– L. *deflagratio*, f. as prec., see -ION.] †**1.** The rapid burning away of anything in a destructive fire –1837. **2.** *Physics.* The action of deflagrating 1666.

1. The fall of a spark on gunpowder, for example, followed by the d. of the gunpowder SIR W. HAMILTON. **2.** The metals are sometimes oxidized by what is called d. 1831.

Deflagrator (de·flăgreᶦtəɹ). 1824. [f. as prec. + -OR 2.] An apparatus for producing deflagration, *esp.* a voltaic arrangement for producing intense heat.

Deflate (dĭflēᶦ·t), *v.* 1891. [f. DE- I. 6 + -*flate* of INFLATE.] **1.** *trans.* To release the air from. Also *fig.* **2.** To reduce an inflated currency 1919. Hence **Defla·tion.**

Deflect (dĭfle·kt), *v.* 1555. [– L. *deflectere* bend aside, f. *de-* DE- I. 1, 2 + *flectere* bend.] **I.** *trans.* **1.** To bend down 1630. **2.** To bend to one side, or from a straight line 1630; *fig.* 1555. **3.** To turn *to* something different from its natural quality or use 1630.

1. They pray..with their knees deflected under them 1630. **2.** If we look at an object through a prism, the rays of light coming from it are deflected HARLAN. *fig.* To d. the judgment by hope or fear LECKY.

II. *intr.* To turn to one side or from a straight line 1646; *fig.* 1612.

At some parts of the Azores it [the needle] deflecteth not, but lyeth in the true meridian SIR T. BROWNE. *fig.* The Mind..can, every moment, d. from the line of truth and reason WARBURTON.

Deflected (dĭfle·ktėd), *ppl. a.* 1828. [f. prec. + -ED¹.] **1.** Turned aside; bent to one side 1860. **2.** *Zool.* and *Bot.* Bent downwards; = DEFLEXED 1828. var. **Defle·ct.** E.B. BROWNING.

Deflection; see DEFLEXION.

Deflective (dĭfle·ktiv), *a.* 1813. [f. DEFLECT *v.* + -IVE. (Better *deflexive.*)] Having the quality of deflecting, as *d. forces.*

Deflector (dĭfle·ktəɹ). 1837. [f. as prec. + -OR 2.] That which deflects; *e.g.* (*a*) a deflecting magnet; (*b*) a diaphragm for deflecting a current of air, gas, etc.

Deflexed (dĭfle·kst), *ppl. a.* 1826. [f. earlier *deflex* adj. (– L. *deflexus*, pa. pple. of *deflectere* DEFLECT) + -ED¹.] *Zool.* and *Bot.* Bent downwards; deflected. var. **De·flex.**

Defl·exible, *a.* 1796. [f. L. *deflex-* (see next) + -IBLE.] Capable of being deflected. Hence **Deflexibi·lity.**

Deflexion, deflection (dĭfle·kʃən). 1603. [– late L. *deflexio*, f. L. *deflex-*, pa. ppl. stem of *deflectere* DEFLECT; see -ION. Cf. Fr. *déflexion* (XVI). The sp. *deflection*, now common, is taken from the verb DEFLECT.] **1.** The action of bending down; bent condition; a bend or curve 1665. **2.** The action of turning, or state of being turned from a straight line or regular course; the amount of such deviation; a turn or deviation 1605. **3.** The turning of a word or phrase aside from its actual form, application, or use 1603. **4.** *Electr.*, etc. The turning of a magnetic needle away from its zero; the measured amount of this 1646. **5.** *Optics.* The bending of rays of light from the straight line. See DIFFRACTION. 1674. **6.** *Naut.* The deviation of a ship from her true course 1706.

1. The deflection of a beam supporting a lateral weight 1879. **2.** The great deflection of the coast southward from Cape Wrath MERIVALE. A deflection from simplicity MOZLEY. **3.** A deflexion of a word 1659.

Deflexionize, -ed, -ation; see DE- II. 1.

Deflexure (dĭfle·ksiŭɹ, -fle·kʃŭɹ). *rare.* 1656. [f. L. *deflex-* (see DEFLEXION) + -URE.] Deflexion; the condition of being bent (down or away).

Deflorate (dĭflōᵊ·rĕt, de·florĕt), *a.* 1828. [– late L. *defloratus*, pa. pple. of *deflorare*; see next, -ATE².] **1.** *Bot.* Past the flowering state; as anthers that have shed their pollen, etc. **2.** = DEFLOWERED 1883.

Defloration (deflorēⁱ·ʃən). ME. [– (O)Fr. *défloration* or late L. *defloratio*, f. *deflorat-*, pa. ppl. stem of *deflorare*, f. *de-* DE- I. 6 + *flos, flor-* flower; see -ION.] **1.** The act of deflowering a virgin. **2.** The culling of the choice parts of a book ME.

2. The *deflorations* or MSS. containing excerpts 1890.

Deflore, deflour, obs. ff. DEFLOWER.

†Deflou·rish, *v.* 1494. [– OFr. *de(s)flouriss-*, extended stem of *de(s)flourir* (mod. *défleurir*); see DE- I. 6, FLOURISH *v.*] **1.** *trans.* To deflower; also *fig.* –1538. **2.** *intr.* To cease to flourish 1656.

†Deflow·, *v.* [f. DE- I. 1 + FLOW *v.* after L. *defluere* flow down or away.]. *intr.* To flow down. SIR T. BROWNE.

Deflower (dĭflauᵊ·ɹ), *v.* ME. [– OFr. *deflourer*, earlier *de(s)flo(u)rer* (mod. *déflorer*) – Rom. **disflorare*, for late L. *deflorare*, f. *de-* DE- I. 6 + *flos, flor-* FLOWER.] **1.** *trans.* To deprive (a woman) of her virginity; to violate, ravish. Also *fig.* **†2.** To cull from (a book) its choice parts –1781. **3.** To deprive of flowers 1630.

1. *fig.* Actual discovery (as it were) rifles and deflowers the newness and freshness of the object SOUTH. Hence **Deflow·erer.**

Defluent (de·fluĕnt). *rare.* 1652. [– *defluent-*, pres. ppl. stem of L. *defluere*, f. *de-* DE- I. 1 + *fluere* flow; see -ENT.]

A. *adj.* Flowing down, decurrent.

B. *sb.* That which flows down (from a main body). So **†De·fluency,** fluidity (*rare*).

†Defluous (de·fluəs), *a. rare.* 1727. [f. L. *defluus* flowing down (f. *defluere*: see prec.) + -OUS; see -UOUS.] Flowing down; also, falling off –1882.

†Deflux (dī·flɒks), *sb.* 1599. [– L. *defluxus*, f. *deflux-*, pa. ppl. stem of *defluere*; see prec.] **1.** A flowing down; defluxion –1710. **2.** *concr.* An effluence (*rare*) –1682.

Defluxion (dĭflɒ·kʃən). 1549. [– Fr. *défluxion* or late L. *defluxio*, f. as prec.; see -ION.] **†1.** A flowing down –1832. **2.** *Path.* The flow or discharge accompanying a cold or inflammation; a running at the nose; catarrh. Now *rare.* 1576. **†3.** That which flows down –1633; *fig.* an effluence –1678.

Defœdation; see DEFEDATION.

†Defoi·l, *v.* [– Fr. *défeuiller*, OFr. *des-, deffueiller*, f. *des-, de-* DE- I. 6 + *feuille* leaf. Cf. late L. *defoliare* (see next).] *trans.* = DEFOLIATE *v.* P. Holland.

Defoliate (dĭfōᵘ·lieⁱt), *v.* 1793. [– *defoliat-*, pa. ppl. stem of late L. *defoliare*, f. *de-* DE- I. 6 + *folium* leaf; see -ATE³.] *trans.* To strip of leaves; also *fig.* So **Defo·liate** *a.* having cast or lost its leaves (*rare*). **Defolia·tion,** loss or shedding of leaves. **Defo·liator,** that which defoliates; an insect which strips trees of their leaves.

Deforce (dĭfōᵊ·ɹs), *v.* ME. [– AFr. *deforcer* = OF. *deforcier*, f. *des-, de-* (DE- I. 6) + *forcier, forcer* to FORCE. Cf. ENFORCE, etc.] **1.** *Law.* To keep (something) by force (*from* the rightful owner) 1470. **2.** To keep (a person) forcibly out of the possession *of* his property 1531. **3.** *Sc. Law.* To prevent by force (an officer of the law) from executing his official duty 1461.

2. He [Stephen] deforced Mawd..of her right 1586. Hence **Defo·rcement. Defo·rcer. Defo·rciant,** one who keeps another wrongfully out of possession of an estate. **†Deforcia·tion.**

Deforest (dĭfǫ·rėst), *v.* 1538. [f. DE- II. 2 + FOREST *sb.*; cf. DE-AFFOREST, DISAFFOREST, DISFOREST.] **1.** *Law.* To make no longer a forest; = DISAFFOREST 1, DISFOREST 1. **2.** *gen.* To clear of forests or trees 1880. Hence **Deforesta·tion.**

Deform (dĭfǭ·ɹm), *a. arch.* ME. [– L. *deformis*, f. *de-* DE- I. 6 + *forma* shape; cf. Fr. *†déforme.* See DIFFORM *a.*] Deformed; hideous.

Sight so d. what heart of rock could long Driey'd behold MILT. *P. L.* XI. 494. **†Defo·rmly** *adv.*

Deform (dĭfǭ·ɹm), *v.*¹ ME. [– OFr. *difformer, de(s)former* (mod. *difformer, déformer*) – med.L. *difformare*, Rom. **disformare*, L. *deformare*, f. DIS-, DE- I. 6 + *forma* FORM *sb.*] **1.** *trans.* To mar the beauty or excellence of; to disfigure, deface (*lit.* and *fig.*) 1450. **2.** To mar the form of; to misshape ME. **3.** To alter the form of; in *Physics*, to change the normal shape of 1702. **¶4.** Obs. var. of DIFFORM *v.*

1. He..deformed the country with ruine and spoile HAYWARD. **2.** Cheated of Feature by dissembling Nature, Deform'd, vnfinish'd *Rich. III*, I. i. 20. Hence **Defo·rmable** *a.* deformed; capable of being deformed; hence **Deformabi·lity. Defo·rmer,** one who or that which deforms.

†Deform, *v.*² *rare.* ME. only. [– L. *deformare* form, fashion, f. *de-* DE- I. 3 + *forma* FORM *sb.*] To form, fashion.

Deformation (dīfǫɹmēⁱ·ʃən). ME. [–(O)Fr. *déformation* or L. *deformatio* (med.L. *diff-*), f. *deformat-*, pa. ppl. stem of *deformare*; see DEFORM *v.*¹, -ION.] **1.** The action (or result) of deforming; disfigurement, defacement. **2.** Alteration of form for the worse; (often opp. to *reformation*) 1546. **3.** *Physics.* Alteration of shape; an altered form *of* 1846.

3. The d. of the solar disc by refraction 1869.

Deformed (dĭfǭ·ɹmd), *ppl. a.* ME. [f. DEFORM *v.*¹ + -ED¹.] **†1.** Marred in appearance –1632. **2.** Marred in shape, misshapen; unshapely. Now chiefly of persons. ME. **3.** Shapeless –1677. **4.** *fig.* Perverted; morally ugly 1555. Hence **Defo·rmed-ly** *adv.*, **†-ness.**

Deformity (dĭfǭ·ɹmĭti). ME. [– OFr. *deformité* (*deff-, desf-*) – L. *deformitas*, f. *deformis* misshapen; see DEFORM *a.*, -ITY. Cf. DIFFORMITY.] **1.** The quality or condition of being DEFORMED 1450. **2.** Bodily misshapenness or malformation ME. **3.** An instance of deformity; *spec.* a bodily malformation ME. *transf.* A deformed being or thing 1698. **4.** *fig.* Moral ugliness or crookedness ME. **¶5.** Misused for DIFFORMITY 1531.

1. Disease [small-pox], and its consequent effects, d. 1805. **2.** Edmunde..surnamed Crowke backe.. for his deformytye FABYAN. **3.** The tumour..is merely a d. S. COOPER. **4.** The corruption and deformitie of our nature 1561. The deformities of the representative system MACAULAY.

Deforse, etc., obs. ff. DEFORCE, etc.

Defo·ssion. 1753. [– mod. L. *defossio*, f. L. *defodere* inter.] The punishment of burying alive. (Dicts.)

†Defou·l, defoi·l, *v.* [ME. *defoule* (with unexpl. var. *defoyle*) – OFr. *defouler, defuler*, f. *dé-* DE- I. 1 + *fouler* tread; see FOIL *v.*¹, FULL *v.*², and DEFILE *v.*¹] **1.** *trans.* To trample under foot; tread down –1574. **2.** To crush (*lit.* and *fig.*) –1548. **3.** To deflower, debauch –1596. **4.** To violate (laws, holy places, etc.); to profane –1614. **5.** To render foul; to defile. Also *fig.* –1611. **6.** To make unsightly. ME. only. Hence **†Defou·l, defoi·l** *sb.* oppression; defilement.

†Defrau·d, *sb.* ME. [f. next, after FRAUD *sb.*] = DEFRAUDATION –1800.

Defraud (dĭfrǭ·d), *v.* ME. [– OFr. *defrauder* or L. *defraudare*, f. *de-* DE- I. 3 + *fraudare* cheat, f. *fraus, fraud-* FRAUD.] **1.** To take or withhold from (a person) by fraud what is his by right: to cheat, cozen, beguile. Also *absol.* **2.** *fig.* To deprive or cheat (a thing) of what is due to it (*arch.*) 1497.

1. To d. citizens of their rights 1880. **2.** Here beggar pride defrauds her daily cheer, To boast one splendid banquet once a year GOLDSM. Hence **Defrau·dment.** ? *Obs.*

Defrauda·tion. 1502. [– OFr. *defraudation* or late L. *defraudatio*, f. *defraudat-*, pa. ppl. stem of L. *defraudare*; see prec., -ION.] The action (or an act) of defrauding; cheating.

Defray (dĭfrēⁱ·), *v.* 1543. [– Fr. *défrayer*, f. *dé-* DE- I. 6 + *†frai, †frait* (usu. pl. *frais, †fres*) expenses, cost :– med.L. *fredum, -us* fine for breach of the peace.] **†1.** To pay out, spend –1613. **2.** To discharge by paying; to meet, settle 1570. Also *fig.* **3.** To meet the expense of; pay for. Now *rare* or *arch.* 1581. **†4.** To reimburse (a person); to entertain free of charge –1858.

2. Money to d. their charges FULLER. *fig.* Can Night d. The wrath of thundring Joue SPENSER *F.Q.* I. v. 42. **4.** The State will d. you all the time you stay BACON. Hence **†Defray·,** *sb.* defrayal. **Defray·able** *a.* **Defray·al,** the action of defraying. **Defray·er. Defray·ment,** defrayal.

Defrock (dĭfrǫ·k), *v.* 1581. [– Fr. *défroquer*, f. *dé-* DE- I. 6 + *froc* FROCK.] To deprive of the priestly garb; to unfrock.

Deft (deft), *a.* ME. [ME. *defte*, var. of DAFT.] **†1.** = DAFT 1 (*rare*). (ME. only.) **2.** Apt, skilful, dexterous, clever or neat in action ME. **3.** Neat, trim; handsome. Still *dial.* 1579. **4.** Quiet. Still *dial.* 1763.

2. To see the lame so d. At that cup service CHAPMAN. Of d. tongue CARLYLE. **3.** By the messe, a d. lass HEYWOOD. Hence **De·ft-ly** *adv.*, **-ness.**

Defunct (dĭfɒ·ŋkt). 1548. [– L. *defunctus*, pa. pple. of *defungi* discharge, perform, finish, f. *de-* DE- I. 3 + *fungi* perform. Cf. (O)Fr. *défunt.*]

A. *adj.* Having ceased to live; deceased, dead. Also *fig.* 1599.

The Organs, though d. and dead before, Breake vp their drowsie Graue *Hen. V*, IV. i. 21. The ghost of a d. absurdity COLERIDGE

B. *sb. The d.*: the deceased; hence, with *pl.* (*rare*), a dead person 1548.

Defunction (dĭfɒ·ŋkʃən). *rare.* 1599. [– late L. *defunctio*, f. *defunct-*, pa. ppl. stem of *defungi*; see prec., -ION.] Dying, death. *Hen. V*, I. ii. 58.

†Defu·nctive, *a. rare.* [f. as prec., see -IVE.] Of or pertaining to dying, as *d. music.* SHAKS.

Defuse, -ed, -edly, Defusion, -ive, obs. ff. DIFFUSE, etc.

†**Defy·**, *sb.* 1580. [– Fr. *défi*, f. *défier*; see next.] Declaration of defiance; challenge –1734.

Defy (dĭfəi·), *v.*[1] [ME. *defye, deffie* – (O)Fr. *défier* (earlier *des-, def-*) :– Rom. **disfidare*, f. L. *dis-* (see DE- I. 6) + *fidus* trustful, rel. to *fides* FAITH.] †**1.** *trans.* To renounce faith, allegiance, or affiance to; to declare hostilities against; to send a declaration of defiance to –1568. **2.** To challenge to combat (*arch.*) ME. **3.** *trans.* To challenge to a contest or trial of skill. Const. *to* and *inf.* 1674. **4.** To set at defiance; to set at nought ME. †**5.** To reject, renounce, disdain, revolt at –1738. †**6.** *intr.* To have distrust *of.* [OFr. *difier de.*] –1613.

2. The knyghtes in the Castel defyen yow MALORY. **3.** Defying the Ocean Gods to compete BOWEN. **4.** Ha, thou fortune, I the defie GOWER. The fortress defied their attacks THIRLWALL. **5.** To d. a bribe GAY.

†**Defy·**, *v.*[2] ME. [Origin unkn.] **1.** *trans.* and *intr.* To digest –1542. **2.** *trans.* To concoct; to dissolve. (ME. only.)

‖**Dégagé** (degaʒe), *a.*; fem. **-ée.** 1697. [Fr., pa. pple. of *dégager* set free, f. *dé-* DE- I. 6, after *engager* ENGAGE.] Easy, unconstrained.

Degarnish (dĭgā·miʃ), *v. rare.* By-form of DISGARNISH; see DE- I. 6.

Degela·tion. *rare.* [f. Fr. *dégeler.*] Thawing. (Dicts.)

†**Dege·nder,** *v.* 1539. [alt., after GENDER *sb.*, of contemporary *degener* – Fr. *dégénérer* – L. *degenerare* DEGENERATE.] *intr.* To degenerate –1597. var. †**Dege·ner.**

Degeneracy (dĭdʒe·nĕrăsi). 1664. [f. next; see -ACY.] The condition or quality of being degenerate; something that is degenerate (*rare*).

This grand D. of the Church HY. MORE. The cathedral of Sens is a sad d. from ours ALFORD.

Degenerate (dĭdʒe·nĕrĕt), *a.* 1494. [– L. *degeneratus*, pa. pple. of *degenerare*; see next, -ATE[2].]

A. as *pa. pple.* = degenerated. ? *Obs.*

B. as *adj.* **1.** Having lost the qualities proper to the kind; having declined to a lower type; hence, declined in character or qualities; debased, degraded 1494. Also *fig.* of things. **2.** *transf.* Characterized by degeneracy 1651.

1. Thou art degenerat, & growen out of kynde FABYAN. How then art thou turned into the d. plant of a strange vine *Jer.* 2:21. Penguins..a d. duck SIR T. HERBERT. Any d. form of active faith MORLEY. **2.** These d. days POPE. Hence **Dege·nerate-ly** *adv.*, **-ness** (*rare*).

Degenerate (dĭdʒe·nĕrēꞋt), *v.* 1545. [– *degenerat-*, pa. ppl. stem of L. *degenerare* depart from its race or kind, f. *degener* debased, ignoble, f. *de-* DE- I. 2 + *genus, gener-* kind; see -ATE[3].] **1.** *intr.* To lose the qualities proper to the kind; to fall away from ancestral excellence; hence, to decline in character or qualities, become of a lower type 1553. Also *transf.* and *fig.* of things. †**2.** To show a degeneration or an alteration *from* –1739. †**3.** *trans.* To cause to degenerate –1811.

1. When men d., and by sinne put off the nature of man T. TAYLOR. Plants for want of Culture, d...sometimes so far as to change into another kind BACON. **2.** Gods! how the son degenerates from the sire POPE. Hence **Dege·nerative** *a.* of the nature of, or tending to degeneration.

Degeneration (dĭdʒenĕrēꞋ·ʃən). 1481. [– Fr. *dégénération* or late L. *degeneratio*, f. as prec.; see -ION.] **1.** The process of degenerating; declining to a lower stage of being; degradation of nature 1607. **b.** *Biol.* A change of structure by which an organism, or an organ, assumes the form of a lower type 1848. **c.** *Path.* A morbid change in the structure of parts 1851. **2.** Degeneracy 1481. †**3.** That which has degenerated –1748.

1. Capable..of D. into any thing harmful COWLEY. Such a d. may take place simply from want of use CARPENTER. Fatty d. 1883. **3.** The Degenerations and Counterfeits of Benevolence HARTLEY.

Degenerescence (-e·sĕns). 1882. [– Fr. *dégénérescence*, f. *dégénérer*; see DEGENERATE *v.*, -ESCENT, -ENCE.] Tendency to degenerate; the process of degeneration.

†**Dege·nerous,** *a.* 1597. [f. L. *degener* (see DEGENERATE *v.*) + -OUS, after GENEROUS, of which it is, in some senses, treated as a derivative.] **1.** Degenerate; characterized by degeneration –1734. **2.** *transf.* and *fig.* of things (*esp.* organisms or organic products) –1748.

1. An upstart and d. race NORTH. A d. feare DANIEL, age BOYLE. Hence †**Dege·nerously** *adv.*

Dege·rm, *v.* [DE- II. 2.] *trans.* To remove the germ from (*e.g.* wheat). So **Dege·rminator,** a machine with iron discs for splitting the grains of wheat and removing the germ. (Dicts.)

Deglaze, *v.*; see DE- II. 2.

†**Deglo·ry,** *v. rare.* 1610. [DE- II. 2.] To deprive of its glory –1653.

†**Deglute** (dĭglū·t), *v.* 1599. [– L. *deglut(t)ire* swallow down, f. *de-* DE- I. 1 + *glut(t)ire* swallow.] *trans.* To swallow down. Also *absol.*

Deglu·tinate, *v.* 1609. [– *deglutinat-*, pa. ppl. stem of *deglutinare* unglue, f. *de-* DE- I. 6 + *glutinare* glue; see -ATE[3].] †**1.** *trans.* To unglue; to loosen or separate (things glued together) –1727. **2.** To extract the gluten from 1889. Hence **Deglutina·tion.**

Deglutition (dī:gluti·ʃən). 1650. [– Fr. *déglutition* or mod.L. *deglutitio*, f. *deglutit-*, pa. ppl. stem of *deglut(t)ire*; see DEGLUTE, -ION.] The action of swallowing. Also *fig.*

In a city feast..what d. PALEY. Hence **Degluti·tious** *a.* pertaining or tending to d. (*rare*). So **Deglu·titory** *a.* pertaining to d.; swallowing (*rare*).

De:go·rder. 1880. [f. DEG(REE) + ORDER.] *Math.* The pair of numbers signifying the degree and order of any form.

†**Dego·rge,** *v.* 1493. [– Fr. *dégorger* (OFr. *des-*), f. *gorge* GORGE *sb.*[1]; see DE- I. 6.] = DISGORGE –1737.

Degradation[1] (degrădēꞋ·ʃən). 1535. [–(O)Fr. *dégradation* or eccl. L. *degradatio*, f. *degradat-*, pa. ppl. stem of *degradare*; see DEGRADE, -ION.] **1.** Deposition from some rank, office, or position of honour as an act of punishment; as, the d. of an ecclesiastic, a knight, a military officer, a graduate of a university. **2.** Lowering in honour, estimation, social position, etc.; the state of being so lowered 1752. **3.** Lowering in character or quality; moral or intellectual debasement 1697. **4.** Reduction to an inferior type or stage of development. Also *attrib.* 1850. **b.** *spec. Biol.* Reduction to a less perfect organic condition; degeneration 1849. **c.** *Bot.* A change in the substance of plants, resulting in the formation of degradation-products (see quots.) 1875. **d.** *Physics.* The conversion of (energy) to a form less capable of transformation 1871. **5.** A lowering in strength, amount, etc. 1769. **6.** *Geol.* The wearing down of rocks, strata, etc., by atmospheric and aqueous action 1799.

1. An..active statesman, exposed to the vicissitudes of advancement and d. JOHNSON. **2.** The d. of the poor-house JEVONS. **3.** The d. of marrying a man she did not love 1866. **4.** *D. products*: products which have no further use in the building up of the structures of plants, *e.g.* gum, etc. **5.** The d. in the value of silver A. SMITH. **6.** The chalk..yields rather easily to d. PHILLIPS. Hence **Degrada·tional** *a.* manifesting structural degradation.

Degradation[2] (dī:grădēꞋ·ʃən). 1706. [In sense 1 – Fr. *dégradation* – It. *digradazione*, f. *digradare* come down by degrees. Cf. GRADATION.] **1.** The gradual lowering of colour or light in a painting; *esp.* that which gives the effect of distance. ? *Obs.* †**2.** Diminution by degrees; the part so reduced –1730.

Degrade (dĭgrēꞋ·d), *v.* ME. [– (O)Fr. *dégrader* – eccl. L. *degradare*, f. *de-* DE- I. 1 + *gradus* rank, degree.] **1.** *trans.* To reduce from a higher to a lower rank, to depose *from* (†*of*) a position of honour or estimation. **2.** To lower in estimation, character, or quality; to reduce in price, strength, purity, tone, etc. 1500. **3. a.** *Biol.* To reduce to a lower organic type. **b.** *Physics.* To reduce (energy) to a form less capable of transformation. 1862. **4.** *Geol.* To wear down (rocks, etc.) by surface abrasion or disintegration 1812. **5.** *intr.* To descend to a lower grade or type; to degenerate 1850. **6.** *Cambridge Univ.* To put off entering the examination in honours for the degree of B.A. for one year 1829.

1. His censure was to be degraded both from her ministry and degrees taken in the University 1628. **2.** How low avarice can d. a man GOLDSM. To d. prices COBDEN. **5.** And throned races may d. TENNYSON. Hence **Degra·der. Degra·dingly** *adv.*

Degraded (dĭgrēꞋ·dĕd), *ppl. a.* 1483. [f. prec. + -ED[1].] **1.** Lowered in rank, position, reputation, character, etc.; debased. **2. a.** *Biol.* Showing structural or functional degradation 1862. **b.** *Geol.* Worn down 1869. **3.** Of colour: Toned down 1877.

1. A d. race of men MAX-MÜLLER, priest 1885. **2.** A d. form of life H. DRUMMOND.

Degra·ded, *a.* 1562. [f. DE- I. + L. *gradus* step + -ED[2].] *Her.* Of a cross: Set on steps or degrees.

†**Degra·dement.** 1641. [– Fr. †*dégradement*, f. *dégrader*; see DEGRADE, -MENT.] Degradation, abasement. MILTON.

†**De·gravate,** *v.* 1574. [– *degravat-*, pa. ppl. stem of L. *degravare*, f. *de-* DE- I. 1 + *gravare* to burden; see -ATE[3].] *trans.* To weigh down, burden, load –1727. Hence †**Degrava·tion.**

Degree (dĭgrī·), *sb.* [ME. *degre* – (O)Fr. *degré* :– Rom. **degradus*, f. L. *de-* DE- I. 1 + *gradus* step, GRADE.]

I. 1. A step in an ascent or descent; one of a flight of steps; a rung of a ladder. (*Obs.* exc. in *Her.*) Also *transf.* of anything resembling a step 1611. **2.** *fig.* A step or stage in a process, etc. ME. **3.** A step in direct line of descent; in *pl.* the number of such steps, determining the proximity of blood in collateral descendants of a common ancestor ME. **4.** A stage or position in the scale of dignity or rank; relative social or official rank or station; a rank or class of persons. ? *Obs.* ME. **5.** Manner, way, wise; relation, respect ME. **6.** A step or stage in intensity or amount; the relative intensity, measure, or amount of a quality, attribute, or action. (Cf. sense 2.) ME. **b.** *Crim. Law.* Relative measure of criminality, as in *Principal in the first*, or *second d.* In *U.S. Law*, A grade of crime. 1676.

1. He saw a ladder whyche had ten degrees or stappes CAXTON. *Jul. C.* II. i. 26. **2.** Which recognizance is the first d. to amendment 1550. Phr. *By degrees*: by little and little, gradually. **3.** *Prohibited* or *forbidden degrees*: degrees of consanguinity and affinity within which marriage is not allowed. **4.** Knyȝte, squiere, ȝoman and knaue, Iche mon in thayre degre ME. **6.** Misprision in the highest d. *Twel. N.* I. v. 61. Differing but in d., of kind the same MILT. *P. L.* v. 490. Phr. *To a d.* (colloq.): to an undefined, but serious, extent. *To the last d.*: to the utmost measure.

II. Spec. and techn. senses. **1.** A stage of proficiency in an art, craft, or course of study; *esp.* An academical rank conferred by a university or college as a mark of proficiency in scholarship; honorary distinction ME. **2.** *Gram.* Each of the three stages (POSITIVE, COMPARATIVE, SUPERLATIVE) in the comparison of an adj. or adv. (Cf. I. 6.) 1460. **3.** *Geom.* (*Astron., Geog.*, etc.) A unit of measurement of angles or circular arcs, being an angle equal to the 90th part of a right angle, or an arc equal to the 360th part of the circumference of a circle (which subtends this angle at the centre) ME. **b.** *transf.* A position as measured by degrees (chiefly of latitude) 1647. **4.** *Thermometry.* **a.** A unit of temperature varying according to the scale in use. **b.** Each of the marks denoting degrees on the scale of a thermometer, or the interval between two successive marks. 1727. **5.** *Mus.* Each of the successive lines and spaces on the stave; also applied to tone or interval 1674. †**6.** *Arith.* A group of three figures taken together in numeration –1677. **7.** *Alg.* The rank of an equation or expression as determined by the highest power of the unknown or variable quantity, or the highest dimensions of the terms which it contains 1730.

3. b. He knew the Seat of Paradise, Could tell in what D. it lies BUTLER *Hud.* I. i. 174.

Degree (dĭgrī·), *v.* 1614. [f. prec. sb.] †**1.** *trans.* To lead or bring on by degrees –1670. **2.** To confer a degree upon. *nonce-use.*

‖**Degu** (de·gu). 1843. [Native name.] *Zool.* A S. Amer. genus *Octodon* of hystricomorphous or porcupine-like rodents.

Degust (dĭgʊ·st), *v. rare.* 1623. [– L. *degustare*, f. *de-* DE- I. 3 + *gustare* to taste; in mod. use – Fr. *déguster*.] To taste. Also *absol.*

Degustate (dĭgʊ·steˈt), *v. rare.* 1599. [– *degustat-*, pa. ppl. stem of L. *degustare*; see prec., -ATE³.] = prec. Hence **Degusta·tion,** the action of degusting.

‖**Déhaché** (deha·ʃe), *a.* 1766. [obs. Fr., f. DE- I. 1, 2 + *hacher* to cut.] *Her.* = COUPED, q.v.

Dehisce (dĭhi·s), *v.* 1657. [– L. *dehiscere*, f. *de-* DE- I. 2 + *hiscere*, inceptive of *hiare* gape. Cf. HIATUS.] *intr.* To gape; in *Bot.* to burst open, as seed-vessels.

Dehiscence (dĭhi·sĕns). 1828. [– mod.L. *dehiscentia* (Linnæus), f. as prec.; see -ENCE.] Gaping, opening by divergence of parts; in *Bot.* the bursting open of capsules, fruits, anthers, etc. in order to discharge their mature contents. Also *fig.* and *gen.* So **Dehi·scent** *a.* gaping open; in *Bot.* opening as seed-vessels.

Deho·nestate, *v. rare.* 1663. [– *dehonestat-*, pa. ppl. stem of L. *dehonestare* to dishonour, f. *de-* DE- I. 6 + *honestus* HONEST; see -ATE³.] *trans.* To dishonour, disparage. Hence **Dehonesta·tion,** dishonouring, dishonour.

‖**Dehors** (dəhō·r). 1701. [OFr. *dehors* prep., mod.Fr. adv. and sb.]

A. *prep.* (*Law.*) Outside of; not within the scope of.

†**B.** *sb.* (*Fortif.*) All sorts of separate outworks, made for the better security of the main works. (Dicts.)

Dehort (dĭhǫ·ɹt), *v.* Now *rare.* 1533. [– L. *dehortari* dissuade, f. *de-* DE- I. 2 + *hortari* exhort.] To use exhortation to dissuade from; to advise against. Also *absol.*

Wherby we doe perswade..disswade..exhorte, or dehorte..any man 1553. Croker dehorts me from visiting Ireland SOUTHEY. So **Dehorta·tion,** earnest dissuasion. **Deho·rtative** *a.* dehortatory; *sb.* a dehortative address or argument. **Deho·rtatory** *a.* characterized by dehortation; †*sb.* a dehortatory address. **Deho·rter.**

Dehumanize (dĭhiū·mănəiz), *v.* 1818. [DE- II. 1.] *trans.* To deprive of human attributes. Turner's face was a good deal de-humanized MOORE.

†**Dehu·sk,** *v. rare.* 1566. [DE- II. 2.] To deprive of the husk.

Dehydrate (dĭˌhəi·dreˈt), *v.* 1876. [f. DE- II. 2 + Gr. ὕδωρ water + -ATE³.] *Chem.* **1.** *trans.* To deprive of water, or of its constituents. **2.** *intr.* To lose water as a constituent 1886. Hence **Dehydra·tion,** the removal of water, or of its constituents, in a chemical combination.

Dehydrogenate (dĭˌhəi·droˌdʒĕneˈt), *v.* 1850. [DE- II. 1.] = next.

Dehydrogenize (dĭˌhəi·droˌdʒĕnəiz), *v.* 1878. [DE- II. 1.] *Chem.* To deprive of its hydrogen; to remove hydrogen from. Hence **Dehy·drogeniza·tion.**

Deicide[1] (dī·isəid). 1653. [– eccl.L. *deicida*, f. L. *deus* god + *-cida* -CIDE¹; so Fr. *déicide* (XVII).] The killer of a god.

Deicide[2] (dī·isəid). 1611. [See prec., -CIDE².] The killing of a god. Hence **De·icidal** *a.* of or pertaining to d.

Deictic (dəi·ktik), *a.* Also **deiktic.** 1828. [– Gr. δεικτικός, f. δεικτός, vbl. adj. of δεικνύναι to show. A purely academic word.] Directly pointing out, demonstrative; in *Logic*, applied to reasoning, and opp. to *elenctic*, which proves indirectly. So †**Dei·ctical** *a.* †**Dei·ctically** *adv.*

Deific (dīˌi·fik), *a.* 1490. [– (O)Fr. *déifique* or eccl.L. *deificus* (Tertullian), f. L. *deus* god + *-ficus* -FIC.] Deifying, making divine; *loosely*, divine, godlike. So †**Dei·fical.**

Deification (dīˌifikēˈ·ʃən). ME. [– eccl. L. *deificatio*, f. *deificat-*, pa. ppl. stem of *deificare*; see DEIFY, -ION.] The action of deifying; deified condition; a deified embodiment. **b.** Absorption into the divine nature 1856.

Deiform (dī·ifǭɹm), *a.* 1642. [– med.L. *deiformis*, f. L. *deus* god; see -FORM.] **1.** Godlike in form. **2.** Conformable to the nature of God; godlike 1654. Hence **Deifo·rmity,** d. quality.

Deify (dī·ifəi), *v.* ME. [– (O)Fr. *déifier* – eccl.L. *deificare*, f. L. *deus* god; see -FY.] *trans.* To make a god of; to exalt to the position of a deity; to enrol among the gods. **b.** To render godlike ME. **c.** To treat, regard, or adore as a god 1590.

[They] were both ystellyfyed In the heauen and there defyed LYDG. **b.** No vertue more deified a Prince then Clemencie SIR T. HERBERT. **c.** The old man deifies prudence JOHNSON. Hence **De·ifier. De·ifying** *vbl. sb.* and *ppl. a.*

Deign (dēˈn), *v.* ME. [– OFr. *degnier*, *deigner*, (also mod.) *daigner* :– L. *dignare*, *-ari* deem worthy, f. *dignus* worthy.] **1.** *intr.* To think it worthy of oneself (*to do* something); to vouchsafe, condescend. Also †*impers.* **2.** *trans.* with *simple obj.* **a.** To condescend to give or bestow, to vouchsafe. (Now *esp.* with *reply*, *answer*, in neg. sentences.) 1589. †**b.** To vouchsafe to accept. (Opp. to *to disdain.*) –1661. †**3.** To dignify (a person) *with.* [= L. *dignari.*] –1648.

1. Would he daine to wed a Countrie Lasse GREENE. **2.** Nor would we deigne him buriall of his men *Macb.* I. ii. 60. **b.** Thy pallat then did daine The roughest Berry, on the rudest Hedge *Ant. & Cl.* I. iv. 63.

†**Dei·gnous,** *a.* ME. [app. short f. *dedeignous*, DISDAINOUS; cf. DAIN *v.*] Disdainful, haughty –1643.

‖**Dei gratia.** [L.] By the grace of God; see GRACE.

Deil (dīl, dīl). 1500. [Sc.] **1.** The Devil. **2.** A mischievously wicked fellow 1786.

Deinosaur, Deinothere, etc.; see DINO-.

De-insularize, -integrate, etc.; see DE- II. 1.

‖**Deipara** (dīˌi·pără). 1664. [Late L., f. *deus* + *-parus*, *-a* bearing; a L. equiv. of Gr. θεοτόκος.] A title of the Virgin Mary, 'Mother of God'. So **Dei·parous** *a.* bearing a god.

Deipnosophist (dəipnǫ·sŏfist). 1656. [– Gr. δειπνοσοφιστής, f. δεῖπνον dinner + σοφιστής a master of his craft.] A master of the art of dining: taken from δειπνοσοφισταί, the title of the Greek work of Athenæus, in which a number of learned men discuss dinners, literature, and miscellaneous topics of every kind.

Deis(e, obs. f. DAIS.

Deism (dī·iz'm). 1682. [f. L. *deus* god + -ISM, after next; cf. Fr. *déisme* (Pascal).] The doctrine or belief of a deist; usually, belief in the existence of a God, with rejection of revelation; 'natural religion'.

D. being the very same with old Philosophical Paganism BENTLEY.

Deist (dī·ist). 1621. [– Fr. *déiste* (XVI), f. L. *deus* god + *-iste* -IST.] One who acknowledges the existence of a God upon the testimony of reason, but rejects revealed religion.

(The term was originally opposed to *atheist*, and was interchangeable with *theist* even in the end of the 17th c.)

In speaking of a d. they fix their attention on the negative, in speaking of a theist on the positive aspect of his belief 1880. Hence **Dei·stic** *a.* of the nature of or pertaining to deists or deism. **Dei·stical** *a.* (in same sense); also, tending to deism; **-ly** *adv.*

†**De·itate,** *ppl. a.* [– *deitatus*, pa. pple. of eccl.L. *deitare*, tr. Gr. θεοῦν deify; see -ATE².] Deified. CRANMER.

Deity (dī·iti). ME. [– (O)Fr. *déité* – eccl.L. *deitas* (Augustine), rendering Gr. θεότης, f. θεός god; see -TY¹.] **1.** The estate or rank of a god; godhood; godship; *esp.* with *poss. pron.* **b.** The divine nature of God; Godhood; the Godhead. ME. **2.** *concr.* A divinity, a divine being, a god. Also *fig.* ME. **3.** (*with capital.*) A supreme being as creator of the universe; *the Deity*, the Supreme Being, God. (*Esp.* as a term of Natural Theology.) 1647.

1. The Goddes themselues (Humbling their Deities to loue) *Wint. T.* IV. iv. 26. **b.** The fader the sone & the holy ghost, one essence of deite 1502. **2.** The chief d., the sun SULLIVAN. *fig.* Tobacco (England's bainefull D.) 1630. **3.** Men spoke of 'the Deity', as a sort of first cause of all things, and..had lost sight of the Personal God PUSEY. Hence **De·ityship.**

Deje·ct, *ppl. a. Obs.* or *arch.* ME. [– L. *dejectus*, pa. pple. of *deicere*; see next.] **1.** *pa. pple.* Thrown down; †cast away. **2.** *ppl. a.* DEJECTED 1528; abased 1510. Hence **Deje·ctly** *adv.*

Deject (dĭˌdʒe·kt), *v.* ME. [– *deject-*, pa. ppl. stem of L. *deicere*, f. *de-* DE- I. 1 + *jacere* throw.] **1.** *trans.* To cast down; to overthrow. *arch.* or *Obs.* †**2.** To cast away, reject –1633. †**3.** *fig.* To lower in condition or character, to abase –1691. †**4.** To reduce the strength of, weaken –1684. **5.** To depress in spirits; to cast down, dispirit, dishearten. (The ordinary current sense.) 1581.

3. Being loath to d. them whom he had once aduanced 1601. **5.** Good Authours d. me too-too much, and quaile my courage FLORIO *Montaigne.* So ‖**Deje·cta** *sb. pl.* excrements. **Deje·ctant** *a. Her.*, bending down. **Deje·cter.**

Dejected (dĭˌdʒe·ktėd), *ppl. a.* 1581. [f. prec. + -ED¹.] **1.** *lit.* Cast down (*arch.*) 1682; in *Her.* bent downwards 1889. †**2.** Lowered in estate, condition, or character; abased, lowly –1721. **3.** Downcast, low-spirited 1581. Also *transf.*

3. To-day glad—to-morrow d. LYTTON. *transf.* With a drooping head and d. pace SCOTT. Hence **Deje·cted-ly** *adv.*, **-ness.**

Dejection (dĭˌdʒe·kʃən). ME. [– L. *dejectio*, f. *deject-*; see DEJECT *v.*, -ION.] **1.** *lit.* The action of casting down; the fact of being cast down 1681. †**2.** *fig.* A casting down; abasement, humiliation –1659. **3.** Depression of spirits; dejected condition 1450. †**4.** Lowering of force or strength –1732. **5.** *Med.* Fæcal discharge 1605. **6.** That which is dejected 1727.

2. Adoration implies submission and d.; so that, while we worship, we cast down ourselves PEARSON. **3.** What besides Of sorrow and d. and despair Our frailtie can sustain MILT. *P.L.* XI. 301. **6.** Fæcal dejections 1849. Igneous dejections [from a volcano] MURCHISON. So †**Deje·ctive** *a.* characterized by, or betokening, d.; purgative.

Dejectory (dĭˌdʒe·ktəri), *a.* 1640. [f. DEJECT *v.* + -ORY²; cf. *dejecta* (see DEJECT *v.*).] *Med.* Capable of promoting evacuation of the bowels; aperient.

Dejecture (dĭˌdʒe·ktiŭɹ). 1731. [f. as prec. + -URE.] Matter discharged from the bowels; excrement.

†**De·jerate,** *v.* 1607. [f. L. *dejerare* take an oath, f. DE- I. 3 + *jurare.*] *intr.* and *trans.* To swear solemnly –1641. So †**Dejera·tion.**

Dejeune, dejune. *Obs.* or *arch.* 1630. [For earlier *desjeune*, DISJUNE, q.v.] = next.

‖**Déjeuner,** †**déjeuné** (deʒöne). 1787. [Fr. *déjeuner* (also †*déjeuné*), subst. use of the infin. *déjeuner* break one's fast.] The morning meal; breakfast. (In France, often = luncheon.)

De jure; see DE I. c.

Dekadarchy, -drachm, Dekarch, etc.; see DECA-.

Dekle, var. of DECKLE.

Del, obs. f. DEAL *sb.*¹, and of DOLE, *sb.*²

Dela·bialize, *v.* [DE- II. 1.] To deprive of its labial character. SWEET.

†**Dela·ce,** *v. rare.* [– Fr. *délacer* (OFr. *des-*, see DE- I. 6), f. *lacer* to lace.] To untie, undo. HOWELL.

Delacerate, etc., obs. f. DILACERATE, etc.

Delacrima·tion. Also **delacry-.** 1623. [– L. *delacrimatio*; see DE- I. 1, LACHRYMATION.] Weeping (*obs.*); a superabundant flow of an aqueous or serous humour from the eyes; epiphora.

Delacta·tion. 1727. [f. DE- I. 6 + LACTATION.] The act of weaning; **b.** 'artificial arrest of the secretion of milk' (*Syd. Soc. Lex.*).

Delaine (dĭlēˈ·n). 1840. [Short for *muslin delaine*, Fr. *mousseline de laine* lit. 'woollen muslin'.] A light textile fabric for women's dresses; orig. of wool, now usually of wool and cotton.

Delaminate (dĭlæ·mineˈt), *v.* 1877. [f. DE- I. 1, 2 + L. *lamina* thin plate, layer + -ATE³.] *trans.* and *intr.* (*Biol.*) To split into separate layers. Hence **Delamina·tion,** the process of delaminating; *spec.* applied to the formation of the layers of the BLASTODERM, q.v.

†**Dela·pse,** *sb. rare.* 1630. [– L. *delapsus*; see next.] Downfall, descent –1657.

Delapse (dĭlæ·ps), *v.* ? *Obs.* 1526. [– *delaps-*, pa. ppl. stem of L. *delabi*, f. *de-* DE- I. 1 + *labi* slip, fall.] *intr.* To fall or slip down, descend, sink (*lit.* and *fig.*).

Nature is delapsed into that dotage and folly 1651. So †Dela·psion, *spec.* in *Path.* = prolapsus.

†**Delassa·tion.** *rare.* 1692. [– med.L. *delassatio*, f. *delassat-*, pa. ppl. stem of L. *delassare* tire out, f. *de-* DE- I. 3 + *lassare* to weary; see -ION.] Fatigue –1727.

Delate (dĭlēⁱ·t), *v.* 1515. [– *delat-*, stem of functional pa. pple. of L. *deferre*; see DEFER *v.*², -ATE³.] †**1.** *trans.* = DEFER *v.*² 1. –1626. †**2.** = DEFER *v.*² 2. –1875. †**3.** To hand down or over; to refer –1858. **4.** To accuse, impeach; to inform against; to denounce to a tribunal 1515; to report (an offence, etc.) 1582. **5.** To relate 1639.

1. To try exactly the time wherein Sound is delated BACON. **4.** To d. sinners from the pulpit JOHNSON. To punish the crimes delated vnto him 1605.

Delate, obs. f. DILATE, DELETE.

Delation (dĭlēⁱ·ʃən). 1578. [– L. *delatio*, f. as DELATE *v.*; see -ION.] †**1.** Conveyance (to a place) –1626. **2.** Handing down, transference. *Obs.* (exc. in *Rom. Law*). 1681. **3.** Informing against; accusation, denouncement 1578.

1. It is certain that the D. of Light is in an Instant BACON.

Delator (dĭlēⁱ·təɹ). 1572. [– L. *delator*, f. as prec.; see -OR 2.] An informer, a secret or professional accuser. Hence †**Dela·tory** *a.* of the nature of delation.

Delay (dĭlēⁱ·), *sb.* ME. [– (O)Fr. *délai*, f. the vb.; see next.] **1.** The action of delaying; putting off; procrastination; loitering. **2.** The fact of being delayed; hindrance to progress 1748.

1. The Lawes d. *Haml.* III. i. 72. Fabius thou, whose timely delays gave strength to the state BOWEN. **2.** There will be a d. of a day JOWETT. Phr. *Without d.*: without loitering, at once.

Delay (dĭlēⁱ·), *v.*¹ ME. [– OFr. *delayer*, var. of *deslaier*, presumably f. *des-* DIS- + *laier* to leave.] **1.** *trans.* To put off; to defer, postpone. **2.** To impede the progress of; to retard, hinder ME. **3.** *intr.* To put off action; to linger, loiter 1509.

1. My Lord delayeth his comming *Matt.* 24:48. Delaying as the tender ash delays To clothe herself TENNYSON. **2.** Joy and Grief can hasten and d. Time STEELE. **3.** So spake th' Eternal Father.. nor delaid the winged Saint After his charge receivd MILT. *P.L.* v. 247. Hence **Delay·er** (now *rare*), one who (or that which) delays. **Delay·ingly** *adv.* †**Delay·ment,** delaying; delay.

†**Delay·,** *v.*² 1530. [– Fr. *délayer*, in OFr. *desleier* :– Rom. **disligare*, f. L. *dis-* DIS- + *ligare* bind.] **1.** To ALLAY; to temper –1624. **2.** To mitigate, assuage –1603. **3.** To soak (*rare*) –1580.

‖**Del credere** (del krē·dĕre), *attrib.* and *adv. phr.* 1797. [It. = 'of belief, of trust'.] *Comm.* A phrase expressing the obligation undertaken by a factor, broker, or commission merchant, when he guarantees and becomes responsible for the solvency of the persons to whom he sells. Hence *del credere agent, account*, etc.

Del credere commission: the additional premium charged by the factor for this guarantee.

‖**Dele** (dī·li). 1841. [L. *dele*, 2nd sing. pres. imper. act. of *delēre* DELETE.] 'Delete (the letter, etc. marked)'. (Commonly written ϑ.)

Dele, obs. f. DEAL. *sbs.*¹ and ³, *v.*

‖**Deleatur** (dīli,ēⁱ·tǒɹ). 1602. [L. = 'let it be deleted'.] A written mark on a printed proof-sheet directing something to be omitted; hence *fig.*

D., therefore, wherever you meet it EVELYN.

Deleble, var. of DELIBLE.

Delectable (dĭle·ktăb'l), *a.* ME. [– (O)Fr. *délectable* – L. *delectabilis*, f. *delectare* to DELIGHT; see -ABLE.] Affording delight; delightful. (Now used seriously in poetry only, or elevated prose).

Trees of God, D. both to behold and taste MILT. *P.L.* VII. 539. Hence **Delectabi·lity,** d. quality. **Dele·ctableness. Dele·ctably** *adv.*

Delectate (dĭle·kteⁱt, dī·lekteⁱt), *v. rare.* 1802. [– *delectat-*, pa. ppl. stem of L. *delectare*; see prec., -ATE³.] *trans.* To delight. (Affected or humorous.)

Delectation (dīlektēⁱ·ʃən). ME. [– (O)Fr. *délectation* – L. *delectatio*, f. as prec.; see -ION.] The action of delighting; delight, enjoyment. Also *transf.* (Now restricted to the lighter kinds of pleasure).

‖**Delectus** (dĭle·ktǒs). 1828. [L., f. *delect-*, pa. ppl. stem of *deligere* choose out, f. *de-* DE- I. 2 + *legere* choose.] A selection of passages, *esp.* Latin and Greek, for translation.

Delegable (de·lĭgăb'l), *a.* 1660. [f. L. *delegare* to DELEGATE + -BLE.] Capable of being delegated.

Delegacy (de·lĭgăsi). 1533. [f. DELEGATE *sb.*, after *prelate, prelacy*; see -ACY.] **1.** The action or system of delegating; commission or authority given to act as a delegate. **2.** A body or committee of delegates; †a meeting of such a body 1621.

Delegant (de·lĭgănt). 1627. [– *delegant-*, pres. ppl. stem of L. *delegare*; see DELEGATE *v.*, -ANT.] One who delegates; in *Civil Law*, one who, to discharge a debt, assigns his own debtor to his creditor, as debtor in his place.

Delegate (de·lĭgĕt), *sb.* ME. [– L. *delegatus*, subst. use of pa. pple. of *delegare*, f. *de-* DE- I. 2 + *legare* send on a commission; see -ATE¹. Cf. OFr. *delegat* (mod. *délégué*).] **1.** A person sent or deputed to act for or represent another or others; a deputy, commissioner. **2.** *spec.* A commissioner appointed by the crown under the great seal to hear and determine appeals from the ecclesiastical courts 1554. **b.** *Oxford Univ.* A member of a permanent committee entrusted with some branch of University business 1604. **3.** *U.S.* The representative of a Territory in Congress, where he has a seat and the right of speech, but no vote 1825. **b.** *House of Delegates*: (*a*) the lower house of the General Assembly in Virginia, West Virginia, and Maryland; (*b*) the lower house of the General Convention of the Protestant Episcopal Church.

Delegate (de·lĭgĕt), *ppl. a.* 1530. [– L. *delegatus*, pa. pple.; see prec., -ATE².] Delegated.

Delegate (de·lĭgeⁱt), *v.* 1530. [– *delegat-*, pa. ppl. stem of L. *delegare*; see prec., -ATE³.] **1.** *trans.* To send or commission (a person) as a deputy or representative, with power to act for another; to depute 1623. **2.** To entrust or commit (authority, etc.) to another as an agent or deputy 1530; †*loosely*, to assign –1774. **3.** *Civil Law.* To assign to a creditor as debtor in one's place 1818.

1. Will any man..think it reasonable my Lord Keeper should, *ad placitum*, d. whom hee will to keep the Seale 1641. **2.** Those bodies..to whom the people have delegated the power of legislation T. JEFFERSON. I wish we could d. to women some of this work HELPS. Hence **Delegatee·,** the party to whom a debtor is delegated by the delegant. †**De·legative** *a.* having the attribute of delegating; of delegated nature.

Delegation (delĭgēⁱ·ʃən). 1611. [– L. *delegatio*, f. as prec.; see -ION.] **1.** The action of delegating or fact of being delegated (see DELEGATE *v.*) 1612. **2.** A charge or commission given to a delegate 1611. **3.** A delegated body; a number of persons sent or commissioned to act as representatives 1818. **4.** *Civil Law.* The assignment of a debtor by his creditor to a creditor of the delegant, to act as debtor in his place and discharge his debt 1721. **5.** A letter, etc. not negotiable and unstamped, used by bankers and others for the transfer of a debt or credit 1882. ‖**b.** A share-certificate. [Fr. *délégation.*] 1882.

3. The Jersey d...presented to congress a number of the counterfeits H. PHILLIPS. **5. b.** The English government intended purchasing 200,000 Suez Canal delegations 1882.

Delegator (de·lĭgeⁱtəɹ). 1875. [– late L. *delegator*, f. as prec.; see -OR 2.] One who delegates, a delegant. Hence **De·legatory** *a.* of or relating to delegation; of the nature of delegated power; †holding delegated authority.

‖**Delenda** (dĭle·ndă), *sb. pl.* 1645. [L., plur. of *delendum*, gerundive of *delēre* DELETE.] Things to be deleted.

†**Dele·niate,** *v. rare.* 1623. [irreg. f. L. *delenire* soften, soothe; see -ATE³.] To soothe, mitigate –1657.

Delete (dĭlī·t), *v.* 1495. [– *delet-*, pa. ppl. stem of L. *delēre* blot out, efface.] †**1.** *trans.* To destroy, do away with –1851. **2.** To strike out, erase, expunge 1605. Also *fig.*

2. Here..the *and* must be deleted F. HALL. So †**Dele·te** *pa. pple.* deleted.

Deleterious (delĭtīᵊ·riəs), *a.* 1643. [f. med.L. *deleterius* – Gr. δηλητήριος noxious, + -OUS. Cf. Fr. *délétère* (XVI).] Physically or morally harmful or injurious; noxious.

'Tis pity wine should be so d. BYRON. Politics is a d. profession EMERSON. var. †**Delete·rial** *a.* Hence **Delete·rious-ly** *adv.*, **-ness.**

†**Deletery** (de·lĭtĕri), *a.* Also *erron.* **-ory, -ary.** 1576. [– med.L. *deleterius*; see prec.]

A. *adj.* Deleterious, poisonous –1684.

A certain deletary and poysonous quality 1657.

B. *sb.* **1.** A deleterious drug; a poison. Also *fig.* –1653. **2.** That which destroys the effect of anything noxious; an antidote. [Assoc. w. L. *delēre.*] –1660.

2. Deleteries of sin and instruments of repentance JER. TAYLOR.

Deletion (dĭlī·ʃən). 1590. [– L. *deletio*, f. *delet-*, pa. ppl. stem of *delēre* DELETE; see -ION.] **1.** The action of effacing or destroying; destruction. Now *arch.* 1606. **2.** The action of deleting; the fact of being deleted; a deleted passage, an erasure 1590.

1. A total d. of the sin JER. TAYLOR. **2.** The d. was initialed in the margin 1884.

Deletive (dĭlī·tiv), *a.* [f. as prec. + -IVE.] Having the property of deleting. EVELYN.

Deletory (dĭlī·təri). 1612. [f. as prec. + -ORY².]

A. *adj.* That is used to delete, effacing.

B. *sb.* That which destroys or effaces. (Cf. DELETERY *sb.* 2.) 1647.

Confession..as a d. of sin JER. TAYLOR.

Delf¹ (delf). Now *local.* [ME. *delf*, late OE. *dælf* for *delf*, app. aphet. f. *ġedelf* digging, ditch, f. *delfan* DELVE.] **1.** That which is delved or dug; as, a pit; a trench; a quarry; a mine. †**2.** That which is or may be dug into; as, a bed of any earth or mineral –1706. **3.** *Sc.* A sod 1812; †in *Her.* a square repr. a sod, used as an abatement –1688. †**4.** A thrust of the spade –1688. Also *attrib.*

1. The fens are divided by embanked upland rivulets or 'delphs' 1851. Quarries or Delfes of Stone or Slate 1588.

Delf², **delft** (delf, delft). Also **delph.** 1714. [– Du. *Delf*, now *Delft*, a town of Holland, named from its chief canal, known as *delf, delve* 'ditch'; cf. prec.] A kind of glazed earthenware made at Delf or Delft in Holland; originally called *Delf ware.* Also *attrib.*

Delian (dī·liăn), *a.* 1623. [f. L. *Delius* (Gr. Δήλιος) + -AN.] Of or belonging to Delos, an island in the Grecian archipelago, the reputed birthplace of Apollo and Artemis.

D. problem, the problem of finding the side of a cube having double the volume of a given cube (*i.e.* of finding the cube root of 2); so called from the answer of the oracle of Delos, that a plague raging at Athens should cease when Apollo's altar, which was cubical, should be doubled.

†**Deli·bate,** *v.* 1623. [– *delibat-*, pa. ppl. stem of L. *delibare*, f. *de-* DE- I. 2 + *libare* to taste; see -ATE³.] *trans.* To take a little of, taste, sip; also *fig.* –1660. Hence †**Deliba·tion,** a taste or slight knowledge *of* something; a portion extracted.

†**Deli·ber,** *v.* late ME. [– Fr. *délibérer* (XV) or L. *deliberare*; see DELIBERATE *v.*] **1.** *intr.* To deliberate, consider –1545. **2.** *trans.* To determine, resolve –1580.

Deli·berant. *rare.* 1673. [– *deliberant-*, pres. ppl. stem of L. *deliberare*; see DELIBERATE *v.*, -ANT¹.] One who deliberates.

Deliberate (dĭli·bĕrĕt), *a.* 1548. [– L. *deliberatus*, pa. pple. of *deliberare*; see next, -ATE².] **1.** Well weighed or considered; carefully thought out; done of set purpose; studied; not hasty or rash. **2.** Of persons: Characterized by deliberation; considering carefully; not hasty or rash 1596. **3.** Leisurely, slow, not hurried 1600.

1. Such as..in stead of rage D. valour breath'd MILT. *P.L.* I. 554. **2.** O these d. fooles *Merch. V.* II. ix. 80. **3.** D. in his movements 1895. Hence **Deli·berate-ly** *adv.*, **-ness.**

Deliberate (dĭli·bĕreⁱt), *v.* 1550. [– *deliberat-*, pa. ppl. stem of L. *deliberare*, f. *de-* DE- I. 3 + *librare* weigh, f. *libra* scales; see -ATE³.] †**1.** *trans.* To weigh in the mind; to consider carefully with a view to decision; to think over. (Now *to d. upon.*) –1829. **2.** *intr.* To use consideration with a view to decision; to think carefully; to take time for consideration. Const. †*of, on, upon*, etc. 1561. †**3.** To resolve, determine –1633.

2. Two daies the King deliberated vpon an

answer 1624. The woman that deliberates is lost ADDISON.

Deliberation (dĭlibĕrēⁱ·ʃən). ME. [– OFr. *deliberacion* (later and mod. *-tion*) – L. *deliberatio*, f. as prec.; see -ION.] **1.** The action of deliberating; careful consideration with a view to decision. **2.** The consideration and discussion of the reasons for and against a measure by a number of councillors 1489; †a conference –1648. **†3.** A resolution or determination –1653. **4.** Deliberateness of action ME.; absence of hurry; leisureliness 1855.

1. To close tedious d. with hasty resolves JOHNSON. **2.** The deliberations of the Royalist Convention MACAULAY. **4.** Hee treds with great d. EARLE.

Deliberative (dĭli·bĕrĕtiv). 1553. [– Fr. *délibératif, -ive*, or L. *deliberativus*, f. as prec.; see -IVE.]

A. *adj.* **1.** Pertaining to deliberation; having the function of deliberating. **2.** Characterized by deliberation 1659.

1. Erecting itself into a d. body BURKE. **2.** The slower operations of d. reason KAMES. Hence **Deli·berative-ly** *adv.*, **-ness.**

†B. *sb.* A discussion of some question with a view to settlement; a deliberative discourse; a matter for deliberation –1650.

In deliberatiues the point is what is good and what is euill BACON.

Deli·berator. 1782. [– L. *deliberator*, f. as prec.; see -OR 2.] One who deliberates.

Delible (de·lĭb'l), *a.* 1610. [– L. *delebilis* f. *delēre*; see DELETE *v.*, -BLE. Sp. assim. to -IBLE as in *indelible*.] Capable of being deleted or effaced (*lit.* and *fig.*).

Delicacy (de·likăsi). ME. [f. DELICATE *a.*; see -ACY.]

I. The quality of being DELICATE. **†1.** The quality of being addicted to sensuous delights; voluptuousness, luxuriousness, daintiness –1741. **†2.** Luxury –1725; gratification –1667. **†3.** The quality of being delightful; beauty, daintiness, pleasantness –1650. **4.** Exquisite fineness of texture, substance, finish, etc.; soft or tender beauty 1586. **5.** Tenderness of constitution or health 1632. **6.** The quality or condition of requiring nice handling 1785. **7.** Exquisite fineness of feeling, observation, etc.; sensitiveness 1702. **8.** Exquisite nicety of skill, expression, touch, etc. 1675. **9.** A refined feeling of what is becoming, modest, or proper; sensitiveness; delicate regard for the feelings of others 1712. **†10.** Fastidiousness –1793.

2. He Rome brende for his delicasie CHAUCER. **4.** A man. .in whom strong making took not away d., nor beauty fierceness SIDNEY (J.). **5.** The d. of her sex 1632, of her Constitution ADDISON. **6.** Negociations of the utmost d. (*mod.*). **7.** The d. of his sense of right and wrong MACAULAY. **8.** D. of expression 1683, of colouring DRYDEN. **9.** A false D. is Affectation, not Politeness STEELE.

II. 1. A thing which gives delight; *esp.* a dainty viand 1450. **2.** A delicate trait, observance, or attention 1712. **3.** A nicety 1789.

Delicate (de·likĕt). ME. [– (O)Fr. *délicat* or L. *delicatus*, of unkn. origin; see -ATE².]

A. *adj.* **I.** = DAINTY *a.* **1.** Delightful, charming, pleasant, nice; *esp.* pleasing to the palate, dainty. **†2.** Characterized by sensuous delight; luxurious, voluptuous, effeminate –1737; of persons, given to pleasure or luxury –1640. **†3.** Self-indulgent, indolent –1601. **†4.** Softly reared; dainty; effeminate –1688. **†5.** Fastidious, nice, dainty –1796.

1. The ayre is d. *Macb.* I. vi. 10. A most fresh and d. creature *Oth.* II. iii. 20. D. meats M. PATTISON. **2.** Soft and d. desires *Much Ado* I. i. 305.

II. 1. Fine or exquisite; soft, slender, or slight 1533; of colour, subdued 1822. **2.** Subtle in its fineness 1692. **3.** Tender, fragile 1568; feeble in constitution; weakly ME. **4.** *fig.* Requiring nice handling; critical; ticklish 1742.

1. D. gauze 1825, sea-ferns LOWELL, meats GEO. ELIOT, machines EMERSON. A d. blue light TYNDALL. **2.** The most d. differences BAIN. **3.** D. mural-Fruit EVELYN. In very d. health MACAULAY.

III. 1. Fine in power of perception, feeling, appreciation, etc.; finely sensitive 1533. **2.** Finely skilful 1589; †finely ingenious –1673. **3.** Finely sensitive to what is becoming, or to the feelings of others 1634; of actions, etc., characterized by feelings of delicacy 1818.

1. A d. ear RUSKIN, conscience MANNING. **2.** So d. with her needle *Oth.* IV. i. 199. *Lear* IV. vi. 188. Hence **De·licate-ly** *adv.*, **-ness.**

B. *sb.* **†1.** One who is luxurious, dainty, or fastidious –1709. **2.** A thing that gives pleasure; *esp.* a choice viand, a delicacy 1450.

‖**Delicatesse** (delikăte·s). 1698. [Fr. *délicatesse*, f. *délicat* delicate.] Delicacy.

‖**Delicatessen** (de:likăte·sən). orig. *U.S.* 1889. [G. *delikatessen* – Fr. (see prec.).] Delicacies or relishes for the table; esp. *attrib.* in *d. shop, store.* Also *ellipt.* = d. shop.

†Deli·ce. ME. [– (O)Fr. *délice*, pl. *délices* :– L. *delicium* n. sing., *deliciæ* fem. pl., delight, etc.] **1.** Delight; *esp.* sensual or worldly pleasure –1685. **2.** A delight; a delicacy –1779. ¶Spenser stresses *de·lices.*

†Deli·ciate, *v. rare.* 1633. [– *deliciat-*, pa. ppl. stem of late L. *deliciari* luxuriate, f. L. *deliciæ*; see prec., -ATE³. Cf. OFr. *delicier.*] *intr.* To take one's pleasure, revel, luxuriate –1678.

Delicious (dĭli·ʃəs), *a.* ME. [– OFr. *delicious* (mod. *délicieux*) – late L. *deliciosus* (Augustine), f. L. *delicia, -iæ*; see DELICE, -OUS.] **1.** Affording great pleasure or enjoyment. (Now, less dignified than 'delightful'.) **2.** Highly pleasing to the bodily senses, *esp.* to the taste and smell ME. **†3.** Addicted to sensuous indulgence; voluptuous, luxurious –1681.

1. A green d. plain FARRAR. A d. joke KINGSLEY. **2.** The soft d. air MILT. *P.L.* II. 400. **3.** Festival and d. Tables JER. TAYLOR. Hence **Deli·ciously** *adv.* **Deli·ciousness,** the quality of being d. (now *esp.* to the senses); luxury.

Delict (dĭli·kt). 1523. [– L. *delictum*, subst. use of n. of *delictus*, pa. pple. of *delinquere*; see DELINQUENT.] A violation of law or right; an offence, a delinquency.

In flagrant d.: tr. L. *in flagrante delicto*, in the very act of committing the offence. Hence **Deli·ctual** *a.* of or belonging to a d. (*rare*).

Deligation (deligēⁱ·ʃən). 1661. [f. DE- I. 3 + LIGATION.] *Surg.* **†a.** Bandaging; a bandage –1857. **b.** The tying of an artery, etc., with a ligature 1840. So **De·ligated** *ppl. a.* tied with a ligature.

Delight (dĭləi·t), *sb.* [ME. *delit* – OFr. *delit*, f. stem of *delitier* :– L. *delectare* allure, charm, frequent. of *delicere.* The sp. with *-gh-* on the anal. of native words like *light* dates from XVI.] **1.** The fact or condition of being delighted; pleasure, joy, or gratification felt in a high degree. **2.** Anything which affords delight ME. **3.** Delightfulness. Now *poet.* ME. **4.** = TURKISH *delight* 1870.

1. Sounds, and sweet aires, that giue d. and hurt not *Temp.* III. ii. 145. When he hath a delite in that that he doeth KINGESMYLL. **2.** Daphnis, the Fields' D. DRYDEN. **3.** She was a Phantom of d. WORDSW. Hence **Deli·ghtless** *a.* **Delightsome** *a.*, **-ly** *adv.*, **-ness.** (Now only literary.)

Delight (dĭləi·t), *v.* [– OFr. *delitier*; see prec.] **1.** *trans.* To give great pleasure or enjoyment to; to please highly. Also *absol.* **2.** *intr.* (for *refl.*) To be highly pleased, take great pleasure, rejoice ME. Also *refl.* **†3.** *trans.* To enjoy greatly –1618.

1. But for I. .was so besy you to delyte CHAUCER. **2.** The labour we d. in physicks paine *Macb.* II. iii. 55. I will d. my selfe in thy statutes *Ps.* 119:16. **Deli·ghtable** *a.* affording delight (*rare*). **Deli·ghter,** one who takes delight *in.* **Deli·ghtingly** *adv.*

Delighted (dĭləi·tėd), *ppl. a.* 1603. [f. DELIGHT *v.* and *sb.* + -ED.] **1.** Highly pleased or gratified 1687. **†2.** Attended with delight; delightful –1747.

2. If Vertue no d. Beautie lack *Oth.* I. iii. 290. Hence **Deli·ghtedly** *adv.*

Delightful (dĭləi·tfŭl), *a.* 1530. [f. DELIGHT (*delite*) *sb.* + -FUL.] **1.** Affording delight; highly pleasing, charming. **†2.** Experiencing delight; delighted *with* –1687.

1. Rimmon, whose d. Seat Was fair Damascus MILT. *P.L.* I. 467. D. books LOWELL. Hence **Delightful-ly** *adv.*, **-ness.**

Delimit (dĭli·mit), *v.* 1852. [– Fr. *délimiter* – L. *delimitare*, f. *de-* DE- I. 3 + *limitare*; see LIMIT *v.*] *trans.* To mark or fix the limits of; to define, as a limit or boundary.

Delimitate (dĭli·miteⁱt), *v.* 1884. [– *delimitat-*, pa. ppl. stem of L. *delimitare*; see prec., -ATE³.] = prec. So **Deli·mitative** *a.* having the function of delimiting.

Délimitation (dĭlimitēⁱ·ʃən). 1836. [– Fr. *délimitation* – L. *delimitatio*, f. as prec.; see -ION.] Determination of a limit or boundary; *esp.* of the frontier of a territory.

†Deli·ne, *v.* 1589. [– L. *delineare.* Cf. ALINE *v.*] = DELINEATE *v.* 1, 2. –1734.

Delineate (dĭli·ni,eⁱt), *v.* 1559. [– *delineat-*, pa. ppl. stem of L. *delineare* outline, sketch out, f. *de-* DE- I. 3 + *lineare* draw lines, f. *linea* LINE *sb.*²] **1.** *trans.* To trace out by lines, trace the outline of. **2.** To trace in outline, sketch out; 'to make the first draught of' (J.) 1613. **3.** To draw, portray 1610. **4.** *fig.* To portray in words 1618.

1. To d. a triangle BERKELEY. **2.** To d. a proposal MARVELL, a process REID, constitution JOWETT. **4.** When I d. him without reserve BOSWELL. Hence **Deli·neable** *a.* capable of being delineated (*rare*). **†Deli·neament,** delineation. **Deli·neate** *ppl. a.* delineated (*arch.* or *poet.*).

Delineation (dĭlini,ēⁱ·ʃən). 1570. [– late L. *delineatio*, f. as prec.; see -ION. Cf. Fr. *délinéation.*] **1.** The action of tracing out by lines; *concr.* a drawing, diagram, or figure. **2.** The action of tracing in outline something to be constructed; a sketch, plan, rough draft. Usu. *fig.* 1581. **3.** Pictorial representation; *concr.* a picture 1594. **4.** The action of portraying in words 1603. **†5.** Lineal descent (*rare*) 1606.

2. I call it only a D., or rude draught WOLLASTON. **4.** My delineations of the heart are from my own experience COWPER. var. **†Deli·neature.**

Delineator (dĭli·ni,eⁱtəɹ). 1774. [f. DELINEATE + -OR 2.] **1.** One who delineates 1782. **2.** An instrument for tracing outlines. Hence **Deli·neatory** *a.* belonging to delineation.

†Delini·tion. *rare.* [irreg. f. L. *delinere* besmear (pa. ppl. stem *delit-*); see -TION.] The action of smearing. HY. MORE.

†Deli·nquence. 1682. [– eccl.L. *delinquentia*, f. as DELINQUENT; see -ENCE.] The fact of being a delinquent; culpable failure in duty –1832.

Delinquency (dĭli·ŋkwĕnsi). 1636. [f. as prec.; see -ENCY.] **1.** The quality of being a delinquent; failure in or violation of duty; guilt 1648. **2.** (with *pl.*) An act of delinquency; a fault; an offence, misdeed.

2. From these Delinquencies proceed greater crimes 1651.

Delinquent (dĭli·ŋkwĕnt). 1484. [– *delinquent-*, pres. ppl. stem of L. *delinquere* be at fault, offend, f. *de-* DE- I. 3 + *linquere* leave; see -ENT.]

A. *adj.* Failing in, or neglectful of, a duty or obligation; guilty of a misdeed or offence 1603. Also *transf.*

B. *sb.* **1.** One who fails in duty or obligation; more generally, an offender 1484. **2.** *Eng. Hist.* A name for those who assisted Charles I or Charles II in levying war, 1642–1660.

2. Hereupon, they [the Commons] call'd whom they pleased, Delinquents CLARENDON.

†De·liquate, *v.* 1669. [f. DE- I. 3 + LIQUATE *v.*] **1.** *trans.* To melt down 1673. **2.** *intr.* To deliquesce –1800. Hence **†Deliqua·tion.**

Deliquesce (delikwe·s), *v.* 1756. [– L. *deliquescere* melt away, dissolve, f. *de-* DE- I. 3 + *liquescere*, inceptive of *liquēre* be liquid; cf. -ESCENT.] **1.** *Chem.* To melt or become liquid by absorbing moisture from the air, as certain salts. **2.** *Biol.* To melt away, as some parts of fungi, etc., in the process of growth or of decay 1836. **3.** *gen.* To melt away (*lit.* and *fig.*). (Mostly *humorous.*) 1858.

1. This pot-ash. .deliquesces a little in moist air 1780.

Deliquescence (delikwe·sĕns). 1800. [f. DELIQUESCENT; see -ENCE.] The process of deliquescing or melting away; the liquid or solution resulting from this process.

The English. .hurry to the seaside with red, perspiring faces, in a state of combustion and d. HAWTHORNE. So **Delique·scency,** the quality of being deliquescent (*rare*).

Deliquescent (delikwe·sĕnt), *a.* 1791. [– *deliquescent-*, pres. ppl. stem of L. *deliquescere*; see DELIQUESCE, -ENT.] **1.** *Chem.* That deliquesces; melting or becoming liquid by absorption of moisture from the air. **2. a.**

Biol. Melting away in the process of growth or decay 1874. **b.** *Bot.* Dissolved into ramifications, as the trunk of the White Elm, etc. 1866. **3.** *joc.* Dissolving (in perspiration) 1837.

1. Mild fixed alkali is..d. 1791. **3.** The dusty and d. pedestrian 1876.

†**Deli·quiate,** *v.* 1782. [irreg. f. L. *deliquare* DELIQUATE, or f. DELIQUIUM².] *intr.* = DELIQUATE 2, DELIQUESCE –1854. So †**Deliquia·tion.**

Deliquium¹ (dǐli·kwiǒm). *arch.* 1621. [– L. *deliquium* want, defect (in med.L. offence, transgression), f. *delinquere, deliqu-*; see DELINQUENT.] **1.** Failure of the vital powers; a swoon. Also *fig.* †**2.** A failure of light, as in an eclipse –1671. **3.** Confused with next 1711.

†**Deli·quium².** 1641. [f. DELIQUATE *v.*, with L. ending as in *effluvium.*] = DELIQUESCENCE –1823.

Deli·racy. *rare.* [f. DELIRATE; see -ACY.] Delirium. SOUTHEY. So **Deli·rament,** †**Deli·rancy** (in same sense). †**Deli·rant** *a.* raving, mad.

†**Deli·rate,** *v. rare.* [– *delirat-*, pa. ppl. stem of L. *delirare*; see DELIRE *v.*, -ATE³.] *trans.* = DELIRIATE; *intr.* = DELIRE 2. P. HOLLAND.

Deliration (delirēⁱ·ʃən). 1600. [– L. *deliratio*, f. as prec.; see -ION.] Delirium, aberration of mind; madness. Also *fig.*

An earnestness..which..drove him into the strangest incoherences, almost delirations CARLYLE.

†**Deli·re,** *v.* ME. [– L. *delirare*; see DELIRIUM. In sense 2 perh. partly – Fr. *délirer.*] **1.** *intr.* To go wrong, err –1633. **2.** To go astray from reason; to be delirious or mad, to rave –1675.

2. O how green Youth delires QUARLES. So †**Deli·rement** = *delirament.*

Deliriant (dǐli·riănt), *a.* 1883. [f. DELIRIUM + -ANT, after *stimulant*, etc.] *Med.* Having power to produce delirium. Also as *sb.* So **Delirifa·cient** *a.* and *sb.*

†**Deli·riate,** *v.* 1658. [f. DELIRIUM + -ATE³.] *trans.* To make delirious –1711.

Delirious (dǐli·riəs), *a.* 1599. [f. as next + -OUS.] **1.** Affected with delirium, *esp.* as a result or symptom of disease; wandering in mind 1706. **2.** *transf.* and *fig.* Frantic, 'mad' 1599.

1. A d. patient 1871, manner 1809. **2.** D. with delight 1855. The d. screech..of a railway train CARLYLE. Hence **Deli·rious-ly** *adv.*, **-ness.**

Delirium (dǐli·riǒm). Pl. **-iums, -ia.** 1599. [– L. *delirium*, f. *delirare* deviate, be deranged, f. *de-* DE- I. 2 + *lira* ridge between furrows.] **1.** A disordered state of the mental faculties resulting from disturbance of the functions of the brain, and characterized by incoherent speech, hallucinations, restlessness, and frenzied excitement. **2.** *fig.* Excitement as of one delirious; frenzied rapture; wildly absurd thought or speech 1650.

2. The gorgeous d. of gladiatorial shows GEO. ELIOT. **D. tremens.** [mod. Medical L. = trembling delirium.] A species of d. resulting from the abuse of alcohol, and characterized by tremblings and delusions.

†**Deli·rous,** *a.* 1656. [f. L. *delirus* (f. *delirare*) + -OUS; see prec.] = DELIRIOUS –1722.

Delit, earlier f. DELIGHT. So †**Delitable** *a.* delectable. †**Delitably** *adv.* †**Deli·te** *a.* delightful (*rare*).

Delitescence (delite·sĕns). 1776. [f. DELITESCENT; see -ENCE.] **1.** The condition of lying hid; concealment, seclusion. **2.** *Med.* **a.** The sudden disappearance of inflammation by resolution. **b.** = INCUBATION. var. **Delite·scency.**

Delitescent (delite·sĕnt, dī-), *a.* 1684. [– *delitescent-*, pres. ppl. stem of L. *delitescere* hide away, lurk, f. *de-* DE- I. 2 + *latescere*, inceptive of *latēre* lie hid; see -ESCENT.] Lying hid, latent.

Deli·ver, *a. Obs.* or *arch.* ME. [– OFr. *delivre, deslivre*, f. *delivrer*; see next.] †**1.** Free, at liberty. (ME. only.) **2.** Free from all impediments; active, nimble, quick in action ME. †**3.** Delivered (of a child) –1460.

2. Light and deliuer, voyde of al fatness 1472.

Deliver (dǐli·vəɹ), *v.*¹ ME. [– (O)Fr. *délivrer* :– Gallo-Rom. **deliberare*, f. *de-* DE- I. 3 + *liberare* LIBERATE.] **1.** *trans.* To set free, liberate, rescue, save. Const. *from, out of,* †*of.* †**2.** To free, rid, divest, clear *of, from* –1677; *transf.* to dispel (pain, etc.); to relieve –1610. **3.** To disburden *of* the fœtus; in *pass.*, to give birth to a child or offspring. Rarely said of beasts. (The active is late.) ME. †**b.** *pass.* Of the offspring: To be brought forth (*lit.* and *fig.*) –1604. **4.** To unload. ? *Obs.* 1793. **5.** *refl.* To disburden *oneself of* what is in one's mind; to discourse ME. †**6.** To dispose of quickly; *refl.* to make haste –1530. **7.** To give up entirely, surrender, yield ME. **8.** To hand over to another's possession or keeping; *spec.* to give or distribute to the proper person or quarter; to present (an account, etc.). Const. *to*, or with dative. ME. **b.** *Law.* To give or hand over formally; see DELIVERY 1574. **9.** To give forth, send forth, emit; to discharge, launch; to cast, throw, project 1586. **10.** To give forth in words, utter, pronounce 1576. †**11.** *trans.* To declare, communicate, report, make known; to state, affirm; to set forth, describe –1800. **12.** *Pottery* and *Founding.* To set free from the mould. Also *intr.* 1782.

1. Fro temptacioun deliure me CHAUCER. **2.** Phr. *To d. a gaol*: to clear it of prisoners in order to bring them to trial at the assizes. **3.** She is, something before her time, deliuer'd *Wint. T.* II. ii. 25. There are many Euents in the Wombe of Time, which wilbe deliuered *Oth.* I. iii. 378. **5.** To d. oneself against a bill STEELE. **7.** See them deliuered ouer To execution *Rich. II*, III. i. 29. **8.** To d. a message 1843, a letter 1881, bill of costs 1892, deed WILLIAMS. **9.** To d. water 1633, a harpoon MEDWIN, an assault 1864. Phr. *To d. battle*: to begin an attack. **10.** To d. a course of lectures 1804, judgment 1882. Hence **Deli·verable** *a.* that can be delivered; to be delivered.

†**Deli·ver,** *v.*², var. of DELIBER *v.*

Deliverance (dǐli·vərăns). ME. [– (O)Fr. *délivrance*, f. *délivrer*; see DELIVER *v.*¹, -ANCE.] **1.** The act of setting free, or fact of being set free; liberation, release, rescue. †**2.** The bringing forth of offspring; delivery –1660. †**3.** The action of giving up; surrender –1568. †**4.** The action of handing over, transferring, or delivering; delivery –1631. †**5.** Sending forth, discharge 1626. †**6.** Utterance, enunciation, delivery –1609. †**7.** The action of setting forth in words, or that which is set forth; statement, narration, communication ME. **8.** *Sc. Law.* Judgement delivered; any judicial or administrative order ME.; verdict 1660. †**9.** Deliverness ME.

1. Our d. from the bondage of sin HOBBES. The next generall gaoles deliveraunce 1487. **4.** *Writ of second d.* (Law): a writ for re-delivery to the owner of goods distrained or unlawfully taken. **7.** The recorded deliverances of the Founder of Christianity MILL.

Deliverer (dǐli·vərəɹ). ME. [– OFr. *delivrere*, f. *délivrer* DELIVER *v.*¹; see -ER² 3.] **1.** One who sets free or releases; a liberator. **2.** One who hands over, commits, surrenders, etc. 1531. **3.** One who utters, sets forth, etc. (*rare*) 1597.

1. Thy great d., who shall bruise The Serpents head MILT. *P.L.* XII. 149. So **Deli·veress,** a female d. (*rare*).

Deli·verly, *adv. Obs.* or *arch.* ME. [f. DELIVER *a.* + -LY².] **1.** Lightly, nimbly, quickly. **2.** Deftly 1530. ¶As *adj.* (erron.) SCOTT.

2. Carry it sweetly and d. 1612. So †**Deli·verness,** lightness, nimbleness, quickness.

Delivery (dǐli·vəri). 1480. [– AFr. *delivree*, subst. use of fem. pa. pple. of *delivrer*, see DELIVER *v.*¹, -Y³.] †**1.** The action of setting free; release, rescue, deliverance –1784. **2.** The being delivered of, or bringing forth, offspring; child-birth 1577. Also *fig.* **3.** The act of giving up possession of; surrender 1513. **4.** The action of handing over anything to another; in *Law, esp.* the formal transfer of a deed by the grantor 1480. **5.** The act of delivering (a missile, a blow, etc.); throwing or bowling of a ball 1702. †**6.** 'Use of the limbs' (J.); action, bearing, deportment –1771. **7.** Utterance, or manner of utterance or enunciation 1581. †**8.** = DELIVERANCE 7. –1653.

3. The d. of the Castell Hall, of powder and stores 1780. **4.** The d. of goods 1799, of letters 1838, a telegram 1879, possession CRUISE, a deed R. COKE. **6.** The duke had the neater limbs and freer d. WOTTON (J.). **7.** A grave, serious d. PEPYS.

Dell¹ (del). [OE. *dell* = MLG., MDu. *delle* (Du. *del*), MHG. *telle* (G. dial. *telle*) :– Gmc. **daljō*, f. **dal-* (see DALE¹).] †**1.** A deep hole, a pit –1783. **2.** A small deep natural hollow or vale ME.

2. A green and silent spot, amid the hills, A small and silent d. COLERIDGE.

Dell² (del). *Rogues' Cant. arch.* 1567. [Origin unkn.] A wench.

‖**Della Crusca** (de:ˌla kru·ska). [It. *Accademia della Crusca*, lit. Academy of the bran or chaff.] The name of an Academy established at Florence in 1582, mainly to sift and purify the Italian language; whence its name, and its emblem, a sieve. Hence **Della-Cru·scan** *a.* of or pertaining to the Academy della Crusca, or its methods; also, applied to an artificial school of English poetry, started at the end of the 18th c.; *sb.* any one of these.

Delocalize (dǐlōᵘ·kăləiz), *v.* 1855. [DE- II. 1.] To detach from its locality, or from local limitations.

‖**Deloo** (dǐlū·). 1861. [Native name (Dor language).] A N. African antelope, akin to the duykerbok.

Delph, var. of DELF.

Delphian (de·lfiăn). 1625. [f. *Delphi* place name + -AN.] Of or relating to Delphi, a town of Phocis, in Greece, and to the sanctuary and oracle of Apollo there; hence, of or relating to the Delphic Apollo; and *transf.* oracular. So **De·lphic, De·lphical** *a.*

Delphin (de·lfin). ME. [– L. *delphin*, *delphinus* – Gr. δελφίς, later δελφίν; see DAUPHIN, DOLPHIN.]

†**A.** *sb.* **1.** = DOLPHIN –1633. **2.** *Chem.* Short for *delphinin*: A neutral fat found in the oil of several species of dolphin; called also *phocenin.*

B. *adj.* **1.** [attrib. use of L. *delphini* in phr. *ad usum Delphini.*] Of or pertaining to the Dauphin of France, and to the edition of the Latin classics, prepared 'for the use of the dauphin', son of Louis XIV. 1775. **2.** *Chem.* A bad form of DELPHINE, DELPHININE.

De·lphine, *a.* and *sb.* Var. of DELPHIN *a.*, DELPHININE *a.*, DELPHININE *sb.*

Delphinic (delfi·nik), *a.* [f. DELPHIN *sb.* 2 + -IC.] In *d. acid*, an acid discovered in dolphin-oil; it is identical with inactive valeric acid. A salt of it is a **De·lphinate.**

Delphinine (de·lfinəin), *sb.* 1830. [f. mod.L. *Delphinium* the genus Larkspur + -INE⁵.] *Chem.* A poisonous alkaloid obtained from the seeds of *Delphinium staphisagria*, STAVESACRE. Called also **Delphi·nia.**

De·lphinine, *a.* [f. L. *delphinus* DELPHIN + -INE¹.] Of the nature of a dolphin: in *Zool.*, of or pertaining to the *Delphininæ* or subfamily of Cetacea, containing the Dolphins and Porpoises.

‖**Delphinium** (delfi·niǒm). 1664. [– mod.L. *delphinium* – Gr. δελφίνιον larkspur, f. δελφίν DELPHIN.] *Bot.* A genus of plants, N.O. *Ranunculaceæ*, comprising the common Larkspur and other species. In horticultural use the name for the cultivated species and varieties.

De·lphinoid. [– Gr. δελφινοειδής, f. δελφίν DELPHIN; see -OID.] *Zool.*

A. *adj.* Like or related to a dolphin; belonging to the *Delphinoidea*, a division of the Cetacea, which includes the dolphins and seals.

B. *sb.* A member of the *Delphinoidea.*

Delphinoidine (delfinoi·dəin). 1883. [f. as DELPHININE *sb.* + -OID.] *Chem.* An amorphous alkaloid obtained from the same source as delphinine.

‖**Delphinus** (delfəi·nǒs). 1672. [L., = 'dolphin'.] In *Zool.*, the cetacean genus containing the Dolphin, etc.; in *Astron.*, an ancient northern constellation, figured as a dolphin.

Delta (de·ltă). ME. [Gr. δέλτα (– Phœnician *daleth*).] **1.** The fourth letter of the Greek alphabet, having the form of a triangle (Δ), and the power of D. **2.** A Δ-shaped tract of alluvial land enclosed and traversed by the diverging mouths of a river; as the d. of the Nile, the Ganges, etc. 1790. **3.** *Electr.* In a three-phase alternator, the triangular figure formed by connecting the three wires of the transmitting circuit to the junction of the three coils; *attrib.* as *d. connection, current* 1902.

Comb.: **d.-metal,** an alloy of copper, zinc, and iron named in allusion to its *three* constituents; **d. rays** (or *δ-rays*), rays of low penetrative power emitted by radioactive substances. **Deltaic** (deltēⁱ·ik) *a.* pertaining to, or forming a d.; of the nature of a d.

‖**Deltidium** (delti·diŏm). 1851. [mod.L. dim. of Gr. δέλτα, in reference to its shape.] *Conch.* The triangular space between the beak and the hinge of brachiopod shells.

Deltohedron (deltohī·drǫn). 1879. [f. Gr. δελτο-, as comb. f. next, + ἕδρα base.] *Crystall.* A solid figure the surface of which is formed by twenty-four deltoids.

Deltoid (de·ltoid), *a.* (*sb.*) 1741. [– Fr. *deltoïde*, or mod.L. *deltoides* (Linnæus) – Gr. δελτοειδής; see DELTA, -OID.] **1.** Like the Greek letter Δ in shape; triangular; *esp.* in *Bot.*, of a leaf 1753. **2.** Of the nature of the delta of a river 1837. So **Deltoi·dal** *a.*

1. *D. muscle* (Anat.): the large muscle of triangular shape which forms the prominence of the shoulder.

B. *sb.* The deltoid muscle. Also in L. form *deltoides, deltoideus* 1758.

The d., which caps the shoulder like an epaulette O. W. HOLMES.

‖**Delubrum** (dĭlⁱū·brŏm). 1665. [L., f. *deluere* wash off, cleanse.] **1.** A temple, shrine, or sanctuary. **2.** *Eccl. Archit.* A church furnished with a font; a font 1665.

†**Delu·ce, dely·s.** 1450. Short for *flower deluce* (Fr. *fleur de lis*, OFr. *lys*; see FLEUR-DE-LIS), *i.e.* lily-flower, the ensign of the Bourbons –1594.

Delude (dĭlⁱū·d), *v.* 1450. [– L. *deludere* play false, mock, f. *de-* DE- I. 4 + *ludere* to play, f. *ludus* play, game.] †**1.** *trans.* To play with (any one) to his injury or frustration; to mock; to defraud *of* –1697. **2.** To befool the mind or judgement of, so as to cause what is false to be accepted as true; to cheat, deceive, beguile; to impose upon 1450. †**3.** To frustrate the purpose of; to elude –1680.

2. As arrant imposters as ever deluded the credulous world T. BROWN. **3.** The 7. of June she againe deluded us, after two houres chase SIR T. HERBERT. Hence **Delu·der.**

Deluge (de·liudʒ), *sb.* ME. [– (O)Fr. *déluge*, alt., after pop. formations in *-uge*, of earlier *duluve, delouve* – L. *diluvium* DILUVIUM.] **1.** A great flood or overflowing of water, an inundation. (Often used hyperbolically.) **2.** *spec.* The great Flood in the time of Noah ME. **3.** *fig.* and *transf.* ME.

1. Together with earthquakes, deluges also, and inundations of the sea P. HOLLAND. **3.** Drowned in the d. of erroure EDEN. A fiery D., fed With ever-burning Sulphur unconsum'd MILT. *P.L.* I. 68.

Deluge (de·liudʒ), *v.* 1649. [f. the sb.] **1.** *trans.* To flow over in a deluge; to flood, inundate. Also *absol.* (Often used hyperbolically.) **2.** *fig.* and *transf.* 1654.

1. Sufficient to d. the World, and drown Mankind DE FOE. Deluged in tears MME. D'ARBLAY. **2.** At length Corruption, like a gen'ral Flood.. Shall d. all POPE. Deluged with pamphlets W. IRVING.

†**Delu·mbate,** *v. rare.* 1609. [– *delumbat-*, pa. ppl. stem of L. *delumbare* to lame in the loin, f. *de-* DE- I. 6 + *lumbus* loin; see -ATE³.] To lame, maim, emasculate –1624.

‖**Delundung** (de·ləndɒŋ). 1840. [Native name.] The weasel-cat of Java and Malacca, belonging to the civet family.

Delusion (dĭlⁱū·ʒən). ME. [– late L. *delusio*, f. *delus-*, pa. ppl. stem of *deludere*; see DELUDE, -ION.] **1.** The action of deluding (see DELUDE *v.* 1, 2); the fact or condition of being deluded. **2.** Anything that deceives the mind with a false impression; a deception; a fixed false opinion with regard to objective things, *esp.* as a form of mental derangement 1552. †**3.** Evasion 1606.

1. God shall send them strong d., that they should believe a lie 2 *Thess.* 2:11. **2.** A juglers d. 1638. The poor fellow was only labouring under a d. 1874. Hence **Delu·sional** *a.* of the nature of, or characterized by, d. **Delu·sionist,** one given to deluding; one given up to delusions.

Delusive (dĭlⁱū·siv), *a.* 1605. [f. as prec. + -IVE.] **1.** Having the attribute of deluding, characterized by delusion; deceptive. **2.** Of the nature of a delusion 1645.

1. D. appearances JOHNSON, promises PRESCOTT. **2.** Of what d. worth The bubbles we pursue LONGF. Hence **Delu·sive-ly** *adv.*, **-ness.** So **Delu·sory** *a.* of deluding quality; delusive.

De luxe; see LUXE.

Delve (delv), *sb.* 1590. [Partly a var. of DELF *sb.*, partly f. DELVE *v.*] **1.** That which is delved; excavation, pit, den; = DELF *sb.*¹ 1. **2.** A depression; a wrinkle 1811. **3.** An act of delving 1869.

1. The very tigers from their delves Look out MOORE. Logs and roots innumerous He gathered in a d. upon the ground SHELLEY.

Delve (delv), *v.* [OE. *delfan* = OFris. *delva*, OS. *bi-delban* (Du. *delven*), OHG. *bi-telban* :– W.Gmc. **delb- *dalb- *dulb-*.] **1.** *trans.* To dig; to turn up (ground) with a spade OE. Also *fig.* and *transf.* **2.** To make by digging, excavate (*arch.*) OE. Also *transf.* and *fig.* †**3.** To put in by digging –1735. **4.** To dig *up* or *out of* (*arch.* or *dial.*) OE. †**5.** To penetrate as by digging –1450. **6.** *absol.* or *intr.* To labour with, or as with, a spade; to dig; to drudge (*arch.* or *poet.*, and *dial.*) OE. **7.** Of a road, etc.: To dip sharply 1848.

1. They delved the soil, they wove the fleece 1845. *fig.* What's his name, and Birth?..I cannot d. him to the roote *Cymb.* I. i. 28. **2.** *fig.* Time..delues the paralels in beauties brow SHAKS. *Sonn.* lx. **6.** Where frigid learning delves In Aldine folios O. W. HOLMES. Hence **De·lver,** one who delves (*lit.* and *fig.*).

Dem, *v.*; formerly **demn.** ME. Minced form of DAMN; so **demd** for *damned.*

Demagnetize (dĭmæ·gnĕtəiz), *v.* 1842. [DE- II. 1.] **1.** To deprive of magnetic quality. †**2.** To free from mesmeric influence; to demesmerize 1850.

1. Hot air traversing the discs and rolls demagnetizes the discs 1887. Hence **Dema:gnetiza·tion.**

Demagogic, -al (de:măgǫ·gik, -gǫ·dʒik, -ăl), *a.* 1734. [– Gr. δημαγωγικός, f. δημαγωγός DEMAGOGUE; see -IC, -ICAL.] Of, pertaining to, or like a demagogue.

Demagogism, -goguism (de·măgǫgiz'm). 1824. [f. DEMAGOGUE + -ISM.] The practice and principles of a demagogue.

Demagogue (de·măgǫg), *sb.* 1648. [– Gr. δημαγωγός, f. δῆμος people + ἀγωγός leader, f. ἄγειν lead. Cf. Fr. *démagogue.*] **1.** In ancient times, a leader of the people as against other parties in the state 1651. **2.** In bad sense: A leader of a popular faction, or of the mob; an unprincipled or factious mob orator or political agitator.

2. He despised the mean arts and unreasonable clamours of demagogues MACAULAY. Hence **De·magoguery** (*U.S.*), demagogism. **De·magogy,** the action or quality of a d.

Demain(e, early ff. DOMAIN, DEMESNE.

Demand (dĭmɑ·nd), *sb.* ME. [– (O)Fr. *demande*, f. *demander*; see next.] **1.** An act of demanding or asking by virtue of right or authority; a peremptory request or claim; also *transf.*, that which is demanded. Also *fig.* **2.** The action of demanding 1602. **3.** *Law.* The action or fact of demanding in legal form; a legal claim·1485. **4.** 'The calling for a thing in order to purchase it' (J.); in *Pol. Econ.* a call for a commodity on the part of consumers, combined with the power to purchase; called also *effectual demand.* Correl. to *supply.* 1776. **5.** An urgent requirement 1790. **6.** A request; a question (*arch.*) ME. **7.** *attrib.*, as *d. note*, a note payable on d.; also, a formal request for payment 1866.

1. A desire that Whitelocke would putt down his demands in writing 1654. *fig.* A d. of nature BUTLER. **2.** Phr. *On* (†*at*) *d.*: (payable) on request, claim, or presentation. **4.** The English, finding a great d. for tobacco in Europe 1780. Phr. *In d.*: sought after, in request. **5.** The demands of a profession destroy the elasticity of the mind JOWETT.

Demand (dĭmɑ·nd), *v.* ME. [– (O)Fr. *demander* :– L. *demandare* hand over, entrust (in med.L., demand, request), f. *de-* DE- I. 3 + *mandare* commission, order.] **1.** *trans.* To ask for with legal right or authority 1489. **2.** *spec.* in *Law.* To make formal claim to (real property) as the rightful owner 1485. **3.** To ask for peremptorily, imperiously, or urgently; †to ask (*esp.* in transl. from Fr., etc.) 1484. **4.** *fig.* Said of things: To call for of right, or as necessary 1703. **5.** To ask authoritatively to know 1548; † to ask (a person) to inform one (*of, how*, etc.) –1722. †**6.** With cogn. obj.: To ask (a question, etc.) –1605. **7.** *intr.* To ask, make inquiry ME.

1. I d. my Liberty, being freed by the jury 1670. **3.** They demanded a King HOBBES. The offenders are demanded to justice FULLER. **4.** Government..demands skill, patience, energy, long and tenacious grip MORLEY. **5.** Then the prieste shall demaunde the name of the child *Bk. Com. Prayer.* *Cymb.* III. vi. 92. **7.** Heare..I will d. of thee, and declare thou vnto me *Job* 42:4. Hence **Dema·ndable** *a.* that may be demanded or claimed. **Dema·ndant,** one who demands; *spec.* in *Law*, the plaintiff in a real action; *gen.* any plaintiff or claimant. **Dema·nder.** †**Dema·nderess,** a female demandant.

Dema·ndative, *a.* [f. *demandat-*, pa. ppl. stem of L. *demandare*; see prec., -IVE.] Of the nature of a legal claim; made by the demandant. BENTHAM.

Demarcate (dī·maɹkeⁱt), *v.* 1816. [Back-formation from DEMARCATION; see -ATE³.] To mark out the limits of; to mark off *from*; to determine, as a boundary or limit; to define (*lit.* and *fig.*).

To d. a region 1882, a frontier 1884, Reproduction from Growth LEWES.

Demarcation (dīmaɹkēⁱ·ʃən). Also **demarkation.** 1727. [orig. in the phr. *line of demarcation* (Sp. *linea de demarcación* = Pg. *linha de demarcação*), – Sp. *demarcación* (Pg. *demarcação*), f. *demarcar* mark out the bounds of, f. *de-* DE- I. 3 + *marcar* MARK *v.*; see -ATION.] The action of marking the limits of, or of marking off; delimitation; separation. Usu. in phr. *line of d.* Also *fig.*

As early as the 4th of May (1493) the celebrated bull was signed by Pope Alexander VI, which established 'to all eternity' the line of d. between the Spanish and Portuguese possessions 1849. The lines of d. between the species LYELL.

Demarch (dī·maɹk). 1642. [– L. *demarchus* – Gr. δήμαρχος, f. δῆμος DEME *sb.*² + ἀρχός leader.] The chief magistrate of an Attic deme. In mod. Greece: The mayor of a commune. So **De·marchy,** the office of a d.; a popular government; the municipal body of a Greek commune.

‖**Démarche** (dema·rʃ). (In mod. Dicts. **demarch.**) 1658. [Fr., f. *démarcher* take steps, f. *dé-* DE- I. 3 + *marcher* MARCH *v.*²] Walk, step; proceeding, manner of action.

Demark (dĭmā·ɹk), *v.* 1834. [Deduced from DEMARCATION after MARK *v.*] = DEMARCATE.

Dematerialize (dīmătīᵊ·riăləiz), *v.* 1884. [DE- II. 1.] *trans.* To deprive of material character or qualities; *intr.* to become dematerialized.

†**Deme,** *sb.*¹ [OE. *dēma, dēma* = OHG. *tuomo*; see DEEM *v.*, DOOM *v.*] A judge, arbiter, ruler –ME.

Deme (dīm), *sb.*² 1833. [– Gr. δῆμος; see DEMOS.] **1.** A township or division of ancient Attica. In mod. Greece: A commune. **2.** *Biol.* Any undifferentiated aggregate of cells, plastids, or monads 1883.

†**Demea·n,** *sb.* 1450. [f. DEMEAN *v.*¹] **1.** Bearing, behaviour, demeanour –1756. **2.** Treatment (of others). SPENSER.

1. Another Damsell modest of demayne SPENSER.

Demean (dĭmī·n), *v.*¹ ME. [– (O)Fr. *démener* lead, exercise, practise, *se démener* behave :– Rom. **deminare*, f. L. *de-* DE- I. 3 + L. *minare* drive (animals), orig. urge on with threats (L. *minari* threaten).] †**1.** *trans.* To conduct; to manage, deal with, employ –1640; to express (sorrow, etc.) –1607. **2.** *refl.* To comport oneself. (The only existing sense.) ME. Also *fig.* of things.

1. As our obdurat Clergy have with violence demean'd the matter MILT. **2.** To d. himself like a Gentleman SHAFTESB. To have a vigilant eye how Bookes d. themselves as well as men MILT. Hence †**Demea·nance,** demeanour. var. †**Demeine.**

Demean (dĭmī·n), *v.*² 1601. [f. DE- I. 1 + MEAN *a.*, after *debase.*] *trans.* To lower; esp. *refl.* to lower or humble oneself.

Could a girl so far d. herself as to ask for love W. BLACK. To d. herself to a common carpenter GEO. ELIOT.

Demean, Demeane, earlier ff. DEMESNE.

Demeanour (dĭmī·nəɹ). Also **-or** (*U.S.*). 1494. [f. DEMEAN *v.*¹, prob. by association with †*havour* HAVIOUR.] **1.** Conduct, mode of proceeding, management; practice, behaviour. **2.** Manner of comporting oneself towards others; bearing. (The usual current sense.) 1509.

1. A commission..to examine Lord Shaftsb[ury's] demeanours 1677. **2.** With Goddess-like d. forth she went MILT. *P.L.* VIII. 59. Gravity and almost apathy of d. J. H. NEWMAN.

||**Démêlé** (dеmę·le). 1661. [Fr.; = quarrel, etc.] Debate, contention, quarrel.

Demembration (dīmembrēⁱ·ʃən). 1597. [– med.L. *demembratio*, f. *demembrat-*, pa. ppl. stem of late L. *demembrare*; see DISMEMBER, -ION. Cf. OFr. *demembration*.] The cutting off of a limb; mutilation; dismemberment. (Chiefly in *Sc. Law*.)

||**Demembré.** *Her.* 1727. [Fr.] = DISMEMBERED.

Dement (dīme·nt), *a.* (*sb.*) 1560. [– Fr. *dément* or L. *demens, -ment-* insane, f. *de-* DE- I. 6 + *mens, ment-* mind.] Demented. *Obs.* or *arch.* *sb.* One demented 1888.

Dement (dīme·nt), *v.* 1545. [– OFr. *dementer* or late L. *dementare*, f. *demens*; see prec.] To put out of one's mind, drive mad, craze. So **Deme·ntate** *v.* (in same sense); **Dementa·tion,** the action of dementing; the being demented. Hence **Deme·nted** *ppl. a.* crazed; affected with dementia. **Deme·ntedness.**

||**Dementia** (dīme·nʃiă). 1806. [L., f. *demens* DEMENT *a.*] **1.** *Med.* [tr. Fr. *démence* (Pinel).] A species of insanity characterized by failure or loss of the mental powers. **2.** *gen.* Infatuation 1877. var. †**De·mency.**

†**Deme·ntie,** *sb.* 1594. [– Fr. †*démentie* (mod. *démenti*), f. *démentir* (OFr. *des-*) give the lie to, f. *dé-, des-* (DE- I. 6) + *mentir* lie.] The giving any one the lie. [Now only as Fr., *démenti* (demañti).]

Demerara (demĕrēᵊ·ră, demĕrā·ră). 1848. The name of a region of British Guiana, used to designate a kind of raw cane-sugar, originally and chiefly brought from Demerara, the crystals of which have a yellowish-brown colour.

†**Deme·rge,** *v.* 1610. [– L. *demergere* sink, submerge, f. *de-* DE- I. 1 + *mergere* plunge, dip.] *trans.* To plunge, immerse –1669.

Demerit (dīme·rit), *sb.* ME. [– OFr. *de(s)merite* or L. *demeritum*, f. *demerit-*, pa. ppl. stem of *demereri* merit, deserve, f. *de-* DE- I. 3 + *mereri* MERIT *v.*] †**1.** Merit, desert; a deserving act –1731. **2.** Desert in a bad sense: quality deserving blame; ill-desert; censurable conduct: opp. to *merit* 1509; †a blameworthy act (usu. in *pl.*) –1637. Also *transf.* of things. †**3.** That which is merited (*esp.* for ill doing); desert –1728.

1. Your demerites are so ferre aboue all prayses of man UDALL. **2.** Mine is the merit, the d. thine DRYDEN. *transf.* The merits or demerits of hereditary royalty 1832.

Demerit (dīme·rit), *v.* *Obs.* or *arch.* 1538. [– *demerit-*, pa. ppl. stem of L. *demereri*, see prec.; partly after Fr. *démériter*.] †**1.** *trans.* To merit, deserve (*esp.* evil) –1711. †**2.** To disparage –1643. **3.** To fail to merit 1654. †**4.** *intr.* To merit blame, deserve ill –1734.

1. To d. pains 1538, the fauour of God T. TAYLOR, blame 1619. **4.** For he was..the kings servant already, and had not demerited NORTH. Hence **Deme:rito·rious** *a.* ill-deserving; †undeserving (*rare*).

Demersal (dīmə̄·ɹsăl), *a.* 1889. [f. as next + -AL¹ 1.] Sinking to or living at the bottom of the sea.

†**Demerse** (dīmə̄·ɹs), *v.* 1662. [– *demers-*, pa. ppl. stem of L. *demergere*; see DEMERGE.] *trans.* To immerse, submerge –1691. Hence **Deme·rsion** (*rare*) 1692.

Deme·smerize, *v.* 1855. See DE- II. 1.

Demesne (dīmēⁱ·n, dīmī·n). ME. [– AFr., OFr. *demeine*, later AFr. *demesne*, subst. use of adj., of or belonging to a lord, :– L. *dominicus* of a lord or master; cf. DOMAIN. For the insertion of the unetymological *-s-* cf. MESNE.]

I. Possession. **1.** *Law.* Possession (of real estate) as one's own ME. †**2.** *transf.* and *fig.* Possession; dominion, power –1747.

1. *To hold in d.* (*tenere in dominico*), i.e. in one's own hands as possessor by free tenure. (See II. 1.) *In his d. as of fee* (*in dominico suo ut de feodo*): in possession as an estate of inheritance. (Not applied to things incapable of physical possession.) *In ancient d.*: see below.

II. An estate possessed. **1.** An estate held in demesne: land possessed and held by the owner himself, and not held of him by any subordinate tenant. **b.** In mod. use, The land immediately attached to a mansion, and held along with it for use or pleasure; the park, chase, home-farm, etc. ME. **2.** The territory or dominion of a sovereign or state; a DOMAIN ME.; landed property; usu. *pl.* estates, lands 1584. **3.** *fig.* A district, region, territory; DOMAIN 1592. †**4.** *pl.* Means –1650.

1. *Royal D.*: the Crown-lands. *Ancient d.*: a d. possessed from ancient times; *spec.* the ancient d. of the crown, *i.e.* that property which belonged to the king at the Norman Conquest, as recorded in Domesday-book. Hence *tenants in ancient d.*, etc. **2.** A Gentleman..Of fair demeanes *Rom. & Jul.* III. v. 182. **3.** One wide expanse..That deep-browed Homer ruled as his d. KEATS.

III. *attrib.* or as *adj.* Of or pertaining to a demesne (II. 1); demesnial, as *d. lands* ME.

Demesnial (dīmēⁱ·niăl, -mī·niăl), *a.* 1857. [f. prec., after *manorial*, etc.; see -IAL.] Of or pertaining to a demesne.

Demi (de·mi), *sb., a., pref.* ME. [– Fr. *demi* :– med.L. *dimedius* half, for L. *dimidius*. Cf. DEMY.]

A. As separate word. (Formerly also **demy.**) **I.** *adj.* (or *adv.*) Half; half-sized, diminutive. Now *rare*.

†**II.** as *sb.* A half. Chiefly *ellipt.* –1761.

B. Demi- in combination: half, semi-, half-sized, curtailed.

1. In *Heraldry*, etc., as *d.-lion, -man*; *d.-belt*, etc.; **d.-vol,** a single wing of a bird used as a bearing.

2. In *Costume*, as *d.-robe, -train*; †**d.-crown,** a coronet.

3. In *Arms* and *Armour*, as **d.-brassard, -gardebras,** a piece of plate-armour for the upper arm at the back; **-chamfron,** a chamfron covering part only of the face of the horse; **-cuirass,** a corslet of iron, which only partly protected the body, front and back; **-jambe,** a piece covering the front of the leg; **-mentonniere,** a chin-piece for the tilt covering the left side only; **-pauldron,** the smaller form of shoulder-plate used in the end of the 15th c.; **-pike** = HALF-PIKE; **-placard, -placate** = *demi-cuirass*; **-suit,** the suit of light armour used in and after the 15th c.; **-vambrace,** a piece of plate-armour protecting the outside of the fore-arm.

4. In *Artillery*, as *d.-bombard*; †**d.-cannon,** a gun formerly used, of about 6½ inches bore; †**-culverin,** a cannon formerly in use, of about 4½ inches bore; †**-hake,** †**-haque,** a smaller form of HAKE or HACKBUT.

5. In *Fortif.*, as **d.-bastion,** a work with one face and one flank, like half a bastion; **-caponier,** a construction across the ditch, having but one parapet and glacis; **-distance** (of polygons), the distance between the outward polygons and the flank; **-gorge,** half of the gorge or entrance to the bastion, taken from the angle of the curtain to the centre of the bastion; **-parallel,** short entrenchments thrown up between the main parallels of attack, to protect the guards of the trenches; **-revetment,** a revetment or retaining wall for the face of a rampart, which is carried only as high as the cover in front, leaving the rest as an earthen rampart at the natural slope.

6. In *Military tactics*, the *Manège*, etc., as **d.-brigade,** a regiment of infantry and artillery, under the first French Republic (Littré); **-volte,** one of the seven artificial motions of a horse: a half-turn made with the forelegs raised.

7. In *Weights, Measures, Coins*, etc., as †*d.-barrel*, †*-groat*; **d.-ame,** half an AAM; **-farthing,** a copper coin of Ceylon, of the value of half a farthing.

8. With names of stuffs, etc., as †**d.-castor,** a mixture of beaver's and other fur; a hat made of this.

9. *Mus.* †**d.-cadence,** an imperfect cadence, a half-close; †**-crochet,** a quaver; †**-ditone,** a minor third (see DITONE); †**-quaver,** a semiquaver; **-semiquaver,** a note of half the value of a semiquaver; the symbol for this note, resembling a quaver, but with three hooks; **-semitone,** a quarter-tone; **-tone** = SEMITONE.

10. With names of material or geometrical figures: Half-, semi-; as **d.-circle,** a semicircle; an instrument of semicircular form for measuring angles; *d.-column, -cylinder*, etc.; **-octagonal,** of the shape of half an octagon; †**d.-sphere** = hemisphere.

11. With ordinary class-nouns, as †**d.-island,** †**-isle,** a peninsula; †**-male,** a eunuch; **-tint** (? *Obs.*), a half-tint; *d.-wolf*.

12. With nouns of action, state, etc., as **d.-metamorphosis** (*Entom.*), partial metamorphosis, hemimetabolism; **-toilet,** half evening (or dinner) dress.

13. With adjs.: as *d.-Norman, -official*; **d.-equitant** (*Bot.*) = OBVOLUTE. (*Semi-* is now usual with most of these.)

14. With vbs., etc.: as †*d.-deify*, †*-natured*.

Demi-bath (de·mibɑþ). 1847. [tr. Fr. *demi-bain*.] A bath in which the body can be immersed only up to the loins.

Demigod (de·migǫd). 1530. [DEMI- 11: tr. L. *semideus*.] *Mythol.* A being partly of divine nature, as the offspring of a god and a mortal, or a man raised to divine rank; a minor or inferior deity. So **De:migo·ddess** (*rare*).

†**De·migrate,** *v.* 1623. [– *demigrat-*, pa. ppl. stem of L. *demigrare*, f. *de-* DE- I. 2 + *migrare* MIGRATE; see -ATE³.] *intr.* To migrate –1651. Hence †**Demigra·tion.**

Demijohn (de·mi,dʒǫn). 1769. [prob. – Fr. *dame-jeanne* (XVII, †*dame-jane*), with early assimilation to DEMI- and later to the proper name *John*; prop. 'Lady Jane'.] A large bottle with bulging body and narrow neck, usually cased in wicker- or rush-work.

Demi-lance (de·mi,lɑns). 1489. [– Fr. *demie lance*; cf. DEMI- 3.] **1.** A lance with a short shaft, used in the 15th and 16th centuries. **2.** A light horseman armed with a demi-lance. Hence **Demi-la·ncer** = DEMI-LANCE 2.

Demilune (de·milⁱūn), *sb.* (*a.*) 1727. [– Fr., in XVI–XVII *demie lune* half moon; cf. DEMI- 10.] †**1.** *gen.* A half-moon, a crescent 1734. **2.** *Fortif.* An outwork resembling a bastion with a crescent-shaped gorge, to protect a bastion or curtain 1727. **3.** *Physiol.* A granular mass of protoplasm, of semilunar form, found in the salivary glands 1883.

B. *adj.* Semilunar 1885.

||**Demi-mondaine** (dəmi,moñdę̄n). 1894. [Fr.; f. next.] A woman of the demi-monde.

||**Demi-monde** (dəmi,mōñd, de·mi,mǫnd). 1855. [Fr., 'half-world' (Alexandre Dumas *fils*, 1824–95).] The class of women of doubtful reputation and social standing, upon the outskirts of society. (Improp. extended to courtesans in general.)

†**Demi-o·stade, -ostage.** 1537. [– OFr. *demie ostade*, f. *demi, -e* half + *ostade* (XIV) – Eng. WORSTED.] A stuff: app. half-worsted half linen, linsey-woolsey –1882.

Demi-pique (de·mi,pīk), *a.* (*sb.*) 1695. [f. DEMI- 3 + *pique*, erron. var. of PEAK *sb.*² Not connected with Fr. *demi-pique*, which was a *half-pike* or *sponson*.] **A.** *adj.* Of a saddle: 'Half-peaked'; having a peak of about half the height of that of the older war-saddle. **B.** *sb.* A demi-pique saddle. Hence **De·mi-piqued** *a.* half-peaked.

†**De:mi-pu·ppet.** [DEMI- 10.] A dwarf puppet. *Temp.* v. i. 36.

Demi-rep (de·mi,rep). 1749. [f. DEMI- 11 + *'rep*, for *reputation*'. Cf. also *reputable*.] A woman of doubtful reputation or chastity.

That character which is vulgarly called a demi-rep, that is to say, a woman..whom every body knows to be what no body calls her FIELDING. Hence **Demire·pdom.**

||**De·mi-sang.** 1797. [Fr.] *Law.* Half-blood.

Demise (dīməi·z), *sb.* 1509. [– AFr. **demise*, subst. use of fem. pa. pple. of OFr. *de(s)mettre* (mod. *démettre*) dismiss, (*refl.*) resign, abdicate.] **1.** *Law.* Conveyance or transfer of an estate by will or lease. **2.** Transference or devolution of sovereignty; usu. in phr. *d. of the crown* 1689. **3.** Transferred to the death or decease which occasions the demise; hence, pop., = Decease, death 1754. Also *fig.*

2. That King James..had by d. abdicated himself and wholly vacated his right EVELYN. **3.** The early d. of this favourite friend of science 1799.

Demise (dīməi·z), *v.* 1480. [f. prec. sb.] **1.** *Law.* To give, grant, convey, or transfer by will or by lease. **b.** To convey or transfer (a title or dignity); *esp.* said of the transmission of sovereignty, as by abdication or death 1670. †**2.** *gen.* To convey; to 'lease' –1660. †**3.** To dismiss –1615. **4.** *intr.* To resign the crown; to die, decease (*rare*) 1727.

1. To let and demyse fermes ther for the terme of vij yere and undir 1495. To d. the crown 1892. **2.** What Honour, Canst thou d. to any childe of mine *Rich. III*, IV. iv. 247.

De·mi-sea:son, *a.* 1890. [– Fr. *demi-saison*

(also used).] Of costume: Of a style intermediate between that of the past and that of the coming season.

Demi-semi (de·mi,se·mi), *a.* 1805. [f. DEMI- 13 + SEMI half.] *lit.* Half-half, *i.e.* quarter: usu. a contemptuous diminutive.

Demi-sheath (de·mi,ʃīþ). [Cf. DEMI- 3.] *Entom.* A half-sheath; *i.e.* one of the two channelled organs of which the tubular sheaths, covering the ovipositors or stings of insects, are composed.

Demiss (dǐmi·s), *a.* 1572. [– L. *demissus* let down, dejected, pa. pple. of *demittere* DEMIT *v.*[1]] †**1.** Submissive, humble; also in bad sense, Abject, base –1649. †**2.** Hanging down, downcast –1634. **3.** *Bot.* Depressed, flattened.

1. Like a most demisse And abiect thrall SPENSER. With demisse reverence 1612. Hence †**Demi·ss-ly** *adv.*, **-ness.**

Demission[1] (dǐmi·ʃən). 1638. [– L. *demissio*, f. *demiss-*, pa. ppl. stem of *demittere*; see DEMIT *v.*[1], -ION.] **1.** Abasement, degradation. Now *rare*. †**2.** Dejection, depression –1719. †**3.** *lit.* Lowering –1741.

2. Heaviness and d. of spirit NORRIS.

Demi·ssion[2]. 1577. [– Fr. *démission*, in OFr. *desmission*, answering to med.L. **dismissio*, for *dimissio*, whence DIMISSION, DISMISSION. In Eng. the *de-* is taken as DE- I.] **1.** The action of putting away or letting go from oneself, giving up, or laying down (*esp.* a dignity or office). **2.** Dismission (*rare*) 1811.

1. The queenes d. of hir crowne HOLINSHED.

†**Demi·ssive,** *a.* 1622. [f. *demiss-*, pa. ppl. stem of L. *demittere* DEMIT *v.*[1] + -IVE.] = DEMISS 1, 2. –1763. Hence **Demi·ssively** *adv.*

†**Demi·ssory,** *a.* Var. of DIMISSORY; cf. DEMIT *v.*[2]

Demit (dǐmi·t), *v.*[1] 1556. [– L. *demittere* let or send down, f. *de-* DE- I. 1 + *mittere* send.] **1.** To send, put, or let down; to lower 1646. †**2.** *fig.* To bring down; to humble, abase –1688.

2. By taking on him the nature of man..he demitted, or humbled himselfe 1656.

Demi·t, *v.*[2] 1529. [– Fr. *démettre*, in OFr. *desmettre*, f. *des-*, *dé-* :– L. *dis-* + *mettre*; taking the place of L. *dimittere*; cf. DISMISS. Chiefly *Sc.*] **1.** To dismiss (*arch.*). †**2.** To put away, let go –1678. **3.** To give up, lay down (an office, etc.); to abdicate 1567. Also *absol.* †**4.** To send out –1756.

3. The Ritualists will neither submit nor d. 1880.

Demiurge (de·miɒ̄ɹdʒ, dǐ-mi-). 1678. [– eccl.L. *demiurgus* – Gr. δημιουργός handicraftsman, artisan, f. δήμιος public (see DEMOS) + *εργ- work.] **1.** A name for the Maker of the world, in the Platonic philosophy; in the Gnostic system, conceived as a being subordinate to the Supreme Being, and sometimes as the author of evil. **2.** *Gr. Hist.* A magistrate in certain Greek states, and in the Achæan league 1844. Hence **Demiu·rgic,** †**-al** *a.* of or pertaining to the D. or his work; creative.

Demi-vill. *rare.* ME. [AFr. *demie vile.*] *Constit. Hist.* A half-vill or town; the half of a vill as a political unit.

Demobilize (dǐmōᵘ·biləiz), *v.* 1882. [– Fr. *démobiliser* (1870); see DE- II. 1, MOBILIZE.] To reduce from a mobilized condition; to disband. Abbrev. **demob** (dǐmǫ·b) 1920. Hence **Demo:biliza·tion,** the action of demobilizing, reduction of forces to a peace footing.

Democracy (dǐmǫ·krăsi). 1574. [– (O)Fr. *démocratie* – late L. *democratia* – Gr. δημοκρατία; see DEMOS, -CRACY.] **1.** Government by the people; that form of government in which the sovereign power resides in the people, and is exercised either directly by them or by officers elected by them. In mod. use often denoting a social state in which all have equal rights. 1576. **b.** A state or community in which the government is vested in the people as a whole 1574. Also *fig.* **2.** That class of the people which has no hereditary or special rank or privilege; the common people 1827. **3.** *U.S. politics.* The principles, or the members, of the Democratic party 1825.

1. Those ancient whose resistless eloquence Wielded at will that fierce democraty MILT. *P.R.* IV. 269.

Democrat (de·mo,kræt). 1790. [– Fr. *démocrate*, f. *démocratie* (see prec.), after *aristocrate* ARISTOCRAT.] **1.** An adherent or advocate of democracy; *orig.* opp. to *aristocrat* in the French Revolution of 1790. **2.** *U.S.* A member of the Democratic party; see DEMOCRATIC 2. 1798. **3.** *U.S.* A light four-wheeled cart with several seats, one behind the other 1873. Also *attrib.*(*rare*).

1. Napoleon, in his first period, was a true d. CARLYLE.

Democratic (demo,kræ·tik), *a.* 1602. [– (O)Fr. *démocratique* – med.L. *democraticus* – Gr. δημοκρατικός, f. δημοκρατία DEMOCRACY; see -IC.] **1.** Of the nature of, or characterized by, democracy; advocating or upholding democracy. **2.** *U.S. politics.* (With capital D.) Name of the political party originally called *Anti-Federal* and afterwards *Democratic-Republican*, which favours strict interpretation of the Constitution, and the least possible interference with local and individual liberty; opp. to the *Republicans* (formerly called *Federals* and *Whigs*). **b.** Pertaining to the Democratic party, as 'a D. measure'. 1800.

1. Aristocratick gouernment nor Democratick pleas'd 1602. Hence **Democra·tical** *a.* (in sense 1); **-ly** *adv.*

Democratism (dǐmǫ·kræt,iz'm). 1793. [f. DEMOCRAT + -ISM.] Democracy as a principle or system. So †**Demo·cratist,** a democrat.

Democratize (dǐmǫ·krătəiz), *v.* 1798. [– Fr. *démocratiser*, f. *démocrate*, *démocratie*; see -IZE.] To make or become democratic. Hence **Demo:cratiza·tion,** the action of democratizing.

Democritean (dǐmǫ:kritī·ăn), *a.* 1617. [f. L. *Democriteus* (Gr. Δημοκρίτειος) + -AN.] Of, pertaining to, or after the style of Democritus, the Greek philosopher (known as 'the laughing philosopher'), or of his atomistic or other theories. So **Democri·tic,** †**-al** *a.* in same sense; †**Demo·critism,** the practice of Democritus in laughing at everything.

Demo·ded, *ppl. a.* 1887. [f. Fr. *démodé* + -ED[1].] That has gone out of fashion. So ‖**Démodé** (demōᵘ·de, ‖demode) [Fr.], demoded.

‖**Demodex** (dī·modeks). 1876. [mod.L.; f. Gr. δημός fat + δήξ wood-worm.] *Zool.* A genus of parasitic mites, including *D. folliculorum*, which infests the hair follicles and sebaceous follicles of man and domestic animals.

Demogorgon (dī:mogǭ·ɹgən). 1590. [late L., of uncertain origin. First mentioned by the Scholiast (Lactantius or Lutatius Placidus, ? c 450) on Statius *Theb.* iv. 516, as the great nether deity invoked in magic. Hence perh. a disguised Oriental name.] Name of a mysterious and terrible infernal deity.

Orcus and Ades, and the dreaded nam^ Of D. MILT. *P.L.* II. 965.

Demography (dǐmǫ·grăfi). 1880. [f. Gr. δῆμος people + -GRAPHY; cf. Fr. *démographie* (1878).] That branch of anthropology which treats of the statistics of births, deaths, diseases, etc. Hence **Demo·grapher,** one versed in d. **Demogra·phic** *a.* of or pertaining to d.

Demoid (dī·moid), *a.* 1884. [– Gr. δημοειδής vulgar, f. δῆμος people; see -OID.] Used of a type of animal or plant which by its commonness, etc. characterizes a region or a period of time.

‖**Demoise·lle.** 1520. [Fr., see DAMSEL.] **1.** A young lady, a maid, a girl. **2.** *Zool.* The Numidian Crane (*Anthropoides virgo*); so called from its elegance of form 1687. **3.** *Zool.* A dragon-fly 1844.

Demolish (dǐmǫ·liʃ), *v.* 1570. [– *démoliss-*, lengthened stem of (O)Fr. *démolir* – L. *demoliri*, f. *de-* DE- I. 1 + *moliri* construct, f. *moles* mass; see MOLE *sb.*[3], -ISH[2].] **1.** *trans.* To destroy by disintegration of the fabric of; to pull or throw down, reduce to ruin. †**b.** *intr.* with passive sense (*rare*) –1706. **2.** *fig.* To make an end of. Also *joc.* 1620.

1. To d. a partition wall 1641, the images in cathedrals MACAULAY. **2.** To d. a doctrine BERKELEY. Hence **Demo·lishable** *a.* **Demo·lisher. Demo·lishment** (now *rare*), the act of demolishing; demolished state or (*pl.*) †remains.

Demolition (demǫli·ʃən, dī-). 1549. [– (O)Fr. *démolition* – L. *demolitio*, f. *demolit-*, pa. ppl. stem of *demoliri*; see prec., -ION.] **1.** The action of demolishing; the fact or state of being demolished 1610; *pl.* demolished remains, ruins 1638. **2.** *fig.* Destruction, overthrow 1549.

1. The d. of the mass-house by Lincoln's Inn JOHNSON. **2.** The d. of rights and privileges 1775. Hence **Demoli·tionist,** one who aims at or advocates d.

Demon (dī·mən). Also **dæmon.** ME. [– med.L. *demon*, L. *dæmon* – Gr. δαίμων divinity, genius; cf. (O)Fr. *démon*. In both senses repr. L. *dæmonium*, Gr. dim. δαιμόνιον.] **1.** *Gr. Myth.* (= δαίμων): A being of a nature intermediate between that of gods and men; an inferior divinity, spirit (including the souls of deceased persons). Often written *dæmon* for distinction. 1569. **b.** Sometimes, An attendant spirit; a genius ME. **2.** An evil spirit 1706. **b.** *gen.* A malignant being of superhuman nature; a devil ME. Also *transf.* (of persons, animals, or agencies personified), and *fig.* Also *attrib.*

1. In Homer, there is scarcely any distinction between gods and dæmons GROTE. **b.** O Anthony! ..Thy Dæmon, that thy spirit which keepes thee, is Noble, Couragious, high vnmatchable *Ant. & Cl.* II. iii. 19. **2.** They sacrificed unto demons, which were no God R. V. *Deut.* 32:17. *transf.* The grim d. of a bull-dog 1821. *fig.* The d. of intemperance 1895. Hence **De·moness,** a female d.; a she-devil. **Demo·nial** *a.* of or relating to, or of the nature of, a d. or demons (*rare*). **Demo:nia·lity,** the nature of demons; demons collectively (*rare*). **Demo·nian** *a.* = demonial. †**Demo·nianism,** the doctrine of demoniacal possession. †**Demo·niast,** one who has dealings with demons, or with the devil (*rare*).

Demonetization (dǐmǫ:nĭtəizē[i]·ʃən). 1852. [f. next.] The action of demonetizing, or condition of being demonetized.

Demonetize (dǐmǫ·nĭtəiz), *v.* 1852. [– Fr. *démonétiser* (1793), f. *dé-* DE- I. 6 + L. *moneta* MONEY; see -IZE. Cf. MONETIZE.] *trans.* To deprive of standard monetary value; to withdraw from use as money.

Demoniac (dǐmōᵘ·niæk). ME. [– (O)Fr. *démoniaque* – eccl.L. *dæmoniacus*, f. *dæmonium*; see DEMON, -AC.]

A. *adj.* **1.** Possessed by an evil spirit. **2.** Of or pertaining to demons 1642. **3.** Befitting a demon; devilish 1820. **4.** = DEMONIC 2. 1844.

1. I hold him certeinly demoniack CHAUCER. **2.** The Demoniack legion MILT. **3.** D. scorn HAZLITT. **4.** The d. element in man 1844. So **Demoni·acal** *a.* (in senses 1–3).

B. *sb.* **1.** One possessed by an evil spirit ME. †**2.** *Eccl. Hist.* One of an Anabaptist sect, who hold that the devils will be saved at the last. (Dicts.)

1. And helyth the demonyackes or madde folk CAXTON.

Demonic (dǐmǫ·nik), *a.* Also **dæm-.** 1662. [– late L. *dæmonicus* – Gr. δαιμονικός, f. δαίμων; see DEMON, -IC.] **1.** Of, belonging to, or of the nature of, an evil spirit; devilish. **2.** Of, relating to, or of the nature of, supernatural power or genius = Ger. *dämonisch* (Goethe). (Usu. spelt *dæmonic* for distinction.) 1798.

1. D. delusions 1738. **2.** The Dæmonic Dickens: as pure an instance of genius as ever lived FITZGERALD. var. **Demo·nical** *a.* (in sense 1). Now *rare.*

Demonifuge (dǐmǫ·nifiūdʒ). *nonce-wd.* 1790. [f. L. *dæmon* (DEMON) + -FUGE.] A charm against demons.

Demonism (dī·mǫniz'm). Also **dæ-.** 1669. [f. DEMON + -ISM.] Belief in, or doctrine of, demons.

A belief in d. and witchcraft 1891. So **De·monist,** a believer in, or worshipper of, demons.

Demonize (dī·mǫnəiz), *v.* 1821. [f. as prec. + -IZE.] **1.** *trans.* To make into, or like, a demon. **2.** To subject to demoniacal influence 1864. Hence **De:moniza·tion,** the action of making into, or like, a demon.

Demono-, bef. a vowel **demon-,** repr. Gr. δαιμονο-, comb. f. Gr. δαίμων DEMON: as in **Demono·cracy,** the rule of demons. **Demono·graph(er,** a writer on demons. **Demono·graphy. Demono·later,** a worshipper of demons. **Demono·latry.** †**Demono·machy,** fighting with a demon. †**Demono·magy,** magical art relating to demons. †**De·monoma:ncy,** divination by the help of demons. **De:monoma·nia,** a mental disease in which the patient fancies himself possessed by a demon. So **Demono·pathy.** †**Demo·nomist,** a believer in, or worshipper of, demons. †**Demo·nomy,** demon-worship.

Demonology (dīmǒnǫ·lŏdʒi). Also dæ-. 1597. [f. DEMONO- + -LOGY.] That branch of knowledge which treats of demons, or of beliefs about demons; a treatise on demons. So **Demono·loger, Demono·logist,** one versed in d. **Demonolo·gic, -al** *a.*; **-ly** *adv.*

†**Demono·manie.** 1623. [– Fr. *démonomanie*; see DEMONO-, -MANIA.] Foolish belief in demons –1638.

De-monopolize (dīmǫ̆nǫ·pǒləiz), *v.* 1878. [DE- II. 1.] To destroy the monopoly of, withdraw from monopoly.

Demonry (dī·mənri). 1851. [f. DEMON + -RY.] Demoniacal influence or practices.

Demonship (dī·mənʃip). *rare.* 1638. [f. as prec. + -SHIP.] The rank or condition of a demon.

Demonstrable (dīmǫ·nstrăb'l, de·mǫ̆nstrăb'l), *a.* ME. [– L. *demonstrabilis*; see DEMONSTRATE *v.*, -BLE.] **1.** Capable of being shown or made evident; *occas.* = Evident (*obs.*). **2.** Capable of being proved conclusively 1551.

2. It being so mathematically d. that [etc.] HY. MORE. Hence **Demonstrabi·lity, Demo·nstrableness,** d. quality or condition. **Demo·nstrably** *adv.*

†**Demo·nstrance.** ME. [– OFr. *demonstrance*, f. *demonstrer*; see DEMONSTRATE *v.*, -ANCE.] **1.** A pointing out; indication –1704. **2.** Demonstration, proof –1646.

†**Demo·nstrate,** *ppl. a.* 1509. [– L. *demonstratus*, pa. pple. of *demonstrare*; see next, -ATE[2].] Demonstrated –1707. As *sb.* A demonstrated proposition 1655.

Demonstrate (dīmǫ·nstreⁱt, de·mǫ̆nstreⁱt), *v.* 1552. [– *demonstrat-*, pa. ppl. stem of L. *demonstrare*, f. *de-* DE- I. 3 + *monstrare* to show; see -ATE[3].] †**1.** *trans.* To point out, indicate; to set forth –1684. †**2.** To manifest, show, display –1803. **3.** To describe and explain by help of specimens, or by experiment; also *absol.* to teach as a demonstrator 1683. **4.** To show or make evident by reasoning; to establish the truth of by deduction; to prove indisputably 1571. Also *absol.* Of things: To prove 1601. **5.** *intr.* To make a military (or other) demonstration 1827.

3. The anatomist demonstrates, when he points out matters of fact cognisable by the senses 1856. **4.** Archimedes demonstrates..that the proportion of the Diameter unto the Circumference is as 7 almost unto 22 SIR T. BROWNE. **5.** The habit of demonstrating with bands and banners BRYCE.

Demonstration (demǫ̆nstrēⁱ·ʃən). ME. [– OFr. *demonstracion* (later and mod. *-tion*) or L. *demonstratio*, f. as prec.; see -ION.] †**1.** The action of demonstrating; exhibition, manifestation; an instance of this –1668. **b.** An illustration; a sign –1684. **2.** A display, show, manifestation 1556. **3.** The action or process of making evident by reasoning; proving indisputably by deduction or by practical proof; also (with *pl.*) a series of propositions proving an asserted conclusion ME. **b.** That which serves as proof ME. **4.** *Rom. Law.* The statement of the cause of action by the plaintiff at the outset 1864. **5.** The exhibition and explanation of specimens and operations as a method of instruction. Also *attrib.* 1807. **6.** *Mil.* A show of military force or of offensive movement 1835. **7.** A public manifestation of feeling; often taking the form of a procession and mass-meeting 1839.

2. Did your letters pierce the queen to any d. of grief *Lear* IV. iii. 12. **3.** A d. is either *Direct* or *Indirect*. In the latter case we prove the conclusion by disproving the contradictory, or shewing that the conclusion cannot be supposed untrue JEVONS. Phr. *To d.*: conclusively. **b.** The Circulation of the Blood is a D. of an Eternall Being 1659. **6.** He made last year a d. against Julalabad 1835. **7.** Then, besides 'ovations', there are 'demonstrations', the Q. E. D. of which is not always very easy to see 1861. Hence **Demonstra·tional** *a.* of or pertaining to d. **Demonstra·tionist,** one who takes part in a d.

Demonstrative (dīmǫ·nstrătiv), *a.* and *sb.* ME. [– (O)Fr. *démonstratif, -ive* – L. *demonstrativus*, f. as prec.; see -IVE.]

A. 1. Having the function or quality of demonstrating; making evident; illustrative. **2.** *Rhet.* Setting forth with praise or censure 1553. **3.** Provable by demonstration 1612. **4.** Characterized by outward expression (of the feelings, etc.) 1819. **5.** Teaching by the exhibition and description of examples or experiments (*rare*) 1814.

1. A d. proof..of the fecundity of His wisdom and Power RAY. Logic..is a purely d. science BOWEN. **2.** The oracion d. standeth either in praise or dispraise of some one man, or of some one thyng 1553. **3.** A d. truth 1798. **4.** Englishmen are much less d. than the men of most other European nations DARWIN.

B. *sb. Gram.* An adjective or pronoun having the function of pointing out the particular thing referred to, as *that, this,* etc. 1530. Hence **Demo·nstrative-ly** *adv.*, **-ness.**

Demonstrator (de·mǫ̆nstrēⁱtəɹ). 1611. [– L. *demonstrator*, f. as prec.; see -OR 2. Partly after Fr. *démonstrateur.*] **1.** One who or that which demonstrates, points out, or proves. **2.** An assistant to a professor of science, who does the practical work of exhibiting and describing examples or experiments 1684. **3.** One who takes part in a public demonstration 1870. Hence **Demo·nstratory** *a.* that has the property of demonstrating.

Demorage, obs. f. DEMURRAGE.

Demoralization (dīmǫ:rələizēⁱ·ʃən). 1809. [f. next + -ATION.] The action of demoralizing; demoralized state.

His army is in a state of utter d. and disorganization 1877.

Demoralize (dīmǫ·răləiz). *v.* 1793. [– Fr. *démoraliser* (f. DE- II. 1 + MORAL *a.*), a word of the French Revolution; see -IZE.] **1.** *trans.* To corrupt the morals or moral principles of. **2.** To lower or destroy the MORALE of: applied *esp.* to an army, etc.; also *transf.* 1848.

2. The long series of English victories had.. demoralized the French soldiery J. R. GREEN. The market became demoralized 1894.

‖**Demos** (dī·mǫs). Occas. **demus,** *pl.* **-i.** 1776. [– Gr. δῆμος people.] **1.** = DEME[2] 1. **2.** The people or commons of an ancient Greek state; hence, the populace; often personified 1831.

2. Celtic D. rose a Demon, shriek'd and slaked the light with blood TENNYSON.

Demosthenic (demǫsþe·nik), *a.* 1846. [– Gr. Δημοσθενικός.] Of or pertaining to Demosthenes, the Athenian orator; like Demosthenes or his style of oratory. So **Demosthene·an, Demosthe·nian** *adjs.*

Demot (dī·mǫ̆t). [– Gr. δημότης, f. δῆμος DEME[2]. See -OT[2].] A member of a Greek deme. GROTE.

Demotic (dīmǫ·tik), *a.* 1822. [– Gr. δημοτικός popular, f. δημότης; see prec., -IC.] **1.** Of or belonging to the people: *spec.* applied to the popular and simplified form of the ancient Egyptian script (as dist. from the *hieratic*): called also *enchorial.* Also *absol.* = The d. character or script. **2.** *gen.* Popular, vulgar. Somewhat *rare.* 1831.

†**Demou·nt,** *v.* 1533. [– Fr. *démonter*; cf. DISMOUNT.] To dismount.

Dempne, obs. f. DAMN.

Dempster (de·mᵖstəɹ). [ME. *demestre*, in form fem. of *demere* deemer; see -STER. Cf. DEEMSTER.] †**1.** A judge; a DEEMSTER (2). (ME. only.) **2.** *Sc.* 'The officer of a court who pronounced doom or sentence definitively as directed by the clerk or judge' (Jamieson). *Hist.* 1513.

†**Demulce** (dīmʊ·ls), *v.* 1530. [– L. *demulcēre*; see next.] To soothe or mollify; to soften or make gentle –1831. var. (irreg.) †**Demu·lceate.**

Demulcent (dīmʊ·lsĕnt). 1732. [– *demulcent-*, pres. ppl. stem of L. *demulcēre* stroke caressingly, f. *de-* DE- I. 3 + *mulcēre* stroke, appease; see -ENT.] *adj.* Soothing, lenitive, mollifying, allaying irritation. *sb.* A demulcent medicine.

†**Demu·lsion.** 1623. [f. *demuls-*, pa. ppl. stem of L. *demulcēre*; see prec., -ION.] The action, or a means, of soothing. FELTHAM.

Demur (dīmɒ̄·ɹ), *sb.* ME. [– (O)Fr. *demeure*, f. *demeurer*; see next.] †**1.** Delay, waiting –1675; abode –1673. †**2.** Hesitation; pause; state of irresolution –1824. **3.** The act of demurring 1639. †**4.** *Law* = DEMURRER[1] –1713.

3. After a little d., he accepted the offer DICKENS.

Demur (dīmɒ̄·ɹ), *v.* ME. [– OFr. *demourer*, (also mod.) *demeurer* :– Rom. **demorare*, for L. *demorari*, f. *de-* DE- I. 3 + *morari* delay.] †**1.** *intr.* To linger, tarry, wait –1653; to abide –1550. †**2.** *trans.* To cause to tarry; to put off, delay –1682. †**3.** *intr.* To hesitate; to suspend action; to pause in uncertainty –1818. **b.** *trans.* To hesitate about –1730. **4.** *intr.* To make scruples or difficulties; to take exception *to* (occas. *at, on*). (The current sense.) 1639. **b.** *trans.* To object to 1827. **5.** *Law.* (*intr.*) To put in a DEMURRER 1620.

1. Yet durst they not demoure nor abyde vpon the campe 1550. **3.** King Edwine demurred to embrace Christianity FULLER. **b.** Let none d. Obedience to her will 1730. **4.** My host at first demurred..but I insisted TYNDALL. **b.** I d. the inference 1876.

Demure (dīmiūᵊ·ɹ), *a.* ME. [perh. (with muting of *-é* as in ASSIGN *sb.*[2]) – AFr. *demuré*, OFr. *démoré*, pa. pple. of *demorer* (mod. *demeurer*) remain, stay (see prec.), but infl. by OFr. *mur, meür* grave (mod. *mûr*) :– L. *maturus* ripe, MATURE. For the development of meaning cf. *staid.*] †**1.** Calm, still. (ME. only.) **2.** Sober, grave, serious; reserved in demeanour ME. **3.** Affectedly or constrainedly grave or decorous 1693.

2. A face d. and sage BALE. Sober, steadfast, and d. MILT. **3.** This Gentleman, and his d. Psalm-singing Fellows SHADWELL. Demurest of the tabby kind GRAY. Hence **Demu·re-ly** *adv.*, **-ness.**

†**Demu·re,** *v. rare.* [f. prec.] *intr.* ? To look demurely. *Ant. & Cl.* IV. xv. 29.

Demu·rity. *rare.* 1483. [f. DEMURE *a.* + -ITY.] **1.** Demureness. **2.** A demure character or person. (Cf. *oddity.*) LAMB.

Demurrable (dīmɒ̄·răb'l), *a.* 1827. [f. DEMUR *v.* or *sb.* + -ABLE.] That may be demurred to; to which exception may be taken.

Demurrage (dīmʊ·rėdʒ). 1641. [– OFr. *demorage, demourage*, f. *demorer*; see DEMUR *v.*, -AGE; in sense 2, f. DEMUR *sb.* and *v.*] †**1.** Stay; delay; hesitation; pause –1823; detention –1817. **2.** *Comm.* **a.** Detention of a vessel by the freighter beyond the time agreed on; the payment made in respect of this 1641. **b.** A charge for detention of railway trucks 1858. **c.** A charge of $1\frac{1}{2}d.$ per ounce made by the Bank of England in exchanging gold or notes for bullion 1875.

2. If the Delay was occasioned by the Merchant, he shall be obliged to pay for the Days of D., to the Captain 1755.

Demurral (dīmɒ̄·răl). *rare.* 1810. [f. DEMUR *v.* + -AL[1].] The action of demurring; demur.

Demurrant (dīmʊ·rănt). 1529. [– OFr. *demourant*; see DEMUR *v.*]

A. *adj.* †**1.** Abiding, staying, resident –1587. †**2.** Delaying 1633.

B. *sb.* One who demurs, or puts in a demurrer 1809.

Demurrer[1] (dīmʊ·rəɹ). 1533. [– AFr. *demurrer*, subst. use of infin.; see DEMUR *v.*, -ER[4].] **1.** *Law.* A pleading which, admitting the facts as stated in the opponent's pleading, denies that he is legally entitled to relief, and thus stops the action until this point be determined 1547; *transf.* = DEMUR *sb.* 3. 1599. †**2.** = DEMUR *sb.* 2. –1645.

Demurrer[2] (dīmɒ̄·rəɹ). 1711. [f. DEMUR *v.* + -ER[1].] One who demurs.

Demy (dimǝi·), *sb.* (and *a.*) Pl. **demies.** ME. [Early f. DEMI- half, retained for the separate word. The uses are all elliptical.] †**1.** A gold coin current in Scotland in the 15th century: app. orig. the half-mark. †**2.** 'A short close vest' (Fairholt) –1599. **3.** *Paper Manuf.* A certain size of paper. (Properly *adj.*; *ellipt.* as *sb.* = demy paper.) 1546.

D. printing paper measures $17\frac{1}{2} \times 22\frac{1}{2}$ inches; d. writing paper $15\frac{1}{2} \times 20$.

4. A foundation scholar at Magdalen College, Oxford (so called because their 'commons' was orig. half that of a Fellow) 1486. Hence **Demy·ship,** a scholarship at that College.

Den (den), *sb.*[1] [OE. *denn*, corresp. to MLG., MDu. *denne* low ground (WFlem. *den* threshing-floor), OHG. *tenni* (G. *tenne*) floor, threshing-floor :- Gmc. **danjam*, **danjō*; rel. to DEAN[2].] **1.** The lair or habitation of a wild beast. **2.** A cavern ME. **3.** *transf.* and *fig.* A place of retreat or abode ME.; a room unfit for human habitation 1837; a small room or lodging in which a man can be alone (*colloq.*) 1771. **4.** A dingle. *Sc. local.* 1552. †**5.** *Anat.* A cavity, hollow –1683.

1. Then the beastes goe into dennes: and remaine in their places *Job* 37:8. **2.** [They] lurked in dennes and wholes secretly HALL. **3.** A d. of thieves *Matt.* 21:13. The frightful dens of some of the Manchester operatives 1840. A small d. for me in particular SCOTT.

Den[2], in *good den*; see GOOD-DEN.

Den (den), *v.* ME. [f. DEN *sb.*[1]] *intr.* To live or dwell in (or as in) a den; to hide oneself in a den 1610.

The sluggish saluages, that d. belowe G. FLETCHER.

†**Dena·me**, *v.* 1555. [f. DE- I. 3 + NAME *v.*, after OFr. *denomer*, L. *denominare*.] To denominate –1640.

Denar, denare (dī·nāɹ, dinā·ɹ, -ēᵊ·ɹ). 1547. [var. of ME. *dener* – AFr. *dener* = (O)Fr. *denier*; see DENIER[3].] A coin: the Roman DENARIUS; the It. *denaro*; the East Indian DINAR, q.v.

Denarcotize; see DE- II. 1 and NARCOTIZE.

‖**Denarius** (dīnēᵊ·riǒs). Pl. **-ii** (-i,əi). ME. [L. (ellipt. for *denarius nummus* coin containing ten asses), f. *deni* by tens, distributive of *decem* ten. Cf. DENIER[3], DENAR.] **1.** An ancient Roman silver coin, orig. of the value of ten asses (about eightpence) 1579. **2.** A gold coin (*d. aureus*), worth 25 silver denarii 1661. **3.** A (silver) pennyweight ME. ¶In English reckoning used for 'penny', and abbreviated *d.*

†**Denary, denarie**, *sb.*[1] 1449. [– L. *denarius*; see prec.] = DENARIUS, the Roman penny –1674.

Denary (dī·nări), *a.* and *sb.*[2] 1577. [– L. *denarius* containing ten; see DENARIUS, -ARY[1].]

A. *adj.* Having ten as the basis of reckoning; decimal 1848.

†**B.** *sb.* **1.** The number ten; a decad –1682. **2.** A tithing 1577.

Denationalize (dīnæ·ʃənăləiz), *v.* 1807. [f. Fr. *dénationaliser* (a word of the French Revolution); see DE- II. 1.] *trans.* To deprive (a person, etc.) of nationality; to divest (a country) of national character.

The attempt to . . d. the education of the infant poor 1839. Hence **Dena:tionaliza·tion**, the action of denationalizing, denationalized condition.

Denaturalize (dīnæ·tiŭrăləiz), *v.* 1800. [DE- II. 1.] **1.** To deprive of its original nature; to make unnatural. **2.** To deprive of the status and rights of a natural subject or citizen; the opposite of *naturalize* 1816.

1. The lyrical ballad . . is almost always denaturalized by culture PALGRAVE. **2.** The Duque d'Aveiro, having been degraded and denaturalized previous to condemnation KEATINGE. Hence **Dena:turaliza·tion**, the action of denaturalizing; denaturalized condition.

Denature (dīnēⁱ·tiŭɹ), *v.* 1685. [– Fr. *dénaturer*, OFr. *des-*, f. *des-*, *dé-* (DE- I. 6) + *nature*; cf. DISNATURE.] †**1.** *trans.* To render unnatural. **2.** To alter (*e.g.* tea, etc.) so as to change its nature 1878.

2. The denatured nature of London milk 1878.

Denay, obs. var. of DENY *v.* and *sb.*

Dendrachate, etc.; see under DENDRO-.

Dendriform (de·ndrifǫɹm), *a.* 1847. [f. Gr. δένδρον + -FORM.] Of the form of a tree; branching; arborescent.

Dendrite (de·ndrəit). Also in L. form **dendrites** (dendrəi·tīz), pl. **dendritæ** (-tī). 1727. [– Fr. *dendrite* – Gr. δενδρίτης pertaining to a tree, f. δένδρον tree; see -ITE[1].] **1.** A tree- or moss-like marking or figure, found on or in some stones or minerals; a stone or mineral so marked. **2.** A crystalline growth of branching or arborescent form, as of some metals under electrolysis 1882. Hence **Dendri·tic, -al** *a.* resembling d.; tree-like; having tree-like markings.

Dendro-, bef. a vowel **dendr-**, comb. f. Gr. δένδρον tree: as in:

De·ndrachate [see ACHATE *sb.*[1]], a variety of agate with tree-like markings. **De·ndrocœl, -cœle** *a.* [Gr. κοιλία], *Zool.* having a branched or arborescent intestine; belonging to the division *Dendrocœla* of Turbellarian worms; so **Dendrocœ·lan, Dendrocœ·lous** *adjs.*, in same sense. **De:ndrocola·ptine** *a.* [Gr. κολάπτειν to peck], *Ornith.* belonging or allied to the genus of birds *Dendrocolaptes* or S. American treecreepers. **Dendrode·ntine**, 'the form of branched dentine seen in compound teeth, produced by the inter-blending of the dentine, enamel, and cement' (*Syd. Soc. Lex.*). **De·ndrodont** [Gr. ὀδοντ-] *a.*, having, or consisting of, teeth of dendritic internal structure; *sb.* a dendrodont fish. **De·ndrolite**, a petrified or fossil tree or part of a tree. **Dendro·meter**, an instrument for measuring trees. **Dendro·philous** *a.*, tree-loving; in *Bot.* growing on or twining round trees. **De·ndrostyle**, *Zool.* one of the four pillars by which the syndendrium is suspended from the umbrella in the *Rhizostomidæ*.

Dendrobe (de·ndrōᵘb). 1882. [– mod.L. *Dendrobium*, f. Gr. δένδρον tree + βίος life; cf. MICROBE.] Name of a genus of epiphytal orchids.

Dendrodic (dendrǫ·dik), *a.* 1854. [f. Gr. δενδρώδης tree-like + -IC.] Of the form of a tree; *dendritic*. So **De·ndroid, -al** *a.*

Dendrology (dendrǫ·lŏdʒi). 1708. [f. DENDRO- + -LOGY.] The study of trees; the part of botany which treats of trees. So **Dendrolo·gic, -al, Dendro·logous** *adjs.* belonging to d. **Dendro·logist**, one versed in d.

Dene (dīn), *sb.*[1] Var. of DEAN *sb.*[2] a (wooded) vale.

Dene (dīn), *sb.*[2] Also **den.** ME. [The meaning suggests affinity with LG. (whence G.) *düne* and Du. *duin* sand-hill on the coast (see DUNE).] A bare sandy tract by the sea; a low sand-hill.

†**De·negate**, *v.* 1623. [– *denegat-*, pa. ppl. stem of L. *denegare*; see DE- I. 3, NEGATE.] To deny –1652. Hence **Denegation,** †refusal; denial. So **Dene·gatory** *a.* (*rare*).

Dene-hole, Dane-hole (dī·n-, dēⁱ·n,hōᵘl). Also **Danes' hole.** 1768. [perh. repr. OE. **Denahol*, f. *Dena*, gen. of *Dene* Danes + *hol* HOLE *sb.*; assoc. by later archæologists with DENE *sb.*[2] and DEN *sb.*[1]] The name of a class of excavations, found in chalk-formations in England and France, consisting of a shaft sunk to the chalk, and there widening out into one or more chambers, used probably for concealment in time of war.

Dengue (deŋ·ge). Also **d.-fever, denga.** 1847. [– W. Indian Sp. *dengue* – Swahili *denga*, *dinga*, the full name being *ka dinga pepo*, lit. a kind of cramp plague (evil spirit). The word was identified with Sp. *dengue* fastidiousness, prudery, with mocking reference to the stiffness of the neck and shoulders characteristic of the disease; cf. the synon. W. Indian Negro *dandy* (of the same origin) and *giraffe*.] An infectious eruptive fever, commencing suddenly, and attended with excruciating pains, especially in the joints, with great prostration and debility, but rarely fatal. Also called *Dandy*, and *Breakbone fever*.

Deni·able, *a.* 1548. [f. DENY *v.* + -ABLE.] That can be denied.

Denial (dīnəi·ăl). 1528. [f. DENY *v.* + -AL[1].] **1.** The act of saying 'no'; refusal of anything asked or desired. **2.** The asserting (of anything) to be untrue or untenable; contradiction; also, the denying of the existence or reality of a thing 1576. **3.** Refusal to acknowledge; a disowning, disavowal 1590. **4.** *Law.* †**a.** = DENIER[2] 1628; **b.** The opposing of a plea, claim, or charge advanced 1728.

1. Deniall of buriall 1631. *A d. of one's self* = SELF-DENIAL. **2.** The d. of the suppressed premiss WHATELY, of abstract ideas JOWETT. **3.** A denyall of the Soveraign Power HOBBES. var. †**Deni·ance.**

Denier[1] (dīnəi·əɹ). ME. [f. as prec. + -ER[1].] One who denies.

†**Denier**[2]. 1532. [subst. use of Fr. *dénier* inf., to DENY; see -ER[4].] *Law.* The act of denying or refusing –1642.

Denier[3] (dīnīᵊ·ɹ, ‖dənye·). *Obs.* or *arch.* ME. [– (O)Fr. *denier* :- L. *denarius*; cf. DENAR and see DENARIUS.] **1.** A French coin, the twelfth of the sou; orig. of silver; but from 16th c. a small copper coin. Hence, a very small sum. †**2.** Used as tr. L. *denarius* –1606. †**3.** A pennyweight –1706. **4.** A unit of weight, equal to about 8⅓ troy grains, by which silk yarn is weighed and its fineness estimated 1839. Hence **Denie·r** *v. trans.*, to ascertain the fineness of (silk yarns) in deniers. **Denie·rer.**

1. My Dukedome to a Beggerly d. SHAKS.

Denigrate (de·nigreⁱt), *v.* Now *rare*. 1526. [– *denigrat-*, pa. ppl. stem of L. *denigrare*, f. *de-* DE- I. 3 + *nigrare* blacken, f. *niger* black; see -ATE[3].] **1.** *trans.* To blacken, make black or dark 1623. **2.** *fig.* To blacken, defame.

2. This he spake, not to honour Christ, but to d. him TRAPP. Hence **Denigra·tion, De·nigrator,** one who or that which blackens.

Denim (dĭni·m, de·nim). 1695. [Short f. *serge de Nim* – Fr. *serge de Nîmes* or *Nismes*, serge of Nîmes in southern France. Cf. DELAINE.] A name orig. of a kind of serge; now in U.S. of a coloured twilled cotton material used for overalls, hangings, etc.

Denitrate (dīnəi·treⁱt), *v.* 1863. [DE- II. 1.] To free from nitric or nitrous acid. **Denitra·tion. Deni·trator,** an apparatus for this.

Denitrify (dīnəi·trifəi), *v.* 1891. [DE- II. 1.] To deprive of nitrous or hyponitric acid. Hence **Deni·trifier,** a denitrifying agent. **Deni:trifica·tor,** an apparatus used in sulphuric acid works to remove the nitrous vapours from the sulphuric acid previously nitrated in the Gay-Lussac tower. var. **Deni·trize.**

†**De·nizate**, *v.* 1604. [– *denizat-*, pa. ppl. stem of AL. *denizare*, *denizatio* (XVI–XVII), f. DENIZ(EN; see -ATE[3].] *Law.* To constitute a denizen –1628. Hence **Deniza·tion.**

†**Denize**, *v.* 1577. [f. DENIZ(EN, and prob. repr. an AFr. **denizer*; see prec.] **1.** To make (a person) a denizen –1708. **2.** *fig.* To naturalize (a word, a custom, etc.) 1594.

Denizen (de·nizĕn). [Late ME. *deynseyn* – AFr. *deinzein*, f. OFr. *deinz* within :- late L. *de intus* (from within) + *-ein* :- L. *-aneus*. The trisyllabic form (XV) was due to assimilation to *citizen*.]

A. 1. One who dwells within a country, as opp. to *foreigners*. Now *rare* in *lit.* sense. **b.** *transf.* and *fig.* Used of persons, animals, and plants. Chiefly *poet.* or *rhet.* 1474. **2.** By restriction: One who lives habitually in a country but is not a native-born citizen; an alien admitted to citizenship by royal letters patent 1576. Also *transf.* and *fig.* 1548.

1. The Charter of London . . is the birthright of its own Denisions, not Strangers GURNALL. **b.** Winged denizens of the crag SCOTT. **2.** *fig.* Denisens in heauen UDALL. Hence **De·nizenship.**

B. *adj.* or *attrib.* 1483.

Denizen (de·nizĕn), *v.* 1556. [f. prec. sb.] **1.** To make a denizen; to admit (an alien) to residence and rights of citizenship. Usu. *fig.* 1577. **2.** To furnish with denizens; to people with settlers from without (*rare*).

1. The old denisoned wordes 1556. The cholera . . is denizened among us SOUTHEY.

Dennet (de·nét). 1818. [Supposed to be f. the surname *Dennet*.] A light open two-wheeled carriage akin to a gig; fashionable c1818–1830.

Denominable (dīnǫ·minăb'l), *a.* 1658. [– med.L. *denominabilis*, f. L. *denominare* DENOMINATE *v.* + -BLE.] That may be named.

Deno·minant, *sb. rare.* 1889. [– *denominant-*, pres. ppl. stem of L. *denominare*; see DENOMINATE *v.*, -ANT[1].] = DENOMINATOR 3.

Denominate (dīnǫ·minĕt), *ppl. a.* and *sb.* 1579. [– L. *denominatus*, pa. pple. of *denominare*; see next, -ATE[2].]

A. *pa. pple.* Named, denominated. *Obs.* or *arch.*

†**B.** *adj. Arith.* Said of a number: CONCRETE, q.v.; opp. to *abstract* –1674.

†**C.** *sb.* **1.** A name, denomination 1638. **2.** *Gram.* A denominative –1654.

Denominate (dīnǫ·mineⁱt), *v.* 1552. [– *denominat-*, pa. ppl. stem of L. *denominare*, f. *de-* DE- I. 3 + *nominare* to name; see -ATE[3].] **1.** *trans.* To give a name to; to name (orig. *from* or *after* something). Now usually: To call (a thing) . . . †**2.** To give a name to; to characterize; to constitute –1817. †**3.** To denote –1792.

1. This is what the world..Denominates an itch for writing COWPER. **2.** Our general course of life must d. us wise or foolish JOHNSON.

Denomination (dǐnǫminēⁱ·ʃən). ME. [– OFr. *denominacion* (later and mod. *-tion*) or L. *denominatio*, f. as prec.; see -ION.] **1.** The action of naming *from* or *after* something; naming; calling by a name. **2.** A characteristic name given to a thing or class of things; that which anything is called; an appellation, designation, title ME. **3.** *Arith.* A class of one kind of unit in any system, distinguished by a specific name ME. **4.** A class, sort, or kind distinguished by a specific name 1664. **5.** *spec.* A religious sect or body designated by a distinctive name 1716.

2. The tribes of gypsies, jockies, or cairds—for by all these denominations such banditti were known SCOTT. **3.** Weight in which the smallest D. is a Grain 1725. **5.** All sects and denominations FRANKLIN.

Denominational (dǐnǫ:minēⁱ·ʃənăl), *a.* 1838. [f. prec. + -AL¹.] Belonging to, or of the nature of, a denomination; sectarian.

Under the dominion of the new law d. schools are the rule M. ARNOLD. Hence **Denomina·tionalism,** adherence to d. principles or a d. system (*e.g.* of education). **Denomina·tionalist,** an adherent of these. **Denomina·tionalize** *v.* to make d. **Denomina·tionally** *adv.* according to a d. method.

Denominative (dǐnǫ·minětiv). 1589. [– late L. *denominativus*; see DENOMINATE *v.*, -IVE; in *Gram.*, after Priscian's tr. of Gr. παρώνυμος. Cf. Fr. *dénominatif* (XV).]

A. *adj.* **1.** Characterized by giving a name to something 1614; connotative 1638. **†2.** Having a distinctive name (*rare*) 1677. **3.** *Gram.* Formed or derived from a noun 1783.

2. The least d. part of time is a minute 1677. **3.** D., that is, derived of a noun, as from *dens* comes *dentatus* 1783. Hence **Deno·minatively** *adv.*

B. *sb.* **†1.** A denominative term –1599. **2.** *Gram.* A word derived from a noun 1638.

Denominator (dǐnǫ·mineⁱtəɹ). 1542. [– Fr. *dénominateur* (in mathematical sense XV) or med.L. *denominator*, f. as prec.; see -OR 2.] **1.** One who or that which gives a name to something. Now *rare.* 1577. **2.** *Arith.* and *Alg.* The number written below the line in a vulgar fraction, which gives the denomination or value of the parts into which the integer is divided; the corresponding expression in an algebraical fraction, denoting the *divisor*. (Correl. to *numerator.*) 1542. Also *fig.* **3†.** An abstract noun denoting an attribute 1599.

1. The City of Lincoln, the chief d. of the County HEYLIN.

Denotable (dǐnōᵘ·tăb'l), *a.* 1682. [f. DENOTE *v.* + -ABLE.] That can be denoted or marked.

†Denotate (dī·noteⁱt), *v.* 1597. [– *denotat-*, pa. ppl. stem of L. *denotare*; see DENOTE *v.*, -ATE³.] = DENOTE 1–4. –1653.

Denotation (dǐnotēⁱ·ʃən). 1532. [– Fr. *dénotation* or L. *denotatio*, f. as prec.; see -ION.] **1.** The action of denoting; expression by marks, signs, or symbols; indication; (with *a* and *pl.*) a mark; a sign. **2.** A designation 1631. **3.** The signification of a term 1614. **4.** *Logic.* That which a word *denotes*, as dist. from its *connotation*; the individuals to which a word applies; extension 1843.

3. Time hath brought the word *knaue* to a d. of ill qualities SELDEN.

Denotative (dǐnōᵘ·tătiv), *a.* 1611. [f. as prec. + -IVE; see -ATIVE.] Having the quality of denoting; designative, indicative.

Proper names are preeminently d. LATHAM. Hence **Deno·tatively** *adv.*

Denote (dǐnōᵘ·t), *v.* 1592. [– (O)Fr. *dénoter* or L. *denotare*; see DE- I. 3, NOTE *v.*²] **†1.** *trans.* To note down; to describe –1697. **2.** To mark; to mark out; to distinguish by a mark 1598. **3.** To be the visible sign of; to indicate 1592. **4.** To signify; to stand for 1668; **b.** to express by a symbol 1871. **5.** *Logic.* To be a name of; to be predicated of. (Used by Mill.) 1843.

2. Sun Dialls, by the shadow of a stile or gnomon denoting the hours of the day SIR T. BROWNE. **3.** We keep the sea, which denotes a victory PEPYS. Thou hast enough Denoted thy concern SMOLLETT. **4. b.** D. by (X) the area of the path of P. 1882.

Denotement (dǐnōᵘ·tměnt). 1622. [f. DENOTE *v.* + -MENT.] The fact of denoting; *concr.* a token, sign.

Denotive (dǐnōᵘ·tiv), *a.* 1830. [f. as prec. + -IVE.] Serving to denote.

‖**Dénouement** (denū·mań). 1752. [Fr., f. *dénouer* (earlier *des-*) untie, f. *des-*, *dé* (DE- I. 6) + *nouer* knot.] Unravelling; *spec.* the final unravelling of the plot in a drama, etc.; the catastrophe; *transf.* the issue of a complication, difficulty, or mystery.

Denounce (dǐnau·ns), *v.* ME. [– OFr. *denoncier* (mod. *dénoncer*) :– L. *denuntiare* give official information, f. *de-* DE- I. 3 + *nuntiare* make known, report.] **1.** To give formal, authoritative, or official information of; to proclaim, announce, to publish. Also †*transf.* of things. **2.** To proclaim by way of a threat or warning 1632. **3.** To proclaim (a person) to be (something). *Obs.* or *arch.* ME. **4.** To inform against, delate, accuse 1485. **5.** To utter denunciations against 1664. **6.** To give formal notice of the termination of (a treaty, etc.). [So Fr. *dénoncer*.] 1842.

1. Geving thanks..at the Cocke-crowing, because at that time the coming of the day is denounced BIBLE (Douay) *Ps.* 118, comm. His look denounc'd Desperate revenge MILT. *P. L.* II. 106. **2.** To d. fire and desolation T. BROWN. **3.** To d. a man as a public enemy DIXON. **4.** Archdeacons..shall..d. such of them as are negligent..to the Bishop AYLIFFE. **5.** To d. a man as an upstart BRYCE.

Hence **Denou·ncement,** the action of denouncing; denunciation. **Denou·ncer,** one who denounces.

De novo; see DE 1 d.

†Densa·tion. 1615. [– L. *densatio*, f. *densat-*, pa. ppl. stem of *densare* make thick, f. *densus*; see next, -ION.] Condensation –1729.

Dense (dens), *a.* 1599. [– Fr. *dense* or L. *densus* thick, dense, crowded. Orig. in techn. use, as in mod.Fr.] **1.** Having its constituent particles closely compacted together; thick, compact. **2.** *fig.* Profound, intense, impenetrable, crass 1732. **3.** *Photogr.* Of a negative: Opaque in the developed film, so that the lights and shades are well contrasted.

1. D. fog 1860, tufts 1776. A d. crowd 1836. **2.** D. ignorance 1877. Hence **De·nse-ly** *adv.*, **-ness.**

Denshire (de·nʃəɹ), *v.* 1607. [Syncopated f. *Devonshire*.] *trans.* To clear or improve (land) by burning the turf, stubble, etc., and spreading the ashes; = BURN-BEAT.

Densimeter (densi·mǐtəɹ). 1863. [f. L. *densus* dense + -METER.] An apparatus for measuring the density or specific gravity of a substance.

Density (de·nsǐti). 1603. [– Fr. *densité* or L. *densitas*, f. *densus*; see DENSE, -ITY.] **1.** The quality or condition of being dense, thickness; closeness of consistence. **2.** *Physics.* The degree of consistence of a substance, measured by the quantity of matter in a unit of bulk 1665. **b.** *Electr.* The quantity of electricity per unit of volume or area 1873. **3.** Degree of aggregation 1851. **4.** *Photogr.* Opaqueness of the developed actinized film in a negative 1879.

Dent (dent), *sb.*¹ ME. [In senses 1 and 2, var. of DINT *sb.*; in sense 3, f. DENT *v.*] **†1.** = DINT *sb.* 1. –1603. **†2.** = DINT *sb.* 2. –1600. **3.** A hollow or impression made by a blow or by pressure; a DINT 1565.

1. Ase hit were a d. of þonder ME. **3.** Taking his Hammer, he again beat out the d. 1691.

Dent, *sb.*² 1552. [– Fr. *dent* tooth.] **†1.** An indentation in the edge of anything –1700. **2.** A tooth, in various technical uses 1703.

Dent, *ppl. a.* 1450. [Short for *dented.*] **†1.** Embossed. **†2.** *Her.* INDENTED 1610.

D. corn: variety of Indian corn having a dent in each kernel (*U.S.*).

Dent, *v.* ME. [prob. aphet. f. INDENT.] **1.** *trans.* To make a dent in; to indent. **2.** To impress with a stroke or impact 1450. **3.** *intr.* To enter or sink *in*, so as to make a dent. **b.** To become indented. ME. **†4.** To aim a penetrating blow (*at*) 1580.

1. Armour dented at Cressy 1881. **2.** The tracks of horses' hoofs deeply dented in the road W. IRVING.

Dental (de·ntăl). 1594. [– late L. *dentalis*, f. L. *dens*, *dent-* tooth; see -AL¹.]

A. *adj.* **1.** Of or pertaining to the teeth, or to dentistry; of the nature of a tooth 1599. **2.** *Phonology.* Pronounced by applying the tip of the tongue to the front upper teeth, as t, d, n, etc. 1594.

1. *D. formula*, a concise tabular statement of the dentition of a mammal; the numbers of teeth in the upper and the lower row are written above and below a horizontal line: see DENTITION 2.

B. *sb.* **1.** *Phonology.* A dental consonant 1794. **2.** *Arch.* = DENTIL 1761. **3.** *Zool.* A mollusc of the genus *Dentalium* or family *Dentaliidæ*; a tooth-shell 1678. Hence **Denta·lity,** d. quality. **De·ntalize** *v.* to make d. **Dentiliza·tion.**

Dentary (de·ntări). 1830. [– late L. *dentarius*, f. L. *dens*, *dent-* tooth; see -ARY¹. Cf. Fr. *dentaire.*]

A. *adj.* Of, pertaining to, or connected with the teeth; dental.

B. *sb.* A bone forming part of the lower jaw in Vertebrates below *Mammalia*, and bearing the teeth when these are present 1854.

‖**Dentata** (dentēⁱ·tă). 1727. [L. fem. of *dentatus* 'toothed' (sc. *vertebra*); see next.] *Anat.* = AXIS¹ 2.

Dentate (de·ntět), *a.* 1810. [– L. *dentatus* toothed, f. *dens*, *dent-* tooth; see -ATE².] Having teeth or tooth-like projections; toothed. In *Bot. spec.* of leaves having sharp teeth directed outwards. Hence **De·ntately** *adv.* **Denta·tion,** the condition or fact of being d. So **De·ntated** *ppl. a.*

Denta·to-, comb. f. of L. *dentatus*, prefixed to other adjs. in the sense 'dentately —', 'dentate and —'.

Dented (de·ntėd), *ppl. a.* ME. [f. DENT *v.* and *sb.* + -ED.] **†1.** Bent inward; incurved –1607. **2.** Having dents, indented, toothed 1552.

De·ntel. 1850. [– Fr. *dentelle* (obs. in this sense).] = DENTIL.

Dentelated, -ella- (de·ntėleⁱtėd), *ppl. a.* 1797. [After Fr. *dentelé.*] Having small teeth; finely indented.

Dentelle (dente·l, Fr. dãṅtę·l). 1859. [– Fr., f. *dent* tooth; see -EL².] ‖**1.** Lace [Fr.]. **2.** *Book-binding.* A tooling resembling lace. Also *attrib.*

Denti-, comb. f. L. *dens*, *dent-* tooth, *dentes* teeth.

De·ntifactor, a machine for making artificial teeth. **Dentila·bral** *a.*, having relation to teeth and lips. **Dentili·ngual** *a.*, of or formed by teeth and tongue; also as sb. (*sc.* consonant or sound). **Denti·parous** *a.*, producing teeth. **De·ntiphone,** an instrument for conveying sound to the inner ear through the teeth, an AUDIPHONE.

Denticete (de·ntisīt), *a.* 1855. [f. DENTI- + L. *cetus* whale.] Toothed (as a whale).

Denticle (de·ntik'l), *sb.* ME. [– L. *denticulus*; see DENTICULE.] **1.** A small tooth or tooth-like projection. **2.** *Arch.* = DENTIL 1674. So **Denti·cular** *a.* resembling, or of the nature of, a small tooth; (*Arch.*) having dentils. **Denti·culate** *a.* finely toothed; (*Arch.*) denticular. **Denti·culated** *ppl. a.*

Denticulation (denti:kiulēⁱ·ʃən). 1681. [f. L. *denticulus* (see next) + -ATION.] The condition of being denticulate; usu. *concr.* an instance of this; a series of small teeth (mostly in *pl.*).

Denticule (de·ntikiul). 1563. [– L. *denticulus*, dim. of *dens*, *dent-* tooth; see -CULE. Cf. Fr. *denticule* in same sense.] = DENTIL b.

Dentiform (de·ntifǫɹm), *a.* 1708. [f. DENTI- + -FORM.] Of the form of a tooth; odontoid.

Dentifrice (de·ntifris). 1558. [– Fr. *dentifrice* – L. *dentifricium*, f. *dens*, *dent-* (cf. DENTI-) + *fricare* to rub.] A powder or other preparation for rubbing or cleansing the teeth.

Dentigerous (denti·dʒěrəs), *a.* 1839. [f. DENTI- + -GEROUS.] Bearing teeth.

Dentil (de·ntil). 1663. [– Fr. †*dentille*, fem. dim. of *dent* tooth; see DENTAL, DENTICULE.] *Arch.* Each of the small rectangular blocks, resembling a row of teeth, under the bed-moulding of the cornice in the Ionic, Corinthian, Composite, and sometimes Doric, orders. **†b.** *transf.* The member of the entablature in which the dentils (when present) are cut –1789. Also *attrib.*

De·ntilated, *ppl. a.* [var. of DENTELATED,

after DENTIL.] 'Formed like teeth; having teeth'. So **Dentila·tion,** 'dentition' (Worcester); denticulation, perforation of postage stamps.

Dentile (de·ntil). 1864. [var. of DENTIL.] *Conchol.* A small tooth or tooth-like projection.

Dentine (de·ntīn). 1840. [f. L. *dens, dent-* TOOTH + -INE⁴.] *Anat.* The hard tissue, resembling bone but usually denser, which forms the chief constituent of the teeth. Hence **De·ntinal** *a.* pertaining to or of the nature of d.

Dentiro·ster. *rare.* 1847. [– Fr. *dentirostre* – mod.L. *dentirostris* (Cuvier), f. DENTI- + L. *rostrum* beak.] *Ornith.* A member of the *Dentirostres* or Passerine birds having a tooth or notch on each side of the upper mandible. By later naturalists restricted to the Turdoid or thrush-like *Passeres* or *Insessores.* Hence **Dentiro·stral, Dentiro·-strate** *adjs.* belonging to the *Dentirostres*; having a toothed beak.

De·ntiscalp. 1656. [– L. *dentiscalpium* toothpick, f. DENTI- + *scalpere* scrape.] An instrument for scaling teeth.

Dentist (de·ntist). 1759. [– Fr. *dentiste,* f. *dent* tooth; see -IST.] One whose profession it is to treat diseases of the teeth, extract them, insert artificial ones, etc.; a dental surgeon. Hence **Denti·stic, -al** *a.* of, pertaining to, or of the nature of, a d. (*rare*). **De·ntistry,** the profession or practice of a d.

Dentition (denti·ʃən). 1615. [– L. *dentitio,* f. *dentit-,* pa. ppl. stem of *dentire* teethe; see -ION.] **1.** The production or cutting of the teeth; teething. **2.** The arrangement of the teeth proper to an animal 1849.

Dento-, an incorrect comb. f. L. *dent-* tooth, as in **Dento-li·ngual,** etc.; see DENTI-.

De·ntoid, *a. rare.* 1828. [irreg. f. L. *dens, dent-* tooth + -OID.] Dentiform, ODONTOID.

De·nture¹. *rare.* 1685. [f. DENT *v.* + -URE.] Indentation, indent.

Denture² (de·ntiŭɹ). 1874. [– Fr. *denture,* f. *dent* tooth; see -URE.] A set of (artificial) teeth.

Denucleate, -ed; see DE- II. 1.

Denudate (dĭniū·dĕt, de·niudĕt), *a.* 1866. [– L. *denudatus,* pa. pple. of *denudare*; see DENUDE, -ATE².] Denuded; naked, bare.

Denudate (de·niudeˈt, dĭniū·deˈt), *v.* 1627. [– *denudat-,* pa. ppl. stem of L. *denudare*; see DENUDE, -ATE³.] = DENUDE.

Denudation (deniudēˈ·ʃən). 1584. [– late (eccl.) L. *denudatio* uncovering, laying bare, f. *denudat-,* pa. ppl. stem of *denudare*; see next, -ION. Cf. (O)Fr. *dénudation.*] **1.** The action of making naked or bare; denuded condition. Also †*fig.* **2.** *Geol.* The laying bare of an underlying rock or formation through the *erosion* of that which lies above it by the action of water, ice, etc. 1811. So **Denu·dative** *a.* having the quality of denuding.

Denude (dĭniū·d), *v.* 1513. [– L. *denudare,* f. *de-* DE- I. 3 + *nudare* to bare, f. *nudus* nude.] *trans.* To make naked or bare; to strip *of* covering; *spec.* in *Geol.*: To lay bare (a rock, etc.) by the wearing away of that which lies above it. Also *fig.*

Rapidly denuded by rain and rivers A. R. WALLACE.

†**Denu·mberment.** 1455. [–(O)Fr. *dénombrement,* f. *dénombrer* to number – late L. *denumerare* (cl. L. *di-*), f. *de-* DE I. 3 + *numerare*; see NUMBER *v.,* -MENT.] The act of numbering; an enumeration –1657.

Denu·merant. 1859. [– *denumerant-,* pres. ppl. stem of late L. *denumerare*; see prec., -ANT¹.] *Math.* The number expressing how many solutions a given system of equations admits of.

Denumeration (dĭniū:mĕrēˈ·ʃən). 1623. [f. DE- I. 3 + NUMERATION, or f. late L. *denumerare*; see prec., -ATION.] **1.** †Enumeration; arithmetical calculation (*rare*); the determination of the denumerant. **2.** 'A present paying down of money' (Bailey).

Denunciant (dĭnɒ·nsiănt, -ʃiănt), *a.* 1837. [– *denuntiant-,* pres. ppl. stem of L. *denuntiare*; see DENOUNCE, -ANT¹.] Denouncing.

Denunciate (dĭnɒ·nsiˌeˈt, -ʃieˈt), *v.* 1593. [– *denunciat-,* pa. ppl. stem of L. *denuntiare*; see DENOUNCE, -ATE³.] To denounce; to utter denunciation against.

He only enunciated and denunciated DE MORGAN. So **Denu·nciative** *a.* characterized by denunciation.

Denunciation (dĭnɒ:nsiˌēˈ·ʃən). 1548. [– (O)Fr. *dénonciation* or L. *denunciatio,* f. as prec.; see -ION.] †**1.** Public announcement. **2.** Announcement of evil, punishment, etc., in the manner of a warning or menace 1563. **3.** Accusation before a public prosecutor 1588. **4.** Public condemnation or inveighing against 1842. **5.** The action of denouncing a treaty, etc. 1885.

1. D. of Bannes before matrimony BP. HALL. **2.** The prophet. by the d. of miseries, weakened the alacrity of the multitude WHISTON.

Denunciator (dĭnɒ·ns-, dĭnɒ·nʃieˈtəɹ). 1474. [– Fr. *dénonciateur* or L. *denunciator,* f. as prec.; see -OR 2.] One who denounces or utters denunciations; in *Civil Law*: One who lays an information against another. Hence **Denu·nciatory** *a.* of or pertaining to denunciation (in various senses); denouncing, accusing, arraigning, condemning.

Denutrition (dĭniutri·ʃən). 1876. [DE- I. 6, or II. 3.] The opposite to nutrition; reversal of the nutritive process; in *Med.* treatment by deprivation of nourishment. Also *attrib.*

Deny (dĭnəi·), *v.* [ME. *denie* – tonic stem-form *deni-* of OFr. *deneier, denoier,* later (also mod.) *dénier* :– L. *denegare,* f. *de-* DE- I. 3 + *negare* say no, refuse.] **1.** To contradict or gainsay; to declare (anything stated) to be untrue or untenable, or not what it is stated to be. Also *absol.* **2.** *Logic.* To assert the contradictory of (opp. the truth of (opp. to *affirm*) ME. **3.** To refuse to admit the truth of (opp. to *assert* or *maintain*) 1630; to reject as non-existent 1621. **4.** To refuse to acknowledge; to disown, repudiate, renounce ME. **5.** To refuse or withhold; to refuse to give or grant ME. Also *fig.* **6.** To say 'no' to ME. †**7.** To refuse permission to; to forbid (*to do, the doing* of) –1759. †**8.** To refuse to take –1725.

1. To d. a charge FIELDING. **2.** I d. your Maior 1 *Hen. IV,* II. iv. 544. **3.** To d. the apparition of ghosts SIR W. HAMILTON, Witches BURTON. **4.** He could not d. his own hand and seal MACAULAY. **5.** To d. just requests MARLOWE, a place to art JOWETT. **6.** The poor were never at their need denaid GREENE. Too well to d. Company, and too ill to receive them STEELE. Phr. *To d. oneself*: to withhold from oneself the gratification of desire; to practise self-abnegation. Hence **Deny·** *sb.* act of denying or refusing. **Deny·ingly** *adv.* in a way that denies or refuses.

Deobstru·ct, *v.* 1653. [f. DE- I. 6 + OBSTRUCT *v.* Cf. med.L. *deobstruere* to free from obstruction.] *trans.* To clear of obstruction.

Deobstruent (diˌǫ·bstruĕnt). 1691. [f. DE- I. 6 + OBSTRUENT.]

A. *adj.* That removes obstructions by opening the natural passages or pores of the body 1718.

B. *sb.* A deobstruent medicine or substance.

Deo·culate, *v.* [f. DE- II. 1 + L. *oculus* eye + -ATE³.] To deprive of eyes, or of eyesight. LAMB.

Deodand (dī·odænd). 1523. [– law Fr. *deodande* – AL. *deodanda, -um,* i.e. *Deo danda, -um* that is to be given to God, dat. of *deus* God, gerundive of *dare* give.] A thing to be given to God; *spec.* in *Eng. Law,* a personal chattel which, having been the immediate occasion of the death of a person, was forfeited to the Crown to be applied to pious uses. (Abolished in 1846.) **b.** *loosely.* A sum taken in lieu of the deodand 1831.

‖**Deodar** (dī·odāɹ). 1842. [– Hindi *dē' odār, dēwdār* :– Skr. *devadāru,* f. *devás* divine + *dāru* wood, timber.] A species of cedar (*Cedrus deodara*), found native in the Western Himalayas, and now largely grown as an ornamental tree in England. Also applied in India to other trees.

†**Deodate** (dī·odeˈt). 1600. [– L. *deo datum* given to God; in sense 2 = *a deo datum* given by God; cf. DEODAND.]

A. *sb.* **1.** A thing given to God. HOOKER. **2.** A gift from God. G. HERBERT.

B. *adj.* Given by God. GAYTON.

Deodorant (diˌōᵘ·dŏrant), *sb.* 1869. [f. as next + -ANT².] A deodorizer.

Deodorize (diˌōᵘ·dŏrəiz), *v.* 1856. [f. DE- II. 1 + L. *odor* ODOUR + -IZE.] *trans.* To deprive of (bad) odour. Also *fig.* Hence **Deodoriza·tion,** removal of (bad) smell. **Deo·dorizer.**

†**Deo·nerate,** *v.* 1623. [f. DE- II. 1 + ONERATE.] To disburden –1651.

Deontology (dī:ǫntǫ·lŏdʒi). 1826. [f. Gr. δέον, δεοντ- that which is binding, duty, n. pres. pple. of δεῖ it is binding, it behoves + -LOGY.] The science of duty or moral obligation.

Ethics has received the more expressive name of d. BENTHAM. Hence **De:ontolo·gical** *a.* of, pertaining to, or according to d. **De:onto·logist,** one who treats of d.

Deoperculate (dīˌopɔ̄·ɹkiŭlĕt), *a.* 1866. [irreg. f. DE- II. 3 + OPERCULATÉ *a.*] *Bot.* Having lost the operculum: said of the capsules of mosses, etc. So **Deope·rculate** *v.* to shed the operculum.

†**Deoppilate** (diˌǫ·pileˈt), *a.* 1620. [f. DE- II. 1 + OPPILATE.] *trans.* To free from obstruction; *absol.* to remove obstructions –1710. So **Deo·ppilant** *a.* that removes obstructions; **Deoppila·tion,** the removal of obstructions; **Deo·ppilative,** *a.* deobstruent; *sb.* a deobstruent.

Deordination (diˌǫɹdinēˈ·ʃən). Now *rare.* 1596. [– late L. *deordinatio,* f. *de-* DE- I. 6 + L. *ordinatio*; see -ATION. Cf. DISORDAIN.] **1.** Departure from or violation of (moral) order; disorder. **2.** Departure from the normal 1686.

†**Deo·sculate,** *v. rare.* 1623. [f. L. *deosculari*; see DE- I. 3, OSCULATE.] To kiss affectionately. Hence †**Deoscula·tion,** kissing.

De-ossify, -fication; see DE- II. 1.

Deoxidate (diˌǫ·ksideˈt), *v.* 1799. [DE- II. 1.] *Chem.* To remove the oxygen from; *intr.* to undergo deoxidation. Hence **Deoxida·-tion,** the removal of oxygen from an oxide or other compound.

Deoxidize (diˌǫ·ksidəiz), *v.* 1794. [DE- II. 1.] *Chem.* = DEOXIDATE. Hence **Deoxidiza·tion, Deo·xidizer.**

Deoxygenate (diˌǫ·ksidʒĕneˈt), *v.* 1799. [DE- II. 1.] *Chem.* To deprive of (free) oxygen; also = DEOXIDATE. Hence **Deoxygena·tion.**

Deoxygenize (diˌǫ·ksidʒĕnəiz), *v.* 1881. [DE- II. 1.] *Chem.* = DEOXYGENATE.

Deo·zonize, *v.* 1874. [DE- II. 1.] To deprive of ozone.

†**Depai·nt,** *ppl. a.* [ME. *depeint* – (O)Fr. *dépeint,* pa. pple. of *dépeindre* :– L. *depingere*; see DE- I. 3, PAINT *v.*] Depicted; ornamented; coloured. Chiefly as *pa. pple.* –1557.

†**Depaint** (dĭpēˈ·nt), *v.* ME. [f. prec.] **1.** *trans.* To paint; to depict; to delineate –1748. Also *fig.* **2.** To depict in words or by comparison –1808. **3.** To adorn with or as with painted figures –1706. **4.** To stain –1600.

1. Apelles could not d. Motion 1659. **2.** Her lips you may in sort d. By cherries ripe 1771. **4.** Few siluer drops her vermile cheekes d. 1600. Hence †**Depai·nter,** one who or that which depaints.

†**Depai·r,** *v.* 1460. [– OFr. *des-, depeirer* despoil, f. *des-, de-* (DE- I. 6) + *-peirer* :– L. *pejorare* make (later, become) worse, f. *pejus* worse. Cf. APPAIR, IMPAIR *v.*] To impair, injure, dilapidate –1568.

Depaire no Church, nor auncient acte 1568.

†**Depardieu·,** *interj.* ME. [– OFr. *de par Dieu.*] In God's name; by God; used as an asseveration –1634.

Depart (dĭpā·ɹt), *v.* ME. [– (O)Fr. *départir* :– Rom. **de-,* **dispartire,* for L. *dispertire* divide; see DE- I. 6, PART *v.*]

I. †**1.** *trans.* To divide into parts –1551; *intr.* to become divided –1577. †**2.** *trans.* To part among persons; to share; *occas.* to bestow, impart –1651. Also *absol.* †**3.** *trans.* To separate –1677. †**4.** *trans.* To sever, break off (a connection, etc.) –1579. Also *intr.* (for *refl.*).

2. They departed my rayment among them N.T. (Geneva) *John* 19:24. **3.** Till death vs departe *Bk. Com. Prayer.* **4.** Ye departed the loue bitwene me and my wyf MALORY.

II. †**1.** *intr.* To go asunder; to separate from each other –1641. **2.** *intr.* To go away (*from*);

to take one's leave. (The current sense, but chiefly literary.) ME. **b.** To set out, start. Opp. to *arrive*. (Now commonly to *leave*.) 1489. †**c.** To go away *to* or *into* –1611. **3.** *intr.* To leave this world, die. (Now only *to d. from* (*this*) *life*.) 1501. **4.** *trans.* To quit. Now *rare*, exc. in phr. *to d. this life* (= prec.) ME. †**5.** To send away –1614. **6.** *intr.* To withdraw, deviate; to desist (*from*) ME.

2. The Learned Leaches in despair d. DRYDEN. The train departs at 6.30 1895. **3.** Lord, now lettest thou thy servant d. in peace *Luke* 2:29. **4.** The soules of men departing this life HOOKER. **6.** They d. from received opinions BP. BERKELEY. Phrases. †**D. with, a.** To go away from (*rare*). **b.** To part with; to give up; to give away. So **D. from,** in sense b.

Hence †**Depa·rtable, -ible** *a.* separable; divisible. **Depa·rtingly** *adv.*

†**Depart,** *sb.* ME. [– (O)Fr. *départ*, f. *départir* (see prec.); partly treated as directly from the Eng. verb.] **1.** The act of departing; parting; death –1840. **2.** *Old Chem.* The separation of one metal from another with which it is alloyed –1751.

1. At my d. I gaue this to Iulia *Two Gent* V. iv. 96. **2.** The chymists have a liquor called water of d. BACON (J.).

Departer[1] (dĭpā·ɹtəɹ). ME. [f. DEPART *v.* + -ER[1]. In sense 2 perh. – Fr. †*départeur* (OFr. *departeör*).] **1.** One who departs (see DEPART *v.*). †**2.** *Old Chem.* One who separates a metal from an alloy 1656.

†**Depa·rter**[2]. 1628. [subst. use of AFr. inf. *departer*, = (O)Fr. *départir* DEPART *v.*; see -ER[4].] *Law.* = DEPARTURE 5. –1751.

†**Departition** (dīpaɹti·ʃən). ME. [f. DEPART *v.*, on L. analogies; see -ITION. Cf. AL. *departitio* dissolution of Parliament (XIV).] **1.** Distribution, partition 1530. **2.** Separation –1485. **3.** Departure –1485. var. †**Depa·rtison.**

Department (dĭpā·ɹtmĕnt). [– (O)Fr. *département*, f. *départir*; see DEPART *v.*, -MENT.] †**1.** = DEPARTURE 1, 2. –1677. **2.** 'Separate allotment; province or business assigned to a particular person' (J.); hence, A separate division of a complex whole, *esp.* of activities or studies; a branch, province 1735. **b.** *spec.* One of the separate divisions or branches of state or municipal administration 1769. **3.** One of the districts into which France is divided for administrative purposes 1792. **b.** A part, section, region (*rare*) 1832.

2. Perfection in every d. of writing but one—the dramatic FOOTE. The D. of War, of State, etc. (*U.S.*) The Paymaster General's D. **4.** *attrib.* **d. store** (orig. *U.S.*), a large shop dealing in a variety of articles. Hence **Departme·ntal** (dī-) *a.* of or pertaining to a d. **Departme·ntally** *adv.* **Departme·ntalism,** attachment to departmental methods.

Departure (dĭpā·ɹtiŭɹ). 1523. [– OFr. *departeüre*, f. *departir*; see DEPART *v.*, -URE.] †**1.** Separation, parting –1643. **2.** The action of going away 1533; decease, death (*arch.*) 1558. **3.** *transf.* and *fig.* Withdrawal, divergence, deviation (from a path, standard, etc.) 1694. **4.** The action of starting on a journey; *spec.* the starting of a railway train from a station. Also *attrib.* (Opp. to *arrival.*) 1540. Also *fig.* **5.** *Law.* A deviation in pleading from the ground taken by the same party in an antecedent plea 1548. **6.** *Navigation.* **a.** The distance by which a ship in sailing departs east or west from a given meridian 1669. (Abbrev. *dep.*) **b.** The bearing of an object on the coast, taken at the commencement of a voyage, from which the dead reckoning begins 1669.

2. D. from this happy place MILT. The time of my d. is at hand 2 *Tim.* 4:6. **3.** D. from evil TILLOTSON, from truth 1832. **4.** The d. side of the station 1887. Phr. *New d.*: a fresh start; the beginning of a new course of procedure. **6.** We took a new D. from thence [Isle of Ascension] 1699.

Depascent (dĭpæ·sĕnt), *a. rare.* 1651. [– *depascent-*, pres. ppl. stem of L. *depascere* eat up, consume, f. *de-* DE- I. 3 + *pascere* feed, pasture; see -ENT.] Consuming.

Depasture (dĭpɑ·stiŭɹ), *v.* 1586. [f. DE- I. 1 + PASTURE *v.*; cf. prec.] **1.** *trans.* To consume the produce of (land) by grazing upon it; to use for pasturage. Also *fig.* 1596. **2.** *intr.* To graze 1586. **3.** *trans.* To pasture or feed (cattle) 1713.

3. A right of depasturing cattle on the land of another 1844. The run will d. about 4000 sheep 1844. Hence **Depa·sturage, Depa·sture** *sb.*

†**Depa·triate,** *v.* 1688. [– *depatriat-*, pa. ppl. stem of med.L. *depatriare* (also *des-*) leave home, f. *de-* DE- I. 2 + L. *patria* fatherland; see -ATE[3].] *intr.* To expatriate oneself –1797.

Depau·perate, *ppl. a.* 1460. [– med.L. *depauperatus*, pa. pple. of *depauperare* impoverish; see next, -ATE[2].] †Made poor; †impoverished; in *Bot.*, etc. = DEPAUPERATED.

Depauperate (dĭpǭ·pĕreᶦt), *v.* 1623. [– *depauperat-*, pa. ppl. stem of med.L. *depauperare*, f. L. *de-* DE- I. 3 + *pauperare* make poor, f. *pauper* poor; see -ATE[3].] To render poor, impoverish; to reduce in quality, vigour, or capacity.

Bishops..had..depauperated many of the sees CARTE. Hence **Depau·perated** *ppl. a.* impoverished; in *Bot.*, etc., stunted or degenerate from or as if from want of nutriment. **Depau:pera·tion.** var. **Depau·perize** *v.*[1]

De-pauperize (dīpǭ·pĕraiz), *v.*[2] 1863. [f. DE- II. 1 + PAUPERIZE *v.*] To free from pauperism; to DISPAUPERIZE.

†**Depe,** *v.* [OE. *dēpan* = OFris. *dēpa*, OS. *dōpian* (Du. *doopen*), OHG. *toufen* (G. *taufen*), Goth. *daupjan* baptize, f. Gmc. **deup-* **daup*; see DEEP, which influenced this word in ME.] **1.** To immerse, baptize –ME. **2.** To submerge, plunge deeply, dip –1565.

Depe, obs. f. DEEP *a.* and *v.*

†**Depea·ch,** *sb.* 1528. [– Fr. *dépêche*, f. the vb.; see next.] Dispatch; a message or messengers sent off –1624.

†**Depea·ch,** *v.* 1474. [– OFr. *depechier* (mod. *dépêcher*) disembarrass, expedite; cf. IMPEACH. Superseded by DISPATCH *v.*] To dispatch –1655.

Depectible, misprint in J. for DEPERTIBLE (Bacon, *Sylva* §857).

†**Depe·culate,** *v.* 1641. [– *depeculat-*, pa. ppl. stem of L. *depeculari* despoil, f. *de-* DE- I. 3 + *peculari* PECULATE; see -ATE[3].] *trans.* To plunder by peculation: said of public officials –1648. Hence †**Depecula·tion.**

†**Depei·nct, depinct,** *v.* 1579. [Intermediate forms between DEPAINT, *depeint*, and DEPICT; cf. OFr. *depeinct*, var. of *depeint*, and It. *depinto*.] = DEPICT –1690.

†**Depe·l, depell,** *v.* 1533. [– L. *depellere* drive out, f. *de-* DE- I. 1, 2 + *pellere* drive.] To drive away, expel –1788.

†**Depe·ncil,** *v.* 1631. [f. DE- + PENCIL *v.*] *trans.* To inscribe with a pencil or brush; *fig.* to depict –1766.

Depend (dĭpe·nd), *v.* ME. [– (O)Fr. *dépendre* – Rom. **dependere*, for L. *dependēre*; see DE-. I. 1, PEND *v.*] **1.** *intr.* To hang down, be suspended. (Now literary.) 1510. **2.** *intr. fig.* To be contingent on, or conditioned by. Const. *on, upon,* †*of*, occas. *from, to, in.* ME. **3.** To belong to as something subordinate 1500. **4.** To rest entirely *on, upon* (†*of*) for support, or what is needed 1548. **5.** To rely in mind, count *on, upon* (†*of*, etc.) 1500. **b.** *ellipt.* with following cl.: = 'to depend upon it' (*colloq.*) 1700. †**6.** To wait in suspense or expectation *on, upon* –1704. **7.** To be in suspense or undetermined. (Usu. in pres. pple. = pending.) ME. †**8.** To impend –1719.

1. As on your boughes the ysicles d. SPENSER. **2.** Small things whereunto greater doe d. BALDWIN. Phr. *That depends* (ellipt.): *i.e.* on circumstances. **3.** Hereupon a story depends FULLER. **4.** Well directed labour is all we have to d. on HT. MARTINEAU. **5.** Faith Miss, d. upon it, I'll give you as good as you bring SWIFT. **6.** The hearer on the speaker's mouth depends DRYDEN. **7.** Bills of supply were still depending MACAULAY. Hence **Depe·ndable, -ible** *a.* that may be depended on; trustworthy. **Depe·ndably** *adv.* **Depe·nder,** †a dependant; one who depends *on* something.

Dependant, -dent (dĭpe·ndĕnt), *sb.* 1523. [– Fr. *dépendant*, pres. pple. of *dépendre*; see prec., -ANT[1], -ENT. The sp. *-ent*, after L., is less usual in the sb.; cf. *defendant*, etc.] †**1.** A subordinate part, appurtenance, dependency –1837. **2.** A person who depends on another for support, position, etc.; a retainer, subordinate, servant 1588.

1. With all incidentes, circumstaunces, dependentes or connexes HALL. **2.** His own numerous family and dependants CLARENDON.

Dependence, -ance (dĭpe·ndĕns). 1535. [– (O)Fr. *dépendance*, f. *dépendre*; see prec., -ANCE, -ENCE. The form in *-ance* is rare after 1800.] †**1.** The action of hanging down; *concr.* something that hangs down (*rare*) 1697. **2.** The relation of having existence conditioned by the existence of something else; the fact of depending *upon* something else 1535. **3.** The condition of a dependant; subjection, subordination. (Opp. to *independence*.) 1614. †**4.** *concr.* That which is subordinate to, connected with, or belonging to, something else –1794; a retinue (usu. *-ance*) –1692. **5.** The condition of resting in faith or expectation (upon something); reliance, confidence or trust 1627; *transf.* object of confidence or trust (? *obs.*) 1754. **6.** The condition of waiting for settlement; pending, suspense. (Now only legal.) 1605. †**b.** A quarrel 'depending' or awaiting settlement –1820.

2. The chain of d. which runs throughout creation TYNDALL. **3.** To free the Crown from its d. upon Parliament J. R. GREEN. **5.** Living..in d. on the will of God JOWETT. Your honour, your piety, are my just d. RICHARDSON. **6.** Nothing herein .. shall affect any action now in d. 1874.

Dependency, -ancy (dĭpe·ndĕnsi). 1594. [f. as prec.; see -ANCY, -ENCY.] **1.** The condition of being dependent; contingent logical or causal connection; = prec. 2. 1597. **2.** The relation of a thing (or person) to that by which it is supported; = prec. 3. 1594. †**3.** = prec. 5 (*rare*) –1677. **4.** Something dependent or subordinate; an appurtenance 1611; †a retinue –1701; a dependent or subordinate place or territory 1684. †**5.** = prec. 6 b. –1632.

1. Such a dependancy of thing, on thing *Meas. for M.* V. 1. 62. **3.** The d. of Ireland upon the crown of England SWIFT. **4.** A thorough sifting of this subject, and its dependencies 1852. The earth, and its dependencies T. BURNET. That Sheffield which now, with its dependencies, contains a hundred and twenty thousand souls MACAULAY.

Dependent, -ant (dĭpe·ndĕnt), *a.* ME. [orig. *dependant* – Fr. *dépendant*; now usually *dependent*, after L.] **1.** Hanging down. **2.** That depends *on* something else; having its existence contingent on, or conditioned by, that of something else 1594. **3.** That depends *on* something else for support or what is needed 1643. **4.** Subordinate, subject; opp. to *independent* 1616. †**5.** Impending (*rare*). SHAKS.

1. D. leaves 1880. **2.** Effects d. on the same.. Causes 1664. **3.** D. upon strangers 1791, on charity TROLLOPE. **4.** D. colonies of England BRIGHT. *D. variable* (Math.): one whose variation depends on that of another variable (the *independent variable*). **5.** *Tr. & Cr.* II. iii. 21. Hence **Depe·ndently** *adv.*

Depeople (dĭpī·p'l), *v. arch.* 1611. [– Fr. *dépeupler*, after PEOPLE. See DE- I. 6, DISPEOPLE.] To depopulate.

†**Depe·rdit, -ite.** 1608. [– L. *deperditus*, pa. pple. of *deperdere* destroy, ruin, f. *de-* DE- I. 3 + *perdere* destroy, lose.]

A. *adj.* Lost, abandoned –1642.

B. *sb.* Something lost or perished 1802. Hence **Depe·rditely** *adv.* So **Deperdi·tion,** loss, destruction by wasting away (*rare*).

Deperition (dīpĕri·ʃən). *rare.* 1793. [f. DE- I. 3 + L. *perire* perish + -TION, perh. after *deperdition* (see prec.).] Perishing, total wasting away.

Depe·rsonalize, *v.* 1866. [DE- II. 1.] To deprive of personality.

†**Depe·rtible,** *a.* 1626. [Latinized form of *departible* (see DEPART *v.*).] Divisible.

†**Dephlegm** (dĭfle·m), *v.* 1660. [– med. or mod.L. **dephlegmare* (whence also Fr. *déflegmer*); see next.] = DEPHLEGMATE.

†**Dephlegmate** (dĭfle·gmeᶦt), *v.* 1668. [– *dephlegmat-*, pa. ppl. stem of med. or mod.L. **dephlegmare*; see DE- I. 6, PHLEGM, -ATE[3].] *Old Chem.* To free (a spirit or acid) from phlegm or watery matter; to rectify –1789; *fig.* to purify BURKE. Hence †**Dephlegma·tion. De·phlegmator,** an apparatus for dephlegmation.

Dephlogi·sticate, *v.* 1775. [f. DE- II. 1 + PHLOGISTICATE *v.*] †**1.** *trans. Old Chem.* To deprive of PHLOGISTON, q.v. –1788. **2.** To relieve of inflammation 1842. Hence **Dephlogi·sticated** *ppl. a.* (*esp.* in *dephlogisticated air*, Priestley's name for oxygen); **Dephlogi:stica·tion.**

Dephosphorize (dīfǫ·sfǒrəiz), *v.* 1878. [DE- II. 1.] To free from phosphorus. Hence **Dephosphoriza·tion.**

†**Depi·ct,** *ppl. a.* ME. [– L. *depictus*, pa. pple. of *depingere*; see next.] Depicted –1598.

Depict (dĭpi·kt), *v.* 1631. [– *depict-*, pa. ppl. stem of L. *depingere* portray, f. *de-* DE- I. 3 + *pingere* paint.] **1.** *trans.* To draw, figure, or represent in colours; to paint; also, to figure anyhow. Also *transf.* and *fig.* **2.** To represent or portray in words; to describe graphically 1740.

1. The history of the Bible..depicted in needle work FULLER. **2.** No language can d. the chaos at its base KANE. Hence **Depi·cter, -or,** one who depicts. So **Depi·ction,** the action of depicting; painted representation; graphic description. **Depi·ctive** *a.* having the quality of depicting.

Depi·cture, *sb.* 1500. [f. next.] Depiction.

Depicture (dĭpi·ktiŭɹ), *v.* 1593. [f. DE- I. 3 + PICTURE *v.* Superseded by DEPICT *v.*] **1.** = DEPICT *v.* 1, 2. **2.** *fig.* To picture to one's own mind; to imagine 1775.

1. A paradise or garden was depictured on the ground GIBBON.

Depilate (de·pileˡt), *v.* 1560. [– *depilat-*, pa. ppl. stem of L. *depilare*, f. *de-* DE- I. 3 + *pilare* deprive of hair, f. *pilus* hair; see -ATE³.] **1.** To remove the hair from; to make bare of hair. †**2.** To decorticate (*rare*) 1620. Hence **Depila·tion,** the action of stripping, or condition of being void, of hair; †pillage. **Depi·latory** *a.* having the property of removing hair; var. †**Depi·lative;** *sb.* a depilatory agent or substance.

Depilous (de·piləs), *a.* 1646. [f. L. *depilis* hairless (cf. prec.) + -OUS. (Rare type of formation, but cf. *scurrile, scurrilous*).] Deprived or void of hair.

Deplane (dīplēˡ·n), *v.* 1923. [f. DE- II. 2 + PLANE *sb.*³ 1 e.] To alight from an aeroplane.

Deplete (dĭplī·t), *v.* 1807. [– *deplet-*, pa. ppl. stem of L. *deplēre*, f. *de-* DE- I. 6 + *-plēre* fill.] **1.** To reduce the fullness of; to empty out, exhaust 1859. **2.** *Med.* To relieve the system or vessels when overcharged, as by blood-letting or purgatives 1807.

1. To d. a garrison of troops 1880. So **Deple·te** *a.* emptied out, exhausted. **Deple·tive** *a.* characterized by depletion; *sb.* a drug which produces depletion. **Deple·tory** *a.* depletive.

Depletion (dĭplī·ʃən). 1656. [– Fr. †*déplétion* or late L. *depletio* (earlier *depletura*) blood-letting, f. as prec.; see -ION. In sense 1, f. prec. + -ION.] **1.** The action of depleting, or condition of being depleted; exhaustion. **2.** *Med.* The relieving of overcharged vessels of the body 1735.

Deplorable (dĭplōᵊ·răb'l), *a.* 1612. [– Fr. *déplorable* or late L. *deplorabilis*, f. *deplorare*; see DEPLORE, -BLE.] To be deplored or lamented; lamentable, very sad, grievous, miserable, wretched. Now chiefly used of events, conditions, circumstances.

The storie of Your most d. fortune MASSINGER. A d. want of sense COTTON. Hence **Deplo:rabi·lity,** the quality of being d.; a d. matter (*rare*). **Deplo·rableness. Deplo·rably** *adv.*

†**Deplo·rate,** *a.* 1529. [– L. *deploratus*, pa. pple. of *deplorare*; see DEPLORE, -ATE².] Given up as hopeless; desperate –1695.

In a d. or desperate dropsie 1615.

Deploration (dĭploᵊrēˡ·ʃən). 1490. [– L. *deploratio*, f. *deplorat-*, pa. ppl. stem of *deplorare*; see next, -ION.] **1.** The action of deploring; lamentation 1533. †**2.** Deplorable condition. CAXTON.

Deplore (dĭplōᵊ·ɹ), *v.* 1559. [– (O)Fr. *déplorer* or It. *deplorare* – L. *deplorare*, f. *de-* DE- I. 3 + *plorare* wail, bewail.] **1.** To weep for, bewail, lament; to grieve over, regret deeply 1567; to tell with grief (SHAKS.). **2.** *intr.* To lament. ? *Obs.* 1632. †**3.** *trans.* To give up as hopeless (*rare*) –1729.

1. He..left me here his losse for to d. SPENSER. **3.** To stay with the patient after the disease is deplored BACON. Hence **Deplo·rer. Deplo·ringly** *adv.*

Deplored (dĭplōᵊ·ɹd, -rĕd), *ppl. a.* 1559. [f. prec.; tr. L. *deploratus.*] **1.** Lamented. †**2.** Given up as hopeless; DEPLORATE –1655. Hence **Deplo·red·ly** *adv.*, **-ness.**

Deploy·, *sb.* 1796. [f. next.] *Mil.* The action or evolution of deploying. So **Deploy·ment** (in same sense).

Deploy (dĭploi·), *v.* 1477. [– Fr. *déployer* :– L. *displicare* unfold (later also, explain), also late L. *deplicare* unfold, explain, f. *de-*, *dis-* (see DE- I. 6) + *plicare* fold.] †**1.** (in Caxton) To unfold, display. **2.** *Mil.* To spread out (troops) so as to form a more extended line of small depth 1786. Also *intr.* of a body of troops. Also *fig.*

2. *intr.* The right wing, having deployed into line, began to advance WELLINGTON.

Deplumate (dīplˡū·mĕt), *a.* 1883. [– med.L. *deplumatus*, pa. pple. of *deplumare*; see DEPLUME, -ATE².] Stripped of feathers, deplumed. So **Deplu·mated** *ppl. a.* 1727.

Deplumation (dīplˡumēˡ·ʃən). 1611. [– Fr. †*déplumation*, or f. next + -ATION.] The action of depluming, or condition of being deplumed; loss of feathers, plumes, or (*fig.*) of honours, etc.; in *Path.*, a disease of the eyelids which causes the eyelashes to fall off.

Deplume (dĭplˡū·m), *v.* ME. [– Fr. *déplumer*, OFr. *desplumer*, or med.L. *deplumare*; see DE- I. 6, PLUME *v.*] **1.** *trans.* To strip of feathers; to pluck the feathers off. **2.** *fig.* To strip or deprive of honour, wealth, or the like 1651.

1. Thus was the Roman Eagle deplumed, every Bird has its own Feather N. BACON. **2.** His favourite amusement of depluming me GIBBON.

Depolarize (dĭpōᵘ·lărəiz), *v.* 1818. [DE- II. 1.] *trans.* To deprive of polarity; to reverse or destroy the effect of polarization. **a.** *Optics.* To change the direction of polarization of (a polarized ray) so that it is no longer arrested by the analyser in a polariscope 1819. **b.** *Electr.*, etc. To deprive of polarity. Also *fig.* 1860. Hence **Depolariza·tion,** the action or process of depolarizing. **Depo·larizer,** an instrument for producing depolarization.

Depolish (dĭpǫ·liʃ), *v.* 1873. [DE- II. 1.] *trans.* To remove the polish from.

Depone (dĭpōᵘ·n), *v.* Chiefly *Sc.* 1533. [– L. *deponere* lay aside, put down, in med.L., testify, f. *de-* DE- I. 1 + *ponere* place.] †**1.** *trans.* To lay down (an office, etc.) –1843. **2.** To state or declare upon oath; to DEPOSE 1549. **3.** *intr.* To declare upon oath; to testify. Also *fig.* 1640.

2. Andr. Martin..Depones, that he was present in the house GLANVILL. **3.** He could not d. to one fact against the accused 1835.

Deponent (dĭpōᵘ·nĕnt). 1528. [– *deponent-*, pres. ppl. stem of L. *deponere*; see prec., -ENT.]

A. *adj. Gram.* Of verbs: Passive or middle in form but active in meaning.

Both form and meaning were orig. reflexive (e.g. *utor* I serve myself, etc.). What was *laid aside* was not a passive meaning, as formerly supposed, but the reflexive sense.

B. *sb.* **1.** A deponent verb 1530. **2.** One who deposes or makes a deposition under oath; one who gives written testimony to be used as evidence in a court of justice, etc. 1548. So †**Depo·ner.**

Depo·pularize, *v.*; see DE- II. 1.

Depo·pulate, *ppl. a.* 1531. [– L. *depopulatus*, pa. pple. of *depopulare* in its med.L. sense; see next, -ATE².] Laid waste; deprived (wholly or partly) of inhabitants. Used †**a.** as *pa. pple.*; **b.** as *adj.* (now *arch.* or *poet.*).

Depopulate (dĭpǫ·piŭleˡt), *v.* 1545. [– *depopulat-*, pa. ppl. stem of L. *depopulare*, *-ari* ravage, f. *de-* DE- I. 3 + *populare*, *-ari* lay waste (f. *populus* people), in med.L., depopulate; see -ATE³.] †**1.** *trans.* To ravage, lay waste –1670. **2.** To deprive wholly or partly of inhabitants; to reduce the population of 1594. Also *transf.* and *fig.* †**3.** To thin –1798. **4.** *intr.* To become less populous 1761. †**5.** *trans.* To destroy, cut off –1650.

2. The late Plague, which did much d. this kingdom 1690. **4.** The kingdom was depopulating from the increase of enclosures HUME. Hence **Depopula·tion,** the action of depopulating; depopulated condition. **Depo·pulator,** one who †ravages or depopulates a district or country.

†**Depo·rt,** *sb.* 1477. [– OFr. *deport*, *des-*, diversion, pleasure, etc.; see DISPORT *sb.* and next.] **1.** = DISPORT. **2.** Behaviour, deportment –1740.

Deport (dĭpōᵊ·ɹt), *v.* 1474. [In branch I, – OFr. *deporter*, f. *de-* DE- I. 3 + *porter* carry :– L. *portare*. In branch II – Fr. *déporter* – L. *deportare* (see DE- I. 2).]

I. †**1.** *trans.* To bear with; to spare –1481. †**2.** *refl.* To abstain, forbear –1613. **3.** To bear oneself; to behave 1598.

3. He so prudently deported himself that.. FULLER.

II. *trans.* To carry away, remove; *esp.* to remove into exile, to banish 1641. **b.** In Indian use, to detain (a political offender) 1909.

Hence **Deportee·**, *spec.* in Indian use = DÉTENU.

Deportation (dīpoɹtēˡ·ʃən). 1595. [– late L. *deportatio*, f. *deportat-*, pa. ppl. stem of L. *deportare*; see DEPORT *v.* II, -ION. Cf. Fr. *déportation.*] The action of carrying away; forcible removal, *esp.* into exile; transportation.

Wholesale deportations to Cayenne 1860.

Deportment (dĭpōᵊ·ɹmĕnt). 1601. [– (O)Fr. *déportement*; see DEPORT *v.* I, -MENT.] Manner of conducting oneself; conduct (*of* life); behaviour; carriage, bearing, address. Also *fig.*

His air, his mien, his d., charm'd me so SHADWELL.

Deporture, in Dicts., error for DEPARTURE (Speed, *Hist. Great Brit.* IX. xxiv).

Deposable (dĭpōᵘ·zăb'l), *a.* 1643. [f. DEPOSE *v.* + -ABLE.] That may be deposed; liable to be deposed.

Deposal (dĭpōᵘ·zăl). ME. [prob. – AFr. *deposaille*; see next, -AL¹.] = DEPOSITION I. 3.

Depose (dĭpōᵘ·z), *v.* ME. [– (O)Fr. *déposer*, based on L. *deponere* DEPONE, f. *de-* DE- I. 2 + *ponere* to place; see POSE *v.*¹] **1.** *trans.* To lay down; to DEPOSIT (*arch.*). Also †*fig.* **2.** To put down from office, or authority; *esp.* to dethrone. (The prevailing sense.) ME. †**3.** To take away; also to remove (opp. to *impose*) –1617; to divest (a person *of*) –1681. **4.** To testify; to testify to; *esp.* to give evidence upon oath in a court of law, to make a deposition (*trans.* and *intr.*) ME. †**5.** *causally.* To examine on oath; to cite as a witness. *pass.* To bear witness. –1721.

1. A paper which he solemnly deposed on the high altar MILMAN. **2.** He was deposed from his kyngly trone COVERDALE *Dan.* 5:20. **3.** *Rich. II*, IV. i. 192. **4.** He deposed to having fastened up the house at eleven o'clock 1862. When our memory deposes otherwise J. H. NEWMAN. **5.** Grant thou hadst a thousand witnesses To be deposed they heard it MASSINGER. Hence **Depo·ser,** one who puts down another from office, etc.; one who makes a statement on oath.

Deposit (dĭpǫ·zit), *sb.* 1624. [– L. *depositum*, subst. use of neut. of pa. pple. of *deponere*; see DEPONE, DEPOSE.] **1.** Something laid up in a place, or committed to the charge of a person, for safe keeping. Also *fig.* 1660. **b.** *spec.* A sum of money deposited in a bank 1753. **c.** Something committed to another person's charge as a pledge 1737. **2.** The state of being deposited; in phr. *on*, *upon*, †*in d.* 1624. **3.** Something deposited, laid, or thrown down; *esp.* matter precipitated from a fluid medium, or collected in one place by natural process. In *Mining*, an accumulation of ore, *esp.* of a somewhat casual character, as in pockets. 1781. **4.** The act of depositing; cf. prec. senses, and DEPOSIT *v.* 1773. **5.** A depository, a depot. (Chiefly *U.S.*) 1719.

3. Recent deposites of sandstone, clay, and gypsum 1836. **4.** A d. of white powder soon takes place 1823. *Comb.* **d.-receipt,** a receipt for anything deposited, *spec.* for money deposited with a banker at a stated rate of interest.

Deposit (dĭpǫ·zit), *v.* Also †**deposite.** 1624. [– Fr. †*dépositer* or med.L. *depositare*, f. L. *depositum*; see prec.] **1.** *trans.* To lay, put, or set down 1671; *intr.* to be laid down or precipitated, to settle (*rare*) 1831. †**2.** *fig.* (*trans.*) To lay aside, give up; to lay down (one's life, etc.) –1804. **3.** To place in a repository; to commit to the charge of any one for safe keeping or as a pledge; *spec.* to place in a bank at interest 1659. Also *fig.*

1. He deposited his reckoning FIELDING. She flies to some neighbouring pool, where she deposites her eggs GOLDSM. [The water] deposits more or less of the matter which it holds in suspension HUXLEY. **3.** The silver..deposited in the bank BERKELEY. *fig.* Christianity is..a trust, deposited with us in behalf of others BUTLER.

Depositary (dĭpǫ·zitări), *sb.* 1605. [– late L. *depositarius*, f. *deposit-*, pa. ppl. stem of *deponere*; see DEPOSIT *sb.*, -ARY[1]. Cf. (O)Fr. *dépositaire.*] **1.** A person with whom anything is lodged in trust; a trustee; one to whom anything is committed or confided. In *Law*, a bailee of personal property, to be kept for the bailor without recompense. 1605. **2.** = DEPOSITORY 1. 1797.

1. They [Jews]..are the Depositaries of these.. Prophecies ADDISON. I am the sole d. of my own secret, and it shall perish with me 'JUNIUS'.

Depositary, *a. rare.* 1839. [f. DEPOSIT *sb.* + -ARY[1].] **1.** *Geol.* Belonging to or of the nature of a deposit. **2.** Receiving deposits, as a bank 1886.

Depositation (dĭpǫzitēi·ʃən). Chiefly *Sc.* 1622. [f. med.L. *depositare*; see DEPOSIT *v.*, -ATION.] The action of depositing; a deposit.

Depositee (dĭpǫ:zitī·). 1676. [f. DEPOSIT *v.* + -EE[1]; correl. to *depositor.*] A person with whom something is deposited.

Deposition (dĭpozi·ʃən, dep-). ME. [– (O)Fr. *déposition* – L. *depositio*, f. *deposit-*, pa. ppl. stem of *deponere*; see DEPOSIT *sb.*, -ION.]

I. 1. The taking down of the body of Christ from the cross; a representation of this 1526. †**2.** The action of laying down or putting aside or away; usu. *fig.* –1748. **3.** The action of deposing from a position of dignity or authority; degradation; dethronement ME. **4.** The giving of testimony upon oath in a court of law, or the testimony so given; *spec.* a statement in answer to interrogatories, constituting evidence, taken down in writing to be read in court as a substitute for the production of the witness 1494. **b.** *trans.* and *fig.* Testimony, statement; allegation 1587.

II. 1. The action of depositing, laying down, or placing in a position of rest; *spec.* interment [med.L. *depositio*], or placing of a saint's body or relics in a new resting-place 1659. **2.** The placing of something in a repository, or in the hands of a person for safe keeping; *concr.* a deposit 1592. **3.** Precipitation; a deposit, precipitate, sediment 1797.

1. The d. of the eggs by these insect cuckoos 1875. **3.** The crystallization, precipitation, and d. of these solids KIRWAN.

Depositor (dĭpǫ·zitəɹ). 1624. [f. DEPOSIT *v.* + -OR 2.] One who or that which deposits; *spec.* one who deposits money in a bank.

Depository (dĭpǫ·zitəri). 1656. [– med.L. *depositorium*, f. *deposit-*, pa. ppl. stem of L. *deponere*; see DEPOSIT *sb.*, -ORY[1].] **1.** A place in which things are deposited for safe keeping; a storehouse, a repository 1750. **2.** = DEPOSITARY *sb.* 1. Usu. *fig.* 1656.

1. The Jewel Tower..the d. of the Regalia H. AINSWORTH. **2.** I think well of her judgment in chusing you to be the d. of her troubles JOHNSON.

†‖**Depositum** (dĭpǫ·zitŏm). Pl. **-a, -ums.** 1582. [L.; see DEPOSIT *sb.*] **1.** = DEPOSIT *sb.* 1 c (*lit.* and *fig.*) –1745. **2.** = DEPOSIT *sb.* 5 (*lit.* and *fig.*) –1796.

Depositure (dĭpǫ·zitiŭɹ). *rare.* 1635. [orig. var. of DEPOSITION II. 1; see -URE.] The action of depositing or placing.

Depot (de·pou, dĭpōu·, dī·pou). Also **depôt, dépôt.** 1794. [– Fr. *dépôt*, OFr. *depost* – L. *depositum*; see DEPOSIT *sb.*] †**1.** The act of depositing –1836. †**2.** = DEPOSIT *sb.* 1, 3. –1850. **3.** *Mil.* **a.** A place where military stores are deposited. **b.** The head-quarters of a regiment, where and whence supplies are received and distributed. **c.** A station where recruits are assembled and drilled, and where soldiers who cannot join their regiments remain. **d.** *attrib.* Applied to a portion of a regiment left at home when the rest are on foreign service. 1798. **e.** A place of confinement for prisoners of war 1806. **4.** A place where goods are deposited or stored 1802. **5.** *U.S.* A railway station 1842.

†**De·pravate,** *ppl. a.* 152.. [– L. *depravatus*, pa. pple. of *depravare*; see DEPRAVE, -ATE[2].] Depraved, corrupted –1665. So †**De·pravate** *v.* = DEPRAVE.

Depravation (dīprăvēi·ʃən, dep-). 1526. [– L. *depravatio*, f. *depravat-*, pa. ppl. stem of *depravare*; see next, -ION. Cf. Fr. *dépravation.*] **1.** The action or fact of making or becoming depraved, bad, or corrupt; deterioration, degeneration, *esp.* moral degeneration 1561. **2.** The being depraved; corruption 1577. †**3.** Depravation or corruption (of a text, etc.) –1849. †**4.** Detraction, calumny –1606.

1. The total Loss of Reason is less deplorable than the total D. of it COWLEY. **4.** A meere deprauation and calumny without all shadowe of truth BACON.

Deprave (dĭprēi·v), *v.* ME. [– (O)Fr. *dépraver* or L. *depravare*, f. *de-* DE- I. 3 + *pravus* crooked, perverse, wrong.] **1.** To make bad; to pervert; to deteriorate, corrupt. Now *rare*, exc. as in sense 2. **2.** *spec.* To make morally bad. (The current sense.) 1482. †**3.** To represent as bad; to vilify, defame, disparage –1667. Also *absol.* †**4.** To become bad or depraved. FULLER. ¶Formerly often erron. for DEPRIVE.

1. To d. the text 1663, the voice of a singer JOHNSON, our money NEAL. **2.** Vicious indulgence..depraves the inward constitution and character BUTLER. Hence **Depra·ved-ly** *adv.*, **-ness. Depra·vement** (*arch.*), depravation; †misinterpretation. **Depra·ver,** one who depraves, corrupts, or vilifies.

Depravity (dĭpræ·vĭti). 1641. [alt. of PRAVITY after DEPRAVE; in theol. use superseding *pravity* and *depravation.*] The quality or condition of being depraved or corrupt: †perverted quality –1758; moral perversion 1646; *Theol.* the innate corruption of human nature due to original sin (often *total depravity*) 1757; a depraved act or practice 1641.

Both the elect and the non-elect come into the world in a state of total d. and alienation from God, and can, of themselves, do nothing but sin J. H. BLUNT.

†**De·precable,** *a.* 1633. [f. DEPRECATE + -ABLE, on the anal. of *separate, separable.* Cf. late and med.L. *deprecabilis* open to entreaty.] That may be, or to be, deprecated –1648.

Deprecate (de·prĭkeit), *v.* 1624. [– *deprecat-*, pa. ppl. stem of L. *deprecari*, f. *de-* DE- I. 2 + *precari* pray; see -ATE[3].] **1.** To pray against (evil); to seek to avert by prayer; to pray for deliverance from (*arch.*) 1628. **2.** To plead earnestly against; to express earnest disapproval of 1641. †**3.** To beseech (a person) –1822. Also †*absol.* †**4.** To invoke (evil) –1790.

1. Wise men still d. these mens kindnesses 1628. **2.** To d. such a method of proceeding OUSELEY, panic 1882. Hence **De·precatingly** *adv.*

Deprecation (deprĭkēi·ʃən). 1556. [– L. *deprecatio*, f. as prec.; see -ION. Cf. (O)Fr. *déprécation.*] †**1.** Intercessory prayer. [So in L.] **2.** Prayer for the averting or removal (*of* evil, etc.) 1596. **3.** Earnest desire that something may be averted or removed; earnest disapproval of 1612. †**4.** Imprecation (*rare*) –1804.

2. D. of Gods displeasure 1673. **3.** A look of d. GEO. ELIOT. So **De·precative** *a.* deprecating; of or pertaining to d.

De·precator. 1656. [– L. *deprecator* intercessor, f. as prec., see -OR 2.] One who deprecates; †a petitioner.

Deprecatory (de·prĭkeitəri), *a.* 1586. [– late L. *deprecatorius*, f. L. *deprecator*; see prec., -ORY[2].] **1.** Serving to deprecate; that prays for deliverance from or aversion of evil. **2.** Deprecating anticipated disapproval 1704. Also as †*sb.* [*sc.* word or expression.] –1734.

1. D. Rites to avert Evil 1738. **2.** A d. laugh 1872.

Depreciate (dĭprī·ʃieit), *v.* 1646. [– *depreciat-*, pa. ppl. stem of late L. *depretiare* (med.L. *deprec-*), f. *de-* DE- I. 1 + *pretium* price; see -ATE[3].] **1.** *trans.* To lower in value, lessen the value of; *spec.* to lower the market value of; to reduce the purchasing power of (money). **2.** To represent as of less value; to undervalue, belittle 1666. Also *absol.* **3.** *intr.* To fall in value, to become of less worth 1790.

1. To d. the esteeme and value of miracles SIR T. BROWNE, our Silver Standard 1719. **2.** I don't like to hear you d. yourself DICKENS. **3.** Conditions which caused property to d. 1884. Hence **Depre·ciatingly** *adv.* **Depre·ciative** *a.* depreciatory. **Depre·ciator.**

Depreciation (dĭprī:ʃi,ēi·ʃən). 1767. [f. prec. + -ION.] **1.** Lowering of value; fall in the exchangeable value (of money). **2.** Lowering in estimation: disparagement 1790.

Depreciatory (dĭprī·ʃiătəri), *a.* 1805. [f. as prec. + -ORY[2].] Tending to depreciate.

†**Depre·dable,** *a.* 1640. [f. next + -ABLE; cf. DEPRECABLE.] Liable to be preyed upon –1656.

Depredate (de·prĭdeit), *v.* 1626. [– *depredat-*; see next, -ATE[3].] †**1.** *trans.* To prey upon; to plunder, pillage –1677; *fig.* to consume by waste –1662. **2.** *intr.* To make depredations. (*affected.*) 1797.

1. *fig.* [Exercise] maketh the Substance of the Body..less apt to be Consumed and Depredated by the Spirits BACON. Hence **De·predator,** one who, or that which, depredates. **Depre·datory** (also de·prĭ-) *a.* characterized by depredation.

Depredation (deprĭdēi·ʃən). 1483. [– Fr. *déprédation* – late L. *depredatio*, f. *depredat-*, pa. ppl. stem of *deprædari*, f. *de-* DE- I. 3 + *prædari* to plunder; see -ION.] The action of making a prey of; plundering, pillaging; also, †plundered or pillaged condition. Also *fig.*

Habits of d. JOHNSON. *fig.* [They] perished..by the depredations of the lava LYELL.

†**Depre·dicate,** *v. rare.* 1550. [DE- I. 3.] To proclaim aloud; celebrate –1674.

†**Deprehend** (deprĭhe·nd), *v.* 1523. [– L. *deprehendere*, f. *de-* DE- I. 2; see APPREHEND.] **1.** *trans.* To seize, capture; to arrest, apprehend –1834. **2.** To take in the act –1677. **3.** To detect –1683.

2. Touching the woman deprehended in adultery WHITGIFT. **3.** The Motions..are Invisible..but yet they are to be deprehended by Experience BACON.

†**Deprehe·nsible,** *a.* 1653. [– late L. *deprehensibilis*, f. as next; see -BLE.] Capable of being detected –1660.

†**Deprehe·nsion.** 1527. [– L. *deprehensio*, f. *deprehens-*, pa. ppl. stem of L. *deprehendere*; see DEPREHEND, -ION.] The action of catching in the act; detection; arrest –1649.

Depress (dĭpre·s), *v.* ME. [– OFr. *depresser* – late L. *depressare*, frequent. f. *depress-*, pa. ppl. stem of L. *deprimere* press down, f. *de-* DE- I. 1 + *premere* press.] †**1.** *trans.* To put down by force –1675. **2.** To press down (in space). Often more widely: To lower. 1526. **3.** *fig.* To put down, bring low, humble (now *rare*) 1526; †to keep down –1861. †**4.** To depreciate, disparage –1791. **5.** To render weaker or less; to render dull or languid 1647. **6.** To cast down mentally, dispirit. (The chief current use.) 1621. †**7.** *Alg.* To reduce to a lower degree or power –1816.

2. Alternately raising and depressing the piston 1822. **4.** To d. the credit of others HOOKER. **5.** When the trade is depressed, and when wages and interest are low JEVONS. To d. the voice SCOTT. **6.** This house depresses and chills one DICKENS. Hence **Depre·ssant** *a.* sedative; *sb.* a sedative. **Depre·ssible** *a.* **Depre·ssingly** *adv.*

Depressed (dĭpre·st, *poet.* dĭpre·sĕd), *ppl. a.* Also **deprest.** ME. [f. prec. + -ED[1].] **1.** Pressed or forced down 1609. **2.** Lowered in position, force, amount, or degree ME. **3.** Having a flattened or hollowed form, as if produced by downward pressure; *spec.* said of convex things which are flattened vertically (opp. to COMPRESSED); *e.g.* a *d. arch* 1753. **4.** Brought low, oppressed, etc.; *esp.* in low spirits 1621. Hence **Depre·ssedly** *adv.*

Depression (dĭpre·ʃən). ME. [– (O)Fr. *dépression* or L. *depressio*, f. *depress-*; see DEPRESS, -ION.] **1.** The action of pressing down, or fact of being pressed down; usu. more widely: The action of lowering, or process of sinking; the condition of being lowered. Also *fig.* 1656. **2.** *spec.* **a.** *Astron.* (*a*) The angular distance of a star, the pole, etc., below the horizon (opp. to *altitude*); the angular distance of the visible horizon below the true horizontal plane, the DIP of the horizon. (*b*) The apparent sinking of the celestial pole towards the horizon as the observer travels towards the equator. ME. **b.** *Surg.* The operation of couching for cataract 1851. **3.** A depressed formation on a surface; a hollow, a low place or part 1665. **4.** A lowering in quality, vigour, or amount; the state of being lowered; in mod. use *esp.* of trade 1793. **b.** A lowering of the column of mercury in the barometer or of the atmospheric pressure thereby measured; *spec.* in *Meteorol.* a CYCLONE, q.v. 1881. **5.** Dejection 1665. **†6.** *Alg.* Reduction to a lower degree or power –1823.

4. The d. of the public funds 1793. **5.** He found her in a state of deep d. GEO. ELIOT.

Depressive (dĭpre·siv), *a.* 1620. [– Fr. *dépressif, -ive* or med.L. *depressivus*, f. as prec.; see -IVE.] Tending to press or force down. Also *fig.* Hence **Depre·ssiveness.**

Depressor (dĭpre·səɹ). 1611. [– L. *depressor*, f. as prec.; see -OR 2.] **1.** One who or that which depresses (see the vb.). **2.** *Anat.* and *Phys.* **a.** A muscle which depresses or pulls down the part to which it is attached; also *attrib.*, as *d. muscle.* **b.** *D. nerve*: a branch of the vagus, the stimulation of which lowers the pressure of the blood. 1615.

†Depressure (dĭpre·ʃ'ŭɹ). 1621. [f. as prec. + -URE.] = DEPRESSION 1, 3, 4. –1774.

†De·priment, *a. rare.* 1713. [– *depriment-*, pres. ppl. stem of L. *deprimere*; see DEPRESS, -ENT.] Depressing, as *d. muscles* –1721. As *sb.* That which depresses 1624.

†Depri·sure. *rare.* 1648. [f. †*deprise* v. – Fr. *dépriser* DISPRIZE; see -URE.] Depreciation.

Deprivable (dĭprəi·văb'l), *a.* 1593. [f. DEPRIVE *v.* + -ABLE.] Liable to be deprived; subject to deprivation.

They [the Bishops]..are..depriuable 1593.

Deprival (dĭprəi·văl). 1611. [f. as prec. + -AL[1] 2.] The act of depriving; DEPRIVATION.

Deprivation (deprivēi·ʃən). 1533. [– med. (eccl.) L. *deprivatio*, f. *deprivat-*, pa. ppl. stem of *deprivare*; see next, -ION.] **1.** The action of depriving or fact of being deprived; dispossession, loss. **2.** *spec.* The action of depriving of an office, dignity, or benefice; *esp.* the depriving of an ecclesiastic of a benefice or preferment 1551.

1. D. of Ecclesiastical Burial 1731. So **Depri·vative** *a.* of or characterized by d.

Deprive (dĭprəi·v), *v.* ME. [– OFr. *depriver* – med. (eccl.) L. *deprivare*, f. *de-* DE- I. 3 + L. *privare* deprive.] **1.** To divest, bereave, dispossess *of*, †*from*. **2.** To divest of office; to inflict (*esp.* ecclesiastical) deprivation upon ME. **3.** To keep out *of*; to debar *from* ME. **†4.** To take away; to remove –1654.

1. Thee I have missed, and thought it long, depriv'd Thy presence MILT. *P.L.* IX. 857. **2.** The Bp...depriv'd him for three years HEARNE. **3.** I am depriued of the residue of my yeeres *Isa.* 38:10. **4.** 'Tis honour to d. dishonour'd life SHAKS. Hence **†Depri·vement,** deprivation. **Depri·ver.**

De profundis; see DE.

†Depro·me, *v. rare.* 1652. [– L. *depromere*, f. *de-* DE- I. 2 + *promere* bring forth. See PROMPT *a.*] To draw out or forth –1657. var. **†Depro·mpt** (*rare*).

†Depro·strate, *a. rare.* [DE- I. 3.] Extremely prostrate. G. FLETCHER.

Deprotestantize, deprovincialize; see DE- II. 1 and *protestantize*, etc.

Depth (depþ). late ME. [prob. based on ME. *depness* deepness + -TH[1] (cf. WIDTH). Superseded or supplemented OE. *dīepe*, DEEP *sb.*]

I. 1. Measurement from the top downwards, from the outer part inwards, or from front to back. **2.** The quality of being DEEP 1526. **3.** *fig.* Profundity, penetration 1590; intensity 1624. **4.** *Logic.* = COMPREHENSION, q.v. 1864.

1. Alle these thre dymensions..that is to seye lengthe, brede and depthe LYDG. Serried Shields in thick array Of d. immeasurable MILT. *P.L.* I. 549. **2.** Because it had no d. of erth TINDALE *Matt.* 13:5. **3.** D. of knowledge BP. HALL. A man of extraordinary d. HEARNE. To sound the d. of this knauerie *Tam. Shr.* V. i. 141. D. of silence 1624, of shadow S. ROGERS.

II. Concrete senses. **1.** A deep water; a deep part of the sea (usu. in *pl.*; now *poet.* and *rhet.*) late ME.; †the DEEP –1611. **2.** A deep place in the earth, etc.; *pl.* the lowest part of a pit, etc. (*rhet.*) 1523. **3.** An abyss; the deep or remote part. Usu. *pl.* (*poet.* and *rhet.*) 1613. **4.** The inmost part. Also *pl.* late ME. **5.** The middle part 1605. **6.** *fig.* The inmost, remotest, or extreme part. Now often *pl.* late ME.

1. The depths haue couered them *Exod.* 15:5. **2.** The depths of Hell DRYDEN. **3.** The Depths of Heav'n above, and Earth below DRYDEN. Measureless depths of air LONGF. **4.** In d. of woods embrac'd POPE. **5.** The d. of Winter BOLTON. **6.** The depths of unrecorded time SHELLEY.

Phr. *Beyond* or *out of one's d.*: *lit.* in water too deep for one to touch bottom without sinking; *fig.* beyond one's powers or understanding. *attrib.* **d. bomb, charge,** a bomb to be exploded at a given depth. Hence **De·pthless** *a.* unfathomable; shallow.

De·pthen, *v.* 1587. [f. prec. + -EN[5].] = DEEPEN.

†Depu·cel, -elle, *v.* ME. [– Fr. †*dépuceler* (OFr. *des-*), f. *dé-, des-* (DE- I. 6) + *pucelle* PUCELLE.] *trans.* To deflower –1483. var. **†Depu·celate** (*rare*).

†Depu·dorate, *v.* [f. DE- II. 1 + L. *pudor* shame + -ATE[3].] To make shameless. CUDWORTH.

†Depu·lse, *v.* 1555. [– L. *depulsare* thrust away; see DE- I. 2, REPULSE *v.*] *trans.* To drive or thrust away –1623. So **†Depu·lsion,** the action of driving or thrusting away. **†Depu·lsive** *a.* averting; prophylactic. **†Depu·lsory** *a.* depulsive.

Depurant (dĭpiūə·rănt, de·piu-), *a.* 1875. [– *depurant-*, pres. ppl. stem of med.L. *depurare*; see next, -ANT[1].] Purifying; *Med.* Having the quality of purifying the blood or other fluids of the body. Also as *sb.*

Depurate (dĭpiūə·rēit, de·piu-), *v.* 1620. [– *depurat-*, pa. ppl. stem of med.L. *depurare*, f. *de-* DE- I. 3 + *purare* purify, f. *purus* pure; see -ATE[3].] To make or become free from impurities. Also *fig.*

Sufficient to d. the blood 1751.

So **†Depu·rate** *ppl. a.* purified, cleansed, clarified. **Depura·tion,** the action or process of freeing from impurities: in *Med.* the removal of impurities from the humours or fluids of the body. **Depu·rative, de·purative** *a.* depurant; *sb.* a depurant. **De·purator,** an agent or apparatus that purifies. **Depu·ratory** *a.* (*sb.*) = *depurative.*

†Depu·re, *v.* ME. [– (O)Fr. *dépurer* or med.L. *depurare*; see prec.] = DEPURATE *v.* –1873.

Depurition, bad f. DEPURATION.

Deputable (dĭpiū·tăb'l, de·piŭ-), *a.* 1621. [f. DEPUTE *v.* + -ABLE.] Capable of being, or fit to be, deputed.

Deputation (depiutēi·ʃən), *sb.* ME. [– late L. *deputatio*, f. *deputat-*, pa. ppl. stem of L. *deputare*; see DEPUTE *v.*, -ION.] **†1.** *gen.* Appointment (to an office, function, etc.) –1650. **2.** *spec.* Appointment to act on behalf of another; delegation 1552. **†3.** An appointment by the lord of the manor to the office and rights of a gamekeeper; a document conveying this –1815. **4.** A person or body of persons appointed to go on a mission on behalf of another or others. (The chief current use.) 1732.

2. That we Feed them our selves, and not by Proxy or D. 1698. **4.** A d. of the Houses waited on the King D'ISRAELI. Hence **Deputa·tional** *a.* of or belonging to a d.

Deputative (de·piŭtēitiv), *a.* 1625. [– late L. *deputativus*, f. as prec.; see -IVE.] Characterized by deputation; of the nature of a deputy.

De·putator. *rare.* 1669. [mod.L., f. as prec. + -OR 2.] One who deputes another to act for him.

Depute (de·piut), *ppl. a.* and *sb.* Now only *Sc.* ME. [– (O)Fr. *député*, pa. pple. of *députer* (repr. late L. *deputatus*); for the muting of final *-é* cf. ASSIGN *sb.*[2]]

†A. as *pa. pple.* Deputed; imputed; appointed, assigned; see DEPUTE *v.* –1623.

B. *sb.* = DEPUTY ME.

Depute (dĭpiū·t), *v.* ME. [Partly – (O)Fr. *députer* – L. *deputare* destine, assign, f. *de-* DE- I. 2 + *putare* consider; partly based on DEPUTE *sb.*] **†1.** *trans.* To appoint –1683. **†2.** To impute, ascribe –1592. **†3.** To consign –1483. **4.** To assign (a charge); now *spec.* to commit (authority, etc.) to a deputy or substitute 1495. **5.** *spec.* To appoint as one's substitute, delegate, or agent; to ordain to act on one's behalf 1552.

1. He deputed two howres for the matters of Asie LD. BERNERS. **4.** The Devil may d. such and such powers..to his confederates DE FOE. **5.** To d. Cassio in Othellos place *Oth.* IV. ii. 226.

Deputize (de·piŭtəiz), *v.* 1730. [f. next + -IZE.] **1.** To appoint as a deputy. Chiefly *U.S.* **2.** *intr.* To act as a deputy 1869.

Deputy (de·piŭti), *sb.* ME. [var. of DEPUTE *sb.*, with final syllable of the Fr. retained; see -Y[5].] **1.** A person appointed to act for another or others; a substitute, lieutenant, vicegerent. Also *fig.* **2.** A person elected to represent a constituency; a member of a representative legislative assembly 1600. **3.** *attrib.*, etc. Deputed; acting or appointed to act instead of ..; vice-.. 1548.

1. For the Greek lecture, the reader therof..got a d. to do it WOOD. *General d.* (Law): a person authorized to act for another in the whole of his office, but having no interest in the office. *Special d.*: a person similarly authorized to exercise some special function only. Phr. *By d.*: by another person in one's stead. **2.** *Chamber of Deputies*: the second house in the national assembly of France, and some other countries. **3.** Singing women escorted by d. husbands MACAULAY. Hence **De·putyship,** the office, term of office, or position of a d.

†Dequa·ntitate, *v.* [f. DE- II. 1 + L. *quantitas, -at-* quantity + -ATE[3].] To diminish the quantity of. SIR T. BROWNE.

Deracinate (dĭræ·sineit), *v.* 1599. [– Fr. *déraciner* (OFr. *des-*), f. *dé-* DE- I. 6 + *racine* root; see -ATE[3].] To tear up by the roots; to eradicate.

The Culter rusts, That should d. such Sauagery *Hen. V*, V. ii. 47. Hence **Deracina·tion.**

†Derai·gn, *sb.* ME. [– AFr. *dereine*, f. *dereiner*; see next.] The action of vindicating one's right, *esp.* by wager of battle; hence, a duel –1658. So **Derai·gnment**[1] (in same sense).

Derai·gn, *v.*[1] Now *Hist.* [ME. *dereine, deraine* – AFr. *derainer, dereiner*, OFr. *derais-, dereisnier* – Rom. **derationare*, f. *de-* (see DE- I. 6) + *ratio* account, reason. Cf. ARRAIGN *v.*[1]] *trans. Law.* To justify, vindicate, *esp.* by wager of battle; to contest; to challenge; to determine.

To d. battle (*combat*, etc.): †**a.** To maintain (a wager of battle, etc.); †**b.** To do battle; whence, to set the battle in array; †**c.** To dispose (troops, etc.) in battle array. (Elizabethan archaisms.)

†Derai·gn, *v.*[2] 1500. [– OFr. *desregner*, var. of *desrengier* (mod. *déranger*) put out of ranks, DERANGE.] **1.** To derange –1706. **2.** *passive.* To be discharged from (religious) orders –1661. Hence **†Derai·gnment**[2], discharge from a religious order.

Derail (dĭrēi·l), *v.* 1850. [– Fr. *dérailler*, f. *dé-* DE- II. 2 + *rail* RAIL *sb.*[2] First gen. used in U.S.] To run or cause to run off the rails, as a locomotive. Hence **Derai·lment,** the fact of leaving or being thrown off the rails.

Derange (dĭrēi·ndʒ), *v.* 1776. [– Fr. *déranger* (OFr. *desregner, desrengier* DERAIGN *v.*[2]), f. *dé- des-* DE- I. 6 + *rang* RANK *sb.* Not in Johnson, who considered the word to be French.] **1.** *trans.* To disturb or destroy the arrangement of; to throw into confusion; to disarrange 1777. **2.** To disturb the normal state, working, or functions of; to cause to act abnormally 1776. **3.** To disorder the mind or brain of 1825. **4.** To disturb 1848.

1. This letter deranged all the projects of James MACAULAY. **2.** Habits..which tend..to d. the animal functions SIR B. BRODIE. **3.** Minds deranged by sorrow MACAULAY. Hence **Dera·nged** *ppl. a.* disordered, disarranged; insane.

Derangement (dĭrēi·ndʒmĕnt). 1737. [– Fr. *dérangement*, f. *déranger*; see prec., -MENT.] The act of deranging, or fact of being deranged; disorder; confusion; insanity.

Derate (dĭrēi·t), *v.* 1928. [f. DE- II. 2 + RATE *sb.*[1]] To diminish the burden of rates upon.

Deray (dĭrēi·), *sb. arch.* [ME. *derai, desrai* – AFr. *derai*, OFr. *desrai*, etc., f. next.] **1.** †Disorder –1513; disarray, confusion (*mod. archaism*) 1831. **†2.** Violence, insolent ill-treatment –1550. **3.** Disorderly mirth 1500.

†Deray (dĭrēi·), *v.* ME. [– AFr. *deraier*, OFr. *desreer* (see DISRAY) :– Rom. **desredare* put into disorder, f. *de-* (DE- I. 6) + *-redare*; see ARRAY *v.*] *refl.* and *intr.* To act in a disorderly manner; to rage.

Derby (dā·ɹbi, dǝ·ɹbi). The name of a town (in OE. *Dēorabȳ, Dēorbȳ*) and shire of England, and of an earldom named from the shire. See also DARBY. Hence **1.** Name of an annual horse-race, founded in 1780 by the twelfth Earl of Derby, and run at the Epsom races, usually on the Wednesday before, or the second Wednesday after, Whitsunday. **b.** Hence *attrib.* and in *comb.*, as **D. day,** the day on which the Derby is run. Also *transf.* **2.** Short for *D. hat*: a stiff felt hat with a rounded crown and narrow brim (*U.S.*) 1888. **3.** *Plastering.* See DARBY 5. 1823.

Derbyshire (dā·ɹbi-, dǝ·ɹbiʃǝɹ). [In OE. *Dēorbȳ-scīr, Dēorbī-scīr.*] The shire or county of Derby in England. Hence **1. D. neck:** goitre 1802. **2. D. spar, †drop:** fluor-spar 1772.

†Der-do·ing, *ppl. a.* A pseudo-archaism, app. from *dare-do* (cf. DERRING-DO), in the sense 'Doing daring deeds'. SPENSER.

†Dere, *sb.* ME. [f. DERE *v.*, or a continuation of OE. *daru* (see next) with the vowel assim. to that of the verb.] Harm, *esp.* in phr. *to do* (*a person*) *d.* –1674.

†Dere, *v.* [OE. *derian* = OFris. *dera*, OS. *derian*, OHG. *terren* :– WGmc. **darjan*, f. **daro* str. fem., OE. *daru* hurt, OHG. *tara.*] **1.** *trans.* To hurt. Also *absol.* –1613. **2.** To trouble, vex, incommode –1674.

Dereign(e, dereine, var. DERAIGN *v.*

Derelict (de·rilikt). 1649. [– L. *derelictus*, pa. pple. of *derelinquere*, f. *de-* DE- I. 3 + *relinquere* leave.]

A. *adj.* **1.** Forsaken, abandoned, left by the possessor or guardian; *transf.* said of land left dry by the sea. **2.** Guilty of dereliction of duty; delinquent (*U.S.*) 1864.

1. A sort of d. possession, to be seized by the occupant HALLAM. *fig.* So as to seize upon the vacant, unoccupied, d. minds of his friends BURKE.

B. *sb.* **1.** That which is abandoned or deserted; *esp.* a vessel abandoned at sea 1670. **2.** One guilty of dereliction of duty (*U.S.*) 1888.

1. I was a D. from my cradle SAVAGE. So **†Dereli·ct** *v.* to abandon, forsake (*rare*).

Dereliction (derili·kʃǝn). 1597. [– L. *derelictio*, f. *derelict-*, pa. ppl. stem of *derelinquere*; see prec., -ION. Cf. Fr. †*déréliction.*] **1.** The action of leaving or forsaking (with intention not to resume); the condition of being forsaken or abandoned. Now *rare.* **b.** *fig.* The leaving of land by the sea; *concr.* the land thus left 1767. **2.** In mod. use implying a reprehensible abandonment or neglect; chiefly in phr. *d. of duty* 1778. **b.** Hence *absol.* Failure in duty, delinquency 1830. **†3.** Failure, cessation; fainting –1807.

1. Imposts..by long d. apparently obsolete BRYCE. Lands newly created..by the alluvion or d. of the sea BLACKSTONE. **2.** A d. of every opinion and principle that I have held BURKE.

Dereligionize; see DE- II. 1.

Dereling, -yng, obs. ff. DARLING.

†Dereli·nquish, *v.* [f. RELINQUISH, after L. *derelinquere*; see DERELICT.] To relinquish utterly, abandon –1799.

†Derf, *sb.* [app. shortened from OE. *ġedeorf*, f. *deorfan* to labour; see DERVE.] Trouble, hurt.

†Derf, *a.* (*adv.*) ME. [app. – ON. *djarfr* bold, etc.] Bold; audacious; sturdy; painful; dreadful; difficult –16... **†De·rfful** *a.* ? = DERF *a.* **†De·rf-ly** *adv.*, **-ness.**

Deric (de·rik), *a.* 1878. [f. Gr. δέρος skin + -IC.] *Biol.* Pertaining to, or constituting, the skin.

Deride (dǐrǝi·d), *v.* 1530. [– L. *deridere*, f. *de-* DE- I. 3 + *ridere* laugh, laugh at.] **1.** To laugh at in contempt; to laugh to scorn; to make sport of, mock. **†2.** *intr.* To laugh scornfully –1675.

1. And the rulers also..derided him *Luke* 23:35. He justly derides the absurd reverence for antiquity GIBBON. Hence **Deri·der. Deri·dingly** *adv.*

Derisible (dǐri·zib'l), *a.* 1657. [– late L. *derisibilis*, f. as next; see -BLE. In mod. use f. DERISION, on the analogy of *vision, visible.*] To be derided; worthy of derision.

Derision (dǐri·ʒǝn). ME. [– (O)Fr. *dérision* – late L. *derisio*. f. *deris-*, pa. ppl. stem of *deridere*; see prec., -ION.] **1.** The action of deriding; ridicule, mockery. **2.** *concr.* An object of ridicule; a laughing-stock 1539.

1. Scorne and d. neuer comes in teares *Mids. N.* III. ii. 123. But now they that are younger than I have me in d. *Job* 30:1. **2.** His word was a reproach and a d. to the profane 1612.

Derisive (dǐrǝi·siv), *a.* 1662. [f. prec., or as prec., + -IVE, after *decision, decisive*; but cf. OFr. *derisif, -ive.*] Characterized by derision; scoffing, mocking, as *d. cheers.* Hence **Deri·sive-ly** *adv.*, **-ness.**

Derisory (dǐrǝi·sǝri), *a.* 1618. [– late L. *derisorius*; see DERISION, -ORY[2].] = prec.

Derivable (dǐrǝi·văb'l), *a.* 1640. [f. DERIVE *v.* + -ABLE.] Capable of being derived (see DERIVE *v.*); †transmissible –1716; obtainable 1711; deducible 1653; traceable *from* (a source) 1682.

The income d. from a capital sum of..twenty-six millions 1884. Hence **Derivabi·lity** (*rare*). **Derivably** *adv.* in a derivative manner.

Derival (dǐrǝi·văl). *rare.* 1871. [f. DERIVE *v.* + -AL[1].] Derivation.

Derivant (dǐrǝi·vănt). 1876. [f. as prec. + -ANT[1].]

A. *adj. Med.* = DERIVATIVE 1 b.

B. *sb. Math.* Applied to derived function of a special kind.

Derivate (de·rivĕt). 1494. [– *derivat-*, pa. ppl. stem of L. *derivare*; see DERIVE, -ATE.]

A. as *pa. pple.* and *a.* Derived.

B. *sb.* Anything derived 1660. So **†Dè·rivate** *v. rare.* = DERIVE *v.* (*trans.* and *intr.*).

Derivation (derivēⁱ·ʃǝn). 1530. [– Fr. *dérivation* or L. *derivatio*, f. as prec.; see -ION.] **†1.** The leading or carrying a current of water, or the like, *from* a source, *to* another part; *concr.* a branch of a river, etc. which does this –1835. **b.** The action of leading away (in a current); diversion; an instance of this; in *Electr.* a fault 1855. **c.** *Med.* The withdrawal of inflammation, etc., from a diseased part of the body, by blistering, cupping, etc. 1600. **†2.** Transmission; communication –1699. **3.** The action of drawing, obtaining, or deducing from a source 1660. **4.** Extraction, origin, descent 1599. **5.** A derivate, a derivative 1641. **6.** *Gram.* Origination as a derivative 1530; the tracing of the origin of a word from its root or radical elements 1596. **7.** *Math.* The operation of passing from any function to any derivative function; *spec.* differentiation 1816. **8.** *Biol.* The theory of evolution of organic forms 1874.

1. The fleet passed from the Euphrates into an artificial d. of that river GIBBON. **3.** There was no real d. of English law from Normandy FREEMAN. **4.** *Hen. V*, III. ii. 141. **5.** The Father is the whole substance, but the Son a d. MILTON. **6.** The d. of the word Substance favours the idea we have of it LOCKE. Hence **Deriva·tional** *a.* **Deriva·tionist,** (*Biol.*) one who holds the theory of d. of organic types; one who occupies himself with the d. of words.

Derivative (dǐri·vătiv). 1530. [– Fr. *dérivatif* – L. *derivativus* (Priscian), f. as prec.; see -IVE, -ATIVE.]

A. *adj.* **1.** †Characterized by transmission –1640. **b.** *Med.* Producing derivation; see DERIVATION 1 c. 1851. **2.** Of derived character or nature 1530. **3.** Of or pertaining to a theory of derivation; derivational 1871.

2. A secondary and d. kind of Fame STEELE. *D. circulation*, term applied to the direct communication which exists between arteries and veins in some parts of the body, so that all the blood does not necessarily pass through the capillaries of these parts (*Syd. Soc. Lex.*). A d. word L. MURRAY, conveyance 1848.

B. *sb.* **1.** A thing of derived character 1593. **2.** *Gram.* Any word which is not a primitive word or root 1530. **3.** *Math.* A function derived from another; *spec.* a differential coefficient 1674. **4.** *Mus.* A chord derived from a fundamental chord, *esp.* by inversion; also, the (assumed) root, from the harmonics of which a chord is derived 1828. **5.** *Med.* A method or agent that produces DERIVATION (q.v., 1 c) 1843.

1. The third deriuatiue of Delicacie, is sloth NASHE. Hence **Deri·vative-ly** *adv.*, **-ness** (*rare*).

Derive (dǐrǝi·v), *v.* ME. [– (O)Fr. *dériver* or L. *derivare*, f. *de-* DE- I. 2 + *rivus* brook, stream.]

I. Transitive senses. **†1.** To conduct *from* a source, etc., *to* or *into* a channel, place, etc.; to convey through a channel –1805. **†2.** To draw off, divert the course of; *spec.* in *Med.*, cf. DERIVATION 1 c. –1771. **†3.** To carry (a channel of any kind) –1777. **4.** *transf.* and *fig.* To convey from one to another, as by transmission, descent, etc.; to hand on (*Obs.* or *arch.*) 1526. Also †*refl.* **†5.** To cause to come –1808. **6.** To draw, fetch, obtain. Const. *from*, rarely †*out of.* 1561. Also *refl.*; also *absol.* **b.** *Chem.* To obtain (a compound) from another, as by partial replacement 1868. **7.** To obtain by reasoning; to gather, deduce 1509. **8.** *refl.* To come *from* something as its source 1662. Also *passive* (in same sense) ME. **9.** *trans.* To trace or show the derivation, origin, or pedigree of; to state a thing to be derived *from* 1600.

4. Parents..rich enough to d. unto him the hereditary infirmity of the gout FULLER. **6.** O that estates, degrees, and offices, Were not deriu'd corruptly *Merch. V.* II. ix. 42. Sculpture may d. its Pedegree from the infancy of the World EVELYN. *absol.* The grantee whom he derives from BURKE. **7.** Rules..derived from nature 1624. **8.** *pass.* A Participle is an Adjective derived of a Verb WESLEY. **9.** To d. dream from drama JOHNSON, religion from myths 1874.

II. Intrans. senses. **1.** To have its derivation *from*, rarely *out of* ME. **2.** To proceed (*to* a receiver, etc.) 1559.

1. The Family he derives from 1684. The words *Comus* and *Encomium* d. thence 1866. **2.** Puritanism..derives to this country directly from Geneva M. PATTISON.

Hence **†Deri·vement** (*rare*), derivation; that which is derived. **Deri·ver.**

Derk(e, -ly, etc., obs. ff. DARK, -LY, etc.

Derm (dǝɹm). 1835. [– Gr. δέρμα skin; cf. Fr. *derme.*] *Anat.* The layer of tissue forming the true skin or corium of an animal.

‖Derma (dǝ·ɹmă). 1706. [mod.L. – Gr.] *Anat.* = prec. Hence **De·rmad** *adv.* toward the skin. **De·rmal** *a.* pertaining to the skin in general; cutaneous; *occas.*, pertaining to the derma, as opp. to *epidermal.* **Derma·tic, De·rmic** *adjs.* of or relating to the skin; dermal. **De·rmatoid, De·rmoid** *adjs.* resembling or of the nature of skin; *occas.*, dermal.

‖Dermaptera (dǝɹmæ·ptĕră), *sb. pl.* 1835. [f. Gr. δέρμα skin + πτερόν wing; in mod. Fr. *dermaptère.*] *Entom.* An order of orthopterous insects, comprising the Earwigs. Hence **Derma·pteran** *a.* belonging to the D.; *sb.* one of the D.; **Derma·pterous** *a.* belonging to the D.

De·rmat-, de·rmato-, comb. stem of Gr. δέρμα, δερματ- skin, hide, leather, as in

‖Dermata·lgia *Path.*, neuralgia of the skin. **Dermatine** (dǝ·ɹmătin), *a.* [Gr. δερμάτινος] Dermatic. **‖Dermati·tis,** inflammation of the skin. **Dermatobra·nchia;** see DERMO-. **De·rmatogen** *Bot.*, the primordial cellular layer in the embryo plant, from which the epidermis is developed. **Dermato·graphy** [-GRAPHY], description of the skin. **Dermato·logy** [-LOGY], the branch of science which treats of the skin and its diseases; hence **Dermatolo·gical** *a.*, **Dermato·logist.** **‖Dermato·lysis** [Gr. λύσις], a relaxed and pendulous condition of the skin. **‖Dermatomyco·sis** [Gr. μύκης fungus], skin-disease caused by a vegetable parasite, *e.g.* ringworm. **‖Dermatono·sis** [Gr. νόσος], skin-disease. **Dermato·pathy** [Gr. πάθος], skin-disease. **De·rmatophyte** = DERMO-(*phyte*). **De·rmatopla:sty** [Gr. πλαστός], 'the remedying of skin defects by a plastic operation' (*Syd. Soc. Lex.*). **Dermato·ptera** = DERMAPTERA. **De·rmatopsy,** 'skin-vision', sensitiveness of the skin to light. **Dermato·ptic** *a.* [Gr. ὀπτικός] *Zool.*, having 'skin-vision'. **‖Dermatorrhœ·a** [Gr. ῥοία], a morbidly increased secretion from the skin. **‖Dermatosclero·sis** [Gr. σκλήρωσις], induration of the skin; sclerodermia. **‖Dermato·sis,** the formation of bony plates or scales in the skin; also a skin-disease (*Syd. Soc. Lex.*). **Dermatoske·leton** = DERMO- (*skeleton*). **Dermato·tomy** = DERMO-(*tomy*). **‖Dermatozo·a** [Gr. ζῷον], animal parasites of the skin; hence **‖Dermatozoöno·sis,** skin-disease caused by animal parasites.

‖Dermestes (dǝɹme·stīz). 1802. [irreg. f. Gr. δέρμα + ἐσθίειν eat.] *Entom.* A genus of beetles (the type of the family *Dermestidæ*), the larvæ of which are very destructive to leather and other animal substances. Hence **Derme·stid** *a.* belonging to the family *Dermestidæ*; *sb.* one of this family. **Derme·stoid** *a.* resembling the genus *D.*; belonging to the *Dermestidæ*.

‖**Dermis** (dɔ̄·ɹmis). 1830. [mod.L., after Gr. ἐπιδερμίς EPIDERMIS.] *Anat.* = DERM.

Dermo-, repr. Gr. δερμο-, shortened comb. f. δέρμα, δέρματ-, skin, etc. (as in δερμόπτερος); hence

Dermobranchia (dɔ̄ɹmoˌbræ·ŋkiă), **-branchia·ta** [BRANCHIA] *Zool.*, a group of molluscs, having external gills in the form of dorsal membranous tufts; hence **Dermobra·nchiate** *a.* **Dermoga·stric** *a.* [Gr. γαστήρ], pertaining to the skin and stomach, as in *d. pores*, etc. **Dermo·graphy** = DERMATOGRAPHY. **Dermohæmal** (-hī·măl) *a.*, pertaining to the skin of the hæmal or ventral aspect of the body; applied to the ventral fin rays of fishes, in their relation to the hæmal arch. **Dermohæ·mia**, hyperæmia of the skin. **Dermohu·meral** *a.*, pertaining to the skin and humerus, as in the *d. muscle* in some animals. **Dermo·logy, Dermomyco·sis**; see DERMATO-. **Dermomu·scular** *a.*, of skin and muscle. **Dermoneu·ral** *a.*, pertaining to the skin of the neural or dorsal aspect of the body; applied to the dorsal fin rays of fishes, in their relation to the neural arch. **Dermopa·thic, -o·pathy**; see DERMATO-. **De·rmophyte** [Gr. φυτόν], a parasitic vegetable growth in the skin; hence **Dermophy·tic** *a.* ‖**Dermo·ptera** *pl.* [Gr. δερμόπτερος] *Zool.*, a sub-order of Insectivora, containing the *Galeopithecus* or Flying Lemur of the Moluccas (from the wing-like extension of skin, which enables them to take flying leaps). **Dermo·pterous** *a.*, having membranous wings (or fins). **Dermoptery·gian** *a.*, having membranous fins. **Dermorhy·nchous** *a.* [Gr. ῥύγχος snout], having the bill covered by an epidermis, as in the duck. **Dermoscle·rite** [Gr. σκληρός hard], a mass of spicules in the outer layer of the tissue of some Actinozoa. **Dermoske·leton,** the external bony, shelly, crustaceous, or coriaceous integument of many invertebrates and some vertebrates (*e.g.* crabs, tortoises); hence **Dermoske·letal** *a.* **Dermo·tomy** [Gr. -τομια], the anatomy of the skin.

†**Dern.** [OE. *derne, dierne* = OFris. *dern*, OS. *derni*, OHG. *tarni* :– WGmc. **darnja.*]
A. *adj.* Secret; dark; private –1460.
B. *sb.* A secret –ME.; secrecy –1508; a secret place –1500. Hence †**Derne** *adv.* †**De·rnly** *adv.* darkly; dismally (SPENSER). †**De·rnful** *a.* dreary. (A pseudo-archaism.)

Dern, var. of DARN = DAMN.

†**Dern, darn,** *v.* Now *dial.* [OE. *diernan* = OS. *dernian*, OHG. *tarnen* :– WGmc. **darnjan*, f. **darnja*; see DERN *sb.*] †**1.** *trans.* To hide –ME. Also *refl.* and *intr.* †**2.** To cause to hide, run to earth –1637.

Dernier (dɔ̄·ɹniəɹ, ‖dęrnye), *a.* 1602. [– Fr. *dernier*, OFr. *derrenier*, f. *derrein*; see DARREIN.] Last, ultimate, final. *Obs.*, exc. in *d. ressort*, †*resort*, last refuge; *orig.* last court of appeal; *the* (or *le*) *d. cri* [lit. the last cry], the very latest fashion.

Dero·be, *v. rare.* 1841. [DE -II. 1.] To doff.

De·rogate, *ppl. a.* Now *rare.* ME. [– L. *derogatus*, pa. pple. of *derogare*, see next, -ATE².] †**1.** *pa. pple.* Abrogated in part; lessened in authority, etc. –1587. **2.** *adj.* Debased 1605. Hence †**De·rogately** *adv.* (*Ant. & Cl.* II. ii. 33.)

Derogate (de·rŏgeᶦt), *v.* 1513. [– *derogat-*, pa. ppl. stem of L. *derogare*, f. *de-* DE- I. 2 + *rogare* ask, question, propose (a law); see -ATE³.] †**1.** *trans.* To repeal or abrogate in part; to destroy or impair the force and effect of; to lessen the extent of –1677. †**2.** To detract from; to disparage, depreciate –1642. **3.** To take away (something *from*) so as to lessen or impair (*arch.*) 1561. Also *absol.* or *intr.* **4.** *intr.* To do something derogatory to one's rank or position; to degenerate 1611.

2. To d. the author of the booke BILLINGSLEY. **3.** Not to d. credit from your owne word BINGHAM. To d. from the Authority of the Ancients 1640, from Pompey ADDISON. **4.** I do not d. In loving Romney Leigh E. B. BROWNING. Hence **De·rogator.**

Derogation (derŏgēᶦ·ʃən). 1450. [– Fr. *dérogation* or L. *derogatio* (only in sense 'partial abrogation of a law'), f. as prec.; see -ION.] **1.** The partial abrogation or repeal of a law, etc. 1548. **2.** Impairment of the power or authority *of*; detraction *from* 1450. **3.** Lowering in value or estimation, disparagement, depreciation 1520. **4.** Falling off in character or excellence; loss of rank 1838.

1. New and subtile inuentions in d. of the Common Law COKE. **2.** Papal usurpations, to the d. of the Crown CARTE. **4.** He might pretend surely to his kinswoman's hand without d. THACKERAY.

Derogative (dĭrǫ·gătiv), *a.* 1477. [– Fr. †*derogatif, -ive* or late L. *derogativus*, f. as prec.; see -IVE.] Tending to derogation; derogatory.

Derogatory (dĭrǫ·gătəri), *a.* 1502. [– late L. *derogatorius*, f. as prec.; see -ORY².] **1.** Having the character of derogating (see DEROGATE *v.* 1). Const. *to, from,* †*of.* **2.** Lowering in honour or, estimation; depreciatory 1563.

1. Provided there be nothing contain'd in the Law..d. from his supreme power HOBBES. **2.** Conduct..d. to his rank JAMES.

†*D. clause*: a clause in a will, deed, etc., by which the right of subsequently altering or cancelling it is abrogated, and the validity of a later document, doing this, is made dependent on the correct repetition of the clause and its formal revocation. Hence **Dero·gatori-ly** *adv.*, **-ness.**

Derotremate (derotrī·mĕt), *a.* 1849. [– mod.L. *derotrematus* (in neut. pl. *Derotremata* name of the group), f. Gr. δέρη neck + τρῆμα, -ματ- boring.] *Zool.* Of or pertaining to the *Derotremata*, a group of urodele batrachians, having gill-slits. So **Derotre·matous** *a.* **De·rotreme** *a.* and *sb.*

Derout (dĭrau·t), *sb.* 1644. [– Fr. *déroute*, f. *dérouter*, OFr. *des-*; see DE- I. 6, ROUT *sb.*², *v.*⁵] An utter ROUT. So **Derou·t** *v.* to put completely to flight.

Derrick (de·rik), *sb.* 1600. [From the surname of a hangman at Tyburn *c*1600; orig. the Du. *Dirk, Dierryk, Diederik* = G. *Dietrich* Theodoric.] †**1.** A hangman; hanging; the gallows. (Cf. *Jack Ketch.*) –1656. **2.** A contrivance for hoisting or moving heavy weights, consisting of a spar or boom set up obliquely, with its head steadied by guys, and furnished with suitable tackle and purchases; orig. used on board ship. **b.** A kind of crane (in full *d.-crane*) in which the jib is pivoted to the foot of the central post; a 'jib and tie' crane. 1727.

Derring do, derring-do. *pseudo-archaism.* ME. [f. *durran, dorren* DARE, and *don, do*, pres. inf. of DO *v.*] *lit.* Daring to do (CHAUCER *Troylus* V. 837); but misconstrued as a substantive phrase, and taken to mean, Daring action or feats, desperate courage. So †**Derring doers,** daring doers (SPENSER).

Derringer (de·rindʒəɹ). *U.S.* 1856. [f. the inventor's surname.] A small pistol with large bore, very effective at short range. Also *attrib.*

Derry (de·ri). 1553. A meaningless word used in refrains of songs; *hence* a set of verses.

Derth(e, obs. f. DEARTH.

Deruralize; see DE- II. 1.

†**Derve,** *v.* [ME. *derven* str. and weak; the str. vb. app = OE. *deorfan* labour.] **1.** *intr.* To labour. (Only in OE.) **2.** *trans.* To trouble, hurt, molest –ME.

Dervish (dɔ̄·ɹviʃ). 1585. [– Turk. *derviş* – Pers. *darvēsh, darvish* poor, a religious mendicant. (The native Arabic equiv. is *faḳīr* poor, poor man.)] A Moslem friar, who has taken vows of poverty and austere life.

Des- in obs. words; see DEC-, DESC-, DESS-, DIS-.

Des-, *prefix.* Regular Romanic form of L. *dis-*; in mod.Fr. *dés-* bef. a vowel or silent *h*, otherwise *dé-* (OFr. *descharge*, mod. *décharge*). Occas. repr. a late L. *de-ex-*, for L. *ex-*. Early OFr. words passed into English with the prefix in the form *des-* (*descharge*, ME. *descharge*), but have all a later form in DIS-, under which they are here treated. See also DISPATCH.

‖**Descamisado** (deskamisā·do). 1823. [Sp.; = shirtless. Cf. *sans-culotte.*] A nickname for the ultra-liberals in the Spanish revolutionary war of 1820–23. Also *transf.*

Descant (de·skænt), *sb.* Also **dis-.** ME. [orig. *deschaunt* – OFr. *deschant* (mod. *déchant*) – med.L. *discantus* part-song, refrain, f. *dis-* asunder, apart + *cantus* song; see DIS-, CHANT *sb.*]

I. *Mus.* Now *Hist.*, or *poet.* **1.** A melodious accompaniment to the *plainsong*, sung or played above it: the earliest form of counterpoint. **2.** The soprano or highest part of the score in part-singing 1569. **3.** *gen.* A melodious strain 1576. **4.** Musical composition, harmony; also, a harmonized composition 1565. **5.** An instrumental prelude, consisting of variations on a given theme 1644.

1. The merry Larke hir mattins sings aloft; The Thrush replyes; the Mavis d. playes SPENSER. **3.** The birds in vain their amorous d. join GRAY. **5.** And then a low sad d. rung, As prelude to the lay he sung SCOTT.

II. Transf. uses. †**1.** Variation from that which is typical or customary –1712. **2.** Varied comment on a theme; a comment; †*occas.*, censorious criticism 1594; a disquisition 1622.

1. Running, Leaping, and Dancing, the descants on the plain song of walking FULLER. **2.** With merry descants on a nation's woes COWPER.

Descant (deskæ·nt), *v.* 1510. [prob. f. the sb.; so OFr. *deschanter* (mod. *déchanter*).] **1.** *Mus.* To play or sing an air in harmony with a fixed theme; *gen.* to warble 1538. **2.** *intr.* To comment, enlarge (*upon, on*) 1510. †**3.** *trans.* To comment on; *occas.* to carp at –1649.

2. He used to d. critically on the dishes which had been at table BOSWELL. Hence **Desca·nter.**

Descend (dĭse·nd), *v.* ME. [– (O)Fr. *descendre* :– L. *descendere*, f. *de-* DE- I. 1 + *scandere* climb.]

I. Intr. senses. **1.** To move or pass from a higher to a lower place; to come or go down, fall, sink. (The general word; the opposite of *ascend.*) Also *fig.* †**b.** To disembark; to alight –1600. **c.** *Astron.*, etc. To move towards the horizon; to move southwards ME. **2.** *transf.* To slope downwards ME. **3.** To come down with or as a hostile force; to fall violently *upon* ME. **4.** To proceed to something subsequent in time or order, or (*esp.*) from generals to particulars ME. **5.** To come down; to condescend, stoop (*to do* something); usually in a bad sense 1554. **6.** *Mus.* To go down the scale 1597. **7.** To come *of*, spring *from* (an ancestor or ancestral stock) ME. Also *fig.* **8.** *intr.* To come down by way of inheritance 1486. Also *transf.* of personal qualities, etc.

1. The moist droppes of the rein Descenden into middel erthe GOWER. *fig.* Sleep nor quiet upon my eyes descended 1871. **c.** The setting Sun Slowly descended MILT. *P.L.* IV. 541. Phr. †*To d. into* or *within oneself*: to betake oneself to deep consideration. **3.** That the Turke woulde d. upon the realme of Naples 1600. **5.** Wordsworth..descends to such babyisms 1829. **7.** We are descended of ancient Families STEELE. **8.** The Crowne..descended on her GOUGE.

II. Trans. senses. †**1.** To cause to descend –1677. **2.** To go or come down; to pass downwards over, along, or through 1607.

2. To d. the Hill MILT., the steps 1891.

Descendance, -ence (dĭse·ndăns). Now *rare.* 1599. [– (O)Fr. *descendance* or med.L. *descendentia*; see prec., -ANCE, -ENCE.] **1.** = DESCENT 7. **2.** *concr.* Descendants. (App. a corruption.) var. †**Desce·ndancy, -ency.**

Descendant, -ent (dĭse·ndănt). 1572. [– (O)Fr. *descendant*, pres. pple. of *descendre*; see DESCEND, -ANT, -ENT. The spelling is now always *-ant.*]

A. *adj.* **1.** Descending (*rare*) 1644; *Her.* descending towards the base of the shield 1572. **2.** Descending or originating from an ancestor; also *fig.* 1594.

2. Were not wise sons descendent of the wise POPE.

B. *sb.* **1.** One who is descended from an ancestor; issue (in any degree) 1600. Also *fig.* and *transf.* †**2.** *Astron.* The part of the heavens which at any moment is descending below the horizon (opp. to the ASCENDANT) 1690.

1. Abraham's descendents according to the flesh 1729.

Descendental (dĭsende·ntăl), *a. nonce-wd.* 1850. [f. prec., after *transcendental.*] That descends to matter of fact; realistic.

†**Desce·nder**¹. 1485. [– AFr. *descender* used subst.; see -ER⁴.] *Law.* Descent; title of descent –1768.

Descender² (dĭse·ndəɹ). 1667. [f. DESCEND *v.* + -ER¹.] One who or that which descends; in *Typogr.* a letter that descends below the line.

Descendible, -able (dĭse·ndĭb'l, -ăb'l), *a.* 1495. [In XV *-able* – OFr. *descendable*; subseq. refash. after L. analogies; see -ABLE, -IBLE.] **1.** That descends or may descend to an heir. **2.** Capable of being descended; down which one may go (*rare*) 1730. Hence **Descendibi·lity** (*rare*).

Descending (dǐse·ndiŋ), *ppl. a.* 1642. [f. DESCEND *v.* + -ING[2].] **1.** *lit.* Moving downwards 1700. **2.** *transf.* Directed downwards, as *d. aorta, colon*, etc. 1737; *spec.* in *Her.* (see DESCENDANT *a.* 1). **3.** *fig.* Proceeding to what is lower in position or value, or later in order; *Math.*, of series: Proceeding from higher to lower quantities or powers 1642.

D. node (Astron.): that node of a planet's orbit at which it passes from north to south of the ecliptic. Hence **Desce·ndingly** *adv.*

Descension (dǐse·nʃən). Now *rare*. ME. [– OFr. *descension* – L. *descensio*, f. *descens-*, pa. ppl. stem of *descendere*; see DESCEND, -ION.] **1.** The action of descending; descent (*lit.* and *fig.*) Now *rare*. †**2.** Lineage –1523. †**3.** A coming down from dignity or high station; condescension –1692. †**4.** *Old Chem.* A method of distillation, in which the vapour was forced to distil downwards –1751. †**5.** *Astron.* The setting, or descent below the horizon, of a celestial body –1726. †**6.** *Astrol.* The part of the zodiac in which a planet had least influence (opp. to *exaltation*) –15..

5. *Right d., oblique d.* of a celestial body: the degree of the celestial equator, reckoned from the first point of Aries, which sets with it in a right, or oblique, sphere. Hence **Desce·nsional** *a.* of or pertaining to d. (*rare*).

Descensive (dǐse·nsiv), *a.* 1611. [f. L. *descens-* (see prec.) + -IVE.] **1.** Having the quality of descending (*lit.* and *fig.*); opp. to *ascensive*. **2.** *Gram.* Diminishing the force 1854.

†**Desce·nsory**, *sb.* ME. [– med.L. *descensorium*, whence OFr. *descensoir*, f. as prec.; see -ORY[1].] *Old Chem.* A vessel used for distillation by DESCENT –1678. So †**Desce·nsory** *a.* relating to, or of the nature of, distillation by descent.

Descent (dǐse·nt). ME. [– (O)Fr. *descente*, f. *descendre* DESCEND, after *attente, vente* from *attendre, vendre*.] **1.** The action of descending; downward motion (of any kind). Also *fig.* †**b.** *Old Chem.* = DESCENSION 4. –1751. **2.** *concr.* A downward slope, a declivity 1591; a means of descending, a way leading downwards 1634; †the lowest part. *Lear* V. iii. 137. **3.** A sudden hostile invasion or attack, *esp.* from the sea 1600. **4.** *fig.* A coming down to a lower state or condition; fall, decline, sinking; progress downwards to that which is subordinate 1667; a stage or step downward (? *obs.*) 1589. **5.** A fall, lowering (of the pitch of sound, temperature, or the like) 1581. **6.** The action of proceeding in sequence, discourse, or argument, to what is subsequent; subsequent part or course; succession 1642. **7.** The fact of descending from an ancestor or ancestral stock; lineage ME. Also *transf.* (in *Biol.* extended to origination of species) and *fig.* †**8.** A line of descent, lineage –1618; a descendant (*lit.* and *fig.*); also, issue –1667. **9.** A stage in the line of descent; a generation 1513. **10.** *Law.* The passing of (real) property to the heir or heirs without disposition by will; transmission by inheritance ME. Also *transf.* and *fig.*

1. The d. to Avernus 1866. **2.** At the d. of the mount of Olives *Luke* 19:37. **3.** Argyle was threatening a d. upon Scotland SCOTT. **4.** Her birth was by manie degrees greater than mine, and my woorth by manie discents lesse than hers GREENE. **8.** Our d.. Which must be born to certain woe, devourd By Death at last MILT. *P.L.* x. 979. **9.** Euen twelue descents after the flood 1593.

Describe (dǐskrəi·b), *v.* 1513. [– L. *describere* write down, copy off, f. *de-* DE- I. 1 + *scribere* write. Superseded DESCRIVE *v.*, exc. in Sc.] †**1.** To write down –1667. **2.** To set forth in words by reference to characteristics; to give a detailed or graphic account of. (The ordinary current sense.) 1513. **3.** To set forth in delineation; to represent, picture, portray. *Obs.* or *arch.* 1526. **4.** To delineate, trace the outline of 1552. **5.** To form or trace by motion 1559. **6.** To mark off or distribute into parts. *Josh.* 18:6. ¶**7.** = DESCRY *v.*[1] 1574.

2. D. we next the Nature of the Bees DRYDEN. **3.** A Gladiatore.. admirably described in Marble 1620. **4.** A triangle.. described vpon a line 1570. **5.** The most northely circle which the Sonne describeth 1559. Hence **Descri·bable** *a.* **Descri·ber.**

Describent (dǐskrəi·bĕnt). 1704. [– *describent-*, pres. ppl. stem of L. *describere*; see prec., -ENT.]

A. *adj.* 'Describing, marking out by its motion' (Ash).

B. *sb. Geom.* A point, line, or surface, generating by its motion a line, surface, or solid.

Descrier (dǐskrəi·əɹ). 1599. [f. DESCRY *v.* + -ER[1].] One who descries.

Descri·pt, *ppl. a.* 1665. [– L. *descriptus*, pa. pple. of *describere* DESCRIBE.] Described; apportioned; inscribed, engraved.

Description (dǐskri·pʃən). ME. [– (O)Fr. *description* – L. *descriptio*, f. *descript-*, pa. ppl. stem of *describere* DESCRIBE; see -ION.] †**1.** The action of writing down. CAXTON. **2.** The action of setting forth in words by mentioning characteristics; verbal representation or portraiture ME.; (with *pl.*) a graphic or detailed account ME.; in *Logic*, a definition by non-essential attributes 1628. **3.** The combination of qualities or features that marks out or describes a particular class; hence, a sort, species, kind, or variety 1596. †**4.** Pictorial representation (*rare*) –1646. **5.** *Geom.* **a.** The describing of a geometrical figure; see DESCRIBE *v.* 4. ?*Obs.* 1655. **b.** Tracing out or passing over a certain course or distance 1706.

2. For her owne person, It beggard all discription *Ant. & Cl.* II. ii. 203. **3.** A friend of this d. SHAKS. A d. of vehicle, peculiar.. to Cuba 1844.

Descriptive (dǐskri·ptiv), *a.* 1751. [– late L. *descriptivus*, f. as prec.; see -IVE. Cf. Fr. *descriptif, -ive*.] Having the quality or function of describing; serving to describe; characterized by description.

D. words JOHNSON, poets HAZLITT, Anatomy 1896. A name d. of its construction HUXLEY. Hence **Descri·ptive-ly** *adv.*, **-ness.**

Descri·ve, *v.* Now only *Sc.* ME. [– OFr. *descrivre* (mod. *décrire*) :– L. *describere* DESCRIBE. See next.] = DESCRIBE *v.*, q.v.

Descry (dǐskrəi·), *v.* ME. [In senses 1, 2 – OFr. *descrier* cry, publish, DECRY. In senses 3, 4, app. through identification with †*descrie* (– OFr. *descrire*), var. of DESCRIVE *v.*] †**1.** To cry out, announce (*rare*) 1440; to make known –1660; to bewray –1670. †**2.** To cry out against, challenge to fight –1480; to decry (see DECRY *v.* 1, 2) –1677. **3.** To catch sight of, *esp.* from a distance; to espy ME. **4.** To discover by observation ME. Also *absol.* †**5.** To investigate, explore –1742.

1. His purple robe he [Alectus] had thrown aside lest it should d. him MILT. **3.** At intervals we descried a maple W. BLACK. **4.** *absol.* Still Hills and Vallies as far as we could d. 1670. **5.** The house of Ioseph sent to d. Bethel *Judg.* 1:23. Hence †**Descry·, discry** *sb.* cry, war-cry; perception from a distance.

†**De·secate**, *v.* 1623. [– *desecat-*, pa. ppl. stem of L. *desecare* cut off, cut away, f. *de-* DE- I. 2 + *secare* cut; see -ATE[3].] *trans.* To cut off, cut away; to cut free –1651.

Desecrate (de·sǐkre[i]t), *v.* 1674. [f. DE- II. 1 + stem of *con-secrate*. L. *desecrare* or *desacrare* meant to consecrate.] *trans.* To take away its sacred character from; to treat as not sacred; to profane 1677. **b.** To dedicate or devote *to* something evil 1825. **c.** To dismiss from holy orders (*arch.*) 1674.

To d. Sunday J. H. NEWMAN. **b.** To d. a spot to Satan SIR J. STEPHEN. **c.** The [Russian] clergy cannot suffer corporal punishment without being previously desecrated 1800. Hence **De·secrate** *ppl. a.* **De·secrater, -or. Desecra·tion. De·secrative** *a.*

De:segmenta·tion. 1878. [DE- II 1.] *Zool.* Union of two or more segments of a body into one. So **Dese·gmented** *ppl. a.*

Dese·nsitize, *v.* 1904. [f. DE- II. 1, after *sensitize*.] To reduce or destroy the sensitiveness esp. of a photographic plate, etc.

Desert (dǐzɔ̄·ɹt), *sb.*[1] ME. [– OFr. *desert, deserte*, subst. derivatives of *deservir* DESERVE.] **1.** Deserving; merit or demerit. **b.** Meritoriousness ME **2.** That in conduct or character which deserves reward or punishment. Usu. in *pl.* (often = 1.) ME. **b.** A good deed or quality; a merit. ? *Obs.* 1563. **3.** That which is deserved, whether good or evil ME.

1. What constitutes d.?..a person is understood to deserve good if he does right, evil if he does wrong MILL. To behold d. a beggar borne SHAKS. **2.** To do to each according to his deserts MILL. **3.** I shall nother ete nor drynke tyll thou hast thy dysert LD. BERNERS. Hence **Dese·rtful** *a.* deserving. ? *Obs.* **Dese·rtfully** *adv.* **Dese·rtless** *a.*

Desert (de·zəɹt), *sb.*[2] ME. [– (O)Fr. *désert* – eccl.L. (Vulg.) *desertum*, subst. use of neut. of *desertus* abandoned, left waste, pa. pple. of *deserere* leave, forsake.] **1.** An uninhabited and uncultivated tract of country; a wilderness; now *esp.* a desolate and barren region, waterless and treeless, with but scanty herbage :– *e.g.* the *D. of the Sahara*, etc. Also *transf.* and *fig.* †**2.** *abstractly.* Desert condition; desolation –1523.

1. In our lande is also a grete deserte or forest 1511. The D...a wild waste of pebbly soil STANLEY. *fig.* To roam the howling desart of the main POPE.

Comb.: **d.-chough,** a bird of the genus *Podoces*, family *Corvidæ*, found in Central Asia; **-falcon,** a species of falcon inhabiting deserts, a member of the sub-genus *Gennæa*, allied to the peregrines; **-ship,** 'ship of the d.', the camel or dromedary; **-snake,** a serpent of the family *Psammophidæ*, a sand-snake.

Desert (de·zəɹt), *a.* ME. [– (O)Fr. *désert* – L. *desertus* (see prec.). Now apprehended as an attrib. use of the sb.] **1.** Deserted (*arch.*) 1480. **2.** Unpeopled, desolate, lonely ME. **3.** Barren, waste; of the nature of a desert ME. Also *fig.*

2. When Deucalion hurl'd His Mother's Entrails on the desart World DRYDEN. **3.** The Countrey.. is desart, sterile and full of loose sand SIR T. HERBERT.

Desert (dǐzɔ̄·ɹt), *v.* 1603. [– Fr. *déserter* – late L. *desertare*, f. L. *desertus*; see DESERT *sb.*[2]] **1.** *trans.* To abandon, forsake, relinquish; to depart from. **2.** To forsake (a person, cause, etc. having moral or legal claims upon one); *spec.* of a soldier or sailor: To run away from (the service, his colours, etc.) 1647. **3.** *intr.* To forsake one's duty, one's post, or one's party; *spec.* of a soldier, etc.: To run away from the service without permission 1689.

1. His slacken'd hand deserts the lance it bore POPE. To d. a ship 1790. **2.** A husband deserts his wife if he wilfully absents himself from her society, in spite of her wish 1891. **3.** The fourth regiment deserted in a body 1792. Hence **Dese·rtedness,** deserted condition.

Deserter (dǐzɔ̄·ɹtəɹ). 1635. [f. DESERT *v.* + -ER[1], after Fr. *déserteur*.] **1.** One who forsakes a person, place, or cause; usually with implied breach of duty. **2.** *esp.* A soldier or seaman who quits the service without permission 1667.

Desertion (dǐzɔ̄·ɹʃən). 1591. [– (O)Fr. *désertion* – late L. *desertio*, f. *desert-*, pa. ppl. stem of L. *deserere*; see DESERT *sb.*[2], -ION.] **1.** The action of deserting, forsaking, or abandoning, *esp.* a person or thing that has moral or legal claims to the deserter's support; occas. simply, departure from a place. **2.** *Law.* The wilful abandonment of an employment or of duty; *esp.* such abandonment of the military or naval service 1712. **3.** Deserted condition 1751; †in *Theol.*, spiritual despondency. SOUTH (J.).

1. The D. of this Island by the Romans 1683. **2.** Ranks thinned by frequent desertions THIRLWALL.

Desertness (de·zəɹtnĕs). ME. [f. DESERT + -NESS.] Desert condition.

†**Dese·rtrice.** *rare.* [f. DESERTER, after Fr. types; see -TRICE.] A female deserter. MILTON. So **Dese·rtress, Dese·rtrix.**

Deserve (dǐzɔ̄·ɹv), *v* ME. [– OFr. *deservir* (mod. *desservir*) :– L. *deservire* serve zealously or well, f. *de-* DE- I. 3 + *servire* SERVE.] **1.** To merit by service; to become entitled to or worthy of. *Obs.* or *arch.* **2.** To have acquired, and thus to have, a rightful claim to; to be entitled to; to be worthy to have. (Now the ordinary sense.) ME. **3.** *absol.* or *intr.* To be entitled to recompense; to merit, be worthy. Often in phr. *to d. ill* or *well of.* ME. †**4.** *trans.* To earn, win –1628. †**5.** To serve; to benefit –1634. †**6.** *trans.* To pay back, requite –1525.

1. 'Tis not in mortals to Command Success, But we'll do more, Sempronius; we'll D. it ADDISON. **2.** Mr. Ho...deserves a better fate than to be ever of the loosing side 1668. Books..which d. to last EMERSON. **3.** That he, who best deserves, alone may reign DRYDEN. Hence **Dese·rved** *ppl. a.* rightfully earned; merited; † = *Deserving* ppl. a. (SHAKS. *Cor.* III. i. 292.) **Dese·rved-ly** *adv.*, **-ness. Dese·rver,** one who deserves (*esp.* well). **Dese·rving** *vbl. sb.* desert, merit; *ppl. a.* that deserves (*esp.* well); **-ly** *adv.*

†Dese·sperance, -aunce. [– OFr. *desesperance*; see DIS-, ESPERANCE, and cf. DESPERANCE.] Despair –1460.

Deshabille; see DISHABILLE.

Desiccant (de·sikănt, dĭ·sikănt). 1676. [– *desiccant-*, pres. ppl. stem of L. *desiccare*; see next, -ANT[1].] *adj.* Having the property of drying; serving to dry 1775. *sb.* A drying agent.

Desiccate (de·sikeⁱt, dĭ·sikeⁱt), *v.* 1575. [– *desiccat-*, pa. ppl. stem of L. *desiccare*, f. *de-* DE- I. 3 + *siccare* make dry, f. *siccus* dry; see -ATE[3].] **1.** To make quite dry; to deprive thoroughly of moisture; to dry up. Also *fig.* **2.** *intr.* To become dry (*rare*) 1679.

1. Wine helpeth to digest and d. the moisture BACON. Desiccated Soup 1884. So **De·siccate** *ppl. a.* (*arch.*). Hence **Desicca·tion,** the action of desiccating; desiccated condition.

Desiccative (de·sikeⁱtiv, dĭ·sikătiv). ME. [– late L. *desiccativus*, f. as prec.; see -IVE. Cf. OFr. *desiccatif, -ive.*] *adj.* Having the tendency or quality of drying up 1541. *sb.* A desiccant.

Desiccator (de·sikeⁱtəɹ, dĭ·sikătəɹ). 1837. [f. DESICCATE + -OR 2.] One who or that which desiccates; a name applied to a chemical apparatus used to dry substances decomposed by heat or by exposure to the air; also, to contrivances for desiccating milk, fruit, etc.

De·siccatory, *a.* 1800. [f. as prec. + -ORY[2].] Desiccative.

†Desi·derable, *a.* ME. [– L. *desiderabilis*, f. *desiderare*; see DESIDERATE *v.*, -BLE.] To be desired; desirable –1675. Hence **†Desi·derably** *adv.*

Desiderata, pl. of DESIDERATUM, q.v.

†Desi·derate. 1640. [– L. *desideratus*, pa. pple. of *desiderare*; see next, -ATE[2].] *adj.* Desired; desirable. *sb.* A desideratum –1670.

Desiderate (dĭsi·dĕreⁱt), *v.* 1645. [– *desiderat-*, pa. ppl. stem of L. *desiderare*, f. *de-* DE- I. 1, 2 + base **sider-*, as in *considerare* CONSIDER; see -ATE[3], DESIRE *v.*] *trans.* To desire with a sense of want or regret; to feel the want of; to miss.

In an evening I d. the resources of a family or a club GIBBON. The great step which is now desiderated in education SOUTHEY.

Desideration (dĭsi:derēⁱ·ʃən). 1525. [– L. *desideratio*, f. as prec.; see -ION.] **1.** The action of desiderating. **†2.** Desideratum (*rare*) 1836.

Desiderative (dĭsi·dĕrĕtiv). 1552. [– late L. *desiderativus*, f. as prec.; see -IVE.]

A. *adj.* **1.** Having or denoting desire; pertaining to desire 1655. **2.** *Gram.* Of a verb, etc.: Formed from another verb to express a desire of doing the act thereby denoted; pertaining to such a verb 1552.

B. *sb. Gram.* A desiderative verb, verbal form, or conjugation 1751.

‖**Desideratum** (dĭsi:dĕrēⁱ·tŏm). Pl. **-ata.** 1652. [L., subst. use of n. sing. of pa. pple. of *desiderare* DESIDERATE.] Something for which a desire is felt; something wanting and required or desired.

The explanation of them was still a d. in geology PLAYFAIR.

‖**Deside·rium.** 1715. [L.; f. *desiderare* DESIDERATE.] An ardent desire or wish; a longing, properly for a thing once possessed and now missed; a sense of loss.

†Desidio·se, *a.* 1727. [– L. *desidiosus* slothful; see -OSE[1].] = next –1822.

†Desi·dious, *a.* 1540. [f. as prec. + -OUS; see -IOUS.] Idle, slothful –1656. Hence **†Desi·diousness.**

Desight (dĭsəi·t). 1834. [prob. orig. a var. of *dessight*, DISSIGHT.] A thing unsightly, an eyesore. So **Desi·ghtment,** disfigurement (*rare*).

Design (dĭzəi·n), *sb.* 1588. [– Fr. †*desseing* (mod. *dessein, dessin*), f. *desseigner* to DESIGN.]

I. 1. A plan or scheme conceived in the mind of something to be done; the preliminary conception of an idea that is to be carried into effect by action; a project 1593; 'a scheme formed to the detriment of another' (J.) 1704. **2.** Purpose, aim, intention 1588. **3.** The thing aimed at 1657. **4.** Contrivance in accordance with a preconceived plan; adaptation of means to ends; prearranged purpose; as, the *argument from d.* 1665. **5.** In a bad sense: Crafty contrivance; an instance of this (*arch.*) 1704.

1. The d. of insurrection MACAULAY. He had no d. upon your pocket LYTTON. **2.** With d. to besiege it 1734. Phr. *By* (†*out of, on, upon*) *d.*; purposely. **3.** If Milk be thy D.; with plenteous Hand Bring Clover-grass DRYDEN.

II. 1. A preliminary sketch for a work of art; the plan of a building, or part of it, or of a piece of decorative work, after which the structure or texture is to be completed; a delineation, pattern 1638. **2.** The combination of details which go to make up a work of art; artistic idea as executed; a piece of decorative work, an artistic device 1644. Also *transf.* of literary work 1875. **3.** The art of picturesque delineation and construction 1638.

2. To admire the designs on the enamelled silver centres GEO. ELIOT. **3.** *Arts of d.*: those in which d. plays a principal part, as painting, sculpture, architecture, engraving. *School of d.*: a school in which the arts of d. are specially taught.

Design (dĭzəi·n), *v.* 1548. [– Fr. *désigner* indicate, designate, and L. *designare* DESIGNATE *v.*]

I. [after L. *designare.*] **†1.** To mark out; to indicate –1668. **2.** To DESIGNATE (*arch.*) 1603. **3.** To appoint or assign. *Obs.* exc. in *Sc. Law.* –1701. **4.** To set apart in thought for some one 1664. **5.** To destine to a fate or purpose 1593.

2. The writer..is not named or designed 1874. **4.** What present I had designed for her DE FOE.

II. [allied to DESIGN *sb.* I.] **1.** To plan, plan out 1548. **2.** To purpose, intend 1655. Also *intr.* (*rare*). **3.** To have in view 1677. **4.** *intr.* and quasi-*pass.* (usu. with *for*): To intend to go or start 1644.

1. He can suspend the laws himself designed S. ROGERS. **2.** Not for obscurity designed DRYDEN. **4.** They d. to Bristol 1688.

III. [allied to DESIGN *sb.* II.] **1. †a.** To sketch. **b.** To trace the outline of, delineate. (App. implied in DESIGNMENT.) 1570. **c.** To make the preliminary sketch of; to make the plans and drawings necessary for the construction of 1697. **2.** To plan and execute; to fashion with artistic skill or decorative device 1666. **3.** *intr.* **a.** To draw, sketch. **b.** To form or fashion a work of art; less widely, to devise artistic patterns 1662.

2. The Roman bridges were designed on the same grand scale as their aqueducts 1865.

Designable, *a.* 1644. [In sense 1 – med.L. *designabilis*; in sense 2, f. prec. + -ABLE.] **†1.** (de·signăb'l) That can be distinctly marked out –1716. **2.** (dĭzəi·năb'l) Capable of being designed.

Designate (de·signĕt), *ppl. a.* 1646. [– L. *designatus*, pa. pple. of *designare*; see next, -ATE[2].] Marked out for office, etc.; appointed, but not yet installed, as in *bishop d.*

Designate (de·s-, de·zigneⁱt), *v.* 1791. [– *designat-*, pa. ppl. stem of L. *designare*, f. *de-* DE- I. 3 + *signare* to mark, SIGN; see -ATE[3]. *Designate* takes up the senses of the L. vb. not expressed by DESIGN *v.*] **1.** *trans.* To point out, indicate; to specify 1801. **2.** To point out by a name or description; to name, denominate 1818. **3.** To appoint, nominate for duty or office; to destine to a purpose or fate 1791.

1. To d. faults 1801, limits N. WEBSTER. **2.** Miriam is almost always designated as the 'prophetess' STANLEY. **3.** A clause designating the successor by name MACAULAY. So **De·signative** *a.* having the quality of designating. **De·signator,** one who designates or points out; in *Rom. Antiq.*, an officer who assigned to each person his rank and place in public shows and ceremonies. **De·signatory** *a.* of or pertaining to a designator or designation.

Designation (des-, dezignēⁱ·ʃən). ME. [– (O)Fr. *désignation* or L. *designatio*, f. as prec.; see -ION.] **1.** The action of marking or pointing out; indication; *concr.* a distinctive mark. **2.** The action of appointing or nominating; the being nominated; appointment, nomination 1605. **3.** The action of devoting by appointment to a particular purpose or use; an act of this nature (*arch.*) 1637. **†4.** Purpose, intention, design –1763. **5.** A descriptive name, an appellation; *spec.* in *Law*, the statement of profession, trade, residence, etc., for purposes of identification 1824.

2. The *quasi* d. of Eadward to the crown FREEMAN. **3.** To make various designations of their profits BLACKSTONE. **5.** The name Argeioi..as a d. of the army before Troy GLADSTONE.

Designed (dĭzəi·nd), *ppl. a.* 1586. [f. DESIGN *v.* + -ED[1].] †Marked out; planned, purposed; drawn, outlined; fashioned according to design. Hence **Desi·gnedly** *adv.* on purpose.

Designer (dĭzəi·nəɹ). 1649. [f. as prec. + -ER[1].] **1.** One who designs or plans; in bad sense, a plotter, schemer, intriguer. **2.** One who makes an artistic design or plan of construction; *spec.* one who makes designs or patterns for the manufacturer or constructor 1662.

Designful (dĭzəi·nful), *a.* 1677. [f. DESIGN *sb.* + -FUL.] Full of design; intentional. Hence **Desi·gnfulness,** d. quality.

Designing (dĭzəi·niŋ), *vbl. sb.* 1618. [-ING[1].] The action of DESIGN *v.*; marking out; planning, etc.; plotting, scheming.

Desi·gning, *ppl. a.* 1653. [-ING[2].] **1.** That designs, plans, etc. **2.** Scheming, crafty, artful 1671. Hence **Desi·gningly** *adv.*

Designless (dĭzəi·nlĕs), *a.* 1643. [f. DESIGN *sb.* + -LESS.] Void of design or plan. Hence **Desi·gnlessly** *adv.*

†Desi·gnment. 1570. [f. DESIGN *v.* + -MENT.] = DESIGNATION, DESIGN –1738.

Desiliconize (dīsi·likŏnəi:z), *v.* 1881. [f. DE- II. 1.] To free from silicon.

Desilver (dīsi·lvəɹ), *v.* 1864. [DE- II. 2.] To remove the silver from, free from silver.

Desilverize (dīsi·lvərəiz), *v.* 1872. [f. prec. + -IZE.] To extract the silver from (lead, etc.). Hence **Desilveriza·tion.**

Desinence (de·sinĕns). 1599. [– Fr. *désinence* – med.L. *desinentia*, f. *desinent-*, pres. ppl. stem of L. *desinere* leave off, close; see -ENCE.] Termination, close; in *Gram.* a suffix or ending of a word. Hence **Desine·ntial** *a.* pertaining to, or of the nature of a d.

Desinent (de·sinĕnt), *a.* ? *Obs.* 1605. [– *desinent-*; see prec., -ENT.] Forming the end, terminal; closing.

Their upper parts human..their d. parts fish B. JONS.

Desipience (dĭsi·piĕns). 1656. [– L. *desipientia*, f. *desipere* be foolish; see -ENCE.] Folly; foolish trifling, silliness. var. **Desi·piency.** So **Desi·pient** *a.* foolish, silly; playing the fool (*rare*).

Desirable (dĭzəiᵊ·răb'l), *a.* (*sb.*) ME. [– (O)Fr. *désirable*, f. *désirer*, after L. *desiderabilis*; see DESIRE *v.*, -ABLE]. **1.** Worthy to be desired; to be wished for. In early use: Pleasant, delectable, excellent. **†2.** To be regretted 1650. **3.** *sb.* That which is desirable 1645.

1. Horsemen riding vpon horses, all of them desireable young men *Ezek.* 23:12. No evil is in its self d., or to be chosen STILLINGFL. Hence **Desi:rabi·lity. Desi·rableness. Desi·rably** *adv.*

Desire (dĭzəiᵊ·ɹ), *sb.* ME. [– (O)Fr. *désir*, f. *désirer*; see next.] **1.** The fact or condition of desiring; that emotion which is directed to the attainment or possession of some object from which pleasure or satisfaction is expected; longing, craving; a wish. **2.** *spec.* Physical appetite; lust ME. **†3.** = DESIDERIUM. Chapman. **4.** A wish as expressed; a request, petition ME. **5.** *transf.* That which one desires or longs for ME.

1. Desyre To be clepyd lorde or syre R. BRUNNE. **2.** That satiate yet vnsatisfi'd d. *Cymb.* I. vi. 47. **4.** The House hath been in conference with the Lords upon their d. MARVELL. **5.** The d. of all nations shall come *Haggai* 2:7. Hence **Desi·reful** *a.* (now *rare*), †desirable; desirous; eager; **†-ness. Desi·reless** *a.*

Desire (dĭzəiᵊ·ɹ), *v.* ME. [– (O)Fr. *désirer* :– L. *desiderare*; see DESIDERATE *v.*] **1.** *trans.* To have a strong wish for; to long for, crave.

2. *intr.* (or *absol.*) To have or feel a desire ME. †**3.** *trans.* Of things: To require, need, demand –1607. **4.** To long for (something lost); to desiderate 1557. **5.** To express a wish for; to request ME. †**6.** To request to be told –1708. †**7.** To invite –1606.

1. Do not all men d. happiness JOWETT. You d. your child to live TENNYSON. **4.** And now his chair desires him here in vain TENNYSON. **5.** I.. thereupon desired to have the Council's letters ABP. PARKER. He desires me to dine with him again on Sunday SWIFT.

Hence **Desi·red** *ppl. a.* wished for, etc. (see above): †desiderated; †desirous [= L. *cupidus*]. **Desi·redly** *adv.* in a desired manner; †according to one's own desire. **Desi·redness. Desi·ringly** *adv.*

Desirous (dĭzəiᵊ·rəs), *a.* ME. [– AFr. *desirous*, OFr. *-eus* (mod. *désireux*) :– Rom. **desiderosus*; see prec., -OUS.] **1.** Having desire or longing; characterized by desire; wishful, desiring; *occas.*, covetous. †**2.** Eager, ardent (*esp.* in deeds of arms) –1485. †**3.** Exciting desire; desirable –1728.

1. The Grecians being d. of learning A. V. *Transl. Pref.* 4. Owre men..were desyrous to see the towne EDEN. **3.** Places d. to be in BUNYAN. Hence **Desi·rous-ly** *adv.*, **-ness** (now *rare*).

Desist (dĭzi·st), *v.* 1509. [– (O)Fr. *désister* – L. *desistere*, f. *de-* DE- I. 2 + *sistere*, reduplicated f. *stare* stand.] **1.** *intr.* To cease *from*; to stop, leave off, forbear 1530. †**2.** *trans.* To discontinue –1784.

1. I counsayle you desyst from this purpose PALSGR. Request that he would d. in his gallantries to me GOLDSM. **2.** Thou foole d. thy wordes vayne 1509. Hence **Desi·stance, -ence,** the action of desisting; cessation, discontinuance of action. **Desi·stive** *a.* ending (*rare*).

Desition (dĭsi·ʃən). 1612. [– late and med.L. *desitio* cessation, f. *desit-*, pa. ppl. stem of L. *desinere* leave off, cease; see DESINENCE, -ION.] Termination or cessation of being; ending.

†**Desitive** (de·sitiv). *rare.* 1725. [f. as prec. + -IVE.]

A. *adj. Logic.* Having reference to the ending of any thing, as *d. propositions.*

B. *sb.* A desitive proposition.

Desk (desk), *sb.* [Late ME. *deske* – med.L. *desca*, prob. based on Pr. *desc*, *desca* basket or It. *desco* table, butcher's block :– L. *discus* quoit, dish, disc. See DISCUS, and cf. DAIS, DISH *sb.*] **1.** A table, board, or the like, usually with a sloping surface, intended to serve as a rest for a book, writing paper, etc., while reading or writing. Often qualified, as *litany-*, *music-*, *writing-desk*, etc. **b.** In mod. use often a portable box or case, for writing materials, letters, etc. 1548. †**c.** In early use, also a shelf, case, or press for books –1717. **2.** In a church or chapel: A sloping board on which books used in the service are laid. Hence (*esp.* in U.S.), a pulpit. 1449. **3.** *fig.* Used for the functions or office of the occupant of a desk 1581; also for clerical or office work 1797.

Comb.: **d.-cloth,** a cloth to cover a reading-d. or lectern; **-knife,** an eraser; **-work,** work at a d., as clerk, book-keeper, etc.

†**Desk,** *v.* 1509. [f. the sb.] **1.** To fit up with desks. **2.** To place in or as in a desk –1670.

Desma (de·smă). Pl. **-mata, -mas.** 1857. [– Gr. δέσμα.] **1.** A bandage; a ligament. **2.** A kind of spicule which unites with others to form the skeletal framework in some sponges.

‖**Desman** (de·smăn). 1774. [Fr. and G., from Sw. *desman-råtta* musk-rat, f. *desman* musk.] *Zool.* An aquatic insectivorous mammal, of the genus *Myogale*, nearly allied to the shrew; esp. *M. moschata*, the musk-rat, which inhabits the rivers of Russia. *M. pyrenaica* is a species found in the Pyrenees.

Desmid (de·smid). 1862. [– mod.L. *Desmidium* (generic name), f. Gr. type *δεσμίδιον, dim. of δεσμός band, chain. See -ID².] *Bot.* A plant of the genus *Desmidium*, or order *Desmidiaceæ* of microscopic unicellular algæ; so called because sometimes found united in chains. Hence **Desmidia·ceous** *a.* of the N.O. *Desmidiaceæ*, containing the desmids; **Desmi·dian** *a.* of the desmids; *sb.* a desmid; **Desmidio·logy,** the scientific study of desmids; **Desmidio·logist.**

Desmine (de·smin). 1811. [f. Gr. δέσμη bundle + -INE⁵.] *Min.* = STILBITE.

Desmo- (de·smo), comb. f. Gr. δεσμός bond. Hence

Desmo·brya *pl.* [Gr. βρύον; see BRYOLOGY], name for a group of ferns; hence **Desmo·bryoid** *a.*, belonging to or like the *Desmobrya*. **De·smodont** *a.* and *sb.* [Gr. ὀδοντ-], belonging to, or one of, the *Desmodonta*, a group of bivalve molluscs. **Desmo·gnathous** *a.* [Gr. γνάθος], having the type of palatal structure shown in the *Desmognathæ*, a group of birds, in which the maxillo-palatine bones are united across the median line; so **Desmo·gnathism,** this type of palatal structure. **Desmo·graphy** *Anat.*, a description of the ligaments of the body. **Desmo·logy,** 'the anatomy of the ligaments of the body; also, a treatise on bandages' (*Syd. Soc. Lex.*). **Desmo·pathy,** disease of the ligaments. **Desmope·lmous** *a.* [Gr. πέλμα sole of the foot], *Ornith.*, having the plantar tendons connected, as some birds, so that the hind toe cannot be moved independently of the front toes. **Desmo·stichous** *a.* [Gr. στίχος row], belonging to or like the *Desmosticha*, a group of echinoids having the ambulacra equal and bandlike. **Desmo·tomy** [Gr. -τομια], the dissection of ligaments.

Desmoid (de·smoid), *a.* 1847. [f. Gr. δεσμός band and δέσμη bundle + -OID.] Resembling a bundle. **a.** *Path.* Applied to the fibrous tissue of certain tumours. **b.** *Zool.*, etc. Ligamentous; tendinous.

†‖**Deso·bligeant.** 1768. [– Fr. *désobligeante* fem. (sc. *voiture*).] A chaise so called in France from its holding but one person. Cf. *sulky.* –1770.

Desocialize, -ation; see DE- II. 1.

‖**Désœuvré** (dezö·vre), *a.* 1750. [Fr.] Unoccupied; languidly idle. So **Désœuvrement,** lack of occupation.

Desolate (de·sŏlĕt), *ppl. a.* ME. [– L. *desolatus*, pa. pple. of L. *desolare* abandon, f. *de-* DE- I. 3 + *solus* alone; see -ATE².]

†**A.** as *pa. pple.* Brought to desolation; see DESOLATE *v.* ME. only.

B. *adj.* **1.** Left alone, lonely ME. †**2.** Destitute *of*, lacking. With *inf.*: Without means *to.* –1720. **3.** Destitute of inhabitants; uninhabited, deserted ME. **4.** In a ruinous condition; neglected; laid waste; bare, barren; cheerless ME. **5.** Comfortless; forlorn, disconsolate; wretched ME. †**6.** Destitute of good quality, abandoned. (Occas. confounded with *dissolute.*) –1782. Also *absol.*

1. He which hath no wif..lyveth helples, and is al d. CHAUCER. **2.** The place..was d. of inhabitants DE FOE. **3.** So d. stode Thebes and so bare CHAUCER. **4.** No man thinks of walking in this d. place DICKENS. **5.** Gyue confort to a d. hert CAXTON. **6.** Unhappy men of d. and abandoned principles 1782. Hence **De·solate-ly** *adv.*, **-ness.**

Desolate (de·sŏleⁱt), *v.* ME. [– *desolat-*, pa. ppl. stem of L. *desolare*; see prec., -ATE³.] **1.** *trans.* To deprive of inhabitants, depopulate. **2.** To lay waste; to make bare, barren, or unfit for habitation ME. **3.** To leave alone, abandon; to make desolate 1530. **4.** To make comfortless 1530.

1. As if the city had been desolated by the plague LYELL. **2.** The revolutions of Nature which had desolated France 1796. **4.** Desolated by continuous despair 1887. Hence **De·solator, -er,** one who or that which makes desolate. †**De·solatory** *a.* having the quality or tendency of desolating (*rare*).

Desolation (desolēⁱ·ʃən). ME. [– late L. *desolatio*, f. as prec.; see -ION. Perh. partly through French.] **1.** The action of desolating or laying waste; utter devastation. Also *personified.* **2.** The condition of being left desolate; ruined state; dreary barrenness ME.; a thing or place in this condition 1611. **3.** Solitariness, loneliness 1588. **4.** Deprivation of comfort; dreary sorrow; grief ME.

2. Yon dreary Plain, forlorn and wilde, The seat of d. MILT. *P. L.* I. 181. This house shall become a d. *Jer.* 22:5. **3.** You have liu'd in d. heere, Vnseene, vnuisited *L. L. L.* V. ii. 357. **4.** Euerie thing about you, demonstrating a careless d. *A. Y. L.* III. ii. 400.

De:sophi·sticate, *v.* 1827. [DE- II. 1.] To free from sophistication. Hence **Desophistica·tion.**

Desoxalic (desǫksæ·lik), *a.* 1868. [– Fr. *désoxalique*; see DES-, OXALIC *a.*] *Chem.* Formed by the deoxidation of oxalic acid.

D. acid, a synonym of racemo-carbonic acid, $C_5H_6O_8$. Hence **Deso·xalate,** a salt of this acid.

Desoxy-. 1882. [f. as prec.] *Chem.* Without oxygen, deoxidated.

Despair (dĭspēᵊ·ɹ), *sb.* [ME. *despeir*, *dis-* – AFr. **despeir* (see next), for OFr. *desespeir* (mod. *désespoir*).] **1.** The action or condition of despairing; hopelessness. Also *personified.* **2.** That about which there is no hope 1605.

1. It becomes no man to nurse d. TENNYSON. Hollow-eyed Abstinence, and lean D. COWPER. **2.** People..The meere despaire of Surgery, he cures *Macb.* IV. iii. 152. Hence **Despai·rful** *a.* hopeless, desperate.

Despair (dĭspēᵊ·ɹ), *v.* [ME. *despeire*, *dis-* – *despeir-*, tonic stem of OFr. *desperer* :– L. *desperare* to despair, f. *de-* DE- I. 6 + *sperare* to hope.] **1.** *intr.* To give up hope; to be without hope. Const. *of*, rarely †*in*, *to* with *inf.* ME. Also †*refl.* in same sense. †**2.** *trans.* To cast into despair (*rare*) –1618. †**3.** *trans.* = *despair of* in sense 1. –1773.

1. As long as you hope, I will not d. STEELE. His life was despaired of 1718. **3.** *Macbeth.* I bear a charmed Life.. *Macduff.* Dispaire thy Charme *Macb.* V. viii. 13. Hence **Despai·red** *ppl. a.* †desperate; †despaired of. **Despai·rer. Despai·ringly** *adv.*

Desparple, obs. var. of DISPARPLE *v.*

Despatch, var. of DISPATCH.

†**Despe·che,** *v.* 1531. [var. of DEPEACH, q.v.] To send away, get rid of, dispatch –1550.

De:speci·ficate, *v. rare.* 1872. [DE- II. 1.] To deprive of its specific character. Hence **Despecifica·tion.**

Inaptitude and *ineptitude* have been usefully despecificated; and only the latter now imports 'folly' F. HALL.

†**Despect** (dĭspe·kt), *sb.* 1624. [– L. *despectus*, f. *despicere* look down upon; see next. Cf. DESPITE *sb.*] A looking down upon; contempt –1834. So †**De·spection.**

Despe·ctant, *ppl. a.* 1688. [– *despectant-*, pres. ppl. stem of L. *despectare*, frequent. of *despicere*; see prec., -ANT¹.] *Her.* Looking downwards.

†**Despee·d,** *v.* 1611. [f. DE- I. 2 + SPEED *v.*] To send with speed; to dispatch.

Despend, -pence; see DISP-.

†**De·speracy.** 1628. [f. DESPERATE; see -ACY.] Desperateness –1800.

Desperado (despĕrēⁱ·do). 1610. [refash., after Sp. words in -ADO, of DESPERATE *sb.*] = DESPERATE *sb.* 1, 2.

†**Desperance.** ME. [– OFr. *desperance*, f. *desperer* to DESPAIR; see -ANCE, and cf. DESESPERANCE.] Despair –1560.

Desperate (de·spĕrĕt). 1483. [– L. *desperatus*, pa. pple. of *desperare* despair of, f. *de-* DE- I. 6 + *sperare* hope for, f. *speres*, OL. pl. of *spes* hope.]

A. *adj.* **1.** Despairing, hopeless (*arch.*). **2.** Of conditions, etc.: That leaves little or no room for hope 1555. †**3.** Of things (and persons): Given up as hopeless; irretrievable –1871. **4.** Of persons: Driven to desperation. Hence, Reckless, violent, ready to risk or do anything. 1489. **5.** Of actions, etc.: Characterized by the recklessness of despair; applied *esp.* to those done in the last extremity 1579; †involving serious risk –1654. †**6.** Outrageous, extravagant –1661. **7.** Of such a quality as to be despaired of; 'awful' 1604.

1. I am d. of obtaining her *Two Gent.* III. ii. 5. D. sobs DISRAELI. **2.** D. diseases EDEN. **3.** His d. game FULLER. **4.** Want makes Men d. 1718. **5.** His look denounc'd D. revenge MILT. *P.L.* II. 107. Marriage is a d. thing SELDEN. **6.** The desparate Principles..of Quakers SANDERSON. **7.** D. sots and fools POPE. Hence **De·sperate** *v.* to render d. (*rare*). **De·sperate-ly** *adv.*, **-ness.**

B. *sb.* †**1.** A person in despair –1622. †**2.** One ready for any desperate deed –1718.

C. *adv.* Hopelessly; usually (*colloq.* and *dial.*) as an intensive: Excessively, 'awfully' 1636.

Desperation (despĕrēⁱ·ʃən). ME. [– OFr. *desperation* – L. *desperatio*, f. *desperat-*, pa. ppl. stem of *desperare*; see prec., -ION.] **1.** The action of despairing or losing all hope; the condition of having utterly lost hope; despair. Now *rare.* **2.** *spec.* Despair leading to recklessness, or recklessness arising from despair. (Cf. DESPERATE *a.* 4, 5.) 1531.

1. Horrour of deathe..and disperation of æternal blisse 1588. **2.** Needy and hungry to d. EMERSON.

Despicable (de·spikăb'l), *a.* 1553. [– late L. *despicabilis*, f. *despicari* look down upon,

f. *de-* DE- I. 1 + **specari*, from same root as *specere* look; see -ABLE.] **1.** To be looked down upon or despised; vile, contemptible; †wretched. †**2.** Contemptuous –1775.

1. All things with them are d. and vile EDEN. These poor d. wretches 1635. **2.** I have a very d. opinion of the present age 1662. Hence **Despicabi·lity, De·spicableness,** d. quality, worthlessness. **De·spicably** *adv.*

†Despi·ciency. 1623. [– L. *despicientia*, f. *despicere*; see DESPISE, -ENCY.] Looking down upon or despising; contempt –1672.

Despiritualize, *v.*; see DE- II. 1.

Despisable (dĭspəi·zăb'l), *a.* [In ME. *despisa·ble* – OFr., f. stem *despis-* of *despire* DESPISE.] = DESPICABLE *a.* 1 (now *rare*), †2. Hence **†Despi·sableness.**

Despisal (dĭspəi·zăl). 1650. [f. DESPISE *v.* + -AL[1] 2.] The act of despising; contempt.

Despise (dĭspəi·z), *v.* ME. [– *despis-*, pres. stem of OFr. *despire* :– L. *despicere*, f. *de-* DE- I. 1 + *specere* look.] **1.** *trans.* To look down upon; to view with contempt; to scorn or disdain. †**2.** To treat with contempt –1557; †*fig.* of things, to set at nought –1666.

1. He is despised and reiected of men *Isa.* 53:3. **2.** *fig.* [The fire]..despised all the resistance [which] could be made by the strength of the buildings STILLINGFL. Hence **†Despi·se** *sb.* despite, contempt. **†Despi·sedness. Despi·ser. Despi·singly** *adv.*

Despite (dĭspəi·t), *sb.* ME. [– OFr. *despit* (mod. *dépit*) :– L. *despectus* looking down (upon), f. *despect-*, pa. ppl. stem of *despicere*; see prec.] **1.** The looking down upon anything; contempt, scorn, disdain. *Obs.* or *arch.* **2.** Action that shows contemptuous disregard; insulting action; outrage, injury, contumely ME.; †defiance –1719. **3.** (with *pl.*) An outrage, etc. ME. **4.** Evil feeling, anger. In later use, *esp.* aversion; settled ill-will; SPITE. ME.

1. Any attribute that is given in despight HOBBES. Phr. †*To have in d.* **2.** Whi hast thou don despit to Chivalrye CHAUCER. **4.** Rancorous d. 1846.

Phr. **In d. of.** †**a.** In contempt of. †**b.** In open defiance of. **c.** Notwithstanding the opposition of. **d.** Notwithstanding. **e.** *In his, her, one's,* etc. *d.*: in the prec. senses. **f.** In later use often **d. of** (senses c, d); whence DESPITE *prep.*, rarely *in d.*

Despite (dĭspəi·t), *v. arch.* ME. [– OFr. *despiter* (mod. *dépiter*) :– L. *despectare*, frequent. of *despicere*; see prec.] **1.** To show contempt for, set at nought; to do despite to. †**2.** To provoke to anger; to spite –1658. †**3.** *intr.* To show despite –1736.

1. Reason..Despiteth love, and laugheth at her Folly DRAYTON.

Despite (dĭspəi·t), *prep.* 1593. [Shortened from *despite of*, orig. *in despite of*; see DESPITE *sb.*] In spite of.

Despiteful (dĭspəi·tful), *a.* 1450. [f. DESPITE *sb.* + -FUL.] †**1.** Contemptuous; insulting –1676. **2.** Cruel; malignant; spiteful 1470.

2. I shalbe called foolishe, curious, despitefull, and a sower of sedition KNOX. The hainous and despightfull act Of Satan done in Paradise MILT. *P. L.* X. 1. Hence **Despi·teful-ly** *adv.*, **–ness.**

Despiteous (despi·tiəs), *a.* late ME. [alt., after PITEOUS, of next.] **1.** *orig.* = DESPITOUS (*arch.*). **2.** Spiteful, malevolent, cruel; later, merciless, DISPITEOUS 1510.

1. The proud, d. rich man MORRIS. **2.** Dispitious torture *John* IV. i. 34. Hence **†Despi·teously** *adv.*

†Despitous, *a.* ME. [– AFr. *despitous*, OFr. *despitos* (mod. *dépiteux*), f. *despit* DESPITE *sb.* + *-os* -OUS.] **1.** *orig.* Full of despite; hence insulting, vexing –1494. **2.** Cruel; malevolent –1578. Hence **†Despitously** *adv.*

Despoil (dĭspoi·l), *sb.* ME. [– OFr. *despoille*, f. the vb.; see next.] **1.** The action of despoiling (*arch.*) 1483. †**2.** *concr.* SPOIL –1619.

Despoil (dĭspoi·l), *v.* [ME. *despuile, -spoile,* – OFr. *despoill(i)er, despuillier* (mod. *dépouiller*) :– L. *despoliare*, f. *de-* DE- I. 6 + *spolia* (see SPOIL *sb.*).] **1.** *trans.* To plunder, rob. **2.** To deprive violently *of*; to rob ME. †**3.** *spec.* To strip of clothes; to undress –1700. †**4.** To strip of value or use; to SPOIL –1685. †**5.** To carry off by violence –1604.

1. The Ebrues well dispoile the Egypcyens MORE. **2.** Theeues ..dispoiling him of his apparell KNOLLES. Despoild of Innocence MILT. *P. L.* IX. 411. **3.** He bad That wommen schuld despoilen hir right there CHAUCER. Hence **Despoi·ler. Despoi·lment.**

Despoliation (dĭspōᵘ:liₗēⁱ·ʃən). 1657. [– late L. *despoliatio*, f. *despoliat-*, pa. ppl. stem of L. *despoliare*; see prec., -ION. Cf. OFr. *despoliation.*] The action of despoiling; despoilment.

Despond (dĭspǫ·nd), *v.* 1655. [– L. *despondēre* give up, resign, abandon, f. *de-* DE- I. 2 + *spondēre* promise.] *intr.* To lose heart or resolution; to become depressed by loss of confidence or hope. (Dist. from *despair* as not expressing entire hopelessness.) Occas. with *of.*

Though he d. that sows the grain 1696. Desponding of their Art DRYDEN. Hence **Despo·nd** *sb.* despondency (*arch.*). **Despo·nder** (*rare*). **Despo·ndingly** *adv.*

Despondence (dĭspǫ·ndĕns). 1676. [f. prec. + -ENCE.] The action of desponding; also (less correctly) = DESPONDENCY.

Bear up thyself..from fainting and d. HALE.

Despondency (dĭspǫ·ndĕnsi). 1653. [f. as prec. + -ENCY.] The condition of being despondent; dejection of spirits through loss of resolution or hope.

The d. with which the Greeks viewed the situation THIRLWALL.

Despondent (dĭspǫ·ndĕnt), *a.* 1699. [f. as prec. + -ENT.] **1.** Characterized by despondency; labouring under mental depression. **2.** Of or belonging to despondency 1844.

1. A d. sinner 1699. **2.** A d. gesture DICKENS, attitude 1888. Hence **Despo·ndently** *adv.*

†Despo·nsate, *a.* 1471. [– L. *desponsatus*, pa. pple. of *desponsare*, frequent. of *despondēre* betroth, f. *de-* DE- I. 2 + *spondēre* promise.] **1.** Betrothed, espoused 1483. **2.** *fig.* (*Alch.*) Chemically combined 1471. So **†Desponsa·tion.**

†Despo·nsories, *sb. pl.* 1626. [– Sp. *desposorios* espousal, f. *desposar* affiance :– L. *desponsare* (after which the Eng. word was modified). Chiefly used in relation to the proposed Spanish marriage of Charles I.] **1.** Betrothal –1659. **2.** A document formally declaring a betrothal –1670.

†Despo·se. *v. rare.* 1587. [– OFr. *desposer*, occas. var. of *deposer*; see DE- 6, DEPOSE.] To depose, lay down –1603.

Despot (de·spǭt). 1562. [– Fr. *despote*, earlier †*despot* – med.L. *despota* – Gr. δεσπότης master, lord.] **1.** *Hist.* A word which, in its Greek form, meant 'master' or 'lord'; in Byzantine times it was used of the Emperor, and, later, of various subordinate rulers, also as a form of address. **2.** An absolute ruler of a country; hence, any ruler who governs absolutely or tyrannically; any person who exercises tyrannical authority; a tyrant, oppressor 1781.

2. Hast thou..returned..A d. big with power obtained by wealth COWPER. Under the primeval despots of Egypt EMERSON. So **De·spotat, -ate,** the dominion of a Greek d. under the Turks; a principality.

Despotic, -al (despǫ·tik, -ăl), *a.* 1608. [– (O)Fr. *despotique* – Gr. δεσποτικός, f. δεσπότης; see prec., -IC, -ICAL.] Of, pertaining to, or of the nature of a despot, or despotism; arbitrary, tyrannical. Hence **Despo·tical-ly** *adv.*, **†-ness.**

Despotism (de·spǭtiz'm). 1727. [– Fr. *despotisme*; see DESPOT, -ISM.] **1.** The rule of a despot; despotic government; the exercise of absolute authority. Also *fig.* **2.** A political system under the control of a despot; a despotic state; an arbitrary government 1856.

1. The simplest form of government is d. BURKE. *fig.* The d. of the senses EMERSON. **2.** Your empire is a d. exercised over unwilling subjects JOWETT. So **De·spotist,** an advocate of d. **De·spotize** *v. intr.* to act the part of a d.

†Despou·se, *v.* ME. [f. L. *desponsare* betroth, on the model of *espouse*; see DESPONSATE, ESPOUSE *v.*] To betroth; to marry. Also *fig.* –1609. Hence **†Despou·sage,** betrothal; espousal.

Despraise, Despread, Desprize; see DIS-.

Despumate (dĭspiū·meⁱt, de·spiumeⁱt), *v.* 1641. [– *despumat-*, pa. ppl. stem of L. *despumare* skim (off), f. *de-* DE- I. 6 + *spuma* foam, froth, scum; see -ATE[3].] **1.** *trans.* To skim; to clarify by removing the scum. **2.** *intr.* (for *refl.*) To throw off its froth or scum; to become clarified by this process 1733. **3.** *trans.* To throw off as froth 1733. Hence **Despu·mat(ed** *ppl. a.* clarified. **Despuma·tion,** clarification; the expulsion of impure matter from the fluids of the body; the matter despumated. So **†Despu·me** *v.* to clear of froth or scum; *intr.* to foam.

Desquamate (de·skwămeⁱt), *v.* 1727. [– *desquamat-*, pa. ppl. stem of L. *desquamare* scale (off), f. *de-* DE- I. 6 + *squama* scale; see -ATE[3].] †**1.** *trans.* To take the scales off; to scale, peel –1740. **2.** *intr.* To scale off 1828. Hence **Desquama·tion,** the removal of scales or any scaly crust; a coming off in scales, *esp.* that of the epidermis; exfoliation; that which comes off. So **Desqua·mative** *a.* tending to or characterized by desquamation. **Desqua·matory** *a.* of or pertaining to desquamation; *sb.* a desquamatory trepan.

†Dess, *sb.* 1552. [– OFr. *deis, dais*; see DAIS.] **1.** Obs. f. DAIS. **2.** A desk –1596.

Dessert (dĕzō·ɹt). 1600. [– Fr. *dessert* masc., *desserte* fem., pa. ppl. deriv. of *desservir* remove what has been served at table, f. *des-* DIS- I. 4 + *servir* SERVE.] A course of fruit, sweetmeats, etc. served after a dinner or supper; 'the last course at an entertainment' (J.). **b.** In U.S. often including pies, etc. 1848.

Such eating, which the French call desert, is unnaturall 1600. *Comb.*: **d.-spoon,** that used for the d.; it is intermediate in size between a tablespoon and a tea-spoon.

‖**Dessiatine, desyatin** (de·syătīn). 1799. [– Russ. *desyatina* lit. 'tithe'.] A Russian superficial measure of about 2.7 acres.

Destemper, obs. f. DISTEMPER.

†De·stin, destine, *sb.* 1575. [– Fr. *destin* masc. or OFr. *destine* fem., f. *destiner* DESTINE.] = DESTINY *sb.* –1616. Hence **†De·stinable** *a.* fixed by destiny; fated, fatal. **†De·stinably** *adv.* **†De·stinal** *a.* of, pertaining, or according to destiny.

†De·stinate, *ppl. a.* ME. [– *destinatus*, pa. pple. of L. *destinare*; see DESTINE *v.*, -ATE[2].] **1.** Fated –1659. **2.** Intended, designed –1671.

Destinate (de·stineⁱt), *v.* Now *rare.* 1490. [– *destinat-*, pa. ppl. stem of L. *destinare*; see DESTINE *v.*, -ATE[3].] To DESTINE, ordain, or design.

That name that God..did d. and appoynt vnto hym UDALL. So †**De·stinate** *ppl. a.* destined.

Destination (destinēⁱ·ʃən). 1598. [– (O)Fr. *destination* or L. *destinatio*, f. as prec.; see -ION.] **1.** The action of destining to a particular use, purpose, or end; the fact of being destined. **b.** *trans.* The end or purpose for which a person or thing is destined 1656. **2.** *spec.* The fact of being bound for a particular place; hence, short for *place of d.*; the intended end of a journey or course. (Now the usual sense.) 1787.

1. Our d. for society KAMES. A d. above the objects, the employments, and the abilities of this world MOZLEY. **2.** 'It [the fleet] has as many destinations' he [Nelson] said 'as there were countries' SOUTHEY.

Destine (de·stin), *v.* ME. [– (O)Fr. *destiner* – L. *destinare* make firm, establish, f. *de-* DE- I. 3 + **stanare* settle, fix, f. *stare* stand.] **1.** *trans.* To ordain, appoint (definitely). *Obs.* (or merged in 3.) **2.** To appoint, to predetermine by an unalterable decree. Now chiefly in *pass.*; often without any definite reference to predetermination. (Usu. with *inf.*) ME. **3.** To set apart in intention for a particular purpose, use, end, etc.; to design, devote, allot. (Usu. in *pass.*) 1530.

2. Yf god destyneth hym, he shall wynne the pryse CAXTON. He was, however, not destined to escape so easily PEACOCK. **3.** Phr. *To be destined*: to be bound (*for* a particular place). Hence **De·stined** *ppl. a.* foreordained, fated (now often merely = 'that is (or was) to be'); intended; *spec.* bound to a particular place.

Destiny (de·stĭni), *sb.* ME. [– (O)Fr. *destinée* – Rom. subst. use of fem. pa. pple. of prec. L. vb.; see -Y[5].] **1.** That which is destined to happen; FATE. **2.** That which is destined to happen to a particular person or thing; (one's) FATE ME. **3.** In weakened sense: Ultimate condition. (Also in *pl.*) 1555. **4.** The power or agency by which events are unalterably predetermined; divine preordination; invincible necessity; FATE. (Often personified.) ME. **5.** *Mythol.* The goddess of destiny; *pl.* the three Parcæ ME.

2. Oh, I was borne to it, it was my destonie 1583. *Merch. V.* II. ix. 83. **3.** Their children also had little better d. 1665. **4.** The force Of ruthless D. COWPER. **5.** Seuen faire branches.. Some..by the destinies cut *Rich. II*, I. ii. 15. Hence **De·stinism,** fatalism. **De·stinist,** a believer in d. †**De·stiny** *v.* to destine, foreordain; to prognosticate.

†**Desti·tuent,** *a.* [– *destituent-*, pres. ppl. stem of L. *destituere*; see next, -ENT.] Wanting, lacking. JER. TAYLOR.

Destitute (de·stitiut), *a.* (*sb.*) ME. [– L. *destitutus* forsaken, pa. pple. of *destituere*, f. *de-* DE- 1, 2 + *statuere* set up, place.] †**1.** Abandoned; forsaken, forlorn –1755. **2.** †Deprived or bereft *of* –1492; devoid *of*, entirely lacking *in* 1500. **3.** Bereft of resources, 'in want and misery'; now, without the means of bare subsistence, in absolute want 1535. **4.** *sb.* One who is destitute 1737.

1. Great houses long since built Lye d. and wast 1592. **2.** A barren waste d. of trees and verdure JOWETT. **3.** He will regard the prayer of the d. *Ps.* 102:17. The deep curses which the d. Mutter in secret SHELLEY. Hence **De·stitute-ly** *adv.*, **-ness.**

Destitute (de·stitiut), *v.* Now *rare.* *Pa t.* **-ed,** †**destitute.** 1530. [Partly f. prec., partly repr. L. *destituere* forsake, abandon; see prec.] †**1.** *trans.* To forsake, abandon, leave to neglect –1673. **2.** To deprive, bereave *of*; to render destitute 1540. **3.** *spec.* To deprive of office. [mod.Fr. *destituer.*] 1653. **4.** To lay waste 1593. †**5.** To frustrate, disappoint –1619.

1. To forsake or d. a Plantation, once in Forwardnesse BACON. **3.** Let not the Patriarch think..to d. or depose me 1716. **5.** Offended, when his expectation is destituted 1619.

Destitution (destitiū·ʃən). ME. [– (O)Fr. *destitution* – L. *destitutio*, f. *destitut-*; see DESTITUTE *a.*, -ION.] †**1.** The action of deserting or forsaking –1727. **2.** Deprivation of office 1554. **3.** The condition of being destitute (see DESTITUTE *a.* 1, 2) ME. **4.** *spec.* The condition of being destitute of resources; want of the necessaries of life 1600.

3. D. in these [food and clothing] is such an impediment HOOKER. **4.** Left in a state of d. COBDEN.

‖**Destour, dastur** (dĕstūᵊ·ɹ). 1630. [Pers. *dastūr* prime minister :– Pahlavi *dastōbār.*] A chief priest of the Parsees.

De·strer, de·strier (de·strəɹ, -iəɹ, destrīᵊ·ɹ). *arch.* ME. [– AFr. *destrer*, (O)Fr. *destrier* :– Rom. **dextrarius* (sc. *caballus* horse), f. L. *dext(e)ra* (see DEXTER), the knight's charger being led by the squire with his right hand.] A war-horse, a charger.

Destroy (dĭstroi·), *v.* [ME. *destru(e), destrui(e), destrie, destroie* – OFr. *destruire* (mod. *détruire*) :– Rom. **destrugere*, for L. *destruere*, f. *de-* DE- I. 6 + *struĕre* pile up.] **1.** To pull down or undo, as a building; to demolish. †**2.** To lay waste –1611; to ruin (men) –1621. **3.** To undo, break up, reduce into a useless form, consume, or dissolve. (Now the leading sense.) ME. **b.** To render useless 1542. **4.** To deprive of life; to kill ME. **5.** To put an end to; to do away with ME. **6.** To counteract 1729.

1. The cite of rome shulde haue be dystroyed CAXTON. Like a Torrent, which..destroies all 1659. **2.** That same tyme attila destroyed Italye CAXTON. **3.** To d. Skiffs 1700, old houses 1798, works on alchemy 1884. **b.** With Blites d. my Corn DRYDEN. **4.** To d. Priam's innocent people BOWEN. **5.** And thou destroyest the hope of man *Job* 14:19. To d. a contingent remainder CRUISE. Hence **Destroy·able** *a.* **Destroy·ingly** *adv.*

Destroyer (dĭstroi·əɹ). late ME. [f. prec. + -ER¹.] One who or that which destroys. **b.** abbrev. of TORPEDO-BOAT *destroyer* 1893.

Destructible (dĭstrɒ·ktib'l), *a.* 1755. [– Fr. *destructible* or late L. *destructibilis*, f. as next; see -IBLE.] Capable of being destroyed; liable to be destroyed. Hence **Destructibi·lity, Destru·ctibleness,** d. quality.

Destruction (dĭstrɒ·kʃən). ME. [– (O)Fr. *destruction* – L. *destructio*, f. *destruct-*, pa. ppl. stem of *destruere*; see DESTROY, -ION.] **1.** The action of destroying (see the vb.); demolition; devastation; havoc; slaughter. Often *personified.* **2.** The fact or condition of being destroyed; ruin ME. **3.** A cause or means of destruction 1526.

1. The dystrucyon of Jerusalem 1520. The d. of clouds 1813, of beasts of prey 1894. D. and death say, We have heard the fame thereof with our ears *Job* 27:22. **2.** In horrible d. thus laid low MILT. **3.** The d. of the poore is their pouertie *Prov.* 10:15.

Destructionist (dĭstrɒ·kʃənist). 1807. [f. prec. + -IST.] **1.** A partisan of a policy of destruction, *esp.* of an existing political system or constitution. (Chiefly dyslogistic.) 1841. **2.** *Theol.* One who believes in the final annihilation of the wicked; an annihilationist.

Destructive (dĭstrɒ·ktiv). 1490. [– (O)Fr. *destructif, -ive* – late L. *destructivus*, f. as DESTRUCTION; see -IVE.]

A. *adj.* Having the quality of destroying; tending to destroy; pernicious, deadly, annihilative. Const. *to, of.* (In political and philosophical use opp. to *constructive* and *conservative.*) **b.** *Logic.* Applied to conjunctive syllogisms and dilemmas, in which the conclusion negatives a hypothesis in one of the premisses.

D. distillation; see DISTILLATION.

B. *sb.* **1.** A destructive agent, instrument, or force; a destructive proposition or syllogism 1640. **2.** A destructionist. (Chiefly dyslogistic.) 1832. Hence **Destru·ctively** *adv.* **Destru·ctiveness,** tendency to destroy; in *Phren.* a propensity having a bump allotted to it.

Destructor (dĭstrɒ·ktəɹ). 1691. [f. as prec. + -OR 2.] **1.** A destroyer. **2.** A furnace for the burning of refuse 1881.

†**Destru·ctory,** *a.* and *sb.* 1614. [As adj., app. f. as prec. + -ORY²; as sb. – med.L. *destructorium* refutation.] = DESTRUCTIVE –1644.

Desubstantiate (dĭ,sɒbstæ·nʃi,eⁱt), *v.* 1884. [DE- II.1; see SUBSTANTIATE.] To deprive of substance.

Desudation (dĭsiudēⁱ·ʃən). 1727. [– late L. *desudatio*, f. *desudat-*, pa. ppl. stem of L. *desudare* sweat greatly (cf. *sudatio* heavy sweat); see -ION.] *Med.* A profuse and inordinate sweating.

Desuetude (de·swĭtiud). 1623. [– Fr. *désuétude* or its source, L. *desuetudo*, f. *desuet-*, pa. ppl. stem of *desuescere* disuse, become unaccustomed, f. *de-* DE- I. 6 + *suescere* be wont.] †**1.** A discontinuance of the use or practice (*of*); disuse; †cessation *from* –1706. **2.** The state of disuse 1637.

1. By a d. and neglect of it BOYLE. **2.** Rights which had .. passed into d. GREEN.

Desulphur (disɒ·lfəɹ), *v.* 1874. [DE- II. 2.] To free from sulphur. So **Desu·lphurate** *v.* (in same sense); **Desulphura·tion. Desu·lphurize** *v.*; **Desulphuriza·tion.**

Desulphuret (disɒ·lfiŭret), *v.* 1878. [DE- II. 2.] To deprive of sulphurets or sulphides.

Desultory (de·sɒltəri), *a.* 1581. [– L. *desultorius* pertaining to a vaulter, superficial, f. *desultor*, f. *desult-*, pa. ppl. stem of *desilire* leap down, f. *de-* DE- I. 1 + *salire* leap; see -ORY².] **1.** Skipping about, jumping from one thing to another; devious; wavering (*lit.* and *fig.*). **2.** Unmethodical 1740; random 1704; motley (*rare*) 1842.

1. I shot at it but it was so d. that I missed my aim G. WHITE. **2.** This makes my reading wild and d. WARBURTON. Some d. project HAZLITT. var. **Desulto·rious** *a.* (in sense 1). Hence **De·sultori-ly** *adv.*, **-ness.**

†**Desu·me,** *v.* 1564. [– L. *desumere* pick out, f. *de-* DE- I. 2 + *sumere* take.] To take (*from* some source); to borrow –1697.

Desynonymize (dĭ,sinǫ·nimaiz), *v.* 1817. [f. DE- II. 2 + SYNONYM + -IZE.] **1.** *trans.* To differentiate words previously synonymous; to free from synonyms. **2.** *intr.* To cease to be synonymous 1862. Hence **Desyno:nymiza·tion,** the process of desynonymizing.

Detach (dĭtæ·tʃ), *v.* 1684. [– Fr. *détacher*, earlier †*destacher*, f. *des-, dis-* DIS- I. 1 + stem of *attacher* ATTACH.] **1.** *trans.* To unfasten and separate; to disengage, disunite (*lit.* and *fig.*) 1686. **2.** *Mil.* and *Naval.* To separate and dispatch on special service. Also *transf.* 1684. **3.** *intr.* (for *refl.*) To disengage and separate oneself 1842.

1. [It] only tends..to d. me from the restlessness of human pursuits LAMB. **2.** During this the front line detaches skirmishers 1796. **3.** Detaching, fold by fold, From those still heights, and slowly drawing near TENNYSON. Hence **Detachabi·lity. Deta·chable** *a.* capable of being detached. **Deta·ched** *ppl. a.* separated; unattached, standing apart, isolated. **Deta·chedly** *adv.*

Detachment (dĭtæ·tʃmĕnt). 1669. [– Fr. *détachement*, f. *détacher*; see prec., -MENT.] **1.** The action of detaching (see DETACH *v.*). **2.** *concr.* That which is detached; *esp.* a portion of an army or navy taken from the main body and employed on some special service 1678. **3.** A standing aloof from objects or circumstances 1798.

1. They confirm the d. of the dauphine with 25,000 men to the Rhine 1693. **2.** A. D. of Actors from Drury Lane CIBBER. **3.** The d. of a saint J. H. NEWMAN. The d. of the United States from the affairs of the Old World BRYCE.

Detail (dĭ·teⁱl, dĭtēⁱ·l), *sb.* 1603. [– Fr. *détail*, f. *détailler*, f. *dé-* DE- I. 3 + *tailler* cut in pieces.] **1.** The dealing with matters item by item. **2.** A minute account; a detailed narrative or description of particulars 1695. **3.** An item, a particular; a minute or subordinate portion of any whole 1786. Also as *collective sing.* **4.** *Mil.* **a.** The distribution in detail of the Daily Orders first given in general; hence, the list or table showing the general or particular distribution of duty (*general* or *particular d.*) for the whole force or for any part of it 1703. **b.** The detailing or telling off a small party for a special duty; *concr.* the small body thus detailed 1708.

1. *In d.*, item by item; part by part, circumstantially. He [Brian Boru] defeated his enemies in d. 1887. **3.** The whole d. of private life MILL. The d. of a single weedy bank laughs the carving of ages to scorn RUSKIN. The d. is otherwise denominated the *working drawings* P. NICHOLSON. **4.** Details had gone to the front after the wounded 1885.

Detail (as prec.), *v.* 1637. [– Fr. *détailler*; see prec.] **1.** *trans.* To deal with, relate, or describe minutely or circumstantially; to give particulars of; to enumerate, mention, or relate in detail. Also *absol.* **2.** *Mil.* To appoint or tell off for a particular duty 1793. Also *transf.*

1. Certain peculiarities to be detailed hereafter SCRIVENER. Hence **Detailed** *ppl. a.* stated circumstantially; abounding in details; minute, circumstantial. **Detailer.**

Detain (dĭtēⁱ·n), *v.* [Late ME. *deteine* – *detein-*, tonic stem of (O)Fr. *détenir* :– Rom. **detenēre*, for L. *detinēre*, f. *de-* DE- I. 2 + *tenēre* hold.] **1.** *trans.* To keep in confinement or custody 1485. **2.** To keep back, withhold. ? *Obs.* 1535. †**3.** To keep, retain –1774; to hold, hold down –1780. **4.** To keep from proceeding; to keep waiting; to stop. (The ordinary current sense.) 1592.

2. To d. servants wages 1535. **3.** To d. one's eyes too long upon the same object GOLDSM. **4.** The business which then detained him PALEY. Hence †**Detai·n** *sb.* detention. **Detai·nable** *a.* **Detai·nal,** detention (*rare*). **Detai·nment** (now *rare*).

Detainer¹ (dĭtēⁱ·nəɹ). 1531. [f. prec. vb. + -ER¹.] One who or that which DETAINS.

Detai·ner². 1619. [– AFr. *detener*, inf. used subst., = (O)Fr. *détenir*; see DETAIN, -ER⁴.] *Law.* The action of detaining, withholding, or keeping in one's possession; *spec.* **a.** The (wrongful) detaining of goods taken from the owner for distraint, etc. 1619. **b.** The detaining of a person; *esp.* in custody or confinement 1640. **c.** A process authorizing the sheriff to detain a person already in his custody 1836.

Phr. *Forcible d.*; the 'violently taking or keeping possession, with menaces, force, and arms, of lands and tenements, without the authority of law' (Blackstone).

Deta·nt, var. of DETENT, q.v.

Detect (dĭte·kt), *ppl.a. arch.* ME. [– L. *detectus*, pa. pple. of *detegere*; see next.] Detected; disclosed; open.

Detect (dĭte·kt), *v. pa. pple.* †**Dete·ct, Detected.** 1447. [– *detect-*, pa. ppl. stem of L. *detegere*, f. *de-* DE- I. 6 + *tegere* to cover.] †**1.** *trans.* To uncover, lay bare, expose, display –1739. †**2.** To expose (a person); to inform against, accuse –1645. **3.** To find out, discover (a person) being or doing something 1581. **4.** To discover the presence, existence, or fact of (something apt to elude notice) 1756. **5.** *Wireless.* To rectify, as in a detector.

1. Secret Confession, wherein Men do d. their sins in the Priests ear FOXE. **2.** *Meas. for M.* III. ii. 129. **3.** To d. a baker in selling short weight BENTHAM. **4.** We d. all the shades of meaning GODWIN. Hence **Dete·ctable, -ible** *a.*

Detection (dǐte·kʃən). 1471. [– late L. *detectio*, f. as prec.; see -ION.] †**1.** Exposure, revelation of what is concealed; accusation –1807. **2.** Discovery (of what is unknown or hidden) 1619.

2. It is easy for the author of a lie, however malignant, to escape d. JOHNSON.

Detective (dǐte·ktiv). 1843. [f. DETECT *v.* + -IVE, after *elect, elective*, etc.]

A. *adj.* Serving to detect; employed for the purpose of detection; as the *d. police.*

B. *sb.* One whose occupation it is to discover matters artfully concealed; particularly (and as short for *d. policeman*, or the like) a member of the police force employed to investigate specific cases, etc. 1856.

Detector (dǐte·ktəɹ). Also **-er.** 1541. [f. DETECT *v.* + -ER[1], -OR 2. Cf. late L. *detector.*] He who, or that which, detects; *esp.* an instrument or device for detecting anything liable to escape observation, abnormal, or the like; as, an arrangement in a lock by which any attempt to tamper with it is indicated; a low-water indicator for a boiler; a coherer.

†**Dete·nebrate,** *v.* 1646. [f. DE- II. 1 + L. *tenebræ* darkness, *tenebrare* darken; see -ATE[3].] To free from darkness –1656.

Detent (dǐte·nt). 1688. [– Fr. *détente*, OFr. *destente*, f. *destendre* (mod. *détendre*) slacken, f. *des-* DIS- (privative) + *tendre* stretch. In Eng. assoc. with L. *detinēre, detent-* DETAIN.] A stop or catch in a machine which checks or prevents motion, and the removal of which brings some motor at once into action; as, in guns, an oscillating tongue to carry the sear over the half-cock; in clocks and watches, the catch which regulates the striking; etc.

‖**Détente** (detãnt). 1908. [Fr., 'loosening, relaxation'.] The easing of strained relations.

Detention (dǐte·nʃən). 1552. [– Fr. *détention* or late L. *detentio*, f. *detent-*, pa. ppl. stem of L. *detinēre*; see DETAIN *v.*, -ION.] **1.** Keeping in custody or confinement; arrest 1570. **2.** The keeping back of what is due or claimed 1552. **3.** Holding in one's possession or control; retention. ? *Obs.* exc. in *Law.* 1626. **4.** A keeping from going on or proceeding 1600.

1. Her [Q. Mary's] d. under safe custody 1570. **3.** The depositary has mere d., the depositor has possession 1875. Phr. *House of d.*: a lock-up.

‖**Détenu** (detənü). 1803. [Fr.; pa. pple. of *détenir* used subst.] A person detained in custody; *spec.* a political prisoner in India.

He was a *d.* for eleven years at Verdun 1815.

Deter (dǐtɔ̄·ɹ), *v.* 1579. [– L. *deterrēre*, f. *de-* DE- I. 2 + *terrēre* frighten.] **1.** *trans.* To restrain *from* acting or proceeding by any consideration of danger or trouble. †**2.** To terrify –1634.

1. That degree of severity which is sufficient to d. others 1766. When my own Face deters me from my Glass PRIOR. Hence **Dete·rment,** the action or fact of deterring; a deterring circumstance.

Deterge (dǐtɔ̄·ɹdʒ), *v.* 1623. [– Fr. *déterger* (Paré) or L. *detergēre*, f. *de-* DE- I. 2 + *tergēre* wipe.] To wash off or out; chiefly *Med.*, to clear away foul or offensive matter from the body, from an ulcer, etc.

Detergent (dǐtɔ̄·ɹdʒěnt). 1616. [– *detergent-*, pres. ppl. stem of L. *detergēre*; see prec., -ENT. Cf. Fr. *détergent.*]

A. *adj.* Cleansing, purging.

B. *sb.* Anything that cleanses 1676. Hence **Dete·rgency,** d. quality.

Deteriorate (dǐtīᵊ·riŏreⁱt), *v.* 1572. [– *deteriorat-*, pa. ppl. stem of late L. *deteriorare*, f. *deterior* worse; see -ATE[3].] **1.** *trans.* To make worse; to lower in quality or value; to worsen. **2.** *intr.* To become worse; to become impaired in quality or value; to degenerate 1758.

1. Not onely not bettered, but much deteriorated O. WALKER. To d. the value of property 1847. **2.** Under such conditions the mind rapidly deteriorates GOLDSM. Hence **Dete·riorative** *a.* causing or tending to deterioration. **Dete·riorator.**

Deterioration (dǐtīᵊ:riŏrēⁱ·ʃən). 1658. [– Fr. *détérioration* – late L. *deterioratio*, f. as prec.; see -ION.] The process of growing or making worse; a deteriorated condition. Hence **Deteriora·tionist,** one who holds d., not progress, to be the order of things.

Deterio·rity. *rare.* 1692. [f. L. *deterior* worse + -ITY, after *inferiority.*] Poorer or lower quality; worseness.

†**Dete·rm,** *v.* ME. By-form of DETERMINE *v.* –1647.

Determinable (dǐtɔ̄·ɹminăb'l), *a.* [In ME. – OFr. *determinable* fixed, determinate – late L. *determinabilis* (Tertullian) finite; in mod. use, f. DETERMINE + -ABLE.] †**1.** Fixed, definite –1646. **2.** Capable of being determined, authoritatively decided, definitely limited, or definitely ascertained 1485. **3.** Liable to come to an end; terminable (*esp.* in *Law*) 1584.

2. Matters d. by your common law 1845. Relations..not d. with Certainty and Precision HARTLEY. **3.** In Lease for 99 years, d. on one, two, or three Lives 1707. Hence **Determinabi·lity,** d. quality. **Dete·rminably** *adv.*

Dete·rminacy. *rare.* 1873. [f. DETERMINATE *a.*; see -ACY.] Determinateness.

Determinant (dǐtɔ̄·ɹminănt). 1610. [– *determinant-*, pres. ppl. stem of L. *determinare*; see DETERMINE, -ANT[1]; as sb. (*Math.*), tr. mod.L. *determinans* (Gauss, 1802), whence Fr. *déterminant* (Cauchy).]

A. *adj.* Determining; that determines; determinative.

B. *sb.* One who or that which determines. **1.** In *University Hist.* (repr. med.L. *determinans*). A determining Bachelor; see DETERMINATION 3. 1864. **2.** A determining factor or agent 1686. **3.** *Math.* The sum of the products of a square block or matrix of quantities, each product containing one factor from each row and column, and having the plus or minus sign according to the arrangement of its factors in the block 1843.

A determinant is commonly denoted by writing the matrix with a vertical line on each side, thus— $\begin{vmatrix} a_1 & a_2 & a_3 \\ b_1 & b_2 & b_3 \\ c_1 & c_2 & c_3 \end{vmatrix}$

Hence **Determina·ntal** *a. Math.*, relating to determinants.

Determinate (dǐtɔ̄·ɹminět), *ppl. a.* ME. [– L. *determinatus*, pa. pple. of *determinare*; see DETERMINE, -ATE[2].]

A. as *pa. pple.* = DETERMINED. *Obs.* or *arch.*

My bonds in thee are all d. SHAKS.

B. *adj.* **1.** Definitely limited; definite, fixed; clearly defined; distinct ME. **b.** *Math.* Having a fixed value or magnitude 1722. **c.** *Bot.* Of inflorescence: Definite, centrifugal 1880. **2.** Settled, fixed, so as not to vary 1526. **3.** Finally determined upon; definitive 1533. **4.** Intended 1586. **5.** Fixed in mind or purpose, determined, resolute 1587.

1. The clear and d. meaning of my words BERKELEY. **b.** *D. problem*, is that which has but one, or at least but a certain number of solutions E. CHAMBERS. A *d. number* is that referred to some given unit; as a ternary, or three *Ibid.* **2.** A d. form of praiyng 1559. **3.** No d. reply could be given to the letter WELLINGTON. **4.** Men of d. minds and courage 1598. Hence **Dete·rminate-ly** *adv.*, **-ness.**

†**Dete·rminate,** *v.* 1563. [– *determinat-*, pa. ppl. stem of L. *determinare*; see DETERMINE, -ATE[3].] *trans.* To determine; to end –1788. Also *intr.*

Determination (dǐtɔ̄:ɹminēⁱ·ʃən). ME. [– (O)Fr. *détermination* – L. *determinatio*, f. as prec.; see -ION.] **1.** A bringing, or coming, to an end; ending; termination; *esp.* in *Law*, the cessation of an estate or interest of any kind 1483. **2.** Judicial or authoritative decision or settlement ME. **3.** The resolving of a question or maintaining of a thesis in a scholastic disputation; *spec.* in University history, the name of certain disputations which complete the taking of the degree of B.A. *Obs.* exc. *Hist.* 1665. **4.** The determining of bounds; delimitation; definition 1594; in *Logic*, the rendering of a notion more definite by the addition of attributes; also, a determining attribute 1644. **5.** The action of definitely ascertaining the position, nature, amount, etc. (*of* anything) 1677; the result of this 1570. **6.** Decisive or determining bias (*lit.* and *fig.*) 1660; *spec.* a tendency or flow of the blood, etc., to a particular part 1737. **7.** *Metaph.* The definite direction of the mind or will towards an object or end, by some motive 1685. **8.** The mental action of coming to a decision; the result of this; a fixed intention 1548. **9.** Determinedness, resoluteness 1822.

1. The d. of an estate tail CRUISE. **4.** The d. of the parties who are admissible 1866. **5.** On the D. of the Orbits of Comets 1793. Astronomical determinations 1857. **6.** Heavy bodies have a d. towards the centre of the earth E. CHAMBERS. **7.** Dr. Hutcheson, considering all the principles of action as so many determinations or motions of the will REID. **9.** Never was..operation executed with greater..d. 1853.

Determinative (dǐtɔ̄·ɹminětiv). 1655. [– Fr. *déterminatif, -ive* or late L. *determinativus*, f. as prec.; see -IVE.]

A. *adj.* **1.** Serving or tending to determine, decide, or fix. **2.** Serving to limit or fix the extent, specific kind, or character of anything: said of attributes or marks 1697.

1. D. of the character of life HOLLAND. **2.** The term..is d. and limits the subject to a particular part of its extension WATTS.

B. *sb.* **1.** A determinative agent 1832. **2.** That which serves to define the character or quality of something else; *e.g.* in *hieroglyphic writing*, an ideographic sign annexed to a word phonetically represented; in *Gram.*, a demonstrative word 1862.

1. A restraint or d. from wrong 1832.

Hence **Dete·rminatively** *adv.* so as to determine; †determinately. **Dete·rminateness.**

Determinator (dǐtɔ̄·ɹmineⁱtəɹ). 1556. [– late L. *determinator*, f. as prec.; see -OR 2.] He who or that which DETERMINES (see the vb.); a determiner.

Determine (dǐtɔ̄·ɹmin), *v.* ME. [– (O)Fr. *déterminer* – L. *determinare* bound, limit, fix, f. *de-* DE- I. 3 + *terminare* TERMINATE.]

I. 1. *trans.* To put an end to; to end. (Now chiefly in *Law.*) 1483. **2.** *intr.* (for *refl.*) To come to an end; to expire ME.; to end *in* (*arch.*) 1605. **3.** *trans.* †To set bounds to, limit –1732; in *Logic*, to limit by adding differences 1838; †to limit *to* –1691.

1. To d. an estate 1845. **2.** The head..determines in a snout 1767. **3.** It determines his power CROMWELL.

II. 1. *trans.* To settle or decide ME. **2.** *intr.* To come to a judicial decision; to decide. †Const. *of* (*on*). ME. †**3.** To lay down decisively or authoritatively –1486. †**4.** To fix beforehand; to ordain, decree –1758. **5.** *trans.* To fix or decide causally 1651. **6.** To decide upon (one of several) 1659. †**7.** To conclude from reasoning, investigation, etc. –1814. **8.** *trans.* To ascertain definitely; to fix as known 1650. **9.** *Geom.* (*trans.*) To define the position of 1840. **10.** To resolve a question (*determinare quæstionem*), or maintain a thesis, *esp.* in a disputation by which a student entered upon the degree of B.A.; hence, *absolutely*, to perform the exercises of DETERMINATION (sense 3). *Obs.* exc. *Hist.* 1570.

1. Let the lawes of Rome d. all. *Tit. A.* I. i. 407. **4.** For evil is determined against our master 1 *Sam.* 25:17. **5.** Not the seller, but the buyer, determines prices HOBBES. **6.** To d. the first passengers by lot 1771. **8.** To d. the velocity of a Glacier TYNDALL.

III. 1. *trans.* To give a terminus or aim to; to direct; to impel *to* ME. Also *fig.* **2.** *intr.* To take its course, go, tend *to* (*arch.*) 1651. **3.** *trans.* To bring to the determination or resolution (*to do* something) 1672. †Also *refl.* [= Fr. *se déterminer.*] –1701. **4.** *intr.* (for *refl.*) To resolve definitely (*to do* something) 1450.

1. Accidental impulses d. us to different paths JOHNSON. **2.** They all d. and concentre there SANDERSON. **3.** These reflections determined me MRS. SHELLEY. **4.** Phr. *To be determined*: to be finally and firmly resolved.

Hence **Dete·rmined** *ppl. a.* (in various senses of the vb.); resolute; not to be moved from one's purpose; of actions, etc., showing determination. **Dete·rmined-ly** *adv.*, **-ness.**

Determiner[1] (dǐtɔ̄·ɹminəɹ). 1530. [f. prec. + -ER[1].] **1.** He who or that which determines, in various senses. **2.** = DETERMINANT B. 1. *Obs.* exc. *Hist.* 1574.

Determiner[2]. 1450. [AFr. *determiner* inf. used subst.; see -ER[4].] *Law.* The final determining of a judge or court of justice; in *oyer and d.*, a var. of *terminer*. *Obs.* exc. *Hist.*

Determinism (dĭtɔ̄·ɹminiz'm). 1846. [f. DETERMINE *v.* + -ISM. Cf. Fr. *déterminisme.*] **1.** The doctrine that human action is not free but necessarily determined by motives. **2.** *gen.* The doctrine that everything that happens is determined by a necessary chain of causation 1876. So **Dete·rminist** *sb.* one who holds the doctrine of d.; *a.* of or pertaining to d. **Determini·stic** *a.* of or pertaining to d. or determinists.

†**Deterra·tion.** 1686. [f. L. *de-* DE- I. 1 + *terra* earth + -ATION.] The carrying down of the surface of the earth from hills and higher grounds into the valleys, by rain, land-slips, etc.; cf. DEGRADATION[1] 6. –1704.

Deterrence (dĭte·rĕns). 1861. [f. next; see -ENCE.] Preventing by fear.

Deterrent (dĭte·rĕnt). 1829. [– *deterrent-*, pres. ppl. stem of L. *deterrēre*; see DETER, -ENT.]

A. *adj.* Deterring; serving or tending to deter, as *d. weather*.

B. *sb.* Something that deters 1829.

Detersion (dĭtɔ̄·ɹʃən). 1607. [– late L. *detersio*, f. *deters-*, pa. ppl. stem of *detergere*; see DETERGE, -ION.] The action of cleansing (a sore, etc.).

Detersive (dĭtɔ̄·ɹsiv). 1586. [– Fr. *détersif*, *-ive*, f. as prec.; see -IVE.]

A. *adj.* **1.** Cleansing; tending to cleanse 1601. **2.** *Med.* and *Surg.* Detergent 1586.

B. *sb.* A cleansing agent; a detergent 1634. Hence **Dete·rsive-ly** *adv.*, **-ness.**

Detest (dĭte·st), *v.* 1533. [– L. *detestari* denounce, renounce, f. *de-* DE- I. 4 + *testari* bear witness, call to witness, f. *testis* witness; perh. partly back-formation from DETESTATION.] †**1.** *trans.* To curse, calling God to witness; to denounce, execrate –1745. **2.** To hate or dislike intensely; to abhor, abominate 1535. ¶Misused for *attest*, *protest*, *testify*.

1. All posteritie shall..with execrations d. thy fact 1632. **2.** A fashion shee detests *Twel. N.* II. v. 220. The Justice of the Land detesteth that the Judge should himself be an Accuser FULLER. var. †**Dete·state** *v.* (*rare*). Hence **Dete·ster.**

Detestable (dĭte·stăb'l), *a.* 1461. [– (O)Fr. *détestable* or L. *detestabilis*; see prec., -ABLE.] **1.** To be detested; intensely hateful; execrable, abominable. **2.** quasi *adv.* Detestably 1610.

1. That d. sight SPENSER *F. Q.* I. i. 26. The d. ornamentation of the Alhambra RUSKIN. Hence **Dete·stableness,** d. quality. **Dete·stably** *adv.*

Detestation (dĭtestē̆·ʃən). ME. [– (O)Fr. *détestation* – L. *detestatio*, f. *detestat-*, pa. ppl. stem of *detestari*; see DETEST, -ION.] †**1.** Public execration (of a thing) –1683. **2.** The mental state of detesting; intense dislike or hatred; abhorrence 1526. **3.** *concr.* That which is detested 1728.

2. His d. of priests and lawyers JOWETT. **3.** Thou art grown the d. of all thy party SWIFT.

Dethrone (dĭþrōᵘ·n), *v.* 1609. [f. DE- II. 2 + THRONE *sb.*] To remove from the throne; to depose. Also *transf.* and *fig.*

Authoritie to de-Throan and de-Crowne Princes 1609. Love, by dethroning Reason..doth kill the Man BOYLE. Hence **Dethro·nement,** deposition from kingly authority. **Dethro·ner.** var. †**Dethroni·ze;** whence †**Dethroniza·tion,** dethronement.

Detinue (de·tiniū). 1563. [– OFr. *detenue*, subst. use of fem. pa. pple. of *detenir* DETAIN with assimilation to L. *detinēre*.] *Law.* The act of detaining (see DETAIN *v.* 2); *spec.* unlawful detention of a personal chattel belonging to another. *Obs.* exc. in *action*, etc., *of d.*

Action of d.: an action at law to recover a personal chattel (or its value) wrongfully detained by the defendant. So *writ of d.* Also *d.* = action or writ of d.

Detonate (de·tŏnē̆ⁱt, dī-), *v.* 1729. [– *detonat-*, pa. ppl. stem of L. *detonare*, f. *de-* DE- I. 3 + *tonare* to thunder; see -ATE[3]. Partly back-formation from DETONATION.] **1.** *intr.* To explode with sudden loud report; cf. DETONATION. Also *fig.* **2.** *trans.* To cause to explode with sudden loud report 1801.

1. Saltpeter..detonates, or makes a noise in the fire 1729. Hence **De·tonative** *a.* having the property of detonating. **De·tonator,** that which detonates, as a percussion-cap; a railway fog-signal. var. †**De·tonize** *v.*; whence, †**Detoniza·tion.**

Detonating (de·tŏneⁱtiŋ), *ppl. a.* 1808. [f. prec. + -ING[2].] That detonates. **a.** Explosive, as *d. gas*; **b.** That is used in producing detonation, as *d. primer, tube*; **c.** *esp.* That explodes, or is used in explosion, by percussion, as *d. hammer, powder*.

D. bulb, the small glass bulb also called *Prince Rupert's drop*, which flies to pieces on a slight scratch.

Detonation (detŏnē̆ⁱ·ʃən, dī). 1677. [– Fr. *détonation*, f. *détoner* – L. *detonare* DETONATE; see -ION.] The action of detonating. **1.** The noise produced by the sudden liberation of gas in connection with chemical decomposition or combination; hence, explosion accompanied with a sudden loud report. **2.** *gen.* A loud noise as of thunder; also, the action of causing a substance to detonate 1727. Also *fig.*

2. The great Crater..testified by its loud detonations [etc.] LYELL.

†**Detort** (dĭtǭ·ɹt), *v.* 1550. [– *detort-*, pa. ppl. stem of L. *detorquere*, f. *de-* DE- I. 2 + *torquere* twist.] **1.** *trans.* To turn aside from the purpose; to twist, wrest, pervert. (Freq. in 17th c.) 1555. **2.** To derive by perversion 1605. Hence **Deto·rtion, -sion** (? *Obs.*), the action of detorting; distortion.

Detour, ‖**détour** (dĭtūᵊ·ɹ, ‖detūr). 1738. [– Fr. *détour* change of direction, f. *détourner* turn away.] A deviation from the direct road; a roundabout way, course, or proceeding. Now usu. *lit.*

To avoid these ruts we make long detours W. BLACK.

Detract (dĭtræ·kt), *v.* 1449. [– *detract-*, pa. ppl. stem of L. *detrahere* draw off, take away, disparage, f. *de-* DE- I. 2 + *trahere* draw.]

I. 1. *trans.* To take away, withdraw 1509. **2.** *absol.* or *intr.* To take away a portion. Usu. *to d. from.* 1592. **3.** *trans.* To take reputation from; to disparage, belittle, traduce. Now *rare.* 1449. Also †*absol.*

1. That first great grief which..detracts something from the buoyancy of the youngest life DISRAELI. **3.** To..d. his greatest actions B. JONS.

II. †**1.** *trans.* To draw away (*from* an action, etc.); *refl.* and *intr.* To withdraw –1802. †**2.** To draw out, protract –1641; *absol.* or *intr.* To delay –1592.

III. = DETRECT. †*trans.* To draw back from, decline; to give up –1606.

Hence †**Detracta·tion** (*rare*) = DETRACTION 2. **Detra·cter** = DETRACTOR. **Detra·ctingly** *adv.*

Detraction (dĭtræ·kʃən). ME. [– (O)Fr. *détraction* – L. *detractio*, f. as prec.; see -ION.] **1.** †A taking away, deduction, withdrawal –1817; a detracting *from* (merit, etc.) 1633. **2.** The action of detracting from a person's merit or reputation; the utterance of what is injurious to his reputation; depreciation, defamation, calumny, slander. (The prevalent sense.) ME. †**3.** Protraction (*of time*) –1637.

1. Let it be no d. from the merits of Miss Tox DICKENS. **2.** Enuies abhorred childe, D. 1599. Hence †**Detra·ctious** *a.* given to d.

Detractive (dĭtræ·ktiv), *a.* 1490. [– OFr. *detractif*, *-ive* or med.L. *detractivus*, f. as prec.; see -IVE.] **1.** Conveying, of the nature of, or given to, detraction. **2.** Tending to detract *from* 1654. Hence **Detra·ctiveness.**

Detractor (dĭtræ·ktəɹ). Also **-ter.** ME. [– AFr. *detractour*, (O)Fr. *détracteur* or L. *detractor* slanderer, f. as prec.; see -OR 2.] **1.** One who detracts; a defamer, traducer, calumniator. ‖**2.** *Anat.* A DEPRESSOR muscle. ? *Obs.* 1811.

1. Every fashion has its detractors DORAN. So **Detra·ctory** *a.* = DETRACTIVE 1. Hence **Detra·ctress,** a female d.

Detrain (dĭtrē̆ⁱ·n), *v.* 1881. [f. DE- II. 2 + TRAIN *sb.*[1] 8; cf. ENTRAIN *v.*[2]] To alight or discharge from a railway train. Hence **Detrai·nment.**

†**Detray·**, *v.* 1509. [– OFr. *detrai-*, pres. stem of *detraire* :– L. *detrahere*; see DETRACT.] = DETRACT *v.* 1, 2. –1520.

†**Detre·ct**, *v.* 1542. [– L. *detrectare* decline, detract from, frequent. of *detrahere*; see prec.] = DETRACT *v.* I.3., III. –1630. Hence **Detracta·tion,** declinature (*rare*).

†**Detre·nch,** *v.* ME. [– OFr. *detrenchier* cut away, cut off, f. *dé-* DE- I. 2 + *trenchier* cut; see TRENCH *v.*] To cut through –1500; to cut up –1489; *fig.* to retrench 1654.

Detriment (de·trimĕnt), *sb.* ME. [– (O)Fr. *détriment* or L. *detrimentum*, f. pret. stem *detrī-* of *deterere* wear away, f. *de-* DE- I. 2 + *terere* rub; see -MENT.] **1.** Loss or damage done to, or sustained by, any person or thing; that which causes a loss 1504. **2.** *Astrol.* The position or condition of a planet when in the sign opposite its house; a condition of weakness 1632. **3.** *Her.* Eclipse (of sun or moon) 1610. **4.** *pl.* Certain small charges made by colleges and similar societies upon their members 1670.

1. To the great D. of our own natural Subjects 1529. Hence **De·triment** *v.* to cause loss or damage to.

Detrimental (detrime·ntăl). 1656. [f. prec. sb. + -AL[1].]

A. *adj.* Causing loss or damage; prejudicial.

B. *sb.* A person or thing that is prejudicial; in *Society slang*, a younger brother of the heir of an estate; an ineligible suitor 1831. Hence **Detrime·ntally** *adv.*

Detrital (dĭtrəi·tăl), *a.* 1832. [f. DETRITUS + -AL[1].] *Physiog.* Of or pertaining to detritus.

Detrited (dĭtrəi·tĕd), *ppl. a.* 1697. [– L. *detritus* DETRITUS + -ED[1].] **1.** Worn down. **2.** *Geol.* Formed as detritus 1853.

Detrition (dĭtri·ʃən). 1674. [– med.L. *detritio* 'detrimentum' (Du Cange), f. *detrī-*; see next, -TION.] The action of wearing away by rubbing.

D. has made it as smooth as the shingle pebbles on our shores 1890.

Detritus (dĭtrəi·tŏs). 1795. [– L. *detritus* rubbing away, f. *detrī-*; see DETRIMENT. In sense 2, after Fr. *détritus* (which superseded the more correct *détritum*).] †**1.** Wearing away or down by detrition –1802. **2.** Matter produced by the detrition of exposed surfaces, *esp.* material eroded and washed away by aqueous agency; a mass of this nature 1802. Also *transf.* and *fig.*

1. The effects of waste and *d.* PLAYFAIR. **2.** The quantity of d. brought down by the rivers PLAYFAIR. *fig.* The loose d. of thought, washed down to us through long ages 1849.

Detrude (dĭtrū·d), *v.* 1548. [– L. *detrudere* thrust away or down, f. *de-* DE- I. 1, 2 + *trudere* thrust.] **1.** *trans.* To thrust or force down (*lit.* and *fig.*). **2.** To thrust out or away (*lit.* and *fig.*) 1555. Hence **Detru·sion,** the action of detruding (*lit.* and *fig.*)

Detruncate (dĭtrɒ·ŋkeⁱt), *v.* 1623. [– *detruncat-*, pa. ppl. stem of *detruncare* lop off; see DE- I. 2, TRUNCATE *v.*] *trans.* To shorten by lopping off a part (*lit.* and *fig.*); to cut short. Hence **Detrunca·ted** *ppl. a.* = TRUNCATED. **Detrunca·tion,** the action of cutting off or cutting short; the being cut short (*lit.* and *fig.*).

Detrusor (dĭtrū·səɹ). 1766. [mod.L., f. *detrus-*, pa. ppl. stem of L. *detrudere* DETRUDE; see -OR 2.] *Anat.* A name for the muscular coat of the bladder, by the contraction of which the urine is expelled.

†**Detruss** (dĭtrɒ·s), *v.* 1475. [– Fr. *détrousser*, OFr. *des-* despoil, f. *dé-*, *des-* DE- I. 6 + *trousse(s)* baggage; see TRUSS *sb.*] To spoil, plunder (of baggage) –1598.

Dette, etc., obs. ff. DEBT, etc.

Detumescence (dĭtiume·sĕns). 1678. [f. L. *detumescere*, f. *de-* DE- I. 6 + *tumescere* swell; see -ENCE.] Subsidence from swelling, or (*fig.*) from tumult.

Detur (dī·tɒ̆ɹ). 1836. [L. = 'let there be given'.] A prize of books given annually at Harvard College, U.S., to meritorious students: so called from the first word of the accompanying Latin inscription.

†**Detu·rb,** *v.* 1609. [– L. *deturbare* thrust down, f. *de-* DE- I. 1 + *turbare* disturb, disorder.] To drive down; to thrust out –1657. var. †**Detu·rbate** (*rare*).

†**Detu·rn,** *v.* 1450. [– Fr. *détourner* (OFr. *destorner*; see DISTURN), f. *dé-*, *des-* DE- I. 6 + *tourner* TURN.] *trans.* To turn away or aside –1745.

†**Detu·rpate,** *v.* 1623. [– L. *deturpat-*, pa. ppl. stem of *deturpare* make unsightly; see -ATE[3].] To make, or become, vile or base –1833. Hence †**Deturpa·tion.**

Deuce[1] (diūs). 1481. [– OFr. *deus* (mod. *deux*) :– L. *duos*. For the sp. *-ce*, for earlier *-s*, cf. *peace*, etc.] **1.** The *two* at dice or cards 1519. **2.** *Tennis*. [= It. *a due*, Fr. *à deux de jeu*.] A term denoting that the two sides have each gained three points (called 40) in a game, in which case *two* successive points must be gained in order to win the game 1598. *Comb.*: **d.-ace,** two and one (*i.e.* a throw that turns up two with one die and ace with the other); hence, a poor throw, bad luck, etc.; **d. game,** the game won, which makes the score in games level when each side has won more than five; so **d. set.**

Deuce[2] (diūs). *colloq.* or *slang*. 1651. [– LG. *duus* (in *de duus!*, *wat de duus!*) = G. *daus* (in *der daus!*, *was der daus!*), prob. to be ult. identified with prec. as a dicer's exclamation on making the lowest throw, viz. a two.] Bad luck, plague; in imprecations, etc. **b.** The spirit of mischief, the devil 1694. **c.** As an exclam. of incredulous surprise; also, as an emphatic negative 1710.

b. The very d. is in them COWPER. **c.** The d. he is! married to that vengeance SWIFT. Hence **Deuced** (diūst, diū·sėd) *a.* plaguy, confounded; devilish; often advb.; **Deu·cedly** *adv.*

†**Deusan, deuzan.** 1570. [– Fr. *deux ans* two years.] = APPLE-JOHN –1741.

Deu·tero-, bef. a vowel **deuter-,** – Gr. δευτερο-, comb. f. δεύτερος second, as in δευτεραγωνιστής one who plays second, etc. Hence, **Deuterocano·nical** *a.*, of, pertaining to, or constituting a second or secondary canon; opp. to *protocanonical*. **Deutero·gamist** [see next], one who marries a second time, or who upholds second marriages. **Deutero·gamy** [Gr. γάμος], marriage after the death of a first husband or wife. **Deuteroge·nic** *a.* [Gr. γένος], of secondary origin; in *Geol.* applied to rocks derived from the primary or protogenic rocks. **Deutero-Isaiah,** a second or later Isaiah, to whom some attribute chapters 40–46 of Isaiah. **Deuterome·sal** *a.* [Gr. μέσος] *Entom.*, applied to certain cells in the wings of hymenopterous insects, now usually called the first and third discoidal and first apical cells. **Deutero-Nicene** *a.*, belonging to the second Nicene council. **Deutero·pathy** [Gr. -πάθεια] *Med.*, a secondary affection, sympathetic with or consequent upon another; hence **Deuteropa·thic** *a.*, of or pertaining to deuteropathy. **Deutero·scopy** [Gr. -σκοπία, σκοπιά], †the second view; †an ulterior meaning; second sight (*rare*). **Deutero·stoma** [Gr. στόμα] *Biol.*, a secondary blastopore; hence **Deuterosto·matous** *a.*, having a secondary blastopore. **Deuterozo·oid** (*Biol.*), a secondary zooid produced by gemmation from a zooid.

Deutero·nomist. 1862. [f. next + -IST.] The writer of Deuteronomy, or of the parts of it which do not consist of earlier documents. Hence **Deuteronomi·stic** *a.* of the nature or style of the writer of Deuteronomy.

Deuteronomy (diūtĕrǫ·nŏmi, diū·tĕrǫnǫmi). ME. [– eccl.L. *Deuteronomium* – Gr., f. δεύτερος + νόμος. The name is taken from the words of the LXX in Deut. 17:18 τὸ δευτερονόμιον τοῦτο second law, a mistr. of the Heb., = 'a duplicate of this law'.] The fifth book of the Pentateuch, which contains a repetition, with parænetic comments, of the Decalogue, etc. Hence **Deuterono·mic, -al** *a.* of or pertaining to, or like, the book of D.

†**Deuterosy.** *rare*. 1641. [– eccl.L. *deuterosis* – Gr. δευτέρωσις repetition.] A 'tradition of the elders' among the Jews –1650.

Deuto-, bef. a vowel **deut-,** shortened f. DEUTERO-, used

1. In *Chemistry* to distinguish the second in order of the terms of any series. Thus **Deuto·xide,** that which comes next to the *protoxide*, containing the next smallest quantity of oxygen. **2.** In *Biology*; as **Deutence·phalon** [Gr. ἐγκέφαλος], the second of the three primary cerebral vesicles of the embryo. Hence **Deutencepha·lic** *a.* ‖**Deutoma·la** [L. *mala* jaw], the second pair of jaws of the Myriapoda; hence **Deutoma·lar** *a.* **Deuto·merite** [Gr. μέρος], the second or posterior cell of a dicystid gregarine, as dist. from the *protomerite*. **Deu·toplasm** [Gr. πλάσμα], Reichert's term for the food-yolk of the meroblastic egg, *e.g.* the yellow yolk of a bird's egg; hence **Deutopla·smic, -pla·stic** *a.* of, pertaining to, or like, deutoplasm; **Deu:toplasmi·genous** *a.* producing deutoplasm; **Deutopla·smogen,** that which is converted into deutoplasm. **Deutosco·lex** [Gr. σκώληξ], a daughter-cyst of a scolex or cystic worm. **Deutote·rgite** [L. *tergum*], the second dorsal segment of the abdomen of insects. **Deuto·vum** [L. *ovum*], *pl.* **-ova,** a secondary egg-cell; also called *metovum*, and after-egg.

‖**Deutzia** (diū·tsiă, doi·tsiă). 1837. [mod.L. (1781), f. name of J. *Deutz* of Amsterdam; see -IA[1].] *Bot.* A genus of shrubs (N.O. *Saxifragaceæ*), natives of China and Japan, cultivated for their white flowers.

‖**Deva** (dēⁱ·vă). 1819. [Skr., 'a god', *orig.* 'a shining one', f. **div-* shine.] A god; one of the good spirits of Hindu mythology.

Deva·lue, *v.* 1918. [DE- II. 1.] To reduce or annul the value of. So **Deva·luate** *v.* (1898), **-a·tion.**

‖**Devanagari** (dēⁱ:vă,nā·gărī). 1781. [Skr., lit. 'divine town script', f. *dēvás* god + *nāgarī* (an earlier name of the alphabet), f. *nāgaran* town.] The formal alphabet in which the Sanskrit is written. Also called *Nagari*. Used both as *adj.* and *sb.*

Devance (dĭva·ns), *v.* 1485. [– (O)Fr. *devancer*, f. *devant* before, in front, after *avant*, *avancer*. Became obs. in XVII, but was revived in XIX.] To forestall; to get ahead of; to outstrip.

†**Deva·nt, devau·nt.** ME. [– (O)Fr. *devant* prep. and adv., before, in front, f. Gallo-Rom. *de abante* from in front; see AVAUNT *adv.*]

A. *adv.* In front 1609.

B. *sb.* Front –1599.

Deva·porate, *v.* 1787. [f. DE- II. 1 + EVAPORATE *v.*] To condense or become condensed. Hence †**Devapora·tion.**

Devastate (de·văsteⁱt), *v.* 1634. [– *devastat-*, pa. ppl. stem of L. *devastare*, f. *de-* DE- I. 3 + *vastare* lay waste; superseded older †*devast*. Rare till XIX.] To lay waste, ravage, render desolate.

A succession of cruel wars had devastated Europe MACAULAY. var. **Deva·st** (now *rare*). Hence **De·vastative** *a.* having the quality of devastating. **De·vastator,** he who or that which devastates.

Devastation (devăstēⁱ·ʃən). 1603. [– Fr. *dévastation* or late L. *devastatio*, f. as prec.; see -ION.] **1.** The action of devastating; devastated condition; laying waste; ravages. **2.** *Law*. Waste of the property of a deceased person by an executor or administrator 1670.

1. The great Devastations made by the Plague HALE.

‖**Devastavit** (dīvæstēⁱ·vit). 1651. [L.; 'he has wasted'.] *Law*. A writ that lies against an executor or administrator for waste of the testator's estate; also, the offence of such waste.

Deve, obs. f. DEAVE *v.* to deafen.

Devel (de·v'l), *sb. Sc.* 1786. [Origin unkn.] A stunning blow. Hence **De·vel** *v.* to strike with such a blow; **De·veller,** a boxer.

Develop (dĭve·lŏp), *v.* Also **develope.** 1592. [– (O)Fr. *développer* (OFr. also *desveloper* DISVELOP) :– Rom. vb. f. L. *dis-* DIS- I. 1 + **volup-*, **velup-* (as in OFr. *voloper* envelop, Pr. *volopar*, It. *viluppare* wrap up); ult. origin unkn.] **1.**† *trans.* To unfold, unroll; to unfurl –1868. **b.** *Geom.* To flatten out (a curved surface); to change the form of (a surface) by bending 1879. †**2.** To unveil; to unfold; to disclose –1837. **3.** To unfold more fully, bring out all that is contained in 1750; in *Mil.*, to open gradually (an attack) 1883. **4.** *Math.* To change the form of a mathematical function or expression without changing the value 1871. **5.** To bring forth from a latent or elementary condition 1813; in *Photogr.*, to bring out and render visible (the latent image produced by actinic action upon a sensitive surface); to apply to (the plate, etc.) the treatment by which this is effected. Also *absol.* 1845. **6.** *trans.* To cause to grow (what exists in the germ); to evolve 1839. Also *transf.* and *refl.* **7.** *intr.* (for *refl.*) To unfold itself, grow from a germ; to grow into a fuller, higher, or maturer condition 1843.

3. To d. the latent excellencies..of our art SIR J. REYNOLDS, an idea HARE, property 1890. **5.** We thus d. both attraction and repulsion TYNDALL. **6.** They grow, or in modern phraseology they are developed ARGYLL. Forces have been at work, developing in each great continent animal forms peculiar to itself 1880. *transf.* Fresh powers.. which..d. further resources HT. MARTINEAU. It is astonishing what ambulatory powers he can d. HELPS. **7.** London developed into the general mart of Europe J. R. GREEN. The time swine fever takes to d. 1891.

Developable (dĭve·lŏpăb'l), *a.* (*sb.*) 1816. [f. prec. + -ABLE.] **1.** Capable of being developed or developing 1835. **2.** *sb.* (*Math.*) A developable surface; a ruled surface in which consecutive generators intersect (Salmon).

Developer (dĭve·lŏpəɹ), *v.* 1833. [f. as prec. + -ER[1].] He who or that which develops; in *Photogr.*, a chemical agent by which photographs are developed.

Development (dĭve·lŏpmĕnt). Also **-ope-.** 1756. [f. as prec. + -MENT, after Fr. *développement*.]

I. 1. A gradual unfolding; a fuller working out of the details of anything. Also quasi-*concr.* that in which this is realized. **2.** Evolution; the production of a natural force, energy, or new form of matter 1794. **3.** The growth of what is in the germ; the condition of that which is developed; EVOLUTION 1844. **4.** Growth from within 1836. **5.** A developed or well-grown condition 1851. **6.** The developed result or product 1845.

2. The d. of heat 1794. **3.** The d. of buds and flowers SIR B. BRODIE. *D. theory* or *hypothesis* (*Biol.*): the doctrine of Evolution; *esp.* as taught by Lamarck (died 1829). **6.** The butterfly..is the d. of the grub J. H. NEWMAN.

II. Techn. uses. **1.** *Geom.* The unbending of any curved surface into a plane, or of a non-plane curve into a plane curve 1800. **2.** *Math.* The process of expanding any expression into another of equivalent value or meaning; the expanded form itself 1816. **3.** *Photogr.* The process of developing a photograph (see DEVELOP *v.* 5) 1845. **4.** *Mus.* The unfolding of the capacities of a musical phrase or subject by modifications of melody, harmony, etc.; *esp.* in a sonata; the part of a movement in which this takes place. Also *attrib.* 1880.

Hence **Deve:lopme·ntal** *a.* of or pertaining to d.; evolutionary. **Developme·ntally** *adv.* **Deve·lopmentist** (*nonce-wd.*), an evolutionist.

†**Devenu·state,** *v. rare*. 1653. [– *devenustat-*, pa. ppl. stem of L. *devenustare* disfigure, f. *de-* DE- I. 6 + *venustus* beautiful; see -ATE[3].] To deprive of beauty.

Devest (dĭve·st), *v. arch.* 1563. [– OFr. *devester*, *des-*, *devestir*. Now DIVEST (q.v.), exc. in sense 4.] †**1.** *trans.* To unclothe, undress –1649. †**2.** To strip *of* anything that covers –1809. Also †*fig.* †**3.** To take off; to put off, lay aside –1765. Also †*refl.* **4.** *Law*. To take away (a right, etc. vested in any one), to alienate 1574; †to dispossess of any right, etc. –1810.

2. And Aaron of his Ephod to d. DRYDEN. Hence **Deve·sture,** the action of devesting (*rare*).

†**Deve·x,** *a.* (*sb.*) ME. [– L. *devexus*, pa. pple. of *devehere*, f. *de-* DE- I. 1 + *vehere* carry.] **1.** Bent down, sloping downward –1669. **2.** *sb.* = DEVEXITY 1627.

†**Deve·xity.** 1601. [– L. *devexitas*, f. as prec.; see -ITY.] Downward incline; concavity –1618.

†**De·viant,** *ppl. a. rare*. ME. [– *deviant-*, pres. ppl. stem of late L. *deviare*; see DEVIATE *v.*, -ANT[1].] **1.** Deviating –1623. **2.** That diverts 1471.

†**De·viate,** *ppl. a. rare*. 1560. [– *deviatus*, pa. pple. of late L. *deviare*; see next, -ATE[2].] Turned out of the way; remote –1638.

Deviate (dī·vi,eⁱt), *v.* 1633. [–*deviat-*, pa. ppl. stem of late L. *deviare*, f. *de-* DE- I. 2 + *via* way; see -ATE[3].] **1.** *intr.* To turn aside from the course or track; to turn out of the way; to swerve 1635. Also *fig.* **2.** *trans.* To turn (any one) out of the way, divert, deflect (*lit.* and *fig.*) 1660.

1. Neither stand still, nor go back, nor d. QUARLES. *fig.* Shadwell never deviates into sense DRYDEN. **2.** To let them d. him from the right path COTTON. Hence **De·viative** *a.* causing or tending to deflexion. **De·viator. De·viatory** *a.* deviating.

Deviation (dīvi,ēⁱ·ʃən). 1603. [– Fr. *déviation* – med.L. *deviatio*, f. as prec.; see -ION.] **1.** The action of deviating; turning aside from a track; swerving, deflexion 1646. †**b.** *Astron.* The deflexion of a planet's orbit from the plane of the ecliptic: attributed in the Ptolemaic astronomy to an oscillatory motion of the deferent –1727. **c.** *Comm.* Voluntary departure from the intended course of a vessel without sufficient cause

1809. **2.** Divergence from the straight line, from the mean, or standard position; variation, deflexion; the amount of this 1675. **3.** *fig.* Divergence *from* any course, method, rule, standard, etc. (The usual sense.) 1603. †**b.** Deviation from rectitude –1831. †**c.** A digression –1713.

2. *D. of the compass*: the deflexion of the needle of a ship's compass, owing to the magnetism of the iron in the ship, etc. *Conjugate d.* (*Path.*): see CONJUGATE *a.* **3.** A d. from the plain accepted meaning of words W. GROVE.

Device (dǐvəi·s). [ME. *devis* (later *devise* – OFr. *devise* fem.) – OFr. *devis* m. – Rom. deriv. of L. *divis-*, pa. ppl. stem of *dividere* DIVIDE; cf. DEVISE *v.* Spelling with *-ce* from XV.] **1.** The action, or faculty, of devising; invention, ingenuity. Now *arch.* and *rare.* (orig. *devis*). ME. **b.** Design (*arch.*) ME. †**2.** Purpose (orig. *devis*) –1548. **3.** Will, pleasure, inclination, desire (orig. *devis*) ME. †**4.** Opinion, notion; *occas.* advice –1594. †**5.** Talk, chat. [Fr. *devise.*] –1610. **6.** Something devised; an arrangement, plan, contrivance; often an underhand contrivance; a plot, stratagem, trick ME. **7.** *concr.* The result of contriving; an invention, contrivance ME. **8.** Something fancifully devised ME. **9.** *spec.* An emblematic figure or design, *esp.* one borne by a particular person, etc., as a heraldic bearing, etc.: usually accompanied by a motto ME.; also, a motto or legend borne with or in place of such a design 1724.

1. Gold, or silver, or stone, graven by art and man's d. *Acts* 17:29. 'Tis Plate of rare deuice *Cymb.* I. vi. 189. **3.** We will walk after our own deuices *Jer.* 18:12. **6.** By this happy d...[they] screen themselves PRIESTLEY. **7.** Devices for baling cut hay KNIGHT. **8.** A dyvyse of goold for mastres Margret 1465. Ballad, jest, and riddle's quaint d. BEATTIE. Masques and devices, welcome SHIRLEY. **9.** The deuice he beares vpon his shield Is a blacke Ethyope, reaching at the sunne. The word, *Lux tua vita mihi* SHAKS. *Per.* II. ii. 19. A banner with the strange d., 'Excelsior' LONGF. Hence **Devi·ceful** *a.* full of d.; ingenious, curious (now *rare*). **Devi·cefully** (†**devisefully**) *adv.* **Devicefulness.**

Devil (de·v'l, de·vil), *sb.* [OE. *dēofol* = OFris. *diovel*, OS. *diubul*, *-al* (Du. *duivel*), OHG. *tiufal* (G. *teufel*), ON. *djǫfull*, Goth. *diabaulus*, *-bulus*. The Goth. forms were directly – Gr. διάβολος (used in LXX to render Heb. *Śāṭān* SATAN), prop. accuser, slanderer, f. διαβάλλειν slander, traduce, f. διά across + βάλλειν throw. The other Gmc. forms were – Chr.L. *diabolus*.] **1.** *The Devil* [repr. Gr. ὁ διάβολος of the LXX and N.T.]: In Jewish and Christian theology, the supreme spirit of evil, the tempter and spiritual enemy of mankind, the foe of God and holiness, Satan. (In this sense without a pl.) **b.** In pl. applied to 'the Devil and his angels'; see Matt. 25:41. **c.** As tr. Heb. = 'satyrs', *Rev.* 18:2. **2.** = DEMON (sense 2), q.v. OE. Also *fig.*; see BLUE DEVIL. **3.** Hence, generically, A fiend, a demon. Also applied to the idols or false gods of the heathen. OE. **4.** *transf.* A malignantly wicked man; in ME. occas. a giant OE. **b.** In later use, a term of reprobation; also used playfully 1601. **c.** A term of contempt or pity (chiefly with *poor*). [So in It., Fr., etc.] 1698. **d.** Applied to a vicious beast 1834. **5.** *spec.* *Printer's d.*: the errand-boy in a printing office 1683. **b.** A junior legal counsel who does professional work for another, usually without fee 1849. **6.** *fig.* Applied to qualities 1604. **7.** Used (usu. with qualifications) as the name of various animals, on account of their characteristics 1636. **8.** A name of various instruments, machines, etc., *esp.* such as work with sharp teeth or spikes 1831. **9.** A name for various highly-seasoned broiled or fried dishes; also for hot ingredients 1786. **10.** A form of firework; a cracker, squib 1742. **11.** A moving sand-spout in Eastern countries 1835. **12.** *Naut.* 'The seam which margins the waterways on a ship's hull' (Smyth). **13.** *predic.* Something as bad as the devil 1710. Also *attrib.*

1. All gathers up in a person, in the d., who has a kingdom, as God has a kingdom TRENCH. The d. appears himself, Armed and accoutred, horns and hoofs and tail BROWNING. **2.** Devils they adore for deities MILT. *P. L.* I. 373. He hath a deuill and is mad *John* 10:20. **4.** Haue I not chosen you twelue, and one of you is a deuill *John* 6:70. **6.** The diuell drunkennesse *Oth.* II. iii. 297. Evans bowled steadily, but without much 'd.' 1884. **7.** *Tasmanian d.*, a carnivorous marsupial of Tasmania (*Sarcophilus ursinus*); *Sea D.*, the DEVIL-FISH. **8.** To the paper factory, where they have a horrid machine they call the d., that tears everything to bits O. W. HOLMES. **9.** Another holds a curry or d. in utter abomination W. IRVING. **13.** These Southern girls are the d. 1885.

Phrases, etc. *To go to the d.*: to go to perdition. So *to wish* any one *at the d.*, etc. *Who, what, how, where, when the d.*: expressions of impatience, irritation, surprise, etc. Used interjectionally in same sense, and, prefixed to a sb., to express strong negation.

In proverbs, etc. **a.** *The d. to pay*: supposed to refer to bargains made by wizards, etc., with Satan, and the inevitable payment in the end. **b.** *To play the d.*: to act diabolically, do mischief. **c.** *The d. among the tailors*: a row going on; also a game.

Comb.: **d.-bird,** a name of various birds, *esp.* the Swift, and the Brown Owl of Ceylon; **-bolt,** a sham bolt: 'a bolt with false clenches, often introduced into contract-built ships' (Smyth); **-carriage, -cart,** one for moving heavy ordinance; **d.-in-a-bush,** a garden flower, *Nigella damascena*, with horned capsules peering from a bush of finely-divided involucre; **d. on two sticks,** a double cone made to spin in the air by means of a string attached to two sticks held in the hand; **-shrieker, -skriker,** the Swift (*local*); **-tree,** an apocynaceous tree (*Alstonia scholaris*) of India, Africa, and Australia, having a powerfully bitter bark and milky juice; **-wood,** *Osmanthus americanus*, N.O. *Oleaceæ*, a small N. American tree with wood of extraordinary toughness and heaviness; **-worship,** the cult of the d., or of a demon; so **-worshipper, -worshipping; -wort,** a plant.

b. Special phrases. **Devil's advocate** [L. *advocatus diaboli*], one who urges the devil's plea against the canonization of a saint, etc.; hence, one who advocates the wrong side, or injures a cause by his advocacy; **devil's bones,** dice; **devil's cow,** a black beetle; **devil's darning-needle** (*U.S.*) = *devil's needle* (see also c.); **devil's dirt, devil's dung,** asafœtida; **devil's dozen:** see DOZEN; **devil's finger,** a belemnite; **devil's fingers,** the star-fish; **devil's needle,** the dragon-fly; **'Devil's Own',** the 88th Foot (*the Devil's own Connaught boys*); also the Inns of Court Rifle Corps of Volunteers; **devil's tattoo:** see TATTOO; **devil's toe-nail,** a belemnite.

c. in popular names of plants: **devil's apple,** the thorn-apple (*Datura stramonium*); **devil's apron,** a U.S. name of species of *Laminaria* and other seaweeds with a large dilated lamina; **devil's club** (*U.S.*), a prickly araliaceous plant, *Fatua horrida*; **devil's cotton,** an East Indian tree, *Abroma*, the fibres of which are made into cordage; **devil's darning-needle,** *Scandix pecten-veneris*; **devil's ear** (*U.S.*) a species of wake-robin (*Arum*); **devil's fig,** the prickly pear; **devil's leaf,** a virulent species of stinging nettle, *Urtica urentissinta*, found in Timor.

Hence **De·vildom,** the rule of the (or a) d.; the domain of the d.; the condition of devils. **De·vil-ess,** a she-devil. **De·vilet,** a little d., in various senses; the Swift. **De·vilhood,** the condition and estate of a d. **De·viling,** a young d.; the Swift (*local*). **De·vilism,** devilish quality; d.-worship. **De·vilize** *v.* to make a d. of; †*intr.* to act as a d. **De·vilkin,** an imp; also *fig.* **De·vil-like** *a.* and *adv.* †**De·villy, devily** *a.* = DEVILISH. **De·vilment,** mischief; a devilled dish; a devilish device. **De·vilry,** †a demon; diabolical art; devilish mischief; *joc.* reckless mischief, hilarity, or daring; demonology; devils collectively. **De·vilship,** the office or condition of a d. **De·viltry** = DEVILRY.

Devil (de·v'l, de·vǐl), *v.* 1652. [f. the sb.] †**1.** To play the devil with. **2.** *trans.* To grill with hot condiments 1800. **3.** *intr.* To act as devil to a lawyer (see DEVIL *sb.* 5 b) 1864. **4.** To tear to pieces (rags, etc.) with a devil (see DEVIL 8).

De·vil-dodger. *joc.* 1791. [See DODGE *v.*] One who tries to dodge the devil; also, a nickname for (ranting) preachers.

De·vil-fish. 1814. A name of various large and formidable fishes, etc.; *esp.* **a.** A large pediculate fish (*Lophius piscatorius*), also called ANGLER (q.v.). **b.** in U.S., a gigantic species of eagle-ray, *Ceratoptera vampyrus*, having expanded sides, the expanse of which is sometimes 20 feet. Less commonly, **c.** The Californian grey whale. **d.** The piranha of Uruguay. **e.** The octopus, cuttle-fish, or other cephalopod.

Devilish (de·v'liʃ), *a.* 1494. [f. DEVIL *sb.* + -ISH[1].] **1.** Having the nature or character of the devil; diabolical, execrable. **2.** Of or belonging to the devil 1526. **3.** *loosely.* Violent; extremely bad; enormous, excessive 1612. **4.** *adv.* Very 1612.

1. A diuelish knaue *Oth.* II. i. 249. D. whisperings 1827. **2.** Devilishe instigacion HALL. Hence **De·vilish-ly** *adv.*, **-ness.**

†**Devi·lity.** 1589. [f. as prec., after *civility*, etc.] Devilism –1609.

De·vil-may-ca·re. 1837. [The exclam. used attrib.] Wildly reckless; careless and rollicking.

Devil's-bit. 1450. [tr. med.L. *morsus diaboli.*] *Herb.* **1.** A species of Scabious (*Scabiosa succisa*); also *Devil's-bit Scabious.* **2.** *transf.* (in U.S.) *Chamælirium luteum*, the Blazing Star, N.O. *Liliaceæ.*

Devil's books. 1729 (Swift). Colloquial expression for playing-cards.

Devil's claw. **1.** *Naut.* **a.** A very strong split hook made to grasp a link of a chain cable, and used as a stopper. **b.** A grapnel. **2.** *Conchol.* A Scorpion shell (*Pteroceras scorpio*) from the Indian Ocean.

Devil's coach-horse. 1840. The large rove-beetle (*Goerius olens*), so called from its defiant attitude when disturbed.

Devil's dust. 1840. The flock made of old cloth by the machine called a devil; shoddy. (Orig. the dust made in this process.)

Devil's guts. 1670. *Herb.* A name of the Dodder (*Cuscuta*), from its pale slender stems which wind round and strangle other plants.

Devil's milk. 1578. [tr. G. *Teufelsmilch.*] A name given to plants with acrid milky juice; *e.g.* the Sun-Spurge (*Euphorbia helioscopia*) and Petty Spurge (*E. peplus*).

†**Devi·nct,** *ppl. a. rare.* 1573. [– L. *devinctus*, pa. pple. of *devincire* bind fast, f. *de-* DE- I. 3 + *vincire* bind.] Bounden –1643.

Devious (dī·viəs), *a.* 1599. [f. L. *devius* (f. *de-* DE- I. 2 + *via* way) + -OUS.] **1.** Lying out of the way; remote, sequestered. **2.** Departing from the direct way; following a winding or erratic course 1628. **3.** *fig.* Erring, straying 1633. **4.** quasi-*adv.* 1782.

1. These d. and untrodden ice-fields KANE. **2.** A shoal of d. minnows LOWELL. Hence **De·vious-ly** *adv.*, **-ness.**

†**Devi·rginate,** *v.* 1583. [– *devirginat-*, pa. ppl. stem of L. *devirginare*, f. *de-* DE- I. 6 + *virgo, virgin-* virgin; see -ATE[3].] *trans.* To deprive of virginity; to deflower. Also *fig.* –1680. So †**Devi·rginate** *ppl. a.* Hence **Devirgina·tion. Devi·rginator** (*rare*).

Deviscerate (dǐvi·sĕrē[i]t), *v. rare.* 1727. [f. DE- II. 1, after EVISCERATE.] To disembowel, eviscerate. Hence **Deviscera·tion.**

Devise (dǐvəi·z), *v.* ME. [– (O)Fr. *deviser* divide, dispose, design, etc. – Rom. **divisare*, f. *divis-*, pa. ppl. stem of *dividere* DIVIDE. Cf. DEVICE.] †**1.** *trans.* To divide –1483. †**2.** To assign, appoint, order, direct (*absol.* or *trans.*) –1606. **3.** *Law.* To give by will. Now only of realty, but formerly = bequeath. ME. **4.** To order the plan or design of; to plan, contrive, think out, frame, invent. (The chief current sense.) ME. Also *absol.* **5.** *trans.* In a bad sense: To plot, scheme (*arch.*) ME.; to feign, invent (*arch.*) 1513; also *absol.* †**6.** *trans.* (or *absol.*) To contrive successfully; to 'manage' –1592. †**7.** To prepare with skill, purvey. (Also *absol.*) –1500. †**8.** *trans.* (or *absol.*) To conceive; to conjecture –1814. †**9.** *intr.* (or *trans.* with *obj. cl.*) To think, deliberate –1599. †**10.** To consider, scan –1509; to discern –1620. †**11.** To recount –1570. Also †*intr.* (or *absol.*). †**12.** To confer, converse, talk. [So in mod.Fr.] *refl.* and *intr.* –1614.

4. The moost..delicate dysshes, that can or may be deuysed for a kynge 1526. Speake all good you can deuise of Cæsar *Jul. C.* III. i. 246. **5.** For thirtie pence he did my death d. G. HERBERT. D. fair pleas for delay BOWEN. **12.** *intr.* Let us..a little d. of those evils [etc.] SPENSER. Hence **Devi·sable** *a.* that can be devised, bequeathed, or contrived. **Devi·sal** (*rare*), the act of devising; contrivance, invention. **Devi·ser,** one who devises; a contriver, inventor, etc.

Devise (dǐvəi·z), *sb.* 1542. [– OFr. *devise* (see DEVICE) – med. L. *divisa* (also *divisio*) testament, f. fem. pa. pple. of L. *dividere* DIVIDE.] The act of devising by will; a testamentary disposition of real property; the clause in a will conveying this. (Cf. DEVISE *v.* 3.)

Devisee (dĭvəi:zī·). 1542. [f. DEVISE *v.* + -EE[1].] *Law.* The person to whom a devise is made. (Correl. to *devisor.*)

Devisor (dĭvəi·zǭɹ). 1542. [– AFr. *devisour*, f. (ult.) (O)Fr. *deviser* DEVISE. Formerly used in all senses of the vb.] One who makes a devise. (Correl. to *devisee.*)

Devitalize (dĭvəi·tăləiz), *v.* 1849. [DE- II. 1.] *trans.* To deprive of vitality or vital qualities. Hence **Devi:taliza·tion.**

†**Devita·tion.** *rare.* 1614. [– L. *devitatio*, f. *devitat-*, pa. ppl. stem of *devitare*, f. *de-* DE- I. 3 + *vitare* shun; see -ION.] Shunning; exhortation to shun: opp. to *invitation* –1623. So †**Devi·te** *v. trans.*, to shun; to ask not (*to do*). LAMB.

Devitrify (dĭvi·trifəi), *v.* 1832. [DE- II. 1; app. after Fr. *dévitrifier.*] *trans.* To deprive of vitreous qualities; to cause (glass, etc.) to become opaque, hard, and crystalline in structure. Hence **Devi:trifica·tion,** the action or process of devitrifying.

Devocalize (dĭvōᵘ·kăləiz), *v.* 1877. [DE- II. 1.] *trans.* To make (a vowel, etc.) voiceless or non-sonant. Hence **Devocaliza·tion.**

†**De·vocate,** *v. rare.* 1570. [– *devocat-*, pa. ppl. stem of L. *devocare*, f. *de-* DE- I. 1, 2 + *vocare* call.] *trans.* To call down –1633. Hence †**Devoca·tion,** a calling down or away.

Devoid (dĭvoi·d), *a.* ME. [orig. pa. pple. of DEVOID *v.*, short for *devoided.*] **1.** With *of*: Empty, void, destitute; entirely without. (Orig. participial, like *bereft.*) **2.** Without *of*: Void, empty. SPENSER.

1. He lay speechless, deuoid of sence and motion KNOLLES.

†**Devoid,** *v. rare.* ME. [– OFr. *devoidier*, *-vuidier* (mod. *dévider*), f. *de-* DE- I. 3 + *voider*, *vuider* VOID *v.*] **1.** *trans.* To cast out; to void –1509. †**2.** To make void or empty –1548.

Devoir (dĕvwǭ·ɹ, de·vwǭɹ), *sb.* [ME. *dever* – AFr. *dever*, OFr. *deveir* (mod. *devoir*) :– L. *debēre* owe. The ME. pronunc. was dəvē·r, later de·vər, which is continued in ENDEAVOUR.] **1.** One's duty. (Chiefly in phr. *to do one's d.*) *arch.* †**2.** One's utmost or best –1671. †**3.** Service due to any one –1742. **4.** A dutiful act of civility or respect; usu. in *pl.* 14.. †**5.** *pl.* Moneys due; dues –1641.

4. I beseech your ladyship instruct me where I may tender my devoirs DRYDEN.

Devolute (de·vŏlⁱūt), *v. rare.* 1534. [– *devolut-*, pa. ppl. stem of L. *devolvere*; see DEVOLVE.] *trans.* To pass by devolution; to DEVOLVE. So †**De·volute** *ppl. a.* devolved.

Devolution (devoliū·ʃən). 1545. [– late L. *devolutio* (in med.L. sense), f. as prec.; see -ION.] **1.** Rolling down; descending or falling with or as with a rolling motion. **2.** *Biol.* (opp. to EVOLUTION): Degeneration 1882. **3.** The causing of anything to descend or fall *upon*; the handing (of anything) on to a successor 1621. **4.** *spec.* The delegation of portions or details of duties to subordinate officers or committees 1780.

1. This..D. of Earth and Sand from the Mountains WOODWARD. *fig.* A long d. of years 1651. 3. A d. of the right of election for that turn BLACKSTONE. A d. of the crown HALLAM. 4. To lighten the cares of the central Legislature by judicious d. T. JEFFERSON.

Devolve (dĭvǫ·lv), *v.* ME. [– L. *devolvere*, f. *de-* DE- I. 1 + *volvere* roll.]

I. *trans.* **1.** To roll down; to cause to descend with rolling motion; also to unroll, unfurl (*arch.*). **2.** *fig.* To cause to pass *to* or fall *upon* (a person) 1538. **3.** *spec.* To delegate to deputies duties for which the responsibility belongs to the principal 1633.

1. His Thames, With gentle course devolving fruitful Streams M. PRIOR. He spake of virtue.. And..Devolved his rounded periods TENNYSON. 3. To d. on others the weight of government HUME.

II. *intr.* **1.** To roll or flow down or on (*lit.* and *fig.*) 1579. **2.** *fig.* To pass to the next in natural or conventional order 1555. **3.** Of persons: **a.** To come *upon* as a charge. **b.** To sink gradually. ? *Obs.* 1748.

2. The Empire thus deuolued to Dioclesian SPEED. Upon him would d. the chief labour TYNDALL.

Devonian (dĭvōᵘ·niăn), *a.* (*sb.*) 1612. [f. med.L. *Devonia*, f. *Devon* (OE. *Defena-sćīr*); see -AN, -IAN.] **1.** Of or belonging to Devonshire. **b.** as *sb.* A native or inhabitant of Devonshire. **2.** *Geol.* Name of a system of rocks lying below the Carboniferous and above the Silurian formations; hence, of or pertaining to this formation and its geological period. 1837. var. **Devo·nic** *a.* (*rare*).

Devonport; see DAVENPORT.

Devonshire, *v.*; see DENSHIRE.

†**Devora·tion.** 1528. [– OFr. *devoration* or late L. *devoratio*; see DEVOUR, -ATION.] The action of devouring or consuming –1614.

‖**Devo·ta.** [It. and Sp., fem. of DEVOTO.] A female devotee. EVELYN.

†**Devo·tary.** 1646. [– med.L. *devotarius*, *-aria*; see next, -ARY[1].] A votary; a devotee –1670.

Devote (dĭvōᵘ·t), *a.* and *sb. arch.* ME. [– (O)Fr. *dévot* or L. *devotus*, pa. pple. of *devovere* DEVOTE *v.* As sb. repl. by DEVOTEE, or occas. identified with mod.Fr. *dévote* fem. Cf. DEVOUT.]

A. *ppl. a.* = DEVOTED.

B. *adj.* = DEVOUT 1625.

C. *sb.* A devotee 1630.

Devote (dĭvōᵘt), *v.* 1586. [– *devot-*, pa. ppl. stem of L. *devovere*, f. *de-* DE- I. 3 + *vovere* vow.] **1.** To appropriate by, or as if by, a vow; to set apart or dedicate solemnly or formally; to consecrate (*to*). **2.** To give up, addict, apply zealously or exclusively (*to*); *esp.* refl. *to devote oneself* 1604. **3.** To consign to destruction; to pronounce a curse upon 1647.

1. No deuoted thing that a man shall deuote vnto the Lord *Lev.* 27:28. To d. property to charity 1802. 2. D. this day to mirth ROWE. [He] who devotes himself to some intellectual pursuit JOWETT. Hence **Devo·tement,** the action of devoting, or fact of being devoted; dedication. **Devo·ter,** †a devotee (*rare*); one who devotes (Dicts.). †**Devo·tress,** a female devotee. var. †**Devou·t** *v.*

†**Devoté.** Erron. f. DEVOTE *sb.*, with pseudo-Fr. spelling. FIELDING.

Devoted (dĭvōᵘ·tėd), *ppl. a.* 1594. [f. DEVOTE *v.* + -ED[1].] **1.** Vowed; dedicated, consecrated. **2.** Characterized by devotion 1600. **3.** Doomed 1611.

2. Sir, your very d. SHERIDAN. 3. Round our d. heads the billows beat M. PRIOR. Hence **Devo·tedly** *adv.*, **-ness.**

Devotee (devotī·). 1645. [f. DEVOTE *v.* or *a.* + -EE[1], after *assignee*, etc. Repl. DEVOTE *sb.*] **1.** *gen.* One who is zealously devoted to a party, cause, pursuit, etc.; a votary 1657. **2.** *spec.* One characterized by religious devotion, *esp.* of an extreme or superstitious kind.

1. A d. of vegetarianism BURTON. 2. He grew older, became..from a profligate a d. J. HARRIS. Hence **Devotee·ism,** the principles or practice of a d.

Devotion (dĭvōᵘ·ʃən), *sb.* ME. [– (O)Fr. *dévotion* or L. *devotio*, f. as DEVOTE *v.*; see -ION.]

I. In religious use; from eccl.L. through OFr. **1.** The fact or quality of being devoted to religious observances, etc.; reverence, devoutness ME. **2.** Religious worship or observance. **b.** *spec.* An act of worship; now only in *pl.* **c.** A form of worship, for private use. ME. †**3.** An oblation; alms –1662. **4.** The action of devoting; solemn dedication, consecration. (A Renaissance sense.) 1502.

1. A journey of D. to Rome PRIDEAUX. Devocion..to Cupido CHAUCER. 2. A splendid book of devotions FREEMAN.

II. In non-religious use; from ancient L. through It. and Fr. **1.** The quality of being devoted to a person, cause, etc. 1530. †**2.** Devoted service; disposal –1839. †**3.** That to which anything is devoted; object, purpose –1646. **4.** The action of applying to a particular use or purpose 1861.

1. This fervid d. to art in Charles D'ISRAELI. 2. Phr. *To be at the d. of*, to be entirely devoted to. 3. *Rich. III*, IV. i. 9. 4. The d. of a few pages to it M. PATTISON.

Hence †**Devotionair** (*rare*), var. of *Devotionary*. **Devo·tional** *a.* of, pertaining to, of the nature of, or characterized by, d. **Devo·tionalist,** one given to d. **Devotiona·lity. Devo·tionally** *adv.* †**Devo·tionary** *a.* pertaining to d.; *sb.* a DEVOTEE. **Devo·tionist,** a devotionalist.

†**Devoto** (dĭvōᵘ·to), *sb.* Pl. **-oes, -o's, -os;** also (as in It.) **-i.** 1599. [– It. and Sp. *devoto* :– L. *devotus*; see DEVOTE *a.* and *sb.* Cf. DEVOTA.] A devotee –1712. var. (or ? misprint) †**Devo·tor.**

Devour (dĭvau̇ᵊ·ɹ), *v.* ME. [– *devour-*, tonic stem of (O)Fr. *dévorer* – L. *devorare*, f. *de-* DE- I. 3 + *vorare* swallow.] **1.** To swallow or eat up voraciously, as a beast of prey. **2.** Of human beings: To eat greedily, consume or make away with, as food; to eat like a beast ME. **3.** To consume destructively; to waste, destroy, swallow up ME. **4.** To take in greedily the sense of (a book, etc.) 1581; to look upon with avidity 1621; to swallow (chagrin, etc.) 1650. **5.** Of things: To absorb 1500.

1. Turned, as a wolf to d. the lambs SEWEL. 3. This thy son..which hath devoured thy living with harlots *Luke* 15:30. Time hath devoured it [the Monument] SIR T. HERBERT. The quicksand that devours all miserie MARSTON. 4. With eager Eyes devouring..The breathing Figures of Corinthian Brass DRYDEN. Hence **Devou·rable** *a.* that can be devoured; consumable. **Devou·rer,** one who or that which devours. †**Devou·ress,** a female devourer. **Devou·ringly** *adv.* **Devou·rment,** the action of devouring.

Devout (dĭvau̇·t), *a.* and *sb.* [ME. *devot*, *devout* – (O)Fr. *dévot* – L. *devotus*; see DEVOTE *a.* and *sb.*] **A. 1.** Devoted to divine worship or service; reverential in religious exercises; pious, religious; †*gen.* devoted (*to* a person or cause) –1659. **2.** Of actions, etc.: Showing or expressing devotion ME. **3.** Earnest, sincere, hearty 1828.

1. A shorte orison, saide with good devouute herte 1450. *gen.* The most d. friend of the Church 1659. 2. Uplifted hands, and eyes d. MILT. *P. L.* XI. 863.

B. *sb.* †**1.** A devotee –1675. **2.** The devotional part (of a composition, etc.). MILT.

Hence **Devou·tly** *adv.* in a d. manner; earnestly, sincerely.

†**Devou·tful,** *a.* 1597. [irreg. f. DEVOUT *a.* + -FUL.] Full of devoutness; pious –1604.

As painfull Pilgrim in deuoutfull wise 1598. So †**Devou·tless** *a.* without devoutness.

Devoutness (dĭvau̇·tnės). ME. [f. DEVOUT *a.* + -NESS.] The quality of being devout; religiousness, piety.

†**Devo·ve,** *v.* 1567. [– L. *devovere*; see DEVOTE *v.*] To devote –1808.

†**Devow·,** *v.* 1579. [– Fr. *dévouer*, f. DE- I. 2, 3 + *vouer* to VOW after L. *devovere* DEVOTE *v.*] **1.** *trans.* To dedicate or give up by vow –1609. **2.** To devote –1632. **3.** To disavow (*rare*) 1610.

Devu·lgarize, *v.* 1868. [DE- II. 1.] *trans.* To free from vulgarity.

Shakespeare, and Plutarch's 'Lives', are very devulgarizing books 1868.

Dew (diū), *sb.* [OE. *dēaw* = OFris. *dāw*, OS. *dau* (Du. *dauw*), OHG. *tou* (G. *tau*), ON. *dǫgg* (gen. *dǫggvar*) :– Gmc. **dauwaz*, *-am.*] **1.** The moisture deposited in minute drops upon any cool surface by the condensation of the vapour in the atmosphere; plentiful in the early morning. (Formerly supposed to fall softly from the heavens.) **2.** *fig.* Something likened to dew: **a.** as coming with refreshing power or falling gently ME.; **b.** as characteristic of the morning of life 1535. **3.** *transf.* Applied to moisture generally, *esp.* that which exudes from any body ME. **4.** *attrib.* and *comb.* ME.

1. Our day is gone, Clowds, Dewes, and Dangers come *Jul. C.* V. iii. 64. The d. was falling fast WORDSW. 2. The continuall deawe of thy blessinge *Bk. Com. Prayer* 1559. The timely d. of sleep MILT. *P. L.* IV. 614. Thou hast the d. of thy youth *Ps.* 110:3. 3. The night of d. that on my cheekes downe flowes *L. L. L.* IV. iii. 29. *Mountain-d.*, a term for whisky illicitly distilled on the mountains. 4. Knotgrass, d.-besprent MILT. *Comus* 540. D.-impearled flowers DRAYTON. D.-lit eyes TENNYSON. Hence **Dew·less** *a.*

Dew (diū), *v.* [ME. *dewen*, repr. OE. **dēawian* = OS. **daujan*, OHG. *touwōn* (G. *tauen*), ON. *dǫggva* :– Gmc. **dauwōjan*, f. **dauw-* DEW *sb.*] †**1.** *intr.* To give or produce dew; *impers.* to fall as dew (cf. *it rains*, etc.) –1726. **2.** *trans.* To wet with or as with dew; to bedew; to moisten ME. †**3.** To cause to fall as dew –1593.

2. Cold sweat Dew'd all my face OTWAY. [Music] Every sense in slumber dewing SCOTT.

Dew, obs. for DUE.

||**Dewan** (dīwā·n). Also **diwan,** etc. 1690. [– Arab. – Pers. *dīwān* orig. a register for fiscal purposes.] In India: **a.** The head financial minister of a state. **b.** The prime minister of a native state. **c.** The chief native officer of certain Government establishments. **d.** In Bengal, a native servant in charge of a house of business or a large domestic establishment. Hence **Dewa·nship** = next.

||**Dewani, dewanny, dewaunee** (dīwā·ni). 1783. [– Pers. *dīwānī* the office or function of *dīwān*; see prec.] The office of dewan; *esp.* the right of collecting the revenue in Bengal, Behar, and Orissa, ceded to the E. I. Company by Shāh 'Alam in 1765. Also used occas. for the territory in question.

Dew-berry (diū·beri). 1578. [f. DEW *sb.* + BERRY.] A species of blackberry or bramble-berry: in Great Britain *Rubus cæsius*; in N. America *R. canadensis*, differing from the British plant in its fruit. The name is applied to both the fruit and the shrub. In mod. dialects (and ? in Shaks.), the name is applied to the Gooseberry.

Feede him with Apricocks and Dewberries *Mids. N.* III. i. 169.

Dew-claw (diū·klǭ). 1576. [prob. f. DEW *sb.* + CLAW *sb.*] **1.** The rudimentary inner toe or hallux (not reaching the ground) sometimes present in dogs. **2.** The false hoof of deer and other ungulates 1576.

Dewdrop (diū·drǫp). 1590. [f. DEW *sb.* + DROP *sb.*] A drop of dew.

Dew-fall (diū·fǭl). 1622. [f. DEW *sb.* + FALL *sb.*] The deposition of dew; the time when this begins, in the evening.

†**Dewitt, De-Witt** (dīwi·t), *v.* 1689. [f. John and Cornelius *De Witt*, Dutch statesmen, who were murdered by a mob in 1672.] *trans.* To lynch –1888.

Dewlap (diū·læp). Also *erron.* **dew-clap.** ME. [f. DEW *sb.* + LAP *sb.*[1], perh. after ON. **dǫggleppr* (ODa. *doglæp*).] The fold of loose skin which hangs from the throat of cattle. Also *transf.*; and *joc.* of pendulous folds of flesh about the human throat (*Mids. N.* II. i. 50). Hence **Dew·lapped** *a.* having a d.

Dew-point (diū·point). 1833. That point of atmospheric temperature at which dew begins to be deposited.

Dew·-pond. 1877. A shallow pond, usu. artificial, fed by the condensation of water from the air, occurring on downs having no other adequate water-supply.

Dew-ret (diū·ret), *v.* Also **-rot, -rate.** 1710. [f. DEW *sb.* + RET *v.*] To ret or macerate (flax, hemp, etc.) by exposure to the dew and atmospheric influence instead of by steeping in water.

†**Dewtry.** 1598. [Cf. Marathi *dhutra, dhotrā*, dial. *dhutrō*.] The Thorn-apple, *Datura stramonium*; a stupefying drug or drink prepared from this –1711.

Dew-worm (diū·wɒ̄ɹm). 1599. [f. DEW *sb.* + WORM.] The common earth-worm; in OE. ring-worm.

Dewy (diū·i), *a.* [OE. *dēawiġ*, f. *dēaw* DEW *sb.*; see -Y[1]. Not in ME.] **1.** Characterized by, or abounding with, dew; affected by the influence of dew OE. **2.** *transf.* Moistened as with dew. In *Bot.* Covered as with dew. 1577. **3.** Dewlike, moist OE. **4.** Of dew (*poet.*) 1820. **5.** *fig.* Falling gently, vanishing, as the dew (*poet.*) 1611.

1. From Noon to d. Eve MILT. *P. L.* I. 743. Twilight's d. tints S. ROGERS. **2.** Her faire deawy eies SPENSER *F. Q.* III. ii. 34. **5.** Till dewie sleep Oppressed them MILT. *P. L.* IX. 1044. Hence **Dew·ily** *adv.* **Dew·iness,** d. quality (*lit.* and *fig.*).

Dexiocardia (de:ksi,okā·ɹdiă). 1866. [f. Gr. δεξιός on the right side + καρδία heart.] An anomaly of development in man in which the heart is on the right side.

Dexiotropic (de:ksi,otrǫ·pik), *a* 1883. [f. as prec. + Gr. -τροπος turning + -IC.] Turning or turned to the right, as the spire of some shells; opp. to *leiotropic.* var. **De·xiotrope.**

Dexter (de·kstəɹ), *a.* (*sb.* and *adv.*). 1562. [– L. *dexter*, a compar. formation from base **dex-*, whence Gr. δεξιός on the right hand.]

A. *adj.* **1.** Belonging to or situated on the right side; right; *esp.* in *Her.* the opposite of SINISTER. †**2.** = DEXTEROUS –1659.

1. In a representation of a coat of arms, that part of the shield which appears on the *left* side [of a spectator] is called the Dexter, and that on the *right*, the Sinister CUSSANS.

B. *sb.* The right 1814.

C. *adv.* On or to the right. POPE.

†**Dexte·rical,** *a.* 1607. [irreg. f. L. *dexter* (see prec.) + -IC + -AL[1].] Dexterous –1644.

Dexterity (dekste·rĭti). 1527. [– Fr. *dextérité* – L. *dexteritas*; see DEXTER, -ITY.] **1.** Manual skill, neat-handedness; hence, address in the use of the limbs and in bodily movements 1548. **2.** Mental adroitness or skill; cleverness, address, ready tact. In a bad sense: Sharpness. 1527. †**3.** Handiness, conveniency –1614. **4.** *lit.* Right-handedness (*rare*) 1882.

1. Able to handle his Peece with due dexteritie GARRARD. **2.** My admirable dexteritie of wit *Merry W.* IV. v. 120. Dexteritie to cheat and deceive GALE.

Dexterous, dextrous (de·kstĕrəs, de·kstrəs), *a.* 1605. [f. L. *dexter* DEXTER + -OUS.] †**1.** = DEXTER 1. –1678. †**2.** Handy. BACON. **3.** Deft or nimble of hand; hence skilful in the use of the limbs and in bodily movements 1635. **4.** Having mental adroitness or skill; expert in contrivance or management; clever 1622. †In a bad sense: Clever, crafty –1715. **5.** Of things: Characterized by dexterity; clever 1625. **6.** Right-handed (*mod.*).

3. A dextrous archer GIBBON. **4.** Dextrous in Letters MABBE, in business SOUTHEY. Dexterous in the management of temporal affairs MRS. JAMESON. **5.** Dexterous conduct SYD. SMITH. var. †**Dexte·rious.** Hence **De·xterously, de·xtrously** *adv.*; var. †**Dexte·riously. De·xterousness, de·xtrousness.**

Dextrad (de·kstræd), *adv.* and *a.* 1803. [f. L. *dextra* right hand + -AD II.] To or toward the right side of the body; dextrally.

Dextral (de·kstrăl), *a.* 1646. [– med.L. *dextralis*; see prec., -AL[1].] **1.** Situated on the right side of the body; right, as opp. to *left.* **2.** *Conchol.* Of a gastropod shell: Having the whorl ascending from left to right (*i.e.* of the external spectator) 1847. Hence **Dextra·lity,** the condition of having the right side differing from the left, also, right-handedness. **De·xtrally** *adv.* to the right, as opp. to the left.

Dextrane (de·kstrēⁱn). [f. DEXTRO- + -ANE.] *Chem.* An amorphous dextro-rotatory gummy substance, $C_6H_{10}O_5$, found in unripe beetroot, and formed in the lactic fermentation of sugar.

Dextrer(e, dextrier; see DESTRER.

Dextrin (de·kstrin). Also **-ine.** 1838. [– Fr. *dextrine*, f. L. *dextra* on the right hand; see next and -IN[1]. Named from its property of turning the plane of polarization 138·68° to the right.] *Chem.* A soluble gummy substance into which starch is converted when subjected to a high temperature, or to the action of dilute alkalis or acids, or of diastase. Called also *British gum* and *Leiocome.*

Dextro-, comb. f. L. *dexter, dextra*, in the sense '(turning or turned) to the right', chiefly with reference to the property of causing the plane of a ray of polarized light to rotate to the right. Hence:

a. Dextrogyre (de·kstro,dʒəiᵊɹ), *a.* [L. *gyrus*, Gr. γῦρος circuit], circling to the right. **Dextro·gy·rate** *a.*, characterized by turning the plane of polarization to the right, as a *dextrogyrate crystal.* **Dextrogy·rous** *a.* = *dextrogyre.* **Dextro-rota·tion,** rotation to the right. **Dextro-ro·-tatory** *a.*, dextrogyrous.

b. Dextro-co·mpound, a chemical compound which causes dextro-rotation. **Dextro-glu·cose** = DEXTROSE. **Dextro-race·mic, Dextro-tarta·ric acid,** the modifications of racemic and tartaric acid which cause dextro-rotation.

Dextrorse (dekstrǭ·ɹs), *a.* 1864. [– L. *dextrorsum, dextrorsus.*] Turned toward the right hand. (Used by the earlier botanists as = 'to the right hand of the observer'; by modern as = 'to the right hand of the plant', which is to the left of the external observer.) var. **Dextro·rsal** (*rare*).

Dextrose (de·kstrōᵘs). 1869. [f. L. *dexter, dextra* (see DEXTRO-) + -OSE[2].] *Chem.* The form of GLUCOSE which is dextro-rotatory to polarized light; dextro-glucose; ordinary glucose or grape-sugar.

Dextrous; see DEXTEROUS.

Dey[1] (dēⁱ). Now *dial.* [OE. *dǣġe*, corresp. to ON. *deigja* maid, female servant. The primitive meaning is 'kneader'. Cf. DAIRY, LADY.] **1.** A woman having charge of a dairy; in early use, also, female servant. Hence, **2.** A man having similar duties 1483. *Comb.*: **d.-house,** a dairy; **-maid,** a dairy-maid; **-wife, -woman,** a dairy woman.

||**Dey**[2] (dēⁱ). 1659. [– Fr. *dey* – Turk. *dayı* maternal uncle, also a friendly title for middle-aged or old people, *esp.* among the Janissaries.] The titular appellation of the commanding officer of the Janissaries of Algiers, who in 1710 deposed the pasha, and became sole ruler. (Disused after the French conquest of 1830.)

Dey, obs. f. DIE *sb.* and *v.*

Deynt, Deynte, -tie, etc.; see DAINT, etc.

Dezincation (dīzinkēⁱ·ʃən). 1891. [f. DE- II. 1 + ZINC *v.* + -ATION.] The removal of zinc from an alloy or composition.

Dezincify, dezinkify (dīzi·ŋkifəi), *v.* 1874. [f. DE- II. 1 + ZINCIFY.] To remove zinc from an alloy or composition.

Dezymotize (dīzəi·mŏtəiz), *v.* 1884. [f. DE- II. 1 + ZYMOTIC + -IZE.] To free from disease-germs.

Dh-, in the English spelling of East Indian words, represents the Indian dental sonant-aspirate, written *dha*, also the lingual sonant-aspirate, *ḍha*. It has also been extended erroneously to words having simple *da* dental or *ḍa* lingual, and to words not really Indian, as *dhooly*, etc.

||**Dhak** (dhāk). Also **dhawk.** 1825. [Hindi *ḍhāk*.] An East Indian tree *Butea frondosa*, N.O. *Leguminosæ*, noted for its brilliant flowers.

||**Dhal,** var. of DAL Indian pulse.

||**Dharna, dhurna** (dhɒ·rna). 1793. [Hindi *dharnā* placing, act of sitting in restraint, f. Skr. *dhṛ* to place.] A mode of compelling payment or compliance with a demand, by sitting at the debtor's door, and there remaining without tasting food till the demand shall be complied with; this action is called 'sitting (in) dharnā'.

||**Dhobi** (dhō·bi). 1860. [Hindi *dhōbī*, f. *dhōb* washing.] A native washerman in India.

||**Dhole** (dhōᵘl). 1827. [Origin unkn.] The wild dog of the Deccan in India.

||**Dhoney, doney** (dōᵘ·ni). Also **doni.** 1582. [– Tamil *thōni* (pronounced *dōni*); cf. Pers. *dōnī* a yacht.] A small native sailing vessel of Southern India.

Dhooley, -lie, erron. ff. DOOLIE, a litter.

||**Dhoti, dhootie** (dhōᵘ·ti, dhū·ti). 1622. [Hindi *dhōtī*.] The loin-cloth worn by Hindus.

Dhourra, dhurra = DURRA, Indian millet.

||**Dhow, dow** (dau). 1802. [Original language unkn.] A native vessel used on the Arabian Sea, generally with a single mast, and of 150 to 200 tons burden; more widely, applied to all Arab vessels.

Dhurrie, durrie (dɒ·ri). 1880. [Hindi *darī*.] A kind of cotton carpet of Indian manufacture, usually made in rectangular pieces, and used for sofa-covers, curtains, and the like.

Di- (di, dəi), *pref.*[1], repr. L. *dī*, short form of *dis-*, used in L. before *b, d, g* (usually), *l, m, n, r, s* + cons., *v*, and sometimes before *j*. In ME. often varying with *de-*, whence *defer, devise*, etc., f. L. *differre, divisa*, etc. For its force in composition see DIS-.

Di- (dəi, di), *pref.*[2], repr. Gr. δι- for δίς twice. Hence, **1.** Entering into numerous Eng. words, mostly technical, as *dichromic*, etc.; in Nat. Hist. *Diandria*, etc.; in *Cryst. ditetrahedron*, etc. **2.** As a living prefix, used in *Chem.* in the general sense 'twice, double', but with special applications, expressing the presence of two atoms, equivalents, molecules, formulas, as the case may be.

Di-, *pref.*[3], the form of DIA- used bef. a vowel, as in *di-optric*, etc.

Dia-, *pref.*[1], bef. a vowel **di-,** repr. Gr. δια-, δι-, the prep. διά through, during, across, by. [orig. *δϝιγα, from root of *δϝο, δύο two, and so related to δίς, and L. *dis-* a-two.] Much used in the senses 'through, thorough, thoroughly, apart'.

Dia-, *pref.*², in medical terms. The Gr. phrases διὰ τεσσάρων (in full τὸ διὰ τεσσάρων φάρμακον medicament made up of four ingredients), διὰ πέντε and the like, were treated in Latin as words, thus *diatessaron*, *diapente*, etc., and later formations of the same kind were added to the number. Of these a few, *e.g.* DIACHYLUM, survive in modern use.

Diabantite (dəiăbæ·ntəit). 1875. [irreg. f. DIABASE (as if = Gr. διάβας, διαβαντ- having crossed over) + -ITE¹ 2 b.] *Min.* A chlorite-like mineral occurring in diabase and giving to this rock its green colour.

Diabase (dəi·ăbēˈs). 1836. [– Fr. *diabase* (improp. for *dibase* 'rock with two bases'); abandoned, and in 1842 re-introduced by Hausmann, perh. with some reference to Gr. διάβασις transition.] *Min.* Brongniart's original name for DIORITE; now applied to a fine-grained, compact, crystalline granular rock, consisting essentially of augite and a triclinic feldspar, with some chloritic matter; a variety of the class of rocks called greenstone and trap. Also *attrib.* Hence **Diaba·sic** *a.* pertaining to or resembling d.

Diabaterial (dəi:ăbătīə·riăl), *a. rare.* 1784. [f. Gr. διαβατήρια (sc. ἱερά) offerings before crossing + -AL¹.] Pertaining to the crossing of a frontier or river.

Diabetes (dəiăbī·tīz). 1562. [– L. *diabetes* – Gr. διαβήτης lit. 'a passer through, a siphon', f. διαβαίνειν go through.] †**1.** A siphon 1661. **2.** *Med.* A disease characterized by the immoderate discharge of urine containing glucose, and accompanied by thirst and emaciation.

Sometimes called *Diabetes mellitus*, to distinguish it from *Diabetes insipidus* which is characterized by an absence of saccharine matter. (In 18th c. with *the* or *a.*) var. †**Di·abete.** **Diabetic** (dəiăbe·tik, -ī·tik) *a.* pertaining to d. or its treatment (var. **Diabe·tical**); affected with d.; *sb.* one who suffers from d.

Diablerie (di,ā·bləri). Also **-ery.** 1751. [– Fr. *diablerie*, f. *diable* DEVIL; see -ERY.] **1.** Dealings with the devil; sorcery or conjuring; devilry. **2.** Devil-lore 1824.

‖**Diablotin** (diablotęṅ). 1812. [Fr., dim. of *diable* DEVIL.] An imp.

Diabolic (dəiăbǫ·lik). ME. [– (O)Fr. *diabolique*, Chr.L. *diabolicus*, f. *diabolus* DEVIL; see -IC.]

A. *adj.* **1.** Of, pertaining to, or resembling the devil; having to do with the devil; pertaining to witchcraft or magic. **2.** Of the nature of the devil; fiendish; inhumanly wicked 1483.

1. A diabolike instrument 1533. D. pow'r MILT., aspect 1862, possession 1871. **2.** No d. delight 1876.

†**B.** *sb.* An agent of the devil –1638; a person possessed by a devil –1825. var. **Diabo·lical** *a.* and *sb.* Hence **Diabo·lical-ly** *adv.*, **-ness.**

Dia·bolifuge. [f. L. *diabolus* DEVIL + -FUGE.] Something that drives away the devil. O. W. HOLMES.

Diabolify (dəiăbǫ·lifəi), *v.* 1647. [f. as prec. + -FY.] To make a devil of; to represent as a devil.

Diabolism (dəi,æ·bǫliz'm). 1614. [f. Gr. διάβολος + -ISM.] **1.** Dealing with the devil; sorcery, witchcraft. **2.** Conduct or action worthy of the devil; devilry 1681. **3.** Doctrine as to devils; worship of the devil 1660. **4.** The character or nature of a devil 1754. So **Dia·bolist**, a teacher of d. **Dia·bolize** *v.* to render, or represent as, diabolical; to subject to diabolical influence.

Diabolo (diæ·bǒlo). 1907. [It., = devil.] The game 'the devil-on-two-sticks' (see DEVIL).

Diabolology (dəi:ăbǫlǫ·lǒdʒi). 1875. [f. Gr. διάβολος DEVIL + -LOGY.] Doctrine of the devil; devil-lore. var. **Diabo·logy.**

Diabolonian (dəi:ăbǫlōᵘ·niăn). 1682. [f. L. *diabolus*, after *Babylonian*, etc.] 'One of the host of Diabolus (the Devil) in his assault upon Mansoul' (Bunyan); also as *adj.*

†**Di:acatho·licon.** 1562. [So in OFr. and med.L., repr. Gr. διὰ καθολικῶν composed of general or universal (ingredients). See DIA-².] Old term for a laxative electuary; hence, a universal remedy or appliance –1665.

Diacaustic (dəiăkǭ·stik). 1704. [f. Gr. διά DIA-¹ + καυστικός burning; see CAUSTIC. Cf. Fr. *catacaustique.*]

A. *adj.* **1.** *Math.* Of a surface or curve: Formed by the intersection of refracted rays of light. †**2.** *Med.* 'Formerly applied to a double convex lens or burning glass' (Mayne).

B. *sb.* **1.** *Math.* A diacaustic curve or surface; a caustic by refraction 1727. †**2.** *Med.* A double convex lens used to cauterize.

Dia·cetate. *Chem.* See DI-² 2, ACETATE.

Dia·cetin. *Chem.* See DI-² 2, ACETIN.

Diachænium (dəiăkī·niǒm). 1870. [mod. L., f. DI-² + L. *achænium* ACHENE.] *Bot.* = CREMOCARP.

†‖**Diachore·sis.** 1706. [Gr. διαχώρησις excretion.] *Med.* The act or faculty of voiding excrements –1721. Hence **Diachore·tic** *a.*

Diachylon, -lum (dəi,æ·kilǫn, -lǒm), **diaculum** (dəi,æ·kiŭlǒm). ME. [– OFr. *diaculon*, *-chilom* – late L. *diachylon*, for L. *diachȳlōn*, repr. Gr. διὰ χυλῶν composed of juices; see DIA-², CHYLE.] Orig., a kind of ointment composed of vegetable juices; now a name for lead-plaster, *emplastrum plumbi*, made by boiling together litharge (lead oxide), olive oil, and water. It adheres when heated.

†**Dia·chyma.** 1866. [f. Gr. δια- (see DIA-¹) + χύμα that which is poured out.] *Bot.* = PARENCHYMA.

Diacid (dəi,æ·sid), *a.* 1866. [See DI-² 2.] *Chem.* Capable of combining with two acid radicals.

Diaclasite (dəi,æ·klăsəit). 1850. [f. G. *diaklas*, f. Gr. διακλάειν + -ITE¹ 2b; on account of its easy cleavage.] *Min.* A bisilicate of iron and magnesium.

†‖**Diacodium** (dəiăkoᵘ·diǒm). Also **-dion.** 1564. [med. and mod.L., repr. Gr. διὰ κωδειῶν (a preparation) made from poppy-heads; see DIA-².] A syrup prepared from poppy-heads, used as an opiate –1829.

Diacœlosis (dəi:ăsīlōᵘ·sis). 1888. [f. DIA-¹ + Gr. κοίλωσις hollow, belly.] *Biol.* The separation of the cœlome into several sinuses, as in leeches, etc.

Diaconal (dəi,æ·kǒnăl), *a.* 1611. [–eccl.L. *diaconalis*, f. *diaconus* DEACON; see -AL¹. Cf. (O)Fr. *diaconal.*] Of or belonging to a DEACON.

Diaconate (dəi,æ·kǒnět). 1727. [– eccl.L. *diaconatus*, f. as prec.; see -ATE¹. Cf. Fr. *diaconat.*] **1.** The office or rank of deacon. **2.** The time during which any one is a deacon 1880. **3.** A body of deacons 1891.

‖**Diaco·nicon.** Also **-um.** 1727. [Gr. διακονικόν, n. adj. f. διάκονος DEACON; see- IC.] *Eccl. Antiq.*, etc. A building or room adjoining the church, where vestments, ornaments, etc., used in the church service are kept; a sacristy, a vestry.

‖**Diacope** (dəi,æ·kopi). 1586. [Gr. διακοπή gash, cleft, f. διακόπτειν cut through.] †**1.** *Gram.* Tmesis –1678. **2.** *Surg.* A cut, fissure, longitudinal fracture; usually an oblique incision made in the cranium by a sharp instrument, without the piece being removed.

Diacoustics (dəiăkau·stiks). 1683. [See DI-³.] The science of refracted sounds; diaphonics. So **Diacou·stic** *a.* pertaining to d. (Dicts.)

Diacrante·ric, *a.* 1883. [f. Gr. διά (see DIA-¹) + κραντῆρες the wisdom teeth + -IC.] Having the posterior teeth more widely separated than the anterior, as some snakes. So **Diacrante·rian** *a.*

‖**Dia·crisis.** 1684. [mod.L. – Gr., f. διακρίνειν to separate; *spec.* mark a crisis in a fever. Cf. Fr. *diacrise.*] **a.** The act of separation or secretion. **b.** 'A critical evacuation'. **c.** = DIAGNOSIS. Hence **Diacrisio·graphy,** 'a description of the organs of secretion' (*Syd. Soc. Lex.*).

Diacritic (dəiăkri·tik). 1699. [– Gr. διακριτικός, f. διακρίνειν distinguish; see DIA-¹, CRITIC *a.*]

A. *adj.* Serving to distinguish, distinctive; in *Gram.* applied to signs or marks used to distinguish different sounds or values of the same letter or character; *e.g.* è, é, ê, ë, etc.

B. *sb. Gram.* A diacritic sign or mark 1866. So **Diacri·tical** *a.* diacritic; also, capable of distinguishing. **Diacri·tically** *adv.*

Diactinic (dəi,ækti·nik), *a.* 1867. [f. DI-³ + ACTINIC.] *Optics.* Having the property of transmitting the actinic rays of light. So **Dia·ctinism,** d. condition.

‖**Diadelphia** (dəiădeˑlfiă). 1762. [mod.L. (Linnæus 1735), f. Gr. δι- DI-² + ἀδελφός brother + -IA¹.] *Bot.* The seventeenth class in the Linnæan Sexual system, including plants with stamens normally in two bundles. Hence **Diade·lphian** *a.*

Diadelphic (dəiăde·lfik), *a.* 1847. [f. as prec. + -IC.] **a.** *Bot.* = DIADELPHOUS. **b.** *Chem.* Of a compound: Having the elements combined in two groups 1866.

Diadelphous (dəiăde·lfəs), *a.* 1807. [f. as prec. + -OUS.] *Bot.* Of stamens: United by the filaments so as to form two bundles. Of plants: Having the stamens so united.

Diadem (dəi·ădem). ME. [– (O)Fr. *diadème* – L. *diadema* – Gr. διάδημα regal fillet of the Persian kings, f. διαδεῖν bind round.] **1.** A crown. (Now chiefly *poet.* and *rhet.*) **b.** *spec.* A band or fillet of cloth, worn round the head, originally by Eastern monarchs, as a badge of royalty 1579. **c.** *Her.* Applied to the circles which close on the top of the crowns of sovereigns, and support the mound 1727. **2.** *fig.* Royal or imperial dignity, sovereignty ME. **3.** *fig.* and *transf.* 1526. **4.** Short for *d.-monkey.*

1. Diocletian..ventured to assume the d...It was no more than a broad white fillet set with pearls, which encircled the emperor's head GIBBON. **3.** The crescent moon, the d. of night, Stars countless COWPER.

Comb.: **d.-lemur,** a species of *Indris*; **-monkey,** *Cercopithecus diadematus*; **-spider,** the garden spider, *Epeira diadema.*

Di·adem, *v.* ME. [f. prec. sb.] *trans.* To adorn with or as with a diadem; to crown. Chiefly in *pa. pple.*

And every stalk is diadem'd with flowers SIR W. JONES. The Judge that comes in mercy..To d. the right NEALE. So **Di·ademated** *ppl. a.* diademed. ? *Obs.*

‖**Diadoche** (dəi,æ·dǒki). 1706. [Gr. διαδοχή succession.] Succession; *spec.* in *Med.* the exchange of one disease into another of different character and in a different situation.

Diadochian (dəiădōᵘ·kiăn), *a.* 1881. [f. Gr. διάδοχος succeeding, successor (cf. prec.) + -IAN.] Belonging to the *Diadochi* or Macedonian generals among whom the empire of Alexander the Great was divided after his death.

†**Di·adrom, -ome.** 1661. [– Gr. διαδρομή a running across.] A vibration of a pendulum –1690.

Diæresis (dəi,e·rīsis, -īə·rīsis). Also **dieresis.** 1611. [– late L. *diæresis* – Gr. διαίρεσις, f. διαιρεῖν divide.] **1.** The division of one syllable into two, as in *aër*, etc. 1656. **b.** The sign [¨] marking such a division, or placed over the second of two vowels, to indicate that they are to be sounded separately 1611. **2.** *Prosody.* The division made in a line or a verse when the end of a foot coincides with the end of a word 1844. **3.** *Surg.* Separation of parts normally united, as by a wound or burn, lancing, etc. 1706.

Diæretic (dəi,ěre·tik). Also **dieretic.** 1640. [– Gr. διαιρετικός divisible, f. διαιρεῖν; see prec., -IC.]

A. *adj.* Of, pertaining to, or by means of diæresis or division.

B. *sb.* A caustic agent 1721.

Diageotropic (dəiă,dʒī,otrǫ·pik), *a.* 1880. [f. DIA-¹ + GEOTROPIC.] *Bot.* Characterized by diageotropism. Hence **Di:ageo·tropism** (*Bot.*), the tendency in parts of plants to grow transversely to the earth's radius.

Diaglyph (dəi·ăglif). *rare.* 1864. [f. stem of Gr. διαγλύφειν carve in intaglio.] An intaglio. Hence **Diagly·phic** *a.* pertaining to or of the nature of an intaglio.

Diagnose (dəiăgnōᵘ·z), *v.* 1861. [f. next.] *trans.* To make a diagnosis of; to identify by careful observation. Also *absol.*

Diagnosis (dəiăgnōᵘ·sis). Pl. **-oses.** 1681. [– mod.L. – Gr. διάγνωσις, f. διαγιγνώσκειν distinguish, discern, f. διά DIA-¹ + γιγνώσκειν perceive.] **1.** *Med.* Determination of the nature of a diseased condition; identification of a disease by investigation of its symptoms and history; also, the formal statement of this. Also *transf.* and *fig.* **2.** *Biol.*, etc. Distinctive characterization in precise terms (*of* a genus, species, etc.) 1853.

1. *transf.* Our d. of the character of a person 1868. **2.** The 'Genera Piscium' contains well-defined diagnoses of 45 genera 1880.

Diagnostic (dəiăgnǫ·stik). 1625. [– Gr. διαγνωστικός able to distinguish, ἡ διαγνωστική (sc. τέχνη) the art of distinguishing diseases; see prec., -IC. Cf. Fr. *diagnostique*.]

A. *adj.* **1.** Of or pertaining to diagnosis. **2.** Of value for purposes of diagnosis; specially characteristic, distinctive 1650.

B. *sb.*; occas. in *collect. pl.* **diagnostics. 1.** = DIAGNOSIS 1. 1625. **2.** A distinctive symptom or characteristic 1646.

Hence **Diagno·stically** *adv.* by means of diagnosis, with reference to diagnosis. **Diagno·sticate** *v.* = DIAGNOSE *v.* **Di:agnosti·cian,** one skilled in diagnosis. var. **Diagnost** (*rare*).

Diago·meter. 1863. [– Fr. *diagomètre*, f. Gr. διάγειν carry across; see -METER.] *Electr.* An instrument for measuring the electro-conductive power of various substances.

Diagonal (dəi,æ·gŏnăl). 1541. [– L. *diagonalis*, f. Gr. διαγώνιος from angle to angle, f. διά across, DIA-[1] + γωνία angle; see -AL[1]. Cf. (O)Fr. *diagonal*.]

A. *adj.* **1.** *Geom.* Extending, as a line, from any angular point of a quadrilateral or multi-lateral figure to a non-adjacent angular point. Hence *gen.* Extending from one corner to the opposite corner. **2.** More loosely: Having an oblique direction; inclined at an angle other than a right angle (usually about 45°) 1665. **3.** Marked with diagonal lines, or having some part placed diagonally 1679.

3. *D. cloth*: a twilled fabric having the edges d., *i.e.* running obliquely to the lists. *D. couching* (in needlework): couching in which the stitches form a zigzag pattern. *D. scale*: a scale marked with equidistant parallel lines crossed at right angles by others at smaller intervals, and having one of the larger divisions additionally crossed by parallels obliquely placed: used for measurement of small fractions of the unit of length.

Comb.: **d.-built** *a.*, (a boat or ship) having the outer skin consisting of two layers of planking making angles of about 45° with the keel in opposite directions; **-planed** *a.*, (a crystal) having facets situated obliquely; **-wise** *adv.* = DIAGONALLY.

B. *sb.* **1.** *Geom.* A diagonal line 1571; a diagonal line of things arranged in a square or other parallelogram (*e.g.* of squares on a chess-board); a part of any structure, as a beam, etc., placed diagonally 1837. **2.** = *d. cloth* (see A. 3) 1861.

So **Dia·gonalize** *v.* to move in a d. (*rare*). **Dia·gonally** *adv.* var. †**Dia·gony** *sb.*

†**Diago·nial.** 1624. [f. Gr. διαγώνιος (see prec.) + -AL[1].] = DIAGONAL; also diagonally opposite; *fig.* diametrically opposed –1678.

Both d. contraries MILT.

Diagram (dəi·ăgræm), *sb.* 1619. [– L. *diagramma* – Gr. διάγραμμα, f. διαγράφειν mark out by lines, f. διά DIA-[1] + γράφειν write. See -GRAM.] **1.** *Geom.* A figure composed of lines, serving to illustrate a statement or to aid in a demonstration 1645. **2.** An illustrative figure giving an outline or general scheme of an object and its various parts 1619. **3.** A graphic representation of the course or results of any action or process or its variations. (Often with defining word prefixed, as *indicator-d.* (in the steam-engine, etc.) †**4.** After Gr. usage: A list; a detailed inscription; also, 'the title of a booke' (Cockeram) –1662. †**5.** A musical scale –1751.

2. *Floral d.* (Bot.): a linear drawing showing the position and number of the parts of a flower as seen on a transverse section. Hence **Di·agram** *v.* to make a d. of (*rare*). **Di:agramma·tic** *a.* having the form or nature of a d.; of or pertaining to diagrams. **Diagramma·tically** *adv.* in the form of a d.; with diagrammatic representation.

Diagrammatize (dəiăgræ·mătəiz), *v.* 1884. [f. Gr. διαγραμματ-, stem of διάγραμμα DIAGRAM + -IZE.] To put into the form of a diagram.

Diagraph (dəi·ăgrɑf). 1847. [– Fr. *diagraphe*, f. stem of Gr. διαγράφειν; see DIAGRAM, -GRAPH.] **1.** An instrument for drawing mechanically projections of objects. **2.** A combined protractor and scale used in plotting. So **Diagra·phic,** †**-al** *a.* of or pertaining to drawing or graphic representation. **Diagra·phics,** the art of drawing.

‖**Diagry·dium.** ME. [Late L., a corruption of Gr. δακρύδιον 'a kind of scammony', dim. of δάκρυ. In Fr. *diagrède*.] *Pharm.* A preparation of scammony.

Diaheliotropic (dəiă,hī:liotrǫ·pik), *a.* 1880. [f. DIA-[1] + HELIOTROPIC.] *Bot.* Of a plant-organ: Growing transversely to the direction of incident light. So **Diahelio·tropism,** a tendency in plants to do this.

Dial (dəi·ăl), *sb.* late ME. [– med.L. *diale* dial of a clock (XIV, XV), n. of adj. **dialis*, implied by *dialiter* daily, f. L. *dies* day; see -AL[1]. Cf. OFr. *dial* masc., wheel in clock that completes one turn daily.] **1.** An instrument serving to tell the hour of the day, by means of the sun's shadow upon a graduated surface; a SUN-DIAL. **2.** With qualifying words: *e.g. declining, horizontal, vertical, nocturnal* (= MOON-DIAL), etc. 1605. †**3.** A time-piece of any kind –1676. Also *fig.* **4.** The face of a clock or watch. Cf. *dial-plate*. 1575. **5.** A †mariner's or miner's compass 1523. **6.** An external face on which revolutions, pressure, etc., are indicated by an index-finger or otherwise, as in a gas-meter, etc. 1747. **b.** The human face (*slang*) 1811. **7.** A lapidary's instrument for holding a gem while exposed to the wheel 1875. Also *attrib.*

Comb.: **d.-bird,** an Indian bird (*Copsichus saularis*); also extended to the genus *Copsichus*; **-lock,** a lock furnished with dials, having pointers which must be set in a given way before the bolt will move; **-piece, -plate,** the face-plate of a d.; *spec.* (in *Clock-making*) the sheet of metal, glass, etc. on the face of which the hours, etc. are marked; **-writer,** a typewriter with a d.

Dial (dəi·ăl), *v.* 1653. [f. prec. sb.] **1.** To measure as with a dial 1821. **2.** To survey with the aid of a miner's dial 1653. **3.** To mark as the plate of a dial 1817. **4.** To indicate on a dial (a number required, e.g. on an automatic telephone). Also *absol.* to make a call in this way. 1922.

Dialect (dəi·ălekt). 1551. [– Fr. *dialecte* or L. *dialectus* – Gr. διάλεκτος discourse, way of speaking, f. διαλέγεσθαι hold discourse, f. διά DIA- + λέγειν speak.] **1.** Manner of speaking, language, speech; *esp.* one peculiar to an individual or class; phraseology, idiom 1579. **2.** A variety of a language arising from local peculiarities. (In relation to modern languages usually *spec.* A variety of speech differing from the standard language; a provincial method of speech.) Also, more widely, a language in its relation to the family to which it belongs. 1577. †**3.** = DIALECTIC *sb.*[1] 1. –1698.

1. By corruption of speech they false d. and misse-sound it NASHE. A Babylonish D., Which learned Pedants much affect BUTLER *Hud.* I. i. 93. **2.** The Durham d. is the same as that spoken in Northumberland HALLIWELL. **3.** Logike otherwise called Dialecte 1551. Hence **Diale·ctal** *a.* belonging to or of the nature of a d. **Diale·ctally** *adv.* in dialect; argumentatively.

Dialectic (dəiăle·ktik), *sb.*[1] ME. [– (O)Fr. *dialectique* or L. *dialectica* – Gr. διαλεκτική subst. use (sc. τέχνη art) of fem. of διαλεκτικός. The L. *dialectica* was also treated as a n. pl., whence Eng. *dialectics*; see -IC 2.] **1.** The art of critical examination into the truth of an opinion: in earlier Eng. use, a synonym of LOGIC as applied to formal rhetorical reasoning; logical disputation. Also in pl. form **Dialectics. 2.** In modern Philosophy: Applied by Kant to the criticism which shows the mutually contradictory character of the principles of science, when employed to determine objects beyond the limits of experience (*e.g.* the soul, the world, God); by Hegel (a.) to the process of thought by which such contradictions are seen to merge themselves in a higher truth that comprehends them; and (b.) to the world-process, which, in his view, is but the thought-process on its objective side, and develops similarly by a continuous unification of opposites 1798.

Dialectic (dəiăle·ktik), *a.* and *sb.*[2] 1640. [– L. *dialecticus* – Gr. διαλεκτικός, f. διάλεκτος; see DIALECT.]

A. *adj.* **1.** Of, pertaining to, or of the nature of logical disputation 1650. **2.** Addicted to logical disputation 1831. **3.** = DIALECTAL 1813.

B. *sb.*[2] [The adj. used absol.] One who pursues the dialectic method; a critical inquirer after truth; a logical disputant 1640.

Hence **Diale·ctical** *a.* = DIALECTIC *a.*; dialectal; *sb.* = DIALECTIC *sb.*[1] 1. **Diale·ctically** *adv.* by means of d.; as regards dialect.

Dialectician (dəi:ălekti·făn). 1693. [– Fr. *dialecticien* (Rabelais).] **1.** One skilled in dialectic; a logician. **2.** A student of dialects 1848.

1. An art that..might help the subtile d. to oppose even the man he could not refute BOLINGBROKE.

Diale·ctics, *sb. pl.*; see DIALECTIC *sb.*[1] 1.

Dialectology (dəiălektǫ·lŏdʒi). 1879. [See -LOGY.] The study of dialects; that branch of philology which treats of dialects. Hence **Dialecto·loger, Dialecto·logist. Dialecto-lo·gical** *a.*

Dialing; see DIALLING.

Dialist (dəi·ălist). 1652. [f. DIAL *sb.* + -IST.] A maker of dials; one skilled in dialling.

‖**Diallage**[1] (dəi,æ·lădʒi). 1706. [mod.L. – Gr. διαλλαγή interchange.] *Rhet.* A figure by which arguments, after being considered from various points of view, are all brought to bear upon one point.

Diallage[2] (dəi·ălĕdʒ). 1805. [– Fr. *diallage*, f. Gr. διαλλαγή (see prec.), named by Haüy 1801, from its dissimilar cleavages.] *Min.* A grass-green variety of pyroxene, of lamellar or foliated structure: formerly applied also to hypersthene, bronzite, etc.

‖**Diallelon** (dəiăli·lǫ[u]n). 1837. [mod.L., f. Gr. δι' ἀλλήλων through or by means of one another.] *Logic.* Definition in a circle, *i.e.* by means of the term to be defined.

‖**Diallelus** (dəiăli·lǒs). 1837. [mod.L., f. Gr. (τρόπος) διάλληλος reasoning in a circle; see prec.] *Logic.* Reasoning in a circle.

Dialler, dialer (dəi·ăləɹ). 1747. [f. DIAL *sb.* + -ER[1].] One who surveys mines by the aid of a dial.

Dialling, dialing (dəi·ăliŋ), *vbl. sb.* 1570. [f. DIAL *sb.* and *v.* + -ING[1].] **1.** The art of constructing dials. †**b.** The measurement of time by dials. **2.** The use of a dial in mining 1670.

Di-a·llyl. 1869. [DI-[2].] *Chem. sb.* The organic radical allyl in the free state, C_6H_{10} = $C_3H_5.C_3H_5$; see ALLYL. *attrib.* Containing two equivalents of allyl.

Dialogic, -al (dəiălǫ·dʒik, -ăl), *a.* 1601. [– late L. *dialogicos* – Gr. διαλογικός, f. διάλογος DIALOGUE; see -IC, -ICAL.] Of, pertaining to, or of the nature of dialogue. Hence **Dialo·gically** *adv.*

Dialogism (dəi,æ·lŏdʒiz'm). 1580. [– late L. *dialogismos* – Gr. διαλογισμός f. διαλογίζεσθαι DIALOGIZE; see -ISM. Cf. Fr. *dialogisme*.] **1.** *Rhet.* The discussion of a subject under the form of a dialogue. **2.** A conversational phrase or speech; a DIALOGUE 1623. **3.** *Logic.* A form of argument having a single premiss and a disjunctive conclusion 1880.

Dialogist (dəi,æ·lŏdʒist). 1660. [– late L. *dialogista* – Gr. διαλογιστής, f. διάλογος; see DIALOGUE, -IST. Cf. Fr. *dialogiste*.] **1.** One who takes part in a dialogue 1677. **2.** A writer of dialogues. Hence **Dialogi·stic, -al** *a.* having the nature or form of dialogue; taking part in a dialogue; argumentative. **Dialogi·stically** *adv.*

Dialogite (dəi,æ·lŏdʒəit). Erron. **diall-.** 1826. [– Gr. διαλογή doubt, selection; see -ITE[1] 2b.] *Min.* A rose-red carbonate of manganese; = *rhodochrosite*.

Dialogize (dəi,æ·lŏdʒəiz), *v.* 1601. [– Gr. διαλογίζεσθαι converse, debate, f. διάλογος; see next, -IZE.] *intr.* To converse, or carry on a dialogue (*with*).

Dialogue (dəi·ălǫg), *sb.* ME. [– OFr. *dialoge* (mod. *dialogue*) – L. *dialogus* – Gr. διάλογος conversation, discourse, f. διαλέγεσθαι converse. See DIALECT.] **1.** A conversation between two or more persons; a colloquy; (without *pl.*) conversation. **2.** A literary work in the form of a conversation between two or more persons ME.; (without *pl.*) literary composition of this nature 1589.

1. Feare you not my part of the D. SHAKS.

Dialogue (dəi·ălǫg), *v.* 1597. [f. prec. sb.] **1.** *intr.* To hold a dialogue 1607. Also *transf.* and *fig.* **2.** *trans.* To express in the form of a dialogue 1597.

2. And dialogu'd for him what he would say SHAKS. Hence **Dia·loguer** (*rare*), = DIALOGIST 1. **Di·aloguist,** a writer of dialogue.

Di·al-plate. 1690. [f. DIAL *sb.* + PLATE.] = DIAL *sb.* 4.

Dialu·ric, *a.* 1845. [f. DI-[2] + AL(LOXAN + URIC.] *Chem.* In *d. acid*, $C_4N_2H_4O_4$, an acid obtained by hydrogenizing alloxan.

Dialy- (dəi:ăli) – Gr. διαλυ-, stem of διαλύειν, used with the sense 'separated', or 'non-united'. Thus:

Dialyca·rpel [see CARPEL], 'an ovary or fruit with ununited carpels' (*Syd. Soc. Lex.*). **Dialyca·rpous** *a.* [Gr. καρπός], having the carpels distinct. **Dialype·talous** *a.*, having the petals distinct. **Dialyphy·llous** *a.* [Gr. φύλλον], having the leaves distinct. So **Dialyse·palous, Dialysta·minous** *adjs.*, having the sepals, the stamens, distinct.

Dialyse, -ze (dəi·ăləiz), *v.* 1861. [f. DIALYSIS, after *analyse.*] *Chem.* To separate the crystalloid part of a mixture from the colloid, in the process of chemical dialysis. Hence **Di·aly:sable, -zable** *a.* capable of separation by dialysis. **Dia·lysate** (*Chem.*), that portion of a mixture that remains after dialysis. **Dia·lysa:tor, Di·alyser, -zer,** an apparatus for effecting dialysis; a vessel formed of parchment or animal membrane floated on water, through which the crystalloids pass, leaving the colloids behind.

Dialysis (dəi,æ·lisis). Pl. **-lyses.** 1586. [– L. *dialysis* – Gr. διάλυσις, f. διαλύειν part asunder, f. διά DIA-[1] + λύειν set free.] †**1.** *Rhet.* **a.** A statement of disjunctive propositions. **b.** = ASYNDETON. –1823. †**2.** *Gram.* = DIÆRESIS 1. –1818. †**3.** *Med.* Dissolution of strength –1883. **4.** *Path.* Solution of continuity 1811. **5.** *Chem.* The process of separating the soluble crystalloid substances in a mixture from the colloid by means of a dialyser 1861.

Dialytic (dəiăli·tik), *a.* 1846. [– Gr. διαλυτικός able to dissolve, f. διαλύειν; see prec., -IC.] Of or pertaining to DIALYSIS, in various senses.

D. telescope: one in which achromatism is effected by means of two lenses separated and placed at some distance from each other. Hence **Dialy·tically** *adv.* by way of dialysis.

Di:ama·gnet. 1864. [DIA- *pref.*[1]] = DIAMAGNETIC *sb.*

Diamagnetic (dəi:ămægne·tik). 1846. [DIA- *pref.*[1]]

A. *adj.* **1.** Exhibiting the phenomena of DIAMAGNETISM; opp. to *magnetic* or *paramagnetic.* **2.** Belonging or relating to diamagnetic bodies, or to diamagnetism 1846.

B. *sb.* A diamagnetic body or substance 1846. Hence **Diamagne·tically** *adv.* in the manner of a d. body, or of diamagnetism.

Diamagnetism (dəi:ămæ·gnĕtiz'm). 1850. [DIA- *pref.*[1]] **a.** The phenomena exhibited by a class of bodies, which, when freely suspended and acted on by magnetism, take up a position transverse to that of the magnetic axis, *i.e.* lie (approximately) east and west; the force to which these are attributed; the quality of being diamagnetic. **b.** That branch of science which treats of diamagnetic bodies and phenomena.

Diamagnetize (dəi:ămæ·gnĕtəiz), *v.* 1877. [DIA- *pref.*[1]] To render diamagnetic. Hence **Diama:gnetiza·tion.** (Dicts.)

Diama:gneto·meter. 1886. [f. DIAMAGNET(ISM + -METER.] An instrument for measuring diamagnetic force.

‖**Diamanté** (diăma·nte). 1904. [Fr., pa. ppl. formation on *diamant* DIAMOND.] Material scintillating with powdered crystal, etc. Also *attrib.*

Di:amanti·ferous, *a.* 1878. [f. after Fr. *diamantifère*, f. *diamant* DIAMOND; see -FEROUS.] Diamond-producing.

Diamantine (dəiămæ·ntin). 1591. [– Fr. *diamantin*, f. *diamant* DIAMOND; see -INE[1].] **A.** *adj.* **1.** Consisting of, or of the nature of, diamond; producing diamonds 1605. †**2.** Adamantine –1649. **B.** *sb.* A preparation of adamantine or crystallized boron, used as a polishing powder for steel work 1884.

Diamesogamous (dəi:ămėsǫ·găməs), *a.* [f. Gr. διάμεσον the intervening part + γάμος marriage + -OUS.] *Bot.* Of flowers: Fertilized by the intervention of some external agency, as that of insects or of wind.

Diameter (dəi,æ·mĭtəɹ). ME. [– (O)Fr. *diamètre* – L. *diametrus, -os* – Gr. διάμετρος (sc. γραμμή line) diagonal, diameter, f. διά DIA-[1] + μέτρον measure.] **1.** *Geom.* A straight line passing through the centre of a circle (or sphere), and terminated at each end by its circumference (or surface). Hence, a chord of any conic (or of a quadric surface) passing through the centre; also, a line passing through the middle points of a system of parallel chords, in a curve of any order. Also *gen.* **2.** The transverse measurement of any geometrical figure or body; width, thickness ME. **b.** *Archit.* The transverse measurement of a column at its base, taken as a unit of measurement for the proportions of an order 1604. **c.** Whole extent from side to side or from end to end 1602.

2. c. [Slander], whose whisper o'er the world's d... Transports his poison'd shot *Haml.* IV. i. 41.

Diametral (dəi,æ·mĭtrăl). 1555. [– (O)Fr. *diamétral* – late L. *diametralis*, f. *diametrus*; see prec., -AL[1].]

A. *adj.* **1.** Of or relating to a diameter; of the nature of a diameter. †**2.** = DIAMETRICAL 2. –1768.

Phr. †*D. number* (Arith.), one that is the product of two factors the sum of whose squares is a square; thus $3^2 + 4^2 = 5^2$; then $3 \times 4 = 12$ is a d. number. *D. plane*: (*a*) *Geom.* a plane passing through the centre of a solid; (*b*) *Cryst.* a plane passing through two of the axes of a crystal.

†**B.** *sb.* A diametral line, diameter –1676.

Hence **Dia·metrally** *adv.* in the way of a diameter; †directly; diametrically (*lit.* and *fig.*).

Diametric (dəiăme·trik), *a.* 1802. [f. next by substitution of -IC for -ICAL (q.v.).] **1.** Relating to or of the nature of a diameter 1868. **2.** Of opposition, etc.: = DIAMETRICAL 2.

Diametrical (dəiăme·trikăl), *a.* 1553. [f. Gr. διαμετρικός (f. διάμετρος DIAMETER) + -AL[1]; see -ICAL.] **1.** Of or pertaining to a diameter; passing through or along a diameter; diametral. **2.** Of opposition, etc.: Direct, entire, complete (like that of the ends of a diameter). Usu. *fig.* 1613. †**b.** Directly opposed –1734.

2. b. The Revolution was very quick and d. NORTH. Hence **Diame·trically** *adv.* in the manner or direction of a diameter; directly, entirely.

Diamide (dəi·ăməid). 1866. [DI-[2].] *Chem.* An amide formed on the type of two molecules of ammonia, the hydrogen of which is replaced by one or more acid radicals.

Diami·do-. *Chem.* See DI-[2] and AMIDO-.

Diamine (dəi·ăməin). 1866. [DI-[2].] *Chem.* An amine derived from two molecules of ammonia the hydrogen of which is replaced by one or more basic radicals, as *Ethene-diamine*

$$\left.\begin{matrix}NH_2\\NH_2\end{matrix}\right\}C_2H_4.$$

Diamond (dəi·ămənd, dəi·mənd), *sb.* [ME. *diama(u)nt* – (O)Fr. *diamant* – med.L. *diamas, diamant-*, alt. of L. *adamas* ADAMANT, prob. through a pop. form **adimas* (whence OFr. *aïmant*, mod. *aimant* lodestone), and by association with words in DIA-.] **1.** A very hard and brilliant precious stone, consisting of pure carbon crystallized in regular octahedrons and allied forms, and either colourless or variously tinted. It is the hardest substance known. (For TABLE, ROSE, and BRILLIANT cutting, see these words.) †**b.** = ADAMANT –1667. **c.** *Her.* In blazoning by precious stones, the name for the tincture *sable* 1572. **2.** *transf.* (usu. with distinguishing epithet) 1591. **3.** *fig.* ME. **4.** A tool consisting of a small diamond set in a handle; a *glazier's*, or *cutting d.* 1697. **5.** A diamond-shaped figure, *i.e.* a plane figure in the form of a section of an octahedral diamond; a rhomb (or a square) placed with its diagonals vertical and horizontal; a lozenge 1496. **b.** *spec.* A figure of this form printed on a playing card; a card of the suit so marked 1594. **c.** The figure formed by the four bases in base-ball; hence, the whole field (*U.S.*) 1894. **6.** *Printing.* The second smallest standard size of roman or italian type, a size smaller than pearl. Also *attrib.* [– Du. *diamant*: so named by its introducer.] 1778.

This line is a specimen of the type called Diamond.

7. *attrib.* Made or consisting of diamond, as *d. lens*, etc. 1553; †hard as diamond, adamantine –1659; set with a diamond or diamonds, as *d. button, clasp, ring*, etc. **8.** *attrib.* or *adj.* Of the shape of a diamond (see sense 5), as *d. fret, netting*, etc.; having a head of this shape, as *d. dibber*, etc. 1598; having a surface cut into facets 1717.

1. b. His vaunting foe, Though huge, and in a Rock of D. Armd MILT. *P. L.* VI. 364. **2.** *Bristol d.* (see BRISTOL). **3.** Each puny wave in diamonds roll'd O'er the calm deep SCOTT.

Phrases. **a.** *Black d.*: (*a*) a d. of a black or brown colour; (*b*) *pl.* a playful name for coal. **b.** *Rough d.*: a d. before it is cut and polished; hence *fig.* a person of high intrinsic worth, but rude and unpolished. **c.** *D. cut d.*: an equal match in sharpness, finesse, etc.

Combs.: **d.-bird,** an Australian shrike of the genus *Pardalotus*, esp. *P. punctatus*; **-borer** = *diamond-drill* (*b*); **-breaker** = *diamond-mortar*; **-broaching,** broached hewn-work done with a d.-hammer; **-crossing,** a crossing on a railway where two lines of rails intersect obliquely without communicating; **-drill,** (*a*) one armed with one or more diamonds for boring hard substances; (*b*) a drill for boring rocks, having a head set with rough diamonds; **-dust** = *diamond-powder*; **-hammer,** a mason's hammer furnished with pyramidal pick points for stone-dressing; **-knot** (*Naut.*), a kind of ornamental knot worked with the strands of a rope; **-mortar,** a steel mortar used for crushing diamonds; **-plaice,** the common plaice (*local*); **-plough,** (*a*) a d.-pointed instrument for engraving upon glass; (*b*) a small plough having a mould-board and share of a d. shape; **-powder,** the powder produced by grinding or crushing diamonds; **d. rattlesnake,** a rattle-snake (*Crotalus adamanteus*) having d.-shaped markings; **-tool,** a metal-turning tool whose cutting edge is formed by facets; **-weevil** = DIAMOND-BEETLE; **-wheel,** a metal wheel used with d.-powder and oil in grinding hard gems.

Di·amond, *v.* 1751. [f. prec. sb.] To adorn with or as with diamonds.

He plays, dresses, diamonds himself H. WALPOLE. Hence **Di·amonded** *a.* adorned with or as with diamonds; having the figure of a diamond.

Di·amond-back. 1819. [Short for next.] **A.** *adj.* = next.

B. *sb.* **a.** The Diamond-back Moth. **b.** The Diamond-backed Turtle.

Di·amond-backed, *a.* 1895. [f. DIAMOND *sb.* + BACKED.] Having the back marked with lozenge-shaped figures.

Diamond-backed turtle or *terrapin*, the fresh-water tortoise of the Atlantic coast of N. America, *Malaclemmys palustris.*

Di·amond-beetle. 1806. A South American beetle, *Curculio* (*Entimus*) *imperialis*, having elytra studded with brilliant sparkling points.

Di·amond-cut, *a.* 1637. **1.** Cut into the shape of a diamond. **2.** Cut with facets like a diamond, as *diamond-cut glass* 1703.

Di·amond-cutter. 1722. A lapidary who cuts and polishes diamonds. So **Di·amond-cutting** *sb.*

Diamondi·ferous *a.* 1870. [f. DIAMOND, after *diamantiferous.*] Diamond-producing.

Dia·mondize, *v.* 1599. [f. as prec. + -IZE.] To bedeck with or as with diamonds.

Diamond-point. 1874. **1.** A stylus tipped with a fragment of diamond, used in engraving, etc. **2.** *Railways.* Usually in *pl.* The set of points at a diamond crossing; in *sing.* one of the acute angles formed by two rails at such a crossing 1881. Also *attrib.*

Diamond-snake. 1814. Any snake having diamond-shaped markings, *esp.* **a.** a large Australian serpent, *Morelia spilotes*; **b.** a venomous Tasmanian serpent, *Hoplocephalus superbus.*

‖**Diamorphosis** (dəiămǫ·ɹfŏsis, -mǫɹfōᵘ·sis). 1861. [mod.L. – Gr.] **1.** 'The building up of a body to its proper form' (*Syd. Soc. Lex.*). ¶**2.** *erron.* for DIMORPHISM.

Dia·myl. 1850. [DI-[2].] *Chem.* **a.** *sb.* The organic radical AMYL in the free state, $C_{10}H_{22} = C_5H_{11}.C_5H_{11}$. **b.** *attrib.*, etc. Containing two equivalents of amyl.

Dia·mylene. *Chem.* See DI-[2] and AMYLENE.

†**Di·an.** 1591. [– Fr. *diane* – Sp. *diana*

reveille, f. *dia* day.] A trumpet-call or drum-roll at early morn. Also *attrib.*

The bee..Beating the d. with its drums MARVELL.

Diana (dəiˌæ·nă, dəiˌēⁱ·nă), anglicized DIAN (dəi·ăn). ME. [– L. *Diana*; also *diane* (XIII–XVI) – (O)Fr. *Diane.*] **1.** An Italian divinity, the moon-goddess, patroness of virginity and of hunting; subseq. identified with the Greek Artemis, and so with Oriental deities. **b.** *poet.* The moon ME. **2.** In early Chemistry a name for silver 1706.

1. Or on Dianaes Altar to protest For aie, austerity and single life *Mids. N.* I. i. 89. **b.** Meek Dian's crest BYRON.

Diana monkey, *Cercopithecus diana,* a large African monkey, with a white crescent marked on its forehead.

‖**Diandria** (dəiˌæ·ndriă). 1753. [mod.L. (Linnæus 1735), f. DI-² after MONANDRIA.] *Bot.* The second class in the Linnæan sexual system, comprising all plants having two stamens. So **Dia·ndrous** *a.* belonging to the class Diandria; two-stamened.

Dianodal (dəiănōᵘ·dăl), *a.* 1870. [f. DIA-¹ + NODE + -AL¹.] *Math.* Passing through nodes.

Dianoetic (dəiăno,e·tik). 1677. [– Gr. διανοητικός, f. διανοεῖσθαι think; see -IC.] *Metaph.*

A. *adj.* Of or pertaining to thought; intellectual.

B. *sb.* Applied by Sir W. Hamilton to denote the operations of the discursive faculty 1836. Hence †**Dianoe·tical** *a.*; **-ly** *adv.*

Di:anoia·logy. [f. Gr. διάνοια intelligence + -LOGY.] *Metaph.* That portion of logic which deals with dianoetic or demonstrative propositions (Sir W. Hamilton).

‖**Dianthus** (dəiˌæ·nþŏs). 1849. [f. Gr. Διός of Jupiter + ἄνθος flower.] *Bot.* A genus of caryophyllaceous flowering plants, which includes the pinks and carnations; one of these. Hence **Dia·nthine,** name of an aniline dye.

‖**Diapa·lma.** 1646. [med.L., f. *dia-* DIA-² + L. *palma* palm. Cf. Fr. *diapalme.*] *Pharm.* A desiccating plaster composed originally of palm oil, litharge, and sulphate of zinc, now of white wax, emplastrum simplex, and sulphate of zinc.

Di·apase. 1591. = DIAPASON (*poet.*).

Diapasm (dəi·ăpæz'm). *arch.* 1599. [– L. *diapasma* – Gr., f. διαπάσσειν sprinkle over.] A scented powder for sprinkling over the person.

Diapason (dəiăpēⁱ·zən), *sb.* ME. [– L. *diapason* – Gr. διαπασῶν, i.e. διὰ πασῶν (sc. χορδῶν), more fully ἡ διὰ πασῶν χορδῶν συμφωνία the concord through all the notes (of the scale). Cf. (O)Fr. *diapason.*] †**1.** The interval of an octave; the consonance of the highest and lowest notes of the musical scale –1787. †**2.** *fig.* Complete concord or harmony –1719. **3.** More or less vaguely extended, with the idea of 'all the tones or notes' (see quots.) 1501. **4.** *transf.* and *fig.* **a.** A rich outburst of sound 1589. **b.** Entire compass, reach 1851. **5.** A fixed standard of musical pitch; as in Fr. *diapason normal.* Also *fig.* 1875. **6.** The name of two stops in the organ, the *Open D.*, and the *Closed* or *Stopped D.*, so called because they extend through the whole compass of the instrument; also the name of other stops 1519. Also *attrib.*

2. A d. of vows and wishes BURTON. **3.** A full-mouth'd d. swallows all CRASHAW. Through all the compass of the Notes it ran, The D. closing full in Man DRYDEN. **4. a.** The D. of thy threates GREENE. **b.** The whole d. of joy and sorrow HELPS. Hence †**Diapa·son** *v.* (*intr.* and *trans.*) to resound sonorously; (*intr.*) to maintain accord *with.*

‖**Diapedesis** (dəi:ăpɪdī·sis). 1625. [mod.L. – Gr. διαπήδησις, f. (ult.) δια- through + πηδᾶν leap, throb.] *Path.* The oozing of blood through the unruptured walls of the blood-vessels.

†**Diapente** (dəiăpe·nti). ME. [– OFr. *diapente* – late L. *diapente* – Gr. διὰ πέντε through five; cf. DIAPASON, and DIA-².] **1.** *Mus.* The consonance or interval of a fifth –1787. **2.** *Pharm.* A medicine composed of five ingredients –1800; *transf.* punch –1741.

Diaper (dəi·ăpəɹ), *sb.* ME. [– OFr. *diapre,* earlier *diaspre* – med.L. *diasprum* – Byzantine Gr. δίασπρος, f. διά DIA-¹ + ἄσπρος white. The orig. meaning of the Gr. word is uncertain.] **1.** The name of a textile fabric; now, usually, a linen fabric, woven with patterns showing up by opposite reflections from its surface, and consisting of lines crossing diamond-wise, with the spaces filled up by parallel lines, leaves, dots, etc. **2.** A towel, napkin, or cloth of this material; a baby's napkin 1596. **3.** The geometrical or conventional pattern or design forming the ground of this fabric, or any similar pattern 1830. **b.** *Her.* A similar style of ornamentation used to cover the surface of a shield and form the ground 1634. Also *attrib.*

2. Let one attend him vvith a siluer Bason.. Another beare the Ewer: the third a D. *Tam. Shr.* I. i. 57.

Diaper (dəi·ăpəɹ), *v.* ME. [f. prec.; cf. (O)Fr. *diaprer, diapré.*] **1.** *trans.* To diversify the surface of with a diaper pattern; *transf.* and *fig.* to variegate. **2.** *intr.* To do diaper-work; to flourish 1573.

1. *fig.* The rayes Wherewith the sunne doth d. the seas W. BROWNE. Hence **Di·apering** *vbl. sb.* the production of a diaper pattern; a diaper pattern; diaper-work.

Diaphane (dəi·ăfēⁱn). 1561. [– (O)Fr. *diaphane* – med.L. *diaphanus*; see next.]

†**A.** *adj.* = DIAPHANOUS –1824.

B. *sb.* **1.** A transparent body or substance; a transparency 1840. **2.** A silk stuff, having transparent coloured figures 1824.

Hence †**Di·aphaned** *ppl. a.* made diaphanous. **Dia:phane·ity,** †**Diapha·nity,** the quality of being diaphanous. ‖**Dia·phanie,** a French process for the imitation of stained glass. **Diaphano·meter,** an instrument for measuring transparency, *esp.* that of the atmosphere. **Dia·phanoscope,** †a contrivance for viewing transparent positive photographs; also, an instrument used for the examination of internal organs by means of an electric light introduced into the abdomen. **Diaphano·scopy.**

Diaphanous (dəiˌæ·fănəs), *a.* 1614. [f. med.L. *diaphanus,* f. Gr. διαφανής, f. διά DIA-¹ + φαίνειν, φαν- to show; see -OUS.] Permitting light and vision to pass through; perfectly transparent.

Such a d. pellucid dainty body as you see a Crystal-Glasse is HOWELL. **Dia·phanous-ly** *adv.*, **-ness.**

Diaphemetric (dəiˌæ:fīme·trik), *a.* 18.. [f. Gr. δια- (DIA-¹) + ἁφή touch + -METRIC.] Relating to the measurement of the comparative tactile sensibility of parts, as *d. compasses.*

Diaphonic, -al (dəiăfǫ·nik, -ăl), *a.* 1775. [f. as DIAPHON-Y + IC, -AL¹; see -ICAL.] **1.** Of or pertaining to DIAPHONY 1822. **2.** = DIACOUSTIC. Hence **Diapho·nics,** (?*Obs.*) = DIACOUSTICS.

Diaphony (dəiˌæ·fŏni). 1656. [– late L. *diaphonia* – Gr. διαφωνία discord, f. διάφωνος, f. δια- apart + φωνεῖν to sound.] *Mus.* †**1.** Discord. **2.** The most primitive form of harmony, in which the parts proceeded by parallel motion in fourths, fifths, and octaves: the same as ORGANUM 1834.

‖**Diaphoresis** (dəi:ăforī·sis). 1681. [Late L. – Gr. διαφόρησις perspiration, f. διαφορεῖν, f. διά DIA-¹ + φορεῖν carry.] Perspiration, *esp.* that produced artificially.

Diaphoretic (dəi:ăfore·tik). 1563. [– late L. *diaphoreticus* – Gr. διαφορητικός, f. διαφόρησις perspiration; see prec., -IC.]

A. *adj.* Having the property of promoting perspiration; sudorific. var. †**Diaphore·tical** *a.*

B. *sb.* A medicinal agent doing this 1656.

Diaphragm (dəi·ăfræm), *sb.* ME. [– late L. *diaphragma* (also used) – Gr. διάφραγμα, f. διά DIA-¹ + φράγμα fence, φράσσειν fence in, hedge round.]

I. *Anat.* The septum or partition, partly muscular, partly tendinous, which in mammals divides the thoracic from the abdominal cavity; the midriff.

II. Transferred uses. **1.** *gen.* Applied to anything resembling the diaphragm in nature or function 1660. **2. a.** *Zool.* A partition separating the successive chambers of certain shells 1665. **b.** *Bot.* A septum or partition occurring in the tissues of plants; a transverse partition in a stem or leaf 1665. **3.** *Mech.* A thin lamina or plate serving as a partition, or for some specific purpose; also *transf.* 1665.

Hence **Diaphra·gmal** *a.* diaphragmatic. ‖**Diaphragma·lgia** [Gr. -αλγια], pain in the d. **Di:aphragmatic** *a.* of or pertaining to the d.; of the nature of a d.; **Diaphragma·tically** *adv.* by means of the d. ‖**Diaphragmati·tis, -mi·tis,** inflammation of the d. **Diaphra·gmatocele,** hernia of the d.

Di·aphragm, *v.* 1879. [f. prec.] *trans.* To fit or act upon with a diaphragm.

To d. down in *Optics*: to reduce the field of vision of (a lens, etc.) by means of an opaque diaphragm with a central aperture.

Diaphysis (dəiˌæ·fisis). 1831. [– Gr. διάφυσις growing through, f. διά DIA-¹ + φύσις growth.] **1.** *Anat.* 'The shaft of a long bone, as distinct from the extremities' (*Syd. Soc. Lex.*). **2.** *Bot.* 'A præternatural extension of the flower, or of an inflorescence' (*Treas. Bot.*) 1866.

‖**Diaplasis** (dəiˌæ·plăsis). 1704. [mod.L. – Gr. διάπλασις setting of a limb, f. διαπλάσσειν to form, mould.] *Surg.* The setting of a dislocated limb. Hence †**Diaplas·tic** *a.* good for a dislocated limb; also as *sb.*

†‖**Dia·pnoe.** 1681. [mod.L. – Gr. διαπνοή (Galen).] *Med.* An insensible perspiration on the skin –1706. Hence **Diapno·ic** *a.* producing this.

Diapophysis (dəiăpǫ·fisis). Pl. **-physes.** 1854. [f. Gr. δια- + ἀπόφυσις APOPHYSIS.] *Anat.* A term applied to a pair of exogenous segments of the typical vertebra, forming lateral processes of the neural arch. Hence **Diapophy·sial** *a.* of or belonging to a d.

‖**Diaporesis** (dəi:ăporī·sis). 1678. [mod.L. – Gr. διαπόρησις being at a loss.] *Rhet.* A figure, in which the speaker professes to be at a loss, which of two or more courses, statements, etc., to adopt.

Diarch (dəi·aɹk), *a.* 1884. [f. Gr. δι- DI-² + ἀρχή origin.] *Bot.* Proceeding from two distinct points of origin: said of the primary xylem of the root.

Diarchy (dəi·aɹki). 1835. [f. Gr. δι- DI-² + -αρχία rule, after *monarchy.*] A government by two rulers. **b.** Revived, esp. in the form **dyarchy,** in reference to the reformed Indian constitution of 1919. Hence **Dia·rchal, Dia·rchic (dy-)** *adjs.*

Diarian (dəiˌēᵊ·riăn). 1774. [f. DIARY *sb.* + -AN.]

A. *adj.* Of or pertaining to a diary; †journalistic. *var.* **Dia·rial** *a.*

B. *sb.* The writer of a diary (*rare*) 1800.

Diarist (dəi·ărist). 1818. [f. DIARY *sb.* + -IST.] One who keeps a diary. Hence **Diari·stic** *a.* of the style of a d.; of the nature of a diary. So **Di·arize** *v. intr.*, to write a record of events in a diary.

Diarrhœa (dəiărī·ă). Also **diarrhea.** ME. [– late L. *diarrhœa* (Cælius Aurelianus) – Gr. διάρροια (Hippocrates), f. διαρρεῖν flow through, f. διά DIA-¹ + ῥεῖν flow.] A disorder consisting in the too frequent evacuation of too fluid fæces, sometimes attended with griping pains. Also *transf.*

transf. He..was troubled with a d. of words H. WALPOLE. Hence **Diarrhœ·al, Diarrhœ·ic Diarrhœ·tic, -rhe·tic** *adjs.* of, pertaining to, or of the nature of d.

Diarthrodial (dəiˌaɹþrōᵘ·diăl), *a.* 1830. [f. DI-³ + ARTHRODIAL.] *Anat.* Pertaining to or characterized by diarthrosis.

Diarthrosis (dəiˌaɹþrōᵘ·sis). 1578. [f. DI-³ + *arthrosis* (see ARTHRO-).] *Anat.* The general term for all forms of articulation which admit of the motion of one bone upon another; free arthrosis.

Diary (dəi·ări), *sb.* 1581. [– L. *diarium* daily allowance, (later) journal, diary, in form subst. use of n. of *diarius* daily (which, however, is not pre-mediæval), f. *dies* day; see -ARY¹.] **1.** A daily record of events or transactions, a journal; specifically, a daily record of matters affecting the writer personally. **2.** A book prepared for keeping a daily record; also, applied to calendars containing daily memoranda 1605.

1. Diaries of wind and weather PLOT. **2.** This is my d., Wherin I note my actions of the day B. JONS.

Diary (dəi·ări), *a.* 1592. [– med.L. *diarius* (see prec.), whence Fr. *diaire* (XVI).] **1.** Lasting for one day; ephemeral 1610. †**2.** Daily –1623.

1. *D.-fever*, a fever lasting one day (*Syd. Soc. Lex.*).

†Di·ascord. 1605. [med.L. *diascordium* (also used), for *diascordion*, from Gr. διὰ σκορδίων (a preparation) of scordium; see DIA-².] *Pharm.* A medicine made of the dried leaves of *Teucrium scordium* and many other herbs –1820.

Diaskeuast (dəiăskiu·æst). Also **diasceuast.** 1822. [– Gr. διασκευαστής reviser of a poem, interpolator.] A reviser; used *esp.* in reference to old recensions of Greek writings. So ‖**Diaskeu·asis** [Gr.], revision, recension.

†Dia·sper. 1582. [– med.L. *diasprum.*] = JASPER –1638.

‖**Diaspora** (dəi,æ·spŏră). 1876. [– Gr. διασπορά, f. διασπείρειν disperse, f. διά DIA-¹ + σπείρειν sow, scatter.] The Dispersion; cf. John 7:35, Jas. 1:1, 1 Pet. 1:1. Hence *transf.* (The term originated in Deut. 28:25.)

Diaspore (dəi·ăspŏᵊɹ). 1805. [mod. f. Gr. διασπορά; see prec. So named from its strong decrepitation when heated.] *Min.* Native hydrate of aluminium, an orthorhombic, massive, or sometimes stalactitic mineral, varying in colour from white to violet.

Diastaltic (dəiăstæ·ltik), *a.* 1774. [– Gr. διασταλτικός, in music 'able to expand or exalt the mind'; in sense 2 (where it appears to be taken as = 'transmissive'), after PERISTALTIC.] **1.** *Greek Mus.* Dilated, extended: applied to certain intervals. **2.** *Phys.* Applied to the actions termed reflex, as taking place through the spinal cord 1852.

Diastase (dəi·ăstēⁱs). 1838. [– Fr. *diastase* – Gr. διάστασις; see next.] *Chem.* A nitrogenous ferment formed in a seed or bud (*e.g.* in potatoes) during germination, and having the property of converting starch into sugar. Hence **Diasta·sic** *a.* diastatic.

‖**Diastasis** (dəi,æ·stăsis). 1741. [mod.L. – Gr. διάστασις separation, f. διά DIA-¹ + στάσις placing, setting.] *Path.* Separation of bones without fracture, or of the fractured ends of a bone.

Diastatic (dəiăstæ·tik), *a.* 1881. [– Gr. διαστατικός separative.] Pertaining to or of the nature of diastase. Hence **Diastatically** *adv.*

Diastem (dəi·ăstem). 1694. [– Gr. διάστημα; see next.] In ancient Gr. music, an interval.

‖**Diastema** (dəiăstī·mă). Pl. **diastemata.** ME. [Late L. – Gr. διάστημα space between.] **1.** *Mus.* = prec. **2.** *Zool.* and *Anat.* A space between two teeth, or two kinds of teeth 1854. Hence **Di:astema·tic** *a.* characterized by intervals (*rare*).

Diaster (dəi,æ·stəɹ). Also **dy-.** 1882. [f. Gr. δι- DI-² twice + ἀστήρ star.] *Biol.* The double star of chromatin filaments which forms the penultimate stage in the division of a single cell-nucleus into two. Hence **Dia·stral** *a.*

‖**Diastole** (dəi,æ·stoli). 1578. [– late L. *diastole* – Gr. διαστολή separation, expansion, dilatation, f. διαστέλλειν, f. διά DIA-¹ + στέλλειν to place.] **1.** *Phys.* The dilatation or relaxation of the heart, an artery, etc., rhythmically alternating with the *systole* or contraction. Also *fig.* **2.** *Gr.* and *L. Prosody.* The lengthening of a syllable naturally short 1580. **3.** *Gr. Gram.* A mark (originally semicircular) used to indicate separation of words; still occas. used, in the form of a comma, to distinguish ὅ,τι, ὅ,τε, neut. of ὅστις, ὅστε, from ὅτι, ὅτε.

1. *fig.* There must be a systole and d. in all inquiry GEO. ELIOT. **Diasto·lic** *a.* of or pertaining to d.

Diastrophism (dəi,æ·strofizm). 1881. [f. Gr. διαστροφή distortion, dislocation, f. (ult.) διά + στρέφειν to turn; see -ISM.] *Geol.* A general term for the action of the forces which have dislocated the earth's crust, and produced the greater inequalities of its surface. Hence **Diastro·phic** *a.* of or pertaining to d.

Diastyle (dəi·ăstəil). 1563. [– L. *diastylus* – Gr. διάστυλος 'having space between the columns'; also – Gr. διαστύλιον the intercolumnar space; f. διά through + στῦλος pillar.]

A. *adj.* Of a colonnade, etc.: Having the intercolumnar intervals each of three (or four) diameters (in the Doric order, of 2⅔).

B. *sb.* Such a colonnade, etc., or such an intercolumnar interval.

Diasyrm (dəi·ăsəɹm). 1678. [– late L. *diasyrmos* – Gr. διασυρμός disparagement.] *Rhet.* A figure expressing disparagement or ridicule.

‖**Diatessaron** (dəiăte·sărǫn). ME. [– late L. *diatessaron*, f. Gr. διὰ τεσσάρων through, i.e. composed of, four (cf. DIA-²).] **†1.** *Gr. Mus.* The interval of a fourth –1857. **†2.** *Pharm.* A medicine composed of four ingredients –1698. **3.** A harmony of the four Gospels 1803.

†Diathermal (dəiăþə̄·ɹmăl), *a.* 1835. [f. DIA-¹ + THERMAL.] = DIATHERMANOUS.

Diathermancy (dəiăþə̄·ɹmănsi). 1837. [– Fr. *diathermansie* (Melloni 1833), f. Gr. διά through + θέρμανσις heating. The Eng. ending is assim to -ANCY.] **†1.** *orig.* = THERMOCHROSY; also called *heat-colour.* **2.** Now: The property of being diathermic or diathermanous; pervious to radiant heat (var. **Diathe·rmacy**) 1837.

Diathermane·ity. *rare.* 1835. [– Fr. *diathermanéité*, f. *diathermane*; cf. prec.] = prec. 2. So **†Diathe·rmanism** (in same sense).

Diathermanous (dəiăþə̄·ɹmănəs), *a.* 1834. [f. Fr. *diathermane* (cf. prec.) + -OUS.] Having the property of freely transmitting radiant heat; pervious to heat-rays. (Corresp. to *diaphanous* in relation to light.)

Diathe·rmic, *a.* 1840. [– Fr. *diathermique*, f. Gr. διά through + θέρμη, θερμόν heat; see -IC.] = prec. So **Diathe·rmous** *a.*

Diathermo·meter. 1883. [f. Gr. διά through + θερμόν heat + -METER.] An instrument for measuring the thermal resistance of a body.

Di·athermy. 1910. [f. Gr. διά + θέρμη, θερμόν heat + -Y³.] Application of electric currents to produce heat in the deeper tissues of the body.

‖**Diathesis** (dəi,æ·þĭsis). Pl. **-theses** (-īz). 1651. [mod.L. – Gr. διάθεσις disposition, f. διατιθέναι arrange.] *Med.* A permanent condition of the body which renders it liable to certain special diseases.

The epileptic d. 1879. *fig.* The intellectual d. of the modern world MAINE. Hence **Diathe·tic** *a.* of, pertaining to, or arising from d.; constitutional.

Diatom (dəi·ătǫm). 1845. [– mod.L. *Diatoma*, f. Gr. διάτομος, f. διατέμνειν to cut through.] A member of the genus *Diatoma*, or of the *Diatomaceæ*, an order of microscopic unicellular Algæ, with siliceous cell-walls, and the power of locomotion. The genus *Diatoma* has the frustules, or individual cells, connected by their alternate angles so as to form a kind of zig-zag chain: hence the name. Hence **Di:atoma·ceous** *a.* of or pertaining to the order *Diatomaceæ*; (*Geol.*) consisting of the fossil remains of diatoms. **Diatoma·cean, Diato·mean,** a diatomaceous plant, a diatom.

Diatomic (dəiătǫ·mik), *a.* 1869. [f. DI-² + ἄτομος ATOM + -IC.] *Chem.* Consisting of, or having, two atoms; occas. used as = divalent.

Diatomin (dəi,æ·tŏmin). 1882. [f. mod.L. *Diatoma* DIATOM + -IN¹.] The buff-coloured pigment which colours diatoms.

Diatomous (dəi,æ·tŏməs), *a.* 1847. [f. Gr. διάτομος cut through + -OUS.] *Min.* 'Having crystals with one distinct diagonal cleavage.' (Dicts.)

Diatonic (dəiătǫ·nik), *a.* 1597. [– (O)Fr. *diatonique* or its source, late L. *diatonicus* – Gr. διατονικός proceeding through, i.e. at the interval of, a tone, f. διά DIA-¹ + τόνος TONE; see -IC.] **1.** *Gr. Mus.* That scale (the others being CHROMATIC and ENHARMONIC) in which the interval of a tone was used, the tetrachord being divided into two whole tones and a semitone (as in each half of the modern diatonic scale) 1603. **2.** In modern music, denoting the scale which in any key proceeds by the notes proper to that key without chromatic alteration. Also *fig.* Hence **Diato·nically** *adv.* in a d. manner. **Dia·tonism,** diatonic system.

Diatribe (dəi·ătrəib), *sb.* 1581. [– Fr. *diatribe* – L. *diatriba* – Gr. διατριβή employment (of time), study, discourse.] **1.** A discourse, disquisition (*arch.*). **2.** A dissertation directed against some person or work; a bitter and violent criticism; an invective 1804.

2. A rambling, bitter d. on the . . sufferings of the labourers 1850. Hence **Di·atribist,** one who writes or utters a d.

‖**Diaulos** (dəi,ǭ·lǫs). 1706. [Gr. δίαυλος double pipe, f. δι- DI-² + αὐλός pipe.] *Gr. Antiq.* **1.** A double course, in which the racers returned to the starting point. **2.** The double flute.

Diazeuctic (dəiăziū·ktik), *a.* 1698. [– Gr. διαζευκτικός disjunctive.] Disjunctive; applied, in ancient Gr. Music, to the interval of a tone separating disjunct tetrachords; also to the tetrachords.

Diazo- (dəi,æ·zo). 1873. [f. DI-² + AZO-.] *Chem.* A formative of the names of compounds derived from the aromatic hydrocarbons, which contain two atoms of nitrogen combined in a peculiar way with phenyl (C_6H_5), as *d.-benzine, -naphthaline,* etc. Also used *attrib.*, as in *diazo compounds, reaction,* etc.

‖**Diazoma** (dəiăzōᵘ·mă). 1706. [L. – Gr. διάζωμα girdle, partition, etc.] **1.** *Gr. Theatre.* A semicircular passage through the auditorium, parallel to its outer border, and cutting the radial flights of steps at a point about half-way up. **†2.** *Anat.* The midriff –1883.

Diazotize (dəi,æ·zŏtəiz). 1889. [f. DIAZO- + -IZE, after AZOTE.] *Chem.* To convert into a diazo compound.

Dib, *sb.* Usu. in *pl.* **dibs.** 1730. [Earlier *dib-stones*, perh. f. DIB *v.*²] **1.** *pl.* A children's game played with pebbles or the knucklebones of sheep; also the pebbles or bones so used. **2.** A counter used in playing at cards. **3.** *pl.* Money (*slang*) 1812. **4.** = DIBBLE (*dial.*) 1891.

Dib, *v.*¹ Now *dial.* ME. [prob. modified form of DIP *v.*, with duller sound.] = DIP *v.*

Dib, *v.*² 1609. [f. DAB *v.*¹, with weaker vowel.] **1.** *trans.* To dab lightly. **2.** *intr.* To tap lightly 1869. **3.** *intr.* = DAP *v.*¹, DIBBLE *v.*² 2. 1681. **4.** To dibble 1891.

Dibasic (dəibēⁱ·sik), *a.* 1868. [DI-².] *Chem.* Having two bases, or two atoms of a base. *D. acid*: one containing two atoms of displaceable hydrogen. See BIBASIC. Hence **Dibasi·city,** d. quality.

Dibber (di·bəɹ). 1736. [f. DIB *v.*² + -ER¹.] **1.** An instrument for dibbling; a dibbler. **2.** *Mining.* The pointed end of an iron bar used for making holes (*U.S.*) 1871.

Dibble (di·b'l), *sb.* 1450. [app. conn. w. DIB *v.*²; see -LE 1.] An instrument used to make holes in the ground for seeds, bulbs, or young plants.

Dibble (di·b'l), *v.*¹ 1583. [f. prec. sb.] **1.** *trans.* To make a hole in with or as with a dibble; to sow or plant by this means. **2.** *intr.* To use a dibble; to bore holes in the soil 1895. Hence **Di·bbler,** one who or that which dibbles.

Dibble (di·b'l), *v.*² 1622. [perh. f. DABBLE with lighter vowel, but cf. DIB *v.*² 3.] **1.** *intr.* = DABBLE *v.* 2. **2.** = DIB *v.*² 3, DAP *v.* 1. 1658.

Dib-hole. 1833. [app. f. *dib*, var. of DUB.] *Mining.* = SUMP.

Diblastula (dəiblæ·stiŭlă). 1890. [f. DI-² + mod.L. *blastula* BLASTULE.] *Embryol.* That stage of the embryo at which it consists of a vesicle enclosed in a double layer of cells; = GASTRULA.

Dibrach (dəi·bræk). *rare.* [– late L. *dibrachys* – Gr. δίβραχυς, f. δι- DI-² + βραχύς short.] In Gr. and L. prosody: A foot consisting of two short syllables; a pyrrhic.

Dibranchiate (dəibræ·ŋkiĕt). 1835. [– mod.L. *dibranchiata*, f. Gr. δι- (DI-²) + βράγχια gills of fishes; see -ATE².] *Zool.*

A. *adj.* Belonging to the *Dibranchiata*, an order of cephalopods having two branchiæ or gills.

B. *sb.* One of the *Dibranchiata*.

Dibs (pl.); see DIB *sb.*

Di·bstones, *sb. pl.* 1692. [See DIB *sb.*] A children's game; the same as *dibs* or *dabstones*.

Dibu·tyl, Dibutyro-. *Chem.* See DI-².

Dicacity (dikæ·sĭti). *arch.* 1592. [- L. *dicacitas* raillery, f. *dicax, dicac-* sarcastic (f. *dic-*, stem of *dicere* speak); see -ITY.] A jesting habit of speech; raillery; pertness; talkativeness.

Given to the humor of dicacitie and iesting BACON.

Dicæology (dəisi,ǫ·lŏdʒi). Also **dice-.** 1656. [- L. *dicæologia* - Gr. δικαιολογία plea in defence; see -LOGY.] †**1.** A description of jurisdiction 1664. **2.** *Rhet.* Justification.

Dicalcic (dəikæ·lsik), *a.* 1863. [DI-² 2.] *Chem.* Containing two equivalents of calcium.

Dicarbo-, bef. a vowel **dicarb-.** *Chem.* See DI-².

Dicarbon (dəikā·ɹbǫ̆n), *a.* 1869. [DI-².] *Chem.* Containing or derived from two atoms of carbon, as the *d.* series of hydrocarbons.

Dica·rbonate. *Chem.* See DI-².

Dicast (di·kæst). Also **dikast.** 1822. [- Gr. δικαστής judge, juryman, f. δικάζειν judge, f. δίκη judgement.] *Gr. Antiq.* One of the 6,000 citizens chosen annually in ancient Athens to try cases in the several law-courts. Hence **Dica·stic, dik-,** of or belonging to a d. or dicasts.

Dicastery (dikæ·stĕri). Also **dikastery.** 1822. [- Gr. δικαστήριον.] One of the courts of justice in which the dicasts sat; the court or body of dicasts.

Dicatalectic (dəi:kætăle·ktik), *a.* [DI-².] *Pros.* Doubly catalectic; wanting a syllable both in the middle and at the end. (Dicts.)

Dice (dəis), *sb.*, pl. of DIE *sb.*, q.v. Much more used than the singular *die*. *Comb.* **d.-coal,** a species of coal easily splitting into cubical fragments; **-shot** = *die-shot* (see DIE).

Dice (dəis), *v.* ME. [f. prec.] **1.** To play with dice; *trans.* to throw *away* by dicing. **2.** To cut into dice: *esp.* in cookery ME. **3.** To mark or ornament with a pattern of cubes or squares; to chequer 1688.

Dice-box. 1552. The box from which dice are thrown in gaming; used typically for gaming.

‖**Dicentra** (dəise·ntră). 1866. [mod.L., f. Gr. δίκεντρος, f. δι- two + κέντρον spur.] *Bot.* A genus of plants (N.O. *Fumariaceæ*) having drooping heart-shaped flowers; several species are cultivated in the flower-garden, esp. *D. spectabilis* (also called *Dielytra*).

Dicephalous (dəise·făləs), *a.* 1808. [f. Gr. δικέφαλος (f. δι- DI-² + κεφαλή head) + -OUS.] Having two heads, two-headed.

Dicer (dəi·səɹ). ME. [f. DICE *v.* or *sb.* + -ER¹.] One who plays or gambles with dice.

As false as Dicers Oathes *Haml.* III. iv. 45.

Dicerous (dəi·sĕrəs), *a. rare.* 1826. [irreg. f. Gr. δίκερως, f. 'δι- two + κέρας horn.] *Entom.* Having two horns, antennæ, or tentacles.

†**Dich.** *rare.* A corrupt word, app. meaning *do it*. *Timon* I. ii. 73.

‖**Dichasium** (dəikē¹·ziŏm). Pl. **-ia.** 1875. [mod.L., f. Gr. δίχασις a division.] *Bot.* A biparous cyme. Hence **Dicha·sial** *a.* belonging to or of the nature of a d.

‖**Dichastasis** (dəikæ·stăsis). 1864. [f. Gr. δίχα asunder + στάσις standing.] 'Spontaneous subdivision' (Webster). Hence **Dicha·stic** *a.* capable of undergoing d.

Dichlamydeous (dəiklămi·diəs), *a.* 1830. [f. Gr. δι- DI-² + χλαμύς, χλαμυδ- cloak; see -EOUS.] *Bot.* Having two envelopes (calyx and corolla).

Dichloride (dəiklōə·rəid, -rid). 1825. [DI-².] *Chem.* A compound of two atoms of chlorine with an element or radical, as mercury dichloride $HgCl_2$.

Dicho-, - Gr. διχο-, comb. f. δίχα in two, asunder, separately. (The ι is short in Greek.)

Dichogamous (dəikǫ·găməs), *a.* 1859. [f. DICHO- + Gr. -γαμος married, γάμος wedding + -OUS.] *Bot.* Said of those hermaphrodite plants in which the stamens and pistils (or analogous organs) mature at different times, so that self-fertilization is impossible. So **Dicho·gamy,** the condition of being d.

Dichord (dəi·kǭɹd). 1819. [- Gr. δίχορδος.] An instrument having two strings. **b.** An instrument having two strings to each note.

Dichoree (dəi:korī·). 1801. [- L. *dichoreus* - Gr. διχόρειος, f. δι- DI-² + χορεῖος CHOREE.] *Pros.* A foot consisting of two chorees or trochees.

Dichotomic (dəikotǫ·mik), *a.* 1873. [f. as DICHOTOMOUS + -IC.] Relating to or involving dichotomy. Hence **Dichoto·mically** *adv.*

Dichotomist (dəikǫ·tŏmist). 1592. [f. DICHOTOMY + -IST.] One who dichotomizes.

Dichotomize (dəikǫ·tŏməiz), *v.* 1606. [f. DICHOTOMY + -IZE.] **1.** *trans.* To divide into two parts or sections; *esp.* in reference to classification; †*loosely*, to divide. **2.** *intr.* (for *refl.*) To divide into two continuously; *spec.* used of the branching of a stem, root, etc. 1835.

1. That great citie might well be dichotomized into cloysters and hospitals BP. HALL. Hence **Dicho·tomized** *ppl. a.* divided into two branches; *Astron.* said of the moon when exactly half her disc is illuminated.

Dichotomous (dəikǫ·tŏməs), *a.* 1690. [f. late L. *dichotomos* - Gr. διχότομος cut in half (see next) + -OUS.] Divided or dividing into two.

The division of arteries is usually d. 1842. Hence **Dicho·tomously** *adv.*

Dichotomy (dəikǫ·tŏmi). 1610. [- mod.L. *dichotomia* - Gr. διχοτομία a cutting in two; see DICHO-, -TOMY.] **1.** Division of a whole into two parts; *spec.* in *Logic*, etc.: Division of a class or genus into two lower mutually exclusive classes or genera. **2.** *Astron.* That phase of the moon, etc., at which exactly half the disc appears illuminated 1686. **3.** *Bot.*, *Zool.*, etc. A form of branching in which each successive axis divides into two 1707.

1. What is called d. by contradiction, *e.g.* that 'everything must either be red or not red' 1877.

Dichotriæne (di:ko,trəi,ī·n). 1887. [f. DICHO- + Gr. τρίαινα trident.] *Zool.* A dichotomous triæne; a three-forked sponge spicule, having each fork dividing into two.

Dichro-. In comb. = DICHROIC.

Dichroic (dəikrō̆u·ik), *a.* 1864. [f. Gr. δίχροος (f. δι- two + χρώς colour) + -IC.] Having or showing two colours; *spec.* applied to doubly-refracting crystals that exhibit different colours when viewed in different directions. So **Di·chroism,** the quality of being d. Hence **Dichroi·stic** *a.* dichroitic.

Dichroite (dəi·kro,əit). 1810. [f. Gr. δίχροος (see prec.) + -ITE¹ 2 b.] *Min.* A synonym of IOLITE, from its often exhibiting dichroism. Hence **Dichroi·tic** *a.* of, or of the nature of, d.; dichroic.

Dichromate (dəikrōu·mĕt). 1864. [DI-².] *Chem.* A double CHROMATE (q.v.), as *potassium d.* $K_2 . CrO_4 . CrO_3$. (Also *bichromate.*)

Dichromatic (dəikromæ·tik), *a.* 1847. [f. Gr. δι- DI-² + χρωματικός CHROMATIC.] Having or showing two colours; *spec.* of animals: Presenting, in different individuals, two different colours or systems of coloration. So **Dichro·matism,** the quality or fact of being d.

Dichromic (dəikrōu·mik), *a.* 1854. [f. Gr. δίχρωμος (f. δι- DI-² + χρῶμα colour) + -IC.] **1.** Relating to or including (only) two colours; applied to the vision of colour-blind persons including only two of three primary colour-sensations. **2.** DICHROIC 1877.

Dichronous (dəi·krŏnəs), *a.* 1883. [- late L. *dichronus* - Gr. δίχρονος (f. δι- DI-² + χρόνος time) + -OUS.] **1.** *Gr.* and *L. Pros.* Having two times or quantities; common. **2.** *Bot.* 'Having two periods of growth in the year' (*Syd. Soc. Lex.*).

Dichroscope (dəi·kro,skōup). 1857. [f. Gr. δίχροος two-coloured + -SCOPE.] An instrument for observing or testing the dichroism of crystals, etc. Hence **Dichrosco·pic** *a.*

Dicing (dəi·siŋ), *vbl. sb.* 1456. [f. DICE *v.* + -ING¹.] **1.** Gambling with dice; dice-play. **2.** *Book-binding.* A method of ornamenting leather in squares or diamonds. Also *attrib.* (in sense 1).

Dick (dik), *sb.*¹ 1553. [Playful f. *Ric-*, contr. of Norman Fr., AFr. *Ricard*, L. *Ricardus* = *Richard*; cf. HICK *sb.*¹] **1.** A familiar form of *Richard*. Hence generically = fellow, lad, man. **2.** *slang.* A riding whip 1873.

1. *Tom, D., and Harry*: any three (or more) of the populace taken at random.

Dick, *sb.*² *dial.* 1847. [app. conn. w. DICKY *sb.* 8.] A leather apron.

Dick, *sb.*³ *dial.* 1736. [Cf. DIKE and DITCH.] A ditch; a dike.

Dick, *sb.*⁴ *slang.* 1860. Abbrev. of *dictionary*; hence, Long words.

Dick, *sb.*⁵ *slang.* 1861. [Short for *declaration*; cf. DAVY.] In *To take one's d.* = to take one's declaration.

Dickens (di·kĕnz). *slang* or *colloq.* 1598. [prob. a fanciful use of the personal name *Dickens*, f. *Dicken*, *Dickon*, dim. of *Dick*; see DICK *sb.*¹] The deuce, the devil.

I cannot tell what (the dickens) his name is SHAKS.

Dickensian (dike·nziăn), *a.* 1856. [See -IAN.] Of or pertaining to Charles Dickens, or his style.

Dicker (di·kəɹ), *sb.*¹ [ME. *dyker* (whence med.L. *dicra*, Domesday Book), pointing to an OE. **dicor*, corresp. to MLG. *dēker*, MHG. *techer*, (also mod.) *decher* :- WGmc. **decura* - L. *decuria* set of ten; see DECURION, DAKER.] The number of ten; half a score; being the customary unit of exchange, *esp.* in hides or skins; hence a lot of (ten) hides. Also †*transf.*

A dycker of hydes tanned 1526. *transf.* A whole d. of wit SYDNEY.

Dicker (di·kəɹ), *sb.*² *U.S.* 1823. [f. DICKER *v.*] The action or practice of dickering; petty bargaining.

Dicker, *v.* *U.S.* 1845. [perh. f. DICKER *sb.*¹; see quot.] *intr.* To trade or barter; to truck; to bargain in a petty way. Also *trans.*

The white men who penetrated to the semi-wilds [of the West] were always ready to d. and to swap F. COOPER.

Dicky, dickey (di·ki), *sb. colloq.*, *slang*, and *dial.* 1753. [Some of the senses are evidently applications of *Dicky*, dim. (see -Y⁶) of DICK *sb.*¹ (cf. also DICK *sb.*²); of others the relationship is obscure.] **1.** *Naut.* An officer acting in commission 1867. **2.** A (male) donkey 1793. **3.** A small bird (also DICKY-BIRD) 1851. †**4.** An under petticoat -1878. †**5.** A worn-out shirt (*slang*) 1781. **6.** A detached shirt-front 1811. **7.** A shirt collar. (*New England.*) 1858. **8.** A covering worn to protect the dress during work; *e.g.* a leather apron; a child's bib; a 'slop'; an oil-skin suit 1847. **9.** The seat in a carriage on which the driver sits; also one at the back for servants, etc., or for the guard of a mail-coach 1801. **b.** An extra seat at the back of a two-seater motor-car 1912.

Di·cky, dickey, *a.* *slang* or *colloq.* 1812. [perh. orig. f. *Dick* in phr. 'I am as queer as Dick's hatband' (Grose); see -Y¹.] Sorry, poor; unsound, shaky, queer.

‖**Diclesium** (dəiklī·ziŏm). 1857. [mod.L., f. Gr. δι- (DI-²) + κλῆσις closing.] *Bot.* A dry indehiscent fruit consisting of an achene enclosed within the indurated base of the adherent perianth.

Diclinic (dəikli·nik), *a.* 1864. [f. Gr. δι- + κλίνειν to incline + -IC.] *Cryst.* Having the lateral axes at right angles to each other, but both oblique to the vertical axis.

Diclinism (dəi·kliniz'm). 1882. [f. as next + -ISM.] *Bot.* The condition of being DICLINOUS.

Diclinous (dəi·klinəs), *a.* 1830. [f. mod.L. *Diclines* pl. (f. Gr. δι- DI-² + κλίνη bed) + -OUS. So Fr. *dicline.*] *Bot.* Having the stamens and pistils on separate flowers. Also said of the flowers (= unisexual).

Dicoccous (dəikǫ·kəs), *a.* 1819. [f. DI-² + Gr. κόκκος grain (see COCCUS) + -OUS.] *Bot.* Splitting into two cocci; see COCCUS 2.

Dicondylian (dəikǫndi·liăn), *a.* 1883. [f. Gr. δικόνδυλος (cf. CONDYLE) + -IAN.] *Zool.* Of a skull: Having two occipital condyles.

Dicotyledon (dəi:kǫtilī·dən). 1727. [mod. L. pl. *cotyledones* (Ray); see DI-², COTYLEDON.] *Bot.* A flowering plant having two cotyledons or seed-lobes. Hence **Di:cotyle·donary, Di:cotyle·donous** *adjs.* having two cotyledons; belonging to the class of Dicotyledons; of or belonging to a dicotyledonous plant.

Dicrotic (dəikrǫ·tik), *a.* 1811. [f. Gr. δίκροτος double-beating + -IC; in mod.Fr. *dicrote.*] *Phys.*, etc. Of the pulse (or a tracing of its motion): Exhibiting a double beat or wave for each beat of the heart. **b.** Of or pertaining to a dicrotic pulse or tracing, as a *d.notch* or *wave.* vars. **Dicro·tal, Di·crotous.** So **Di·crotism,** the quality of being d.

Dict (dikt), *sb. arch.* ME. [– OFr. *dict* (mod. *dit*) or L. *dictum,* pa. pple. n. of *dicere* say.] A saying or maxim.

Dicta, pl. of DICTUM.

Dictaphone (di·ktăfōᵘn). 1907. [irreg. f. DICTATE + -PHONE.] A proprietary name for a machine which records and reproduces words spoken into it.

Dictate (di·ktĕt), *sb.* 1594. [– L. *dictatum,* subst. use of n. pa. pple. of *dictare,* usu. in pl. *dictata* rules, precepts.] †**1.** That which is dictated –1826; DICTATION –1678. †**2.** A DICTUM –1728; a maxim –1682. **3.** An authoritative direction delivered in words 1618. **b.** Often applied to the monitions of a written law, conscience, reason, nature, experience, self-interest, etc. 1594.

3. I could not receive such dictates without horror JOHNSON. Every man will obey the dictates of Reason and Nature GIBBON.

Dictate (diktēⁱ·t, di·kteⁱt), *v.* 1592. [– *dictat-*, pa. ppl. stem of L. *dictare,* frequent. of *dicere* say.] **1.** *trans.* To put into words which are to be written down; to pronounce *to* a person (something which he is to write). Also *absol.* **2.** *trans.* To prescribe; to lay down authoritatively; to order in express terms 1621. **3.** *intr.* To use or practise dictation; to lay down the law, give orders 1651.

1. He dictated them while Bathurst wrote 1783. 2. They dictated the conditions of peace GIBBON. Of all that Wisdom dictates, this the drift COWPER. 3. To cavil, censure, d., right or wrong POPE.

Dictation (diktēⁱ·ʃən). 1656. [– late L. *dictatio,* f. as prec.; see -ION.] **1.** The act of dictating 1727. Also *attrib.* **2.** Authoritative utterance or prescription 1656; arbitrary command 1856. **3.** Something dictated 1841.

1. I will write out the charm from your d. JOWETT. 2. It would have probably been unsafe for the crown to attempt d. or repression FROUDE.

Dictative (diktēⁱ·tiv, di·ktĕtiv), *a.* 1768. [f. DICTATE *v.* + -IVE; cf. med.L. *dictativus.*] Of the nature of dictation.

Dictator (diktēⁱ·təɹ). ME. [– L. *dictator*; see DICTATE *v.*, -OR 2.] **1.** A ruler or governor whose word is law; an absolute ruler of a state; *esp.* one invested with absolute authority in seasons of emergency. Also *transf.* **2.** A person exercising absolute authority of any kind or in any sphere 1605. **3.** One who dictates to a writer 1617.

1. As in old Rome, when the D. was created, all inferiour magistracies ceased BURTON. 2. The dictators of behaviour, dress, and politeness SWIFT. Hence **Dicta·torate,** the office of a d.

Dictatorial (diktătōᵊ·riăl), *a.* 1701. [f. L. *dictatorius* (f. *dictator*; see prec.) + -AL¹; see -ORIAL.] **1.** Of, pertaining, or proper to a dictator. **2.** Pertaining to or characteristic of dictation; inclined to dictate; overbearing in tone 1704.

1. D. power 1701. 2. By violent measures, and a d. behaviour SWIFT. Hence **Dictato·rially** *adv.* **Dictato·rialness.** So †**Dictato·rian** *a.* of, proper to, or characteristic of a dictator. var. **Di·ctatory** *a.*; whence **Di·ctatorily** *adv.*

Dictatorship (diktēⁱ·təɹʃip). 1586. [See -SHIP.] **1.** The office or dignity of a dictator. **2.** Absolute authority in any sphere 16...

Dictatress (diktēⁱ·trĕs). 1784. [f. DICTATOR + -ESS¹.] A female dictator (*lit.* and *fig.*). So **Dicta·trix.**

Dictature (diktēⁱ·tiŭɹ). 1553. [– L. *dictatura*; see DICTATE *v.*, -URE.] **1.** = DICTATORSHIP. **2.** A collective body of dictators 1759.

†**Di·ctery.** *rare.* [– L. *dicterium* witty saying.] A witty saying. BURTON.

Diction (di·kʃən). 1542. [–(O)Fr. *diction* or L. *dictio* saying, mode of expression, (later) word, f. *dict-*, pa. ppl. stem of *dicere* say.] †**1.** A word –1697. †**2.** A phrase, locution –1709. †**3.** Speech; verbal description –1602. **4.** The manner in which anything is expressed in words 1700. **5.** *Mus.* Rendition of words in singing, as regards pronunciation, etc.

3. *Haml.* v. ii. 123. 4. Almost all fancy the d. makes the poet HARE. Absolute accuracy of d. and precision of accent in prose RUSKIN.

†**Dictiona·rian.** *rare.* 1846. [f. as next + -AN.] The maker of a dictionary.

Dictionary (di·kʃənări). 1526. [– med.L. *dictionarium* (sc. *manuale* MANUAL *sb.*) and *dictionarius* (sc. *liber* book), f. L. *dictio* phrase, word; see DICTION, -ARY¹.] **1.** A book dealing with the words of a language, so as to set forth their orthography, pronunciation, signification, and use, their synonyms, derivation, and history, or at least some of these; the words are arranged in some stated order, now, usually, alphabetical; a word-book, vocabulary, lexicon. **2.** By extension: A book of information or reference on any subject or branch of knowledge, the items of which are arranged alphabetically; as a D. of *Architecture, Biography,* of *the Bible,* of *Dates,* etc. 1631. Also *fig.* Also *attrib.*

1. Neither is a d. a bad book to read..it is full of suggestion,—the raw material of possible poems and histories EMERSON. 2. *fig.* Burnet was..a living d. of English affairs MACAULAY.

Dictograph (di·ktŏgrɑf). 1907. [orig. proprietary name, irreg. f. L. *dictum* thing said + -GRAPH.] An instrument designed to record in one room sound made in another.

‖**Dictum** (di·ktŏm). Pl. **dicta, dictums.** 1670. [L.; see DICT.] A saying: usu. a formal and authoritative pronouncement 1706. **b.** *Law.* An expression of opinion by a judge on a matter of law 1776. **c.** A current saying 1826. **d.** An award 1670.

A d. of Johnson's 1787. **c.** The *d.* that truth always triumphs MILL. **d.** *D. of Kenilworth,* an award made in 1266 between King Henry III and the barons who had taken arms against him.

Dictyogen (di·ktioˌdʒen, diktəi·ŏˌdʒen). 1846. [f. Gr. δίκτυον net + -GEN, after ENDOGEN, etc.] *Bot.* Lindley's name for those plants which have a monocotyledonous embryo and reticulated leaf-veins.

Dicy·an(o)-. [f. DI-² + CYANO-.] *Chem.* Combined with two equivalents of the radical cyanogen, CN, replacing two of hydrogen, chlorine, etc.

Dicyanide (dəisəi·ănəid). 1863. [DI-².] *Chem.* A compound containing two equivalents of cyanogen (CN) united to an element or dyad radical, as *mercuric d.* $Hg(CN)_2$.

Dicya·nogen. *Chem.* [DI-².] Cyanogen in the free form.

Dicynodont (dəisi·nŏdǫnt). 1854. [f. Gr. δι- two + κυν- dog + ὀδοντ- tooth.] *Palæont.* A fossil reptile having no teeth except two long canines in the upper jaw. *adj.* Having this character.

The typical genus is *Dicynodon,* order *Dicynodontia.* Hence **Dicynodo·ntian** *a.*

Did, pa. t. of DO *v.*, q.v.

‖**Didache** (di·dăkī). 1885. Gr. διδαχή, in the title Διδαχὴ τῶν δώδεκα ἀποστόλων Teaching of the twelve apostles, the name of a Christian treatise of the beginning of the second century.

Didactic (didæ·ktik, dəi-). 1644. [– Gr. διδακτικός, f. stem διδακ- of διδάσκειν teach, perh. after Fr. *didactique*; see -IC.]

A. *adj.* Having the character or manner of a teacher; characterized by giving instruction; instructive, preceptive.

B. *sb.* †**1.** A didactic author or treatise –1835. **2.** *pl.* The science or art of teaching 1846.

2. Life is rather a subject of wonder, than of didactics EMERSON. So **Dida·ctical** *a.* (*rare*). **Dida·ctically** *adv.* **Dida·cticism,** the practice or quality of being d. **Didacti·city** (*rare*), d. quality.

Didactive (didæ·ktiv), *a.* 1711. [irreg. f. Gr. διδακτός taught, or that can be taught + -IVE, after words from L. like *active.*] = DIDACTIC.

Didactyl, -yle (dəidæ·ktil), *a.* 1819. [irreg. f. DI-² + Gr. δάκτυλος finger.] *Zool.* Having two fingers, toes, or claws. var. **Dida·ctylous.**

Didal(l, obs. ff. DIDLE.

Didapper (dəi·dæ:pəɹ). ME. [Reduced f. DIVE-DAPPER.] **1.** = DABCHICK. **2.** Applied ludicrously to a person 1589.

Didascalic (didæ̆skæ·lik), *a.* 1609. [– L. *didascalicus* – Gr. διδασκαλικός instructive, f. διδάσκαλος teacher; see -IC.] Of the nature of a teacher or of instruction; didactic. Hence **Didasca·lics** *sb. pl.* = DIDACTICS. So **Dida·scalar** *a.* didactic. *nonce-wd.*

Didder (di·dəɹ), *v.* Now *dial.* ME. [Related to DODDER *v.* and dial. *dadder,* of symbolic origin. Cf. DITHER.] *intr.* To tremble, quake, shake, shiver.

Diddest, rare f. *didst,* 2nd sing. pa. t. of DO *v.*

Diddle (di·d'l), *v.*¹ *colloq.* or *dial.* 1632. [app. parallel to DIDDER. Cf. DADDLE.] †**1.** *intr.* = DADDLE. **2.** To move from side to side by jerks; to shake 1786. **3.** *trans.* To jerk from side to side 1893.

Diddle (di·d'l), *v.*² *colloq.* 1806. [In sense 2 prob. back-formation from *diddler,* f. name of Jeremy Diddler (in J. Kenney's farce, 'Raising the Wind', 1803).] **1.** To waste time in mere trifling 1826. **2.** *trans.* **a.** To swindle; to 'do'. **b.** To do for, ruin; to kill. 1806. Hence **Di·ddler,** a mean swindler or cheat.

Diddle- in comb. 1523. [conn. w. DIDDLE *v.*¹, *v.*²]

D.-daddle, 'stuff and nonsense'. **D.-dee,** the shrub *Empetrum rubrum.* **D.-diddle,** the sound or action of fiddling. **Diddledum,** used contemptuously for something trifling.

†**Di-decahe·dral,** *a.* 1805. [DI- *pref.*² 1.] *Crystall.* Having the form of a ten-sided prism with five-sided bases, making twenty faces in all.

Didelphian (dəide·lfiăn), *a.* 1847. [f. mod. L. *Didelphia,* f. Gr. δι- DI-² + δελφύς womb; see -AN.] *Zool.* Belonging to the subclass *Didelphia* of the class *Mammalia,* characterized by a double uterus and vagina, and comprising the single order of Marsupials. So **Dide·lphic, Dide·lphine, Dide·lphous** *adjs.* in same sense. **Didelph, Dide·lphid,** a member of the subclass *Didelphia,* or of the family *Didelphidæ* (opossums). **Dide·lphoid** *a.* double, as the uterus in the *Didelphia.*

Didine (dəi·dəin), *a.* 1885. [f. mod.L. *didus* the dodo + -INE¹.] *Zool.* Belonging to the family *Didídæ* of birds, akin to the dodo.

Didle (dəi·d'l), *sb. local.* 1490. [Origin unkn.] A sharp triangular spade, used for clearing out ditches, etc. So **Di·dle** *v.* (*local*), to clean out the bed of (a river or ditch); *intr.* to work with a didle.

Dido (dəi·do). *U.S. slang.* 1843. [Origin unkn.] A prank, a caper; a shindy, *esp.* in phr. *to cut* (*up*) *didoes.*

†**Di-do:decahe·dral,** *a.* 1805. [DI- *pref.*² 1.] *Crystall.* Having the form of a twelve-sided prism, with six planes in each base, or twenty-four faces in all.

Didonia (dəidōᵘ·niă). 1873. [From the story of Dido, who bargained for as much land as a hide would cover, and cut the hide into a long narrow strip so as to inclose a large space.] *Math.* The curve which, on a given surface and with a given perimeter, contains the greatest area.

Didrachm (dəi·dræm). 1548. [– late L. *didrachmon, -ma* – Gr. δίδραχμον, f. δι- DI-² + δραχμή DRACHMA.] An ancient Greek silver coin; a two-drachma piece; see DRACHMA. Hence **Didra·chmal** *a.* of the weight of two drachmæ: applied to the stater.

Didst, 2nd sing. pa. t. of DO *v.*

†**Didu·ce,** *v.* 1578. [– L. *diducere* draw apart, sunder, f. *di-* DI-¹ + *ducere* draw. Sometimes confused with DEDUCE.] **1.** *trans.* To pull away or apart –1696. **2.** To dilate, expand –1657. Hence †**Didu·ction.**

Diduce, -ment, obs. (erron.) ff. DEDUCE, -MENT.

Diductively, obs. (erron.) f. DEDUCTIVELY.

Didymate (di·dimĕt), *a.* 1843. [f. mod.L. *didymus* – Gr. δίδυμος twin + -ATE².] *Zool.*, etc. = DIDYMOUS.

†‖**Di·dymis.** Pl. **-es.** 1543. [Arbitrary or erron. shortening of Gr. ἐπιδιδυμίς (Galen); see EPIDIDYMIS.] = EPIDIDYMIS –1883.

Didymium (didi·miŏm). 1842. [mod.L.

f. Gr. δίδυμος adj. twin + -IUM; so called from its close association with lanthanum.] *Chem.* A rare metal, found only in association with cerium and lanthanum. Symbol Di.

Didymous (di·didiməs), *a.* 1794. [f. Fr. *didyme* adj. (– Gr. δίδυμος adj. twin) + -OUS.] *Bot.*, etc. Growing in pairs, paired, twin.

‖**Didynamia** (didinēⁱ·miă). 1753. [mod.L. (Linnæus 1735), f. Gr. δι- DI-² + δύναμις power, strength; see -IA¹.] *Bot.* The fourteenth class in the Linnæan Sexual System of plants, containing those with four stamens in pairs of unequal length, whence the name. Hence **Di·dynam**, a plant of this class; **Didyna·mian** *a.* didynamous.

Didynamous (dəidi·năməs, did-), *a.* 1794. [f. as prec. + -OUS.] *Bot.* Of stamens: Arranged in two pairs of unequal length. Of a flower or plant: Belonging to the Linnæan class *Didynamia.*

Die (dəi), *sb.* Pl. **dice** (dəis), **dies** (dəiz). [ME. *dē, dee*, pl. *dēs, dees* – (O)Fr. *dé*, pl. *dés* :– L. (Rom.) *datum*, subst. use of n. pa. pple. of *dare* give (cf. DATE *sb.*²), *spec.* play, as in *calculum dare* play a 'man'.]

I. With pl. *dice.* **1.** A small cube, having its faces marked with spots numbering from one to six, used in games of chance by being thrown from a box or the hand. **b.** *pl.* The game played with these. **2.** *fig.* Hazard, chance, luck 1548. **3.** A small cubical segment of anything ME.

2. I haue set my life vpon a cast, And I will stand the hazard of the Dye *Rich. III*, v. iv. 10. Phr. *The d. is cast*: the course of action is irrevocably decided. **3.** Turnips and carrots cut in dice MRS. RAFFALD.

II. With pl. *dies.* **1.** A cubical block; in *Arch.* the cubical portion of a pedestal, between the base and cornice; = DADO 1. 1664. **2.** An engraved stamp (often one of two) for impressing a design or figure upon some softer material, as in coining money, striking a medal, embossing paper, etc. 1699. **3.** A name of mechanical appliances:

spec. **a.** One of two or more pieces (fitted in a *stock*) to form a segment of a hollow screw for cutting the thread of a screw or bolt. **b.** The bed-piece serving as a support for metal from which a piece is to be punched, and having an opening through which the piece is driven. **c.** *Shoe-making*, etc. A shaped knife for cutting out blanks of any required shape or size: cf. DIE *v.*² 1812.

4. *Sc.* A toy 1808.

attrib. and *Comb.*, as *die-shaped* a.; **d.†-shot,** shot of cubical form; **-sinker,** an engraver of dies for stamping; so **-sinking**; **-stock,** the stock or handle for holding the dies used in cutting screws (see II. 3 a).

Die (dəi), *v.*¹ Pa. t. and pple. **died** (dəid), pres. pple. **dying** (dəi·iŋ). [ME. *deȝen, deye*, either (i) repr. OE. **dīeġan*, **dēġan* = OS. *dōian*, OHG. *touwen* (MHG. *töuwen*), ON. *deyja* :– Gmc. **dawjan*, f. **daw-*, repr. also in DEAD *a.*, DEATH; or, as is more likely (ii) immed. derived from ON. *deyja.*]

I. Of man and sentient beings. **1.** *intr.* To lose life, cease to live, suffer death; to expire. Const. with *of, by, from, through*; also *for* a cause, object, etc., *for* the sake of one, *in* a state or condition, etc. **2.** To suffer the pains of death; to face death ME. **3.** *Theol.* To suffer spiritual death; 'To perish everlastingly' (J.); cf. DEATH. **4.** To languish, pine away with passion; *to d. for*, to desire excessively 1591.

1. In the day thou eat'st, thou di'st MILT. *P. L.* VII. 544. He shall dye a Fleas death *Merry W.* IV. ii. 158. Phr. *To d. the death*: to suffer death, to be put to death. *To d. in one's bed, in one's shoes, in harness* (*i.e.* in full work), *in the last ditch* (*i.e.* to fight till the last extremity). **2.** I d. daily 1 *Cor.* 15:31. **4.** Deare, I d. As often as from thee I goe DONNE. I am dying for a drink 1897.

II. 1. Of plants, or organized matter: To cease to be subject to vital forces; to pass into a state of decomposition ME. **2.** *fig.* Of substances: To become dead, flat, vapid, or inactive 1612. **3.** Of actions, institutions, states, or qualities: To come to an end; to go out, as a candle or fire; to pass out of memory ME. **4.** To pass gradually away (*esp.* out of hearing or sight) 1704. **5.** To pass by dying (*into* something else) 1633; in *Archit.* to merge *into*; to terminate gradually *in* or *against* 1665.

1. My heart seemed to d. within me SMOLLETT. The shining daffodils d. TENNYSON. **3.** So dies my reuenge *Much Ado* v. i. 301. Art, which cannot d. SHELLEY. **4.** I hear soft music die along the grove POPE. **5.** The day dyes into night BP. HALL.

Die, *v.*² 1703. [f. DIE *sb.*] *trans.* To furnish with a die; to mould or shape with a die.

Die·-away, *a.* 1802. [from the phr. *to die away.*] That dies away or seems to die away; languishing.

‖**Dieb** (dīb). 1829. [– Arab. *ḏi'b* 'wolf'.] *Zool.* A North African Jackal (*Canis anthus*).

Die·-back, *sb.* 1886. [From the phr. *to die back.*] The name for a disease affecting orange trees in Florida, etc., in which the tree dies from the top downward.

Diecious, etc., var. DIŒCIOUS, etc.

Diedral, var. DIHEDRAL.

‖**Diegesis** (dəiˌidʒī·sis). 1829. [– Gr. διήγησις narrative.] A narrative; a statement of the case.

†**Diego** (dyē·go). 1611. [Sp. *Diego* James, the patron saint of Spain.] **1.** A Spaniard; cf. DAGO. (Also *attrib.*) –1687. **2.** A Spanish sword –1867. **3.** A variety of pear. EVELYN.

Die·-hard. 1844. [from the phr. *to die hard.*]

A. *adj.* That resists to the last.

B. *sb.* One that dies hard; *esp.* an extremely conservative politician, etc.; *spec.* (*pl.*) an appellation of the 57th Regiment of Foot in the British Army.

Dielectric (dəiˌile·ktrik). 1837. [DI-³.]

A. *sb.* A substance or medium through or across which electric force acts without conduction; a non-conductor; an insulating medium.

B. *adj.* **1.** Non-conducting 1871. **2.** Relating to a dielectric medium, or to the transmission of electricity without conduction 1863.

‖**Diencephalon** (dəiˌense·fălǫn). 1883. [mod.L., f. Gr. δι-, δια- + ἐγκέφαλον brain. Repr. G. *zwischenhirn.*] = THALAMENCEPHALON. Hence **Diencepha·lic** *a.* pertaining to the d.

Dieresis, dieretic, var. DIÆRESIS, -ETIC.

‖**Dies** (dəi·īz). 1607. [L. 'day'.] Used in:

a. Dies iræ, 'day of wrath', the first words, and hence the name, of a Latin hymn on the Last Judgement, used as the sequence at a mass of requiem.

b. Dies non (short for *dies non juridicus*), in *Law*, a day on which no legal business is transacted, or which is not reckoned for some particular purpose.

Diesel (dī·zəl). 1894. *D. engine*, a type of oil-engine invented by R. *Diesel* of Munich.

‖**Diesis** (dəi·ĕsis). Pl. **dieses** (īz). ME. [– L. *diesis* – Gr. δίεσις quarter-tone, f. διιέναι send through, f. διά DIA-¹ + ἱέναι send.] **1.** *Mus.* **a.** In ancient Gr. music, the Pythagorean semitone (ratio 243:256). **b.** Now, the interval equal to the difference between three major thirds and an octave (ratio 125:128); usually called *enharmonic d.* **2.** *Printing.* The sign ‡, usually called 'double dagger' 1706.

Diet (dəi·ĕt), *sb.*¹ ME. [– (O)Fr. *diète* – L. *diæta* – Gr. δίαιτα course of life.] †**1.** Way of living or thinking –1656. **2.** *esp.* Way of feeding ME. **3.** Prescribed course of food, restricted in kind or quantity; regimen ME. **4.** Food; the victuals in daily use ME. **5.** †An allowance of food –1671; board (now *Hist.*) 1455. †**6.** Allowance for the expenses of living –1651.

2. A meat d. is far from satisfying LIVINGSTONE. **3.** To preach d. and abstinence to his patients JOHNSON. **4.** The Athletick D. was of pulse SIR T. BROWNE.

Comb.: **d.-bread,** special bread prepared for invalids and others; **-kitchen,** a charitable establishment which provides proper food for the helpless poor.

Diet (dəi·ĕt), *sb.*² ME. [– med.L. *diēta* day's journey, allowance, work, wages; assoc. w. L. *dies* day.] †**1.** A day's journey. Chiefly Sc. (So Fr. *journée.*) –1651. **2.** *Sc.* An appointed date or time; *spec.* the day on which a party is cited to appear in court. (So OFr. *journée.*) 1568. **3.** *Sc.* A session of any assembly occupying a day or part of one 1587. **4.** A conference, congress, convention. (So OFr. *journée.*) 1450. **5.** *spec.* The English name (from the end of the 16th c.) of the former *Reichstag* of the (German) Roman Empire, and of the federal or national assemblies of Switzerland, Poland, Hungary, etc.; later of the *Bundestag* of the Germanic Confederation (1815–66); applied also to the existing *Reichstag* or Imperial Parliament of the Austro-Hungarian and German Empires, and the *Landtag* or local parliament of their constituent states, and sometimes to the parliamentary assemblies of other states of Eastern Europe, of Japan, etc. 1565. **6.** The metal scraped or cut from gold and silver plate assayed day by day at the Mint, and retained for the purpose of trial 1700. Hence **Die·tal** *a.* of or belonging to a d.

Di·et, *v.* ME. [f. DIET *sb.*¹, after OFr. *dieter*, med.L. *diætare.*] **1.** *trans.* To feed; to put to a specified diet. Also *fig.* **2.** To prescribe or regulate the food of (a person, etc.) in nature or quantity ME. **3.** To board 1635. **4.** *intr.* To take one's meals; to feed (*on*) 1566. **5.** To regulate oneself as to diet 1660.

1. He that taught Abel how to d. Sheep 1655. **2.** Full power. . to pill. . d. . . and poultice all persons FOOTE. **4.** At what ordinary. . do they d. FULLER. Hence **Di·eter** (now *rare*), one who diets himself or others.

Dietary (dəi·ĕtări). ME. [– med.L. *dietarium*, f. *dieta*; see DIET *sb.*¹, -ARY¹.]

A. *sb.* **1.** A course of diet prescribed; a book prescribing such a course. **2.** An allowance and regulation of food, as in a hospital, workhouse, or prison 1838.

B. *adj.* Pertaining to diet, or a dietary 1614.

Dietetic (dəiˌĕte·tik). 1541. [– L. *diæteticus*, – Gr. διαιτητικός, f. δίαιτα; see DIET *sb.*¹, -IC.]

A. *adj.* Of or pertaining to diet, or to the regulation of the kind and quantity of food to be eaten 1579. var. †**Diete·tical** *a.* Hence **Diete·tically** *adv.*

B. *sb.* **1.** One who studies dietetics 1759. **2.** **Dietetics,** less usually **dietetic:** The part of medicine which relates to diet.

Diethene- (dəiˌe·pīn). *Chem.* See DI-².

Diethyl (dəiˌe·pil). 1850. [DI-².] *Chem.* **1.** as *sb.* A name for the group C_4H_{10} (*butyl hydride* or *butane*), considered as a double molecule of the radical ethyl. **2.** in *Comb.* Denoting two equivalents of the monad radical ethyl (C_2H_5), replacing two atoms of hydrogen in a compound, as *die·thylami·ne* $NH(C_2H_5)_2$.

Dietic (dəiˌe·tik). 1659. [f. DIET *sb.*¹ + -IC.]

A. *adj.* = DIETETIC *a.* 1716. So **Die·tical** *a.*

†**B.** *sb.* A dietetic article or application.

Dietine (dəi·ĕtīn). 1669. [– Fr. *diétine*, lit. 'little diet', f. *diète* DIET *sb.*² 5 + dim. suff. *-ine.*] A subordinate diet; in Polish Hist., a provincial diet which elected deputies for the national diet.

Dietist (dəi·ĕtist). 1607. [f. DIET *sb.*¹ + -IST.] One who professes or practises dietetics. So **Dieti·cian, dieti·tian.**

Dietrichite (dī·trikəit). 1882. [f. *Dietrich*, a German chemist + -ITE¹ 2b.] *Min.* A fibrous alum, containing zinc and other bases.

†**Dieugard(e.** ME. [– Fr., f. Fr. phr. *Dieu vous garde* 'God keep you'.] The salutation 'God preserve you!'; a spoken salutation, as contrasted with a nod –1656.

Dif-, prefix of L. origin, = *dis-* before *f*, as in *differre.* In Romanic it became *def-*, whence in OFr. *de-*; this occas. appears in Eng., as *defer* from L. *differre*, OFr. *defferer*, etc. Usually, however, the L. form is used in Eng. For its force, see DIS-.

Diffame, etc., etymol. f. DEFAME, etc., still occas. used.

Diffarreation (difæriˌēⁱ·ʃən). 1623. [– L. *diffarreatio*, f. *dif-* DIF- + *farreum* spelt-cake; see CONFARREATION.] *Rom. Antiq.* An ancient Roman mode of dissolution of marriage, the undoing of confarreation.

Differ (di·fəɹ), *v.* ME. [– (O)Fr. *différer* defer, be different – L. *differre* in same senses, f. *dif-* DIF- + *ferre* carry. Thus L. *differre* has given two Eng. vbs. DEFER *v.*¹ and *differ.*] [**1.** The earlier form of DEFER *v.*¹ in all senses.] **2.** *trans.* To make unlike, different, or distinct; to cause to vary; to differentiate. Now *unusual.* **3.** *intr.* To be not the same; to be unlike, distinct, or various: two (or more) things are said to differ (absolutely, or *from each other*), one thing differs *from* another ME. **4.** *intr.* To be at variance; to disagree. Const. *with*; also *from* (*esp.* when followed by *in*). 1563. †**b.** To express disagreement; to dispute; to quarrel (*with*) –1737.

2. That differed it from the cases wherein the Court had gone some lengths CRUISE. **3.** One star differeth from another star in glory 1 *Cor.* 15:41. The same man, in divers times, differs from himselfe HOBBES. **4.** I d. with him totally 1809. She may..d. from me in opinion J. H. NEWMAN. **b.** We'll never d. with a crowded pit ROWE. Hence **Di·ffer** *sb.* (*Sc.* and *dial.*) = DIFFERENCE *sb.*

Difference (di·fĕrĕns), *sb.* ME. [– (O)Fr. *différence* – L. *differentia*; see DIFFERENT, -ENCE.] **1.** The condition, quality, or fact of being different or not the same; dissimilarity, distinction, diversity; disagreement *between* two or more things. **b.** (with *a* and *pl.*) An instance of unlikeness; a point in which things differ ME. **2.** *Math.* The quantity by which one quantity differs from another; the remainder left after subtracting one quantity from another ME. **b.** *spec.* The amount of increase or decrease in the price of stocks and shares between certain dates 1717. **3.** A diversity of opinion, sentiment, or purpose; hence, a dispute, a quarrel ME. **4.** A mark, device, or feature, which distinguishes one thing or set of things from another. Now *rare*, exc. as in b and c. 1481. **b.** *Her.* An alteration of or addition to a coat of arms, to distinguish a junior member or branch from the chief line 1450. **c.** *Logic.* = DIFFERENTIA 1551. †**d.** *transf.* A division, class, or kind –1682. **5.** A discrimination viewed as conceived by the subject ME. Also *attrib.*

1. D. is of two kinds as oppos'd either to identity or resemblance HUME. **3.** With full power to concert all matters in d. GOLDSM. **4.** An absolute gentleman, full of most excellent differences *Haml.* v. ii. 112. **b.** Oh you must weare your Rew with a d. *Haml.* IV. v. 183. **5.** He vysyted the seek folke without dyfference CAXTON.

Di·fference, *v.* 1450. [f. prec.] †**1.** *intr.* To be different (*rare*) –1483. †**2.** *trans.* To make different –1675. **3.** To differentiate (*from* something else). Freq. in *pass.* 1598. **4.** To discriminate. Const. *from.* (Now *rare.*) 1570. Also †*absol.* **5.** *Math.* To calculate the difference of. †**b.** To take the differential of. 1670.

3. Every individual has something that differences it from another LOCKE.

†**Di·fferency.** 1607. [See DIFFERENCE *sb.*, -ENCY.] = DIFFERENCE *sb.* –1812.

Different (di·fĕrĕnt), *a.* (*sb.*, *adv.*) ME. [– (O)Fr. *différent* – *different-*, pres. ppl. stem of L. *differre*; see DIFFER, -ENT.]

A. *adj.* **1.** Having unlike attributes; not of the same kind; not alike; of other nature, form, or quality. Const. *from*, also *to*, *than*, †*against*, †*with*. **2.** Not identical, distinct 1651. **3.** *slang.* Out of the ordinary, special, *recherché* 1912.

1. Persons d. in state and condition PETTIE. Much d. from the man he was *Com. Err.* v. i. 46. Elected for very d. merits than those of skill in war GOLDSM. **2.** At d. times ADDISON. Hence **Di·fferent-ly** *adv.*, **-ness** (*rare*).

B. *sb.* †**1.** = DIFFERENCE *sb.* 3 (*rare*) –1606. **2.** That which is different (*rare*) 1581.

C. as *adv.* = *Differently*. Now vulgar.

‖**Differentia** (difĕre·nʃiă). Pl. **-iæ** (-i,ī). 1827. [L.; see DIFFERENCE *sb.*] *Logic.* The attribute by which a species is distinguished from all other species of the same genus; a distinguishing mark.

Differe·ntiable, *a. rare.* 1863. [f. DIFFERENTIATE + -ABLE, after similar pairs, e.g. *deprecate*, *deprecable*; *depreciate*, *depreciable*.] Capable of being differentiated.

Differential (difĕre·nʃăl). 1647. [– med. and mod.L. *differentialis*, f. L. *differentia*; see DIFFERENCE *sb.*, -IAL.]

A. *adj.* **1.** Of or relating to difference; exhibiting or depending on a difference. **2.** Constituting a specific difference; special 1652; relating to specific differences 1875. **3.** *Math.* Relating to infinitesimal differences (see B. 1) 1702. **4.** *Physics* and *Mech.* Relating to, depending on, or exhibiting the difference of two (or more) measurable physical qualities 1768. **b.** Applied esp. to mechanism enabling a motor car's rear wheels to revolve at different rates when turning a corner 1902.

1. D. duties in favour of colonial timber ROGERS. **2.** The great D. marks of the Distemper CHEYNE. D. diagnosis 1875. Phr. **3.** *D. calculus*: a method of calculation which treats of the infinitesimal differences between consecutive values of continuously varying quantities, and of their rates of change as measured by such differences. *D. equation*: an equation involving differentials. **4.** *D. gear, gearing*: a combination of toothed wheels communicating a motion depending on the difference of their diameters or of the number of their teeth. *D. pulley*: a pulley having a block with two rigidly connected wheels or sheaves of different diameters, the chain or rope unwinding from one as it winds on the other. *D. screw*: a screw having two threads of different pitch; one of which unwinds as the other winds. *D. thermometer*: a thermometer consisting of two air-bulbs connected by a bent tube partly filled with a liquid, the position of the column of liquid indicating the difference of temperature between the two bulbs. *D. winding*: the method of winding two insulated wires side by side in an electric coil, through which currents pass in opposite directions.

B. *sb.* **1.** *Math.* The infinitesimal difference between consecutive values of a continuously varying quantity; either of the two quantities (usually considered to be infinitesimal) whose ratio constitutes a differential coefficient 1704. **2.** *Biol.* A distinction or distinctive characteristic of structure: opp. to *equivalent* 1883. **3.** *Comm.* A differential charge; see A. 1. 1890.

Differentially (difĕre·nʃăli), *adv.* 1644. [f. as prec. + -LY².] **1.** Distinctively, specially; see DIFFERENTIAL A. 2. **2.** In relation to the difference of two measurable quantities; in two different directions; see DIFFERENTIAL A. 4. 1862.

Differentiate (difĕre·nʃi,eⁱt), *v.* 1816. [– *differentiat-*, pa. ppl. stem of med.L. *differentiare*, f. L. *differentia*; see -ATE³.] **1.** To make different; to constitute the difference in or between; to distinguish 1853. **2.** *Biol.*, etc. To make different in the process of development, *esp.* for a special function or purpose; to make unlike by modification; to specialize. (Chiefly in *pass.*) 1858. Also *intr.* (for *refl.*) **3.** *trans.* To ascertain the difference in or between 1876. **4.** *Math.* To obtain the differential or the differential coefficient of 1816.

1. Genius differentiates a man from all other men DE QUINCEY. **2.** 'Protoplasm'..which is not yet differentiated into 'organs' CARPENTER. Hence **Differe·ntiator,** he who or that which differentiates.

Differentiation (difĕrenʃi,ēⁱ·ʃən). 1802. [f. prec. + -ION.] **1.** The action of differentiating, or condition of being differentiated (see prec. 1, 2); *spec.* in *Biol.* the process, or the result of the process, by which in the course of development a part, organ, etc. is modified into a special form, or for a special function; specialization; also the gradual production of differences between the descendants of the same ancestral types 1855. **2.** The action of ascertaining a difference (see prec. 3) 1866. **3.** *Math.* The operation of obtaining a differential or differential coefficient 1802.

1. He [the naturalist] justly considers the d. and specialisation of organs as the test of perfection DARWIN.

†**Di·fferingly,** *adv.* 1602. [f. *differing*, pres. pple. of DIFFER + -LY².] Differently –1691.

†‖**Difficile, -il** (difi·sil, di·fisil), *a.* 1477. [Fr. *difficile* – L. *difficilis*, f. *dis-* DIF- + *facilis* easy. See FACILE, DIFFICULT *a.*] Difficult; hard to do –1665; hard to understand –1637; of persons, hard to persuade or satisfy –1855. Hence **Diffici·leness,** the quality of being d.

†**Diffici·litate,** *v. rare.* 1611. [app. f. DIF- + FACILITATE, on Latin analogy.] To render difficult –1648.

Difficult (di·fikŏlt), *a.* Comp. **difficulter,** superl. **difficultest** (now *rare*). ME. [Back-formation from DIFFICULTY, from which a form †*difficul* (XV–XVII) was also derived, and used beside †*difficil* (see DIFFICILE).] **1.** Not easy; requiring effort or labour; troublesome, hard, puzzling. **2.** Of persons: Not easy to get on with 1589; hard to induce or persuade; obstinate 1502.

1. How d. a thing it is, to love, and to be wise, and both at once 1608. Knowledge..is d. to gain WORDSW. Great things, and d., which thou knowest not *Jer.* 33:3. **2.** My temper is d. THACKERAY. var. †**Difficul.** Hence **Di·fficult-ly** *adv.*, †**-ness** (*rare*).

Di·fficult, *v.* Now *local.* 1608. [– Fr. †*difficulter* – med.L. *difficultare*, f. *difficultas* DIFFICULTY.] †**1.** *trans.* To render difficult, impede –1818. **2.** To embarrass. Usu. *pass.* (*Sc.* and *U.S.*) 1686. var. †**Di·fficultate** in sense 1 (*rare*).

Difficulty (di·fikŏlti). ME. [– L. *difficultas*, f. *dis-* DIF- + *facultas* FACULTY; partly through Fr. *difficulté*.] **1.** The quality, fact, or condition of being difficult; the character of an action that requires labour or effort; hardness to be accomplished; the opposite of *ease* or *facility* ME. **b.** The quality of being hard to understand 1529. **2.** with *a* and *pl.* An instance of this quality; that which is difficult; often *spec.* a pecuniary embarrassment (usu. in *pl.*) ME. **3.** Reluctance; demur. *Obs.* exc. in phr. *to make a d.*; formerly †*to make d.*, *i.e.* to show reluctance. 1513.

1. If aught..in the shape Of d. or danger could deterre Me MILT. *P. L.* II. 449. The d. and obscurity of the phrase FARRAR. **2.** They mistake difficulties for impossibilities SOUTH. Difficulties in revelation J. H. NEWMAN. Mr. Brunton..is in 'difficulties' (civilized plural for debt) F. A. KEMBLE.

Diffidation (difidēⁱ·ʃən). 1731. [– med.L. *diffidatio*, f. *diffidare* renounce an alliance, etc., f. Rom. **disfidare*; see DEFY *v.*¹ So OFr. *diffidation*. See -ATION.] The undoing of relations of faith, allegiance, or amity; declaration of hostilities; DEFIANCE.

They sent a..letter of d., in which they renounced their allegiance 1807.

Diffide (difəi·d), *v.* Now *rare.* 1532. [– L. *diffidere* to mistrust, f. *dis-* DIF- + *fidere* to trust.] *intr.* To have or feel distrust. (The opposite of *confide*.) Also †*trans.*

Diffidence (di·fidĕns). 1526. [– Fr. †*diffidence* or L. *diffidentia*; see next, -ENCE.] (The opposite of CONFIDENCE.) **1.** Want of confidence; mistrust, distrust, doubt. Now *rare*. **2.** Distrust of oneself; want of confidence in one's own ability, worth, or fitness; modesty, shyness 1709.

1. A d...of his judgment or his virtue JAS. MILL. **2.** Speak, tho' sure, with seeming d. POPE. var. †**Di·ffidency.**

Diffident (di·fidĕnt), *a.* 1598. [– *diffident-*, pres. ppl. stem of L. *diffidere*; see DIFFIDE, -ENT.] (The opposite of CONFIDENT.) **1.** Wanting confidence (*in*); distrustful, mistrustful (*of*). **2.** Wanting in self-confidence; distrustful of oneself; timid, shy, modest, bashful. (The usual current sense.) 1713.

1. In the constancie of his people he was somewhat d. RALEGH. **2.** He [Dr. Johnson] never.. meant to terrify the d. MME. D'ARBLAY. Hence **Di·ffident-ly** *adv.*, †**-ness** (*rare*).

†**Diffla·tion.** 1568. [– *difflat-*, pa. ppl. stem of L. *difflare*, f. *dis-* DIF- + *flare* to blow; see -ION. Cf. Fr. †*difflation*.] Blowing asunder or dispersion by blowing –1763.

Diffluence (di·fluĕns). 1633. [f. next; see -ENCE.] **1.** The flowing apart or abroad; dispersion by flowing. Also *fig.* **2.** Dissolution into a liquid state 1847. So †**Di·ffluency,** diffluent condition.

Diffluent (di·fluĕnt), *a.* 1618. [– *diffluent-*, pres. ppl. stem of L. *diffluere* flow apart or away, f. *dis-* DIF- + *fluere* flow; see -ENT.] Characterized by flowing apart or abroad; fluid; deliquescent. Also *fig.*

†**Difform** (difǭ·ɹm), *a.* 1547. [– (O)Fr. *difforme* or med.L. *difformis*, for L. *deformis*; see DIF-, DEFORM *a.*] **1.** Of diverse forms; differing in shape –1677. **2.** Without symmetry; not uniform; of irregular form –1845.

1. A confused Mixture of d. qualities NEWTON. **2.** If the Parts be dissimilar, then the Substance is d. 1707.

†**Difformity** (difǭ·ɹmĭti). 1530. [– Fr. *difformité* or med.L. *difformitas*, f. *difformis*; see prec., -ITY.] **1.** Want of uniformity between things –1857. **2.** Want of conformity *with* or *to* –1677.

Diffra·ct, *a.* 1883. [– L. *diffractus*, pa. pple. of *diffringere*; see next.] *Bot.* Of lichens:

'Broken into *areolæ* with distinct interspaces'.

Diffract (difræ·kt), *v.* 1803. [– *diffract-*, pa. ppl. stem of L. *diffringere*; see next.] *trans.* To break in pieces, break up; in *Optics*, To deflect and break up (a beam of light) at the edge of an opaque body or through a narrow aperture. Also *fig.*

Diffraction (difræ·kʃən). 1671. [– Fr. *diffraction* or mod.L. *diffractio* (Grimaldi 1665), f. *diffract-*, pa. ppl. stem of L. *diffringere* break in pieces, f. *dis-* DIF- + *frangere* break; see -ION.] *Optics.* The breaking up of a beam of light into a series of light and dark spaces or bands, or of coloured spectra, due to interference of the rays when deflected at the edge of an opaque body or through a narrow aperture. **b.** *Acoustics.* An analogous phenomenon occurring in the case of sound-waves passing round the corner of a large body.

D. grating, a plate of glass or polished metal ruled with very close equidistant parallel lines, producing a spectrum by diffraction of the transmitted or reflected light.

Diffractive (difræ·ktiv), *a.* 1829. [f. as DIFFRACT *v.* + -IVE.] Tending to diffract. Hence **Diffra·ctively** *adv.*

Diffranchise, error for DISF- in J.

Diffu·gient, *ppl. a.* [– *diffugient-*, pres. ppl. stem of L. *diffugere*, f. *dis-* DIF- + *fugere* flee; see -ENT.] Dispersing. THACKERAY.

Diffusate (difiū·zět). 1850. [f. DIFFUSE *v.* + -ATE[1]; cf. FILTRATE *sb.*] *Chem.* The crystalloid portion of a mixture which passes through the membrane in the process of chemical dialysis.

Diffuse (difiū·s), *a.* ME. [– Fr. *diffus* or L. *diffusus* extensive, ample, prolix, pa. pple. of *diffundere* pour out or abroad, f. *dis-* DIF- + *fundere* pour.] †**1.** Confused; vague, doubtful –1602. **2.** Spread out in space; widespread, dispersed. Also †*fig.* 1643. **3.** Of a style: Using many words to convey the sense; verbose: opp. to *concise* or *condensed* 1742.

1. A mater to me doubtfull and d. 1560. **2.** D. typography JOHNSON, inflammation 1874. **3.** Too strong and concise, not d. enough for a woman JANE AUSTEN. Hence **Diffu·se-ly** *adv.*, **-ness.**

Diffuse (difiū·z), *v.* 1526. [– *diffus-*, pa. ppl. stem of L. *diffundere*; see prec.] †**1.** To pour out as a fluid with wide dispersion; to shed –1734. **2.** To pour or send forth as from a centre of dispersion; to spread widely, shed abroad, disperse, disseminate 1526; *fig.* to dissipate 1608. **3.** To extend or spread out (the body, etc.) freely (*arch.* and *poet.*) 1671. **4.** *intr.* (for *refl.*) To be or become diffused, to spread abroad (*lit.* and *fig.*) 1653. **5.** *Physics.* To intermingle, or (*trans.*) cause to intermingle, by diffusion 1808. †**6.** To distract. *Lear* I. iv. 2.

1. *Temp.* IV. i. 79. **2.** D. thy riches among thy friends JOHNSON. To d. geniality around one MASSON. **3.** See how he lies at random, carelessly diffused MILT. *Sams.* 118. Hence **Diffu·sed** (-zd, *poet.* -ėd) *ppl. a.* **Diffu·sed-ly** *adv.*, **-ness.** **Diffu·ser**, one who or that which diffuses.

Diffusible (difiū·zib'l), *a.* Also **-able.** 1782. [f. as prec. + -IBLE.] Capable of being diffused. Hence **Diffusibi·lity**, capacity of being diffused; *esp.* in *Physics*, as a measurable quality of gases and fluids. So **Diffu·sibleness.**

Diffusio·meter. 1866. [f. DIFFUSION 4 + -METER.] An apparatus for measuring the rate of diffusion of gases. var. **Diffusi·-meter.**

Diffusion (difiū·ʒən). ME. [– L. *diffusio*, f. *diffus-*; see DIFFUSE *v.*, -ION.] **1.** The action of diffusing; the condition of being diffused; a spreading; dispersion; wide distribution. **2.** *fig.* Spreading abroad, dispersion, dissemination (of abstract things) 1750. **3.** Of writing, etc.: Diffuseness; copiousness of language ME. **4.** *Physics.* The spontaneous molecular interpenetration of two fluids without chemical combination 1808. Also *attrib.*

2. The universal d. of learning among a people HUME. **3.** His d., and affluence of conversation BOSWELL.

Diffusive (difiū·siv), *a.* 1614. [– med.L. *diffusivus*, f. as prec.; see -IVE.] **1.** Having the quality of diffusing, or of being diffused; characterized by diffusion (*lit.* and *fig.*). †**2.** Of a body of people: As consisting of members in their individual capacity. (Common in 17th c.) –1718. **3.** = DIFFUSE *a.* 3. (Occas. in good sense: Copious, full.) 1699.

1. D. of knowledge MILT. Leaven hath..a d. faculty BP. HALL. The strength of some d. thought TENNYSON. **3.** He is less d. and more pointed than usual L. STEPHEN. Hence **Diffu·sive-ly** *adv.*, **-ness.** **Diffu·sivity** = DIFFUSIBILITY.

Dig (dig), *v.* Pa. t. and pple. **dug** (dɒg), formerly **digged** (digd). [ME. *digge*, perh. :– OE. **dīcigian*, f. *dīc* DITCH *sb.*; superseded *delve* and *grave.*]

I. *intr.* **1.** 'To work in making holes or turning the ground' (J.); to make an excavation; to work with a spade or similar tool. Also *transf.* and *fig.* **b.** *spec.* To study hard and closely at a subject (*U.S.*) 1789. **2.** To make one's way *into* or *through* by digging; to make an excavation *under* 1535.

1. Digge about þe vyne rotis WYCLIF. They [ants] dug deeper and deeper to deposite their eggs GOLDSM.

II. *trans.* **1.** To penetrate and turn up (the ground, etc.) with a spade or similar tool ME. Also *transf.* **2.** *spec.* To break up and turn over (the soil) with a mattock, spade, or the like, as an operation of tillage ME. **3.** To make (a hole, mine, etc.) by the use of a spade or the like; to form by digging; to excavate ME. **4.** To obtain or extract by excavation. Const. *from*, *out of*. ME. †**5.** To put and cover up (in the ground, etc.) by digging; to bury –1647. **6.** To thrust or force *in* or *into* 1553. **7.** To spur vigorously; to thrust, stab, prod 1530.

1. Sone of man, d. the wal WYCLIF *Ezek.* 8:8. **2.** It [a vineyard] shall not be pruned nor digged; but there shall come up briers and thorns *Isa.* 5:6. **3.** Digge my graue thy selfe 2 *Hen. IV*, IV. v. 111. **4.** I with my long nayles will digge thee pig-nuts *Temp.* II. ii. 172.

In comb. with adverbs. **D. down. a.** To cause to fall by digging. **b.** To lower or remove by digging. **D. in. a.** To put in and cover up by digging. **b.** To drive in deeply. **c.** Also *fig.* To establish oneself in a position. **D. out. a.** To extract or remove by digging. **b.** To excavate. **c.** *intr.* To depart (*U.S. colloq.*). **D. up. a.** To take or get out of the ground, etc., by digging. **b.** To break up or open by digging. **c.** To break up and open the soil of, by digging.

Dig, *sb.* 1674. [f. prec. vb.] **1.** An act of digging 1887. **2.** A definite quantity to be dug out 1890. **3.** A tool for digging 1674. **4.** A thrust, a sharp poke, as with the elbow, fist, etc. 1819. Also *fig.* **5.** A diligent or plodding student (*U.S. slang*) 1849. **6.** = DIGGING 4. 1893.

Digallic (dəigæ·lik), *a.* 1877. [DI-[2].] *Chem.* In *D. acid*, which contains two molecules of gallic acid, minus one equivalent of water.

Digamist (di·gămist). 1656. [f. as DIGAMY + -IST.] A man or woman who has married a second time.

Digamma (dəigæ·mă). 1698. [– L. *digamma* – Gr. δίγαμμα, f. δι- twice + γάμμα: so called from its shape Ϝ, resembling two gammas (Γ) set one above the other.] The sixth letter of the original Greek alphabet, corresponding to the Semitic *waw* or *vau*, which was afterwards disused. It was a consonant, probably equivalent to English *w*. So **Diga·mmate** *a.*, **-ated** *ppl. a.* having the d.; formed with a figure like the d.

Digamous (di·gămǝs), *a.* 1864. [f. late L. *digamus* (– Gr. δίγαμος, f. δι- twice + γάμος marriage) + -OUS.] **1.** Married a second time; of the nature of digamy. **2.** *Bot.* = ANDROGYNOUS 1883.

Digamy (di·gămi). 1635. [– late L. *digamia* – Gr. διγαμία, f. δίγαμος; see prec., -Y[3].] **1.** Digamous condition or state; second marriage. †**2.** = BIGAMY 1. –1766.

Digastric (dəigæ·strik), *a.* and *sb.* 1696. [– mod.L. *digastricus* (also used), f. Gr. δι- DI-[2] + γαστήρ belly; see -IC.] *Anat.*

A. *adj.* **1.** Having two parts swelling like bellies; *spec.* applied to muscles having two fleshy bellies with a tendon between 1721. **2.** Of or pertaining to the digastric muscle of the lower jaw; see B. 1831.

B. *sb.* A muscle of the lower jaw, fleshy at its extremities, and tendinous at its middle 1696.

Digeneous (dəi,dʒī·niəs), *a.* 1883. [f. Gr. διγενής of double or doubtful sex (f. δι- DI-[2] + γένος, γενε- sex) + -OUS.] **1.** Bisexual. **2.** Of or pertaining to the *Digenea*, a division of the trematode worms or flukes.

Digenesis (dəi,dʒe·nėsis). 1876. [– mod.L., f. Gr. δι- DI-[2] + γένεσις generation.] *Biol.* Successive generation by two different processes, as sexual and asexual. So **Digene·tic** *a.* relating to or characterized by d.

Digenite (di·dʒĭnəit). 1850. [f. Gr. διγενής of doubtful kind + -ITE[1] 2b.] *Min.* A variety of CHALCOCITE or copper-glance.

Digenous (di·dʒĭnəs), *a.* 1884. [irreg. f. Gr. διγενής (see DIGENEOUS) + -OUS.] Of two sexes, bisexual. Hence **Di·geny**, sexual reproduction.

†**Di·gerent.** *rare.* 1477. [– *digerent-*, pres. ppl. stem of L. *digerere*; see DIGEST *v.*, -ENT.]

A. *adj.* Digesting –1755.

B. *sb.* A medicine which promotes digestion or suppuration –1867.

Digest (dəi·dʒest), *sb.* ME. [– L. *digesta* 'matters methodically arranged', n. pl. of *digestus*, pa. pple. of *digerere* divide, distribute, dissolve, digest, f. *di-* DI-[1] + *gerere* carry.] **1.** A digested collection of statements; a methodically arranged compendium or summary of written matter 1555. **2.** *Law.* An abstract of some body of law, systematically arranged 1626; *spec.* the body of Roman laws compiled from the earlier jurists by order of Justinian ME. †**3.** = DIGESTION –1602.

1. His [Milton's] d. of scriptural texts MACAULAY. **2.** The Digests of the Jewish Law 1652.

Digest (di,dʒe·st, dəi-), *v.* 1450. [– *digest-*, pa. ppl. stem of L. *digerere*; see prec.] †**1.** *trans.* To divide and dispose –1675; to disperse –1727. **2.** To dispose methodically; to reduce into a systematic form, usually with condensation; to classify 1482. **3.** To settle and arrange methodically in the mind; to think over 1450. **4.** To prepare (food) in the stomach and intestines for assimilation by the system; see DIGESTION 1. 1483. Also *absol.* **b.** *intr.* (for *refl.*) To undergo digestion, as food 1574. **c.** *trans.* To cause or promote the digestion of 1607. **5.** *fig.* and *transf.* (from 4) 1576. **6.** To bear without resistance; to 'swallow, stomach' 1553; to get over the effects of (*arch.*) 1576. **7.** To obtain mental nourishment from 1548. †**8.** To mature, *esp.* by the action of heat. Also *fig.* –1708. †**9.** *trans.* To cause to suppurate; also *absol.* to promote suppuration –1767. Also †*intr.* (for *refl.*) **10.** *trans.* To prepare by boiling; to dissolve by the aid of heat and moisture 1616. Also *intr.* (for *refl.*).

2. The Civil Law is digested into general Heads HALE. **3.** To d. a plan for keeping accounts SMEATON. **4.** *absol.* Each has to..d. for himself CLOUGH. **5.** Most of them [leaves] were not able to d. the third fly DARWIN. The Hapsburgs.. have not digested Bosnia completely yet 1889. **6.** To d. a wanton attack W. IRVING, a loss COLERIDGE. **7.** Read, marke, learne, and inwardly digeste them *Bk. Com. Prayer.* **10.** D. the bark in alcohol 1838. Hence †**Dige·st, Dige·sted** *ppl. adjs.* **Dige·stedly** *adv.*

Digester (didʒe·stəɹ, dəi-). Also **-or.** 1578. [f. prec. + -ER[1], -OR 2.] He who or that which digests; *esp.* a strong close vessel in which bones or other substances are dissolved by the action of heat.

Digestible (didʒe·stĭb'l, dəi-), *a.* Also **-able.** ME. [–(O)Fr. *digestible* – L. *digestibilis*, f. as DIGEST *v.*; see -IBLE.] Capable of being digested. Hence **Dige·stibleness. Dige·stibly** *adv.*

Digestion (didʒe·styən, dəi-). ME. [–(O)Fr. *digestion* – L. *digestio*, f. as prec.; see -ION.] **1.** The process whereby the nutritive part of food is, in the stomach and intestines, rendered fit to be assimilated by the system. Also *transf.* and *fig.* **2.** The power or faculty of digesting food ME. **3.** *fig.* The action of digesting; see DIGEST *v.* 1610. **4.** *Chem.* †**a.** The operation of maturing by the action of gentle heat –1677. **b.** The operation of dissolving a substance by the action of heat and moisture 1610. †**5.** *Surg.* The process of maturing an ulcer, etc.; disposition to healthy suppuration –1830. †6. The action of methodizing and reducing to order; the result of this; a DIGEST –1754.

1. Things sweet to tast, proue in d. sowre *Rich. II*, I. iii. 236. *transf.* Whether they [Drosera]. . have the power of d. DARWIN. *fig.* I devoured them [books] with appetite, if not d. W. IRVING. D. of a wrong STERNE. 2. Our digestion would be better, if our dishes were fewer NASHE.

Digestive (didʒe·stiv, dəi-). ME. [– (O)Fr. *digestif, -ive* or L. *digestivus*, f. as prec.; see -IVE.]

A. *adj.* **1.** Having the function of digesting; engaged in or pertaining to digestion 1532. **2.** Promoting digestion; digestible 1528. **3.** Promoting suppuration.

1. The d. powers 1725, organs 1837, cavity 1841. 2. D. cheese, and fruit there sure will be B. JONS. Applying only a d. warmth 1799.

B. *sb.* **1.** Anything promoting digestion of food ME. **2.** A substance which promotes suppuration in a wound, etc.; digestive ointment 1543.

Hence **Dige·stive-ly** *adv.*, **-ness.**

†Dige·story. 1612. [– late L. *digestorius*, f. as prec.; see -ORY[2].]

A. *adj.* = DIGESTIVE.

B. *sb.* A vessel or organ of digestion –1774.

†Dige·sture. 1565. [f. as prec. + -URE, after *gesture*.] = DIGESTION 1, 2. –1700.

Di·ggable, *a.* 1552. [f. DIG *v.* + -ABLE.] That can be digged.

Digger (di·gəɹ). ME. [f. DIG *v.* + -ER[1].] **1.** One who or that which digs. **2.** *spec.* A miner; *esp.* one who searches for gold 1531. **b.** One of a tribe of N. American Indians who live chiefly on roots 1837. **c.** *Eng. Hist.* A section of the Levellers in 1649, who began to dig and plant the commons 1649. **3.** An instrument for digging; the digging part of a machine 1686. **4.** A division of Hymenopterous insects, also called *Digger-wasps* 1847.

Comb.: **d.-wasp** (see sense 4).

Digging (di·giŋ), *vbl. sb.* 1538. [f. DIG *v.* + -ING[1].] **1.** The action of DIG *v.*, in various senses; an instance of this 1552. **2.** *concr.* The materials dug out 1559. **3.** A place where digging is carried on; in *pl.* (occas. taken as *sing.*) applied to mines, and especially to gold-fields 1538. **4.** *colloq.* in *pl.* Lodgings, quarters 1838.

3. *Wet-diggings* and *Dry-diggings* are terms in gold districts, for mines near rivers or on the higher lands as the case may be FARMER *Americanisms*.

Dight (dəit), *v.* Now *arch.* and *dial.* [OE. *dihtan* direct, compose, write, etc., corresp. to MLG., MDu. *dichten* compose, contrive (Du. *dichten* invent, compose), OHG. *tihtōn, dihtōn* (G. *dichten*) write, compose verses, ON. *dikta* compose in Latin, invent, contrive – L. *dictare* appoint, prescribe, DICTATE, in med.L. write, compose.] **†1.** *trans.* To dictate OE.; to ordain –1558; to order –1522; to deal with, treat –1650; *spec.* to have to do with sexually ME.; to dispose of –1535. **†2.** To compose –1607; to do –1596. **3.** †To put in order –1500; to equip ME.; to dress, array ME.; to make ready, or proper (revived in poet. and romantic use) ME.

1. 'Who checks at me, to death is d.' SCOTT. 3. The hall. .With rich array and costly arras d. SPENSER *F. Q.* I. iv. 6. Orion, in golden panoply d. BOWEN. To d. him for earth or for heaven 1821. Hence **Di·ghter** (now *dial.*), one who or that which dights.

Digit (di·dʒit), *sb.* ME. [– L. *digitus* finger, toe.] **1** One of the terminal divisions of the hand or foot; a finger or toe 1644. **2.** A finger's breadth, three-quarters of an inch 1633. **3.** *Arith.* Each of the numerals below ten (originally counted on the fingers); any of the nine, or (including the cipher, 0) ten Arabic figures ME. **4.** *Astron.* The twelfth part of the diameter of the sun or moon; used in expressing the magnitude of an eclipse 1591.

1. We find among reptiles, all the combinations of digits, from five to one, taken between two pairs of hands or claws 1802. 4. Ye Sun. .was darkned 10 digits ½ HEARNE. Hence **†Di·git** *v.* to point out with the finger.

Digital (di·dʒităl). ME. [– L. *digitalis*, f. *digitus* DIGIT; see -AL[1].]

A. *adj.* **1.** Of or pertaining to a finger, or to the fingers or digits 1656. **2.** Resembling a finger or the impression made by one 1831. **3.** Having digits 1833.

2. The D. Cavity R. KNOX. 3. The d. feet 1887.

B. *sb.* **†1.** = DIGIT *sb.* 3. ME. only. **2.** A finger (*joc.*) 1840. **3.** A key played with the finger in a piano or organ 1878.

Digitalic (didʒitæ·lik), *a.* 1858. [f. DIGITALIS + -IC.] Of or pertaining to digitalis; in *d. acid*, an acid obtained from the foxglove, crystallizing in white acicular prisms.

Digitaliform (-tæ·lifǫɹm), *a.* 1859. [f. mod.L. *digitalis* DIGITALIS + -FORM.] *Bot.* Of the form of the corolla of the foxglove.

Digitalin (di·dʒitălin). 1837. [f. DIGITALIS + -IN[1].] *Chem.* The substance or substances extracted from the leaves of the foxglove, as its active principle. (Originally named *digitalia, digitaline.*)

‖**Digitalis** (didʒitē[i]·lis). 1664. [mod.L. (Fuchs, 1542), subst. use (sc. *herba* plant) of L. *digitalis* pertaining to the finger, after G. *fingerhut* thimble, foxglove, lit. 'finger-hat'.] **1.** *Bot.* A genus of plants of the N.O. *Scrophulariaceæ*, including the foxglove (*D. purpurea*). **2.** A medicine prepared from the foxglove 1799.

Digitally (di·dʒităli), *adv.* 1832. [f. DIGITAL *a.* + -LY[2].] By means of or with respect to the fingers.

Digitate (di·dʒitět), *a.* 1661. [– L. *digitatus*, f. *digitus* DIGIT + *-atus* -ATE[2].] **1.** *Zool.* Having divided digits or toes. **2.** Divided into parts resembling fingers; *spec.* in *Bot.* of leaves, etc.: Having deep radiating divisions, as the compound leaves of the horse-chestnut 1788. Hence **Di·gitately** *adv.* So **Di·gitated** *a.* (in same senses).

Digitate (di·dʒite[i]t), *v.* 1658. [In sense 1 f. med.L. *digitare* point at, indicate, f. L. *digitus* DIGIT; see -ATE[3].] **†1.** *trans.* To point out with or as with the finger (*rare*). **2.** *intr.* To become divided into finger-like parts 1796.

Digitation (didʒitē[i]·ʃən). 1658. [f. DIGITATE *v.* or *a.*; see -ATION.] **†1.** A touching, or pointing, with the finger –1800. **2.** Division into fingers or finger-like processes; *concr.* one of these processes 1709.

Digiti- (di·dʒiti), comb. f. L. *digitus* (see DIGIT *sb.*).

Di·gitiform *a.* digitate. **Di:gitine·rvate, -ne·rved, -ne·rvous** *adjs.*, *Bot.* having the ribs of the leaf radiating from the top of the leaf-stalk. **Di:gitipa·rtite** *a.* having more than five lobes of a similar character.

Digitigrade (di·dʒitigrē[i]:d). 1833. [– Fr. *digitigrade*, in mod.L. *digitigrada* (Cuvier 1817), f. L. *digitus* DIGIT + *-gradus* going, walking.]

A. *adj.* Walking on the toes; *spec.* in *Zool.* belonging to the tribe *Digitigrada* of Carnivora. (Opp. to PLANTIGRADE.)

B. *sb.* A digitigrade animal. (Chiefly in *pl.*) 1835. Hence **Di·gitigra:dism,** d. condition.

Digitize (di·dʒitəiz), *v. rare.* 1704. [f. DIGIT + -IZE.] To treat in some way with the fingers; to finger; as, *to d. a pen.*

Digito-, shortened from *digitalis*, as in *digito·lein*, a fat obtained from digitalis leaves; etc.

†Digla·diate, *v.* 1656. [– *digladiat-*, pa. ppl. stem of L. *digladiari* contend fiercely, f. *di-* DI-[1] + *gladius* sword; see -ATE[3].] *intr.* To cross swords; to contend. So **Digladia·tion** (now *rare*), fighting with swords (*lit.* and *fig.*).

Diglot, Diglott (dəi·glǫt), *a.* 1863. [– Gr. δίγλωττος, f. δι- DI-[2] + γλῶττα tongue.] Using or expressed in two languages, bilingual; also as *sb.* A diglot book or version. So **Di·glottism,** the use of words derived from two languages.

Diglyph (dəi·glif). 1727. [– Gr. δίγλυφος doubly indented, f. δι- DI-[2] + γλύφειν carve.] *Archit.* A projecting face or tablet with two vertical grooves or channels.

†Dignation (dignē[i]·ʃən). 1450. [– L. *dignatio*, f. *dignat-*, pa. ppl. stem of *dignare*, *dignari* think worthy, deign; see -ION. Cf. OFr. *dignation*.] The action of deeming worthy; honour conferred –1737.

†Digne, *a.* ME. [– (O)Fr. *digne* :– L. *dignus* worthy.] **1.** Of high worth or desert; honourable –1578. **2.** Worthy, deserving. Const. *of* (*to*), or *inf.* –1643. **3.** Becoming fit. Const. *to, unto, of, for.* –1549. **4.** Haughty, disdainful (in ME. only). Hence **†Di·gnely** *adv.*

Dignification (di:gnifikē[i]·ʃən). Now *rare.* 1577. [– med.L. *dignificatio*, f. *dignificat-*, pa. ppl. stem of late L. *dignificare*; see DIGNIFY, -ION. Cf. OFr. *dignification*.] The action of dignifying, or fact of being dignified.

Dignified (di·gnifəid), *ppl. a.* 1667. [f. DIGNIFY + -ED[1].] **1.** Invested with dignity; exalted 1763. **†2.** Ranking as a dignitary (*esp.* ecclesiastical) –1860. **3.** Marked by dignity; stately, noble, majestic 1812. Hence **Di·gnifiedly** *adv.*

Dignify (di·gnifəi), *v.* 1526. [– Fr. †*dignifier* (OFr. *dignefier*) – late L. *dignificare*, f. L. *dignus* worthy; see -FY.] **1.** *trans.* To make worthy or illustrious; to confer dignity or honour upon; to ennoble, honour. **b.** In lighter use: To give a high-sounding name or title to 1750. **†2.** To confer a title of honour upon –1727.

1. Such a Day. .Came not, till now, to dignifie the Times 2 *Hen. IV*, I. i. 22. To d. letters with the title of Walpoliana H. WALPOLE. Hence **Di·gnifier.**

Dignitary (di·gnitări). 1672. [f. DIGNITY, after *propriety, proprietary*; see -ARY[1].]

A. *sb.* One holding high rank or office, *esp.* ecclesiastical.

B. *adj.* Of, belonging to, or invested with a dignity (*esp.* ecclesiastical) 1715.

Dignity (di·gnĭti). [ME. *dignete, dignite* – OFr. *digneté*, (also mod.) *dignité* – L. *dignitas*, f. *dignus* worthy; see -ITY.] **1.** The quality of being worthy or honourable; worth, excellence; †desert. **2.** Honourable or high estate, position, or estimation; honour; rank ME. Also *fig.* **b.** *collect.* Persons of high estate or rank 1548. **3.** An honourable office, rank, or title; *transf.* a dignitary ME. **4.** Nobility of aspect, manner, or style; becoming stateliness, gravity 1667. **5.** *Astrol.* A situation of a planet in which its influence is heightened ME. **¶6.** [Fantastic rendering of Gr. ἀξίωμα.] An axiom. SIR T. BROWNE.

1. It is of the essence of real d. to be self-sustained H. TAYLOR. 2. Gyuyng somewhat to the dygnyte of presthode T. STARKEY. *collect.* I cannot see the d. of a great kingdom. .imprisoned or exiled, without great pain BURKE. 3. *transf.* These filthy dreamers. speake euill of dignities *Jude* 8. 4. In every gesture dignitie and love MILT. *P. L.* VIII. 489.

†Digno·sce, *v.* 1639. [– L. *dignoscere* recognize apart, f. *di-* DI-[1] + (*g*)*noscere* know.] To distinguish, discern (*trans.* and *intr.*) –1676.

†Digno·tion. 1578. [f. *dignot-*, pa. ppl. stem of L. *dignoscere* (see prec.) + -ION. Cf. med.L. *dinotio* perception.] The action of distinguishing or discerning; a distinguishing sign –1658.

Digoneutic (dəigoniū·tik), *a.* 1889. [f. DI-[2] + Gr. γονεύειν beget; cf. *monogoneutic*, *polygoneutic* (see POLY-).] *Entom.* Producing two broods in a year. Hence **Digoneu·tism,** d. condition.

Digonous (di·gonəs, dəi-), *a.* 1788. [f. mod.L. *digonus* (f. Gr. δι- DI-[2] + -γωνος angled) + -OUS. Cf. TRIGONOUS.] *Bot.* Having two angles.

Di·gram. 1864. Proposed synonym of DIGRAPH. Webster.

Digraph (dəi·grɑf). 1788. [f. DI-[2] + -GRAPH.] A group of two letters expressing a simple sound, as *ea* in *head*, etc. Hence **Digra·phic** *a.*

Digress (digre·s, dəi-), *v.* 1530. [– *digress-*, pa. ppl. stem of L. *digredi*, f. *di-* DI-[1] + *gradi* to step, walk, f. *gradus* step.] **1.** *intr.* To go aside from the track; to diverge, deviate, swerve 1552. Also †*fig.* **†2.** To diverge from the right path; to transgress –1640. **3.** To deviate from the subject in discourse or writing. (Now the prevailing sense.) 1530.

1. I find myself in Bond Street. .I d. into Soho, to explore a bookstall LAMB. *fig.* Digresse good sir from such lewd songs 1603. 2. So man. .digressed and fell 1640. 3. I have too long digressed, and therefore shall return to my subject SWIFT. Hence **†Digress** *sb.* = DIGRESSION 2. **Digre·sser.**

Digression (digre·ʃən, dəi-). ME. [– (O)Fr. *digression* or L. *digressio*, f. as prec.; see -ION.] **1.** The action of digressing (*lit.* and

†*fig.*). (Now *rare* in *lit.* sense.) 1552. **2.** Deviation from the subject in discourse or writing; an instance of this. (The most frequent sense.) ME. **3.** *Astron.*, etc. Deviation from a particular line, or from the mean position; deflexion; *e.g.* of an inferior planet from the sun 1646.

1. Then my d. is so vile, so base, That it will liue engrauen in my face SHAKS. **2.** It were a long disgression Fro my matere CHAUCER. Hence **Digre·ssional** *a.* of, pertaining to, or characterized by d.

Digressive (digre·siv, dəi-), *a.* 1611. [– late L. *digressivus*, f. as prec.; see -IVE.] Characterized by, or given to, digression; of the nature of digression. Hence **Digre·ssive-ly** *adv.*, **-ness.**

‖**Digue.** 1523. [Fr.] = DIKE.

‖**Digynia** (dəidʒi·niă). 1762. [mod.L., (Linnæus 1735), f. DI-[2] + Gr. γυνή wife; see -IA[1].] *Bot.* The second Order in many classes of the Linnæan Sexual System, comprising plants having two pistils. Hence **Digy·nian, Digy·nious** *adjs.* belonging to the order *D.*; **Di·gynous** *a.* having two pistils.

Dihedral (dəihī·drăl), *a.* 1799. [f. next + -AL[1].] **1.** *Cryst.* Having or contained by two planes or plane faces. **2.** *Math.* Of the nature of a dihedron 1893.

1. *D. angle*, the inclination of two planes which meet at an edge; also, the angle formed by any two meeting or intersecting planes or plane faces, *spec.* the angle formed by the wing pairs of an aeroplane. Also as *sb.* = d. angle.

Dihedron (dəihī·drǫn). 1888. [f. Gr. δι- DI-[2] + ἕδρα seat, base, after *tetrahedron*, etc.] *Math.* The portion of two superposed planes bounded by (or contained within) a regular polygon.

‖**Dihe·lios.** Also **dihelium.** 1727. [mod.L., f. DI-[3] + Gr. ἥλιος sun.] *Astr.* Kepler's name for that ordinate of the ellipsis, which passes through the focus, wherein the sun is supposed to be placed. E. CHAMBERS.

Dihexagonal (dəi:heksæ·gŏnăl), *a.* 1864. [DI-[2].] *Cryst.* Having twelve angles, of which the first, third, fifth,.. eleventh, are equal to one another, and the second, fourth, sixth,.. twelfth, are equal to one another, but those of the one set not equal to those of the other.

Di-hexahe·dron. 1888. [DI-[2].] *Cryst.* A six-sided prism with trihedral summits, making twelve faces in all. Also occas., a double hexagonal pyramid. So †**Di-hexahedral** *a.* having twice six faces.

Dihydrite (dəihəi·drəit). 1868. [f. Gr. δι- DI-[2] + ὕδωρ water + -ITE[1] 2b.] *Min.* A variety of pseudo-malachite or native phosphate of copper, containing two equivalents of water.

Diiamb (dəi,əiæ·mb). 1753. [– late L. *diiambus* – Gr. διίαμβος, f. δι- DI-[2] + ἴαμβος IAMBUS.] *Pros.* A metrical foot consisting of two iambs (◡—◡—).

Di-iodide (dəi,əi·ŏdəid). 1873. [DI-[2].] *Chem.* A compound of two atoms of iodine with a dyad element or radical.

†**Diju·dicant.** *rare.* 1661. [– *dijudicant-*, pres. ppl. stem of L. *dijudicare*; see next, -ANT[1].] One who dijudicates –1691.

Dijudicate (dəi,dʒū·dikeⁱt), *v.* Now *rare.* 1607. [– *dijudicat-*, pa. ppl. stem of L. *dijudicare*, f. *di-* DI-[1] + *judicare* to judge; see -ATE[3].] To judge; to determine, decide; *trans.* to judge of; to pronounce judgement on, decide. Hence **Dijudica·tion** (now *rare*).

‖**Dika** (dəi·kă). 1859. [W. African name.] In *d.-bread*, a cocoa-like substance, prepared from the fruit of a species of mango-tree. *D.-fat, -oil*, the fatty substance of d.-bread.

Di·k-dik. 1895. A small African antelope.

Dike, dyke (dəik), *sb.* ME. [– ON. *dík*, *díki* or MLG. *dīk* dam, MDu. *dijc* ditch, pool, mound, dam (Du. *dijk* dam); see DITCH. In sense 1 first recorded from northern and eastern texts, in which it is prob. of Norse origin, in sense 4 prob. orig. from the Low Countries in connection with drainage works.] **1.** †A DITCH –1575; a hollow dug out to hold or conduct water. **2.** Hence, any water-course or channel 1616. †**3.** Any hollow dug in the ground; a pit, cave, etc. –1475. **4.** An embankment 1487; a wall or fence ME. Also *fig.* **5.** An embankment to prevent inundations 1635; a raised causeway 1480. Also *fig.* **6.** (*Northumb.*) A fissure in a stratum, filled up with deposited or intrusive rock 1789. Hence, in *Geol.* A mass of mineral matter, usually igneous rock, filling up a fissure in the original strata 1802.

2. Whole sheets descend of sluicy Rain, The Dykes are fill'd DRYDEN. **5.** The land here is lower than the waters; for which reason they have the strongest dams or dykes in the whole country 1756. *fig.* The last dike of the prerogative 'JUNIUS'.

Dike, dyke, *v.* [OE. had *dīcian*; but the ME. vb. is a new formation.] **1.** *intr.* To make a dike; to dig ME. **3.** *trans.* To provide with a dike or dikes, in various senses ME. **3.** To place (flax or hemp) in a dike or water-course to steep 1799.

1. He wolde dyke and delue..for euery poure wight CHAUCER. Hence **Di·ker, dy·ker,** one who constructs or works at dikes; *Sc.* one who builds enclosure walls (without mortar).

Di·ke-grave. 1563. [– MDu. *dijcgrave*, f. *dijk* dike + *graaf* earl.] In Holland, an officer who has charge of the dikes or sea-walls; in England (*esp.* Lincolnshire) = DIKE-REEVE. Now only *dial.*

Di·ke-reeve, dyke-. 1665. [f. DIKE *sb.* + REEVE; perh. an alteration of prec.] An officer who has charge under the Court of Sewers of the drains, sluices, and sea-banks of a district of fen or marsh-land in England.

†**Dila·cerate,** *ppl. a.* 1602. [– L. *dilaceratus*, pa. pple. of *dilacerare*; see next, -ATE[2].] Rent asunder, torn –1649.

Dilacerate (di-, dəilæ·sĕreⁱt), *v.* 1604. [– *dilacerat-*, pa. ppl. stem of L. *dilacerare*, f. *di-* DI-[1] + *lacerare* tear, lacerate; see -ATE[3].] *trans.* To tear asunder, tear in pieces. Also *fig.* Hence **Dila:cera·tion**, the action of dilacerating; the being dilacerated.

Dila·ctic, *a.* 1863. *Chem.* See DI-[2] 2 and LACTIC.

Dilambdodont (dəilæ·mdodǫnt), *a.* [f. Gr. δι- DI-[2] + λάμβδα the letter lambda, Λ + ὀδούς, ὀδοντ- tooth.] *Zool.* Having oblong molar teeth with two Λ- or V-shaped ridges.

Dilamination (dəilæminēⁱ·ʃən). 1849. [f. DI-[1] + L. *lamina* thin plate, layer + -ATION.] *Bot.* Separation into laminæ, or splitting off of a lamina.

†**Dila·niate,** *v.* 1535. [– *dilaniat-*, pa. ppl. stem of L. *dilaniare* tear in pieces, f. *di-* DI-[1] + *laniare* tear; see -ATE[3].] To rend or tear in pieces –1653. Hence †**Dilania·tion.**

Dila·pidate, *ppl. a. Obs.* or *arch.* 1590. [– L. *dilapidatus*, pa. pple. of *dilapidare*; see next, -ATE[2].] = DILAPIDATED.

Dilapidate (dilæ·pideⁱt), *v.* Also **de-.** 1570. [– *dilapidat-*, pa. ppl. stem of L. *dilapidare*, f. *di-* DI-[1] + *lapis, lapid-* stone; see -ATE[3].] **1.** *trans.* To bring (a building) into a state of decay or of partial ruin. Also *fig.* **2.** *fig.* To waste, squander (a benefice or estate) 1590. **3.** *intr.* To become dilapidated; to fall into ruin, decay, or disrepair 1712.

1. Dilapidated.., to obtain stones to build a house 1706. **2.** Those who by overbuilding their houses have dilapidated their lands FULLER. **3.** The church of Elgin..was..suffered to d. JOHNSON. Hence **Dila·pidated** *ppl. a.* fallen into ruin or disrepair; ruined, broken down (*lit.* and *fig.*). **Dila·pidator.**

Dilapidation (dilæ:pidēⁱ·ʃən). Also **de-.** ME. [– late L. *dilapidatio*, f. as prec.; see -ION.] **1.** The action of dilapidating; the condition of being in ruins or in disrepair (*lit.* and *fig.*) 1460. **2.** *Law.* The action of pulling down, allowing to decay, or in any way impairing ecclesiastical property belonging to an incumbency ME.; also, *loosely*, the sums charged to make good such damage incurred during an incumbency 1553. **3.** The falling of stones or masses of rock from mountains or cliffs by natural agency 1794; *concr.* debris 1816.

1. The d. of the national resources MALTHUS, of buildings 1886. The wretched delapidation of the Holy Sepulchre 1860. **2.** She hath heard widowes complain of dilapidations OVERBURY.

Dilatable (dəilēⁱ·tăb'l, di-), *a.* 1610. [f. DILATE *v.* + -ABLE.] Capable of being dilated; expansible. Hence **Dila:tabi·lity, Dila·tableness,** capacity of being dilated.

Dilatancy (dəilēⁱ·tănsi, di-). 1885. [f. next; see -ANCY.] The property of dilating or expanding; *spec.* that of expanding in bulk with change of shape, exhibited by granular masses.

Dilatant (dəilēⁱ·tănt, di-). 1841. [In A, f. DILATE *v.*[2] + -ANT[1]. In B – Fr. *dilatant.*]

A. *adj.* Dilating; expansive.

B. *sb.* **a.** A substance having the property of dilating. **b.** A surgical instrument used for dilating.

Dilatate (dəi·lĕtĕt), *ppl. a.* 1846. [– L. *dilatatus*, pa. pple. of *dilatare*; see DILATE *v.*[2], -ATE[2].] *Zool.* Dilated.

Dilatation (dəilĕtēⁱ·ʃən). ME. [– OFr. *dilatation* – late L. *dilatatio*, f. *dilatat-*, pa. ppl. stem of L. *dilatare*; see DILATE *v.*[2], -ION. Largely superseded by DILATION[2].] **1.** The action or process of dilating; the condition of being dilated; expansion, enlargement. (Chiefly in *Physics* and *Physiol.*) **b.** *concr.* A dilated form, formation, or part of any structure 1833. **2.** The spreading abroad (of abstract things) (*arch.*) ME. **3.** The action or practice of dilating upon a subject; amplification ME.

3. What needeth gretter dilatacioun CHAUCER.

Dilatator (dəi·lĕtēⁱ:təɹ). 1611. [– mod.L. *dilatator*, f. as prec.; see -OR 2. Cf. Fr. *dilatateur.*] **a.** *Anat.* A muscle which dilates a part; also *attrib.* **b.** *Surg.* An instrument for dilating an opening.

Dilatatory (dəilēⁱ·tătŏri). 1611. [– mod.L. *dilatatorium*, after Fr. *dilatatoire*; see prec., -ORY[1].] *Surg.* An instrument for dilating a part or organ.

†**Dila·te,** *v.*[1] ME. [– OFr. *dilater* defer, etc. – late L. *dilatare* defer, postpone, frequent. of L. *differre* DEFER. Cf. DILATORY.] **1.** *trans.* To delay, defer –1620. **2.** To protract, prolong, lengthen –1658.

Dilate (di-, dəilēⁱ·t), *v.*[2] ME. [– (O)Fr. *dilater* – L. *dilatare* (trans.) spread out, f. *di-* DI-[1] + *latus* wide.] **1.** *trans.* To make wider or larger; to expand, amplify, enlarge 1528. Also *fig.* †**2.** To spread abroad (*lit.* and *fig.*) –1719. **3.** *intr.* (for *refl.*) To become wider or larger; to spread out, widen, enlarge, expand 1636. Also *fig.* †**4.** *trans.* To relate at length; to enlarge or expatiate upon –1801. **5.** *intr.* To discourse or write at large. Const. †*of, on, upon.* 1560.

1. All thynges .are dilated by heate EDEN. **3.** The pupil has the property of contracting and dilating HARLAN. **5.** She proceeded to d. upon the perfections of Miss Nickleby DICKENS.

Dilate (dəilēⁱ·t), *a. arch.* 1471. [– L. *dilatus*, pa. pple. of *deferre* DEFER (see DILATE *v.*[1]), but used in sense of L. *dilatatus* (see DILATE *v.*[2]). See -ATE[2].] = DILATED, widely extended or expanded.

Dilated (dəilēⁱ·tėd), *ppl. a.* 1450. [f. DILATE *v.*[2] + -ED[1].] Widened, distended, etc.; see the vb.; in *Her.* opened or extended, as a pair of compasses. Hence **Dila·tedly** *adv.*

Dilater (dəilēⁱ·təɹ). 1605. [f. DILATE *v.*[2] + -ER[1]. Now mostly supplanted by DILATOR.] One who or that which dilates; *spec.* = DILATATOR.

†**Dila·tion**[1]. ME. [– OFr. *dilacion*, (mod. †*dilation*) – L. *dilatio* delay, procrastination, f. *dilat-*, pa. ppl. stem of *deferre* DEFER. Cf. DILATE *v.*[1], -ION.] Delay, procrastination –1665.

Dilation[2] (dəilēⁱ·ʃən, di-). 1598. [improp. f. DILATE *v.*[2], as if *dilate* contained the suffix -ATE[3]. See DILATATION.] = DILATATION 1–3.

The beauty of its d. and contraction SOUTHEY. Frivolous terms, and dilations cut away 1851.

Dilative (dəilēⁱ·tiv), *a.* 1528. [f. DILATE *v.*[2] + -IVE.] **1.** Having the property of dilating or expanding (*trans.* and *intr.*) 1634. †**2.** Serving to diffuse (the food) –1634.

Dilatometer (dəiletǫ·mǐtəɹ). 1882. [f. as prec. + -METER.] An instrument for measuring the dilatation or expansion of a liquid by heat. Hence **Dilatome·tric** *a.*

Dilator (dəilēⁱ·təɹ), *sb.* 1688. [f. DILATE *v.*[2] + -OR 2. Cf. DILATER.] One who or that which dilates: *spec.* = DILATATOR. Also *attrib.*

Dilatory (di·lătəri). 1535. [– late L. *dilatorius* delaying, f. L. *dilator* delayer, f. *dilat-*, pa. ppl. stem of *differre* DEFER; see -ORY[1].]

A. *adj.* **1.** Tending to cause delay; made for the purpose of gaining time. **2.** Given to or characterized by delay; slow, tardy 1604.

1. This d. sloth and trickes of Rome *Hen. VIII*, II. iv. 237. Phr. *D. plea* (in *Law*), a plea put in for the sake of delay. **2.** A d. man 1742, blockade 1843.

B. *sb. Law.* A dilatory plea; see A. 1563.

†Dildo[1]. Also **dildoe.** 1610. [Origin unkn.] A word used in the refrain of ballads –1698. *Comb.*: **d.-glass,** a cylindrical glass.

†Dildo[2]. 1696. [prob. the same word as prec., from its cylindrical form like a 'dildo-glass'.] A tree or shrub of the genus *Cereus* (N.O. *Cactaceæ*) –1756.

†Dilection (dile·kʃən). ME. [– (O)Fr. *dilection* or eccl.L. *dilectio* (Christian) love, f. *dilect-*, pa. ppl. stem of L. *diligere* esteem highly, love. Cf. DILIGENT.] **1.** Love, affection –1683. **2.** Choice; *esp.* in *Theol.* = ELECTION 3. –1656.

Dilemma (dile·mă, dəi-), *sb.* 1523. [– L. *dilemma* – Gr. δίλημμα, f. δι- DI-[2] + λῆμμα assumption, premiss.] **1.** In *Rhet.* A form of argument involving an adversary in choice between two (or, *loosely*, more) alternatives, both equally unfavourable to him. (The alternatives are the 'horns' of the dilemma.) Hence in *Logic*, A hypothetical syllogism having one premiss conjunctive and the other disjunctive. **2.** Hence, popularly: A choice between two (or, *loosely*, several) alternatives, which are equally unfavourable; a position of doubt or perplexity 1590.

1. A d., that Bishop Morton..used, to raise up the benevolence to higher rates..'That if they met with any that were sparing, they should tell them that they must needs have, because they laid up; and if they were spenders, they must needs have, because it was seen in their port and manner of living' BACON. **2.** In the d. of a swimmer among drowning men, who all catch at him EMERSON. Hence **Dile·mma** *v.* to place or †be in a d. (*rare*). **Dilemma·tic, -al** *a.* of the nature of, or relating to, a d. **Dilemma·tically** *adv.* **Dile·mmist** (*rare*), one who bases his position upon a d.; name of a Buddhist school of philosophy.

Dilettant (di·lĕtɑːnt), *a.* and *sb.* 1851. [var. of next.] = next.

‖**Dilettante** (dilĕtæ·nti, It. dīlet,ta·nte). Pl. **-ti** (-tī), rarely **-es.** 1733. [It., subst. use of pres. pple. of *dilettare* :– L. *delectare* DELIGHT; see -ANT[1].] **1.** A lover of the fine arts; orig. = *amateur*; in later use, one who interests himself in an art or science merely as a pastime and without serious study. **2.** *attrib.* Amateur 1774; of, pertaining to, or characteristic of a dilettante 1753.

1. [The Romans] cared for art as dilettanti; but no schools either of sculpture or painting were formed among themselves FROUDE. **2.** A d. painter T. L. PEACOCK. D. work CARLYLE.

Hence **Diletta·nte** *v.*, **Diletta·ntize** *v.*, to play the d. **Diletta·ntish** *a.*, also **-teish,** somewhat like a d. **Diletta·ntism,** *also* **-teism,** the practice or method of a d.; the quality or character of dilettanti. **Diletta·ntist,** characterized by dilettantism.

Diligence[1] (di·lidʒĕns). Also **†Di·ligency.** ME. [– (O)Fr. *diligence* – L. *diligentia*, f. *diligent-*; see DILIGENT, -ENCE.] **1.** The quality of being diligent; industry, assiduity. **†2.** Speed, dispatch –1781. **†3.** Careful attention, heedfulness, caution –1795. **4.** *Law.* The attention and care due from a person in a given situation 1622. **5.** *Sc. Law.* The process by which persons, lands, or effects are attached on execution, or in security for debt; also, the warrant issued to enforce the attendance of witnesses, or the production of documents 1568.

1. The carefull toile and d. of the Bee B. GOOGE. **3.** Phr. *To do* or *have d.*, to take care, take heed.

Diligence[2] (di·lidʒĕns; Fr. diliʒāṅs). 1742. [– Fr. *diligence* (XVIII), short for *carrosse de diligence* 'coach of speed'; cf. DILIGENCE[1] 2.] A public stage-coach; *esp.* in France and abroad.. Also *attrib.*

Diligent (di·lidʒĕnt), *a.* ME. [– (O)Fr. *diligent* – L. *diligens, -ent-* assiduous, attentive, pres. pple. of *diligere* esteem highly, love, choose, take delight in; see -ENT.] **1.** 'Constant in application, persevering in endeavour, assiduous', industrious; 'not idle, not negligent, not lazy' (J.). **2.** Of actions, etc.: Constantly or steadily applied; prosecuted with activity and perseverance; assiduous ME. **†3.** Attentive, careful –1756. **†4.** as *adv.* = diligently –1590.

1. Thei wer d. in here seruice ME. **2.** In diligente labourynge 1500. **3.** A very d. and observing person DAMPIER. Hence **Di·ligent-ly** *adv.*, **†-ness** (*rare*).

Dill (dil), *sb.* [OE. *dile* and *dyle*, corresp. to OS. *dilli* (Du. *dille*), OHG. *tilli, dilli* (G. *dill* from LG.), and MDu. *dulle*, MHG. *tülle*, ON. *dylla*; of unkn. origin.] An umbelliferous annual plant, *Anethum graveolens*, cultivated for its carminative fruits or 'seeds'. Also called ANET.

Dill, *v. n. dial.* 1450. [rel. to *dill* adj., ME. var. of DULL *a.* Cf. ON. *dilli* (intr.) trill, lull.] To soothe, lull, quiet down.

‖**Dillenia** (dilī·niă). 1753. [f. name of J. J. *Dillenius*, professor of botany at Oxford 1728–47; see -IA[1].] *Bot.* A genus of plants, typical of the N.O. *Dilleniaceæ*, natives of India and the Eastern peninsula, consisting of lofty forest trees with handsome flowers. Hence **Dillenia·ceous** *a.* **Dille·niad,** a member of this N.O.

Di·lligrout. Now *Hist.* 1662. [Origin unkn.] A kind of pottage, of which a mess was offered to the Kings of England on their coronation-day by the lord of the manor of Addington in Surrey, being the service by which the manor was held.

Dilling (di·liŋ). Now *dial.* 1584. [Origin unkn.] Darling; the last born of a family; *dial.* the weakling of a litter.

†Di·llue, *v.* 1671. [– Cornish *dyllo* send forth.] *Mining.* To finish the dressing of (tin-ore) by shaking it in a fine sieve in water –1778. Hence **Dilluing-sieve.**

Dilly[1] (di·li). 1786. [abbrev. of DILIGENCE[2].] **†1.** A public stage-coach –1818. **2.** Applied also to other vehicles, *esp.* carts, trucks, etc., used in agriculture 1850.

Di·lly[2]. *colloq.* 1845. [Origin unkn.] A call to ducks; hence, a duck.

Di·lly[3]. 1878. Short f. DAFFODILLY.

Di·lly[4]. 1895. [Shortened from *Sapodilla.*] In *Wild D.*, a small sapotaceous tree, *Mimusops sieberi*, found in the W. Indies, etc.

Dilly-dally (di·li,dæ·li), *v.* 1741. [redupl. of DALLY *v.*] *intr.* To loiter in vacillation, to trifle. Hence **Di·lly-da·lly** *†sb., a.*

Dilogical (dəilǫ·dʒikăl), *a.* 1633. [f. Gr. δίλογος doubtful + -ICAL.] Of double meaning; equivocal. So **Di·logy,** the use of an equivocal expression; the expression so used.

†Dilu·cid, *a.* 1640. [– L. *dilucidus* clear, bright, f. *dilucēre*, f. *di-* DI-[1] + *lucēre* shine.] Clear to the sight; lucid, plain –1671. var. **†Dilu·cidate** *ppl. a.* Hence **Dilu·cidly** *adv.*

†Dilu·cidate, *v.* 1538. [– *dilucidat-*, pa. ppl. stem of late L. *dilucidare* make clear, f. *dilucidus*; see prec., -ATE[3].] *trans.* To elucidate –1764. So **†Dilucida·tion. †Dilu·ci·dity,** lucidity.

Diluent (di·l[1]u,ĕnt). 1721. [– *diluent-*, pres. ppl. stem of L. *diluere* wash away; see DILUTE *v.*, -ENT.]

A. *adj.* Diluting; serving to attenuate or weaken by the addition of water, etc. 1731.

B. *sb.* **1.** That which dilutes, dissolves, or makes more fluid 1775. **2.** *spec.* A substance serving to increase the proportion of water in the blood 1721.

2. Diluents, as Water, Whey, Tea ARBUTHNOT.

Dilute (di-, dəil[1]ū·t), *ppl. a.* 1605. [– L. *dilutus*, pa. pple. of *diluere*; see next.] **1.** Watered down 1658; washed-out 1665. **2.** *fig.* Weak, paltry 1605.

Dilute (di-, dəil[1]ū·t), *v.* 1555. [– *dilut-*, pa. ppl. stem of L. *diluere* wash away, dissolve, f. *di-* DI-[1] + *-luere*, comb. form of *lavare* wash.] **1.** *trans.* To dissolve, or make thinner or weaker by the addition of water; to reduce the strength of by admixture 1664. **2.** To weaken the brilliancy of (colour) 1665. **3.** *fig.* To weaken 1555. **4.** *intr.* (for *refl.*) To suffer dilution; to become attenuated 1764.

1. Replenish it with wine Diluted less COWPER. **2.** The chamber was dark, lest these colours should be diluted and weakened by the mixture of any adventitious light NEWTON (J.) Hence **Dilu·tedly** *adv.*, **-ness. Dilu·ter.**

Dilution (di-, dəil[1]ū·ʃən). 1646. [f. prec. + -ION.] **1.** The action of diluting. **2.** Dilute condition 1805. **3.** That which is diluted 1861.

Diluvial (dil[1]ū·viăl), *a.* 1656. [– late L. *diluvialis*, f. *diluvium* flood, DELUGE; see DILUVIUM, -AL[1].] **1.** Of or pertaining to a deluge or flood, *esp.* to the Noachian Flood. **2.** *Geol.* Produced by or resulting from a general deluge or periods of catastrophic action of water 1816; of or pertaining to DILUVIUM 1823. Hence **Dilu·vialist,** one who attributes certain geological features to a universal deluge.

Diluvian (dil[1]ū·viăn), *a.* Also **de-.** 1655. [f. as prec. + -AN.] Of or pertaining to a deluge; *esp.* the Noachian Flood. Hence **Dilu·vianism,** a theory which attributes certain phenomena to a universal deluge.

†Dilu·viate, *v.* 1599. [– *diluviat-*, pa. ppl. stem of L. *diluviare* inundate, f. *diluvium*, *-ies* flood; see next, -ATE[3].] To flow in a deluge.

‖**Diluvium** (dil[1]ū·viŏm). 1819. [L., rel. to *lavare* wash (cf. DILUTE *v.*).] Applied to superficial deposits apparently due to some extraordinary movement of the waters; such were at first attributed to the Noachian deluge, whence the name.

†Dilu·vy. ME. [– L. *diluvium*; cf. -Y[4].] = DELUGE *sb.* –1546.

Dim (dim). [OE. *dim(m)* = OFris. *dim*, ON. *dimmr*, rel. to synon. OHG. *timbar* (MHG., mod. dial. *timmer*), OSw. *dimber*, OIr. *dem* black, dark.]

A. *adj.* **1.** Faintly luminous, not clear; somewhat dark, obscure, gloomy. (Opp. to *bright* or *clear.*) Also *fig.* **2.** Not clear to the sight; indistinct, faint; misty, hazy OE. Also *fig.* **3.** Of colour: Not bright; dull; dusky; lustreless ME. **4.** Not seeing clearly ME.; *fig.* dull of apprehension 1729. Also *transf.* of sound, etc.

1. A d. religious light MILT. *Pens.* 160. *fig.* Hope grew pale and d. SHELLEY. **2.** Egypt d. in the distance STANLEY. *fig.* A memory d. 1871. **3.** Violets d. *Wint. T.* IV. iv. 119. **4.** Jacob.. somewhat d. for age 1577. *fig.* The understanding is d., and cannot by its natural light discover spiritual truth 1729.

B. *sb.* Dimness; obscurity; dusk ME.

Comb.: **d.-eyed, -sighted,** etc.

Dim, *v.* ME. [f. DIM *a.*] **1.** *intr.* To grow or become dim. **2.** *trans.* To make dim, obscure, or dull; to render less distinct; to becloud (the eyes) ME. Also *fig.*

1. Suddenly mine eyes began to d. 1607. **2.** Windows dimmed with armorial bearings W. IRVING. *fig.* To d. a conqueror's triumph 1659.

Dim., dimin. (*Mus.*), abbrev. of DIMINUENDO.

†Dima·ne, *v.* 1610. [– L. *dimanare* flow different ways, spread abroad, f. *di-* DI-[1] + *manare* flow.] *intr.* To flow forth *from*; to originate *from* –1657.

Dimaris (di·măris). 1827. *Logic.* The mnemonic term designating the third mood of the fourth syllogistic figure, in which a particular affirmative major premiss (*i*), and a universal affirmative minor (*a*), yield a particular affirmative conclusion (*i*).

Dimastigate (dəimæ·stigĕt), *a.* [f. DI-[2] + Gr. μαστιγ- (μάστιξ) whip; see -ATE[2].] *Zool.* Having two flagella, as certain Infusoria (*Dimastiga*).

Dimble (di·mb'l). Now *dial.* 1589. [perh. conn. w. DIM or DINGLE.] A deep and shady dell, a dingle.

Dime (dəim), *sb.* ME. [– (O)Fr. *dime*, *†disme* :– L. *decima* tithe, subst. use (sc. *pars* part) of fem. of *decimus* tenth.] **1.** A tenth part, a tithe. Now *Hist.* **2.** A silver coin of the United States, of the value of 10 cents, or $\frac{1}{10}$ dollar 1786. **3.** *attrib.* Costing a dime; as in *d. novel*, a cheap sensational story.

Dimension (dime·nʃən), *sb.* late ME. [– Fr. *dimension* (XV) – L. *dimensio*, f. *dimens-*, pa. ppl. stem of *dimetiri* measure out, f. *di-* DI-[1] + *metiri* measure.] **†1.** The action of measuring, measurement –1793. **2.** Measurable extent of any kind, as length, breadth, thickness, area, volume; measure, magnitude, size. (Now usu. in pl.) Also *fig.* 1529. **†b.** Extension in time –1677. **3. a.** *Geom.* A mode of linear measurement, or extension, in a particular direction ME. **b.** *Alg.* A term for the (unknown or variable) quantities contained in any product as factors; any power of a quantity being of the dimensions denoted by its index. (Thus x^3, x^2y, xyz are each of three dimensions.) The number of dimensions corresponds to the DEGREE of a quantity or equation. 1557. †4. Measurable form or frame; *pl.* material parts; proportions –1667.

1. Things infinite, I see, Brooke no d. GREENE. 2. Greatness of d. is a powerful cause of the sublime BURKE. 3. The three dimensions of a body, or of ordinary space, are length, breadth, and thickness (or depth); a surface has only two dimensions (length and breadth); a line only one (length). O.E.D. 4. Hath not a Iew hands, organs, dementions *Merch. V.* III. i. 62.

Comb.: **d.-lumber, -timber, -stone,** *i.e.* that which is cut to specified dimensions; **-work,** masonry built of d.-stones. (Chiefly *U.S.*)

Hence **Dime·nsion** *v.* to measure or space out (*rare*). **Dime·nsioned** *ppl. a.* having a particular d., or dimensions. **Dime·nsionless** *a.* without d., or dimensions; of no (appreciable) magnitude; vast.

Dimensional (dime·nʃənăl), *a.* 1816. [f. prec. sb. + -AL[1].] **1.** Of or pertaining to dimension. **2.** *Geom.* Of or relating to (a specified number of) dimensions 1875. Hence **Dimensiona·lity,** d. quality.

Dimensive (dime·nsiv), *a.* Now *rare.* 1563. [– med.L. *dimensivus*; see DIMENSION, -IVE.] †**1.** Having, or related to, physical dimension –1694. †**2.** Serving to measure the dimensions of something –1610. **3.** Dimensional (*rare*) 1845.

2. All Bodies have their measure and their space, But who can draw the Soul's d. Lines DAVIES.

†‖**Dime·nsum.** 1630. [late L. *dimensum* measure, (later) measured quantity, subst. use of n. pa. pple. of L. *dimetiri*; see DIMENSION.] A measured portion; a fixed allowance –1643.

†**Dimensura·tion.** 1593. [f. DI-[1] + MENSURATION.] Measuring out or off –1677.

Dimeran (di·mĕrăn). 1847. [f. mod.L. *dimera*, n. pl. of *dimerus* (see DIMEROUS) + -AN.] *Entom.* A member of the division *Dimera* of hemipterous insects, having the tarsi two-jointed.

Dimerous (di·mĕrəs), *a.* 1826. [f. mod.L. *dimerus*, f. Gr. διμερής bipartite, + -OUS.] Consisting of two parts or divisions: applied to the tarsus of an insect, leaves, etc. So **Di·merism,** d. condition or constitution.

Dimeta·llic, *a.* 1861. [DI-[2].] *Chem.* Containing two equivalents of a metal.

Dimeter (di·mĭtəɹ). 1589. [– late L. *dimeter, dimetrus* adj., *dimetrus* sb. – Gr. δίμετρος of two measures, f. δι- twice + μέτρον measure.] *Pros.* A verse consisting of two measures, *i.e.* either two feet or four feet.

Dimethyl (dəime·þil). 1869. [DI-[2].] *Chem.* A name of Ethane (C_2H_6), regarded as two molecules of the radical methyl (CH_3). Also *attrib.*

Dimetient (dəimī·ʃiĕnt). 1571. [– *dimetient-*, pres. ppl. stem of L. *dimetiri*; see DIMENSION, -ENT.]

A. *adj.* †**1.** That measures across through the centre –1729. **2.** *Math.* That expresses the dimension 1842.

†**B.** *sb.* (Short for *d. line.*) = DIAMETER –1690.

Dimetric (dəime·trik), *a.* 1868. [f. Gr. δι- DI-[2] + μέτρον measure + -IC.] *Cryst.* = TETRAGONAL.

Dimication (dimikēⁱ·ʃən). Now *rare.* 1623. [– L. *dimicatio*, f. *dimicat-*, pa. ppl. stem of *dimicare* fight; see -ION.] Fighting; contention.

Dimidiate (dimi·diĕt, dəi-), *a.* 1768. [– L. *dimidiatus*, pa. pple. of *dimidiare*; see next, -ATE[2].] **1.** Divided into halves; halved, half. **2.** *Bot.* and *Zool.* **a.** Of an organ: Having one part much smaller than the other, so as to appear to be wanting. **b.** Split in two on one side, as the calyptra of some mosses. **c.** *Zool.* Relating to the lateral halves of an organism: applied to hermaphrodites having one side male and the other female. 1830.

Dimidiate (dimi·dieⁱt, dəi-), *v.* 1623. [– *dimidiat-*, pa. ppl. stem of L. *dimidiare* halve, f. *dimidium* half; see -ATE[3].] **1.** *trans.* To divide into halves; to reduce to the half. **2.** *Her.* To cut in half; to represent only half of (a bearing) 1864. Hence **Dimi:dia·tion,** the action of dimidiating; dimidiated condition.

Diminish (dimi·niʃ), *v.* ME. [Blending of earlier DIMINUE and MINISH.] **1.** To make (or cause to appear) smaller; to lessen; to reduce in magnitude or degree. (The opp. of *enlarge, increase, augment, magnify.*) **2.** To lessen in estimation, or power; to put down, degrade; to belittle (*arch.*) 1560. †**3.** To take away *from*; hence *gen.* to take away, subtract –1627. Also †*absol.* †**4.** To deprive in part *of* –1762. **5.** *Mus.* †To make gradually softer. Also, To lessen (an interval) by a semitone. 1674. **6.** *intr.* To become less or smaller; to lessen, decrease 1520; in *Arch.* to taper 1715.

1. Perauenture it diminysshed theyr payne in hell 1526. 2. I will d. them, that they shall no more rule over the nations *Ezek.* 29:15. 3. Neither add anything nor d. 1533. 4. If now then the builders. . be diminished of their wages 1559. 6. Crete's ample fields d. to our eye POPE.

Hence **Dimi·nishable** *a.*, **-ness. Dimi·nisher** (*rare*). **Dimi·nishingly** *adv.* **Dimi·nishment** (now *rare*), the action of diminishing; diminution.

Diminished (dimi·niʃt), *ppl. a.* 1607. [f. prec. + -ED[1].] **1.** Made smaller, lessened; see the vb. **2.** Lowered in estimation, etc. (see DIMINISH *v.* 2); now only in phr. from Milton 1667. **3.** *Mus.* Of an interval: Less by a chromatic semitone than a perfect, or than a minor, interval of the same name 1727.

1. Phr. *D. arch.*, an arch which is less than a complete semicircle. *D. bar* in *Joinery*, the bar of a sash that is thinnest on the inner edge. *D. column*, a column decreasing in diameter from the base upwards. 2. O thou [sun]. . at whose sight all the Starrs Hide their diminisht heads MILT. *P. L.* IV. 35.

†**Diminue,** *v.* ME. [– (O)Fr. *diminuer* – L. *diminuere* break up small. See DIMINISH.] = DIMINISH *v.* –1568.

‖**Diminuendo** (dimi:nu,e·ndo). 1775. [It., 'diminishing'; see prec.] *Mus.* A direction: To be gradually decreased in volume of sound (usu. indicated by the abbrev. *dim.* or *dimin.* or the sign >). As *sb.* Such a decrease; a passage of this description. Also *transf.* and *fig.* Also as *vb.* (Opp. to CRESCENDO.)

†**Dimi·nuent,** *a. rare.* 1608. [– *diminuent-*, pres. ppl. stem of L. *diminuere*; see DIMINUE, -ENT.] Diminishing –1657.

†**Diminu·te,** *a.* 1450. [– L. *diminutus*, pa. pple. of *diminuere*; see DIMINUE.] Diminished, lessened; incomplete –1731. Hence †**Diminu·tely** *adv.* So **Dimi·nute** *v.* to lessen, belittle (*rare*).

Diminution (diminiū·ʃən). ME. [– (O)Fr. *diminution* – L. *diminutio*, f. *diminut-*, pa. ppl. stem of *diminuere*; see DIMINUE, -ION.] **1.** The action of diminishing or making less; the process of becoming less; reduction in magnitude or degree. †**2.** Extenuation –1659. †**3.** Lessening of honour or reputation; depreciation, belittling –1734. †**4.** Curtailment, abatement –1675. **5.** *Mus.* The repetition of a subject in notes of half or a quarter the length of the original: opp. to *augmentation* 1597. **6.** *Her.* The defacing of part of an escutcheon; later, = DIFFERENCE 1610. **7.** *Law.* An omission in the record of a case sent up to a higher court 1657. **8.** *Archit.* The tapering of a column, etc.; also, the amount of this tapering in the whole length 1706.

1. Change by addition or d. HOOKER. 3. I shall not much regard the worlds opinion or d. of me *Eikon Bas.* 49. 8. [The] turret. . ends with a fine d. 1766.

Diminutival (dimi:niutəi·văl), *a.* (*sb.*) 1868. [f. next + -AL[1].] *Gram.* Of, pertaining to, or of the nature of, a diminutive. As *sb.* A diminutival suffix 1880.

Diminutive (dimi·niūtiv). ME. [– (O)Fr. *diminutif, -ive* – late L. *diminutivus*, f. *diminut-*; see DIMINUTION, -IVE.]

A. *adj.* **1.** *Gram.* Expressing diminution; denoting something little. (Opp. to *augmentative.*) 1580. †**2.** Making less or smaller –1711. †**3.** Depreciative –1791. **4.** Characterized by diminution; hence, of less size than the ordinary; small, little. Now, usu. = minute, tiny. 1602.

2. Anything d. of. . national Liberty SHAFTESB. 4. Small, almost d., in stature 1870.

B. *sb.* **1.** *Gram.* A derivative denoting something small of the kind ME. **2.** *Her.* A smaller ordinary corresponding in form and position to the larger, but of less width 1572. **3.** A diminutive thing or person 1606. †**4.** *Med.* Something that abates the violence of a disease –1621.

1. Babyisms and dear diminutives TENNYSON. 3. Pestred with such water-flies, diminutiues of Nature SHAKS. Hence **Dimi·nutive-ly** *adv.*, **-ness.**

†**Dimi·ss,** *v.* 1543. [– *dimiss-*, pa. ppl. stem of L. *dimittere*; see DIMIT.] = DISMISS *v.* –1729.

†**Di·missaries,** *sb. pl.* 1494. [perh. – mod. or med.L. **demissarius* (pl. *-arii* 'hangers-down'), f. L. *demissus* hanging down, descending, pa. pple. of *demittere*; see prec., -ARY[1]. Perh. a schoolman's (jocular) latinization of some contemp. Eng. word, as †*pendants.*] Testicles –1577.

†**Dimi·ssion.** 1494. [– L. *dimissio*, f. *dimiss-*, pa. ppl. stem of *dimittere*; see DIMISS, DIMIT, -ION.] **1.** = DEMISSION[2] 1. –1568. **2.** = DEMISE *sb.* 1. 1495. **3.** Dismissal, discharge –1823.

Dimissory (di·misəri), *a.* (*sb.*). Also **de-.** ME. [– late L. *dimissorius* (in *litteræ dimissoriæ*), f. *dimiss-*; see prec., -ORY[2].]

A. †**1.** Pertaining to dismission or leave-taking; valedictory –1656. **2.** *Eccl. D. letter* (usu. in pl. *letters d.*): **a.** Formerly, a letter from a bishop dismissing a clergyman from one diocese and recommending him to another. **b.** A letter from a bishop, authorizing the bearer as a candidate for ordination. 1583.

†**B.** *sb.* = Letters dimissory; see prec. –1725.

†**Dimi·t,** *v.* 1495. [– L. *dimittere* send away, dismiss, etc., f. *di-* DI-[1] + *mittere* send; in Branch II, a var. of DEMIT *v.*[1]]

I. 1. *trans.* = DEMIT *v.*[2], in various senses –1678. **2.** *intr.* Of a river: To debouch 16. . .

II. *trans.* To send, put, or let down, lower –1671; *fig.* to abase 1655.

Dimity (di·mĭti). ME. [– It. *dimito* or med.L. *dimitum* – Gr. δίμιτος, f. δίς DI-[2] + μίτος thread of the warp; the origin of the final *-y* is unknown.] A stout cotton cloth, woven with raised stripes and fancy figures; used undyed for beds and hangings, and sometimes for garments. *attrib.* Made of dimity 1639.

Dimly (di·mli), *adv.* [ME., f. DIM *a.* + -LY[2].] In a dim manner; in or with a dim light; obscurely; faintly.

Di·mmer. 1822. [f. DIM *v.* + -ER[1].] One who or that which dims; *spec.* a device for reducing the brilliance of a light; also, a dim lamp.

Dimmish (di·miʃ), *a.* 1683. [f. DIM *a.* + -ISH[1].] Somewhat dim. So **Di·mmy** *a.* more or less dim.

Dimness (di·mnės). [OE. *dimnis*, f. DIM *a.* + -NESS.] The quality of being dim.

In proof of the d. of our internal light JOHNSON.

Dimorph (dəi·mǫɹf). [Back-formation from DIMORPHOUS.] One of the two forms of a dimorphous substance; as 'aragonite and calcite are dimorphs'.

Dimo·rphic, *a.* 1859. [f. as next + -IC.] Existing or occurring in two distinct forms.

Dimorphism (dəimǭ·ɹfiz'm). 1832. [f. next + -ISM.] The condition of being DIMORPHIC. **a.** *Cryst.* The property of assuming two distinct crystalline forms, not derivable from each other. **b.** *Biol.* The occurrence of two distinct forms of flowers, leaves, etc., on the same plant or in the same species; or of two forms distinct in structure, size, colouring, etc., among animals of the same species 1859. **c.** *Philol.* The existence, in one language, of a word under two different forms, or of doublets 1877.

Dimorphous (dəimǭ·ɹfəs), *a.* 1832. [f. Gr. δίμορφος (f. δίς- DI-[2] + μορφή form), + -OUS.] = DIMORPHIC. (Mostly in *Chem.* and *Min.*)

Dimple (di·mp'l), *sb.* ME. [prob. repr. OE. **dympel*, corresp. to OHG. *tumphilo* (MHG. *tümpfel*, G. *tümpel*) deep place in water, f. Gmc. **dump-*, perh. nasalized form of **dup-* **deup-* DEEP *a.* Cf. DUMP *sb.*[3]] **1.** A small hollow or dent, formed in the surface of some part of the human body, *esp.* in the cheeks or chin. **2.** *transf.* Any slight surface depression 1632.

1. The Valley, The pretty dimples of his Chin, and Cheeke *Wint. T.* II. iii. 101. 2. In a d. of the hill 1815. Hence **Di·mply** *a.* full of dimples.

Di·mple, *v.* 1602. [f. prec. sb.] **1.** *trans.* To mark with, or as with, dimples. **2.** *intr.* To break into dimples or ripples, to form dimples 1700.

1. With whirlpools dimpl'd DRYDEN. 2. As shallow streams run dimpling all the way POPE. Hence **Di·mplement,** a dimpling (*rare*).

Di·m-si·ghted, *a.* 1561. Having dim sight (*lit.* and *fig.*).

Dimyary (di·miări). 1835. [f. mod.L. *dimyarius* (*Dimyaria* name of group), f. Gr. δι- twice + μῦς muscle; see -ARY¹.]

A. *adj.* Double-muscled: said of those bivalve molluscs which have two adductor muscles for closing the shell. Also **Dimyarian** (dimi,ēə·riăn) *a.*

B. *sb.* A d. bivalve.

Din (din), *sb.* [OE. *dyne* (:– *duniz) and *dynn*, corresp. to OHG. *tuni*, ON. *dynr* (:– *dunjaz, -uz).] A loud noise; *esp.* a continued confused and resonant sound, which stuns or distresses the ear.

Ile..make thee rore, That beasts shall tremble at thy dyn *Temp.* I. ii. 371. I have a perpetual d. in my head and..hear nothing aright COWPER.

Din, *v.* Pa. t. and pple. **dinned** (dind). [OE. *dynian* = OS. *dunian*, MHG. *tünen* roar, rumble, ON. *dynja* come rumbling down :– Gmc. *dunjan; see prec.] †**1.** *intr.* (In OE. and ME.) To sound, resound –1513. **2.** *trans.* To assail with din 1674. **3.** To make to resound; to utter continuously so as to deafen or weary 1724. **4.** *intr.* To make a din; to give forth deafening or distressing noise 1794.

2. To have my ears dinned by him and his dotards 1786. 3. This hath often been dinned in my ears SWIFT. 4. The bag-pipe dinning on the midnight moor WORDSW.

‖**Dinanderie** (dināndəri). 1863. [Fr.; f. *Dinant*, formerly *Dinand*, in Belgium, 'wherein copper kettles, etc., are made'.] Kitchen utensils of brass, made at Dinant; extended recently to the brass-work of the Levant and India.

‖**Dinar** (dīnā·ɹ). 1634. [– Arab., Pers. *dīnār* – late Gr. δηνάριον – L. DENARIUS.] A name of various oriental coins: applied to the gold mohur; also to the staple silver coin corresponding to the modern rupee; in Persia a coin of account.

Dindle (di·nd'l, di·n'l), *v.* Now only *Sc.* and *n. dial.* ME. [prob. imit.; cf. dial. *dingle*, TINGLE *v.*; TINKLE *v.*¹] **1.** *intr.* To tinkle; *trans.* to thrill with sound. **2.** *intr.* To be in a state of vibration from some sound, shock, or percussion 1470. **3.** *intr.* To tingle, as with cold or pain 1483. Hence **Di·ndle** *sb.*¹ a thrill, a tingle.

Di·ndle, *sb.*² *dial.* 1787. A name of various yellow Composite flowers; *e.g.* common and corn sow-thistles, hawkweeds, dandelions, etc.

Dine (dəin), *v.* [– OFr. *di(s)ner* (mod. *dîner*) :– Rom. *disjunare, for *disjejunare break one's fast. Cf. DISJUNE.] **1.** *intr.* To eat the principal meal of the day; to take DINNER. Const. *on, upon, off.* †**2.** *trans.* To eat –1485. **3.** To provide with a dinner; to entertain at dinner; to accommodate for dining purposes ME.

1. They rose & herd masse, & dynid LD. BERNERS. Phr. *To d. with Duke Humphrey* (see O. E. D.). 2. 'Now, maister,' quod the wyf, 'What wil ye dine?' CHAUCER. 3. As much bread as would d. a sparrow ROWLEY. Hence **Dine** *sb.* (now *dial.*), the act of dining; dinner.

Diner (dəi·nəɹ). 1807. [f. prec. + -ER¹.] **1.** One who dines; a dinner-guest 1815. **b.** **Diner-out:** one who is in the habit of dining from home 1807. **2.** *U.S.* A railway dining car 1890.

1. A brilliant diner out, though but a curate BYRON.

†**Dine·tic,** †**-al,** *a. rare.* 1646. [f. Gr. δινητός whirled round + -IC, + AL¹.] Of or belonging to rotation; rotatory –1691.

Ding (diŋ), *v.*¹ *arch.* or *dial.* ME. [prob. of Scand. origin; cf. ON. *dengja* hammer, whet a scythe, OSw. *dängia*, Da. *dænge* beat, bang.] **1.** *intr.* To deal heavy blows; to knock, hammer, thump (? *n. dial.*). **2.** *trans.* To beat, knock; to thrash, flog. (Now *dial.*) ME. **3.** *fig.* To beat, surpass 1724. **4.** To dash or violently drive (a thing) *away, down, in, out, over,* etc. ME. †**5.** *intr.* (for *refl.*) To precipitate oneself, dash, press, drive –1627; to fling, to bounce –1712. **6.** In imprecations: = DASH *v.* 1822.

2. *To d. to death* ME. **3.** Duns dings a' *Sc. Prov.* **4.** Ready..to d. the book a coits distance from him MILT. **5.** They..drive at him as fast as they could d. DRAYTON. Rain dinging on night and day 1663. Hence **Ding** *sb.*¹ *dial.*, the act of dinging.

Ding (diŋ), *v.*² 1582. [imit., but influenced by prec. and DIN *v.*] **1.** *intr.* To sound as metal when heavily struck 1820. **2.** *intr.* To speak with wearying reiteration 1582.

1. Sledge hammers were dinging upon iron all day long DICKENS.

¶*To d. into the ears*, 'to drive or force into the ears', unites this with DING *v.*¹ and DIN *v.*

Hence **Ding** *sb.*² and *adv.*, used as an imitation of the sound of a bell, etc.

Ding-dong (di·ŋdǫ·ŋ). 1560. [imit.]

A. *adv.*, or without constr. **1.** An imitation of the sound of a bell. **2.** With a will 1672.

B. *sb.* **1.** The sound of a bell, a repeated ringing sound; a jingle of rhyme 1560. **2.** *Horol.* An arrangement for indicating the quarters of the hour by the striking of two bells of different tones. Also *attrib.* 1822.

C. *adj.* **1.** Of or pertaining to the sound of bells or the jingle of rhyme 1792. **2.** Vigorously maintained, downright, desperate 1864.

Ding-dong theory of language, the theory which refers the primitive elements of language to phonetic expression naturally given to a conception as it first thrilled through the brain, just as a sonorous body when struck naturally emits sound.

Di·ng-do·ng, *v.* 1659. [imit.] *intr.* To ring as a bell, or like a bell; also *fig.*

‖**Dinghy, dingey** (di·ŋgi). Also **dingy.** 1810. [– Hindi *ḍiṅgī, ḍeṅgī.* The sp. with *gh* is used to indicate pronunc. with **g.**] **1.** Orig., a native rowing-boat in use upon Indian rivers. **2.** Hence, a small rowing-boat; *spec.* **a.** a small extra boat in men-of-war; etc., **b.** a small pleasure rowing-boat 1836.

Dingle (di·ŋg'l), *sb.* ME. [Of unkn. origin; cf. DIMBLE.] A deep dell or hollow; now usually, one that is closely wooded; also, a deep narrow cleft between hills (RAY). Hence **Di·ngly** *a.*

Di·ngle-da·ngle. 1598. [redupl. f. DANGLE.]

A. *adv.* In a dangling manner.

B. *sb.* A dangling to and fro; *concr.* a dangling appendage 1622.

C. *adj.* Swinging, dangling 1693.

‖**Dingo** (di·ŋgo). 1789. [Native name; cf. *jūnghō* (George's River), *jūgūng* (Turuwul, Botany Bay).] The wild or semi-domesticated dog of Australia, *Canis d.*

†**Dingthrift** (di·ŋþrift). ME. [f. DING *v.*¹ + THRIFT.] **1.** A spendthrift –1598. **2.** An obsolete game. ME. only.

The Ding-thrifts proverbe is, Lightly come, lightly goe 1624.

Dingy (di·ndʒi), *a.* 1736. [perh. to be referred ult. to OE. *dynġe* dung, manured land, f. *dung* DUNG; see -Y¹. Not recognized by Dr. Johnson.] **1.** *dial.* Dirty. **2.** Of a dark and dull colour or appearance; blackish or dusky brown; now usually, dirty as from smoke, grime, dust, etc., or deficiency of daylight 1751. Also *fig.*

2. His clothes getting dingier..summer by summer W. BLACK. *fig.* D. acquaintances THACKERAY. Hence **Di·ngi-ly** *adv.*, **-ness.**

Dinic (di·nik). *rare.* 1721. [f. Gr. δῖνος a whirling + -IC.]

A. *adj.* Relating to dizziness. So **Di·nical** *a.*

B. *sb.* A remedy for dizziness.

Dining (dəi·niŋ), *vbl. sb.* ME. [f. DINE *v.* + -ING¹.] The action of DINE *v.*; a dinner. Also in *comb.* with sense 'used for dining', as *d.-hall, -room, -table,* etc.

Dinitro- (dəinəi·tro). Bef. a vowel **dinitr-.** 1869. [f. DI-² + NITRO-.] **1.** Having two equivalents of the radical NO_2 taking the place of two atoms of hydrogen. **2.** **D.-cellulose,** a substance $C_6H_8(NO_2)_2O_5$, analogous to *gun-cotton* (*trinitro-cellulose*), produced by the action of a mixture of nitric and sulphuric acids on cotton. Also called *soluble pyroxylin.*

Dink (diŋk), *a. Sc.* and *n. dial.* 1508. [Of unkn. origin; cf. next.] Decked out; trim. Hence **Di·nkly** *adv.* So **Dink** *v.* (*Sc.*) to dress finely.

Dinky (di·ŋki), *a.* orig. *dial.* and *U.S. colloq.* 1858. [f. prec. + -Y¹.] Neat, trim, dainty.

Dinmont (di·nmənt). *Sc.* and *n. dial.* ME. [f. unknown element + *mont* MONTH.] A wether between the first and second shearing.

Dinner (di·nəɹ), *sb.* [ME. *diner* – OFr. *di(s)ner* (mod. *dîner*), subst. use of inf.; see DINE *v.*, -ER⁴.] The chief meal of the day, eaten originally, and still by many, about midday (cf. Ger. *Mittagessen*), but now, by the fashionable classes, in the evening; particularly, a repast given publicly in some one's honour, or the like. Also *attrib.*

Comb.: **d.-jacket,** a dress-coat without tails worn in the evening, esp. at dinner; **-wagon,** a tray with shelves beneath, supported by four legs, usually on castors, for the service of a dining-room.

Hence **Di·nnerless** *a.* without d. **Di·nnerly** *a.* of or pertaining to d.; *adv.* in a manner appropriate to d. **Di·nnery** *a.* characterized by d. or dinners.

Dinner (di·nəɹ), *v.* 1748. [f. DINNER *sb.*] **1.** *intr.* To dine, have dinner. **2.** *trans.* To entertain at dinner; to provide dinner for 1822.

‖**Dinoceras** (dəinǫ·sĕrēs). 1872. [mod.L., f. Gr. δεινός terrible + κέρας horn.] A genus of extinct ungulated quadrupeds (*Dinocerata*) of huge size, and having apparently three pairs of horns. Hence **Dino·cerate** *a.* related to the d.

Dinomic (dəinǫ·mik), *a.* 1863. [f. Gr. δι- twice + νομός district + -IC.] Belonging or restricted to two divisions (of the globe).

‖**Dinornis** (dəinǭ·ɹnis). 1843. [mod.L., f. Gr. δεινός terrible + ὄρνις bird.] A genus of recently extinct birds of great size, remains of which have been found in New Zealand; the moa of the Maori. Hence **Dinorni·thic, Dino·rnithine** *adjs.*

Dinosaur, deino- (dəi·nŏsǭɹ). 1841. [– mod.L. *dinosaurus* (Owen, 1841), f. Gr. δεινός terrible + σαῦρος lizard.] A member of an extinct race of Mesozoic Saurian reptiles (group *Deinosauria*), some of which were of gigantic size; the remains resemble birds in some respects, in others mammals. Hence **Dinosau·rian** *a.* and *sb.*

Dinothere, deino- (dəi·nŏþīəɹ). 1835. [– mod.L. *dinotherium* (Kaup, 1829), f. Gr. δεινός terrible + θηρίον wild beast.] A member of a genus of extinct proboscidean quadrupeds of great size, whose remains exist in the miocene formations of Europe and Asia. Hence **Dinothe·rian** *a.*

Di·nsome, *a. Sc.* 1724. [f. DIN *sb.* + -SOME¹.] Full of din; noisy.

Dint (dint), *sb.* [OE. *dynt*, reinforced in ME. by the related ON. *dyntr* (*dyttr*), *dynta.* Cf. DENT *sb.*¹, DUNT.] †**1.** A stroke or blow –1837. **2.** The dealing of blows; hence, force of attack or impact (*lit.* and *fig.*); violence, force. Now *rare*, exc. in phr. *By d. of*: by force of. ME. **3.** A mark made by a blow or by pressure; an indentation. Also *fig.* 1590.

1. With d. of Sword, or pointed Spears DRYDEN. Like thunders d. 1600. 2. The d. of pitty *Jul. C.* III. ii. 198. We..Earned, by d. of failure, triumph BROWNING. 3. Nor d. of hoof, nor print of foot BYRON. Hence **Di·ntless** *a.*

Dint (dint), *v.* [ME. – ON. *dynta* (*dytta*) dent; see prec.] †**1.** *trans.* To strike or knock –1649. †**2.** *intr.* To make a dint *in* something (*rare*) –1590. **3.** *trans.* To mark with dints 1597; to impress with force 1631.

Dinumera·tion. 1626. [– L. *dinumeratio*; see DI-¹, NUMERATION.] **1.** The act of numbering one by one. **2.** *Rhet.* = APARITHMESIS.

Diobol (dəi,ō^u·bǫl). 1887. [– Gr. διώβολον, f. δι- DI-² + ὀβολός OBOL.] *Numism.* A silver coin of ancient Greece equal to two obols.

Diocesan (dəi,ǫ·sĭsăn). late ME. [– Fr. *diocésain* – late L. *diocesanus*; see next, -AN.]

A. *adj.* Of or pertaining to a diocese, as *d. synods* 1450.

B. *sb.* **1.** One in charge of a diocese; the bishop of a diocese ME. **2.** One of the clergy or people of a diocese 1502.

1. Prelates who were statesmen rather than diocesans 1881. 2. Humble diocesans of old Bishop Valentine LAMB.

Diocese (dəi·ǒsės, -sīs). Also †**diocess(e.** [ME. *diocise* – OFr. *diocise* (mod. *diocèse*) – late L. *diocesis*, for L. *diœcesis* governor's jurisdiction, district, (eccl.) diocese – Gr. διοίκησις administration, government, (Roman) province, (eccl.) diocese, f. διοικεῖν keep house, administer.] †**1.** Administration (*Sc.*) 1596. **2.** A division of a country under a governor; a province. Now *Hist.* 1494. **3.** *Eccl.* The sphere of jurisdiction of a bishop; the district under the pastoral care of a bishop. (The ordinary sense in English.) ME. Also *transf.* and *fig.* Hence †**Diocesener** = DIOCESAN *sb.* 2.

†**Dioce·sian,** *a.* and *sb.* 1686. [– med.L. *diocesianus*, f. *diocesis* DIOCESE; see -AN, -IAN. Cf. OFr. *dyocesiien.*] = DIOCESAN.

Diodon (dəi·ǒdǫn). 1776. [mod.L., f. Gr. δι- DI-² + ὀδούς, ὀδοντ- tooth. So Fr. *diodon* (XVIII).] *Zool.* A genus of globe-fishes, having the jaws tipped with enamel, forming a tooth-like tubercle in the centre of the beak above and below.

Di·odont. [See prec.; cf. *mastodon, mastodont.*] *adj.* Having two teeth: *spec.* of or pertaining to the *Diodontidæ*, of which *Diodon* is the typical genus; *sb.* a fish of this family. So **Diodo·ntoid.** (Dicts.)

‖**Diœcia** (dəi,ī·ʃiă). 1753. [mod.L., f. Gr. δι- DI-² + οἶκος house + -IA¹. Cf MONŒCIA.] *Bot.* The twenty-second class in the Sexual System of Linnæus, comprising plants which have male and female flowers on separate individuals. Hence **Diœ·cian** *a.* = DIŒCIOUS.

Diœcious (dəi,ī·ʃ ͥəs), *a.* 1748. [f. prec. + -OUS.] **1.** *Bot.* Of plants: Having the unisexual male and female flowers on separate plants. **2.** *Zool.* Having the two sexes in separate individuals 1826. Hence **Diœ·cious-ly** *adv.*, **-ness.** So **Diœ·cism,** d. condition. **Dioi·cous** *a.*

Diogenes (dəi,ǫ·dʒėnīz). 1802. A Greek CYNIC philospher, who showed his contempt for the amenities of life by living in a tub.

D.-crab, a species of W. Indian hermit crab, which chooses an empty shell for its residence. **D.-cup,** the cup-like cavity formed in the palm of the hand by arching the fingers, etc. Hence **Dioge·nic, -al** *a.* of, pertaining to, or of the nature of D.

†**Di·onise.** 1483. [– OFr. *dionise* – med.L. *dionysia* = L. *dionysias* (Pliny) – Gr. διονυσιάς, f. Διόνυσος (see next).] A precious stone, black, with streaks of red, reckoned, by mediæval writers, a preservative against drunkenness –1855.

Dionysiac (dəi,ǒni·siæ̆k). 1827. [– late L. *Dionysiacus* – Gr. Διονυσιακός, f. Διόνυσος god of wine; see -AC.]

A. *adj.* Of or pertaining to Dionysus, or to his worship 1844.

B. *sb. pl.* The Dionysiac festivals or *Dionysia*, celebrated periodically in ancient Greece.

Dionysian (dəi,ǒni·siăn), *a.* 1607. [Sense 1 f. L. *Dionysius*, adj. f. *Dionysus* (see prec.); senses 2–4 f. proper name *Dionysius*; see -AN, -IAN.] **1.** = DIONYSIAC 1610. **2.** Pertaining to or characteristic of the Elder or Younger Dionysius, tyrants of Syracuse, notorious for cruelty 1607. **3.** Pertaining to Dionysius the Little, an abbot of the 6th century, to whom is ascribed the method of dating events from the birth of Christ 1727. **4.** Of Dionysius the Areopagite (Acts 17:34) 1885.

3. *D. period*, a period of 532 Julian years, after which the changes of the moon recur on the same days of the year; introduced for calculating the date of Easter.

Diophantine (dəi,ofæ·ntin, -əin), *a.* 1700. [f. proper name *Diophantus* + -INE¹.] *Math.* Of or pertaining to Diophantus of Alexandria, a celebrated mathematician; *spec.* applied to problems involving indeterminate equations, and to a method of solving them (*D. analysis*).

Diophysite, -ism, improp. ff. DIPHYSITE, DYOPHYSITE, etc.

Diopside (dəi,ǫ·psəid). 1808. [– Fr. *diopside* (Haüy, 1801), irreg. f. Gr. δι- DI-² + ὄψις appearance, aspect, but viewed by later authors as f. δίοψις view through (DI-³).] *Min.* = PYROXENE; now restricted to the transparent varieties.

Dioptase (dəi,ǫ·ptē ͥs). 1804. [– Fr. *dioptase* (Haüy, 1801), irreg. f. Gr. δίοπτος transparent.] *Min.* A translucent silicate of copper, crystallizing in six-sided prisms, called emerald copper ore.

Diopter (dəi,ǫ·ptəɹ). Also **dioptra.** 1594. [– Fr. *dioptre* – L. *dioptra* – Gr. διόπτρα.] **1.** An ancient form of theodolite 1613. **2.** = ALIDADE 1594. †**3.** A surgical speculum –1872. **4.** = DIOPTRIC *sb.* 2. 1890.

Dioptric (dəi,ǫ·ptrik). 1635. [– Gr. διοπτρικός pertaining to the use of the διόπτρα; see prec., -IC. Cf. Fr. *dioptrique* adj. and sb.]

A. *adj.* †**1.** Of the nature of, or pertaining to, a DIOPTER (sense 1) –1681. **2.** Assisting vision by means of refraction (as a lens, etc.) 1653. **3.** Relating to dioptrics (see B. 3); *esp.* (of a telescope, etc.), refractive, refracting. (Opp. to CATOPTRIC.) 1672. †**4.** Capable of being seen through –1860.

3. *D. system*, in lighthouses, 'that in which the rays issuing from the flame are collected and refracted in a given direction by a lens placed in front of the light.'

B. *sb.* **1.** = DIOPTER 1. 1849. **2.** A unit for expressing the refractive power of a lens, being the power of a lens whose focal distance is one metre 1883. **3.** *pl.* **Dioptrics:** that part of Optics which treats of the refraction of light. (Opp. to CATOPTRICS.) 1644.

Hence **Dio·ptrical** *a.* = DIOPTRIC *a.*; of or belonging to dioptrics; skilled in dioptrics. **Dio·ptrically** *adv.* by means of refraction.

Diorama (dəi,orɑ·mă). 1823. [f. Gr. δι-, δια- through (DI-³) + ὅραμα that which is seen, f. ὁρᾶν see. Cf. PANORAMA.] A mode of scenic representation in which a picture, some portions of which are translucent, is viewed through an aperture, the sides of which are continued towards the picture; the light, which is thrown upon the picture from the roof, may be diminished or increased at pleasure. Also, the building in which such views are exhibited. Hence **Diora·mic** *a.* (better *dioramatic*) of the nature of, or pertaining to, a d.

Diorism (dəi·ǒriz'm). *rare.* 1664. [– Gr. διορισμός logical division, f. διορίζειν draw a boundary through.] The act of defining; distinction, definition: in Hy. More = distinctive application. So †**Diori·stic, -al** *a.* serving to define or distinguish. †**Dioristically** *adv.*

Diorite (dəi,ǒrəit). 1826. [– Fr. *diorite* (Haüy), irreg. f. Gr. διορίζειν distinguish (cf. prec.) + *-ite* -ITE¹ 2 b.] *Min.* A variety of GREENSTONE, consisting of hornblende combined with a triclinic feldspar (albite or oligoclase). Hence **Diori·tic** *a.* of the nature of, or containing, d.

‖**Diorthosis** (dəi,ǫɹþō ͧ·sis). 1704. [mod.L., f. Gr. διόρθωσις, f. ὀρθός straight.] The act of setting straight: **a.** in *Surg.*, the straightening of crooked or fractured limbs. **b.** The recension of a literary work. Hence **Diortho·tic** *a.* corrective.

Dioscoreaceous (dəi,ǫskō ͤ:ri,ē ͥ·ʃəs), *a.* [f. mod.L. *Dioscoreaceæ*, f. *Dioscorea*, the typical genus, containing the yams; see -ACEOUS.] *Bot.* Of or belonging to the N.O. *Dioscoreaceæ* of Monocotyledons.

‖**Diosma** (dəi,ǫ·smă). 1794. [mod.L., f. Gr. δῖος divine + ὀσμή odour.] *Bot.* A genus of S. African heath-like plants (N.O. *Rutaceæ*), with strong balsamic odour.

‖**Diosmosis** (dəi,ǫsmō ͧ·sis). Also **di·osmose.** 1825. [mod.L., f. Gr. δι- DI-² + OSMOSIS; cf. END-, EXOSMOSIS.] = OSMOSIS. Hence **Diosmo·tic** *a.*

‖**Diota** (dəi,ō ͧ·tă). 1857. [L. *diota* – Gr. διώτη two-eared.] *Gr.* and *Rom. Antiq.* A vessel with two ears or handles.

Diothelism, -ite, irreg. ff. DITHELISM, DYOTHELISM, etc.

†‖**Dio·ti, dihoti.** 1651. [Gr. διότι, f. διὰ (τοῦτο) ὅτι for the reason that.] A wherefore –1734.

Diotrephes (dəi,ǫ·trifīz). 1626. The name of a man mentioned in 3 John 9, 10. Hence used typically of persons loving to have the pre-eminence in the church. Hence **Diotrephe·sian, Diotre·phian, Diotre·phic** *adjs.*

Dioxide (dəi,ǫ·ksəid). 1847. [DI-².] *Chem.* An oxide containing two equivalents of oxygen with one of the metal or metalloid, as *Carbon d.* CO_2.

Dip (dip), *v.* Pa. t. and pple. **dipped, dipt,** pr. pple. **dipping.** [OE. *dyppan* :– Gmc. **dupjan*, f. **dup-* **deup-* (see DEEP *a.*).]

I. Trans. **1.** To put down or let down for a moment *in* or *into*; to immerse; to plunge. Also *fig.* **b.** To immerse in a colouring solution; to dye 1667. **2.** To immerse in baptism; to baptize by immersion (now usu. *contemptuous*). Also *absol.* OE. **3.** To suffuse with moisture 1634; to dip into (*rare*) 1842. **4.** To obtain or take *up* by dipping 1602. **5.** *transf.* To lower or let down for a moment, as if dipping in a liquid; *spec.* to lower and then raise (a flag) as a salute, or (a sail) in tacking 1776. **6.** *fig.* To immerse, involve (*in* any affair) 1627; to involve in debt; to mortgage 1640.

1. To d. children in cold water MULCASTER, a garment in bloud HOBBES. With..colours dipt in Heav'n MILT. *P. L.* v. 283. **3.** A cold shuddering dew Dips me all over — *Comus* 802. But, ere he dipt the surface, rose an arm TENNYSON. **4.** To d. up shrimps CAREW, water MISS MITFORD. **5.** To-day, 'dipping the flag' is an act of courtesy 1894. **6.** Sr Steph. Fox is dipt 70,000ll deepe in that concerne 1671. Never d. thy Lands DRYDEN.

II. Intrans. **1.** To plunge down a little into water, etc., and quickly emerge. Const. *in, into, under.* ME. **2.** To plunge one's hand (or a ladle or the like) into water, a receptacle, etc., and take something out 1697. **3.** = DAP *v.* 1799. **4.** *transf.* To sink, drop, or extend downwards, as if dipping into water ME. **5.** To have a downward inclination; to be inclined to the horizon: *spec.* of the magnetic needle, and in *Geol.* of strata 1665. **6.** To go into a subject deeply 1755, or cursorily 1682.

1. Her yards would d. into the water 1830. **2.** Phr. *To d.* (*deeply*, etc.) *into one's purse, means*, etc. **4.** The Sun's rim dips; the stars rush out COLERIDGE. Two turreted precipice blocks D., like walls, to the wave BOWEN. **6.** When I dipt into the future far as human eye could see TENNYSON. I have not attentively read him, but only dipp'd here and there GRAY.

Dip (dip), *sb.* 1599. [f. DIP *v.*] **1.** An act of dipping; see various senses of the vb. **2.** Depth of submergence (*e.g.* of a paddle-wheel); depth below a particular level; depth of a vessel, etc. 1793. **3.** *Astron.* and *Surveying.* The apparent depression of the horizon due to the observer's elevation 1774. **4.** The angle which the direction of the magnetic needle at any place makes with the horizon 1727. **5.** Downward slope of a surface; *esp.* in *Mining* and *Geol.* the downward slope of a stratum or vein, estimated by its angle of inclination to the horizon 1708. **6.** A hollow to which the surrounding high ground dips 1789. **7.** = *Dip-candle* 1815. **8.** A sweet sauce for puddings, etc. (*local Eng.* and *U.S.*) 1825. **9.** *Thieves' slang.* A pickpocket; also pocket-picking 1859.

1. A d. in the horse pond JAMES, into a book JAS. GRANT. To keep the signal at the d. MARKHAM. **6.** We saw groves and villages in the dips of the hills BECKFORD.

Comb.: **d.-bucket,** a bucket contrived to turn easily and dip into water; **-candle,** a candle made by dipping a wick into melted tallow; **-circle,** a dipping-needle having a vertical graduated circle for measuring the amount of the d.; **-head,** a heading driven to the d. in a coal-mine in which the beds have a steep inclination; **-net,** a small net with a long handle, used to catch fish by dipping in the water; **-pipe,** a valve arranged to dip into water or tar, and form a seal; a seal-pipe; **-sector,** an instrument on the principle of the sextant, used to ascertain the d. of the horizon; **-splint,** a kind of friction-match.

Dipartite (dəipā·ɹtəit), *a.* 1825. [f. DI-¹ + L. *partitus*, pa. pple. of *partire* divide.] Divided into various parts. So **Diparti·tion.**

Dipa·schal, *a.* 1840. [DI-².] Including two passovers.

Dipchick, var. of DABCHICK.

Dipetalous (dəipe·tăləs), *a.* 1707. [f. mod.L. *dipetalus* (f. Gr. δι- DI-² + πέταλον PETAL) + -OUS.] *Bot.* Having two petals.

Diphen- in chemical terms; see DI-² 2, PHEN-.

Diphenyl (dəife·nil). 1873. [f. DI-² + PHENYL.] *Chem.* An aromatic hydrocarbon, $C_6H_5.C_6H_5$, having twice the formula of the radical PHENYL. Also *attrib.*

Diphtheria (difþiə·riă). 1857. [– mod.L. – Fr. *diphthérie*, substituted by Pierre Bretonneau (of Tours, d. 1862) for his earlier *diphthérite*; see next.] *Path.* An acute and highly infectious disease, characterized by inflammation of a mucous surface, and by an exudation therefrom which results in the formation of a false membrane. Its chief seat is the mucous membrane of the throat and air passages.

Hence **Diphthe·rial, Diphthe·rian** *adjs.* of or belonging to d. **Diphthe·ric** *a.* diphtheritic.

Diphtheritis (difþĕrəi·tis). Also || (Fr.) **diphtherite.** 1826. [– Fr. *diphthérite* (now *diphthérie*; see prec.), f. Gr. διφθέρα or διφθερίς skin, hide + *-ite* -ITIS. So mod. L. *diphtheritis* and G. *diphtheritis.*] = DIPHTHERIA. Hence **Diphtheri·tic** *a.* of the nature of, belonging to, or connected with diphtheria; affected with diphtheria. So **Di·phtheroid** *a.* resembling diphtheria.

Diphthong (di·fþǫŋ), *sb.* 1483. [In early use often *dipthong* – Fr. *diphtongue*, †*dypthongue* – L. *diphthongus* (late *dipthongus*) – Gr. δίφθογγος, f. δι- DI-² + φθόγγος voice, sound.] A union of two vowels pronounced in one syllable; the combination of a sonantal with a consonantal vowel. **b.** Often applied to a combination of two vowel characters, prop. termed DIGRAPH, and applied to the ligatures *æ*, *œ* of the Roman alphabet 1587. Also *attrib.*

I and *u* according to our English pronunciation of them, are not properly Vowels, but Diphthongs WILKINS. **b.** When the two letters represent a simple sound, as *ea*, *ou*, in *head* (hed), *soup* (sūp), they have been termed an *improprer d.*: properly speaking these are *monophthongs* written by *digraphs.* O.E.D.

Hence **Di·phthong** *v.* to sound as, or make into, a d. **Diphtho·ngal** *a.* of, belonging to, or of the nature of, a d. **Diphtho·ngic** *a.* diphthongal. **Di·phthongize** *v.* to turn into, or (*intr.*) form, a d. **Di:phthongiza·tion,** the changing of a simple vowel into a d. **Diphtho·ngous** *a.* diphthongal (*rare*).

Diphy-, – Gr. διφυ- from διφυής of double nature or form, double, bipartite: as in

Di·phycerc [Gr. κέρκος tail], *Ichth.* a diphycercal fish. **Diphyce·rcal** *a.*, having the tail divided into two equal halves by the caudal spine. **Di·phycercy,** diphycercal condition. **Di·phyid,** *Zool.* a member of the *Diphyidæ*, a family of Hydrozoa furnished with a pair of swimming-bells. **Di·phyodont** *a.* [Gr. ὀδοντ-], having two sets of teeth; consisting (as teeth) of two sets; as *sb.* a diphyodont animal. **Diphyzo·oid, diphyo-,** *Zool.* a free-swimming organism consisting of a group of zooids detached from a colony of Hydrozoa of the order *Siphonophora.*

Diphyllous (dəifi·ləs), *a.* 1788. [f. mod.L. *diphyllus* (f. Gr. δι- DI-² + φύλλον leaf) + -OUS.] *Bot.* Having two leaves (or sepals).

Diphyo-; see DIPHY-.

Diphysite (di·fisəit), *sb.* (*a.*) [– late Gr. (v) διφυσίτης, pl. -ῖται; see DYOPHYSITE, MONOPHYSITE.] *Theol.* One who held the doctrine **(Di·physiti:sm),** of two distinct natures in Christ, a divine, and a human; opp. to MONOPHYSITE.

Diplarthrous (diplā·ɹþrəs), *a.* 1887. [f. Gr. διπλόος double + ἄρθρον joint + -OUS.] *Zool.* Having the carpal or tarsal bones double articulated, *i.e.* the several bones of one row alternating with those of the other, as in ungulate mammals: opp. to *taxeopodous.* So **Dipla·rthrism,** d. condition.

Diplasic (diplæ·zik, dəi-), *a.* 1873. [f. Gr. διπλάσιος twofold + -IC.] *Pros.* Double, twofold; having the proportion of two to one, as in *d. ratio*, = Gr. διπλασίων λόγος.

||**Diple** (di·plī). 1656. [Gr. διπλῆ (sc. γραμμή line).] A marginal mark of this form >, to indicate various readings, rejected verses, a paragraph, etc.

||**Diplegia** (dəiplī·dʒiă). 1883. [f. DI-², after HEMI-, PARAPLEGIA.] *Path.* Paralysis of corresponding parts on both sides of the body. Hence **Diple·gic** *a.* relating to d., or to corresponding parts on both sides.

Dipleidoscope (dipləi·dǫskōᵘp). 1843. [f. Gr. διπλόος double + εἶδος form, image + -SCOPE.] An instrument consisting of a hollow triangular prism, with two sides silvered and one of glass, used for determining the meridian transit of a heavenly body by the coincidence of the two images formed by single and double reflection.

||**Dipleura** (dəiplūə·ră), *sb. pl.* 1883. [mod. L., neut. of *dipleurus*, f. Gr. δι- DI-² + πλευρά side (of the body).] *Biol.* Organic forms with bilateral symmetry having a single pair of antimeres. Hence **Dipleu·ral** *a.* zygopleural with only two antimeres. **Dipleu·ric** *a.* exhibiting bilateral symmetry.

Dipleurobranchiate (dəiplūə:roˌbræ·ŋkiĕt), *a.* [f. mod.L. *Dipleurobranchia* (f. Gr. δι- DI-² + πλευρά side + βράγχια gills) + -ATE².] See -IA².] *Zool.* Having the characters of the *Dipleurobranchia* or *Inferobranchiata*, nudobranchiate gastropods having foliaceous branchiæ situated in a fold on each side of the shell-less body.

Diplex (dəi·pleks), *a.* 1878. [Altered f. *duplex* after DI-².] *Telegr.* Characterized by the passing of two messages simultaneously in the same direction.

Diplo- (di·plo), bef. a vowel **dipl-,** comb. f. Gr. διπλό-ος, διπλοῦς, twofold, double: as in

Diplobacte·ria *sb. pl.*, bacteria consisting of two cells. **Diplobla·stic** *a.*, *Biol.* having two germinal layers, the hypoblast and epiblast. **Diploca·rdiac** *a.*, *Zool.* having the heart double, *i.e.* with the right and left halves completely separate, as in birds and mammals. **Diploce·phaly,** monstrosity consisting in having two heads. ||**Diploco·ccus,** *Biol.* a cell formed by conjugation of two cells. **Diplo·dal** *a.* [Gr. ὁδός], *Zool.* of sponges, having both canals, prosodal and aphodal, well developed. **Diplo·docus** [Gr. δοκός beam], a genus of gigantic extinct herbivorous dinosaurs. **Diploga·ngliate** *a.*, having ganglia arranged in pairs. **Diploge·nesis,** the production of double parts instead of single ones; hence **Diplogenetic** *a.*; **Diploge·nic** *a.*, 'producing two substances; partaking of the nature of two bodies' (Craig). **Di·plograph,** an instrument for writing double, *i.e.* in relief for the blind and in the ordinary manner, at the same time; so **Diplogra·phical** *a.*, of or pertaining to writing double; also **Diplo·graphy. Diploneu·ral** *a.*, *Anat.* supplied by two nerves of separate origin, as a muscle; **Diploneuro·se** *a.*, *Zool.* belonging to the *Diploneura* (= *Articulata*); **Diploneu·rous** *a.*, 'having two nervous systems; also, belonging to the *Diploneura*' (*Syd. Soc. Lex.*). **Diplopla·cula,** *Embryol.* a placula composed of two layers; hence **Diplopla·cular, Diplopla·culate** *a.* **Di·plopod** *a.* and *sb.*, *Zool.* belonging to the order of *Diplopoda* (= *Cheilognatha*) of Myriapods, having two pairs of limbs on each segment of the body; a member of this order; hence **Diplo·podous** *a.* **Diplo·pterous** *a.*, *Entom.* belonging to the family *Diploptera* (the true wasps), which have the fore wings folded when at rest. **Diplospondy·lic** *a.*, *Zool.* said of a vertical segment having two centra, or of a vertebral column having twice as many centra as arches, as in fishes and batrachians; hence **Diplospondy·lism. Diplo·stichous** *a.*, arranged in two rows. **Diplosy·ntheme** = DISYNTHEME.

||**Diploe** (di·ploˌī). 1696. [mod.L., f. Gr. διπλόη doubling, fold, overlapping of the bones of the skull (Hippocrates), f. διπλόος double.] **1.** *Anat.* The light porous or cancellated bone-tissue lying between the inner and outer tables of the skull. **2.** *Bot.* = DIACHYMA 1866. Hence **Diploe·tic** (bad form), **Diplo·ic** *adjs.* belonging to the d.

Diploid (di·ploid). [f. Gr. διπλόος double + -OID.] *Cryst.* A solid belonging to the isometric system, contained within twenty-four trapezoidal planes.

Diploidion (diploˌi·diǫn). 1850. [– Gr. διπλοΐδιον, dim. of διπλοΐς, -ιδ- double cloak.] *Gr. Antiq.* A chiton or tunic worn by women, having the part above the waist double with the outer fold hanging loose. So **Diplois** (di·ploˌis), in same sense.

Diploma (diplōᵘ·mă), *sb.* Pl. **-as,** occas. **-ata.** 1645. [– L. *diploma* – Gr. δίπλωμα, -ματ- folded paper, f. διπλοῦν to double, fold, f. διπλόος double.] **1.** A state paper, an official document; a charter; *pl.* historical or literary muniments. **2.** A document conferring some honour, privilege, or licence; *esp.* that given by a university or college, testifying to a degree taken by a person, and conferring upon him the rights and privileges of such degree, as to teach, practise medicine, etc. Also *attrib.*, as *d. picture*, one given to a society of art by a member on his election. Hence **Diplo·ma** *v.* to furnish with a d. Chiefly in *ppl. a.* **Diplomaed.**

Diplomacy (diplōᵘ·măsi). 1796. [– Fr. *diplomatie*, f. *diplomatique*, after *aristocratie*, *-cratique.* See -ACY.] **1.** The management of international relations by negotiation; the method by which these relations are adjusted and managed by ambassadors and envoys; the business or art of the diplomatist; skill or address in the conduct of international intercourse and negotiations. †**2.** The diplomatic body. [= Fr. *diplomatie.*] –1806. **3.** Skill in intercourse of any kind 1848. **4.** = DIPLOMATIC *sb.* 3 (*rare*) 1870.

1. As d. was in its beginnings, so it lasted for a long time; the ambassador was the man who was sent to lie abroad for the good of his country STUBBS. **3.** The lady thought it better to attain her ends by d. 1896.

Diplomat (di·plomæt). Also **-ate.** 1813. [– Fr. *diplomate*, back-formation from *diplomatique*, after *aristocrate*, *-cratique.*] One employed or skilled in diplomacy.

†**Di·plomate,** *v.* 1660. [f. DIPLOMA + -ATE³.] To invest with a degree, privilege, or title by diploma –1738.

[**Diplomatial:** error in Dicts. for DIPLOMATICAL.]

Diplomatic (diplomæ·tik). 1711. [– mod.L. *diplomaticus* (in Mabillon's 'De re diplomatica', 1681), f. L. *diploma*, *-mat-*; see DIPLOMA, -IC. In senses 2 and 3 of the adj. – Fr. *diplomatique.* In B. 1 and 2, subst. uses of the adj.; in 3 – Fr. *diplomatique*, based on mod.L. *diplomaticus.*]

A. *adj.* **1.** Of or pertaining to official or original documents, charters, or manuscripts; textual. **2.** Of the nature of official papers connected with international relations 1780. **3.** Of, pertaining to, or connected with the management of international relations; of or belonging to diplomacy 1787. **4.** Showing address in negotiations or intercourse of any kind 1826.

1. *D. copy*, an exact reproduction of an original. **3.** *D. body* (Fr. *corps diplomatique*), the body of ambassadors, envoys, and officials attached to the foreign legations at any seat of government. **4.** Conduct which is wily and subtle, without being directly false or fraudulent, is styled 'd.' 1877.

B. *sb.* **1.** = DIPLOMATIST 1791. **2.** The diplomatic art. Also in pl. **diplomatics.** 1794. **3.** The science of diplomas, which has for its object to decipher old writings, to ascertain their authenticity, their date, signatures, etc. Also in *pl.* 1803.

2. Our ministers are not great in diplomatics. var. **Diploma·tical** = DIPLOMATIC *a.* 1, 3; *sb.* 1. Hence **Diploma·tically** *adv.* **Diplomati·cian** (*rare*), diplomatist.

Diplomatics; see DIPLOMATIC B. 2, 3.

Diplomatist (diplōᵘ·mătist). 1815. [f. Fr. *diplomate*, or L. stem *diplomat-* + -IST.] One engaged in official diplomacy. **b.** One characterized by diplomatic address.

Diplomatize (diplōᵘ·mătəiz), *v.* 1670. [f. *diplomat-*, stem of L. *diploma* DIPLOMA + -IZE. In II a new formation from *diplomat*, *-ic*, *-ist.*]

I. *trans.* To invest with a diploma (*rare*).

II. 1. *intr.* To act or serve as a diplomat; to use diplomatic arts 1826. **2.** *trans.* To act diplomatically towards (*rare*) 1855. Also with *out of.*

||**Diplopia** (diplōᵘ·piă). Also **diplopy.** 1811. [mod.L., f. DIPLO- + Gr. ὤψ eye + -IA¹. Cf. AMBLYOPIA, MYOPIA.] *Phys.*, etc. An affection of the eyes, in which objects are seen double. Hence **Diplopic** (diplǫ·pik) *a.* pertaining to d.

Diplostemonous (diplostī·mǒnəs), *a.* 1866. [f. DIPLO- + Gr. στήμων warp, taken as = στῆμα stamen + -OUS.] *Bot.* Having the stamens in two series, or twice as many as the petals. So **Diploste·mony,** d. condition.

||**Diplozoon** (diplozōᵘ·ǫn). Pl. **-zoa.** 1835. [f. DIPLO- + Gr. ζῷον animal.] *Zool.* A genus of trematode worms, parasitic on the gills of fishes; the mature organism is double, and X-shaped.

Dipneumonous (dipniū·mǒnəs), *a.* [f. mod.L. *dipneumonus* (f. Gr. δι- DI-² + πνεύμων lung) + -OUS.] *Zool.* Having two respiratory organs; said of the *Dipneumona* or two-lunged fishes, and of the *Dipneumones* or two-lunged spiders; also of a group of Holothurians.

Dipneustal (dipniū·stăl), *a.* [f. mod.L. *Dipneusta* (f. Gr. δι- DI-² + πνευστός, πνεῖν breathe) + -AL¹.] *Zool.* = DIPNOAN.

Dipnoan (di·pno,ăn). 1883. [f. mod.L. *Dipnoi* (see DIPNOOUS) + -AN.] *Zool.*

A. *adj.* Belonging to the *Dipnoi*, a sub-class of fishes having both gills and lungs.

B. *sb.* A member of this sub-class. var. **Di·pnoid** *a.* and *sb.*

Dipnoous (di·pno,əs), *a.* Also *erron.* **dipnous.** 1811. [f. mod.L. *dipnous*, pl. *Dipnoi* a sub-class of fishes (– Gr. δίπνοος with two breathing apertures, f. δι- DI-² + πνοή breathing, breath) + -OUS.] **1.** *Zool.* Having both gills and lungs, as a dipnoan fish 1881. **2.** *Path.* Of a wound: Having two openings for air, etc. 1811.

Dipody (di·pŏdi). 1844. [– late L. *dipodia* (also used) – Gr. διποδία, f. δίπους, διποδ- two-footed; see -Y³.] *Pros.* A double foot; two feet making one measure. Hence **Dipo·dic** *a.* of the nature of a d.

Dipolar (dəipōᵘ·lăɹ), *a.* 1864. [DI-².] Of or pertaining to two poles; having two poles.

Dipolarize, etc. 1837. [DI-².] Used by some instead of DEPOLARIZE, etc.

‖**Diporpa** (dəipǭ·ɹpă). Pl. **-æ.** 1888. [mod.L., f. Gr. δι- DI-² + πόρπη tongue of a buckle.] *Zool.* The solitary immature form of a DIPLOZOON.

Dipper (di·pəɹ). ME. [f. DIP. *v.* + -ER¹.] **1.** One who dips, in various senses: *spec.* one who immerses something in a fluid 1611. **2.** One who uses immersion in baptism; *esp.* an Anabaptist or Baptist 1617. **3.** A name of birds which dip or dive in water. **a.** The Water Ouzel, *Cinclus aquaticus*; also other species, as, in N. America, *C. mexicanus*. **b.** *locally* in England: The Kingfisher. **c.** = DABCHICK. ? *Obs.* **d.** in *U.S.* The buffle, *Bucephala albeola*. ME. **4.** That which dips up water, etc.; *spec.* a ladle consisting of a bowl with a long handle 1801. **b.** in *U.S.* A name for the configuration of seven bright stars in Ursa Major. *Little D.*: the seven bright stars in Ursa Minor. 1858. **5.** *Photogr.* An apparatus for immersing negatives in a chemical solution 1859. **6.** A receptacle for oil, varnish, etc., fastened to a palette 1859.

1. I became also a lounger in the Bodleian library, and a great d. into books W. IRVING.

attrib. and *comb.*: **d.-bird** (see 3 a); **-clam** (*U.S.*), a bivalve mollusc, *Mactra solidissima*; **-gourd** (*U.S.*), a gourd used as a d. (sense 4).

Hence **Di·pperful** (*U.S.*), as much as fills a d.

Dipping (di·piŋ), *vbl. sb.* ME. [f. DIP *v.* + -ING¹.] **1.** The action of DIP *v.* **2.** *concr.* A liquid preparation in which things are dipped; a wash for sheep; dubbing for leather (*Sc.*) 1825.

attrib. and *comb.*: **d.-frame,** a frame used in dipping tallow candles, and in dyeing; **-well,** the receptacle in front of an isobath inkstand.

Di·pping-nee:dle. 1667. [See DIP *v.* II. 5 and *sb.* 4.] A magnetic needle mounted so as to move in a vertical plane about its centre of gravity, and thus indicate by its dip the direction of the earth's magnetism. So *d.-compass* = *dip-circle*.

Dippy (di·pi), *a. slang.* 1922. [Origin unkn.] Mad, crazy.

†**Diprisma·tic,** *a.* 1821. [DI-².] *Min.* Doubly prismatic.

Dipropargyl (dəiprǫpā·ɹdʒil). 1875. [DI-² 2.] *Chem.* A hydrocarbon isomeric with benzene, having the constitution of a double molecule of the radical Propargyl (CH ≡ $C.CH_2$); a pungent, mobile, highly refractive liquid.

‖**Diprotodon** (dəiprōᵘ·tŏdǫn). 1839. [mod. L., f. Gr. δι- DI-² + πρῶτος first + ὀδούς, ὀδοντ- tooth. Cf. DIODON, DIODONT.] *Palæont.* A genus of huge extinct marsupials, having two incisors in the lower jaw. So **Dipro·todont** *a.* having the dentition of the genus *D.*; *sb.* a marsupial of this genus.

Dipsacaceous (dipsăkēⁱ·ʃəs), *a.* [f. mod.L. *Dipsacaceæ* (f. *Dipsacus* – Gr. δίψακος teasel) + OUS. See -ACEOUS.] *Bot.* Belonging to the N.O. *Dipsacaceæ*, containing the teasels and their allies. var. **Dipsa·ceous** *a.*

Dipsadine (di·psădəin), *a.* [f. *dipsad-*, stem of L. DIPSAS, + -INE¹.] *Zool.* Of or belonging to the family of non-venomous snakes, *Dipsadinæ*, to which belongs the genus *Dipsas* (DIPSAS 2 a).

‖**Dipsas** (di·psæs). Pl. **dipsades** (di·psădīz). ME. [L. – Gr. διψάς, orig. adj., causing thirst, f. δίψα thirst.] **1.** A serpent whose bite was fabled to produce a raging thirst. **2.** *Zool.* **a.** A tropical genus of non-venomous serpents. **b.** A genus of fresh-water bivalves of the family *Unionidæ*, or river-mussels. 1841.

Dipsetic (dipse·tik). 1847. [– Gr. διψητικός provoking thirst, f. διψᾶν to thirst, f. δίψα thirst; see -IC.]

A. *adj.* Producing thirst.

B. *sb.* A medicine that produces thirst.

‖**Dipsomania** (dipsomēⁱ·niă). 1843. [f. Gr. διψο-, comb. form of δίψα thirst + -MANIA.] A morbid and insatiable craving, often paroxysmal, for alcohol. Also applied to persistent drunkenness. Hence **Dipsoma·niac** *sb.* a person affected with d.; *a.* affected with d. So **Dipsomani·acal** *a.*

Dipsopathy (dipsǫ·păþi). 1883. [f. as prec. + -PATHY, after *homœopathy*.] The treatment of disease by abstinence from liquids.

‖**Dipso·sis.** 1851. [f. Gr. δίψα thirst + -OSIS; the regular Gr. word was δίψησις.] *Med.* A morbid degree of thirst.

‖**Di·ptera,** *sb. pl.* 1819. [mod.L., – Gr. δίπτερα (Aristotle), n. pl. of δίπτερος two-winged (f. δι- DI-² + πτερόν wing) used subst. (sc. ἔντομα insects).] *Entom.* The two-winged flies, a large order of insects having one pair of membranous wings, with a pair of halteres or poisers representing a posterior pair. Examples are the common house-fly, the gnats, gad-flies, etc.

Diptera·ceous, *a.* 1849. [f. mod. Bot.L. *Dipteraceæ*, f. *Dipter-* contr. of *Dipterocarpus* DIPTEROCARP; see -ACEOUS.] *Bot.* Of or belonging to the N.O. *Dipteraceæ* (*Dipterocarpeæ*); see DIPTEROCARP. So **Di·pterad,** a plant of this order.

Dipteral (di·ptĕrăl), *a.* 1812. [f. L. *dipteros* (Vitruvius) – Gr. δίπτερος (see DIPTERA), + -AL¹.] **1.** *Arch.* Having a double peristyle. var. †**Dipte·ric** *a.* **2.** *Entom.* = DIPTEROUS 1828.

Di·pteran, *a.* and *sb.* 1842. [f. as DIPTERA + -AN.] **1.** *adj.* = DIPTEROUS. **2.** *sb.* A dipterous insect.

Di·pterist. 1872. [f. DIPTERA + -IST.] One who studies the *Diptera*.

Dipterocarp (di·ptĕro,kāɹp). 1876. [– mod.L. *Dipterocarpus*, f. Gr. δίπτερος two-winged + καρπός fruit.] *Bot.* A member of the genus *Dipterocarpus* or N.O. *Dipterocarpeæ*, comprising E. Indian trees characterized by two wings on the summit of the fruit, formed by enlargement of two of the calyx-lobes. Cf. DIPTERACEOUS. So **Dipteroca·rpous** *a.* belonging to this genus or order.

Diptero·logy. 1881. [f. DIPTERA + -LOGY.] That branch of entomology which relates to the *Diptera*. Hence **Di:pterolo·gical** *a.* **Diptero·logist** = DIPTERIST.

‖**Di·pteros.** 1706. [Gr. δίπτερος (sc. ναός) two-winged (temple).] *Archit.* A building with double peristyle.

Dipterous (di·ptĕrəs), *a.* 1773. [f. mod.L. *dipterus* (see next) + -OUS.] **1.** *Entom.* Two-winged; of, pertaining to, or resembling the DIPTERA. **2.** *Bot.* Having two wing-like processes, as certain fruits, seeds, etc. 1851.

‖**Di·pterus.** 1842. [mod.L. – Gr. δίπτερος two-winged. See DIPTERA.] *Palæont.* A genus of Palæozoic dipnoous fishes, having two dorsal fins, opposite the ventral and anal respectively. Hence **Dipte·rian** *a.* and *sb.* belonging to, or a member of, this genus.

Dipterygian (diptĕri·dʒⁱăn), *a.* 1847. [f. mod.L. *Dipterygii* (f. Gr. δι- DI-² + πτερύγιον fin) + -AN.] *Ichth.* Having (only) two fins, as certain fishes. Also **Diptery·gious** *a.*

Diptote (di·ptōᵘt), *sb.* and *a.* 1612. [– late L. *diptota* – Gr. δίπτωτα, n. pl. of δίπτωτος, f. δι- DI-² + πτωτός falling (πτῶσις case).] *Gram.* **1.** *sb.* A noun having only two cases. **2.** *adj.* Having only two cases.

Diptych (di·ptik). 1622. [– late L. *diptycha* – late Gr. δίπτυχα pair of writing-tablets, n. pl. of δίπτυχος, f. δι- DI-² + πτυχή fold.] **1.** Anything folded, so as to have two leaves; *esp.* a two-leaved, hinged, writing tablet of metal, ivory, or wood, having its inner surfaces covered with wax for writing with the stylus. **2.** *Eccl.* (in *pl.*) Tablets containing a list of those, living and dead, who were commemorated by the early Church at the celebration of the eucharist. Hence, the list of such names; the intercessions in the course of which the names were introduced. 1640. **3.** An altar-piece or painting composed of two leaves which close like a book 1852. So **Di·ptychous** *a.* double-folded.

‖**Dipus** (dəi·pŭs). 1799. [mod.L. – Gr. δίπους two-footed, f. δι- DI-² + πούς foot.] *Zool.* **a.** The typical genus of the jerboas. **b.** A small marsupial quadruped of Australia, *Chæropus castanotis*.

Dipyre (dipəiᵊ·ɹ). 1804. [mod. (Haüy, 1801) – L. *dipyrus* twice burned, Gr. δίπυρος twice baked, f. δι- DI-² + πῦρ fire: so named because when heated it exhibits both phosphorescence and fusion.] *Min.* A silicate of alumina with small proportions of the silicates of soda and lime, occurring in square prisms.

Dipyrenous (dəipirī·nəs), *a.* 1866. [f. Gr. δι- DI-² + πυρήν fruit-stone + -OUS.] *Bot.* Containing two fruit-stones.

Diradiation (dəirēⁱdiēⁱ·ʃən). 1706. [DI-¹.] The diffusion of rays from a luminous body.

Dircæan (dəɹsī·ăn), *a.* 1730. [f. L. *Dircæus*, f. *Dirce*, Gr. Δίρκη a fountain in Bœotia.] Of or belonging to the fountain of Dirce: used of Pindar, called by Horace *Dircæus cygnus* the D. swan; Pindaric, poetic.

Dirdum (dǝ̄·ɹdəm). *Sc.* and *n. dial.* ME. [Cf. Gael. *diurdan, durdan* anger, snarling, Ir. *deardan* storm, tempest.] **1.** Uproar. **2.** Outcry; blame 1709.

Dire (dəiᵊɹ). 1567. [– L. *dirus* fearful, ill-boding.]

A. *adj.* 'Dreadful, dismal, mournful, horrible, terrible, evil in a great degree' (J.).

All monstrous, all prodigious things..Gorgons and Hydra's and Chimera's d. MILT. *P. L.* II. 628. His direst foe COWPER. D. necessity C. BRONTË.

†**B.** *sb.* **1.** Direness 1660. **2.** *pl.* = L. *Diræ*, Furies 1610.

Direct (dire·kt, dəi-), *v.* ME. [prob. based immed. on pa. pple. *direct* (Chaucer) – L. *directus*, pa. pple. of *dirigere, derigere* straighten, direct, guide, f. *dis-* DI-¹, *dē-* DE- I. 3 + *regere* put straight, rule.] **1.** *trans.* To write (something) directly or specially *to*; to address; *spec.* in mod. usage, To write the direction on (a letter or the like) 1588. Also *absol.* **2.** To address (speech) *to* any one (*arch.*) 1459. **3.** To put or keep straight, or in right order. Also *absol.* 1509. **4.** *trans.* To cause (a thing or person) to move or point straight *to* or *towards* a place; to aim; to make straight (a way) *to*; to turn (the eyes, attention, etc.) straight *to* 1526. **5.** *trans.* To regulate the course of; to guide, conduct; to advise 1559. **6.** To give authoritative instructions to; to ordain, order, or appoint (a person) *to do* a thing, (a thing) *to be done* 1598. **b.** *intr.* or *absol.* To give directions; to order, appoint, ordain 1655.

1. D. to me at Mr. Hipkis's, Ironmonger in Monmouth BURKE. 2. In the morning will I d. my prayer vnto thee *Ps.* 5:3. 3. *absol.* Wisedom is profitable to d. *Eccles.* 10:10. 4. I directed my Sight as I was ordered ADDISON. To d. attention to TYNDALL. 5. Some God d. my judgement *Merch. V.* II. vii. 14. 6. I'le first d. my men what they shall doe with the basket *Merry W.* IV. ii. 98. *absol.* Who can d., when all pretend to know GOLDSM.

Hence †**Dire·ctedly** *adv.* directly.

Direct (dire·kt, dəi-), *a.* and *adv.* ME. [– L. *directus*; see prec.]

A. *adj.* **1.** Straight; undeviating in course; not circuitous or crooked. **2.** Perpendicular to a given surface, etc.; not oblique 1563. **3.** *Astron.* Of the motion of a planet, etc.: Proceeding in the order of the zodiacal signs, in the same direction as the sun in the ecliptic, *i.e.* from west to east; also said of the planet, etc. Opp. to *retrograde*. ME. **4.** Straightforward, uninterrupted, immediate; *spec.* of succession: Lineal, as opp. to *collateral*; as a *d. heir* or *ancestor* 1548. **5.** Without circumlocution or ambiguity; straightforward; downright 1530. **6.** Without intervening agency; immediate 1596.

2. Phr. *D. fire* (Mil.), fire which is perpendicular to the works attacked. **5.** *A.Y.L.* v. iv. 90. *Oth.* III. iii. 378. **6.** *All's Well* III. vi. 9. *D. narration*: not modified by being reported in the third person. *D. action*, action which takes effect without intermediate instrumentality, as in the *d.-action* or *d.-acting steam-engine*, without the intervention of a working-beam between the piston-rod and the crank; also, the exertion of pressure on the community by strikes, etc., instead of on Parliament through representatives. *D. current* (Electr.), a current running in one direction only (abbrev. *D.C.* or *d.c.*). *D. tax*: see TAX *sb.* 1. **b.** Of or pertaining to the work and expenses actually incurred during production as distinct from subsidiary work and overhead charges; also, applied to labour employed for the construction of works directly (without the intervention of a contractor) 1895.

B. *adv.* = DIRECTLY, q.v. Also in *comb.*

Direct (dire·kt), *sb.* 1615. [app. f. DIRECT *v.*] **1.** *gen.* A direction. **2.** *Mus.* A sign (*w*) placed on the stave at the end of a page or line to indicate the position of the following note 1674.

Directer; see DIRECTOR.

Direction (dire·kʃən, dəi-). ME. [– Fr. *direction* or L. *directio*, f. *direct-*, pa. ppl. stem of *dirigere*; see DIRECT *v.*, -ION.] **1.** The action or function of directing, aiming, guiding, instructing, or administering; conduct; instruction; management, administration 1509. †**2.** Administrative faculty –1636. **3.** = *Directorate* 1710. †**4.** Arrangement, order. Chiefly in *to take* or *set d.* –1548. **5.** with *a.* and *pl.* An instruction how to proceed; an order, a precept 1576. **6.** The action of directing or addressing a letter, or the like; the superscription or address upon a letter or parcel sent, indicating for whom it is intended, and where it is to be taken 1524. **7.** The particular course or line pursued by any moving body, as defined by the region or point towards which it is directed; the relative point towards which one moves, turns the face, the mind, etc.; the line towards any point or region 1665. Also *fig.*

1. A Souldier, fit to stand by Caesar And giue d. *Oth.* II. iii. 128. She felt the need of d. GEO. ELIOT. **2.** *Rich. III*, v. iii. 16. **5.** He..took little or nothing but by the Doctors directions 1654. The stage d. STRUTT. Proper directions for finding me in London GOLDSM. **6.** My d. is—care of Andrew Bruce, merchant, Bridge-street BURNS. **7.** These terms—north and south, east and west.. indicate definite directions HUXLEY. The d. of a force is the line in which it acts 1879. He has gone in the d. of Paris 1896. *fig.* New directions of enquiry JOWETT.

Hence **Dire·ctional** *a.* of or relating to d. in space.

†**Dire·ctitude.** Humorous blunder, app. for *discredit*. *Cor.* IV. v. 222.

Directive (dire·ktiv, dəi-), *a.* (*sb.*) 1594. [– med.L. *directivus*, f. *direct-* (see DIRECTION) + *-ivus* -IVE. Cf. (O)Fr. *directif, -ive*. In sense 4 – med.L. *directivum*.] **1.** Having the quality or function of directing; see DIRECT *v.* **2.** Having the quality, function, or power of directing motion 1625. †**3.** Subject to direction (*rare*) –1606. †**4.** *sb.* That which directs –1654.

1. Laws being rules d. of our actions BP. BERKELEY. **2.** It is..d., not motive, altering the direction of other forces, but not..initiating them W. GROVE. **3.** *Tr. & Cr.* I. iii. 356. Hence **Dire·ctive-ly** *adv.*, **-ness.**

Directly (dire·ktli), *adv.* ME. [f. DIRECT *a.* + -LY².] **1.** In a direct manner; in a straight line of motion; straight 1513. Also *fig.* **b.** *Math.* Opp. to *inversely* 1743. **2.** At right angles to a surface; not obliquely 1559. **3.** Completely, exactly, just ME. **4.** Without the intervention of a medium; immediately; by a direct process or mode 1526. **5.** Immediately (in time); straightway 1602. **b.** *colloq.* as *conj.* As soon as, the moment after. (Ellipt. for *d. that, as,* or *when.*) 1795.

1. To run d. on *Jul. C.* IV. i. 32. *fig.* I asked him his opinion d., and without management BURKE. **2.** Take a quadrant..and set it d. upright 1559. **3.** The wind..is d. contrary 1863. I find no decision d. in point 1891. **4.** A universal primeval language revealed d. by God to man MAX-MÜLLER. **5.** I will come d. 1896. **b.** Iodine and phosphorus combine d. they come into contact 1837.

Directness (dire·ktnės). 1598. [f. as prec. + -NESS.] The quality of being direct (*lit.* and *fig.*).

‖**Directoire** (dire·ktwāɹ), *a.* and *sb.* 1878. [Fr.; see DIRECTORY *sb.* 5.] (A style of dress) imitating that prevalent at the time of the French Directory.

Director (dire·ktəɹ). Also (from XVI) **-er.** 1477. [– AFr. *directour* – late L. *director* governor, ruler (whence also Fr. *directeur* XVI); see DIRECT *v.*, -OUR, -ER², -OR 2.] **1.** One who or that which directs, rules, or guides; a guide, a conductor; a superintendent. **b.** *spec.* A member of a board appointed to direct the affairs of a commercial corporation or company 1632. **c.** *Eccl.* (chiefly in *R.C.Ch.*) A spiritual adviser 1669. **2.** One who or that which causes something to take a particular direction 1632. **b.** *Surg.* A grooved probe for guiding a cutting-instrument 1667. **c.** A metallic rod in a non-conducting handle for applying electric current to a part of the body 1795.

Comb.: **d.-circle** (of a conic), the locus of intersection of tangents at right angles to each other; **-plane,** a fixed plane used in describing a surface, analogous to the line called a DIRECTRIX.

Hence **Dire·ctorate,** the office of a d., or of a body of directors; management by directors; *concr.* a board of directors. **Directo·rial** *a.* of, pertaining to, or of the nature of a d., or of direction; of or pertaining to a body of directors. **Directo·rially** *adv.* †**Dire·ctorize** *v.* to bring under the authority of a directory (*rare*). **Dire·ctorship,** the office or position of a d., guiding.

Directory (dire·ktŏri), *a.* 1450. [– late L. *directorius* that directs, directive, f. *director*; see prec., -ORY².] Serving or tending to direct; directive, guiding. **b.** *spec.* Applied *esp.* to a statute or part of a statute which operates as advice or direction.

b. There was no necessity ..to comply with the d. provisions of the Act as to delivery of copies 1884.

Directory (dire·ktŏri), *sb.* 1543. [– late L. *directorium* guidance, directory, guide-book, etc., subst. use of n. sing. of *directorius*; see prec., -ORY¹.] **1.** Something that serves to direct; *esp.* a book of rules or directions. **2.** *Eccl.* A book containing directions for the order of public or private worship, *e.g.* that compiled in 1644 by the Westminster Assembly 1640. **3.** A book containing one or more alphabetical lists of the inhabitants of any locality, or of classes of them, with their addresses, occupations etc. 1732. †**4.** *Surg.* = DIRECTOR 2 b. –1764. **5.** *Fr. Hist.* [tr. Fr. *Directoire.*] The executive body in France during part of the revolutionary period (Oct. 1795—Nov. 1799) 1796.

Directress (dire·ktrės). Also **directoress.** 1586. [f. DIRECTOR + -ESS¹.] A female who directs. Also *fig.* var. †**Dire·ctrice.**

Directrix (dire·ktriks). Pl. **-ices.** 1622. [– med.L. *directrix*, f. late L. *director*; see -TRIX.] **1.** = DIRECTRESS. **2.** *Geom.* †**a.** = DIRIGENT *sb.* 3. **b.** A fixed line used in describing a curve or surface; *spec.* the straight line the distance of which from any point on a conic bears a constant ratio to the distance of the same point from the focus. 1702.

Direful (dəiᵊ·ɹfŭl), *a.* 1583. [f. DIRE *a.* (or *sb.*) + -FUL.] Fraught with dire effects; dreadful, terrible.

Prodigies of d. import MERIVALE. Hence **Di·reful-ly** *adv.*, **-ness.**

†**Dire·mpt,** *ppl. a.* [– L. *diremptus*, pa. pple. of *dirimere* separate, divide, f. *dir-*, DIS- 1 + *emere* take.] Distinct, divided. STOW. So †**Dire·mpt** *v.* to separate, divide; to break off.

Diremption (dire·mᵖʃən). Now *rare.* 1623. [– L. *diremptio*, f. *dirempt-*, pa. ppl. stem of *dirimere*; see prec., -ION.] A forcible separation, *esp.* of man and wife.

Direness (dəiᵊ·ɹnės). 1605. [f. DIRE *a.* + -NESS.] The quality of being dire.

†**Dire·ption.** 1483. [– L. *direptio*, f. *dirept-*, pa. ppl. stem of *diripere* snatch away, f. *di-* DI-¹ + *rapere* tear away. Cf. Fr. †*direption.*] The action of pillaging, snatching away, or dragging apart violently –1828. So †**Direpti·tiously** *adv.* by way of pillaging.

Dirge (dɔ̄ɹdʒ), *sb.* ME. [orig. *dirige*, the first word of the antiphon *Dirige, Domine, Deus meus, in conspectu tuo viam meam*, Ps. 5:8.] **1.** In the Latin rite: The first word of the antiphon at Matins in the Office of the Dead, used as a name for that service. **2.** *transf.* A funeral song; a song of mourning. Also *fig.* 1500. **3.** A funeral feast 1730.

2. D. at an end, the departed is placed in the funeral bed BOWEN. *Comb.*: **d.-ale,** an ale-drinking at a funeral. Hence **Di·rgeful** *a.* full of lamentation, mournful.

‖**Dirhe·m.** 1788. [Arab. *dirham* – L. *drachma*; see DRACHM.] An Arabian measure of weight, orig. 44·4 grains troy; in Egypt at present = 47·661 troy grains. Also a small silver coin of the same weight, used still in Morocco, and worth about 4*d.* English.

Dirige (di·ridʒi), original f. DIRGE.

†**Dirigent** (di·ridʒĕnt). 1617. [– *dirigent-*, pres. ppl. stem of L. *dirigere*, see DIRECT *v.*, -ENT.]

A. *adj.* **1.** That directs. **2.** *Pharm.* Formerly applied to certain ingredients in prescriptions which were held to guide the action of the rest –1860. **3.** *Geom.* Applied to the line along which the describing line, or surface, is carried in the genesis of any figure 1704.

B. *sb.* **1.** = DIRECTOR 1. 1756. **2.** *Pharm.* A dirigent ingredient 1854. **3.** *Geom.* A dirigent line 1706.

Dirigible (di·ridʒĭb'l), *a.* and *sb.* 1581. [f. L. *dirigere* DIRECT *v.* + -IBLE; in sense 2 replacing earlier *dirigeable* (c1880) – Fr. *dirigeable* (1870).] **1.** *adj.* Capable of being directed or guided, as a *d. balloon*. **2.** *sb.* A dirigible airship. Also *attrib.* 1907.

Dirigo-motor (di:rigo,mōᵘ·tŏɹ), *a.* [irreg. f. L. *dirig-*, stem of *dirigere* DIRECT *v.* + MOTOR *a.*] *Physiol.* That both produces and directs muscular motion. H. SPENCER.

Diriment (di·rimĕnt), *a.* 1848. [– *diriment-*, pres. ppl. stem of L. *dirimere*; see DIREMPT, -ENT.] That nullifies; chiefly in *d. impediment*, one that renders marriage null and void from the beginning.

†**Di·rity.** [– L. *diritas*, f. *dirus*; see DIRE, -ITY.] Direness. HOOKER.

Dirk (dɔ̄ɹk), *sb.* 1602. [Earliest in Sc. *durk, dowrk*; the present sp. was popularized by Johnson; of unkn. origin.] A kind of dagger or poniard: *spec.* the dagger of a Highlander. *Comb.* **d.-knife,** a large clasp-knife with a d.-shaped blade. Hence **Dirk** *v.* to stab with a d.

Dirk(e, -ness, obs. ff. DARK, -NESS.

Dirl, *v. Sc.* and *n. dial.* 1513. [Modification of THIRL *v.*] **1.** *trans.* To pierce, to thrill. **2.** *intr.* To vibrate; to tingle 1715; to ring 1823. So **Dirl** *sb.* a thrill or vibration.

Dirt (dɔ̄ɹt), *sb.* [ME. *drit* – ON. *drit*, corresp. to MDu. *drēte* (Du. *dreet*), rel. to the vbs. OE. *ġedrītan* = ON. *drita*, MDu. *driten* (Du. *drijten*). The present metathesized form appears XV.] **1.** Ordure; EXCREMENT. **2.** Unclean matter, such as soils any object by adhering to it; filth. Also *fig.* ME. **3.** Mud; soil, earth, mould; brick-earth (*colloq.*) 1698; in *Mining, quarrying*, etc., useless material, rubbish 1799; *esp.* the material from which gold, etc. is separated 1857. **4.** Dirtiness; uncleanness in action or speech 1774; meanness 1625.

2. The spoiling of my clothes and velvet coat with d. PEPYS. *fig.* The wealth was all like d. under my feet DE FOE. He has too much land: keep it, d. BEAUM. & FL. **4.** The Turkish steamer ..was in a beastly state of d. GEN. GORDON. Honours..thrown away upon d. and infamy MELMOTH.

Phrases. *To cast, throw,* or *fling d.*: to asperse with scurrilous or abusive language. *To eat d.*: to submit to degrading treatment.

Comb.: **d.-bed,** *Geol.* a stratum consisting of ancient vegetable mould; *spec.* a bed of dark bituminous earth, occurring in the lower Purbeck series of the Isle of Portland; **-bird,** a local name of the skua, *Stercorarius crepidatus*; **-cheap** *a.* (*adv.*), as cheap as d.; exceedingly cheap; **-eater,** one who eats d. (see next); **-eating,** the eating of some kinds of earth or clay as food, practised by some savage tribes; a disorder of the nutritive functions characterized by a morbid craving to eat earth; **-pie,** a mud pie; **-track,** a course made of cinders, etc. for motor-cycle racing, or of earth for flat-racing.

Hence **Dirt** *v. trans.* to dirty.

Dirty (dɔ̄·ɹti), *a.* 1530. [f. DIRT *sb.* + -Y¹.] **1.** Soiled with dirt; foul, unclean; mixed with dirt; that makes dirty. **2.** Morally unclean; 'smutty' 1599; despicable 1670; basely earned 1742. **3.** Repulsive, hateful, despicable 1611. **4.** Of the weather: Foul, muddy; at sea, wet and squally 1660. **5.** Of colour: Inclining to black, brown, or dark grey 1665.

1. A beastly Towne and durtie streets 1630. D. coal 1894, drudgery GOLDSM. **2.** One of Swift's d. volumes 1850. A d. trick 1674. D. and dependent bread COWPER. Phr. *To do the d.*: to play a dirty trick. **3.** Those Who worship durty Gods *Cymb.* III. vi. 55. Hence **Di·rtily** *adv.* **Di·rtiness.** **Di·rty** *v.*, to make or become dirty or unclean.

Dirty Allan. 1771. = *Dirt-bird* (see DIRT).

†**Diru·ption.** *rare.* 1656. [– L. *diruptio*, f. *dirupt-*, pa. ppl. stem of *dirumpere* burst or break asunder. Cf. DISRUPTION.] Breaking or rending asunder –1680.

Dis- (ME. also **dys-**) *prefix*, of L. origin. [repr. L. *dis-*, which was rel. to *bis*, orig. **dvis* = Gr. δίς, from *duo*, δύο, the primary meaning being 'two ways, in twain'. It was reduced to *dī-* before some voiced consonants, as in *dīligere* (see DILIGENT), *dīrigere* DIRECT *v.*, *dīvidere* DIVIDE, became *dir-* between vowels in *dirimere* (see DIRIMENT), was assim. before *f*, as in *differre* DIFFER, *difficilis* DIFFICULT, but retained its full form before *p*, *t*, *c*, and *s*.] In English, *dis-* appears (1) as repr. L. *dis-* in words adopted from L.; (2) as repr. OFr. *des-* (mod.Fr. *dé-*, *dés-*), the inherited form of L. *dis-*; (3) as repr. late L. *dis-*, Rom. *des-*, substituted for L. *de-*; (4) as a living prefix, used with words without respect to their origin.

I. As an etymological element. In the senses:

1. 'In twain, in different directions, apart, asunder', hence 'abroad, away'; as in *discern*, *dilapidate*, *divide*, etc. **2.** 'Between'; as in *dijudicate*, etc. **3.** 'Separately, singly'; as in *dinumerate*, etc. **4.** With privative sense; as in *disjoin*, *dissuade*, etc. **5.** As an intensive, with verbs having already a sense of undoing; as in *disalter*, *disannul*, etc.

II. As a living prefix, with privative force, sometimes replacing earlier *mis-*, as in *disfortune*, *dislike*.

6. Forming compound verbs, etc.; as in DISESTABLISH, DISOWN, etc. **7.** With sbs., forming verbs, etc. in the senses: **a.** To strip of, free or rid of; as in DISFROCK, DISPEOPLE, etc. **b.** To deprive of the character, rank, or title of; as in DISBISHOP, DISCHURCH, etc. **c.** To turn out from the place or receptacle implied; as in DISBAR, DISBENCH, etc. **d.** To undo or spoil; as in DISCOMPLEXION. **8.** With adjs., forming verbs in the sense of: To undo or reverse the quality expressed by the adj.; as in DISABLE, etc. **9.** With a sb., forming another expressing the opposite, or denoting the lack, of (the thing in question); as in DISEASE, DISHONOUR, etc. **10.** Prefixed to adjs., with neg. force; as in DISHONEST, etc.

Disability (disăbi·lĭti). 1580. [f. DIS- 9 + ABILITY.] **1.** Want of ability; inability, incapacity, impotence (now *rare* in *gen.* sense); pecuniary inability 1624. **2.** Incapacity in the eye of the law, or created by the law; legal disqualification 1641.

1. His disabilitie to performe his promise LUPTON. Disabilities for making a good book 1824. **2.** The next legal d. is want of age BLACKSTONE.

†**Disa·ble**, *a.* ME. [DIS- 10.] Unable; incapable; impotent –1649. Hence †**Disa·bleness**, incapacity; disabled state.

Disable (disē^i·b'l), *v.* 1485. [DIS- 8.] **1.** *trans.* To render unable or incapable; to deprive of ability, physical or mental, to incapacitate. Const. *from*, †*to*, *for.* 1548. **b.** *spec.* To render incapable of action or use by injury, etc.; to cripple 1491. **2.** *spec.* To incapacitate legally; to pronounce legally incapable 1485. **3.** To pronounce incapable; hence, to disparage, depreciate (*arch.*) 1529. †**4.** To make or pronounce of no force –1693.

1. b. My writeing hand hath been disabled by a sprain HEARNE. **2.** Papists, by the Act of Settlement, are disabled to inherit the crown 1678. **3.** *A.Y.L.* IV. i. 34. Hence **Disa·blement.** **Disa·bler**, one who or that which disables.

Disabuse (disăbiū·z), *v.* 1611. [f. DIS- 7a + ABUSE *sb.*] To free from ABUSE (q. v.); to relieve from fallacy or deception; to undeceive.

Wise and disabused persons JER. TAYLOR. [Man] still by himself abus'd, or dis-abus'd POPE.

†**Disacce·ptance.** 1642. [f. †*disaccept* decline + -ANCE.] Refusal to accept –1720.

Disaccommodate (disăkǫ·mŏdē^it), *v.* ? *Obs.* 1611. [DIS- 6.] To put to inconvenience, to incommode. Hence **Disacco:mmoda·tion.** ? *Obs.*

Disaccord (disăkǭ·ɹd), *sb.* 1809. [f. DIS- 9 + ACCORD *sb.* Cf. (O)Fr. *désaccord.*] The reverse of accord; disagreement.

Disaccord (disăkǭ·ɹd), *v.* late ME. [– Fr. *désaccorder*, f. *des-* DIS- 4 + *accorder* ACCORD *v.*] *intr.* To be out of accord; to disagree; to refuse assent. Hence **Disacco·rdance** (*rare*). So **Disacco·rdant** *a.* (*rare*).

Disaccustom (disăkʊ·stəm), *v.* 1484. [– OFr. *desaco(u)stumer* (mod. *désaccoutumer*), f. *des-* DIS- 4 + *acostumer* ACCUSTOM.] **1.** *trans.* To render no longer customary; to break off (a habit, etc.) (*arch.*). **2.** To cause (a person) to lose a habit. Const. *to*, †*from.* 1530.

Disaci·dify, *v. rare.* [DIS- 6.] To free from acidity.

Disacknowledge (disæknǫ·lėdʒ), *v.* 1598. [DIS- 6.] To refuse to acknowledge; to disown.

Disacquai·nt, *v.* ? *Obs.* 1548. [DIS- 6.] To make no longer acquainted; to render unfamiliar. So **Disacquai·ntance.** ? *Obs.*

Disacryl (disæ·kril). 1863. [f. DIS- implying disintegration + ACRYL.] *Chem.* A white flocculent substance into which acrolein changes when kept for some time. Also called *disacrone*. Also *attrib.*

†**Disadju·st**, *v. rare.* 1611. [DIS- 6.] To undo the adjustment of; to unsettle –1747.

†**Disado·rn**, *v. rare.* 1598. [DIS- 6.] To deprive of adornment –1729.

†**Disadva·nce**, *v.* [ME. *disavaunce* – OFr. *desavancer* repel, push back, f. *des-* DIS- 4 + *avancer* to ADVANCE.] To check the advance of; to draw back; to lower. Also *fig.* –1659.

Disadvantage (disædva·ntėdʒ), *sb.* [ME. *des-*, *disadvauntage* – (O)Fr. *désavantage*, f. *des-* DIS- 4 + *avantage* ADVANTAGE.] **1.** Absence of advantage; an unfavourable condition or circumstance 1530. **2.** Detriment, loss, or injury to interest; prejudice to credit or reputation ME.

1. Martius we have at d. fought And did retyre to win our purpose *Cor.* I. vi. 49. Every condition has its disadvantages JOHNSON. **2.** They speake there..to the d. of our nation NAUNTON. He sold to d. JOHNSON. Hence **Disadva·ntage** *v.* to cause d. to. †**Disadva·ntageable** *a.* prejudicial.

Disadvantageous (disæ:dvăntē^i·dʒəs), *a.* 1603. [f. DIS- 10 + ADVANTAGEOUS, perh. after Fr. *désavantageux.*] Attended with disadvantage; unfavourable, prejudicial; depreciative. ? *Obs.*

The English were in a streight d. place MILT. A d. Character SWIFT. Hence **Disadvanta·geously** *adv.*, **-ness.**

†**Disadve·nture.** [Late ME. *disaventure* – OFr. *desaventure*, f. *des-* DIS- 4 + *aventure* ADVENTURE.] Mishap, misfortune –1638. Hence †**Disadve·nturous** *a.* unfortunate, disastrous.

Disadvi·se, *v.* 1636. [DIS- 6.] To give advice against; to dehort *from*.

Disaffect (disăfe·kt), *v.*[1] 1621. [f. DIS- 6 + AFFECT *v.*[1]] **1.** *trans.* To lack affection for; to dislike. ? *Obs.* **2.** To alienate the affection of; to make unfriendly or less friendly; *spec.* to discontent or dissatisfy, as subjects with the government; to make disloyal. (Mostly in *pass.*) 1641.

2. You..began to raise Cain by disaffecting the other workmen 1893.

†**Disaffe·ct**, *v.*[2] 1625. [f. DIS- 6 + AFFECT *v.*[2]] To affect in an evil manner; to disorder, derange –1688.

It disaffects the bowels HAMMOND.

Disaffected (disăfe·ktėd), *ppl. a.* 1632. [f. DISAFFECT *v.*[1], [2] + -ED[1].] **1.** Evilly affected; estranged in affection; almost always *spec.* Unfriendly to the government, disloyal. †**2.** Affected with disease, disordered –1665. Hence **Disaffe·ctedly** *adv.*, **-ness.**

Disaffection (disăfe·kʃən). 1605. [f. DIS- 9 + AFFECTION, or f. DISAFFECT *v.*[1], [2], after AFFECTION.] **1.** Absence or alienation of affection or good will; *esp.* toward the government. †**2.** Physical disorder or indisposition –1741.

1. Nor any dis-affection to the state Where I was bred B. JONS.

†**Disaffe·ctionate**, *a. rare.* 1636. [DIS- 10.] Wanting in affection; disloyal –1796.

Disaffirm (disăfə̄·ɹm), *v.* 1531. [DIS- 6.] *trans.* To contradict, deny, negative: the contrary of to AVER 1548. **b.** *Law.* To annul or reverse (a decision, etc.); to repudiate (a settlement or agreement): the contrary of CONFIRM.

Disaffirmance (disăfə̄·ɹmăns). 1610. [f. prec. + -ANCE, after AFFIRM, AFFIRMANCE.] The action of disaffirming; negation; annulment, repudiation.

A Demonstration in d. of any thing that is affirmed HALE. So **Disaffirma·tion.** **Disaffi·rmative** *a.*

Disafforest (disăfǫ·rėst), *v.* 1598. [– AL. *disafforestare*, f. *dis-* DIS- 4 + *afforestare* AFFOREST. Cf. synon. DEAFFOREST, DEFOREST, DISFOREST.] *trans.* To free from the operation of the forest laws; to reduce from the legal state of forest to that of ordinary land.

The whole inclosed with a Pale, and disaforested 1725. Hence **Disafforesta·tion.** **Disaffo·restment.**

Disa·ggregate, *v.* 1828. [f. DIS- 6. Cf. Fr. *désagréger.*] **1.** To separate (an aggregate) into its component particles. **2.** *intr.* (for *refl.*) To separate from an aggregate 1881. Hence **Disaggrega·tion.**

Disagree (disăgrī·), *v.* 1494. [– (O)Fr. *désagréer*, f. *des-* DIS- 4 + *agréer* AGREE.] **1.** *intr.* To differ; not to AGREE, correspond, or harmonize. Const. *with*, †*to*, †*from*. **2.** To differ in opinion; to dissent 1559. **3.** To refuse to accord or agree. Const. *to*, *with*, †*from*. 1495. **4.** To be at variance, to dispute or quarrel 1548. **5.** Of food, climate, etc.: To conflict in operation or effect; to be unsuitable. Const. *with.* 1563.

1. Tradition..disagreeing to the Scripture BP. STILLINGFL. **2.** Who shall decide when Doctors d. POPE. **3.** I shall move to d. to that clause GLADSTONE. **4.** Men onely d. Of creatures rational MILT. *P. L.* II. 497. **5.** So plain a dish Could scarcely d. SHELLEY. Hence **Disagre·er** (*rare*).

Disagreeable (disăgrī·ăb'l), *a.* (*sb.*) ME. [– (O)Fr. *désagréable*, f. *des-* DIS- 4 + *agréable* AGREEABLE.] †**1.** Not in agreement. Const. *to*, *with.* –1766. **2.** Not in accordance with one's taste or liking; exciting displeasure or disgust 1698. **3.** Of persons: Unamiable; offensive 1710. **4.** *sb.* A disagreeable †person, thing, or experience 1781.

2. In regard to d...things, prudence does not consist in evasion..but in courage EMERSON. **2.** A very d. man 1825. **4.** The disagreeables of life C. BRONTË. Hence **Disagree:abi·lity**, unpleasantness. **Disagree·ableness**, the quality of being d. **Disagree·ably** *adv.* in a d. manner or degree.

†**Disagree·ance.** 1548. [f. DISAGREE *v.*, after contemporary *agreeance*. Cf. OFr. *desagreance.*] = DISAGREEMENT –1597.

Disagreement (disăgrī·mĕnt). 1495. [f. DISAGREE *v.*, after AGREEMENT.] **1.** Want of agreement or harmony; difference; discordance 1576. **2.** Refusal to agree or assent 1495. **3.** Difference of opinion; dissent 1576. **4.** Quarrel, dissension, strife 1589. **5.** Unsuitableness to the constitution 1702. **6.** An unpleasantness. [Fr. *désagrément.*] *rare.* 1778.

†**Disallie·ge**, *v. rare.* [f. DIS- 6 + **alliege*, deduced from ALLEGIANCE.] To alienate from allegiance. MILTON.

Disallow (disălau·), *v.* ME. [– OFr. *desalouer*, f. *des-* DIS- 4 + *alouer* ALLOW.] To refuse to ALLOW (in various senses). †**1.** *trans.* To refuse to laud; to blame –1656. **2.** To refuse to sanction; to disapprove of (*arch.*) 1494. Also †*intr.* with *of*. †**3.** To refuse to accept with approval –1660. Also †*intr.* with *of*. **4.** To refuse to admit (intellectually) ME. **5.** To refuse to grant 1555. **6.** To forbid the use of 1563.

1. Like errour which wise men disalowe 1510. **2.** The auditor also disallowed the refreshments the committee had 1892. **3.** What followes if we d. of this *John* I. i. 16. **4.** To d. a hypothesis RAY. **5.** To d. a claim 1841. **6.** He utterly disallowes all hote Bathes in melancholy BURTON. Hence †**Disallow·able** *a.* not to be allowed. **Disallow·ance**, the action of disallowing; disapproval, rejection, prohibition; in †*Mus.*, an irregularity. **Disallow·er.**

Disally (disǎləi·), *v. rare.* 1671. [DIS- 6.] To free from alliance.

†**Disalte·rn,** *v. rare.* [f. DIS- 5 + L. *alternare.*] *trans.* To alter for the worse. QUARLES.

Disamis (di·sǎmis). 1551. *Logic.* The mnemonic term for the second mood of the third syllogistic figure, in which a particular affirmative major premiss (*i*), and a universal affirmative minor (*a*), yield a particular affirmative conclusion (*i*).

†**Disana·logy.** *rare.* 1610. [DIS- 9.] Want of analogy –1641.

Disanchor (disæ·ŋkəɹ), *v.* 1470. [– OFr. *desancrer*, f. *des-* DIS- 4 + *ancrer* ANCHOR *v.*] **1.** *trans.* To loosen (a ship) from its anchorage 1477. **2.** *intr.* To weigh anchor.

†**Disange·lical,** *a.* 1687. [DIS- 10.] The reverse of angelical –1736.

Disanimate (disæ·nimeᶦt), *v.* 1583. [f. DIS- 6 + ANIMATE *v.*, prob. after Fr. *désanimer.*] **1.** To deprive of life 1646. **2.** To deprive of spirit; to discourage, dishearten.

2. Disanimated at disasters C. MATHER. Hence **Disa:nima·tion.**

Disannex (disǎne·ks), *v.* 1495. [– OFr. *desannexer*; see DIS- 1, ANNEX. Cf. mod.L. *disannexus.*] *trans.* To separate (that which is annexed); to disjoin.

To d. from the Provostship of the College (Oriel) a canonry of Rochester 1869. Hence **Disannexa·tion.**

Disannul (disǎnʊ·l), *v.* 1494. [DIS- 5.] **1.** To cancel and do away with; to bring to nothing, abolish, annul. †**2.** To deprive by the annulment of one's title; *fig.* to do out *of*. Const. *from, of.* –1613.

1. Wilt thou also d. my judgment *Job* 40:8. Hence **Disannu·ller. Disannu·lment.**

Disanoint (disǎnoi·nt), *v.* 1648. [DIS- 6.] To undo the anointing of; as, *to d. a king.*

†**Disappa·rel,** *v.* 1580. [f. DIS- 6 + APPAREL *v.*; cf. OFr. *des(a)pareillier.*] To deprive of apparel; to disrobe, undress. Also *fig.* –1655.

The Cup..does d. the soul FELTHAM.

Disappear (disǎpiᵊ·ɹ), *v.* 1530. [f. DIS- 6 + APPEAR, after Fr. *disparaître.*] **1.** *intr.* To cease to appear or be visible; to vanish from sight; to be traceable no farther. **2.** To cease to be present, to depart; to pass away, be lost 1665.

1. The vysion disapered incontynent PALSGR. A moraine..disappearing at the summit of the cascade TYNDALL. **2.** As duly as the swallows d. COWPER. Hence **Disappea·rance,** the action of disappearing. **Disappea·rer.**

†**Disappe·ndancy, -ency.** *rare.* 1760. [DIS- 9.] *Law.* The condition of being disappendant; an instance of this.

†**Disappe·ndant, -ent,** *a.* 1642. [DIS- 10.] *Law.* The opposite of APPENDANT; detached from being an appendancy –1760.

Disappoint (disǎpoi·nt), *v.* 1494. [–(O)Fr. *désappointer*, f. *des-* DIS- 4 + *appointer* APPOINT *v.*] **1.** *trans.* To undo the appointment of; to dispossess, deprive. *Obs.* (exc. as *nonce-wd.*) 1586. **2.** To frustrate the expectation of; to defeat, balk, or deceive in fulfilment of a desire. Const. †*of, in, with.* 1494. †**3.** To break off (what has been appointed); to fail to fulfil an appointment with –1633. **4.** To undo or frustrate anything appointed or determined; to defeat; to balk, foil, thwart 1579; †to undo, destroy –1712.

2. [They] were miserably disappointed of their expectations 1697. **4.** The wary Trojan shrinks, and, bending low Beneath his buckler, disappoints the blow POPE. To d. expectations LADY M. W. MONTAGU, good works STEELE. Hence **Disappoi·ntingly** *adv.*

Disappoi·nted, *ppl. a.* 1552. [f. prec. + -ED¹.] **1.** Having one's expectations frustrated; foiled, thwarted. †**2.** Improperly equipped; unprepared –1659.

2. Cut off euen in the Blossomes of my Sinne, Vnhouzzled, d., vnnaneld *Haml.* I. v. 77.

Disappointment (disǎpoi·ntmĕnt). 1614. [f. DISAPPOINT *v.* + -MENT; cf. Fr. *désappointement.*] **1.** The fact of disappointing; the frustration or non-fulfilment of expectation, intention, or desire; an instance of this. **2.** The state of being disappointed 1756. **3.** *ellipt.* A thing or person that disappoints 1765.

1. Hope will predominate in every mind, till it has been suppressed by frequent disappointments JOHNSON. **2.** No one ever lays one [a newspaper] down without a feeling of d. LAMB.

Disappreciate (disǎprī·ʃiˌeᶦt), *v.* 1828. [DIS- 6.] To regard with the reverse of appreciation; to undervalue. So **Disappre·ciation.**

Disapprobation (disæ·probēᶦ·ʃən). 1647. [DIS- 9.] The act or fact of disapproving; moral condemnation; disapproval.

Disapprobative (disæ·prŏbeᶦtiv), *a.* 1824. [DIS- 10.] Characterized by or expressing disapprobation. So **Disa·pprobatory** *a.*

Disappropriate (disæprōᵘ·priˌĕt), *ppl. a.* 1613. [– med.L. *disappropriatus*, pa. pple. of *disappropriare*; see next, -ATE².] Deprived of appropriation; severed from connection with a religious corporation.

Disappropriate (disæprōᵘ·priˌeᶦt), *v.* 1645. [– *disappropriat-*, pa. ppl. stem of med.L. *disappropriare*; see DIS- 4, APPROPRIATE *v.*] **1.** *trans.* To dissolve the appropriation of 1656. †**2.** To render no longer the private property or possession of any one. MILT.

1. A Bill for the disappropriating of the Rectory appropriate to Preston 1656. Hence **Disappropria·tion,** the action of rendering disappropriate.

Disapproval (disǎprū·vǎl). 1662. [f. next + -AL¹.] The act or fact of disapproving; moral condemnation; disapprobation.

Disapprove (disǎprū·v), *v.* 1481. [f. DIS- 4 + APPROVE *v.*] †**1.** *trans.* To prove to be untrue or wrong –1793. **2.** To feel or express disapprobation of 1647. Also *intr.* with *of*, †*to* (*rare*).

2. Why must I hear what I d., because others see what they approve STEELE. Hence **Disappro·vable** *a.* **Disappro·ver,** one who disapproves. **Disappro·vingly** *adv.* in a disapproving manner.

Disard, obs. or arch. f. DIZZARD.

Disarm (disǎ·ɹm), *v.* ME. [– (O)Fr. *désarmer*, f. *des-* DIS- 4 + *armer* ARM *v.*] **1.** *trans.* To deprive of arms; to take the arms or weapons from. Const. *of.* 1481. Also *intr.* (for *refl.*) **2.** *trans.* To deprive of means of attack or defence 1602. **3.** To reduce to the customary peace footing. Usu. *absol.* or *intr.* (for *refl.*) 1727. **4.** *fig.* To deprive of power to injure or terrify; to divest of aversion, suspicion, or the like; to render harmless. Const. *of*, †*from.* ME.

1. A proclamation for disarming papists BLACKSTONE. He may be disarmed by the 'Left Parry' 1833. **3.** On the conclusion of peace it is usual for both sides to d. 1727. **4.** Conscious security disarms the cruelty of the monarch GIBBON. Hence **Disa·rm** *sb.* the act of disarming (an opponent). **Disa·rmer.**

Disarmament (disǎ·ɹmǎmĕnt). 1795. [f. prec. + -MENT, after Fr. *désarmement.*] The action of disarming; *esp.* reduction to the customary peace footing.

Disa·rmature. [f. DISARM *v.*, after ARMATURE.] The action of disarming. SIR W. HAMILTON.

Disarrange (disǎrēᶦ·ndʒ), *v.* 1744. [DIS- 6; cf. Fr. *désarranger.*] *trans.* To undo the arrangement of; to put into disorder. Hence **Disarra·ngement,** the fact of disarranging; disorder.

Disarray (disǎrēᶦ·), *sb.* ME. [– AFr. **desarei*, OFr. *desaroi* (mod. *désarroi*); see DIS- 4, ARRAY *sb.*] **1.** The condition of being out of array or regular order; disorder, confusion. **2.** Imperfect or improper attire (*arch.*) 1590.

1. They..put hem to flyght and disaraye CAXTON.

Disarray (disǎrēᶦ·), *v.* 1470. [f. DIS- 6 + ARRAY *v.*, perh. after OFr. *desareer, desareier, -oier*, f. *desaroi*; see prec.] **1.** *trans.* To throw out of array or order; to disorganize. (Chiefly of military array.) **2.** To strip or spoil of personal array; to disrobe 1483; to strip *of* any adjunct 1579.

1. At the first skirmish the enemies were disaraied HOLLAND. **2.** That witch they disaraid, And robd of roiall robes SPENSER *F. Q.* I. viii. 46. My song, its pinions disarrayed of might, Drooped SHELLEY. Hence †**Disarray·ment** (*rare*), the fact of disarraying; derangement.

†**Disarre·st,** *v.* 1528. [– OFr. *desarrester* or med.L. *disarrestare*; see DIS- 4, ARREST *v.*] To set free from arrest –1643.

Disarticulate (disaɹti·kiŭleᶦt), *v.* 1830. [DIS- 6.] To disjoint or become disjointed; to separate at the joints. Hence **Disarticula·tion. Disarti·culator,** he who or that which disarticulates.

†**Disasse·nt,** *v.* ME. [– OFr. *desassentir*, f. *des-* DIS- 4 + *assentir* ASSENT *v.*] *intr.* To disagree –1692. Hence †**Disasse·nt** *sb.* dissent. †**Disasse·nter.**

†**Disassidu·ity.** 1613. [DIS- 9.] Want of assiduity; slackness –1635.

Disassimilation (disǎsi:milēᶦ·ʃən). 1880. [DIS- 9.] The process which reverses assimilation; in *Physiol.* the transformation of assimilated substances into less complex and waste substances; catabolism. So **Disassi·milate** *v.* to transform by catabolism.

Disassociate (disǎsōᵘ·ʃiˌeᶦt), *v.* 1603. [DIS- 6.] To free or detach from association; to dissociate, sever. Const. *from* (*with*). So **Disasso:cia·tion,** dissociation.

Disaster (dizɑ·stəɹ), *sb.* 1590. [– Fr. *désastre* or its source It. *disastro*, f. *dis-* DIS- 4 + *astro* (:– L. *astrum*) star. Cf. *ill-starred.*] †**1.** An unfavourable aspect of a star or planet; 'an obnoxious planet' –1635. **2.** Anything ruinous or distressing that befalls; a sudden or great misfortune, or mishap; a calamity. Also †*attrib.*

1. Disasters in the sun *Haml.* I. i. 118. **2.** The day's disasters in the morning's face GOLDSM. A record of d. 1896. Hence †**Disa·sterly** *adv.* in an ill-starred manner.

†**Disa·ster,** *v.* 1580. [f. prec. sb.] *trans.* To bring disaster upon; to strike with calamity; to ruin, afflict, endamage –1812.

At his disastred iourney made into Barbary 1598.

Disastrous (dizɑ·strəs), *a.* 1586. [– Fr. *désastreux* – It. *disastroso*; see DISASTER *sb.*, -OUS.] †**1.** Stricken with or subject to disasters; ill-starred, ill-fated; unfortunate –1790. **2.** Foreboding disaster, unpropitious, ill-boding (*arch.*) 1603. **3.** Of the nature of a disaster; fraught with disaster; calamitous 1603.

1. Always desastrous in love MARSTON. **2.** Some dysastrous aspect of the Planets 1648. **3.** Heavy rains followed by d. floods LYELL. Hence **Disa·strous-ly** *adv.*, **-ness.**

†**Disatti·re,** *v.* 1598. [DIS- 6.] To divest of attire; disrobe –1677.

†**Disaugme·nt,** *v.* 1611. [DIS- 6.] To diminish –1635.

†**Disauthe·ntic,** *a.* 1591. [DIS- 10.] Not authoritative –1619.

†**Disau·thorize,** *v.* 1548. [DIS- 6.] To strip of authority; to make or treat as of no authority –1689.

Disavai·l, *v.* ? *Obs.* ME. [DIS- 6.] †**1.** *intr.* To be prejudicial –1549. **2.** *trans.* To disadvantage 1471. Hence †**Disavai·l** *sb.* disadvantage.

Disavaunce, Disaventure, obs. ff. DISADVANCE, DISADVENTURE.

†**Disavou·ch,** *v.* 1597. [DIS- 6.] = DISAVOW –1679.

Disavow (disǎvau·), *v.* ME. [– (O)Fr. *désavouer*, f. *des-* DIS- 4 + *avouer* AVOW *v.*¹] **1.** *trans.* To refuse to avow; to disclaim knowledge of, responsibility for, or approbation of; to disown, repudiate. †**2.** To refuse to acknowledge as true; to deny –1660. †**3.** To decline –1660.

1. Melfort never disavowed these papers MACAULAY. **2.** Yet can they never..d. my blood Plantagenet's FORD. **3.** They..d. to have any further dealing with worldly contentments FULLER. Hence **Disavow·al,** the action of disavowing; repudiation, denial. †**Disavow·ance,** disavowal (*rare*). **Disavow·er,** one that disavows. †**Disavow·ment,** disavowal (*rare*). †**Disavow·ry,** disavowal.

Disband (disbæ·nd), *v.* 1591. [– Fr. †*desbander* (mod. *dé-*), f. *des-* DIS- 1 + *bande* BAND *sb.*³] **1.** *trans.* To break up (a company); to dismiss from service; †to discharge. †**2.** To let loose, turn off or out, send away –1790. †**3.** To break up the constitution of, dissolve –1793. **4.** *intr.* (for *refl.*) To break up as a body of soldiers; to break rank, fall into disorder, disperse; to leave military service 1598. †**5.** To dissolve; to separate, retire from association –1697.

1. The Marquiss of Huntley..disbanded his forces BP. GUTHRY. **2.** And therfore..she [the wife] ought to be disbanded MILT. **4.** I commanded our men not to d., but pursue them SIR F. VERE. **5.** When both rocks and all things shall

d. G. HERBERT. Hence **Disba·ndment,** the action or fact of disbanding.

†**Disba·r,** *v.*[1] 1565. [f. DIS- 1 + BAR *v.*; see DEBAR.] = DEBAR *v.* –1598.

Disbar (disbā·ɹ), *v.*[2] 1633. [f. DIS- 7 + BAR *sb.*[1]] To expel from the bar; to deprive of the status and privileges of a barrister. Hence **Disba·rment.**

†**Disbark** (disbā·ɹk), *v.*[1] 1552. [– Fr. †*desbarquer* (mod. *débarquer*; see DEBARK *v.*[1]), f. *des-* DIS- 4 + *barque* BARK *sb.*[2]] = DEBARK *v.*[1] –1842.

Disba·rk, *v.*[2] 1578. [f. DIS- 7 a + BARK *sb.*[1]; cf. DEBARK *v.*[2]] = DEBARK *v.*[2]

†**Disba·se,** *v. rare.* 1592. [f. DIS- 5 + BASE *v.*[1]] = DEBASE –1601.

Before I will d. mine honour so GREENE.

†**Disbeco·me,** *v.* 1632. [f. DIS- 6 + BECOME *v.*] *trans.* To misbecome –1639.

Disbelief (disbǐlī·f). 1672. [DIS- 9; superseded MISBELIEF (XIII).] The action or an act of disbelieving; mental rejection of a statement; positive unbelief.

Our belief or d. of a thing does not alter the nature of the thing TILLOTSON (J.). A d. in ghosts 1865.

Disbelieve (disbǐlī·v), *v.* 1644. [DIS- 6; superseded MISBELIEVE (XIV).] **1.** *trans.* Not to believe or credit; to refuse credence to. Also *absol.* or *intr.* **2.** *intr.* with *in*: Not to believe in 1834.

Plutarch disbelieved Phanias BENTLEY. It does not rest with any man to determine what he shall believe or what he shall d. CARPENTER. Hence **Disbelie·ver.**

Disbe·nch, *v.* 1607. [DIS- 7 c.] †**1.** To displace from a bench or seat. *Cor.* II. ii. 75. **2.** To deprive of the status of a bencher 1874.

†**Disbe·nd,** *v.* 1607. [f. DIS- 6 + BEND *v.*; cf. OFr. *desbender*, var. of *desbander* (mod. *débander*) in same sense.] To unbend, relax –1632.

†**Disbi·nd,** *v. rare.* 1638. [DIS- 6.] To unbind, to loose.

†**Disbla·me,** *v.* ME. [– OFr. *desblasmer*, f. *des-* DIS- 4 + *blasmer* BLAME *v.*] To free from blame, exculpate –1656.

Disbody (disbǫ·di), *v.* 1646. [DIS- 7.] = DISEMBODY. Hence **Disbo·died** *ppl. a.* disembodied.

†**Disbo·gue,** *v. rare.* 1600. [f. Sp. *desbocar* = *desembocar*, whence DISEMBOGUE. See DIS- 4.] *intr.* = DISEMBOGUE –1628.

Disbosca·tion. 1726. [– med.L. *disboscatio*, f. *dis-* DIS- 4 + *boscus, boscum* wood; see BOSK, -ATION.] The clearing away of woods; the conversion of wooded land into arable or pasture.

Disbowel (disbau·ĕl), *v.* ME. [DIS- 7 a.] = DISEMBOWEL (*lit.* and *fig.*).

Disbranch (disbra·nʃ), *v.* 1575. [DIS- 7 a.] **1.** *trans.* To cut or break off the branches of. **2.** To cut or break off, as a branch; to sever 1605.

Disbud (disbɒ·d), *v.* 1725. [DIS- 7 a.] To remove the buds of; to deprive of (superfluous) buds.

Disburden, -burthen (disbɔ̄·ɹd'n, -bɔ̄·ɹð'n), *v.* 1531. [DIS- 7 a.] **1.** *trans.* To remove a burden from; to relieve of a burden (*lit.* and *fig.*). **2.** *trans.* To get rid of (a burden); to discharge, unload 1586. Also *refl.* **3.** *intr.* (for *refl.*) To discharge its load 1667.

1. I am disburthened and eased of many cares FLEMING. **2.** Obtaining an excuse for disburdening his wrath upon her 1828. **3.** Where Nature.. by disburd'ning grows More fruitful MILT. Hence **Disbu·rdenment, -bu·rthenment,** the act of disburdening; the being disburdened.

†**Disbu·rgeon,** *v. rare.* 1601. [DIS- 7 a.] = DISBUD.

Disburse (disbɔ̄·ɹs), *v.* 1530. [– OFr. *desbourser* (mod. *débourser*, whence DEBURSE), f. *des-* DIS- 4 + *bourse* PURSE.] **1.** *trans.* To pay out or expend; to pay or defray; also *absol.* †**2.** *fig.* To spend, give out or away –1671.

1. Bid my wife D. the summe, on the receipt thereof *Com. Err.* IV. i. 38. Hence †**Disbu·rse** *sb.*, **Disbu·rsement,** the act or fact of disbursing; money paid out; expenditure. **Disbu·rser.**

Disburthen; see DISBURDEN.

Disc, var. sp. of DISK, now usual.

†**Disca·binet,** *v.* [DIS- 7.] To disclose, as cabinet secrets. MILT.

Discage (diskē·dʒ), *v.* 1649. [DIS- 7 c.] To let out as from a cage; to uncage.

Discal (di·skăl), *a.* 1848. [f. L. *discus* + -AL[1].] Of, pertaining to, or of the nature of, a disc; discoid.

Discalceate (diskæ·lsi,ĕt). 1658. [– L. *discalceatus* unshod, f. *dis-* DIS- 4 + *calceatus*, f. *calceus* shoe; see -ATE[2].]

A. *ppl. a.* Barefooted.

B. *sb.* A barefooted friar or nun.

†**Disca·lceate,** *v. rare.* 1623. [– *discalceat-*, pa. ppl. stem of late L. *discalceare*; see prec., -ATE[3].] To pull off the shoes. Hence †**Discalcea·tion,** the action of taking off the shoes.

Discalced (diskæ·lst), *ppl. a.* 1631. [An abbreviated var. of *discalceated* (= DISCALCEATE *ppl. a.*), after Fr. *déchaux*, repr. a pop. L. **discalceus.*] = DISCALCEATE *ppl. a.*

†**Discamp** (diskæ·mp), *v.* 1574. [– It. *scampare*, with *dis-* for *s-*; cf. DECAMP.] **1.** *intr.* To raise or break up a camp; to decamp. Also *fig.* –1693. **2.** *trans.* To remove or abandon (a camp); to force to abandon a camp –1658.

†**Disca·ndy,** *v. rare.* [DIS- 6.] *intr.* To melt or dissolve out of a candied condition. SHAKS.

Disca·nonize, *v.* 1605. [DIS- 6.] †**1.** To exclude from the canon –1660. **2.** To undo the canonization of 1797. Hence **Dis-canoniza·tion.**

Discant, var. of DESCANT.

Discapa·citate, *v. rare.* 1660. [DIS- 6.] To deprive of capacity, to incapacitate.

Discard (diskā·ɹd), *v.* 1586. [f. DIS- 7 c + CARD *sb.*[2], after Fr. †*descarter*, †*decarter*, whence DECARD.] **1.** *Cards.* To throw out (a card) from the hand. Also *absol.* 1591. **2.** To cast off, cast aside, reject 1598. **3.** To dismiss from employment, service, or office; to discharge 1586.

2. We have.. discarded our faith in astrology and witches SIR B. BRODIE. **3.** My man.. is a sad dog; and the minute I come to Ireland I will d. him SWIFT. Hence **Disca·rdment,** the action of discarding (*rare*). †**Disca·rdure,** discardment.

Di·scard, *sb.* 1744. [f. prec. vb.] **1.** *Cards.* The act of discarding; also, the card discarded. **2.** That which is discarded (*rare*) 1892.

†**Disca·rnate,** *a. rare.* 1661. [f. DIS- 4 + L. *caro, carn-* flesh or late L. *carnatus* fleshy; see -ATE[2].] Stripped of flesh, as *d. bones.*

Discase (diskē·s), *v. arch.* 1596. [DIS- 7 a.] To remove the case of; to uncase, unsheathe, undress. Also *intr.* (= *refl.*)

†**Disca·tter,** *v.* [ME. *descater*, f. DE- 6 + SCATTER *v.*; later assim. to words in DI-[1], DIS-.] *trans.* To scatter abroad, disperse –1635.

†**Disce·de,** *v.* 1650. [– L. *discedere* depart, f. *dis-* DIS- 1 + *cedere* go.] *intr.* To depart, deviate –1665.

Discept (dise·pt), *v. rare.* 1652. [– L. *disceptare* contend, f. *dis-* DIS- 2, 3 + *captare* try to catch.] *intr.* To dispute, debate; to express difference of opinion, differ.

Permit me to d. 1818. So †**Discepta·tor** (*rare*).

Disceptation (diseptē·ʃən). *arch.* ME. [– OFr. *disceptation* or L. *disceptatio*, f. *disceptat-*, pa. ppl. stem of *disceptare*; see prec., -ION.] Disputation, debate.

Discern (dizɔ̄·ɹn), *v.* ME. [– (O)Fr. *discerner* – L. *discernere*, f. *dis-* DIS- 1 + *cernere* to separate.] †**1.** *trans.* To separate as distinct –1645. **2.** To recognize as distinct; to separate mentally (*arch.*) 1483. **3.** *intr.* To recognize the difference; to discriminate *between* (*arch.*) ME. **4.** *trans.* To distinguish (one thing or fact) by the intellect; to perceive distinctly ME.; *intr.* to judge *of* 1622. Also *absol.* **5.** *trans.* To distinguish by the sight (or other senses); to make out ME. Also †*intr.* or *absol.* (*rare*). ¶**6.** Formerly sometimes used for DECERN 1494.

2. To discerne the truthe from that whiche is false 1551. **4.** His swift pursuers from Heav'n Gates d. Th' advantage MILT. *P. L.* I. 326. **5.** We could d. no trace of rupture [in the ice] TYNDALL. Hence †**Disce·rnance,** difference, discernment. **Disce·rner. Disce·rning** *vbl. sb.* discrimination, discernment; *ppl. a.* showing discernment; penetrating. **Disce·rningly** *adv.*

Discernible (dizɔ̄·ɹnĭb'l), *a.* 1561. [orig. *-able*, f. DISCERN + -ABLE; later conformed to late L. *discernibilis*; see prec., -ABLE, -IBLE.] **1.** Capable of being discerned; perceptible. †**2.** Distinguishable (*from* something else) –1670.

1. When I behold with mine eyes some small scarce d. Graine or Seed HOOKER. A d. weight 1794. A d. state of danger JER. TAYLOR. Hence **Disce·rnibleness. Disce·rnibly** *adv.*

Discernment (dizɔ̄·ɹnmĕnt). 1586. [f. DISCERN *v.* + -MENT. Cf. Fr. *discernement.*] **1.** The act of discerning 168.. **2.** The faculty of discerning; discrimination; judgement; keenness of intellectual perception; penetration, insight 1586. †**3.** The act of distinguishing; a distinction –1648.

2. His d. was expressed in the choice of this important post GIBBON.

Discerp (disɔ̄·ɹp), *v.* Now *rare.* Pa. t. and pple. **discerped, discerpt.** 1482. [– L. *discerpere* tear in pieces, f. *dis-* DIS- 1 + *carpere* pick, pluck, etc.] **1.** To pluck or tear asunder, pull to pieces. Also *fig.* **2.** To pluck or tear off, sever 1655. So †**Disce·rpible** *a.* = DISCERPTIBLE.

Discerptible (disɔ̄·ɹptĭb'l), *a.* 1736. [f. *discerpt-*, pa. ppl. stem of L. *discerpere*; see prec., -IBLE.] Capable of being plucked asunder, or divided into parts. Hence **Discerptibi·lity,** divisibility.

Discerption (disɔ̄·ɹpʃən). Now *rare.* 1647. [– late L. *discerptio* (Vulg.), f. as prec.; see -ION.] **1.** The action of pulling to pieces; also *fig.* **2.** The action of tearing off, severance; *concr.* a portion torn off or severed 1688.

Disce·rptive, *a. rare.* [f. as prec. + -IVE.] Having the quality of dividing or separating; tending to pull to pieces.

†**Discession.** 1521. [– L. *discessio*, f. *discess-*, pa. ppl. stem of *discedere*; see DISCEDE, -ION.] Departure; secession; separation –1622.

Discharge (dis,tʃā·ɹdʒ), *v.* [ME. *descharge* – OFr. *descharger* (mod. *décharger*) :– Rom. **discarricare*; see DIS- 4, CHARGE *v.*]

I. 1. *trans.* To unload (a ship, etc.); to rid of a charge or load; to disburden. (Also *absol.*, and *intr.* for *refl.*) **b.** To disburden (a weapon) by letting fly the missile with which it is charged; to fire off. Also *absol.* 1555. **c.** *Electr.* (*trans.*) To rid of an electric charge 1748. Also *transf.* and *fig.* (Now *rare.*) **2.** *fig.* To relieve of (an obligation or charge); to exonerate; to release *from* ME. †**b.** *refl.* To relieve oneself of an obligation by fulfilling it –1705. **3.** *trans.* To relieve of a charge or office; (more usually) to dismiss from office, etc.; to cashier. Const. *from*, †*of.* 1476. †**4.** *trans.* To clear of a charge or accusation; to exculpate, acquit –1742. **5.** To dismiss (one charged with an offence); to release from custody, liberate 1556. **b.** To send away, let go 1586. **6.** To charge not to do; to prohibit, forbid. (Chiefly *Sc.*) 1570. **7.** *Archit.* To relieve (some part) of pressure by distributing it over adjacent parts 1667.

1. To d. a Bark 1712, muskets and blunderbusses WESLEY, a Leyden phial 1794, the Earth of its Moisture 1712. **2.** Phr. *To d. a bankrupt*: to release him from further legal liability for debts contracted before his bankruptcy. **3.** The duke of Yorke was discharged of the office of Regent F. HALL. To be discharged of employment EVELYN. **4.** To d. a constable of suspicion FIELDING. **5.** To d. a prisoner 'JUNIUS', a jury 1893. **7.** The arched ceilings.. are made of cane, to d. the Walls 1715.

II. 1. To remove (that with which anything is charged); to clear out, send out or forth, emit 1479. Also *refl.*; *esp.* of a river, to disembogue (also *intr.*) 1600. **2.** *trans.* †To remove (a charge, obligation, etc.): to get rid of –1778; in *Law*, to cancel, annul (an order of a court) 1798. **3.** To clear off, or acquit oneself of, by fulfilment or performance; to pay 1525; †to pay for –1842. **4.** To acquit oneself of, perform (a charge, office, function, etc.) 1548. **5.** *Dyeing*, etc. To remove (the dye) *from* a textile fabric, etc. **b.** To print (a fabric) with a pattern by discharging parts of the ground colour 1727.

1. To d. cargo R. H. DANA, a shot SHAKS., a dart POPE, a stroke GOLDSM., choler 1600, water 1833. **2** To d. a duty 1741. **3.** I will d. my bond SHAKS. To d. one's debts HALLAM, the Jew SHAKS. A shilling to d. his chair SWIFT. **4.** Neglygent in dyschargeinge theyr office LATIMER. **5.** Wash the Ethiop white, d. the leopard's spots CHURCHILL.

Hence **Discha·rger,** one who or that which discharges; *spec.* an apparatus for producing a charge of electricity; a *discharging rod.*

Discharge (disˌtʃā·ɹdʒ), *sb.* 1460. [f. prec.; cf. OFr. *descharge* (mod. *décharge*).] **1.** The act of freeing from or removing a charge or load; unloading (*of* a vessel, etc.); removal (*of* a cargo, etc.) 1580. **2.** The act of discharging a weapon or missile; firing off a fire-arm, letting fly an arrow, etc. Also *fig.* 1596. **3.** The act of sending out or pouring forth; emission, ejection; the rate or amount of emission 1600; *concr.* that which is emitted or poured forth 1727. **4.** The act of freeing from obligation, liability, or restraint; exoneration; exculpation; dismissal; liberation 1460. **b.** *concr.* Something that frees from obligation; as, a legal document; an acquittance; a certificate 1495. **5.** The act of clearing off a pecuniary liability; payment 1611. **6.** Fulfilment, execution 1610. **7.** †Dismissal; in *Law*, dismissal or reversal of an order of court 1677. **8.** *Archit.* The relieving some part of a building of pressure; *concr.* a contrivance for effecting this 1703. **9.** *Dyeing.* The removing the colour with which a textile fabric is charged; *concr.* a mixture used for this purpose 1836.

3. *spec.* (*Electr.*) The emission or transference of electricity between two bodies positively and negatively charged, when placed in contact or near each other. **4.** Phr. *D. of a bankrupt*: release from further legal liability for debts contracted before his bankruptcy. His receiving a d. from guilt 1836. There is no d. in that warre *Eccles.* 8:8. Death, who sets all free, Hath paid his ransom now and full d. MILT. *Sams.* 1573. **5.** A penny Cord..of what's past, is, and to come, the d. *Cymb.* V. iv. 173. **6.** The d. of our duty 1675.

Discharm (disˌtʃā·ɹm), *v.* 1480. [– OFr. *descharmer, de-,* f. *des-* DIS- 4 + *charmer* to CHARM.] *intr.* and *trans.* To undo, or free from the influence of, a charm.

Dischevel, etc., obs. f. DISHEVEL, etc.

†**Dischu·rch,** *v.* 1629. [DIS- 7.] **1.** *trans.* To cause to be no longer a church; to unchurch –1656. **2.** To exclude from the church 1651.

†**Disci·de,** *v.* 1494. [– L. *discidere* cut in pieces, f. *dis-* DIS- 1 + *cædere* cut.] To cut asunder; to cut off or away (*lit.* and *fig.*) –1679.

Disciferous (disi·fĕrəs), *a.* 1883. [f. L. *discus* + -FEROUS.] *Bot.* Bearing a disc or discs.

Discifloral (disiflōᵊ·răl), *a.* 1873. [f. L. *discus* DISK + *-florus* flowering, flowered + -AL¹.] *Bot.* Having flowers with the receptacle enlarged into a conspicuous disc surrounding the ovary: *spec.* applied to a series of orders of polypetalous exogens (*Discifloræ*).

Disciform (di·sifǫɹm), *a.* 1830. [f. as prec. + -FORM.] Discoidal.

Disci·nct, *a. rare.* 1647. [– L. *discinctus*, pa. pple. of *discingere* ungird.] Ungirt (*lit.* and *fig.*).

†**Disci·nd,** *v.* 1640. [– L. *discindere*, f. *di-* DI-¹ + *scindere* tear, rend.] To sever, separate –1691.

Disciple (disəi·p'l), *sb.* [OE. *discipul* – L. *discipulus* learner, f. *discere* learn; reinforced in ME. by OFr. *deciple*; later conformed to the L. sp.] **1.** One who attends upon another for the purpose of learning from him; a pupil or scholar. **a.** A follower of Christ during his life; *esp.* one of the Twelve. **b.** In the N.T., an early Christian; hence *absol.*, a Christian ME. **c.** A follower of any (religious) teacher OE. **d.** *gen.* A scholar or pupil. (Now *arch.*, *rhet.* or *joc.*) 1489. **2.** One who belongs to any 'school' ME. **3.** *pl.* The name of a denomination of Christians, a branch of the Baptists; called also Campbellites. (Chiefly in U.S.) 1858.

Hence †**Disci·plehood, Disci·pleship,** the condition or state of a d. †**Disci·pless,** a female d.

Disci·ple, *v.* Now *rare* or *arch.* 1492. [f. prec. sb.] †**1.** *trans.* To teach, train –1681 **2.** To make a disciple of 1647. †**3.** To subject to discipline; to chastise, correct –1651.

1. He..was Discipled of the brauest *All's Well* I. ii. 28. **2.** Go out with Zeal, D. all Mankind KEN.

Disciplinable (di·siplinăb'l), *a.* 1542. [– late L. *disciplinabilis*, f. *disciplinare* instruct; see DISCIPLINE *sb.*, -ABLE. Cf. Fr. *disciplinable.*] **1.** Amenable to discipline or teaching; docile. †**2.** Disciplinary –1677. **3.** Subject to discipline or correction 1870.

3. D. offences 1870. Hence **Disciplinableness.**

Disciplinal (di·siplinăl, disiplǝi·năl), *a.* 1628. [In sense 1 – late L. *disciplinalis*; in sense 2, f. DISCIPLINE *sb.* + -AL¹.] †**1.** = DISCIPLINABLE 1. **2.** Of, belonging to, or of the nature of discipline 1853.

Di·sciplinant. 1620. [– Sp. *disciplinantes* (pl.), or It. *disciplinanti* (pl.), f. med.L. *disciplinare* to scourge; see -ANT¹.] One who subjects himself to a course of discipline; *spec.* a flagellant.

Disciplinarian (di:siplinēᵊ·riăn). 1585. [f. as DISCIPLINARY + -AN; see -ARIAN.]

A. *adj.* **1.** *Ch. Hist.* Of or pertaining to the Disciplinarians 1593. **2.** Of or pertaining to discipline 1640.

1. The D. or Presbyterian party was extinct 1889.

B. *sb.* **1.** *Ch. Hist.* One of the English Puritans, who favoured the Genevan or Presbyterian ecclesiastical polity or discipline 1585. **2.** One who enforces discipline 1639. **3.** An advocate of strict discipline 1746.

1. All sectaries pretend to scripture; papists, anabaptists, disciplinarians SANDERSON.

Disciplinary (di·siplinări), *a.* 1593. [– med.L. *disciplinarius*, f. L. *disciplina*; see -ARY¹.] **1.** Relating to ecclesiastical discipline. **2.** Pertaining to or promoting discipline 1598. **3.** Pertaining to mental training 1644. †**4.** Acquired by learning (*rare*) –1658.

2. All these restrictions are merely d. 1866. **3.** An excellent d. instrument for the formation of character J. MARTINEAU.

†**Di·sciplinate,** *v.* 1586. [– *disciplinat-*, pa. ppl. stem of late L. *disciplinare* teach, train; see -ATE³.] To subject to instruction or discipline –1647. Hence **Di·sciplina:tory, Discipli·natory** *a.* tending to promote discipline.

Discipline (di·siplin), *sb.* ME. [– (O)Fr. *discipline* – L. *disciplina*, f. *discipulus* DISCIPLE.] †**1.** Instruction imparted to disciples or scholars; teaching; learning; education –1615. **2.** A branch of instruction; a department of knowledge ME. **3.** The training of scholars and subordinates to proper conduct and action by instructing and exercising them in the same; mental and moral training; also used *fig.* ME. **b.** *spec.* Training in the practice of arms and military evolutions; drill. Formerly, more widely: The art of war. 1489. **4.** A trained condition 1509. **5.** The order maintained and observed among persons under control or command 1667; a system of rules for conduct 1659. **6.** *Eccles.* The system by which order is maintained in a church; the procedure whereby this is carried out; the exercise of penal measures by a Christian Church 1549. **b.** *spec.* The ecclesiastical polity of the Puritan or Presbyterian party (thence styled DISCIPLINARIANS) in the 16th and 17th c. 1574. **7.** Correction; chastisement; in religious use, the mortification of the flesh by penance; also, a beating, or the like ME. Hence *transf.* A whip or scourge 1622. †**8.** Medical regimen (*rare*) 1754.

1. *Tr. & Cr.* II. iii. 31. **2.** Professors of arts and disciplines at Paris BURTON. **3.** Certainely wife and children are a kind of d. of humanity BACON. A man not ignorant in the disciplyne of warre EDEN. **4.** Sound-headed men, Of proper d., and excellent mind 1827. **5.** The lawless Troops, which d. disclaim DRYDEN. The d. of workshops, of schools, of private families MACAULAY. Submitted to an almost monastic d. M. PATTISON. **7.** With a rope's-end..he continued this d. c1790. On the floor lay a d., or penitential scourge SCOTT.

Di·scipline, *v.* ME. [– (O)Fr. *discipliner* or late and med.L. *disciplinare*, f. L. *disciplina* DISCIPLINE.] **1.** *trans.* To subject to discipline; in earlier use, to educate, train; later, *esp.* to bring under control. **b.** *spec.* To train in military exercises and prompt action in obedience to command; to drill 1598. **c.** To subject to ecclesiastical discipline 1828. **2.** To inflict penitential discipline upon; hence, to chastise, thrash, punish ME.

1. Disciplined in the school of adversity BURGON. **2.** Ha's he disciplin'd Auffidius soundly *Cor.* II. i. 139. Hence **Di·sciplíner,** one who disciplines.

Discipular (disi·piŭlăɹ), *a.* 1859. [f. L. *discipulus* DISCIPLE + -AR¹.] Of, belonging to, or of the nature of, a disciple.

Discission (disi·ʃən). 1647. [– late L. *discissio*, f. *disciss-*, pa. ppl. stem of L. *discindere* DISCIND.] *Surg.* An incision into a tumour or cataract. *Obs.* in gen. sense.

Disclaim (disklēⁱ·m), *v.* 1560. [– law AFr. *desclaim-*, tonic stem of *desclamer* (AL. *disclamare*), f. *des-* DIS- 4 + *clamer* CLAIM.] **1.** *intr. Law.* To renounce a legal claim. Const. †*in* the thing, †*out of* or *from* the claim of the other party. 1574. †**2.** *intr.* To disavow all part *in* –1637; to proclaim one's renunciation of, or dissent *from* –1644. **3.** *trans. Law.* To renounce a legal claim to; to repudiate a connection with 1595. **4.** To disavow any claim to or connection with; to disown formally 1593. **5.** To refuse to admit; to renounce 1659; †to refuse –1805. †**6.** To cry out upon the claims of –1659. **7.** *trans. Her.* To declare not to be entitled to bear arms; to 'make infamous by proclamation' 1634.

1. The lord may disclaime..which signifieth utterly to renounce the seignory COKE. **3.** An executor may, before probate, d. the executorship WHARTON. **4.** Sir, shee's yours, Or I disclaime her ever HEYWOOD. **5.** The troops..disclaimed the command of their superiors GIBBON. **6.** Phr. †*To d. against*: to DECLAIM against. Hence †**Disclaim** *sb.* an act of disclaiming.

Disclaimer¹ (disklēⁱ·məɹ). 1579. [– AFr. *disclaimer*, subst. use of inf.; see prec., -ER⁴.] **1.** *Law.* The action of disclaiming, renouncing, or relinquishing a legal claim; a formal refusal to accept an estate, trust, duty, etc. **2.** *gen.* A disavowal of claims or pretensions 1790. **3.** *Her.* A proclamation of persons not entitled to bear arms 1854.

Disclaimer². 1702. [f. DISCLAIM *v.* + -ER¹.] One who disclaims.

Disclamation (disklămēⁱ·ʃən). 1592. [– med.L. *disclamatio*, f. *disclamat-*, pa. ppl. stem of *disclamare*; see DISCLAIM, -ION.] Renunciation, repudiation, disclaimer.

†**Discla·nder,** *sb.* ME. [– AFr. **desclandre*, deriv. of OFr. *esclandre* :– eccl. L. *scandalum*; see ESCLANDRE.] **1.** Malicious speech bringing opprobrium on any one; slander –1562. **2.** Public disgrace or opprobrium; scandal –1532.

†**Discla·nder,** *v.* [ME. *desclandre*, f. prec. sb.] **1.** *trans.* To slander –1530. **2.** To bring into public disgrace or opprobrium –1483.

†**Discloa·k,** *v.* 1599. [DIS- 6 or 7 a.] To take off the cloak of; to unrobe –1677.

†**Disclo·se,** *sb.* 1548. [f. DISCLOSE *v.*; cf. CLOSE *sb.*²] = DISCLOSURE –1625.

Disclose (disklōᵘ·z), *v.* ME. [– OFr. *desclos-*, pres. stem of *desclore* :– Gallo-Rom. **disclaudere*; see DIS- 4, CLOSE *v.*] †**1.** *trans.* To open up; to unfasten –1596; to hatch (an egg) 1626. Also *intr.* **2.** *trans.* To uncover; to remove a cover from and expose to view ME.; to uncover (a young bird, etc.) from the egg; to hatch; also *fig.* Rarely, to lay (eggs). 1486. †**3.** To discover –1611. **4.** To open up to the knowledge of others; to reveal ME. Also †*intr.* for *refl.*

1. It [a rosebud] discloseth it selfe and spreadeth abroad B. GOOGE. **2.** The parting deep disclos'd her sand TATE & BRADY. Anon as patient as the female Doue, When that her golden Cuplet are disclos'd *Haml.* V. i. 310. **4.** Tell me your Counsels, I will not d. 'em *Jul. C.* II. i. 298.

Hence **Disclo·sed** *ppl. a.* in the senses of the vb.; in *Her.* with wings expanded: said of all birds that are not birds of prey. **Disclo·ser,** one who or that which discloses.

Disclosure (disklōᵘ·ʒⁱŭɹ). 1598. [f. prec. + -URE, after CLOSURE.] **1.** The action of disclosing, opening up to view, or revealing; discovery, exposure. **2.** That which is disclosed; a revelation 1825.

1. A public d. of his motives THIRLWALL. The d. of the insect from the pupa KIRBY. **2.** Preparing him for the d. 1825.

Discloud (disklau·d), *v.* 1600. [DIS- 7 a.] To free or clear from clouds; to reveal.

†**Disclou·t,** *v.* [DIS- 7 a.] To take out of a clout. BP. HALL.

†**Disclu·sion.** *rare.* 1656. [– L. *disclusio*, f. *disclus-*, pa. ppl. stem of *discludere* separate

by shutting up apart; infl. in sense by DISCLOSE *v.*] 'Emission' (J.) –1668.

Disco- (disko), comb. f. Gr. δίσκος quoit, DISK: as in:

Discobla·stic *a.* [Gr. βλαστός germ], *Embryol.* (of an ovum), having discoidal segmentation of the formative yolk. **Di·scocarp** [Gr. καρπός], *Bot.* (*a*) a fruit consisting of a number of achenes within a hollow receptacle, as in the rose; (*b*) the disc-liek fructification of discomycetous fungi and gymnocarpous lichens; hence **Discoca·rpous** *a.*, relating to, or having, a discocarp. **Discoce·phalous** *a.* [Gr. κεφαλή], *Zool.* belonging to the sub-order *Discocephali* of fishes, having a sucking-disc on the head. **Discoda·ctyl(e, Discoda·ctylous** *adjs.* [Gr. δάκτυλος], *Zool.* having toes dilated at the end so as to form a disc, as a tree-frog. **Discomyce·tous** *a.*, *Bot.* belonging to the order *Discomycetes* of Fungi, having a disc-shaped hymenium or *discocarp*. **Discopla·cental, Discoplacenta·lian** *adjs.*, *Zool.* belonging to the section *Discoplacentalia* of mammals, having a disc-shaped placenta. ||**Discopo·dium,** *Bot.* 'the foot or stalk on which some kinds of disks are elevated'. **Disco·podous** *a.*, *Zool.* having the foot shaped as a disc; belonging to the section *Discopoda* of Gastropods. **Discosto·matous** *a.*, *Zool.* pertaining or belonging to the class *Discostomata* of *Protozoa*, containing the sponges and collar-bearing monads.

†**Discoa·st,** *v.* 1598. [DIS- 6.] **1.** *intr.* To withdraw from the coast or side. **2.** *fig.* To withdraw, depart 1677.

1. Discoasting from England to the coast of Fraunce 1598. **2.** Never willingly to discost from truth and equity BARROW.

||**Discobolus** (diskǫ·bǒlǒs). 1727. [L. – Gr. δισκόβολος, f. δίσκος DISCUS + *bol, var. base of βάλλειν throw.] *Class. Antiq.* A thrower of the DISCUS; an ancient statue representing a man in the act of throwing the discus.

†**Discohe·rent,** *a.* 1600. [DIS- 10.] Without coherence –1675.

Discoid (di·skoid). 1794. [– Gr. δισκοειδής, f. δίσκος; see DISCUS, -OID.]

A. *adj.* **1.** Disc-shaped; (more or less) flat and circular; in *Conchol.* used of spiral shells of which the whorls lie in one plane 1830. **2.** *Bot.* Of composite flowers: Having, or consisting of, a disc only, with no ray, as in Tansy 1794. So **Discoi·dal** *a.*

B. *sb.* A body resembling a disc in shape; in *Conchol.* a discoid shell. Cf. A. 1. 1828.

Discolith (di·skoliþ). 1875. [f. DISCO- + -LITH.] *Biol.* A kind of coccolith of the form of a flattened disk. (Cf. CYATHOLITH.)

Discolor (di·skɒləɹ, -kǫlǒɹ), *a.* 1866. [– L. *discolor* variegated, f. *dis-* DIS- 1 + *color* COLOUR *sb.*] Of different colours; also, of a different colour from some other part or organ. So **Disco·lorous** *a.*

Discolor, *v.*: see DISCOLOUR.

Discolorate (diskɒ·lərēⁱt), *v. rare.* 1651. [– *discolorat-*, pa. ppl. stem of med.L. *discolorare*; see DISCOLOUR, -ATE³.] *trans.* = DISCOLOUR *v.* 1.

Discoloration, discolouration (diskɒlər-, -kǫlǒrēⁱ·ʃən). 1642. [– Fr. †*discoloration* (mod. *dé-*) or med.L. *discoloratio*, f. as prec.; see -ION.] The action of discolouring or condition of being discoloured; alteration or loss of colour; discolourment. **b.** *concr.* A discoloured marking; a stain. **Discoloriza·tion** (*rare*).

Discolour, discolor (diskɒ·ləɹ), *v.* ME. [– OFr. *descolorer* or med.L. *discolorare*, f. *dis-* DIS- 4 + L. *colorare* COLOUR *v.*; in sense 3 – L. *discolor* DISCOLOR *a.*] **1.** *trans.* To alter the proper colour of; *esp.* to make of a dingy or unnatural colour; to stain, tarnish. Also *fig.* **2.** *intr.* (for *refl.*) To become discoloured; to lose or change colour. Also *fig.* 1641. †**3.** *trans.* To render of different colours, or different in colour –1665.

1. We shall your tawnie ground with your red blood D. *Hen. V*, III. vi. 171. *fig.* Some whimsey in the brain..which discoloured all experience to its own shade STEVENSON. So **Disco·lour, disco·lor** *sb.* (now *rare*), discoloured state; loss or change of colour; discoloration, stain. Hence **Disco·loured, -lored** *ppl. a.* altered from the natural colour; †without colours (*nonce-use*); variegated; differently coloured, the one from the other. **Disco·lourment,** discoloration.

Discomfit (diskɒ·mfit), *v.* [ME. *disconfite*, based on pa. pple. *disconfit* (XIII) – OFr. *desconfit*, pa. pple. of *desconfire* (mod. *déconfire*) :– Rom. **disconficere*, f. *dis-* DIS- 4 + L. *conficere* put together, destroy, consume.] **1.** *trans.* To undo in battle; to defeat completely; to rout. **2.** *gen.* To defeat the plans or purposes of; to foil. **b.** To throw into perplexity, confusion, or dejection; to disconcert ME.

1. Hys men..which wer in maner disconfit, and redy to flye 1548. **2.** Wel go with me, and be not so discomfited *Tam. Shr.* II. i. 164. Dombey was quite discomfited by the question DICKENS. Hence †**Disco·mfit** *sb.* discomfiture. **Disco·mfiter,** one who or that which discomfits.

Discomfiture (diskɒ·mfitiŭɹ). ME. [– OFr. *desconfiture* (mod. *dé-*), f. *desconfit*; see prec., -URE.] The action of discomfiting, or fact of being discomfited: **a.** Complete defeat, overthrow, rout; **b.** Defeat or frustration of plans or hopes; **c.** Complete disconcertment.

Sad tidings..Of losse, of slaughter, and d. 1 *Hen. VI*, I. i. 59. To rely upon promises..would end in regret and d. 1828. The d. of the questioner 1885.

Discomfort (diskɒ·mfəɹt), *sb.* [ME. *disconfort* – OFr. *desconfort* (mod. *dé-*), f. *desconforter*; see next.] †**1.** Undoing of courage; discouragement –1551. †**2.** Absence of comfort or gladness; distress, grief, sorrow, annoyance –1847. **3.** Now: The condition of being uncomfortable; uneasiness 1841.

2. In solitude there is not only d. but weakness also SOUTH. **3.** The great d. which attends..a heavy dinner 1842. The troops..had many discomforts to endure MACAULAY.

Discomfort (diskɒ·mfəɹt), *v.* [ME. *desconfort, discom-* – OFr. *desconforter* (mod. *dé-*), f. *des-* DIS- 4, 9 + *conforter*; see COMFORT *v.*] †**1.** *trans.* To deprive of courage; to dishearten, dismay –1706. **2.** To deprive of comfort or gladness; to distress, grieve, sadden. *Obs.* or *arch.* ME. **3.** Now: To make uncomfortable or uneasy 1856. ¶Formerly often used for DISCOMFIT, q.v.

1. My Lord, you doe d. all the Hoste *Tr. & Cr.* V. x. 10. **3.** The Registrar..was discomforted by a pair of tight boots 1893. Hence **Disco·mforter.**

Discomfortable (diskɒ·mfəɹtăb'l), *a.* ME. [– OFr. *desconfortable*, f. *desconforter*; see prec., -ABLE.] **1.** Causing discomfort; destroying comfort or happiness. *Obs.* (exc. as in 2). **2.** Wanting in material comfort; causing physical discomfort 1607. **3.** Uncomfortable, uneasy 1844.

2. Pacing to and fro in his d. house STEVENSON. Hence **Disco·mfortableness.**

Discommend (diskǒme·nd), *v.* 1494. [DIS- 6.] **1.** *trans.* To express disapprobation of: the opposite of COMMEND. **2.** To speak of dissuasively: the opposite of RECOMMEND 1533. **3.** To cause to be unfavourably viewed or received. ? *Obs.* 1579.

1. Who else shall d. her choice PATMORE. **2.** Savanarola discommends Goats flesh BURTON. Hence **Discomme·ndable** *a.* worthy of censure; †not to be recommended. †**Discomme·ndableness. Disco:mmenda·tion.**

†**Discommi·ssion,** *v.* 1622. [DIS- 7.] To deprive of a commission –1659.

†**Disco·mmodate,** *v.* 1610. [prob. alt. f. INCOMMODATE.] = next –1649.

Discommode (diskǒmōᵘ·d), *v.* 1721. [– Fr. †*discommoder*, var. of *incommoder*; see INCOMMODE, on which *discommode* may be directly based.] To put to inconvenience; to disturb, trouble.

†**Discommo·dious,** *a.* 1540. [f. DIS- 10 + COMMODIOUS, or var., with change of prefix, of INCOMMODIOUS.] Causing trouble or inconvenience; disadvantageous, troublesome –1668. Hence †**Discommo·dious-ly** *adv.*, †**-ness.**

Discommodity (diskǒmǫ·dĭti). 1513. [f. DIS- 9 + COMMODITY, or var., with change of prefix, of INCOMMODITY.] The quality of being discommodious; (with *a* and *pl.*) a disadvantage, inconvenience.

Discommon (diskǫ·mən), *v.* 1478. [f. DIS- 7, 8 + COMMON *sb.* and *a.*; cf. also COMMON *v.*] †**1.** *trans.* To cut off from membership of a community; *esp.* to disfranchise; to excommunicate –1655. **2.** At Oxford and Cambridge: To deprive (a tradesman) of the privilege of dealing with undergraduates 1530. **3.** To deprive of the right of common; see COMMON *sb.* Also *fig.* **b.** To deprive of the character of a common 1597.

Discommons (diskǫ·mənz), *v.* 1852. [f. DIS- 7 a + COMMONS *sb. pl.*] **1.** To deprive of commons in a college 1856. **2.** = DISCOMMON 2.

Discommune (diskǫ·miŭn), *v.* 1590. [f. DIS- 6 + COMMUNE *v.*, or DIS- 7 a + COMMUNE *sb.*, after med.L. *discommunicare.*] †**1.** *trans.* To cut off from community or fellowship –1659. **2.** = DISCOMMON 2. 1677. So †**Discommu·nion,** exclusion from communion or fellowship.

Discommunity (diskǒmiŭ·nĭti). *rare.* [DIS- 9.] Absence of community; the quality of not having something in common. DARWIN.

†**Disco·mpanied,** *ppl. a. rare.* 1599. [f. DIS- 4 + *companied*, pa. pple. of COMPANY *v.* Cf. OFr. *descompaignier.*] Destitute of company, unaccompanied –1618.

If she bee alone, now, and d. B. JONS.

†**Discomple·xion,** *v. rare.* [DIS- 7 d.] To spoil the complexion or aspect of. SHIRLEY.

Discompli·ance. *rare.* [DIS- 9.] Non-compliance. PEPYS.

Discompose (diskǒmpōᵘ·z), *v.* 1483. [DIS- 6.] **1.** *trans.* To destroy the composure or calmness of; to ruffle, agitate. **2.** To disturb the order or arrangement of; to disarrange, disorder, unsettle. Now *rare.* 1611. †**3.** To displace, discard –1640.

1. Better for Us..That never passion discompos'd the mind POPE. No Wind..the Air to d. COWLEY. **2.** Eve, With Tresses discompos'd MILT. *P. L.* V. 10. Hence **Discompo·sed-ly** *adv.*, **-ness.** †**Discomposi·tion.** †**Discompo·sture,** discomposure.

Discomposure (diskǒmpōᵘ·ʒⁱŭɹ). 1641. [f. prec., after COMPOSURE.] **1.** The fact or condition of being discomposed; disorder; †indisposition; †dismemberment. **2.** Agitation, perturbation 1647. †**3.** Want of harmony; dissension (*rare*) –1673.

2. There was an air of d. about his whole person SCOTT.

Discompt, obs. f. DISCOUNT.

†**Disco·ncert,** *sb. rare.* 1668. [f. DIS- 9 + CONCERT *sb.*] Want of concert; disunion, disagreement in action –1839.

Disconcert (diskǒnsə̄·ɹt), *v.* 1687. [– Fr. †*desconcerter* (mod. *dé-*), f. *des-* DIS- 4 + *concerter* CONCERT *v.*] **1.** *trans.* To put out of concert; to throw into confusion, derange; now *esp.* to disarrange measures or plans concerted. **2.** To disturb the complacency or self-possession of; to ruffle, put out 1716.

1. An unforeseen accident disconcerted all his measures W. ROBERTSON. **2.** He never..disconcerts a puny satirist with unexpected sarcasms JOHNSON. Hence **Disconce·rtion, Disconce·rtment,** the action of disconcerting; the being disconcerted.

†**Discondu·ce,** *v.* [DIS- 6.] To be nonconducive *to.* DONNE. Hence †**Discondu·cive** *a.* not conducive (*rare*).

†**Disconfo·rmable,** *a.* 1603. [DIS- 10.] Unconformable –1823.

Disconformity (diskǒnfǭ·ɹmĭti). 1602. [DIS- 9.] The opposite of conformity or practical agreement; nonconformity.

D. with Rome in the keeping of Easter 1639. Conformity or d. to usage MILL.

Discongru·ity. ? *Obs.* 1624. [DIS- 9.] Absence of congruity; disagreement, inconsistency; incongruity. So †**Disco·ngruous** *a.* wanting in congruity (*rare*).

Disconnect (diskǒne·kt), *v.* 1770. [DIS- 6.] **1.** To sever the connection of or between; to disunite, separate. Const. *with, from.* **2.** To separate into disconnected parts. *Obs.* exc. in *pa. pple.* 1790.

1. To d. the drains of the defendants from the sewer 1892. **2.** They shall not induce me to d. my army WELLINGTON. Hence **Disconne·cted** *ppl. a.* having no connection; detached; separate; incoherent. **Disconne·cter, -or. Disconne·ction, -ne·xion,** the action of disconnecting (*rare*); the being disconnected or unconnected; separation; disconnectedness.

†**Disconse·nt,** *v.* 1530. [f. DIS- 4 + CONSENT *v.*] *intr.* To refuse consent; not to consent; to dissent. Const. *with, from.* –1641.

Disconsider (diskǫnsi·dəɹ), *v. rare.* 1887. [DIS- 6.] To bring into disrepute. So **Disconsidera·tion.**

†**Disco·nsolacy.** 1653. [f. DISCONSOLATE *a.*; see -ACY.] Disconsolate state –1677.

Disconsolance, -cy, errors for prec. in Dicts. (Worcester, etc.).

Disconsolate (diskǫ·nsŏlĕt), *a.* ME. [– med.L. *disconsolatus*, f. L. *dis-* DIS- 4 + *consolatus*, pa. pple. of *consolari* CONSOLE *v.*] **1.** Destitute of consolation; unhappy, comfortless; inconsolable. **2.** Of places or things: Causing or manifesting discomfort; dismal, cheerless, gloomy ME.

1. A poor d. widow 1704. On the nigh-naked tree the robin piped D. TENNYSON. **2.** The d. darkness of our winter nights RAY. Hence †**Disco·nsolate** *v.* to make d.; to deprive of consolation. **Disco·nsolate-ly** *adv.*, **-ness. Disco·nsolation.**

†**Disco·nsonant,** *a.* 1630. [DIS- 10.] Out of agreement or harmony; discordant –1806. Hence †**Disco·nsonancy.**

Discontent (diskǫnte·nt), *sb.*[1] 1588. [DIS- 9.] **1.** Want of content; dissatisfaction of mind 1591; †vexation –1678. †**2.** *transf.* An occasion of discontent; a grievance. (Usu. in *pl.*) –1620.

1. Now is the Winter of our D. Made glorious Summer by this Son of Yorke *Rich. III*, I. i. 1. Some inward d. at the ingratitude of the times BACON. **2.** An ill Liuer is my d. 1620. Hence **Disconte·ntful** *a.* full of d. (*arch.*).

Disconte·nt, *a.* and *sb.*[2] 1494. [DIS- 10; cf. Fr. †*descontent.*]

A. *adj.* **1.** Not content; dissatisfied, discontented. Const. *with, to* with *inf.* 1500. **2.** Vexed –1655.

1. He..withdrew, disconcerted and d. M. PATTISON.

B. *sb.*[2] A discontented person; a malcontent. Now *rare.* 1596.

Fickle Changelings, and poore Discontents SHAKS.

Disconte·nt, *v.* 1494. [DIS- 6; cf. Fr. †*descontenter.*] **1.** *trans.* To deprive of contentment; to make unquiet in mind; to dissatisfy. (Now chiefly in pa. pple.) 1549. **2.** To vex. *Obs.* or *arch.* 1494. Hence †**Discontenta·tion** = DISCONTENT *sb.*[1] **Disconte·nted-ly** *adv.*, **-ness.** †**Disconte·ntive** *a.* feeling, showing, or causing discontent. **Disconte·ntment** = DISCONTENT *sb.*[1]

Discontigu·ity. 1676. [DIS- 9.] Discontinuity of parts.

†**Disconti·nual,** *a.* ME. [DIS- 10.] **1.** = DISCONTINUOUS –1611. **2.** *Math.* Said of *proportion*: = DISCONTINUED –1706.

Discontinuance (diskǫnti·niu,ăns). ME. [– AFr. *discontinuaunce*, OFr. *-ance*, f. *discontinuer*; see DISCONTINUE, -ANCE.] **1.** The action of discontinuing; interruption of continuance; cessation; intermission. †**2.** A (temporary) ceasing to be in a place; absence –1677. †**3.** *Law.* An interruption of a right of possession or right of entry, consequent upon a wrongful alienation by the tenant in possession for a larger estate than he was entitled to –1768. **4.** *Law.* The interruption of a suit, or its dismissal, by reason of the plaintiff's omission of formalities necessary to keep it pending 1540.

1. The cause of the d. of the works at Lisbon WELLINGTON. The d. of agriculture 1875. **4.** The devil..is an unwearied sollicitor, and will not lose his claim by d. SANDERSON.

Discontinuation (diskǫnti:niu,ēⁱ·ʃən). 1611. [– (O)Fr. *discontinuation* – med.L. *discontinuatio*, f. *discontinuat-*, pa. ppl. stem of *discontinuare*; see next, -ION.] **1.** = DISCONTINUANCE 1. **2.** *concr.* A breach of continuity 1728.

1. The d. of the houses T. A. TROLLOPE.

Discontinue (diskǫnti·niu), *v.* ME. [– (O)Fr. *discontinuer* – med.L. *discontinuare*, f. L. *dis-* DIS- 4 + *continuare* CONTINUE.] **1.** *trans.* To cause to cease; to cease from (an action); to break off, put a stop to, give up 1479. Also *ellipt.* To cease to take, pay, etc. (*mod.*). †**2.** To cease to frequent, occupy, or inhabit 14... **3.** *Law.* **a.** To dismiss or abandon (a suit, etc.) 1487. †**b.** To alienate land in such a manner as operates to the discontinuance of the heir in tail –1818. †**4.** To interrupt, disrupt, sunder –1751. **5.** *intr.* To cease to continue; to stop 1555; †to cease to reside –1677. †**6.** To become disrupted 1626.

1. [He] begg'd that they would d. their visits 1726. To d. a subscription 1896. **4.** Solid bodies ..being once discontinued, are not easily consolidated again CUDWORTH. **5.** To d. a while from labour BARET. And thou, euen thyselfe, shalt d. from thine heritage that I gaue thee *Jer.* 17:4.

Hence **Disconti:nuee·**, one to whom an estate is aliened to the discontinuance of the heir in tail. **Disconti·nuer,** one who discontinues; †an absentee. **Disconti·nuo:r** (*Law*), the tenant in tail whose alienation of an estate has caused a discontinuance.

Discontinuity (diskǫntiniū·ĭti). 1570. [– med.L. *discontinuitas*, f. *discontinuus*; see next, -ITY.] The quality or state of being discontinuous; want of continuity; interrupted condition; (with *pl.*) a break or gap 1794.

Discontinuous (diskǫnti·niu,əs), *a.* 1667. [– med.L. *discontinuus* (f. L. *dis-* DIS- 4 + *continuus* continuous) + -OUS. Cf. Fr. *discontinu.*] †**1.** Producing discontinuity; gaping –1703. **2.** Not continuous; having interstices or breaks; interrupted, intermittent 1718.

1. The griding sword with d. wound Pass'd through him MILT. **2.** Wide spread the d. ruins lie ROWE.

Phr. *D. function* (Math.): one that varies discontinuously, and whose differential coefficient may therefore become infinite. Hence **Disconti·nuous-ly** *adv.*, **-ness.**

Disconve·nience, *sb.* ME. [f. DIS- 9 + CONVENIENCE, or var., with change of prefix, of INCONVENIENCE.] †**1.** Incongruity, inconsistency –1660. †**2.** Unfitness –1598. **3.** Incommodity; (with *pl.*) an inconvenience. Now *dial.* 1553. var. †**Disconve·niency.** Hence **Disconve·nience** *v.* to inconvenience (*dial.*).

Disconve·nient, *a.* ME. [f. DIS- 10 + CONVENIENT, or var., with change of prefix, of INCONVENIENT.] †**1.** Incongruous; unsuitable –1660. **2.** Disadvantageous. Now *dial.* 1450.

Discophoran (diskǫ·fŏrăn). 1878. [f. mod.L. *Discophora*, n. pl. of *discophorus*, – Gr. (f. δίσκος discus + -φορος bearing), taken in sense 'bearing a disc'; see -AN.] *Zool.*

A. *adj.* **1.** Belonging to the subclass *Discophora* of Hydrozoa, comprising the jelly-fishes. **2.** Belonging to the order *Discophora* of suctorial worms, synonymous with *Hirudinea* or leeches.

B. *sb.* One of the *Discophora.* Also **Di·scophore.** So **Disco·phorous** *a.* of or pertaining to the *Discophora.*

Discoplacental, etc.; see DISCO-

Discord (di·skǫɹd), *sb.* [ME. *des-, discord* – OFr. *descord, discord* (mod. *discord* m., *discorde* fem.), f. *des-, discorder*; see DISCORD *v.*] **1.** Absence of concord or harmony; dissension; diversity. **2.** *Mus.* (The opposite of CONCORD.) **a.** Dissonance. **b.** A combination of notes not in harmony with each other; a chord which requires to be resolved or followed by some other chord. **c.** The interval between two notes forming a discord. **d.** A single note which is dissonant with another, or with others of a chord. 1440. **3.** A clashing of sounds, a confused noise; a harsh or unpleasing sound 1590.

1. An Age of d. and continuall strife 1 *Hen. VI*, V. v. 63. Merry and tragicall..How shall wee finde the concord of this d. *Mids. N.* V. i. 60. **3.** So musicall a d., such sweet thunder *Mids. N.* IV. i. 123. Hence **Disco·rdful** *a.* quarrelsome.

†**Di·scord,** *a. rare.* ME. [– (O)Fr. *discord*, f. L. *discors, discord-*; see next.] Discordant –1606.

Discord (diskǭ·ɹd), *v.* ME. [– OFr. *descorder*, (also mod.) *discorder* – L. *discordare* be at variance, f. *discors, discord-* discordant, f. *dis-* DIS- 4 + *cor, cord-* heart.] **1.** *intr.* To disagree; also, to dissent *from.* **2.** Of things (chiefly): To be different (*from*), discordant (*with*) ME.; of sounds, to jar, clash ME.

1. We discorded commonly on two points CARLYLE. **2.** The one [sound] jarring or discording with the other BACON.

†**Discordable,** *a.* ME. [– OFr. *des-, discordable* – L. *discordabilis*, f. *discordare*; see prec., -ABLE.] Characterized by discord, discordant –1549.

Discordance (diskǭ·ɹdăns). ME. [– OFr. *des-*, (also mod.) *discordance* – med.L. *discordantia*, f. L. *discordare*; see DISCORD *v.*, -ANCE.] **1.** The fact of being discordant; disagreement. **2.** Discord of sounds ME.

1. The d. between the action and the law HOBBES. So **Disco·rdancy,** the condition or quality of being discordant; discord of sounds.

Discordant (diskǭ·ɹdănt), *a.* ME. [– OFr. *des-*, (also mod.) *discordant*, pres. pple. of *discorder*; see DISCORD *v.*, -ANT[1]. Cf. late L. *discordans.*] **1.** Not in accord, not in harmony; at variance; disagreeing, differing; incongruous. Const. *to, from, with.* **2.** Of sound: Inharmonious, dissonant, jarring ME.

1. The reasons and resolutions are, and must remain d. HOBBES. A d. family JOHNSON. **2.** War, with d. notes and jarring noise CONGREVE. Hence **Disco·rdant-ly** *adv.*, **-ness.**

†**Di·scordous,** *a.* [f. L. *discors, discord-* DISCORD *a.*, or Eng. DISCORD *sb.*, + -OUS.] Full of discord. BP. HALL.

Discorporate (diskǭ·ɹpŏrĕ͡ⁱt), *v. rare.* 1683. [DIS- 6.] **1.** *trans.* To deprive of corporate character. **2.** To separate from a corporate body 1891. So **Disco·rporate** *ppl. a.* (*rare*).

†**Discorrespo·ndent,** *a. rare.* 1654. [DIS- 10.] Lacking in congruity. So †**Discorrespo·ndency.**

Discost, var. of DISCOAST *v. Obs.*

†**Discostate** (diskǫ·stĕt), *a.* 1849. [f. DIS- 1 + COSTATE.] *Bot.* Of leaves: Having radiately divergent ribs.

Discostomatous; see DISCO-.

†**Discou·nsel,** *v.* 1477. [– OFr. *desconseillier* (mod. *déconseiller*), f. *des-* (DIS- 4) + *conseillier* COUNSEL *v.*] = DISADVISE 1, 2. –1631.

Discount (di·skaunt), *sb.* 1622. [– Fr. †*descompte* (earlier *desconte*), f. *descompter*; see next.] †**1.** An abatement or deduction from the amount or from the gross reckoning of anything. (Also *fig.*) –1798. **2.** *Commerce.* **a.** A deduction made for payment before it is due, or for prompt payment, of a bill or account; any deduction or abatement from the nominal value or price 1690. **b.** The interest charged for discounting a bill of exchange or promissory note 1633. **3.** The act of discounting a bill, etc. 1839.

2. Here's ready Money: Speak, what D. 1702. The *true* d. is less than the banker's or *mercantile* d. 1881.

Phrases. *At a d.*: at less than the nominal value; below par; *fig.* in low esteem, depreciated. *Banker's* or *mercantile d.*: interest on the amount of a bill for the time it has to run. *True d.*: interest on the present worth of a bill.

Comb.: **d.-broker,** one whose business is to cash notes or bills of exchange at a d.; also *d. accommodation, business, house*; (in sense 2a) *d.-bookseller.*

Discount (diskau·nt, di·skaunt), *v.*[1] 1629. [– Fr. †*descompter* (mod. *décompter*), or direct from It. (*di*)*scontare*; see DIS- 4, COUNT *v.*] †**1.** *trans.* To reckon as an abatement or deduction from a sum due –1726; to deduct –1828. **2.** To give or receive the present worth of (a bill or note) before it is due 1694. **3.** *fig.* **a.** To leave out of account; to disregard. **b.** To deduct from. **c.** To part with a future good for some present consideration. **d.** *esp.* To make allowance for exaggeration in. **e.** To take (an event, etc.) into account beforehand. 1702.

1. That the said provisions may be discounted upon the pay of the said army 1645. **3.** Of the three opinions (I d. Brown's), under this head, one supposes [etc.] SIR W. HAMILTON. To d. statements made by the natives 1883. To *d.* news 1882. Hence **Discou·ntable** *a.* that may be discounted.

†**Discount,** *v.*[2] *rare.* 1655. [DIS- 1.] To reckon separately –1662.

Discountenance (diskau·ntĭnăns), *v.* 1580. [f. DIS- 4 or 7 + COUNTENANCE *sb.*; partly after Fr. †*descontenancer.*] †**1.** To put another countenance on, to mask (*rare*) 1587. **2.** To put out of countenance, put to shame, disconcert, abash 1580. **3.** To withdraw one's countenance from, set the countenance against; to show disapprobation of; to discourage 1589.

2. How would one look from his majestic brow.. D. her despised MILT. *P. R.* II. 218. He appeared much discountenanced at this last part of my narrative CARLYLE. **3.** Duels are neither quite discountenanc'd, nor much in vogue STEELE. Hence **Discou·ntenancer.**

Discountenance (diskau·ntĭnăns), *sb. arch.* 1580. [Partly – OFr. *descontenance*; partly f. DIS- 9 + COUNTENANCE *sb*, after the vb.] **1.** The act or fact of discountenancing; unfavourable aspect, disapprobation shown. **†2.** The state of being put out of countenance; abashment –1656.

1. He thought that the estimation of Cato was altogether the d. of his [own] power and greatnesse NORTH.

Discounter (diskau·ntəɹ). 1732. [f. DISCOUNT *v.*[1] + -ER[1].] One who discounts a bill or note; see DISCOUNT *v.* 2.

Discouple (diskɒ·p'l), *v.* 1489. [– OFr. *descupler* (mod. *découpler*), f. *des-* DIS- 4 + *coupler* COUPLE *v.*] To disunite what is coupled, to uncouple. Also *intr.* (for *refl.*).

Discour, -coure, obs. ff. DISCOVER *v.*

†Discou·rage, *sb.* 1500. [DIS- 9.] Want or failure of courage; discouragement –1611.

Discourage (diskɒ·rėdʒ), *v.* 1481. [– OFr. *descouragier* (mod. *décourager*), f. *des-* DIS- 4, 7 + *courage* COURAGE.] **1.** *trans.* To deprive of courage; to lessen the courage of; to dishearten, dispirit. The opposite of *encourage*. Also †*transf.* and *fig.* **2.** *transf.* To lessen or repress courage for; to discountenance, express disapproval of, 'throw cold water on' 1641. Also †*intr.* (for *refl.*).

1. I think no Slow of Despond would d. me BUNYAN. To d. from a task 1756. **2.** Idleness should of all things be discouraged BERKELEY. Hence **Discou·rageable** *a.* capable of being discouraged; to be discouraged (*rare*). **Discou·rager,** one who or that which discourages. **Discou·ragingly** *adv.*

Discouragement (diskɒ·rėdʒmĕnt). 1561. [– OFr. *descouragement* (mod. *dé-*); see prec., -MENT.] **1.** The action or fact of discouraging 1600. **2.** The fact or state of being discouraged; want of spirit or confidence; depression of spirit with regard to effort. (The more usual sense.) 1561. **3.** That which discourages; a deterrent influence 1612.

1. His..d. of that pest of society, Attorneys H. WALPOLE. **2.** Terrour and d. 1561. **3.** The books..are full of..discouragements from vice SWIFT.

Discourse (diskōᵊ·ɹs), *sb.* [ME. *discours* – L. *discursus* running to and fro, (late) intercourse, (med.) argument, f. *discurs-*, pa. ppl. stem of *discurrere*, f. *dis-* DIS- 1 + *currere* run; assim. in form to COURSE *sb.*] **†1.** Onward course; = COURSE –1612. **†2.** 'The act of the understanding, by which it passes from premises to consequences' (J.); reasoning, ratiocination; reason, rationality. (*Obs.* or *arch.*) ME. **3.** Communication of thought by speech; talk, conversation (*arch.*) 1559. **†b.** The faculty of conversing –1641. **c.** (with *a* and *pl.*) A talk; a conversation (*arch.*) 1632. **†4.** Narration; a narrative –1647. **5.** A spoken or written treatment of a subject at length; a dissertation, treatise, sermon, or the like. (The prevailing sense.) 1581. **†6.** Familiar intercourse –1602. **†b.** Conversancy (*in*) –1604.

1. The naturall d. of the sunne ELYOT. **2.** Phr. †*D. of reason*: process or faculty of reasoning; A beast that wants d. of Reason *Haml.* I. ii. 150. **3.** Ample enterchange of sweet D. *Rich. III*, v. iii. 99. I have had a long d. with my father DE FOE. **5.** Authors who have published Discourses of Practical Divinity ADDISON. His discourses in the pulpit MACAULAY. **6.** If you be honest, and fair, your Honesty should admit no d. to your Beautie *Haml.* III. i. 108.

Discourse (diskōᵊ·ɹs), *v.* 1547. [f. DISCOURSE *sb.*; partly after Fr. *discourir.*] **†1.** *intr.* To run or travel over a space, region, etc.; *transf.* to extend –1555. **†2.** *intr.* 'To pass from premises to conclusions' (J.); to reason –1700. Also †*trans.* **3.** *intr.* To hold discourse, to talk, converse; to discuss a matter, confer 1559. Also *fig.* **4.** *intr.* To speak or write at length on a subject 1564. **5.** *trans.* To go through in speech; to treat of in speech or writing; to talk over; to talk of; to tell (*arch.*) 1563. **b.** To utter 1602. **6.** *trans.* To converse with; to talk to; to discuss a matter with; to address. (*Obs.* or *arch.*) 1677.

3. *fig.* She speakes, yet she sayes nothing, what of that? Her eye discourses *Rom. & Jul.* II. ii. 13. **4.** To d. for two hours without intermission BUCKLE. **5. b.** Giue it breath with your mouth, and it will d. most excellent Musicke *Haml.* III. ii. 374. **6.** A Friend whom I discoursed on this Point LOCKE. Hence **Discou·rser,** one who discourses. **†Discou·rsist,** one who reasons.

†Discou·rsive, *a.* 1588. [f. DISCOURSE *v.* + -IVE; cf. DISCURSIVE.] **1.** Of or pertaining to discourse or reason; rational –1678. **2.** Discursive –1613. **3.** Disposed to converse; talkative; communicative –1669. **b.** Of the nature of dialogue; conversational –1716.

2. Thou..In thy d. thought, dost range as farre W. BROWNE. **3.** See how these vain D. Bookmen talk DANIEL. **b.** Interlaced with Dialogue or D. Scenes DRYDEN. Hence **†Discou·rsively** *adv.*

†Discou·rt, *v.* 1585. [DIS- 7 b.] To dismiss from court –1722.

Discourteous (diskōᵊ·ɹtyəs, -kɒ̄·ɹtyəs), *a.* 1578. [DIS- 10.] Void of or lacking in courtesy; uncivil, rude. Hence **Discou·rteous-ly** *adv.*, **-ness.**

Discourtesy (diskōᵊ·ɹtési, -kɒ̄·ɹ-). 1555. [DIS- 9.] The opposite of courtesy; rude or uncivil behaviour; incivility; an instance of this.

Some jealousies and discurtesies passed lately betweene them and the Pope 1599.

†Discou·rtship. *rare.* [DIS- 9.] = DISCOURTESY. B. Jonson.

†Di·scous, *a.* 1706. [– mod.L. *discosus*, f. *discus* DISK; see -OUS.] Having a disc or discs; discoid –1794.

†Disco·venant, *v.* 1650. [f. DIS- 6 + COVENANT *v.* 1, or DIS- 7 a + COVENANT *sb.*] *trans.* To dissolve covenant with; to exclude from a covenant –1861.

Discover (diskɒ·vəɹ), *v.* ME. [– OFr. *descovrir* (mod. *découvrir*) :– late L. *discooperire*, f. *dis-* DIS- 4 + *cooperire* COVER *v.*] **†1.** *trans.* To remove the covering from –1628. **†2.** To remove (anything serving as a cover) –1618. **3.** To disclose or expose to view (anything covered up or previously unseen), to reveal, show. Now *rare.* 1450. **4.** To disclose to knowledge; to make known (*arch.*) ME. **†5.** To reconnoitre. Also *absol.* –1600. **6.** To reveal the identity of; hence, to betray (*arch.*) ME. **†7.** To exhibit, display –1771. **8.** To obtain sight or knowledge of for the first time; to find out 1555; to catch sight of, descry 1576. **†9.** To explore –1850. **†10.** *intr.* To make discoveries; to look; to see –1821. **†11.** *trans.* and *intr.* To distinguish –1796.

1. If the house be discouered by tempest [etc.] COKE. **3.** From those flames No light, but only darkness visible Serv'd only to d. sights of woe MILT. *P. L.* I. 64. **4.** Secrets which Time will d. 1662. **6.** Mercy, and that ye nat discouere me CHAUCER. **7.** The remaining Bones discovered his Proportions SIR T. BROWNE. **8.** Harvey discovered the circulation of the blood 1783. He discovered that he had made a mistake 1892. Now when we had discovered Cyprus, we left it on the left hand *Acts* 21:3. Hence **Disco·verer,** one who discovers (*esp.* in senses 3, 5, 8).

Discoverable (diskɒ·vərăb'l), *a.* 1572. [f. prec. vb. + -ABLE.] Capable of being discovered; discernible, perceptible, ascertainable.

Its effects ..are everywhere d. JOHNSON. Hence **Discoverabi·lity,** d. quality. **Disco·verably** *adv.*

Disco·vert. ME. [– OFr. *descovert* (mod. *découvert*), pa. pple. of *descovrir*; see DISCOVER.]

A. *adj.* **†1.** Uncovered, exposed –1525. **2.** *Law.* Of an unmarried woman or a widow: Not covert, not under the cover, authority, or protection of a husband; cf. COVERT *a.* 1729.

†B. *sb.* An uncovered or exposed state –1592.

Phr. †*In* or *at d.*, off one's guard. [OFr. *à descovert.*]

Discoverture (diskɒ·vəɹtiŭɹ). 1818. [f. prec. + -URE, after COVERTURE.] *Law.* The state of being discovert, or not under coverture; cf. COVERTURE.

Discovery (diskɒ·vəri). 1553. [f. DISCOVER + -Y[3], after *recover, recovery*; repl. *discovering* vbl. sb.] **†1.** The action of uncovering or fact of becoming uncovered 1658. **2.** The action of disclosing or divulging; revelation 1586; in *Law*, disclosure by a party to an action, at the instance of the other party, of facts or documents necessary to maintain his own title 1715. **b.** The unfolding of the plot of a play, poem, etc. 1727. **3.** The finding out or bringing to light of that which was previously unknown; making known; an instance of this 1553; †exploration, reconnaissance –1774. **†4.** Indication that brings anything to light –1705. **5.** That which is discovered, found out, revealed, or brought to light 1632.

2. Resolved..to make a D. of the whole affair 1737. **3.** Show me..a discoverer who has not suffered for his d...whether a Columbus or a Galileo LANDOR. **5.** No indication that the mariner's compass was a recent d. 1837.

†Discra·dle, *v. rare.* 1634. [DIS- 7 c.] *trans.* To turn out of a cradle. *intr.* (for *refl.*) To emerge from the cradle.

Discreate (diskri,ēi·t), *v.* 1570. [DIS- 6.] *trans.* To uncreate, annihilate, reduce to chaos.

Thou hast set thine hand to unmake and d. SWINBURNE. Hence **Discrea·tion,** the undoing of creation.

Discredit (diskre·dit), *sb.* 1565. [f. DIS- 9 + CREDIT *sb.*, after It. *discredito*, Fr. *discrédit.*] **1.** Loss or want of credit; disrepute, reproach; an instance of this. **2.** Loss or want of belief or credit; disbelief, distrust 1647.

1. Such conduct brings d. on the name of Athens JOWETT. **2.** The answers..[threw] d. upon his previous evidence 1868. The course of the discount market depends upon credit or d. 1885.

Discredit (diskre·dit), *v.* 1559. [f. DIS- 6 + CREDIT *v.*, after It. *discreditare*, Fr. *discréditer.*] **1.** *trans.* To refuse to credit; to disbelieve. **2.** To show to be unworthy of belief; to destroy confidence in 1561. **3.** To injure the credit or reputation of; to bring into discredit or disrepute 1579.

1. A statement which there is no reason to d. 1815. **2.** The idea is..discredited by modern science J. MARTINEAU. **3.** Henry is said to have been discredited for the death of Thomas FREEMAN. Hence **†Discre·ditor,** one who discredits anything (*rare*).

Discreditable (diskre·dităb'l), *a.* 1640. [f. DIS- 10 + CREDITABLE.] The reverse of CREDITABLE; injurious to reputation; disreputable, disgraceful. Hence **Discre·ditably** *adv.*

Discreet (diskrī·t), *a.* [ME. *discret(e* – (O)Fr. *discret, -ète* – L. *discretus* separate (see DISCRETE), which in late L. and Rom. took over the meaning of *discretio* DISCRETION.] **1.** Showing discernment in the guidance of one's own speech and action; judicious, circumspect, cautious; often *esp.* silent when speech is inconvenient. **2.** In *Sc.* well-spoken, well-behaved 1782. **†3.** Rare 16th c. spelling of DISCRETE, q.v.

1. A wife ought to be discret 1569. You are a d. man, and I make no doubt can keep a secret W. IRVING. A d. silence 1883. Hence **Discree·tly** *adv.*, **-ness.**

Discrepance (di·skrĭpăns, diskre·păns). ME. [– OFr. *discrepance* – L. *discrepantia*, f. as next; see -ANCE.] **1.** The fact of being discrepant; disagreement, difference. **†2.** Distinction, difference –1611. **†3.** Variation, change (of action) (*rare*) 1560.

1. Betwixt us and our Prince there is no d. BAILLIE. **2.** Ther hath bene euer a d. in vesture of youthe and age ELYOT. var. **Discrepancy.**

Discrepant (di·skrĭpănt, diskre·pănt). 1524. [– *discrepant-*, pres. ppl. stem of L. *discrepare* be discordant, f. *dis-* DIS- 1 + *crepare* creak; see -ANT[1].]

A. *adj.* **1.** Exhibiting difference; dissimilar, discordant, inharmonious, inconsistent. Const. *from*, †*to*. **†2.** Apart in space (*rare*) –1818.

1. Wherin he is moste d. from brute beastes ELYOT. **2.** Further d. than heaven and ground 1649.

†B. *sb.* A dissentient. JER. TAYLOR.

Discrete (diskrī·t), *a.* Also **†discreet.** ME. [– L. *discretus*, pa. pple. of *discernere* separate, DISCERN. A doublet of DISCREET.] **1.** Separate, detached from others, distinct. Opp. to *continuous*. **b.** *Pathol.* Separate, not coalescent or confluent 1854. **2.** Consisting of individual parts; discontinuous 1570. **†3.** *Gram.* and *Logic.* Of conjunctions: adversative. Of propositions: discretive –1664. **4.** *Metaph.* Detached from the material, abstract 1854.

1. Of distinct and d. vnits DEE. *D. tones* (Mus.): tones separated by fixed intervals of pitch, as the notes of a piano. **2.** *D. quantity*, quantity composed of distinct units, as the rational numbers.

Dist. from *continuous quantity* = magnitude. *D. proportion* = DISCONTINUED proportion. **3.** A d. sentence, is, which hath a d. conjunction; as, *although, yet, notwithstanding,* etc. 1654. Hence **Discre·te-ly** *adv.*, **-ness.**

Discrete, early f. DISCREET.

†Discre·te, *v.* 1646. [– *discret-*, pa. ppl. stem of L. *discernere*; see prec.] To divide into discrete parts; to separate distinctly –1858.

Discretion (diskre·ʃən). ME. [– (O)Fr. *discrétion* – L. *discretio* separation, distinction, (later) discernment, f. as prec.; see -ION.]

I. Separation, disjunction, distinction 1590.

Mind..has no discretion of parts or capacity of division or determination from without 1892.

II. [In late L. sense.] **1.** The action of discerning or judging; judgement; discrimination ME. **†2.** The faculty of discerning –1651. **3.** Liberty or power of deciding, or of acting according to one's own judgement; uncontrolled power of disposal ME.; in *Law*, the power to decide, within the limits allowed by positive rules of law, as to punishments, remedies, or costs, and generally to regulate matters of procedure and administration 1467.

1. Y refer all to your d. MARY Q. SCOTS. **3.** As to the form of worship, a large d. was left to the clergy MACAULAY. That the costs of references.. should be in the d. of the arbitrators 1891.

Phr. *At d.*, as one thinks fit, chooses, or pleases.

III. [Cf. DISCREET.] **1.** The quality of being discreet; discernment; prudence, sagacity, circumspection, sound judgement ME. **2.** *Sc.* Propriety of behaviour 1782. **†3.** A title formerly applied to bishops, etc. Cf. *your worship, your honour*. –1555.

1. D. of Speech is more than Eloquence BACON. Phr. *Age of, years of, d.*: the time of life at which a person is presumed to be capable of exercising d.; in *Eng. Law* the age of fourteen.

Hence **Discre·tional** *a.* discretionary. **Discre·tionally** *adv.* **Discre·tionary** *a.* pertaining or left to d.; †discreet. **Discre·tionarily** *adv.*

Discretive (diskrī·tiv). 1588. [– late L. *discretivus* (Priscian) serving to distinguish, f. as prec.; see -IVE. Cf. OFr. *discretif, -ive.*]

A. *adj.* **1.** = DISJUNCTIVE. **†2.** Serving to distinguish or discriminate; diacritic –1819.

†B. *sb.* A disjunctive conjunction or proposition –1725.

Hence **Discre·tive-ly** *adv.*, **-ness.**

†Discri·minable, *a. rare.* 1730. [f. DISCRIMINATE *v.* + -ABLE, after *separate, separable.*] Capable of being discriminated –1813.

Discri·minal, *a. rare.* 1842. [– late L. *discriminalis* serving to divide or separate, f. L. *discrimen* division, separation; see -AL¹.] Of the nature of a distinction or division.

D. line in *Palmistry*: the line between the hand and the arm.

Discriminant (diskri·minănt). 1836. [– *discriminant-*, pres. ppl. stem of L. *discriminare*; see DISCRIMINATE *v.*, -ANT¹.]

A. *adj.* **1.** Discriminating. **2.** *Math.* Implying equal roots or a node (cf. B.). *D. relation*, a one-fold relation between parameters determining a nodal point.

B. *sb. Math.* The eliminant of the *n* first derived functions of a homogeneous function of *n* variables. Hence **Discrimina·ntal** *a.* relating to a d.

Discriminate (diskri·minĕt), *a.* 1626. [– L. *discriminatus*, pa. pple. of *discriminare*; see next, -ATE².] **1.** Distinct, discriminated (*arch.*). **2.** Marked by discrimination: opp. to *indiscriminate* 1798.

2. Much may be done by d. charity MALTHUS. Hence **Discri·minate-ly** *adv.*, **-ness.**

Discriminate (diskri·mineit), *v.* 1628. [– *discriminat-*, pa. ppl. stem of L. *discriminare*, f. *discrimen, -min-* distinction, f. *discernere* DISCERN; see CRIME, -ATE³.] **1.** To make or constitute a difference in or between; to differentiate. **2.** To perceive or note the difference in or between; to distinguish 1665. **3.** *intr.* or *absol.* To make a distinction 1774.

1. Capacities which d. one individual from another GROTE. **2.** To d. the goats from the sheep BARROW. **3.** Phr. *To d. against*: to make an adverse distinction with regard to. To d. against certain imports from the United States 1885.

Discri·minating, *ppl. a.* 1647. [f. prec. + -ING².] **1.** That discriminates (sense 1). **2.** That discriminates (sense 2) 1792.

1. A d. mark of a disease 1797. **2.** A d. judgment 1794. Phr. *D. duty* or *rate*: one that varies according to the country or place of origin of goods, or according to the persons rated; a differential duty or rate. Hence **Discri·minatingly** *adv.*

Discrimination (diskriminēi·ʃən). 1646. [– late L. *discriminatio*, f. as DISCRIMINATE *v.*; see -ION.] **1.** The action of discriminating or distinguishing; a distinction (made with the mind or in action) 1648; the condition of being discriminated or distinguished. ? *Obs.* 1699. **2.** Something that discriminates or distinguishes; a distinction; a distinguishing mark. Now *rare* or *Obs.* 1646. **3.** The faculty of discriminating; the power of observing differences accurately, or of making exact distinctions 1814. **†4.** = RECRIMINATION. *Obs. rare.* –1684.

1. To make a d. between the Good and the Bad 1705. **3.** His character was touched with yet more d. by Flora SCOTT.

Discriminative (diskri·minĕtiv), *a.* 1638. [f. as DISCRIMINATE *v.* + -IVE.] **1.** Serving to discriminate; distinctive, distinguishing 1677. **2.** Characterized by discriminating; discerning 1638. **b.** *transf.* of things 1826. **c.** Differential 1872.

1. The d. Mark of a True Christian HALE. **2.** D. Providence HY. MORE. A more d. censure FOSTER. Heavy d. duties 1872. Hence **Discri·minatively** *adv.* So **Discri·minatory** *a.* (*rare*).

Discri·minoid. 1879. [f. after DISCRIMINANT; see -OID.] *Math.* A function of which the vanishing expresses the equality of all the integrating factors of a differential equation. Hence **Discri·minoidal** *a.*

†Discri·minous, *a. rare.* 1666. [– late L. *discriminosus* dangerous, f. L. *discrimen*; see DISCRIMINATE *v.*, -OUS.] Critical, hazardous –1727.

Discrive, obs. f. DESCRIVE.

Discrown (diskrau·n), *v.* 1586. [f. DIS- 6 + CROWN *v.* or DIS-7 + CROWN *sb.*] To deprive of a crown; *spec.* to depose; also *transf.* and *fig.*

To crown or d. its Monarchs KINGLAKE. Discrowning sovereign reason MORLEY.

†Discru·ciate, *v.* 1600. [– *discruciat-*, pa. ppl. stem of L. *discruciare*, f. *dis-* DIS- 5 + *cruciare* torment; see EXCRUCIATE *v.*, -ATE³.] **1.** *trans.* To torture, excruciate –1660. **2.** *nonce-use.* To solve (a crux or riddle) 1745.

2. Pray d. what follows SWIFT.

†Discuba·tion. [f. DIS- 1 as var. of ACCUBATION; cf. L. *cubatio, accubatio.*] Reclining at meals. COWLEY.

†Discu·bitory, *a. rare.* [f. *discubit-*, pa. ppl. stem of L. *discumbere*; see DISCUMB, -ORY².] Adapted for reclining. SIR T. BROWNE.

Disculpate (diskɒ·lpeit), *v.* 1693. [– *disculpat-*, pa. ppl. stem of med.L. *disculpare*; see -ATE³, and cf. EXCULPATE.] *trans.* To clear from blame or accusation; to exculpate.

Being faithful and just, with the testimony of things to d. him NORTH. Hence **Disculpa·tion.**

†Discu·mb, *v. rare.* 1683. [– L. *discumbere* recline, f. *dis-* DIS- 1 + *cumbere* lie down.] *intr.* To recline (at table) –1699. So **†Discu·mbency,** the reclining posture at meals. **†Discu·mbent** *a.* reclining; *sb.* one who reclines at table; one lying ill in bed.

Discumber (diskɒ·mbəɹ), *v.* 1725. [f. DIS- 6 + CUMBER *v.*; cf. OFr. *descombrer* (mod. *décombrer*).] To relieve; to disencumber.

Discure, obs. f. DISCOVER *v.*

†Discu·rrent, *a.*¹ 1599. [DIS- 10.] Not current.

†Discu·rrent, *a.*² 1656. [– *discurrent-*, pres. ppl. stem of L. *discurrere*; see next, -ENT.] Running hither and thither –1710.

Discursion (diskō·ɹʃən). *rare.* 1535. [– OFr. *discursion* or late L. *discursio*, f. *discurs-*, pa. ppl. stem of L. *discurrere* run hither and thither, f. *dis-* DIS- 5 + *currere* run; see -ION.] **†1.** The action of running or moving to and fro –1684. Also *fig.* **2.** = DISCOURSE *sb.* 2. 1603. So **†Discu·rsist,** one who practises discoursing.

Discursive (diskō·ɹsiv), *a.* 1599. [– med.L. *discursivus*, f. *discurs-*; see prec., -IVE.] **1.** Running hither and thither (*rare* in *lit.* sense) 1626. **2.** *fig.* Passing rapidly or irregularly from subject to subject; rambling, digressive; ranging over many subjects 1599. **3.** Passing from premisses to conclusions; ratiocinative. (Cf. DISCOURSE *v.* 2.) Often opp. to *intuitive.* 1608.

2. A most vivid, though very d. and garrulous, history of the time FREEMAN. **3.** Reason..D., or Intuitive MILT. *P. L.* v. 488. The..D. Faculty.. has only one operation, it only compares SIR W. HAMILTON. Hence **Discu·rsive-ly** *adv.*, **-ness.**

Discursory (diskō·ɹsŏri), *a. rare.* 1581. [– med.L. *discursorius*, f. as prec.; see -ORY².] **†1.** Of the nature of discourse or reasoning –1614. **2.** Discursive 1881.

†Discu·rtain, *v.* 1616. [DIS- 6 or 7 a.] *trans.* To unveil –1659.

‖**Discus** (di·skɒs). 1656. [L. – Gr. δίσκος quoit.] **1.** *Class. Antiq.* A disc of heavy material used in ancient Greek or Roman athletic exercises; a quoit. Also, *ellipt.*, the game of hurling the discus. **†2.** = DISK in various technical senses –1706.

Discuss (diskɒ·s), *v.* ME. [– *discuss-*, pa. ppl. stem of L. *discutere* dash to pieces, disperse, dispel, in Rom. investigate, f. *dis-* DIS-1 + *quatere* shake.] **†1.** *trans.* To drive away, disperse (*lit.* and *fig.*) –1651; to shake off; also to set free –1590. **2.** *Med.* To dissipate, dispel, or disperse (humours, etc.) (*arch.*) 1533. Also *intr.* (for *refl.*). **†3.** *trans.* To investigate; to try (as a judge) –1613. **†4.** To decide (as a judge) –1771. **†5.** To make known, declare. (This sense is obscure.) –1632. **6.** To investigate or examine by argument; to sift; to debate. (Now the ordinary sense.) 1450. Also *absol.* **7.** To try the quality of (food or drink); to consume. (*Somewhat joc.*) 1815. **8.** *Civil Law.* To 'do DILIGENCE' or exhaust legal proceedings against (a debtor), *esp.* against the person primarily liable, before proceeding against a surety 1681.

1. All regard of shame she had discust, And meet respect of honor putt to flight SPENSER *F. Q.* III. i. 48. **5.** Art thou a Gentleman? What is thy Name? discusse *Hen. V*, IV. iv. 5. **6.** Several schemes were proposed and discussed MACAULAY. **7.** To d. slices of cold boiled beef SCOTT, port wine MARRYAT. Hence **†Discu·ss** *sb.* = DISCUSSION. **Discu·ssable, -ible** *a.* capable of being discussed. **Discu·sser,** one who or that which discusses.

Discussion (diskɒ·ʃən). ME. [– (O)Fr. *discussion* – L. *discussio*; see prec., -ION.] **†1.** Examination, trial (by a judge); judicial decision –1526. **2.** Examination (*of* a matter) by arguments for and against; debate; a disquisition in which a subject is treated from different sides 1556. **3.** Investigation of the quality of food, etc. by consumption of it (*joc.* and *colloq.*) 1862. **†4.** *Med.* The dissipation or dispersal of humours, etc. –1758. **5.** *Civil Law.* The exhaustion of legal proceedings against a debtor, *esp.* against the person primarily liable, before proceeding against a person secondarily liable 1681.

2. D. is no prejudice but an honour to the truth HY. MORE. This d. is one of the least satisfactory in the dialogues of Plato JOWETT. **3.** The d. of a bottle of port 1870. Hence **Discu·ssional** *a.* of the nature of or pertaining to d.

Discussive (diskɒ·siv). 1580. [– med.L. *discussivus*, f. as prec.; see -IVE.]

A. *adj.* **†1.** *Med.* = DISCUTIENT *a.* –1727. **†2.** Having the quality of settling; decisive –1644. **3.** Pertaining to debate 1644.

†B. *sb. Med.* A DISCUTIENT –1671. Hence **†Discu·ssively** *adv.*, **†-ness.**

†Discu·stom, *v.* 1502. [– OFr. *descostumer*, f. *des-*, DIS- 4 + *costumer*; see CUSTOM *v.*] = DISACCUSTOM –1677.

Discutient (diskiū·ʃiĕnt). 1612. [– *discutient-*, pres. ppl. stem of L. *discutere*; see DISCUSS *v.* 2, -ENT.]

A. *adj.* Having the quality of discussing or dissipating morbid matter; resolvent.

B. *sb.* A discutient agent 1655.

Disdain (disdēi·n), *sb.* [ME. *desdeyne*, earlier *de-* – OFr. *desdeign*, AFr. *dedeigne* (mod. *dédain*) f. *desdeignier*; see next.] **1.** The feeling entertained towards anything unworthy of notice or beneath one's dignity; scorn, contempt. **†2.** Indignation; anger arising from offended dignity; dudgeon

–1677. †3. Loathing, aversion; †*transf.* loathsomeness –1655.

1. Disdaine and Scorne ride sparkling in her eyes, Mis-prizing what they looke on *Much Ado* III. i. 51. 2. The great person..took the neglect in huge d. BARROW. 3. *transf.* Most lothsom, filthie, foul, and full of vile disdaine SPENSER *F. Q.* I. i. 14. Hence †**Disdai·nish** *a.* inclined to be scornful; †**-ly** *adv.* †**Disdai·nous** *a.* disdainful; indignant; †**-ly** *adv.*

Disdain (disdēi·n), *v.* ME. [– OFr. *desdeignier* :– Rom. **disdignare*, for late L. *dedignare*, cl. L. *-ari*, f. *de-* DE- I. 6 + *dignari*, *-are* DEIGN.] 1. *trans.* To think unworthy of oneself, or of one's notice; to regard with contempt; to scorn ME.; to think (anything) unworthy *of* 1591. †2. To be indignant, angry, or offended at; to be indignant *that* –1796. †3. *intr.* To be moved with indignation, take offence. Const. *at* (rarely *against*, *of*, *on*). –1634. †4. *trans.* To move to indignation or scorn –1817.

1. He laid against me..that I did d. everi mans cumpani G. HARVEY. 2. Ingratitude, which I disdaine as Hell LITHGOW. Disdaining that the enemies of Christ should abound in wealth 1796. Hence **Disdai·nable** *a.* worthy of disdain (*rare*). **Disdai·ner.**

Disdainful (disdēi·nful), *a.* 1542. [f. DISDAIN *sb.* + -FUL.] 1. Full of or showing disdain; scornful, contemptuous, proudly disregardful. †2. Indignant, displeased; inimical (*rare*) –1550. †3. Hateful; that is the object of disdain –1586.

1. Vnder disdainfull brow WYATT. D. of private ends 1874. Hence **Disdai·nful-ly** *adv.*, **-ness.**

†**Disdecei·ve,** *v.* 1622. [DIS- 6.] To undeceive –1649.

†**Disde·ify,** *v. rare.* [DIS- 6.] To deprive of deity. FELTHAM.

Disdein(e, -deigne, -deyn(e, obs. ff. DISDAIN.

‖**Disdiaclasis** (disdəi,æ·klăsis). 1883. [mod. L., irreg. f. Gr. δίς twice (see DI-[2]) + διάκλασις breaking-up of light-rays.] *Optics.* Double refraction.

Disdiaclast (disdəi·ăklæst). 1867. [– mod.L. *disdiaclastus*; see next.] Brücke's term for one of the minute doubly-refracting particles of striated muscular tissue.

Disdiacla·stic, *a. rare.* 1670. [f. mod.L. *disdiaclastus* doubly refracting, irreg. f. Gr. δίς twice (see DI-[2]) + διακλαστός, vbl. adj. of διακλᾶν break in two, f. κλᾶν break. See prec., -IC.] Doubly refracting: applied to crystals; also, of the nature of disdiaclasts.

†**Disdiapa·son.** 1609. [– L. *disdiapason* 'twice through all (the chords)' – Gr. δὶς διὰ πασῶν; see DIAPASON.] *Mus.* The interval of a double octave; a fifteenth –1774.

Disease (dizī·z), *sb.* [ME. *di-*, *desese* – AFr. *des-*, *disease*, OFr. *desaise*, f. *des-* DIS- 4, 9 + *aise* EASE *sb.*] †1. Absence of ease; uneasiness; inconvenience, annoyance; disturbance; trouble –1623; a cause of discomfort –1712; molestation –1493. 2. A condition of the body, or of some part or organ of the body, in which its functions are disturbed or deranged. Also applied to plants. **a.** *gen.* Illness, sickness ME. **b.** An ailment 1526. 3. *fig.* A morbid condition (of mind or disposition, of the affairs of a community, etc.); an evil affection or tendency 1509.

1. Doth sleep thus seize Thy powers, affected with so much dis-ease CHAPMAN. Phr. †*To do d. to*, to molest. 2. The legions of Augustus melted away in d. and lassitude GIBBON. Diseases, desperate growne, By desperate appliance are releeued *Haml.* IV. iii. 9. 3. Bad Latin was a catching d. in that age FULLER.

Phrases. *Addison's d.*, a structural d. of the suprarenal capsules, resulting in anæmia and loss of strength, and commonly characterized by a bronzed discoloration of the skin; first described by Thomas Addison (1793–1860). BRIGHT'S D., FRENCH *d.*, POTATO *d.*, etc.: see these words.

Hence **Disea·seful** *a.* †fraught with discomfort; morbid, diseased (now *rare*); causing or tending to d. †**Disea·sefulness.** **Disea·sement,** †the action of depriving, or condition of being deprived, of ease; ailment (*nonce-use*). †**Disea·sy** *a.* annoying, troublesome; morbid.

Disease (disī·z), *v.* ME. [– AFr. **diseaser*, *-eeser*, *-aeser*, for OFr. *desaaisier*, f. *desaise* sb., after *aaisier*, *aiser* to ease.] †1. *trans.* To deprive of ease; to trouble, incommode –1697; to disturb (from quiet, etc.) –1653. 2. To bring into a morbid or unhealthy condition; to infect with disease. Usu. in pa. pple. 1467. Also *fig.*

1. What racking cares dis-ease a monarch's bed CONGREVE. 2. Evil Ministers D. the Commonwealth 1680.

Diseased (dizī·zd), *ppl. a.* 1467. [f. prec. + -ED[1].] Affected with disease. Now usually of the bodily organs or fluids: In a disordered state, infected. **b.** Characterized by disease; pertaining to disease; morbid 1574. Also *fig.*

His miracles which hee did on them that were d. *John* 6:2. Hence **Disea·sed-ly** *adv.*, **-ness.**

Disedge (dise·dʒ), *v.* 1611. [DIS- 7 a.] To take the edge off; to blunt, dull.

Served a little to d. The sharpness of that pain TENNYSON.

Disedify (dise·difəi), *v.* 1526. [DIS- 6]. *trans.* To do the reverse of edifying; to shock or weaken the piety of. Hence **Dise:difica·-tion.**

Diselder, *v.*; see DIS- 7 b, ELDER *sb.*[2]

Diselectrify (disĭle·ktrifəi), *v.* 1876. [DIS- 6.] *trans.* To render non-electric.

†**Dis-e·lement,** *v.* 1612. [DIS- 7 c.] *trans.* To put out of its element –1727.

Diselenide (dəi,se·lĕnəid), etc., *Chem.*; see DI-[2] 2.

Disembark (disĕmbā·ɹk), *v.* 1582. [– Fr. *désembarquer*, Sp. *desembarcar*, or It. *disimbarcare*; see DIS- 4, EMBARK.] 1. *trans.* To put ashore from a ship; to land. 2. *intr.* To go on shore from a ship; to land 1582.

1. I must vnto the Road, to dis-embarque Some necessaries *Two Gent.* II. iv. 187. 2. Touching Breton Sands, they disembark'd TENNYSON. Hence **Disembarka·tion,** †**Disemba·rkment,** the action of disembarking.

Disembarrass (disĕmbæ·răs), *v.* 1726. [f. DIS- 6 + EMBARRASS *v.*, prob. after Fr. †*désembarrasser* (mod. *débarrasser*). See DEBARRASS.] *trans.* To free from embarrassment, encumbrance, or complication; to rid; to relieve; to disentangle.

We may at once d. ourselves of those formidable terms—'absolute' and 'unconditioned' E. CONDER. Hence **Disemba·rrassment,** disembarrassing or being disembarrassed.

†**Disembay·,** *v.* 1651. [f. DIS- 6 + EMBAY *v.*[1]] To bring out of a bay.

Disembellish (disĕmbe·liʃ), *v.* 1611. [DIS- 6.] To deprive of embellishment or adornment.

Disembi·tter, *v. rare.* [DIS- 6.] To free from bitterness. ADDISON.

Disembody (disĕmbǫ·di), *v.* 1714. [DIS- 6.] 1. *trans.* To separate (as a spirit) from the body; to free (anything) from that in which it is embodied. 2. To discharge from military embodiment 1762.

1. Our souls, when they are disembodied..will.. be always sensible of the divine presence ADDISON. Hence **Disembo·diment,** the action of disembodying; disembodied state.

Disembogue (disĕmbōu·g), *v.* 1595. [Also (XVI, XVII) *disemboque*, *disemboak* – Sp. *desembocar*, f. *des-* DIS- 4 + *embocar* run into a creek or strait, f. *en-* IN-[1] + *boca* mouth. See DISBOGUE, EMBOGUE.] †1. *intr.* To come out of the mouth of a river, strait, etc. into the open sea –1633. 2. *intr.* Of a river, lake, etc.: To flow out at the mouth; to empty itself; to flow *into*. Also *fig.* and *transf.* 1598. 3. *trans.* Of a river, lake, etc.: To discharge its waters at the mouth; *refl.* to empty itself. Also *fig.* and *transf.* 1610. †**b.** To drive out –1632.

2. The Danube disembogues into the Euxine by seven mouths GOLDSM. The presses of Europe are still disemboguing into the ocean of literature DE QUINCEY. 3. Paris disembogues itself to witness, with grim looks, the *Séance Royale* CARLYLE. Hence †**Disembo·gue** *sb.* place of disemboguing. **Disembo·guement,** action or place of disemboguing.

Disembo·som, *v.* 1742. [DIS- 6.] To separate from the bosom; to reveal; *refl.* and *intr.* to unburden oneself.

Disembow·el, *v.* 1603. [In sense 1, intensive (see DIS- 5) of EMBOWEL 1; in sense 2, f. DIS- 6 + EMBOWEL 2. Cf. DISBOWEL, and see DISEN-, DISEM-.] 1. To remove the bowels or entrails of; to eviscerate. Also *fig.* 2. To take out of the bowels 1703.

2. So her disembowell'd web Arachne..spreads 1703. Hence **Disembo·welment,** the act of disembowelling.

Disembow·er, *v.* 1856. [DIS- 6.] To set free from a bower.

†**Disembra·ce,** *v.* 1638. [DIS- 6.] *trans.* To refrain or withdraw from embracing; also, to undo embracing –1775.

†**Disembra·ngle,** *v.* 1726. [DIS- 6.] To free from complication.

Disembroi·l, *v.* 1622. [f. DIS- 6 + EMBROIL *v.*[2] Cf. Sp. *desembrollar.*] To free from embroilment or confusion; to disentangle.

To d. a Subject that seems to have perplexed even Antiquity 1741.

Disembu·rden, -bu·rthen, *v.* 1790. [See DISEN-.] = DISBURDEN.

Disemic (dəi,sī·mik), *a.* [f. late L. *disemus* disyllabic – Gr. δίσημος of doubtful quantity (f. δι- DI-[2] + σῆμα sign) + IC.] In *Gr.* and *L. Prosody*: Of the value of two moræ or units of time.

Disemploy (disĕmploi·), *v. rare.* 1618. [DIS- 6.] *trans.* To cease to employ, throw out of employment. Hence **Disemploy·ed** *ppl. a.* unemployed. **Disemploy·ment,** absence or withdrawal of employment (*rare*).

Disempow·er, *v. rare.* 1813. [DIS- 6.] To deprive of power conferred.

Disemprison, var. DISIMPRISON.

Disen-, disem-. Verbs in *dis-* are sometimes in sense negative or privative of those in *em-*, *en-*: e.g. *en-franchise*, *dis-franchise*; generally, however, verbs in *em-* or *en-* have *dis-* prefixed, as in *dis-embarrass*, *dis-engage*, *dis-entwine*. Occas., as in *disemburden*, forms in *disen-*, *disem-* may occur even when there is no verb in *em-* or *en-*.

Disenable (disĕnēi·b'l), *v.* 1604. [DIS- 6.] To render unable or incapable; the reverse of *enable*.

I am constitutionally disenabled from that vice LAMB.

Disena·ct, *v. rare.* 1651. [DIS- 6.] To repeal.

Disena·mour, *v.* 1598. [f. DIS- 6 + ENAMOUR. Cf. Fr. *désenamourer* and It. *disinnamorare.*] To free from being enamoured.

Disenchai·n, *v. rare.* 1849. [f. DIS- 6 + ENCHAIN. Cf. Fr. *désenchaîner.*] To set free from chains or restraint.

Disenchant (disĕn,tʃɑ·nt), *v.* 1586. [– (O)Fr. *désenchanter*, f. *des-* DIS- 4 + *enchanter* ENCHANT.] To set free from enchantment, magic spell, or illusion.

A noble stroke or two Ends all the charms, and disenchants the grove DRYDEN. Hence **Disencha·nter.** **Disencha·ntment,** the action of disenchanting; disenchanted state. **Disencha·ntress.**

Disencha·rm, *v. rare.* 1651. [DIS- 6.] To deliver from a charm.

†**Disenclo·se,** *v. rare.* 1611. [DIS- 6.] To throw open (that which is enclosed) –1669.

†**Disencou·rage,** *v.* 1626. [DIS- 6.] To DISCOURAGE –1803. Hence †**Disencou·ragement,** disheartenment.

Disencrease; see DISINCREASE.

Disencumber (disĕnkɒ·mbəɹ), *v.* 1598. [f. DIS- 6 + ENCUMBER, prob. after (O)Fr. *désencombrer*. Cf. DISCUMBER.] To relieve or free of encumbrances.

Disencumbered from my villatick bashfulness JOHNSON. Hence **Disencu·mberment** (*rare*). †**Disencu·mbrance,** deliverance or freedom from encumbrance.

Disendow (disĕndau·), *v.* 1861. [DIS- 6.] To deprive of endowments. Hence **Disendow·ment,** the action or fact of disendowing, as, *the d. of the Irish Church.*

Disenfra·nchise, *v.* 1626. [DIS- 6.] 1. To DISFRANCHISE 1664. †2. [f. DIS- 5, or error.] To set free, enfranchise (*rare*) –1654. Hence †**Disenfra·nchisement.**

Disengage (disĕngēi·dʒ), *v.* 1611. [f. DIS- 6 + ENGAGE *v.*, prob. after Fr. *désengager.*] 1. To free from engagement, pledge, contract, or obligation. *Obs.* exc. as *pa. pple.* 2. To loosen from that which holds fast, adheres, or entangles; to detach, liberate, free 1662. Also *fig.* 3. *intr.* (for *refl.*) To free oneself, get loose 1646. 4. *intr. Fencing.* To pass the point of one's blade smartly to the opposite side of the opponent's sword, so as to free it for a thrust 1684.

1. Are you disengaged this evening DICKENS. 2. It slowly decomposes the water, combining with

its hydrogen and disengaging its oxygen HUXLEY. To d. great principles from capricious adjuncts GROTE. 3. The left Troop..must d...before it can move 1832. Hence **Disenga·ge** *sb.* (*Fencing*), the action of disengaging.

Disengaged (disėngēⁱ·dʒd), *ppl. a.* 1621. [f. prec. + -ED¹.] Set free from engagement, ties, or prepossession; detached; not engaged; at liberty. Hence **Disenga·gedness.**

Disengagement (disėngēⁱ·dʒmĕnt). 1650. [f. DISENGAGE + -MENT, after ENGAGEMENT or Fr. *désengagement.*] The action of disengaging or fact of being disengaged *from* (anything).

A noble D. from the World JER. COLLIER. The d of a quantity of nitrous gas 1791. Mental d. FERRIER. To parry the d. ROLAND.

Disenme·sh, *v. rare.* 1868. [DIS- 6.] To free from meshes, disentangle.

Disenno·ble, *v.* 1645. [DIS- 6.] To deprive of nobleness; to render ignoble.

An unworthy behaviour.. disennobles a man ADDISON.

†Diseno·rm, *v.* [f. DIS- 6 or 8 + ENORM.] To make conformable to a norm or standard. QUARLES.

†Disenro·l, *v. rare.* [f. DIS- + ENROL; cf. Fr. †*desenrouller.*] To remove from a roll. DONNE.

Disenshrou·d, *v. rare.* 1835. [DIS- 6.] To set free from or as from a shroud.

Disensla·ve, *v.* Also **†disin-.** 1649. [DIS- 6.] To set free from enslavement; to liberate from slavery.

Such an one as should d. them from the Roman yoke SOUTH.

Disentail (disėntēⁱ·l), *v.* Also **†disin-.** 1641. [DIS- 6.] **1.** *Law.* To free from entail; to break the entail of; see ENTAIL *sb.*² 1848. **†2.** To divest *of.* Hence **Disentai·l** *sb.*, **Disentai·lment,** the act of disentailing.

Disentangle (disėntæ·ŋg'l), *v.* Also **†disin-.** 1598. [DIS- 6.] **1.** *trans.* To free from that in or with which a thing is entangled; to disengage, extricate. Const. *from,* †*of.* Also *fig.* **2.** To bring out of a tangled state; to unravel, untwist 1805. Also *fig.* **3.** *intr.* (for *refl.*) To become disentangled; to disentangle oneself 1607.

1. To d. our line from the water-lillies J. WILSON. To d. our minds from..prejudices BP. BERKELEY. To d. facts from the mass of fable 1874. **2.** To d. the knots of my harness KANE. **3.** This skein won't d. 1896. Hence **Disenta·nglement,** the fact of disentangling; disentangled state.

†Dise·nter, *v.* 1629. [f. DIS- 6 + ENTER *v.* 2.] To eject, oust –1631.

Disenthra·l, -ll, *v.* Also **†disin-.** 1643. [DIS- 6.] To set free from enthralment or bondage; to liberate from thraldom. Hence **Disenthra·lment,** emancipation from thraldom.

Disenthrone (disėnþrōᵘ·n), *v.* Also **†disin-.** 1608. [DIS- 6.] To put down from a throne; to depose from royal dignity or authority; to dethrone. Hence **Disenthro·nement,** dethroning.

Disentitle (disėntəi·t'l), *v.* Also **†disin-.** 1654. [DIS- 6.] To deprive of title or right (*to* something).

Every ordinary offence does not d. a son to the love of his father SOUTH.

Disentomb (disėntū·m), *v.* 1626. [DIS- 6.] To take out of the tomb. Also *transf.* and *fig.*

A mummy. which we saw disentombed 1877. Hence **Disentombment** (-tū·m,mĕnt), the act of disentombing.

†Disentrai·l, *v.* 1596. [f. DIS- 7a + ENTRAIL *sb.*¹] To draw forth from the entrails or inward parts –1692.

Disentra·mmel, *v.* 1866. [DIS- 6.] To free from its trammels.

Disentra·nce, *v.* 1663. [DIS- 6.] To arouse from or as from a trance.

Disentwi·ne, *v.* 1814. [DIS- 6.] To free from being entwined; to untwine (*lit.* and *fig.*). Also *intr.* (for *refl.*)

Disenve·lop, -e, *v.* Also **†disin-.** 1632. [f. DIS- 6 or 7 + ENVELOP *v.* or ENVELOPE *sb.*] To free from that in which it is enveloped; to unfold.

Disepalous (dəise·păləs), *a.* 1841. [f. DI-¹ + mod.L. *sepalum* SEPAL + -OUS.] *Bot.* Having or consisting of two sepals.

†Disequa·lity. 1602. [f. *disequal* (XVII), after EQUALITY.] Inequality, disparity –1655.

Disequili·brium. 1840. [DIS- 9.] Absence or destruction of equilibrium. So **Disequili·brate, Disequi·librize** *vbs.* to throw out of balance; **Disequilibra·tion.**

†Dise·rt, *a.* ME. [– L. *dis(s)ertus* skilful in speaking, pa. pple. of *disserere* discuss, discourse, f. *dis-* DIS- 1 or 2 + *serere* interweave, connect, compose.] Well-spoken, eloquent –1675. Hence **†Dise·rtly** *adv.*

†Disespou·se, *v. rare.* [DIS- 6.] To undo the espousal or betrothal of. MILT.

Disestablish (disėstæ·bliʃ), *v.* 1598. [DIS- 6.] To deprive of the character of being established; *spec.* to deprive (a church) of especial State connection and support.

Disesta·blishment. 1806. [f. prec. + -MENT.] The act of disestablishing; *spec.* the withdrawal of especial State patronage and control from a church.

From the establishment of Christianity under Constantine, to the beginnings of its d. under Pope Leo X 1806.

Disesteem (disėstī·m), *sb.* 1603. [f. DIS- 9 + ESTEEM *sb.* Cf. Fr. †*désestime*: see next.] The action of disesteeming, or position of being disesteemed; low estimation or regard.

Pastorals are fallen into D. DRYDEN.

Disestee·m, *v.* 1594. [f. DIS- 6 + ESTEEM *v.*, perh. after Fr. †*désestimer.*] **1.** *trans.* To regard with the reverse of esteem; to hold in low estimation, slight, despise. Also *intr.* with *of.* **†b.** To take away the estimation of (*rare*) 1637. **†2.** with *subord. cl.*: To think or believe otherwise than (*rare*) 1677.

1. Strange notes to like, and d. our own DANIEL. Opinions disesteem'd, Impostures branded B. JONS. Hence **Disestee·mer,** one who disesteems.

†Dise:stima·tion. 1619. [f. DIS- 9 + ESTIMATION, after prec.] = DISESTEEM *sb.* –1677.

‖**Diseuse** (dī·zǒz). 1896. [Fr., fem. = talker; see DISOUR.] A female artiste who entertains with monologue. Also less freq. masc. **Diseur.**

†Dise·xercise, *v. rare.* [DIS- 6.] To put out of exercise. MILTON.

Disfa·me, *sb. rare.* 1460. [f. DIS- 9 + FAME *sb.*¹ In early use – OFr. *des-, disfame* f. *des-, disfamer* DEFAME. *v.*] Disrepute; defamation. So **†Disfa·me** *v.* to defame.

Disfashion (disfæ·ʃən), *v.* 1535. [DIS- 6.] To mar or undo the fashion of; to disfigure.

Gluttony..disfashioneth the body MORE.

Disfavour, -or (disfēⁱ·vəɹ), *sb.* 1533. [f. DIS- 9 + FAVOUR *sb.*, prob. after Fr. †*desfaveur.*] **1.** Unfavourable regard, dislike, disapproval. **†2.** An act or expression of dislike or ill will –1647. **3.** The condition of being unfavourably regarded 1581.

1. The kynges disfauoure is like yᵉ roaringe of a Lyon COVERDALE *Prov.* 19:12. **2.** To dispense favours and disfavours CLARENDON. **3.** Phr. *To be (live,* etc.) *in d., to bring, come, fall,* etc. *into d.*

Disfa·vour, -or, *v.* 1535. [DIS- 6.] **1.** *trans.* To regard or treat with the reverse of favour; to discountenance; to treat with disapprobation 1570; †to dislike –1740. **†2.** To mar the countenance or appearance of; to disfigure –1607.

1. Countenanced or disfavoured according as they obey SWIFT. Hence **Disfa·vourer** (*rare*), one who disfavours.

†Disfa·vourable, *a.* 1561. [DIS- 10.] Unfavourable; adverse. **†Disfa·vourably** *adv.*

Disfeature (disfī·tiŭɹ), *v.* 1659. [DIS- 7 a or d. Cf. DEFEATURE.] To mar the features of; to disfigure, deface.

Disfe·llowship, *sb.* 1608. [DIS- 9.] Exclusion from fellowship. So **Disfe·llowship** *v.* to exclude from fellowship; to excommunicate. (Now *U.S.*)

Disfigura·tion. 1653. [f. DISFIGURE + -ATION. Cf. OFr. *desfiguration.*] = DISFIGUREMENT.

Disfigure (disfi·giŭɹ), *v.* ME. [– OFr. *desfigurer* (mod. *dé-*) – Rom. **disfigurare,* f. L. *dis-* DIS- 4 + *figura* FIGURE *sb.*] **1.** *trans.* To mar the figure or appearance of; to deform, deface. Also *fig.* **†2.** To disguise –1713. **†3.** *techn.* To carve (a peacock) –1706.

1. Disfiguring not Gods likeness, but thir own MILT. *P. L.* XI. 521. Diction disfigured by foreign idioms MACAULAY. **2.** And me so wel d... That.. ther shal no man me knowe CHAUCER. Hence **†Disfigure** *sb.* disfigurement. **Disfi·gurer,** one who or that which disfigures.

Disfi·gurement. 1634. [f. prec. vb. + -MENT.] **1.** The action of disfiguring; the fact or condition of being disfigured; defacement, deformity. **2.** Something that disfigures; a deformity, defacement 1641.

2. A dial is not necessarily a d. to a tower 1874.

Disfle·sh, *v.* 1620. [DIS- 7 a.] To deprive of flesh; also, to disembody.

Disfoliaged; see DIS- 7 a, etc.

Disforest (disfǫ·rėst), *v.* 1502. [– AL. **disforestare* (cf. *disforestatio* 1307), f. *dis-* DIS- 4 + *foresta* FOREST. Cf. DEFOREST.] **1.** *trans.* = DISAFFOREST. Also *fig.* **2.** To clear of forests or trees 1668. Hence **Disforesta·tion.**

Disform (disfǭ·ɹm), *v. rare.* 1527. [f. DIS- + FORM *v.*; cf. DIFFORM, DEFORM.] **†1.** To mar the form, character, or condition of; to deform –1658. **2.** To alter the form of; *intr.* (for *refl.*) to lose its form (*rare*) 1868.

2. They seem to form, d., and re-form before us, like the squares of coloured glass in the kaleidoscope GLADSTONE.

†Disfo·rmity. *rare.* 1494. [var. of DEFORMITY, DIFFORMITY; cf. prec.] **a.** = DEFORMITY. **b.** = DIFFORMITY. –1600.

†Disfo·rtune. *rare.* 1529. [var. of earlier MISFORTUNE; see DIS- II. Cf. OFr. *desfortune.*] Misfortune –1592.

†Disfra·me, *v.* 1629. [DIS- 6.] To undo the frame or framing of –1644.

Disfranchise (disfræ·ntʃiz, -əiz), *v.* 1467. [DIS- 6.] To deprive of the rights and privileges of a free citizen of a borough, city, or country, or of some franchise previously enjoyed. Also *transf.* and *fig.*

He..shalbe dysfranchesed opynly at Carfox 1535. The decayed burghs were disfranchised, and their members given to the counties LD. BROUGHAM. Wise men are timerous in the disfranchising of their judgement 1646. Hence **Disfra·nchisement,** the action of disfranchising or fact of being disfranchised.

†Disfri·ar, *v.* 1599. [DIS- 7 b.] To deprive of the order of a friar; also *refl.* –1639.

Disfro·ck, *v.* 1837. [f. DIS- 7 a + FROCK *sb.*] To deprive of the clerical garb and character; to unfrock.

Disfu·rnish, *v.* 1531. [– OFr. *desfournir,* f. *des-* DIS- 4 + *fournir* FURNISH.] To deprive of that wherewith it is furnished; to strip of furniture, etc.; to render destitute (*of*).

These poore habiliments, Of which, if you should here d. me, You take the sum and substance that I haue *Two Gent.* IV. i. 14. Hence **Disfu·rnishment.** So **†Disfu·rniture,** disfurnishment.

†Disga·ge, *v.* 1594. [– Fr. †*desgager* (mod. *dé-*), f. *des-* DIS- 4 + *gager* pledge etc., see GAGE *v.*] To release from pledge or pawn; to disengage –1603.

†Disga·llant, *v. rare.* 1599. [f. DIS- 8 + GALLANT *a.*] To deprive of courage; to dispirit –1640.

Disgarland (disgā·ɹlănd), *v.* 1616. [DIS- 7 a.] To divest of a garland or garlands.

Disgarnish (disgā·ɹniʃ), *v.* 1450. [– OFr. *desgarnir* (mod. *dé-*), f. *des-* DIS- 4 + *garnir* GARNISH *v.*] To deprive of that which garnishes or furnishes; to disfurnish, despoil.

The front..was..disgarnished of troops SIR W. NAPIER.

Disga·rrison, *v.* Now *arch.* 1594. [DIS- 7 a.] To deprive of a garrison.

Disgavel (disgæ·vĕl), *v.* 1683. [f. DIS- 7 a + *gavel* (GAVELKIND) *sb.*] To relieve from the tenure of GAVELKIND.

Disgene·ric, *a.* [DIS- 10.] Of different genera (opp. to *congeneric*).

†Disglo·rify, *v. rare.* 1577. [DIS- 6.] To deprive of glory; to treat with dishonour –1671.

†Disglo·ry. 1547. [DIS- 9.] The opposite of glory; dishonour –1577.

Disgorge (disgǭ·ɹdʒ), *v.* 1477. [– OFr. *desgorger* (mod. *dé-*), f. *des-* DIS- 4, DE- I. 6 + *gorge* throat, GORGE *sb.*¹] **1.** *trans.* To eject or throw out from, or as from, the gorge or throat; to vomit forth (what has been swallowed); *esp.* to give up what has been wrongfully appropriated. Also *absol.* **2.** *trans.* To discharge or empty; also *refl.* 1592. **†3.** *Farriery.* To dissipate an engorgement –1753.

1. Jonah's whale swallowed and disgorged him night after night MISS THACKERAY. D. thy care, abandon feare 1587. Some mode..to make the French Generals d. the church plate which they have stolen WELLINGTON. *absol.* The river Nile.. disgorging at seaven mouthes Into the Sea MILT. *P.L.* XII. 158. **2.** Several vessels were disgorging themselves HAWTHORNE. Hence **Disgo·rgement. Disgo·rger.**

†**Disgo·spel,** *v.* [DIS- 7 a.] To deprive of the gospel or gospel character; to oust the gospel from life. MILTON.

†**Disgou·t,** *v.* 1611. [DIS- 7 a.] To free from gout –1748.

Disgown (disgau·n), *v.* 1734. [DIS- 7 a.] To strip (any one) of his gown, and thus of his degree or office. Also *intr.* (for *refl.*)

Disgrace (disgrē^i·s), *sb.* 1581. [– Fr. *disgrâce* – It. *disgrazia*, f. *dis-* DIS- 4 + *grazia* GRACE *sb.*] **1.** The disfavour of one in a powerful position; the state of being out of favour and honour; †a disfavour; an affront –1739. †**2.** The disfavour of Fortune; adverse fortune –1697; a misfortune –1748. **3.** Dishonour in public estimation; ignominy, shame 1593. †**4.** Opprobrium, reproach, disparagement –1676. **5.** That which brings into dishonour 1590.

1. I heare Macduffe liues in d. *Macb.* III. vi. 23. The interchange continually of favours and disgraces BACON. **3.** Tito shrank..from d. GEO. ELIOT. **4.** Then Hector him with words of great d. Reproved HOBBES. **5.** I found the two disgraces..are, first, disloyalty to Church and State, and, second, to be born poor EMERSON.

Disgrace (disgrē^i·s), *v.* 1549. [– Fr. *disgracier* – It. *disgraziare*; see prec.] †**1.** *trans.* To undo or mar the grace of; to disfigure –1781. †**2.** To put out of countenance –1591. **3.** To put out of grace or favour; to dismiss from (royal, etc.) favour 1593. †**4.** To cast shame or discredit upon –1715. †**5.** To speak of dishonouringly; to disparage, revile –1720. **6.** To be a disgrace or shame to; to reflect dishonour upon 1593.

3. Queensbury was disgraced for refusing to betray the interests of the Protestant religion MACAULAY. **4.** They never vse reason so willingly as to d. reason HOOKER. **6.** I could finde in my heart to d. my mans apparell, and to cry like a woman *A. Y. L.* II. iv. 4. Hence †**Disgra·cement,** the action of disgracing; that which causes disgrace. **Disgra·cer,** one who or that which disgraces; †an opprobrious reviler.

Disgraceful (disgrē^i·sfŭl), *a.* 1591. [f. DISGRACE *sb.* + -FUL.] †**1.** Void of grace, unpleasing –1702. **2.** Full of, or fraught with, disgrace; shameful, dishonourable 1597. **3.** Inflicting disgrace, degrading, opprobrious 1608.

2. Stained with black d. crimes DANIEL. **3.** Such d., such contemptible punishment FOOTE. Hence **Disgra·ceful-ly** *adv.*, **-ness.**

‖**Disgracia, -grazia.** 1739. [Sp. *desgracia* (-grāþya), It. *disgrazia* (-gratsya).] An unpleasant accident.

Disgracious (disgrē^i·ʃəs), *a.* 1594. [– Fr. *disgracieux*, f. *dis-* DIS- 4 + *gracieux* GRACIOUS.] **1.** Ungracious, unkind. ? *Obs.* 1598. †**2.** In disfavour; disliked –1611. †**3.** Disgraceful 1615. **4.** Uncomely 1870. Hence †**Disgra·ciously** *adv.*

†**Disgra·cive,** *a. rare.* 1602. [irreg. f. DISGRACE *v.* + -IVE; cf. *coercive*.] Conveying or tending to disgrace –1627.

Disgradation (disgrădē^i·ʃən). ? *Obs.* 1727. [f. DISGRADE *v.*] = DEGRADATION[1] 1.

Disgrade (disgrē^i·d), *v.* ME. [– OFr. *desgrader*, var. of *degrader* DEGRADE. See DE- 6.] = DEGRADE *v.* 2.

†**Disgra·duate,** *v.* 1528. [DIS- 7 b.] Deprive of rank, a dignity, etc. –1550.

Disgregate (di·sgrĭgē^it), *v.* 1593. [– *disgregat-*, pa. ppl. stem of late L. *disgregare*, f. *dis-* DIS- 1 + *gregare* collect (in a flock), f. *grex, greg-* flock; see -ATE[3].] †**1.** To separate (*from*). **2.** To disintegrate 1603. †**3.** To scatter (the visual rays); hence, to confuse (the sight) –1645. Hence **Disgrega·tion,** disintegration, dispersal; *spec.* in *Chem.* separation of the molecules of a substance by heat, etc.

†**Disgross** (disgrō^u·s), *v.* 1611. [– OFr. *desgrosser*, later *-ir* (mod. *dé-*) in same sense, f. *des-* DIS- 4 + *gros* thick, GROSS *a.*] To make finer or less gross –1823.

If bullion be..disgrost into wire or lace PETTY.

Disgruntle (disgrʊ·nt'l), *v.* 1682. [f. DIS- 5 + GRUNTLE *v.* To put into ill humour; to chagrin, disgust. Chiefly in *pa. pple.*

Disguise (disgəi·z), *v.* [ME. *des-, degise*, etc. – OFr. *desguis(i)er* (mod. *déguiser*), f. Rom. *des- (see DE- I. 6, DIS-) + *guisa – Frankish *wīsa*. See GUISE.] †**1.** *trans.* To change the usual or natural guise or fashion of; *esp.* of dress –1563. †**2.** To transform; to disfigure –1697. **3.** To change the dress and appearance of so as to conceal identity; to conceal the identity of by dressing *as* or *in*. (Now the leading sense.) ME. Also *refl.* **4.** To exhibit (anything) in a false light; to colour, to misrepresent ME. **5.** To conceal or hide by a false show, or the like 1591. **6.** To intoxicate (with liquor) 1562.

2. Faces..disguised in death DRYDEN. **3.** Disguised in the habit of a Turk KNOLLES. Disguised as a monk 1896. **4.** To d. and put off a bad commodity 1732. **5.** A feint to d. the real intention 1853. **6.** Three cuppes full at once shall oft dysgyse thee 1562. Hence **Disgui·sed-ly** *adv.*, **-ness. Disgui·ser,** one who disguises; †a masker.

Disguise (disgəi·z), *sb.* ME. [f. prec. vb.] †**1.** New or strange fashion (*esp.* of an ostentatious kind) –1594. **2.** Altered fashion of dress and appearance intended to conceal identity; the state of being thus disguised ME. Also *fig.* **3.** A garb assumed in order to deceive 1596. Also *transf.* and *fig.* **4.** Any artificial manner assumed for deception 1632. **5.** The act or practice of disguising 1603. †**6.** A masque –1630. **7.** 'Disorder by drink' (J.) 1606.

2. The banished Kent; who, in d., Follow'd his enemy king, and did him service *Lear* V. iii. 220. A blessing in d. 1896. **3.** Ned, where are our disguises 1 *Hen. IV*, II. ii. 78. **5.** Hence false tears, deceits, disguises POPE. **6.** Masques (which they then called Disguises) BACON. Hence **Disgui·seless** *a.*

Disgui·sement. 1580. [f. DISGUISE *v.* + -MENT. Cf. OFr. *desguisement* (mod. *dé-*).] **1.** The fact of disguising, or of being disguised 1583. **2.** That which disguises; a disguise 1580. **3.** *pl.* Additions that change the appearance; bedizenments 1638.

†**Disgui·sy,** *a.* ME. [– OFr. *desguisié*, *deguisié*, pa. pple. of *de(s)guisier*; see DISGUISE *v.*, -Y[5].] Disguised, altered from familiar guise, mode, or appearance –1430.

Disgu·lf, -gu·lph, *v.* 1635. [DIS- 7 c.] To discharge as from a gulf.

Disgust (disgʊ·st), *sb.* 1598. [– Fr. *desgoust* (mod. *dégoût*), f. *desgouster* (mod. *dégoûter*), or It. *disgusto*, f. *disgustare*; see DIS- 4, GUSTO.] **1.** Strong distaste for food, drink, medicine, etc.; nausea, loathing 1611. (Formerly in milder sense.) **2.** Strong repugnance excited by that which is loathsome or offensive; profound instinctive dissatisfaction 1611. †**3.** An outbreak of mutual ill-feeling; a quarrel –1761. †**4.** That which causes repugnance; an annoyance. *Obs.* –1807.

1. To this day the [hare]..is an object of d. in certain parts of Russia 1885. **2.** He soon retreated in d. across the Alps S. AUSTIN. **3.** Some disgusts happen'd 'twixt Rustan and his brother SIR T. HERBERT. **4.** Some disgusts which she had received from the States HUME. Hence **Disgu·stful** *a.* causing disgust; nauseous; displeasing; disgusting; full of disgust. **Disgu·stful-ly** *adv.*, **-ness.**

Disgust (disgʊ·st), *v.* 1601. [– Fr. *desgouster* or It. *disgustare*; see prec.] †**1.** *trans.* To have a strong distaste for or repugnance to –1752. **2.** To offend the senses or sensibilities of 1650; *absol.* to be very distasteful 1756.

2. The remedy..disgusts the palate 1650. Want of the usual proportions in men and other animals is sure to d. BURKE. Hence **Disgu·sted** *ppl. a.* †distasteful; feeling disgust. **Disgu·ster** (*rare*). **Disgu·sting-ly** *adv.*, **-ness.**

Dish (diʃ), *sb.* [OE. *disć* plate, bowl, platter, corresp. to OS. *disk* (Du. *disch*) table, OHG. *tisc* plate (G. *tisch* table), ON. *diskr* (perh. – OE.) – L. *discus* quoit, (Vulg.) dish, disc (of a sundial); see DISCUS and cf. DAIS, DESK.] **1.** Any open vessel used to hold food at meals. Often restricted to those of oval, square, or irregular shape, as distinguished from *plates*. **b.** A hollow vessel of wood or metal, used for drinking, and also *esp.* as a receptacle for alms; a cup ME. **2.** The food served on or in a dish; a distinct variety of food 1526. **3.** As much as will fill or make a dish; a dishful 1596. Also *fig.* **4.** *transf.* Any shallow concave receptacle 1633. **5.** A dish-like concavity; *e.g.* a depression in a field, etc. 1810. **6. a.** *Tin-mining.* A gallon of ore ready for the smelter. **b.** *Lead-mining.* A measuring box for lead ore; by statute fixed to contain fifteen pints of water. **c.** Also, the proportion of ore paid as royalty to the mine land-lord, etc. 1531. †**7.** A quoit; quoit-playing –1552.

1. She brought forth butter in a lordly d. *Judg.* 5:25. I know him as the beggar knows his d. 1605. **2.** Let's carue him, as a D. fit for the Gods *Jul. C.* II. i. 173. **3.** The Boat returned with a good d. of Fish DAMPIER. He sate him pensive o'er a d. of tea BYRON. *fig.* Roger..had a D. of Chat with her MOTTEUX.

Comb.: **d.-cloth, -clout, -rag, -towel,** a cloth, clout, etc. used for washing dishes; **-wash,** the greasy water in which dishes have been washed; **-washer,** a scullion or scullery-maid; the pied or water wagtail (*Motacilla alba*); **-water** = *dish-wash*; also *attrib.*

Dish (diʃ), *v.*[1] 1586. [f. DISH *sb.*] **1.** *trans.* To put into a dish, ready for table. Also with *up*. Also *fig.* **2.** To make concave like a dish; to hollow *out* 1805. **3.** *intr.* To be or become concave; to cave in 1669. **4.** *intr.* Of a horse: To move the fore-feet in his trot with a scooping motion 1863. **5.** *trans. slang.* To 'do for'; to cheat, circumvent. [From the notion of meat being *done*, and *dished*.] 1798.

1. Jemima, d. up MARRYAT. To d. up a story DORAN. **3.** We had much trouble with our wagon, the wheel dishing frequently 1886. **5.** I believe it [the House of Commons] to be completely used up. Reform has dished it DISRAELI.

Dish, *v.*[2] *Sc.* 1821. [var. of Sc. *dush*, itself perh. a modification of DASH *v.*] To push violently, thrust.

Dishabilitate (dis,hăbi·lite^it), *v.* 1662. [DIS- 6.] *Sc. Law.* To incapacitate, disqualify. Hence **Dishabilita·tion.**

Dishabille (disăbī·l, -bi·l). 1673. [Earliest forms *déshabillé*, etc. – Fr. *déshabillé*, subst. use of pa. pple. of *déshabiller* undress, f. *des-* DIS- 4 + *habiller* dress. For the muting of final *-é* cf. DEFILE *sb.*] **1.** Undress; the state of being dressed in a negligent style 1684. **2.** A garment of a negligent style 1673. Also *transf.* and *fig.*

1. To surprise his mistress in d. 1684. **2.** [Pepys] sets down his thoughts in a most becoming d. MISS MITFORD.

†**Dis,ha·bit,** *v. rare.* [DIS- 6.] To dislodge. SHAKS. *John* II. i. 220

†**Dis,ha·bited,** *ppl. a.* 1577. [f. Fr. *déshabité* without inhabitants + -ED[1].] Uninhabited; deserted of inhabitants –1602.

The d. towns afford them rooting CAREW.

Dis,habi·tuate, *v.* 1868. [f. DIS- 6 + HABITUATE *v.*, prob. after Fr. *déshabituer* in same sense.] To render unaccustomed.

Dis,hable, obs. f. DISABLE *v.*

Dishallow (dis,hæ·lo^u), *v.* 1552. [DIS- 6.] To undo the hallowing of; to profane.

God hateth the dishallowing of the Sabboth LATIMER.

Disharmonious (d ,hāɹmō^u·niəs), *a.* 1659. [f. DIS- 10 + HARMONIOUS, after *disharmony*.] **1.** Not in harmony or agreement. **2.** Of sounds: Discordant 1683.

Disharmonize (dis,hā·ɹmŏnəiz), *v.* 1801. [f. DIS- 6 + HARMONIZE, after next.] **1.** To put out of harmony; to make discordant. **2.** *intr.* To be out of harmony 1863.

Disharmony (dis,hā·ɹmŏni). 1602. [DIS- 9, prob. after *discord*.] **1.** Want of harmony or agreement. Also with *a* and *pl.* **2.** Discord, dissonance 1655.

1. D. of mind and tongue CARLYLE. Hence **Disharmo·nic,** †**-al** *a.*

Dis,hau·nt, *v.* (Chiefly *Sc.*) 1584. [– Fr. †*deshanter*; see DIS- 4, HAUNT *v.*] To cease to haunt; to absent oneself from.

†**Dis,hea·rt,** *v.* 1603. [DIS- 7 a.] = next –1616.

Dishearten (dis,hā·ɹt'n), *v.* 1599. [f. DIS- 6 + HEARTEN, or f. prec. + -EN[5], after *hearten*.] To deprive of heart or courage; to dispirit. Also with †*from*, or †*to* and *inf.*

Their former losse dishartned them so much WARNER. Hence **Dis,hea·rtenment.**

†**Dis,hei·r,** *v. rare.* 1607. [DIS- 7 b.] **1.** To deprive of one's inheritance. **2.** To deprive of an heir. DRYDEN.

Dishelm (dis,he·lm), *v.*¹ 1477. [f. DIS- 7 a + HELM *sb.*¹, after OFr. *desheaulmer*, in same sense.] To deprive of one's helmet. *intr.* for *refl.* To take off one's helmet.
Sir Raynold dishelmed the Englisshe knyght LD. BERNERS.

Dishelm (dis,he·lm), *v.*² [DIS- 7 a.] To deprive of the helm or rudder.

Disherison (dis,he·rizən), *sb.* ME. [orig. *disheriteson* – OFr. *des(h)eriteisun, -eison*, f. *des(h)eriter*; see next, -ISON.] The action of depriving of, or cutting off from, an inheritance; disinheritance.
Improvident alienations..to the d. of the lawful heirs WILLIAMS.

†**Disherit** (dis,he·rit), *v.* ME. [– OFr. *deseriter* (mod. *déshériter*) – Rom. **desheretare*, f. *des-* DIS- 4 + **heretare*, for late L. *hereditare*. Superseded by DISINHERIT.] To deprive or dispossess of an inheritance; to disinherit. Const. *of* (rarely *from*). Also *fig.* –1795. So †**Dis,he·ritance,** disinheritance. †**Dis,-he·ritor,** one who disinherits.

†**Dishe·vel,** *a.* ME. [var. of DISHEVELY, with muted *-é* as in ASSIGN *sb.*², DEFILE *sb.*] Without coif or head-dress; hence, with the hair unkempt. Sometimes app.: In dishabille. –1470.

Dishevel (diʃe·vĕl), *v.* 1598. [prob. chiefly a back-formation from DISHEVELLED. Cf. Fr. †*descheveler* (mod. *dé-*).] **1.** To loosen and throw about in disorder (hair and the like); to let (the hair) down. †**2.** *intr.* (for *refl.*) To hang loose or in disorder 1638.
1. The Peacock when he's viewed disheuels his faire traine 1618.

Dishevelled, -eled (diʃe·vĕld), *ppl. a.* 1450. [f. late ME. *dischevel(y*, f. *dischevelee*, (see DISHEVEL *a.* and next), f. OFr. *deschevelé*, pa. pple. of *descheveler*, f. *des-* DIS- 1 + *chevel* hair; see -ED¹.] †**a.** = DISHEVEL *a.* –1653. **b.** With disarranged dress 1612. Also *transf.*
1. She, so disheuld blusht SIDNEY. The dishevelled fair hastily following FIELDING. Our hair dischiveld, not platted nor crisped 1638. Hence **Dishe·velment,** d. condition.

†**Dishe·vely, -elee,** *ppl. a.* ME. [– OFr. *deschevelé*; see prec., -Y⁵.] = DISHEVEL *a.* –1450.

Dishful (di·ʃful). ME. [See -FUL.] As much as a dish will contain.

Dishing (di·ʃiŋ), *vbl. sb.* 1679. [f. DISH *v.*¹ + -ING¹.] The action of the verb DISH; oblique position of the spokes of a wheel.

Dishome (dis,hōᵘ·m), *v.* 1880. [DIS- 7 c.] To deprive of a home.

Dishonest (disǫ·nėst), *a.* ME. [– OFr. *deshoneste* (mod. *déshonnête*) – a Romanic form with *des-* for L. *dehonestus*; see DE- I. 6, DIS- 4.] †**1.** Entailing dishonour or disgrace; dishonourable, shameful –1760. †**2.** Unchaste, lewd, filthy –1734. †**3.** Ugly, hideous –1725. **4.** Of actions, etc.: Not straightforward or honourable, underhand; now, fraudulent, knavish 1611. **5.** Of persons: Wanting in honesty; disposed to cheat or defraud; thievish 1751.
1. The galowes and..dyshonest dethe CAXTON. **2.** *Hen. V*, I. ii. 50. **3.** Enormous beasts d. to the eye POPE. **4.** To get d. gaine *Ezek.* 22:27. D. artifices BUTLER. **5.** Imposed upon..by d. brethren JORTIN. Hence **Disho·nestly** *adv.*

†**Disho·nest,** *v.* ME. [– OFr. *deshonester* – a Rom. form with *des-* for L. *dehonestare*; see DE- I. 6, DIS- 4.] **1.** To bring dishonour –1670. **2.** To defame –1615. **3.** To defile –1652.
3. To deflour Virgins, d. Matrons FOXE.

Dishonesty (disǫ·nėsti). ME. [– OFr. *deshoneste*, mod. *déshonnêteté*, f. Rom. **deshonestus* for L. *dehonestus*; see DISHONEST *a.*] †**1.** Dishonour, discredit, shame; also with *pl.* –1596. †**2.** Unchastity, lewdness –1639. †**3.** Shameful appearance, ugliness, deformity –1535. **4.** Lack of probity; disposition to deceive, defraud, or steal. Also, a dishonest act. 1599.
1. We renounce the hidden things of dishonestie 2 *Cor.* 4:2. **4.** I neuer knew profit in dishonestie 1616.

Dishonour, -honor (disǫ·nəɹ), *sb.* ME. [– OFr. *deshonor* (mod. *déshonneur*) – Rom. **dishonor*; see DIS- 4, HONOUR.] **1.** The reverse of honour; the withholding of honour due to any one; a state of shame or disgrace; ignominy, indignity. Also with *a* and *pl.* **2.** A cause or source of shame, a disgrace 1553. **3.** *Comm.* Refusal or failure to honour or pay (a bill of exchange, etc.) 1834.
1. He would rather dye..then live in dishonor COGAN. **2.** His little daughter, whose sweet face He kissed..Becomes d. to her race TENNYSON. **3.** Notice of d. should be given to each indorser CRUMP.

Dishonour, -or (disǫ·nəɹ), *v.* ME. [–(O)Fr. *déshonorer* – med.L. *dishonorare*, f. L. *dis-* DIS- 4 + *honorare* HONOUR *v.*] **1.** *trans.* To deprive of honour; to treat with indignity; to violate the honour or respect due to any one. **2.** To violate the honour or chastity of; to defile ME. **3.** To bring dishonour upon, by one's conduct, etc.; to disgrace 1568. †**4.** To strip *of* what is an honour –1700. **5.** *Comm.* To refuse or fail to accept or pay (a bill of exchange, etc.) 1811.
1. To Value a man..at a low rate, is to D. him HOBBES. **3.** America..dishonours herself by tolerating slavery 1848. **4.** His scalp..dishonour'd quite of hair DRYDEN. Hence **Disho·noured, -ored,** *ppl. a.* **Disho·nourer, -orer.**

Dishonourable, -honorable (disǫ·nŏrăb'l), *a.* 1533. [orig. f. DISHONOUR *v.*; partly f. DIS- 10 + HONOURABLE.] **1.** Entailing dishonour; ignominious, base. **2.** Of persons: **a.** Disesteemed (*rare*). **b.** Devoid or negligent of honour; unprincipled, base 1611.
1. And peepe about To finde our selues d. Graves *Jul. C.* I. ii. 138. **2.** He that is honoured in pouertie, how much more in riches, and he that is d. in riches, how much more in pouertie *Ecclus.* 10:31. Hence **Disho·nourableness. Disho·nourably** *adv.*

Dis,ho·rn, *v.* 1598. [DIS- 7 a.] To deprive of horns.

Dis,ho·rse, *v.* 1859. [DIS- 7 c.] To unhorse.

Dishouse (dis,hau·z), *v.* 1586. [f. DIS- 6 or 7 + HOUSE *v.* or *sb.*] **1.** To oust from a house; also, to deprive of a habitation. **2.** To clear (ground) of houses 1640.
1. Make them melt as the dishowsed snaile 1586.

†**Dis,hu·mour,** *sb.* 1712. [DIS- 9.] Ill humour –1795. So †**Dis,hu·mour** *v.* to put out of humour.

Disillu·minate, *v. rare.* 1865. [DIS- 6.] To deprive of illumination; to darken.

Disillusion (disilⁱū·ʒən), *sb.* 1598. [DIS- 5 and 9. With sense 2 cf. Fr. *désillusion* (XIX).] †**1.** [DIS- 5.] Illusion, delusion –1603. **2.** [DIS- 9.] The action of freeing or becoming freed from illusion; the condition of being freed from illusion; disenchantment. Hence **Disillu·sion** *v.* to free from illusion, disenchant. **Disillu·sionize** *v.* to disillusion. **Disillu·sionment,** the action of disillusioning, or fact of being disillusioned.

Disillu·sive, *a.* 1878. [After *illusive.*] Tending to disillusion.

Disima·gine, *v.* 1647. [DIS- 6.] To imagine not to be.

Disimmu·re, *v.* 1611. [DIS- 6.] To set free from confining walls; to liberate.

†**Disimpa·rk,** *v.* 1609. [DIS- 6.] To turn out of a park, to free from the enclosure of a park –1675.

Disimpa·ssioned, *ppl. a.* Also **disem-.** 1861. [DIS- 10.] Freed or free from passion.
That pale soft sweet disempassioned moon BROWNING.

Disimpri·son, *v.* Also **disem-.** 1611. [f. DIS- 6 + IMPRISON. Cf. Fr. †*désemprisonner.*] To release from imprisonment or confinement.
'All History is an imprisoned Epic'..says Sauerteig there. I wish he had disimprisoned it in this instance CARLYLE.

Disimpro·ve, *v.* 1642. [DIS- 6.] To do the reverse of improving; to render worse in quality. *intr.* To grow worse. Hence **Disimpro·vement,** a change for the worse.

Disinca·rcerate, *v.* 1665. [DIS- 6.] = DISIMPRISON. Hence **Disincarcera·tion.**

Disinclination (disinklinēⁱ·ʃən). 1647. [DIS- 9.] Want of inclination or liking; slight dislike or aversion; indisposition.
His d. to the church CLARENDON. A d. from having recourse to unjust extremities 1813.

Disincline (disinkləi·n), *v.* 1647. [DIS- 6.] To deprive of inclination; to make indisposed, averse, or unwilling. *intr.* To incline not (*to do* something).
It served..to d. them from any reverence or affection to the queen CLARENDON. [He] felt disinclined for any more sleep 1888.

Disinclose, obs. var. of DISENCLOSE.

†**Disinco·rporate,** *ppl. a.* 1605. [DIS- 10.] Disunited or separated from a body, corporation, or society –1681.

Disincorporate (disinkǭ·ɹpŏreⁱt), *v.* 1697. [f. DIS- 6 + INCORPORATE *v.* Cf. Fr. *désincorporer* (XVII).] **1.** To undo the incorporation of, to dissolve (a corporation). **2.** To separate from a corporation or body 1701. Hence **Disincorpora·tion.**

†**Disincrea·se,** *v.* ME. [DIS- 6.] To decrease, diminish –1430.

Disincru·stant. 1878. [– Fr. *désincrustant*, f. *désincruster* remove incrustation from, f. *des-* DIS- 4 + *incruster*; see ENCRUST 4, -ANT¹.] Something that removes or prevents incrustation.

Disindivi·dualize, *v.* 1839. [DIS- 6.] To divest of individuality.

Disinfect (disinfe·kt), *v.* 1598. [– Fr. *désinfecter* (XVI), f. *des-* DIS- 4 + *infecter* INFECT *v.*] †**1.** To rid of an infection or infectious disease (*rare*) –1722. **2.** To cleanse from infection; to destroy the germs of disease in 1658. Also *absol.*
2. The best mode of disinfecting the clothes of scarlatina patients 1844. Hence **Disinfe·cter, -or,** he who or that which disinfects. **Disinfe·ction,** the action of disinfecting; destruction of the germs of infectious diseases.

Disinfe·ctant. 1837. [– Fr. *désinfectant*, pres. pple. of *désinfecter*; see prec., -ANT¹.] **1.** *adj.* Having the property of disinfecting 1875. **2.** *sb.* An agent having this property.

Disinfla·me, *v. rare.* 1611. [DIS- 6.] To make no longer inflamed; to deprive of ardour.

Disinge·nious, etc., 17th c. error for DISINGENUOUS, etc.

Disingenuity (di:sindʒėniū·ĭti). 1647. [f. next.] = DISINGENUOUSNESS (now more usual). Also with *a* and *pl.*

Disingenuous (disindʒe·niu,əs), *a.* 1655. [DIS- 10.] The opposite of *ingenuous*; lacking in frankness, insincere, morally fraudulent.
A D. Speaker 1718. The d. shift of a protest HALLAM. Hence **Disinge·nuously** *adv.*

Disinge·nuousness. 1674. [f. prec. + -NESS.] The quality of being disingenuous; insincerity, unfairness.
D. and double-dealing JANE AUSTEN.

†**Disinha·bit,** *v.* 1530. [DIS- 6.] To dispeople –1818. Hence †**Disinha·bited** *ppl. a.* without inhabitants.

Disinhe·rison. Also **disen-.** 1543. [f. DIS- 9: cf. next, DISHERISON.] = DISHERISON.

Disinherit (disinhe·rit), *v.* Also **disen-.** 1450. [f. DIS- 6 + INHERIT, superseding DISHERIT.] To deprive or dispossess of an inheritance; 'to cut off from an hereditary right' (J.); to prevent (a person) from coming into possession of a property or right which in the ordinary course would devolve upon him as heir. Also *fig.*
He was disinherited and turned out of his father's house HOOK. And thou, fair moon.. Stoop thy pale visage through an amber cloud, And d. Chaos, that reigns here MILT. *Comus* 334. Hence **Disinhe·ritable** *a.* liable to be disinherited. **Disinhe·ritance,** dispossession from an inheritance.

Disinhume (disinhiū·m), *v.* Also **disen-.** 1821. [DIS- 6.] To unbury, exhume.

Disintail, etc.; see DISENTAIL.

Disi·ntegrable, *a.* 1796. [f. DISINTEGRATE; see -ABLE.] Capable of being disintegrated.

Disi·ntegrant. 1855. [f. as prec. + -ANT¹.] **1.** *adj.* Disintegrating, or becoming disintegrated. **2.** *sb.* A disintegrating agent.

Disintegrate (disi·ntĭgreⁱt), *v.* 1796. [DIS- 6.] **1.** *trans.* To separate into its component parts or particles; to reduce to fragments, break up, destroy the cohesion or integrity of. Also *fig.* **b.** To separate as particles *from* the whole mass 1873. **2.** *intr.* To become disintegrated 18...
1. Marlites..are not disintegrated by exposure to the atmosphere KIRWAN. To d. the Homeric poems GLADSTONE. **2.** The Church itself was fast disintegrating FROUDE. Hence **Disi·ntegrative** *a.* tending to d. **Disi·ntegrator,** a machine for reducing substances to powder.

Disintegra·tion. 1796. [f. prec. + -ATION.] The action or process of disintegrating, or the condition of being disintegrated; breaking up; destruction of cohesion or integrity; *spec.* in *Geol.*, the wearing down of rocks by atmospheric influences. Also *fig.*

The d. of clay-slate rocks THOMSON, of nations HT. MARTINEAU, of Roman society MERIVALE.

Disinte·grity. 1785. [DIS- 9.] Want of entireness; disintegrated condition.

Disinter (disintə̄·ɹ), *v.* 1611. [– Fr. *désenterrer*; see DIS- 4, INTER *v.*] To take out of the earth in which it is buried; to unbury, exhume. Also *transf.* and *fig.*

†**Disinteress,** *v.* Pa. pple. **-essed, -est.** 1622. [– Fr. *désintéresser*; see DIS- 4, INTEREST. Superseded by DISINTEREST *v.*] = DISINTEREST *v.* –1655. So †**Disintere·ssment,** disinterestedness.

Disinterest, *sb.* 1658. [DIS- 9.] **1.** That which is contrary to interest or advantage; prejudice. Now *rare.* 1662. †**2.** Disinterestedness –1805.

1. Whatever..tends to the D. of the Public, is evil NORRIS.

Disi·nterest, *v.* Now *rare.* 1612. [DIS- 6; superseding DISINTERESS.] **1.** To rid or divest of interest or concern; to detach from the interest or party of. **2.** To render disinterested 1681.

Disinterest, var. of DISINTERESSED *ppl. a.*

Disi·nterested, *ppl. a.* 1612. [f. DISINTEREST *v.* + -ED[1], or f. DIS- 10 + INTERESTED.] **1.** Without interest or concern. ? *Obs.* **2.** Not influenced by interest; now always, Unbiased by personal interest 1659.

1. A careless d. spirit is not part of his character 'JUNIUS'. **2.** His d. kindness to us LIVINGSTONE. Hence **Disi·nterested-ly** *adv.*, **-ness.**

Disi·nteresting, *ppl. a.* 1737. [f. DIS- 10 + INTERESTING *ppl. a.*] Uninteresting.

Disinte·rment. 1790. [f. DISINTER *v.* + -MENT.] The action of disinterring; exhumation; something disinterred.

Disinthrall, Disinthrone; see DISEN-.

Disi·ntricate, *v.* 1598. [DIS- 6.] To free from intricacy; to disentangle, unravel, extricate.

†**Disinu·re,** *v.* 1613. [DIS- 6.] To disaccustom –1644.

God..dis-inuring his chosen Israel from his wonted call JACKSON.

Disinve·st, *v.* 1630. [DIS- 6.] To deprive of that with which one is invested; to strip, divest (*lit.* and *fig.*). Hence **Disinve·stiture, Disinve·sture,** the action of disinvesting; disinvested state.

Disinvi·gorate, *v.* *rare.* [DIS- 6.] To enervate. SYD. SMITH.

†**Disinvi·te,** *v.* 1580. [DIS- 6.] To retract or cancel an invitation to –1665. Hence †**Disinvita·tion,** the opposite of an invitation.

Disinvo·lve, *v.* 1611. [DIS- 6.] To free from an involved condition; to unfold; to disentangle.

Disja·sked, -et, -it, *ppl. a.* *Sc.* 1816. [perh. a corruption of *dejected.*] Dilapidated; decayed (*lit.* and *fig.*).

Disject (disdʒe·kt), *v.* 1581. [– *disject-*, pa. ppl. stem of L. *disicere* throw asunder, f. *dis-* DIS- 1 + *jacere* throw.] To cast or break asunder; to scatter. Hence **Disje·ction,** forcible dispersion, rout.

‖**Disjecta membra.** *Lat. phr.* An alteration of Horace's *disjecti membra poetæ*, used as = Scattered remains.

Disjoin (disdʒoi·n), *v.* ME. [– *desjoign-*, pres. stem of OFr. *desjoindre* (mod. *dé-*) :– L. *disjungere*, f. *dis-* DIS- 4 + *jungere* JOIN.] **1.** To undo the joining of; to disunite; to separate; to sunder 1483. †**2.** To disjoint –1612. **3.** *intr.* (for *refl.*) To part, become separate 1592.

1. Deserts and..mountaines disjoyning the provinces 1601. That mariage therfore God himself dis-joyns MILT. **3.** Till breathlesse he disioynd, and backward drew SHAKS.

†**Disjoi·nt,** *sb.* ME. [– OFr. *desjointe*, *dis-*separation, division, rupture, subst. use of fem. of pa. pple. of *desjoindre*; see prec.] A disjointed or out-of-joint condition; a dilemma, fix –1553.

What wyght þat stont in swych disioynte CHAUCER.

†**Disjoi·nt,** *ppl. a.* ME. [– OFr. *desjoint*, pa. pple. of *desjoindre*; see DISJOIN *v.*] **1.** Disjointed, out of joint –1717. **2.** In a dilemma 1500. **3.** Disjoined; separate –1660.

Disjoint (disdʒoi·nt), *v.* ME. [orig. f. DISJOINT *ppl. a.*, but in some uses treated as f. JOINT *sb.*] **1.** *trans.* To put out of joint; to destroy the connection and arrangement of; to dislocate, dismember. Also *fig.* **2.** To disjoin, disunite 1533. **3.** To separate joint from joint; to take in pieces at the joints 1587. Also *absol.* **4.** *intr.* (for *refl.*) To be disjointed; to suffer dislocation; to go out of joint; to come in pieces 1605.

1. To d. the frame of society PUSEY. *fig.* A writer of taste..disjointing the order of his ideas GIBBON. **2.** Great Britain, disjointed from her colonies T. JEFFERSON. **3.** Like watches by unskilfull men Disjoynted LOVELACE. A good Carver..cuts up, disjoints, and uncases with incomparable Dexterity STEELE. Hence **Disjoi·nted** *ppl. a.* separated joint from joint; disjoined. **Disjoi·nted-ly** *adv.*, **-ness.**

Disjoi·ntly, *adv.* 1621. [f. DISJOINT *ppl. a.* + -LY[2].] **1.** Separately; disjunctly: opp. to *conjointly* 1634. **2.** Disconnectedly 1621.

Disjudication, error in Dicts. for DIJUDICATION.

Disjunct (disdʒʊ·ŋkt), *a.* 1594. [– L. *disjunctus*, pa. pple. of *disjungere*; see DISJOIN *v.*] **1.** Disjoined, separated; †distant. Now *rare* exc. in techn. senses.) 1599. †**2.** *Math.* = DISCONTINUOUS –1597. **3.** *Mus.* (Opp. to CONJUNCT.) 1694. **4.** *Logic.* etc. †**a.** = DISJUNCTIVE. **b.** = DISCRETE. **c.** Applied to the alternative members of a disjunctive proposition. 1608.

3. *D. tetrachords*, tetrachords separated by an interval of a tone. Hence †**Disju·nctly** *adv.*

Disjunction (dis,dʒʊ·ŋkʃən). ME. [– OFr. *disjunction* (mod. *disjonction*) or its source, L. *disjunctio*, f. *disjunct-*; see prec., -ION.] **1.** The action of disjoining or condition of being disjoined; separation, disunion. **2.** *Logic*, etc. The relation of the terms of a disjunctive proposition; hence, a disjunctive proposition; an alternative 1588.

1. Death being..a d. of the Soul from the Body HY. MORE.

Disjunctive (dis,dʒʊ·ŋktiv). 1570. [– L. *disjunctivus*, f. *disjunct-*; see prec., -IVE.]

A. *adj.* **1.** Having the property of disjoining; characterized by separation. **2.** *Logic*, etc. Involving a choice between two (or more) things or statements; alternative 1584. **3.** *Gram.* Applied to conjunctions that express an alternative or imply an adversative relation between the clauses which they connect 1628.

2. *D. proposition*, one in which it is asserted that one or other of two (or more) statements is true. *D. syllogism*, one in which the major premiss is d., and the minor affirms or denies one of the alternatives stated in the major; *loosely*, any syllogism containing a d. premiss. **3.** The d. conjunctions..which bear this contradictory name, because, while they disjoin the sense, they conjoin the sentences J. HARRIS.

B. *sb.* **1. a.** *Logic.* A disjunctive proposition; see A. 2. Hence generally, **b.** An alternative 1533. **2.** *Gram.* A disjunctive conjunction; see A. 3.

Hence **Disju·nctively** *adv.* alternatively, adversatively.

Disju·ncture. ME. [– med.L. *disjunctura*, f. as prec.; see -URE. Cf. OFr. *desjointure.*] The fact of disjoining or disjoined condition; disjunction; breach. Also *fig.*

Disjune (disdʒū·n), *sb.* Chiefly *Sc. arch.* 1491. [– OFr. *desjeün* (mod. dial. *déjun*), f. *desjeüner* (mod. *déjeûner*) break fast, breakfast, f. *des-*, *dé-* (DE- I. 6) + *jeün* (mod. *jeun*) fasting :– L. *jejunus.*] = DÉJEUNER.

Disk, disc (disk). 1664. [– Fr. *disque* or its source L. DISCUS.] **1.** = DISCUS 1. Now *Hist.* 1715. **2.** A thin circular plate of any material 1803. **3.** Anything resembling a circular plate 1711. **4.** *spec.* The (apparently flat) surface or face of the sun, the moon, or a planet, as it appears to the eye 1664. Also *transf.* **5.** *Bot.* A round and flattened part in a plant. *spec.* **a.** A collection of tubular florets in the flower-head of *Compositæ*. **b.** An enlargement of the torus or receptacle of a flower, below or around the pistil. **c.** The flat surface of a leaf, etc. (In these senses always spelt *disk.*) 1727. **6.** *Zool.* A roundish flattened part in an animal body. *spec.* **a.** The central rounded and flattened part containing the oral opening in Echinoderms, Cœlenterates, etc. **b.** The set of feathers surrounding the eye of an owl. **c.** The flat locomotive organ or 'foot' of a gastropod. 1761. **7.** *Anat.* Applied to various round flat structures, as *blood-disks, intervertebral disks*, etc. **8.** A phonograph or gramophone record 1888.

1. In empty air their sportive jav'lins throw, Or whirl the disk POPE.

attrib. and *comb.*: **d.-armature,** an armature wound so that its coils lie in the form of a d.; **-barrow,** a flat circular barrow or tumulus; **-dynamo,** a dynamo furnished with a d.-armature; **-engine, -steam-engine,** a type of rotary engine in which the steam acts upon a revolving or oscillating d.; **-owl,** the barn-owl; **-valve,** a valve formed by a circular d., with a rotary or reciprocating motion; **-wheel,** a kind of worm-wheel in which the spur-gear is driven by a spiral thread in the face of the d.

Hence **Disked** *a.* having or showing a d. (*rare*). **Di·skless** *a.*

†**Dis,ki·ndness.** 1596. [DIS- 9.] Unkindness; unfriendliness. Also with *a* and *pl.* –1774.

†**Dis,kno·w,** *v.* [DIS- 6.] To fail to know, to ignore. SYLVESTER.

†**Disla·de,** *v.* *rare.* 1609. [DIS- 6.] *trans.* To unlade, unload –1649.

†**Disla·dy,** *v.* [DIS- 7 b. Cf. Fr. †*desdamer* in same sense.] To deprive of the rank of a lady. B. JONS.

Dislea·f, -lea·ve, *v.* 1598. [DIS- 7 a.] To strip of leaves.

†**Disle·al,** *a.* [– It. *disleale.*] Disloyal. SPENSER *F. Q.* II. v. 5.

Disli·kable, *a.* 1843. [f. DISLIKE *v.* + -ABLE.] Capable of being disliked; exciting dislike, as *d. qualities.*

Dislike (disləi·k), *sb.* 1577. [f. DISLIKE *v.*] †**1.** Displeasure, disapproval (as directed to some object) –1742. **2.** The contrary feeling to liking; distaste, aversion, repugnance. Also with *a* and *pl.* 1597. †**3.** Discord, disagreement –1632.

1. A letter from the government, in d. of such proceedings PENN. **2.** We need not show d. too coarsely LYTTON. Away with these weake dislikes BP. HALL. **3.** *Tr. & Cr.* II. iii. 236. Hence †**Disli·keful** *a.* unpleasant; characterized by d.

†**Disli·ke,** *a.* 1596. [DIS- 10.] Unlike, dissimilar –1644.

Dislike (disləi·k), *v.* 1555. [f. DIS- 6 + LIKE *v.*[1]; superseded MISLIKE.] †**1.** *trans.* (Only in 3rd pers.) To displease, annoy –1814. †**2.** *intr.* To be displeased or dissatisfied (*with*); to disapprove (*of*) –1677. **3.** *trans.* Not to like; to regard with aversion; to have an objection to. (The opposite of LIKE *v.*; and so less strong than *hate.*) 1594. †**b.** To express aversion to –1667.

1. Ile do 't, but it dislikes me *Oth.* II. iii. 49. **3.** I may neither choose whom I would, nor refuse whom I d. *Merch. V.* I. ii. 26. I neuer heard any Souldier d. it *Meas. for M.* I. ii. 18. Hence **Disli·ker.**

Disli·kelihood. *rare.* [DIS- 9.] Improbability. SCOTT.

†**Disli·ken,** *v.* [f. DISLIKE *a.* + -EN[5], after *like, liken.*] To make unlike; to disguise *Wint. T.* IV. iv. 666.

†**Disli·keness.** 1623. [f. DISLIKE *a.* + -NESS, or f. DIS-9 + LIKENESS.] Unlikeness –1690.

Dislimb (disli·m), *v.* 1662. [DIS- 7 a.] *trans.* To cut off the limbs of; to tear limb from limb.

Dislimn (disli·m), *v.* 1606. [f. DIS- 6 + LIMN.] **1.** *trans.* To obliterate the outlines of; to efface, blot out. **2.** *intr.* (for *refl.*) To become effaced, to vanish 1832.

1. That [clowd] which is now a Horse, euen with a thoght The Racke dislimes, and makes it indistinct, As water is in water *Ant. & Cl.* IV. xiv 10.

Dislink (disli·ŋk), *v.* 1610. [f. DIS- 6 + LINK *v.*] To unlink, uncouple, separate (things that are linked) (*lit.* and *fig.*).

†**Dislive** (disləi·v), *v.* 1598. [app. f. DIS- 7 a or c + LIFE.] To deprive of life; to kill –1631.

Disload (dislōᵘ·d), *v.* 1568. [DIS- 6.] *trans.* and *intr.* To unload, disburden.

Dislocable (di·slŏkăb'l), *a.* *rare* [f. DISLOCATE *v.* + -ABLE.] Displaceable. BENTHAM.

Dislocate (di·slŏkeⁱt), *v.* 1605. [prob. back-formation from DISLOCATION (first in medical sense), but cf. earlier †*dislocate* ppl. a.

(c1400).] **1.** *trans.* To put out of its proper (or former) place; to displace. Now *rare.* 1623. **2.** To put out of proper position in relation to contiguous parts 1660. **b.** *spec.* To put (a bone) out of joint; to 'put out' (a joint or limb) 1605. Also *fig.*

1. A plant may be dislocated from an old, and removed to a new bed HOLLAND. **2.** These hands ..are apt enough to d. and tear Thy flesh and bones *Lear* IV. ii. 65. *fig.* He contrived to d. all their military plans T. JEFFERSON. So **Di·slocate** *ppl. a.*

Dislocation (dislǒkēⁱ·ʃən). late ME. [– OFr. *dislocation* or med.L. *dislocatio*, f. *dislocat-*, pa. ppl. stem of *dislocare*, f. *dis-* DIS- 1 + L. *locare* place; see -ION.] **1.** Displacement; *spec.* displacement of a bone from its natural position in the joint; luxation. **b.** *Geol.* A displacement in a stratum or series of strata caused by a fracture with upheaval or subsidence; a fault 1695. **c.** *Mil.* The distribution of troops to a number of garrisons, camps, etc. 1808. **2.** *fig.* Displacement of parts; disarrangement; a disordered state 1659.

2. The utter d. of society PUSEY.

Dislodge (dislǫ·dʒ), *v.* 1450. [– OFr. *dislog(i)er*, f. *des-* DIS- 4 + *logier*, (also mod.) *loger* LODGE *v.*] **1.** *trans.* To remove or turn out of a place of lodgement; to displace 1500. †**b.** *Mil.* To shift the position of (a force) –1670. **c.** *Mil.* To drive (a foe) out of his position 1450. **2.** *intr.* (for *refl.*) To go away from one's lodging or abode; to remove 1489.

1. To d. a wilde Bore SIR T. HERBERT, a Ministry J. W. CROKER, a stone STEPHEN. To d. the Spaniards from their fortifications 1783. **2.** Many of the inhabitants of Paris began to d. HUME. Hence †**Dislo·dge** *sb.* dislodgement. **Dislodgement, -lodgment,** the act of dislodging; displacement.

†**Disloi·gn,** *v.* [– OFr. *desloignier*, f. *des-* DIS- 1 + *loin* far.] To remove to a distance. SPENSER *F. Q.* IV. x. 24.

†**Dislo·ve.** 1533. [DIS- 9.] Unfriendliness, hatred –1823.

Disloyal (disloi·ăl), *a.* 1477. [– OFr. *desloial* (mod. *déloyal*), f. *des-* DIS- 4 + *loial* LOYAL.] Not loyal; unfaithful to the obligations of friendship or honour, to the marriage tie, etc. (now *rare*); wanting in loyalty to the government or constituted authority; perfidious, treacherous.

Thou do'st suspect That I haue been disloyall to thy bed *Rich. II*, V. ii. 105. Executed by your Lordship as seditious and disloyall PRYNNE.

Disloyalty (disloi·ălti). 1481. [f. prec. + -TY¹, or f. DIS- 9 + LOYALTY. Cf. OFr. *desloyau(l)té* (mod. *déloyauté*).] The quality of being disloyal; now *esp.* Violation of allegiance or duty to one's sovereign, state, or government.

Dislustre (dislɒ·stəɹ), *v.* 1638. [DIS- 7 a.] **1.** To deprive of lustre; to dim, sully. **2.** *intr.* To lose its lustre 1890.

Dismai·l, *v. arch.* 1450. [– OFr. *desmailler*, f. *des-* DIS- 4 + *maille* MAIL *sb.*¹] To divest of mail; to break the mail off.

Dismal (di·zmăl). ME. [– AFr. *dis mal* (XIII) :– med.L. *dies mali* evil days.]

†**A.** *sb.*¹ (The original use.) The *dies mali*, evil, unlucky days, of the mediæval calendar, called also *dies Ægyptiaci*; hence, Evil days (generally), days of gloom, the days of old age –1400.

A waytiþ not þeis Egipcian daies, þat we call dysmal 1400.

B. *adj.* [orig. attrib. use of A.] †**1.** Of days: Of or belonging to the *dies mali*; unlucky –1618. †**2.** Of other things; Unlucky, sinister, malign, fatal –1632. **3.** Disastrous, calamitous. (Now *rare.*) 1592. **4.** Causing dismay; dreadful; now, Causing gloom; depressing, miserable 1588. **5.** Such as causes gloom or depression; sombre, dreary, or cheerless 1617. **6.** (Subjectively) gloomy or miserable 1705.

1. An ugly feend, more fowle than dismall day SPENSER. **4.** Dire is the conflict, d. is the din POPE. **5.** Blacke is not knowne among them, they say tis dismall and a signe of hell and sorrowe SIR T. HERBERT. The dismallest howlings of the wolves DE FOE. **6.** Wrote d. letters to the Court BP. BURNET.

C. *sb.*² [Ellipt. or absol. use of B.] †**1.** A dismal person; *e.g.* a funeral mute –1708. †**2.** *pl.* Mourning garments –1778. **3.** *pl.* Low spirits 1762. **4.** A local name of tracts of swampy land on the eastern sea-board of the U.S. 1763.

Hence **Disma·lity,** d. quality or state; an instance of this. **Di·smalize** *v.* to make d. **Di·smally** *adv.*, **-ness.**

Disman (dismæ·n), *v.* 1627. [DIS- 7.] †**1.** *trans.* To deprive of what constitutes the man –1651. **2.** To deprive of men. KINGLAKE.

Dismantle (dismæ·nt'l), *v.* 1579. [– OFr. *desmanteler* (mod. *dé-* in mil. sense), f. *des-* DIS- 4 + *manteler* fortify.] †**1.** *trans.* To divest of a mantle or cloak (*lit.* and *fig.*) –1691. Also †*intr.* (for *refl.*). **2.** To deprive *of* (clothing, covering, equipment, or fortifications); *esp.* to strip (a fortress) of its defences, (a vessel) of its rigging, etc. 1601. **3.** To render useless for its purpose; to pull down, take to pieces, destroy 1579.

1. Muffle your face, Dis-mantle you *Wint. T.* IV. iv. 666. **2.** Houses..dismantled of their roofs 1879. **3.** The gun was dismounted..the carriage dismantled and conveyed piecemeal to the opposite shore 1853.

Hence **Disma·ntlement.**

†**Disma·rch,** *v.* 1596. [– OFr. *desmarchier* (mod. *démarcher*) retire, etc., f. *des-* DIS- 4 + *marchier* MARCH *v.*²] *intr.* To march or fall back, to retreat –1635.

†**Disma·rry,** *v. rare.* [– OFr. *desmarier* (mod. *dé-*), f. *des-* DIS- 4 + *marier* MARRY *v.*] To annul the marriage of. LD. BERNERS.

Disma·rshall, *v. rare.* [DIS- 6.] To derange, throw into confusion. DRUMM. OF HAWTH.

†**Disma·sk,** *v.* 1588. [– Fr. †*desmasquer* (mod. *dé-*), f. *des-* DIS- 4 + *masquer* MASK *v.*³] To divest of a mask or covering; to unmask –1651.

Dismast (dismɑ·st), *v.* 1747. [DIS- 7 a; cf. Fr. *démâter* (XVII).] To deprive of masts; to break down the masts of.

A furious storm..dismasted his ship PRESCOTT. Hence **Disma·stment,** the action of dismasting.

†**Dismaw·,** *v.* 1620. [DIS- 7 c.] To empty out from the maw.

Dismay (dismēⁱ·), *sb.* 1590. [f. DISMAY *v.*] Utter loss of moral courage or resolution in prospect of danger or difficulty; faintness of heart from terror or inability to cope with the situation; †dismaying influence or operation (SPENSER *F. Q.* V. 88. 50).

Yet would he not for all his great d. Give over to effect his first intent SPENSER *F.Q.* II. xi. 41. Hence **Dismay·ful** *a.* appalling; **-ly** *adv.*

Dismay (dismēⁱ·), *v.* ME. [– OFr. **desmaier, demaier* :– Rom. **dismagare* deprive of power, f. L. *dis-* DIS- 4 + Gmc. **mag-* be able, MAY *v.*¹] **1.** *trans.* To deprive of moral courage at the prospect of peril or trouble; to appal or paralyse with fear or apprehension; utterly to discourage, daunt, or dishearten. *refl.* †To be filled with dismay. †**2.** To defeat by sudden onslaught –1596. †**3.** *intr.* To become utterly discouraged or faint-hearted –1596.

1. The enemies were dispersed and dismayed GIBBON. **2.** SPENSER *F.Q.* VI. x. 13. **3.** 1 *Hen. VI*, III. iii. 1. Hence **Dismay·edness,** dismayed condition. **Dismay·er.** †**Dismay·ment,** dismay.

Disme (dəim), var. of DIME *sb.* and *v.*

†**Dismea·surable,** *a.* 1474. [– OFr. *desmesurable*, f. *des-* DIS- 4 + *mesurable* MEASURABLE.] Beyond measure. Hence †**Dismea·surably** *adv.*

†**Dismea·sured,** *a.* 1483. [f. DIS- 10 + *measured*, repr. OFr. *desmesuré* (mod. *dé-*).] **1.** Unmeasured; unrestrained –1585. **2.** In false measure 1574.

Dismember (disme·mbər), *v.* ME. [– OFr. *desmember* (mod. *dé-*) :– Rom. **desmembrare*, f. *des-* DIS- 4 + L. *membrum* MEMBER *sb.*] **1.** *trans.* To deprive of limbs or members; to cut off the limbs or members of; to tear or divide limb from limb. Also *transf.* and *fig.* †**2.** To cut off, sever from the body –1694. Also †*fig.* and *transf.* **3.** [f. DIS- 7 b + MEMBER.] To cut off from membership 1649.

1. Fowls obscene dismember'd his remains POPE. To d. (= carve) a Hern 1804. Italy.. poor Italy lies dismembered, scattered asunder, not appearing in any protocol or treaty as a unity at all CARLYLE. **3.** The new members.. were soon dismembered by vote of the house NORTH. Hence **Disme·mberer,** one who or that which dismembers.

Disme·mbered, *ppl. a.* 1552. [f. prec. + -ED¹.] In the senses of the vb.; *spec.* in *Her.* Depicted without limbs or members; or, with the members separate from the body as if just cut off.

Disme·mberment. 1658. [f. as prec. + -MENT. Cf. OFr. *desmembrement* (mod. *dé-*).] **1.** The act of dismembering (*lit.* and *fig*). 1751; quasi-*concr.* a detached part formed by separation from the main body 1830. **2.** Cutting off from membership 1658.

1. The present violent d. and partition of Poland 1772. Aversion..to the d. of their country from the Aragonese monarchy PRESCOTT. var. †**Dismembra·tion.**

Di·smembrator. 1877. [Goes with contemp. *dismembrate*, f. DISMEMBER + -ATE³; see -OR 2.] Something that disintegrates or dismembers; *spec.* an apparatus for separating flour from bran, after crushing in a roller mill.

†**Disme·rit,** *v.* 1484. [f. DIS- 6 or 7 a + MERIT *v.* or *sb.*] To deprive of or lose merit; cf. DEMERIT *v.* –1629.

†**Disme·ttled,** *ppl. a. rare.* 1650. [DIS- 7 a.] Deprived of mettle; spiritless.

Dismiss (dismi·s), *v.* Pa. t. and pple. **dismissed,** †**-mist.** 1477. [First in *pa. pple.*, repr. OFr. *desmis* (mod. *démis*) :– med.L. *dismissus*, for L. *dimissus*, pa. pple. of *dimittere*, f. *di-* DI-¹ + *mittere* send; see DIMISS, which *dismiss* superseded.] **1.** *trans.* To disperse, dissolve; to disband 1582. Also *intr.* (for *refl.*). **2.** *trans.* To send away (a person); to bid or allow to depart 1548. Also *transf.* of things. **3.** To send away or remove from office, employment, or position 1477. **4.** To discard, reject. Also *absol.* 1610. **5.** To put away, get rid of 1592. **6.** To have done with (a subject), bring to an end; hence to treat of summarily 1698. **7.** *Law.* †**a.** *refl.* (with *of* or *inf.*) To free or exclude oneself from a burden or advantage –1642. **b.** To send out of court, reject (a claim or action) 1607.

1. The boys may d. 1809. **2.** Please you dismisse me, eyther with I, or no 3 *Hen. VI*, III. ii. 78. **3.** *spec.* in the army and navy, not debarring from further employment in public service otherwise than in the army (or navy): cf. CASHIER *v.* 2. To be dismissed of the court LYLY. Dismist the treasury 1692. **5.** He, smiling, said, D. your Fear DRYDEN. Hence †**Dismi·ss** *sb.* a dismissal. **Dismi·ssible, -able** *a.*

Dismissal (dismi·săl). 1806. [f. DISMISS *v.* + -AL¹; cf. *committal*, etc. A recent word, repl. the more regular DISMISSION.] = next.

Dismission (dismi·ʃən). 1547. [f. as prec. + -ION, after Fr. †*desmission* (mod. *dé-*; see DEMISSION²).] **1.** The action of dismissing or sending away in various directions 1646. **2.** Permission to go, leave to depart; earlier, formal leave-taking 1608. **3.** Deprivation of office, dignity, or position; discharge from service 1547. **4.** Liberation, discharge 1609. **5.** Rejection, discarding 1611. **6.** Putting aside from consideration 1742.

1. The Diet..had this Day a final D. 1711. **3.** To be punished by d. from the public service MACAULAY.

Dismissive (dismi·siv), *a.* 1645. [f. as prec. + -IVE.] Tending to dismiss; valedictory.

Dismissory (dismi·səri), *a.* (*sb.*) 1647. [var. of DIMISSORY (XIV, XVI), after DISMISS.] = DIMISSORY.

†**Dismi·t,** *v.* ME. [– med.L. *dismittere*, for cl.L. *dimittere* DIMIT. Cf. OFr. *desmetre*.] **1.** *trans.* To send away; to let go. **2.** *refl.* To divest oneself of; to relinquish –1496.

†**Dismo·rtgage,** *v.* [DIS- 7 a.] To free from mortgage. HOWELL.

Dismount (dismau·nt), *v.* 1544. [f. DIS- 6 + MOUNT *v.*, prob. after OFr. *desmonter*, etc., med.L. *dismontare*.]

I. *intr.* **1.** To come down from a height; to descend 1579. **2.** To get down, alight (*from* a horse, etc.; formerly, *from* a vehicle) 1588.

1. The bright Sunne gynneth to d. SPENSER. **2.** Neither yet in the day of battell ought he to d. 1598.

II. *trans.* **1.** To come down from; to get off, alight from (a horse, etc.) 1589. **2.** (*causal*) To unseat, unhorse 1599. **3.** To remove from that on or in which it has been mounted, set, or enclosed; to take (mechanism) to pieces 1544. **4.** To set, put, or bring down; to lower. ? *Obs.* 1597. †**5.** *fig.* (largely from 2) –1718.

1. He straight dismounts his throne QUARLES. **3.** One of our Ships..had dismounted Two of their Batteries 1707. *Twel.N.* III. iv. 244. **5.** But Superstition dismountes all this [Sense, Philosophy, Piety, etc.] BACON. Hence **Dismou·nt** *sb.* an act or method of dismounting.

Disna, *Sc.* = does not; see DO *v.*

†**Disna·tural,** *a.* ME. [– OFr. *desnaturel*, f. *des-* DIS- 4 + *naturel* NATURAL.] Contrary to nature –1677.

Disna·turalize, *v.* 1704. [f. DIS- 6 + NATURALIZE.] = DENATURALIZE *v.* 1, 2.

Disnature (disnē^i·tiŭɹ), *v.* 1450. [– OFr. *desnaturer* (mod. *dé-*). See DIS- 4, NATURE.] †**1.** *intr.* To get into or be in a disordered condition. CAXTON. **2.** *trans.* To render unnatural 1450.

Disnest (disne·st), *v. rare.* 1596. [DIS- 7 c.] To dislodge from, or as from, a nest; to void (as a nest) *of* its occupants.

Disobedience (disobī·diĕns). ME. [– OFr. *desobediance*, from a Rom. formation for eccl.L. *inobœdientia*; see DIS- 4, OBEDIENCE.] The fact or condition of being disobedient; neglect or refusal to obey; violation of a command or of a prohibition; an instance of this.

Adam..And Eve..the worlde dampned..By d. HAWES. So †**Disobe·diency,** †**Disobei·sance.**

Disobedient (disobī·diĕnt), *a.* ME. [– OFr. *desobedient*, from a Rom. formation for eccl. L. *inobœdiens*, f. *inobœdire*; see DIS- 4, OBEDIENT.] Withholding obedience; refusing or failing to obey; not observant of authoritative command; guilty of breach of prescribed duty; refractory, rebellious. **b.** *transf.* Intractable, stubborn 1588.

These were not loving subjects, but d. rebels SCOTT. *transf.* D. to any medicine 1588. Hence **Disobe·diently** *adv.* So †**Disobei·sant.**

Disobey (disobē^i·), *v.* ME. [– (O)Fr. *désobéir* – Rom. **desobedire*, for eccl. L. *inobœdire*; see DIS- 4, OBEY.] **1.** *intr.* To be disobedient. **2.** *trans.* [The obj. repr. an earlier dative.] To refuse or neglect to obey (any one); to neglect wilfully, transgress, or violate, the commands or orders of; to refuse submission to ME.

1. The wish to d. is already disobedience RUSKIN. **2.** Ther might nothing hem d. GOWER. Him who disobeys Me disobeys MILT. *P.L.* V. 611. To d. a father 1797, God and the law JOWETT. Hence **Disobey·er,** one who disobeys; a rebel.

†**Disobliga·tion.** 1616. [DIS- 9.] **1.** Freedom or release from obligation –1770. **2.** A slight –1788. **3.** The fact or feeling of being disobliged –1754; a grudge 1754.

†**Diso·bligatory,** *a.* 1649. [DIS- 10.] Not binding; releasing from obligation.

Disoblige (disobləi·dʒ), *v.* 1603. [– (O)Fr. *désobliger* :– Rom. **desobligare*, f. *des-* DIS- 4 + *obligare* OBLIGE.] †**1.** *trans.* To release from duty or engagement. Const. *of, from.* –1678. **2.** To refuse or neglect to oblige; not to consult or comply with the wishes of; hence, to put a slight upon, affront 1632. **3.** To inconvenience, incommode, annoy 1668.

1. To d. themselves of their greatest duty DRUMM. OF HAWTH. **2.** Colonel Lesley..being lately disobliged (as they called it) by the King, that is, denied somewhat he had a mind to have CLARENDON. **3.** I must..get our disobliging neighbours turned out MRS. CARLYLE. Hence **Disobli·gement** = DISOBLIGATION 1, 2. **Disobli·ging-ly** *adv.*, **-ness.**

Disobstru·ct, *v.* ? *Obs.* 1611. [DIS- 6.] = DEOBSTRUCT.

†**Diso·ccident,** *v.* [f. DIS- 6, after DISORIENT.] To throw out of reckoning as to the west; to confuse as to the points of the compass. MARVELL.

Disoccupa·tion. 1834. [f. DIS- 9 + OCCUPATION; cf. Fr. *désoccupation* (XVII).] Lack of occupation, unoccupied condition.

Disomatous (dəisō^u·mătəs), *a.* 1857. [f. Gr. *δισώματος* double-bodied (f. *δι-* DI-² + *σῶμα, σωματ-* body) + -OUS.] Having two bodies.

†**Disopi·nion.** 1598. [DIS- 9.] **1.** Adverse or mean opinion (*of*) –1705. **2.** Difference of opinion; dissent (*rare*) –1640.

†**Diso·ppilate,** *v.* 1577. [f. DIS- 6 + OPPILATE. Cf. Fr. *désopiler.*] *Med.* = DEOPPILATE –1652.

Disorb (disǭ·ɹb), *v.* 1606. [f. DIS- 7 a, c, + ORB *sb.*¹] **1.** *trans.* To remove from its orb. **2.** To deprive of the orb, as a symbol of sovereignty 1863.

†**Diso·rdain,** *v.* ME. only. [– OFr. *desordener* disorder, degrade (mod. *désordonner*), Rom. formation from *des-* DIS- 4 + L. *ordinare*; see ORDAIN.] **1.** To deprive of orders. **2.** To disorder, derange. Hence †**Diso·rdained** *ppl. a.* disordered; immoderate.

†**Diso·rdeine, diso·rdeny,** *a.* ME. [– OFr. *desordené*, pa. ppl. of *desordener*; see prec. For the muted *-é* in *disordeine* cf. ASSIGN *sb.*²; for *-eny*, see -Y⁵.] Inordinate, excessive; disorderly –1450.

Disorder (disǭ·ɹdəɹ), *sb.* 1477. [f. next, after Fr. *désordre.*]

1. Absence or undoing of order; confusion; confused state or condition. †**b.** Irregularity. POPE. **2.** (with *a* and *pl.*) An irregularity 1574; *spec.* †an irregularity of conduct; a misdemeanour –1772. **3.** Disturbance, commotion, tumult 1532. †**4.** Disturbance of mind –1838. **5.** An ailment, disease. (Usually weaker than DISEASE, and not implying structural change.) 1704.

1. Light shon, and order from d. sprung MILT. *P.L.* III. 713. Boughs..twined in picturesque d. 1839. **b.** POPE *Ess. Crit.* 152. **2.** The disorders which attended the retreat SIR W. NAPIER. **3.** To prevent all d. the train-bands kept a guard on both sides of the way 1628. **4.** *John* III. iv. 102. **5.** A slight d. in my eye COWPER.

Disorder (disǭ·ɹdəɹ), *v.* 1477. [app. modification after ORDER *v.* of *disordeine* DISORDAIN.] **1.** *trans.* To put out of order; to throw into confusion; to disarrange, derange, upset. Also †*intr.* (for *refl.*). †**2.** *trans.* To make morally irregular; to corrupt –1585. †**b.** *refl.* To violate moral order; to break loose from restraint; to go to excess –1654. †**3.** *trans.* To disturb the mind or feelings of; to discompose –1819. **4.** To derange the functions of; to 'upset' 1526. †**5.** = DISORDAIN 1. –1681. **6.** [f. DIS- 6 + ORDER *v.*] To countermand 1643.

1. With..tresses all disordered MILT. *P.L.* X. 914. **4.** The east wind..never fails to d. my head BP. BERKELEY. This climate is apt to d. the liver 1896. Hence **Diso·rdered** *ppl. a.* disarranged; †irregular; deranged; morbid. **Diso·rdered-ly** *adv.*, **-ness.**

Disorderly (disǭ·ɹdəɹli), *a.* 1585. [f. DISORDER *sb.* + -LY¹.] **1.** Characterized by disorder, or absence of order; in a state of disorder; confused, irregular, untidy 1632. **2.** Violating moral order, constituted authority, or recognized rule; lawless; unruly; tumultuous, riotous 1585. **b.** *spec.* in *Law.* Violating public order or morality; constituting a nuisance; *esp.* in *d. house* 1744. †**3.** Affected with disorder of the bodily functions; morbid 1655.

1. A d. and confused chaos BP. BERKELEY. **2.** Charged with being drunk and d. 1896. Phr. *D. person*, one guilty of one of a number of offences against public order as defined by various Acts of Parliament 1744. *absol.* as *sb.* a d. person. Hence **Diso·rderliness, Diso·rderly** *adv.*

†**Diso·rdinance.** ME. [– OFr. *desordenance*, f. *desordener*; see DISORDAIN, -ANCE.] Disorder, confusion, irregularity –1502.

†**Diso·rdinate,** *a.* ME. [– med.L. *disordinatus* inordinate, for cl.L. *inordinatus*; see DIS- 4, ORDINATE *a.*] **1.** Not conformed to what is right, befitting, or reasonable; inordinate –1693. **2.** = DISORDERLY *a.* 1. (Only in De Quincey.)

1. D. gestures 1577. A Prince..d. in eating 1574. Hence †**Diso·rdinately** *adv.*

†**Disordina·tion.** 1626. [– med.L. *disordinatio* disarrangement, f. *disordinat-*, pa. ppl. stem of *disordinare*; see DISORDAIN, DISORDINATE, and -ION.] = DEORDINATION –1684.

Disorga·nic, *a.* [DIS- 10.] Without organic constitution. CARLYLE.

Diso:rganiza·tion. 1794. [– Fr. *désorganisation* (1764); see next, -ATION.] The action of disorganizing, or condition of being disorganized; loss or absence of organization.

The total d. of society HT. MARTINEAU.

Disorganize (disǭ·ɹgănəiz), *v.* 1793. [– Fr. *désorganiser* (1764), f. *des-* DIS- 4 + *organizer* ORGANIZE. This word and its congeners date in Eng. from the French Revolution.] To destroy the organization of; to break up the organic connection of; to throw into confusion or disorder.

Their ever memorable decree of the 15th of December, 1792, for disorganizing every country in Europe BURKE. Hence **Diso·rganizer.**

†**Diso·rient,** *v.* 1655. [– Fr. *désorienter*, f. *des-* DIS- 4 + *orienter* ORIENT *v.*] *trans.* To turn from the east; to cause to lose one's bearings; to put out –1835.

Disorientate (disō^ə·riĕnte^i t), *v.* 1704. [DIS- 6.] *trans.* To turn from an eastward position; *pa. pple.* not facing due east. Also *fig.*

It has a chancel..strangely disorientated towards the south 1853. Hence **Disorienta·tion.**

Di·sour. Now *Hist.* ME. [– OFr. *disour* (mod. *diseur*), f. *dire, dis-* say; see -OUR. Cf. DISEUSE.] A (professional) story-teller; a jester.

Disown (disō^u·n), *v.* 1620. [f. DIS- 6 + OWN *v.* Not conn. w. OE. *unnan* to grant.] †**1.** *trans.* To cease to own; to give up, renounce. **2.** To refuse to acknowledge as one's own, or as connected with oneself; not to own; to repudiate, disclaim 1649. †**3.** To refuse to acknowledge or admit; to deny –1726.

2. To own or d. books 1649. Their Mufti..disowns the Emperor's Authority 1726. **3.** The Court no longer d. his..Majesty's arrival 1710. Hence **Disow·nment,** the act of disowning, renunciation.

†**Diso·xidate,** *v.* 1801. [DIS- 6.] *Chem.* = DEOXIDATE –1817. Hence **Disoxida·tion** = DEOXIDATION.

†**Diso·xygenate,** *v.* 1800. [DIS- 6.] *Chem.* = DEOXYGENATE –1831. Hence **Disoxygena·tion** = DEOXYGENATION.

†**Dispa·ce,** *v.* 1588. [perh. f. DI-¹ + It. *spaziare* to walk.] *intr.* and *refl.* To walk or move about –1610.

Long time he did himselfe d. There round about SPENSER.

†**Dispai·nt,** *v.* [DIS- 1.] To paint diversely. SPENSER *F. Q.* II. ix. 50.

†**Dispai·r,** *v.* 1598. [DIS- 6.] *trans.* To separate from being a pair.

†**Dispa·nd,** *v.* 1656. [– L. *dispandere* spread out, f. *dis-* DIS- 1 + *pandere* spread.] *trans.* To spread abroad, to expand –1732.

Dispansive (dispæ·nsiv), *a.* 1883. [f. *dispans-*, pa. ppl. stem of L. *dispandere* (see prec.) + -IVE, after *expansive.*] A term applied to a system of lenses with negative focal distance; opp. to *collective. Syd. Soc. Lex.*

†**Dispa·radise,** *v. rare.* 1593. [DIS- 7 c.] To turn out of paradise. Also *fig.* –1623.

†**Dispa·rage,** *sb.* [ME. *desparage* – OFr. *desparage* unworthy marriage, f. *des-* DIS- 4 + *parage* equality of rank :– Rom. **paraticum*, f. L. *par* equal; see PEER *sb.*, -AGE.] **1.** Inequality of rank in marriage; an unequal match –1596. **2.** Disparagement –1615.

1. Her friends..dissuaded her from such a d. SPENSER *F.Q.* IV. viii. 50.

Disparage (dispæ·rĕdʒ), *v.* ME. [– OFr. *desparagier*, f. *desparage*; see prec.] †**1.** *trans.* To match unequally; to degrade by an unequal match –1781. **2.** To lower in esteem ME. †**3.** To lower in position or dignity; to cast down –1716. **4.** To treat slightingly; to undervalue; to vilify 1536.

1. Moch was this fayr damysel dysparaged sith that she was maryed ayenst al the comune assent of England CAXTON. **2.** The place oft-times disparages; As, to put the Arke of God into a Cart BP. HALL. **3.** I am disparaged and disheartened by your commendations POPE. **4.** It is the fashion..to d. negative logic MILL. Hence **Dispa·rageable** *a.* †tending to d.; to be disparaged. **Dispa·rager,** a detractor. **Dispa·ragingly** *adv.*

Disparagement (dispæ·rĕdʒmĕnt). 1486. [– OFr. *desparagement*, f. *desparagier*; see prec., -MENT.] †**1.** Marriage to one of inferior rank; the disgrace or dishonour involved in this –1585. **2.** Lowering of value, honour, or estimation; dishonour, indignity, disgrace, discredit 1486. **3.** Depreciation, detraction, undervaluing 1591.

1. He..thought that match a fowle d. SPENSER. **2.** Passed sentence may not be recal'd But to our honours great d. *Com. Err.* I. i. 149. **3.** A strong bias towards..the d. of the Britons 1859.

Disparate (di·spărĕt). 1586. [orig. – L. *disparatus*, pa. pple. of *disparare* separate,

f. *dis-* DIS- 1 + *parare* prepare. In use often assoc. w. *dispar* unequal (cf. DISPARITY). Cf. Fr. *disparate*.]

A. *adj.* **1.** Essentially different or diverse in kind; dissimilar, unlike, distinct. In *Logic*, used of things or concepts having no obvious common ground or genus in which they are correlated. 1608. **2.** Unequal 1764.

1. As remote in their nature..as any two d. things we can propose or conceive; number and colour T. BURNET. **2.** Between ages so very d. LAMB.

B. *sb.* Chiefly *pl.* Things so unlike that they cannot be compared with each other 1586.

Hence **Di·sparate-ly** *adv.*, **-ness.**

†**Dispa·rish,** *v.*[1] ME. [– *disparaiss-*, lengthened stem of Fr. *disparaître*; see DISAPPEAR.] *intr.* To disappear –1632.

Dispa·rish, *v.*[2] 1593. [DIS- 7.] To oust from one's parish; also, to deprive of the status of a parish.

†**Dispa·rison.** 1609. [f. COMPARISON by substitution of prefix DIS- 9 to express the opposite.] Depreciatory comparison –1647.

†**Dispari·tion.** 1594. [– Fr. *disparition*, f. *disparaître* disappear, after *apparition*.] Disappearance –1773.

Disparity (dispæ·rĭti). 1555. [– Fr. *disparité* – late L. *disparitas*; see DIS- 4, PARITY.] **1.** Inequality or dissimilarity in respect of age, amount, number, or quality; want of parity 1597. **2.** The quality of being unlike or different. Also with *pl.* An instance or form of this. 1555.

1. A wife..fit for him without d. 1651. **2.** The disparities and differences [of men] NORTH.

Dispark (dispā·ɹk), *v.* 1542. [f. DIS- 7 b + PARK *sb.*; cf. Fr. †*desparquer*, mod. *déparquer*.] *trans.* To divest of the character of a park; to throw open (park-land), or convert (it) to other uses. Also *transf.* and *fig.*

You haue..Dis-park'd my Parkes, and fell'd my Forrest Woods *Rich. II*, III. i. 23. He thereupon disparks his Seralio, and flyes thence SIR T. HERBERT.

†**Dispa·rkle, -pa·rcle,** *v.* 1449. [app. a corrupt form of DISPARPLE.] = DISPARPLE –1661.

†**Dispa·rple,** *v.* ME. [– OFr. *desparpelier*, *-peillier*, *-pillier*, f. Rom. **des-* (DIS-) + **parpaliare*, f. **parpilio*, **parpalio*, app. an alt. form of L. *papilio* butterfly.] *trans.* To scatter abroad, disperse –1615. Also *intr.* (for *refl.*).

Dispart (dispā·ɹt), *sb.* 1578. [Of doubtful origin; prob. f. DISPART *v.*[1], but there are chronological difficulties.] **1.** The difference between the semi-diameter of a gun at the base ring and at the swell of the muzzle 1588. **2.** *concr.* A sight-mark placed on the muzzle of a gun, to make the line of sight parallel to the bore; called also *d.-sight* 1578.

1. Every Gunner before he shootes must trulie disparte his Peece, or give allowance for the disparte 1588.

Dispart (dispā·ɹt), *v.*[1] 1590. [– It. *dispartire* divide, part, or L. *dispartire* distribute, divide; see DIS- 1, PART *v.*; superseded *depart* in the corresp. senses.] **1.** *trans.* To part asunder, to cleave. **2.** To separate, sever 1633. **3.** To divide into parts; to distribute 1629. **4.** *intr.* To part asunder 1633. †**5.** *D. with*: to part with (*pseudo-arch.*) SCOTT.

1. The Sea..fled, Disparted by the wondrous Rod WESLEY. **2.** Till death d. the union SOUTHEY. **4.** The broken heav'ns d. P. FLETCHER.

Dispa·rt, *v.*[2] 1587. [f. DISPART *sb.*] **1.** *trans.* To estimate the dispart in (a gun); to make allowance for this in taking aim. **2.** To furnish with a dispart 1669.

Dispa·ssion, *sb.* 1692. [DIS- 9.] Freedom from passion; dispassionateness; †apathy. So †**Dispa·ssion** *v.* to free from passion. Chiefly in *ppl. a.* **Dispa·ssioned.**

Dispassionate (dispæ·ʃənĕt), *a.* 1594. [DIS- 10.] Free from the influence of passion; calm, composed, cool; impartial. Said of persons, their faculties, and actions.

The wise and dis-passionate among them 1594. A d. fairness towards older faiths J. R. GREEN. Hence †**Dispa·ssionate** *v.* to free from passion (*rare*). **Dispa·ssionate-ly** *adv.*, **-ness.**

Dispassioned; see DISPASSION *v.*

Dispatch, despatch (dispæ·tʃ), *v.* 1517. [– It. *dispacciare* or Sp. *despachar*, f. *dis-*, *des-* DIS- 4 + base of It. *impacciare* hinder, stop, Sp., Pg. *empachar* impede, embarrass; this base is of obscure origin and difficult to relate directly with that of the synon. OFr. *empechier* (mod. *empêcher* prevent) IMPEACH, OFr. *depechier* (mod. *dépêcher*), whence DEPEACH *v.*, which was superseded by *dispatch*.]

I. *trans.* **1.** To send off post-haste or with expedition. The word regularly used for the sending of messengers, messages, troops, mails, express trains, etc. **2.** To dismiss (a person) after settling his business; to get rid of. Now *rare.* **3.** To get rid of by putting to death; to kill 1530. **4.** To rid oneself promptly of (a piece of business, etc.); to get through 1533; to dispose of (food) quickly (*colloq.*) 1711. †**5.** To remove; to get rid of –1726. †**6.** To rid (a person, etc. *of, from*) –1641.

1. We..dispached that poste..reservyng thys to be written by my selff at laysor 1517. **3.** We are peremptory to dispatch This Viporous Traitor *Cor.* III. i. 286. **4.** To my office, where dispatched some business PEPYS. **5.** Dispatching some by death, and other by banishment GRAFTON. **6.** *Haml.* I. v. 75.

II. *intr.* †**1.** (for *refl.*) To start promptly –1712. **2.** To make haste (*to do something*), be quick (*Obs.* or *arch.*) 1581. †**3.** (*absol.* from I. 4.) To settle a business; to get through, have done (*with*) –1666.

1. And now dispatch we toward the Court 2 *Hen. IV*, IV. iii. 82. Hence **Dispa·tcher,** †**Dispa·tchment,** the act of dispatching, dispatch.

Dispatch, despatch (dispæ·tʃ), *sb.* 1550. [f. the verb, or – It. *dispaccio*, Sp. *despacho*; superseded DEPEACH *sb.*]

I. 1. The sending off (of a messenger, letter, etc.) 1600. †**2.** Official dismissal; congé –1698. **3.** Making away with by putting to death; killing 1576. **4.** The getting (of business, an affair, etc.) out of hand; (prompt or speedy) settlement 1581. Also, Promptitude in dealing with affairs 1607. **b.** Speed, expedition 1573. †**5.** The act of getting rid (of something) –1653.

1. The d. of a French Embassy to England FROUDE. **2.** *Lear* II. i. 127. **4.** Clerk-like 'despatch of business' 1837. Dispatch is no mean Virtue in a Statesman 1680.

II. Concr. and transf. senses. **1.** A written message sent off speedily; *spec.* an official communication relating to public affairs 1582. **2.** An agency for the quick transmission of goods, etc.; a conveyance by which goods, etc., are dispatched 1694.

1. Excepting upon very important occasions I write my dispatches without making a draft WELLINGTON.

attrib. and *comb.*: **d.-boat,** a swift vessel used in d. duty; **-box,** a box for carrying dispatches; **-rider,** *esp.* motor-cyclist or horseman carrying dispatches; **-tube,** a tube in which letters, etc., are transported by a current of air. Hence **Dispa·tchful** *a.* having the quality of dispatch-ing; speedy, expeditious (*Obs.* or *arch.*).

Dispathy, obs. f. DYSPATHY.

Dispauper (dispǭ·pəɹ), *v.* 1631. [DIS- 7 b.] To deprive of the privileges of a pauper; to disqualify from suing *in formâ pauperis*, i.e. without payment of fees.

Dispau·perize, *v.* 1833. [DIS- 6.] To free from the state of pauperism; to free from paupers.

Dispeace (dispī·s). 1825. [DIS- 9. Orig. *Sc.*] The absence or reverse of peace; uneasiness (of mind): dissension, enmity.

Scotland had elements of d. 1873.

†**Dispee·d,** *v.* 1603. [app. – It. †*dispedire* (mod. *spedire*) dispatch, f. DIS-[1], but in Eng. assoc. w. SPEED *v.* Cf. DESPEED.] *trans.* To send off (promptly); *refl.* to get away quickly –1814.

Dispel (dispe·l), *v.* 1631. [– L. *dispellere*, f. *dis-* DIS- 1 + *pellere* drive.] *trans.* To drive away in different directions or in scattered order; to disperse by force, dissipate. Also *intr.* (for *refl.*).

He..gently rais'd Their fainted courage, and dispel'd their fears MILT. *P.L.* I. 530. Melt and d., ye spectre-doubts CAMPBELL. Hence **Dispe·ller,** he who or that which dispels.

Dispence, var. of DISPENSE.

Dispe·nd, *v. Obs.* or *arch.* Pa. t. and pple. **dispended, dispent.** [ME. *des-*, *dispend* – OFr. *despendre* expend – L. *dispendere* weigh out, pay out, f. *dis-* DIS- 1 + *pendere* weigh.] **1.** *trans.* To pay away, expend, spend. **2.** *pass.* To be exhausted or spent; to come to an end ME. **3.** To waste, squander ME. **4.** To DISPENSE ME.

1. To d. shot, time 1582, money 1680, oaths SWIFT. **2.** Til hese issue male be dispended 1452. So †**Dispe·nder** = DISPENSATOR.

Dispendious (dispe·ndiəs), *a.* 1557. [In sense 1 – L. *dispendiosus* hurtful (f. *dispendium*); in sense 2 – Fr. *dispendieux* (XVIII) expensive.] †**1.** Hurtful. **2.** Expensive; extravagant 1727. So ‖**Dispe·ndium** [L.] Loss; expenditure; expense.

Dispensable (dispe·nsăb'l), *a.* 1533. [– med.L. *dispensabilis*, f. L. *dispensare*; see DISPENSE *v.*, -ABLE. Cf. Fr. *dispensable* (XVI).] **1.** *Eccl.* Subject to dispensation. **2.** Allowable, excusable. ? *Obs.* 1589. **3.** That can be done without; unessential; unimportant 1649. Hence **Dispensabi·lity. Dispe·nsableness.** var. †**Dispe·nsible** *a.* (in senses 1, 2).

Dispensary (dispe·nsări). 1699. [subst. use of med.L. *dispensarius* adj., f. L. *dispensare*; see DISPENSE *v.*, -ARY[1]. Cf. DISPENSATORY *sb.*] **1.** A place in which medicines are dispensed. *spec.* A charitable institution, where medicines are dispensed and medical advice given gratis, or for a small charge. †**2.** *transf.* A collection of the drugs, etc., mentioned in the pharmacopœia –1774. †**3.** = DISPENSATORY 1. –1725.

Di·spensate, *v. rare.* 1701. [– *dispensat-*, pa. ppl. stem of L. *dispensare*; see DISPENSE *v.*, -ATE[3].] = DISPENSE.

Conceptions of widely dispensated happiness W. IRVING.

Dispensation (dispensē¹·ʃən). ME. [– (O)Fr. *dispensation* – L. *dispensatio*, f. *dispensat-*, pa. ppl. stem of *dispensare*; see DISPENSE *v.*, -ION.]

I. 1. The action of dispensing or dealing out; distribution; economical disposal. **2.** The process of dispensing medicines or medical prescriptions 1646.

1. The d. of this grace unto all men SELDEN.

II. 1. The action of administering, ordering, or managing; the system by which things are administered. [From the L. use of *dispensatio* as tr. Gr. οἰκονομία in N.T., etc.] **2.** Stewardship (*arch.*) ME. **3.** Ordering, management; *esp.* the ordering of events by divine providence ME.; with *a* and *pl.* 1652. **4.** *Theol.* A religious order or system, conceived as a stage in a progressive revelation, expressly adapted to a particular nation or age, as the *patriarchal*, *Mosaic*, *Christian d.*; also, the age 1643.

3. Mysterious dispensations of Providence DICKENS.

III. 1. *Eccl.* The granting of licence by a pope, archbishop, or bishop, to a person, to do what is forbidden, or omit what is enjoined by ecclesiastical law, etc.; the licence so given ME. Also *transf.* and *fig.* **2.** *Law.* The relaxation or suspension of a law in a particular case 1607. **3.** *transf.* Exemption from any obligation, fate, etc.; remission. ? *Obs.* 1653. **4.** The action of dispensing *with* anything 1593.

2. A way of preventing the King's d. with Acts 1667. **3.** A d. from ceremonious visits JOHNSON.

Hence **Dispensa·tional** *a.* pertaining to d., or to a d.

Dispe·nsative, *a.* (*sb.*) 1528. [– late L. *dispensativus*, f. as prec.; see -IVE. Cf. (O)Fr. *dispensatif*, *-ive*.] †**1.** Administrative, official; pertaining to a dispensator –1656. **2.** Giving dispensation; dispensatory 1621. Hence **Dispe·nsatively** *adv.*

Di·spensa:tor. Now *rare.* ME. [– AFr. *dispensatour*, OFr. *-teur* – L. *dispensator*, f. as prec.; see -OR 2.] One who dispenses; a dispenser, a distributor. †**b.** A steward –1698. So **Dispensa·trix,** a female d.

Dispe·nsatory, *sb.* 1566. [– med.L. *dispensatorium* store-room, pantry, pharmacopœia, subst. use of the adj.; see next.] **1.** A book in which medicinal substances, their composition, method of preparation, and use are described; a pharmacopœia. Also *fig.* †**2.** = DISPENSARY 1. –1799.

Dispe·nsatory, *a.* 1635. [In sense 1 – late L. *dispensatorius*, f. *dispensator*; see DISPENSATOR, -ORY[1]. Sense 2 is from med.L. eccl. use.] †**1.** = of or pertaining to the office of a dispensator, or steward, or to administration –1679. **2.** That gives dispensations 1647. Hence **Dispe·nsatorily** *adv.* by dispensation.

†Dispe·nse, *sb.* [ME. *des-, dispense* – OFr. *despense* – med.L. *dispensa*, subst. use of fem. sing. of pa. pple. of *dispendere*; see next. In sense 4, prob. from the vb.] **1.** The act of spending –1664; *pl.* expenses –1718; money to spend –1652. **2.** The act of bestowing liberally –1596. **3.** = SPENCE 1622. **4.** = DISPENSATION III. 1. –1777.

Dispense (dispe·ns), *v.* ME. [– OFr. *despenser* – L. *dispensare* weigh out, disburse, frequent. of *dispendere*; see DISPEND.]

I. from L. in classical senses. **1.** *trans.* To deal out, distribute; to bestow in portions; †to spend (time, talents) –1649. **2.** *Med.* To make up (medicine); to put up (a prescription) 1533.

1. To d. favours and disfavours 1647, equity 1894.

II. from med.L. *dispensare* in eccl. use. **1.** *intr.* To deal dispensatorily, to use dispensatory power ME. **†2.** *trans.* To relax the law in reference to (some thing or person) ME. **3.** To dissolve, relax, or release by dispensation 1532. **†4.** To do without; = *D. with* –1647. **†5.** *intr.* To make amends *for*. SPENSER *F. Q.* I. iii. 30.

1. When he dispenseth he sheweth the case whereon he dispenseth to be contained under the meaning of the law HARPSFIELD. **2.** The Pope, dispensing all things for money 1566. **3.** Thy holy vow dispensed MASSINGER. Dispensed from all necessity of providing for himself JOHNSON.

Phr. **D. with.** [Orig. = med.L. *dispensare cum aliquo* (*ut possit*), etc.] **a.** To exempt, excuse (a person) from doing something; †to compound with, for an offence, etc. (*rare*). **b.** To give special exemption or relief from; to relax or set aside the obligation of; to do away with; to do without. **†c.** To grant a dispensation for (something illegal or irregular); †to do with, put up with.

Hence **Dispe·nser,** one who dispenses, deals out, or administers. **Dispe·nsing** *vbl. sb.* and *ppl. a.*; also *attrib.*, as in *dispensing power*.

†Dispe·nsive, *a.* 1590. [f. *dispens-*, pa. ppl. stem of L. *dispendere*; see DISPEND, -IVE. Assoc. w. DISPENSE *v.*] **1.** Given to spending or distributing –1677. **2.** Subject to dispensation. MARLOWE.

Dispeople (dispī·p'l) *v.* 1490. [– OFr. *despeupler* (mod. *dé-*) – Rom. formation on L. *dis-* DIS- 4 + *populus* PEOPLE.] **1.** = DEPOPULATE 2. **†2.** [DIS- 7 b.] To cut off from being a people –1687.

1. Some cruell Lord..could..d. a whole parish 1649. *transf.* We will d. all the elements To please our palates RANDOLPH. Hence **Dispeo·pler,** one who or that which dispeoples.

†Disperge, *v.* 1530. [– L. *dispergere*; see DISPERSE. Cf. OFr. *disperger*.] = DISPERSE v. –1657.

Dispe·rmous, *a.* 1760. [f. DI-² + Gr. σπέρμα, -ματ- seed + -OUS.] *Bot.* Having two seeds. var. **Dispe·rmatous.**

Disperple, obs. var. of DISPARPLE *v.*

Dispersal (dispə̄·ɹsăl). 1821. [f. DISPERSE *v.* + -AL¹.] = DISPERSION.

Disperse (dispə̄·ɹs), *v.* 1450. [– *dispers-*, pa. ppl. stem of L. *dispergere* scatter, f. *dis-* DIS- 1 + *spargere* strew. Cf. Fr. *disperser* (XV).] **1.** *trans.* To scatter in all directions; to rout. **2.** To spread about; to send to, or station apart at, various points. *Esp.* in *pa. pple.* 1529. **b.** *intr.* (for *refl.*) To go different ways 1672. **†3.** *trans.* To divide, dispart –1600. **4.** To distribute from a source or centre 1555. **5.** To spread about; to diffuse 1576. **6.** To dissipate 1563. Also *intr.* **7.** *trans. Optics.* Of a refractive medium: To scatter (rays of light) 1654.

1. Her feet d. the powdery snow WORDSW. **2.** Dispersed throughout the museums of Europe YEATS. **4.** Wee..find Charles Butler guiltie of dispersing bad monie 1693. **6.** At length the sonne..Disperst those vapours that offended vs *Com. Err.* I. i. 90. Hence **Dispe·rsed-ly** *adv.*, **-ness. Dispe·rser,** one who or that which disperses.

Dispersion (dispə̄·ɹʃən). ME. [– late L. *dispersio* scattering; in sense 1 spec. of the diaspora, f. *dispers-*, pa. ppl. stem of L. *dispergere*; see prec., -ION. Cf. (O)Fr. *dispersion*.] **1.** The action of dispersing or scattering abroad; the state of being dispersed. **2.** The action of diffusing; diffusion 1664. **3.** *Med.* The removal of inflammation, etc., from a part; dissipation 1753. **4.** *Optics.* The divergence of the different-coloured rays of a beam of composite light when refracted by a prism or lens, or when diffracted, so as to produce a spectrum; *esp.* in reference to its amount 1727. Also *attrib.*

1. I conceiv'd that our d. was a necessary circumstance to be fulfil'd BEN ISRAEL. Phr. *The D.*: The Jews living dispersed among the Gentiles after the Captivity (John 7:35); = DIASPORA.

Dispersive (dispə·ɹsiv), *a.* 1627. [f. DISPERSE + -IVE. Cf. (O)Fr. *dispersif, -ive*.] Having the character or quality of dispersing; in *Optics*, having the quality of causing the different-coloured rays of light to diverge; see DISPERSION 4. 1802. Hence **Dispe·rsive-ly** *adv.*, **-ness,** d. quality.

Dispersonate (dispə̄·ɹsǒneˈt), *v.* 1624. [f. DIS- 6 + L. *persona* mask, person + -ATE³.] To divest of personality. So **Dispe·rsonalize** *v.*

Dispersonify (dispəɹsǫ·nifəi), *v.* 1846. [DIS- 6.] To represent or regard as impersonal. Hence **Disperso:nifica·tion.**

Dispe·tal, *v.* 1863. [DIS- 7 a.] To strip of petals.

Disphenoid (dəisfī·noid). 1895. [DI-² 1.] *Cryst.* A solid figure contained by eight isosceles triangles.

†Dispi·cion. 1510. [app. a perversion of DISPUTISOUN by association w. L. *dispicere* investigate, etc. Cf. contemp. †*dispicience* in same sense.] Disputation –1553.

Dispie·ce, *v.* 1477. [– OFr. *despiecer* (mod. *dépiécer*), earlier *despecier*, f. *des-* DIS- 1 + *piece* PIECE.] To divide into pieces.

Dispirit (dispi·rit), *v.* 1642. [DIS- 7 a.] **†1.** *trans.* To deprive of essential quality; to weaken; to deprive (liquor) of its spirit –1713. **2.** To lower the spirits of, depress 1647. **†3.** To extract and transfuse the essence of. FULLER.

1. He that has dispirited himself by a debauch COLLIER. **2.** To d. the sufferer from future exertions COMBE. Hence **Dispi·ritment.**

Dispirited (dispi·ritĕd), *ppl. a.* 1647. [f. prec. + -ED¹.] **†1.** Deprived of essential quality; spiritless –1758. **2.** Cast into low spirits; disheartened, dejected 1647.

1. Flat, D., or Dead Drink 1700. **2.** A few unarmed, d. men 1741. Hence **Dispi·rited-ly** *adv.*, **-ness.**

Dispiteous (dispi·tiəs), *a.* 1803. [orig. var. of DESPITEOUS; now taken as f. DIS- 10 + PITEOUS.] Pitiless, merciless. Hence **Dispi·teous-ly** *adv.*, **-ness.**

Displace (displēˈ·s), *v.* 1551. [f. DIS- 6 + PLACE; partly after Fr. †*desplacer* (mod. *dé-*), f. *des-* DIS- 1, 4 + *place* sb., *placer* vb. place.] **1.** *trans.* To shift from its place; to put out of the proper or usual place. **2.** To remove from a position, dignity, or office 1553. **3.** To oust from its place and occupy it instead 1774.

1. Thy diadem displaced, thy sceptre gone COWPER. **2.** King Solomon displaced Abiathar the high preest FOXE. **3.** To d. by regular garrisons the troops of the Thakurs 1844. In three years..this weed..absolutely displaced every other plant on the ground A. R. WALLACE. Hence **Displa·ceable** *a.* that may be displaced. **Displa·cer,** one who or that which displaces; *Pharm.* a PERCOLATOR.

Displacement (displēˈ·smĕnt). 1611. [f. prec. + -MENT; in sense 1 perh. – Fr. †*desplacement* (mod. *dé-*).] **1.** The act of displacing or fact of being displaced. **2.** *Physics.* The amount by which anything is displaced; the difference between the initial position of a body and a subsequent position 1837. **3.** = REPLACEMENT 1868. **b.** *Hydrostatics.* The displacing of a liquid by a body immersed in or floating on it; the amount or weight of fluid so displaced by a floating body, *e.g.* a ship 1802. **c.** *Pharm.* = PERCOLATION 1883.

1. His d. from the Regency of France SPEED. A vertical d. of the strata 1880. **3.** The d. of human labor through..machinery 1880. **b.** Her total length is 320 feet..with a d. of 11,407 tons 1876.

Displacency (displēˈ·sĕnsi). Now *rare.* 1652. [– med.L. *displacentia*, for L. *displicentia*; see DISPLICENCY; or alt. of this after COMPLACENCY. Cf. DISPLEASANCE.] The condition of being displeased with something; displeasure, dissatisfaction, dislike. (The reverse of *complacency*.) var. **†Displa·cence.**

Displant (displa·nt), *v.* 1491. [– Fr. †*desplanter* (mod. *dé-*) :– Rom. **desplantare*, f. **des-* DIS- 1 + L. *plantare* plant.] **1.** *trans.* To remove (a plant) from the ground; to uproot. Also †*fig.* **†2.** To undo the settlement or establishment of (a 'plantation' or colony) –1660.

1. *fig.* He must..d. vices, and plant the contrarie vertues 1612. **2.** All those countryes, which..had bene planted with English, were shortly displanted and lost SPENSER. Hence **†Displanta·tion.**

†Displa·t, *v.* [DIS- 6 or 7 a.] *trans.* To unplait. HAKEWILL.

Display (displēˈ·), *v.* ME. [– OFr. *despleier* (mod. *déployer* DEPLOY), earlier *desplier* :– L. *displicare* scatter, (med.L.) unfold, unfurl, f. *dis-* DIS- 1, 4 + *plicare* fold.] **1.** *trans.* To unfold, expand, spread out; to unfurl (a banner, sail). Now *Obs.* exc. as influenced by sense 3. **†b.** *Mil.* = DEPLOY *v.* 2. –1610. **2.** To lay or place with the limbs extended; to extend (a limb, wing, etc.). *spec.* in *Her.*; see DISPLAYED 2. ME. **3.** To open up to view, exhibit to the eyes, show ME.; in *Printing*, to make more prominent by larger type, spacing, etc. 1888. **4.** To unfold or exhibit to other senses, or to the mind; to make manifest 1575. **5.** *esp.* To exhibit ostentatiously; to make a show of 1628. Also †*intr.* (for *refl.*) *Lear* II. iv. 41. **6.** *trans.* To allow to be seen, to betray 1602. **†7.** To depict, describe; to expound; to unfold (a tale) –1808. **†8.** *Med.* To disperse. TOPSELL. **¶9.** To discover, descry. [As if 'to unfold to one's own view'.] 1590.

1. [He] displaid his sails to a prosperous west wind EARL MONM. **3.** More recently the Royal Banner has always displayed the Arms of England 1864. **4.** Their labour to d. QUARLES. To d. insubordination 1885. **5.** These few good parts hee has, hee is no niggard in displaying 1628. **6.** He began to d...some token of suspition 1632. Hence **Display·er.**

Display·, *sb.* 1583. [f. prec. vb.] **1.** The act of displaying; exhibition, manifestation 1680; †a description –1714. **2.** An exhibition, a show 1665. **3.** Show, ostentation 1816. **4.** *Printing.* The selection and arrangement of types so as to call attention to a word, line, etc. 1824.

1. An occasion for the d. of his powers FROUDE. **2.** The d. of dahlias 1845. **3.** Fatal to the man of letters, fatal to man, is the lust of d. EMERSON.

Comb.: **d.-letter, -type,** a letter or type used for displaying printed matter; **-stand,** a stand, rack, or shelf, etc. for displaying goods.

Displayed (displēˈ·d), *ppl. a.* ME. [f. prec. vb. + -ED¹.] **1.** Unfolded, unfurled, spread open to view; expanded, as wings, leaves, etc. 1578. **2.** *Her.* Having the wings expanded: said of a bird of prey ME.

†Di·sple, *v.* 1492. [app. f. DISCIPLINE *sb.* or *v.*] *trans.* To subject to discipline; *esp.* as a religious practice –1641.

Bitter Penaunce, with an yron whip, Was wont him once to d. every day SPENSER *F. Q.* I. x. 27.

†Displea·sance. ME. [– OFr. *desplaisance* (mod. *dé-*), f. *desplaisant*; see next, -ANCE, and cf. PLEASANCE.] The fact of being displeased; displeasure, dissatisfaction, annoyance; a cause or instance of this –1590.

†Displea·sant, *a.* ME. [– OFr. *desplaisant*, pres. pple. of *desplaire*; see next, -ANT¹.] **1.** That displeases; unpleasant, disagreeable –1668. **2.** Displeased –1709. Hence **†Displea·sant-ly** *adv.*, **†-ness.**

Displease (displī·z), *v.* ME. [– *desplais-*, pres. stem of OFr. *desplaisir*, *desplaire* (mod. *déplaire*); see DIS- 4, PLEASE.] **1.** *intr.* To cause displeasure, dissatisfaction, or dislike. **2.** *trans.* [The object repr. an earlier dative.] To be displeasing or disagreeable to; to offend, annoy, vex ME.

1. Ev'n spring displeases, when she shines not here POPE. **2.** He put them al to deth that displesid him CAXTON. The world, in the main, displeaseth me ARBUTHNOT. *fig.* My mirth is much displeas'd, but pleas'd my woe *Meas. for M.* IV. i. 13. Hence **Displea·sed-ly** *adv.*, **†-ness. Displea·sing-ly** *adv.*, **-ness.**

Displeasure (disple·ʒˈŭɹ), *sb.* 1470. [In XV, *des-*, *displaisir* – OFr. *desplaisir*, subst.

use of infin., see prec.; later conformed to PLEASURE.] **1.** The fact or feeling of being displeased or offended; a feeling varying in intensity from dissatisfaction or disapproval to indignation 1484. **†2.** The opposite of pleasure; discomfort, unhappiness; sorrow, trouble –1875. **b.** with *a* and *pl.* –1686. **3.** That which causes offence or trouble; injury; a wrong, an offence (*arch.*) 1470. **†4.** A disagreement –1576.

1. An indication of the d. of Heaven FROUDE. Phr. *To take (a) d.*; to take umbrage. **2.** When good is proposed, its absence carries d. or pain with it LOCKE. **3.** Hast thou delight to see a wretched man Do outrage and d. to himself *Com. Err.* IV. iv. 119. **4.** During the d. between him and Earle Godwin LAMBARDE. Hence **Displea·surable** *a.* disagreeable (*rare*). **Displea·sure** *v.* to cause d. to (*arch.*).

Displenish (disple·niʃ), *v. Sc.* 1639. [f. DIS- 6 + PLENISH.] To deprive of furniture, supplies, or (farm) stock. Hence **Disple·nishment.**

†Di·splicence. 1605. [– L. *displicentia*, f. *displicēre*; see DISPLEASE, -ENCE.] Displeasure, dissatisfaction –1736.

Displicency (di·splisĕnsi). 1640. [f. as prec.; see -ENCY. Cf. DISPLACENCY.] = DISPLACENCY.

†Displo·de, *v.* 1667. [– L. *displodere* burst asunder, f. *dis-* DIS- 1 + *plaudere* clap.] *trans.* To discharge with an explosion; *intr.* to explode –1812. So **†Displo·sion,** the action of disploding. **†Displo·sive** *a.* eruptive.

Displume (displū·m), *v.* 1480. [f. DIS- 7 a + PLUME *sb.*] **†1.** *trans.* Of birds: To cast (their feathers). CAXTON. **2.** = DEPLUME *v.* (*lit.* and *fig.*) 1606.

2. Wastes where the wind's wings break Displumed by daylong ache SWINBURNE. *fig.* Humblenes may flaring Pride d. SYLVESTER.

†Dispoi·nt, *v.*[1] 1483. [– OFr. *despointier*, f. *des-* DIS- 4 + *-pointier* in *apointier* to APPOINT.] **1.** To dismiss, discard; to deprive *of* –1489. **2.** To disappoint. Const. *of.* –1565.

Dispoi·nt, *v.*[2] [DIS- 7 a.] To deprive of the point. SYLVESTER.

Dispond: see DESPOND.

Dispondee (dəispǫ·ndī). 1706. [– late L. *dispondeus* (also used) – Gr. δισπόνδειος; see DI-[2], SPONDEE.] A double spondee. Hence **Disponda·ic** *a.*

Dispone (dispōu·n), *v.* Chiefly *Sc.* ME. [– L. *disponere* arrange, dispose, etc., f. *dis-* DIS- 1 + *ponere* place; see DISPOSE *v.*] **†1.** *trans.* To set in order –1588. **†2.** To dispose *to* or *for* (something); to incline –1613. **†3.** To dispose of –1580. **4.** *Sc. Law.* To make over or convey officially or in legal form 1555. **†5.** *intr.* or *absol.* To make disposition, arrange –1605.

Hence **Dispo:nee·**, the person to whom a conveyance is made. **Dispo·ner,** the person who conveys property.

Disponent (dispōu·nĕnt), *a.* 1613. [– *disponent-*, pres. ppl. stem of L. *disponere*; see prec., -ENT.] Disposing; inclining towards a particular end.

Disponge, var. f. DISPUNGE.

Dispo·pe, *v.* 1622. [DIS- 7 b.] To deprive of the popedom.

Disport (dispōə·ɹt), *sb. arch.* ME. [– OFr. *desport*, f. *desporter*; see next.] **1.** Diversion; relaxation; amusement (*arch.*). **2.** A pastime, game, sport (*arch.*) ME. **†3.** Merriment –1801.

Disport (dispōə·ɹt), *v.* ME. [– AFr. *desporter* (mod. *déporter* DEPORT), f. *des-* DIS- 1 + *porter* carry.] **†1.** *trans.* To divert (from sadness, etc.); to amuse –1665. **2.** *refl.* To cheer, divert oneself; now *esp.* to play wantonly, frolic, gambol ME. **3.** *intr.* (for *refl.*) = prec. 1480. **†4.** *trans.* To turn away (*rare*) 1450.

1. All the way we sail'd . . we were disported by Whales SIR T. HERBERT. **2.** Whilst he disported himself at the court of France DRUMM. OF HAWTH. **3.** I her caught disporting on the greene SPENSER. Hence **Dispo·rtive** *a.* inclined to d. (*rare*). **Dispo·rtment** = DISPORT *sb.*

Disposable (dispōu·zăb'l), *a.* 1643. [f. DISPOSE *v.* + -ABLE.] **1.** Inclinable (*to* something) (*rare*) 1652. **2.** Capable of being disposed of; capable of being put to some use; at (some one's) disposal 1643.

2. A disposeable surplus BURKE. D. as literary ware MASSON.

Disposal (dispōu·zăl). 1630. [f. DISPOSE *v.* + -AL[1]; superseding DISPOSE *sb.*] The act or faculty of disposing. **†1.** The action of arranging, ordering, or regulating by right of power or possession; control, direction; ordinance, appointment, dispensation –1710. **2.** The action of disposing of, settling, or definitely dealing with 1648. **3.** The action of giving or making over; bestowal, assignment 1660. **4.** Power or right to dispose of; control, command, management; usu. in phr. *at (in) one's d.* 1630. **5.** = DISPOSITION I. 1. 1828.

1. Tax not divine d. MILT. *Sams.* 210. **2.** Directions about the d. of your money GAY. **3.** The right of d. is suspended 1845. **4.** A very pretty young Lady, in her own d. STEELE.

Dispose (dispōu·z), *v.* ME. [– (O)Fr. *disposer*, f. *dis-* DIS- 1 + *poser* place, set in order, settle (see POSE *v.*[1]), after L. *disponere*, whence directly DISPONE.] **I.** *trans.* **1.** To place suitably, adjust; to arrange in a particular order ME.; to put away; to put in place, distribute (now *rare*) ME.; †to assign, appoint –1697. **†2.** To regulate; to order, control, direct –1677. **†3.** To bestow, make over; to deal out, distribute –1818. **4.** To make fit or ready; to fit, prepare (*to do*, or *to* or *for* something) (*arch.*) ME. **5.** To give a tendency or inclination to; to incline, make prone (*to*, or *to do* something) ME.

1. The sterres . . ben disposed in signis of bestes CHAUCER. The town is . . handsomely disposed 1777. Ye Gods, to better Fate good Men d. DRYDEN. **2.** I wyll d. this mater as I shall thynke best PALSGR. **4.** Therefore will we d. our selves to suffer FLEMING. **5.** Not that I imagine geometry disposeth men to infidelity BERKELEY. They ate Lettuse after supper . . to d. them selves to sleepe 1599.

II. *intr.* To make arrangements; to ordain, appoint ME.; †to make terms 1606.

You did suspect She had dispos'd with Cæsar *Ant. & Cl.* IV. xiv. 123.

Phr. **To d. of:** †**a.** = sense I. 2. **b.** To deal with definitely; to get rid of; to get done with, finish. **c.** To make over by way of sale or bargain, sell.

Dispo·se, *sb.* ? *Obs.* 1590. [f. prec.; superseded by DISPOSAL.] **†1.** = DISPOSITION I. 1. 1603. **†2.** = DISPOSAL 1. –1671. **†3.** = DISPOSAL 4. –1741. **†4.** = DISPOSAL 3. –1673. **5.** †Mental constitution or inclination –1628; air, pose (*rare*) 1601.

2. The unsearchable d. Of Highest Wisdom MILT. *Sams.* 1746. **5.** He hath a person, and a smooth d., To be suspected *Oth.* I. iii. 403.

Disposed (dispōu·zd), *ppl. a.* ME. [f. as prec. + -ED[1].] **1.** Arranged, appointed, prepared, etc.; see DISPOSE *v.* 1, 4. **†2.** In a (specified) condition of body or health –1694. **3.** Having a (particular) disposition or turn of mind ME. **4.** Inclined ME.; *†ellipt.* inclined to merriment –1616. Hence **Dispo·sed-ly** *adv.*, **-ness.**

†Dispo·sement. 1583. [f. as prec. + -MENT.] Disposition, disposal –1679.

Disposer (dispōu·zəɹ). 1526. [f. as prec. + -ER[1].] One who or that which disposes; see DISPOSE *v.* 1, 5.

My author and D., what thou bidst Unargu'd I obey MILT. *P. L.* IV. 635.

†Dispo·sit, *v. rare.* [– *disposit-*, pa. ppl. stem of L. *disponere*; see next.] To deposit. GLANVILL.

Disposition (dispozi·ʃən). ME. [– (O)Fr. *disposition* – L. *dispositio*, f. *disposit-*, pa. ppl. stem of *disponere*; see DISPONE, -ION; not a deriv. of DISPOSE, but assoc. with it in form through the adoption of Fr. *-poser* as repr. L. *-ponere.*]

I. 1. The action of setting in order, or condition of being set in order; arrangement, order; relative position 1541. **2.** Arrangement (of affairs, measures, etc.), *esp.* for the accomplishment of a purpose; plan; complexion of affairs ME. **3.** = DISPOSAL 1. ME. **4.** The action of disposing of; *spec.* in *Law*, the action of disponing; power of disposing of: *esp.* in phr. *at (in) one's d.* (= DISPOSAL 4) ME.

1. The divers d. of the clouds FULKE. *D.* . . in Architecture, is the just placing of all the several Parts of a Building, according to their proper Order E. PHILLIPS. **2.** I craue fit d. for my Wife . . With such Accomodation and besort As leuels with her breeding *Oth.* I. iii. 237. The military dispositions of Julian were skilfully contrived GIBBON. **4.** The choice of action or of repose is no longer in our d. GIBBON.

II. †1. *Astrol.* The situation of a planet in a horoscope –1590. **2.** Turn of mind ME. **3.** The state or quality of being disposed (*to*, or *to do* something); inclination (occas. = desire, intention); the condition of being (well or ill) disposed *towards* ME. **†b.** Mood, humour –1764. **†4.** Physical constitution –1813. **5.** Physical aptitude, or tendency (*to*, or *to do* something) ME. **†6.** Physical condition –1732; normal condition (*rare*) –1632.

2. [The] saturnine dispositions of the English 1779. **3.** Testiness is a d. or aptness to be angry LOCKE. **5.** The different dispositions of wool, silk, etc. to unite with the colouring particles 1791.

Hence **Disposi·tional** *a.* relating to d. (*rare*). **Disposi·tioned** *ppl. a.* having a (specified) d.

Dispositive (dispǫ·zitiv), *a.* 1483. [f. (O)Fr. *dispositif, -ive* or med.L. *dispositivus*, f. as prec.; see -IVE.] **†1.** Characterized by special disposition (*rare*). CAXTON. **2.** That disposes or inclines: often opp. to *effective* 1612. **3.** Relating to control or disposal 1613. **†4.** Of or pertaining to natural disposition –1681.

2. Some causes are dispositiue, adiuuant, or impetrant 1624. Hence **Dispo·sitively.** ?*Obs.*

Dispositor (dispǫ·zitəɹ). 1598. [– L. *depositor*, in med.L. sense, f. as prec.; see -OR 2.] *Astrol.* 'The lord of a sign in its relation to another planet.'

Dispossess (dispŏze·s), *v.* 1494 [– OFr. *despossesser*, f. *des-* DIS- 4 + *possesser* POSSESS.] **1.** *trans.* To put out of possession; to deprive of the possession *of*; to dislodge, oust. Also *transf.* and *fig.* **†2.** To cast out, or rid *of* (an evil spirit) –1845.

1. His father and grandfather had been too powerful for the house of Vicenza to d. them H. WALPOLE. Hence **Disposse·ssion,** the action of dispossessing or fact of being dispossessed; in *Law* = OUSTER; exorcism. **Dispossessor,** one who dispossesses.

Dispo·st, *v.* 1577. [f. DIS- 7 + POST *sb.*; cf. Fr. †*desposter* dispossess, *déposter* dislodge from a post or position.] To deprive of a post.

Disposure (dispōu·ʒ'ŭɹ). Now *rare.* 1569. [f. DISPOSE *v.* + -URE.] **1.** = DISPOSITION I. 1, 2. 1625. **†2.** = DISPOSAL 1. –1689. **3.** = DISPOSAL 2, 3. 1649. **†4.** = DISPOSAL 4. –1693.

Dispraise (disprēi·z), *sb.* 1509. [f. DIS- 9 + PRAISE *sb.*, or f. DISPRAISE *v.* after PRAISE *sb.*] **1.** The action or fact of dispraising; blame, censure. **2.** with *a* and *pl.* An instance or a cause of blame 1535.

1. In praise and in d. the same TENNYSON.

Dispraise (disprēi·z), *v.* ME. [– OFr. *despreisier* – Rom. **despretiare*, for L. *depretiare* DEPRECIATE. See DISPRIZE *v.*] **1.** *trans.* To speak of with disparagement, or disapprobation; to blame, censure. **†2.** To depreciate, despise –1500.

1. Foxes d. the grapes they cannot reach 1612. *absol.* When he intends to praise or d., he will doe it to the purpose FULLER. Hence **†Disprai·sable** *a.* worthy of dispraise. **Disprai·ser.**

Dispread, disspread (dispre·d), *v. arch.* 1590. [DIS- 1.] To spread about or out; to extend, open out. Also *intr.* (for *refl.*).

A vine on wall dispred G. SANDYS. She is the centre from whence all the light Dispreads HAN. MORE. Hence **Disprea·der,** one who spreads abroad.

Dispre·judice, *v.* [DIS- 7 a.] To free from prejudice. 1654.

Disprepa·re, *v.* [DIS- 6.] To render unprepared. HOBBES.

†Dispre·ss, *v.* 1605. [f. DIS- 1 + PRESS *v.*] To press apart –1627.

Disprince; see DIS- 7 b.

Disprison (dispri·z'n), *v.* [DIS- 7 c.] To set free from prison. LYTTON.

Disprivilege (dispri·vilĕdʒ), *v.* 1617. [DIS- 7 a (or 6).] **1.** To deprive (a person) of privilege. **†2.** To undo the privilege of 1622.

†**Dispri·ze**, *sb.* 1560. [f. next, or – OFr. *despris*, f. *desprisier* (see next).] Disparagement, contempt –1636.

Disprize (disprəi·z), *v. Obs.* or *arch.* 1480. [– OFr. *desprisier*, var. of *despreisier*; see DISPRAISE *v.*] **1.** *trans.* To depreciate, undervalue (*arch.*). †**2.** To dispraise, decry –1621.

†**Disprofe·ss**, *v.* [DIS- 6.] To renounce the profession of. SPENSER.

Dispro·fit, *sb. Obs.* or *arch.* 1494. [DIS- 9.] Disadvantage; †a disadvantage –1671.

Dispro·fit, *v. Obs.* or *arch.* 1483. [DIS- 6.] **1.** *trans.* To bring disadvantage to. †**2.** *intr.* (for *refl.*) To fail to profit 1561.

†**Dispro·fitable**, *a.* 1548. [f. DIS- 10 + PROFITABLE. Cf. Fr. †*desprofitable*.] Unprofitable; detrimental –1572.

Disproof (disprū·f). 1531. [f. DIS- 9 + PROOF *sb.*, after DISPROVE.] The proving of a thing not to be what is asserted; refutation; the evidence constituting this. Also with *a* and *pl.*

Allegations..susceptible of specific d. SYD. SMITH.

†**Dispro·perty**, *v. rare.* [DIS- 7 b.] To deprive of property; to dispossess. *Cor.* II. i. 264.

Disproportion (disprop̄ōᵊ·ɹʃən), *sb.* 1555. [f. DIS- 9 + PROPORTION *sb.*, after Fr. *disproportion*.] Want of proportion in number, quantity, size, etc.; lack of symmetry or due relation between things or parts; the condition of being out of proportion. Also with *a* and *pl.*

Let there be no great d. in age FULLER. A leg too long, or some other d. JOWETT.

Dispropo·rtion, *v.* 1593. [f. the sb., after Fr. *disproportionner*.] To render or make out of due proportion.

To shape my Legges of an vnequall size, To d. me in euery part 3 *Hen. VI*, III. ii. 160. Statutes that d. punishment to crime LYTTON. Hence **Dispropo·rtionable** *a.* out of due proportion. **Dispropo·rtionableness. Dispropo·rtionably** *adv.*

Dispropo·rtional. 1609. [f. prec. sb. + -AL[1].] **a.** *adj.* = DISPROPORTIONATE. **b.** *sb.* A disproportional quantity or number 1696.

a. It is very d. to the Understanding of childhood LOCKE. Hence **Disproportiona·lity**, the quality of being d. **Dispropo·rtionally** *adv.*

Dispropo·rtionate, *a.* 1555. [f. DIS- 10 + PROPORTIONATE *a.*, after Fr. *disproportionné*.] Out of proportion; failing to observe or constitute due proportion; inadequately or excessively proportioned. Const. *to*.

A long repentance is a d. price to pay for a short enjoyment WOLLASTON. So †**Dispropo·rtionated.** Hence **Dispropo·rtionate-ly** *adv.*, **-ness.**

†**Dispro·priate**, *v.* [f. as the opposite of APPROPRIATE *v.* by substitution of DIS- 6.] To deprive of the ownership *of*; to dispossess. PURCHAS.

Disprovable (disprū·văb'l), *a.* 1548. [f. DISPROVE *v.* + -ABLE.] †**1.** To be disapproved –1579. **2.** Capable of being disproved; refutable 1685.

Dispro·val. *rare.* 1614. [f. as prec. + -AL[1].] The act of disproving; disproof.

Disprove (disprū·v), *v. Pa. ppl.* **disproved, disproven.** ME. [– OFr. *desprover*, f. *des-* DIS- 4 + *prover* PROVE.] **1.** *trans.* To prove to be false or erroneous; to refute, rebut, invalidate. **2.** To convict (a person) of falsehood or error; to refute, confute. ?*Obs.* 1589. †**3.** To disapprove. Also *intr.* with *of*. –1824.

1. There is a mighty difference between not proven and disproven CHALMERS. **2.** *Oth.* V. ii. 172. Hence **Dispro·ver**, a refuter; †a disapprover.

Disprovi·de, *v. arch.* 152.. [DIS- 6.] To fail to provide for; to leave unprovided.

†**Dispu·nct**, *a.* [f. DIS- 4 + *punct-*, extracted from *punctilio*. Cf. *in punto* (see PUNTO[1]) = *in point*, in order, correctly.] The reverse of punctilious; discourteous. B. JONS.

Dispunct (dispʊ·ŋkt), *v. rare.* 1563. [– *dispunct-*, pa. ppl. stem of L. *dispungere* lit. 'to prick here and there', f. *dis-* DIS- 1 + *pungere* prick.] To mark off with points or pricks of the pen; to erase; to distinguish. Hence †**Dispu·nction**, erasure.

Dispunge (dispʊ·ndʒ), *v.* Also **-sponge.** 1606. [In sense 1, f. *di-*, DIS- 1 + *spunge* SPONGE *v.*; in sense 2, var. of EXPUNGE by substitution of DIS-.] **1.** To discharge as from a squeezed sponge (*arch.*). †**2.** To delete, expunge –1662.

1. Oh Soueraigne Mistris of true Melancholly, The poysonous dampe of night d. vpon me *Ant. & Cl.* IV. ix. 12. **2.** Thou..that has dispong'd my score 1639.

Dispunishable (dispʊ·niʃăb'l), *a.* 1577. [– AFr. *dispunishable*, f. DIS- 10 + PUNISHABLE.] Free from liability to penalty; not punishable.

†**Dispu·rpose**, *v. rare.* 1607. [f. DIS- 7 d + PURPOSE *sb.*] To defeat of its purpose.

†**Dispu·rse**, *v.* 1593. [Altered from DISBURSE.] = DISBURSE –1649.

†**Dispurvey·**, *v.* ME. [– OFr. *desporveeir*, f. *des-* DIS- 4 + *porveeir* provide; see PURVEY.] To rob or strip of provision; to render destitute –1609. Hence †**Dispurvey·ed** *ppl. a.* †**Dispurvey·ance** (*rare*).

Disputable (di·spiutăb'l, dispiū·tăb'l), *a.* 1548. [– Fr. *disputable* or L. *disputabilis*, f. *disputare* DISPUTE *v.* + *-abilis* -ABLE.] **1.** That may be disputed; liable to be called in question, contested, or controverted; questionable. †**2.** Disputatious 1600.

1. This is a matter d. in Schooles 1587. **2.** He is too disputeable for my companie *A. Y. L.* II. v. 36. Hence **Disputableness. Disputably** *adv.*

†**Disputa·city.** 1660. [irreg. f. DISPUTATIOUS; see -ACITY.] = DISPUTATIOUSNESS –1711.

Disputant (di·spiutănt). 1612. [– *disputant-*, pr. ppl. stem of L. *disputare*; see DISPUTE *v.*, -ANT[1].]

A. *adj.* Disputing; engaged in controversy 1671.

B. *sb.* One who disputes; *esp.* a public controversialist 1612.

Disputants are rarely..good judges MILL.

Disputation (dispiutēⁱ·ʃən). 1450. [– Fr. *disputation* – L. *disputatio*, f. *disputat-*, pa. ppl. stem of *disputare*; see DISPUTE *v.*, -ION. Repl. DISPUTISOUN.] **1.** The action of disputing or debating; controversial argument; debate, discussion. **b.** *spec.* An exercise in which parties formally sustain, attack, and defend a thesis, as in the mediæval universities 1551. †**2.** A dissertation –1615. †**3.** Doubt –1689. †**4.** ? Interchange of ideas. SHAKS.

1. In the heat of d. JOHNSON. **4.** 1 *Hen. IV*, III. i. 206.

Disputatious (dispiutēⁱ·ʃəs), *a.* 1660. [f. prec.; see -OUS. Cf. *ostentatious, vexatious*.] Characterized by, or given to, disputation; contentious.

The wine rendered me loquacious, d., and quarrelsome SCOTT. Hence **Disputa·tious-ly** *adv.*, **-ness.**

Disputative (dispiū·tătiv), *a.* 1579. [– late L. *disputativus*, f. *disputat-* (see DISPUTATION) + *-ivus* -IVE. See -ATIVE.] **1.** Given to disputation; disputatious. †**2.** That is the subject of dispute; controversial –1708. **3.** Pertaining to disputation 1664.

1. The cavils of the d. 1788. **2.** D. elections LUTTRELL. Hence **Dispu·tative-ly** *adv.*, **-ness.**

Dispute (dispiū·t), *v.* [ME. *des-, dispute* – OFr. *desputer*, (also mod.) *disputer* – L. *disputare* estimate, discuss, (Vulg.) contend in words, f. *dis-* DIS- 1 + *putare* reckon, consider.]

I. *intr.* **1.** To contend with opposing arguments or assertions; to discuss, argue, hold disputation; often, to debate with heat, to altercate. †**2.** To contend with arms, or the like; to strive, struggle –1828.

1. Thou disputes like an Infant: goe whip thy Gigge SHAKS. The Emperor told Josephine that he disputed like a devil on these two points EMERSON.

II. *trans.* **1.** To debate, discuss, or argue ME. †**2.** To maintain by disputation; to argue or contend –1713. **3.** To argue against, contest, controvert 1513. **4.** To oppose, contest, resist 1605. **5.** To contend for or contest a prize, victory, etc. 1654.

1. I will not d. what Gravity is RAY. **3.** My right there is none to d. COWPER. He would D. the Devil upon that Question 1687. **4.** They.. seemed resolved to d. his landing 1748. **5.** To d. in arms every inch of ground FREEMAN. Hence **Dispu·ter.**

Dispute (dispiū·t), *sb.* 1594. [f. the vb.] **1.** The act of arguing against, controversy, debate 1638. **2.** An argumentative contention, a controversy; also, in weakened sense, a difference of opinion; freq., a heated contention, a quarrel 1611; †a logical argument 1594. †**3.** Strife; a fight or struggle –1745.

1. That once was in the heat of d. WESLEY. Phr. *In d.*: that is disputed. *Beyond, out of, past, without d.*: indisputably. Hence †**Dispu·teful** *a.* disputatious (*rare*).

†**Dispu·tisoun.** ME. [– OFr. *desputeisun*, etc., early – L. *disputatio* DISPUTATION, with popular type of suffix, see -ISON. Superseded by DISPUTATION.] = DISPUTATION –1450.

Disqualification (diskwǫ:lifikēⁱ·ʃən). 1711. [f. DISQUALIFY; see -FICATION.] **1.** The action of disqualifying; *spec.* legal incapacitation; also, the being disqualified 1770. **2.** That which disqualifies; a ground or cause of incapacitation 1711.

1. D. to hold any office 1789. **2.** I hope you don't think good looks a d. for the business DICKENS.

Disqualify (diskwǫ·lifəi), *v.* 1718. [DIS- 6.] *trans.* To deprive of the qualifications required for some purpose; to render unqualified; to unfit, disable. **b.** *spec.* = DISABLE *v.* 2. 1732.

My common illness is of that kind which utterly disqualifies me from all conversation; I mean my deafness SWIFT.

Disquantity (diskwǫ·ntĭti), *v.* 1605. [DIS- 7 a.] To deprive of quantity; to diminish.

†**Disqua·rter**, *v.* [irreg. f. DIS- 1 (or Gr. δ(ι)s) + QUARTER *v.*] To halve or divide the quarters of. QUARLES.

Disquiet (diskwəi·ĕt), *v.* 1530. [DIS- 6.] To deprive of quietness, bodily or mental; to disturb, alarm; to make uneasy or restless.

Yee euery man..disquieteth himself in vayne COVERDALE *Ps.* 38:5. Hence †**Disqui·etal** (*rare*), the action of disquieting. **Disqui·eter.**

Disquiet (diskwəi·ĕt), *a.* Now *rare.* 1587. [DIS- 10.] The reverse of quiet; restless, uneasy, disturbed. Hence **Disqui·et-ly** *adv.* in a d. or †disquieting manner; **-ness. Disqui·etude,** disquieted condition or state; restlessness, disturbance; also with *a* and *pl.*

Disquiet (diskwəi·ĕt), *sb.* 1574. [f. DISQUIET *a.* and *v.*] Absence of bodily or mental quietness; disturbance; uneasiness, anxiety; restlessness. Also with *a* and *pl.* (*arch.* or *Obs.*) Hence †**Disqui·etful** *a.* †**Disqui·etive** *a.* tending to d. †**Disqui·etous** *a.* disquieting.

†**Disqui·parancy.** 1697. [– med.L. *disquiparantia*, for *disæquiparantia*, f. DIS- 4 + late L. *æquiparantia*; cf. EQUIPARATION.] *Logic.* The relation of two correlates which are heteronymous, *i.e.* denoted by different names, as father and son: opp. to *equiparancy*. So **Disquipara·tion** (*rare*).

Disquisition (diskwizi·ʃən). 1605. [–(O)Fr. *disquisition* – L. *disquisitio*, f. *disquisit-*, pa. ppl. stem of *disquirere*, f. *dis-* DIS- 1 + *quærere* seek; see -ITION.] **1.** Diligent or systematic search; investigation 1608; †*ellipt.* a subject for investigation –1660. **2.** A treatise or discourse in which a subject is investigated and discussed at some length; less correctly, an elaborate dissertation *on* a subject 1647.

1. In this d. into human conduct J. HARRIS. **2.** Puzzling them with scholastical craggy disquisitions TRAPP. Hence **Disquisi·tional** *a.* of the nature of a d. **Disquisi·tionist,** the author of a d.

Disquisitive (diskwi·zitiv), *a.* 1647. [f. L. *disquisit-* (see prec.) + -IVE.] Characterized by disquisition; given to research or investigation; inquiring.

A man of great d. powers 1772.

Disquisitor (diskwi·zitəɹ). 1766. [– med.L. *disquisitor*, f. as prec.; see -OR 2.] One who makes disquisition; an investigator. Hence **Disquisito·rial** *a.* of or belonging to a d.; inquiring (*rare*). So **Disqui·sitory** *a.* (*rare*).

†**Disra·nge**, *v.* 1485. [– OFr. *desrangier*, *-rengier*, f. *des-* DIS- 4 + *ranc, renc*, mod. *rang*. See RANK *sb.*, RANGE *v.*[1]] To

disarrange; *refl.* and *intr.* to fall out of rank –1775.

Disrank (disræ·ŋk), *v.* 1597. [DIS- 7 c.] †**1.** To throw out of rank or into disorder –1654. Also †*transf.* and *fig.* **2.** To reduce to a lower rank; to degrade 1599.

Disrate (disrēⁱ·t), *v.* 1811. [DIS- 7 a.] To reduce to a lower rating or rank. Also *fig.*

†**Disray·**, *sb.* ME. [var. of *desray*, DERAY *sb.*; see DIS-.] = DERAY, DISARRAY –1610.

†**Disray·**, *v.* ME. [var. of *desray*, DERAY *v.*; see DIS-.] **1.** = DISARRAY *v.* 1. –1631. **2.** = DISARRAY *v.* 2. –1608.

Disrealize (disrī·ăləiz), *v.* *rare.* 1889. [DIS- 6.] To divest of reality; to idealize.

†**Disrea·son**, *v.* 1622. [Anglicized from OFr. *desraisnier* or its latinized form *disrationare*; see DERAIGN *v.*[1]] To prove, assert, vindicate; = DERAIGN *v.*[1]

Disrecommendation (disre:kǒmendēⁱ·ʃən). 1752. [DIS- 9.] The reverse of a recommendation; that which is unfavourable to any one's claims.

In a Government where trifling qualities are no d. H. WALPOLE.

Disregard (disrĭgā·ɹd), *sb.* 1665. [DIS- 9.] Want of regard; neglect; in earlier use often, slighting, undue neglect; later, the treating of anything as of no importance.

A d. of fame ADDISON, of historical accuracy JOWETT. Hence **Disrega·rdful** *a.* neglectful; **-ly** *adv.*

Disregard (disrĭgā·ɹd), *v.* 1641. [DIS- 6.] To treat without regard. **1.** In earlier use, *esp.*, to treat without due regard; to neglect unduly, slight 1641. **2.** In later use, *esp.*, to treat as of no importance, to pay no attention to 1793.

1. To make all the people d. and despise the Gospel BAXTER. **2.** To d. public opinion 1703, idle rumours MACAULAY, symptoms DICKENS. So **Disrega·rdant** *a.* disregarding. Hence **Disrega·rder.**

†**Disre·gular,** *a.* [DIS- 10.] Irregular. EVELYN.

Disrelish (disre·liʃ), *sb.* 1625. [f. DISRELISH *v.*; or f. DIS- 9 + RELISH *sb.*] Distaste, aversion, some degree of disgust.

Men..have an extreme d. to be told of their duty BURKE.

Disrelish (disre·liʃ), *v.* 1548. [f. DIS- 6 or 7 a + RELISH *v.* or *sb.*] †**1.** *trans.* To destroy the relish of; to render distasteful –1760. **2.** To find not to one's taste; to regard with disfavour; to dislike 1604. †**3.** To prove distasteful to –1708. **4.** *intr.* To be distasteful 1631.

2. Her delicate tendernesse wil..disreelish and abhorre the Moore *Oth.* II. i. 236. Hence †**Disre·lishable** *a.*

Disremember (disrĭme·mbəɹ), *v.* Chiefly *dial.* 1836. [DIS- 6.] To fail to remember; to forget (*trans.* and *absol.*).

Disrepair (disrĭpēᵊ·ɹ). 1798. [DIS- 9.] The being in bad condition for want of repairs.

All spoke neglect and d. SCOTT.

†**Disrepo·rt.** *rare.* [DIS- 9.] Evil report. FULLER.

Disreputable (disre·piŭtăb'l), *a.* (*sb.*) 1772. [f. DIS- 10 + REPUTABLE, after *disrepute.*] **1.** The reverse of reputable; such as to bring into disrepute; discreditable. **2.** In bad repute; not respectable 1828. **3.** *sb.* A disreputable person 1853.

1. D. to his character as a Clergyman 1795. **2.** A few d. individuals DISRAELI. **Disre·putably** *adv.*

Disreputa·tion. *Obs.* or *arch.* 1601. [DIS- 9.] **1.** Privation or loss of reputation; bringing into disrepute; dishonour, disgrace 1601; †a discredit –1751. †**2.** The condition of being in disrepute –1770.

1. He will..bring d. on the institution T. JEFFERSON.

Disrepute (disrĭpiū·t), *sb.* 1653. [DIS- 9.] Loss or absence of reputation; ill repute.

It brings the administration of justice into d. BUCKLE.

†**Disrepu·te,** *v.* 1611. [DIS- 6.] *trans.* To disesteem; to bring into discredit; to defame; to bring an evil name upon (by one's conduct) –1697.

You quote us the Homilies..I think you d. them BP. MONTAGU.

Disrespect (disrĭspe·kt), *sb.* 1631. [f. DIS- 9 + RESPECT *sb.*; or perh. f. next.] Want of respect, courteous regard, or reverence; †an instance of this –1714.

My memory fails me, if I have mentioned their names with d. 'JUNIUS'.

Disrespe·ct, *v.* 1614. [DIS- 6.] *trans.* The reverse of *to respect*; to have or show no respect or reverence for.

If he love the one he must d. the other BP. HALL. Hence **Disrespe·cter** (*rare*).

Disrespectable (disrĭspe·ktăb'l), *a.* 1813. [DIS- 10.] The opposite of respectable; not worthy of respect. Hence **Disrepe:ctabi·lity,** the quality of being d.

Disrespectful (disrĭspe·ktfŭl), *a.* 1677. [f. DIS- 10 + RESPECTFUL, after *disrespect.*] The opposite of respectful; full of or manifesting disrespect.

I must say nothing..that is d. or undutiful RICHARDSON. Hence **Disrespe·ctful-ly** *adv.*, **-ness.**

†**Disrespe·ctive,** *a.* 1623. [f. DIS- 10 + RESPECTIVE, after *disrespect.*] = DISRESPECTFUL –1736.

†**Disrespo·ndency.** 1657. [DIS- 9.] Absence of response.

†**Disre·st.** 1567. [DIS- 9.] Disquiet, unrest –1726.

†**Disre·verence,** *v.* 1529. [DIS- 6 or 7 a.] To treat with irreverence; to deprive of reverence –1670.

Disrobe (disrōᵘ·b), *v.* 1581. [f. DIS- 6 or 7 a + ROBE *v.* or *sb.*, perh. after OFr. *desrober* in same senses.] **1.** *trans.* To divest of a robe or garment; to undress, strip. Also *transf.* and *fig.* 1590. **2.** *refl.* and *intr.* To undress.

1. D. the Images *Jul. C.* I. i. 69. And thou disroab'd of all thy dignitie 1592. Hence **Disro·ber.**

Disroof (disrū·f), *v.* 1837. [DIS- 7 a.] To unroof.

Disroot (disrū·t), *v.* 1612. [DIS- 6.] To pull up by the roots; to uproot; *transf.* to dislodge from the place where it is fixed.

Daun..could not have disrooted Friedrich this season CARLYLE.

†**Disrou·t,** *v.* 1525. [– OFr. *desrouter* (mod. *dé-*), f. *des-* DIS- 4 + OFr. *route* band, company. Cf. ROUT *v.*[5]] To put, or be put, to rout –1630.

Disru·ddered, *ppl. a.* *rare.* 1788. [DIS- 7 a.] Deprived of the rudder.

†**Disru·ly,** *a.* *rare.* 1570. [– OFr. *desrieulé* (mod. *déréglé*); see DIS- 4, RULE *v.*, -Y[5].] Unruly. Hence †**Disru·lily** *adv.* in an unruly manner.

Disrump (disrɒ·mp), *v.* 1581. [– L. *disrumpere*, f. *dis-* DIS- 1 + *rumpere* break.] To break up, DISRUPT (*trans.* and *intr.*).

Disrupt (disrɒ·pt), *ppl. a.* 1730. [– L. *disruptus*, pa. pple. of *disrumpere*; see prec.] Chiefly as poetic *pa. pple.* = disrupted.

Disrupt (disrɒ·pt), *v.* 1657. [– *disrupt-*, pa. ppl. stem of L. *disrumpere*; see prec.] **1.** *intr.* To burst asunder. TOMLINSON. **2.** *trans.* To break or burst asunder; to shatter 1817. Also *fig.*

2. The attempt..to d. the government 1879. Hence **Disru·pter, -or,** one who breaks up.

Disruption (disrɒ·pʃən). 1646. [– L. *disruptio*, f. as prec.; see -ION.] **1.** The action of rending or bursting asunder; forcible severance. **2.** A disrupted condition or part 1760.

1. At the sudden d. of the masses of rock above 1816. **2.** In the time of weakness and d. 1852.

Phr. *The D.*: the great split in the Established Church of Scotland, 18th May, 1843, when 451 ministers left that Church and formed themselves into the Free (Protesting) Church of Scotland. Hence **Disru·ptionist,** one who favours d.

Disruptive (disrɒ·ptiv), *a.* 1842. [f. DISRUPT *v.* + -IVE.] **1.** Causing or tending to disruption; bursting or breaking asunder. **2.** Produced by disruption; eruptive 1870.

1. The speedy development of d. tendencies STUBBS. **2.** The d. character of these rocks PAGE. Hence **Disru·ptive-ly** *adv.*, **-ness.**

Disrupture (disrɒ·ptiŭɹ), *sb.* 1796. [f. DISRUPT *v.*, after *rupture.*] = DISRUPTION. Hence **Disru·pture** *v.* to break off or asunder; to divide by a rupture.

Diss (dis). 1855. [– Arab. *dīs.*] The Algerian name for a Mediterranean grass, *Ampelodesma* (*Arundo*) *tenax*, used for making cordage, etc.

Dissatisfaction (dissætisfæ·kʃən). 1640. [DIS- 9.] The fact or condition of being dissatisfied; discontent; 'want of something to complete the wish' (J.); a cause of this.

The d. you take at the ways of some good men CROMWELL. The d. of being obliged to return home, without [etc.] 1702.

Dissatisfactory (dissætisfæ·ktŏri), *a.* 1610. [DIS- 10.] Not satisfactory; causing dissatisfaction; unsatisfactory; 'unable to give content' (J.).

Things which..were d. to her Subjects 1610. Hence **Dissatisfa·ctoriness.**

Dissatisfy (dissæ·tisfəi), *v.* 1666. [DIS- 6.] To deprive of satisfaction, to render unsatisfied; to fail to fulfil the desires or wishes of; to displease, discontent. Also *absol.*

Since they [the advantages of life] are not big enough to satisfy, they should not be big enough to d. COLLIER (J.).

†**Dissa·vage,** *v.* [DIS- 8.] To tame, to civilize. CHAPMAN.

Dissceptre (disse·ptəɹ), *v.* 1591. [DIS- 7 a.] To deprive of the sceptre, or of kingly authority.

†**Dissea·son,** *v.* 1583. [DIS- 6.] To take away the flavour of –1621.

Disseat (dissī·t), *v.* 1612. [f. DIS- 6 or 7 c + SEAT *v.* or *sb.*] To remove from or as from a seat; to unseat.

The disseated Parliament-men 1648.

Dissect (disse·kt), *v.* 1607. [– *dissect-*, pa. ppl. stem of L. *dissecare*, f. *dis-* DIS- 1 + *secare* cut.] **1.** *trans.* To cut asunder, cut in pieces, divide by cutting. **2.** *spec.* To cut up (an animal, a plant, etc.) for the purpose of displaying the position, structure, and relations of the various internal parts; to anatomize 1611. **3.** *transf.* and *fig.* To take to pieces, so as to lay bare every part; to analyse; to criticize in detail 1631.

1. Hee that dissected Gordions knot SIR T. HERBERT. **2.** Anatomists d. and mangle, To cut themselves out work to wrangle BUTLER, *Hud.* **3.** To d. the human mind JOWETT. Hence **Disse·ctible** *a.* (*rare*).

Disse·cted, *ppl. a.* 1634. [f. prec. + -ED[1].] **1.** That has been cut up, or divided into pieces; as, a *d. map.* **2.** Cut into many deep lobes; much divided; as, a *d. chin, leaf*, etc. 1652.

Disse·cting, *vbl. sb.* 1767. [f. as prec. + -ING[1].] The action of DISSECT *v.*

Comb.: **d.-forceps, -knife, -microscope, -room** (*i.e.* used in anatomical dissection); **-clerk,** one employed in analysing invoices and accounts.

Disse·cting, *ppl. a.* 1854. [f. as prec. + -ING[2].] That dissects. *D. aneurism*, one in which the blood passes between the inner and middle and the outer coats of the artery.

Dissection (disse·kʃən). 1581. [f. DISSECT *v.* + -ION, perh. partly – med.L. *dissectio*, Fr. *dissection.*] †**1.** The action of cutting asunder or in pieces; division by cutting –1784. **2.** *spec.* The methodical cutting up of an animal or plant for examination of its structure 1605. **3.** The action of separating anything into its elements for the purpose of critical examination 1642. **4.** *concr.* Anything which is the result or produce of dissecting 1581.

2. For hundreds of years..the d. of human bodies was impeded, and anatomists were confined to the d. of dead animals HUXLEY.

Disse·ctive, *a.* 1860. [f. DISSECT *v.* + -IVE.] Serving to dissect.

Dissector (disse·ktəɹ). Also **-er.** 1578. [– mod.L. *dissector*, f. *dissect-*; see DISSECT *v.*, -OR 2.] One who dissects, *esp.* anatomically.

Disseise, disseize (dissī·z), *v.* ME. [– AFr. *disseisir*, OFr. *dessaisir* dispossess; see DIS- 4, SEIZE.] *Law.* To put out of actual seisin or possession; to dispossess (a person) of his estates, etc., usually wrongfully or by force; to oust. Const. *of* (†*from*). Also *transf.* and *fig.*

Where..personnes..be dysseased..from their lawful inheritance 1540. They..With gentle sleep their fear and care disseised HOBBES.

Hence **Dissei:see·, -zee·,** one who is disseised of his estate: correl. to *Disseisor.* **Dissei·sor, -zor,** one who disseises another of his lands, etc. **Dissei·soress.** †**Dissei·sure, -zure** = next.

Disseisin, -zin (dissī·zin), *sb.* ME [– AFr. *disseisine*, OFr. *dessaisine*; see DIS- 4, SEISIN.] *Law.* The act or fact of disseising;

privation of seisin; usually, the wrongful dispossession of the lands, etc., of another: since 15th c. not used of personalty. †**Dissei·sin** *v.* = prec.

Dissel-boom (di·s'l,būm). *S. Afr.* 1858. [Du., f. *dissel* shaft + *boom* beam, boom.] The pole of a wagon.

Dissemblance (dise·mblăns). *arch.* 1463. [In sense 1 – OFr. *dessemblance.* (mod. *dis-*), f. *dessembler*; see DISSEMBLE *v.*², -ANCE. In sense 2, a var. of earlier †*dissimulance*, after *dissemble.*] **1.** Want of resemblance. **2.** The action of dissembling, dissimulation 1602.

2. No time .. is this for bravery As little for d. SOUTHEY.

Dissemble (dise·mb'l), *v.*¹ [Late ME. *dissemile, -immil*, alt. of DISSIMULE *v.*, through *dissimble*, and assoc. w. SEMBLANCE.] **1.** *trans.* To alter or disguise the semblance of so as to deceive; to give a false semblance to; to cloak or disguise by a feigned appearance 1513. †**2.** To disguise –1697. **3.** To pretend not to see or notice; to ignore 1500. **4.** *absol.* or *intr.* To conceal one's intentions, opinions, etc. under a feigned guise; 'to use false professions, to play the hypocrite' (J.) 1523. †**5.** *trans.* To feign, pretend, simulate –1813.

1. That we shoulde not d. nor cloke them [our sins] before the face of Almighty God. *Bk. Com. Prayer.* **2.** *Twel. N.* IV. ii. 4. **3.** Learn to d. wrongs ROWE. **4.** The subtle fiend. . Dissembled, and this answer smooth return'd MILT. *P. R.* I. 467. D. not with me thus SOUTHEY. Hence **Disse·mbler**, one who dissembles; a deceiver, hypocrite. **Disse·mblingly** *adv.*

†**Disse·mble,** *v.*² *rare.* 1586. [– OFr. *des-, dissembler*, f. *des-* DIS- 4 + *sembler* be like, seem.] To be unlike, resemble not. So †**Disse·mblable** *a.* unlike, dissimilar.

Disse·mbly. *nonce-wd.* A perversion of *assembly. Much Ado* IV. ii. 1.

Disseminate (dise·minеⁱt), *v.* 1603. [– *disseminat-*, pa. ppl. stem of L. *disseminare*, f. *dis-* DIS- 1 + *semen, semin-* seed; see -ATE³.] **1.** *trans. lit.* To scatter abroad, as in sowing seed; to spread here and there; to disperse, so as to deposit in all parts; †to distribute –1668. **b.** In *pa. pple.* and *pass.* used of diffused situation, without implying the action 1677. **2.** *fig.* To spread abroad, diffuse, promulgate 1643.

1. The mistletoe is disseminated by birds DARWIN. The pantheists supposed life to be disseminated through all the interstices of matter 1869. **2.** To d. a Doctrine 1670, opinions BP. WATSON, knowledge 1802. So **Disse·minative** *a.* having the quality of disseminating or of being disseminated. **Disse·minator,** one who or that which disseminates.

Dissemination (dise:minēⁱ·ʃən). 1646. [– L. *disseminatio*, f. as prec.; see -ION.] The action of disseminating; the fact or condition of being disseminated; dispersion, diffusion, promulgation.

The extensive d. of the Scriptures 1829.

Dissension (dise·nʃən). ME. [– (O)Fr. *dissension* – L. *dissensio*, f. *dissens-*, pa. ppl. stem of *dissentire*; see DISSENT *v.*, -ION. From XV freq. spelt *-tion.*] **1.** Disagreement in opinion, *esp.* such as produces contention; discord; an instance of this. †**2.** *Med.* Physical disturbance producing ailment –1725. †**3.** = DISSENT *sb.* 3. –1807.

1. But first among the priests d. springs MILT. *P. L.* XII. 352. There were dissensions. . existing within the Church, as well as without J. H. NEWMAN.

Dissensious; see DISSENTIOUS.

Dis,se·nsualize, *v.* [DIS- 6.] To free from sensual quality or elements. LOWELL.

Dissent (dise·nt), *v.* ME. [– L. *dissentire*, f. *dis-* DIS- 1 + *sentire* feel, think. Cf. Fr. *dissentir* (XV).] **1.** *intr.* Not to assent; to disagree with or object to an action. Const. *from*, †*to.* **2.** To think differently, disagree, differ *from*, †*with* 1536; *spec.* to differ from the doctrine or worship of a church, *esp.* the Church of England 1553. †**3.** To be at variance –1743. †**4.** To differ in sense, or meaning, or in any other respect –1659.

1. Some lords entred their reasons for dissenting to the order 1696. **2.** The Methodists have hitherto been accused of dissenting from the Church of England SYD. SMITH. Hence **Disse·ntingly** *adv.*

Dissent (dise·nt), *sb.* 1585. [f. prec.] **1.** Difference of opinion or sentiment; disagreement; †dissension 1596. **2.** Disagreement with a proposal; the opposite of *consent* 1651. **3.** *spec.* Difference of opinion in regard to religious doctrine or worship 1585; separation from an established church, *esp.* the Church of England; non-conformity 1772. †**4.** Want of agreement; difference of sense, nature, etc. –1638.

2. The opposite Lords. . desired they might enter their dissents PEPYS. **3.** D., not satisfied with toleration, is not conscience, but ambition BURKE. **4.** The Consent and D. between Visibles and Audibles BACON.

Dissentaneous (disentēⁱ·niəs), *a.* 1623. [f. L. *dissentaneus* (f. *dissentire* DISSENT *v.*) + -OUS.] Disagreeing, discordant; at variance *with*; contrary *to.* var. †**Disse·ntany** *a.*

†**Dissenta·tion.** 1613. [irreg. f. DISSENT *v.* + -ATION.] Dissension –1623.

Dissenter (dise·ntəɹ). 1639. [f. DISSENT *v.* + -ER¹.] **1.** One who dissents in any matter: one who disagrees with any opinion, resolution, or proposal 1647. **2.** One who dissents in matters of religious belief and worship 1639; one who separates himself *from* any specified church 1663, *esp.* from the communion of the Established Church of England 1679. Usu. with capital D. (Sometimes restricted to those who disagree with the principle of national or state churches.)

2. Its discipline is. . so easy, that it allows more freedom to dissenters than any of the sects would allow it DRYDEN. Do you take me for a D., you rascal FIELDING. Hence **Disse·nterism,** the principles and practice of Dissenters.

†**Disse·ntiate,** *v.* [irreg. f. L. *dissentire* DISSENT *v.* + -ATE³.] *trans.* To move to dissension. FELTHAM.

Dissentient (dise·nʃⁱĕnt). 1621. [– *dissentient-*, pres. ppl. stem of L. *dissentire*; see DISSENT *v.*, -ENT.]

A. *adj.* Differing or disagreeing in opinion; *esp.* dissenting from the opinion or sentiment of the majority 1651.

B. *sb.* One who differs or disagrees in opinion. Hence **Disse·ntience** (*rare*).

Dissentious (dise·nʃəs), *a.* Now *rare.* 1560. [f. DISSENSION (and therefore better *dissensious*); see -IOUS. Cf. Fr. †*dissentieux, -cieux.*] Of, pertaining to, or characterized by, dissension; *esp.* given to dissension, quarrelsome. Hence †**Disse·ntiously** *adv.*

†**Disse·ntive,** *a.* [f. DISSENT *v.* + -IVE.] Inclined to dissent. FELTHAM.

Dissepiment (dise·pimĕnt). 1727. [– L. *dissæpimentum*, f. *dissæpire*, f. *dis-* DIS- 1 + *sæpes* hedge; see -MENT.] *Bot.* and *Zool.* A partition in some part or organ; a septum. *spec.* **a.** *Bot.* A partition separating the cells of a syncarpous ovary or fruit. **b.** *Zool.* One of the horizontal plates connecting the vertical septa in corals. Hence **Dissepime·ntal** *a.*

Dissert (disə·ɹt), *v.* 1623. [– *dissert-*, pa. ppl. stem of L. *disserere* treat, examine, discourse, f. *dis-* DIS- 1 + *serere* join, connect, join words in composition.] †**1.** *trans.* To discuss, examine –1721. **2.** *intr.* To make a dissertation. (Now *affected.*) 1657.

2. 'Tis always with a moral end That I d. BYRON.

Dissertate (di·səɹteⁱt), *v.* 1766. [– *dissertat-*, pa. ppl. stem of L. *dissertare* discuss, debate, frequent. of *disserere*; see prec., -ATE³.] = prec. 2. (Unusual.)

Dissertation (disəɹtēⁱ·ʃən). 1611. [– L. *dissertatio*, f. as prec.; see -ION.] †**1.** Discussion –1709. **2.** = DISCOURSE *sb.* 5. 1651.

2. A D. concerning Man HOBBES. Hence **Disserta·tional** *a.* belonging to or of the nature of a d. **Disserta·tionist,** one who makes a d.

Di·ssertator. 1698. [– late L. *dissertator* disputant, f. as prec.; see -OR 2.] One who makes a dissertation.

Disserve (disə·ɹv), *v.* 1618. [In sense 1, f. DIS- 6 + SERVE *v.*, prob. after (O)Fr. *desservir* in same sense; in sense 2 after mod. Fr. in the sense 'clear the table'.] **1.** *trans.* To do the contrary of *to serve*; to serve badly, do an ill turn to. **2.** To clear a table 1816.

1. In what sort the said Duke had disserved him and abused his trust 1618.

Disservice (disə·ɹvis), *sb.* 1599. [f. DIS- 9 + SERVICE¹. Cf. Fr. *desservice* (XVI) in same sense.] The contrary of *service*; the rendering of an ill service or ill turn; injury, detriment; an injury.

The making of religion a notional thing hath been of infinite d. BP. BERKELEY. Hence **Disse·rviceable** *a.* unhelpful, hurtful, detrimental. **Disse·rviceableness,** d. quality. **Disse·rviceably** *adv.*

†**Disse·ttle,** *v.* 1635. [DIS- 6.] *trans.* To unsettle, disturb –1692. Hence **Disse·ttlement,** the action of dissettling; dissettled condition.

Dissever (dise·vəɹ), *v.* ME. [– AFr. *des(c)everer*, OFr. *dessevrer* (mod., techn. *desseuvrer*) :– late L. *disseparare*, f. *dis-* DIS- 1 + *separare* SEPARATE *v.* See SEVER.] **1.** *trans.* To separate; to divide, disjoin, sever, part. **2.** To divide into parts ME.; †to break up –1615. **3.** *intr.* To separate, part ME.

1. Disseueringe the bishoprick of Chester. . from the iurisdiction of Canterbury 1541. **2.** The very name of Crumwell was able to d. insurrections 1615. Hence **Dissevera·tion,** disseverance. **Disse·verment,** the action of dissevering; disseverance.

Disseverance (dise·vĕrăns). ME. [– OFr. *dessevrance*, f. *dessevrer*; see prec., -ANCE.] The action of dissevering; separation.

Dissha·dow, dish-, *v. rare.* 1610. [DIS- 7 a.] To free from shadow.

Dissheathe (dis,ʃī·ð), *v. rare.* 1614. [DIS- 6.] To unsheathe. (Also *intr.* for *refl.*)

†**Disshi·p,** *v. rare.* 1557. [f. DIS- 6 + SHIP *v.*] To remove from a ship.

†**Disshi·ver,** *v.* 1586. [f. DIS- 1 + SHIVER *v.*¹] To shatter or become shattered –1638.

Disshroud (dis,ʃrau·d), *v. rare.* 1577. [f. DIS- 6 or 7 a + SHROUD *v.*¹ or *sb.*¹] To deprive of a shroud; *fig.* to expose.

Dissidence (di·sidĕns). 1656. [– Fr. *dissidence* or L. *dissidentia*; see next, -ENCE.] Disagreement (in opinion, character, etc.); difference, dissent.

Dissenting for the mere pleasure of d. 1891. var. †**Di·ssidency.**

Dissident (di·sidĕnt). 1534. [– Fr. *dissident* or *dissident-*, pres. ppl. stem of L. *dissidēre* disagree, f. *dis-* DIS- 1 + *sedēre* sit; see -ENT.]

A. *adj.* Disagreeing (in opinion, character, etc.); at variance, different. Const. *from.*

A forme of prayer d. from the common 1617. D. ejected Priests CARLYLE.

B. *sb.* One who disagrees; a dissentient 1789; a dissenter 1790.

The scruples of such dissidents from public opinion are real 1826.

Dissight (dissəi·t disəi·t). 1710. [DIS- 9.] An unsightly object, an eyesore. So **Dissi·ghtly** *a.* unsightly (*rare*).

Dissilient (dissi·liĕnt), *a.* 1656. [– *dissilient-*, pres. ppl. stem of L. *dissilire* fly apart, f. *dis-* DIS- 1 + *salire* leap; see -ENT.] Leaping asunder, springing apart; *spec.* in *Bot.* bursting open with force, as, a *d. pericarp.* Hence **Dissi·liency,** d. quality (*rare*).

†**Dissili·tion.** 1660. [f. *dissilit-*, pa. ppl. stem of L. *dissilire* (see prec., -ION), or on the analogy of similar formations; cf. RESILIENT, RESILITION.] A leaping or springing apart; a bursting –1685.

Dissimilar (disi·milăɹ), *a.* (*sb.*) 1621. [f. DIS- 10 + SIMILAR, after L. *dissimilis*, Fr. *dissimilaire.*] **1.** Not similar or alike; different in appearance, properties, or nature; unlike. Const. *to* (occas. *from, with*). **2.** *sb.* (in *pl.*) Dissimilar things 1654.

1. A new picture. . it was d. to all the others C. BRONTË. Hence **Dissimila·rity,** unlikeness, difference; an instance of this. **Dissi·milarly** *adv.*

Dissimilate (disi·mileⁱt), *v. rare.* 1841. [f. DIS- 4 + L. *similis*, after ASSIMILATE *v.*] To make or become unlike. Hence **Dissi·milative** *a.* tending to or causing dissimilation; *spec.* in *Biol.* katabolic.

Dissimilation (disimilēⁱ·ʃən). 1830. [f. prec., after *assimilation.*] The action of making, or process of becoming, unlike: opp. to ASSIMILATION. *spec.* **a.** *Philol.* The differentiation of two identical sounds occurring near each other in a word, by change of one of them, as in It. *pelegrino* from L. *peregrinus*. **b.** *Biol.* Katabolism.

Dissimile (disi·mili), *sb.* 1682. [– L. *dissimile*, n. of *dissimilis*, after SIMILE.] The opposite of 'simile'; a comparison or illustration by contrast.

Dissimilitude (disimi·litiūd). 1532. [– L. *dissimilitudo*, f. *dissimilis* unlike; see -TUDE.] **1.** The condition of being unlike; unlikeness, dissimilarity; diversity; an instance of this. **†2.** *Rhet.* A comparison by contrast –1751.

1. D. of life and diuersitie of maners 1564.

†Dissi·mulate, *a.* 1450. [– L. *dissimulatus*, pa. pple. of *dissimulare*; see next, -ATE².] Dissembled, feigned, pretended –1653.

Dissimulate (disi·miŭleⁱt), *v.* 1533. [– *dissimulat-*, pa. ppl. stem of L. *dissimulare*; see DIS- 4, SIMULATE *v.*] **†1.** *trans.* To pretend not to see, pass over (*rare*). **2.** To conceal or disguise under a feigned appearance; to dissemble 1610. Also *intr.* Hence **Dissi·mulative** *a.* given to or marked by dissimulation (*rare*). **Dissi·mulator,** a dissembler.

Dissimulation (disi:miulēⁱ·ʃən). ME. [– (O)Fr. *dissimulation* – L. *dissimulatio*, f. as prec.; see -ION.] The action of dissimulating; concealment under a feigned semblance; feigning, hypocrisy; an instance of this (*arch.*).

Let loue be without d. *Rom.* 12:9. Simulation is a Pretence of what is not, and D. a Concealment of what is STEELE. Smooth D., skilled to grace A devil's purpose with an angels' face COWPER.

†Dissi·mule, *v.* ME. [– (O)Fr. *dissimuler* – L. *dissimulare*; see DISSIMULATE *v.* Hence DISSEMBLE *v.*¹] **1.** *trans.* = DISSEMBLE *v.*¹ 1–5. –1636. ¶ **2.** In the later Wycliffite version repr. *dissimulare* of the Vulgate, where the sense of the original is 'linger' and 'leave off'. Hence **†Dissi·muler, †-our** = DISSEMBLER.

†Dissi·new, *v. rare.* 1640. [DIS- 7 a.] To deprive of sinew or vigour –1641.

†Di·ssipable, *a.* 1603. [– L. *dissipabilis*, f. *dissipare*; see next, -ABLE. Cf. Fr. †*dissipable*.] That can be dissipated –1710. Hence **†Dissipabi·lity.**

Dissipate (di·sipeⁱt), *v.* 1532. [– *dissipat-*, pa. ppl. stem of L. *dissipare*, f. *dis-* DIS- 1 + **supare*, **sipare* throw; see -ATE³.] **1.** *trans.* To scatter; to cause to go off in all directions; to disperse 1534. Also *intr.* (for *refl.*). **†2.** *trans.* To scatter in defeat –1789. **3.** To dispel by dispersion (mist, clouds, etc.); to cause to disappear 1532. Also *fig.* and *transf.* **b.** *intr.* To pass away by dispersion; to disappear 1626. **4.** *trans.* To disintegrate or dissolve completely, undo, annul 1555. Also *intr.* (for *refl.*). **5.** *trans.* To scatter or consume wilfully (money, faculties); to squander 1682. **6.** *trans.* To distract by variety of objects; to fritter away 1683. **7.** *intr.* To practise dissipation; to engage in frivolous or (now usually) dissolute pleasures 1836.

3. They will clerely d. and discusse the myst MORE. [It] has dissipated the Fears of that People STEELE. *intr.* Libels neglected quickly.. disipat to ayr HOWELL. 4. Shall the Heavens and Earth be wholly dissipated and destroyed RAY. 6. Thought may be dissipated into a number of aperçus 1883. Hence **†Di·ssipate, Di·ssipated** *ppl. adjs.* dispersed, scattered, wasted, frittered away; given to dissipation, dissolute. **Di·ssipater,** one who or that which dissipates. **Di·ssipative** *a.* tending to d. **Dissipati·vity** (in *Physics*), a quantity expressing the rate of dissipation of energy; called also *dissipation-function*.

Dissipation (disipēⁱ·ʃən). 1545. [– (O)Fr. *dissipation* or L. *dissipatio*, f. as prec.; see -ION.] **†1.** The action of dissipating or dispersing; dispersed condition –1760. **2.** The wasting of a substance, or form of energy, through continuous dispersion 1615. **3.** Complete disintegration or dissolution 1597. **4.** Squandering, waste 1639. **5.** Distraction of the mental faculties from concentration on serious subjects; diversion, amusement; also with *a* and *pl.* 1733. **6.** Waste of the moral and physical powers by vicious indulgence in pleasure; intemperate or dissolute mode of living 1784.

1. Foule d. follow'd, and forc't rout MILT. *P. L.* VI. 598. 3. The d. of the whole frame of Nature into disjoynted dust HY. MORE. 4. There had been such a d. of treasure BP. BURNET. 5. Change of place..inevitably produces d. of mind JOHNSON. 6. He died young, worn out by d. 1894.

†Di·ssite, *a.* 1600. [– L. *dissitus* lying apart, remote, f. *dis-* DIS- 1 + *situs* placed, situate.] Situated apart –1657.

Britaine..Far d. from this world of ours P. HOLLAND.

†Disslander, var. of DISCLANDER.

Dissociable (see below), *a.* 1603. [In sense 1, f. DIS- 10 + SOCIABLE; in sense 2 – L. *dissociabilis*; in sense 3 – Fr. *dissociable*.] **1.** (dissōᵘ·ʃăb'l) The reverse of sociable; unsociable. **2.** That tends to separate. (*rare*) 1835. **3.** (disōᵘ·ʃⁱăb'l) Separable 1833.

1. They came in two by two..matched in the most d. Manner ADDISON. Hence **Dissociabi·lity** (*rare*), **Disso·ciableness,** unsociableness.

Dissocial (dissōᵘ·ʃăl), *a.* 1762. [DIS- 10.] Disinclined or unsuitable for society; unsocial.

Hatred and other d. passions KAMES. Hence **Disso·cialize** *v.* to render d.

Disso·ciate, *ppl. a. rare.* 1548. [– L. *dissociatus*, pa. pple. of *dissociare*; see next, -ATE².] Dissociated.

Dissociate (disōᵘ·ʃi,eⁱt), *v.* 1611. [– *dissociat-*, pa. ppl. stem of L. *dissociare*, f. *dis-* DIS- 1 + *sociare* join together, f. *socius* companion; see -ATE³.] **1.** *trans.* To cut off from association or society; to sever, disunite. Const. *from.* **b.** *Chem.* To separate the elements of, *spec.* by heat 1869. **2.** *intr.* (for *refl.*) To cease to associate 1866.

1. Our very wants and desires, which first bring us together, have a tendency likewise to d. us TUCKER. Hence **Disso·ciative** *a.* causing dissociation or decomposition.

Dissociation (disōᵘʃi,ēⁱ·ʃən, -si,ēⁱ·ʃən). 1611. [– Fr. *dissociation* or L. *dissociatio*, f. as prec.; see -ION.] **1.** The action of dissociating or the condition of being dissociated; disunion. **2.** *Chem.* Decomposition, *spec.* by the action of heat. Hence *d.-point*, the temperature at which such decomposition takes place.

1. It will add infinitely to the d., distraction, and confusion of these confederate republics BURKE.

Dissoluble (di·sǫliub'l, disǫ·liub'l), *a.* 1534. [– (O)Fr. *dissoluble* or L. *dissolubilis*, f. *dissolvere*; see DIS- 1, SOLUBLE.] **1.** Separable into elements or atoms; capable of being destroyed by complete decomposition. **†2.** Soluble in a liquid –1809. **3.** Capable of being loosened, unfastened, or (*fig.*) undone 1600. **4.** That may be dissolved, as an assembly 1642.

1. How then should the Gods Being atomic not be d. TENNYSON. Hence **Disso:lubi·lity, †Disso·lubleness,** the quality of being d.

Dissolute (di·sŏlⁱut), *a.* (*sb.*) ME. [– L. *dissolutus* loose, disunited, pa. pple. of *dissolvere* DISSOLVE.] **†1.** Disjoined, disunited –1651. **†2.** Relaxed, enfeebled –1816. **†3.** Slack, negligent, remiss –1619. **4.** †Loose, wanton –1713; lawless in style (now *rare*) 1566. **5.** Lax in morals, loose-living; licentious, profligate, debauched. The current sense. 1513. **6.** *sb.* A dissolute person (*rare*) 1608.

4. The d. dulness of English Flamboyant RUSKIN. 5. Belial, the dissolutest Spirit that fell MILT. *P. R.* II. 150. Hence **Di·ssolute-ly** *adv.*, **-ness.**

Dissolution (disŏlⁱū·ʃən). ME. [– (O)Fr. *dissolution* or L. *dissolutio*, f. *dissolut-*; see prec., -ION.] **1.** Separation into parts or constituent elements; disintegration, decomposition. **2.** Reduction from the solid to the fluid form; liquefaction; formerly, also, = fusion 1598. **3.** Solution in a liquid. ? *Obs.* 1558; †result of this; a solution –1707. **†4.** Hurtful relaxation or weakening –1683. **5.** The condition of being loose from due restraint; †excess; laxity of behaviour or morals; dissoluteness (*arch.*) ME. **†b.** with *pl.* An instance of this –1653. **6.** The relaxation of any tie, bond, or binding power 1534. **7.** The breaking up of an assembly, association, or constituted body of persons 1535. **8.** Termination of life; death, decease 1522. **9.** The action of bringing or condition of being brought to an end 1528. **†10.** Solution (of a question, etc.) (*rare*) 1549.

1. The d. of flesh, skin, and bones BUTLER. 2. The d. of the great snow FULLER. 6. The cause of dissolucion of their amitie and league 1548. 7. A d. is the civil death of the parliament BLACKSTONE. The d. of the monasteries LD. BROUGHAM, of the Huguenot party J. R. GREEN. 8. The disolucion and seueraunce of the soule fro the body MORE. 9. That realm were like to come to d. 1528. Hence **Dissolu·tionism,** the doctrine of dissolutionists. **Dissolu·tionist,** one who advocates d.

Dissolutive (di·sŏlⁱutiv), *a.* Now *rare.* ME. [– med.L. *dissolutivus*, f. as prec.; see -IVE. Cf. Fr. *dissolutif, -ive* (XVI).] **1.** Having the property of dissolving. **2.** Pertaining to, or of the nature of, dissolution 1886.

Disso·lvable, *a.* Also **-ible.** 1541. [f. DISSOLVE *v.* + -ABLE; repl. (in part) DISSOLUBLE.] **1.** Capable of being separated into its elements; decomposable. **2.** Capable of being liquified or melted. ? *Obs.* 1653. **3.** Of a connection, society, etc.: Terminable, destructible 1681.

1. You are but men..and your substance but d. clay 1661. 2. D., by Water, or by Fire 1668. 3. A mere partnership d...by mutual consent LOWELL. Hence **Dissolvabi·lity, Disso·lvableness.**

†Disso·lvative, *a. rare.* 1577. [f. next + -ATIVE.] **a.** Having the property of dissolving. **b.** That tends to dissolve readily –1580.

Dissolve (dizǫ·lv), *v.* ME. [– L. *dissolvere*, f. *dis-* DIS- 1 + *solvere* loosen, SOLVE.] **I.** *trans.* **1.** To put asunder the parts of; to reduce to its formative elements; to disintegrate, decompose. (Now *rare.*) **2.** To liquefy by means of heat, moisture, etc.; to fuse (now *rare*); to melt; to melt (*in* something), make a SOLUTION of ME. Also *fig.* **†3.** To relax, enfeeble –1563. **4.** To loosen, release (*lit.* and *fig.*) (*arch.*) ME. **†5.** To release from life; usu. in *pass.* to die, depart –1736. **6.** To cause to vanish; to bring to nought, destroy ME. **†7.** *Med.* To dissolve (humours), reduce (swellings), assuage (pains, etc.) –1657. **8.** To break up, dismiss, disperse; to terminate the existence of (now *esp.* of Parliament) 1494. Also *ellipt.* = *d. parliament.* 1868. **9.** To undo (a tie, etc.); to bring to an end (a relation) ME.; †to sunder –1611. **10.** To destroy the authority, force, or influence of; to annul, abrogate 1526. **11.** To solve (a question, etc.) 1549. **12.** *Cinema.* To cause (a picture) to fade away. Also *intr.* 1912.

2. Before the Sunne hath..dissolved the yce HAKLUYT. *fig.* Dissolv'd in Pleasures PENN, tears 1800, Speech CARLYLE. 4. As the soft touch dissolved the virgin zone THOMSON. 6. Each gay phantom was dissolv'd in air SIR W. JONES. 8. To d. his armye 1548, Parliament 1548, a religious house 1586. 9. To d. a jointure BLACKSTONE, marriage LANE, partnership 1896. 10. To frustrate and d. these magic spells MILT. *Sams.* 1149.

II. *intr.* **1.** To become disintegrated; to vanish gradually, come to an end ME. **2.** To become liquefied; to fuse; to melt; to melt (*in* something), forming a SOLUTION 1450. Also *fig.* **3.** Of an assembly, etc.: To break up; to disperse; to lose its corporate character 1513. **4.** To lose its binding force 1611.

1. The great Globe it selfe, Yea, all which it inherit, shall dissolue *Temp.* IV. i. 154. 2. While Mountain Snows d. against the Sun DRYDEN. *fig.* I am almost ready to dissolue (= faint away), Hearing of this *Lear* V. iii. 203. 4. The charme dissolues apace SHAKS. Hence **Disso·lve** *sb.* (cf. sense 12 above). **Disso·lver. Disso·lvingly** *adv.*

Dissolvent (dizǫ·lvĕnt). 1646. [– *dissolvent-*, pr. ppl. stem of L. *dissolvere*; see DISSOLVE, -ENT. Cf. Fr. *dissolvant* (XVI).] **A.** *adj.* Having the power to dissolve; solvent 1665.

B. *sb.* One who or that which dissolves. **1.** *spec.* A substance having power to dissolve other substances; a solvent, a menstruum; †formerly, in *Med.*, a substance which dissolves morbid concretions, etc. 1646. **2.** *gen.* and *fig.* 1835.

1. Fire—the only Catholic D. RAY. 2. Wine is the great d. of distrust 1835.

Dissonance (di·sŏnăns). 1571. [– (O)Fr. *dissonance* or late L. *dissonantia*, f. as next; see -ANCE.] **1.** The quality or fact of being dissonant; an inharmonious or harsh sound or combination of sounds; a DISCORD 1597. *spec.* in *Mus.* A combination of tones causing beats (cf. BEAT *sb.*[1] 6); also, a note which in combination with others produces a harsh effect 1660. **2.** Want of concord or harmony (between things) 1571.

1. The..roar..filled the air with barbarous d. MILT. *Comus* 548. So †**Di·ssonancy.**

Dissonant (di·sŏnănt), *a.* (*sb.*) 1490. [– (O)Fr. *dissonant* or L. *dissonant-*, pres. ppl. stem of *dissonare* disagree in sound, f. *dis-* DIS- 1 + *sonare* SOUND *v.*[1]] **1.** Disagreeing or discordant in sound, inharmonious; harsh-sounding 1573. **2.** Disagreeing, discordant, different, in any respect. Const. *from, to* (rarely *with*). 1490. **3.** *sb.* A harsh sound of speech 1579.

1. D. and iarring dittyes G. HARVEY. **2.** Opinions not altogether d. from the Scriptures PURCHAS. The interests..before that time jarring and d., were..adjusted BURKE. Hence **Di·ssonantly** *adv.*

†**Di·ssonate,** *a.* 1548. [– L. *dissonatus*, pa. pple. of *dissonare*; see prec., -ATE[2].] = DISSONANT –1781.

Disspirit, obs. f. DISPIRIT.

†**Dissta·te,** *v.* 1605. [DIS- 7.] To remove from its state; to deprive of state –1647.

Dissuade (diswēi·d), *v.* 1513. [– L. *dissuadēre*, f. *dis-* DIS- 4 + *suadēre* advise, urge; cf. Fr. *dissuader.*] **1.** *trans.* To give advice against. ? *Obs.* **2.** To advise or exhort (a person) against; to dehort (*from*). ? *Obs.* 1534. **3.** To draw a person *from* a course or action by suasion 1576.

1. My friends..With mild entreaties my design d. POPE. **2.** Some disswaded him to hunt that day; but he resolved to the contrary CAMDEN. **3.** I have tried what is possible to d. him MISS BURNEY. Hence **Dissua·der,** one who dissuades.

Dissuasion (diswēi·ʒən). 1526. [– (O)Fr. *dissuasion* or L. *dissuasio*, f. *dissuas-*, pa. ppl. stem of *dissuadēre*; see prec., -ION.] The action, or an act, of dissuading; advice or exhortation against something; dehortation.

Ev'n thy Dissuasions me persuade COWLEY.

Dissuasive (diswēi·siv). 1609. [f. as prec. + -IVE. Cf. Fr. *dissuasif, -ive.*]

A. *adj.* Tending to dissuade; dehortatory; as. *d. ejaculations.*

B. *sb.* A dissuasive speech or argument; that which tends or is intended to dissuade 1629. Hence **Dissua·sive-ly** *adv.*, **-ness.**

†**Dissua·sory,** *a.* and *sb.* 1555. [– late L. *dissuasorius*, f. L. *dissuasor*, f. as prec.; see -ORY[2].] = DISSUASIVE –1844.

Dissunder (dissɒ·ndəɹ), *v.* 1580. [DIS- 1 or 5.] *trans.* To sunder, sever, dissever.

Th' Aethiops, far dissunder'd in their seat CHAPMAN.

†**Disswee·ten,** *v.* 1622. [DIS- 6.] *trans.* To deprive of sweetness –1667.

Dissyllabic, -able, etc.; see DISYLLABIC, -ABLE, etc.

Dissymmetric, -al (dissime·trik, -ăl), *a.* 1867. [DIS- 10.] **a.** The opposite of symmetrical. **b.** Symmetrical, but in opposite directions, like the two hands.

Dissymmetry (dis,si·mĕtri). 1845. [DIS- 9.] **a.** Lack or absence of symmetry. **b.** Symmetry between two objects, disposed in opposite directions, such as the two hands, etc.

Distad (di·stæ̆d), *adv.* 1803. [f. DIST(ANT + -AD II; cf. DEXTRAD.] In the direction of the end or distal part of a limb, etc.

Distaff (di·staf). Pl. **distaffs,** †**distaves.** [OE. *distæf*, a peculiarly Eng. word (the Continental word being repr. by ROCK *sb.*[2]), f. the base of MLG. *dise, disene* distaff, bunch of flax (LG. *diesse*), rel. to DIZEN; the second element is STAFF *sb.*[1]] **1.** A cleft staff about 3 feet long, on which, in the ancient mode of spinning, wool or flax was wound. **2.** Used as the type of women's work ME.; hence, for the female sex, female authority; also, the female branch of a family; a female heir 1494.

1. Wymen comynly do not entremete but to spynne on the distaf CAXTON. Phr. †*To have tow on one's d.*: to have work in hand. **2.** Some say the Crozier, some say the Distaffe was too busie HOWELL.

attrib. and *Comb.*, as **d. side,** the female branch of a family; **distaff's** or **St. Distaff's day,** the day after the Feast of the Epiphany, on which day (Jan. 7) women resumed their spinning after the holidays; also called *rock-day*, a d. being called a *rock*; **d. thistle,** a name of *Carthamus lanatus* (*Cirsium lanatum*), from its woolly flowering stems.

Distain (distēi·n), *v. arch.* ME. [– OFr. *desteign-*, pres. stem of *desteindre* (mod. *déteindre*) :– Rom. **distingere*; see DIS- 1, TINGE *v.*] **1.** *trans.* To imbue or stain with a colour different from the natural one; to discolour, dye. **2.** *transf.* and *fig.* To defile; to sully, dishonour ME.

1. The tears that so d. my cheeks MARLOWE. **2.** A soul distain'd by earth and gold SHENSTONE.

Distal (di·stăl), *a.* 1808. [irreg. f. DIST(ANT + -AL[1], after *dorsal*, etc.] *Anat.* Situated away from the centre of the body, or from the point of origin (said of the distant part or of the extremity of a limb or organ); terminal. Opp. to *proximal*. Also *transf.* Hence **Di·stally** *adv.*

Distance (di·stăns), *sb.* ME. [– OFr. *destance*, (also mod.) *distance* – L. *distantia*; see DISTANT, -ANCE.]

†**I.** [from OFr. *destance* discord, quarrel.] The condition of being at variance; discord; dispute, debate –1752; with *a* and *pl.* –1666.

They were in suche vnyte, that there was no dystaunce amonge them LD. BERNERS.

†**II.** [from L. *distantia* difference.] Difference, diversity –1556.

III. [f. L. *distantia*, Fr. *distance*, in the sense of 'being apart in space'.] **1.** The fact or condition of being far off in space; remoteness 1594. **2.** The space lying between any two objects; the space to be passed over before reaching an object; an intervening space ME. **3.** Techn. applications of 2. **a.** *Mil.* The space between man and man when standing in rank; also that between the ranks 1635. **b.** *Fencing.* A set space to be kept between two combatants 1592. **c.** *Racing.* The space measured back from the winning-post which a horse must have reached, in a heat-race, when the winning horse has covered the whole course, in order not to be 'distanced' 1674. †**d.** *Mus.* An interval –1797. **e.** See also FOCAL *d.*, POLAR *d.*, ZENITH *d.* **4.** *fig.* Remoteness in likeness, relationship, allusion, degree, or the like; 'ideal disjunction' (J.) 1667. **5.** Remoteness in intercourse 1597; hence **a.** Aloofness, excessive reserve 1660; **b.** Deference 1689. **6.** *ellipt.* A point or place at a distance, the region in the distance 1782. **b.** *Painting*, etc. The distant part of a landscape 1706. **7.** *ellipt.* The 'space' of time between two events ME.

1. 'Tis d. lends enchantment to the view CAMPBELL. **2.** Within jumping d. TYNDALL. **3.** In these times you stand on d.: your Passes, Stoccado's, and I know not what *Wint. T.* II. i. 233. **4.** The mistake..I conceive to have been an effect of mental d. MAINE. **5.** With safest d. I mine honour shielded SHAKS. A..courteous Prince..without state or d. 1660. I hope your modesty Will know, what d. to the crown is due DRYDEN. Phr. *To keep one's d.* **6.** Viewed from a d. COWPER. A trumpet in the d. pealing news TENNYSON. Phr. *Middle d.* (in *Painting*): the part of a landscape midway between the foreground and the remote region. **7.** An apprehension not to be mentioned, even at this d. of time, without shame MACAULAY.

Comb.: **d.-flag** (*Racing*), a flag held by the man who is stationed at the d.-post; **-judge,** a judge stationed at the **d.-post,** a post (or flag) placed at the fixed 'distance' in front of the winning-post in a heat-race, to note what horses are 'distanced', through failing to reach this before the winner passes the winning-post.

Di·stance, *v.* 1578. [f. prec. sb. Cf. (O)Fr. *distancer.*] **1.** *trans.* To place at a distance; to eloign. **2.** To make to appear distant 1695. †**3.** *intr.* To be distant (*rare*) –1658. **4.** *trans.* To outstrip or leave behind in a race. Also *fig.* 1642. **b.** *Racing.* To beat by a distance; see DISTANCE *sb.* III. 3 c. 1674.

1. This insight..distances those who share it from those who share it not EMERSON. **2.** Mountains, which the ripe Italian air distances with a bloom like that on unplucked grapes LOWELL. **4.** [He] had distanced all his competitors LEVER.

Distanced (di·stănst), *ppl. a.* 1644. [f. prec. + -ED[1].] †**1.** Put at a distance; remote –1672. **2.** Left behind, outstripped as in a race 1713. **b.** *Racing.* Beaten by a distance; see DISTANCE *sb.* III. 3 c. 1737.

Distancy (di·stănsi). *rare.* 1628. [f. L. *distantia* DISTANCE *sb.*; see -ANCY.] Distantness.

Distant (di·stănt), *a.* ME. [– (O)Fr. *distant* or *distant-*, pres. ppl. stem of L. *distare*, f. *dis-* DIS- 1 + *stare* stand.] **1.** Separate or apart in space. **2.** Widely separated; far apart, not close together 1548. **3.** Standing, lying, or taking place afar off; remote 1590. **4.** Far apart or remote in time 1603. **5.** *transf.* and *fig.* Remote in relations other than those of space and time 1538. †**6.** Different –1710. **7.** Reserved in intercourse; standing aloof; not intimate 1709.

1. One board had two tenons, equally d. one from another *Exod.* 36:22. **2.** D. from thy blest abode 1760. **3.** Earth's d. ends POPE. D. vision HARLAN. **4.** Written..at d. times BP. BERKELEY. **5.** I haven't the most d. idea SHERIDAN. By d. analogy ARGYLL. Not a sister, but a more d. kinswoman FREEMAN. **7.** The d. Behaviour of the Prude STEELE.

So †**Dista·ntial** *a.* distant; differing. Hence **Di·stant-ly** *adv.*, **-ness.**

Distaste (distēi·st), *sb.* 1598. [f. DIS- 9 + TASTE *sb.*[1], after OFr. *desgoust* (mod. *dégoût*), It. *disgusto* DISGUST *sb.*] **1.** Disrelish or dislike of food or drink; nausea. Now *rare.* **2.** Disinclination, dislike 1598. †**3.** Unpleasantness; annoyance, discomfort –1711. †**4.** Offence –1731. †**5.** Mutual aversion, quarrel –1697.

2. An aversion more resembling a d. than a conviction J. MARTINEAU. **3.** Prosperity is not without many Feares and Distastes BACON.

Distaste (distēi·st), *v.* Now *rare.* 1586. [f. DIS- 6 + TASTE *v.*, after OFr. *desgouster* (mod. *dégoûter*), It. (*di*)*sgustare* DISGUST *v.*] **1.** *trans.* To have no taste for, disrelish, dislike; to regard with aversion or displeasure. †**2.** To offend the taste of; to disgust –1678. Also †*absol.* or *intr.* **3.** *trans.* To displease, offend 1597; †*intr.* to cause displeasure or offence; to be distasteful –1654. †**4.** *trans.* (as f. DIS- 7 a + TASTE *sb.*[1]) To destroy or spoil the taste or savour of –1650.

1. Distasting wholesome meat well dressed FULLER. [He] should d. the society of his class 1805. **2.** Let it [the Physicke] distast me so it heale me 1636. Poysons, Which at the first are scarce found to d. *Oth.* III. iii. 327. **3.** Yet loth in anything to d. the King SIR T. HERBERT. Hence †**Dista·stive** *a.* feeling or expressing distaste; disgusting, offensive; also as *sb.* †**Dista·sture,** loathing of food; nausea; vexation.

Distasteful (distēi·stfŭl), *a.* 1607. [f. DISTASTE *sb.* + -FUL.] **1.** Disagreeable to the taste; causing disgust; nasty 1611. **2.** Causing dislike; disagreeable, offensive 1607. †**3.** Full of dislike; showing dislike; malevolent –1646.

1. The green d. fruit DRYDEN. **2.** D. truth DRYDEN. **3.** After distastefull lookes..They froze me into Silence *Timon* II. ii. 220. Hence **Dista·steful-ly** *adv.*, **-ness.**

Distemonous (dəistī·mŏnəs), *a.* 1883. [f. Gr. δι-, DI-[2] + στήμων stamen + -OUS.] *Bot.* Having two stamens; = DIANDROUS.

Distemper (diste·mpəɹ), *v.*[1] Now *rare.* ME. [– late L. *distemperare*, f. L. *dis-* DIS- 4 + *temperare* proportion or mingle duly, TEMPER *v.*] †**1.** *trans.* To temper improperly; to disturb or derange the due proportion of. (ME. only.) **2.** To disturb or disorder the humour (formerly, the due proportion of the four humours), temper, or feelings of; to render ill-humoured or ill at ease; to upset. (Now *rare.*) ME. **3.** To disorder or derange the bodily or mental condition of; to render unhealthy or diseased; to sicken ME. †**b.** *spec.* To intoxicate –1679. **4.** *transf.* and *fig.* To disorder the condition of; to derange 1494. †**5.** To deprive (a metal) of 'temper' (*rare*) 1795.

3. Vainely distempering himselfe about idle and frivolous questions BP. HALL. **4.** This variable composition of mans bodie hath made it as an Instrument easie to d. BACON. **5.** The malignancie of my fate, might perhaps d. yours *Twel. N.* II. i. 5.

Diste·mper, *v.*[2] ME. [– OFr. *destremper* or late L. *distemperare* soak, macerate, f. L. *dis-* DIS- 1 or 5 + *temperare* mingle, qualify, TEMPER *v.*] †**1.** *trans.* To treat with water or other liquid; to dilute; to steep –1667. **2.** *transf.* and *fig.* To dilute; to allay (*arch.*) 1592. **3.** *Painting.* To paint in distemper 1873.

2. Jealousy..Distempering gentle Love in his desire, As air and water do abate the fire SHAKS.

Distemper (diste·mpəɹ), *sb.*[1] 1555. [f. DISTEMPER *v.*[1], partly f. DIS- 9 + TEMPER *sb.*] †**1.** 'A disproportionate mixture of parts'; distempered condition –1644. †**2.** A disordered condition of the air, climate, weather, etc.; inclemency –1856. **3.** Derangement of the 'humour' or 'temper' (formerly regarded as due to disturbance in the bodily 'humours'; cf. TEMPER, TEMPERAMENT); ill temper, ill humour; disaffection. (Now assoc. w. sense 4.) 1555. **4.** Deranged condition of the body or mind (formerly regarded as due to disproportion in the four humours); ill health, illness, disease 1598; with *a* and *pl.* 1648. **b.** *spec.* A catarrhal affection of dogs. Also applied to other diseases of animals. 1747. †**c.** Intoxication –1650. **5.** *transf.* and *fig.* Derangement, or disorder (*esp.* in a state) 1605.

2. Exposed to theeves, vermin, and distempers of weather 1655. **3.** Good my Lord, what is your cause of d. *Haml.* III. ii. 351. **4.** Eccentricity Nowise amounting to d. BROWNING. Such plenty of wine as to cause d. 1607. **5.** In these sad times of our Civill Distempers 1647.

Diste·mper, *sb.*[2] 1632. [f. DISTEMPER *v.*[2], after Fr. †*destrempe* (mod. *détrempe*).] *Painting.* A method of painting in which the colours are mixed with some glutinous substance soluble in water, executed usually upon a ground of chalk or plaster mixed with gum (*d.-ground*): mostly used in scene-painting and in the decoration of walls. Also applied to the pigments and to the ground.

†**Diste·mperance.** ME. [– OFr. *des-, distemperance*, etc. – late L. *distemperantia*, f. *dis-* DIS- 4 + L. *temperantia* TEMPERANCE.] = DISTEMPERATURE –1620.

Diste·mperate, *a. arch.* ME. [– late L. *distemperatus*, f. *dis-* DIS- 4 + L. *temperatus* TEMPERATE.] †**1.** Of the air or elements: Not temperate –1647. †**2.** Of the bodily 'humours': Not properly tempered; diseased; ill-conditioned –1658. **3.** Immoderate; intemperate. ? *Obs.* 1557. Hence †**Diste·mperately** *adv.*

Distemperature (diste·mpĕrătiŭɹ). Now *arch.* 1531. [– med.L. **distemperatura*, f. *dis-* DIS- 4 + L. *temperatura* TEMPERATURE. Cf. OFr. *destrempëure.*] **1.** Distempered condition of the air or elements; inclemency, unwholesomeness. **2.** Distempered condition of the 'humours'; disorder, ailment 1533. **3.** Disturbance of mind or temper 1571. Also *transf.* and *fig.* **4.** Excess (*esp.* of heat or cold; cf. sense 1); intemperance 1572.

1. The temperature or d. of the regions ELYOT. **2.** A huge infectious troope Of pale distemperatures *Com. Err.* V. i. 82. **3.** What I uttered through the d. of my passion WARBURTON.

†**Diste·mperment.** 1582. [f. DISTEMPER *v.*[1] + -MENT.] Distempered condition (of the air or humours) –1661.

†**Diste·mperure.** ME. [– OFr. *destemprure, -trempure*; see DISTEMPER *v.*[1], -URE.] = DISTEMPERATURE.

Distend (diste·nd), *v.* ME. [– L. *distendere*, f. *dis-* DIS- 1 + *tendere* stretch. Cf. Fr. *distendre* (XVI) in sense 3.] †**1.** *trans.* To stretch asunder; to spread out. Also *fig.* –1834. †**2.** *intr.* To stretch out, extend –1638. **3.** *trans. spec.* To swell out or enlarge by pressure from within, as a bladder; to expand, dilate by stretching 1650. Also *transf.* and *fig.* **4.** *intr.* To increase in bulk by internal stretching; to swell out, expand 1667.

3. May thy Cows their burden'd Bags d. DRYDEN. **4.** Now his heart Distends with pride MILT. *P. L.* I. 573. †**Diste·ndible** *a.* capable of being distended.

Distensible (diste·nsĭb'l), *a.* 1828. [f. L. *distens-* (see next) + -IBLE.] Capable of being distended or dilated. Hence **Distensibi·lity,** d. quality.

Distension (diste·nʃən). 1607. [– L. *distensio*, later var. of *distentio*, f. *distent-, distens-*, pa. ppl. stem of L. *distendere* DISTEND; see -ION. Cf. (O)Fr. *distension.*] **1.** The action of distending; distended condition; expansion by stretching or swelling out. **2.** Extension; straining, racking. ? *Obs.* 1625.

Distensive (diste·nsiv), *a. rare.* 1836. [f. L. *distens-* (see prec.) + -IVE.] Distensible.

†**Diste·nt,** *sb.* 1613. [– L. *distentus* distension, f. pa. ppl. stem of *distendere* DISTEND. See DISTENSION.] Distension; breadth –1659.

Distent (diste·nt), *ppl. a.* 1590. [– L. *distentus*, pa. pple. of *distendere* DISTEND. See DISTENSION.] †**1.** Extended –1773. **2.** Swollen out 1605.

Distention, var. of DISTENSION.

Dister; see DISTERR.

†**Diste·rminate,** *v.* 1599. [– *disterminat-*, pa. ppl. stem of L. *disterminare*, f. *dis-* DIS- 1 + *terminare* TERMINATE *v.*] To separate as a boundary does; to bound, divide –1676.

So †**Diste·rminate** *a.* separated, marked off, divided. †**Distermina·tion,** separation as by boundaries; division.

†**Diste·rr,** *v.* [f. DIS- 7 c + L. *terra* land.] To banish from one's country; to exile. HOWELL.

Disthene (di·sþīn). 1808. [f. Gr. δι- DI-[2] + σθένος strength.] = CYANITE 1. Named from its different electrical properties in two different directions.

Disthrone (disþrōu·n), *v.* 1591. [DIS- 7 c.] To dethrone. Also *fig.* So †**Disthro·nize** *v.*

Distich (di·stik), *sb.* Pl. **distichs,** †**distiches.** 1553. [– L. *distichon* – Gr. δίστιχον, subst. use (sc. μέτρον metre) of n. of δίστιχος of two rows or verses, f. δι- DI-[2] + στίχος row, line of verse.] A couple of lines of verse, usually making complete sense; a couplet.

By far the greater number of verses in the poetry of the Old Testament consist of Distichs 1891.

Distich (di·stik), *a. rare.* 1788. [– L. *distichus* – Gr. δίστιχος of two rows or verses; see prec.] = DISTICHOUS.

Distichal (di·stikăl), *a.* (*sb.*) 1778. [f. L. *distichus* (see prec.) + -AL[1].] **1.** *Pros.* Consisting of two lines of verse. **2.** *Zool.* Applied to certain joints in the arm of a crinoid; also as *sb.* 1879.

‖**Distichiasis** (distikəi·ăsis). 1875. [mod. L., f. Gr. διστιχία double row, f. δίστιχος; see DISTICH *sb.*, -ASIS.] *Path.* A malformation in which the eyelid has a double row of eyelashes.

Distichous (di·stikəs), *a.* 1753. [f. L. *distichus* adj. (see DISTICH *a.*) + -OUS.] Disposed in two opposite rows; two-ranked; formerly, sometimes = dichotomous. Hence **Di·stichously** *adv.*

Distil, distill (disti·l), *v.* Infl. **distilled, -illing.** ME. [– (partly through (O)Fr. *distiller*) L. *distillare*, for *destillare* drip or trickle down, f. *de-* DE- 1 + *stillare*, f. *stilla* a drop.] **1.** *intr.* To trickle down or fall in drops; to exude. **b.** To pass or flow gently (chiefly *fig.*) 1609. **c.** To drip *with* 1714. **2.** *trans.* To let fall or give forth in drops ME. **3.** *transf.* and *fig.* To give forth or impart in minute quantities; †to instil ME. **4.** To subject to the process of distillation (see DISTILLATION 3) ME.; to extract the essence of by distillation ME.; to transform or convert *into* by distillation 1636. *absol.* 1611. Also *fig.* **5.** To obtain, extract, produce, or make, by distillation ME. Also *fig.* **6.** *intr.* To undergo distillation; to drop, pass, or condense from the still ME. †**7.** To melt, dissolve (*lit.* and *fig.*) –1719.

1. Soft showers distill'd, and suns grew warm in vain POPE. My speach shall distill as the deaw *Deut.* 32:2. **2.** His dewie locks distill'd Ambrosia MILT. *P. L.* V. 56. **3.** Distilling healing virtue into bitter waters 1841. **4.** The Water..Looke thou dystyll B. GOOGE. An herb destill'd, and drunk G. HERBERT. **5.** *fig.* Siren tears, Distill'd from limbecks foul as hell within SHAKS. **7.** Swords by the lightning's subtle force distill'd ADDISON. Hence **Disti·llable** *a.* capable of being distilled (*lit.* and *fig.*). So **Di·stillate** *sb.* the product of distillation. **Disti·lment,** the process, or produce, of distillation.

Distillation (distilēi·ʃən). ME. [– L. *destillatio* a dripping down, catarrh, f. *destillat-*, pa. ppl. stem of *destillare*; see prec., -ION.] **1.** The action of falling or flowing down drop by drop. †**2.** *Path.* A defluxion of rheum –1755. **3.** The action of converting any substance into vapour by means of heat, and of again condensing this by means of an alembic, retort and receiver, or a still and refrigeratory; and, generally, the operation of separating by means of fire, and in closed vessels, the volatile from the fixed parts of any substance ME. Also *transf.* and *fig.* **4.** *concr.* The product of distilling 1598. Also *fig.*

3. *Dry* or *destructive d.*, the decomposition of a substance by strong heat in a retort, and the collection of the volatile matters evolved, as in the destructive d. of coal in gas-making. *Fractional d.*, the separation of two or more volatile liquids having different boiling-points, so that they pass over at different temperatures and can be collected separately.

†**Di·stillator.** 1576. [f. as prec. + -OR 2. Cf. Fr. *distillateur* (XVI).] A distiller –1659.

Distillatory (disti·lătŏri). 1460. [– med.L. *distillatorius*, f. as prec.; see -ORY[2], and cf. Fr. *distillatoire* (XVI). In sense 2 – med.L. *distillatorium* (XIV) alembic; see -ORY[1].] **a.** *adj.* Pertaining to, or employed in, distillation 1576. †**b.** *sb.* An apparatus for distillation; a still, etc. –1736.

Distiller (disti·ləɹ). 1577. [f. DISTIL *v.* + -ER[1].] **1.** One who or that which distils; *spec.* one who extracts alcoholic spirit by distillation. Also *fig.* **2.** An apparatus for distilling salt water at sea; a *Distilling condenser* 1885.

Distillery (disti·ləri). 1677. [f. prec.; see -ERY.] †**1.** = DISTILLATION 3. –1807. **2.** The establishment or works in which the distilling of spirits is carried on 1759.

Distinct (disti·ŋkt), *ppl. a.* ME. [– L. *distinctus*, pa. pple. of *distinguere* DISTINGUISH. Cf. (O)Fr. *distinct* (XIV).]

A. as *pa. pple.* **1.** Distinguished, differentiated –1667. †**2.** Divided –1526.

B. *adj.* **1.** = DIFFERENT *a.* 2. ME. **b.** Not confounded with each other, or with something else 1674. **2.** Possessing differentiating characteristics; different in quality or kind; not alike. Const. *from.* 1523. **3.** Clearly perceptible or discernible by the senses or the mind; plain, definite ME. **4.** Marked; decorated, adorned. (A Latinism, chiefly *poetic.*) 1596.

1. A large Feather..contains neer a million of d. parts 1665. The worker from the work d. was known POPE. **2.** Holiness..is quite d. from vindictiveness 1836. **3.** D. the shaggy mountains lie, D. the rocks SCOTT. The d. expression of thoughts TYNDALL. A d. loss to the stage 1887. **4.** The place..was dight With divers flowres d. with rare delight SPENSER.

†**Disti·nct,** *v.* ME. [– OFr. *di-, destincter*, f. *distinct* (see prec.).] = DISTINGUISH; in *pa. pple.* sometimes = DISTINCT *a.* –1583.

Distinction (disti·ŋkʃən). ME. [– (O)Fr. *distinction* – L. *distinctio*, f. *distinct-*, pa. ppl. stem of *distinguere.* See DISTINGUISH, -ION.] †**1.** Division, partition; separation –1729; punctuation; a point or stop –1637. †**2.** One of the parts of a whole; a division, section; a class, category –1848; class (in relation to status); rank, grade –1763. **3.** The action of distinguishing; the perceiving, noting, or making a difference between things; discrimination. Also with *a* and *pl.* ME. **4.** The condition of being different; difference; a difference ME. **5.** The faculty of distinguishing. ? *Obs.* 1606. †**6.** The condition of being distinct; distinctness –1712. **7.** Something that distinguishes; a distinguishing mark, quality, or characteristic ME. **8.** The treating with special consideration or honour; also with *a* and *pl.* 1715. **9.** Excellence or eminence that distinguishes from others; elevation of character, rank, or quality 1699.

1. The d. of chapters and verses now in use BOYLE. **3.** They rend and tear the scriptures with their distinctions TINDALE. Without d. of rank or creed 1891. **4.** Denying a d. of persons in the Godhead 1731. **7.** The capital is the great d. of this order RICKMAN. **8.** The distinctions..paid us by our betters GOLDSM. **9.** Various persons of d. had come there in his train SCOTT. The book.. has..d. 1891. Hence **Disti·nctional** *a.* of the nature of d. (*rare*).

Distinctive (disti·ŋktiv). 1583. [f. as prec. + -IVE.]

A. *adj.* **1.** Having the quality of distinguishing; characteristic, distinguishing. **2.** Having the power of discriminating; discriminative; discerning (*rare*) 1646. **3.**

Having a distinct character or position (*rare*) 1867. **4.** *Heb. Gram.* Applied to accents used, instead of stops, to separate clauses 1874.
1. Papist and Protestant now became d. names D'ISRAELI.
B. *sb.* **1.** A characteristic 1816. **2.** *Heb. Gram.* A distinctive accent; see A. 4. 1874. Hence **Disti·nctive-ly** *adv.*, **-ness.**

Distinctly (disti·ŋktli), *adv.* ME. [f. DISTINCT *a.* + -LY².] †**1.** In a distinct or separate manner; separately –1737. **2.** Clearly, plainly; without confusion or obscurity ME.; in mod. use (chiefly with adjs. or adjectival phrases): Unmistakably, decidedly, indubitably 1858.
2. I remember a masse of things, but nothing d. SHAKS. An object which was d. not political 1858.

Distinctness (disti·ŋktnės). 1654. [f. as prec. + NESS.] **1.** The condition or quality of being distinct; separateness; individuality 1668. **2.** The condition or quality of being clear: **a.** as a quality of the object 1668; **b.** as a quality of perception or thought 1654.
1. The soul's..incorporeity or d. from the body CUDWORTH. **2.** The absence of all scientific d. of thought WHEWELL.

†**Disti·nctor.** 1577. [f. DISTINCT *v.* + -OR 2.] One who draws distinctions.

†**Disti·ngue,** *v.* ME. [– (O)Fr. *distinguer* or L. *distinguere*; see DISTINGUISH.] = DISTINGUISH.

‖**Distingué** (dīstẹ̄·nge), *a.* 1813. [Fr., pa. pple. of *distinguer*; see next.] Distinguished; having an air of distinction.

Distinguish (disti·ŋgwiʃ), *v.* 1561. [irreg. f. Fr. *distinguer* or L. *distinguere* + -ISH². Cf. EXTINGUISH.]
I. *trans.* **1.** †To divide or separate –1729; to class, classify 1581. **2.** To mark as different or distinct; to separate by distinctive marks; to differentiate 1576. **b.** To mark; to characterize 1600. **3.** To recognize as distinct or different; to separate mentally; to perceive the difference between; to draw a distinction between 1561. †**b.** To make a distinction in or with respect to –1748. **4.** To perceive distinctly or clearly; to 'make out'; to recognize 1593. **5.** To single out; to honour with special attention (*arch.*) 1607. **6.** To make conspicuous, or eminent in some respect. Now usu. *refl.* or *pass.* 1600.
1. The inhabitants were..distinguished into artisans and soldiers GOLDSM. **2.** By the first [Ciuilitie] we are distinguished from bruit-beasts led by sensualitie A. V. *Transl. Pref.* **3.** I can d. gold, for example, from iron BP. BERKELEY. **4.** No man could d. what he said SHAKS. *Lucr.* 1785. **6.** He had distinguished himself on every frontier of the empire GIBBON.
II. *intr.* **1.** To make or draw a distinction; to perceive the difference between things; to discriminate. Const. *absol.*, or (usually) with *between.* 1604. †**2.** *intr.* (for *refl.*) To become distinguished or differentiated (*rare*) 1649.
1. Since I could d. betwixt a Benefit, and an Iniurie *Oth.* I. iii. 314. Phr. *To d. upon* = I. 3 b. Hence **Disti·nguisher.**

Distinguishable (disti·ŋgwiʃăb'l), *a.* 1597. [f. prec. + -ABLE.] **1.** Capable of being distinguished, separated, or discriminated. **2.** Capable of being divided or classified; divisible 1658. **3.** Discernible, perceptible 1611. †**4.** Worthy of distinction; noteworthy –1824. †**5.** Distinctive (*rare*) 1665.
1. Whatever objects are different are d. HUME. **2.** A simple idea is not d. into different ideas LOCKE. Hence **Disti·nguishably** *adv.*

Distinguished (disti·ŋgwiʃt), *ppl. a.* 1609. [f. DISTINGUISH *v.* + -ED¹.] †**1.** Individually distinct –1813. †**2.** Clearly perceived; clear; pronounced –1782. †**3.** Differentiated from others; special, distinctive –1813. **4.** Possessing distinction; remarkable, eminent; celebrated; of high standing. (Now almost always of persons.) 1714. **b.** = DISTINGUÉ 1748.
4. Four or five d. guests, including the Conservative Premier MRS. H. WARD. **b.** Mr. Cleveland was tall and d. DISRAELI. Hence **Disti·nguishedly** *adv.* in a d. manner; with distinction.

Disti·nguishing, *ppl. a.* 1670. [f. as prec. + -ING².] **1.** Constituting a difference; distinctive, characteristic; sometimes, That renders distinguished 1686. **2.** Discriminating 1697. †**3.** That confers special favour –1719.
1. Very probably I shall be ordered to hoist a D. Pendant NELSON. It is Mr. N's d. merit that [etc.] 1893. Hence **Disti·nguishingly** *adv.*

Disti·nguishment. ? *Obs.* 1586. [f. DISTINGUISH *v.* + -MENT.] **1.** Distinction; also *concr.* something serving to distinguish. †**2.** Clear discernment 1642.

†**Disti·tle,** *v.* [DIS- 7 a.] To deprive of title. B. JONS.

‖**Di·stoma, Di·stomum.** 1851. [mod. L., f. Gr. δίστομος, -ον, double-mouthed. *Distoma* has pl. *distomata*; *distomum*, pl. *distoma.*] *Zool.* A genus of digenetic *Trematoda*, parasitic worms or flukes, having two suckers (whence the name). So **Disto·matous** *a.* belonging to the genus *D.* var. **Di·stome.**

†**Disto·rt,** *ppl. a.* 1588. [– L. *distortus*, pa. pple. of *distorquere*; see next.] Distorted; wry, awry –1642.

Distort (distǭ·ɹt), *v.* 1586. [– *distort-*, pa. ppl. stem of L. *distorquere*, f. *dis-* DIS- 1 + *torquere* twist.] †**1.** *trans.* To twist or wrench to one side, or out of the straight position –1720. **2.** To put out of shape or position by twisting or drawing awry; to change to an unnatural shape 1634. **3.** *fig.* To give a twist to (the mind, thought, views); to pervert (statements, facts) 1586.
1. Headlong he falls, and..Distorts his neck GAY. **2.** To d. the limbs JOHNSON. A mirror which distorts the features 1896. **3.** Words..distorted from their common use GLANVILL. Hence **Disto·rted-ly** *adv.*, **-ness. Disto·rter. Disto·rtive** *a.* having the quality of distorting.

Distortion (distǭ·ɹʃən). 1581. [– L. *distortio*, f. as prec.; see -ION.] **1.** The action of distorting, or condition of being distorted, or twisted awry or out of shape; *spec.* a condition of the body or a limb, in which it is twisted out of the natural shape. **b.** *Math.* and *Optics.* Any change of shape not involving breach of continuity 1879. **c.** *concr.* A distorted form or image 1820. **2.** A twisting or writhing movement; a contortion 1718. **3.** The twisting or perversion of words, facts, history, etc. 1650.
1. The d. or writhing of the mouth MULCASTER. Hence **Disto·rtionist,** a caricaturist; an acrobat who distorts his body.

Distra·ct, *ppl. a. arch.* ME. [– L. *distractus*, pa. pple. of *distrahere*, f. *dis-* DIS- 1 + *trahere* draw, drag.] **1.** = DISTRACTED †1, 3, 4. †**2.** Drawn away; having the attention diverted –1553.

Distract (distræ·kt), *v.* ME. [– *distract-*, pa. ppl. stem of L. *distrahere*, pull asunder; see prec.] **1.** *trans.* To draw asunder or apart; to separate, divide (*lit.* and *fig.*) 1585. **2.** To turn aside, or in another direction; to divert. (Now only in *to d. the attention, the mind*, or the like.) ME. **3.** To draw in different directions; to perplex or confuse; to cause dissension or disorder in 1597. **4.** To throw into a state of mind in which one knows not how to act 1583. †**5.** To derange the intellect of; to drive mad –1791.
1. A kingdom..divided and distracted into factions ABP. SANDYS. **2.** [This] distracts the mind from the sense of danger CARPENTER. **3.** How is his tongue distracted between the Spirit of God and the spirit of gold FULLER. **4.** I am at present distracted with doubts DICKENS. **5.** This is a poore mad soule. pouerty hath distracted her 2 *Hen. IV*, II. i. 116. Hence †**Distra·ct** *sb.* a distraction. QUARLES. †**Distra·ctful** *a.* fraught with distraction. **Distra·ctingly** *adv.* **Distra·ctive** *a.* of distracting quality or tendency, **-ly** *adv.*

Distracted (distræ·ktėd), *ppl. a.* 1590. [f. DISTRACT *v.* + -ED¹.] †**1.** Drawn apart; divided –1642. **2.** Driven hither and thither; agitated 1632. **3.** Mentally drawn to different objects; perplexed or confused 1633. **4.** Much confused or troubled in mind 1602. **5.** Deranged in mind; crazy, mad. Now *rare* in lit. sense. 1590.
2. A d. Sea 1725. **3.** The d. affairs of that kingdom 1799. **5.** It [Bethlem] was an Hospital for d. people HOWELL. Hence **Distra·cted-ly** *adv.*, **-ness.**

†**Distra·ctile,** *a.* 1709. [– L. *distract-* (see DISTRACT *v.*) + -ILE.] Capable of being drawn asunder or stretched, extensible. (Cf. *contractile.*) –1835.

Distraction (distræ·kʃən). 1450. [– (O)Fr. *distraction* or L. *distractio*, f. as prec.; see -ION.] †**1.** A drawing or being drawn asunder; forcible division or severance –1838. **2.** Diversion of the mind or attention (usually in adverse sense) 1450; an instance of this; something that distracts the attention 1614. **3.** The fact or condition of being drawn or pulled in different directions 1598; disorder or confusion caused by internal dissension 1642. **4.** Violent perturbation of mind 1606. †**5.** Mental derangement; craziness, insanity –1794.
2. That you may attend vpon the Lord without d. 1 *Cor.* 7:35. **3.** To settle the Peace of the Kingdom, and compose the present Distractions 1642. **4.** The Princess loves you to d. 1802. **5.** In the d. of this madding fever SHAKS. Hence †**Distra·ctious** *a.* fraught with distractions.

Distrain (distrēⁱ·n), *v.* ME. [– OFr. *destreign-*, pres. stem of *destreindre* :– L. *distringere* draw asunder, f. *di-* DIS- 1 + *stringere* draw tight.]
I. General senses: all *Obs.* †**1.** To compress, grasp tightly –1600. †**2.** *fig.* To hold in its grasp, as disease, etc. –1618. †**3.** To constrain or compel (a person *to do* something). (Hence the legal sense II. 1.) –1400. †**4.** To strain out, express –1634. †**5.** To tear off; to rend asunder –1590.
3. Who destreyns þe to swere ofte ME. **5.** That same net..neither guile nor force might it distraine SPENSER *F. Q.* II. xii. 82.
II. *Law.* **1.** *trans.* †To constrain or force (a person) by the seizure and detention of a chattel or thing, to perform some obligation; to punish by such seizure for non-performance of an obligation ME. In later usage: To levy a distress upon (a person) in order by sale of the chattels to obtain satisfaction for a debt, *esp.* for arrears of rent 1768. **2.** *absol.* or *intr.* To levy a distress. Const. *for*; also *upon, on* a person or thing. ME. **3.** *trans.* To seize (chattels, etc.) by way of distress; to levy a distress upon (*arch.*) 1531.
1. To make sommons, and distreyne for lacke of appearaunce all and every Tenant of the sayd Abbot GRAFTON. **2.** To distreyne for the same rentes in the seid Maners 1512.
Hence †**Distrai·n** *sb.* distraint; restraint. **Distrai·nable** *a.* liable to distraint; capable of being distrained for. **Distrai:nee·**, one who is distrained. **Distrai·ner, -or,** one who levies a distress. **Distrai·nment,** the action of distraining; distraint.

Distraint (distrēⁱ·nt). 1730. [f. prec. vb. after *constrain, constraint*(see CONSTRAINT *sb.*).] The action of distraining (in the legal sense); DISTRESS.
Payment of taxes..was enforced by d. J. R. GREEN.

Distrai·t, *a.* ME. [– OFr. *destrait*, pa. pple. of *destraire* (mod. *dis-*) DISTRACT *v.*] †**1.** Distracted in mind –1450. **2.** Absent-minded. [from mod. Fr., with Fr. fem. *distraite.*]

Distraught (distrǭ·t), *ppl. a. arch.* ME. [alt. of DISTRACT *ppl. a.* by assim. to †*straught*, pa. pple. of STRETCH.] **1.** = DISTRACTED 4. **2.** = DISTRACTED 5. †**3.** *lit.* Pulled asunder, drawn in different directions –1642.
1. I lay awake D. with warring thoughts L. MORRIS. **2.** D., and mad with terror *Rom. & Jul.* IV. iii. 49. **3.** His greedy throte..in two d. SPENSER *F. Q.* IV. vii. 31.

†**Distrau·ghted,** *ppl. a.* 1572. [alt. f. DISTRACTED *ppl. a.*; see prec.] = DISTRACTED –1603.

†**Distrea·m,** *v. rare.* 1630. [DIS- 1.] To stream down or away –1750.
O'er that virtuous blush distreams a tear SHENSTONE.

Distress (distre·s), *sb.* ME. [– OFr. *destres(c)e, -esse* (mod. *détresse*) :– Gallo-Rom. **districtia* (cf. *angustia* ANGUISH *sb.*, f. *angustus*), f. pa. ppl. stem of L. *distringere* DISTRAIN.] **1.** The action or fact of straining or pressing tightly; strain, stress; *fig.* pressure employed to produce or (less usually) prevent action; compulsion; restraint. Now *dial.* **2.** Anguish or affliction affecting the body, spirit, or community ME. **b.** *Naut.* The condition of a ship when it requires immediate assistance 1659. **c.** Exhausted condition under extreme physical strain 1861. **3.** *Law.* The action of distraining; the legal seizure and detention of a chattel, orig. for the purpose of constraining the owner to do some act; later, in order out of the proceeds of its sale to satisfy some debt or claim, *esp.* for rent unpaid ME. **4.** The chattel or chattels thus seized ME.

2. Sorrow and hearts d. MILT. *P. L.* XII. 613. They fired four Guns as Signals of D. 1745. **3.** The Phocians not meaning so to lose their Rent, made a distresse by strong hand RALEGH. **4.** If..no distresse sufficient there can be founde 1512.

Comb.: **d.-gun, -rocket,** signals of a ship in d.; **-sale,** a sale of distrained goods; **-warrant,** a warrant authorizing a d.

Distress (distre·s), *v.* *Pa. t.* and *pa. pple.* **distressed;** also **distrest.** ME. [– AFr. *destresser*, OFr. *-ecier*, f. the sb. Aphetic STRESS.] **1.** *trans.* To subject to severe strain or pressure; to put to sore straits; now *esp.* to afflict or exhaust. Also *transf.* and *fig.* †**2.** To crush in battle –1796. **3.** To constrain by force or suffering ME. **4.** To cause pain or anxiety to; to afflict, vex, make miserable 1586. †**5.** To rob; to plunder –1568. **6.** To levy a distress upon ME.

1. Wee are troubled on euery side, yet not distressed 2 *Cor.* 4:8. **3.** Men who can neither be distressed nor won into a sacrifice of duty 1788. Hence **Distre·ssed-ly** *adv.*, **-ness. Distre·ssingly** *adv.*

Distre·ssful, *a.* 1591. [f. DISTRESS *sb.* + -FUL.] **1.** Fraught with, causing, or involving distress; †gained by severe toil SHAKS. **2.** Of persons, their actions, etc.: Full of distress; sorely distressed 1601.

1. Distressefull Warre 1 *Hen. VI*, V. iv. 126. D. uncertainty 1860. **2.** The most d. districts 1883. Hence **Distre·ssful-ly** *adv.*, **-ness.**

Distributable (distri·biutăb'l), *a.* 1654. [f. DISTRIBUTE *v.* + -ABLE. Cf. med.L. (Logic) *distributibilis.*] Capable of being distributed.

Distributary (distri·biutări). 1541. [f. DISTRIBUTE *v.* + -ARY¹.]

A. *adj.* †**1.** Distinct, several. **2.** Distributive 1846.

B. *sb.* Something whose function is to distribute; *e.g.* branch canals 1886.

†**Distri·bute,** *pa. pple.* ME. [– L. *distributus*, pa. pple. of *distribuere*; see next.] Distributed –1562.

Distribute (distri·biut), *v.* 1460. [– *distribut-*, pa. ppl. stem of L. *distribuere*, f. *dis-* DIS- 1 + *tribuere* grant, assign.] **1.** *trans.* To deal out or bestow in portions or shares among many; to allot or apportion as his share to each. †To dispense, administer (justice, etc.) –1746. **2.** To spread or disperse abroad through a space or over a surface; more loosely, to spread, scatter. (In *pass.* often with no idea of motion; cf. *diffused*, etc.) 1511. **3.** To divide and arrange 1553. **4.** To divide and place in classes or other divisions; to classify 1664; †in *Arith.* = DIVIDE –1729. **5.** To separate and allocate to distinct places. *spec.* in *Printing.* To remove (type that has been set up) from the forme, and return each letter into its proper box in the case. Also *absol.* 1615. **6.** *Logic.* To employ (a term) in its full extension 1827. **7.** *Gram.* To make distributive 1876.

1. To distribut in almes to an hundred poore men an hundred pence 1574. *absol.* Distributing to the necessity of Saints *Rom.* 12:13. **2.** To d. ink over the form 1875. **6.** The middle term ..must be distributed once, at least, in the premises WHATELY. Hence **Distributee·** (*Law*), a person to whom a share falls in the distribution of an intestate estate. **Distri·buter, -or,** one who distributes.

Distribution (distribiū·ʃən). ME. [–(O)Fr. *distribution* or L. *distributio*, f. as prec.; see -ION.] **1.** The action of distributing, dealing out, or bestowing in portions among a number; apportionment, allotment. **b.** *Pol. Econ.* (*a*) The dispersal among consumers of commodities produced: opp. to *production.* (*b*) The distribution of the aggregate produce of any society among its individual members. 1848. **2.** The action of spreading abroad or dispersing to or over every part of a space or area; the condition or mode of being so dispersed or located 1589. **3.** The orderly dividing of a mass into parts: division and arrangement; classification 1605. **4.** *Logic.* †**a.** = DIVISION –1725. **b.** More recently, The application of a term to each and all of the individuals included in its denotation or extension 1827. **5.** *Rhet.* A figure whereby an orderly division or enumeration is made of the principal qualities of a subject 1553. **6.** *Archit.* The arrangement of the parts of a building, *esp.* of the interior divisions 1727. **7.** *Printing.* The action or process of distributing type 1727. **8.** *Steam-engine.* 'The steps or operations by which steam is supplied to and withdrawn from the cylinder at each stroke of the piston; viz. admission, suppression or cutting off, release or exhaust, and compression of exhaust steam prior to the next admission' (Webster 1864).

1. All shall be set right at the final d. of things BUTLER. The laws of Production and D. MILL. The unequal d. of the fruits of industry 1896. **2.** This Order..has such and such a geographical d. 1885. **3.** The d. of land into parishes EMERSON. Hence **Distribu·tional** *a.* **Distribu·tionist,** one who advocates a system of d. (*rare*).

Distributive (distri·biŭtiv). 1475. [–(O)Fr. *distributif, -ive* or late L. *distributivus*, f. as prec.; see -IVE.]

A. 1. Having the property of distributing; dispensing, bestowing, or dealing out in portions; given to distribution. **2.** Having a tendency to diffusion 1627. **3.** Of, belonging to, or arising from, distribution 1531. **4.** Expressing distribution; *spec.* in *Gram.* Having reference to each individual of a number or class 1520. **5.** *Logic.* Referring to each individual of a class separately: opp. to *collective* 1725. **6.** *Math.* Operating upon every part in operating upon the whole; as *d. formula, function*, etc. 1855.

3. *D. justice*, one of the two divisions of Justice, according to Aristotle (the other being COMMUTATIVE). Hence, applied to that part of substantive law, which is concerned with the determination of rights. **4.** *D. adjectives*, the words *each, either, neither, every. D. numerals*, in Latin, *singuli*, one by one, *bini*, two by two, etc.

B. *sb.* **1.** *Gram.* A distributive word; see A. 4. 1530. †**2.** That which is distributed 1635. Hence **Distri·butive-ly** *adv.*, **-ness.**

†**Distri·ct,** *a.* 1526. [– L. *districtus* strict, severe, pa. pple. of *distringere*; see next.] Strict; severe; exact –1700. †**Distri·ctly** *adv.*

District (di·strikt), *sb.* 1611. [– Fr. *district* – med.L. *districtus* (power of) exercising justice, territory involving this – *district-*, pa. ppl. stem of L. *distringere*; see DISTRAIN, STRICT.] †**1.** *Law.* The territory under the jurisdiction of a feudal lord –1670. **2.** A portion of territory marked off or defined for some special administrative or official purpose; *e.g.* a *police, postal*, or *registration d.*, etc. 1664. **3.** *spec.* **a.** A division of a parish, having its own church or chapel, etc. 1818. **b.** A subdivision of a county, having an Urban or Rural District Council 1895. **c.** In British India: A division or subdivision of a province or presidency, having at its head a 'Magistrate and Collector', or 'Deputy-Commissioner' 1776. **d.** In U.S. used in specific and local senses: *e.g.* a political division = election constituency, as an *assembly, congressional*, or *senate d.* 1800. **e.** An allotted sphere of operation; *esp.* a section of a parish allotted to a lay visitor, working under the clergyman 1863. Also †*fig.* **4.** A tract of country of vaguely defined limits; a region, locality, quarter 1712.

4. A purely agricultural d. 1896.

attrib. and *Comb.*, in sense 'of, belonging to, or allotted to a particular d.'; as *d.-chapel*, etc.; *d.-judge*, etc. **D.-attorney** (U. S.), the local prosecuting officer of a d.; **-council,** the local council of an Urban or Rural D. as constituted by the Parish Councils Act of 1894; hence **-councillor; -court** (U.S.), a court of limited jurisdiction, having cognizance of certain causes within a d., presided over by a d.-judge; **d. visitor,** a person who does parochial work in a district under a clergyman's direction.

Di·strict, *v.* 1828. [f. prec. sb.] To divide into districts.

†**Distri·ction.** 1450. [– late L. *districtio* severity, rigour, f. *district-*, pa. ppl. stem of L. *distringere*; see DISTRICT *sb.*, -ION. Cf. OFr. *distriction.*] Strictness, severity, rigour –1660.

‖**Distringas** (distri·ŋgæs). 1467. [L., = 'thou shalt distrain', being the first word of the writ.] *Law.* The name of a writ bidding the sheriff distrain in certain cases.

‖**Distrix** (di·striks). 1811. [mod.L., f. Gr. δίς twice (DI-²) + θρίξ hair.] *Med.* A disease of the hair, in which it splits at the end.

†**Distrou·ble,** *v.* ME. [– OFr. *destro(u)bler*, f. *des-* DIS- 5 + *tro(u)bler* TROUBLE *v.*] To disturb (greatly) –1609.

†**Distru·ss,** *v.* ME. [– OFr. *destro(u)sser* unpack (mod. *détrousser*), f. *des* DIS- 4 + *tro(u)sser* TRUSS *v.*] *trans.* To strip or plunder; hence, to rout. Also *fig.* –1548.

Distrust (distrɒ·st), *sb.* 1513. [f. DIS- 9 + TRUST *sb.*; cf. next.] **a.** Absence or want of trust; lack of confidence, faith, or reliance; doubt, suspicion. **b.** Loss of credit 1667. **c.** Breach of trust 1667.

1. Eche..in such hatred and d. of other MORE. Foul d. and breach Disloyal on the part of Man MILT. Hence †**Distru·stless** *a.* confident; unsuspecting.

Distrust (distrɒ·st), *v.* ME. [f. DIS- 6 + TRUST *v.*, after Fr. *défier* (cf. DEFY *v.*¹) or L. *diffidere.*] †**1.** *intr.* with *of, in, to*: To be without confidence in –1671. **2.** *trans.* To do the opposite of trusting; to withhold trust from; to put no trust in, or reliance on 1548; to entertain doubts concerning 1586. †**3.** with *infin. phr.* or *cl.*: To suspect –1707.

2. To d. mine eyes *Twel. N.* IV. iii. 13. He..distrusted his ministers GIBBON. Not distrusting mine health 2 *Macc.* 9:22. I shall not d. to be acquitted of presumption MILT. Hence **Distru·ster.**

Distrustful (distrɒ·stfŭl), *a.* 1591. [f. DISTRUST *sb.* + -FUL.] **1.** Full of distrust in oneself or others; wanting in confidence, diffident; doubtful, suspicious, incredulous. **2.** Causing or giving rise to distrust 1618.

1. Faith fortifieth the heart against d. fears TRAPP. Hence **Distru·stful-ly** *adv.*, **-ness.**

Distu·ne, *v.* 1484. [DIS- 6 or 7.] To put out of tune.

Disturb (distɔ̄·ɹb), *v.* [ME. *desto(u)rbe* – OFr. *desto(u)rber* – L. *disturbare*, f. *dis-* DIS- 5 + *turbare* disorder, disturb, f. *turba* tumult, crowd.] **1.** *trans.* To agitate and destroy (quiet, etc.); to break up the quiet, tranquillity, or rest of; to stir up, trouble, disquiet; to agitate 1599; to unsettle 1664. **2.** To agitate mentally, discompose the peace of mind or calmness of; to trouble, perplex ME. **3.** To interfere with the settled course or operation of; to interrupt, hinder, frustrate ME. **4.** *Law.* To deprive of the peaceful enjoyment or possession *of* 1541.

1. No Nonconforming Sects d. his Reign DE FOE. An image in the lake Which rains d. SHELLEY. **2.** Disturbed by a dream JOHNSON. **3.** Praise..may much d. The bias of the purpose COWPER. **4.** An action against a stranger for disturbing the plaintiff in his pew 1870. Hence †**Distu·rb** *sb.* an act of disturbing; a thing that disturbs; disturbance. **Distu·rbedly** *adv.*

Disturbance (distɔ̄·ɹbăns). ME. [– OFr. *desto(u)rbance*, f. *desto(u)rber*; see prec., -ANCE.] **1.** The interruption of tranquillity, peace, rest, or settled condition; agitation (physical, social, or political). **2.** Interruption of mental tranquillity; discomposure ME. **3.** Interference with the due course of any action or process; molestation ME. **4.** *Law.* The hindering or disquieting the owners in their regular and lawful enjoyment of an incorporeal hereditament 1598.

1. Innumerable Disturbances on Earth through Femal snares MILT. The..election passed off without any d. H. WALPOLE. Storms or atmospheric disturbances 1875. **2.** To any ones disturbaunce and vexation 1576. **3.** That he may let the ship sail on without d. ADDISON. **4.** D. of (1) franchise, (2) common, (3) ways, (4) tenure, and (5) patronage WHARTON. Hence †**Distu·rbancy,** state of d. (*rare*).

Disturbant (distɔ̄·ɹbănt). 1617. [– *disturbant-*, pres. ppl. stem of L. *disturbare*; see DISTURB, -ANT¹. Cf. AFr. *destourbant.*] **a.** *adj.* That disturbs; agitating. **b.** *sb.* A disturber 1865.

†**Disturba·tion.** 1529. [– med.L. *dis-, desturbatio* (whence OFr. *destorbeson*) interference (in cl. L., destruction), f. *disturbat-*, pa. ppl. stem of L. *disturbare*; see DISTURB, -ION.] = DISTURBANCE –1658.

Disturber (distɔ̄·ɹbəɹ). ME. [– AFr. *destourbour* (OFr. *destorbëor*), f. *destourber* DISTURB; see -ER² 3.] **1.** A person or thing that disturbs or disquiets; one who causes tumult or disorder; a troubler. **2.** *Law.*

(also *disturbor.*) One who disquiets or hinders another in the lawful enjoyment of his right 1498.

1. Only one man, a common d., behaved amiss WESLEY.

Disturbor; see DISTURBER 2.

†**Distu·rn,** *v.* ME. [– OFr. *desto(u)rner* (mod. *détourner*, whence DETURN), f. *des-*, *dé-* (DE- I. 6) + *to(u)rner* TURN *v.*] *trans.* To turn aside or away; to avert, divert, pervert –1631.

Distyle (dəi·stəil), *sb.* (*a.*) 1840. [f. DI-[2] + Gr. στῦλος column: so Fr. *distyle* sb.] *Archit.* A porch having two styles or columns. Also as *adj. D. in antis*: two circular pillars between two square piers.

Disulphate (dəisʊ·lfět). 1838. [DI-[2].] *Chem.* **1.** A salt containing two equivalents of sulphuric acid to one of base. **2.** A sulphate containing a hydrogen atom replaceable by a basic element or radical (*Cent. Dict.*). **3.** A salt of disulphuric acid, a pyrosulphate 1877.

Disulphide (dəisʊ·lfəid). 1863. [DI-[2].] *Chem.* A compound in which two atoms of sulphur are united with another element or a radical, as *carbon d.*, CS_2.

Disulpho- (dəisʊ·lfo). 1868. [See DI-[2] and SULPHO-.] *Chem.* In composition, denominating acids derived from two molecules of sulphurous acid. Hence **Disulpho·nic** *a.*

Disu·lphuret. 1854. [See DI-[2].] = DISULPHIDE.

Disulphuric (dəisʊlfiūə·rik), *a.* 1875. *Chem.* [DI-[2].] In *d. acid*, the same as pyrosulphuric or Nordhausen sulphuric acid, $H_2S_2O_7 = 2(SO_2OH) + O$. (So called because the molecule represents two molecules of sulphuric acid deprived of one of water.)

Dis,u·niform, *a.* 1687. [DIS- 10.] Without uniformity.

Disunion (disyū·niən). 1598. [DIS- 9.] **1.** Rupture of union; separation; disjunction. **2.** Absence or want of union; disunited condition; dissension 1601.

1. Foreigners would..believe..that we are on the very verge of d.; but the fact is otherwise G. WASHINGTON. 2. Ages of d. and disaster CHALMERS.

Disunionist (disyū·niənist). 1846. [f. prec. + -IST.] One who works for disunion; *spec.* in U.S., for a dissolution of the Union of the States.

Disunite (disyunəi·t), *v.* 1560. [DIS- 6.] **1.** *trans.* To undo the union of; to disjoin 1598; to set at variance, alienate 1560. **2.** *intr.* (for *refl.*) To separate oneself; to part; to fall or come asunder 1675.

1. A corner-stone, that unites things most disunited DONNE. Goe on both hand in hand, O Nations never to be dis-united MILT. 2. The several joints of the body politick do separate and d. SOUTH. Hence **Dis,uni·ter** (*rare*).

Disu·nity. 1632. [DIS- 9.] Want of unity; a state of separation; dissension.

†**Dis,u·sage.** 1475. [f. DISUSE *v.*, after *usage*; cf. Fr. †*désusage.*] = DISUSE *sb.* 1. –1712. So **Disu·sance** (*rare*).

Disuse (disyū·s), *sb.* 1552. [DIS- 9.] **1.** Discontinuance of use, practice, or exercise; †unaccustomedness –1792; desuetude 1699. †**2.** Uselessness. FELTHAM.

1. Strange they [fashions] be by reason of d. P. HOLLAND. Through long d. of solitude SWIFT.

Disuse (disyū·z), *v.* ME. [f. OFr. *desuser*, f. *des-* DIS- 6 + *user* USE *v.*] †**1.** *trans.* To disaccustom. Chiefly in *pass.* Const. *from*, *of*, *to*, or *infin.* –1791. **2.** To cease to use; to discontinue the use or practice of 1487. †**3.** To misuse, abuse –1440.

1. With Bion long disus'd to play 1791. 2. Which lawe by negligence is disused 1487. Hence †**Dis,u·ser**, lapse of use.

Disuti·lity. 1879. [DIS- 9.] Injuriousness, harmfulness.

Disutilize (disyū·tiləiz), *v.* 1856. [DIS- 6.] To deprive of utility, render useless.

Disvalue (disvæ·liu), *v.* Now *rare.* 1603. [DIS- 6.] To make or treat as of no value, depreciate, disparage. Hence †**Disvalua·tion,** †**Disva·lue** *sbs.* depreciation, disparagement.

†**Disva·ntage.** 1591. [f. DIS- 9 + VANTAGE *sb.*] = DISADVANTAGE –1619. Hence †**Disvanta·geous** *a.* disadvantageous (*rare*).

†**Disve·lop,** *v.* 1592 [– OFr. *desveloper* (mod. *développer*); see DEVELOP.] To DEVELOP, display heraldically –1755.

†**Disve·nture.** 1612. [– Sp. *desventura*, f. *des-* DIS- 4 + *ventura* VENTURE *sb.*] A misadventure –1718.

Disvi·sage, *v. rare.* 1603. [– OFr. *desvisager* (mod. *dé-*), f. *des-* DIS- 4 + *visage* VISAGE *sb.*] To deface, disfigure.

†**Disvi·sor,** *v.* 1548. [DIS- 7 a.] To uncover (a visored face) –1621.

†**Disvou·ch,** *v.* [DIS- 6.] = DISAVOUCH. *Meas. for M.* IV. iv. I.

†**Diswa·rn,** *v. rare.* 1607. [DIS- 1.] To warn off *from* –1622.

Diswa·rren, *v.* 1727. [DIS- 7 b.] To make no longer a warren.

†**Diswea·pon,** *v.* 1602. [DIS- 7 a.] To deprive of weapons. Also *fig.*

†**Diswe·re.** ME. [f. DIS- 5 + †*were* doubt, hesitation.] Doubt –1500.

†**Diswi·t,** *v.* 1599. [DIS- 7 a.] To deprive of wit –1627. Hence **Diswi·tted** *ppl. a.*

†**Diswo·nt,** *v.* 1600. [DIS- 6.] To render unaccustomed or unused –1635. Hence **Diswo·nted** *ppl. a.* unwonted, unaccustomed.

†**Diswo·rkmanship.** [DIS- 9.] Defective workmanship. HEYWOOD.

†**Diswo·rship,** *sb.* ME. [DIS- 9.] The withholding of esteem, regard, or honour; a disgrace, a dishonour –1644. So †**Diswo·rship** *v.* to do d. or dishonour to; to dishonour. †**Diswo·rshipful** *a.* dishonourable.

†**Diswo·rth,** *v. rare.* [DIS- 7 a.] To render worthless. FELTHAM.

Disyllabic, dissyllabic (dəi-, disilæ·bik), *a.* 1637. [– Fr. *dissyllabique* (XVI), f. L. *disyllabus* adj.; see DISYLLABLE. The sp. with *ss* was regular XVI–XVIII, the etymol. sp. with *s* being first favoured XIX, and now preferred by scholars.] Consisting of two syllables. var. †**Di·syllabe, dissyllabe.** Hence **Disylla·bically, diss-** *adv.*

Disyllabize, diss- (dəi-, disi·lăbəiz), *v.* 1870. [f. L. *disyllabus*; see next, -IZE.] To make disyllabic. So **Disylla·bify, diss-** *v.* Hence **Disy·llabism, diss-,** disyllabic character or state.

Disyllable, dissyllable (dəi-, disi·lăb'l), *sb.* (*a.*) 1589. [– Fr. *disyllabe* – L. *disyllabus* adj. – Gr. δισύλλαβος of two syllables, f. δι- DI-[2] + συλλαβή SYLLABLE *sb.*] A word, or metrical foot, consisting of two syllables; as *adj.* = DISYLLABIC.

Disyntheme (dəisi·nþīm). 1879. [f. DI-[2] + *syntheme* (see SYN-).] *Math.* A system of groups of elements, each group being so formed that each element occurs just twice among all the groups. Thus 1·2, 2·3, 3·4, 1·4 is a duadic d.—that is, one composed of pairs.

Disyoke (disyōᵘ·k), *v. rare.* 1847. [DIS- 6.] To unyoke; to free from the yoke.

Dit, *sb. arch.* 1590. [app. taken by Spenser from ME. *dit* = DITE *sb.*, and mispronounced.] A ditty; see DITE *sb.*

Dit (dit), *v.* Now *Sc.* or *dial.* [OE. *dyttan* close, shut :– **duttjan*, prob. rel. to *dott* small lump, clot, plug; see DOT *sb.*[1], DOTTLE.] *trans.* To stop up, shut; to fill *up*.

Dit, early f. DITE *sb.*

‖**Dita** (dī·tă). 1876. [Native name.] The bark of *Echites* (*Alstonia*) *scholaris*, of the Philippine Islands. Usu. **d.-bark.**

Dital (dəi·tăl). 1816. [f. It. *dito* finger, after *pedal*.] A thumb key, by which the pitch of a guitar- or lute-string can be raised a semitone.

†**Dita·tion.** 1612. [– med.L. *ditatio*, f. *ditat-*, pa. ppl. stem of L. *ditare* enrich.] Enrichment –1659.

Ditch (ditʃ), *sb.* [OE. *dīć*, corresp. to OFris., OS. *dīk* ditch, dike (Du. *dijk*), MHG. *tīch* (G. *teich* pond, pool), ON. *diki* ditch, DIKE; a word of the Baltic coast, of unkn. origin.] **1.** A long and narrow hollow dug in the ground; a trench, a fosse. **2.** *esp.* Such a hollow dug out to receive or conduct water ME.; hence, rhetorically, any watercourse or channel 1589. †**3.** Any hollow dug in the ground; a pit, cave, etc. –ME. **4.** = DIKE 4. Now only *dial.* 1568.

1. Rather a d. in Egypt Be gentle graue vnto me *Ant. & Cl.* V. ii. 57. 2. A Caue or D., which alwaies was full of water 1582. *Comb.* **d.-water,** the stagnant or foul water that collects in a d.

Ditch (ditʃ), *v.* ME. [f. prec.; not repr. OE. *dīćian* dig, make an embankment.] **1.** *intr.* To construct a ditch or ditches. **2.** *trans.* To surround with a ditch ME. **3.** To dig ditches or furrows in for purposes of drainage, etc. ME. **4.** To clean out (a ditch); to cast up and repair (the banks of a ditch) 1576. **5.** To throw into or as into a ditch, *esp.* to throw (a train) off the line or track 1877.

3. Set two men to d. the five roods HOWITT. 5. The engine was ditched and turned on its side (U.S.) 1881.

Ditcher (di·tʃəɹ). ME. [f. prec. + -ER[1].] **1.** One who makes and repairs ditches. **2.** A ditching-machine 1862.

†**Dite,** *sb.* (After 1500 only *Sc.*) ME. [– (O)Fr. *dit* (:– L. *dictum*) saying, maxim, etc., subst. use of pa. pple. of *dire* :– L. *dicere* say.] **1.** A written or spoken composition –1578. **2.** A song, a ditty –1567. **3.** Diction. *Sc.* –1549.

†**Dite,** *v.* ME. [– OFr. *ditier*, *diter* write, compose :– L. *dictare*, frequent. of *dicere* say. Occas. aphet. form of *endite* (see INDITE).] **1.** *trans.* To compose or put in words; to indite. (Also *absol.*) –1603. **2.** = DICTATE *v.* –1643. **3.** To summon, indict –1775. Hence †**Di·tement,** a composition; an indictment. †**Di·ter,** one who indites or indicts.

Diter, obs. f. *Dighter*; see DIGHT.

Ditetragonal (dəitĭtræ·gŏnăl), *a.* 1879. [DI-[2] 1.] *Cryst.* Having eight angles, of which the first, third, fifth, and seventh are equal, and also the second, fourth, sixth, and eighth, but those of the one set are not equal to those of the other; as a *d. pyramid* or *prism*.

†**Di-tetrahe·dral,** *a.* 1805. [DI-[2] 1.] *Cryst.* Having the form of a tetrahedral prism with dihedral summits.

Dithecous (dəiþī·kəs), *a.* 1880. [f. Gr. δι-, DI-[2] + θήκη case + -OUS.] *Bot.* Consisting of two cells; bilocular. var. **Dithe·cal.**

Ditheism (dəi·þi,iz'm). 1678. [DI-[2].] Belief in two supreme gods; religious dualism; *esp.* the belief in two independent antagonistic principles of good and evil, as in Zoroastrianism and Manicheism. So **Di·theist,** one who holds the doctrine of d. **Di:thei·stic, -al** *a.*

Dither (di·ðəɹ), *v.* 1649. [Phonetic var. of DIDDER, q.v.] *intr.* To tremble, quake, quiver (*dial.*). **b.** To vacillate (*colloq.*). Also as *sb.* Hence **Dithering-grass,** *Briza media.*

Dithionic (dəiþəiǫ·nik, diþiǫ·nik), *a.* 1854. [f. DI-[2] + θεῖον sulphur + -IC. (The formative *-thionic* is used for a group of compounds containing H_2O_6, in combination with two or more atoms of sulphur.)] In *d. acid*, $H_2S_2O_6$, a dibasic acid not isolated in the pure state, but forming crystallizable salts, called **Dithi·onates.**

Dithyramb (di·þiræmb). 1603. [– L. *dithyrambus* (also used) – Gr. διθύραμβος.] *Gr. Antiq.* A Greek choric hymn, originally in honour of Dionysus or Bacchus, vehement and wild in character; a Bacchanalian song; hence, *transf.* a poem, speech, or writing having this character.

1. The Dithyrambe with clamours dissonant P. HOLLAND. *transf.* What dithyrambs he went into about eating and drinking GEO. ELIOT.

Dithyrambic (diþiræ·mbik). 1603. [– L. *dithyrambicus* – Gr. διθυραμβικός; see prec., -IC.]

A. *adj.* Pertaining to, or like, a dithyramb; composing dithyrambs; *transf.* wild, vehement.

Priests..howling chaunt these Dithyrambik charms 1611.

B. *sb.* A dithyrambic verse; a dithyramb; something like a dithyramb in style; a writer of a dithyramb 1646.

†**Dition** (di·ʃən). 1538. [– OFr. *dicion*, *dition* – L. *dicio*, (less correctly) *ditio*. Cf. CONDITION *sb.*] Rule, dominion –1654; a dominion –1685. Hence †**Di·tionary** *a.* and *sb.* (one) under dominion.

Ditokous (di·tokəs), *a.* [f. Gr. διτόκος (f. δι- DI-² + τόκος offspring) + -OUS.] **a.** Having twins. **b.** Laying only two eggs at a clutch. **c.** Producing young of two kinds. (In recent Dicts.)

Ditolyl (dəitǭᵘ·lil). 1877. [DI-².] *Chem.* An aromatic hydrocarbon, a crystalline substance of the composition $2(C_6H_4.CH_3)$; see TOLYL.

Ditone (dəi·tōᵘn). 1609. [– late L. *ditonum* – Gr. δίτονον the ancient major third, n. of δίτονος, f. δι- DI-² + τόνος TONE *sb.*] *Mus.* An interval containing two whole tones; *esp.* the Pythagorean major third.

Ditrematous (dəitrī·mătəs), *a.* [f. mod.L. *Ditremata* n. pl. (f. Gr. δι- DI-² + τρῆμα, τρηματ- opening) + -OUS.] *Zool.* Of or pertaining to the *Ditremata*, a division of gastropod molluscs, having the external male and female orifices far apart; also, having the anal and genital orifices distinct, as in *Ditrema*, a genus of fishes.

Ditremid (dəitrī·mid). [– mod.L. *Ditremidæ* sb. pl. f. *Ditrema*; see prec., -ID³.] *Zool.* A fish of the family *Ditremidæ*, of which *Ditrema* is the typical genus.

Di-tri-, short for *di- or tri-*, *di- and tri-*, in composition, as *di-trichotomous* = dichotomous or trichotomous.

Ditriglyph (dəitrəi·glif). 1727. [– Fr. *ditriglyphe*, f. *di-* DI-² + *triglyphe* TRIGLYPH.] *Arch.* **1.** 'The space between two triglyphs.' **2.** A space between columns of the Doric order, admitting the use of two triglyphs in the frieze, between those over the columns 1791. So **Ditrigly·phic** *a.* having two triglyphs in the space over the intercolumniation.

Ditrigonal (dəitri·gŏnăl), *a.* 1878. [DI-².] *Cryst.* Having (dihedral) angles, of which the first, third, and fifth are equal, and also the second, fourth, and sixth, but those of the one set are not equal to those of the other.

Ditrochee (dəitrōᵘ·kī). 1855. [– late L. *ditrochæus* – Gr. διτρόχαιος, f. δι- DI-² + τροχαῖος TROCHEE. Oftener used in the L. form.] *Pros.* A foot consisting of two trochees; a double trochee. So **Ditroche·an** *a.* containing two trochees.

Ditroite (di·troˌəit). 1868. [f. *Ditro* in Transylvania + -ITE¹ 2 b.] *Min.* A rock composed of orthoclase, elæolite, and sodalite.

Ditt, obs. f. DIT *sb.* and *v.*

Dittander (ditæ·ndəɹ). ?*Obs.* 1578. [Of the same origin as DITTANY; the terminal part is unexpl.] **1.** A name for Pepperwort, *Lepidium latifolium* 1578. †**2.** Dittany of Crete –1658.

Dittany (di·tăni). [Late ME. *ditane*, *diteyne* – OFr. *ditan*, *ditain* :– med.L. *dictamus*, for L. *dictamnus*, *-um* – Gr. δίκταμνον, reputed to be f. Δίκτη the mountain in Crete, a well-known habitat of the plant. The trisyllabic form (*detany*) appears XV; it depends on med.L. *ditaneum*, late L. *dictamnium*.] **1.** A labiate plant, *Origanum dictamnus*, called also *D. creticus* or Dittany of Crete. **b.** *fig.* (From the supposed power of Cretan dittany to expel weapons.) 1623. †**2.** *Marrubium pseudodictamnus*, also called Bastard Dittany –1671. **3.** The English name for the genus *Dictamnus* (N.O. *Rutaceæ*); esp. *D. fraxinella* (Bastard Dittany), and *D. albus* (White Dittany) 1605. †**4.** Erron. for DITTANDER 1. –1578. **5.** In U.S. applied to *Cunila mariana* (N.O. *Labiatæ*) 1676.

1. *fig.* The shaft sticks still in thee;..None but the Sovereign D. of thy Saviour's Righteousness can drive it out BP. HALL.

Dittay (di·te, di·ti). 1470. [– OFr. *dité*, *ditté*, the same word as DITTY.] *Sc. Law.* The ground of indictment against a person for a criminal offence; also, the indictment.

Ditto (di·to). 1625. [– It. *ditto*, Tuscan var. of *detto* said :– L. *dictus*, pa. pple. of *dicere* say.] †**1.** Said month –1677. **2.** Hence, The aforesaid, the same; used, in accounts and lists (often in the form *d°*, *do.*, or as two dots or commas, or a dash), to avoid repetition; hence in commercial, office, and colloquial language 1678. **3.** Hence as *sb.* **a.** A duplicate; the like 1776. **b.** Cloth of the same material; chiefly pl., in *suit of dittos*: a suit of clothes of the same material throughout 1755. Hence **Di·tto** *v.* to match.

Dittography (ditǫ·grăfi). 1874. [f. Gr. διττός double + -GRAPHY.] In *Palæography*, etc.: Double writing; unintentional repetition of a letter, or series of letters, by a copyist. So **Di·ttograph**, a letter or series of letters thus repeated; **Dittogra·phic** *a.* of the nature of a dittograph.

Dittology (ditǫ·lŏdʒi). 1678. [– Gr. διττολογία repetition of words, f. as prec.; see -LOGY.] A twofold reading or interpretation.

†**Di·tton.** 1572. [– Fr. *dicton* (in XVI pron. *diton*) :– L. *dictum* DICTUM.] A phrase, an expression; *esp.* a motto or proverb –1653.

Ditty (di·ti), *sb.* [ME. *dite*, *ditee* – OFr. *dité* composition, treaty :– L. *dictatum*, subst. use of n. pa. pple. of *dictare* express in language, compose. Cf. DICTATE *sb.*, DITE *sb.*, -Y⁵.] †**1.** = DITE *sb.* 1. (ME. only.) **2.** A song, lay; now, a short simple song ME.; †any composition in verse –1614. †**3.** The words of a song; also, the leading theme or phrase; hence, Subject, theme, burden –1672.

2. The lark..doth welcome daylight with her d. SHAKS. **3.** There vvas no great matter in the dittie, yet yᵉ note was very vntunable *A.Y.L.* V. iii. 36. Hence †**Di·tty** *v. intr.* to sing a d.; *trans.* to sing as a ditty; also, to fit words to (music); **Di·ttied** *ppl. a.*

Di·tty-bag. 1860. [Origin unkn.] A bag used by sailors to contain their smaller necessaries. So **Di·tty-box**, a box used similarly by fishermen.

Diureide (dəiˌ¹ūᵊ·rīˌəid). 1877. [DI-².] *Chem.* A compound of two urea-residues with an acid radical.

‖**Diuresis** (dəiˌ¹urī·sis). 1681. [mod.L., f. Gr. διά through (DI-³) + οὔρησις urination; see next.] *Med.* Excretion of urine, esp. when excessive.

Diuretic (dəiˌ¹ure·tik). ME. [– (O)Fr. *diurétique* or late L. *diureticus* – Gr. διουρητικός, f. διουρεῖν urinate, f. διά (DI-³) + οὖρον urine; see -IC.]

A. *adj.* Having the quality of exciting (excessive) discharge of urine; †of persons, urinating excessively –1812.

B. *sb.* A substance having diuretic qualities ME. var. †**Diure·tical** *a.* (*sb.*)

†**Diu·rn(e**, *a.* ME. [– L. *diurnus*; see next.] = DIURNAL *a.* –1603.

Diurnal (dəiˌǝ̄·ɹnăl). ME. [– late L. *diurnalis*, f. L. *diurnus* daily, f. *dies* day; see -AL¹. Cf. JOURNAL.]

A. *adj.* **1.** Performed in one day; daily. **2.** Of or belonging to each day; daily (*arch.*) 1594. **3.** Of or belonging to the day; day-: opp. to *nocturnal*. In *Zool.*, *spec.* of animals active by day only 1623. **4.** Lasting for a day only; ephemeral (*rare*) 1866.

1. The D. Motion of the Sun DRYDEN. **2.** D. prints 1815. The Laird's d. visits SCOTT. **3.** D. birds J. G. WOOD. The d. position [of leaves or petals] 1875.

B. *sb.* **1.** *Eccl.* A service-book containing the day-hours, except matins 1550. **2.** A day-book, diary; *esp.* a journal (*arch.*) 1600. **3.** A newspaper published daily, or (*loosely*) at short periodical intervals 1640. **4.** A diurnal bird, butterfly, or moth. (In recent Dicts.) Hence **Diu·rnalist**, a writer of a d. **Diu·rnally** *adv.*

Diurna·tion. 1836. [f. L. *diurnus* daily + -ATION, after *hibernation*.] The habit of sleeping or remaining quiescent during the day.

Diuturnal (dəiˌ¹utǝ̄·ɹnăl), *a.* Now *rare.* 1599. [– med.L. *diuturnalis*, f. L. *diuturnus*, f. *diu* long, for a long time; or f. contemp. †*diuturn* + -AL¹.] Of long duration, lasting. var. †**Diutu·rn.**

Diutu·rnity. Now *rare.* ME. [– L. *diuturnitas*, f. *diuturnus* of long duration; see prec., -ITY.] Long duration; lastingness.

‖**Div** (dīv). 1777. [Pers. :– Zend *daēva* = Skr. *deva* god; see DEVA.] An evil spirit or demon of Persian mythology.

‖**Diva** (dī·va). 1883. [It. :– L. *diva* goddess.] A distinguished female singer, a prima donna.

Divagate (dəi·văgeⁱt), *v.* 1599. [– *divagat-*, pa. ppl. stem of L. *divagari*, f. *di-* DI-¹, DIS- 1 + *vagari* wander.] *intr.* To wander about; to stray from one place or subject to another.

So does a child's balloon d. upon the currents of the air STEVENSON. Hence **Divaga·tion.**

Divalent (dəi·vălĕnt, di·v-) *a.* 1869. [f. DI-² twice + *valent-*, pres. ppl. stem of L. *valēre* be worth; see -ENT and cf. VALENCY.) *Chem.* Having two combining equivalents; also *bivalent*. Formerly *dyad*.

Divan (divæ·n). 1586. [– Fr. *divan* or It. *divano* – Turk. *dīvān* – Arab. *dīwān* – Pers. *dīvān* collection of poems, register, etc., court, council chamber, (cushioned) bench. Cf. DEWAN, DOUANE.] **1.** An Oriental council of state; *spec.* in Turkey, the privy council of the Porte 1586; a council in general 1619. **2.** The hall where the Turkish divan is held; a court of justice; a council-chamber 1597. **3.** A continued step, or raised part of the floor, against the wall of a room, often cushioned, so as to form a sofa or couch 1702. **4.** A room entirely open at one side 1678. **5.** A smoking-room furnished with lounges; hence, a cigar-shop 1848. ‖**6.** A name for a collection of poems; *spec.* a series of poems by one author, the rimes of which usually run through the whole alphabet 1823.

1. In this councell called diuan..audience is open to euery one 1586. **6.** The most important diwans are those of..Hafiz, Saadi, and Jami 1877.

†**Divapora·tion.** 1612. [f. EVAPORATION by substitution of prefix.] The driving out of vapours by heat; evaporation.

Divaricate (di-, dəivæ·rikeⁱt), *v.* 1623. [– *divaricat-*, pa. ppl. stem of L. *divaricare*, f. *dis-* DI-¹ + *varicare* stretch (the legs) asunder, f. *varicus* straddling. See VARICOSE, -ATE³.] **1.** *intr.* To stretch or spread apart; to branch off or diverge; in *Bot.* and *Zool.* to diverge widely. **2.** *trans.* To stretch or open wide apart or asunder 1672. **3.** To cause to spread or branch out in different directions. ? *Obs.* 1670.

1. At the spot where these two [roads] divaricated, the horseman stopped JAMES. So **Divari·cate** *a.* widely divergent; *spec.* applied (in *Bot.* and *Zool.*) to branches which diverge from the stem, etc., almost at right angles. **Diva·ricately** *adv.* Hence **Divarica·tion**, the action of stretching apart; spreading out, divergence; *transf.* divergence of opinion; *concr.* the point at which branching takes place; that which divaricates. **Diva·ricator**, a muscle which draws parts asunder, as that which opens the shells of Brachiopods.

†**Divast**, *a.* [Incorrect f. *devast* (see DEVASTATE).] Devastated. 1677.

Dive (dəiv), *v.* Pa. t. **dived;** *U.S.* and *Eng. dial.* **dove.** [OE. had: (1) the strong vb. *dūfan*, pa. t. *dēaf*, pl. *dufon*, intr. duck, dive, sink (obs. bef. 1300); (2) the weak vb. *dȳfan*, *dȳfde* dip, submerge: f. Gmc. **daub-* **deub-* **dub-*, parallel to **daup-* **deup-* **dup-* DEEP *a.*, DIP *v.* The mod. dial. pa. t. *dove* is app. a new formation, after *drive*, *drove*, etc.]

I. *intr.* **1.** To plunge (usually head-foremost) into or under water or other liquid. Also *transf.* **2.** To penetrate with the hand *into*; *slang* to pick pockets 1700. **3.** *fig.* To enter deeply or plunge *into* (a matter) 1583. **4.** To dart out of sight, disappear 1844.

1. [The cormorant] from a vast height drops down to d. after its prey GOLDSM. *transf. Timon* IV. i. 2. The fierce soul to darkness dived and hell POPE.

II. *trans.* [In early use OE. *dȳfan.*] **1.** To dip or plunge (a person or thing) *in*, or *into* a liquid, or the like (*arch.*) OE.; to plunge (the hand, etc.) *into* 1590. Also †*transf.* and *fig.* **2.** To penetrate or traverse by diving. Now *rare.* 1615. **3.** *slang.* To pick (pockets). B. JONSON.

2. The Curtii bravely dived the gulf of flame DENHAM. He dives the hollow, climbs the steep EMERSON.

Dive (dəiv), *sb.* 1700. [f. prec. vb.] **1.** The act of diving (*lit.* and *fig.*). Also *transf.* **2.** In *U.S.* An illegal drinking-den, or place of low resort, often situated in a cellar, or the like 1882.

2. Opium-smoking dives 1883.

Di·ve-dap, -dop. Now *dial.* [OE. *dūfedoppa*, f. *dūfan* to dive + *doppa*, agent-n. f. ablaut stem *dēop-*, *dup-* (*dop-*) dip. *Dyve-* replaced *dūfe-* when the strong form of the vb. became obs.; see DIVE.] = next.

Di·ve-dapper. 1559. [f. prec.; assim. to agent-nouns in -ER¹.] = DIDAPPER; also applied to other diving waterfowl.

†**Dive·ll,** *v.* 1627. [– L. *divellere* rend asunder, f. *di-*, *dis-* DIS- 1 + *vellere* tear.] To tear or rend asunder –1801.

Divellent (di-, dəive·lĕnt), *a.* 1782. [– *divellent-*, pres. ppl. stem of L. *divellere*; see prec., -ENT.] Drawing asunder; decomposing, separative.

Dive·llicate, *v.* 1638. [f. L. *di-*, *dis-* DIS- 1 + *vellicat-*, pa. ppl. stem of *vellicare*, from *vellere*; see prec., -ATE³.] To pull to pieces. Also *fig.*

Diver (dəi·vəɹ). 1506. [f. DIVE *v.* + -ER¹.] **1.** One who, or that which, dives under water. **b.** *fig.* One who dives into a subject, etc. 1624. **2.** A water bird that dives. **a.** *spec.* Any of the *Colymbidæ*, as the *Great Northern D.*, the *Red-throated D.*, etc. **b.** The grebe. **c.** Various *Anseres*: *Black D.*, the common scoter, *Dun D.*, the female and young male merganser. 1510. **3.** A pick-pocket 1608.

1. Dyvers, and Fishers for Pearls WOODWARD. **b.** A d. into causes WOTTON.

†**Di·verb.** 1621. [perh. a latinization of *by-word*, the Eng. prefix being repr. by L. *di-*, *dis-*, DI-¹, DIS- 1.] A proverb, byword; a proverbial expression –1689.

You may define *ex ungue leonem*, as the d. is BURTON.

†**Dive·rberate,** *v.* 1609. [– *diverberat-*, pa. ppl. stem of L. *diverberare*, f. *di-* DIS- 1 + *verberare* scourge; see -ATE³.] *trans.* To cleave asunder; to strike through –1656. Hence **Diverbera·tion,** beating.

Diverge (divə̄·ɹdʒ, dəi-), *v.* 1665. [– med.L. *divergere*, f. L. *di-* DIS- 1 + *vergere* bend, incline; see VERGE *v.*²] **1.** *intr.* To proceed in different directions from a point or from each other: opp. to CONVERGE. **b.** *transf.* and *fig.* To take different courses; to turn off *from* a track or course; to differ in opinion or character; to deviate from a normal form or state 1856. **2.** *trans.* To cause (lines or rays) to branch off in different directions; to deflect 1748.

1. The mountains here d., in a fan-like form KEATINGE. Hence **Dive·rgement,** divergence.

Divergence (divə̄·ɹdʒĕns, dəi-). 1656. [f. prec. + -ENCE, perh. after Fr. *divergence*.] **1.** The action of diverging; also *ellipt.* for *amount* or *degree of d.* **2.** *transf.* and *fig.* Continuous deviation from a standard or norm 1839. **3.** *Math.* In fluid motion, the decrement of density at any point. So **Dive·rgency,** divergent quality or state; also = DIVERGENCE 1.

Divergent (divə̄·ɹdʒĕnt, dəi-), *a.* 1696. [f. as prec. + -ENT, perh. after Fr. *divergent*.] **1.** Proceeding in different directions from each other or from a common point; diverging. **2.** *transf.* and *fig.* Differing from each other or from a standard or norm 1801. **3.** Of, pertaining to, or produced by, divergence 1831. **4.** *Math.* = DIVERGING 2. 1837.

1. *D.*, a Term in Opticks said of the Beams, which having suffered the Refraction, separate one from the other E. PHILLIPS. **2.** Thence arise d. opinions SOUTHEY. **3.** *D. squint*: strabismus in which the axes of the eye diverge. Hence **Dive·rgently** *adv.*

Dive·rging, *ppl. a.* 1706. [-ING².] **1.** Proceeding in different directions from a common point, so as to become more and more widely separate; turning off from the straight course. **2.** *Math.* Applied to a series, the sum of whose terms becomes indefinitely greater as more and more are taken. (Opp. to CONVERGENT.) 1795. Hence **Dive·rgingly** *adv.*

Divers (dəi·vəɹz), *a.* ME. [– (O)Fr. *divers*, fem. *diverse* :– L. *diversus* orig. 'turned different ways', pa. pple. of *divertere* DIVERT.] †**1.** Different in character or quality; not of the same kind. Now repl. by DIVERSE. –1691. †**2.** Differing from what is right, good, or profitable; perverse, adverse –1581. **3.** (always *pl.*) Various, sundry, several; more than one, some number of. (Thus *variety* gradually becomes *indefinite number*.) ME. Also *absol.* and with *of*. †**4.** as *adv.* Diversely –1720.

1. Whether it be lawful to beare Arms for the Service of a Prince that is of d. Religion 1625. **3.** At sundry times and in d. manners *Heb.* 1:1. Seised in fee of d. freehold lands 1827. **4.** MILT. *P.L.* IV. 234. Hence **Di·versly** *adv.*

Diverse (di-, dəivə̄·ɹs dəi·vəɹs), *a.* ME. [Identical in origin w. prec., in later use differentiated from it in form and pronunc. (cf. *adverse*, *inverse*), with restriction to the sense of the orig. Latin.] **1.** = DIVERS 1. **2.** Multiform, varied, diversified 1541. †**3.** = DIVERS 2. –1483. †**4.** Distracting. (In SPENSER.) †**5.** = DIVERS 3. (rare in this spelling after 1700.) –1728. Also *absol.* †**6.** *adv.* = DIVERS 4. –1729.

1. With habits so d., we may well expect [etc.] 1841. **2.** The d. Moon WYATT. **5.** Collected out of d. Authenticall Records 1601. [It] hath been excellently handled by d. BACON. Hence **Diverse-ly** *adv.*, **-ness** (now *rare*).

†**Dive·rse,** *v.* ME. [– OFr. *diverser* change, vary – med.L. *diversare*, frequent. of L. *divertere* DIVERT.] **1.** To render, be, or grow, diverse –1634. **2.** *intr.* To turn aside (*rare*) 1590.

2. The Redcrosse Knight diverst: but forth rode Britomart SPENSER *F. Q.* III. iii. 62.

Diversi-, comb. element, f. L. *diversus* DIVERSE: as in

Diversiflo·rate, -flo·rous *adjs.*, bearing flowers of different kinds. **Diversifo·liate, -fo·lious** *adjs.*, having leaves of different kinds. **Dive·rsiform** *a.*, of diverse forms. †**Diversi·volent** *a.*, desiring strife or differences (*rare*).

Diversification (divə̄·ɹsifikēⁱ·ʃən, dəi-). 1603. [– med.L. *diversificatio*, f. *diversificat-*, pa. ppl. stem of *diversificare*; see next, -ION. Cf. OFr. *diversification*.] The action of diversifying; the process of becoming diversified; the fact of being diversified; a diversified condition, form, or structure.

The minuter diversifications are called varieties KIRWAN.

Diversify (divə̄·ɹsifəi, dəi-), *v.* 1481. [– OFr. *diversifier* – med.L. *diversificare* render unlike, f. L. *diversus* DIVERSE; see -FY.] **1.** *trans.* To render diverse, different, or varied, in form or qualities; to give variety to; to variegate, vary, modify 1490. †**2.** *intr.* or *absol.* To produce diversity or variety. Also *intr.* (for *refl.*) –1815.

1. The bones of the body..be deuersyfyed in dyuers maners R. COPLAND. We diversifie our selves from him [God] FELTHAM. Hence **Dive·rsifiable** *a.* capable of being diversified (*rare*). **Diversifiabi·lity.**

Diversion (divə̄·ɹʃən, dəi-). 1600. [– late L. *diversio* turning away, f. *divers-*, pa. ppl. stem of L. *divertere* DIVERT; see -ION. The mil. use may be immed. – Fr. *diversion* or It. *diversione*.] **1.** The turning aside (*of* any person or thing) from any course, object, or occupation; a turning aside of one's course or attention; deviation, deflexion. **2.** *Mil.* A manœuvre to draw off the enemy's attention from a particular operation, by an attack in an unexpected quarter 1647. **3.** *spec.* The turning away of the thoughts, attention, etc., from fatiguing or sad occupations; distraction, recreation, amusement. Also with *a* and *pl.* 1648.

1. Fearing the d. of trade 1872. A d...from this rectitude, this uprightness DONNE. The d... was the suggestion of a treaty proposed by the enemy BURKE. **3.** Among the in-door diversions were draughts, chess, etc. 1875.

Diversity (divə̄·ɹsĭti, dəi-). ME. [– (O)Fr. *diversité* – L. *diversitas*, f. *diversus*; see DIVERSE, -ITY.] **1.** The condition of being diverse; difference, unlikeness. Also with *a* and *pl.* †**b.** Divers manners or sorts –1610. †**2.** Perversity, evil, mischief –1523.

1. Diversitie of circumstance may alter the case RALEGH. **b.** Mo diuersitie of sounds, all horrible SHAKS.

†**Dive·rsory,** *sb.* ME. [– med.L. *diversorium*, for cl. L. *deversorium* lodging, inn, f. *devers-*, pa. ppl. stem of *devertere* turn aside, lodge; see -ORY¹. Cf. OFr. *diversoire*.] A place to which one turns in by the way –1681.

Dive·rsory, *a. rare.* 1864. [f. *divers-*; see prec., -ORY².] Serving to divert, divertive.

Divert (divə̄·ɹt, dəi-), *v.* ME. [– Fr. *divertir* – L. *divertere*, f. *dī-* DI-¹ + *vertere* turn.] **1.** *trans.* To turn aside from its direction or course; to deflect; to turn *from* one destination *to* another 1548. Also †*refl.* **2.** *intr.* (for *refl.*) To deviate, digress (*lit.* and *fig.*). Now *arch.* ME. †**3.** (?) To turn awry. *Tr. & Cr.* I. iii. 99. **4.** To draw off (a person) *from* a course, etc.; to distract (the mind, attention, etc.) 1600. **5.** To draw away from fatiguing or serious occupations; to entertain, amuse 1662. Also *refl.* (now *rare*). †**6.** To while away (time) –1773.

1. The old Channel..for diverting the Thames 1699. Persevering labour, not diverted from one object to another SIR B. BRODIE. **4.** Less profitable amusements d. their attention COWPER. **5.** I had neither Friends or Books to d. me STEELE. Hence **Dive·rter. Dive·rtible** *a.* (*rare*). **Dive·rting-ly** *adv.*, **-ness.** †**Dive·rtment,** diversion.

†**Dive·rticle.** 1570. [– L. *diverticulum*; see next.] **1.** A by-way or bypath; a turning out of the course. Also *fig.* –1782. **2.** = DIVERTICULUM 2. 1847.

‖**Diverticulum** (dəivəɹti·kiŭlŏm). Pl. **-a.** 1647. [L. MS. var. (hence med.L.) of *deverticulum* by-way, f. *devertere* turn down or aside, f. *de-* DE- I. 1 + *vertere* turn; see -CULE.] †**1.** A by-way; a means of exit –1695. **2.** A smaller side-branch of any cavity or passage; in *Anat.* applied to a blind tubular process 1819. Hence **Diverti·cular** *a.* pertaining to or like a d. **Diverti·culate(d** *a.* having a d.

‖**Divertimento** (d*i*vert*i*me·nto). Pl. **-ti** (-*ti*), **-tos.** 1759. [It.] †**a.** Diversion, amusement. **b.** *Mus.* = DIVERTISSEMENT 2.

†**Divertise,** *v.* Also **-ize.** 1597. [f. Fr. *divertiss-*, lengthened stem of *divertir*; cf. *advertise*. Stressed by Bailey *dive·rtise*; Johnson has *diverti·se*.] = DIVERT 4, 5. Chiefly *refl.*: To enjoy oneself, make merry –1696. So ‖**Dive·rtissant** *a.* diverting.

Divertisement (divə̄·ɹtizmĕnt). *arch.* 1642. [– Fr. *divertissement*, f. as prec.; see -MENT.] **1.** = DIVERSION 3. **2.** = DIVERTISSEMENT 2. 1667.

1. Some for d., and some for businesse HOBBES.

‖**Divertissement** (divęrtismaṅ). 1728. [See prec.] **1.** An entertainment 1804. **2.** A short ballet or other entertainment given between acts or longer pieces (= Fr. *entr'acte*); †a piece of music on given *motifs* (Grove).

Divertive (divə̄·ɹtiv, dəi-), *a.* Now *rare.* 1598. [f. DIVERT *v.* + -IVE.] Tending to divert; distractive, amusing, entertaining.

Greatly d. to the inward man 1831.

‖**Dives** (dəi·vīz). ME. [L., = rich, rich man.] **1.** Commonly taken as the proper name of the rich man in the parable (see Luke 16); and used generically for 'rich man'. **2.** *Law. D. costs*; costs on the higher scale 1849.

Divest (dive·st, dəi-), *v.* 1605. [refash. of DEVEST on L. models in *di-*. Cf. med.L. *dis-*, *di-*, *devestire*.] **1.** *trans.* To unclothe; to strip *of* clothing, or of any covering, ornament, etc. 1795. **2.** *fig.* To strip *of* possessions, rights, or attributes; to denude, deprive; occas., to free, rid. Also *refl.* 1605. **3.** To put off. Now *rare.* 1639. **4.** *Law.* To take away (property, etc., vested in any one); to DEVEST (Sense 4) 1789.

2. [Monkeys] can never be divested of a mischievous disposition 1769. **3.** I will d. all fear BROWNING. Hence **Dive·sted** *ppl. a.* (loosely used for: Devoid *of*). **Dive·stible** *a.* capable of being divested. **Dive·stment,** divestiture.

Dive·stitive, *a.* 1802. [f. as next + -IVE.] Having the property of divesting.

Ablative, or say d. facts BENTHAM.

Divestiture (dive·stitiŭɹ, dəi-). 1601. [– med.L. *divestitura* (*dis-* Niermeyer), f. *divestit-*, pa. ppl. stem of *divestire*; see DIVEST, -URE.] **1.** Deprivation of a possession or right; dispossession; alienation. **2.** Putting off of clothing; also *fig.* 1820. var. **Dive·sture.**

Divet, var. of DIVOT.

Dividable (divəi·dăb'l), *a.* 1587. [f. DIVIDE *v.* + -ABLE.] **1.** Capable of being divided; divisible. †**2.** Having the function of dividing. *Tr. & Cr.* I. iii. 105.

Dividant, var. of †DIVIDENT.

Divide (divəi·d), *v.* ME. [– L. *dividere*, f. *dis-* DI-¹ + **videre*. Cf. DEVISE *v.*]

I. *trans.* **1.** To separate into parts, or into smaller groups; to split up, cleave; to break or cut asunder. **2.** To separate into branches ME. **3.** To separate or mark out into parts (in fact or in thought). Most freq. in *pass.*; sometimes nearly = to consist of (so many) parts. ME. **4.** To separate into classes; to class, classify 1551. **5.** To separate *from*; to cut off, sunder, part ME. **6.** To establish or constitute a boundary between (*lit.* and *fig.*) ME. **7.** To separate in opinion, feeling, or interest; to set at variance; to distract ME. **8.** To distribute among a number; to deal out, dispense ME.; to share 1526; to direct to different things 1611. **9.** *Math.* To perform the process of DIVISION on; also *absol.* ME.; to be a divisor of 1709. **10.** To part (a legislative assembly, etc.) into two groups in order to ascertain the number voting on each side of a question. Also *absol.* and *intr.* 1554. †**11.** *Mus. trans.* To perform with divisions; *intr.* to perform divisions; to descant –1618.

1. And the king said, D. the living chiId in two 1 *Kings* 3:25. Phr. *To d. the hoof*: to have cloven hoofs. (A Hebraism.) **3.** A ruler divided into inches and small parts 1665. Thir songs D. the night MILT. *P. L.* IV. 688. **5.** The sick were divided from the rest 1700. **6.** What thin partitions Sense from Thought d. POPE. **7.** There shall be five in one house divided, three against two, and two against three *Luke* 12:52. **8.** God divided the land of Canaan among the Israelites HOBBES. He stood, This way and that dividing the swift mind, In act to throw TENNYSON.

II. *intr.* (See also I. 9, 10, 11.) **1.** *absol.* To make separation or distinction (*between*) ME. **2.** *intr.* (for *refl.*) To become divided, undergo division; to become separated; to part; to cleave, break up, go to pieces; to branch 1526.

1. Diuide with reason betweene Self-loue, and Society BACON. **2.** Loue cooles, friendship falls off, brothers diuide *Lear* I. ii. 15. [The river] divides and sub-divides HUXLEY.

Divi·de, *sb.* 1642. [f. prec. vb.] **1.** Division. **2.** In U.S., etc.: A ridge or line of high ground forming the division between two river valleys or systems; a watershed 1807.

Divi·ded, *ppl. a.* 1565. [f. DIVIDE *v.* + -ED¹.] **1.** Separated into parts; in *Bot.* (of leaves, etc.) cut into segments. **2.** Situated apart; separate 1658. **3.** Discordant; split into factions 1594. **4.** Distributed among a number; directed to different objects 1607. Hence **Divi·ded-ly** *adv.*, **-ness.**

Dividend (di·vidĕnd). Also *erron.* †**dividente, -ent.** 1477. [– AFr. *dividende* – L. *dividendum*, subst. use of n. gerundive of *dividere* DIVIDE.] **1.** *Math.* A number or quantity which is to be divided by another. (Correl. to DIVISOR.) 1542. **2.** A sum of money to be divided among a number of persons; *esp.* the total sum payable as interest on a loan, or as the profit of a joint-stock company 1623. **3.** *transf.* A portion or share of anything divided; *esp.* the share that falls to each distributee 1477. †**4.** The action of dividing; distribution –1726.

2. *To declare a d.*: see DECLARE *v.* **3.** A very liberal d. of praise JOHNSON. A testatrix gave to trustees certain bank stock, upon trust to pay the dividends to [etc.] 1827.

†**Di·vident.** 1450. [– *divident-*, pres. ppl. stem of L. *dividere*; see DIVIDE *v.*, -ENT.] **A.** *adj.* **1.** Distributive 1660. **2.** Separate. (In Shaks. *divi·dant.*) *Timon* IV. iii. 5.

B. *sb.* One who or that which DIVIDES; in *Arith.* = DIVISOR –1656.

Divident, -e; see DIVIDEND.

Divider (divəi·dəɹ). 1526. [f. DIVIDE *v.* + -ER¹.] **1.** One who or that which divides, or separates a whole into parts 1591. **2.** One who distributes; one who shares something with another 1526. †**3.** One who classifies –1610. **4.** One who or that which causes division 1643. **5.** *pl.* Dividing compasses, worked by means of a screw; a pair of compasses with steel points 1703.

2. Who made me a judge or a d. over you *Luke* 12:14. **4.** Hate is of all things the mightiest d. MILT. Money, the great d. of the world SWIFT.

Divi·ding, *ppl. a.* 1620. [f. as prec. + -ING².] That divides (see the vb.).

D. engine, a machine for graduating a circle, or for cutting the circumference of a wheel into a number of teeth. *D.ridge* = DIVIDE *sb.* 2. Hence **Divi·dingly** *adv.*

‖**Divi-divi** (di·vidi·vi). 1843. [Carib.] The curled pods of *Cæsalpinia coriaria*, a tree of tropical America; they are highly astringent, and much used in tanning. Also the tree.

Dividual (divi·diuăl), *a.* (*sb.*) 1598. [f. L. *dividuus* + -AL¹.]

A. 1. Separable; separate. **2.** Divisible; divided into parts 1619. **3.** Distributed among a number; shared 1667.

†**B.** *sb.* **1.** That which is dividual 1668. **2.** *Math.* One of the parts of the dividend, each of which yields successively one term of the quotient –1811. Hence **Divi·dually** *adv.* separately.

Dividuous (divi·diu,əs), *a.* *rare.* 1766. [f. as prec. + -OUS.] = DIVIDUAL A 1, 2.

†**Di·vinail.** ME. [– OFr. *de-*, *divinail*, *-aille*, f. *deviner*; see DIVINE *v.*, -AL¹ 2.] **1.** Divining, divination –1484. **2.** A riddle –1483.

Divination (divinēⁱ·ʃən). ME. [– (O)Fr. *divination* or L. *divinatio*, f. *divinat-*, pa. ppl. stem of *divinare*; see DIVINE *v.*, -ION.] **1.** The action or practice of divining; the foretelling of future events or discovery of what is hidden or obscure by supernatural or magical means. Also with *a* and *pl.*, an exercise of this, a prophecy, an augury. **2.** Successful conjecture or guessing 1597. ¶*catachr.* Divine condition. P. HOLLAND.

1. The flying of birds, which doe geue a happy d. to things to come SIR T. NORTH. **2.** 2 *Hen. IV* I. i. 88.

Di·vinator. ? *Obs.* 1607. [– late L. *divinator*, f. as prec.; see -OR 2.] One who divines; a diviner; soothsayer. So **Divinato·rial** *a.* conjectural (*rare*). **Divi·natory** *a.* prophetic; conjectural.

Divine (divəi·n), *a.* and *sb.*¹ [ME. *devine*, *divine* – OFr. *devin*, fem. *-ine*, later (by assim. to L. sp.) *divin* – L. *divinus*, f. *divus* godlike, god, rel. to *deus* god.]

A. 1. Of or pertaining to God or a god ME. **2.** Given by or proceeding from God ME. **3.** Addressed, or devoted to God; religious, sacred ME. **4.** Partaking of the nature of God; godlike; celestial ME.; †beatified –1632. **5.** More than human, excellent in a superhuman degree. Said of persons and things. 1470. **6.** Connected or dealing with divinity or sacred things. ? *Obs.* 1548. †**7.** Foreboding, prescient. [A Latinism.] 1667.

1. D. acts R. W. DALE. **2.** The d. right of kings 1640. An irresistible d. impulse SEELEY. **3.** Like prayers d. SHAKS. *D.Office*, *Service*: see OFFICE 6 a, SERVICE¹ III. 4b. **4.** Or flocks, or herds, or human face d. MILT. *P. L.* III. 40. **5.** 1 *Hen. VI*, I. vi. 4. Blackness sits On the divinest wits H. VAUGHAN. **7.** Yet oft his heart, d. of something ill, Misgave him MILT. *P. L.* IX. 845.

†**B.** *sb.*¹ **1.** Divine service –1606. **2.** Divinity, theology –1400. **3.** DIVINATION. (ME. only.) **4.** Divine nature. (ME. only.)

Divine (divəi·n), *sb.*² [ME. *devine* – OFr. *devin* (:– L. *divinus* soothsayer), later *divin* theologian, after med.L. *divinus* doctor of divinity, theologian; subst. use of prec.] †**1.** A diviner, soothsayer; a seer –1587. **2.** Formerly, any ecclesiastic, clergyman, or priest; now, a theologian ME.

2. It is a good Diuine that followes his owne instructions *Merch. V.* I. ii. 16.

Divine (divəi·n), *v.* [ME. *devine* – (O)Fr. *deviner*, f. *devin* DIVINE *sb.*², after L. *divinare* foretell, predict.]

I. *trans.* †**1.** To make out by supernatural or magical insight; hence, to interpret, explain, make known –1625. **2.** To conjecture, guess ME. **3.** To have presentiment of (things to come); hence *gen.* to predict by intuition ME. †**4.** To point out, foreshow, prognosticate –1847. †**5.** To render divine; to divinize –1622.

2. Nor cou'd I d. the Meaning of it 1696. **3.** To shun the danger that his Soule diuines *Rich. III*, III. ii. 18. **4.** A certain magick rod divines Whene'er the soil has golden mines SWIFT.

II. *intr.* **1.** To use or practise divination; to soothsay ME. **2.** To foretell by divine or superhuman power (*arch.*) ME. **3.** To conjecture ME.

1. You shal not d., nor observe dreames BIBLE (Douay) *Lev.* 19:26. **3.** Something from Cyprus, as I may diuine *Oth.* I. ii. 39. Whereon d. you, Sir GREENE. Hence †**Divi·nement,** divination.

Divinely (divəi·nli), *adv.* 1582. [f. DIVINE *a.* + -LY².] In a divine manner. **1.** By or as by the agency of God 1594. **2.** As or like God; in a godlike manner; with an excellence more than human 1582. †**3.** In a holy manner –1682.

1. As some d. gifted man TENNYSON. **2.** Shee fair, d. fair, fit love for Gods MILT. *P. L.* IX. 489.

Divineness (divəi·nnės). 1579. [-NESS.] **1.** The quality or state of being divine. **2.** Superhuman or supreme excellence 1580.

Diviner (divəi·nəɹ). [ME. *de-*, *divinour* – AFr. = OFr. *devinĕor*, etc., corresp. to L. *devinator*; see DIVINE *v.*, -ER² 3. In sense 2, after OFr. *divin* DIVINE *sb.*² Till 1500 stressed *de·vinou·r*, *de·vinou·r.*] **1.** One who practises divination; a successful conjecturer. †**2.** A theologian –1552.

1. The deuynour had told hym that he shold deye within fyue dayes CAXTON. A notable D. of Thoughts LOCKE. So **Divi·neress,** a female d.

†**Divinesse.** 1594. [Compressed var. of *divineness*. Cf. †*prones(se* proneness.] **a.** Divination. **b.** Divineness, divinity. –1605.

Diving (dəi·viŋ), *vbl. sb.* ME. [f. DIVE *v.* + -ING¹.] The action of DIVE *v.*

Comb. **d.-bell,** a strong heavy vessel, originally bell-shaped, with the bottom open, in which persons may descend into deep water, respiration being sustained by compressed air, or by fresh air from above.

Di·ving, *ppl. a.* 1602. [-ING².] That dives. *Comb.*: **d.-buck** or **goat,** a S. African antelope (*Cephalophus mergens*); **-duck,** the golden-eye duck (*Clangula glaucion*); **-pigeon,** the black guillemot (*Uria grylle*); **-spider,** *Argyroneta aquatica*, which lives in a nest under water.

Divinify (divi·nifəi), *v.* 1633. [f. L. *divinus* DIVINE *a.* + -FY, after *deify*.] To render or regard as divine; to divinize.

Divi·ning, *vbl. sb.* (*ppl. a.*) ME. [f. DIVINE *v.* + -ING¹,².] The action of DIVINE *v.*; also *attrib.*

D.-rod, a rod used in divination; *spec.* a forked stick, by means of which certain persons claim to be able to discover water and minerals underground. See *Dowsing-rod* (DOWSE).

†**Divi·nister.** [f. DIVINE *v.*; see -ISTER.] A diviner. CHAUCER.

Divinity (divi·nĭti). [ME. *de-*, *divinite* – (O)Fr. *divinité* – L. *divinitas* (in Vulgate tr. Gr. θειότης and θεότης), f. *divinus*; see -ITY.] **1.** The character or quality of being divine; divineness; divine nature; Deity, Godhead. **2.** *concr.* A divine being; a god, a deity ME. Also *fig.* **3.** Divine quality, virtue, or power 1510. **4.** The science of divine things; the science that deals with the nature and attributes of God, His relations with mankind, etc.; theology; the theological faculty ME. Also *transf.* †**5.** = DIVINATION 1 (*rare*) –1601.

1. The veil is rent. That hides d. from mortal eyes COWPER. **2.** There's a Diuinity that shapes our ends, Rough-hew them how we will *Haml.* V. ii. 10. **3.** There is Diuinity in odde Numbers *Merry W.* V. i. 3. **4.** *Hen. V*, I. i. 38. *attrib.* **d. calf,** dark-brown binding with blind tooling. Hence **Divi·nityship,** the status of a d.; skill in d. (STERNE).

Divinize (di·vinəiz), *v.* 1656. [– Fr. *diviniser* (XVI), f. *divin* DIVINE *a.*; see -IZE.] To make or †become divine. Hence **Diviniza·tion,** the action of divinizing, or condition of being divinized.

†**Divi·se,** *a.* ME. [– L. *divisus*, pa. pple. of *dividere* DIVIDE *v.* Cf. OFr. *devis.*] Divided; separate, distinct –1677.

Divisible (divi·zib'l), *a.* (*sb.*) 1552. [–(O)Fr. *divisible* or late L. *divisibilis*, f. *divis-*, pa. ppl. stem of L. *dividere*; see DIVIDE *v.*, -IBLE.] **1.** Capable of being divided into parts (actually or in thought). **2.** *Math.* Capable of being divided without remainder (*by*) 1709.

1. Every particle of matter is infinitely d. PRIESTLEY. Hence **Divisibi·lity, Divi·sibleness,** d. quality. **Divi·sibly** *adv.*

Division (divi·ʒən). [ME. *de-*, *divisioun*, etc. – OFr. *de-*, *divisiun* (mod. *division*) – L. *divisio*, f. as prec.; see -ION.]

I. As an action or condition. **1.** The action of dividing or state of being divided into parts; partition; separation. **2.** The action of distributing among a number; distribution, sharing ME. †**3.** The action of distinguishing; distinction –1611. **4.** Disagreement, variance, dissension; a disagreement ME. **5.** *Math.* The action or process of finding how many times one quantity or number is contained in another; the inverse of multiplication; a rule or method for doing this ME. **6.** *Logic*, etc. Separation of a genus into species; classification. Also, less strictly, **b.** Enumeration of the parts of a whole, called *partible d.* **c.** Distinction of the various meanings of a term, called *nominal d.* 1551. †**7.** *Mus.* The execution of a rapid melodic passage, originally conceived as the dividing of each of a succession of long notes into several short ones; such a passage itself; often nearly = DESCANT *sb.* –1840. **8.** The separating of the members of a legislative body, etc., into two groups, in order to count their votes 1620.

1. The D. of Time into Hours, Days, and Weeks 1726. **2.** Phr. *D. of labour*, the d. of a process or employment into parts, each of which is performed by a particular person. **4.** Mark them which cause divisions..and avoid them *Rom.* 16:17. **5.** Phr. *Long d.* (in *Arith.*), the method in which the steps of the operation are successively written down. *Short d.*, the method adopted when the divisor is 12 or less, in which the quotient is set down directly, without writing down the steps of the operation. **7.** Ditties.. Sung by a faire Queene..With ravishing Diuision to her Lute SHAKS. **8.** Negatived without a d. 1794.

II. What produces, or is produced by, division. **1.** What divides or marks separation; a partition ME. **2.** One of the parts into which anything is **or** may be divided; a portion, section ME. *spec.* **b.** A portion of a country, etc., as marked off for some political, administrative, or other purpose 1640. **c.** *Mil.* and *Naut.* A portion of an army or fleet, under one commanding officer; also, a definite portion of a squadron or battalion (see quots.); also, a portion of a ship's company appropriated to a particular service 1597. **d.** *Nat. Hist.* A section of a larger group in classification: used widely, as the divisions of a kingdom, class, order, family, or genus 1833.

2. The leafe jagged in five divisions like a starre B. GOOGE. *Division*—In its strict sense, the fourth part of a Squadron 1832. Two or three battalions are usually formed into a brigade, two brigades into a division 1879. **e.** A grade of clerk in the Civil Service 1876. **f.** One of the three grades of imprisonment 1865. **Divi·sional** *a.* of the nature of d.; pertaining to d.; of or belonging to a d. or portion. **Divi·sionally** *adv.* **Divi·sionary** *a.* divisional (*rare*). †**Divi·sioner**, one who makes a d.

Divisive (divəi·siv), *a.* 1603. [– late L. *divisivus*, f. as prec.; see -IVE. Cf. Fr. *divisif*, *-ive* (XVI).] **1.** Causing or expressing division or distribution; analytical. **2.** Producing or tending to division, dissension, or discord 1642.

2. Vanity is of a d., not of a uniting nature CARLYLE. Hence **Divi·sive-ly** *adv.*, **-ness.**

Divisor (divəi·zəɹ). ME. [– Fr. *diviseur* or L. *divisor*, f. as prec.; see -OR 2.] *Math.* A number or quantity by which another is to be divided. (Correl. to DIVIDEND.) **b.** One that divides another exactly; a measure, factor 1557.

Common d. = common measure or factor.

Divisory (divəi·zŏri), *a.* 1614. [– med.L. *divisorius*, f. as prec.; see -ORY[2].] Pertaining to distribution among a number.

Divorce (divōᵊ·ɹs), *sb.* ME. [– (O)Fr. *divorce* – L. *divortium* separation, divorce, f. *divortere*, var. of *divertere* DIVERT.] **1.** Legal dissolution of marriage by a court or other competent body, or according to forms locally recognized. **2.** *transf.* and *fig.* Complete separation; disunion of things closely united ME. †**3.** That which causes divorce –1607. Also *attrib.*

1. D. *a mensa et thoro* (from bed and board), now, since 1857, called 'judicial separation'. **2.** To suffre devorce or departyng betwene his soule and his body 1532. **3.** SHAKS. *Ven. & Ad.* 932.

Divorce (divōᵊ·ɹs), *v.* ME. [– (O)Fr. *divorcer* – late L. *divortiare*, f. *divortium*; see prec.] **1.** *trans.* To dissolve the marriage contract between, by process of law; to separate by divorce *from* 1494. Also *refl.* and *intr.* **2.** *trans.* To put away (a spouse). Also *fig.* ME. **3.** To dissolve (a marriage or union) (*arch.*) 1580. **4.** *fig.* To separate; to sever ME.

2. *fig.* Say March may wed September And time d. regret SWINBURNE. **4.** Divorced from matter, where is life TYNDALL. Hence **Divo·rceable** *a.* that can or may be divorced. **Divo:rcee·** (also as Fr. *divorcé(e)*, a divorced person. **Divo·rcement,** divorce; complete separation. **Divo·rcer. Divo·rcive** *a.* (also **-sive**), causing or leading to divorce.

Divot (di·vət). *Sc.* and *n. dial.* 1536. [orig. Sc. *deva(i)t, devot, diffat, defett, divat, duvat*; of unkn. origin.] A slice of earth with the grass growing on it, a turf, a sod: used for roofing cottages, etc.; in *Golf*, a piece of turf cut out in making a stroke.

†**Divu·lgate**, *ppl. a.* ME. [– L. *divulgatus*, pa. pple. of *divulgare*; see DIVULGE, -ATE[2].] Made public. (Chiefly used as pa. pple. = divulged.) –1574.

Divulgate (dəi·vɒlgeᶦt), *v.* 1530. [– *divulgat-*, pa. ppl. stem of L. *divulgare*; see next, -ATE[3].] To DIVULGE. **Di·vulgater, -ator. Divulga·tion. Di·vulgatory** *a.* tending to publish (*rare*).

Divulge (divɒ·ldʒ, dəi-), *v.* 1460. [– L. *divulgare*, f. *di-* DIS- 1 + *vulgare* publish, propagate, f. *vulgus* common people. The pronunc. with -dʒ is prob. due to the sp. *-ge*.] †**1.** *trans.* To make publicly known –1791; to publish –1709. **2.** To declare or tell openly (something private or secret); to disclose, reveal 1602. †**3.** *transf.* To make common, impart generally. [A Latinism.] (*rare*) 1667. **4.** *intr.* (for *refl.*) To become publicly known (*rare*) 1602.

1. Among the Danai thy dreams divulging COWPER. **2.** Command him to d. the crimes confessed to him 1797. **3.** MILT. *P. L.* VIII. 583. Hence **Divu·lgement**, the act of divulging; also, †*concr.* in *pl.* **Divu·lgence,** disclosure. **Divu·lger.**

†**Divu·lse**, *v.* 1602. [– *divuls-*, pa. ppl. stem of L. *divellere*; see DIVELL.] *trans.* To tear apart or asunder –1691. So **Divu·lsive** *a.* tending to tear apart or asunder.

Divulsion (divɒ·lʃən, dəi-). 1603. [– Fr. *divulsion* or L. *divulsio*, f. as prec.; see -ION.] The action of tearing, pulling, or plucking asunder; the condition of being torn apart *from*. Also *fig.*

Others [islands] are made by d. from some continent 1684.

Diwan; see DEWAN, DIVAN.

Dixie[1] (di·ksi). 1879. **(dechsie).** [– Hind. *degchī* – Panjabi *dekachī*, Hindi *degćī*, all – Pers. *degcha*, dim. of *deg* pot, saucepan.] An iron pot or kettle for tea or stew.

Dixie[2] (di·ksi). 1861. [Origin unkn.] The Southern U.S. Also *Dixie Land.*

‖**Dixit** (di·ksit). 1628. [L., = he has said; see IPSE DIXIT.] An utterance (quoted as) already given.

‖**Dizain** (dizēᶦ·n). 1575. [Fr. *dizain* (XV), f. *dix* ten.] A poem or stanza of ten lines.

‖**Dizdar, disdar** (dī·zdāɹ). 1768. [Pers. and Turkish.] The warden of a castle or fort.

Dizen (dəi·z'n, di·z'n), *v.* 1530. [f. base repr. by the first syll. of DISTAFF; cf. MDu. *disen*, perh. the immed. source. See -EN[5].] †**1.** *trans.* To dress (a distaff) with flax, etc., for spinning –1575. **2.** To dress, *esp.* to attire or array with finery, deck *out* (*up*), bedizen. Also *transf.* and *fig.* 1619.

2. Lasses..Sate dizen'd up 1706. Like a tragedy-queen he has dizen'd her [Comedy] out GOLDSM. Hence **Di·zenment.**

Dizz (diz), *v.* 1632. [Back-formation from DIZZY *a.*, after *craze, crazy*, etc.] To make dizzy or giddy.

†**Dizzard** (di·zăɹd). 1529. [perh. modified f. DISOUR; in sense 2 app. assoc. w. DIZZY.] **1.** = DISOUR –1618. **2.** An idiot, a blockhead –1886. Also *attrib.* Hence **Di·zzardly** *a.*

Dizzy (di·zi), *a.* [OE. *dysiġ* = OFris. *dusig*, MDu. *dosech, dösech*, LG. *dusig, dösig* giddy, OHG. *tusic* foolish, weak, f. WGmc. **dus-*, found also in OE. *dys(e)lić* foolish, LG. *dusen* be giddy, and with *l*-suffix in LG. *dusel* giddiness, MDu. *dūselen* (Du. *duizelen*) be giddy or stupid; see -Y[1].] **1.** Foolish, stupid. Now only *dial.* **2.** Having a sensation of vertigo in the head, with proneness to fall; giddy ME. **3.** Mentally or morally unsteady, giddy 1501. **4.** Producing giddiness 1605. **5.** Arising from giddiness; reeling 1715. **6.** *fig.* Whirling with mad rapidity 1791.

2. I daunce up and down tyll I am dyssy SKELTON. **3.** At thy heels the d. multitude MILT. *P. R.* II. 420. **4.** He began..to climb..towards that d. pinnacle MACAULAY. **5.** Lost in a d. mist the warrior lies POPE. Hence **Di·zzily** *adv.* **Di·zziness.**

Dizzy (di·zi), *v.* [In sense 1, from OE. *dysiġan*, etc., to be foolish; in the trans. sense, f. prec. adj.] †**1.** *intr.* To act foolishly or stupidly –ME. **2.** *trans.* To make dizzy or giddy; to cause to reel 1501. **3.** To bewilder or confuse mentally 1604.

2. You turn my head, you d. me COWLEY. **3.** A vision to d. and appal J. H. NEWMAN.

Dj-, repr. the Arabic letter *jīm*, = English *j* (dʒ), in Arabic, Turkish, or Berber words, which have come to us through a French channel; *e.g.* **djerid** or **djereed, djin,** etc. For these see under J; for **djowr**, see GIAOUR.

Do (dū), *v.*, *pa. t.* **did** (2nd *pers. sing.* **didst,** †**didest**); *pa. pple.* **done;** *pres. pple.* and *vbl. sb.* **doing.** In the *Present Indicative*: 1*st pers. sing.* **do**; 2*nd pers. sing.* **doest** (now confined to the principal vb.), **dost** (usu. auxiliary); 3*rd pers. sing.* **does** (*arch.* **doth, doeth,** now *liturg.* and *poet.*); *pl.* **do.** [OE. *dōn*, corresp. to OFris. *duā*, OS. *dōn* (Du. *doen*), OHG. *tuon* (G. *tun*); the WGmc. verb is based on a widespread. IE. **dhō- *dhē *dhə-*, repr. by Skr. *dádhāmi* put, lay, Gr. τίθημι I place, L. *facere* make, do. Cf. DEED *sb.*, DOOM *sb.*]

I. *trans.* **1.** To put, place (*lit.* and *fig.*). Now only *dial.* †**2.** *refl.* To put oneself; to proceed, go. Also †*intr.* –ME. **3.** To bestow, impart, render, give (a thing to a person); to cause by one's action (a person) to have (something) OE. **4.** To put forth (action or effort); to perform; to perpetrate; to execute OE. **5.** To perform duly, carry out OE.; †to deliver (a message, etc.) –1707. **6.** (In *pa. pple.* and *perf. tenses.*) To accomplish, finish, bring to a conclusion ME. **7.** To put forth (diligence, etc.) in effecting something ME. **8.** To bring into existence by one's action 1580. **9.** To operate upon or deal with in any way; *e.g.* to clean 1515; to prepare. as food, lessons, a review, etc. 1660; to play the part of 1599; to 'do for' ME.; to swindle (*slang*) 1641; to go over as a tourist (*colloq.*) 1830; to serve out (a term of punishment) 1865; etc. **10.** To render *into* another language or form of composition 1660.

1. Take a gallon..of pure water, and d. it into a pot 1600. Phr. *To d. to death*: orig. to put to death; now, often implying a protracted process (*arch.*). **3.** It..did me a great deal of good WOOD. To d. him right He was a Man indeed ROWE. **4.** He did neuer doe a more pleasing deed A.V. *Transl. Pref.* 2. Phr. *To d. good, evil, right, wrong*, etc. We knew not what to d. with this poor girl DE FOE. **5.** Thy will be done *Matt.* 6:10. To d. penance STUBBS. **6.** When dinner is done SWIFT. **7.** Phr. *To d. one's best, devoir, diligence, endeavour, might*, etc. **8.** The sun is a painter. He does the photograph 1860. **9.** To d. a room 1883, pastry 1897, a sum (*mod.*), Andromache FOOTE, the amiable DICKENS, a mile a minute 1890, Cologne 1854, time 1889. **10.** He did his sentences out of English into Johnsonese MACAULAY.

II. *intr.* **1.** To put forth action; to act (in some specified way). Now a leading sense of the vb. OE. **2.** To perform deeds; to work ME.; *euphem.* to copulate 1601. **3.** In perfect tenses: To make an end ME. **4.** To fare, get on ME.; *spec.* to be in health 1463. **5.** To 'work'; to do what is wanted; to succeed, answer, or serve; to be fitting; to suffice 1596.

1. Send me word how ye wyll that I doo there in *Paston Lett.* **2.** Let's meet, and either d. or die FLETCHER. **3.** Ha done with words SHAKS. **4.** The farmers were doing badly 1832. Flax does well after wheat 1847. All..asked him 'how the Marquess did?' DISRAELI. **5.** That will d., thank you 1897.

III. Causal and auxiliary uses. †**1.** With *that* and subord. clause: To cause (*that* a person or thing shall do something) –ME. **2.** With *obj.* and *infin.*: To make or cause a person, etc., to do something OE. **3.** Put as a substitute for a verb just used, to avoid repetition OE. **4.** As a *Periphrastic Auxiliary* of the present and past Indicative.

a. In *Affirmative* sentences, orig. = the simple tense; still retained, where the order of pronoun and verb is inverted, and now the normal *Emphatic* form of the present and past Indicative OE. **b.** In *Interrogative* sentences, now the normal form ME. **c.** In *Negative* sentences, now the normal form with *not* 1489. **d.** In *Negative Interrogative* sentences, now the normal form 1581.

5. As auxiliary of the *Imperative*:

a. In the Imperative *positive*, adding force; in earlier times, merely periphrastic OE. **b.** In *do but*—, perh. not auxiliary, but = *ne do but, do nought but*—: cf. BUT *conj.* 1604. **c.** In the Imperative *negative do not*, colloq. contracted *don't* (dō"nt), is now the normal form.

2. Phr. †*To d. him die*: to make him die, to put him to death. *To d.* (one) *to wit, know*, or *understand*: to cause (one) to know; to give (one) to understand; to inform. **3.** He speaks as well as you do 1879. I chose my wife, as she did her wedding-gown GOLDSM. **4. a.** The flowers she most did love LONGF. How bitterly did I repent 1897. I *do* wish you would let me sleep 1890. **b.** What *do* you mean MRS. STOWE. **c.** We d. not know (*mod.*). **d.** Didn't you stop SHERIDAN. **5. a.** D., d. be calm 1884. **b.** D. but hear me GOLDSM. **c.** Don't you speak DICKENS.

IV. Special uses.

†**1. Do,** the imperative, was used absol. = Go on! Go it! (Cf. L. *age.*) –1610. **2. To do,** the dative infin., after the verb *to be*, also after a *sb.* = Proper or necessary to be done, hence, †the thing to be done. *What's to do?* What is the matter? ME. Hence, as a *subst. phr.* = ADO *sb.*, business, fuss 1570. *To have to do*, to have business, or concern. *To have to do with*: to have business or dealings with. **3. Doing,** the pres. pple. = in action, at work, busy ME. **b.** *To be doing* ME. *Nothing doing*: nothing going on; no prospect of business or success. **4. Done,** the pa. pple., is used *esp.* in the sense 'finished'; hence, in dating an official document, in accepting a wager, etc. 1596.

V. With prepositions.

†**1. D. after** —. To act in obedience to or compliance with. **2. D. by** —. To act towards or in respect of: see BY *prep.* **3. D. for** —. To act for or in behalf of; to attend to (now *colloq.*); to ruin, destroy, wear out entirely (*colloq.*). **4. D. to** —, **unto** —. To behave to; to treat. **5. D. with** —. To deal with; to manage with. **6. D. without** —. To d. one's business without; to dispense with.

VI. With adverbs. (Chiefly *trans.* with *passive.*)

1. D. away. †To put away, dismiss; to put an end to, destroy; also, later, *d. away with* (intr.), in same sense. **2. D. in.** To bring disaster upon, to kill (*slang*). **3. D. off.** To put off; to DOFF (*arch.*); to sketch, hit off. **4. D. on.** = DON *v.* (*arch.*). **5. D. out.** †To put out; to clean out; *to d.* (any one) *out of*: to deprive of, *esp.* by sharp practice. **6. D. over.** To overlay, cover, coat. **7. D. up.** To raise; *refl.* to arise; to repair, restore; to wrap up (a parcel); to disable, tire out (chiefly in *pa. pple.*); to ruin financially (*colloq.*). †**8. D. way** (in imperative): to put away; *absol.* to cease. †**9. D. withal.** *intr.* To d. to the contrary; to help it. (In neg. and interrog. sentences.)

Do (dū), *sb.*[1] 1599. [f. DO *v.*] †**1.** Stir, fuss, ADO –1708. (Common in XVII.) **2.** The action of doing or that which is done; deed, action, business. Now *rare* or *arch.* 1631. **b.** *colloq.* A performance, entertainment, jollification 1828. **3.** A cheat, swindle, imposture 1835. ¶See also DERRING-DO.

Do (dōu), *sb.*[2] 1754. [It. (XVII).] *Mus.* The syllable now commonly used in solmization instead of UT, to denote the first note (key-note) of the scale (*movable Do*); or in some cases the note C, the key-note of the 'natural scale' (*fixed Do*). (In *Tonic Sol-fa* commonly *doh.*)

Do., abbrev. of DITTO.

‖**Doab, duab** (dōu·āb, dū·āb). 1803. [– Hind. – Pers. *dō-āb*, i.e. *dō* two + *āb* water.] The tongue or tract of land between two confluent rivers.

The Doab, Entre Rios, or Mesopotamia, bounded by the rivers Obi and Irtish LATHAM.

Doable (dū·ăb'l), *a.* 1449. [f. DO *v.* + -ABLE.] Capable of being done.

Do-all (dū·ǫl). 1633. [f. DO *v.* + ALL.] A factotum.

Dunstan was the Doe-all at Court, being the Kings Treasurer, Chancellour, Counsellour, Confessour, all things FULLER.

Doand, obs. f. *doing*, pr. pple. of DO *v.*

Doat, -er, -ing, etc.; see DOTE *v.*, etc.

Dobber (dǫ·bəɹ). *U.S. local.* 1809. [– Du. *dobber* float, cork.] The float of an angler's fishing-line.

Dobbin (dǫ·bin). 1596. [The proper name *Dobbin* (dim. of *Dob*, altered forms of *Robin, Rob*) as a pet name.] **1.** An ordinary draught horse; *contempt.*, a jade. **2.** [perh. a distinct word.] A small drinking-vessel 1792.

Dobby, dobbie (dǫ·bi). 1691. [perh. playful application of proper name *Dobbie* (f. as prec.).] **1.** A silly old man, a dotard (*dial.*). **2.** A household sprite or apparition; a brownie (*dial.*) 1811. **3.** *Weaving.* A small Jacquard attachment to a loom for weaving small figures 1878.

Dobchick(in, obs. ff. DABCHICK.

‖**Do·bla.** Now *Hist.* 1829. [Sp.] An obs. Sp. gold coin.

Dobson (dǫ·bsən). *U.S.* 1889. An angler's name for the larva of *Corydalus cornutus*.

Do·bule. 1864. [– mod.L. *Dobula* (Gesner).] *Ichthyol.* A N.Amer. species of dace.

Docent (dōu·sĕnt). 1639. [– *docent-*, pr. ppl. stem of L. *docēre* teach. See -ENT.]

A. *adj.* Teaching.

B. *sb.* In some American universities, etc., a recognized teacher not on the salaried staff 1880.

‖**Docetæ** (dosī·tī), *sb. pl.* 1818. [med.L. – Gr. Δοκηταί, f. δοκεῖν seem, appear.] *Eccl. Hist.* A sect of heretics, who held that Christ's body was either a phantom, or of celestial substance. Hence **Doce·tic** *a.* of or pertaining to the D. **Doce·tism,** the doctrine or views of the D. **Doce·tist. Doceti·stic** *a.*

Dochmiac (dǫ·kmiæ̆k). 1775. [– late L. *dochmiacus* – Gr. δοχμιακός, f. synon. δόχμιος oblique.] *Gr. Pros.*

A. *adj.* Of the nature of a *dochmius*; composed of *dochmii*, i.e. of pentasyllabic feet of which the typical form is ∪ — — ∪ —.

B. *sb.* A foot or verse of this description.

Docible (dǫ·sib'l), *a.* ? *Obs.* 1549. [– Fr. †*docible* or late L. *docibilis*, f. *docēre* teach; see -IBLE.] **1.** Apt to be taught or trained; teachable; tractable. **2.** Capable of being imparted by teaching 1659.

1. Their tenderest and most d. age MILT. Hence **Docibi·lity** (?*Obs.*), **Do·cibleness** (?*Obs.*), capacity or aptness for being taught; teachableness.

Docile (dōu·səil, dǫ·sil), *a.* 1483. [– L. *docilis*, f. *docēre* teach; see -ILE. Cf. Fr. *docile* (XVI).] **1.** Apt to be taught or trained; teachable; tractable. **2.** *transf.* of things: Yielding readily to treatment; tractable 1795.

1. The d. mind may soone thy precepts know B. JONS. **2.** The d. wax 1881, ores 1884. Hence **Do·cilely** *adv.*

Docility (dosi·lĭti). 1560. [– L. *docilitas*, f. *docilis*; see prec., -ITY. Cf. Fr. *docilité* (XV).] Docile quality; aptness to be taught; amenability to training or treatment; tractability, obedience.

The elephant..whose d. is exhibited unto us in the theaters P. HOLLAND.

Docimasy (dǫ·simăsi). 1802. [– Gr. δοκιμασία, f. δοκιμάζειν examine. Cf. Fr. *docimasie.*] **1.** *Gr. Antiq.* A judicial inquiry (*esp.* at Athens) into the character and antecedents of aspirants for public office or citizenship. **2.** The art or practice of assaying metallic ores 1802. **3.** The art of ascertaining the properties and purity of drugs; also of ascertaining certain physiological facts. Hence **Docima·stic** *a.* of or pertaining to d., *esp.* to the assay of metals; proving by experimental tests.

Docimology (dǫsimǫ·lŏdʒi). 1847. [f. Gr. δόκιμος examined, tested + -LOGY.] A treatise on the art of assaying metals, etc.; see prec.

Do·city. *dial.* 1682. [Supposed to be alt. f. *docility.*] Docility; gumption.

Dock (dǫk), *sb.*[1] [OE. *docce*, corresp. to MDu. *docke-blaederen* (whence G. *dockenblätter*), ODa. *ådokke* (= OE. *ēadocce* water-dock).] The common name of various species of the genus *Rumex* (N.O. *Polygonaceæ*), coarse weedy herbs with thickened rootstock, sheathing stipules, and panicled racemes of inconspicuous greenish flowers. Without qualifying word usually the common dock (*R. obtusifolius*). **Yellow Dock** is *R. crispus*. Also applied to other coarse plants of similar habit.

Phr. *In d., out nettle*, orig. a charm uttered to aid the cure of nettle-stings: †hence, a proverbial expression for changeableness. *Comb.* **d.-cress,** nipplewort.

Dock (dǫk), *sb.*[2] ME. [perh. identical with OE. *docca* (or *-e*) in *fingerdoccan* finger-muscles, and corresp. to Fris. *dok* bunch, ball (of twine, etc.), (M)LG. *dokke* bundle of straw, OHG. *tocka* (south G. *docke*) doll.] **1.** The solid fleshy part of an animal's tail. **2.** A piece of leather harness covering the clipped tail of a horse; also, the crupper of a saddle or harness ME. **3.** A cut end of anything, *e.g.* of hair, (?) of a tree-trunk. Now *dial.* 1573. †**4.** [f. DOCK *v.*[1]] The act of docking –1751.

Dock (dǫk), *sb.*[3] 1513. [– MLG., MDu. *docke* (mod. *dok*), of unkn. origin.] †**1.** The bed (in the sand or ooze) in which a ship lies dry at low water –1633. †**2.** An artificial inlet, to admit a boat, etc. –1719. **3.** An artificial basin excavated, built round with masonry, and fitted with flood-gates, into which ships are received for repair, loading, etc. 1552. **4.** (Often *pl.*) A range of dock-basins (sense 3) together with the adjoining wharfs, warehouses and offices (*commercial docks*). **b.** A DOCKYARD (*naval docks*). 1703. **5.** *Railways.* An enclosure in a platform into which a single line of rails runs and terminates.

3. *Dry* or *graving d.*, a narrow basin into which a single vessel is received, and from which the water is then let out, leaving the vessel dry for repairing, etc. *Wet d.*, a large water-tight enclosure in which the water is maintained at the level of high tide, so that vessels remain constantly afloat in it. *Floating d.*, a large floating structure that can be used like a dry d. **4.** Cuttle lived.. near the India Docks DICKENS. *Comb.* **d.-warrant,** a warrant given to the owner of goods warehoused in a d.

Dock (dǫk), *sb.*[4] 1586. [prob. at first a word of rogues' cant and identical w. the word repr. by Flem. *dok* cage, fowl-pen, rabbit-hutch.] The enclosure in a criminal court in which the prisoner is placed at his trial.

attrib. **d. brief,** a brief undertaken by a barrister in court for a prisoner in the d. without means.

Dock (dǫk), *v.*[1] ME. [f. DOCK *sb.*[2]] **1.** *trans.* To cut short in some part, *esp.* in the tail, hair, or the like. **2.** *transf.* and *fig.* To cut short, curtail; to deprive *of* some part ME. **3.** To cut away, cut off; also = DAG *v.*[1] 3. ME.

1. His tope was doked lyk a preest biforn CHAUCER. His [a dog's] tail must then be docked JOHNSON. **2.** To d. wages by rent 1889. Phr. *To d. the entail* (Law): to cut off or put an end to the entail; also *fig.*

Dock (dǫk), *v.*[2] 1514. [f. DOCK *sb.*[3]] **1.** *trans.* To take, bring, or receive (a ship) into a dock (see DOCK *sb.*[3]). **2.** To furnish or lay out with docks 1757.

1. And see my wealthy Andrew dockt in sand *Merch. V.* I. i. 27.

Dockage (dǫ·kĕdʒ). 1708. [f. DOCK *sb.*[3] + -AGE.] Charges made for the use of docks; also, dock accommodation; the berthing of vessels in docks.

Docker (dǫ·kəɹ). 1762. [f. as prec. + -ER[1].] **1.** A dweller in or near a dock; *spec.* an inhabitant of Devonport. **2.** A labourer in the docks 1887.

Docket (dǫ·kĕt), *sb.* Also †**docquet(t.** 1483. [Of unkn. origin; perh. f. DOCK *v.*[2] + -ET; also spelt *dogget* (XV–XVII); cf. AL. *doggetum* (XV) docket, summary.] **1.** A brief, summarized statement; an abstract; a digest, minute. Now *Hist.* 1483. **2.** *spec.* The abstract of the contents of proposed Letters-patent, written upon the King's bill which authorized the preparation of such letters, and also copied into a Register or Docket-book 1552. **3.** *Law.* A memorandum or register of legal judgements 1668. **4.** *Law.* A list of causes for trial, or of names of persons having causes pending. Hence phr. *On the d.* (U.S.) 1790. **5.** An endorsement on a document, briefly indicating its contents or subject; a label; a written direction, a ticket 1706. **6.** A warrant from the Custom House on entering goods, certifying the payment of the duty 1712.

Phr. †*To strike a d.*: to issue a fiat in bankruptcy; to make a man a bankrupt.

Do·cket, *v.* 1615. [f. prec. sb.] †**1.** *trans.* To furnish with a docket –1833. **2.** *Law.* To make an abstract of (judgements, etc.) and enter them in a list or index 1692. **3.** To endorse (a letter, etc.) with a short note of its contents, writer, date, etc. 1750. Also *transf.* and *fig.*

3. Whatever letters and papers you keep, d. and tie them up in their respective classes CHESTERF.

Dockyard (dǫ·kˌyāɹd). 1704. [f. DOCK *sb.*[3] + YARD.] An enclosure in which ships are built and repaired, and all kinds of ships' stores are brought together; *esp.* a Government establishment of this character.

Docoglossate (dǫkoglǫ·sět), *a.* 1884. [f. mod. L. *Docoglossa* (f. Gr. δοκός balk, bar + γλῶσσα tongue) + -ATE[2].] *Zool.* Of or pertaining to the *Docoglossa*, a group of gastropod molluscs having transverse rows of beam-like teeth on the lingual ribbon.

Docquet(t, obs. f. DOCKET.

Doctor (dǫ·ktəɹ), *sb.* ME. [– OFr. *doctour* – L. *doctor* teacher, f. *doct-*, pa. ppl. stem of *docēre* teach.] **1.** A teacher, instructor; one who inculcates learning, opinions, or principles. (Const. *of.*) Now *rare.* **2.** One skilled in, and therefore competent to teach, any branch of knowledge; an eminently learned man (*arch.*) ME. Also †*transf.* **3.** *spec.* applied to: *The Doctors of the Church*, certain early 'fathers' distinguished by their eminent learning. **b.** The leading Schoolmen. ME. **4.** One who, in any faculty, has attained to the highest degree conferred by a University; a title originally implying competency to teach such subject, but now merely a certificate of the highest proficiency therein. (Now often conferred by Universities as an honorary compliment.) ME. **5.** Hence: A learned divine ME.; one learned in the law ME. **6.** *spec.* A doctor of medicine; *pop.* any medical practitioner ME. Also *fig.* **7.** *transf.* Any mechanical appliance for curing or removing defects, regulating, adjusting, or feeding 1796. **8.** A fish of the genus *Acanthurus*: also called *d.-fish, surgeon-fish* 1833. **9.** *Naut.* A ship's cook 1860. **10.** *Old slang.* A loaded die 1700.

1. These new Doctors of the rights of men BURKE. **2.** Who shall decide, when Doctors disagree POPE. **6.** So liv'd our Sires, ere doctors learn'd to kill DRYDEN. **7.** (*Calico-printing.*) The cleaning-d., which wipes clean the surface of the roller 1874. The superfluous colour is.. wiped off by the colour doctors 1875.

Doctor (dǫ·ktəɹ), *v. colloq.* 1599. [f. prec. sb.; in sense 1 – med. (scholastic) L. *doctorare*, 'doctorem facere'. So OFr. *doctorer.*] **1.** *trans.* To confer the degree of Doctor upon; to make a Doctor. **2.** To treat, as a doctor; to administer medicine or treatment to 1737; also *transf.* **3.** *fig.* To tamper with, adulterate, sophisticate 1774. **4.** *intr.* To practise as a physician 1865.

2. Brodie..sent me off to d. myself 1832. **3.** To d. wines 1820, dice DE QUINCEY, narratives 1866. Hence **Do·ctoral, Docto·rial** *adjs.* of or belonging to a d.; †holding the position of a d. **Do·ctorally** *adv.* **Do·ctorly** *a.* like or befitting a d.

Doctorate (dǫ·ktǒrět), *sb.* 1676. [– med.L. *doctoratus*, f. L. *doctor* + *-atus* -ATE[1].] The degree of doctor.

Doctorate (dǫ·ktǒreᶦt), *v.* Now *rare.* 1611. [– *doctorat-*, pa. ppl. stem of med.L. *doctorare*, f. L. *doctor*; see DOCTOR *sb.*, -ATE[3].] *trans.* To confer the degree of Doctor upon; also *absol.*

Doctoress; see DOCTRESS.

Do·ctorize, *v. rare.* 1600. [f. DOCTOR *sb.* + -IZE.] To confer the degree of Doctor upon; to doctor. Hence **Doctoriza·tion.** (Dicts.)

Doctors' Commons. 1680. [See COMMONS.] The common table of the Association or College of Doctors of Civil Law in London; hence, the buildings occupied by these as an incorporated Society; and now the name of the site of these, to the south of St. Paul's Cathedral.

Literary references to Doctors' Commons in later times usually refer to the registration, etc. of wills, to marriage licences, or to divorce proceedings.

Doctorship (dǫ·ktəɹʃip). 1586. [-SHIP.] **1.** = DOCTORATE *sb.* **2.** The position, character, or function of a DOCTOR 1598.

Doctress (dǫ·ktrės), **doctoress** (dǫ·ktǒrės). 1549. [f. DOCTOR *sb.* + -ESS[1], after Fr. †*doctoresse.*] **1.** A female doctor. (Now only when sex is emphasized.) **2.** *joc.* A doctor's wife or daughter 1748.

†**Do·ctrinable,** *a.* [– OFr. *doctrinable* or med.L. *doctrinabilis*, f. *doctrinare* teach; see -ABLE.] Fit for instruction; instructive. SIDNEY.

Doctrinaire (dǫktrinēᵊ·ɹ). 1820. [– Fr. *doctrinaire*, f. *doctrine* DOCTRINE + *-aire* -ARY[1].]

A. *sb.* **1.** *Fr. Hist.* One of a constitutionalist party which arose in France soon after 1815, having for their object to reconcile authority and liberty, royalty and national representation. **2.** Hence, One who tries to apply some doctrine without sufficient regard to practical considerations; a pedantic theorist. (Often used as a term of reproach by practical men.) 1831.

B. *adj.* Pertaining to, or of the character of, a doctrinaire; merely theoretical or speculative 1834. Hence **Do:ctrinai·rism,** the principles or practice of a d.

Doctrinal (dǫ·ktrinăl, dǫktrəi·năl), *a.* and *sb.* 1450. [As adj. – late L. *doctrinalis*; as sb., after OFr. *doctrinal*, med.L. *doctrinale* (subst. use of n. of the adj.); see DOCTRINE, -AL[1].]

A. *adj.* **1.** Of or pertaining to doctrine; containing doctrine. †**2.** Serving to teach or instruct –1641.

1. He had some d. opinions which they liked not CLARENDON. **2.** In the nature of a doctrinall instrument HOOKER.

B. *sb.* †**1.** The title of a text-book on grammar by Alex. de Villedieu; hence, any text-book –1653. **2.** *pl.* Matters of doctrine or instruction 1619.

Hence **Doctrinally** *adv.* in a d. manner; by way of, or in respect of, teaching.

Doctrinarian (dǫktrinēᵊ·riăn). 1747. [– mod.L. **doctrinarius*, f. med.L. *doctrinare* teach; see -ARY[1], -ARIAN.] **a.** *sb.* = DOCTRINAIRE *sb.* **b.** *adj.* = DOCTRINAIRE *a.* Hence **Doctrina·rianism,** doctrinairism.

Do·ctrinate, *v. arch.* 1631. [– *doctrinat-*, pa. ppl. stem of med.L. *doctrinare* instruct, f. *doctrina* DOCTRINE; see -ATE[3].] *trans.* To teach or instruct; *absol.* to give instruction *on.*

Doctrine (dǫ·ktrin), *sb.* ME. [– (O) Fr. *doctrine* – L. *doctrina* teaching, learning, f. *doctor*; see DOCTOR *sb.*, -INE[4].] †**1.** The action of teaching or instructing; a lesson, a precept –1710. **2.** That which is taught. **a.** A body of instruction or teaching ME. **b.** *esp.* That which is laid down as true concerning a particular department of knowledge, as religion, politics, science, etc.; a belief, theoretical opinion; a dogma ME. **3.** A body or system of principles; a theory; a science, or department of knowledge. ? *Obs.* 1594. †**4.** Erudition –1601. †**5.** Discipline (*rare*) –1533.

1. He..said unto them in his d., Hearken *Mark* 4:2. **2.** The d. of the equality of all men BURKE. *Monroe d.* (U.S. politics): the principles of policy put forward in the Message of President Monroe to Congress, 2 Dec. 1823, the effect of which is that the United States will regard as an unfriendly act any attempt by any European Power to interfere with for the purpose of controlling, or to plant new colonies in, any part of the American continent. **3.** The d. of comets CHATHAM. **4.** *All's Well* I. iii. 247. Hence **Do·ctrinism,** adherence to, or setting forth of, d. So **Do·ctrinist,** one who does this.

Document (dǫ·kiumĕnt), *sb.* 1450. [–(O)Fr. *document* – L. *documentum* lesson, proof, etc., in med.L., written instrument, official paper, f. *docēre* teach; see -MENT.] †**1.** Teaching, instruction, warning –1793. †**2.** A lesson; an admonition, a warning –1800. †**3.** That which serves to show or prove something; evidence, proof –1847. **4.** Something written, inscribed, etc., which furnishes evidence or information upon any subject, as a manuscript, title-deed, coin, etc. 1727.

2. Even bad pictures supply him with useful documents SIR J. REYNOLDS. **3.** A d. of Fortunes instabilitie RALEGH. **4.** These frescoes..have become invaluable as documents MRS. JAMESON. Hence **Do:cume·ntal** *a.*

Do·cument, *v.* 1648. [f. prec. sb.] †**1.** *trans.* To teach, instruct –1739; to give a lesson to –1802. **2.** To furnish with documents; to provide (a ship) with the papers required to manifest its ownership and cargo 1807.

1. I am finely documented by my own daughter DRYDEN.

Documentary (dǫ:kiume·ntări), *a.* 1802. [f. DOCUMENT *sb.* + -ARY[1].] **1.** Of the nature of or consisting in documents. **2.** Evidential (*rare*). CARLYLE. **3.** Relating to teaching (*rare*) 1871.

1. Fragments of Letters and other d. scraps CARLYLE.

Documentation (dǫ:kiumentēᶦ·ʃən). 1754. [f. DOCUMENT *v.* + -ATION.] † **1.** Admonition, 'lecturing' –1844. **2.** The furnishing of a ship with papers 1844. **3.** Use of documentary evidence and authorities 1888.

†**Do·cumentize,** *v.* 1599. [f. DOCUMENT *sb.* + -IZE.] *trans.* To teach, give a lesson to; also, to furnish with evidence –1754.

Dod, *sb.*[1] and *interj. dial.* 1676. Orig. a deformation of *God.*

Dod (dǫd), *sb.*[2] *dial.* 1661. [cogn. w. Du. *dodde* in same sense.] The Reed-Mace or Cat's-tail, *Typha latifolia.*

Dod, dodd, *sb.*[3] *n. dial.* 1878. [rel. to DOD *v.*[1]] A rounded summit or eminence.

Dod (dǫd), *v.*[1] Now *dial.* [ME. *dodden*, from same root as DOD *sb.*[3] Cf. DODDY.] To make the top or head of (anything) blunt, rounded, or bare; hence, to clip, poll, lop, etc.

Dod, *v.*[2] Now *dial.* 1661. [var. of Sc. and n. dial. *dad* in same sense.] *trans.* To beat, knock.

†**Do·ddard.** *rare.* [app. f. DOD *v.*[1] + -ARD; cf. *pollard.*] A tree that has lost its head of branches by decay. Also *attrib.* DRYDEN.

Do·dded, *ppl. a. n. dial.* ME. [f. DOD *v.*[1] + -ED[1].] Polled, lopped; hornless; awnless.

Dodder (dǫ·dəɹ), *sb.* [ME. *doder*, corresp. to MLG. *dod(d)er*, MHG. *toter* (G. *dotter*).] **1.** The common name of the genus *Cuscuta*, N.O. *Convolvulaceæ*, comprising slender leafless plants, like masses of twining threads, parasitic on flax, clover, thyme, furze, etc. **2.** = DOD *sb.*[2] *dial.*

Dodder (dǫ·dəɹ), *v.* 1617. [var. of or parallel form to dial. †*dadder.*] **1.** *intr.* To tremble or shake from frailty. **2.** To move unsteadily, totter 1819. **Do·dderer. Do·ddering** *vbl. sb.* and *ppl. a.*; **Do·ddering-grass,** quaking-grass. **Do·ddery** *a.*

Doddered (dǫ·dəɹd), *ppl. a.* 1697. [app. orig. a deriv. of DOD *v.*[1]; cf. DODDARD.] **1.** Having lost the top or branches, *esp.* through age or decay; hence, remaining as a decayed stump: a conventional epithet of old oaks. Johnson's erroneous explanation 'Overgrown with dodder', has added, in lit. usage, a vague notion of some kind of parasitical accretion accompanying decay. **2.** *dial.* Shattered, infirm 1847.

1. Sere-wood, and firs, and d. oaks DRYDEN.

Doddle (dǫ·d'l), *v.* 1653. [var. of DADDLE *v.*; cf. also DODDER *v.*, and with sense 2 TODDLE *v.*] †**1.** *trans.* To shake, nod (the head). **2.** *intr.* To toddle; to totter; to dawdle 1761.

Doddy, doddie (dǫ·di), *sb. Sc.* 1808. [f. DOD *v.*[1]] A cow or bull without horns; *attrib.* = DODDED.

†**Doddypoll** (dǫ·dipōᵘl). ME. [app. f. DOTE *v.*, referred to DOD *v.*[1]; cf. *roundhead.*] A stupid person; blockhead, fool –1767.

Dodeca-, dodec-, Gr. δώδεκα twelve, a comb. form, as in:

Dode·cadrachm [Gr. δραχμή], an ancient Greek coin worth 12 drachmas. **Dode·cagon** [Gr. -γωνος, γωνία], *Geom.* a plane figure having twelve sides and twelve angles. ‖**Do:decagy·nia** [Gr. γυνή], *Bot.* a Linnæan order of plants having either eleven or twelve pistils; hence, **Dode·cagyn,** a plant of this order; **Dodecagy·nian, -gy·nious, Dodeca·gynous** *adjs.* **Dodecahe·dral** *a.* [see next], having the form of a dodecahedron; twelve-sided. **Do:decahe·dron** [Gr. ἕδρα], *Geom.* a solid figure having twelve faces. **Dodeca·merous** *a.* [Gr. μέρος], consisting of twelve parts or divisions. ‖**Dodeca·ndria** [Gr. ἀνδρ-, ἀνήρ], *Bot.* the eleventh class in the Linnæan system, comprising plants having from twelve to nineteen stamens, not cohering; hence, **Dodeca·nder,** one of the *Dodecandria*; **Dodeca·ndrian** *a.*, belonging to that class; **Dodeca·ndrous** *a.*, having twelve stamens. **Do·decane,** *Chem.* a paraffin of the composition $C_{12}H_{26}$. **Do:decape·talous** *a.*, *Bot.* having twelve petals. **Do·decarchy** [Gr. -αρχία], government by twelve; a ruling body of twelve. **Do:decase·mic** *a.* [Gr. -σημος, σῆμα], *Pros.* consisting of twelve units of time, as a *d. foot.* **Do·decastyle** [Gr. στῦλος], a portico or colonnade of twelve columns. **Do:decasy·llable,** *Pros.* a line or word of twelve syllables; hence, **Do:decasylla·bic** *a.*, of or containing twelve syllables.

†**Dodecate·mory.** 1603. [– Gr. δωδεκατημόριον, f. δωδέκατον twelfth + μόριον portion.] *Astron.* A twelfth part; applied chiefly to each of the twelve divisions of the Zodiac –1751.

Dode·cuplet. 1880. [f. DODEC(A- + ending of *octuplet*; see OCTUPLE.] *Mus.* 'A group of twelve notes to be played in the time of eight' (Stainer and Barrett).

Dodge (dǫdʒ), *v.* 1568. [Of unkn. origin.] **1.** *intr.* To move to and fro, or backwards and forwards; to shuffle 1704; †to use shifts (*with* a person, etc.) so as to baffle or catch him –1816. †**2.** *intr.* To be off and on in one's speech and action; to parley, palter, haggle –1763. **3.** *trans.* To play fast and loose with; to baffle by shifts; to trifle with 1573. **4.** To avoid or elude by changes of position, shifts, etc. 1680. **5.** To follow stealthily 1727. **6.** *trans.* and *intr.* (*dial.*) To jog 1802.

1. The King..had been dodging with Essex eight or ten days DE FOE. Dodging behind the mizzen mast 1756. **2.** With Fate's lean tipstaff none can d. PRIOR. **3.** He dodged me with a long and loose account TENNYSON. **5.** I will d. your steps 1840. Hence **Do·dgy** *a.* evasive, tricky, artful. **Do·dgily** *adv.* **Do·dginess.**

Dodge (dǫdʒ), *sb.* 1575. [f. prec. vb.] **1.** The act of slipping aside and eluding; the slip, the go-by. Now *dial.* **2.** A shifty trick 1638. **3.** *colloq.* and *slang.* A clever expedient or contrivance (cf. *trick*); vulgarly extended to a machine, a natural phenomenon, etc. 1842.

2. 'It was all false, of course?' 'All, sir,' replied Mr. Weller, 'reg'lar do, sir; artful d.' DICKENS. **3.** The alternation of green and corn crops is a good d. 1842.

Dodger (dǫ·dʒəɹ). 1568. [f. DODGE *v.* + -ER[1].] **1.** One who dodges; in early use, *esp.* a haggler; later, *esp.* one who practises artful dodges. **2.** *U.S.* A hard-baked corn-cake 1852. **3.** *U.S.* A small handbill 1884. So **Do·dgery,** trickery.

†**Dodipole,** var. DODDYPOLL.

Dodkin (dǫ·dkin). [Late ME. *doydekin, doykyn* – MDu. *doytkin*, dim. of *duit, deuyt*; see DOIT.] = DOIT, q.v. Hence, any small coin. Now *Hist.*

Do·dman. Now *dial.* 1550. [Of unkn. origin.] A snail; called also *hodman-dod.*

Dodo (dōᵘ·do). 1628. [– Pg. *doudo* simpleton, fool.] An extinct bird, *Didus ineptus*, of the order *Columbidæ*, formerly inhabiting Mauritius; it had a massive clumsy body, and small wings, useless for flight.

Dodonæan, -ean (dōᵘdonī·ăn), *a.* 1569. [– L. *Dodonæus* – Gr. Δωδωναῖος – Δωδώνη Dodona; see -EAN.] Of or pertaining to Dodona in ancient Epirus, or its oracle of Zeus situated in a grove of oaks. Also †**Dodo·nian.**

†**Dodra·ntal,** *a. rare.* 1656. [– L. *dodrantalis*, f. *dodrans, -ant-* nine-twelfths of a weight or measure; see -AL[1].] 'Of nine ounces or nine inches in length or weight' (Blount).

Doe (dōᵘ). [OE. *dā*, of unkn. origin.] **1.** The female of the fallow deer; also, of allied animals, as the reindeer. **2.** The female of the hare or rabbit 1607. Also *attrib.*, as *d.-buck*, a male deer.

Doe, obs. f. DO, DOUGH.

Doer (dū·əɹ). ME. [f. DO *v.* + -ER[1].] **1.** One who performs some act or deed. **2.** One who acts for another; an agent; a factor; an attorney. Now only *Sc.* 1465. **3.** An animal or plant that does or thrives (well or ill) 1865.

1. Talkers are no good dooers *Rich. III*, I. iii. 352.

Does, 3rd pers. sing. pres. ind. of DO *v.*

Doeskin (dōᵘ·skin). 1456. [f. DOE + SKIN.] **1.** The skin of a doe; also, a kind of leather made from this. **2.** A closely-cut thick black cloth, twilled, but dressed so as to show little of the twill. (Cf. BUCKSKIN.) 1851.

Doest (dū·ėst), 2nd pers. sing. pres. ind. of Do *v.*

Doff (dǫf), *v.* Pa. t. and pple. **doffed** (dǫft). ME. [Fused form of *do off.* In XIX freq. in lit. use.] **1.** *trans.* To put off or take off, as clothing, the hat, etc. Also †*intr.* with *with. absol.* To raise one's hat (*rare*). **2.** *refl.* To undress oneself. Also *fig.* Now only *dial.* 1697. **3.** *transf.* and *fig.* To put off, lay aside; hence, to get rid of 1592. †**4.** To put (any one) *off* (with an excuse, etc.); to turn aside –1659.

1. Thou weare a Lyons hide! d. it for shame *John* III. i. 128. **3.** He sometimes d'offeth his owne nature and puts on theirs B. JONS. **4.** *Oth.* IV. ii. 176 (Qo. 1).

Doffer (dǫ·fəɹ). 1825. [f. prec. + -ER[1].] One who or that which doffs. **1.** In a carding machine, a comb or revolving cylinder which strips off cotton or wool from the cards; a *doffing-cylinder.* **2.** A worker who removes the full bobbins or spindles 1862.

Dog (dǫg), *sb.* [Late OE. *docga* (once in a gloss); previous history unkn. Introduced into continental langs. usually, in early instances, with the attribute 'English'. In Gmc. langs., the generic name was *hund*; see HOUND.] **1.** A quadruped of the genus *Canis*, of which wild species are found in various parts of the world, and numerous breeds, varying greatly in size, shape, and colour, occur in a more or less domesticated state in almost all countries. These are referred by zoologists to a species *C. familiaris*; but their common origin is disputed. **b.** *esp.* A dog used for hunting; a hound ME. **c.** *fig.* ME. **d.** With qualifications, as BANDOG, BULL-DOG, CUR-*dog*, etc., q.v. ME. **2.** The male of this species; opp. to BITCH. Also, a male fox. 1577. **3.** Of a person: **a.** in contempt: A worthless, surly, or cowardly fellow. (Cf. CUR.) ME. **b.** playfully: A gallant; a fellow, chap. Usu. with *adj.*, as *sad, sly*, etc. 1618. **c.** = BULL-DOG 2. 1847. **4.** *Astron.* The name of two constellations, the Great and Little D. (*Canis Major* and *Minor*); see DOG-STAR 1551. **5.** Short for DOG-FISH 1674. **6.** A name for various mechanical devices used for gripping or holding, such as:

a. A grappling-iron for raising the monkey of a pile-driver, or clutching and withdrawing tools used in well-boring or mining. **b.** A grappling-iron with a fang which clutches an object, as a log, etc. to be hoisted, or to be secured in position for sawing. **c.** A projection or tooth acting as a detent, *e.g.* in a lock; a catch or click which engages the teeth of a ratchet-wheel. **d.** An adjustable stop placed in a machine to change direction of motion (Webster).

7. One of a pair of irons for supporting burning wood in a fireplace; a *fire-d.*; = ANDIRON; also, a rest for the fire-irons 1596. **8.** *attrib.*, etc. = canine 1565; = male 1555; = bastard, as *d.-Latin* 1611; with certain adjs. = As..as a d. (cf. DOG-CHEAP) 1552.

1. *fig.* Cæsars Spirit..Shall..Cry hauocke, and let slip the Dogges of Warre *Jul. C.* III. i. 273. **3.** You spurn'd me such a day; another time You cald me d. *Merch. V.* I. iii. 129. I was an unfortunate d. DE FOE.

Phrases, etc. *To the dogs*; to destruction or ruin; as in *to go, send, throw to the dogs. Fight d., fight bear*: *i.e.* till one be overcome. *A hair of the d. that bit you*: formerly thought a specific for the bite of a mad d.; hence allusively, *esp.* of more drink to take off the effects of drunkenness. *To lead a dog's life*: *i.e.* a life of misery, or of miserable subserviency. *Whose d. is dead?* What's the matter? Also in many other proverbs and phrases.

Comb.: **a.** †**d.-ape,** a d.-faced baboon, CYNOCEPHALUS; **-belt,** in *Coal-mining*, a belt worn round the waist, used for drawing sledges, etc. in the workings; †**-chance** = *dog-throw*; **-grate,** a detached fire-grate standing in a fireplace upon supports called dogs; **-iron** = sense 7; **-nap,** a short nap taken while sitting; **-power,** the mechanical power exerted by a d., as in turning a spit, etc.; †**-spasm** = CYNIC spasm; **-stopper** *Naut.*, a strong rope clenched round the mainmast, and used to relieve the deck-stopper when the ship rides in a heavy sea (Smyth); **-stove** = *dog-grate*; **-tent,** a small tent, having a resemblance to a dog's kennel; **-throw,** the lowest throw at dice (L. *canis, canicula*); **-town** (*U.S.*), a colony of prairie dogs.

b. *Comb.* with *dog's*: **Dog's body,** a sailor's name for dried pease boiled in a cloth; †**dog's face,** a term of abuse; **dog's sleep, trick,** see DOG-SLEEP, -TRICK.

c. In names of animals (*a*) resembling dogs in some respect, or (*b*) infesting dogs: as **d.-badger,** 'one resembling the d. in his feet'; **-bat,** one having a head like a dog's; **-flea,** a species of flea (*Pulex serraticeps*) infesting dogs; **-guts,** the fish *Harpodon nehereus*, also called BUMMALO; **-louse,** a kind of louse infesting dogs; also = *dog-tick*; **-tick,** a tick of the genus *Ixodes* infesting dogs.

d. In names of plants (frequently denoting a worthless sort, or one unfit for human food): as **d.-blow,** in Nova Scotia, the Ox-eye daisy; **dog('s) cabbage,** *Thelygonum cynocrambe*, a succulent herb of the Mediterranean; **d.-daisy,** the common Daisy, *Bellis perennis*; also, locally, and in books, the Ox-eye Daisy; **-lichen,** *Peltidea canina*, formerly used as a cure for hydrophobia; **dog('s)-parsley,** *Æthusa cynapium*, also called Fool's Parsley; **dog('s)-wheat,** *Triticum caninum* = DOG-GRASS.

Dog (dǫg), *v.* Pa. t. and pple. **dogged** (dǫgd). 1519. [f. prec. sb.] **1.** *trans.* To follow like a dog; to follow pertinaciously or closely; to pursue, track. Also *fig.* **2.** *intr.* or *absol.* To follow close 1519. **3.** *trans.* To drive or chase with, or as with, a dog or dogs 1591. **4.** To fasten by means of a dog (see DOG *sb.* 6) 1591. **5.** *U.S. slang.* Used in imprecations. Cf. DOG-GONE. 1860.

1. The Bayliffs dog'd us hither to the very door WYCHERLEY. Famine dogs their footsteps SOUTHEY.

Dogal (dōᵘ·găl), *a.* 1848. [– It. *dogale.*] Of or pertaining to a doge.

‖**Dogana** (dogā·nă). 1645. [It.; see DOUANE.] A custom-house (in Italy); also, customs (in Italy and Spain).

‖**Dogare·ssa.** 1820. [It., irreg. fem. of *doge.*] The wife of a doge.

Dogate (dōᵘ·geⁱt). 1727. [– Fr. *dogat* – It. (Venetian) *dogato*, f. *doge*; see -ATE[1].] The office of a DOGE.

Dogbane; see DOG'S-BANE.

Dogberry[1] (dǫ·gberi). 1551. [DOG *sb.* 8 d.] The drupe of the Wild Cornel or DOGWOOD; the shrub itself. Also, in Nova Scotia, the mountain-ash.

Do·gberry[2]. The constable in *Much Ado about Nothing*; thence, allusively, an ignorant consequential official.

Dogbolt, dog-bolt (dǫ·gbōᵘlt). 1465. [Of unkn. origin.] †**1.** Some kind of bolt or blunt-headed arrow; ? one of little value that might be shot at any dog –1612. †**2.** A term of contempt; = 'mean wretch' –1690. **3.** The bolt of the cap-square over the trunnion of a gun 1867.

Dog-bramble. Also **dog's-.** 1567. [DOG *sb.* 8 d.] A name for various thorny shrubs; *esp.* a kind of currant, *Ribes cynosbati.*

†**Dog-brier.** 1530. [tr. L. *sentis canis*, Gr. κυνόσβατος.] The wild brier –1682.

Dog-cart. 1668. **1.** A small cart drawn by dogs. **2.** A cart with a box under the seat for sportsmen's dogs; now, an open vehicle, with two transverse seats back to back, the hinder of these originally made to shut up so as to form a box for dogs.

Dog-cheap, *adv.* and *pred. a. arch.* 1526. [See DOG 8.] Extremely cheap; also *fig.*

Dog-days, *sb. pl.* 1538. [tr. L. *dies caniculares*; see CANICULAR.] **1.** The days about the time of the heliacal rising of the Dog-star; noted as the hottest and most unwholesome period of the year. Rarely in *sing.*

Variously calculated, as depending on the greater dog-star (Sirius) or the lesser (Procyon); and on the heliacal, or the cosmical rising of either of these (both of which also differ in different latitudes); and their duration has been variously reckoned at from 30 to 54 days. In the latitude of Greenwich, the cosmical rising of Procyon now takes place about July 27, that of Sirius about Aug. 11. The heliacal rising is some days later. In current almanacs the dog-days begin July 3, and end Aug. 11.

2. *fig.* A time in which malignant influences prevail 1555. Also *attrib.*, **dog-day.**

†**Dog-draw.** 1598. *Forest Law.* The act of drawing after or tracking venison illegally killed or wounded, by the scent of a dog led with the hand –1708.

‖**Doge** (dōᵘdʒ). 1549. [– Fr. *doge* – It. *doge* – Venetian *doze* :– L. *ducem*, nom. *dux.*] The chief magistrate in the republics of Venice and Genoa. Also *transf.* and *fig.* Hence **Do·geless** *a.* without a d.

Dog-ear, var. of DOG'S-EAR.

Dog-faced (dǫ·gfēⁱst), *a.* 1607. Having a face like a dog's.

Dog-fennel. Also **dog's-.** 1523. [From its smell, and fennel-like leaves.] Stinking Camomile, *Anthemis cotula.*

Do·g-fish, dogfish. 1475. [DOG *sb.* 8 c.] **1.** One of various small sharks of the families *Squalidæ* (*Spinacidæ*), *Galeorhinidæ* (*Carchariidæ*), and *Scylliidæ*, or these collectively; *esp.* the Large and Small Spotted Dogfish (*Scyllium catulus*, *S. canicula*), and in New England, the Picked Dogfish (*Squalus acanthias*). **b.** Applied also to the mud-fish (*Amia calva*); to the blackfish (*Dallia pectoralis*); and to the mud-puppy (*Necturus maculatus*). **2.** *fig.* Opprobriously of persons 1589.

Dog-fisher. The Otter. WALTON.

Dog-fly. ? ME. An English tr. of Gr. κυνάμυια; identified by some writers with British flies troublesome to dogs.

Dog-fox. 1576. **1.** A male fox (see DOG *sb.* 2). **2.** Applied also to certain small burrowing animals of the genus *Canidæ*, as the CORSAC.

Dogged (dǫ·gėd), *a.* (*adv.*) ME. [f. DOG *sb.* + -ED²; cf. CRABBED.] **1.** *gen.* Like a dog. **b.** Of or pertaining to a dog, canine. Now *rare*. **2.** Currish; cruel; surly; sullenly obstinate. Also †*transf.* of things. ME. **3.** Obstinate, stubborn; pertinacious. (The current use.) 1779.

1. Now..Doth d. warre bristle his angry crest, And snarleth in the gentle eyes of peace *John* IV. iii. 149. 2. My wife in a d. humour for my not dining at home PEPYS. 3. A d. veracity JOHNSON. Hence **Do·gged-ly** *adv.*, **-ness.**

Dogger[1] (dǫ·gəɹ). ME. [– MDu. *dogger* trawler, fishing-boat (Du. *dogger* cod-fisher).] **1.** A two-masted fishing vessel with bluff bows, used in the North Sea deep-sea fisheries. **2.** Short for *Dogger Bank* 1887. *Comb.*: **D. Bank,** name of a shoal in the North Sea; **d.-man,** one of the crew of a d.

Dogger[2] (dǫ·gəɹ). 1670. [perh. a deriv. of DOG.] **1.** *dial.* A kind of ironstone found in nodules. **2.** *Geol.* A sandy ironstone of the Lower Oolite; applied to part of the Jurassic series 1822.

Doggerel (dǫ·gərĕl), **doggrel** (dǫ·grĕl). ME. [In earliest use adj. in *rym dogerel*, presumably f. DOG (with contemptuous implication as in *dog Latin*, †*dog rime* XVII) + *-erel*; see -REL.]

A. *adj.* An epithet applied to burlesque verse of irregular rhythm; or to mean, trivial, or undignified verse. *transf.* Bastard, burlesque.

This may wel be Rym dogerel quod he CHAUCER.

B. *sb.* Doggerel verse 1630; a piece of doggerel 1857.

He has a happy talent at d. ADDISON. A d. always had a curious fascination for him [Browning] 1892.

Doggery (dǫ·gəri). 1611. [f. DOG *sb.* + -ERY.] †**1.** Obscene language. **2.** Dog-like or mean behaviour 1844. **3.** Dogs collectively. Used by Carlyle as tr. Fr. *canaille*. 1843. **4.** *U.S.* (*vulgar*). A low drinking saloon 1860.

Dogget, obs. f. DOCKET.

Doggish (dǫ·giʃ), *a.* ME. [f. DOG *sb.* + -ISH¹.] **1.** Pertaining to or like a dog 1530. **2.** Currish; malicious; snappish. Now *rare*. ME. Hence **Do·ggish-ly** *adv.*, **-ness.**

Doggo (dǫ·go), *adv. slang.* 1893. [app. f. DOG + *-o* as in *billy-o*, *beano*, etc.] *To lie* (etc.) *d.*: to lie quiet, to remain hid.

Dog-gone (dǫ·ggǫn). *U.S. slang.* Also **dog on.** 1851. [app. development of earlier *dog on it* (etc.), of obscure origin, as euphem. substitute for *God damn it*. Cf. Sc. *dagone!* deuce take it!] **A.** *vb.* Used imperatively: 'hang!' **B.** *adj.* or *pa. pple.* = C. 1851. **C. Dog-goned** *adj.* or *pa. pple.* 'darned' 1860.

Dog-grass, dog's-grass. 1597. [DOG *sb.* 8 d.] A name for Couch-grass, *Triticum repens*, and for *T. caninum*; also, locally for *Cynosurus*.

Doggy, doggie (dǫ·gi), *sb.* 1825. [-Y⁶.] **1.** A little dog; a pet name for a dog. **2.** *Coal-mining* (*colloq.*) A man employed by the BUTTY (q.v.) as his underground manager.

Doggy (dǫ·gi), *a.* ME. [f. DOG *sb.* + -Y¹; cf. *horsy*.] †**1.** Malicious; vile –1583. **2.** Of or pertaining to a dog 1869. **3.** Addicted to dogs, as *d. men* 1859.

Dog-head. 1607. †**1.** A kind of ape with a head like a dog's; the CYNOCEPHALUS. **2. a.** The head of a nail formed by a rectangularly projecting shoulder. (Cf. DOG-NAIL.) 1793. **b.** The hammer of a gun 1812. So **Dog-headed** *a.* (in sense 1).

Dog-hole. 1579. A hole fit only for a dog; a vile or mean dwelling or place.

Dog-hook. 1571. †**1.** A hook used for leading a dog –1631. **2.** A wrench for uncoupling boring-rods; a spanner. **b.** An iron bar with a bent prong for grappling logs, etc.

Dog-hutch. 1830. A hutch for a dog; a DOG-HOLE.

Do·g-in-the-ma·nger. 1573. A churlish person who will neither use a thing himself not let another use it; in allusion to the fable of the dog in a manger and the hay.

Dog-Latin. Bad Latin; see DOG *sb.* 8.

†**Dog-leech.** 1529. [LEECH *sb.*¹] **1.** A veterinary surgeon who treats dogs –1831. **2.** A quack –1652.

Dog-legged (dǫ·glegd), *a.* 1703. *Archit.* Applied to a staircase, without a well-hole, the successive flights of which form a zigzag; also, to a variety of golf-hole.

Dogma (dǫ·gmă). Pl. **dogmas, dogmata.** 1638. [– L. *dogma* philosophical tenet – Gr. δόγμα, -ματ- opinion, tenet, decree, f. δοκεῖν seem, seem good, think.] **1.** That which is held as an opinion; a belief; a tenet or doctrine; sometimes, depreciatingly, an arrogant declaration of opinion. **2.** The body of opinion formulated and authoritatively stated; tenets or principles collectively; doctrinal system 1791.

1. Our dogmata and notions about justification 1652. 2. The present..is a revolution of doctrine and theoretick d. BURKE.

Dogmatic (dǫgmæ·tik). 1605. [– late L. *dogmaticus* – Gr. δογματικός; see prec., -IC. Cf. Fr. *dogmatique* (XVI).]

A. *adj.* **1.** Pertaining to the setting forth of opinion; didactic (*rare*) 1678. **2.** Of, pertaining to, or of the nature of, dogma or dogmas; doctrinal 1706. **3.** Proceeding upon *a priori* principles accepted as true 1696. **4.** Of persons, writings, etc.: Asserting dogmas or opinions in an authoritative or arrogant manner 1681.

1. He is no longer interrogative but d. JOWETT. 2. Dogmatick jargon learnt by heart GAY. 3. D. philosophy 1696. 4. He wrote against dogmas with a spirit perfectly d. D'ISRAELI.

B. *sb.* †**1.** A dogmatic philosopher or physician –1771. †**2.** A dogmatic person. HOBBES. **3.** Chiefly in *pl.* form **Dogmatics:** A system of dogma; *spec.* dogmatic theology 1845.

So **Dogma·tical** *a.* (*sb. pl.*). Hence **Dogma·tical-ly** *adv.*, **-ness. Dogmati·cian,** a professor of dogmatics.

Dogmatism (dǫ·gmătiz'm). 1603. [– Fr. *dogmatisme* or late L. *dogmatismus*; see DOGMA, -ISM.] **1.** Positive assertion of dogma or opinion; dogmatizing; positiveness in the assertion of opinion. **2.** With *pl.* A dogmatic tenet or system (*rare*) 1803. **3.** *Philos.* A system of philosophy based upon principles dictated by reasoning alone; opp. to *scepticism*. More generally, a way of thinking based upon principles which have not been tested by reflection. 1858.

1. Where there is most doubt, there is often the most d. PRESCOTT. 3. What Kant meant we may best understand if we consider how he opposes Criticism to two other forms of philosophy, D. and Scepticism 1877.

Dogmatist (dǫ·gmătist). 1541. [– Fr. *dogmatiste* or late L. *dogmatistes* – Gr. δογματιστής, f. δογματίζειν; see next, -IST.] **1.** One who dogmatizes, or lays down particular dogmas; *esp.* one who does this positively or arrogantly; a dogmatic person 1654. †**2.** A propounder of new opinions –1797. **3.** A philosopher or a physician of the dogmatic school (see DOGMATIC *a.* 3) 1541.

1. I expect but little success of all this upon the d., his opinion's assurance is paramount to argument GLANVILL.

Dogmatize (dǫ·gmătəiz), *v.* 1611. [– (O)Fr. *dogmatiser* or late L. *dogmatizare* – Gr. δογματίζειν lay down as one's opinion, decree, f. δόγμα; see DOGMA, -IZE.] **1.** *intr.* To make dogmatic assertions; to speak authoritatively or imperiously *upon* without reference to argument or evidence; †to teach new opinions –1696. **2.** *trans.* To deliver as a dogma. Now *rare*. 1621.

1. Prompt to impose, and fond to d. POPE. Hence **Do·gmatizer.**

Dog-nail. 1703. A nail having a large and slightly countersunk head; also a large nail with a head projecting on one side.

Dog-rose. 1597. [tr. med.L. *rosa canina*, repr. L. *cynorrodon* (Pliny), Gr. κυνόροδον.] A species of wild rose (*Rosa canina*), with pale red flowers, frequent in hedges.

Do·g's-bane, do·g-bane. 1597. [See BANE.] A name for plants reputed to be poisonous to dogs, chiefly of the orders *Asclepiadaceæ* and *Apocynaceæ*.

Do·g's-ear, *sb.* 1725. [Cf. next.] The corner of a leaf of a book, etc. turned over like a dog's ear, by careless use, etc.

Dog's-ear, *v.* Also **dog-ear.** 1659. [Cf. prec.] To disfigure a book by turning down the corners of the leaves.

Dog-shore. 1805. [SHORE *sb.*²] Each of two blocks of timber used to prevent a ship from starting off the slips while the keel-blocks are being removed in preparation for launching.

Dog-skin. 1676. The skin of a dog, or the leather made from it. Also *attrib.* So †**Dog's-leather.** 2 *Hen. VI*, IV. ii. 26.

Dog-sleep. 1613. †**1.** Feigned sleep –1711. **2.** A light or fitful sleep, easily interrupted 1708.

Dog's letter. 1636. [tr. L. *canina littera* (Persius I. 109).] The letter R, as resembling in sound the snarl of a dog.

Dog's-meat, dog's meat. 1593. **1.** Food for dogs, prepared from horse-flesh, offal, etc. **2.** *transf.* and *fig.* Carrion; offal 1606. Also *attrib.*

Dog's-tail. Also **dog-tail.** 1753. [tr. Bot.L. *Cynosurus*.] **1.** (Usu. **Dog's-tail Grass.**) A genus of grasses, *Cynosurus*, and chiefly the species *C. cristatus*, which has the flowers in each panicle all pointing one way, like the hairs of a dog's tail. **2.** = CYNOSURE 1. 1867.

Do·g-star. 1579. [After Gr. κύων, L. *canicula* (*canis*).] The star Sirius, in the constellation of the Greater Dog, the brightest of the fixed stars. Also, Procyon (the Lesser Dog-star).

The Dogge starre, which is called Syrius, or Canicula reigneth 1579.

Do·g-stone. 1640. A stone used for a millstone.

Do·gstones. 1597. [tr. med.L. *Testiculus canis*; from the shape of the tubers.] A name for various British species of Orchis.

Do·g's-tongue. Also **dog-.** 1530. [tr. L. *cynoglossum*.] The genus *Cynoglossum* of boraginaceous plants, esp. Hound's-tongue. (From the shape of the leaves.)

Dog's-tooth. Also **dog-.** 1578. [tr. med.L. *dens canis*.] **1.** (Now **Dog's-** or **Dog-tooth Violet.**) The genus *Erythronium* of liliaceous plants, esp. *E. dens-canis*; so called from the teeth on the inner segments of the perianth. **2.** A species of grass, *Cynodon dactylon* 1600. ¶See also DOG-TOOTH.

Dog-tired, *a.* 1809. [See DOG *sb.* 8.] Tired out.

Dog-tooth. Also **dog's-.** ME. **1.** A canine tooth; see CANINE *a.* **2.** *Archit.* A pointed moulding resembling a projecting tooth, frequent in mediæval architecture. Also *attrib.* 1836.

Dog-tooth spar: a variety of calcite, crystallizing in pointed scalenohedral forms. Hence **Dog-tooth** *v.* to decorate with dog-tooth moulding.

Dog-tree. 1548. [app. as bearing DOG-BERRIES, q.v.] **1.** The common Dogwood. **2.** Locally applied to the Spindle-tree, the Elder, and the Guelder-Rose 1703.

Dog-trick. ? *Obs.* 1540. A low, treacherous, or spiteful trick; an ill turn.

Dog-trot. 1664. An easy trot like that of a dog. Also †*fig.*

Dog-vane. 1769. *Naut.* 'A small vane, made of thread, cork, and feathers, or buntin, placed on the weather gunwale to show the direction of the wind' (Smyth). Hence, *joc.* A cockade.

Dog-violet. Also **dog's violet.** 1778. [tr. Bot. L.] The common name of *Viola canina*.

Dog-watch. 1700. [Cf. DOG-SLEEP.] *Naut.* The name of the two short or half watches, one from 4 to 6 p.m., and the other from 6 to 8 p.m.

Dog-weary, *a.* 1596. = DOG-TIRED.

Dog-whelk. 1856. [See WHELK.] A name of univalve molluscs of the genus *Nassa*.

Dogwood (dǫ·gwud). 1617. [lit. *wood* of the DOG-TREE, q.v.] **1.** The wild Cornel, *Cornus sanguinea*, common in English woods and hedgerows; also, other species of the genus *Cornus*; *esp.*, in N. America, *C. florida*, a tree bearing large white or pink flowers, and scarlet berries 1676. **2.** Applied to various other shrubs and trees; as, in Jamaica, to various species of *Piscidia*; in England, improp., to the Spindletree, Guelder Rose, Woody Nightshade, etc. 1725. **3.** The wood of any of these; *esp.* that of *C. sanguinea*, which is close and smooth-grained 1664. Also *attrib.*

White D., Guelder Rose and *Piscidia erythrina*.

Dohter, -or, -ur, obs. ff. DAUGHTER.

Doiled, doilt, *ppl. a. Sc.* 1513. [perh. var. of †*dold* ppl. a., of unc. origin.] Stupid; crazed.

Doily (doi·li), *a.* or *sb.* 1678. [From surname *Doiley* or *Doyley*.] †**1.** *attrib.* or *adj.* The name of a woollen stuff for summer wear –1714. **2.** *sb.* (Orig. **D.-napkin.**) A small ornamental napkin used at dessert 1711.

1. Some D. Petticoats, and Manto's we have DRYDEN.

Doing (dū·iŋ), *vbl. sb.* ME. [f. DO + -ING[1].] **1.** The action of the verb DO; *euphem.* copulation. **2.** A deed, act, action, performance, transaction, etc. Usu. (now always) *pl.* ME. **3.** *pl.* (*U.S.*) Adjuncts of a dish, fancy dish 1838; *gen.* adjuncts, etceteras, anything that is needed or is 'about' 1915. Also *ppl. a.*

2. Even a child is known by his doings *Prov.* 20:11.

Doit (doit). 1594. [– MLG. *doyt* = MDu. *duit, deuyt*. See DODKIN.] **1.** A small Dutch coin formerly in use; hence, a very small coin or sum 1728. **2.** *transf.* and *fig.* A very small part *of* anything; a bit, jot; *esp.* in *not to care a d.* 1660.

Doi·ted, *a. Sc.* ME. [perh. var. of *doted*, pa. pple. of DOTE *v.*, but *oi* is obscure.] Having the faculties impaired.

Doitkin = DODKIN, q.v.

Dokimastic, -asy, var. ff. DOCIMASTIC, -ASY.

†**Dola·bre.** *rare.* 1474. [– L. *dolabra* pickaxe, f. *dolare* to chip.] An adze. Hence **Do·labrate** *a. Bot.* = DOLABRIFORM.

Dolabriform (dolæ·brifǫɹm), *a.* 1753. [f. L. *dolabra* (see prec.) + -FORM.] Axe-shaped, cleaver-shaped; in *Bot.* applied to some fleshy leaves; in *Entom.*, to joints of antennæ, etc.

‖**Dolce far niente** (do·ltʃe fār nie·nte). 1814. [It.; = 'sweet doing nothing'.] Delightful idleness. Also *attrib.*

Doldrum (dǫ·ldrǒm). Usu. in pl. **doldrums.** 1811. [prob. orig. dial. or slang, f. *dol* DULL *a.*, perh. after *tantrum*.] †**1.** *slang.* A dullard –1824. **2.** pl. *The doldrums.* **a.** Dumps, low spirits 1811. **b.** The condition of a ship which is becalmed 1824. **c.** A nonplussed condition 1871. **3.** *spec.* A region near the equator, where the trade winds neutralize each other. (App. due to taking the state 'in the doldrums' for a locality.) 1855.

Dole (dōᵘl), *sb.*[1] [OE. *dāl* :– Gmc. **dailaz*; see DEAL *sb.*[1]] †**1.** The state of being divided –ME. †**2.** = DEAL *sb.*[1] 1. –1573. **b.** *Mining.* A portion of ore 1823. **c.** = DALE[2] 1. –1787. **3.** A share, portion, lot (*arch.*) ME. **4.** Lot in life; destiny (*arch.*) 1500. **5.** Distribution; *esp.* of charitable gifts ME. **6.** That which is doled out ME. **b.** *The d.*: relief paid to the unemployed 1919. †**7.** Dealing, intercourse –1561. Also *attrib.*

3. What d. of honour Flies where you bid it *All's Well* II. iii. 176. **4.** Happy man be his d., say I 1 *Hen. IV*, II. ii. 79. **5.** Large doles of death FLETCHER. A d. every Sunday, of 21 two-penny loaves 1778. **6.** Recipients of the ordinary d. of grain MERIVALE.

Comb.: **d.-beer,** beer given as alms; **-land, -meadow, -moor,** common land, moor, etc. in which several have portions indicated by landmarks, but not divided off; **-window,** one at which doles were distributed.

Dole, dool, dule (dōᵘl, dūl), *sb.*[2] *arch.* and *dial.* ME. [– OFr. *dol, doel, duel* (mod. *deuil*) mourning :– pop.L. *dolus*, f. L. *dolēre* grieve.] **1.** Grief, sorrow. **2.** Mourning, lamentation; chiefly in phr. *To make d.* ME. **3.** That which excites grief or pity; a grief, sorrow ME. †**4.** *transf.* Mourning garments –1734. **5.** A funeral. Now *dial.* 1548. †**6.** A company of doves 1486.

1. Earth's..joy and dole E. B. BROWNING. **2.** She died. So that day there was dole in Astolat TENNYSON.

Dole, *sb.*[3] 1563. [– L. *dolus* deceit, etc.] †**1.** Guile, deceit –1839. **2.** *Sc. Law.* Corrupt, malicious, or evil intent 1753.

Dole, *sb.*[4], var. of DOOL[1].

Dole, *v.*[1] 1465. [f. DOLE *sb.*[1]] **1.** *trans.* To give as a dole. **2.** To give *out* in small quantities; to portion *out* in a niggardly manner 1749. †**3.** To deal *about, around* –1766.

2. This comfort..she doled out to him in daily portions FIELDING. **3.** Compensations most liberally doled about to one another 1766.

Dole, *v.*[2] ? *Obs.* ME. [– OFr. *doleir, doloir*, mod. (*se*) *douloir* :– L. *dolēre*.] **1.** *intr.* To sorrow, grieve, lament –1668. †**2.** *trans.* To mourn, bewail 1567. †**3.** To grieve B. JONS.

1. The doling of the dove W. E. AYTOUN.

Dole; see DOOL, DOWEL, DULL.

†**Do·leance.** 1489. [– Fr. *doléance*, in OFr. *do(u)liance*, f. *doleier* grieve, f. *duel* grief; see DOLE *sb.*[2]] **1.** Grieving; grief –1639. **2.** Complaining, complaint –1656.

Doleful (dōᵘ·lfŭl), *a.*[1] ME. [f. DOLE *sb.*[2]] **1.** Full of or attended with dole or grief; distressful, sorrowful. **2.** Expressing grief, mourning, or suffering ME. Also as *sb.* (*pl.*) *colloq.*

1. Regions of sorrow, d. shades MILT. *P. L.* I. 65. The d. Ariadne so..forsaken stood COWLEY. **2.** A d. face 1865. Hence **Do·leful-ly** *adv.*[1], **-ness.**

Do·leful, *a.*[2] *rare.* 1617. [f. DOLE *sb.*[3]] Crafty, malicious. Hence **Do·lefully** *adv.*[2]

Dolent (dōᵘ·lĕnt), *a. arch.* 1450. [–(O)Fr. *dolent* – Gallo-Rom. **dolentus*, f. *dolent-*, pres. ppl. stem of L. *dolēre* grieve; see -ENT.] Grieving; sorrowful.

Dolerin(e (dǫ·lĕrin). 1863. [– Fr. *dolérine*, f. as next, with *-ine* = -ITE[1] 2b; see -INE[5].] *Min.* A gneissoid rock in the Alps, consisting of talc and feldspar.

Dolerite (dǫ·lĕrəit). 1838. [– Fr. *dolérite* (Haüy), f. Gr. δολερός deceptive; see -ITE[1] 2 b. So named from the difficulty of discriminating its constituents.] *Min.* A mineral allied to basalt, containing feldspar (labradorite) and augite. Hence **Doleri·tic** *a.*

Dolesome (dōᵘ·lsǒm), *a.* Now *rare.* 1533. [f. DOLE *sb.*[2] + -SOME[1].] = DOLEFUL *a.*[1] Hence **Do·lesome-ly** *adv.*, **-ness.**

Dolf, -en, obs. pa. t. and pple. of DELVE.

Dolichocephalic (dǫ:likoˌsĭfæ·lik), *a.* 1849. [f. Gr. δολιχός long + κεφαλή head + -IC.] *Ethnol.* Long-headed; applied to skulls of which the breadth is less than four-fifths of the length: opp. to BRACHYCEPHALIC. var. **Dolikhokephalic.** So **Dolichoce·phali** *sb. pl.* [mod.L.], men with d. skulls. **Dolichoce·phalism,** the quality of being d. **Dolichoce·phalous** *a.* = DOLICHOCEPHALIC. **Dolichoce·phaly** = *dolichocephalism.*

‖**Dolichurus** (dǫlikiūᵊ·rǒs). [mod.L. – Gr. δολιχουρος long-tailed.] *Gr.* and *L. Pros.* A dactylic hexameter with a redundant syllable in the last foot. Hence **Dolichu·ric** *a.*

Do·-little. 1586. [f. DO *v.* + LITTLE.] *sb.* One who does little; a lazy person. *adj.* Doing little; lazy.

‖**Dolium** (dōᵘ·liǒm). 1483. [L.] **1.** *Rom. Antiq.* A large earthenware jar or vessel, for holding wine, oil, or dry commodities; hence, in mod. use, a cask. **2.** *Zool.* A genus of gastropod molluscs, having a ventricose shell; also called *tun.*

Doll (dǫl), *sb.* 1560. [Pet-form of *Dorothy*, with *l* for *r* as in *Hal, Sal, Moll*, for *Harry, Sarah, Mary*.] **1.** A female pet, a mistress. **2.** A girl's toy-baby 1700. **3.** *transf.* A pretty but silly woman 1841.

2. I'll carry you and your d. too GARRICK. **3.** A sturdy lad..is worth a hundred of these city dolls EMERSON. **4.** *Comb.* **doll's house,** a miniature toy house for dolls; hence, a diminutive dwelling-house. Hence **Doll** *v.* to dress up finely (*colloq.*).

Dollar (dǫ·ləɹ). 1533. [– early Flem., LG. *daler* (Du. *daalder*) – G. *taler* (formerly also *thaler*), short for *Joachimst(h)aler*, applied to a silver coin made from metal obtained in *Joachimst(h)al* (i.e. 'Joachim's valley') in the Erzgebirge, Germany.] **1.** English name for the German *thaler*; *esp.* the unit of the German monetary union (1857–73) equal to 3 marks (about 2*s.* 11*d.*). Also of the *rigsdaler* of Denmark, etc. **2.** English name for the peso or Spanish piece of eight (*i.e.* eight reales), largely used in the British N. American Colonies at the time of their revolt 1581. **3.** The standard unit of the gold and silver coinage of the United States, containing 100 cents; = about 4*s.* 1½*d.* Eng. Also a coin of the same value in some British colonies. Sometimes abbreviated *dol.*, but usually represented by the dollar-mark $ before the number. 1785. **4.** Also a name for various foreign coins of corresponding value; as the *peso* of Mexico, etc., the *piastre* of Arabia, the *yen* of Japan, etc. 1882. **b.** *slang.* A five-shilling piece.

Phrases. *Pillar d.*, a silver coin of Spain, bearing a figure of the Pillars of Hercules: cf. sense 2. *Trade d.*, a silver d. of 420 grains formerly coined by the U.S. mint for purposes of trade with eastern Asia.

Comb.: **d.-bird,** an Australian bird of the genus *Eurystomus*, having a large round white spot on its wing; **-fish, a.** *Vomer setipinnis*, called also *moonfish*; **b.** *Stromateus triacanthus*, called also *butter-* and *harvest-fish.*

Dollop (dǫ·ləp). 1573. [perh. of Scand. origin (cf. Norw. dial. *dolp* lump).] †**1.** *Farming.* A clump of grass, weeds, etc. in a field –1825. **2.** *colloq.* or *vulg.* A large quantity; a clumsy lump 1812.

Dolly (dǫ·li), *sb.*[1] 1610. [f. DOLL + -Y[6].] **1.** A pet-form of *Dorothy*. **2.** †A female pet (*slang*). **b.** A slattern (*dial.* or *colloq.*) 1648. **3.** A pet name for a child's doll 1790. **4.** Applied to contrivances fancied to resemble a doll:

a. *dial.* A wooden appliance with two arms, and legs or feet, used to stir clothes in the wash-tub, called a *d.-tub*. Also applied to an apparatus for agitating and washing ore in a vessel. **b.** *Pile-driving.* A block set on the top of a pile to act as a buffer between it and the ram; a punch. **c.** *Austral. Goldfields.* An appliance like a pile-driver, used to crush quartz. **d.** A tool used in forming the head of a rivet. *Comb.* **d.-shop,** a marine store, frequently having a black doll hanging outside as a sign, and often serving as a low pawn-shop.

‖**Dolly** (dǫ·li), *sb.*[2] *Anglo-Ind.* 1860. [– Hindi *ḍālī*.] An offering of fruit, flowers, sweetmeats, etc., presented usually on a tray.

Dolly (dǫ·li), *a.* 1852. [f. DOLL + -Y[1].] **1.** Like a doll; babyish. **b.** *Games.* Designating an easy catch, etc. 1895.

Dolly (dǫ·li), *v. dial.* and *techn.* 1831. [f. DOLLY *sb.*[1] 4.] **a.** To stir, as clothes, ore, etc. with a dolly. **b.** *Gold-mining.* To crush (quartz) with a dolly; to obtain (gold) by this process; of the quartz: To yield (so much gold) by this method 1894.

Dolly Varden. 1872. [From the character in Dickens's *Barnaby Rudge*.] **a.** A print dress with a large flower pattern, worn with the skirt gathered up in loops. **b.** A large hat, with one side bent downwards, and abundantly trimmed with flowers. **c.** A Californian species of trout.

Blue eyes look doubly blue Beneath a Dolly Varden A. DOBSON.

Dolman (dǫ·lmăn). 1585. [In sense 1 – Fr. *doliman*; in sense 2 – Fr. *dolman* – G. *dolman* – Magyar *dolmany*; all ult. – Turk. *dolama*.] **1.** A long robe open in front, with narrow sleeves, worn by the Turks. **2.** The uniform jacket of a hussar, worn like a cape with the sleeves hanging loose 1883. **3.** A mantle with cape-like appendages instead of sleeves, worn by women 1872.

Dolmen (dǫ·lmen). 1859. [– Fr. *dolmen*, prob. repr. inexactly Cornish *tolmēn* 'hole of stone', misapplied to the *cromlech*.] French name for a CROMLECH.

Dolomite (dǫ·lŏməit). 1794. [– Fr. *dolomite*, also *dolomie*, f. name of Sylvain *Dolomieu*, French geologist (1750–1802); see -ITE[1] 2 b.] *Min.* A native double carbonate of lime and magnesia, occurring crystalline, and in granular masses, white or coloured, called *d. marble*; a rock consisting of this. **b.** pl. *The Dolomites* = the d. mountains; *spec.* those of Southern Tyrol. Hence **Dolomi·tic** *a.* of the nature of or containing d. **Do·lomitize** *v.* (also **Do·lomize**), to convert into d. **Dolomitiza·tion** (also **Dolomiza·tion**), conversion into d.

Dolor, var. of DOLOUR.

†Dolori·ferous, *a.* 1599. [f. late L. *dolorifer*, f. L. *dolor* pain + *-fer*; see -FEROUS.] = next –1638.

Dolorific (dǫlǒri·fik), *a.* Now *rare.* 1634. [– med.L. *dolorificus*, f. as prec.; see -FIC.] Causing pain; grievous.

Dolorous (dǫ·lŏrəs), *a.* ME. [– OFr. *doleros* (mod. *douloureux*) – late L. *dolorosus*, f. as prec.; see -OUS.] **1.** Painful. **2.** Causing grief; distressful; doleful, dismal 1450. **3.** Of persons, etc.: Full of or expressing sorrow; sad, distressed 1513.

1. A very d. thirst 1731. **2.** The death of therle was d. to all Englishmen 1548. **3.** Many a d. groan MILT. Hence **Do·lorous-ly** *adv.*, **-ness.**

Dolose (dolōu·s), *a.* 1832. [– L. *dolosus*, f. *dolus* DOLE *sb.*[3]; see -OSE[1].] *Law.* Characterized by criminal intention; intentionally deceitful.

Dolour, dolor (dōu·ləɹ, dǫ·ləɹ). ME. [– OFr. *dolor, dolour* (mod. *douleur*) :– L. *dolor* pain, grief; see -OUR, -OR 1.] **†1.** Physical suffering, pain; a pain, a disease –1720. **2.** Mental suffering ME.; *pl.* griefs, sorrows (now *rare*) 1611. **†3.** Lamentation, mourning –1634. **†4.** Indignation. [as in L.] –1644.

2. Pitifully behold the dolour of our heart 1544. **3.** *To make dolour*: to mourn.

Dolphin (dǫ·lfin). ME. [Three types of form have been current: (i) *delfyn, delphin* (XIV–XVII): see DELPHIN; (ii) *dolphyn* (XV, XVI) – OFr. *daulphin*: see DAUPHIN; (iii) *dolfyn, dolphin*, app. Eng. alterations of (ii).] **1.** A cetaceous mammal (*Delphinus delphis*), frequently confounded with the porpoise. **2.** The dorado (*Coryphæna hippuris*), a fish celebrated for its rapid changes of hue when dying 1578. **3.** *Astron.* A northern constellation, *Delphinus* ME. **4.** A figure of a dolphin, in painting, sculpture, etc. ME. **5.** Applied to various contrivances fancifully likened to a dolphin 1704.

a. In early artillery, each of two handles cast solid on a cannon nearly over the trunnions. **b.** *Naut.* (*a*) A spar or block of wood with a ring-bolt at each end for vessels to ride by. (*b*) A mooring-post or bollard placed along a quay, wharf, or beach. (*c*) A wreath of plaited cordage fastened about a mast or yard. **c.** *Gr. Antiq.* A heavy mass of lead, etc. suspended from a yard at the bow of a war-vessel, to be dropt into an enemy's ship.

6. A black species of aphis or plant-louse (*Aphis fabæ*), very destructive to bean-plants; also called *collier* and *d.-fly* 1731. **†7.** = DAUPHIN –1708.

1. Like Orion on the Dolphines backe *Twel. N.* I. ii. 15. **2.** Parting day Dies like the D., whom each pang imbues With a new colour. . The last still loveliest BYRON.

Comb.: **d.-flower,** the Larkspur (*Delphinium*); **-fly** = sense 6; **-striker** (*Naut.*), a short gaff spar fixed vertically under the bowsprit; also called *martingale.*

Hence **†Dolphine·t,** a female d. SPENSER.

Dolt (dōult), *sb.* 1543. [prob. rel. to †*dold* stupid, numb, and *dol(l*, var. of DULL *a.*] **1.** A dull stupid fellow; a blockhead, numskull. **2.** *attrib.* or as *adj.* Doltish, stupid. *Comb.* as **†d.-head,** a dolt. 1679.

1. Oh Gull, oh d., As ignorant as durt *Oth.* V. ii. 163. Hence **†Dolt** *v.* to make a d. of; *intr.* to act like a d. **Do·ltish** *a.* like a. d.; thick-headed. **Do·ltish-ly** *adv.*, **-ness.**

Dolven, obs. pa. pple. of DELVE *v.*

‖**Dom**[1] (dǫm). 1716. [In sense 1, – Pg. *dom*, = Sp. *don* :– L. *dominus*. In sense 2, short for L. *dominus* master. Cf. DON *sb.*[1], DAN[1].] **1.** In Portugal and Brazil, a title of dignity conferred only by Royal authority 1727. **2.** A title prefixed to the names of certain R.C. ecclesiastical dignitaries and monks 1716. **3.** *Dom Pedro* (*U.S.*): a game at cards, a variation of DON, q.v. 1887.

‖**Dom**[2] (dōm). 1861. [G., – L. *domus* (*Dei*) house (of God); cf. DOME.] A cathedral church.

-dom, *suffix.* [OE. *-dōm* = OS. *-dōm* (Du. *-dom*), OHG. *-tuom* (G. *-tum*); suffixal use of OE. *dōm* judgement, statute, jurisdiction, DOOM, OHG. *tuom* position, condition, dignity.] Frequent in OE. as a suffix to sbs. and adjs. Now a living suffix, with the sense of 'condition, state, dignity'; also of 'domain, realm' (*fig.*).

†Do·mable, *a. rare.* 1623. [– OFr. *domable* or L. *domabilis*, f. *domare* to tame; see -ABLE.] Tamable. Hence **†Do·mableness.**

Domage, -eable, etc., obs. ff. DAMAGE, etc.

Domain (domēi·n), *sb.* ME. [– Fr. *domaine*, alt., by association with L. *dominus* (see DOMINION), of OFr. *demaine, demeine* DEMESNE.] **†1.** = DEMESNE 1. Also *attrib.* in *d. lands.* –1630. **2.** A heritable property; estate or territory held in possession; lands; dominions 1601. **b.** *transf.* Sphere of activity or dominion 1727. **3.** *fig.* A sphere of thought or action; field, province, etc. 1764.

2. These are in the nature of a d. and inheritance, and fall to the next heire in succession P. HOLLAND. *transf.* He was lord of his library, and seldom cared for looking out beyond his domains LAMB. **3.** The d. of Art CARLYLE, of Science 1864.

Phr. *Eminent d.*: ultimate or supreme lordship; the superiority of the sovereign power over all property in the state, whereby it is entitled to appropriate any part required for the public advantage, compensation being made to the owner.

Hence **Domai·nal, Doma·nial** *adjs.* of, pertaining, or relating to d., or to a d.

Domal (dōu·măl), *a.* 1716. [– med.L. *domalis* (*domalia* household goods), f. L. *domus* house (in med.L. planetary house); see -AL[1].] **1.** *Astrol.* Of or pertaining to a house. **2.** Domestic 1728.

Dōm-bōc, OE. form of DOOMBOOK.

Domdaniel (dǫmdæ·niĕl). 1801. [– Fr. *domdaniel*, app. f. Gr. δῶμα Δανιήλ, or L. *domus Danielis* hall or house of Daniel.] A fabled submarine hall where a magician met his disciples; used by Carlyle in the sense of 'infernal cave'.

Chief Enchanter. . in the D. of Attorneys CARLYLE.

Dome (dōum), *sb.* Also **†dosme, doom.** 1513. [In sense 1, – L. *domus* house; in other senses, – Fr. *dôme* – It. DUOMO, (dial. *domo*) house, house of God, cathedral, cupola, – L. *domus.*] **1.** A house, a home; a mansion. Now chiefly *poet.* **†2.** = DOM[2]. –1753. **3.** A rounded vault forming the roof of a building or chief part of it; a cupola 1656. **4.** *transf.* Anything resembling a dome or rounded vault 1727. **5.** Technical uses:

a. *Manuf.* The cover of a reverberatory furnace. **b.** *Cryst.* A trimetric, monoclinic, or triclinic prism, whose faces and edges are parallel to one of the secondary axes. **c.** *Railways.* The raised conical part of the boiler of a locomotive engine, the *steam-d.*; the raised roof of a railway carriage. **d.** *Watch-making.* The back part of the inner case of a watch.

1. Dated at my D., or rather Mansion place in Lincolneshire 1553. **4.** A bed, with a d. to it COMBE. The d. of the sky MRS. RADCLIFFE. Imbower'd vaults of pillar'd palm. . the d. Of hollow boughs TENNYSON. Tabor with its rounded d. STANLEY.

Dome, *v.* 1876. [f. prec. sb.] **1.** To cover with or as with a dome. **2.** To make dome-shaped 1879. **3.** *intr.* To rise or swell as a dome 1887.

1. [He] domes the red-plow'd hills With loving blue TENNYSON.

Dome, obs. f. DOOM, DOUM.

Domed (dōumd), *a.* 1775. [f. DOME *sb.* or *v.*] **1.** Dome-shaped; vaulted. **2.** Having a dome or domes 1855.

†Domes-booke. = DOMESDAY *Book.*

Domesday (dōu·mzdēi, dū·mzdēi). ME. spelling of DOOMSDAY, day of judgement, now used as a historical term, in the following:

D. Book, colloq. *D.*; the name of the record of the Great Inquisition or Survey of the lands of England, their extent, value, ownership, and liabilities, made by order of William the Conqueror in 1086. Also *transf., fig.*, and allusively.

The booke. . to be called D., bicause (as Mathew Parise saith) it spared no man, but iudged all men indifferently, as the Lord in that great day will do LAMBARDE.

Domestic (dome·stik). 1521. [– (O)Fr. *domestique* – L. *domesticus*, f. *domus* house, with ending as in *rusticus* RUSTIC, etc.]

A. *adj.* **†1.** Housed –1681; intimate, at home –1750. **2.** Of or belonging to the home, house, or household; household, home, family 1611. **3.** Of or pertaining to one's own country or nation; internal, inland, home 1545; indigenous; home-grown, home-made 1660. **4.** Of animals: Living in or near the habitations of man; tame, not wild 1620; †of men: Not nomad 1632. **5.** Attached to home; domesticated 1658.

1. He was. . domestick. . with all CLARENDON. **2.** D. joy GOLDSM., life D'ISRAELI, servants DICKENS. **3.** D. Trade 1719, policy MACAULAY, woollens and flannels URE. **4.** Domesticke or tame Ducks VENNER. **5.** It is praiseworthy and right to be d. J. H. NEWMAN.

B. *sb.* **†1.** A member of a household (*lit.* and *fig.*) –1737. **2.** A household servant 1613. **†3.** An inhabitant of the same country –1682. **4.** *pl.* Articles of home produce or manufacture, *esp.*, in U.S., home-made cotton cloths 1622.

2. His Domesticks are all in Years, and grown old with their Master ADDISON.

Hence **†Dome·stical** *a.* domestic; familiar, homely; *sb.* = DOMESTIC *sb.* 1, 2. **Dome·stically** *adv.* in a d. manner; with regard to d. affairs.

Domesticate (dome·stikeit), *v.* 1639. [– *domesticat-*, pa. ppl. stem of med.L. *domesticare*, f. L. *domesticus*; see prec., -ATE[3].] **1.** *trans.* To cause to be at home; to naturalize. Also *transf.* and *fig.* **2.** To make domestic; to attach to home and its duties 1748. **3.** To tame or bring under control; *transf.* to civilize 1641. **†4.** *intr.* (for *refl.*) To live at home (*with*); to take up one's abode –1812.

1. D. yourself there [at Naples] CHESTERF. **2.** [They] easily become domesticated 1863. **3.** To d. a savage people EARL MONM., the dog DARWIN. So **†Dome·sticant** *a.* making its home (*rare*). Hence **Dome·sticated** *ppl. a.* **Dome:stica·tion,** the action of domesticating; domesticated condition. **Dome·sticator,** one who domesticates.

Domesticity (dōumesti·sīti). 1721. [f. DOMESTIC *a.* + -ITY. Cf. Fr. *domesticité*, late L. *domesticitas.*] **1.** The quality or state of being domestic; family life; devotion to home; homeliness. **2.** *pl.* Domestic arrangements 1824.

Dome·sticize, *v.* 1656. [f. DOMESTIC + -IZE.] *trans.* = DOMESTICATE.

Domett (dǫ·mėt). 1835. [perh. from a proper name.] 'A kind of plain cloth of which the warp is cotton and the weft woollen' (Booth).

Domeykite (domēi·kəit). 1850. [After *Domeyko*, a Chilean mineralogist + -ITE[1] 2 b.] *Min.* A native arsenide of copper of a greyish or tin-white metallic appearance.

Domic, -al (dōu·mik, -ăl), *a.* 1823. [f. DOME *sb.* + -IC, -ICAL.] **1.** Of, pertaining to, or like a dome. **2.** Characterized by domes or dome-like structure 1861.

Domicile (dǫ·misil, -səil), *sb.* 1477. [– (O)Fr. *domicile* – L. *domicilium*, f. *domus* house.] **1.** A place of residence or ordinary habitation; a house or home. Also *transf.* and *fig.* **2.** *Law.* The place where one has his permanent residence, to which, if absent, he has the intention of returning 1766; residence 1835. **3.** *Comm.* The place where a bill of exchange is made payable 1892.

Do·micile (see prec.), *v.* 1809. [f. prec. sb.] **1.** To establish in a domicile or fixed residence. Also *transf.* and *fig.* **2.** *Comm.* To make (a bill, etc.) payable at a certain place 1809. **3.** *intr.* (for *refl.*) To dwell 1831.

†Domici·liar. *rare.* 1655. [– med.L. **domiciliaris* (cf. *domicillaris canonicus* in Du Cange), f. L. *domicilium* + *-aris* -AR[1]. See next.]

A. *adj.* Of or pertaining to one's domicile.

B. *sb.* Short for *d. canon*, a canon of a minor order having no voice in a chapter 1761.

Domiciliary (dǫmisi·liări), *a.* 1790. [– Fr. *domiciliaire* (see -AR[2]) – med.L. *domiciliarius*, f. L. *domicilium* DOMICILE + *-arius* -ARY[1].] **1.** Pertaining to or connected with a domicile. **2.** *Zool.* Of or pertaining to the general integument occupied in common by infusoria, and the like. (Dicts.)

1. *D. visit*, a visit to a private dwelling, by official persons, in order to search or inspect it.

Domiciliate (dǫmisi·liˌeit), *v.* 1778. [f. L. *domicilium*, after Fr. *domicilier*; see -ATE[3].] **1.** *trans.* To establish in a place of residence; to domicile. Also *intr.* (for *refl.*). **†2.** To domesticate (animals) (*rare*) –1816. Hence

Do:micilia·tion, the action of domiciliating; domestication (*rare*).

Domiculture (dǫ·mikɒltiŭɹ). *rare.* 1860. [f. L. *domus* house, after *agriculture*.] The art of housekeeping, cookery, etc.; domestic economy.

†**Do·mify,** *v.* ME. [– Fr. *domifier* (XVI) in same sense – med.L. *domificare* build houses, f. L. *domus* house; see -FY.] *Astrol. trans.* To divide (the heavens) into twelve houses; to locate (the planets) in their respective houses –1751.

‖**Domina** (dǫ·mină). 1706. [L. = mistress, lady.] †**1.** A lady of rank. **2.** The superior of a nunnery 1751.

Dominance (dǫ·minăns). 1819. [f. next; see -ANCE.] The fact or position of being dominant; ascendancy, sway. So **Do·minancy,** dominant quality.

Dominant (dǫ·minănt). 1532. [– (O)Fr. *dominant* – *dominant-*, pres. ppl. stem of L. *dominari* DOMINATE; see -ANT.] **A.** *adj.* **1.** Exercising chief authority or rule; ruling, governing; most influential. **2.** Occupying a commanding position 1854. **3.** *Mus.* [cf. B. b.] Relating to or based upon the dominant 1819. **4.** In Mendelism, of a marked parental character transmitted to a hybrid descendant 1900.

1. An odde feaverish sickness d. in the Universitie WOOD. **2.** To take possession of the d. parts of the globe 1854.

Phr. *Rom. Law. D. land, tenement*: 'the tenement or subject in favour of which a servitude exists or is constituted' (Bell). Hence **Do·minantly** *adv.*

B. *sb. Mus.* **a.** In eccl. modes, the reciting note of a tone. **b.** The fifth note of the scale of any key 1819.

Dominate (dǫ·mineⁱt), *v.* 1611. [– *dominat-*, pa. ppl. stem of L. *dominari* bear rule, f. *dominus* lord, master; see -ATE³.] **1.** *trans.* To bear rule over, command, sway; to master. **2.** *intr.* To be dominant (*over*) 1818. **3.** *trans.* To command as a height; also *fig.* 1833.

1. Hee that..can d. his passions 1613. **2.** Republicanism dominates within and without CARLYLE. **3.** This hill..dominates the plain BOSW. SMITH.

Domination (dǫminēⁱ·ʃən). ME. [– (O)Fr. *domination* – L. *dominatio*, f. as prec.; see -ION.] **1.** The action of dominating; lordly rule, sway, or control; ascendancy. †**2.** The territory under rule; a dominion –1654. **3.** *pl.* The fourth of the nine orders of angels in the Dionysian hierarchy. Cf. DOMINION 4. ME.

1. The Lordship and d. over thys yle 1585. **2.** His subiectes of his said dominacion of Wales 1535. **3.** Thrones, Dominations, Princedoms, Vertues, Powers MILT. *P. L.* v. 601.

Dominative (dǫ·minĕtiv), *a.* 1599. [– (O)Fr. *dominatif, -ive* or med.L. *dominativus*, f. as prec.; see -IVE.] **1.** Of lordly authority. †**2.** Of predominant importance –1655.

Dominator (dǫ·mineⁱtəɹ). 1450. [orig. – (O)Fr. *dominateur*, later –, or assim. to, L. *dominator*, f. as prec.; see -OR 2.] One who or that which dominates; a ruler.

Jupiter..Lord of the ascendant, and great d. GAULE.

†**Domine** (dǫ·mini), *sb.* 1566. [voc. case of L. *dominus*. Cf. DOMINIE.] **1.** Lord, master: a term of address to the clergy or members of the professions –1675. **2.** A clergyman or parson; *spec.* = DOMINIE 2, q.v. –1711.

†**Do·mine,** *v.* 1470. [– (O)Fr. *dominer* – L. *dominari*; see DOMINATE.] *trans.* To rule, DOMINATE –1509; *intr.* to prevail –1614.

Domineer (dǫminīᵊ·ɹ), *v.* 1588. [– Du. *domineren* – Fr. *dominer*; see prec., -EER.] **1.** *intr.* To rule arbitrarily or despotically; to tyrannize. Now usually, To lord it; †to play the master –1764. †**2.** To feast riotously. [Du. *domineren* feast luxuriously.] –1691. †**3.** To prevail –1725. **4.** To tower (*over, above*) 1658. **5.** *trans.* To govern imperiously, tyrannize over 1764; to tower over 1812.

1. Oligarchies, where a few rich men d. BURTON. He rants and domineers, He swaggers and swears DRYDEN. **2.** Goe to the feast, reuell and domineere *Tam. Shr.* III. ii. 226. **5.** The entrenchments.. were domineered within pistol shot 1812. Hence **Dominee·r** *sb.* a domineering air or manner. **Do:minee·rer** (now *rare*), a tyrant, despot. **Dominee·ring** *vbl. sb.* and *ppl. a.* despotic; overbearing, insolent; †dominant. **Dominee·ring-ly** *adv.*, **-ness.**

Dominial (domi·niăl), *a.* 1727. [f. DOMINION + -AL¹.] Of or pertaining to ownership.

Dominical (domi·nikăl), 1540. [– (O)Fr. *dominical* or late L. *dominicalis*, f. *dominicus*, f. *dominus* lord, master; see -ICAL.]

A. *adj.* **1.** Of or pertaining to the Lord (Jesus Christ); Lord's; as *D. day, year* 1553. **2.** Of or pertaining to the Lord's day [eccl. L. *dominica* (*dies*)]; Sunday –1623. Also *fig.* †**3.** Belonging to a demesne [med.L. *dominicum*] –1640.

2. Grave D. Postures COWLEY. *D. letter*: the letter used to denote the Sundays in a particular year. The seven letters A, B, C, D, E, F, G are used in succession to denote the first seven days of the year (Jan. 1–7), and then in rotation the next seven days, and so on, so that, *e.g.* if the 3rd Jan. be a Sunday, the d. letter for the year is C. Leap year has two D. letters, one for the days preceding Feb. 29, the other for the rest of the year. *fig.* For all Cromwells Nose weares the Dominicall Letter [in allusion to the printing of the D. letter in red] 1647.

B. *sb.* †**1.** *Eccl.* A garment or veil for Sundays [med.L. *dominicale*] –1751. †**2.** Short for *D. letter* –1686. †**3.** The Lord's day –1673.

2. My red Dominicall, my golden letter SHAKS.

Dominican (domi·nikăn). 1632. [– med.L. *Dominicanus* (whence Fr. *dominicain*), f. *Dominicus*, L. form of the name of *Domingo* de Guzman (St. Dominic); see -AN.] **A.** *adj.* Of or pertaining to St. Dominic or to the order of preaching friars (and nuns) founded by him 1680. **B.** *sb.* A friar of this order; a Black friar.

Dominie (dǫ·mini). Also **domine.** 1612. [sp. of L. *domine* (see DOMINE *sb.*), prob. – Du. *dominee.*] **1.** A schoolmaster, pedagogue. (Chiefly *Sc.*) **2.** In U.S., the title of a pastor of the Dutch Reformed Church; whence, of ministers or parsons of other churches. (Usu. pronounced, after Du., dōᵘ·mini.) 1824.

Dominion (dǒmi·nyən). ME. [– OFr. *dominion* – med.L. *dominio*, f. *dominium* property, f. *dominus* lord, master.] **1.** The power or right of governing and controlling; sovereign authority; sovereignty; rule; control. Also *fig.* **2.** The domains of a feudal lord. **b.** The territory subject to a king or a ruler, or under a particular government or control. Often in *pl.* 1512. Also *fig.* **3.** *Law.* Ownership, property; right of possession. [= *dominium* in Rom. Law.] 1651. **4.** = DOMINATION 3. (Usu. in *pl.*) 1611.

2. *The Old D.*, a popular name in U.S. for Virginia. **b.** Applied to countries outside England or Great Britain under the sovereignty or suzerainty of the English crown; (*b*) (usu. with cap.) designating the larger self-governing British dominions; the title was given *spec.* to Canada in 1867 (1 July; anniversary called *D. day*) and to New Zealand in 1907 (28 Sept.). In the Statute of Westminster (1931) the term includes the Dominion of Canada, the Commonwealth of Australia, the Dominion of N. Zealand, the Union of S. Africa, the Irish Free State, and Newfoundland. **3.** *Eminent D.* (cf. DOMAIN). **4.** *Col.* 1:16.

‖**Domi·nium.** 1823. A term of Roman law, rendered 'lordship', 'ownership', 'property', etc., often retained in legal use: cf. DOMINION 3.

Domino (dǫ·mino). Pl. **-oes.** 1719. [– Fr. *domino* a hood worn by priests in winter; cf. Sp. *domino* a masquerade garment. Derived in some way from L. *dominus*.] **1.** A kind of loose cloak, chiefly worn at masquerades, with a small mask covering the upper part of the face; *occas.*, the half-mask itself. Also *fig.* **2.** A person wearing a domino 1749. **3.** One of 28 rectangular pieces of ivory, bone, or wood, having the under side black, and the upper equally divided by a cross line into two squares, each either blank or marked with pips from one to six in number. *pl.* A game played with these, (usually) by placing corresponding ends in contact, the player who has the lowest number of pips remaining being the winner. 1801. **b.** *interj.* An ejaculation of completion 1882.

Domitable (dǫ·mităb'l), *a. rare.* 1677. [f. L. *domitare*, frequent. of *domare* tame, + -ABLE.] Tamable.

Domite (dōᵘ·məit). 1828. [f. *Puy de Dôme* in Auvergne; see -ITE¹ 2 b.] *Min.* A light-grey variety of trachyte.

Dom Pedro; see DOM¹ 3.

Don (dǫn), *sb.*¹ 1523. [– Sp. *don* :– L. *dominus.* See DAN, DOM¹.] **1.** A Spanish title, formerly confined to men of high rank, but now an appellation of courtesy. **2.** A Spanish lord or gentleman; a Spaniard 1610. **3.** *transf.* A distinguished man; a leader; an adept (*colloq.*) 1634. **4.** Hence, in the English Universities: A head, fellow or tutor of a college 1660. †**5.** = DAN¹, DOM¹ 2 (*rare*) 1600. **6.** More fully, *D. Pedro*, a game at cards 1873.

2. I never turn'd my back upon D. or devil yet TENNYSON. **3.** The great dons of wit DRYDEN. **4.** An introduction to two Oxford dons BURGON.

†**Don,** *sb.*² *rare.* 1524. [– Fr. *don* :– L. *donum.*] A gift.

Don (dǫn), *v. arch.* 1567. [contr. from *do on*; see DO *v.*] **1.** *trans.* To put on (anything worn, etc.). The opposite of DOFF. **2.** *refl.* To dress oneself. Chiefly *n. dial.* 1801.

1. She donned the garment of a nun 1879.

‖**Doña** (do·nʸa), **dona** (dōᵘ·nă). 1622. [Sp. *doña*, Pg. *dona* :– L. *domina* mistress, lady. Cf. DONNA.] **1.** A (Sp. or Pg.) lady. Also prefixed to the name as a courtesy title. **2.** *slang.* (*dona*, also vulgarly *donah, doner.*) A woman, a sweetheart 1873.

Donary (dōᵘ·nări). 1582. [– L. *donarium* offering, f. *donum* gift; see -ARY¹.] A gift; a votive offering.

†**Donat,** var. of DONET.

Do·natary. 1818. [var. of DONATORY, prob. after (O)Fr. *donataire* – med.L. *donatarius.*] The donee of a gift; a DONATORY: spec. in *Sc. Law.*

Donate (donē̆ⁱ·t), *v.* (Chiefly *U.S.*) 1845. [Back-formation from next.] **1.** *trans.* To make a donation of; hence (in U.S.) to give, grant. **2.** To present *with* 1862.

Donation (donēⁱ·ʃən). ME. [– (O)Fr. *donation* – L. *donatio*, f. *donare* donate, f. *donum* gift.] **1.** The action or faculty of giving; presentation; grant. **2.** *Law.* The action or contract by which a person transfers the ownership of a thing from himself to another, as a free gift 1651. **3.** That which is presented; a gift 1577.

1. Many principal church livings are in the d. of the crown SWIFT. **3.** The commissioners had anticipated that the donations would fall off 1895.

Donatism (dǫ·nătiz'm). 1588. [f. as next; see -ISM.] The principles of the Donatists.

Donatist (dǫ·nătist). 1460. [– late L. *Donatista*, f. *Donatus* (of uncertain identity); see -IST.] One of a sect of Christians, named after Donatus, which arose in North Africa in 311; they claimed to be the only true and pure church, and maintained that the baptisms and ordinations of others were invalid. Also *attrib.* or *adj.* Hence **Donati·stic, -al** *a.* pertaining to Donatism or the Donatists.

Donative (dǫ·nătiv). ME. [– L. *donativum* largesse, f. *donat-*, pa. ppl. stem of *donare* (see DONATION) + *-ivum* -IVE.]

A. *adj.* Of the nature of a donation; *esp.* of a benefice: Vesting or vested by donation; opp. to PRESENTATIVE 1559.

B. *sb.* **1.** A donation, gift, present; a largess ME. **2.** *spec.* A benefice which the founder or patron can bestow without presentation to or investment by the ordinary 1564.

1. The Romane Emperors custome was at certaine solemne times to bestow on his Souldiers a Donatiue HOOKER.

Donator (donēⁱ·təɹ). 1449. [orig. – AFr. *donatour* = (O)Fr. *donateur* – L. *donator*, f. as prec.; see -OR 2. In mod. use f. DONATE + -OR 2.] One who makes a donation; a donor.

Donatory (dǫ·nătəri). 1617. [– med.L. *donatorius*, f. as prec.; see -ORY¹.] The recipient of a donation.

Do-naught; see DO-NOUGHT.

Done (dɒn), *ppl. a.* (*sb.*) ME. [pa. pple. of DO *v.*] Performed, executed, finished, ended, settled; also, used up, worn out; see DO *v.*

Donee (dōᵘnī·). 1523. [f. DONOR; see -EE¹.] One to whom anything is given; *esp.* in *Law*, (*a*) one to whom anything is given gratuitously; (*b*) one to whom land is conveyed in fee tail; (*c*) one to whom a power is given for execution.

†**Do·net, do·nat.** ME. [– OFr. *donet, donnat* – L. *Donatus*.] An introductory Latin grammar; orig. that of Ælius Donatus; hence, any introductory treatise –1535.

Dong (dǫŋ), *v.* 1587. [Echoic.] *intr.* To sound as a large bell. So **Dong** *sb.* (or without construction), the sound itself.

‖**Donga** (dǫ·ŋgă). *S. Afr.* 1879. [Bantu.] A ravine or watercourse with steep sides.

Doni, var. of DHONEY.

Donjon (dɒ·ndʒən, dǫ·ndʒǫ̆n), arch. sp. of DUNGEON, q.v.; now usual in sense 1, 'The great tower or innermost keep of a castle'.

Donkey (dǫ·ŋki). 1785. [In early use pron. so as to rhyme with *monkey*, whence the proposed derivations from DUN and from the proper name *Duncan* (cf. DICKY, NEDDY).] **1.** An ass. (Now in general use, exc. in scriptural language, and in Nat. Hist.) **2.** *transf.* A stupid or silly person 1840.

Comb.: **d.-boy, -man,** one in charge of a d., or of a d.-engine; **-engine,** a small steam-engine, usually for subsidiary purposes, as feeding the boilers, etc.; hence *d.-boiler*; **-pump,** an auxiliary steam-pump; **d.'s years,** a very long time (*slang*).

‖**Donna** (dǫ·nă, It. do·nna). 1670. [It. :– L. *domina*, fem. of *dominus* DON *sb.*[1] Cf. DOÑA, DONA.] A lady; a title of honour or courtesy for an Italian lady.

Prima d.: the principal female singer in an opera.

Donnish (dǫ·niʃ), *a.* 1835. [f. DON *sb.*[1] + -ISH[1].] Of the character of a (college) don; pedantically stiff in manner. Hence **Do·nnishness.** So **Do·nnism,** d. action or manner.

Donnot; see DO-NOUGHT.

Donor (dōᵘ·nəɹ, -ǭɹ). 1494. [– AFr. *donour*, OFr. *doneur* :– L. *donator*; see DONATIVE, -OR 2.] One who gives or presents; *esp.* in *Law*, one who grants an estate, or power for execution. Correl. of DONEE.

The doctrine..that a freehold interest in possession must pass instantly from d. to donee DIGBY.

Do-nothing (dū·nɒːþiŋ). 1579.

A. *sb.* One who does nothing; an idler.

B. *adj.* Characterized by doing nothing; idle, indolent, as *do-nothing folk* 1832. Hence **Dono·thingism, Dono·thingness,** the habit or practice of doing nothing; idleness, indolence.

Do-nought (dū·nǫ̆t), **donnot** (dǫ·nǫ̆t). Now usu. *dial.* 1594. [app. f. *do nought.*] = DO-NOTHING; also, a good-for-nothing.

Donship (dǫ·nʃip). 1626. [f. DON *sb.* + -SHIP.] The personality of a don; the possession of the title 'don'.

Don't (dōᵘnt), colloq. contr. of *do not*. Also as *sb.* = Prohibition, and *vb.*

Donzel (dǫ·nzĕl). *arch.* 1592. [– It. *donzello* – Rom. *dominicello*, dim. of L. *dominus*. See DON *sb.*[1], DAMSEL.] A young gentleman not yet knighted; a squire, a page.

Doo, Sc. form of DOVE.

‖**Doob** (dūb). 1810. [Hindi *dūb* = Skr. *dūrvā*.] The dog's-tooth grass (*Cynodon dactylon*).

Doodah (dū·dā). *slang.* 1915. *All of a d.*, in a flutter of excitement.

Doodle (dū·d'l), *sb. colloq.* 1628. [– LG. *dudel-* in *dudeltopf, -dopp* simple fellow.] A noodle. Hence **Doo·dle** *v.*[1] (*dial.*) to befool, cheat.

Doodle (dū·d'l), *v.*[2] Chiefly *Sc.* 1816. [– G. *dudeln* in same sense; cf. *dudelsack* bag-pipe.] To play (the bagpipes). Also **D.-sack,** a bagpipe.

Dook, obs. and Sc. f. DUCK *v.*

Dool[1] (dūl), **dole** (dōᵘl). ME. [corresp. to OFris. *dōl* (Du. *doel*) aim, mark.] **1.** A boundary or landmark, consisting of a post, a stone, or an unploughed balk of land. **2.** *Sc.* (dül). The goal in a game 1550. Also *attrib.*

Dool[2], var. of DOLE *sb.*[2] grief, etc.

‖**Doolie, dooly** (dū·li). 1625. [– Hindi *dōlī*, dim. of *dōlā* swing, cradle, litter :– Skr. *dōlā*, f. *dul-* swing.] A rudimentary litter or palanquin used by the lower classes in India, and as an army ambulance. Also *attrib.*, as *d.-bearer.*

Doom (dūm), *sb.* [OE. *dōm* = OFris., OS. *dōm*, OHG. *tuom*, ON. *dómr*, Goth. *dōms* :– Gmc. **dōmaz* lit. that which is set or put, f. **dō-* place, set, DO *v.* For the sense-development cf. Gr. θέμις law (*θε- place), L. *statulum* STATUTE.] **1.** A statute; *gen.* an ordinance. Now *Hist.* **2.** A judgement; a sentence; mostly in adverse sense OE. †**3.** Private judgement, opinion –1624; discernment –1697. **4.** Fate, lot, destiny. (Rarely in good sense.) ME. **b.** Final fate, ruin, death 1600. **5.** Judgement, trial (*arch.*) OE. **6.** The last Judgement (*arch.*) ME. †**7.** Justice; equity; righteousness. (Chiefly in versions of Scripture.) –1587. †**8.** Power, authority; *esp.* to judge –ME.

1. The first Dooms of London provide especially for the recovery of cattle J. R. GREEN. **2.** O! Partial Judge, Thy D. has me undone 1709. **3.** With..unerring D., He sees what is, and was, and is to come DRYDEN. **4.** The doome of Destiny SHAKS. The minister's d. was sealed J. R. GREEN. **6.** What will the Line stretch out to' th' cracke of Doome SHAKS. Phr. *Day of d.*: the day of judgement; †*transf.* the last day of one's life.

Comb.: **d.-ring** (*Archæol.*), a ring of stones delimiting the old Norse courts of judgement; **-tree,** a tree on which the condemned were hanged.

Hence **Doo·mful** *a.* fraught with d.; fateful.

Doom (dūm), *v.* 1450. [f. prec. sb.] **1.** *trans.* To pronounce judgement or sentence upon. *arch.* exc. as in 2. **2.** To pronounce judgement or sentence against; to condemn *to* 1588. **3.** To destine or consign to some (adverse) fate or lot 1602. **4.** *U.S.* (*local*). To judge and assess the tax payable by a person who has made no returns 1816. **5.** To decree; to fix as a sentence or fate; to adjudge 1588. **6.** *intr.* To give judgement (*arch.*) 1591.

2. Tribunes with their tongues d. men to death *Tit. A.* III. i. 47. **3.** Hopes..doomed to disappointment TYNDALL. **5.** The Emperor in his rage will doome her death *Tit. A.* IV. ii. 114. Hence **Doo·mage** (*U.S. local*), assessment in default. **Doo·mer.**

Doombook (dū·mbuk). Also **dome-, domes-, dooms-.** [OE. *dōm-bōc* book of dooms.] A book or code of (Old Teutonic) laws; *spec.* that attributed to King Alfred. Also *transf.*

Doomsday (dū·mzdēⁱ). [OE. *dōmes dæġ*, i.e. gen. of DOOM, DAY; cf. DOMESDAY.] **1.** The judgement day. **b.** *transf.* A day of judgement or trial. Also, a day of final dissolution. 1579. **2.** = DOMESDAY. **3.** *attrib.* 1649.

1. Hit myght laste til Domesday ME. Why then Al-soules day is my bodies d. *Rich. III*, V. i. 12.

Doo·msman. [Early ME. *domes man*, man of judgement; see DOOM *sb.*] A judge, deemster.

Doomster (dū·mstəɹ). ME. [var. of *demester*, DEMPSTER, DEEMSTER, after DOOM *sb.* and *v.*] **1.** A judge, doomer (*arch.*). **2.** *Sc.* = DEMPSTER 2. 1609.

Door (dōᵊɹ). [(i) OE. *duru* (fem. *u-stem*) = OFris. *dure*, OS. *duru*; (ii) OE. *dor* (n. *a-stem*) = OS. *dor*, (O)HG. *tor* gate, Goth. *daur*; Gmc. **dur-* :– IE. **dhur-*, which is repr. also by L. *foris*, Gr. θύρα, Skr. *dur*, *dvār*.] **1.** A movable barrier of wood or other material, usually turning on hinges or sliding in a groove, and serving to close or open a passage into a building, room, etc. **b.** Indicating the room or house to which the door belongs 1669. **2.** The passage into a building or room; a doorway ME. **3.** *fig.* A means of entrance or exit OE.

1. Doors and windows barred fast 1509. Having taken offices a few doors off 1885. **2.** They..met the iealous knaue their Master in the doore *Merry W.* III. v. 103. **3.** Phr. *To open a d. to* or *for*; *to close the d. upon* etc.

Phrases **a.** *In doors*: within doors, in or into the house. *Next d.* (*to*): in the next house (to); hence *fig.* very near (to). *Out of door(s*: out of the house; in the open air; hence *fig.* out of place, irrelevant. *Within door(s*: in a house or building, indoors. *Without doors*: out of doors.

b. *To lay, lie,* or *be at the d. of*: to impute, or be imputable or chargeable to. *To darken a d.*: see DARKEN. *To keep open doors*: see OPEN.

attrib. and *Comb.* **a.** attrib. as *d.-arch, -curtain, -handle, -knocker, -ring*, etc. **b.** objective and obj. genitive, as *d.-banging, -opener*, etc.

Comb.: **d.-alarm,** a device attached to a d., to give an alarm when the d. is opened; **-case,** the case lining a doorway, in which the d. is hung; **-cheek** (now *n. dial.*), a d.-post; **-frame,** (*a*) a d.-case; (*b*) the structure forming the skeleton of a panelled d.; **-keeper, doo·rkeeper,** one who keeps or guards a d., a janitor, porter; **-mat; -nail,** a large-headed nail, with which doors were formerly studded: now chiefly in *dead, deaf, dumb, dour as a d.-nail*; **-plate,** a plate on a d., giving the name, etc. of the occupant; **-post,** one of the jambs of a d.; **-sill,** the sill or threshold of a d.; **-stead,** a place for a d.; **-step,** the step at the threshold of a d., raised above the level of the ground outside; **-stone,** a flagstone before a d.; **-stop,** a device to stop a d. from opening too widely; also, the slip of wood against which it shuts in its frame; **-weed,** a name for *Polygonum aviculare*; **-yard** (*U.S.*), a yard or garden-patch about the d. of a house.

Dooring, error for *door-ring*; see above.

Doo·rless, *a.* ME. [-LESS.] Having no door.

Doo·rward. *arch.* [OE. *duruweard*, f. *duru* DOOR + *weard* warden, keeper.] A door-keeper. In *Sc. Hist.* = warder of the palace.

Doo·rway. 1799. The opening or passage which a door serves to close or open; a portal.

†**Dop,** *sb.*[1] 1599. [f. DOP *v.*] A curtsy, dip –1825.

Dop, *sb.*[2] 1700. [– Du. *dop* shell, husk, cover.] **1.** A pupa case. **2.** A copper cup into which a diamond is cemented for cutting or polishing 1764. **3.** Cape brandy made from grape-skins 1894.

†**Dop,** *v.* [ME. *doppe*, repr. OE. **doppian*, whence frequent. *doppettan* dip, immerse, baptize, f. Gmc. **deup- *daup- *dup-*; see DIP, DEEP.] To duck, dip –1692.

Dope (dōᵘp), *sb.* 1880. orig. *U.S.* [– Du. *doop* sauce, f. *doopen* dip, mix, adulterate.] **1.** Any thick liquid or semi-fluid used as a lubricant or absorbent. **b.** A surface dressing, e.g. varnish for aeroplanes 1912. **3.** A preparation of opium or other narcotic, esp. for doctoring horses; any narcotic (*d.-fiend*, a drug addict) 1889. **4.** Information about a racehorse's condition; hence, fraudulent information and information generally 1901. Hence **Dope** *v.* to drug, 'doctor', apply 'dope' to (a fabric); *fig.* to make, find, or work *out*.

Do·ppelga:nger. 1895. [– G. *doppelgänger*.] = DOUBLE-GANGER, q.v.

†**Dopper.**[1] ME. [f. DOP *v.* + -ER[1].] A didapper.

Dopper[2] (dǫ·pəɹ). 1620. [– Du. *dooper*, f. *doopen* dip; see DOPE.] A (Dutch) Baptist.

Dopplerite (dǫ·plərəit). 1863. [f. *Doppler*, a German physicist + -ITE[1] 2b.] *Min.* A hydrocarbon, amorphous and jelly-like when fresh, and elastic when dried, looking like black pitch.

Dor, dorr (dǭɹ), *sb.*[1] [OE. *dora*; cf. MLG. *dorte* drone; prob. imit.] An insect that flies with a loud humming noise. †**1. a.** A humble-bee or bumble-bee. **b.** A drone bee. **c.** A hornet. **d.** *fig.* A drone. –1681. **2.** *spec.* **a.** The common black dung-beetle (*Geotrupes stercorarius*), which flies after sunset. **b.** The cockchafer. **c.** The rosebeetle. Also vaguely, other species of beetles. 1450. Also † *fig.*

Comb.: **d.-bee, -beetle** (see 1, 2); **-bug** (*U.S.*), a name for various beetles; **-fly** (see 1, 2); **-hawk,** the night-jar.

†**Dor,** *sb.*[2] 1552. Also **dorre.** [Goes with DOR *v.*[1]; perh. – ON. *dár* scoff, in phr. *draga dár at* make game of.] Mockery, 'making game' –1855.

[He] brings home the dorre upon himself MILT.

†**Dor,** *v.*[1] Also **dorre.** 1570. [Goes with DOR *sb.*[2]; perh. – ON. *dára* mock, make sport of.] To make game of, mock, befool –1675.

Phr. *To d. the dotterel*: to hoax a simpleton: cf. DARE *v.*[2]

†**Dor(r,** *v.*[2] 1601. [Cf. Sc. and n. dial. *dirr* deaden.] To make dim (in colour).

Dora (dōᵊ·rā). 1918. Joc. personification, from its initials, of the *D*efence *O*f the *R*ealm *A*ct (August 1914), which gave the Government wide powers in time of war.

‖**Dorado** (dorā·do). 1604. [– Sp. *dorado* :– *deauratus*, pa. pple. of late L. *deaurare* gild over. See DORY *sb.*[1]] **1.** A fish (*Coryphæna hippuris*); also called *dolphin*. **2.** A southern constellation, also called Xiphias or the Sword-fish 1819. †**3.** *fig.* A rich man.

Dorcas (dǭ·ɹkăs). 1847. Name of a woman mentioned in Acts 9:36; hence, *D. society*, a ladies' association in a church for making and providing clothes for the poor.

Doree, dorey, var. of DORY.

Dor-fly, dorhawk; see DOR *sb.*[1]

‖**Doria, dorea** (dōᵊ·riă). 1696. [Hindi *doriyā* striped.] A kind of striped Indian muslin.

Dorian (dōᵊ·riăn), *a.* 1603. [f. L. *Dorius* – Gr. *Δώριος* of Doris; see -IAN] **A.** Of Doris or Doria, a division of ancient Greece.
D. mode in *Mus.*, an ancient Grecian mode, characterized by simplicity and solemnity; also, the first of the authentic ecclesiastical modes.
B. *sb.* A native or inhabitant of Doris 1662.

Doric (dǫ·rik). 1569. [– L. *Doricus* – Gr. *Δωρικός*; cf. prec. and see -IC.] **A.** *adj.* **1.** = DORIAN; of or pertaining to the Dorians; of a dialect, etc.: Broad; rustic. **2.** *Archit.* The name of one of the three Grecian orders (Doric, Ionic, Corinthian), of which it is the oldest, strongest, and simplest 1614.
1. With eager thought warbling his D. lay MILT.
B. *sb.* **1.** The Doric dialect of ancient Greek 1837. **b.** A broad or rustic dialect of English, Scotch, etc. 1870. **2.** The Doric order of architecture 1812.
Hence **Do·ricism**, a D. form of expression.

Dorism (dōᵊ·riz'm). 1698. [– Gr. *Δωρισμός* speaking Doric, f. *Δωρίζειν*; see next; -ISM.] **1.** The Dorian character of culture 1870. **2.** A Doricism.

Dorize (dōᵊ·rəiz), *v.* 1678. [– Gr. *Δωρίζειν*; see prec., -IZE.] **1.** *intr.* To imitate Doric manners, language, etc. **2.** *trans.* To render Doric in manners, etc. 1846.

Dorking (dǭ·ɹkiŋ), *a.* (*sb.*) 1840. [f. *Dorking* in Surrey.] Name of a breed of poultry of a long square form, and possessing five toes.

Dormancy (dǭ·ɹmănsi). 1789. [f. next; see -ANCY.] Dormant condition; cf. next.
The d. of any such prerogative 1789.

Dormant (dǭ·ɹmănt). ME. [– (O)Fr. *dormant*, pres. pple. of *dormir* :– L. *dormire* sleep; see -ANT.]
A. *adj.* **1.** Sleeping, lying asleep or as asleep; hence, *fig.* intellectually asleep 1623. **b.** Of plants: With development suspended 1863. **c.** *Her.* In a sleeping attitude 1500. **2.** In a state of inactivity; quiescent; in abeyance 1601. **3.** Fixed, stationary, as *d. tree* ME. **4.** *D. window*, also *d.* = DORMER 2. 1651.
1. In dry weather they [Mosses] are often completely d. 1863. **2.** A d. claim 1792, volcano HUXLEY. Phr. *D. commission, credit, warrant, writing*, etc., one drawn out in blank, to be filled up when required to be used. *D. partner*, a sleeping partner, who takes no part in the working of a concern. **3.** *D. table*, one fixed to the floor (*arch.*).
B. *sb.* †**1.** A fixed horizontal beam; a sleeper; a summer. More fully *d. tree* (see A 3). –1665. **2.** = DORMER window; see A. 4.

Dormer (dǭ·ɹməɹ). 1592. [– OFr. *dormēor*, f. *dormir* sleep + *-ēor* -ER² 3.] **1.** A dormitory. Now *Hist.* 1605. **2.** A projecting vertical window in the sloping roof of a house. Also *d.-window*. (Orig. the window of a dormitory.) 1592. †**3.** = DORMANT *sb.* 1. –1825. Hence **Do·rmered** *a.* having dormers.

‖**Dormeuse** (dormö̆·z). 1734. [Fr.; fem. of *dormeur*, lit. 'sleeper'.] †**1.** A nightcap –1753. **2.** A travelling-carriage adapted for sleeping in 1825.

Dormient (dǭ·ɹmiĕnt), *a.* 1643. [– *dormient-*, pres. ppl. stem of L. *dormire* sleep; see -ENT.] Sleeping, dormant.

Dormition (dǫɹmi·ʃən). 1483. [– Fr. *dormition* – L. *dormitio*, f. *dormit-*, pa. ppl. stem of *dormire* sleep; see -ION.] Sleeping; falling asleep; *fig.* death (of the righteous).

Do·rmitive. 1593. [– Fr. *dormitif, -ive*, f. as prec.; see -IVE.] **A.** *adj.* Causing sleep. **B.** *sb.* A soporific; a narcotic 1619.

Dormitory (dǭ·ɹmitŏri), *sb.* 1485. [– L. *dormitorium*, subst. use of n. of *dormitorius*, f. as prec.; see -ORY¹.] **1.** A sleeping-chamber; *spec.* a room containing a number of beds, or a gallery or building divided into cells or chambers with beds, as in a monastery, schools, etc. **2.** *fig.* A resting-place 1634. †**3.** A cemetery, vault, grave –1775.
3. We obtained a D. for his Body among the Armenian Christians SIR T. HERBERT.

Dormouse (dǭ·ɹmaus). ME. [Of unkn. origin.] **1.** A small rodent of a family intermediate between the squirrels and the mice; *esp.* the British species *Myoxus avellanarius*, noted for its hibernation. **2.** *transf.* A sleepy person 1568. **3.** *attrib.* Sleepy 1601.
2. A d. against the Devil MILT. **3.** Your d. valour SHAKS.

Dormy (dǭ·ɹmi), *a.* 1887. [Of unkn. origin.] *Golf.* Of a player: As many 'up' as there are holes to play; thus, *d. one*, etc.

Dornick (dǭ·ɹnik). 1489. Applied to certain fabrics originally manufactured at *Doornick*, a Flemish town (in French called Tournay), and used for hangings, carpets, vestments, etc. Also, 'A species of linen cloth used in Scotland for the table' (J.).
(In the latter sense, referred erron. to *Dornoch* in Scotland.)

Dorothy Perkins (dǫ·rəþi pə̄·ɹkinz). 1904. [Personal name.] A climbing rose bearing clusters of double pink flowers.

†**Dorp.** 1570. [– Du. *dorp* = OE. *þorp.*] A (Dutch) village; formerly: = THORP.
No neighb'ring D., no lodging to be found DRYDEN.

Dorr, var. of DOR *sb.*¹ and *v.*²

Dorsad (dǭ·ɹsæd), *adv.* 1803. [f. L. *dorsum* + -AD II.] *Anat.* Towards the back.

Dorsal (dǭ·ɹsăl), *a.* (*sb.*) 1541. [– (O)Fr. *dorsal* or late L. *dorsalis*, for L. *dorsualis*, f. *dorsum* back; see -AL¹. Cf. DOSSAL.]
A. †**1.** Having a back: of a knife with one edge. **2.** *Anat.* **a.** (*Zool.*) Pertaining to, or situated on or near, the back of an animal, as *d. fin, nerves, vertebræ*. (Opp. to VENTRAL.) 1727. **b.** (*Zool.* and *Bot.*) Pertaining to, or situated on the back (*i.e.* upper, outer, convex, or hinder surface) of any organ or part 1808. **3.** *gen.* Forming a ridge like the back of an animal 1827.
3. The great d. range that in Turkey corresponds to the Apennines G. DUFF. Hence **Do·rsally** *adv.*
B. *sb.* **1.** *Anat.* Short for *d. fin.* or *d. vertebra* 1834. **2.** *Eccl.* = DOSSAL b. 1870.

†**Dorse,** *sb.*¹ 1524. [– L. *dorsum* back; cf. med.L *dorsum* back of document (cf. ENDORSE).] **1.** = DOSSAL b. **2.** The back of a book or writing –1691.
2. Books..richly bound with gilt dorses WOOD.

Dorse (dǭɹs), *sb.*² 1610. [– LG. *dorsch* = ON. *torskr* codfish.] A young cod. (Formerly supposed to be a distinct species, and named *Gadus* (or *Morrhua*) *callarias*.)

Dorsel; see DOSSAL, DOSSEL.

Dorser; see DOSSER¹.

Dorsi- (dors-), comb. f. L. *dorsum* back = 'back-; of, to, on the back'. (Sometimes used improperly where DORSO- is the correct form.) Hence:
Dorsibra·nchiate *a.*, having gills on the back; belonging to the order *Dorsibranchiata* of Annelids; *sb.* a dorsibranchiate annelid. **Do·rsigrade** *a.*, walking upon the backs of the toes, as certain armadillos. **Dorsime·dian** *a.*, situated in the middle line of the back. **Dorsime·sal, dorsome·sal** *a.* [see next] = prec. **Dorsime·son** [Gr. *μέσον*], the middle line of the back. **Dorsispi·nal** *a.*, pertaining to the spinous processes of the vertebræ.

Dorsiferous (dǭɹsi·fĕrəs), *a.* 1727. [irreg. f. DORSI- + -FEROUS.] **1.** *Bot.* Bearing the fructification (as a fern) upon the back (*i.e.* under side) of the frond. **2.** = DORSIPAROUS b. 1755. **3.** = next.

Dorsigerous (dǫɹsi·dʒĕrəs), *a.* 1839. [irreg. f. DORSI- + -GEROUS.] Carrying the young upon the back, as a species of opossum.

Dorsiparous (dǭɹsi·părəs), *a.* 1727. [f. DORSI- + -PAROUS.] **a.** *Bot.* = DORSIFEROUS. **b.** *Zool.* Hatching the young upon the back, as certain toads.

Dorsi-ventral; see DORSO-*ventral*.

Dorso-, dors-, stem and comb. f. L. *dorsum* back, used in comb. in the sense 'back and —' (and sometimes improperly, where *dorsi-* is the correct form). Hence:
Dorso-abdo·minal, dorsabdo·minal *a.*, relating to the back and abdomen. **Dorsola·teral** *a.*, relating to the back and the side. **Dorso-ve·ntral** *a.*, (*a*) = *dorsabdominal*; (*b*) *Bot.* having dorsal and ventral halves of different internal structure, as most monosymmetrical organs; whence **Dorso-ve·ntrally** *adv.*, in a dorso-ventral direction or situation.

‖**Do·rsolum, -ulum.** 1826. [mod. L., dim. of *dorsum.*] *Entom.* A piece of the exoskeleton of an insect situated between the collar and scutellum.

‖**Dorsum** (dǭ·ɹsŏm). 1782. [L., = back.] **1.** The back of an animal. **b.** The upper, outer, or convex surface of an organ or part. 1840. **2.** A ridge of high ground (*nonce-use*) 1782.

Dortour, dorter (dǭ·ɹtəɹ). Now *Hist.* ME. [– OFr. *dortour* (mod. *dortoir*) :– L. *dormitorium* DORMITORY; see -OUR.] A dormitory.

Dory (dōᵊ·ri), *sb.*¹ ME. [– Fr. *dorée*, subst. use of fem. pa. pple. of *dorer* gild :– late L. *deaurare*, f. *de-* DE- + *aurare* gild, f. *aurum* gold.] A fish, *Zeus faber*. Also called JOHN DORY, q.v.

Dory (dōᵊ·ri), *sb.*² *W. Indies* and *U.S.* 1798. [Of unkn. origin.] A small flat-bottomed boat much used in sea-fisheries.

Dosage (dōᵘ·sėdʒ). 1867. [f. DOSE *v.* or *sb.* + -AGE. Cf. Fr. *dosage.*] **1.** The administration of medicine in doses 1876. **2.** The operation of dosing; addition of a dose or doses, *e.g.* to wine, etc.

Dose (dōᵘs), *sb.* 1600. [– Fr. *dose* – late L. *dosis* DOSIS – Gr. *δόσις* giving, gift, portion of medicine (Galen), f. *διδόναι* give.] **1.** *Med.* A definite quantity of a medicine given or prescribed to be given at one time. **2.** *transf.* and *fig.* A definite quantity of something regarded as analogous to medicine in use or effect; a definite amount of some ingredient added to wine to give it a special character 1607.
1. To administer doses of bark MACAULAY. **2.** To repeat and daily increase the d. of flattery MERIVALE.

Dose (dōᵘs), *v.* 1654. [f. prec.; cf. Fr. *doser.*] **1.** *trans.* To divide into, or administer in, doses 1713. **2.** To administer doses to; to physic 1654. Also *transf.*
2. A bold, self-opinioned physician..who shall d., and bleed, and kill him *secundum artem* SOUTH.

Dōsimeter (dosi·mĭtəɹ). 1881. [f. DOSE *sb.* + -METER.] An apparatus for measuring doses or the like.

Dosimetric (dǫsime·trik), *a.* 1881. [f. as prec. + -METRIC.] Relating to the measurement of doses. So **Dosi·metry**, the measurement of doses.

Dosio·logy, doso·logy. 1678. [irreg. f. DOSE or DOSIS + -LOGY.] The science of the doses in which medicine should be given.

‖**Do·sis.** 1543. [Late L., see DOSE *sb.*] = DOSE *sb.*

†**Doss,** *sb.*¹ 1482. [– OFr. *dos* :– pop. L. *dossum* for L. *dorsum* back.] = DOSSAL b. –1533.

Doss (dǫs), *sb.*² *slang.* 1789. [prob. same word as prec., see DOSS *v.*²] **1.** A bed; *esp.* a bed in a common lodging-house. **2.** Sleep 1858.
Comb.: **d.-house,** a common lodging-house.

Doss (dǫs), *v.*¹ Now *dial.* 1583. [Cf. MDu. *dossen*, intensive of *dosen, doesen* strike with violence and noise.] **1.** *intr.* To push with the horns, as a bull; *trans.* to toss. **2.** *Sc.* To throw *down* with force 1745.

Doss, *v.*² *slang.* 1785. [Goes with DOSS *sb.*²] *intr.* To sleep; *esp.* to sleep at a 'doss-house'.

Dossal, dossel (dǫ·săl, -ĕl). 1658. [Early forms †*dosel*, †*dorsel* – med.L. *dossale*, n. of *dossalis*, for *dorsalis*; see DORSAL. Cf. OFr. *dossal, dossel*. The ME. word was DOSSER¹.] **a.** An ornamental cloth forming a cover for the back of a seat (*arch.*). **b.** *Eccl.* An ornamental cloth hung at the back of the altar or at the sides of the chancel.

†**Dossel.** Also **dorsel.** 1755. [app. var. of DOSSER¹ and of its var. *dorser*, with substitution of suffix -EL.] = DOSSER¹ 2. –1827.

Dosser¹ (dǫ·səɹ), **dorser** (dǭ·ɹsəɹ). Now *Hist.* [ME. *doser, dorser* – OFr. *dossier* (in mod.Fr. back of a seat, DOSSIER, etc.) – med. L. *dorsarium, dossarium* in same sense, f. *dossum, dorsum* (cf. DOSSAL) + *-arium* -ARY¹.] **1.** = DOSSAL b. **2.** A pannier ME.

Do·sser². *slang.* 1866. [f. DOSS *v.*² + -ER¹.] One who frequents a 'doss-house'.

Dossier (dǫ·sieⁱ). 1880. [– Fr. *dossier* bundle of papers in a wrapper having a label on the back (XVII), f. *dos* back (:– L. *dorsum*) + *-ier* -ARY¹.] A bundle of papers referring to some matter.

Dossil (dǫ·sil). ME. [– OFr. *dosil, doisil*, mod. *doisil, douzil* :– Gallo-Rom. *duciculus* (med.L. *duciculus, ducillus, docillus*), f. L. *ducere* lead, conduct.] †**1.** A plug for a barrel, a spigot –1483. **2.** A plug of lint or rag for stopping a wound, etc.; a pledget 1575. **3.** A roll of cloth for wiping ink from the surface of a copper-plate in printing 1874.

Dost (dɒst), 2 sing. pres. ind. of DO *v.*, q.v.

Dot (dǫt), *sb.*[1] [OE. *dott* (once) head of a boil, perh. in continuous colloq. use (cf. DOTTLE), but not recorded again until XVI in sense 2, when its appearance may be due to Du. *dot* knot.] †**1.** The head of a boil. (Only OE.) **2.** A small lump, clot. Now *dial.* 1570. **3.** A minute spot, speck, or mark 1674. **4.** A minute roundish mark made with or as with a pen 1748. **5.** Specifically:

Orthogr. **a.** A point used in punctuation. **b.** The point over the letters i and j. **c.** A point placed over, under, or by a letter or figure to modify its value 1740. **d.** *Mus.* a point placed after, over, or under a note, after a rest, or before or after a double bar.

6. A little child or other creature 1859. **7.** The act by which a dot is made 1858.

4. A small island..represented in the general chart..only by a d. 1748. **6.** Troops of children, from little dots of four and five..to big girls SALA.

Comb.: **d.-and-dash** *a.*, formed by dots and dashes, as the Morse alphabet, etc.; **-stitch,** a stitch used in making dots in embroidery; **-wheel,** a toothed wheel mounted in a handle, which when rolled over a surface produces a dotted line.

‖**Dot** (dǫt), *sb.*[2] 1855. [– (O)Fr. *dot* – L. *dos, dot-*, f. **do-* give.] A woman's marriage portion, of which the annual income alone is under her husband's control. Cf. DOTE *sb.*[2]

Some little difficulty about the *dot* 1870.

Dot (dǫt), *v.*[1] 1740. [f. DOT *sb.*[1]] **1.** *trans.* To mark with a dot or dots. **2.** To cover or diversify as with minute spots 1818. **3.** To scatter like dots or specks 1816. **4.** *intr.* To make a dot or dots 1755.

1. *D. in*, to fill in with dots. *To d. the i's* (*fig.*): to particularize minutely; [He] dotted our 'i's' and crossed our 't's'..about the lack of men in the Navy 1896. **2.** The whole Channel was dotted with our cruisers MACAULAY.

Phr. *To d. down*, to write down compendiously.

Dot, *v.*[2] *rare.* 1887. [– (O)Fr. *doter*, f. *dot* DOT *sb.*[2] The historical Eng. form was *dote* (XVI).] *trans.* To dower with a marriage portion.

Dotage (dōᵘ·tėdʒ). ME. [f. DOTE *sb.*[1] or *v.* + -AGE. Cf. Fr. *radotage*, f. *radoter.*] **1.** The state of one who dotes, now *esp.* through old age; feebleness of mind; folly; second childhood; senility. Also *transf.* **2.** The action or habit of doting upon any one; foolish affection; excessive fondness ME.; that which is doted upon 1662.

1. The world is in its d. 1766. Rabbinical dotages 1825. **2.** Merlyn felle in a dottage on the damoisel MALORY. You shall..Become Jove's d. 1662.

Dotal (dōᵘ·tăl), *a.* 1513. [– Fr. *dotal* or L. *dotalis*; see DOT *sb.*[2], -AL[1].] Pertaining to a dower, dowry, or woman's marriage portion.

†**Do·tant.** [f. DOTE *v.* + -ANT. Cf. Fr. *radotant.*] = DOTARD. *Cor.* V. ii. 47.

Dotard (dōᵘ·tăɹd). ME. [f. DOTE *v.* + -ARD.]

A. *sb.* **1.** An imbecile; now, usually, one who is in his dotage. †**b.** One who dotes (*on* something) 1602. †**2.** (? a different word) A tree that has lost its top or branches, and of which the decayed trunk alone remains –1725.

1. Thou were an olde dooterd and a foole CAXTON.

B. *adj.* [*sb.* used *attrib.*] **1.** Imbecile; in senile decay ME. †**2.** Of a tree; Remaining as a decayed trunk without branches –1787. Hence **Do·tardly** *a.* foolish.

Dotarie, obs. f. DOTERY.

Dotation (dotē̆ⁱ·ʃən). ME. [– (O)Fr. *dotation* or med.L. *dotatio*, f. *dotat-*, pa. ppl. stem of L. *dotare*; see -ION.] The action of endowing; endowment.

A general d. of the poorer citizens MERIVALE.

†**Dote,** *sb.*[1] ME. [app. based on MDu. *dote* folly.] **1.** A dotard –1630. **2.** Dotage 1610.

Dote (dōᵘt), *sb.*[2] *arch.* 1515. [– Fr. †*dote*, var. of *dot* DOT *sb.*[2]] **1.** A woman's marriage portion. †**2.** *fig.* (Usu. in *pl.*) A natural gift –1656.

Dote, doat (dōᵘt), *v.* [ME. *dotie* (perh. OE. **dotian*), corresp. to MDu. *doten* be silly (whence OFr. *redoter*, mod. *radoter*). In senses 1 and 2 mostly *dote*, also *doat* (from XVI), esp. in sense 3.] **1.** *intr.* To be silly, deranged, or out of one's wits; to act or talk foolishly. **2.** Now *esp.* To be weak-minded from old age ME. **3.** To be infatuatedly fond *of*; to be foolishly in love. Const. †*of, upon, on.* 1477. **4.** To decay, as a tree. Now *dial.* ME. †**5.** *trans.* To cause to dote; to befool, infatuate –1611. †**6.** To say or think foolishly –1612.

1. Doting about questions, and strifes of wordes 1 *Tim.* 6:4. **2.** The parson..is now old and doates 1710. **3.** You doate on her, that cares not for your loue *Two Gent.* IV. iv. 87. Hence **Do·ted, doa·ted** *ppl. a.* †dotard; †infatuated; of a tree, decayed inside (*dial.*). **Do·ter, doa·ter,** one who dotes. †**Do·tery, doterie,** doting.

Doth (dɒþ), arch. 3 sing. pres. ind. of Do *v.*

Do·ting, doating, *vbl. sb.* ME. [f. DOTE *v.* + -ING.[1]] The action of DOTE *v.*; an instance of this.

Do·ting, doating, *ppl. a.* 1489. [f. as prec. + -ING[2].] That dotes; weak-minded; foolishly fond; of trees, decaying from age. Hence **Do·tingly** *adv.*

Do·tish, doatish, *a. arch.* 1509. [f. DOTE *sb.*[1] + -ISH[1].] Silly, childish.

Dottard, obs. or dial. f. DOTARD, sense 2.

Dotted (dǫ·tėd), *ppl. a.* 1772. [f. DOT *v.*[1] and *sb.*[2] + -ED.] **1.** Formed of dots. **2.** Marked with or as with dots 1821. **3.** Furnished with a dot 1837.

1. A d. line 1772. **2.** The back-ground..is d. or stippled 1821. **3.** Thus a double dotted minim is equal to three crotchets and a quaver 1837.

Dotter (dǫ·təɹ), *sb.* 1832. [f. DOT *v.*[1] + -ER[1].] One who or that which dots; *spec.* a hand-instrument used in embossing letters for the blind.

Put on the eyes [in bird's-eye maple] by dabbing with the d. 1873.

Dotterel (dǫ·tərĕl), **dottrel** (dǫ·trĕl). ME. [f. DOTE *v.*: see -REL.] **1.** A species of plover (*Eudromias morinellus*): said to be so simple that it readily allows itself to be taken. **2.** A silly person (*dial.*) ME. **3.** A doddered tree (*dial.*) 1568.

1. This dotrell is a lytell fonde byrde, for it helpeth in maner to take it selfe 1526. **2.** Old idle dottrels tayles 1547.

Dottle (do·t'l). 1440. [f. DOT *sb.*[1] + -LE.] †**1.** A plug –1743. **2.** A plug of tobacco left unsmoked in a pipe 1825.

Dotty (dǫ·ti), *a.* 1812. [f. DOT *sb.*[1] + -Y[1].] **1.** Consisting of dots; dot-like. **2.** Of unsteady gait. Hence *fig.* Silly. 1870.

Do·ty, *a. dial.* 1883. [rel. to DOTE *v.* 4, DOTARD 2.] Of wood: Decayed.

‖**Douane** (du,a·n, dwan). 1656. [Fr. *douane* – It. *doana, dogana* – Turk. *duwan*, Arab. *dīwān* DIVAN.] A custom-house. Hence ‖**Douanier** (dwanye), a custom-house officer (in France or, by extension, elsewhere).

‖**Douar, dowar** (dū·aɹ). 1829. [– N. Afr. Arab. *dūwar*, after Fr. *douar.*] A group of Arab tents arranged in a circle round an enclosure for the cattle.

Doub, var. of DOOB.

Double (dɒ·b'l), *a.* (*adv.*) ME. [– OFr. *doble, duble*, later and mod. *double* :– L. *duplus* DUPLE.]

A. *adj.* **1.** Consisting of two combined; twofold; forming a pair, coupled. Often with a sing. sb., = 'two' or 'a couple of' with pl. sb. ME. **b.** Doubled; bent, 'doubled up' 1450. **c.** Having some essential part double 1469. **d.** Of flowers: Having the number of petals doubled or more by conversion of stamens and carpels into petals 1578. **2.** Having a twofold relation; of two kinds; dual; occas. = ambiguous ME. **3.** Twice as much or many; multiplied by two. Const. *of*; also *ellipt.* = twice. ME. **4.** Of (or about) twice that denoted by the simple word; of extra size, strength, amount 1472. **b.** *Mus.* Sounding an octave lower in pitch 1674. **c.** *Mil.* Applied to a pace in marching 1833. **5.** Acting in two ways at different times; characterized by duplicity; false, deceitful ME.

1. Like to a d. cherry..Two louely berries molded on one stem *Mids. N.* III. ii. 209. A d. knock DICKENS. **b.** Bent d. with pain 1897. **2.** Fye on doble entendement, and cloked adulacion HALL. **3.** Let a d. portion of thy spirit be vpon me 2 *Kings* 2:9. **4.** Sengle bere, and othir that is dowbile 1500. D. foolscap, 27 by 17 URE. A new coin, to be called a D.-Florin 1887. Phr. *D. time* (Mil.): formerly, a pace of 150 steps in the minute; at present (1896), in the British Army, one of 165 steps of 33 inches to the minute. **5.** He was d. in love and nothing pleyne CHAUCER. He was..either very d. or very inconstant BP. BURNET.

Phrases. *D.-acting* ppl. a. acting in two directions, by two methods, etc.; *spec.* of a steam-engine, worked by application of steam power on both sides of the piston. So *D. action. D. algebra*: algebra which deals with two sets of quantities or relations. *D. change* (Bell-ringing): one in which two pairs of bells change places. *D. cone* (Archit.): a moulding composed of truncated cones joined base to base and top to top. *D. consonant* (Phonology): two instances of the same consonant coming together, as in *wholly*; also = *double letter* (*a*) below. *D. feast* (Eccl.): one on which the antiphons are recited in full before and after psalms and canticles. *D. first* (Univ. colloq.): a place in the first class in each of two final examinations in different subjects; one who takes such a place. *D. letter*: (*a*) a letter denoting two sounds, as *x* (= *ks*); (*b*) in *Printing*, two letters combined in one type as ff, fi. *D. point*: in the Higher Geometry, a point common to two branches of a curve, or at which the curve has two tangents; a node, cusp, or conjugate point; also an analogous point on a curved surface. *D. snipe*, the greater snipe, *Gallinago major. D. spar*, a name for Iceland spar, as being double-refracting. *D. star* (Astron.): two stars so near as not to be separately visible without a telescope. *D.-stopping* (Mus.): the simultaneous sounding of two (stopped) notes on two strings of a violin, etc.; notes so played are called *d.-stops. To work d. tides*; see TIDE. *D. time*: see 4 (quots.). *D. U*: name of the letter W.

¶ Also in other phrases, as *d. bar, curvature, entry, Gloucester, refraction, shuffle*, etc., etc., for which see the sbs.

B. *adv.* **1.** To twice the amount or extent; in two ways; twice, twice over, DOUBLY; in a couple ME. †**2.** After a numeral: = (so many) times; -fold. (Occas. pleonastic, as *sevenfold d.* = sevenfold.) –1698.

1. Words brought into the world, to make men see d. HOBBES. To ride d. 1599. To carry d. 1678.

Phr. *D. or quit(s* (Gambling): an expression implying that the stake already due is either to be doubled, or to be cancelled, on the next issue; hence *fig.*

C. Double- in comb.

1. Double *adj.* in parasynthetic combs., e.g. *d.-barred* (having a d. bar or two bars), *-chinned, -eyed*, etc.; **d.-brooded,** producing two broods in the year or season, as some insects; **-footed,** †(*a*) two-footed; (*b*) = *diplopod* (see DIPLO-); **-fronted** d.-faced; **-leaded,** having the lines of type widely separated by means of d. leads; **-lived,** having two lives or manners of life; †amphibious, etc.

2. Double *adj.* in comb. with sbs., forming **a.** adjs., as *d.-action, -shift*, etc. **d.-beat valve,** (*a*) a valve in a pump affording two openings for the water; (*b*) a device in a steam-engine consisting of two connected conical valves between which steam is admitted so as to equalize the upward and downward pressure; also called *d.-seat valve.* **b.** sbs. arising out of the absol. or ellipt. use of those preceding, as D.-FACE, etc. **c.** sbs., as **d.-ripper, -runner** (*U.S.*), two sleds connected by a plank, used by boys for coasting downhill; etc.

3. Vbs. formed from *double* adv. in comb. with vbs. (or from *double* adj. with sbs.), as *d.-arm, -bar* (to secure with d. bars), *-bolt, -damn*, etc.

4. Double *adv.* in comb.: **a.** with pa. pples. or ppl. adjs., as *d.-distilled, -stitched*, etc.; **d.-cut,** of a file = CROSS-CUT *a.* 2; **-hung,** of sashes, those of which the window contains two, each movable separately; **-ironed,** loaded with irons on both legs; **-milled,** of cloth, milled twice to make it closer and thicker; **-sunk,** of a dial, having recesses for the hour hand and the seconds hand; **-worked,** of a tree, twice budded or grafted. **b.** with pres. pples. or ppl. adjs., as *d.-refracting*, etc. **c.** with adjs., as *d.-concave, -convex*, etc. **d.** with agent-nouns, as **d.-breather,** an animal that breathes through two nostrils.

Double (dɒ·b'l), *sb.* ME. [In branch I, the adj. used ellipt.; in II, noun of action from DOUBLE *v.*]

I. 1. A double quantity; twice as much or many. **2.** A thing that is an exact repetition of another. †**a.** A duplicate (*of* a writing). Chiefly *Sc.* –1752. **b.** A counterpart. **c.** *spec.* A wraith. 1798. **3.** Technical senses:

a. *Bell-ringing.* A change, in which two pairs of bells change places. **b.** Double-headed shot. **c.** *pl.* A kind of thick narrow black ribbons for shoe-strings. **d.** Accidental duplication of a word or passage. **e.** *Mil.* A double pace: see DOUBLE *a.* 4 c. **f.** *Lawn Tennis.* A game played by two a side; also two faults in succession. **g.** An actor or singer who takes two parts in the same piece, as in case of absence of another performer. **h.** *Whist.* A game in which one side scores five before the other scores three. **i.** Often ellipt.; e.g. = *double bed, feast, flower, line, star*, etc.

1. Ten, which is the d. of five JOWETT. **2.** The fetch or d. of the Göttingen student HONE. **3. e.**

The men cheering, broke out into a d., and at last into a regular race RUSSELL. **h.** That's two doubles and the rub DICKENS.

II. 1. A fold; a folded piece of stuff. ? *Obs.* 1602. **2.** A sharp turn in running, as of a hunted hare; also, of a river; *fig.* an evasive turn or shift 1592.

1. Rowled up in seaven-fould doubles Of plagues MARSTON. **2.** Phr. *To give one the d.*, i.e. the slip.

Double (dʊ·b'l), *v.* [ME. *doble, duble* – OFr. *dobler, dubler* (mod. *doubler*) :– late L. *duplare*, f. L. *duplus*; see DOUBLE *a.*] **1.** *trans.* To make double; to make twice as much, as many, or as great; to multiply by two; to put two in place of one. Also *absol.* **2.** *intr.* (for *refl.*) To increase twofold ME.; of flowers, to become double 1882. †**3.** *trans.* To repeat; to redouble; to make a duplicate of (*Sc.*) –1805. †**b.** *intr.* or *absol.* To speak with repetition of sounds (*rare*) –1621. **4.** *Mil.* **a.** *trans.* To increase (ranks or files) to twice their length by marching others up into them. **b.** *intr.* Of ranks or files: To march up into the other ranks or files so as to double them 1598. **c.** *trans.* (*colloq.*) To couple *with* 1837. **5.** *Mil. intr.* To go 'at the double' 1890. **6.** *trans.* To line or add a second layer of material to ME. **7.** To bend over, so as to bring the two parts into contact or proximity; to fold; to close, clench (the hand or fist). Often with *up*. ME. Also *intr.* (for *refl.*). **8.** *Naut.* (*trans.*) To sail round or to the other side of (a cape or point) 1548; *intr.* to get round. **9.** *intr.* To turn sharply in running; to turn back on one's course 1596; *fig.* to make evasive turns or shifts. ? *Obs.* 1530.

1. I doubled my pace DE FOE. To d. a vowel ROBY. Phr. *To d. a part*: to act as the double of or substitute for another player; also *fig.* **2.** The circulation doubled 1882. **3.** This knaues tongue begins to d. 2 *Hen. VI*, II. iii. 94. **7.** The page is doubled down DRYDEN. Phr. *To d. up*: to make to bend, as by a blow; hence *fig.* to cause to collapse (*slang.*). **8.** To d. the Cape of Good Hope 1665. Phr. (*intr.*) *To d. upon* (Mil., etc.): to get round so as to enclose between two fires. **9.** See how he doubles, like a hunted hare DRYDEN. *fig.* Why hast thou dealt thus craftely And doubled so with mee 1578.

Double-banked (-bæŋkt), *a.* 1697. [parasynth. f. *double bank* + -ED².] **a.** Having pairs of opposite oars pulled by rowers on the same bench; or, having two rowers at each oar. **b.** *Double-banked frigate*: one carrying guns on two decks; a **Double-banker. Double-bank** *v.*, to provide thus with rowers; also *transf.* and *absol.*

Double-barrelled, -eled, *a.* 1709. Of a fire-arm: Having two barrels; *fig.* double, twofold.

Double-bass (dʊ·b'l,bēⁱ·s). 1727. [f. DOUBLE *a.* 4 + BASS *sb.*³, after It. *contrabasso* CONTRABASS.] The largest and deepest-toned instrument of the violin class.

Double-bitt, *v.* 1833. [See BITT.] *Naut.* To pass (a cable) twice round the bitts, or round two pairs of bitts.

Double-bitted, *a.* 1816. [See BIT *sb.*¹] Having two bits.

Double-breasted, *a.* 1701. Of a coat, etc.: Having the two sides of the breast made alike, so as to button on either side.

Double-cro·ss, *sb. slang.* 1874. [f. DOUBLE *a.* + CROSS *sb.* 18.] An act of treachery to both parties, esp. by pretended collusion with each; also more widely. Hence **Double-cross** *v.*, **-crosser.**

Dou·ble-dealer. 1547. [f. next.] One who acts with duplicity.

Dou·ble-dealing, double dealing, *vbl. sb.* 1529. [See DOUBLE *a.* 5.] Action marked by duplicity. Also as *ppl. a.*

Double-decker. *colloq.* [parasynth. f. *double deck* + -ER¹.] 'A ship with two decks above the water-line.' Also, A street-car having seats on top as well as inside.

Double-dye, *v.* 1602. [f. DOUBLE *adv.* + DYE *v.*] To dye twice; *fig.* to stain deeply, as, *a double-dyed scoundrel.*

Double-e·nder. 1865. **1.** Anything having two ends alike; *spec.* a gun-boat rounded fore and aft (*U.S.*). **2.** A cross-cut sawing machine with two adjustable circular saws, for sawing both ends of timber.

‖**Double entendre** (dūbl ãntãndr). 1673. [– Fr. (rare) †*double entendre*, for usual *double entente* 'double understanding'.] A double meaning; a word or phrase having a double sense, *esp.* as used to convey an indelicate meaning.

Double-face. 1892. **a.** (As two words) 'Duplicity'; double-dealing. **b.** (*dou·ble-face*) A double-faced person 1892.

Double-faced (-fēⁱst), *a.* 1575. **1.** Having two faces or aspects; of a fabric, finished on both sides 1589. **2.** *fig.* Facing two ways; insincere.

2. Double-fac'd men God abhorreth 1577.

Dou·ble-ganger (-gæŋəɹ). 1830. [Semi-anglicization, by Scott and C. Kingsley, of G. *doppelgänger* 'double-goer, -walker' = Du. *dubbelganger*.] The apparition of a living person; a double, a wraith.

Dou·ble-ha·nded, *a.* 1611. **1.** Two-handled. **2.** Having two hands; *fig.* capable of two applications 1665.

Dou·ble-hea·ded, *a.* 1542. Having a double head or two heads, two-headed (*lit.* and *fig.*).

Double-headed shot: a shot consisting of two balls joined together. *Double-headed snake* = AMPHISBÆNA 2.

Double-hea·der. *U.S.* 1869. [parasynth. f. *double head* + -ER¹.] **a.** A kind of firework. **b.** A railway train having two engines.

Dou·ble-hea·rted, *a.* 1552. [See DOUBLE *a.* 5.] Having a double heart; deceitful, dissembling.

Dou:ble-lo·ck, *v.* 1592. *trans.* To lock by two turns of the key

Bid Suspicion double-lock the door SHAKS.

Double meaning, *sb.* 1551. = DOUBLE ENTENDRE. So **Dou·ble-meaning** *a.*

Dou·ble-mi·nded, *a.* 1552. Having two minds; undecided or wavering in mind; †also, formerly, Having two meanings.

A double minded man is vnstable in all his ways *Jas.* 1:8.

Doubleness (dʊ·b'lnes). ME. [f. DOUBLE *a.* + -NESS.] **1.** The quality or state of being double or two-fold. **2.** The character of being double in action or conduct; duplicity, treachery ME.

Dou·ble-qui·ck, *a.* (*sb.*, *adv.*) 1822. **a.** *adj. Mil.* Applied to the quickest step next to the run; see DOUBLE *a.* 4 (quots.). **b.** *sb.* Double-quick pace or time; = DOUBLE *sb.* 3 e; also *gen.* **c.** *adv.* In double-quick time.

In the U.S. army, Double-quick time is identical with the 'double time' now in force in the British Army, for which see DOUBLE *a.* 4 (quots.).

Doubler¹ (dʊ·bləɹ). Now *dial.* ME. [– AFr. *dobler, dubler* = OFr. *dob-, doublier* kind of dish, etc. :– med.L. *duplarium*, f. L. *duplus* double + *-arium* -ARY¹.] A large plate or dish.

Doubler² (dʊ·bləɹ). 1552. [f. DOUBLE *v.* + -ER¹. Cf. Fr. *doubleur*.] One who or that which makes double; *esp. Electr.* A machine intended to multiply, by repeated doubling, a very small quantity of electricity, till it became sufficient to affect an electrometer, give sparks, etc.

Double-reef, *v.* 1703. *trans.* To reduce the spread of (a sail) by taking in two reefs.

Double-shot, *v.* 1824. To load with a double quantity of shot. Also *fig.*

Doublet (dʊ·blėt). ME. [– OFr. *doublet*, f. *double*; see DOUBLE *a.*, -ET.] **1.** A close-fitting body-garment, with or without sleeves, worn by men from the 14th to the 18th centuries. Now *Hist.* **2.** One of two things precisely alike; one of a pair or couple; a duplicate copy; *pl.* twins. *spec.* **b.** *Philol.* One of two words (in the same language) representing the same ultimate word but differentiated in form, as *cloak* and *clock*, etc. **c.** *Printing.* = DOUBLE *sb.* 3 d. **3.** *Gaming.* (*pl.*) **a.** The same number turning up on both the dice at a throw 1450. †**b.** An old game at tables or backgammon –1684. **4.** A pair or couple 1816; *spec.* a combination of two simple lenses 1831. **5.** A counterfeit jewel composed of two pieces of 'crystal' cemented together with a layer of colour between them, or of a thin slice of a gem cemented on a piece of glass or inferior stone 1449.

1. Phr. *D. and hose*; *esp.* as the typical masculine attire; also as a sort of undress, or dress for active pursuits. †*Iron* or *stone d.*: a prison.

Doubleton (dʊ·b'ltən). *Cards.* 1906. [After *singleton*.] Two cards only of one suit in a hand.

†**Double-tongue.** ME. [DOUBLE *a.* 5.] **1.** Duplicity of speech. (Prop. two words.) ME. only. **2.** *Herb.* The shrub *Ruscus hypoglossum* –1601.

Double-tongued (-tʊŋd), *a.* ME. [DOUBLE *a.* 5, -ED¹.] Deceitful or insincere in speech.

Thou art but a double-tongued Christian DE FOE.

Doubling (dʊ·bliŋ), *vbl. sb.* ME. [-ING¹.] **1.** Twofold increase; multiplication by two. **b.** 'The second distillation of low wines' (Knight). **2.** *concr.* The lining of a garment; *esp.* in *Her.* 1572. **3.** *Naut.* **a.** A piece of timber fitted on to the bitts; fir-lining. **b.** The lining of a ship with an extra layer of planking; also, the extra layer. **c.** *pl.* That part of a mast between the trestletrees and the cap. 1769. **4.** *Building.* 'The double course of shingles or slates at the eave of a house' (Knight). **5.** The folding of anything; a fold 1634. **6.** A sudden turn in running; *fig.* an evasion; double-dealing 1573.

Doubloon (dʊblū·n). 1622. [– Fr. *doublon* or its source, Sp. *doblón*, augm. f. *doble* DOUBLE; see -OON.] A Spanish gold coin, orig. = 2 pistoles; now = £1.

‖**Doublure** (dublü·r). 1886. [Fr. 'lining', f. *doubler* to line; see -URE.] An ornamental lining, usually of leather, on the inside of a book-cover.

Doubly (dʊ·bli), *adv.* ME. [f. DOUBLE *a.* + -LY².] **1.** In two ways, or twice as much. **2.** With duplicity ME.

1. Here we synnen doubli WYCLIF. D. sorry 1789. **2.** Let him not deale d. with vs 1585.

Doubt (daut), *sb.* [ME. *dut(e, doute* – OFr. *dote, dute* (mod. *doute*), f. *douter*; see next.] **1.** The (subjective) state of uncertainty as to the truth or reality of anything. With *pl.*: A feeling of uncertainty as to something. **b.** The condition of being (objectively) uncertain; a state of affairs giving occasion to uncertainty ME. †**2.** A doubtful matter or point; a difficulty –1693. †**3.** Apprehension, dread, fear –1659; danger, risk –1596.

1. Your wordes bring me in a d. 1559. Modest D. is cal'd The Beacon of the wise *Tr. & Cr.* II. ii. 16. **b.** To give the defendant the benefit of the d. 1892. **3.** They dare not, for dought of Kyng Charlemayne LD. BERNERS. Well approv'd in many a d. SPENSER.

Phrases. *To make d.*: to doubt, to be uncertain. *No d.*: doubtless. *Without d.*: certainly; †fearlessly.

Doubt (daut), *v.* Pa. t. and pple. **doubted.** ME. [– OFr. *doter, duter* (mod. *douter*) :– L. *dubitare* waver, hesitate. The latinized sp. with *b* appears XV, following Fr. †*doubter*.]

I. 1. *intr.* To be in doubt; to be undecided in opinion or belief. **2.** *trans.* To be uncertain or divided in opinion about; to call in question; to mistrust ME. †**3.** To hesitate, scruple, delay; with *infin.* –1743.

1. Hee that never doubted, scarce ever well-beleeved 1633. **2.** Doctors d. that *Merry W.* V. v. 183. It was never doubted but that one partner might bind the rest 1817. **3.** Mr. Locke hath not doubted to assert [etc.] FIELDING.

II. 1. *trans.* To dread, fear, be afraid ME. **2.** In weakened sense: To apprehend; to suspect (*arch.*) 1509. †**3.** *refl.* To fear; to be afraid. [= OFr. *se douter*.] –1820. †**4.** To be in fear; to be afraid *of* –1587. †**5.** *impers.* To make (a person) afraid –1625.

1. I d., I d., I have been beguiled SCOTT. **2.** They doubted some sinister motive PRESCOTT. I d. that Thackeray did not write the Latin epitaph TROLLOPE. **5.** The virtues of the valiant Caratach, More doubts me than all Britain FLETCHER. So **Dou·btable** *a.* doubtful, questionable; redoubtable. †**Dou·btance,** doubt; dread. Hence **Dou·bter. Dou·bting** *a.*, **-ly** *adv.*, **-ness.**

Doubtful (dau·tfŭl), *a.* ME. [f. DOUBT *sb.* + -FUL.] **1.** Of things: Involved in doubt; uncertain; indistinct, ambiguous. **b.** Of uncertain issue 1562. **c.** Of questionable character 1838. **d.** *Pros.* That may be either long or short 1871. **2.** Of persons: Divided or unsettled in opinion; in doubt; undetermined, hesitating 1509. †**3.** To be feared; dread –1556. †**4.** Giving cause for apprehensions –1776. †**5.** Full of fear; apprehensive –1791. **6.** as *sb.* A doubtful person or thing 1589.

1. Whether he were a God or man, is doubtful GALE. The d. Chance of War MANLEY. She never employed d. agents or sinister measures PRESCOTT. **2.** The king was d., and could not resolve DE FOE. He was d. of the prospects of the rebellion FROUDE. **4.** The d. and dangerous situation of the empire GIBBON. **5.** I hear things which make me d. and anxious BURKE. Hence **Dou·btful-ly** *adv.*, **-ness.**

Doubtless (dau·tlės). ME. [f. DOUBT *sb.* + -LESS.]

A. *adj.* Free from doubt; undoubted, indubitable; †free from apprehension.

Pretty childe, sleepe doubtlesse, and secure SHAKS.

B. *adv.* Without doubt; unquestionably, certainly (now generally concessive) ME.; often in a weaker sense; = No doubt 1664.

Of good things, the greater good is most excellent? D. BP. BERKELEY. So **Dou·btlessly** *adv.*

†**Dou·btous, doutous,** *a.* ME. [– OFr. *doutous* (mod. *douteux*), f. *doute*; see DOUBT *sb.*, -OUS.] **1.** Doubtful –1532. **2.** Doubting –1490. **3.** Fraught with terror –1500.

‖**Douc** (duk). 1774. [– Fr. *douc* – Cochin *douc, dok* monkey.] A species of monkey (*Semnopithecus nemeus*) found in Cochin China.

Douce (dus), *a.* ME. [– OFr. *dous* (mod. *doux*), fem. *douce* :– L. *dulcis* sweet.] †**1.** Sweet, pleasant –1614. **2.** Quiet, steady, sedate. *Sc.* and *n. dial.* 1728.

1. Y-born in d. fraunce ME. **2.** A d. woman she was, civil to the customers SCOTT.

Doucepere; see DOUZEPERS.

Doucet (dū·sėt), **dowset** (dau·sėt). ME. [– OFr. *doucet*, subst. use of *doucet, doucette* adj., dim. of *doux, douce* sweet (see prec.). Cf. DULCET.] †**1.** A sweet dish –1640. †**2.** A kind of flute –1450. **3.** *Hunting.* (*pl.*) The testicles of a deer 1611.

‖**Douceur** (dusö̆r). ME. [– Fr. *douceur*, earlier †*dousour*, etc. :– Rom. **dulçōre*, for late L. *dulcor, -cor-* sweetness. In ME. app. naturalized.] †**1.** Sweetness and pleasantness of manner; amiability –1793. †**2.** A complementary phrase or speech –1807. **3.** A gratuity; a bribe 1763.

3. Her lord has..added..little douceurs..to her jointure 1763.

Douche (duʃ, dūʃ), *sb.* 1766. [– Fr. *douche* – It. *doccia* conduit pipe, f. *docciare* pour by drops :– Rom. **ductiare*, f. L. *ductus* DUCT.] A jet or stream of water, or the like, applied to some part of the body, generally for medicinal purposes; the application of this; an instrument for administering it. Hence **Douche** *v.* to administer a d. to.

‖**Doucine** (dusī·n). 1726. [Fr.] *Archit.* = *Cyma recta*; see CYMA.

Doucker, obs. f. DUCKER.

Dough (dōᵘ), *sb.* [OE. *dāg* = OFris. *deeg*, MLG. *dēch* (Du. *deg*), OHG. *teic* (G. *teig*), ON. *deig*, Goth. *daigs* :– Gmc. **daiʒaz*, f. **daiʒ-* :– IE. **dhoigh-* **dheigh-* **dhigh-* smear, knead.] **1.** A mass consisting of flour or meal moistened and kneaded into a paste, ready to be baked into bread, etc.; paste of bread. **2.** Any soft pasty mass 1559. **3.** *U.S. slang.* Money 1851.

1. (*My*) *cake is d.*: my project has failed. See *Tam. Shr.* V. i. 145. *Comb.*: **d.-brake, -kneader, -maker, -mixer,** machines for kneading and mixing d.; **-head** (*U.S.*), a fool; **-raiser,** 'a pan in a bath of heated water, to maintain a temperature in the d. favorable to fermentation' (Knight).

Dou·gh-baked, *ppl. a.* Now *dial.* 1592. [f. DOUGH *sb.* + BAKE *v.*] Imperfectly baked, so as to remain doughy; hence, imperfect; deficient in intellect, etc.; feeble, 'soft'.

Dou·gh-bird. *local U.S.* The Eskimo curlew (*Numenius borealis*).

Dou·gh-boy. 1685. **1.** A boiled flour dumpling. **2.** *U.S.* An infantry soldier 1867.

Dou·gh-face, doughface. *U.S.* 1833. **1.** A face resembling dough. **2.** One who is easily moulded or worked upon; formerly, in U.S. politics, applied to Northern politicians who were unduly compliant to the South, in the matter of slavery, etc. 1834. So **Dou·gh-faced** *a.*

Doughnut (dōᵘ·nɒt). *local Eng.* and *U.S.* 1809. A small cake made of dough, and fried or boiled in lard.

Dough-trough (dōᵘ·trǫf). ME. A trough or vessel in which dough is placed to rise; also = *dough-raiser*; see DOUGH *sb.*

Doughty (dau·ti), *a.* [Late OE. *dohtiġ*, repl. *dyhtiġ* (ME. *dühti*), corresp. to MLG., MDu. *duchtich* (Du. *duchtig*), MHG. *tühtic* (G. *tüchtig* brave); f. Gmc. **duʒ-*; see DOW *v.*¹] Capable, virtuous; valiant, formidable: now somewhat arch., and often joc.

Kyng Arthur was..bolde and doubty of body CAXTON. Of his duchtie Deidis and Justice done 1535. Hence **Dou·ghtily** *adv.* **Dou·ghtiness.**

Doughy (dōᵘ·i), *a.* 1601. [f. DOUGH *sb.* + -Y¹.] Of the nature of dough; like dough 1601.

All the unbak'd and dowy youth of a nation *All's Well* IV. v. 3. Hence **Dou·ghiness.**

Doulocracy, var. of DULOCRACY..

Doum (daum, dūm). Also **doom.** 1801. [– Arab. *dawm, dūm.*] A palm (*Hyphæne thebaica*) found in Egypt, having a dichotomously divided trunk, and an edible fruit about the size of an apple. Usu. **d.-palm.**

Dour (dūr), *a. Sc.* and *n. dial.* ME. [prob. – Gael. *dúr* dull, stupid, obstinate = (M)Ir. *dúr*, which may be – L. *durus* hard.] **1.** Hard, stern. **2.** Obstinate, sullen 1470.

1. A d. and hard lyfe 1596. **2.** D. men 1572. Hence **Dou·r-ly** *adv.*, **-ness.**

Doura, var. DURRA, Indian millet.

Douse (daus), *sb.* 1625. [f. DOUSE *v.*¹] A dull heavy blow.

Douse (daus), *v.*¹ 1559. [perh. rel. to similar and partly synon. MDu., LG. *dossen*, Du. *doesen*, G. dial. *dusen* beat, strike.] †**1.** *trans.* To strike, punch –1736. **2.** *Naut.* To strike (a sail); to lower or slacken suddenly or in haste; to close (a porthole) 1627. **3.** To doff 1785. **4.** (? a different word.) To dout (a light) 1785. **5.** To stop 1887.

2. D. the ports 1802. **4.** Phr. *Dowse the glim* (slang) = put out the light. Hence **Dou·ser,** a heavy blow.

Douse (daus), *v.*² 1600. [prob. imit. (cf. *souse*), but poss. identical with prec.] †**1.** *trans.* To plunge vigorously in water or the like –1662. **2.** To throw water over; to drench 1606. **3.** *intr.* To plunge or be plunged in water 1603. Hence **Dou·ser,** one who drenches.

Douse, Douser, etc.; see DOWSE, etc.

Dousing-chock, -rod; see under DOWSE *v.*

Dout (daut), *v.* Now *dial.* 1526. [Fused f. *do out*; see DO *v.*] *trans.* To put out (a fire or light). Hence **Dout** *sb.* an extinguisher. **Dou·ter,** one who or that which douts.

‖**Douzaine** (duzē·n). 1682. [Fr. = DOZEN, q. v.] *Channel Islands.* A body of twelve men representing a parish. Hence **Douzainier** (dūzēniᵊ·ɹ), one of such a body.

†**Douzepers** (dū·zəpēᵊɹs), *sb. pl.* ME. [– OFr. *douze per(s*, mod. *douze pairs* twelve peers. In Eng. finally treated as one word, with a singular.] In the *Romances*, the twelve peers or paladins of Charlemagne. In *History*, applied to the twelve great peers, spiritual and temporal, of France. (See Du Cange s.v. *Pares Franciæ*.). Also *transf.*

Dove (dɒv). [ME. *duve, douve, dofe* – ON. *dúfa* = OFris. *dūve*, OS. *duba*. (Du. *duif*), OHG. *tūba* (G. *taube*), Goth. *dūbo* :– Gmc. **dūbōn*, presumed to be imit. of the bird's note.] **1.** A bird of the *Columbidæ*, or pigeon family.

Formerly applied to all the species of pigeon native to or known in Britain; but now often restricted to the Turtle-dove, and its congeners. The dove, as the type of gentleness and harmlessness, occupies an important place in Christian symbolism.

2. *fig.* and *transf.* (see quots.) ME. **3.** An image of a dove as a symbol of innocence, etc.; also, the vessel enclosing the pyx, formerly used in the East and in France 1513.

1. Voices of the well-contented doves TENNYSON. **2.** Holy Spirit, heavenly D. WATTS. He will be a d. of peace to your ark LYTTON. She is coming, my d., my dear TENNYSON.

Comb.: **d.-colour,** a warm grey with a tone of pink or purple; **-dock,** the coltsfoot; **-flower** = *dove-plant*; **dove's-foot,** the plant *Geranium molle*, and some other small species of cranesbill; **-hawk,** the *d.-coloured falcon* or hen-harrier (*Circus cyaneus*); **-plant,** an orchid of Central America, *Peristeria elata*; **-tick,** a blind mite parasite on pigeons.

Dove (dōᵘv), occas. pa. t. of DIVE *v.*

Dovecot, -cote (dɒ·vkǫt). ME. [f. DOVE *sb.* + COT *sb.*¹, COTE *sb.*¹] A house for doves or pigeons; usually placed at a height above the ground, with openings, and internal provision for roosting and breeding. Also *fig.*

Like an Eagle in a Doue-coat *Cor.* V. vi. 115.

Do·ve-ey:ed, *a.* 1717. Having eyes like a dove; meek, or soft-eyed; as, *Dove-eyed Hope.*

Do·vehouse. ME. A house for doves; a dovecot. Also *attrib.*

Dovekie (dɒ·vki). 1821. [Sc. dim. of *dove*] An Arctic bird, the Black Guillemot.

Dovelet (dɒ·vlėt). 1825. A little dove.

Dovelike (dɒ·vləik), *a.* and *adv.* 1577. Like a dove; after the manner of a dove.

Thou..Dove-like satst brooding on the vast Abyss MILTON.

Dover's powder. 1854. [Name of Thomas Dover (d. 1742).] A pharmaceutical preparation of opium and ipecacuanha.

Dovetail (dɒ·vtēᵊl), *sb.* 1565. **1.** Something in the shape of a dove's tail; *spec.* a tenon cut in the shape of a dove's tail spread, to fit into a mortise of corresponding shape; also, a mortise shaped to receive such a tenon 1674. **2.** = *D. joint*: A joint composed of these.

Comb.: **d.-moulding,** *Archit.* a moulding arranged in the form of a series of figures like dovetails; **-saw,** a saw employed in making dovetails.

Do·vetail, *v.* 1657. [f. prec. sb.] **1.** *trans.* To fit together or join by means of dovetails. Const. *in, into, to.* **2.** *fig.* To adjust exactly so as to form a continuous whole 1815. **3.** *intr.* To fit into each other, so as to form a compact and harmonious whole 1817.

Dovey (dɒ·vi). 1769. [f. DOVE + -Y⁶.] A term of affection: cf. LOVEY.

†**Do·vish,** *a.* 1537. [-ISH.¹] Of or pertaining to the dove; dovelike –1546.

Doveyshe simplicitie, serpentlike wysdome 1546.

Dow (dau), *v.*¹ Now *Sc.* and *n. dial.* [One of the orig. Gmc. preterite-present verbs (see CAN, DARE, MAY); OE., OS. *dugan* be worth, competent, strong, OHG. *tugan* (G. *taugen*), ON. *duga*, Goth. **dugan*; see DOUGHTY.] †**1.** *intr.* To be good, strong, virtuous. Only OE. †**2.** To be valid, or of value; to be good for anything –1788. †**3.** To avail. Chiefly *impers.* –1590. †**4.** To become, behove. Usually *impers.* –ME. **5.** To be able (to do something) ME. **6.** To thrive, prosper 1674.

5. I never dowed to bide a hard turn o' wark in my life SCOTT.

†**Dow,** *v.*² ME. [– (O)Fr. *douer* :– L. *dotare*, f. *dos, dot-* dowry, rel. to *dare* give.] **1.** = ENDOW 2. –1483. **2.** To invest *with* –1450. **3.** To bequeath. CHAUCER.

Dow, earlier f. DHOW, q. v.

Dowable (dau·ab'l), *a.* 1535. [– AFr. *dowable*, f. (O)Fr. *douer* DOW *v.*²] Capable of being endowed; entitled to dower.

Dowager (dau·ėdʒəɹ). 1530. [– OFr. *douag(i)ere*, f. *douage* dower, f. *douer* portion out (see DOW *v.*²).] A widow who is in the enjoyment of some title or some property that has come to her from her deceased husband. Often added to the title so enjoyed, as *princess-, queen-d., d.-duchess*, etc. **b.** *familiarly.* An elderly lady of dignified demeanour 1870.

I haue a Widdow Aunt, a d., Of great reuennew *Mids. N.* I. i. 157. Hence **Dow·agerism,** the condition of a d.

Dowcet(e, obs. ff. DOUCET, DULCET.

Dowd (daud), *sb.*¹ ME. [Of unkn. origin.] A person whose dress and appearance are devoid of smartness and brightness.

Dowd, *sb.*² Now *dial.* 1749. [Of unkn. origin.] A woman's cap or night-cap.

Dowdy (dau·di). 1581. [f. DOWD *sb.*¹ + -Y⁶.]

A. *sb.* A woman or girl unattractively dressed, without smartness or brightness.

The Duchesse of Albemarle, who is ever a plain homely d. PEPYS.

B. *adj.* Shabbily dull in colour or appearance; without brightness or freshness 1676.

A dress..d. with age TROLLOPE. A shy, d. young woman 1869. Hence **Dow·dily** *adv.* **Dow·diness. Dow·dyish** *a.* somewhat d. **Dow·dyism,** d. character or quality.

Dowel (dau·ėl), *sb.* ME. [– MLG. *dovel*, corresp. to OHG. *tubili* (MHG. *tübel*; G. *döbel*, after LG.). Cf. THOLE *sb.*] **1.** A headless pin, peg, or bolt, of wood, metal, etc., serving to fasten together two pieces of wood, stone, etc., by penetrating into the substance of both pieces. **2.** A plug of wood

driven into a wall to receive nails. [Ger. *döbel, dübel.*]
Comb.: **d.-bit,** a boring-tool of semi-cylindrical form terminating in a conoidal edge; a *spoon-bit*; **-joint,** a junction formed by means of dowels; **-pin** = sense 1; **-pointer,** a tool for pointing the ends of dowels. Hence **Dow·el** *v.* to fasten with dowels.

†**Dower,** *sb.*[1] ME. [Cf. OFr. *douvre*, var. of *douve* ditch, dyke.] A burrow (of rabbits, or the like) –1490.

Dower (dau·əɹ), *sb.*[2] ME. [– OFr. *douaire* – med.L. *dotarium*, f. L. *dos, dot-* dowry, *dotare* endow; see Dow *v.*[2]; -ary[1].] **1.** The portion of a deceased husband's estate which the law allows to his widow for her life. **2.** = Dowry 2, †3. ME. **3.** *fig.* Endowment ME.
1. Her part and dowyer of my godes ME. **2.** Choose thou thy husband, and Ile pay thy d. Shaks. **3.** A mortal Song we sing, by d. Encouraged of celestial power Wordsw. *Comb.*, as **d.-house, -land.**

Dower (dau·əɹ), *v.* 1605. [f. Dower *sb.*[2]] **1.** *trans.* To give a dowry to; to endow. **2.** To endow *with* any gift, talent, or power 1793. **3.** *intr.* To take or receive dower 1848.
2. Dower'd with the hate of hate, the scorn of scorn Tennyson.

†**Dow·eress.** 1519. [f. Dower *sb.*[2] + -ess[1].] A widow holding a dower –1823.

Dowerless (dau·əɹlės), *a.* 1605. [f. Dower *sb.*[2] + -less.] Portionless.

Dowie, dowy (dau·i, do·wi), *a. Sc.* and *n. dial.* 1508. [= xvi *dolly*. Prob. a deriv. of ME. *dol, doll* Dull.] Dull and lonely, dreary, dismal.

Dowl (daul). Now *dial.* ME. [perh. rel. to Down *sb.*[2]] One of the filaments of a feather; down, fluff.

Dowlas (dau·lăs). 1529. [f. *Daoulas* or *Doulas*, SE. of Brest in Brittany. Cf. Lockram.] †**a.** A coarse kind of linen, much used in the 16th and 17th centuries. **b.** A strong calico, now made in imitation of this. Also *attrib.*
Doulas, filthy Doulas 1 *Hen. IV*, III. iii. 79.

†**Dowment.** 1552. [f. Dow *v.*[2] + -ment.] Endowment; the giving of dower –1628.

Down (daun), *sb.*[1] [OE. *dūn* = OFris. *dūne*, OS. *dūna* (Du. *duin*; cf. Dune), a word of the LG. area, perh. – OCelt. (Gaulish) **dūnom*, whence (O)Ir. *dún* fort, W. †*dīn* fort, cogn. w. OE. *tūn* Town.] †**1.** A hill –1653. **2.** An open expanse of elevated land; *spec.* in *pl.*, the treeless undulating chalk uplands of the south and south-east of England; serving chiefly for pasturage; also, similar tracts elsewhere ME. **3.** A sand-hill, Dune 1523. **4.** *The Downs*: the part of the sea within the Goodwin Sands, off the east coast of Kent, a famous rendezvous for ships. (It lies opposite the eastern end of the North Downs.) 1460. **5.** Applied to a breed of sheep raised on the chalk downs of England. Cf. Southdown. 1831.
2. My boskie acres, and my vnshrubd downe *Temp.* IV. i. 81. By dale and d. We dwell Scott. **3.** Over the downs of sand by the sea side Carte. **4.** Sir Simon Mondford..was appoynted to kepe the downes, and the five Portes 1548.

Down (daun), *sb.*[2] ME. [– ON. *dúnn*, whence LG. *dune*, G. *daune*.] **1.a.** The first feathering of young birds. **b.** The fine soft under plumage of fowls, used for stuffing beds, pillows, etc. Also *fig.* **2.** Hence, **a.** The hair as it first shows itself on the face 1580. **b.** The pubescence on some plants and fruits; the soft feathery pappus of some seeds ME. **c.** Any feathery or fluffy substance 1626.
1. Of downe of pure doves white Chaucer. *fig.* Must I break from the d. of thy embraces, To put on steel Ford. **2.** The callow d. began To shade my chin Dryden.
attrib. and *Comb.*, as *d.-bed, -pillow*, etc.; **d.-tree,** the cork-wood, *Ochroma lagopus*; **-weed,** *Filago germanica.*

Down, *sb.*[3] 1611. [Down *adv.*, used subst., or ellipt. for 'downward motion'.] †**1.** The burden of a song –1656. **2.** A descent; a reverse of fortune. Usu. in phr. *ups and downs*. 1710. **3.** *colloq.* A tendency to be 'down *upon*' 1893. **4.** A cry of *down with* 1889.

Down (daun), *a.* 1565. [Down *adv.*, used attrib., or by ellipsis of some ppl. wd.] **1.** Directed downwards; descending; of a train or coach: Going down, *i.e.* in Great Britain, away from London. Hence *transf.* 1851. **2.** Downcast, dejected. *Obs.* (exc. predic.) 1645.
1. To cross the line to the d. platform 1885.

Down (daun), *adv.* [In late OE. *dūne, dūn*, aphet. f. *adūne* Adown, q.v.] **1.** In a descending direction (real or imaginary); from above, or towards that which is below; from a higher to a lower place or position; to the ground. Also vaguely in *up and d.*, often = to and fro; see Up. **2.** In a low or lower situation or position or one conventionally viewed as lower; on the ground ME. **3.** Into or in a fallen, sitting, or overthrown position or posture ME. **4.** Prostrate with sickness; ill 1710. **5.** Below the horizon ME. **6.** Below the surface or to the bottom of water 1659. **7.** Downstairs, or to the dining-room, to dinner 1592. **8.** Down the throat 1582. **9.** In reference to payment: (Laid) upon the table or counter; (paid) at the instant 1557. **10.** In writing: with *write, note, set*, etc. See the vbs. 1576. **11.** From an earlier to a later time ME. **12.** To or at a lower amount, rate, or price 1573. **13.** Into or in a lower or inferior condition, low spirits, a state of depression, defeat, or the like ME. **14.** To a smaller bulk or finer consistency 1675. **15.** Into or in a state of subsidence 1590. **16.** Into a weaker quality 1816. **17.** *slang.* Aware, wide-awake 1812. **18.** With ellipsis of a verb, *e.g.* of *come, go, sit, kneel, lie* ME.; of *go*, in sense 'be swallowed' (*lit.* and *fig.*) 1580; of *put*, etc. 1820; so *d. with*; also used in ballad refrains, without meaning 1598.
1. He a lighted downe of his horse Hall. In our journey d. Goldsm. To go d. from Oxford 1897. **2.** The tide was d. 1894. **3.** Fold it d. 1669. Four d. and three to play 1894. **4.** We have now about 50 men d. 1712. **5.** The sun had gone d. 1849. **6.** When Kempenfelt went d. Cowper. **8.** A bitter potion that is soon d. 1660. **9.** For a lump sum d. 1894. **10.** *Much Ado* IV. ii. 17. **11.** D. from the time of Moses 1662. **12.** Cutting d. his salary Macaulay. **13.** Who can rayse him, that Fortune will have downe Drayton. **14.** He..melted it [New Coll. plate] downe Wood. **15.** D. dropt the breeze Coleridge. **18.** Downe therefore, and beg mercy of the Duke Shaks.
Phrases. **D. on. a.** Aware of, 'up to' (*slang*). **b.** *To be d. on* (*upon*): to fall upon, attack (from a superior position); to treat severely. **D. east** (*U.S.*): into or in the eastern sea-coast districts of New England, *esp.* Maine. Also as *adj.* and *sb.* Hence **D. easter. D. south:** into or in the south; in *U.S.* into or in the Southern States. **D. to the ground** (*colloq.*): completely.
¶ For **Down-** in comb., see Downcast, Downcome, etc.

Down (daun), *prep.* 1508. [Down *adv.* construed with an object.] **1.** In a descending direction along, through, or into; from a higher to a lower part of 1508; at a lower part of 1769. **2.** To (or at) what is regarded as a lower part of; along the course or extent of 1674. **3.** The prep. and its object may be used as an advb. or attrib. phrase; as in *d.-river, -stream, -town* 1645.
1. Such notes as..Drew iron tears d. Pluto's cheek Milt. Three miles d. the river De Foe. **2.** Phr. *D. town*: Into the town; down in the town. *D.* (*the*) *wind*: see Wind.

Down, *v.* 1682. [f. Down *adv.* 18; see above.] **1.** *trans.* To bring, put, throw, or knock down 1778. **2.** *intr.* To descend 1825. **3.** *To d. upon, on*: to fall upon as from a superior position 1852. **4.** *To d. with*: to put down; to have done with 1682.
1. His horse had downed him three times Surtees. **4.** Except they d. with their Dust 1682.

Down and out, *adj. phr.* orig. *U.S.* 1889. Completely without resources. Also as *sb.*

†**Downbea·r,** *v.* ME. *trans.* To bear down, press down, cause to sink; also *fig.* –1834.

Downcast (daunka·st), *v.* ME. [f. Down *adv.* + Cast *v.*] To cast down (*lit.* and *fig.*); to demolish; to dispirit. (Now only *poet.*)

Downcast (dau·nkast), *sb.* ME. [f. Down *adv.* + Cast *sb.*; cf. prec.] **1.** The act of casting down (*lit.* and *fig.*); demolition; downward cast (of the eyes, etc.); in *Geol.* = Downthrow 2. **2.** The throwing down of a current of air into a coal-mine, etc.; *attrib.* in *d. shaft*, the shaft by which this is done, also *ellipt.* called the *down-cast* 1816.
1. I saw the respectful d. of his eyes Steele.

Downcast (dau·nkast), *ppl. a.* 1602. [f. Down *adv.* + Cast *ppl. a.*; also f. Downcast *v.*] **1.** Cast down; ruined, destroyed; *fig.* dejected. **2.** Of looks, etc.: Directed downwards; dejected 1633.
1. A few looked d. 1832. **2.** With d. eyes Freeman.

Downcome (dou·n,kɒm), *sb.* 1513. [f. Down *adv.* + Come *v.*; cf. *income*.] **1.** The act of coming down (*lit.* and *fig.*); downfall; humiliation; in *Hawking*, a swoop down. **2.** *Metallurgy.* (See quot.) 1881.
2. *Downcome*, the pipe through which tunnel-head gases from iron blast-furnaces are brought down to the hot-blast stoves and boilers, when these are below the tunnel-head (Raymond). So **Dow·n-coming** (in sense 1).

Down-draught (dau·ndraft). 1849. A descending current of air.

Downfall (dau·nfǫl). ME. **1.** Sudden descent; a fall (of rain, snow, etc.) 1450. †**2.** A steep descent, precipice; an abyss, etc. –1822. **3.** Fall from high estate; ruin. (The current use.) ME. **b.** *concr.* (*pl.*) Ruins 1602. **4.** *attrib.* Descending 1793.
1. The sonne knowyng no downe falle 1450. **2.** Dreadfull downfalls of unheeded rocks Dryden. **3.** Histories of the downfal of kingdoms Johnson. So **Dow·n-fallen** *ppl. a.* **Dow·nfalling** *ppl. a.*

Down grade, down-grade. 1885. [See Grade.] *lit.* A downward gradient (on a railway, etc.); hence *fig.* a downward course in morals, etc. Also *attrib.*

†**Down-gyved,** *ppl. a.* [See Gyve *sb.*] Hanging down like fetters. *Haml.* II. i. 80.

Dow·nhaul (-hǭl). 1669. [f. Down *adv.* + Haul *v.*] *Naut.* A rope to pull down a sail when shortening sail. Also *attrib.*

Downhearted (-hāɹtėd), *a.* 1774. [See Down *adv.* 13.] Having the heart down; low-spirited (*colloq.*).

Downhill.
A. *sb.* (dau·nhill). [f. Down *adv.*] The downward slope of a hill; a declivity, descent (*lit.* and *fig.*) 1591.
B. *adv.* (daunhi·l). [f. Down *prep.*] Down the slope of a hill; on a decline; downwards (*lit.* and *fig.*) 1659.
C. *adj.* (dau·nhil). Sloping or descending downwards; declining. (Also *fig.*) 1727.
sb. The d. of life 1853. *adv.* A very short cut, and all d. *adj.* The d. side of life Cowper.

Dow·nland. 1842. [f. Down *sb.*[1]; cf. OE. *dūnland*.] Land forming downs; hilly pasture-land.

†**Dow·nlooked** (-lukt), *a.* 1641. [See Down *a.* 1.] Having downward looks; guilty-looking; demure –1814.

Dow·n-lying, *vbl. sb.* 1526. **a.** Lying down, going to bed. **b.** Lying-in of a woman, confinement (*n. dial.*).

Downmost (dau·nmoust). 1790. Superlative degree of Down *adv.* and *adj.*

Dow·npour (-pōəɹ), *sb.* 1811. A pouring down; *esp.* a heavy, continuous fall (of rain, etc.).

Downright (daunrəi·t). ME. [Aphetic f. Adownright, f. Adown *adv.* + Right *adj.* and *adv.*]
A. *adv.* (Stressed *dow·nright* before, *downri·ght* following, the word it qualifies.) †**1.** Straight down; vertically downwards –1763. **2.** Absolutely, out and out ME. †**3.** In a straightforward manner; plainly –1684. †**4.** Straightway, straight –1712.
2. Killed four d., and wounded several 1724. **4.** Mrs. Bull. fell down right into a fit Arbuthnot.
B. *adj.* (Usu. stressed *dow·nright*.) **1.** Descending straight downwards; vertical 1530. **2.** *fig.* **a.** Direct, straightforward. Of persons: Plain and direct (sometimes to bluntness). *Obs.* or *arch.* 1603. **b.** Nothing less than.., mere, absolute, thorough 1565.
2. A certain d. honesty 1875. A d. atheist 1856.
C. *sb.* (*dow·nright.*) [The *adj.* used *ellipt.*] †**1.** A perpendicular 1674. **2.** (*pl.*) A quality of wool 1793.
Hence **Downri·ght-ly** *adv.* (*rare*), **-ness.**

Dow·nrush (-rɒʃ). 1855. Rapid descent.

Dow·nset, *a.* 1847. *Her.* Of a fess: Broken so that the one half is set lower than the other by its whole width.

Downside (dou·nsəid). 1683. The under side. Also *advb.*

Dow·nshare, corrupt f. Denshire.

Downstairs. Less freq. **downstair.** 1596. **a.** *adv. phr.* (daunstēə·ɹz). On or to a lower floor or (*fig.*) the lower regions. **b.** *attrib.* or *adj.* (dau·nstēᵊɹ(z) 1819. **c.** *sb.* (daunstēᵊ·ɹz). The downstairs part of a building; the lower regions 1843.

†**Dow·nsteepy,** *a.* [STEEPY.] Steeply descending. FLORIO.

Downthrow (dau·nþrōᵘ). 1615. **1.** A throwing or being thrown down (*rare*). **2.** *Geol.* The depression of strata below the general level on one side of a fault 1858.

Downtrodden (dauntrǫ·d'n), *pa. pple.* and (dau·ntrǫ:d'n), *ppl. a.* 1568. **1.** Trampled down. **2.** Crushed by oppression or tyranny 1595.

The..d. vassals of perdition MILT. var. **Dow·ntrod** *ppl. a.*

Downward (dau·nwǫɹd). ME. [f. ADOWN *adv.* + -WARD; orig. aphet. f. ADOWNWARD.]

A. *adv.* **1.** Towards a lower place or position; towards what is below; with a descending motion. **2.** *fig.* Towards that which is lower in order, or inferior in any way ME. **b.** Onward from an earlier to a later time 1611.

1. A drope..fallyth dounwarde by his owne heuvynesse TREVISA. Looking d. 1855. **2.** Things seem to tend d. EMERSON. From Solon d. GROTE.

†**B.** *prep.* = DOWN *prep.* 1 (*rare*) ME. only.

C. *adj.* **1.** Directed towards that which is lower; descending; inclined downard (*lit.* and *fig.*) 1552. **2.** Lying or situated below; lower (*rare*) ME.

1. The d. track DRYDEN. Steps in a d. scale FREEMAN.

Downwards (dau·nwǫɹdz), *adv.* ME. [See -WARDS.] = DOWNWARD *adv.*

Downweigh (daunwēⁱ·), *v.* 1600. *trans.* To weigh down; to outweigh; to depress.

The gloom..downweighs My spirit MOIR.

†**Down weight, down-weight.** 1524. Full or good weight. *attrib.* Of full weight. Also *fig.* –1698.

Downy (dau·ni), *a.*[1] 1671. [f. DOWN *sb.*[1] + -Y[1].] Characterized by downs.

A..rolling, d. country MOTLEY.

Downy (dau·ni), *a.*[2] 1548. [f. DOWN *sb.*[2] + -Y[1].] **1.** Of the nature of or like down 1578. **2.** Made or consisting of down 1592. **3.** Covered with down 1548. **4.** *transf.* Soft as down 1602. **5.** *slang.* [See DOWN *adv.* 17.] Wide-awake, knowing 1821.

1. Thick d. feathers R. H. DANA. **2.** D. pillows 1712. **3.** D. Peaches DRYDEN. **4.** Shake off this Downey sleepe, Deaths counterfeit *Macb.* II. iii. 81. Hence **Dow·nily** *adv.* (*rare*). **Dow·niness.**

Dowress; see DOWERESS.

Dowry (dauə·ri). ME. [– AFr. *dowarie* = (O)Fr. *douaire*; see DOWER *sb.*[2]] †**1.** = DOWER 1. –1841. **2.** The portion given with the wife; the dot ME. †**3.** A present given by a man to or for his bride –1611. **4.** *fig.* A gift of nature or fortune; an endowment ME.

3. Aske mee neuer so much dowrie and gift..but giue mee the damsell to wife *Gen.* 34:12.

†**Dow·sabel.** 1590. An English form (through Fr.) of the female name *Dulcibella*. Applied generically to a sweetheart, ladylove; cf. DOLL. –1675.

Dowse (dauz), *v.* Also **douse.** 1691. [Of unkn. origin.] *intr.* To use the divining-rod in search of water or mineral veins. Hence **Dow·sing** *vbl. sb.* **Dowser** (dau·zəɹ), one who uses the dowsing-rod. **Dowsing-rod,** the rod or twig used by dowsers. **Dowsing-cheek, -chock,** one of several pieces fayed athwart the apron and lapped on the knight-heads or inside stuff above the upper deck (Weale).

Dowve, obs. f. DOVE.

Doxastic (dǫksæ·stik), *a.* 1794. [– Gr. δοξαστικός conjectural, f. δοξάζειν conjecture; see -IC.] Of, pertaining to, or depending on opinion.

Doxology (dǫksǫ·lŏdʒi). 1649. [– med.L. *doxologia* – Gr. δοξολογία, f. δόξα glory + -λογια -LOGY.] †**a.** Thanksgiving. **b.** A short formula of praise to God; *spec.* the *Gloria in excelsis* or 'Greater d.', the *Gloria Patri* or 'Lesser d.', or some metrical formula, *e.g.* 'Praise God from whom all blessings flow', etc. Hence **Doxolo·gical** *a.* pertaining to or of the nature of a d. **Doxo·logize** *v. intr.* to say the d.; *trans.* to address a d. to.

Doxy[1] (dǫ·ksi). 1530. [orig. rogues' cant; of unkn. origin.] A beggar's trull; hence, *slang,* a paramour, prostitute; *dial.* a sweetheart.

Do·xy[2]. *colloq.* 1730. [Terminal element of *orthodoxy* and *heterodoxy* used joc. (with ref. to DOXY[1]) as a word.] Opinion (*esp.* in theological matters). (Cf. *-ism.*)

'Orthodoxy, my Lord,' said Bishop Warburton ..'is my d.,—heterodoxy is another man's d.'

‖**Doyen** (dwayęṅ). ME. [Fr.; see DEAN[1].] †**1.** A commander of ten. ME. only. **2.** The senior member of a body 1670.

Doyley, -ly; see DOILY.

Doze (doᵘz), *v.* 1647. [Perhaps earlier in dialects. The trans. sense = Da. *døse* make dull, drowsy, etc.] †**1.** *trans.* To stupefy; to make drowsy or dull; to confuse –1818. **2.** *intr.* To sleep drowsily; to be half asleep; to nod. Also *fig.* 1693. **3.** *trans.* (with *away, out*). To pass (time) in dozing 1693.

1. The tobacco had..dozed my head DE FOE. **2.** I have been dozing over a stupid book SHERIDAN. **3.** We d. away our hours 1693. Hence **Doze** *sb.* a short slumber. **Dozed** *ppl. a.* stupefied; drowsy; of timber, decayed inside; doted. **Do·zer,** one who dozes.

Dozen (dɒ·z'n), *sb.* ME. [– OFr. *dozeine, -aine* (mod. *douzaine*); Rom. deriv. with *-ēna* (as in L. *decena, centena,* etc. group of 10, 100, etc.) of **do(t)ze* :– **dōdece* :– L. *duodecim* 12.] **1.** A group or set of twelve. Orig. as a sb., with *of*; in sing., without *of* = twelve. (Abbrev. *doz.*) †**2.** A kind of kersey. (Usu. in *pl.*) –1721. †**3.** Corruptly, a tithing, or group of ten households (AFr. *dizeyne,* Fr. *dizaine*) –1672.

1. A d. of Knives 1726. Six d. pencils 1897. Phr. *Baker's d.* (see BAKER), *devil's, long, printer's d.,* thirteen. *Round d.,* a full d. *To talk nineteen to the d.*: to talk very fast. Hence **Do·zener,** (*a*) a member of a tithing; (*b*) the head of a dozen; (*c*) a local name for constables. **Do·zenth** *a. colloq.* = TWELFTH.

Dozy (dōᵘ·zi), *a.* 1693. [f. DOZE *v.* + -Y[1].] **1.** Drowsy. **2.** Of timber or fruit: In incipient decay; sleepy 1882. Hence **Do·zily** *adv.* **Do·ziness.**

†**Do·zzle,** *v.* [frequent. of DOZE *v.*; see -LE.] *trans.* To stupefy. HACKET.

Dr., abbrev. of *Debtor* (in *Book-keeping*), *Doctor.*

Drab (dræb), *sb.*[1] 1515. [perh. from Du. or LG.; cf. Du. *drab* dregs, LG. *drabbe* thick dirty liquid, mire, *drabbig* muddy. Cf. DRABBLE.] **1.** A slatternly woman. **2.** A strumpet 1530. **3.** (?a different word.) *Salt-making.* A wooden case into which the salt is put when it is taken out of the boiling pan 1753.

Drab (dræb), *sb.*[2] and *a.* 1541. [prob. alt. of †*drap* cloth (as in *drab-de-Berry* for DRAP-DE-BERRY) – OFr. *drap* – late L. *drappus,* perh. of Celt. origin. See DRAPE *v.*]

A. *sb.* A kind of hempen, linen, or woollen cloth.

B. *adj.* Of a dull light brown or yellowish-brown 1775; *fig.* dull; wanting brightness 1880.

C. *sb.* [the adj. used absol.] **1.** Drab colour; cloth of this colour; also, in *pl.* = drab breeches 1821. **2.** Name for a group of moths 1819.

Drab (dræb), *v.* 1602. [f. DRAB *sb.*[1]] *intr.* To whore. Also *to d. it.* Hence †**Dra·bber,** a whoremonger.

Drabbet (dræ·bėt, dræ̆be·t). 1851. [f. DRAB *sb.*[2] + -ET.] A drab twilled linen.

Drabbish (dræ·biʃ), *a.*[1] 1566. [f. DRAB *sb.*[1] + -ISH[1].] Sluttish.

Dra·bbish, *a.*[2] 1842. [f. DRAB *a.* + -ISH[1].] Somewhat drab in colour.

Drabble (dræb'l), *v.* ME. [– LG. *drabbelen* walk or paddle in water or mire; cf. DRAB *sb.*[1], -LE.] **1.** To make or become wet and dirty by contact with muddy water or mire. **2.** *Angling.* (*intr.*) To fish for barbel, etc. with a rod and a weighted line 1799. Hence **Drabble-tail,** a draggle-tail.

Drabbler, drabler (dræ·bləɹ). 1592. [f. DRABBLE *v.,* from its position.] *Naut.* A piece of canvas, laced to the bottom of the bonnet of a sail, to give it greater depth.

‖**Dracæna** (drăsī·na). 1823. [mod.L. – Gr. δράκαινα, fem. of δράκων dragon.] *Bot.* A genus of *Liliaceæ,* containing the dragon-tree *Dracæna draco,* and other ornamental species.

Drachm (dræm). See also DRAM. [Late ME. *dragme* – OFr. *dragme* or late L. *dragma,* var. of L. *drachma* – Gr. δραχμή, Attic weight and coin.] **1.** An ancient Greek silver coin, the DRACHMA. Its average value was 9¾*d.* English. (Also DRACHMA.) Hence, the Arabic DIRHEM. **2.** A weight about equal to that of the coin; now, in Apothecaries' weight = 60 grains, or ⅛ of an ounce, in Avoirdupois = 27⅓ grains, or $\frac{1}{16}$ of an ounce. (Spelt *drachm* or *dram.*) Also, the Arabic DIRHEM. ME. **3.** *fig.* A very little 1635.

‖**Drachma** (dræ·kmă). Pl. **-mas,** also **-mæ.** 1579. [– L. – Gr. δραχμή DRACHM.] **1.** = DRACHM 1. Also, the Jewish quarter-shekel. **b.** A silver coin of modern Greece = Fr. *franc,* It. *lira* 1882. **2.** = DRACHM 2. 1527.

† **Dracin, -ine.** *Chem.* = DRACONIN.

Draco·nian, *a.* 1876. [f. as DRACONIC; see -IAN] = DRACONIC 1, 2.

Draconic (drăkǫ·nik), *a.* 1680. [f. L. *draco, -ōn-* DRAGON or the proper name *Draco,* Gr. Δράκων + -IC.] **1.** Of, pertaining to, or characteristic of Draco, archon at Athens in 621 B.C., or the severe code of laws attributed to him; harsh, severe, cruel 1708. **2.** Pertaining to, or of the nature of, a dragon 1680. **3.** *Astron.* = DRACONTIC 1876. var. †**Draco·nical** *a.* Hence **Draco·nically** *adv.*

Dra·conin, -ine. 1837. [f. L. *draco, -ōn-* dragon + -IN[1], -INE[5],] *Chem.* The colouring matter in *Dragon's blood.*

‖**Draconites** (drækŏnəi·tīz). 1579. [L. *draconitis,* f. *draco, -ōn-* DRAGON.] A precious stone fabled to be taken out of the head of a dragon.

Draconi·tic, *a. Astron.* = DRACONTIC. (In recent Dicts.)

Dracontic (drăkǫ·ntik), *a.* 1727. [f. Gr. δρακοντ-, stem of δράκων + -IC.] *Astron.* Pertaining to the moon's nodes; see DRAGON'S-HEAD, -TAIL.

Dracontine (drăkǫ·ntəin), *a.* 1806. [irreg. f. Gr. δράκων, δρακοντ- + -INE[1].] Of the nature of, or belonging to, a dragon.

‖**Dracunculus** (drăkɒ·ŋkiŭlŏs). 1706. [L., dim. of *draco* DRAGON.] **1.** The Guinea-worm, *D.* (*Filaria*) *medinensis.* **2.** *Ichthyol.* A fish, a dragonet of the genus *Callionymus* 1752. **3.** *Bot.* A herbaceous genus of *Araceæ,* containing the GREEN *dragon* or DRAGONS 1706.

Drad, obs. f. DREAD *a.* and *v.*

Dradge, obs. or dial. f. DREDGE.

Draff (draf). [Early ME. *draf,* perh. repr. OE. **dræf* = MLG., MDu. *draf,* OHG. **trab,* pl. *trebir* (G. *treber, träber* husks, grains), ON. **draf* (Icel. *draf,* Norw. *drav* mash).] Refuse, lees, dregs; hog's-wash; *spec.* brewer's grains. Also *transf.* and *fig.*

The d. of servile food MILT. *Sams.* 573. The brood of Belial, the draffe of men MILT. Hence **Dra·ffish, Dra·ffy** *adjs.* worthless.

Dra·ffsack. Now *dial.* ME. [f. DRAFF + SACK *sb.*] A sack of draff or refuse; also *fig.* a big paunch; lazy glutton. Hence †**Dra·ffsacked** *ppl. a.* stuffed with draff; worthless.

Draft (druft), *sb.* 1494. A modern phonetic spelling of DRAUGHT *sb.,* now established in the following senses: **1.** The turn of the scale in weighing; hence a deduction from the gross weight allowed for this (= CLOFF, q.v.). **2.** The drawing off or selection of a party from some larger body for some special purpose; *spec.* in military use 1703; the body so drawn off 1756. **3.** The drawing of money by an order in due form. Also DRAUGHT, q.v. 1633. **b.** A bill or cheque drawn; sometimes, *spec.* an order drawn by one branch of a firm upon another, or by one department of an office upon another 1745. Also *fig.* **4.** A plan, sketch, or drawing, *esp.* of a work to be executed. More often DRAUGHT, q.v. 1697. **5.** A rough sketch of a writing or document, from which the final or fair copy is made 1528. **6.** *Masonry.* Chisel-dressing at the margin of the surface of a stone to serve as a guide for the levelling of the surface. Also DRAUGHT, q.v. **b.** 'The degree of deflexion of a mill-stone-furrow from a radial direction' (*Cent. Dict.*). **7.** *attrib.* **a.** Drafted from the flock, as *d. ewe.* **b.** Drawn up as a rough form whence a fair copy can be made. **c.** *D.-cattle, -horses*; see DRAUGHT.

2. I am..convinced. all the drafts [will] quit the service G. WASHINGTON. **3.** *fig.* So great a d.

on our patience 1869. **5.** The d. of the petition BURKE. **7.** A d. will 1879.

Draft (draft), *v.* 1714. [f. prec. sb. Still spelt DRAUGHT in some senses.] **1.** *trans.* To draw out and remove from a larger body for some special purpose. Chiefly in *Mil.* use, and in *Stock-farming.* **b.** *gen.* To draw off or away 1742. **2.** To draw up in a preliminary form. Rarely *draught.* 1828. **3.** *Masonry.* To cut a draught (or draft) on a stone 1878.

1. The..Corps out of which they have been drafted 1724. **2.** The Duke..read me a letter.. which he had drafted J. W. CROKER. Hence **Dra·fter**, one who drafts (animals, a document, etc.).

Draftsman (dra·ftsmæn). 1663. [var. sp. of DRAUGHTSMAN.] **1.** One who makes drawings or designs. **2.** One who drafts a document, *esp.* a legal document or a parliamentary bill or clause 1759. Hence **Dra·ftsmanship.**

Drag (dræg), *v.* 1440. [Obscurely developed from OE. *dragan* DRAW, or – cogn. ON. *draga* (Sw. *draga*, Da. *drage*).]

I. 1. *trans.* To draw or pull (that which is heavy or resists motion); to haul; hence to draw with force or violence; to draw slowly and with difficulty; to trail. Also *intr.* for *refl.* = *passive.* **2.** *fig.* Said of other than physical force or local motion 1596. **3.** *intr.* To lag behind 1494. **4.** *intr.* To trail; to move with friction on the ground or surface 1666. **5.** To protract or continue tediously; usu. *d. on* 1697. **6.** *intr.* To progress slowly and painfully; to become tedious by protraction 1735.

1. Or Captive drag'd in Chains MILT. *P. L.* VI. 260. To d. one foot after the other 1897. *To d. the anchor* (Naut.): to trail it along the bottom after it is loosened from the ground. **2.** Phr. *To d. in* (*into*), to introduce (a subject) in a forced manner, or unnecessarily. **3.** The Chorus dragged 1863. **4.** To raise the Door that it d. not MOXON. **5.** 'Tis long since I..have dragg'd a ling'ring life DRYDEN. **6.** The day drags through BYRON.

II. To use or put a drag to. **1.** *trans.* To draw some contrivance over the bottom of (a river, etc.); to dredge; to sweep with a drag-net; to search by means of a drag or grapnel. Also *fig.* 1577. *absol.* 1530. **2.** To break up with a drag or heavy harrow 1722. **3.** To put a drag upon (wheels, etc.) 1829.

1. *fig.* While I dragg'd my brains for such a song TENNYSON. Hence **Dra·gger**, one who drags.

Drag (dræg), *sb.* See also DRUG *sb.*[2] ME. [f. prec., or partly – MLG. *dragge* grapnel.] **1.** Something heavy that is used by being dragged along the ground or over a surface. **a.** A heavy kind of harrow for breaking up ground ME. **b.** A rough kind of sledge 1576. **c.** A kind of vehicle; often = BREAK; in strict English use, a sort of private stage-coach, with seats inside and on the top 1755. **2.** Something used to pull a weight or obstruction. †**a.** A hook or the like with which anything is forcibly pulled –1789. **b.** A DRAGNET 1481. **c.** An apparatus for dredging, also for collecting oysters from the bed 1611. **d.** An apparatus for recovering objects, the bodies of drowned persons, etc., from the bottom of rivers or pools 1797. **3.** Something that drags or hangs heavily, so as to impede motion. **a.** *Naut.* 'Whatever hangs over a ship, or hinders her sailing' (Kersey). **b.** A drag-anchor (see below). **c.** An iron shoe, or other device, for retarding the rotation of a carriage wheel 1797. **d.** *fig.* A heavy obstruction to progress 1857. **4.** Techn.: **a.** *Masonry.* A thin plate of steel indented on the edge, used in working soft stone 1823. **b.** *Founding.* The bottom part of a flask; called also *drag-box* 1864. **5.** *Hunting.* **a.** The line of scent left by a fox, etc.; the trail 1735. **b.** Any strong-smelling thing used to leave an artificial scent; *e.g.* a red-herring, etc. 1841. **c.** = *drag-hunt* 1851. **6.** The action or fact of dragging; slow, heavy, impeded motion; progress against resistance 1813; the amount by which anything drags 1864; in *Billiards*, retarded motion given to the cue-ball 1873.

1. c. Behind her came..a d., or private stage-coach, with four horses THACKERAY. **2. b.** They catch them in their net, and gather them in their d. *Hab* 1:15. **3. c.** Gently down hill. Put on the d. SYD. SMITH. **5. a.** As the D. or Trail mends, cast off more Dogs that you can confide in 1741. **6.** Working with pleasure, and not with any d. 1887. *attrib.* and *Comb.*: **d.-anchor,** a floating frame of wood, or of spars clothed with sails, used to keep the ship's head to the wind in a gale or when dismasted; a drift-anchor; **-bar, -bolt, -chain, -hook, -spring,** those by which locomotive engines, tenders, and trucks are connected; **-box,** (*a*) see 1 c; (*b*) see 4 b; **-hound,** one of a pack used to hunt with a d. (sense 5 b); **-hunt,** a hunt in which a d. (sense 5 b) is used; also, a club for the prosecution of this sport; **-link,** a link for connecting the cranks of two shafts, in marine engines; **-man,** one who uses a drag-net; **-rake,** a large rake, for raking after the cart in hay and corn harvest; **-sheet** = *drag-anchor*; **-twist,** a spiral hook at the end of a rod, for cleaning bore-holes.

Drag-chain (-tʃēⁱn). 1791. **1.** A chain used to retard the motion of a vehicle; *esp.* one with a large hook to hitch on the hind wheel. Also *fig.* **2.** The strong chain by which railway wagons, etc. are coupled.

‖**Dragée** (draʒe). 1866. [Fr.; see DREDGE *sb.*[2]] A sugar plum containing a drug; now often, a chocolate drop.

Draggle (dræ·g'l), *v.* 1513. [dim. and frequent of DRAG *v.*; see -LE.] **1.** To wet or befoul by allowing to drag through mire or wet grass; to make wet, limp, and dirty; †to trail (through the dirt) –1723. **2.** *intr.* (for *refl.*) To trail (on the ground), hang trailing 1594. **3.** *intr.* To come on or follow slowly and stragglingly 1577.

1. The wet day draggles the tricolor CARLYLE. **3.** With heavy hearts they draggled at the heels of his troop W. IRVING. Hence **Dra·ggle** *sb.* the action of draggling (*rare*).

Draggle-haired, *a.* [After next.] With hair hanging wet and untidy. DICKENS.

Draggle-tail (dræ·g'lˌtēⁱl). 1596. [f. DRAGGLE *v.* + TAIL *sb.*[1]] **1.** A draggle-tailed person. **2.** *pl.* Skirts that drag on the ground in the mud 1858. **3.** *attrib.* = next 1707.

Dra·ggle-tailed, *a.* 1654. Having a tail or skirt that trails on the ground in mud and wet.

Drag-hook. 1530. **1.** A hook used for dragging. **2.** The hook of a drag-chain.

Dragman[1]; see DRAG *sb.*

Dragman[2], obs. f. DRAGOMAN.

Dra·g-net. 1541. [Cf. OE. *drægnet*, Sw. *dragg-not*; see DRAY *sb.*[1]] A net which is dragged along the bottom of a river, etc., as in fishing; also one used to sweep the ground game off a field. Also *fig.*

Dragoman (dræ·gŏmăn). Pl. **-mans, -men.** ME. [– Fr. †*drogueman* (now *drogman*) – It. *dragomano* – med.Gr. δραγόμανος – Arab. *tarjumān* (see TRUCHMAN), f. *tarjama* interpret (see TARGUM), – Aramaic *targēm* interpret, – Assyrian *targumānu* interpreter. See also TRUCHMAN.] An interpreter; strictly applied to a guide in countries where Arabic, Turkish, or Persian is spoken. Also *transf.*

Cirus..All vnpurueyed of drogeman or of guide LYDG. Hence **Dra·gomanate**, the office of a d. **Dragoma·nic** *a.*

Dragon (dræ·gən). ME. [– (O)Fr. *dragon* – L. *draco*, *-ōn-* – Gr. δράκων.] †**1.** A huge serpent or snake; a python –1849. **2.** A mythical monster, part serpent, part crocodile, with strong claws, and a scaly skin; it is generally represented with wings, and sometimes as breathing out fire. The heraldic dragon combines reptilian and mammalian form with the addition of wings. ME. **3.** In the Bible versions repr. *draco* of the Vulgate and δράκων of the Septuagint, where the Hebr. has (*a*) *tannin* a great sea- or water-monster, also a large serpent; or (*b*) *tan*, now understood to be the jackal ME. **4.** An appellation of Satan, the 'Old Serpent' ME.; *transf.* a fiend 1508. **5.** An appellation of Death (*arch.*) 1500. **6.** A fierce violent person; *esp.* a duenna 1755. **7.** A figure of the mythical creature ME. **8.** *Astron.* The constellation *Draco* 1551; †the part of the moon's path which lies south of the ecliptic –1594; †applied to a shooting star with a luminous train –1774. †**9.** = DRAGOON *sb.* 1, 2. –1867. **10.** *Zool.* A lizard of the genus *Draco*, having on each flank a broad wing-like membrane, which enables it to make long leaps in the air 1819. **11.** *Ichthyol.* (Also *d.-fish.*) **a.** = DRAGONET 2. †**b.** The ANGLER, *Lophius.* 1661. **12.** = DRAGOON *sb.* 3. 1867. **13.** (Also *Green D.*) The plant *Dracunculus vulgaris*; = DRAGONS, DRAGONWORT 1538. †**14.** A disease of the eye in horses –1720. **15.** *attrib.* Of or as of a dragon; dragon-like 1606.

1. Hee..Now D. grown..Huge Python MILT. *P. L.* X. 529. **2.** His Armes spred wider than a Dragons Wings 1 *Hen. VI*, I. i. 11. Saint George that swindg'd the D. *John* II. i. 288. Swift, swift, you Dragons of the night (*i.e.* those which drew the chariot of Cynthia or the moon) *Cymb.* II. ii. 48. Phr. *Like a d.*: fiercely, violently. **3.** The lion and the d. [*R. V.* serpent] shalt thou trample under feet *Ps.* 91:13. It shall be an habitation of dragons [*R. V.* jackals] and a court for owls *Isa.* 34:13. **7.** *D. china*, a kind of porcelain decorated with designs of dragons. **15.** Cynthia checks her d. yoke MILT. *Pens.* 59.

Comb.: **d. arum,** the plant *Dracunculus vulgaris* (sense 13); **d.-beam, -piece,** 'a beam bisecting the wall-plate, for receiving the heel or foot of the hip-rafters' (P. Nicholson); **-fish** (see sense 11); **-shell,** a species of concamerated limpet; **-stone,** DRACONITES; †**-water,** a medicinal preparation popular in 17th c.

Comb. with *dragon's*. **a.** In names of plants, as **dragon's-claw, -herb** (= DRAGONWORT); **-mouth,** the Snapdragon. **b. Dragon's belly** (*Astron.*), that part of a planet's orbit most remote from the nodes, that is, from the dragon's head and tail; **dragon's skin,** a familiar term among miners, etc., for the stems of *Lepidodendron*; **dragon's teeth,** the teeth of the d. fabled to have been sown by Cadmus, whence sprang armed men.

Dragonade; see DRAGONNADE.

Dragoness (dræ·gŏnės). 1634. [-ESS[1].] A female or she dragon (*lit.* and *fig.*).

Dragonet (dræ·gŏnėt). ME. [– Fr. *dragonet*, dim. of *dragon* DRAGON; see -ET.] **1.** A small or young dragon. **2.** A fish of the genus *Callionymus*, esp. *C. dracunculus* 1769. **3.** A S. American lizard, *Crocodilurus.*

Dra·gon-fly, dragon fly. 1626. The common name for neuropterous insects of the group *Libellulina*, characterized by a long, slender body, large eyes, and two pairs of large reticulated wings, and by their strong, swift flight.

Dra·gonish, *a.* 1530. [-ISH[1].] Of the nature or shape of a dragon.

Dragonnade (drægŏnēⁱ·d). *sb.* Also **dragonade, dragoonade.** 1715. [– Fr. *dragonnade*, f. *dragon* DRAGOON *sb.* 2; see -ADE.] In *pl.*, a series of persecutions directed by Louis XIV against French Protestants, in which dragoons were quartered upon them. Hence, any persecution carried on with the help of troops. (Rare in *sing.*)

The dragoonades of Claverhouse SPURGEON.

Dra·gon-root. 1621. †**1.** The root of dragonwort or dragons. **2.** In *U.S.*, the tuberous roots of species of *Arisæma*; also, the plants themselves 1866.

†**Dra·gons.** [Late ME. *dragance* – OFr. *dragance*, var. of *dragonce* :– late L. *draconlia*, for L. *dracontium* – Gr. δρακόντιον, f. δράκων, -οντ- DRAGON.] The plant, *Dracunculus vulgaris* –1757.

Dragon's blood. 1599. A bright red gum or resin, an exudation upon the fruit of a palm, *Calamus draco.* Formerly applied also to the inspissated juice of the dragon-tree, *Dracæna draco*, and to exudations from *Pterocarpus draco*, *Croton draco*, etc. Also *attrib.*

Dragon's head. 1509. [See DRAGON 8.] **1.** *Astron.* The ascending node of the moon's orbit with the ecliptic (marked ☊). *Her.*, the name of the tincture *tenné* or tawny, in blazoning by the heavenly bodies 1706. **2.** *Herb.* The name of a genus of plants, *Dracocephalum* 1753.

Dragon's tail. 1605. [See DRAGON 8.] **1.** *Astron.* The descending node of the moon's orbit with the ecliptic (marked ☋) 1605. *Her.*, the name of the tincture *murrey* or *sanguine*, in blazoning by the heavenly bodies 1706. **2.** *Palmistry.* The discriminal line 1678.

Dra·gon-tree. 1611. The monocotyledonous plant *Dracæna draco* (N.O. *Liliaceæ*).

†**Dra·gonwort.** 1565. **1.** = DRAGONS –1607. **2.** *Small d.*: the common Arum or Wake-robin 1674. **3.** The Snakeweed (*rare*) 1656.

Dragoon (drăgū·n), *sb.* 1622. [– Fr. *dragon* DRAGON; see -OON.] †**1.** A kind of carbine. So called from its 'breathing fire'. –1659. **2.** Orig., a mounted infantryman armed with a dragoon (sense 1); now a name for certain regiments of cavalry 1622. **b.** A rough and fierce fellow 1712. **3.** A variety of pigeon 1725. *Comb.* **d.-bird,** a Brazilian bird (*Cephalopterus ornatus*), called also *umbrella-bird*.

Dragoo·n, *v.* 1689. [f. prec., after Fr. *dragonner*; cf. DRAGONNADE.] **1.** *trans.* To force or drive by the agency of dragoons; to persecute, as in the DRAGONNADES. **2.** To force (*into* a course) by rigorous and harassing measures 1689.

1. To D. all Men into the Kings Religion 1692. **2.** He dragooned men into wisdom GODWIN.

Dragoonade; see DRAGONNADE.

†Dragoo·ner. 1639. [prob. – Fr. *dragonnier* (unrecorded in this sense).] **1.** = DRAGOON *sb.* 2. –1705. **2.** A horse ridden by a dragoon 1642. **3.** [f. DRAGOON *v.*] A rigid persecutor –1826.

Dragsman (dræ·gzmæn). 1812. **1.** The driver of a drag. **2.** One employed to drag a river-bed, etc. 1896.

Dra·g-staff (-stɑf). 1769. A trailing pole hinged to the rear of a vehicle to check backward movement in going uphill.

†Drail, *v.* 1598. [app. var. of TRAIL *v.*] **1.** *trans.* To drag or trail along –1664. **2.** *intr.* To draggle, move laggingly –1716.

Drain (drēⁱn), *v.* [OE. *drēahnian, drēhnian* prob. f. **drēaʒ-* :– Gmc. **drauʒ-* (see DRY *a.*).] **†1.** *trans.* To strain through any porous medium –1667. **2.** To draw or carry *off* or *away* gradually 1538. Also *transf.* and *fig.* **3.** To drink to the last drops 1602. **4.** *intr.* Of liquid: To trickle *through*; to flow gradually *off* or *away* 1587. **5.** *trans.* To withdraw the water or moisture from gradually; to leave dry by withdrawal of moisture 1577. **6.** To drink dry 1697. **7.** *transf.* and *fig.* To exhaust; to deprive gradually of resources, strength, etc. 1660. **8.** *intr.* To become dry by percolation or flowing away of moisture 1664.

1. Salt-water drayned through twenty vessels BACON. **2.** The streams..are now drained drie FULLER. He..permitted those of Rome to exhaust and d. the wealth of England 1625. **3.** He dreines his draughts of Renish downe *Haml.* I. iv. 10. **5.** Ile dreyne him drie as Hay *Macb.* I. iii. 18. **6.** They had drained the cup of life to the dregs DICKENS.

Drain (drēⁱn), *sb.* 1552. [f. DRAIN *v.*] **1.** That by which liquid is drained; *esp.* an artificial channel or conduit for carrying off water, sewage, etc.; in *Surgery*, a tubular instrument used to draw off the discharge from a wound or abscess 1834. **2.** The act of draining; drainage; now only *fig.* constant or gradual outlet or withdrawal 1721. **3.** *slang.* A drink 1836. **4.** *pl.* Dregs from which liquid has been drained; *dial.* brewers' grains from the mash-tub 1820.

1. Through these Fens run great Cuts or Dreyns 1696. The main d. of the country is the Wale nullah 1876. **2.** A sad d. upon my time MOORE. A d. on the revenue 1849. *attrib.* and *Comb.*, as *d.-pipe, -tile*, etc.; **d.-cock,** a cock for draining the water out of a boiler; **-trap,** a trap on a d. to prevent the escape of sewer-gas; **-well,** 'a pit sunk through an impervious stratum of earth to reach a pervious stratum and form a means of drainage for surface water' (Knight).

Drainage (drēⁱ·nėdʒ). 1652. [f. DRAIN *v.* + -AGE.] **1.** The action of draining. Also *fig.* **2.** A system of drains, artificial or natural 1878. **3.** That which is drained off by a system of drains; sewage 1834.

attrib. and *Comb.*, as *d.-area, -district, -shaft*; **d.-tube** (*Surg.*), a small tube, with lateral perforations, passed through a cannula into the cavity to be drained.

Drainer (drēⁱ·nəɹ). 1598. [f. as prec. + -ER¹.] **1.** One who drains; *esp.* one who constructs field-drains 1611. **2.** That which drains; a drain; a vessel for draining moist substances.

Drai·ning, *vbl. sb.* 1565. [f. DRAIN *v.* + -ING¹.] The action of DRAIN *v.*

attrib. and *Comb.*, as *d.-brick, -tile, -well*, etc.

Drai·nless, *a.* 1817. [f. DRAIN *sb.* or *v.* + -LESS.] Exhaustless.

Drake¹ (drēⁱk). [OE. *draca* = OFris., MLG., MDu. *drake* (Du. *draak*), OHG. *trahho* (G. (MG.) *drache*) :– WGmc. **drako* – L. *draco* DRAGON. Sense 3 is from LG.] **1.** = DRAGON 2. *Obs.* or *arch.* **†b.** = DRAGON 1. (OE. only.) **†2.** A fiery meteor; see FIRE-DRAKE 2. –1610. **3.** A small sort of cannon. Now *Hist.* 1625. **4.** Angler's name for species of *Ephemera* 1658. **5.** A beaked galley. (Cf. ON. *dreki*.) 1862. *Comb.* **d.-shot** from sense 3.

Drake² (drēⁱk). ME. [To be referred, with G. dial. (LG.) *drake, drache*, to WGmc. **drako* (**dreko*) of obscure origin, which forms the second element of OHG. *antrahho, antrehho* (G. *enterich*), the first element of which is OHG. *anut, enit* (G. *ente*) = OE. *ened* duck.] The male of birds of the duck kind. Also *attrib.* *Comb.* **d.-stone,** a flat stone thrown along the surface of water so as to graze it and rebound.

Drake, obs. f. DRAWK.

Dram (dræm), *sb.¹* ME. [– OFr. *drame* or med.L. *drama*, vars. of *dragme, dragma*; see DRACHM.] **†1.** = DRACHM 1. –1526. **2.** A weight; = DRACHM 2. Also the Arabic DIRHEM. **3.** A fluid dram (= ⅛ fluid ounce) of medicine, etc.; hence, **b.** A small draught of spirits or the like. 1590. Hence **dram-shop,** a liquor shop (1761). **4.** *fig.* = DRACHM 3. 1566. **5.** *Canada* and *U.S.* A section of a raft of staves. (? A distinct word.) 1878.

4. Having not one d. of learning HEARNE. Hence **Dram** *v.* to tipple; *trans.* to ply with drams.

Dram, *sb.²* 1663. [Short for *Drammen*.] Timber from Drammen in Norway. Also *attrib.*

Drama (drā·mă). 1515. [– late L. *drama* – Gr. δρᾶμα, f. δρᾶν do, act, perform. Earlier *drame*, as in Fr.] **1.** A composition in prose or verse, adapted to be acted on the stage, in which a story is related by means of dialogue and action, and is represented with accompanying gesture, costume, and scenery, as in real life; a play. **2.** With *the*: The dramatic branch of literature; the dramatic art 1661. **3.** A series of actions or course of events having dramatic unity, and leading to a final catastrophe 1714.

1. I cannot for the stage a d. lay, Tragic or comic B. JONS. **2.** The received Rules of the D. ADDISON. The lover of the Elizabethan d. M. PATTISON. **3.** The awful d. of Providence now acting on the moral theatre of the world BURKE.

Dramatic (drămæ·tik), *a.* (*sb.*) 1589. [– late L. *dramaticus* – Gr. δραματικός, f. δρᾶμα, δραματ-; see DRAMA, -IC.]

A. 1. Of, pertaining to, or connected with the, or a, drama; dealing with or employing the forms of the drama. So **Drama·tical** *a.* (now *rare*). **2.** Characteristic of, or appropriate to, the drama; theatrical 1725.

1. A d. critic 1885. **2.** The destruction of a great and ancient institution is an eminently d. thing 1878.

B. *sb.* **†1.** A dramatic poet –1741. **2.** *pl.* The drama 1684.

Drama·tically, *adv.* 1652. [f. as prec.; see -ICAL, -LY².] In a dramatic manner; from a dramatic point of view; with theatrical effect.

Drama·ticle, -icule. 1813. [f. late L. *drama, dramat-* with dim. suffix; see -CULE.] A miniature or insignificant drama.

‖**Dramatis personæ** (dræ·mătis pəɹsōᵘ·nī). Abbrev. *dram. pers.* 1730. [L. 'persons of the drama'.] The characters of a play (*lit.* and *fig.*).

Dramatist (dræ·mătist). 1678. [f. Gr. δρᾶμα, δράματ- DRAMA + -IST.] A writer of dramas or dramatic poetry; a playwright.

Dramatize (dræ·mătəiz), *v.* 1780. [f. as prec. + -IZE.] **1.** *trans.* To convert into a drama; to put into dramatic form, adapt for the stage. **2.** To represent dramatically 1823. **3.** *intr.* To admit of dramatization 1819.

1. To d. the Lady of the Lake SCOTT. **3.** The story would d. admirably 1836. Hence **Dra:matiza·tion,** conversion into drama; a dramatized version.

Dramaturge (dræ·mătɒ̄ɹdʒ). 1870. [– Fr. *dramaturge* – Gr. δραματουργός, f. δραματ- + -εργος worker. Cf. THAUMATURGE.] = DRAMATURGIST.

Fate is the d.; necessity Allots the parts SYMONDS. So **Dramatu·rgic, -al** *a.* pertaining to dramaturgy.

Dra·maturgist. 1825. [f. as prec. + -IST.] A composer of a drama.

Dra·maturgy. 1801. [– Gr. δραματουργία composition of dramas (see DRAMATURGE), prob. after G. *dramaturgie*.] **1.** Dramatic composition; the dramatic art. **2.** Theatrical acting 1837.

Drank, pa. t. of DRINK.

[**Drank,** erron. f. DRAWK.]

†Drap-de-Berry. Also as three words. [Fr.; = cloth of Berry.] 1619. A kind of woollen cloth, coming from Berry in France –1818.

Your rotten French camlets now, or your drab-de-berries SCOTT.

Drape (drēⁱp), *v.* ME. [– OFr. *draper*, f. *drap* cloth :– late L. *drappus*, perh. of Celt. origin. See DRAB *sb.²*] **†1.** *trans.* To weave into cloth –1683. Also *absol.* **2.** To cover with, or as with, cloth; to hang, dress, or adorn with drapery 1847. Also *transf.* and *fig.* **3.** To adjust artistically. Also *intr.* for *refl.* 1862. **†4.** To reprimand. [Cf. DRESS *v.*] TEMPLE.

1. Flanders doth d. Cloth for thee of thine own Wool 1683. **2.** A red gown draped with old Spanish lace 1882. *fig.* Draped in solemn inanities FROUDE. Hence **Dra·ping** *vbl. sb.*

Drape (drēⁱp), *sb.* 1665. [f. Fr. *drap* and DRAPE *v.*] **a.** Cloth, drapery. **b.** Draping.

Draper (drēⁱ·pəɹ), *sb.* ME. [– AFr. *draper*, (O)Fr. *drapier*, f. *drap* cloth; see DRAPE *v.*, -ER² 2.] **1.** Orig. One who made (woollen) cloth. Subseq., A dealer in cloth, whence, now, in other textile fabrics. **2.** In comb. = *seller*; see ALE-*draper*. So **†Dra·per** *v. rare*, to weave into cloth; *absol.* to drape.

Drapery (drēⁱ·pəri), *sb.* ME. [– (O)Fr. *draperie*, f. *drap* cloth, *drapier* DRAPER; see -ERY.] **1.** Cloth or textile fabrics collectively. **2.** The business of a draper; †cloth-making; now, the sale of cloth, etc. 1488. **3.** The artistic arrangement of clothing in painting or sculpture 1610. **4.** The stuff with which anything is draped; clothing or hangings of any kind; *esp.* the clothing of the human figure in sculpture or painting. Also *fig.* 1686. Also *attrib.*

3. Attitude without action..dress without d. 1811. **4.** To dispose the d., so that the folds shall have an easy communication, and gracefully follow each other SIR J. REYNOLDS. Nature is stripped of all her summer d. HOWITT. Hence **Dra·pery** *v.* to cover with, or as with, d. **Dra·peried** *ppl. a.*

†Dra·pet. 1590. [– It. *drappetto*, dim. of *drappo* cloth.] A covering –1799.

Drastic (dræ·stik), *a.* 1691. [– Gr. δραστικός active, effective, f. δρᾶν do.] **1.** *Med.* Of medicines: Acting with vigour, violent. Also as *sb.* **2.** *transf.* Vigorously effective; violent 1808.

1. D. purgatives 1789, remedies 1836. **2.** So d. a measure MILL. Hence **Dra·stically** *adv.*

Drat (dræt), *int.* 1815. [Aphetic f. *od-ra·t* (Fielding) i.e. OD, minced form of God, and RAT *v.²*] An exclam. of angry vexation; = 'Hang', 'dash', 'confound'. Hence **Drat** *v.* **Dratted** *ppl. a.*

Drat, obs. 3rd pers. sing. pres. of DREAD *v.*

Draught (drɑft), *sb.* [Early ME. *draht*, if not in OE., – ON. *drahtr, dráttr*, later reinforced from MDu. *dragt* = OHG. *traht* (G. *tracht*), abstr. sb. f. Gmc. **dragan* draw. See DRAFT.]

I. 1. The action, or an act, of drawing or pulling, *esp.* of a vehicle, plough, etc.; pull, traction. (rarely *draft.*) **2.** That which is drawn. **†a.** A load. ME. only. **b.** A quantity drawn: used as a specific measure 1740. **3.** Something used in drawing or pulling, as harness for horses 1483. **4.** A team of horses or oxen, together with what they draw. Now *dial.* 1523.

1. The Hertfordshire wheel-plough..is of the easiest d. MORTIMER. **2.** *Draught*..sixty-one pounds weight of wool HALLIWELL.

II. *fig.* Drawing, attraction; inclination (*arch.*). (also †*draft.*) ME.

III. 1. The act of drawing a net for fish ME. **2.** The take in one drawing of the net. (rarely *draft.*) ME. **3.** A measure of weight of eels, = 20 lbs. 1859.

1. For he was astonished..at the d. of the fishes which they had taken *Luke* 5:9.

IV. †1. The drawing of a bow; also, a bow-shot –1605. **†2.** The sweep of a weapon –1460. **3.** The drawing of a saw through a block of wood or stone; hence a measure of sawyer's work ME. **4.** See DRAFT 1. 1494.

V. 1. The drawing of liquid into the mouth or down the throat; an act of drinking; the quantity drunk at one pull. (rarely *draft.*) ME. **2.** A dose of liquid medicine; a potion 1656. **3.** Inhaling of smoke or vapour; that which is inhaled at one breath 1621. **4.** *fig.* The drinking in of something by the mind or soul. (Cf. DRINK *v.*) 1560.

1. Our morning d. MASSINGER. 2. Fee the doctor for a nauseous d. DRYDEN. Phr. *Black d.*: a purgative consisting of an infusion of senna with sulphate of magnesia and extract of liquorice. (Also *fig.*) 4. Make the d. of life sweet or bitter JOHNSON.

VI. The action of drawing out to a greater length; that which is drawn out or spun, a thread ME.

VII. *Naut.* The action of drawing or displacing (so much) water; the depth of water which a vessel draws. (sometimes *draft.*) 1601.

A..Vessel..For shallow d. and bulke vnprizable *Twel. N.* v. i. 58.

VIII. †**1.** The action of moving along; course, going –1485. †**2.** A move at chess, etc. [Fr. *trait* :– L. *tractus.*] –1656. **3.** *pl.* A game played by two persons on a chequer-board, simpler than chess, all the pieces being of equal value and moving alike diagonally. (In U.S. called *checkers*, in Scotl. *dambrod.* (rarely †*drafts.*) ME. **b.** One of the pieces: = DRAUGHTSMAN. (Usu. in *pl.*) 1894.

IX. 1. A current, stream, flow 1601; in *Hydraulics*, the area of an opening for a flow of water. (also *draft.*) 1874. **2.** A current of air, *esp.* in a room or a chimney. (occas. *draft.*) 1768.

2. *Natural d.*: the current of air that passes through the fire in a steam boiler, etc., without mechanical aid, as dist. from *blast, forced d.*, that artificially increased either by rarefying the air above the fire or by compressing it below.

X. †**1.** The drawing of a line or mark with a brush, pen, pencil, etc.; the mark so made; a stroke. [Fr. *trait.*] –1662. †**2.** Delineation, drawing –1734. †**3.** That which is drawn or delineated. (rarely *draft.*) –1796. †**b.** Representation in sculpture; a sculptured figure –1686. **4.** *spec.* A sketch, preparatory to a work of art 1573. Also *fig.* **5.** A sketch in words. (occas. *draft.*) 1503. **6.** A plan.. Also DRAFT 4, q.v. **7.** See DRAFT 5. 1528. †**8.** Something drawn up; a scheme; a plot. (rarely *draft.*) –1731.

4. Like the first d. of a painter FULKE. 5. Thus I have, in a short d., given a view of our original Ideas LOCKE. 7. What I wrote in the first d. of this work T. BURNET.

XI. 1. See DRAFT 2. 1703. **2.** *Comm.* See DRAFT 3. 1633.

1. Draughts of labourers were employed in Spain 1872.

XII. †**1.** *fig.* Derivation; something derived –1561. †**2.** An extract –1601. **3.** The action of drawing liquor from a vessel; readiness to be so drawn ME. **4.** A mild blister, etc., that 'draws' 1828. **5.** *Masonry*, etc. See DRAFT 6. 1859.

XIII. †**1.** (?) A cesspool or sink –1703. †**2.** A privy –1681.

XIV. *attrib.* **a.** Of beasts: Used for draught or drawing. (also *draft.*) 1466. **b.** Of sheep: Drafted from the flock. **c.** Of liquor: On draught; as *d. ale, beer*, etc. 1893. **d.** Of a document: Drawn up as a rough copy. (Commonly DRAFT, q.v. 7b.) 1878.

Comb.: **d.-board,** the board on which the game of draughts is played; **-box,** an air-tight tube by which the water from an elevated wheel is conducted to the tail-race; **-engine,** the engine over the shaft of a coal-pit or mine; **-hook,** one of the hooks of iron fixed on the cheeks of a cannon carriage, used for drawing a gun backwards or forwards; †**-hound,** a hound used for tracking by scent; †**-house,** a privy (= sense XIII. 2); **-line,** a line on a ship marking the depth of water she draws; **-net,** a net that is drawn for fish; **-spring,** a spring inserted between the trace and the wagon, etc., so as to relieve the strain of starting; **-way,** a way along which something is drawn; a passage for a current of air.

Draught (draft), *v.* 1714. [f. DRAUGHT *sb.*] **1.** *trans.* = DRAFT *v.* 1. **2.** To make a plan or sketch of; to design. (occas. *draft.*) 1828. **3.** To cut a draught upon. (Also DRAFT *v.* 3.) 1848. **4.** *Weaving.* To draw (the threads of the warp) through the heddles of the loom.

1. The commander..shall d. off an equal number of men..to supply their places 1758.

For other senses see DRAFT *v.*

†**Drau·ght-bridge.** ME. = DRAWBRIDGE –1543.

Draughtsman (dra·ftsmæn). Pl. **-men.** See also DRAFTSMAN. 1663. [f. *draught's* + MAN.] **1.** A man employed or skilled in making drawings or designs. **2.** One who draws up, or makes a draft of, legal or other documents. Now oftener DRAFTSMAN, q.v. 1759. **3.** One of the pieces used in the game of draughts; var. *draughtman* 1894.

1. The d. of the Survey 1875. 2. The actual d. of the Report 1887. Hence **Drau·ghtsmanship.**

Draughty (dra·fti), *a.* 1602. [f. DRAUGHT *sb.* + -Y[1].] **1.** Abounding in currents of air, as, a *d. room* 1846. †**2.** Rubbishy; filthy (*rare*) 1602. Hence **Drau·ghtiness.**

Drave, obs. or arch. pa. t. of DRIVE *v.*

Dravidian (drăvi·diăn), *a.* and *sb.* 1856. [f. Skr. *Dravida*, province of S. India, + -IAN.] Name of a race of S. India and Ceylon, and the group of agglutinative languages spoken by them.

Draw (drǭ), *v.* Pa. t. **drew** (drū); pa. pple. **drawn** (drǭn). [OE. *dragan* = ON. *draga* draw, pull, and (in the sense 'bear, carry', 'wear') OFris. *draga*, OS. *dragan* (Du. *dragen*), OHG. *tragan* (G. *tragen*), Goth. (*ga*)*dragan.*]

I. Of simple traction. (The most general word for this.) **1.** *trans.* To cause to move toward oneself by the application of force; to pull. Also *absol.* Also *refl.*, and *intr.* for *passive.* **2.** To pull after one; move (a thing) along by traction ME. Also *absol.*, and *intr.* for *passive.* **3.** *transf.* To convey in a vehicle; to cart; to haul ME. ***In specific applications.*** **4.** To drag (traitors) at a horse's tail, or on a hurdle, to the place of execution ME. †**5.** To pull or tear *in pieces, asunder* –1700. **6.** To cause to shrink; to distort ME. Also *intr.* for *refl.* †**7.** To mend (a rent) –1611. ****With specific objects.*** **8.** To pull up (a sail, etc.), pull out (a bolt, etc.), haul in (a net), etc. ME. **9.** To bend (a bow); also, to pull back (the arrow) on the string. Also *absol.* ME. **10.** To pull (a curtain, veil, etc.) over something, or aside or off from it. Also *fig.* ME. Also *intr.* for *refl.* = *passive.* **11.** Of a ship, etc.: To displace (so much depth of water); to sink so deep in floating. [So Fr. *tirer seize pieds d'eau*, etc.] 1555. **12.** In *Cricket*, To divert (the ball) to the 'on' side by a slight turn of the bat 1857. *****In transf. and fig. applications.*** **13.** *trans.* To cause to come, move, or go (from or to some place, position, or condition). *Obs.* exc. in assoc. with other senses. ME. †**14.** To lead (a ditch, wall, etc.) from one point to another. (L. *ducere.*) –1796. †**15.** To render; to translate –1569. †**16.** *fig.* **a.** To adduce. **b.** To attribute. **c.** To pervert, wrest. –1704. †**17.** *Arith.* To add (*to, together*); to subtract (*out of*); to multiply (*into, in*) –1811.

1. A Shark..drew him under Water 1700. The rope drew taut 1886. 2. A locomotive drawing a long train of wagons 1897. Phr. *To d. with*: to be in like case with SHAKS. 4. After the fassyon of treytours to be drawen, hanged and quartred HALL. 6. The face smiling, but drawn and fixed SWINBURNE. 9. A certaine man drew a bow at a venture 1 *Kings* 22:34. Phr. *To d. a bead*; see BEAD *sb.* *To d. bit, bridle, rein*: to pull up: also *fig.* 10. When the curtens were drawne, all the people might see it 1631. Phr. *To d. the cloth*: to 'clear away' after a meal. (Now *arch.*) 13. Phr. *To d. into example, precedent, comparison*, etc.

II. Of attraction, drawing in or together. **1.** To take in (air, etc.) into the lungs; to breathe; to cause (a draught) to enter ME. **2.** *absol.* or *intr.* To produce or admit of a draught; said of a chimney, a cigar, etc. 1758. **3.** To attract, as a magnet; to contract (rust, heat, etc.: also *fig.*) ME. **4.** *fig.* To attract by moral force, persuasion, inclination, etc.; to lead, entice, turn (*to, into*, or *from* a course, condition, etc.) ME. Also *absol.* **5.** To induce (*to do* something) 1568. **6.** To bring together. *Obs.* exc. as assoc. with other senses. 1568. Also *intr.* for *refl.* **7.** To bring about as a result, entail, bring on ME. **8.** To cause to fall *upon* ME.

1. Swoln with wind and the rank mist they d. MILT. *Lycidas* 126. 2. The fire does not d. well 1833. 3. Bras draweth soone ruste ME. 4. I was drawn..therunto through the FLEMING. MILT. *P. L.* II. 308. Mr. Emerson always draws LOWELL. 7. The interest that drawes the freehold BACON. 8. The occasion [that] drew this mischiefe upon him 1628.

III. Of extraction, withdrawal, removal. **1.** To pull out, take out, extract ME. Also *absol.* **2.** To pull or take out one of a number of things ('lots') ME.; to obtain or select by lot 1709. **3.** To separate or select from a group or heap; *spec.* to separate (seeds) from the husks ME. **4.** To drag or force (a badger or fox) from his hole 1834. †**5.** To withdraw (stakes, a horse, etc.) –1857. **6.** To leave undecided (a game, etc.). [? = *withdraw.*] 1837. **7.** To raise, as water from a well, etc. ME. **8.** To cause (liquid) to flow from a vessel through an opening, blood from a wound, etc. Also *absol.* to draw liquor. ME. **9.** To extract (a liquor, etc.) by suction, pressure, infusion, or distillation 1550. Also *absol.* (of the teapot), and *intr.* (of the tea). **10.** *Med.* To cause a flow of (blood, etc.) to a particular part; to promote suppuration. Also *absol.* (of a poultice or blister). ME. **11.** To drain off (water); also *absol.*, and *intr.* (for *refl.*) 1607. **12.** To take, obtain, or derive *from* a source ME. Also *intr.* or *absol.* **13.** To elicit, evoke. *spec.* in *Cards.* To cause (a card or cards) to be played out. ME. **14.** *colloq.* To rouse to action, speech, or anger; to 'fetch'; to exasperate 1860. **15.** To deduce 1576. **16.** To extract something from, draw out the contents of; to drain 1576; to draw out the viscera of; to disembowel ME. **17.** To draw a net through or along (a river, etc.) for fish ME. **18.** *Hunting.* To search (a wood, etc.) for game. Also *absol.* 1583. **19.** *colloq.* To 'pump' (a person) 1857.

1. He would have drawn the cork 1828. To d. stumps at cricket 1850, two cards 1870. To d. [= thin] an onion bed 1897. *absol.* D. (*sc.* the sword), if you be men *Rom. & Jul.* I. i. 69. 2. Phr. *To d. cut(s, lot(s*: see CUT *sb.*[1], LOT *sb.* The jury is drawn very fairly KEATINGE. 6. To d. a battle 1878. 8. I will entertaine Bardolfe: he shall d.; he shall tap *Merry W.* I. iii. 11. Their Stings d. Blood DRYDEN. Phr. *To d. it mild*: (*a*) *lit.* in reference to beer; (*b*) to refrain from exaggeration. 9. Oil of sweet Almonds newly drawn 1747. 12. The stocke from whence he draweth his descent FLEMING. [He] drew his salary quarterly 1850. 13. He draws all the trumps and wins all the tricks H. H. GIBBS. 16. To d. an oven PEPYS. To pluck and d. a Goose CULPEPPER. 18. Phr. *To d.* (a covert) *blank*: to search it without success; also *to d. a blank* (with allusion to drawing a blank in a lottery).

IV. Of tension, extension, protection. **1.** To pull out to a greater length or size; to stretch, distend, extend; to spin (a thread). Also *absol.*, and *intr.* for *refl.* ME. Also *fig.* **2.** *techn.* **a.** To make (wire) by drawing a piece of metal through holes of diminishing size. **b.** To flatten out (metal). **3.** *Naut. intr.* Of a sail: To swell out tightly with the wind 1627.

1. The Skin drew or stretch'd like a Piece of Doe-Leather 1747. *fig.* The anguish..is too long drawn 1885.

V. Of delineation or construction by drawing. **1.** To trace (a line, figure, etc.) by drawing a pencil, pen, or the like, across a surface ME. **2.** To make by drawing lines; to design, delineate; †to model 1526. Also *fig.* ME. Also *absol.* or *intr.* 1530. †**3.** To devise; to set in order, arrange –1663. **4.** To frame (a document, bill, cheque, etc.) in due form; to write out ME. Also *fig.* **5.** To frame, formulate, institute (comparisons, distinctions, etc.) 1789.

1. Like figures drawn upon a dial plate COWPER. Phr. *To d. a line* (*fig.*): to fix a limit or boundary. 2. To d. cartoons on wood 1861. *fig.* To d. a character ADDISON. 4. Clarke, d. a deed of gift *Merch. V.* IV. i. 394. She should d. bills upon me DE FOE. Phr. *To d. against*, to issue drafts in consideration of (value placed in the drawee's hands). 5. I..avoided drawing comparisons between your son and F. 1802.

VI. *refl.* and *intr.* Of motion, moving oneself. †**1.** *refl.* *To d. oneself*: to move oneself, come, go *to* or *towards*; to withdraw *from* –1618. †**2.** *intr.* To move, come, go –1808. **b.** Now only, To move *towards* a place, to come near, approach, to come *together*, to withdraw to one side ME. Also *fig.* **3.** To draw near or approach in time ME. **4.** *Hunting.* Of a hound: To track game by the scent. **b.** To move slowly towards the game after pointing. 1589. **5.** *Racing.* Gradually to gain *on* or get *away from* an antagonist 1823.

2. Our men immediately..drew together in a body DAMPIER. *fig.* To d. to age CAXTON. 3. To d. to a conclusion 1821. 5. Phr. *To d. level*: to come up with an antagonist.

Comb. with adverbs. See also simple senses and adverbs. **D. back: a.** *Comm.* To recover (the whole or part of the duty on goods) upon exportation; see DRAWBACK *sb.* **b.** *intr.* To move backwards from one's position; also *fig.* **D. in: a.** *trans.* To contract; to cause to shrink. **b.** To inhale. **c.** *fig.* To inveigle, entice; to ensnare. **d.** Of a day or evening: To draw to a close. Also of a succession of days: To become gradually shorter. **D. off: a.** *trans.* To withdraw (troops) from a position; *intr.* to withdraw. **b.** To divert (the mind, etc.). **c.** *trans.* To convey away (liquid) by a tap, a channel, or the like. Also *intr.* (for *refl.*). **D. on: a.** To bring on. **b.** To lead on. **c.** *intr.* To advance, approach. **d.** *Hunting.* = sense VI. 4. **D. out: a.** *trans.* To extract. **b.** *Mil.* To lead out of camp or quarters; also *intr.* for *refl.*; to extend in line; to detach from the main body. **c.** To stretch; to flatten out (metal). **d.** *fig.* To protract. **e.** To elicit. **f.** To induce to talk (*colloq.*). **g.** To draw up; to make out; to delineate. **h.** *intr.* To become longer. **i.** *Racing.* To get gradually further ahead. **D. over:** To convert to one's party or interest. **D. up: a.** *refl.* To assume an erect attitude. **b.** To bring or come to a stand. **c.** To set in array, as troops. Also *intr.* for *refl.* **d.** To frame, write out in proper form. **e.** To come up *with*, come close *to*. **f.** To take up *with*.

Draw (drǭ), *sb.* 1663. [f. DRAW *v.*] **1.** An act of drawing; see DRAW *v.* **2.** Anything having power to draw a crowd (*colloq.*) 1881. **3.** Drawing of lots; a raffle 1755. **4.** A drawn game or match 1871. **5.** 'That part of a bridge which is raised up, swung round, or drawn aside (*U.S.*)' (Webster). **6.** A thing or person employed to draw a person out. Also, one who is easily drawn out (*slang*). 1811.

Draw-, the verb-stem in comb.:

a. used attrib. = drawing-, used for, in, or by drawing: as

d.-arch, a movable arch in a bridge; a draw-bridge arch; **-bench,** a machine in which wire or strips of metal are reduced in thickness by drawing through gauged apertures, also called *drawing-bench*; **-bolt,** a coupling-pin of a railway wagon; **-bore,** a pin-hole through a tenon, so bored that the pin shall draw the parts together; hence **d.-bore** *v.*; **-dock,** a creek or inlet in the bank of a navigable river into which boats or barges can be run; **-gear,** (*a*) harness for draught animals; (*b*) the apparatus by which railway carriages and trucks are connected together in a train; **-head,** the head of a draw-bar in a railway-carriage; **-kiln,** a lime-kiln so constructed that the burned lime is drawn at the bottom; **-link,** a link connecting railway carriages or trucks; **-loom,** the loom used in figure-weaving, in which the strings through which the warps are passed were pulled by a d.-boy; **-rod,** a rod connecting the d.-bars of railway carriages; **-shave,** a drawing-knife for shaving spokes, etc.; **-spring,** the spring between a d.-bar and the truck or carriage; **-tap,** a tap for emptying a pipe, cistern, etc.; **-tube,** the compound tube, one part sliding within the other, which carries the object-glass and eye-piece of a microscope.

b. governing an object: as

d.-blood, he who or that which draws blood.

Draw·able, *a.* 1647. Capable of being drawn.

Drawback (drǭ·bæk). 1618. [f. phr. *to draw back.*]

A. *sb.* †**1.** One who draws back or retires. **2.** An amount paid back from a charge previously made; *esp.* a certain amount of excise or import duty remitted when the commodities on which it has been paid are exported; orig., the action of drawing back a sum paid as duty 1697. **3.** A deduction 1753. **4.** A hindrance, disadvantage 1720.

3. A..d. from the utility of their compilations 1837. 4. Roman citizenship had its drawbacks 1865.

B. *adj.* That is, or has to be, drawn back; as *d.-lock* 1703.

Draw-bar (drǭ·bāɹ). 1839. The bar that bears the draw-links or couplings by which railway carriages and trucks are connected in a train.

Draw·-boy. 1731. The boy who pulled the cords of the harness in figure-weaving; hence, the piece of mechanism by which this is now done.

Draw·bridge. ME. [f. DRAW-; see also DRAUGHT-BRIDGE.] **1.** A bridge hinged at one end and free at the other, which may be drawn up and let down so as to prevent or permit passage over it, or allow passage through the channel which it crosses.

The original form was the *lifting d.*, used to span the foss of a castle or fortification, or the inner part of it; in more recent times a *swing-* or *swivel-bridge* which revolves horizontally is much employed; see also BASCULE. A d. to permit the passage of vessels sometimes forms a small section of a long permanent bridge.

2. A movable bridge or gangway on a ship, etc. 1856.

Drawcansir (drǭkæ·nˌsəɹ). Also **Draw·-cansir.** 1672. [Burlesque alt. of *Almanzor* of Dryden's 'Conquest of Granada' (1670–2), perh. designed to suggest *draw* and *can* (of liquor).] Name of a blustering, bragging character in Villiers's burlesque 'The Rehearsal', who in the last scene enters a battle and kills all the combatants on both sides: hence allusively, and *attrib.*

Such a D., as to cut down both friend and foe TUCKER.

Draw·-cut, *sb.* 1833. A cut made by a drawing movement.

Drawee (drǭˌī·). 1766. [See -EE[1].] The person on whom a draft or bill of exchange is drawn.

Drawer[1] (drǭ·əɹ). ME. [f. DRAW *v.* + -ER[1]]. **1.** One who, or that which, draws; see DRAW *v.* **2.** *spec.* One who draws liquor; a tapster at a tavern 1567. **3.** One who draws a draft, bill of exchange, or legal document 1682. **4.** One who makes a drawing; a draughtsman 1579.

Drawer[2] (drǭ^əɹ). 1580. [f. DRAW *v.* + -ER[1], after (O)Fr. *tiroir*, f. *tirer* draw.] A box-shaped receptacle, fitting into a space in a cabinet or table, so that it can be drawn out horizontally. **b.** *pl. Drawers* = *Chest of drawers*: a piece of furniture made to contain a number of drawers, arranged in tiers.

Drawers (drǭ^əɹz), *sb. pl.* 1567. [f. DRAW *v.* + -ER[1]; of low origin.] A garment for the lower part of the body and legs; now usually under-hose worn next the skin.

Draw-file (drǭ·fəil), *v.* 1884. [f. DRAW- used advb.] *trans.* To file longitudinally, without lateral movement.

Draw·gate. 1791. A sluice-gate.

Draw-glove. ME. †**1.** (Also *draw-gloves.*) An old parlour game, also called *drawing (of) gloves*, which consisted in a race at drawing off gloves when certain words were spoken. **2.** An archer's drawing-glove.

Drawing (drǭ·iŋ), *vbl. sb.* ME. [f. DRAW *v.* + -ING[1].] **1.** *gen.* The action of DRAW *v.* q.v. **b.** *concr.* That which is drawn, or obtained by drawing. *spec.* in *pl.*, the amount of money taken in a shop, or drawn in the course of business. 1883. **2.** The formation of a line by drawing some tracing instrument from point to point of a surface; representation by lines; delineation, as dist. from painting; the draughtsman's art 1530; *transf.* the arrangement of the lines which determine form 1753. **3.** That which is drawn; a delineation by pen, pencil, or crayon; a sketch 1668. **4.** *Textile Manuf.* A name given to a number of operations from combing to spinning, to reduce the thickness of the sliver of wool by drawing the warp through the reed 1831.

Comb.: **a.** In various senses, as **d.-awl,** an awl having an eye near the point, so as to carry a thread through the hole bored; **-bench,** a bench or table in the mint on which strips of metal are drawn to the same thickness for coining; also a bench on which a cooper works with his d.-knife; **-bridge** = DRAWBRIDGE; **-frame,** a machine in which the slivers from the carding machine are drawn out and attenuated; **-glove,** a glove worn by archers on the right hand in drawing the bow; **-machine,** a machine through which strips of metal are drawn to be made thin and even, etc.; **-press,** a machine for cutting and pressing sheet metal into a required shape, as for pans, etc.; **-table,** a table extensible by drawing out slides or leaves. **b.** Of or pertaining to delineation, as **d.-block,** a block composed of leaves of drawing-paper, adhering at the edges, so as to be removable one by one; **-board,** a board on which paper is stretched for drawing on; **-book,** a book for drawing in; **-compass, -es,** a pair of compasses having a pencil or pen in place of one of the points; **-paper,** stout paper of various kinds for drawing on; **-pen,** an instrument adjustable by a screw to draw ink lines of varying thicknesses; **-pin,** a flat-headed pin used to fasten d.-paper to a board, desk, etc.

Draw·ing, *ppl. a.* ME. [f. as prec. + -ING[2].] **1.** *gen.* That draws, in various senses 1576. **2.** *spec.* Draught- 1551. **3.** That draws out purulent or foreign matter from a wound, etc. ME. †**4.** Attractive –1669. Hence †**Draw·ingly** *adv.* in a slow manner.

Draw·ing-knife. 1737. **a.** A tool, consisting of a blade with a handle at each end, for shaving or scraping a surface. **b.** A farrier's instrument. **c.** A tool used to make an incision on the surface of wood along which the saw is to follow, to prevent the teeth of the saw from tearing the wood.

Draw·ing-master. 1779. A teacher of drawing.

Drawing-room (drǭ·iŋˌrūm). 1642. [Shortening of *withdrawing-room* (XVI; very common in XVII); †*drawing-chamber* is earlier (XVI).] **1.** *orig.* A room to withdraw to; *spec.* a room reserved for the reception of company, and to which the ladies withdraw after dinner; now sometimes used for an important reception room. **b.** The company assembled in a drawing-room 1841. **2.** A levee held in a drawing-room; the reception at which ladies are presented at court 1711.

1. The gentlemen..rejoin the ladies in the drawing-room, and take coffee EMERSON. 2. There was a drawing-room to-day at court SWIFT.

Drawk, drauk (drǭk). ME. [– med.L. *drauca*, whence OFr. (mod. dial.) *droue.*] A kind of grass growing as a weed among corn; app. orig. brome-grass (*Bromus secalinus*); but also confounded with cockle, darnel, and wild oats.

Draw-knife. 1703. = DRAWING-KNIFE.

Drawl (drǭl), *v.* 1597. [prob. orig. vagrants' cant – E.Fris., LG., Du. *dralen* delay, linger. DRAIL, of similar date, was used in the same senses.] **1.** *intr.* To crawl or drag *along*. Now *rare*. **2.** *intr.* To speak slowly, as from indolence or affectation 1598. **3.** *trans.* To utter with lazy slowness: chiefly with *out* 1663. **4.** To cause to pass *on* or *away*, or move along slowly or laggingly; to drag *out*, *on*, etc. 1758.

2. Such a drawling-affecting rogue *Merry W.* II. i. 145. 4. The Chancery would d. it out till [etc.] COBBETT. Hence **Draw·ler. Draw·lingly** *adv.*

Drawl, *sb.* 1760. [f. prec. vb.] The action of drawling; a slow indolent utterance.

†**Draw·-latch,** *sb.* ME. [f. DRAW *v.* + LATCH *sb.*] **1.** A string by which a latch is drawn or raised 1614. **2.** A thief who enters by drawing up the latch; a sneaking thief –1607. **3.** A lazy laggard –1610.

Drawn (drǭn), *ppl. a.* ME. [f. DRAW *v.*] **1.** In the senses of the vb. **2.** Of a sword: Pulled out of the sheath, naked ME. **3.** Of a battle or match: Undecided 1610. **4.** Traced, as a line. Chiefly in *comb.* 1571. **5.** Disembowelled 1789. **6.** Subjected to tension 1879. **7.** Gathered, in needle-work 1852.

Draw·-net. 1624. = DRAG-NET; also 'a net with large meshes for catching the larger varieties of fowls'.

Draw·n-work. Also **drawn-thread work.** 1595. Ornamental work done in textile fabrics by drawing out some of the threads of warp and woof, so as to form patterns.

Draw·-plate. 1832. A steel plate pierced with graduated apertures through which wire or metal is drawn to be reduced in thickness.

Draw·-well. ME. **1.** A deep well from which water is drawn by a bucket suspended to a rope. †**2.** A deep drawer. STERNE.

Dray (drēⁱ), *sb.*[1] [Late ME. *dreye, draye* (AL. *dreia*), corresp. formally to OE. *dræġe* (also *dræġnet*) drag-net, f. base of *dragan* DRAW *v.* Cf. MLG. *drage* bier, litter (G. *trage* hand-barrow, litter).] †**1.** A sled or cart without wheels –1552. **2.** A low cart without sides for carrying heavy loads: *esp.* that used by brewers 1581. **3.** *attrib.* and *Comb.*, as **d.-cart** = sense 2; **d.-horse,** a large and powerful horse used for drawing a d.

Dray, drey (drēⁱ), *sb.*[2] *local.* 1607. [Of unkn. origin.] A squirrel's nest.

Drayage (drēⁱ·ėdʒ). 1791. [f. DRAY *sb.*[1] +

-AGE.] **a.** Conveyance by dray. **b.** The charge for this.

Dray·man. 1581. A man who drives a (brewer's) dray.

Drazel (dræ·z'l). Now *dial.* 1674. [Of unkn. origin; cf. DROSSEL.] A slut.

Dread (dred), *v.* [Early ME. *drēden*, aphetic f. OE. *adrǣdan* (cf. ADREAD), late form of *ondrǣdan* = OS. *antdrādan*, OHG. *intrātan*, f. *ond-*, *and-* (as in ANSWER) + a WGmc. base of obscure origin.] **1.** *trans.* To fear greatly; to regard with awe or reverence. **2.** To look forward to with terror ME. †**3.** *intr.* (or *absol.*) To be greatly afraid or apprehensive –1840; also *refl.* †**4.** *trans.* To cause to fear; to affright –1681.

1. MILT. *P. L.* I. 464. **2.** Leaves look pale, dreading the winter's near SHAKS. **3.** D. not, nor be dismayed 1 *Chr.* 22:13. Hence †**Drea·dable** *a.* to be dreaded. **Drea·der**, one who dreads.

Dread (dred), *sb.* ME. [f. prec. vb.] **1.** Extreme fear; deep awe or reverence; apprehension as to future events. Rarely in *pl.* **2.** An object of fear, reverence, or awe ME. †**3.** Doubt, risk of the thing proving otherwise –1556.

1. The drede of god FISHER. Suspicion ripened into d. WORDSW. **2.** Vna his dear dreed SPENSER *F. Q.* I. vi. 2. Their once great d., captive and blind before them MILT. *Sams.* 1473.

†**Dread** (dred), *a.* ME. [Aphetic f. ADRAD, assim. to prec.] Afraid, frightened –1450.

Dread (dred), *ppl. a.* [ME. pa. pple. of DREAD *v.*] **1.** Feared greatly; hence, to be feared; dreadful. **2.** Held in awe; awful, revered ME.

1. Death or aught then Death more d. MILT. *P. L.* IX. 969. **2.** Most Dredde Soverayne Lord ME. Your d. command *Haml.* III. iv. 109.

Dreadful (dre·dfŭl). ME. [f. DREAD *sb.* + -FUL.]

A. *adj.* †**1.** Full of dread, fear, or awe; fearful; reverential –1659. **2.** Inspiring dread or reverence; terrible; awful ME. **3.** In mod. colloq. use often a strong intensive = Exceedingly bad, great, long, etc.

2. Harsh resounding Trumpets dreadfull bray *Rich. II*, I. iii. 135. **3.** The parting was d. 1864.

B. *adv.* = Dreadfully. (Now *vulgar.*) 1682.

C. *sb.* A story of crime written in a morbidly exciting style; a journal or print of such a character (*colloq.*) 1884.

Hence **Drea·dfully** *adv.* in a d. manner; *colloq.* = EXCEEDINGLY.

Drea·dingly, *adv.* 1589. [f. *dreading* + -LY².] With dread.

Drea·dless. ME. [See -LESS.]

A. *adj.* Void of dread or fear; fearless. Const. *of.* †**b.** Exempt from apprehension of danger; secure (*rare*) –1622.

With d. confidence 1854. **b.** That which makes death so..dreadlesse to a beleeuer S. WARD.

†**B.** *adv.* Without doubt of mistake; doubtless –1535.

Hence **Drea·dless-ly** *adv.*, **-ness.**

†**Drea·dly**, *a.* ME. only. [f. DREAD *sb.* + -LY¹.] = DREADFUL 1, 2.

Dreadly (dre·dli), *adv.* ME. [f. DREAD *a.* + -LY².] **1.** Dreadfully. **2.** With dread or awe (*rare*) 1674.

1. D. sweeping thro' the vaulted sky 1751. So **Drea·dness** (now *rare*).

Dreadnought (dre·dnǫt). 1806.

A. *adj.* Dreading nothing, fearless 1836.

B. *sb.* **1.** A thick coat worn in very inclement weather; also, the cloth of which such garments are made. **2.** Name of a recent type of battleship 1908.

†**Dream**, *sb.*¹ [OE. *drēam* = OS. *drōm* mirth, noise :- WGmc. *draum-; see next.] **1.** Joy, gladness, mirth –ME. **2.** Music; noise –ME.

Dream (drīm), *sb.*² [ME. *drēm*, identical in form with prec., but corresp. in sense to OFris. *drām*, OS. *drōm* (Du. *droom*), OHG. *troum* (G. *traum*), ON. *draumr.* The relation between this and the prec. word is undetermined.] **1.** A train of thoughts, images, or fancies passing through the mind during sleep; a vision during sleep; the state in which this occurs. **2.** *fig.* A vision of the fancy indulged in when awake (*esp.* as being unreal or idle); a reverie, castle-in-the-air; cf. DAY-DREAM 1581. Also *transf.*

1. He intepretid þe kynges dremes ME. Striving, as is usual in dreams, without ability to move JOHNSON. **2.** These may seem..but Golden Dreams 1697.

†**Dream**, *v.*¹ [OE. *drēman*, *dryman* = OS. *drōmian*, f. WGmc. *draum-, OE. *drēam* DREAM *sb.*¹] *intr.* To make a musical or joyful noise –ME.

Dream (drīm), *v.*² Pa. t. **dreamed** (drīmd), **dreamt** (dremt). [Appears XIII with DREAM *sb.*², q.v.] **1.** *intr.* To have visions and imaginary sense-impressions in sleep ME. **2.** *trans.* To behold, imagine, or fancy, in, or as in, a dream ME. **3.** *intr.* with *of*, †*on*: To think *of* even in a dream; to have any conception *of*; to conceive, imagine. Chiefly in neg. sentences. 1538. **4.** *intr.* To fall into reverie; to form imaginary visions *of* (unrealities) 1533. **5.** *intr. fig.* To hover or hang dreamily or drowsily 1842. **6.** *To d. away* or *out*: to pass or spend in dreaming 1590.

1. Jacob..Dreaming by night under the open Skie MILT. *P. L.* III. 514. **2.** Said he not so? Or did I dreame it so *Rom. & Jul.* V. iii. 79. He dreamed that God spake to him HOBBES. Come now, and let me d. it truth M. ARNOLD. **3.** *Haml.* I. v. 168. **4.** He also dreaming after the empire KNOLLES. **5.** Mist..dreamed along the hills HAWTHORNE. **6.** Foure nights wil quickly dreame away the time *Mids. N.* I. i. 8. Hence **Drea·mingly** *adv.*

Dreamer (drī·məɹ). ME. [f. DREAM *v.*² + -ER¹.] **1.** One who dreams; a visionary; an idle speculator. **2.** A puff-bird.

1. He is a D., let vs leaue him *Jul. C.* I. ii. 24.

Dreamery (drī·məri). 1838. [f. DREAM *sb.*² + -ERY.] Dreaming, dreaminess.

Drea·mful, *a.* 1552. [f. DREAM *sb.*² + -FUL.] Full of dreams; dreamy, as *d. slumber.* Hence **Drea·mfully** *adv.*

Dream-hole. 1559. [app. f. DREAM *sb.*¹ 2.] One of the holes or slits left in the walls of steeples, towers, barns, etc.

Dreamland. 1834. [f. DREAM *sb.*² + LAND *sb.*] The land which one sees in dreams; an ideal or imaginary land.

They are real, and have a venue in their respective districts in d. LAMB.

Drea·mless, *a.* 1605. [See -LESS.] Without or free from dreams. Hence **Drea·mlessly** *adv.*

Dreamy (drī·mi), *a.* 1567. [f. DREAM *sb.*² + -Y¹.] **1.** Abounding in dreams. **2.** Given or pertaining to reverie 1809. **3.** Dream-like; vague, indistinct; misty, dim, cloudy 1848.

1. A d. slumber KANE. **2.** D. moods 1845. **3.** A d. recollection JOWETT. Hence **Drea·mily** *adv.* **Drea·miness.**

†**Drear**, *sb.* 1563. [Back-formation from DREARY *a.*] Dreariness, sadness, gloom –1775.

Drear (drīᵊɹ), *a.* Chiefly *poet.* 1629. [Short for DREARY *a.*] = DREARY 3, 4.

A d. and dying sound MILT. *Nativity* 193.

Drearihead (drīᵊ·rihed). *arch.* ME. [See -HEAD.] Dreariness. So **Drea·rihood.**

†**Drea·ring.** [irreg. f. *drear*, *dreary.*] Sorrowing, grief. SPENSER.

Dreary (drīᵊ·ri), *a.* [OE. *drēoriġ*, f. *drēor* gore :- Gmc. *dreuzaz, f. *dreuz- *drauz-, whence also OE. *drēosan* drop, fall, OS. *driosan*, Goth. *driusan*, and OS. *drōr*, OHG. *trōr*, ON. *dreyri* gore, blood, MHG. *trūrec* (G. *traurig* sorrowful).] †**1.** Gory –1590. †**2.** Cruel, dire, horrid, grievous –1600. **3.** Of persons, etc.: Sad, doleful, melancholy. *Obs.* or *arch.* OE. **4.** Dismal, gloomy; repulsively dull. (The ordinary current sense.) 1667.

3. Al drery was his cheere and his lookyng CHAUCER. **4.** Seest thou yon d. Plain..The seat of desolation MILT. *P. L.* I. 180.

Hence **Drea·rily** *adv.* **Drea·riment**, d. or dismal condition or the expression of it. **Drea·riness.** **Drea·risome** *a.* of a d. character.

Dreche; see DRETCH *v.*

Dredge (dredʒ), *sb.*¹ 1471. [Earliest as Sc. *dreg*, perh. – MDu. *dreghe* 'harpago', 'verriculum', but the final cons. of the Eng. word suggests a native origin.] An instrument for collecting and bringing up objects by dragging. **a.** *orig.* A drag-net for taking oysters, etc. **b.** An apparatus for collecting marine objects for scientific investigation. **c.** A dredging machine. Also *attrib.*

Dredge, *sb.*² [ME. *drag(g)e*, *dragie* (XIV-XV) – OFr. *dragie*, (also mod.) *dragée*, in med. L. *drageia*, *dragetum*, *-ata*; referred by some to L. *tragemata* – Gr. τραγήματα spices. Senses 2, 3 prob. a different word.] †**1.** A sweetmeat; cf. DRAGÉE –1616. **2.** A mixture of grains, *esp.* of oats and barley, sown together ME. **3.** *Mining.* Ore of a mixed quality 1875. *Comb.* **d.-malt**, malt made of oats and barley.

Dredge, *v.*¹ 1508. [Goes with DREDGE *sb.*¹] **1.** *trans.* To collect and bring up by means of a dredge. Also *fig.* **2.** *intr.* To make use of a dredge 1681. **3.** *trans.* To clean out the bed of (a river, etc.) with a dredging apparatus 1844.

Dredge, *v.*² 1596. [f. DREDGE *sb.*²] **1.** *trans.* To sprinkle with powder, *esp.* flour; *orig.* to sprinkle with a powder of mixed spices, sugar, etc. **2.** To sprinkle *over* anything 1648. Hence **Dre·dging** *vbl. sb*; *attrib.* as *dredging-box.*

Dredger¹ (dre·dʒəɹ). 1508. [f. DREDGE *v.*¹ + -ER¹.] **1.** One who uses a dredge. **2.** A boat employed in dredging for oysters 1600. **3.** A dredging machine; see quot. 1863.

3. *D.*, vessels fitted with iron buckets and machinery for deepening rivers or bars [etc.] 1892.

Dre·dger². Also **drudger.** 1666. [f. DREDGE *v.*²] A box with a perforated lid for sprinkling powder over anything, as a *flour d.*

Dree (drī), *v.* Now *Sc.* and *n. dial* or *arch.* [OE. *drēogan* perform, endure, f. Gmc. *dreuʒ- *drauʒ- *druʒ-, repr. by Goth. *driugan* do military service and ON. *drýgja* perpetrate, practise. Revived as a literary archaism by Sir Walter Scott.] **1.** To do, endure, suffer. **2.** *intr.* To endure, last, hold out ME.

1. *To d. one's weird*: to suffer one's destiny. Hence **Dree** *sb.* suffering. Mostly a mod. archaism.

Dree, dreigh (drī, drīχ), *a.* Now *Sc.* and *n. dial* or *arch.* [ME. *dreȝ*, *dregh*, corresp. to ON. *drjúgr* enduring, lasting; f. stem of DREE *v.*] Long; tedious; persistent; difficult to surmount; dreary, doleful.

Dreg, *sb.* Chiefly in pl. **dregs** (dregz). ME. [prob. of Scand. origin; cf. ON. pl. *dreggjar*, MSw. *dräg* 'fæx', Sw. pl. *drägg.*] **1.** (Usu. pl.) The sediment of liquors; grounds, lees, feculent matters. Also *fig.* †**2.** *transf.* Fæces, refuse; corrupt or defiling matters –1668. **3.** *fig.* The refuse 1531. **4.** Small remnant, residue; hence, a small quantity or drop 1577.

1. Phr. *To drink to the dregs.* **3.** The very dregs of the population 1876. **4.** A d. of the Romish superstitution 1789. Hence **Dre·ggish, Dre·ggy** *adjs.* of the nature of dregs; feculent; foul; polluted. Also *transf.* and *fig.*

Dreint, obs. pa. t. and pple. of DRENCH *v.*

Drench (drenʃ), *sb.* [OE. *drenć* :- Gmc. *draŋkiz, f. *draŋk-, ablaut var. of *driŋk- DRINK *v.*; corresp. to OS. *dranc*, OHG. *tranc(h)* (G. *trank*), ON. *drekka*, Goth. *dragk.*] †**1.** Drink; a draught –ME. **2.** *spec.* A potion. From 1600 often (after 3): A large draught, or one forcibly given. OE. **3.** A draught of medicine administered to an animal 1552. **4.** The act of drenching; such a quantity as drenches 1808.

2. A d. of sack B. JONS. **4.** A d. of rain 1893.

Drench (drenʃ), *v.* [OE. *drenćan* = OFris. *drenza*, OS. *drenkian* (Du. *drenken*), OHG. *trenchen* (G. *tränken*), ON. *drekkja*, Goth. *dragkjan* :- Gmc. *draŋkjan.] **1.** *trans.* To make to drink; now *spec.* to administer a draught of medicine forcibly to. †**2.** To submerge, drown –1621. †**3.** *intr.* To sink, to be drowned –1570. **4.** *trans.* To steep, soak, saturate ME. **5.** To wet through and through 1549. †**6.** *fig.* To drown, immerse, plunge, overwhelm –1818.

4. Good Shepherds after Sheering d. their Sheep DRYDEN. **5.** Dark wood-walks drench'd in dew TENNYSON.

Drench; see DRENG.

Dre·ncher. 1755. [f. DRENCH *v.* + -ER¹.] One who or that which drenches; a drenching shower; an apparatus for administering a drench.

Dreng (dreŋ). Also **drench.** [Late OE. *dreng* – ON. *drengr* young man, lad, fellow (Sw. *dräng* man, servant, Da. *dreng* boy, apprentice).] *Eng. Hist.* A free tenant (specially) in ancient Northumbria, holding by a tenure partly military, partly servile. So **Dre·ngage**, the tenure or service of a d.

†**Drent.** ME. Pa. pple. of DRENCH *v.* –1579.

Dresden (dre·zdən). 1752. Name of a town in Saxony designating a white porcelain of elaborate and delicate kind. Also allusively.

Dress (dres), *v.* Pa. t. and pple. **dressed, drest.** ME. [– (O)Fr. *dresser* :– Rom. **directiare*, f. L. *directus* DIRECT *a.*]

I. †**1.** *trans.* To make straight or right –1672. †**2.** To place or set in position; to put on –1530. **3.** *Mil.* **a.** *trans.* To draw up (troops) in proper alignment 1746. **b.** *intr.* To form in proper alignment 1796. **4.** *trans.* To make ready or prepare. *Obs.* exc. as transf. from 5. ME. †**b.** *refl.* and *intr.* –1596. **5.** To array, attire; to deck with apparel; in later use, to clothe ME. **b.** *refl.* (and pass.) To attire oneself with attention to effect; *spec.* to put on dress-clothes; also, simply, to put on one's clothes 1641. **c.** *intr.* in reflexive sense 1703. **6.** To array, equip; to adorn ME. **7.** To treat (a person) properly, *esp.* with deserved severity; hence, to chastise; to reprimand. (Now usually with *down.*) ME. **8.** To treat with remedies or curative appliances 1471. **9.** To treat or prepare (things) in a proper manner; to cleanse, purify, trim, smooth, etc. 1480. **10.** To remove (anything) in the process of preparing, etc. 1701. **11.** Spec. and techn. uses (see quots.) ME.

2. A coroun on hir heed thay han i-dressed CHAUCER. **3.** The battalion dressed its ranks with precision KINGLAKE. **b.** Soldiers d. by one another in ranks STOCQUELER. **5.** Some light housewife..dressed like a May-lady BURTON. I was up and dressed at seven MRS. CARLYLE. **b.** He was come back to d. himself for a ball JOHNSON. Phr. *To d. up*: to attire elaborately. *To d. out*: to deck out with dress. **6.** *To d. a ship*: to deck it out with flags, etc. **7.** He would d. my jacket, an [etc.] 1785. **8.** He had his wound dressed 1850. **10.** Kill your pig, d. off the hair MRS. RAFFALD. **11. a.** To prepare for use as food: We d. them with carp sauce T. SHERIDAN. **b.** To do up (the hair): Her hair dressed *à la negligence* PEPYS. **c.** To till, cultivate, prune, tend: In planting and dressing the vines DE FOE. †**d.** To train or break in: That horse, that I so carefully haue drest *Rich. II*, v. v. 80. **e.** To groom or curry: D. your horse twice a day, when hee rests MARKHAM. **f.** To curry, as leather. **g.** To finish, as cloth. **h.** To cleanse from chaff: Corn Threshed, Winnowed, and Dressed PRIDEAUX. **i.** To prepare (ore) for smelting by removing the non-metallic portion: Apparatus used for dressing the inferior copper ores 1851.

II. To direct. †**1.** *trans.* To make straight the course of; to direct, guide –1591. †**2.** *refl.* and *intr.* To direct one's course; to repair; to proceed, go –1572. †**3.** To ADDRESS (speech or a writing) *to* any one –1664.

Dress (dres), *sb.* 1565. [f. prec. vb.] †**1.** The act of dressing –1778. **2.** Personal attire: orig. that proper to some special order of person or to some ceremony or function; later, merely: Clothing, costume 1606. **b.** With *a* and *pl.*: A lady's robe or gown made not merely to clothe but also to adorn 1638. Also *transf.* and *fig.* **3.** *techn.* The arrangement of the furrows on the face of a millstone 1870.

2. Phr. *Full d.* (or, simply, *d.*): the elaborate apparel proper to a public ceremony, a dinner, etc. *fig.* Eloquence, the d. of our thoughts BOYLE.

attrib. and *Comb.* **a.** Of, for, or pertaining to apparel, or to a woman's d., as *d.-goods, -gown, -skirt*, etc.; **d.-guard**, an appliance fixed to a cycle, etc., to prevent injury to d. from the wheels; **-improver** = BUSTLE *sb.*[2] **b.** Characterized by, or pertaining to, 'full dress', as *d.-ball, -coat, -shoes, -suit, -sword, -uniform*, etc.; **d.-circle**, a circular row of seats in a theatre, etc., the spectators in which were originally expected to be in dress-clothes.

Dresser[1] (dre·səɹ). ME. [– OFr. *dresseur, dreçor* (mod. *dressoir*; cf. med.L. *directorium*), f. *dresser* prepare; see -ER[2].] **1.** A sideboard or table in a kitchen on which food is or was dressed. **2.** A kind of kitchen sideboard surmounted by rows of shelves on which plates, dishes, etc., are ranged 1552. **3.** *U.S.* A dressing- or toilet-table 1906.

2. Dressers..with brilliant copper..vessels 1859.

Dre·sser[2]. 1520. [f. DRESS *v.* + -ER[1].] **1.** One who dresses (see the vb.). **2.** One who attires another 1625. **3.** One who attires himself (or herself) elegantly, or in a specified way 1679. **4.** A surgeon's assistant in a hospital, whose duty it is to dress wounds, etc. 1747. **5.** Any appliance used in dressing things; *e.g.* a shoemaker's tool, a plumber's mallet, a tool for dressing the furrows on a millstone, etc. 1600.

2. A former d. of the Queen's 1884.

Dre·ssing, *vbl. sb.* ME. [f. as prec. + -ING[1].] **1.** The action of the vb. **2.** Applied to various techn. processes. See the vb. 1540. **3.** *ironically.* A beating; chastisement, castigation 1769. **4.** *concr.* That which is used in the preceding actions and processes; that with which any thing or person is dressed: *e.g.*

a. *Cookery.* The seasoning substance used in cooking; stuffing; the sauce, etc., used in preparing a dish, a salad. **b.** Personal decorations; vestments, dress; trimmings. **c.** *Agric.* Manure or compost spread over or ploughed into land. **d.** *Surg.* The remedies, bandages, etc., with which a wound or sore is dressed. **e.** *Arch.* Projecting mouldings on a surface. **f.** Glaze, size, or stiffening used in the finishing of textile fabrics; etc.

1. There is no elaborate d. for dinner here MRS. CARLYLE. **3.** For this he got a very severe d. from Ld. North 1769. Blucher..got a genuine d. down 1876.

attrib. and *Comb.* **a.** Employed in or connected with attiring the person, as *d.-bag, -block, -gown, -jacket, -maid, -robe, -room, -table*, etc.; **d.-bell, -gong**, one rung as the signal for dressing for dinner. **b.** Pertaining or appropriated to the treatment of various articles, as *d.-machine, -shed*, etc.; **d.-floors**, a surface works where the tin stuff as it comes from the shaft of the mine is first crushed, and then washed, in order to separate the tin from alien matter.

†**Dre·ssing-board.** ME. A board on which anything (*esp.* food) was dressed; a dresser –1700.

Dre·ssing-case. 1819. A case of toilet utensils; also formerly called a *dressing-box*.

Dress-maker (dre·s,mē¹kəɹ). 1828. A (female) maker of dresses.

Dre·ss-making, *vbl. sb.* 1837. The action or occupation of making (women's) dresses.

Dressy (dre·si), *a.* 1768. [f. DRESS *sb.* + -Y[1].] **1.** Attentive to dress; given to showy dressing. **2.** Of garments: Stylish 1818.

1. I am a d. man THACKERAY. **2.** A d. boot 1845. Hence **Dre·ssiness.**

Drest, var. pa. t. and pple. of DRESS.

†**Dretch,** *v.* [OE. *dreċċ(e)an*; not in other Gmc. langs.] *trans.* To afflict, torment, vex; in ME. *esp.* to trouble in sleep –1485.

Drevel(l, -ill, -yll, var. of DRIVEL *sb.*[1]

Drew (drū), pa. t. of DRAW *v.*

Drey, obs. f. DRY, DRAY[1]; var. of DRAY[2].

Dreynt, obs. pa. t. and pple. of DRENCH *v.*

†**Drib,** *v.* 1523. [Modification of DRIP *v.*] **1.** To fall in drops; also *fig.* **2.** *trans.* To let fall in or as in drops or driblets –1599; to defalcate 1693; to lead one by little and little *into* 1700. **3.** To shoot (an arrow) so that it falls short or wide –1592. Hence **Drib** *sb.* a DRIBLET.

Dribble (dri·b'l), *v.* 1565. [frequent. of DRIB *v.*; see -LE. With sense 4 (perh. a different word) cf. Du. *dribbelen* toddle, trip.] **1.** *trans.* To let flow or fall in driblets (*lit.* and *fig.*) 1589. **2.** *absol.* or *intr.* To slaver, as a child or an imbecile; to DRIVEL 1673. **3.** *intr.* To flow down in small quantities; to trickle 1599. Also *transf.* and *fig.* **4.** *trans.* In *Football*, etc.: To keep (the ball) moving along the ground in front of and close to one by successive short pushes. Also *absol.* 1863. †**5.** *Archery.* = DRIB *v.* 3. –1615.

1. Dribling Almes by Art WARNER. **3.** *transf.* The Reichs Army kept dribbling in CARLYLE.

Dribble, *sb.* 1680. [f. prec. vb.] **1.** A small trickling stream; a small drop of liquid. Also *transf.* and *fig.* **2.** *Football.* An act of dribbling (sense 4) 1889.

1. *transf.* The little d. of Commerce STEPHEN.

Dribbler (dri·bləɹ). 1835. [f. as prec. + -ER[1].] One who dribbles; *e.g.* at football.

Driblet, dribblet (dri·blėt), *sb.* 1591. [f. DRIB *v.* + -LET.] **1.** 'A small sum, odd money in a sum' (J.) 1632. **2.** A petty quantity or part 1678. **3.** A DRIBBLE (of liquid) 1860.

1. We..pay in Driblets, or else never pay QUARLES. **3.** A d. of sour milk 1860.

Drie, obs. f. DREE *v.*, DRY.

Dried (drəid), *ppl. a.* ME. [f. DRY *v.* + -ED[1].] Deprived of moisture, desiccated. Often with *up.* Also *fig.*

Drier, dryer (drəi·əɹ). 1528. [f. as prec. + -ER[1].] **1.** One who or that which dries. **2.** (*dryer*) A desiccating substance or apparatus 1840.

Drier, driest, [see -ER[3], -EST] comp. and superl. of DRY *a.*

Drift (drift), *sb.* ME. [orig. – ON. *drift* snow-drift (= sense II. 2); later – MDu. *drift* drove, course, current = OFris. *drift* in *urdrift* expulsion, MHG., G. *trift* passage for or of cattle, pasturage, drove; f. base of DRIVE.]

I. 1. The act of driving; propulsion, impulse, impetus. (Now *rare.*). **b.** *Forest Law.* The driving of the cattle within a forest to one place on a particular day, for the determination of ownership, levying of fines, etc. 1540. †**c.** *Arch.* The horizontal thrust of an arch –1823. **2.** The condition of being driven, as by a current; the action of drifting; a slow course or current. Also *fig.* 1562. **b.** *Naut.* The deviation of a ship from its course in consequence of currents 1671. **c.** *Aeronautics.* The horizontal component of the aerodynamic pressure on all exposed surfaces of an aeroplane in flight 1896. **3.** *fig.* Natural or unconscious course; tendency 1549. **4.** The conscious direction of action or speech to some end; the end itself; purpose, object, aim. (Now *rare.*) 1526. **b.** Meaning, tenor, scope. Now the usual sense. 1526. †**5.** A scheme, plot, device –1674.

1. As the whele gothe by drifte of water 1523. **2.** A considerable Frost and d. of Ice..that Winter 1721. **3.** The general d. of affairs on the Continent 1891. **4.** My sole d. is to be useful COWPER. **b.** The main d. and scope of these pamphlets FULLER.

II. That which is driven. **1.** A drove, herd, flock, †flight of birds. *Obs.* or *dial.* 1450. **2.** A shower (of rain, dust, snow, etc.) driven by the wind ME. **b.** An accumulation of snow, sand, etc., driven together by the wind. Also *transf.* ME. **3.** Floating matter, a log, a mass of wood, etc., driven by currents of water 1600. **4.** *Geol.* (*a*) Any superficial deposit caused by a current of water or air; (*b*) *spec.* (*the D.*) Pleistocene deposits of glacial and fluvio-glacial detritus; diluvium 1839. **5.** A set of fishing-nets. **b.** A large kind of net, extended by weights at the bottom and floats at the top, and allowed to float with the tide; a *d.-net.* 1834. **6.** *techn.* **a.** A tool used for driving or ramming something (*e.g.* for driving piles) 1552. **b.** A steel tool for enlarging or shaping a hole in a piece of metal; a *drift-pin* 1874. **c.** *pl. Ship-building.* Those parts where the sheer is raised, and where the rails are cut off and ended by scrolls 1711. **d.** *Ship-building.* The difference between the size of a bolt and the hole into which it is driven, or between the circumference of a hoop and that of the mast on which it is to be driven 1792.

1. Whole driftes of quailes BP. HALL. **2.** The city lies Beneath its d. of smoke TENNYSON. **3.** Some log perhaps upon the waters swam, An useless d. DRYDEN.

III. 1. *gen.* A track (*poet.* and *rare*) 1711. **2.** *Mining.* A passage driven or excavated horizontally; *esp.* one driven in the direction of a mineral vein 1653. **3.** = DRIFTWAY 1 (*local*) 1686. **4.** *S. Afr.* A ford 1849.

IV. *Naut.* Length of rope paid out before a fastening is made; length that a tackle will reach from its fixed point; distances so estimated 1860.

Comb.: **d.-anchor**, a floating wooden frame or the like, used to keep the ship's head to the wind in a gale or when dismasted; **-bolt**, a long punch used for driving out other bolts; **-keel** = BILGE-KEEL; **-net** = sense II. 5 (also *attrib.*); **-pieces**, solid pieces, fitted at the drifts, to form scrolls (see II. 6c); **-pin, -punch** = sense II. 6b; **-weed**, (*a*) sea-weed drifted on shore by the waves; (*b*) the gulf-weed (*Sargassa baccifera*) and tangle (*Laminaria digitata*).

Drift, *v.* 1600. [f. prec. sb.] **1.** *intr.* To move as driven or borne along by a current; to be driven into heaps by the wind. Also *transf.* and *fig.* **2.** *trans.* To drive or carry along, as by a current of water or air; to blow into heaps 1618. **3.** *trans.* To cover with drifts; also *intr.* for *refl.* 1851. †**4.** To drive at, aim at –1618. **5.** *Mech.* To form or enlarge a hole with a DRIFT (II. 6b) 1869. **6.** *Mining.*

intr. To excavate a DRIFT (III. 2); *trans.* to excavate a drift in 1864.

1. To d. with the current SCOTT. *fig.* Content to let things d. 1885. 2. To be drifted into civil war FROUDE. 3. When Winter drifts the fields With snow MOIR. Hence **Dri·fting** *vbl. sb.* the action of the vb.; also *concr.* that which is drifted.

Driftage (dri·ftėdʒ). 1768. [f. DRIFT *v.* + -AGE.] 1. The process or operation of drifting 1862. 2. *concr.* Drifted material 1768.

Drift-ice, 1600. [f. DRIFT *sb.*] Detached pieces of ice drifting with the ocean currents, etc.

Driftland; see DROF-LAND.

Driftless (dri·ftlės), *a.* 1806. [f. DRIFT *sb.* + -LESS.] 1. Having no drift or purpose; aimless. 2. *Geol.* Free from drift 1873.

Driftway, drift-way (dri·ft,wēⁱ). 1611. [f. DRIFT *sb.* + WAY *sb.*] 1. A lane or road along which cattle are driven; a drove-way. 2. *Naut.* Lee-way 1721. 3. *Mining,* etc. = DRIFT *sb.* III. 2. 1843.

Drift-wood, dri·ftwood. 1633. Wood floating on, or cast ashore by, the water.

[We] made a fire..with the drift-wood R. H. DANA.

Drifty (dri·fti), *a.* 1571. [f. DRIFT *sb.* + -Y¹.] †1. Wily. 2. Characterized by drifts, of the nature of a drift 1730.

Drill (dril), *sb.*¹ 1641. [Of unkn. origin; see DRILL *v.*²] A (? trickling) rivulet; a rill.

Springs..Whose Drils our plants with moisture feed 1641.

Drill (dril), *sb.*² 1611. [f. DRILL *v.*³; sense 1 prob. – Du. *dril, drille* in same sense.] 1. An instrument for drilling or boring; *e.g.* a pointed steel tool for boring holes in metal, stone, and other hard substances; a drilling machine, etc. 2. A shell-fish which bores into the shells of young oysters; a borer 1886. 3. Style in which a hole is drilled 1849. 4. *Mil.* The action or method of instructing in military evolutions; military exercise or training; with *a* and *pl.* such an exercise 1637. 5. A drill-master 1814. 6. *fig.* Rigorous discipline; exact routine 1815.

1. The ordinary miner's d. is a bar of steel, with a chisel-shaped end RAYMOND. 4. A company of soldiers..at d. 1859. 6. D. in Latin grammar, ..cricket, boating, wrestling EMERSON.

attrib. and *Comb.* a. Pertaining to a d. (sense 1), as **d.-press,** 'a machine for drilling holes in metal, the drill being pressed to the metal by the action of a screw' (Webster); **-stock,** the hold-fast for a metal d.; etc. b. Pertaining to or connected with military d.,as *d.-master*; **d.-sergeant,** a non-commissioned officer who trains soldiers in military evolutions.

Drill (dril), *sb.*³ 1644. [prob. native name; cf. MANDRILL.] A W. Afr. baboon, *Cynocephalus leucophæus.*

Drill, *sb.*⁴ 1727. [perh. a use of DRILL *sb.*¹] 1. A small furrow in which seed is sown; a ridge having such a furrow on its top; also, the row of plants thus sown. 2. A machine for sowing seed in drills, drawing furrows, and covering the seed when sown 1731.

Comb.: **d.-barrow,** a barrow-like contrivance for sowing in drills; **-harrow,** a harrow used between the drills for extirpating weeds; **-machine, -plough** = sense 2.

Drill (dril), *sb.*⁵ 1743. Shortening of DRILLING *sb.*

Drill, *v.*¹ Now *dial.* ME. [Of unkn. origin.] 1. *trans.* and *absol.* To delay, put off. Also with *away, on, out.* 2. To entice (a person) *on* from point to point; and so = to put off 1669. Also with *in, into*; *on, along, out of.* 3. To slip away, vanish by degrees (*dial.*) ME.

1. This accident hath drilled away the whole summer SWIFT. 2. She drilled him on to Five and Fifty and..she will drop him in his old Age ADDISON.

†**Drill,** *v.*² 1603. [app. var. of THRILL *v.*; related to DRILL *sb.*¹] To flow in a small stream or in drops; to trickle; to drip. Also *transf.* and *fig.* –1638.

Drill, *v.*³ 1622. [– MDu. *drillen* bore, turn in a circle, brandish = MLG. *drillen* roll, turn, whence (M)HG. *drillen* turn, round off, bore, drill soldiers.] 1. *trans.* To pierce or bore with or as with a drill; to perforate 1649. 2. To make or bore (a hole, etc.) by drilling 1669. 3. *trans.* To turn round and round. *Obs.* or *dial.* 1681. 4. *trans.* To train or exercise in military evolutions. [Prob. f. sense 3.] 1626. Also *intr.* for *refl.* and *pass.* 5. *transf.* and *fig.* To train or instruct as with military rigour and exactness 1622. 6. To regulate exactly 1877. b. To impart by strict method 1863.

4. He [Frederick the Great] drilled his people as he drilled his grenadiers MACAULAY. 5. He had drilled her in all that she should do W. BLACK.

Drill, *v.*⁴ 1740. [f. DRILL *sb.*⁴] 1. *trans.* To sow in drills; to raise (crops) in drills. 2. To plant (ground) in drills 1785.

2. He drilled two acres of land with this barley 1894.

Driller (dri·ləɹ). 1652. One who or that which drills.

Drilling (dri·liŋ), *sb.* 1640. [alt. of G. *drillich,* earlier †*drilich* – L. *trilix, trilic-* triple-twilled, f. *tri-* three + *licium* thread.] A coarse twilled linen or cotton fabric. Also *attrib.*

Drilling (dri·liŋ), *vbl. sb.* 1639. [f. DRILL *v.*³ + -ING¹.] 1. Boring; perforation 1698. 2. Training in military evolutions. Also *transf.*

Drily, *adv.*; see DRYLY.

Drink (driŋk), *v.* Pa. t. **drank** (dræŋk); pa. pple. **drunk** (drɒŋk). [OE. *drincan* = OFris. *drinka,* OS. *drinkan* (Du. *drinken*), OHG. *trinkan* (G. *trinken*), ON. *drekka,* Goth. *drigkan* :– Gmc. **dreŋkan.*]

I. Trans. senses. 1. To take (liquid) into the stomach; to swallow down, imbibe. Also with *off, out, up,* expressing exhaustion of the liquid. Also *transf.* and *fig.* 2. *transf:* To absorb (moisture); to suck. Often with *up* or *in.* 1530. 3. *fig.* esp. with *in*: To take into the mind; to listen to, or contemplate with rapture 1592. †4. To inhale (tobacco smoke, etc.) –1781. 5. To swallow down the contents of ME. 6. To spend in drinking 1492.

1. I ne're drank sacke in my life SHAKS. *fig.* Dire sorrow drinkes our blood SHAKS. 2. Let the purple Vi'lets d. the Stream DRYDEN. 3. To d. in the beauty of the scene 1859. 4. The first who smoked, or, (as they called it), drank tobacco publickly PENNANT. 5. Phr. *To d. the cup of joy, sorrow,* etc.: see CUP *sb.* (II. 2). 6. He drinks his whole earnings 1897.

II. Absol. and intr. senses. 1. *absol.* To swallow down or imbibe liquid, for nourishment or quenching of thirst OE. 2. To take intoxicating liquor, either convivially, or to gratify appetite; to indulge therein to excess; to tipple; *spec.* to be a habitual drunkard 1440. 3. *intr.* To have a specified flavour when drunk. [Fr. *se boire,* refl. for pass.] 1607. †4. *fig.* To experience, endure, pay the penalty; to taste the cup of suffering (*trans.* and *absol.*) –1677.

1. Having sufficiently eaten and drunken RUSKIN. Phr. *To d. deep*: to take a large draught, either once or habitually. 2. I have been drinking hard 1611. Poor woman! her husband drinks 1897.

Phr. *To d. to* (a person): †a. To hand beverage for his use. The cup presented was first sipped by the one who offered it, and hence b. To salute by drinking; to invite (any one) to d. by drinking first; to d. in his honour; to d. in honour of (anything desired), with good wishes for its furtherance.

Drink (driŋk), *sb.* [OE. *drinc* and *drinca,* f. *drincan* to DRINK.] 1. Liquid swallowed for assuaging thirst or taken into the system for nourishment. Also *fig.* and *transf.* 2. A beverage OE. 3. *spec.* Intoxicating alcoholic beverage OE. 4. A draught or portion of liquid OE.

1. For d. the Grape She crushes MILT. *P. L.* v. 344. 2. Hiss drinnch wass waterr ORMIN. 3. I doe not speake to thee in Drinke 1 *Hen. IV,* II. iv. 458. [He] shall drink neither wine nor strong d. *Luke* 1:15. 4. A d. of milk KINGSLEY.

Comb.: **d.-offering,** an offering of wine or other liquid poured out in honour of a deity; **-money, -penny,** a gratuity to be spent on d.

Drinkable (dri·ŋkăb'l). 1611. [-ABLE.] a. *adj.* That may be drunk, suitable for drinking. b. *sb.* (usu. *pl.*) That which may be drunk, liquor 1708. Hence **Dri·nkableness.**

Drinker (dri·ŋkəɹ). OE. [f. DRINK *v.* + -ER¹.] 1. One who drinks; *spec.* one who drinks to excess; a drunkard. 2. (In full **d.-moth.**) A large European moth, *Lasiocampa* (*Odonestis*) *potatoria,* so called from its long suctorial proboscis 1682.

1. His father was a hard d. 1897.

Dri·nk-hail. Now *Hist.* [Early ME. *drinc hæil, drinc hail,* f. DRINK *v.* in imper. + HAIL *a.* = ON. *heill* HAIL *a.*] The customary reply to a pledge in early English times. The cup was offered with the salutation *wæs hail* 'health or good luck to you' (see WASSAIL), to which the reply was *drinc hail* 'drink health or good luck'.

Drinking (dri·ŋkiŋ), *vbl. sb.* ME. [f. DRINK *v.* + -ING¹.] 1. The action or habit denoted by the vb. DRINK; *spec.* the use of intoxicating liquor, *esp.* to excess. 2. An occasion of drinking; a carousal 1515.

Comb. a. with sense 'used for d.'; as *d.-bowl, -cup, -horn, -water,* etc. b. used for the sale or consumption of drink; as *d.-booth, -house, -room, -saloon.*

Dri·nkless, *a.* ME. [See -LESS.] Without drink or liquor; dry.

Drip (drip), *v.* 1440. [– MDa. *drippe* (Da. *dryppe*), f. Gmc. **drupp-* (see DROP).] 1. *trans.* To let fall in drops. 2. *intr.* To have moisture or liquid falling off in drops 1508. 3. *intr.* To fall in drops 1670.

1. The lofty barn..Which from the thatch drips fast a shower of rain SWIFT. 2. Pine branches.. dripping with moisture STEPHEN. 3. The rain ..came through..and dripped from the ceiling TYNDALL.

Drip (drip), *sb.* 1440. [f. prec. vb.] †1. A falling drop –1552. 2. The act or fact of dripping 1669. 3. That which drips; *pl.* drippings 1707. 4. *Arch.* A projecting member of a cornice, etc., from which the rain-water drips and so is thrown off from the parts below; also, a *drip-joint* 1664.

2. On the ear Drops the light d. of the suspended oar BYRON. Phr. *Right of d.* (Law): an easement which entitles the owner of a house to let the water from his eaves drip on his neighbour's land.

attrib. and *Comb.*, as **d.-joint,** a mode of uniting two sheets of metal in roofing where the joint is with the current, so as to form a water conductor (Knight).

Dri·p-drop, *sb.* 1848. [redupl. of DRIP or DROP.] Continuous dripping with alternation of sound.

Dri·pping, *vbl. sb.* 1440. [f. DRIP *v.* + -ING¹.] 1. The fall of liquid in drops; the liquid so falling. 2. *spec.* The melted fat which drips from roasting meat. Formerly often in *pl.* 1463. *Comb.* **d.-pan,** a pan used to catch the d. (sense 2).

Dripple (dri·p'l), *v.* 1821. [Fusion of DRIP and DRIBBLE.] 1. *intr.* = DRIBBLE *v.* 3; but connoting a brisker motion. 2. = DRIP *v.* 3. 1822.

Dripstone (dri·pstoᵘn). 1812. 1. A moulding or cornice over a door, window, etc., to throw off the rain. Also *attrib.* 2. A filter composed of porous stone 1858.

Drive (drəiv), *v.* Pa. t. **drove** (drōᵘv); *arch.* **drave** (drēⁱv). Pa. pple. **driven** (dri·v'n). [OE. *drīfan* = OFris. *drīva,* OS. *drīban* (Du. *drijven*), OHG. *trīban* (G. *treiben*), ON. *drífa,* Goth. *dreiban* :– Gmc. **drīban.*]

I. 1. *trans.* To force to move on before one, or flee away from one; to urge on or impel with violence. *transf.* To constrain to go or flee 1510. Also *fig.* 2. To chase, pursue; also *fig. Obs.* or *arch.* ME. b. To impel game, etc., into nets, traps, or a small area where they can be killed, etc. 1753. 3. With the area as verbal object ME. 4. *spec.* To urge onward and direct the course of (a vehicle or the animal which draws it, a railway train, etc.) ME.; hence, to convey in a vehicle 1662; *absol.* to act as driver; also, to go in a carriage driven or directed by oneself. Also *intr.* for *pass.* of the vehicle. 1592.

1. We droue them to flyghte EDEN. *transf.* Hope of imployment drives him up to London 1615. 2. Grouse and partridge driving 1883. 3. To d. the forests: see DRIFT *sb.* I. 1b. To d. a rocky hill for a tiger BAKER. 4. Where Chineses d. With sails and Wind thir canie Waggons light MILT. *P. L.* III. 438. If they do not like the price, they d. off LANDOR.

II. 1. To cause to move along; to propel, carry along OE. 2. To throw, cast, send, or impel in any direction OE. 3. To force, impel, or expel, by a blow or thrust. Also *fig.* ME. Also *intr.* for *refl.* or *pass.* of a nail, ball, etc. 1703. 4. To cause to penetrate, as a tunnel, etc.; *spec.* in *Mining,* to excavate horizontally (also *absol.*): dist. from SINK *v.* (III. 3) 1485. 5. *intr.* (Also *to let d.*): To aim a blow or a missile *at*; *trans.* to aim (a blow) ME. 6. To spread or beat out thin. (Now only in *Painting.*) ME. 7. To set going, supply motive power for 1596.

1. Their ships were driuen on shore 1582. 3. [He] drove his heels into the horse's sides 1816. 5. Driving at him with her stool 1752. 6. When colour is spread thinly and rapidly, it is.. 'driven' 1859. 7. A dynamo driven by belting from the engine 1891. Phr. *To d. a quill* 1793.

III. 1. To impel forcibly; to force (*to, into, from* some action, state, etc.) ME. **2.** To urge on to action; to force to work; to overtask 1645.

1. To d. a girl to a decision W. BLACK, a man out of his senses 1879. 2. To d. a committee GRAY.

IV. *trans.* To carry on vigorously, push (a trade, etc.); to carry through or out; to conclude (a bargain) OE.

V. †**1.** *trans.* To pass (time); to cause (the time) to pass –1697. **2.** To protract (time, etc.); hence, to defer. Also *absol.* ME.

1. To d. the tedious Hours away DRYDEN. 2. To d. a thing to the last minute 1897 (*colloq.*).

†**VI.** To deduce, infer –1674.

VII. *intr.* **1.** To run or come with violence; to dash, rush, hasten OE. Also *fig.* **2.** To drift ME.; to fish with a drift-net 1677. **3.** *fig.* To tend 1460; with *at*: To aim at, mean 1579.

1. They..ran away as fast as they could d. DAMPIER. 2. The clouds that drove before the wind THOMSON. 3. What can he be driving at now FOOTE.

Drive (drəiv), *sb.* 1697. [f. prec. vb.] **1.** The action or an act of driving; see the vb. **b.** An excursion in a carriage driven or directed by oneself 1785. **c.** A forcible blow or stroke in various games; in *Cricket* one which sends the ball back nearly straight 1857. **d.** (orig. *U.S.*) An organized effort to collect money for a special purpose 1890. **2.** A carriage road; also, a course over which game is driven 1816. **3.** *Mining.* = DRIFT *sb.* III. 2. 1864. **4.** *Type-founding.* = STRIKE *sb.* 11. 1874.

1. Phr. *Full d.*: at full speed. *fig.* The constant d. of work 1854. *Whist-drive*: see WHIST *sb.*[2]

Drive-, the vb.-stem used in *Comb.*: **d.-bolt** = *drift-bolt* (see DRIFT *sb.*); **-pipe,** a pipe conveying water for driving machinery; **-screw,** a kind of screw driven by a hammer; **-shaft,** a shaft for communicating motion so as to drive machinery; **-wheel** = DRIVING-WHEEL.

†**Dri·vel**, *sb.*[1] [Early ME.: app. of LG. origin; cf. MDu. *drevel* scullion, etc.] **1.** A drudge, a menial servant –1580. **2.** Hence: **a.** An imbecile. (Cf. *driveller.*) –1597. **b.** A dirty or foul person –1596.

Drivel (dri·v'l), *sb.*[2] ME. [f. next.] = SLAVER *sb.*[1] (now rare); *fig.*, twaddle (1852).

Drivel (dri·v'l), *v.* [ME. *drevele, dryuele*, repr. OE. *dreflian*, in pr. pple. glossing med.L. *reumaticus* rheumy; a var. †*dravele* points to an OE. **dræflian*; cf. DRAFF, -LE.] **1.** *intr.* To let saliva or mucus flow from the mouth or nose, as infants and idiots do; to slaver. Also †*trans.* †**2.** *intr.* To flow as saliva from the mouth; to flow ineptly from the lips; also *transf.* of water, etc. –1784. **3.** *transf.* To talk childishly or idiotically; to rave. Also *trans.*, and with *away, on.* ME.

3. Droning and dreaming and drivelling to a Multitude SWIFT. Hence **Dri·veller, -eler,** one who drivels or slavers; a drivelling idiot. **Dri·velling, -eling** *vbl. sb.* and *ppl. a.*

Driven (dri·v'n), *ppl. a.* 1579. [pa. pple. of DRIVE *v.*] **1.** See the vb. **2.** Of snow: Drifted. Of feathers or down: Separated from the heavier by a current of air. 1579.

2. As white as the d. snow LYLY. My thrice-driven bed of Downe *Oth.* I. iii. 232.

Driver (drəi·vəɹ). ME. [f. DRIVE *v.* + -ER[1].] **1.** *gen.* One who drives (see the vb.). **2.** *spec.* **a.** One who drives cattle 1483. **b.** One who drives a vehicle or the animal that draws it; a coachman, cabman, etc.; also, one who drives a locomotive 1450. **c.** The overseer of a gang of slaves 1796. **3.** A tool or appliance for driving:

a. A tool used in driving on the hoops of casks. **b.** *Weaving.* The piece of wood which drives the shuttle through the shed of the loom. **c.** A tamping-iron. **d.** = DRIFT *sb.* II. 6b. **e.** A tool for driving out the piece of a metal plate in punching. **f.** *Golf.* The *play-club.* 1674.

4. A boat used in fishing with a drift-net 1664. **5.** *Naut.* A SPANKER, a fore-and-aft sail used at the aftermost part of a ship 1867. **6.** A part of machinery which communicates motion to other parts; the driving-wheel of a locomotive, etc. 1831.

1. Solicitors and Drivers of Bargains 1570.

Comb.: **d.-ant,** a species of ant (*Anomma arcens*) found in W. Africa, so called because they drive before them every living creature; **-boom** (*Naut.*), the boom on which the d. (sense 5) is set.

Driveway (drəi·v,wēⁱ). Chiefly *U.S.* 1875. [f. DRIVE *v.* + WAY.] A way along which something is driven; a carriage drive.

Driving (drəi·viŋ), *vbl. sb.* ME. [-ING[1].] The action of DRIVE *v.*

attrib. and *Comb.* **a.** Relating to, adapted for, or devoted to driving (in a carriage), as *d. clubs*, etc. **b.** In names of mechanical contrivances used for driving, as *d.-block, -bolt*, etc.; *esp.* of parts of machinery communicating motion to other parts, as *d.-axle, -band, -belt, -gear, -pulley, -shaft*; also **d.-iron,** an iron used in golf for playing longish approaches.

Dri·ving, *ppl. a.* ME. [-ING[2].] **1.** Impelling, actuating. **2.** Moving along rapidly, *esp.* before the wind 1601.

1. The ability of its journals is the d. force EMERSON. 2. Perpetual Sleet, and d. Snow DRYDEN.

Phr. †*D. notes* (*Mus.*): syncopated notes, so named as being driven or prolonged through the accent.

Dri·ving-box. 1794. **1.** The box on which the driver of a carriage sits. **2.** The journal-box of a driving-axle 1874.

Driving-wheel. 1838. **a.** A wheel which communicates motion. **b.** Each of the large wheels of a locomotive engine, to which the power is transmitted through the connecting-rod and crank. **c.** The wheel of a bicycle, etc. to which the force is directly applied. Also *fig.*

Drizzle (dri·z'l), *sb.* 1554. [Goes with DRIZZLE *v.*] Fine spray-like rain.

Drizzle (dri·z'l), *v.* 1543. [prob. f. ME. *drēse*, OE. *drēosan* fall = OS. *driosan*, Goth. *driusan* (cf. DREARY); see -LE.] **1.** *intr.* To rain in fine spray-like drops; *impers.* to fall, as rain, in fine drops 1566. †**2.** *trans.* To shed in fine spray-like drops –1642. **3.** To wet with minute drops (*rare*) 1810.

1. These tears, that d. from mine eyes MARLOWE. It is even drizzling a little CARLYLE. 2. *Jul. C.* II. ii. 21. 3. Drizzled by the ceaseless spray, The wizard waits SCOTT.

Drizzly (dri·zli), *a.* 1697. [f. DRIZZLE + -Y[1].] Of the nature of, or characterized by drizzling.

During Winter's drisly Reign DRYDEN.

Drof(e, droff(e, obs. ff. *drove*; see DRIVE *v.*

†**Drof-land.** 1660. [f. ME. *drōf*, OE. *drāf*, DROVE, driving + LAND.] *Old Law.* Land held by the service of driving, as of the lord's cattle from place to place, or to and from markets, fairs, and the like –1664. var. (*erron.*) **Driftland.**

Drogher (drōᵘ·gəɹ). Also **droger, drogger.** 1756. [– obs. Fr. *drogueur* ship that fished and dried herring and mackerel – Du. *drogger* drier, f. *droogen* to dry.] A W. Indian coasting vessel; hence used of other slow clumsy coasting craft. Also *attrib.*

Drogoman, droguemann, vars. of DRAGOMAN.

Drogue (drōᵘg). 1725. [Of unkn. origin.] **1.** *Whale-fishing.* A contrivance attached to the end of a harpoon line to check the progress of a whale. **2.** *Naut.* A hooped canvas bag towed at the stern of a boat to prevent it from broaching to 1875.

Droh, obs. pa. t. of DRAW *v.*

†**Droil,** *sb.* 1579. [Goes with the vb. Prob. influenced by *toil, moil.* Cf. the vb.] **1.** A drudge –1668. **2.** Drudgery –1645.

†**Droil,** *v.* 1591. [perh. rel. to Du. *druilen* loiter, slumber.] **1.** *intr.* To drudge, slave –1660. **2.** *trans.* To subject to drudgery. QUARLES.

Droit[1] (droit, or as Fr., drwa). 1480. [– (O)Fr. *droit* :– Rom. **drectum*, L. *directum*, subst. use of n. of *directus* DIRECT *a.*] **1.** A right; hence, that to which one has a legal claim; a due; a perquisite; *pl.* dues, duties 1481. †**2.** Law, right, justice; a law –1536.

1. *Droits of Admiralty*: certain rights or perquisites, as the proceeds arising from the seizure of enemies' ships, wrecks, etc., formerly belonging to the Court of Admiralty, but now paid into the Exchequer. Hence **Droitsman,** the collector of droits.

†**Droit**[2]. 1601. [Of unkn. origin.] The four hundred and eightieth part of a grain troy, one twenty-fourth of a mite –1858.

Droitural (droi·tiŭrăl), *a.* 1850. [f. Fr. *droiture* (see next) + -AL[1].] *Law.* Relating to a right to property, as dist. from possession.

†**Droi·ture.** *rare.* [– (O)Fr. *droiture* – med.L. *drectura* for L. *directura*; see DIRECT *a.*, -URE.] Uprightness. CAXTON.

Droll (drōᵘl), *sb.* 1645. [– Fr. *drôle* (see next), orig. a sb., perh. – MDu. *drolle* (mod. *drol*) little chap.] **1.** A funny or waggish fellow; a merry-andrew, buffoon, humorist. †**2.** A farce; an enacted piece of buffoonery; a puppet-show –1818. †**3.** Jesting; burlesque writing or style –1842. **4.** *attrib.*, as †*d.-house*, a place where drolls were acted 1706.

1. Very merry we were, Sir Thomas Harvy being a very drolle PEPYS.

Droll, *a.* 1623. [– Fr. *drôle*, earlier *drolle* (XVI). See prec.] **1.** Intentionally facetious, amusing, comical. **2.** Unintentionally amusing; queer, quaint, odd, funny 1753.

1. The d. inventions of Hogarth 1789. 2. A d. sort of house SCOTT. Hence **Dro·lly** *adv.*

Droll, *v.* 1654. [– Fr. †*drôler*, play the wag, f. *drôle*; see prec.] **1.** *intr.* To make sport; to jest; to play the buffoon. **2.** *trans.* To jest (a thing) *away, off,* †(a person) *out of* or *into*; to bring *forth* like a jester 1663.

1. Whitelocke drolled with them 1654. 2. Men that will not be reasoned into their senses, may yet be laughed or drolled into them L'ESTRANGE. Hence †**Dro·ller,** †**Dro·llist,** a jester; **Dro·llingly** *adv.*

Drollery (drōᵘ·ləri). 1597. [– Fr. *drôlerie*, f. *drôle*; see prec., -ERY.] **1.** The action of a droll; waggery 1653. **2.** Something humorous or funny: †**a.** A puppet-show; a puppet –1847; †**b.** a caricature –1641; **c.** a facetious story 1654. **3.** Droll quality; quaint humour 1742.

1. An affected humour of d. GLANVILL. 2. That fatal d. called a representative government DISRAELI. 3. The rich d. of 'She Stoops to Conquer' MACAULAY.

Dromæognathous (drǫmi,ǫ·gnăþəs), *a.* 1867. [f. *Dromæus*, generic name of the emu (– Gr. δρομαῖος swift-running) + γνάθος jaw; see -OUS.] *Ornith.* Having the bones of the palate arranged as in the emu and its allies. Hence **Dromæo·gnathism,** d. quality.

Dromedary (drɒ·m-, drǫ·mĕdări). ME. [– AFr. **dromedarie*, OFr. *dromedaire* (mod. *dromadaire*), or late L. *dromedarius* (Vulg.) for **dromadarius* (sc. *camelus* camel), f. *dromas, dromad-* (– Gr. δρομάς, -αδ- runner) + *-arius* -ARY[1].] **1.** A light and fleet breed of the camel, usually of the Arabian or one-humped camel, specially trained for riding. See CAMEL. †**2.** = DROMOND –1568. †**3.** A stupid, bungling fellow –1785. **4.** *attrib.*, as *d. camel*, etc. 1553.

1. The Dromidory..will ride above 80 miles in the day LITHGOW. Hence **Dromeda·rian** *a.* of the nature of a d.; *sb.* a rider of a d.; also **Dro·medarist.**

Dromic, -al (drǫ·mik, -ăl), *a.* 1850. [– Gr. δρομικός, f. δρόμος race-course; see -IC, -ICAL.] Of, pertaining to, or of the form of a race-course; applied to the basilican type of Eastern churches.

Dromioid (drǫ·mi,oid), *a.* (*sb.*) 1852. [f. mod.L. *Dromia* + -OID.] **a.** Having the form of a *Dromia*, a genus of Anomourous Crustacea, closely allied to the true crab. **b.** *sb.* A crustacean of this genus.

Dro·mograph. 1883. [f. Gr. δρόμος course + -GRAPH.] An instrument for measuring the speed of the blood current. Also *attrib.*

Dromond (drǫ·mǫnd, drɒ·mənd). Also **dromon.** *Hist.* and *arch.* ME. [– AFr. *dromond*, OFr. *dromon(t)*, late L. *dromo*, *dromōn-* – late Gr. δρόμων large many-oared vessel.] A very large mediæval ship. Used both in war and commerce.

The great d. swinging from the quay MORRIS.

‖**Dromornis** (dromǭ·ɹnis). Also **Dromæornis.** 1872. [f. Gr. δρόμος course, race, or mod.L. *Dromæus* emu + ὄρνις bird.] A genus of extinct Australian ratite birds allied to the emu.

‖**Dromos** (drǫ·mǫs). 1850. [Gr. δρόμος race-course, avenue, f. vbl. stem δρεμ- run.] *Archæol.* An avenue or entrance-passage to a building, often between rows of columns or statues.

Alleys of..sphinxes form the approach or d. 1850.

Drone (drō^{u}n), *sb.*[1] [OE. *drān, drǣn*, corresp. to OS. *drān, dreno*, MLG. *drāne, drōne* (LG. *drōne*), (with *e*-grade) OHG. *treno* (MHG. *tren(e*, G. dial. *träne*), prob. f. **dran-* **dren-* **drun-* boom. The OE. forms gave normally ME. and mod. dial. *drane*; the form *drone* (XV), common to Sc. and Eng., is – (M)LG. *drōne*.] **1.** The male of the honey-bee. It is a non-worker. **2.** *fig.* A non-worker; an idler, a sluggard 1529.

1. Some against hostile drones the hives defend GAY. **2.** A Droan of a Husband OTWAY.

Comb.: **d.-beetle** = DOR-*beetle*; **-fly**, a dipterous insect, *Eristalis tenax*, resembling the drone-bee.

Hence **Dro·nage**, the condition of a d.

Drone (drō^{u}n), *sb.*[2] 1500. [app. f. DRONE *v.*[1]] **1.** A continued monotonous humming or buzzing sound, as that of the bass of the bagpipe, etc. Also *transf.* **2.** A bagpipe 1502. **3.** The bass pipe of a bagpipe. (The modern Highland bagpipe has three drones.) 1592. **4.** The tone emitted by the drone of a bagpipe 1596.

1. Ever..thrumming the d. of one plaine song MILT. *transf.* The d. of her voice MME. D'ARBLAY. **4.** As Melancholly as..the D. of a Lincolnshire Bagpipe 1 *Hen. IV*, I. ii. 85. *attrib.* The d.-pipe of an humble-bee COWPER.

Drone (drō^{u}n), *v.*[1] 1500. [f. DRONE *sb.*[1], or *sb.*[2], sense 2.] **1.** *intr.* To give forth a continued monotonous sound; to hum or buzz; to talk in a monotonous tone. **2.** *trans.* To emit in a dull monotonous tone. Also with *out*. 1614. †**3.** [f. DRONE *sb.*[2]] To smoke (a pipe) (as if playing on a bagpipe). B. JONS.

1. Beetles d. along the hollow lane KINGSLEY. **2.** Penitents..droning their dirges THACKERAY.

Drone, *v.*[2] 1509. [f. DRONE *sb.*[1]] **1.** *intr.* To proceed sluggishly or indolently. **2.** *trans.* To pass *away*, drag *out* sluggishly 1739.

2. To d. out manhood in measuring cloth LYTTON.

Drongo (drǫ·ŋgo). 1841. [– Malagasy *drongo*.] A name orig. of a Madagascar bird, *Dicrurus* (*Edolius*) *forficatus*; subseq. extended to the numerous other species of *Dicruridæ*, also called **D.-shrikes.**

D. cuckoo, a species of the cuckoo genus *Surniculus*, a native of Nepal.

†**Dronkelew**, *a.* [ME. *drunke(n)lew, dronkelew(e)*, f. DRUNKEN + -LEWE. Cf. OSTLEW.] Drunken –1532.

Dronish (drō^{u}·niʃ), *a.* 1580. [f. DRONE *sb.*[1] + -ISH[1].] Like a drone; sluggish, inactive. Hence **Dro·nish-ly** *adv.*, **-ness.** So **Dro·ny** *a.*

† ‖**Dronte** (drǫ·nt). [Du. and Fr. *dronte*.] A name of the DODO, q.v.

Drool (drūl), *v. dial.* and *U.S.* 1847. [contr. f. DRIVEL *v.*] = DRIVEL *v.*

Droop (drūp), *v.* [ME. *drupe, droupe* – ON. *drúpa* hover, hang the head for sorrow (cf. *drúpr* drooping spirits), f. Gmc. **drūp-*; see DROP *sb.*] **1.** *intr.* To hang or sink down, as from weariness, etc.; to bend or incline downward. **2.** To sink; to decline, draw to a close. Now only *poet.* ME. **3.** To decline in vital strength; to languish, flag ME. Also *transf.* and *fig.* **4.** To become dispirited or despondent ME. **5.** *trans.* To let hang or sink down; to bend downwards; to cast down 1583.

1. Thus droupes this loftie Pyne 2 *Hen. VI*, II. iii. 45. **2.** Laborious til day d. MILT. *P. L.* XI. 178. **3.** *fig.* The rate of interest droops BON. PRICE. **4.** Why droop'st, my soul? Why faint'st thou in my breast P. FLETCHER. **5.** I cannot veil, or d. my sight TENNYSON. Hence **Droop** *sb.* the act or fact of drooping. **Droop** *a.* (*rare*) = drooping; *esp.* in combs., as *d.-headed.* **Droo·per**, one that droops. **Droo·pingly** *adv.* in a drooping manner.

Droopy (drū·pi), *a.* [Early ME. *drupi*, referred to DROOP *v.*, but perh. repr. an ON. **drúpag-*, f. *drúpr* (see prec.).] Dejected, drooping.

Drop (drǫp), *sb.* [OE. *dropa*, whence ME. *drope* = OS. *dropo*, ON. *dropi* :– Gmc. **dropon*; beside OE. **droppa*, whence ME. *droppe* (and the present form) = OHG. *tropfo* (G. *tropfen*) :– Gmc. **droppon*; f. **drup-*, weak grade of the base of DROOP; cf. DRIP.]

I. The orig. sb. **1.** The smallest quantity of liquid that falls in a spherical form; a globule. Also *fig.* **2.** *ellipt.* or *absol.*: = tear-drop; also drop of blood, sweat, etc. OE. **3.** In dispensing, etc. the smallest separable quantity of a liquid 1772. **4.** *pl.* Medicine to be taken in drops. Rarely *sing.* 1726. **5.** The smallest appreciable quantity ME. Also *transf.* and *fig.* **6.** *spec.* A small quantity of drink 1700. †**7.** A spot of colour; also *fig.* –1674. **8.** Anything resembling a drop of liquid in size, shape, or pendent character. **a.** A pendant, as an ear-drop; a glass pendant of a chandelier, etc. 1502. **b.** *Arch.* The frusta of cones used as an ornament under the triglyphs, and also in the under part of the mutuli, of the Doric Order 1696. †**c.** Small shot 1752. **d.** A sugar-plum, orig. of spherical form 1836. **e.** Applied to flowers with pendent blossoms, as the fuchsia (*dial.*), and in comb., as *snow-d.* 1664.

1. Why raine falleth in round drops W. FULKE. *fig.* To preserve thy sweets Unmix'd with drops of bitter COWPER. Phr. *D. serene*, tr. L. *gutta serena*, an old name for amaurosis. **2.** They would be faithful to him to the last d. DE FOE. **5.** Phr. *A d. in the* (*a*) *bucket* or *the ocean*: an inappreciable addition. **6.** I..had a d. too much J. PAYN. **8.** Phr. (*Prince*) *Rupert's Drops*: glass drops with long and slender tails, which burst to pieces, on the breaking off those tails in any parts (E. Chambers).

II. Secondary sb., f. DROP *v.* **1.** The action or an act of dropping; an abrupt fall or descent 1637. Also *fig.* **2.** That which drops or is used for dropping; *e.g.* in a theatre, the painted curtain let down between the acts; also called *act-d.*, and *d.-curtain* 1779. **3.** A small platform or trap-door on the gallows, which is let fall from under the feet of the condemned 1796. **4.** A contrivance for temporarily lowering a gas-jet (Webster). **b.** A movable plate covering the key-hole of a lock. **c.** The slit of a letter-box (*U.S.*) 1870. **5.** The distance through which anything drops; *e.g.* a criminal when hanged 1879. **6.** The depth to which anything sinks or is sunk below the general level 1794.

1. The d. of the woodland fruit's begun BROWNING. *fig.* A d. in exchanges 1884, in the temperature 1897. **3.** The d. fell. They were executed in their irons 1813.

attrib. and *Comb.* (See also DROP-.) **a.** Of, pertaining to, or consisting of a d. or drops, as *d.-earring, -pearl*, etc. **b.** Special comb.: **d.-black**, a superior quality of bone-black ground in water, formed into drops, and dried; **-dry**, *a.*, water-tight; **-meter**, an instrument for measuring out liquid d. by d.; **-sulphur, -tin**, *i.e.*, that granulated by being dropped in a molten state into cold water.

Drop (drǫp), *v.* Pa. t. and pple. **dropped, dropt.** [OE. *dropian, droppian*, f. prec.]

I. Intr. senses. **1.** To fall in drops. **2.** = DRIP *v.* 2. ME. **3.** To fall like a drop ME. **4.** To fall exhausted, wounded, or dead ME.; of a setter, etc.: To squat down at the sight of game 1870. **5.** To fall *into* some condition 1654; *fig.* to die (cf. *d. off*) 1654. **6.** To come to an end; to fall through 1697. **7.** To sink, become depressed 1729. **8.** To descend with the tide or a light wind 1772; to let oneself fall *behind* or *to the rear* 1823. **9.** To come or go casually; to fall upon 1633.

1. The crystal tide that from her two cheeks.. Dropt SHAKS. **3.** The shell opens, and the nut drops out 1660. *fig.* His words like Honey dropped from his tongue HOBBES. **4.** Tho' thousands of their Men dropt, they would not give ground an Inch 1700. **5.** To d. into oblivion PRIDEAUX. **6.** The matter was let d. HEARNE. **7.** Prices dropped afterwards 1866. **8.** The Resolution..dropped down the river COOK. Phr. *To d. astern*: to slacken a ship's way, so as to let another pass.

II. Trans. senses. **1.** To let fall or shed in drops; to distil. Also *fig.* ME. **2.** To sprinkle with or as with drops; to bedrop (*arch.*) ME. **3.** To let fall (like a drop or drops). Also *fig.* ME. **4.** To let fall in birth; to give birth to. Also *absol.* 1622. **5.** To let fall (words, a hint, etc.); to utter casually or by the way 1611; to let (a letter, etc.) fall into the letter-box; hence, to send (a note, etc.) in an informal way 1777. **6.** *slang.* To part with (money) 1676. **7.** To cause to fall by a blow or shot 1726. **8.** To set down; also, to leave (a packet) at a person's house 1796. **9.** To omit in pronunciation or writing 1864. **10.** To let droop 1842. **11.** To let move gently with the tide 1805. **b.** *To d. astern*: to leave in the rear 1867. **12.** *Football.* To obtain (a goal) by a drop-kick 1882. **13.** To have done with; to break off acquaintance with 1605.

1. To d. many a teare 1626. **2.** Their wav'd coats dropt with Gold MILT. *P. L.* VII. 406. **3.** Phr. *To d. anchor*: to let the anchor down, to cast anchor. **4.** At the time the ewes d. KEATINGE. **5.** D. not thy word against the house of Isaac *Amos* 7:16. **6.** We played hazard..And I dropped all the money I had THACKERAY. **8.** [He] promised to d. us at the Shetland Islands KANE. **9.** He does not d. his *h*'s O. W. HOLMES. **13.** She will d. him in his old Age ADDISON.

Phr. *To d. a curtsy*: to make a curtsy by lowering the body.

Comb. with adverbs. See also simple senses and advs. **D. away.** *intr.* To fall away drop by drop or one by one. **D. in.** *intr.* **a.** To pay a casual visit. **b.** To come in at intervals. **c.** To become vacant. **d.** To fall in *with.* **D. off.** *intr.* **a.** To withdraw one by one, or by degrees. **b.** To fall asleep. **c.** To die. **d.** To become less frequent *in.* **D. out.** *intr.*, to disappear from one's place in a series or order. **D. short.** *intr.* **a.** To fall short; usu. with *of.* **b.** *colloq.* or *slang.* To die.

Drop-, the vb.-stem used in *Comb.*

a. *attrib.* with sb., in the sense of 'dropping', 'used in dropping', 'arranged so as to drop', forming sbs. or adjs.; as **d.-arch** (*Arch.*), one having a radius shorter than the breadth of the arch; **-bar** (*Printing*), a bar or roller for running the sheet into the machine; **-curtain** = DROP *sb.* II. 2; **-fly** (*Angling*) = DROPPER 3; **-hammer** = *drop-press*; **-handle** *a.*, applied to a form of needle-telegraph instrument which is operated by a handle directed downward; **-lamp, -light** (*U.S.*), a portable gas-burner, connected with the gas-fittings by a flexible tube, usually in the form of a lamp, which can stand on a table; **-press**, a machine for embossing, punching, etc., consisting of a weight guided vertically, to be raised by a cord and pulley worked by the foot, and to drop on an anvil; called also *d.-hammer*; **-shutter**, a device consisting of a slide operated by a spring or the like; used in instantaneous photography to secure very brief exposure; **-table**, a machine for lowering weights, and *esp.* for removing the wheels of locomotives. **b.** In vbl. comb. with object, as **d.-seed**, a grass that readily drops its seed, spec. *Muhlenbergia diffusa.*

‖**Dropax** (drō^{u}·pæks). ? *Obs.* 1621. [med.L. – Gr. δρῶπαξ pitch-plaster, f. δρέπειν pluck. Also *dropace* (XVII) – Fr. †*dropace*.] A pitch-plaster, a depilatory.

Drop-kick. 1857. [See DROP-.] *Football.* A kick made by dropping the ball from the hands, and kicking it the very instant it rises.

Dro·plet. 1607. [See -LET.] A minute drop.

Drop-letter. *U.S.* 1844. A letter posted in any place merely for local delivery.

†**Dro·p-meal**, *adv.* [OE. *drop-mǣlum*; see -MEAL.] In drops, drop by drop.

As the cloud dissolves drop-meal upon the earth TRAPP.

Dropped, dropt, *ppl. a.* 1600. [f. DROP *v.* + -ED[1].] **a.** See the vb. **b.** Of eggs: Fried or poached, 'dropped into the frying pan' (Jam.) 1824.

Dropper (drǫ·pəɹ). 1700. [f. DROP *v.* + -ER[1].] **1.** One who or that drops; *spec.* one who drops seeds into the holes made by a dibbler. **2.** A dog that drops (see DROP *v.* I. 4); a setter. **3.** *Angling.* A fly adjusted to a leader above the stretcher fly. Also *drop-fly, d.-fly* 1746. **4.** A pendant 1825. **b.** A glass tube for dropping liquid 1889. **c.** A branch vein which drops off from the main lode 1864.

Dropping (drǫ·piŋ), *vbl. sb.* OE. [f. DROP *v.* + -ING[1].] **1.** The action of DROP *v.* **2.** That which drops; dripping, etc. ME. **3.** Dung of animals. (Now only *pl.*) 1596.

attrib. and *Comb.*, as **d.-bottle**, a bottle used to supply fluid in small quantities; **-tube**, the tubulated stopper of the d.-bottle; **-well**, a well formed by the dropping of water from above.

Dropping, *ppl. a.* ME. [f. as prec. + -ING[2].] **1.** That drops. **2.** Desultory, not continuous, as *a d. fire* 1708. Hence **Dro·ppingly** *adv.*

Dro·p-scene. 1815. Used loosely for *drop* or *act-drop* (DROP *sb.* II. 2); also for the final scene of a drama in real life.

Dropsical (drǫ·psikăl), *a.* 1678. [f. DROPSY + -ICAL, after *hydropical*.] **1.** Of, pertaining to, or like dropsy 1688. **2.** Affected with or subject to dropsy. Also *transf.* and *fig.*

1. D. symptoms 1846. Hence **Dro·psically** *adv.*

Dropsied (drǫ·psid), *a.* 1601. [f. DROPSY + -ED².] Having the dropsy; swollen with or as with water; as *the d. clouds* (DRAYTON).

Dropsy (drǫ·psi), *sb.* (*a.*) ME. [aphet. f. ME. *i-, ydropsy* HYDROPSY, q.v.] **1.** *Med.* A morbid accumulation of watery fluid in the serous cavities or the connective tissue of the body. Also *transf.* of young trout and of succulent plants. Also *fig.* †**2.** *attrib.* or *adj.* = DROPSICAL –1683.

†**Drop vie, drop-vie,** *vbl. phr.* or occas. *v.* 1598. [f. DROP *v.* + VIE *sb.*] To drop coins or the like in rivalry; to view –1616.

Dropwise (drǫ·pwəiz), *adv.* 1673. [See -WISE.] Drop by drop.
The spring..trickling d. from the cleft TENNYSON.

Dropwort (drǫ·pwɒɹt). 1538. [f. DROP *sb.* + WORT¹; cf. the L. name *filipendula, i.e.* pendulous threads.] A name of plants; esp. *Spiræa filipendula,* and other species of Spiræa.

‖**Droshky** (drǫ·ʃki), **drosky** (drǫ·ski). Also **droitzschka, droshka, -ke.** 1808. [– Russ. *drózhki*, pl., dim. of *drógi* wagon, hearse; prop. pl. of *drogá* perch of a vehicle.] Prop., a Russian low four-wheeled carriage, in which the passengers sit astride a narrow bench, their feet resting on bars near the ground; hence *transf.*; in some German towns the name of the ordinary fiacre.

Drosometer (drosǫ·mĭtəɹ). 1825. [f. Gr. δρόσος dew + -METER.] An instrument for measuring the quantity of dew deposited.

Dross (drǫs), *sb.* [OE. *drōs* = MDu. *droes(e* dregs; cf. OE. *drōsna* (gen. pl.), MLG. *drōsem*, MDu. *droesen(e* (Du. *droesem*), OHG. *truosana* (G. *drusen*) dregs, lees.] **1.** The scum thrown off from metals in smelting. **b.** An alloy formed in the zinc-bath by the action of the zinc on the iron articles dipped 1884. Also *fig.* **2.** Dreggy, impure, or foreign matter mixed with any substance ME. Also *fig.* **3.** *gen.* Refuse; rubbish; worthless, impure matter ME.
2. *fig.* The Dregs and Lees of the Earth, and Drosse of Mankinde 1677. **3.** All treasures and all gain esteem as d. MILT. *P.R.* III. 23. Hence **Dross** *v.* to free from d. **Dro·ssless** *a.* free from d.

†**Dro·ssel, drosell.** 1581. [Cf. DRAZEL.] A sloven, a slut –1617.

Drossy (drǫ·si), *a.* ME. [f. DROSS *sb.* + -Y¹.] Of metals, etc.: Full of dross; of the nature of dross; dreggy, feculent. Also *transf.* and *fig.*
Thin brass or d. lead MORRIS. Hence **Dro·ssiness.**

Drou, drough, drouȝ, obs. pa. t. of DRAW *v.*

Drought (draut), **drouth** (drauþ, *Sc.* drūþ). [Late OE. *drūgaþ*, f. *drūȝ-, base of *drȳȝe* DRY *a.*; cf. (M)LG. *drogede*, (M)Du. *droogte*, f. *droog* dry. For the Sc. and north. *drouth*, cf. *highth* HEIGHT, and see -TH¹.] **1.** The quality of being dry; aridity, lack of moisture (*arch.*). **2.** *spec.* Dryness of the weather or climate; lack of rain. ME. †**3.** Parched land, desert –1671. **4.** Thirst (*arch.* and *dial.*) ME.
1. The burning drouth Of that long desert TENNYSON. **2.** The tender dew after drouth SWINBURNE. **3.** MILT. *P.R.* III. 274. **4.** His carcass, pined with hunger and with droughth MILT. *P.R.* I. 325.

Droughty (drau·ti), **drouthy** (drau·þi, *Sc.* drū·þi), *a.* 1603. [f. prec. + -Y¹.] **1.** Dry, without moisture; arid. Also *fig.* **2.** Characterized by drought 1605. **3.** Thirsty; addicted to drinking 1626.
1. Out of the droughty rocke Moses..bringeth forth water 1643. **2.** Drouthy weather SCOTT. **3.** The dusty, drouthy wayfarers 1879. Hence **Drou·ghtiness.**

†**Droumy,** *a. rare.* 1605. [perh. conn. w. Sc. DRUMLY.] Turbid –1640.

Drouth, drouthy, var. of DROUGHT, -Y.

Drove (drōᵘv), *sb.* [OE. *drāf*, f. gradation-var. *ai of *drīfan* DRIVE.] †**1.** The action of driving. (Only OE.) **2.** A number of beasts, as oxen, sheep, etc., driven in a body; a herd, flock OE.; *transf.* a crowd, multitude, shoal OE. Also *fig.* of things. **3.** Locally: **a.** A road along which horses or cattle are driven 1664. **b.** A channel for drainage or irrigation OE. **4.** A stone-mason's chisel with a broad face 1825.
2. A d. of sheep LYTTON. His finny d. SPENSER. A great d. of Heresies..broke loose among them 1692. **3.** The major rode in the middle of the D. (so our fen roads are called) 1829. *Comb.* **d.-road,** an ancient road along which there is a free right of way for cattle, but which is not kept in repair.

Drove, *v.*¹ 1632. [f. DROVE *sb.*, or back-formation from DROVER.] To follow the occupation of a drover (*trans.* and *intr.*).

Drove, *v.*² 1825. [f. DROVE *sb.* 4.] *trans.* To dress (stone) in parallel lines with a DROVE (sense 4).

Drove, pa. t. (and obs. pa. pple.) of DRIVE *v.*

Drover (drōᵘvəɹ). ME. [f. DROVE *sb.* + -ER¹.] **1.** One who drives droves of cattle, sheep, etc., to market; a dealer in cattle. **2.** A boat used for fishing with a drift-net 1465.
1. Why that's spoken like an honest Drouier: so they sel Bullockes *Much Ado* II. i. 201.

Drovy (drōᵘ·vi), *a.* Now *dial.* ME. [f. OE., ME. *drōf* turbid, troubled, or the deriv. vb., ME. *drōve* trouble, disturb; see -Y¹.] Turbid.

Drow, obs. pa. t. of DRAW *v.*

Drown (draun), *v.* [ME. (orig. north.) *drun(e, droun(e*, pointing to an OE. **drūnian*, rel. to ON. *drukna* be drowned :- **druŋknan*, f. **druŋk-*, var. of **driŋk-* DRINK. Superseded DRENCH.] **1.** *intr.* To suffer death by suffocation under water, etc.; †to sink (as a ship) –1523. (Now *unusual.*) **2.** *trans.* To suffocate by submersion in water, etc. Also said of the water. ME. Also *fig.* †**3.** To sink in water; to send to the bottom –1632. **4.** To lay under water, etc.; to submerge, inundate; to drench ME. **5.** *transf.* and *fig.* To overwhelm, to overpower (sound, etc.); to smother ME.
2. He..was prively drouned in a But of Malvesey HALL. *fig.* They d. themselves in drink 1659. **4.** When the Fens are drowned 1696. Phr. *To d. out*: to stop (works, etc.) or drive (people, etc.) from their houses by flooding. **5.** Yells drowned his voice FROUDE. Hence **Drow·nage** (*rare*), drowning. **Drow·ner,** one who, or that which, drowns. **Drow·ningly** *adv.* so as to d.

Drowse (drauz), *v.* 1573. [Back-formation from DROWSY.] **1.** *intr.* To be drowsy; to be heavy with or as with sleep; to be half asleep. Also *fig.* **2.** *trans.* To render drowsy; to make heavy or inactive, as with sleep 1600.
1. I drowsed..but I anon wakened PEPYS. *fig.* Let not your prudence..d. TENNYSON. **2.** Nations drows'd in peace KEATS.

Drowse, *sb.* 1814. [f. prec. vb.] The action of drowsing; the state of being half asleep.

Drowsy ((drau·zi), *a.* 1529. [prob. based on the stem of OE. *drūsian* be languid or sluggish, f. **drūs-*, var. of base of *drēosan* fall. Cf. DREARY.] **1.** Inclined to sleep; heavy with sleepiness; half asleep, dozing 1530. **2.** Caused or characterized by sleepiness 1529. **3.** Soporific 1590. **4.** *fig.* Dull, inactive; lethargic 1570.
1. A d. watchman's footsteps DICKENS. **2.** D. Diseases, called Coma [etc.] CULPEPPER. **3.** A d. posset MIDDLETON. **4.** The dead and drowsie fier SHAKS. *Comb.* **d.-head,** a person of a sluggish disposition. Hence **Drow·sihead, Drow·sihood,** drowsiness. **Drow·sily** *adv.* in a d. manner. **Drow·siness,** d. state; also *fig.*

Drowte, drowth, obs. var. DROUGHT.

Droyl, Droyt, obs. ff. DROIL, DROIT.

Drub (drɒb), *v.* 1634. [ult. repr. Arab. *ḍaraba* strike, beat, hit, pronounced *ḍrab* in N. Africa.] **1.** *trans.* To beat with a stick or the like, to cudgel; in early use, *spec.* to bastinado; also, to beat in a fight. Also *transf.* and *fig.* **2.** To beat the ground, stamp (*trans.* and *intr.*) 1855.
1. He is almost drubd (with many terrible bastinadoes on the soles of his feet) to death SIR. T. HERBERT. He was most confoundedly drubb'd just now FIELDING. **2.** Drubbing with her little feet THACKERAY. Hence **Drub** *sb.* a stroke with a cudgel; a thump. **Dru·bber,** one who drubs or beats. **Dru·bbing** *vbl. sb.* a beating, a thrashing.

Drudge (drɒdʒ), *sb.* 1494. [prob. f. the verb, which is, however, first recorded 50 years later.] One employed in mean, servile, or distasteful work; a hack; a hard toiler.
Lexicographer, a writer of dictionaries; a harmless d. [etc.] JOHNSON.

Drudge (drɒdʒ), *v.* 1548. [poss. a continuation with extended meaning of ME. *drugge* drag or pull heavily (but the pronunc. of *gg* in this word is uncertain). See DRUG *v.*¹] **1.** *intr.* To perform mean or servile tasks; to work slavishly; to toil at distasteful work. **2.** *trans.* To subject to drudgery (*rare*) 1847.
1. College-tutors do indeed work; they d. M. PATTISON. Phr. *To d. out*, to perform as drudgery; *to d. away, over*, to pass in drudgery. Hence **Dru·dger,** one who drudges. **Dru·dgingly** *adv.*

Drudgery (drɒ·dʒəri). 1550. [f. DRUDGE *sb.* + -ERY.] The occupation of a drudge; mean, servile, or wearisome toil; distasteful work. Also *attrib.*
A servant with this clause Makes drudgerie divine G. HERBERT. The d. of his Dictionary BOSWELL.

†**Druery, drury,** ME. [– OFr. *druerie* love, friendship, f. *dru*, fem. *drue* lover, dear friend.] **1.** Love, *esp.* sexual love; courtship; *often*, illicit love –1460. **2.** A love-token, keepsake –1560. **3.** A sweetheart –1450. **4.** A beloved thing, a treasure. (Only ME.)

Drug (drɒg), *sb.*¹ [Late ME. *drogges, drouges*, pl. – (O)Fr. *drogue(s*, of much disputed origin.] **1.** An original, simple, medicinal substance, organic or inorganic, used by itself, or as an ingredient in Medicine, or, formerly, in the arts generally. In early use always *pl.* **b.** *spec.* A narcotic or opiate 1902. **2.** A commodity which is no longer in demand, and so is unsaleable. (Now usu. *a d. in the market.*) 1661.
1. Tea and other Drugs 1682. What d. can make A wither'd palsy cease to shake? TENNYSON. **2.** Horses in Ireland are a D. TEMPLE. A wife's a d. now; mere tar-water..but nobody takes it MURPHY. They told me poetry was a mere d. 1824. **3.** *Comb.* **d.-store** (*U.S.*), a druggist's shop, also dealing in toilet requisites, stationery, etc. 1845. Hence **Dru·ggy** *a.* of, pertaining to, or resembling drugs.

Drug, *sb.*² 1677. [Allied to DRUG *v.*¹; cf. DRAG *sb.*] A low truck for the carriage of timber, etc.

Drug, *sb.*³ var. of DROGUE.

Drug, *v.*¹ Now *dial.* [ME. *drugge* drag or pull heavily, of unkn. origin. See DRUDGE *v.*] To drag.

Drug (drɒg), *v.*² 1605. [f. DRUG *sb.*¹] **1.** *trans.* To mix or adulterate with a drug. **2.** To administer drugs to, *esp.* for the purpose of stupefying or poisoning 1730; to administer something nauseous to 1667. **3.** *intr.* To take drugs habitually 1895.
1. I haue drugg'd their Possets, That Death and Nature doe contend about them *Macb.* II. ii. 7. **2.** Whom he has drugg'd to sure repose 1730. With pleasure drugg'd, he almost long'd for woe BYRON.

Drug, Druggery, etc., obs. ff. DRUDGE, etc.

Drugger (drɒ·gəɹ). 1594. [f. DRUG *sb.*¹, and DRUG *v.*²] †**1.** A dealer in drugs –1845. **2.** One who administers a drug 1836.

Druggery (drɒ·gəri). 1535. [– Fr. *droguerie*, f. *drogue* drug.] **1.** Drugs collectively. **2.** A place where drugs are kept 1865.

Drugget (drɒ·gėt). 1580. [– Fr. *droguet*, of unkn. origin.] **1.** Formerly, a kind of stuff, all of wool, or half wool, half silk or linen, used for wearing apparel. **b.** Now, a coarse woollen stuff used for floor-coverings, etc. **2.** †A garment of drugget; a floor-cloth of drugget 1713. **3.** *attrib.* 1580.
2. He was married in a plain d. STEELE. **3.** A d. petticoat W. BLACK. Hence **Dru·ggeting** = sense 1 b.

Druggist (drɒ·gist). 1611. [– Fr. *droguiste*; see DRUG *sb.*¹, -IST.] One who deals in drugs. In Scotl. and U.S. the name for a pharmaceutical chemist.

Druid (drū·id), *sb.* (*a*). 1563. [– Fr. *druide* or its source L. pl. *druidæ, druides*, Gr. δρυΐδαι – Gaulish *druides.*] **1.** One of an order of men among the ancient Celts of Gaul and Britain, who, according to Cæsar, were priests, but in native Irish and Welsh legend were magicians, soothsayers, and the like. (The Eng. use follows the L. sources.) Orig. always in *pl.* **2.** Hence: **a.** A priest, chaplain. **b.** A philosophic bard. 1710. **c.** One of certain officers of the Welsh Gorsedd 1884. **3.** *attrib.* Druidic 1670.
1. Mona was a sacred place of the Druids 1892. **2.** *United Ancient Order of Druids*, a secret benefit society founded in London in 1781, and having now numerous lodges or *groves* in most English-speaking countries. **3.** *D. stones, sandstones*, greywethers, of which Stonehenge is constructed. Hence **Dru·idess,** a female D.; a

Druidical prophetess. **Dru·idism,** the religious and philosophical system of the Druids.

Druidic, -al (drui·dik, -ăl), *a.* 1755. [f. prec.; see -IC, -ICAL.] Of or pertaining to the Druids.

Circles of upright stones, like those which in Europe are termed Druidical PRICHARD.

Drum (drɒm), *sb.*[1] 1541. [Shortening of †*drom(b)slade*, †*drombyllsclad* (XVI) DRUMSLADE, alt. f. LG. *trommelslag* drum-beat, f. *trommel* drum + *slag* beat.] **1.** A percussive musical instrument, consisting of a hollow cylinder or hemisphere of wood or metal, with a head of tightly stretched membrane at one or both ends, to be beaten with a stick. Also *fig.* and *transf.* **b.** *Zool.* Applied to the hollow hyoid bone of the howling monkey 1817. **2.** The sound of the instrument, or any similar sound 1646. **3.** *Mil.* One who plays the drum; a drummer. Also, †a small party sent with a drum to parley with the enemy. 1577. **4.** Anything resembling a drum in shape or structure.

a. The tympanum of the ear 1615. **b.** *Machinery.* A cylinder round which a belt passes or is wound 1776. **c.** A cylinder or cask for steaming printed fabrics in order to fix the colour. **d.** The cylindrical case for the spring of a car-brake. **e.** A cylindrical chamber used in heating apparatus 1888. **f.** A doffer in a carding-machine.

5. *Arch.* **a.** The vase of the Corinthian and Composite capitals 1727. **b.** The block of stone composing one section of the shaft of a column (Gwilt). **c.** The upright part under or above a cupola 1837. **6.** *techn.* **a.** A sieve 1706. **b.** A cylinder of canvas used as a storm-signal 1867. **c.** The cylindrical part of an urn or the like. **7.** A cylindrical box or receptacle for fruit, fish, etc. 1812. **8.** An evening assembly of fashionable people at a private house; a rout. Later, an afternoon tea-party. Cf. KETTLEDRUM. 1745. **9.** More fully **d.-fish:** Any of various sciænoid fishes which make a drumming noise; as, the 'salt-water d.' (*Pogonias chromis*) found on the Atlantic coast; the 'fresh-water d.' (*Haplodinotus grunniens*) of the Mississippi, etc.; the 'branded d.' or 'sea-boss' (*Sciæna ocellata*) of the Gulf States 1676.

1. And sodainly strake up a Dromme or Drounslade HALL. The large d., beaten at both ends, is called a *double-d.* KNIGHT. *Bass d.* = *double-drum.* **2.** Phr. *John D.'s entertainment*: a rough reception, turning an unwelcome guest out of doors. *All's Well* III. vi. 41. **8.** We went last night to a d. at Rothschild's 1824.

attrib. and *Comb.*: **d.-armature,** a dynamo-armature in the form of a rotating hollow cylinder; **-curb,** a cylindrical curb of iron or wood to support the brickwork of a shaft; **-fire,** continuous rapid artillery fire; †**-room,** the room in which a d. or rout is held; **-sieve,** a sieve enclosed in a d.-like box, for sifting fine substances; **-wheel,** (*a*) a cylinder round which a rope is coiled; (*b*) a water-raising current-wheel made in the form of a d., a tympanum.

Drum, *sb.*[2] 1725. [– Gael. and Ir. *druim* back, ridge.] A ridge or 'rigg', a long narrow hill often separating two parallel valleys. Hence *Geol.* A long narrow ridge of 'drift' formation.

Drum, *v.* 1583. [f. DRUM *sb.*[1]] **1.** *intr.* To beat on or as on a drum 1583. **b.** Applied to the strong beating of the heart 1593. **2.** Of birds or insects: To make a hollow reverberating sound, as by the quivering of the wings 1813. **3.** To sound like a drum; to resound 1638. **4.** 'To go about, as a drummer does, to gather recruits, to secure partisans, customers, etc.; with *for*' (Webster). **5.** *trans.* To summon by or as by beat of drum; to beat *up* as by drumming; *colloq.* to obtain by solicitation 1606. **6.** To expel publicly by beat of drum 1766. **7.** To din or drive *into* by persistent repetition 1820. **8.** To perform (a tune) on or as on a drum 1864.

1. [Her] foot was drumming on the carpet SALA. **2.** Flies and gnats d. around you 1873. **6.** Another is drummed out of a regiment MACAULAY. **7.** To d. a doctrine into the public mind MILL.

Drumble, *sb.* Now *dial.* 1575. [var. of *dumble* DUMMEL.] An inert or sluggish person; a drone.

Drumble, *v.* Now *dial.* 1579. [f. prec.] **1.** *intr.* To be sluggish; to move sluggishly 1598. †**2.** *intr.* To drone, to mumble –1596.

1. Look, how you d. *Merry W.* III. iii. 156.

†**Drumbler, drumler.** 1598. [– early mod. Du. *drommeler* a kind of ship.] A small fast vessel used as a transport, etc. –1630.

Dru·mhead. 1622. [f. DRUM *sb.*[1] + HEAD *sb.*] **1.** The skin or membrane stretched upon a drum. **2.** The tympanic membrane 1664. **3.** The circular top of a capstan, into which the capstan bars are fixed 1726. **4.** A flat-topped variety of cabbage 1797. **5.** *attrib.*, as *d. court-martial*, a court-martial round an up-turned drum, for summary trial of offences during military operations. So *d. law, discipline.*

Drumlin (drɒ·mlin). 1833. [app. for *drumling*, dim. of DRUM *sb.*[2]] = DRUM *sb.*[2]

Drumly (drɒ·mli), *a.* Orig. *Sc.* 1513. [app. a nasalized var. of ME. †*drubly* in same sense. Cf. DROUMY.] **1.** Of the sky or day: Troubled; cloudy. Also *fig.* **2.** Of water, etc.: Turbid; not clear 1570. Also *fig.* and *transf.*

Dru·m-major. 1598. [See MAJOR *sb.*] †**1.** The first or chief drummer in a regimental band. **b.** A non-commissioned officer who has command of the drummers. **c.** An officer of a band or drum-corps, who leads and directs it on the march. †**2.** *joc.* A large drum or rout 1753.

Drummer (drɒ·məɹ). 1573. [f. DRUM *v.* + -ER[1].] **1.** One who beats a drum for military or other purposes; one who plays the drum in a band. **2.** *fig.* A commercial traveller. See DRUM *v.* 4 and 5 (*U.S.*) 1827. **3.** A drum-fish. **b.** The large W. Indian cockroach (*Blatta gigantea*), which drums its head against the woodwork of houses as a sexual call. **c.** A rabbit. 1725.

Dru·mming, *vbl. sb.* 1583. [See -ING[1].] **1.** The action of DRUM *v.* **2.** Fishing for drum-fish (*U.S.*) 1889.

Drummond light. 1854. The lime-light, or oxyhydrogen light (invented by Capt. T. *Drummond*, R.E., *c*1825), wherein a blow-pipe flame, *e.g.* of combined oxygen and hydrogen, impinges on a piece of pure lime, and renders it incandescent.

†**Drumslade, dromslade.** 1527. [See DRUM *sb.*[1]] **1.** A drum –1635. **2.** A drummer –1777. Hence †**Dru·mslager** = sense 2.

Drumstick (drɒ·mstik). 1589. **1.** The stick with a knobbed end used in beating a drum. **2.** *transf.* (in reference to shape.) **a.** The lower joint of the leg of a fowl 1764. **b.** *U.S.* The stilt-sandpiper.

Drungar (drɒ·ŋgăɹ). *Hist.* 1619. [– med. L. *drungarius*, f. late L. *drungus* a body of soldiers; see -AR[2].] The commander of a troop.

The great drungaire of the fleet GIBBON.

Drunk (drɒŋk), *ppl. a.* and *sb.* ME. [pa. pple. of DRINK *v.*, earlier DRUNKEN. Now only in the predicate, exc. in Sc. and n. dial.] **A. 1.** Overcome by or as by alcoholic liquor; intoxicated. Also *fig.* †**2.** Drenched; soaked with moisture –1697. **3.** = DRUNKEN 5. 1884.

1. She was blind d. SIMS. D. with opium 1585, with tobacco 1698. *fig.* D. with success J. R. GREEN. **2.** I will make mine arrows d. with blood *Deut.* 32:42.

B. *sb.* (*colloq.*) **1.** A drinking-bout 1862. **2.** A drunken person; a case or charge of being drunk 1882.

Drunkard (drɒ·ŋkărd). 1530. [prob. – MLG. *drunkert*, f. *drunken*; cf. MDu. *dronker*, Du. *dronkaard*, whence early mod. Fr. *dronquart*; see -ARD.] One addicted to drinking, *esp.* to excess; an inebriate, a sot.

As drunckards..they staggring reele 1586.

Drunken (drɒ·ŋkĕn), *ppl. a.* OE. [pa. pple. of DRINK *v.*; cf. DRUNK. Sc. *drucken* is from Norse.] **1.** Intoxicated. Also *transf.* and *fig.* **2.** Habitually intemperate. (The more usual current sense.) 1548. **3.** Proceeding from or pertaining to drink or drunkenness 1591. **4.** *transf.* Soaked with moisture ME. **5.** *fig.* Of a thing: Unsteady; off the vertical 1786.

1. Ye fare as folkes that dronken ben of ale CHAUCER. D. with cold KANE. **2.** Stephano, my d. butler *Temp.* v. i. 277. **3.** To take up a d. brawl MASSINGER. **4.** The d. Field DRYDEN. Hence **Dru·nkenly** *adv.*

Drunkenness (drɒ·ŋkĕn,nĕs). OE. [f. prec. + -NESS.] **1.** The state of being drunk; intoxication; the habit of drinking to excess. **2.** *fig.* Intoxication of the mind or spirit.

1. D. is frequently a disease 1871. **2.** The d. of factious animosity MACAULAY. vars. †**Dru·nkenship,** †**Dru·nkness,** †**Dru·nkship.**

Drupaceous (drupēⁱ·ʃəs), *a.* 1822. [f. mod. L. *drupa*; see next and -ACEOUS.] *Bot.* Of the nature of a drupe, or bearing drupes; belonging to the *Drupaceæ.*

Drupe (drūp). 1753. [– L. *drūpa, druppa* over-ripe olive, specialized in mod. botanical L. (*Linnæus*) – Gr. δρύππα olive. Cf. Fr. *drupe.*] *Bot.* A stonefruit; a fleshy or pulpy fruit enclosing a stone or nut having a kernel, as the olive, plum, cherry.

Drupel (drū·pĕl). 1835. [– mod.L. *drupella*, dim. of *drupa* DRUPE; see -EL.] *Bot.* A little drupe: such as those of the blackberry. So **Dru·pelet, Dru·peole.**

Drupose (drū·pōᵘs). 1872. [f. DRUPE + -OSE[2].] *Chem.* A substance ($C_{12}H_{20}O_8$) produced together with glucose, by the action of boiling moderately diluted hydrochloric acid on glycodrupose, the stony concretions found in pears.

Druse[1] (drūz). 1811. [– Fr. *druse* – G. *druse* weathered ore = MLG. *drūse, drose*, Du. *droes.*] *Min.* A crust of small crystals lining the sides of a cavity in a rock; also, the cavity. Hence **Dru·sy** *a.* lined with minute crystals.

Druse[2], **druze** (drūz), *sb.* (*a.*) 1786. [– Fr. *Druse* – Arab. *durūz* pl. of *darzī.*] One of a political and religious sect of Moslem origin, inhabiting the region round Mount Lebanon. Hence **Dru·sian, -ean** *sb.* (*obs.*) and *a.*

Druxy (drɒ·ksi), *a.* 1589. [Earlier *dricksie*, f. †*drix* decayed wood, of unkn. origin.] Of timber: Having decayed spots concealed by healthy wood.

Dry (drəi), *a.* [OE. *drȳġe* :– **drūȝiz*, rel. to (M)LG. *dröge, dreuge*, MDu. *drōghe* (Du. *droog*) :– **drauȝiz*, f. Gmc. **drauȝ-* **dreuȝ-* **drūȝ-* (not in IE.).]

I. As a physical quality. **1.** Destitute of moisture; arid; of the eyes, free from tears. **b.** Of a season or climate: Free from or deficient in rain ME. **2.** That has lost its natural moisture; dried, parched, withered OE.; dried up ME. **3.** Of persons: Wanting drink; thirsty. (Now vulgar.) *transf.* Causing thirst. ME. **4.** Not yielding liquid; of cows, etc.: Not yielding milk ME. **5.** Not under, in, or on water (see also DRY LAND) ME. **6.** Of bread, etc.: Without butter 1579. **7.** Solid, not liquid; also *transf.* 1688. **8.** Of wines, etc.: Not sweet or fruity 1700. **9.** Of copper, tin, or lead: Not sufficiently de-oxidated in refining 1875. **10.** Not associated or connected with liquid; *esp.* (*Med.*) not marked by a discharge of matter, phlegm, etc., as diseases, etc. ME. †**11.** Of a blow, or a beating: prop., That does not draw blood; also vaguely = Hard, stiff, severe –1774.

1. Among whome was not oon drie eye 1562. A d. year 1897. **2.** D. fish from Newfoundland 1677. Some small Rivers..are d. at certain seasons DAMPIER. **3.** *transf.* It's d. work 1897. **4.** D. milch cows 1658. A d. inkstand 1874. **5.** Further d. arches on each shore 1798. The tide leaves them d. 1816. **7.** D. wares, as Corn, Seeds, [etc.] HUTTON. Phr. *D. measure*, measure of capacity for non-liquids. **8.** Where's the old d. wine? THACKERAY. **10.** A d. death *Temp.* I. i. 72. **b.** Of a country, legislation, etc. (orig. *U.S.*): tee-total, prohibiting sale of intoxicants; also, deprived of intoxicants by prohibition 1888.

II. Fig. senses. **1.** Feeling or showing no emotion ME. **2.** Of a jest or sarcasm: Uttered in a matter-of-fact tone; of humour: Apparently unconscious; used also of the humorist; in early use, ironical 1542. †**3.** Yielding no fruit, result, or satisfaction; barren, jejune, unfruitful –1680; of persons: Miserly, uncommunicative –1689. **4.** Lacking embellishment; bare; matter-of-fact 1626. **5.** Insipid. (*fig.* from food.) 1621. **6.** *Art.* Stiff and formal in outline; lacking in softness; frigidly precise 1716. **7.** Of money, rent, etc.: Paid in hard cash. [Cf. Fr. *argent sec.*] 1574. **8.** *Dry light* (see Heraclitus, ed. Bywater 30): 'Light' untinged by prejudice or fancy 1625.

1. Noted for an address so cold, d., and distant [etc.] HUME. **2.** [He] was something of a..d. joker SCOTT. **4.** A long catalogue of d. facts

DARWIN. **6.** A hard and d. manner of execution 1876. **8.** The d. light of every day LOWELL.

Combs. **a.** Parasynthetic, as **d.-eyed** *a.*, having d. eyes, tearless. **b.** Adverbial, in sense 'in a d. way: without the use of liquid; without drawing blood'; as **d.-cupping,** see CUPPING; **-cure** *v.*, to cure meat, etc. by salting and drying; **-salt** *v.* = *dry-cure.* **c.** Special attributive combs.: **d.-bob** (see BOB *sb.*[3]); also as *vb.*; **-bone** (*U.S.*), a name for the silicate and other ores of zinc; **-bones,** a familiar name for a thin and withered person; **-castor,** 'a kind of beaver, called also *parchment-beaver'* (Webster); †**-ditch** *v.*, to work at without result, like one digging a ditch into which no water flows; **-fly** *a.* and *v.* (*Angling*), used to describe a method of fishing in which an artificial fly floats lightly on the water; **-march,** a boundary line not formed by water; **d. pack,** see PACK *sb.*[1] 8; **-plate** (*Photogr.*), a sensitized plate which may be exposed to the action of light in a d. state; **-point** (*Engraving*), (*a*) a sharp-pointed needle used for engraving without acid on a copper plate from which the etching-ground has been removed; (*b*) this process of engraving, or an engraving so executed; hence **-point** *v.*; †**-rent,** a RENTSECK; **-stone** *a.*, used of a dike built without mortar; **-stove,** a stove for plants, with d. heat; **d. wall,** a wall built without mortar. Hence **Dry·ish** *a.* somewhat d.

Dry, *sb.* ME. [subst. use of prec.] **1.** Dry state, *esp.* of the atmosphere. **2.** That which is dry; *spec.* dry land ME. **3.** A drying-house 1876. **4.** *Masonry.* A fissure in a stone, rendering it unfit to support a load 1825. **5.** (orig. *U.S.*) A prohibitionist 1918.

Dry (drəi), *v.* Pa. t. and pple. **dried** (drəid). [OE. *dryġan* trans. (beside *drūgian* intr.), f. *drȳġe* DRY *a.*] **1.** *trans.* To make dry by any means; to rid or deprive of moisture; to desiccate. **2.** *intr.* To become dry; to lose or be exhausted of moisture ME.; of moisture, to disappear by evaporation, exhaustion, or draining ME. †**3.** To be thirsty –1541. **4.** *trans.* To render a cow dry; *intr.* to become dry 1780.

1. Thei dryen it at the Sonne MAUNDEV. To d. all teares 1551. The water. .was now dried away DAMPIER. **2.** It [a sandbank] drys at Low-Water 1705. Great Seas haue dried *All's Well* II. i. 143.

Comb. **D. up.** *trans.* **a.** To suck, draw, or take up moisture entirely. **b.** To exhaust of its moisture. (Chiefly in *pass.*) **c.** *intr.* Of moisture: To disappear entirely. Of a source: To become quite dry. **d.** (*slang*) To cease talking; also *gen.* to cease.

Dryad (drəi·æd). Pl. **dryads;** also in L. form **Dryades** (drəi·ădīz). late ME. [–(O)Fr. *dryade* – L. *Dryades*, pl. of *Dryas* – Gr. Δρυάς, Δρυάδης, f. δρῦς tree; see -AD.] *Gr.* and *L. Mythol.* A nymph supposed to inhabit trees; a wood-nymph. Also *transf.*

transf. The palm, the loftiest d. of the woods BYRON. Hence **Drya·dic** *a.* of, pertaining to, or resembling a d.

Dryasdust (drəi·æzdɒst). 1820. [i.e. *Dry as dust.*]

A. *sb.* Name of a fictitious person to whom Sir W. Scott dedicates some of his novels; hence, a writer or student of antiquities, statistics, etc., who occupies himself with dry details.

B. *adj.* Extremely dry 1872.

†**Dry-beat,** *v.* 1567. [See DRY *a.* I. 11.] To inflict dry blows upon –1667.

Drydenian (drəidī·niăn), *a.* 1687. [See -IAN.] Characteristic, or in the style, of John Dryden. So **Dry·denism,** a D. phrase, etc.

Dry dock, dry-dock. 1627. See DOCK *sb.*[3] Hence **Dry-dock** *v.* to place in a dry dock for repairs.

Dryer, var. of DRIER, freq. in techn. senses.

†**Dry·fat, dry-fat.** Also as two wds. 1526. [f. DRY *a.* + FAT *sb.*[1] = *vat.*] A large vessel used to hold dry things (as opp. to liquids) –1677.

†**Dry·-fist.** 1604. [Cf. DRY *a.* II. 3.] A niggardly person. So †**Dry·-fi:sted** *a.* niggardly.

Dry-foot (drəi·fut), *adv.* Also as two wds. ME. **1.** Without wetting the feet. †**2.** *To draw* or *hunt dry-foot*: to track game by the mere scent of the foot –1651. Also as *adj.*

2. *Com. Err.* IV. ii. 39. Hence **Dry·-foo:ted** *a.* in sense 1; *fig.* ?passing lightly over a difficulty.

Dry·-fou:nder, *v.* 1611. = FOUNDER *v.* Chiefly in pa. pple.

Dry goods. 1708. A name (chiefly in U.S.) for textile fabrics; articles of drapery, mercery, etc. (as opp. to groceries). Also *attrib.*

Drying (drəi·iŋ), *vbl. sb.* ME. [f. DRY *v.* + -ING[1].] **1.** The action of DRY *v.* **2.** *attrib.* and *Comb.* Used in or for drying something, as *d.-box, -floor, -ground, -room, -yard,* etc. 1502.

Dry·ing, *ppl. a.* ME. [f. as prec. + -ING[2].] **1.** That dries or renders dry; having the quality of abstracting moisture; as, *a d. wind.* **2.** Becoming dry; drying quickly; *spec.* of oils 1758.

2. Some oils, by the absorption of oxygen, become what are termed 'd. oils' 1865.

Dry land. ME. [See DRY *a.* I. 5.] Land not under water; land as opp. to sea. Also *attrib.*

Dryly, drily (drəi·li), *adv.* ME. [f. DRY *a.* + -LY[2]. The better spelling is *dryly*; cf. *shyly, slyly,* etc.] In a dry manner; see DRY *a.* II. 1, 2, 4–6.

Dryness (drəi·nės). ME. [f. as prec. + -NESS.] The quality or condition of being dry; see DRY *a.*

Dry-nurse, *sb.* 1598. [Cf. DRY *a.* I. 4.] A woman who looks after a child, but does not suckle it (opp. to *wet-nurse*). Also *fig.* of a man who 'coaches' another in his duties. Hence **Dry-nurse** *v.* to bring up by hand, without the breast; to play the dry-nurse to (*lit.* and *fig.*).

Dry rot, dry-rot. 1795. A decayed condition of timber in confined situations, in which it becomes brittle and crumbles to a dry powder; caused by various fungi, or by slow chemical processes. Also, any fungus causing this. Also *fig.* of hidden moral or social disintegration. Hence **Dry-rot** *v.* to affect with dry rot. **Dry-rotten** *ppl. a.*

Drysalter (drəi·sǭltəɹ). 1707. [app. f. *dry salt,* after *salter.*] A dealer in chemical products used in the arts, drugs, gums, etc.; occas. also in oils, sauces, pickles, etc. Hence **Dry·sa:ltery,** the store or business of a d.; the articles dealt in by a d. (*sing.* and *pl.*).

Dry-shod (drəi·ʃǫd), *a.* 1535. [= *dry shoed,* with dry shoes.] Without wetting the feet. (With *go, walk,* etc.)

Dryster (drəi·stəɹ). ? ME. [f. DRY *v.*; see -STER.] A workman or woman employed in drying something, *e.g.* the grain in a kiln.

Dryth (drəiþ). Also **drith(e.** Now *s. dial.* 1533. [f. DRY *a.* + -TH[1], after *warmth,* etc.] Dryness, dry condition; drought.

D.T. (dī·tī·), also **D.T.'s:** see D III. 1858.

Duad (diū·æd). 1660. [– Gr. δυάς, δυαδ- the number two (see -AD), prob. infl. by L. *duo*; the normal repr. of the Gr. is DYAD.] A combination of two; a couple, a pair. Hence **Dua·dic** *a.* relating to or consisting of duads.

Dual (diū·ăl). 1607. [– L. *dualis*, f. *duo* two; see -AL[1].]

A. *adj.* **1.** Of or pertaining to two. **2.** Twofold, double 1654.

1. *D. number* (Gram.), the inflected form expressing two or a pair. **2.** Truth is often of a d. character TYNDALL.

B. *sb. Gram.* The d. number 1650.

Dualin (diū·ălin). Also **-ine.** 1874. [f. DUAL + -IN[1], -INE[5].] *Chem.* A powerful explosive consisting of 20 parts of nitre mixed with 30 of fine sawdust, and 50 of nitroglycerin. Also *d.-dynamite.*

Dualism (diū·ăliz'm). 1794. [f. DUAL + -ISM, after Fr. *dualisme.*] **1.** The state of being dual; twofold division; duality 1831. **2.** *Gram.* The fact of expressing two in number 1874. **3.** A system of thought which recognizes two independent principles. *spec.* **a.** *Philos.* The doctrine that mind and matter exist as independent entities; opp. to *idealism* and *materialism.* **b.** The doctrine that there are two independent principles, one good and the other evil. **c.** *Theol.* The (Nestorian) doctrine that Christ consisted of two personalities. 1794. **4.** *Chem.* The theory, now abandoned, that every compound is constituted of two parts having opposite electricities 1884.

1. A d. between knowing and being, between the 'me' and the 'not me' 1877. **3.** The d.—the existence of matter as the source of evil apart from God—finds a distinct expression in the *Wisdom of Solomon* FARRAR.

Dualist (diū·ălist). 1661. [Sense 2, after contemp. PLURALIST, PLURALITY; sense 1, after Fr. *dualiste.* See DUAL, -IST.] **1.** One who holds a doctrine of dualism or duality 1822. †**2.** A holder of two offices (*rare*). FULLER.

Dualistic (diūăli·stik), *a.* 1801. [f. prec. + -IC, after Fr. *dualistique.*] **1.** Pertaining to, or of the nature of, dualism. **2.** Dual 1832.

1. Berzelius raised the structure of d. chemistry, which asserted that every compound. .must be constituted of two parts, of which one is positively and the other negatively electrified 1884. Hence **Duali·stically** *adv.*

Duality (diu,æ·lĭti). ME. [– late L. *dualitas* dual nature, f. L. *dualis*; see DUAL, -ITY. Cf. Fr. *dualité* (XVI). In sense 2, app. after PLURALITY 2; see DUALIST.] **1.** The fact of being dual; twofold condition. †**2.** The holding of two benefices together –1647.

Dualize (diū·ăləiz), *v.* 1838. [f. DUAL + -IZE.] To make or regard as two.

Dually (diū·ăli), *adv.* 1650. [See -LY[2].] In a dual capacity; in the dual number.

Duan (dū·ăn). 1765. [Gael and Ir.] A poem or song; a canto.

Till what is call'd, in Ossian, the fifth D. BYRON.

Duarchy (diū·ăɹki). 1586. [f. L. *duo* (or irreg. f. Gr. δύο) two, after *monarchy,* etc.] A government by two; a diarchy.

Dub (dɒb), *sb.*[1] *Sc.* and *n. dial.* 1500. [Of unkn. origin.] **1.** A muddy or stagnant pool; a puddle. (Chiefly *Sc.*) **2.** A deep dark pool in a river or stream. (*n. dial.*) 1535.

Dub (dɒb), *sb.*[2] 1572. [Mainly echoic.] **1.** A beat, or the sound, of a drum. **2.** A blow 1664. Hence **Dub-a-dub,** the sound made in beating a drum: used advb., as *sb.*, or as *adj.*; also as *vb.*

Dub (dɒb), *sb.*[3] *East Ind.* 1781. [Telugu *dabba.*] A small copper coin; = 20 cash.

Dub (dɒb), *v.*[1] [Late OE. **dubbian*, in phr. *dubbade tō rīdere* 'dubbed to knight' – AFr. *duber*, aphetic f. *aduber*, OFr. *adober* (mod. *adouber*) equip with armour, repair, mend; of unkn. origin.] **1.** To confer knighthood by a stroke of a sword. **2.** To invest with a dignity or new title. (Often *joc.*) ME. **3.** To style, nickname (now usu. in pleasantry) 1599. †**4.** To dress, array, adorn –1570. **5.** *Angling.* To dress (a fly, or a hook and line *with* a fly) 1450. **6.** To cut off the comb and wattles of (a cock) 1570. **b.** To trim or crop (hedges, etc.) 1634. **7.** To dress (cloth) 1801. **8.** To smear with fat or grease, as leather 1611. **9.** To trim with an adze 1711. **10.** To beat blunt or flat 1879.

1. Whan my Kyng had doubed me a Knight 1559. So he him dubbed SPENSER *F. Q.* VI. ii. 35. **2.** A Man of wealth is dubb'd a Man of worth POPE. **4.** Dobbed in his diademe 1450.

Dub, *v.*[2] 1513. [Echoic. Cf. EFris. *dubben* butt, beat, strike.] **1.** *trans.* To thrust; now implying a somewhat blunt thrust or poke; *intr.* to make a thrust, to poke (*at*) 1833. **2.** Used *intr.* and *trans.* of the beating or sound of a drum. Also *Dub-a-dub* (DUB *sb.*[2]), *rub-a-dub.*

2. With trumpets sounding, and with dubbing drums 1588.

Dub, *v.*[3] *slang.* 1840. [Of unkn. origin.] *intr. To d. up*: to pay up.

‖**Dubash** (duba·ʃ). *E. Ind.* 1698. [– Hindi *dōbāshī*, f. *dō* two + *bhāshā* language.] An (Indian) interpreter or commissionaire.

‖**Dubba, dubber** (dɒ·bə). *E. Ind.* 1698. [Urdu *dabbah* vessel made of raw skins.] A leather bottle or skin bag, used chiefly in India for holding oil, ghee, and other liquids.

Dubbing, *vbl. sb.* ME. [f. DUB *v.*[1] + -ING[1].] **1.** The act of dubbing, as a knight, etc.; see DUB *v.*[1] 1, 2. **2.** *Angling.* The materials used in dressing a fly 1676. **3.** A preparation of grease for softening leather and making it waterproof. Also *dubbin.* 1781. **4.** The act of smoothing, etc.; *spec.* working timber with an adze 1823.

Dubiety (diubəi·ĭti). 1750. [– late L. *dubietas*, f. *dubium* doubt; see -ITY.] The state or quality of being dubious; doubtfulness; also, an instance of this.

The twilight of d. never falls upon him LAMB.

Dubiosity (diūbiǫ·sĭti). 1646. [f. as next + -ITY; see -OSITY.] = DUBIOUSNESS; with *pl.*, a doubtful matter.

Men swallow falsities for truths, dubiosities for certainties SIR T. BROWNE.

Dubious (diū·biəs), *a.* 1548. [– L. *dubiosus*, f. *dubium* doubt; see -OUS.] **1.** Objectively doubtful; uncertain, undetermined; ambiguous, vague. **b.** Of uncertain issue 1635. **c.** Of questionable character 1860. **2.** Subjectively doubtful; wavering or fluctuating in opinion; hesitating 1632.

1. A d. honour A. P. STANLEY. **b.** In d. Battel MILT. *P. L.* I. 104. **c.** In very d. company 1884. **2.** Fluctuations of a d. Will NORRIS. Hence **Du·bious-ly** *adv.*, **-ness**, d. quality.

Dubitable (diū·bitǎb'l), *a.* 1624. [– L. *dubitabilis*, f. *dubitare* doubt; see -ABLE. Cf. OFr. *dubitable.*] Liable to doubt or question. Hence **Du·bitably** *adv.*

†**Dubitancy.** 1648. [– OFr. *dubitance*, f. as DUBITATION; see -ANCY.] Doubt, hesitation, uncertainty –1669.

Dubitant (diū·bitǎnt), *a.* 1821. [– *dubitant-*, pres. ppl. stem of L. *dubitare* doubt; see -ANT.] Doubting; having doubts. *absol.* One who doubts.

Dubitate (diū·bite[i]t), *v. rare.* 1827. [– *dubitat-*, pa. ppl. stem of L. *dubitare* doubt; see -ATE[3].] *intr.* To doubt, hesitate, waver.

If..he were to loiter dubitating, and not come CARLYLE.

Dubitation (diūbitē[i]·ʃən). 1450. [– (O)Fr. *dubitation* – L. *dubitatio*, f. as prec.; see -ION.] The action of doubting; doubt; a doubt.

Dubitative (diū·bitǎtiv), *a.* 1615. [–(O)Fr. *dubitatif, -ive* or late L. *dubitativus*, f. as prec.; see -IVE.] Inclined to doubt; expressing doubt or hesitancy. Hence **Du·bitatively** *adv.*

Duboisine (diuboi·sǝin). 1883. [See -INE[5].] *Chem.* An alkaloid obtained from an Australian shrub (*Duboisia myoporioides*), having qualities similar to those of hyoscyamine.

Ducal (diū·kǎl), *a.* 1494. [– Fr. *ducal*, f. *duc* DUKE; see -AL[1].] **a.** Of or pertaining to a duke or dukedom (also, a doge). **b.** Of the rank of duke, as *d. families* 1796.

Laws, which are for the most part the d. customs of Normandy BLACKSTONE. Hence **Du·cally** *adv.* in a d. manner; as a d.

Ducape (diukē[i]·p). 1678. [Of unkn. origin.] 'A plain-wove stout silk fabric of softer texture than *Gros de Naples*' (Beck).

Ducat (dɒ·kǎt). ME. [– It. *ducato* or its source, med.L. *ducatus* DUCHY.] **1.** A gold (or silver) coin of varying value, formerly in use in most European countries. First issued by Roger II of Sicily, as Duke of Apulia. The gold ducat was worth about 9*s.* 4*d.*; the silver ducat of Italy about 3*s.* 6*d.* **2.** *loosely.* A piece of money; *pl.* Money, cash 1775.

Ducatoon (dɒkǎtū·n). 1611. [– Fr. *ducaton* – It. *ducatone*, f. *ducato*; see prec., -OON.] A silver coin formerly current in some European states, worth from 5*s.* to 6*s.* sterling.

‖**Duces tecum** (diū·sīz tī·kɒm). 1617. [L. phrase: more fully *sub pœna duces tecum*, 'Under penalty thou shalt bring with thee'.] *Law.* A writ commanding a person to produce in court documents, etc. required as evidence.

Duchess (dɒ·tʃes). ME. [–(O)Fr. *duchesse* – med.L. *ducissa*, f. L. *dux, duc-*; see DUKE, -ESS[1]. Spelt *dutchess* from XVI to early XIX.] **1.** The wife or widow of a duke. **b.** A lady holding a DUCHY in her own right. **2.** *slang.* A woman of imposing appearance. [Cf. Fr. *duchesse.*] 1700. **3.** A size of roofing slate, 24 by 12 inches 1823.

1. *Hen. VIII*, II. iii. 38.

‖**Duchesse** (dɒ·tʃés, ‖düʃe̦s). 1878. [Fr. (see prec.).] A kind of satin, also of Brussels pillow-lace. *D. dressing chest*, etc., a dressing-table with a swing glass; so *d. toilet set*, a set of covers for a dressing-table.

Duchy (dɒ·tʃi). ME. [– (i) OFr. *duché* fem., later form of *duchée* :– Rom. **ducitas, -itat-*, f. *dux, duc-* (see DUKE, -ITY) and (ii) (O)Fr. *duché* m. :– med.L. *ducatus* (see -ATE[1]). See -Y[5].] **1.** The territory ruled by a duke or duchess. **2.** *attrib.* **a.** *gen.*, as *d. rights.* **b.** *spec.* Of or relating to the Royal duchies of Cornwall and Lancaster; as *d. land, tenement*, etc.; **chamber**, the court room at Westminster of **d.-** the **d.-court** of Lancaster, having equitable jurisdiction over lands holden of the Crown in right of the d.

Duck (dɒk), *sb.*[1] [OE. *duce* or *dūce*, f. base of **dūcan* dive; see DUCK *v.*] **1.** A swimming bird of the genus *Anas* and kindred genera of the family *Anatidæ.*

Without addition, the word is applied to the common *domestic d.*, a domesticated form of the *wild d.* or MALLARD. In its widest technical sense, the name includes golden-eyes, pintails, scoters, sheldrakes, teal, widgeons, and other related groups; the geese, though *Anatidæ*, are not usually called 'ducks'.

b. *spec.* The female of this fowl: the male being the DRAKE ME. **2.** *transf.* A term of endearment 1590. **3.** Short for *lame d.*; see sense 6. **4.** A boy's game, also called *duck-stone*; a stone used in this game, and occas. a player 1821. **5.** *Cricket.* Short for DUCK'S EGG 1868. **6.** *Lame d.*: a disabled person or thing: *spec.* (*Stock Exchange*): a defaulter. Also *d.* 1761. **7.** *Bombay d.* = BUMMALO 1860. **8.** *attrib.* 1884.

1. Though thou canst swim like a Ducke, thou art made like a Goose *Temp.* II. ii. 136.

Comb.: **d.-boards**, a narrow slatted path laid over wet ground; **-legged** *a.*, having unusually short legs; so *duck-legs*; **-shot**, shot of a size for shooting wild ducks; **-weight**, a d. of stone or clay used as a weight in ancient Assyria and Babylonia. **b. d.-ant**, the termite; **-eagle**, a S. Afr. species of eagle; **-mole**, the Duck-billed Platypus; **-mud**, Crow-silk; **-snipe** (Bahamas), the willet, *Symphemia semipalmata*; **-wheat** = D.-BILL wheat; etc.

Duck, *sb.*[2] 1554. [f. DUCK *v.*] **1.** A dip 1843. **2.** A rapid jerky lowering of head or body.

2. The ducks and nods Which weak minds pay to rank LAMB.

Duck, *sb.*[3] 1640. [– (M)Du. *doek* linen, linen cloth = OFris., OS. *dōk*, OHG. *tuoh* (G. *tuch*), of unkn. origin.] **1.** A strong untwilled linen (or later, cotton) fabric, lighter and finer than canvas; used for small sails and men's (*esp.* sailors') clothing. **2.** *pl.* Trousers of duck 1825. **3.** *attrib.* 1849.

Duck (dɒk), *v.* [ME. *douke, dūke*, repr. OE. **dūcan* = OFris. *dūka*, MLG., MDu. *dūken* (Du. *duiken*), OHG. *tūhhan* (G. *tauchen*). The short vowel is evidenced XVI; cf. *suck.*] **1.** *intr.* To plunge or dive, or suddenly go down under water, and emerge again. Also *fig.* **2.** To bend or stoop quickly; to bob; hence *fig.* to cringe, yield; so, *to d. under* 1530. **3.** *trans.* To plunge momentarily *in*, *into*, or *under* water or other liquid ME. **4.** To lower (the head) suddenly for a moment; to jerk down 1598.

1. (To avoid their Darts) he sometimes ducked HEYLIN. **2.** To d. at the whiz of a cannon-ball POPE. Law ducks to Gospel here BROWNING. **3.** I say, d. her in the loch, and then we will see whether she is witch or not SCOTT. **4.** We ducked our heads, and hurried 1884.

Duck and Drake. 1583. [From the motion of the stone over the water.] A pastime consisting in throwing a flat stone or the like over the surface of water so that it shall skip as many times as possible before sinking. (Often in *pl.*) Also *fig.* Also *attrib.*

Phr. *To make ducks and drakes of* or *with, to play (at) duck and drake with*: to throw away idly and carelessly; to handle recklessly; to squander.

Du·ck-bill, *sb.* 1556. [f. DUCK *sb.* + BILL *sb.*[2]] **a.** Short for *duck-bill wheat*; red wheat. **b.** = Duck-billed platypus; see below 1840. Hence **Duck-billed,** *a.* having a bill like a duck's. **Duck-billed platypus,** the *Ornithorhynchus* of Australia, a monotrematous mammal having a horny beak like a duck's bill; **duck-billed speculum,** a speculum flattened like a duck's bill.

Ducker (dɒ·kǝɹ). 1475. [f. DUCK *v.* + -ER[1]. In sense 2 = Du. *duiker*, Ger. *taucher* diver (bird).] **1.** A person who ducks; a diver 1483. **2.** A diving-bird; *spec.* the little grebe or dabchick 1475. **3.** 'A cringer' (J.).

Duck-hawk. 1812. [f. DUCK *sb.*[1] + HAWK.] **1.** Eng. name of the marsh harrier or moor-buzzard (*Circus æruginosus*). **2.** *U.S.* The American variety of the peregrine falcon (*Falco peregrinus* var. *anatum*) 1884.

Ducking (dɒ·kiŋ), *vbl. sb.*[1] 1539. [f. DUCK *v.* + -ING[1].] **a.** Immersion in water 1581. **b.** Prompt bending of the head or body.

Du·cking, *vbl. sb.*[2] 1577. [f. DUCK *sb.*[1] + -ING[1].] The catching or shooting of wild ducks.

Du·cking-pond. 1607. [f. DUCKING *vbl. sb.*[1] and [2].] **a.** A pond on which ducks may be hunted or shot. **b.** A pond for the ducking of offenders.

Du·cking-stool. 1597. A chair at the end of an oscillating plank, in which scolds, etc., or dishonest tradesmen, were tied and ducked in water, as a punishment.

Du·ckling. 1440. [-LING[1].] A young duck.

Duck's bill. 1601. The bill of a duck. Applied to surgical instruments, etc., of this shape.

Comb., as **duck's-bill bit,** a form of bit for use in a brace in wood-boring; **duck's-bill limpet,** a limpet of the genus *Parmophorus.*

Duck's egg. Also **duck egg.** ME. **a.** The egg of a duck; hence, **b.** in *Cricket*, the score of zero or '0'; no runs. **c.** The colour of the egg of a duck; used *attrib.* 1876.

Duck's meat, duckmeat. 1538. = next.

Du·ckweed. 1440. A name for plants of the genus *Lemna*, which float on still water, and cover the surface like a green carpet.

Ducky (dɒ·ki). 1819. [f. DUCK *sb.*[1] + -Y[6].] A term of endearment; as *adj.*, an emotional epithet of commendation.

Duct (dɒkt). 1650. [– L. *ductus* leading, etc., in med.L. aqueduct, f. *duct-*, pa. ppl. stem of *ducere* lead.] †**1.** The action of leading; lead –1684. †**2.** Course, direction –1718. †**3.** A stroke drawn or traced or the tracing of it (cf. L. *ductus litterarum*) –1796. **4.** A conduit, channel, or tube for conveying water, etc. 1713. **5.** *Phys.* A tube or canal in the animal body. Now restricted to the vessels conveying the chyle, lymph, and secretions. 1667. **b.** *Bot.* One of the vessels of the vascular tissue of plants 1858. **Du·ctless** *a.*

Ductile (dɒ·ktil, -ǝil), *a.* ME. [– OFr. *ductile* or L. *ductilis*, f. as prec.; see -ILE.] **1.** Malleable; flexible, not brittle. Still freq. in lit. use. **b.** That may be drawn out into wire or thread, tough. (The current techn. use.) 1626. **2.** That may be led or drawn; tractable, pliant; plastic 1622. Also *fig.*

1. All Bodies D. (as Metals that will be drawne into Wire) BACON. **2.** D. wax POPE, language 1842, streams 1834. The man was in truth childishly soft and d. MRS. H. WARD. var. **Du·ctible** (now *rare*). Hence **Du·ctile-ly** *adv.*, **-ness** (*rare*). **Ductili·meter,** an instrument for measuring the ductility of metals.

Ductility (dɒkti·lĭti). 1654. [f. DUCTILE + -ITY. Cf. Fr. *ductilité.*] **1.** Capability of being extended by beating, drawn into wire, worked upon, or bent. Also *fig.* **2.** Tractableness, docility 1654.

†**Du·ction.** ME. [– L. *ductio*, f. *duct-*, pa. ppl. stem of *ducere* lead; see DUCT, -ION.] The action of leading or bringing (*lit.* and *fig.*) –1696.

Ductor (dɒ·ktǝɹ, -ǭɹ). 15... [– L. *ductor* leader, f. as prec.; see -OR 2.] **1.** A leader. **2.** *Printing.* A roller which conveys the ink from the ink-fountain to the distributing-rollers. Also *d.-roller.* 1851.

†**Du·cture.** 1644. [f. *duct-* (see prec.) + -URE, after *fracture*, etc.] **1.** Leading –1716. **2.** Movement in some direction –1691. **3.** A duct 1670.

Dud (dɒd). Chiefly *pl.* **duds** (dɒdz). *colloq.* and *dial.* ME. [Of unkn. origin. Cf. AL. *dudde* (pl.), 1307.] **1.** Usually (now always) *pl.* = Clothes. (depreciatory or joc.) **b.** 'Things' 1662. **2.** *pl.* Rags, tatters. (Rarely *sing.*) 1508. **3.** A counterfeit thing; a futile person or thing 1825; also as *adj.* 1903. Hence **Du·ddery** (*dial.*), a place where woollen cloth is sold or made.

Dudder (dɒ·dǝɹ), *v.* Now *dial.* 1658. [var. of DIDDER.] *intr.* To shudder, shiver.

Dude (diūd). *U.S.* 1883. [prob. – G. dial. *dude* fool (cf. LG. *dudenkop* 'stupid head').] A name given in ridicule to a man who is ultra-fastidious in dress, speech, deportment, and 'form'; hence, an exquisite, a dandy; as, *a social d., a club d.*, etc. Hence **Dudine** (-ī·n), a female d.; **Du·dish** *a.*

Dudeen (dudī·n). Also **dudheen,** etc. 1841. [– Ir. *dúidín*, dim. of *dúd* pipe.] Irish name for a short clay tobacco-pipe.

†**Dudgen.** 1589. [perh. same as DUDGEON *sb.*[1]] **A.** *sb.* Trash 1592. **B.** *adj.* **1.** Mean, poor –1593. **2.** ? Ordinary, homely –1618.

Dudgeon (dɒ·dʒǝn), *sb.*[1] ME. [*Digeon* in AFr. (XIV); of unkn. origin.] †**1.** A kind of wood (according to Gerarde, boxwood) used by turners, *esp.* for handles of knives, daggers, etc. –1660. †**2.** The hilt of a dagger made of this. SHAKS. **3.** Hence **d.-dagger,** and later **d.:** A dagger with a d.-haft; also, a butcher's steel (*arch.*) 1581.

Dudgeon (dɒ·dʒən), *sb.*[2] 1573. [Of unkn. origin.] A feeling of anger or resentment; ill humour. Usu. in phr. *in d.*, and *esp.* with *high, great, deep.*
I hope you are not going out in d., cousin CONGREVE.

Due (diū). [ME. *dew, du(e* – OFr. *dëu* (mod. *dû*, fem. *due*) :– Rom. **debutus*, for L. *debitus* (cf. DEBIT), pa. pple. of *debēre* owe.]
A. *adj.* **1.** That is owing or payable, as a debt. †**2.** Belonging or falling *to* by right –1655. **3.** That ought to be given or rendered; merited ME. **4.** Such as ought to be; fitting; proper; rightful ME. **5.** Such as is requisite or necessary; adequate ME. **6.** To be ascribed or attributed; owing to, caused by, in consequence of (*rare* bef. 19th c.) 1661. **7.** Under engagement or contract to be ready or arrive (at a defined time) 1833.
1. Three thousand Ducats d. vnto the Iew SHAKS. **3.** Silent, not wanting d. respect, the crowd CRABBE. **4.** In d. Form 1728, time BUDGELL, course 1876. **5.** Upon d. consideration LD. BROUGHAM. **6.** The difficulty..is really d. to our ignorance JOWETT. **7.** The train is d. in London at 5 a.m. 1897. *Comb.*, etc., as **d.-bill** (*U.S.*), a brief written acknowledgement of a debt, not made payable to order, like a promissory note; **d. date,** the date on which a bill falls d.; so †**d. day.** Hence **Due·ness.**
B. *adv.* **1.** = DULY, in various senses. (*arch.*) 1597. **2.** With reference to the points of the compass: Properly; right, straight; directly. (Orig. *Naut.* Allied to A. 4.) 1601.
2. There lies your way, d. West *Twel. N.* III. i. 145.

Due (diū), *sb.* ME. [– Fr. *du* (now *dû*), subst. use of pa. pple. of *devoir* owe :– L. *debēre*; see prec.] †**1.** That which is due; a debt –1682. **2.** That which is due to any one legally or morally 1582. **3.** That which is due by any one 1738. **4.** *spec.* A legal charge, toll, tribute, fee, or the like. Chiefly in *pl.* 1546. †**5.** Duty –1697. †**6.** A right –1669. **7.** *Naut.* What is duly or thoroughly done: in phr. *for a full d.* = for good and all 1830.
1. *Timon* II. ii. 16. **2.** To cheat the hangman of his d. 1612. Phr. *To give the devil his d.*: to do justice to a person one dislikes. **6.** *Of* (*by*) *d.*, by right: The key of this infernal Pit by d...I keep MILT.

†**Due,** *v.*[1] ME. [var. of DOW *v.*[2]; cf. ENDUE.] To endow –1591.

†**Due,** *v.*[2] *rare.* [f. DUE *a.*] *impers.* To be due. DRAYTON.

Dueful (diū·fŭl), *a. arch.* [Coined by Spenser from DUE *a.*; cf. *rightful.*] Due, appropriate.

Duel (diū·ĕl), *sb.* 1591. [– It. *duello* or L. *duellum*, arch. form of *bellum* war, used in med.L. for judicial single combat, whence also Fr. *duel* (XVI).] **1.** A regular fight between two persons; *esp.* one prearranged and fought with deadly weapons, usu. in the presence of two witnesses called seconds, to settle a quarrel or point of honour 1611. **2.** Duelling as a practice 1615. **3.** Any contest between two persons or parties 1591.
1. They fought a Duell, that is, a single combat in a field hard by Spira CORYAT. **3.** A d. in the form of a debate COWPER. Hence **Du·elsome** *a.* inclined to duelling THACKERAY.

Duel (diū·ĕl), *v.* 1645. [f. prec.] **1.** *intr.* To fight a duel. †**2.** *trans.* To encounter or kill in a duel –1716. Hence **Du·eller, dueler,** a duelist. **Du·elling, dueling** *vbl. sb.* the fighting of duels; also *attrib.*

Duellist, duelist (diū·ĕlist). 1592. [f. DUEL *sb.* + -IST, after Fr. *duelliste* or It. *duellista.*] One who fights duels, or practises duelling. Also *fig.*
The blind wrestling of controversial duellists FROUDE.

‖**Duello** (due·lo). 1588. [It.; = DUEL.] **1.** Duelling as a custom; the code of duellists. †**2.** A duel (*lit.* and *fig.*) –1826.
1. But observes not the lawes of the D. OVERBURY.

Duenna (diu,e·nă). 1668. [Sp. *dueña* (dwe·nʸă), formerly spelt *duenna* :– L. *domina.*] **1.** The chief lady in waiting upon the queen of Spain. **b.** An elderly woman, half governess, half companion, having charge over the girls of a Spanish family 1681. **2.** Any elderly woman whose duty it is to watch over a young one; a chaperon 1708.
2. Guarded by a dragon-like d. 1877.

Duet, duett (diu,e·t), *sb.* 1740. [– G. *duett* or It. *duetto*, f. *duo* two; see DUO, -ET.] *Mus.* A composition for two voices or two performers. Hence **Due·t, -ett** *v. intr.* to perform a d.

‖**Duettino** (diuettī·no). 1839. [It.; dim. of next.] 'A duet of short extent and concise form' (Grove).

Duetto (due·tto). 1724. [It.; dim. of *duo* a duet; see DUO.] = DUET.

Duff (dɒf), *sb.*[1] 1840. [north. var. of DOUGH.] **a.** Dough, paste (*dial.*). **b.** A flour pudding boiled in a bag.

Duff (dɒf), *sb.*[2] *local.* 1844. [Possibly same word as prec., but more prob. echoic.] **1.** *Sc.* The spongy part of a loaf, a turnip, etc. **b.** 'A soft spongy peat' (Jam.). **2.** *Sc.* and *U.S.* The decaying vegetable matter which covers forest ground 1844. **3.** Coal-dust; slack. Also *d.coal.* 1865.

Duff (dɒf), *v.*[1] *slang* or *colloq.* 1838. [perh. back-formation from DUFFER *sb.*[1]] **1.** *trans.* To 'fake up'. **2.** *Australia.* To alter the brands on (stolen cattle); to steal (cattle), altering the brands 1869.

Duff, *v.*[2] 1897. [f. DUFFER *sb.*[2]] *Golf.* To perform (a shot) badly. Also *fig.*

‖**Duffada·r.** *E. Ind.* 1800. [– Urdu (– Pers.) *daf'a-dār*, commander of a small body of cavalry or infantry.] A petty officer of native police; a non-commissioned officer (= corporal) in regiments of Irregular Cavalry.

Duffel, duffle (dɒ·f'l). 1677. [f. *Duffel*, name of a town in Brabant.] **1.** A coarse woollen cloth having a thick nap or frieze. **2.** *U.S.* Change of flannels; a sportsman's outfit 1884. **3.** *attrib.* 1699.
1. Let it be of duffil grey WORDSW.

Duffer (dɒ·fəɹ), *sb.*[1] 1756. [conn. w. DUFF *v.*[1]] **1.** One who sells trashy articles as valuable, upon false pretences. **2.** A pedlar or hawker 1795. **3.** [f. DUFF *v.*[1]] One who 'fakes up' sham articles 1851. **b.** *Australia.* One who duffs cattle 1889.
1. Duffers, who vend pretended smuggled goods MAYHEW.

Du·ffer, *sb.*[2] *colloq.* and *slang.* 1842. [Possibly alt. of Sc. *doofart, dowfart* stupid or dull person, f. *douf, dowf* dull, spiritless, app. identical w. †*douffe* sb., perh. – ON. *doufr* DEAF.] **1.** *colloq.* A person without practical ability or capacity. Also, generally, a stupid or foolish person. **2.** *slang.* Any article that is no good; *esp.* counterfeit coin 1875.

Du·ffer, *v.* 1885. [f. prec.] *intr.* Of a mine: To prove no good, give *out.*

Duffing (dɒ·fiŋ), *ppl. a. slang.* 1851. [f. DUFF *v.*[1] + -ING[2].] **1.** That passes off a worthless article as valuable 1862. **2.** Rubbishy and offered as valuable 1851. **3.** Duffer-like 1881.

Duffle; see DUFFEL.

Dufoil (diū·foil). 1688. [f. L. *duo* + FOIL *sb.*[1], cf. *trefoil*, etc.] *Her.* A two-leaved flower; = TWAYBLADE.

Dufrenite (diufre·nəit). [Named 1833 after M. *Dufrénoy*, a French mineralogist, + -ITE[1] 2 b.] *Min.* Hydrous phosphate of iron, occurring in greenish nodules and fibrous masses.

‖**Dufter** (dɒ·ftəɹ). *E. Ind.* 1776. [– Urdu – Arab., Pers. *daftar* record – Gr. διφθέρα skin.] **a.** A bundle of official papers; a register, record. **b.** A business office. **Dufterda·r,** a Turkish officer of finance 1599.

Dug (dɒg), *sb.*[1] 1530. [Of unkn. origin.] The pap or udder of female mammalia; also the teat or nipple. As applied to a woman's breast, now contemptuous.

†**Dug,** *sb.*[2] 1607. *Angling.* A kind of red worm used as a bait. Also *d.-worm.* –1674.

Dug (dɒg), *ppl. a.* 1715. [pa. pple. of DIG *v.*] Obtained by digging, etc.; see the vb.

Dugong (dū·gɒŋ). 1800. [ult. – Malay *dūyong*, recorded (1751) as *dugung* and adopted as *dugon(g.*] A large herbivorous mammal (*Halicore dugong*, order *Sirenia*) of the Indian seas.

Dug-out. 1819. [See *dig out*, DIG *v.*]
A. *ppl. a.* Hollowed out by digging 1886.
B. *sb.* (chiefly *U.S.*) **1.** A canoe made by hollowing out the trunk of a tree 1819. **2.** A rough dwelling formed by an excavation (usually in a slope or bank), roofed with turf, canvas, etc. 1855. **b.** *spec.* A roofed shelter used in trench warfare 1904. **3.** A superannuated officer in temporary service (chiefly *Army slang*) 1912. Also *transf.*

‖**Duiker, duyker** (dəi,kəɹ). 1777. [Du. *duiker* diver; cf. DUCKER.] In full *duikerbok*: A small S. Afr. antelope, *Cephalopus mergens*, which plunges through the bushes when pursued.

Duke (diūk), *sb.* [ME. *duc, duk* – (O)Fr. *duc* – L. *dux, duc-* leader, rel. to *dūcere* lead.] †**1.** A leader; a captain or general; a chief, ruler –1591. **2.** In some European countries: A sovereign prince, the ruler of a duchy ME. †**b.** As tr. DOGE –1820. **c.** Cf. GRAND DUKE. **3.** In Great Britain and some other countries: A hereditary title of nobility, ranking next below that of a prince ME. **4.** Name of a kind of cherry 1664. **5.** *pl. slang.* The hand or fist 1879.
1. Jesus Crist d. of our batel WYCLIF. **2.** Thy father was the D. of Millaine and A Prince of power *Temp.* I. ii. 58. The D., and the Senators of Venice greet you *Oth.* IV. i. 230. **3.** *Royal d.*, a d. who is a member of the royal family, taking precedence of other dukes. Hence **Duke** *v. intr.* (also to *d. it*), to play the d., act as a d. **Du·keling,** a petty d.; a duke's child. **Du·keship,** the office or dignity of a d.; also (*joc.*) as a title.

Dukedom (diū·kdəm). 1460. [See -DOM.] **1.** The territory ruled by a duke; a duchy. **2.** The office or dignity of a duke 1534.

Dukery (diū·kəri). 1565. [See -ERY, -RY.] **1.** †A dukedom –1596. **b.** A duchy. (Now only as *nonce-wd.*) 1855. **2.** The residence or estate of a duke; *spec.* (usually *pl.*) a district in Nottinghamshire containing several ducal estates 1837.

‖**Dulcamara** (dɒlkămēᵊ·ră). 1578. [med.L., f. L. *dulcis* sweet + *amara* bitter (sc. *herba*).] *Herb.* and *Pharm.* The Woody Nightshade or Bittersweet, *Solanum dulcamara.* Hence **Dulcama·rin,** *Chem.* the glucoside $C_{22}H_{34}O_{10}$, obtained from d.

†**Dulca·rnon.** ME. [– med.L. *dulcarnon*, corrupted from Arab. *ḏū-l-ḳarnayn* two-horned.] A dilemma (= med.L. *cornutus*, CORNUTE *sb.*); a non-plus; *at d.*, at one's wit's end –1534.

†**Dulce** (dɒls), *a.* 1500. [– L. *dulcis* sweet, or a refash. of DOUCE after the L., through the intermediate *doulce.*] Sweet –1709. Also as *adv.* **Du·lce-ly** *adv.*, **-ness.**

Dulce, *sb.* 1659. [f. prec.] †**1.** Sweetness, gentleness –1728. ‖**2.** [Sp.] A sweet substance; must 1870.

†**Dulce,** *v.* 1579. [refash. from *douce, dulce* v., aphetic f. ADDULCE; cf. DULCE *a.*] *trans.* To sweeten; to soften, soothe –1610.

Dulcet (dɒ·lsĕt). ME. [refash., after L. *dulcis*, of orig. *doucet* – (O)Fr. *doucet*, dim. of *doux*, fem. *douce*; see -ET.]
A. *adj.* **1.** Sweet to the taste or smell. (*Obs.* or *arch.*) **2.** Sweet to the eye, ear, or feelings; pleasing; soothing. Now chiefly of sounds. ME.
1. D. creams MILT. *P. L.* V. 347. **2.** My d. frinde 1567. D. Symphonies and voices sweet MILT.
B. *sb.* †**1.** A dulcet note 1575. †**2.** ? = DOUCET 3. **3.** † = DOUCET 2. **b.** An organ stop resembling the Dulciana, but an octave higher in pitch 1876.

Dulcian (dɒ·lsiăn). 1852. [app. anglicized form of next. Cf. OFr. *doulçaine, doulcine, doucine* 'a sort of flute':] *Mus.* = BASSOON 2.

‖**Dulciana** (dɒlsiɑ·nă). 1776. [– med.L. *dulciana* 'instrumenti musici genus' (Du Cange), f. L. *dulcis* sweet. Cf. prec.] *Mus.* An 8-foot organ stop of a soft string-like tone.

Dulci·fluous, *a. rare.* 1727. [f. late L. *dulcifluus* (f. L. *dulcis* sweet + *-fluus* flowing) + -OUS.] Sweetly or softly flowing.

Dulcify (dɒ·lsifəi), *v.* 1599. [– L. *dulcificare*, f. *dulcis* sweet; see -FY. Cf. Fr. *dulcifier* (XVII).] **1.** *trans.* To render sweet to the taste. †**2.** *Old Chem.* To wash the soluble salts out of; to neutralize the acidity of –1789. Also †*intr.* for *pass.* **3.** To sweeten in temper; to mollify; to appease 1669. Hence **Du:lcifica·tion.**

†**Dulci·loquy.** *rare.* 1623. [= med.L. *dulciloquium*, f. L. *dulcis* sweet + *loqui* speak.] A soft manner of speaking (Dicts.).

Dulcimer (dɒ·lsimər). 1475. [– OFr. *doulcemer, -mele*, corresp. to Sp. †*dulcemele*, It. *dolcemelle*, supposed to represent L. **dulce melos* sweet song.] **a.** A musical instrument, having strings of graduated lengths stretched over a sounding board, which are struck with two hammers held in the hands. **b.** Sometimes applied erron. to wind-instruments, as in *Dan.* 3:10, where 'bagpipe' would be more correct. 'Psaltery' in the same passage signifies 'dulcimer'. 1567.

‖**Dulcinea** (dɒlsi·niˌă, dɒlsinī·ă). 1748. [Sp., f. *dulce* sweet.] The name of Don Quixote's mistress; hence, A mistress, sweetheart.

[**Dulciness**, in Dicts., an error for DULCENESS.]

Dulcite (dɒ·lsəit). 1863. [f. L. *dulcis* sweet + -ITE[1] 4 b.] *Chem.* A saccharine substance ($C_6H_{14}O_6$), isomeric with mannite, obtained from various plants, and known in the crude state as Madagascar manna. Called also **Dulcin, Dulcitol, Dulcose.**

Du·lcitude. 1623. [– L. *dulcitudo*, f. *dulcis* sweet; see -TUDE.] Sweetness. So †**Du·lcity.**

†**Dulcorate** (dɒ·lkoreⁱt), *v.* 1566. [– *dulcorat-*, pa. ppl. stem of late L. *dulcorare*, f. *dulcor* sweetness; see -ATE[3].] To sweeten, DULCIFY –1675. Hence **Dulcora·tion.**

Duledge (diū·lėdʒ). 1721. [Cf. DOWEL.] A dowel or peg for connecting the felloes of the wheels of gun-carriages.

‖**Dulia** (duləi·ă). Also **douleia.** 1617. [med.L. – Gr. δουλεία slavery, servitude, f. δοῦλος slave.] Servitude, service; *spec.* the inferior kind paid by Roman Catholics to saints and angels; opp. to LATRIA.

Dull (dɒl), *a.* ME. [– MLG., MDu. *dul*, corresp. to OE. *dol* stupid (:– **dulaz*), OS. (Du.) *dol*, OHG. *tol* (G. *toll*).] **1.** Not quick in intelligence; obtuse, stupid. In early use, occas.: Fatuous, foolish. **2.** Wanting sensibility. In dial. use, *esp.* Hard of hearing. ME. Of pain, etc.: Indistinctly felt 1725. **3.** Slow in motion or action; not brisk ME. **4.** Of persons, or their mood: Depressed; listless; not lively or cheerful ME. **5.** Causing depression or ennui 1590. **6.** Not sharp or keen; blunt (in *lit.* sense) ME. **7.** Of physical qualities: Not clear, vivid, or intense; obscure; muffled; flat. **b.** Of the weather: Gloomy, overcast ME.

1. Dulle are þi wittes LANGL. A d. child HT. MARTINEAU. **2.** When I..sleepe in d. cold Marble SHAKS. A d. pain 1725. **3.** A d. Sailer DAMPIER, boy HAZLITT. D. trade FAWCETT, Consols 1895. **4.** You are d. to Night; prithee be merry STEELE. **5.** A d. Campaign 1798, curate 1838. **6.** Thy sithe is d. G. HERBERT. **7.** Is not their Clymate foggy, raw, and d. SHAKS. The dawn was d. 1860.

Comb., as *d.-looking*; parasynthetic, as *d.-brained, -browed, -eyed, -headed, -hearted, -sighted, -witted*; also †**d.-house,** a mad-house.

Dull (dɒl), *v.* ME. [f. DULL *a.*; rel. to DILL *v.*] **1.** *trans.* To render sluggish or inert; to stupefy. †**2.** To render dull of mood; the opposite of to enliven –1611. **3.** To render less sensitive or less intense 1552. **4.** To take off the sharpness of, to blunt ME. **5.** To make dim or indistinct; to tarnish. Also *fig.* ME. **6.** *intr.* To become stupid, inert, blunt, dim, etc. ME. †**7.** To grow listless; to tire *of*. (ME. only.)

1. D. not Deuice, by coldnesse and delay SHAKS. **2.** I would not d. you with my song SHAKS. **3.** To d. the sight LYTE, the inward pain TENNYSON. **4.** How quickly the edge of their valour was dulled SOUTH. **6.** The day had dulled somewhat W. BLACK

Dullard (dɒ·lăɹd). ME. [prob. – MDu. *dull-, dollaert*; see DULL *a.*, -ARD.]

A. *sb.* A stupid or dull person; a dolt, a dunce.

B. *adj.* Stupid, dull 1583.

Du·ller. *rare.* 1611. [f. DULL *v.* + -ER[1].] One who or that which dulls.

†**Du·ll-head.** 1549. A slow-witted person; a fool –1624.

Dullish (dɒ·liʃ), *a.* ME. [f. DULL *a.* + -ISH[1].] Somewhat dull.

Dullness, dulness (dɒ·lnės). ME. [f. DULL *a.* + -NESS. The former spelling is the more analogical.] The state or quality of being DULL, q.v.

Dully (dɒ·lˌli), *adv.* ME. [f. DULL *a.* + -LY[2].] In a dull manner (see DULL *a.*).

Honest joggtrot men, who go on smoothly and d. GOLDSM.

Dulness; see DULLNESS.

Dulocracy (diulǫ·krăsi). Also **dou-.** 1656. [– Gr. δουλοκρατία, f. δοῦλος slave; see -CRACY.] Government by slaves.

Dulse (dɒls). 1684. [– Ir., Gael. *duileasg*, = W. *delysg, dylusg*.] An edible seaweed, *Rhodymenia palmata*, having bright red, deeply divided fronds. Also, locally, *Iridæa edulis.*

Duly (diū·li), *adv.* ME. [f. DUE *a.* + -LY[2].] In DUE manner, order, form, or season; see quots.

Rent d. paid STEELE. The Man..who d. weighs an Hour YOUNG. Persons duely qualified 1769.

Duma (dū·mă). [Russ., = thought, council.] In Russia, an elective municipal council; *spec.* the elective legislative council of state of 1905–17.

Dumb (dɒm), *a.* (*sb.*) [OE. *dumb* = OFris., OS. *dumb* (Du. *dom*) stupid, OHG. *tumb* stupid, deaf (G. *dumm* stupid), ON. *dumbr*, Goth. *dumbs* mute; of unkn. origin.] **1.** Destitute of the faculty of speech. Also *fig.* **2.** That does not or will not speak; silent; reticent ME. **3.** Unaccompanied by speech 1538. **4.** Not emitting sound; silent, mute; unheard 1606. **5.** Applied to contrivances which take the place of a human agent. See DUMB-WAITER. 1782. **6.** Silent to the understanding; meaningless; stupid. Now *rare.* 1531. **b.** *U.S. colloq.* (cf. G. *dumm*, Du. *dom*) Foolish, stupid. (Chiefly of persons.) 1823. **7.** Lacking something normally belonging to things of the name 1638. †**8.** Lacking brightness; dull. DE FOE.

1. A dum mouthe SKELTON. The tongue of the dumbe [shall] sing *Isa.* 35:6. *Deaf and d.*: see DEAF *a.* *To strike d.* to deprive for the moment of the faculty of speech. **2.** This Spirit dumbe to vs, will speake to him *Haml.* I. i. 171. **3.** *D. crambo*; see CRAMBO. *D. cake*, a cake made in silence on St. Mark's Eve, by maids, to discover their future husbands. Excellent d. discourse *Temp.* III. iii. 39. **4.** All the while his whip is d. WORDSW. Its thunder made the cataracts d. SHELLEY. *D. peal*: a muffled peal of bells. **6.** 'Twas not dumbe chance SIR T. BROWNE. **7.** *D. ague*, one in which the paroxysms are obscure.

†**B.** *absol.* or as *sb.* **1.** A dumb person –1596. **2.** A state or fit of dumbness –1678.

Comb.: **d.-chalder** or **cleat,** a metal cleat, bolted to the back of the stern-post for one of the rudder-pintles to rest on (Smyth); **d. iron,** either of the two forward ends of the frame-side members of a motor chassis; **-scraping,** 'scraping wet-docks with blunt scrapers' (Smyth); **d. sheave,** a sheaveless block having a hole for a rope to be reeved through; **-tooling** (*Bookbinding*) = *blind tooling*; **d. well,** a well sunk into a porous stratum, to carry off surface water or drainage; a *blind* or *dead* well.

Dumb, *v.* ME. [f. prec. adj.] †**1.** *intr.* To become dumb. (ME. only.) **2.** *trans.* To render dumb, silent, or unheard 1608.

Dumb barge. 1869. [DUMB *a.* 7.] A barge without mast or sails, as a Thames lighter.

Dumb-bell (dɒ·mbel), *sb.* 1711. **1.** Formerly, An apparatus, like that for swinging a church-bell, but without the bell, 'rung' for exercise. **2.** A short bar, weighted at each end with a roundish knob; used in pairs, and swung for exercise 1785. **3.** An object of the shape of a dumb-bell; *e.g.* certain crystals found in the urine; also, a diplococcus 1864.

Dumb cane. 1696. A W. Indian araceous plant, *Dieffenbachia seguine*, which, when chewed, swells the tongue and destroys the power of speech.

Dumbfound, dumfound (dɒmfau·nd), *v.* 1653. [app. f. DUMB *a.* + (CON)FOUND.] *trans.* To strike dumb; to confound; to nonplus. Hence **Dumb-, dumfou·nder** *v.* in same sense.

Dumble-, in names of insects, app. = DUMMEL, but varying with *bumble-, humble-.*

Dumbledore, dumble-dore (dɒ·mb'lˌdǭ³ɹ). *local.* 1787. [f. DUMBLE- + DOR *sb.*[1]] A humble- or bumble-bee; also *dial.* a cockchafer.

Dumbly (dɒ·mli), *adv.* 1552. [See -LY[2].] In a dumb manner; speechlessly, mutely.

Dumbness (dɒ·mnės). ME. [f. DUMB *a.* + -NESS.] Dumb quality or condition; inability to speak; silence, muteness.

There was speed in their dumbnesse SHAKS.

Dumb show. 1561. **1.** Formerly, A part of a play represented by action without speech. **2.** Significant gesture without speech 1588.

2. Expressing in dumb Show those Sentiments [etc.] ADDISON.

Dumb-waiter. 1755. [See DUMB *a.* 7.] **1.** An upright pole with revolving trays or shelves for holding dishes, cruets, etc. **2.** (*U.S.*) A movable frame or lift, by which dishes, etc. are passed from one room or story of a house to another 1864.

Dumdum (dɒ·mdɒm). 1897. [*Dum Dum*, name of military station and arsenal near Calcutta.] orig. *Dum Dum bullet*: A soft-nosed bullet which expands on impact.

Dumfound, -er, var. DUMBFOUND, -ER.

Dummel (dɒ·mĕl), *a. dial.* 1570. [app. f. DUMB.] Stupid, dull. Also *sb.*

†**Du·mmerer.** 1567. [f. DUMB *a.*] *Cant.* A beggar who pretended to be dumb –1834.

Dummy, dumby (dɒ·mi), *sb.* 1598. [f. DUMB *a.* + -Y[6]. Cf. BLACKY, etc.] **1.** A dumb person (*colloq.*). **2.** At *Whist*, An imaginary player whose hand is exposed, and played by his partner; a game so played 1736. **b.** *Bridge.* The partner of the player who makes the first call in the accepted declaration, or his hand 1895. **3.** A person who has no active part in affairs; a dolt, blockhead 1796. **4.** One who is a mere tool of another 1866. **5.** A counterfeit object, as a sham package, a lay figure, etc. for showing clothes, a baby's indiarubber teat; etc. 1845. **6.** *attrib.* or *adj.* Counterfeit, sham 1843.

2. *Double d.*: a game in which two hands are exposed so that each of the two players manages two hands. **5.** Phr. *To give* or *sell the d.* (Rugby Football): to deceive an opponent by feigning to pass the ball. **6.** *D. whist*: see 2.

Dump (dɒmp), *sb.*[1] 1523. [prob. of LG. or Du. origin and a fig. use of MDu. *domp* exhalation, haze, mist, rel. to DAMP.] †**1.** A fit of abstraction, a reverie; perplexity; absence of mind. (Often in *pl.*) –1698. **2.** A fit of melancholy or depression; now only in *pl.* (*colloq.* and *joc.*): Low spirits 1529. †**3.** A mournful or plaintive melody or song; a tune; *occas.*, a kind of dance –1852.

1. [They] were in a great dumpe and perplexitie J. HOOKER. **2.** His head, like one in doleful d., Between his knees BUTLER. **3.** Some good old dumpe that Chaucers mistresse knew SIDNEY.

Dump, *sb.*[2] 1770. [app. identical with the first element in *dumpling*.] A familiar term for objects of a dumpy shape.

a. A leaden counter, used by boys in games. **b.** A name of certain small coins; *esp.* a coin worth 1*s.* 3*d.* formerly current in Australia; hence (*slang* or *colloq.*) a small coin or amount; in *pl.* money. **c.** A bolt or nail used in ship-building (also *d.-bolt, -nail*). **d.** A globular sweetmeat, a bull's-eye.

Dump, *sb.*[3] *local.* 1788. [perh. from Norse; cf. Norw. *dump* pit, pool.] A deep hole in the bed of a river or pond.

Dump, *sb.*[4] 1825. [f. DUMP *v.*[1]] **1.** (Chiefly *U.S.*) A pile or heap of refuse, etc. dumped or thrown down 1871. **b.** A temporary depôt of ammunitions of war, etc.; hence, material deposited for use later, or the place of such deposit 1915. **2.** (Chiefly *U.S.*) A place where refuse, *esp.* from a mine or quarry, is dumped 1872. **3.** A dull, abrupt blow; a thud; a bump 1825.

Dump (dɒmp), *v.*[1] ME. [perh. from Norse; cf. Da. *dumpe*, Norw. *dumpa* fall suddenly, fall plump. But in mod. use partly echoic; cf. *thump*.] †**I.** *intr.* and *trans.* To plunge (down) ME. **II. 1.** *trans.* (Chiefly *U.S.*) To throw down in a lump or mass, as in tilting anything out of a cart; to shoot (rubbish, etc.); to fling down or drop with a bump. Also *fig.* 1828. **b.** To throw on the market in large quantities and at low prices; to send (surplus goods) to a foreign market for sale at low prices 1884. **c.** To deposit in or as in a dump (DUMP *sb.*[4] 1 b) 1919. **2.** *intr.* To strike with a thud 1832. **3.** *trans.* To compress (wool-bales), as by hydraulic pressure. (*Australia.*) 1872.

Hence **Du·mping** *vbl. sb.*; *concr.* that which is dumped; *attrib.* used for dumping, as *d.-bucket, -cart, -ground*, etc.

†**Dump,** *v.*² 1530. [f. DUMP *sb.*¹] **1.** *intr.* To fall into a reverie; to muse. **b.** To be in the dumps. –1590. **2.** *trans.* To cast into melancholy, grieve, cast down –1614.

Du·mpage. *U.S.* 1864. [f. DUMP *v.*¹ + -AGE.] The work of dumping; the privilege of dumping on a particular spot; the fee paid for the privilege.

Dumper (dɒ·mpəɹ). *U.S.* 1881. [-ER¹.] **a.** One who dumps. **b.** A dumping-cart or truck.

Dumpish (dɒ·mpiʃ), *a.* 1545. [f. DUMP *sb.*¹ + -ISH¹.] †**1.** Slow-witted; inert; insensible –1682. **2.** Dejected; in the dumps 1562. Hence **Du·mpish-ly** *adv.*, **-ness.**

Dumple (dɒ·mp'l), *v. rare.* 1625. [perh. f. DUMP *sb.*², or DUMPY *a.*², after *crumple*; see -LE.] To bend or compress into a dumpy shape.

Dumpling (dɒ·mpliŋ). 1600. [app. f. DUMP *sb.*² + -LING¹; *dumpling*, however, is recorded very much earlier.] **1.** A pudding consisting of a mass of dough, more or less globular in form, either plain and boiled, or inclosing fruit and boiled or baked. **2.** A dumpy animal or person 1617.

Dumpty (dɒ·mpti), *a.* (*sb.*) 1847. By-form of DUMPY *a.*²

Dumpy (dɒ·mpi), *a.*¹ 1618. [f. DUMP *a.*¹ + -Y¹.] Dejected.

Dumpy (dɒ·mpi), *a.*² (*sb.*) 1750. [f. DUMP *sb.*² + -Y¹.]

A. Short and stout; as, *d. level* (Surveying), a spirit-level having a short telescope with a large aperture.

B. *sb.* **a.** A dumpy person or animal; *spec.* one of a breed of short-legged fowls. **b.** Short for *d. level*; see above 1808.

Dun (dɒn), *a.* [OE. *dun(n* = OS. *dun* date-brown, nut-brown, prob. rel. to OS. *dosan*, OHG. *tusin* (cf. DUSK); prob. not of Celtic origin.] **1.** Of a dull or dingy brown colour; now *esp.* dull greyish brown, like the hair of a mouse. **2.** Dark, dusky (from absence of light); murky. (Chiefly *poet.*) ME.

1. Its d. or iron-grey colour HUXLEY. **2.** D. Night has veil'd the solemn view COLLINS.

Comb.: **d.-bar,** a d.-coloured moth (*Cosmia trapezina*) having two bars on the fore-wings; **d. cow** (*local*), the shagreen ray, *Raia fullonica*; **d. cur** (*local*), the pochard = DUN-BIRD. Hence **Du·nness. Du·nnish** *a.*

Dun (dɒn), *sb.*¹ ME. [subst. use of prec.] **1.** Dun colour 1568. **2.** A dun horse. Formerly, a quasi-proper name for any horse. ME. **3.** *Angling.* A name for various dusky-coloured flies 1681.

Phr. *D.* [the horse] *is in the mire*, i.e. things are at a stand-still CHAUCER.

Dun, *sb.*² 1628. [abbrev. of †*dunkirk* privateer; see DUNKIRK.] **1.** One who duns. **2.** An act of dunning, *esp.* for debt; a demand for payment 1673.

1. An Vniversitie Dunne..Hee is a sore beleaguerer of Chambers EARLE.

‖**Dun,** *sb.*³ Also **doon.** 1605. [Ir. and Gael. *dun* (dun), hill, hill-fort, W. *din.*] An ancient hill-fortress or fortified eminence.

Dun (dɒn), *v.*¹ [OE. *dunnian*, f. *dun(n*, DUN *a.*] *trans.* To make dun, dusky, or dingy. **b.** In New England, To cure (codfish) in a particular way, by which they become of a dun colour, and are termed *dunfish* 1828.

†**Dūn,** *v.*² ME. [– ON. *duna* thunder, give a hollow sound, whence also DIN *sb.* and *v.*] *intr.* = DIN *v.* 1. –1483.

Dun (dɒn), *v.*³ 1626. [f. DUN *sb.*²] **1.** *trans.* To press repeatedly and persistently, to importune; *esp.* for money due. **2.** *transf.* To pester, plague 1659. **3.** Assoc. w. DIN *v.* 1753.

1. I dunn'd him for money and could not get it 1681.

Dun-bird. 1766. [f. DUN *a.* + BIRD.] The pochard, *Fuligula ferina.*

Dunce (dɒns), *sb.* 1527. [From John *Duns* Scotus, the scholastic theologian, called the Subtle Doctor, who died in 1308. The *Duns-men* or *Dunses* were a predominating sect, until the 16th c., when the system was discredited by the humanists and the reformers.] †**1.** The name *Duns* used attrib. –1641. †**2.** A copy of the works of Duns Scotus; a text-book embodying his teaching; a gloss by him or after his manner –1633. **3.** An adherent of Duns Scotus; a hair-splitting reasoner; a cavilling sophist. Now *Hist.* 1577. †**4.** A pedant –1642. **5.** One who shows no capacity for learning; a dullard, blockhead 1577.

1. †*Duns man* = sense 3. **4.** A d., void of learning but full of books FULLER. **5.** Blockhead! d.! ass! coxcomb ARBUTHNOT.

Hence †**Dunce** *v.* to puzzle; to make a d. of. **Du·ncedom,** the domain of dunces; a dunce's condition or character; dunces collectively. **Du·ncely** *adv.* as a d., or †a follower of Duns Scotus. **Du·ncery, dunsery,** the practice or character of a †Scotist, or of a d. **Du·ncical** *a.* (now *rare*), of or pertaining to duncery. **Du·ncify** *v.* to make a d. of (*rare*). **Du·ncish** *a.* d.-like.

Dunch (dɒnʃ), *v. Sc.* and *n. dial.* ME. [Of unkn. origin.] *trans.* To push with a short rapid blow; now *esp.* to jog with the elbow. So **Dunch** *sb.*

Dunch, *a.* Now *dial.* 1574. [Of unkn. origin; cf. DUNNY.] **1.** Deaf. **2.** Blind 16.. **3.** Heavy, as bread 1842.

Dunciad (dɒ·nsiæ̆d). 1728. [f. DUNCE *sb.*; see -AD.] The epic of dunces; a poem by Pope. Also, the commonwealth of dunces.

Dunder (dɒ·ndəɹ). 1793. [Also *dander* (see DANDER *sb.*³), f. Sp. *redundar* overflow.] The lees or dregs of cane-juice, used in the W. Indies in the fermentation of rum.

Dunderbolt, dial. f. THUNDERBOLT.

Dunderhead (dɒ·ndəɹhed). 1625. [perh. to be assoc. with dial. *dunner* resounding noise.] A ponderously stupid person; a numskull. Hence **Du·nder-headed** *a.* So **Du·nderpate.**

Dun-diver. 1678. [f. DUN *a.* + DIVER 2.] **a.** The female and young male of the goosander (*Mergus merganser*). **b.** *U.S.* The ruddy duck.

Dundreary (dɒndrīᵊ·rĭ). Name of a character in T. Taylor's comedy *Our American Cousin* (1858); *D. whiskers,* long side whiskers without a beard.

Dune (diūn). 1790. [– (O)Fr. *dune* – MDu. *dūne* (Du. *duin*) = OE. *dūn* DOWN *sb.*¹] A mound, ridge, or hill of wind-drifted sand, esp. on the sea-coast.

By the aid of embankments and the sand dunes of the coast LYELL.

Du·nfish, dun-fish. *U.S. local.* 1828. [f. DUN *a.*] Cod cured by dunning (see DUN *v.*¹).

Dung (dɒŋ), *sb.* [OE. *dung* = OFris. *dung*, MDu. *dung(e*, OHG. *tunga* manuring (G. *dung* manure); cf. Sw. *dynga* muck, dung, Da. *dynge* heap, pile, Icel. *dyngja* heap, dung; of unkn. origin.] **1.** Manure. **2.** (As constituting the usual manure.) The excrement of animals: as *cow-, horse-d.*, etc. ME. Also *transf.* and *fig.*

Comb.: **d.-bath** (Dyeing), a mixture of d., usually that of cows, with chalk in warm water, used to remove superfluous mordant from printed calico; **-beetle,** the dor-beetle; also, any of the group of beetles which roll up balls of d.; **-bird,** (*a*) the hoopoe; (*b*) = *dung-hunter*; **-chafer** = *dung-beetle*; **-fly,** a two-winged fly of the genus *Scatophaga*, feeding in ordure; **-hunter, -teaser,** the Dirt-bird or Dirty Allan.

Dung (dɒŋ). *v.* [OE. *dyngian*, f. *dung* (prec.). In ME. assim. to, or formed anew from, the sb.] **1.** *trans.* To manure with dung. **2.** *intr.* Of animals: To eject excrement 1470. **3.** *Calico-printing.* To immerse in a dung-bath in order to remove superfluous mordant 1836.

‖**Dungaree** (dɒ·ŋgărī). **Also dungeree.** 1696. [Hindi *dungrī.*] A kind of coarse inferior Indian calico; *pl.* overalls of such material.

Du·ng-cart. ME. A cart used to convey manure.

Dungeon (dɒ·ndʒən), *sb.* ME. [– (O)Fr. *donjon* :– Gallo-Rom. **domnio, -ōn-* 'lord's tower' or 'mistress tower' (in med.L. *dangio, dunjo, donjo*, etc.), f. L. *dominus* master, lord.] **1.** The great tower or keep of a castle. (Now usually spelt **donjon.**) **2.** A strong close cell; a deep dark vault ME. Also *transf.* and *fig.*

1. The noble tour of Ylion That of the citee was the cheef d. CHAUCER. **2.** Beneath the castle I could discern vast dungeons BP. BERKELEY. A d. of learning (*mod. Sc.*). *Comb.*: **d.-keep, -tower** = sense 1.

Dungeon (dɒ·ndʒən), *v.* 1615. [f. prec. sb.] *trans.* To shut *up* in or as in a dungeon. Hence **Du·ngeoner,** one who or that which dungeons.

Du·ng-fork. ME. **1.** A kind of pitchfork used to lift or spread dung. **2.** *Entom.* A fæcifork.

Dunghill (dɒ·ŋhil), *sb.* ME. **1.** A heap of dung or refuse. **2.** *transf.* and *fig.*, *esp.* as the type of the basest station 1526. **3.** *attrib.* Of or pertaining to a dunghill; fit for a dunghill; cowardly, as the *d. cock* ME.

1. Mud hovels, with their dunghills..around them LEVER. **2.** The condition from which this son of a d. sprung 1768. Out, d.! dar'st thou braue a Nobleman SHAKS. *Comb.*: **d.-cock, -fowl, -hen,** common barndoor fowls, as dist. from the game-cock, etc.

Dungy (dɒ·ŋi), *a.* ME. [See -Y¹.] **1.** Of the nature of dung; abounding in dung 1606. **2.** Filthy or vile as dung.

1. Our dungie earth alike Feeds Beast as Man *Ant. & Cl.* I. i. 35.

‖**Duniwassal** (dū·ni,wa·săl). 1565. [– Gael. *duine uasal*, i.e. *duine* man, *uasal* gentle- or noble-born.] A (Highland) gentleman of secondary rank; a cadet of a family of rank.

Dunker (dɒ·ŋkəɹ), **Tunker** (tɒ·ŋkəɹ). 1756. [– G. *dunker*, dial. var. of *tunker*, f. *dunken, tunken* (cf. OHG. *dunkōn*, MHG. *tunken, dunken*, G. *tunken*); see -ER¹. So (*U.S.*) *dunk* dip.] A member of a body of German-American Baptists, who administer baptism only to adults, and by triple immersion. var. **Du·nkard.**

Dunkirk (dɒ·nkəɹk). 1602. [Cf. DUN *sb.*²] Name of a town on the coast of French Flanders; hence, a privateer from that town. Also *transf.* and *fig.* Hence **Du·nkirker,** a D., or one of its crew.

Dunlin (dɒ·nlin). 1531. [prob. for **dunling*, f. DUN *a.* + -LING¹. Cf. DUNNOCK.] The red-backed sandpiper (*Tringa alpina*). Also an Amer. species (*T. pacifica*).

Dunnage (dɒ·nĕdʒ), *sb.* [In AL. *dennagium* (XIII); *dennage* (XIV), *donage* (XV), *dynnage* (XVII), *dunnage* (XVIII); perh. conn. w. AL. *dennare, deniare* (XIV) stow, which could, however, be a back-formation from *dennagium.*] *Naut.* Brushwood, mats, or any light material, stowed among and beneath the cargo of a vessel to keep it from injury by chafing or wet. Hence **Du·nnage** *v.* to stow or secure with d. Also *intr.*

Dunner (dɒ·nəɹ). 1700. [f. DUN *v.*³] One who duns another, *esp.* for money due; a dun.

Dunnock (dɒ·nŏk). 1475. [app. f. DUN *a.* + -OCK; from its brown plumage. Cf. DUNLIN.] **1.** The hedge-sparrow (*Accentor modularis*). **2.** (form *dinnick*) The Wryneck (*local*) 1863.

Du·nny, *a. dial.* 1708. [Of unkn. origin; cf. DUNCH *a.*] Dull of hearing, deaf; stupid. Hence **Du·nniness.**

Duns, dunse, etc., obs. ff. DUNCE, etc.

Dunstable (dɒ·nstăb'l). 1549. [A town in Bedfordshire.] †**1.** *attrib.* in phr. *D. way*, app. referring orig. to the road from London to Dunstable, a part of the Roman Road called Watling Street; used proverbially as a type of directness and plainness –1744. †**b.** Hence as *adj.*: Direct, plain, downright –1817. †**c.** as *sb.* in phr. *Plain* (or *downright*) *D.*: plain language –1824. **2.** *attrib.* Made at D., or in the D. manner, as a kind of straw plait 1849.

1. As plain as D. Road FULLER. That's the plain d. of the matter, Miss! RICHARDSON.

Dunstone (dɒ·n,stōᵘn). 1777. [f. DUN *a.*] *Geol.* Stone of a dun or dull brown colour; as magnesian limestone, ironstone, sandstone, and sometimes dolerite.

Dunt (dɒnt), *sb. Sc.* and *dial.* ME. [perh. a var. of DINT *sb.*] **a.** A firm but dull-sounding blow, **b.** A beat of the heart 1768.

Dunt (dɒnt), *v. Sc.* and *dial.* 1570. [f. prec.] **1.** To knock with a dull sound. Also *absol.* and *intr.* **2.** *intr.* Of the heart: To beat violently 1724.

Dunter (dʊ·ntəɹ). *local.* 1693. [f. DUNT *v.*] **1.** The eider-duck. Also *d.-goose, -duck.* **2.** A porpoise 1825.

||**Duo** (dū·o). 1590. [It. *duo* (whence Fr. *duo* duet) – L. *duo* two.] *Mus.* A duet.

Duo-, L. *duo* = Gr. δύο (*dyo*), 'two'; a combining form. Sometimes improp. used for BI- (or in Gr. words DI-); *e.g.* **Duoca·meral** = bicameral; **Du·oglott** = diglott; etc.

Duode·cagon, -he·dron = DODECAGON, -HEDRON.

Duodecahe·dral, *a.* = DODECAHEDRAL.

Duodecim-, L. *duodecim* twelve, an initial element; *e.g.* in **Duodeci·mfid** *a.* [L. *-fidus* cleft], divided into twelve parts.

Duodecimal (diuˌode·simăl). 1714. [f. L. *duodecimus* twelfth + -AL¹. Cf. DECIMAL.]

A. *adj.* Relating to twelfth parts or to the number twelve; proceeding by twelves 1727.

B. *sb.* **Duodecimals,** a method of multiplying together quantities given in feet, inches, etc., without reducing them to one denomination; also called *cross-multiplication.*

||**Duodecimo** (diūˌode·simo) 1658. [L. (*in*) *duodecimo* in a twelfth (*sc.* of a sheet).] **1.** The size of a book, or of a page of a book, in which each leaf is one-twelfth of a sheet: usu. abbreviated 12mo. **2.** A volume of this size 1712. **3.** *attrib.* or *adj.* 1777.

2. The Author of a D. ADDISON. **3.** Lady Betty.. was taking the dust..in a sort of d. phaeton SHERIDAN.

Duode·cuple, *a.* [f. L. *duodecim* twelve, after DECUPLE.] Twelvefold. ARBUTHNOT.

Duodenal (diūˌodī·năl), *a.* 1843. [f. DUODENUM + -AL¹.] Pertaining or relating to the duodenum.

Duode·nal, *sb.* 1874. [f. DUODENE + -AL¹.] *Mus.* The symbol of the root of a DUODENE.

Duodenary (diuˌodīnări). 1681. [– L. *duodenarius* containing twelve; see -ARY¹.]

A. *adj.* **1.** *Arith.* Pertaining to twelve; proceeding by twelves 1857. **2.** *Mus.* Relating to duodenes 1874.

1. The d. system of calculation 1890.

B. *sb.* †**1.** A period of twelve years 1681. **2.** *Mus.* A keyboard constructed according to duodenes 1874.

Duodene (diū·odīn). 1874. [f. med.L. *duodena* a group of twelve, f. L. *duodeni* twelve each.] *Mus.* Name for a group of twelve notes having certain fixed relations of pitch, in a proposed scheme for obtaining exact intonation on a keyboard instrument.

||**Duodenum** (diūˌodī·nʊ̆m). ME. [med.L. (so called from its length, = *duodenum digitorum* space of twelve fingers' breadth), f. *duodeni* (see prec.).] *Anat.* The first portion of the small intestine immediately below the stomach, terminating in the jejunum. Hence **Duodeni·tis,** inflammation of the d.; **Duodeno·stomy** [Gr. στόμα], **Duodeno·tomy** [Gr. -τομία], the opening of the d. through the abdominal walls, to introduce food.

Duologue (diū·ŏlǫg). 1864. [irreg. f. L. *duo* or Gr. δύο two, after *monologue.*] A dialogue; *spec.* a dramatic piece spoken by two actors. Also *attrib.*

||**Duomo** (dwōmo). 1549. [It.; see DOME *sb.*] A cathedral church (in Italy); cf. DOM².

Vignettes..Of tower or d., sunny-sweet TENNYSON.

Dup (dʊp), *v. dial.* or *arch.* 1547. [contr. from *do up*; cf. *don, doff*, etc.] *trans.* To open. *Haml.* IV. v. 51.

Dupable (diū·păb'l), *a.* Also **dupeable.** 1833. [f. DUPE *v.* + -ABLE.] Capable of being duped. Also as *sb.*

Dupe (diūp), *sb.* 1681. [– Fr. *dupe*, earlier †*duppe*, said (XV) to be a cant term; joc. application of dial. *dupe* hoopoe (of obscure origin) from the bird's stupid appearance.] One who allows himself to be deluded; a victim of deception.

The ready d. of astrologers and soothsayers SCOTT.

Dupe, *v.* 1704. [f. DUPE *sb.*, after Fr. *duper.*] *trans.* To make a dupe of; to delude; to cheat.

I will not concur to d. and mislead a senseless multitude. Hence **Du·per,** a deluder. **Du·pery,** the act or practice of duping; duped condition.

Du·pion. ? *Obs.* 1828. [– Fr. *doupion* = It. *doppione*, f. *doppio* double.] 'A double cocoon formed by two silk-worms' (Simmonds).

Duplation (diuplēⁱ·ʃən). ME. [– late L. *duplatio*, f. *duplat-*, pa. ppl. stem of L. *duplare* double; see -ION.] The operation of doubling.

Duple (diū·p'l). 1542. [– L. *duplus*, f. *duo* two.]

A. *adj.* Double, twofold. *Obs.* in *gen.* sense: in *Math.* applied to the proportion of two quantities one of which is double the other; in *Mus.*, to time having two beats in the bar.

†**B.** *sb.* = DOUBLE *sb.* 1. –1787. So †**Du·ple** *v.* to double. Hence †**Du·plet,** doublet. DRYDEN.

Duplex (diū·pleks), *a.* 1817. [– L. *duplex*, f. *duo* two + *plic-* fold.] **1.** Composed of two parts; twofold. **2.** *Electric Telegraphy.* **a.** Applied to any system by which two messages can be sent along the same wire at the same time. **b.** Now restricted to systems in which two messages are sent simultaneously in opposite directions: opp. to DIPLEX, q. v. 1873.

1. *D. escapement*, one in which the escape-wheel has both spur and crown teeth; *d. gas-burner*, one having two jets so arranged as to combine the two flames into one; *d. lamp*, one with two wicks; *d. lathe*, one having a cutting-tool at the back opposite to that in front, and in an inverted position.

Du·plex, *v.* 1880. [f. prec. 2.] *Electric Telegraphy.* To render duplex; to arrange (a wire or cable) so that two messages can be sent along it at the same time.

Duplexity (diuple·ksĭti). *rare.* [f. DUPLEX *a.* + -ITY.] The quality of being double; doubleness; = DUPLICITY 2.

Duplicate (diū·plikĕt). ME. [– L. *duplicatus*, pa. pple. of *duplicare*, f. *duplus* double; see -ATE².]

A. *adj.* **1.** Double, twofold, consisting of two corresponding parts. **2.** Double, doubled 1548. **3.** That is the counterpart of something; said of any number of copies or specimens 1812.

3. The d. copy of Florio, which the British Museum purchased EMERSON. Phr. *D. proportion, ratio*: the proportion or ratio of squares, in relation to that of the radical quantities.

B. *sb.* [the adj. used absol.] **1.** One of two things exactly alike, so that one is the double of the other; *esp.* that which is made from or after the other. **a.** A second copy of a letter or official document, having the legal force of the original. **b.** The second copy of a bill drawn in two parts; a 'second of exchange'. **c.** A pawnbroker's ticket. 1532. **2.** *gen.* A thing which is the exact double of another reckoned the original; one of two or more specimens exactly or virtually alike 1701.

1. Two duplicats thereof to be signed 1575. **2.** We will part with duplicates [of coins] HEARNE. As if a man should suddenly encounter his own d. LAMB. Phr. *In d.*: in two exactly corresponding copies.

Duplicate (diū·plikeⁱt), *v.* 1623. [– *duplicat-*, pa. ppl. stem of L. *duplicare*; see prec., -ATE³.] **1.** *trans.* To double; to make double or twofold; to redouble. **2.** To make or provide in duplicate; to repeat 1860. Also †*intr.* for *refl.* **3.** *Eccl.* (*absol.*) To celebrate the Eucharist twice in one day 1865.

2. To provide against the possibility of a breakdown..all the vital parts are duplicated 1880.

Duplication (diūplikēⁱ·ʃən). ME. [– (O)Fr. *duplication* or L. *duplicatio*, f. as prec.; see -ION.] **1.** The action of doubling. **b.** The repetition of an action or thing; division into two by natural growth or spontaneous division 1590. **2.** A duplicate copy or version; a counterpart 1872. **3.** *Civil* and *Canon Law.* A pleading on the part of the defendant in reply to the replication 1622. †**4.** *Anat.* A folding, a doubling; *concr.* a fold –1748. **5.** *Eccl.* 'A second celebration of the Eucharist by the same priest on the same day' 1866.

1. The d. of their joys JER. TAYLOR. Phr. *D. of the cube* (Math.): the problem of finding the side of a cube having double the volume of a given cube; see DELIAN *a.*

Duplicative (diū·plikĕtiv). 1870. [f. as prec. + -IVE.] **a.** *adj.* Having the quality of doubling; producing two instead of one. **b.** *sb.* A doubling addition 1884.

Du·plica:to-, comb. f. L. *duplicatus*, prefixed to adjs. in the sense 'doubly'; *esp.* in *Bot.*, as *d.-dentate, -pinnate*, applied to toothed, etc. leaves of which the teeth are themselves again dentate, etc.

Duplicator (diū·plikeⁱtəɹ). 1894. [f. DUPLICATE *v.* + -OR 2.] A machine for producing copies. Also *attrib.*

Duplicature (diū·plikeⁱtiūɹ). 1686. [– Fr. *duplicature*, f. as prec. + *-ure* -URE.] A doubling; a fold. (Chiefly in *Anat.*)

Duplicidentate (diū:pliside·ntĕt), *a.* [f. L. *duplici-* (comb. f. *duplex*) + DENTATE.] *Zool.* Belonging to the *Duplicidentata*, a division of rodents characterized by two pairs of upper incisor teeth.

Duplicity (diūpli·sĭti). ME. [– (O)Fr. *duplicité* or late L. *duplicitas*, f. *duplex*, *duplic-* DUPLEX; see -ITY.] **1.** The quality of being double in action or conduct; deceitfulness, double-dealing. (The most usual sense.) **2.** *lit.* The quality of being double; doubleness 1589. **3.** *Law.* Double pleading 1848.

1. The d. of the King's conduct D'ISRAELI *Chas. I*, I. vi. 206. **2.** The d. of Saturn's ring 1867.

Duppa, dupper, var. DUBBA.

Duppy (dʊ·pi). 1774. [Afr.] Name among W. Ind. Negroes for a ghost or spirit.

Dura (diūᵊ·ră). 1882. [L. adj. fem.] **1.** Short for DURA MATER. **2.** = DURAMEN.

Durability (diūᵊrăbi·lĭti). ME. [– Fr. †*durabilité* – late L. *durabilitas*, f. *durabilis*; see next, -ITY.] The quality of being durable (senses 1 and 2).

Durable (diūᵊ·răb'l), *a.* ME. [– (O)Fr. *durable* – L. *durabilis*, f. *durare* last, ENDURE; see -ABLE.] **1.** Capable of continuing in existence; persistent; permanent. **2.** Able to withstand change, decay, or wear ME. †**3.** Able to endure toil, etc. –1616.

1. D. remedie 1450, compunction HUME, designs ALISON. **2.** Inscriptions are more d. incised than in relief 1874. **Du·rableness** (*rare*). **Du·rably** *adv.*

Dural (diūᵊ·răl), *a.* 1888. [f. DURA (*dura mater*) + -AL¹.] Of or pertaining to the dura mater.

Duralumin [diuræ·liumin). 1910. [Trade name; – G., f. *Düren* (in the Rhineland) + *alumin(ium* ALUMINIUM.] A light aluminium alloy, remarkable for its strength and hardness, used esp. in aircraft building.

||**Dura mater** (diūᵊ·ră mēⁱ·təɹ). ME. [med.L. = hard mother; lit. tr. of Arab.; 'mother', etc. in Arab. being used to indicate relations between things.] The dense, tough, outermost membranous envelope of the brain and spinal cord.

||**Duramen** (diurēⁱ·men). 1837. [– L. *duramen* hardness, f. *durare* harden.] The heart-wood of an exogenous tree.

Durance (diūᵊ·răns). 1494. [– OFr. *durance*, f. *durer*; see next -ANCE.] †**1.** Duration; lastingness –1698. †**2.** Lasting quality –1847. †**3.** A stout durable cloth. (Cf. DURANT *sb.*) –1709. **4.** Endurance (of toil, etc.) (*arch.*) 1579. **5.** Forced confinement, imprisonment; constraint. Now *esp.* in phr. *in d. vile.* 1513.

2. The d. of a granite ledge EMERSON. **4.** Hardinesse..acquired by practise of their bodies to d. SPEED. **5.** St. Paul being at d. in Rome SANDERSON. var. †**Durancy** (*rare*) in sense 1.

Durant (diūᵊ·rănt). 1455. [– (O)Fr. *durant* pres. pple. of *durer*; see DURE *v.*, -ANT.]

†**A.** *adj.* Lasting, continuous; current –1653.

B. *sb.* A variety of tammy, called by some 'everlasting' 1766.

||**Durante** (diuræ·nti), *pres. pple.* and *prep.* 1556. The abl. sing. of L. pres. pple. *durans*, used in absol. constructions. **a.** In L. phr. *durante beneplacito*, during pleasure; *d. vita*, during life 1621. †**b.** Hence, in Eng. context, = DURING –1832.

Duration (diurēⁱ·ʃən). ME. [– OFr. *duration* – med.L. *duratio*, f. *durat-*, pa. ppl. stem of L. *durare* harden, endure; see DURE *v.*, -ION.] **1.** Lasting, continuance in time; the continuance of time; the time during which anything continues. †**b.** Durableness –1753. †**2.** Hardening –1657.

1. The peace will probably be of short d. COWPER. The average d. of human life..[in] great cities 1862.

||**Durbar** (dʊ̄·ɹbāɹ). *E. Ind.* 1609. [– Urdu – Pers. *darbār* court.] **1.** A public audience or levee held by a native prince, or by a British

governor or viceroy in India. **2.** The hall or place of audience 1793.
1. The Maharanee held durbars daily 1862. A grand D. was held..by Mr. Crosthwaite the Commissioner at Mandalay 1887.

Dure (diūᵊɹ), *v. arch.* and *dial.* ME. [– (O)Fr. *durer* – L. *durare* harden, endure, f. *durus* hard.] **1.** *intr.* To last; to continue (*arch.*) †**2.** To extend in space –1500. †**3.** *trans.* To endure –1598. Hence †**Du·reful** *a.* lasting. †**Du·reless** *a.* transient.

Dure (diū·ᵊɹ), *a. arch.* ME. [– (O)Fr. *dur* – L. *durus* hard.] **1.** Hard. (*lit.* and *fig.*) †**2.** *Mus.* Sharp. [So formerly Fr. *dur.*] 1609.
Blows with bils most d. was delt *Flodden F.* viii. 80.

Dureresque (dürĕre·sk), *a.* 1860. [See -ESQUE.] In the style or manner of Albert Dürer (1471–1528), famous both as painter and as engraver on copper and on wood.

Duress, duresse (diure·s, diūᵊ·rés), *sb.* ME. [– OFr. *duresse* :– L. *duritia*, f. *durus* hard; see -ESS².] †**1.** Hardness; severity; hardiness of endurance; firmness –1651. †**2.** Harsh treatment; affliction –1673. **3.** = DURANCE 5. ME. **4.** Constraint; in *Law*, Constraint illegally exercised to force a person to perform an act 1596.
3. What, then, is the degree of duresse which is to constitute imprisonment WELLINGTON. **4.** The man was under duresse, and his act not voluntary, but imposed upon him by force TUCKER. Hence †**Du·ress** *v.* to subject to d. †**Dure·ssor,** he who subjects another to d.

†**Duret.** [Of unkn. origin.] A kind of dance. BEAUM. & FL.

‖**Dure·tto.** Also **-etta, ette.** 1619. [It., dim. of *duro* hard.] A coarse stout stuff. Also *attrib.* –1660.

‖**Durgah** (dɒrgā). *E. Ind.* 1793. [Pers. *dargāh* royal court.] In India, The shrine of a (Moslem) saint.

‖**Durian** (durī·ăn, diūᵊ·riăn). 1588. [Malay *durian*, f. *dūrī* thorn, prickle.] The oval or globular fruit of *Durio zibethinus*, N.O. *Sterculiaceæ*; it has a hard prickly rind and luscious cream-coloured pulp, of a strong civet odour, but agreeable taste; also, the tree.

During (diūᵊ·riŋ), *pres. pple.* and *prep.* (*conj.*) ME. †**1.** The pres. pple. of DURE *v.* = enduring, lasting, continuing; used in Fr. and Eng. as tr. L. *durante* in absolute constructions; thus L. *vita durante*, OFr. *vie durant*, Eng. *life during*, while life lasts –1545. Hence, **2.** *prep.* Throughout the whole continuance of; in the course of ME. †**3.** *conj.* While, until. (Also *d. that.*) (*rare*) –1693.
2. Trees may live d. the world 1670. D. the course of seven hundred years HUME. D. the night the rain changed to snow TYNDALL. Hence †**Du·ringly** *adv.* lastingly; for a long time.

†**Du·rity.** 1543. [– L. *duritas*, f. *durus* hard; see -ITY.] Hardness (*lit.* and *fig.*) –1795.

Durmast (dō·ɹmɑst). 1791. [perh. orig. an error for *dunmast*, i.e. DUN *a.* + MAST *sb.*²] A variety of oak (*Quercus pubescens*, or *Q. sessiliflora*). Usually *d.-oak.*

†**Du·rous,** *a. rare.* 1666. [f. L. *durus* hard + -OUS.] Hard.

†**Duroy** (dŭroi·). 1619. [Of unkn. origin.] A kind of coarse woollen fabric; akin to *tammies*. (Not the same as *corduroy.*) –1807.

‖**Durra, dhurra** (du·ră). 1798. [– Arab. *ḏur(r)a.*] A kind of corn, Indian Millet. Also *attrib.*

Durst, pa. t. (and *dial.* pa. pple.) of DARE *v.*¹

Dusk (dɒsk). [Early ME. *dosk* (later *dusk*, in *dusked* (Chaucer), repr. OE. *dox* dark, swarthy (:– *duskaz :– *dhuskos, whence L. *fuscus* dark, dusky), and its deriv. *doxian* become dark in colour; rel. to OS. *dosan*, OHG. *tusin* darkish (of colour), dull. Cf. DUN *a.*]
A. *adj.* (Now more often *dusky.*) **1.** Dark from absence of light; dim, gloomy, shadowy; blackish; dusky ME. †**2.** Obscure, veiled from sight or understanding –1583.
1. Vapour and Exhalation, d. and moist MILT.
B. *sb.* **1.** The quality of being dusk; that which is dusk; duskiness; gloom 1700. **2.** The darker stage of twilight at night or in the morning 1622.
1. In the d. of thee [Old Yew] TENNYSON. **2.** In the duske of the evening MABBE.

Dusk, *v.* ME. [f. DUSK *a.*; OE. *doxian*, early ME. *doskin*, later *dusken*. See prec.] To make or (*intr.*) become dusky or dark. Also *fig.*
Dusked hise eyen two and failled breeth CHAUCER. That shadow which dusketh the light of the Moone P. HOLLAND. So **Du·sken** *v. rare*, in same senses.

Duskish (dɒ·skiʃ), *a.* 1530. [See -ISH¹.] Somewhat dusk or dusky, as *a d. red*. Hence **Du·skish-ly** *adv.*, **-ness.**

Dusky (dɒ·ski), *a.* 1558. [f. DUSK *a.*; see -Y¹ 2.] **1.** Somewhat black or dark in colour; darkish. **2.** Somewhat dark or deficient in light; dim, obscure 1580. **3.** *fig.* Gloomy, melancholy 1602.
1. No duskie vapour did bright Phœbus shroude GREENE. **2.** The duskie hour Friendliest to sleep MILT. *P. L.* v. 667. **3.** That d. scene of horror, that melancholy prospect BENTLEY. Hence **Du·skily** *adv.* **Du·skiness.**

‖**Dusserah** (dɒsē·rā). 1799. [– Hindi *dasahrā.*] The tenth day of a Hindu annual festival occurring in the month of Ashvin (September–October).

Dust (dɒst), *sb.* [OE. *dūst* = OFris. *dūst*, MDu. *donst*, *dūst* (LG. *dust*, Du. *duist* meal-dust, bran), ON. *dust*. The primary notion appears to be 'that which rises in a cloud, as dust, smoke, vapour'; cf. OHG. *tun(i)st* wind, breeze, LG. *dunst* vapour.] **1.** Earth or other solid matter so comminuted as to be easily raised and carried in a cloud by the wind; any substance pulverized; powder. (Rarely in *pl.*) Often extended to include ashes, etc., from a house. **2.** With *a* and *pl.* **a.** A minute particle of dry matter 1593. **b.** in *Cookery*, etc., a small pinch of something powdery 1784. **c.** (With *a*) A cloud of dust floating in the air 1570. **3.** *transf.* and *fig.* That to which anything is reduced by disintegration; *spec.* the ashes of a dead body. Also in phrases denoting the condition of being dead and buried. OE. **b.** Denoting a condition of humiliation ME. **c.** As the type of that which is worthless ME. **4.** *fig.* (from 2c.) Confusion, disturbance, turmoil 1570. **b.** Hence (*slang* or *colloq.*) A disturbance, row, shindy 1753. **5.** *slang.* Money, cash 1607. **6.** = DUST-BRAND. **7.** *attrib.* 1580.
1. To clense houses of duste TREVISA. Showers, which..laid the d. WESLEY. **2.** A graine, a d., a gnat, a wandering haire *John* IV. i. 93. A d. of grated nutmeg 1784. **3.** The Noble d. of Alexander *Haml.* V. i. 225. The Power..that rais'd us from the d. MILT. *P. L.* IV. 416. **4.** That quarrel and raise a D. about nothing T. BROWN. **5.** He.. is not willing to down with his d. 1691.
Phrases. *To shake the d. off one's feet* (see Matt. 10:14, etc.). *To throw d. in the eyes of*: to make blind to the actual facts of the case. *To bite the d.*: to fall to the ground; *esp.* to fall wounded or slain.
Comb.: **d.-bin, du·stbin,** a receptacle for the d. and refuse of a house; **-chamber** (in an ore-roasting furnace), a closed chamber in which the heavier products of combustion are collected; **-colour,** a dull light brown; **-cover, -jacket,** a paper cover in which a book is issued; **-guard,** a contrivance to keep off d. from the axle and bearings of a wheel, etc.; **-hole,** a hole or bin in which d. and refuse are collected; **-louse,** an insect of the genus *Psocus*; **-pan,** a utensil into which d. is swept from a floor, etc.; **-shoot,** a place where d. and refuse are shot; **-storm,** a tempest in which large clouds of d. are carried along.

Dust, *v.* ME. [f. prec. sb.; cf. ON. *dusta* to dust.] †**1.** *intr.* To be dusty. ME. only. †**2.** To reduce, or (*intr.*) crumble, to dust –1686. **3.** *trans.* To sprinkle with dust or powder 1592. Also *intr.* for *refl.* **4.** To make dusty 1530. **5.** To strew as dust 1790. **6.** To free from dust 1568. **7.** To brush, shake, or rub off as dust 1775. **8.** To ride or go quickly; also, *to d. it.* (Now *U.S. slang* or *colloq.*) 1655.
6. Phr. *To d. a person's coat, jacket*, etc.: to beat him soundly (*colloq.*).

Dust-box. 1581. A box from which dust, *i.e.* fine sand or powder, is sprinkled on something (*e.g.* on writing, etc.)

Dust-brand. 1861. [f. DUST *sb.* + BRAND *sb.*] A disease of corn, in which the ears become filled with a black powder; *smut.*

Duster (dɒ·stəɹ). 1576. [f. DUST *v.* or *sb.* + -ER¹.] **1.** One who, or that which, dusts or removes dust. **2.** An apparatus for sifting dry poisons upon plants to kill insects. **3.** A light cloak or wrap worn to keep off dust. Chiefly *U.S.* 1864.

Dusting (dɒ·stiŋ), *vbl. sb.* 1623. [f. DUST *v.* + -ING¹.] **1.** The action of DUST *v.* **2.** A beating, thrashing; also (*Naut.*) rough weather (*colloq.* or *slang*) 1799. **3.** *attrib.*, as *d.-brush, -cloth, -powder*, etc. 1667.

Dustless (dɒ·stlės), *a.* 1618. [-LESS.] Free from dust.

Dustman (dɒ·stmæ̆n). 1707. [f. as prec. + MAN.] **1.** A man whose occupation is to remove dust and refuse from dust-bins, etc. **2.** *slang.* A preacher who uses violent action; a 'cushion-thumper' 1877.

‖**Dustoor** (dɒstū·ᵊɹ). *E. Ind.* 1680. [– Urdu – Pers. *dastūr* councillor, custom.] **a.** Custom, usage, fashion. **b.** Customary commission; var. ‖**Dustoo·ry.**

†**Dust-point.** 1611. A boy's game in which 'points' were laid in a heap of dust, and thrown at with a stone –1675.

‖**Dustuck, dustuk** (dɒ·stɒk). *E. Ind.* 1748. [– Urdu – Pers. *dastak.*] A passport.

Dusty (dɒ·sti), *a.* [OE. *dūstiġ*; see DUST *sb.*, -Y¹.] **1.** Full of, abounding with, or strewn with dust ME. **2.** Consisting of dust; powdery 1552. **3.** Of colour, etc.: As if strewn with dust. Also *advb.* 1676. **4.** *fig.* Mean, worthless; now only in slang phr. *not so d.* 1893. *Comb.* **d. miller,** (*a*) the auricula (*Primula auricula*), from the fine powder on the leaves and flowers; (*b*) a kind of artificial fly. Hence **Du·stily** *adv.* **Dustiness.**

Dutch (dɒtʃ). ME. [– MDu. *dutsch*, *duutsch*, *duutsc* Hollandish, Netherlandish, or even German, in early mod.Du. *duytsch*, now *duitsch*, 'German', OHG. *diutisc*, popular, national, vulgar. Since 1600 the term 'Dutch' has been gradually restricted in England to the Netherlanders, with whom the English came most in contact.]
A. *adj.* **1.** Of or pertaining to the people of Germany; German; Teutonic. Now *Hist.* 1460. **2.** Of, pertaining to, or characterizing the 'Low Dutch' people of Holland and the Netherlands 1606. **3.** Of or belonging to the Dutch; native to, or coming from Holland 1592. **4.** Characteristic of or attributed to the Dutch; often used in derision or contempt 1608.
1. *High D.*, of or pertaining to the South Germans, High German; *Low D.*, of or pertaining to the Germans of the sea-coast, and of the north and north-west, including the Netherlands and Flanders. **2.** The collection of pictures of the D. school 1838. A D. love for tulips TENNYSON. **3.** Late as the D. clock showed it to be DICKENS. **D. cheese,** a small round cheese made from skim milk. **D. clinker,** a kind of brick used for paving stables and yards, being exceedingly hard. **D. foil, gold, gilt, gilding, leaf, metal,** a very malleable alloy of 11 parts of copper and 2 of zinc, beaten into thin leaves, forming a cheap imitation of gold-leaf. **D. liquid, oil,** Ethylene dichloride, $2(CH_2Cl)$, a thin oily liquid, having a sweetish smell and taste. **D. Rushes,** a species of *Equisetum* or Horse-tail used for polishing; shave-grass. **4.** *D. auction, bargain, concert, courage, nightingale*, etc.: see AUCTION, BARGAIN, etc.
B. *sb.*¹ [The adj. used ellipt.] **1.** The German language. *Obs.* exc. in *High D.* = German; *Low D.* = Low German, including Netherlandish. **2.** The language of Holland and the Netherlands 1706. *Double* (†*high*) *D.*: gibberish 1789. **3.** *The D.* †**a.** The Germans. **b.** The people of Holland and the Netherlands. 1577.

Dutch (dɒtʃ), *sb.*² *slang.* 1889. [abbrev. of DUCHESS.] A costermonger's wife (*old d.*).

Dutch, *v.* 1763. [f. prec. adj.] To clarify and harden (quills) by plunging them in heated sand, or rapidly passing them through a fire.

Dutchify (dɒ·tʃifəi), *v.* 1680. [f. DUTCH *a.* + -FY.] To make Dutch or Dutch-like.

Dutchman (dɒ·tʃmæ̆n). ME. †**1.** A German –1788. **2.** An inhabitant of Holland or the Netherlands 1596. **3.** A Dutch ship 1657.
1. *Much Ado* III. ii. 33. **2.** Phr. *I'm a D.*, i.e. I'm not myself: as an alternative clause to an assertion (*colloq.*). **3.** *Flying D.*: A legendary or spectral ship supposed to be seen near the Cape of Good Hope; also, its captain, said to have been condemned to sail the seas for ever. *Comb.*: **Dutchman's breeches,** (*a*) in U.S., the plant *Dicentra cucullaria*; (*b*) *Naut.* a very small patch of blue

sky often seen when a gale is breaking; **Dutchman's laudanum,** a climbing shrub allied to the Passion-flower, *Passiflora murucuja*; also, a narcotic prepared from this; **Dutchman's pipe,** (*a*) a climbing shrub, *Aristolochia sipho*; (*b*) the nest of the S. Amer. wasp.

Duteous (diū·tiəs), *a.* 1593. [f. DUTY + -OUS; cf. *beauteous.*] Characterized by the performance of duty to a superior; dutiful, submissive, obedient.

A daughter d. DRYDEN. **Du·teous-ly** *adv.*, **-ness.**

Dutiable (diū·ti,āb'l), *a.* 1774. [See -ABLE.] Liable to duty; on which a duty is levied; as *d. articles.*

Dutied (diū·tid), *a. U.S.* 1771. [f. DUTY + -ED².] Subjected to duty.

Dutiful (diū·tifŭl), *a.* 1552. [See -FUL.] **1.** Full of duty, *i.e.* that which is due to a superior; rendering the services and attention that are due. †**2.** Relating to duty (*rare*) 1588.

1. With all duetifull respect unto your Lordship 1590. D. and loyal subjects of the King 1844. Hence **Du·tiful-ly** *adv.*, **-ness.**

Duty (diū·ti). ME. [– AFr. *deweté, dueté,* f. *du(e)* DUE *a.*; see -TY¹.] **1.** The action and conduct due to a superior; homage; reverence, due respect. †**2.** That which is owing to any one; (one's) due; a debt –1642. **3.** A payment due and enforced by law or custom 1489. *spec.* †**a.** Payment for the services of the church. Chiefly *pl.* (repl. by *dues*). –1562. **b.** A payment to the public revenue; *esp.* one levied upon the import, export, manufacture, or sale of certain commodities. Applied to payments under the heads of customs, excise, licences, stamp-duties, death-duties, inhabited house duty. 1474. **4.** Action, or an act, that is due by moral or legal obligation; that which one ought or is bound to do. (The chief current sense.) ME. **b.** Absolutely: Moral obligation. (Occas. personified.) 1579. **5.** Business, office, function ME. **6.** *Mech.* The measure of effectiveness of an engine, expressed by units of work done per unit of fuel 1827.

1. Our d. to your Honour *Haml.* I. ii. 252. **2.** Take that which is thy d. TINDALE *Matt.* 20:14. To pay their d. unto nature, as their creditor 1540. **3.** By taxes they [the American colonists] mean internal taxes; by duties they mean customs FRANKLIN. **4.** England expects that every man will do his d. NELSON. Stern Daughter of the Voice of God! O D. WORDSW. **5.** *Ministerial* or *clerical d.*, or simply *d.*: the regular ministration and service of a clergyman. *Military d.*: appointed military service (now, where no enemy is to be engaged). Phr. *On d.*: officially engaged. So *Off d. Comb.*: **d.-free** *a.* (and *adv.*), free of d.; **-paid** *a.*, on which customs or excise-d. has been paid.

Duumvir (diu,ʊ·mvəɹ). Pl. **-virs,** or as L. **-viri** (-virəi). 1600. [L., sing. derived from gen. pl. *duum virum* of *duo viri* two men.] *Rom. Hist.* One of the *duumviri* or pairs of coequal magistrates, etc. in Rome and in her coloniæ and municipia. Also *transf.*

Here is a compact of iniquity between these two duumvirs [Wheler and Hastings] BURKE.

Hence **Duu·mviral** *a.* of or pertaining to duumvirs. **Duu·mvirate,** the joint office of duumvirs; a coalition of two men; a pair of officials.

‖**Duvet** (düve). 1758. [Fr.] A quilt of eiderdown or swansdown.

Dux (dɒks). 1808. [L.] **1.** A leader, chief; *spec.* the head pupil in a class: chiefly in Scotland. **2.** *Mus.* The subject of a fugue (the answer being called *comes*) 1819.

Duyker; see DUIKER.

Dwale (dwēˡl), *sb.* ME. [prob. from Scandinavian; cf. Da. *dvale* dead sleep, stupor, *dvaledrik* soporiferous draught.] †**1.** A stupefying or soporific drink. (Prob. the infusion of Belladonna.) –1606. **2.** The Deadly Nightshade, *Atropa belladonna* ME. †**3.** In *Her.* occas. used for *sable* –1751.

Dwang (dwæŋ). *Sc.* 1842. [Cf. Du. *dwang* force, compulsion, restraint.] *Arch.* 'A term used in Scotland to denote the short pieces of timber employed in strutting a floor' (Gwilt).

Dwarf (dwǭɹf). Pl. **-fs.** [OE. *dweorg, dweorh* = OFris. *dwirg,* MDu. *dwerch* (Du. *dwerg*), OHG. *twerg* (G. *zwerg*), ON. *dvergr* :– Gmc. **dwerʒaz.*]

A. 1. A human being much below the ordinary stature or size; a pygmy. **2.** *transf.* Of animals and plants 1664.

B. *adj.* Of or pertaining to a dwarf; dwarfish; pygmy 1634. Also *transf.* of plants, animals, etc. *Comb.* **d.-wall,** any low wall; *spec.* one which forms the basis of a railway, or which supports the joists under a floor.

Hence **Dwa·rfish** *a.* d.-like; of a size below the average; pygmy, puny. **Dwa·rfish-ly** *adv.*, **-ness. Dwa·rfling,** a small d. **Dwa·rfy** *a.* dwarfish.

Dwarf (dwǭɹf), *v.* 1626. [f. prec. sb.] **1.** *trans.* To render dwarf or dwarfish; to stunt in growth. Also *transf.* and *fig.* **2.** To cause to look or seem small (*lit.* and *fig.*) 1850. **3.** *intr.* To become dwarf or dwarfed 1833.

1. [We] d. them and stay their growth BACON. The incessant repetition of the same hand-work dwarfs the man EMERSON. **2.** An immense chandelier..dwarfing the apartments DISRAELI.

Dwell (dwel), *v.* Pa. t. and pple. **dwelt,** now rarely **dwelled.** [OE. *dwellan* lead astray, corresp. to OS. *bi-dwellian* hinder, MDu. *dwellen* stun, perplex, OHG. *twellen* (MHG. *twellen*) delay, harass, ON. *dvelja* trans. delay, intr. and refl. tarry, stay; f. Gmc. **dwel-* **dwal-* **dwul-.*] †**1.** *trans.* To lead into error; to stun, stupefy –ME. †**2.** To hinder, delay. (Only OE.) †**3.** *intr.* To tarry; to desist from action –1485. **4.** To abide for a time, in a state, place, or condition (*arch.*) ME. **5.** *To d. on, upon,* †*in*: to spend time upon or linger over; now *esp.* to treat at length or with insistence; also, to sustain (a note) in music. (The most frequent use in speech.) 1513. †**6.** To last; to remain (ME. only). **7.** To remain as in a permanent residence; to have one's abode; to reside. (Now usu. repl. by *live* in spoken use.) ME. †**8.** *trans.* To inhabit –1799. †**9.** To cause to abide *in* 1667.

4. Ile rather d. in my necessitie *Merch. V.* I. iii. 157. **5.** [Plato] is constantly dwelling on the importance of regular classification JOWETT. **7.** The King that dwelleth in Heaven HOBBES. *fig.* Farewel happy Fields Where Joy for ever dwells MILT. *P. L.* I. 250. **9.** MILT. *P. L.* XII. 487.

Dweller (dwe·ləɹ). ME. [f. as prec. + -ER¹.] One who dwells (in a place); an inhabitant, resident. Also with *on.*

The rude dwellers on the mountain-heights COWPER.

Dwelling (dwe·liŋ), *vbl. sb.* ME. [f. as prec. + -ING¹.] **1.** The action of DWELL *v.* **2.** *concr.* A place of residence; a dwelling-place, habitation, house. Also *fig.* ME.

2. Good will To future men, and in thir dwellings peace MILT. *P. L.* VII. 183. *fig.* Enclosed in the narrow d. of the mind 1655. *Comb.*, etc.: **d.-house,** a house occupied as a place of residence; **-place,** a place of abode.

Dwindle (dwi·nd'l), *v.* 1596. [A frequent. f. DWINE *v.*; see -LE.] **1.** *intr.* To become smaller and smaller; to shrink, waste away, decline. **b.** *fig.* To degenerate 1678. **2.** *trans.* To cause to shrink 1661.

1. Man seems the only growth that dwindles here GOLDSM. *fig.* In thy old age to d. to a Whig T. BROWN. **2.** These Monsters..have dwindled the Wolf into a Fox 1679. Hence **Dwi·ndler.**

Dwi·ndle, *sb. rare.* 1779. [f. prec.] The process of dwindling; *concr.* a dwindled object.

Dwine (dwəin), *v.* Now *Sc., dial.,* and *arch.* [OE. *dwīnan* waste away =(M)LG., MDu. *dwīnen,* ON. *dvīna.* Cf. DWINDLE *v.*] *intr.* To waste or pine away. **b.** *trans.* To cause to pine away (*rare*) 1597.

Dwt., abbrev. for PENNYWEIGHT; see D.

Dyad (dəi·æd). 1675. [– late L. *dyas, dyad-* – Gr. δυάς, δυαδ-, f. δύο two; see -AD. Cf. DUAD.] **1.** The number two; a group of two. **2.** *spec.* **a.** *Chem.* An atom, radical, or element that has the combining power of two units, *i.e.* of two atoms of hydrogen 1865. **b.** *Biol.* A secondary unit consisting of an aggregate of monads 1883. **c.** *Pros.* A group of two lines having different rhythms 1885. **3.** *attrib.* or as *adj.* = DYADIC 1869.

Dyadic (dəiæ·dik), *a.* 1727. [– Gr. δυαδικός of the number two; see prec., -IC.] **a.** Of or pertaining to a dyad. **b.** *Chem.* Of the atomic constitution of a dyad 1873.

Phr. *D. arithmetic*: binary arithmetic, in which the radix is 2.

Dyakis-dodecahedron (dəi·ǎkis,dōᵘ:dīkă hī·drǫn). 1881. [f. Gr. δυάκις twice + DODECAHEDRON.] *Cryst.* = DIPLOID.

Dyarchy; see DIARCHY.

Dyas (dəi·æs). 1876. [Gr. δυάς (see DYAD), after TRIAS.] *Geol.* A name for the Permian system. Hence **Dya·ssic** *a.*

Dye (dəi), *sb.* [OE. *dēah, dēag,* rare ME. *dēh*; the present word is a new formation on the vb. (XVI).] **1.** Colour produced by, or as by, dyeing; tinge, hue. Also *fig.* **2.** A material used for dyeing; *esp.* colouring matter in solution OE.

1. *fig.* Wings and crests of rainbow dyes J. WILSON. *fig.* Crimes..of the blackest d. MACKINTOSH.

Comb.: **d.-bath, -beck,** the vessel containing the dyeing liquid; also the colouring matter contained in it; **-house,** the building in which a dyer carries on his work; **-stuff, -ware,** a substance which yields a d.; **-wood,** wood yielding a d.; **-works,** works in which dyeing is carried on.

Dye (dəi), *v.* Pa. t. and pple. **dyed;** pr. pple. **dyeing.** [OE. *deagian,* of unkn. origin. Not recorded again till late XIV (Chaucer).] **1.** *trans.* To tinge with a colour or hue; to fix a colour in the substance of; to colour, stain. **2.** *intr.* for *pass.* To take a colour (well or badly) in the process of dyeing 1897.

1. My hands with blood of innocence are dy'd GAY. The most usual stuffs..which are required to be dyed, are wool, silk, cotton, and linen 1816. Phr. *To d. in (the) wool, in grain,* to d. while the material is in the raw or primitive state, and therefore more lastingly; hence *dyed-in-the-wool* adj. (*fig.*).

Dye, obs. f. DIE *v.* and *sb.*

Dyeing (dəi·iŋ), *vbl. sb.* Also formerly **dying.** OE. [f. DYE *v.* + -ING¹.] The process of impregnating with colour; *esp.* the fixing of colours in solution in textiles, etc.

Dyer (dəi·əɹ). ME. [f. as prec. + -ER¹.] One whose occupation is to dye cloth, etc.

Comb., etc.: **dyer's broom, whin,** *Genista tinctoria,* also called **dyer's greenweed,** *Dyer's weed,* and *woadwaxen*; **dyer's moss,** archil; **Dyer's weed,** a name for plants that yield a dye: *esp.* Yellow-weed or Weld, *Reseda luteola*; also Dyer's greenweed or Woadwaxen, and Dyer's woad, *Isatis tinctoria.*

Dyer, obs. f. *dier,* one who dies.

Dygogram (dəi·gogræm). 1862. [contr. for Dynamo-gonio-gram, 'force and angle diagram'.] A diagram showing the variation of the horizontal component of the force of magnetism exerted upon the ship's compass-needle by the iron in the ship's composition while making a circuit or curve.

Dying (dəi·iŋ), *vbl. sb.* ME. [f. DIE *v.*¹ + -ING¹.] **1.** Ceasing to live, expiring, decease, death. Also *transf.* and *fig.* **2.** *attrib.* Of, belonging to, or relating to dying or death, as *d. bed, command, day, declaration,* etc. 1580.

Dy·ing, *ppl. a.* ME. [f. as prec. + -ING².] Departing from this life; at the point of death; mortal. Also *transf.* and *fig.* Hence **Dy·ing-ly** *adv.* in a d. manner, in d.; **-ness;** d. quality.

Dyke, etc., a frequent sp. of DIKE, etc.

Dynactino·meter. ? *Obs.* 1851. [f. Gr. δύν(αμις power + ἀκτίς (ἀκτιν-) ray + -METER; cf. ACTINOMETER.] An instrument for measuring the intensity of the photogenic rays, and for computing the power of object-glasses.

†**Dy·nam.** 1847. [– Fr. *dyname* (also *dynamie*), f. Gr. δύναμις power, force.] Whewell's proposed term for expressing a pound or other unit, in estimating the effect of mechanical labour.

Dynameter (dəi-, dinæ·mĭtəɹ). 1828. [f. Gr. δύνα(μις + -METER.] = DYNAMOMETER 2. Hence **Dyname·tric, -al** *a.* pertaining to a d.

Dynamic (dəi-, dinæ·mik). 1817. [– Fr. *dynamique* (Leibnitz, 1692) – Gr. δυναμικός, f. δύναμις force; see -IC.]

A. *adj.* **1.** Of or pertaining to force producing motion; often opp. to *static* 1827. **2.** Of or pertaining to force in action; active 1862. Also *transf.* and *fig.* **3.** Of, according to, or pertaining to DYNAMICS: as the *d.* theory of the tides 1838. **4.** *Med.* Functional, as opp. to *organic* 1834. **5.** In the Kantian philosophy: Relating to the reason of existence of an object of experience. **6.** Relating to the existence or action of some force or forces 1817.

1. According to the d. view..heat is regarded as a motion TYNDALL. 2. A mere capacity..potential but not d. TYNDALL. 5. *D. relations*, the relations of substance and accident, of cause and effect, and of substances acting on each other. 6. *D. theory of Kant*, a theory according to which matter was constituted by attraction and repulsion.

B. *sb.* **1.** = DYNAMICS, q. v. 1873. **2.** = Dynamic theory; see A. 6. 1884. **3.** Energizing force 1894.

Dynamical (dəi-, dinæ·mikăl), *a.* 1812. [See prec., -ICAL.] **1.** = DYNAMIC *a.* 1–4. **2.** Applied to inspiration conceived as an endowing with divine power 1841. **3.** Of or pertaining to DYNAMISM (sense 1) 1845. Hence **Dyna·mically** *adv.* in the way of a force in action or motion; from the point of view of dynamics.

Dynami·city. *Chem.* [f. DYNAMIC + -ITY; see -ICITY.] = VALENCY or ATOMICITY. (Mod. Dicts.)

Dynamics (dəi-, dinæ·miks). 1788. [Pl. of DYNAMIC; see -IC 2.] **1.** The branch of Physics which treats of the action of Force; in earlier use restricted to *Kinetics*, and thus opp. to *Statics*, but more recently taken as including both. Also called DYNAMIC. **b.** That branch of any science in which force or forces are considered 1843. **2.** *transf.* The moving physical or moral forces in any sphere, or the laws by which they act 1833.

2. The great storehouse of our spiritual d. J. MARTINEAU.

Dynamism (dəi·n-, di·nămiz'm). 1831. [f. Gr. δύναμις power, force + -ISM.] **1.** A philosophical theory, which seeks to explain the phenomena of the universe by some immanent force or energy; *esp.* the doctrine of Leibnitz that all substance involves force 1857. **2.** The mode of being of force or energy 1831. **3.** *Med.* 'The theory of the origin of disease from change or alteration of vital force' (*Syd. Soc. Lex.*). Hence **Dy·namist,** one who holds the doctrine of d. **Dynami·stic** *a.*

‖**Dynamitard.** 1882. [f. DYNAMITE, after Fr. *communard*. (Not in recognized Fr. use.)] = DYNAMITER.

Dynamite (dəi·nămait, di·n-), *sb.* 1867. [f. Gr. δύναμις + -ITE[1] 4a, by Alfred Nobel the inventor.] **1.** A high explosive prepared from nitro-glycerine mixed, for safety, with some inert absorptive substance. **2.** *attrib.*, as *d. outrage*; **d. cruiser,** a cruiser armed with d. guns; **d. gun,** a pneumatic gun for throwing d. shells, or the like. 1880.

Hence **Dynami·tic, -al** *a.* **Dynami·tically** *adv.* **Dy·namiti:sm,** the principles or practice of the dynamiter; the use of d., etc., as a means of attacking a government, nation, or person.

Dy·namite, *v.* 1881. [f. prec. sb.] *trans.* To wreck by the explosion of dynamite; to mine or charge with dynamite.

Dynamiter (dəi·nămaitər, di·n-). 1883. [f. prec. + -ER[1], perh. after Fr. *dynamiteur.*] One who employs dynamite, etc., for unlawful purposes; *esp.* as a means of attacking a government, nation, or person.

Dynamize (dəi·n-, di·nămaiz), *v.* 1855. [See -IZE.] *Med.* To endow with power. In *Homœopathy*, To increase the power of (medicines) by trituration or succussion. Hence **Dynamiza·tion.**

Dynamo-, from Gr. δύναμις 'power, force', a combining form, as in **D.-electric** *a.*, pertaining to current (formerly called dynamic) electricity; also, pertaining to the conversion of dynamical into electrical energy, as *d.-electric machine*; etc.

Dynamo (dəi·nămo), *sb.* Pl. **-os.** 1882. [Short for *dynamo-machine*, itself short for *dynamo-electric-machine* (1867).] *Electr.* A machine for converting mechanical power into electric energy, by setting conductors (usually coils of copper wire) to rotate in a magnetic field.

Dynamogeny (dəin-, dinămǫ·dʒĭni). 1887. [f. DYNAMO- + -GENY.] Production of increased nervous activity; dynamization of nerve-force. So **Dynamoge·nesis,** in same sense. **Dynamoge·nic** *a.*

Dynamograph (dəi·n-, di·nămograf). 1851. [f. DYNAMO- + -GRAPH.] An instrument for recording the amount of force exerted.

Dynamometer (dəin- dinămǫ·mĭtəɹ). 1810. [– Fr. *dynamomètre* (1805); see DYNAMO-, -METER.] **1.** Any instrument for measuring the amount of energy exerted by an animal, or expended by a motor in its work, or by the action of any mechanical force. **2.** An instrument for measuring the magnifying power of a telescope 1832. Hence **Dynamome·tric, -al** (also **dynami-**) *a.* of or pertaining to the measurement of force; **Dynamo·metry,** the measurement of force.

Dynast (di·n-, dəi·næst). 1631. [– L. *dynastes* – Gr. δυναστής, f. δύνασθαι be able or powerful.] One in power; a ruler, lord, potentate, *esp.* a hereditary ruler; a member or founder of a dynasty. Hence **Dyna·stic, -al** *a.* of, pertaining to, or connected with a dynasty or dynasties. **Dyna·stically** *adv.* **Dyna·sticism,** the dynastic principle; the system of ruling dynasties.

Dynastidan (din-, dəinæ·stidăn). 1835. [f. mod.L. *Dynastidæ*, f. *Dynastes* as a generic name. See -ID[3], -AN.] *Entom.* A member of the *Dynastidæ*, a family of large beetles including the *Dynastes* or Hercules-beetle.

Dynasty (di·năsti, dəi-). 1460. [– Fr. *dynastie* or late L. *dynastia* – Gr. δυναστεία power, domination, f. δυναστής; see DYNAST, -Y[3].] **1.** Lordship, sovereignty, power; régime. Now *rare.* 1613. **2.** A succession of rulers of the same line or family 1460. Also *transf.* and *fig.*

Dyne (dəin). 1873. [– Fr. *dyne*, taken from Gr. δύναμις force.] *Physics.* The unit of force in the centimetre-gramme-second (C.G.S.) system, *i.e.* the force which, acting for one second on a mass of one gramme, gives it an acceleration of one centimetre per second per second.

Dyophysite (dəi,ǫ·fizəit). 1860. [– late Gr. δυοφυσῖται, f. δύο two + φύσις nature. See DIPHYSITE.] *Theol.* A holder of the doctrine of the coexistence of two natures, the divine and the human, in Christ; opp. to the Monophysites. Hence **Dyophysi·tic** *a.*

Dyothelete, -ite (dəi,ǫ·pĭlīt, -əit). 1848. [f. Gr. δύο + θελητής: lit. a 'two-willer'.] *Theol.* **a.** *adj.* Holding the doctrine that Christ had two wills, a divine and a human. **b.** *sb.* One who holds this doctrine; an opponent of MONOTHELETISM.

Dyphone (dəi·fōᵘn). 1676. [f. Gr. δύο two + -PHONE.] *Mus.* The 'double lute', invented by Thomas Mace in 1672.

Dys-, obs. spelling of DIS-, in many words.

Dys- (dis), *prefix*, repr. Gr. δυσ- [=Skr. *dus-*, Gmc. *tuz-, OHG. *zūr-* (Ger. *zer-*), ON. *tor-*, OE. *tō-* in *to-break*, etc.] 'inseparable prefix, opp. to εὖ [see EU-], with notion of *hard, bad, unlucky*, etc.; destroying the good sense of a word, or increasing its bad sense' (Liddell and Scott).

Dysgenesis (-dʒe·nĭsis) [Gr. γένεσις, difficulty in breeding; *spec.* a condition of hybrids in which they are sterile among themselves, but capable of producing (sterile) offspring with either of the parental races; so **Dysgenesic** (-dʒĭne·sik) *a.* **Dysphonia** (-fōᵘ·niă), **Dysphony** (di·sfŏni) [Gr. δυσφωνία], difficulty of speaking arising from affection of the vocal organs; hence **Dysphonic** (-fǫ·nik) *a.* **Dystocia** (-tōᵘ·siă), **Dystokia,** erron. **-tochia** (-tǫ·kiă) [Gr. δυστοκία], difficult or painful childbirth; hence **Dysto·cial** *a.* **Dystome** (di·stoᵘm), **Dystomic** (distǫ·mik), **Dystomous** (di·stŏməs) *adjs.* [Gr. δύστομος], *Min.* having imperfect fracture; cleaving with difficulty. See also O.E.D.

Dysæsthesia (disėsþī·siă). 1706. [mod.L. – Gr. δυσαισθησία (Galen), f. δυς- DYS- + -αισθησία in ἀναισθησία; cf. ÆSTHESIS, ANÆSTHESIA.] *Path.* Difficulty or derangement of sensation, or of any bodily senses.

†**Dyscra·se,** *v.* ME. [f. *dyscrasie* DYSCRASY. Later, viewed as conn. w. CRAZE *v.*] To affect with a dyscrasy; to distemper, disorder –1610.

‖**Dyscrasia** (diskrēⁱ·siă). ME. [Late L. – Gr. δυσκρασία bad temperament (of body, air, etc.), f. δυς- DYS- + κρᾶσις mixing, tempering; see -IA[1].] = DYSCRASY. Hence **Dyscra·sic** *a.*

Dyscrasite (di·skrăsəit). Also **dis-.** 1852. [f. Gr. δυσκρασία bad mixture (see prec.) + -ITE[1] 2 b.] *Min.* Antimonial silver, a native alloy of silver and antimony in various proportions.

Dyscrasy (di·skrăsi). ME. [– OFr. *dyscrasie* or late L. DYSCRASIA. Cf. EUCRASY.] A bad or disordered condition of the body (originally ascribed to a disproportionate mixture of the 'humours'); morbid diathesis; distemper. Also *fig.*

Sin is but a disease and D. in the soul CUDWORTH.

Dysenteric, †-al (disente·rik, -ăl), *a.* 1601. [– L. *dysentericus* – Gr. δυσεντερικός, f. δυσεντερία; see next, -IC, -ICAL.] **1.** Belonging to or of the nature of dysentery. **2.** Affected with dysentery 1677.

1. D. diarrhœa 1846. 2. Twelve d. patients GOOD.

Dysentery (di·sentĕri). ME. [– OFr. *dissenterie* or L. *dysenteria* – Gr. δυσεντερία, f. δυσέντερος, f. δυσ- DYS- + ἔντερα bowels; see -Y[3].] Inflammation of the mucous membrane and glands of the large intestine, attended with griping pains, and mucous and bloody evacuations.

Dyslogistic (dislodʒi·stik), *a.* Also erron. **dis-.** 1802. [f. DYS- + stem of *eu-logistic.*] Having a bad connotation; opprobrious; opp. to *eulogistic.*

The d. names, by which it pleases each side to denominate its opponents 1887. Hence **Dyslogi·stically** *adv.*

Dysluite (di·slu,əit). 1821. [f. DYS- + Gr. λύειν loose, dissolve + -ITE[1] 2b.] *Min.* A variety of gahnite or zinc spinel, containing manganese: it is difficult to decompose.

Dyslysin (di·slisin). 1851. [f. DYS- + Gr. λύσις solution + -IN[1].] *Chem.* 'A substance got from bilin digested with dilute hydrochloric acid with alcohol'; it is almost insoluble.

‖**Dysmenorrhagia** (di:smenorēⁱ·dʒiă). 1885. [See DYS-.] = next.

‖**Dysmenorrhœa** (-rī·ă). Also **-rhea.** 1810. [See DYS-.] *Path.* Difficult or painful menstruation.

Dysmerism (di·smĕriz'm). 1881. [f. Gr. δυσ- (DYS-) + μερισμός division.] *Biol.* The aggregation of unlike parts in the formation of an organism. Hence **Dysmeri·stic** *a.* having the character of such an aggregation. **Dysmerogenesis** (di:smĕro,dʒe·nĕsis), the formation of an organism by successive production of parts which are unlike; hence **Dy:smerogene·tic** *a.*

Dysodyle, -ile (di·sodəil). 1809. [– Fr. *dysodyle* (Cordier 1808), f. Gr. δυσώδης ill-smelling + *-yle* -YL. Cf. CACODYL.] *Min.* A very inflammable hydrocarbon, yellow, and of foliated structure, which burns with a fetid odour.

Dyspathy (di·spăþi). *rare.* 1603. [– Fr. †*dispathie*, taken as the opposite of Gr. συμπάθεια sympathy.] The opposite of *sympathy*; antipathy; disagreement of feeling or sentiment.

‖**Dyspepsia** (dispe·psiă). Also **dyspe·psy** (now less usual). 1706. [– L. *dyspepsia* – Gr. δυσπεψία, f. δύσπεπτος; see next, -IA[1].] Difficulty or derangement of digestion; indigestion: applied *esp.* to disorder of the stomach, usually involving weakness, loss of appetite, and depression of spirits.

A French writer calls d. 'the remorse of a guilty stomach' 1862.

Dyspeptic (dispe·ptik), *a.* (*sb.*) 1694. [f. Gr. δύσπεπτος difficult of digestion, f. δυσ- DYS- + πεπτός cooked, digested, after Gr. πεπτικός able to digest.]

A. †**1.** Difficult of digestion. **2.** Of or belonging to dyspepsia; also *fig.* 1809. **3.** Subject to or suffering from dyspepsia 1822.

2. D. symptoms 1875. *fig.* No d. politics 1894.

B. *sb.* A person subject to or suffering from dyspepsia 1822. Hence **Dyspe·ptical** *a.* (*rare*). **Dyspe·ptically** *adv.*

‖**Dysphagia** (disfēⁱ·dʒiă) Rarely **dysphagy** (di·sfădʒi). 1783. [mod.L., f. DYS- + Gr. -φαγία eating.] *Path.* Difficulty of swallowing (as a symptom of some affection). Hence **Dyspha·gic** *a.*

‖**Dyspnœa** (dispnī·ă). 1681. [– L. *dyspnœa* – Gr. δύσπνοια, f. δυσ- DYS- + πνοή breathing; see -A 4.] *Path.* Difficulty of breathing. Hence **Dyspnœ·al** *a.* of or belonging to d.; **Dyspnœ·ic** *a.* of the nature of or affected with d.

Dysporomorph (di·spǒromǭ:ɹf). [f. *Dysporus* name of a genus of gannets + -μορφος -FORM.] *Zool.* A bird of the division *Dysporomorphæ*, including the pelicans, gannets, cormorants, etc. So **Dy:sporomo·rphic** *a.*

Dysteleology (di:steli,ǫ·lǒdʒi). 1874. [– G. *dysteleologie* (Häckel), f. DYS- privative + *teleologie* TELEOLOGY.] The doctrine of purposelessness in nature (opp. to TELEOLOGY); the study of functionless rudimentary organs as bearing on this doctrine. Hence **Dy:steleolo·gical** *a.* relating to d. **Dy:steleo·logist.**

Dysury (di·siŭri). ME. [– OFr. *dissurie* (mod. *dysurie*) or late L. *dysuria* – Gr. δυσουρία, f. δυσ- DYS- + οὖρον urine.] *Path.* Difficult or painful urination. So **Dysu·ric** *a.* pertaining to or affected with d.

Dyvour (dəi·vəɹ). *Sc.* ? *Obs.* 1508. [Of unkn. origin.] A bankrupt; hence *gen.* one in debt; a beggar.

‖**Dzeren** (dzī^ə·ren). Also **-on, -in.** 1834. [Mongolian, f. *dzĕr* reddish-yellow.] The Mongolian antelope, *Procapra gutturosa.*

‖**Dziggetai, dzh-** (dzi·gĕtai, dʒ-). 1793. [– Mongolian *dschiggetai*, var. of *tchikketei* (long-)eared, f. *tchikki* ear.] A species of equine quadruped, *Equus hemionus.* It approaches the mule in appearance.

E

E (ī), the fifth letter of the Roman and English Alphabet, repr. historically the Semitic ה (= *h*), but adopted by the Greeks (and from them by the Romans) as a vowel. In pronunc. it probably varied from the 'mid-front' (*e*) to the 'low-front' (*ę*) vowels of Bell's system.

For its principal sounds in standard English see KEY TO THE PRONUNCIATION.

The silent *e*, due primarily to the ME. obscure *-e*, is still retained: (1) To indicate that the vowel in the syllable is long; *e.g.* in *wine* (wəin), *paste* (pēⁱst), etc. (2) When otherwise *v*, or, after consonants, *l*, or *r* would end the word. (3) To soften the sound of a preceding *c* or *g*. (4) After *s* or *z* preceded by a cons., as in *pulse, furze*, etc. (5) In words like *infinite, rapine*, etc., and in words adopted from Fr. (6) In certain anomalous cases, as *are, were, come, done, gone, some, one, none.*

II. Besides serial order (5th) in the alphabet, or as a vowel (2nd), E, e, or *e* signifies *spec.* **1.** *Mus.* The 3rd note of the diatonic scale of C major. Also the scale or key which has that note for its tonic. **2.** In *Logic*: a universal negative. **3.** E. The second class of rating on Lloyd's books. Cf. A. IV. **4.** In *Math.* e or *e*. **a.** The quantity 2·71828.., the base of Napier's system of logarithms. **b.** The ECCENTRICITY of an ellipse. **5.** In *Electr. e* stands for the electromotive force of a single cell, E for the sum of such forces. **6.** In *Chem.* E = the element Erbium.

III. *Abbreviations.* E. = **1.** Various proper names, as Edward, etc.; Engineer(s) in C.E., R.E., etc. **2.** East, a point of the compass. **3.** E.E., E. & O.E. (*Comm.*) = *errors (and omissions) excepted.* **4.** E.M. = Earl Marshal. **5.** *e.g.* = Lat. *exempli gratia* for example.

E-, *prefix*, L. *ē*, shortened form of *ex-* out of; see EX-¹.

Ea (ī·ă). *dial.* 1781. [repr. OE. *ēa* river; see Æ *sb.*¹] A river, running water. Also *attrib.*

They rowed away for Crowland, by many a mere and many an e. KINGSLEY.

Each (ītʃ), *a.* and *pron.* [OE. *ǣlć* = OFris. *ellik, elk, ek*, MLG. *ellik*, MDu. *elic, ellic*, (M)LG., (M)Du. *elk*, OHG. *eogilīh* (G. *jeglich*) :– WGmc. phr. **aiwō ʒalīkaz* 'ever alike'; see AY *adv.*, ALIKE *a.* For loss of *l* cf. *such, which.*]

I. As adj. used *attrib.* Every (one of two or more) regarded separately. **a.** followed immediately by a sb. **b.** with *one* used absol. (Now usually repl. by *every one*, or by *each* absol.) OE.

a. E. night we die, E. morn are born anew YOUNG. **b.** Every e. one respectively 1631.

II. Absol. (quasi-*pron.*) **1.** With reference to a sb. going before, or followed by *of*. Occas. (erron.) with pl. vb. OE. **2.** Distributing a pl. subj. or obj. OE.

1. All and e. . . Did join in the pursuit COWPER. E. has his own place J. H. NEWMAN. **2.** His majesty's heirs and successors, e. in his time and order BURKE. Phr. *E. other = one another.* (Now a compound (cf. Du. *elkander*); but orig. *other* was governed by a vb., prep. or sb., as still in occas. in *e. to other*, etc.)

†**Ea·ch-whe·re.** ME. [f. EACH + WHERE.] Everywhere –1649.

†**Ea·di**, *a.* [OE. *ēadiǵ* = OS. *ōdag*, OHG. *ōtag*, ON. *auðigr*, Goth. *audags*; see -Y¹.] **1.** Wealthy –ME. **2.** Fortunate –ME.

Eadish, obs. f. EDDISH.

Eager (ī·gəɹ), *a.* ME. [– AFr. *egre*, (O)Fr. *aigre* :– Rom. **acrum*, for L. *acer, acr-*.] †**1.** Pungent, acrid, keen; sharp; severe –1601. Also *fig.* †**2.** *spec.* Acid, tart –1727. †**3.** Of metals: Brittle –1766. †**4.** Of persons, etc.: Strenuous, ardent, impetuous; fierce –1733. Also *transf.* **5.** Full of keen desire or appetite; impatiently longing; impatient ME.; of actions, etc.: Manifesting alacrity or impatient desire 1697. †**6.** *spec.* Hungry –1766.

1. A. . more egre medicine CHAUCER. *fig.* The bitter clamour of two e. tongues *Rich. II*, I. i. 49. **2.** It doth posset And curd like Aygre droppings into Milke *Haml.* I. v. 69. **4.** Egre as is a Tygre CHAUCER. **5.** E. of fame 1695, for war 1769, about your coming BURKE, in plundering the baggage MORSE. E. controversy 1853.

So †**Ea·ger** *v.* to excite, irritate; also *refl.* **Ea·ger-ly** *adv.*; **-ness**, the state or quality of being e.; keenness of appetite or desire.

Eagle (ī·g'l), *sb.* late ME. [– AFr. *egle*, (O)Fr. *aigle* :– L. *aquila.*] **1.** Any of the larger diurnal birds of prey which are not Vultures. Two species of Eagle are natives of Britain; the Golden Eagle (*Aquila chrysaetus*), mainly confined in these islands to the mountainous parts of Scotland and Ireland; and the Sea, or White-tailed Eagle (*Haliaetus albicilla*), found on the coasts of the same countries. The emblematic bird of the United States is the Bald or White-headed Eagle (*H. leucocephalus*). Also *fig.* **2.** A figure of the bird used for any purpose: **a.** as an ensign in the Roman army, and as an ensign and badge by France under the empire ME. **b.** as an armorial bearing; *esp.* of the Holy Roman Empire, and of the Austrian, French, German, and Russian empires ME. **3.** Anything made in the form of an eagle; as a lectern in a church; a clasp for a belt; etc. 1766. **4.** The constellation *Aquila* 1551. **5.** A coin bearing an image of the bird; *spec.* a base coin current at the accession of Edward I; a U.S. gold coin, value ten dollars. *Double-e.*: a U.S. coin worth twenty dollars. 1753. **6.** *Golf.* A hole played in two strokes under par or bogey 1922.

1. These moyst Trees, That haue out-liu'd the E. *Timon* IV. iii. 224. Can I make my eye an Eagle's BROWNING. *fig.* Russia's famish'd eagles SHELLEY.

Comb.: **a.** attrib. as *e.-eye, -speed*, etc.; **b.** objective, as *e.-bearer*; **c.** parasynthetic, as *e.-sighted, -winged* adjs. Also **e.-eyed** *a.*, having an eye like an e.; keen-sighted (*lit.* and *fig.*); **-fisher**, the Osprey; **-hawk**, a S. Amer. bird of prey of the genus *Morphnus* (not in Eng. use); **-owl**, a nocturnal bird of prey (*Bubo ignavus*), the largest European owl; **-ray, -skate**, a species of skate, *Myliobates marginata*; **-stone** = AETITES, q. v.

Eaglet (ī·glėt). 1572. [f. prec. + -ET, after Fr. *aiglette*, †*eglette.*] A young eagle.

Ea·gle-wood. 1712. [tr. Fr. *bois d'aigle*, a perversion of Malayalam *aγil*, or some other vernacular form of Skr. *aguru.*] = AGALLOCH, CALAMBAC.

Eagre (ēⁱ·gəɹ, ī·gəɹ). 1612. [Of unkn. origin.] A tidal wave of unusual height in a narrowing estuary; = BORE *sb.*³

Eam, obs. var. of EME, uncle.

†**Ean**, *v.* [OE. *ēanian.*] Of ewes: To bring forth lambs –1750. Hence **Ea·nling**, a young lamb.

-ean, formerly often with parallel forms in *-æan, -eian, -ian*, suffix repr. L. *-æus, -ēus* (corresp. to Gr. -αῖος, -ειος), *-eus*, compounded with -AN; e.g. *Eurōpæus* EUROPEAN, *Eurīpidēus Euripidean* (Εὐρωπαῖος, Εὐριπίδειος), med.L. *empyreus, -æus* (ἐμπύριος) EMPYREAN; the use in ANTIPODEAN is irregular.

Ear (īᵊɹ), *sb.*¹ [OE. *ēare* = OFris. *āre*, OS., OHG. *ōra* (Du. *oor*, G. *ohr*), ON. *eyra*, Goth. *ausō* :– Gmc. **auzo·n*, **au·son*, f. **aus-* :– IE. **ous-*, whence also L. *aures, -is*, Gr. οὖς, ὠς.] **1.** The organ of hearing in men and animals. Its parts are (1) the *external ear*, consisting of the pinna and the meatus or passage leading thence to (2) the *middle ear*, or tympanum, separated from the external meatus by a membrane called the *membrana tympani*; (3) the *internal ear*, or labyrinth. **2.** The external ear OE. **3.** The internal and middle ear, together or separately ME. **4.** With reference to its function: The organ of hearing OE. Also *transf.* and *fig.* of the mind, heart, etc. **5.** *transf.* Used in *sing.* and *pl.* for: The sense of hearing, auditory perception ME. **6.** (in *sing.*) The faculty of discriminating sounds, and recognizing musical intervals 1526. **7.** Voluntary hearing, favourable attention 1503. **8.** Any object resembling the external ear in shape or position; as, †an auricle of the heart; the handle of a pitcher; the projecting part of anything by which it is hung, as a bell, lifted, as a pile-driver, or handled, as a mortar-shell, a composing-rule, etc. **9.** *Bot.* and *Conch.* = AURICLE 2. 1688.

1. In the lowest animals the e. is reduced to a sack filled with a special fluid 1861. **2.** The jewel That trembles in her e. TENNYSON. Phr. *About one's ears*: said of a shower of missiles, a falling house, etc. Also *fig. Button e.*: in dogs an ear falling forward and hiding the inside. *Rose e.*, one folding at the back, and disclosing the inside. *Over (head and) ears, up to the ears*: *fig.* deeply immersed *in. To set (persons) by the ears*: to put them at variance. †*(Not to dare) for one's ears* (in allusion to the loss of ears as a punishment). **4.** They say Walls have Ears (*i.e.* there may be listeners anywhere) SHELTON. *fig.* The ears of fame 1864. Phr. *To incline one's ear(s, lend an e. To bow down one's e.*: to listen graciously. *To be all ears*: to be eagerly attentive. **6.** I have no E. for Musick STEELE. **7.** Phr. *to give e. To have (win, gain) a person's e.*

attrib. and *Comb.* **a.** attrib., as *e.-drum, -lobe*, etc.; *e.-jewel*, etc.; *e.-douche, -speculum, -syringe*, etc.; **b.** objective, as *e.-protector, -catching, -deafening, -piercing, -splitting*, etc.

Special comb.: **e.-bob** (now *vulg.* or *joc.*) = EAR-DROP; **-brisk** *a.*, quick at pricking up his ears, said of a horse; **-brush** = AURILAVE; **-cap,** a covering for the ears against the cold; **-chamber,** the cavity of the internal e.; **-cough,** a cough excited by irritation of the external ear; **-drop,** (*a*) a pendant worn in the e.; (*b*) the flower of the common fuchsia; †**-finger,** the little finger, often put in the e.; **-flap,** the lobe of the e.; the external e. generally; **-lap,** the lobe of the e.; **-lock,** a lock of hair over or above the e.; **-phone,** a headphone; **-pieces, -plate,** part of a helmet covering the e.; **-shell,** one of the *Haliotidæ*, called also *sea-ears*; also, *Auris marina*, a genus of shell-fish; †**shrift,** auricular confession; †**-sore** (cf. EYE-SORE); **-sore** *a.* (*dial.*), irritable, ill-tempered; **-stone,** an otolith; **-string** (cf. *heart-strings*); **-worm** ? = EARWIG; **-wort,** a plant, *Dysophila auricularis*, supposed to cure deafness.

Ear (īᵊɹ), *sb.*² [OE. *ēar* (Northumb. *æhher*) = OFris. *ār*, OS. *ahar* (Du. *aar*), OHG. *ahir, ehir* n. (G. *ähre* fem.), ON. *ax*, Goth. *ahs* :– Gmc. **aχuz*, **ahiz*, rel. to L. *acus, acer-*, husk, chaff.] A spike or head of corn; the part of a cereal plant which contains its flowers or seeds.

Barley was in the e. *Ex.* 9:31.

†**Ear,** *sb.*³ *rare.* 1460. [f. EAR *v.*¹] The action of ploughing –1693.

Ear (īᵊɹ), *v.*¹ Now *arch.* [OE. *erian* = OFris. *era*, OS. *erian*, OHG. *erren*, ON. *erja*, Goth. *arjan*, f. IE. **ar-*, repr. also by L. *arare.*] **1.** *trans.* To plough, till; also with *up.* Also *absol.* **2.** *transf.* and *fig.* ME.

2. Make the Sea serue them; which they eare and wound With keeles *Ant. & Cl.* I. iv. 49.

Ear (īᵊɹ), *v.*² ME. [f. EAR *sb.*²] *intr.* Of corn: To come into ear.

Ea·r-ache. 1789. [f. EAR *sb.*¹] Pain in the drum of the ear; otalgia.

Ear-cockle (īᵊ·ɹkǫ:k'l). 1836. [f. EAR *sb.*² + COCKLE in some sense.] A disease of wheat, etc., caused by vibriones in the seed.

Eared (īᵊɹd), *ppl. a.*¹ ME. [f. EAR *sb.*¹ + -ED².] **a.** Furnished with ears (in various senses); in *Bot.* = AURICULATE. **b.** With defining word: Having (large, open, etc.) ears 1514.

E. owl: a species with ear-like tufts on the head.

Eared (īᵊɹd), *ppl. a.*² ME. [f. EAR *sb.*² and *v.*² + -ED.] Of corn, etc.: Having ears; that has come into ear. In *Her.* having ears of a certain tincture.

†**Ea·ring,** *vbl. sb.*¹ ME. [f. EAR *v.*¹ + -ING¹.] Ploughing; a ploughing –1616.

Ea·ring, *vbl. sb.*[2] 1547. [f. EAR *v.*[2] + -ING[1].] The coming into ear. Also *concr.*

Earing (ī³·riŋ), *sb.* 1626. [f. EAR *sb.*[1] + -ING[1] or RING *sb.*[1]] 'One of a number of small ropes employed to fasten the upper corner of a sail to the yard' (Adm. Smyth). Also *attrib.*

Earl (ɔ̄ɹl), *sb.* [OE. *eorl* = OS., OHG. *erl*, ON. *jarl*, of unkn. origin. Cf. JARL.] †**1.** A man of noble rank, as dist. from a *ceorl* CHURL. Only in OE. **b.** In OE. poetry: A warrior, a man. **2.** In late OE.: A Danish under-king (see JARL); hence, later, the governor of one of the great divisions of England, as Wessex, Mercia, etc. (In this sense = ALDERMAN.) *Obs.* exc. *Hist.* **3.** After the Norman Conquest taken as = L. *comes* COUNT *sb.*[2] †**a.** Applied to all feudal nobles and princes bearing the Romanic title of Count; also *Hist.* to the officers called *comites* ME. **b.** *spec.* In England, Scotland, and Ireland, a title of nobility ranking next below that of marquis and next above that of viscount and corresponding to the European *Count* OE.

Earldom (ɔ̄·ɹldəm). OE. [f. prec. + -DOM.] The territory governed by an earl (*Obs.* exc. *Hist.*); the rank or dignity of an earl.

Others with Titles and new Earldoms caught DRYDEN.

Earless (ī³·ɹlės), *a.* 1611. [f. EAR *sb.*[1] + -LESS.] **1.** Having no ears, as human beings, drinking vessels, bivalve shells, etc. **2.** Without the sense of hearing; without an ear for music; also *poet.* where nothing is heard 1802.

2. In some deep dungeon's e. den WORDSW.

Earlet (ī³·ɹlėt). 1609. [f. EAR *sb.*[1] + -LET.] †**1.** An ear-ring. **2.** Anything resembling a small ear (see EAR *sb.*[1] 8) 1668.

Ea·rl Ma·rshal. ME. A high officer of state, formerly the deputy of the CONSTABLE as judge of the court of chivalry. The title was originally 'marshal'. The office is now hereditary in the line of the Dukes of Norfolk, who, as such, preside over the Heralds' College, appoint its officers, and undertake certain purely ceremonial duties.

Earlship. [f. EARL + -SHIP. Sense 1 is OE. *eorlsćipe.*] †**1.** Manliness; nobility, lordship. OE. only. **2.** The dignity or office of an earl (*Hist.*) 1792.

Early (ɔ̄·ɹli), *a.* [ME. *earlich*, f. the adv., after ON. *árligr.*] **1.** Near to the beginning of a period of time, as morning, night, the year, a lifetime: opp. to *late.* **2.** Belonging or relating to the initial stage of an epoch, of the history of a people, of the world, of a science, etc.; ancient 1672. **3.** Connected with the initial part of any continuous action, etc.; also, timely, done or taking place before it is too late. In compar. and superl. = former, foremost (in time). 1767. **b.** Of future events, etc.: Not remote, near at hand 1857. **4.** Near the beginning in serial order 1707.

1. The e. Village Cock *Rich. III*, v. iii. 209. Ev'n in this e. Dawning of the Year DRYDEN. E. rest, rising COWPER. E. Purple Orchis 1861. E. training JOWETT. **2.** While yet in e. Greece she sung COLLINS. E. philosophers 1794, engravers 1821, fathers of the Church MACAULAY. **3.** No prospect of an e. peace 1857. **4.** The e. chapters of the book 1891.

Phr. **e. closing,** designating a movement for the reduction of hours of labour, (later) a system of closing business premises early one day in the week 1847; **E. English** (*Arch.*): the style of English architecture succeeding the Norman, characterized by pointed arches and lancet windows.

Hence †**Ea·rlily** *adv.* **Ea·rliness.**

Early (ɔ̄·ɹli), *adv.* [OE. (late Northumb.) *ǣrlīće*, beside *ārlīće*, f. *ǣr* ERE + *-līće* -LY[2], after ON. *árliga.*] **1.** Near the beginning of a period of time (see EARLY *a.* 1). **2.** Far back in date, anciently ME. **3.** In the initial part of any continuous action, etc. Also, in good time, before it is too late. 1655. **4.** Near the beginning in serial order 1891.

1. What misaduenture is so earely vp SHAKS.

Ea·r-mark, *sb.* 1523. [f. EAR *sb.*[1] + MARK *sb.*[1]] **1.** A mark in the ear of a sheep or other animal, serving as a sign of ownership. **2.** *transf.* and *fig.* A stamp, mark of ownership, identifying mark 1577.

2. Fanatick Money hath no Ear-mark MARVELL.

Ea·r-mark, *v.* 1591. [f. prec. sb.] *trans.* To mark in the ear as a sign of ownership or identity. **b.** To assign (money, etc.) to a definite purpose 1890.

Sums ear-marked..for the extinction of licences 1890.

Earn (ɔ̄ɹn), *v.*[1] [OE. *earnian* = MLG. *arnen*, OHG. *arnēn*, *arnōn* reap :- WGmc. **aznōjan*, **aznæjan*, f. **aznu*, rel. to OE. *esne* labourer, man, OHG. *esni*, Goth. *asneis* hired labourer.] *trans.* To render an equivalent in labour for; hence, to obtain or deserve as the reward of labour. In early use: To deserve. **b.** Of qualities or actions: To procure as a direct consequence *for* a person 1596.

1. These praises..have been dearly earned 'JUNIUS'. Do they all e. wages HT. MARTINEAU. **b.** The stern justice of his rule earned the hatred of the disorderly baronage J.R.GREEN.

Earn, *v.*[2] 1674. Now *dial.* [Same as ME. *erne*, rel. to RUN *v.* Cf. RENNET *sb.*[1]] To curdle (*intr.* and *trans.*).

†**Earn,** *v.*[3] 1579. [app. a var. of YEARN *v.*[1]; cf. dial. *ear* for *year.*] **1.** *intr.* To desire strongly –1596. **2.** To grieve –1651. **3.** Of hounds, etc.: To utter a prolonged cry.

Earn, var. of ERNE, eagle.

Earnest (ɔ̄·ɹnėst), *sb.*[1] [OE. *eornust*, *-ost* = MLG. *ernest*, OHG. *ernust* (G. *ernst*), f. **ern-*, repr. also in ON. *ern* brisk, vigorous, Goth. *arniba* safely; of unkn. origin.] †**1.** Ardour in battle; more widely, intense desire –ME. **2.** Seriousness, as opp. to jest OE.

2. But in good e., madam, speak 1570. This caitiff, never worth my e., and now not seasonable for my jest MILT.

Earnest (ɔ̄·ɹnėst), *sb.*[2] ME. [Earliest forms *ernes*, *eernes*; prob. alt., with assim. to -NESS, of synon. and contemp. *erles*; see ARLES. Assim. to *ernest* (= prec.) appears XV.] Money in part payment, *esp.* for the purpose of binding a bargain. Also *fig.* a foretaste, instalment, pledge, of what is to come.

E. given me of something further intended in my Favour STEELE. *Comb.*, *e.-money*, etc.

Earnest (ɔ̄·ɹnėst), *a.* (*adv.*) [OE. *eornost(e)* = OFris. *ernst*, MLG. *ernest.*] **1.** Of persons: Serious; usually in emphatic sense, intensely serious, in purpose, feeling, conviction, or action; sincerely zealous. Of words or actions: Proceeding from intense conviction. Also *trans.* **2.** Of things: Demanding serious consideration; weighty 1544.

1. I..haue been An e. aduocate to plead for him *Rich. III*, I. iii. 87. We ought to giue the more e. heede *Hebr.* 2:1. *transf.* Life is e. LONGF. **2.** E. and weightie matters ASCHAM.

†**B.** *adv.* = Earnestly –1791.

Hence **Ea·rnest-ly** *adv.* in an e. manner; **-ness.**

†**Ea·rnest,** *v.* [f. EARNEST *sb.*[1] or *a.*] To use in earnest; to render earnest –1603.

†**Ea·rnestful,** *a.* ME. [f. EARNEST *sb.*[1] + -FUL.] = EARNEST *a.* 1, 2. –1563.

†**Ea·rnest-pe·nny.** 1508. [f. EARNEST *sb.*[2] + PENNY.] A piece of money paid as earnest to bind a bargain –1760. Also *fig.*

Ea·rnful, *a.* Now *dial.* 1500. [app. a var. of YEARNFUL; see EARN *v.*[3]] Anxious, full of yearning; sorrowful. Hence **Ea·rnfully** *adv.*

Earning (ɔ̄·ɹniŋ), *vbl. sb.*[1] OE. [f. EARN *v.*[1] + -ING[1]; in OE. *earnung*, *ġearnung.*] **1.** The action of EARN *v.*[1]; *concr.* in pl. that which is earned by labour, or invested capital 1732. †**2.** The fact of deserving; what one deserves –ME. †**3.** *pl.* Gain, profit –1675.

1. The earnings of the peasant MACAULAY. The gross earnings of railways 1888.

†**Ea·rning,** *vbl. sb.*[2] [f. EARN *v.*[3] + -ING[1].] = YEARNING –1711.

Earning (ɔ̄·ɹniŋ), *vbl. sb.*[3] *dial.* 1615. [f. EARN *v.*[2] + -ING[1].] **1.** The action of EARN *v.*[2] 1782. **2.** Rennet. Also *attrib.* Also **e.-grass** = BUTTERWORT.

Ea·r-pi:ck, -pi:cker. 1483. [f. EAR *sb.*[1]] An instrument for clearing the ear of wax, etc.; also *fig.*

†**Ea·r-rent.** 1610. [perh. orig. f. EAR *sb.*[3]] ?Some kind of agricultural rent. Used punningly by B. Jons. for loss of ears in the pillory. –1624.

Ea·r-ring, earring. OE. [f. EAR *sb.*[1]] **1.** A ring worn in the lobe of the ear for ornament, etc.; often, a pendant or drop. **2.** *dial.* The common fuchsia.

Earsh. Now *dial.* 1622. [A slurred pronunc. of EDDISH. See ARRISH.] **a.** A stubble field. **b.** Eddish.

Earshot (ī³·ɹʃǫt). 1607. [f. EAR *sb.*[1]; after *bowshot*, etc.] The distance at which the voice may be heard; hearing.

Earth (ɔ̄ɹþ), *sb.*[1] [OE. *eorþe* = OFris. *erthe*, OS. *ertha* (Du. *aarde*), OHG. *erda* (G. *erde*), ON. *jǫrð*, Goth. *airþa* :- Gmc. **erþō.*] **I. 1.** The ground as a mere surface, or as a solid crust. **2.** The hole or hiding-place of a burrowing animal, as a fox, etc. Also *fig.* 1575. **3.** The soil as suited for cultivation OE. **4.** *Electr.* Connection of a wire conductor with the earth, either accidental (with leakage of current) or intentional (as for providing a return path for a telegraph current, etc.) 1870.

1. They kneele, they kisse the E. *Wint. T.* v. i. 109. Who under e. on human kind avenge Severe, the guilt of violated oaths COWPER. **2.** Frighted hare fled to cover, or fox to e. DE FOE. **3.** Fatty e. 1751.

II. The world we live on. **1.** The dry land OE. **2.** The world as including land and sea; as dist. from the (material) heaven OE. **3.** The world as the abode of mortals; freq. opp. to heaven and hell. In poet. and rhet. use often without the article. OE. Also *transf.* of the inhabitants of the world 1549. **4.** The world as a sphere, orb, or planet ME.; †*transf.* –1841.

1. God clepid the drie erthe WYCLIF *Gen.* 1:10. **3.** Those that haue knowne the E. so full of faults *Jul. C.* I. iii. 45. The whole e. was of one language *Gen.* 11:1. What on e. is the matter 1891. **4.** *transf.* He affirmed..the Moon [to be] an e., having Mountains [etc.] CUDWORTH.

†**III.** A country, land; a portion of the earth's surface –1628.

This blessed plot, this e., this Realme, this England *Rich. II*, II. i. 50.

IV. 1. The material of which the surface of the ground is composed, soil, mould, dust, clay OE. **2.** Used for: The body. Cf. *dust*, *clay.* 1600. **3.** Earth as one of the four (or more) so-called 'elements' ME. **4.** *Chem.* Applied to certain metallic oxides, *e.g.* magnesia, alumina, zirconia, and the 'alkaline earths', baryta, lime, strontia 1728.

2. Poore soule the center of my sinfull e. SHAKS. *Sonn.* cxlvi. **3.** You should not rest Betweene the elements of ayre and e. *Twel. N.* I. v. 294.

attrib. and *Comb.*: **e.-bags** = *sand-bags* (Adm. Smyth); **-balls,** truffles; †**-bath,** a medical bath in which the patient was buried up to the shoulders in e. or mud; **-battery** (*Electr.*), a battery formed by burying two voltaic elements some distance apart; **-bed,** a bed upon the ground; the grave; **-bob,** a maggot, the larva of the beetle; **-chestnut** = EARTH-NUT; **-closet,** a closet in which e. is used as a deodorizing agent; **-current** (*Electr.*), an irregular current due to the e., which renders telegraph wires temporarily useless; †**-dog,** a terrier; **-flax,** ?asbestos; **-gall,** the Lesser Centaury; **-hog** = AARD-VARK; **-house,** an underground dwelling; *fig.* the grave; **-hunger,** a disease characterized by a morbid craving for eating e.; *fig.* greed of land or territory; **-oil,** petroleum; **-pillar** (*Geol.*), a pillar-like mass of earth, sometimes capped with a stone; **-plate** *Electr.*), a metal plate buried in the e., connected with a telegraph battery; **-sack** = *earth-bag*; **-shine** = E.-LIGHT; †**-shrew,** the Shrew-mouse; **-smoke,** the plant Fumitory; **-spring,** in electrical machines a spring connected with the e.; **-star,** a fungus so called from its shape when lying on the ground; **-stopper,** one who stops up the earths of foxes; **-table** (*Arch.*), the plinth of a wall, the projecting course immediately above the ground; **-tongue** (*Bot.*), the genus *Geoglossum*; **-wave,** a seismic wave in the crust of the e.; **-wolf,** tr. Du. AARD-WOLF, q. v.

†**Earth,** *sb.*[2] [OE. **erþ*, WS. *ierþ* :- **arþiz*, f. Gmc. *ar-*; see EAR *v.*[1], -TH[1].] The action of ploughing –1813.

Earth (ɔ̄ɹþ), *v.* ME. [f. EARTH *sb.*[1]] **1.** *trans.* To commit to the earth; to bury. Now *dial.* **2.** To hide in the earth; to cover *up* with earth. Also *intr.* (for *refl.*). Also *fig.* 1648. **3.** *trans.* To conceal in a hole or burrow 1619; *intr.* (for *refl.*) of the fox, etc.: To run to his earth 1622. **4.** *trans.* To drive (a fox, etc.) to his earth. Also *fig.* 1575. **5.** *Electr.* To connect (a conductor) with the earth 1888.

1. Though earthed be his corps, yet florish shall his fame 1557. **2.** Seeds thrive When earth't BENLOWES. E. up the plants frequently 1796. **3.** Perhaps some Fox had earth'd there 1634. **4.** We e. and digge a Badgerd TURBERV.

Ea·rth-apple. OE. [f. EARTH *sb.*[1]] **1.** In OE. ? A cucumber. **2.** ? The potato [tr. Fr. *pomme de terre*]. Mod. Dicts.

Ea·rth-board. 1649. [f. EARTH *sb.*[1] or [2] + BOARD.] The mould-board of a plough.

Ea·rth-born, *ppl. a. poet.* or *rhet.* 1603. **1.** Born by emerging from the earth, as the Titans, etc. Also = AUTOCHTHONOUS. **2.** Of earthly or mortal race 1667. **3.** Of things: Produced by or arising from the earth 1702.

1. Cadmus and his earth-born men JOWETT. **2.** Creatures..earth-born perhaps, Not Spirits MILT. *P. L.* iv. 360 **3.** Earth-born Pride ROWE.

†Ea·rth-din. OE. [f. EARTH *sb.*[1] + DIN.] An earthquake –1483.

Earthen (ə̄·ɹþ'n), *a.* ME. [f. EARTH *sb.*[1] + -EN[4].] **1.** Made of earth; made of baked clay. **2.** *transf.* and *fig.* Characteristic of the earth; merely material c1600.

Earthenware (ə̄·ɹþ'nˌwēᵊɹ). 1673. [f. EARTHEN *a.* + WARE *sb.*[2]; formerly as two words.] **1.** Vessels, etc., made of baked clay; in *pl.* kinds of earthenware. **2.** The material of which such vessels are made 1799. **3.** *attrib.* 1812.

Earthfast (ə̄·ɹþfɑst), *a.* OE. [f. EARTH *sb.*[1] + FAST *a.*] Fixed in the ground.

Earthiness (ə̄·ɹþinės). ME. [f. EARTHY *a.* + -NESS.] **1.** The quality of being earthy; the properties characteristic of earth; †*concr.* earthy matter –1693. **2.** *fig.* = EARTHLINESS 1. 1670.

Ea·rth-light. 1833. *Astron.* The light reflected from the earth upon the dark half of the moon; = *earth-shine.*

Earthliness (ə̄·ɹþlinės). 1535. [f. EARTHLY *a.* + -NESS.] **1.** The quality of being earthly or terrestrial; worldliness as opp. to *heavenliness* 1583. **†2.** = EARTHINESS 1. –1642.

1. Each stain of e. Had passed away SHELLEY.

†Ea·rthling, *sb.*[1] [OE. *yrþling*; see EARTH *sb.*[2], -LING[1].] A ploughman –1714.

Earthling (ə̄·ɹþliŋ), *sb.*[2] 1593. [f. EARTH *sb.*[1] + -LING[1].] **1.** An inhabitant of the earth. **2.** A worldling 1615.

2. Beyond your earthlings gold and siluer mines 1615.

Earthly (ə̄·ɹþli), *a.* [OE. *eorþlić*, f. EARTH *sb.*[1] + -LY[1].] **1.** Pertaining to the earth, terrestrial. Now usually opp. to *heavenly.* **b.** As an expletive; = on earth 1753. **†2.** Existing or living in or on the ground –1658. **3.** = EARTHY 1, 2. *arch.* or *Obs.* ME. **†4.** = EARTHEN (*rare*) –1533.

1. The pageant pomp of e. man SCOTT. Of no e. use ROGERS. *Not an e.*: not an e. chance. **2.** A Scepter, or an E. Sepulchre 3 *Hen. VI*, I. iii. 17. *Comb.*: **e.-minded** *a.*, having the affections set on the things of the e.; whence **-mindedness; -wise** *adv.*, in an e. manner.

†Ea·rth-mad. *rare.* [OE. *eorþmata* for *eorþmaþa*, f. *eorþe* EARTH *sb.*[1] + *maþe* a worm (see MATHE).] An earthworm –1601.

Ea·rth-nut. OE. **1.** The roundish tuber of an umbelliferous plant (*Bunium flexuosum*, including *B. bulbocastanum*), called also *Earth-chestnut* and *Pig-nut.* **2.** Applied also to the truffle (*Tuber*), the ARACHIS, the *Œnanthe pimpinelloides*, and the Heath Pea 1548.

Earthquake (ə̄·ɹþkwēˈk). ME. [f. EARTH *sb.*[1] + QUAKE *sb.* Superseded EARTH-DIN.] **1.** A shaking of the ground; usually *spec.* a convulsion of the earth's surface produced by volcanic or similar forces within the crust. Also *fig.* **2.** *attrib.*, as *e.-shock, -voice, -wave*, etc. 1821.

1. *fig.* In this age, wherein there is an e. of ancient hospitals FULLER. This social and political e. BRIGHT.

†Ea·rthquave. ME. [f. EARTH *sb.*[1] + †*quave*; see QUAVER *v.*] = EARTHQUAKE –1541.

Earthward (ə̄·ɹþwəɹd), *adv.* ME. [See -WARD.] Towards the earth.

Earthwork (ə̄·ɹþwǒɹk). 1633. [f. EARTH *sb.*[1] + WORK *sb.*] A bank or mound of earth used as a rampart or fortification.

Earthworm (ə̄·ɹþwǒɹm). 1591. [f. EARTH *sb.*[1] + WORM.] **1.** A worm that lives in the ground, *esp.* one of the genus *Lumbricus.* **2.** *fig.* A mean grovelling person 1594.

Earthy (ə̄·ɹþi), *a.* 1555. [See -Y[1].] **1.** Of the nature of earth; resembling, characteristic of, or consisting of earth. Of minerals: Without lustre, friable, and roughish to the touch; also, containing earth, as in *E. Cobalt*, etc. **†2.** Having the properties of the 'element' earth; heavy, gross –1677. Also *fig.* **3.** *Chem.* Pertaining to an 'earth' or 'earths' (see EARTH IV. 4); in mod. use, pertaining to the class of metallic oxides so named 1718. **4.** Pertaining to the ground, or to what is below it; dwelling inside the earth 1665. **5.** Dwelling or existing on the earth: opp. to *heavenly* 1595.

1. Starry roofe and e. floore SIDNEY. **2.** *fig.* Her e., and abhor'd commands *Temp.* I. ii. 273. **4.** Those e. spirits black and envious are DRYDEN. **5.** The impious race Of e. giants, that would heaven outface CHAPMAN.

Ea·r-tru:mpet. 1776. A straight or convoluted conoidal tube, used by persons partially deaf, to collect and intensify sounds.

Ea·r-wax. ME. [f. EAR *sb.*[1]] A viscid secretion which collects in the external meatus of the ear.

Earwig (īᵊ·ɹwig), *sb.* [OE. *ēarwicga*, f. *ēare* EAR *sb.*[1] + *wicga* earwig, prob. rel. to WIGGLE *v.*; cf. synon. ME. *arwygyll*, dial. *arrawiggle.*] **1.** An insect, *Forficula auricularia*, which is supposed to creep into the ear. **†2.** *fig.* A whisperer, flatterer, parasite –1758.

2. The earwigs of royalty 1758.

Earwig (īᵊ·ɹwig), *v.* 1837. [f. the sb.] **a.** To pester by private importunities. **b.** To bias by secret communications; to insinuate oneself into the confidence of.

Each secretary of state is sure to be earwigged by a knot of sturdy beggars 1839.

Ea·r-wi:tness. 1594. [f. EAR *sb.*[1]] One whose testimony is based upon his own hearing.

Strabo himself was an ear-witness of this 1734.

Ease (īz), *sb.* ME. [– AFr. *ese*, OFr. *eise*, (also mod.) *aise* †elbow-room, †favourable occasion, convenience :– Rom. **adjaces* for *adjacens*, subst. use of pres. pple. of L. *adjacēre* (see ADJACENT).] **†1.** Opportunity, means or ability –1500. **2.** Comfort, convenience; *formerly* also, enjoyment. Also with *an* and *pl.* (obs.) ME. **3.** Absence of pain or discomfort; freedom from annoyance ME. **4.** Rest; leisure; in bad sense, idleness, sloth ME. **b.** Facility; *esp.* in phr. *with e.* 1610. **c.** Unconcern; absence of hesitation 1808. **5.** Freedom from constraint; an unconstrained position; *esp.* in *Mil.* phr., *To stand at e.* 1802. **6.** Freedom from awkwardness in social behaviour 1750. **7.** Relief; alleviation 1542. Also with *an* and *pl.* (obs.) ME.

2. The e., and benefit the Subjects may enjoy HOBBES. A condition of e. and fortune EMERSON. Phr. *To take one's e.*: to make oneself comfortable. **3.** E. of bodie 1597, of Mind STEELE, heart BURKE. **4.** E. breedeth vice 1577. **6.** A certain graceful e. marks him as a man who knows the world MACAULAY. **7.** Sudden e. from pain BUTLER. Phr. *Chapel of E.*; see CHAPEL.

Phrases (senses 1–6). *At e., at one's e.*: in comfort, without anxiety or annoyance, unconstrained, unembarrassed; formerly also, well-to-do. *Ill at e.*: uncomfortable, uneasy.

Ease (īz), *v.* ME. [orig. – OFr. *aisier*, *aaisier*, f. phr. *a aise* at ease; later directly f. the sb.] **1.** *trans.* To give ease to; to comfort, disburden; †to benefit, help. Also *refl.* Also (rarely) *absol.* **2.** To relieve, lighten, set free (a person, etc.) *of*, †*from* a burden, anxiety, etc. ME. **b.** *joc.* To deprive *of* 1609. **3.** To lighten (a burden, etc.); to lessen (an inconvenience); to assuage (pain, etc.) ME. **b.** *poet.* To relax (labour) 1715. **4.** To facilitate (*rare*) 1632. **5.** To relax slightly; to shift a little, make to fit 1891. **6.** *Naut.* Often with *away, down, off*: to slacken (a rope, sail, etc.). *E. her!* (in a steam vessel): reduce the speed of the engine. *E. the helm!*: put the helm down a few spokes in a head sea. (Adm. Smyth.)

1. Some scruple rose, but thus he eas'd his thought POPE. The declared intention of easing the dissenters HUME. **2.** E. your bosoms of a fear so vain POPE. **3.** Is there no play To e. the anguish of a torturing houre? SHAKS. **4.** With mutual wing Easing thir flight MILT. Hence **Ea·seless** *a.*

Easeful (ī·zful), *a.* ME. [See -FUL.] **1.** That gives ease, comfort, or relief. **2.** Unoccupied; indolent 1611.

1. E. Death KEATS. **2.** Giving the best of their grain to the easefull and idle RALEGH. Hence **Ea·seful-ly** *adv.*, **-ness.**

Easel (ī·zĕl, ī·z'l). 1634. [– Du. *ezel* = G. *esel* ass. Cf. HORSE *sb.* II. 2.] A wooden frame to support a picture during its execution, or for exhibition. *Comb.* **e.-picture, -piece,** one painted at the e., or small enough to stand on an e.

Easement (ī·zmĕnt). ME. [– OFr. *aisement*, f. *aisier* EASE *v.*; see -MENT.] **1.** The process or means of giving or obtaining ease or relief; alleviation; †redress of grievances. Now somewhat *rare.* **2.** Advantage, convenience, comfort; furtherance; formerly also, enjoyment (*arch.*) ME. **b.** Accommodation ME. **3.** The right or privilege of using something not one's own; *esp.* in *Law.* (See quot.) 1463.

1. I certainly stand in need of every kind of relief and e. BURKE. **3.** If the purposes for which the land of another is used merely tend to the more convenient enjoyment of another piece of land, the right is called an e. 1876.

Easily (ī·zili), *adv.* Formerly compared **easilier, -est.** ME. [f. EASY *a.* + -LY[2].] **1.** Comfortably; without pain, anxiety, or disturbance. **2.** Freely ME. **†3.** Without hurry. Also, quietly. –1695. **4.** With little labour or difficulty ME. **5.** With little resistance or reluctance 1649. **†6.** After *but*: Indifferently, poorly –1536.

1. Persons seeking only to live e. 1562. **2.** Sir, your wit ambles well; it goes e. *Much Ado* V. i. 159. **4.** Nothing is more e. broken than a mans word HOBBES. **5.** To catch Distempers e. STEELE.

Easiness (ī·zinės). ME. [f. EASY *a.* + -NESS.] **1.** The state or quality of being EASY (see quots.). **†2.** The being easily influenced; in bad sense, credulity –1797.

1. The e. we enjoy when asleep RAY. E. of Behaviour RICHARDSON, of wit D'ISRAELI. Ruin'd by his E. and Neglect 1699. E. of conquest 1800, of temper BUTLER. **2.** Persons..who practised upon their e. 1674.

Ea·ssel, *adv. Sc.* 1810. [Obscurely f. next.] Eastward, easterly.

East (īst). [OE. *ēast-* in comps. (e.g. *Ēastangle* East-Anglians) = OFris. *āst*, OS., OHG. *ōst* (Du. *oost*, G. *ost*), repr. Gmc. **austo-* (with suffix **-no-* in OE. *ēastan*, OS., OHG. *ōstana*, ON. *austan* from the east); as adv. prob. shortening of **ēaster* = OS., OHG. *ōstar*, ON. *austr* toward the east :– Gmc. **austro-*; f. IE. base **aus-*, as in L. *aurora* (:– **ausōsa*), *auster* (cf. AUSTRAL), Gr. (Æolic) αὔως dawn, αὔριον (:– **ausrion*) to-morrow; cf. Skr. *ushâs* morning, dawn.]

A. *adv.* **†1.** [repr. OE. *ēastan.*] From the east –ME. **2.** [repr. OE. *ēast.*] In the direction of the part of the horizon where the sun rises; in the direction of that point of the horizon which is 90° to the right of the north point; also *due e.* OE. **3.** quasi-*sb.* with *from, on*, etc. ME.

B. *sb.* **1.** subst. use of A. 2. The portion of the horizon or the sky near the place of the sun's rising; that one of the cardinal points near which the sun rises ME. **2.** The orient; the eastern part of a country, district, or town ME. **3.** = East wind 1763.

1. The gentle day..Dapples the drowsie E. with spots of grey *Much Ado* V. iii. 27. **2.** Where the gorgeous E...Showrs on her Kings Barbaric Pearl MILT. *P. L.* II. 3. **3.** Where the sharp e. for ever..blows SHENSTONE.

C. as *adj.* That is in, near, or towards the east; oriental, easterly ME.

An E. window welcomes the infant beams of the Sun FULLER. *Comb.*: **E.-south-east, E.-north-east:** the points of the compass distant 22½° from due E.; **E.-by-South, E.-by-North:** the points distant 11¼° from due E.

East (īst), *v.* 1858. [f. prec.] **a.** *intr.* To move towards the east. **b.** *refl.* To orientate; to find one's true position.

Ea·st-cou:ntry. 1701. An eastern country; in 18th c. *spec.* the region of the Baltic; cf. EASTLAND. Also *attrib.*

Ea:st-e·nd. OE. The easterly part of anything. Now often *spec.* The eastern part of London. Hence **Ea:st-e·nder.**

Easter (ī·stəɹ), *sb.* [OE. *ēastre*, mainly pl. *ēastron*, also *ēastro, -a* = OFris. *āsteron*, OHG. *ōstarūn* (G. *Ostern* pl.); derived by Bede from the name of a goddess whose feast was celebrated at the vernal equinox, *Ēostre*, Northumb. var. of *Ēastre* :– Gmc. **Austrōn*, cogn. w. Skr. *usrā* dawn (see EAST).] **1.** A festival of the Christian Church, commemorating the resurrection of Christ, and corresponding to the Jewish passover, whence its name in most European langs. (Gr. πάσχα – Heb. *pésaḥ*, L. *pascha*, Fr. *Pâques*, It. *Pasqua*). It is observed on the first Sunday after the calendar full moon—*i.e.* the 14th day of the calendar moon—which happens on or next after 21 March. Applied colloq. to the week commencing with Easter Sunday. †2. The Jewish passover –1611. 3. *attrib.*, as *e.-holidays*, *-Sunday* (*-Monday*, etc.), *-tide*, *-time*, *-week*, etc. ME.

2. Intending after E. to bring him foorth *Acts* 12:4. *Comb.*: **e.-dues,** money payable at E. to the parson of a parish by the parishioners; **-eggs,** eggs painted in bright colours, which it was (and, now, again is) customary to present to friends at E.; **-offering** = *easter-dues*; formerly also the paschal sacrifice.

†**Ea·ster,** *a.* ME. [perh. continuing OE. compar. *ēasterra* (cf. ON. *austarr* more to the east).] Nearest the east; eastern –1816.

Ea·ster-da·y. [OE. *Ēasterdæġ*, f. *Ēaster-*, comb. f. *Ēastron* EASTER.] Easter Sunday.

Ea·stering, *ppl. a. rare.* 1876. [perh. f. EASTER *a.* + -ING².; cf. *westering.*] Shifting eastward.

Ea·sterling. Now *Hist.* 1534. [app. f. EASTER *a.* + -LING¹, prob. after Du. *oosterling.* In AFr. and AL. *sterling(us*, *esterling(us* appear in XIII but only in the sense of 'sterling penny' or 'pennyweight', not as the name of the Easterlings or Hanse merchants. See STERLING.] A native of the east. 1. *spec.* A native of the Baltic coasts; chiefly applied to the citizens of the Hanse towns. Hence *E. money.* b. [tr. AL. *esterlingus.*] The weight of the easterling or sterling penny; a pennyweight 1605. 2. *gen.* An inhabitant of an eastern country or district; also, a member of the Eastern Church (*arch.*) 1561.

Easterly (ī·stəɹli). 1548. [prob. f. EASTER *a.* + -LY¹; cf. Du. *oosterlijk.*]

A. *adj.* 1. Situated towards the east. 2. Coming from the east 1559.

1. E. towns..are more wholesome than the westerly 1655.

B. *adv.* In an eastern position or direction; from the east 1635.

†**Ea·stermost,** *a.* 1555. [f. EASTER *a.* + -MOST.] = EASTERNMOST –1832.

Eastern (ī·stəɹn). [OE. *ēasterne* = OS., OHG. *ōstroni*, ON. *austrœnn* :– Gmc. **austrōnja-*, f. **austro-* (see EAST).]

A. *adj.* 1. Of or pertaining to the east; dwelling in the East; Oriental OE. 2. Lying or directed towards the east 1593. 3. Coming from the east (*poet.*) OE.

1. E. priests POPE. An e. tale MORLEY. 2. The e. sky TYNDALL. E. voyages ADDISON.

B. *sb.* An inhabitant of the East OE. b. A member of the Eastern Church 1865.

Hence **Ea·sterner,** an inhabitant of one of the eastern or New England states of U.S. 1864.

Easternmost (ī·stəɹnməst, -moᵘst), *a.* 1830. [f. prec. + -MOST.] Situated farthest to the east.

Ea:st I·ndia. *Obs.* exc. *attrib.* 1634. Formerly used = (*The*) EAST INDIES.

East India Company, a company formed for carrying on an East Indian trade, *esp.* the English company incorporated in 1600. *E. Indiaman*, a ship of large tonnage engaged in the East India trade.

Ea:st I·ndian. 1553. [f. prec. + -AN.]

A. as *adj.* 1. Of or pertaining to the East Indies. 2. In Anglo-Ind. use; = EURASIAN *a.* 1831. B. as *sb.* A Eurasian 1831.

Ea:st I·ndies. 1598. A term including Hindustan, Further India, and the islands beyond. Opp. to the *West Indies* or Central American islands.

They shall be my East and West Indies, and I will trade to them both *Merry W.* I. iii. 79.

Easting (ī·stiŋ), *vbl. sb.* 1628. [f. EAST + -ING¹.] 1. *Naut.* 'The course made good, or gained to the eastward' (Adm. Smyth). 2. An approach to an easterly direction; a shifting or veering eastwards; easterly direction 1855.

Eastland (ī·stlænd). OE. [f. EAST + LAND *sb.*] An eastern country or district; †*spec.* the lands bordering on the Baltic. Also *attrib.*

Eastward (ī·stwəɹd). [OE. *ēastewearde* adv.; hence as adj. XV.] A. *adv.* 1. In an eastern direction. 2. quasi-*sb.* 1695.

1. Turne thee E. 1 *Kings* 17:3. 2. To sail to the e. 1828. var. **Ea·stwards** *adv.*

B. *adj.* That moves or looks eastward ME.

The..e. posture in prayer SCHAFF.

Hence **Ea·stwardly** *adv.* in an eastern direction; from an eastern quarter. Also as *adj.*

East wind. 1. (OE. *ēastanwind*) A wind blowing from the east 1398. 2. A player in the game of mah jong 1922.

Easy (ī·zi). ME. [– AFr. *aisé*, OFr. *aisié* (mod. *aisé*), pa. pple. of *aisier* put at ease; see EASE *v.*, -Y⁵.]

A. *adj.* †1. At liberty, having opportunity or means (to do something). ME. only. 2. Characterized by ease or rest; comfortable, quiet ME. 3. Free from pain or discomfort ME. 4. Free from constraint or stiffness; without trace of effort; smooth 1483. 5. Not hard pressed; not hurried, gentle ME. 6. Free from care, or apprehension 1692. 7. = EASY-GOING 1649. 8. Comfortably off 1701. 9. Conducive to ease ME. 10. Presenting few difficulties; offering little resistance ME. 11. Of persons, etc.; Soon yielding, compliant; credulous 1611. 12. That is obtained with ease 1697. 13. Not oppressive; not burdensome ME.; †of persons: Not exacting; lenient; not difficult to get on with –1727. †14. Indifferent; slight –1648. 15. Loosely fitting 1594. 16. *Comm.* (opp. to *tight*) Of a commodity: Not much in demand. Of the market: Showing little firmness in prices. 1888.

2. To make life e. BEVERIDGE. 3. After an opiate he became easier 1809. 4. Easie and obliging conversation BP. BURNET. An e. Writer STEELE. E. and unstudied writing 1884. Phr. *Free and e.* (see FREE AND EASY). 5. Under e. sail 1834. Of e. motion 1852. 6. I made her e. on that point DE FOE. An e. conscience 1885. 8. In e. circumstances 1879. 9. E. cushions 1879. 10. This easie truth HOBBES. E. of access H. WALPOLE. It is e. to make a solitude and call it peace MORLEY. 11. An easie King deserves no better Fate DRYDEN. Phr. *Lady of e. virtue.* 12. He obtained an e. pardon 1856. 13. On the easiest terms PEPYS. A generous and easie Governour BENTLEY. In e. confinement 1855. 16. The money-market is e. 1891.

Phr. *Honours e.* (Whist): 'honours divided'.

B. *adv.* In an EASY manner. Now mostly *colloq.* ME.

Phr. *To take it e.*, to do no more than one must. *E. ahead!*: (steam) at a moderate speed. *Easy all!* (in Boating): stop (rowing)! Hence as *sb.* A short rest. *To stand e.*: (of a squad, etc., standing at ease) to relax still further.

Ea·sy chai·r, ea:sy-chai·r. 1707. A chair adapted for ease or repose, often with arms and padded.

Ea·sy-go·ing, *ppl. a.* 1674. Of a horse: Having an easy gait. Hence *fig.* That takes things easily; comfort-loving; indolent.

Eat (īt), *v.* Pa. t. **ate, eat** (ēⁱt, et, it). Pa. pple. **eaten** (ī·t'n). [OE. *etan* = OFris. *eta*, OS. *etan* (Du. *eten*), OHG. *ezzan* (G. *essen*), ON. *eta*, Goth. *itan* :– Gmc. **etan*; f. IE. base **ed-*, whence L. *edere*, Gr. ἔδειν.] 1. *trans.* To masticate and swallow as food. Used also of liquid food, for which a spoon is used. Also *transf.* and *fig.* Also with *of* in partitive sense. 2. *intr.* To consume food, take a meal OE. Also quasi-*trans.* 3. *intr.* with pass. force (chiefly with *adj.* or *adv.*) 1601. 4. *trans.* To devour, consume; to feed destructively upon (*lit.* and *fig.*) OE. 5. *trans.* To gnaw, pierce 1611; also *transf.* of the slow action of frost, rust, cancer, corrosives, the waves, etc. 1555. Also *absol.* 6. To make (a hole, etc.) by fretting or corrosion (*lit.* and *fig.*) 1697. 7. *intr.* To make a way by gnawing or corrosion (*lit.* and *fig.*) 1606. 8. *Naut. trans.* and *intr.* (See quots.) 1769.

1. They..eate rootes for breade SIR T. NORTH. We eat excellent cream EVELYN. Lest..thou eate of his sacrifice *Ex.* 34:15. Phr. *To e. one's terms*: to qualify for being called to the Bar by eating dinners three or more times during each of twelve terms in the Hall of an Inn of Court. *To e. one's words*: to retract humbly. See also HUMBLE PIE. 2. There should be temperance..in eating EMERSON. Phr. quasi-*trans. To e.* (a person) *out of house and home.* 3. If the cakes at tea e. short and crisp GOLDSM. 4. That they may..eate every herbe of the land *Ex.* 10:12. Phr. *To e. one's* (*own*) *heart*: to suffer from silent grief or vexation. 5. *transf.* The Rose..eaten with the canker LYLY. 7. Has not the desire of wealth so eaten into our hearts J. H. NEWMAN. 8. *Sourdre au vent*, to hold a good wind; to claw or e. to windward FALCONER. *To e. the wind out of a vessel*: to steal to windward of her by very keen seamanship. Hence **Ea·ter.**

Eat, *sb.* [OE. *æt* = OFris. *ēt*, OS. *āt*, OHG. *āz*; in mod. use f. prec.] †1. That which is eaten –1609. b. Now freq. in pl. *U.S.* 1889. 2. The action of eating; a meal –ME. Phr. *On the eat* (U.S.) 1879.

Eatable (ī·tăb'l). 1483. [See -ABLE.]

A. *adj.* In a state fit to be eaten.

B. *sb.* An article of food. Chiefly in *pl.* 1672.

Eatage (ī·tėdʒ). *n. dial.* 1641. [f. EAT *v.* + -AGE.] 1. Grass available only for grazing; *esp.* the aftermath. 2. The right of using for pasture 1857.

Eath, eith (īð, īþ). *Obs.* exc. *Sc.* [OE. *ēaþe* adv. = OS. *ōðo*, OHG. *ōdo*, ON. *auð-*; OE. *īeþe*, *ȳþe* adj. = OS. *ōði*, OHG. *ōdi.*] A. *adj.* Easy. B. *adv.* Easily OE. var. †**Ea·thly** *a.* and *adv.*

Eating (ī·tiŋ), *vbl. sb.* ME. [f. EAT *v.* + -ING¹.] 1. The action or habit of taking food. Also, a meal. 2. Corrosion 1691. 3. *attrib.*, as *e.-apple*, etc. ME.

Comb. **e.-house,** a house for e., *esp.* one in which meals are supplied; a restaurant.

‖**Eau** (*o*). 1823. [Fr.; = 'water'.] Hence: **E.-de-Cologne,** a perfume, originally made at Cologne. **E.-de-vie** [lit. 'water of life'], the French name for brandy.

Eave (īv). 1580. [f. EAVES, treated as pl.] Used as sing. of EAVES. Hence **Eave** *v.* to shelter under eaves. **Eaved** *ppl. a.* provided with eaves.

Eaver (ī·vəɹ). Now *dial.* 1732. [Of unkn. origin.] Rye grass.

Eaves (īvz). [OE. *efes*, corresp. to OFris. *ose*, MLG. *ovese*, Flem. *oose*, MDu. *ovese*, *ose*, OHG. *obasa*, *-isa*, MHG. *ob(e)se* (G. dial. *obsen*) eaves, porch, ON. *ups*, Goth. *ubizwa* 'στοά' :– Gmc. **obaswa*, **obiswa*, prob. f. **ob-* of OVER *adv.*] 1. The projecting edge of a roof, etc., which overhangs the side. 2. *transf.* Anything that projects or overhangs slightly; *poet.* the eyelids ME.

1. With minute-drops from off the e. MILT. *Pens.* 130. 2. Closing e. of wearied eyes I sleep TENNYSON.

Comb.: **e.-board** (also *eave-board*), **-catch, -lath,** an arris fillet, when used to raise the slates at the e. of a building (Gwilt); **-martin,** the House Martin (*Hirundo urbica*).

Ea·vesdrip, -drop, *sb.* [ME. *evesdroppes*, prob. – ON. *upsardropi*, corresp. to OE. *yfæsdrypæ*, WFris. *oesdrip*, *-drup*, Flem. *oosdrup* eaves; see DRIP *v.*, DROP *sb.*] The dripping of water from the eaves of a house; the space of ground on which such water falls.

Eavesdrop (ī·vzdrǫp), *v.* 1606. [Back-formation from *eavesdropper.*] *intr.* To stand within the 'eavesdrop' of a house in order to overhear secrets; hence, to listen secretly to private conversation. Also *trans.* To listen secretly to; to listen to the secrets of.

It is not civil to e. him SHIRLEY. We must not peep and e. at palace-doors EMERSON. Hence **Ea·vesdropper,** one who eavesdrops.

‖**Ebauchoir.** [Fr., f. *ébaucher* sketch out.] a. A large chisel used by sculptors to rough-hew their work. b. A large hatchel or comb used by ropemakers.

Ebb (eb), *sb.* [OE. *ebba* = (M)LG., (M)Du. *ebbe* (Du. *eb*) :– WGmc. **abjo*, *-ō-*, f. **ab-* (see OF), as if meaning 'a running off or away'.] 1. The reflux of the tide; the return of tide-water towards the sea. 2. *transf.* and *fig.* Decline, decay; a change to a worse state ME. 3. *attrib.* and *Comb.*, as *e.-tide*, etc. 1699. 4. [perh. a distinct word.] The Common Bunting, *Emberizia miliaria* (*dial.*) 1802.

1. During the freshets the e. and flow are little felt 1832. 2. Not coueting to make of my floudde, another manes ebbe 1555. Private and public Virtue were at the lowest E. 1763. Hence **E·bbless** *a.*

†**Ebb,** *a.* ME. [orig. the sb. used attrib.] 1. Shallow. With *of*: Short –1747. 2. Near the surface; also as quasi-*adv.* –1794.

Ebb (eb), *v.* [OE. *ebbian* (f. EBB *sb.*) = (M)LG., (M)Du. *ebben.*] 1. *intr.* To flow back or recede, as the water of the sea or a tidal river. Also *transf.* 2. *fig.* To take a backward course; to decay, decline; to fade or waste away ME. 3. *trans.* To hem in (fish) with stakes and nets at the ebb-tide 1827.

1. The sea will ebbe and flow *L. L. L.* IV. iii. 216. *transf.* [He] eyed The life-blood e. in crimson tide SCOTT. 2. After full sea, our hopes ebde too 1633.

Ebdomade, -ary, obs. ff. HEBDOMAD, -ARY.

Ebe·neous, *a.* [f. late L. *ebeneus* + -OUS.] Of the nature of ebony (Mod. Dicts.).

Ebenezer (ebĕnī·zəɹ). 1758. [Heb. *'eben*

hā-'ēzer 'stone of the help'.] **1.** The name of the memorial stone set up by Samuel after the victory of Mizpeh; see 1 *Sam.* 7:12. Used in fig. phrases, with allusion to the sentiment 'Hitherto hath the Lord helped us'. **2.** Occas. adopted by Methodists, Baptists, etc. as the name of a meeting-house. Hence, contemptuously, A 'dissenting chapel' 1856.

Ebionite (ī·biŏnəit). 1650. [– med.L. *ebionita*, f. Heb. *'ebyôn* poor; see -ITE¹ 1.] One of a body of 1st c. Christians, later, a sect, who held that Jesus was a mere man, and that the Mosaic law was binding upon Christians. Hence **E:bioni·tic** *a.* pertaining to the Ebionites or their doctrine; **E·bioni:-tism,** the tenets of the Ebionites; also **E·bionism. E·bionize** *v. intr.* to adopt Ebionitism.

Eblis (e·blīz). Also **Eblees.** 1786. [Arab.] In Moslem demonology, the chief of the jinns; Satan.

Eboe (ī·bo). 18? . A W. Indian name for the Negroes of Benin. ? Hence *attrib.* **E.-tree** (*Dipteryx eboensis*), a tree of Central America, yielding **E. oil.**

Ebon (e·bən). [Late ME. *eban* (XV) – OFr. *eban* (also *ebaine*, mod. *ébène*) = med.L. *ebanus*, var. of L. *ebenus, hebenus* – Gr. ἔβενος ebony tree, of Sem. origin.]

A. *sb.* **1.** = EBONY. Now only *poet.* †**2.** The tree, *Diospyros ebenus*, which provides ebony –1623.

1. India black e. and white iv'ry bears DRYDEN.

B. *attrib.* and *adj.* (chiefly *poet.* or *rhet.*) 1592.

Deaths e. dart SHAKS. As blind as E. night HEYWOOD. The tough shaft of heben wood SCOTT.

Ebonist (e·bŏnist). 1706. [f. EBONY + -IST. Cf. Fr. *ébéniste*.] A worker or dealer in ebony and ornamental woods.

Ebonite (e·bŏnəit). 1861. [f. as prec. + -ITE¹ 4a.] = VULCANITE. Also *attrib.*

Ebonize (e·bŏnəiz), *v.* 1880. [f. as prec. + -IZE.] To make (furniture, etc.) look like ebony.

Ebony (e·bŏni). 1573. [Earliest *hebeny*, alt. f. *eben(e, heben(e* (XVI–XVII), latinizing vars. of EBON; the *-y* is perh. after IVORY.] **1.** A hard black wood, obtained from various species of the N.O. *Ebenaceæ*, esp. *Diospyrus ebenus*, a native of Ceylon, Madagascar, and Mauritius, and *Diospyrus melanoxylon*, a native of Coromandel. **b.** The wood of *Brya ebenus*, a native of Jamaica. Also the trees. **2.** As the type of intense blackness 1834. **3.** *attrib.* 1598.

‖**Eboulement.** [Fr. *éboulement*, f. *ébouler* crumble.] **1.** *Fortif.* The crumbling or falling of the wall of a fortification. **2.** *Geol.* A landslide.

Ebracteate, -ated (ibræ·kti,ĕt, -eᶦtėd). 1830. [– mod.L. *ebracteatus*, f. *e-* E- + *bractea* BRACT; see -ATE², -ED¹.] *Bot.* Destitute of bracts.

Ebra·cteolate, *a.* 1870. [– mod.L. *ebracteolatus*; cf. prec.] *Bot.* Not furnished with bracteoles.

Ebraick, Ebrew; see HEBRAIC, HEBREW.

Ebriety (ībrəi·ėti). 1582. [– Fr. *ébriété* or L. *ebrietas*, f. *ebrius* drunk; see -ITY.] The state or habit of intoxication; drunkenness. Also *fig.*

fig. The e. of constant amusement JOHNSON.

‖**Ebrillade.** 1753. [Fr.] *Manège.* A check of the bridle by a jerk of one rein, given to a horse when he refuses to turn.

Ebriosity (ībri,ǫ·sĭti). *rare.* 1646. [– L. *ebriositas*, f. *ebriosus* + *-itas* -ITY; see -OSITY.] Habitual intoxication; exhilaration.

Ebrious (ī·briəs), *a.* 1569. [f. L. *ebrius* + -OUS.] **a.** Addicted to drink; tipsy. **b.** Characteristic of the intoxicated state. var. **E:brio·se** (*joc.*). Hence **E·briously** *adv.*

Ebu·lliate. *rare.* 1599. [Badly f. L. *ebullire*; see next, -ATE³.] *trans.* and *intr.* To boil; to bubble out.

Ebullience (ĭbɒ·liens). 1749. [f. next; see -ENCE.] An issuing forth in agitation, like boiling water; overflow; effervescence. So **Ebu·lliency,** ebullient quality (*lit.* and *fig.*).

Ebullient (ĭbɒ·liĕnt). 1599. [– *ebullient-*, pres. ppl. stem of L. *ebullire*, f. *e-* E- + *bullire* BOIL *v.*; see -ENT.] **1.** That boils; agitated, as if boiling. **2.** Characterized by heat; causing heat and agitation 1620. **3.** *fig.* Bubbling over, overflowing, enthusiastic 1664.

2. They engender e. humors VENNER. The E. Ague 1684. **3.** Commentaries..e. with subtlety 1844. Hence **Ebu·lliently** *adv.*

Ebullioscope (ĭbɒ·lio,skōᵘp). 1880. [– Fr. *ébullioscope*, f. L. *ebullire* boil up; see prec., -SCOPE.] An instrument for ascertaining the strength of distilled liquors by observing the boiling point and the atmospheric pressure.

Ebullition (ebɒli·ʃən). 1534. [– late L. *ebullitio*, f. *ebullit-*, pa. ppl. stem of *ebullire*; see prec., -ION.] **1.** The process of boiling; the state of agitation occasioned by boiling 1594. Also *transf.* †**b.** *Path.* A state of agitation in the blood or 'humours' due to heat –1753. **2.** The action of rushing forth in a state of agitation or boiling; said of water, fire, lava, etc. 1599. **3.** *fig.* A sudden outburst, as of war, passion, sentiment, etc. 1534.

3. Ebullitions of genius JOHNSON, of jealousy 1796.

Eburin (ī·biūrin). [f. L. *ebur* ivory + -IN¹.] A substance made of ivory or bone dust mixed with albumen or ox blood and subjected to pressure.

Eburnation (ībɒɹnēᶦ·ʃən). 1840. [f. L. *eburnus* made of ivory + -ATION.] *Path.* 'The act or process of becoming hard and dense like ivory' (*Syd. Soc. Lex.*). So **E·burnated** *ppl. a.*

Eburnean, -ian (ībɒ̄·ɹnĭăn), *a.* 1656. [f. L. *eburneus* made of ivory + -AN, -IAN.] Made of or resembling ivory.

Ebu:rnifica·tion. *rare.* 1878. [f. as EBURNATION; see -FICATION.] = EBURNATION.

Ecalcarate (īkæ·lkărĕt), *a.* 1819. [f. E- + L. *calcar* spur + -ATE².] *Bot.* Without a spur.

Ecardine (īkā·ɹdəin). 1878. [f. E- + L. *cardo, cardin-* + -INE¹.] A mollusc which has no hinge.

‖**Écarté** (ekarte). 1824. [Fr., pa. pple. of *écarter* discard, f. *é-* E- + *carte* CARD *sb.*²] A game of cards for two persons, played with a pack from which the cards from 2 to 6 are excluded. The players may discard any or all of the cards dealt, and replace them from the pack; hence the name. Also *attrib.*

Ecaudate (ikǭ·deᶦt), *a.* 1840. [f. E- + CAUDATE.] **1.** *Zool.* That has no tail, or a very short one 1847. **2.** *Bot.* 'Spikeless, without a stem' (Paxton).

‖**E·cbasis.** 1706. [Gr. ἔκβασις, f. stem of ἐκβαίνειν go out, digress.] 'A going out, an Event; also a Rhetorical Figure call'd Digression' (Phillips).

Ecbatic (ekbæ·tik), *a.* 1836. [– Gr. ἐκβατικός, f. as prec.; see -IC.] *Gram.* Of a clause or conjunction: Denoting a mere result or consequence, as dist. from a purpose or intention.

[The use of ἵνα is sometimes] e. 1836.

‖**Ecblastesis** (ekblæstī·sis). 1866. [mod.L. – Gr. ἐκβλάστησις shooting or budding forth.] *Bot.* The production of buds within flowers, or in inflorescences.

‖**Ecbole** (e·kbŏlī). 1753. [mod.L. – Gr. ἐκβολή, f. ἐκβάλλειν throw out.] *Rhet.* A digression, in which a person is introduced speaking his own words (Webster).

Ecbolic (ekbǫ·lik). 1753. [As if – Gr. ἐκβολικός, f. ἐκβολή expulsion.] **a.** *adj.* That promotes the expulsion of the fœtus 1877. **b.** *sb.* [sc. *drug.*]

Ecca:leobi·on. 1839. [Gr. ἐκκαλέω βίον (in sense 'I evoke life') as one word.] An egg-hatching apparatus.

‖**Ecce** (e·ksi). 1596. Latin for 'lo!' or 'behold!' Used in *Ecce signum!* behold a sign (1 *Hen. IV*, II. iv. 187). Also **Ecce Homo,** 'Behold the Man' (*John* 19:5); hence *sb.*, a picture of Christ wearing the crown of thorns.

Eccentric (ekse·ntrik). 1551. [– late L. *eccentricus*, f. Gr. ἔκκεντρος, f. ἐκ out, EX-² + κέντρον CENTRE *sb.*; see -IC. Cf. (O)Fr. *eccentrique.*]

A. *adj.* **1.** Of a circle: Not concentric with another circle (const. *to*); †*fig.* having little in common –1670. **2.** That has its axis, its point of support, etc., not centrally placed 1647. **3.** Not centrally placed; not passing through the centre 1849. **4.** Of orbital motion: Not referable to a fixed centre; not circular. Of a curve, an elliptic, etc., orbit: Deviating from a circular form. Also *transf.* of planets, etc. 1642. **5.** *fig.* Regulated by no central control; irregular, anomalous, capricious; of persons, etc., odd, whimsical 1630.

1. *fig.* His owne endes, which must needes be often eccentrique to the endes of his Master or State BACON. **2.** That..contrivance the e. wheel 1831. **4.** A comet moves round the sun...in..a very e. ellipse SIR J. HERSCHEL. Phr. *E. anomaly*: the true (as opp. to the mean) anomaly of a planet moving in an e. orbit. **5.** The eccentrick aberration of Charles the Second BURKE. That great, though..e. genius 1836.

B. *sb.* **1.** [= *e. circle, orb.*] In Ptolemaic astronomy: A circle or orb not having the earth precisely in its centre. Now *Hist.* 1561. **2.** *Mech.* A circular disc fixed on a revolving shaft, some distance out of centre, working freely in a ring (the *e. strap*), which is attached to a rod called an *e. rod*, by means of which the rotating motion of the shaft is converted into a backward and forward motion. (Earlier *e. circle, motion*; see A. 2.) 1827. **3.** An irregular, odd, or whimsical person 1832.

attrib. and *Comb.*, as *e.-hook, -rod*, etc.: **e.-hoop, -ring, -strap,** the ring in which the e. revolves. **b.** = worked by an e. wheel or dependent on an e. arrangement, as *e.-arbor, -chuck, -gear, -pump*, etc.

So **Ecce·ntrical** (in sense A. 1); also *fig.*; exceptional, irregular. Hence **Ecce·ntrically** *adv.*

Eccentricity (eksentri·sĭti). 1551. [f. prec. + -ITY.] **1.** The quality of being abnormally centred; of not being concentric; of not having the axis in the centre. †**2.** Distance from the centre –1837. **3.** Of a curve: Deviation from circular form 1696. **b.** as a measurable quantity: The ratio of the focal distance (of any point in the curve) to the distance from the directrix 1726. **4.** The quality or habit of deviating from what is customary; irregularity, oddity, whimsicality. Also with *a* and *pl.* 1657.

‖**Ecchymoma** (ekimōᵘ·mă). 1541. [mod.L. – Gr. ἐκχύμωμα; see next, -OMA.] *Path.* A tumour formed by an effusion of blood under the skin.

Ecchymosed (e:kimōᵘ·st, -ōᵘ·zd), *ppl. a.* 1834. [– Fr. *ecchymosé*, f. *ecchymose*, Fr. form of next.] *Path.* Affected with ecchymosis.

‖**Ecchymosis** (ekimōᵘ·sis). 1541. [mod.L. – Gr. ἐκχύμωσις, f. ἐκχυμοῦσθαι extravasate blood; see -OSIS.] *Path.* 'A blotch caused by extravasation of blood below the skin' (*Syd. Soc. Lex.*). So **Ecchymo·tic** *a.* of the nature of e.

Eccles (e·k'lz). 1881. [Name of a town in Lancashire.] *E. cake*, a round cake of pastry filled with a currant mixture.

‖**Ecclesia** (eklī·ziă, -ʒᶦă). *Hist.* 1577. [Chr. L. *ecclesia* – Gr. ἐκκλησία assembly, (eccl.) church, f. ἐκκλητός, pa. ppl. adj. of ἐκκαλεῖν, f. ἐκ out, EX-² + καλεῖν call, summon.] A regularly convoked assembly; *esp.* the general assembly of Athenian citizens. Later, the regular word for CHURCH, q.v. Hence †**Eccle·sial** *a.* ecclesiastical. (Freq. in Milton.) **Eccle·siarch,** a ruler of the church.

Ecclesiast (eklī·zi,æst). ME. [– Chr. L. *ecclesiastes* – Gr. ἐκκλησιαστής one who takes part in an ECCLESIA (= sense 3 below), in LXX. rendering Heb. *ḳōheleṯ* one who addresses a public assembly.] **1.** 'The Preacher', *i.e.* Solomon. †**2.** An ecclesiastic. CHAUCER. **3.** A member of the Athenian Ecclesia 1849.

Ecclesiastes (eklī:ziæ·stīz). ME. [– Gr. ἐκκλησιαστής; see ECCLESIA.] The title of a book of the O.T., written in the person of Solomon, or prop. the designation of Solomon considered as the author of the book.

Ecclesiastic (eklī:ziæ·stik). 1483. [– Fr. *ecclésiastique* or Chr. L. *ecclesiasticus* – Gr. ἐκκλησιαστικός, f. ἐκκλησιαστής (see prec.), ult. f. ἐκκλησία ECCLESIA.]

A. *adj.* (Now *rare*) **1.** Of or pertaining to the church; opp. to *civil* or *secular*. **2.** Of persons, etc.: Clerical, as opp. to *lay*, as *e. attire* 1603.

1. E. terms 1638, writers 1678, architecture 1856.

B. *sb.* **1.** A clergyman, person in orders, a 'churchman' as dist. from a 'layman' 1651. †**2.** *pl.* Matters ecclesiastical. **b.** The science of church government (*rare*) –1738.

Ecclesia·stical, *a.* 1538. [f. prec. + -AL¹; see -ICAL.] **1.** = ECCLESIASTIC A. 1. **2.** Of or pertaining to the church as consisting of the clergy 1538. **3.** quasi-*sb.* Matters ecclesiastical; *pl.* matters concerning the church 1641.

1. *E. Commission, Commissioners*: a body of commissioners for administering certain portions of the revenues of the Church of England. *E. Courts*: courts for administering e. law and maintaining the discipline of the Church of England. *E. law*: the law, derived from Canon and Civil law, which e. courts administer. *E. judge*: a judge of an e. court. **2.** †*E. State(s*, the provinces formerly ruled by the Pope as Head of the Roman Church; = *States of the Church, Papal States.*
Hence **Ecclesia·stically** *adv.*

Ecclesiasticism (eklīːziæ·stisiz'm). 1862. [f. as prec. + -ISM.] Ecclesiastical spirit, or principles of action.

Ecclesio·graphy. 1881. [f. *ecclesio-*, comb. f. ECCLESIA + -GRAPHY.] A descriptive treatise on the church.

Ecclesiolatry (eklīːzi‚ǫ·lătri). 1847. [f. as prec. + -LATRY.] Worship of the church, church forms, and church traditions.

Ecclesiology (eklīːzi‚ǫ·lǒdʒi). 1837. [f. as prec. + -LOGY.] **a.** The science of church building and decoration. **b.** A treatise on churches.

The first phase of e. was simple antiquarianism FREEMAN. Hence **Eccle:siolo·gic, -al** *a.* of or pertaining to e.; **-ally** *adv.* **Eccle:sio·logist,** a student of e.

Eccoprotic (ekoprǫ·tik). 1656. [– Gr. ἐκκοπρωτικός, f. ἐκκοπροῦν, f. ἐκ EX-² + κόπρος dung.] **a.** *adj.* Mildly purgative. **b.** *sb.* A mild aperient.

Eccrinology (ekrinǫ·lǒdʒi). [– Fr. *eccrinologie*, f. Gr. ἐκκρίνειν secrete; see -LOGY.] *Phys.* 'The doctrine of, or a treatise on, the secretions' (Syd. Soc. Lex.).

‖**Eccrisis** (e·krisis). 1706. [mod.L. – Gr. ἔκκρισις secretion, f. ἐκκρίνειν secrete.] *Med.* Old term for an excretion; also the thing excreted.

Eccritic (ekri·tic), *a.* 1681. [– Gr. ἐκκριτικός having the power of secretion or excretion.] *Med.* 'A remedy which promotes discharges, as an emetic, or a cathartic' (Webster).

Ecderon (e·kdĕrǫn). 1859. [irreg. – Gr. ἐκ + δέρος, δέρμα skin.] Huxley's term for the outer part of the skin and skin-like structures. Opp. to ENDERON. Hence **Ecdero·nic** *a.*

‖**Ecdysis** (e·kdisis). 1854. [mod.L. – Gr. ἔκδυσις, f. ἐκδύειν put off.] The action of shedding or casting off an integument, as in serpents, caterpillars, Crustacea, etc. Also *concr.* that which is cast off.

Echelon (eʃəlon, e·ʃĕlǫn). Also **echellon.** 1796. [– Fr. *échelon*, f. *échelle* ladder :– L. *scala* SCALE *sb.*³ See -OON.] **1.** 'A formation of troops in which the successive divisions are placed parallel to one another, but no two on the same alignement' (Stocqueler). Also *attrib.* **2.** A division marching in e. 1808.

Echelon (e·ʃĕlǫn), *v.* 1860. [f. prec., or – Fr. *échelonner*.] *trans.* To arrange (troops) in the form of an echelon. Also *fig.*

†**Echene·is.** *rare.* Also **echineis.** 1594. [Gr. ἐχενηΐς, f. ἔχειν to hold + ναῦς (dat. νηΐ) ship, from its supposed power of holding back a ship.] The Remora, or Sucking-fish, which has on the crown of its head an oblong flat sucker –1774.

Echeveria (etʃivīᵊ·riă). 1840. [After M. *Echeveri*, draughtsman of the *Flora Mexicana*. See -IA¹.] A handsome genus of succulent plants allied to the house-leek (N.O. *Crassulaceæ*).

‖**Echevin** (eʃəvæṅ). 1766. [Fr. *échevin*.] The French or Belgian equivalent of an English alderman.

‖**Echidna** (ĭki·dnă). 1847. [mod.L. – Gr. ἔχιδνα viper.] *Zool.* A genus of Australian toothless burrowing monotremate mammals (family *Echidnidæ*), as large as hedgehogs and like them. The best known species is *E. hystrix*, the Porcupine Ant-eater. So **Echi·dnine,** the essential principle of the poison of the viper.

Echinal (ĭkəi·năl, e·kinal), *a.* [f. ECHINUS + -AL¹.] Of or belonging to a sea-urchin. LYELL.

Echinate (e·kinĕt), *a.* 1668. [– L. *echinatus*, f. *echinus* hedgehog; see -ATE².] **1.** *Bot.* Furnished with bristles or prickles. **2.** *Zool.* Resembling a sea-urchin 1846. So **E·chinated** *ppl. a.*

Echinid (ĭkəi·nid). 1835. [– mod.L. *Echinidæ*, f. *Echinus*; see -ID³.] *Zool.* Any member of the *Echinus* family. As pl. mod.L. **Echi·nida;** also **Echi·nidans.**

Echinite (e·kinəit). 1750. [f. ECHINUS + -ITE¹ 2 a.] A fossil echinoderm. Hence **Echini·tal** *a.* pertaining to or like an e.

Echino- (ĭkəi·no, e·kino), before a vowel **echin-**, comb. f. Gr. ἐχῖνος hedgehog, sea-urchin.

Echinococcus (-kǫ·kǒs) [Gr. κόκκος seed-grain], *Zool.* a former genus of ACEPHALOCYSTS or hydatids, now known to be the higher larval form of a species of tapeworm. *Tænia echinococcus* (formerly *T. nana*). †**Echi·nod** [Gr. ὀδούς], the fossil tooth of the sea-urchin.

Echinoderm (ĭkəi·no, e·kinodəɹm). 1835. [f. ECHINO- + Gr. δέρμα, δέρματ- skin.] A member of the class *Echinodermata*; hence **Echinode·rmal** *a.* = ECHINODERMATOUS.

‖**Echinodermata** (-dɔ̄·ɹmătă), *sb. pl.* [f. Gr. δέρμα (δέρματ-) skin], a class of animals formerly included in the *Radiata*, but now placed in the sub-kingdom *Annuloida*, comprising Sea-urchins, Sea-cucumbers, etc. The skin of the typical species is covered with spines. **Echinode·rmatous** *a.*, belonging to or like the echinodermata.

Echinoid (e·kinoid). 1851. [f. ECHINUS + -OID.]

A. *adj.* Like, or having the characteristics of, an Echinus or Sea-urchin.

B. *sb.* An individual of the Order *Echinoidea* (Class *Echinodermata*), characterized by a shell composed of calcareous plates, and locomotion by suckers and spines 1864.

Echinulate (ĭki·niŭlĕt), *a.* 1846. [f. L. *echinus* + dim. suff. -ULE + -ATE², after ACICULATE.] Having or covered with small prickles. So **Echi·nuliform** *a.* in the form of, or like, small prickles.

Echinus (ĭkəi·nǒs). ME. [– L. – Gr. ἐχῖνος hedgehog, sea-urchin.] *Zool.* **1.** The Sea-urchin; a genus of animals (Order *Echinoidea*, Class *Echinodermata*), inhabiting a spheroidal shell built up from polygonal plates, and covered with rows of sharp spines. (The sense 'hedgehog' is not in Eng. use.) **2.** *Arch.* The ovolo moulding next below the abacus of the capital of a column. [So in Gr. and L.] 1563.

Echites (ĭkəi·tīz). ME. [– Gr. ἐχίτης, f. ἔχις viper.] †**1.** A precious stone, dark-green, red, or violet, with fabulous properties; cf. AETITES –1731. **2.** *Bot.* A genus of climbing plants (N.O. *Apocynaceæ*) 1731.

Echo (e·koᵘ), *sb.* Pl. **echoes,** rarely **echos.** ME. [– (O)Fr. *écho* or L. *echo* – Gr. ἠχώ, rel. to ἠχή sound.] **1.** A repetition of sounds, due to the reflection of the sound-waves by some obstacle; hence *concr.* a secondary or imitative sound, as dist. from the original sound. **2.** The cause of this personified, *e.g.* in Gr. Myth. as an Oread 1592. **3.** An artifice in verse, by which one line repeats the concluding syllables of the preceding line. Hence, this kind of verse. Also *attrib.*, as in *e. verse.* 1633. **4.** *fig.* A repetition or close imitation (*e.g.* of a writer's thoughts or style); an enfeebled reproduction; and the like 1622. Also *transf.* of a person. **5.** *Mus.* = *e. organ, stop* (see below) 1711. **6.** *Whist* and *Bridge.* A conventional indication given to a partner of the number of cards held in a suit led, etc. 1862.

1. Echoes softly flung from rock and hill BRYANT. Phr. *To applaud to the e.*: *i.e.* so vociferously as to produce echoes. **2.** *Rom. & Jul.* II. ii. 162. **3.** But are there cares and businesse with the pleasure? *Echo*, Leisure G. HERBERT. *Comb.* **e. organ,** one of the divisions of a large organ, containing soft stops (**e. stops**) for echo effects. Hence **Echo·ic** *a.* of the nature of an e. **E·choism,** the formation of words imitative of sounds. **E·choist,** one who repeats like an e. **E·choize** *v.* to form words imitative of sounds. **E·choless** *a.* (*lit.* and *fig.*).

Echo (e·koᵘ), *v.* 1559. [f. the sb.] **1.** *intr.* To resound with an echo. Also *fig.* 1596. **b.** Of a sound; To be repeated by echoes, reverberate, resound; hence *fig.* of rumours, fame, etc. 1559. **2.** *trans.* To repeat by echo 1855. Also *transf.* of light. **3.** *fig.* To play the echo to; to repeat the words of, imitate the style or sentiments of; to resemble 1604. Also *absol.* and *intr.* **4.** *Whist* and *Bridge.* (Cf. ECHO *sb.* 6) 1862.

1. And at every Roar it gave, it made all the Valley Eccho BUNYAN. That sound echoed and reverberated from innumerable cavities among the rocks DE FOE. **2.** A sound echoed from many sides BAIN. **3.** Posterity have echoed these censures KEIGHTLEY. *intr.* Now e. vnto me, and sing, Thou myne HEYWOOD. Hence **E·choer. E·choingly** *adv.*

Echo·meter. 1736. [– Gr. ἦχος sound + -METER. Cf. Fr. *échomètre*.] *Mus.* A graduated scale for measuring the duration of sounds and ascertaining their intervals and ratios. So †**Echo·metry.**

‖**Éclair** (eⁱklēᵊ·ɹ). 1870. [Fr., lit. lightning.] A small pastry filled with cream and iced.

†**Eclaircise,** *v. rare.* 1754. [Back-formation from next, with assim. to *-ise*, -IZE.] *trans.* To clear up.

‖**Éclairci·ssement.** 1673. [Fr., f. *éclairciss-*, lengthened stem of *éclaircir* clear up; see -MENT. Very common in XVIII.] A clearing up of what is obscure, unknown, or misunderstood; an explanation.

When the e. comes there will be a scene THACKERAY.

Eclampsia, eclampsy (eklæ·mpsiă, -si). 1866. [mod.L. – Fr. *eclampsie* (XVIII), irreg. – Gr. ἔκλαμψις sudden development (Galen), f. ἐκλάμπειν shine forth.] *Path.* 'Epileptiform convulsions dependent on some actual disturbance of the nervous centres caused by anatomical lesion' (*Syd. Soc. Lex.*). So **Ecla·mptic** *a.*; also, *erron.*, **ecla·mpsic.**

‖**Éclat** (ekla·). 1674. [Fr., f. *éclater* burst out.] †**1.** Brilliancy, radiance, dazzling effect –1835. †**2.** Ostentation; publicity; *concr.* public exposure, scandal –1823. **3.** Lustre of reputation; celebrity, renown. In 19th c. often disparaging. 1742. **b.** Conspicuous success; acclamation 1741.

2. He was then a man of e., had many servants CLARENDON. With the view of saving an é. BYRON. **3.** A diplomatist of great é. BYRON. **b.** We get on with great é. BYRON. So ‖**Eclat** *v.* to make or become known (*rare*).

Eclectic (ekle·ktik). 1683. [– Gr. ἐκλεκτικός, f. ἐκλέγειν select, f. ἐκ out EX-² + λέγειν choose.]

A. *adj.* **1.** In ancient use, epithet of a class of philosophers who 'selected such doctrines as pleased them in every school' (Liddell and Scott). In mod. times applied similarly, *e.g.* to V. Cousin and others. **2.** That borrows or is borrowed from various sources. Of persons, etc.: Broad, not exclusive. 1847. **3.** Made up of selections. **b.** That selects. 1814.

1. Some e. system of belief 1796. The E. school of thought MORLEY. **2.** The e. phraseology [of] the Shepherd's Calendar 1879. **3. b.** His mind was in the best sense e. GLADSTONE. Hence **Ecle·tical** *a.*

B. *sb.* **a.** An adherent of the Eclectic school of philosophy 1856. **b.** One who follows the eclectic method 1817.

Eclecticism (ekle·ktisiz'm). 1835. [f. prec. + -ISM.] The eclectic philosophy; the eclectic method in speculation or practice.

†**Ecle·gme.** 1605. [– med.L. *eclegma*, for L. *ecligma* – Gr. ἔκλειγμα, f. ἐκλείχειν lick out. Cf. ELECTUARY.] *Med.* Old term for a linctus, or semifluid medicine, which is licked off the spoon –1710.

Eclipse (ĭkli·ps), *sb.* ME. [– OFr. *eclipse*, †*esclipse* (mod. *éclipse*) – L. *eclipsis* – Gr. ἔκλειψις, f. ἐκλείπειν be eclipsed, leave its place, fail to appear, f. ἐκ EX-² + λείπειν leave.] **1.** *Astron.* An interception or obscuration of the light of the sun, moon, or other luminous body, by the intervention of some other body, either between it and the eye, or between the luminous body and that illuminated by it; as of the moon, by passing through the earth's shadow; of the sun, by the moon coming between it and the observer; or of a satellite, by entering the shadow of its primary. **b.** *transf.* Absence of light, temporary or permanent 1526. **2.** *fig.* Obscuration, obscurity; dimness; loss of splendour 1598.

1. Phr. *Annular, partial, total e.*: see these adjs. These late Eclipses in the Sun and Moone portend no good to vs *Lear* I. ii. 112. *transf.* Blind among enemies. . Irrecoverably dark, total e. MILT. *Sams.* 80. **2.** God oftentimes leaves the brightest men in an e. FULLER. **b.** Of birds: Change to duller plumage 1838.

Eclipse (ĭkli·ps), *v.* ME. [– (O)Fr. *éclipser*, f. *éclipse* (prec.); cf. med.L. *eclipsare*.] †**1.** *intr.* To suffer eclipse –1667. Also †*fig.* **2.** *trans.* To cause the obscuration of; said of a heavenly body. Also *transf.* **3.** *fig.* To throw into the shade, *esp.* by surpassing; to obscure, deprive of lustre 1581; †to hide *from* –1653.

1. When the moon eclipses the sun to us, the earth is eclipsed to the moon 1832. **2.** The splendour of the House of Argyle had been eclipsed MACAULAY. Hence **Ecli·psable** *a.* **Ecli·pser.**

Ecli·psis. 1538. [– Gr. ἔκλειψις (see ECLIPSE *sb.*). In sense 1 perh. confused w. *ellipsis*.] †**1.** An omission of words needful fully to express the sense –1589. **2.** In *Irish Grammar*: 'The suppression of the sounds of certain radical consonants, by prefixing others of the same organ' 1845.

Ecliptic (ĭkli·ptik). ME. [– L. *eclipticus* – Gr. ἐκλειπτικός, f. ἐκλείπειν; see ECLIPSE *sb.*, -IC. Cf. Fr. *écliptique*.]

A. *adj.* Of or pertaining to an eclipse 1609. Also *fig.*

Phr. *E. limits*, the limits within which an eclipse is possible. *E. conjunction*, a conjunction of sun and moon which results in a solar eclipse. †*E. circle, line, way* = ECLIPTIC *sb.*

B. *sb.* **1.** The great circle of the celestial sphere which is the apparent orbit of the sun. So called because eclipses can happen only when the moon is on or near this line. Occas. = plane of the ecliptic. 1635. **2.** The great circle on the terrestrial sphere which at any given moment lies in the plane of the celestial ecliptic 1819. Hence **Ecli·ptical** *a.*, **-ly** *adv.*

Eclogite (e·klŏdʒəit). 1852. [f. Gr. ἐκλογή selection + -ITE[1] 2 b.] *Min.* A metamorphic rock, consisting of granular garnet and hornblende, with grass-green smaragdite; so called because the constituents do not exist together in primitive rocks.

Eclogue (e·klǫg). *c* 1430. [– L. *ecloga* short poem – Gr. ἐκλογή selection, esp. of poems, f. ἐκλέγειν; see ECLECTIC.] A short poem of any kind, *esp.* a pastoral dialogue, *e.g.* Virgil's Bucolics.

†**Eco·d,** *int.* 1733. [var. of EGAD, *egod*, AGAD.] Used as a mild oath –1865.

Ecology, œco- (ĭkǫ·lŏdʒi). 1873. [– G. *ökologie* (Haeckel), f. Gr. οἶκος house (used for 'habitat'): see -LOGY.] The science of the economy of animals and plants; that branch of biology which deals with the relations of living organisms to their surroundings, their habits and modes of life, etc. Hence **Ecolo·gical** *a.* **Eco·logist.**

Economic (īkonǫ·mik). ME. [– (O)Fr. *économique* or L. *œconomicus* – Gr. οἰκονομικός; see ECONOMY, -IC.]

A. *adj.* **1.** †Pertaining to household management (*arch.*) –1791. **b.** Relating to pecuniary position 1831. **2.** Relating to Political Economy 1835. **b.** Practical, industrial 1861. †**3.** = ECONOMICAL 2. –1801. **4.** *Theol.* Pertaining to economy of truth 1851 **5.** Pertaining to a dispensation. Cf. ECONOMY II. 1817.

1. a. Oeconomicke or household order 1603. **2.** E. problems, subjects, force (*mod.*). **b.** E. applications of electricity 1891. **3.** E. of her smiles 1801.

B. *sb.* †**1.** *sing.* Housekeeping –1609. **2.** *pl.* (after L. *œconomica*, Gr. τὰ οἰκονομικά a treatise attributed to Aristotle.) The science of †household, rural, and *esp.* political economy 1792. **3.** Financial or material condition (*mod.*).

2. The London school of Economics 1895. **3.** The oppression has gone..into the economics of Ireland CARLYLE.

Economical (īkonǫ·mikăl), *a.* 1577. [f. as prec. + -AL[1]; see -ICAL.] **1.** = ECONOMIC *a.* 1, 2, 4, 5. Now *rare.* **2.** Saving, thrifty (cf. ECONOMY 1) 1780.

1. The e. writers of antiquity GIBBON. **2.** An œconomical constitution is a necessary basis for an œconomical administration BURKE. [Pope's] e. habits STEPHEN. Hence **Econo·mically** *adv.*

Economist (ĭkǫ·nŏmist). 1586. [f. Gr. οἰκονόμος (see ECONOMY) + -IST.] **1.** One who practises economy (see ECONOMY 1); hence, **a.** A housekeeper (*arch.*). **b.** A thrifty and effective manager *of* money, time, etc. 1710. **2.** A student of, or writer upon, political economy 1804. **b.** One of the French school dubbed *Les Economistes* 1776.

1. a. The perfect e., or mistress of a household RUSKIN. **b.** A rigid e. of time 1841. **2. a.** Facts which form a special study of the e. ROGERS.

Economize (ĭkǫ·nŏməiz), *v.* 1648. [f. as prec. + -IZE.] †**1.** *intr.* To govern a household. **2.** *trans.* To use sparingly; to save *from* 1820. **3.** *intr.* To practise thrift (*in* a thing) 1790. **4.** *trans.* To turn to account 1832.

4. [Machinery's] object is to e. force supplied from without 1872. Hence **Eco:nomiza·tion,** the action of economizing. **Eco·nomi:zer,** one who, or that which, economizes; in *Mech.* any appliance that effects a saving, *esp.* of heat or fuel.

Economy (ĭkǫ·nŏmi). 1530. [– (O)Fr. *économie* or L. *œconomia* – Gr. οἰκονομία, f. οἰκονόμος manager of a household, steward, f. οἶκος house; see -NOMY.]

I. 1. Management of expenditure: orig. of household (*arch.*), later of any, expenses; often specialized, as *Domestic, Naval, Rural*, etc. **2. Political Economy** [tr. Fr. *économie politique*]: orig. The art of managing the resources of a people and of its government (Adam Smith); later, The theoretical science of the laws of production and distribution of wealth (McCulloch). 1767. **3.** Careful management, frugality, of labour, money, time, etc. Also in *pl.* Savings. 1670.

1. Yconomie, or Howsolde keepynge 1530. His Equipage and Oeconomy had something in them ..sumptuous STEELE. The Œconomy of a Commonwealth HOBBES. Dockyard E. and Naval Power 1863. **3.** The e. shown by nature in her resources is striking DARWIN. Saved from bankruptcy by economies 1876.

II. 1. *Theol.* The divine government of the world; *esp.* = DISPENSATION, as the *Mosaic, Jewish, Christian e.* 1664. **2.** *Theol.* Judicious handling, *i.e.* tactful presentation, of doctrine (a tr. of Gr. οἰκονομία as used by the Fathers) 1833. Hence, by confusion (begun by Voltaire) with sense I. 3: *E. of truth* = A (discreditable) reticence 1796.

1. The scheme of the divine e. 1814. **2.** An œconomy of truth..a sort of temperance BURKE.

III. *fig.* Organization, like that of a household, in a product of art, in the mind or body, nature or society 1592.

Œconomy of the fable MILT. The e. of the body 1660, of the brain 1704. Phr. *The animal, vegetable e.; the e. of nature, of society.*

‖**Écorché.** [Fr., pa. pple. of *écorcher* strip the bark off, flay.] An anatomical subject with the skin removed so as to display the muscles for study.

‖**Écossaise.** 1863. [Fr.] A lively dance tune, formerly in $\frac{3}{4}$ slow time, now in $\frac{2}{4}$ time.

Ecostate (īkǫ·stēt), *a.* 1866. [f. E- *pref.* + L. *costa* rib + -ATE[2].] *Bot.* Having no central rib.

‖**Écoute** (ekut). 1815. [Fr., f. *écouter* listen.] *Mil.* An excavation in which a miner listens for the working of the enemy's miners.

‖**E·cphasis,** also **E·cphrasis.** 1706. [Gr.] 'A plain declaration'.

‖**Ecphone·ma,** ‖**Ecphone·sis,** exclamation (Puttenham): Greek rhetorical terms now found only in Dicts.

‖**Ecphora** (e·kfŏră). 1715. [Gr. ἐκφορά, f. ἐκφέρειν, f. ἐκ out + φέρειν bear.] *Arch.* 'The projecture of a member or moulding of a column' (Gwilt).

Ecphore (e·kfoər), *v.* 1914. [– Gr. ἐκφορεῖν dig out, f. ἐκ out + φορεῖν, frequent. of φέρειν (see prec.).] *Psycho-analysis.* To evoke or revive by means of a stimulus.

†**Ecphra·ctic,** *a.* 1657. [– late Gr. ἐκφρακτικός, f. ἐκφράσσειν remove obstructions.] Aperient, deobstruent. Also as quasi-*sb.* –1883.

‖**Écraseur** (ekrazör). 1859. [Fr., f. *écraser* to crush.] *Surg.* A blunt chain-saw, tightened by a screw, etc., for removing piles, polypi, etc.

‖**Ecroulement.** 1820. [Fr., f. *écrouler* crumble, collapse.] The fall of a mass of rock, a building, etc. Also *fig.*

‖**Ecru** (ekrü), *a.* *sb.* 1869. [Fr., = 'raw, unbleached'.] The colour of unbleached linen.

‖**Ecstasis** (e·kstăsis). 1621. [mod.L. – Gr. ἔκστασις; see next.] = next 2, 3.

Ecstasy (e·kstăsi). ME. [– OFr. *extasie* – (with assim. to sbs. in *-sie*, L. *-sia*; mod. *extase*) late L. *extasis* – Gr. ἔκστασις, f. ἐκστα-, stem of ἐξιστάναι put out of place, f. ἐκ out EX-[2] + ἱστάναι to place.] **1.** The state of being beside oneself with anxiety, astonishment, fear, or passion. **2.** *Path.* †**a.** Any morbid state characterized by unconsciousness, as swoon, trance, catalepsy, etc. –1647. **b.** A nervous state in which the mind is absorbed in a dominant idea, and becomes insensible to surrounding objects 1866. **3.** In mystical writers, the state of rapture in which the soul, liberated from the body, was engaged in the contemplation of divine things. Now *Hist.* 1652. **b.** The state of trance supposed to accompany prophetic inspiration; hence, Poetic frenzy or rapture 1670. **4.** Rapture, transport; rapturous delight 1526. †**b.** An outburst (of feeling, etc.) –1725.

1. Our words will but increase his e. MARLOWE. **2. a.** The Ministers of the State..like men in an Extasy..had no speech or Motion CLARENDON. **3. a.** The Emigration of humane Souls from the bodie by E. HY. MORE. **b.** Certaine women in a kind of ecstasie foretold of calamities to come MILT. In mood Of minstrel e. SCOTT. **4.** In the e. of my joy DE FOE. *transf.* The e. of the monk's terror SCOTT.

E·cstasy, *v.* 1624. [f. the sb.] †**1.** *trans.* To throw into a state of frenzy or stupor. Only in *pass.* –1670. **2.** To raise to a high state of feeling; now *esp.* to enrapture 1624.

2. The crowd was again ecstasied T. HARDY.

Ecstatic (ekstæ·tik). 1630. [– Fr. *extatique* – Gr. ἐκστατικός, f. ἐκστα-; see ECSTASY *sb.*, -IC.]

A. *adj.* Of the nature of ecstasy; characterized by or producing ecstasy. Of persons: Subject to trance, catalepsy, rapturous emotion, etc. (See ECSTASY *sb.* 1, 2, 4.)

1. In e. fit MILT. In trance extatic POPE. In e. pain FALCONER, idolatry DISRAELI. Minds of a visionary and e. nature 1878.

B. *sb.* **1.** One who is subject to fits of ecstasy (see ECSTASY *sb.* 2, 3) 1659. **2.** *pl.* Sarcastically used for: Transports 1819.

2. Ecstatics, again, might be spared 1865. Hence **Ecsta·tical** *a.* (*arch.*). **Ecsta·tical-ly** *adv.*, †**-ness.**

‖**Ectasia** (ektēⁱ·ziă). 1876. [mod.L., f. as next with irreg. substitution of suffix *-ia*.] *Path.* A dilatation; = ANEURISM.

‖**E·ctasis.** 1706. [mod.L. – Gr. ἔκτασις, f. ἐκτείνειν stretch out.] **1.** *Gram.* A figure whereby a short syllable is made long. **2.** *Path.* Any morbid condition of dilatation 1879.

Ecteron, -onic, bad ff. ECDERON, -ONIC.

Ectethmoid (ekte·þmoid), *a.* 1882. [f. ECTO- + ETHMOID.] *Anat.* External to the ethmoid; prefrontal.

‖**Ecthlipsis** (ekþli·psis). 1657. [mod.L. – Gr., f. ἐκθλίβειν squeeze out.] *Pros.* 'Crushing out, in verse, of a syllable ending in *m* before an ensuing vowel' (Roby).

‖**Ecthyma** (ekþəi·mă). 1834. [mod.L. – Gr. ἔκθυμα, f. ἐκθύειν break out as heat or humours'.] Same as *Impetigo.*

Ecto- (e·kto), comb. form, repr. Gr. ἐκτο-, stem of ἐκτός *adv.*, outside:

E·ctoblast [Gr. βλαστός], the membrane composing the walls of a cell. **E:cto-cu·neiform** *a.*, of or pertaining to one of the bones of the tarsus; see CUNEIFORM. **E·ctocyst** [Gr. κύστις], the cell encasing each individual of a colony of Polyzoa. **E·ctoderm** [Gr. δέρμα], the outer layer of the blastoderm, called also *epiblast*; also, the outer layer of the body of the Cœlenterata; hence **Ectode·rmal, -mic** *adjs.* **Ectoge·nesis,** the production of structures or bodies outside the organism. **E:ctopa·rasite,** any parasite which derives its nourishment from the skin. **E·ctoplasm** [Gr. πλάσμα], the outer firm layer of the body of an Amœba, or the like; opp. to *endoplasm*; hence **E:ctopla·smic** *a.* **E:ctopro·ctous** *a.* [Gr. πρωκτός], belonging to the *Ectoprocta*, an order of *Polyzoa* having the anus outside the mouth-tentacles. **E:cto-pte·rygoid** *a.* [see PTERYGOID], situated externally to the pterygoid; of or relating to an ectopterygoid bone. **E·ctosarc** [Gr. σάρξ, σαρκός], *Zool.* the outer transparent sarcode-layer of certain rhizopods, such as the Amœba. **Ectosto·sis** [f. Gr. ὀστέον, after ἐξόστωσις], an external growth of bone. **Ectozo·on** (pl. **-a**) [Gr. ζῷον], any parasitic insect that infests the surface of the body; opp. to *Entozoon.*

-ectomy (e·ktŏmi), repr. Gr. ἐκτομή excision, in surgical terms denoting an operation for the removal of a part, as HYSTERECTOMY, TONSILLECTOMY.

‖**Ecto·pia.** 1847. [mod.L., f. Gr. ἔκτοπος out of place. See -IA[1].] *Path.* 'Displacement; anomaly of situation or relation' (*Syd. Soc. Lex.*).

‖**Ectro·pion, -um.** 1685. [mod.L. *ectropium*, Gr. ἐκτρόπιον everted eyelid, f. ἐκ out + τρέπειν turn.] *Path.* An outward bending; *esp.* applied to eversion of the eyelid.

Ectrotic (ektrǫ·tik), *a.* 1866. [– Gr. ἐκτρωτικός pertaining to abortion.] *Med.* Tending to cause abortion of the fœtus. Also tending to produce the abortion of a disease.

Ectypal (e·ktipăl), *a.* 1642. [f. next + -AL¹.] Of or pertaining to an ectype; of the nature of a copy; opp. to *archetypal*.

Ectype (e·ktəip). 1642. [– Gr. ἔκτυπον, n. of ἔκτυπος worked in relief, f. ἐκ out + τύπος figure. See TYPE *sb.*] **1.** An impression of a seal or medal. ? *Obs.* 1662. **b.** *fig.* A copy: *esp.* as opp. to *archetype* or *prototype* 1646. **2.** *Arch.* An object in relievo or embossed 1876.

1. *fig.* The Complex Ideas of Substances are Ectypes, Copies too; but not perfect ones LOCKE.

Ectypography (ektipǫ·grăfi). 1870. [f. Gr. ἔκτυπος (see prec.) + -GRAPHY.] A method of etching in which the lines on the plate are produced in relief.

‖**Écu** (ekü). 1704. [Fr. :– L. *scutum*; so called from the three fleurs-de-lis stamped on the coin as on a shield.] A French silver crown piece. Now, a French five-franc piece.

Ecumenacy, -ic, -ical, etc.; see ŒCUMEN-.

Eczema (e·kzĭmă). 1753. [mod.L. – Gr. ἔκζεμα, f. ἐκζεῖν boil over, (of disease) break out, f. ἐκ out, EX-² + ζεῖν boil.] *Path.* 'A.. non-contagious, simple inflammation of the skin, characterized by the presence of itching papules and vesicles which discharge a serous fluid, or dry up' (*Syd. Soc. Lex.*). Hence **Ecze·matous** *a.*, **-ly** *adv.*

†**Ed-,** *prefix.* [OE. *ed-* = OFris. *et-*, OHG. *et(a)-*, ON. *ið-*, rel. to L. *et* and Gr. ἔτι yet, Gaulish *etic* and Goth. *iþ* then, but.] Freq. in OE., occas. in ME., with the general sense of 'back' or 'again' (= L. *re-*).

-ed, *suffix*¹, in OE. *-ed*, *-ad*, *-od* (*-ud*), in ME. *-ed* (*-id*, *-yd*), the formative of the pa. pple. of wk. vbs. The ppl. suffix proper is *-d* :– Gmc. *-ðaz :– IE. *-tós; cf. Gr. -τός and L. *-tus*. **1.** The written spelling is usually *-ed*, although the pronunc. is now normally vowelless (d), or after a voiceless cons. (t), as in *robed* (rōᵘbd), *hoped* (hōᵘpt). From 16th to 18th c. the suffix was often written *-t*, when so pronounced, as in *jumpt*, *whipt*, *stept*, and this is still occasionally done.

2. In 15th, 16th, and 17th c. the suffix was added to adapted forms of L. pples., e.g. *situated*, and to ppl. adjs. in *-ate* – L. *-atus*, e.g. *bipinnate(d*, *dentate(d*, without difference of meaning.

3. Some of the adjs. formed by the addition of *-ed* to sbs. may be examples of this suffix.

-ed, *suffix*², OE. *-ede* = OS. *-ôdi* :– Gmc. *-ōðja-, is appended to sbs. in order to form adjs., with the sense 'possessing, provided with, characterized by'; *e.g.* in *toothed*, *moneyed*, *jaundiced*, etc. As to pronunciation, this suffix follows the same rules as -ED¹.

Edacious (ĭdēⁱ·ʃəs), *a.* 1819. [f. L. *edax*, *edac-* (f. *edere* eat) + -OUS; see -ACIOUS.] Of or relating to eating; voracious; *fig.* greedy.

E. Flunkies CARLYLE. The e. tooth of Time LOWELL.

Edacity (ĭdæ·sĭti). 1626. [f. as prec. see -ITY.] **1.** The quality of being edacious; capacity for eating. (Now *joc.*) †**2.** Corrosive quality 1657.

Edaphodont (e·dăfodǫnt), *a.* 1854. [– mod.L. *edaphodus*, f. Gr. ἔδαφος floor + ὀδούς, ὀδόντ- tooth; so named from the shape of the teeth.] *Palæont.* A fish of the fossil genus *Edaphodus*, found in deposits ranging from the Cretaceous to the Eocene.

‖**Edda** (e·dă). 1771. [Of disputed etym.; either from the name of the great-grandmother in the poem 'Rigsþul' or f. ON. *óðr* poetry.] Applied to: **a.** A miscellaneous handbook to Icelandic poetry written *c* 1230, and called since 1642 Snorre's Edda, or the Younger or Prose Edda. **b.** A collection (made *c* 1200) of ancient ON. poems, named 'Elder or Poetic Edda' or 'Edda of Sæmund', and erroneously ascribed to the Icel. historian Sæmund (*d.* 1133). Hence **Edda·ic, E·ddic** *a.* of, pertaining to, or resembling the Eddas.

Edder (e·dəɹ), *sb.* Now *dial.* 1523. [Doubtfully identified w. OE. *eodor*, *eder* enclosure.] Osiers, and the like, used for interlacing hedge stakes at the top. Hence **Edder** *v.*, also **ether**, to interlace or bind (a hedge) at the top with osiers, etc. **E·ddering** *vbl. sb.* the materials used in doing this.

Edder, obs. and dial. f. ADDER *sb.*¹, EIDER.

Eddish (e·diʃ). See also EARSH, ARRISH. [Formally identified w. OE. *edisc* park, enclosed pasture; the discrepancy of sense is a difficulty, but cf. OE. *edischenn* quail, perh. 'stubble-hen'.] †**1.** OE. *edisc*: A park or enclosed pasture for cattle. **2.** Grass (also clover, etc.) which grows again; aftermath. **b.** Stubble; a stubble-field. 1468. **3.** *attrib.* as in *e.-grass* OE.

Eddoes (e·doᵘz). 1685. [A Gold Coast word.] *Bot.* The tuberous stems of various araceous plants, as *Colocasia esculenta*, etc. *Eddy-root*: the root of the taro (*Colocasia macrorhiza*).

Eddy (e·di), *sb.* 1455. [prob. f. base of OE. *ed-* again, back; see ED- *prefix*. Cf. ON. *iða* of same meaning.] The water that runs contrary to the direction of the tide or current; a circular motion in water, a small whirlpool. Also *transf.* of wind, fog, dust, etc. Also *fig.*

The madness of the straiten'd stream Turns in black eddies round THOMSON. Circling eddies of fog DICKENS. *fig.* The eddies of the royal history STANLEY.

Eddy (e·di), *v.* 1730. [f. prec. sb.] **1.** *intr.* To move in an eddy or eddies. (*lit.* and *fig.*) 1810. **2.** *trans.* To whirl round in eddies. Also with *in*: To collect as into an eddy (*rare*).

1. Eddying in almost viewless wave SCOTT. The vapour..eddying wildly in the air TYNDALL. **2.** The circling mountains e. in From the bare wild the dissipated storm THOMSON.

E·ddy-wind. 1626. A wind that moves in an eddy.

‖**Edelweiss** (ē·dĕlvəis). 1862. [f. G. *edel* noble + *weiss* white.] *Bot.* An Alpine plant, *Gnaphalium leontopodium* or *L. alpinum*, remarkable for its white woolly flower, growing at high altitudes on the Swiss mountains.

Edematose, -ous, var. ff. ŒDEMATOSE, -OUS.

Eden (ī·d'n). ME. [– L. (Vulg.) *Eden*, Gr. (LXX) Ἠδήν – Heb. *'ēden*, assoc. with the word meaning 'delight'.] **1.** The first abode of Adam and Eve, Paradise. **2.** *transf.* and *fig.* A delightful abode, a paradise ME.

2. This sceptred Isle..This other E., demy paradise *Rich. II*, II. i. 42. Hence **Edenic** (ide·nik) *a.* of or pertaining to E. **E·denize** *v.* to make like E.; to admit into E. or Paradise.

Edental (ide·ntăl), *a.* 1845. [f. E- + L. *dens*, *dent-* tooth + -AL¹.] = next.

‖**Edenta·ta,** *sb. pl.* 1834. [mod.L. *edentata* (sc. *animalia*), n.pl. of pa. pple. of L. *edentare* render toothless.] *Zool.* An order of Mammalia characterized by the absence of front teeth; represented by the Ant-eater, Armadillo, Sloth, etc.

Edentate (ide·ntĕt). 1828. [– L. *edentatus*; see prec. -ATE².]

A. *adj.* Characterized by the absence of front teeth; belonging to the *Edentata*. Occas. = 'toothless'.

He is not truly e., but has teeth 1885.

B. *sb.* **1.** in *pl.* = EDENTATA 1835. **2.** *joc.* One who has lost his teeth. KINGSLEY.

Edentulous (ide·ntiŭləs), *a.* 1782. [f. L. *edentulus* toothless + -OUS.] Having no teeth, toothless.

Edge (edʒ), *sb.* [OE. *eċġ* = OFris. *egg*, OS. *eggia* (Du. *egge*), OHG. *ekka* (G. *ecke*), ON. *egg* :– Gmc. *aʒjō, f. *aʒ- :– IE. *ak- be sharp or pointed, as in L. *acies* edge, Gr. ἀκίς point.] **1.** The thin sharpened side of a cutting instrument or weapon. Hence **b.** A cutting weapon OE. **c.** Sharpness ME. **2.** *fig.* Power to cut or wound; trenchancy; keenness (of desire, etc.) 1593. **3.** The crest of a narrow ridge ME.; *fig.* a sharp dividing line; a critical position or moment 1597. **4.** The line in which two surfaces, *e.g.* of a polyhedron, meet abruptly 1823. **5.** Any relatively thin terminating border, as of a coin, a book, etc. 1677. **6.** A bounding line; a border; also, the part adjacent thereto. Also *fig.* ME. **7.** The brink or verge (of a precipice, etc.) ME.

1. [They] escaped the e. of the sword *Heb.* 11: 34. A tool with a fine e. GODWIN. **c.** The knife has no e. 1891. **2.** Abate the e. of Traitors, Gracious Lord *Rich. III*, V. v. 35. The e. of law SHERIDAN, of appetite 1830. Phr. *On e.*: full of eagerness, ready. *To set the teeth on e.*: 'to cause an unpleasant tingling in the teeth' (J.); also *fig.* **3.** *fig.* The perilous e. Of battel MILT. *P. L.* I. 276. **5.** The milled e. of a shilling, the top e. of a book 1891. **6.** From e. to e. A th' world *Ant. & Cl.* II. ii. 117. *fig.* On the e. of winter JOHNSON. **7.** *fig.* Phr. *On the e. of*: on the point of (doing something).

attrib. and *Comb.*

a. locative, as *e.-moulding*, *-gilt* adj., etc. **b.** objective, as *e.-cutting*. **c.** advb., as *e.-view*. Also **e.-joint,** a joint made by two edges, forming a corner; **-mill,** an ore-grinding or oil-mill in which the stones travel on their edges; **-rail,** (*a*) one form of rail-road rail, which bears the rolling stock on its edge (Knight); (*b*) a guard rail placed by the side of the main rail at a switch; **-roll,** a brass wheel used hot, in running an e. ornament, on a book cover (Knight); **-shot** *a.*, having an e. planed, as a board; **-wheel,** a wheel travelling on its e. in an annular or circular bed (Knight).

Edge (edʒ), *v.* ME. [f. EDGE *sb.*; see also EGG *v.*¹] **1.** *trans.* To give an edge to (a weapon, etc. or tool). **b.** *transf.* and *fig.* To give keenness or incisive force to 1599. †**2.** = EGG *v.* (but usu. with more direct reference to the sb.); also, to stimulate –1648. Also with *on.* **3.** To set (the teeth) on edge. Now *dial.* ME. **4.** To furnish with a border or edging 1555. **5.** *intr.* To move edgeways; to advance by almost imperceptible movements. Chiefly *Naut.* 1624. **6.** *trans.* To move by insensible degrees; to insinuate *into* a place 1677.

1. *fig.* With spirit of Honor edged More sharper then your Swords *Hen. V*, III. v. 38. To e. the appetite BLAIR. **2.** This..will Encourage and e., Industrious and Profitable Improuements BACON. **4.** Haunted spring and dale Edged with poplar pale MILT. A balustrade which edges it quite round EVELYN. **5.** They..stood edging in for the shore DE FOE. **6.** Every one edging his chair a little nearer W. IRVING. Phr. *To e. in* (a word, etc.): to get in edgeways.

Edge-bone, corruption of AITCH-BONE, q.v.

Edgeless (e·dʒlĕs), *a.* 1617. [See -LESS.] That has no edge.

His sword, which he carried neither edgeles, nor in vaine 1617.

†**E·dgeling, -long,** *adv.* ME. [f. EDGE *sb.* + -LING, -LONG.] **a.** With the edge. **b.** On the edge. –1611.

b. A dye that stands edgeling, so as tis doubtfull what chance it will yeeld COTGR.

Edge-tool, edged tool. ME. **1.** In early use, Any implement having a sharp cutting edge, as a knife or a sword; now (in lit. sense) restricted to industrial tools, as chisels, etc., also (with defining adj. *heavy*) axes, etc. Also *attrib.* **2.** *fig.*; *esp.* in phr. *play* or *jest with edge tools* 1579.

E·dge-ways, -wise, (rarely) **-way.** 1566. [f. EDGE *sb.* + -WAYS, -WISE.] **1.** With the edge towards the spectator. **2.** Of motion: With the edge foremost 1794. **3.** On the edge. SMEATON.

2. *fig.* Phr. *To get a word*, etc. *in edgeways*, etc.

Edging (e·dʒiŋ), *vbl. sb.* ME. [f. EDGE *v.* + -ING¹.] †**1.** The setting on edge (of the teeth). ME. only. **2.** The putting an edge or border to anything. Also *attrib.*, as in *e.-lace*, *-tile*, etc. 1580. **3.** *concr.* That which forms an edge to anything, as the fringe, trimming, etc. on the edge of a garment, a border round a flower-bed, etc. 1664.

Edgy (e·dʒi), *a.* 1775. [f. EDGE *sb.* + -Y¹.] **1.** Sharp, cutting. Also *fig.* **2.** Of a painting: Having the outlines too hard 1825.

1. E. splinters RUSKIN. **2.** Less e...than previous works 1868. Hence **E·dginess.**

Edible (e·dib'l). 1611. [– late L. *edibilis*, f. *edere* eat; see -IBLE.] **A.** *adj.* That is suitable for food. **B.** *sb.* Anything edible, an article of food. (Chiefly in *pl.*) Hence **Edibi·lity, E·dibleness,** the quality of being e.

Edict (ī·dikt). ME. [– L. *edictum*, subst. use of pa. pple. n. of *edicere* proclaim, f. e- E- + *dicere* say, tell. In 16th and 17th c. stressed on the last syllable.] That which is proclaimed by authority as a rule of action; an order issued by a sovereign to his subjects; an ordinance or proclamation having the force of law; *esp.* the edicts of the Roman emperors, and of the French monarchs. Also *fig.*

fig. The generall Edicts of nature HOOKER.

Phr. *E. of Nantes*, an edict issued by Henry IV of France, granting toleration to the Protestants; revoked by Louis XIV.

Edictal (ĭdi·ktăl), *a.* 1814. [– late L. *edictalis*, f. *edictum*; see prec. -AL[1].] Of or pertaining to an edict or edicts; consisting of edicts.

The e. rights of patronus 1875. **Edi·ctally** *adv.*

†**Edi·ficant,** *a.* 1642. [– *ædificant-*, pres. ppl. stem of L. *ædificare*; see next, -ANT.] Edifying –1655.

†**Edi·ficate,** *a.* 1470. [– L. *ædificatus*, pa. pple. of *ædificare*; see next, -ATE[2].] Built up –1560.

Edification (e:dĭfikēⁱ·ʃən). ME. [– L. *ædificatio* (in Vulg. rendering Gr. οἰκοδομή), f. *ædificat-*, pa. ppl. stem of *ædificare* build; see EDIFY, -ION.] **1.** Building (now *rare*) 1549; †*concr.* a building –1584. Also *fig.* **2.** *fig.* A building up in faith and holiness of life (cf. 1 *Cor.* 14.) ME.; mental or moral improvement; instruction (now often *ironical*) 1660.

2. To the e. of God's people 1651. That he might distribute his e. in equal proportions 1857.

Edi·ficative, *a.* ? *Obs.* ME. [– med.L. *edificativus*, f. as prec.; see -IVE.] Edifying.

Edificatory (e·difikeⁱtəri). 1649. [– late L. *ædificatorius*, f. as prec.; see -ORY[2].] Intended or proper for edification.

Edifice (e·dĭfis). ME. [– (O)Fr. *édifice* – L. *ædificium*, f. *ædis, ædes* dwelling. See next.] **1.** A (large and stately) building, as a church, palace, fortress. Also *transf.* and *fig.* †**2.** Style of building. NORTH.

1. *fig.* The corner-stone of Comte's e. MORLEY. Hence **Edifi·cial** *a.* pertaining to, or of the nature of, an e.

Edify (e·difəi), *v.* ME. [– (O)Fr. *édifier* – L. *ædificare*, f. *ædis, ædes* dwelling, orig. hearth + *-ficare* -FY.] **1.** *trans.* To build; to construct, set up (now *rare*). †**b.** To build over –1596. †**2.** *fig.* To build up, establish –1781. †**3.** *intr.* To take form, grow, prosper –1662. **4.** *trans.* To build up in faith and holiness; to strengthen. Also *absol.* ME. **b.** To instruct, improve (occas. *ironical*) 1534. †**5.** *intr.* To profit spiritually or mentally –1800.

1. To take timber to edifie the house againe 1641. Edified out of the Rib of Adam SIR T. BROWNE. **2.** He secretly edified the throne of his successors GIBBON. **4.** To edifie the conscience that is weake DRAYTON. **b.** *Twel. N.* V. i. 298. Hence **E·difier** (*rare*). **E·difying** *ppl. a.* that tends to moral and spiritual improvement; now often *ironical.* **E·difyingly** *adv.*

Edile, var. of ÆDILE.

Edingtonite (e·diŋtə̆nəit). 1825. [f. the surname *Edington* + -ITE[1] 2 b.] *Min.* A greyish white translucent mineral, consisting chiefly of the silicates of alumina, baryta, etc.

Edit (e·dit), *v.* 1791. [Partly – Fr. *éditer* publish, edit (itself based on *édition*); partly back-formation from EDITOR.] †**1.** To publish, give to the world. Chiefly in pa. pple. **2.** To prepare an edition of, *e.g.* 'to e. (the works of) Horace,' etc. **b.** To prepare, set in order for publication (literary material). Sometimes euphemistically for: To garble, 'cook'. **c.** To be or act as the EDITOR of (a newspaper, etc.). 1793.

2. b. The folly of attempting to 'e.' the news 1885.

Edition (ĭdi·ʃən). 1551. [– (O)Fr. *édition* – L. *editio*, f. *edit-*, pa. pple. stem of *edere* put forth, f. *e-* EX-[1] + *dare* put.] †**1.** Publication –1663. †**2.** The action of producing; hence, birth, creation, origin, kind, fashion –1677. **3.** *concr.* **a.** One of the differing forms in which a literary work is published. **b.** The whole number of copies printed from the same set of types and issued at one time. 1570. Also *fig.*

2. Barons of late e. EARL MONM. **3. a.** Above 60 editions of the Orlando Furioso were published in the 16th century HALLAM. **b.** The latest e. of the evening paper 1891. Hence †**Edi·tioner** (*rare*) = EDITOR.

‖**Editio princeps** (ĭdi·ʃio pri·nseps). 1802. [mod.L., = first edition.] The first printed edition of a book.

Editor (e·ditəɹ). 1649. [– L. *editor* producer, exhibitor, f. *edit-*; see EDITION.] †**1.** A publisher (cf. Fr. *éditeur*). **2.** One who edits (a text, newspaper, etc.) 1712.

2. This blunder-headed e. of *Bell's Messenger* COBBETT.

Editorial (editōᵊ·riăl). 1744. [f. prec. + -IAL.] **A.** *adj.* Of or pertaining to an editor; characteristic of an editor; as *e. criticism, prophecy*, etc. **B.** *sb.* A newspaper article written by, or by the direction of, the editor 1864. Hence **Edito·rially** *adv.* in an e. manner or capacity.

E·ditorship. 1782. [See -SHIP.] The duties, functions, and office of an editor; editorial superintendence.

Editress (e·ditrės). 1799. [f. EDITOR + -ESS[1].] A female editor.

†**Edi·tuate,** *v.* 1646. [f. L. *ædituat-*, ppl. stem of *æditua ri*, f. *æditu us*, tr. Gr. νεωκόρος in *Acts* 19:35.] To keep, as a temple.

E·domitish, *a.* 1641. [f. *Edomite* descendant of Esau or Edom, inhabitant of Edom + -ISH[1].] Pertaining to Edom: characteristic of the Edomites. In 17th c. sometimes used with reference to Ps. 137:7.

Edriophthalmian (e:driˌǫfþæ·lmiăn). 1877. [f. mod.L. *Edriophthalma* sb. pl. (irreg. f. Gr. ἕδρα seat + ὀφθαλμός eye) + -IAN.] **a.** *adj.* Belonging to or resembling the *Edriophthalma*, or sessile-eyed Crustacea (including the Prawns, Shrimps, etc.). **b.** *sb.* An individual of that order. So **E:driophtha·lmous** *a.*

Educable (e·diŭkăb'l), *a.* 1845. [f. EDUCATE *v.* + -ABLE. Cf. Fr. *éducable.*] Capable of being educated. Hence **E:ducabi·lity.**

Educate (e·diŭkeⁱt), *v.* 1588. [– *educat-*, pa. ppl. stem of L. *educare*, rel. to *educere* EDUCE; see -ATE[3].] *trans.* or *absol.* †**1.** To rear, bring up –1818. **2.** To bring up from childhood, so as to form habits, manners, mental and physical aptitudes 1618. **b.** To provide schooling for 1588. **3.** To train generally 1849. **4.** To train so as to develop some special aptitude, taste, or disposition. Const. *to*, also *inf.* 1841.

2. Mountaines, among which he had been educated BOLTON. **b.** It costs 8*d.* a week to e. a child 1863. **3.** The question is, not what to teach, but how to e. KINGSLEY. **4.** Our ears are educated to music by his rhythm EMERSON. I had..to e... our party DISRAELI.

Educated (e·diŭkeⁱtėd), *ppl. a.* 1670. [f. prec. + -ED[1].] That has received education; instructed, trained, etc.; see the vb. Often qualified, as *half-, over-, well-*, etc. Also *transf.*

Education (ediŭkēⁱ·ʃən). 1531. [– (O)Fr. *éducation* or L. *educatio*, f. as EDUCATE *v.*; see -ION.] †**1.** The process of nourishing or rearing –1661. **2.** The process of bringing up (young persons); the manner in which a person has been brought up. *Obs.* exc. with notion of 3. 1531. **3.** The systematic instruction, schooling or training given to the young (and, by extension, to adults) in preparation for the work of life. Also, the whole course of scholastic instruction which a person has received. Often qualified, as *classical, legal, medical, technical*, etc. 1616. Also *fig.* **4.** Hence, Culture or development of powers, formation of character. Often qualified, as *intellectual, moral*, etc. 1860. **5.** *attrib.*, as *E. Society*, etc. 1662.

2. The beste forme of e. or bringing up of noble children ELYOT. **3.** If you consent to put your clerical e., or any other part of your e., under their direction or control BURKE. *fig.* The e. of the world TEMPLE. **4.** It confounds e. with the knowledge of facts, whereas it really is the possession of method ROGERS.

Hence **Educa·tional** *a.* †due to e.; of, pertaining to, or concerned with e. **Educa·tionally** *adv.* **Educa·tionalist, Educa·tionist,** a student of the science or methods of e.; an advocate of e.

Educative (e·diŭkĕtiv), *a.* 1844. [f. EDUCATE *v.* + -IVE.] **1.** Of or pertaining to education 1856. **2.** Tending to educate, as, an *educative* knowledge.

Educator (e·diŭkeⁱtəɹ). 1566. [orig. – L. *educator*; see EDUCATE *v.*, -OR 2 b. In mod. use, directly from the verb.] One who or that which educates. Hence **E·ducatress,** a female e.

Educe (ĭdiū·s), *v.* ME. [– L. *educere*, f. *e-* EX-[1] + *ducere* lead.] †**1.** *pass.* To be led forth, as a river, a blood-vessel –1578. †**2.** *Med.* To draw forth so as to remove –1658. **3.** To bring out, elicit, develop 1603. **b.** *Chem.* To disengage from a compound; contrasted with *produce* 1805. **4.** To evoke, give rise to 1665.

3. Chaos was that ancient slime, out of which all things were educed GALE. Notions..which we e. from experience SIR W. HAMILTON. Hence **Edu·cible** *a.* that may be educed.

Educt (ī·dɒkt). 1799. [– L. *eductum*, pa. pple. n. of *educere* EDUCE.] That which is educed. **1.** *Chem.* A body separated by decomposition from another; as dist. from *product.* **2.** A result of inference or of development 1816.

Eduction (ĭdɒ·kʃən). 1649. [– L. *eductio*, f. as prec.; see -ION.] †**1.** A leading or putting forth or out –1659. †**2.** *Med.* Removal by drawing forth –1710. **3.** The action of educing. Also *concr.* = EDUCT. 1655. **4.** *Steam-engine.* **a.** = EXHAUST. **b.** Short for *e.-valve.* 1782.

4. An e. valve..to let the steam escape to the condenser 1859.

Eductive (ĭdɒ·ktiv), *a.* 1657. [– med.L. *eductivus*, f. as prec.; see -IVE.] Tending to educe.

Eductor (ĭdɒ·ktəɹ). 1794. [– L. *eductor*, f. as prec., see -OR 2.] He who, or that which, educes.

Edulcorate (ĭdɒ·lkŏrĕt), *ppl. a. rare.* 1810. [– med.L. *edulcoratus*, pa. pple. of *edulcorare*; see next, -ATE[2].] Softened, sweetened.

Edulcorate (ĭdɒ·lkŏreⁱt), *v.* 1641. [– *edulcorat-*, pa. ppl. stem of med.L. *edulcorare*, f. *e-* EX-[1] + late L. *dulcor* sweetness, f. *dulcis* sweet; see -ATE[3].] †**1.** To make sweet –1710. **2.** To free from harsh and acrid properties; to purify, soften 1641. **3.** *Chem.* To free from soluble particles by washing, etc. 1660.

2. Experiments for edulcorating vicious train-oil 1762. Hence **Edu:lcora·tion,** the action or process of washing away particles soluble in water.

Edulcorator (ĭdɒ·lkoreⁱtəɹ). 1669. [f. prec. + -OR 2.] One who, or that which, edulcorates.

Edward (e·dwəɹd). 1598. The 'angel' of Edward IV, or the 'noble' of Edward III.

E. shovelboard, a broad shilling of Edward VI, used in the game of Shovel-board. *Merry W.* I. i. 158.

Edwardian (edwǭ·ɹdiăn), *a.* and *sb.* 1861. [-IAN.] **1.** Pertaining to (the reigns of) the first three Edwards (1272–1377). **2.** Belonging to the reign of Edward VI (1547–1553) 1866. **b.** Belonging to (an alumnus of) a school of the foundation of Edward VI, St. Edward's School, Oxford, or King Edward VII Schools 1873. **c.** (A person) of the reign of Edward VII (1901–1910) 1908. Also **Edwa·rdine** (-əin) *a.* belonging to the acts of Edward VI's reign.

Ee, *north.* and *esp. Sc.* f. EYE.

-ee, *suffix*[1], correl. to *-or*; orig. – *-é* of certain AFr. pa. pples.; used chiefly in technical terms of Eng. law, denoting usually the indirect object of the vbs. from which they are derived; as *vendee*, the person to whom a sale is made; etc. In a few words, as *bargee, devotee*, the use is app. arbitrary.

2. *-ee* also appears in the Eng. spelling of certain sbs. adopted from mod.Fr. ppl. sbs. in *-é*, as *debauchee, refugee.*

-ee, *suffix*[2], usu. with a dim. force, as in *bootee, coatee.* In other words, as *goatee, settee*, its meaning is vague. ¶In *dungaree, jamboree, marquee, puttee*, the source of the *-ee* is different.

Eel (īl). [OE. *ǣl* = OFris. *ēl*, OS., OHG. *āl* (Du., G. *aal*), ON. *áll* :– Gmc. *ǣlaz*, of unkn. origin.] **1.** The name of a genus (*Anguilla*) of soft-finned osseous fishes, resembling snakes in appearance; including the Common or Sharp-nosed Eel (*A. anguilla*), and the Broad-nosed Eel or GRIG (*A. latirostris*). **b.** A name for the *Murænidæ*, comprising the true eels with other genera, notably the CONGER. **2.** Applied to other fishes resembling eels in form 1705. **3.** The pop. name for the *Entozoa* found in vinegar and in sour paste 1746.

1. An old yeele is wholsomer than a yong COGAN. †*Salt e.*: a rope's end used for flogging. PEPYS. **2.** *Electric e.*: = GYMNOTUS. *Nine-eyed e.*: the River Lamprey.

Comb.: **e.-backed** *a.*, applied to horses having 'black lists along their backs'; **-basket,** a trap of basket-work with funnel-shaped entrance for catching eels; **-buck** (see Buck *sb.*[4]); **-fork** = EEL-SPEAR; **-grass** (*U.S.*), a name for GRASS-*wrack* (*Zostera marina*), and for other grass-like weeds; **-pot** = *eel-buck*; **-ware**, *Ranunculus fluitans*; **-weel** (erron. *-wheel*) = *eel-buck*.

Ee·l-bed. 1483. A pond for eels; *transf.* a bivouac on swampy ground.

Eel-fare (ī·lfēᵊɹ). 1533. [FARE *sb.*[1] 2.] **a.** The passage of young eels up a river. **b.** A brood of young eels.

Ee·l-pout. [OE. *ǣlepūta*; see EEL, POUT *sb.*[1]] **1.** = BURBOT. **b.** = BLENNY. **2.** ? = EEL-*ware* 1736.

Ee·l-skin. 1562. [f. EEL + SKIN.] The skin of an eel. Also *attrib.*, as in **eel-skin dress,** a tight-fitting dress.

Ee·l-spear. 1555. [f. EEL + SPEAR.] A pronged instrument for spearing eels.

Eely (ī·li), *a.* 1655. [f. EEL + -Y[1].] Eel-like.

Een, obs. and dial. pl. of EYE.

E'en, contr. form of EVEN *sb.* and EVEN *adv.*

-een[1], terminal element in names of fabrics, now usu. denoting one inferior to or coarser than that denoted by the original word; it represents Fr. *-ine*, as in *ratteen* XVII (– Fr. *ratine*), *camleteen* XVIII (– Fr. *camelotine*); *velveteen* (XVIII) was modelled on *ratteen*, *sateen* (XIX) is a modification thereafter of *satin*.

-een[2], *suffix*, repr. Ir. dim. ending *-in*, as in *buckeen* (XVIII), *caubeen*, *colleen*, *dudeen*, *mavourneen* (XVIII), *spalpeen*, *squireen*.

Eer, obs. f. ERE, before.

-eer, *suffix*, repr. Fr. *-ier* (= L. *-iarius*, and often replacing *-air* :– L. *arius*), in sense 'one who is concerned with', 'one who deals in', often with a contemptuous implication.

E'er, var. of EVER.

Eerie, eery (ī·ri), *a.* ME. [orig. north. Eng. and Sc. *eri*, *ery*; deriv. from ME. *erȝ*, *arȝe* cowardly, timid (OE. *earg*) would suit the earliest sense, but the vowel of the stem is not appropriate, and the ending (*-ie*, -Y[1]) would be difficult to account for.] **1.** Fearful, timid. In mod. use, expressing the notion of a vague superstitious uneasiness. **2.** Fear-inspiring; gloomy, strange, weird 1792.

2. Night comes dark and eerie 1795. Hence **Ee·rily** *adv.* **Ee·riness,** a vague sense of fear; superstitious dread. **Ee·risome** *a.* weird, gloomy.

Eete(n, eette, obs. ff. pres. t., pa. t. and pa. pple. of EAT.

Ef (ef). Name of the letter F, q.v.

Ef-, *pref.*, repr. L. pref. *ex-* used before *f.*

Effable (e·făb'l), *a.* 1637. [– Fr. †*effable* or L. *effabilis*, f. *effari* utter, f. *ex-* EF- + *fari* speak; see -ABLE.] That can be uttered, or expressed in words. Now only *arch.*

Efface (efē¹·s), *v.* 1490. [– (O)Fr. *effacer*, f. *es-* (see ES-, EF-) + *face* FACE *sb.*] **1.** To rub out, obliterate; more widely, to cause to disappear 1611. **2.** To expunge, erase. Now only in fig. sentences. 1737. **3.** To wipe out; to blot out, obtain oblivion for; to abolish 1490. **4.** *fig.* To reduce to insignificance; also *refl.* [after Fr. *s'effacer*] 1716.

1. So coin grows smooth..Till Cæsar's image is effaced at last COWPER. **2.** Fluent Shakespeare scarce effac'd a line POPE. **3.** All my sins e. WESLEY. **4.** As a politician he has completely effaced himself 1891. Hence **Effa·ceable** *a.* **Effa·cement. Effa·cive** *a.* (*nonce-wd.*), disposed or tending to e.

||**Effaré** (efa·re), *a.* 1738. [Fr. pa. pple. of *effarer* agitate.] *Her.* Salient.

†**Effa·scinate,** *v.* 1616. [– *effascinat-*, pa. ppl. stem of L. *effascinare*, f. *ex-* EF- + *fascinare*; see FASCINATE.] = FASCINATE –1678. So †**Effa:scina·tion,** = FASCINATION.

†**Effa·te.** 1650. [– L. *effatum*, subst. use of pa. pple. n. of *effari* speak out, f. *ex-* EF- + *fari* speak.] A saying, dictum, maxim –1690.

Effect (efe·kt), *sb.* ME. [– OFr. *effect* (mod. *effet*) or L. *effectus*, f. *effect-*, pa. ppl. stem of *efficere* work out, f. *ex-* EF- + *facere*, *fic-* make, do.] **1.** Something caused or produced; a result, consequence. Correl. w. CAUSE. **b.** Efficacy ME. **c.** *Mech.* The amount of work done in a given time 1812. **2.** Purport, drift, tenor ME. †**3.** An outward manifestation; a phenomenon –1656. **b.** A (happy) combination of colour or form in a picture, a landscape, etc. 1884. †**4.** Something attained or acquired by an action 1602. **b.** *pl.* Goods and chattels, movable property; also, funds in the bank to meet drafts 1704. **5.** Operative influence 1668. **b.** The state or fact of being operative 1771. **6.** The impression produced on the mind 1736. **7.** Accomplishment 1483. †**b.** Reality, fact –1674.

1. We know not at all what death is in itself; but only some of its effects BUTLER. **b.** This Tree is.. of Divine e. To open Eyes MILT. *P. L.* IX. 865. **c.** Phr. *Useful e.*: the net result, after allowance made for friction, etc. **2.** Phr. *To this* or *that e.*, *to the e. that.* **3.** What effects of passion shows she *Much Ado* II. iii. 112. **4.** *Haml.* III. iii. 54. **b.** Sale of household effects 1891. **5.** Speeches which will have an e. upon the courts JOWETT. **b.** Phr. *To give e. to*: to render operative. *To take e.*: to become operative. **7.** Phr. *To bring to e.*, *to carry into e.* **b.** *Tr. & Cr.* V. iii. 109. Phr. *In e.*: formerly = in fact, in reality; in mod. use, virtually, substantially. Hence **Effe·ctless** *a.*

Effect (efe·kt), *v.* 1589. [f. prec. sb.] **1.** *trans.* To bring about; to accomplish. **b.** To make (*arch.*) 1791. †**2.** To give effect to; to fulfil –1660. †**3.** *absol.* and *intr.* To have an effect, be effectual –1660. ¶**4.** Confused with AFFECT 1494.

1. To e. a marriage SHAKS., Peace 1792, a cure JOWETT. Phr. *To e. a sale, an insurance*; hence, to *e. a policy* (of insurance). **2.** *Tr. & Cr.* V. x. 6.

Hence **Effe·cter, -or,** one who or that which effects. **Effe·ctible** *a.* capable of being effected. †**Effe·ction,** production; performance; in *Geom.* a construction, a proposition.

Effective (efe·ktiv). ME. [– L. *effectivus*, f. as prec.; see -IVE. Cf. (O)Fr. *effectif*, *-ive.*]

A. *adj.* †**1.** That is concerned in the production *of* –1684; having the power of acting upon objects –1652. †**2.** Concerned with, or having the function of, effecting –1607. **3.** That has an effect 1760; *spec.* said of that portion of an agency or force which is actually brought to bear on an object 1798. **4.** Efficient ME.; striking 1853. **5.** Fit for work or service, as soldiers, etc. 1684. **6.** Actual, *de facto*; opp. to *potential*, *nominal* 1786.

3. An e. voice in legislation ADAM SMITH. *E. range*: the range within which a missile or fire-arm is e. *E. faith, love* (Theol.): that bears fruit in action. **4.** An e. speaker 1836. **5.** Army of 60,000 on paper; of e. more than 50,000 CARLYLE. Phr. *E. charge*: the expenditure on e. forces, as dist. from pensions, etc. **6.** The collection of an e... revenue BURKE. Phr. *E. money*, coin as dist. from paper money.

B. *sb.* †**1.** An efficient cause –1686. **2.** *Mil.* An effective soldier. (See A. 5.) Usually *pl.* 1722. **b.** *collect. sing.* The effective part of an army 1885.

2. The garrisons..consist of 1000 Effectives 1722.

Hence **Effe·ctively** *adv.* in an e. manner; †in fact; virtually, decisively, completely. **Effe·ctiveness,** the quality of being e.

†**Effectress** (efe·ktrĕs). 1601. [f. *effecter*, *-or* (see EFFECT *v.*) + -ESS[1].] A female effecter –1662. So ||**Effe·ctrix** [sc. *causa*, *vis*], an efficient cause or power.

Effectual (efe·ktiŭăl), *a.* ME. [– med.L. *effectualis*, f. L. *effectus* EFFECT *sb.*; see -AL[1].] **1.** That produces its intended effect, or answers its purpose. †**2.** = EFFECTIVE, q.v. –1689. **3.** Of prayers: Earnest, urgent ME. †**4.** ? Actual –1655. †**5.** To the point, pertinent, conclusive –1677.

1. To make complaints rather e. than loud BURKE. Phr. *E. calling* (Theol.): 'the word of God's Spirit, whereby..he doth persuade and enable us to embrace Jesus Christ' *Shorter Catech.* *E. demand* (Pol. Econ.): demand 'sufficient to effectuate the bringing of the commodity to market' (Adam Smith). **5.** A speedy and e. answer 1625.

Hence **Effectua·lity,** e. quality. **Effe·ctually** *adv.* so as to answer the purpose; †earnestly; †explicitly; †in effect; †in fact. **Effe·ctualness** (now *rare*), efficacy.

Effectuate (efe·ktiu,e¹t), *v.* 1580. [– *effectuat-*, pa. ppl. stem of med.L. *effectuare*, f. as prec.; see -ATE[3].] *trans.* To bring to pass; to carry into effect, accomplish.

To e. a desire SIDNEY, a Cure CHEYNE, purpose JOHNSON, an intention CRUISE, a conclusion (*mod.*).

Hence **Effe:ctua·tion,** accomplishment, fulfilment.

†**Effe·ctuous,** *a.* ME. [f. late L. *effectuosus* (f. as prec.) + -OUS. Cf. OFr. *effectueux.*] = EFFECTUAL *a.* 1, 3. –1655. Hence †**Effe·ctuous-ly** *adv.*, †**-ness.**

†**Effei·r,** *sb.* ME. [Sc. var. of AFFAIR, q. v.] **1.** A 'cause' –1605. **2.** Appearance; show; ceremony –1818.

Effeir, effere (in Sc. efī·r), *v. n. dial.* ME. [Usual Sc. spelling of AFFEIR, AFFERE.] **1.** *impers. intr.* To fall by right, appertain, be proper or meet. *Obs.* exc. in Sc. law phr. 'as effeirs'. †**2.** As *personal* vb. To pertain properly –1820.

2. In all that effeirs to war SCOTT.

Effeminacy (efe·minăsi). 1602. [f. next + -ACY.] **1.** Effeminate quality; unmanly weakness, softness, or delicacy. †**2.** Addiction to women –1671.

2. But foul e. held yok't Her Bond-Slave MILT.

Effeminate (efe·minĕt). ME. [– L. *effeminatus*, pa. pple. of *effeminare* make feminine, f. *ex-* EF- + *femina* woman; see -ATE[2].]

A. *adj.* **1.** That has become like a woman: **a.** Unmanly, enervated; self-indulgent; delicate or over-refined. **b.** Of things: Characterized by, or proceeding from, effeminacy 1579. †**c.** Gentle, compassionate –1594. †**d.** Of music, odours, etc.: Soft, voluptuous –1692. †**2.** Addicted to women –1589.

1. a. An e. persone neuer hathe spirite to any hie or noble dedes LD. BERNERS. **b.** I scorn those e. revenges 1685. **c.** *Rich. III*, III. vii. 211.

B. *sb.* An effeminate person 1597.

This wanton young e. [Richard II] DANIEL.

Hence **Effe·minately** *adv.* in an unmanly manner or style; †through addiction to women (MILT. *Sams.* 562). **Effe·minateness,** e. quality or condition.

Effeminate (efe·mine¹t), *v.* ME. [– *effeminat-*, pa. ppl. stem of L. *effeminare*; see prec., -ATE[3].] †**1.** *trans.* To represent as a woman (*rare*) –1739. **2.** To make womanish or unmanly; to enervate 1551. **3.** *intr.* To become womanish; to grow weak, languish ME.

2. Luxurious living..Effeminates fools in body SHADWELL. **3.** In a slothfull peace both courages will e., and manners corrupt BACON.

Effemination (efe:minē¹·ʃən). ? *Obs.* 1650. [– late L. *effeminatio*, f. as prec.; see -ION.] The process of making or of becoming effeminate.

Effeminize (efe·minəiz), *v.* Now *rare.* 1612. [f. EFFEMINATE *a.* + -IZE.] *trans.* To render effeminate.

||**Effendi** (efe·ndi). 1614. [– Turk. *efendi* – mod.Gr. ἀφέντης (pronounced *aféndi*), voc. of ἀφέντης (*aféndis*) :– Gr. αὐθέντης lord, master. See AUTHENTIC.] A Turkish title of respect, chiefly applied to officials and to professional men.

Efferent (e·fĕrĕnt). 1856. [– *efferent-*, pres. ppl. stem of L. *efferre*, f. *ex-* EF- + *ferre* bear; see -ENT.] *Phys.* **a.** *adj.* Conveying outwards; as *e. vessels*, *nerves*. Opp. to AFFERENT. **b.** *sb.* That which carries outwards 1876.

†**E·fferous,** *a. rare.* 1614. [f. L. *efferus* very fierce (f. *ex-* EF- + *ferus* fierce) + -OUS.] Fierce, violent –1657.

Effervesce (efəɹve·s), *v.* 1702. [– L. *effervescere*, f. *ex-* EF- + *fervescere*, inceptive of *fervēre* be hot, boil; see -ESCENT.] †**1.** *intr.* 'To generate heat by intestine motion' (J.). **2.** To give off bubbles of gas, *esp.* as the result of chemical action 1784. Of the gas itself: To issue forth in bubbles 1830. Also *fig.*

2. *fig.* A number of..juveniles..were effervescing in all those modes of..gambol and mischief MRS. STOWE. Hence **Efferve·scible** *a.* capable of producing effervescence; *fig.* ready to e. **Efferve·scive** *a.* tending to effervescence.

Effervescence (efəɹve·sĕns). 1651. [f. as next; see -ENCE.] †**1.** The action of boiling up; heated agitation of the particles of a fluid –1710. **2.** The action of bubbling up as if boiling; the rise of bubbles of gas from a fluid; *esp.* as the result of chemical action 1684.

2. That e. observed in the mixture of acids and alkalies BERKELEY. *fig.* The e. of invention JOHNSON. So **Efferve·scency,** effervescent state or condition.

Effervescent (efəɹve·sĕnt), *a.* 1684. [– *effervescent-*, pres. ppl. stem of L. *effervescere*; see EFFERVESCE, -ENT.] †**1.** That is in a state of bubbling heat. **2.** That has the property of rising in bubbles 1875. Also *fig.*

2. *fig.* Nonsense e. with animal spirits MACAULAY.

Effet, obs. or dial. f. EFT *sb.*

Effete (efī·t), *a.* 1621. [– L. *effetus* exhausted as by bearing young, f. *ex-* EF- + *fetus* bearing (see FŒTUS).] †**1.** Of animals: That has ceased to bring forth offspring

–1774. Also *fig.* **2.** *transf.* Of substances; That has lost its special quality or virtue; exhausted, worn out 1662. **3.** *fig.* Of systems, etc.: That has exhausted its vigour; incapable of efficient action 1790.

3. They find the old governments e., worn out BURKE. Your e. English aristocrat 1857. Hence **Effe·teness.**

†**E·fficace,** *sb.* ME. [– OFr. *efficace* sb. – L. *efficacia*, f. *efficax* (see next).] **a.** Efficacy. **b.** Effect. **c.** Active duty. –1712.

Efficacious (efikēⁱ·ʃəs), *a.* 1528. [f. L. *efficax, efficac-*, f. *efficere* accomplish (see EFFICIENT): see -ACIOUS.] That produces, or is certain to produce, the intended effect; effective. (Not said, in prose, of personal agents.)

Lesse e., that is, in plain English ineffectual 1651. Hence **Effica·cious-ly** *adv.*, **-ness.**

Effica·city. ME. [– (O)Fr. *efficacité* – L. *efficacitas*, f. *efficax*; see prec., -ITY.] = next.

Efficacy (e·fikăsi). 1527. [– L. *efficacia*, f. *efficax*; see EFFICACIOUS, -Y³.] **1.** Capacity to produce effects; power to effect the object intended. (Not used of personal agents.) †**2.** A mode of effecting a result. LOCKE. †**3.** Effect –1633.

1. An act, not..beyond the e. of the Sun SIR T. BROWNE. E. in a distemper BP. BERKELEY. The e. of mirth JOHNSON.

Efficience (efi·ʃĕns). ? *Obs.* 1669. [– L. *efficientia*; see EFFICIENT, -ENCE.] The exercise of efficient power.

Efficiency (efi·ʃĕnsi). 1593. [f. as prec.; see -ENCY.] **1.** The fact of being an efficient cause. Now only in philosophical use. †**b.** Production, causation, creation –1678. **2.** Efficient power, effectiveness, efficacy 1633.

2. The greatest dissemination of power consistent with e. MILL. The e. of labour FAWCETT.

Efficient (efi·ʃĕnt). ME. [– *efficient-*, pres. ppl. stem of L. *efficere* accomplish, f. *ex-* EF- + *facere* make, do; see -ENT. Cf. (O)Fr. *efficient.*]

A. *adj.* **1.** Making, causing to be; that makes (a thing) to be what it is. **2.** Productive of effects; operative. Of persons: Adequately skilled and active. 1787.

1. The common e. cause of beauty BURKE. **2.** An e. government 1787. An expert and e. workman 1850.

B. *sb.* †**1.** 'The cause which makes effects to be what they are' (J.). Common in 17th c. –1804. **2.** *Mil.* An efficient soldier; a volunteer qualified for service 1864.

1. The E. or Author of it, is..God himselfe 1649. Hence **Effi·ciently** *adv.* †as by an e. cause; in an e. manner.

†**Effie·rce,** *v.* [f. EF- + FIERCE.] To render fierce. SPENSER *F. Q.* III. xi. 27.

Effi·gial, *a. rare.* 1715. [f. L. *effigies* EFFIGY + -AL¹. Cf. med.L. *effigialis.*] Of the nature of an effigy.

Effigiate (efi·dʒiˌeⁱt), *v.* Now *rare.* 1608 [– *effigiat-*, pa. ppl. stem of late L. *effigiare*, f. *effigies*; see EFFIGY, -ATE³.] To present a likeness of; to portray. Also *fig.* Also with *into* (obs.).

To effigiat the Emperour Nero 1628. Hence **Effi:gia·tion,** the action of representing; a representation.

‖**Effigies** (efi·dʒiˌīz). *arch.* 1600. [L.] Now EFFIGY, q.v.

Effigy (e·fidʒi). 1539. [– L. *effigies*, f. *effig-*, stem of *effingere*, f. *ex-* EF- + *fingere* fashion. ¶Not before XVIII in sing. form, which is based on the L. abl.; earlier pl. *effigies* and phr. *in effigie* (4 syll.) belong to L. *effigies*, which was in common use XVI–XIX.] A likeness, portrait, or image. Now chiefly applied to a sculptured figure or to a habited image; also to a portrait on coins.

Phrases. *In e.*: under the form, or by means of, a representation; also *fig. To execute, hang, burn in e.*: to treat thus an image of any one, as an indication of the treatment popularly desired for the original; formerly also done in the case of a criminal who had fled from justice.

†**Effla·gitate,** *v. rare.* 1641. [– *efflagitat-*, pa. ppl. stem of L. *efflagitare*, f. *ex-* EF- + *flagitare* demand; see -ATE³.] To demand eagerly –1676.

†**Effla·te,** *v. rare.* 1634. [– *efflat-*, pa. ppl. stem of L. *efflare*, f. *ex-* EF- + *flare* blow; see -ATE³.] To puff out.

Efflation (eflēⁱ·ʃən). 1578. [– late L. *efflatio*, f. as prec.; see -ION. Cf. OFr. *efflation.*] **1.** A blowing out; expulsion of breath. **2.** *concr.* That which is blown or breathed forth 1862.

Effloresce (eflore·s), *v.* 1775. [– L. *efflorescere*, f. *ex-* EF- + *florescere*, inceptive of *florēre* bloom, f. *flos, flor-* flower; see -ESCENT.] **1.** To bloom, burst forth into or as into flowers. **2.** *Chem.* **a.** Of a crystalline substance: To change over the surface, or throughout, to 'flowers' or fine powder, owing to loss of water on exposure to the air 1788. **b.** Of a salt: To come to the surface, and there crystallize 1820. **c.** Of the ground, a wall, etc.: To become covered with a powdery crust of saline particles left by evaporation 18.. **3.** *fig.* To blossom out; to become manifest 1834.

3. A disposition..to e. into extremely tall talk 1864.

Efflorescence (eflore·sĕns). 1626. [f. *efflorescent-*, pres. ppl. stem of L *efflorescere* (see prec.); see -ENCE. Partly – Fr. *efflorescence* (XVI).] **1.** The process, or period, of flowering. Also *fig.* **2.** *Path.* 'A morbid redness, or rash of the skin' (*Syd. Soc. Lex.*) 1684. **3.** *Chem.* The process of efflorescing (see EFFLORESCE 2); the powdery deposit which results from this 1667.

1. *fig.* His impertinent e. of Rhetorick MARVELL. So †**Efflore·scency** (in senses 1 *fig.* and 3).

Efflorescent (eflore·sĕnt), *a.* 1818. [f. as prec.; see -ENT.] **1.** *Bot.* That is efflorescing or blooming. **2.** Resembling, or forming, an efflorescence; also *fig.*

Efflower (eflauᵊ·ɹ), *v. rare.* 1875. [– Fr. *effleurer* in same sense.] To deprive a skin of its epidermis with a blunt knife.

Effluence (e·flⁱuĕns). 1603. [– (O)Fr. *effluence* or med.L. *effluentia*, f. as next; see -ENCE.] **1.** A flowing out (*esp.* of light, magnetism, *etc.*). Also *transf.* and *fig.* 1628. **2.** *concr.* That which flows forth; an emanation. Also *fig.* 1603.

1. A moist e. of vapours 1635. *transf.* That stormful e. towards the Frontiers CARLYLE. **2.** Colour is an e. of form JOWETT. So †**E·ffluency.**

Effluent (e·flⁱuĕnt). 1726. [– *effluent-*, pres. ppl. stem of L. *effluere*, f. *ex-* EF- + *fluere* flow; see -ENT. Cf. (O)Fr *effluent.*]

A. *adj.* That flows forth or outwards, as an *e. drain.*

B. *sb.* **a.** A stream flowing from a larger stream, lake, etc. **b.** The outflow from a sewage tank. 1859.

Effluve (eflⁱū·v). 1881. [– Fr. *effluve* in same sense – L. EFFLUVIUM.] *Electr.* The diffusion of electricity from an electrified body by radiation or atmospheric conduction.

†**Efflu·viable,** *a.* [f. EFFLUVIUM + -ABLE.] That can pass off in effluvia. BOYLE.

†**Efflu·viate,** *v.* 1664. [f. EFFLUVIUM + -ATE³.] *trans.* To throw off effluvium; also *absol.* and *intr.* –1693.

Effluvious (eflⁱū·viəs), *a.* 1668. [f. next + -OUS.] Of the nature of an effluvium.

Effluvium (eflⁱū·viŏm). Pl. **-ia,** †**-iums.** 1646. [– L. *effluvium*, f. *effluere*, f. *ex-* EF- + *fluere* flow.] †**1.** A flowing out, an issuing forth –1704. **2.** *esp.* The (real or supposed) outflow of material particles too subtle to be perceived by the senses; *concr.* a stream of such particles. (*Obs.* in gen. sense.) 1646. **b.** An exhalation affecting the sense of smell; *pop.* a noxious or disgusting exhalation 1656. ¶**3.** In sense 2, the pl. *effluvia* has been ignorantly treated as a sing., with pl. *effluvias* or *effluviæ* 1652.

2. The Effluvia of the Load-stone BOYLE. Quick effluvia darting through the brain POPE.

Efflux (e·flɒks), *sb.* 1641. [– med.L. *effluxus* in same sense, f. L. *effluere*; see EFFLUENT.] **1.** A flowing outwards; often opp. to *afflux* or *influx*. Also *attrib.* Hence, a channel of outflow. Also *fig.* 1649. **2.** The lapse (of time, etc.); hence, expiry 1647. **3.** *concr.* That which flows out; an emanation 1647.

2. In e. of time N. BACON. The e. in 1877 of the time within which the turnpike trust was limited 1884. Hence †**Efflu·x** *v.* to flow forth (*rare*).

Effluxion (eflɒ·kʃən). 1621. [– (O)Fr. *effluxion* or late L. *effluxio*, f. as prec.; see -ION.] **1.** The action or process of flowing out; an out-flow. Also *fig.* 1646. **2.** = EFFLUX 2. 1621. **3.** = EFFLUVIUM 1626.

2. The partnership..having expired by e. of time 1868. So †**Efflu·xive** *a.* outflowing (*rare*).

†**Effo·liate,** *v. rare.* 1671. [f. EF- + FOLIATE *v.*] To open into leaf. Hence (with different sense) **Effolia·tion,** removal of leaves.

Efforce (efōᵊ·ɹs), *v.* 1512. [– Fr. *efforcer*; see EFFORT.] †**1.** *refl.* To make an effort (= Fr. *s'efforcer*) –1543. **2.** To force open, to gain by force. SPENSER. **3.** To force out (*rare*) 1855. Hence **Effo·rced** *ppl. a.* uttered with effort.

Efform (efǭɹm), *v.* 1578. [– late L. *efformare* in same sense; see EF-, FORM *v.*] To shape, fashion. Hence †**Efforma·tion.** †**Effo·rmetive** *a.* **Effo·rmer.**

Effort (e·fǭɹt), *sb.* 1489. [– (O)Fr. *effort*, earlier *esforz* nom., f. *esforcier* (mod. *efforcer*) :– Rom. **exfortiare*, f. L. *ex-* EF- + *fortis* strong. See FORCE *sb.*¹] †**1.** Power; also *pl.* powers, properties –1680. **2.** A strenuous exertion of power, physical or mental; a laborious attempt; a struggle 1489. **b.** In oratory, etc.: An achievement 1857.

2. The panting Courser..Makes many a faint E. SOMERVILLE. It required a considerable e. TYNDALL. Hence †**Effo·rt** *v.* to strengthen. **E·ffortless** *a.* making no e. **E·ffortlessly** *adv.*

†**Effo·ssion.** *rare.* 1657. [– late L. *effossio*, f. *effoss-*, pa. ppl. stem of L. *effodere*, f. *ex-* EF- + *fodere* dig; see -ION.] The action of digging out –1714.

Effraction (efræ·kʃən). 1840. [– Fr. *effraction* – med.L. *effractio*, f. *effract-*, pa. ppl. stem of L. *effringere*, f. *ex-* EF- + *frangere* break; see -ION.] Breaking open (a house); burglary.

A riot, with e. and murder MILMAN.

Effranchise (efra·ntʃəiz), *v.* 1864. [In 1864 Webster and mod. dicts. A var. of AFFRANCHISE, ENFRANCHISE.] To invest with franchises or privileges.

†**Effray·,** *v.* ME. [– Fr. *effrayer*; see AFFRAY *v.*] **1.** *t.ans.* To frighten –1596. **2.** To frighten away; to scare 1588. Hence **Effray·able** [? misprint for EFFROYABLE] *a.* frightful.

†**E·ffrenate,** *a.* 1561. [– L. *effrenatus*, pa. pple. of *effrenare*, f. *ex-* EF- + *frenum* bridle; see -ATE².] Unbridled; violent in action –1657. So †**Effrena·tion.**

†**Effro·nt,** *v. rare.* 1643. [(1) Back-formation from next; (2) – OFr. *effronter* (see next).] **1.** *trans.* To free from bashfulness. **2.** To put to confusion 1649.

†**Effro·nted,** *ppl. a.* 1598. [f. Fr. *effronté* + -ED¹; see next.] Shameless, unblushingly insolent –1641. Hence †**Effro·ntedly** *adv.* Also (irreg.) †**Effro·ntuous** *a.* characterized by effrontery (North).

Effrontery (efrɒ·ntĕri). 1715. [– Fr. *effronterie*, f. *effronté* shameless :– Rom. **exfrontatus*, f. **exfrons*, for late L. *effrons* barefaced, f. *ex-* EF- + *frons, front-* forehead; see FRONT, -ERY.] Shameless audacity, unblushing insolence.

The happy inheritance of impregnable e. SMOLLETT.

†**Effu·de,** *v.* 1634. [incorr. – L. *effundere.*] To pour out –1657.

Effulge (efɒ·ldʒ), *v.* 1729. [– L. *effulgēre*; see next.] **1.** *intr.* To shine forth brilliantly. Also *fig.* (now humorously pedantic.) 1735. **2.** *trans.* To flash forth (*lit.* and *fig.*).

1. *fig.* He effulges with the sun in velveteen jacket and breeches 1828.

Effulgence (efɒ·ldʒĕns). 1667. [– late L. *effulgentia*, f. as next + *-ia* -Y³; see -ENCE.] The quality of being effulgent, splendid radiance (*lit.* and *fig.*).

On thee Impresst the e. of his Glorie abides MILT.

Effulgent (efɒ·ldʒĕnt). *a.* 1738. [– *effulgent-*, pres. ppl. stem of L. *effulgēre*; see EF-, FULGENT.] Shining forth brilliantly; diffusing intense light; radiant.

He is upborne by an e. cloud 1852. Hence **Efful·gently** *adv.*

†**Effu:mabi·lity.** [f. L. *effumare*, or next, + -ABLE + -ITY, after words in *-ability.*] Capability of being converted into vapour. BOYLE.

†**Effu·me,** *v. rare.* [– L. *effumare* emit smoke, f. *ex-* EF- + *fumare* to smoke.] To puff out (smoke). B. JONSON. So †**Effuma·tion,** the action of converting into vapour; *concr.* a vapour emitted.

Effund (efʊ·nd), *v.* ME. [– L. *effundere*, f. *ex-* EF- + *fundere* pour.] *trans.* To pour out (*lit.* and *fig.*).

†**Effu·se,** *sb. rare.* 1593. [f. the vb.] Effusion –1631.

Much e. of blood 3 *Hen. VI*, II. vi. 28.

Effuse (efiū·s), *a.* 1530. [– L. *effusus*, pa. pple. of *effundere*; see next.] **1.** Poured out freely; chiefly *transf.* and *fig.* overflowing, unrestrained. ? *Obs.* **2.** *Bot.* Of an inflorescence: Spreading loosely, *esp.* on one side 1870. **b.** *Conch.* Having the lips separated by a groove 1842.

1. No wanton waste amidst e. expence YOUNG.

Effuse (efiū·z), *v.* ME. [– *effus-*, pa. ppl. stem of L. *effundere*; see EFFUND.] *trans.* To pour forth or out; †to shed (blood); in *pass.* to be extravasated. Also *transf.* and *fig.* Also *absol.*

My pitying eye..effus'd a plenteous stream POPE. *fig.* A palpable tranquillity had been effused abroad GALT. Hence **Effu·sedly** *adv.* unrestrainedly (*rare*).

Effusion (efiū·ʒən). ME. [– (O)Fr. *effusion* or L. *effusio*, f. as prec.; see -ION.] **1.** A pouring out; †shedding (of tears, blood, etc.). **b.** *Path.* The escape of any fluid out of its natural vessel, and its lodgement elsewhere 1732. **2.** *transf.* and *fig.* (see quots.) ME. **3.** *concr.* That which is poured out; *esp.* a speech, or the like. Now often *contemptuous.* 1779.

1. E. of wine JER. TAYLOR, of lava HERSCHEL. Phr. †*E. of spirits* (see ANIMAL SPIRITS): the supposed cause of fainting. **2.** E. of treasure RALEGH, of joy 1778, of His [Christ's] Spirit FARRAR. **3.** Here ended this wild e. SCOTT.

Effusive (efiū·siv), *a.* 1662. [f. L. *effus-* (see EFFUSE *v.*) + -IVE.] **1.** Pouring out, overflowing. Of emotions, etc.: Demonstrative. **2.** That gives outlet to emotion. BAIN.

1. The floor Wash'd with th' e. wave POPE. Peel..was not e.; he did not pour out his emotions MCCARTHY. Hence **Effu·sive-ly** *adv.*, **-ness.**

‖**Efreet** (e·frīt). 1841. var. of AFREET.

Eft (eft), *sb.* [OE. *efeta*, of unkn. origin. The form NEWT is now more used.] A small lizard. Now chiefly applied to the Greater Water-Newt (*Triton cristatus*), of the order *Salamandridæ*.

†**Eft,** *a. superl.* **eftest.** [Origin and meaning uncertain.] ?Ready, apt. *Much Ado* IV. ii. 38.

†**Eft** (eft), *adv.* [OE. *eft* = OFris., OS. *eft*, MLG., MDu. *echt*, ON. *ept*, *eft* :– Gmc. **aftiz*, comp. adv., f. **aft-*; see AFTER *adv.*] **a.** Again –1651. **b.** Afterwards –1559.

Eftsoons (eftsū·nz), *adv. Obs.* or *arch.* Also **eftsoon.** [OE. *eftsōna*, f. *eft* EFT *adv.* + *sōna* SOON; extended with advb. *-s* XIV.] †**1.** A second time, again –1637. †**2.** Again, moreover –1601. **3.** Afterwards, soon after; forthwith ME. †**4.** From time to time, repeatedly –1720.

Egad (ĭgæ·d), *interj.* 1673. [prob. f. A *interj.* + GOD (cf. AGAD), but now assoc. w. *By God!*] Used as a softened oath.

Ega·lity. late ME. [– Fr. *égalité*, f. *égal*; see next, -ITY.] = EQUALITY. Re-coined by TENNYSON. So **Egalita·rian** *a.* that asserts e.

†**E·gall,** *a.* late ME. [– (O)Fr. *égal* – L. *æqualis* EQUAL.] = EQUAL –1596. Hence †**E·gal-ly** *adv.*, †**-ness.**

E·gence. *rare.* [– late L. *egentia*, f. L. *egēre* be in need; see -ENCE.] Need. J. GROTE.

Eger, obs. f. EAGER *a.*, EAGRE.

Egest (ĭdʒe·st), *v.* 1607. [– *egest-*, pa. ppl. stem of L. *egerere* to void, f. *e-* EX- + *gerere* carry.] *trans.* To pass off, expel; *esp.* from within the body, as excrement, perspiration, etc. Hence **Ege·stive** *a.* pertaining to egestion.

‖**Egesta** (ĭdʒe·stă), *sb. pl.* 1787. [L., subst. use of n. pl. of *egestus*, pa. pple. of *egerere*; see prec.] Excreta.

Egestion (ĭdʒe·stʃən). ME. [– L. *egestio* voiding, f. *egest-*, pa. ppl. stem of *egerere*; see prec., -ION. Cf. OFr. *egestion.*] †**1.** The action of emptying out. ME only. **2.** *Phys.* The passing off of excreta from within the body; excrement 1607.

Egg (eg), *sb.* late ME. [– ON. *egg*; superseding ME. *ey* :– cognate OE. *ǣg* = OS., OHG. (Du., G.) *ei*, Crim.-Goth. *ada* (Goth. **addi-*) :– Gmc. **ajjaz* n., prob. ult. rel. to L. *ovum*, Gr. ᾠόν.] **1.** The oval body laid by the female of birds and other animal species, and containing the germ of a new individual, enclosed within a shell or strong membrane. **b.** *spec.* A hen's egg OE. **2.** *fig.* That which contains the germ of anything; usu. in a bad sense 1645. **3.** *transf.* An oval 1589.

1. Thinke him as a Serpents egge *Jul. C.* II. i. 32. **b.** They are vp already, and call for Egges and Butter 1 *Hen. IV*, II. i. 64. **2.** Phr. *To crush in the e.*

Phrases. *To have all one's eggs in one basket*: to risk all one's property on a single venture. *To tread upon eggs*: to walk on delicate ground. *A bad e.*: a person or thing that comes to no good 1853. So *Good e.* (U.S.), used as a commendatory exclamation.

Comb.: **a.** attrib., as *e.-basket*, *-cup*, *-spoon*, etc. **b.** objective, as *e.-beater*, *-boiler*, etc. **c.** similative, as *e.-bald*, *-shaped*, etc.

Special comb.: **e. and anchor, e. and tongue, e. and dart (mouldings),** varieties of the ECHINUS, produced by the alternation of vertical with e.-shaped ornaments; **e.-apple,** the fruit of the E.-plant (*Solanum melongena*); **-bag,** (*a*) the ovary; (*b*) = *egg-case*; **-bird,** a species of tern (*Hydrochelidon fuliginosum*); **-bound** *ppl. a.*, said of fowls unable through weakness or disease to expel their eggs; **-case,** the silken cocoon in which spiders enclose the tubes in which the females lay their eggs; **-cell,** the cell or germ from which an ovum or an individual is subsequently developed; **-dance,** a dance blindfold among eggs; also *fig.*; **-flip** = EGG-NOG; **-glass,** (*a*) a glass for holding an e.; (*b*) a sand-glass for timing the boiling of an e.; †**-hot,** 'a hot drink made of beer, eggs, sugar, and nutmeg'; **-plum,** an egg-shaped plum of a light yellow colour; **-pop** (*U.S.*), ? a kind of *egg-flip*; **-pouch, -sac** = *egg-case*; **-Saturday,** the Saturday before Shrove Tuesday (Nares); **-slice,** a slice for removing omelets or fried eggs from the pan; **-stone** = OOLITE; **-sucker,** a bird, the Toucan; **-Sunday,** the Sunday before Shrove Tuesday; **-trot** = *egg-wife's trot*; **-urchin,** the name of species of ECHINUS; †**-wife,** a woman who offers eggs for sale; hence **e.-wife's trot,** her pace in riding to market.

Egg (eg), *v.*[1] ME. [– ON. *eggja* (Da. *egge*), EDGE *v.*] *trans.* To incite, encourage; to provoke, tempt. *Obs.* exc. with *on.* 1566.

A man which sharpens his enemy with taunts, when he would e. him to fight 1593. Schemers and flatterers would e. him on THACKERAY. Hence **E·gger** *sb.*[1]

Egg (eg), *v.*[2] 1833. [f. the sb.] **a.** To cover with yolk of egg. **b.** To pelt with (rotten) eggs. **c.** *intr.* To collect (wild fowls') eggs.

a. To see a sweetbread egged and crumbed 1864. Hence **E·gger** *sb.*[2] (in sense c).

Egger (e·gəɹ), *sb.*[3] 1705. [app. f. EGG *sb.* + -ER[1].] A collector's name for moths, *esp.* the Oak Egger-moth (*Bombyx quercus*).

†**E·ggment.** ME. only. [f. EGG *v.* + -MENT.] Incitement.

Egg-nog(g (e·g-nǫ·g). 1825. [f. EGG *sb.* + NOG *sb.*[2]] A drink in which eggs are stirred up with hot beer, cider, wine, or spirits.

E·gg-plant. 1767. A name for the *Solanum esculentum*, now including both the white-fruited variety and the purple-fruited Aubergine.

E·gg-shell. ME. [f. EGG *sb.* + SHELL.] The shell or external covering of an egg; often as a type of worthlessness or of fragility. **b.** *attrib.*, as in *egg-shell china*: a very thin and delicate porcelain ware.

Eglandular (ĭglæ·ndiŭlăɹ), *a.* 1870. [See E- *pref.*] *Bot.* That has no glands. So **Egla·ndulose** *a.* (in same sense).

Eglantine (e·glăntəin, -tin). ME. [– Fr. *églantine*, f. OFr. *aiglent* :– Rom. **aculentus*, f. (after *spinulentus* thorny), *acus* needle, *aculeus* prickle, sting.] **1.** The Sweet-briar; also *attrib.* ¶**2.** In Milton: ? The honeysuckle.

1. Quite ouer-cannoped with..E. *Mids. N.* II. i. 252. **2.** Through the sweetbrier or the vine, Or the twisted e. MILT. *L'Allegro* 48.

Eglatere (eglătīᵊɹ). ME. [– AFr. *eglanter*, (O)Fr. *églantier*, OFr. also *aiglentier*, f. *aiglent* (see prec.) + *-ier* (:– L. *-arium*) -ER[2] 2.] = prec. Now only *poet.*

Eglogue, obs. f. ECLOGUE.

†**Eglomerate** (ĭglǫ·mĕreⁱt), *v.* 1656. [f., by substitution of E- (EX-[1]) for AG-, as the opposite of contemp. AGGLOMERATE *v.* wind into a ball.] To unwind. (Dicts.)

E·gma. A blunder for ENIGMA. *L.L.L.* III. i. 73.

‖**Ego** (e·go, ĭ·go). 1824. [L., the pron. I. The pronunc. (ĭ·go) is obsolete in England.] *Metaph.* The *I*; the conscious thinking subject, as opp. to the *non-ego* or object. Also *joc.* for 'self'.

In every act of consciousness we distinguish a self or ego 1829. Hence **E.-hood,** individuality, **Ego·ical** *a.* of or pertaining to egotism.

Egoism (e·g-, ĭ·goˌiz'm). 1785. [– Fr. *égoisme* – mod.L. *egoismus*; see prec., -ISM.] **1.** *Metaph.* The belief, on the part of an individual, that there is no proof that anything exists but his own mind: chiefly applied polemically to philosophical systems supposed to involve this conclusion. **2.** *Ethics.* The theory which regards self-interest as the foundation of morality. Also, in practical sense: Regard to one's own interest; systematic selfishness. (Latterly opp. to *altruism.*) **b.** with *an* and *pl.* 1795. **3.** The habit of looking upon all questions chiefly in their relations to oneself. Also, self-opinionativeness. 1840. **4.** = EGOTISM 1. 1807.

Egoist (e·g-, ĭ·goˌist). 1785. [– Fr. *égoiste*; see prec., -IST.] **1.** An adherent of EGOISM (sense 1). **2.** A systematically selfish man 1879. **3.** = EGOTIST. Also quasi-*adj.* 1794.

3. I will turn e., and tell you *my* adventures LYTTON. Hence **Egoi·stic, -al** *a.* pertaining to, or of the nature of, EGOISM (senses 1–3). **Egoi·stically** *adv.*

E·goistry. *nonce-wd.* [f. prec. + -RY.] = EGOISM. Shaftesb.

Egoity (egōᵘ·iti). 1651. [f. EGO + -ITY, after SEITY (– med.L. *seitas*).] Self-hood; that which forms the essence of the individual.

Egomania (egomēⁱ·niă). *orig. joc.* 1825. [f. EGO + -MANIA.] Morbid egotism.

†**E·gomism.** *rare.* 1730. [– Fr. *égomisme*, f. *ego* EGO + *-isme* -ISM, with unexplained *-m-*.] The belief of one who considers himself the only being in existence –1856.

Egophony, var. of ÆGOPHONY.

Egotheism (egoþī·iz'm). *rare.* 1856. [f. Gr. ἐγώ + θεός God + -ISM.] The (mystical) identification of oneself with the deity.

Egotism (e·g-, ĭ·gŏtiz'm). 1714. [f. EGO + -ISM, with intrusive *-t-*; hence Fr. *égotisme.*] **1.** The too frequent use of the word *I*; hence, the practice of talking about oneself and one's doings. **2.** Self-conceit; also, selfishness 1800.

1. The e. of personal narrative KANE. **2.** His [Napoleon's] absorbing e. was deadly to all men EMERSON.

Egotist (e·g-, ĭ·gŏtist). 1714. [f. as prec. + -IST.] One who uses the word *I* too often; one who thinks or talks too much of himself. Also *attrib.* Hence **Egoti·stic, -al** *a.* pertaining to, or characterized by, egotism. **Egoti·stically** *adv.*

Egotize (e·g-, ĭ·gŏtəiz), *v.* 1789. [f. EGOTISM; see -IZE.] *intr.* To talk or write egotistically.

Egranulose (ĭgræ:niŭlōᵘ·s), *a.* 1884. [f. E- + GRANULOSE.] Without granules.

Egre, obs. f. EAGER.

Egregious (ĭgrī·dʒⁱəs, -dʒiəs), *a.* 1534. [– L. *egregius* surpassing, illustrious, f. *e-* EX-[1] + *grex, greg-* flock; see -IOUS.] †**1.** Prominent, projecting 1578. **2.** Remarkable: †**a.** (in a good sense) Distinguished, excellent, renowned –1738. **b.** (in a bad sense) Gross, flagrant 1573.

2. a. E. Ransome SHAKS, doctrine MILT. An e. mathematician HOBBES. **b.** E. Liars and Impostors MILT. An e. exercise of tyranny HUME. Hence **Egre·giously** *adv.* in an e. manner (now only in a bad sense). **Egre·giousness,** excellence.

Egremoigne, -moyn, obs. ff. AGRIMONY.

Egress (ĭ·gres), *sb.* 1538. [– L. *egressus*, f. *egress-*, pa. ppl. stem of *egredi* go out, f. *e-* EX-[1] + *gradi* to step.] **1.** A going out, or the right or liberty of going out. Also *attrib.* **b.** *Astron.* The end of an eclipse or transit 1706. **2.** A channel of exit, an outlet. Also *fig.* 1604.

1. Free ingress e, and regresse 1543. Gates of burning Adamant..prohibit all e. MILT. *P. L.* II. 437. A lane..an e. from which was shut up 1817.

Egress (ĭgre·s), *v.* 1578. [f. the sb.] *intr.* To issue, to go forth. Hence **Egre·ssion,** the action of going out or issuing forth. **Egre·ssive** *a.* tending to go forth.

Egret (e·grėt, ĭ·grėt). ME. [– AFr. *egrette*, (O)Fr. *aigrette* – Pr. *aigreta*, f. stem of *aigron*, corresp. to (O)Fr. *héron* HERON; see -ET.] **1.** The Lesser White Heron. Also *attrib.*, as in *e.-heron.* **2.** = AIGRETTE 3. 1794. **3.** *attrib.*, as †**e.-monkey,** a hypothetical species of ape, called by Linnæus *Simia aygula* 1802.

1. An egript..is all white as the swanne, with legs like to an hearnshaw HAKLUYT.

Egrimonie, -y, obs. ff. AGRIMONY.

†**E·grimony.** *rare.* 1626. [– L. *ægrimonia*, f. *æger* sick; see -MONY.] Deep sorrow. (Dicts.)

Egriot, var. of †AGRIOT, a kind of cherry.

Egritude, obs. var. of ÆGRITUDE.

Egurgitate (ɪ̆gɒ̄·ɹdʒiteɪt), *v. rare.* 1656. [f. after REGURGITATE, with substitution of prefix.] To vomit forth; also *fig.*

Egyptian (ɪ̆dʒi·pʃən). ME. [f. *Egypt* + -IAN.]

A. *adj.* **1.** Belonging or relating to Egypt; also *fig.*, as in *E. bondage, darkness*, etc. ME. **2.** = GIPSY (*joc.*) 1749.

Phrases. **a.** *Bot.* **E. Bean:** perh. the fruit of *Nelumbium speciosum.* **E. Lotus** = *Nymphæa lotus.* **E. Thorn:** *Cratægus pyracantha.* **b.** *Min.* **E. Jasper,** †**pebble:** a brown mottled Jasper from Egypt.

B. *sb.* **1.** A native of Egypt. Often *fig.* (cf. *Ex.* 12:36) ME. **2.** = GIPSY 1514. **3.** *pl.* Short for *E. stocks* (*rec.*).

Hence **Egy·ptianize** *v.* [see -IZE] 1664.

Egyptology (ɪ̆dʒiptǫ·lǒdʒi). 1859. [f. *Egypt* + -LOGY.] The study of Egyptian antiquities. Hence **Egypto·loger, Egypto·logist** (also **Égy·ptologue**), one versed in E. **Egyptolo·gical** *a.* of, pertaining to, or devoted to E.

Eh (ē, ēɪ), *interj.* 1567. [ME. *ey*; of instinctive origin.] **1.** An exclam. of sorrow. Cf. AH a. **2.** An interjectional particle of inquiry, often inviting assent 1773. **3.** *Eh?*: colloq. or vulgar = What did you say? 1837.

Ehlite (ēɪ·ləit). 1868. [f. *Ehl* near Lenz on the Rhine + -ITE[1] 2b.] *Min.* A variety of Pseudomalachite.

Eident (əi·dĕnt), *a. Sc.* 1591. [var. of IDENT.] Diligent, attentive *to.*

Eider (əi·dəɹ). 1743. [– Icel. (ON.) *æðr*, gen. *æðar* in *æðarfugl* eider-duck, (Icel.) *æðardún* (see next).] **1.** A species of duck, *Somateria mollissima*, of northern regions, that lines its nest with EIDER-DOWN; also *King-e.* (*Somateria spectabilis.*). Chiefly *attrib.*, as in *e.-duck*, etc. **2.** The down itself 1766. **3.** *attrib.* or *adj.* Resembling eider-down 1791.

Ei·der-down. 1774. [– Icel. *æðardún*; see prec., DOWN *sb.*[2]] **1.** The small soft feathers from the breast of the eider-duck. Also *attrib.* **2.** = *eider-down quilt.*

Eidograph (əi·dǒgrɑf). 1801. [f. Gr. εἶδος form + -GRAPH.] An instrument for reproducing drawings on any scale.

‖**Eidolon** (əidōᵘ·lǫn). Pl. occas. **-a.** 1828. [Gr. εἴδωλον IDOL.] An (unsubstantial) image, spectre, phantom. Hence **Eido·loclast** [f. Gr. κλάστης], an image-breaker.

†**Eidoura·nion.** 1825. [f. Gr. εἶδος form + οὐρανός heaven.] A mechanical contrivance for representing the motions of the heavenly bodies; cf. ORRERY –1829.

Eigh (ēɪ), *interj. dial.* [Cf. EH, EY.] An exclam. of wonder or asseveration.

Eight (ēɪt). [OE. *ehta* (*eahta, ahta*) = OFris. *achta, acht(e*, OS., OHG. *ahto* (Du., G. *acht*), ON. *átta*, Goth. *ahtau* :– Gmc. **axtō* :– IE. **oktō*, whence also L. *octo*, Gr. ὀκτώ, Skr. *aṣṭáu.*] The cardinal number next after seven; symbols 8 or viii.

A. as *adj.* (see quots.).

E. years 1513. Phr. *An e. days* (= a week) *Luke* 9:28. *ellipt.* We breakfast at e. 1891. *Piece of e.* (*reals*): the Spanish dollar. (Now *Hist.*).

B. as *sb.* **1.** The number eight ME. **2.** A set of eight persons or things, as, *the e. of hearts, the Oxford e.* Phr. *In eights*: in lines of e. syllables. 1598. **3.** The figure (8); hence anything in the form of an 8. 1607.

Comb., as *e.-sided*, etc.; *e.-day* adj., *-fold* adj. and adv.; **e.-day clock,** one that goes for e. days without winding up; **-oar** *a.* (of a boat) manned by e. rowers; also as sb.

Eight, obs. f. AIT.

Eighteen (eɪtī·n, ēɪ·tīn), *a.* (*sb.*) [OE. *e(a)htatēne*, corresp. to OFris. *achtatīne*, OS. *ahtotian* (Du. *achttien*), OHG. *ahtozehan* (G. *achtzehn*), ON. *átján*; see -TEEN.] **1.** The cardinal number next after seventeen; symbols 18 or xviii. **2.** quasi-*sb.* = **e.-pounder** 1833.

Syxe and twelue makyth eyghtene TREVISA.

Comb.: **e.-knot** *a.*, (a vessel) capable of doing e. knots; **-penny** *a.*, worth or costing e.-pence; also quasi-*sb.*; **-pounder,** a gun throwing an eighteen-pound shot.

Eightee·nmo. 1858. [Eng. reading of 18mo. See -MO.] Colloq. for OCTODECIMO.

Eighteenth (eɪtī·nþ, ēɪ·tīnþ), *a.* [ME. *eȝtetenþe*, repl. OE. *e(a)htotēoþa*; cf. OFris. *ahtatīnda, ahtendesta, achtiensta*, ON. *átjándi.*] **1.** Next in order after the seventeenth. **2.** *E. part*: one of eighteen equal parts of anything. Hence **Eightee·nthly** *adv.*

Eighth (ēɪtþ). [Formerly *eight*, etc. OE. *e(a)htoþa* = OFris. *achte*, OHG. *ahtodo* (G. *achte*) :– Gmc. **axtoþan*, f. **axtō*; see EIGHT, -TH[2].]

A. *adj.* **1.** That comes next in order to the seventh. Also *ellipt.*, as the *e. of April.* **2.** *E. part*: one of eight equal parts of anything 1523.

B. *sb.* **1.** = *eighth part* 1557. †**2.** *Mus.* = OCTAVE –1706. Hence **Ei·ghthly** *adv.* in the e. place.

Eightieth (ēɪ·tiėþ), *a.* (*sb.*) ME. [f. EIGHTY; see -TH[2].] The ordinal number answering to the cardinal eighty.

Ei·ght-squa·re. *Obs.* exc. *Naut.* 1538. [f. EIGHT + SQUARE *a.*, after *four-square.*] Having eight equal sides; octagonal.

Eighty (ēɪ·ti), *a.* (*sb.*) [ME. *eȝteti*, repl. OE. *hunde(a)htatiġ*; see -TY[2].] **1.** The cardinal number equal to eight tens; symbol 80 or lxxx. Also *ellipt.*, as in *now over e.* **2.** quasi-*sb.* **a.** The age of eighty years. **b.** *The eighties*: the years between eighty and ninety in a century. 1835.

Eigne (ēɪn), *a.* 1586. [Erroneous sp. of AYNE.] *Law* First-born, eldest; see AYNE.

Phr. *E. title*: a prior title. *E. estate*: one that is entailed.

Eikon, var. of ICON.

Eild (īld), *a. Sc.* 1822. [perh. var. of YELD *a.*] Of a cow: Not giving milk; dry.

Eild, var. of ELD *sb.* and *v.*

Eir(e, obs. f. AIR, EYRE, HEIR.

Eirenarch (əirī·nāɹk). 1641. [– Gr. εἰρηνάρχης, f. εἰρήνη peace + ἄρχης -ARCH.] An officer charged with the preservation of the public peace.

Eirenic, irenic (əirī·nik), *a. rare.* 1878. [– Gr. εἰρηνικός, f. εἰρήνη peace; see -IC.] Tending to peace.

‖**Eirenicon** (əirī·nikǫn). 1865. [– Gr. εἰρηνικόν, n. sing. of εἰρηνικός; see prec.] A proposal tending to reconcile differences.

Eiry, var. of AERIE, EERIE.

†**Ei·sell.** [Late OE. *aisile, eisile* – OFr. *aisil*, f. L. *acetum* vinegar, with unexpl. ending.] Vinegar –1634.

Woo't drinke vp Esile, eate a Crocodile SHAKS.

‖**Eisteddfod** (eɪste·ðvod). 1822. [W., 'session', f. *eistedd* sit.] A congress of (Welsh) bards.

Either (əi·ðəɹ, ī·ðəɹ), *a.* (*pron.*) and *adv.* [OE. *ǣġþer*, contr. f. *ǣġ(e)hwæþer* = OFris. *ēider*, MLG., MDu. *ed(d)er* (as adv.), OHG. *eogihwedar* (MHG. *iegeweder*) :– Gmc. phr. **aiwo ȝixwaþaraz*, i.e. 'ever each of two'; see AY *adv.*, WHETHER, and cf. EACH.]

A. *adj.* (*pron.*) **1.** Each of the two. †**b.** with pl. sb.: = 'both' –1608. †**2.** *absol.* as *pron.* –1759. **b.** Sometimes = each (of more than two) 1588. **3.** One or other of the two ME. **4.** *absol.* as *pron.* 1548. **b.** Sometimes = any one (of more than two) 1616.

1. There was a huge fireplace at e. end of the hall SCOTT. **2.** How different has been the fate of e. GOLDSM. **b.** At e. of the three corners HOWELLS. **3.** Spirits when they please Can e. Sex assume MILT. *P. L.* I. 424. **4.** E. causes loss CRUMP. **b.** The furtherance of all or e. of these three HIERON.

B. as *adv.* (*conj.*) †**1.** In OE. and early ME. = BOTH. **2.** Introducing alternatives ME. †**3.** = OR –1611. **4.** As an alternative, 'which you please'. **b.** In neg. or interrog. sentences: 'Any more than the other'. ME.

2. I never thought treson to your Highnes. ayther in woorde or dede T. CROMWELL. **3.** E. [*R.V.*, Or] how canst thou say to thy brother *Luke* 6:42. **4.** *To.* Wilt thou set thy foote o' my necke? *An.* Or o' mine e. *Twel. N.* II. v. 206. **b.** Thy sex cannot help that e. SCOTT.

Ejaculate (ɪ̆dʒæ·kiŭleɪt), *v.* 1578. [– *ejaculat-*, pa. ppl. stem of L. *ejaculari*, f. *e-* EX-[1] + *jaculari* dart, f. *jaculum* dart, javelin, f. *jacere* throw; see -ATE[3].] **1.** *trans.* To dart forth; to throw out suddenly and swiftly, eject. *Obs.* exc. *spec.* Also †*transf.* and *fig.* **2.** To utter suddenly (a short prayer; now a short exclamation). Also *absol.* 1666.

1. They [Porcupines] have..prickles..which they e. 1661. *spec.* To e. its venom into the wound 1816. **2.** But where can the Prince be? he kept ejaculating CARLYLE. Hence **Eja·culative** *a.* of the nature of an ejaculation.

Ejaculation (ɪ̆dʒæ:kiulēɪ·ʃən). 1603. [– Fr. *éjaculation*, f. *éjaculer* – L. *ejaculari*; see prec., -ATION.] †**1.** The action of ejaculating (missiles, water, etc.) –1818. **2.** The sudden ejection or emission (of seeds, fluids, etc.) 1603. **3.** *transf.* and *fig.* **a.** The emission of rays, occult influence, etc. **b.** The hasty utterance of prayers, emotional exclamations, etc. 1625. **4.** *concr.* A short hasty emotional utterance 1624.

3. a. There seemeth to be acknowledged, in the Act of Enuy an Eiaculation..of the Eye BACON. **4.** Ejaculations of welcome F. A. KEMBLE.

‖**Eja·culator.** 1727. [mod.L., f. *ejaculari*; see EJACULATE, -OR 2.] *Phys.* Applied to two muscles of the genitals, which ejaculate the seminal fluid.

Ejaculatory (ɪ̆dʒæ·kiŭlătəri), *a.* 1644. [f. EJACULATE + -ORY[2].] **1.** †Adapted for, or concerned in, ejection 1655. †**2.** Given to ejaculation. QUARLES. **3.** Of the nature of or resembling an ejaculation 1644. **4.** quasi-*sb.* = EJACULATION 4 (*rare*) 1883.

1. E. ducts 1751. **3.** E. passages 1644, prayers 1698, petitions SMOLLETT.

Eject (ī·dʒekt), *sb.* 1878. [– L. *ejectum*, n. pa. pple. of *e(j)icere* (see next), after *object, subject.*] Something (*viz.* an inferred sensation or mental state) which is neither an actual nor a possible object of one's own consciousness.

My neighbour's mind, feelings, motions are ejects to me; they can never be objects C. L. MORGAN.

Eject (ɪ̆dʒe·kt), *v.* 1555. [– *eject-*, pa. ppl. stem of L. *e(j)icere*, f. *e-* EX-[1] + *jacere* throw.] **1.** To throw out from within; also *transf.* and *fig.* 1598. **2.** To expel, drive out *from* any place or position 1555. **3.** To expel from a dignity or office. Also, To evict *from*; *esp.* in *Law.* 1570.

1. A Diana ejecting a fountain EVELYN. **3.** If they can prove their Ministers fit to be ejected, let them there prove it BAXTER. Hence **Eje·ctive** *a.* that has the function or power of ejecting; pertaining to an eject. **Eje·ctively** *adv.*

‖**Ejectamenta** (ɪ̆dʒe:ktăme·ntă), *sb. pl.* 1863. [pl. of L. *ejectamentum*, f. *ejectare*, frequent. of *e(j)icere* EJECT *v.*; see -MENT.] *Geol.* Substances ejected by eruptive forces.

Ejection (ɪ̆dʒe·kʃən). 1566. [– (O)Fr. *éjection* or L. *ejectio*, f. *eject-*; see EJECT *v.*, -ION.] **1.** The action of casting out from within. Formerly *spec.* in *Phys.* 1613. **b.** *concr.* Something ejected: *spec.* by a volcano 1654. **2.** Expulsion from a place or position; also from office or possessions; †exile (*rare*) 1566.

1. E. of ashes 1813, of gas 1881. **2.** Exorcisme (that is to say, of e. of Devills by Conjuration) HOBBES.

Ejectment (ɪ̆dʒe·ktmĕnt). 1567. [– legal AFr. *ejectement*; see EJECT *v.*, -MENT.] **1.** *Law.* The act or process of ejecting a person from his holding; hence, more widely, = EJECTION 2. **2.** 'An action at law whereby a person ousted or amoved from an estate for years may recover possession thereof' (Tomlins); the original writ in this action 1697. †**3.** *pl.* [after L. *ejectamenta.*] Things cast up or out. SIR T. BROWNE.

Ejector (ɪ̆dʒe·ktəɹ). 1640. [f. EJECT *v.* + -OR 2.] **1.** *gen.* One who ejects (*lit.* and *fig.*); *spec.* in *Law*, one who ejects a person from his holding. **2.** Any portion of machinery, etc., which ejects; *e.g.* an appliance for discharging empty cartridge cases from a firearm; etc. Also *attrib.* 1874.

2. *E.-condenser* (steam-engine), a form of condenser worked by the exhaust steam from the cylinder.

†**Ejula·tion.** 1619. [– L. *ejulatio*, f. *ejulat-*, pa. ppl. stem of *ejulare* wail; see -ION.] Wailing, lamentation –1708.

Eke (īk), *sb.* Now *dial.* [OE. *ēaca* increase = OFris. *āka*, ON. *auki*, f. same base as EKE *v.*] **1.** An addition. In OE., A reinforcement (of troops). **2.** *spec.* **a.** A tag to a bell-rope; also *attrib.* 1549. **b.** A cylinder on which a beehive is placed to add to its capacity 1857.

Eke (īk), *v.* ME. [OE. **ēacan* (implied in *ēacen*, pa. pple.; cf. *ēacian* intr., increase) = OFris. *āka*, OS. *ōkian*, ON. *auka*, Goth. *aukan*, rel. to L. *augēre* increase, Gr. αὔξειν, f. base **aug-*. The ME. vb. may have been partly from EKE *sb.*] **1.** *trans.* To increase, add to. Also *absol.* Now *dial.* †**2.** To add. Also *absol.* –1733.

1. Some patch'd dog-hole ek'd with ends of wall POPE. Phr. *To e. out*: to supplement (const. *with*); *esp.* to make to last, or to suffice, by additions, by economy, by makeshifts, or the like.

Eke (īk), *adv. arch.* [OE. *ēc*, *ēac* = OFris. *āk*, OS. *ōk* (Du. *ook*), OHG. *ouh* (G. *auch*), ON., Goth. *auk*; referred by some to IE. **au* again + **ge*, emphatic particle (cf. Gr. αὖ γε again), by others to EKE *v.*] Also, too, moreover; in addition.

E. therto he was right a mery man CHAUCER.

Ekebergite. 1822. [f. Sw. traveller *Ekeberg* + -ITE[1] 2 b.] *Min.* A variety of scapolite.

†**E·ke-name.** ME. [f. EKE *sb.* + NAME *sb.*; cf. ON. *aukanafn*. See NICKNAME *sb.*] An additional name, a NICKNAME, q. v. –1483.

Eking (ī·kiŋ), *vbl. sb.* ME. [f. EKE *v.* + -ING[1].] **1.** The action of EKE *v.* **2.** An augmentation ME. **3.** *Naut.* **a.** 'A piece of wood fitted..to make good a deficiency in length, as the end of a knee or the like.' **b.** 'The carved work under the lower part of the quarter-piece, at the aft part of the gallery.' ADM. SMYTH.

-el, *suffix*[1], repr. OE. *-el*, *-ela*, *-ele* (Gmc. **-ilaz*, **-ilon*, **-ilōn*); in mod.Eng. retained only after *v*, *th*, *ch*, *n*, as in *hovel*, *brothel*, etc. See -LE.

-el, *suffix*[2], – OFr. *-el* (mod.Fr. usu. *-eau*), *-elle*, repr. L. *-ello-*, *-ella-*; used to form diminutives, as (from the masc. *-el*), *tunnel*, etc.; (from the fem. *-elle*) *chapel*, etc.

2. In Eng. wds. adapted from Fr., *-el* may also stand for Fr. *-el* :– L. *-ali-* (see -AL), as in *vowel*; for Fr. *-eil* :– L. *-iculo-*, as in *apparel*; or for Fr. *-il* :– L. *-ile*, as in *kennel*.

Ela (ē·lā·). Now *Hist.* 1580. [f. E + LA *sb.*] *Mus.* The highest note of Guido's scale. Often *fig.* as a type of something 'high-flown'.

Why God-a-mercy..this is a note above E La SCOTT.

Elaborate (ilæ·bŏrĕt). 1581. [– L. *elaboratus*, pa. pple. of *elaborare*, f. *e-* EX-[1] + *labor* LABOUR *sb.*; see -ATE[2].]

†**A.** as *pa. pple.* = ELABORATED.

B. as *adj.* **1.** Produced by labour; also = ELABORATED. *Obs.* or *arch.* 1592. **2.** Worked out minutely; highly finished 1621. Also *transf.* of persons: Painstaking 1649.

2. An e. letter DAVENANT, contrivance DARWIN, study MORLEY. *transf.* An e. Collector 1728.

Hence **Ela·borate-ly** *adv.*, **-ness.**

Elaborate (ilæ·bŏreⁱt), *v.* 1607. [– *elaborat-*, pa. ppl. stem of L. *elaborare*; see prec., -ATE[3].] **1.** To produce or develop by labour; to work out in detail 1611. **2.** *transf.* Of nature, etc.: To produce from elements or sources; to fashion or develop; also, to transmute *into* a developed product 1607.

1. The objects of landscape may be either elaborated or suggested RUSKIN. **2.** Honey..is elaborated by the Bee BOYLE. The animal spirits are elaborated from the blood BP. BERKELEY.

Hence **Ela·borated** *ppl. a.* worked up; worked out in detail, finely wrought, etc. **Ela·borative** *a.* that has the property of elaborating. **Ela·borator.**

Elaboration (ilæ:borēⁱ·ʃən). 1578. [– L. *elaboratio* (in med.L. also = 'extraction', *Alch.*), f. as prec.; see -ION.] **1.** The process of elaborating (see ELABORATE *v.* 1); the state of being elaborated 1612. **2.** The production by natural agencies of chemical substances from their elements or sources; *spec.* in *Phys.* the formation of animal or vegetable tissues, or the process of assimilation of alimentary substances after their reception into the body 1578. **3.** *concr.* 1765.

1. The e. of his [Virgil's] verse GLADSTONE. **2.** Milk is a chyle which..has received but a light E. 1677. **3.** Science is an e. 1856.

Elaboratory (ilæ·bŏrătəri). 1652. [f. ELABORATE *v.* (sense 2) + -ORY[1], after LABORATORY.] = LABORATORY. Now *Hist.* Also *transf.*

transf. The functions of leaves are to..act as elaboratories 1845.

Elæo-, comb. f. Gr. ἔλαιον oil (properly olive-oil); as in **Elæopten(e** (eli,ǫ·ptīn), also **ela-** [Gr. πτηνός volatile], the liquid part of a volatile oil, as dist. from stearoptene; etc.

Elæolite (ilī·ŏləit). Also **elao-.** 1816. [f. Gr. ἔλαιον olive-oil + -LITE.] *Min.* A variety of nephelite occurring massive, or in large crystals, and having a greasy lustre.

Elaic (ilē·ik), *a.* 1845. [irreg. f. as prec. + -IC.] *Chem.* = OLEIC.

Elaidic (ele,i·dik), *a.* 1865. [f. as prec. + *-idic* (i.e. -IDE + -IC).] *Chem.* Designation of an acid $C_{18}H_{34}O_2$, derived from elaic (oleic) acid. So **Ela·idate,** a salt of e. acid. **Ela·idin,** a solid isomeric modification of olein, produced by the action of nitrous acid.

Elain (ilē·in). 1810. [irreg. f. as prec. + -IN[1].] = OLEIN.

†**Ela·mp,** *v.* [app. suggested by Gr. ἐκλάμπειν shine forth.] To shine forth. G. FLETCHER.

‖**Élan.** 1880. [Fr., f. *élancer*; see next.] An impetuous rush (*e.g.* of troops); also (*abstr.*), ardour, dash.

Elance (ilā·ns), *v.* ? *Obs.* 1718. [– Fr. *élancer*, f. *é-* EX-[1] + *lancer*; see LAUNCH *v.*] *trans.* To launch; to cast or throw (a lance or dart). Also *fig.* Also *intr.* for *refl.*

Thy unerring Hand elanc'd..another Dart M. PRIOR.

Eland (ī·lănd). 1786. [S. Afr. use of Du. *eland* elk – G. *elend* (more fully *elentier*) – Lith. *élnis*.] A very large S. Afr. Antelope (*Boselaphus oreas*), much prized for its flesh. Also *attrib.*

Elanet (e·lănėt). 1880. [app. f. mod.L. *elanus* + -ET.] A species of kite, *Elanus melanopterus*.

Elao-; see ELÆO-.

Elaphine (e·lăfəin), *a.* 1835. [– Gr. ἔλαφος deer + -INE[1].] Belonging to or like the stag.

‖**Elaps** (ī·læps). [mod.L. – Gr. ἔλαψ var. of ἔλλοψ; see ELLOPS.] A genus of venomous S. African garter snakes.

Elapse (ilæ·ps), *v.* 1644. [– *elaps-*, pa. ppl. stem of L. *elabi* slip away; see E-, LAPSE *v.*] **1.** *intr.* Of time: To slip or glide away, expire. (Perfect tenses occas. with *be.*) †**2.** *trans.* To suffer to pass by –1709. †**3.** *intr.* To lapse –1769.

1. Fourteen months were now elapsed 1792.

Ela·pse, *sb. arch.* 1677. [f. prec. vb.] **1.** A flowing out or away; also *fig.* **2.** Lapse, slipping away 1793. So †**Ela·psion** (*rare*).

†**Ela·rgement.** [perh. erron. f. ENLARGEMENT.] = ENLARGEMENT. Hy. More.

Elasmobranch (ilæ·zmobræŋk). 1872. [– mod.L. *elasmobranchii*, f. Gr. ἐλασμός metal beaten out + βράγχια gills.] *Zool.* One of the *Elasmobranchii* or *Chondropterygii*, a class of fishes marked by the cartilaginous nature of the bones, and the absence of sutures in the cranium, as the Shark, Sturgeon, Ray, etc. Also *attrib.* or *adj.* var. **Elasmobra·nchiate.**

Elastance (ilæ·stăns). 1890. [irreg. f. ELASTIC + -ANCE.] *Electr.* The capacity of a dielectric for opposing an electric charge or displacement.

Elastic (ilæ·stik). 1653. [– mod.L. *elasticus* – Gr. ἐλαστικός, f. ἐλα- stem of ἐλαύνειν drive.]

A. *adj.* †**1.** Pertaining to, causing, or characterized by, spontaneous expansion. Now merged in 2. –1669. **2.** That spontaneously resumes its normal bulk or shape after contraction, dilatation, or distortion by external force. Also of motions, forces, etc.: Characteristic of an elastic body. 1674. **b.** *fig.* Not permanently or easily depressed; buoyant 1778. **3.** *pop.* That can be stretched without permanent alteration of size or shape 1781. **b.** *fig.* Flexible, accommodating 1859. †**4.** Propulsive. 1712.

2. His e. bow COWPER. Phr. *E. limit*: the extent to which the particles of a body may be relatively displaced without fracture or other permanent alteration. *E. fluids*: still often used spec. for gases, though the mod. definition applies perfectly to liquids. **b.** This e. little urchin CARLYLE. **3.** *fig.* A very e. conscience 1891. Phr. *E. tissue* (Anat.): a variety of areolar or connective tissue. †*E. gum* [= Fr. *gomme élastique*]: india-rubber. *E. web*: cloth woven with india-rubber threads so as to stretch. *E. boots*: boots with elastic web at the sides.

B. *sb.* Elastic cord or string, usually woven with india-rubber 1863.

Hence †**Ela·stical** *a.* elastic. **Ela·stically** *adv.*

Ela·sticin. 1878. [f. ELASTIC + -IN[1].] 'The substance composing the elastic fibres of connective tissue' (*Syd. Soc. Lex.*).

Elasticity (ī-, elæsti·sĭti). 1664. [f. as prec. + -ITY.] **1.** The quality of being elastic (see ELASTIC A. 1, 2). **2.** *fig.* Capacity for resisting or overcoming depression 1678; flexibility, accommodatingness 1858.

1. The e. or tension of steam MRS. SOMERVILLE. The e. of the spine DARWIN. **2.** Our old men have lost the e. of youth JOWETT. There is no e. in a mathematical fact O. W. HOLMES.

Elastin (ilæ·stin). 1875. [contr. f. ELASTICIN.] = ELASTICIN. (*Syd. Soc. Lex.*).

Elate (ilēⁱ·t), *a.* [ME. *elat* – OFr. *elat* proud; later – L. *elatus*, pa. pple. of *eferre*; see next, -ATE[2].] †**1.** Lifted (*rare*) 1730. **2.** *fig.* **a.** Exalted, lofty ME. **b.** Of persons: In high spirits, exultant, flushed (with success, etc.) 1647.

1. With upper lip e., he grins 1730. **2.** **a.** A fortune more E. 1610. Of an e. spirit SELDEN. **b.** An army e. with victory CLARENDON.

Ela·te, *v.* 1578. [– *elat-* pa. ppl. stem of L. *efferre*, f. *ex-* EF- + *ferre* BEAR *v.*[1]; see -ATE[3].] †**1.** *trans.* To lift on high, elevate –1772. Also *fig.* **2.** To exalt the spirits of; to stimulate, excite; also, to make proud. Also *absol.* 1619.

1. Sometimes they e. a finger, smile and pray to Mahomet SIR T. HERBERT. **2.** Elated with the glory of Martyredome 1619. The wine..elateth me LONGF. Hence **Ela·ted-ly** *adv.*, **-ness.** †**Ela·tement,** elatedness. **Ela·ter**[1], one who or that which elates.

Elater[2] (e·lătəɹ). 1653. [mod.L. – Gr. ἐλατήρ driver, f. ἐλα-, stem of ἐλαύνειν drive.] †**1.** The expansive property inherent in air or gases; hence, = 'spring', 'elasticity'. Also *fig.* **2.** *Zool.* Linnæus' name for the family *Elateridæ* of beetles, possessing the power of springing upward from a supine position, in order to fall on their feet; also, a beetle of this family, a skip-jack 1802. **3.** *Bot.* An elastic spiral filament, or elongated cell, serving to disperse the sporules when ripe, as in certain Liverworts, Horsetails, etc. 1830.

1. Persons..having the e. or spring of their own natures to facilitate their iniquities SIR T. BROWNE.

Elaterin (ilæ·tĕrin). Also **elatine.** 1830. [f. ELATERIUM + -IN[1].] *Chem.* The active principle of Elaterium ($C_{20}H_{28}O_5$).

†**Ela·terist.** 1661. [f. ELATER[2] + -IST.] One who explains certain phenomena as due to ELATERY –1674.

Elaterite (ilæ·tĕrəit). 1826. [f. ELATER[2] + -ITE[1] 2b.] *Min.* A brown hydrocarbon, usually soft and elastic like india-rubber; elastic bitumen.

‖**Elaterium** (elătīᵊ·riɒm). 1578. [L. – Gr. ἐλατήριον, f. ἐλα-, stem of ἐλαύνειν to drive.] †**1.** A purgative. **2.** A precipitate from the juice of the Squirting Cucumber (*Ecballium agreste*, *Momordica elaterium*), acting as a drastic purgative and emetic 1578. †**3.** = ELATER[2]. (Dicts.).

Elaterometer (ilæ·tĕrǫ·mĭtəɹ). [– Fr. *élatéromètre*; see ELATER[2], -METER.] An instrument for indicating the pressure of confined air or steam. KNIGHT.

†**E·late:ry.** 1653. [f. ELATER[2] + -Y[3].] The elastic force of the air –1676.

Elation (ilē·ʃən). ME. [– OFr. *elacion*, and (later) its source L. *elatio*, f. *elat-*; see ELATE *v.*, -ION.] †**1.** (after L.) **a.** Lifting. **b.** Carrying out (*e.g.* of a dead body) (*rare*). –1697. **2.** Elevation of mind arising from success, etc.; pride, vainglory ME. **3.** Elevation of spirits. (The usual current sense.) 1750. **b.** with *an* and *pl.* 1870.

2. Riches exposes a Man to..a foolish E. of Heart ADDISON. **3.** These praises give me but very little E. 1804.

Ela·tive, *a. rare.* 1595. [f. ELATE *v.* + -IVE.] That elates (*lit.* and *fig.*).

†**Elayl** (e·lĕıil). 1865. [irreg. f. Gr. ἔλαιον olive-oil + -YL.] *Chem.* = ETHYLENE.

Elbow (e·lboᵘ). [OE. *el(n)boga* = MDu. *elleboghe* (Du. *elleboog*), OHG. *elinbogo* (G. *ellenbogen*), ON. *ǫlnbogi* :- Gmc. **alinobogon*, f. **alinā* arm (cf. ELL¹) + **bogon* BOW *sb.*¹] **1.** The bend of the arm; the outer part of the joint at the bend of the arm. †**b.** The analogous part in the shoulder or hock of quadrupeds –1789. **2.** *transf.* Anything resembling an elbow. **a.** A sharp bend in the course of a river, road, etc. 1591. **b.** A forward or outward projection 1626. **c.** *Mech.* An angle in a tube, etc.; a piece of piping bent at an angle to join two long straight pieces 1777. **d.** *Arch.* The upright side which flanks any panelled work, as in windows below the shutters, etc. (Gwilt); the projections on the side of stalls (Parker). †**3.** *transf.* An arm of a chair, made to rest the elbow –1784.

1. A pair of Gloves Up to his Elbows ETHEREGE. **2. a.** The elbows of serpentine rivers H. WALPOLE. **3.** A great Chair with elbows 1679.

Phrases. *At the elbow(s*: very near; in close attendance; also *fig. E. in the hawse* (Naut.): a cross in the hawse, when a ship, being moored in a tideway, swings twice the wrong way. *To be out at elbow(s*: to have a coat worn out at the elbows, to be ragged, poor, in seedy condition.

attrib. and *Comb.*, as *e.-cushion*, etc.; also **e.-chair,** a chair with elbows (see 3); **-grease** (*joc.*), vigorous rubbing; hard physical labour of any kind; **-joint,** (*a*) the hinge-joint connecting the fore and the upper arm; (*b*) = ELBOW 2 c; **-piece,** (*a*) a piece of armour covering the juncture of the plates meeting at the e.; (*b*) a piece of tubing forming an e.; **-room,** room to move one's elbows; hence, free scope.

Elbow (e·lboᵘ), *v.* 1605. [f. prec. sb.] **1.** *trans.* To thrust with the elbow; to jostle; also *fig.* Also with *off, out of.* †**2.** *absol.* and *intr.* To push right and left with the elbow; also *fig.* –1885. **3.** quasi-*trans.* To make (one's way) by elbowing 1833. **4.** *intr.* To go out of the direct way, zigzag 1804. **5.** 'To jut out in angles' (J.).

1. Must our Sides be elbowed, our Shins broken 1710. They [the Dutch] would e. our own Aldermen off the Royal Exchange MACAULAY. **3.** To e. his way into the bank 1833.

Elbowed (e·lboᵘd), *ppl. a.* 1825. [f. ELBOW *sb.* + -ED².] **a.** Having elbows or bends. **b.** Provided with elbow-rests, as a seat. **c.** Bent into the shape of an elbow.

‖**Elchee** (e·ltʃi). Also **elchi, eltchi.** 1828. [Turk. *elçi*, f. *el* a (nomad) tribe, hence the representative of the *el.*] An ambassador.

Eld (eld), *sb.* [OE. (Anglian) *eldu*, (WS.) *ieldu* = OFris. *elde*, OS. *eldi*, OHG. *elti*, ON. *elli* :- Gmc. **alð-* (WGmc.), **alþ-*; see OLD.] **1.** The age of a person. Now *dial.* †**2.** Full age; majority –1529. **3.** Old age OE. †**b.** Old men; senate, aristocracy –1592. **4.** Antiquity, the olden time ME. †**5.** A secular period –1513.

1. Gamelyn, that yong was of elde ME. **3.** Who scorns at e., peels off his own young hairs B. JONS. **4.** Lands that contain the monuments of E. BYRON.

Eld (eld), *a. poet.* and *arch.* 1619. [repr. ME. *eld(e*, OE. (WS.) *eald* :- WGmc. **alða*; see prec., OLD. In mod. writers prob. f. ELD *sb.*] = OLD, q.v.

†**Eld,** *v.*¹ [OE. (WS.) *ealdian*, f. *eald* old; cf. OFris. *aldia*, OHG. *altēn*, Goth. *us-alþan* grow old.] To grow or make old –1536.

†**Eld,** *v.*² [OE. *eldan* (WS. *ieldan*) delay :- WGmc. *alðjan*; see OLD.] *trans.* and *intr.* To defer, delay –ME.

Elder (e·ldəɹ), *sb.*¹ [OE. *ellærn*, ME. *eller, eldre*, corresp. to MLG. *ellern, elderne, elhorn, alhorn*, prob. orig. an adj. formation like (O)HG. *ahorn* maple (corresp. to L. *acernus* of maple).] **1.** A low tree or shrub, *Sambucus nigra* (N.O. *Caprifoliaceæ*), called, for distinction, the Common or Black-berried Elder; bearing umbel-like corymbs of white flowers. The young branches are full of pith. **2.** Extended to other species of the genus *Sambucus*; in N. America applied chiefly to *S. canadensis.* **b.** In names of plants superficially resembling the Elder, as **Dwarf E.,** Goutweed (*Ægopodium podagraria*); **Marsh** or **Marish E.**; etc.

1. My heart of E. *Merry W.* II. iii. 30. **2. Dwarf E., Ground E., Dog E.** (*S. ebulus*) = DANEWORT. *attrib.* and *Comb.*, as **e.-berry,** the fruit of the e.; **-gun,** a pop-gun made of a hollow shoot of e.; **-moth,** *Uropteryx sambucata.*

Elder (e·ldəɹ), *a.* and *sb.*² [OE. *eldra, -e* (*ieldra, -e*) = OFris. *alder, elder*, OS. *aldira*, OHG. *altiro, eltiro* (G. *älter*), ON. *ellri*, Goth. *alþiza*; see ELD *sb.* and *a.*, OLD, -ER³.]

A. *adj.* The comparative degree of OLD *a.*; formerly = the mod. OLDER, but now differentiated. **1.** That has lived or existed longer; senior. Now used without *than*, chiefly as denoting the senior of two; otherwise *arch.* †**2.** Of longer standing, prior; senior –1800. **3.** Ancient, earlier, former ME.

1. The said Wil. Rycroft yelder 1478. How much more e. art thou then thy lookes *Merch. V.* IV. i. 251. **E. statesman,** in Japan, one of the *genro* ('old men') retired statesmen and nobles who are consulted by the Emperor; also *transf.* **2.** An e. title 1642. Phr. *E. hand* (Cards): the first player. **3.** The giant race of e. times SOUTHEY.

B. *sb.* An elder person (*lit.* and *fig.*) †**1.** A parent [cf. mod.G. *eltern* pl.]; a forefather; hence, a predecessor. Usu. in *pl.* –1557. **2.** One who is old or older, a senior. Usu. in *pl.* ME. **3.** A member of a senate, governing body or class, consisting of men (supposed to be) venerable for age. Now chiefly *Hist.* ME. **4.** *Eccl.* = PRESBYTER 1526. **b.** In the Presbyterian churches, one of a class of lay officers who, with the minister, compose the Session, and manage the church affairs.

2. I know my duty to my elders *Tam. Shr.* II. 7. **3.** The reverend elders nodded o'er the case POPE. **4.** That thou..shuldest ordeyne elders in every citie TINDALE *Titus* 1:5.

E·lderling. *rare.* 1606. [f. ELDER *sb.*² + -LING¹.] †**1.** Contemptuously for ELDER *sb.*² 4. **2.** An elderly person 1863.

Elderly (e·ldəɹli), *a.* 1611. [f. ELDER *a.* + -LY¹.] **1.** Somewhat old, verging on old age. **2.** Of or pertaining to an elderly person 1674.

1. E. Fops, and superannuated Coquets BUDGELL.

Eldern (e·ldəɹn), *a.*¹ ME. [f. ELDER *a.* + -EN⁴; an unusual application of the suffix; cf. OLDEN.] †**1.** Elderly –1818. **2.** Belonging to earlier times (*arch.*) ME.

Eldern (e·ldəɹn), *a.*² 1842. [f. ELDER *sb.*¹ + -EN⁴.] Made of elder.

Eldership (e·ldəɹʃip). 1549. [f. ELDER *a.* and *sb.*² + -SHIP.] **1.** The position of being elder; seniority. **2.** The office of elder in a church; the body of elders; a presbytery 1557.

1. My claim to her by E. I prove DRYDEN.

Eldest (e·ldėst), *a. superl.* [OE. *eldest* (*ieldest*) = OFris. *eldest*, OHG. *altist* (G. *ältest*), ON. *ellztr*, Goth. *altista*; see ELDER *a.*, -EST.] †**1.** Most aged. Also *absol.* (quasi-*sb.*). Replaced by OLDEST. –1611. **2.** First-born, or oldest surviving. Also quasi-*sb.* OE. **3.** Earliest; most ancient (*arch.*) OE.

2. The Erle of Ruttlandes eldyste daughter 1536. **3.** The primall e. curse *Haml.* III. iii. 37. Phr. *E. hand* (Cards): the first player; the right of playing first.

†**E·ldfather.** [OE. (WS.) *ealdfæder*, f. *eald*, ELD *a.* + FATHER *sb.*; cf. G. *altvater* ancestor.] **1.** A grandfather; a forefather –1460. **2.** A father-in-law –1634.

E·lding. Now *dial.* ME. [– ON. *elding*, f. *eldr* fire. Cf. Da. *ilding.*] Fuel.

E·ldmother. Now *dial.* [OE. (WS.) *ealdmōdor*; see ELDFATHER.] †**1.** A grandmother –ME. **2.** A mother-in-law; also, a stepmother ME.

‖**El Dorado** (e:ldoɹā·do). 1596. [Sp. *el* the, *dorado* gilded, pa. pple. of *dorar* gild.] A fictitious country (or city) abounding in gold, believed by the Spaniards to exist upon the Amazon within the province of Guiana. Also *fig.*

Unspoil'd Guiana, whose great Citie Geryon's Sons Call El Dorado MILT. *P. L.* XI. 411.

Eldress (e·ldrės). 1640. [f. ELDER *sb.*² + -ESS¹.] A female ELDER.

Eldritch (e·ldritʃ, e·lritʃ), *a. Sc.* 1508. [Of Sc. origin; poss. from attrib. use of OE. **ælf-*, **elfrīce* 'fairy realm' (see ELF *sb.*, RICH).] Weird, unnatural, hideous.

Eleatic (eliˌæ·tik). 1695. [f. L. *Eleaticus*, f. *Elea*, an ancient Greek city in S. W. Italy.]

A. *adj.* Pertaining to Elea or its inhabitants; *spec.* of the philosophy of Xenophanes, Parmenides, and Zeno, who lived or were born there.

The dialectal movement emanated..from the E. school GROTE. Hence **Elea·ticism.**

B. *sb.* An Eleatic philosopher.

Elecampane (e:lĭkæ̆mpēⁱ·n). 1533. [ult. – med.L. *enula campana*, i.e. *enula* for L. *inula* – Gr. ἑλένιον, and *campana* prob. 'of the fields' (cf. CHAMPAIGN).] **1.** A perennial composite plant (*Inula helenium*), with large yellow radiate flowers and bitter aromatic leaves and root; formerly used as a tonic and stimulant. **2.** A sweetmeat flavoured with the root of this plant 1806. **3.** *attrib.* 1610.

2. I don't know how he spent it except in hardbake and alycompaine THACKERAY.

Elect (ĭle·kt). ME. [– L. *electus*, pa. pple. of *eligere*, f. *e-* EX-¹ + *legere* choose.]

A. *adj.* **1.** Picked out, chosen; also, chosen by preference; select. Also *absol.* **2.** *spec.* in *Theol.* Chosen by God, *esp.* for eternal life. Often *absol.* 1526. **3.** Chosen to an office or dignity. Now usually, Chosen, but not installed in office. 1643.

1. The e. o' th' Land *Hen. VIII*, II. iv. 60. **2.** The blessed Spirits e. MILT. *P. L.* III. 136. **3.** The Bishop e. AYLIFFE. So *The bride e.* 1891.

B. *sb.* †**1.** One of the elect (see A. 2) –1646. †**2.** One that has been chosen for an office or function; often *spec.* = *bishop e.* (see A. 3) –1709.

1. Saule..was an e. 1584. **2.** Johne Guthre, e. of Ross 1491.

Elect (ĭle·kt), *v. Pa. t.* and *pple.* **elected.** 1494. [– *elect-*, pa. ppl. stem of L. *eligere*; see prec.] †**1.** *trans.* To pick out, choose. Also *absol.* –1802. **2.** To choose in preference to an alternative. In legal use often *absol.* 1509. **3.** To choose by vote for any office or position 1494. **4.** *Theol.* Of God: To choose as recipients of favour, *esp.* of eternal life. Also *absol.* 1617.

1. 1 *Hen. VI*, IV. i. 4. **2.** The daughter..was..incompetent to e. to take the estate as land or money J. POWELL. He must therefore e. CRUISE. **3.** They resolved to e. an Inter-Rex 1743.

Hence **Ele·ctable** *a.* able or qualified to be elected. **Ele:ctee·**, one chosen or elected.

†**Ele·ctant.** [– *electant-*, pres. ppl. stem of L. *eligere*; see prec., -ANT.] One who has power of choosing. TUCKER

Electary, var. of ELECTUARY.

†**Ele·ctic,** bad f. ECLECTIC.

Election (ĭle·kʃən). ME. [–(O)Fr. *élection* – L. *electio*, f. *elect-*; see ELECT *v.*, -ION.] **1.** The action of choosing for an office, dignity, or position; usually by vote. **b.** *spec.* The choice by popular vote of members of a representative assembly, *e.g.* the House of Commons 1648. **2.** The exercise of deliberate choice ME.; †the faculty of discriminative selection –1602. **3.** *Theol.* The exercise of God's sovereign will in preferring some of His creatures, *esp.* as recipients of eternal life ME. †**b.** *concr.* The body of the elect (*rare*) 1611. **4.** *Astrol.* The selection of times as fit for any particular business; a time so selected. Now *Hist.* ME. †**5.** The choosing of things for special purposes, as simples, etc. –1751.

1. In a large society the e. of a monarch can never devolve to the wisest GIBBON. **b.** Phr. *General e.*: a simultaneous e. of representatives all over the country; opp. to *by-election.* **2.** Disseisins of incorporeal hereditaments are only at the e. and choice of the party injured CRUISE. **3.** The e. of God went to the shepherd, not to the tiller of the ground BACON. **b.** The e. hath obtained it *Rom.* 11:7. **5.** An e. of apt words, and a right disposition of them DRYDEN.

attrib. and *Comb.*, as *e.-address*, etc.; also **e.-committee,** a committee formed to promote the e. of a particular candidate.

Hence **Ele·ctional** *a.* relating to (astrological) e. (*rare*).

Electioneer (ĭle:kʃənīᵊ·ɹ), *v.* 1789. [f. ELECTION + -EER.] *intr.* To busy oneself in (political) elections. Hence **Ele:ctionee·rer.**

Elective (ĭle·ktiv). 1530. [– (O)Fr. *électif, -ive* – late L. *electivus*, f. as ELECT *v.*; see -IVE.]

A. *adj.* **1.** Appointed by election; derived from or dependent on election. **2.** Having the power of election 1632. **3.** Pertaining to election; based upon the principle of election 1642. †**4.** Pertaining to, or proceeding from, choice –1775. †**5.** = ECLECTIC. Hy. More. **6.** Of physical forces and agencies: Having a tendency to operate on certain objects in preference to others 1766. Also *fig.*

1. E. Kings RALEGH. An e. sway MILT. 2. An e. body LD. BROUGHAM. 3. The e. constitution of the new clergy of France MACKINTOSH. The E. Franchise CARLYLE. 4. E. actions HOBBES. 6. Phr. *E. affinity*, also, formerly, *e. attraction*: a tendency to combine with some things and not with others. Light..which has been sifted..by e. absorption TYNDALL.

†**B.** *sb.* An elected representative (*rare*) 1701. Hence **Ele·ctively** *adv.* by choice. **Elec-ti·vity,** the act or property of selection.

†‖**Ele·cto.**· 1609. [Sp.; pa. pple. of *elegir* ELECT.] A leader chosen by mutineers –1650.

Elector (ǐle·ktəɹ). 1467. [– (O)Fr. *électeur*, L. *elector*; see ELECT *v.*, -OR 2.] **1.** One who has the right to vote in an election. **b.** *spec.* In Great Britain and Ireland, one who has the parliamentary vote; in U.S., one of those chosen by the several states to elect the President and Vice-President. **2.** One of the Princes of Germany formerly entitled to take part in the election of the Emperor 1529. Hence **Ele·ctorship,** the state or condition of an e.

Electoral (ǐle·ktŏrăl). 1675. [f. prec. + -AL[1].]

A. *adj.* **1.** Relating to, composed of, or holding rank as, electors. ¶**2.** = ELECTIVE 1 (*rare*) 1849.

1. Austria had..friends in the e. college S. AUSTIN.

†**B.** *sb.* = ELECTOR –1707.

Hence **Ele·ctorally** *adv.* with reference to electors or elections.

Electorate (ǐle·ktŏrĕt). 1675. [f. as prec. + -ATE[1], after Fr. *électorat.*] **1.** The dignity of a German Elector. **b.** The dominions of an Elector. **2.** The whole body of electors 1879. So †**Electora·lity** (in sense 1) (*rare*).

Electorial (ǐlektō·riăl). 1790. [f. as prec. + -IAL.] = ELECTORAL.

†**Ele·ctral,** *a.* 1673. [f. L. *electrum* + -AL[1].] = ELECTRICAL –1708.

†**Ele·ctre.** Also **electar.** ME. [– L. *electrum* – Gr. ἤλεκτρον in same senses.] **1.** An alloy of gold and silver; also *attrib.* –1656. **2.** Amber. Also *attrib.* –1632.

Electress (ǐle·ktrĕs). Also **ele·ctoress.** 1618. [f. ELECTOR + -ESS[1].] **1.** The wife of a German Elector of the Empire. **2.** A female elector 1869.

Electric (ǐle·ktrik). 1646. [– mod.L. *electricus*, f. L. *electrum* – Gr. ἤλεκτρον amber; see -IC.]

A. *adj.* **1.** Possessing the property (first observed in amber) of developing electricity. **b.** Charged with electricity. **2.** Of the nature of, or pertaining to, electricity; producing, produced by, or operating by means of, electricity 1675. **3.** *fig.* 1793.

1. By Electrick bodies, I conceive..such as conveniently placed unto their objects attract all bodies palpable SIR T. BROWNE. 2. From e. fire (= *fluid*)..spirits may be kindled FRANKLIN. 3. The e. flash, that from the melting eye Darts the fond question COLERIDGE.

Phr. **e. arc,** the luminous electrified space between the points of two electrodes through which a current of electricity is passing; **e. atmosphere,** the space round electrical bodies within which they manifest their special properties; **e. chair,** a chair used for electrocution; **e. current,** the flow of electricity through a conducting body from the positive to the negative pole, or from a high to a low potential; **e. eel** = GYMNOTUS; **e. fishes,** certain fishes that can give electric shocks; **e. fluid,** Franklin's term for a (supposed) all-pervading fluid, the cause of electricity; **e. force,** the force with which electricity tends to move matter; **e. ray** = TORPEDO *sb.*[1]; **e. resistance,** opposition to the passage of an e. current; **e. spark,** the luminous discharge from the conductor of an electrical machine to a pointed body presented to it; **e. tension,** the strain or pressure exerted upon a dielectric in the neighbourhood of an electrified body.

Also, in names of instruments for developing, measuring, illustrating, or applying electricity, and of machines, etc., actuated or controlled by electricity, as in *e. clock, governor, heater, railway, telegraph*, etc.; **e. battery** (see BATTERY); **e. candle,** a form of electric-light apparatus in which the carbon pencils are parallel and separated by a layer of plaster of Paris; **e. chimes,** three bells suspended on a metal rod, rung by electricity; **e. column,** a form of the voltaic pile; **e. harpoon,** one in which a bursting charge is exploded by electricity; **e. indicator,** one indicating magnetic currents; **e. log,** a ship's log registering by electricity; **e. machine,** usu. *spec.* a machine for developing frictional electricity; **e. regulator,** one for stopping or starting a machine by electro-magnetic circuit; **e. switch,** a commutator; **e. wires,** those of the electric telegraph.

B. *sb.* **1.** A substance in which the electric force can be excited and accumulated by friction 1646. **2.** *Positive* (*negative*) *electrics*: = electro-positive (-negative) substances 1842.

Electrical (ǐle·ktrikăl), *a.* 1635. [f. prec. + -AL[1]; see -ICAL.] **1.** = ELECTRIC A. 1. **2.** Relating to or connected with electricity; also, of the nature of electricity. (The mod. sense). Also more usual than *electric* in *electrical machine, electrical eel.* 1747. **3.** *fig.* 1775.

3. The atmosphere becomes e. SHERIDAN. Hence **Ele·ctrically** *adv.* (*lit.* and *fig.*).

Electrician (ǐlek-, elektri·ʃăn). 1751. [f. as prec. + -IAN.] One who studies, or is versed in, electricity; one who deals with electrical apparatus.

Electricity (ǐlek-, elektri·sĭti). 1646. [f. ELECTRIC + -ITY.] **1.** In early use, The property (first discovered in amber) of attracting light bodies when excited by friction; also, the state of excitation produced by friction. Subseq., the name given to the common cause of this phenomenon and of many others, *e.g.* the electric spark, lightning, the galvanic current, etc. This cause Franklin considered to be a subtle fluid diffused through all bodies, which, when in excess of the normal, constituted 'positive electricity', when in defect, 'negative electricity'. The view now current is that electricity is a peculiar condition of the molecules of a body or of the ether surrounding them, developed by friction, etc. (see below); but the term 'electric fluid' is still in popular use. **2.** *fig.* 1791. **3.** The branch of electricity which deals with the nature and phenomena of electrical action 1734.

1. E. may be called into activity by mechanical power (= *frictional e.*), by chemical action (= *galvanic e.*), by heat (= *thermal e.*), and by magnetic influence (= *magnetic e.*) MRS. SOMERVILLE. 2. The natural e. of youth LOWELL.

Phrases. With adjs. denoting (*a*) the source or mode of production, as *frictional, galvanic, induced, thermal, vital, voltaic*; (*b*) the place of development, as *animal, atmospheric, organic*; (*c*) the quality, as *active, constant, free, negative, positive. Vitreous, resinous e.*: older synonyms for positive and negative electricity, which were first observed as resulting from the friction of glass and of resinous bodies respectively.

Electricize (ǐle:ktrisəi·z), *v. rare.* 1872. [f. as prec. + -IZE.] = ELECTRIFY *v.* 1.

Ele·ctric li·ght. 1843. **a.** *gen.* Light produced by electrical action. **b.** *spec.* The same as used for illumination. It is commonly produced by the incandescence of a metallic or carbon filament, or by the arc formed by the passing of electricity between two carbon points.

Electrification (ǐle:ktrĭfikē[i]·ʃən). 1748. [f. ELECTRIFY; see -FICATION.] The act of electrifying, or the state of being charged with electricity.

Electrify (ǐle·ktrifəi), *v.* 1747. [f. ELECTR(IC + -FY.] **1.** *trans.* To charge with electricity, or pass the electric current through; to subject to an electric shock or current. **b.** To introduce electric power into (railways, etc.) 1900. **2.** *fig.* To startle, rouse, excite, as though with an electric shock 1752.

1. To e. the body 1796, quicksilver SIR J. HERSCHEL. 2. Those heights of courage which e. an army and ensure victory BURKE. An audience is electrified EMERSON.

†**Electrine,** *a.* 1677. [See ELECTRUM, -INE[2].] **1.** Resembling what exists in amber, electric. HY. MORE. **2.** Made of ELECTRUM.

Electrize (ǐle·ktrəiz), *v.* 1746. [f. ELECTR(IC + -IZE; cf. Fr. *électriser.*] = ELECTRIFY. Hence †**Electri·zable** *a.* **Ele:ctriza·tion.**

Electro (ǐle·ktro), *sb.* or *v. colloq.* 1864. Short for **a.** ELECTRO-PLATE *v.*, ELECTRO-PLATING *vbl. sb.*; **b.** ELECTROTYPE *sb.* and *v.*

Electro- (ǐle·ktro), comb. f. Gr. ἤλεκτρον, taken as meaning 'electricity'; hence:

Ele:ctroballi·stic *a.*, relating to the art of timing by electricity the flight of projectiles. **Ele:ctro-bio·scopy** [see BIO- + *-scopy*], the examination of an animal body by means of a galvanic current, to discover muscular contractions as evidence of life. **Ele:ctro-ca·pillary** *a.*, having reference to the influence of electricity on capillary tubes under certain conditions. **Ele:ctro-che·mic, -al** *a.*, pertaining to electricity and chemistry jointly. **Ele:ctro-chro·nograph,** an instrument for recording electrically exact instants of time. **Ele:ctro-depo·sit** *v.*, to deposit by means of electricity; hence **-depo·sit, -deposi·tion,** this process; **-depo·sitor,** one who does this. **Ele:ctro-fu·sion,** the fusion of metals by means of electricity. **Ele:ctro-ge·nesis** [see -GENESIS], the state of tetanoid spasm that supervenes in the muscles highly stimulated by galvanism, when the current is withdrawn; so **Ele:ctroge·nic** *a.*, pertaining to electrogenesis. **Ele:ctro-gi·ld** *v.*, to gild by means of an electric current; hence **-gilding** *vbl. sb.*, **-gilt** *ppl. adj.* **Ele:ctro-kine·tic** *a.* [see KINETIC], having reference to electricity in motion. **Ele:ctro-ma·ssage,** kneading the body or a limb with a combined roller and small galvanic machine. **Ele:ctro-meta·llurgy,** the application of electrolysis to the deposition of thin coatings of metals; hence **-metallu·rgic, -al** *a.* **Ele:ctro-mu·scular** *a.*, having reference to the relations between electricity and muscular contraction. **Ele:ctro-ne·gative** *a.*, pertaining to, or producing, negative electricity. **Ele:ctro-patho·logy,** the science of morbid conditions as revealed by electricity. **Ele:ctro-po·lar** *a.*, applied to a cylindrical conductor when, on being electrified by induction, the ends become polar. **Ele:ctro-po·sitive** *a.*, pertaining to, or producing, positive electricity. **Ele:ctropu·ncture** = GALVANOPUNCTURE. **Ele:ctrosynthe·tic** *a.*, causing chemical composition by means of the galvanic current; hence **Ele:ctrosynthe·tically** *adv.* **Ele:ctro-tele·graphy** = electric telegraphy; hence **Ele:ctro-te·legraphic** *a.* **Ele:ctro-therapeu·tics,** the treatment of disease by electricity. **Ele:ctro-the·rapy** [Gr. θεραπεία healing], = *electro-therapeutics.* **Ele:ctro-the·rmancy,** also **Ele·ctro-the:rmy** [as if – Gr. -θερμία], the science of the electricity developed by heat. **Ele·ctroti:nt** [cf. AQUATINT], a mode of engraving, the design being drawn on copper-plate and transferred by means of an electric bath. **Ele:ctro-vi·tal** *a.*, having reference to the relations of electricity and the vital actions; hence **Ele:ctro-vi·talism.**

Electro-biology (ǐle:ktro,bəi,ǫ·lŏdʒi). 1849. [f. prec. + BIOLOGY.] **1.** The branch of electricity which deals with the electrical phenomena of living beings. **2.** A form of hypnotism, in which unconsciousness was induced by causing the patient to gaze steadily at a small disc of zinc or copper; also, 'animal magnetism' generally 1850. Hence **Ele:ctrobiolo·gical** *a.* **Ele:ctrobio·logist.**

Electrocute (ǐle·ktrŏkiūt), *v.* 1889. [orig. †*electricute*, back-formation from †*electricution* (1889), f. *electri(cal exe)cution* (1888); re-formed after ELECTRO-.] *trans.* To put to death by means of a powerful electric current. Hence **Electrocu·tion.**

Electrode (ǐle·ktrōd). 1834. [f. ELECTRIC + Gr. ὁδός way, after *anode, cathode.*] One of the poles of a galvanic battery. See ANODE and CATHODE.

Electrodynamic, -al (ǐle:ktro,dəinæ·mik, -ăl), *a.* 1832. [f. ELECTRO- + DYNAMIC, -AL[1].] Pertaining to the force excited by one magnetic current upon another. Hence **Ele:ctro-dyna·mics,** the science of the mutual influence of electric currents. **Ele:ctrody·namism** = *electro-dynamics.* **Ele:ctro-dynamo·meter,** an instrument for measuring e. force.

Electrograph (ǐle·ktrograf). 1840. [f. as prec. + -GRAPH.] †**1.** An instrument for producing electrotypes. **2.** An instrument for registering electrical conditions; the automatic record of an electrometer 1881.

Electrolier (ǐle:ktrŏlī[ə]·ɹ). 1882. [f. ELECTRO-, after *chandelier.*] A cluster of electric lamps.

Electrology (ǐ-, elektrǫ·lŏdʒi). [f. as prec. + -LOGY.] The science of electricity. Hence **Electrolo·gic, -al** *a.*

Electrolysis (ǐ-, elektrǫ·lĭsis). 1839. [f. as prec. + -LYSIS.] **1.** Chemical decomposition by galvanic action; also, the science of this. **2.** *Surg.* The breaking up of tumours, also of calculi, by galvanic action 1867.

Electrolyte (ǐle·ktrŏləit). 1834. [f. as prec. + Gr. λυτός loosed, f. λύειν loose.] 'A body which can be or is being decomposed by ELECTROLYSIS' (*Syd. Soc. Lex.*). Hence **Ele:ctroly·tic, -al** *a.* pertaining to, or capable of, electrolysis. **Ele·ctroly·tically** *adv.*

Electrolyze (ĭle·ktrŏləiz), *v.* 1834. [f. prec., after *analyze*, etc.] *trans.* To treat by ELECTROLYSIS (senses 1, 2). Hence **Ele:ctroly·zable** *a.* capable of being electrolyzed. **Ele:ctrolyza·tion,** the process of electrolyzing.

Electro-magnet (ĭle:ktro,mæ·gnėt). 1831. [f. ELECTRO- + MAGNET.] A piece of soft iron surrounded by a coil of wire, through which a current of electricity may be passed, rendering the iron temporarily magnetic.

The first simple electro-magnet was made by Sturgeon [of Manchester] 1879.

Hence **Ele:ctro-magne·tic, -al** *a.* pertaining to electro-magnetism. **Ele:ctro-magne·tically** *adv.* **Ele:ctro-magne·tics,** the science of electro-magnetism. **Ele:ctro-ma·gnetism,** the phenomena of the production of magnetism by the electric current; also, the influence of a magnet on the electric current.

Electrometer (ĭlek-, elektrǫ·mĭtəɹ). 1749. [f. as prec. + -METER.] An instrument for determining the quality and quantity of electricity. Hence **Ele:ctrome·tric, -al** *a.* **Electro·metry,** measurement of electricity by the e.

Electromotion (ĭle:ktro,mōᵘ·ʃən). 1803. [f. as prec. + MOTION *sb.*] The motion of a galvanic current; also, recently, mechanical motion produced by electricity.

Electromotive (ĭle:ktro,mōᵘ·tiv). 1806. [f. ELECTRO- + MOTIVE *a.*]

A. *adj.* Pertaining to electromotion.

Phr. *E. force*: orig., the force exhibited in the voltaic battery; in mod. use, the difference of potential which is the cause of electric currents.

B. *sb.* [after *locomotive.*] A locomotive engine with electricity for its motive power 1887.

Electromotor (ĭle:ktro,mōᵘ·təɹ). 1827. [f. as prec. + MOTOR.]

A. *sb.* Orig., a metal serving as a voltaic element. In mod. use, a machine for applying electricity as a motive power.

B. *attrib.* or *adj.* = ELECTROMOTIVE.

‖**Electron**[1] (ĭle·ktrǫn). 1856. [– Gr. ἤλεκτρον.] = ELECTRUM 2.

Electron[2] (ĭle·ktrǫn). 1891. [f. ELECTRIC + *-on* of *anion, cation, ion.*] *Physics.* The smallest supposed component of matter, associated with (or consisting of) an invariable charge of negative electricity. Hence **Electro·nic** *a.*

Electrophorus (ĭlek-, elektrǫ·fŏrŭs). 1778. [mod.L., f. ELECTRO- + Gr. -φορος that bears or produces; see -PHORE.] An instrument, invented by Volta, for generating static electricity by induction. Anglicized as **Ele·ctrophore.**

Electroplate (ĭle·ktropleⁱt), *v.* 1870. [f. ELECTRO- + PLATE *v.* 2.] *trans.* To coat with silver by electrolysis. Hence **Ele·ctropla:ter,** one who electroplates. **Ele·ctropla:ting** *vbl. sb.* So **Ele·ctro-plate** *sb.* the ware produced by electroplating.

Electroscope (ĭle·ktroskōᵘp). 1824. [f. as prec. + -SCOPE.] An instrument for ascertaining the presence and quality of electricity. Hence **Ele:ctrosco·pic** *a.* measured by the e.

Electrostatic, -al (ĭle:ktro,stæ·tik, -ăl), *a.* 1867. [f. as prec. + STATIC, -AL[1], after *hydrostatic, -al.*] Pertaining to static electricity. Hence **Electrostatics,** the theory of static electricity.

‖**Electrotonus** (ĭlek-, elektrǫ·tŏnŭs). 1860 [mod.L., f. ELECTRO- + TONUS.] The modified condition of a nerve subjected to a constant current of electricity. Anglicized as **Ele·ctrotone.** So **Ele:ctroto·nic** *a.* relating to or characterized by e.; also applied by Faraday to the peculiar electrical state characteristic of a secondary circuit in the electro-magnetic field. **Ele:ctrotoni·city,** the condition produced by electrotonizing. **Electro·tonize** *v.* to produce e.

Electrotype (ĭle·ktrotəip). 1840. [f. as prec. + -TYPE.] **1.** A copy of a thing formed by the deposition of copper on a mould by galvanic action; also *attrib.* **2.** The process of electrotyping 1840.

1. An e. seal 1840. E. cuts 1880. **2.** The E. in America 1840.

Ele·ctrotype, *v.* 1847. [f. prec. sb.] *trans.* To copy in electrotype. Also *fig.* Hence **Ele·ctroty:per. Ele·ctroty:pist.**

Electrum (ĭle·ktrŏm). ME. [– L. *electrum* – Gr. ἤλεκτρον in same senses. Cf. ELECTRE.] †**1.** Amber –1794; also *fig.* of tears 1591. **2.** = ELECTRE 1. Also *attrib.* ME. **b.** *Min.* Native argentiferous gold containing from 20 to 50 per cent. of silver 1555. **3.** An alloy of copper, zinc, and nickel. URE.

1. *fig.* It was her masters death That drew e. from her weeping eyes GREENE.

Electuary (ĭle·ktiŭări). ME. [– late L. *electuarium*, prob. altered deriv. of synon. Gr. ἐκλεικτόν, f. ἐκλείχειν lick up. Cf. ECLEGME.] A medicine, consisting of a powder or other ingredient mixed with honey, jam, or syrup. Also *fig.*

‖**Eledone** (elĭdōᵘ·ni). 1835. [mod.L. – Gr. ἐλεδώνη a kind of polypus.] A cephalopod of the tribe *Octopoda.*

Eleemosynary (e:lĭ,ĭ,mǫ·sinări). 1620. [– med.L. *eleemosynarius*, f. Chr. L. *eleemosyna* ALMS; see -ARY[1].]

A. *adj.* **1.** Of or pertaining to alms or almsgiving; charitable 1630. **2.** Supported by alms 1654. **3.** Of the nature of alms; gratuitous 1620.

1. These her eleemosinary acts RISDON. **2.** The flock of e. doves HAWTHORNE. **3.** E. relief C. BRONTË.

†**B.** *sb.* **1.** One who lives upon alms. Also *fig.* –1673. **2.** = ALMONER[1] (*rare*) –1809. **3.** = ALMONRY 1688. Hence **Eleemo·synarily** *adv.* charitably, by way of charity.

Elegance (e·lĭgăns). 1510. [– Fr. *élégance* – L. *elegantia*; see next, -ANCE.] **1.** The state or quality of being elegant; refined grace or propriety; tasteful correctness; ingenious simplicity, neatness: said of form, movement, manners, style, formulæ, scientific demonstrations, etc. **2.** *concr.* That which is elegant; an instance or kind of elegance 1676.

1. With untutored e. she dressed CRABBE. E., by which I always mean precision and correctness LANDOR. **2.** A nice contriver of all elegances EVELYN. So **E·legancy** (*esp.* in sense 2).

Elegant (e·lĭgănt), *a.* 1485. [– (O)Fr. *élégant* or L. *elegant-*, pres. ppl. stem of **elegare*, rel. to *eligere* to select; see ELECT, -ANT.] **1.** Tastefully ornate in dress. **2.** Characterized by refinement, grace, or propriety 1658. **3.** Of scientific processes, formulæ, etc.: Neat 1668. **4.** Of persons: Correct and delicate in taste. Now only in *e. scholar.* 1667. **5.** Graceful, polite, appropriate to persons of cultivated taste 1705. **6.** *U.S.* Excellent, first rate 1772.

2. An e. poem BURKE. An e. bedroom 1859. **3.** An e. Composition for a troublesome..Cough 1710. An e. chess problem 1891. **4.** Thou art exact of taste, And e. MILT. *P.L.* IX. 1018. **5.** Phr. *E. arts*; nearly = 'fine arts'. Eminent for..e. literature JOHNSON.

Hence **E·legantly** *adv.*

‖**Elegante** (ele·gant). 1806. [Fr. *élégante*, fem. of *élégant* ELEGANT.] A fashionable lady.

Elegiac (elĭdʒəi·ǣk). 1581. [– Fr. *élégiaque* or late L. *elegiacus* – Gr. ἐλεγειακός, f. ἐλεγεία, ἐλεγεῖον ELEGY; see -AC.]

A. *adj.* **1.** *Pros.* Appropriate to elegies; as, the *e. distich*, consisting of a (dactylic) hexameter and pentameter; *e. verse* (sometimes applied to the pentameter separately) 1586. **2.** Of the nature of an elegy; pertaining to elegies; hence, mournful, plaintive, melancholy 1644. var. **Elegi·acal** (in both senses).

2. E. griefs, and songs of love E. B. BROWNING. Phr. *E. poet*: one who writes **a.** in e. metre; **b.** in a pensive strain.

B. *sb.* †**a.** An elegiac poet 1581. **b.** *pl.* Elegiac verses 1774.

Ele·giast. [f. ELEGY, after *ecclesiast*, etc.] A writer of elegies. GOLDSM.

†**Ele·gious,** *a.* [f. as prec. + -OUS.] Resembling an elegy; hence, lugubrious, mournful. QUARLES.

Elegist (e·lĭdʒist). 1774. [f. as prec. + -IST.] The writer of an elegy.

Elegit (ĭlĭ·dʒit). 1503. [L.; = 'he has chosen'; from the words in the writ.] *Law.* A writ of execution, issued on the election of a judgement creditor, by which the creditor is put in possession of (formerly half) the goods and lands of a debtor, until his claim is satisfied. Also, the right secured by this writ, as in 'tenant by *elegit*'.

Elegize (e·lĭdʒəiz), *v.* 1702. [f. ELEGY + -IZE.] **1.** *intr.* To write an elegy; to write in an elegiac strain. **2.** *trans.* To write an elegy upon 1809.

2. The bard who soars to elegise an ass BYRON.

Elegy (e·lĭdʒi). 1514. [– Fr. *élégie* or L. *elegia* – Gr. ἐλεγεία, f. ἔλεγος mournful poem; see -Y[3].] **1.** A song of lamentation, *esp.* a funeral ode. **2.** Any species of classical poetry written in elegiac verse 1600. **3.** Poetry, or a poem, written in elegiacs. †**b.** An elegiac distich. 1589.

1. Their name, their years..The place of fame and e. supply GRAY. **2.** They gave the name of e. to their pleasantries as well as lamentations SHENSTONE.

Eleme (e·lĭmi). 1879. [– Turk., = 'something sifted or selected'.] *Comm.* Epithet of a kind of dried figs from Turkey.

Element (e·lĭmĕnt, *sb.* ME. [– (O)Fr. *élément* – L. *elementum*, esp. pl., principles, rudiments, letters of the alphabet, used as tr. Gr. στοιχεῖον step, element, etc.]

I. Component part. **1.** One of the simple substances of which all material bodies are compounded: as, **a.** In ancient philosophy, Earth, water, air, and fire. Now *Hist.* †**b.** In prescientific chemistry, Water, air, oil, salt, earth, or as variously enumerated –1765. **c.** In mod. chemistry, Any of seventy or more substances which are provisionally taken to be simple bodies, as having hitherto resisted analysis 1813. **2.** More widely: One of the relatively simple parts of any complex substance; in *pl.* the 'raw material' of anything ME. **3.** The bread and wine used in the Eucharist. Chiefly *pl.* 1593. **4.** *Phys.* A definite small portion of an organic structure 1841. **b.** One of the essential parts of any scientific apparatus. *Voltaic e.*: usu. = CELL II. 2c, but occas. = *electrode.* 1831. **5.** A constituent portion of an immaterial whole 1599. **6.** One of the facts or conditions necessary to determine the result of a process, calculation, deliberation, or inquiry 1812. **7.** *Math.* An infinitesimal part of a magnitude of any kind; a differential 1727.

2. The Elements Of whom your swords are temper'd may as well Wound the loud windes *Temp.* III. iii. 61. **5.** These simple Elements of Magnitude, Figure, Site, and Motion CUDWORTH. The elements of feudalism FREEMAN. It had its usual e. of (= consisting of) cant KINGSLEY. **6.** The elements of their [comets'] orbits PLAYFAIR, of a crystal 1878.

II. The four elements. **1.** Used as a general name for earth, water, air, and fire (see I, 1); now merely a survival ME. Also *fig.* †**2.** The sky; ? also, the air –1714. †**b.** ? One of the celestial spheres of ancient astronomy; also (rarely) one of the heavenly bodies themselves –1604. **3.** *pl.* Atmospheric agencies 1555. **4.** That one of the four elements natural to any particular class of living things. Hence *transf.* and *fig.* the surroundings natural to anything, or forming its proper sphere of activity. 1598.

1. The foure elementes menace alle men that thanke not god CAXTON. Those who drink the pure e. G. WHITE. Fire as 'the devouring e.' 1886. **2. b.** *Oth.* III. iii. 464. **3.** Daunted by the elements PRESCOTT. **4.** She workes by Charmes.. beyond our e. *Merry W.* IV. ii. 186. My proper e. of prose LAMB. Phr. *in, out of* (*one's*) *e.*

III. Primordial principle, source of origin (*rare*) 1655.

One God, one law, one e. TENNYSON.

IV. *pl.* †The letters of the alphabet. Hence, the 'A, B, C' of learning; also, the first principles of an art or science. ME.

†**E·lement,** *v.* ME. [f. prec. sb.] **1.** *trans.* To compound of (the four) elements –1647. Also *fig.* **2.** To instruct in the rudiments of learning –1662.

Elemental (elĭme·ntăl), *a.* 1519. [– med.L. *elementalis* (XIII); see ELEMENT *sb.*, -AL[1].] **1.** Of or pertaining to the four elements, or to any one of them. †**2.** Composed of, or produced by, the (four) elements, material, physical –1646. †**3.** Applied to fire: **a.** Material. **b.** As a pure element –1755. **4.** Pertaining to the forces of nature 1821. Also *fig.* †**5.** Pertaining to the sky –1627. **6.** Of the nature of an ultimate constituent 1555. **7.** Constituent 1639. **8.** Relating to rudiments; elementary. Now *rare.* 1577.

1. All subsists by e. strife POPE. 2. The slaying of an elemental life MILT. 4. E. worship of the grossest kind MERIVALE. *fig.* The freedom and e. grandeur of Byron MORLEY. 6. The primitive e. operations of thought 1863. 8. E. truths 1855.

Hence **Eleme·ntalism** (*nonce-wd.*), worship of the elementary powers of nature. †**E:lementa·lity,** the fact of being an element. **Eleme·ntally** *adv.*

Elementaloid (elĭme·ntăloid), *a.* 1885. [f. prec. + -OID.] *Chem.* Like an element; having the appearance of an element.

Elementary (elĭme·ntări). ME. [– L. *elementarius*, f. *elementum*; see ELEMENT, -ARY[1].] **1.** = ELEMENTAL 1. Now *rare.* 1549. †**2.** = ELEMENTAL 2. –1750. †**3.** Applied to air, fire, water, earth: **a.** Physical. **b.** As pure elements. –1794. **4.** = ELEMENTAL 4, which is now more used 1739. Also *fig.* †**5.** Congenial 1760. **6.** = ELEMENTAL 6. 1622. **b.** *Math.* Of the nature of an element or infinitesimal part 1882. **7.** Of the nature of elements; rudimentary, introductory 1542.

1. E. war—deluges and earthquakes 1856. 4. The e. god of fire H. WALPOLE. 6. The e. substances of which rocks are composed 1813. 7. Phr. *E. books, writers, schools.*

Hence **Eleme·ntarily** *adv.* **Eleme·ntariness,** also †**E:lementa·rity,** the quality of being e.

†**E·lementate,** *v.* 1650. [orig. in pa. ppl. form *elementated* – med.L. *elementatus* composed of elements (XII), whence mod.L. *elementare*; f. L. *elementum* ELEMENT; see -ATE[2,3].] *trans.* **a.** To impregnate with an element; to compound out of elements. **b.** To be elements or an element of (a substance). ASHMOLE.

†**Eleme·ntish,** *a.* 1580. [See -ISH[1].] Material, physical –1646.

Elemi (e·lĭmi). 1543. [In full *gum elimi*, mod.L. *gummi elimi*, prob. of Oriental origin. So Fr. *élémi*, Sp. *elemi.*] A resin obtained from various trees, as *Canarium commune* (Manilla), *Icica icicariba* (Brazil), *Elaphrium elemiferum* (Mexico), used in plasters, ointments, and the manufacture of varnishes. Also *attrib.*

Elemin (e·lĭmin). 1868. [f. prec. + -IN[1].] *Chem.* A crystalline body extracted from elemi; also, a transparent colourless oil obtained from elemi by distilling with water.

†**Elench** (ĭle·ŋk). 1529. [– L. *elenchus* (see next); cf. OFr. *elenche.*] **1.** *Logic.* A syllogism in refutation of a syllogistic conclusion; hence, more widely, a logical refutation –1631. **b.** A sophistical argument; a fallacy –1689. **2.** An index 1563. Hence **Ele·nchic, -al,** *a.* = ELENCTIC, -AL. **Ele·nchically** *adv.* †**Ele·nchize** *v.* to use the elenchus. B. JONS.

‖**Elenchus** (ĭle·ŋkŏs). *Pl.* **elenchi.** 1663. [L. – Gr. ἔλεγχος argument of disproof or refutation.] **1. a.** *Logic.* = ELENCH 1. **b.** *Socratic e.*: the Socratic method of eliciting truth by cross-examination. †**2.** = ELENCH 2.

Elenctic, -al (ĭle·ŋktik, -ăl), *a.* 1833. [– Gr. ἐλεγκτικός, f. ἐλέγχειν refute; see prec., -IC, -ICAL.] Pertaining to elenchus; concerned with cross-examination.

E·lenge, *a.* Now *dial.* [OE. *ǣlenge*, f. Æ- + **lenge* (cf. LENG).] †**1.** Very long, tedious –ME. **2.** Remote, lonely; dreary ME. Hence †**E·lengenesse.**

†**E·lephancy.** 1547. [– L. *elephantia*, var. of ELEPHANTIASIS.] = ELEPHANTIASIS –1657.

Elephant (e·lĭfănt). [ME. *olifaunt*, later (w. assim. to L.) *elifant*, etc. – OFr. *olifant*, *elefant* (mod. *éléphant*) – Rom. **olifantus*, alt. of L. *elephantus*, *-phans* – Gr. ἐλέφας, ἐλεφαντ- ivory, elephant, prob. of alien origin.] **1.** A huge quadruped of the Pachydermate order, having long curving ivory tusks and a prehensile proboscis. Only two species now exist, the Indian and the African; the former of which (the largest of extant land animals) is often used as a beast of burden. Also *fig.* †**2. a.** Ivory [after L. *elephantus*]. **b.** A horn of ivory [after OFr. *olifant*]. –1725. †**3.** A species of lizard mentioned by Pliny –1608. †**4.** [after Pg. *elephante.*] = ELEPHANTA –1703. **5.** (more fully **e.-paper**): A size of drawing paper measuring 28 × 23 inches. *Double e.*, one measuring 40 × 26½ inches. 1702. **6.** *attrib.* 1774.

1. *fig.* Shall the E. Aiax carry it thus *Tr. & Cr.* II. iii. 2. Phr. *White e.*: a burdensome or costly possession (given by the kings of Siam to obnoxious courtiers in order to ruin them). *To see the e.* (U.S.): to see life or the world. 2. **a.** Polished E. DRYDEN.

Comb: **e.-bed,** a stratum at Brighton containing remains of *Elephas primigenius*, etc.; **-beetle,** some S. Amer. beetle, prob. *Dynastes neptunus*; also applied to the Afr. species *Goliathus giganteus* and *G. cacicus*; **-fish,** the *Chimæra callorhynchus*, named from the proboscis-like process on its nose; **-leg** = ELEPHANTIASIS; **-paper** (see 5); **-seal,** a species of seal (*Macrorhinus proboscideus*), the males of which have the snout somewhat prolonged; also called **Sea elephant; -shrew,** *Macroscelides typicus*, a long-snouted burrower of Southern Africa; **-tusk,** the tooth-shell.

b. Also in the names of plants, as **e.-apple,** *Feronia elephantum*, of the family *Aurantiaceæ*; **-creeper,** *Argyreia speciosa*; **elephant's ear,** the Begonia; **elephant's foot,** a species of Yam (*Testudinaria elephantipes*); **elephant's grass,** a kind of reed-mace (*Typha elephantum*); **elephant's-trunk-plant,** *Martynia proboscidea*; **elephant's vine,** *Cissus latifolia.*

Elepha·nta. Also (erron.) **elephanter.** 1725. [– Pg. *elephante*, fem. *-ta.*] A name, originally Portuguese, for violent storms which attend the termination, or, some say, the setting in, of the Monsoon.

Elephantiac (elĭfæ·ntiæk) 1868. [– L. *elephantiacus*, f. *elephantia*; see ELEPHANCY, -AC.] One who has elephantiasis.

‖**Elephantiasis** (e:lĭfăntəi·ăsis). 1581. [L. – Gr. ἐλεφαντίασις, f. ἐλέφας; see ELEPHANT, -ASIS.] *Med.* One of various skin diseases, which make the part affected resemble an elephant's hide. The best known is *E. Arabum*, called also Elephant, or Barbadoes, Leg, which indurates and darkens the skin of the leg.

Elephantic (elĭfæ·ntik). 1491. [– late L. *elephanticus*, f. *elephas*; see ELEPHANT, -IC.] **a.** *adj.* = ELEPHANTINE. Now *rare.* 1598. †**b.** *sb.* = prec.

Elephantine (elĭfæ·ntəin, -tin), *a.* 1630. [– L. *elephantinus* – Gr. ἐλεφάντινος; see ELEPHANT, -INE[1].] **1.** Pertaining to an elephant; resembling an elephant (usually in size or gait); huge, unwieldy, clumsy. **2.** *Rom. Antiq.* Made of ivory 1751.

1. Phr. *E. epoch* (Geol.): the period marked by the abundance of huge pachydermata. Misshapen e. bodies 1630. Ungraceful e. play 1860. 2. Phr. *E. books*: books composed of ivory tablets, wherein were recorded the acts of the Roman emperors and of the senate.

Elephantoid, -al (elĭfæ·ntoid, -ăl), *a.* 1841. [f. ELEPHANT + -OID.] **a.** Elephant-like. **b.** Of or belonging to elephant-like animals.

E·lephantry. 1747. [f. ELEPHANT, after *cavalry*. Cf. *camelry* (see CAMEL).] Troops mounted on elephants.

Eleusinian (eliusi·niăn). 1643. [– L. *Eleusinius* – Gr. Ἐλευσίνιος + -AN.] Belonging to Eleusis in Attica. *E. mysteries*: the mysteries of Demeter there celebrated; also *fig.*

Eleu·therarch. *rare.* 1813. [f. Gr. ἐλεύθερος free + -ARCH.] The chief of an (imaginary) secret society, 'the Eleutheri'.

Eleuthe·rian, *a. rare.* 1623. [– Gr. ἐλευθέριος (f. ἐλεύθερος free) + -AN.] The title of Zeus as protector of political freedom.

Eleuthero- (ĭliū·pəro), comb. f. Gr. ἐλεύθερος free:

Eleu:theroma·nia [see -MANIA], frantic zeal for freedom. So **Eleu:theroma·niac** *a.* Also in botanical compounds, as **Eleu:therope·talous** [Gr. πέταλον], **-phy·llous** [Gr. φύλλον], **-se·palous** [see SEPAL] *adjs.* having the petals, leaves, sepals, free, *i.e.* distinct, not cohering.

†**E·levable,** *a.* [– med.L. *elevabilis*, f. L. *elevare*; see ELEVATE *v.*, -ABLE.] That can be elevated. HY. MORE.

Elevate (e·lĭvět), *pa. pple.* and *ppl. a.* ME. [– L. *elevatus*, pa. pple. of *elevare*; see next, -ATE[2].] Used as pa. pple. of ELEVATE *v.*; also = ELEVATED *ppl. a.* From 18th c. only *poet.*

Apart..In thoughts more e. MILT. *P. L.* II. 559.

Elevate (e·lĭve[i]t), *v.* 1497. [– *elevat-*, pa. ppl. stem of L. *elevare*, f. *e-* EX-[1] + *levare* lighten, raise; see -ATE[3].] †**1.** *trans.* To lessen the weight of; to depreciate –1788. **2.** To raise, lift up higher. Also *fig.* 1497. **b.** To hold up to view, as the Host 1637. †**c.** Of heat: To evaporate or sublime –1715. **3.** *transf.* To raise (the voice) 1618. **4.** To direct upwards; also *fig.* 1611. **b.** *Gunnery.* To raise the axis of (a gun, etc.) to an angle with the horizon 1692. **5.** To exalt in rank or status 1509. **6.** To raise morally or intellectually 1624. **7.** To elate, exhilarate (now *rare*) 1634. **b.** *spec.* of the effects of liquor (*joc.* or *slang*) 1704.

2. To e. a bucket LARDNER. **b.** To e. the Host for adoration 1660. 4. **b.** The mortar must be more elevated 1769. 5. To e. a plebeian 1835. 6. Books which e. the Mind above the World STEELE. 7. **b.** We were all elevated above the use of our legs 1704.

Elevated (e·lĭve[i]tĕd), *ppl. a.* 1553. [f. prec. + -ED[1].] **1.** Raised up; at a high level. Also *fig.* and *transf.* **2.** Exalted in character; lofty, sublime 1604. **3. a.** Elated. **b.** Slightly intoxicated (*joc.* or *slang*). 1624.

1. E. lakes GOLDSM. Phr. *E. railway*: a railway raised on pillars above the street-level; so *e. train.* 2. One of the most e. passages in Plato JOWETT.

Hence **E·levated-ly** *adv.*, **-ness.**

Elevation (elĭvē[i]·ʃən). ME. [– (O)Fr. *élévation* or L. *elevatio*, f. *elevat-*; see ELEVATE *v.*, -ION.]

I. 1. The action of lifting up, raising aloft, or directing upwards 1526. Also †*fig.* and *transf.* **2.** *concr.* A swelling; an eminence 1543. †**3.** Sublimation; vaporization by heat –1677. **4.** The action of raising in rank or dignity; the being elevated in rank 16..

1. But the land is subject also to local elevations and depressions HUXLEY. The E. [of the Host] 1884. *transf.* E. of voice 1668, of the Pulse 1725, of temperature 1882. 4. A sudden e. in life HARE.

II. 1. Of angular magnitude: **a.** *Astron.* The altitude of the pole, or of any heavenly body, above the horizon. Also in *Dialling*, the angle made by the gnomon with the horizon (= the latitude of the place). ME. **b.** The angle made with the horizontal by any line of direction; *spec.* the angle at which a gun is elevated 1692. **2.** A particular altitude above a given level 1732. **3.** *concr.* A drawing of a building, etc., made in projection on a vertical plane 1731. **4.** Height, loftiness (*lit.* and *fig.*) 1639.

2. Snow at the higher elevations TYNDALL. 4. E. of style WOTTON (J.), of character 1868. A building of imposing e. 1891.

Elevator (e·lĭve[i]təɹ). 1646. [mod.L. *elevator*, f. as prec.; see -OR 2. In mod. use f. ELEVATE *v.*] One who or that which elevates. **1.** *Anat.* A muscle which raises a limb or an organ 1646. **2.** *Surg.* 'An instrument for raising any depressed portions of bone. Also, an instrument used in Dentistry for the removal of stumps of teeth' (*Syd. Soc. Lex.*). **3. a.** A machine used for raising corn or flour to an upper storey. **b.** *U.S.* A large building (containing one or more of these machines) used for the storage of grain. **c.** A lift, hoist, ascending chamber. 1825. **4.** *Aeronautics.* **a.** An elevating screw. **b.** A rudder device for lifting or steering an aircraft vertically. 1871.

Elevatory (e·lĭve[i]təri). 1612. [In B. – mod.L. **elevatorium*, or after Fr. *élévatoire* (XVI); see prec., -ORY[1]; in A., f. ELEVATE *v.* + -ORY[2].]

A. *adj.* Of or pertaining to elevation; that tends to elevate (*lit.* and *fig.*) 1833.

B. *sb.* = ELEVATOR 2.

†**Ele·ve.** Now only as Fr. 1736. [– Fr. *élève*, f. *élever* bring up.] A pupil –1829.

Eleven (ĭle·v'n). [OE. *endleofon*, *-lufon*, *ellefne*, ME. *endleven(e*, *elleven(e* = OFris. *andlova*, *elleva*, *al-*, *elvene*, OS. *elleban*, OHG. *einlif* (Du., G. *elf*), ON. *ellifu*, Goth. *ainlif* :– Gmc. **ainlif-*, f. **ainaz* ONE + **lif-* (appearing also in TWELVE), quasi 'one left (over ten)'.] The cardinal number next after ten; symbols 11 and xi.

A. *adj.* **1.** With sb. expressed. **2.** With ellipsis of sb. ME.

2. About a leuen [*sc.* hours] of the clocke UDALL.

B. as *sb.* **1.** The abstract number eleven ME. **2.** A set of eleven persons; *esp.* a side at cricket or football 1800.

Eleventh (ĭle·v'nþ). ME. [f. ELEVEN + -TH[2], a new formation superseding OE. *endleofeþa*, itself a new formation on *endleofon*, superseding previous *endlyfta*, *ællefta* = OFris. *andlofta*, *ellefta*, OS. *ellifto*, OHG. *einlifto* (Du. *elfde*, G. *elfte*), ON. *ellifti* :– Gmc. **ainliftōn.*]

A. *adj.* **1.** That comes next after the tenth. **2.** *E. part:* one of eleven equal parts of anything 1797. †3. *Mus.* The interval of an octave and a fourth 1597.

1. Phr. *E. hour*: the latest possible time (see *Matt.* 20); Though at the e. hour Thou hast come SOUTHEY.

B. *sb.* = *eleventh part*; see A. 2. 1557.

Hence **Ele·venthly** *adv.*; also quasi-*sb.*

Elf (elf), *sb.* [OE. *elf*, non-WS. var. of **ielf*, late *ylf* = MDu. *elf* :– **albiz*, parallel to **albaz*, whence OE. *ælf* = OS., MLG. *alf*, MHG. *alp* (G. *alp* nightmare), ON. *álfr.*] **1.** *Mythol.* The name of a class of supernatural beings, believed to be of dwarfish form, and to possess magical powers, which they exercised either to the help or the hurt of mankind. Now a mere synonym of FAIRY. †**b.** Sometimes dist. from fairies: (*a*) as a subject species; (*b*) as more malignant; also *fig.* 1587. **2.** *transf.* A diminutive being; a dwarf; a mischievous child 1530. **b.** A tricksy, sometimes a malicious, creature 1553. †**3.** A knight of Spenser's 'faerie land'.

1. Ye Elves of hils, brooks, standing lakes and groues *Temp.* v. i. 33.

Comb. **a.** appositive, as *e.-child*, a changeling; **b.** attributive as *e.-land*, etc. Also **e.-arrow, -bolt,** a flint arrow-head (see ELF-SHOT); also, a belemnite; **-dart** = ELF-SHOT 1; **-dock,** the Elecampane; **-fire,** *ignis fatuus*; **-knot** = ELF-LOCK; **-stone** = ELF-SHOT 2; **-wort** = *elf-dock.*

†**Elf,** *v. rare.* [f. ELF *sb.*] To tangle (hair) as an elf might do. *Lear* II. iii. 10.

Elfin (e·lfin). 1596. [f. ELF *sb.*, poss. suggested by ME. *elvene*, gen. pl. of *elf*, and infl. by *Elphin*, a character of Arthurian romance.] **A.** *adj.* Pertaining to elves; of elfish nature or origin. Also *transf.*

An e. storm from faery land KEATS.

B. *sb.* **1.** An ELF, or urchin 1596. †**2.** *Sc.* ?Elf-land –1802.

Elfish (e·lfiʃ), *a.* 1542. [f. ELF + -ISH[1].] Pertaining to elves; weird, spectral; tricksy, mischievous; †intractable.

The e. light COLERIDGE. Our e. rogue Myouk KANE.

Elf-lock. 1592. [f. ELF + LOCK *sb.*[1]] Hair tangled, *esp.* by Queen Mab: 'which it was not fortunate to disentangle' (Nares).

E·lf-shot. 1681. [f. ELF + SHOT *sb.*[1] Cf. G. *hexenschuss.*] **1.** Disease, supposed to be due to the agency of elves. **2.** A flint arrow-head, 'supposed to be shot by fairies at cattle' (Pennant) 1769.

Eliasite (ǐlǝi·ǎsǝit). 1852. [f. a mine called *Elias* at Joachimsthal + -ITE[1] 2b.] *Min.* Hydrous oxide of uranium, like gum in appearance.

†**Elicit** (ǐli·sit), *a.* 1624. [– L. *elicitus*, pa. pple. of *elicere*; see next.] *Philos.* Of an act: Evolved immediately from an active power or quality; opp. to *imperate* –1693.

Not..the..elicite acts of conscience, but the imperate, commanded and externall acts 1646.

Elicit (ǐli·sit), *v.* 1641. [– *elicit-*, pa. ppl. stem of L. *elicere* draw forth by trickery or magic, f. *e-* EX-[1] + *lacere* deceive.] **1.** *trans.* To draw forth (what is latent or potential). Also *fig.* **2.** To educe (principles, etc.) *from* data; to draw out (information), evoke (a response, etc.), *from* a person 1677.

1. They e...the innate sense of right and wrong J. H. NEWMAN. **2.** He could not e. a syllable from him on the subject 1822. So †**Eli·citate** *v.* (in same sense) HY. MORE. **Eli:cita·tion.** Hence †**Eli·citive** *a.* pertaining to, or of the nature of, elicit acts. **Eli·citor.**

Elide (ǐlǝi·d), *v.* 1593. [– L. *elidere* crush out, f. *e-* EX-[1] + *lædere* dash.] †**1.** *trans.* To destroy (the force of evidence) –1688. **2.** To strike out, suppress 1847. **3.** *Gram.* To omit (a vowel, or syllable) in pronunciation 1796.

3. Some sounds elided, others exaggerated 1851.

†**E·ligent.** 1670. [– *eligent-*, pres. ppl. stem of L. *eligere*; see -ENT.] = ELECTOR –1688.

Eligibility (e:lǐdʒibi·lǐti). 1650. [f. next; see -ITY. Cf. med.L. *eligibilitas* (XIV).] **1.** The quality of being eligible. **2.** *concr.* in *pl.* Eligible courses of action; qualities that render eligible 1660.

1. E. to a fellowship 1815.

Eligible (e·lǐdʒib'l), *a.* 1561. [– Fr. *éligible* – late L. *eligibilis*, f. *eligere* choose; see -IBLE.] **1.** Fit or proper to be chosen (for an office, etc.). †**2.** Subject to appointment by election –1739. **3.** That deserves to be chosen; desirable, suitable 1603. **b.** That is a matter of choice 1769. **4.** quasi-*sb.* in *pl.* Eligible persons or things 1844.

3. The most e. manner of doubling Cape Horn ANSON. E. property 1871. Hence **E·ligibly** *adv.*

Eliminant (ǐli·minǎnt). 1876. [– *eliminant-*, pres. ppl. stem of L. *eliminare*; see next, -ANT[1].] **A.** *adj.* Expulsive; throwing off by the excretions 1876. **B.** *sb. Math.* The result of eliminating *n* variables between *n* homogeneous equations of any degree 1881.

Eliminate (ǐli·mineit), *v.* 1568. [– *eliminat-*, pa. ppl. stem of L. *eliminare* thrust out of doors, expel, f. *e-* EX-[1] + *limen, limin-* threshold; see -ATE[3].] **1.** *trans.* To put out of doors, expel. Now *joc.* **2. a.** *Phys.* To get rid of (waste matter, etc.), *esp.* by excretion. **b.** *Chem.* To disengage, expel (a constituent). 1794. **3.** *gen.* To expel, get rid of 1714. **b.** *fig.* To treat as non-existent 1850. **4.** *Algebra* To get rid of (one or more quantities) from an equation 1845. ¶**5.** Incorrectly used for: To disengage, isolate, disentangle; hence, to elicit, deduce 1843.

3. To e. middle men and intermediate profits 1861, the supernatural 1871. *fig.* Eliminating him from the argument THACKERAY. **5.** The roots indeed e. nourishment from the soil 1872. Hence **Eli·minable** *a.* **Eli·minative** *a.* that eliminates or tends to e. (rare). **Eli·minator** *spec.* an apparatus which eliminates a battery by enabling a wireless set to be worked from a mains current.

Elimination (ǐli:minēi·ʃǝn). 1601. [f. prec.; see -ATION.] †**1.** The action of turning out of doors or expelling –1809. **2.** *gen.* Expulsion, casting out, getting rid of 1627. **3.** *Phys.* The process of throwing off (waste matter, etc.) from the tissues 1855. Also *transf.* and *fig.* **4.** *Algebra.* The act or process of eliminating (one or more quantities) from an equation or set of equations 1845. ¶**5.** *catachr.* (See ELIMINATE *v.* 5.) 1869.

†**Eli·nguate,** *v.* [– *elinguat-*, pa. ppl. stem of L. *elinguare*, f. *e-* EX-[1] + *lingua* tongue; see -ATE[3].] To deprive of the tongue. DAVIES.

†**Eli·ngued,** *a.* [f. L. *elinguare* (prec.) + -ED[1].] Deprived of the tongue; hence *fig.* speechless, dumb. FELTHAM.

Eliquate (e·likweit), *v.* 1621. [– *eliquat-*, pa. ppl. stem of L. *eliquare* (in late L. and med.L., liquefy, dissolve), f. *e-* EX-[1] + *liquare* melt, dissolve, liquefy; see -ATE[3].] †**1.** *trans.* **a.** To melt (by heat), fuse. **b.** To liquefy. **c.** To cause to flow freely. –1710. **2.** To separate by fusion, smelt 1879.

Eliquation (elikwēi·ʃǝn). 1651. [– late L. *eliquatio*, f. as prec.; see -ION.] †**1.** The action or process of liquefying; liquefaction –1757. **2.** *Metall.* The process of separating the different parts of ores or alloys by the different degrees of heat required to melt them 1753.

†**Eli·quidate,** *v. rare.* [See E- *pref.*] To make clear. HARINGTON.

Elision (ǐli·ʒǝn). 1581. [– late L. *elisio*, f. *elis-*, pa. ppl. stem of L. *elidere*; see ELIDE, -ION.] **1.** The action of dropping out or suppressing, as a letter or syllable in pronunciation, a passage in a book, etc. **2.** A breaking (so as to make a gap) by mechanical force 1760.

Phr. †*E. of the air*: a cutting, dividing, or attenuating of the air, formerly assigned as the cause of sound. Hence **Eli·sional** *a.* pertaining to e. (*rare*).

Elisor (e·lizǝr), *sb.* ME. [– OFr. *esliseor*, later *elisour*, f. *e(s)lis-*, stem of *esliser* choose, elect. See next.] †**1.** = ELECTOR –1529. **2.** *Law.* One of two persons appointed in certain cases to select a jury 1628.

‖**Élite** (eli·t), *sb.* 1823. [Fr., subst. use of fem. of pa. pple. †*e(s)lit* of *élire*, †*eslire* :– Rom. **exlegere*, for L. *eligere* ELECT.] The choice part or flower (of society, etc.).

The é. of the Russian nobility 1848.

Elixate (ǐli·k-, e·likseit), *v.* 1623. [– *elixat-*, pa. ppl. stem of L. *elixare* boil thoroughly; see -ATE[3].] **1.** To boil, seethe; to extract by boiling. **2.** To steep (in water); to macerate 1657. Hence **Elixation,** the action of seething; digestion.

†**Eli·xed,** *ppl. a. rare.* 1602. [f. L. *elixus* (cf. prec.) + -ED[1].] **a.** Boiled; hence, distilled. **b.** Macerated. –1666.

Elixir (ǐli·ksǝɹ), *sb.* ME. [– med.L. *elixir* (Roger Bacon) – Arab. *al-'iksir*, perh. f. *al* AL-[2] + Gr. ξηρίον desiccative powder for wounds, f. ξηρός dry.] **1.** *Alchemy.* A preparation by the use of which it was hoped to change the baser metals into gold. Occas. = 'the philosopher's stone'. Also *e-stone.* Also *transf.* and *fig.* **2.** A supposed drug or essence capable of indefinitely prolonging life. More fully, *E. of life* (tr. med.L. *elixir vitæ*). 1605. **3.** A strong extract or tincture. Now *Hist.* 1597. **b.** *fig.* The quintessence of a thing 1638.

2. To toy with magic, and pursue the e. of life DIXON. **3. b.** A pure elixar of mischief MILT. Hence †**Eli·xir** *v.* to distil as an e.; to work upon as by an e. (*rare*). Also *absol.* †**Eli·xirate** *v.* to distil; to refine, purify.

†**Elixi·viate,** *v. rare.* 1674. [f. E- *pref.* + LIXIVIATE.] *trans.* To clear from lixivium or lye; to refine –1756.

Elizabethan (ǐli:zǎbī·þǎn). 1817. [See -AN.] **A.** *adj.* Belonging to, or in the style of, the period of Queen Elizabeth; *esp.* of architecture, literature, etc.

B. *sb.* A poet, dramatist, statesman, etc., of the period of Queen Elizabeth 1881.

Elk[1] (elk). 1486. [prob. repr. OE. *elh, eolh,* with k for χ as in dial. *dwerk* (OE. *dweorh*) DWARF, *fark* (OE. *fearh*) FARROW *sb.*, *felk* (OE. *felh*) FELLOE, *selk* (OE. *seolh*) SEAL *sb.*[1]] **1.** The largest existing animal of the deer kind (*Alces malchis*). The American variety is also called MOOSE. **2.** Applied also to the 'Irish Elk', an extinct species of deer (*Cervus megaceros*); and to the Wapiti (*Cervus canadensis*) 1884. **3.** The ELAND or Cape-elk 1731.

Comb.: **e.-nut,** *Hamiltonia oleifera*; **-wood,** *Magnolia macrophylla.*

†**Elk**[2]. 1541. [Of unkn. origin.] A kind of yew, of which bows were made –1607.

†**Elk**[3] (elk). 1552. [Of unkn. origin.] The Wild Swan (*Cygnus ferus*). Also the Wild Goose (*Anas anser*). –1839.

Ell[1] (el). [OE. *eln* = OFris. (*i*)*elne*, OS. *elina*, MDu. *elne, elle* (Du. *el*), OHG. *elina* (G. *elle*), ON. *ǫln* (*aln-*), Goth. *aleina*, orig. 'arm', 'forearm', cogn. w. L. ULNA, Gr. ὠλένη ELBOW. For *ll* from *ln* cf. dial. *kill* KILN, MILL *sb.*[1]] **1.** A measure of length varying in different countries. The English ell = 45 in.; the Scotch = 37.2 in.; the Flemish = 27 in. Now only *Hist.* †**2.** = ELL-WAND –1768.

Ell[2] (el). *dial.* and *U.S.* 1875. [var. of *ele* AISLE.] = L (the letter) I. 1a.

Ellagic (elæ·dʒik). 1810. [– Fr. *ellagique*, f. *ellag*, anagram of *galle* gall-nut; see -IC. Cf. GALLIC *a.*[2]] In *e. acid*: $C_{14}H_8O_9$; orig. obtained from oak-galls; found also in bezoar, whence called also *bezoartic acid.* Hence **E·llagate,** a salt of ellagic acid.

†**E·llan.** 1613. [Earlier *elan* – Fr. *élan* – G. *elend*; see ELAND.] The Elk –1682.

Ellebore, -bory, obs. ff. HELLEBORE.

Elleck (e·lěk). 1862. [Of unkn. origin.] A fish: the Red Gurnard, *Trigla cuculus.*

†**Ellinge,** var. of ELENGE *a.*

Ellipse (eli·ps). 1753. [– Fr. *ellipse* – L. *ellipsis* – Gr. ἔλλειψις; see next.] **1.** A plane closed curve in which the sum of the distances of any point from the two foci is a constant quantity. **2.** *transf.* An object or figure bounded by an ellipse. Also *fig.* 1857. **3.** *Gram.* = ELLIPSIS 2 (*rare*) 1843.

1. The dark Earth follows wheel'd in her e. TENNYSON.

‖**Ellipsis** (eli·psis). Pl. **ellipses** (-siz). 1570. [– L. *ellipsis* (Quintilian) – Gr. ἔλλειψις defect, ellipse, grammatical ellipsis, f. ἐλλείπειν leave out, fall short, fail, f. ἐν IN + λείπειν leave.] **1.** = ELLIPSE 1, 2. Now *rare.* **2.** *Gram.* The omission of one or more words in a sentence, which would be needed to express the sense completely; *concr.* an instance of this 1612. †**3.** Formerly applied to the dash (—) as indicating the omission of letters in a word 1824.

Ellipsograph (eli·psǒgrɑf). [f. ELLIPSE + -GRAPH.] An instrument for describing ellipses.

Ellipsoid (eli·psoid). 1721. [f. as prec. + -OID.]

A. *sb.* A solid of which all the plane sections through one of the axes are ellipses, and all other sections ellipses or circles.

Phr. *E. of revolution*: a solid generated by the revolution of an e. round one of its axes.

B. *adj.* Having the nature or shape of an ellipse 1861. So **Ellipsoi·dal** *a.*

Elliptic (eli·ptik). 1726. [– Gr. ἐλλειπτικός defective, f. ἐλλείπειν; see ELLIPSIS, -IC.] **1.** That has the form of an ellipse; pertaining to ellipses. **2.** *Gram.* Characterized by ELLIPSIS (sense 2).

1. *E. chuck*: a chuck for oval or elliptic turning. *E. compass(es*: an instrument for drawing ellipses. *E. integrals* (Math.): a class of integrals discovered by Legendre in 1786, as the result of the investigation of e. arcs. *E. functions* (Math.): certain specific functions of e. integrals.

Comb., as *e.-lanceolate, a.*, etc., having a form intermediate between e. and lanceolate, etc.

Hence **Elli·ptical** *a.* **Elli·ptically** *adv.*

Ellipticity (elipti·sĭti). 1753. [f. prec. + -ITY.] Elliptic form; degree of deviation (of an orbit, etc.) from circularity, (of a spheroid) from sphericity.

The e. of the earth..has been found to be 1/299 BREWSTER.

Elliptograph. = ELLIPSOGRAPH.

‖**Ellops** (e·lǫps). *Obs.* in actual use. 1601. [– Gr. ἔλλοψ or ἔλοψ.] **1.** A kind of serpent. MILT. *P. L.* x. 526. **2.** A kind of fish mentioned by ancient writers 1601.

Ell-wand (e·lwǫnd). Chiefly *Sc.* and *n. dial.* ME. [f. ELL + WAND.] **1.** An ell-measure: sometimes used for 'yard-measure' 1500. †**2.** = ULNA. ME. only. **3.** *Sc.* The group of stars called Orion's Belt 1513.

Elm (elm). [OE. *elm*, corresp. to MLG., OHG. *elm(boum, elmo* (MHG. *elme, ilme*, G. dial. *ilm*), and, with vowel variation, ON. *álmr* (Sw., Norw. *alm*), L. *ulmus*.] **1.** Any of the trees belonging to the genus *Ulmus, esp.*, in England, *Ulmus campestris*; in Scotland, *Ulmus montana* or *Ulmus suberosa*; in U.S. the White Elm (*Ulmus americana*) OE. **2.** The wood of these trees 1823.

1. The E. delights in a sound, sweet and fertile Land EVELYN. *Comb.*, chiefly *attrib.*, as *e.-tree*, *-wood*, etc.; **e.-balm**, the fluid contained in elm-galls; **-gall**, that produced on elms by the puncture of *Aphis ulmi*. Hence **E·lmen** *a.* (now *arch.*), of or pertaining to elms or elm-wood. **E·lmy** *a.* consisting of or abounding in elms.

†**Elne, e·llen,** *sb.* [OE. *eilen*, corresp. to OS. *ellian*, OHG. *ellen, -ian*, Goth. *aljan*, and (str. fem.) ON. *eljan*.] Strength, courage (also, in OE., zeal). So †**E·lne** *v.* to strengthen, comfort.

†**Eloca·tion.** *rare.* 1619. [f. specific application of L. *elocare* hire out, lease, f. *e-* EX-[1] + *locare* place, let or hire. Cf. LOCATION, LOCATE.] **1.** Removal from a person's control. BP. HALL. **2.** *fig.* Alienation (of mind).

Elocular (ĭlǫ·kiŭlăɹ), *a.* 1864. [f. E- + LOCULUS 2 + -AR[1].] *Bot.* Without partitions or separate cells.

Elocution (elŏkiū·ʃən). 1509. [– L. *elocutio*, f. *elocut-*, pa. ppl. stem of *eloqui* speak out; see ELOQUENT, -ION.] †**1.** Oratorical or literary expression; literary style as dist. from matter –1844. †**2.** Eloquence, oratory; in *pl.* harangues –1791. **3.** Oral utterance 1623. **4.** The art of public speaking as regards delivery, pronunciation, tones, and gestures; manner or style of oral delivery. [= L. *pronuntiatio.*] Also *attrib.* 1613.

1. Elocucion is an appliyng of apte wordes and sentences to the matter 1553. **2.** Both e. and address in arms COWPER. **3.** Whose taste..Gave e. to the mute MILT. *P. L.* IX. 747. **4.** True theatrical e. CIBBER. Hence **Elocu·tionary** *a.* of or pertaining to e. **Elocu·tionist**, a master of e.

Elocutive (ĭlǫ·kiŭtiv), *a.* 1627. [f. as prec. + -IVE.] Pertaining to utterance or eloquence. FELTHAM.

Elo·ge. 1566. [– Fr. *éloge* – L. *elogium*; see next.] †**1.** An encomium –1802. **2.** A funeral oration; a discourse in honour of a deceased person 1725.

2. Pronouncing the E. of his old master into whose place he now ascends 1861. So †**E·logist,** one who pronounces an e.

†‖**Elo·gium.** 1570. [L., = short saying or formula, epitaph, altered – Gr. ἐλεγεῖον ELEGY; app. confused with EULOGIUM, EULOGY.] = next –1789.

†**E·logy.** 1605. [Anglicized f. prec.] **1.** An explanatory inscription, *e.g.* on a tombstone –1663. **2.** A characterization; *esp.* a eulogy –1740. **3.** A biographical notice –1652. **4.** A funeral oration –1689.

‖**Elohim** (elōᵘ·him, -hĭm)). 1605. [Heb. *'ĕlōhîm*; = 'gods', but often construed as sing.] One of the Hebrew names of God, or of the gods. Hence **Elohi·mic** *a.* using the word *Elohim* instead of *Yahveh* (*rare*).

Elohist (elōᵘ·hist). 1862. [f. ELOH(IM + -IST.] A name for the author (or authors) of those parts of the Hexateuch in which *Elohim* is used as the name of God instead of *Yahveh* (pop. *Jehovah*). Hence **Elohi·stic** *a.* of or pertaining to the E.; using ELOHIM instead of *Yahveh*.

Eloin, eloign (ĭloi·n), *v.* 1535. [– OFr. *esloignier* (mod. *éloigner*) :– Rom. **exlongiare*, for late L. *elongare*; see next.] †**1.** To remove to a distance (*lit.* and *fig.*) –1692. **2.** *Law.* To convey or remove out of the jurisdiction 1558. **3.** To remove, carry off (property) 1622.

1. From worldly cares himselfe he did esloyne SPENSER *F. Q.* I. iv. 20. **2.** The sheriff may return that he is eloigned BLACKSTONE. Hence **Eloi·ner** (*Law*). †**Eloi·nment, eloi·gnment**, distance; removal to a distance.

†**Elo·ng,** *v.* ME. [– late L. *elongare* remove, withdraw, prolong, f. *e-* EX-[1] + *longē* far off, *longus* long.] **1.** *trans.* To make longer; to retard –1610. **2.** To remove, separate *from.* Also *fig.* –1609.

Elongate (ī·lǫŋgeᶦt, ĭlǫ·ŋgeᶦt), *v.* 1540. [– *elongat-*, pa. ppl. stem of late L. *elongare*; see prec., -ATE[3].] †**1.** *trans.* and *intr.* To remove *from* –1656. **2.** *Astron.* (*intr.*) To recede apparently from the sun; said, *e.g.* of a star or planet 1646. **3.** *trans.* To lengthen, prolong 1578. **4.** *Bot.* (*intr.*) To grow in length; to be lengthy 1801.

Elongate (ĭlǫ·ngĕt), *a.* 1828. [f. late L. *elongatus*, pa. pple. of *elongare*; see prec., -ATE[2].] Lengthened, extended; *esp.* in *Bot.* and *Zool.* long in proportion to its breadth.

Lip e...narrowing towards the point STARK. Hence **E·longato-**, comb. form, as in **e.-conical, -ovate, -triangular** *adjs.*, having the form of a lengthened cone, egg, triangle.

Elongation (ĭlongēᶦ·ʃən). ME. [– late L. *elongatio*, f. *elongat-*; see ELONGATE *v.*, -ION.] **1.** *Astron.* The angular distance of a planet from the sun, or of a satellite from its primary. †**2.** Removal to a distance; hence, remoteness; also *fig.* –1787. **3.** The action or process of elongating 1731. **4.** *Surg.* **a.** An imperfect luxation, when the ligaments are lengthened, but the bone is not displaced 1676. **b.** 'The extension of a limb for the purpose of reducing a dislocation' (*Syd. Soc. Lex.*). **5.** The state of being elongated; that which is elongated 1751.

2. His e. and further removal from Court 1654. **3.** E. of the boughs on the lee side 1828. **5.** The e. of the image WHEWELL.

Elope (ĭlōᵘ·p), *v.* 1596. [– AFr. *aloper*, perh. f. ME. **alope(n*, pa. pple. of **alepe* run away, f. A- *pref.* 1 + LEAP *v.*] **1. a.** *Law.* Of a wife: To run away from her husband with a paramour. **b.** More frequently said of a woman running away from home with a lover for the purpose of being married. 1628. **2.** *gen.* To run away, abscond 1596. Also *transf.* and *fig.*

1. If the wife e. from her husband she shall lose her dower COKE. We..must e. methodically, madam GOLDSM. Hence **Elo·per.**

Elopement (ĭlōᵘ·pmĕnt). 1641. [f. prec. + -MENT. Cf. AFr. *alopement*.] The action of eloping (see ELOPE *v.*).

‖**Elops** (ī·lǫps). [mod.L. – Gr. ἔλοψ; see also ELLOPS.] *Zool.* A genus of fishes of the Herring family.

Eloquence (e·lŏkwĕns). ME. [– (O)Fr. *éloquence* – L. *eloquentia*, f. as next; see -ENCE.] **1.** The action, practice, or art of speaking or writing with fluency, force, and appropriateness, so as to appeal to the reason or move the feelings. Also *fig.* †**2.** Verbal expression in general –1659. **3.** The quality of being eloquent ME. **4.** = RHETORIC 1623.

1. His e. was irresistibly impressive GROTE. *fig.* Her tears her only e. S. ROGERS. **3.** A Scantling of Jacks great e. SWIFT. So †**E·loquency** (in sense 3).

Eloquent (e·lŏkwĕnt), *a.* ME. [– (O)Fr. *éloquent* – L. *eloquent-*, pres. ppl. stem of *eloqui* speak out, f. *e-* EX-[1] + *loqui* speak; see -ENT.] **1.** Of persons: Possessing or exercising the power of fluent, forcible, and appropriate expression. Also *transf.* and *fig.* **2.** Of utterances or style: Characterized by forcible and appropriate expression ME.

1. E. speakers are enclined to Ambition HOBBES. *fig.* Her dark eyes—how e. S. ROGERS. Hence **E·loquently** *adv.* So †**Elo·quious** *a.* (*rare*).

Eloquential (elŏkwe·nʃăl), *a. rare.* 1711. [f. L. *eloquentia* ELOQUENCE + -AL[1].] Pertaining to eloquence; rhetorical.

Elrage, -aige, -ich, -itch, var. ff. ELDRITCH.

Elroquite (elrǫ·kəit). 1882. [f. *El Roque*, name of an island in the Caribbean Sea + -ITE[1] 2b.] *Min.* An apple-green to grey silicate of aluminium and iron.

-els, *suffix*, common in OE. See -LE.

Else (els), *adv.* [OE. *elles* = OFris. *elles, -is*, MDu. *els*, OHG. *elles, alles*, OSw. *äljes* (Sw. *eljest*), gen. sing., corresp. to Goth. *aljis*, of Gmc. **aljaz*, cogn. w. L. *alius*, Gr. ἄλλος.] **1.** A synonym of *other*, used with pronominal words or phrases, which in mod. use it follows. Also inflected, as in *somebody else's*, etc. (*colloq.*). **2.** = 'in (some, any, what, etc.) other manner, place, or time' ME. †**3.** By other means –1471; = *elsewhither* –1591. **4.** In another case; otherwise; if not; also preceded by *or* OE. **b.** *idiomatically.* = 'If it is not believed'. Now *rare* or *dial.* 1590. †**5.** quasi-*conj.* If only, provided that, so long as. (Cf. Ger. *anders.*) ME. only.

1. Shall he nede any thynge elles 1532. What do they e., but scrape and scramble..for these things BARROW. **2.** Here more than anywhere e. MORLEY. **3.** *Two Gent.* IV. ii. 125. **4.** E. how should any one be saved J. H. NEWMAN. Speak fair words, or e. be mute SHAKS.

Hence †**Elsewhat** *pron.* something or anything else.

Elsewhere (e·lsˌhwēᵊ·ɹ), *adv.* OE. [f. ELSE + WHERE.] **1.** At some other point; in some other place. **2.** = next 1513.

1. Here as well as e. SCOTT. **2.** If used ill..we go e. GOLDSM.

Elsewhither, *adv. ? arch.* OE. [f. ELSE + WHITHER.] To some other place, in some other direction; †whithersoever.

Send to the town or e. to buy bread 1616. The dusty fugitives must shrink e. CARLYLE.

Elsewise (e·lsˌwəiz), *adv.* 1548. [See WISE *sb*[1].] Otherwise.

Elsin (e·lsin). Now *n. dial.* ME. [app. – MDu. *elsen(e* (Du. *els*) :– Gmc. **alisno*, etc., f. same base as AWL.] An awl.

†**Elu·cid,** *a.* [f. E- + LUCID.] That gives out light. BOYLE.

Elucidate (ĭlᶦū·sideᶦt), *v.* 1568. [– *elucidat-*, pa. ppl. stem of late L. *elucidare*, f. *e-* EX-[1] + *lucidus* LUCID; see -ATE[3].] To render lucid; now only *fig.* to throw light upon, explain. Also *absol.*

The merit of elucidating the text MACAULAY. Hence **Elu·cidative** *a.* tending to e. **Elu·cidator. Elu·cidato:ry** *a.* that elucidates or tends to e.

Elucidation (ĭlᶦū:sidēᶦ·ʃən). 1570. [– med.L. *elucidatio*, f. as prec.; see -ION.] **1.** The action or process of elucidating. **2.** That which serves to elucidate; an explanation, demonstration, illustration 1667.

1. Documents..and the notes..added for their e. FROUDE.

†**Elu·ctate,** *v.* [– *eluctat-*, pa. ppl. stem of L. *eluctari* struggle out, f. *e-* EX-[1] + *luctari* struggle.] To struggle forth. HACKET.

†**Elucta·tion.** 1627. [– late L. *eluctatio*, f. as prec.; see -ION.] The action of struggling forth; *fig.* escape through struggle –1682.

†**Elu·cubrate,** *v.* 1623. [– *elucubrat-*, pa. ppl. stem of L. *elucubrare* compose by lamp-light.] To produce by the use of midnight oil –1656. Hence †**Elu·cubrator.**

Elucubration (ĭlᶦū:kiubrēᶦ·ʃən). 1643. [– late L. *elucubratio*, f. as prec.; see -ION.] †**1.** The action of composing by candle-light –1697. **2.** *concr.* Any literary composition 1664.

Elude (ĭlᶦū·d), *v.* 1538. [– L. *eludere*, f. *e-* EX-[1] + *ludere* play.] †**1.** To befool; also, to baffle –1656. **2.** *trans.* To escape by dexterity or stratagem 1634. **3.** To evade compliance with or fulfilment of 1651. **4.** To escape adroitly from; to evade 1667.

2. The wary Trojan, bending from the blow Eludes the death POPE. To e. an argument D'ISRAELI. **3.** To e. a Treaty STEELE, the obligation of an oath 1769. **4.** The glittering gem.. ever eludes the grasp 1859. Hence **Elu·der. Elu·dible** *a.*

E·lul. [Heb.] The 6th month of the Heb. sacred, the 12th of the civil year, nearly = September.

Elumbated (ĭlɒ·mbeˈtėd), *ppl. a.* Now only *joc.* 1731. [f. L. *elumbis* (f. *e-* Ex-¹ + *lumbus* loin) + -ATE³ + -ED¹.] Weakened in the loins.

Elusion (ĭlˈū·ʒən). 1550. [– late L. *elusio* deception, trickery, f. *elus-*, pa. ppl. stem of L. *eludere*; see ELUDE, -ION.] †**1.** The action of befooling; *concr.* an illusion –1695. **2.** The action of escaping dexterously from, evading (now *rare*) 1624; *absol.* †an evasion; †evasiveness 1617.

Elusive (ĭlˈū·siv), *a.* 1719. [f. as prec. + -IVE.] That eludes or seeks to elude; also *fig.* *fig.* Guérin's e., undulating, impalpable nature M. ARNOLD. Hence **Elu·sive-ly** *adv.*, **-ness.**

Elusory (ĭlˈū·səri), *a.* 1646. [– med.L. *elusorius*, f. as prec.; see -ORY².] Tending to elude; evasive; deceptive.
E. tergiversations 1646. An e. problem 1856.

†**Elu·te,** *v.* 1731. [– *elut-*, pa. ppl. stem of L. *eluere*, f. *e-* Ex-¹ + *luere* wash.] To wash out, cleanse.

Elution (ĭlˈū·ʃən). 1612. [– late L. *elutio*, f. as prec.; see -ION.] *Chem.* Washing from impurity.
All these starches are prepared by e. 1870.

Elutriate (ĭlˈū·tri,eˈt), *v.* 1731. [– *elutriat-*, pa. ppl. stem of L. *elutriare* wash out; see -ATE³.] *trans.* To decant; to purify by straining; in *Chem.* to separate the lighter from the heavier particles of a mixture by washing.
Hence **Elu:tria·tion,** the action of elutriating.

‖**Eluvies** (ĭlˈū·vi,ĭz). 1710. [L., = a washing away of impurities, f. *eluere*; see ELUTE.] **a.** 'The humour discharged in leucorrhœa; an inordinate discharge of any kind'. **b.** 'The effluvium from a swampy place' (Hooper).

Eluvium (ĭlˈū·viŏm). 1882. [mod.L., f. *e* + *luere*, after ALLUVIUM.] *Geol.* Accumulations of débris whether atmospheric or carried by wind-drift. Hence **Elu·vial** *a.* pertaining to, or of the nature of, e.

Eluxate (ĭlɒ·kseˈt), *v.* 1731. [f. E- + LUXATE *v.*] To put out of joint. Hence **Eluxa·tion.**

Elvan (e·lvăn). 1791. [Referred to Corn. *elven* spark.] **1.** The Cornish name for intrusive rocks of igneous origin, such as quartz-porphyry, whinstone, etc. Also *attrib.* **2.** A dike of this rock. MURCHISON. Hence **E·lvanite** (*Min.*) = ELVAN. **Elvani·tic** *a.*

Elve, obs. var. of ELF.

Elver (e·lvəɹ). 1640. [var. of *eelvare*, southern form of EEL-FARE.] A young eel, *esp.* a young conger or sea-eel.

Elves, pl. of ELF.

Elvish (e·lviʃ), *a.* ME. [f. ELF + -ISH¹.] **1.** Of or pertaining to elves; supernatural, weird. **2.** Elf-like in behaviour: †**a.** Spiteful. **b.** Tricksy (cf. ELFISH). ME.
2. He semeth eluyssh by his contenance CHAUCER.

†**Ely·chnious,** *a.* [f. Gr. ἐλλύχνιον lampwick + -OUS.] Of the nature of a wick. SIR T. BROWNE.

Elysian (ĭli·ziăn, -ʒiăn), *a.* 1579. [f. ELYSIUM + -AN.]
A. 1. Of or pertaining to Elysium. **2.** *fig.* Of the nature of, or resembling, what is in Elysium; beatific, glorious 1750.
1. E. joys MASSINGER. Phr. *E. fields* = ELYSIUM 1.
B. as *sb.* = ELYSIUM. Marlowe.

Elysium (ĭli·ziŏm, -ʒiŏm). 1599. [– L. *Elysium* – Gr. Ἠλύσιον (sc. πεδίον plain).] **1.** The abode assigned to the blessed after death in Greek mythology. Also *transf.* of other states of the departed. **2.** *fig.* A place or state of ideal happiness 1599.
2. The wretched Slaue all Night sleepes in Elizium *Hen. V*, IV. i. 291.

Elytriform (eli·trifǭɹm), *a.* 1835. [f. as next + -FORM.] That has the form of elytra.

Elytrigerous (elitri·ʒĕrəs), *a.* 1877. [f. *elytri-*, comb. f. ELYTRUM + -GEROUS.] That has or bears elytra.

Elytrin (e·litrin). [f. ELYTRON + -IN¹.] 'The form of chitin which composes the elytra of insects' (*Syd. Soc. Lex.*).

Elytroid (e·litroid), *a.* 1864. [– Gr. ἐλυτροειδής; see next, -OID.] Resembling an elytron, sheath-like.

Elytron (e·litrǫn). Pl. **elytra.** 1774. [– Gr. ἔλυτρον a sheath.] **1.** The outer hard wing-case of a coleopterous insect. **2.** One of the shield-like dorsal plates of some annelids 1841. **3.** 'A term for the vagina' (*Syd. Soc. Lex.*).

E·lytrum. 1816. [mod.L. – prec.] = ELYTRON.

Elzevir (e·lzĭvəɹ). 1710. **1.** The name (properly *Elzevier*, latinized *Elzevirius*) of a family of printers at Amsterdam, Leyden, etc. (1592–1680), famous chiefly for their editions of the classics. Used *attrib.* or as *adj.*, *e.g.* in *E. edition*; also formerly applied to books published in the style of the Elzeviers. Also *absol.* a book printed by one of them. **2. E. letter, type. a.** The style of type of the small Elzevir editions of the classics. **b.** Now used for a special type—ELZEVIR TYPE.
Hence **Elzevi·rian** *a.* of or pertaining to the Elzeviers; published by or in the style of the Elzeviers; quasi-*sb.* one who collects or fancies E. editions.

Em (em). The name of the letter M. In *Printing*, the square of the type 'm', used as the unit for measuring the amount of printed matter in a line, page, etc.

'Em (əm), *pron.* ME. Orig. a form of HEM, dat. and accus. 3rd pers. pl. Now regarded as an abbrev. of *them.* Still in colloq. use.

Em-, *prefix*, the form taken by EN-¹,², bef. *b*, *p*, and (frequently) *m*. Nearly all the Eng. words with this prefix have (or have had) alternative forms with IM-¹. Hence:
1. Transitive vbs. **a.** f. *em-* + sb., as **empanoply,** to array in complete armour; etc. **b.** f. *em-* + sb. or adj., as **embeggar,** to bring into a state of beggary; etc. **2.** Verbs f. *em-* + verb, with intensive force, as †**embias. 3.** Ppl. adjs. f. *em-* + sb. + *-ed*, as **embastioned,** etc.

†**Ema·cerate,** *v. rare.* 1610. [– L. *emaceratus*, f. *e-* intensive + *maceratus*, pa. pple. of *macerare*; see MACERATE.] *trans.* = EMACIATE *v.* –1669. Hence †**Ema:cera·tion. a.** = EMACIATION. **b.** = MACERATION.

Emaciate (ĭmēˈ·ʃi,ĕt), *ppl. a.* 1675. [– L. *emaciatus*, pa. pple. of *emaciare*; see next, -ATE².] Emaciated.

Emaciate (ĭmēˈ·ʃi,eˈt), *v.* 1646. [– *emaciat-*, pa. ppl. stem of L. *emaciare*, f. *e-* Ex-¹ + *macies* leanness; see MACERATE, -ATE³.] To make or †become lean or wasted in flesh.
Consumption may e. the dimpled cheeks HERVEY. Hence **Ema·ciated** *ppl. a.* made lean, atrophied; also *fig.* **Ema:cia·tion,** the action of emaciating; emaciated state.

†**Ema·culate,** *v.* 1623. [– *emaculat-*, pa. ppl. stem of L. *emaculare* clear from spots, f. *e-* Ex-¹ + *macula* spot.] *trans.* To free from spots or blemishes, emend –1656.

†**Emai·led,** *ppl. a.* 1480. [app. f. OFr. *emaillié* (mod. *émaillé*) enamelled + -ED¹; see ENAMEL.] ? Embossed (with a raised pattern).

Emanant (e·mănănt), *ppl. a. arch.* 1614. [– *emanant-*, pres. ppl. stem of L. *emanare*; see next, -ANT.] That emanates or issues from a source.
Filling eminent places, with e. poisons 1614.

Emanate (e·măneˈt), *v.* 1788. [– *emanat-*, pa. ppl. stem of L. *emanare*, f. *e-* Ex-¹ + *manare* flow.] **1.** *intr.* To flow forth, issue *from*, as a source. **2.** To flow forth, issue, originate, from a source 1818. **3.** *trans.* To emit, send out (*lit.* and *fig.*) (*rare*) 1797.
1. His destruction..emanating from himself LAMB. **2.** Fissures..from which mephitic vapours emanated LYELL.

Emanation (emănēˈ·ʃən). 1570. [– late L. *emanatio*, f. as prec.; see -ION.] **1.** The process of flowing forth, issuing, or proceeding from as a source (*lit.* and *fig.*). **b.** The action of emitting. Cf. EMANATE *v.* 3. 1742. **2.** That which emanates; an efflux; *spec.* a beam, flash, ray of light 1646. Also *fig.* **3.** A person or thing produced by emanation from the Divine Essence 1650.
1. The E. of the Son BP. BURNET. The pantheistic doctrine of e. 1880. **2.** The powerful emanations of the loadstone GOLDSM. Gaseous emanations 1836. A direct e..from the first principles of morals MILL.
Hence **Emana·tional** *a.* pertaining to the theory of e., as dist. from creation.

E·manatist. *rare.* 1838. [f. EMANATION + -IST.] A believer in EMANATION. Hence **E:manati·stic** *a.*

Emanative (e·mănetiv), *a.* 1651. [f. as prec. + -IVE.] **1.** Tending to emanate (see EMANATE *v.* 1–3); of the nature of an emanation; due to emanation. **2.** Relating to or connected with the theory of EMANATION 1839. Hence **E·manatively** *adv.*

Emanatory (e·mănătəːri), *a.* 1659. [f. as prec. + -ORY².] **a.** Derivative. **b.** Pertaining to the theory of EMANATION.

Emancipate (ĭmæ·nsipĕt), *ppl. a.* 1605. [– L. *emancipatus*, pa. pple. of *emancipare*; see next, -ATE².] = EMANCIPATED. Now usu. *poet.*

Emancipate (ĭmæ·nsipeˈt), *v.* 1625. [– *emancipat-*, pa. ppl. stem of L. *emancipare*, f. *e-* Ex-¹ + *mancipium*; see -ATE³.] **1.** *trans.* In *Rom. Law*: To set free (a child or wife) from the *patria potestas* 1651. **2.** *gen.* To set free from control; to release from civil, moral, or intellectual restraint 1625. Also *transf.* and *fig.* †**3.** To deliver into subjection; to enslave (because emancipation in Rom. Law was effected by fictitious sale) –1752.
1. The Son discharged from Paternal Power is emancipated MAINE. **2.** Emancipated from our civil disabilities HT. MARTINEAU. Emancipated from modern Puritanism KINGSLEY. Hence **Ema·ncipative** *a.* that has the property of emancipating. **Ema·ncipator,** one who emancipates (*lit.* and *fig.*). **Ema·ncipato:ry** *a.* that has the function or the effect of emancipating.

Emancipation (ĭmæːnsipēˈ·ʃən). 1631. [– L. *emancipatio*, f. as prec.; see -ION. Cf. (O)Fr. *émancipation.*] **1.** *Rom. Law.* The action of setting free from the *patria potestas* 1651. **2.** The action of setting free from slavery; and hence, generally, from civil disabilities 1797. Also *transf.* and *fig.* of intellectual, moral, or spiritual fetters 1631.
2. The e. of the Catholicks BURKE. The national e. from superstition WARTON.
Hence **Ema:ncipa·tionist,** an advocate of the e. of any class, *esp.* of slaves.

Emancipist (ĭmæ·nsipist). *Australian.* 1834. [f. EMANCIPATE + -IST.] An ex-convict, who has served his term.

Emandibulate (īmændi·biŭlĕt), *ppl. a.* 1826. [f. E- + MANDIBULATE *a.*] *Entom.* Destitute of mandibles.

†**Ema·ne,** *v.* 1656. [– (O)Fr. *émaner* or L. *emanare*; see EMANATE.] = EMANATE *v.* –1817.

Emarcid (ĭmā·ɹsid), *a.* 1661. [– med.L. *emarcidus*, f. *e-* Ex-¹ intensive + L. *marcidus*; see MARCID.] †**1.** Drooping, limp (*rare*). **2.** *Bot.* Withered, flaccid, wilted. (Dicts.).

Emarginate (ĭmā·ɹdʒinĕt), *a.* 1794. [– L. *emarginatus*, pa. pple. of *emarginare*; see next, -ATE².] **1.** Notched at the margin, as a leaf, shell, etc. **2.** *Crystall.* Having the edges of the primitive form cut off.

Emarginate (ĭmā·ɹdʒineˈt), *v.* 1656. [– *emarginat-*, pa. ppl. stem of L. *emarginare* remove the edge of, f. *e-* Ex-¹ + *margo*, *margin-* edge, border; see -ATE³.] **1.** *trans.* To remove the margin of. **2.** *Optics.* Of the effects of unequal refraction: To double the contour lines of (an object embedded, *e.g.* in a jelly) 1881. Hence **Ema:rgina·tion,** the state of being emarginate.

Emasculate (ĭmæ·skiŭlĕt), *a.* (quasi-*sb.*) 1622. [– L. *emasculatus*, pa. pple. of *emasculare*; see next, -ATE².] Emasculated.

Emasculate (ĭmæ·skiŭleˈt), *v.* 1607. [– *emasculat-*, pa. ppl. stem of L. *emasculare* castrate, f. *e-* Ex-¹ + *masculus* male; see -ATE³.] **1.** *trans.* To deprive of virility, to castrate 1623. **2.** *transf.* and *fig.* To deprive of strength and vigour; to weaken, make effeminate; to enfeeble 1607. **b.** *esp.* To take the vigour out of (literary compositions) by removing what is indecorous 1756. †**3.** To turn woman. SIR T. BROWNE.
2. b. I..consented to e. my poems KINGSLEY. Hence **Ema·sculator.** (Dicts). **Ema·sculato:ry** *a.* that tends to emasculation.

Emasculation (ĭmæːskiŭlēˈ·ʃən). 1623. [f. prec.; see -ATION.] **1.** The action of depriving of virility; the state of impotence. **2.** *fig.* The depriving of masculine vigour; prudish expurgation of a literary work 1654.

Embace, obs. var. of EMBASE.

Embale (embēⁱ·l), *v.* 1727. [f. EM- + BALE *sb.*[3] Cf. (O)Fr. *emballer.*] To do up into bales; also *fig.* So †**Emba·ll** *v.*[1] HAKLUYT.

Emball (embǭ·l), *v.*[2] 1580. [f. EM- + BALL *sb.*[1]] **1.** *trans.* To encompass with a sphere. **2.** To invest with the ball as an emblem of royalty. (Or ? indecent.) *Hen. VIII,* II. iii. 47.

Embalm (embā·m), *v.* [ME. *embaume* – (O)Fr. *embaumer,* f. *en-* EM- + *baume* BALM *sb.*] **1.** To impregnate (a dead body) with spices, to preserve it from decay. **2.** *fig.* To preserve from oblivion; to keep in honoured remembrance 1675. **3.** †**a.** To anoint with aromatic spices, oil, etc. **b.** To make balmy. ME.

1. They imbalmed him and he was put in a coffin in Egypt *Gen.* 50: 26. **2.** That..elegance of language in which he has embalmed so many BOSWELL. **3.** The buxom air, imbalm'd with odours MILT. *P. L.* II. 842. Hence **Emba·lmer,** he who or that which embalms; *esp.* one who embalms dead bodies. **Emba·lmment,** the act of embalming; a preparation used for this.

Embank (embæ·ŋk), *v.* Also **im-.** 1649. [f. EM- + earlier synon. BANK *v.*[1]] **1.** *trans.* To enclose, confine, or protect by banks 1700. †**2.** *intr.* Of a ship: To run aground 1649. **3.** To cover with embankments 1872.

Embankment[1] (embæ·ŋkmĕnt). 1786. [f. prec. + -MENT.] **1.** The action of embanking 1874. **2.** A mound, bank, or the like, for confining a river, etc., within bounds 1786. **3.** A long earthen bank or mound 1810.

3. A vast e., over which the canal is carried 1810.

†**Emba·nkment**[2]. *rare.* 1813. [f. EM- + BANK *sb.*[3] + -MENT.] A banking speculation; a bank account.

‖**Embaphium** (embæ·fiŏm). 1715. [mod. L. – Gr. ἐμβάφιον, f. ἐμβάπτειν dip in.] *Med.* A small vessel in which food or medicine is put or measured, or in which it is dipped.

Embar (embā·ɹ), *v.* 1480. [– (O)Fr. *embarrer,* f. *em-* EM- + *barrer* BAR *v.*] **1.** *trans.* To enclose within bars; to imprison. Also *fig.* (*arch.*) 1594. **2.** To arrest, stop; to interrupt. ? *Obs.* 1577. †**b.** *Law.* = BAR *v.* 5 –1599. †**3.** To debar *from* an action –1603. †**4.** To lay under embargo –1649. †**5.** To break in the bars of (a helmet). CAXTON.

1. Fast embar'd in mighty brazen wall SPENSER *F. Q.* I. vii. 44. **2.** To e. all farther trade for the future BACON. Hence †**Emba·rment.**

‖**Embarcade·ro.** *rare.* 1850. [Sp., f. *embarcar* embark.] A wharf, quay.

Embarcation, var. of EMBARKATION.

†**Emba·rge,** *sb.* 1574. [– Sp. *embargo*; see EMBARGO *sb.*] = EMBARGO –1656.

†**Emba·rge,** *v.* 1600. [f. prec. sb.] *trans.* To lay under an embargo; to sequestrate; to arrest –1657. Hence †**Emba·rgement.**

Embargo (embā·ɹgo), *sb.* 1602. [– Sp. *embargo,* f. *embargar* arrest, impede :– Rom. **imbarricare,* f. L. *in-* IM-[1], EM- + *barra* BAR *sb.*[1]] **1.** A prohibitory order, forbidding the ships within a country's ports to sail; generally issued in anticipation of war. **2.** A suspension of commerce, either general or particular, imposed by municipal law 1658. **3.** *transf.* and *fig.* A prohibition, impediment 1692.

1. An e...is daily expected 1758. **2.** An e. on the export of provisions ERSKINE MAY.

Embargo (embā·ɹgo), *v.* 1650. [f. prec. sb.] **1.** To forbid (a vessel) to leave a port; to lay under an embargo 1755. Also *fig.* **2.** To requisition for the service of the state 1755. **3.** To seize, confiscate 1650.

Embark (embā·ɹk), *v.* 1550. [– Fr. *embarquer,* f. *en-* EM- + *barque* BARK *sb.*[2]] **1.** *trans.* **a.** To put on board ship. **b.** Of the ship: To take on board. **2.** *transf.* and *fig.* 1584. **3.** *intr.* (for *refl.*) To go on board ship (*lit.* and *fig.*) 1580. **4.** To engage *in* a business or undertaking 1649.

1. b. The Osborne will..e. the Prince 1885. **2.** To e. money in an ironwork HT. MARTINEAU. **3.** A restless impulse urged him to e. SHELLEY. **4.** To e. in the most disastrous of wars ROGERS.

Embarkation (embaɹkēⁱ·ʃən). 1645. [f. prec. + -ATION. In sense 3 – Fr. *embarcation* – Sp. *embarcacion.*] **1.** Embarking. †**2.** *concr.* A body of troops embarked –1757. †**3.** A vessel, boat –1807.

1. The E. of the Army CLARENDON. **2.** Another and much greater e. followed BURKE. So †**Emba·rkage. Emba·rkment** (in sense 1), now *rare.*

Embarque, obs. var. of EMBARK.

Emba·rras, *sb.* 1664. [– Fr. *embarras,* f. *embarrasser*; see next.] **1.** Embarrassment. Now only as Fr. (aṅbara) in phr. *e. de choix, e. de richesse* so much choice, wealth, as to be embarrassing. **2.** *U.S.* A place in a river made difficult by accumulation of driftwood 1814.

Embarrass (embæ·răs), *v.* 1672. [– Fr. *embarrasser* – Sp. *embarazar* – It. *imbarrazzare,* f. *imbarrare* EMBAR.] **1.** To encumber, hamper, impede (movements, actions, persons) 1683. **b.** *pass.* Of persons: To be encumbered with debts; to be 'in difficulties'. **2.** To perplex (in thought) 1672. **3.** To render difficult; to complicate (a question, etc.) 1736.

1. The state of the rivers..will e. the enemy WELLINGTON. **2.** Such a circumstance may e. an operator 1824. **3.** This case will [not] be embarrassed by that decision CRUISE. Hence **Emba·rrassedly, Emba·rrassingly** *advs.*

Embarrassment (embæ·răsmĕnt). 1676. [f. prec. + -MENT. Cf. Fr. †*embarrassement.*] **1.** Embarrassed state or condition, *esp.* of pecuniary affairs, circumstances, etc. **b.** Perplexity, confusion of thought; hesitation; constraint arising from bashfulness or timidity 1774. **2.** Something which embarrasses. In *pl.* often = 'pecuniary difficulties'. 1729.

1. A state of e. and threatened bankruptcy BRIGHT. **2.** There was e. on the maiden's part SCOTT. **2.** The embarrassments of that humble household TRENCH.

Embarrel; see EM- *prefix* and BARREL.

†**Emba·rren,** *v.* 1627. [f. EM- + BARREN.] *trans.* To make barren –1808.

†**Em:barrica·do,** *v.* 1603. [f. Sp. *embarricado* sb. barricade.] = BARRICADE *v.* –1630.

†**Embase** (embēⁱ·s), *v.* 1551. [var. of ABASE, DEBASE by substitution of the prefix EM-.] To lower in position or direction –1644. Also *fig.* **2.** To lower in rank, condition, etc.; to humiliate; to degrade. Also *refl.* –1820. **3.** To depreciate (*lit.* and *fig.*) –1698. **4.** To debase (coin) by a mixture of alloy (*lit.* and *fig.*) –1752.

1. When God..Embast the Valleys and embost the Hills SYLVESTER. **2.** It is..selfishness that 'embases and embrutes' L. HUNT. **4.** It will imbase even the purest metal in man FELTHAM. Hence †**Emba·sement.**

Embassade (embăsēⁱ·d). ? *Obs.* 1480. [occas. var. of AMBASSADE, q. v.] **1.** = AMBASSADE 1–3. **2.** quasi-*adv.* On an embassy (*rare*) 1525.

Embassador (embæ·sădəɹ). Var. of AMBASSADOR; now *obs.* in England, but in U.S. still preferred. Cf. EMBASSY. So **Embassadorial** *a.* ambassadorial. †**Embassadress,** ambassadress. †**Embassadry,** ambassadry.

Embassage (e·mbăsĕdʒ). *arch.* 1526. [var. (freq. in mod. archaistic use) of AMBASSAGE, q. v. In ordinary use repl. by EMBASSY.] = EMBASSY 1–3.

Carneades the philosopher came in e. to Rome BACON.

†**Emba·ssiate.** ME. only. [var. of AMBASSIATE, q. v.] = EMBASSY.

Embassy (e·mbăsi). 1579. [var. of AMBASSY (and now almost the only current form), – OFr. *ambassé, -axée, -asée,* corresp. to Pr. *ambaissada,* OSp. *ambaxada,* It. *ambasciata,* med.L. *ambasc(i)ata* (f. Rom. **ambactiare*; see AMBASSADOR); see -Y[5].] **1.** The function or position of an ambassador; also, the sending of ambassadors. **2.** Hence †**a.** The message or business; **b.** The official residence, of an ambassador. 1595. **3.** The ambassador and his retinue, with their surroundings 1671.

3. Embassies from regions far remote MILT.

Embastardize, mod. var. of IMBASTARDIZE.

Embathe, imbathe (em-, imbēⁱ·ð), *v. poet.* 1593. [f. EM-, IM-[1] + BATHE.] To bathe, immerse; to bedew, drench.

Embattle (em-, imbæ·t'l), *v.*[1] ME. [– OFr. *embataillier,* f. *en-* EM- + *bataille* BATTLE *sb.*] **1.** *trans.* To set in battle array. Also (Spenser) to arm (an individual) for battle. ME. Also *fig.* **2.** *refl.* To form in order of battle 1450. Also †*intr.* for *refl.* **3.** = EMBATTLE *v.*[2] Also *fig.* ME.

1. One in bright armes embatteiled full strong SPENSER *F. Q.* II. v. 2. As a General..mustereth and embattaileth his troops BARROW. **3.** Fear builds castles and embattles cities 1830.

Embattle (embæ·t'l), *v.*[2] ME. [f. EM- + OFr. *bataillier*; see BATTLEMENT.] *trans.* To furnish with battlements.

Licenses to e. manor-houses 1851. Hence †**Emba·ttle** *sb.*, **Emba·ttlement** = BATTLEMENT.

Embattled (embæ·t'ld), *ppl. a.*[1] 1475. [f. EMBATTLE *v.*[1] + -ED[1].] **1.** Drawn up in battle array, marshalled for battle. Also *transf.* and *fig.* **2.** Covered with troops in battle array. Also *fig.* 1593. **3.** Fortified 1765.

1. Bondage threatened by the e. East WORDSW. The e. legions of ignorance HALLAM. **2.** Castor glorious on th' e. plain POPE.

Embattled (embæ·t'ld), *ppl. a.*[2] ME. [f. EMBATTLE *v.*[2] + -ED[1].] **1.** *Arch.* Furnished with battlements, crenellated. **2.** Having an edge shaped like a battlement; crenellated; *spec.* in *Her.* ME.

1. An embatelid Waulle now sore yn ruine LELAND. **2.** His comb..Enbateled as it were a castel wall CHAUCER.

Embay (embēⁱ·), *v.*[1] 1583. [f. EM- + BAY *sb.*[2]] **1.** *trans.* To lay within a bay. Also, To force into or detain within a bay. 1600. **2.** To enclose (as in a bay); to shut in; also *fig.*

1. He found himself embayed within a mighty head of land C. MATHER. **2.** Embayed by the ice COOK.

†**Embay·,** *v.*[2] *poet.* 1590. [f. EM- + *bay* bathe.] *trans.* To bathe; hence, to drench. Also *fig.* –1762.

fig. In the warme sunne he doth himselfe e. SPENSER.

Embayment (embēⁱ·mĕnt). 1815. [f. EMBAY *v.*[1] + -MENT.] **1.** The action of forming into a bay; *concr.* a bay. **2.** A bay-like recess 1848.

2. The deep e. of her favourite window 1848.

†**Embeam** (embī·m), *v.* 1610. [f. EM- + BEAM *sb.*] *trans.* To cast beams upon, irradiate –1652.

Embed, imbed (em-, imbe·d). 1778. [f. EM-, IM- + BED *sb.* (*Embed* is now usual.)] **1.** *trans.* To fix firmly in a surrounding mass of material. Also *fig.* and *transf.* **2.** Said of the surrounding mass: To enclose firmly. Also *fig.* 1853.

1. Insects..imbedded in the gum-copal LIVINGSTONE. *transf.* Nemi, imbedded in wood, Nemi inurned in the hill CLOUGH. Hence **Embe·dment,** the action of embedding; embedded state; *concr.* something which embeds.

†**E·mbelif.** ME. [– OFr. phr. *en belif* obliquely.] **a.** *adv.* Obliquely. CHAUCER. **b.** *adj.* Oblique –1413.

Embellish (embe·liʃ), *v.* ME. [f. *embelliss-,* lengthened stem of (O)Fr. *embellir,* f. *en-* EM- + *bel* beautiful; see -ISH[2].] **a.** To render beautiful (*obs.* in gen. sense). **b.** To beautify with adventitious ornaments; to ornament. **c.** *fig.* Often = to dress up (a narration) with fictitious additions 1447.

b. Bridles..embellished with bits of yellow gold STRUTT. **c.** Events..probably..much..embellished 1801. Hence **Embe·llisher.**

Embe·llishment. 1623 [f. prec. + -MENT Cf. (O)Fr. *embellissement.*] **1.** The action or process of embellishing; decoration, adornment. **2.** That which embellishes or beautifies (*lit.* and *fig.*); an ornament, decoration; also, an exaggeration.

1. They might not tend to the E. of my paper ADDISON. **2.** Abatement is made for poetical embellishments FULLER.

Ember[1] (e·mbəɹ). [OE. *æmyrġe, æmerġe* = MLG. *ēmere,* OHG. *eimuria* pyre (MHG. *eimere*), ON. *eimyrje* (Da. *emmer,* Sw. *mörja*) embers :– Gmc. **aimuzjōn.* For intrusive *b* cf. *slumber.*] A small piece of live coal or wood in a smouldering fire. Chiefly in *pl.*: The smouldering ashes of a fire. Also *fig.*

They heat it [flesh] a little upon imbers of coales HAKLUYT. Hence **E·mbered** *ppl. a.* strewn with, or burnt to, embers.

Ember[2] (e·mbəɹ). Now only *attrib.* and in *Comb.* [OE. *ymbren,* which may be an alt. of *ymbryne* period, revolution of time, f. *ymb* about, around + *ryne* course (f. **run* RUN *v.*); but the possibility that it is based partly on eccl. L. *quatuor tempora* is suggested by the form of G. *quatember.*] The English name of the four periods of fasting and prayer (L. *quatuor tempora*) in the four seasons of the year. Each of these occupies three days, called *E. days*, and the weeks in which they occur are called *E. weeks*. The Council of Placentia (A.D. 1095) appointed for Ember days the Wednesday, Friday, and Saturday next following (1) the first Sunday in Lent, (2) Whitsunday, (3) 14 Sept., (4) 13 Dec.

†**1.** As *sb.*; = *E.-day* –1573. **2.** *attrib.* and *Comb.*, as *e.-day, -fast, -tide*, etc.; **e.-eve**, the vigil of an E. day OE. var. **E·mbering.**

Ember³. Also **imber, immer, emmer,** etc. 1744. [– Norw. *emmer(-gaas).*] A variety (*Colymbus immer*) of the Northern Diver or Loon (*Colymbus glacialis*) to which the name is sometimes given. Chiefly in *Comb.*, as *e.-goose*, etc.

†**Embe·tter,** *v.* 1583. [f. EM- + BETTER *a.*] To make better –1680.

Embezzle (embe·z'l), *v.* 1469. [– AFr. *embesiler*, f. *en-* EN-¹ + *besiler* in same sense (whence BEZZLE *v.*) = OFr. *besillier* maltreat, ravage, destroy; of unkn. origin.] †**1.** *trans.* To make away with; *esp.* to carry off secretly for one's own use –1750. †**b.** To mutilate, tamper with (a document, etc.) –1691. †**2.** To impair, diminish –1670; to squander –1770. **3.** To divert to one's own use in violation of trust or official duty. (The only current sense.) 1585.

1. b. To imbezill or corrupt a Record 1671. **2.** He hath embeazled his estate BURTON. **3.** Bellasys, the English General, embezzled the stores MACAULAY. Hence **Embe·zzler.**

Embezzlement (embe·z'lmĕnt). 1548. [f. EMBEZZLE + -MENT; in AFr. (XV) *embesilement.*] The action of embezzling. †**a.** In senses of EMBEZZLE 1, 2. **b.** Fraudulent appropriation of property entrusted to one.

†**Embi·llow,** *v. rare.* 1625. [f. EM- + BILLOW.] *trans.* To raise in billows.

Embind (embəi·nd), *v.* Also **im-.** 1628. [f. EM- + BIND.] *trans.* To confine, hold fast.

Embitter (embi·təɹ), *v.* Also **im-.** 1603. [f. EM- + BITTER *a.*] **1.** *trans.* To make bitter. Now *rare* in *lit.* sense. Also *fig.* **2.** *fig.* To make more bitter or painful 1642. **3.** *fig.* To render virulent, intensely hostile, or discontented; to exacerbate 1634.

1. Brewers e. their beers with hops 1834. *fig.* It would e. all the sweets of life STEELE. **2.** His actual misery was embittered by the recollection of past greatness GIBBON. To e. Peoples minds one against another BP. BURNET.

Hence **Embi·tterer. Embi·tterment,** the action of embittering; embittered state.

†**Embla·dder,** *v. rare.* 1662. [f. EM- + BLADDER.] **a.** To blister. **b.** To confine in a bladder 1664.

†**Embla·nch,** *v.* ME. [– OFr. *emblanchir*, f. *en-* EM- + *blanchir* whiten; see BLANCH *v.*¹] *trans.* To whiten (*fig.*) –1662.

Emblaze (emblē·z), *v.*¹ Also **im-.** 1634. [f. EM- + BLAZE *sb.*¹] **1.** *trans.* To light up, cause to glow. **2.** To set in a blaze. Also *fig.* 1728.

1. Th' unsought Diamonds..e. the forehead of the Deep MILT. *Comus* 733. **2.** Where nearer suns e. its veins COLLINS.

Emblaze (emblē·z), *v.*² Also **im-.** 1522. [f. EM- + BLAZE *v.*²] †**1. a.** *trans.* To describe heraldically. **b.** To set forth by means of heraldic devices. –1781. **2.** To adorn with heraldic devices. Hence, to make resplendent. 1522. **3.** To inscribe inconspicuously 1590. **4.** To celebrate, render famous or infamous 1596.

2. With crowns of gold emblased SKELTON. **3.** Where stout Hercules Emblaz'd his trophies on two posts of brass GREENE. Hence **Embla·zer.**

Emblazon (emblē·zən), *v.* 1592. [f. EM- + BLAZON *v.*] **1.** *trans.* To inscribe or portray conspicuously, as on a heraldic shield; to adorn *with* heraldic devices, words, etc. (*lit.* and *fig.*). Occas. influenced by EMBLAZE *v.*¹ 1593. **2.** To celebrate, extol; to render illustrious.

1. God..emblazond the aire with the tokens of his terror NASHE. **2.** Heraulds to emblazen his Progresse GAULE.

Hence **Embla·zoner. Embla·zonment,** the action of EMBLAZON *v.*; *concr.* that which is emblazoned.

Emblazonry (emblē·zənri). 1667. [f. prec. vb. + -RY.] **1.** The art of emblazoning; *concr.* heraldic devices collectively. **2.** Display of gorgeous colours; brilliant representation or embellishment (*lit.* and *fig.*) 1805.

1. With bright imblazonrie, and horrent Arms MILT. **2.** The Sun..with his gold-purple e. CARLYLE.

Emblem (e·mblĕm), *sb.* Also **embleme.** ME. [– L. *emblema* inlaid work, raised ornament – Gr. ἔμβλημα, -ματ-, insertion, f. ἐμβλη-, ἐμβάλλειν throw in, insert, f. ἐν- EM- + βάλλειν throw.] †**1.** An ornament of inlaid work –1775. †**2.** A drawing or picture expressing a moral fable or allegory; a fable or allegory such as might be expressed pictorially –1736. **3.** An object, or a picture of one, representing symbolically an abstract quality, an action, a class of persons, etc. 1601. **b.** In wider sense: A symbol, type 1631. **4.** A figured object used symbolically, as a badge 1616.

2. An E. is but a silent parable QUARLES. **3.** His sicatrice an E. of warre heere on his sinister cheeke *All's Well* II. i. 44. **b.** The evening is an e. of autumn JOHNSON. **4.** National emblems..a crescent, a lion, an eagle..on an old rag of bunting EMERSON.

Emblem (e·mblĕm), *v.* 1584. [f. prec.] *trans.* To be the emblem of; to express, symbolize, suggest.

All Christianism..is emblemed here CARLYLE.

Emblematic, -al (emblĕmæ·tik, -ăl), *a.* 1644. [f. Gr. ἔμβλημα, -ματ- (see EMBLEM *sb.*) + -IC, after Fr. *emblématique*; see -ATIC, -ICAL.] Pertaining to, of the nature of, or serving as, an emblem; symbolical, typical.

Clothes..are Emblematic..of a manifold cunning Victory over Want CARLYLE. Hence **Emblema·tically** *adv.* **Emblema·ticize** *v.* to impart an e. character to (*rare*).

Emblematist (emble·mătist). 1646. [f. as prec. + -IST.] One who delineates or writes emblems.

Emblematize (emble·mătəiz), *v.* 1615. [f. as prec. + -IZE.] **1.** *trans.* To serve as an emblem of. **2.** Of persons: To represent by means of an emblem 1830.

1. The goose and little goslings should e. a Quaker poet that has no children LAMB.

Emblement (e·mblĭmĕnt). 1495. [– OFr. *emblaement*, f. *emblaer, emblaier*, (also mod.) *emblaver* sow with corn, f. *blé* corn.] *Law.* 'The profits of sown land'; occas. used more largely for grass, fruit, etc.

†**Emble·mish,** *v.* ME. [f. EM- + BLEMISH *v.*] *trans.* To damage, injure; also, to deface –1671.

Emblemize (e·mblĕməiz), *v.* 1646. [f. EMBLEM + -IZE.] *trans.* To represent emblematically. So †**E·mblemist** = EMBLEMATIST.

†**Embli·ss,** *v. rare.* ME. [f. EM- + BLISS.] To make happy –1797.

†**Embloo·m,** *v.* 1528. [f. EM- + BLOOM *sb.*¹] To cover with bloom –1729.

Emblossom, im- (em-, imblǫ·səm), *v.* 1766. [f. EM-, IM-¹ + BLOSSOM *sb.*] To load or cover with blossoms.

Embodiment, im- (em-, imbǫ·diment). 1828. [f. EMBODY *v.* + -MENT.] **1.** The action of embodying; embodied state (*lit.* and *fig.*) 1858. **2.** *concr.* That in which anything is embodied; the 'vesture' *of* (a soul); the concrete expression (of an idea, a principle, etc.); the incarnation (of a quality, sentiment, etc.).

2. Works of art..the visible e. of the divine JOWETT.

Embody, im- (em-, imbǫ·di), *v.* 1548. [f. EM-¹ + BODY *sb.*, after L. *incorporare*. The form *embody* is now usual.] **1.** *trans.* To put into a body. **2.** To give a material or concrete character or form to 1634. **3.** To unite into one body; to incorporate 1601. †**4.** *Chem.*, etc. **a.** *trans.* To form into one body. **b.** *intr.* for *refl.* To draw together, solidify. –1710. **5.** *intr.* (for *refl.*) To form or join a body or company 1648.

1. A pale, small person, scarcely embodied at all HAWTHORNE. **2.** The custom having been embodied in law GROTE. **3.** Livius..embodied the population of the town ARNOLD. The measure embodies..the six points..of the charter 1869. **5.** [He] commanded the Horse to E. within the Lines 1681. Hence **Embo·dier.**

Embog (embǫ·g), *v.* Also **embogue.** 1602. [f. EM- + BOG *sb.*¹] *trans.* To plunge into a bog.

†**Embo·gue,** *v.* 1603. [app. – Sp. *embocar*, f. *em-* EM- + *boca* mouth.] = DISEMBOGUE. Hence †**Embo·guing** *vbl. sb.* the place where a lake or river discharges its waters.

†**Emboi·l,** *v.* [f. EM- + BOIL *v.*] *trans.* To cause to boil with rage; *intr.* to be in a boil. SPENSER.

||**Emboîtement** (aṅbwatmaṅ). 1854. [Fr.; f. *emboîter*, f. *en-* + *boîte* box.] **1.** *Anat.* The fitting of a bone into another. **2.** *Biol.* Buffon's term for the hypothesis that successive generations proceed from germs, and contain the germs of all future generations. **3.** The closing up of a number of men in order to secure the front rank from injury. (Dicts.)

Embolden, im- (em-, imbōᵘ·ldən), *v.* 1571. [f. EM-, IM-¹ + BOLDEN.] To render bold or more bold; to incite, encourage.

Thus I embold'nd spake MILT. *P. L.* VIII. 434. So †**Embo·ld** *v.* Hence **Embo·ldener.**

||**Embole** (e·mbŏlī). 1811. [mod.L. – Gr. ἐμβολή a putting in.] *Med.* †**1.** The reducing of a dislocated limb. **2.** A plug or wedge (*Syd. Soc. Lex.*). **3.** = EMBOLUS (*Syd. Soc. Lex.*).

Embolic (embǫ·lik), *a.* 1866. [f. EMBOLUS + -IC.] *Path.* Relating to or caused by an embolus.

†**Embolimæ·al,** *a. rare.* 1677. [f. Gr. ἐμβολιμαῖος, of same meaning (cf. EMBOLISM) + -AL¹.] Intercalary. So †**Embolimæ·an, -ar.**

Embolism (e·mbŏliz'm). ME. [– late L. *embolismus* – Gr. ἐμβολισμός, f. ἐμβάλλειν throw in, f. ἐν EM- + βάλλειν throw; see -ISM. Cf. Fr. *embolisme* intercalation (XV).] **1.** *Chronol.* An intercalation or insertion of a day or days in the calendar, to complete a period. *concr.* The time intercalated. **2.** *Path.* The occlusion of a blood-vessel by an embolus 1855.

1. The year of the Mahometans consists of twelve lunar months..no e. being employed to adjust it to the solar period 1788.

Hence †**Emboli·smal, Emboli·smic** *adjs.* that pertains to e.; intercalary.

||**Embolismus** (emboli·zmŏs). ME. [L.; see prec.] †**1.** *Chronol.* **a.** The excess of the solar over the lunar year of twelve synodical months. **b.** Intercalation. –1796. **2.** In the Gr. liturgy: A prayer inserted after the concluding petitions of the Lord's Prayer. SHIPLEY.

Embolite (e·mbŏləit). 1850. [f. Gr. ἐμβόλιον a thing inserted + -ITE¹ 2 b, 'because between the chlorid and bromid of silver' (Dana).] *Min.* A chloro-bromide of silver, $Ag_5Br_2Cl_3$. Also *attrib.*

||**Embolon** (e·mbŏlǫn). 1878. [Gr. ἔμβολον peg, stopper.] *Path.* = EMBOLUS 2.

||**Embolus** (e·mbŏlŏs). 1669. [L. *embolus* piston of a pump – Gr. ἔμβολος peg, stopper.] †**1.** *Mech.* Something inserted, as a wedge; *esp.* the piston of a syringe –1739. **2.** *Path.* 'The body which causes EMBOLISM' (*Syd. Soc. Lex.*). **3.** *Anat.* 'The osseous axis of the horns of the *Ruminantia cavicornia*' (*Syd. Soc. Lex.*).

Emboly (e·mbŏli). 1877. [– Gr. ἐμβολή with assim. to -Y³; cf. Fr. *embolie.*] = INVAGINATION: **a.** *Surg.* A particular operation for hernia. **b.** *Phys.* The process of formation of the *gastrula* by involution of the wall of the single-layered segmented ovum.

||**Embonpoint** (aṅboṅpwaṅ). 1751. [– Fr. phr. *en bon point* 'in good condition'.]

A. *sb.* Plumpness (*complimentary* or *euphemistic*).

B. as predicative *adj.* Plump, of well-nourished appearance 1806.

†**Embo·rder,** *v.* Also **im-.** 1530. [f. EM- + BORDER *sb.* Cf. OFr. *emborder.*] **a.** To furnish with a border; to edge. **b.** To set as a border. –1667.

Embosom, im- (em-, imbu·zəm), *v.* 1590. [f. EM-, IM-¹ + BOSOM *sb.*] **1.** *trans.* To take to, or place in, the bosom; to cherish; to embrace. Chiefly *fig.* Now *rare.* **2.** *transf.* To enclose, conceal, shelter, in the bosom. †**b.** *refl.* Of a river: To pour itself *into* the bosom. 1685.

1. Anger rests Embosom'd..in foolish brests QUARLES. **2.** My..home Which oaks e. SHENSTONE. Deep sleep embosometh their jaded limbs SINGLETON.

†**Embo·ss,** *sb.* [f. EMBOSS *v.*¹] A boss-like projection. EVELYN.

Emboss (embǫ·s), *v.*¹ ME. [– OFr. **embocer*, Fr. †*imbocer* (XVI), *embosser* (Cotgr.), f. *en-* EM- + *boce, bosse* BOSS *sb.*¹] **1.** *trans.* to cause to bulge; to cover with protuberances 1460. **2.** *spec.* To carve or mould in relief.

Also *fig.* (The prevailing mod. sense) ME. **b.** To adorn with figures, etc. in relief; to represent in relief. Also of the figures, etc.: To stand out as an ornament upon. ME. **3.** To ornament with or as with bosses; hence, to decorate sumptuously 1578.

1. Botches and blaines must all his flesh imboss MILT. *P. L.* XII. 180. **2.** Fleur-de-lis embossed out of the stone EVELYN. **b.** The rich bronze which embossed its gates PRESCOTT. **3.** Berries that imboss the bramble COWPER.

Hence **Embo·sser. Embo·ssing** *vbl. sb.* the action of the vb., as in *e.-press*, etc.

Embo·ss, *v.*^{2} [– OFr. *emboscher*, var. of *embuschier* AMBUSH *v.*] †**1.** *intr.* To plunge into a wood or thicket –1680. †**2.** To drive (a hunted animal) to extremity –1768. †**3.** In *pass.* To be exhausted; *hence*, to foam at the mouth –1651. **4.** *trans.* To cover with foam (*arch.*) 1531.

4. Embossed with foam..The labouring Stag strained full in view SCOTT.

†**Embo·ss,** *v.*^{3} 1590. [perh. f. EN- + BOSS *sb.*^{3}] *trans.* To encase (in armour); to plunge (a weapon) *in* an enemy's body. Also *fig.* in *pass.* To be wrapped (in ease). –1621.

Embossed (embǫ·st), *ppl. a.* ME. [f. EMBOSS *v.*^{1} + -ED^1.] **1.** Carved or moulded in relief, etc. (see EMBOSS *v.*^{1}) 1541. **2.** Covered with bosses; richly decorated 1591. †**3.** hump-backed. ME. only. †**4.** Bulging, swollen; *fig.* of style –1646. **5.** *Bot.* 'Projecting in the centre like the boss of a shield' (*Syd. Soc. Lex.*).

1. The e. alphabet for the blind 1849. **4.** 1 *Hen. IV*, III. iii. 177.

Embossment (embǫ·smĕnt). 1610. [f. as prec. + -MENT.] †**1.** The action of embossing 1801. **2.** *concr.* A figure carved or moulded in relief; embossed ornament. Now *rare.* Also *attrib.*, as in *e.-map.* 1620. **3.** *gen.* A bulging 1610. So **Embo·sture** [after *sculpture*].

Embottle; see EM- *pref.* and BOTTLE *sb.*

‖**Embouchement** (aṅbuʃmaṅ, embū·ʃment). 1844. [Fr.; see next.] **a.** The mouth (of a river). **b.** *Phys.* The point at which one vessel leads into another.

‖**Embouchure** (aṅbuʃūr). 1678. [Fr., f. *s'emboucher* refl., discharge itself by a mouth, f. *en* EM-^{1} + *bouche* mouth; see -URE.] **1.** The mouth of a river or creek. Also *transf.* of a valley. 1792. **2.** *Mus.* The mouthpiece of a wind instrument 1834. **3.** *Mus.* 'The disposition of the lips, tongue, and other organs necessary for producing a musical tone' (Grove).

Embound, im- (em-, imbau·nd), *v. poet. arch.* 1595. [f. EM-, IM-^{1} + BOUND *sb.*] *trans.* To set bounds to; to confine.

Embow (embō^u·), *v.* ME. [f. EM- + BOW *sb.*^{1}] **1.** To bend or curve into a bow. **2.** *Arch.* To arch, vault 1481. **3.** To englobe, encircle 1605.

2. The pillared vestibule..the roof embowed WORDSW. Hence **Embow·ed** *ppl. a.* bent into a bow; *Her.* bent or curved; *Arch.* arched, vaulted; also, projecting outward, as in a bow-window. †**Embow·ment,** vaulting BACON.

Embowel (embau·ĕl), *v.* 1521. [In sense 1 – OFr. *emboweler*, alt. (by substitution of *em-* for *es-*) of *esboueler*, f. *es-* EX-^{1} + *bouel* BOWEL. In sense 2, f. EM- + BOWEL.] **1.** *trans.* = DISEMBOWEL. Also *transf.* and *fig.* †**2.** To put, convey, into the bowels. Usu. *transf.* and *fig.* –1634.

1. Imbowell'd will I see thee by and by 1 *Hen. IV*, v. iv. 109. W^{ch} made me..send for a chirurgeon from York to e. him 1640. All was embowelled and enwombed in the waters DONNE. Hence **Embow·eller. Embow·elment,** the action of disembowelling; the inward parts of a thing.

Embower, im- (em-, imbau^ə·ɹ, -bau·əɹ), *v.* 1580. [f. EM-, IM-^{1} + BOWER *sb.*^{1}] **1.** To shelter, enclose, as in a bower; also *absol.* †**2.** *intr.* for *refl.* To lodge as in a bower –1610.

1. Him..Whom Sion holds embowered SIDNEY. **2.** Small Birds in their wide boughs embowring SPENSER. Hence **Embow·erment,** the action of embowering.

†**Embow·l,** *v. rare.* 1580. [f. EM- + BOWL *sb.*^{1}] To make, or grow, into the form of a globe –1886.

Embox (embǫ·ks), *v.* 1611. [f. EM- + BOX *sb.*^{2}] To set in or as in a box.

Embrace (embrē^i·s), *sb.* 1592. [f. EMBRACE *v.*^{2} Superseding earlier EMBRACEMENT.] The action of clasping in the arms, pressing to the bosom. (Sometimes *euphem.* of sexual intercourse.) Also *transf.* and *fig.*

Armes, take your last e. *Rom. & Jul.* v. iii. 113. Pride..by whose embraces she had two daughters JOHNSON.

†**Embra·ce,** *v.*^{1} *rare.* ME. [f. EM- + BRACE *sb.*^{1}] To put (a shield) on the arm –1592.

Embrace (embrē^i·s), *v.*^{2} ME. [– OFr. *embracer* (mod. *embrasser*) :– Rom. **imbracchiare*, f. L. *in* IM-^{1} + *bracchium* arm, pl. *bracchia*; see EM-, BRACE *sb.*^{2}] **1.** *trans.* To clasp in the arms, usually as a sign of affection. Used also of sexual embraces. Also *absol.* **2.** *fig.* †**a.** To compass, gain –1475. †**b.** To accept as a friend –1635. **c.** To accept eagerly; now chiefly, to avail oneself of ME. **d.** To accept, submit to 1591. †**e.** To cultivate (a virtue, etc.) –1623. **f.** To adopt (a course of action, a doctrine etc.). Formerly also, to take (a path). 1639. **g.** To attach oneself to (a cause, etc.) 1720. †**h.** To take in hand –1818. **3.** To encircle; to clasp, enclose (*lit.* and *fig.*) ME. **4.** To include, comprise 1697. **5.** To take in with the eye or mind; also with these as subject 1831.

1. The frere..her embracith in his armes narwe CHAUCER. You will say, she did e. me as a husband *Much Ado* IV. i. 50. **2. c.** E. we then this opportunitie 1 *Hen. VI*, II. i. 13. **d.** Thurio give backe, or else e. thy death *Two Gent.* V. iv. 126. **f.** To e. the monastic life FREEMAN. **g.** To e. the Reformed faith SMILES. **3.** You'l see your Rome embrac'd with fire SHAKS. **4.** To e. all the cases in a single formula 1891.

Hence **Embra·ceable** *a.* inviting an embrace; so **Embra·ceably** *adv.* **Embra·ced** *ppl. a.* (*Her.*) braced or bound together. **Embra·cive** *a.* given to embracing THACKERAY.

Embrace (embrē^i·s), *v.*^{3} 1475. [app. back-formation from EMBRACER^2.] *Law.* To attempt to influence (a jury, etc.) corruptly. Also *absol.*

†**Embra·ce,** *v.*^{4} 1475. [f. EM- + BRACE *sb.*^{2}] To fix with a brace; to fasten, fit close –1596.

Embracement (embrē^i·smĕnt). 1485. [– OFr. *embracement*, f. *embracer*; see EMBRACE *v.*^{2}, -MENT.] **1.** = EMBRACE *sb.* †**2.** An undertaking –1662. **3.** A clasping, enclosure; also *fig.* 1599. **4.** *fig.* Willing acceptance 1535.

1. After embracements and teares MILT. **4.** The favorable embracements of Gods word 1535.

Embracer^1 (embrē^i·səɹ). 1547. [f. EMBRACE *v.*^{2} + -ER^1.] One who embraces (see EMBRACE *v.*^{2} 1, 2).

Embracer^2 (embrē^i·səɹ). 1495. [– AFr., OFr. *embraseor* instigator, f. *embraser* set on fire; see EMBRASE. For the sense development cf. ENTICE.] *Law.* One who attempts to influence a jury corruptly.

Embracery (embrē^i·sĕri). 1450. [f. prec. + -ERY.] *Law.* The offence of influencing a jury illegally and corruptly.

†**Embrai·d,** *v.*^{1} 1481. [f. EM- + BRAID *v.*^{2} Cf. the var. ABRAID.] *trans.* To upbraid. Also, to taunt one with. –1582.

†**Embrai·d,** *v.*^{2} 1491. [f. EM- + BRAID *v.*^{1}] *trans.* **a.** To fasten on like braid. **b.** To plait; to intertwine –1596.

Embranchment (embra·nʃmĕnt). 1830 [– Fr. *embranchement* in same senses; see EM-, BRANCH *sb.*, -MENT.] A branching off or out, as of an arm of a river, etc.; a branch, ramification. Also *fig.*

Embrangle, im- (em-, imbræ·ŋg'l), *v.* 1664. [f. EM-, IM-^{1} + BRANGLE *v.*] *trans.* To entangle, perplex.

Embrangled in inexplicable difficulties BP. BERKELEY. Hence **Embra·nglement.**

†**Embra·se,** *v.* 1480. [– (O)Fr. *embraser*, f. *braise* hot charcoal; cf. BRAISE, BRAZIER^2.] To set on fire. Also *fig.* –1605.

†**Embra·sure,** *sb.*^{1} [f. EMBRACE *v.*^{2} + -URE.] = EMBRACE. Shaks.

Embrasure (embrē^i·ʒ^{i}ŭɹ), *sb.*^{2} Also **embrazure.** 1702. [– Fr. *embrasure*, f. *embraser*, varying with *ébraser*, level off, slope door or window opening from within; of unkn. origin; see -URE.] **1.** A bevelling inwards of the sides of an aperture for a window or door 1753. **2.** *Mil.* An opening widening from within made in an epaulement or parapet, so that a gun can be fired through it 1702. **3.** *attrib.* 1809.

1. They put me in a chair in the e. of the window CARLYLE. Hence **Embra·sure** *v.* to furnish with embrasures.

Embrave (embrē^i·v), *v.* 1579. [f. EM- + BRAVE *a.*] †**1.** To make brave; to adorn splendidly –1736. **2.** To render courageous 1648.

The faded flowres her corse embraue SPENSER.

†**Embrea·ch,** *v.* 1581. [f. EM- + BREACH *sb.*] *intr.* To enter a breach; *trans.* to make a breach in –1610.

Embread, var. of EMBRAID *v.*^{2}

Embrea·stment. [f. EM- + BREAST + -MENT, after *embankment.*] A swelling of the ground. COLERIDGE.

Embreathe (embrī·ð), *v.* 1529. [f. EM- + BREATHE *v.*; cf. IMBREATHE.] **1.** *trans.* To breathe *into*; to inspire *with*. Also, to give breath to. **2.** To inhale (*fig.*). M. ARNOLD.

Hence **Embrea·thement** (*rare*) = INSPIRATION.

Embrew, obs. f. IMBRUE.

†**Embri·ght,** *v.* 1598. [f. EM- + BRIGHT *v.* or *a.*] To make bright –1766.

Embri·ghten, *v.* 1610. [f. EM- + BRIGHTEN.] = BRIGHTEN.

†**Embroca·do,** *v.* [f. EM- + *brocado* = BROCADE, q.v.] ? To adorn with or as with brocade. FELTHAM.

Embrocate (e·mbrŏke^{i}t), *v.* 1612. [– *embrocat-*, pa. ppl. stem of med.L. *embrocare*; see next, -ATE^3.] *Med. trans.* To bathe or foment (a diseased part) with liquid.

Embrocation (embrokē^i·ʃən). 1543. [– (O)Fr. *embrocation* or med.L. *embrocatio*, f. *embrocat-*, pa. ppl. stem of *embrocare*, f. late L. *embroc(h)a* – Gr. ἐμβροχή lotion; see -ATION.] †**1.** The action of embrocating –1634. **2.** A liquid used for embrocating a diseased part; now usu. one applied by rubbing; a liniment 1610.

He bathed the doctors face with an e. SMOLLETT.

†**Embro·ch(e,** *sb.* 1585. [– late L. *embrocha, -che*; see prec.] = EMBROCATION 2. –1657. So †**Embro·che** *v.* = EMBROCATE.

Embroglio, bad f. IMBROGLIO. Scott.

Embroider (embroi·dəɹ), *v.* ME. [Earlier also *embro(u)der*, extension of *embroude* – AFr. *enbrouder*, f. *en-* EM- + OFr. *brouder*, *broisder* (mod. *broder*) – Gmc. **brusdan*; the form *broid-* is partly due to blending with BROID *v.*] **1.** *trans.* To ornament with, or (†*transf.*) as with, needlework; to work in needlework upon cloth, etc. Also *absol.* **2.** *fig.* †To dignify –1667; †to set forth floridly –1648; to embellish with rhetoric or with exaggerations 1614.

1. The women..e...for the embellishment of their persons BERKELEY. **2.** He had embroidered his own story with some marvellous legends H. WALPOLE. Hence **Embroi·derer. Embroi·deress.**

Embroidery (embroi·dəri). late ME. [– AFr. *enbrouderie*; see prec., -ERY.] **1.** The art of embroidering; also *attrib.* **2.** Embroidered work or material 1570. **3.** *fig.* of any showy or adventitious ornamentation 1640. **4.** *transf.* Any ornament or marking compared in appearance to needlework 1644. ¶**5.** An embroidery manufactory. BURKE.

2. Saphire, pearle, and rich embroiderie *Merry W.* v. v. 75. **3.** All the e. of poetic dreams COWPER. **4.** An e. of daisies and wild flowers SCOTT.

†**Embroi·l,** *sb.* 1636. [f. EMBROIL *v.*^{2}] = EMBROILMENT –1788.

†**Embroi·l,** *v.*^{1} *rare.* [f. EM- + BROIL *v.*^{1}] To burn up –1726.

Embroil (embroi·l), *v.*^{2} 1603. [– Fr. *embrouiller*; see EM-, BROIL *sb.*^{1} and *v.*^{2}] **1.** *trans.* To bring into confusion and disorder; to render unintelligible. **2.** To throw into uproar or tumult 1618. **3.** To entangle in dissension or hostility *with* (any one); to bring into a state of discord 1610.

1. The former..are so embroil'd with Fable ADDISON. **2.** More to e. the deep THOMSON. **3.** [They] embroiled him with the House of Commons 1680. Hence **Embroi·ler.**

Embroilment (embroi·lmĕnt). 1609. [f. prec. + -MENT. Cf. Fr. *embrouillement.*] **1.** The action of embroiling 1622. **2.** A tumult 1609; a state of variance 1667. **3.** A state of entanglement or confusion 1856.

2. He was not apprehensive of a new e. BURNET.

Embronze; see EM- *pref.* and BRONZE *sb.*

†**Embrow·d, embraw·d,** *v.* ME. [f. EM- + BROWD *v.*] *trans.* To embroider –1555.

Embrown (embrau·n), *v.* 1667. [f. EM- + BROWN *a.*; cf. Fr. *embrunir*, used in sense 1.] **1.** To make dusky. Chiefly *poet.* **2.** To make brown. Also (occas.) *intr.* for *refl.* 1725.
1. The air, Imbrown'd with shadows CARY. **2.** The Smith's hardy and embrowned countenance SCOTT.

Embrue, var. of IMBRUE.

Embrute, var. of IMBRUTE.

Embryo (e·mbri,o). 1590. [– late L. *embryo*, *-io*, mistaken form arising from taking *embryon* as a sb. in *-ōn*, *-ōnis*; – Gr. ἔμβρυον new-born animal, fœtus, f. ἐν EM-¹ + βρύειν swell, grow.]
A. *sb.* **1.** The offspring of an animal before its birth (or emergence from the egg); in the case of man, the fœtus before the fourth month of pregnancy. **2.** *Bot.* 'The rudimentary plant contained in the seed' (*Syd. Soc. Lex.*) 1728. **3.** *fig.* A thing in its rudimentary stage; a germ 1601. **4.** *attrib.* 1835.
3. The project itself was but an E. 1601. Phr. *In e.*: in an undeveloped stage; There a chancellor in e. SHENSTONE. *Comb.*: **e.-bud**, 'an adventitious bud, when enclosed in the bark, as in the cedar of Lebanon' (*Syd. Soc. Lex.*); **-cell**, the first cell of the fecundated animal ovum; **-sac**, *Bot.* a cavity in the archegonium of a plant, within which the e. is produced.
B. *adj.* [The sb. used attrib.] That is still in germ; unformed, undeveloped, as *e. patriots* 1684.
Hence **E·mbryoi:sm**, the state of being an e.

Embryoctony (embri,ǫ·ktŏni). [f. Gr. ἐμβρυοκτόνος that kills the fœtus; see -Y³.] 'The destruction of the fœtus in the womb' (*Syd. Soc. Lex.*).

Embryoferous (embri,ǫ·fərəs), *a.* 1859. [f. EMBRYO + -FEROUS.] *Biol.* That bears or contains an embryo.

Embryogenesis (e:mbri,odʒe·nėsis). 1830. [f. as prec. + GENESIS.] *Biol.* 'The origin and formation of the embryo; and the science thereof' (*Syd. Soc. Lex.*). Hence **E:mbryogene·tic** *a.* pertaining to e.

Embryogeny (e:mbri,ǫ·dʒĕni). 1835. [f. as prec. + -GENY.] = prec. Hence **E:mbryoge·nic** *a.* embryogenetic.

Embryography (embri,ǫ·grăfi). [f. as prec. + -GRAPHY.] 'The description of the fœtus or embryo' (*Syd. Soc. Lex.*).

Embryology (embri,ǫ·lŏdʒi). 1859. [f. as prec. + LOGY.] *Biol.* The science relating to the embryo and its development.
Against the belief in such abrupt changes, e. enters a strong protest DARWIN.
||Hence **E:mbryolo·gic**, **-al** *a.*; **-ly** *adv.* **Embryologist**, one who studies or is versed in e.

Embryon (e·mbri,ǫn), *sb.* (*a.*) Pl. **embrya, embryons.** 1592. [mod.L. – Gr. ἔμβρυον; see EMBRYO.] The original form of EMBRYO; now *rare*, and only in techn. use.
Hence **E·mbryonal** *a.* of or pertaining to an e. **E·mbryona:ry** *a.* relating to an e.

Embryonate (e·mbri,ŏnĕt), *a.* 1669. [f. prec. + -ATE².] †**1.** = EMBRYONATED –1675. †**2.** = *embryonal* 1693. **3.** 'Having an embryo in germ' (*Syd. Soc. Lex.*). Hence in *Bot.* **E. plants**, plants which possess seeds.

†**E·mbryonated**, *ppl. a.* 1652. [f. as prec. + -ED¹.] Of chemical and mineral bodies: Found with or embedded (like embryos) in other bodies –1676.

Embryonic (embri,ǫ·nik), *a.* 1849. [f. as prec. + -IC.] Pertaining to, or like, an embryo; *fig.* immature, undeveloped.
fig. Every Englishman is an e. chancellor EMERSON. So **Embryo·tic** *a.* (*lit.* and *fig.*).

Embryotomy (embri,ǫ·tŏmi). 1721. [– late L. *embryotomia* – Gr. ἐμβρυοτομία; see EMBRYON, -TOMY.] 'The cutting up of the *fœtus in utero* into pieces in order to effect its removal' (*Syd. Soc. Lex.*).

†**E·mbryous**, *a. rare.* 1677. [f. EMBRYO + -OUS.] Of or pertaining to an embryo; in germ; undeveloped. (Dicts.)

†**Embu·ll**, *v.* 1480. [f. EM- + BULL *sb.*²] *trans.* To publish in a bull, issue a bull against; to affix the Papal (or other) seal to –1589.

Embus (embʋ·s), *v.* 1915. [f. EM- + BUS, after ENTRAIN *v.*²] To go or take on board a bus.

Embush, obs. f. of AMBUSH.

†**Embu·sy**, *v.* 1484. [f. EM- + BUSY *a.*] To occupy –1693.

Eme. *Obs.* exc. *dial.* [OE. ēam = OFris. ēm, MDu. *oem* (Du. *oom*), OHG. ōheim (G. *oheim*).] An uncle; also *dial.* a gossip.
Didna his e. die..wi' the name of the Bluidy Mackenyie SCOTT.

Emeer(e, var. ff. EMIR.

Emend (ĭme·nd), *v.* ME. [– L. *emendare*, f. *e-* EX-¹ + *menda* fault.] **1.** *trans.* To free from faults, correct. Also *intr.* for *refl.* Now *rare.* **b.** *esp.* To remove errors from (a text), emendate 1768. **2.** = MEND –1480.
1. b. Pisistratus..did..collect, arrange, and e. poems LYTTON. Hence **Eme·ndable** *a.* **Eme·nder.** †**Eme·ndment** (*rare*), = AMENDMENT.

†**Emendate**, *a.* 1654. [– L. *emendatus*, pa. pple. of *emendare*; see prec., -ATE².] Emended, corrected –1677. Hence †**Emendately** *adv.*

Emendate (ī·mendē¹t), *v.* 1876. [– *emendat-*, pa. ppl. stem of L. *emendare*; see prec., -ATE³.] To remove errors and corruptions from (a text).
Hence **E·mendator.** **Eme·ndatory** *a.* †corrective; pertaining to EMENDATION 2.

Emendation (īmĕndē¹·ʃən). 1536. [– L. *emendatio*, f. as prec.; see -ION.] †**1.** *gen.* Correction, reformation –1677. **2.** Improvement by alteration and correction; *esp.* of literary and artistic products, methods, systems, etc.; an instance of this 1586. **b.** *esp.* The correction (usually by conjecture) of corruptions in a text; an instance of this 1622.
1. The e. of the Church R. COKE. **2.** A better E. of the Calendar 1665. **3.** The emendations being more often wrong than right DOWDEN.

†**Eme·ndicate**, *v.* 1611. [– *emendicat-*, pa. ppl. stem of L. *emendicare*, f. *e-* EX-¹ + *mendicare* beg.] To obtain by begging –1681.

Emerald (e·mərăld). [ME. *emeraude* – OFr. *e(s)meraude* (mod. *émeraude*) :– Rom. **smaralda*, *-o*, alteration of L. *smaragdus* – Gr. σμάραγδος SMARAGDUS.] **1.** A precious stone of bright green colour; in mod. use applied only to a variety of beryl (see BERYL *sb.*). **2.** *Her.* Eng. name for the colour *vert* 1527. **3.** *transf.* = *emerald-green.* **4.** *Printing.* A size of type intermediate between nonpareil and minion:

Emerald type.

5. *attrib.* **a.** Simple *attrib.*, as in *an e. ring* 1877. **b.** quasi-*adj.*, as in *e. meadow* 1598. **c.** Similative, as in *e.-bright*, *-green*, etc. 1614.
1. The fourth an emeralde (= Heb. *nōphek*, LXX ἄνθραξ, Vulg. *carbunculus*) TINDALE *Rev.* 31:19.
Comb.: †**e. copper** (*Min.*) = DIOPTASE; **e. green**, a vivid light-green pigment, prepared from the arseniate of copper; **E. Isle**, a name given to Ireland on account of its verdure; **e. moth** (*Entom.*), a name of certain bright green moths, *e.g.* those of the genus *Hipparchus*; **e. nickel** (*Min.*), a native hydrocarbonate of nickel.

Emeraldine (e·mərăldin, –əin). 1855. [f. prec. + -INE¹.]
A. *adj.* Like an emerald in colour.
B. *sb.* A dye formed from aniline treated with hydrochloric acid and chlorate of potassium; aniline-green.

†**Emeras.** 1631. [Of unkn. origin.] One of a pair of small escutcheons affixed to the shoulders of an armed knight.

Emerge (ĭmɔ̄·ɹdʒ), *v.* 1563. [– L. *emergere*, f. *e-* EX-¹ + *mergere* dip, MERGE.] †**1.** *intr.* To rise by virtue of buoyancy *from* or *out of* a liquid –1721. **2.** To come up out of a liquid in which (the subject) has been immersed. Also *transf.* to rise *from* (under) the earth. 1640. **3.** To come forth into view, issue, appear 1563.
2. The Ocean out of which [Gt. Britain] emerged EMERSON **3.** To e. from the crowd JOHNSON. The satellite..will e...after..occultation SIR J. HERSCHEL. *fig.* To e. into distinct notice FROUDE. Here emerges the question as to [etc.] M. PATTISON. Hence †**Eme·rgement** NORTH.

Emerge, bad sp. of IMMERGE *v.*

Emergence (ĭmɔ̄·ɹdʒĕns). 1649. [– med.L. *emergentia*, f. *emergent-*, pres. ppl. stem of L. *emergere*; see prec., -ENCE. Cf. Fr. *émergence.*] **1.** The rising out of the water 1833. **2.** The process of issuing from concealment, confinement, etc. (*lit.* and *fig.*) 1755. **3.** An unforeseen occurrence; a sudden occasion (hence erron. used for 'urgent want'). Now repl. by EMERGENCY. 1649. **4.** *Bot.* An outgrowth on leaves or stems which arises from the sub-epidermic tissue 1882.
1. The e. of the land 1875. **2.** The e. of refracted light 1704. A glacier's e. from the valley KANE.

Emergency (ĭmɔ̄·ɹdʒĕnsi). 1631. [f. as prec.; see -ENCY.] **1.** = EMERGENCE 1. Now *rare.* 1646. †**2.** = EMERGENCE 2. –1762. †**3.** The sudden or unexpected occurrence (of a state of things, etc.) –1776. **4.** *concr.* A juncture that arises or 'crops up'; a sudden occasion (hence erron. used for 'pressing need') 1631; in *pl.* †casual profits. **5.** *attrib.* or *adj.* Used, issued, called upon, or arising in an emergency. *E. man*: spec. (in Ireland) a bailiff's officer, recruited for special service, *esp.* in evictions.
3. The e. of war..on the frontiers GIBBON. **4.** Relief on sudden emergencies 1764.

Emergent (ĭmɔ̄·ɹdʒĕnt). 1528. [– *emergent-*, pres. ppl. stem of L. *emergere*; see EMERGE, -ENT.]
A. *adj.* **1.** Rising out of a surrounding medium, *e.g.* water; also *fig.* 1627. **2.** That is in process of issuing forth; also *fig.* 1619. **3.** Casually or unexpectedly arising (*arch.*) 1593. ¶**4.** Used (imprŏp.) for 'urgent', 'pressing' 1706.
1. *fig.* Hope, still e., still contemns the wave SHENSTONE. **2.** The e. rays will be collected to a focus IMISON. *fig.* Declining all e. controversys 1619. E. parties J. H. NEWMAN. **3.** Directions vpon e. occasions DIGBY.
B. *sb.* †**1.** An outcome –1656. †**2.** = EMERGENCY 3. –1720. **3.** *Science.* That which is produced by a combination of causes, but cannot be regarded as the sum of their individual effects. Opp. to *resultant.* 1874.
Hence **Eme·rgently** *adv.*

Emerick, emeril(l, obs. ff. EMERY.

†**Eme·rit**, *v.* [– *emerit-*, pa. ppl. stem of L. *emerēri*; see EMERITUS.] *trans.* To earn by service. FAIRFAX.

Emerited (ĭme·ritėd), *ppl. a. arch.* 1664. [f. prec. + -ED¹.] = EMERITUS *a.*; *hence*, skilled, experienced.

||**Emeritus** (ĭme·ritŏs). 1823. [L. *emeritus*, pa. pple. of *emerēri* earn (one's discharge) by service, f. *e-* EX-¹ + *merēri* deserve; see MERIT.]
A. *adj.* Honourably discharged from service; that has retired from an office.
An e. Professor of Moral Philosophy DE QUINCEY.
B. *sb.* One who has retired from active service or occupation; an e. professor (Dicts.)

†**E·merods**, *sb. pl.* ME. [var. of HÆMORRHOID¹.] = HÆMORRHOID¹ 1. Still occas. used in allusions to 1 *Sam.* 5:6, 7.

Emersed (ĭmɔ̄·ɹst), *ppl. a.* 1686. [f. L. *emersus* (pa. pple. of *emergere* EMERGE), + -ED¹.] Standing out from a medium, *e.g.* water.

Emersion (ĭmɔ̄·ɹʃən). 1633. [– late L. *emersio*, f. *emers-*, pa. ppl. stem of L. *emergere* EMERGE; see -ION.] **1.** The appearing (of what has been submerged) above the surface of the water 1667. **2.** The action of issuing from concealment, etc.). Somewhat *rare.* 1763. †**3.** A coming into notice –1680.
1. The Immersion and E. of the Globe 1667. **2.** The e. of a satellite of Jupiter JOHNSON. **3.** The e. of the New Jerusalem into Being 1680.

Emery (e·məri). 1481. [– Fr. *émeri*, *émeril*, var. of †*esmeril* – It. *smeriglio* :– Rom. **smericulum*, f. med.Gr. σμηρί, Gr. σμίρις, σμύρις polishing powder.] **1.** A coarse variety of corundum, used for polishing metals, stones, and glass. **2.** *attrib.*, as *e. stone.*
Comb.: **e.-cloth, -paper**, cloth or paper covered with e.-powder, used for polishing or cleaning metals, etc.; **-powder**, ground e., hence a *vb.*, to rub with e.-powder; **-stick**, 'a stick of wood round which E. paper is glued'; **-wheel**, a wheel coated with e., and used for polishing.

||**Emesis** (e·mĭsis). 1875. [Gr. ἔμεσις, f. ἐμεῖν vomit.] *Path.* Vomiting.

Emetia (ĭmĭ·tiă). 1830. [f. Gr. ἔμετος vomiting + -IA¹.] = EMETINE.

Emetic (ĭme·tik). 1657. [– Gr. ἐμετικός, f. ἔμετος vomiting, f. ἐμεῖν vomit; see -IC.]
A. *adj.* Having power to cause vomiting; *fig.* sickening, mawkish 1670.
fig. Richardson..in his e. history of Pamela 1770.
B. *sb.* A medicine that excites vomiting.
Hence **Eme·tical** *a.* = EMETIC *a.*, **-ly** *adv.*

Emetine (e·mĭtəin). 1819. [f. Gr. ἔμετος (see prec.) + -INE⁵.] *Chem.* An alkaloid obtained from the root of *Cephaëlis ipecacuanha.*

Emeto-cathartic (e:mĭto,kăþā·ɹtik). 1879. [f. *emeto-*, comb. form of Gr. ἔμετος vomiting.] *Med.* **a.** *adj.* Able to induce both purging and vomiting. **b.** *sb.* [*sc.* substance.]

Emetology (emĭtǫ·lŏdʒi). 1847. [f. as prec. + -LOGY.] *Med.* 'The doctrine of, or a treatise on, vomiting and emetics' (*Syd. Soc. Lex.*).

Emeu, Emew, vars. of EMU.

‖**Émeute** (emö̆t). 1862. [Fr. :– Rom. **exmovita*, subst. use of fem. pa. pple. of **exmovēre* (see EMOTION).] A popular rising or disturbance.

†**Emfo·rth.** ME. only. [f. *em* EVEN *adv.* + FORTH.] **a.** *adv.* Equally. **b.** *prep.* **1.** According to; in proportion to. **2.** Equally with.

†**E·micant,** *a.* [– *ēmicant-*, pres. ppl. stem of L. *emicare*; see next, -ANT.] That darts or flashes forth. BLACKMORE.

†**E·micate,** *v. rare.* 1657. [– *emicat-*, pa. ppl. stem. of L. *emicare* spring forth, flash out; see -ATE³.] *intr.* To spring forth, appear. Also *fig.* –1708. Hence †**Emica·tion,** flying off in small particles, as sparkling liquors; shining forth.

Emiction (ĭmi·kʃən). 1666. [– *emict-*, pa. ppl. stem of med.L. *emingere*, f. *e-* EX-¹ + *mingere* urinate; see -ION.] **1.** The voiding of urine 1847. **2.** Urine.

Emictory (ĭmi·ktəri). [f. as prec.; see -ORY.] **a.** *adj.* Diuretic. **b.** *sb.* A diuretic. (Dicts.)

Emigrant (e·migrănt). 1754. [– *emigrant-*, pres. ppl. stem of L. *emigrare*; see EMIGRATE *v.*, -ANT. Cf. Fr. *émigrant.*]

A. *sb.* One who leaves his own country to settle (permanently) in another. Also *attrib.* as in *e.-ship.* **b.** *spec.* = ÉMIGRÉ 1792.

The noise of embarking emigrants EMERSON.

B. *adj.* That emigrates. Also (of birds) migratory. 1794.

†**Emi·grate,** *a.* [– L. *emigratus*, pa. pple. of *emigrare*; see next, -ATE².] That has migrated (from the body). GAYTON.

Emigrate (e·migreⁱt), *v.* 1778. [– *emigrat-*, pa. ppl. stem of L. *emigrare*, f. *e-* EX-¹ + *migrare* MIGRATE; see -ATE³.] **1.** *intr.* To quit one country, etc. to settle in another. **2.** *trans.* To cause or assist to do this 1870.

1. They don't e., till they could earn their livelihood..at home 1778.

Emigration (emigrēⁱ·ʃən). 1649. [– late L. *emigratio*, f. *emigrat-*; see prec., -ION. Cf. Fr. *émigration.*] **1.** The action of departing out of a particular place or set of surroundings. **2.** *esp.* The departure of persons from their native country, to settle permanently in another. Also *attrib.*, as in *e.-agent.* 1677. **3.** Emigrants collectively 1863.

1. The E. of humane Souls from the bodies by Ecstasy MORE. **2.** Those melancholy emigrations ..from the Islands..of Scotland 1791. Hence **Emigra·tional** *a.* pertaining to e. **Emigra·tionist,** an advocate of e.

Emigrator (e·migreⁱtəɹ). *rare.* 1837. [f. EMIGRATE *v.* + -OR 2.] = EMIGRANT.

Emigratory (e·migreⁱtəri), *a.* 1839. [f. as prec. + -ORY².] **1.** Of animals: = MIGRATORY (*rare*). **2.** Engaged in emigrating; pertaining to emigration 1854.

‖**Émigré.** 1792. [Fr. pa. pple. of *émigrer*, EMIGRATE.] A French emigrant; *esp.* one of those Royalists who fled at the time of the French Revolution.

Eminence (e·minĕns). 1603. [– L. *eminentia*, f. as next; see -ENCE. Cf. (O)Fr. *éminence.*]

I. 1. †Height; an elevated position 1658. †**2.** A prominence. Chiefly in *Anat.* –1743. **3.** A rising ground, hill. Also *fig.* 1670.

3. There is a battery..on an e. ANSON. *fig.* We..speak..of Age As of a final E. WORDSW.

II. 1. Distinguished superiority as compared with others in rank, station, character, attainments, or the possession of any quality, good or bad 1603. **2.** As a title of honour, now borne only by Cardinals 1653. †**3.** An eminent quality; a distinction –1659. †**4.** Eminent measure –1710.

1. Satan by merit rais'd to that bad e. MILT. *P. L.* II. 6. Surgeons of e. 1800. E. in science M. PATTISON. **3.** So several eminences met in this worthy man FULLER. **4.** Men..who had no one Quality in any E. STEELE. So **E·minency** (in same senses).

Eminent (e·minĕnt), *a.* ME. [– *eminent-*, pres. ppl. stem of L. *eminēre* project; see -ENT. Cf. (O)Fr. *éminent.*] **1.** High, towering above other things; projecting, prominent. Also *fig.* 1541. **2.** Of persons: **a.** Exalted in rank or station 1603. **b.** Distinguished in character or attainments 1611. †**3.** Of things or places; Chief, important; especially useful –1748. **4.** Remarkable in degree; signal, noteworthy ME. ¶Confused with IMMINENT. 1600.

1. Upon an high mountain and e. *Ezek.* 17:22. **2. a.** A certain e. rajah BURKE. **b.** E. cooks are paid 1200*l.* a-year HT. MARTINEAU. E. as a speaker GROTE. **4.** His success was e. DISRAELI. Phr. *Right of e. domain*: see DOMAIN.

Eminently (e·minĕntli), *adv.* 1610. [f. prec. + -LY².] In an eminent manner. †**1.** On high –1675. †**2.** Conspicuously –1774. **3.** In an eminent degree 1641. **4.** *Philos.*, etc. In a higher sense than *formally* (*i.e.* according to the definition of things) 1640.

Emir (emīᵊ·ɹ, ī·məɹ). 1625. [– Fr. *émir* – Sp. *emir* – Arab. *'amīr* AMEER. See ADMIRAL.] **1.** A Saracen or Arab prince, or governor of a province; a military commander 1632. **2.** A title of honour borne by the descendants of Mohammed.

2. Mahomet's..kinsmen in greene Shashes, who are called Emers PURCHAS. Hence **Emi·rate,** the jurisdiction or government of an e.

Emissary (e·misări), *sb.*¹ and *a.* 1625. [– L. *emissarius* scout, spy, f. *emiss-*, pa. ppl. stem of *emittere* EMIT; see -ARY¹.]

A. *sb.* A person sent out on a mission to promote the interests of his employer. (Usually in a bad sense, implying something odious or underhand in the mission or its manner.) Also *fig.* **b.** = SPY. (Dicts.)

I am endeavouring to get information by emissaries WELLINGTON. Hence **E·missaryshi:p** B. JONS.

B. *adj.* **1.** That is sent forth 1659. **2.** *Phys.* Of small vessels: Sent forth from a main trunk 1831.

1. The High-Priest..offered the e. (= scape-)goat 1833.

Emissary (e·misări), *sb.*² 1601. [– L. *emissarium* outlet, f. as prec.; see -ARY¹.] An outlet, channel, duct. Also *fig.* *Obs.* exc. in *Rom. Antiq.*

Without any emissaries, tunnels, or holes HOLLAND. *fig.* The common e. of scandal SWIFT.

Emissile (ĭmi·sil), *a.* 1732. [f. L. *emiss-* (see prec.) + -ILE.] That can be thrust out, as *emissile* cornua in snails.

Emission (ĭmi·ʃən). 1607. [– L. *emissio*, f. as prec.; see -ION. Cf. (O)Fr. *émission.*] †**1.** *gen.* The action of sending forth –1827. †**2.** The issuing (of a book, notice, etc.) –1779. **3.** The setting in circulation (of bills, notes, shares, etc.). Also *concr.* 1773. **4.** The action of giving off or sending out (of light, heat, gases, etc.). Also *fig.* 1619. **5.** *concr.* That which is emitted 1664. **6.** *Phys.* = L. *emissio seminis* 1646.

4. The e. of fragrance 1859, of sparks of light 1871. Phr. *Theory of e., E. theory*: the theory that light consists of imponderable particles emitted from luminous bodies.

†**Emissi·tious,** *a.* [f. L. *emissicius* sent out (f. as prec.) + -OUS; see -ITIOUS¹.] Prying, inquisitive, as *emissitious* eyes. BP. HALL.

Emissive (ĭmi·siv), *a.* 1657. [f. as prec.; see -IVE. With sense 1, cf. Fr. *émissif*, -IVE.] **1.** Having power to EMIT (sense 1) 1870. †**2.** That is emitted –1737.

1. Phr. *E. theory*: = *Emission theory.* Hence **Emissi·vity,** emissive or radiating power of heat or light 1880.

Emissory (ĭmi·səri). 1858. [f. as prec. + -ORY¹; cf. EMISSARY *sb.*²] = EMISSARY *sb.*²

Emit (ĭmi·t), *v.* 1626. [– L. *emittere*, f. *e-* EX-¹ + *mittere* send.] (Not used with personal obj.) **1.** *trans.* To send forth, discharge, exude, give off. †**2.** To throw out as an offshoot –1756. **3.** To utter 1753. †**4.** To issue, publish –1847. **5.** To issue formally and by authority (now *esp.* paper currency, bills, etc.) 1649. †**6.** To discharge (a missile) 1720.

1. To e. effluvia BENTLEY, light 1794, threads (as spiders) TODD, flames MRS. JAMESON, fluid 1879. **3.** To e. sound TYNDALL, thoughts CARLYLE.

So †**Emi·ttent** *a.* that emits. Hence **Emi·tter.**

Emmantle, var. of IMMANTLE.

Emmarble (emā·ɹb'l), *v.* Also **en-.** 1596. [f. EM- + MARBLE *sb.*] *trans.* To turn into marble (*fig.*); to sculpture in marble; to adorn with marble.

Emmarvel (emā·ɹvĕl). Also **en-.** 1740. [f. EM- + MARVEL *sb.* or *v.*] *trans.* To fill with wonder.

Emmenagogue (emī·năgǫg). 1702. [f. Gr. ἔμμηνα menses (f. ἐν EM- + μην- month) + ἀγωγός drawing forth, f. ἄγειν to lead.] *Med.*

†**A.** *adj.* Having power to promote the menstrual discharge –1830. Hence **Emme:nago·gic** *a.* (in same sense).

B. *sb.* Agents which promote the menstrual discharge 1731.

Emmenology (emīnǫ·lŏdʒi). 1742. [f. as prec. + -LOGY.] A treatise on, or the doctrine of, menstruation. Hence **Emme:nolo·gical** *a.* relating to menstruation.

Emmet (e·mĕt). [repr. OE. *ǣmete* wk. fem. (see ANT). The OE. *ǣ* became in ME. *ā* or *ē*, whence ME. *āmete* (*amt* ANT), and *ēmete* (EMMET) respectively.] An ANT. Chiefly *dial.* *Comb.* **e.-hunter** (*dial.*) the Wryneck.

Emmetrope (e·mĕtrōᵘp). 1875. [f. as next.] *Phys.* One whose sight is emmetropic.

‖**Emmetropia** (emĕtrōᵘ·piă). Also **Emme·tropy.** 1864. [mod.L., f. Gr. ἔμμετρος in measure + ὤψ (ὠπ-) the eye + -IA¹.] *Phys.* The normal condition of the refractive media of the eye in which parallel rays come to a focus upon the retina when the eye is at rest and passive. So **Emmetro·pic** *a.* characterized by e.

Emmew, var. of INMEW *v.*

Emmove, var. of ENMOVE *v.*

Emodin (e·mŏdin). 1858. [f. mod.L. (*Rheum*) *emodi*, Turkey rhubarb (f. Gr. Ἠμωδός the Himalaya) + -IN¹.] *Chem.* A constituent of rhubarb root. Its formula is $C_{40}H_{30}O_{13}$.

Emollescence (imǫle·sĕns). 1794. [f. late L. *emollescere* (L. *mollescere*, f. *mollis* soft); see -ESCENCE.] *Chem.*, etc. 'A state of softening; the softened condition of a melting body before it fuses' (*Syd. Soc. Lex.*).

Emolliate (ĭmǫ·li,eⁱt), *v.* 1802. [irreg. f. L. *emollire* + -ATE³, after *emaciate*, etc.] To soften, render effeminate. PINKERTON. So †**Emo·lliative** *a.* that tends to e. (*rare*).

Emollient (ĭmǫ·li,ĕnt). 1643. [– *emollient-*, pres. ppl. stem of L. *emollire*, f. *e-* EX-¹ + *mollis* soft; see -ENT.] **a.** *adj.* That can soften or relax. Also *fig.* **b.** *sb.* A softening application. Chiefly in *pl.* 1656.

Emolli·tion. ? *Obs.* 1619. [f. *emollit-*, pa. ppl. stem of L. *emollire* (see prec.) + -ION.] The action of softening. Also *fig.*

Emolument (ĭmǫ·liŭmĕnt). 1480. [– (O)Fr. *émolument* or L. *emolumentum*, *emoli-* gain, orig. prob. 'payment to a miller for the grinding of corn', f. *emolere* grind up, f. *e-* EX-¹ + *molere* grind; see MILL, -MENT.] **1.** Profit or gain from station, office, or employment; dues; remuneration, salary. †**2.** Advantage –1756.

1. Certain..emoluments unto the said benefice due 1480. Hence †**Emolume·ntal** (*rare*), **Emo:lume·ntary** *adjs.* profitable, advantageous.

†**Emo·ng,** *prep.* and *adv.* ME. [var. of AMONG.] = AMONG –1571. Hence †**Emo·nges(t** *prep.* = AMONGST.

Emony (e·mǒni). 1644. [Aphetic f. *anemone* (taken as *an emony*).] = ANEMONE.

Emotion (ĭmōᵘ·ʃən). 1579. [– Fr. *émotion*, f. *émouvoir* excite, move the feelings of, after *mouvoir*, *motion.*] †**1.** A moving out, migration –1695. †**2.** A (physical) moving, stirring, agitation –1822. †**3.** *transf.* A popular movement, tumult –1757. **4.** *fig.* Any vehement or excited mental state 1660. **b.** *Psychology.* A mental feeling or affection (*e.g.* of pain, desire, hope, etc.), as dist. from cognitions or volitions. Also *abstr.* 'feeling'. 1808.

4. The emotions of humanity JER. TAYLOR. **b.** He..almost denounces me..for referring Religion to the region of E. TYNDALL. Hence **Emo·tioned** *ppl. a.* stirred by e.

Emotional (ĭmōᵘ·ʃənăl), *a.* 1847. [f. prec. + -AL¹.] **1.** Connected with the feelings or passions. **2.** Liable to, or easily affected by, emotion; having the capacity for emotion. Also as quasi-*sb.* 1857.

1. The e. weaknesses of humanity FROUDE. Hence **Emo:tiona·lity**, e. character or temperament. **Emo·tionally** *adv.* in an e. manner; with reference to the emotions.

Emotionalism (ĭmōᵘ·ʃənăliz'm). 1865. [f. prec. + -ISM.] Emotional character; *esp.* the habit of cultivating or of weakly yielding to emotion.

The religion of e. [is] represented by the negro 1883.

Emotionalist (ĭmōᵘ·ʃənălist). 1866. [f. as prec. + -IST.] **a.** One who bases his theory of conduct on the emotions. **b.** Contemptuously: One who is foolishly emotional, or who appeals (discreditably) to the emotions of others.

a. Mill writes..as if he were a mere e. 1866.

Emotionalize (ĭmōᵘ·ʃənăləiz), *v. rare.* 1879. [f. as prec. + -IZE.] To render emotional; to deal with emotionally.

A pious family, where religion was not..emotionalised FROUDE.

Emotive (ĭmōᵘ·tiv), *a.* 1735. [– *emot-*, pa. ppl. stem of L. *emovēre* (see next) + -IVE.] **1.** †**a.** Causing movement. **b.** Tending or able to excite emotion. **2.** Pertaining to emotion 1830. Hence **Emo·tively** *adv.* emotionally. **Emo·tiveness.**

Emove (ĭmū·v), *v. rare.* ME. [– L. *emovēre*, f. *e-* EX-¹ + *movēre* MOVE.] *trans.* †**a.** To move (to an action). **b.** To excite emotion in.

b. Kindly raptures them e. THOMSON.

Empa·cket, *v. rare.* 1825. [See EM-, PACKET.] *trans.* To pack up SCOTT.

Empæstic (empī·stik), *a.* 1850. [– Gr. ἐμπαιστική (τέχνη), f. ἐμπαίειν beat in, emboss.] In phr. *E. art*: the art of embossing.

Empair, Empale, etc.; see IMP-.

†**Empa·le**, *v.* 1604. [f. EM- + PALE *a.*] To make pale –1664.

The heart's still perfect; though empaled the face 1604.

†**Empa·nel**, *sb.* 1501. [f. next.] A list of jurors; a panel –1775.

Empanel, im- (empæ·nĕl), *v.* 1487. [– AFr. *empaneller*; see EM-, PANEL.] *trans.* To enter (the names of a jury) on a panel or official list; to constitute or enroll (a body of jurors).

Jurors duly empannelled and sworn BURKE. Hence **Empa·nelment**, the action of the vb.

†**Empa·nnel**, *v. rare.* 1620. [f. EM- + PANEL *sb.* 2.] To put a pack-saddle upon –1881.

Empanoply; see EM-, PANOPLY.

Emparadise, Empark, etc.; see IMP-.

†**Empa·sm.** *rare.* 1657. [f. Gr. ἐμπάσσειν sprinkle on.] A powder to be sprinkled on the body to mask the smell of sweating; also for other purposes.

Empassion, Empawn, etc.; see IMP-.

Empathy (e·mpăþi). *Psychol.* 1912. [Rendering, after Gr. ἐμπάθεια, of G. *einfühlung* (Lipps), f. *ein* IN *prep.* + *fühlung* feeling; see EM-, -PATHY.] The power of projecting one's personality into, and so fully understanding, the object of contemplation.

Empennage (empe·nédʒ). 1909. [Fr., f. *empenner* feather (an arrow).] An arrangement of stabilizing planes at the stern of an aeroplane or airship; also, the tail-surfaces or tail-plane.

†**Empeo·ple**, *v.* 1582. [f. EM- + PEOPLE.] **1.** *trans.* To fill with people –1631. **2.** *nonce-use.* To establish as the population. SPENSER.

Emperess(e, Emperice, obs. ff. EMPRESS.

†**Empe·rish**, *v. rare* 1530. [app. f. Fr. *empirer* worsen (f. *pire* worse), formally assoc. with PERISH.] *trans.* To make worse, impair –1593.

I deeme thy braine emperished bee Through rustie elde SPENSER. Hence †**Empe·rishment.**

†**E·mperize**, *v. rare.* 1598. [f. EMPERY + -IZE.] *trans.* and *intr.* To rule as an emperor –1601.

Emperor (e·mpərəɹ). [ME. *emperere*, *emperour* – respectively OFr. *emperere*, nom. and *emperour*, *-eor*, acc. (mod. *empereur*), semi-pop. – L. *impera·tor*, *imperato·rem*, f. *imperare* command, f. *in* IM-¹ + *parare* prepare, contrive; see -OR 2.] **1.** The sovereign of an Empire: a title considered superior in dignity to that of 'king'. Also *transf.* and *fig.* †**2.** In the etymol. sense = 'commander'. **b.** *Rom. Antiq.* As tr. L. *imperator* in its republican sense (now repl. by the L. word). –1741. **3.** *attrib.*, as *e.-king*, etc. ME.

1. The grete Cham..is the gretteste Emperour of alle the parties beȝonde MAUNDEV. Otton the emperour 1529. The E. of Russia was my Father *Winter's T.* III. ii. 120. Since Buonaparte's time the title of E...has ceased to have any particular meaning FREEMAN. **2.** Cicero was saluted E. 1741.

Comb.: **e.-moth** (*Saturnia pavonia minor*); **Purple E.**: a butterfly, *Apatura iris*, also called †**E. of the Woods**, and perh. †**E. of Morocco.** Hence **E·mperorshi:p**, the office, dignity, or reign of an e.

Empery (e·mpĕri), *sb.* Now usu. *poet.* ME. [– OFr. *emperie*, *empirie* – L. *imperium* EMPIRE.] **1.** †The dignity or dominion of an emperor –1588. **b.** Absolute dominion 1548. †**c.** Legitimate government (= L. *imperium*) –1642. **2.** The territory of an emperor, or of a powerful ruler: also *fig.* 1550.

1. b. The only God of emperie and of might DRAYTON. **2.** *fig.* More than her e. of joys KEATS.

Empetrous (e·mpĭtrəs), *a.* [f. Gr. ἔμπετρος growing on rocks + -OUS.] *Zool.* Of seals, and other short-limbed animals: Lying directly upon the ground.

†**Empha·se**, *v.* [f. EMPHASIS.] ? To lay emphasis upon. B. JONS.

Emphasis (e·mfăsis). Pl. **emphases.** 1573. [– L. *emphasis* – Gr. ἔμφασις, orig. (mere) appearance, f. *ἐμφα- in ἐμφαίνειν exhibit, f. *en* EM-² + φαίνειν show (see PHASIS).] †**1.** (The Gr. and L. sense.) A figure of speech in which more is implied than is actually said; a meaning conveyed by implication –1764. **2.** Vigour of expression. Now as *transf.* from 4. 1573. **3.** Force of feeling, action, etc. 1602. **4.** Stress of voice laid on a word or phrase to indicate its implied meaning, or simply to mark its importance 1613. **5.** *transf.* Stress laid upon, or importance assigned to, a fact or idea 1687. **6.** Prominence 1872. †**7.** A mere appearance. WHARTON.

2. Tertullian doth add the greater E. to his Arguments BP. STILLINGFL. **3.** *Haml.* V. i. 278. **4.** The e. is wrongly placed JOWETT. **5.** My laying e. on the previous effect of the vaccine inoculation 1805. **6.** The bones which mark the features.. lose their e. BLACKIE. var. †**E·mphasy.**

Emphasize (e·mfăsəiz), *v.* Also **-ise.** 1828. [f. EMPHASIS + -IZE.] To impart emphasis to; to lay stress upon; to add force to; to bring into special prominence.

Gesticulation goes along with speech..to e. it TYLOR.

Emphatic (emfæ·tik), *a.* 1708. [– late L. *emphaticus* – Gr. ἐμφατικός; see EMPHASIS, -IC. Cf. Fr. *emphatique.*] **1.** Forcibly expressive; bearing the stress in pronunciation. **2.** Of persons: That expresses himself with emphasis of voice, gesture, or language 1760. **3.** Of actions, etc.: Strongly marked 1846.

1. The e. representation of Scripture 1836. Accented or..e. syllables HALLAM. **2.** A little e. man DICKENS. **3.** Still more e. honours PRESCOTT. Hence **Empha·tical** *a.* (now *rare*), in senses 1–3; also, †merely apparent. **Empha·tically** *adv.* in an e. manner, forcibly; decisively; †suggestively; †merely in appearance. **Empha·ticalness** (*rare*).

Emphractic, †-al (emfræ·ktik, †-ăl). 1678. [– late L. *emphracticus* – Gr. ἐμφρακτικός, f. ἐμφράττειν obstruct; see -IC.] *Med.* **a.** *adj.* Having power to obstruct 1727. **b.** *sb.* A medicine which shuts up the pores of the skin.

Emphrensy, obs. var. of ENFRENZY.

‖**Emphysema** (emfisī·mă). 1661. [Late L. – Gr. ἐμφύσημα, f. ἐμφυσᾶν puff up.] *Med.* A swelling caused by the presence of air in the connective tissue. So **Emphyse·matous** *a.* of the nature of e.; pertaining to e.

Emphyteusis (emfitiū·sis). 1618. [– late L. *emphyteusis* – Gr. ἐμφύτευσις, lit. 'implanting', f. ἐμφυτεύειν implant.] *Law.* A perpetual right in a piece of another's land.

An e. or hereditary lease 1878. Hence **Emphyteu·tic, -al** *a.* of the nature of, or held by, e.

‖**Emphyteuta** (emfitiū·tă). 1708. [Late L. – Gr. ἐμφυτευτής, f. ἐμφυτεύειν; see prec.] *Law.* 'A tenant of land which was subject to a fixed perpetual rent' (Maine). So †**Emphyteu·ticary**, in same sense.

Empicture (empi·ktiūr), *v.* Also **en-, im-.** 1520. [f. EM- + PICTURE.] To represent in a picture, portray.

Empierce, im- (em-, impīᵊ·ɹs), *v.* 1578. [f. EM- IM-¹ + PIERCE *v.*] *trans.* To pierce through keenly; to transfix (*lit.* and *fig.*).

†**Empi·ght**, *v.* ME. [pa. t. and pa. pple. of **empitch*, f. EM- + PITCH *v.*¹] Fixed in, implanted. Also *intr.* for *refl.* –1746.

Empire (e·mpəiᵊɹ), *sb.* ME. [– (O)Fr. *empire*, earlier *emperie* (see EMPERY) – L. *imperium*, rel. to *imperator* EMPEROR.] **1.** Supreme and extensive political dominion. **2.** *trans.* and *fig.* Absolute sway, supreme control ME. **3.** = EMPERORSHIP 1606. **4.** Government by an emperor or emperors, and the period during which it existed 1834. **5.** An extensive territory (*esp.* an aggregate of many states) ruled over by an emperor, or by a sovereign state ME. Also *transf.* and *fig.* (Cf. *realm.*) **6.** A sovereign state 1532.

1. The establishment of the British e. in India 1845. **2.** Thy blood and vertue Contend for E. in thee *All's Well* I. i. 72. **4.** The Consulate and the E. 1866. **5.** The approximate population of the British E. is now 321,000,000 *Whitaker's Almanack* 1887. Phr. *The E.*: often *spec.* (*esp.* before 1804) the 'Holy Roman' or 'Romano-Germanic' empire; (*b*) Great Britain with its colonies and dependencies; the British Empire.

Order of the British Empire: an order, open to both men and women, instituted by George V in 1917 to reward services rendered to the Empire, whether at home or abroad.

Comb. **E. City, State:** in U.S., a name for the City and State of New York. **E. Day,** 24th May. Hence †**E·mpire** *v.* to rule as an emperor.

Empiric (empi·rik). 1541. [– L. *empiricus* sb. – Gr. ἐμπειρικός, f. ἐμπειρία experience, f. ἔμπειρος skilled, f. ἐν EM- + πεῖρα trial, experiment; see -IC. Cf. (O)Fr. *empirique.* In XVII usu. (e·mpĭrik).]

A. *adj.* = EMPIRICAL (chiefly in senses of the use as *sb.*) 1605.

B. *sb.* **1.** One of the sect of ancient physicians called *Empirici* (Ἐμπειρικοί), who drew their rules of practice only from experience 1541. **b.** One who, in matters of science, relies solely upon observation and experiment. Also *fig.* 1578. **2.** One who practises physic or surgery without scientific knowledge; a quack, a charlatan. Also *transf.* 1562.

Empirical (empi·rikăl), *a.* 1569. [f. prec. + -AL¹.] **1.** *Med.* Based on, or guided by, the results of observation and experiment only. **2.** That practises physic or surgery without scientific knowledge; quack 1680. **3.** *gen.* That is guided by mere experience, without knowledge of principles. Often *transf.* from 2: Charlatan. 1751. **4.** Pertaining to, or derived from, experience 1649.

2. A..Tinker e. to the Body of Man BUTLER. E. drugs 1839. Hasty and e. measures 1861. **4.** An e. law then, is an observed uniformity, presumed to be resolvable into simpler laws, but not yet resolved into them MILL. Hence **Empi·rically** *adv.*

Empiricism (empi·risiz'm). 1657. [f. EMPIRIC + -ISM.] **1.** *Med.* The method or practice of an EMPIRIC; ignorant and unscientific practice; quackery. Also *transf.* **2.** The use of empirical methods in any art or science. **b.** *Philos.* The theory which regards experience as the only source of knowledge. 1803. **3.** *concr.* An empirical conclusion 1846.

So **Empi·ricist**, one who upholds philosophical e., or one who follows empirical methods.

Empirism (e·mpiriz'm). 1716. [– Fr. *empirisme*, f. *empirique* EMPIRIC; see -ISM.] = EMPIRICISM 2 b. Hence **Empiri·stic** *a.* pertaining to e.

Emplacement (emplēⁱ·smĕnt). 1802. [– Fr. *emplacement*, f. *en-* EM- + *place* PLACE; see -MENT.] **1.** The action of placing in a position; placed condition 1869. **2.** Position; site (*rare*) 1802. **3.** *Mil.* A platform for guns, with epaulements to protect the gunners 1811.

Hence **Empla·ce** *v.* (*rare*) to put into position.

Empla·ne, *v.* 1923. [f. EM- + PLANE *sb.*³] To take or go on board an aeroplane.

†**Empla·ster**, *sb.* ME. [– OFr. *emplastre* (mod. *emplâtre*) – L. *emplastrum* plaster; also, in budding trees, – Gr. ἔμπλαστρον plaster or salve.] **1.** *Med.* or *Surg.* = PLASTER. Also *fig.* –1809. **2.** = EMPLASTRATION 1, q.v. –1656.

†**Empla·ster**, *v.* ME. [– OFr. *emplastrer* (mod. *emplâtrer*), f. *emplastre* (see prec.). In sense 2 – L. *emplastrare*, f. *emplastrum* (see

prec.).] **1.** To cover with a plaster; to plaster over; also *fig.* **b.** To spread on as a plaster. –1633. **2.** To bud trees; see EMPLASTRATION 1. –1656.

1. Als fair as ye his [Solomon's] name emplastre, He was a lecchour CHAUCER.

†**Empla·stic.** 1618. [– Fr. *emplastique* (XVI) or its source late L. *emplasticus* – Gr. ἐμπλαστικός; see EMPLASTER *sb.*, -IC.] **A.** *adj.* Fit to be used as a plaster; *hence*, adhesive, glutinous. Also, that stops up the pores. –1756. **B.** *sb.* An adhesive or glutinous substance –1751.

†**Emplastra·tion.** ME. [– L. *emplastratio*, f. *emplastrat-*, pa. ppl. stem of *emplastrare*; see EMPLASTER *v.*, -ION. Cf. Fr. *emplastration* (XVI).] **1.** A mode of budding trees; so called from the piece of bark surrounding the bud, like a plaster on the tree –1745. **2.** The application of a plaster –1633.

Emplead, obs. f. IMPLEAD.

Emplection, bad f. EMPLECTON.

Emplectite (emple·ktəit). 1857 [f. Gr. ἔμπλεκτος inwoven + -ITE[1] 2 b, from its appearance.] *Min.* A sulphide of bismuth and copper, occurring in bright tin-white needle-shaped crystals.

‖**Emple·cton.** 1708. [mod.L. – Gr. ἔμπλεκτον; see prec.] *Arch.* 'A kind of masonry, in which the outsides of the wall are ashlar, and the interval filled up with rubble' (Liddell and Scott).

Emplore, obs. f. IMPLORE.

Employ (emploi·), *sb.* 1666. [f. next; cf. Fr. *emploi.*] †**1.** = EMPLOYMENT 1. –1829. **2.** The state or fact of being employed 1709. **3.** That on which a person or thing is employed; occupation 1678.

2. Phr. *In, out of, e.*; *in the e. of* (the person employing).

Employ (emploi·), *v.* 1460. [– (O)Fr. *employer* :– Rom. *implicare*, for L. *implicari* be involved (in) or attached (to), pass. of *implicare* enfold, involve; see IMPLY.] **1.** *trans.* To apply to a purpose; to use as a means or instrument, or as material. **b.** To make use of (time, etc.); 'to fill with business' (J.) 1481. **2.** To use the services of for some special business; to have or maintain in one's service 1584. **3.** To find work or occupation for; in *pass.* often merely to be occupied. Also *refl.* 1579. †**4.** = IMPLY in various senses –1626.

1. Imploy your chiefest thoughts to courtship *Merch. V.* II. viii. 43. **b.** Having ten days at my disposal..I was anxious to e. them TYNDALL. **2.** Lessing..was employed by Voltaire..in the Hirschel case MORLEY. Scott & Co., employing nine men six months RAYMOND. **3.** He was imploy'd in drinking SWIFT. Speculations to e. our curiosity BERKELEY. Hence **Employ·able** *a.*

‖**Employé** (anplwaye). 1834. [Fr., pa. pple. of *employer* EMPLOY *v.*] One who is employed; *esp.* one employed for wages or a salary by a business house or by government. Hence also **Employée**, a female e.

Employee (ėmploi·*i*, emploi,*ī*·). 1854. [f. EMPLOY *v.* + -EE[1]. Cf. prec.] = prec. Also in U.S. **Employ(e.**

Employer (emploi·əɹ). 1599. [f. as prec. + -ER[1].] One who employs; *spec.* one who employs servants, workmen, etc. for wages.

Employment (emploi·mėnt). 1593. [f. EMPLOY *v.* + -MENT.] **1.** The action of employing; the state of being employed 1598. †**b.** Service –1603. **2.** That on which (one) is employed; business; occupation; a commission 1597. †**b.** The use to which a thing is put –1658. †**3.** A position in the public service –1734.

1. The hand of little Imployment hath the daintier sense *Haml.* V. i. 77. **b.** *John* I. i. 198. **2.** The excuse of not finding e. HOBBES. **b.** *Rich. II*, I. i. 90.

Emplume (empl*i*ū·m), *v.* Also **im-.** 1623. [– (O)Fr. *emplumer*, f. *en-* EM- + *plume* feather.] To adorn with or as with plumes. Hence **Emplu·med** *ppl. a.*

Emplunge, obs. var. of IMPLUNGE.

Empocket (empǫ·kėt), *v. arch.* Also **im-.** 1728. [f. EM- + POCKET *sb.*] *trans.* To put into one's pocket.

Empoison (empoi·zən, -z'n), *v.* ME. [– OFr. *empoisoner* (mod. *-nn-*), f. *en-* EM- + *poison* POISON *sb.*] †**1.** *trans.* To administer poison to. Also *absol.* –1670. †Also *transf.* and *fig.* –1667. **2.** To put poison into; also, to dip in poison. Now *rhet.* 1602. **3.** *fig.* To vitiate as with poison; to envenom; to embitter ME.

3. *fig.* How much an ill word may impoison liking SHAKS. Hence **Empoi·soner.** *Obs.* or *arch.* **Empoi·sonment,** the act of poisoning or fact of being poisoned (*Obs.* or *arch.*); the action of tainting with, or as with, poison.

Emporetic (empore·tik), *a.* [– L. *emporeticus* – Gr. *ἐμπορητικός for -ευτικός; see next.] *Antiq.* Pertaining to trade. *E. paper:* a coarse kind of papyrus used for wrapping up parcels.

†**Emporeu·tic.** 1612. [– Gr. ἐμπορευτικός, f. ἐμπορεύεσθαι trade, f. ἔμπορος trader; see next.] **A.** *adj.* Of or pertaining to trade. **B.** *sb.* **a.** *sing.* The emporeutic art. **b.** *pl.* Articles made for sale.

Emporium (empōᵊ·riŏm). Pl. **-iums, -ia.** 1586. [– L. *emporium* – Gr. ἐμπόριον, f. ἔμπορος merchant, f. ἐν EM- + vbl. stem πορ- περ- journey.] **1.** A place in which merchandise is collected or traded in; a principal centre of commerce, a mart. **b.** A pompous name for: A shop 1839. Also *transf.* and *fig.* †**2.** 'The common sensory of the brain' (Bailey).

1. The e., or general market, for the goods of all the different countries whose trade it carries on ADAM SMITH. **b.** Emporiums of splendid dresses DICKENS. var. †**E·mpory.** Hence †**Empo·rial** *a.* pertaining to, or of the nature of, an e.

†**Empo·rtment.** [– (O)Fr. *emportement*, f. *emporter* carry away; see -MENT.] A fit of passion. NORTH.

†**Empo·ver,** *v. rare.* 1474. [– OFr. *empoverer*, also *empov(e)rir* (mod. *empauvrir*); see IMPOVERISH.] To impoverish –1528.

Empoverish, obs. f. IMPOVERISH.

Empower (empau·ᵊr), *v.* Also **im-.** 1654. [f. EM- + POWER.] **1.** *trans.* To invest legally or formally with power; to authorize, license. **2.** To impart power (*to do* something); to enable, permit 1681. Also †*refl.* with *over.*

1. To e. (a person) to erect a Colledge 1654, to levy troops MOTLEY. **2.** Much less can he e. others to do Miracles SCOTT. Hence **Empow·erment,** the action of empowering; the state of being empowered.

†**Emprent,** *v.* Used as tr. L. *impetrare* to obtain by request. CHAUCER.

Empress (e·mprės), *sb.*[1] [ME. *emperice, emperesse* – OFr. *emperesse*, f. *emperere* EMPEROR; see -ESS[1].] **1.** The consort of an emperor. Also, a female sovereign of an empire. **2.** A female exercising absolute power. Chiefly *transf.* and *fig.* ME.

2. The pale-faced Empresse of the night HABINGTON. *Comb. E.-cloth:* a woollen fabric resembling merino, but untwilled. (App. not an Eng. trade term.)

†**E·mpress,** *sb.*[2] 1593. [var. of IMPRESS *sb.*[1]] A motto or significant device. Also *attrib.* –1688.

†**Empre·ss,** *v.* ME. [– (O)Fr. *empresser* (in OFr. senses 'subject to pressure, crowd in'), f. *en-* EM- + *presser* PRESS *v.* Cf. IMPRESS *v.*[1]] To press, oppress. Also *intr.* to crowd *into.* –1475.

‖**Empressement** (anprę·sman). 1749. [Fr.] Effusive cordiality.

†**Empri·me,** *v. rare.* 1575. [Of unkn. origin.] To separate a deer from the herd.

Emprint, obs. f. IMPRINT *sb.* and *v.*

Emprise, emprize (emprəi·z), *sb. arch.* ME. [– (O)Fr. *emprise* :– Rom. **imprensa*, subst. use of pa. pple. fem. of **imprendere* undertake, f. *in-* EM-, IM-[1] + *pre(he)ndere* take. Superseded by ENTERPRISE.] **1.** An undertaking, an (adventurous or chivalrous) enterprise. **2.** *abstr.* Enterprise, prowess ME. †**3.** Renown –1500; estimation. ME. only.

1. To fighten in this emprise CHAUCER. Dare first The great emprise BROWNING. **2.** Giants of mightie Bone and bould emprise MILT. *P. L.* xi. 642.

†**Empri·se,** *v.* ME. [f. prec. sb.] *trans.* To undertake –1608. Hence **Empri·sing** *ppl. a.* enterprising, adventurous.

Emprison, obs. f. IMPRISON.

‖**Emprosthotonos** (emprǫsþǫ·tǫnǫs). 1657. [mod. L. – Gr., f. ἔμπροσθεν before + τόνος a stretching.] *Path.* 'A condition in tetanus in which the body is drawn forwards by excessive action of the anterior muscles of the trunk' (*Syd. Soc. Lex.*).

Hence **Empro:sthoto·nic** *a.* characterized by e.

Empt (empt), *v.* Now *dial.* [OE. *ǣmtian*, f. *ǣmta, ǣmetta* leisure; see EMPTY *a.* and *v.*] †**1.** To be at leisure. Only in OE. **2.** To make or †become empty (*lit.* and *fig.*) ME. **3.** To pour forth or carry out 1606.

Emptiness (e·mptinės). 1533. [f. EMPTY *a.* + -NESS.] **1.** The condition of being empty or void of contents or of specified contents; *concr.* void space, a vacuum. **2.** Want of solidity or substance; inability to satisfy desire; unsatisfactoriness; vacuity, hollowness 1695. **3.** Want of knowledge; lack of sense; inanity 1658.

1. No idea of the e. of London 1747. Neglect and e. of form 1875. **2.** The E. of Ambition 1710.

Emption (e·mpʃən). 1461. [– L. *emptio*, f. *empt-*, pa. ppl. stem. of *emere* purchase; see -ION. Cf. OFr. *emption.*] **1.** The action of buying, as in *right of emption.* **2.** *Rom. Law*, Purchase (L. *emptio*, as correl. of *venditio*) 1555. Hence **E·mptional** *a.* that can be purchased.

‖**Emptor** (e·mptoɹ, -əɹ). 1875. [L., f. as prec.; see -OR 2.] A purchaser.

†**E·mptory.** 1641. [– med.L. *emptorium*, f. as prec.; see -ORY[1].] A mart –1676.

Empty (e·mpti). [OE. *ǣmtiġ, ǣmet(t)iġ*, f. *ǣmetta* leisure :– **ǣmōtiþa*, perh. f. negative *ā-* + *mōt-* meeting (see MOOT *sb.*). See EMPT *v.*]

A. *adj.* †**1.** At leisure. Also, unmarried. Only in OE. **2.** Containing nothing; void of contents or of specified contents; opp. to *full.* Also *fig.* OE. **3.** *transf.* †**a.** Destitute of money. (Only contextual.) –1724. **b.** Wanting food. Now *colloq.* 1593. †**c.** Of the body: Emaciated; of the pulse: Weak –1707. **4.** Of space, etc.: Unoccupied. Also *fig.* OE. **5.** Without anything to bring or carry ME. **6.** Lacking knowledge and sense; frivolous, foolish 1611. **b.** Of things: Wanting solidity and substance; unsatisfactory, vain, meaningless ME.

2. The e. vessel makes the greatest sound *Hen. V*, IV. iv. 73. We..are of ourselves emptie of all good BP. HALL. **4.** And dead mens cries do fill the emptie aire 2 *Hen. VI*, V. ii. 4. Dauids place was emptie 1 *Sam.* 20 : 25. **5.** E. camels MARLOWE. Vessels..e., or loaded with Masts 1714. *fig.* A hollow form with e. hands TENNYSON. **6.** A very e. and unprepared design CLARENDON. **b.** Weighs.. solid pudding against e. praise POPE. Hence **E·mptily** *adv.*

B. *sb.* An empty truck or wagon; an empty box, case, etc. which has contained goods 1865.

Empty (e·mpti), *v.* 1526. [f. EMPTY *a.*; cf. OE. *ġeǣmtiġian.*] **1.** *trans.* To make empty; to remove the contents of. Also with †*in, into, upon.* **b.** To drain away, pour off. Also *fig.* 1578. **2.** To discharge *of.* Chiefly *transf.* and *fig.* 1526. Also *refl.* of persons. **3.** *refl.* Of a river, etc.: To discharge itself *into* 1555. Also *intr.* for *refl.* (now chiefly in *U.S.*). **4.** *intr.* To become empty 1633.

1. E. the woolly Rack DRYDEN. **2.** All The Chambers emptied of delight TENNYSON. **3.** The Veins..e. themselves into the Heart HOBBES. Hence **E·mptier.**

E·mpty-ha·nded, *a.* 1613. [See EMPTY *a.*] Bringing no gift; carrying nothing away; chiefly in phrases, *To come, go*, etc. *empty-handed.*

E·mptying, *vbl. sb.* 1605. [f. EMPTY *v.* + -ING[1].] **1.** The action of making empty. **2.** *concr.* **a.** What is emptied out of any vessel; also *fig.* **b.** *pl.* Yeast. *U.S.* 1650.

Empurple (empɔ̆·ɹp'l), *v.* Also **im-.** 1590. [f. EM- + PURPLE.] *trans.* To make purple; to redden; to robe in purple (*rare*).

The violets..impurple not the winter DRUMM. OF HAWTH.

Empusa (empiū·ză). Also **empuse.** 1603. [– Gr. Ἔμπουσα.] **1.** A hobgoblin or spectre. **2.** *Bot.* A genus of the family *Entomophthoreæ.*

†**Empu·zzle,** *v.* [f. EM- + PUZZLE *sb.* or *v.*] To puzzle. SIR T. BROWNE.

Empyema (empi,*ī*·mă). 1615. [– late L. *empyema* – Gr. ἐμπύημα, f. ἐμπυεῖν suppurate, f. ἐν EM- + πύον PUS.] *Path.* **1.** 'A collection of pus in the cavity of the pleura,

the result of pleurisy' (*Syd. Soc. Lex.*). **2.** More widely: Suppuration (*rare*) 1866.
Hence †**Empye·matous**, †**Empyema·tic** *adjs.*, belonging to or suffering from e.

Empyesis (empi,ī·sis). [mod.L. – Gr. ἐμπύησις, f. as prec.] *Path.* A pustular eruption.

Empyreal (empi·rĭăl, empirī·ăl, -pəi-), *a.* 1481. [– med.L. *empyreus* (late L. *empyrius*), as sb. n. -*eum* (sc. *cælum* heaven) – Gr. ἐμπύριος, as sb. n. -ιον (Proclus), f. ἐν EM- + πῦρ fire; see -AL[1].] **1.** Of or pertaining to the EMPYREAN. Also *fig.* **b.** Of or pertaining to the sky, celestial 1744. **2.** Fiery; composed of pure fire. Also *fig.* 1601. †**3.** *Chem.* Capable of supporting combustion –1812.
1. Go soar with Plato to th' e. sphere POPE. **3.** Phr. *E. air*: Scheele's name for oxygen. var. †**Empyre**.

Empyrean (empi·rĭăn, empirī·ăn, -pəi-). Also **empyræan.** 1614. [f. as prec.; see -EAN.]
A. *adj.* Of or pertaining to the sphere of fire or highest heaven. Also *fig.*
Drenched in e. light WORDSW.
B. *sb.* **1.** The highest heaven. Anciently, the sphere of pure fire; in Christian use, the abode of God and the angels. Also *fig.* 1667. **2.** *transf.* **a.** The visible heavens 1808. **b.** Cosmic space 1880.
1. Divine Interpreter sent Down from the E. MILT.

†**Empyre·um.** Also **empyræum.** 1647. [– med.L. *empyreum*; see EMPYREAL.] = EMPYREAN B. 1. –1777.

Empyreuma (empirū·mă). Pl. **-mata.** 1641. [– Gr. ἐμπύρευμα live coal covered with ashes, f. ἐμπυρεύειν set on fire, f. ἐν EM- + πῦρ fire.] †**1.** 'Heat left by the fire in the burned part' (J. Steer) –1656. **2.** The burnt smell imparted by fire to organic substances 1641. var. †**Empyreu·m(e.** Hence **Empy:reuma·tic, -al** *a.* pertaining to, or having the quality of, e., as *empyreumatic oil.* **Empyreu·matize** *v.* to taint with an e.

Empyrical (empi·rikăl), *a. rare.* [f. Gr. ἔμπυρος + -IC + -AL[1].] **a.** Of or pertaining to burning. **b.** 'Containing the combustible principle of coal' (Smart 1847).

†**Empyro·sis.** *rare.* 1677. [– Gr. ἐμπύρωσις, f. as EMPYREUMA; see -OSIS.] A general fire, conflagration.

Emrod(e, obs. var. of EMERALD.

Emu (ī·miu). Also **emeu, emew.** 1613. [Earliest forms *emia, eme*, later *emeu, emew*, orig. – Pg. *ema*. Cf. Fr. *émeu* (1698), *émou*, Du. *emoe*.] †**1.** = CASSOWARY 1. –1656. †**2.** ? The American Ostrich, *Rhea americana*. [Perh. an error.] –1796. **3.** A genus (*Dromæus*) of birds, peculiar to the Australian continent. The best known species is *D. novæ-hollandiæ*. The Emu and Cassowary are closely allied. 1842. *Comb.* **e.-wren,** an Australian bird, *Stipiturus* (or *Malurus*) *malacurus*, of the family *Sylviidæ*.

†**E·mulable,** *a. rare.* 1693. [f. EMULATE *v.* + -ABLE.] Worthy of emulation.

†**E·mulate.** [– L. *æmulatus*, pa. pple. of *æmulari*; see -ATE[2] and cf. next.] Ambitious. *Haml.* I. i. 82.

Emulate (e·miŭleit), *v.* Also †**æm-.** 1589. [– *æmulat-*, pa. ppl. stem of L. *æmulari*, f. *æmulus* rival; see -ATE[3].] **1.** *trans.* To strive to equal or rival; to imitate with the object of equalling or excelling; to vie with, rival. †**2.** *intr.* To strive in a spirit of rivalry. Const. *inf.* –1649. †**3.** To desire to rival; *hence*, to be jealous of –1654. †**4.** To spur (*rare*) 1804.
1. Contemn the bad, and E. the best DRYDEN. I see how thine eye would e. the diamond SHAKS.

Emulation (emiulēi·ʃən). Also †**æm-.** 1552. [– L. *æmulatio*, f. as prec.; see -ION. Cf. (O)Fr. *émulation*.] **1.** The endeavour to equal or surpass others in actions or qualities; also, the desire to equal or excel. †**2.** Ambitious rivalry; contention or ill will between rivals –1651. †**3.** Jealousy; dislike of those who are superior –1771.
1. This Faire æmulation, & no envy is B. JONS. **2.** The dissension and e. that I have seen..between private captains for vainglory 1588. **3.** For E. ever did attend Upon the Great DRAYTON.

Emulative (e·miŭlĕtiv), *a.* 1593. [f. EMULATE *v.* + -IVE.] Characterized by, or tending to, emulation or rivalry. Const. *of.* Also *fig.* 1748.
Noble minds, e. of perfection 1748. Hence **E·mulatively** *adv.*

Emulator (e·miŭleitəɹ). Also †**æm-.** 1589. [– L. *æmulator*; see EMULATE *v.*, -OR 2.] One who emulates, in good or bad sense.
An enuious e. of every mans good parts SHAKS. A diligent e. of Grocyn..was..Linacre HALLAM.

†**E·mulatory,** *a. rare.* 1621. [f. prec.; see -ORY[2].] Of the nature of emulation, as *emulatory officiousness* –1627.

†**E·mulatress.** *rare.* 1620. [f. as prec. + -ESS[1].] A female emulator –1741. So †**Emula·trix.**

†**E·mule,** *v. rare.* Also **æm-.** 1816. [– L. *æmulari* EMULATE.] = EMULATE *v.*

Emulge (ĭmɒ·ldʒ), *v.* 1681. [– L. *emulgēre* milk out.] *trans.* To drain (secretory organs).

Emulgence (ĭmɒ·ldʒĕns). *rare.* 1674. [f. as next; see -ENCE.] The action of milking out.

Emulgent (ĭmɒ·ldʒĕnt). 1578. [– *emulgent-*, pres. ppl. stem of L. *emulgēre* milk out; see -ENT.]
A. *adj.* That 'milks out'; *esp.* applied to the vessels of the kidneys.
B. *sb.* = *Emulgent vessels* 1612.

Emulous (e·miŭləs), *a.* ME. [f. L. *æmulus* + -OUS.] **1.** Desirous of rivalling, imitating, obtaining. Also, formerly, of things (*rare*). **2.** Filled with emulation 1617. †**3.** Covetous of praise or power; also, envious –1660. **4.** Proceeding from emulation or rivalry 1535.
1. Of other excellence not e. MILT. *P. L.* VI. 822. **2.** Æmulous the royal robes they lave POPE. **3.** He is not e., as Achilles is *Tr. & Cr.* II. iii. 243. **4.** E. extravagance 1782. Hence **E·mulous-ly** *adv.*, **-ness.**

Emulsic (ĭmɒ·lsik), *a.* [f. EMULSIN + -IC.] *Chem.* Related to EMULSIN.

Emulsify (ĭmɒ·lsifəi), *v.* 1859. [f. L. *emuls-* (see EMULSION) + -FY.] To convert into an emulsion. Also *absol.*
To e. bromide of silver in liquid gelatine 1881. So **Emu·lsionize** *v.* Hence **Emu:lsifica·tion,** the action of the vb.; *spec.* the last stage of fatty degeneration. **Emu·lsifier,** an emulsifying agent.

Emulsin (ĭmɒ·lsin). 1838. [f. EMULSION + -IN[1].] *Chem.* A neutral substance contained in almonds; called also *synaptase*.

Emulsion (ĭmɒ·lʃən). 1612. [– Fr. *émulsion* or mod.L. *emulsio*, f. *emuls-*, pa. ppl. stem of L. *emulgēre* milk out; see -ION.] †**1.** The action of emulging (*fig.*) 1658. **2.** A milky liquid obtained by bruising almonds, etc. in water. **b.** *Pharm.* 'A milky liquid, consisting of water holding in suspension minute particles of oil or resin by the aid of some albuminous or gummy substance' (*Syd. Soc. Lex.*). 1612. Also *attrib.* **3.** *Photog.* A mixture of light-sensitive silver salts suspended in collodion or gelatin for coating plates, films, etc. 1877.

Emu·lsive, *a.* 1861. [f. L. *emuls-* (see prec.) + -IVE.] That has the nature of an EMULSION.

†**Emu·nct,** *a. rare.* 1679. [– L. *emunctus*, pa. pple. of *emungere* (see next). The L. phr. *emunctæ naris homo* a man of 'keen scent' (*fig.*) gave rise to the use of the pple. in sense 'acute'.] Of the judgement: Keen –1697. So †**Emu·nction** (*rare*), the wiping of the nose; whence *transf.* of clearing any of the passages of the body.

Emunctory (ĭmɒ·ŋktəri). 1547. [– med.L. *emunctorius* (sb. -*ium* as in B), f. *emunct-*, pa. ppl. stem of L. *emungere* wipe or blow the nose; see -ORY[1,2].] *Phys.* **A.** *adj.* **a.** Of or pertaining to the blowing of the nose. **b.** That conveys waste matters from the body 1858. **B.** *sb.* A cleansing organ or canal. Also *fig.* 1601.

†**Emu·nge,** *v.* 1664. [– L. *emungere* wipe or blow the nose.] *trans.* To wipe or clean out; *fig.* to cheat –1846.

†**Emusca·tion.** 1664. [f. L. *emuscare* cleanse from moss (f. *muscus* moss); see -ATION.] The action of cleansing from moss. Also *fig.* –1679.

En (en). 1785. [The name of the letter N.] *Printing.* The half-square, formerly of the type 'n', half the width of an EM.

‖**En** (aṅ). Fr. prep., = in, as (a), used in various phr., many of which are current in Eng., as **en déshabillé**, in undress; **en famille**, among one's family; **en garçon**, as a bachelor; **en pension**, as a boarder; **en règle**, in due form; **en route** (see ROUTE *sb.* 4); **en suite** (see SUITE 4). See also EN BLOC.

En-, *prefix*[1], the form assumed in Fr. (Pr., Sp., Pg.) by L. *in-* (see IN-). In Eng., used chiefly in words adapted from Fr.
A. 1. Before *b* and *p*, and occas. before *m*, it is now (since 17th c.) changed to *em-*. **2.** In ME. (as in OFr.) *en-*, *em-*, freq. became *an-*, *am-* (cf. AMBUSH), whence *a-* A- 10 (see APPAIR, APPRAISE). Conversely, *a-* often became *en-* (*em-*), as in *embraid*. **3.** From 14th c. onwards IN- (IM-) has taken the place of *en-* (*em-*); and the converse has also occurred. Hence much difficulty in determining in a particular word whether the prefix *en-* or *in-* is Fr., Lat., or purely Eng. in origin.
B. The applications of the prefix in Fr. (Pr., Sp., Pg.), and hence in Eng., are mainly those of the L. *in-*; viz. to form vbs. from sbs., adjs., or from other vbs.
1. Verbs formed by prefixing *en-* to a sb.
a. With sense 'to put into or on what is denoted by the sb.':
†**Enambush; enchair; enchannel; †encoach; †engaol; †enkennel; enkerchief; enkernel; enmagazine; enniche; †enseat; enshadow; enshawl; †enshelter; †enslumber; †enstage; enwall; enzone;** etc.
b. With sense 'to put what is denoted by the sb. into or on' (a person or thing):
†**Encowl; endiadem; enmoss; †ensilver; †enspangle; †entackle; enverdure;** etc.
2. Verbs formed by prefixing *en-* to a sb. or adj., with sense 'to bring into a certain condition or state':
†**Enanger; †encanker; †encinder; encommon; endiaper; †endrudge** (*refl.*); †**enfavour; †enfierce; †enfort; enfoul; enfree; enfreedom; enfroward; †engallant; †engarboil; engloom; engolden; †enlength; †enripe; †ensafe; †ensober; entempest; envineyard; †enwoman; †enwrack;** etc.
b. Verbs formed (with sense as above) on adjs. or sbs. with prefix *en-* and suffix -EN[5], as ENLIVEN, ENLIGHTEN.
3. Verbs, mostly transitive, formed by prefixing *en-* to a verb, with additional sense of *in*, or simply intensive; also vbs. formed as in 2 b.
†**Encheck, †enchequer**, to arrange chequerwise; †**enclog; †endamnify; †endart; †endazzle; enfasten; †enfester; †enfreeze; engladden; †enhedge; †enlengthen; †enmix; †enquicken; †enrive; †enstrengthen† †entwist; †enwallow** *intr.*; †**enwiden; enwrite; †enyoked;** etc.

En-, *prefix*[2], the form taken by the Gr. ἐν. (Before *b*, *m*, *p*, *ph*, it becomes *em-*; before *l*, *r* it becomes *el-*, *er-* respectively.)

en, *suffix*[1] :– Gmc. *-*īnam*, formally the neut. of *-*īnaz* -EN[4], is used to form dims. from sbs., as in CHICKEN, etc.

-en, *suffix*[2] :– WGmc. -*innja*, repr. Gmc. *-*inī*, *-*injō*, is used to form feminines, as in VIXEN, the only surviving instance of this. It is also added to the stem of a vb., or of a verbal-abstract sb., as in BURDEN, etc.

-en, *suffix*[3], the ME. form of OE. -*an*, the termination of the nom., accus., and dat. pl. of wk. sbs. Hence the termination -*en* became a formative of the pl., as in *ox-en*, and was also added to the remains of other old plurals, as in *brethren, children, kine*.

-en, *suffix*[4] (reduced to -*n* after *r* in unstressed syllables) :– Gmc. *-*īnaz*, = Gr. -ινος, L. -*inus* (see -INE[1]), added to noun-stems to form adjs. with sense 'pertaining to, of the nature of'. In literary English the use of these adjs. is largely superseded by the attrib. use of the sb., as in 'a gold watch'. In a few cases (e.g. *wooden, woollen, earthen, wheaten*) they are still familiarly used.

-en, *suffix*[5], forming verbs. **1.** from adjs., as *darken, deepen*, etc. **2.** from sbs. The majority of these (e.g. *heighten, lengthen, strengthen*, etc.) appear first in mod.Eng., and follow the analogy of verbs f. adjs. LISTEN (OE. *hlystnian* :– WGmc. **hlusinôjan*) is an exception. **3.** In one or two cases (e.g. *waken*) the suffix -*en* represents Gmc. -*na*-, the formative of the present stem in some strong verbs.

-en, *suffix*⁶, forming the regular ending of pa. pples. of strong verbs; OE. *-en*, corresp. to OS., OHG. *-an* (Du., G. *-en*), ON. *-inn*, *-enn*, Goth. *-ans*. Usu. passive in meaning, but active meanings are shown in *mistaken* (also pass.), *outspoken*.

Enable (enē·b'l), *v.* ME. [f. EN-¹ + ABLE *a.*; cf. ABLE *v.*] †**1.** To invest with legal status –1721. **2.** To empower; to give legal power or licence to 1526. **3.** To make able (to be or to do something); to strengthen; to supply with means, opportunities, or the like 1460. †**4.** To regard as competent –1596. †**5.** To make possible; also, to make effective –1675. †**6.** *intr.* for *refl.* To become able (*rare*) ME.

1. She was restored and enabled in blood STRYPE. **2.** Congress cannot e. a state to legislate 1824. **3.** Exercise to e. the body MULCASTER. A solitude.. which enabled him to work better there MORLEY. Hence †**Ena·blement,** the action or means of enabling. **Ena·bler.** **Ena·bling** *ppl.a.* that enables: chiefly of legislative enactments.

†**Ena·ct,** *sb.* 1467. [f. next.] That which is enacted; *fig.* a purpose, resolution (*Tit. A.* IV. ii. 118) –1588.

Enact (enæ·kt), *v.* ME. [f. EN-¹ + ACT *sb.* and *v.*, after med.L. *inactare*, *inactitare*.] †**1.** (from ACT *sb.*) To enter among the *acta* or public records, or in a chronicle –1641. **2.** Of a legislative authority: To make into an act; hence, to ordain, decree 1464. †**3.** To declare officially –1715. †**4.** (from ACT *v.*) To actuate, influence –1647. **5.** To represent on or as on the stage; to act the part of, play; also *fig.* ME. †**6.** To bring into act, perform –1616. †**7.** *intr.* To act –1684.

2. Wouldst thou His laws of fasting disanull? E. good cheer G. HERBERT. **5.** I did e. Julius Cæsar *Haml.* III. ii. 108. To e. the philosopher DE QUINCEY. Hence †**Ena·ct** = *enacted* pa. pple. **Ena·ctable** *a.* **Ena·cting** *ppl.a.* that enacts; *spec.* in *enacting clauses* (of a statute), viz. those in which new provisions are enacted (opp. to *declaratory*). **Ena·ctive** *a.* enacting. **Ena·ctor,** one who enacts (a law); one who enacts (a part, scene, transaction, etc.). **Ena·ctory** *a.* enacting. †**Ena·cture,** ? fulfilment (*Haml.* III. ii. 207 *Qos.*).

Enaction (enæ·kʃən). 1630. [f. prec. + -ION.] = ENACTMENT 1, 2.

Enactment (enæ·ktmĕnt). 1817. [f. ENACT *v.* + -MENT, superseding ENACT *sb.*, ENACTION.] **1.** The action of enacting (a law); the state of being enacted. **2.** That which is enacted; an ordinance, a statute; one of the provisions of a law 1821.

1. The e. of the Six Articles MILMAN. **2.** Enactments for the regulation of trade J. R. GREEN.

†**Ena·ge,** *v.* 1593. [f. EN-¹ + AGE.] To make or cause to look old –1631.

Enaliosaur (enæ·li,osǭ:ɹ). 1863. [f. Gr. ἐνάλιος of the sea + σαῦρος lizard.] A 'marine lizard'; a name for the gigantic fossil reptiles forming the orders *Sauropterygia* and *Ichthyopterygia*. Hence **Ena:liosau·rian** *a.* and *sb.*

Enallage (enæ·lădʒi). 1583. [– late L. *enallage* – Gr. ἐναλλαγή, f. base of ἐναλλάσσειν, f. ἐν EN-² + ἀλλάσσειν exchange, f. ἄλλος other.] *Gram.* The substitution of one grammatical form for another, *e.g.* of sing. for pl., present for past tense, etc.

†**Ena·luron.** 1562. [perh. – AFr. phr. **en aileron*.] *Her.* A bordure charged with birds. (According to Porny the word is an adv., = '*orlé*, or in manner of a bordure'.) –1766.

‖**Enam** (ĭnā·m). Also **enaum, inam.** 1803. [Pers. (Arab.); lit. 'favour'.] In India: A grant of land free of the land-tax due to the State; also, the land so held. So ‖**Ena:mda·r,** one who holds an e.

Enambush; see EN- *prefix*¹ 1.

Enamel (enæ·mĕl), *sb.* 1463. [f. ENAMEL *v.*; see AMEL *sb.*] **1.** A semi-opaque variety of glass, applied by fusion to metallic surfaces, either to ornament them in colours, or to form a surface for encaustic painting; now also as a lining for cooking utensils, etc. **b.** *fig. esp.* with reference to the hardness and polish of enamel 1680. **c.** A glassy bead formed by the blowpipe. **d.** In recent use, any composition employed to form a smooth hard coating on any surface. **2.** *Phys.* [after Fr. *émail.*] The substance which forms the hard glossy coating of the teeth; the similar substance coating the bony scales of ganoid fishes 1718. **3.** A work executed in enamel 1861. **4.** *transf.* Any smooth and lustrous surface-colouring 1600. **5.** *attrib.*, as *e.-colour*, *-painting*, etc. 1754.

1. b. None of the hard and brilliant e. of Petrarch in the style MACAULAY. **4.** On the green e. of the plain Were shown me the great spirits CARY. *Comb.*: **e.-painting,** painting by fusing vitrifiable colours laid on a metal surface; **-paper,** paper covered with a glazed metallic coating. Also (in dental anatomy), **e.-cell,** one of the cells of the *enamel-organ*, sometimes called collectively 'enamel-membrane'; **-germ,** a portion of thickened epithelium, which develops into the **e.-organ.**

Enamel (enæ·mĕl), *v.* ME. [– AFr. *enameler*, *enamailler*, f. *en* EN-¹ + *amail*; see AMEL.] **1.** *trans.* To inlay, cover, or portray with ENAMEL. **b.** *transf.* To variegate like enamelled work; to beautify with varied colours 1650. †**c.** *fig.* To adorn magnificently; to impart an additional splendour to –1670. **2.** To cover with a glossy coating resembling enamel. **b.** To make smooth (the skin of the face) with cosmetics 1868.

1. Brende golde..enaumaylde with azer ME. And therin imagery grauen & enamelyd FABYAN. **b.** Spring ne'er enamell'd fairer meads than thine SHENSTONE. **2.** To e. cardboard, leather, etc. 1891. Hence **Ena·meller, -eler. Ena·melist,** an artist in enamel.

Enamellar, -elar (enæ·mĕlăɹ), *a.* [f. ENAMEL *sb.* + -AR¹.] Of or like enamel; smooth, glossy. (Dicts.)

Enamelling, -eling (enæ·mĕliŋ), *vbl. sb.* 1449. [f. ENAMEL *v.* + -ING¹.] The action or process of covering or adorning with enamel; *concr.* anything so treated. Also *fig.* and *attrib.*

fig. A fair enamelling of a terrible danger 15..

‖**Enamora·do.** [Sp.] = INAMORATO. Sir T. HERBERT.

†**Ena·morate,** *v. rare.* 1591. [– *innamorat-*, pa. ppl. stem of It. *innamorare*.] *trans.* To inspire with love –1711. Hence **Ena:mora·tion.**

†**Ena·morate.** 1607. [– It. *innamorato*; see prec.] **a.** *adj.* Enamoured. **b.** *sb.* A lover –1711.

Enamour (enæ·məɹ), *v.* ME. [– (O)Fr. *enamourer* (cf. It. *innamorare*, Sp. *enamorar*), f. *en* EN-¹ + *amour* love.] **1.** *trans.* To inspire with love. Chiefly *pass.* Also *fig.* **2.** To charm, delight, fascinate. Chiefly *pass.* Const. *of*, †*on*, †*with*. 1590.

1. Me-thought I was enamoured of an Asse *Mids. N.* IV. i. 82. **2.** Mine eare is much enamored of thy note *Mids. N.* III. i. 141. Hence **Ena·mourment.**

Enantiopathy (enæ·nti,ǫ·păþi). 1852. [f. Gr. ἐναντίος opposite + *-pathy*, after *allopathy*.] *Med.* = ALLOPATHY; the treatment of disease by contraries. Hence **Ena:ntiopa·thic** *a.*

Enantiosis (enæ:nti,ōᵘ·sis). 1657. [mod.L. – Gr. ἀντίωσις opposition.] *Rhet.* A figure in which the opposite is meant to what is said; irony.

†**Enarch** (enā·ɹtʃ), *v.* ME. [f. EN-¹ + ARCH *sb.*, in late ME. prob. – OFr. *enarchier*.] To build in the form of an arch; to arch in or over; in *Her.* of a chevron: To have an arch within its inner angle –1631. Hence **Ena·rched** *ppl. a.*

Enargite (enā·ɹdʒəit). 1852. [f. Gr. ἐναργής clear (from its cleavage being apparent) + -ITE¹ 2 b.] *Min.* A black sulph-arsenide of copper, of metallic lustre.

†**Ena·rm,** *v.* ME. [– OFr. *enarmer* arm, equip, f. *en* EN-¹ + *armer* ARM *v.*¹] = ARM *v.* –1588.

Enarm, var. of INARM, to embrace.

†**Enarration.** 1563. [– L. *enarratio*; see E-, NARRATION. Cf. OFr. *enarration*.] **1.** An exposition –1647. **2.** A description, a detailed narrative –1826.

Enarthrodial (enaɹþrōᵘ·diăl), *a.* 1836. [f. EN-¹ + ARTHRODIA + -AL¹.] *Anat.* Of the nature of, or belonging to, the ball-and-socket joint.

Enarthrosis (enaɹþrōᵘ·sis). 1634. [– Gr. ἐνάρθρωσις jointing in, f. ἔναρθρος jointed. Cf. EN-², ARTHROSIS.] *Anat.* The jointing of the head of a bone into a socket; the ball-and-socket joint.

Enascent (ĭnæ·sĕnt), *a. rare.* 1745. [– *enascent-*, pres. ppl. stem of L. *enasci*; see E-, NASCENT.] That is just coming into being. Also *fig.*

†**Enatant,** *a. rare.* [– *enatant-*, pres. ppl. stem of L. *enatare* float up, f. *e-* EX-¹ + *natare* swim; see -ANT.] Floating up, coming to the top. So †**Enata·tion,** a swimming out.

Enate (ī·nĕt), *a.* 1666. [– L. *enatus*, pa. pple. of *enasci*, f. *e-* EX-¹ + *nasci* be born; see -ATE².] *Phys.* That has grown out, as the apophysis of a bone. So **Ena·tion** (*Bot.*), outgrowth.

†**Enau·nter,** *conj. rare.* ME. [var. of *an, in, on aunter*, Fr. *en aventure*. See ADVENTURE *sb.*¹] In case that; lest by chance. SPENSER.

Enb-, obs. spelling of EMB-.

†**Enbai·ssing,** *vbl. sb.* [Corrupt var. of *abaissing*. See ABASH *v.*] Abashment. CHAUCER.

Enbibe, enbibing, obs. ff. IMBIBE, etc.

‖**En bloc** (aṅ blok), *adv. phr.* 1877. [Fr.] In a block, as a whole. Also *attrib.*

‖**Enca·dré.** 1817. [Fr., pa. pple. of *encadrer* frame. See CADRE.] *Crystall.* Having 'facets which form kinds of squares around the planes of a more simple form already existing in the same species' (R. Jameson).

Encænia (ensī·niă). Also † **encenia.** ME. [– L. *encænia* – Gr. (τὰ) ἐγκαίνια dedication festival, f. ἐν EN-² + καινός new.] †**1.** A renewal; a dedicatory festival. ME. only. **2.** The anniversary festival of the dedication of a temple or church ME. **3.** The annual Commemoration of founders and benefactors at Oxford 1691.

Encage, in- (en-, inkē·dʒ), *v.* 1593. [f. EN-¹, IN-² + CAGE *sb.*; cf. (O)Fr. *encager*.] To confine in, or as in, a cage. Hence †**Enca·gement** (*rare*).

Encalendared, modernized spelling of †INCALENDARED.

Encamp (enkæ·mp), *v.* Also †**in-.** 1549. [f. EN-¹ + CAMP *sb.*²] **1.** *trans.* To form into or settle in a camp. Also *intr.* for *refl.* **2.** *transf.* (*intr.* and *pass.*) To lodge in the open in tents or the like 1725.

1. Bid him encampe his Souldiers where they are SHAKS. **2.** We followed up the stream..encamping each night DE FOE. Hence †**Enca·mper** (*rare*).

Encampment (enkæ·mpmĕnt). Also **in-.** 1598. [f. prec. + -MENT.] **1.** The action of encamping, or state of being encamped 1686. **2.** The place where troops are encamped in tents, huts, etc.; a CAMP. Also *attrib.* and *fig.* 1598. **b.** *transf.* The temporary quarters of a body of men on the march, travellers, etc. Also *fig.* 1725. †**3.** A Masonic meeting –1878.

1. A square of about seven hundred yards was sufficient for the e. of twenty thousand Romans GIBBON. **2. b.** Signs of a small Indian e. 1825.

Encanker; see EN- *pref.*¹ 2.

Encanthis (enkæ·nþis). 1586. [– Gr. ἐγκανθίς, f. ἐν + κανθός corner of the eye.] *Med.* A small red excrescence growing in the inner corner of the eye.

Encapsulate, -ation, var. ff. INCAPSULATE, -ATION.

Encapsule (enkæ·psiul), *v.* 1877. [See EN-¹.] *Phys.* To enclose in a capsule; cf. CAPSULE 2.

†**Enca·ptive,** *v.* 1592. [f. EN-¹ + CAPTIVE *a.*] To make into a captive; to enthral –1605.

†**Enca·rdion.** [– Gr. ἐγκάρδιον the heart of wood.] *Bot.* 'The pith of vegetables' (*Syd. Soc. Lex.*).

Encarnadine, var. of INCARNADINE.

Encarnalize (enkā·ɹnăləiz), *v.* Also **in-.** 1847. [f. EN-¹ + CARNALIZE.] To put in flesh and blood; also *fig.* Also, to make gross, sensual.

fig. So incarnalise The strong idea H. COLERIDGE.

‖**Enca·rpa,** *sb. pl.* 1662. [L. *encarpa* – Gr. ἔγκαρπα, n. pl. of ἔγκαρπος; see next.] *Arch.* Festoons of fruit (as an ornament).

Encarpus (enkā·ɹpŏs). [– Gr. ἔγκαρπος containing fruit, taken as = prec.] *Arch.* 'The festoons on a frieze; consisting of fruit, flowers, leaves, etc.' (Gwilt).

Encase, in- (eŋ-, iŋkē·s), *v.* 1633. [f. EN-¹, IN-² + CASE *sb.*² Cf. Fr. *encaisser*.] **1.** *trans.* To put into or enclose within a case 1727. **2.** To overlay, surround, hem in; also, to cover, invest 1633.

1. A little soul is encased in a large body JOWETT. Hence **Enca·sement,** also **in-,** that which encases; in *Biol.* = EMBOÎTEMENT.

Encash (enkæ·ʃ), *v.* 1861. [f. EN-¹ + CASH *sb.*¹; cf. Fr. *encaisser.*] **1.** To convert into cash; to CASH. **2.** To receive in cash, realize 1861.
2. The communication of the revenue encashed 1879. Hence **Enca·shable** *a.* **Enca·shment,** the action of encashing; *concr.* the sum received in cash.

†**Encau·ma.** 1708. [– Gr. ἔγκαυμα result of burning in.] **1.** 'The scoria of silver' (*Syd. Soc. Lex.*). **2.** A deep foul ulceration of the cornea. (Dicts.) **3.** The mark, or a vesicle, resulting from a burn.

Encaustic (enkǭ·stik). 1601. [– L. *encausticus* (Pliny) – Gr. ἐγκαυστικός, f. ἐγκαίειν burn in; see EN-², CAUSTIC. Cf. Fr. *encaustique.*]
A. *adj.* Pertaining to, or produced by, the process of burning in: **a.** chiefly with reference to the ancient method of painting with wax colours, and fixing by heat; **b.** applied occasionally to enamelling, painting on pottery, etc. 1656. Also *transf.* and *fig.*
Phr. *E. brick, tile*: one decorated with patterns in different coloured clays, inlaid in the brick, and burnt with it.
B. *sb.* [– Gr. ἐγκαυστική τέχνη.] **1.** The art or process of encaustic painting (see A) 1601. †**2.** A pigment or glaze applied by burning in 1662.
Hence **Encau·stically** *adv.* in e.

†**Encave,** *v.* [– (O)Fr. *encaver*, f. *en* EN-¹ + *cave* cellar.] To put into a cellar. *Oth.* IV. i. 82.

-ence, *suffix.* [– Fr. *-ence* – L. *-entia*, forming abstr. sbs. on ppl. stems in *ent-*, e.g. *sapient-em, sapient-ia.* See also -ANCE.] In sense, words in *-nce* are partly nouns of action, as in OFr., partly of state or quality, as in L.

‖**Enceinte** (aṅsæṅt), *sb.* 1708. [Fr. :– L. *incincta*, pa. pple. fem. of *incingere* gird in.] An enclosure; chiefly in *Fortif.*
The 'enceinte' or 'body of the place' is the main enclosure of the fortress 1879.

‖**Enceinte** (aṅsæṅt), *a.* 1602. [Fr. :– med.L. *incincta* 'ungirded', f. L. *in-* IN-³ + *cincta*, fem. pa. pple. of *cingere* gird.] Of women: Pregnant.

Encens(e, obs. ff INCENSE.

‖**Encephala** (ense·fălă), *sb. pl.* 1854. [mod.L., f. Gr. ἐν EN-² + κεφαλή head; see -A 4.] *Zool.* A division of Mollusca, viz. those which have a distinct brain.
Hence **Ence·phalous** *a.* belonging to the E.

Encephalic (ensĭfæ·lik), *a.* 1831. [f. Gr. ἐγκέφαλος brain + -IC.] Pertaining to the brain or ENCEPHALON.

Encephalitis (ensefăləi·tis). 1843. [f. as prec. + -ITIS.] *Path.* Inflammation of the brain; now chiefly of the brain-substance, as dist. from its membranes. Hence **Encephali·tic** *a.*

Encephalocele (ense·făloṣīːl). 1835. [f. as prec. + Gr. κήλη tumour.] *Med.* Hernia of the brain.

Encephaloid (ense·făloid), *a.* 1846. [– Fr. *encéphaloïde* (Laennec), f. as prec. + -OID.] *Path.* Resembling the brain or brain-structure; the distinctive epithet of soft cancer.

Encephalon (ense·fălǫn). 1741. [– Gr. (τὸ) ἐγκέφαλον what is within the head.] *Anat.* What is within the skull; the brain.

Encephalopathy (ensefălǫ·păþi). 1866. [f. Gr. ἐγκέφαλος brain + -PATHY.] *Path.* Disease of the brain in general. Hence **Encephalopa·thic** *a.* pertaining to e.

‖**Encephalos** (ense·fălǫs). *rare.* 1708. [Gr.] = ENCEPHALON.

Enchafe (enˌtʃēⁱ·f), *v.* [ME. *enchauf*, alt. f. ESCHAUFE, whence ACHAFE. See A- 10.] To make or grow hot or warm; also *fig.*

Enchain (enˌtʃēⁱ·n), *v.* ME. [– (O)Fr. *enchaîner* :– Gallo-Roman **incatenare*, f. *in* EN-¹ + *catena* CHAIN *sb.*] **1.** To put in, or bind with, chains 1491. **2.** *fig.* To fetter 1751; to hold fast; to bind 1658. †**b.** *intr.* for *refl.* To become closely united. ME. only. †**3.** To link together –1768.
2. Enchained by rules HALLAM. Rachel's acting ..enchained me with interest C. BRONTË.
Hence **Enchai·nment,** the action of enchaining; enchained state.

Enchair, Enchannel; see EN- *pref.*¹ 1.

Enchant (enˌtʃɑ·nt), *v.* ME. [– (O)Fr. *enchanter* :– L. *incantare*, f. *in* EN-¹ + *cantare* sing (see CHANT *v.*).] **1.** *trans.* To exert magical influence upon; to bewitch. Also, to endow with magical powers or properties. Also *fig.* †**2.** *fig.* To influence as if by a charm; to hold spellbound; in bad sense, to delude –1678. **3.** To charm, enrapture 1592.
1. Cockering mothers inchant their sonnes to make them rod-free FULLER. Enchanted amulets 1772. **3.** Bid me discourse, I will e. thine ear SHAKS. Hence **Encha·nted** *ppl.a.* bewitched; invested with magical powers or properties; charmed. **Encha·nting** *ppl.a.* that enchants; charming. **Encha·ntingly** *adv.*

Enchanter (enˌtʃɑntəɹ). ME. [– OFr. *enchanteor, -our* (mod. *-eur*) :– late L. *incantator, -ōr-*; see -ER² 3. In mod. use apprehended as f. ENCHANT + -ER¹.] One who enchants, uses magic; formerly also, a conjurer.
By this means I knew the foul e. MILT. *Comus* 645. **Enchanter's nightshade,** *Circæa lutetiana.*

†**Encha·ntery.** *rare.* ME. [– OFr. *enchanterie*, f. *enchanteor*; see prec., -ERY.] Magic –1591.

Enchantment (enˌtʃɑ·ntmĕnt). ME. [– (O)Fr. *enchantement*; see ENCHANT, -MENT.] **1.** The action of enchanting, or of using magic or sorcery. **2.** *fig.* Alluring or overpowering charm; enraptured condition; (delusive) appearance of beauty 1678.
1. With thyne inchantment [A.V. sorceries] were deceaved all nations TINDALE *Rev.* 18:23. **2.** 'Tis distance lends e. to the view CAMPBELL.

Enchantress (enˌtʃɑ·ntrĕs). ME. [– (O)Fr. *enchanteresse*; see ENCHANTER, -ESS¹.] **1.** A female who uses magic; a sorceress. Also *fig.* **2.** *fig.* A bewitching woman 1713.
1. Endor, famous by reason of the Inchantresse RALEGH.

†**Encha·rge,** *sb.* [– OFr. *encharge*, f. *enchargier*; see next.] An injunction. 1595.

Encharge (enˌtʃā·ɹdʒ), *v.* Also **in-**. ME. [– OFr. *enchargier* (mod. †*encharger*), f. *en* EN-¹ + *charge* CHARGE *sb.*] †**1.** *trans.* To impose as a charge or duty –1828. †**2.** To enjoin *to* do something –1681. **3.** To burden, entrust *with* 1640.
3. Encharging them with the flocke over which Christ hath made them Bishops BP. HALL.

†**Encha·rm,** *v.* Also **in-**. 1480. [– OFr. *encharmer*, f. *en* EN-¹ + *charme* CHARM *sb.*¹] To throw a charm over; to enchant –1611.

†**Encha·se,** *v.*¹ ME. [– OFr. *enchacier*, f. *en* EN-¹ + *chacier* CHASE *v.*¹] To drive away; to hunt, pursue –1741. Hence †**Encha·se** *sb.* chase; hunting (*rare*).

Enchase (enˌtʃēⁱ·s), *v.*² 1463. [– (O)Fr. *enchâsser* enshrine, set (gems), encase, f. *en* EN-¹ + *châsse*; see CHASE *sb.*²] **1.** To set *in*; also, to serve as a setting for 1534. **2.** To set (gold, etc.) *with*. Also *transf.* and *fig.* 1589. **3.** To inlay *with* 1640. **4.** To adorn with figures in relief. Hence, to engrave. 1463. **5.** *transf.* and *fig.* To adorn as with engraved figures 1590. **6.** To enshrine *in*. [The orig. Fr. sense.] Also *fig.* 1615. †**7.** To shut in, enclose –1715. **8.** To 'let in' to a 'chase' or mortice. Also *transf.* and *fig.* 1611.
1. A gold ring with a ruby enchased 1877. **2.** Whose floore with Stars is gloriously inchased DRAYTON. **4.** Wherein is enchased many a fayre sight SPENSER. **6.** Enchased in a crystal covered with gold EVELYN. *fig.* Thy bright Idea in my Heart E. KEN.
Hence †**Encha·sement,** setting, frame. **Encha·ser,** one who enchases or engraves metal. So ‖**Enchâssure** [Fr.] (*rare*), the casing of a relic.

Encha·sten, *v.* [See EN-¹.] To make chaste. 1800.

†**Enchea·son.** ME. [– OFr. *encheson, encheison*, f. *encheoir*, lit. fall in, hence be in fault.] Occasion, cause, reason –1642.

†**Enchea·t,** *sb.* ME. [– OFr. *encheoite*, f. *encheoir* fall in; cf. prec. and ESCHEAT *sb.*] Revenue from escheats or confiscations –1494.

Encheck, Enchequer: see EN- *pref.*¹ 3.

Encheer (enˌtʃīᵊ·ɹ), *v.* 1605. [f. EN-¹ + CHEER *v.*] To cheer.

‖**Enchei·ria.** [Gr. ἐγχειρία.] Method of manipulation. NEWTON.

Enchesoun, variant of ENCHEASON.

†**Enche·st,** *v.* Also **in-**. 1632. [f. EN-¹ + CHEST *sb.*¹] To enclose in, or as in, a chest.

Enchiridion (enkəiri·diǫn). 1541. [– late L. *enchiridion* – Gr. ἐγχειρίδιον, f. ἐν EN-² + χείρ hand + -ίδιον dim. suff.] A handbook or manual.

Enchisel; see EN- *pref.*¹ 2.

‖**Enchondroma** (enkǫndrōᵘ·ma). *Pl.* **-mata.** 1847. [mod. L., f. Gr. ἐν in + χόνδρος cartilage + -OMA.] *Path.* A cartilaginous tumour. Hence **Enchondro·matous** *a.*

Enchorial (enkǭ·riăl), *a.* 1822. [f. Gr. ἐγχώριος in or of the country (f. ἐν in + χώρα country) + -AL¹.] That belongs to, or is used in, a particular country; used *esp.* of the popular (as dist. from the hieroglyphic and the hieratic) writing of the ancient Egyptians; = DEMOTIC. In general sense now *rare.*

†**Enchro·nicle,** *v.* 1513. [See EN-¹.] To enter in a chronicle –1593.

†**Enchu·rch,** *v.* 1681. [See EN-¹.] To form into a church –1702.

Encincture (ensi·ŋktiŭɹ), *v.* 1821. [f. EN-¹ + CINCTURE *sb.*] To surround with, or as with, a girdle. Also as *sb.* (*rare*), enclosure; an enclosure.

Encinder; see EN- *pref.*¹ 2.

Encipher (ensəi·fəɹ), *v.* 1577. [f. EN-¹ + CIPHER *sb.*] *trans.* To write in cipher; also, to combine in a monogram *with*.

Encircle (ensɔ̄·ɹk'l), *v.* ME. [f. EN-¹ + CIRCLE.] **1.** To enclose in a circle, surround; also, to surround *with*. Also *transf.* and *fig.* **2.** To make a circling movement round 1598.
1. Great Britaine..encircled by the Sea HOWELL. *fig.* Satire and censure encircled his throne GOLDSM. **2.** Hermes..Her brows encircled with his serpent-rod PARNELL. Hence **Enci·rcler** (*rare*).

†**Encla·ret,** *v.* [See EN-¹.] To tinge with claret. HERRICK.

Enclasp (enkla·sp), *v.* Also **in-**. 1596. [f. EN-¹ + CLASP *sb.* and *v.*] To hold in or as in a clasp.

‖**Enclave** (enklēⁱ·v, aṅkla·v), *sb.* 1868. [Fr., f. (O)Fr. *enclaver* :– pop.L. **inclavare*, f. *in* EN-¹ + *clavis* key.] A piece of territory entirely shut in by foreign dominions. Also *fig.*

Encla·ve, *a.* 1661. [– Fr. *enclavé*, pa. pple. of *enclaver* dovetail; see prec.] *Her.* Of the border of an ordinary: Having a contour like that of a dovetail joint.

†**Enclea·r,** *v.* 1509. [f. EN-¹ + CLEAR *a.*] **1.** To make clear –1556. **2.** To light up (*lit.* and *fig.*) –1580.

Enclitic (enkli·tik). 1656. [– late L. *encliticus* (Priscian) – Gr. ἐγκλιτικός, f. ἐγκλίνειν lean on, f. ἐν EN-² + κλίνειν LEAN *v.*¹ See -IC.] *Gram.*
A. *adj.* That 'leans its accent on the preceding word' (Liddell and Scott): in Gr. grammar applied to words which have no accent, and which usually modify the accent of the word they follow. Hence applied analogously to the L. particles *-que, -ve, -ne*, etc., and to similar unemphatic words in mod. langs.
B. *sb.* An enclitic word 1663.
B. When we say 'Give me content', the *me* in this case is a perfect enclitick J. HARRIS.
So †**Encli·tical** *a.* **Encli·tically** *adv.* **Encli·ticism,** accentual leaning on another word.

Enclog; see EN- *pref.*¹ 2.

†**Encloi·ster,** *v.* 1596. [f. EN-¹ + CLOISTER *sb.* Cf. (O)Fr. *encloîtrer.*] To shut up in or as in a cloister; to immure –1710.

†**Enclo·se,** *sb. rare.* 1484. [f. next.] = ENCLOSURE –1648.

Enclose, in- (en-, inklōᵘ·z), *v.* ME. [– (O)Fr. *enclos(e)*, pa. pple. of *enclore* :– pop.L. **includere*, f. L. *includere* INCLUDE. English usage favours *enclose.*] **1.** *trans.* To surround so as to bar ingress or egress. **b.** To fence in (common land) with a view to appropriation. Also *fig.* 1503. **2.** To seclude, imprison. ?*Obs.* ME. **3.** To insert within a frame, case, envelope, receptacle, or the like. Also *fig.* ME. **4.** To surround, bound on all sides; to contain ME. **5.** Of an army, etc.: To hem in on all sides 1601.
2. The nuns live in community, but are not enclosed SHIPLEY. **3.** Onix stones enclosed in ouches of gold *Ex.* 39:6. **4.** Two straight lines cannot e. a space 1762. **5.** *Jul. C.* V. iii. 27. Hence †**Enclo·sement** (*rare*) = ENCLOSURE.

Encloser (enklōᵘ·zəɹ). ME. [f. prec. + -ER¹.] **1.** One who encloses; *esp.* one who appropriates common land 1597. †**2.** As tr. L. *clusor* (Vulg.), for Heb. *masgēr*, a smith. ME. only.

Enclosure (enklōᵘ·ʒ'ŭɹ, -ʒəɹ). Also **in-**. 1538. [– legal AFr., OFr. *enclosure*; see

ENCLOSE *v.*, -URE.] **1.** The action of enclosing; *spec.* the action of surrounding (land) with a fence; the action of thus appropriating common land. Also *attrib.*, as in *Enclosure Act.* Also *fig.* **2.** The state of being enclosed (see ENCLOSURE *v.* 2) 1816. **3.** That which encloses, as a fence, barrier, wall, envelope 1556. **4.** That which is enclosed: **a.** A space included within boundaries 1580. **b.** Anything enclosed within an envelope (*mod.*).

Enclothe (enklōu·ð), *v.* 1831. [f. EN-[1] + CLOTHE *v.*] To clothe, invest.

Encloud (enklau·d), *v.* 1591. [f. EN-[1] + CLOUD *sb.*] To envelop in a cloud; to overshadow.

Encoach; see EN- *pref.*[1] 1 a.

Enco·ffin, *v.* Now *rare.* 1598. [f. EN-[1] + COFFIN.] To put in or as in a coffin. Hence **Enco·ffinment.**

Encolden; see EN- *pref.*[1] 3.

Encollar; see EN- *pref.*[1] 2.

Enco·lour, *v.* 1648. [See EN-[1].] To colour, tinge.

Encolure (enkolʼiūə·ɹ). [Fr.; the neck of an animal.] Used by Browning for: The mane (of a horse).

Encomiast (enkōu·mi,æst). 1610. [– Gr. ἐγκωμιαστής, f. (ult.) ἐγκώμιον ENCOMIUM.] One who composes or utters an encomium; a panegyrist. So †**Encomia·ster.**

Encomiastic (enkōu:mi,æ·stik). 1599. [– Gr. ἐγκωμιαστικός; see prec., -IC.] **a.** *adj.* Commendatory, eulogistic. †**b.** *sb.* A eulogistic discourse –18... So **Enco:mia·stical** *a.*; **-ly** *adv.* (*rare*).

Encomium (enkōu·miɒ̆m). *Pl.* **-iums**; (now *rarely*) **-ia.** 1589. [– L. *encomium* – Gr. ἐγκώμιον eulogy, subst. use (sc. ἔπος speech) of n. of adj., f. ἐν EN-[2] + κῶμος revel. Cf. COMIC.] A formal or high-flown expression of praise; a panegyric.

Many..encomia of ancient famous men JOWETT. vars. †**Enco·mion**, †**Enco·my.**

Encommon; see EN- *pref.*[1] 2.

†**Enco·mpany**, *v.* 1494. [– OFr. *encompaignier*, var. of *accompaignier* (mod. *accompagner*); see EN-[1], ACCOMPANY.] **1.** *trans.* To accompany –1533. **2.** To associate. Const. *to.* LD. BERNERS.

Encompass (enkɒ·mpăs), *v.* Also †**in-.** 1553. [f. EN-[1] + COMPASS *sb.*] **1.** To encircle, surround, bound on all sides 1555. **2.** Of persons: To form a circle about. Also *fig.* Also *absol.* 1555. †**3.** To go all round (anything) –1784. **4.** To surround entirely; to contain 1553. †**5.** To 'get round'. SHAKS.

1. The mountains encompassing Borrowdale 1872. **2.** Encompass'd by his faithful guard TENNYSON. **5.** *Merry W.* II. ii. 158. Hence **Enco·mpasser** (*rare*). **Enco·mpassment** (*rare*), the action of encompassing; encompassed state.

Encorbellment (enkǭ·ɹbĕlmĕnt). 1886. [f. EN-[1] + CORBEL + -MENT, after Fr. *encorbellement.*] *Arch.* The continuous projection of each horizontal course over the one immediately below it.

Encore (aṅkǫ·r, often ǫŋkōə·ɹ). 1712. [– Fr. *encore*, of disputed origin. Not used abroad in the Eng. sense.]

A. *interj.* Again, once more: used by spectators or auditors to demand the repetition of a song, piece of music, or the like.

Loud shouts of 'encore' roused him HONE.

B. *sb.* A call for the repetition of a song, etc.; the repetition itself. Also *attrib.* 1763.

Enco·re, *v.* 1748. [f. prec.] To call for a repetition of (a song, etc.), or by (a performer).

They encored it RICHARDSON. The wretches.. encored him [Sir Charles] without mercy 1754.

†**Enco·rpore**, *v.* ME. [– OFr. *encorporer* – late L. *incorporare*; see INCORPORATE.] **1.** *intr.* in *Alchemy*: To amalgamate –1470. **2.** To insert in a body of documents. LD. BERNERS.

Encounter (enkau·ntəɹ), *sb.* ME. [– (O)Fr. *encontre*, f. *encontrer*; see next.] **1.** A meeting face to face; a meeting in conflict; *hence*, a battle, skirmish, duel, etc. **2.** A coming upon, *esp.* undesignedly or casually. Const. *of, with.* 1656. †**b.** An amatory meeting. SHAKS. †**3.** Style of address, behaviour. SHAKS. **4.** Occurrence (*rare*) 1870. †**5.** *Rhet.* = ANTITHESIS. Puttenham.

1. This keene e. of our wittes SHAKS. The e. with death 1853. **a.** There was a constant risk of an e. which might have produced several duels 1859.

Encounter (enkau·ntəɹ), *v.* ME. [– OFr. *encontrer* (mod. *rencontrer*) :– Rom. **incontrare*, f. *in-* EN-[1] + *contra* against.] **1.** *trans.* To meet as an adversary; to confront in battle. Also *fig.* Also †*intr.* with *with.* †**2.** *trans.* To go counter to, oppose; to contest. Also *absol.* –1786. †**3.** *trans.* To be opposite in position or direction to 1610. **4.** To come upon, *esp.* casually. Occas. *absol.* Also *fig.* ME. Also †*intr.* with *with.* **5.** To meet with; to face resolutely 1814. Also †*intr.* with *with.* †**6.** To go to meet; also *fig.* SHAKS. †**7.** To address –1590.

1. They challenge, and e. Breast to Breast DRYDEN. **2.** To e. his [God's] Word GOLDING. **4.** We never met before, and never..may again e. BYRON. **5.** The Royal Society..encountered fierce hostilities D'ISRAELI. **6.** I will e. darknesse as a bride SHAKS. Hence †**Encou·nterer**, one who or that which encounters; a 'forward' person (*Tr. & Cr.* IV. v. 58).

Encourage (enkɒ·rėdʒ), *v.* 1483. [– (O)Fr. *encourager*; see EN-[1], COURAGE *sb.*] **1.** *trans.* To inspire with courage, animate, inspirit 1490. **2.** To embolden 1538. **b.** To incite, instigate; to recommend 1483. **3.** To stimulate; to countenance; in bad sense, to abet 1668. **b.** To allow or promote the growth of; to foster 1677.

1. Jack was incouraged at this success STEELE. **2.** To be encouraged to do the like EDEN. **b.** To e. individuals to make right or wrong for themselves JOWETT. **3.** Paying them [tradesmen] is only encouraging them SHERIDAN. **b.** To e. the Iron Manufacture 1677.

Hence **Encou·rager. Encou·raging** *ppl. a.* that encourages or tends to e. **Encou·ragingly** *adv.*

Encouragement (enkɒ·rėdʒmĕnt). Also †**in-.** [– (O)Fr. *encouragement*; see prec., -MENT.] The action or process of encouraging, the being encouraged; that which serves to encourage.

[Plato] gives no e. to individual enthusiasm JOWETT. The e. of saving 1883.

Encover, in- (en-, inkɒ·vəɹ), *v. rare.* 1520. [f. EN-[1], IN-[2] + COVER *v.*] To cover completely.

Encowl; see EN- *pref.*[1]

Encradle (enkrēi·d'l), *v.* 1596. [See EN-[1].] To lay in a cradle.

Where he encradled was In simple cratch SPENSER.

Encratism (e·nkrătiz'm). 1885. [f. next + -ISM.] The doctrine and practice of the Encratites.

Encratite (e·nkrătəit). Usu. in *pl.* 1587. [– late L. *encratita*, pl. *-æ* – patristic Gr. ἐγκρατῖται pl. (Hippolytus), f. ἐγκρατής continent + -ιτης -ITE[1] 1.] One of an early Christian sect that abstained from flesh, wine, and marriage.

Encrease, etc.; see INCREASE.

Encrimson (enkri·mzən), *v.* Also **in-.** 1773. [f. EN-[1] + CRIMSON.] To make or dye crimson; also *fig.*

Encrinital (enkrinəi·tăl), *a.* 1847. [f. ENCRINITE + -AL[1].] **1.** *Geol.* Of, pertaining to, or resembling, Encrinites. **2.** Containing Encrinites 1876. vars. **E·ncrinal, Encri·nic.**

Encrinite (e·nkrinəit). 1808. [f. ENCRINUS + -ITE[1] 2 b.] *Geol.*, etc. A fossil crinoid; formerly, *occas.*, any crinoid. Hence **Encrini·tic** *a.* containing fossil Encrinites.

‖**Encrinus** (e·nkrinɒ̆s). 1762. [mod.L. *encrinus* (Harenberg, 1729) 'stone-lily', f. Gr. ἐν EN-[2] + κρίνον lily.] *Zool.* †**a.** = ENCRINITE. **b.** A particular (extinct) genus of crinoids, the type of the family *Encrinidæ.* †**c.** One of certain extant animals resembling the fossil encrinus; *esp.* the *Pennatula encrinus* of Linnæus. Hence **E·ncrinoid** *a.* resembling an Encrinite.

†**Encri·sp**, *v. rare.* ME. [See EN-[1].] *trans.* To curl crisply –1523.

†**Encroa·ch**, *sb. rare.* 1611. [f. next.] Encroachment –1716.

Encroach (enkrōu·tʃ), *v.* ME. [– OFr. *encrochier* seize, fasten upon, f. *en* EN-[1] + *crochier* to crook, f. *croc* hook – ON. *krókr* CROOK *sb.*] †**1.** *trans.* To seize, acquire wrongfully. Also *absol.* –1606. **2.** *intr.* To trench or intrude usurpingly (*esp.* by insidious or gradual advances) on the territory or rights of another. Also *transf.* and *fig.* of things: To make gradual inroads on. Const. *on, upon*; also *simply.* 1534. **3.** *intr.* To intrude beyond natural or conventional limits. Also †*refl.* 1555.

2. Bie littell and littell engroched on the sowthe partes of the Ile 1534. The sea encroched upon these cliffs SMEATON. **3.** A state which encroaches beyond the boundaries of sleep 1830.

Hence **Encroa·cher. Encroa·chingly** *adv.*

Encroachment (enkrōu·tʃmĕnt). 1523. [f. ENCROACH *v.* + -MENT; in AFr. (1437) *encrochement.*] The action of encroaching.

Encrochment, when the Lord hath gotten and seised of more rent or seruices of his tenant then of right is due 1613. The encroachments of error SIR T. BROWNE, of the waves 1878.

Encrown (enkrau·n), *v.* 1486. [f. EN-[1] + CROWN *sb.*] To put a crown on; to crown. Hence †**Encrow·nment.**

Encrust, in- (en-, inkrɒ·st), *v.* 1641. [– Fr. *incruster* (XVI) – L. *incrustare*, f. *in* IN-[2] + *crusta* CRUST *sb.* The Eng. var. *encrust* is evidenced much later, but is favoured in actual use.] **1.** *trans.* To ornament by overlaying with a crust of something precious. **2.** To cover with a crust or thin coating. Also *fig.* 1733. **3.** To form into a crust, as snow 1726. Also *intr.* for *refl.* **4.** *intr.* To form or deposit a crust *upon* 1725. **5.** To shut up as within a crust (*rare*) 1711.

1. A staircase encrusted with jasper MACAULAY. **2.** Such..waters..incrust vessels in which they are contained 1756. **5.** Tho' I should..In Alps of Ice encrusted, freeze KEN. Hence **Encru·stment,** that which is deposited as a crust; an outer encrusted layer or shell.

†**Encu·mber**, *sb.* ME. [– (O)Fr. *encombre*, f. *encombrer*; see next.] The state of being encumbered; an encumbrance –1642.

Encumber (enkɒ·mbəɹ), *v.* ME. [– (O)Fr. *encombrer* block up :– Rom. **incombrare*; see EN-[1], CUMBER *v.*] **1.** *trans.* To hamper, embarrass *with* or *as* a clog or burden. Also *fig.* †**2.** To entangle *in* –1720. †**3.** To cause trouble to –1605. **4.** To burden with debts, etc.; *esp.* to charge (an estate) with a mortgage 1593. **5.** To load or fill *with* what obstructs or is superfluous; to block up; also *fig.* ME.

1. They marched heavily armed and encombered HOLLAND. To e. branches of trade with high duties 1842. **2.** And lefte his scheep encombred in the myre CHAUCER. **4.** Encumbered with much serving 1593, with debt BERKELEY. Hence **Encu·mberer. Encu·mberingly** *adv.* **Encu·mberment** (now *rare*) = ENCUMBRANCE.

Encumbrance (enkɒ·mbrăns). ME. [– OFr. *encombrance*, f. *encombrer*; see prec., -ANCE.] †**1.** Encumbered state or condition; trouble, molestation –1559. **2.** *concr.* That which encumbers; a burden, clog; a useless addition; an annoyance 1535. **3.** A person dependent on another for support 1742. **4.** *Law.* 'A claim, lien, liability attached to property; as a mortgage, etc.' (Wharton) 1626.

2. To hire incumbents or rather incumbrances for life-time MILT. **3.** Phr. *Without e.* = 'having no children'. Hence **Encu·mbrancer**, one who has a legal claim on an estate.

†**Encu·mbrous**, *a.* ME. [– OFr. *encombros*, f. *encombre*; see ENCUMBER *sb.*, -OUS.] Cumbersome, distressing –1694.

Encurl (enkɒ̄·ɹl), *v.* Also **in-.** 1647. [f. EN-[1] + CURL.] To twist, entwine.

Encurtain (enkɒ̄·ɹtėn, -t'n), *v.* ME. [– OFr. *enco(u)rtiner*, f. *en* EN-[1] + *co(u)rtine* CURTAIN.] **1.** To surround with, or as with, a curtain. †**2.** *Fortif.* To flank with a wall 1598.

-ency, – L. *-entia*, a suffix signifying properly quality or state. Where the same word exists in both the *-ence* and the *-ency* forms, the former is usually restricted to action or process, the latter to quality; cf. *coherence* and *coherency.* See also -ANCY.

Encyclic (ensəi·klik). 1824. [– late L. *encyclicus*; see next.] = ENCYCLICAL.

Encyclical (ensəi·klikăl). 1616. [f. late L. *encyclicus*, f. Gr. ἐνκύκλιος circular, general, f. ἐν EN-[1] + κύκλος circle; see -ICAL.]

A. *adj.* **1.** *Antiq.* Used as tr. Gr. ἐγκύκλιος (παιδεία); *i.e.* general (education); cf. ENCYCLOPÆDIA. **2.** Of eccl. letters: Circular, intended for many. Now chiefly of letters issued by the pope. 1647.

2. The apostolical vicars put forth an e. letter forbidding the people..to take the oath 1805.

B. *sb.* An encyclical letter; see A. 2. 1837.

Encyclopædia, -pedia (ensəi:klopī·diă). Also **-pedy.** 1531. [– mod.L. – spurious Gr. ἐγκυκλοπαιδεία (in MSS. of Quintilian 'Inst.' I. x. 1, Pliny 'Nat. Hist.' pref.), for ἐγκύκλιος (see prec.) παιδεία 'general education'.] **1.** The circle of learning; a general course of instruction. **2.** A work containing information on all branches of knowledge, usually arranged alphabetically 1644. **b.** Occas. applied *spec.* to the French 'Encyclopédie ou Dictionnaire raisonné des Sciences, des Arts, et des Métiers' (1751–1765) 1773. **3.** A work containing exhaustive information on some one art or branch of knowledge, arranged systematically 1801.

Hence **Ency:clopæ·diac, -al** *a.* = ENCYCLOPÆDIC. **Ency:clopæ·dial** *a.* pertaining to an encyclopædia.

Encyclopædian (ensəi:klopī·diăn), *a.* 1837. [f. prec. + -AN.] **a.** Embracing the circle of knowledge, or a wide range of subjects. **b.** Of the nature of or resembling an encyclopædia.

Encyclopædic, -pedic (ensəi:klopī·dik), *a.* 1824. [f. as prec. + -IC.] Of, pertaining to, or resembling an encyclopædia; hence, embracing all branches of learning; full of information, comprehensive.

Affectation of e. knowledge MERIVALE. An e. statistician 1872. So **Ency:clopæ·dical, -pe·dical.**

Encyclopædism, -pedism (ensəi:klopī·diz'm). 1833. [f. as prec. + -ISM.] **1.** Encyclopædic learning. **2.** The doctrines of the Encyclopædists 1835.

Encyclopædist, -pedist (ensəi:klopī·dist). 1651. [f. as prec. + -IST.] **1.** One who compiles, or writes in, an encyclopædia; *esp.* one of the writers of the French *Encyclopédie* (see ENCYCLOPÆDIA 2 b) 1796. **2.** One who takes all knowledge for his province 1871.

1. What Steam-engine..did these Encyclopedists invent for mankind CARLYLE.

Encyclopædize, -pedize (ensəi:klǫ·pidəiz), *v.* 1824. [f. as prec. + -IZE.] *trans.* To arrange as an encyclopædia. **b.** To describe in an encyclopædia.

Encyst (ensi·st), *v.* 1845. [f. EN-[1] + CYST.] To enclose in a cyst; only in *pa. pple.* and *refl.*

Encystation (ensistēⁱ·ʃən). 1869. [f. prec. + -ATION.] = ENCYSTMENT.

Encysted (ensi·stėd), *ppl. a.* 1705. [f. as prec. + -ED[1].] That is contained in a cyst or sac. Also *fig.*

E. Tumors 1705. The e. venom, or poison-bag, beneath the adder's fang COLERIDGE.

Encystment (ensi·stmĕnt). 1865. [f. as prec. + -MENT.] **a.** 'The condition of an encysted tumour' (*Syd. Soc. Lex.*). **b.** *Biol.* The process of becoming surrounded by a cyst.

End (end), *sb.* [OE. *ende* = OFris. *enda, -e,* OS. *endi* (Du. *einde*), OHG. *enti* (G. *ende*), ON. *endir, endi,* Goth. *andeis,* f. Gmc. **andja-* :– IE. **antjó*; cf. Skr. *ántas* end, boundary, death.]

I. 1. The extremity or outermost part of a portion of space or of anything extended in space; utmost limit. *Obs.* exc. in *ends of the earth.* **b.** A limit of multitude OE. †**2.** A quarter (of the world, of a country or town) –1450. **3.** One of the two extremities of a line or of the length of anything; that part of anything which includes either of its two extremities ME. **b.** ?*transf.* In the game of Bowls: The part of a game which is played from one end of the green 1688. **4.** The surface which bounds an object at either of its extremities 1526. **5.** A piece broken, cut off, or left; a fragment, remnant 1481. †Also *fig.* **6.** *techn.* **a.** *Coal-mining.* The furthest part of a working 1865. **b.** Naut. *Cable's e.*, or simply *end*: the last length of a cable. *Rope's e.*: a short length of rope, bound at the ends with thread. *Bitter e.* (see BITTER). **c.** *A shoemaker's e.*: = WAX-END. **d.** *Textiles.* (*a*) *Card.-e.*: a sliver or carding. (*b*) A worsted yarn in a Brussels carpet. 1875.

1. The towns e. GREENE. Earth's distant ends POPE. **b.** There was no e. to the advantages MILL. **3.** At the tables ende LD. BERNERS. Mutton-chops off the worst e. JOHNSON. Phr. *From e. to e.* **4.** The ends of a cask 1891. **5.** A broker's shop that hath ends of everything BACON. Phr. *Odds and ends* (see ODDS 7). **6.** I beat him, and then went up in to fetch my rope's e. PEPYS.

II. 1. Limit of duration; termination, conclusion OE. **b.** Latter part ME. **2.** Termination of existence; destruction, abolition; death, mode or manner of death OE. **3.** Ultimate state. Chiefly in Biblical phrases. OE. †**4.** A termination of doubt or debate; a settlement –1543. †**5.** Completion of an action; accomplishment of a purpose –1679. **6.** Event, issue, result ME. **7.** Intended result; aim, purpose ME. **8.** Final cause 1534.

1. To his Life's E. ADDISON. From year's e. to year's e. TREVELYAN. **b.** In e. of Autumne *Merch. V.* I. iii. 82. **2.** A Swan-like e., Fading in musique *Merch. V.* III. ii. 44. There would be an e. of all civil government LOCKE. **3.** *Ps.* 37:37. **6.** The e. still crownes the deed HEYWOOD. **7.** I have no e. to serve but truth BERKELEY. **8.** The flower is the e. or proper object of the seed RUSKIN.

Phrases. **1. a.** *At the e.*: at last. *In the e.*: ultimately. *To an e.*: consecutively, all through. **b.** *On e.* (see also AN-END): consecutively; in an upright position. **c.** *Without e.* (ME. *buten ende*): for ever; also in adj. sense, endless. *World without e.*: see WORLD I. 6. **d.** *E. for e.*: each end in place of the other; chiefly *Naut.* to reverse (a rope); to upset (a boat). *E. to e.*: lengthwise. **e.** *E. on*: with the end directly towards the eye, or towards any object; opp. to *broadside on. E. up*: with the end uppermost. **f.** *No e.*: a vast quantity or number (*colloq.*). Also (*slang*) as adv. = 'immensely'.

2. Proverbial phrases. *To have at one's fingers'* or *tongue's e.*: to know by heart. *At a loose e.*: with no fixed occupation. *To make both, two, ends meet*: to live within one's income. *To come to the e. of one's tether*: see TETHER *sb. To keep one's e. up*: to sustain one's part in an undertaking or performance.

Comb., chiefly *attrib.* with sense 'placed at the e.' or 'last used'; as *e.-man, -parlour, -wall,* etc.: also **e.-bulb,** the terminal expansion of a nerve; **-gatherer,** a collector of refuse wool; **-grain,** (*attrib.*) (of wood), placed with the e. of the grain turned outwards; **-iron,** a movable plate in a kitchen range which enlarges or contracts the grate; **-paper** (*Bookbinding*), a sheet of paper folded and pasted to the first or last leaf of a book; **-plate,** the extreme fibres of a muscle or nerve; **-shake,** a freedom of motion in a spindle at its e.; **-stone,** one of the plates of a watch-jewel supporting a pivot; **-stopping** (of blank verse), a division of the lines such that they end with a pause; so **-stopped** *ppl. a.*; **-wool,** refuse wool.

End (end), *v.*[1] [OE. *endian* = OFris. *endia,* OS. *endion* (Du. *einden*), OHG. *entōn* (G. *enden*), ON. *enda.*]

I. *Trans.* †**1.** To finish, complete –1738. **2.** To conclude, come to a termination of ME. Also *absol.*; *esp.* with reference to speech. **3.** To put an end to OE. †**b.** To kill (a person) –1623.

1. Pray e. what you began POPE. **2.** Not then the drudging Hind his Labour ends DRYDEN. *absol.* To e. with a motion 1891. **3.** To e. strife 1808. **b.** This Sword hath ended him 1 *Hen. IV*, V. iii. 9.

II. Intr. **1.** To come to an end. Also with *in* or *by.* OE. **2.** To die. Now *rare.* ME. **3.** To terminate, have its end or extremity 1611.

1. All's well that ends well, yet *All's Well* V. i. 25. **2.** Thus Thisbie ends *Mids. N.* V. i. 353. **3.** The promontory..ends in the Lizard 1877.

End, *v.*[2] Now *dial.* 1607. [perh. dial. var. or corruption of INN *v.*, infl. by END *v.*[1]] *trans.* To put (corn, etc.) into a (barn, etc.); to get in. Also *fig.*

I..holpe to reape the Fame Which he did e. all his *Cor.* V. vi. 37.

E·ndable, *a.* 1693. [f. END *v.*[1] + -ABLE.] That can be ended. (Dicts.)

End-all (e·nd-ǭl). 1605. [f. END *v.*[1] + ALL.] That which ends all. Now *dial.*, exc. as in *Macb.* I. vii. 5.

Endamage (endæ·mėdʒ), *v.* ME. [f. EN-[1] + DAMAGE *sb.*, or – OFr. **endamagier.*] *trans.* To inflict damage or injury upon; to prejudice, hurt; to spoil (a thing).

Nor was Christianity endamaged by all that fury BP. BURNET. Hence †**Enda·mageance** (*rare*), injury. **Enda·magement,** the action of endamaging; endamaged state; injury.

Endamnify; see EN- *pref.*[1] 3.

Endanger (endēⁱ·ndʒəɹ), *v.* 1477. [f. EN-[1] + DANGER *sb.*] †**1.** To subject (a person) to the will of another –1579. †**2.** *pass.* To be liable to punishment by another –1596. †**3.** To put in peril. Const. *of, to* with *inf.* –1737. †**4.** To cause the danger of (something untoward) –1796. †**5.** To chance, risk –1771. **6.** To put in danger. (The only mod. sense.) 1509.

4. Such ill Courses as will e. his Ruin 1716. **5.** To e. being benighted ADDISON. **6.** To e. the liberties of the country 'JUNIUS'. Hence **Enda·ngerer. Enda·ngerment,** the action of putting in danger; endangered condition.

†**Enda·rk,** *v. rare.* ME. [f. EN-[1] + DARK *a.*] To render dark; to dim –1631. So †**Enda·rken** *v.*

†**Ende.** [OE. *ened* = MDu. *aent,* MLG. *an(e)t,* OHG. *anut* (G. *ente*), ON. *ǫnd* :– Gmc. **anuðiz,* cogn. w. L. *anas, anat-.*] A duck –1475.

Endear (endīᵊɹ), *v.* 1580. [f. EN-[1] + DEAR *a.*, after Fr. *enchérir* (f. *en* + *cher* dear).] †**1.** *trans.* To enhance the price or value of; also, to exaggerate –1803. **2.** To render dear; to create affection for (a person or thing). (The mod. sense.) 1611. †**3.** To hold dear –1711. †**4.** To win the affection of. Also, to deepen (affection). –1704.

1. All Victualls and other Provision endeared 1618. **2.** Endeared by long companionship 1879. Hence **Endea·rance** (*rare*), the action of endearing or state of being endeared. †**Endea·redly** *adv.*, †**-ness. Endea·ring** *ppl. a,* inspiring or manifesting affection. **Endea·ringly** *adv.*

Endearment (endīᵊ·ɹmĕnt). 1612. [f. ENDEAR *v.* + -MENT.] **1.** The action of endearing or the fact of being endeared; *concr.* something that endears 1663. **2.** An action or utterance expressive of affection; a caress. Also *abstr.* 1702. †**3.** Affection –1821.

2. His Indearments and Tenderness to his Lady RICHARDSON. **3.** Pledges of conjugal e. HERVEY.

Endeavour (ende·vəɹ), *sb.* ME. [f. the verb.] **1.** The action of endeavouring; effort directed to attain an object; a strenuous attempt. †**2.** *Philos.* Used by Hobbes: = L. *conatus* (see quot.) –1667.

1. On his high e. The light of praise shall shine WORDSW. Phr. *To do one's endeavour(s*: to do all one can; My best endeuors shall be done herein *Merch. V.* II. ii. 182. **2.** These small beginnings of Motion, within the Body of Man..are commonly called E. HOBBES.

Endeavour (ende·vəɹ), *v.* ME. [f. phr. *put oneself in dever* (*devoir*), after Fr. *se mettre en devoir* do one's utmost. See DEVOIR.] †**1.** *refl.* To exert oneself –1655; †*trans.* to exert (one's power, etc.) –1642. †**2.** *intr.* for *refl.* To exert oneself; to direct one's efforts –1624. **3.** *intr.* To try, strive, make an effort for a specified object; to attempt strenuously. (The only mod. sense.) 1594. **4.** *trans.* To use effort for; to attempt (now *arch.*) 1581; †to try to fulfil (a law) MILT.

3. To e. to compromise matters FROUDE. To e. at eminence JOHNSON, after more riches MILL. **4.** To e. the extirpation of Popery CLARENDON. Hence **Endea·vourer,** one who endeavours; an aspirant; also *spec.*, a member of the Christian Endeavour Society founded in U.S. in 1881. †**Endea·vourment,** endeavour.

Endebt, -ed; see IND-.

Endeca-, incorrect f. HENDECA-; as in:
Ende·cagon, a plane figure of eleven sides; **Endeca·gynous** *a.* (*Bot.*), having eleven pistils; **E:ndecaphy·llous** *a.*, having eleven leaflets; **E:ndecasylla·bic** *a.*, having eleven syllables; **E:ndecasy·llable,** a verse of eleven syllables.

Ended (e·ndėd), *ppl. a.* 1598. [f. END *v.* and *sb.* + -ED.] **1.** That has come to an end. **2.** [f. END *sb.*] That has its end (of a certain kind), or (so many) ends.

Endeictic (endəi·ktik), *a.* 1655. [– Gr. ἐνδεικτικός probative, indicative, f. ἐνδεικνύναι point out. Cf. APODEICTIC, DEICTIC.] Serving to show or demonstrate: a term used in ancient classifications of the Platonic dialogues.

†**Endei·gn,** *v.* [– OFr. (*s'*)*endaignier* (mod. *s'indigner*) :– L. *indignari*; see INDIGNANT.] *intr.* To be indignant. WYCLIF.

Endemial (endī·miăl), *a.* 1672. [f. Gr. ἐνδήμιος (see next) + -AL[1].] = ENDEMIC *a.*

Endemic (ende·mik). 1662. [– Fr. *endémique* or mod. L. *endemicus* – Gr. ἔνδημος, ἐνδήμιος pertaining to a people, native, f. ἐν EN-[1] + δῆμος people.]

A. *adj.* Peculiar to a people or to a district: *esp.* **a.** Of plants and animals: Having their habitat in a (specified) district; opp. to *exotic.* **b.** Of disease: Habitually prevalent in a certain country, and due to permanent local causes.

Famines are periodical or e. in Hindostan 1776.

B. *sb.* An endemic disease. Also *fig.*

Hence **Ende·mical** *a.* endemic. **Ende·mically** *adv.* **Endemi·city,** the quality or fact of being e.

†**Ende·nize**, *v.* Also **in-**. 1598. [Altered f. ENDENIZEN, with assim. to verbs in -IZE.] **1.** *trans.* = ENDENIZEN 1. –1687. **2.** To remove into another order of being; to translate. Hence, to metamorphose. –1633. Hence **Endeniza·tion** (*rare*).

Endenizen (ende·nizən), *v.* 1592. [f. EN-[1] + DENIZEN.] **1.** *trans.* To make a denizen of; to naturalize, enfranchise. Also *transf.* and *fig.* †**2.** *intr.* To become a denizen or citizen 1598.

Endent, -ure; see INDENT, etc.

Ender (e·ndəɹ), *sb.* ME. [f. END *v.* + -ER[1].] He who or that which ends.

Myn hertes lady, e. of my lyf CHAUCER.

Enderma·tic, *a.* [f. as next.] = next.

Endermic, -al (endə̄·ɹmik, -ăl), *a.* 1831. [f. Gr. ἐν EN-[2] + δέρμα, δέρματ- skin + -IC, -ICAL. Cf. Fr. *endermique*.] That acts on, or through, the skin.

He administers it by the e. method; that is, applied in the form of a salve on a part deprived of the epidermis 1831. Hence **Ende·rmically** *adv.* by the e. method.

Enderon (e·ndĕrǫn). 1859. [irreg. f. Gr. ἐν + δέρος, δέρμα skin.] *Phys.* Huxley's term for the inner derm or true skin, or any homologous structure. Opp. to ECDERON. Hence **Endero·nic** *a.*

†**Endiablee**, *v.* [– Fr. *endiabler*, f. *diable* DEVIL.] To put a devil into. NORTH. So †**Endia·blement**, diabolical possession (*rare*).

Endiadem, Endiaper; see EN- *pref.*[1]

Endict, obs. f. INDICT.

Ending (e·ndiŋ), *vbl. sb.* OE. [f. END *v.*[1] + -ING[1].] **1.** The action of END *v.*[1]; termination, conclusion, completion; †death, etc. Also *attrib.* **2.** Concluding part; *esp.* that of a word, metrical line, piece of music, etc.; also, an inflexional or formative suffix 1599.

1. Time is our tedious song should here have e. MILT.

Endite, etc., obs. f. INDICT, INDITE, etc.

Endive (e·ndiv). ME. [– (O)Fr. *endive* – late L. *endivia* – med.Gr. ἴνδιβι – L. *intibum* – Gr. ἔντυβον.] The name of two species of Chicory, *Cichorium intybus* or Wild Endive, and (*esp.*) *C. endivia*, N.O. *Compositæ*. The leaves of the latter are commonly blanched and used as salad, etc.

Endless (e·ndlės). [OE. *endelēas*; see END *sb.*, -LESS.]

A. *adj.* **1.** Having no end of duration; unending, eternal. Also *hyperbolically* for: Interminable; incessant. **2.** Having no end in space; boundless, infinite; †bottomless ME. **3.** Of immaterial things: Limitless, infinite ME. †**4.** Fruitless. FLETCHER.

1. E. night SHAKS., day STEELE, feast TENNYSON, platitudes 1872. **2.** E. Labyrinths COWLEY, passages 1864, miles of moor W. BLACK. **3.** Endeles wisdom WYCLIF.

Phrases. *E. band, cable, chain, strap*: one whose ends are joined for the purpose of continuous motion. *E. screw*: a short length of screw revolving on an axis, used to give continuous motion to a toothed wheel.

†**B.** *adv.* **a.** In an infinite degree. **b.** For ever. –ME. Hence **E·ndless-ly** *adv.*, **-ness**.

Endlong (e·ndlǫŋ). ME. [orig. OE. *andlang* prep. (see ALONG), replaced by ME. *endelong*, f. *ende* END *sb.* + LONG.]

A. *prep.* From end to end of; through or over the length of; along (as opp. to *across*). Chiefly of *place*.

The rede blood Ran endelong the tree CHAUCER.

B. *adv.* **1.** At one's whole length; horizontally. Now *n. dial.* ME. **2.** Lengthwise, as dist. from *crosswise* or *athwart* (*arch.*) ME. †**3.** Right along, straight on or through –1700. **4.** On end, vertically 1600.

2. Galloping..crossways and e. SCOTT. **3.** Spurring at full speed, ran e. on DRYDEN.

C. *adj.* †**1.** Extended lengthwise –1541. **2.** (from B. 4.) Set on end, perpendicular (*rare*) 1716.

E·ndmost, *a. rare.* 1775. [f. END *sb.* + -MOST.] Nearest to the end, furthest, most distant.

Endo- (e·ndo; bef. two unstressed syllables endǫ·), also **end-**, *prefix*, comb. f. Gr. ἔνδον within; as in:

E·ndarteri·tis, E·ndo-arteri·tis [see ARTERITIS], *Path.* inflammation of the inner coat of an artery. **E:ndocho·rion** [see CHORION], *Anat.* the inner layer of the chorion. **E·ndochrome**, the colouring matter of vegetable cells except when green. **E·ndocrane** [Gr. κρανίον; also in L. form *endocra·nium*], the inner surface of the skull. **E·ndocyst** [see also CYST and ECTOCYST], the body-wall within the cell in Polyzoa. **Endogna·thal** *a.* [Gr. γνάθος], *Zool.* that is placed within the jaw; *endognathal palp*, a palpiform appendage in certain Crustacea. **E:ndolary·ngeal** *a.* [cf. LARYNGEAL], pertaining to the interior of the larynx. **E·ndolymph** [see LYMPH], *Anat.* the fluid contained in the membranous labyrinth of the ear. **Endome·trial** *a.*, pertaining to **E:ndometri·tis** [Gr. μήτρα womb + -ITIS], *Path.* inflammation of the lining membrane of the womb. **Endo·metry** [see -METRY], *Med.* the measurement of an internal part. **E·ndomorph** [Gr. μορφή form], *Min.* a mineral enclosed within another. **Endopa·rasite**, *Zool.* an animal that lives and finds food in the internal organs of another; hence **E:ndoparasi·tic** *a.* **E·ndophragm** [Gr. φράγμα partition], **a.** *Bot.* a transverse diaphragm or septum; **b.** *Zool.* the chitinous covering of the neural canal in the thorax of some Crustacea; hence **Endophra·gmal** *a.* **Endophy·llous** *a.* [Gr. φύλλον], evolved from within a sheath, as the young leaves of monocotyledons. **E·ndoplasm** [Gr. πλάσμα something moulded], the inner soft layer of the body of an Amœba, or the like (cf. ECTOPLASM). **E·ndoplast** [Gr. πλαστός formed], 'a large proto plasmic corpuscle in the external parenchyma of the body of the Infusoria' (*Syd. Soc. Lex.*); hence **Endopla·stic** *a.*; **Endopla·stule** [see -ULE], 'a bright rod-like mass lying in the interior or outside of the endoplast of Protozoa; supposed to be a male sexual organ' (*Syd. Soc. Lex.*). **Endopleu·ra** [Gr. πλευρά side), *Bot.* the internal covering of a seed. Hence **Endopleu·rite**, *Zool.* the portion of the apodeme of the thorax in Crustacea, which arises from the interepimeral membrane connecting each pair of somites. **Endo·podite** [Gr. πούς, ποδός foot + -ITE], 'the innermost of the two processes appended to the basal process of the hinder limbs of some of the Crustacea' (*Syd. Soc. Lex.*). **E·ndor(r)hiz** [Gr. ῥίζα root], *Bot.* 'the sheath-enclosed radicle of an endorrhizous plant' (*Syd. Soc. Lex.*). Hence **Endor(r)hi·zal, -ous** *adjs.* **E·ndosarc** [Gr. σάρξ, σαρκός flesh], *Zool.* the inner sarcode-layer of certain rhizopods, as the Amœba. **E·ndoscope** [see -SCOPE], *Med.* 'an instrument so arranged as to give a view of some internal part of the body through a natural canal' (*Syd. Soc. Lex.*). Hence **Endosco·pic** *a.* **Endo·scopy. E:ndoske·letal** *a.*, of or pertaining to the **E:ndoske·leton** [see SKELETON], *Anat.* the interior framework of the *Vertebrata*, consisting of bone and cartilage. **E·ndosperm** [Gr. σπέρμα], *Bot.* the nutritive element, or albumen, enclosed with the embryo in many seeds; hence **Endospe·rmic** *a.* **E·ndospore** [Gr. σπορά sowing], *Bot.* **a.** the inner coat of a spore in lichens; **b.** a spore formed inside a theca; hence **E:ndospo·rous** *a.* having spores contained in a case. **Endoste·rnite** [Gr. στέρνον], *Zool.* the portion of the apodeme in the thorax of Crustacea which arises from the intersternal membrane. **Endo·steum** [mod.L., f. Gr. ὀστέον bone], *Anat.* the internal periosteum; hence **Endo·steal** *a.*; **Endo·steally** *adv.* **Endo·stoma** [Gr. στόμα], *Zool.* a plate which supports the labrum in certain Crustacea. **E·ndostome** [see prec.], *Bot.* the orifice in the inner integument of an ovule. **Endosto·sis** [Gr. ὀστέον, an internal growth of bone. **E·ndostyle** [Gr. στῦλος column], *Zool.* 'a rigid, hollow, rod-like structure on the floor of the ventral groove of *Tunicata*' (*Syd. Soc. Lex.*); hence **Endosty·lic** *a.* **Endothe·ca** [Gr. θήκη case], **a.** *Zool.* the inner layer of the wall of the sac of the gonosome of the *Hydrozoa*; **b.** *Bot.* the inner membrane of the wall of the cells of the anther. Hence **Endothe·cal** *a.*, (dissepiments) horizontal plates growing inwards from the septa of a corallite (*Syd. Soc. Lex.*). **Endothe·lium** [Gr. θηλή nipple], *Phys.* the layer of cells lining a blood-vessel or serous cavity (cf. EPITHELIUM); hence **Endothe·lial** *a.*; **Endothe·lioid** *a.*

Endocardial (endokā·ɹdiăl), *a.* 1847. [f. ENDO- + *cardial* (see CARDIAC).] *Phys.* **a.** That is within the heart. **b.** Relating to the endocardium.

Endocarditis (e:ndo,kaɹdəi·tis). 1836. [f. next + -ITIS.] *Med.* Inflammation of the lining membrane of the heart. Hence **Endocardi·tic** *a.*

‖**Endocardium** (endokā·ɹdiŏm). 1872. [mod.L., f. Gr. ἔνδον (ENDO-) + καρδία heart, after *pericardium*.] *Phys.* The membrane lining the cavities of the heart.

Endocarp (e·ndokāɹp). 1830. [f. ENDO- + Gr. καρπός fruit.] *Bot.* The inner layer of a pericarp.

Endocrine (e·ndokrəin). 1913. [orig. adj., f. ENDO- + κρίνειν separate.] *Anat.* A ductless gland. Hence **Endocrino·logy** [-OLOGY].

Endoderm (e·ndodə̄ɹm). 1835. [f. ENDO- + Gr. δέρμα skin.] **1.** *Bot.* **a.** The cellular face of the liber. **b.** The inner layer of the wall of a vegetable cell. **2.** *Biol.* **a.** The inner layer of the blastoderm. **b.** The lining of the interior cavity of the *Cœlenterata* 1861. Hence **Endode·rmal, Endode·rmic** *adjs.*; **Endode·rmis** [after *epidermis*], *Bot.*

Endogamy (endǫ·gămi). 1865. [f. as prec. + Gr. γάμος marriage, after *polygamy*.] The custom of marrying only within the limits of a clan or tribe. Hence **Endo·gamic, Endo·gamous** *adjs.*

Endogen (e·ndodʒėn). 1842. [– Fr. *endogène* (De Candolle, 1813); see ENDO-, -GEN.] *Bot.* A plant in which new wood is developed in the interior of the stem, which is not differentiated into wood and bark; opp. to EXOGEN. Also *fig.* Hence **E:ndogene·ity**, the fact of being ENDOGENOUS. (A bad formation.)

Endogenous (endǫ·dʒĭnəs), *a.* 1830. [f. prec. + -OUS.] **a.** Growing from within. **b.** *Path.* Of a contagion: Passing direct from the sick body to the sound. **c.** Of or pertaining to an ENDOGEN. Hence **Endo·genously** *adv.*

Endorse (endǭ·ɹs), *sb.* 1572. [app. f. next.] *Her.* A vertical division of a shield, one-eighth (or one-fourth) of the breadth of a PALE.

Endorse, in- (en-, indǭ·ɹs), *v.* 1547. [– med.L. *indorsare*, f. L. *in* IN-[2] + *dorsum* back. Superseded earlier ENDOSS. Commercial and literary use favours *endorse*, legal *indorse*. Commercial and literary use favours *endorse*, legal *indorse*.] **1.** *trans.* To write on the back of (a document); *spec.* in *Comm.* to sign one's name on the back of (a bill, promissory note, or cheque). **2.** *fig.* To confirm, countenance, as by an endorsement 1847. **b.** To declare one's approval of, 'crack up' (a person or thing). *U.S.* 1914. **3.** To load the back of (an animal) *with*. (Merely literary.) 1671. **4.** *Her.* In pa. pple. *endorsed*. **a.** = ADDORSED. **b.** Of a pale: Placed between two endorses. **c.** Of wings: Thrown backwards 1500.

1. A bundle of letters..indorsed..'Letters from the Old Gentleman' 1709. To e. a bill ROGERS, a chauffeur's licence 1865. **2.** This conclusion I unhesitatingly indorse CARPENTER. **3.** Elephants indorsed with towers MILT. *P. R.* III. 329. Hence **Endo·rsable**, also **in-** *a.*, that may or can be endorsed. **Endorsee·**, also **in-**, one to whom a note or bill is endorsed, or assigned by endorsement. **Endo·rser, indorser**, occas. **-or**, one who endorses (*lit.* and *fig.*).

Endorsement, in- (en-, indǭ·ɹsmĕnt). 1547. [f. prec. + -MENT.] **1.** The action of endorsing; *concr.* a signature, memorandum, or remark endorsed upon a document. **2.** *fig.* Confirmation, ratification, approving testimony 1633.

1. By his E. he made it his own Bill 1682. **2.** This doctrine..bears the e. of the very highest names 1879.

Endosmic (endǫ·zmik), *a.* 1865. [f. ENDO- + Gr. ὠσμός (see ENDOSMOSE) + -IC.] Of or pertaining to endosmosis. So **Endosmo·dic** *a.* (*rare*).

Endosmometer (endǫ̆zmǫ·mĭtəɹ). 1836. [f. as prec. + -METER.] An instrument for exhibiting and measuring endosmosis.

Endosmose (e·ndǫzmōᵘs). 1829. [– Fr. *endosmose* (Dutrochet), f. Gr. ἔνδον (ENDO-) + ὠσμός thrusting, pushing, + *-ose* -OSIS.] = next. Hence **Endosmo·sic** *a.* of or pertaining to e.

Endosmosis (endǫ̆zmōᵘ·sis). 1836. [alt. of prec. on Eng. analogies; see -OSIS.] *Phys.*, etc. The passage of a fluid inwards through a porous septum, to mix with another fluid on the inside of it. So **Endosmo·tic** *a.* of or pertaining to e.

Endosperm, -spore, etc.; see ENDO-.

†**Endo·ss**, *v.* [– (O)Fr. *endosser*, f. *en* EN-[1] + *dos* back. Cf. med.L. *indossare*. Repl. by ENDORSE.] **1.** = ENDORSE *v.* 1. –1613. **2.** To inscribe or portray on any surface –1596.

2. Her name in euery tree I will endosse SPENSER.

Endoubt; see EN- *pref.*[1] 2.

Endow (endau·), *v.* ME. [– legal AFr. *endouer*, f. *en* EN-[1] + (O)Fr. *douer* :– L. *dotare*, f. *dos*, *dot-* dowry, rel. to *dare* give.] **1.** *trans.* To give or assure †a dowry, or dower, to. Formerly with *of*. 1535. **2.** To enrich with

property; to provide a permanent income for 1460. 3. *fig.* To enrich or furnish *with* any gift ME.
1. The wife..shall bee endowed of the thirde parte of such landes. tr. *Littleton's Tenures.* 2. With all my worldly goods I thee e. *Bk. Com. Prayer.* To e. an Hospital 1638, a dog EMERSON. 3. To be endowed with ample priviledges 1661, with life and organisation 1872, speech MORLEY. Hence **Endow·er,** one who endows. †**Endow·ry** = DOWRY.

Endowed (endau·d), *ppl. a.* 1700. [f. prec. + -ED[1].] In senses of the vb. Chiefly of societies or institutions: Possessing a permanent income from gifts or bequests.
They are schools e.; with exhibitions..for the education of youth 1700.

†**Endow·er,** *v.* 1606. [– OFr. *endouairer,* f. *en* EN-[1] + *douaire* DOWER.] To dower (a woman); also *fig.* –1654.

Endowment (endau·mĕnt). 1460. [f. ENDOW *v.* + -MENT.] 1. The action of endowing (see ENDOW *v.*). 2. *concr.* The property or fund with which a society, institution, etc. is endowed 1597. †3. Property, possessions (*rare*) –1816. 4. A gift, power, capacity, or the like, with which a person is endowed 1610.
2. Alms and endowments, the usual fruits of a late penitence BURKE. 3. These women's worldly endowments SCOTT. 4. The King's rare natural Endowments 1610.

Endrudge; see EN- *pref.*[1] 2.

†**E·ndship.** 1589. [f. END *sb.* + -SHIP. Cf. *township.*] A small suburb –1701.

Endue, in- (en-, indiū·), *v.* ME. [orig. – (O)Fr. *enduire* (i) :– L. *inducere* lead in (INDUCE); (ii) a new formation f. *en* EN-[1] + *duire* :– L. *ducere* lead; by crossing with L. *induere* put on (a garment), clothe, the word became partly synon. with *endow* and *invest.*] †1. To induct into a living, or into a lordship –1460. †2. Of a hawk: To digest. Hence *transf.* Also *fig.* –1618. †3. To lead on; to bring up, educate –1604. 4. To put on as a garment; to clothe; to cover. Also *transf.* ME. 5. To invest, endow, supply *with* anything; *esp.* with a power or quality, a spiritual gift, etc. ME.
4. Endu'd with robes of various hue DRYDEN. To e. his heavy mail LYTTON. 5. Leah said, God hath endued me with a good dowry *Gen.* 30: 20. We are endued with capacities of action, of happiness, and misery BUTLER. Hence †**Endue·ment,** the action of enduing; that with which one is endued.

Endungeon (endɒ·ndʒən), *v.* 1599. [See EN-[1] *pref.*] To put into or shut up in a dungeon. Hence *transf.*

Endurable (endiūᵊ·răb'l), *a.* 1607. [f. ENDURE *v.* + -ABLE.] 1. That can be endured or put up with 1800. 2. Durable (*rare*). Hence **Endu:rabi·lity** (*rare*). **Endu·rableness** (*rare*).

Endurance (endiūᵊ·răns). 1494. [– (O)Fr. *endurance,* f. *endurer*; see ENDURE, -ANCE.] 1. The fact, the habit or the power of enduring; *absol.* long-suffering, patience 1667. 2. Duration. Also, power of lasting. 1494. 3. That which is endured; a hardship 1555.
1. Ease out of pain Through labour and e. MILT. 3. Heauie Burthens and Endurances BACON.

Endurant (endiūᵊ·rănt), *a.* 1866. [f. next + -ANT. Cf. Fr. *endurant.*] That endures or is capable of enduring. Const. *of.*
Doing good, and e. of evil NEALE.

Endure (endiūᵊ·ɹ), *v.* ME. [– (O)Fr. *endurer* :– L. *indurare* harden, f. *in* EN-[1] + *durus* hard.] †1. To harden. Hence *fig.* to make callous. Also, to strengthen. –1600. 2. *intr.* To last. Also, to persist, hold out. ME. 3. *trans.* To undergo, bear, support, sustain; *prop.* to undergo without giving way. Also *absol.* ME. 4. To suffer without resistance, submit to, tolerate 1475. †5. Of things: To permit of (*arch.*) –1823.
2. His lordship and power in this worlde may not long e. EARL RIVERS. Highe wodes and forestes that endured to the cyte of Constances LD. BERNERS. 3. To e. exile, or ignominy, or bonds, or pain MILT. *P. L.* II. 206. To e. the whole weight of the imperial army DE FOE. 4. Brutus baite not me, Ile not e. it SHAKS. For how can I e. to see the evil that shall come unto my people *Esther* 8: 6. 5. I have that to say..which will not e. your presence SCOTT.
Hence †**Endu·rement,** the action of enduring; hardship. **Endu·rer.** †**Endu·ring** *prep.* = DURING. **Endu·ring-ly** *adv.*, **-ness.**

End-way(s, -wise (endwēⁱ, -wēⁱz, -wəiz), *adv.* 1575. [f. END *sb.* + -WAY(S, WISE *sb.*[1]] 1. Of position: With the end uppermost, foremost, or towards the spectator. Also *Endways on.* 1657. 2. Of motion: a. End on, continuously. (Now *dial.*) 1575. b. End foremost 1765. c. Lengthwise; also quasi-*adj.* 1790.

-ene, *suffix,* in *Org. Chem.* the termination of names of hydrocarbons, e.g. *benzene, camphene,* etc. In systematic nomenclature, proper to compounds of the olefine group, with formula C_nH_{2n}, and widely used for hydrocarbons of any type with at least one double bond.

†**E·necate,** *v.* 1657. [– *enecat-,* pa. ppl. stem of L. *enecare,* f. *e* EX-[1] + *necare* kill. See -ATE[3].] To kill outright –1665. Hence †**Eneca·tion.**

En échelon; see ECHELON.

Ened, var. of ENDE.

Eneid, var. of ÆNEID.

Enema (e·nĭma, enī·mă). Pl. **enemas;** (techn.) **enemata.** 1681. [– late L. *enema* – Gr. ἔνεμα, f. ἐνιέναι send or put in, inject, f. ἐν EN-[2] + ἱέναι send.] 1. *Med.* A liquid or gaseous substance (either medicinal or alimentary) injected into the rectum; a clyster, an injection. Also *attrib.* 2. Short for 'enema-apparatus'.

Enemy (e·nĕmi.) ME. [– OFr. *enemi* (mod. *ennemi*) :– L. *inimicus,* f. *in-* IN-[3] + *amicus* friend.]
A. *sb.* 1. One that hates, and wishes or seeks to injure another; an adversary, opponent. Also *transf.* and *fig.* 2. One of a hostile army or nation ME. 3. The hostile force. Also, a hostile ship. 1601.
1. The man of the world, that worst e. of the world MORLEY. Phr. *The e.*: the Devil. *fig.* So mak'st thou faith an e. to faith *John* III. i. 263. 2. A rebel is not an e. BLACKSTONE. 3. They strike at the e. in his..most vulnerable part BURKE.
B. *adj.* †1. Hostile, unfriendly –1726. 2. Of or pertaining to an ENEMY (sense 2); hostile. Now *rare.* ME.
1. I have been shipwrackt, yet am not e. with the sea or winds SIR T. BROWNE. 2. E. goods 1793.

Enemy, dial. corruption of ANEMONE.

†**Ene·nt, ene·ntes,** *prep.* ME. [var. of ANENT.] = ANENT –1516.

Enepidermic (enepidə̄·ɹmik), *a.* [f. EN-[2] + EPIDERMIS + -IC.] *Med.* Of or pertaining to applications to the skin.

Energetic (eneɹdʒe·tik), *a.* 1651. [– Gr. ἐνεργητικός active, f. ἐνεργεῖν operate, effect, f. ἐν EN-[2] + ἔργον work.] †1. Operative. GREW. 2. Powerfully operative 1651. 3. Characterized by energy 1796.
1. A being eternally energetick 1701. 2. An energetick remedy 1651. 3. Active and e. respiration 1842. The world belongs to the e. EMERSON. So **Energe·tical.** Hence **Energe·tically** *adv.* **Energe·tics** *sb. pl.* the science of ENERGY.

†**Ene·rgiatype.** 1845. [f. late L. *energia* (see ENERGY) + TYPE.] = FERROTYPE –1859.

Energic, †-al (enə̄·ɹdʒik, -ăl), *a.* 1665. [f. ENERGY + -IC, -AL[1]. Cf. Fr. *énergique.*] †1. = ENERGETIC 2. –1753. 2. = ENERGETIC 3. Now *rare.* 1702. 3. *nonce-uses.* (see quots.) 1796.
2. Cæsar, astute, e., press'd the war 1876. 3. E. reason COLERIDGE. The e. faculty that we call Will 1859.

‖**Energico** (ęnę·rdʒiko), *adv.* [It.] *Mus.* A direction: With energy. In mod. Dicts.

Energize (e·neɹdʒəiz), *v.* 1752. [f. ENERGY + -IZE. Cf. Fr. †*énergiser.*] 1. *trans.* To rouse into energy, or supply with energy 1753. 2. *intr.* To be in active operation; to put forth energy 1752.
1. Faith will e. us for any sort of work 1875. 2. We exist only as we energise SIR W. HAMILTON. Hence **E·nergizer,** he who or that which energizes.

Energumen (enəɹgiū·mĕn). 1702. [– late L. *energumenus* – Gr. ἐνεργούμενος, pa. pple. of ἐνεργεῖν work in or upon, f. ἐν EN-[2] + ἔργον work.] 1. One possessed by a devil; a demoniac 1706. 2. An enthusiast, a fanatical devotee 1702.
1. If there was ever an *Energumene*..there is a devil speaking with that woman's tongue SCOTT.

Energy (e·nəɹdʒi). 1599. [– Fr. *énergie* or late L. *energia* – Gr. ἐνέργεια (Aristotle), f. ἐν EN-[2] + ἔργον work; see -Y[3].] 1. Force or vigour of expression 1599. 2. Exercise of power, operation, activity; †*concr.* an effect 1626. †b. Effectual operation –1725. 3. Vigour of action, utterance, etc. Hence: The capacity and habit of strenuous exertion. 1809. 4. Power actively and efficiently exerted. Occas. in *pl.* 1665. b. *pl.* Activities 1742. 5. Ability or capacity to produce an effect 1677. 6. *Physics.* The power of doing work possessed by a body or system of bodies. (First used by Young to denote *actual, kinetic,* or *motive e.* (cf. sense 4); but now including *potential, static,* or *latent e.,* or *e. of position.* Also differentiated as *mechanical, molecular, chemical, electrical,* etc.) 1807.
1. The Liturgy, admired for its e. and pathos EMERSON. 2. Naturalization had a retrospective e. 1798. 3. He took his measures with his usual e. MACAULAY. 4. The disturbing e. of the planets MRS. SOMERVILLE. b. The troublesome energies of Parliament MAY. 5. The e. and power of church music ATTERBURY. 6. 'The term e. may be applied..to the product' (now *half* the product) 'of the mass or weight of a body, into the square of the number expressing its velocity' T. YOUNG. Phr. *Conservation of e.* (see CONSERVATION). In every case in which e. is lost by resistance, heat is generated THOMSON & TAIT.

Enervate (ĭnə̄·ɹvĕt), *a.* 1603. [– L. *enervatus,* pa. pple. of *enervare*; see next, -ATE[2].] 1. Wanting in strength or force; debilitated, spiritless, weak. 2. *Bot.* Ribless.

Enervate (e·nəɹveⁱt), *v.* 1610. [– *enervat-,* pa. ppl. stem of L. *enervare,* f. *e* E- + *nervus* sinew; see -ATE[3].] †1. *trans.* To cut the tendons of; chiefly *spec.* to hamstring, hough (a horse) –1751. †2. To emasculate. J. H(EALEY). 3. To weaken physically; now only of things that impair nervous tone 1668. 4. To weaken mentally or morally; to destroy the capacity of for action. Also *transf.* of sentiments, expressions, etc. 1614. †5. To render ineffectual –1836.
3. The conquerors were enervated by luxury GIBBON. 4. The tendency of abstract thought.. to e. the will M. PATTISON. 5. To e. the force and vigour of all divine injunctions 1702. Hence **E·nervator.**

Enervation (enəɹvēⁱ·ʃən). 1555. [– late L. *enervatio,* f. as prec.; see -ION. Cf. Fr. *énervation.*] †1. = L. *enervatio,* used as tr. Gr. ἀπονεύρωσις (see quot.) –1751. 2. The action of enervating; enervated state 1555.
1. The fibres of the recti of the abdomen..are intersected by several nervous places, called by the antients, enervations: though they be real tendons CHAMBERS *Cycl.* s.v. 2. A love for knowledge without e. of character GROTE.

†**Ene·rve,** *v.* 1613. [– (O)Fr. *énerver* – L. *enervare* ENERVATE *v.*] = ENERVATE *v.* –1799.

†**Ene·rvous,** *a. rare.* 1677. [f. L. *enervis* (f. *e* E- + *nervus* sinew) + -OUS.] Without nerve or strength; powerless, futile –1734.

Eneuch, eneugh, Sc. f. ENOUGH.

†**Enew·,** *v.* 1486. [– OFr. *enewer, eneauer,* f. *en* EN-[1] + *eau* (:– L. *aqua*) water.] Of a hawk: To drive (a fowl) into the water. (In SHAKS. *Meas. for M.* III. i. 91, erron. *emmew.*) –1612.

Enface (enfēⁱ·s), *v.* 1861. [f. EN-[1] + FACE *sb.,* after ENDORSE.] *trans.* To write or print on the face of. Hence **Enfa·cement,** what is written or printed on the face of a bill or note.

†**Enfa·mish,** *v.* ME. [Altered f. AFFAMISH; EN-[1].] *trans.* To famish –1491. Hence †**-ment.**

‖**Enfant terrible** (aṅfaṅ tę·ribl). 1851. [Fr. 'terrible child'.] A child who embarrasses his elders by his remarks; also *transf.*

†**Enfa·rce,** *v.* ME. [– OFr. *enfarcir* – L. *infarcire,* f. *in* IN-[2] + *farcire* stuff.] To stuff. Also *fig.* –1624.

Enfect, obs. f. INFECT *a.* and *v.*

Enfeeble (enfī·b'l), *v.* ME. [– OFr. *enfeblir, -lier,* f. *en* EN-[1] + *feble* FEEBLE. Cf. AFFEEBLE.] *trans.* To make feeble.
So much hath..paine Infeebled me MILT. *P. L.* IX. 488. Hence **Enfee·blement. Enfee·bler** (*rare*).

†**Enfee·blish,** *v.* ME. [– *enfebliss-,* lengthened stem of OFr. *enfeblir*; see prec., -ISH[2].] To make or become feeble –1576.

Enfe·lon, *v. Obs.* or *arch.* 1475. [– OFr. *enfelloner, -ir,* f. *en* EN-[1] + *felon* furious. See FELON *a.* and *sb.*[1]] To make furious, infuriate.
Like one enfelon'd or distraught SPENSER.

Enfeoff (enfe·f), *v.* ME. [– AFr. *enfeoffer* (AL. *enfeoffare*), OFr. *enfeffer*, f. *en* EN-[1] + *fief* FIEF.] **1.** *trans.* To invest with a fief; to put in possession of the fee-simple or fee-tail of lands, tenements, etc. Also *absol.* Also *transf.* and *fig.* **2.** *fig.* To hand over as a fief; to give up entirely 1596.

2. The skipping King..Enfeoff'd himselfe to Popularitie SHAKS.

Enfeoffment (enfe·fmĕnt). 1460. [f. prec. + -MENT.] **a.** The action of enfeoffing. **b.** The deed or instrument by which a person is enfeoffed. **c.** The fief. **d.** The possession of a fief.

Enfester; see EN- *pref.*[1] 3.

Enfetter (enfe·təɹ), *v.* Also **in-**. 1604. [See EN-[1].] To put into fetters (*lit.* and *fig.*); to enslave *to*.

His Soul is so enfetter'd to her Loue *Oth.* II. iii. 351.

Enfever (enfī·vəɹ), *v.* 1799. [See EN-[1].] To throw into a fever; *fig.* to incense.

Enfief (enfī·f), *v. rare.* 1861. [f. EN-[1] + FIEF.] = ENFEOFF.

Enfield (e·nfīld). 1858. A village in Middlesex, near which is a Government manufactory of small-arms. Used *attrib.*, as in *E. rifle*, etc.

Enfierce; see EN- *pref.*[1] 2.

Enfilade (enfilēi·d), *sb.* 1705. [– Fr. *enfilade*, f. *enfiler* thread on a string, pierce or traverse from end to end, f. *en* EN-[1] + *fil* FILE *sb.*[2]; see -ADE.] †**1.** A suite of rooms, whose doorways are opposite each other; also, a vista, as between rows of trees, etc. –1805. **2.** *Mil.* A fire from artillery or musketry which sweeps a line of works or men from end to end. Also *attrib.* in *e. fire.* 1796.

Enfilade (enfilēi·d), *v.* 1706. [f. prec.] †**1.** *trans.* To set (trees) so as to form an enfilade 1725. **2.** *Mil.* To subject to an enfilade; to rake (a line of works or troops, a road, etc.) from end to end with a fire in the direction of its length 1706. Also *transf.*

2. The bridge..was enfiladed by the enemy's cannon PRESCOTT.

†**Enfi·le**, *v.* ME. [– Fr. *enfiler*; see ENFILADE *sb.*] **1.** To put on a string or thread –1675. **2.** *Her.* In pa. pple. (See quot.) 1830.

2. When the head of a man or beast, or any other charge, is placed on the blade of a sword, the sword is said to be enfiled with whatever is borne upon it 1830.

†**Enfi·re**, *v.* 1513. [f. EN-[1]. + FIRE *sb.*] *trans.* To set on fire. Also *fig.* –1855.

Enflesh (enfle·ʃ), *v.* Also **in-**. 1548. [See EN-[1], IN-[2].] *trans.* **a.** To make into flesh. **b.** To cause a growth of flesh upon. **c.** To plant in the flesh, to ingrain. **d.** To give a form of flesh to.

Enflower (enflauə·ɹ), *v.* 1523. [See EN-[1].] To cover or deck with flowers.

These odorous and enflower'd fields B. JONS.

Enfold, in- (en-, infōu·ld), *v.*[1] *Pa. pple.* occas. **infold, enfolden.** 1579. [f. EN-[1], IN-[2] + FOLD *sb.* and *v.*] **1.** *trans.* To wrap up, envelop *in* or *with*. Also said of the garment, etc. Also *fig.* 1592. **2.** To encompass; to clasp, embrace. Also *fig.* 1596. †**3.** = INVOLVE –1646. **4.** To shape as a fold or folds; formerly *fig.* to render involved 1605.

1. The oak is enfolded in the acorn TRENCH. *fig.* Night enfolds the day 1867. **2.** [Vines] with lusty stems Their elms infolding SINGLETON. **4.** The rim is infolded DARWIN. Hence **Enfo·lder, infolder. Enfo·ldment,** enfolding; that which enfolds.

Enfold (enfōu·ld), *v.*[2] *rare.* 1683. [f. EN-[1] + FOLD *sb.*[1]] To shut up in a fold.

†**Enfo·llow**, *v. rare.* ME. [See EN-[1].] **a.** *trans.* To follow after; *fig.* to imitate. **b.** *intr.* To follow on; to result –1485.

†**Enfo·rce**, *sb.* ME. [f. next.] Effort, exertion –1671.

A pretty enterprise of small e. MILTON.

Enforce (enfōə·ɹs), *v.* ME. [– OFr. *enforcier*, (also mod.) *enforcir* :– Rom. **infortiare*, **infortire*, f. *in-* IN-[2] + *fortis* strong. Cf. AFFORCE.]

I. †**1.** *trans.* To strengthen physically or morally; to reinforce, encourage –1685. †**2.** To add force to –1775. **3.** To press home; to urge; †to emphasize 1449. †**4.** *refl.* To exert oneself, strive –1693. †**5.** *intr.* for *refl.* To strive, attempt –1595.

1. To e. the Towns of Flanders by..our Troops TEMPLE. **3.** In order to e. what he had said JOHNSON.

II. †**1.** *trans.* To drive by force *to* or *from* –1664. †**2.** To press hard upon; also *fig.*; also *intr.* in same sense –1662. †**3.** To overcome by violence; also *fig.* –1631. **4.** To compel, constrain 1509.

1. As swift as stones Enforced from the old Assyrian slings *Hen. V*, IV. vii. 65. **2.** *Jul. C.* IV. iii. 112. **3.** To e. a woman CAXTON, a town 1579. **4.** To inforce a Borrower to pay LOCKE.

III. 1. To produce, impose, effect by force 1531. **2.** To compel the observance of; to support by force (a claim, etc.) 1603.

1. To e. a brawle B. JONS., a tear 1812, obedience to an order 1844, payment KINGSLEY. **2.** To e. a precept GOLDSM., a demand 1841.

Hence **Enfo·rceable** *a.* that can be enforced; also, †forcible. **Enfo·rcedly** *adv.* **Enfo·rcer. Enfo·rcingly** *adv.*

Enforcement (enfōə·ɹsmĕnt). Also **in-**. 1475. [– OFr. *enforcement*; see prec., -MENT.] **1.** The action of enforcing (see ENFORCE *v.*); *concr.* a reinforcement 1587. **2.** Constraint, compulsion; a constraining or compelling influence. Now *rare.* 1475. **3.** The forcible exaction of a payment, an action, etc.; the compelling the fulfilment of (a law, obligation, etc.); †*concr.* a means of enforcing, a sanction 1597.

1. What inforcements..to perswade men GOLDING. And his e. of the Citie Wiues *Rich. III*, III. vii. 8. The Prince of Conde was sent..with a great E. TEMPLE. **2.** Tuneless numbers, wrung By sweet e. KEATS. **3.** The Rewards and Punishments..established as the Enforcements of his Law LOCKE. An e. of domestic discipline SCOTT.

Enforcible, var. of ENFORCEABLE.

†**Enfo·rcive**, *a.* 1606. [f. ENFORCE *v.* + -IVE.] Tending to enforce; forcible, urgent –1693. Hence †**Enfo·rcively** *adv.*

†**Enfo·rest**, *v.* 1619. [– med.L. *inforestare*, f. *in* IN-[2] + *foresta* FOREST. Cf. AFFOREST.] To turn into forest –1662.

Enform, etc.; see INFORM, etc.

Enfort; see EN- *pref.*[1] 2.

†**Enfortu·ne**, *v.* [See EN-[1].] To invest with a quality. CHAUCER.

†**Enfou·lder**, *v.* [app. f. EN-[1] + OFr. *fouldre* (mod. *foudre*) thunderbolt.] In **Enfou·ldred** *ppl. a.* ?black as a thunder-cloud. SPENSER.

Enframe (enfrēi·m), *v.* Also **in-**. 1848. [See EN-[1], IN-[2].] To enclose in or as in a frame.

†**Enfra·nch**, *v.* 1581. [– AFr. *enfraunchir*, f. as next.] = ENFRANCHISE –1633.

Enfranchise (enfræ·ntʃiz, -tʃəiz), *v.* 1514. [f. *enfranchiss-*, lengthened stem of OFr. *enfranchir*, f. *en* EN-[1] + *franc*, *franche* free, FRANK. Cf. AFFRANCHISE.] **1.** To set free; to release from slavery or serfdom, confinement, or obligatory payments or legal liabilities 1531. †**2.** To make free of a municipality or corporation. Also *fig.* –1655. **3.** To invest (a city or town) with municipal rights. Now *chiefly* to invest with the right of representation in Parliament. 1564. **4.** To admit to political rights; now *esp.* to the electoral franchise 1683. **5.** To naturalize; also *fig.* ?*Obs.* 1601.

1. Phr. *To e. a copyhold* or *leasehold*: to convert it into freehold. **3.** Verolam-cestre was at this time enfranchised FULLER. **5.** By enfranchising strange forein words 1668. Hence **Enfra·nchiser,** one who or that which enfranchises.

Enfranchisement (enfræ·ntʃizmĕnt). Also †**in-**. 1595. [f. prec. + -MENT.] **1.** Liberation from imprisonment, servitude, or political subjection. Also *fig.* **2.** Admission to the freedom of a city or body politic; admission to political rights. **b.** The conferring of privileges (*esp.* of the electoral franchise) upon a town. 1628. **3.** The conversion of copyhold or leasehold lands into freehold 1876.

Enfree, -freedom, -freeze, etc.; see EN-[1].

Enfrenzy (enfre·nzi), *v.* 1656. [See EN-[1].] To throw into a frenzy.

Enfroward; see EN-[1] 2.

†**Enfu·me**, *v.* 1601. [– (O)Fr. *enfumer* :– L. *infumare*, f. *in-* IN-[2] + *fumus* smoke.] To expose to the action of smoke –1658.

Engage (engēi·dʒ), *sb.* 1589. [f. next.] †**1.** Bargain; also, entanglement, peril –1626. **2.** In Sword-exercise: The preliminary movement in which combatants cross swords 1833.

Engage (engēi·dʒ), *v.* 1525. [– (O)Fr. *engager* :– Rom. **invadiare*, f. *in-* EN-[1] + **wadium* GAGE *sb.*[1], WAGE.]

I. †**1.** To pledge or pawn; to mortgage –1669. **2.** *fig.* To pledge (one's life, honour, etc.); also, to expose to risk. Now *rare.* 1568. †**3.** To make (a person) security for (a debt, etc.) –1651. **4.** To bind by promise, or by legal or moral obligation; *spec.* to betroth 1603. **b.** *pass.* To have made an appointment, etc. 1885. **5.** To bespeak 1753. **6.** *intr.* for *refl.* To pledge oneself 1613. †**7.** *trans.* To lay under obligation; in *pass.* to be committed *to* –1667. **8.** To urge, induce. Now *rare.* 1647. **9.** To gain, win over, as an adherent or helper (*arch.*) 1697. **10.** To attract, charm, fascinate. Also *absol.* Now *rare.* 1711.

2. This to be true, I do e. my life *A. Y. L.* V. iv. 172. **3.** *Merch. V.* III. ii. 264. **4.** I am engaged for to-morrow 1891. **5.** To e. Balmat as guide TYNDALL, rooms, box-seats, etc. (*mod.*). **6.** More than I e. for JANE AUSTEN. **8.** O..example high! InGaging me to emulate MILT. *P. L.* IX. 963. **9.** To e. poetry in the cause of virtue 1779.

II. 1. a. To entangle. ?*Obs.* 1602. **b.** *Arch.* To fasten, attach. In *pass.* of a pillar: To be partly let into a wall in the rear. 1766. **c.** *Mech.* (*intr.* for *refl.*) of a cog-wheel, etc.: To gear *with* 1884. †**2.** *trans.* To cause to penetrate *into* a country, a defile, etc.; also *refl.* and *intr.* –1693. †**3.** To involve, mix up *in*, also occas., *into*, *to*, *with*. Also *intr.* for *refl.* –1796. **4.** To attract and hold fast 1642. **5.** *trans.* To occupy, employ. Now usu. *pass.* 1648. **6.** *intr.* for *refl.* 'To embark in any business' (J.) 1646. **7.** *trans.* Of combatants: To interlock (weapons). Also *absol.* 1697. **8. a.** To bring into conflict *with* the enemy 1668. **b.** *intr.* for *refl.* To enter into combat (*with*); also *fig.* 1647. **9.** = 'engage with' (see 8); also (now *rarely*) *fig.* 1698.

1. a. *Haml.* III. iii. 69. **4.** Her form..engaged the eyes of the whole congregation in an instant STEELE. **5.** Engaged with my guitar 1847. **6.** To e. in politics JOWETT. **8. a.** He had taken care not to e. the whole of his troops 1891. **9.** These monsters, Critics! with your darts e. POPE.

Engaged (engēi·dʒd), *ppl. a.* 1615. [f. prec. + -ED[1].] **1.** †Entangled. †**b.** Obliged. **c.** Locked in fight. **d.** Betrothed. **2.** (See quots.)

1. b. Not as an e. person, but indifferently WALTON. **2.** *E. column*, one partly let into a wall in the rear. *E. wheels* (Mech.), wheels in gear with each other. Hence †**Enga·gedness.**

Engagement (engēi·dʒmĕnt). Also †**in-**. 1624. [– (O)Fr. *engagement*, f. *engager*; see ENGAGE *v.*, -MENT.] **1.** The action of engaging, in various senses (see ENGAGE *v.*). **2.** The state, condition, or fact of being engaged; *spec.* betrothal 1642. **3.** A formal promise, agreement, undertaking, covenant 1624; an appointment 1806; in *pl.* pecuniary liabilities 1848. †**4.** Moral or legal obligation; a tie –1794; attachment, prepossession, bias (*rare*) –1708. **5.** A battle, encounter; †a single combat 1665. †**6.** *concr.* An inducement, motive –1698.

2. Your account of your daughter's e. DICKENS. **3.** Mr. A. B. is unable to meet his engagements 1891. **5.** We daily expect to hear of an E. between the Swedish and Danish Fleets 1710.

Engager (engēi·dʒəɹ). 1650. [f. ENGAGE *v.* + -ER[1].] **1.** One who engages; *esp.* one who enters into an engagement or agreement; †a guarantor 1653. **2.** *spec.* One of those who approved of the secret treaty or engagement negotiated at Carisbrooke in 1647 between Charles I and the Scottish commissioners. *Obs.* exc. *Hist.* 1650.

Engaging (engēi·dʒiŋ), *ppl. a.* 1673. [f. as prec. + -ING[2].] That engages; †obliging; †absorbing; winning, attractive.

Phr. *E.* and *disengaging machinery* (Mech.): that in which one part is alternately united to or separated from another part, as occasion may require (Nicholson). Hence **Enga·ging-ly** *adv.*, †**-ness.**

Engallant, -gaol, -garboil, etc.; see EN- *pref.*[1]

Engarland (engā·ɹlănd), *v.* 1581. [f. EN-[1] + GARLAND *sb.* Cf. Fr. *enguirlander*.] To encircle with or as with a garland.

†**Enga·rrison**, *v.* 1612. [f. EN-[1] + GARRISON *sb.*] To serve as a garrison in; to protect by a garrison; to station as a garrison (*pass.* only) –1775.

†**Enga·strimyth.** 1598. [– Fr. *engastrimythe* – Gr. ἐγγαστρίμυθος, f. ἐν EN-[2] + γαστρί, dat. of γαστήρ belly + μῦθος speech.] A ventriloquist –1708. Hence **Engastrimy·thic** *a.*

Engem (endʒe·m), *v. rare.* 1630. [f. EN-[1] + GEM *sb.*] To set with, or as with, gems; to bejewel.

†**Enge·nder,** *sb.* 1528. [– OFr. *engendre*; see next.] The action of engendering; *concr.* offspring, produce –1647.

Engender (endʒe·ndəɹ), *v.* ME. [– (O)Fr. *engendrer* :– L. *ingenerare*, f. *in-* EN-[1] + *generare* GENERATE *v.*] **1.** *trans.* Of the male: To beget: Const. *on, of.* Now *rhet.* or *fig.* †**2.** Of the female: To conceive, bear –1683. **3.** To produce, give existence to ME. †**4.** *absol.* To copulate. Const. *with.* Also *fig.* –1826. †**5.** *intr.* To breed, be produced, develop. Also *fig.* –1865.

1. When a man..engenders his like..it is no Miracle HOBBES. **3.** Reptiles ingendered in the putrid waters 1777. Taxes..destroy industry, engendring despair HUME. Heat engendered by friction TYNDALL. **5.** Thick clouds are spread, and storms e. there DRYDEN. Hence **Enge·nderer. Enge·nderment.**

Engendrure (endʒe·ndriŭɹ). *arch.* ME. [– OFr. *engendr(e)ure*, f. *engendrer*; see prec., -URE.] †**1.** The action of engendering –1555. **2.** Descent, origin ME. var. **Enge·ndure** (a bad form).

Engild (engi·ld), *v.* ME. [f. EN-[1] + GILD *v.*[1]] To gild; also *fig.*

Faire Helena; who more engilds the night SHAKS.

Engine (e·ndʒin), *sb.* ME. [– OFr. *engin* :– L. *ingenium* natural quality, disposition, or temper, talents, genius, clever device, f. *in* IN-[2] + *gen-* root of *gignere* beget.] †**1.** Mother wit; genius. (Stressed *engi·ne*) –1820. †**2.** Ingenuity; also, artfulness, trickery –1650. †**3.** An instance or product of ingenuity; a contrivance, plot; a snare, wile (cf. GIN *sb.*[1]); also, an appliance, means –1781. **4.** A mechanical contrivance, machine, implement, tool; also short for *beer-*, *fire-*, *garden-e.*, etc. (see FIRE-, GARDEN-, etc.). Also *fig.* of persons and things. ME **5.** *spec.* **a.** A machine or instrument used in warfare ME. †**b.** An engine of torture –1689. †**6.** As tr. L. *machina* (see MACHINE *sb.*) –1654. **7.** = STEAM-ENGINE. (The prevailing sense.) 1816. **8.** Applied also to analogous machines, including in themselves the means of generating power, as *caloric-*, *gas-e.*, etc. 1891.

1. A man hath sapiences thre, Memorie, engin, and intellect also CHAUCER. **3.** The hidden engines, and the snares that lie So undiscovered QUARLES. **4.** Our modern e., the microscope 1664. An e. to grind knives and scissars ARBUTHNOT. *fig.* Empson and Dudley, the wicked engines of Henry VII BLACKSTONE. Two great engines, punishment and reward BENTHAM. **6.** Phr. *E. of the world* (after L. *machina mundi* Lucretius): the 'universal frame'. **7.** His iron might the potent e. plies CLOUGH.

attrib. and *Comb.*: **a.** attrib., as *e. room*, etc.; **b.** objective, as *e.-driver*, etc.; also **e.-lathe,** a lathe worked by machinery; **-sized (paper)**, sized by a machine, not by hand; **-turning,** the engraving of symmetrical patterns upon metals by machinery.

Engine (e·ndʒin), *v.* ME. [orig. – OFr. *enginier* :– med.L. *ingeniare*, f. *ingenium* (see prec.); later, f. ENGINE *sb.*] †**1.** *trans.* To contrive, plan. Also *absol.* with inf. –1611. †**2.** To take by craft, ensnare. Only in ME. †**3.** To put on the rack ME.; to assault with engines 1613. **4.** To supply with engines 1868.

3. Enemies to e. and batter our walls T. ADAMS.

Engineer (endʒiniə·ɹ), *sb.* [ME. *engyneour* – OFr. *engigneor*, *-our* (mod. *ingénieur*) :– med.L. *ingeniator*, *-ōr-*, f. *ingeniare*, f. *ingenium*. In XVI the forms from OFr. were superseded by *en-*, *inginer*, either after mod.Fr. or – It. *ingegnere*, a distinct formation :– Rom. **ingenarius*; the ending was later assim. to -IER, -EER[1].] †**1.** One who contrives, designs, or invents; an inventor, a plotter –1702. **2.** One who designs and constructs military †engines or works. Also *fig.* ME. **3.** One who designs and constructs works of public utility. (From 18th c. also *Civil E.*, dist. orig. from 2, but now from 4.) Often specialized, as *electrical*, *gas*, *mining*, *railway*, *telegraph e.* 1606. **4.** A contriver or maker of engines (see ENGINE *sb.*); now spec. *mechanical e.* 1575. **5.** One who manages an engine; now in England only a marine engine; in U.S. often applied to the driver of a locomotive 1839.

Engineer (endʒiniə·ɹ), *v.* 1681. [f. prec. sb.] **1.** *intr.* To act as an engineer. **2.** *trans.* To employ the art of the engineer upon; to construct or manage as an engineer 1843. **b.** *fig.* To contrive, plan, superintend. Also (U.S.) to carry through a measure or enterprise. 1873.

2. The roads are admirably engineered OLMSTED. **b.** The corner in grain engineered..in Chicago 1882.

Engineering (endʒiniə·riŋ), *vbl. sb.* 1720. [f. prec. + -ING[1].] **1.** The work done by, or the profession of, an engineer. Often specialized as *civil*, *mechanical*, *military e.*; *agricultural*, *electrical*, *gas*, *hydraulic*, *railway*, *sanitary*, *telegraph e.*; see ENGINEER *sb.* 2–4. 1702. **b.** *fig.* Contriving, manœuvring 1780. **2.** *attrib.* 1739.

1. b. Party e. and the trickery of elections 1884. **2.** E. slang BYRON.

Engineership (endʒiniə·ɹʃip). 1649. [See -SHIP.] The business or position of an engineer.

†**Enginee·ry.** [f. ENGINEER *sb.* + -Y[3].] The science of engineering. SMEATON.

Engineman (e·ndʒinmǣn). 1835. [f. ENGINE *sb.* + MAN *sb.*] One who works or attends to an engine (see ENGINE *sb.*).

Enginery (e·ndʒinəri, -nri). 1605. [f. ENGINE *sb.* + -(E)RY.] †**1.** The art of constructing engines (see ENGINE *sb.*), or military works. Also *attrib.* –1672. **2.** Engines collectively; machinery; engines of war. Often *fig.* 1641. **3.** The work of an engine. Also *fig.* 1804.

2. In hollow Cube, Training his devilish Enginrie MILT. *P. L.* vi. 553.

†**E·nginous,** *a.* ME. [– OFr. *engi(g)nos*, *-eus* :– L. *ingeniosus*; see INGENIOUS.] **1.** Clever, crafty; deceitful –1615. **2.** Of or of the nature of, an engine (*lit.* and *fig.*) –1630.

1. Open force, or projects e. CHAPMAN. **2.** Some e. strong words B. JONS.

Engird (engə̄·ɹd), *v.* *Pa. pple.* **engirt.** 1566. [f. EN-[1] + GIRD *v.*[1]] To surround with, or as with, a girdle.

Engirdle (engə̄·ɹd'l), *v.* 1602. [f. EN-[1] + GIRDLE *v.*] = prec.

†**Engi·rt,** *v.* 1590. [f. EN-[1] + GIRT *v.*] **1.** To gird *with.* Also *simply.* –1634. **2.** To surround as a girdle does –1742; to enclose or hem in –1634.

2. The wat'ry zone Ingirting Albion W. BROWNE.

Engiscope; see ENGYSCOPE.

Engladden; see EN- *pref.*[1] 3.

England (i·ŋglănd). [OE. *Engla land*, lit. 'the land of the Angles'; see ENGLISH, ANGLE[3].] †**1.** The territory of the Angles. Only in OE. **2.** The southern part of the island of Great Britain. Occas. loosely: Great Britain. Often: The English (or British) nation or state. OE. Also *transf.* **3.** Short for *The King of England*, also for the English, or a portion of them, as in 'Young England' (see YOUNG) 1595. Hence **E·nglander** (*rare*), an Englishman.

‖**Englanté,** *a.* 1731. [Fr., f. *en-* EN-[1] + *gland* acorn.] *Her.* Bearing acorns. (Dicts.)

Engle, obs. f. INGLE.

†**Englei·m,** *v.* ME. [f. EN-[1] + †*gleim* slime.] To make slimy; to set fast with, or as with, slime. Also to clog, surfeit –1470.

English (i·ŋgliʃ). [OE. *englisc*, occas. *ænglisc* prop. pertaining to the Angles, but in the earliest examples, pertaining to the group of Germanic peoples known collect. as *Angelcynn* (Bede's *gens Anglorum*), lit. 'race of Angles'; also adj. and sb., of their language. See ANGLE *sb.*[3], -ISH[1].]

A. *adj.* **1.** Of or belonging to the *Angelcynn* ('Angle-kin' = Bede's *gens Anglorum*); or, later, to the pre-Norman inhabitants of England or their descendants. Now only *Hist.* **2.** Of or belonging to England or its inhabitants ME. **b.** *ellipt.* = 'English people, soldiers', etc. 1599. **3.** *transf.* Marked by the characteristics of an Englishman 1539. **4.** As the designation of a language (see B. 1). Hence: Belonging to, written or spoken in, the English language. OE.

2. Phr. †*E. Disease* (*Malady*), *E. Melancholy*: the spleen. **3.** He will find the design to be truly E., that is, sincere and honest 1695. **4.** The E. Classics MACAULAY.

B. *sb.* **1.** The English language. Also *attrib.*, as *E. scholar.* OE. **b.** The 'English' of any special period, district, or author ME. †**2.** Means of expression in English; the English word or equivalent (*for*) –1679. **3.** *transf.* The plain sense (*of*) 1645. **4.** *Printing.* **a.** A size of type intermediate between Great Primer and Pica.

English type.

b. *Old E.*: a form of Black Letter, now occas. used for ornamental purposes.

1. Wych I purpose now to declare On (= *in*) ynglysh BOKENHAM. Phr. *The king's, the queen's E.* (cf. 'to deface the king's coin). **b.** The *Old E.* period, that ending about 1100–1150. The *Middle E.* period, that ending about 1450, when the period of *Modern E.* begins. The term *Old E.* is also popularly applied to all obsolete forms of the language. **2.** Myn Englissh eek is insufficient CHAUCER. **3.** When they unmask cant, they say, 'The E. of this is', etc. EMERSON.

English (i·ŋgliʃ), *v.* ME. [f. prec. adj.] **1.** To translate into English. †**2.** To describe in plain English –1671. **3.** To make English, to anglicize 1824.

1. I Englishe it thus WYCLIF. **2.** Those gracious Acts..may be english'd more properly Acts of feare MILT. **3.** Clive—he..Conquered and annexed and Englished 1880. Hence †**E·nglishable** *a.* (Dicts.) **E·nglisher,** one who translates into English.

Englishism (i·ŋgliʃiz'm). *rare.* 1855. [See -ISM.] The characteristics of the English; English ways or manifestations; attachment to what is English.

Englishly (i·ŋgliʃli), *adv.* Now *rare.* 1529. [See -LY[2].] In an English manner; †in English; like an Englishman or Englishmen.

Englishman (i·ŋgliʃmǣn). [OE. *Engliscmon*, f. ENGLISH *a.* + MAN *sb.*] A man who is English by descent, birth, or naturalization.

Englishry (i·ŋgliʃri). 1470. [In AFr. *englescherie*, AL. *englescheria* (XII) – ME. *englisch*; see -(E)RY.] **1.** The fact of being an Englishman 1620. **2.** That part of the population, *esp.* in Ireland, that is of English descent. *Hist.* 1470. **b.** English people; an English quarter (*rare*) 1867.

1. *Presentment of E.* (Law): the offering of proof that a slain person was an Englishman, in order to escape the fine levied (in Norman times) upon the hundred for the murder of a Norman.

E·nglishwoman. 1530. [f. ENGLISH *a.* + WOMAN *sb.*] A woman who is English by descent, birth, or naturalization.

Englobe (englōᵘ·b), *v.* Also †**in-.** 1611. [f. EN-[1] + GLOBE] To form into a globe; also, to enclose in, or as in, a globe. Usu. *fig.*

Engloom; see EN- *pref.*[1] 2.

†**Englue·,** *v.* ME. [– (O)Fr. *engluer*, f. *en* EN-[1] + *glu* GLUE.] **1.** To fasten down with, or as with, glue; *fig.* to connect closely –1475. **2.** To ensnare, fascinate. Only in ME.

Englut (englʌ·t), *v. arch.* 1491. [In sense 1 – OFr. *englotir* (mod. *engloutir*) :– late L. *inglut(t)ire* gulp down; in sense 2 f. EN-[1] + GLUT *v.*] **1.** To swallow; to gulp down. **2.** To glut, satiate (*lit.* and *fig.*) 1571.

1. Inveterate wolf! whose gorge ingluts more prey, Than any beast beside CARY.

‖**Engobe** (engōᵘ·b). 1857. [Fr.] A white coating of pipe-clay, used to cover pottery.

Engolden; see EN- *pref.*[1] 2.

Engore (engōə·ɹ), *v.*[1] 1593. [f. EN-[1] + GORE *sb.*[1]] To steep in gore; to make gory.

†**Engo·re,** *v.*[2] *rare.* 1590. [f. EN-[1] + GORE *v.*[1]] To gore, wound deeply; *fig.* to infuriate. SPENSER.

Engorge (engǭ·ɹdʒ), *v.* 1515. [– OFr. *engorgier* feed to excess (mod. *engorger* obstruct, congest), f. *en* EN-[1] + *gorge* throat; see GORGE.] **1.** *trans.* To gorge, feed or fill to excess; chiefly *refl.* Also *transf.* in *pass.* **2.** To put into the gorge; to devour greedily. Also *transf.* and *fig.* 1541.

1. *transf.* These vessels are congested, or engorged with blood 1869. **2.** Prepare not to ingorge The eternal Pyramids 1798. Hence **Engo·rger.**

Engorgement (engǭ·ɹdʒmĕnt). 1611. [– Fr. *engorgement*, orig. in obs. sense 'action of engorging', now only in the sense 'congestion, blocking, clogging'; see prec., -MENT.] **a.** The action of engorging. **b.** Engorged state; esp. *Path.* congestion (of a tissue or organ) with blood, secretions, etc.

‖**Engouement** (aṅgūmaṅ). 1848. [Fr.; lit. 'obstruction in the throat'.] Unreasoning fondness.

Engouled (engū·ld), *a.* [f. Fr. *engoulé*, pa. pple. of *engouler* gobble up, f. *en* EN-[1] + OFr.

goule (mod. *gueule*) throat.] *Her.* An epithet of bends, crosses, saltires, etc.: Entering the mouths of animals. var. (in mod. Dicts.) **engoulée.**

Engrace (engrēi·s), *v.* Also †**in-.** 1610. [f. EN-[1] + GRACE *sb.*] †**a.** To introduce into favour –1641. **b.** To put grace into. PUSEY.

†**Engra·ff, in-,** *v.* ME. [f. EN-[1], IN-[2] + GRAFF *v.*] = ENGRAFT *v.* 1, 2. –1739. Hence **Engra·ffment** = ENGRAFTMENT.

Engraft, in- (en, ingra·ft), *v.* 1585. [f. EN-[1], IN-[2] + GRAFT *v*[1].] **1.** *trans.* To insert (a scion of one tree) as a graft *into* or *upon* (another). Also *absol.* 1677. **b.** *transf.* To set firmly in. SMEATON. **2.** *fig.* To implant; to incorporate; to superadd 1585. **3.** To graft (a tree) 1794. †**4.** = INOCULATE 3. 1717.

2. This word..would root out vice and ingraft virtue ABP. SANDYS. To e. trade on a national bank BP. BERKELEY. **4.** The boy was engrafted last Tuesday 1717. Hence **Engrafta·tion** (*rare*).

Engraftment (engra·ftmĕnt). Also **in-.** 1647. [f. prec. + -MENT.] **1.** The action of engrafting (*lit.* and *fig.*); also *concr.* a graft. †**2.** = INOCULATION 2. 1722. †**3.** The issuing of additional stock in a trading company –1776. So †**Engra·fture,** also **in-,** the action of engrafting; engrafted state.

Engrail (engrēi·l), *v.* ME. [– OFr. *engresler* (mod. *engrêler*), f. *en* EN-[1] + *gresle* (*grêle*) hail, the marks being compared to hailstones.] **1.** To indent the edge of with curvilinear notches; *spec.* in *Her.* Mainly in pa. pple. **2.** *transf.* To give a serrated appearance to; †to render prickly 1576. †**3.** To indent –1602. †**4.** ?To variegate –1611. **5.** *Occas.* To ornament *with* (metal) (*poet.*) 1814.

1. They also e. the bend itself 1864. **2.** Hills with peaky tops engrail'd TENNYSON. **5.** The car Engrailed with brass W. BRYANT. Hence **Engrai·led** *ppl.a.* in the senses of the vb.; *spec.* in *Her.* curvilinearly notched, as an ordinary. †**Engrai·ling** *vbl. sb.* the action of the vb.; *concr.* an engrailed edge. **Engrai·lment,** the state of being engrailed; the engrailed circle round the margin of a coin, etc.

Engrain, in- (en-, ingrēi·n), *v.* ME. [Sense 1 – OFr. *engrainer* to dye, f. phr. *en graine* (whence Eng. *in grain*); sense 2 f. EN-[1] + GRAIN *sb.*[1] IV. In the ppl. a. usually spelt *in-*.] **1.** *trans.* To dye with kermes or cochineal; hence, to dye in fast colours, dye in grain. Also *transf.* and *fig. Obs.* or *arch.* **2.** To work into the fibre or minute structure of a thing. Chiefly *fig.* of habits, convictions, tastes, etc. 1641. **3.** *nonce-use.* To form a granular surface on 1862.

1. Hire robe..of red scarlet engreyned LANGL. **2.** The stain hath become engrained by time SCOTT. *fig.* The feeling..so deeply engrained in human nature MAX-MÜLLER. Hence **Engrai·ned, in-** *ppl. a.* in the senses of the vb.; *fig.* incorrigible. †**Engrai·ner, in-.**

†**Engra·ndize, -ise,** *v.* 1625. [– *engrandiss-*, lengthened stem of Fr. †*engrandir* – It. *ingrandire*; cf. AGGRANDIZE.] *trans.* To make great, increase in estimation, etc. –1670.

Engrapple, obs. var. of INGRAPPLE *v.*

Engra·sp, *v.* 1593. [See EN-[1].] To embrace, grasp; also *fig.*

Engrave (engrēi·v), *v. Pa. pple.* **engraved, engraven.** 1509. [f. EN-[1] + GRAVE *v.*[1], after Fr. †*engraver*.] †**1.** *trans.* To sculpture –1614. **2.** †To cut into (*rare*). **b.** To mark by incisions. 1590. **3.** To carve upon a surface; hence, to record by incised letters; also *fig.* 1542. **b.** *fig.* To impress deeply, fix indelibly 1509. **4.** To represent by incisions upon wood, metal, stone, etc., with the view of reproducing by printing 1667.

1. Lysippus engraued Vulcan with a streight legge LYLY. **2. b.** This fruit, whose gleaming rind engrav'n 'For the most fair' TENNYSON. **3.** Crimes..ingraven in some Plate of Iron or Brass BUNYAN. **b.** To e. them on his memory OUSELEY. **4.** Maps..engraven in Copper PETTY. Hence †**Engra·vement,** the action of engraving; that which is engraved; also *fig.* a record, trace.

Engrave, var. of †INGRAVE, to entomb.

†**Engra·ven,** *v.* 1605. [perh. alt. of ENGRAVE, due to anal. of vbs. with prefix EN-[1] and suffix -EN[5].] = ENGRAVE –1713.

Engraver (engrēi·vəɹ). 1586. [f. ENGRAVE *v.* + -ER.[1]] **1.** One who engraves; *spec.* one who engraves pictures on metal or wood from which to take prints. **2.** A graver (*rare*) 1821. So †**Engra·very,** the art or work of the e.; also *concr.* engravings, (*rarely*) an engraving.

Engraving (engrēi·viŋ), *vbl. sb.* 1601. [f. as prec. + -ING[1].] **1.** The action of ENGRAVE *v.*; the art of the engraver. **2.** *concr.* That which is engraved; an engraved figure or inscription (*rare*) 1611. **3.** An impression from an engraved plate 1803.

2. The worke of an engrauer in stone; like the engrauings of a signet *Exod.* 28:11.

†**Engrea·ten,** *v.* 1614. [f. EN-[1] 2b + GREAT *a.* + -EN[5].] To make great –1684.

†**Engre·ge,** *v.* ME. [– OFr. *engregier* :– Rom. **ingreviare*, f. *in* EN-[1] + **grevis* for L. *gravis* heavy. See AGGREGE.] To make heavy; hence, to harden (the heart, etc.); also, to aggravate –1600.

†**Engrie·ve,** *v.* ME. [– OFr. *engrever* :– Rom. **ingrevare*, f. *in* EN-[1] + **grevis* for L. *gravis* heavy (whence L. *ingravare*). Cf. prec.] **1.** To cause grief to; also *absol.* –1626. **2.** To aggravate –1592. **3.** To make a grievance of. HOLINSHED.

Engroove, in- (en-, ingrū·v), *v.* 1842. [f. EN-[1], IN-[2] + GROOVE *sb.* or *v.*] *trans.* To work into a groove, or form a groove in.

Let the change which comes be free To ingroove itself with that which flies TENNYSON.

Engross (engrōu·s), *v.* ME. [– AFr. *engrosser* and AL. *ingrossare*; in sense 1, f. *en* IN + OFr. *grosse*, med.L. *grossa* large writing; in senses 2–4, f. phr. *en gros* and *in grosso* in the lump, wholesale.] **1.** To write in large letters; now usually, to write in a large, fair, legal hand; *hence*, to express in legal form. Also *absol.* †**b.** To include in a list –1660. **2.** To buy up wholesale; *esp.* to buy up the whole, or as much as possible, of (a commodity) for the purpose of 'regrating'. Now *Hist.* ME. **3.** *transf.* and *fig.* †To collect from all quarters (also with *up*); to monopolize 1596. **4.** To occupy wholly, absorb 1602. **5.** To render gross, dense, or bulky. Also *intr.* for *refl.* 1561. †**6.** *Mil.* To add to the numbers of (an army); also, to draw up (a battalion) in a compact body –1654.

1. For engrossing his will, twice unto paipar, after unto parchment 1591. **b.** T'ingross their names within his Register QUARLES. **2.** Forestallyng, regratyng..ingrossing of marchaundise CRANMER. **3.** To e. the sovereign powers 1832, the conversation BUCKLE. **4.** If man alone e. not Heaven's high care POPE. The degree in which self-love engrosses us BUTLER. **5.** To e. the body 1587, the minde 1628, a bill 1663. **6.** They went on in ingrossing the Militia HOWELL. Hence **Engro·ssedly** *adv.* **Engro·ssing-ly** *adv.*, **-ness.**

Engrosser (engrōu·səɹ), *vbl. sb.* 1460. [f. prec. + -ER[1].] **1.** †One who buys in large quantities; †a forestaller; a monopolist. **2.** One who copies (a document) in large, fair characters 1607.

Engrossment (engrōu·smĕnt). 1526. [f. as prec. + -MENT.] **1.** The action of engrossing; also that which is engrossed; also *fig.* **2.** The state or fact of being engrossed 1837.

1. An e. of grain 1818, of a charter PALGRAVE. **2.** Amidst the e. of other studies CAIRNS.

Enguard; see EN- *pref.*[1] B. 3.

Engulf, in- (engʊ·lf), *v.* 1555. [f. EN-[1], IN-[2] + GULF; cf. Fr. †*engoulfer*.] *trans.* To swallow up in, or as in, a gulf; *transf.* to bury completely. Also *refl.* and *intr.* for *refl.*

They were engulfed by chance in the great sea EDEN. Hence **Engu·lfment.**

Engyscope (e·ndʒiskōup). Also (badly) **engiscope.** 1684. [f. Gr. ἐγγύς near at hand + -SCOPE.] In 17th and 18th c.: = MICROSCOPE; subseq. restricted to reflecting microscopes.

Enhalo (enhēi·lo), *v.* 1842. [f. EN-[1] + HALO.] To surround with, or as with, a halo.

Enhance (enha·ns), *v.* ME. [– AFr. *enhauncer*, prob. alt. of OFr. *enhaucier* :– Rom. **inaltiare*, f. *in* EN-[1] + *altus* high.] †**1.** *trans.* To lift, raise, set up –16.. Also †*fig.* **2.** To raise in degree, heighten, intensify 1559; to make to appear greater ME. **3.** To raise, increase (prices, charges, etc.) 1542. Also †*intr.* to rise –1671. **4.** To raise or increase *in* price, value, importance, attractiveness, etc. Also †*simply.* 1526.

1. Who, nought agast, his mightie hand enhaunst SPENSER. *fig.* To inhaunce with favours this thy reign DRUMM. OF HAWTH. **2.** To e. an injury RAY, delights GIBBON, the infirmity of Philip 1832. **3.** Taxes and customs daily enhansed 1649. **4.** Base Mony, may easily be enhansed, or abased HOBBES.

†**Enha·ppy,** *v.* 1626. [See EN-[1] B. 2.] To make happy or prosperous –1742.

†**Enha·rbour,** *v.* 1596. [f. EN-[1] + HARBOUR *sb.*[1] or *v.*] To harbour within itself; to dwell in, as in a harbour –1616.

Enharden (enha·ɹd'n), *v.* ?*Obs.* 1502. [f. EN-[1] + HARDEN *v.*] To make hard, harden (*fig.*); to embolden (*rare*).

†**Enha·rdy,** *v.* 1483. [f. EN-[1] + HARDY *a.*] To make hardy, embolden –1525.

Enharmonic, -al (enhaɹmǫ·nik, -ăl), *a.* 1603. [– late L. *en(h)armonicus* – Gr. ἐναρμονικός, f. ἐν EN-[2] + ἁρμονία HARMONY; see -IC.] *Mus.* **1.** Pertaining to that scale of Greek music which proceeded by quarter tones and major thirds. **2.** Pertaining to, or concerned with, intervals smaller than a semitone; *esp.* with reference to the interval between those notes (belonging to different keys) which in instruments of equal temperament are rendered by the same tone; *e.g.* between G♯ and A♭. 1794.

2. Phr. *E. change* or *modulation*: that in which 'advantage is taken of the fact that the same notes can be called by different names, which lead..into unexpected keys' (Parry). Hence **Enharmo·nically** *adv.* **Enharmo·nics** *sb.pl.* e. music.

†**Enhau·lse,** *v.* [– OFr. *enhau(l)cier*; see ENHANCE.] = ENHANCE. P. HOLLAND.

†**Enhau·nt,** *v.* ME. [– Fr. †*enhanter*, f. *en* EN-[1] + (O)Fr. *hanter* to HAUNT.] **1.** *trans.* To practise. WYCLIF. **2.** To haunt; *intr.* to keep company *with* –1658.

†**Enha·zard,** *v.* 1562. [f. EN-[1] + HAZARD *sb.*] To expose to hazard, to risk –1611.

Enhearse, in- (en-, inhō·ɹs), *v.* 1600. [f. EN-[1], IN-[2] + HEARSE *sb.*] To put into, or as into, a hearse.

Enhearten (enhā·ɹt'n), *v.* Now *rare.* Also †**in-.** 1610. [f. EN-[1] B. 2b + HEARTEN *v.*] To make courageous; to strengthen, cheer.

Enhea·ven, in-, *v.* 1652. [See EN-[1].] To place in or as in heaven.

Enhedge; see EN- *pref.*[1] B. 3.

†**Enho·rt,** *v.* ME. [– OFr. *en(h)orter* :– L. *inhortari*, f. *in* IN-[2] + *hortari* exhort.] *trans.* To encourage, incite. Also with sb. as obj.: To recommend. –1483. Hence †**Enho·rtment,** an exhortation.

†**Enhui·le,** *v.* [– OFr. *enhuilier*, f. *en* EN-[1] + *huile* oil.] = ENOIL. P. HOLLAND.

Enhungered (enhʊ·ŋgəɹd), *ppl. a.* 1480. [Alteration of AHUNGERED, ANHUNGERED by substitution of EN-[1] for the prefix.] Hungry.

For he was sore enhongred 1480.

Enhydrite (enhəi·drəit). 1812. [f. as next + -ITE[1] 2b.] A mineral containing water occluded in its cavities. Hence **Enhydri·tic** *a.* of the nature of an e., as *enhydritic agates.*

Enhydrous (enhəi·drəs), *a.* 1812. [f. Gr. ἔνυδρος (ἐν EN-[2] + ὕδωρ water) + -OUS.] Containing water or other fluid.

Enhypo·statize, *v. rare.* [f. EN-[2] + HYPOSTATIZE.] To unite in one hypostasis or 'person'. SCHAFF.

Enigma (ĭni·gmă). 1539. [– L. *ænigma, -mat-* – Gr. αἴνιγμα, f. base of αἰνίσσεσθαι speak allusively or obscurely, f. αἶνος apologue, fable.] **1. a.** A riddle. †**b.** An obscure or allusive speech; a parable. (Now only *transf.* from a.). **2.** *fig.* Something as puzzling as an enigma 1605.

1. a. Some e., some riddle, come, thy Lenuoy begin SHAKS. **2.** A person both God and Man, an ænigma to all Nations, and to all Sciences JER. TAYLOR. Hence †**Eni·gmatist,** one who writes, or speaks in enigmas. **Eni·gmatize** *v.* †to symbolize; to render enigmatical; *intr.* to make, or talk in, enigmas.

Enigmatic, -al (ĭnigmæ·tik, -ăl), *a.* 1576. [– Fr. *énigmatique* or late L. *ænigmaticus*; see prec., -ATIC, -ICAL.] Pertaining to, of the nature of, or containing, an enigma; ambiguous, obscure, perplexing. Of persons: Mysterious.

He saw the figure of the enigmatic Jew GEO. ELIOT. Hence **Enigma·tically** *adv.* ambiguously, obscurely.

Enigmato-, comb. f. ENIGMA, as in **Enigmato·grapher** [Gr. -γράφος], a maker or explainer of enigmas. **Enigmato·graphy** [Gr. -γραφία], the making or collecting of enigmas.

Enigmato·logy [see -LOGY], the study of enigmas.

Enisle, in- (en-, inəi·l), *v.* 1612. [f. EN-¹, IN-² + ISLE.] **a.** To make into an isle 1630. **b.** To place or settle on an isle; *fig.* to isolate, sever.

a, Mine eyes en-isle themselves with floods DRUMM. OF HAWTH. **b.** An inisled kingdom of fisherfolk 1880.

Enjail, in- (en-, indʒēi·l), *v.* 1631. [f. EN-¹, IN-² + JAIL. See also ENGAOL.] To shut up in, or as in, a jail.

†**Enja·mb,** *v.* 1600. [– Fr. *enjamber* stride over, go beyond, encroach, f. *en* EN-¹ + *jambe* leg.] To encroach.

Enjambment (endʒæ·mbmĕnt). Also **enjambement.** 1837. [– Fr. *enjambement,* f. *enjamber*; see prec., -MENT.] *Pros.* The continuation of a sentence beyond the second line of a couplet.

It [the couplet] was turned by enjambements into something very like rhythmic prose SAINTSBURY.

Enjewel (endʒ¹ū·ĕl), *v.* 1648. [See EN-¹.] To adorn with jewels; to adorn as a jewel does.

Faire injewel'd May Blowne out of April HERRICK.

Enjoin (endʒoi·n), *v.* ME. [– *enjoi(g)n-,* stem of (O)Fr. *enjoindre* :– L. *injungere* join, attach, impose, f. *in* EN-¹ + *jungere* JOIN.] †**1.** *trans.* To join together –1684. **2.** In early use: To impose (a penalty, duty, etc.); said *esp.* of a spiritual director. Hence: To prescribe authoritatively and with emphasis. ME. †**b.** To impose rules on (oneself). BACON. **3.** To prohibit, forbid. Now only in *Law*: To prohibit or restrain by an INJUNCTION. 1589.

2. The Lords..have enjoyned their clerks secrecy MARVELL. The pope..enjoined him to return to his duties FROUDE. **3.** To e. an action 1814, a person from infringing a right BOWEN.

Hence **Enjoi·ner, Enjoi·nment.**

Enjoy (endʒoi·), *v.* ME. [– OFr. *enjoier* give joy to, *refl.* enjoy, f. *en* EN-¹ + *joie* JOY, or – OFr. *enjoïr* enjoy, rejoice, f. *en-* + *joïr* :– L. *gaudēre.*] †**1.** *intr.* To be in a joyous state; to rejoice –1549. †**2.** *trans.* To put into a joyous condition –1610. **b.** *refl.* To experience pleasure, be happy 1656. **3.** *trans.* To possess, use, or experience with delight; also, to relish. Also *absol.* 1462. **4.** To have the use of, have for one's lot 1460. †**b.** To have one's will of (a woman) –1667.

2. b. Creatures are made to e. themselves, as well as to serve us HY. MORE. To e. oneself at the seaside 1891. **3.** No one can long Enyoy plesure T. STARKEY. **4.** To hold and e. the same as a place of inheritance CRUISE. At best she enjoys poor health 1834. Hence **Enjoy·able** *a.* capable of being enjoyed; affording pleasure. **Enjoy·ably** *adv.* **Enjoy·er.**

Enjoyment (endʒoi·mĕnt). 1553. [f. prec. + -MENT.] **1.** The action or state of enjoying anything. Also, the possession and use of something which affords pleasure or advantage. Const. *of.* **2.** Gratification, pleasure; *concr.* that which gives pleasure 1665.

1. Injoyment of many Lands MANLEY, of one's legal rights MACAULAY. **2.** Food, drink, sleep, and the like animal enjoyments BP. BERKELEY.

†**Enke·nnel,** *v.* 1577. [See EN-¹.] To lodge as in a kennel –1603.

Enkindle (enki·nd'l), *v.* 1548. [f. EN-¹ + KINDLE *v.*¹] **1.** *trans.* To cause to blaze up. Chiefly *fig.* (to excite passions, war, etc.) 1583. **2.** To set on fire. In lit. sense *Obs.* 1548. **b.** *transf.* To light up 1870. †**3.** *intr.* To take fire; to burst forth in flame –1747.

1. To e. rage JOHNSON. **2.** Inkindled to an indeauour of good BP. HALL. Hence **Enki·ndler.**

Enlace (enlē¹·s), *v.* ME. [– OFr. *enlacier* (mod. *enlacer*) :– Rom. **inlaciare*, f. *in* IN-² + **laciare*, f. **lacium*, for L. *laqueus* noose. In later use taken as f. EN-¹ + LACE *sb.*] **1.** *trans.* To lace about, encircle tightly with, or as with, lace; *transf.* to enfold, embrace. **2.** To interlace, entangle. Also *fig.* ME.

1. They will e. him in the coils of their red tape 1877. Hence **Enla·cement.**

†**Enla·rd,** *v.* 1556. [f. EN-¹ + LARD.] *trans.* **a.** To lard –1606. **b.** = INTERLARD –1621.

Enlarge (enlā·ɹdʒ), *v.* ME. [– OFr. *enlarger, -ir,* f. *en* EN-¹ + *large* LARGE. Some of the uses are due to (O)Fr. *eslargir,* mod. *élargir* set free.] **1.** *trans.* To make larger; to increase the size of; to extend the limits of; to magnify, exaggerate. **b.** *Photog.* To reproduce on a larger scale. Also *absol.* 1871. **2.** *fig.* To extend the scope of 1553; to widen, to expand 1665; †to grant or obtain an extension of time for (an action, a lease, an order, etc.) –1863. **3.** *intr.* for *refl.* To increase or widen in extent, bulk, or scope. Also *refl.* ME. **4.** *intr.* for *refl.* To speak at large, expatiate 1659. **5.** To set at large, release. Now *arch.* or *U.S.* 1494. †**6.** To bestow liberally. [So OFr. *enlarger*; cf. L. *largiri.*] –1657.

1. That..his honour [might be] inlarged FLEMING. Any Prince willing to enlarge his Territories PETTY. Report generally inlarges matters 1728. Phr. †*To e. on* (intr.): to add to (a plan); to amplify (a hint). **2.** To e. the Christian fayth EDEN, the legal operation of an instrument 1884, our conceptions of Time MCCOSH. Phr. *To e. the heart*: now usu., to increase its capacity for affection. *To e. an estate* (Law): to convert a lease for years or a life-interest into a fee-tail or fee-simple. **4.** I shall e. upon the point BUTLER, *Hud.* II. ii. 68. **5.** He was enlarged upon sureties 1878.

Hence **Enla·rgeable** *a.* **Enla·rgeableness. Enla·rged** *ppl. a.* increased, expanded, set free; also *fig.* liberal. †**Enla·rgedly** *adv.* †**Enla·rgedness. Enla·rger. Enla·rgingly** *adv.*

Enlargement (enlā·ɹdʒmĕnt). 1540. [f. ENLARGE *v.* + -MENT.] **1.** The action of enlarging; an increase in extent, capacity, magnitude, or amount 1564. **b.** *Photog.* (Cf. ENLARGE *v.* 1b.) 1871. **2.** The widening or expanding of the mind, of a person's sympathies, affections, etc.; the quality of being enlarged in mind, etc. 1806. **3.** Expatiation on a subject (*arch.*) 1659. **4.** Release from confinement, limitation, or bondage 1540; liberty (*arch.*) 1611.

3. I restrain my pen from all e. 1765. **4.** The e. of the deer 1875, of Mr. Parnell from prison 1883.

Enleague (enlī·g), *v.* 1602. [f. EN-¹ + LEAGUE *sb.*² or *v.*] *trans.* To unite in, or as in, a league.

Enlength, -en; see EN- *pref.*¹ B. 2, 3.

Enlevement (enlī·vmĕnt, an̄lęvman̄). 1769. [– Fr. *enlèvement,* f. *enlever* carry off or away.] *Sc. Law.* An abduction.

Ele(v)en, -enth, obs. ff. ELEVEN, -TH.

†**Enlight** (enləi·t), *v.* [OE. *inlihtan,* f. *in-* + *lihtan* to shine (see LIGHT *v.*²); subseq. f. EN-¹ + LIGHT *v.*²] To shed light upon, illuminate. Also *fig.* and *absol.* –1709.

Enlighten (enləi·tən), *v.* ME. [orig. f. prec. + -EN⁵; later f. EN¹ + LIGHTEN *v.*², or LIGHT *sb.* + -EN⁵.] †**1.** *trans.* To put light into, make luminous –1763. **2.** To illuminate; to give light to. Also *absol.* Now *poet.* or *rhet.* 1611. †**3.** To light –1817. **4.** *fig.* To impart knowledge, wisdom, or spiritual light to; to instruct. In mod. colloq. use: To inform. 1577.

2. His lightnings inlightned the world *Ps.* 97:4. Shadow and sunshine..darkning and enlightning..ev'ry spot COWPER. **4.** [The Seuentie] were..enlightened by propheticall grace A.V. *Pref.* To e. their minds JOHNSON. Hence **Enli·ghtener,** one who or that which enlightens. (Rare exc. *fig.*)

Enlightened (enləi·t'nd), *ppl. a.* 1611. [f. prec. + -ED¹.] †**1.** Blazing, light-giving –1803. **2.** Illuminated 1638. **3.** Possessed of mental light; instructed, well-informed; free from superstition or prejudice 1663. Hence **Enli·ghtenedness.**

Enlightenment (enləi·t'nmĕnt). 1669. [f. as prec. + -MENT.] **1.** The action of enlightening; enlightened state. Only in *fig.* sense. **2.** [after G. *Aufklärung.*] Shallow and pretentious intellectualism, unreasonable contempt for authority and tradition, etc.; applied *esp.* to the spirit and aims of the French philosophers of the 18th c. 1865.

2. The individualistic tendencies of the age of E. 1889.

†**Enli·mn,** *v.* 1453. [f. EN-¹ + LIMN. See ENLUMINE.] *trans.* To illuminate (a book); also, to paint in bright colours –1603.

Enlink (enli·ŋk), *v.* 1560. [f. EN-¹ + LINK *sb.*² or *v.*] *trans.* To fasten as with links; to connect closely (*lit.* and *fig.*).

Enlist (enli·st), *v.* Also †**in-.** 1698. [f. EN-¹ + LIST *sb.*⁵ or *v.*⁴, perh. after Du. *inlijsten* inscribe on a list or register.] **1.** *trans.* To enrol on the list of a military body; to engage as a soldier. **2.** *transf.* and *fig.* To secure the support or aid of; to make available for a purpose 1753. **3.** *intr.* for *refl.* To have one's name inscribed in a list of recruits; to engage for military service. Also *transf.* and *fig.* 1776.

2. It was clever to inlist on his side those venerable prejudices 1826. To e. the aunt as his friend DISRAELI. **3.** A bounty to induce men to e. 1865.

Enlistment (enli·stmĕnt). 1765. [f. prec. + -MENT.] **1.** The action of enlisting men for military service; the action of engaging for military service. Also *fig.* and *attrib.* **2.** 'The document by which a soldier is bound' (Webster). ?*U.S. only.*

†**Enli·ve,** *v.* 1593. [f. EN-¹ + LIFE, after LIVE *v.*] = next –1659.

Enliven (enləi·v'n), *v.* 1633. [Extended form of prec., after words in -EN⁵.] †**1.** *trans.* To give or restore life to; to animate –1732. **2.** To give fuller life to; to inspirit, invigorate; to quicken 1644. **3.** To make lively, cheer; to relieve the monotony of; to brighten 1691.

2. To inliven Trade 1677, to e. old trees PLOT, the circulation 1799. **3.** To e. Morality with Wit ADDISON. A sage to consult, rather than a companion to e. DIBDIN. Hence **Enli·vener,** one who or that which enlivens. **Enli·venment,** the action of enlivening; the being enlivened; that which enlivens.

Enlock (enlǫ·k), *v.* Also **in-.** 1596. [f. EN-¹ + LOCK *v.*] To lock up, shut in, hold fast. Also *fig.*

†**Enlu·mine,** *v.* ME. [– (O)Fr. *enluminer* – med.L. *inluminare* (for L. *illuminare*) light up, limn, f. *in* IN-² + *lumen, lumin-* light. See LIMN.] **1.** To light up, illuminate; also *fig.* –1596. **2.** To illuminate (MSS.) –1525.

†**Enlu·re,** *v.* 1486. [f. EN-¹ + LURE *sb*¹. Cf. ALLURE *v.*] To entice by a lure; also *fig.* –1613.

†**Enlute,** *v.* ME. [f. EN-¹ + LUTE *v.*²] *Alch.* To stop or cement with clay –1584.

Enmagazine; see EN- *pref.*¹ B. 1a.

†**Enma·nché, emma·nché.** 1586. [–¹ Fr. *emmanché,* f. *en*-EM- 1 + *manche* handle.] *Her.* **1.** Of the field: = *barry-pily.* (Not in Eng. use.) **2.** Of a chief: Having 'lines drawn from the upper edge of the chief on the sides' (Bailey).

Enmarble, etc.; see EMM-.

‖**En masse** (an̄mas). 1802. [Fr.] In a mass or body; all at once.

Enmesh, emm-, imm- (enme·ʃ, eme·ʃ, ime·ʃ), *v.* 1604. [f. EM- 1 + MESH *sb.*] *trans.* To catch or entangle in, or as in, meshes.

I got immeshed in a network of turns unknown C. BRONTË. Hence **Enme·shment,** entanglement.

Enmew, var. of INMEW.

Enmity (e·nmĭti). ME. [– OFr. *enemi(s)tié* (mod. *inimitié*) :– Rom. **inimicitas, -tat-,* f. L. *inimicus*; see ENEMY, -ITY.] **1.** The disposition or the feelings of an enemy; ill-will, hatred. **2.** The condition of being an enemy; a state of mutual hostility ME. Also *transf.*

1. For enymyte and hate are contrary to frendship and concorde CAXTON. **2.** An age at e. with all restraint LOCKE (J.).

Enmoss; see EN- *pref.*¹ B. 1b.

†**Enmu·ffle,** *v.* [f. EN-¹ + MUFFLE *v.*] To muffle up. FLORIO.

E:nneacontahe·dral, *a. rare.* 1817. [f. Gr. ἐννεάκοντα (erron. for ἐνενήκοντα) ninety + ἕδρα base + -AL¹.] Of a crystal: Having ninety faces.

Ennead (e·niæ̆d). 1653. [– Gr. ἐννεάς, ἐννεαδ-, f. ἐννέα nine; see -AD.] †**1.** The number nine 1655. **2.** A set of nine; *spec.* one of the six divisions in Porphyry's collection of Plotinus' works, each of which contains nine books. Hence **Ennea·dic** *a.* pertaining to an e.

Enneaeteric (e:nĭă,ĭte·rik), *a.* [f. Gr. ἐννέα nine + ἔτος year, after τριετηρίς cycle of three years; see -IC.] Consisting of nine years. GROTE.

Enneagon (e·nĭ,ăgǫn). 1660. [f. Gr. ἐννέα nine + -GON.] *Geom.* A plane figure with nine angles. Hence **Ennea·gonal** *a.* having nine angles.

Enneagynous (enĭæ·dʒinəs), *a.* [f. Gr. ἐννέα nine; see -GYNOUS.] *Bot.* Having nine pistils. (Dicts.)

Enneahedral (e:nĭăhī·drăl), *a.* 1802. [f. Gr. ἐννέα nine + ἕδρα base + -AL¹.] Having nine faces.

Ennea·ndrian, *a.* [f. mod.L. *enneandria*, one of the Linnæan classes (f. as next) + -AN.] *Bot.* = next.

Enneandrous (enĭæ·ndrəs), *a.* 1870. [f. Gr. ἐννέα nine + ἀνδρ- male + -OUS.] *Bot.* Having nine stamens.

Enneapetalous (e:nĭăpe·tăləs), *a.* 1847. [f. Gr. ἐννέα nine + πέταλον leaf + -OUS.] *Bot.* Having nine petals. So **Enneaphy·llous** *a.* [Gr. φύλλον], having nine leaves. **Ennease·palous** *a.* [see SEPAL], having nine sepals. **Enneaspe·rmous** *a.* [Gr. σπέρμα], having nine seeds.

Enneatic, -al (enĭæ·tik, -ăl), *a. rare.* 1751. [f. Gr. ἐννέα + -ATIC (+ -AL[1]).] Occurring once in nine times, days, years, etc.; ninth. Phr. †*Enneatical day*: every ninth day of a disease. †*Enneatical year*: every ninth year of life.

†**Ennew·,** *v.*[1] ME. [f. EN-[1] + NEW.] To make new or anew –1623.

†**Ennew·,** *v.*[2] ME. [– OFr. *ennuer*, f. *en* EN-[1] + *nuer* to shade (cf. Fr. *nuance* XVII), f. (O)Fr. *nue* cloud.] *trans.* To shade; to graduate (colours). Also *fig.* –1573.

Enniche; see EN- *pref.*[1] B. 1a.

Ennoble (enō͡ᵘ·b'l), *v.* 1502. [– (O)Fr. *ennoblir*; see EN-[1], NOBLE.] **1.** To give the rank of nobleman to 1594. **2.** To impart nobility to; to dignify, elevate, refine 1502. †**3.** To render illustrious or conspicuous –1775.

1. His [Columbus'] family was ennobled 1791. **2.** The Son of God..ennobling all that he touches TRENCH. **3.** Bear Thy death ennobl'd by Ulysses' spear POPE. Hence **Enno·blement,** the action of ennobling; the state or fact of being ennobled; †that which ennobles. **Enno·bler. Enno·blingly** *adv.* var. †**Enno·blish,** †**Enno·blize.**

†**Ennoy·,** var. of ANNOY *sb.* and *v.*

‖**Ennui** (aṅnüi), *sb.* 1758. [Fr. :– L. phr. *in odio*; see ANNOY *sb.*] Mental weariness and dissatisfaction arising from want of occupation, or lack of interest.

Ennui, *v.* 1805. [f. prec. sb.; only in pa. pple.] To affect with ennui; to bore, weary. They [animals] rejoice, play, are ennuied as we are 1805.

‖**Ennuyé** (aṅnüiye), *a.* 1757. [Fr., pa. pple. of *ennuyer*, f. *ennui*; see prec.] Affected with ennui. As quasi-*sb.* (also *fem.* **-ée**), one who is troubled with ennui.

†**Eno·date,** *v.* 1656. [– *enodat-*, pa. ppl. stem of L. *enodare*, f. *e* EX-[1] + *nodus* knot; see -ATE[3].] To free from knots; *fig.* to unravel, make clear –1681. Hence †**Enoda·tion.**

†**Eno·de,** *v. rare.* 1623. [– L. *enodare*; see prec.] To untie (a knot); *fig.* to solve (a riddle) –1684.

†**Enoi·l,** *v.* ME. [f. EN-[1] + OIL *sb.* Cf. ANOIL, ENHUILE.] To anoint, or mix, with oil –1647.

Enoint, obs. f. ANOINT.

Enology; see ŒNOLOGY.

Enomotarch (enǫ·mŏtaɹk). 1623. [– Gr. ἐνωμοτάρχης, f. ἐνωμοτία (see next) + -αρχης; see -ARCH.] *Gr. Antiq.* The commander of an ENOMOTY.

Enomoty (enǫ·mŏti). 1623. [– Gr. ἐνωμοτία band of sworn soldiers, f. ἐν EN-[2] + ὀμνύναι swear.] *Gr. Antiq.* A division in the Spartan army.

Enoptromancy (enǫ·ptromænsi). Also (erron.) **enopto-.** 1855. [f. Gr. ἔνοπτρον mirror + -MANCY.] Divination by means of a mirror.

Enorganic (enǫɹgæ·nik), *a.* [f. EN-[2] + ORGANIC.] Inherent in the organism. SIR W. HAMILTON.

Enorm (ĭnǭ·ɹm). 1481. [– Fr. *énorme* or L. *enormis*; see ENORMOUS.] †**1.** Abnormal, extravagant –1734. †**2.** Outrageous –1639. **3.** Abnormally large (*arch.*) 1581.

†**Eno·rmious,** *a.* 1545. [f. L. *enormis* + -OUS; see ENORMOUS.] = ENORMOUS –1665.

Enormity (ĭnǭ·ɹmĭti). 1475. [– (O)Fr. *énormité* – L. *enormitas*, f. *enormis*; see next, -ITY.] **1.** Deviation from a normal standard or type; *esp.* from moral or legal rectitude. In later use: Monstrous wickedness. 1538. **2.** *concr.* That which is abnormal; an irregularity; a crime; in later use, a monstrous offence 1475. **3.** Excess in magnitude. (An incorrect use.) 1792.

1. Deeds of peculiar e. and rigour W. ROBERTSON. Other enormities Catiline had been guilty of FROUDE.

Enormous (ĭnǭ·ɹməs), *a.* 1531. [f. L. *enormis* (f. *e* EX-[1] + *norma* pattern) + -OUS.] †**1.** Deviating from ordinary rule or type; abnormal; hence, monstrous –1818. †**2.** Of persons, deeds, etc.: Disorderly. Hence, excessively wicked, outrageous. –1827. **3.** Extraordinary in size or quality; huge, vast, immense. (The only current sense.) 1544.

1. E. appetite VENNER, bliss MILT., faith POPE. **2.** Oh great corrector of e. times 1612. E. wickedness, guilt SOUTHEY. **3.** E. woe 1827, cracks and fissures 1836. Hence **Eno·rmous-ly** *adv.*, **-ness.**

†**Eno·rn,** *v.* ME. [var. of ANORN.] = ANORN –1513.

Eno·rthotrope. [f. Gr. ἐν EN-[2] + ὀρθός upright + -τροπος turning.] A toy; a card on which confused objects are transformed into regular figures or pictures, by causing it to revolve rapidly. (Dicts.)

Enostosis (enǫstō͡ᵘ·sis). 1874. [f. Gr. ἐν EN-[2] + ὀστέον bone + -OSIS, after EXOSTOSIS.] *Anat.* A bony tumour growing inward into the medullary canal of a bone.

Enough (ĭnʊ·f). [OE. *ġenōg, ġenōh* = OFris. *enōch*, OS. *ginōg* (Du. *genoeg*), OHG. *ginuog* (G. *genug*), ON. *gnógr*, Goth. *ganōhs* :– Gmc. **ʒanōʒaz*, rel. to OE. *ġenēah*, OHG. *ginah*, Goth. *ganah* it suffices.]

A. *adj.* **1.** Sufficient in quantity or number: used in concord with sb., which it usually follows, or predicatively. **2.** *absol.* in *sing.* That which is sufficient OE. **b.** *ellipt.* = 'Enough has been said,' etc.; quasi-*interj.*; also with *of* ME.

1. With payne and trauayle anough LD. BERNERS. Prisoners mo than Inough 1500. It is ynough, holde now thy hande COVERDALE 2 *Sam.* 24:16. **2.** I have had e. of fighting DE FOE.

B. *adv.* (In mod. Eng. *enough* normally follows the word it qualifies.) **1.** Sufficiently; in a quantity or degree that satisfies or is effectual OE. **2.** In vaguer sense. **a.** With intensive, or slightly intensive, force OE. **b.** Belittling what is conceded 1606.

1. He [Dauid] himselfe was olde, and had lyued ynough COVERDALE 1 *Chr.* 23:1. Good e. for me JOWETT. **2. a.** This poynte is..metely playn inough MORE. Phr. *Aptly e., oddly e.* **b.** A good e. man in his way MRS. CARLYLE.

Enounce (ĭnau·ns), *v.* 1805. [– Fr. *énoncer* – L. *enuntiare* ENUNCIATE, after *announce*, *pronounce*.] **1.** *trans.* = ENUNCIATE 1. **2.** To state publicly, proclaim 1807. **3.** To utter, pronounce; cf. ENUNCIATION 1829.

3. The student should be able to e. these [sounds] independently A. M. BELL. Hence **Enou·ncement.**

Enow (ĭnau·), *a.* and *adv.*[1] Now only *arch.* [repr. *ġenōge*, nom. and acc. pl. of OE. *ġenōg* ENOUGH; in literary use as the pl. of *enough* at least till XVIII (later in Sc. writers and dial.).] = ENOUGH *a.* and *adv.*

Enow (ĭnau·), *adv.*[2] *dial.* [perh. short for *e'en* (= *even*) *now*, or for *the now*.] Just now (*Sc.*); presently.

Enp-; see EMP-.

‖**En passant** (aṅ pasaṅ), *adv.* 1665. [Fr.] In passing; by the way.

†**Enqua·rter,** *v.* 1622. [f. EN-[1] + QUARTER *sb.*] **1.** To put into quarters; to billet. Also *absol.* –1673. **2.** *Her.* To quarter –1635.

Enquere, obs. var. of ENQUIRE, INQUIRE.

Enquicken; see EN- *pref.*[1] B. 3.

Enquire (enkwəiᵊ·ɹ), *v.* An alternative form of INQUIRE; used *esp.* in the sense 'to ask a question'. Hence **Enquirer, Enquiry,** etc., for which see IN-.

†**Enra·ce,** *v. rare.* 1577. [f. EN-[1] + RACE *sb.*[2]] To introduce into a race; to implant –1596.

Enrage (enrē͡ᵢ·dʒ), *v.* 1502. [– (O)Fr. *enrager*, f. *en-* EN-[1] + *rage* RAGE *sb.*] †**1.** *intr.* To be distracted. Const. *for.* –1557. †**2.** To rage –1782. †**3.** *Pa. pple.* Maddened; inspired. Also, affected with rabies. –1719. **4.** *trans.* To put into a rage; to exasperate; also *absol.* 1589. †**5.** *transf.* To cause heat or fever in –1693.

3. His love, perceiving how he is enraged, Grew kinder SHAKS. **4.** Question enrages him *Macb.* III. iv. 118. **5.** To e. the blood 1626, a wound 1635. Hence **Enra·ged-ly** *adv.*, **-ness. Enra·gement,** the action of enraging; enraged state or condition; †rapture.

†**Enrai·l,** *v.* 1523. [f. EN-[1] + RAIL *sb.*[2] and *v.*[2]] To enclose with, or as with, a railing –1607.

†**Enra·nge,** *v.* [f. EN-[1] + RANGE *sb.*[1] and *v.*[1]] **1.** To arrange. **2.** To range or ramble in. ? In Spenser only.

Enra·nk, *v.* 1591. [f. EN-[1] + RANK *sb.*] To set in ranks, or in order (of battle).

‖**En rapport** (aṅrapǫr). 1818. [Fr.] In relation (*with*); in mesmeric 'rapport'; see RAPPORT.

Enrapt (enræ·pt), *pa. pple.* 1606. [f. EN-[1] + RAPT.] Carried away in an ecstasy; hence, absorbed in contemplation, enraptured. ¶Sometimes undistinguishable from *enwrapt* (fig.).

Enrapture (enræ·ptiŭɹ), *v.* 1740. [f. EN-[1] + RAPTURE.] **1.** To throw into a poetic rapture 1742. **2.** To delight greatly.

Enravish (enræ·viʃ). Now *rare.* 1596. [f. EN-[1] + RAVISH.] To transport with delight; to enrapture. Hence †**Enra·vishingly** *adv.* **Enra·vishment,** enravished condition; ecstasy.

Enregiment (enre·dʒ'mĕnt), *v.* 1831. [– Fr. *enrégimenter*, f. *en* EN-[1] + *régiment* REGIMENT *sb.*] To form into, or as into, a regiment; hence, to discipline.

Enregister (enre·dʒistəɹ), *v.* 1523. [– (O)Fr. *enregistrer*, f. *en* EN-[1] + *registre* REGISTER *sb.*[1]] **1.** *trans.* To enter in a register or official record. Also *transf.* and *fig.* (Revived in recent use as a gallicism.) **2.** To put on record as law 1651.

Hence **Enregistra·tion,** the registering, on the brain, of previous actions, so that performance becomes automatic or instinctive 1922. †**Enre·gistry,** the action of enregistering.

†**Enrheu·m,** *v.* 1666. [– OFr. *enrheumer* (mod. *enrhumer*), f. *en* EN-[1] + *rheume* (mod. *rhume*); see RHEUM[1].] *trans.* To affect with rheum; to give a cold to.

Enrich (enri·tʃ), *v.* ME. [–(O)Fr. *enrichir*, f. *en-* EN-[1] + *riche* RICH.] **1.** *trans.* To make rich with material, or (*fig.*) mental or spiritual, wealth. Also *absol.* **2.** To add to the valuable contents of. Also *fig.* 1579. **3.** To make (the soil, etc.) rich; to fertilize 1601. **4.** To make rich with (costly) decoration. Also *fig.* 1601. **5.** To make richer; to heighten 1620.

1. To enrych the Corowne FORTESCUE. *fig.* E. them with thy heauenly grace *Bk. Com. Prayer.* **2.** E. thy cofers LYLY. *fig.* The English tongue is mightily enriched 1598. **4.** The hilt and scabbard were gold enriched with diamonds SWIFT. Hence **Enri·cher. Enri·chingly** *adv.*

Enrichment (enri·tʃmĕnt). 1626. [f. prec. + -MENT.] **1.** The action or process of enriching; the condition of being enriched; *concr.* that which enriches. **2.** *spec.* The ornament used for enriching a building, etc. 1664.

†**Enridged,** *ppl. a.* Thrown into ridges, ridged. *Lear* IV. vi. 71, *Qo.* 1 & 2.

Enring (enri·ŋ), *v. poet.* 1589. [f. EN-[1] + RING *sb.*[1]] *trans.* To put within a ring; to encircle.

The female Iuy so Enrings the barky fingers of the Elme SHAKS.

Enripen (enrəi·p'n), *v. rare.* 1631. [See EN-[1] B. 2b.] To mature.

Enrive; see EN- *pref.*[1] B. 3.

Enrobe (enrō͡ᵘ·b), *v.* 1593. [f. EN-[1] + ROBE *sb.* Cf. (O)Fr. *enrober.*] To put a robe upon, dress in a robe. Also *transf.* and *fig.*

Enro·ckment. 1846. [– Fr. *enrochement* in same sense.] A mass of large stones thrown into water at random to form the bases of piers, breakwaters, etc.

Enrol, enroll (enrō͡ᵘ·l), *v.* [ME. *enrolly*, – OFr. *enroller* (mod. *enrôler*), f. *en* EN-[1] + *rolle* ROLL *sb.*[1]] **1.** To write, inscribe the name of, on a roll, list, or register. **2.** To place upon a list; *esp.* to enlist, incorporate in the ranks of an army; to levy (an army) 1576. **3.** To enter among the rolls, *i.e.* upon the records of a court 1495. **4.** To record (*lit.* and *fig.*); also to celebrate 1530. **5.** To form into rolls; to wrap up *in* or *with*; also *transf.* and *fig.* 1530.

1. Our Sea-men..were carefully enroll'd 1691. **2.** Enrolled among the wittes BARROW, as guards to the Caliph J. H. NEWMAN. **3.** Indentures.. inrolled in your Courte of the Chauncery of recorde 1495. Hence **Enro·ller.**

Enrolment (enrōᵘ·lměnt). 1535. [f. prec. + -MENT.] **1.** The action of enrolling; the process of being enrolled 1552. **2.** The action of recording in official archives; *esp.* registration 1535. **b.** *concr.* An official entry; a record 1603.

Enroot (enrū·t), *v.* Only in pa. pple. 1490. [f. EN-¹ + ROOT *sb.*] **1.** To fix by the root; *fig.* to implant deeply in the mind. **2.** To entangle root by root. 2 *Hen. IV*, IV. i. 207.

Enrough (enrɒ·f), *v.* 1601. [f. EN-¹ B. 2 + ROUGH *a.*] To make (the sea) rough; also *fig.*

†**Enrou·nd,** *v.* ME. [f. EN-¹ + ROUND *sb.*¹] To surround –1600.

‖**En route** (aṅrūt). [Fr.] On the way; see ROUTE.

Ens (enz), *sb. Pl.* **entia** (e·nʃiă). 1581. [Late L. *ens* (Boethius), subst. use of n. of pres. pple. formed from *esse* be, on the supposed anal. of *absens* ABSENT, to render Gr. ὄν being, pres. pple. n. of εἶναι be.] **1.** *Philos.* **a.** A being, entity, as opp. to an attribute, quality, etc. 1614. **b.** An entity as an abstract notion 1581. †**2.** = ESSENCE –1730. †**b.** *Alch.* 'The most efficacious Part of any natural Mixt Body' (Kersey) –1715.

1. a. Men have needlessly multiplied *Entia* HALE.

Ensafe; see EN-¹ B. 2.

Ensample (ensɑ·mp'l), *sb. arch.* ME. [– AFr. *ensa(u)mple*, alt. of OFr. *assample, essemple* EXAMPLE.] = EXAMPLE.

An ensampelle of deseytte ME. As ye haue vs for an e. *Phil.* 3:17. Making them [Sodom and Gomorrah] an e. vnto those that after should liue vngodly 2 *Pet.* 2:6.

†**Ensa·mple,** *v.* ME. [f. prec. sb.] **1.** To exemplify –1599. **2.** To give an example to. Also, to model (something) *by, upon.* –1654. Hence †**Ensa·mpler,** a copy, pattern.

Ensanguine (ensæ·ŋgwin), *v.* 1667. [f. EN-¹ + L. *sanguis, -in-* blood. Cf. med. L., It. *insanguinare.*] To stain with blood. Also *fig.* and *transf.*

Th' ensanguind Field MILT. *P. L.* XI. 654. Ensanguined fury 1806, hue BARHAM.

Ensate (e·nseᵗt), *a.* 1830. [– mod. L. *ensatus*, f. L. *ensis* sword + -ATE².] *Bot.* Sword-shaped.

†**Ensca·le,** *v.* [perh. f. EN-¹ + SCALE (in music).] *trans.* ?To attune. G. DANIEL.

†**Ensche·dule,** *v.* [f. EN-¹ + SCHEDULE *sb.*] To insert in a schedule; to schedule. SHAKS.

Ensconce (enskǫ·ns), *v.* 1590. [f. EN-¹ + SCONCE *sb.*³ Cf. OFr. *esconser* conceal, shelter.] †**1.** *trans.* To furnish with earthworks –1752. †**2.** To shelter within or behind a fortification; also *transf.* and *fig.* –1734. Also †*intr.* for *refl.* **3.** To conceal or place securely. Chiefly *refl.* 1598.

3. I will e. mee behinde the Arras SHAKS. Ensconcing themselves in the warm chimney-corner DICKENS.

Enseal (ensī·l), *v. arch.* ME. [– OFr. *enseeler*, f. *en* EN-¹ + *seel* SEAL *sb.*² Cf. ASSEAL.] *trans.* To put a seal upon; to confirm by sealing.

fig. For every thing he said there, Seemed as it inseald were 1500.

†**Ensea·m,** *v.*¹ 1450. [alt., through confusion with next, of OFr. *essaïmer* (mod. *essimer*), f. *es-* Es- (:– L. *ex-*) + *saïm* fat; see next, SEAM *sb.*³] To cleanse or become clear of superfluous fat: said of a hawk, and later a horse –1774.

†**Ensea·m,** *v.*² 1562. [– OFr. *ensaïmer* (mod. *ensimer*, †*ensémer*), f. *en* EN-¹ + *saïm* fat; see prec., SEAM *sb.*³] To load with grease –1602.

In the ranke sweat of an enseamed bed SHAKS.

Enseam (ensī·m), *v.*³ 1605. [f. EN-¹ + SEAM *sb.*¹ and *v.*] †**1.** To sew or stitch up in. **2.** To mark as with a seam 1611.

2. His lechery inseam'd upon him BEAUM. & FL.

†**Ensea·m,** *v.*⁴ *rare.* 1596. [Origin unexpl.; cf. ME. *in same, inseme* together, and ON. *semja* put together.] **a.** To include. **b.** To introduce to company 1607.

†**Ensea·r,** *v.* [f. EN-¹ + *sear* SERE *a.*] *trans.* To dry up. *Timon* IV. iii. 187.

Ensearch (ensɔ̄·ɹtʃ), *v. Obs.* or *arch.* [ME. *encerche, enserche* – OFr. *encerchier, -serchier*, f. *en* EN-¹ + *cerchier* (mod. *chercher*) SEARCH *v.*] *trans.* and *intr.* To search; to seek (for); to inquire (into). Hence **Ensea·rcher.**

†**Enseel** (ensī·l), *v. rare.* 1486. [f. EN-¹ + SEEL *v.*²] To stitch up the eyelids of (a hawk).

Ensemble (aṅsāṅb'l). ME. [– (O)Fr. *ensemble* :– Rom. *insemul, for L. *insimul*, f. *in* IN-² + *simul, semul* at the same time.] †**A.** *adv.* Together, at the same time –1528. ‖**B.** *sb.* (Only as Fr.) All the parts of anything taken together so that each is considered only in relation to the whole; the general effect. Also **Tout ensemble** (tutaṅsāṅb'l) in same sense. 1703. **b.** *Mus.* The united performance of all voices or all instruments in a piece of concerted music, or of a chorus and orchestra; also the manner in which this is done 1844.

†**Ense·mble,** *v.* ME. [– OFr. *ensembler*, f. as prec. Cf. ASSEMBLE *v.*¹] To bring together, assemble –1533.

They ensembled themselfe together MORE.

Ensepulchre (ense·pɒ̆lkəɹ), *v.* 1820. [f. EN-¹ + SEPULCHRE.] To put into a sepulchre; to entomb. Also *transf.*

Cities..ensepulchred beneath the flood 1827.

Enshadow, Enshawl; see EN- *pref.*¹ B. 1a.

Ensheath(e (enʃī·þ, -ð), *v.* 1593. [f. EN-¹ + SHEATH, SHEATHE.] To enclose in, or as in, a sheath.

Enshelter; see EN- *pref.*¹ B. 1a.

†**E·nshield,** *a.* 1603. [app. = *enshielded*, pa. pple. of next.] ?Shielded, concealed.

These blacke Masques Proclaime an e. beauty *Meas. for M.* II. iv. 80.

Enshield (enʃī·ld), *v. rare.* 1855. [f. EN-¹ + SHIELD *v.*] To guard as with a shield.

Enshrine (enʃrəi·n), *v.* Also †**in-.** 1583. [f. EN-¹ + SHRINE *sb.*] **1.** *trans.* To enclose in, or as in, a shrine. **2.** To serve as a shrine for. Also *fig.* 1621.

1. We will e. it as a holy relic MASSINGER. **2.** The greatest God of all My brest inshrines 1621.

Enshroud (enʃrau·d), *v.* 1583. [f. EN-¹ + SHROUD *sb.*¹] To cover as with a shroud; to envelop, hide completely.

They lurk enshrouded in the vale of night CHURCHILL.

Ensient (ensie·nt), *a.* 1827. *Law.* Later sp. of *enseint* = ENCEINTE *a.*

Ensiform (e·nsifǭɹm), *a.* 1541. [f. L. *ensis* sword + -FORM.] *Biol.* Sword-shaped. (Often said of leaves.)

E. cartilage, a cartilage appended to the sternum.

Ensign (e·nsəin). ME. [– (O)Fr. *enseigne* :– L. *insignia*; see INSIGNIA.] †**1.** A signal; a battle-cry. Chiefly *Sc.* –1513. **2.** A sign or token (*arch.*) 1474. **3.** An emblem, badge 1579. **4.** *esp.* A badge or symbol of office or dignity; chiefly *pl.* = L. *insignia*; also, heraldic bearings 1513. **5.** A naval or military standard; a banner; *spec.* in British nautical use, a flag with a white, blue, or red field, and the union in the corner ME. Also *transf.* †**6.** A company, troop, serving under one banner –1650. **7.** The soldier who carries the ensign (see ANCIENT *sb.*²). Formerly a commissioned officer of the lowest rank in the infantry, now a sub-lieutenant. 1513. **8.** †**a.** Midshipman (tr. Fr. *enseigne de vaisseau*) 1708. **b.** In the U.S. navy, a commissioned officer of the lowest rank 1886.

2. We see no Ensigns of a Wedding here B. JONS. **3.** Those ensigns of authority, the keys MISS MITFORD. **4.** Having in his hands the Ensigne meet..A Golden Scepter and a Crown of Bays HOBBES. **5.** We are wont to fight cheerfully under this e. abroad BP. HALL. Hence **E·nsigncy,** †**E·nsignship,** the rank or position of an e. *Comb.* †**E.-bearer** = ENSIGN 7.

Ensign (ensəi·n), *v. Obs.* exc. *Her.* 1474. [– OFr. *ensignier*, (also mod. = point out, teach) *enseigner* :– med. L. *insignare*, for L. *insignire* mark, distinguish, f. *in* IN-² + *signum* SIGN *sb.*] †**1.** *trans.* To indicate. Also *absol.* –1576. †**2.** To direct *to* an object; to instruct; to teach –1598. **3.** To mark with a distinctive sign or badge; *esp.* in *Her.* with a crown, coronet, or mitre. *Obs.* in gen. sense. 1572.

3. Henry but join'd the roses, that ensign'd Particular families B. JONS. Archbishops..e. their Shields with their Mitres 1864.

†**Ensi·gnment.** ME. [– (O)Fr. *enseignement*, f. *enseigner*; see prec., -MENT.] **1.** Instruction; a lesson; also a means of instruction –1600. **2.** = ENSIGN 4. –1611.

Ensilage (e·nsilėdʒ), *sb.* 1881. [– Fr. *ensilage*, f. *ensiler* – Sp. *ensilar*, f. *en* EN-¹ + *silo*; see SILO, -AGE.] **1.** The process of preserving green fodder in a silo or pit, without previously drying it. **2.** The fodder thus preserved 1881. **3.** *attrib.* 1883.

2. About 3 in. of the e. was found to be mouldy 1882.

Ensilage (e·nsilėdʒ), *v.* 1883. [f. prec. sb.] To subject to the ensilage process. So **E·nsilate.**

Ensile (ensəi·l), *v.* 1883. [– Fr. *ensiler*; see ENSILAGE *sb.*] *trans.* To put into a silo for preservation; to convert into ensilage.

The ensiling of immature fodder 1885. Hence **E·nsilist,** one who preserves his crops by ensilage.

Ensilver; see EN- *pref.*¹ B. 1b.

†**Ensi·ndon,** *v.* [f. EN-¹ + SINDON.] To wrap in a sindon or linen cloth. DAVIES.

Ensisternal (ensistɔ̄·ɹnăl), *a.* [f. L. *ensis* sword + STERNUM + -AL¹.] 'Relating to the ensiform cartilage' (*Syd. Soc. Lex.*).

Ensky (enskəi·), *v.* 1603. [See EN-¹.] To place in the sky or in heaven; *pass.* only. *Meas. for M.* I. iv. 34.

Enslave (enslēⁱ·v), *v.* 1643. [f. EN-¹ + SLAVE.] *trans.* To reduce to slavery; to make a slave of. Also *transf.* and *fig.*

Prevent them from..enslaving their brethren, of whatever complexion MORSE. *fig.* All spirits are enslaved which serve things evil SHELLEY. Hence **Ensla·vement. Ensla·ver.**

Enslumber; see EN- *pref.*¹ B. 1a.

Ensnare (ensnē³·ɹ), *v.* Also **in-.** 1593. [f. EN-¹ + SNARE.] *trans.* To catch in a snare. Chiefly *transf.* and *fig.*

She ensnar'd Mankind with her faire looks MILT. *P. L.* IV. 717. Hence **Ensna·rement. Ensna·rer.**

†**Ensna·rl,** *v.* 1593. [f. EN-¹ + SNARL *sb.*¹] To entangle in, or as in, a snarl or ravelled knot –1675.

Ensober; see EN- *pref.*¹ B. 2.

†**Enso·phic,** *a.* 1693. [f. late Heb. *'ēn sōp̄* 'without an end' + -IC.] *Cabbala.* Infinite.

Enso·rcell, *v.* 1541. [– (O)Fr. *ensorceler*, f. *ensorcerer, f. *en-* EN-¹ + *sorcier* SORCERER.] *trans.* To bewitch.

†**Enso·rrow,** *v.* [ME. *insorwen*, f. IN-¹ + *sorwen* SORROW *v.*; in XVI f. EN-¹ + SORROW *sb.*] To sorrow or render sorrowful –1603.

Ensoul, in- (en-, insōᵘ·l), *v.* 1633. [f. EN-¹, IN-² + SOUL.] **1.** *trans.* To take into the soul. **2.** To infuse a soul into; to dwell in as a soul 1652.

Enspangle; see EN-¹ B. 1b.

Ensphere (ensfī³·ɹ), *v.* Also **in-.** 1612. [f. EN-¹, IN-² + SPHERE.] **1.** To place in, or as in, a sphere; to enclose. **2.** To make into a sphere. Also *fig.* 1640.

1. His ample shoulders in a cloud enspher'd Of fierie chrimsine CHAPMAN. Hence **Ensphe·rement.**

Enstamp (enstæ·mp), *v.* 1611. [f. EN-¹ + STAMP *v.*] To stamp, imprint (marks, etc.) *on* anything. Also *fig.*

On the other side were enstamped the towers of Zion C. MATHER.

Enstate; see INSTATE.

Enstatite (e·nstătəit). 1857. [f. Gr. ἐνστάτης adversary (from its refractory nature) + -ITE¹ 2b.] *Min.* A variety of diallage, varying from greyish-white to olive-green and brown. Hence **Enstati·tic** *a.*

†**Enstee·p,** *v.* [f. EN-¹ + STEEP *v.*] To station under water. *Oth.* II. i. 70.

†**Enstore,** *v.* ME. [Partly var. of †*astore* v., infl. by L. *instaurare* repair; partly f. EN-¹ + STORE *sb.* or *v.*] **1.** *trans.* To repair (tr. L. *instaurare*). WYCLIF. **2.** To store *with* –1633.

Enstrengthen; see EN-¹ B. 3.

†**Ensty·le,** *v.* 1599. [f. EN-¹ + STYLE *sb.* or *v.*] To style, name –1648.

Ensue (ensiū·), *v.* ME. [– OFr. *ensiw-, ensu-*, stem of *ensivre* (mod. *ensuivre*) :– Rom. *insequere, for L. *insequi*, f. *in* IN-² + *sequi* follow.] †**1.** *trans.* To follow. Also *absol.* and *intr.* –1626. †**2.** *fig.* To imitate; to conform to (advice, inclination, etc.) –1599. **3.** †To pursue –1569; *fig.* to seek after (*arch.*) 1483. **4.** †*trans.* To succeed, be subsequent to –1649; *intr.* to be (immediately) subsequent; to arise subsequently 1485. **5.** †To result from –1754; *intr.* to result 1483. **6.** *intr.* To follow as a conclusion. Usu. *impers.* Now *rare.* 1581.

3. *fig.* Let him seke peace and e. it COVERDALE *Ps.* 33: 14. **4.** *intr.* Now dreadful deeds Might have ensu'd MILT. *P. L.* IV. 991. **5.** *intr.* From the wound ensued no purple Flood DRYDEN. **6.** *A.Y.L.* I. iii. 36. Hence †**Ensu·able** *a.* following naturally or logically, sequent. †**Ensu·ant** *a.* **Ensu·er. Ensu·ing** *ppl. a.* and †quasi-*prep.* †**Ensu·ingly** *adv.*

‖**En suite** (añ swī·t, Fr. añ süi·t), *adv.* So as to form a suite; see SUITE.

†**Ensu·rance;** see INSURANCE.

Ensure (enʃūə·ɹ), *v.* ME. [– AFr. *enseürer*, alt. of OFr. *asseürer* ASSURE.] †**1.** *trans.* To convince –1674. †**2.** To pledge one's credit to –1642. †**3.** To warrant; to guarantee –1738. †**4.** To betroth –1606. **5.** To secure, make safe 1704. †**6.** *Comm.* To INSURE –1747. **7.** To make certain, ASSURE 1742. Hence **Ensu·rer.**

Enswathe, in- (enswēi·ð), *v.* 1597. [f. EN-[1], IN-[2] + SWATHE *sb.*[2] or *v.*] To bind or wrap in a swathe or bandage. Also *transf.* and *fig.*

fig. Inswathed sometimes in wandering mist TENNYSON. Hence **Enswa·thement.**

Ensweep; see EN- *pref.*[1] B. 3.

†**Enswee·ten,** *v.* 1607. [f. EN-[1] B. 2b + SWEETEN *v.*] To sweeten. Also *fig.* –1640.

Ensynopticity (e:nsinǫpti·sĭti). [f. EN-[2] + SYNOPTIC + -(I)TY.] A capacity for taking a general view of a subject. WHATELY.

-ent, *suffix,* – Fr. *-ent* – L. *-ent-* stem of the ending of pr. pples. of vbs. of the 2nd, 3rd, and 4th conjugation. In sense the words in *-ent* are primarily adjs., sometimes ppl., as *obsolescent*, etc., and some are used as sbs., meaning an agent, personal or material, as *president, regent, coefficient, aperient*, etc.

Entablature (entæ·blătiŭɹ). 1611. [– (partly through Fr. *entablement*; see next), It. *intavolatura* boarding, f. *intavolare* board up, f. *in* EN-[1] + *tavola* TABLE *sb.*] **1.** *Arch.* That part of an order which is above the column; including the architrave, the frieze, and the cornice. **2.** *Mech.* **a.** In the marine steam-engine: A strong iron frame supporting the paddle-shaft. **b.** The platform which supports the capstan. 1867. Hence **Enta·blatured** *ppl. a.* furnished with an e.

Entablement (entēi·b'lmĕnt). 1664. [– Fr. *entablement*, f. *entabler*, f. *en* EN-[1] + *table* TABLE *sb.*; see -MENT.] **a.** = prec. **b.** The platform or series of platforms supporting a statue and placed above the dado and the base.

†**Enta·ch, ente·ch,** *v.* ME. [– OFr. *entachier, entechier*, f. *en-* EN-[1] + *tache, teche* spot, etc.] **1.** To stain; to infect –1509. **2.** To imbue with any quality. Only in ME.

Entackle; see EN-[1] B. 1b.

†**Entai·l,** *sb.*[1] ME. [– (O)Fr. *entaille*, f. *entailler* ENTAIL *v.*[1]; cf. It. *intaglio*.] **1.** Ornamental carving –1530. **2.** *transf.* Cut, fashion of a garment; shape; figure, stature –1570.

1. Carven in Cristall by crafte of Entaile ME. Phr. (Persons) *of entaile*: of quality.

Entail (entēi·l), *sb.*[2] ME. [f. ENTAIL *v.*[2]] **1.** *Law.* The action of entailing; the state of being entailed. **2.** *transf.* and *fig.* **a.** The securing (an office, etc.) to a predetermined line of successors; a predetermined order of succession ME. **b.** The transmission, as an inalienable inheritance, of qualities, conditions, etc. 1706. **c.** Necessary sequence 1662. **d.** *concr.* That which is entailed 1822.

1. To his heires male by an especial Entaile aforesaid POWEL. Phr. *To break, cut (off) the e.* **2. b.** An intail of dependence is a bad reward of merit BURKE.

†**Entai·l,** *v.*[1] ME. [– OFr. *entaillier*, (mod. *entailler*) :– med.L. *intalliare*, f. *in-* EN-[1] + *talliare* cut; see TAIL *v.*[2], TALLY *sb.*[1]] **1.** *trans.* To carve; to ornament with carvings; to represent by carving –1637. **2.** To engrave in intaglio (*rare*) –1587. **3.** To cut into 1601.

2. Costlie stones alreadie intailed for seales 1577.

Entail (entēi·l), *v.*[2] ME. [f. EN-[1] + AFr. *taile* TAIL *sb.*[2] or *taillé* TAIL *a.*] **1.** *Law.* To convert into 'fee tail' (*feudum talliatum*); to settle (land, an estate, etc.) on a number of persons in succession, so that it cannot be dealt with by any one possessor as absolute owner. **2.** *transf.* and *fig.* To bestow as if by entail 1509. †**3.** *gen.* To tack on, attach –1713. **4.** To impose (labour, expense, etc.) *upon* a person 1665. **5.** *simply.* To necessitate; to involve logically 1829.

1. They cannot sell them [houses], because they are entailed 1856. **2.** The benefits of the Gospell are intayled vpon them alone 1630. **5.** A conquest which brought with it no evil and entailed no regret 1829.

Hence **Entai·lable** *a.* **Entai·ler. Entai·lment.**

†**Enta·lent,** *v.* ME. [– OFr. *entalenter*, f. *en* EN-[1] + *talent* (– L. *talentum* a weight, that which inclines the balance, hence) inclination.] To inspire with desire or passion; to excite –1616.

†**E·ntally,** *adv.* 1691. [– *ent-*, stem of late L. *ens* (see ENS) + -AL[1] + -LY[2], after *really*, etc.] Really.

†**Enta·me,** *v.*[1] ME. [– (O)Fr. *entamer* cut into, broach, etc. :– eccl.L. *intaminare* pollute; cf. CONTAMINATE. See ATTAME.] **1.** To make a cut into; also *fig.* –1490. **2.** *fig.* To open –1500.

Enta·me, *v.*[2] 1600. [f. EN-[1] 2a + TAME *a.*] To make or †become tame. *A. Y. L.* III. v. 48.

Entangle (entæ·ŋg'l), *v.* 1555. [f. EN-[1] + TANGLE *sb.* or *v.*] **1.** To catch or impede with a tangle; to involve in coils, network, or the like, or in anything from which extrication is difficult. **b.** *esp.* To ensnare. Also *fig.* 1568. †**c.** *intr.* To become entangled –1673. **2.** *fig.* To involve in difficulties; to embarrass; to perplex, bewilder 1540. **3.** To make tangled; to twist, interlace, or mix up in a tangle; *fig.* to complicate (a subject, etc.) 1555.

1. Lest she should e. her Feet in her Petticoat ADDISON. Entangled in the meshes of political parties D'ISRAELI, in the defiles of the mountains PRESCOTT. **2.** Entangled in a complimentary speech 1833. **3.** The obscure and intangl'd Wood of Antiquity MILTON. Hence **Enta·ngler.**

Entanglement (entæ·ng'lmĕnt). 1637. [f. prec. + -MENT.] **1.** The action of entangling; the fact or condition of being entangled, confused medley 1687. **2.** That which entangles 1637.

‖**Entasis** (e·ntăsis). 1753. [mod.L. – Gr. ἔντασις, f. ἐντείνειν to strain.] **1.** *Arch.* An almost imperceptible swelling of the shaft of a column 1827. †**2.** *Path.* 'Old term for tonic spasm' (*Syd. Soc. Lex.*). Hence †**Enta·tic,** also (erron.) †**Enta·stic,** *adjs.* of or pertaining to e.

Enta·ssment. [– Fr. *entassement*, f. *en-* EN-[1] + *tas* heap.] A heap, accumulation. (Dicts.)

Entelechy (ente·lĕki). Also **entelecheia, entelechia.** 1603. [– late L. *entelechia* – Gr. ἐντελέχεια, f. ἐν EN-[2] + τέλει, dat. of τέλος end, perfection + ἔχειν be in a (certain) state; see -Y[3].] **1.** In Aristotle's use: The condition in which a potentiality has become an actuality. **2. a.** That which gives form or perfection to anything. **b.** The soul, as opp. to the body. 1603. **3.** A monad in the system of Leibnitz 1877.

‖**Entellus** (ente·lŏs). 1843. [Proper name; see Virg. *Æn.* v. 437–472.] *Zool.* An E. Indian species of monkey of the genus Semnopithecus.

Entemple (ente·mp'l), *v.* 1603. [f. EN-[1] + TEMPLE *sb.*[1]] To enclose as in a temple.

†**Ente·nder,** *v.* 1594. [f. EN-[1] + TENDER *a.*] To make tender; to weaken –1765.

‖**Entente** (añtā·nt). 1877. [Fr.] An understanding; most freq. used as a shortening of ‖**Entente cordiale** (1844). **b.** A group of states or powers connected by an entente cordiale.

†**E·nter,** *sb.* ME. [f. the vb.] The action, power, or right of entering; *concr.* a passage –1588.

Enter (e·ntəɹ), *v.* ME. [– (O)Fr. *entrer* :– L. *intrare*, f. *intra* within.]

I. *intr.* (Often conjugated with *be.*) **1.** To go or come into; to pass within the boundaries of. Also *fig.* **b.** *simply.* To make entry. ME. **2.** *Law.* To make entry (into lands); to take possession 1523. **3.** To penetrate *into*; to be plunged deeply. Also †*fig.* ME. **4.** To become a member in a society, etc. ME. †**5.** To come into a state or condition –1710. **6.** To make a beginning, engage. Const. *in* (arch.), *into.* 1450. †**b.** Of a period, state of things, etc.: To begin –1688.

1. We..entered into a noble forest MARRYAT. **b.** The Air..entring by the Furnace-pipes EVELYN. **3.** The iron entered into his soul BIBLE (Great) *Ps.* 105:18. **5.** Entre thou into the ioye of thi lord WYCLIF *Matt.* 25:21. **6.** E. not into iudgement with thy seruant *Ps.* 143:2.

II. *trans.* (formerly occas. conjugated with *be.*) **1.** To go or come into or within; to step upon (a path, a bridge) ME. **b.** To take up one's abode in. *Meas. for M.* I. ii. 182. **c.** To force an entrance into 1586. **2.** To pierce; to penetrate 1613. **3.** To become a member of (*mod.*). **4.** To begin 1515. **5.** To come into a state or condition; to embrace (a profession). *Obs.* exc. in *To e. religion.* 1563. **6.** To turn to a particular place in (a mathematical table). Still in *Naut.* use. 1593.

1. To e. a Gaol STEELE, a carriage DICKENS. **3.** Phr. *To e. the army, the church, a university.* **5.** To e. wedlocke 1576, the profession of a monke SPEED.

III. To cause to enter. **1.** *trans.* To put or bring into something (*arch.*); also †*fig.* 1523. **2.** To instruct initially; to initiate; to train; to put (a young dog) on the scent of 1481. **3.** To put *into*, insert, introduce. Now chiefly *techn.* ME. **4.** To put into a list in writing, a description, a record; to write down ME. **b.** To hand in at the Custom House a statement of the amount and value of (goods exported or imported). Also, to register (a vessel) as arriving or leaving. 1634. **c.** To insert by name on the list of competitors. Also *intr.* 1684. **5.** To admit; to engage; to procure admission for. Also *refl.* and *intr.* for *refl.* 1651.

1. *fig.* Baptism..enters us into covenant with God 1658. **2.** To e. children in the Rudiments of the Latin Tongue ELLWOOD. To e. young hounds to fox 1875. **3.** To e. shot or shell and ram home 1859. **4.** To e. his answer on the records BURKE. Phr. *To e. up*: **a.** To enter in regular form. **b.** *Law.* To cause (judgement, etc.) to be written down on the records of a court. *To e. an action, caveat, writ*, etc.: to bring it before the court in due form, usu. in writing. *To e. a protest*: to record a protest on the minutes; hence *gen.* to protest. **5.** He was entred into Ch. Ch. WOOD. He therefore entered himself as a clerk to a solicitor 1870.

Comb. (with preps.). **To e. into** (†**in**): **a.** To take upon oneself; as, *to e. into matrimony*, etc. **b.** To become a party to; to bind oneself by; as, *to e. into a treaty*, etc. (See also RECOGNIZANCE, SECURITY.) **c.** To consider. †**d.** To intermeddle with. **e.** To take an interest in. **f.** To form part of; to be a constituent element in. **g.** In Bible phrase, *To e. into* (another's) *labours*: to reap where another has sown. **To e. on, upon: a.** (*Law.*) To make an entry into (land); to assume possession of. **b.** To take the first steps upon or in; also *fig.* **c.** To begin to deal with (a subject).

Enter-, entre-, *prefix,* – (O)Fr. *entre-* :– L. *inter* (see INTER-), with senses 'between', 'among', 'mutually'. Since *c*1650 this prefix has ceased to be used to form new words, and the compounds in which it occurs are either obs. or have been refashioned with *inter-*.

Enteradenography, -ology; see ENTERO-.

Enterate (e·ntĕrĕt), *a.* 1877. [– mod.L. *enteratus*, f. Gr. ἔντερα bowels; see -ATE[2].] *Zool.* Having an intestine distinctly separated from the outer body-wall.

†**E·nterclose, i·nter-.** ME. [– OFr. *entreclos*, in med.L. *interclausum*, f. *entre* ENTER- + *clos* CLOSE *sb.*[1]] **1.** A partition. TREVISA. **2.** *Arch.* ?A screen, partition; a space partitioned off –1853.

†**Enterfea·t.** 1614. [– Fr. *entrefaite*, f. †*s'entrefaire* do (something) to one another. See ENTER-, FEAT *sb.*] *pl.* Deeds (of arms) on both sides –1662.

Enteric (ente·rik), *a.* 1869. [– Gr. ἐντερικός, f. ἔντερον intestine; cf. Fr. *entérique.*] *Anat.*, etc. Of or pertaining to the intestines. *E. fever*: typhoid fever.

b. *Pharm.* Of or designating a medicinal preparation that becomes disintegrated in the intestines after passing through the stomach unaltered.

Entering (e·nteriŋ), *vbl. sb.* ME. [f. ENTER *v.* + -ING[1].] **1.** The action of the vb. †**2.** An entrance; a door, etc.; an opening –1541. **3.** *attrib.* esp. *Naut.* with reference to the means of entrance to a vessel, as *e.-port, -rope*, etc.; and *Mech.*, as *e.-chisel*, etc.

Enteritis (entĕrəi·tis). 1808. [f. Gr. ἔντερον intestine + -ITIS.] *Path.* Inflammation of the (small) intestines.

†**Enterme·te,** *v.* ME. [– OFr. *entremetre* (mod. *-mettre*), repr. L. *intermittere* and *intromittere*. Cf. INTERMIT *v.*[1],[2], INTROMIT.] **1.** *refl.* To intermeddle; to have dealings. Also, to undertake *to* (do something). Also *intr.* for *refl.* –1548. **2.** To put (oneself) *between* 1541.

†**Entermi·se.** 1490. [– (O)Fr. *entremise,* f. *entremettre*; see prec.] **a.** Business. **b.** Interposition. –1638.

Entero- (e·ntĕro, entĕrǫ·, bef. a vowel sometimes *enter-*), comb. f. Gr. ἔντερον intestine: as in

Enteradeno·graphy [see ADENOGRAPHY], *Anat.* 'a description of the intestinal glands' (*Syd. Soc Lex.*). **Enteradeno·logy** [see ADENOLOGY], *Anat.*, etc. 'an account of the intestinal glands' (*Syd. Soc. Lex.*). **E·nteroce:le** [Gr. κήλη tumour], *Surg.* a hernial tumour whose contents are intestine. Hence **Enteroce·lic** *a.* **E:nteroepi·plocele** [see EPIPLOCELE], *Surg.* a hernia in which portions of intestine and omentum are both protruded. **E:nteroga·strocele,** *Surg.* an abdominal hernia containing intestine. **Entero·graphy,** 'a description of the intestines' (*Syd. Soc. Lex.*). **E:nterohy·drocele** [see HYDROCELE], *Surg.* 'intestinal hernia conjoined with hydrocele' (*Syd. Soc. Lex.*). **E·nteroli:te,** altered f. **E·nteroli:th** [Gr. λίθος], *Path.* a stony concretion in the intestines. **Entero·logy** [+ -LOGY], *Anat.* a treatise on, or the science of, the intestines. **Entero·pathy** [Gr. -παθεια, f. πάθος], *Path.* intestinal disease. **E:nteropla·sty** [Gr. πλάστης fashioner + -Y[3]], *Surg.* the restoration by plastic operation of a solution of continuity of the intestine. **Entero·tomy** [Gr. -τομια cutting], *Surg.* the opening of the intestine to release its contents or to remove a foreign body.

Enterodelous (e:ntęrodī·ləs), *a.* 1847. [f. mod.L. *enterodela* sb. pl., f. ENTERO- + Gr. δῆλος manifest + -OUS.] *Biol.* Having an intestine plainly visible; applied to certain Polygastria.

‖**Enteron** (e·ntĕrǫn). 1878. [mod.L. – Gr. ἔντερον intestine.] The alimentary canal.

Enteropneustal (e:ntĕro,pniū·stăl), *a.* 1877. [f. ENTERO- + Gr. πνευστ-, f. πνέειν breathe + -AL[1].] Of or pertaining to the *Enteropneusta*, worm-like animals having the breathing apparatus borne on the intestinal canal.

†**Enterpa·rlance.** 1603. [– OFr. *entreparlance,* f. *entreparler*; see ENTER-, PARLANCE.] A conference –1643. So †**Enterpa·rle** *v.* to confer. †**Enterpa·rley.**

Enterprise (e·ntəɹprəiz), *sb.* ME. [– (O)Fr. *entreprise,* subst. use of pa. pple. fem. of *entreprendre,* later var. of *emprendre,* whence *emprise* EMPRISE.] **1.** A design of which the execution is attempted; a piece of work taken in hand; now only, a bold, arduous, or dangerous undertaking. **2.** Disposition to engage in undertakings of difficulty, risk, or danger; daring spirit 1475. †**3.** Management –1803.

1. The enterprizes of fancy 1814. Those enterprises which we call joint-stock undertakings HELPS. **2.** Times of national e. 1783. Contempt for his lack of e. FREEMAN.

Enterprise (e·ntəɹprəiz), *v.* *arch.* 1450. [Partly f. prec.; partly f. Fr. *entrepris* pa. pple.] **1.** *trans.* To take in hand, attempt, run the risk of (*arch.*) 1485. †**2.** *intr.* To make an attempt, form a design, make an attack (*upon*) –1813.

1. This was enterprized by a Prince, who [etc.] LOCKE. To e. a road RUSKIN. **2.** Be sure of the court, before you e. any other where J. UDALL. Hence **Enterpri·ser,** one who attempts an undertaking; †an adventurer.

Enterprising (e·ntəɹprəiziŋ), *ppl. a.* 1611. [f. prec. + -ING[2].] That undertakes. In early use, foolhardy, also scheming; now, full of enterprise.

An enterprizing foole needs little wit 1611. A company of e. Venetian merchants J. H. NEWMAN. Hence **Enterpri·singly** *adv.*

†**Entertai·n,** *sb.* 1591. [f. next; cf. Fr. *entretien.*] = ENTERTAINMENT –1686.

Entertain (entəɹtē[i]·n), *v.* 1475. [Late ME. *enterteine,* repr. tonic stem of (O)Fr. *entretenir* :– Rom. *intertenēre, f. *inter* among + *tenēre* hold.] †**1.** *trans.* To hold mutually –1578. †**2.** To keep in a certain state or condition –1714. **3.** To keep up, maintain. *Obs.* or *arch.* 1475. †**4.** To keep in one's service; to be at the charges of; to hire; to retain –1771. †**5.** To support; to provide sustenance for –1771. †**6.** To deal with; to treat in a (specified) manner –1662. **7.** To engage, keep occupied the attention of. Hence, to discourse to *of* something. 1598. †**b.** To occupy (time) –1673. **8.** To engage agreeably the attention of; to amuse. Now often *ironical.* Also *refl.* and *absol.* 1626. †**9.** To accommodate –1721. **10.** To receive as a guest; to show hospitality to. Also *absol.* 1490. **11.** †To give reception to; to receive –1710; to admit to consideration 1614; to harbour; to cherish; to experience 1576. †**12.** To encounter (*rare*) –1634. †**13.** To take upon oneself; to engage in –1719.

3. To e. Discourse SOUTHEY, a correspondence MILMAN. **4.** With princely wagies dyd me enterteyne 1559. Sweet Lady, entertaine him for your Seruant *Two Gent.* II. iv. 110. **7.** To entertaine him with hope *Merry W.* II. i. 68. **b.** The weary time she cannot e. SHAKS. **8.** My favourite occupations..now cease to e. LAMB. **11.** To e. a novell opinion BP. HALL, thoughts of Death BOYLE, the Addresses of a Man STEELE. To e. resentment LANGHORNE, a purpose SCOTT. Hence **Entertai·nable** *a.* capable of being received into the mind. **Entertai·ner.**

Entertaining (entəɹtē[i]·niŋ), *ppl. a.* 1659. [f. prec. + -ING[2].] †**1.** Affording sustenance (*rare*) 1691. **2.** Interesting; now chiefly, amusing 1697. †**3.** Hospitable (*rare*) 1659.

Entertainment (entəɹtē[i]·nmĕnt). 1531. [f. as prec. + -MENT.] †**1.** The action of taking into service; service, employment –1662. Also †*concr.* pay, wages –1709. †**2.** Support; sustenance –1761. †**3.** Treatment –1660. **4.** Occupation (of time). Now *rare.* 1551. **5.** The action of occupying attention agreeably; that which affords interest or amusement; *esp.* a public performance of a varied character 1612. †**6.** Accommodation –1721. †**7.** Reception; manner of reception –1692. **8.** The action of receiving a guest 1594. **b.** *concr.* Hospitable provision for the wants of a guest (now *arch.*) 1540. **c.** A meal; *esp.* a banquet. Now *rare.* 1607. **9.** The action of receiving, of taking into consideration, or of harbouring 1586.

1. The Saxons..desirous of intertainment to serue in warres HOLINSHED. **3.** The savage e. He met with in it [the World] BOYLE. **4.** *L. L. L.* V. i 126. **5.** An Oration..to giue the visitours intertainment 1612. Importunate for dramatic entertainments EMERSON. **7.** *Ant. & Cl.* III xiii. 140. **8.** Hezekiah's e. of them with gladness 1649. **b.** Great deal of company, but poor e. PEPYS. *Comb* **Entertainment tax** 1918.

Enterta·ke, *v.* [See ENTER-] *trans.* To entertain. SPENSER.

Entertissued, var. of INTER-.

†**E·nthean,** *a.* 1635. [f. Gr. ἔνθεος (see ENTHEOS) + -AN.] Divinely inspired –1652.

†**E·ntheasm.** 1751. [f. ENTHEOS + *-asm,* after ENTHUSIASM.] = ENTHUSIASM. So †**Enthea·stic, -al** *a.* agitated by a divine energy. †**Enthea·stically** *adv.*

†**E·ntheate,** *a.* Also **entheat.** 1630. [– L. *entheatus* (Martial), f. *entheos* (see next) + *-atus* -ATE[2].] Possessed by a god –1640.

†‖**E·ntheos, -us.** 1594. [– L. *entheos, -us* – Gr. ἔνθεος divinely inspired, f. ἐν EN-[2] + θεός god. See ENTHUSIASM.] An indwelling divinity; inspiration –1782.

Enthetic (enþe·tik), *a.* 1867. [– Gr. ἐνθετικός, f. ἐνθε- aorist stem of ἐντιθέναι put in.] *Med.* Put in; introduced from without. Said *esp.* of syphilitic diseases.

Enthral(l (enþrǭ·l), *v.* Also **in-.** 1576. [f. EN-[1] + THRALL *sb.*] To hold in thrall; to enslave. Also *fig.* now chiefly in sense 'to hold spellbound by pleasing qualities'.

Ingrateful Cæsar who could Rome e. COWLEY. *fig.* So is mine eye enthralled to thy shape *Mids. N.* III. i. 142. Hence **Enthra·ldom** (*rare*), the condition of being enthralled. **Enthra·ller. Enthra·lment,** the action of enthralling; slavery. Chiefly *fig.*

†**Enthri·ll,** *v.* 1559. [f. EN-[1] + THRILL *v.*] *trans.* To pierce –1593.

Enthrone (enþrōᵘ·n), *v.* Also **in-.** 1606. [f. EN-[1] + THRONE, repl. †*enthronize* (XIV). Cf. OFr. *entrosner,* mod. †*enthroner* (COTGR.).] **1.** *trans.* To seat on a throne; *esp.* to set (a king, bishop, etc.) on a throne as a formal induction to office; to invest with regal or episcopal authority. Also *fig.* **2.** To set as on a throne; to exalt 1699.

1. [The] Bishop of Norwich was..enthroned as Primate 1876. *fig.* There pride, enthroned in misty errours, dwels 1628. Hence **Enthro·nement,** the action of enthroning; the fact of being enthroned. **Enthro:niza·tion,** enthronement. var. **Enthro·nize** (*Obs.* exc. *arch.*).

Enthuse (enþiū·z), *v.* orig. *U.S.* slang. 1859. [Back-formation from ENTHUSIASM.] To make or grow enthusiastic.

Enthusiasm (enþiū·zi,æ̆z'm). 1603. [– Fr. *enthousiasme* or late L. *enthusiasmus* – Gr. ἐνθουσιασμός (Plato), f. ἐνθουσιάζειν be inspired or possessed by the god, f. ἔνθους, ἔνθεος inspired, f. ἐν EN-[2] + θεός god. Cf. ENTHEOS.] †**1.** Possession by a god, supernatural inspiration, prophetic or poetic ecstasy –1807. †**b.** Poetical fervour –1781. **2.** Fancied inspiration; a conceit of divine favour or communication. In 18th c. often: Ill-regulated religious emotion or speculation (*arch.*). 1660. **3.** Rapturous intensity of feeling on behalf of a person, cause, etc.; passionate eagerness in any pursuit. (The current sense.) 1716.

1. Doth he think they knew it by E. or Revelation from Heaven BAXTER. **2.** Everywhere the history of religion betrays a tendency to e. 1841. **3.** E. is very catching, especially when it is very eloquent 1817.

Enthusiast (enþiū·zi,æ̆st). 1609. [– Fr. *enthousiaste* or eccl. L. *enthusiastes* designation of a sect – eccl. Gr. ἐνθουσιαστής. See prec.] †**1.** One who is (really or seemingly) possessed by a god. Also *fig.* –1700. **2.** †**a.** *Eccl. Hist.* One of a sect of 4th c. heretics who laid claim to special revelations –1639. **b.** *gen.* One who imagines himself to receive special divine communications 1609. **3.** One who is full of enthusiasm (see ENTHUSIASM 3). Occas., A visionary self-deluded person. 1764. **4.** *attrib.* or *adj.* 1681.

2. b. It is the believing those to be Miracles which are not, that constitutes an E. WESLEY. **3.** Paracelsus..an astrological e. 1793.

Enthusiastic (enþiū:zi,æ·stik). 1603. [– Gr. ἐνθουσιαστικός, f. ενθουσιάζειν; see prec., -IC.]

A. *adj.* †**1.** Pertaining to, or of the nature of, possession by a deity. Also *fig.* –1849. †**2.** Characterized by mystical delusions in religion; *transf.* quixotic –1775. **3.** Of the nature of, characterized by, ENTHUSIASM 3. 1786.

2. *transf.* An e. contempt of interest JOHNSON. **3.** E. admirers of literature LANE. Hence **Enthusia·stical** *a.* (in same senses). **Enthusia·stically** *adv.*

†**B.** *sb.* = ENTHUSIAST 1, 2b. –1707.

Enthymematic, -al (e:nþimīmæ·tik, -ăl), *a.* 1588. [– Gr. ἐνθυμηματικός, f. ἐνθύμημα; see next, -IC.] Of, pertaining to, or containing, an enthymeme; consisting of enthymemes.

Enthymeme (e·nþimīm). 1588. [– L. *enthymema* (also used) – Gr. ἐνθύμημα, f. ἐνθυμεῖσθαι consider, reflect, infer, f. ἐν EN-[2] + θυμός passion, courage, mind.] †**1.** *Rhet.* An argument based on probable premisses, as dist. from a demonstration –1841. **2.** *Logic.* A syllogism with one premiss unexpressed; as, *Cogito, ergo sum.* (A misapprehension of 'imperfect syllogism' applied to 1.) 1588.

2. The common form of Argumentation is E., which consists of but two propositions 1870.

Entice (entəi·s), *v.* ME. [– OFr. *enticier,* prob. :– Rom. **intitiare,* f. L. *in* EN-[1] + **titius,* for L. *titio* firebrand, as if 'set on fire, add fuel to'. Cf. ATTICE.] †**1.** *trans.* To stir up, instigate –1628. **2.** To allure, attract by the hope of pleasure or profit; *esp.* to allure insidiously or adroitly. Also *absol.* ME.

2. My son, if sinners e. thee, consent thou not *Prov.* 1:10. Beer mingled with Honey, to e. the Wasps EVELYN. Hence †**Enti·ceable** *a.* seductive. **Enti·cer. Enti·cing** *ppl.a.* alluring. **Enti·cingly** *adv.*

Enticement (entəi·smĕnt). ME. [– OFr. *enticement,* f. *enticier*; see prec., -MENT.] †**1.** Incitement; *concr.* that which incites –1587. **2.** The action of alluring or attracting; attractive quality; *concr.* a means or method of enticing; an allurement 1549.

2. What inticement is there in common profane Swearing BENTLEY.

Entier, Entierty, obs. ff. ENTIRE, etc.

Entify (e·ntifəi), *v. rare.* 1882. [f. *ent-*, stem of late L. *ens* (see ENS) + -FY. Cf. ENTALLY.] To make into an entity, attribute objective existence to. Hence **Entifica·tion.**

Entire (entəiᵊ·ɹ). [ME. *enter, entier* – AFr. *enter,* (O)Fr. *entier,* fem. *-ière* :– Rom **inte·gro*, for L. *i·ntegrum* (nom. *integer*), f. *in* IN-² + **tag-*, base of *tangere* touch.]

A. *adj.* **I. 1.** Whole; with no part excepted. **2.** Complete; †perfect ME. †**b.** Applied about 1722 to 'porter' –1839. **3.** Thorough, total ME. †**b.** Of persons: Wholly devoted; unreserved –1718. **4.** Unbroken, intact; undiminished 1601. **b.** *spec.* Not castrated 1834. **c.** Of persons: Not fatigued, fresh. [So L. *integer.*] (*arch.*) 1590. **5.** Of one piece; continuous; in *Bot.*, etc., without notches or indentations 1590. †**6.** Homogeneous; unmixed –1699.

1. A day e. MILT. The e. Creation WESLEY. Phr. *E. tenancy* (Law): a sole possession in one man. E. control of a business 1891. **2.** An e. farm 1804. **3.** E. liberty of conscience MACAULAY. **b.** It is best to be courteous to all; e. with few BP. HALL. **4.** With all the Fortifications e. 1727. Apprehension, Memory, Reason, all e. BUTLER. **5.** Of one entyre and perfect Chrysolite *Oth.* v. ii. 144. Last segment of the abdomen e. or notched STARK. Phr. *Rank e.* (Mil.): *i.e.* forming an unbroken body.

II. †1. Morally whole, blameless –1779. †**2.** Of integrity; honest, upright –1707. †**3.** Of feelings, etc.: Unfeigned, sincere –1716. †**4.** ? Inward. SPENSER *F. Q.* IV. viii. st. 48.

B. *sb.* **1.** The whole. Now *rare.* 1597. **2.** Entirety 1622. **3.** An entire horse 1881. **4.** Short for *entire beer*; see A. I. 2 b. 1825.

Hence **Enti·rely** *adv.* in an e. state or manner. **Enti·reness,** the quality, state, or condition of being e.

Entirety (entəiᵊ·ɹti). 1548. [– (O)Fr. *entièreté* :– L. *integritas, -tat-*, f. *integer*; see prec., -TY¹.] **1.** The state or condition of being entire; in *Law*, the entire and undivided possession of an estate. **2.** The whole; the sum total 1856.

1. The Christian Church taken in its e. ROBERTSON. They shall not haue the land by entierties, but by moities ioyntly 1613.

Entitative (e·ntitĕtiv), *a.* 1600. [– med.L. *entitativus* (in phr. *actus entitativus* used by Scotists), f. *entitas*; see ENTITY, -IVE.] **1.** Pertaining to the mere existence of anything. **2.** Having real existence 1862. Hence **E·ntitatively** *adv.*

Entitle (entəi·t'l), *v.* ME. [– AFr. *entitler*, OFr. *entiteler* (mod. *intituler*) – late L. *intitulare*, f. *in* IN-² + *titulus* TITLE.]

I. 1. *trans.* To furnish with a heading, name, or designation (see TITLE *sb.*). †**b.** To ascribe *to* an author –1724. **2.** To speak of by a title or designation ME. †**3.** To write down under titles or headings –1582.

1. I will intitle this boke the Golden boke LD. BERNERS. A booke, entitled to sainct Augustine CRANMER.

II. 1. To furnish with a title *to* an estate. Hence *gen.* to give a rightful claim *to* anything. 1468. †**2.** To regard as having a title *to* something, or as being the agent, cause, or subject of anything –1690. †**b.** To impute (something) *to* –1665.

1. Entitled to any timber felled by the tenant for life CRUISE. Entitled to complain of neglect HT. MARTINEAU. **2. b.** Intitling the Opinion of Intentional Species to Aristotle GLANVILL.

Entitule, obs. var. of INTITULE *v.*

Entity (e·ntĭti). 1596. [– Fr. *entité* or med. L. *entitas*, f. *ent-*, stem of late L. *ens*; see ENS, -TY¹.] **1.** Being, existence, as opp. to non-existence; the existence, as dist. from the qualities or relations, of anything. **2.** That which makes a thing what it is; essence, essential nature 1643. **3.** *concr.* An ENS, as dist. from a function, attribute, relation, etc. 1628. **4.** 'Being' generally 1604.

1. Both Night and Coldnesse..have reall entitie HY. MORE. **3.** An ideal E., like the Utopia BOLINGBROKE.

Ento- (e·nto), *prefix* (bef. a vowel usually *ent-*), repr. Gr. ἐντός within, inside: as in: **E·ntoblast** [Gr. βλαστός sprout], the nucleolus of a cell. **Entocu·neiform** *a.* [see CUNEIFORM], the innermost of the three cuneiform bones. **E·ntocyst** [see CYST], 'the inner layer of the cuticular envelope of the Polyzoa' (*Syd. Soc. Lex.*). **En·toderm** [Gr. δέρμα], the outer layer of the blastoderm, also called *hypoblast.* **Entoga·stric** *a.* [see GASTRIC], pertaining to the interior of the gastric cavity. **Entoglo·ssal** *a.* [Gr. γλῶσσα + -AL], a term applied to one of the bones of the hyoidean arch in some fishes, which supports the tongue. **Entome·tatarse** [mod.L. *metatarsus*], the bones between the tarsus and the toes. **E:ntoperi·pheral** *a.* [see PERIPHERAL], a term applied to feelings initiated within the body, as hunger. **E·ntophyte** [Gr. φυτόν], a plant growing within the substance of other plants or animals; hence **Entophy·tic** *a.* **Entopro·ctous** *a.* [Gr. πρωκτός anus], belonging to the *Entoprocta*, a class of Polyzoa, in which the anus lies within the circle of tentacles. **Entopte·rygoid** *a.* [see PTERYGOID], 'an oblong and thin bone attached to the inner border of the palatine and pterygoid' (Gunther). **Ento·ptic** *a.* [see OPTIC], relating to the appearance of the different internal structures of the eye; hence **Ento·ptics** *sb.* **Entoste·rnal** *a.* [see STERNAL], pertaining to the *entosternum* or median piece of the breastbone, very largely developed in birds. **Ento·tic** *a.* [see OTIC], pertaining to or occurring in the inner ear. **E:ntotympa·nic** *a.* [see TYMPANIC], situated within the tympanum.

Entoil (entoi·l), *v. arch.* 1621. [f. EN-¹ + TOIL *sb.*²] To bring into toils or snares; to entrap. Chiefly *fig.*

So mused awhile, entoyled in woofed fantasies KEATS.

Entomb (entū·m), *v.* 1576. [– OFr. *entomber*, f. *en* EN-¹ + *tombe* TOMB.] **1.** To place in, or as in, a tomb; to bury. **2.** To serve as a tomb for (*lit.* and *fig.*) 1631. Hence **Ento·mbment,** the action of entombing.

Entomic (entǫ·mik), *a.* 1862. [– Gr. ἔντομα (sc. ζῷα) insects, subst. use of n. plur. of ἔντομος cut up + -IC.] Of or pertaining to insects. So **Ento·mical.** (Dicts.)

Entomo- (entŏmǫ·-, entǫ·mŏ-, e:ntŏmo-), comb. f. Gr. ἔντομος adj. 'cut up', in neut. pl. 'insects'; see INSECT.

Entomo·genous *a.* [Gr. -γενής + -OUS], *Bot.* having its growth in the body of insects. **Ento·molite** [Gr. λίθος], *Geol.* a fossil insect. **Entomo·meter** [Gr. μέτρον], an instrument for measuring insects. **Entomo·phagan** [Gr. φαγεῖν + -AN], *Zool.* one of the *Entomophaga* or insect-eaters—in mammals, a division of the *Marsupialia*, in insects of the *Hymenoptera.* **Entomo·phagous** *a.* [Gr. φαγεῖν + -OUS], insect-eating. **Entomo·philous** *a.* [Gr. φίλος + -OUS], *Bot.* used of plants in which fertilization is effected through the agency of insects. **Entomo·stracan** *a.* [Gr. ὄστρακον shell + -AN], *Zool.*, etc. of or belonging to the *Entomostraca*, one of the orders of the *Crustacea*; also as *sb.* So **Entomo·stracous** *a.* **Entomo·tomy** [Gr. -τομία], *Zool.* the science of the dissection of insects; hence **Entomo·tomist,** one who dissects insects.

Entomoid (e·ntŏmoid), *a.* 1835. [f. as prec. + -OID.] Insect-like. Also quasi-*sb.*

Entomology (entŏmǫ·lŏdʒi). 1766. [– Fr. *entomologie* or mod.L. *entomologia*, f. as ENTOMO- + -LOGY.] That branch of natural history which deals with insects.

Hence **E:ntomolo·gical** *a.* of or pertaining to e. or insects. **Entomo·logist,** one who studies e. **Entomo·logize** *v.* to study e.; to collect specimens, or observe the habits of insects.

Entone (entōᵘ·n), *v.* 1485. [Late ME. *entone* – OFr. *entoner* (mod. *entonner*) :– med.L. *intonare*; see INTONE, ENTUNE.] = INTONE.

Entonic (entǫ·nik), *a.* [f. Gr. ἔντονος strained + -IC.] *Med.* 'Having exaggerated action, or great tension' (*Syd. Soc. Lex.*).

†**Ento·rtill,** *v.* 1629. [– Fr. *entortiller* (OFr. *-eiller*), f. *en* EN-¹ + *tortiller* twist.] To entwine, coil –1653. Hence †**Entortilla·tion,** the action of twisting.

Entosthoblast (entǫ·sþoblast). 1884. [f. Gr. ἔντοσθε from within + -BLAST.] A granule within the nucleolus of a nucleated cell.

Entou·r, *v.* 1623. [– Fr. *entourer*; see next.] †**1.** To surround (with a halo or the like) –1653. **2.** *Her.* Said (in *pa. pple.*) of a shield decorated with branches 1847.

‖**Entourage** (ăṅturā·ʒ). 1832. [Fr., f. *entourer* surround, f. *entour* surroundings, subst. use of adv., 'round about'; see -AGE.] Surroundings, environment; *esp.* the set of persons who are in attendance on a superior.

The e. which surrounded Elizabeth FROUDE.

Entozoon (entozōᵘ·ǫn). 1834. [f. ENTO- + Gr. ζῷον animal.] *Zool.* A parasitic animal that lives within another. Also *attrib.* In *pl.* **entozo·a,** an artificial class of animals, taking their name merely from their mode of existence.

Also **Entozo·al** *a.* of or pertaining to the *Entozoa*; also, caused by the presence of *Entozoa.* So **Entozo·ic** *a.* **E:ntozoolo·gically** *adv.* with reference to entozoology. **E:ntozoo·logist. Entozoo·logy,** that part of zoology which treats of the *Entozoa.*

‖**Entr'acte** (ăṅtrakt). 1863. [Fr., f. *entre* between + *acte* act.] **a.** The interval between two acts of a play. **b.** A dance, piece of music, etc. performed between the acts.

†‖**Entra·da.** 1618. [Sp. *entrada.*] Income, revenue –1654.

Entrail (e·ntreⁱl), *sb.*¹ Chiefly in pl. ME. [– (O)Fr. *entrailles* – med.L. *intralia*, alt. of L. *interanea*, subst. use of n. pl. of *interaneus* internal, f. *inter*; see INTERIOR.] †**1.** *collect. sing.* The intestines or internal parts –1652. **2.** *sing.* An internal organ; = L. *viscus* 1483. **3.** *pl.* The internal parts of man or other animals; *spec.* the bowels, the intestines ME. †**4.** *transf.* = 'heart', 'soul' –1790. **5.** The inner parts of anything. Now *rare.* 1490.

4. In her entrayles all malice was enclosed LYDG. **5.** The other entralles of the earth; as Pitch, Chalke, lyme FULBECKE. To look into the entrals of this Sacrament 1655.

†**Entrai·l,** *sb.*² [f. next; cf. AFr. *entrail* 'reticulum'.] The action of ENTRAIL *v.*; a coil. SPENSER.

†**Entrai·l,** *v.* 1577. [– OFr. *entreillier*, f. *en* EN-¹ + *treille* trellis-work.] *trans.* To entwine, interlace –1736.

Entrain (entrēⁱ·n), *v.*¹ 1568. [– (O)Fr. *entraîner*, f. *en* EN-¹ + *traîner* drag. See TRAIN *v.*] *trans.* To drag away with or after oneself. Now *rare.* Also †*fig.*

Yeares entraine me if they please, but backward FLORIO.

Entrai·n, *v.*² 1881. [f. EN-¹ + TRAIN *sb.*¹] To put into or board a railway-train.

Entrammel (entræ·mĕl), *v.* 1598. [f. EN-¹ + TRAMMEL.] To put into trammels; to entangle, fetter.

Entrance (e·ntrăns), *sb.* 1526. [– OFr. *entrance*, f. *entrer* ENTER *v.*; see -ANCE.] **1.** The action of coming or going in; the coming (of an actor) upon the stage 1600. **b.** *fig.* 1526. **c.** Short for *entrance money* 1681. **2.** Power, right, or opportunity of entering (*lit.* and *fig.*) 1576. †**3.** The beginning or commencement; the first part –1765. **4.** *concr.* A door, gate, avenue, passage, etc. for entering. Also, the point at which anything enters or is entered. 1535. **5.** *Naut.* The part of a ship that comes first (in the water); 'the bow of a vessel, or form of the fore-body under the load-water line' (Smyth) 1781. †**6.** The action of entering in a record; an entry –1620. **7.** *attrib.*, as *entrance-hall*, etc. 1681.

1. The e. of the Royal party 1839. They haue their Exits and their Entrances *A.Y.L.* II. vii. 141. **b.** Before they made an e. upon more solemn debates CLARENDON. **2.** Free e. and safe egress LYTTON. **3.** At the E. of the Spring EVELYN. **4.** The e. of a tent SHAKS., of a harbour 1849.

Entrance (entra·ns), *v.* 1593. [f. EN-¹ + TRANCE *v.* 2.] **1.** *trans.* To throw into a trance 1608. **2.** To put 'out of oneself'; to overpower with delight, fear, etc. 1598; to carry away in or as in a trance (*from, to*) 1593.

1. Angel Forms, who lay intrans't MILT. *P.L.* I. 301. **2.** So stand the Sea-men..Entraunch'd with what this man of God recited QUARLES. Hence **Entra·ncedly** *adv.* **Entra·ncement,** the action of entrancing; entranced state. **Entra·ncing** *ppl. a.* transporting. **Entra·ncingly** *adv.*

Entrant (e·ntrănt). 1635. [– Fr. *entrant*, pres. pple. of *entrer* ENTER; see -ANT. Cf. earlier INTRANT.]

A. *sb.* One who or that which enters (see ENTER *v.*). Also *fig.*

B. *adj.* That enters 1640.

Entrap (entræ·p), *v.* 1534. [– OFr. *entrap(p)er*, f. *en* EN-¹ + *trappe* TRAP *sb.*¹] **1.** *trans.* To catch in or as in a trap; to bring unawares into difficulties or dangers; to beguile (*to, into*). **2.** To involve in contradictions 1611.

1. To e. the wild elephant GOLDSM. Manuel.. was..intrapped in the straights of Cilicia, and his

Army miserably cut off 1678. Hence **Entra·pment. Entra·pper. Entra·ppingly** *adv.* so as to e.

Entreasure (entre·ʒiŭɹ), *v.* 1597. [f. EN-¹ + TREASURE *v.*] **1.** To store up in or as in a treasury. †**2.** To stock with treasure. CHAPMAN.

†**Entrea·t,** *sb.* 1485. [f. next.] Entreaty, supplication –1650.

Entreat (entrī·t), *v.* Also **in-** (*arch.*) ME. [– OFr. *entraitier*, f. *en* EN-¹ + *traitier* TREAT *v.*]

I. 1. To treat (a person, etc.) in a (specified) way. *Obs.* or *arch.* †**2.** To handle –1681. †**3.** *intr.* To treat *of* or *upon* –1681. †**4.** *intr.* To treat *with* a person; *of*, occas. *about, for*; also *simply* –1603.

1. Their authors..spitefully entreated as monomaniacs 1864. **4.** To intreat with him of peace KNOLLES.

II. †**1.** *intr.* To plead *for* –1818. **2.** *trans.* To ask earnestly for; chiefly with *clause* as obj. 1600. **3.** To request earnestly; to beseech, implore 1502. †**4.** To prevail on by supplication or solicitation; to persuade by pleading. Also, to induce. –1638.

1. The prisoners entreated for their release JAS. MILL. **2.** To e. of the gods what they will not give 1878. **3.** I e. my reader to think BP. BERKELEY. **4.** God was intreated and Moses prevailed 1638.

Hence †**Entrea·table, intrea·table** *a.* that can be handled; manageable; placable. **Entrea·tableness.** †**Entrea·tance,** also **in-**, treatment; intercession. †**Entrea·ter.** †**Entrea·tful** (*rare*), supplicating. **Entrea·tingly** *adv.* †**Entrea·tive** *a.* of the nature of, or characterized by, entreaty. **Entrea·tment** (now *arch.*), treatment; †negotiation; †conversation.

Entreaty (entrī·ti). 1523. [f. ENTREAT *v.*, after TREATY.] †**1.** Treatment; handling; management –1670. †**2.** Negotiation –1607. **3.** Earnest request, solicitation, supplication 1573.

3. The poore vseth intreaties *Prov.* 18:23.

||**Entrechat** (aṅtrəʃa). 1775. [Fr. – It. (*capriola*) *intrecciata* a complicated caper.] A feat in dancing, in which the dancer leaps from the ground and strikes the heels together a number of times.

||**Entrée** (ăṅtre). 1782. [Fr.] **1.** The action or manner of entering; also, privilege of entrance; admission. **2.** *Cookery.* A made dish, served before the joint 1850. **3.** *Mus.* 'The opening piece (after the overture) of an opera or ballet' (Grove).

†**E·ntremess.** ME. [– OFr. *entremes* (mod. *entremets*), f. *entre* between + *mes* (mod. *mets*) MESS *sb.*] Something served between the courses of a banquet –1708.

||**Entremets** (aṅtrəmę). *pl.* 1475. [– Fr.; see prec.] **1.** Side dishes. **2.** *Antiq.* A spectacular interlude between the courses of a banquet 1863.

Entrench, in- (en-, intre·nʃ), *v.* 1555. [f. EN-¹, IN-² + TRENCH *sb.* and *v.* In recent use *entrench* is favoured.] **1.** *Mil.* To place within a trench; to surround or fortify with trenches. Also *transf.* and *fig.* †**2.** To make by cutting –1601. **3.** *intr.* To encroach or trespass; to TRENCH, q.v. Now *rare.* 1633.

1. Here he found the enemy strongly entrenched BURKE. *fig.* Entrenched within tradition, custom, authority, and law BP. BERKELEY. **2.** *All's Well* II. i. 45. **3.** To e. upon the privileges of parliament 1831.

Entrenchment, in- (en-, intre·nʃmĕnt). 1590. [f. prec. + -MENT.] **1.** The action of entrenching (Dicts.); *concr.* a line of trenches, a post fortified by trenches; *loosely*, a fortification. †**2.** Encroachment, intrusion –1694.

1. The 52nd regiment..carried the e. with the bayonet WELLINGTON. **2.** An e. upon their Prerogative SELDEN.

||**Entrepôt** (aṅtrəpo). 1721. [Fr. (earlier †*entrepost*, †*-pos*), f. *entreposer* store, f. *entre* among + *poser* place; see INTER-, POSE *v.*¹] **1.** Temporary deposit of goods, etc.; chiefly *concr.* a storehouse, depot. Also *fig.* **2.** A commercial centre; a place to which goods are brought for distribution. Also *attrib.*, as in *entrepôt-trade*. 1758. **3.** A mart or place where goods are deposited, free of duty, for exportation.

||**Entrepreneur** (aṅtrəprənör). 1878. [Fr., f. *entreprendre* undertake.] **a.** The director or manager of a public musical institution. **b.** One who gets up entertainments. **c.** *Pol. Econ.* A contractor acting as intermediary between capital and labour 1885.

||**Entresol** (e·ntəɹsǫl, Fr. aṅtrəsol). 1711. [Fr., f. *entre* between + *sol* ground.] A low story placed between the ground floor and the first floor of a building; a mezzanine.

†**Entri·ke,** *v.* ME. [– OFr. *entriquer* :– L. *intricare* entangle; see INTRICATE *a.*, INTRIGUE.] **1.** To ensnare, beguile –1545. **2.** To complicate –1549.

||**Entrochus** (e·ntrŏkŏs). Pl. **entrochi.** 1676. [mod.L., f. Gr. ἐν + τροχός wheel.] *Palæont.* A name for the wheel-like plates of which certain crinoids are composed. Hence **E·ntrochal** *a.* pertaining to, or containing, entrochi. var. **E·ntrochite.** (Dicts.)

||**Entropion, entropium** (entrōᵘ·pi,ǫn, -ŏm). 1875. [mod.L., f. Gr. ἐν EN-², after ECTROPION.] *Path.* Introversion of the eyelids.

Entropy (e·ntrŏpi). 1868. [– G. *entropie* (Clausius, 1865), f. Gr. ἐν EN-² + τροπή transformation; see -Y³.] *Physics.* The name given to one of the quantitative elements which determine the thermodynamic condition of a portion of matter.

A portion of matter at uniform temperature retains its entropy unchanged so long as no heat passes to or from it, but if it receives a quantity of heat without change of temperature, the entropy is increased by an amount equal to the ratio of the mechanical equivalent of the quantity of the heat to the absolute measure of the temperature on the thermodynamic scale. The entropy of a system..is always increased by any transport of heat within the system; hence 'the entropy of the universe tends to a maximum' (Clausius).

Entrust, in- (en-, intrɒ·st), *v.* 1602. [f. EN-¹ + TRUST *sb.* The form *intrust* is obsolescent.] **1.** *trans.* To invest with a trust; to commission or employ (a person) in a manner implying confidence. **2.** To confide the care or disposal of *to*, †*with* 1618.

1. Those entrusted in the fleete to inform us PEPYS. To e. new universities with power to confer degrees M. ARNOLD. **2.** To e. an errand to a boy DE FOE, one's safety to a boat 1891. Hence **Entru·stment**, the action of entrusting; the fact of being entrusted; †that with which one is entrusted.

Entry (e·ntri). [ME. *entre(e)* – (O)Fr. *entrée* :– Rom. **intrata*, subst. use of fem. pa. pple. of L. *intrare* ENTER; see -Y⁵.] **1.** The action of coming or going in or into; the coming (of an actor) upon the stage. Also *transf.* and *fig.* **2.** *Law.* **a.** The actual taking possession of lands and tenements, by entering or setting foot on the same 1491. **b.** An act essential to complete the offence of burglary 1769. **3.** †**a.** A dance introduced between the parts of an entertainment –1675. **b.** *Mus.* = ENTRÉE 3. 1728. †**4.** = ENTRANCE 2. –1615. **5.** *concr.* That by which entrance is made; a door, a gate; a passage; the mouth (of a river). Also *fig.* ME. **b.** *transf.* A passage common to two or more houses; an alley (now *dial.*); also, †an avenue ME. **6.** The action of entering something in a list, record, account-book, etc. Also *concr.* that which is so entered. 1553. **b.** The list of competitors entering (for a race, etc.) 1885. **c.** The entering at the custom-house of the nature and quantity of goods in a ship's cargo 1692. **7.** *attrib.*, as in *entry-clerk*, etc. 1471.

1. Since our e. into the ice KANE. *fig.* To find e. into the mind CHALMERS. **4.** Free entree, egresse, and regresse 1574. **5.** At the entrie of which riuer he stayed his course HAKLUYT. **6.** A notary made an e. of this act BACON. Phr. *Double E.*: the method of bookkeeping in which every item is entered twice, once to the credit of one account in the ledger, and once to the debit of another. *Single E.*: the method in which each item (as a general rule) is entered only in one account. **c.** Phr. *Port of e.*: the port at which imported goods are entered.

†**Entu·ne,** *v.* ME. [var. of ENTONE, as *tune* is of *tone*.] **1.** *trans.* To intone. Also *absol.* –1627. **2.** To bring into tune –1530. Hence †**Entu·ne** *sb.* tune; melody (*rare*).

Entwine, in- (en-, intwəi·n), *v.* 1597. [f. EN-¹, IN-² + TWINE *v.*] **1.** *trans.* To twine, twist, or wreathe together or round 1616; to form by twining 1700. Also *intr.* for *refl.* Also *fig.* **2.** To clasp; to enfold, embrace. Also *fig.* 1633.

1. Intwine..the flesh-like Columbine With Pinckes W. BROWNE. For him may Love the myrtle wreath e. LANDOR. Hence **Entwi·nement.**

Entwist, in- (en-, in,twi·st), *v.* 1590. [f. EN-¹, IN-² + TWIST *v.*] To clasp with, or form into, a twist; to twist in *with*.

†**Entwi·t(e,** *v.* 1542. [Altered f. ATWITE; cf. TWIT.] To twit or twit with –1608.

Enucleate (ĭniū·kli,eⁱt), *v.* 1548. [– *enucleat-*, pa. ppl. stem of L. *enucleare* extract the kernel from, make plain, f. *e* EX-¹ + *nucleus* kernel; see NUCLEUS, -ATE³.] **1.** *fig.* To extract the kernel from; to lay open, clear, explain. **2.** *Surg.* To extract (a tumour, etc.) from its capsule. Also *absol.* 1878.

1. Enucleating the sense which underlies a difficult construction 1859.

Enucleation (ĭniū:kli,ēⁱ·ʃən). 1650. [– Fr. *énucléation* or med.L. *enucliatio*, f. as prec.; see -ION.] **1.** The action of enucleating; unfolding, explanation. **2.** *Surg.* The shelling out of a tumour, etc. from its capsule 1874.

Enula campana; see ELECAMPANE.

Enumerable, erron. f. INNUMERABLE.

†**Enu·merate,** *pa. pple.* 1646. [– L. *enumeratus*, pa. pple. of *enumerare*; see next and -ATE².] = ENUMERATED –1711.

Enumerate (ĭniū·mĕreⁱt), *v.* 1647. [– *enumerat-*, pa. ppl. stem of L. *enumerare*, f. *e* EX-¹ + *numerus* NUMBER *sb.*; see -ATE³.] *trans.* To count, ascertain the number of; more usually, to mention separately, as if for counting; to specify as in a catalogue or list.

The priest pardons no sins but those which are enumerated JER. TAYLOR. The enumerated population of London..was 3,251,804 *Census* 1871. Hence **Enu·merative** *a.* that enumerates; concerned with enumeration. **Enu·merator,** one who enumerates.

Enumeration (ĭniū:merēⁱ·ʃən). 1551. [– Fr. *énumeration* or L. *enumeratio*, f. as prec.; see -ION.] **1.** The action of ascertaining the number of something; *esp.* a census 1577. **2.** The action of specifying seriatim; *concr.* a catalogue, list 1551. **3.** *Rhet.* tr. L. *enumeratio*: A recapitulation, in the peroration, of the heads of an argument.

2. The e. of these circumstances is not to restrict the generality of the enactment 1858.

Enunciable (ĭnɒ·nʃiăb'l), *a.* 1652. [f. ENUNCIATE; see -ABLE. Cf. med.L. *enuntiabilis*.] That admits of being enunciated.

Enunciate (ĭnɒ·nʃi,eⁱt), *v.* 1623. [– *enuntiat-*, pa. ppl. stem of L. *enuntiare*, f. *e* EX-¹ + *nuntiare* ANNOUNCE.] **1.** *trans.* To give definite expression to (a proposition, etc.). **2.** = ENOUNCE 2. 1864. **3.** = ENOUNCE 3. 1759.

1. The dogmas enunciated in the Lambeth articles 1853. **3.** Each enunciates with a human tone 1759. Hence **Enu·nciative** *a.* that serves to e.; declaratory; pertaining to vocal utterance. **Enu·nciatively** *adv.* **Enu·nciator,** one who or that which enunciates. †**Enu·nciatory** *a.* enunciative.

Enunciation (ĭnɒnʃi,ēⁱ·ʃən). 1551. [– (O)Fr. *énonciation* or L. *enuntiatio*, f. *enuntiat-*; see prec., -ION.] The action of enunciating. **1.** The action of giving definite expression to a law, principle, etc.; †a proposition, statement; the form of words in which a proposition, etc. is stated 1628. **2.** Formal declaration or assertion 1551. **3.** The uttering or pronouncing of articulate sounds; manner of utterance 1750.

Enure (eniūᵊ·ɹ), *v.* 1489. [f. EN-¹ + URE¹. Now repl. by INURE *v.*¹, exc. in sense 3.] †**1.** = INURE *v.* 2. –1612. **2.** = INURE *v.* **1.** 1489. **3.** *intr.* Chiefly *Law.* To come into operation; to have effect; to be available; to be applied (to the use of) 1607.

2. Troops enured to toil ADDISON. **3.** The dignity enures only to the grantee for life BLACKSTONE.

||**Enuresis** (eniurī·sis). 1800. [mod.L., f. Gr. ἐνουρεῖν urinate in.] *Path.* Incontinence of urine.

†**Enva·ssal,** *v.* 1605. [f. EN-¹ + VASSAL.] *trans.* To make a vassal of. Also *fig.* –1660. Hence †**Enva·ssalage** (*rare*).

†**Envau·lt,** *v.* 1523. [f. EN-¹ + VAULT *sb.*] To arch over; also, to entomb –1745.

Enveigle; see IN-.

Enveil (envēⁱ·l), *v.* 1555. [f. EN-¹ + VEIL *sb.* Cf. OFr. *envoiler.*] To cover with, or as with, a veil.

Envelop (enve·ləp), *v.* [ME. *envelupe, -ipe* = OFr. *envoluper, -oper* (mod. *envelopper*), f. *in* EN-[1] + **volup-*, **velup-*, of unkn. origin; cf. DEVELOP.] **1.** *trans.* To wrap up in or as in a garment, etc.; to serve as a wrapping or case for 1595. Also *fig.* **2.** To wrap, surround on all sides. Const. *in, with.* Also *fig.* 1474. **b.** *Mil.* To effect the surrounding of (the enemy). †**3.** *catachr.* To line. SPENSER *F. Q.* II. vii. 4.

1. Envoliped in synne CHAUCER, in cotton LYELL, by the earth 1870. **2.** A cloud of smoke envelops either host DRYDEN. Invelloped in vapours 1762.

Envelope (e·nvělo[u]p, ăṅv'lop), *sb.* 1707. [– Fr. *enveloppe*, f. *envelopper*; see prec.] **1.** That in which anything is enveloped; 'a wrapper, integument, covering' (J.) 1715. Also *fig.* **2.** *spec.* The cover of a letter 1714. **3.** *Bot.* The calyx or the corolla, or both together 1830. **4.** *Astron.* The nebulous covering of the head of a comet, the coma 1830. **5.** *Fortif.* 'A work of earth, sometimes in form of a single parapet, and at others like a small rampart' (Stocqueler). **6.** *Math.* The locus of the ultimate intersections of consecutive curves in a system of curves 1871.

Envelopment (enve·ləpmĕnt). 1763. [f. ENVELOP *v.* + -MENT.] The action of enveloping; the state of being enveloped; *concr.* a covering, wrapper. Also *fig.*

Envenom (enve·nəm), *v.* [ME. *envenim, -em* – (O)Fr. *envenimer*, f. *en* EN-[1] + *venim* (mod. *venin*) VENOM.] †**1.** *trans.* To poison by contact, bite, inoculation, etc. Also *absol.* –1725. **2.** To put venom or poison on; to taint with poison; to render noxious ME. **b.** To infuse venom or bitterness into; to embitter, make virulent 1533. **3.** *fig.* To corrupt, vitiate ME.

1. A Toad may envenome outwardly 1665. **2.** To e. arrowes EDEN. To e. thoughtes GRAFTON, a crime 1658, hatred MILL. **3.** A universall tetter of impurity had invenom'd every part MILTON.

Enve·nomed, *ppl. a.* ME. [f. prec. + -ED[1].] **1.** †Charged with venom; smeared with venom; poisoned –1810. **2.** *fig.* Virulent, malignant, embittered ME.

1. As when Alcides..felt th' envenom'd robe MILT.

†**Enve·nomous,** *a.* ME. [– OFr. *envenimeus*, f. *envenimer*; see ENVENOM, -OUS.] Poisonous –1624.

†**Enve·rmeil,** *v.* ME. [– OFr. *envermeillier, -ir*, f. *en* EN-[1] + *vermeil* vermilion-coloured; see VERMEIL.] *trans.* To tinge as with vermilion; to make ruddy –1822.

Enviable (e·nviăb'l), *a.* 1602. [f. ENVY *v.* + -ABLE.] That is to be envied.

An e. mediocrity of fortune CAREW. Hence **E·nviableness. E·nviably** *adv.*

Envier (e·nviəɹ). 1509. [f. ENVY *v.* + -ER[1].] One who envies.

Never bride had fewer enviers 1762.

Envigor, var. INVIGOUR *v.*

†**Envi·ned,** *ppl. a.* [perh. f. AFr. **enviné* in same sense, with play on Fr. (XV) *enviné* †tipsy; f. *en* EN-[1] + *vin* wine.] Stored with wine. CHAUCER.

Envious (e·nviəs), *a.* ME. [– AFr. *envious*, OFr. *envieus* (mod. *-eux*), f. *envie* ENVY *sb.*, after L. *invidiosus*; see -OUS.] **1.** Full of envy, affected or actuated by envy; vexed at the good fortune or qualities of another. Const. †*against*, †*at, of*, †*to* with *sb.* or *inf.* †**2.** Full of ill-will; malicious –1713. †**3.** Full of emulation –1821. †**4.** Grudging, excessively careful –1667. †**5.** Invidious; odious –1640. †**6.** Enviable –1665.

1. Neither be thou enuious at the wicked *Prov.* 24:19. E. of my diamond LYTTON. The e. who but breathe in others' pain BYRON. **3.** Foremost in the e. race KEATS. **4.** No men are so e. of their health JER. TAYLOR. **6.** So e. a place PEPYS. Hence **Enviously** *adv.* **Enviousness.**

Environ, *sb. Obs.* in *sing.* ME. [– OFr. sing. *environ* (see next); in sense 2 – mod. Fr. pl. *environs* (XVII).] †**1.** *sing.* Compass, circuit. Only in ME. **2.** In mod. Eng. *pl.* **Environs** (envəi·rənz, e·nvirənz). The outskirts, surrounding districts, of a town 1665.

2. London and its Environs EVELYN. Hence **Envi·ronage** (*rare*), surroundings. **Envi·ronal** *a.* arising from relations to the environment.

Environ (envəi·rən), *v.* ME. [– OFr. *environer* (mod. *-onner*), f. *environ* surroundings, around, f. *en* IN + *viron* circuit, f. *virer* turn, VEER *v.*[2]] **1.** *trans.* To form a ring round, surround, encircle; to beset; to beleaguer. Also *fig.* of circumstances, dangers, etc. **2.** To envelop, enclose ME. †**3.** To go round in a circle –1647.

1. Ilands environed by the sea GOUGE. Colonel Pride..had environed the house with two regiments HUME. *fig.* What Perils do inviron The Man that meddles with cold Iron BUTLER *Hud.* I. iii. 1. **2.** Gravely-gladsome light environed them LANDOR.

†**Envi·ron.** ME. [f. (O)Fr. *environ*; see prec.]

A. *adv.* Round about; in the neighbourhood –1600.

B. *prep.* Round, about –1450.

Environment (envəi·rənmĕnt). 1603. [f. ENVIRON *v.* + -MENT.] **1.** The action of environing; the state of being environed. **2.** That which environs; *esp.* the conditions or influences under which any person or thing lives or is developed 1827.

2. In such an element with such an e. of circumstances CARLYLE. The organism is continually adapted to its e. 1874.

Environs; see ENVIRON *sb.*

Envisage (envi·zédʒ), *v.* 1820. [– Fr. *envisager*, f. *en-* EN-[1] + *visage* VISAGE.] **1.** *trans.* To look in the face of; also *fig.* **2.** To set before the mind's eye; to contemplate 1837.

1. To e. circumstance, all calm KEATS. **2.** From the very dawn of existence the infant must e. self MCCOSH. Hence **Envi·sagement**, envisaging.

†**Envolume** (envǫ·lium), *v. rare.* 1632. [f. EN-[1] + VOLUME.] To form into, or incorporate with, a volume.

Envolupe(n, obs. f. ENVELOPE *v.*

Envoy (e·nvoi), *sb.*[1] Also (in Fr. form) **l'envoi**; see L'ENVOY. ME. [–(O)Fr. *envoi*, f. *envoyer* send, f. phr. *en voie* on the way.] **1.** The final stanza of a poem containing an address to the reader or the person to whom it is dedicated; the concluding strophe, as of a ballade or chant royal, having a prescribed metrical form (*arch.*). **2.** The action of dispatching a messenger or parcel; hence, a mission, errand (*arch.*) 1795.

Envoy (e·nvoi), *sb.*[2] 1666. [alt. of Fr. *envoyé* (previously used unchanged), subst. use of pa. pple. of *envoyer* send; see prec.] **1.** A public minister sent by one sovereign or government to another for the transaction of diplomatic business. Now *esp.* a minister plenipotentiary, ranking below an ambassador, and above a 'chargé d'affaires'. **2.** An agent, commissioner, deputy, messenger, representative 1696. Hence **E·nvoyship,** the office, position, or function of an e.

Envy (e·nvi), *sb.* [ME. *envie* – (O)Fr. *envie* (which early developed the sense 'desire'), semi-pop. – L. *invidia* malice, ill-will, f. *invidēre* look maliciously upon, grudge, envy, f. *in* upon, against + *vidēre* see.] †**1.** Ill-will, malice, enmity –1707. **b.** as tr. L. *invidia*: Odium, unpopularity –1679. †**2.** Harm, mischief –1460. **3.** Mortification and ill-will occasioned by the contemplation of another's superior advantages ME.; *concr.* the object of envy 1836. **4.** †**a.** Emulation –1635. **b.** A longing for another's advantages 1723. †**5.** Desire; enthusiasm –1607.

1. No lawful meanes can carrie me Out of enuies reach *Merch. V.* IV. i. 10. **3.** E...es joye of oþer mens harme and sorowe of oþer mens welefare 1440. All..saue only hee, Did that they did, in enuy of great Cæsar *Jul. C.* V. v. 70. Enuie striketh most spitefully at the fairest A.V. *Transl. Pref.* 2. The little envies of them [women] to one another DRYDEN. **4. b.** Your success excites my e. 1891.

Envy (e·nvi), *v.*[1] ME. [– (O)Fr. *envier*, f. *envie*; see prec.] **1.** *trans.* To feel envy at the superior advantages of; to regard with discontent another's possession of (some superior advantage). Also in more neutral sense: To wish oneself on a level with (another) in some respect, or possessed of (something which another has). †**2.** To feel a grudge against –1630. †**3.** *trans.* To begrudge; to treat grudgingly. Also *absol.* –1770. †**4.** *intr.* To have envious, grudging, or malevolent feelings 1477.

1. I..owe no man hate, enuie no mans happinesse *A. Y. L.* III. ii. 78. I e. him for walking.. with you MIDDLETON. Ah! much I e. thee thy boys CRABBE. **3.** But that sweet Cordiall..She did to him e. SPENSER *F. Q.* III. v. 50. Antiquity enuieth there should be new additions BACON. **4.** Phr. *To e. at* = senses 1–3; But now I enuie at their libertie SHAKS.

†**Envy·**, *v.*[2] ME. [– OFr. *envier* :– L. *invitare* challenge. Cf. VIE *v.*] **a.** *intr.* To vie. **b.** To vie with, seek to rival –1621.

As thogh the erthe enuye wolde To be gayer than the heuen CHAUCER.

Enwall, in- (en-, inwǭ·l), *v.* 1523. [f. EN-[1], IN-[2] + WALL *sb.*[1]] To enclose within a wall; also, to serve as a wall to. Also *fig.*

Enwallow; see EN- *pref.*[1] B3.

†**Enwhee·l,** *v. rare.* 1604. [f. EN-[1] + WHEEL *sb.*] To encircle –1621.

Enwiden; see EN- *pref.*[1] B3.

Enwind, in- (en-, inwəi·nd), *v.* 1850. [f. EN-[1], IN-[2] + WIND *v.*[1]] *trans.* To wind itself around; to encircle (*lit.* and *fig.*).

Let her great Danube rolling fair E. her isles TENNYSON.

Enwoman; see EN- *pref.*[1] B2.

Enwomb (enwū·m), *v.* 1590. [f. EN-[1] + WOMB.] **1.** *trans.* To make pregnant; also *fig.* **2.** To hold in or as in the womb. ? *Obs.* 1601. **3.** *transf.* To plunge *into*, bury *in*, the womb or bowels of 1591.

Enwrap, in- (en-, inræ·p), *v.* ME. [f. EN-[1], IN-[2] + WRAP *v.*] **1.** *trans.* To wrap, envelop, enfold. Also *transf.* and *fig.* **2.** *fig.* **a.** To contain implicitly 1642. **b.** To wrap in slumber, engross in thought, etc. 1589. †**c.** To involve, implicate (in danger, difficulty, etc.) –1826.

2. b. If such holy song E. our fancy long MILTON. Hence †**Enwra·pment,** also **in-,** *rare*, the action of enwrapping; the being enwrapped; a wrapping, covering.

Enwreathe, in- (en-, inrī·ð), *v.* 1620. [f. EN-[1], IN-[2] + WREATHE *v.*] To surround or encircle with or as with a wreath.

Enzootic (enzo,ǫ·tik). 1880. [f. Gr. ἐν in + ζῷον animal + -IC, after *chaotic*, etc. Cf. Fr. *enzootique.*]

A. *adj.* 'Applied to diseases of cattle peculiar to a district, climate, or season' (*Syd. Soc. Lex.*). **B.** *sb.* An enzootic disease.

Enzyme (e·nzəim). 1881. Also *U.S.* **enzym.** [– G. *enzym* (Kühne, 1876), f. mod. Gr. ἔνζυμος leavened, f. Gr. ἐν EN-[2] + ζύμη leaven.] *Biochem.* Any of a class of complex organic substances that cause chemical transformations of material in plants and animals; formerly called *ferment.* Hence **Enzy·mic** *a.*

Eo-, *prefix*, comb. f. Gr. ἠώς dawn, as in: **Eoli·thic** *a.* pertaining to the earliest age of man that is characterized by the use of worked flint instruments. **Eozoic** (ī,ozō[u]·ik) *a.* [Gr. ζῷον animal], characterized by the earliest appearance of animal life; said of the Laurentian strata and their period.

Eoan (ī,ō[u]·ăn), *a.* 1619. [f. L. *eous* – Gr. ἠῷος, f. ἠώς dawn + -AN.] Of or pertaining to the dawn; eastern.

Eocene (ī·ŏsīn), *a.* 1833. [f. Gr. ἠώς (see EO-) + καινός new.] *Geol.* **1.** The epithet applied to the lowest division of the Tertiary strata, and to the geological period which they represent. Also *fig.* **2.** quasi-*sb.*, as *Upper E.*, etc.

Eol-, Eon, vars. ÆOL-, ÆON.

Eolienne (iō[u]lie·n). 1902. [– Fr. *éolienne*, f. Gr. αἰόλος sheeny.] A fine dress fabric of silk and wool.

Eosin (ī·ŏsin). 1866. [f. Gr. ἠώς dawn + -IN[1].] *Chem.* A red dye-stuff produced by the addition of bromine to a solution of fluorescin in glacial acetic acid. Its potassium salt is used as a rose-coloured dye. Also *attrib.*

-eous, *suffix*, occurring in adjs., is chiefly f. L. *-eus* + -OUS, in the sense 'of the nature of, resembling'.

Eozoic, etc.; see EO- *pref.*

Ep-, *prefix*; see EPI-.

Epacrid (epæ·krid). 1881. [– mod.L. *epacris, -id-*, f. Gr. ἐπί + ἄκρις summit; so named by Forster (1776), because 'generally found on mountain tops'. In sense b, f. mod.L. *Epacrideæ.*] **a.** A plant of the genus *Epacris.* **b.** A plant of the N.O. *Epacrideæ*, consisting of corollifloral dicotyledons, growing in Australia and the Indian Archipelago, and resembling heaths.

Epact (ī·pækt, e·pækt). 1552. [– (O)Fr. *épacte* – late L. *epactæ* pl. – Gr. ἐπακταί (sc. ἡμέραι days), fem. pl. of ἐπακτός, f. ἐπάγειν intercalate.] **1. a.** (Also pl. *epacts*.) The number of days by which the solar exceeds the lunar year of 12 months. **b.** The number of days of the moon's age on the first day of the year (now Jan. 1st, formerly March 1st or 22nd). **2.** Any intercalated day or days (*rare*) 1603.

Epactal (ĭpæ·ktăl, epæ·ktăl), *a.* 1878. [f. Gr. ἐπακτός (see prec.) + -AL[1].] *Anat.* 'Imported; foreign' (*Syd. Soc. Lex.*).

E. bone: the Wormian bone at the superior angle of the occipital bone.

†**Epæne·tic,** *a.* 1675. [– Gr. ἐπαινετικός, f. ἐπαινεῖν praise; see -IC.] Panegyrical –1736.

‖**Epagoge** (epăgōᵘ·gi). [Gr. ἐπαγωγή, f. ἐπάγειν bring in.] *Logic.* The bringing forward of particular instances to lead to a general conclusion; argument by induction. Hence **Epago·gic** *a.* inductive. (Dicts.)

Epagomenic (e:păgome·nik), *a.* 1839. [f. Gr. ἐπαγομένη (sc. ἡμέρα day); see prec., -IC.] Intercalary.

Epalpate (ipæ·lpĕt), *a.* 1884. [f. E- + L. *palpus* PALP *sb.* + -ATE[2]; see EX-[1].] *Entom.* Having no palpi or feelers.

Epalpebrate (ipæ·lpĭbrĕt), *a.* 1884. [f. as prec.; see PALPEBRA.] Having no eyebrows.

Epana-, bef. a vowel *epan-*, comb. f. Gr. ἐπί upon, in addition + ἀνά up, again, occurring in some rhetorical terms, adopted from Gr.

Epa:nadiplo·sis [Gr. δίπλωσις], a figure in which 'a sentence begins and ends with the same word; as Severe to his servants, to his children severe' (Phillips). **E:panale·psis** [Gr. λῆψις], a figure by which the same word or clause is repeated after intervening matter. **Epana·phora** [Gr. φορά] = ANAPHORA. **Epana·strophe** [Gr. στροφή], a figure by which the end-word of one sentence begins the next. **Epa·nodos** [Gr. ὁδός], **a.** the repetition of a sentence in inverse order; **b.** a return to the regular thread of discourse after a digression. **E:panortho·sis** [Gr. ὄρθωσις], a figure in which a word is recalled, in order to substitute a more correct term. Hence **E:panortho·tic** *a.*

Epanthous (epæ·nþəs), *a.* [f. Gr. ἐπί EPI- + ἄνθος flower + -OUS.] *Bot.* Growing upon flowers, as certain fungi. (Dicts.).

Eparch (e·paɹk). 1656. [– Gr. ἔπαρχος, f. ἐπί EPI- + ἀρχός chief, ruler; see -ARCH.] **1. a.** *Hist.* = L. *præfectus* prefect. **b.** The governor of an eparchy in modern Greece. **2.** *Eccl.* A metropolitan (bishop) in the Greek (Russian) Church 1882.

Eparchy (e·păɹki). 1796. [– Gr. ἐπαρχία, f. ἔπαρχος; see prec., -Y[3].] **1.** A district or province under an eparch; in mod. Greece, a division of a monarchy 1838. **2.** In the Russian (Greek) Church: A diocese. Hence **Epa·rchial** *a.*

‖**Epaule** (epǭ·l). 1702. [Fr.] *Fortif.* The shoulder of a bastion, *i.e.* the place where the face and flank meet.

Epaulement (epǭ·lmĕnt). 1687. [– Fr. *épaulement*, f. *épauler* protect (troops) by an epaulement, f. *épaule* shoulder; see -MENT.] *Fortif.* 'A covering mass raised to protect from the fire of the enemy' (Smyth).

Epaulet, epaulette (e·pǫlet). 1783. [– Fr. *épaulette*, dim. of *épaule*; see EPAULE, -ET, -ETTE. The better form is *epaulet*, that in *-ette* is more common.] **1.** A shoulder-piece; an ornament worn on the shoulder as part of a military, naval, or (occas.) civil uniform. **2.** *Entom.* The plate that covers the base of the anterior wings in hymenopterous insects 1834. **3.** = POULDRON, q. v. 1824. **4.** An ornament for the shoulder of a lady's dress 1865.

1. Obliged to borrow from Rothschild, the banker, the epaulettes he wore as Austrian consul 1848. Hence **E·paule:tted** *ppl. a.*

Epaxial (epæ·ksiăl), *a.* 1872. [f. EP- + L. *axis* + -AL[1].] *Anat.* On or above the axis (of the body): said of muscles, cartilages, etc. that lie upon or above the vertebral column viewed horizontally. Hence **Epa·xially** *adv.* in an e. position or direction.

Epencephalon (epense·fălǫn). 1854. [f. EP- + ENCEPHALON.] *Anat.* The anterior of the two enlargements into which the posterior primary vesicle of the brain divides. Also called *hind-brain.* Hence **Epe:ncepha·lic** *a.* pertaining to or covering the e.

Ependyma (epe·ndimă). 1872. [– Gr. ἐπένδυμα, f. ἐπενδύειν, f. ἐπί over + ἐν on + δύειν put. Cf. Fr. *épendyme.*] 'Virchow's name for the lining membrane of the cerebral ventricles and of the central spinal canal' (*Syd. Soc. Lex.*).

Epenthesis (epe·nþĭsis). 1657. [Late L. *epenthesis* – Gr. ἐπένθεσις, f. ἐπενθε-, stem of ἐπεντιθέναι insert, f. ἐπί EPI- + ἐν in + τιθέναι place.] *Gram.* The insertion of a letter or sound in the middle of a word. var. †**Epe·nthesy.**

Epenthetic (epenþe·tik), *a.* 1831. [– Gr. ἐπενθετικός; see prec. and -IC.] Pertaining to epenthesis. Of a letter or sound: Inserted in the middle of a word.

Epergne (ĭpə·ɹn). 1761. [perh. a corruption of Fr. *épargne* saving. The meaning is not accounted for.] A centre-dish for the dinner-table, now often in a branched form, each branch supporting a small dish, or a vase for flowers.

Grand Epergnes filled with fine Pickles 1761.

Epexegesis (epe:ksĭdʒī·sis). 1621. [– Gr. ἐπεξήγησις, f. ἐπεξηγεῖσθαι; see EPI-, EXEGESIS.] The addition of a word or words by way of further elucidation; that which is so added. Hence **Epe:xege·tic, -al** *a.* pertaining to or of the nature of an e. **Epe:xege·tically** *adv.*

Ephah (ī·fă). ME. [Heb. *'ēpāh*, believed to be of Egyptian origin (cf. LXX Gr. οἰφί, Vulgate L. *ephi*).] *Heb. Antiq.* A Hebrew dry measure; = BATH *sb.*[3]; variously said to have contained 4½ to 9 gallons. Also *fig.*

Ephebe (efī·b). 1880. [– L. *ephebus* (also used) – Gr. ἔφηβος, f. ἐπί upon + ἥβη early manhood.] *Gr. Antiq.* A young citizen from eighteen to twenty years of age, which period he spent chiefly in garrison duty. Hence **Ephe·bic** *a.*

Ephectic (efe·ktik), *a.* 1693. [– Gr. ἐφεκτικός, f. ἐπέχειν hold back, suspend (one's judgement).] Characterized by suspense of judgement.

†**Ephe·mera,** *a.* and *sb.*[1] ME. [– med.L. *ephemera* (sc. *febris* fever), fem. of late L. *ephemerus* – Gr. ἐφήμερος lasting only for a day, f. ἐπί EPI- + ἡμέρα day.]

A. *adj.* Of a fever: Lasting only for a day. **B.** *sb.* (sc. *fever*) –1813.

Ephemera (ĭfe·mĕră), *sb.*[2] Pl. **ephemeræ, -as.** 1677. [– mod.L. *ephemera* (sc. *musca* fly); see prec.] *Zool.* An insect that (in its imago) lives only for a day. In mod. entomology, a genus of pseudo-neuropterous insects belonging to the *Ephemeridæ* (Day-flies, May-flies). Also *transf.* and *fig.*

These papers of a day, the Ephemeræ of learning JOHNSON.

Ephemeral (ĭfe·mĕrăl). 1576. [f. (after Fr. *éphémère*) Gr. ἐφήμερος (see prec.) + -AL[1].]

A. *adj.* **1.** Beginning and ending in a day; existing only for a day, or for a few days. **2.** Short-lived, transitory 1639.

1. An e. fever 1866. E. insects HELPS. **2.** Their e. liberty SYD. SMITH. May I, the e., ne'er scrutinize Who made the heaven and earth BROWNING.

B. *sb.* in *pl.* Insects which live only for a day. Also *transf.* of books, persons, etc. 1817.

Hence **Ephe:mera·lity,** e. quality; in *pl.* e. matters. var. †**Ephe·meran** *a.* (in sense A. 1) and *sb.*

Ephe·meric, *a.* [f. EPHEMERA + -IC.] = EPHEMERAL. (Dicts.)

Ephemerid (ĭfe·mĕrid). 1872. [– mod.L. *Ephemeridæ*, f. EPHEMERA *sb.*[2]; see -ID[3].] One of the *Ephemeridæ*; see EPHEMERA[2].

‖**Ephemeris** (ĭfe·mĕris). Pl. **ephemerides** (efĭme·ridīz), formerly used as *sing.* 1551. [– L. *ephemeris* – Gr. ἐφημερίς diary, f. ἐφήμερος daily; see EPHEMERA *a.*] †**1.** A diary, journal –1682. **2.** A table showing the computed (rarely the observed) places of a heavenly body for every day of a given period. †Also, in *pl.* the tabulated positions of a heavenly body for a series of successive days 1551. †**b.** *pl.* A collection of such tables –1635. **3.** A book giving the places of the planets and other astronomical matters in advance for each day of a certain period; an astronomical almanac 1647. †**4.** An almanac or calendar of any kind. (Used in bibliographical works, in *pl.*, as a general heading for Almanacs, Calendars, etc.) –1796. ¶ **5.** *catachr.* = EPHEMERA[2]. 1820.

5. Honour is venerable to us because it is no e. EMERSON. Hence †**Ephe·merist,** one who makes or uses an e.

Ephemeromorph (ĭfe·mĕro,mǭ:ɹf). *rare.* 1874. [f. Gr. ἐφήμερος (see EPHEMERA *sb.*[1]) + μορφή form.] *Biol.* A general name for the lowest forms of life, which are not definitely either animal or vegetable.

Ephemeron (ĭfe·mĕrǫn). *Pl.* **ephemera, -ons.** 1578. [– Gr. (ζῷον) ἐφήμερον, neut. of ἐφήμερος; see EPHEMERA[2].] **1.** An insect, which, in its winged state, lives only for a day. Also *fig.* and *attrib.* 1626. †‖**2.** A plant described by ancient writers –1661. Hence **Ephe·merous** *a.* like an e.; transitory.

Ephesian (ĭfī·ʒăn). ME. [f. L. *Ephesius* (– Gr. ἐφέσιος, f. Ἔφεσος) + -AN.]

A. *adj.* Of or pertaining to Ephesus.

B. *sb.* **1.** An inhabitant of Ephesus ME. †**2.** A boon companion. *Merry W.* IV. v. 19.

Ephesine (e·fĭsin), *a.* 1579. [– late L. *Ephesinus*, f. *Ephesus*; see -INE[1].] Of or pertaining to Ephesus; chiefly *Eccl.*

†**Ephe·stian,** *a.* [f. Gr. ἐφέστιος of the house or family + -AN.] Domestic. URQUHART.

Ephete (e·fīt). *rare.* 1839. [– Gr. ἐφέτης, f. ἐφιέναι impose, etc.] In *pl.* A body of magistrates at Athens. More usu. in L. form *ephetæ*.

Ephialtes (efi,æ·ltīz). 1601. [– Gr. ἐφιάλτης.] Nightmare.

‖**Ephippium** (efi·piǒm). 1841. [– L. *ephippium* horse-cloth, saddle – Gr. ἐφίππιος adj. 'that is for putting on a horse'.] **1.** *Anat.* A saddle-shaped depression of the sphenoid bone 1842. **2.** *Zool.* The envelope enclosing the winter ova of the Daphniidæ (a genus of the Crustaceans). It is probably a development from the carapace.

Ephod (e·fǫd). ME. [– Heb. *'ēpōd.*] **1.** A Jewish priestly garment, without sleeves, slit at the sides below the armpits, fastened with buckles at the shoulders, and by a girdle at the waist. The ephod worn by the priests was of linen; that of the high-priest was of 'gold, purple, scarlet, and byssus'. **2.** *transf.* A typical priestly garment; hence, †the priestly office, etc. 1603.

2. The holy e. made a cloak for gain DRAYTON.

Ephor (e·fǫɹ). 1586. [– Gr. ἔφορος overseer, f. ἐπί upon + root of ὁρᾶν see. Also in L. form *ephori.*] **1.** One of a body of five magistrates at Sparta, elected annually by popular vote, who exercised control over the kings. **2.** In mod. Greece: An overseer 1890. Hence **E·phoral** *a.* of or pertaining to the ephors. **E·phoralty,** the office of e.; the body of ephors. **E·phorship,** term of office as e.

Ephy·driad. [– Gr. ἐφυδριάς, -αδ-, f. ἐπί EPI- + ὕδωρ water.] A water-nymph. L. HUNT.

Epi-, *prefix*, repr. Gr. ἐπι- (bef. an unaspirated vowel ἐπ-, bef. an aspirate ἐφ-, in Eng. EP-, EPH-) in senses 'upon, at, or close upon, on the ground or occasion of, in addition'.

Epibasal (epibē·săl), *a.* 1882. [f. EPI- + BASAL *a.*] *Bot.* Epithet of the upper cell in the oospore of certain cryptogams.

Epiblast (e·piblɑst). 1866. [f. EPI- + -BLAST.] **1.** *Bot.* A small transverse plate found on the embryo of some grasses. **2.** *Biol.* The outermost layer of the wall of the blastoderm when fully formed 1877.

‖**Epiblema** (epiblī·mă). 1870. [mod. L.– Gr. ἐπίβλημα that which is thrown over, f. ἐπί EPI- + βάλλειν throw.] *Bot.* A modified epidermal tissue investing the roots of plants.

Epic (e·pik). 1589. [– L. *epicus* – late Gr. ἐπικός, f. ἔπος; see EPOS, -IC.]

A. *adj.* **1.** Pertaining to that kind of narrative poetry (see EPOS) which celebrates the achievements of some heroic personage of history or tradition. **2.** Such as is described in epic poetry 1847.

1. My poem's E., and is meant to be Divided in twelve books BYRON. Phr. *E. dialect*: that form of the Greek language in which the e. poems were written.

B. *sb.* †1. An epic poet. B. JONS. **2.** An epic poem. Also *transf.* and *fig.* 1706.

2. Phr. *National e.* (transf.): any imaginative work embodying a nation's conception of its own past history, or of incidents in it.

Hence **E·pical** *a.* **E·pically** *adv.* **E·picism,** the mental habit characteristic of the e. poet. **E·picist,** a writer of e. poetry.

Epicalyx (epikæ·liks). 1870. [f. EPI- + CALYX.] *Bot.* A whorl of leaf-like organs surrounding the true calyx in some plants.

Epicarp (e·pikāɹp). 1835. [f. Gr. ἐπί EPI- + καρπός fruit.] *Bot.* In fruits: the outermost layer of the pericarp. Cf. ENDOCARP.

Epicede (e·pisīd). *arch.* 1549. Anglicized f. EPICEDIUM.

‖**Epicedium** (episī·diŏm, -sidəi·ŏm). Pl. **epicedia, -ums.** 1587. [L. *epicedium* – Gr. ἐπικήδειον, subst. use of n. of ἐπικήδειος, f. ἐπί EPI- + κῆδος care, spec. funeral observance.] A funeral ode. Hence **Epice·dial** *a.* elegiac (*arch.*). **Epice·dian** *a.* elegiac, funereal; †*sb.* an epicedium. var. †**Epice·dion.**

Epicene (e·pisīn). 1528. [– late L. *epicœnus* – Gr. ἐπίκοινος, f. ἐπί EPI- + κοινός common.]

A. *adj. Gram.* In L. and Gr. grammar, said of nouns which have but one form to denote either sex. Hence (improp.) *epicene gender.* Loosely, = *common.* Also *transf.* and *fig.* 1601.

fig. In an Epicœne fury B. JONS. An e. creature, a bundle of languid affectations BLACK.

B. *sb.* One who shares the characteristics of both sexes 1609.

E., or The Silent Woman B. JONS. (*title*).

Epicentral (epise·ntrăl), *a.* 1866. [– Gr. ἐπίκεντρος (see EPICENTRUM, which is the immediate source of sense 2) + -AL[1].] **1.** Situated upon a (vertebral) centrum. Also quasi-*sb.* **2.** Pertaining to an epicentrum 1887.

‖**Epicentrum** (epise·ntrŏm). 1879. [mod. L. – Gr. ἐπίκεντρον, adj. neut., f. ἐπί EPI- + κέντρον CENTRE.] The point over the centre: applied in *Seismology* to the point of outbreak of earthquake shocks. var. **E·picentre.**

†**Epicera·stic,** *a. rare.* 1684. [– Gr. ἐπικεραστικός, f. ἐπικεραννύναι to temper.] Emollient. Also as *sb.* in *pl.*

Epicerebral (epise·rībrăl), *a.* [f. EPI- + CEREBRAL.] *Anat.* Situated upon the brain.

‖**Epicheirema** (e:pikəirī·mă). 1721. [mod. L. – Gr. ἐπιχείρημα lit. 'an attempt', f. ἐπιχειρεῖν undertake, f. ἐπί EPI- + χείρ hand.] A name given to a syllogism when to either premiss, or to both, is annexed a reason implying the existence of a prosyllogism. In Aristotle the word denotes a dialectical proof, which is something short of a demonstrated conclusion.

Epichile (e·pikəil). [– mod. L. *epichilium,* f. Gr. ἐπί EPI- + χεῖλος lip, rim.] *Bot.* 'The upper half of the lid of an orchid, when that organ is once jointed or strangulated' (*Treas. Bot.*).

Epichordal (epikǭ·ɹdăl), *a.* [f. EPI- + CHORD + -AL[1].] *Anat.* Situated upon or about the intercranial part of the notochord; applied to certain segments of the brain.

Epichorial (epikōᵊ·riăl), *a.* 1840. [f. Gr. ἐπιχώριος in or of the country + -AL[1].] Proper to a country or district.

The local or e. superstitions from every district DE QUINCEY.

Epichristian (epikri·styăn), *a.* 1840. [f. EPI- + CHRISTIAN.] Pertaining to the age not long after Christ.

‖**Epiclesis, -klesis** (epiklī·sis). 1878. [Gr. ἐπίκλησις, f. ἐπικαλεῖν call upon.] In some Christian liturgies, a part of the prayer of consecration in which the Holy Spirit is invoked.

Epiclinal (epikləi·năl), *a.* [f. Gr. ἐπί EPI- + κλίνη couch + -AL[1].] *Bot.* 'Placed upon the disk or receptacle of a flower' (*Treas. Bot.*).

Epicœle (e·pisīl). 1877. [f. EPI- + Gr. κοιλία the cavity of the belly.] In the Tunicata, a kind of perivisceral cavity, formed by an invagination of the ectoderm. **Epicœ·lous** *a.*

Epicolic (epikǫ·lik), *a.* [f. EPI- + Gr. κόλον COLON + -IC.] *Anat.* Of or pertaining to the region over, or beside, the colon.

Epico·ndyle. 1836. [– Fr. *épicondyle,* mod.L. *epicondylus* (Chaussier, *c*1820); see EPI-, CONDYLE.] *Anat.* The external CONDYLE of the humerus.

Epicoracoid (epikǫ·răkoid). 1839. [f. EPI- + CORACOID.] **A.** *adj.* A bone, or pair of bones, found in reptiles, etc., and forming a continuation of the coracoid. **B.** *sb.* The epicoracoid bone. Hence **Epico:racoi·dal** *a.*

Epicorolline (epiko·rǫlin, -əin), *a.* [f. EPI- + COROLLA + -INE[1].] *Bot.* Inserted in or upon the corolla.

Epicotyl (epikǫ·til). 1880. [f. EPI- + COTYLE.] *Bot.* The stem immediately above the cotyledons.

Epicotyle·donary, *a.* 1884. [f. EPI- + COTYLEDON + -ARY[1].] *Bot.* Immediately above the cotyledons.

Epicranial (epikrēⁱ·niăl), *a.* 1831. [f. EPI- + CRANIUM + -AL[1].] *Anat.* Pertaining to the epicranium.

‖**Epicranium** (epikrēⁱ·niŏm). 1888. [mod. L., f. Gr. ἐπί EPI- + κρανίον CRANIUM.] *Anat.* All that overlies the cranium; the scalp. **b.** In insects: The upper surface of the head.

†‖**Epicra·sis.** [mod.L. – Gr. ἐπίκρασις, f. ἐπικεραννύναι to temper; see EPICERASTIC.] The use of epicerastics. HAKEWILL.

Epicure (e·pikiuɹ), *sb.* 1545. [– med.L. *epicurus,* one whose chief happiness is in carnal pleasure; appellative use of L. *Epicurus,* Gr. Ἐπίκουρος name of an Athenian philosopher *c*300 B.C.] †**1.** A follower of Epicurus; an EPICUREAN –1722. †**b.** *loosely,* One who disbelieves in the divine government of the world and in a future life –1691. †**2.** One who gives himself up to sensual pleasures; a glutton, a sybarite –1774. **3.** One who cultivates a refined taste for the pleasures of the table. (The current sense.) Also *transf.* 1586.

3. *transf.* The little E., the Bee BP. STILLINGFL. An e. in words 1872. Hence †**E·picure** *v.* to indulge as an e.

Epicurean (e:pikiurī·ăn). 1572. [– Fr. *épicurien,* or L. *epicureus* = Gr. ἐπικούρειος, f. Ἐπίκουρος; see prec., -EAN.]

A. *adj.* **1.** Of or pertaining to Epicurus, or to his system of philosophy 1586. **2.** Devoted to the pursuit of pleasure. Now chiefly: Devoted to refined sensuous enjoyment. 1641.

1. It was no E. speech of an Epicure BURTON. The Atomical or E. Hypothesis BP. STILLINGFL. **2.** The sober majesties Of settled, sweet, E. life TENNYSON.

B. *sb.* **1.** A disciple of Epicurus 1605. **2.** One who makes pleasure the object of his life 1572.

1. The very Epicureans allowed the being of gods BP. BERKELEY. **2.** A voluptuary and an e. SCOTT.

†**Epicu·reous, -ious, E·picurish** (*rare*) *adjs.*

Epicureanism (e:pikiurī·ăniz'm). 1751. [f. prec. + -ISM.] **1.** The philosophical system of Epicurus. **2.** Adherence to the principles of Epicurus; hence, devotion to a life of ease and luxury. Also *transf.* 1847.

Epicurism (e·pikiuri:z'm). 1575. [Partly f. L. *Epicurus,* after Fr. *épicurisme*; partly f. EPICURE + -ISM.] **1.** The philosophical system of Epicurus, and allied doctrines; attachment to such doctrines. Now usu. EPICUREANISM. 1575. †**2.** The pursuit of pleasure; sensuality; gluttony –1775. **3.** The disposition and habits of an epicure. Also *transf.* 1619.

2. Epicurisme and Lust Make it [our Court] more like a Tauerne, or a Brothell Than a grac'd Pallace SHAKS. So †**Epicurist** = EPICUREAN *sb.*

†**Epi·curize,** *v.* 1621. [f. L. *Epicurus* (or EPICURE) + -IZE. Cf. late L. *epicurizare* (v.).] **1.** *intr.* To profess or practise the doctrines of Epicurus –1688. **2.** To play the epicure. Const. *on.* Also *fig.* –1711.

Epicycle (e·pisəik'l), *sb.* ME. [–(O)Fr. *épicycle* or late L. *epicyclus* – Gr. ἐπίκυκλος; see EPI-, CYCLE *sb.*] **1.** A small circle, having its centre on the circumference of another circle. Chiefly *Astron.*

In the Ptolemaic system each of the 'seven planets' was supposed to move in an epicycle, the centre of which moved along a greater circle called a deferent. This conception is still oocas. used with reference to the geocentric hypothesis.

2. *Mod. Astron.* The curve described by a planet moving in an epicycle, *i.e.* its geocentric path 1854.

Epicyclic, -al (episi·klik, -ăl), *a.* 1837. [f. prec. + -IC; see -ICAL.] Of or pertaining to epicycles.

Phr. *E. train*: one in which the axes of the wheels revolve around a common centre.

Epicycloid (episəi·kloid). 1790. [f. EPICYCLE + -OID.] A curve generated by a point in the circumference of a movable circle, which revolves on the exterior of a fixed circle; formerly called an *exterior epicycloid,* and dist. from the *interior epicycloid* (now *hypocycloid*). Hence **E:picycloi·dal** *a.* of the form or nature of an e.

Epideictic, -ktic (epidəi·ktik), *a.* Also **epidictic.** 1790. [– Gr. ἐπιδεικτικός, f. ἐπί- EPI- + δεικνύναι to show.] Adapted for display; chiefly of set orations. Hence **Epidei·ctical** *a.*

Epidemic (epide·mik). 1603. [– Fr. *épidémique,* f. *épidémie* (whence EPIDEMY) – late L. *epidemia* – Gr. ἐπιδημία prevalence of a disease, f. ἐπιδήμιος, f. ἐπί EPI- + δῆμος people; see DEMOS, -IC.]

A. *adj.* **1.** Of a disease: 'Prevalent among a people or a community at a special time, and produced by some special causes not generally present in the affected locality' (*Syd. Soc. Lex.*). †**2.** Widely prevalent, universal –1745.

1. E. diseases BACON, fever COWPER. *fig.* The e. terror of an imaginary danger SCOTT. **2.** A toleration of epidemick whordom MILTON.

B. *sb.* An epidemic disease; also *fig.* 1757.

fig. An epidemick of despair BURKE.

var. †**Epide·mial** *a.* (in sense A. 1). Hence **E:pidemi·city,** e. quality.

Epidemical (epide·mikăl), *a.* 1621. [f. prec. + -AL[1]; see -ICAL.] **1.** Epidemic; also, characterized by epidemics. †**2.** = EPIDEMIC A. 2. –1813. Hence **Epide·mical-ly** *adv.*, **-ness.**

Epidemiography (e:pidī:mi,ǫ·grăfi). [f. Gr. ἐπιδήμιος (see EPIDEMIC) + -GRAPHY.] A treatise on, or history of, epidemic diseases. Hence **E:pide:mio·graphist,** a writer on e.

Epidemiology (epidī:mi,ǫ·lŏdʒi). 1873. [f. as prec. + -LOGY.] That branch of medical science which treats of epidemics. Hence **Epide:miolo·gical** *a.* of or pertaining to e. **Epide:mio·logist,** one who studies e.

†**Epidemy.** 1472. [– OFr. *ypidime, impidemie,* (also mod.) *épidémie*; see EPIDEMIC, -Y[3].] An epidemic disease –1809.

Epidendral (epide·ndrăl), *a.* 1882. [f. EPI- + Gr. δένδρον + -AL[1].] *Bot.* That grows upon trees. So **Epide·ndric** *a.*

Epiderm (e·pidəɹm). 1835. [– Fr. *épiderme* – late L. *epidermis,* mod.L. *epiderma.*] = EPIDERMIS. Hence **Epide·rmal** *a.* of or pertaining to the epidermis.

†‖**Epide·rma.** 1582. [mod.L. *epiderma,* alt. of late L. *epidermis,* after Gr. δέρμα skin.] = EPIDERMIS.

Epidermatoid (epidō·ɹmătoid), *a.* [f. as next + -OID.] Resembling an epidermis. (Dicts.)

Epidermatous (epidō·ɹmătəs), *a.* [f. EPI- + Gr. δέρμα (δερματ-) + -OUS.] Pertaining to the epidermis.

Epide·rmic 1830, †**-ical** 1693, *adjs.* [f. EPIDERM + -IC, -ICAL.] Of, pertaining to, or of the nature of an epidermis. **-ically** *adv.*

Epidermis (epidō·ɹmis). 1626. [– late L. *epidermis* – Gr. ἐπιδερμίς (Hippocrates), f. ἐπί EPI- + δέρμα skin.] **1.** *Anat.* The outer (non-vascular) layer of the skin; the cuticle or scarf-skin. **b.** = ECTODERM. (Huxley.) **2.** *Conch.* The outer animal integument of a shell 1755. **3.** *Bot.* 'The true skin of a plant below the cuticle' (*Treas. Bot.*) 1813.

Epidermoid (epidō·ɹmoid), *a.* 1835. [f. EPIDERM + -OID.] Of the nature of epidermis. So **E:pidermoi·dal** *a.*

Epide·rmose. 1847. [f. EPIDERM + -OSE[1].] *Chem.* The insoluble matter in the epidermis.

Epidiascope (epidəi·ăskōᵘp). 1903. [f. EPI- + DIA-[1] + -SCOPE.] A kind of magic lantern for projecting images of both opaque and transparent objects. Hence **Epidiasco·pic** *a.*

Epidictic, obs. f. EPIDEICTIC.

Epididymis (epidi·dĭmis). 1610. [– Gr. ἐπιδιδυμίς, f. ἐπί EPI- + δίδυμοι testicles.] *Anat.* A long narrow structure attached to the dorsal surface of the testicle, and consisting chiefly of coils of the efferent duct. Hence **Epidi·dymal** *a.* pertaining to the e. **E:pididymi·tis,** *Path.* inflammation of the e.

Epidi·orite. [f. EPI- + DIORITE.] *Min.* A mineral differing from diorite in that the hornblende it contains is fibrous.

Epidote (e·pidoᵘt). 1808. [– Fr. *épidote*, f. Gr. ἐπιδιδόναι superadd.] *Min.* A mineral common in many crystalline rocks, consisting largely of the silicate of iron and lime. It usually takes the form of flattened needles, and has a yellowish-green (pistachio) colour. Hence **Epido·tic** *a.* **E:pidoti·ferous** *a.* containing e.

Epigæous, var. of EPIGEOUS.

†**Epiga·ster.** 1653. [– Fr. *épigastre*; see EPIGASTRIUM.] = EPIGASTRIUM.

Epigastric (epigæ·strik), *a.* 1656. [f. EPIGASTRIUM + -IC. Cf. Fr. *épigastrique.*] Of or pertaining to the epigastrium. So **Epiga·strial** *a.*

Epigastriocele (epigæ·striosīːl). [f. Gr. ἐπιγάστριος over the belly + κήλη tumour.] *Path.* An abdominal hernia near the epigastrium.

‖**Epigastrium** (epigæ·striŏm). 1681. [Late L. *epigastrion* – Gr. ἐπιγάστριον, subst. use of n. sing. of ἐπιγάστριος, f. ἐπί EPI- + γαστήρ belly.] *Anat.* 'That part of the abdomen which is immediately over the stomach' (*Syd. Soc. Lex.*).

Epigeal (epidʒī·ăl). = EPIGEOUS. (Dicts.)

Epigee (e·pidʒī). [– Gr. ἐπίγειον (Ptolemy), subst. use of n. sing. of ἐπίγειος adj., f. ἐπί upon, near to + γῆ earth. Cf. PERIGEE.] = PERIGEE. (Dicts.)

Epigene (e·pidʒīn), *a.* 1823. [– Fr. *épigène*, – Gr. ἐπιγενής, f. ἐπί upon, after + -γενής born.] **1.** *Crystall.* Of crystals: Chemically altered in substance subsequently to their formation (Haüy). By some used for *pseudomorphous*. **2.** *Geol.* Produced on the surface of the earth; opp. to *hypogene*. GEIKIE.

Epigenesis (epidʒe·nĭsis). 1807. [f. Gr. ἐπί upon + γένεσις generation. Cf. Fr. *épigénèse.*] *Biol.* The formation of an organic germ as a new product.

Phr. *Theory of e.*: the theory that the germ is brought into existence (by successive accretions), and not merely developed, in the process of reproduction. (The opposite theory is now spoken of variously as the theory of 'preformation', of 'encasement', or of 'emboîtement'.)

Hence **Epige·nesist**, one who holds the theory of e. **E:pigene·tic** *a.* of or pertaining to, or of the nature of, e. **Epigene·tically** *adv.*

Epigenist (ĭpi·dʒĭnist). 1875. [f. EPIGEN(ESIS + -IST.] = EPIGENESIST.

Epigenous (ĭpi·dʒĭnəs), *a.* 1866. [f. as prec. + -OUS.] *Bot.* 'Growing upon the surface of a part, as many fungals on the surface of leaves' (*Treas. Bot.*).

Epigeous (epidʒī·əs), *a.* 1835. [f. Gr. ἐπίγειος (f. ἐπί upon + γῆ earth) + OUS.] Of plants: Growing on the ground.

†**E·piglot.** 1547. Anglicized f. EPIGLOTTIS –1594.

Epiglottis (epiglǫ·tis). 1615. [– Gr. ἐπιγλωττίς, f. ἐπί upon + γλῶττα tongue. Cf. GLOTTIS.] 'The erect, leaf-like cartilage at the root of the tongue, which during the act of swallowing is depressed, and forms a lid, or cover for the glottis' (*Syd. Soc. Lex.*). Hence **Epiglo·ttic, E:piglotti·dean** *adjs.* of or pertaining to the e.

Epigone[1] (e·pigoᵘn). *rare.* 1865. [In pl. – Fr. *épigones* – L. *epigoni* – Gr. ἐπίγονοι, pl. of ἐπίγονος born afterwards, f. ἐπί upon, after + -γονος, f. γίγνεσθαι be born.] One of a succeeding (and less distinguished) generation. Applied *esp.* to the sons of the 'Seven against Thebes'; and hence allusively.

Epigone[2] (e·pigoᵘn). 1866. [– mod.L. *epigonium*, f. Gr. ἐπί upon + γονή, γόνος seed.] *Bot.* The membranous bag which encloses the spore-case of a liverwort or scale-moss when young.

Epigram (e·pigræm). 1538. [– Fr. *épigramme* or L. *epigramma* – Gr. ἐπίγραμμα, f. ἐπί EPI- + γράφειν write.] †**1.** = EPIGRAPH 1. –1699. **2.** A short poem leading up to and ending in a witty or ingenious turn of thought 1538. **3.** A pointed or antithetical saying 1796. **b.** Epigrammatical expression 18 . . .

1. The E., that was written upon the public Sepulchre at Athens BENTLEY. **2.** The force and vertue of an e. is in the conclusion TOPSELL. **3.** He [Bacon] liked. . to generalise in shrewd and sometimes cynical epigrams 1884.

†**E:pigrammata·rian.** 1597. [f. late L. *epigrammatarius* (f. *epigrammat-*; see next) + -AN; see -ARIAN.] A writer of epigrams –1607.

Epigrammatic, -al (e:pigrămæ·tik, -ăl), *a.* 1605. [– late L. *epigrammaticus* adj., f. *epigrammat-*, stem of L. *epigramma* EPIGRAM; see -IC, -ATIC, -ICAL.] Of or pertaining to epigrams; of the nature, or in the style, of an epigram; concise, pointed.

The sting is very e. H. WALPOLE. Smart e. speeches EMERSON. E. terseness BANCROFT. Hence **E:pigramma·tically** *adv.* So **Epigra·mmatism**, e. style. **Epigra·mmatist**, a maker of epigrams.

Epigrammatize (epigræ·mătəiz), *v.* 1691. [f. as prec. + -IZE.] **1.** *intr.* To compose epigrams; to write or speak in an epigrammatic style 1811. **2.** *trans.* To express epigrammatically 1691. **3.** To make the subject of an epigram 1862.

1. Men do not e. . .with the bitterness of Voltaire 1872. Hence **Epigra·mmatizer.**

‖**Epigramme** (epigram). 1736. [Fr.; app. a fanciful use of *épigramme* = EPIGRAM.] A small cutlet, dressed in a certain way.

Epigraph (e·pigrɑf). 1624. [– Gr. ἐπιγραφή, f. ἐπιγράφειν write upon, f. ἐπί upon + γράφειν write.] **1.** An inscription; *esp.* one placed upon a building, tomb, statue, etc., to indicate its name or purpose; a legend on a coin. †**2.** The superscription of a letter, book, etc.; the imprint on a title-page –1826. **3.** The short quotation or motto placed at the commencement of a book, a chapter, etc. 1844.

1. And this E., *Quid me Persequeris* EVELYN. **2.** Geneva was adopted for the e. of the title-page 1812. Hence **E·pigraph** *v.* to furnish with an e. **Epigra·phic, -al** *a.* **Epigra·phically** *adv.*

Epigraphy (ĭpi·grăfi). 1851. [f. prec. + -Y[3]; see -GRAPHY.] **1.** Inscriptions collectively. **2.** The science concerned with the interpretation, classification, etc. of inscriptions. Often, the palæography of inscriptions. 1863. Hence **Epi·grapher, Epi·graphist,** a student of, or authority on, inscriptions.

Epigynous (ĭpi·dʒinəs), *a.* 1830. [f. mod. L. *epigynus* (Jussieu), f. Gr. ἐπί on + γυνή woman (used for 'pistil'); see -OUS.] *Bot.* Placed upon the ovary; growing upon the summit of the ovary. Said of the stamens or corolla. Hence **Epi·gyny,** e. character or quality.

Epihyal (epihəi·ăl), *a.* 1854. [f. EPI- + HY(OID + -AL[1].] *Anat.* That is placed upon the hyoid bone. Applied to the upper part of the hyoid arch; also, to a bone found in certain fishes.

†**E·piky.** 1508. [– med.L. *epikeia, epieikeia* equity (XIV) – Gr. ἐπιείκεια reasonableness. Cf. OFr. *epyeykie.*] Reasonableness, equity –1549.

Epilate (e·pileᶦt), *v.* 1886. [f. Fr. *épiler* (see -ATE[3]), after DEPILATE.] *trans.* To pull out (hair). Hence **Epila·tion.**

†**E·pileny.** [– Gr. ἐπιλήνιον (μέλος), f. ἐπί + ληνός wine-vat.] A song in praise of wine; a drinking song. MOTTEUX.

Epilepsy (e·pilepsi). 1578. [– Fr. *épilepsie* or late L. *epilepsia* – Gr. ἐπιληψία, f. ἐπιλαβ-, stem of ἐπιλαμβάνειν seize upon, attack, f. ἐπί EPI- + λαμβάνειν take hold of.] *Path.* A disease of the nervous system, characterized by paroxysms, in which the patient falls to the ground unconscious, with general spasm of the muscles, and foaming at the mouth; the *falling sickness*. var. †**E·pilency;** whence †**Epile·ntic** *a.*

Epileptic (epile·ptik). 1605. [– Fr. *épileptique* – late L. *epilepticus* – Gr. ἐπιληπτικός; see prec., -IC.]

A. *adj.* **1.** Of, pertaining to, or of the nature of, epilepsy 1608. **2.** Affected with epilepsy 1605.

2. A plague vpon your Epilepticke visage SHAKS.

B. *sb.* **1.** An epileptic person 1651. **2.** In *pl.* Medicines for epilepsy. (Dicts.)

Hence **Epile·ptical** *a.* (in sense A. 1); also *fig.* **Epile·ptiform** *a.* resembling epilepsy. **Epile·ptoid** *a.* resembling, or of the nature of, epilepsy.

Epilobe (e·piloᵘb). 1861. [– mod.L. *epilobium* (also used), f. Gr. ἐπί upon + λοβός lobe, pod, capsule; named with reference to the position of the corolla.] *Bot.* A plant of the genus *Epilobium* (N.O. *Onagraceæ*): *e.g.* the Willow-herb.

†**Epi·logate,** *v.* 1652. [f. Fr. *épiloguer* – med.L. *epilogare*; see EPILOGUE, -ATE[3].] To speak the epilogue of (a play). Hence †**Epiloga·tion,** a final summing up.

†**Epilogism.** 1646. [– Gr. ἐπιλογισμός, f. ἐπιλογίζεσθαι reckon over or in addition; also, EPILOGIZE.] **1.** Computation; *concr.* number reckoned; also, excess in reckoning. **2.** Something said by way of epilogue 1671.

Epilogize (ĭpi·lŏdʒəiz), *v.* 1623. [– Gr. ἐπιλογίζεσθαι, f. ἐπίλογος; see next, -IZE.] *intr.* To serve as an epilogue; also, to write or speak an epilogue. *trans.* To put an epilogue to.

Epilogue (e·pilǫg), *sb.* 1564. [– (O)Fr. *épilogue* – L. *epilogus* – Gr. ἐπίλογος, f. ἐπί EPI- + λόγος speech; see -LOGUE.] †**1.** *Rhet.* The peroration of a speech; a summary 1644. **2.** The concluding part of a literary work; an appendix 1564. **3.** A speech or short poem addressed to the spectators by one of the actors after a play is over. Also *transf.* and *fig.* 1590.

3. No E., I pray you; for your play needs no excuse SHAKS. Hence **Epilo·gic, -al** *a.* pertaining to, or like, an e. **Epi·logist**, the writer or speaker of an e. **E:pilogi·stic** *a.* of the nature of an e.

†**Epiloguize** (ĭpi·lŏgəiz), *v.* 1634. [f. prec. + -IZE.] *intr.* To deliver an epilogue, or speak as though delivering one. *trans.* To put an epilogue to. –1750.

Epimeron (epimīᵊ·rǫn). *Pl.* **epimera.** 1872. [f. Gr. ἐπί upon + μηρός thigh.] *Anat.* That part of the lateral wall of a somite of a crustacean which is situated between the articulation of the appendage and the pleuron. Hence **Epime·ral** *a.* of or pertaining to the e.

Epimyth (e·pimiþ). 1866. [– Gr. ἐπιμύθιον, subst. use of n. of ἐπιμύθιος coming after the fable, f. ἐπί EPI- + μῦθος fable.] The moral of a fable.

Epinasty (e·pinæsti). 1880. [f. EPI- + Gr. ναστός, (f. νάσσειν squeeze close) + -Y[3].] *Bot.* (See quot.)

The term e. . .implies that the upper surface of an organ grows more quickly than the lower surface, and thus causes it to bend down 1880. Hence **Epina·stic** *a.* of the nature of, or influenced by, e.

Epineural (epiniū·răl), *a.* 1866. [f. EPI- + NEURAL.] *Anat.* Situated upon a neural arch, as a spine of a fish's backbone. Also quasi-*sb.*

‖**Epinglette.** 1853. [Fr., dim. of *épingle* pin; see -ETTE.] 'An iron needle with which the cartridge of any large piece of ordnance is pierced before it is primed' (Stocqueler).

Epinician (epini·siăn), *a.* 1652. [f. next + -AN.] Celebrating victory. vars. †**Epini·cial, Epini·kian.**

Epinicion (epini·siǫn). Also **epinikion, epinicium.** 1613. [– Gr. ἐπινίκιον, subst. use of n. of adj. ἐπινίκιος, f. ἐπί upon + νίκη victory.] In Greece, an ode in honour of a victor in the games; also generally.

†‖**Epinyctis** (epini·ktis). 1676. [mod.L. – Gr. ἐπινυκτίς, f. ἐπί EPI- + νύξ night.] *Med.* A pustule which is most painful by night.

Epiotic (epi,ǫ·tik), *a.* 1870. [f. Gr. ἐπί upon + οὖς, ὠτός ear + -IC.] *Anat.* Situated above the ear; epithet of one of the three bones which together form the periotic bone. Also quasi-*sb.*

†**E:pipedo·metry.** 1706. [f. Gr. ἐπίπεδος, in *Geom.* = plane, superficial, + -METRY.] Explained in Dicts. as 'The mensuration of figures standing on the same base'.

Epiperipheral (e:pipĕri·fĕrăl), *a.* [f. EPI- + PERIPHERY + -AL[1].] Of sensations: Externally initiated. H. SPENCER.

Epipetalous (epipe·tăləs), *a.* 1845. [f. EPI- + PETAL + -OUS.] *Bot.* Of stamens: 'United separately to the corolla' (Bentley).

Epiphanous (ĭpi·fănəs), *a.* [f. Gr. ἐπιφανής + -OUS; cf. next.] Resplendent. LAMB.

Epiphany[1] (ĭpi·făni). ME. [- (O)Fr. *épiphanie* - eccl.L. *epiphania* - eccl.Gr. ἐπιφάνια, n. pl. of *ἐπιφάνιος, f. ἐπιφαίνειν to manifest, f. ἐπί EPI- + φαίνειν show; see -Y[3].] *Eccl.* The festival commemorating the manifestation of Christ to the Gentiles in the persons of the Magi; observed on Jan. 6th, the 12th day after Christmas.

Epiphany[2] (ĭpi·făni). 1667. [- Gr. ἐπιφάνεια manifestation, appearance of a divinity, f. ἐπιφανής manifest, f. ἐπιφαίνειν (see prec.).] A manifestation or appearance of some divine or superhuman being. Also *transf.* and *fig.*

An e. of Vishnu F. HALL. Epiphanies of the Grecian intellect DE QUINCEY.

Epipharyngeal (e:pifări·ndʒĭăl), *a.* 1871. [f. Gr. ἐπί upon + φάρυγξ PHARYNX + *-eal* as in PHARYNGEAL.] Situated above the pharynx.

Epiphenomenon (e:pifĭnǫ·mĭnǫ̆n). 1706. [f. EPI- + PHENOMENON.] An additional phenomenon; *Path.* a secondary symptom.

‖**Epiphonema** (e:pifonī·mă). 1579. [L. - Gr. ἐπιφώνημα, f. ἐπιφωνεῖν call to.] **1.** *Rhet.* An exclamatory sentence or striking reflection, which sums up or concludes a discourse or a passage. **2.** Acclamation 1654.

1. The e. to the daughters of Jerusalem 1870. Hence **E:pipho:nema·tical** *a.*, **-ly** *adv.* var. †**E:piphone·me.**

‖**Epiphora** (epi·fŏra). 1657. [L. - Gr. ἐπιφορά a bringing to or upon.] **1.** A sudden afflux of humours; *esp.* a flow of an aqueous or serous humour from the eyes. **2.** *Rhet.* A figure in which one word is repeated impressively at the end of several sentences 1678. **3.** *Logic.* The conclusion of a syllogism or consequent of a hypothesis. (Dicts.)

Epiphragm (e·pifræm). 1854. [- mod.L. *epiphragma* - Gr. ἐπίφραγμα lid, f. ἐπί EPI- + φράγμα fence. Cf. DIAPHRAGM.] **1.** *Zool.* The secretion with which a snail closes the aperture of its shell during hibernation. **2.** *Bot.* A membrane closing the mouth of the spore-case in urn-mosses and fungi 1882.

†**Epiphy:llospe·rmous,** *a.* 1704. [f. EPI- + Gr. φύλλον leaf + σπέρμα seed + -OUS.] *Bot.* Having the seeds on the back of the leaves. Cf. DORSIFEROUS. -1760.

Epiphyllous (epifi·ləs), *a.* 1835. [f. EPI- + Gr. φύλλον leaf + -OUS.] *Bot.* That grows upon a leaf, as *epiphyllous fungi.*

‖**Epiphysis** (epi·fĭsis). Also (in Fr. form) **epiphyse.** *Pl.* **epiphyses.** 1634. [mod.L. - Gr. ἐπίφυσις, f. ἐπί EPI- + φύσις growth.] *Anat.* **1.** An extremity or other portion of a long bone originating in a separate centre of ossification; opp. to APOPHYSIS. **2.** *abstr.* The process of developing such a growth 1862. Hence **Epi·physary, Epiphy·sial** *adjs.* pertaining to, or of the nature of, an e.

Epiphyte (e·pifəit). 1847. [f. Gr. ἐπί upon + φυτόν plant.] **1.** *Bot.* A plant which grows on another plant; usually restricted to those which do not derive nutrition from other plants 1861. **2.** *Path.* A vegetable parasite on the surface of the animal body 1847.

Hence **Epiphy·tal** *a.* having the distinctive property of an e. **Epiphy·tic, -al** *a.* epiphytal. **Epiphy·tically** *adv.* **Epi·phytous** *a.* epiphytal.

Epipleural (epipliūə·răl), *a.* 1866. [f. Gr. ἐπίπλευρος (f. ἐπί upon + πλευρά rib) + -AL[1].] Situated upon a rib. Also quasi-*sb.*

‖**Epiplexis** (epiple·ksis). 1678. [Late L. - Gr. ἐπίπληξις, f. ἐπί upon + πλήσσειν strike.] *Rhet.* A figure of rhetoric which endeavours to convince by a kind of upbraiding. Hence †**Epiple·ctic** *a.* of the nature of e.

‖**Epiploce** (epi·plŏsi). 1678. [mod.L. - Gr. ἐπιπλοκή plaiting together.] *Rhet.* A figure by which one striking circumstance is added, in due gradation, to another. (Dicts.)

Epiplocele (epi·plosīl). 1721. [- Gr. ἐπιπλοκήλη, f. ἐπίπλοον (see next) + κήλη rupture.] *Path.* A hernia in which a part of the omentum is protruded.

Epiploön (epi·plŏ,ǫn). 1541. [mod.L. - Gr. ἐπίπλοον, f. ἐπιπλεῖν sail or float on.] The caul or omentum, a fatty membrane enwrapping the intestines. Hence **Epiplo·ic** *a.* of or pertaining to the e.

Epipodial (epipōᵘ·diăl), *a.* 1877. [f. EPIPODIUM + -AL[1].] Pertaining to or like the epipodium.

Epipodite (epi·pŏdəit). 1869. [f. next + -ITE[1] 3.] *Anat.* A long curved appendage to the basal joint of the anterior limbs of some Crustacea. Hence **Epi:podi·tic** *a.* like an e.

Epipodium (epipōᵘ·diŏm). *Pl.* **-a.** 1866. [mod.L. - Gr. ἐπιπόδιον, subst. use of n. of adj. ἐπιπόδιος, f. ἐπί upon + πούς, ποδ- foot.] **1.** *Zool.* A lobe developed from the lateral and upper surfaces of the foot of some molluscs 1877. **2.** *Bot.* A form of disc consisting of glands upon the stipe of an ovary; also, the stalk of the disc.

Epipolic (epipǫ·lik), *a.* 1845. [f. Gr. ἐπιπολή surface + -IC.] *Physics.* **a.** Of, pertaining to, or taking place upon the surface. **b.** Of or pertaining to epipolism. Hence **Epi·polism,** e. dispersion; = FLUORESCENCE. **Epi·polize** *v.* to change into the e. condition; to cause to exhibit the phenomena of fluorescence.

Epipterous (ĭpi·ptĕrəs), *a.* 1866. [f. Gr. ἐπί upon + πτερόν wing + -OUS.] *Bot.* Of seeds: Bearing wings at the summit.

Epirhizous (epirəi·zəs), *a.* 1866. [f. Gr. ἐπί upon + ῥίζα root + -OUS.] *Bot.* Growing on a root.

†**Epi·rot.** [- Gr. ἠπειρώτης, f. ἤπειρος mainland; see -OT[2].] One who dwells inland. JER. TAYLOR.

Episcleral (episklīə·răl), *a.* 1861. [f. EPI- + Gr. σκληρός hard + -AL[1].] *Anat.* Belonging to or placed upon the sclerotic coat of the eye.

Episcleritis (e:pisklīərəi·tis). 1861. [f. as prec. + -ITIS.] Inflammation of the connective tissue covering the sclerotic coat of the eye.

Episcopable (ĭpi·skŏpăb'l), *a.* 1676. [f. EPISCOPATE *v.* + -ABLE.] Capable of being made a bishop.

Episcopacy (ĭpi·skŏpăsi). 1647. [f. eccl.L. *episcopatus* EPISCOPATE *sb.*, after *prelacy*; see -ACY.] †1. Supervision 1659. **2.** Government of the church by bishops; the system of church government which comprises three distinct orders, bishops, priests, and deacons 1647. **3.** The office, or period of tenure, of a bishop. Now *rare.* 1660. **4.** *concr.* The body of bishops 1757.

3. Aldhelm died..in the fifth year of his e. LINGARD. **4.** An aggressive e. 1885.

Episcopal (ĭpi·skŏpăl). 1485. [- (O)Fr. *épiscopal* or eccl.L. *episcopalis*, f. *episcopus* BISHOP; see -AL[1].]

A. *adj.* **1.** Of or pertaining to a bishop or bishops, or to episcopacy; †advocating episcopacy. **2.** Of a church: Governed by bishops. Often *spec.* (with capital E) of the Anglican Church; also of other bodies, specialized as *Methodist E.*, *Reformed E.*, etc. Hence of buildings: Belonging to such a church. 1752.

1. An E. See 1675. E. government 1704. **2.** The established clergy were e: HUME. The e. chapel 1806.

†**B.** *sb.* = EPISCOPALIAN -1823.

Hence **Epi·scopally** *adv.*

Episcopalian (ĭpi:skopēᵢ·liăn). 1738. [f. prec. + -IAN.]

A. *adj.* **1.** Belonging to an episcopal (*esp.* the Anglican) church 1768. **2.** Of an episcopal character (*rare*) 1822.

B. *sb.* **a.** An adherent of episcopacy. **b.** One who belongs to an episcopal church. 1738.

Hence **Episcopa·lianism**, the principles of an E. as such.

Episcopalism (ĭpi·skŏpăli:zm). [f. as prec. + -ISM.] That theory of church polity which places the supreme authority in the hands of an episcopal or pastoral order, and regards any recognized head of the church who exercises this authority as merely the delegate of this order. Held in the Church of Rome by the Gallicans, but rejected by the Vatican Council in 1870.

†**Epi·scopant.** [- *episcopant-*, pres. ppl. stem of late and med.L. *episcopare*; see EPISCOPATE *v.*, -ANT.] A bishop. MILTON.

†**Episcopa·rian.** 1649. [Modification of *episcopalian*; see -ARIAN.]

A. *adj.* Of or pertaining to episcopacy - 1691.

B. *sb.* An adherent of episcopacy -1691.

Episcopate (ĭpi·skŏpĕt), *sb.* 1641. [- eccl.L. *episcopatus*, f. *episcopus* BISHOP + *-atus* -ATE[1].] **1.** The office or dignity of a bishop. **2.** An episcopal see 1807. **3.** The time a bishop holds office 1868. **4.** The body of bishops 1842.

†**Epi·scopate,** *v.* 1641. [- *episcopat-*, pa. ppl. stem of late L. (be a bishop) and med.L. (be a bishop, make a bishop of) *episcopare*, f. eccl.L. *episcopus* BISHOP; see -ATE[3]. Cf. BISHOP *v.*[1]] To make, or become, a bishop; also, to act as a bishop -1705.

†**Epi·scopici:de.** *rare.* 1692. [f. eccl.L. *episcopus* + -CIDE 2. Cf. med.L. *episcopicida.*] The murdering of a bishop -1751.

Episcopize (ĭpi·skŏpəiz), *v.* 1649. [f. eccl.L. *episcopus* bishop + -IZE; cf. EPISCOPATE *v.*] **1.** *trans.* To make or consecrate (a person) a bishop. Also *absol.* **2.** To rule as a bishop; also *intr.* 1679. **3.** To render Episcopalian 1767. **Epi:scopiza·tion** (*rare*).

Episcopy (ĭpi·skŏpi). 1641. [- Gr. ἐπισκοπία overseeing (whence eccl.L. *episcopia*), f. ἐπίσκοπος overseer; see -Y[3].] †**1.** Survey; superintendence. MILTON. †**2.** Government of the church by bishops. JER. TAYLOR. **3.** The bench of bishops 1874.

Epise·palous, *a.* 1882. [f. EPI- + SEPAL + -OUS.] *Bot.* Growing upon the sepals.

Episiorrhaphy (e:pisəi,ǫ·răfi). 1872. [f. Gr. ἐπίσειον the region of the pubes + -ραφία, f. ῥάπτειν sew.] *Surg.* An operation for the relief of prolapsus uteri by a suture.

Episkeletal (episke·lĭtăl), *a.* 1871. [f. EPI- + SKELETON + -AL[1].] *Anat.* Of muscles: Situated upon the skeleton, *i.e.* epaxial.

Episodal (e·pisōᵘdăl), *a.* 1876. [f. next + -AL[1].] = EPISODIC.

Episode (e·pisoᵘd). 1678. [- Gr. ἐπεισόδιον, subst. use of n. of ἐπεισόδιος coming in besides, f. ἐπί EPI- + εἴσοδος entrance, f. εἰς into + ὁδός way, passage. Cf. Fr. *épisode.*] **1.** In the Old Greek Tragedy, the interlocutory parts interpolated between two choric songs. **2.** An incidental narrative or digression in a poem, story, etc., separable from, but arising naturally out of, the main subject 1679. **3.** *transf.* An incidental passage in a person's life, in a history, etc. 1773. **4.** *Mus.* In ordinary fugues, a certain number of bars allowed to intervene from time to time before the subject is resumed 1869.

3. Like the Glacial e. before mentioned LYELL. Hence **Episo·dial, Episo·dic** *adjs.* of, pertaining to, or of the nature of an e.; incidental; casual. **Episo·dical** *a.* **Episo·dically** *adv.* by way of e.

Epispastic (epispæ·stik). 1657. [- mod.L. *epispasticus* - Gr. ἐπισπαστικός, f. ἐπισπᾶν, f. ἐπί towards + σπᾶν draw; see -IC.]

A. *adj.* Drawing out humours; blistering.

B. *sb.* A blister; a substance used for blistering 1675.

Episperm (e·pispəɹm). [f. EPI- + Gr. σπέρμα seed.] *Bot.* The outer covering of a seed.

Epispore (e·pispōəɹ). 1835. [f. EPI- + SPORE.] *Bot.* The outer membrane on the spore of a lichen or fern.

‖**Epistaxis** (epistæ·ksis). 1793. [mod.L. - Gr. ἐπίσταξις, f. ἐπιστάζειν bleed at the nose.] Bleeding from the nose.

Epistemology (e:pistĭmǫ·lŏdʒi). 1856. [f. ἐπιστημο-, comb. form of Gr. ἐπιστήμη knowledge, f. ἐπιστάναι know (how to do); see -LOGY.] The theory or science of the method or grounds of knowledge. Hence **E:pistemolo·gical** *a.*

†**E:pistemo·nical,** *a.* [f. Gr. ἐπιστημονικός capable of knowledge + -AL[1].] ?Capable of becoming an object of knowledge. CUDWORTH.

Episternum (epistə̄·ɹnŏm). 1855. [f. EPI- + STERNUM.] *Anat.* In mammals, the upper part of the sternum or breast-bone; in other animals, applied to various structures adjoining the breast. Hence **Episte·rnal** *a.* situate upon the sternum; also, pertaining to the e.; of the nature of an e.

‖**Epistho·tonos.** 1811. [erron. formation, after OPISTHOTONOS.] = EMPROSTHOTONOS.

Epistilbite (e:pisti·lbəit). 1826. [f. EPI- + STILBITE.] *Min.* A zeolitic mineral, a hydrous silicate of aluminium, calcium, and sodium.

Epistle (ĭpi·s'l), *sb.* OE. [ME. *epistle* – OFr. *epistle* (mod. *épître*) – L. *epistola* – Gr. ἐπιστολή, f. ἐπιστέλλειν send, esp. as a message, f. ἐπί EPI- + στέλλειν send. OE. *epistole* was directly from L.] **1.** A communication made to an absent person in writing; a letter. Chiefly applied to those letters written in ancient times which rank as literature. Now used only rhetorically, playfully, or sarcastically. **2.** *spec.* A letter from an apostle, forming part of the canon of Scripture ME. **3.** *Eccl. The Epistle:* The extract from an apostolical Epistle read in the Communion Service ME.

1. What seyth also the epistelle of Ouyde CHAUCER. Some obscure Epistles of Loue *Twel. N.* II. iii. 169. *Comb.*: **e.-side** (of the altar), the south side, from which the e. is read. Hence **Epi·stle** *v. trans.* to write as a preface (*rare*); †to write a letter to; to write in a letter. **Epi·stler**, one who writes an e.; also, = EPISTOLER 2.

†**Epistolar** (ĭpi·stŏlăɹ), *a.* 1579. [– L. *epistolaris*, f. *epistola*; see prec., -AR[1].] = EPISTOLARY –1715.

Epistolary (ĭpi·stŏlări), *a.* 1656. [– Fr. *épistolaire* or L. *epistolaris*; see prec., -ARY[2].] **1.** Of or pertaining to letters or letter-writing. **2.** Contained in, or carried on by, letters; of the nature of letters 1706.

1. I seek no e. fame SWIFT. **2.** Intercourse, personal and e. T. JEFFERSON. Hence **Epi:stola·rian** *a.* given to or occupied in letter-writing; *sb.* a letter-writer. var. **Epi·stolatory** *a.* (*arch.*)

Epistole·an. 18.. [irreg. f. L. *epistola* EPISTLE + -EAN.] A writer of epistles or letters.

Epistoler (ĭpi·stŏləɹ). 1530. [In sense 2 – OFr. *epistelier* or med.L. *epistolaris*, *-arius* (see -ER[2] 2); in sense 1 – Fr. †*épistolier.*] **1.** A letter-writer 1637. **2.** *Eccl.* One who reads the epistle.

Epi·stolet. [f. L. *epistola* + -ET. Cf. It. *epistoletta.*] A small epistle. LAMB.

†**Episto·lic**, *a.* 1741. [– Gr. ἐπιστολικός, f. ἐπιστολή; see EPISTLE.] **a.** = EPISTOLOGRAPHIC. **b.** = EPISTOLARY.

Hence †**Episto·lical** *a.* (in sense b).

†**Epi·stolist.** 1743. [f. L. *epistola* + -IST.] One who writes epistles –1853.

Epistolize (ĭpi·stŏləiz), *v.* 1634. [f. as prec. + -IZE.] **1.** *intr.* To write a letter. **2.** *trans.* To write a letter to 1739.

Hence **Epi·stolizable** *a.* that may form the subject of a letter. **Epi:stoliza·tion**, the writing of letters. **Epi·stolizer.**

Epistolographic (ĭpi:stŏlogræ·fik), *a.* 1699. [– Gr. ἐπιστολογραφικός, f. ἐπιστολή EPISTLE; see -GRAPHIC.] Used in the writing of letters; = DEMOTIC, ENCHORIAL, q.v. So **Epi:stolo·grapher, Epi:stolo·graphist**, a writer of letters. **Epi:stolo·graphy**, letter-writing.

Epistom(e (e·pistǫm, e·pistoᵘm). 1852. [– mod.L. *epistoma*, f. Gr. ἐπί upon + στόμα mouth.] *Zool.* An appendage in front of the mouth in Crustacea and certain insects.

‖**Epistrophe** (epi·strǫ̆fi). 1647. [mod.L. – Gr. ἐπιστροφή, f. ἐπιστρέφειν turn about; see EPI-, STROPHE.] *Rhet.* A figure in which each sentence or clause ends with the same word.

E...as 'we are born to sorrow, pass our time in sorrow, end our days in sorrow' 1845.

Epistyle (e·pistəil). 1615. [– Fr. *épistyle* or L. *epistylium* – Gr. ἐπιστύλιον, f. ἐπί EPI- + στῦλος pillar.] *Arch.* = ARCHITRAVE.

Episyllogism (episi·lŏdʒiz'm). 1860. [– mod.L. *episyllogismus*; see EPI- and SYLLOGISM.] *Logic.* A syllogism the major premiss of which is proved by a preceding syllogism, called in this relation the *prosyllogism.*

Epitactic (epitæ·ktik), *a.* 1845. [– Gr. ἐπιτακτικός, f. ἐπιτάσσειν enjoin.] Of the nature of an injunction.

Epitaph (e·pitɑf), *sb.* ME. [– (O)Fr. *épitaphe* – L. *epitaphium* funeral oration – Gr. ἐπιτάφιον, subst. use of n. of adj. ἐπιτάφιος, f. ἐπί EPI- + τάφος obsequies, tomb.] An inscription upon a tomb. Hence, occas., a brief composition written on the occasion of a person's death. Also *transf.* and *fig.*

Such a epitaphie as shall be devised by me or my executours 1520. A Booke of Epitaphes made upon the Death of Sir William Buttes 1583 (*title*).

Epitaph (e·pitɑf), *v.* 1592. [f. prec. sb.] **1.** *trans.* To describe in an epitaph (with *compl.*); to furnish with an epitaph. †**2.** *intr.* To speak or write as in an epitaph –1661.

1. Epitaph'd an honest man 1818. **2.** The commons..e. vpon him as on that Pope, 'He lived as a wolfe, and died as a dogge' BP. HALL. Hence **E·pita:pher**, the writer of an e.

Epitaphial (epitæ·fiăl), *a. rare.* 1862. [f. Gr. ἐπιτάφιος (see EPITAPH) + -AL[1].] Contained in sepulchral inscriptions.

The e. assertions of heathens LOWELL. So **Epita·phian** *a.* (MILTON), **Epita·phic, -al** *adjs.* pertaining to, or of the nature of, an epitaph. **E·pitaphist**, a writer of epitaphs.

‖**Epitasis** (epi·tăsis). 1589. [mod.L. – Gr. ἐπίτασις, f. ἐπιτείνειν intensify, f. ἐπί EPI- + τείνειν stretch.] 'That part of a play where the plot thickens' (Liddell and Scott). Hence †**Epita·tical** *a.* intensive (*rare*). †**Epita·tically** *adv.*

‖**Epithalamium** (e:pipălē[i]·miŏ̆m). Pl. **-iums, -ia.** 1595. [L. – Gr. ἐπιθαλάμιον, subst. use of n. of adj. ἐπιθαλάμιος, f. ἐπί EPI- + θάλαμος bridal chamber.] A nuptial song or poem in praise of the bride and bridegroom.

To sing Epithalamions to our marriage Feasts 1653. Hence **E:pithala·mial** *a.* of the nature of an e. **Epithala·miast** *rare*, a writer of an e. **E:pithala·mic** *a.* of or pertaining to an e. var. †**Epitha·lamy.**

‖**Epitheca** (epiþī·kă). 1861. [f. EPI- + THECA.] *Zool.* A continuous layer surrounding the thecæ in some corals.

Hence **Epithe·cal** *a.* of, or pertaining to, an e. **Epithe·cate** *a.* provided with an e.

‖**Epithelioma** (epiþī:li,ōᵘ·mă). *Pl.* **-mata.** 1872. [mod.L., f. next + -OMA.] *Path.* Epithelial cancer.

‖**Epithelium** (epiþī·liŏ̆m). 1748. [mod.L., f. Gr. ἐπί EPI- + θηλή teat, nipple; see -IUM.] **1.** *Anat.* A non-vascular tissue forming the outer layer of the mucous membrane in animals. **2.** *Bot.* An epidermis consisting of young thin-sided cells, filled with homogeneous transparent colourless sap. (*Treas. Bot.*) 1870.

Hence **Epithe·lial** *a.* of, pertaining to, or of the nature of, e. **Epithe·liate** *v.* to become covered with e., as a wound when beginning to heal. **Epithe·lioid** *a.* resembling e.

Epithem (e·piþĕm), *sb.* 1559. [– med.L. *epithema* – Gr. ἐπίθεμα, -θημα, remedy for external application, f. ἐπί EPI- + τιθέναι place.] *Med.* 'Any kind of moist, or soft, external application' (*Syd. Soc. Lex.*). Hence †**E·pithem** *v.* to put an e. upon. †‖**E:pithema·tion**, a small plaster.

‖**Epithesis.** [Gr. ἐπίθεσις, f. ἐπί EPI- + τιθέναι place; but Tourneur's meaning is obscure.]

And make his heart E. of sinne TOURNEUR.

Epithet (e·piþĕt), *sb.* 1579. [– Fr. *épithète* or L. *epitheton*, subst. use of n. of Gr. ἐπίθετος attributed, pa. ppl. adj. of ἐπιτιθέναι put on or to, f. ἐπί EPI- + τιθέναι place.] **1.** An adjective expressing some quality or attribute regarded as characteristic of a person or thing 1588. **2.** A significant appellation 1579. †**3.** A term, phrase, expression. SHAKS.

1. Hollow, empty—is the e. justly bestowed on Fame GEO. ELIOT. **2.** We..employ the French term ennui, for want of an equally appropriate e. in English SIR B. BRODIE. **3.** *Oth.* I. i. 14. Hence **E·pithet** *v.* to apply an e. to; to term. **Epithe·tic, -al** *a.* †full of epithets; pertaining to, or of the nature of, an e.; **-ly** *adv.* **E·pithetize** *v.* to apply an e. *to* (*rare*).

†‖**Epi·theton.** 1547. [L.; see prec.] **1.** An attribute. BP. HOOPER. **2.** = EPITHET 1, 2. –1720.

†**E·pithyme.** 1585. [– L. *epithymon* – Gr. ἐπίθυμον, f. ἐπί EPI- + θύμον THYME.] *Bot.* The *Cuscuta epithymum* or Dodder, a parasitic plant growing on thyme, etc. –1725.

Epithymetic (e:pi,þime·tik), *a.* Also **epithumetic.** 1631. [– Gr. ἐπιθυμητικός, f. ἐπιθυμεῖν to desire; see -IC.] Connected with desire or appetite. So †**Epithyme·tical** *a.*

†**Epi·tomate**, *v.* 1702. [– *epitomat-*, pa. ppl. stem of late L. *epitomare* abridge, f. L. *epitome*; see next, -ATE[3].] = EPITOMIZE. So **Epi:toma·tic** *a.* [badly f. EPITOME], pertaining to, or of the nature of, an epitome. **Epi·toma:tor**, one who epitomizes a larger work.

Epitome (ĭpi·tŏmi), *sb.* 1529. [– L. *epitome* – Gr. ἐπιτομή, f. ἐπιτέμνειν cut into, cut short; see EPI-, TOME.] **1.** A brief statement of the chief points of a larger work; an abridgement, abstract. **b.** A summary of anything; a compendium 1621. **2.** *transf.* A condensed record or representation in miniature 1593.

1. In general nothing is less attractive than an e. MACAULAY. **b.** To number his virtues is to give an e. of his life MRS. HUTCHINSON. **2.** The world's epitomy, man 1666. Hence †**Epi·tome** *v.* to make an e. **Epito·mic, -al** *a.* of the nature of an e. **Epi·tomist**, one who writes an e.

Epitomize (ĭpi·tŏməiz), *v.* 1599. [f. EPITOME *sb.* + -IZE.] **1.** *trans.* To make an epitome of; to abridge; to summarize; to concentrate. **2.** To comprise in brief 1628. †**3.** To reduce to a smaller scale –1713.

1. To e. Hooker D'ISRAELI, a pamphlet 1868. To e. the evidence of Theism E. CONDER. **2.** A Carpet, a Pan, and a Platter, epitomizes all their Furniture SIR T. HERBERT. Hence **Epi·tomi:zer.**

Epitonic (epitǫ·nik). 1879. [f. Gr. ἐπίτονος on the stretch (f. ἐπιτείνειν put a strain upon) + -IC.] Overstrained.

Epitrite (e·pitrəit). 1609. [– L. *epitritos* (Gellius) – Gr. ἐπίτριτος in the ratio of 4 to 3, lit. with the addition of one-third, f. ἐπί EPI- + τρίτος third.]

†**A.** *adj.* In the ratio of 4 to 3; *spec.* in ancient music.

B. *sb. Pros.* A foot consisting of three long syllables and one short one, and called first, second, third, or fourth epitrite, according as the short syllable stands first, second, third, or fourth 1678.

Epitrochoid (epitrǫ·koid). 1800. [f. Gr. ἐπί EPI- + τροχός wheel + -OID, after *epicycloid.*] *Math.* The curve described by a point rigidly connected with the centre of a circle which rolls on the outside of another circle. Cf. EPICYCLOID. Hence **Epitrochoi·dal** *a.*

‖**Epitrope** (epi·trŏ̆pi). 1657. [late L. – Gr. ἐπιτροπή, f. ἐπιτρέπειν give up, yield, f. ἐπί EPI- + τρέπειν turn.] *Rhet.* A figure by which permission is granted to an opponent, either seriously or ironically, to do what he proposes to do.

Epitympanic (e:pitimpæ·nik), *a.* 1849. [f. EPI- + Gr. τύμπανον drum + -IC.] *Anat.* Pertaining to or forming the uppermost subdivision of the tympanic pedicle which supports the mandible in fishes. Chiefly quasi-*sb.*

‖**Epizeuxis** (epiziū·ksis). 1589. [late L. – Gr. ἐπίζευξις (Rhet.) repetition of a word, f. ἐπιζευγνύναι, f. ἐπί EPI- + ζευγνύναι yoke.] *Rhet.* A figure by which a word is repeated with vehemence or emphasis.

‖**Epizoon** (epizōᵘ·ǫ̆n). *Pl.* **-oa.** 1836. [mod.L., f. Gr. ἐπί upon + ζῷον animal.] *Zool.* A parasite that lives on the exterior of the body of another animal. Opp. to ENTOZOON.

Hence **Epizo·al, Epizo·an** *adjs.* of or pertaining to epizoa. **Epizo·ic** *a.* of or pertaining to epizoa; living upon animals; *sb.* an epizoic disease.

Epizootic (e:pizo,ǫ·tik). 1748. [– Fr. *épizootique*, f. *épizootie*, irreg. f. Gr. ἐπί + ζῷον; see prec.]

A. *adj.* **1.** Of diseases: Temporarily prevalent among animals; opp. to *enzootic* 1865. †**2.** *Geol.* Containing animal remains, as *e. strata* –1840.

B. *sb.* An epizootic disease 1748.

Epizooty (epizōᵘ·ŏti). 1781. [– Fr. *épizootie*; see prec.] An epizootic disease.

Epoch (e·pǫk, ī·pǫk). 1614. [– mod.L. *epocha* – Gr. ἐποχή stoppage, station, fixed point of time, f. ἐπέχειν stop, take up a position, f. ἐπί EPI- + ἔχειν hold, *intr.* be in a certain state. Cf. Fr. *époque* (XVIII).]

I. A point of time. **1.** *Chron.* The initial point assumed in a system of chronology, or in reckoning a series of years; *e.g.* the date of the birth of Christ; an ERA. Now *rare.* **2.** The beginning of a new era or distinctive period in the history of anything 1673. †**b.** The date of origin of anything –1824. **3.** A fixed point of time 1661. **4.** *Astron.* An arbitrarily fixed date for which the elements necessary for computing the place of a heavenly body are tabulated. Also, the heliocentric longitude of a planet at such a date. 1726.

1. In divers..ages, divers epochs of time were used ABP. USSHER. The Epocha of the Olympiads 1726. 2. Men that mark out Epocha's 1673. The epochs of our life EMERSON. b. The year 1629 is reckoned the epocha of long perukes E. NARES. 3. The precise e. on which they [the designs of the court] were to be executed BURKE. Up to the present e. SCRIVENER.

II. A period dated from an epoch in sense I. **1.** Later, a period of history defined by the prevalence of some particular state of things. 1628. **b.** A period in the life of an individual, or in the history of a process 1768. **c.** *Geol.* Any distinct portion of geological time 1802.

Two epochs of terrible civil discord STUBBS. The Addisonian e. 1883. b. Actions unsuitable to the e. of life 1865. c. The glacial e. TYNDALL. *Comb.*: **e.-making** *a.* said chiefly of scientific discoveries or treatises. Hence **E·pochal** *a.* pertaining to, or of the nature of, an e.; e.-making. **E·pochism**, the practice of dividing time into epochs. **E·pochist**, †a philosopher of the Ephectic School; also, one who holds the days of creation in *Genesis* to be epochs.

Epode (e·po^u^d). 1598. [– Fr. *épode* or L. *epodos* – Gr. ἐπῳδός; see EPI-, ODE.] **1. a.** A kind of lyric poem, invented by Archilochus, in which a long line is followed by a shorter one, of metres other than the elegiac; as, the *Epodes* of Horace. **b.** An incantation. **c.** A grave poem. **2.** The part of a lyric song which follows the strophe and antistrophe 1671. Hence **Epo·dic** *a.*

Epoist (e·po͝ist). [Badly f. Gr. ἔπος EPOS + -IST.] A writer of epic poetry. BROWNING.

Eponym (e·pŏnim). 1846. [– Gr. ἐπώνυμος (a) given as a name, (b) giving one's name to a thing or person, f. ἐπί upon + ὄνομα, Æol. ὄνυμα name.] **1.** One who gives, or is supposed to give, his name to a people, place, or institution. Also in L. form **eponymus. b.** *transf.* One whose name is a synonym of something 1873. **2.** *Assyriology.* A functionary who gave his name to his year of office. Cf. EPONYMOUS 2. Also *attrib.* 1864. **3.** [– Gr. ἐπώνυμον.] A distinguishing title 1863.

1. Pelops is the e. or name-giver of Peloponnesus GROTE. b. Charles [the Great]..had become, so to speak, an e. of Empire BRYCE.

Hence **Epony·mic** *a.* of or pertaining to an e.; that is an e. **Epo·nymism**, the practice of referring names of places or peoples to supposed prehistoric eponyms. **Epo·nymist** = EPONYM 1. **Epo·nymize** *v.* to serve as an e. to.

Eponymous (epǫ·nimǝs), *a.* 1846. [f. Gr. ἐπώνυμος (see prec.) + -OUS.] **1.** That gives (his) name to anything. **2.** Giving his name to the year, as did the chief archon at Athens 1857.

1. The e. hero or protagonist of the play SWINBURNE.

Eponymy (epǫ·nimi). 1865. [– Gr. ἐπωνυμία derived or significant name, + ἐπώνυμος; see EPONYM, -Y³.] **1. a.** = EPONYMISM. **b.** Eponymic nomenclature. **2.** The year of office of an (Assyrian) eponym 1875.

Epopee (e·pŏpī). Now *rare.* 1697. [– Fr. *épopée* – Gr. ἐποποιία; see next.] An epic poem; epic poetry. Also *transf.*

transf. A sort of historical e. GROTE.

Epopœia (epopī·ă). *arch.* 1749. [– Gr. ἐποποιία, f. ἔπος word, song + ποιεῖν make.] = EPOPEE. Hence **Epopœ·ist,** one who writes epic poetry.

Epopt (e·pǫpt). 1696. [– late L. *epopta*, – Gr. ἐπόπτης. f. ἐπί EPI- + ὀπ- see.] A beholder; in *Gr. Antiq.* one initiated into the Eleusinian mysteries. Also *transf.* Hence **Epo·ptic** *a.* of or pertaining to an e. var. **Epo·ptist.**

Epos (e·pǫs). 1835. [L. – Gr. ἔπος word, song, f. ἐπ-, stem of εἰπεῖν say.] **1. a.** *collect.* Early unwritten narrative poetry celebrating incidents of heroic tradition 1839. **b.** = EPIC B. 2. 1855. **c.** Epic poetry 1835. **2.** A series of events worthy of epic treatment 1848.

1. a. The ancient E. hardly survived. b. Every age..expects a morn And claims an e. E. B. BROWNING. c. Almost rises into e. CARLYLE.

†Epota·tion. 1627. [f. contemp. *epote* v. (– L. *epotare*) + -ATION.] The drinking up or off –1677.

‖Eprouvette (epruve·t). 1781. [Fr., f. *éprouver* try, test; see -ETTE.] **1.** An apparatus for testing the strength of gunpowder. **2.** A spoon used in assaying metals 1874.

Epsom (e·psǝm). 1770. **1.** *attrib.* and *Comb.*, as **E.-water,** the water of a mineral spring at Epsom in Surrey. **E.-salt** (*colloq.* **-salts**), orig. the salt (chiefly magnesium sulphate) obtained from Epsom-water; now magnesium sulphate however prepared. **2.** Short for Epsom-salt 1803. Hence **E·psomite,** native magnesium sulphate.

Epulary (e·piŭlări), *a.* 1678. [– L. *epularis*, f. *epulum* banquet; see -ARY².] Of or pertaining to a feast or banquet.

Epulation (epiulē^i^·ʃǝn). Now *rare.* 1542. [– L. *epulatio*, f. *epulat-*, pa. ppl. stem of *epulari* feast; see -ION. Cf. Fr. †*épulation.*] The action of feasting.

‖Epulis (epiū·lis). 1859. [mod.L. – Gr. ἐπουλίς, f. ἐπί EPI- + οὖλον gum.] *Path.* A tumour of the gums.

Epulotic (epiulǫ·tik). 1634. [– Gr. ἐπουλωτικός, f. ἐπουλοῦσθαι be scarred over, f. ἐπί EPI- + οὐλή scar.] *Med.*

A. *adj.* Having power to cicatrize 1761.

B. *sb.* in *pl.* Epulotic medicines or ointments.

Epurate (e·piŭre^i^t), *v. rare.* 1799. [f. (O)Fr. *épurer*, f. *pur* pure; see -ATE³.] *trans.* To purify (*lit.* and *fig.*). Hence **Epura·tion.**

Equability (īk-, ekwăbi·līti). 1531. [– L. *æquabilitas*, f. *æquabilis*; see next, -ITY.] **1.** The quality of being equable; freedom from fluctuation or variation. **†2.** Capability of being compared on equal terms –1817. **†3.** Well-balanced condition –1605.

1. Such an equabilitie of mind HOLINSHED. E. of the Sun's motion RAY, of the climate HOOKER.

Equable (ī·k-, e·kwăb'l), *a.* 1643. [– L. *æquabilis*, f. *æquare* make level or equal, f. *æquus*; see EQUAL, -ABLE.] **1.** Uniform, free from fluctuation or variation: said of motions, temperature, the feelings, etc. 1677. **2.** Free from inequalities; uniform throughout; equally proportioned 1692. **†3.** = EQUITABLE. Sir T. Browne.

1. An e. pulse 1799. E. climates MAURY. E. in style JOWETT. 2. A more e. system of taxation THIRLWALL. Hence **E·quableness** = EQUABILITY. **E·quably** *adv.*

Equæval (ikwī·văl), *a.* Also **equiæval.** 1867. [f. L. *æquævus* (f. *æquus* equal + *ævum* age) + -AL¹.] Of equal age; belonging to the same period. So **†Equæ·vous** *a.*

Equal (ī·kwăl). ME. [– L. *æqualis*, f. *æquus* level, even.]

A. *adj.* **1.** Identical in amount, magnitude, number, value, intensity, etc.; neither less nor greater. **2.** Possessing a like degree of a quality or attribute; on the same level in dignity, power, excellence, etc.; having the same rights or privileges. Const. *to, with.* 1526. **3.** Adequate or fit in quantity or degree; adequately fit or qualified. Of persons: Having competent strength, endurance, or ability. Const. *to.* 1674. **4.** Evenly proportioned; uniform in effect or operation 1661. **†5.** [= L. *æquus.*] Fair, equitable, impartial –1769. **6.** Of surfaces: Level, on the same level (*arch.*) 1649. **7.** †Uniform throughout –1793; in *Bot.* symmetrical 1876. **8.** = EQUABLE 1. 1626. **†9.** Of numbers: Even (*rare*) 1806. **†10.** quasi-*adv.* Equally –1659.

1. Three hils, not in equall distaunce GRAFTON. Of equall height DIGBY. Of e. Profit DRYDEN. In nearly e. ratios 1846. 2. Equall in glory to the father 1526. He meant his children to be all e. CRUISE. Phr. *E. voices* (Mus.): voices either all male or all female. 3. To make my commendations e. to your merit DRYDEN. Phr. *E. to the occasion.* 4. The army dreaded his e. and inexorable justice GIBBON. E. laws 1836. Phr. †*It is e. to me* (*whether*): = 'it makes no difference'. 5. E. heauen hath denied that comfort GREENE. 6. The e. plains of fruitful Sicily E. B. BROWNING. 8. Try them by boiling upon an e. fire BACON. An even or e. trot 1761. In a firm and e. tone GIBBON. To keep an oath with an e. mind TENNYSON.

B. *sb.* **1.** One who is equal to another; as, in rank, in power or performance, or †in age 1573. **2.** abstr. *An e.*: a state of equality. Now *dial.* 1596.

1. A minister who never had his e...for wisdom and integrity 1792. 2. SPENSER *F. Q.* v. ii. 34.

Equal (ī·kwăl), *v.* 1586. [f. prec.] **1.** To make equal or level, to equalize 1594. **†2.** To represent as equal; to liken, compare –1805. **3.** *trans.* To be or become equal to; to come up to, match 1590. **4.** To produce or achieve something equal to. Also †*intr.* To cope on equal terms *with* (*rare*). 1597.

1. Cities..equalled with the ground 1629. Those other two equal'd with me in Fate MILT. *P. L.* III. 33. 2. To e. robbery with murder JOHNSON. 3. The golde and the chrystall cannot equall it *Job* 28:17. 4. To e. art with art W. BROOME. *intr.* A Body strong enough..to equall with the King 2 *Hen. IV*, I. iii. 67.

Equalist (ī·kwălist). *rare.* 1661. [f. EQUAL + -IST.] One who asserts the equality of certain (indicated) persons or things.

Equalitarian (ikwǫ:litē^ə^·riăn). 1799. [f. EQUALITY + -ARIAN; cf. *humanitarian*, etc.]

A. *adj.* Of or pertaining to the doctrine of the equality of mankind.

B. *sb.* One who holds this doctrine.

Equality (ikwǫ·līti). ME. [– OFr. *equalité* (mod. *égalité*) – L. *æqualitas*, f. *æqualis*; see EQUAL, -ITY.] **1.** The condition of being equal in quantity, amount, value, intensity, etc.; *esp.* in *Math.* exact correspondence between magnitudes and numbers in respect of quantity (sometimes expressed by the sign =) 1570. **2.** The condition of being equalty; dignity, privileges, power, etc. with others ME. **†3.** Fairness, impartiality, equity; in things, proportionateness –1845. **4.** Evenness, uniformity. Now *rare.* ME.

1. Pleading e. of years COWPER. 3. E. is of the essence of such taxes MCCULLOCH. 4. E. of Motion 1664, temper 1762, wear HT. MARTINEAU.

Equalize (ī·kwăləiz), *v.* 1590. [f. EQUAL + -IZE, partly after Fr. *égaliser.*] **†1.** = EQUAL *v.* 3. –1826. **†2.** To represent as equal; to place on an equality –1751. **3.** To make equal in magnitude or degree 1622. **†4.** To level –1653. **5.** To render uniform 1822. **6.** *intr. Football*, etc. To bring the score to an equality with the opponent's.

1. The Scythians..do e. the grass in multitude 1595. 2. The Virgin..they do at least equalize to Christ HY. MORE. 3. Intending to e. it [Babel] with the Starres SIR T. HERBERT. Those who attempt to level, never e. BURKE. Office of itself does much to e. politicians MACAULAY. 5. To e. the motion of a machine IMISON. Hence **E:qualiza·tion. E·quali:zer**, one who, or that which, makes equal.

E·qualler. *rare.* 1630. [f. EQUAL *v.* + -ER¹.] One who, or that which, makes equal.

Equally (ī·kwăli), *adv.* ME. [f. EQUAL *a.* + -LY².] **1.** To an equal degree or extent. Const. *with*; occas. *as.* 1634. **2.** In equal shares ME. **3.** According to one and the same rule or measure; impartially, justly 1526. **†4.** On a level; uniformly; in a line *with* –1721. **5.** In uniform degree or quantity 1664.

1. And e. of Fear and Forecast void DE FOE. 2. To her other sisters e. between them CRUISE. 3. To deal e. between man and man HOBBES.

Equalness (ī·kwălnės). Now *rare.* 1530. [f. as prec. + -NESS.] **1.** = EQUALITY 1, 2. **†2.** Fairness, equity –1556. **†3.** Evenness, uniformity –1799.

Equanimity (īkwăni·mĭti). 1607. [– L. *æquanimitas*, f. *æquanimis* having an even mind, f. *æquus* even + *animus* mind; see -ITY.] **†1.** Fairness of judgement, impartiality –1752. **2.** Evenness of mind or temper; the quality of being undisturbed by good or ill fortune 1663.

2. To bear odium with e. BURKE.

Equanimous (ikwæ·nimǝs), *a.* 1656. [f. L. *æquanimis* (see prec.) + -OUS.] **1.** Even-tempered; not easily elated or depressed. **†2.** Impartial 1670. Hence **Equa·nimous-ly** *adv.*, **-ness.**

Equant (ī·kwănt). 1621. [– *æquant-*, pres. ppl. stem of L. *æquare*; see next, -ANT.]

A. *adj.* That equalizes. *E. circle* [med.L. *circulus æquans*], in ancient astronomy, a circle imagined in order to reconcile the planetary movements with the hypothesis of the uniform velocity of celestial motion.

B. *sb.* = *E. circle.*

Equate (ikwē^i^·t), *v.* late ME. [– *æquat-*, pa. ppl. stem of L. *æquare* to make equal, f. *æquus*; see EQUAL, -ATE³.] **†1.** To make bodies equal; to balance (*rare*) –1755. **2.** †To take the average of; in *Astr.* to reduce to an average 1633. **3.** *Math.* To state the equality of; to put in the form of an equation 1799. **4.** *transf.* and *fig.* To treat as equivalent 18...

2. To e. solar days, that is to convert apparent into mean time [etc.] 1751. 4. Boudicca might perhaps be equated..with such a Latin name as Victorina J. RHYS.

Equation (ikwēⁱ·ʃən). ME. [– (O)Fr. *équation* or L. *æquatio*. f. as prec.; see -ION.] **1.** The action of making equal or balancing; equilibrium, equality 1656. †*spec.* in *Astrol.* Equal partition. Only in ME. **2.** *Astron.* Reduction to a normal value or position by making compensations for a known cause of irregularity or error. Chiefly *concr.* the quantity added or subtracted for this purpose. 1666. †**3.** *Math.* The act of stating the identity in value of two quantities or expressions –1673. **4.** A formula affirming the equivalence of two quantitative expressions, connected by the sign =. Also *transf.* 1570.

1. Again the golden day resum'd its right, And ruled in just e. with the night ROWE. Phr. *E. of demand and supply, e. of trade*, etc. **2.** The difference between true and mean solar time..is called the e. of time 1854. Phr. *Annual e.*: see ANNUAL. *E. of the centre*: the difference between the mean and the true anomaly of a heavenly body. *E. of the equinoxes*: the difference between the mean and the apparent places of the equinoxes. *E. of time*: the difference between the time shown by a clock (mean time) and that shown by a sundial. *Personal e.*: the correction required in astronomical observations in consequence of greater or less inaccuracy habitual to individual observers. Also *transf. E. of payments*: the process of finding a mean time for the payment in one amount of sums due at different times. **4.** The two chief kinds of equations are: (1) Those which contain symbols denoting one or more unknown quantities. . .(2) Those which indicate a constant relation between variables: as *E. to a curve*, an equation expressing a relation between coordinates or the like, which is constant for every point of the curve; *e. of motions*, etc. Equations are distinguished as *simple, quadratic, cubic*, etc. (or as of the 1st, 2nd, 3rd etc. degree) according to the highest power which they contain of any unknown or variable. O.E.D. Phr. *To solve an e.*: to discover the numerical values of the symbols denoting unknown quantities.

Equational (ikwēⁱ·ʃənăl), *a.* 1864. [f. prec. + -AL¹.] Pertaining to, or involving the use of, equations. Hence **Equa·tionally** *adv.*

Equator (ikwēⁱ·təɹ, -əɹ). ME. [– (O)Fr. *équateur* or med.L. *æquator*, in full *circulus æquator diei et noctis* circle equalizing day and night, f. *æquare*; see EQUATE, -OR 2.] **1.** *Astron.* A great circle of the celestial sphere, whose plane is perpendicular to the axis of the earth. Called also the EQUINOCTIAL, q.v. **2.** *Geog.* A great circle of the earth, in the plane of the celestial equator, and equidistant from the two poles 1612. Also *transf.* 1746.

2. *transf.* The solar e. LOCKYER. Phr. *Magnetic e.* = *Aclinic line* (see ACLINIC). *E. of the magnet*: the portion of the magnet midway between the two poles, which is apparently less magnetic.

Equatorial (īkwătōᵊ·riăl). 1664. [f. prec. + -IAL. Cf. Fr. *équatorial*.]

A. *adj.* Of or pertaining to an equator, *esp.* the terrestrial equator.

Phr. *E. instrument* or *telescope*: a telescope attached by an arm to an axle revolving in a direction parallel to the plane of the equator. By a uniform motion given to this axle the telescope follows the diurnal apparent motion of any point in the heavens to which it is directed. *E. circle*: a graduated circle (also called *hour-circle, right-ascension-circle*) revolving in a plane parallel to the equator, forming part of the e. instrument.

B. *sb.* = *E. instrument*; see A. 1793.

Equerry (e·kwĕri, īkwe·ri). Also *aphet.* †**querry.** 1526. [Earliest forms *esquiry, escuirie* – Fr. †*escu(i)rie* (mod. *écurie* stable), of unkn. origin. Sense 2 seems to be based on OFr. *escuyer d'escuyrie* 'SQUIRE of stables', AFr. *esquire de qurye*. The stress (e·kweri) is favoured, and is due to an imagined connection with L. *equus* horse.] †**1.** The stables of a royal or princely household, or the body of officers in charge of them –1731. **2.** [Short for 'gentleman of the e.' or 'groom of the e.'] †**a.** A groom 1708. **b.** An officer charged with the care of the horses of a royal or exalted personage. At the English Court, an officer of the household, in occasional attendance on the sovereign. 1526.

Hence **E·querryship**, the position of an e.

Equestrial (ikwe·striăl), *a.* Now *rare.* 1553. [f. as next + -AL¹.] = next.

Equestrian (ikwe·striăn). 1656. [f. L. *equestris* belonging to a horseman, f. *eques* horseman, knight, f. *equus* horse; see -IAN.]

A. *adj.* **1.** Of or pertaining to horse-riding. Also, skilled in horse-riding. **2.** Mounted on a horse. Also, representing a person so mounted. 1711. **3.** *Rom. Antiq.* Of or pertaining to the order of *Equites* 1696.

1. Candidates for e. glory JOHNSON. **2.** An e. lady appeared upon the plains 1711. The Antique E. Statute of Marcus Aurelius ADDISON.

B. *sb.* One who rides on horseback; also, one who publicly performs on horseback 1791.

Hence **Eque·striani:sm**, the art or practice of riding on horseback. So **Equestrie·nne**, a female e.

Equi- (ī·kwi-), repr. L. *æqui-*, comb. f. *æquus*, in sense 'equal', or (advb.) 'equally, in an equal degree'. Hence:

E:qui₁anharmo·nic *a.*, *Math.* equally anharmonic: applied when two ranges, each of four points, are projective; **-ly** *adv.* **E:qui₁arti·culate** *a.*, having equal joints with another. **Equiba·lance** *sb.* = EQUILIBRIUM. †**Equiba·lance** *v.*, to counterpoise. **Equicha·ngeable** *a.*, equally varying. **Equico·nvex** *a.*, having two convex surfaces with equal curves. **Equicre·scent** *a.*, having equal increments. **E:quidia·gonal** *a.*, having the diagonals equal. **E:quidiu·rnal** *a. nonce-word*, [tr. Gr. ἰσημερινός], pertaining to the time when days and nights are equal: applied to the equinoctial line. **Equigra·phic** *a.* = HOMALOGRAPHIC. **Equilo·bate** *a.*, having equal lobes. **E:quimome·ntal** *a. Physics*, having equal moments of inertia about parallel axes. †**Equipe·nsate** *v.*, to weigh or esteem equally. **E:quiperio·dic** *a.*, having equal periods. **Equipro·babilism**, the doctrine of the equiprobabilists. **Equipro·babilist**, one of those who hold that of two opinions the less safe may be followed provided it be as probable, or nearly as probable, as the opposite. **Equira·dial** *a.*, having equal radii. **Equira·dical** *a.*, 'equally radical' (W.). **E:quisegme·ntal** *a.*, *Math.* having equal segments. **E:quitange·ntial** *a.*, having a tangent equal to a constant line; said of a certain curve. **Equiva·lue** *v.*, to make or be equal in value. **E·quivalved** *a.*, *Conch.* having both valves alike. †**E:quivelo·city**, equality in velocity. **Equivo·te** (*U.S.*), a tie in voting.

†**Equia·ngle.** 1570. [– Fr. *équiangle* – late L. *equiangulus*; see next.]

A. *adj.* = EQUIANGULAR –1611.

B. *sb. pl.* Equal angles. *By equiangles*: at right angles. 1593. So †**Equia·ngled** *a.*

Equiangular (īkwi₁æ·ŋgiŭlăɹ), *a.* 1660. [f. late L. *equiangulus* (Boethius), f. *equi-* EQUI- + *angulus* ANGLE *sb.*²; see -AR¹.] Having equal angles, as an *e.* figure, mutually *e.*

Phr. *E. spiral*, a name for the logarithmic spiral, in which the angle between the radius vector and the tangent is constant. Hence **E:quia:ngula·rity**, the condition or fact of being e.

Equiaxe (ī·kwi₁æks), *a.* 1810. [– Fr. *équiaxe*, f. *equi-* EQUI- + *axe* AXIS¹.] *Crystall.* Having equal axes. So **E·quiaxed** *a.*

Equicrural (ī:kwi₁krūᵊ·răl), *a.* 1650. [f. late L. *equicrurius* isosceles (tr. Gr. ἰσοσκελής), f. *equi-* EQUI- + *crus, crur-* leg; see -AL¹.] Having equal legs or sides; isosceles. var. †**E·quicrure.**

Equidifferent (īkwi₁di·fĕrĕnt), *a.* 1695. [f. EQUI- + DIFFERENT.] Having equal differences; arithmetically proportional.

Equidistant (īkwi₁di·stănt), *a.* 1570. [– (O)Fr. *équidistant* or med.L. *equidistans, -ant-*; see EQUI-, DISTANT.] **1.** Separated by an equal distance. Also *fig.* 1593. **2.** Of lines: Parallel.

Hence **Equidi·stantly** *adv.* at an equal distance.

Equiform (ī·kwifǭɹm), *a.* [f. EQUI- + -FORM 2.] Having one and the same form. (Dicts.) So **Equifo·rmal** *a.* †**Equifo·rmity**, uniformity. SIR T. BROWNE.

†**Equila·ter.** 1570. [– (O)Fr. *équilatère* or late L. *æquilaterus*, f. *æqui-* EQUI- + *latus, later-* side.]

A. *adj.* Having equal sides –1715.

B. *sb.* A square or cube, or a square or cube number –1636.

Equilateral (īkwi₁læ·tĕrăl), *a.* 1570. [– Fr. *équilateral* or late L. *æquilateralis*, f. as prec.; see -AL¹.] Having all the sides equal.

Phr. *E. arch*: an arch in which the chords of the sides form with the base an e. triangle. *E. hyperbola*, one whose axes are equal. *E. shell*, one in which a transverse line drawn through the apex of the umbo divides the valve into two equal and symmetrical parts. Hence **Equila·terally** *adv.*

Equilibrant (ikwi·librănt). 1883. [– Fr. *équilibrant*, f. *équilibrer*; see next, -ANT.] *Physics.* 'Any system of forces which if applied to a rigid body, would balance a given system of forces acting on it' (Thomson & Tait).

Equilibrate (īkwi₁ləi·breⁱt), *v.* 1635. [– *æquilibrat-*, pa. ppl. stem of late L. *æquilibrare*, f. *æqui-* EQUI- + *libra* balance; see -ATE³.] **1.** *trans.* To bring into or keep in equipoise or equilibrium; to balance. **2.** To counterpoise 1829. **3.** *absol.* and *intr.* To be in a state of equilibrium; to balance. Const. *with.* 1829.

3. The forces neutralise each other and mutually e. 1830. So †**Equili·brate** *a.* equally balanced. **Equili·bratory** *a.* tending to produce equilibrium. var. **Equili·briate** *v.*

Equilibration (īkwi₁ləibrēⁱ·ʃən). 1612. [– late L. *equilibratio*, f. *equilibrat-*; see prec., -ION.] The action of bringing into or keeping in equilibrium; the state of being in equilibrium. Const. *to, with.*

Drowsy equilibrations of undetermined counsel JOHNSON. var. †**Equili·bre.**

Equilibriate (īkwi₁li·bri₁ĕt), *a.* 1649. [f. EQUILIBRIUM + -ATE².] = EQUILIBRATE.

Equilibrist (ikwi·librist, īkwi₁li·-). 1760. [f. as prec. + -IST.] One skilled in feats of balancing; *esp.* a rope-dancer. Hence **E:quilibri·stic** *a.*

Equilibrity (īkwi₁li·brĭti). 1644. [f. EQUILIBRIUM + -ITY.] The state of being equally balanced; equilibrium.

Equilibrium (īkwi₁li·briŭm). 1608. [– L. *æquilibrium*, f. *æqui-* EQUI- + *libra* balance.] **1.** *Physics.* The condition of equal balance between opposing forces; that state of a body in which the forces acting upon it are so arranged that their resultant at every point is zero. **2.** The state of balance between powers of any kind 1677. **b.** The condition of indecision or indifference produced by opposing influences of equal force 1685.

1. The Fluids, pressing equally and easily yielding to each other, soon restore the Æquilibrium 1697. **2.** So to balance their [the Spaniard and the French] Power, as to keep both in an E. 1677. **b.** There is an end of the Doubt or Æquilibrium 1685.

Hence **Equili·brial** *a.* of or pertaining to e.; constructed on the principle of e. **Equili·brious** *a.* that is in a state of e. †**Equili·briously** *adv.* **Equi·librize** *v.* to bring to an e. var. **Equili·brio** [the L. ablative, treated as Eng.]

Equimultiple (īkwi₁mɒ·ltip'l). 1656. [Anglicization of mod.L. *æquimultiplex* (Billingsley); see EQUI-, MULTIPLE.]

†**A.** *adj.* Produced by multiplying by the same number. HOBBES.

B. *sb.* One of a set of numbers or quantities which each have common multiplier. Thus 14 and 28 are equimultiples of 2 and 4. Chiefly *pl.* 1660.

Equine (ī·kwəin), *a.* 1778. [– L. *equinus*, f. *equus* horse; see -INE¹.] Of, pertaining to, or resembling a horse.

The mule is apt to forget all but the e. side of his pedigree LOWELL. So †**Equi·nal** *a.* Hence **Equi·nity.** LANDOR.

Equinoctial (ek-, īkwinǫ·kʃăl). ME. [– (O)Fr. *équinoctial* – L. *æquinoctialis*, f. *æquinoctium*; see EQUINOX, -AL¹.]

A. *adj.* **1.** Pertaining to a state of equal day and night. **2.** Pertaining to the period or point of the equinox 1570; happening about the time of the equinox 1792. **3.** = EQUATORIAL; also, pertaining to the regions near the terrestrial equator 1594.

1. Phr. *E. line, circle* (*road* MILTON), the celestial or terrestrial equator. Cf. B. 1 and 2. *E. point* = EQUINOX 2. **2.** Six houres, which is the one halfe of an Equinoctiall day 1594. The e. rains WELLINGTON, gales LIVINGSTONE. Phr. *E. colure*: see COLURE. *E. month*: a month which includes one of the equinoxes.

B. *sb.* **1.** The celestial equator: so called because, when the sun is on it, day and night are of equal length ME. **2.** The terrestrial equator. Now *rare.* 1584. Also *transf.* and *fig.* †**3.** = EQUINOX –1665. **4.** An equinoctial gale 1748.

2. As if, when you have crossed the e., all the virtues die BURKE. Hence **Equino·ctially** *adv.* in the direction of the e. or equator.

†‖**Equinoctium.** *rare.* Pl. **-ia, -iums.** ME. [L.; see next.] Equinox –1688.

Equinox (ī·k-, e·kwinǫks). 1579. [– (partly through (O)Fr. *équinoxe*) L. *æquinoctium*, in med.L. *-noxium*, f. *æqui-* EQUI- + *nox, noct-* night.] **1.** One of the two periods of the year when day and night are of equal length, owing to the sun's crossing the Equator. Hence, the time of this crossing, that is, the 20 March, and the 22 or 23 September. 1588. **b.** The condition of equality of day and night. Also *fig.* 1604. **2.** One of the two points at which the sun's path crosses the Equator, *viz.* the first points in Aries and Libra 1594. †**3.** = *Equinoctial line* or EQUATOR –1728. †**4.** An equinoctial gale (*rare*) DRYDEN.

1. Live long, nor feel..Our changeful equinoxes TENNYSON.

Equip (ĭkwi·p), *v.* 1523. [– Fr. *équiper* in same sense (XVI, but cf. AFr. *eskipeson* equipment, med.L. *eschipare* man (a vessel), prob. – ON. *skipa* man (a vessel), fit up, arrange, f. *skip* SHIP *sb.*[1]] **1.** *trans.* To fit out (a ship) 1580. **2.** 'To furnish for service' (T.); to provide with what is requisite for action, as arms, instruments, or apparatus. Hence *fig.* Const. *with*. **b.** To finance 1690. **3.** To array; to dress, fit out (*for* a journey) 1695.

1. Equipping the ship for these two different voyages ANSON. **2.** To e. Horses 1605, a man as a writer 1793, a new theory 1879. **3.** It is Dr. Donne, equipped for the expedition to Cales H. WALPOLE.

Equipage (e·kwipĕdʒ), *sb.* 1579. [– Fr. *équipage*, f. *équiper*; see prec., -AGE.] †**1.** = EQUIPMENT –1684. **2.** Furniture, apparatus, or outfit, including all that is needed for an army, a ship, an establishment, a journey or expedition, etc. 1579. †**3.** Uniform, accoutrements –1818; costume, dress, 'get up' –1823. **4.** Articles for personal ornament or use; a case of these 1716. †**5.** Apparatus in general (*lit.* and *fig.*) –1734. †**6.** Formal state or order; ceremonious display –1756. †**7.** Train, retinue, following –1731. **8.** A carriage with or without horses and the attendant servants 1721. †**9.** The crew of a ship [tr. F. *équipage*.] (*rare*) –1751. †**10.** [as if f. EQUI-.] Equal step; also *fig.* –1655.

2. How war may..Move..In all her e. MILT. Our e. for the night 1858. Phr. *Breakfast-, tea-e.*: a breakfast-, tea-service (*arch.*) **7.** The young Prince of Orange, with a splendid E. EVELYN. **8.** Here..roll and rumble all kinds of equipages HAWTHORNE. **10.** To march in e. with better wit W. BROWNE.

†**E·quipage**, *v.* 1590. [f. prec.] **1.** *trans.* To furnish with an equipage; to fit out –1784. **2.** To rank (*trans.* and *intr.*). HEYWOOD.

†**Equiparable**, *a.* 1611. [– OFr. *equiparable* or L. *æquiparabilis*, f. *æquiparare*; see next, -ABLE.] Equal in comparison, equivalent –1695.

†**Equi·parate**, *v.* 1632. [– *equiparat-*, pa. ppl. stem of L. *æquiparare* compare, liken, f. *æquipar*, f. *æqui-* EQUI- + *par* equal; see -ATE[3].] To level; to treat as on the same level –1671.

Equiparation (ikwi:pārēⁱ·ʃən). 1615. [– L. *æquiparatio*, f. as prec.; see -ION.] The action of placing on an equality; †the action of comparing; *concr.* a parallel.

Equipedal (īkwipĭ·dăl), *a.* [f. L. *æquipedus* (see next) + -AL[1].] Having equal feet; *Zool.* having the pairs of feet equal. (Dicts.)

Equipede (ī·kwipīd). 1835. [– L. *æquipedus* or *æquipes, -ped-* adjs., f. *æqui-* EQUI- + *pes, ped-* foot.] *Zool.* Having legs of equal length. Also as *sb.* in *pl.*

†**Equipe·ndent**, *a.* 1640. [f. EQUI- + PENDENT.] Hanging in equipoise –1681. Hence †**Equipe·ndency**.

Equipment (ĭkwi·pmĕnt). 1717. [– Fr. *équipement*, f. *équiper*; see EQUIP, -MENT.] **1.** The action of equipping; the state of being equipped; the manner in which a person or thing is equipped 1748. **2.** *concr.* Anything used in equipping; furniture, outfit, warlike apparatus; necessaries for travelling, etc.; *fig.* intellectual outfit 1717.

1. The e. of an expedition 1809, of Arctic ships EMERSON. **2.** The e. of a female archer STRUTT, of a soldier 1870.

Equipoise (ī·kwipoiz), *sb.* 1658. [f. EQUI- + POISE *sb.*, repl. the phr. *equal poise*.] **1.** Equality or equal distribution of weight; a condition of perfect balance or equilibrium; *esp.* in intellectual, moral, political, or social forces or interests. **2.** A counterpoise; an equivalent force. Chiefly *fig.* 1780.

1. To live in a continual e. of doubt JOHNSON. **2.** The e. to the clergy [*i.e.* the aristocracy] being removed, the Church became so powerful BUCKLE.

Equipoise (ī·kwipoiz), *v.* 1647. [f. prec. sb.] **1.** *trans.* To serve as an equipoise to; to counterbalance 1664. **2.** To place or hold in equipoise 1764. †**3.** *intr.* To balance *with* 1647.

Equipollence (īkwi,pǫ·lĕns). ME. [– OFr. *equipolence* (mod. *équipollence*), f. *equipolent*; see next, -ENCE. Cf. med.L. *equipollentia*.] **1.** Equality of force, power, or signification. **2.** *Logic.* An equivalence between two or more propositions ME. var. **Equipo·llency.**

Equipollent (īkwi,pǫ·lĕnt). ME. [– OFr. *equipolent* (mod. *équipollent*) – L. *æquipollens, -ent-* of equal value, f. *æqui-* EQUI- + *pollēre* be strong.]

A. *adj.* **1.** Of equal power, weight, importance, or significance. *Obs.* of persons. **2.** Identical in meaning or result; equivalent; in *Logic*, said *esp.* of propositions expressing the same thing but differently 1577. Hence **Equipo·llently** *adv.*

1. A considerable and e. muscular force PALEY.

B. *sb.* Something that has equal power, weight, etc.; an equivalent 1611.

Equiponderance (īkwi,pǫ·ndĕrăns). 1775. [f. next; see -ANCE. Cf. Fr. *équipondérance*.] Equality of weight; equilibrium. var. **Equipo·nderancy.**

Equiponderant (īkwi,pǫ·ndĕrănt). 1630. [– *equiponderant-* pres. ppl. stem of med.L. **equiponderare* have equal weight, f. *equi-* EQUI- + *ponderare* weigh; see -ANT. Cf. Fr. *équipondérant*.]

A. *adj.* Of equal weight; evenly balanced.

The quantity of air to a quantity of water e. thereto, is as 1300 to 1. BOYLE. E. strife 'twixt Good and Evil 1882.

B. *sb. pl.* Things of equal weight 1852.

Equiponderate (īkwi,pǫ·ndĕreⁱt), *v.* 1641. [alt. of PREPONDERATE *v.*[1] by substitution of EQUI- for *pre-*.] †**1.** *intr.* To be in equipoise –1822. **2.** *trans.* To counterbalance 1661. **3.** To make well-balanced 1810.

2. Both e. (a pound, suppose) in air 1766. Hence †**Equipo·nderate, Equipo·nderated** *ppl. adjs.* **Equipo·nderation.**

†**Equipo·nderous,** *a.* 1656. [f. EQUI- + L. *pondus, ponder-* weight + -OUS.] Of equal weight or specific gravity; also *fig.* –1729.

†**Equipo·ndious,** *a.* [f. L. *æquipondium* an equal weight, counterpoise (f. *æqui-* EQUI- + *pondus* weight) + -OUS.] Of equal weight on both sides; nicely-balanced. GLANVILL.

Equi·potent, *a. rare.* 1875. [f. EQUI- + POTENT.] Of equal power.

Equipotential (ī:kwi,pote·nʃăl), *a.* 1678. [f. EQUI- + POTENTIAL.] †**1.** Of equal authority. **2.** Having equality of potential 1880.

2. When a potential function exists, surfaces for which the potential is constant are called E. surfaces MAXWELL.

Equirotal (īkwi,rōᵘ·tăl), *a.* 1839. [f. EQUI- + L. *rota* wheel + -AL[1].] **1.** Having fore and hind wheels of equal diameter. **2.** 'Having equal rotation'. (Dicts.)

Equisetaceous (e:kwi,sĭtēⁱ·ʃəs), *a.* 1867. [See EQUISETUM and -ACEOUS.] *Bot.* Belonging to the order *Equisetaceæ*.

Equisetic (ekwisĭ·tik), *a.* 1838. [f. EQUISETUM + -IC.] *Chem.* Derived from Equisetum. *E. acid* = ACONITIC acid.

Equisetum (ekwisī·tǒm). *Pl.* **-ums, -a.** 1830. [– L. *equisetum* (prop. *equisætum*), f. *equus* horse + *sæta* bristle.] *Bot.* The typical genus of the N.O. *Equisetaceæ*; Horsetail. Hence **Equise·tiform** *a.* (Dicts.).

Equison. [– L. *equiso, -ōn-*, f. *equus* horse.] A groom. LANDOR.

Equisonant (īkwisōᵘ·nănt), *a.* [f. EQUI- + SONANT.] *Ancient Mus.* Consonant in the octave. Hence **Equiso·nance.**

Equitable (e·kwităb'l), *a.* 1646. [– Fr. *équitable*, f. *équité* EQUITY, with active meaning of the suffix, as (e.g.) in *charitable*.] **1.** Characterized by equity or fairness: now *rarely* of persons. **2.** Pertaining to the department of jurisprudence called EQUITY; valid in equity as dist. from law 1720.

1. E. Judges BURNET. In all literal and e. construction CROMWELL. Upon e. grounds 1654. **2.** A trust estate..is good as an e. jointure CRUISE. Hence **E·quitableness. E·quitably** *adv.*

Equitant (e·kwitănt), *a.* 1830. [– *equitant-*, pres. ppl. stem of L. *equitare*; see next, -ANT.] *Bot.* Overriding: said of leaves which successively overlap each other according to age, as in the iris.

Equitation (ekwitēⁱ·ʃən). 1562. [– Fr. *équitation* or L. *equitatio, -ōn-*, f. *equitat-*, pa. ppl. stem of L. *equitare*, f. *eques, equit-* horseman, f. *equus* horse; see -ION.] The action, art, or habit of riding on, or as on, horseback; horsemanship.

Broomsticks..the..instruments of their nocturnal e. LOWELL.

Equity (e·kwĭti). ME. [– (O)Fr. *équité* – L. *æquitas*, f. *æquus*; see EQUI-, -ITY.] **1.** *gen.* The quality of being equal or fair; impartiality; even-handed dealing. **2.** That which is fair and right. *rarely* in *pl.* ME. **3.** *Jurisp.* The recourse to general principles of justice (= L. *naturalis æquitas*) to correct or supplement the ordinary law 1574. **4.** In England, Ireland, and U.S., a system of law existing side by side with the common and statute law (together called 'law' in a narrower sense), and superseding these, when they conflict with it 1591. Also *transf.* of analogous systems. **5.** An equitable right, *i.e.* one recognizable in a court of equity. Often in *pl.* 1626. **b.** The ordinary shares of a company as opposed to the preference shares 1904. **6.** *attrib.* 1832.

1. E. was my crowne *Job* 24:14. **2.** To do equyte and justice CAXTON. 3. Chancellors.. moderated the rigour of the law according..to e. 1858. **4.** There are settled and inviolable rules of e., which require to be moderated by the rules of good conscience 1858. In England, e. was formerly administered by a special class of tribunals, of which the Court of Chancery was chief; but since 1873 all the branches of the High Court administer both 'law' and 'equity', it being provided that where the two differ, the rules of e. are to be followed. O.E.D. **5.** The wife's e. to a suitable provision for the maintenance of herself and her children KENT. Phr. *E. of redemption*: the right of a mortgagor who has in law forfeited his estate to redeem it within a reasonable time by payment of the principal and interest. *E. to a settlement*: a wife's equitable right to have settled upon her any properties coming to her after marriage. *Comb.* **e.-draftsman,** a barrister who draws pleadings in e.

†**E·quivale**, *v.* 1608. [– late L. *æquivalēre*; see next.] *trans.* To be equivalent to; to provide an equivalent for –1695.

Equivalence (ĭkwi·vălĕns), *sb.* 1541. – (O)Fr. *équivalence* – med.L. *equivalentia*, f. *æquivalent-*; see next, -ENCE.] **1.** The condition of being equivalent; in *Physics*, equality of energy or effect. **2.** *Chem.* The doctrine that differing fixed quantities of different substances are equivalent in chemical combinations 1880.

1. To reduce propositions to identity or e. LEWES. Phr. *E. of force*: the doctrine that force of one kind becomes transformed into force of another kind of the same value. Hence †**Equivalence** *v. nonce-wd.* to balance. SIR T. BROWNE. **Equi·valency** [see -ENCY] = EQUIVALENCE; *Geol.* correspondence of strata in serial order and characteristics.

Equivalent (ĭkwi·vălĕnt). 1460. [– (O)Fr. *équivalent* – *æquivalent-*, pres. ppl. stem of late L. *æquivalēre*, f. *æqui-* EQUI- + *valēre* be strong.] **A.** *adj.* **1.** Equal in value, power, efficacy, or import; having equal or corresponding significance. *Obs.* of persons. **2.** Tantamount 1639. **3.** Corresponding 1634. **4.** *Chem.* Equal in combining value; having the same degree of quantivalence 1850. Also **Equi-valent** (īkwivēⁱ·lĕnt).

1. No Fair to thine E. or second MILT. *P. L.* IX. 609. To pay an e. penalty JAS. MILL. Here he makes a republic e. to a democracy 1832. **2.** His presence..would be e. to an army of ten thousand men S. AUSTIN. **3.** The Cadi, or some e. officer MORSE. Hence **Equi·valently** *adv.*

B. *sb.* **1.** Something equal in value or worth; also, something tantamount 1502. **2.** A word, expression, sign, etc. of equivalent import 1651. **3. a.** *Chem.* = *e. proportion* (see quot. and A. 4) 1827. **b.** That which corresponds in relative position or function; as, (*Biol.*) analogous and homologous structures; (*Geol.*) a stratum or formation in one country answering to one in another 1839. **c.** *Physics. Mechanical e.*: the amount of mechanical effect resulting from the operation of a force. *Mechanical e. of heat*: taken as, the amount of mechanical energy required to raise 1 lb. of water through 1° C. 1842.

1. Belleisle alone..was a sufficient e. for Minorca 1792. Phr. *The E.* (Eng. Hist.): the sum ordered, by the Act of Union of 1807, to be paid to Scotland as a set-off against additional excise-duties, loss on coinage, etc. **3. a.** The term e. was subsequently introduced to indicate the proportional weights of analogous substances found to be of equal value in their chemical action 1873.

Comb.: **e.-money** (see B. 1, quot.); **e. number** (*Chem.*) atomic weight.

Equivalue; see EQUI- *pref.*

†Equi·vocacy. *rare.* [f. late L. *æquivocus* (see next) + -ACY.] Equivocal character. SIR T. BROWNE.

Equivocal (ikwi·vŏkăl). 1601. [f. late L. *æquivocus* (see EQUIVOQUE) + -AL[1].]

A. *adj.* **†1.** Equal or the same in name but not in reality; nominal –1744. **2.** Having two or more significations equally appropriate; capable of double interpretation; ambiguous 1601. **3.** Of uncertain nature; undecided (chiefly in neg. sentences) 1658. **4.** Of persons, callings, etc.: Doubtful in character; questionable, suspicious 1790.

2. Without ambiguous or equiuocall tearmes FULBECKE. E. sentences SHAKS., answers 1756, proofs 'JUNIUS'. **3.** The sentiments of London were not e. BURKE. Phr. *E. generation*: the (supposed) production of plants or animals without parents: spontaneous generation. *E. chord* (Mus.): one which may be resolved into different keys without changing any of its tones. **4.** A Churchman..whose sanctity was e. H. WALPOLE. An e. mode of life LYTTON.

Hence **Equi:voca·lity**, e. quality; an equivoque. **Equi·vocally** *adv.* **Equi·vocalness**, e. quality.

†B. *sb.* An equivocal word or term; a homonym –1734.

Equivocate (ikwi·vŏkeᶦt), *v.* 1590. [– *æquivocat-*, pa. ppl. stem of late L. *æquivocare*, f. *æquivocus*; see EQUIVOQUE, -ATE[3]. Cf. Fr. *équivoquer* (XVI).] **†1.** *intr.* To have the same sound *with* 1611. **†2.** To use words of more than one sense; to deal in ambiguities –1686. **3.** In bad sense: 'To mean one thing and express another' (J.); to prevaricate 1590. **†4.** *trans.* To evade (an oath, etc.) by equivocation –1649.

3. The witness shuffled, equivocated, pretended to misunderstand the questions MACAULAY. Hence **Equi·vocatingly** *adv.* **Equi·vocator.** **Equi·vocato·ry** *a.* indicating or containing equivocation.

Equivocation (ikwi:vokēᶦ·ʃən). ME. [– late L. *æquivocatio*, f. as prec.; see -ION. Cf. OFr. *equivocation.*] **†1.** The using (a word) in more than one sense; ambiguity of meaning in words –1810. **b.** *Logic.* As = Gr. ὁμωνυμία: The fallacy of using the same term in different senses in a syllogism 1605. **2.** The use of words or expressions susceptible of a double signification, in order to mislead. Also *concr.* 1605.

2. The Subtle difference..Betwixt Æquivocation and a Lye 1634.

Equivoque, -voke (ī·kwi-, e·kwivoᵘk). ME. [– (O)Fr. *équivoque* or late L. *æquivocus*, f. *æquus* equal + *vocare* call.]

†A. *adj.* = EQUIVOCAL –1650.

B. *sb.* **†1.** A thing which has the same name as something different –1660. **2.** An expression capable of more meanings than one; word-play, punning 1614. **3.** Ambiguity of speech. Also *transf.* 1809. **4.** = EQUIVOCATION 2 (*rare*) 1616.

Equivorous (īkwi·vŏrəs), *a. rare.* 1828. [f. L. *equus* horse + -VOROUS.] Feeding on horseflesh.

Er (ɜɹ). 1862. Representing the inarticulate murmur of a hesitant speaker.

-er[1], *suffix*, ME. *-er(e*, *-ar(e*, OE. *-ere*, forming sbs., represents WGer. *-āri* :– OTeut. *-ārja-z*. The relation between Gmc. *-ārja-z* and L. *-arius* is obscure.

1. In its original sense 'a man who has to do with', it designates persons according to their profession or occupation, as in *hatter, slater*, etc. Exceptions to this are *cottager, villager*, and the ike; also a class of words chiefly belonging to mod. colloq. language, and denoting things or actions, as *header, back-hander, fiver*, etc. In some other words, e.g. *Londoner, foreigner, southerner*, *-er* indicates place of origin or residence.

2. The suffix became also a formative of agent-nouns. These normally denote personal (*orig.* male) agents; but they may be things; e.g. *blotter, poker, roller*, etc.

3. In some words, chiefly of Fr. origin, *-er* appears to be a mere extension of earlier words in *-er* denoting trades or offices; e.g. *caterer, fruiterer*, etc.

4. The suffix *-er* is also used to form sbs. serving as adaptations of L. types in *-logus*, *-graphus*; e.g. *chronologer, biographer*, etc.

-er[2], *suffix*, of various origin, occurring in sbs. and adjs. adopted from OFr.

1. ME. *-er*, repr. OFr. *-er*:—L. *-arem*, *-ar*: see -AR, and *sampler*.

2. ME. *-er*, – AFr. *-er* (OFr. *-ier*) in sbs. which descend from L. forms in *-arius*, *-arium* (see -ARY). The sense is 'a person or thing connected with', 'a receptacle for', as in *mariner, garner*, etc.

3. In mod. Eng. *-er* represents occas. other OFr. suffixes, as OFr. *-ëure* (:—L. *-aturam*), e.g. in *border*; and OFr. *-ëor*, now *-oir* (:– L. *-atorium*), e.g. in *laver*. The agent-suffix -OUR (OFr. *-eor*:—L. *-atorem*) is now very often replaced by *-er*.

-er[3], *suffix*, the formative of the comparative degree.

A. In *adjs.* ME. *-er, -ere* (*-ore, -ure*), *-re*, OE. *-ra* (fem., neut. *-re*) represents two different Gmc. suffixes; viz. *-izon-*, and *-ōzon-*, f. the adverbial *-iz, -ōz*: see B. In mod. Eng. the use of *-er* is almost restricted to words of one or two syllables.

B. In *adverbs*. The OE. form was *-or* :– Gmc. *-ōz*, ?f. *-ō* adverbial suffix + *-iz*, corresp. to L. -is in *magis, nimis*. The inflexional comparison still occurs in poetry, as in *keenlier* (Tennyson).

-er[4], *suffix*, the ending of certain AFr. infs. used as sbs.; e.g. *dinner, supper*; *user, waiver*.

-er[5], *suffix*, forming frequent. and iterative vbs., e.g. *chatter, patter, scatter*.

-er[6], *suffix*, in Oxford Univ. slang used in joc. formations, as *brekker* (f. *breakfast*), *footer* (f. *football*), SOCCER.

Era (īᵊ·ră). 1615. [– late L. *æra*, orig. pl. of *æs*, *ær-* copper in the sense 'counters (for calculation)', used as fem. sing. for 'number used as a basis of reckoning', 'item of account', 'epoch from which time is reckoned' (Isidore); see ORE.] **1.** A system of chronology, numbering years from some particular point of time 1646. **2.** = EPOCH I. 1. 1615. **3.** A date, or an event, which begins a new period in the history of anything; an important date. Cf. EPOCH I. 2. 1703. **4.** A period marked by the prevalence of some particular state of things 1741. **b.** = EPOCH II. b, c. 1796. **5.** The approximate date of an event, etc. 1714.

1. Dionysius the Abbot..brought in the Æra of Christ's Incarnation 1646. In the year 570 of our E...the man Mahomet was born CARLYLE. **2.** Some three centuries before our e. HERSCHEL. **3.** The landing of this English Governor was an e. in their lives DIXON. **4.** The polished æra of Queen Anne H. WALPOLE. **b.** The worst e. of architecture 1870.

Eradiate (ĭrēᶦ·di,eᶦt), *v.* 1647. [f. E- + RADIATE *v.*] **1.** *intr.* To shoot forth, as rays of light. **†2.** *trans.* To give forth like or in rays –1794. Hence **Era:dia·tion,** the action of eradiating; also *concr.*

Eradicate (ĭræ·dikeᶦt), *v.* 1564. [– *eradicat-*, pa. ppl. stem of L. *eradicare*, f. *e-* EX-[1] + *radix, radic-* root; see -ATE[3].] **1.** *trans.* To pull or tear up by the roots; to root out. **2.** To extirpate, get rid of 1647.

1. Okes eradicated By a prodigious whirlwind 1635. **2.** In hopes of eradicating mendicancy LECKY. Hence **Era·dicable** *a.* **Era:dica·tion**, the action of eradicating; total destruction; extirpation. **Era·dicator**, one who or that which eradicates. **Era·dicatory** *a.* tending to e.

Eradicative (ĭræ·dikătiv). 1543. [– OFr. *eradicatif, -ive* (f. as prec.; see -IVE), after *palliatif* PALLIATIVE.]

A. *adj.* Tending or serving to root out or expel (disease, etc.). Const. *of*.

†B. *sb.* An eradicative medicine 1654.

Erase (ĭrēᶦ·z, -s), *v.* 1605. [– *eras-*, pa. ppl. stem of L. *eradere*, f. *e-* EX-[1] + *radere* scrape.] **1.** *trans.* To scrape or rub out; to efface, expunge. **2.** *fig.* To obliterate from the mind or memory 1695. **3.** *transf.* To destroy utterly 1728.

1. To e. a letter 1778, a mark 1858, an obnoxious protestation 1863. **2.** To e. events from the memory SIR B. BRODIE. Hence **Era·sable** *a.* **Era·sement.** **Era·sion**, the action of erasing; an instance of it. **Era·sive** *a.* tending to e. (*rare*).

Erased (ĭrēᶦ·zd, -st), *ppl. a.* 1572. [f. prec. + -ED[1].] **1.** In senses of the vb. 1848. **2.** *Her.* Of the head or other part of an animal: Represented with a jagged edge, as if torn off.

Eraser (ĭrēᶦ·zəɹ, -səɹ). [f. as prec. + -ER[1].] One who, or that which, erases; anything used to erase writing, blots, etc.

Erasmian (ĭræ·zmiăn). 1758. [f. *Erasmus*, literary name of the eminent Dutch scholar (1466–1536) + -IAN.] **A.** *adj.* Pertaining to, or after the manner of, Erasmus 1881.

B. *sb.* A follower of Erasmus; *spec.* one who follows the system of pronunciation of ancient Greek advocated by him; opp. to *Reuchlinian*. Hence **Era·smianism,** the doctrines of Erasmus.

Erastian (ĭræ·stiăn). 1651. [f. Thomas *Erastus* (Liebler), Swiss physician and theologian (1524–1583) + -IAN.]

A. *adj.* Of or pertaining to Erastus or his doctrines 1837.

B. *sb.* An adherent of the doctrines attributed to Erastus; one who maintains the theory of the supremacy of the State in ecclesiastical affairs.

Many most respectable persons have been.. Erastians GLADSTONE. Hence **Era·stianism.** **Era·stianize** *v.* to organize (a church) on, or incline to, E. principles.

Erasure (ĭrēᶦ·ʒiŭɹ). 1734. [f. as ERASE + -URE.] **1.** The action of erasing, or an instance of it. **2.** The place where a word or letter has been erased 1891. **3.** Total destruction 1794.

1. The devise to the trustees was not revoked by the e. 1817. **2.** The word was written over an e. 1891. **3.** E. of cities GIBBON.

Erbia (ɜ·ɹbiă). 1869. [mod.L., f. *Ytt*)*erby*, where gadolinite is found, in which it occurs.] *Chem.* One of the three earths formerly called YTTRIA.

Erbium (ɜ·ɹbiŏm). 1843. [mod.L., f. prec.; cf. *sodium* f. *soda*, etc.] The metallic radical of erbia.

Erce-, Erche-, obs. ff. ARCH-.

†Erd, *sb.* [OE. *eard*, cogn. w. OS. *ard* dwelling, OHG. *art* ploughing, ON. *ǫrð* harvest :– Gmc. **arduz*, **ardō*, f. IE. **ar* plough. Cf. EAR *v.*[1]] **1.** Native land; a country –ME. **2.** In OE.: ?State, condition. Hence (in ME.) disposition. So **†E·rde** *v.* to dwell; to be or be found; *trans.* to inhabit.

Erd(e, etc., obs. ff. EARTH, etc.

Ere (ēᵊɹ). [OE. *ǣr* = OFris., OS., OHG. *ēr* (Du. *eer*, G. *eher*), Goth. *airis* :– Gmc. **airiz*, compar. of **air* early.]

A. *adv.* **1.** Early. Now only *Sc.* **†2.** Earlier –1650. **†3.** Rather, in preference –1536. **†4.** Before, formerly; just now –1647.

2. He that commeth after me, was before me because he was yer than I TINDALE *John* 1:15. **4.** He myght not do as he dyd ere 1557.

B. *prep.* **1.** Before (in time) OE. **2.** In the advb. phrases *ere then, ere this*, etc., before then, before this. Also ERELONG, ERENOW, EREWHILE. OE.

1. E're that time CLARENDON.

C. *conj.* **1.** Of time: Before. Also with *ever*. OE. **2.** Rather than OE.

1. Syr, come downe e. my child die *John* 4:49. This heart shal break..Or ere Ile weepe SHAKS.

†D. *adj.* Only in late OE. and ME. = 'early', 'former'.

Ere, var. of †EAR to plough.

Erebus (e·rĭbŏs). 1596. [– L. *Erebus* – Gr. Ἔρεβος, cogn. w. Goth. *riqis* darkness.] *Myth.* Name of 'a place of darkness, between Earth and Hades' (Liddell and Scott); usu. in *dark as E.*

Erect (ĭre·kt), *a.* ME. [– L. *erectus*, pa. pple. of *erigere* set up, f. *e-* EX-[1] + *regere* direct.] **1.** Upright; not bending forward or downward; vertical. Also used *Bot.* and *Her.* in general sense. Also *fig.* **2.** Chiefly participial: **†a.** Of the face: Uplifted, unabashed. **b.** Of the hair, etc.: Rigid, bristling. 1618. **†3.** *fig.* Of the mind: Uplifted; alert –1756.

1. The e. or vertical diameter of the Luminary 1726. *fig.* A spirit as e. as the king's tiara THIRLWALL. **2.** Her front e. with majesty she bore DRYDEN. With Ears and Tail e., neighing he paws the ground SOMERVILLE. **3.** It conduceth much to haue the Sense Intentiue and E. BACON. Hence **Ere·ct-ly** *adv.*, **-ness.**

Erect (ĭre·kt), *v.* ME. [– *erect-*, pa. ppl. stem of L. *erigere*; see prec.] **I. †1.** To direct upwards; to lift up –1696. †2. To raise in consideration; to exalt; elevate to office –1709.

1. E. your Heads, eternal Gates 1696. 2. We have seen. . Monarchs erected and deposed STEELE.

II. 1. To raise, set upright; to prick up (the ears); also *Phys.* (chiefly in pass.) to render turgid and rigid any organ containing erectile tissue 1573. †**b.** *intr.* for *refl.* To straighten oneself. BACON. †**2.** *fig.* To rouse, excite, embolden –1734.

1. Erecting one most like to fall TUSSER.

III. 1. To set up (a building, etc.); to build ME. Also *fig.* Also *absol.* **2.** *Geom.*, etc. To set up (a perpendicular, a figure of the heavens, etc.) 1646. **3.** To set up or found (an office, institution, etc.); to initiate (a project). *Obs.* or *arch.* exc. in *Law.* 1565.

1. To e. a statue SHAKS., a stove EVELYN, a House of Prayer DE FOE, an engine 1825. *fig.* Malebranche erects this proposition LOCKE (J.). 2. On B e. the perpendicular BA 1828. 3. Two Courts of High Commission were erected BUCKLE. Phr. *To e. into* [cf. Fr. *ériger en*]: to form into, set up as; To e. the town into a staple for wool SCOTT. Hence **Ere·ctable** *a.* **Ere·cter**: see ERECTOR.

Erectile (ĭre·ktil), *a.* 1830. [– Fr. *érectile*, f. as prec.; see -ILE.] Capable of being erected or set upright.

E. tissue: a kind of tissue found in animals, capable of being distended and becoming rigid under excitement; also, a similar tissue in vegetables. Hence **Erecti·lity.**

Erection (ĭre·kʃən). 1503. [– Fr. *érection* or L. *erectio*, f. as prec.; see -ION.] †**1.** A lifting up; also, an elevated condition –1692. †**2.** Advancement in condition; elevation to office –1661. **3.** A setting upright; an upright position 1622. **4.** *Phys.* The action of making rigid any organ containing erectile tissue; the condition of being so erected 1594. †**5.** Exaltation, excitement, invigoration –1651. **6.** The action of setting up (a building, column, etc.); *concr.* a building, structure. Also *fig.* 1609. †**7.** *Astrol.* The construction of a figure of the heavens. B. JONS. **8.** Constitution (of an office, institution, etc.). Also with *into.* 1508.

5. It must be a wonderful e. of their spirits, to know that God will be a father of those fatherless CLARENDON.

Ere·ctive, *a.* 1611. [f. ERECT *v.* + -IVE.] Tending to erect or set upright.

Erectopatent (ĭre:kto₁pæ·tĕnt, -pē̆i·tĕnt), *a.* 1848. [f. *erecto-* as comb. f. L. *erectus* ERECT *a.* + PATENT *a.* II. 3.] **a.** *Bot.* Having a position intermediate between erect and spreading. **b.** *Entom.* Having the primary wings at rest and the secondary horizontal.

Erector (ĭre·ktəɹ). Also **-er.** 1538. [f. ERECT *v.* + -OR 2.] **1.** One who, or that which, erects. †**2.** One who sets up a candidate or a pretender –1611. **3.** *Optics.* A tube with two lenses, slipped into the inner end of the draw-tube of a microscope, serving to erect the inverted image; an *erecting-glass* (*mod.*). **4.** A muscle which causes erection in any part. Also *attrib.* as in *erector-muscle.* 1831.

Erelong (ēᵊɹlǫ·ŋ), *adv.* Also as two wds. 1577. [f. ERE *prep.* + LONG *adv.*] Before the lapse of a long time; soon. Of future time; also (*arch.*) of past.

E. he had not only gotten pity but pardon 1586.

‖**Eremacausis** (e:rĭmăkǭ·sis). 1847. [mod. L., f. Gr. ἠρέμα quietly + καῦσις burning, f. καίειν burn.] *Chem.* 'A slow combustion taking place in presence of air and water, and accompanied by a kind of fermentation' (Watts).

Eremite (e·rĭməit). ME. [– OFr. *eremite*, var. of (*h*)*ermite* HERMIT.] **1.** A recluse, an anchoret. Also *transf.* **2.** A (?quasi-religious) mendicant, a vagabond (see HERMIT) 1495.

1. Heremytis. . þat flees þe felaghshipe of men HAMPOLE. *transf.* Who ledst this glorious E. (= 'desert-dweller') Into the Desert MILT. *P. R.* I. 8. Hence †**E·remitage,** the condition, or dwelling, of a hermit. **E·remiteship,** the condition of being a hermit. **E·remitism,** the state of a hermit. (Dicts.)

Eremitic, -al (erĭmi·tik, -ăl), *a.* 1483. [f. prec. + -IC; see -ICAL.] Of or pertaining to an eremite; characteristic of or habitual to an eremite.

Affecting much an Eremiticall and solitarie life 1601. So **E·remitish** *a.* resembling, or befitting, an eremite.

Erenow (ēᵊɹnau·), *adv.* Also as two wds. ME. [See ERE and NOW.] Before this time.

Ereption (ĭre·pʃən). 1633. [– L. *ereptio*, f. *erept-*, pa. ppl. stem of *eripere*, f. *e-* EX¹- + *rapere* seize, snatch.] The action of snatching away.

†**E·rer.** [OE. *ǣrra*, corresp. to OFris. *ērra*, OHG. *ēriro*, Goth. **airiza*; compar. of *ǣr* ERE. See -ER³, ERST.]

A. *adj.* Former –ME.

B. *adv.* **1.** Formerly –ME. **2.** Sooner, in preference –1560.

Erethism (e·rĭþiz'm). 1800. [– Fr. *éréthisme* – Gr. ἐρεθισμός, f. ἐρεθίζειν irritate. See -ISM.] *Path.* Abnormal excitement of an organ or tissue; also *transf.* Hence **Erethi·smic** *a.* resembling e. **Erethi·stic** *a.* relating to e.

Erewhile (eᵊɹ₁hwəi·l), *adv.* ME. [See ERE and WHILE.] A while before, some time ago.

The faces weeping lay That e. laughed the loudest MORRIS. So †**Erewhi·les** *adv.* [see WHILES].

†**Erf¹.** [OE. *erfe* (WS. *ierfe*) inheritance, corresp. to OFris. *erve*, OS. *erbi* (Du. *erf*), OHG. *erbi* (G. *erbe*), ON. *erfi*, OS. *arbi* :- Gmc. **arbjam.*] Cattle –ME.

Erf² (ǝɹf). *S. Afr.* 1887. [– Du. *erf* in same sense, orig. 'inheritance'; see prec.] 'A garden plot, usually containing about half an acre' (Webster).

Erg (ǝɹg). 1873. [– Gr. ἔργον work.] *Physics.* A unit of work or energy in the centimetre-gramme-second system, the work done by a force of one dyne acting in the direction of the force through a distance of one centimetre.

‖**Ergo** (ǝ·ɹgo), *adv.* ME. [L.; = 'therefore'.] *Logic.* A word used to introduce the conclusion of a syllogism. Hence †**E·rgo** *sb.* a conclusion, a conclusive authorization. **E·rgoism,** pedantic adherence to logically constructed rules.

Ergometer (əɹgǫ·mĭtəɹ). 1879. [f. Gr. ἔργον work + -METER.] An instrument for measuring work or energy.

Ergosterol (əɹgǫ·stĕrǫl). 1906. Earlier **ergosterin** (1889). [f. ERGOT + *-sterol* as in CHOLESTEROL: see -OL.] *Biochem.* An inert alchohol derived orig. from ergot, but now obtained from yeast and other sources.

Ergot (ǝ·ɹgǫ̆t), *sb.* 1683. [– Fr. *ergot*, OFr. *ar*(*i*)*got*, *argor* cock's spur, of unkn. origin.] **1.** A diseased transformation of the seed of rye and other grasses, being the *sclerotium* of a fungus (*Claviceps purpurea*), in colour dark-violet, and in form resembling a cock's spur. Also, the disease. **b.** The diseased seed of rye used as a medicine 1860. **2.** *Farriery.* 'A small horny capsule on each side of the claw. . in Ruminants and Pachyderms' (*Syd. Soc. Lex.*). **3.** *Anat.* A projection in the floor of the posterior extremity of the lateral ventricle of the brain; the *hippocampus minor* 1840.

†**E·rgot,** *v. rare.* 1653. [– Fr. *ergoter* (OFr. *argoter*) argue sophistically, quibble, rel. to *argot* cock's spur; see prec.] *intr.* To argue, wrangle –1658. Hence ‖**Ergoteur,** a wrangler.

Ergotic (əɹgǫ·tik), *a.* 1875. [f. ERGOT *sb.* + -IC.] Of, pertaining to, or resulting from ergot.

E. acid: 'a volatile acid said to exist in Ergot of rye' (*Syd. Soc. Lex.*).

Ergotine (ǝ·ɹgǫ̆tin). 1851. [f. as prec. + -INE⁵.] The active principle of ergot of rye. Hence **Ergo·tinine,** 'an unstable alkaloid existing in very small quantity in ergot' (Watts).

Ergotism¹ (ǝ·ɹgǫ̆tiz'm). 1853. [f. as prec. + -ISM. Cf. Fr. *ergotisme.*] **1.** The formation of ergot in grasses. **2.** The disease produced by ergotized grain, when eaten 1869. **3.** Poisoning by ergot 1884.

Ergotism² (ǝ·ɹgǒtiz'm). 1656. [– Fr. *ergotisme* (XVI), f. *ergoter*; see ERGOT *v.*, -ISM.] Arguing, wrangling; also, logical conclusions.

Ergotize (ǝ·ɹgǒtəiz), *v.* 1860. [f. ERGOT *sb.* + -IZE.] To affect with or transform into ergot. Hence **E:rgotiza·tion.**

Eria (īᵊ·riă). 1868. [Assamese *eriya* adj., f. *era* the castor-oil plant.] In *eria silk*: silk obtained from the cocoons of a silkworm (*Phalæna cynthia*), which feeds on the leaves of the castor-oil plant.

‖**Eric** (e·rik). 1586. [Ir. *eiric.*] *Hist.* A blood-fine or pecuniary compensation for the crime of murdering an Irishman.

‖**Erica** (ĭrəi·kă). 1826. [L. – Gr. ἐρείκη heath.] *Bot.* The genus of plants called in Eng. HEATH.

Ericaceous (erikēⁱ·ʃəs), *a.* 1882. [f. L. *erica*; see prec., -ACEOUS.] *Bot.* Belonging to the N.O. *Ericaceæ*, of which the *Erica* is the typical genus. So **Erici·neous** *a.* in same sense.

Ericetal (erĭsī·tăl), *a.* 1876. [f. L. *erica* heath + *-etum* (as in *arboretum*) + -AL¹.] *Bot.* Moorland.

Ericolin (eri·cǒlin). 1876. [f. ERICA + -OL + -IN¹.] *Chem.* A resinous substance found in *Ericaceæ.*

†‖**Eri·geron.** 1601. [Gr. ἠριγέρων, f. ἦρι early + γέρων old man.] Gr. name of the Groundsel –1666.

Erigible (e·ridʒib'l), *a.* 1803. [f. L. *erigere* (see ERECT *v.*) + -IBLE.] Capable of being erected.

Erinaceous (erinēⁱ·ʃəs, *a.* [f. L. *erinaceus* hedgehog + -OUS.] *Zool.* Pertaining to the hedgehog family; of the nature of a hedgehog. (Dicts.)

Eringo, var. of ERYNGO.

Erinite (e·rinəit). 1828. [f. *Erin* ancient name of Ireland + -ITE¹ 2b.] *Min.* A green arseniate of copper found in Ireland and in Cornwall.

Eri·nnic, *a.* [f. L. *Erinnys*, Gr. 'Ερινύς a Fury + -IC.] Characteristic of a Fury. SOUTHEY.

Eriometer (eri₁ǫ·mĭtəɹ). 1829. [f. Gr. ἔριον wool + -METER.] An instrument for measuring by optical means the diameter of small fibres, such as wool, cotton, etc.

Eristic (eri·stik). 1637. [– Gr. ἐριστικός, f. ἐρίζειν wrangle, f. ἔρις, ἐριδ- strife.]

A. *adj.* Of or pertaining to disputation; controversial.

Polemicke and Eristicke discourses 1637. So †**Eri·stical.**

B. *sb.* **1.** One given to disputation; a controversialist 1659. **2.** = Gr. ἡ ἐριστική (τέχνη), the art of disputation 1866.

1. Phr. *The Eristics*: the school of Megara.

Erke, obs. f. IRK.

Erl-king (ǝ·rl₁ki·ŋ). 1797. [tr. Ger. *erlkönig* (lit. alder-king), Herder's (erron.) tr. Da. *ellerkonge* king of the elves.] 'A goblin that haunts the Black Forest in Thuringia.'

†**Erme,** *v.* [ME. *erme*, repr. OE. (Anglian) **erman*, WS. *ierman*, f. *earm* miserable; corresp. to OHG. *erman*, ON. *erma.*] To be or make miserable –1481.

E·rmelin. Now *arch.* 1555. [Immediate source unc.; cf. Fr. *hermeline* (Boiste), *armeline* (Cotgr.), med.L. *armelinus*; see next.] = ERMINE 1, 2.

Ermine (ǝ·ɹmin), *sb.* ME. [– OFr. (*h*)*ermine* (mod. *hermine*) prob. :- med.L. (*mus*) *Armenius* 'Armenian mouse', equiv. to L. *mus Ponticus* (Pliny) 'mouse of Pontus'.] **1.** An animal of the weasel tribe (*Mustela Erminea*), found in northern countries, called in England a *stoat*, whose fur is reddish brown in summer, but in winter wholly white, except the tip of the tail, which is always black. **2.** The fur of the ermine, often with the black tails arranged upon it for the sake of effect; also in *pl.* trimmings, or garments, made of ermine ME. **3.** *fig.* With reference to the ermine worn by judges and peers 1794. **4.** *Her.* A heraldic fur; white marked with black spots of a triangular shape 1562. **5.** *attrib.* 1450; also quasi-*adj.* white as ermine 1610.

1. Fair ermines, spotless as the snows they press 1744. 3. Skilful lawyers. . were rewarded with e. 1856. 5. †*E. cross*: = cross ERMINEE. E. snow 1821.

Comb.: **e. white** *a.*, white as e.; **e. moth** (*Hyponomeuta padellus*), a moth with white wings spotted with black.

Hence **E·rmine** *v.* to clothe with or as with e. **E·rmined** *ppl.a.* trimmed with or made to resemble e.; robed in e., *i.e.* made a judge or a peer.

Erminee (ǝ·ɹmini), *a.* 1736. [– heraldic Fr. (*croix*) *erminée*, f. *ermine.* See -EE¹ 2.]

Her. Composed of four ermine spots placed in the form of a cross.

E·rmines. 1562. [perh. – OFr. *hermines*, pl. of *herminet*, dim. of *hermine* ERMINE.] *Her.* A fur forming the reverse of ERMINE, *i.e.* with white spots on a black ground.

Erminites (ə·ɹminəits). 1562. [– Fr. *herminite.*] *Her.* A heraldic fur resembling ermine, with the addition of a red hair on each side of the spots.

Erminois (əɹminoi·z). 1562. [– OFr. (*h*)*erminois*, f. *hermine* ERMINE.] A heraldic fur, Or with Sable spots.

Ermit(e, Ermitage. obs. ff. HERMIT, -AGE.

†Ern, *v.* [ME. *ernen*, OE. *irnan*, by metath. for *rinnan* run.] *intr.* To run; to flow –1600.

Ern, dial. f. EARN *v.*[1] to glean. So **Ernes** *sb.pl.* gleanings.

Erne (əɹn), *sb.* [OE. *earn* = MLG. *arn, arnt* (Du. *arend*), OHG. *arn*, ON. *ǫrn* :- Gmc. **arnuz.*] An eagle; *esp.* the *Sea-Eagle* (see EAGLE). *Comb.* **e.-stone** = AËTITES.

Erne, obs. f. EARN *v.*[2]

Ernes(se, -ŝt(e, etc., obs. ff. EARNEST.

Erode (ĭrōᵘ·d), *v.* 1612. [– Fr. *éroder*, or L. *erodere*, f. *e-* EX-[1] + *rodere* gnaw.] **1.** To gnaw away; to destroy by slowly eating out. **2.** *Geol.* To wear away; to eat out 1830.

1. The process of ulceration..eroding the middle coat [of the vessel] TODD. **2.** The materials through which the channel is eroded LYELL. Hence **Ero·ded** *ppl. a.* in senses of the vb.; *Bot.* = EROSE.

Erodent (ĭrōᵘ·dĕnt). [– *erodent-*, pr. ppl. stem of L. *erodere*; see prec., -ENT.] **A.** *adj.* 'Applied to medicines which cause erosion' (*Syd. Soc. Lex.*). **B.** *sb.* A substance which erodes. (Dicts.)

†E·rogate, *v.* 1531. [– *erogat-*, pa. ppl. stem of L. *erogare* pay out, f. *e-* EX-[1] + *rogare* ask; see -ATE[3].] *trans.* To pay out, expend. Also *absol.* –1692. Hence **†Eroga·tion,** expenditure; in *pl.* money expended.

Eros (īᵊ·rǫs, e·roᵘz). 1775. Pl. **Erotes** (erōᵘ·tez); **Eroses** (īᵊ·rǫsėz, e·roᵘzėz). [L. *Eros* – Gr. Ἔρως.] Love, the god of love: = CUPID.

Erose (ĭrōᵘ·s). 1793. [– L. *erosus*, pa. pple. of *erodere*; see ERODE.] *Bot.*, etc. Having the margin irregularly denticulated, as if bitten by an animal.

Erosion (ĭroᵘ·ʒən). 1541. [– Fr. *érosion* – L. *erosio*, f. *eros-*; see prec., -ION.] **1.** The action or process of eroding; the state of being eroded; *spec.* in *Geol.* Also *transf.* and *fig.* Also *concr.* **2.** *attrib.* 1879.

2. *E. theory*: the theory which accounts for the contour of the land by superficial denudation. Hence **Ero·sionist,** one who upholds this theory.

Erosive (ĭrōᵘ·siv), *a.* 1830. [f. L. *eros-* (see prec.) + -IVE.] Having the property of eroding.

Eroso- (ĭrōᵘ·so-), comb. f. L. *erosus* (see EROSE) in **Ero:so-de·ntate** *a.*, toothed irregularly, as if bitten; etc.

Erostrate (irǫ·streᶦt). 1866. [f. E- (see EX-[1]) + L. *rostrum* beak + -ATE[2].] *Bot.* Without a beak.

‖Erote·ma. 1589. [Late L. – Gr. ἐρώτημα, f. ἐρωτᾶν to question.] = next.

‖Erotesis (eroti·sis). 1657. [Late L. – Gr. ἐρώτησις, f. ἐρωτᾶν to question.] *Rhet.* A figure in which a speaker, in the form of a question, boldly asserts the opposite of what the question asks; as in 'Shall I be frighted when a madman stares?' Hence **Erote·tic** *a.* interrogatory.

Erotic (erǫ·tik). 1651. [– Fr. *érotique* – Gr. ἐρωτικός, f. ἔρως, ἐρωτ- sexual love.]

A. *adj.* Of or pertaining to the sexual passion; treating of love; amatory.

B. *sb.* An erotic poem; also [= ἐρωτική (τέχνη)], a doctrine or science of love. Hence **†Ero·tical** *a.* **Ero·tically** *adv.* **Ero·ticism,** e. spirit or character. So **E·rotism,** *Path.* sexual excitement; eroticism.

Erotomania (erōᵘ:tomē·niă). 1874. [f. *eroto-*, comb. form of Gr. ἔρως (see prec.) + -MANIA.] *Path.* Melancholy or madness caused by imaginative love or by sexual excitement.

Erpetology, -ist; see HERP-.

Err (əɹ), *v.* [ME. *erre* – OFr. *errer* :- L. *errare* :- **ersare*, rel. to Goth. *airzei* error, *airzjan* lead astray, OS., OHG. *irri* astray (G. *irre*).] **†1.** *intr.* To ramble, roam, stray –1697. **2.** To go astray; to miss, fail (*rare*) ME. **3.** To go wrong in judgement or opinion; to be incorrect ME. **4.** To go astray morally; to sin ME. **†5.** *trans.* To do or go wrong in –1644.

2. We haue erred and strayed from thy wayes, lyke loste shepe *Bk. Com. Prayer.* The arrows e. not from their aim SOUTHEY. **3.** Possibly the man may e. in his judgement of circumstances JER. TAYLOR. **4.** So Manasseh made Iudah..to erre 2 *Chron.* 33:9. Hence **†Err** *sb.* an error, fault; also heresy. **E·rringly** *adv.*

Errable (e·răb'l), *a. arch.* 1665. [– OFr *errable* or med.L. *errabilis*, f. *errare*; see prec., -BLE.] Fallible, liable to err. Hence **Errabi·lity,** liability to err. **†E·rrableness.**

Errabund (e·răbŏnd), *a.* [– L. *errabundus* wandering to and fro (late L. false, erroneous) f. *errare* ERR.] Erratic; as, *e.* guesses. SOUTHEY.

Errancy (e·rănsi). 1621. [f. ERRANT *a.*; see -ANCY.] The condition of erring or being in error.

Mr. Gladstone's e. 1864.

Errand (e·rănd). [OE. *ǣrende* = OFris. *ērende*, OS. *ārundi*, OHG. *ārunti* :- Gmc. **ǣrundjam*, obscurely rel. to ON. *eyrindi, ǫrindi, erindi*; ult. origin unkn.] **†1.** A message; a verbal communication for a third party –1754. **2.** A going with a message or a commission; *esp.* a short journey on which an inferior is sent to convey a message or do something for the sender OE. **3.** The business on which one goes; a purpose, intention ME.

1. Tel your King, from me, this e. 1583. **2.** The Doctor came on a fool's e. 1840. **3.** He had another errant to Persia, than buying of Slaves BENTLEY.

Errant (e·rănt), *a.* (*sb.*) ME. [In branch I – OFr. *errant*, f. (i) OFr. *errer* travel as in quest of adventure – Rom. **iterare*, for L. *itinerare* ITINERATE; (ii) *errer* wander, ERR. In II, see ARRANT. In III, – *errant-*, pr. ppl. stem of L. *errare* ERR.]

I. A. *adj.* **1.** Itinerant, travelling (in quest of adventure, or like a knight-errant) (*poet.*). **†2.** In **bailiff-errant** (see BAILIFF); **justice-errant,** a justice who travels on circuit –1641. Also *gen.*

B. *sb.* A knight-errant, or the like –1643.

II. 1. In phr. *errant* (*arrant*) *thief*: in Chaucer, the leader of a band of thieves; subseq., a notorious thief. *Obs.* exc. as ARRANT. **†2.** As an intensive: Unmitigated; thorough, downright –1776.

2. An errand grosse hypocrite 1619. So e. a whig 1710.

III. Astray, wandering; straying from the proper course, place, or standard ME.

Planets or e. Starres SIR T. BROWNE. The famous beauty and e. lady the Dutchesse of Mazarine 1676. With e. foot 1861.

Hence **†Erra·ntic** *a.* of or pertaining to knights errant. **E·rrantly** *adv.* at random.

Errantry (e·răntri). 1654. [f. prec. + -RY.] The condition of being errant; the condition or characteristics of a knight-errant.

Errata; see ERRATUM.

Erratic (eræ·tik). ME. [– OFr. *erratique* – L. *erraticus*, f. *errat-* pa. ppl. stem of *errare*; see ERR, -IC.]

A. *adj.* **1.** Wandering; first used of the planets, and of certain diseases, as gout, rheumatism, etc. **†2.** Vagrant; nomadic –1816. **3.** Having no fixed course 1841. **4.** Eccentric, irregular 1841.

1. The Erratick [stars] are seven STANLEY. A slow E. Fever 1725. **2.** My erratick industry JOHNSON. Phr. *E. blocks, boulders* (Geol.): masses of rock, that have been transported from their original locality, apparently by glacial action. **3.** E. puffs of wind 1879. **4.** An e. genius 1841.

B. *sb.* **1. †a.** A vagabond. **b.** An eccentric. 1623. **†2.** An erratic star, a planet (*rare*) 1714. **3.** *Geol.* An erratic block 1849.

Hence **Erra·tical** *a.*, **-ly** *adv.*, **-ness.**

Erratum (erēᶦ·tŏm). Pl. **-ta.** 1589. [– L. *erratum*, subst. use of n. pa. pple. of *errare* ERR.] **1.** An error in writing or printing. Also *transf.* **¶2.** In the forms *errata's*, or *erratæs* pl., and *errata* sing. = 'list of errata', with *-es* in *pl.* 1635.

2. A page Fill'd with Errata's of the present age QUARLES.

Errhine (e·rəin), *sb.* (*a*) 1601. [– mod.L. *errhinum* – Gr. ἔρρινον, f. ἐν in + ῥίς, ῥιν- nostril. Cf. Fr. *errhin* adj.] **1.** A medicine to be snuffed up the nose in order to increase the natural secretions and produce sneezing 1626. **†2.** A plug of lint steeped in this for insertion in the nose –1758. **3.** *adj.* Having the action of an errhine 1876.

Erroneous (erōᵘ·niəs), *a.* ME. [– OFr. *erroneus* or f. L. *erroneus* (whence Fr. *erroné*), f. *erro, erron-* vagabond, f. *errare*; see ERR, -EOUS.] **†1.** Wandering, roving; moving aimlessly. Also quasi-*adv.* –1777. **†b.** Straying from the proper course, as an *e.* circulation 1731. **2.** Straying from the moral, or wise course; misguided. *Obs.* or *arch.* 1512. **3.** Containing errors; of the nature of error; mistaken, wrong ME.; faulty in law, vitiated by error (see ERROR) 1495.

1. The Moon, e. in her course 1777. **2.** 'Tis difficult getting of good Doctrine in e. Times BUNYAN. That e. clemency JOHNSON. **3.** E. opinions 1494, spelling 1711. An e. supposition 1822, impression 1845. Hence **Erro·neous-ly** *adv.*, **-ness.**

Error (e·rəɹ). [ME. *errour* – OFr. *errour, errur* (mod. *erreur*) :- L. *error, error-*; see ERR, -OR 1. The form *error* dates from 1753.] **1.** The action of wandering; hence a devious or winding course. Now only *poet.* 1594. **†2.** Chagrin, fury; extravagance of passion –1460. **3.** The condition of erring in opinion; the holding of mistaken beliefs; a mistaken belief; false beliefs collectively. Also *personified.* ME. **4.** Something incorrectly done through ignorance or inadvertence; a mistake ME. **†b** A flaw, malformation; a miscarriage –1791. **c.** *Law.* A mistake in matter of law appearing on the proceedings of a court of record 1495. **d.** *Math.* The difference between an approximate result and the true determination 1726. **5.** A departure from moral rectitude: a transgression ME.

1. His e. by sea, the sack of Troy B. JONS. **3.** In Religion, What damned e., but some sober brow Will blesse it *Merch. V.* III. ii. 78. Phr. *To be, stand in, lead into e.*; *†without e.* = 'doubtless'. **4.** Errors of the press 1710. Phr. *Clerical e.* (see CLERICAL). **b.** *Nature's e.* = L. *lusus naturæ*; Sure, thou art an errour of nature BOSWELL. **c.** *Writ of e.*: a writ brought to procure the reversal of a judgement on the ground of e. (Now, since 1875, limited to criminal cases.) **5.** The errors of a very wild life BERKELEY.

Hence **E·rrorful** *a.* faulty. **E·rrorist,** one who is inclined to e.; one who encourages e. **E·rrorless** *a.* **E·rrorlessness.**

†Ers. ?*Obs.* 1578. [– Fr. *ers*, app. cogn. w. It. *ervo* :- L. *ervum.*] The bitter Vetch (*Ervum ervilia* L.).

Erse (əɹs), *a.* ME. [Early Sc. var. of IRISH.] **†1.** In early Sc. use: = IRISH. **2.** Applied by Sc. Lowlanders to the Highland Gaelic dialect, people, customs, etc. In 18th c. literary use, the Gaelic of Scotland, and occas. of Ireland; now, *occas.*, the Irish Gaelic alone. Nearly *Obs.* Hence **†E·rseman,** one who is E. by birth or descent.

Ersh; = EARSH *dial.*, eddish.

Erst (əɹst). [OE. *ǣrest*, superl. corresp. to *ǣr* ERE = OS. *ērist* (Du. *eerst*), OHG. *ērist* (G. *erst*); see -EST.]

A. *adj.* **†1.** First –ME. **†2.** *absol.* in advb. phrases –1596.

2. Phr. *Now at e.*: now and not sooner. (By Spenser taken erron. as = 'at once'.)

B. *adv.* **†1.** Earliest, soonest –ME. **†2.** In the first place. (Occas. pleonastically before *ere.*) –1587. **†3.** At first, as opp. to *afterwards* –1605. **†4.** Sooner, earlier; *esp.* with negs. –1588. **5. a.** Of old ME. **†b.** Not long ago –1791.

5. b. The..horrid spectacle, Which e. my eyes beheld, and yet behold MILT. *Sams.* 1543.

Erstwhile (ə·ɹst,hwəil), *adv. arch.* 1569. [f. ERST + WHILE.] Some while ago, formerly. Also *adj.* 1901. So **†E·rstwhiles** [see WHILES].

Erubescence (erube·sĕns). *rare.* 1736. [– late L. *erubescentia*, f. as next; see -ENCE.] Erubescent quality or state.

Erubescent (erube·sĕnt), *a.* 1736. [– *erubescent-*, pres. ppl. stem of L. *erubescere*, f. *e-* EX-[1] + *rubescere*, f. *rubēre* be red; see -ESCENT.] Reddening, blushing.

Erubescite (erube·səit). 1850. [f. L. *erubescere* (see prec.) + -ITE[1] 2b.] *Min.* A copper sulphide, purple copper.

‖**Eruca** (ĭrū·kă). *rare.* 1609. [L., = caterpillar.] The larva of a butterfly or the like; a caterpillar. Hence **Eru·ciform** *a.* caterpillar-like.

Erucic (ĭrū·sik), *a.* 1869. [f. L. *eruca* a kind of cabbage + -IC.] *Chem.* Of or pertaining to *eruca.*

E. acid 'an acid ($C_{22}H_{42}O_2$) obtained by the saponification of the fixed oil of white mustard (Sinapis alba)' (Watts).

Eruct (ĭrʊ·kt), *v.* 1666. [– L. *eructare*, f. *e-* EX-[1] + *ructare* belch.] **1.** *intr.* To void wind noisily from the stomach through the mouth. **2.** To emit by eructation; also *fig.* 1774. Hence **Eru·ction** (*rare*).

Eructate (ĭrʊ·ktēit), *v.* Now *rare.* 1638. [– *eructat-*, pa. ppl. stem of L. *eructare*; see prec., -ATE[3].] **1.** *trans.* To belch, vomit forth. Chiefly *transf.* and *fig.* **2.** *intr.* = ERUCT 1.

Eructation (ĭrʊktē·ʃən). 1533. [– L. *eructatio*, f. as prec.; see -ION.] **1.** The action of belching wind from the stomach through the mouth; belching. Also *transf.* and *fig.* **2.** *concr.* That which is belched forth. Also *fig.* 1607.

1. *transf.* The Ætna, whose eructations throw whole stones from its depths 1652.

Erudite (e·rŭdəit). ME. [– L. *eruditus*, pa. pple. of *erudire* instruct, train, f. *e-* EX-[1] + *rudis* rude, untrained; see -ITE[2].]

A. *adj.* **1.** †**a.** Trained. **b.** Learned, scholarly. (Now chiefly sarcastic.) **2.** Of books, etc.: Characterized by erudition 1533.

1. An e. Pedant MARSTON. **2.** E. theology JER. TAYLOR. Hence **E·rudite-ly** *adv.*, **-ness.**

B. *sb.* [So Fr. *érudit.*] An erudite person (*rare*) 1865.

Erudition (erudi·ʃən). ME. [– OFr. *érudition* or L. *eruditio*, f. *erudit-*, pa. ppl. stem of *erudire*; see prec., -ION.] †**1.** The action of training or instructing; education –1749. †**2.** *concr.* Imparted instruction; also, a doctrine, maxim –1574. **3.** †**a.** Trained condition. **b.** Later: Acquired book learning; scholarship. 1530. †**4.** Of a coin: Perfect workmanship –1747.

3. b. Exhibiting a little e. in such a manner as to make it look a great deal MACAULAY. Hence **Erudi·tional** *a.*

†**E·rugate**, *v. rare.* 1656. [– *erugat-*, pa. ppl. stem of L. *erugare* to smooth, f. *e-* EX-[1] + *ruga* wrinkle; see -ATE[3].] *trans.* To take out wrinkles from; to smooth –1657. So †**E·rugate** *ppl. a.* having the wrinkles rubbed out, smooth.

†**Eru·ginous**, *a.* 1646. [– L. *æruginosus*, f. *ærugo* verdigris; see -OUS. Cf. ÆRUGINOUS.] Partaking of the nature or substance of verdigris, or of copper itself; resembling verdigris –1666. var. †**Eru·ginary.**

†**Eru·mp**, *v.* 1657. [– L. *erumpere*, f. *e-* EX-[1] + *rumpere* burst forth.] To break out as an eruption. So **Eru·mpent** *a.* that bursts forth.

Erupt (ĭrʊ·pt), *v.* 1657. [– *erupt-*, pa. ppl. stem of L. *erumpere*; see prec.] **1.** *intr.* Of the teeth: To break through the skin of the gums. **b.** *trans.* To force through the gums 1859. **2.** *intr.* To break out in eruption, be in a state of eruption; to burst forth 1770. **b.** *trans.* To throw out in an eruption 1769.

2. The showers continued to e. 1866. The Don.. erupts into..a large inland lake 1864. **b.** The volcanic rocks of Tuscany..have been chiefly erupted beneath the sea LYELL.

Eruption (ĭrʊ·pʃən). 1555. [– OFr. *éruption* or L. *eruptio*, f. as prec.; see -ION.] **1.** A bursting forth from natural or artificial limits; also *concr.* that which bursts forth. Also *fig.* **2.** An outbreak of volcanic activity 1740. **3.** Of persons: The action of breaking forth from within boundaries; *e.g.* a hostile movement of armed men from a stronghold, or from their own country, etc. Now *rare.* 1615. **4.** *Path.* A breaking out of a rash, or of pimples on the skin; an efflorescence, rash 1596.

1. *concr.* The streets of Naples..paved with the matter of eruptions BERKELEY. *fig. L. L. L.* v. i. 121. **2.** Iceland chronicles give a list of 63 eruptions 1794. **3.** The eruptions of Barbarians BARROW. Hence **Eru·ptional** *a.* of or pertaining to volcanic e.

Eruptive (ĭrʊ·ptiv), *a.* 1646. [f. ERUPT + -IVE.] **1.** Bursting forth. **2.** Of or pertaining to volcanic eruption. Of rocks: Formed or forced up by eruption, showing traces of eruption. 1799. **3.** *Path.* Attended with or producing efflorescence 1790.

1. The sudden glance [lightning]..e. through the cloud 1744. **2.** Crystalline rock, both e. and metamorphic MURCHISON. **3.** Illness of an e. kind 1852. Hence **Eru·ptive-ly** *adv.*, **-ness. Erupti·vity.**

†**Eruptu·rient**, *a.* 1664. [f. L. *erupt-* (see ERUPT) + -URIENT.] On the point of bursting forth –1685.

-ery, *suffix*, ME. *-erie*, forming sbs., orig. in words adopted from Fr., and by extension in other words.

1. The Fr. *-erie* represents: **a.** Com. Rom. *-ari·a*, f. the L. suffix *-ario-* (Fr. *-ier, -er*) + the suffix *-i·a* (Fr. *-ie*, -Y[3]); **b.** the addition of the suffix *-ie* to agent-nouns in OFr. *-ere, -eor* (mod. Fr. *-eur*) :—L. *-ator, -atorem.*

2. The derivs. of sbs. in *-er* and of vbs. denote the place where an employment is carried on, as *bakery, brewery*, etc.; or classes of goods, as *ironmongery*, etc.; with an extension in a general collective sense (= '*-ware*', '*-stuff*'), as in *machinery, scenery.* The wds. formed by adding *-ery* to sbs. signify a state or condition, as *slavery*; or 'that which is connected with the sb.', as *popery*; or often the place where certain animals are kept or plants cultivated, as *swannery, vinery.* In the pl. form the suffix has of late given rise to various jocular nonce-wds.; *e.g.* 'the Fisheries' for the Fisheries Exhibition of 1883, and the like. Cf. 'The Dukeries'.

3. See also the contracted form -RY.

Eryngo (iri·ŋgo). 1596. [– It. or Sp. *eringio* – L. *eryngium* – Gr. ἠρύγγιον, dim. of ἤρυγγος name of the plant.] †The candied root of the Sea Holly (*Eryngium maritimum*), formerly used as an aphrodisiac –1709. Also, the plant itself, or any allied plant. (In this sense in L. form *eryngium.*) 1668. var. †**Ery·nge.**

Erysipelas (erisi·pĭləs). ME. [– L. *erysipelas* – Gr. ἐρυσίπελας, perh. f. base of ἐρυθρός red + πελ- in πέλλα skin.] *Path.* A local febrile disease accompanied by diffused inflammation of the skin; often called St. Anthony's fire, or 'the rose'.

Hence **E:rysi:pela·tic** *a.* of the nature of or resembling e. **E:rysipe·latoid** *a.* resembling e. †**Erysi·pelous**, †**E:rysipe:lato·se** *adjs.* = next.

Erysipelatous (e:rĭsipe·lătəs), *a.* 1646. [f. med.L. *erysipelatus* (f. stem of Gr. ἐρυσίπελας, -ατ-) + -OUS. Cf. Fr. *érysipélateux* (XVI).] Pertaining to, of the nature of, or affected with, erysipelas.

Erythema (eriþī·mă). 1766. [mod.L. – Gr. ἐρύθημα, f. ἐρυθαίνειν be red, f. ἐρυθρός red.] *Path.* A superficial inflammation of the skin, showing itself in rose-coloured patches. Hence **E:rythema·tic, Erythe·matous** *adjs.* of, pertaining to, or of the nature of, e.

Erythrean, -æan (eriþrī·ăn), *a.* [f. L. *erythræus* – Gr. ἐρυθραῖος, f. ἐρυθρός red + -AN.] Red; as in the *E.* main. MILTON.

Erythric (eri·þrik), *a.* 1840. [f. Gr. ἐρυθρός red + -IC.] *Chem.* In *E. acid*: = next.

Erythrin (eri·þrin). 1838. [f. as prec. + -IN[1].] *Chem.* 'An acid ($C_{20}H_{22}O_{10}$) discovered by Heeren in *Rocella tinctoria*; it appears also to be contained in most of the lichens from which archil is prepared' (Watts).

‖**Erythrina** (eriþrəi·nă). 1865. [mod.L., f. as prec.; see -INA[2].] *Bot.* The Coral-tree, a tropical genus of leguminous plants bearing clusters of blood-red flowers.

Erythrine (eri·þrəin). 1837. [f. as prec. + -INE[5].] *Min.* Hydrous cobalt arsenate.

Erythrite (eri·þrəit). 1844. [f. as prec. + -ITE[1] 2b.] **1.** *Min.* **a.** = prec. **b.** 'A flesh-coloured feldspar, containing 3 per cent. magnesia, found in amygdaloid' (Watts). **2.** *Chem.* An organic substance obtainable from erythrin 1865.

Erythro- (eri·þro-) (bef. a vowel *ery·thr-*), comb. f. Gr. ἐρυθρός red, in compounds occurring in *Chem.* and *Min.*, as,

Ery·thro-benze·ne, a red dye obtained from nitrobenzene. **Erythro·lein** [see OLEIN]. **Ery:throli·tmin** [see LITMUS and -IN], 'red substances obtained from litmus' (Watts). **Ery·throphyll** [Gr. φύλλον leaf], the red colouring matter of leaves in autumn; so **Ery:throphy·llin. Ery:throphy·toscope** [Gr. φυτόν plant + -σκοπος] = ERYTHROSCOPE. **Ery:thropro·tid** [see PROTEID], 'a red extractive matter obtained by Mulder from albumin and allied substances.' **Ery:throre·tin** [see RETENE and -IN], 'a resinous constituent of rhubarb-root, soluble with purple-red colours in alkalis' (Watts). **Ery·throscope** [Gr. -σκοπος], an optical contrivance, by which the green of leaves is caused to appear red, while other green objects retain their hue. **Ery·throsi·derite** [Gr. σίδηρος + -ITE], a hydrous chloride of potassium and iron formed by sublimation in the lavas of Vesuvius. **Ery·throzyme** [Gr. ζύμη leaven], 'an azotised substance which exists in madder root, and gives rise to a peculiar transformation of rubian' (Watts).

Erythrogen (eri·þrodʒen). 1846. [f. ERYTHRO- + -GEN.] **1.** *Bot.* A variety of Chromogen, so called because it produces a red colour with acids (*Syd. Soc. Lex.*). **2.** *Chem.* 'A crystalline, fatty substance obtained from diseased bile; so called from the reddish or purple colour of some of its compounds' (Watts).

E·rythroid, *a.* [f. Gr. ἐρυθρός red + -OID.] Of a red colour. (Dicts.)

Es-, *prefix*, = OFr. *es-* :– L. *ex-* out, as in *escape, escheat.* In a few words refashioned, after L., as *esample*, now *example, eschange*, now *exchange*; otherwise obsolete. See also A- *pref.* 9.

†**Esba·tement.** 1475. [– OFr. *esbatement* (mod. *ébattement*), f. *(s')esbatre* divert (oneself), f. *es-* Es- + *batre* beat; see BATE *v.*[1], -MENT.] Amusement; an amusement –1531.

†**Esbay·**, *v.* 1480. [– OFr. *e(s)baïr* (mod. *ébahir*) astound; see ABASH.] *trans.* To dismay –1531.

Escalade (eskălē·d), *sb.* 1598. [– Fr. *escalade* – Sp. *escalada, -ado* (also used in Eng. XVI–XIX), = It. *scalata*, f. med.L. *scalare* SCALE *v.*[3]; see -ADE.] The action of scaling the walls of a fortified place by means of ladders; also *transf.* and *fig.*

The wall had been protected against such an e. by..old bottles STEVENSON. var. **Escala·do** (*arch.*).

Escalade (eskălēi·d), *v.* 1801. [f. prec. sb.] To climb up and get over (a wall, etc.) by means of ladders; to scale. Hence **Escala·der.**

Escalator (e·skălēitəɹ). orig. *U.S.* 1904. [f. stem of ESCALADE *v.* + -ATOR, after *elevator.*] A moving staircase for carrying passengers up and down.

‖**Escallonia** (eskălōu·niă). 1882. [mod.L., f. *Escallon* the discoverer. See -IA[1].] *Bot.* A genus of flowering shrubs (N.O. *Saxifragaceæ*) found in the temperate parts of S. America.

Escallop (eskæ·ləp). 1610. [– OFr. *escalope* shell; see SCALLOP, which is found much earlier.] **1.** = SCALLOP 1. **2.** *Her.* = ESCALLOP-SHELL 1671. **3.** One of a series of segments of circles forming a scalloped edge. Usu. SCALLOP. 1691.

3. The figure of the leaves..divided into so many jags or Escallops RAY. Hence **Esca·lloped** *ppl.a.* = SCALLOPED 1, 2.

Esca·llop-she·ll. 1610. [See prec.] **1.** The shell (usu. one valve) of the escallop 1628. **2.** An imitation of this for ornamental purposes; *e.g.* in the collar of the order of St. Michael 1664. **3.** *Her.* The figure of an escallop borne as a charge 1610.

1. The escalop-shell, the device of St. James, was adopted as the universal badge of the palmer 1846.

†**Esca·ndalize**, *v.* 1574. [– Sp. *escandalizar.*] = SCANDALIZE, q.v. –1640.

Escapade (eskăpē·d). 1653. [– Fr. *escapade* – Pr. or Sp. *escapade*, f. *escapar*; see ESCAPE *v.*, -ADE.] **1.** An act of escaping from confinement; *fig.* an act in disregard of restraint or rules; a prank. †**2.** Of a horse: A fit of plunging and rearing (*rare*). DRYDEN.

1. *fig.* Lord R. Churchill's latest e. 1885.

‖**Escapado** (eskăpā·do). [Sp.] An escaped prisoner. 1881.

Escape (ėskēi·p), *sb.*[1] ME. [In earliest use – OFr. *eschap*, f. *eschaper* (see ESCAPE *v.*); later from the verb.] **1.** The action of escaping, or fact of having escaped from custody, danger, etc.; *spec.* in *Law* (see quot.). **2.** *concr.* A garden plant growing wild 1870. **3.** A means of escape; also, short for FIRE-ESCAPE 1810. **4.** Leakage, as of water, gases, etc. 1874. †**5.** A sally –1796. †**6.** An inadvertence, mistake; a clerical error –1844. †**7.** A transgression (SHAKS.); a peccadillo –1678.

1. What, has he made an e.! which way B. JONS. E. is where one that is arrested commeth to his liberty before that he be delivered by award of any Justice, or by order of Law *Termes de la Ley* 142. 5. *Meas. for M.* IV. i. 63. 7. Rome will despise her for this foul e. *Tit. A.* IV. ii. 113.

Comb.: **e.-pipe**, the pipe through which steam passes from an e.-valve; **-valve** (*Steam-engine*), a relief valve to provide for the exit of steam or water when necessary; **-warrant**, a process addressed to sheriffs, etc., to retake an escaped prisoner; **-wheel**, an *escapement-wheel*.

Escape (ėskēⁱ·p), *sb.*² 1846. [– Fr. *escape*, f. L. *scapus*; see SCAPE *sb.*².] *Arch.* Properly, shaft of a column; occas. = APOPHYGE.

Escape (ėskēⁱ·p), *v.* [ME. – AFr., ONFr. *escaper* (mod. *échapper*) :– Rom. **excappare*, f. L. *ex* EX-¹ + med.L. *cappa* cloak (see CAP *sb.*¹). See also ASCAPE, SCAPE *v.*] **1.** *intr.* To gain one's liberty by flight. **b.** Of fluids, etc.: To issue, find egress 1450. †**2.** *trans.* To effect one's flight from; to free oneself from; to get safely out of –1667. **b.** To issue unawares from (a person, his lips) ME. **3.** *intr.* To flee and get off safely; to avoid any threatened evil; to go unpunished ME. **4.** *trans.* To get clear away from; to succeed in avoiding; to elude ME.

1. Such sure watch layd vpon him that he cannot eskape MORE. **b.** Common electricity escapes when the pressure of the atmosphere is removed MRS. SOMERVILLE. **2. b.** No word of courtesy escaped his lips 1870. **3.** They escaped all safe to land *Acts* 27:44. **4.** To e. the multitude DANIEL, mistakes 1669, suspicion JORTIN, observation 1821. The name of which escapes me DICKENS.

Hence **Esca·pable** *a.* that can be escaped. **Esca·peless** *a.* that cannot be escaped. **Esca·per. Esca·pingly** *adv.*

Escapement (ėskēⁱ·pmĕnt). 1779. [– Fr. *échappement* (1718), f. *échapper*; see prec., -MENT.] **1.** The action of escaping (*rare*) 1824; an outlet 1856. **2.** In a watch or clock, the mechanism which intervenes between the motive power and regulator, and which alternately checks and releases the train, thus causing an intermittent impulse to be given to the regulator. (So named with reference to the regulated escape of the toothed wheel from its detention by the pallet.) 1779. **3.** *Mus.* In a piano action, the contrivance which causes the hammer to rebound after striking 1896. **4.** The mechanism which controls the movement of the carriage in a typewriter.

Escarbuncle (ėskā·ɹbɒŋk'l). 1572. [– OFr. *escarbuncle* (mod. *escarboucle*), f. *es* ES-; see CARBUNCLE.] *Her.* = CARBUNCLE 2.

‖**Esca·rgatoire.** [Mis-spelling of Fr. *escargotière*.] A place for rearing snails. ADDISON.

†**Esca·rmouche,** *sb.* 1475. [– Fr. *escarmouche*; see SKIRMISH *sb.*] A skirmish; a fit of anger –1820.

Escarp (ėskā·ɹp), *sb.* 1688. [– Fr. *escarpe*, – It. *scarpa*; see SCARP *sb.*²] *Fortif.* 'A steep bank or wall immediately in front of and below the rampart. . generally the inner side of the ditch' (Adm. Smyth). Also *transf.*

Escarp (ėskā·ɹp), *v.* 1728. [– Fr. *escarper*, f. *escarpe*; see prec. and SCARP *v.*, which is the more usual.] *trans.* To form into a steep slope or escarp; to furnish with scarps.

The Glacis was all escarp'd upon the live Rock 1728.

Escarpment (ėskā·ɹpmĕnt). 1802. [– Fr. *escarpement*, f. *escarper*; see prec., -MENT.] **1.** Ground cut into the form of an escarp for the purpose of fortification. **2.** *Geol.* 'The abrupt face or cliff of a ridge or hill range' (Page). Also *transf.* 1813.

2. *transf.* A naked e. of ice, twelve hundred feet high KANE.

†**Escarteled, escartelee.** 1688. [f. OFr. *escartelé*, pa. pple. of *escarteler* (mod. *écarteler*) break into quarters, f. *es-* ES- + *quartier* QUARTER; see -ED¹, -EE¹.] *Her.* **1.** Quartered or quarterly. (Dicts.) ¶**2.** Having a square notch. R. HOLME.

-escent, *suffix*, repr. Fr. *-escent* and its source L. *escent-*, pres. ppl. stem of vbs. in *-escere*, chiefly inceptives f. vbs. of state in *-ēre*, e.g. *liquescere* f. *liquēre* be liquid; primarily occurring in adjs. – L. pres. pples. (orig. through Fr.), as *deliquescent*, *effervescent*, *obsolescent*, *putrescent*, the general sense being 'beginning to assume a certain state'; later used to form adjs. from sbs., as in *alkalescent*, f. *alkali*, and in several words describing the play of light and colour, as *fluorescent*, *iridescent*, *opalescent*, *phosphorescent*. The corresp. suffix of infinitives is **-esce**, and of nouns of state **-escence**, less frequently **-escency**.

Eschalot (eʃălǫ·t). 1707. [– Fr. *eschalotte* (now *échalotte*); see SHALLOT.] = SHALLOT.

Eschar (e·skaɹ). 1543. [– Fr. *eschare* or late L. *eschara* – Gr. ἐσχάρα; see SCAR *sb.*²] *Path.* 'A. . dry slough, resulting from the destruction of a living part, either by gangrene, by burn, or by caustics' (*Syd. Soc. Lex.*). Also *transf.* Hence †**E·scharous** *a.* full of eschars; resembling an e.; scabby.

Escharotic (eskărǫ·tik). 1612. [– Fr. *escharotique* or late L. *escharoticus* – Gr. ἐσχαρωτικός, f. ἐσχάρα; see prec., -OTIC.]

A. *adj.* Tending to form an eschar, caustic. **B.** *sb.* An e. drug; a caustic 1655.

Eschatology (eskătǫ·lŏdʒi). 1844. [f. Gr. ἔσχατος last + -LOGY.]. *Theol.* The science of 'the four last things: death, judgement, heaven, and hell'.

E., the science of the last things, is, as a science, one of the most baseless 1879. Hence **Eschato·lo·gical** *a.* of or concerted with e. **Eschato·logist,** one who treats of e.

†**Eschau·fe,** *v.* ME. [– OFr. *eschaufer* (mod. *échauffer*) :– Rom. **excalefare* for L. *excalefacere*, f. *ex-* EX-¹ + *calefacere* make warm. See CHAFE *v.*, ACHAFE.] *trans.* To heat, warm; also *fig.* –1530.

Eschaunge, obs. var. of EXCHANGE.

Escheat (es,tʃī·t), *sb.* [ME. *eschete* – OFr. *eschete* :– **excadecta*, subst. use of pa. pple. of Rom. **excadēre*, for L. *excidere* fall away, escape, etc., f. *ex* EX-¹ + *cadere* fall.] **1.** *Law.* An incident of feudal law, whereby a fief reverted to the lord when the tenant died seised without heir. (See also ATTAINDER.) Hence, the lapsing of land to the Crown (in U.S. to the state), or to the lord of the manor, on the death of the owner intestate without heirs. **b.** In Scotland: Confiscation or forfeiture of property, real or personal 1457. **2.** Property falling by e. to the lord, king, or state ME. **3.** The right of appropriating escheats 1570. †**4.** A writ to recover escheats. Now abolished. –1842. **5.** Forced contribution, plunder; in *pl.* booty. –1609.

1. Escheats were frequent in England, because there was no power of willing away land BUCKLE. **5.** To make one great by others losse is bad excheat SPENSER.

Escheat (es,tʃī·t), *v.* ME. [f. prec. sb.; cf. ACHEAT *v.*] **1.** *trans.* To make an escheat of, confiscate; †*Sc.* to forfeit. Also *transf.* and *fig.* **2.** *intr.* To become an escheat; to revert by escheat to the lord, king, or state. Also *fig.* 1531.

Hence **Eschea·table** *a.* liable to escheat. **Eschea·tage,** the right of succeeding to an escheat. **Eschea·tor,** an officer formerly appointed to take notice of the escheats in his county, and to certify them into the Exchequer; hence **Eschea·torship,** the office of escheator.

†**Eschel** (e·ʃĕl). 1753. [– G. *eschel* zaffre, f. *esche*, dial. var. of *asche* ashes.] A grey substance resembling ashes, used to mix with smalt when in fusion.

†**Eschele.** ME. [– OFr. *eschele*, *eschiele*, *eschiere* (mod. *échelle* section of men, echelon), blending of *échelle* ladder, SCALE *sb.*³ and Frankish **skara* military unit.] A troop (of soldiers) –1460.

†**Esche·ve,** *v.* ME. [– OFr. *eschever*, *-ir*, var. of *achever* ACHIEVE.] = ACHIEVE –1533.

Eschevin, obs. var. of ECHEVIN.

†**Eschew·,** *a.* ME. only. [–·OFr. *eschieu* :– Rom. **skivo*, f. Gmc.; see next; cf. OE. *sceoh* SHY *a.*] Loth, unwilling.

Eschew (es,tʃū·), *v.* ME. [– OFr. *eschiver* (mod. *esquiver* – It.) :– Rom. **skivare* – Gmc. **skeuχ(w)an* (OHG. *skiuhen*, G. *scheuen*), *f.* **skeuχ(w)az* SHY *a.*] **1.** *trans.* To avoid, shun; to abstain carefully from. †**2.** *intr.* To get off, escape –1560.

1. They must not only e. evil but do good in the world BEVERIDGE. **2.** I promit. . That he sall not e. away, nor fle 1560. Hence **Eschew·al,** a keeping clear of (evil). **Eschew·ance,** avoidance. **Eschew·er. Eschew·ment,** eschewance.

†‖**Escho·ppe.** [Fr. (now *échoppe*) :– L. *scalprum*.] A graver. EVELYN.

‖**Eschscholtzia** (eʃǫ·ltsiă). 1857. [mod.L.; named 1821 by Adelbert von Chamisso after J.F. *v. Eschscholtz*, a German botanist; see -IA¹.] *Bot.* A Californian genus of herbaceous plants (N.O. *Papaveraceæ*); *E. californica*, the best-known species, has large bright yellow flowers, saffron-coloured in the centre.

‖**Esclandre** (ęsklāndr'). 1855. [Fr. :– L. *scandalum*; see SCANDAL and SLANDER.] Unpleasant notoriety; a scandalous occurrence; a scene.

†‖**Esclavage** (esklavāʒ). 1758. [Fr., used in same sense.] A necklace composed of rows of gold chains, beads, or jewels, so called as resembling the fetters of a slave –1834.

Escocheon, obs. f. ESCUTCHEON.

Escopette (eskope·t). *U.S.* 1805. [– Sp. *escopeta* (assim. to Fr. *escopette* – It.) – It. *schioppetto*, dim. of *schippo* carbine.] A sort of carbine. var. **Escope·tto.**

Escort (e·skǫɹt), *sb.* 1579. [– Fr. *escorte* – It. *scorta*, subst. use of fem. pa. pple. of *scorgere* guide, conduct.] **1.** *Mil.* A body of armed men accompanying a traveller or travellers for protection, surveillance, or as a mark of honour, or serving as a convoy for baggage, provisions, etc. Also *transf.* **2.** *abstr.* Attendance in the capacity of an e. 1833.

1. The e. of the military chest WELLINGTON. *transf.* The courier and his e. 1847. **2.** To make him desire Cooper's e. HT. MARTINEAU.

Escort (eskǫ·ɹt), *v.* 1708. [– Fr. *escorter* – It. *scortare*; see prec.] *trans.* To act as an escort to; to accompany for the purpose of protection or guidance, or as a civility.

Catharine, escorted by old Henshaw and a groom of the Knight of Kinfauns SCOTT.

Esco·t, *sb.* [AFr. form of SCOT², = OFr. *escot* (mod. *écot*).] = SCOT². JOHNSON.

†**Esco·t,** *v.* [– OFr. *escoter*, f. *escot*; see prec.] To pay a reckoning for, maintain. *Haml.* II. ii. 362.

†**Escou·t,** *sb.* 1560. [– ·OFr. *escoute* fem. (mod. *écoute*) act of listening, sentinel, f. *escouter* (mod. *écouter*) listen; see SCOUT *sb.*²] Look-out 1630; a SCOUT –1603. Also as *v.* HOLLAND.

Escribe (īskrəi·b), *v.* 1558. [f. E- + L. *scribere* write. Cf. SCRIBE *v.*, EXSCRIBE.] †**1.** *trans.* To write or copy out. **2.** *Math.* To describe (a circle) so as to touch one side of a triangle exteriorly, and the other two produced 1870.

†**Escri·me.** *rare.* 1652. [– Fr. *escrime*, f. *escrimer* fence.] Fencing; swordsmanship. So †**Escri·mer,** a fencer, a swordsman.

†**E·script.** 1483. [– OFr. *escript*; see SCRIPT.] A writing; *spec.* a writ –1724.

Escritoire (ęskritwā·r, e·skritwǭɹ). 1706. [– OFr. *escritoire*, orig. masc., in sense 'study' (mod. *écritoire*) :– L. SCRIPTORIUM.] A writing-desk; a bureau, secretary. Hence **Escrito·rial** *a.* COWPER.

Escrod (eskrǫ·d). = SCROD. 18..

Escroll (eskrōᵘ·l). 1610. [– OFr. *escroele*, dim. of *escroe*; see next and SCROLL.] †**1.** *Law* = ESCROW –1736. **2.** *Her.* = SCROLL 1610.

Escrow (eskrōᵘ·). 1598. [– AFr. *escrowe*, OFr. *escroe* scrap, scroll :– med.L. *scroda* – Gmc. **skrauđ-* SHRED *sb.*] *Law.* A deed, bond, or other engagement delivered to a third party to take effect upon a future condition, and not till then to be delivered to the grantee.

†**Escry·,** *sb.* 1483. [f. next. Cf. SCRY *sb.*] **a.** Outcry; notoriety. **b.** Battle-cry (*lit* and *fig.*). –1538.

†**Escry·,** *v.* 1475. [– OFr. *escrier* (mod. *écrier*), f. *es-* ES- + *crier* cry. Cf. ASCRY *v.*, SCRY *v.*] **1.** *intr.* To cry out –1533. **2.** *trans.* To call out to; to invoke –1530. **3.** *trans.* = DESCRY –1625.

Escuage (e·skiuėdʒ). Now *Hist.* 1513. [– AFr., OFr. *escuage*, f. *escu* (mod. *écu*) shield (:– L. *scutum*) + *-age* -AGE. Cf. SCUTAGE.] **1.** A form of feudal tenure (*lit.* shield-service), personal service in the field for forty days in each year. **2.** = SCUTAGE 1577.

‖**Escudero** (eskudē·ro). 1637. [Sp.; f. *escudo* shield.] A shield-bearer; an esquire; hence, an attendant.

Esculapian, var. of ÆSCULAPIAN.

Esculent (e·skiŭlĕnt). 1625. [– L. *esculentus*, f. *esca* food, f. **ed-* of *edere* eat; see -ULENT.]

A. *adj.* Suitable for food, edible. Also as quasi-*sb.* 1626. Hence †**E·sculency,** e. quality.

B. *sb.* Anything fit for food; *esp.* vegetables.

An e. something like the cabbage YEATS.

Esculin(e, var. f. ÆSCULIN.

Escu·rialize, *v. nonce-wd.* 1843. [f. *Escurial* (better *Escorial*), name of the chief palace of the Spanish kings, about 30 miles from Madrid.] *trans.* To subject to influences like those which prevailed at the Escurial.

Escutcheon (eskɒ·tʃən). 1480. [– AFr., ONFr. *escuchon* (OFr. *escusson*, mod. *écusson*) :– Rom. **scutio, -ōn-*, f. L. *scutum* shield.] **1.** *Her.* The shield or shield-shaped surface on which a coat of arms is depicted; also, the shield with the bearings; a representation of this. Also *fig.* †**2.** A hatchment –1820. **3.** Anything shaped like, or resembling, an e., as: **a.** *Arch.* A shield-shaped ornament, chiefly in Gothic buildings 1875. **b.** A name-plate, a keyhole-plate, etc. 1655. **c.** *Naut.* 'The compartment in the middle of a ship's stern, where her name is written' (Smyth). **d.** *Zool.* An oval depression behind the beaks of certain bivalves 1854.

1. *fig.* A dark blot on the e. of the House of Godwine FREEMAN. Phr. *E. of pretence*; the small e. bearing the arms of an heiress placed in the centre of her husband's shield. **2.** Mrs. Veal was ..dead, and her escutcheons were making DE FOE.

-ese, *suffix*, forming adjs. from names of countries and towns; – OFr. *-eis* (mod. *-ois, -ais*) :– Rom. **-ese* :– L. *-ensem*, with the sense 'belonging to, originating in'. These adjs. may be used as sbs. From the use with authors' names, e.g. *Carlylese*, arose JOURNALESE, etc.

Ese, esement, etc., obs. ff. EASE, etc.

Esemplastic (esemplæ·stik), *a.* 1817. [f. Gr. ἐς into + ἕν, neut. of εἷς one + πλαστικός, f. πλάσσειν to mould; an irreg. formation after Ger. *ineinsbildung* forming into one.] Moulding into unity; unifying.

Nor I trust will Coleridge's..word e...ever become current HARE.

Eserine (e·sĕrəin). 1879. [– Fr. *ésérine*, f. *éséré*, native name; see -INE[5].] *Chem.* A crystalline alkaloid obtained from the Calabar bean, the fruit of *Physostigma venenosum*. It is used in ophthalmic surgery to produce contraction in the pupil of the eye.

†**Esguard.** 1616 [– OFr. *esgard* (mod. *égard*) lit. 'look, attention'; see Es- and GUARD.] A tribunal of the Knights of St. John, which settled differences within the order.

Esker (e·skəɹ). 1852. [– Ir. *eiscir.*] *Geol.* An Irish name for ridges of post-glacial gravel.

Esloign, -loin(e, obs. ff. ELOIN.

†**Esmay·le, emayle.** 1589. [– OFr. *esmail* (mod. *émail*); see AMEL.] Enamel –1594.

Esne (e·znĭ). Now *Hist.* [OE. *esne* = OHG. *asni*, Goth. *asneis* day-labourer.] A serf, hireling.

Theow and E. art thou no longer SCOTT.

†**E·snecy.** 1607. [– med.L. *æs-, esnecia*, latinized form of OFr. *ainzneësse* (mod. *aînesse*), f. *ainz* before, earlier (:– Rom. **antius*) = *né* born (:– L. *natus*) + *-esse* -ESS[2]. Cf. PUISNE.] A prerogative allowed to the eldest coparcener to choose first after the inheritance is divided (Dicts.)

Eso- (e·so-), *prefix* [Gr. ἔσω within], comb. form, as in:

Esoenteri·tis [see ENTERITIS], *Path.* inflammation of the intestinal mucous membrane. **Esogastri·tis** [see GASTRITIS], *Path.* inflammation of the mucous lining of the stomach. **Esona·rthex** [see NARTHEX], the inner vestibule of a Greek church.

Esodic (esǫ·dik), *a.* 1850. [f. Gr. ἔσω within + ὁδός way + -IC.] Of nerves: Proceeding to or into the spinal marrow; afferent.

Esophageal, Esophagus, etc.; see ŒS-.

Esoteric (esote·rik). 1655. [– Gr. ἐσωτερικός, f. ἐσωτέρω inner, compar. of ἔσω within, f. ἐς (εἰς) into. See -THER, -IC.]

A. *adj.* **1.** Designed for, or appropriate to, an inner circle of disciples; communicated to, or intelligible by, the initiated only. Hence of disciples. Opp. to EXOTERIC, q.v. **2.** *transf.* Not openly avowed; pertaining to a select circle 1866. **3.** *Phys.* 'Applied to things which relate to, or have origin within the organism' (*Syd. Soc. Lex.*) 1860.

1. A hidden stream of e. truth HALLAM. Phr. *E. Buddhism*: a body of theosophical doctrine handed down by secret tradition among the initiated. **2.** An exoteric and an e. motive 1866.

B. *sb.* **1.** *pl.* (after Gr. τὰ ἐσωτερικά.) Esoteric doctrines or treatises 1711. **2.** One initiated in esoteric doctrines 1655.

So **Esote·rical** *a.*, **-ly** *adv.*

Esoterism (esǫ·tĕriz'm). 1835. [f. Gr. ἐσωτέρω (see prec.) + -ISM.] The holding of esoteric doctrines. var. **Esote·ricism.** So **Eso·terize,** to hold esoteric doctrines (*rare*). **E·sotery,** esoteric doctrine, secret lore.

‖**Esox** (ī·sǫks). 1520. [L.; a Gaulish word.] A large fish mentioned by Pliny, = *lax*, i.e. salmon. In mod. Ichthyology, the Pike.

†**Espa·ce.** 1483. [–(O)Fr. *espace*; see SPACE.] = SPACE –1490.

‖**Espadon.** [Fr. – It. *spadone*, augm. of *spada* sword.] A long two-handed sword used in 15–17th c.

‖**Espagnolette.** 1870. [Fr., f. *espagnol* Spanish; see -ETTE.] A bolt for French casements; also *attrib.*

Espalier (espæ·liəɹ), *sb.* 1662. [– Fr. *espalier* – It. *spalliera*, f. *spalla* shoulder.] **1.** A kind of framework of stakes upon which fruit-trees or shrubs are trained; also the stakes singly 1741. **2.** A fruit-tree or †row of trees so trained 1662. **3.** *attrib.* 1717.

2. Plant your fairest Tulips..under Espaliers EVELYN.

Espalier (espæ·liəɹ), *v.* 1810. [f. prec. sb.] To train as an espalier; also, to furnish with an espalier.

†**Espa·rcet.** 1669. [– Fr. *esparcet, -ette, éparcet*, prob. rel. to OFr. *espass* (mod. *épars*) SPARSE *a.*] A kind of sainfoin –1708.

Esparto (ėspā·ɹto). 1868. [– Sp. *esparto* :– L. *spartum* – Gr. σπάρτον.] A kind of rush (*Macrochloa tenacissima*), called by some Spanish grass, of which paper, and, in Spain, cordage, shoes, and other articles are made. Also called **esparto grass.**

Espathate (ispē·ⁱpet), *a.* 1866. [f. E- (see EX-[1]) + SPATHE + -ATE[2].] *Bot.* Not having a spathe.

Especial (ėspe·ʃăl), *a.* ME. [– OFr. *especial* (mod. *spécial*), – L. *specialis*, f. *species* SPECIES; see -AL[1]. Cf. SPECIAL.] **1.** = SPECIAL, *arch.* or *Obs.* **2.** Pre-eminent, distinguished; exceptional ME. **3.** Pertaining chiefly to one particular person or thing 1855.

1. Phr. †*E. pleading, e. tail.* **2.** My most especiall good friend Sir Peter Hamond KNOLLES. **3.** I must repeat one thing..for your e. benefit JOWETT.

Phr. *In e.*: in particular; especially. Hence **Espe·cially** *adv.* in an e. manner or degree; principally. **Espe·cialness.** †**Espe·cialty,** an e. degree (of anything); in *Law* = SPECIALTY.

†**E·sperance.** ME. [(O)Fr. *espérance*, f. *espérer* hope :– L. *sperare.*] Expectation, hope –1651. Used as a battle-cry 1 *Hen. IV*, v. ii. 97.

Esperanto (espĕræ·nto). 1898. [Pen-name (= Hoping-one) of its inventor, Dr. L. L. Zamenhof.] Name of an artificial language invented for universal use. Hence **Espera·ntist.**

Espial (ėspəi·ăl). ME. [– OFr. *espiaille* action of spying (concr. in pl. 'spies'), f. *espier*; see ESPY *v.*, -AL[1] 2.] **1.** The action of espying or spying; the fact of being espied. †**2.** *concr.* A body of spies; hence (with *pl.*) a spy, scout –1653.

1. The Captain..cut a small hole of e. in the wall DICKENS. **2.** Ful prively he had his espiaille CHAUCER.

‖**Espiègle** (ęspięgl), *a.* 1816. [Fr., shortened from *Ulespiegle* (XVI) – Du. *Ulenspiegel* = G. *Eulenspiegel*, the name of a personage of fiction, renowned for his practical jokes.] Frolicsome, roguish. So ‖**Espièglerie,** roguishness.

Espier (ėspəi·əɹ). ME. [f. ESPY *v.* + -ER[1].] One who espies; †a spy. Hence **Espi·ery,** the action or habit of espying.

†**Espine·l.** 1595. [– Fr. †*espinelle*, later *spinelle*; see SPINEL.] = SPINEL –1677.

†**Espine·tte.** [– Fr. †*espinette* (mod. *épinette*); see SPINET.] = SPINET. Pepys.

Espionage (e·spiŏnėdʒ). 1793. [Fr. *espionnage*, f. *espionner*, f. *espion* SPY *sb.*] The practice or employment of spies.

†**Espi·ritual,** *a.* ME. [– OFr. *espirituel* (mod. *spirituel*) – L. *spiritualis*; see SPIRITUAL.] = SPIRITUAL –1477.

Esplanade (esplănē·ⁱd). 1681. [– Fr. *esplanade* – Sp. *esplanada*, f. *esplanar* :– L. *explanare* flatten out, level; see EXPLAIN, -ADE.] **1.** *Fortif.* **a.** The glacis of the counterscarp, or the sloping of the parapet of the covered way toward the country 1696. **b.** 'An open, level space of ground, separating the citadel of a fortress from the town' (Stocqueler) 1708. **2.** A levelled piece of ground; *esp.* one used for a public promenade 1682; *transf.* a level open space 1681; a grass-plot 1818.

Esplees (esplī·z), *sb. pl.* 1598. [– AFr. *esplez, espletz*, pl. of OFr. *esplet, esploit* revenue :– L. *explicitum.* Cf. EXPLOIT.] The products which ground or lands yield; as the hay of meadows, herbage of pasture, corn of arable, rents, services, etc.; also, the lands, etc. themselves (Wharton).

†**Espo·ntoon.** 1772. [– Fr. *esponton* (XVI) – It. *spuntone*, or var. *sponton.*] = SPONTOON –1838.

†**Espou·sage.** 1549. [– OFr. *espousage*, f. *espouser*; see ESPOUSE *v.*, -AGE.] The action of espousing or betrothing; also, spousehood, marriage –1599.

Espousal (ėspau·zăl), *sb.* Somewhat *arch.* ME. [– OFr. *espousaille*, chiefly *espousailles*, fem. pl. (mod. *épousailles*) :– L. *sponsalia*, subst. use of n. pl. of *sponsalis*, f. *sponsus* SPOUSE *sb.*; see -AL[1] 2.] **1.** In *pl.*, formerly also in *sing.* **a.** The celebration of a marriage. **b.** The formal plighting of troths; betrothal. Also *fig.* **2.** [as if f. the vb.] The action of espousing; hence *fig.* the espousing a cause, a principle, etc. Now *rare.* 1674. †**3.** An espoused person, a husband or wife –1620. **4.** *attrib.* 1598.

1. a. Though it [the childe] were borne but one day after the espousels solemnized *Termes de la Ley*, 1641. **2.** Political reasons forbid the open e. of his cause H. WALPOLE.

†**Espou·se,** *sb.* 1475. [– OFr. *espous, espouse* (mod. *époux, épouse*) :– L. *sponsus, sponsa* betrothed; see next and cf. SPOUSE *sb.*] = SPOUSE –1654. Hence †**Espou·sess,** a bride.

Espouse (ėspau·z), *v.* 1475. [– OFr. *espouser* (mod. *épouser*) :– L. *sponsare*, f. *spons-*, pa. ppl. stem of *spondēre* betroth. Cf. SPOUSE *v.*] †**1.** *trans.* To contract or betroth (*gen.* a woman). Usually said of the parents. –1626. Also †*fig.* **2.** To take as spouse; to marry. Of the father: To give in marriage *to.* Also *transf.* and *fig.* 1475. †**3.** To unite in marriage (*lit.* and *fig.*) SHAKS. Also †*absol.* DRYDEN. **4.** *trans.* To attach oneself to; to take to oneself, make one's own; to adopt, embrace 1622.

1. To a virgine espoused to a man whose name was Ioseph *Luke* 1:27. **2.** On Ascension Day the Duke [of Venice]..solemnly espouseth the sea 1615. **3.** Espous'd to death *Hen. V*, IV. vi. 26. **4.** To e. a quarrel BACON, a Party ADDISON, a cause 1759, a doctrine PRIESTLEY. Hence **Espou·ser.**

‖**Espressivo** (espressī·vo), *adv.* [It.] *Mus.* A direction: With expression.

Espringal. Now *Hist.* 1605. [–(O)Fr. *espringale*, f. *espringuer* spring, dance :– Frankish **springan* SPRING *v.*[1]] A mediæval military engine for throwing stones, bolts, or the like.

†**Espri·se,** *v.* 1474. [– OFr. *espris* (mod. *épris*), pa. pple. of *esprendre* (mod. *éprendre*) in same sense, f. *es-* ES- + *prendre* take.] *trans.* To enkindle (with love, etc.); also *lit.* –1567.

‖**Esprit** (ęspri). 1591. [Fr. – L. *spiritus* SPIRIT.] Sprit, mind; hence, lively wit; cleverness.

Phr. **Esprit de corps** (-ęspri d'kor). [*corps* body.] A spirit of jealous regard for the corporate honour and interests, and for those of each member of the body as belonging to it. **Esprit fort** (ęspri for). Pl. *esprits forts* [Fr. *fort* strong.] A 'strong-minded' person, *esp.* a 'freethinker'.

†**Espy·,** *sb.* ME. [– OFr. *espie*, f. *espier* (see next); see SPY *sb.*, and cf. ESCOUT *sb.*] **1.** Espial; in WYCLIF, 'snare' –1607. **2.** A spy –1656.

Espy (ĕspəi·), *v.* ME. [– OFr. *espier* (mod. *épier*); see SPY *v.*] **1.** †*trans.* To act as a spy upon, to watch; to examine closely. Also, to look out for. –1667. Also *absol.* or *intr.* (*arch*). ME. **2.** trans. To discover by looking out; to catch sight of; to detect ME. **b.** To perceive by chance 1483.

1. Now question me no more, we are espied *Tit. A.* II. iii. 48. He sends angels to e. us in all our ways JER. TAYLOR. **2.** If I could in any place e. a word of promise BUNYAN. **b.** As one of them opened his sack..he espied his money *Gen.* 42:27. Hence †**Espy·ingly** *adv.* insidiously.

Esq., Esqr., abbrevs. of ESQUIRE.

-esque, *suffix,* repr. Fr. *-esque,* – It. *-esco* :– med.L. *-iscus,* forming adjs., with sense 'resembling in style or characteristics', as in *arabesque, burlesque, romanesque,* etc.

Esquire (ĕskwəiᵊ·ɹ), *sb.*[1] 1460. [Early forms *escuyer, -ier* – OFr. *esquier* (mod. *écuyer*) :– L. *scutarius* shield-bearer, f. *scutum* shield. Aphetic SQUIRE is earlier.] **1.** *Chivalry.* A young man of gentle birth, an aspirant to knighthood, who attended on a knight, and carried his shield. Now *arch.* Cf. ARMIGER. 1475. **2.** A title of dignity next in degree below 'knight' 1460.

Esquires, legally so called, are: (1) younger sons of peers and their eldest sons; (2) eldest sons of knights and their eldest sons; (3) chiefs of ancient families (by prescription); (4) esquires by creation or office, as judges, officers, justices of the peace, barristers-at-law; (5) esquires who attend the Knight of the Bath on his installation.

3. A title allowed by courtesy to all who are regarded as gentlemen. In U.S. it belongs officially to lawyers and public officers, and is freely used in the addresses of letters. 1552. **4.** [transf. use of 1.] A gentleman who attends or escorts a lady in public 1824.

Esquire (ĕskwəiᵊ·ɹ), *sb.*[2] 1562. [app. – OFr. *esquire,* unexpl. var. of *esquarre* (mod. *équerre*) SQUARE *sb.*] *Her.* **a.** *Based esquire*: the lower of the halves into which a canton is divided diagonally. Hence, **b.** = GYRON.

Esquire (ĕskwəi·ɹ), *v. rare.* 1652. [f. ESQUIRE *sb.*[1]] To attend (a lady) as a squire.

‖**Esquisse.** 1731. [Fr. – It. *schizzo*; see SKETCH.] The first rough sketch of a picture or design.

Ess. Pl. **esses.** 1540. The name of the letter S; anything S-shaped. See COLLAR *sb.* I.2.

-ess, *suffix*[1], – Fr. *-esse* :– Com. Rom. *-essa* :– late L. *-issa,* – Gr. -ισσα (:– *-ikya*), forming sbs. denoting female persons or animals; as *authoress, actress,* etc. But the agent-nouns in *-er,* and the sbs. indicating profession, etc., are now treated as of common gender, whenever possible.

-ess, *suffix*[2], ME. *-esse,* in sbs. – Fr., repr. OFr. *-esse, -ece* :– L. *-itia,* forming nouns of quality from adjs.; as *duress, largess,* etc.; it is spelt *-es* in *laches, riches.*

Essart (esā·ɹt), *sb.* 1851. [– OFr. *essart*; see ASSART *sb.*] = ASSART *sb.* 1. So **Essa·rt** *v.* = ASSART *v.*

Essay (e·seⁱ), *sb.* 1597. – (O)Fr. *essai,* f. *essayer*; see next. Cf. ASSAY *sb.*] **1.** The action or process of trying or testing; an ASSAY 1598. **2.** An attempt, endeavour 1598. †**3.** A first attempt in learning or practice –1734; a first draft –1739. **4.** A short composition on any particular subject; orig. 'an irregular undigested piece' (J.), but now said of a finished treatise 1597.

1. By way of triall and e. HEYLIN. A small e. of my zeal for..your Majesty CLARENDON. **2.** My second e. at authorship 1865. **4.** For Senacaes Epistles..are but Essaies—that is dispersed Meditations BACON.

Hence **Essaye·tte, E·ssaykin, E·ssaylet,** dims.

Essay (esēⁱ·), *v.* 1483. [alt. of ASSAY *v.* by assim. to Fr. *essayer* :– Rom. **exagiare* weigh, f. late L. *exagium* weighing, balance, f. *exag-,* base of L. *exigere* weigh.] **1.** *trans.* To put to the proof, try; to test the nature, excellence, fitness, etc. of. †**2.** To ASSAY (an ore, etc.) –1816. **3.** To attempt (anything difficult) 1641. **4.** with *inf.* To set oneself, undertake (*to do* something). Also *absol.* 1530.

1. To e. the world 1593, one's powers MACAULAY. **3.** To e. a Task 1712, a method LOWELL. **4.** To e. to dissipate the cloud of error M. ARNOLD. Hence **Essay·er,** one who essays (something); †an essayist.

Essayist (e·seⁱ,ist). 1609. [f. ESSAY *sb.* and *v.* + -IST.] **1.** One who makes trials or experiments. Now *rare.* 1736. **2.** A writer of essays.

2. Meere Essaists! a few loose sentences, and that's all B. Jons.

‖**Esse** (e·*si*). 1592. [L., inf. of *sum,* used subst.] **1.** In phr. *in esse,* in being; opp. to *in posse,* in potentiality. **2.** Essence 1642.

1. Persons..*in esse* at the time when a will is made CRUISE. See also DE BENE ESSE.

†**Essee.** ME. [– eccl.L. *Essæi* pl., Gr. Ἐσσαῖοι. See ESSENE.] = ESSENE –1613.

Essence (e·sĕns), *sb.* ME. [– (O)Fr. *essence* – L. *essentia* (Quintilian, Seneca), f. **essent-,* assumed pres. ppl. stem of *esse* be, on the model of Gr. οὐσία, f. ὀντ-, pres. ppl. stem of εἶναι be.] †**1.** Being viewed as a fact or as a property of something –1688. **2.** *concr.* Something that *is*; an entity. Now only a spiritual entity. 1587. †**b.** In *fifth e.*: an element distinct from the four elements; see QUINTESSENCE –1837. **c.** 'Constituent substance' (J.) ME. †**3.** Specific being, 'what a thing is'; nature, character –1664. **4.** *Metaph.* Substance; the substratum of phenomena; absolute being 1646. **5.** That by which anything subsists 1585. †**6.** Essentiality –1652. **7.** That which constitutes the being of a thing, either (*a*) as a conceptual, or (*b*) as a real, entity (Locke's *nominal* and *real e.*); that by which it is what it is 1667. **8.** *loosely.* The specific difference of anything 1656. **9.** An extract obtained by distillation or otherwise from a plant or drug, and containing its specific properties in a reduced form. In pharmacy, an alcoholic solution of the volatile elements or essential oil. Also *fig.* 1660. **10.** *spec.* A perfume, scent. Somewhat *arch.* 1627.

2. As far as Gods and Heav'nly Essence Can perish MILT. *P. L.* I. 138. Commonwealths are not physical but moral essences BURKE. **c.** So soft and uncompounded is their [Spirits'] E. pure MILT. *P. L.* I. 425. **5.** *Two Gent.* III. i. 182. **7.** We may exactly know the several Ideas that go to make each Law-term, and so their real Nature and E. may be known 1714. The e. of the mind being equally unknown to us with that of external bodies HUME. **9.** *fig.* It [a love-letter] was the e. of nonsense MARRYAT. Hence **E·ssence** *v.* to pour like an e.; to perfume with an e. var. †**E·ssency.**

Essene (esī·n). 1553. [– L. pl. *Esseni.* (Pliny) – Gr. Ἐσσηνοί; presumably of Heb. or Aram. origin.] One of an ancient Jewish sect, remarkable for ascetic practices and a cœnobitical life.

Hence **Esse·nian** *a.* pertaining to, or resembling, the Essenes. **Esse·nic, -al** *a.* of the nature of Essenism. **E·ssenism,** the doctrine and practice of the Essenes, or a tendency thereto.

Essential (ĕse·nʃăl). ME. [– late L. *essentialis* (Augustine); see ESSENCE, -IAL. Cf. OFr. *essentiel.*]

A. *adj.* **1.** Of or pertaining to the essence of anything (see ESSENCE *sb.* 1–4). **2.** Of or pertaining to specific being, or intrinsic nature ME. **3.** Constituting, or forming part of, the essence of anything; necessarily implied in its definition 1546. **b.** Material, important 1770. **4.** Indispensably requisite 1526. **5.** Of the nature of, or resembling, an essence or extract (see ESSENCE 10); in a state of essence 1674.

1. Anye reall and essenciall presence *Bk. Com. Prayer.* E. poetry COLERIDGE. Phr. *E. disease* (Path.), an idiopathic disease. **2.** Phr. *E. difference* (Logic) = 'specific difference', DIFFERENTIA. *E. character*: the marks which distinguish a species, genus, etc. from the others included with it in the next superior division. *E. proposition* (Logic): one which predicates of a subject part of its connotation. *E. form* (Metaph.): see FORM. **3.** By the Law of Nature as an e. right of Sovereignty BRAMHALL. **b.** You have done e. service to the cause 'JUNIUS'. **4.** Silica..is an e. ingredient in mortar 1807. Phr. *E. chord* (Mus.), in early use = *common chord*; later, = FUNDAMENTAL, opp. to *accidental.* **5.** Phr. *E. oil,* a volatile oil, obtained by distillation, and having the characteristic odour of the plant from which it comes; as the oil of turpentine, etc. Now often = 'volatile oil'.

B. *sb.* †**1.** What exists; existence 1667. **2.** That which is essential; an indispensable element or adjunct; a leading point. Orig. only in *pl.* 1513. †**3.** *pl.* Vitals. SOUTH.

1. MILT. *P. L.* II. 93. **2.** 'Well, well', said Glossin, 'no occasion to be particular, tell the essentials' SCOTT.

Hence **Esse·ntial-ly** *adv.,* **-ness.**

Essentiality (ĕse:nʃi,æ·lĭti). 1616. [– late L. *essentialitas*; see prec., -ITY. In mod. use f. prec.] **1.** The quality or fact of being essential 1640. **2.** Essence 1616. **3.** An essential quality (*rare*); also *pl.* essentials 1649.

†**Esse·ntiate,** *v.* 1561. [– *essentiat-,* pa. ppl. stem of med.L. *essentiare,* f. as prec.; see -ATE[3].] **1.** *trans.* To make into an essence or being; to constitute the essence of –1687. **2.** *intr.* To become essence. B. JONS.

†**Essera.** 1706. [mod.L. *essera* (whence Fr. *essère*) – Arab., 'dry scab, itch'.] *Path.* A variety of nettle-rash –1811.

Essoin, essoign (esoi·n), *sb.* ME. [– OFr. *essoine, essoigne,* (AL. *essonium*), f. *essoi(g)ner* :– med.L. *exsoniare,* f. *ex-* EX-[1] + *sonia* lawful excuse – Frankish **sunne,* **sunni*; cf. OHG. *sunnia* hindrance = OS. *sunnea* want, lack, ON. *syn* refusal, denial, Goth. *sunjon* vb. excuse.] **1.** *Law.* The allegation of an excuse for non-appearance in court at the appointed time; the excuse itself. **2.** *gen.* An excuse, parleying, delay ME. ¶**3.** = ESSOINEE. (App. a misunderstanding of AFr. *essonié.*) 1607.

2. SPENSER *F.Q.* I. iv. 20. *Comb.* **e.-day,** the first general return day of the term, on which the court sat to receive essoins.

Essoin (esoi·n), *v.* 1495. [– OFr. *essoignier*; see prec.] **1.** *Law. trans.* To offer an excuse for the non-appearance of in court. **2.** To excuse, let off. QUARLES.

2. Away with wings of time, (I'll not e. thee) 1620. Hence **Essoi:nee·,** a person excused for non-appearance in court. **Essoi·ner,** one who essoins another. **Essoi·nment,** the action of essoining.

Est, obs. var. of EAST.

-est, *suffix,* forming the superl. degree of adjs. and advbs., repr.: (1) OE. *-ost, -ust-, -ast-* :– Gmc. *-*ōstaz*; (2) OE. *-est-, -st-,* with umlaut :– Gmc. *-*istaz.* The Gmc. suffixes are combs. of the two compar. suffixes *-ôz-, -iz-* with OAryan *-to-*; cf. Gr. -ιστο-, Skr. *ishṭha-.* The only surviving umlaut forms are *best, eldest.*

†**Esta·ble,** *v.* ME. [– OFr. *establir*; see next.] = ESTABLISH in various senses –1533.

Establish (ĕstæ·bliʃ), *v.* [ME. *establisse* – *establiss-,* lengthened stem of OFr. *establir* (mod. *établir*) – L. *stabilire,* f. *stabilis* STABLE *a.*; see -ISH[2]. Aphetic STABLISH is earlier.] **1.** To render stable or firm; †to ratify; to confirm, settle; to restore (health) permanently. **2.** To fix, settle, institute or ordain permanently; also with †*to,* †*upon* ME. **3.** To set up on a secure basis; to found 1460. **4.** To place in a secure or permanent position; to set up in business; to settle (a person) in or at a place. Also *refl.* and †*intr.* for *refl.* 1557. **5.** To set up or bring about permanently; to create (a precedent). Also to create for oneself (a reputation, a position). 1597. **6.** To place beyond dispute; to prove 1704. **7.** To place (a church or a religious body) in the position of a state church 1558.

1. To conferme, ratefie and astablishe this my deyd 1537. The great Pensioner's Health seems to be Establish'd 1708. **2.** Behold, I e. my couenant with you *Gen.* 9:9. To e. an edict STRUTT, the lodger franchise GLADSTONE. **3.** To e. Knighthode HAWES, a manufactory 1863, a throne FREEMAN. **4.** To e. Cæsar as a king SHAKS., the daughters of the house 1872. **5.** To e. a price in the market 1801, liberty of worship MACKINTOSH, order DICKENS. Phr. *To e. a suit* (Cards): to give it the command by drawing all the best cards in it which were against the player. **6.** To e. a point FREEMAN, a case 1885. Hence **Esta·blisher.**

Establishment (ĕstæ·bliʃmĕnt). 1481. [f. prec. + -MENT.]

I. 1. The action of establishing; the fact of being established (see the vb.) 1596. †**2.** Established or stable condition –1777; organization, footing –1799. †**3.** That which establishes or strengthens –1646. **4.** Settlement in life; (formerly often) marriage 1684; settled income or provision 1727.

1. The e. of Christianity in any place BUTLER.

II. †**1.** That which is established; a settled constitution or government –1793. **2.** The ecclesiastical system established by law; the *Church E.* 1731. **3. a.** A permanent military, naval, or civil organization. **b.** The quota of officers and men in a regiment, ship, etc. 1689. **4.** An organized staff of employés or servants, including, or occas. limited to, the building in which they are located 1832. **b.** A household, family residence 1803.

2. To meddle with the Church E. 1786. **3. b.** Phr. *Peace E.*, the reduced numbers of an army in a time of peace. So *War E.* The usual e. of officers for ships of the same class 1828.

Phr. *E. of a port* [Fr. *établissement d'un port*]: the interval between the instant of the moon's transit across the meridian on the day of new or full moon, and the subsequent high water.

Hence **Esta:blishmenta·rian** *a.* advocating the principle of an established church; characteristic of those who advocate this principle; *sb.* one who belongs to, or supports the principle of, an established church. **Establishmenta·rianism. Esta·blishmentism,** the principle of a State Church.

‖**Estaca·de.** 1663. [Fr. – Sp. *estacada*, f. *estaca* stake. See -ADE.] *Mil.* A dike of piles in the sea, a river, etc., to check the approach of an enemy. Cf. STOCKADE.

‖**Estafe·tte.** 1792. [Fr. – It. *staffetta*, dim. of *staffa* stirrup – Langobardic **staffa* step.] A mounted courier.

†**Esta·ll,** *v.* 1577. [– OFr. *estaler* place, fix, etc., in AL. *estallare* (XV) assign terms for payment; see STALL *v.*[1]; STALLING *vbl. sb.* 2, INSTALMENT.] *trans.* To arrange the payment of by instalments –1643.

Estamin (e·stămin). 1701. [– OFr. *estamine* (mod. *étamine*) :– Rom. **staminia*, L. *staminea*, subst. use of fem. of adj. *stamineus* made of thread, f. *stamen* thread.] An open woollen fabric, used for making sieves, etc. In 18th c. also applied to a silk fabric.

‖**Estaminet** (estamine). 1848. [– Fr., Walloon *staminé* manger, cow-house, f. *stamo* pole to which a cow is fastened beside the manger in a stall, prob. G. *stamm* stem, trunk.] A café in which smoking is allowed.

Estampede (estæmpī·d), *sb. rare.* [– Sp. *estampida*, -*ido* crash, uproar; see STAMPEDE *sb.*] = STAMPEDE. Marryat. Hence **Estampe·de** *v. trans.* to stampede (cattle, etc.). ‖**Estampede·ro** [Sp.], a stampeded animal. **Estampe·do** *v. intr.* (of cattle, etc.) to run off in a panic.

‖**Estancia** (esta·nsiă, in Sp. -þiă). 1704. [Sp. = 'station' = OFr. *estance* dwelling :– med.L. *stantia*, f. L. *stans, stant-*, pr. pple. of *stare* stand. See STANCE.] A cattle-farm in Spanish America. So ‖**Estancie·ro** [Sp.], the keeper of an e.

†**Esta·ng.** 1628. [– OFr. *estanc*, later *estang* (mod. *étang*); see STANK.] A pool, fish-pond –1673.

†**Esta·ntion.** 1697. [app. a fusion of Sp. *estacion* and ESTANCIA.] A cattle-farm –1707.

Estate (ėstēi·t), *sb.* ME. [– OFr. *estat* (mod. *état*) – L. *status*, f. *stat-*, pa. ppl. stem of *stare* stand. Aphetic STATE *sb.*] **1.** *gen.* State or condition. **b.** A special state or condition. *Obs.* exc. in *Man's, woman's estate.* ME. **2.** Condition as regards worldly prosperity, fortune, etc. (*arch.*) ME. **3.** Status; degree of rank or dignity ME. **4.** Display of one's condition; pomp, STATE. Now *arch.* ME. †**b.** *ellipt.* A canopy, chair, dais, etc., of state –1607. †**5.** A class or order in a community or nation –1643. **6.** An order or class as part of the body politic, participating in the government directly or by representation ME. †**7.** Political constitution, form of government –1670. †**8.** = STATE –1750. **9.** *Law.* The interest which any one has in lands, tenements, or other effects ME. **10.** Property, fortune, capital 1563. **b.** The collective assets and liabilities of a person (*esp.* of a deceased person, a bankrupt, or a *cestui que trust*) 1830. **11.** A landed property; usually, a considerable one. (Now the commonest sense.) 1760.

1. We pray for the good e. of the Catholick Church *Bk. Com. Prayer.* **b.** Phr. *The (holy) e. of matrimony.* **2.** Distressed in mind, body, or e. *Bk. Com. Prayer.* **3.** The e. of a clerke in the chyrche CAXTON. Their [Princes'] high e. *Bk. Com. Prayer.* **4.** Phr. *Cap. of e.* (Her.): see CAP *sb.*[1] **b.** Princes..sitting upon their e. TOPSELL. **6.** Phr. *Third E.*, a designation of the English 'commons', as dist. from the Lords Spiritual and the Lords Temporal. *The Fourth E.*, the Press. **9.** Phr. An *e. upon condition, in fee, for life, of inheritance, tail, from year to year, at will*, etc. *Real e.*, an interest in realty. *Personal e.*, an interest in personalty. **10.** They were..of no great e. OUIDA. **b.** If his [a bankrupt's] e. pay 10*s.* in the pound MCCULLOCH. **11.** Lord of the broad e. and the Hall TENNYSON.

Estate (ėstēi·t), *v.* 1590. [f. prec. sb.] **1.** *trans.* To put into an estate; to endow. Now *rare.* 1609. †**2.** To furnish with an estate or property (*lit.* and *fig.*) –1653. †**3.** To bestow as an estate *on* or *upon* –1669. †**4.** To put into a certain state –1701.

†**Esta·tely.** ME. only. [f. as prec. + -LY[1] and [2].]

A. *adj.* Stately.

B. *adv.* In a stately manner.

Estatesman (ėstēi·tsmæn). 1820. [f. ESTATE *sb.* + MAN; = estate's man; cf. *beadsman, craftsman*, etc.] A perversion of STATESMAN, a Cumberland or Westmorland yeoman.

Esteem (ėstī·m), *sb.* 1450. [– (O)Fr. *estime*, f. *estimer*; see next.] †**1.** Estimate, valuation; estimated value –1680. **2.** Estimation, opinion (? *arch.*) 1588. **3.** Favourable opinion; regard; respect 1611. †**4.** Account; reputation –1824.

1. Of the substance of your realme..I wyll make an esteame SKELTON. **2.** Yourself, held precious in the worlds esteeme *L. L. L.* II. i. 4. **3.** Whist had engaged her maturer e. LAMB. **4.** 1 *Hen. VI*, III. iv. 8.

Esteem (ėstī·m), *v.* 1460. [– (O)Fr. *estimer* – L. *æstimare* (orig.) fix the price of, estimate, the phonetic repr. of which in Fr. was †*esmer* (see AIM *v.*).] †**1.** *trans.* To estimate the value of; to assess, appraise –1776. **2.** To attach value (subjectively) to; to think highly of; to feel regard for, respect 1530. †**b.** *intr.* To have a (specified) opinion *of* –1697. †**3.** *trans.* To estimate. Const. *at, to* (an amount); also *simply.* –1717. †**4.** To judge of –1624. **5.** To consider, hold 1526. †**b.** *intr.* To account *of* –1633; to be of opinion *that* 1548. †**6.** To purpose, aim (*rare*) –1557.

1. What do you esteeme it at *Cymb.* I. iv. 85. **2.** Have much and thou shalt be esteem'd much SKELTON. **5.** Esteeming these virtues to be in me HOBBES. **b.** E. of things as they really are BP. HALL. Hence †**Estee·mable** *a.* = ESTIMABLE. **Estee·mer.** (*Obs.* exc. w. *of.*)

Ester (e·stəɹ). 1852. [– G. *ester* (Gmelin), arbitrary modification of ETHER, perh. recalling the sound of G. *essigäther*, a repr. of the group.] *Chem.* An ethereal salt; a compound of an alcohol radical with an acid.

Esthete, -ic, var. ff. ÆSTHETE, -IC.

†**Esthiomene.** 1541. [– Fr. †*esthiomène* or med.L. *esthiomenus* – Gr. ἐσθιόμενος, pres. pple pass. or middle of ἐσθίειν eat.] *Path.* A gangrenous sore.

Estimable (e·stimăb'l). 1460. [– Fr. *estimable* – L. *æstimabilis*, f. *æstimare*; see ESTEEM *v.*, -ABLE.]

A. *adj.* †**1.** Capable of being estimated or appraised –1805. †**2.** Valuable; of worth –1803. **3.** Worthy of esteem or regard 1698.

2. A pound of mans flesh..Is not so e., profitable neither As flesh of Muttons, Beefes, or Goates *Merch. V.* I. iii. 167. **3.** A lady said of her two companions, that one was more amiable, the other more e. 1698.

†**B.** *sb. pl.* Things estimable. Cf. *valuables.* SIR T. BROWNE.

Hence **E·stimableness. E·stimably** *adv.*

Estimate (e·stimĕt), *sb.* 1563. [f. the verb, or poss. – L. *æstimatus* vbl. sb., f. *æstimare.*] †**1.** The action of valuing or appraising; a valuation; also *fig.* –1677. **b.** Repute –1657. **2.** An approximate calculation based on probabilities; the result of this 1630. **b.** The sum stated by a builder, etc., as that for which he is prepared to execute a specified piece of work 1796.

1. Of my love he makes no e. DEKKER. **2.** There is a design of building a Church..which by e. will cost [etc.] 1702. This e. both of interest and fitness varied from day to day FROUDE.

Estimate (e·stimeⁱt), *v.* 1532. [f. *æstimat-*, pa. ppl. stem of L. *æstimare*; see ESTEEM *v.*, -ATE[3].] †**1.** *trans.* To assign a value to; to appraise, assess. Const. *at.* –1751. **b.** To value (subjectively); to esteem 1597. **2.** To form a notion of (quantities, numbers, magnitudes, etc.) without actual enumeration or measurement; to fix by estimate *at* 1669. †**3.** = ESTEEM *v.* 5 (*rare*) –1794. **4.** To gauge; to judge of 1651.

1. It is by the weight of silver..that men e. commodities LOCKE (J.). To e. securities JOHNSON. **2.** The difference of declination was only estimated 1765. To e. the amount of injury inflicted PRESCOTT, defalcations 1885. **4.** To e. the powers of an author JOHNSON, of Shakespeare LANDOR. Hence **E·stimator. E·stimatory** *a.* for a price or valuation.

Estimation (estimēi·ʃən). ME. [– OFr. *estimation* or L. *æstimatio*, f. as prec.; see -ION.] †**1.** The action of estimating; valuation –1792; estimated value –1775. **2.** Appreciation, esteem 1503; †repute –1828. **3.** The process of forming a notion of without using precise data ME. **4.** Opinion, judgment ME.; †conjecture. 1 *Hen. IV*, 1, iii. 273.

2. An hie estimacion of our self MORE. Phr. *To have* or *hold in e.* How in estimacion a chaste life is 1569. *To grow out of e.* **3.** If a ship sail 8 Miles South in an Hour, by Log or E. STURMY. **4.** The dearest of men in my e. LANE.

Estimative (e·stimătiv), *a.* ME. [– OFr. *estimatif, -ive* or med.L. *estimativus*, f. as prec.; see -IVE.] **1.** Serving for estimating; having the power of estimating. †**2.** Based upon approximate calculation –1651.

1. The errour is not in the eye, but in the e. faculty BOYLE.

‖**Estivage.** 1850. [Fr., f. *estiver* – It. *stivare* :– L. *stipare* pack close. Cf. STEEVE *v.*[2]] The practice of pressing or screwing the cargo into a vessel by means of a capstan machinery, as in American and Mediterranean ports.

Estival, Estivate, Estivation, var. ff. ÆSTIVAL, etc.

‖**Estoc** (e·stǫk). 1830. [Fr.] A kind of short sword. Hence †**Estoca·de,** a blow with an e.; the weapon itself.

Estoil(e (ėstoi·l). 1572. [– OFr. *estoile* star (mod. *étoile*).] *Her.* A charge in the form of a star with wavy points or rays. So **Estoilée** *a.* shaped like a star with wavy rays, as a *Cross Estoilée.*

Estop (ėstǫ·p), *v.* ME. [– AFr., OFr. *estop(p)er, estouper* (mod. *étouper*) stop up, impede (med.L. *estoppare*), :– late L. *stuppare* (implied in *stuppator* caulker), f. L. *stuppa* oakum. See STUFF *sb.*] **1.** *trans.* To stop with or as with a dam, plug, or bar (*arch.*). **2.** *Law.* To impede or bar by ESTOPPEL 1531. **3.** *gen.* To stop, prevent (*rare*) 1876.

2. A man may not deny..that whereof he wilfully estopped or excluded himselfe by deed indented 1594. Hence **Esto·p** *sb.* a stop or stoppage. **Esto·ppage,** stoppage; in *Law*, the condition of being estopped.

Estoppel (ėstǫ·pĕl). 1531. [– OFr. *estoup(p)ail* plug, stopper, f. *estouper*; see prec., -AL[1] 2.] †**1.** An obstruction (to a watercourse) –1638. **2.** *Law.* An impediment or bar to a right of action arising from a man's own act, or where he is forbidden by law to speak against his own deed (Wharton) 1531. †**b.** *gen.* Prohibition 1583.

2. No e. can bind the king 1667.

Estovers (ėstōᵘ·vəɹz), *sb. pl.* 1523. [pl. of AFr. *estover* (AL. *estoverium*), subst. use of *estover*, OFr. *estoveir*, based on L. *est opus* it is necessary. See -ER[4].] 'Necessaries allowed by law' (J.); *esp.* wood for repairs allowed to a tenant from off the landlord's estate; alimony for a widow or for a wife separated from her husband; maintenance for an imprisoned felon. (Cf. BOOT *sb.*[1]).

Phr. *Common of e.*: see COMMON *sb.*

Estrade (ėstrā·d). 1696. [– Fr. *estrade* – Sp. *estrado* carpeted part of a room; see ESTRADO.] A slightly raised platform; a dais.

†**Estra·diot.** 1577. [– Fr. *estradiot* – It. *stradiotto* – Gr. στρατιώτης soldier. See STRADIOT, -OT[2].] One of a class of light cavalry, originally raised in Greece and Albania, who served as mercenaries in the 15th and 16th centuries –1596.

‖**Estrado** (estrā·do). 1588. [Sp. – L. *stratum*, subst. use of n. of pa. pple of *sternere* spread. See STRATUM.] **a.** In Sp. sense: Drawing-room 1748. **b.** = ESTRADE.

Estramazo·ne. [var. of †*stramazon* – It. *stramazzone.*] A slashing cut in fencing. SCOTT.

†**Estrange.** *rare.* ME. [– OFr. *estrange*; see STRANGE *a.*]

A. *adj.* **a.** Distant, reserved. ME. only. **b.** Strange –1587; in *Law*, not privy *to* –1721.

B. *sb.* A stranger, foreigner. ME. only.

Estrange (ėstrēi·ndʒ), *v.* 1485. [– AFr.

estraunger, OFr. *estranger* (mod. *étranger*) :– L. *extraneare* treat as a stranger, f. *extraneus*; see STRANGE *a.*] **1.** *trans.* To remove from what is accustomed; to keep apart from acquaintance with. Const. *from* (arch.). **2.** To render or regard as alien; to remove from the ownership or dominion of any one (*arch.*) 1523. **3.** To alienate in feeling or affection. †Also *intr.* for *refl.* 1494. **†4.** To change from one's usual condition; hence, to put beside oneself, madden –1622. **5.** To disguise (*arch.*) B. JONS.

1. Estranged from politics POPE. The room waits for its master long estranged B. TAYLOR. **2.** He should not e. or cut off all the Churches of God which retained the tradition of old custome M. HANMER. **3.** To e. and alienate the Saints from their God FLAVEL. **4.** Being mad and sodainely estranged and bereft of his wits M. HANMER.

Hence **Estra·ngedness,** alienation in feeling or affection. †**Estrangeful** *a.* foreign in appearance.

‖**Estrangelo, estranghelo** (estræ·ŋėlo). 1730. [Syriac *estrangelō*, thought to be – Gr. στρογγύλος rounded.] An archaic form of the Syriac alphabet. Also *attrib.*

Estrangement (ėstrēⁱ·ndʒmĕnt.) 1660. [f. ESTRANGE *v.* + -MENT.] The action of estranging; the condition of being estranged; alienation.

E. from God's house 1736.

Estranger[1] (ėstrēⁱ·ndʒəɹ). 1623. [f. ESTRANGE *v.* + -ER[1].] One who or that which estranges.

†**Estra·nger**[2]. 1471. [– OFr. *estranger*; see STRANGER.] **1.** One belonging to another nation, family, or district –1641. **2.** *Law.* = STRANGER. –1714.

†**Estra·ngle,** *v.* 1483. [– OFr. *estrangler* (mod. *étrangler*) STRANGLE.] = STRANGLE *v.*

Estrapade (estrăpēⁱ·d). 1730. [– Fr. *estrapade* – It. *strappata*, f. *strappare* pull tight; see -ADE, STRAPPADO.] **1.** The attempt of a horse to get rid of his rider by rearing and kicking. **2.** *Hist.* = STRAPPADO. 1856.

Estray (ėstrēⁱ·). 1581. [– AFr. *estray*, f. *estraier* whence *estray* v. See ASTRAY, STRAY *vs.*]

A. *sb. Law.* 'Any beast not wild, found within any Lordship, and not owned by any man' (Cowell) 1594. Also *transf.*

B. *adj.* That is astray (*rare*).

So **Estray·** *v.* to STRAY (*arch.*).

†**E·stre.** ME. [OFr. *estre* (mod. *être*) being, condition.] **1.** Condition, way of life. ME. only. **2.** *concr.* A place; a region; also *pl.* apartments; inner rooms, or divisions –1485.

Estreat (ėstrī·t), *sb.* ME. [– AFr. *estrete*, OFr. *estraite*, subst. use of fem. pa. pple. of *estraire* :– L. *extrahere* extract.] *Law.* **1.** 'The true extract, copy, or note of some original writing or record, *esp.* of fines, amercements, etc., entered on the rolls of a court to be levied by the bailiff or other officer' (Wharton). **†2.** *transf.* in *pl.* The fines, etc., themselves –1640.

Estreat (ėstrī·t), *v.* 1523. [f. prec.] *trans.* To extract or take out the record of (a recognizance, etc.) and return it to the court of exchequer to be prosecuted.

Estrepe (ėstrī·p), *v.* 1672. [– AFr., OFr. *estreper* (whence AL. *estrepare*) :– L. *extirpare* root up, EXTIRPATE.] *Law. trans.* To commit waste in lands or woods, to the prejudice of the reversioner (Dicts.).

Estrepement (ėstrī·pmĕnt). 1503. [– AFr., OFr. *estrepement*, f. *estreper*; see prec., -MENT.] Wasting of lands; *esp.* waste committed by a tenant for life to the prejudice of the reversioner; 'also, making land barren by continual ploughing' (Wharton).

E·strich, e·stridge. 1450. [– OFr. **estruche, estruce*, var. of *ostruce* OSTRICH.] **†1.** = OSTRICH –1687. **2.** *Comm.* The fine down of the ostrich 1842.

†**E·striche.** [OE. *ēast-rīc*, f. EAST + *rīc* kingdom.] **1.** An eastern kingdom; in OE. *spec.* the East Frankish kingdom –ME. **†2.** *attrib.* in *Estrich board*: applied to timber coming from Norway or the Baltic –1514.

†**E·stuant,** *a.* ME. only. [– *æstuant-*, pres. ppl. stem of L. *æstuare* boil, be inflamed; see -ANT.] Boiling hot. So †**E·stuance,** heat, warmth.

Estuarial (estiuˌēᵊ·riăl), *a.* [f. next + -AL[1].] Of or pertaining to an estuary. So **Estua·rian, E·stuarine** *adjs.* (in same sense).

Estuary (e·stiuări). 1538. [– L. *æstuarium* tidal part of a shore, tidal channel, subst. use (sc. *litus* shore) of n. of **æstuarius* tidal, f. *æstus* swell, surge, tide; see -ARY[1].] **1.** *gen.* A tidal opening; an arm of the sea. **2.** *spec.* The tidal mouth of a great river, where the tide meets the current. STOW. **†3.** A place where liquid boils up –1825. **†4.** A vapour-bath 1657. **5.** *attrib.* 1832.

1. La Plata..is rather an e. of the sea than a river 1880. **2.** Estuaries (a term which we confine to inlets entered both by rivers and tides of the sea) LYELL.

Estuate, -ation, var. ff. ÆSTUATE, -ATION.

‖**Estufa** (estū·fă). 1875. [Sp., corresp. to OFr. *estuve* (mod. *étuve*); see STOVE.] An underground chamber, in which a fire is kept always burning; used as a place of assembly by the Pueblo Indians.

†**Estuo·sity.** 1657. [f. L. *æstuosus* full of heat; see -ITY, -OSITY.] Heated condition –1730.

Esture, var. of ÆSTURE.

Esurience (isiū°·riĕns). 1825. [f. next; see -ENCE.] Hunger; 'neediness and greediness'. So **Esu·riency.**

Esurient (isiū°·riĕnt), *a.* and *sb.* 1672. [– *esurient-*, pres. ppl. stem of L. *esurire* be hungry, desiderative vb. f. *es-*, pa. ppl. stem of *edere* eat; see -ENT.]

A. *adj.* **1.** Hungry. Now often in Juvenal's sense 'needy and greedy'. **¶2.** *catachr.* Gastronomic 1821.

1. An e. unprovided Advocate; Danton by name CARLYLE.

B. *sb.* A greedy person 1691.

†**Esurine.** 1651. [– mod.L. *esurinus*, app. irreg. f. L. *esuries* hunger. See -INE[1].]

A. *adj.* Promoting appetite; also, voracious. Of salts: Corrosive. –1687.

B. *sb.* A medicine which provokes appetite 1775.

-et, *suffix*, forming dims. from sbs., repr. OFr. *-et* masc., *-ete* (mod.Fr. *-ette*) fem. :– Com. Rom. *-itto, -itta*, perh. of non-Latin origin; as in *bullet, fillet, pullet, sonnet*, etc., chiefly Fr. words, the original dim. sense of which is no longer felt.

Etacism (ē·tăsiz'm). 1833. [f. Gr. ἦτα, name of the letter η + -ISM, with *c* after LAMBDACISM.] The Erasmian pronunciation of the Gr. letter η as (ē) or (ę̄), and not as (ī). So **E·tacist,** one who favours e.

‖**Étagère** (etaʒęr). 1858. [Fr., f. *étage* shelf, storey.] A piece of furniture having a number of shelves or stages, one above another, for holding ornaments, etc.

Et cetera, etcetera (etˌse·tĕră). Also **et cætera**; often abbrev. as **etc., &c.** ME. [– L. *et* and, *cetera* (often *cætera*) the rest, n. plur. of *ceterus* remaining over.] **1.** As phr.: And the rest, and so forth, and so on, indicating that other things which can be inferred are included in the statement. **2.** As *sb.* Also pl. **etceteras. a.** A number of unspecified things or (improp.) persons 1656. **b.** *pl.* only: Usual additions, extras, sundries 1817.

Etch (etʃ), *sb.* 1573. [contr. f. EDDISH.] = EDDISH 2, 3.

Etch, *v.*[1] Now *dial.* 1806. [f. prec.] *intr.* To sow an after-crop.

Etch (etʃ), *v.*[2] 1634. [– Du. *etsen* – G. *ätzen* (OHG. *azzen, ezzen*) :– Gmc. **atjan*, causative of **etan* EAT *v.*] **1.** *trans.* To engrave by eating away the surface of with acids; chiefly, to engrave (a metal plate) by this process for the purpose of printing from it. Hence, to copy or represent (figures, designs) by this method. Also *transf.* and *fig.* **2.** *absol.* or *intr.* To practise the art of etching 1634. **3.** To corrode 1664.

1. All the illustrations, which were formerly etched on copper, have been newly etched on steel MRS. JAMESON. **2.** The operation of etching upon glass 1854. Hence **E·tcher,** one who etches.

†**Etch,** *v.*[3] 1682. Var. of obs. *eche* vb., to increase. *To etch out*, to eke out. LOCKE. –1698.

Etching (e·tʃiŋ), *vbl. sb.* 1634. [f. ETCH *v.*[2] + -ING[1].] **1.** The action of ETCH *v.*[2]; the art of the etcher. **2.** *concr.* A copy or representation produced by etching; an impression from an etched plate 1762. **3.** *attrib.*, as *e.-needle*, etc.; **e.-ground,** the composition with which the plate, etc. is covered, preparatory to etching 1790.

1. Prince Rupert..was the inventor of e. HUME.

†**E·ten, e·ttin.** [OE. *eoten, eten* = ON. *jǫtunn* (Sw. *jätte*, Da. *jette*).] A giant –1611.

†**Eteo·stic, eteo·stichon.** [f. Gr. ἔτεος, gen. of ἔτος year + στίχος row; cf. *distich*, †*distichon*] = CHRONOGRAM. B. JONS.

†**Ete·rminable,** *a.* [f. E- (here = IN-[3]) + TERMINABLE.] Without end; eternal. SKELTON.

Eternal (itō·ɹnăl). ME. [– OFr. *eternal*, *-el* (mod. *éternel*) – late L. *æternalis*, f. L. *æternus*, contr. f. *æviternus* EVITERNAL, f. *ævum* age (cf. ÆON); see -AL[1].]

A. *adj.* **1.** Without beginning or end; that has always existed and always will exist; *esp.* of God 1470. **b.** *Metaph.* Not conditioned by time 1651. **2.** Infinite in past duration 1690. **3.** Infinite in future duration. Also *rhet.* ME. **b.** *transf.* Pertaining to eternal things; having eternal consequences 1605. **4.** *familiar.* Perpetual, incessant, always recurring 1787. **5.** Valid through all eternity, immutable 1688. **6.** Infernal, damned. Now *vulgar*. 1601. **7.** quasi-*adv.* 1611.

1. The eternall God is thy refuge *Deut.* 33:27. **3.** Judgment upon the e. soul 1834. Phr. *E. life, death, punishment. rhet.* That eternall citie Rome 1609. **b.** Things of such e. moment LAW. **4.** Sipping her e. tea THACKERAY. **5.** A Treatise concerning E. and Immutable Morality CUDWORTH (*title*). **6.** I will be hang'd, if some eternall Villaine Haue not deuis'd this Slander SHAKS. **7.** To be Boy eternall SHAKS.

B. quasi-*sb.* and *sb.* **1.** *The E.*: God. 1582. **†2.** = ETERNITY, as in phr. *from eternal* –1742. **3.** Eternal things 1649.

1. The lawe whereby the Eternal himselfe doth worke HOOKER. Hence †**Ete·rnalist,** one who believes in the e. duration of the world. †**Eterna·lity,** eternalness. **Ete·rnalize** *v.* to make e. to perpetuate; to immortalize. **Ete·rnal-ly** *adv.*, **-ness.**

Eterne (itō·ɹn), *a.* Now *arch.* (*poet.*) ME. [– OFr. *eterne* – L. *æternus*; see prec.] **1.** = ETERNAL *a.* **2.** *absol.* **†a.** In *fro e.* (= L. *ab æterno*), from eternity. **b.** *The e.*: that which is eternal. **c.** *The E.*: the Eternal.

1. In them, Natures Coppie's not e. *Macb.* III. ii. 38. Hence **Ete·rnify** *v.* to make eternal.

†**Ete·rnish,** *v. pa. pple.* **eternest.** 1579. [f. prec., or – Fr. *éterniser*; see ETERNIZE, -ISH[2].] To make eternal or eternally famous –1594.

Eternity (itō·ɹnĭti). ME. [– OFr. *éternité* – L. *æternitas*, f. *æternus*; see ETERNAL -ITY.] **1.** The quality, condition, or fact of being eternal; eternal existence. **b.** Indefinite continuance ME. **2.** Infinite time; **a.** without beginning or end 1587; **b.** without beginning 1651; **c.** without end ME. **3.** Time felt as endless, or indefinitely remote 1703. **4.** In contrast with *time*. **a.** *Metaph.* (cf. ETERNAL 1 b): Timelessness 1662. **b.** The condition which begins at death; the future life 1602.

1. He wants nothing of a god but E. *Cor.* V. iv. 25. **b.** A desire he had..of æternity and perpetual fame HOLLAND. **2. b.** 'Natural' are those which have been Lawes from all E. HOBBES. **c.** Eternitie, whose end no eye can reach MILT. *P. L.* XII. 556. **4. a.** E. is a permanent now HOBBES. **b.** All that liues must dye, Passing through Nature to E. *Haml.* I. ii. 73.

Eternize (itō·ɹnəiz, ī·təɹnəiz), *v.* 1568. [– Fr. *éterniser* or med.L. *eternizare*; see ETERNE, -IZE.] **1.** *trans.* To make eternal or everlasting 1580. **2.** To make lasting 1568. **3.** To make eternally famous; to immortalize 1610.

1. This other [immortality] serv'd but to e. woe MILT. *P. L.* XI. 60. **2.** To e. quarrels 1716. **3.** Monuments to e. the men who have thus become great BRIGHT. Hence †**Ete·rnizement,** immortal fame. †**Ete·rnizer.**

Etesian (etī·ʒiăn), *a.* (*sb*). 1601. [f. L. *etesius* – Gr. ἐτήσιος annual (f. ἔτος year) + -AN.] **1.** Epithet of certain winds in the region of the Mediterranean, which blow from the N.W. for about 40 days annually in the summer. Hence *transf.* of the trade-winds, monsoons, etc. **†2.** quasi-*sb.* –1684.

Eth- (eþ-). *Chem.* The first syllable of ETHER, used to form names for the members of the bi-carbon or ETHYL series of hydrocarbons.

Ethal (e·þăl). 1839. [f. ETH- + -AL[2].] *Chem.* The same as *Cetyl* or *Cetylic Alcohol* (see CET-). Hence **Etha·lic** *a.*

Ethane (e·þēⁱn). 1866. [f. ETH- + -ANE.] *Chem.* The saturated hydrocarbon, C_2H_6, forming the second member of the series C_nH_{2n+2}; also called *Ethyl hydride* and *dimethyl*; a colourless, inodorous gas.

‖**Ethanim** (e·þănim). 1535. [Heb. (*yéraḥ hā*) *ēṯānīm* mouth of steady-flowing rivers (*ēṯān* ever-flowing).] The 7th month of the Heb. sacred, and 1st of the civil year, called also Tisri.

E·thel, *sb.* Now *Hist.* [OE. *æþel, ēþel, ōþel* = OS. *ōðil*, OHG. *uodal*, ON. *óðal*, f. Gmc. *ōþ- *āþ-. See ATHEL *sb.*[1], ATHELING, ODAL.] Ancestral land or estate, patrimony.

†**E·thel,** var. of ATHEL *a.* Hence **ethelborn** *a.* nobly born.

Etheling, obs. f. ATHELING.

Ethene (e·þīn). 1873. [f. ETH(YL + -ENE.] *Chem.* A fatty hydrocarbon, C_2H_4, forming the second member of the series C_nH_{2n}; known as Ethylene, Olefiant Gas, or Heavy Carburetted Hydrogen. Also *attrib.*

Ether (ī·þəɹ). Also **æther.** ME. [– OFr. *éther* or L. *æther* – Gr. αἰθήρ upper air, f. base of αἴθειν kindle, burn, shine.] **1.** The clear sky; the medium filling the upper regions of space. Now *poet.* or *rhet.* 1587. **2.** In ancient cosmology, an element filling all space beyond the sphere of the moon, and constituting the substance of the stars and planets. It was conceived as a purer form of fire or of air, or as a fifth element. ME. **3.** Air 1713. †**4.** = AURA 2, 3. –1791. **5.** *Mod. Physics.* An elastic and subtle substance believed to permeate all space; the medium through which the waves of light are propagated. Sometimes called *the luminiferous ether.* Also *fig.* Also *attrib.* 1644. **6.** *Chem.* **a.** The colourless, light volatile liquid ($C_4H_{10}O$), resulting from the action of sulphuric acid upon alcohol, and hence known as *Sulphuric ether.* In commercial use the term ether refers to this substance, which is now called technically *Common ether*, or *Ethyl oxide.* It is an anæsthetic and a powerful solvent of fats, etc. 1757. **b.** Hence, the generic name of a class of compounds, formed by the action of acids upon alcohols, divided into (1) *Simple ethers*, which comprise the oxides, sulphides, chlorides, etc. of alcohol radicals; and (2) *Compound ethers*, in which an acid radical replaces the hydrogen of the hydroxyl of an alcohol 1838.

1. All the unmeasured æther flames with light POPE. A land..Where every breath even now changes to e. divine CLOUGH.

Hence **E·theric** *a.* of or pertaining to e. So †**Ethe·rical** *a.* **E:therifica·tion,** the process of converting alcohol into e. **E·theriform** *a.* having the form of e. **E·therify** *v.* to convert into an e. **E·therous** *a.* e.-like.

Ethereal, -ial (iþīᵊ·riăl), *a.* 1513. [f. L. *æthereus, -ius* (– Gr. αἰθέριος) + -AL[1].] **1.** Of the nature of the ether; hence, light, airy, attenuated 1598. **2.** Celestial. Chiefly *poet.* 1667. **3.** Pertaining to the higher region of the atmosphere; also, to the terrestrial atmosphere, relatively to the lower regions 1513. **4.** Spiritlike, impalpable 1647. **5.** *Physics.* Of, pertaining to, or having the nature of 'ether' (see ETHER 5) 1692. **6.** *Chem.* Resembling 'ether' (see ETHER 6), or its qualities 1800. **7.** *absol.* The ethereal principle, the spirit or essence 1661.

2. Go, Heavenly Guest, Ethereal Messenger MILT. *P. L.* VIII. 646. **3.** Near the Confines of Etherial Light..Th' unwary Lover cast his Eyes behind DRYDEN. **4.** Her e. nature seemed to shrink from coarse reality DISRAELI.

Phr. *E. oil* = Essential or Volatile oil.

Hence **Ethe·realism,** e. quality or state (Dicts.). **Ethe:rea·lity, -iality,** the quality of being e. or incorporeal; something that is e. **Ethe·really, -ially** *adv.* **Ethe·realness.**

Etherealize, -ialize (iþīᵊ·riălaiz), *v.* Also **æther-.** 1829. [f. prec. + -IZE.] To make or render ethereal in various senses. Hence **Ethe:realiza·tion, -ialization,** the action or process of etherealizing.

Etherean, -ian (iþīᵊ·riăn), *a. rare.* 1651. [f. as ETHERIAL + -AN.] = ETHEREAL.

Etherene (ī·þĕrīn). Also **-ine.** 1850. [f. ETHER + -ENE.] *Chem.* = ETHYLENE.

Ethereous, -ious (iþīᵊ·rīəs), *a.* 1667. [f. as ETHERIAL + -OUS.] Composed, or of the nature, of ether, or of the upper element of the universe.

Etherin (ī·þĕrin). 1882. [f. ETHER + -IN[1].] *Chem.* A substance which separates, mixed with etherol, from heavy oil of wine when warmed with water. Both etherin and etherol are polymeric with ethylene.

Etherism (ī·þĕriz'm). [f. ETHER + -ISM; cf. *alcoholism.*] 'The successive phenomena developed in the animal body by administration of the vapour of ether' (*Syd. Soc. Lex.*).

Etherize (ī·þĕrəiz), *v.* 1748. [f. ETHER + -IZE.] **1.** To convert (alcohol, etc.) into ether 1828. **2.** To mix or compound with ether 1800. **3.** To put (a patient) under the influence of ether. Also *transf.* 1864. †**4.** = ELECTRIFY. 1748. Hence **E:theriza·tion,** the administration of ether (also *fig.*); the becoming, or being, etherized. **E·therizer,** an apparatus for administering ether.

Etherol (ī·þĕrol). 1876. [f. ETHER + -OL.] *Chem.* See ETHERIN.

Ethic (e·þik). ME. [– Fr. *éthique* or L. *ethicus* – Gr. ἠθικός, f. ἦθος character, pl. manners. See -IC, -ICS.]

A. *adj.* (Now usu. ETHICAL.) **1.** Relating to morals 1581. **2.** Treating of moral questions or of moral science 1589. **3.** Characterized by 'ethos' (see ETHOS 2) 1848.

1. Æthique precepts 1644, doctrine SAVAGE. **2.** E. epistles POPE. Dr. Hutcheson is the principal E. writer of this country [Ireland] MORSE.

B. *sb.* **1.** *sing.* [After (O)Fr. *éthique*, L. *ethice*, Gr. (ἡ) ἠθική (sc. τέχνη).] The or a science of morals ME. **2.** *pl.* **Ethics** [After OFr. *éthiques*, med.L. *ethica* n. pl. – Gr. τὰ ἠθικά.] The science of morals 1602. **b.** A treatise on the science; *spec.* that of Aristotle ME. **3. a.** The moral system of a particular writer or school of thought 1651. **b.** The rules of conduct recognized in certain limited departments of human life 1789. **4.** The science of human duty in its widest extent, including, besides ethics proper, the science of law whether civil, political, or international 1690.

1. An attempt to construct an e. apart from theology 1886. **3. a.** Christian ethics 1855. The zoölogical ethics of Combe MARTINEAU. **b.** Sea rights and sea ethics 1864. The ethics of dining 1870. Church ethics MOZLEY. Medical ethics 1884.

Ethical (e·þikăl), *a.* 1607. [f. prec. + -AL[1].] **1.** = ETHIC *a.* 1, 3. **2.** = ETHIC *a.* 2. 1665. **3.** *Gram.* In *Ethical dative*: the dative when used to imply that a person, other than the subject or object, has an interest in the fact stated.

Hence **E·thical·ly** adv., **–ness.**

Ethician (eþi·ʃăn). *rare.* 1889. [f. ETHIC(S + -IAN.] One versed in ethics. So **E·thicist.** (Dicts.)

Ethicize (e·þisəiz), *v.* 1816. [f. as prec. + -IZE.] **1.** *intr.* To discuss ethics; to moralize. G. COLMAN. **2.** *trans.* To make ethical 1885.

2. The idealizing process which..ethicizes nature MARTINEAU.

Ethico- (e·þiko-], repr. Gr. ἠθικο-, comb. f. ἠθικός; as in **E.-physical, -political, -religious,** pertaining jointly to ethics and physics, politics, or religion.

Ethide (e·þəid). 1865. [f. ETH- + -IDE.] *Chem.* A compound of an element or radical and the monad radical ethyl.

Ethine (e·þəin). 1877. [f. ETH- + -INE[5].] *Chem.* = ACETYLENE.

Ethionic (īþi,ǫ·nik), *a.* 1838. [f. E(THER + Gr. θεῖον sulphur + -IC.] (*Chem.*) *E. acid*: $C_2H_6S_2O_7$ produced by the action of water on *E. anhydride*, $C_2H_4 2SO_3$, formerly called *Sulphate of carbyl*, which is obtained by bringing together olefiant gas and vapour of sulphuric anhydride in a tube.

Ethiop (ī·þi,ǫp). *arch.* ME. [– L. *Æthiops, Æthiopis* – Gr. Αἰθίοψ, Αἰθίοπος Ethiopian, f. αἴθειν burn + ὤψ face. (In Eng. with initial capital.)]

A. *sb.* lit. = ETHIOPIAN; hence, a black. *To wash an* (*the*) *E.* (*white*): to attempt the impossible.

B. *attrib.* and *adj.* **1.** = ETHIOPIAN. 1667. **2.** Black 1600.

2. E. vvords blacker in their effect Then in their countenance *A. Y. L.* IV. iii. 35.

Hence †**Ethiopesse,** a female Ethiopian.

Ethiopian (īþi,ōᵘ·piăn). 1552. [f. *Ethiopia, Æthiopia* (f. L. *Æthiops*; see prec.) + -AN; see -IAN.]

A. *adj.* **1.** Of or belonging to Ethiopia, or to the *Æthiopes.* Often = 'Negro'. **2. a.** *Anthropology.* Name of one of the races of man 1861. **b.** *Biol.* Epithet of one of the biological regions 1880.

1. The E. guards LYTTON, serenades 1861.

B. *sb.* A native of Ethiopia; †a Negro 1552.

Ethiopic (īþi,ǫ·pik), *a.* 1659. [– L. *æthiopicus* – Gr. αἰθιοπικός; see ETHIOP, -IC.] **1.** Of or belonging to Ethiopia. Now only with reference to language. **2.** *absol.* The Ethiopic language 1867.

†**E·thiops.** Also **æ-.** 1706. [– L. *æthiops* lit. 'ETHIOP, negro'.] A name given formerly to certain black or dark-coloured compounds of metals. *E. martial*: the black oxide of iron. *E. mineral*: the black sulphide of mercury, prepared by triturating mercury with sulphur. –1854.

Ethmo- (e·þmo-), comb. f. Gr. ἠθμός sieve, with sense 'pertaining to the ethmoid bone and ——'; as in:

Ethmo-turbinal (plates) or **Ethmo-turbinals** [see TURBINAL], the lateral masses of the ethmoid bone, connected horizontally with each other at the upper surface by the cribriform bone. **Ethmo-vomerine** (plate), 'a cartilaginous plate beneath the front of the fetal brain, from which the ethmoid region of the skull is developed' (Webster).

Ethmoid (e·þmoid). 1741. [– Gr. ἠθμοειδής sieve-like, 'cribriform' (Galen), f. ἠθμός sieve; perh. through Fr. *ethmoïde* (XVI).]

A. *adj.* Sieve-like, finely perforated.

E. bone: a square-shaped cellular bone, situated between the two orbits, at the root of the nose, containing many perforations, through which the olfactory nerves pass to the nose.

B. quasi-*sb.* or *sb.* = *ethmoid bone.*

Hence **Ethmoi·dal** *a.* of or pertaining to the e. bone; ETHMOID.

Ethmose (eþmōᵘ·s). [irreg. f. Gr. ἠθμός sieve + -OSE[2], after *cellulose.*] *Phys.* Cellular tissue.

Ethnarch (e·þnaɹk). 1641. [– Gr. ἐθνάρχης, f. ἔθνος nation + -αρχης -ARCH.] A governor of a people or province. So **E·thnarchy,** the office or dominion of, or the province ruled by, an e.

Ethnic (e·þnik). ME. [– eccl.L. *ethnicus* heathen – Gr. ἐθνικός, f. ἔθνος nation; see -IC. In LXX, etc. τὰ ἔθνη = the (non-Israelitish) nations, Gentiles.]

A. *adj.* **1.** Pertaining to nations not Christian or Jewish; Gentile, heathen, pagan 1470. **2.** Ethnological 1851.

†**B.** *sb.* A Gentile, heathen, pagan –1728.

Hence **E·thnical** *a.* †heathenish; †pagan; ethnological. **E·thnically** *adv.* **E·thnicism,** †heathenism, paganism; in mod. use, the religions of the Gentile nations or their common characteristics.

†**E·thnish,** *a.* 1550. [f. ETHN(IC + -ISH[1], after *heathenish.*] = HEATHENISH. –1563.

Ethnize (e·þnəiz), *v. rare.* 1847. [f. as prec. (see ETHNIC) + -IZE, after *judaize, hellenize.*] To favour Gentile views or practices.

Ethnodicy (eþnǫ·disi). *rare.* 1889. [f. Gr. ἔθνος + -δικία administration of justice, f. δίκη justice.] Comparative jurisprudence as a branch of ethnology.

Ethnogeny (eþnǫ·dʒĭni). [f. Gr. ἔθνος nation; see -GENY.] The branch of ethnology which treats of the origin of races and nations. Hence **Ethnoge·nic** *a.* pertaining to e.

Ethnography (eþnǫ·grăfi). 1834. [f. as prec.; see -GRAPHY.] The scientific description of nations or races of men, their customs, habits, and differences.

E. embraces the descriptive details..of the human aggregates and organizations 1878.

Hence **Ethno·grapher,** one who studies or is versed in e. **Ethnogra·phic, -al** *a.* of or pertaining to e. **Ethnogra·phically** *adv.* **Ethno·graphist,** ethnographer.

Ethnology (eþnǫ·lŏdʒi). 1842. [f. as prec. + -LOGY.] The science which treats of races and peoples, their relations, their distinctive characteristics, etc.

General e.; [viz.] ethics, ethnodicy, and sociology 1889. Hence **Ethno·loger** = ETHNOLOGIST. **Ethnolo·gic, -al** *a.* of or pertaining to e. **Ethnolo·gically** *adv.* **Ethno·logist,** one who studies or is versed in e. **Ethno·logize** *v. intr.* to speculate on ethnological questions.

Ethnomaniac (eþnomēⁱ·niæk). 1863. [f. as prec. + MANIAC.] One who is crazy about racial autonomy.

Ethnopsychology (e:þno,səikǫ·lŏdʒi). 1886. [f. as prec. + PSYCHOLOGY.] The study of the psychology of races and peoples. Hence **E:thnopsycholo·gical** *a.*

Ethology (iþǫ·lŏdʒi). 1656. [– L. *ethologia* – Gr. ἠθολογία, f. ἦθος character; see -LOGY.] †**1.** The portrayal of character by mimicry. (Dicts.) †**2.** The science of ethics; also, a treatise on morals. (Dicts.) **3.** 'The science of character' (J. S. Mill). Hence **Etholo·gic, -al** *a.* pertaining to e. **Etho·logist,** one who practises, studies, or is versed in e.

†**E:thopoe·tic,** *a.* [– Gr. ἠθοποιητικός, f. ἦθος character + ποιητικός, f. ποιεῖν represent.] Intended to represent character or manners. URQUHART.

‖**Ethos** (ī·þǫs). 1851. [mod.L. – Gr. ἦθος character.] **1.** [After Arist. *Rhet.* II. xii–xiv.] The prevalent tone of sentiment of a people or community; the genius of an institution or system. **2.** *Gr. Æsthetics* and *Rhetoric.* Character; ? ideal excellence; in *Gr. Rhet.* often opposed to *pathos,* emotion 1875.

1. The e. of Catholic sacerdotal life 1882. **2.** By e., as applied to the paintings of Polygnotus, we understand a dignified bearing in his figures, and a measured movement throughout his compositions 1875.

Ethyl (e·þil). Also †**ethule.** 1840. [f. ETH(ER + -YL.] The hypothetical radical of the dicarbon series (C_2H_5), the base of common alcohol, ether, and acetic acid, and of a large series of compounds, as *E. hydride* C_2H_6 ($=C_2H_5H$), *E. chloride* C_2H_5Cl, *E. iodide* C_2H_5I, *E. alcohol* C_2H_6O.

Hence **E·thylami:ne,** a compound ($NH_2C_2H_5$) of the ammonia type in which one of the hydrogen atoms of ammonia is replaced by ethyl; called also *e. ammonia.* **E·thylate,** a salt of the radical ethyl, in which ethyl takes the place of the oxygenated group in a metallic salt. **E·thylene,** the diatomic hydrocarbon or olefine of the ethyl series, C_2H_4; also known as Ethene, Olefiant gas, or Heavy Carburetted Hydrogen, an important constituent of coal gas. **Ethy·lic** *a.* of ethyl; = ETHYL used attrib., as in *Ethylic chanate* = Ethyl cyanate = Vinic cyanate.

Etiolate (ī·tioleⁱt). 1791. [f. Fr. *étioler* (see -ATE³) – Norman Fr. (*s'*)*étieuler* grow into haulm, f. *étieule, éteule* (OFr. *esteule*) :– pop.L. **stupila* straw (see STUBBLE).] **1.** *trans.* To blanch or make colourless (a plant) by excluding the light from it. **2.** *transf.* To give a pale and sickly hue to (a human being or his skin) 1842. Also *fig.* **3.** *intr.* To become white or whiter; to blanch; to be whitened by exclusion of sunlight, as plants 1828.

1. Celery is in this manner blanched or etiolated WHEWELL. **2.** *fig.* These industries are sickly, nerveless, and etiolated 1879. Hence **Etiola·tion,** the action of etiolating, or the becoming, or being, etiolated.

Etiolin (ī·tiŏlin). 1882. [f. ETIOL(ATE + -IN¹.] A yellow modification of chlorophyll formed in plants growing in the dark.

Etiological, var. of ÆTIOLOGICAL.

Etiology, var. of ÆTIOLOGY. Hence **Etio·logist,** one who studies etiology, or the science of causes.

Etiquette (e·tiket). 1750. [– Fr. *étiquette,* the primary sense of which is repr. by TICKET.] **1. a.** The prescribed ceremonial of a court; the usages of diplomatic intercourse. **b.** The order of procedure established by custom in the army and navy, in parliament, etc. **c.** The conventional rules of behaviour and ceremonies observed in polite society. **d.** The unwritten code of honour which discountenances certain practices in some of the professions. †**2.** A rule of etiquette. Chiefly *pl.* –1816. **3.** A label (*rare*) 1867.

c. Man is. .a slave. .to e. ROBERTSON.

Etna (e·tnă). Also **ætna.** 1832. [f. the name of the volcano.] A vessel for heating liquids by burning some kind of spirit.

Eton (ī·t'n). *E. College,* a public school for boys, on the Thames opposite Windsor.

E. collar, a broad stiff collar orig. and esp. worn outside the *E. jacket,* a short black broadcloth jacket pointed at the back (so *E. suit,* also called *Etons*). *E. crop,* a fashion of cutting women's hair close to the head all over.

Etonian (itōᵘ·niăn). 1749. [f. ETON + -IAN.] **a.** *adj.* Of or pertaining to Eton or Eton College. **b.** *sb.* One educated at Eton College 1770.

Etrurian (ĭtrūᵊ·riăn). 1623. [f. *Etruria* + -AN.]

A. *adj.* Of or belonging to Etruria.

B. *sb.* A native of Etruria.

Etruscan (ĭtrʊ·skăn). 1706. [f. L. *Etruscus* + -AN.] **A.** *adj.* Of or belonging to ancient Etruria or its people; *absol.* their language. **B.** *sb.* One belonging to the Etruscan people.

Et seq. and the following: see SEQ.

-ette, *suffix,* forming dims., repr. OFr. *-ette* fem.; see -ET.

Ettercap (e·təɹkæp). *Sc.* 1721. [var. f. ATTERCOP.] = ATTERCOP.

Ettle (e·t'l), *v.* Now only *n. dial.* [ME. *atle, et(t)le* – ON. *ætla* (also *etla, atla*) think, conjecture, purpose, destine, apportion, f. Gmc. **ahtō* (OE. *eaht,* OHG. *ahta,* G. *acht*) consideration, attention, f. base of Goth. *aha* mind, *ahma* spirit.] **1.** *trans.* To purpose, plan; to endeavour. **2.** To assign ME. **3.** To direct (speech or actions) to an object; *absol.* or *intr.* to take aim (*at*) ME.; *intr.* to make an effort *at* 1725. **4.** *trans.* To guess, conjecture ME. Hence **E·ttle** *sb.* aim, intent; opportunity.

Etui, etwee (etwī·). 1611. [– Fr. *étui,* OFr. *estui* prison, f. OFr. *estuier* shut up, keep, save. See STEW *sb.*¹, TWEEZE, TWEEZERS.] A case for small articles, as bodkins, needles, toothpicks, etc.; †a case for surgical instruments.

Etymologer (etimǫ·lŏdʒəɹ). 1650. [– Gr. ἐτυμολόγος (whence L. *etymologos,* Varro) student of etymology, f. ἔτυμον ETYMON; see -LOGER.] = ETYMOLOGIST.

‖**Etymologicon** (e:timolǫ·dʒikǫ̆n). 1645. [mod.L. – Gr. ἐτυμολογικόν, n. sing. (sc. βιβλίον book) of ἐτυμολογικός pertaining to ETYMOLOGY; see -IC.] An etymological word-book.

Etymologize (etimǫ·lŏdʒəiz), *v.* 1530. [– med.L. *etymologizare,* f. L. *etymologia*; see next, -IZE.] **1.** *trans.* To give or trace the etymology of; to suggest an etymology for. **2.** *intr.* To study etymology; to suggest etymologies for words 1652. Hence **Etymologiza·tion.**

Etymology (etimǫ·lŏdʒi). 1447. [In XV *ethi-* – OFr. *ethimologie* (mod. *étymologie*) – L. *etymologia* (med. L. *ethym- ethim-*) – Gr. ἐτυμολογία, f. ἐτυμολόγος student of etymology, f. ἔτυμον; see next, -LOGY.] **1. a.** The process of expounding the elements of a word with their modifications of form and sense. Also with *an* and *pl.* 1588. **b.** The facts relating to the formation and derivation (of a word) 1447. †**c.** Etymological sense –1714. **2.** The branch of linguistic science which treats of the origin of words 1646. **3.** *Gram.* The part of grammar which treats of the parts of speech, their formation and inflexions 1592.

1. E. is sometimes a very precarious. .thing WATTS. **c.** This name [widowes]. .hath received one constant E.; 'deprived' or 'destitute' BRATHWAITE.

Hence **E:tymolo·gic, -al** *a.* of, pertaining to, or in accordance with e. **E:tymolo·gically** *adv.* **Etymo·logist,** one who treats of, or is versed in, e.

‖**Etymon** (e·timǫ̆n). 1570. [L. – Gr. ἔτυμον, subst. use of n. sing. of ἔτυμος true.] †**1.** The 'true' or primitive form of a word –1793. **2.** The primary word from which a derivative is formed 1659. †**3.** 'True' or original signification –1834.

1. Blew hath his E. from the high Dutch Blaw 1606. **2.** Logic is nothing more than a knowledge of words, as the Greek e. implies LAMB.

Eu-, *prefix,* repr. Gr. εὐ-, comb. f. ἐύς good, used in neut. εὖ as adv. = well. In Eng. the prefix occurs mostly in words of Gr. derivation, with the senses 'good', 'well', 'easily'.

Euboic (yubōᵘ·ik), *a.* 1667. [– L. *Euboïcus* – Gr. Εὐβοϊκός, f. Εὔβοια Eubœa; see -IC.] Belonging to Eubœa. MILT. *P. L.* II. 546.

Eucairite (yūkēᵊ·rəit, yūkai·rəit). Also **eukairite.** 1822. [f. Gr. εὔκαιρος opportune + -ITE¹ 2 b.] *Min.* A mineral, consisting principally of selenium, copper, and silver; so named because found about the time Berzelius discovered selenium.

Eucalyn (yū·kălin). 1864. [f. EUCALY(PTUS + -IN¹.] *Chem.* A saccharine substance, obtained by the decomposition of melitose, under the influence of yeast.

Eucalyptus (yūkăli·ptŏs). *Pl.* **-i, -uses.** 1809. [mod.L. (L'Heritier, 1788), intended to denote 'well-covered' (f. Gr. εὐ- EU- + καλυπτός covered, f. καλύπτειν cover, conceal), the flower before it opens being protected by a cap.] *Bot.* A genus of plants of the N.O. *Myrtaceæ*; the Gum-tree of Australia; a tree of this kind. **b.** = *e. oil,* an antiseptic and disinfectant 1885. Hence **Eucaly·ptene, Eucalyptin,** a product ($C_{12}H_{18}$), yielded when eucalyptol is heated with phosphoric anhydride and gives up water. **Eucaly·ptol,** a compound contained largely in the volatile oil of *E. globulus.*

Eucharis (yū·kăris). 1866. [– Gr. εὔχαρις gracious, f. εὐ- (see EU-) + χάρις grace.] *Bot.* A South Amer. bulbous plant (N.O. *Amaryllidaceæ*), bearing white bell-shaped flowers. Also *attrib.*

Eucharist (yū·kărist). ME. [– OFr. *eucariste* (mod., with latinized ending, *eucharistie*) – eccl.L. *eucharistia* – eccl. Gr. εὐχαριστία giving of thanks, (earlier) gratitude, f. εὐχάριστος grateful, f. εὐ- EU- + χαρίζεσθαι show favour, give freely, f. χάρις, χαριτ- favour, grace.] **1.** *Eccl.* The sacrament of the Lord's Supper; the Communion. **2.** The consecrated elements, *esp.* the bread 1536. †**3.** The box containing the bread; the pyx –1560. **4.** Thanksgiving 1613.

1. The efficacy of the E. in both kinds was more complete S. AUSTIN. **2.** The corporal presence of our Lord in the E. HOOK. **4.** To pay their e. to the Holy Ghost JER. TAYLOR.

Hence **Euchari·stic, -al** *a.* of, pertaining to, or of the nature of, the E.; of or pertaining to thanksgiving. **Euchari·stically** *adv.* **Euchari·stize** *v.* to affect (the elements) by an act of thanksgiving.

Euchite (yū·kəit). 1585. [– late L. *euchita, eucheta* (Augustine) – Gr. εὐχίτης, εὐχήτης, f. εὐχή prayer; see -ITE¹ 1.] One of a 4th c. sect which believed that perpetual prayer was the only means of salvation. Also applied to later sects holding these views.

†**Euchlo·ric,** *a.* 1811. [f. as next + -IC.] In *Euchloric gas* = EUCHLORINE.

Euchlorine (yū:klōᵊ·rin). 1812. [f. Gr. εὐ- (see EU-) + χλωρός green + -INE⁵. Formed by Davy after CHLORINE.] *Chem.* 'A gaseous mixture of chlorine and oxide of chlorine, obtained by the action of hydrochloric acid on chlorate of potassium' (Watts).

Euchlorite (yū:klōᵊ·rəit). 1876. [f. as prec. + -ITE¹ 2 b.] *Min.* A deep green variety of magnesia mica, found at Chester (Mass.) in 1876.

‖**Euchologion** (yūkolōᵘ·dʒi,ǫn). Also in L. form -um. 1651. [– Gr. εὐχολόγιον, f. εὐχή prayer; see -LOGY.] A prayer-book; also, a book of ritual, primarily that of the Greek Church. vars. †**Eu·chologue, Eucho·logy.**

Euchre (yū·kəɹ), *sb.* 1846. [Early sp. *euker, uker, yuker.* Of unkn. origin.] **1.** A game of cards, of American origin, played by 2, 3, or 4 persons, with a pack of 32 cards (the 2, 3, 4, 5, 6 of each suit not being used). A player may 'pass', but if he plays, and fails to take 3 tricks, he or his side is 'euchred' and the other side gains two points.

The highest card is the knave of trumps, called *right bower,* and the next highest the other knave of the same colour, called *left bower,* but in *Railroad Euchre* an extra blank card called the *joker* is used, which takes any other.

2. An instance of euchreing or being euchred 1880.

1. We had a small game, And Ah Sin took a hand: It was e. The same he did not understand 1870 Hence **Eu·chreist,** a player at e.

Euchre (yū·kəɹ), *v.* 1866. [f. prec. sb.] *trans.* To get the better of (the adversary) by his failure to take three tricks; see the sb. Hence *transf.* to outwit, 'do'.

Euchroite (yū·kro,əit). 1825. [f. Gr. εὔχροος well-coloured (f. εὐ- EU- + χροά colour) + -ITE¹ 2 b.] *Min.* A hydrous arsenate of copper of a bright emerald-green colour.

†**Euchy·mous,** *a.* 1651. [f. late L. *euchymus* = Gr. εὔχυμος well-flavoured, f. εὐ- EU- + χυμός CHYME; see -OUS.] Conducive to a good state of the fluids of the body. So †**Eu·chymy,** a good state of these.

†**Euchyside·rite.** 1823. [f. Gr. εὐ- + χύσις melting + σίδηρος iron + -ITE[1] 2 b.] *Min.* = PYROXENE.

Euclase (yū·klēⁱs). 1804. [– Fr. *euclase,* f. Gr. εὐ- (see EU-) + κλάσις breaking; so named from its easy cleavage.] *Min.* A silicate of aluminium and glucinum occurring in light-green, transparent crystals.

Euclid (yū·klid). 1581. [– Gr. Εὐκλείδης.] A geometer of Alexandria (*c* 300 B.C.): hence, his works, *esp.* the Elements.

Euclidean (yūkli·dĭăn, yūklidī·ăn), *a.* Also **-ian.** 1660. [– L. *Euclideus,* Gr. Εὐκλείδειος + -AN.] Of or pertaining to Euclid; that is according to the principles of Euclid.

Phr. *E. space*: space as known to us, for which the axioms of Euclid are valid, as opp. to hypothetical kinds of space.

Eucolite (yū·kŏləit). 1847. [f. Gr. εὔκολος easily satisfied (f. εὐ EU- + κόλον food) + -ITE[1] 2 b. So named 'because it *contented itself*. . with iron oxide in default of zirconia' (Scheerer).] *Min.* A variety of eudialyte.

Eucrasy (yū·krăsi). 1607. [– med.L. *eucrasia* = Gr. εὐκρασία good temperature, f. εὐ- EU- + κρα-, κεραννύναι mix; see -Y[3].] Such a due mixture of qualities as constitutes health or soundness.

†**Euctical** (yū·ktikăl), *a.* 1638. [f. Gr. εὐκτικός pertaining to prayer + -AL[1].] Pertaining to prayer; supplicatory –1745.

Eudemon, -dæmon (yudī·mən). 1629. [– Gr. εὐδαίμων fortunate, happy, f. εὐ- EU- + δαίμων genius. Sense 2 is of mod. origin.] **1.** *Astrol.* The eleventh house of a celestial figure, so called as the source of many good things 1706. **2.** = AGATHODEMON.

Eudemonic, -dæmonic (yūdĭmǫ·nik), *a.* 1832. [– Gr. εὐδαιμονικός, f. εὐδαιμονία happiness. See -IC.] **1.** Viewed as conducive to happiness 1865. **2.** *pl.* 'The art of applying life to the maximization of wellbeing' (Bentham). So **Eudemo·nical** *a.*

Eudemonism, -dæmonism (yudī·mən-iz'm). 1827. [f. Gr. εὐδαιμονισμός (Aristotle); see prec., -ISM.] That system of ethics which finds the moral standard in the tendency of actions to produce happiness.

Eudemonist, -dæmonist (yudī·mənist). 1818. [f. as prec. + -IST.] One who believes in eudemonism. Hence **Eudemoni·stic, -al** *a.* of or pertaining to eudemonism.

Eude·mony, -dæmony. *rare.* 1730. [– Gr. εὐδαιμονία (see EUDEMONIC).] Happiness, prosperity.

Eudialyte (yudəi·ăləit). 1837. [– Gr. εὐδιάλυτος easily dissolved; see DIALYSE. So named because easy to dissolve in hydrochloric acid.] *Min.* A vitreous bisilicate of zirconium, iron, calcium, sodium, and other elements, occurring in rhombohedral crystals, rose pink or brownish red.

Eudiometer (yūdi,ǫ·mĭtəɹ). 1777. [f. Gr. εὔδιος clear (weather) + -METER.] An instrument for testing the purity of the air, or rather the quantity of oxygen it contains. It is also used, now chiefly, in the analysis of gases.

Hence **Eudiome·tric, -al** *a.* of, pertaining to, or requiring the use of the e. or eudiometry. **Eudiome·trically** *adv.* by the use of the e. **Eudio·metry,** the art or practice of using the e.

Eudipleural (yūdiplūᵊ·răl), *a.* 1878. [f. Gr. εὐ- EU- + δίς twice + πλευρά side + -AL[1].] Having two equal and symmetrical halves.

†**Eue·ctic.** Also **evectic** in Dicts. 1574. [– Gr. εὐεκτική (τέχνη), f. phr. εὖ ἔχειν be well; see -IC.] That part of medical science which teaches how to get a good habit of body. Hence in same sense **Eue·ctics** *pl.*

Euemerism, etc., obs. f. EUHEMERISM, etc.

Euge (yū·dʒi). 1655. [– L. *euge* – Gr. εὖγε well done.] An exclam. of commendation.

Eugenesis (yudʒe·nĭsis). [f. Gr. εὐ- EU- + γένεσις generation.] The quality of breeding well and freely. Hence **Eugene·sic** *a.* having this quality; applied *esp.* to hybrids that are fertile.

Eugenia (yudʒī·niă). 1775. [mod.L.; named in honour of *Eugene,* Prince of Savoy. See -IA[1].] *Bot.* A genus of tropical trees (N.O. *Myrtaceæ*), of which the most important is *E. pimenta* or Allspice Tree. Hence **Euge·nic** (acid), $C_{10}H_{12}O_2$, oxidized essence of cloves. **Eu·genin,** clove-camphor; a crystalline substance deposited from water which has been distilled from cloves. **Eu·genol** = eugenic acid.

Eugenic (yudʒe·nik). 1833. [f. Gr. εὐ- EU- + γεν- produce; see -IC, -ICS.] **A.** *adj.* Pertaining or adapted to the production of fine offspring. **B.** *sb.* in *pl.* The science which treats of this.

Hence **Euge·nically** *adv.* So **Eu·genist,** a student or advocate of eugenics.

‖**Euha·ges, euba·ges,** *sb. pl.* 1609. [L. (Ammianus Marcellinus). The form *euhages* is due to a misreading of Gr. οὐατεῖς, Strabo's rendering of a Gaulish wd. = L. *vates.* The other form is a scribal error.] *Celt. Antiq.* An order of priests, or natural philosophers, among the ancient Celtæ.

Euharmonic (yūhaɹmǫ·nik), *a.* 1811. [f. Gr. εὐ- EU- + ἁρμονία harmony + -IC.] Producing perfect harmony.

Euhemerism (yuhī·meriz'm). 1846. [f. L. *Euhemerus,* Gr. Εὐήμερος, a Sicilian (*c* 316 B.C.), who maintained that the gods of Greek mythology were deified men and women. See -ISM.] The method of interpretation which regards myths as traditional accounts of real incidents in human history. So **Euhe·merist,** one who follows the method of Euhemerus; also *attrib.* **Euhemeri·stic** *a.* inclined to e.; of the nature of, or like, e. **Euhe·merize** *v.* to subject to or to follow the method of Euhemerus.

Eukairite; see EUCAIRITE.

Eulerian (yulīᵊ·riăn), *a.* 1882. [f. *Euler,* the Swiss mathematician (1707–83) + -IAN.] Of, pertaining to, or discovered by, Euler; as *Eulerian constant, function, integral.*

‖**Eulogia** (yulōᵘ·dʒiă). 1751. [Late (eccl.) L. *eulogia* (med.L. also *eulogium*) consecrated bread – eccl.Gr. εὐλογία, in N.T. blessing, praise. See EULOGY.] **a.** *orig.* The Eucharist. **b.** A portion of the consecrated bread reserved for those who were not present at the communion. **c.** In the Greek church, the unconsecrated bread remaining after communion, blessed and given to the non-communicants.

Eulogic, †-al (yulǫ·dʒik, -ăl), *a.* 1656. [f. EULOGY + -IC; see -ICAL.] Pertaining to eulogy; containing praise. Hence **Eulo·gically** *adv.*

Eulogism (yū·lŏdʒiz'm). 1761. [f. EULOGY + -ISM.] A eulogistic speech; eulogistic language.

Eulogist (yū·lŏdʒist). 1808. [f. as prec. + -IST.] One who eulogizes; a panegyrist.

Eulogistic, -al (yulodʒi·stik, -ăl), *a.* 1825. [f. prec. + -IC; see -ICAL.] Pertaining to or conveying eulogy; of the nature of eulogy; commendatory, laudatory; as, *eulogistic inscriptions.*

Hence **Eulogi·stically** *adv.*

Eulogium (yulōᵘ·dʒiŏm). Pl. **-iums;** also **-ia.** 1706. [– med. L. *eulogium* praise, app. blending of L. *elogium* inscription on a tomb, etc., and med.L. *eulogia* praise – Gr. εὐλογία; see EULOGY.] = EULOGY 1 and 1 b.

Eulogize (yū·lŏdʒəiz), *v.* 1810. [f. next + -IZE.] *trans.* To pronounce a eulogy upon; to speak or write in commendation of; to extol.

Eulogy (yū·lŏdʒi). 1591. [– med.L. *eulogium, eulogia* praise; see EULOGIUM.] **1.** A speech or writing in commendation of the qualities, etc., of a person or thing; *esp.* a set oration in honour of a deceased person. **b.** Commendation, praise 1725. †**2.** *Eccl.* = EULOGIA –1782.

Eulysite (yū·lisəit). 1868. [f. EU- + -LYSIS + -ITE[1] 2 b.] *Min.* 'A granular mixture of augite, garnet, and nearly 50 per cent. of a mineral allied to olivine' (Watts).

Eulytin (yū·litin). 1850. [f. Gr. εὔλυτος easily dissolved + -IN[1]. Cf. DYSLUITE.] *Min.* Native silicate of bismuth, usually occurring in brownish crystals with a resinous lustre var. **Eulytite** (yū·litəit).

Eunomy (yū·nŏmi). *rare.* 1721. [– Gr. εὐνομία, f. εὐ- EU- + νομία law; see -Y[3].] A condition of good law well administered.

Eunuch (yū·nŏk), *sb.* ME. [– L. *eunuchus* – Gr. εὐνοῦχος, f. εὐνή bed + *οχ- *εχ- (in ἔχειν keep); the etymol. meaning is therefore 'bedchamber guard'.] **1.** A castrated male person; also, such a person employed as a harem attendant, or charged with important affairs of state. **b.** = CASTRATO 1732. **2.** *attrib.* and *fig.* 1666.

Hence †**Eu·nuch** *v.* to make a eunuch of; also *fig.* †**Eunu·chate** *v.* to castrate; to deprive of virility. SIR T. BROWNE. **Eu·nuchism,** the custom of making eunuchs; the condition of being a eunuch. **Eu·nuchize** *v.* to castrate; to emasculate (*lit.* and *fig.*).

Euodic (yū,ōᵘ·dik), *a.* 1873. [f. Gr. εὐώδης, f. εὐ- EU- + ὠδ- stem of ὄζειν to smell + -IC.] Aromatic; as *euodic aldehyde.*

Euonymus (yu,ǫ·nimŏs). 1767. [mod. use by Linnæus of L. *euonymus* (Pliny) – Gr. εὐώνυμος lucky, f. εὐ- EU- + *ωνυμ-, var. of ὄνομα name.] *Bot.* A genus of shrubs (N.O. *Celastraceæ*), of which the only British species is the Spindle-tree. The bark of an American species (*E. atropurpureus*) is used as a cathartic.

Euosmite (yu,ǫ·zməit). 1868. [f. Gr. εὔοσμος sweet-smelling + -ITE[1] 2 a.] A fossil resin, giving an aromatic odour when burned.

Eupathy (yū·păþi). 1603. [– Gr. εὐπάθεια happy condition of the soul; see EU-, SYMPATHY.] *Stoical Philos.* Good affections of the mind; as, joy, caution, will.

Eupatorine (yupæ·tŏrəin). Formerly also **-in, -ina.** 1838. [f. next + -INE[5].] *Chem.* An alkaloid contained in the flowers and leaves of the water-hemp (*Eupatorium cannabinum*).

‖**Eupatorium** (yūpătōᵊ·riŏm). 1578. [mod.L. – Gr. εὐπατόριον, *Agrimonia eupatorium,* so called from Mithridates Eupator (Gr. Εὐπάτωρ), king of Pontus, who first used it. See -IUM.] *Bot.* A genus of the N.O. *Compositæ,* of which the only British species is *E. cannabinum,* Hemp Agrimony. Also, a plant of the same. So †**Eu·patory,** Hemp Agrimony.

Eupatrid (yupæ·trid, yū·pătrid). *Pl.* **-ids;** also in L. form **-idæ.** 1833. [– Gr. εὐπατρίδης person of noble ancestry, f. εὐ- EU- + πατήρ father.] A member of the first of the three orders in the Athenian Constitution. Hence (rarely) *gen.* A patrician. Also *attrib.*

‖**Eupepsia** (yū·pe·psiă). 1706. [mod.L. – Gr. εὐπεψία digestibility, f. εὔπεπτος; see next.] Healthy action of the digestive organs; good digestion. Anglicized as **Eupepsy.**

Eupeptic (yupe·ptik). 1699. [f. Gr. εὔπεπτος easy of digestion, having a good digestion, f. εὐ- EU- + πέπτειν digest; see -IC.] **A.** *adj.* †**1.** Promoting digestion. EVELYN. **2.** Having a good digestion 1831. **3.** Of, pertaining to, or resulting from, good digestion 1845. **4.** Easy of digestion. (Dicts.)

2. E'en after dinner, e., would rush yet again to his reading CLOUGH. **3.** Wrapt in lazy e. fat CARLYLE.

†**B.** *sb.* Anything that promotes digestion. (Dicts.)

Hence **Eupepti·city,** the state of feeling resulting from eupepsy (Carlyle).

Euphemious (yufī·miəs), *a. rare.* 1853. [f. Gr. εὔφημος; see next, -IOUS.] **a.** = EUPHEMISTIC. **b.** Well reputed.

Euphemism (yū·fĭ,miz'm). 1656. [– Gr. εὐφημισμός, f. εὐφημίζειν speak fair + εὔφημος fair of speech, f. εὐ- EU- + φήμη speaking; see -ISM.] **1.** *Rhet.* A figure by which a less distasteful word or expression is substituted for one more exactly descriptive of what is intended. **2.** An instance of this figure 1793.

2. A shorn crown. . a e. for decapitation FROUDE. var. **Euphemi·smus** (now *rare*).

Euphemistic, -al (yūfĭ,mi·stik, -ăl), *a.* 1856. [f. Gr. εὔφημος (see prec.) + -IST + -IC; see -ICAL.] Pertaining to euphemism; of the nature of, or containing, a euphemism.

Hence **Euphemi·stically** *adv.*

Euphemize (yū·fĭ,məiz), *v.* 1857. [– Gr. εὐφημίζειν; see EUPHEMISM, -IZE.] To speak or speak of euphemistically.

||**Euphonia** (yū:fōᵘ·niă). 1591. [Late L.; see EUPHONY.] = EUPHONY, q.v.

Euphoniad (yufōᵘ·niăd). 1854. [irreg. f. prec.] *Mus.* An instrument said to combine the tones of the organ, clarinet, horn, bassoon, and violin.

Euphonic, -al (yufǫ·nik, -ăl), *a.* 1814. [f. EUPHONY + -IC; see -ICAL.] **1.** Euphonious. **2.** Of or pertaining to euphony 1816.

2. Purely e. influences 1875. Hence **Eupho·nically** *adv.*

Euphonious (yūfōᵘ·niəs), *a.* 1774. [f. as prec. + -OUS.] Full of or characterized by euphony; pleasing to the ear. Hence **Eupho·niously** *adv.* var. **Eu·phonous.**

Euphonism (yū·fŏniz'm). 1774. [f. as prec. + -ISM.] The habit of using euphonious words; a well-sounding combination or expression.

Euphonium (yufōᵘ·niŏm). 1865. [mod.L., f. Gr. εὔφωνος; see EUPHONY, -IUM.] *Mus.* A bass instrument of the Saxhorn family, usually tuned in B♭ or C.

Euphonize (yū·fŏnəiz), *v.* 1774. [f. EUPHONY + -IZE.] *trans.* To render euphonious; to alter for euphony.

Euphonon (yūfōᵘ·nǫ̆n). 1824. [– Gr. εὔφωνον adj. n.; see EUPHONY.] *Mus.* A musical instrument which resembled the upright piano in form and the organ in tone.

Euphony (yū·fŏni). 1623. [– Fr. *euphonie* – late L. *euphonia* – Gr. εὐφωνία, f. εὔφωνος well-sounding, f. εὐ- EU- + φωνή sound, voice; see -Y³.] **a.** The quality of having a pleasant sound; the pleasing effect of sounds free from harshness. **b.** *Philol.* The tendency to ease of pronunciation, formerly explained as an endeavour after a pleasing acoustic effect.

E. then is the mother of many lies HELPS.

||**Euphorbia** (yūfǭ·ɹbiă). ME. [alt. (by assim. to -IA¹) of L. *euphorbea* (Pliny), f. *Euphorbus* name of a physician of Juba II, king of Mauritania, who is said to have named the plant after him.] *Bot.* The name of the Spurge genus (N.O. *Euphorbiaceæ*), comprising many species, secreting a viscid milky juice, and having a peculiar inflorescence. Cf. SPURGE.

The lofty candelabra-shaped euphorbias towering above the copses of evergreens PRINGLE. Hence **Eu:phorbia·ceous** *a.* of the N.O. *Euphorbiaceæ*. **Eupho·rbial** *a.* (Dicts.).

Euphorbine (yufǭ·rbəin). 1838. [f. EUPHORBIA + -INE⁵.] *Chem.* A non-volatile poisonous principle contained in the milky juice of *Euphorbia myrtifolia.*

||**Euphorbium** (yūfǭ·ɹbiŏm). ME. [– L. *euphorbeum* (Pliny), var. of *euphorbea*; see EUPHORBIA, -IUM.] †**1.** = EUPHORBIA. –1767. **2.** A gum resin obtained from certain species of *Euphorbia*, and formerly used as an emetic and purgative.

Euphory (yū·fŏri). 1684. [– Gr. εὐφορία, f. εὔφορος well-bearing, f. εὐ- EU- + φέρειν bear; see -Y³.] Well-bearing or well-being.

Euphotide (yufōᵘ·təid). 1836. [– Fr. *euphotide*, f. Gr. εὐ- EU- + φῶς, φωτ- light + *-ide* -ID³.] *Geol.* 'A crystalline rock consisting essentially of Labrador felspar and diallage, with subordinate intermixtures of hornblende and augite' (Page). Called also GABBRO, q.v.

||**Euphrasia** (yūfrēⁱ·ziă). 1706. [L. form of next.] **1.** *Bot.* = next. **2.** Cheerfulness 1882.

Euphrasy (yū·frăsi). 1475. [– med.L. *euphrasia* – Gr. εὐφρασία cheerfulness – εὐφραίνειν gladden, f. εὐ- EU- + φρήν mind; see -Y³.] *Bot.* A plant, *Euphrasia officinalis* (N.O. *Scrophulariaceæ*), formerly in repute for the treatment of diseases of the eye; = EYE-BRIGHT. Also *fig.*

Michael..purg'd with Euphrasie and Rue The visual Nerve MILT. *P. L.* XI. 414.

Euphroe (yū·fro). Also **uphroe.** 1815. [– Du. *juffrouw* dead-eye, prop. maiden, f. *jong* young + *vrouw* woman. See YUFFROUW.] *Naut.* A crowfoot dead-eye; a long cylindrical block perforated to receive the cords composing the crowfoot.

Euphues (yū·fiu,īz). 1578. [– Gr. εὐφυής well endowed by nature, f. εὐ- EU- + φυ- (be) in φυή growth.] Name of the chief character in John Lyly's books, *Euphues, The Anatomy of Wit* (1578), and *Euphues and his England* (1580). Hence, the book so named.

Euphuism (yū·fiu,iz'm). 1592. [f. prec. + -ISM.] **1.** Properly, the type of diction and style of Lyly's *Euphues,* fashionable in literature and polite conversation in the 16th and beginning of the 17th c. Hence, any similar affectation in writing or speech; high-flown language. **2.** A euphuistic phrase or composition 1871. ¶**3.** Erron. for EUPHEMISM. 1865.

1. That Beautie in Court, which could not Parley Euphueisme, was as little regarded; as shee which now there, speakes not French 1632.

Euphuist (yū·fiu,ist). 1820. [f. as prec. + -IST.] One whose writing or speech is characterized by EUPHUISM.

Elizabeth was the most affected and detestable of Euphuists J. R. GREEN. Hence **Euphuistic, -al** *a.*, **-ly** *adv.* †**Euphuize** *v.* to talk or make like Euphues.

Euphyllite (yufi·ləit). 1849. [f. Gr. εὔφυλλος well-leaved + -ITE¹ 2b.] *Min.* A white hydrous silicate, micaceous in structure.

Eupione (yū·pi,oᵘn). Also **eupion.** 1838. [– Gr. εὐπίων very fat, f. εὐ- EU- + πίων fat; assim. to derivs. in -ONE.] *Chem.* A volatile, oily liquid produced by the distillation of wood, tar, etc.

Euplastic (yuplæ·stik). 1847. [f. Gr. εὔπλαστος easily moulded + -IC.]

A. *adj.* Easily formed into an organic tissue. **B.** *sb.* Euplastic matter. (Dicts.)

||**Eupnœa** (yūpnī·ă). 1706. [mod.L. – Gr. εὔπνοια, f. εὐ- EU- + πνεῖν breathe.] Normal breathing; easy respiration; opp. to *dyspnœa.*

Eupractic (yupræ·ktik), *a.* [f. Gr. εὐ- EU-, πρακ-, πράσσειν act; see -IC.] Inclined to act rightly. CARLYLE.

†**Eupy·rion.** 1827. [f. Gr. εὐ- EU- + πυρεῖον fire-stick, f. πῦρ fire.] A contrivance for obtaining a light easily. Also *fig.*

||**Euraquilo** (yuᵊræ·kwilo). Also **Euroaquilo.** 1582. [Vulg. *euroaquilo* (Acts 27:14), f. L. *Eurus* east wind + *Aquilo* north wind, repr. N.T. Gr. εὐρακύλων (Sin. AB*), and used in the Rhemish N.T. (1582); in A.V. *Euroclydon*, in R.V. *Euraquilo.* See EUROCLYDON.] A stormy NE. or NNE. wind, blowing in the Levant. R.V. *Acts* 27:14.

Eurasian (yūᵊrēⁱ·ʃăn). 1844. [f. *Europe* + *Asia*, or the comp. *Eurasia*, + -AN.] **A.** *adj.* **1.** Of or pertaining to Europe and Asia considered as one continent 1868. **2.** Of mixed European and Asiatic (*esp.* Indian) parentage 1844. **B.** *sb.* A person of mixed European and Asiatic (*esp.* Indian) blood 1845. Cf. ANGLO-INDIAN.

So **Eurasia·tic** *a.* = EURASIAN A. 1.

†**Eure,** *sb.* ME. [– OFr. *eür* destiny (mod. *heur* (good) fortune, good luck) :– L. *augurium* augury, omen.] Destiny; luck –1525. Hence †**Eure** *v.* to destine. †**Eu·rous** *a.* lucky, prosperous.

Eureka (yuᵊrī·kă), *interj.* 1603. [Gr. εὕρηκα, 1st pers. sing. pf. of εὑρίσκειν find.] The exclam. of Archimedes when he found out how to determine (by specific gravity) the proportion of base metal in Hiero's crown. Hence *allusively*, with reference to any discovery. Often *attrib.*

Eurhythmy (yuri·þmi). 1624. [– L. *eur(h)ythmia* proportion – Gr. εὐρυθμία, f. εὐ- EU- + ῥυθμός proportion, RHYTHM; see -Y³.] **1.** *Arch.* Harmony in the proportions of a building. **2.** *Path.* Regularity of the pulse 1721. **3. a.** Rhythmical order or movement; **b.** graceful proportion and carriage of the body 1706. Hence **Eurhy·thmic. A.** *adj.* In or of harmonious proportion, esp. in architecture 1831. **B.** *sb. pl.* A system of rhythmical bodily movements, esp. with the aid of music, used with an educational object 1915.

Euripus (yuᵊrəi·pŏs). *Pl.* **-pi.** 1601. [L. – Gr. εὔριπος, f. εὐ- EU- + ῥιπή rush.] *orig.* The proper name of the channel between Eubœa (Negropont) and the mainland, where the currents are violent and uncertain. Hence *gen.* a strait or sea-channel of this character. Also *transf.* var. †**Euri·pe.** Hence †**Eu·ripize** *v. intr.* to be 'whirled hither and thither' (Sir T. Browne).

Eurite (yuᵊ·rəit). 1844. [– Fr. *eurite* – Gr. εὔρυτος 'flowing plentifully', f. εὐ- EU- + ῥεῖν flow; see -ITE¹ 2 b.] *Min.* 'A variety of syenite occurring near Christiania, of a blue colour and stratified' (Watts). **Euri·tic** *a.*

†**Euro-boreal,** *a.* [f. L. *Euro-* – Gr. Εὐρο-, comb. form of Εὖρος EURUS, + BOREAL.] North-easterly. EVELYN.

Euroclydon (yuᵊrǫ·klidǫ̆n). 1611. [A.V. *euroclydon* (Acts 27:14) – N.T. Gr. εὐροκλύδων (HLP al. pler.); see also EURAQUILO.] = EURAQUILO, q.v. Occas., a tempestuous wind. Also *fig.*

E. bellows down the chimney LOWELL.

Europæo-, -eo- (yuᵊrǒpī·o-), comb. f. L. *Europæus* European in **Europe·o-Asia·tic,** etc.

European (yuᵊrǒpī·ăn). 1603. [– Fr. *européen*, f. L. *europæus*, f. *Europa* – Gr. Εὐρώπη (of unkn. origin), first applied to central Greece, later extended to the whole Greek mainland and then to the land-mass behind it; see -EAN.] **A.** *adj.* Belonging to Europe or its inhabitants; extending over Europe. **B.** *sb.* A native of Europe 1632.

A. *E. plan* (U.S.), the practice at a hotel of charging for lodging and service without inclusion of meals (contrasted with *American plan*) 1847. A scholar of E. celebrity 1897.

Europeanism (yuᵊrǒpī·ăniz'm). 1828. [f. prec. + -ISM.] **a.** Tendency to adopt what is European, *e.g.* ideas, manners, methods, etc. **b.** Anything peculiar to or characteristic of Europe or Europeans.

Europeanize (yūᵊrǒpī·ănəiz), *v.* 1849. [f. as prec. + -IZE.] *trans.* To make European in appearance, habit, mode of life, or extent.

The reaction thus originated in Germany was.. Europeanized by France 1857. Hence **Europe:aniza·tion.**

†||**Eurus** (yūᵊ·rǒs). ME. [L. – Gr. Εὖρος the east wind.] The east wind, ESE. or SE.; the god of the east wind –1727.

Eurycephalic (yūᵊ:ri,sǐfæ·lik), *a.* 1878. [f. Gr. εὐρύς wide + κεφαλή head + -IC.] *Ethnol.* Broad-headed; applied to a subdivision of the brachycephalic races of man.

Eurycerous (yuᵊri·sĕrəs), *a.* 1836. [– Gr. εὐρύκερως, f. εὐρύς broad + κέρας horn + -OUS.] Broad-horned. (Dicts.)

Eurygnathous (yuᵊri·gnăþəs), *a.* 1878. [f. Fr. *eurygnathe* (f. Gr. εὐρύς broad + γνάθος jaw) + -OUS.] Having a broad upper jaw.

Eurypterid (yuᵊri·ptĕrid). 1871. [– mod. L. *Eurypteridæ* pl., f. *Eurypterus* name of the typical genus, f. Gr. εὐρύς broad + πτερόν feather, wing; see -ID³.] *Palæont.* One of a group of fossil Crustacea, abundant in the Silurian and Devonian periods. So named as having a pair of broad swimming appendages, the hindmost of a series attached to the cephalo-thorax.

Eurystomatous (yūᵊri,stǫ·mătəs), *a.* 1878. [f. Gr. εὐρύς broad + στόμα, στοματ- mouth + -OUS.] Wide-mouthed. Chiefly of serpents: Having a distensible mouth.

Eurythmic, etc., var. EURHYTHMIC, etc.

Eusebian (yusī·biăn). 1730. [f. Gr. Εὐσέβιος + -AN.] **A.** *adj.* Of or pertaining to Eusebius, bishop of Nicomedia, leader of the Arians 1882. **b.** Pertaining to Eusebius of Cæsarea, or his historical works 1860.

b. *E. canons*: an arrangement of the contents of the four Gospels into ten classes of passages, according as they occur in one of the evangelists alone or in any one of the possible combinations of two or three out of the four.

B. *sb.* A member of the Eusebian sect 1730.

Euskarian (yūskēᵊ·riăn), *a.* and *sb.* 1864. [f. Basque *Euskara, Eskuara, Uskara*, the Basque language + -IAN.] Basque; used by some ethnologists to designate a pre-Aryan element in Europeans typified by the Basques.

Eusol (yū·sǫl). 1915. [f. *E*dinburgh *U*niversity *sol*ution; assoc. w. EU-.] A solution of free hypochlorous acid used as an antiseptic and bactericide.

Eustachian (yūstēⁱ·kiăn), *a.* 1741. [f. *Eustachius*, latinized f. Bartolomeo *Eustachi* (*c.* 1500–74), Italian anatomist, + -AN.] *Anat.* Of structures discovered by him.

E. tube (occas. *E. canal*): a canal leading from the pharynx to the cavity of the tympanum; hence *E. catheter*, an instrument for inflating the E. tube with air. *E. valve*: a membranous fold at the orifice of the vena cava inferior, which in the fœtus directs the current of blood from this vessel to the foramen ovale and left auricle.

Eustyle (yū·stəil). 1696. [– L. *eustylos* – Gr. εὔστυλος with pillars well placed, f. εὐ- EU- + στῦλος pillar.] *Arch.* **A.** *adj.* Of a colonnade, etc.: Having the space between each successive pair of columns equal to two diameters of a column and a quarter or half diameter. **B.** *sb.* This distance itself.

Eutaxite (yutæ·ksəit). 1879. [f. Gr. εὐ- + τάξις arrangement + -ITE[1] 2 b.] *Geol.* A rock consisting of layers of different kinds of lava lying regularly one above the other. Hence **Eutaxi·tic** *a.* of the nature of e.

†**Eutaxy.** 1614. [– Fr. *eutaxie* – Gr. εὐταξία good arrangement, f. εὐ- EU- + τάσσειν arrange.] Good or established order or arrangement –1677.

‖**Euterpe** (yū·tə·ɹpi). 1866. [mod.L. – Gr. Εὐτέρπη, the Muse of music, f. εὐ- EU- + τέρπειν to delight.] **1.** *Bot.* A genus of graceful palms, sometimes of great height. **2.** *Astron.* The 27th asteroid. Hence **Eute·rpean** *a.* pertaining to E., or to music.

Eutexia (yute·ksiă). 1884. [– Gr. εὐτηξία, f. εὐ- EU- + τήκειν melt.] The quality of melting readily, *i.e.* at a low temperature. Hence **Eute·ctic** *a.* melting readily; *sb.* a eutectic substance.

Euthanasia (yūþănē[i]·siă, -ziă). 1646. [– Gr. εὐθανασία, f. εὐ- EU- + θάνατος death.] **1.** A quiet and easy death. **2.** The means of procuring this. Also *transf.* and *fig.* 1742. **3.** The action of inducing a quiet and easy death 1869.

1. Not a torture death but a quiet e. CARLYLE. **2.** The true e. she discovered. .in the bite of an asp MERIVALE. **3.** An e., an abridgment of the pangs of disease 1869. var. (in sense 1) **Eutha·nasy.**

†**Eu·thymy.** 1623. [– Gr. εὐθυμία, f. εὐ- EU- + θυμός mind.] Cheerfulness of mind –1671.

Eutopia (yūtō[u]·piă). 1556. [f. Gr. εὐ- (see EU-) + τόπος place. First used by Sir T. More, with a play on UTOPIA (f. Gr. οὐ τόπος = nowhere), the country described in his book with that title.] A place of ideal happiness or good order.

Eutrophy (yū·trŏfi). 1721. [– Gr. εὐτροφία, f. εὐ- EU- + τρέφειν nourish.] *Path.* Good nutrition. Hence **Eutro·phic** *a.* promoting nutrition; *sb.* [sc. *medicine*]. (Dicts.)

Eutychian (yuti·kiăn). 1556. [– eccl.L. *Eutychianus*, f. *Eutyches*, Gr. Εὐτυχής; see -IAN.]

A. *adj.* Of, pertaining or adhering to, the doctrine of Eutyches (5th c.), who held that the human nature of Christ was lost in the divine.

B. *sb.* A follower of Eutyches.

Hence **Euty·chianism,** the E. heresy.

Euxenite (yū·ksĭnəit). 1844. [f. Gr. εὔξενος hospitable + -ITE[1] 2 b. So named as harbouring many rare constituents.] *Min.* A mineral found in Norway, consisting mainly of niobate and titanate of yttrium.

Evacuant (ĭvæ·kiŭănt). 1730. [– *evacuant-*, pr. ppl. stem of L. *evacuare*; see next, -ANT.] *Med.*

A. *adj.* That promotes evacuation, cathartic, purgative 1800.

B. *sb.* A purgative, emetic, diaphoretic 1730.

Evacuate (ĭvæ·kiu,e[i]t), *v.* 1526. [– *evacuat-* pa. ppl. stem of L. *evacuare* (Pliny), f. *e-* EX-[1] + *vacuus* empty; see -ATE[3].] **1.** *trans.* To empty, clear out the contents of 1542. Also *fig.* **2.** Of an army: To relinquish the occupation of 1710; also *gen.* to quit, withdraw from 1809. Also *absol.* †**3.** To make void –1785. †**4.** To get rid of (a disease or humour). Also *fig.* –1790. **5.** To void, discharge, throw off, vent. Also *absol.* 1607. **6.** To take out mechanically, leaving a vacuum; to pump out; to exhaust. Also *fig.* *Obs.* exc. in surgical use. 1719. Also *intr.* for *refl.* **7.** To clear out (inhabitants, troops, etc.) 1639.

1. To e. the stomach 1875. *fig.* To e. the mind of all ill thoughts 1653. **2.** The garrison, in a panic, evacuated the fort MACAULAY. **3.** To euacuate a Marriage BACON. **6.** To e. the contents of abscesses 1877. Hence **Eva·cuative** *a.* that evacuates (the bowels); purgative; *sb.* an evacuant. **Eva·cuator,** one who or that which evacuates. †**Eva·cuatory** *a.* and *sb.* (*rare*) = EVACUANT A and B.

Evacuation (ĭvæ:kiu,ē[i]·ʃən). ME. [– late L. *evacuatio*, f. as prec.; see -ION.] **1.** *spec.* **a.** *Med.* The action of depleting or of clearing out by medicine or other artificial means. Now *rare.* **b.** *Phys.* The process of discharging (waste matter) through the excretory organs (now *esp.* from the bowels) 1532; *concr.* evacuated matter 1625. **2.** *gen.* The action of emptying, or of removing so as to make empty. Also *fig.* 1598. †**b.** A depleting (of population, etc.) –1755. **3.** *Mil.* The withdrawal from occupation of a country, etc.; the removal (of a garrison, inhabitants, etc.) 1710. **4.** Cancelling, nullification 1650.

3. *E. day*, the anniversary of the day on which the British army evacuated New York, Nov. 25, 1783.

Evade (ĭvē[i]·d), *v.* 1513. [– Fr. *évader*, – L. *evadere*, f. *e-* EX-[1] + *vadere* go.] **1.** *intr.* To get away, escape. Const. *from, out of.* Now *rare.* **2.** *trans.* To escape by artifice from; to avoid, save oneself from; to elude, avoid encountering 1535. **4.** *absol.* or *intr.* To practise evasion 1716. **5.** *trans.* Of things: To elude, baffle (efforts, vigiliance, etc.) 1716.

2. To e. her father's anger POPE, payment 1832, enquiries 1832, the force of an obligation LD. BROUGHAM. **5.** Some offences e. definition J. MARTINEAU. Hence **Eva·dable** *a.* **Eva·der.** **Eva·dingly** *adv.*

Evagation (ĭvăgē[i]·ʃən). ME. [– Fr. *évagation* or L. *evagatio*, f. *evagat-*, pa. ppl. stem of *evagari*, f. *e-* EX-[1] + *vagari* wander, stray; see -ION.] **1.** The action of wandering away; rambling, roving 1691. †Also *fig.* of the mind, thoughts, etc. –1677. †**2.** A diversion; an extravagance –1649.

Evaginate (ĭvæ·dʒine[i]t), *v.* 1656. [– *evaginat-*, pa. ppl. stem of L. *evaginare* unsheath, f. *e-* EX-[1] + *vagina* sheath; see -ATE[3].] †**a.** To unsheath. **b.** *Phys.* To turn (a tubular organ) inside out; to protrude by eversion. Hence **Eva·ginable** *a.* that can be evaginated, **Evagina·tion,** the action or result of evaginating.

Eval (ī·văl), *a.* *rare.* 1791. [f. L. *ævum* + -AL[1].] Of or pertaining to age; age-long.

Evaluate (ĭvæ·liu,e[i]t), *v.* 1842. [Back-formation, after (O)Fr. *évaluer*, from next. See -ATE[3].] *trans.* **a.** *Math.* To work out the value of; to find a numerical expression for. **b.** *gen.* To reckon up, ascertain the amount of; to express in terms of the known. Hence **Eva·luable** *a.*

Evaluation (ĭvæ:liu,ē[i]·ʃən). 1755. [– (O)Fr. *évaluation*, f. *évaluer*, f. *e-* EX-[1] + OFr. *value*; see VALUE *sb.*, -ATION.] **1.** = VALUATION. Now *rare.* **2.** The action of evaluating 1779.

Evanesce (evăne·s), *v.* 1822. [– L. *evanescere*, f. *e-* EX-[1] + *vanus* empty; see -ESCE.] *intr.* To fade out of sight, disappear; chiefly *fig.*

Evanescence (evăne·sĕns). 1751. [f. next; see -ENCE.] **1.** The process or fact of vanishing away. **2.** Evanescent quality; tendency to vanish away 1830. **3.** *concr.* An evanescent thing (*rare*) 1830.

2. This e. and lubricity of all objects. .lets them slip through our fingers EMERSON.

Evanescent (evăne·sĕnt), *a.* 1717. [– *evanescent-* pres. ppl. stem of L. *evanescere*; see EVANESCE, -ENT.] **1.** That is on the point of vanishing; in *Math.* on the point of becoming zero, infinitesimal. Hence *tranf.*: Imperceptibly minute. **2.** That quickly vanishes; fleeting 1738; in *Bot.* of parts of plants: Not permanent 1776.

1. To render the crime e., or almost nothing WOLLASTON. **2.** A scene Of e. glory COWPER. Hence **Evane·scently** *adv.*

Evangel[1], **evangile** (ĭvæ·ndʒĕl, -il). Now *arch.* or *rhet.* [ME. *evangile* (later assim. to L.) – (O)Fr. *évangile* – eccl.L. *evangelium* – Gr. εὐαγγέλιον (in eccl. use) good news, (in cl. Gr.) reward for bringing good news, f. εὐάγγελος bringing good news, f. εὐ- EU- + ἀγγέλλειν announce (cf. ANGEL).] **1.** The GOSPEL (in various senses); *esp.* the Gospel record; also, one of the Four Gospels. **2.** *pl.* Copies of the Gospels; used to impart sanctity to an oath. Also *attrib.* ME. **3.** *transf.* †Something 'as true as gospel' –1681; a doctrine or principle of saving efficacy 1831. **4.** A message of glad tidings 1842.

1. The spirit of the Evangile R. WILLIAMS, Lukes Evangel GALE. **3.** That. .Merline's prophesies [are] evangels COLVIL.

Evangel[2] (ĭvæ·ndʒĕl). 1593. [– Gr. εὐάγγελος; see prec.] = EVANGELIST.

Evange·lian, *a.* 1808. [f. Gr. (τὰ) εὐαγγέλια (pl. of εὐαγγέλιον) + -AN.] In *E. sacrifice*: tr. Gr. τὰ εὐαγγέλια, the sacrifice offered on receipt of good news.

Evangelic (ĭvăn-, evăndʒe·lik). 1460. [– eccl. L. *evangelicus* – eccl. Gr. εὐαγγελικός; see EVANGEL[1], -IC.]

A. *adj.* **1.** Of or pertaining to the Gospel narrative, to the Four Gospels, or to the Gospel faith, precepts, or dispensation 1502. †**b.** ?Pious 1460. **2.** = EVANGELICAL 2 a, b. 1583.

B. *sb.* †**1.** The *adj.* used *absol.* 1617. †**2.** = EVANGELICAL B. 1, 2. –1812.

Evangelical (ĭvæn-, evændʒe·likăl). 1531. [f. prec. + -AL[1]; see -ICAL.]

A. *adj.* **1.** = EVANGELIC A. 1. **2.** As the designation of a sect or party. **a.** = PROTESTANT. Now only with reference to Germany and Switzerland. 1532. **b.** Applied to those Protestants who hold that the essence of the Gospel consists in the doctrine of salvation by faith in the atoning death of Christ, and deny the saving efficacy of either good works or the sacraments 1791. **3.** Of or pertaining to an evangelist (*rare*) 1651.

1. Phr. *E. prophet*: a designation of Isaiah, as prophetically describing the life of Christ and anticipating Gospel doctrines. **2. b.** The Wesleyans, the orthodox Dissenters of every description, and the Evangelical churchmen may all be comprehended under the generic name of Methodists SOUTHEY.

B. *sb.* **1.** A Protestant; now *esp.* a German Lutheran, or an adherent of the national church of the German Empire 1532. **2.** A member of the evangelical party, *esp.* a Low churchman 1804.

Hence **Evange·licalism,** the doctrines peculiar to the E. party, or adherence to them. **Evange·lical, -ly** *adv.*, **-ness** (*rare*). **Evangeli·city,** the quality of being e. **Evange·licanism, Evange·licism** (*rare*) = EVANGELICALISM.

Evangelism (ĭvæ·ndʒeliz'm). 1626. [f. EVANGEL + -ISM.] **1.** The preaching or promulgation of the Gospel. **2. a.** = EVANGELICALISM (chiefly in hostile use) 1812. **b.** The faith of the Gospel (*rare*) 1842.

Evangelist (ĭvæ·ndʒelist). ME. [– (O)Fr. *évangéliste* – eccl. L. *evangelista* – eccl. Gr. εὐαγγελιστής, f. εὐαγγελίζεσθαι; see EVANGELIZE, -IST.] **1.** One of the writers of the Four Gospels, Matthew, Mark, Luke, and John. †**2.** The book of the Gospels –1713. **3. a.** *gen.* One who preaches the, or a, gospel 1535. **b.** *orig.* One of a class of teachers, mentioned in *Eph.* 4:11 after 'apostles' and 'prophets'; *later*, an itinerant preacher having no fixed pastoral charge; *now*, a layman who does home missionary work ME.

2. We swere on the holy euangelist, by vs corporally touched LD. BERNERS. **3.** The French Revolution found its E. in Rousseau CARLYLE. **b.** Timothie and Titus. .were Euangelists, a degree aboue ordinarie ministers J. UDALL.

Hence **Eva:ngeli·stic** *a.* of or pertaining to the Four Evangelists, or to preachers of the Gospel. **Eva·ngelistship,** the office or dignity of an e.

Evangelistary (ĭvæ:ndʒĕli·stări). 1646. [– med.L. *evangelistarium*, f. eccl. L. *evangelista*; see prec. -ARY[1].] **a.** A book containing the parts of Gospels used in the liturgy. **b.** A copy of the Four Gospels 1865.

Evangelize (ĭvæ·ndʒĕləiz), *v.* ME. [– eccl. L. *evangelizare* – eccl. Gr. εὐαγγελίζεσθαι, f. εὐάγγελος; see EVANGEL[1], -IZE.] †**1.** *intr.* To bring or tell good tidings; *spec.* to preach, proclaim the Gospel –1808. †**2.** *trans.* To proclaim as glad tidings; to preach –1698. **3.** To preach the Gospel to; to win over to the Christian faith 1652. **4.** To make evangelic in spirit or sense 1677.

3. His [Messiah's] Apostles, whom he sends To e. the Nations MILT. *P. L.* XII. 499. Hence **Eva:ngeliza·tion,** the action or process of evangelizing; the condition of being evangelized. **Eva·ngelizer.**

†**Evangely** (ĭvæ·ndʒĕli). [ME. *evangeli(e)* – eccl. L. *evangelium*; see EVANGEL¹.] = EVANGEL¹ 1, 2, 4. –1683.

Evanid (ĭvæ·nid), *a. arch.* 1626. [– L. *evanidus*, rel. to *evanescere*; see EVANESCE, -ID¹.] **1.** Vanishing away; evanescent. **2.** Faint, weak 1646. †**3.** EMPHATICAL, illusory –1751.

1. Those Animal Spirits are of such an E. and Subtile Nature BP. BURNET. **3.** E. colours 1751. Hence †**Eva·nidness.** HY. MORE.

Evanish (ĭvæ·niʃ), *v.* ME. [– *evaniss-*, extended stem of OFr. *evanir* – Rom. **exvanire*; see E-, VANISH.] *intr.* To vanish.

And cares e. like a morning dream A. RAMSAY. Hence †**Eva·nishment, Evani·tion,** disappearance.

Evansite (e·vănzəit). 1864. [f. Brooke *Evans* who brought it from Hungary + -ITE¹ 2 b.] *Min.* A hydrous phosphate of aluminium occurring in white reniform masses.

Evaporable (ĭvæ·pŏrăb'l), *a.* 1541. [– Fr. *évaporable* or med.L. *evaporabilis*; see EVAPORATE, -BLE. In mod. use f. directly on the verb.] Capable of being evaporated. Hence **Evaporabi·lity.**

Evaporate (ĭvæ·pŏrēⁱt), *v.* 1545. [– *evaporat-*, pa. ppl. stem of L. *evaporare*, f. *e-* EX-¹ + *vapor* steam; see -ATE³.] **1.** *trans.* To convert or turn into vapour; to drive off in the form of vapour. Also *fig.* 1555. **2.** *intr.* To become vapour; to pass off in vapour 1567. **3.** *fig.* To pass off like vapour; to be wasted or dissipated; also *joc.* of persons, to become missing 1631. **4.** *trans.* To subject to evaporation; to drive off the liquid part of. Also *absol.* 1646. **5.** *intr.* To part with liquid particles by evaporation 1799. †**6.** *trans.* To emit in the form of vapour; to give vent to, exhale. Also *absol.* and *intr.* –1799.

1. In the leaves much of the water of the sap is evaporated SIR H. DAVY. **3.** These hostile menaces evaporated without effect GIBBON. **4.** E. to the consistence of honey 1799. **6.** *fig.* To e. the Spleen ADDISON.

Hence **Eva·porative** *a.* pertaining to or producing evaporation. **Eva·porator,** one who or that which evaporates; *esp.* an apparatus for drying fruits, etc. var. **Eva·porize** *v.* (in sense 1).

Evaporation (ĭvæ:pŏrēⁱ·ʃən). ME. [– L. *evaporatio*, f. as prec.; see -ION. Cf. (O)Fr. *évaporation.*] **1.** The process of conversion into vapour; the action of passing off in vapour; an instance of this. Also *fig.* **2.** The action of driving off the liquid part of a substance by means of heat; an instance of this 1718. **3.** The action **a.** of exhaling moisture; †**b.** of emitting (breath, etc.); †**c.** of perspiring insensibly. Also *fig.* 1551. **4.** *concr.* The product of evaporation; vapour; the amount evaporated 1533. †**5.** *Med.* Treatment by means of vapour –1610.

1. By e., water is carried up into the air PALEY. **3. a.** E. takes place through the leaves 1887. **4.** *fig.* The vain evaporations of his discontentment FULLER.

Evapori·meter. Also **-ometer.** 1828. [f. prec. + -METER. Cf. Fr. *évaporo-, évaporimètre.*] An instrument for measuring the quantity of a liquid evaporated in a given time; an atmometer.

Evasible (ĭvēⁱ·sĭb'l), *a.* 18.. [f. as next + -IBLE.] That may be evaded.

Evasion (ĭvēⁱ·ʒən). ME. [– OFr. *évasion* – L. *evasio*, f. *evas-*, pa. ppl. stem of *evadere*; see EVADE, -ION.] **1.** The action of evading or escaping, as by artifice or contrivance; escape (now *rare*); dodging, prevarication 1460. **b.** Means of evading; shuffling excuse subterfuge ME. **2.** Going out, exit (*rare*) 1659.

1. Hope of euasion from Purgatorie 1601. E. from the strength of an Argument HY. MORE. The king's licence for the e. of the act J. H. BLUNT. **b.** Evasions and delays 1874.

Evasive (ĭvēⁱ·siv), *a.* 1725. [f. as prec. + -IVE. Cf. Fr. *évasif, -ive.*] **1.** Seeking to evade; shuffling. **2.** Tending to, or characterized by, evasion 1744. **3.** Elusive 1881. **4.** as *sb.* An evasive expression. NORTH.

1. Thus he..Answer'd e. of the sly request POPE. **2.** E. promises of future service SHERIDAN. Hence **Eva·sive-ly** *adv.*, **-ness.** So †**Evaso·rious.** HY. MORE.

Eve (īv), *sb.* ME. [In ME., two-syll. var. of EVEN *sb.* For similar loss of *-n* cf. *clew, game, maid.*] **1.** = EVENING *sb.*¹ *lit.* and *fig. poet.* or *rhet.* **2.** The evening, hence the day, before a Saint's day or church festival, or *gen.* before any date or event ME. **3.** *transf.* The time immediately preceding some action, event, etc. 1780.

1. From Noon to dewy E. MILT. *P. L.* I. 743. **2.** Saint Bartholomewes Eeve HANMER. **3.** The hull on the e. of sinking DUNCAN. Hence †**Eve** *v.* to be the EVE (sense 2) of.

Eve-churr. 1658. [f. prec. + CHURR *sb.*] †**1.** The Mole-Cricket, or Churr-Worm –1668. **2.** The Nightjar 1837.

†**E·veck.** 1585. [Of unkn. origin.] A kind of wild goat –1611.

Evectant (ĭve·ktănt). 1876. [f. L. *evect-* (see EVECTOR) + -ANT.] *Math.* A contravariant formed by operating upon an invariant or contravariant with an evector.

Eve·cted, *ppl. a. rare.* 1861. [f. as prec. + -ED¹.] Of the edge of a tube: Turned outwards, trumpet-shaped.

Evectic, a dictionary spelling of EUECTIC.

Evection (ĭve·kʃən). 1656. [– L. *evectio*, f. *evect-*, pa. ppl. stem of *evehere* carry forth, elevate, f. *e-* EX-¹ + *vehere* carry; see -ION.] †**1.** A lifting up (*rare*) –1659. **2.** *Astron.* **a.** An inequality in the moon's longitude (see quot.) 1706. †**b.** Used for LIBRATION –1796.

2. a. E., an inequality in the motion of the moon, by which, at her quarters, her mean place differs from her true one by about $2\frac{1}{2}$ degrees more than at her conjunction and opposition BONNYCASTLE. Hence **Eve·ctional** *a.* relating or belonging to the e.

Eve·ctor. [f. as prec. + -OR 2.] *Math.* An operator formed by substituting the differential operators d/da_0, d/da_1, d/da_2, etc. for the coefficients a_0, na_1, $\frac{1}{2}n(n-1)a_2$, etc. of a binary quantic.

Eve-jar. 1789. [f. EVE *sb.* + JAR *sb*¹] = EVE-CHURR 2.

Even (ī·v'n), *sb.* [OE. *æfen*, rel. to synon. OFris. *ēvend*, OS. *āband*, MLG., MDu. *āvont* (Du. *avond*), OHG. *āband* (G. *abend*).] **1.** The latter part of the day. **2.** = EVE 2. ME. *Comb.* **e.-fall,** the fall or commencement of the evening.

Even (ī·v'n), *a.* [OE. *efen* = OFris. *even, iven*, OS. *eban* (Du. *even, effen*), OHG. *eban* (G. *eben*), ON. *jafn*, Goth. *ibns* :– Gmc. **eƀnaz*, of unkn. origin.] **1.** Flat, plane, level; **b.** horizontal (now only *Naut.* in phr. (*On*) *an even keel*) ME. **2.** Of surfaces or lines: Uniform, without inequality ME. **3.** Uniform throughout (in quality, etc.) 1821. †**4.** Straight, direct –1602. **5.** Level *with*, †*to* ME.; in the same plane or line with; parallel ME. **6.** Accurately coincident; exactly adjusted ME. †**7.** Exact, precise –1601. **8.** Uniform; free from variations; equable OE. **9.** Equally balanced 1579. **10.** Of accounts, etc.: 'Square' 1551. **11.** Medium ME. **12.** Equal, just OE. †**13.** On a par, on equal terms –1754. **14.** Equal in magnitude, number, quantity, etc. ME. **15.** Divisible integrally by two; opp. to *odd* ME. **16.** Expressible in integers; containing no fractions 1638.

1. E. ground SHAKS. A fair and e. ridge TENNYSON. **2.** Cut close and e. EVELYN. **3.** A light e. tint 1821. **5.** And shall lay thee euen with the ground *Luke* 19: 44. **7.** *All's Well* V. iii. 326. **8.** At a steady e. trot JOHNSON. **9.** The two scales hang e. BENTHAM. **10.** E. rekoning makes lasting friends SOUTH. Phr. *To be e. with*: to be quits with; I will be e. with you for this scorn 1655. **14.** Three even parts 1660. Phr. *Of e. date*: of the same date (in Eng. chiefly legal). **15.** Death..makes these oddes, all euen *Meas. for M.* III. i. 41. **16.** [The price] down to e. money 1891.

Even (ī·v'n), *adv.* [OE. *efne* = OFris. *efne*, OS. *efno* (Du. *even*), OHG. *ebano* (G. *eben*) :– WGmc. **eƀnō*. The form *e'en* (īn) is now *poet.* or *n. dial.*]

†**I. 1.** Evenly; regularly, uniformly –1728. **2.** In exact agreement –1645. **3.** Equally –1577. **4.** Directly, straight; due (east, etc.); directly (contrary, etc.) –1550.

2. I..rather shun'd to go e. with what I heard *Cymb.* I. iv. 47.

II. As an intensive or emphatic particle. **1.** Exactly, precisely, just: **a.** of manner OE.; **b.** of time ME.; †**c.** of place –1578. **2.** Quite, fully (now only *arch.* in *Even to*) OE. **3.** Emphasizing identity (now *arch.*); also formerly epexegetical; = 'namely' OE. **b.** (Chiefly *e'en.*) Before vbs. in sense 'just', 'nothing else but'; also 'forsooth' (L. *scilicet*). Now *arch.* and *dial.* 1553. **4.** Introducing an extreme case of something more general implied (= Fr. *même*). (The prevailing use; not found exc. in Eng.) 1577.

1. E. thus..the warlike god embraced me SHAKS. Let your love e. with my life decay SHAKS. **3.** E. she I meane *Two Gent.* II. i. 49. **b.** I e'en let him out DE FOE. **4.** Make sacred euen his styrrop *Timon* I. i. 82. E. on that memorable occasion, his stay did not exceed two months GIBBON.

Even (ī·v'n), *v.* [OE. *efnan* and (*ġe*)*efnian*, f. *efen* EVEN *a.*] **1.** *trans.* To level; to make even, level, smooth, or †straight ME. †**2.** To level *to, with* –1632. †**3.** To make (a balance) even –1718. †**4.** To make (accounts, etc.) even –1856. **5.** To †make, treat, or represent as equal. Const. *to, with*. Also *absol.* Now chiefly *Sc.* ME. **6.** To liken, compare. Now *dial.* OE. **7.** *intr.* To be equal, comparable, or †in a line *with* ME. **8.** *trans.* To equal (*rare*) 1583; †to act up to *Cymb.* III. iv. 184.

1. And e. the erthe above ME. E. your Ranks 1688. **8.** A daughter who eveneth thee in beauty R. F. BURTON.

Even- (in early combs. repr. Gmc. stem **eƀno-*; in later use combining directly as *adj.* or *adv.*).

1. Chiefly in parasynthetic derivs., as *e.-handed, -tempered*, etc. †**2.** Prefixed to sbs. in sense 'fellow-', L. *co-*, as in *e.-servant*, etc. **3.** In senses of the *adv.* †**a.** = 'Equally', 'similarly', as in *e.-clad, -high, -mighty*, etc. **b.** = 'Evenly', as in *e.-spun*, etc. †**c.** With quasi-prep. sense, in **e.-deed** *adv.*, indeed. **d.** Straight, directly; see EVENDOWN.

†**E·ven-Chri·stian.** [OE. *efncrīsten* = OFris. *ivinkerstena*, OHG. *ebanchristāni.*] A fellow-Christian –1602.

E·vendown. *north.* (Often hyphened, or as two wds.) ME. [f. EVEN *adv.* (sense I. 4) + DOWN *adv.*]

A. *adv.* †**1.** Straight down. **2.** *dial.* Downright; quite 1869.

B. *adj.* **1.** Coming straight down, as rain 1801. **2.** Downright; straightforward 1786.

†**Eve·ne,** *v.* 1654. [– Fr. †*évenir* (OFr. *esvenir*) – L. *evenire* (see EVENT).] *intr.* To happen –1702.

Evener (ī·v'nəɹ). ME. [f. EVEN *v.* + -ER¹.] One who or that which makes even. **b.** An apparatus for equalizing the draught upon two or three horses working abreast.

†**E·venhead, e·venhood.** ME. [OE. **efenhād*, f. *efen* EVEN *a.* + *hād* rank; see -HEAD, -HOOD.] **1.** Equality; equal dignity or rank –1483. Also *concr.* one who or that which is equal –1570. **2.** Impartiality; well-balanced state (of mind) –1496.

Evening (ī·vniŋ), *sb.*¹ [OE. *ǣfnung*, f. *ǣfnian* grow towards night, f. *ǣfen* EVEN *sb.*; see -ING¹.] †**1.** The coming on of even; the time about sunset –ME. **2.** The close of the day; usu., the time from about sunset to bedtime ME. Also *transf.* and *fig.* **3.** An evening spent in a particular way. Cf. Fr. *soirée.* 1870. **4.** *attrib.*, as in *evening-gun*, etc. 1535.

2. I shall fall Like a bright exhalation in the Euening *Hen. VIII*, III. ii. 226. *fig.* The sad e. of a stormy life POPE. Occasional 'evenings out' 1870.

Comb.: **e. dress; e. flower,** a genus of plants (*Hesperantha*, N.O. *Iridaceæ*) with flowers which expand in the e.; **e. primrose:** see PRIMROSE; **e.-star,** (with def. art.) Venus, (with indef. art.) Venus, Jupiter, or Mercury, also *fig.*; **e.-tide** = EVENTIDE.

†**E·vening,** *sb.*² ME. [f. EVEN *v.* + -ING¹.] **1.** The action of making even, level or smooth or ?of comparing –1670. **2.** Equality ME.

†**E·venlong.** ME. [f. EVEN- + LONG *a.*]

A. *adj.* Oblong –1565.

B. *adv.* Straight along; in an oblong form. Only in ME.

Evenly (ī·v'nli), *a.* Now *Sc.* only. [OE. *efenlić*, f. *efen* EVEN *a.* + *-lić* -LY¹. Cf. ON. *iafnligr*, Goth. *ibnaleiks.*] †**1.** Equal –1513. **2.** Even; equitable; level ME.

Evenly (ī·v'nli), *adv.* [OE. *efenliće*; see EVEN *a.*, -LY².] In an even manner or degree; smoothly; †directly; †exactly; uniformly; with equanimity; without inclination to either side; equally.

Evenness (ī·vĕn,nes). [OE. *efenniss*; see EVEN *a.*, -NESS.] The quality or state of being even; smoothness, levelness; uniformity; equability; †equipoise (*lit.* and *fig.*); equitableness; †equality.

To carry a full cup with evennesse 1646. E. of Voice and Delivery STEELE. The e...in a beautiful set of teeth 1878.

†Even-old. [OE. *efeneald*; see EVEN- and OLD.]

A. *adj.* Of the same age.

B. *sb.* One who is of the same age. –1483.

Evensong (ī·vn'sǫŋ). [OE. *ǣfensang*.] **1.** *Eccl.* Before the Reformation, the service (also called *vespers*) celebrated towards sunset. Later, the 'Evening Prayer' of the Church of England, including vespers and compline. **b.** The time of evensong (*arch.*) ME. **2.** *gen.* A song sung in the evening ME.

1. b. Let hir fast till euensong 1486. **2.** Thee, chauntress, oft the woods among I woo, to hear thy even-song MILT.

†Even-star. [OE. *ǣfensteorra*.] Evening-star –1552.

Event (ǐve·nt), *sb.* 1573. [– L. *eventus*, f. *event-*, pa. ppl. stem of *evenire* come out, result, happen, f. *e-* EX-[1] + *venire* come.] **1.** The occurrence *of.* Now chiefly in phr. *In the event of.* 1602. **2.** An incident, occurrence; *esp.* (in mod. use) an occurrence of some importance 1588. **b.** In the doctrine of chances: Any one of the possible (mutually exclusive) occurrences, one of which must happen under stated conditions, and the relative probability of which may be calculated 1838. **c.** One of the items in a programme of sports 1855. **3.** The outcome, issue, of a course of proceedings; that which results from the operation of a cause; a consequence 1573. **†4.** What becomes of (a person or thing); fate –1674.

2. Coming events cast their shadows before CAMPBELL. Phr. *The course of events*: see COURSE. *Quite an e.* (colloq.). **3.** Causes best friended haue the best euent HEYWOOD. The e. of his enterprise was doubtful MACAULAY. **4.** There is one e. to the righteous and to the wicked *Eccl.* 9:2.

†Event, *v.*[1] 1590. [f. L. *event-* (see prec.).] *intr.* To come to pass –1650.

†Eve·nt, *v.*[2] 1559. [– Fr. *éventer*, OFr. *esventer* :– Rom. **exventare*, f. *ex-* EX-[1] + L. *ventus* wind.] **a.** To expose to the air; hence, to cool. **b.** *intr.* for *refl.* To find a vent. –1606.

†Eve·nterate, *v.* [irreg. f. L. *e-* EX-[1] + *venter* belly + -ATE[3]. Cf. Fr. *éventrer*.] *trans.* To open the bowels of; to disembowel. SIR T. BROWNE.

Eventful (ǐve·ntfŭl), *a.* 1600. [See -FUL.] **1.** Full of striking events. **2.** Fraught with important issues 1773. **3.** Eventual. BENTHAM.

1. This strange euentfull historie SHAKS. **2.** Thalaba..waited calmly for the e. day SOUTHEY.

Eventide (ī·v'ntəid). *arch.* [OE. *ǣfentīd*.] The time of evening; evening. Also *fig.*

†Eve·ntilate, *v.* 1623. [– *eventilat-*, pa. ppl. stem of L. *eventilare*, f. *e-* EX-[1] + *ventilare* VENTILATE.] **1.** To expose to the wind or air; to fan; to winnow –1684. **2.** *fig.* To discuss; to VENTILATE –1669.

2. Copiously..elsewhere eventilated 1669. Hence **†Eventila·tion.**

Eventless (ǐve·ntlės), *a.* 1815. [See -LESS; cf. *eventful*.] Without (noteworthy) events.

Eventration (ǐventrēⁱ·ʃən). 1836. [– Fr. *éventration*, f. *éventrer*, f. *é-* EX-[1] + *ventre* belly.] **1.** The action of opening the belly (of an animal) 1875. **2. a.** The condition of a fœtus in which the abdominal viscera are extruded 1860. **b.** 'The condition of a large ventral hernia' (*Syd. Soc. Lex.*). **c.** The escape of a large amount of intestines from an abdominal wound 1847.

Eventual (ǐve·ntiuăl), *a.* 1612. [– L. *eventus* EVENT + -AL[1], after *actual*.] **†1.** Of or pertaining to events; of the nature of an event –1684. **†2.** That happens to exist –1794. **3.** That will arise or take effect in a certain contingency 1683. **4.** Ultimately resulting 1823.

3. Nothing is provided for it, but an e. surplus to be divided with one class of the private demands BURKE. **4.** An e. denial of God's omnipotence FABER.

Eventuality (ǐve:ntiu,æ·lǐti). 1828. [f. prec. + -ITY. Cf. Fr. *éventualité*.] **1.** A possible event; a contingency 1825. **2.** *Phrenol.* The faculty of observing the order of succession in events; the 'organ' of this faculty 1828.

Eventually (ǐve·ntiuăli), *adv.* 1660. [f. as prec. + -LY[2].] **1.** In a certain event 1830; †conditionally –1785. **2.** †In result –1729; in the event, ultimately 1680.

2. Other vices e. do mischief: this alone aims at it as an end BUTLER.

Eventuate (ǐve·ntiu,eⁱt), *v.* First used in U.S. 1789. [f. as EVENTUAL + -ATE[3], after *actuate*.] **1.** *intr.* To have a (specified) event or issue; to turn out; to result *in.* **2.** To be the issue 1834. **3.** *trans.* To bring to the issue 1837.

1. Discussions which eventuated in Acts of Parliament SMILES. Hence **Eve:ntua·tion**, the action of eventuating; realization; issue.

†Ever, *sb.* [OE. *eofor* = OS. *ebur*, OHG. *ebur* (G. *eber*) wild boar, also ON. *iǫfurr* prince :– Gmc. **eburaz*.] A wild boar; **†e. fern,** (*a*) polypody, *Polypodium vulgare*, (*b*) flowering fern, *Osmunda regalis*.

Ever (e·vəɹ), *adv.* [OE. *ǣfre*, a purely Eng. formation of unkn. origin. From the meaning the first syll. is prob. the mutation of *ā* ever, AY, as in EITHER.]

I. Always, at all times; in all cases. **1.** Throughout all time, all past or future time, one's life, etc.; perpetually (*arch.*). **b.** With limiting adv., prep., or conj., as in *ever after* (*-ward*), *before, since* ME. **2.** = ALWAYS 1. *arch.* and *n. dial.* OE. So in *Ever and again, ever and anon* (see AGAIN, ANON). **3.** Constantly; with perpetual recurrence (*arch.*) OE. So with comparatives, *esp.* before *the—the.* **4.** quasi-*sb.* use of 1, in phr. *For ever, for ever and ay* (arch.) ME.

1. He liveth and reigneth e. one God *Bk. Com. Prayer.* **1. b.** The Coffee-houses have e. since been my chief Places of Resort ADDISON. **2.** The Prelate of the Garter..is e. the Bishop of Winchester R. HOLME. And e. and anon some falling shaft Proves his divinity BYRON. **3.** Pedants..will e. be carping STEELE. **4.** It was the fate of Charles, for e. to aim at projects which were..impracticable GOLDSM.

II. At any time; whence: In any case, in any degree. **1.** At any time OE. **2.** On any supposition, at all OE. **a.** In *Ever, e'er a(n* (vulgar) OE. **b.** In comparatively and relative clauses, introduced by *as, than*, by a superlative with *that*, or by *all, the only*, etc. 1523. **c.** For emphasis with the conjs. *as soon as, before, ere, or* (= *ere*) ME. **d.** After interrog. pronouns, advs., etc. (*how, who, what, where, why*) 1595. **3.** In any degree. **a.** In *Ever the* with comparatives (*colloq.*); = 'at all', 'any' 1622. **b.** In *Ever so* = 'in any conceivable degree' 1690; 'vastly' 1858.

1. The first time that e. I remember to have heard the..singing men in surplices in my life PEPYS. **2. a.** A Man of my Turn enjoys a Holiday with as high a Relish as e'er a Prentice-Boy.. within the Bills of Mortality 1746. **b.** As lowd as e're thou canst, cry 1 *Hen. VI*, I. iii. 72. **3. a.** A Mine undiscovered, from which neither the Owner of the Ground or any Body else, are e. the Richer COLLIER.

Combs.: **e.-being** *a.* that always is; **-blessed** *a.* always blessed; to be always adored; **-during** *a.* everlasting.

Everglade (e·vəɹ,gleⁱd). *U.S.* 1827. [Presumably f. EVER (perh. implying 'interminable') + GLADE (with some obscure ref.).] A marshy tract of land mostly under water and covered in places with tall grass; chiefly in *pl.*, as, *the Everglades of Florida.*

Evergreen (e·vəɹgrīn). 1644. [f. EVER *adv.* + GREEN.]

A. *adj.* **1.** Always green; also *fig.* 1796. **2.** Having green leaves all the year through; opp. to *deciduous.* Also *transf.* of the leaves. 1671.

1. E. valleys 1796. **2.** Shade Of laurel ever-green, and branching palm MILT. *Sams.* 1735.

B. *sb.* An evergreen tree or shrub 1644. Also *attrib.*, as in **Evergreen Oak,** the Holm Oak (*Quercus Ilex*).

Everlasting (evəɹla·stiŋ). ME. [f. EVER *adv.* + LASTING.]

A. *adj.* **1.** Lasting for ever; infinite in future (or, contextually, past) duration. **2.** Used hyperbolically or in relative sense; *esp.* as implying weariness or disgust; cf. ETERNAL 4. ME. **3.** That will never wear out 1590. **4.** In plant-names: **a.** Retaining shape and colour when dried; as in *Everlasting Flower*, a name given to the Cudweeds and various species of *Helichrysum.* **b.** Perennial; as in Everlasting Pea (*Lathyrus latifolius*). **5.** quasi-*adv.* Very, excessively (*U.S. slang*) 1832

1. The Primrose way to th' euerlasting Bonfire *Macb.* II. iii. 22. The mightie God, the euerlasting Father *Isa.* 9:6. **2.** See Cromwell, damn'd to e. fame POPE. The e. Din of Mother-in-law 1688. **3.** E. wear 1891.

B. *absol.* (quasi-*sb.*) and *sb.* **1.** *absol.* In phrases *For, to, from everlasting* ME. **2.** *The Everlasting*: God, the Eternal ME. **3.** *sb.* **a.** = DURANCE 1590. **b.** = LASTING 1822. **4.** = Everlasting Flower. See A. 4. 1794.

1. Euen from e. to e. thou art God *Ps.* 90:2. **2.** *Haml.* I. ii. 131. **3. a.** *Com. Err.* IV. ii. 33.

Hence **Everla·sting-ly** *adv.*, **-ness.**

E:ver-li·ving, *a.* 1547. **1.** That lives or will live for ever. Also *fig.* **2.** quasi-*sb.* 1601.

Evermore (evəɹmōᵊ·ɹ), *adv.* Occas. as two wds. ME. [repl. ME. *evermo*, OE. *ǣfre mā*; see MO *adv.*] Emphatic for EVER. **1.** For all future time. *Obs.* exc. *arch.* **2.** Always, at all times, constantly ME. **3.** With negatives expressed or implied: **a.** At any future time 1600. **b.** Ever again, any longer 1832.

1. Lord, euermore giue vs this bread *John* 6:34. **2.** The minde of man desireth euermore to know the truth HOOKER.

†Eve·rse, *v.* ME. [– *evers-*, pa. ppl. stem of L. *evertere* EVERT.] = EVERT –1661.

Eversible (ǐvə·ɹsib'l), *a.* 1877. [f. as prec. + -IBLE.] Capable of being everted or turned inside out.

Eversion (ǐvə̄·ɹʃən). 1470. [– Fr. *éversion* or L. *eversio*, f. *evers-*, pa. ppl. stem of *evertere*; see EVERT, -ION.] **†1.** The action of overthrowing; the condition of being overthrown; an overthrow. *lit.* and *fig.* –1820. **2.** *Path.* and *Phys.* The action of everting or turning (an organ or structure) inside out; the condition of being everted; as, *eversion of the eyelids* = ECTROPION 1751.

Eversive (ǐvə̄·ɹsiv), *a.* 1717. [f. as prec. + -IVE.] Tending to eversion or overthrow. Const. *of.*

A maxim e...of all justice and morality 1792.

Evert (ǐvə̄·ɹt), *v.* 1533. [L. *evertere*, f. *e-* EX-[1] + *vertere* turn.] **†1.** *trans.* To turn upside down. *lit.* and *fig.* –1693. **†2.** To overthrow –1599. Also *fig.* **†3.** To turn aside –1650. **4.** To turn inside out or outwards 1804.

1. The very thought Everts my soul with passion B. JONS. **4.** To e. the eyelid HARLAN.

Evertebral (ivə̄·ɹtǐbrăl), *a.* 1878. [f. E- + L. *vertebra* + -AL[1].] *Anat.* Not vertebral.

The anterior, or e. portion [of the cranium] 1878.

Evertebrate (ivə̄·ɹtǐbrĕt), *a.* and *sb.* 1883. [f. as prec. + -ATE[2].] *Zool.* = INVERTEBRATE.

Evertebrate (ivə̄·ɹtǐbreⁱt), *v.* 1880. [f. as prec. + ATE[3].] To deprive of the backbone.

Every (e·vəri, ev'ri), *a.* (quasi-*pron.*). [OE. *ǣfre ǣlć*, **ǣfre ylć*; see EVER *adv.* and EACH.]

I. As *adj.* used *attrib.* **1.** Each of a group; all taken one by one. Occas. with vb. in *pl.* **†2.** With plural sb.: All severally –1671. **3.** = 'All possible' 1783. **†4.** = ANY; in sentences expressing possibility –1760.

1. In my euerie action to be guided by others experiences *Cymb.* I. iv. 49. Euery the least remembrance 1620. Phr. *Every now and then, every once in a while* [corruption of *ever*, etc.]: from time to time. **2.** *Temp.* V. i. 249. **3.** I feel e. respect for him 1891.

II. *absol.* (quasi-*pron.*). **†1.** Everybody –1502. **2.** Each, or every one, *of* (several). Formerly often with vb. in *pl. Obs.* exc. *Law.* ME. **†3.** = EACH –1485.

1. E. hath of God a propre gift CHAUCER. **2.** To all and e. the children and child of the said intended marriage BENTHAM.

Comb. **1. Every one. †a.** *adj.* = sense I. 1. 1548. **b.** adj. *absol.* (e:vri wʊ·n). Distributing a sb. or pron. going before; or followed by *of.* Often (erron.) w. pl. vb. Occas. = Each (of two). ME. **c.** *pron.* (e·v'ri,wʊn). Everybody; occas. written as one word. The pron. referring to *every one* is often (?unavoidably) *pl.* ME. **¶2.** The form *ever each* (orig. *evereche, everych*) was corrupted into *every each*, and has occas. been used *arch.* by recent writers.

Everybody (e·vəri-, e·v'ri,bǫdi, -bǫ̆di), *pron.* 1530. [f. EVERY + BODY (= *person*).] Every person. Occas. (incorrectly) with *pl. vb.* or *pron.*

Everyday (e·vəri,-, e·vri,deⁱ, eːvri,deⁱ·). ME. [f. EVERY + DAY.]

A. *sb.* Each day in succession; *dial.* a week-day, as opp. to Sunday.

B. *attrib.* **1.** Daily 1647. **2.** Worn on ordinary days, as opp. to Sundays or high-days 1632. **3.** To be met with every day; common 1763.

1. Of e. occurrence 1880. **2.** In his every-day garments DICKENS. **3.** This was no every-day writer JOHNSON.

†E·verydeal. ME. [f. EVERY + DEAL.] **1.** as *sb.* Every part, the whole; also, subjoined to a sb. or sb. pron. for emphasis: Every whit –1560. **2.** as *adv.* Entirely, wholly –1714.

Every one: see EVERY.

Everything (e·vər,-, e·vri,þiŋ), *pron.* ME. [f. EVERY (sense I. 1) + THING.] **1.** = a neut. absol. use of the adj. A current substitute for *all* (absol.), *all things*. Formerly as two wds. **b.** as *pred.* Of supreme importance. *colloq.* **2.** *sb. rare* in *sing.*; in *pl.* (*joc.*) Things of every kind 1797.

2. Patent everythings going of themselves everywhere RUSKIN.

Everyway (e·vəri,-, e·v'ri,weⁱ), *adv.* 1570. [Cf. ALWAY, ANYWAY. Occas. as two wds.] In every way, manner, or direction; in every respect.

You wrong me every way: you wrong me Brutus *Jul. C.* IV. iii. 55.

Everywhen (e·vəri,-, e·v'ri,hweːn), *adv.* 1843. [f. EVERY + WHEN; after *everywhere*.] At all times, always.

Everywhere (e·vəri,-, e·v'ri,hwēᵊɹ), *adv.* [repr. two distinct ME. compounds: 1. *ever-ywhere*, f. EVER + *ywhere* (OE. *ģehwǣr*) anywhere, everywhere; 2. *every-where*, f. EVERY (ME. *everilk*) + WHERE. Formerly often written separately.] **1.** In every place; in every part. **†2.** quasi-*adj.* All-pervading 1674. Hence **Everywhereness,** omnipresence.

Everywhither (e·vəri,-, e·v'ri,hwiːðəɹ), *adv.* ME. [[f. EVERY + WHITHER.] In every direction.

Eves(e, obs. f. EAVES.

E·ve-star. *Obs.* exc. *poet.* ME. [f. EVE *sb.* + STAR *sb.*[1]] = *Evening star*.

Evet(e, evett, obs. ff. EFT *sb.*

†Evibrate, *v. rare.* 1583. [– *evibrat-*, pa. ppl. stem of L. *evibrare*, f. *e-* EX-[1] + *vibrare* brandish; see VIBRATE.] To vibrate, *trans.* and *intr.* Hence **†Evibra·tion.**

Evict (ĭvi·kt), *v.* 1503. [– *evict-*, pa. ppl. stem of L. *evincere* conquer, f. *e-* EX-[1] + *vincere* conquer. Cf. EVINCE.] **1.** *Law.* To recover by a judicial process, or in virtue of a superior title. **2.** To expel by legal process; in recent use, to eject (a tenant) from his holding. Also *transf.* 1536. **†3.** *gen.* To conquer; to overcome –1667. **†4.** To extort by force –1648. **†5.** To confute, refute; to convict or convince *of* –1660. **†6.** To prove –1722; to settle by argument –1660.

1. If land is evicted, before the time of payment of rent on a lease [etc.] TOMLINS. **2.** Two of the principal tenants..were evicted 1889. Hence **Evi·cted** *ppl.a. spec.* (of a farm) from which the tenant has been evicted. **Evi·ctor,** also **-er,** one who evicts.

Eviction (ĭvi·kʃən). 1583. [– late L. *evictio*, f. as prec.; see -ION.] **1.** *Law.* The action of recovering lands or property by legal process. **2.** The action of evicting or dispossessing a person of property, etc. Also *attrib.* 1626. **†3.** *gen.* The action of conquering –1611; of confuting –1703: of eliciting or establishing by argument –1776.

3. Upon E. I shall freely yield 1703. The sole and ultimate end of logic is the e. of truth 1776.

Evidence (e·videns), *sb.* ME. [– (O)Fr. *évidence* – L. *evidentia*, f. as EVIDENT; see -ENCE.] **1.** The quality or condition of being evident; evidentness 1665. **†2.** Manifestation –1611. **3.** That which makes evident; an indication, mark, trace ME. **†4.** Example. Only in ME. **5.** Ground for belief; that which tends to prove or disprove any conclusion ME. **6.** *Law.* Information that is given in a legal investigation, to establish the fact or point in question. Also, *An evidence* = a piece of evidence. 1503. **b.** Statements or proofs admissible as testimony in a court of law 1817. **7.** One who, or that which furnishes proof; a witness; title-deeds. *Obs.* exc. *Hist.* and *Law.* ME.

1. Phr. *In e.* [after Fr. *en évidence*]: actually present; conspicuous; The sister..was in e. 18... **3.** The evidences of ancient glacier action TYNDALL. **5.** Phr. *External, Internal, Moral, Probable E.* (see these adjs.). **6.** Phr. *To call in e.*: to call as a witness. *Circumstantial, Parole, Presumptive, Primâ facie, Verbal*, etc. *E.* (see these adjs.). **7.** Phr. *To turn King's* (*Queen's State's*) *e.*: to appear as a witness for the prosecution against one's accomplices in a crime. var. **†E·vidency** (in senses 1, 3).

Evidence (e·videns), *v.* 1610. [f. prec. sb.] **1.** *trans.* To attest; bear witness to 1619. **†2.** To make evident, demonstrate, prove –1807. **3.** *Law.* **†a.** To give evidence against –1695. **†b.** To relate as a witness –1812. **c.** *intr.* To give evidence 1656. **4.** To manifest 1610.

1. I invoke Heav'n, earth, and men to e. my truth 1721. **3. c.** Her maid..will e. against her 1693. **4.** Expressions evidencing an intention 1876. Hence **†E·videnceable** *a.* that may be evidenced or proved. **†E·videncer,** a witness.

Evident (e·vidĕnt). ME. [– (O)Fr. *évident* or L. *evidens, -ent-*, f. *e-* EX-[1] + pr. pple. of *vidēre* see; see -ENT.]

A. *adj.* **1. †a.** Conspicuous. **b.** Obvious to the sight. **2.** Clear to the understanding or the judgement; obvious, plain ME. **†3.** Indubitable, certain, conclusive –1653.

1. E. marks of small-pox 1806. **2.** Why, this is e. to any formall capacitie *Twel. N.* II. v. 128.

B. *sb.* Something that serves as evidence; *spec.* in *Sc. Law*; usu. in *pl.* title-deeds ME. Hence **E·vident-ly** *adv.*, **-ness.**

Evidential (evide·nʃăl), *a.* 1610. [– med.L. *evidentialis*, f. L. *evidentia*; see EVIDENCE, -AL[1].] **1.** Of, pertaining to, or based upon evidence; relying on evidence; *esp.* the Evidences of Christianity 1654. **2.** Furnishing evidence; of the nature of evidence 1641. **†3.** Resting on documentary evidence. W. FOLKINGHAM.

1. Phr. *E. method, school, system.* Hence **Evide·ntially** *adv.* So **Evide·ntiary** *a.* (in senses 1,2).

†Evigila·tion. 1720. [– eccl. L. *evigilatio*, f. *evigilat-*, pa. ppl. stem of eccl. L. *evigilare*, f. L. *e-* EX-[1] + *vigilare* watch, be awake. See -ION.] Awakening.

Evil (ī·vil). [OE. *yfel* = OS. *ubil*, OFris., MDu. *evel* (Du. *euvel*), OHG. *ubil* (G. *übel*), Goth. *ubils* :– Gmc. **ubilaz*.]

A. *adj.* The antithesis of GOOD. Now little used, exc. in literary English.

I. Bad in a positive sense. **1.** Morally depraved. Also *absol.* *Obs.* as applied to persons. OE. **2.** Doing or tending to do harm. Of an omen, etc.: Boding ill. ME. **3.** Combining senses 1 and 2. OE. **4.** Causing discomfort, pain, or trouble OE.; †hard, difficult –1551. **5.** †Unfortunate, miserable –1614; unlucky, disastrous ME.

1. Ivel men ME. The imagination of mans heart is euil from his youth *Gen.* 8:21. **2.** Evyl ensaumple WYCLIF. Euill counsel 1584. The Owle shriek'd at thy birth, an euill signe SHAKS. **3.** Much evil-will..shall happen unto you COVERDALE. Phr. *The E. One*: the Devil; Deliver us from the e. one R.V. *Matt.* 6:13. A house of e. repute 1894. **4.** Of an evill savour LYTE. **5.** In euill case *Ex.* 5:19, plight RALEGH. To anticipate the e. day 1878. Phr. **Evil eye. a.** A look of ill will. **b.** A malicious or envious look, popularly supposed to inflict material harm; also, the supposed faculty of injuring by a look.

II. Bad in a privative sense: Not good. **†1.** Unsound, corrupt; diseased; unwholesome –1611. **†2.** Inferior –1799.

1. The horse had an euill foote 1591. An euill Diet SHAKS. The water whereof was so evill HAKLUYT. **2.** Appoint when you come to take an e. dinner with me GRINDAL. E. workmanship 1799.

B. *sb.* The adj. used *absol.*

1. That which is the reverse of good, physically or morally; whatever is censurable painful, disastrous, or undesirable OE. **2.** The evil portion or element of anything OE. **3.** Any particular thing that causes harm or mischief, physical or moral ME. **†4.** A wrong-doing, sin, crime. Usu. *pl.* –1614. **†5.** A calamity, disaster, misfortune –1791. **†6.** A disease, malady –1725.

1. All partial E., universal Good POPE. E. haunts The birth, the bridal TENNYSON. The greatest of all mysteries—the origin of e. 1878. **2.** I pray..that thou shouldest keepe them from the euill *John* 17:15. **3.** There are evils to which the calamities of war are blessings BURKE. Phr. *The social e.*: prostitution. **4.** *Rich. III.* I. ii. 76 (Qo.). **6.** †*The falling e.* (=sickness): epilepsy. **King's evil**: scrofula.

Comb., of the *adj.*, as *e.-minded*, etc.; of the *sb.*, as *e.-doer*, etc.

Hence **E·vil-ly** *adv.*, **-ness.**

†Evil (ī·v'l), *adv.* [ME. *uvele* (ü), *ivele*, *evele*, OE. *yfele*, f. *yfel*; see prec.] In an evil manner; ill; harmfully; badly –1841.

Phr. *To speak e.* (OE. *be*) *of*: to speak maliciously *of*; now taken as a *sb.*, but in OE. and ME. an *adv.*

Comb.: **e.-liking,** ill-favoured; **-sounding,** harsh-sounding; **-sained,** lit. 'ill-blessed', *i.e.* accursed.

†E·vil-fa·voured, *a.* 1530. [f. EVIL + FAVOUR + -ED[2].] = ILL-FAVOURED –1612. Hence **†E·vilfa·vouredness.**

Evince (ĭvi·ns), *v.* 1608. [– L. *evincere*; see EVICT.] **†1.** *trans.* To overcome, subdue –1678. **†2.** To convince –1670; to confute –1672. **†3.** To extort by argument or persuasive motives –1658. **†4.** To prove by argument or evidence. Also, *rarely*, To vindicate. Also *absol.* –1767. **5.** To indicate, make evident or manifest 1621.

1. Error by his own arms is best evinc't MILT. *P. R.* IV. 235. **4.** The Accuser complaines, the Witnesse evinceth, the Judge sentences BP. HALL. **5.** His answers..evinced both wisdom and integrity C. BRONTË.

Hence **†Evi·ncement,** the action of evincing; proof. **Evi·ncible** *a.*, also **†-eable,** demonstrable; †convincing. **Evi·ncibly** *adv.* **Evi·ncive** *a.* indicative.

Evirate (ī·vireⁱt), e·vireⁱt), *v.* 1621. [– *evirat-*, pa. ppl. stem of L. *evirare* castrate, f. *e-* EX-[1] + *vir* man; see -ATE[3].] To deprive of virility or manhood. Hence **†E·virate** *ppl. a.* castrated, emasculated. **Evira·tion,** emasculation.

‖**Evirato** (evirā·to). Pl. **-ti.** 1796. [It.; see prec.] = CASTRATO.

†Evi·rtuate, *v.* 1640. [f. (O)Fr. (*s'*)*évertuer* (f. *é-* EX-[1] + *vertu* strength, virtue) + -ATE[3].] **1.** *intr.* To put forth virtue, exert influence; also *refl.* –1675. **2.** *trans.* To deprive of virtue, strength, or power –1644.

Eviscerate (ĭvi·sĕreⁱt), *v.* 1607. [– *eviscerat-*, pa. ppl. stem of L. *eviscerare*, f. *e-* EX-[1] + *viscera* entrails; see -ATE[3].] *trans.* To take out the entrails of; to disembowel; to gut. Also *absol.* 1623. Also *transf.* and *fig.*

A Paper-Warehouse eviscerated by axe and fire. CARLYLE. Hence **Eviscera·tion.**

Evitable (e·vităb'l), *a.* 1502. [f. (O)Fr. *évitable* or L. *evitabilis*, f. *éviter*, *evitare*; see next, -ABLE.] Avoidable. (Now chiefly with neg. contexts.)

†E·vitate, *v.* 1588. [– *evitat-*, pa. ppl. stem of L. *evitare* avoid; see EVITE *v.*, -ATE[3].] = EVITE *v.* –1603. Hence **Evita·tion,** avoidance, shirking.

E·vite, *sb.* [f. *Eve* the first woman + -ITE[1] 1. Cf. ADAMITE.] A name for a woman wearing little clothing. ADDISON.

Evite (ĭvəi·t), *v. arch.* 1503. [– (O)Fr. *éviter* or its source L. *evitare*, f. *e-* EX-[1] + *vitare* avoid, shun.] To avoid, shun. (Now mostly *Sc.*)

†Evite·rnal, *a.* Also **Æviternal.** 1596. [f. L. *æviternus* (whence by contraction *æternus* ETERNAL) + -AL[1]. Cf. Fr. †*evitern-el* (XVI).] = ETERNAL; everlasting –1652. Hence **†Evite·rnally** *adv.* So **Evite·rnity,** eternity, everlastingness.

Evittate (ī,vi·tĕt), *a.* 1866. [f. E- + VITTA + -ATE[2].] *Bot.* Without vittæ or oil-canals.

Evocable (e·vŏkăb'l), *v.* 1. [– Fr. *évocable*, f. *évoquer*; see EVOKE, -ABLE.] That may be called forth.

Evocate (e·vŏkeⁱt), *v.* 1639. [– *evocat-*, pa. ppl. stem of L. *evocare*; see EVOKE, -ATE[3].] **†1.** *trans.* To call forth –1665. **2.** To call up from the dead, from past times 1675. Hence **Evo·cative** *a.* tending to draw forth. **E·vocator,** one who evocates. **Evo·catory** *a.* having the function of evoking.

Evocation (evokēⁱ·ʃən). 1612. [– L. *evocatio*, f. as prec.; see -ION. Cf. (O)Fr. *évocation*.] **†1.** A calling out or forth; *esp.* of spirits –1656. **†2.** Avocation –1810. **3.** The calling out of a cause from a lower to a higher court 1644. **†4.** *Gram.* A. 'reduction of the third person either to the first or second' –1696.

||**Evoe** (ĭvoᵘ·ĭ), *interj.* (*sb.*) Also **evohe.** 1586. [L., prop. disyll., *eu(h)œ* – Gr. εὐοῖ.] The Bacchanalian cry 'Evoe!'

Evoke (ivōᵘ·k), *v.* 1623. [– L. *evocare*, f. *e*- Ex-¹ + *vocare* call; perh. after Fr. *évoquer*.] **1.** *trans.* To call forth; *esp.* to summon up (spirits, etc.) by the use of magic. Also *transf.* and *fig.* **2.** To summon (a cause) from a lower to a higher tribunal 1752.

1. To e. the Queen of the Faires WARTON. To e. sleeping energies EMERSON, a smile MAX-MÜLLER. **2.** Authority to e. causes to Rome HUSSEY.

†**E·volate,** *v. rare.* 1657. [– *evolat*-, pa. ppl. stem of L. *evolare*, f. *e*- Ex-¹ + *volare* fly; see -ATE³.] To fly forth or away. Hence †**Evola·tion.**

Evolute (ĭ·vŏliūt), *v.* orig. *U.S.* 1868. [Back-formation from EVOLUTION.] **1.** *intr.* To develop by evolution. **2.** *trans.* To evolve, develop (*journalese*) 1896.

Evolute (e·vŏliut). 1730. [– L. *evolutus* pa. pple. of *evolvere* roll out; see EVOLVE.] **A.** *adj.* **a.** *Evolute curve* = B. I. **b.** *Bot.* Fully developed 1835.

B. *sb.* **1.** *Math.* A curve which is the locus of the centres of curvature of another curve (its *involute*), or the envelope of all its normals. (So called because the end of a stretched thread unwound from the evolute will trace the involute.) 1730. **2.** The development of a cone or cylinder. SMEATON.

Evolutility (ivǫ:liuti·lĭti). 1884. [f. *evolut*- (see next) + -ILITY; cf. *contractility*.] *Biol.* Capability of manifesting change as a result of the nutritive processes.

Evolution (evŏliū·ʃən, ĭvŏliū·ʃən). 1622. [– L. *evolutio* unrolling of a book, f. *evolut*-, pa. ppl. stem of *evolvere*; see EVOLVE, -ION.] **I. 1.** The process of evolving, unrolling, opening out, or disengaging from an envelope. Also *concr.* 'the series of things unfolded or unrolled' (J.). Also *fig.* 1647. **2.** *Math.* **a.** *Geom.* The unfolding of a curve, so that from it is produced an involute 1700. **b.** *Arith.* and *Alg.* The extraction of any root from any given power; the reverse of involution 1706. **3.** *Biol.* **a.** Of animal and vegetable organisms or their parts: The process of developing from a rudimentary to a complete state 1670. **b.** The hypothesis that the embryo or germ is a development of a pre-existing form, which contains the rudiments of all the parts of the future organism. (Now better called 'the theory of Preformation'.) 1831. **c.** The origination of species conceived as a process of development from earlier forms, and not as due to 'special creation'. Often in phrases *Doctrine, Theory of Evolution.* 1832. **4.** Development or growth as of a living organism (*e.g.* of a polity, science, language, etc.). Also 'growing' as opp. to 'being made'. 1807. **5.** The formation of the heavenly bodies by the concentration and consolidation of cosmic matter 1850. **6.** In recent speculation used in a more general sense, of which 3a, 3c, 4, 5 are regarded as special applications 1862.

1. The e. of the child 1800, the larva 1817, of light and heat LYELL, of an argument 1870. **3. a.** The..e. of this part of the brain 1805. **c.** The e. of one species out of another 1863. **4.** The tardy e. of the British constitution 1807. **6.** E. is an integration of matter and concomitant dissipation of motion; during which the matter passes from an indefinite, incoherent homogeneity to a definite, coherent heterogeneity; and during which the retained motion undergoes a parallel transformation H. SPENCER.

II. *Mil.* and *Naut.* The opening out of a body of troops or squadron of ships; hence *gen.* any tactical movement or change of position 1622. Also *transf.* and *fig.*

Hence **Evolu·tional** *a.* of, pertaining to, or produced by e. **Evolu·tionary** *a.* of, pertaining to, or in accordance with e. or development. **Evolu·tionism,** the theory of e. or development. **Evolu·tionist,** an adherent of evolutionism; also *attrib.* **E:volutioni·stic** *a.* tending to support the doctrine of e.; tending to produce e.

Evolutive (e·vŏliutiv), *a.* 1874. [f. EVOLUT(ION + -IVE. Cf. Fr. *évolutif*, *-ive* in same sense.] Pertaining, tending to, or promoting evolution.

Evolve (ivǫ·lv), *v.* 1641. [– L. *evolvere* unroll, unfold, f. *e*- Ex-¹ + *volvere* roll.] **1.** *trans.* To unfold, unroll; to open out, expand. Usu. *fig.* **2.** To disengage from wrappings; to disentangle 1664. **3.** To give off, emit, as vapours 1800. **4.** To bring out (what exists implicitly or potentially) 1831. **5.** To give rise to 1851. **6.** To produce or modify by evolution (see EVOLUTION 3–6). Also *intr.* for *refl.* 1799.

1. To e. the powers of the mind 1839. **2.** Time.. Evolves their secrets, and their guilt proclaims 1744. **4.** The new diseases that human life Evolves in its progress LONGF. **6.** Societies are evolved in structure and function as in growth H. SPENCER.

Hence **Evo·lvable** *a.*, also **-ible,** that may be evolved. **Evo·lvement,** evolution. **Evo·lvent** *a.* that evolves; *sb.* the involute of a curve. **Evo·lver.**

||**Evo·lvulus.** 1847. [f. L. *evolvere*. Cf. CONVOLVULUS.] *Bot.* A genus of the N.O. *Convolvulaceæ*, containing about 60 species.

†**Evo·mit,** *v.* ME. [– *evomit*-, pa. ppl. stem of L. *evomere* spew out, f. *e*- Ex-¹ + *vomere* to VOMIT.] *trans.* To vomit, eject. Also *transf.* and *fig.* –1714. Hence †**Evomi·tion,** the action of vomiting forth.

Evulgate (ĭvɒ·lgeᶦt), *v.* ? *Obs.* 1563. [– *evulgat*-, pa. ppl. stem of L. *evulgare*, f. *e*- Ex-¹ + *vulgare* spread among the multitude, f. *vulgus* multitude; see -ATE³. Cf. DIVULGATE, DIVULGE.] To make publicly known; to publish. Hence **Evulga·tion,** publishing, publication. So †**Evu·lge** *v.*

Evulsion (ĭvɒ·lʃən). 1611. [– L. *evulsio*, f. *evuls*-, pa. ppl. stem of *evellere*, f. *e*- Ex-¹ + *vellere* pluck; see -ION.] The action of pulling out by force.

||**Evviva** (evˌvī·va). 1887. [It., f. *e* (:– L. *et*) used intensively + *viva*; see VIVA *sb.*¹] The cry 'Long live (the king)'; hence, a shout of applause.

Ew, obs. f. YEW.

Ewe (yū), *sb.* [OE. *ēowu*, corresp. to OFris. *ei*, OS. *ewwi* (MDu. *oie*, Du. *ooi*), LG. *ouw lamm*, OHG. *ouwi*, *ou* (G. *aue*), ON. *ær* :– Gmc. **awi* :– IE. **owi*, repr. also by L. *ovis*, Gr. ὄ(ϝ)ις.] A female sheep. Also *attrib.* *Comb.*: **e.-neck,** a thin hollow neck (in a horse).

Ewe, *v.* 1579. [f. prec.] †**1.** To give birth to (a lamb) –1660. **2.** *trans.* To give a 'ewe-neck' look to 1848.

†**Ew·er**¹. ME. [– OFr. *ewer* (Cotgr. *eauïer*) :– L. *aquarius*, f. *aqua* (OFr. *ewe*, mod. *eau*) water; see -ER² 2.] = EWERER –1601.

Ewer² (yū·əɹ). ME. [– AFr. **ewere*, ONFr. *eviere*, (O)Fr. *aiguière*:– Rom. **aquaria*, fem. (sc. *olla* pot) of *aquarius* pertaining to water, f. *aqua* water; see -ER² 2.] 'A pitcher with a wide spout, used to bring water for washing the hands' (W.). Now, a bedroom water-jug.

Ew·erer. 1450. [f. EWER¹, or next, + ER¹.] A servant who supplied guests, etc. at table with water to wash their hands.

Ewery, ewry (yūᵊ·ri). 1460. [f. EWER² + -Y³; see -ERY.] The apartment or office for ewers, *esp.* in former times, in the royal household.

Ewt(e, obs. f. EFT.

Ex (eks), *prep.* 1845. [– L. *ex* out of (arch. also *ec*). Bef. consonants occas. reduced to *e*.] **1.** In L. phrases, as EX ANIMO, EX OFFICIO, EX PARTE, EXTEMPORE, EX-VOTO, etc., q.v. **2.** *Comm.* **a.** In sense 'out of' (a ship, the warehouse). **b.** In sense 'exclusive of'; *esp.* in phr. *Ex dividend* (*ex div.*, *e. d.*). So *ex new* (*ex n.*, *x. n.*), exclusive of the right to an allotment of new shares or stock.

Ex- *prefix*¹, of L. origin.

1. repr. L. *ex*-, the prep. *ex* (see prec.) in combination.

a. In L. (and hence in English) the form *ex*- appears before vowels and *h*; also before *c*, *p* (usually), *q*, *s*, *t*; before *f* it becomes *ef*- (in inscriptions *ec*-); before other consonants (exc. in *exlex*) *e*. An *s* following the prefix is commonly omitted, exc. in some English scientific terms, as *exsert* (= *exert*), *exsanguineous*, etc. See also Es-. **b.** In English, as in Latin, *ex*- in composition signifies 'out', 'forth', as in *exclude, exit*; 'upward' as in *extol*; 'thoroughly' as in *excruciate*; 'to bring into a certain state' as in *exasperate*; 'to remove, expel, or relieve from' as in *expatriate, exonerate*; 'to deprive of' as in *excoriate*; 'deprived of' as in *exsanguineous*. The non-Latin sense 'destitute of', as in *exalbuminous*, is more usually expressed by *e*- (see E-).

2. Ex- (with hyphen) prefixed to English words.

Prefixed to titles of office or dignity, to designate previous holders of the position. Hence in the sense 'former', 'sometimes', 'quondam', with respect to calling, station, character, or the like.

Ex- *prefix*², of Gr. origin.

The Gr. ἐξ out of, etymologically = L. *ex*- (see prec.), occurs only bef. vowels, as in *exodus*, *exorcize*, etc. Bef. consonants it is replaced by ἐκ- (L. *ec*-).

Exacerbate (egz-, eksæ·səɹbeᶦt), *v.* 1660. [– *exacerbat*-, pa. ppl. stem of L. *exacerbare*, f. *ex*- Ex-¹ + *acerbare* make harsh or bitter, f. *acerbus* harsh, bitter, grievous; see ACERB, -ATE³.] To increase the smart or bitterness of; to embitter, aggravate. Also, to irritate, provoke. Also *intr.* for *refl.*

To e. the growing moodiness of his temper POE.

Exacerbation (egz-, eksæ:səɹbēᶦ·ʃən). 1582. [– late L. *exacerbatio*, f. as prec.; see -ION.] **1.** The action of exacerbating; the condition of being exacerbated; embitterment, irritation. **2.** Increase in severity (of disease, sufferings, etc.). Chiefly *Path.*, a paroxysm (of a fever, etc.); also *transf.* 1625. var. †**Exacerbe·scence** (in sense 2).

†**Exa:cerva·tion.** 1730. [f. late L. *exacervare* (Boethius), f. L. *acervus* heap; see Ex-¹, -ATION.] The action of heaping up. (Dicts.)

Exacinate, *v.* 1656. [– *exacinat*-, pa. ppl. stem of med.L. *exacinare*, f. *ex*- Ex-¹ + L. *acinus* stone of a berry; see -ATE³.] *trans.* To remove kernels from. Hence †**E:xacina·tion.** (Dicts.)

Exact (egzæ·kt), *a.* 1533. [– L. *exactus*, pa. pple. of *exigere* complete, bring to perfection, examine, ascertain, f. *ex*- Ex-¹ + *agere* perform.]

†**I.** Consummate, finished, perfect –1727; of persons, accomplished, refined –1725.

II. 1. Admitting of no deviation 1538. **2.** Accurate in detail, strict 1533. **3.** Perfectly corresponding, strictly correct, accurate 1645. **4.** Precise; not admitting of vagueness or uncertainty 1601. †**5.** As *adv.* = EXACTLY. –1791.

1. The troops were kept in such e. discipline, that [etc.] JAS. MILL. **2.** Suche exacte cyrcumspeccion MORE. Writing [maketh] an exacte man BACON. Our most e. Observer Mr. Flamstead WHISTON. **3.** A piece e. to the life COWLEY. An e. translation PRIESTLEY. **4.** An e. Minute of the Moon EVELYN. Phr. *E. sciences*: those which admit of absolute precision in their results; *esp.* the mathematical sciences.

Exact (egzæ·kt), *v.* 1529. [– *exact*-, pa. ppl. stem of L. *exigere*; see prec.] **1.** To demand and enforce the payment of; to extort. **2.** To require by force or with authority; to insist upon. Const. *from, of.* 1564. **3.** To call for, demand, require. Const. *from, of.* 1592. †**4.** *intr.* To practise exactions. Const. *on, upon.* –1727. **5.** To force out, extract. *arch.* 1639. **6.** *Law.* To call to appear in court 1607.

1. To e. from Passengers..arbitrary..Sums 1703. **2.** To e. an Account of Wealth 1665. To e. Obedience from every creature SHERLOCK. **3.** Their gray hairs e. of us a particular respect 1683. Hence **Exa·cter** = EXACTOR.

Exacting (egzæ·ktiŋ), *ppl. a.* 1583. [f. prec. + -ING².] That exacts; *esp.* that requires too great advantages, exertions, or sacrifices.

Naturally jealous and e. BLACK. Hence **Exa·cting-ly** *adv.*, **-ness.**

Exaction (egzæ·kʃən). ME. [– L. *exactio*, f. *exact*-; see EXACT *v.*, -ION.] **1.** The action of demanding and enforcing payment, performance, etc. **2.** An illegal or exorbitant demand; extortion 1494. **3.** That which is exacted; an arbitrary or excessive impost ME. **4.** *Law.* A calling to appear in court 1816.

1. E. of the forfeiture *Merch. V.* I. iii. 166, of respect 1674. **2.** Tyrannous e. brings on servile concealment BURKE.

Exactitude (egzæ·ktitiud). 1734. [– Fr. *exactitude*, f. *exact*; see EXACT *a.*, -TUDE.] The quality of being exact; †exactness.

Exactly (egzæ·ktli), *adv.* 1533. [f. EXACT *a.* + -LY².] †**1.** In a perfect manner; to perfection; completely –1726. **2.** In an exact manner; accurately; with strict conformity to rule; 'just' 1658. **b.** *colloq.* expressing agreement 1869.

1. Arm'd at all points e., *Cap a Pe* SHAKS. **2.** Let it be..e. weighed 1756. E. the man for the post 1894.

Exactness (egzæ·ktnės). 1564. [f. as prec. + -NESS.] †**1.** Consummate skill; perfection of workmanship –1697. †**2.** Strictness, rigour –1747. **3.** Minute attention to detail; accuracy, precision; †punctuality 1645.

3. Every writer who aims at e. has to begin with definitions WHITNEY.

Exactor (egzæ·ktəɹ). ME. [– L. *exactor*, f. *exact-*; see EXACT *v.*, -OR 2.] **1.** One who exacts; a tax-collector (*arch.*); †an officer of justice –1582; a taskmaster 1563. **2.** One who makes illegal or extortionate exactions ME. **3.** One who insists upon (something) as a matter of right 1619.

3. Unmerciful exactors of adulation JOHNSON. So **Exa·ctress**, a female e. (*rare*).

†**Exa·cuate,** *v.* 1632. [irreg. f. L. *exacuere* (f. *ex-* EX-[1] + *acuere* sharpen) + -ATE[3].] *trans.* To make keen or sharp –1684. Hence †**Exacua·tion.**

†**Exæ·stuate,** *v.* 1657. [– *exæstuat-*, pa. ppl. stem of L. *exæstuare* boil up; see EX-[1], ÆSTUATE.] *trans.* To overheat. Hence †**Exæstua·tion,** a boiling up; fermentation.

Exaggerate (egzæ·dʒĕreᶦt), *v.* 1533. [– *exaggerat-*, pa. ppl. stem of L. *exaggerare*, f. *ex-* EX-[1] + *aggerare* heap up, f. *agger* heap; see -ATE[3].] †**1.** *trans.* To heap or pile up; to accumulate –1677. †**2.** To emphasize –1734. **3.** To magnify beyond the truth. Also *absol.* 1613. **4.** To enlarge abnormally 1850.

1. The water..exaggerating and raising islands and Continents in other parts HALE. **3.** A Friend exaggerates a Man's Virtues ADDISON.

Hence **Exa·ggeratingly** *adv.* **Exa·ggerative** *a.* marked by, or prone to, exaggeration. **Exa·ggerative-ly** *adv.*, **-ness. Exa·ggerator,** one who or that which exaggerates. **Exa·ggerato:ry** *a.* exaggerative.

Exaggerated (egzæ·dʒĕreᶦtėd), *ppl. a.* 1725. [f. prec. + -ED.[1]] **1.** Unduly magnified or inflated. **2.** Abnormally enlarged 1860.

1. Heroes were e. men BUCKLE. **2.** An e. zigzag TYNDALL. Hence **Exa·ggeratedly** *adv.* unduly.

Exaggeration (egzæ:dʒĕrēᶦ·ʃən). 1565. [– L. *exaggeratio*; see EXAGGERATE, -ION.] †**1.** The action of heaping or piling up; also *concr.* the result. HALE. †**2.** The action of emphasizing –1745. **3.** The action of magnifying unduly in words; an instance of this 1565. **4.** *Painting*, etc. A heightened representation of a subject either in design or colouring; *concr.* an exaggerated copy 1734. **5.** Aggravation (of a condition, etc.); also *concr.* 1661.

1. Lakes grow by the e. of Sand by the Sea 1677. **3.** Such exaggerations will be reduced to their just value GIBBON.

†**Exa·gitate,** *v.* 1532. [– *exagitat-*, pa. ppl. stem of L. *exagitare*, f. *ex-* EX-[1] + *agitare* set in motion; see -ATE[3].] **1.** *trans.* To stir up; to AGITATE –1732. **2.** To harass, worry –1677. **3.** To attack violently –1685. **4.** To discuss –1749. Hence †**Exagita·tion,** excitement; discussion.

Exalbuminous (eksælbiū·minəs), *a.* 1830. [f. EX-[1] + L. *albumen*, *-min-* + -OUS.] *Bot.* Having no albumen in the seed. var. **Exalbu·minose.**

Exalt (egzǭ·lt), *v.* ME. [– L. *exaltare*, f. *ex-* EX-[1] + *altus* high. Cf. (O)Fr. *exalter.*] **1.** *trans.* To raise on high; to lift up, elevate. Now *arch.* in physical sense. 1535. **b.** *transf.* To lift up (the voice, etc.) (*arch.*) 1611. **2.** *fig.* **a.** To raise in rank, honour, estimation, power, or wealth ME. †**b.** To elate. Also *intr.* for *refl.* –1708. **c.** To extol. Also *absol.* ME. **d.** To dignify, ennoble 1711. **e.** To stimulate (powers) 1744. †**3.** *Alchemy.* To raise (a substance, etc.) to a higher 'degree'; hence, to refine, mature; to intensify. Also *fig.* –1813. **4.** To heighten (colours) 1842. **5.** *Astrol.* (in *pass.*): To be in the position of greatest influence 1647.

1. *Jul. C.* I. iii. 8. **b.** Against whome hast thou exalted thy voyce 2 *Kings* 19:22. **2. a.** E. him that is low *Ezek.* 21:26. **c.** My tonge shall.. Dewly exalte thy iustice styll 1545. **d.** I shall not lower but e. the Subjects I treat upon STEELE. **3.** *fig.* This is Jacobinism sublined and exalted into most pure..essence BURKE. Hence **Exa·lter.**

†**Exaltate,** *pple.* ME. [– L. *exaltatus*, pa. pple. of *exaltare*; see prec., -ATE[2].] Exalted. –1500.

Exaltation (egzǭltēᶦ·ʃən). ME. [– (O)Fr. *exaltation* or late L. *exaltatio*, f. *exaltat-*, pa. ppl. stem of L. *exaltare*; see EXALT, -ION.] **1.** The action of lifting up or raising on high; the state of being lifted up. *lit.* and *fig.* **2.** *Astrol.* The place of a planet in the zodiac in which it was supposed to exert its greatest influence. Also *fig.* ME. †**3.** *Alchemy*, etc. The action or process of refining or subliming; an instance of this –1751.

1. The E. of this Pope happen'd upon Ascension day 1670. The..e. of our best faculties LAW.

Exalted (egzǭ·ltėd), *ppl. a.* 1594. [f. EXALT *v.* + -ED[1].] **1.** Raised or set up on high; elevated; highly placed. **2.** Impassioned 1712. **3.** Intense; sublime, noble 1601. †**4.** *Chem.*, etc. Refined, sublimed, concentrated. Of flavour, etc.: Strong. –1796.

1. The Great King..from an e. throne beheld the misfortunes of his arms GIBBON. **3.** E. piety BOYLE, powers EMERSON. Hence **Exa·lted-ly** *adv.*, **-ness.**

†**Exa·ltment.** 1660. [f. as prec. + -MENT.] Exaltation –1677.

Exam (egzæ·m). *colloq.* 1877. Short for EXAMINATION.

Examen (egzēᶦ·men). 1606. [– L. *examen* tongue of a balance, *fig.* examination, for **exagmen*, f. **exag-*, *exigere* weigh accurately; see EXACT *v.*] **1.** Examination; investigation. Now *rare.* 1618. †**2.** A critical disquisition –1738. **3.** A test, assay –1765. **4.** The tongue of a balance (*rare*) 1833.

2. An E. of Mr. Pope's Essay, &c. JOHNSON.

Exameter, -tron, obs. ff. HEXAMETER.

Examinable (egzæ·minăb'l), *a.* 1594. [f. EXAMINE *v.* + -ABLE.] Capable of being examined; in *Law*, cognisable.

Examinant (egzæ·minănt). 1588. [– *examinant-*, pr. ppl. stem of L. *examinare*; see EXAMINE, -ANT.]

A. *sb.* **1.** One who examines; an examiner 1620. †**2.** One who is being examined; a deponent; also, an examinee –1812.

†**B.** *adj.* That examines. MILT.

Examinate (egzæ·mině̆t). 1471. [– L. *examinatus*, pa. ppl. of *examinare*; see EXAMINE, -ATE[2].]

†**A.** *ppl.* Examined –1818.

B. *sb.* A person who undergoes examination 1537.

Examination (egzæ:minēᶦ·ʃən). ME. [– (O)Fr. *examination* – L. *examinatio*, f. *examinat-*, pa. ppl. stem of *examinare*; see EXAMINE, -ION.] †**1.** A trial, proof, assay. Also *fig.* –1552. **2.** The action of testing or judging by a standard. Cf. *Self-examination.* ME. **3.** Investigation by inspection or experiment 1630. **4.** Scrutiny 1538. **5.** The process of testing knowledge or ability by questions 1612. **6.** Formal interrogation, *esp.* of a witness, or an accused person 1555. **b.** The depositions of the witness or accused person 1533.

3. Phr. *Post-mortem e.*, autopsy. **4.** Such an account now claims our e. 1878. **5.** To day..I went through part of my e. for Orders 1783. Phr. *Local, Senate-House Examinations* (see these words). **6.** The party is brought before the magistrate for e. 1861. Phr. *E.-in-chief* (Law), that made by the party calling the witness. CROSS-, RE-EXAMINATION: see CROSS-, RE-EXAMINE). **b.** Phr. *To take the e. of*: to interrogate and note down the answers.

Hence **Examina·tional** *a.* of or pertaining to an e. or examinations. **Examina·tionism,** belief in examinations as the test of fitness, knowledge, etc.

Examinator (egzæ·mineᶦtəɹ). 1621. [– late L. *examinator*, f. as prec.; see -OR 2.]

Examine (egzæ·min), *v.* ME. [– (O)Fr. *examiner* – L. *examinare* weigh accurately, f. *examen*, *-min-* tongue of a balance; see EXAMEN.] †**1.** To try, test, assay. Also *fig.* –1440. **2.** To test judicially or critically; to try by a standard ME. **3.** To investigate by inspection or manipulation; to inspect in detail, scan, scrutinize ME. **4.** To inquire into, investigate; to discuss critically ME. **5.** To test (a person) by questioning (see EXAMINATION 5) ME. **6.** To interrogate formally (*esp.* a witness, an accused person) ME. **7.** *intr.* †**a.** To 'see to it' *that*, etc. (*rare*) –1712. **b.** To inquire *into* 1764.

2. E. me O Lord, and proue me; try my reines and my heart *Ps.* 26:2. Doss examined the books, and found the following entry 1776. **4.** To e. whether things be good or euill HOOKER, a theory REID, a plea MORLEY. **5.** I was examined in Hebrew and History *a*1838. Hence **Exa:minee·**, a person under examination. **Exa·mining-ly** *adv.* searchingly.

Examiner (egzæ·minəɹ). 1530. [f. prec. + -ER[1].] **1.** One who looks into the nature or condition of; an investigator 1561. †**2.** One who interrogates; one who conducts an official inquiry –1686. **3.** A person appointed to examine pupils, candidates for a degree, etc. 1715. Hence **Exa·minership.**

Examplar (egzɑ·mplăɹ), Now *rare.* ME. [– OFr. *examplaire*, var. of *exemplaire*, see EXEMPLAR.] **1.** A pattern, model. **2.** †A copy, transcript. **b.** An exemplar of a book. 1475. †**3.** = SAMPLER –1583. Hence †**Exa·mplary** *a.* exemplary.

Example (egzɑ·mp'l). *sb.* ME. [– OFr. *example* (mod. *exemple*), refash. after L. of *essample* (whence ME. *asample*, (XIII) ENSAMPLE, aphetic SAMPLE) – L. *exemplum*, f. **exem-*, *eximere* take out (see EXEMPT).] **1.** A typical instance; a fact, etc. that forms a particular case of a principle, rule, state of things, or the like; a person or thing that illustrates a quality. **b.** *Math.* A problem framed to illustrate a rule 1674. **c.** A specimen (of workmanship). Also a copy of a (rare) book, etc. 1530. **2.** *Logic.* = Gr. παράδειγμα. (See quot.) 1679. **3.** A signal instance of punishment; a person whose fate serves as a deterrent; a warning, caution ME. **4.** A parallel case 1530. **5.** A precedent. *arch.* or *Obs.* 1509. **6.** Action or conduct that induces imitation ME.

1. The will is to Science the first e. of power 1885. **c.** Examples of the great masters 1894. **2.** The E. is an argument which proves some thing to be true in a particular case from another particular case ABP. THOMSON. **3.** Brought to the barre to be punished for e. sake 1631. **4.** A Discipline and Generosity without e. 1707. **6.** Well, you know what e. is able to do WALTON.

Example (egzɑ·mp'l), *v.* ME. [f. prec. sb.] **1.** *trans.* To exemplify; to find or give an instance of. *Obs.* exc. in *pass.* †**2.** To hold forth as an example –1654. †**3.** To furnish a precedent or precedents for; to justify –1595. **4.** To set an example to 1631. †**5.** *intr.* **a.** To serve as a warning 1571. **b.** To quote an example. B. JONS.

1. Of an interest..not in this degree exampled in recent literature CARLYLE. **3.** That I may e. my digression by some mighty president SHAKS.

†**Exa·mpleless,** *a. rare.* 1603. [See -LESS.] Without a precedent; unexampled –1603.

Exanguin, -guious, -guous, etc.: see EXS-.

Exanimate (egz-, eksæ·nimět), *ppl. a.* 1534. [– L. *exanimatus*, pa. pple. of *exanimare*; see next, -ATE[2].] **1.** = INANIMATE. 1552. **2.** Destitute or deprived of animation; spiritless.

1. Ships..stuck with carcases e. SPENSER *F. Q* II. xii. 7. **2.** Out of heart, crest-faln, e. 1668.

†**Exanimate** (egz-, eksæ·nimeᶦt), *v* 1552. [– *exanimat-*, pa. ppl. stem of L. *exanimare* deprive of life, f. *ex* out + *anima* breath of life; see -ATE[3].] **1.** *trans.* To deprive of life, or of animation –1657. **2.** To dispirit –1667. Hence **Exa:nima·tion,** deprivation of life; apparent death from swooning; disheartenment.

‖**Ex animo** (eks æ·nimo). 1612. [L. *ex* from, *animo*, abl. of *animus* soul.] *lit.* From the soul: hence, heartily, sincerely.

Exannulate (eksæ·niŭlět), *a.* 1861. [f. EX-[1] + ANNULUS + -ATE[2].] *Bot.* Having no *annulus* or ring round the sporangium, as certain ferns.

Exanthalose (eksæ·nþălōᵘs). 1837. [f. Gr. ἐξανθεῖν (see next) + ἅλς salt + -OSE[1].] *Min.* 'Native sulphate of sodium' (Watts).

‖**Exanthema** (eksænþī·mă). Pl. **-ata.** 1657. [late L. – Gr. ἐξάνθημα eruption, f. ἐξανθεῖν, f. ἐξ EX-[2] + ἀνθεῖν to blossom, f. ἄνθος blossom.] **1.** *Path.* An efflorescence, or rash such as takes place in measles, smallpox, etc. Also an eruptive disease. Chiefly *pl.* **2.** *Bot.* Eruptive excrescences on leaves

1866. var. **Exa·nthem.** Hence **Exa:nthema·tic, Exanthe·matous** *adjs.* of, pertaining to, or of the nature of, an e. **E:xanthemato·logy,** the doctrine of the exanthemata; a treatise on eruptive fevers.

Exanthine (eksæ·nþəin). 1875. [f. Gr. ἐξανθεῖν (see prec.) + -INE[5].] The Purree or Indian yellow of India.

†**Exa·ntlate,** *v.* 1650. [– *exantlat-*, pa. ppl. stem of L. *exantlare* (more correctly *exanclare*) draw out (a liquid); see -ATE[3].] *trans.* To draw out as from a well; *fig.* to exhaust –1680.

Hence †**Exantla·tion** (only *fig.*).

Exappendiculate (e:ksæpĕndi·kiŭlĕt), *a.* 1870. [f. EX-[1] + L. *appendicula* (APPENDICLE) + -ATE[2].] *Bot.* Having no appendicles.

Exarate (e·ksărĕt), *a.* 1870. [– L. *exaratus*, pa. pple. of *exarare*; see next, -ATE[2].] *Entom.* Applied to a variety of pupa in which the larval skin is simply thrown off.

†**E·xarate,** *v.* 1656. [– *exarat-* pa. ppl. stem of L. *exarare* in same senses, f. *ex-* EX-[1] + *arare* plough; see -ATE[3].] **1.** *trans.* To plough up. **2.** To write or note down –1657. Hence **Exara·tion** (now *rare*).

Exarch (e·ksaɹk). 1588. [– eccl. L. *exarchus* – Gr. ἔξαρχος leader, chief, f. ἐξ EX-[2] + -αρχος -ARCH.] **1.** Under the Byzantine Emperors, the governor of a distant province, as Africa or Italy. **2.** *Eccl.* In the Eastern Church, orig. = 'arch-bishop', 'metropolitan', 'patriarch'; later, a deputy of the patriarch, entrusted with some special charge or mission.

Exarchate (e·ksaɹkeⁱt, eksā·ɹkĕt). 1561. [– med.L. *exarchatus*, f. *exarchus* (see prec.) + *-atus* -ATE[1].] The office, or the province, of an exarch. *var.* †**E·xarchy.**

Exareolate (eks,ărī·ŏlĕt), *a.* 1866. [f. EX-[1] + AREOLA + ATE[2].] *Bot.* Not areolate.

Exarillate (eks,æ·rilĕt), *a.* 1830. [f. EX-[1] + ARIL + -ATE[2].] *Bot.* Not arillate.

Exaristate (eks,ări·stĕt), *a.* 1866. [f. EX-[1] + ARISTA + -ATE[2].] *Bot.* Not aristate.

Exarticulate (eks,aɹti·kiŭlĕt), *a.* 1835. [f. EX-[1] + L. *articulus* joint + -ATE[2].] *Entom.* Not jointed; not consisting of two parts.

Exarticulate (eks,aɹti·kiŭleⁱt), *v.* 1656. [f. as prec. + -ATE[3].] †**a.** To put out of joint. **b.** To amputate at a joint 1884. Hence **E:xarticula·tion,** †dislocation; amputation at a joint.

Exasperate (egza·spĕrĕt), *pa. pple.* and *ppl. a.* 1540. [– L. *exasperatus*, pa. pple. of *exasperare*; see next, -ATE[2].]

†**A.** *pa. pple.* Exasperated –1609.

B. *ppl. a.* **1.** *Bot.* Covered with short stiff points 1866. **2.** In senses of EXASPERATE *v.* 2, 3 (*arch.*) 1601.

2. Swallows which the e. dying year Sets spinning in black circles E.B. BROWNING.

Exasperate (egza·spĕreⁱt), *v.* 1534. [– *exasperat-*, pa. ppl. stem of L. *exasperare*, f. *ex-* EX-[1] + *asper* rough; see -ATE[3].] †**1.** To make harsh or rugged –1765. **2.** To make more fierce or violent 1611. †**b.** To make, or represent as, worse –1750. **3.** To embitter, intensify 1548. **4.** To irritate; to incense 1534. †**5.** *intr.* To become enraged; of things, diseases, etc.: To become worse –1734.

2. To e. and inflame a sore BARROW. **3.** A temper exasperated by disease PRESCOTT. **4.** The poor are exasperated against the rich FRANKLIN. **5.** The Distemper exasperated NORTH. Hence **Exa·sperated** *ppl. a.* in same senses; *Her.* depicted in a furious attitude. **Exa·sperater, -or. Exa·speratingly** *adv.*

Exasperation (egzaspĕrēⁱ·ʃən). 1547. [– L. *exasperatio*, f. as prec.; see -ION.] **1.** Exacerbation 1633. **2.** The action of exasperating. Also, a cause or means of exasperating 1631. **3.** The condition of being exasperated; irritation, violent passion or anger 1547.

1. Iudging..by the e. of the fits WOTTON. **2.** Their ill usage and exasperations of him ATTERBURY. **3.** The e. of his spirits SOUTH.

†**Exau·ctorate,** *v.* 1593. [– *exauctorat-*, pa. ppl. stem of L. *exauctorare* dismiss from service, f. *ex-* EX-[1] + *auctor* AUTHOR; see -ATE[3].] **1.** *trans.* To dismiss from service; to deprive of office, authority, or rank 1623. **2.** To destroy the authority of (a law, etc.) 1593.

1. They did e. and depose the Protector Richard Cromwell W. ROW. Hence †**Exau·ctorate** *ppl. a.* †**Exauctora·tion,** the action of exauctorating.

†**Exau·gurate,** *v.* 1600. [– *exaugurat-*, pa. ppl. stem of L. *exaugurare* profane, f. *ex-* EX-[1] + *augur* AUGUR; see -ATE[3].] **a.** To undo the inauguration of; to make profane –1695. **b.** To augur evil to 1652. Hence †**Exaugura·tion,** the action of unhallowing.

†**Exau·n.** [repr. (ęgzāṅ), pronunc. of Fr. *exempt.*] = EXEMPT *sb.* BUTLER *Hud.*

Exauthorate, -ation, var. ff. EXAUCTORATE, -ATION.

†**Exau·thorize,** *v.* 1546. [– AL. *exauctorizare* depose, degrade; see EX-, AUTHORIZE.] = EXAUCTORATE *v.* Hence †**Exauthoriza·tion.**

Excalcarate (eks,kæ·lkărĕt), *a.* 1884. [var. of ECALCARATE; see EX-[1].] = ECALCARATE.

†**Exca·lceate,** *v.* 1623. [– *excalceat-*, pa. ppl. stem of L. *excalceare*, f. *ex-* EX-[1] + *calceus* shoe; see -ATE[3].] *trans.* To take off the shoes of. Hence †**Excalcea·tion,** the action of taking off the shoes, *e.g.* as a mark of worship.

†**Excalfa·ction.** *rare.* 1607. [– L. *excalfactio*, f. *ex-* EX-[1] + *cal(e)factio*; see CALEFACTION.] Calefaction. Hence †**Excalfa·ctive,** †**Excalfa·ctory** *adjs.* tending to warm; heating.

Excalibur (ekskæ·libəɹ). [– OFr. *Escalibor*, corrupt f. CALIBURN, in Geoffrey of Monmouth (*c*1140) *Caliburnus*. Cf. the name of the Irish sword *Caladbolg*, perh. = 'hard-belly', *i.e.* 'voracious' (Rhys).] The name of King Arthur's sword.

Excamb (ekskæ·mb), *v.* 1629. [– med.L. *excambiare*; see EXCHANGE *v.*] *Sc. Law.* To exchange (land). Also *absol.* var. **Exca·mbie** So **Exca·mbion,** exchange, *spec.* of land.

Excandescence (ekskænde·sĕns). 1684. [– L. *excandescentia*, f. *excandescere* grow white-hot; see -ENCE.] **a.** Heat, the state of growing hot. †**b.** Anger, passion. var. †**Excande·scency.** So **Excande·scent** *a.* white-hot. (Dicts.)

†**Excanta·tion** (ekskæ̆ntēⁱ·ʃən). *rare.* 1580. [alt. of *incantation* by substitution of EX-[1], after L. *excantare* bring out by enchantment, f. *ex-* EX-[1] + *cantare* sing (see CHANT *v.*).] The action of removing (anything) by enchantment –1863.

†**Exca·rnate,** *v.* 1648. [– *excarnat-*, pa. ppl. stem of late L. *excarnare* deprive of flesh, f. *ex-* EX-[1] + L. *caro, carn-* flesh; see -ATE[3].] *trans.* To remove the flesh of –1709. Hence **Exca·rnate** *a.* divested of flesh, or of a human body; opp. to *incarnate*.

Excarnation (ekskaɹnēⁱ·ʃən). 1847. [f. EX-[1] + L. *caro, carn-* flesh + -ATION.] **1.** *Anat.* A method of isolating the blood-vessels after injection, by the agency of putrefaction or immersion in an acid (Craig). **2.** Separation from the flesh and from fleshly conditions 1858.

†**Excarnificate** (ekskaɹni·fikeⁱt), *v.* 1563. [– *excarnificat-*, pa. ppl. stem of L. *excarnificare* tear to pieces, torture, f. *ex-* EX-[1] + *carnificare* cut in pieces; see CARNIFEX, -ATE[3].] *trans.* **a.** To torture, rack. **b.** To do the office of an executioner upon –1664. Hence **Exca:rnifica·tion,** the action of taking away the flesh.

Ex cathedra: see CATHEDRA. Hence **Excathe·dral** *a.* authoritative. †**Excathe·drate** *v.* to condemn authoritatively (HERRICK).

Excavate (e·kskăveⁱt), *v.* 1599. [– *excavat-*, pa. ppl. stem of L. *excavare*, f. *ex-* EX-[1] + *cavare*, f. *cavus* hollow; see CAVE *sb.*, -ATE[3].] **1.** *trans.* To make hollow by removing the inside; to dig out leaving a hollow. **2.** To form (a hole, channel, etc.) by hollowing out 1839. **3.** To lay bare by digging; to unearth. Also *fig.* 1840. **4.** To get out by digging 1848.

1. The ground is excavated in a circular shape, so as to make a pit J. PHILLIPS. **2.** To e. a canal 1873. **5.** Copper was..excavated in this place 1848. Hence **E·xcavate** *ppl. a.*

Excavation (ekskăvēⁱ·ʃən). 1611. [– Fr. *excavation* or L. *excavatio*, f. as prec.; see -ION.] **1.** The action of excavating or of digging out a hollow or hollows in; an instance of this. **2.** An excavated space; a cavity or hollow 1779. **3.** The process of laying bare by excavating; an unearthing 1864.

2. The wine-press was an oblong e. in the rock 1848.

Excavator (e·kskăveⁱtəɹ). 1815. [f. EXCAVATE *v.* + -OR 2.] **1.** One who, or that which excavates. **2.** *spec.* A machine for digging out earth, etc.; also, an instrument for removing the carious parts in a tooth 1864. Hence **Excavato·rial, Exca·vatory** *adjs.* pertaining to excavation.

Excave (eks,kēⁱ·v), *v. rare.* 1578. [– L. *excavare*, f. *ex-* EX-[1] + *cavus* hollow. Cf. (O)Fr. *excaver.*] To scoop or hollow out. Also *absol.*

†**Exce·cate,** *v.* 1540. [– *excæcat-*, pa. ppl. stem of L. *excæcare*, f. *ex-* EX-[1] + *cæcus* blind; see -ATE[3].] To make blind, *lit.* and *fig.* –1665. Hence †**Exce·cate** *ppl. a.* blinded. **Exceca·tion,** punishment by blinding (*arch.*) also †*fig.*

†**Exce·dent.** *rare.* 1655. [– *excedent-*, pr. ppl. stem of L. *excedere*; see next, -ENT.] That which exceeds; excess –1811.

Exceed (eksī·d), *v.* ME. [– (O)Fr. *excéder* – L. *excedere* depart, go beyond, surpass, f. *ex-* EX-[1] + *cedere* go.] **1.** *trans.* To pass out of; to transcend the limits of; to go beyond. *Obs.* or *arch.* **2.** To be greater than; to be too great for ME. **3.** To surpass, outdo ME. †**4.** *intr.* To pass the bounds of propriety or of truth –1815. **5.** To be pre-eminent; to surpass others; to preponderate 1482. **6.** Chiefly in Cambridge use: To have more, or better fare, than usual. Also of the 'commons': To be in extra quantity. 1590.

1. Do not exceede The Prescript of this Scroule *Ant. & Cl.* III. viii. 4. **2.** Such griefe..as did exceede all consolation 1635. Each part exceeds the whole SHELLEY. **3.** How much a Chintz exceeds Mohair POPE. **4.** You cannot possibly e. in your love to him 1758. **5.** Punish so, as pity shall e. DRYDEN.

Hence **Excee·dable** *a.* that may be exceeded. **Excee·der.**

Exceeding (eksī·diŋ), *vbl. sb.* 1480. [f. prec. + -ING[1].] **1.** The action of EXCEED *v.* **2.** *concr.* **a.** *pl.* In Cambridge use: Extra commons allowed on festival occasions. Also *transf.* 1629. †**b.** An excess, a surplus –1833.

Excee·ding, *ppl. a.* and *adv.* 1494. [f. as prec. + -ING[2].]

A. *adj.* †**1.** Going to extremes –1742. **2.** Extremely great, excessive 1547. †**3.** Of surpassing excellence –1599.

3. Christ tooke..our nature vpon him..Oh what an e. thing is this LATIMER.

B. *adv.* = next. Now somewhat *arch.* 1535. My heart is e. heavy *Much Ado* III. iv. 25.

Exceedingly (eksī·diŋli), *adv.* 1470. †**1.** So as to surpass others. **2.** Above measure, extremely 1535.

Excel (ekse·l), *v.* Also †**excell.** ME. [– L. *excellere* be eminent, rise, raise, f. *ex-* EX-[1] + **cellere* rise high, tower. Cf. Fr. *exceller.*] **1.** *intr.* To be superior or preeminent, usu. in good qualities or praiseworthy actions; to surpass others. **2.** *trans.* To be superior to (others) in some respect; usu. in a good sense; to outdo, surpass 1493. **b.** To surpass (another's qualities or work) (*rare*) 1611. †**3.** To be too hard or great for –1703.

1. Vnstable as water, thou shalt not excell *Gen.* 49:4. To e. at a game 1802. **2.** A babe all babes excelling SHELLEY. **3.** She op'nd, but to shut Excel'd her strength MILT. *P. L.* II. 884.

Excellence (e·ksĕlĕns). ME. [– (O)Fr. *excellence* or L. *excellentia*, f. *excellent-*; see EXCELLENT, -ENCE.] **1.** The state or fact of excelling; the possession chiefly of good qualities in an unusual degree; surpassing merit, virtue, etc.; dignity, eminence. **2.** That in which a person excels ME. †**3. a.** An excellent personality –1790. **b.** = EXCELLENCY 3 b. –1796.

1. Sir, you are not ignorant of what e. Laertes is at his weapon *Haml.* V. ii. 143. **2.** The adoration due to your other excellencies LOCKE.

Excellency (e·ksĕlĕnsi). ME. [– L. *excellentia*; see prec., -ENCY.] †**1.** = EXCELLENCE 1. –1783. **2.** = EXCELLENCE 2. 1601. †**3. a.** = EXCELLENCE 3 a. 1688. **b.** As a title of honour. (Applied, formerly, to royal personages, to ladies, and others; now, only to ambassadors, governors (and their wives), and certain other high officers.) 1532.

1. They onely consult to cast him downe from his e. *Ps.* 62:4. 2. Cram'd (as he thinks) with excellencies *Twel. N.* II. iii. 163.

Excellent (e·ksĕlĕnt). ME. [– (O)Fr. *excellent* – L. *excellens*, *-ent-*, pr. pple. of *excellere*; see EXCEL, -ENT.]

A. as *pr. pple.* Excelling.

B. *adj.* **1.** That excels or surpasses in any respect; pre-eminent, superior. *Obs.* or *arch.* ME. †**2.** Excelling in rank or dignity; exalted, highly honourable –1702. **3.** Extremely good. (The current sense.) 1604.

1. The e. brightnesse of the Sunne BLUNDEVIL. Elizabeth..was an e. hypocrite HUME. 2. His Name alone is e. *Ps.* 148:13. 3. An e. song SHAKS., Gard'ner EVELYN, Drink ARBUTHNOT. The e. of the Earth HERVEY.

†**C.** *adv.* Excellently –1756.

Hence **E·xcellently** *adv.* in an e. manner or degree.

†**Exce·lse.** 1568. [– L. *excelsus*, pa. pple. of *excellere* EXCEL.]

A. *adj.* Lofty, high; *esp.* in fig. sense –1657.

B. *sb.* [tr. L. *excelsum*] A high place (*rare*) –1609.

Excelsior (ekse·lsiọɹ). 1778. [L., compar. of *excelsus* high.] ‖**1.** The Latin motto ('higher') on the seal of the State of New York. (The adverbial meaning is not justified.) Hence *attrib.* in *The Excelsior State*, New York. **2.** *U.S.* A trade name for short thin curled shavings of soft wood used for stuffing cushions, mattresses, etc. Also *attrib.* 1868.

†**Exce·lsitude.** 1470. [– late and med.L. *excelsitudo*, f. L. *excelsus* lofty; see -TUDE.] Highness –1599.

Excentral (ekse·ntrăl), *a.* 1847. [f. L. *ex-* + *centrum* + -AL¹.] *Bot.* Out of the centre; ECCENTRIC. (Dicts.)

Excentric, -al, etc.: see ECCENTRIC, -AL.

Except (ekse·pt), *v.* ME. [– *except-*, pa. ppl. stem of L. *excipere*, f. *ex-* EX-¹ + *capere* take. Cf. (O)Fr. *excepter*.] **1.** *trans.* To take or leave out (of any aggregate or whole); to exclude; to omit 1530. **2.** *intr.* To object or take exception 1577. †**3.** *trans.* To object. Const. with simple obj. or cl., *against, to.* –1753. †**4.** To protest against. SHAKS. †**5.** Erron. for ACCEPT –1635.

1. He was excepted from the general pardon BLUNT. The Church excepted, no agent [etc.] BRYCE. 2. I may be allowed to e. to the witnesses brought against me BACON. 3. Others excepted, that this e. was nothing worth FULLER.

Except (ekse·pt). ME. [– L. *exceptus*, pa. pple. of *excipere*; see prec.]

†**A.** *pple.* = EXCEPTED. (Often in nominative absol. following the sb.; = '(being) excepted'.

B. *prep.* **1.** Excepting, with the exception of, save, but. (Orig. the pa. pple. preceding the sb.) ME. †**2.** Leaving out of account; hence, in addition to, besides (*rare*) –1756.

1. The rabble..know nothing of liberty e. the name GOLDSM.

C. *conj.* **1.** (more fully) *Except that* (the only form now used) 1568. **2.** = 'unless', 'if not' ME. *arch.* **3.** Otherwise (or elsewhere, etc.) than 1586.

1. *Rich. II*, I. iv. 6. 2. E. my memory fails me these are all MOXON. No drama..will be [written] e. it be by the same hand SOUTHEY. 3. The city was strongly fortified on all sides, e. here 1894.

Exceptant (ekse·ptănt). 1697. [f. EXCEPT + -ANT.]

A. *adj.* That excepts 1846.

B. *sb.* One who excepts; *esp.* in *Law*, an accused person who excepts to a judge or juror.

Excepting (ekse·ptiŋ). 1549. [f. EXCEPT *v.* + -ING².]

A. *prep.* **1.** quasi-*prep.* = 'If one excepts' 1549. **2.** With the exception of, except 1618.

2. All young Persons, e. my self HALES.

B. *conj.* = EXCEPT C. 1–3. 1641.

Exception (ekse·pʃən). ME. [– (O)Fr. *exception* – L. *exceptio*, f. *except-*; see EXCEPT *v.*, -ION.] **1.** The action of excepting from the scope of a proposition, rule, etc.; the state or fact of being so excepted. Const. *from, to.* **2.** Something that is excepted; a person, thing, or case to which the general rule is not applicable. Const. *to*, †*from.* 1483. **3.** *Law.* [cf. EXCEPT *v.* 2.] **a.** A plea made by a defendant in bar of the plaintiff's action; in *Sc. Law* = DEFENCE. ME. **b.** An objection made to the ruling of a court in the course of a trial 1715. **c.** In Courts of Equity (now *Obs.*): An objection by the plaintiff to the defendant's answer as insufficient. †**4.** *transf.* **a.** A plea tending to evade the force of an opponent's argument –1643. **b.** A formal objection –1689. **5.** Objection, demur, cavil; an instance of this. *Obs.* or arch. 1571.

1. Phr. *The e. proves the rule*: orig. a legal maxim, in full 'Exception proves the rule in the cases not excepted', but now abbreviated and taken in sense 2. 2. Egypt was an e. from the rules of all other countries FULLER. 3. Phr. *Bill of exceptions*: a statement of objections to the ruling or direction of a judge drawn up on behalf of the dissatisfied party, and submitted to a higher Court. 5. To expose themselues to many exceptions and cauillations A.V. *Transl. Pref.* 4. Phr. *To take e. against, at, to*; to object to; also (chiefly with *at*) to take offence at.

Exceptionable (ekse·pʃənăb'l), *a.* 1664. [f. prec. + -ABLE.] **1.** Open to exception or objection. ¶**2.** Occas. misused for EXCEPTIONAL. 1801. Hence **Exce·ptionableness. Exce·ptionably** *adv.*

Exceptional (ekse·pʃənăl), *a.* 1846. [f. as prec. + -AL¹, after Fr. *exceptionnel.*] Of the nature of or forming an exception; unusual.

Documents or records of e. value 1875. Hence **Exce·ptiona·lity**, e. character. **Exce·ptional-ly** *adv.*, **-ness.**

Exce·ptionary, *a. rare.* 1783. [f. as prec. + -ARY¹.] Of, pertaining to, or indicative of, an exception; EXCEPTIONAL.

†**Exce·ptioner.** [f. †*exception* v. + -ER¹.] One who takes exception; an objector. MILTON.

Exceptionless (ekse·pʃənlės), *a.* 1782. [See -LESS.] Without an exception.

A renewed act of..indispensable, e. disqualification BURKE.

Exceptious (ekse·pʃəs), *a.* 1602. [f. EXCEPTION + -OUS, after *captious.*] Disposed to make objections; cavilling, captious.

It is the character of Country ladies to be e., and suspicious of slights CHESTERF. Hence **Exce·ptiousness.**

Exceptive (ekse·ptiv). 1563. [– late L. *exceptivus*, f. *except-*; see EXCEPT *v.*, -IVE.]

A. *adj.* **1.** *Logic*, etc. That excepts something (see quots.). **2.** Of persons, etc.: Disposed to take exception; captious 1621.

1. E. Conjunctions are, if it be not..unless that, etc. 1751. E. propositions JEVONS. An e. clause introduced into the act FROUDE. **Exce·ptively** *adv.*

B. *sb.* [The adj. used *absol.*] *Logic.* An exceptive word or proposition 1563.

†**Exce·ptless,** *a.* [irreg. f. EXCEPT *v.* + -LESS.] Making no exception. *Timon* IV. iii. 502.

Exceptor (ekse·ptŏɹ, -əɹ). 1641. [In sense 2 – late L. *exceptor*; in sense 1 f. EXCEPT *v.* + -OR 2.] †**1.** An objector –1690. **2.** †**a.** A shorthand writer –1732. **b.** *Hist.* A clerk of the Court of Chancery under the later Roman Empire 1728.

†**Exce·rebrate,** *v.* 1621. [– *excerebrat-*, pa. ppl. stem of late L. *excerebrare*, f. *ex-* EX-¹ + *cerebrum* brain; see -ATE³.] **1.** *trans.* To clear out from the brain. **2.** To beat out the brains of. Hence **Excerebra·tion**, the action of beating out the brains; also, the removing of the contents of the skull.

†**Exce·rn,** *v.* 1578. [– L. *excernere*, f. *ex-* EX-¹ + *cernere* sift.] = EXCRETE. –1738. So **Exce·rnment** *a.* = EXCRETORY.

†**Exce·rp,** *v.* 1563. [– L. *excerpere*; see EXCERPT *v.*] = EXCERPT *v.* 1. –1697.

Excerpt (e·ksəɹpt, eksə̄·ɹpt), *sb.* L. *pl.* **excerpta.** 1638. [– L. *excerptum* subst. use of n. of pa. pple. of *excerpere*; see next.] **1.** A passage taken out of a book or manuscript; an extract. **2.** An article from the 'Transactions' of a society, a periodical, etc. printed off separately. Cf. *off-print.* 1883.

Excerpt (eksə̄·ɹpt), *v.* 1536. [– *excerpt-* pa. ppl. stem of L. *excerpere*, f. *ex-* EX-¹ + *carpere* pluck.] **1.** *trans.* To take out as an extract; to extract, quote. Also *absol.* †**2.** To pluck out; to remove. Also *fig.* –1612.

1. He had excerpted..many notes and precedents HEYLIN. Hence **Exce·rption**, the action of excerpting; that which is excerpted. **Exce·rptive** *a.* inclined to e. †**Exce·rptor**, one who excerpts.

Excess (ekse·s). ME. [– (O)Fr. *excès* – L. *excessus*, f. *excess-*, pa. ppl. stem of *excedere* EXCEED.] †**1.** The action of going out or forth; adjournment –1621. †**b.** *fig.* Departure *from* custom, reason, etc. –1738. †**2.** 'Violence of passion' (J.); extravagant feeling –1742. **3.** The action of overstepping (a limit); going beyond (one's rights, decency, moderation, etc.) ME. **4.** Intemperance, *esp.* in eating and drinking ME. **5.** The fact of exceeding something else in amount or degree 1618. **b.** The amount by which this is done 1557. †**c.** Usury. *Merch. V.* I. iii. 63. **6.** The fact or state of being greater in amount or degree than is usual, necessary, or right; an excessive amount or degree (of anything) ME.

1. Phr. †*E. of mind*, ecstasy, trance, stupefaction. 3. The full wrath beside Of vengeful justice bore for our e. MILT. Driven into excesses little short of rebellion 'JUNIUS'. E. of jurisdiction on the part of the House 1891. 4. The excesses of the preceding night BARHAM. 5. When..one or more muscles act in e. of their opponents, a squint is produced HARLAN. Phr. *Spherical e.*: the quantity by which the sum of the degrees in the angles of spherical triangles exceeds 180°. 6. So distribution should vndoo excesse, And each man have enough *Lear* IV. i. 73. Parsimony..is the more pardonable e. of the two ATTERBURY. Hence †**Exce·ss** *a.*, †**Exce·ssful** *a.* = EXCESSIVE.

Excessive (ekse·siv). ME. [– (O)Fr. *excessif*, *-ive* – med.L. *excessivus*, f. as prec.; see -IVE.]

A. *adj.* Characterized by, or exhibiting EXCESS, in various senses.

Excessiue greefe [is] the enemie to the liuing *All's Well* I. i. 65.

†**B.** *adv.* = EXCESSIVELY *adv.* –1796.

Hence **Exce·ssively** *adv.* in an e. manner, amount, or degree. **Exce·ssiveness.**

Exchange (eksˌtʃēⁱ·ndʒ), *sb.* [ME. *eschaunge*, later (by assim. to L.) *exchaunge* – AFr. *eschaunge*, OFr. *eschange* (Fr. *échange*), f. *eschangier* (mod. *échanger*); see ES-, EX-¹, CHANGE *sb.*] **1.** The action, or an act, of reciprocal giving and receiving. **2.** *Law.* 'A mutual grant of equal interests, the one in consideration of the other'. (Blackstone) 1574. **3.** The action of giving or receiving coin for coin of equivalent value, for bullion, or for notes or bills; the trade of a money-changer ME. **4.** The system of transactions by which the debts of individuals residing at a distance from their creditors are settled without the transmission of money, by the use of 'bills of exchange' 1485. **5.** = Bill of Exchange (see BILL *sb.*³) 1485. **6.** = CHANGE ME. **7.** That which is offered or given in exchange, e.g. a newspaper sent in return for another 1490. **8.** A place of exchange; *esp* a building in which the merchants of a town assemble for the transaction of business. Also *fig.* Cf. BURSE, CHANGE. 1569. **b.** = *telephone exchange* (TELEPHONE *sb.*) 1888.

1. E. of gold for silver 1552, of goods for money BLACKSTONE, of prisoners SMYTH, of salutations STANLEY, of commissions 1875, of pieces captured (in *Chess*) 1878. 3. Well couthe he in eschaunge scheeldes [*i.e.* Fr. *écus*] selle CHAUCER. 4. I haue bils for monie by e. From Florence, and must heere [at Padua] deliuer them *Tam. Shr.* IV. ii. 89. Phr. *Par of e.*: the recognized standard value of the coinage of one country in terms of the coinage of another; *e.g.* £1 sterling at par = 25.22½ francs French money. *Rate* or *Course of e.* (also simply *exchange*): (*a*) the price at which foreign bills may be purchased; (*b*) sometimes, the percentage by which this differs from par. (If the price of a foreign bill is above par, *the exchange is against* the country in which the bill is drawn; if below par, *in its favour*). *Arbitration of e.*: see ARBITRATION. 8. Sir Thomas Gresham..named it the Burse, whereunto afterward Queene Elizabeth gave the name of Royall E. 1593.

Exchange (eksˌtʃēⁱ·ndʒ), *v.* ME. [– OFr. *eschangier* (mod. *échanger*) :– Rom. **excambiare*, f. *ex-* EX-¹ + L. *cambiare*; see CHANGE *v.*] **1.** *trans.* To change away; to dispose of by exchange; to give or part with (something) in return. Also *absol.* 1484. **2.** To give and receive reciprocally; to interchange. *Const.* obj. *with* (a person). 1602. **3.** *Mil.*, etc. **a.** To give up a prisoner in return for one taken by the enemy 1726. **b.** *absol.* To pass, by exchange with another officer, *from* or *out of* one regiment *into* another 1787. **4.** *intr.* Chiefly of coin: To be received as an equivalent *for* 1776. **5.** *trans.* To CHANGE. ME.

1. They shall not..e., nor alienate the first fruits of the land *Ezek.* 48:14. Old money exchanged for new CAMDEN. **2.** E. forgiuenesse with me, Noble Hamlet *Haml.* v. ii. 340. **4.** An English sovereign exchanged a little while ago for thirteen rupees 1890.

Exchangeable (eks,tʃēⁱ·ndʒăb'l), *a.* 1575. [f. prec. + -ABLE.] **1.** That may be exchanged. Const. *for.* 1651. †**2.** = COMMUTATIVE 1 (*rare*) 1575.

1. On condition of General Lee being declared e. WASHINGTON. Phr. *E. value*: value estimated by what will be given for a thing. Hence **Exchaːngeabi·lity.**

Exchanger (eks,tʃēⁱ·ndʒəɹ). Also †-**or.** 1531. [f. as prec. + -ER¹.] One who exchanges or makes an exchange; †a banker (*Matt.* 25:27).

Exchequer (eks,tʃe·kəɹ). [ME. *escheker* – AFr. *escheker*, OFr. *eschequier*, earlier *eschaquier* (mod. *échiquier*) :- med.L. *scaccarium* chess-board; f. *scaccus* CHECK *sb.*¹; see -ER² 2. The form with *ex-* (from XV) is due to assoc. with Ex-¹, as in *exchange*, etc. Aphetic CHEQUER.] †**1.** A chess-board –1474. **2.** Under the Norman kings: An office or department of state managed by the Treasurer, the judges of the King's Court, and certain Barons appointed by the King. Its functions, which were both administrative and judicial, were divided later into two distinct branches; see 3, 4. (So called with reference to a table covered with a cloth divided into squares, on which the accounts of the revenue were kept by means of counters.) ME. **3.** (More fully *Court of E., E. of pleas.*) A court of law, historically representing the Anglo-Norman exchequer in its judicial capacity. Its jurisdiction was extended, by a legal fiction, from matters of revenue to all kinds of cases. Its equitable jurisdiction was abolished in 1841. (Now merged in the King's Bench Division.) 1489. **4.** The department of state charged with the receipt and custody of the moneys collected by the revenue departments ME. **5.** Pecuniary possessions in general 1565. Also *fig.* and *joc.*

2. Phr. *Chancellor of the E.*: originally, an assistant to the Treasurer; now, the responsible finance minister of the United Kingdom; see CHANCELLOR. **4.** The e. being so exhausted with the debts of king James CLARENDON. **5.** The..impoverished state of my e. THACKERAY.

Comb.: **e.-bill**, a bill of credit issued by authority of Parliament, bearing interest at the current rate; hence **e.-bill-office**, the office where these are issued and received; **-bond**, a bond issued by the E. at a fixed rate of interest, and for a fixed period; **-tallies**, the notched sticks with which the accounts of the E. were formerly kept.

Exchequer (eks,tʃe·kəɹ), *v.* 1705. [f. prec.] **1.** *trans.* To place in an exchequer (*rare*). **2.** To proceed against in the Court of Exchequer 1809.

Exchequer-chamber. 1494. **1.** The chamber devoted to the business of the royal exchequer. **2.** 'A tribunal of error and appeal' (WHARTON); now merged in the Court of Appeal 1528.

Excide (eksəi·d), *v.* 1758. [– L. *excidere* cut out, f. *ex-* Ex-¹ + *cædere* cut.] *trans.* To cut out. Also *fig.*

Exci·pient. 1726. [– *excipient-*, pr. ppl. stem of L. *excipere* take out, f. *ex-* Ex-¹ + *capere* take; see -ENT.]

†**A.** *adj.* That takes exception.

B. *sb.* **1.** One who takes up in succession (*rare*) 1852. **2.** That ingredient in a compound medicine which takes up or receives the rest, as the syrup in boluses, etc. 1753. **3.** The material or surface that receives the pigments in painting 1855.

Exciple (e·ksip'l), **Excipule** (e·ksipiul), anglicized forms of next.

‖**Excipulum** (eksi·piŭlŏm). 1857. [L., = receptacle, f. *recipere*; see EXCIPIENT, -ULE.] *Bot.* A layer of cells partially enclosing, as a cup, the APOTHECIUM in lichens.

Excise (eksəi·z), *sb.* 1494. [– MDu. *excijs* XV (also *accijs*), perh. related, as by substitution of prefix, to Rom. **accensum*, verbal sb. of *accensare* to tax, f. L. *ad* AC- + *census* tax.] **1.** *gen.* Any toll or tax. **2.** *spec.* 'A duty charged on home goods, either in the process of their manufacture or before their sale to the home consumers' (*Encycl. Brit.*) 1596. Also *transf.* and *fig.* **3.** Payment or imposition of excise 1710. **4.** The government department charged with the collection of the excise. Now known as the Board of Customs and Excise. 1784.

2. *Excise*, a hateful tax levied upon commodities, and adjudged not by the common judges of property, but wretches hired by those to whom e. is paid JOHNSON. *Comb.* **E. duties**, those collected by the Board of Inland Revenue, comprising many improperly so named, *e.g.* the tax for armorial bearings, game licences, etc.

Excise (eksəi·z), *v.*¹ 1578. [– *excis-*, pa. ppl. stem of L. *excidere* EXCIDE.] †**1.** *trans.* = CIRCUMCISE 1. –1650. **2.** To cut off or out. Also *fig.* 1647. **3.** To notch 1578.

2. To e. a tumour, a reference 1884.

Excise (eksəi·z), *v.*² 1652. [f. EXCISE *sb.*] †**1.** *trans.* To impose an excise or tax upon. Also *transf.* and *fig.* –1765. **2.** To force to pay an excise-due; hence, to overcharge 1659.

Exciseman (eksəi·zmæ̆n). 1647. [f. EXCISE *sb.* + MAN.] An officer who collects excise duties and prevents evasion of the excise laws.

Excision (eksi·ʒən). 1490. [– (O)Fr. *excision* – L. *excisio*, f. *excis-*; see EXCISE *v.*¹, -ION.] **1.** The action or process of cutting off or out; extirpation; destruction. Also *fig.* **2.** The action of cutting off from a religious society; excommunication 1647.

1. E. of ears had, indeed, gone out of fashion 1864. The e. of a clause 1884.

Excitability (eksəiːtăbli·lĭti). 1788. [f. next + -ITY.] **1.** The quality of being excitable, or easily excited 1803. **2.** *Phys.* Of an organ or tissue: The capacity of being excited to its characteristic activity by the action of a specific stimulus.

1. Romola..shrank..from the shrill e. of those illuminated women GEO. ELIOT.

Excitable (eksəi·tăb'l), *a.* 1609. [f. EXCITE + -ABLE. Cf. (O)Fr. *excitable.*] Capable of being excited; easily excited. Const. *to.*

Excitant (e·ksitănt, eksəi·tănt). 1607. [f. EXCITE + -ANT, perh. after Fr. *excitant.*]

A. *adj.* That excites or stimulates (see EXCITE *v.*).

B. *sb.* An agent which excites (organs or tissues) to increased vital activity; a stimulant. Also, an agent for inducing electrical action. 1833.

†**E·xcitate,** *v.* 1548. *Pa. t.* **excitate.** [– *excitat-*, pa. ppl. stem of L. *excitare*; see EXCITE, -ATE³.] = EXCITE –1660. Hence **Exci·tative, Exci·tatory** *adjs.*, able or tending to excite.

Excitation (eksitēⁱ·ʃən). ME. [– (O)Fr. *excitation* – late L. *excitatio*, f. as prec.; see -ION.] **1.** The action of exciting (see EXCITE *v.*). **2.** A means of excitement; a stimulus, instigation (*arch.*) 1627. **3.** The state of being excited, excitement. Now *rare.* ME. **4.** *Electr.*, etc. The process of inducing an electric or magnetic condition; also, the condition 1656.

†**Excita·tor.** *rare.* 1688. [f. EXCITATE + -OR 2.] One who, or that which, excites; *spec.* in *Electr.*, an instrument for discharging a Leyden jar, etc., without exposing the operator to the shock.

Excite (eksəi·t), *v.* ME. [– (O)Fr. *exciter* or L. *excitare* frequent. of *exciēre* call out or forth; see Ex-¹, CITE *v.*] **1.** *trans.* To set in motion, stir up, incite. **2.** To rouse up; to call forth or quicken ME. **3.** To induce, elicit, occasion ME. **4.** To move to strong emotion, stir to passion 1850. **5. a.** *Electr.*, etc. To induce electric or magnetic activity in; to set (a current) in motion. **b.** *Photogr.* To sensitize (a plate). 1646.

1. We e. children by praising them WOLLASTON. [He] excited his attendants to resist JAS. MILL. **2.** With Shouts, the Coward's Courage they e. DRYDEN. **3.** To e. an insurrection FROUDE. **4.** The only result..had been to e. the Under-Secretary for India L. STEPHEN. Hence **Exci·tedly** *adv.* **Exci·tive** *a.* tending to e.

Excitement (eksəi·tmĕnt). 1604. [f. EXCITE *v.* + -MENT.] **1.** The action of exciting; the fact of or state of being excited; excitation. Somewhat *rare.* 1830. **2.** *Path.* A state of abnormal activity in any organ 1788. **3.** Something that excites; an incentive *to* action (*arch.*); an occasion of mental excitement 1604.

1. The e. and propagation of motion HERSCHEL. **2.** The e. it [Tractarianism] caused in England NEWMAN.

Exciter (eksəi·təɹ). ME. [f. as prec. + -ER¹.] One who, or that which, excites; *spec.* in *Med.*, a stimulant.

Exciting (eksəi·tiŋ), *ppl. a.* 1811. [f. as prec. + -ING².] That excites. Phr. *E. cause*: (chiefly *Path.*) that which immediately causes disease, etc.; opp. to *predisposing cause.*

Excito-motory (eksəiːtomōᵘ·təri), *a.* 1836. [f. EXCITOR + MOTORY.] *Phys.* Of or pertaining to the spinal group of nerves, composed of the excitor and the motor nerves. Often applied to the reflex actions produced by these. var. **Exciːto-mo·tor.**

Excitor (eksəi·tŏɹ, -əɹ). 1816. [f. EXCITE + -OR 2, after *motor.*] **a.** = EXCITER. **b.** An afferent nerve belonging to the spinal group.

Exclaim (ekskłē·m), *v.* 1570. [– Fr. *exclamer* or L. *exclamare*; see Ex-¹, CLAIM *v.*] **1.** To cry out with sudden vehemence; to cry out from pain, anger, delight, surprise, etc. Rarely with *out.* †**2.** *trans.* To proclaim loudly –1782.

1. What makes you thus exclame 1 *Hen. VI*, IV. i. 83. 'Spoke like an oracle', they all exclaimed COWPER. To e. against inconsistencies 1860. Hence **Exclai·m** *sb.* outcry (*rare*). **Exclai·mer.**

Exclamation (eksklămēⁱ·ʃən). ME. [– (O)Fr. *exclamation* or L. *exclamatio*, f. *exclamat-*, pa. ppl. stem of *exclamare*; see prec., -ION.] **1.** The action of exclaiming; emphatic or vehement outcry; clamour, vociferation. Also, an instance of this. **2.** A loud complaint or protest; a 'vociferous reproach' (J.) ME. †**3.** Proclamation –1631. **4. a.** *Rhet.* = ECPHONESIS. 1552. **b.** *Gram.* = INTERJECTION. 1862.

1. Huge exclamations burst abruptly out STIRLING. **2.** Exclamations against the follies..of those things DE FOE. **4. b.** *Note, point of e.* also (U.S.) *E.-mark* or *point* = *Note of Admiration*; see ADMIRATION.

Exclamative (ekskłæ·mătiv), *a. rare.* 1730. [f. as prec. + -IVE.] Exclamatory. Hence **Excla·matively** *adv.*

Exclamatory (ekskłæ·mătəri), *a.* 1593. [f. as prec. + -ORY².] **1.** That exclaims, or vents itself in exclamation. **2.** Pertaining to exclamation; of the nature of, or containing, an exclamation 1716.

1. An intemperate and e. Sorrow DONNE. **2.** An e. O! GEO. ELIOT. Hence **Excla·matorily** *adv.*

Exclude (ekskłū·d), *v.* ME. [– L. *excludere*, f. *ex-* Ex-¹ + *claudere* shut.] **1.** *trans.* To bar or shut out; to prevent the existence, occurrence, or use of; not to admit of. **2.** To shut off, debar *from*; to preclude 1495. **3.** To leave out, except ME. **4.** To put out, banish, expel ME. **5.** After L. *excludere ova.* To draw or put forth from (a receptacle); to hatch; also *fig.* to give birth to ME.

1. To e. the pouer of the feende ME., lowd noises 1598, all Pittie 1604. **2.** And none but such from mercy I e. MILT *P. L.* III. 202. **4.** They excluded him out of their counsayle ELYOT. **5.** The method of excluding the Fœtus 1754.

Phr. *Law of Excluded Middle, Third* (Logic): the principle that between two contradictories, *e.g.* A and not-A, no third or middle term is possible—we must think of either the one or the other as existing.

Hence **Exclu·der,** one who or that excludes.

Exclusion (ekskłū·ʒən). 1614. [– L. *exclusio*, f. *exclus-*, pa. ppl. stem of *excludere*; see prec., -ION. Cf. (O)Fr. *exclusion.*] **1.** The action of excluding, in various senses; see the verb. **2.** The action of putting or thrusting forth from a receptacle (see EXCLUDE *v.* 5) 1646. †**3.** The action of discharging (excrement). Also *concr.* excrement –1664.

1. His sad e. from the dores of Bliss MILT. The e. of the Bishops out of the House of Lords LUDLOW. Phr. *Method of Exclusion(s)*: the process of discovering a cause, or the solution of a problem, by disproving all but one of the conceivable hypotheses.

Hence **Exclu·sionary** *a.* of, pertaining to, or characterized by e. **Exclu·sioner**, one who upholds e. **Exclu·sionism**, the character, manners, or principles of an exclusionist. **Exclu·sionist,** one who favours e.; esp. (*Eng. Hist*) a supporter of the Exclusion Bill.

Exclusive (ekskl*ū*·siv). 1515. [– med.L. *exclusivus*, f. as prec.; see -IVE. Cf. Fr. *exclusif, -ive*.]

A. *adj.* **1.** That excludes; †debarring from participation; not admitting of the existence or presence of, not including. Also quasi-*adv.* (and *adv.*) So as to exclude. **2.** Excluding all but what is specified 1581. **3.** Single, sole 1790. **4.** Disposed to resist the admission of outsiders to membership of a body, social intercourse, etc. 1822. **b.** Of a pattern exclusively claimed by a particular establishment 1901.

1. An E. Voice 1706. On grounds..not e. of each other BURKE. quasi-*adv.* From 25th Decemb. last e. 1679. **2.** E. propositions WATTS. The English E. particles are, one, only, alone, exclusively, etc. 1864. Phr. *E. dealing*: the practice of dealing only with certain special tradesmen. **3.** The e. channel BURKE. **4.** The literary class is usually proud and e. EMERSON.

B. *sb.* **1.** An exclusive proposition or particle. (Cf. A. 2.) 1533. **2.** An exclusive person 1825.

Hence **Exclu·sively** *adv.* in an e. †sense or manner; solely. **Exclu·siveness. Exclu·sivism,** systematic exclusiveness. **Exclusivist,** one who maintains the e. validity (of a theory).

Exclu·sory (ekskl*ū*·səri), *a.* 1585. [– late L. *exclusorius*, f. as prec.; see -ORY[2].] = EXCLUSIVE A. 1. Const. *of*.

†Exco·ct, *v.* 1563. [– *excoct-*, pa. ppl. stem of L. *excoquere*, f. *ex-* EX-[1] + *coquere* boil, melt.] **1.** To extract by heat –1671. **2.** To drive off the moisture of; to elaborate –1710. Hence **†Exco·ction,** extraction or elaboration by heat.

Excogitate (ekskǫ·dʒiteᵗt), *v.* 1530. [– *excogitat-*, pa. ppl. stem of L. *excogitare* find out by thinking; see EX-[1], COGITATE.] **1.** *trans.* To think out; to contrive, devise. ¶**2.** *intr.* = COGITATE. 1630.

1. We here e. no new, no occult principle SIR W. HAMILTON. Hence **Exco:gita·tion,** the action, or result, of excogitating.

†Excomme·nge, *v.* 1502. [– OFr. *escomengier* (:– eccl. L. *excommunicare*), with *ex-* after the L. See EXCOMMUNICATE *v.*] To excommunicate –1641. Hence **†Excomme·ngement.**

†Exco·mmune, *v.* 1483. [– (O)Fr. *excommunier* – eccl. L. *excommunicare*; see next.] To EXCOMMUNICATE; *transf.* to exclude from –1654.

transf. Poets..were excommun'd Plato's Common Wealth GAYTON.

Excommunicate (ekskǫ̆miū·nikeᵗt), *v.* 1526. [– *excommunicat-*, pa. ppl. stem of eccl. L. *excommunicare*, f. *ex-* EX-[1] + *communis* COMMON, after *communicare* COMMUNICATE; see -ATE[3].] *Eccl.* To cut off from communion; to exclude, by an authoritative sentence, from the communion of the Church, or from religious rites. Also *transf.*

transf. He was excommunicated; put out of the pale of the school LAMB.

Hence **Excommu·nicable** *a.* liable, or deserving, to be excommunicated; punishable by excommunication. **Excommu·nicant,** one who excommunicates or is excommunicated. **Excommu·nicative** *a.* that excommunicates; disposed to e. **Excommu·nicator. Excommu·nicatory** *a.* of or pertaining to excommunication; excommunicative.

Excommunicate (ekskǫ̆miū·nikĕt). 1526. [– eccl. L. *excommunicatus*, pa. pple. of *excommunicare*; see prec., -ATE[2].]

A. *pa. pple.* and *ppl. a.* Excommunicated (*arch.*).

Phr. *E. things* (tr. Heb. *ḥērem*): objects devoted to destruction.

B. *sb.* An excommunicated person 1562. Also *transf.*

Excommunication (ekskǫ̆miūnikē̆ᵗ·ʃən). 1494. [– eccl. L. *excommunicatio*, f. as prec.; see -ION. Cf. (O)Fr. *excommunication*.] **1.** *Eccl.* The action of excluding an offender from the sacraments (*lesser excommunication*), or from all communication with the Church or its members (*greater e.*). Also *transf.* **2.** Short for 'sentence of excommunication' 1647.

2. The Pope fulminated an e. against him KINGSLEY. So **†Excommu·nion.** MILT.

Excoriate (ekskōᵊ·ri,eᵗt), *v.* 1497. [– *excoriat-*, pa. ppl. stem of L. *excoriare*, f. *ex-* EX-[1] + *corium* skin, hide; see -ATE[3].] **†1.** *trans.* To flay –1826. **2.** To remove parts of the skin, etc., from; *esp. Path.* by the use of corrosives, abrasion, etc. 1497. Also *transf.* and *fig.* **3.** To strip or peel off (the skin) 1547.

3. To prevent..the matter..from excoriating the skin GOOCH. Hence **Exco·riable** *a.* that may be rubbed or stripped off. **Exco·riate** *pple. arch.* having the skin or rind rubbed or stripped off.

Excoriation (ekskōᵊ:ri,ēᵗ·ʃən). 1447. [– (O)Fr. *excoriation* or med. L. *excoriatio*, f. as prec.; see -ION.] **1.** The action of excoriating; the state of being excoriated. Also *fig.* **2.** An excoriated place; a sore 1540.

2. He had a grievous e. behind, with riding post 1751.

Excorticate (ekskǭ·ɹtikeᵗt), *v.* 1600. [– *excorticat-*, pa. ppl. stem of late L. *excorticare*, f. *ex-* EX-[1] + *cortex, cortic-* bark, shell; see -ATE[3]. Cf. Fr. *excortiquer*.] *trans.* To pull or strip off the bark or shell from. Also *fig.* Hence **Exco:rtica·tion.**

†Excreation. 1556. [– L. *ex(s)creatio* hawking or coughing up, f. *ex(s)creat-*, pa. ppl. stem of *ex(s)creare*, f. *ex-* EX-[1] + *screare* hawk, hem; see -ION.] The action of coughing or spitting out; expectoration –1620.

Excrement[1] (e·kskrĭmĕnt). 1533. [– Fr. *excrément* or L. *excrementum*, f. *excre-*, pa. ppl. base of *excernere*, f. *ex-* EX-[1] + *cernere* sift; see -MENT.] **†1.** That which remains after sifting; the lees, refuse –1698. **2.** *Phys.* 'That which is cast out of the body by any of the natural emunctories' (*Syd. Soc. Lex.*); *esp.* the alvine fæces 1533. Also *fig.*

†E·xcrement[2]. 1549. [– L. *excrementum*, f. *excrescere* grow out; see EXCRESCE, -MENT.] **1.** That which grows out or forth; an outgrowth. Also *fig.* –1705. **2.** *abstr.* Growth, augmentation –1609.

1. It will please his Grace..to dallie with my e., with my mustachio *L.L.L.* v. i. 109.

Excremental (ekskrĭme·ntăl), *a.*[1] 1574. [f. EXCREMENT[1] + -AL[1].] **†1.** Pertaining to, or consisting of, dregs or refuse matter –1662. **2.** = EXCREMENTITIOUS 2. 1574.

Excreme·ntal, *a.*[2] *rare.* 1644. [f. EXCREMENT[2] + -AL[1].] Of the nature of an outgrowth or excrescence –1656.

Her whitenesse is but an excrementall whitenesse MILT.

Excrementitial (ekskrimenti·ʃăl), *a.* 1620. [f. as next + -AL[1]. Cf. Fr. *excrémentitiel*.] = next.

Excrementitious (ekskrimenti·ʃəs), *a.* 1586. [f. EXCREMENT[1] + -ITIOUS.] **†1.** Of the nature of dregs or refuse matter –1661. **2.** Of the nature of, pertaining to, or arising from excrement 1586. So **†Excreme·ntuous** *a.*

†Excreme·ntive, *a.* [f. EXCREMENT[1] + -IVE.] Fitted to carry off or discharge excrement. FELTHAM.

†Excreme·ntize, *v.* 1670. [f. as prec. + -IZE.] *intr.* To void excrements.

†Excre·sce, -crea·se, *v.* 1570. [– L. *excrescere*, f. *ex-* EX-[1] + *crescere* grow.] *intr.* To grow out or forth; to constitute an excrescence –1691.

Excrescence (ekskre·sĕns). 1533. [– L. *excrescentia*, f. *excrescent-*, pr. ppl. stem of *excrescere* grow out; see prec., -ENCE.] **1.** †The action of growing out or forth. Also, abnormal increase. –1752. **b.** Exuberance (now *rare*). 1629. **2.** A natural outgrowth or appendage 1633. **3.** An abnormal, morbid, or disfiguring outgrowth. Also *transf.* and *fig.* 1548.

1. The e. of Insects HALE. **b.** Excrescences of joy JER. TAYLOR. **3.** Tumours, wens, and preternatural excrescences BP. BERKELEY. So **Excre·scency,** excrescent state or condition; excrescence.

Excrescent (ekskre·sĕnt), *a.* 1609. [– L. *excrescens, -ent-*; see prec., -ENT.] **†1.** That grows out –1843. **2.** Growing abnormally; constituting an excrescence; redundant 1633. **3.** *Gram.* Of a sound in a word: Due only to euphony, and of no etymological value 1868.

2. We pare off such e. blemishes that the body may be perfect T. ADAMS. The e., or the superinduced population 1832. So **Excresce·ntial** *a.* (in sense 2).

†Excre·ssion. 1610. [A non-etymological formation (for EXCRETION[2]) on L. *excrescere*.] An outgrowth; = EXCRETION[2] –1647.

‖**Excreta** (ekskrī·tă). 1857. [L., subst. use of n. pl. of *excretus*, pa. pple. of *excernere* EXCRETE.] Excreted matters; now *esp.* the fæces and urine.

Excrete (ekskrī·t), *v.* 1620. [– *excret-*, pa. ppl. stem of L. *excernere*; see EXCREMENT[1].] **1.** *trans.* To separate and expel from the system; to discharge 1668. Also *absol.* **†2.** Of drugs, etc.: To cause the excretion of –1651.

1. Certain plants e. sweet juice DARWIN. **2.** They loose the belly and e. out choler VENNER. Hence **Excre·tive** *a.* having the power of excreting or promoting excretion.

Excretin (ekskrī·tin). Also **-ine.** 1854. [f. as prec. + -IN[1].] *Chem.* A crystalline body, $C_{20}H_{36}O$, obtained by exhausting fresh excrements with boiling alcohol.

Excretion[1] (ekskrī·ʃən). 1605. [– Fr. *excrétion* or L. *excretio*, f. *excret-*; see EXCRETE, -ION.] **1.** The action or process of excreting. **2.** *concr.* That which is separated and ejected from the body 1630.

1. E. of urine RAY, of the Blood 1732.

†Excre·tion[2]. 1612. [– late L. *excretio*, f. *excret-*, pa. ppl. stem of *excrescere*; see EXCRESCE, -ION.] = EXCREMENT[2], EXCRESCENCE. Also *fig.* –1725.

Excretolic (ekskrĭtǫ·lik), *a.* 1867. [f. EXCRET-IN + -OL + -IC.] *Chem.* In *Excretolic acid*: a fatty acid obtained from the alcoholic extract of human excrements.

Excretory (ekskrī·təri, e·kskrĭtəri). 1681. [f. EXCRETE *v.* + -ORY[2,1].]

A. *adj.* Having the function of excreting; pertaining to excretion.

B. *sb.* An excretory vessel or duct 1715.

†Excri·minate, *v. rare.* 1661. [f. EX- + contemp. CRIMINATE, or its source, L. *criminari, -are*.] *trans.* To clear from an imputation –1796.

Excruciate (ekskrū·ʃi,eᵗt), *v.* 1570. [– *excruciat-*, pa. ppl. stem of L. *excruciare*, f. *ex-* EX-[1] + *cruciare* torment, f. *crux, cruc-* cross; see -ATE[3].] To subject to torture, put on the rack; hence, to cause intense pain or anguish to (often *hyperbolical*).

They..by pining and excruciating their bodies, liue in hell here on earth NASHE. To e. the mind with cares 1655. Hence **Excru·ciable** *a.* liable to, or deserving of, torment. **†Excru·ciate** *ppl. a.* excruciated; excruciating. **Excrucia·tion,** the action of causing or the state of suffering extreme pain.

Excruciating (ekskrū·ʃi,eᵗtiŋ), *ppl. a.* 1664. [f. prec. + -ING[2].] That excruciates or causes extreme pain or anguish; agonizing. Often *hyperbolical.*

E. deaths 1833. An e. chorus 1876. Hence **Excru·ciatingly** *adv.*

Excubant (e·kskiubănt), *a.* [– *excubant-*, pr. ppl. stem of L. *excubare* lie out on guard, f. *ex-* EX-[1] + *cubare* lie down; see -ANT.] Keeping watch. PEACOCK. So **†Excuba·tion,** the action of keeping guard. (Dicts.) **†Excu·bitor,** a sentinel. G. WHITE.

Exculpate (e·kskŏlpeᵗt, ekskɒ·lpeᵗt), *v.* 1656. [– *exculpat-*, pa ppl. stem of med. L. *exculpare*, f. *ex-* EX-[1] + L. *culpa* blame; see -ATE[3].] **1.** *trans.* To free from blame; to clear *from* an accusation or blame. **2.** Of things: **†a.** To justify 1706. **b.** To furnish ground for exculpating 1783.

1. The latter stood exculpated on both charges GROTE. **2. b.** Evidence, which may..tend to..e. every person BURKE. Hence **Excu·lpable** *a.* capable of being exculpated (*rare*). **Excu·lpate** *ppl. a.* declared guiltless. **Exculpa·tion,** the action of exculpating from blame, or from a crime; that which exculpates; an excuse, a vindication. **Excu·lpative, Excu·lpatory** *adjs.* adapted or intended to e.

†Excur (eks,kɒ̄·ɹ), *v. rare.* 1656. [– L. *excurrere* run out, f. *ex-* EX-[1] + *currere* run.] *intr.* To go out or forth; to digress; to go to an extreme –1672.

Excurrent (ekskɒ·rĕnt), *a.* 1826. [– *excurrent-*, pr. ppl. stem of L. *excurrere*; see prec., -ENT.] **1.** That runs out or forth. **2.** Affording an exit 1854. **3.** *Bot.* **a.** (See quot.) 1835. **b.** Projecting beyond the tip or margin, as when the midrib of a leaf is continued beyond the apex 1847.

1. The residue..is carried out by the e. water 1887. **3. a.** Excurrent; in which the axis remains always in the centre, all the other parts being regularly disposed round it; as the stem of abies LINDLEY.

Excurse (ekskɔ̄·ɹs), *v.* 1748. [– L. *excurs-*; see next.] **1.** *intr.* To run off, wander, digress. **2.** To make, or go upon, an excursion 1775. **3.** To journey through. (Dicts.)

Excursion (ekskɔ̄·ɹʃən). 1574. [– L. *excursio*, f. *excurs-*, pa. ppl. stem of *excurrere*; see EXCUR, -ION.] †**1.** The action of running out or forth; escape from bounds; hence formerly *concr.*: Anything that runs out or projects –1852. †**2.** *fig.* An outburst; a sally (of wit); an escapade –1793. †**3.** *Mil.* A sally, sortie, raid –1701. **4.** A journey from any place with the intention of returning to it. Also *fig.* 1665. **b.** *transf.* in *Physics*, etc.: One movement of any body or particle in oscillating or alternating motion; the length of such a movement 1799. **5.** *spec.* A journey for pleasure or health. Now often: A pleasure-trip taken by a number of persons. 1779. **6.** Deviation from a definite path or course; †a digression 1574. **7.** *attrib.* (sense 5) as in *e.-train*, etc. 1850.

1. What roaring flooddes, what e. of riuers 1579. **4.** A long aëronautic e. 1816. *fig.* An e. into the historical domain BRYCE. **5.** A delightful e. on the lake 1832. **6.** Pardon this long e. on this subject BAXTER.

Hence **Excu·rsion** *v. intr.* to make, or go on, an e. **Excu·rsional** *a.* of or pertaining to an e. †**Excu·rsioner**, **Excu·rsionist**, one who goes on an e.; one who travels by an e.-train; also (*colloq.*) an e.-agent. **Excu·rsionize** *v. intr.* to make, or go on, an e.

Excursive (ekskɔ̄·ɹsiv), *a.* 1673. [f. as prec. + -IVE, perh. after *discursive.*] **1.** Of the nature of an excursion. Of reading, etc.: Desultory. **2.** Capable of, or addicted to, excursions; also, digressive 1744.

1. Johnson's e. reading SOUTHEY. **2.** An intelligence..e., vigorous, and diligent JOHNSON. E. black cattle SCOTT. Hence **Excu·rsive-ly** *adv.*, **-ness.**

Excursus (ekskɔ̄·ɹsɒs). Pl. **excursus,** (now usually) **excursuses.** 1803. [– L. *excursus*, f. *excurs-*; see prec.] **1.** A dissertation appended to a work, in which some point is discussed at length. **2.** A digression 1845.

Excurvation (ekskɒɹvēⁱ·ʃən). 1877. [f. EX-¹ + CURVATION.] A curving or bending outwards.

Excurved (ekskɔ̄·ɹvd), *ppl. a.* 1884. [f. EX-¹ + CURVED.] Curved outwards, as antennæ.

Excusable (ekskiū·zăb'l), *a.* ME. [– (O)Fr. *excusable* – L. *excusabilis*; see EXCUSE *v.*, -ABLE.] That may be excused; deserving to be acquitted; admitting of palliation.

The excuseablest kind of pagans HOWELL. An e. curiosity LYTTON. Hence **Excu·sableness. Excu·sably** *adv.*

Excusal (ekskiū·zăl). Now *rare.* 1584. [f. EXCUSE *v.* + -AL¹ 2; cf. *refusal.*] The act or fact of excusing.

†**Excusa·tion.** ME. [– OFr. *excusation*, f. L. *excusatio*, f. *excusat-*, pa. ppl. stem of *excusare*; see EXCUSE *v.* -ION.] **1.** The action of excusing or defending –1677. **2.** Release from a duty, obligation, etc. –1540. **3.** = EXCUSE *sb.* 2, 3. –1662.

Excuse (ekskiū·s), *sb.* ME. [– (O)Fr. *excuse*, f. *excuser*; see next.] **1.** The action of excusing; justification, indulgence; pardon; release. **2.** That which is offered as a reason for being excused; *occas.*, a (mere) pretext 1500. **3.** That which serves to excuse, or to extenuate (a fault or offence); *esp.* in phr. *without e.* 1494.

1. Hence with denial vain and coy e. MILT. *Lycidas* 18. He pray'd e. for mirth broke short SCOTT. **2.** A bad e. is better, they say, then none at all GOSSON. **3.** My Nephewes trespasse..hath the e. of youth SHAKS. Hence **Excu·seless** *a.* without e.

Excuse (ekskiū·z), *v.* [ME. *escuse* (seeES-), *excuse* – OFr. *escuser* (mod. *excuser*) – L. *excusare* free from blame, f. *ex-* EX-¹ + *causa* accusation.]

I. 1. *trans.* To offer an apology for (a person); to seek to extenuate (a fault). Also *absol.* †**2.** To maintain the innocence of (a person); to justify (an action) –1696. **3.** To obtain exemption or release for ME.; †to decline with apologies –1754. †**4.** To screen, exempt, –1711. **5.** To serve as an exculpation for 1538. **b.** In *pass.*: To be held blameless ME.

1. To e. a step, which it is not possible to justify 1793. **3.** Clarence e. me to the King my Brother 3 *Hen. VI*, v. v. 46. **4.** Faults he took upon him to e. others STEELE. **5.** The wife's presence will not e. the husband ADDISON.

II. 1. To accept a plea in exculpation of; to judge indulgently; to overlook, condone ME. **2.** To free from a task, obligation, etc.; to dispense from payment, etc. ME. **3.** 'To remit; not to exact' (J.) 1646.

1. He is totally Excused, for the reason next before alledged HOBBES. E. my glove, Thomas SHERIDAN. Phr. *E. me* (colloq.): used parenthetically to carry off a strong expression, to indicate politely a difference of opinion, in addressing a stranger, or in interrupting the speech of another. **2.** He was excused the entrance-fee 1894. **3.** I beg you to e. my waiting on you for a little while 1726. Hence **E·xcusator**, an excuser; *esp.* a person officially authorized to present an excuse. **Excu·satory** *a.* tending, or intended, to e.; apologetic. **Excu·ser**, one who excuses; one who extenuates (a fault).

†**Excu·ss**, *v.* 1570. [– *excuss-*, pa. ppl. stem of L. *excutere*, f. *ex-* EX-¹ + *quatere* shake.] **1.** *trans.* To shake off, get rid of –1668. **2.** To shake out; hence, to discuss –1726. **3.** *Mod. Civ. Law.* To seize, take in execution 1726.

†**Excu·ssion.** 1607. [– L. *excussio*; f. as prec.; see -ION.] **1.** The action of shaking off or getting rid of –1698. **2.** *Mod. Civ. Law.* Seizure of goods for debt, etc. –1726.

Ex div., abbrev. *Ex dividend*: see EX prep. 2.

Exeat (e·ksiˌæt). 1485. [L.; = 'let (him) go out'; see EXIT.]

‖**A.** In L. use as vb. A stage direction; = later EXIT. (So also **E·xeant,** 'let (them) go out; = later EXEUNT.)

B. *sb.* **1.** A permission to leave the diocese, granted to a priest by the bishop 1730. **2.** A permission for temporary absence, as in colleges, religious houses, etc. 1727.

Execrable (e·ksĭkrăb'l), *a.* ME. [– (O)Fr. *exécrable* – L. *execrabilis* (in act. and pass. senses), f. *ex(s)ecrari*; see next. -ABLE.] †**1.** Expressing or involving a curse; hence, of an imprecation: Fearful –1630. **2.** Deserving to be execrated; detestable; †accursed; †horrifying. Often *hyperbolical.* 1490.

2. That e. Fraternity of Blasphemers BP. BERKELEY. The e. image of this scene 1805. What e. weather 1867. Hence **E·xecrableness. E·xecrably** *adv.*

Execrate (e·ksĭkreⁱt), *v.* 1561. [– *execrat-*, pa. ppl. stem of L. *ex(s)ecrari* curse, f. *ex-* EX-¹ + *sacrare* devote religiously, f. *sacer, sacr-* religiously set apart; see SACRED, -ATE³.] †**1.** *trans.* To pronounce a curse upon; to declare accursed (*rare*) –1691. **2.** To imprecate evil upon; to abhor, detest 1561. **3.** *intr.* To utter curses 1786.

2. To e. the idolatrie of the Chaldeans 1561, their lot COWPER. So **Execra·tion** late ME. **E·xecrative** *a.* of or pertaining to execration; prone to execration; characterized by an execration. **E·xecratively** *adv.* **E·xecrator. E·xecratory** *a.* of or pertaining to execration; of the nature of an execration; †*sb.* 'a formulary of execrations' (Todd.).

Exect, etc.: see EXSECT, etc.

Executant (ekse·kiŭtănt). 1858. [– Fr. *exécutant*, pr. pple. of *exécuter*; see next, -ANT.]

A. *adj.* That performs (music) 1865.

B. *sb.* Any one who executes, or performs; *esp.* a musical performer. Hence **Exe·cutancy,** e. power.

Execute (e·ksĭkiut), *v.* ME. [– (O)Fr. *exécuter* – med.L. *executare*, f. *ex(s)ecut-*, pa. ppl. stem of L. *ex(s)equi* follow up, carry out, pursue judicially, punish, f. *ex-* EX-¹ + *sequi* follow.] **1.** To follow out, carry into effect; to give effect to. **2.** To carry out, perform (a plan, work, movement, etc.) 1477; †to celebrate (religious service, etc.) –1737. **3.** *Law.* To go through the formalities necessary to the validity of. Hence, to complete and give validity to, as by signing, sealing, etc. 1737. **4.** To fulfil, discharge (an office, a function). Also formerly †*absol.* or *intr.* ME. **5.** To carry out the design of (a work of art or skill); to perform (a piece of music) 1735. **6.** To put to death in pursuance of a sentence; hence, †to put to death, kill (*rare*) 1483.

1. To e. the biddyng of the Kyng LYDG., his enuye CAXTON, a Testament 1641, the sentence of the law PRESCOTT. **2.** Moreau executed a change of front ALISON. **3.** To e. a treaty of peace WELLINGTON, a mortgage CRUMP. **5.** I saw executed in marble the Mercury and the Hope B'NESS BUNSEN. **6.** Sir Thomas Blonte and all the other prysoners were executed HALL.

Hence **Exe·cutable** *a.* that can be executed, performed, or carried out. †**E·xecute** *ppl. a.* executed. **E·xecuter** = EXECUTOR 1.

Execution (eksĭkiū·ʃən). ME. [– (O)Fr. *exécution* – L. *ex(s)ecutio*, f. *ex(s)ecut-*; see prec., -ION.] **1.** The action of carrying out or carrying into effect; accomplishment; †the giving effect to. –1652. **2.** The manner in which a plan, piece of music, etc. is executed 1534. **b.** Excellence of execution 1795. **3.** The performance or fulfilment of (an office or function) 1576. †**4.** Executive ability –1601. **5.** Effective action, or its result. Also *fig.* 1588. **6.** *Law.* The due performance of all formalities, as signing, sealing, etc., necessary to give validity to a legal instrument 1776. **7.** The enforcement by the sheriff of the judgement of a court 1503. **b.** Short for *Writ of Execution* 1777. **8.** The infliction of (*esp.* capital) punishment in pursuance of a judicial sentence ME. **9.** 'The ravaging and destroying of a country that refuses to pay contribution' (Smyth). Also *military e.* 1618.

1. His intention and e. are not very near each other JOHNSON. To put the law in e. GOLDSM. **4.** He was a man of much valour and e. HOLLAND. **5.** The shot..did great e. PRESCOTT. **7.** *Writ of e.*: the process under which the sheriff is commanded to execute a judgement. **8.** The small Remainder of his Ears, left after his first E. PRYNNE.

Execu:tionee·ring, *ppl. a.* [f. prec. + -EER + -ING².] That executes (criminals). LAMB.

Executioner (eksĭkiū·ʃənəɹ). 1561. [f. EXECUTION + -ER¹.] **1.** One who executes (a plan, law, justice, †the duties of an office, etc.) 1587. **2.** *gen.* One who carries out a (capital) sentence 1561. **3.** *transf.* and *fig.* One who puts another to death 1594.

Executive (ekse·kiŭtiv). 1646. [– med.L. *executivus*, f. *execut-*; see EXECUTE, -IVE. Cf. (O)Fr. *exécutif*, revived in late XVIII.]

A. *adj.* †**1.** Operative. **2.** †Active, or (U.S.) skilful, in execution 1708. **3.** Pertaining to execution; having the function of executing; *esp.* as concerned with carrying out the laws, decrees, and judicial sentences; opp. to 'judicial' and 'legislative' 1649. **4.** Of or pertaining to the EXECUTIVE (see B. 1) 1811.

3. The e. government could undertake nothing great without the support of the Commons MACAULAY. Hence **Exe·cutively** *adv.*

B. *sb.* **1.** That branch of the government which is charged with the execution of the laws 1790. **b.** The person or persons in whom the supreme executive magistracy of a country or state is vested. Chiefly U.S. 1787. **2.** *transf.* Any administrative body 1868.

1. b. That a national e. to consist of a single person be instituted *Jrnl. Fed. Conv.* (1819) 89.

Executor (eks-, egze·kiŭtəɹ in sense 3, e·ksĭkiutəɹ in sense 1). ME. [– AFr. *execut(o)ur* – L. *executor*, f. as prec.; see -OR 2.] **1.** One who executes or carries out; an agent, doer. Now *rare* exc. in *Law.* †**2.** = EXECUTIONER –1614. **3.** A person appointed by a testator to execute or give effect to his will after his decease. Also *transf.* and *fig.* ME.

1. Such basenes Had neuer like E. *Temp.* III. i. 13. **2.** *Hen. V*, I. ii. 203. Hence **Exe:cuto·rial** *a.* of or pertaining to an e.; executive. **Exe·cutorship.**

Executory (ekse·kiŭtəri). 1483. [– late and med.L. *executorius*, f. *executor*; see prec., -ORY².]

A. *adj.* **1.** Of or pertaining to the execution of a command, decree, law, etc. 1658. **b.** Of a law, etc: In force, operative 1483. **2.** = EXECUTIVE A. 3. 1649. **3.** *Law.* Designed to take or capable of taking effect only at a future time. Opp. to *Executed.* 1592.

1. The question is only e., not declarative 1658. **2.** Mere e. agents of the British Government 1829. **3.** An e. contract BLACKSTONE, trust J. POWELL.

B. *sb.* †**1.** = EXECUTORSHIP (*rare*) 1496. **2.** An executive body (see EXECUTIVE B. 2) 1868.

Executrix (ekse·kiŭtriks). Pl. **-trixes** (triksėz), **-trices** (trisīz). 1502. [– late and med.L. *executrix*, f. *executor*; see -TRIX.] A woman appointed by a testator to execute his will. vars. **Exe·cutress,** †**Exe·cutrice.**

†**Exe·de**, *v.* 1669. [– L. *exedere*, f. *ex-* Ex-[1] + *edere* eat.] *trans.* To eat out, corrode –1754. So **E·xedent** *a.* 'eating up; consuming; ulcerating' (*Syd. Soc. Lex.*).

‖**Exedra, exhedra** (e·ksĭdră, eksī·dră). Pl. **-dræ**. 1706. [L. *exedra* – Gr. ἐξέδρα, f. ἐξ Ex-[2] + ἕδρα place to sit.] **1.** *Ancient Archit.* The portico of the palæstra or gymnasium in which disputations were held; also, in private houses, the pastas or vestibule. **2.** The APSIS, or bishop's throne 1725. **3.** A porch or chapel, or a recess in a wall, which projects 1850.

Exegesis (eksĭdʒī·sis). 1619. [– Gr. ἐξήγησις, f. ἐξηγεῖσθαι interpret, f. ἐξ Ex-[2] + ἡγεῖσθαι guide.] **1.** Explanation, exposition; *esp.* the interpretation of the Scriptures 1823. †**2.** *Algebra.* Extraction of roots out of adfected equations –1796.

Exegete (e·ksĭdʒīt). 1730. [– Gr. ἐξηγητής, f. as prec.] An expounder, interpreter. var. **Exege·tist.**

Exegetic (eksĭdʒe·tik). 1655. [– Gr. ἐξηγητικός; see prec., -IC.]

A. *adj.* Of, pertaining to, or of the nature of, EXEGESIS or interpretation; *esp.* of the Scriptures; expository. Const. *of.*

B. *sb.* **1.** = Gr. ἐξηγητική (τέχνη), the art of interpretation 1838. **2.** *pl.* (after Gr. τὰ ἐξηγητικά) that branch of theology which deals with the interpretation of the Scriptures 1838.

Hence **Exege·tical** *a.* = EXEGETIC A. **Exege·tically** *adv.*

Exembryonate (ekse·mbri,ŏnĕt), *a.* 1866. [f. Ex-[2] + EMBRYON + -ATE[2].] *Bot.* Not containing an embryo, as cryptogams.

Exemplar (egze·mplăɹ), *sb.* [Late ME. *exemplaire* – (O)Fr. *exemplaire* – late L. *exemplarium*, f. L. *exemplum* EXAMPLE; see -AR[2].] **1.** A model for imitation; an example. Formerly also, †a SAMPLER. **2.** An archetype whether real or ideal 1618. **3.** An instance; a parallel 1677. **4.** A type, specimen 1656. **5.** A copy of a book, etc. 1539.

1. Intimate converse with the great E. 1744. **4.** Sisyphus, the legendary e. of cunning THIRLWALL.

†**Exe·mplar**, *a.* 1475. [– late L. *exemplaris*, perh. through (O)Fr. *exemplaire* adj.; see prec., -AR[1].] = EXEMPLARY *a.*, in various senses –1739.

Exemplarily (see EXEMPLARY), *adv.* 1611. [f. EXEMPLARY *a.* + -LY[2].] †**1.** In senses of EXEMPLARY 2, 4 –1703. **2.** By way of deterrent example 1627. **3.** So as to deserve imitation 1611.

2. Some he punisheth e. in the world HAKEWILL. **3.** E. religious DONNE. So **Exemplariness.**

Exemplarity (egzemplæ·rĭti), 1619. [– med.L. *exemplaritas*, f. late L. *exemplaris*; see next, -ITY.] **1.** Exemplariness. †**2.** The quality or fact of acting as a deterrent example –1660.

Exemplary (egze·-, e·gzemplări). 1589. [– late L. *exemplaris*, f. L. *exemplum* EXAMPLE; see -ARY[2].]

A. *adj.* †**1.** Of or pertaining to an example or examples –1822. **2.** That may serve as a type or an illustration 1614. **3.** Fit to serve as a deterrent 1603. **4.** Serving or fit to serve as an example or pattern 1589.

2. The two Cato's are e. instances 1683. **3.** E. severity 1809, damages BRYCE. **4.** An e. parish priest MACAULAY.

†**B.** *adv.* In an e. manner or degree –1772.

†**Exemplary**, *sb.* ME. [– late L. *exemplarium*; see EXEMPLAR *sb.*, -ARY[1].] **1.** A type; a typical instance; an example –1583. **2.** A copy of a book; a transcript (of a writing) –1706.

Exemplification (egze:mplifikē[i]·ʃən). 1542. [– AFr. *exemplification* and med.L. *exemplificatio*, f. *exemplificat-*, pa. ppl. stem of *exemplificare*; see EXEMPLIFY, -FICATION.] **1.** The action of exemplifying; showing or illustrating by example 1548. **2.** That which exemplifies; an illustration; an example 1582. **3.** An attested copy or transcript of a record, etc. 1542.

Exemplificative (egze·mplifikătiv), *a.* 1826. [f. as prec. + -IVE.] Tending to exemplify; furnishing an example.

Exemplify (egze·mplifəi), *v.* ME. [– med.L. *exemplificare*, f. L. *exemplum* EXAMPLE; see -FY. Cf. OFr. *exemplifier*.] †**1.** *trans.* To instruct by example –1513. †**2.** To make an example of –1642. †**3.** To set an example –1673. †**4.** To fashion after an example –1686. †**5.** To adduce as an example –1794. **6. a.** To illustrate by examples; to be or serve as an example of. (The current sense.) ME. **b.** *intr.* To quote instances in illustration 1582. **7.** †To copy –1709; to make an attested copy of (a legal document) under seal 1523.

6. a. The rules I sent you concerning the hyperbola I cannot well e. BARROW. The roads to the Highlands e. the correctness of this remark MCCULLOCH.

Hence **Exe:mplifi·able** *a.* that may be exemplified. **Exe·mplifier.**

Exempt (egze·mpt). ME. [– L. *exemptus*, pa. pple. of *eximere* take out, deliver, free, f. *ex-* Ex-[1] + *emere* take. Cf. (O)Fr. *exempt.*]

A. *pple.* and *adj.* **1.** = *exempted* pa. pple. and ppl. adj. (see EXEMPT *v.*). **2.** Not subject to superior authority; privileged, as an *exempt monastery*. Now *Hist.* 1460. **3.** Freed *from*; not exposed or subject to ME. **4.** Clear, free *from* (a defect, stain, etc.) 1586.

1. Blessed Sleep! in which e. From our tired Selves long hours we lie HOLLAND. **3.** To live e. From Heav'ns high jurisdiction MILT. *P. L.* II. 318. E. from the frost EVELYN, Passions STEELE, public concerns and duties 1794, from serving in the militia 1853. **4.** From custom's evil taint e. and pure SHELLEY.

B. *sb.* **1.** An exempted person 1846. **2.** *Eccl.* A person or establishment not subject to episcopal jurisdiction. Now *Hist.* 1532. **3.** †A sub-officer of cavalry –1739; also, = EXON, q.v. 1700.

Exempt (egze·m[p]t), *v. Pa. pple.* **exempt.** ME. [f. as prec., orig. in pa. ppl. form (see -ED[1] 2). Cf. (O)Fr *exempter*.] †**1.** *trans.* To take out or away; to remove; to single out –1648. †**2.** To omit; to except –1731. †**3.** To debar *from* something –1689. **4.** To grant to (a person, etc.) immunity or freedom from a liability to which others are subject ME.

2. Thy worth and skill exempts thee from the throng MILT. *Sonn.* xiii. **4.** To e. from paying tribute 1573, from the Iurisdiction of the Bishop FULLER, from the general law 1829, military service LANE, the penalties of their crimes FROUDE. So **Exe·mptile** *a.* that may be taken out. †**Exempti·tious** *a.* separable. **Exe·mptive** *a.* tending to procure exemption.

Exemption (egze·m[p]ʃən). ME. [– (O)Fr. *exemption* or L. *exemptio*, f. *exempt-*, pa. ppl. stem of *eximere*; see EXEMPT *a.*, -ION.] **1.** The action of exempting; the state of being exempted. **2.** Immunity from a liability, obligation, penalty, law, or authority; freedom ME. **3.** Freedom, immunity *from* a defect, disadvantage, or weakness 1662.

2. We take Liberty, for an e. from Lawes HOBBES. An e. from punishment already incurred is a pardon BENTHAM. **3.** E. from humane frailty HEYLIN.

‖**Exence·phalus** (eks,ense·fălŏs). *Pl.* **-li.** 1884. [mod.L., f. Gr. ἐξ out + ἐγκέφαλος brain.] A term for 'a monstrosity in which the brain lies wholly or chiefly outside the cranial cavity at the back of a very flattened head' (*Syd. Soc. Lex.*).

Exenterate (ekse·ntĕrē[i]t), *v.* 1607. [– *exenterat-*, pa. ppl. stem of L. *exenterare*, f. after Gr. ἐξεντερίζειν, f. ἐξ Ex-[2] + ἔντερον intestine; see -ATE[3].] To take out the entrails or internal parts of; to eviscerate, disembowel. Now only *fig.* or *transf.*

transf. They unlawfully e. and eate out the bowels of poore mens purses 1612. Hence **Exe·nterate** *ppl. a.* exenterated. **Exentera·tion**, the action or process of exenterating.

Exenteritis (eks,entĕrəi·tis). 1847. [f. Ex-[2] + ENTERITIS.] *Path.* Inflammation of the outer coat of the intestines.

Exequatur (eksĭkwē[i]·tŏɹ). 1788. [L., 'let him perform', 3rd. pers. sing. pres. subj. of *exequi* EXECUTE.] **1.** An official recognition of a consul or commercial agent by the government of the country to which he is accredited, authorizing him to exercise his functions. **2.** An authorization granted by a sovereign for the publication of Papal bulls, etc. Hence, the necessity of such authorization. 1859.

Exequy (e·ksĭkwi), now always in pl. **exequies** (e·ksĭkwiz). ME. [– OFr. *exequies* – L. acc. *exsequias*, nom. *-iæ* funeral procession or ceremonies, f. *exsequi* follow after, accompany.] Funeral rites; *occas.*, funeral train, bier. Formerly *sing.*; with *pl.* in sense 'funerals'.

The E. of Joan Queen of Spayne WOOD. His exequies were solemnized with great pomp 1771. Hence **Exe·quial**, †**Exe·quious** *adjs.* of or pertaining to a funeral.

†**Exerce**, *v.* Chiefly *Sc.* ME. [– (O)Fr. *exercer* – L. *exercēre*; see next.] **1.** *trans.* To EXERCISE –1578. **2.** To employ; to discipline, train –1596. So †**Exe·rcent** *a.* exercising, practising.

Exercise (e·ksəɹsəiz), *sb.* ME. [– (O)Fr. *exercice* – L. *exercitium*, f. *exercēre* keep busy or at work, practise, etc.] **1.** The action of exercising; the condition of being in active operation. †**2.** Habitual employment –1738. **3.** The practice (of virtues or vices, or of any particular kind of conduct); the execution of (functions) ME. **4.** The performance of rites and ceremonies, worship, etc. 1658. †**5.** The training or drilling of scholars, troops, etc. –1819. **6.** Practice for the sake of training or improvement, either bodily, mental, or spiritual; also, a painful mental struggle (now *rare*) ME. **7.** Bodily exertion with a view to its effect on the subject, *esp.* in the way of health ME. **8.** That which is done for the sake of attaining proficiency, for training body or mind, or as a test of proficiency or skill 1533. **9.** A religious observance; an act of worship; a discourse 1560. **10.** A formal act or ceremony on some special occasion (*U.S.*) 1863.

1. Their conversation is merely an e. of the tongue BP. BUTLER. The e. of the judge's discretion 1890. **3.** The e. of Trades HOBBES, of cruelty 1773. **4.** The E. of the Confession of Auxbourgh 1658. **5.** A Camp of e. 1819. **6.** An army of e. was assembled on the Gwalior frontier STOCQUELER. **7.** By e... the health of man is preserued ELYOT. Phr. *Horse-*, *open air*, *walking*, etc., *e.* **8.** The public exercises for a degree EMERSON. To prepare their lessons and exercises for the following day HEWLETT. attrib. *e. book.*

Exercise (e·ksəɹsəiz), *v.* ME. [f. prec. sb.] **1.** *trans.* To put in operation; to employ, apply, make use of. **2.** To employ habitually, practise (now only *refl.* and *pass.*) ME. †to till (the ground) –1697. **3.** To train by practice; to drill (soldiers, etc.); to put (the limbs, the body) through a course of movements for the sake of strength or health ME.; †to habituate –1607. **4.** To give employment to; to tax the attention, feelings, or powers of; *esp.* to harass, vex, worry 1538. **5.** To carry on, carry out, perform ME.; to fulfil (functions); to exert, possess (dominion, jurisdiction, force, etc.) 1590. **6.** *absol.* or *intr.* for *refl.* †**a.** To ply one's calling –1565. †**b.** To perform one's office *upon* –1703. **c.** To go through exercises; to drill 1606. **d.** To take exercise 1655. **7.** *intr.* To conduct or take part in a religious exercise; to expound Scripture. Now *Hist.* 1561.

1. That right of Punishing, which is exercised in every Common-wealth HOBBES. To e. a trust for sale 1891. **2.** A people exercised in arms GIBBON. **3.** To e. the body with some labour 1557. To e. all one's powers CARLYLE. **5.** To e. Heroic Games MILT., pasture GOLDSM., oppression JAS. MILL, an influence on politics SMILES. Hence **E·xerci:sable**, †**-ible** *a.* capable of being exercised; as, an office, power, right, etc. **E·xerciser**, one who or that which exercises; *esp.* an apparatus for exercising the limbs, etc.

Exercitation (egzə̄:ɹsitē[i]·ʃən). ME. [– L. *exercitatio*, f. *exercitat-*, pa. ppl. stem of *exercitare*, frequent. of *exercēre*; see EXERCISE *sb.*, -ION.] **1.** EXERCISE, in various senses; practice. **2.** An exercise or display of skill; *esp.* a written or spoken disquisition, essay, discourse 1632.

1. Asclepiades [held the soul to be] an e. of the senses FLORIO. **2.** The superb exercitations of Bossuet M. ARNOLD.

†**Exercite**, *sb.*[1] 1485. [– OFr. *exercite* – L. *exercitus*, f. *exercēre*; see EXERCE.] An army –1550.

†**Exe·rcite**, *sb.*[2] 1485. [– OFr. *exercite* exercise, f. *exerciter* – L. *exercitare*, frequent. of *exercēre*; see EXERCE.] = EXERCISE *sb.*, in various senses – 1533. So †**Exercite** *v. trans.* to exercise.

‖**Exercitor** (egzə·ɹsitǫɹ). 1850. [L., f. *exercēre*, pa. ppl. stem *exercit-*; see -OR 2.]

Rom. Law. The person entitled to the daily profits of a ship. Hence **Exercito·rian** *a.*

Exergue (e·ksɔ̄ɹg, egzɔ̄·ɹg). 1697. [– Fr. *exergue* (J. de Bie, 1636), – med.L. *exergum*, f. Gr. ἐξ outside + ἔργον work; prob. intended as a quasi-Gr. rendering of Fr. *hors-d'œuvre.*] *Numism.* A small space on the reverse of a coin or medal, below the principal device, for the date, engraver's initials, or the like. Also, what is there inscribed. Hence **Exe·rgual** *a.*

Exert (egzɔ̄·ɹt), *v.* 1660. [– *exert-*, pa. ppl. stem of L. *ex(s)erere* put forth, f. *ex-* Ex-[1] + *serere* bind, entwine, join.] †**1.** *trans.* To thrust forth; to push out or up; to emit –1708; to exhibit, reveal –1743. **2.** To bring into vigorous action; to exercise, bring to bear 1681. †**3.** To perform, practise –1757.

1. Apple Trees..e. themselves in air DRYDEN. **2.** I should have exerted every nerve for Mr. Laurens BURKE. All bodies are capable of exerting electrical attraction 1816. Phr. *To e. oneself*: to employ one's powers; to use efforts; to strive. Also †*intr.* (for *refl.*). Hence **Exe·rtive** *a.* tending to e. or rouse to action.

Exertion (egzɔ̄·ɹʃən). 1668. [f. prec. + -ION.] †**1.** The action of putting forth; manifestation –1796. **2.** The action or habit of exerting, exercising, or putting into operation. Const. *of.* 1677. **3.** The action of exerting oneself; effort 1777.

1. A proper e. of cheerfulness 1768. **2.** The full e. of one's faculties BURKE. A skilful e. of strength and address SCOTT. **3.** Unequal to the e. of pleading 1876. var. †**Exe·rtment** (*rare*).

Exes (e·ksėz). *pl. colloq.* 1865. [abbrev.] Expenses.

†**Exe·sion.** 1646. [– late L. *exesio*, f. *exes-*, pa. ppl. stem of L. *exedere*; see EXEDE, -ION.] The action of exeding –1684.

Exestuate, -ation, vars. of EXÆSTUATE, -ATION.

‖**Exeunt** (e·ksi,ɒnt), *v.* 1485. [L.; = 'they go out'; see EXIT.] A stage direction (*orig.* **Exeant**) = 'Here two or more actors leave the stage'. So in *Exeunt omnes* 'all go out'.

Exfetation (eksfitē[i]·ʃən). Also **-fœt-.** 1858. [f. Ex-[1] + L. *fetare* impregnate + -ATION.] *Med.* 'Imperfect fetation in some organ exterior to the uterus' (Hoblyn).

Exfoliate (eksfōᵘ·li,eⁱt), *v.* 1612. [– *exfoliat-*, pa. ppl. stem of late L. *exfoliare* strip of leaves, f. *ex-* Ex-[1] + L. *folium* leaf; see -ATE[3].] **1.** *trans.* **a.** *Path.* To cast off in the form of 'leaves' or scales. **b.** *Surg.* To remove the surface of by exfoliation. **2.** *intr.* To come off in layers or scales; to peel off 1676. **3.** *trans.* To unfold the leaves of; to open out 1808.

2. Down with a frozen heel; the bone exfoliating KANE. Before the blowpipe it [anhydrite] does not e. like gypsum DANA. Hence **Exfo:lia·tion,** the action or process of exfoliating; that which is exfoliated; a coat or layer in the stem of a tree. **Exfo·liative** *a.* capable of causing, or favourable to, exfoliation; *sb.* something that causes exfoliation.

Exh-. In words beginning with these letters, the *h* is usually silent. To avoid repetition the more frequent pronunciation is alone indicated.

†**Exhalate,** *v.* 1598. [– *exhalat-*, pa. ppl. stem of L. *exhalare*; see EXHALE *v.*[1], -ION.] **1.** *trans.* To evaporate; to produce by evaporation –1643. **2.** *intr.* = EXHALE *v.*[1] 2, 6. –1623.

Exhalation (eksălē[i]·ʃən). ME. [– L. *exhalatio*, f. as prec.; see -ION.] **1.** The action or process of exhaling, breathing forth, or throwing off in the form of a vapour; evaporation. Const. *of.* **2.** *concr.* That which is exhaled; a mist, vapour, etc.; an emanation or effluvium ME. **3.** A body of (usually enkindled) vapour; a meteor (*arch.*) 1561.

2. Nero's golden house had risen like an e., and like an e. it disappeared MERIVALE. Pulmonary and cutaneous exhalations 1869. **3.** The star of the shepherds was a meteoric e. FARRAR.

Exhale (egz-, eks,hē[i]·l), *v.*[1] ME. [– (O)Fr. *exhaler* – L. *exhalare*, f. *ex-* Ex-[1] + *halare* breathe.] **1.** *trans.* To breathe out; to send up (fumes, vapour, etc.); to give off in vapour. Also *fig.* 1628. **2.** *intr.* To pass off into the air; to be given off as vapour; to evaporate. Also *fig.* ME. **3.** *Phys.* and *Path.* Of animal fluids: To ooze through a membrane or blood-vessel. Also in *pass.* ME. **4.** *trans.* To draw up or drive off in vapour; to evaporate. Also *fig.* 1588. **5.** To breathe or blow forth from within. Also *fig.* 1589. **6.** *intr.* To make an expiration; opp. to INHALE. 1863.

1. Weight..exhaled by insensible Transpiration 1664. **2.** For ofte of it [the floode] exaleth myst impure ME. *fig.* His Hopes exhal'd in empty Smoke DRYDEN. **4.** Yon Light..is some Meteor that the Sun exhales *Rom. & Jul.* III. v. 13. **5.** I could not e. my wrath before his grace 1867.

Hence **Exha·lable** *a.* that can be exhaled or evaporated. **Exha·lant** *a.* that exhales; *sb.* an exhalant vessel or organ. **Exha·lement,** exhalation.

†**Exha·le,** *v.*[2] 1594. [f. Ex-[1] + HALE *v.*[1]] To drag out or draw forth or up –1647.

†**Exha·nce,** *v.* 1450. [alt. of ENHANCE, after words beginning with *ex-*.] = ENHANCE. –1667.

Exhaust (egzǭ·st), *sb.* 1848. [f. EXHAUST *v.*] The process or means of exhausting. **1. a.** *Steam-engine.* The exit of steam from the cylinder after propelling the piston; the passage through which it escapes; EDUCTION. **b.** The expulsion of combustion products from the cylinder of an internal-combustion engine, the products so expelled, the valve or pipe by which they escape 1896. **c.** The process of exhausting (a vessel) of air; the degree to which exhaustion is carried 1880. **2.** The production of an outward current of air by creating a partial vacuum; also, any apparatus for effecting this 1852.

attrib. and *Comb.* (chiefly in sense 1 a), as *e.-passage, -pipe, -valve*; also **e.-fan,** a fan for producing a current by creating a vacuum; **e. injector,** an injector for feeding a steam-boiler with water, worked by e. steam; **e.-port,** the opening in the slide-valve of a steam-engine for the escape of e. steam (= *e.-passage*); **-steam,** the waste steam discharged from the cylinder of a steam-engine.

Exhaust (egzǭ·st), *v.* 1533. [– *exhaust-*, pa. ppl. stem of L. *exhaurire*, f. *ex-* Ex-[1] + *haurire* draw (water), drain.] **1.** *trans.* To draw off or out (now only air); *lit.* and *fig.* 1540. **2.** To use up completely; to expend or account for all of 1533. **3.** To empty by drawing the contents off or out; to drain; to empty *of* 1614. Also *intr.* of steam. **4.** To draw out all that is essential or interesting in (a subject, etc.) 1704. **5.** To drain of strength, resources, etc.; to weary out, enfeeble greatly 1631.

2. Whatever relief was given..the same was soon exhausted BURKE. To e. all the possible combinations MILL. **3.** A tube which could be exhausted of air TYNDALL. **4.** To e. the history of the Roman Republic M. PATTISON. **5.** The Kingdome was much exhausted of men and mony GOUGE.

Hence †**Exhau·st** *pa. pple.* and *ppl. a.* exhausted. **Exhau·stedly** *adv.* **Exhau·ster,** one who, or that which, exhausts; *spec.* in *Gas-making*, a contrivance for pumping the gas in a continuous flow out of the retorts. **Exhau·stible** *a.* that can be exhausted; whence **Exhau:stibi·lity. Exhau·stingly** *adv.*

Exhaustion (egzǭ·stʃən). 1646. [– late L. *exhaustio*, f. as prec.; see -ION.] **1.** The action or process of exhausting; the condition of being exhausted. **b.** *spec.* (*Steam-engine*) The discharge of waste steam from the cylinder 1782. **2.** *Chem.* 'Applied to any process, such as percolation, whereby the active constituents of a drug [etc.] are removed in solution, leaving it exhausted' (*Syd. Soc. Lex.*). **3. a.** *gen.* A process of proof by exhausting all conceivable hypotheses, except one, relating to the question 1877. **b.** *Method of Exhaustions* (Math.): an application of **a.,** as in proving the equality of two magnitudes, by showing that if one is supposed to be greater or less than the other a *reductio ad absurdum* is involved 1685.

1. The e. of the air incumbent on the water BOYLE. The rapid sale and e. of a work KNOX. E...is an occasional cause of death after severe operations 1877. vars. †**Exhau·stment** (*rare*). †**Exhau·sture.**

Exhaustive (egzǭ·stiv), *a.* 1786. [f. EXHAUST *v.* + -IVE.] **1.** Tending to exhaust 1818. **2.** Characterized by exhausting; complete, comprehensive.

2. An e. survey GLADSTONE. Phr. *E. method* = EXHAUSTION 3 a. **Exhau·stive-ly** *adv.*, **-ness.**

Exhaustless (egzǭ·stlės), *a. poet.* and *rhet.* 1712. [f. EXHAUST *v.* + -LESS.] Inexhaustible.

Exhedra, var. of EXEDRA.

Exheredate (eks,he·rĭdeⁱt), *v.* Now *rare.* 1552. [– *exheredat-*, pa. ppl. stem of L. *exheredare*, f. *ex-* Ex-[1] + *heres, hered-* heir; see -ATE[3].] *trans.* To disinherit. Also *fig.* Hence **Exhereda·tion,** †**Exheredita·tion,** disherison.

Exhibit (egzi·bit), *sb.* 1626. [– L. *exhibitum*, n. sing. of pa. pple. of *exhibēre*; see next.] **1.** *Law.* **a.** Any writing identified in court, and marked by the Examiner accordingly. **b.** Any document (or object) produced in court and referred to and identified in written evidence. **2.** Anything exhibited or presented to view; *esp.* an object, or collection of objects, in an exhibition 1862. **3.** A showing, display 1654.

2. An e. in the Peruvian section 1876.

Exhibit (egzi·bit), *v.* 1490. [– *exhibit-*, pa. ppl. stem of L. *exhibēre*, f. *ex-* Ex-[1] + *habēre* hold.] †**1.** *trans.* To offer; to administer (an oath) –1657; †to furnish; hence to defray (expense) –1654; †*intr.* to provide maintenance; to give an exhibition –1868. **2.** *trans.* (*Med.*) To administer (a remedy, etc.) 1601. **3.** To submit for inspection or consideration; *esp.* to produce, put in (a document) in a court of law, to append as an exhibit to written evidence 1529. **4.** To expose to view; to show; *esp.* to show publicly for the purpose of amusement or instruction, or in a competition; *rarely*, to perform in public 1573.

2. To e. Scammony for a purgation P. HOLLAND. **3.** Accept this Scrowle..Which..we doe exhibite to your Maiestie 1 *Hen. VI*, III. i. 151. To e. a charge of high treason against the duke CLARENDON. **4.** To e. a solo on the violin 1845.

Hence †**Exhi·bit** *pa.pple.* exhibited. **Exhi·bitable** *a.* **Exhi·biter, -or** (now more usual).

Exhibition (eksibi·ʃən). ME. [– (O)Fr. *exhibition* – late L. *exhibitio*, f. as prec.; see -ION.] †**1.** Maintenance, support –1711. †**2.** A pension, salary; a gift –1741. **3.** An endowment for a term of years given to a student in a school, college, or university. Cf. BURSARY, SCHOLARSHIP. 1525. **4.** *Med.* The administration of a remedy 1785. **5.** The action of exhibiting, submitting for inspection, displaying, or holding up to view 1663; *concr.* something that is exhibited 1786. **6.** A public display (of works of art, manufactures, etc.); also, the place of the display 1761. **7.** The examination of the pupils of a school or college; an instance of this (*U.S.*) 1829.

5. An e. of presumption MRS. JAMESON. Phr. *To make an e. of oneself* (colloq.): to show oneself in an unfavourable aspect.

Hence **Exhibi·tional** *a.* of or pertaining to an e. **Exhibi·tioner,** one who holds an e. at a university; one who exhibits. **Exhibi·tionism,** indecent exposure of the person, esp. as a manifestation of sexual perversion; also *fig.* and *gen.* tendency towards display or extravagant behaviour; so **Exhibi·tionist.**

Exhibitive (egzi·bitiv), *a.* 1596. [orig. – mod. (theol.) L. *exhibitivus*, f. as prec.; see -IVE.] Having the property of exhibiting or showing forth. Const. *of.* Hence **Exhi·bitively** *adv.*

Exhibitory (egzi·bitəri). 1607. [– late and med.L. *exhibitorius*, f. as prec.; see -ORY[2].]

A. *adj.* Intended to exhibit or cause to be exhibited; of or pertaining to exhibition 1772.

†**B.** *sb.* A procedure with regard to the exhibition of remedies 1607.

Exhilarant (egzi·lărănt). 1803. [– Fr. *exhilarant* – pr. ppl. stem of L. *exhilarare*; see next, -ANT[1].]

A. *adj.* That exhilarates; exhilarating 1866. **B.** *sb.* An exhilarating medicine.

Exhilarate (egzi·lăreⁱt), *v.* 1540. [– *exhilarat-*, pa. ppl. stem of L. *exhilarare*, f. *ex-* Ex-[1] + *hilaris* cheerful; see -ATE[3].] **1.** *trans.* To make cheerful or merry; to cheer, enliven, gladden. †**2.** *intr.* To become cheerful 1620.

1. To e. the spirits with a glass of wine SMOLLETT. Hence **Exhi·larating** *ppl. a.* cheering, inspiriting. **Exhi·laratingly** *adv.* **Exhi·larative** *a.* tending to e. **Exhi·larator.**

Exhilaration (egzi:lărē[i]·ʃən). 1623. [– late L. *exhilaratio*, f. as prec.; see -ION.] **1.** The action or means of exhilarating; an enlivening influence. **2.** Exhilarated condition 1626.

2. E. hath some Affinity with Joy BACON.

Exhort (egzǭ·ɹt), *v.* ME. [– (O)Fr. *exhorter* or L. *exhortari*, f. *ex-* Ex-[1] + *hortari* encourage.] **1.** *trans.* To admonish earnestly; to urge by words to laudable conduct. Of circumstances, etc.: To serve as an incitement. Also *absol.* **2.** With *obj.* a thing: To recommend earnestly 1500.

1. Examples, gross as earth, e. me *Haml.* IV. iv. 46. (Qq.) *absol.* He that exhorteth, to his exhorting R.V. *Rom.* 12:8. **2.** What I exhorte Not herde is 1500.

Hence †**Exho·rt** *sb.* exhortation. **Exho·rtative** *a.* of, pertaining to, or containing exhortation: intended to e. **Exho·rtatory** *a.* exhortative.

Exhortation (egzǭɹtēi·ʃən). ME. [– (O)Fr. *exhortation* or L. *exhortatio*, f. *exhortat-*, pa. ppl. stem of *exhortari*; see prec., -ION.] **1.** The action or process of exhorting, of earnestly admonishing or urging to what is good and laudable. **2.** A set speech delivered for the purpose of exhorting; a discourse 1450.

2. The E. before the Communion 1704.

Exhorter (egzǭ·ɹtəɹ). 1513. [f. EXHORT *v.* + -ER[1].] **1.** One who exhorts or urges on to action 1552. **2.** *spec.* In various churches, a person appointed to give religious exhortation under the direction of his pastor.

Exhumate (e·ks,hiumeit), *v.* 1548. [– *exhumat-*, pa. ppl. stem of med.L. *exhumare*; see next, -ATE[3].] = EXHUME *v. lit.* and *fig.* Hence **Exhuma·tion,** the action or process of removing a body from beneath the ground.

Exhume (eks,hiū·m), *v.* 1783. [– Fr. *exhumer* – med.L. *exhumare*, f. *ex-* Ex-[1] + *humus* ground.] **1.** *trans.* To dig out or remove (something buried) from beneath the ground; *transf.* and *fig.* to unearth. **2.** To remove the overlying soil from (*rare*) 1872.

Exibilate, exiccate, etc.; see EXS-.

Exies (e·ksiz). 1816. [Sc. and north. f. of ACCESS.] **a.** An ague fit. **b.** Hysterics. SCOTT.

‖**Exigeant** (ęksiʒaṅ), *a.* 1803. [Fr.; cf. EXIGENT.] Exacting. Also in fem. **Exigeante** (ęksiʒaṅt).

Exigence (e·ksidʒĕns). 1589. [– (O)Fr. *exigence* and late L. *exigentia*, f. *exigent-*; see EXIGENT *a.*, -ENCE.] **1.** The state or fact of being exigent; urgent want; need, necessity. †**b.** = EXIGENCY 2. –1818. **2.** A case demanding immediate action or remedy; an emergency; an extremity 1643.

1. In time of e. 1691. **2.** Falstaff. . is equal to any e. 1863.

Exigency (e·ksidʒĕnsi). 1581. [– late L. *exigentia*; see prec., -ENCY.] **1.** Pressing state (of circumstances); stringency (of requirements) 1769. **b.** Pressing necessity; in *pl.* pressing needs, straits 1630. **2.** That which is needed; demands, needs, requirements 1581.

2. The various e. of times and occasions *Bk. Com. Prayer.* The exigencies of theology 1857.

Exigent (e·ksidʒĕnt), *a.* and *sb.*[1] ME. [As adj. – *exigent-*, pr. ppl. stem of L. *exigere*; see EXACT *v.*, -ENT. As sb. – OFr. *exigent*, subst. use of the adj.]

A. *adj.* **1.** Requiring immediate action or aid; pressing, urgent 1670. **2.** Requiring too much; exacting 1828.

1. That e. cry for help CLARENDON. **2.** A love that clings not, nor is e. H. TAYLOR.

†**B.** *sb.*[1] **1.** A state of pressing need; an occasion that requires immediate action or remedy; an extremity, strait –1729; end, last extremity –1631. **2.** *pl.* Needs, requirements –1677.

1. The duke seeing himselfe to be driuen to such an e. HOLINSHED. These Eyes. . Waxe dimme, as drawing to their E. 1 *Hen. VI*, II. v. 9. **2.** The present exigents of the Kingdom CHAS. I.

†**E·xigent,** *sb.*[2] 1464. [XV *exigend* – AFr. *exigende* – med.L. *exigenda*, gerundive of L. *exigere*; see prec.] *Law.* A writ commanding the sheriff to summon the defendant to appear upon pain of outlawry; also called *writ of e.* –1768.

†**Exi·genter.** 1512. [– AFr. *exigenter*, f. *exigente, exigende*; see prec., -ER[2].] *Law.* An officer of the Court of Common Pleas (in 18–19th c., of the Court of King's Bench) who made out all exigents –1837.

‖**Exigi facias** (e·ksidʒəi fēi·ʃiæs). 1577. [L.; lit. 'that you cause to be exacted'.] = EXIGENT *sb.*[2]

Exigible (e·ksidʒib'l), *a.* 1610. [– Fr. *exigible*, f. *exiger*; see EXACT *v.*, -IBLE.] That may be exacted; demandable.

There is no part of our debt e. at this time T. JEFFERSON.

Exiguity (eksigiū·iti). 1623. [– L. *exiguitas*, f. *exiguus*; see next, -ITY.] The condition of being exiguous; scantiness; smallness, littleness.

Exiguous (egzi·giu,əs), *a.* 1651. [f. L. *exiguus* scanty in measure or number, f. *exigere* weigh exactly; see EXACT *v.*, -UOUS.] Scanty in size or number; extremely small, diminutive. Hence **Exi·guousness.**

Exile (e·ksəil, e·gzəil), *sb.*[1] ME. [– (O)Fr. *exil*, latinized refash. of earlier *essil* – L. *exilium* banishment, f. *exul* exiled person.] **1.** Enforced removal from one's native land according to an edict or sentence; banishment; also *gen.* prolonged voluntary absence from one's native land. Also *transf.* and *fig.* †**2.** Waste; ruin –1618.

1. He was put to exyle in to yᵉ yle of Sardeyn 1529. Her cite and landes of Cartage are all dystroied and tourned in exyll CAXTON.

Exile (e·ksəil), *sb.*[2] ME. [prob. – (O)Fr. *exilé*, pa. pple. of *exiler* EXILE *v.* Muting of the final syll. as in ASSIGN *sb.*[2] infl. by L. *exul.*] A banished person; one compelled by circumstances to reside away from his native land. Also *transf.* and *fig.*

Tit. A. III. i. 285. *transf.* An e. from the paternal roof 1820.

Exile (e·ksəil, e·gzəil), *a.* ?*Obs.* ME. [– L. *exilis* thin, lank. Cf. Fr. †*exile.*] **1.** Slender, shrunken, thin: small. **2.** Meagre; poor ME.

Exile (e·ksəil, e·gzəil), *v.* ME. [– OFr. *exil(i)er* (mod. *exiler*), refash. of *essilier* – late L. *exiliare*, f. L. *exilium* EXILE *sb.*[1]] **1.** To compel (a person) by decree or enactment to leave his country; to banish. Also *trans.* and *fig.* †**2.** *gen.* To banish, expel –1700. †**3.** To devastate, bring to ruin. Cf. EXTERMINATE. –1533.

1. The emperour exyled Iohan. . into the yle of Pathmose 1493. **3.** He. . exiled diuerse townes LD. BERNERS. Hence **E·xilement,** banishment, exile. †**Exiler.**

Exilic (egz-, eksi·lik), *a.* 1888. [f. EXILE *sb.*[1] + -IC.] Of or pertaining to exile; *esp.* to that of the Jews in Babylon. So **Exi·lian** *a.* 1882.

†**Exili·tion.** 1646. [irreg. f. L. *ex(s)ilire* jump up or forth + -ITION.] A leaping up or forth –1711.

Exility (eksi·liti). 1528. [– L. *exilitas*, f. *exilis* thin, lank; see -ITY.] **1.** Thinness, slenderness, meagreness 1528; †poverty –1774. **2.** Tenuity; subtlety 1626.

Eximious (egzi·miəs), *a.* Now *rare.* 1547. [f. L. *eximius*, 'set apart', select, choice, f. *eximere*; see EXEMPT *a.*, -OUS.] Excellent, distinguished, eminent. Hence †**Exi·miously** *adv.*

†**Exi·nanite,** *v.* 1555. [– *exinanit-*, pa. ppl. stem of L. *exinanire* make empty, f. *ex-* Ex-[1] + *inanis* empty.] **1.** *trans.* To make of none effect –1661. **2.** To reduce to emptiness; to humble –1624.

Exinanition (eksi:năni·ʃən). Now *rare.* 1603. [– L. *exinanitio*, f. as prec.; see -ION.] **1.** The action of emptying or exhausting; emptied or exhausted condition. **2.** Humiliation 1612.

1. Fastings to the e. of spirits JER. TAYLOR.

Exindusiate (eksindiū·si,ĕt), *a.* 1866. [f. EX-[1] + INDUSIUM + -ATE[2].] *Bot.* Not having an indusium.

Exi·nguinal (eksi·ŋgwinăl). 1884. [f. EX-[1], + L. *inguen*, *-in-* groin + -AL[1].] *Entom.*

A. *adj.* Situated outside the groin.

B. *sb.* 'The second segment or trochanter of the limbs of the Arachnida' (*Syd. Soc. Lex.*).

Exintine (eksi·ntin, -təin). 1852. [f. L. *ex-* EX-[1] + *intus* within + -INE[1].] 'The membrane of the pollen grain which lies between the *Extine* and the *Intine*' (*Syd. Soc. Lex.*).

Exion. Blunder for 'action'. 2 *Hen. IV*, II. i. 32.

Exist (egzi·st), *v.* 1602. [prob. back-formation from EXISTENCE. Fr. *exister* is later (Descartes, 1637). But *existere* is recorded in late and med.L. as an auxiliary 'to be', in Lactantius (IV), Gregory (VI), and later.] **1.** To be, to have objective being 1605. **2.** To have being in a specified mode. With advb. phr. or *as.* Also, to subsist, occur. 1602. **3.** To live 1828. **4.** To continue to be 1790.

1. To conceive the world. . to have existed from eternity SOUTH. **2.** A space of a foot existed between the ice and the water TYNDALL. **4.** How does he contrive to e. here 1797.

Hence **Exi·ster** (*rare*). **Exi:stibi·lity,** also **-ability,** capability of existing. **Exi·stible** *a.* (*rare*) capable of existing. **Exi·sting** *ppl. a.*

Existence (egzi·stĕns). ME. [– (O)Fr. *existence* or late L. *existentia*, f. *ex(s)istent-*, pr. ppl. stem of L. *ex(s)istere* emerge, be visible or manifest, f. *ex-* Ex-[1] + *sistere* take up a position; see -ENCE.] †**1.** Reality; opp. to *appearance.* Only in ME. **2.** Being; the fact or state of existing ME.; continuance in being 1736; life 1634. **3.** A mode of existing 1763. **3.** *concr.* All that exists 1751; a being, an entity 1605.

2. Matter is not necessary to the Soul's e. GLANVILL. We know not at all upon what the e. of our living powers depends BUTLER. A wretched e. DICKENS. **4.** An enumeration of Existences, as the basis of Logic MILL. var. †**Exi·stency** (in senses 2, 4).

Existent (egzi·stĕnt). 1561. [– *existent-*; see prec., -ENT.] **A.** *adj.* **1.** That exists, existing; having being. Also *absol.* **2.** Now existing; present-day 1791.

1. There is but one necessarily e. Being 1734. **2.** Types of e. Frenchmen RUSKIN. Hence **Exi·stently** *adv.*

B. *sb.* An existent person or thing 1644.

Existential (egziste·nʃăl), *a.* 1693. [– late L. *existentialis*, f. *existentia*; see EXISTENCE, -AL[1].] **1.** Of or pertaining to existence. **2.** *Logic.* Of a proposition: Predicating existence 1837. **Existe·ntially** *adv.*

†**Existima·tion.** 1538. [– L. *existimatio*, f. *existimat-*, pa. ppl. stem of *existimare*, f. *ex-* Ex-[1] + *æstimare*; see ESTEEM *v.*, -ION.] = ESTIMATION 2, 4, –1712.

Exit (e·ksit). 1538. [In senses 1, 2, – 3rd pers. sing. ind. of L. *exire*, f. *ex-* Ex-[1] + *ire* go; in senses 3, 4, mainly – L. *exitus*, f. pa. ppl. stem of *exire.*] **1.** Replacing EXEAT, q.v. **2.** *sb.* The departure of a player from the stage. Also *transf.* and *fig.*; *esp.* departure from the scene of life; death. 1588. **3.** A going out or forth; liberty to go out; egress 1659. **4.** An outlet; esp. said of the doors affording exit from a public building 1695.

2. They haue their Exits and their Entrances SHAKS. He scorn'd an E. by the common means FELTHAM. **4.** An enclosure. . which. . had no e. JOWETT. Hence **E·xit** *v. intr.* to make one's e.; *fig.* to die.

Exitial (egzi·ʃăl), *a.* ?*Obs.* 1534. [– L. *exitialis* destructive, f. *exitium* destruction.] Hurtful; destructive to life, fatal. So †**Exi·tious** *a.*

†**E·xiture.** ME. [– OFr. *exiture* or med.L. *exitura* abscess, passage out, f. *exit-*, pa. ppl. stem of L. *exire* go out; see EXIT, -URE.] **1.** Passage out or forth –1615. **2.** A running abscess. [So in OFr.] –1657.

Exitus (e·ksitŏs). 1664. [– L. *exitus*, f. as prec.] †**1.** A going out or forth; a departure –1706. **2.** *Path.* A prolapsus 1811; also, 'the termination of a disease' (*Syd. Soc. Lex.*) 1884.

‖**Ex-libris** (eks ləi·bris). Used also as *pl.* 1880. [L.; lit. 'out of the books' (of ——).] An inscription, label, or stamp indicating the owner of a book; *esp.* a book-plate or the like. Hence **Ex-librist,** one who collects these.

Exo- (e·kso, bef. two unstressed syllables eksǫ-), *prefix* (bef. a vowel sometimes *ex-*), repr. Gr. ἔξω without; as in:

Exoca·rdial *a.*, *Phys.* pertaining to the exterior of the heart. **E·xocarp** [Gr. καρπός] = PERICARP. **Exocœ·lar** *a.* [see CŒLOME], pertaining to the outer side of the body-cavity. **E·xoderm** [Gr. δέρμα] = ECTODERM; also the external crust of the body of an insect. **E:xogene·tic** *a.* [Gr. γενετικός, f. γένεσις], that arises from without. **Exona·rthex** [see NARTHEX], the outer vestibule of a Greek church. **Exopa·thic** *a.* [Gr. πάθος], (of disease) originating outside the body. **Exophy·llous** *a.* [Gr. φύλλον], (of dicotyledons) having the young leaves naked, i.e. not enclosed in a sheath. **E·xoplasm** [Gr. πλάσμα], the outermost layer of the cuticular protoplasm of some Protozoa. **Exo·podite** [Gr. ποδ-, πούς], 'the outermost of the two processes appended to the basal process of the hinder limbs of some of the Crustacea' (*Syd. Soc. Lex.*); hence **Exopodi·tic** *a.* **Exo·ptile** *a.*

[Gr. πτίλον feather], *Bot.* having a naked plumule. **Exo(r)rhi·zal** *a.* [Gr. ῥίζα root], *Bot.* (of plants) having the radicle naked; also **Exorrhi·zous** *a.* **Exosco·pic** *a.* [Gr. -σκοπος], viewing from the outside; hence **Exosco·pically** *adv.* **Exoske·letal** *a. Anat.* of or pertaining to the **Exoske·leton,** the external integument, whether bony, or calcified, or leathery; also *fig.* **E·xosperm** [Gr. σπέρμα]. **E·xospore** [see SPORE], *Bot.* the outer coat of a spore or oosphere in fungi or lichens; hence **Exospo·ral** *a.* pertaining to an exospore; **Exospo·rous** *a.* having its spores on the outer surface of the sporangium. **E·xostome** [Gr. στόμα], *Bot.* the aperture in the outer integument of the ovule. **Exothe·ca** [Gr. θήκη case], *Zool.* the hard exterior wall of the gonosome of the Hydrozoa; hence **Exothe·cal** *a.* **Exothe·cium,** *Bot.* 'the cuticular or outer layer of the anther' (*Syd. Soc. Lex.*).

Exoccipital (eks₁ǫksi·pităl). 1847. [f. EXO- + L. *occiput, -pit-* OCCIPUT + -AL¹.]

A. *adj.* That is outside the occipital bone.

B. *sb. pl.* Those parts of the occipital bone which form the sides of the foramen magnum and support the condyles 1854.

Exoculation (eks₁ǫkiulēⁱ·ʃən). 1630. [– med.L. *exoculatio*, f. *exoculat-*, pa. ppl. stem of L. *exoculare*, f. *ex-* EX-¹ + *oculus* eye; see -ION.] The action of putting out the eyes; blinding.

Exode (e·ksoᵘd), *sb.*¹ Also **exod.** ME. [Anglicized f. EXODUS; in sense 1 through (O)Fr. *Exode.*] †**1.** = EXODUS 1. ME. only. **2.** = EXODUS 2. (*rare*) 1751.

Exode (e·ksōᵘd), *sb.*² 1684. [– Fr. *exode* – L. *exodium*; see EXODIUM.] = EXODIUM 1, 2.

Exodic (eksǫ·dik), *a.* 1850. [f. Gr. ἔξοδος way out, issue + -IC.] **1.** Of or pertaining to an exodus. (Dicts.). **2.** *Phys.* Proceeding from the spinal marrow 1850.

Exodist (e·ksǫdist). *rare.* 1849. [f. EXODUS + -IST.] **1.** One who makes an exodus 1883. **2.** An emigrant 1849.

‖**Exodium.** 1600. [L. – Gr. ἐξόδιον, n. sing. of ἐξόδιος pertaining to an exit, f. ἔξοδος; see next.] **1.** *Gr. Drama.* The end or catastrophe of a play 1842. **2.** *Rom. Drama.* A comic interlude or farce following something more serious.

Exodus (e·ksǒdǒs). OE. [– eccl.L. *Exodus* – Gr. ἔξοδος, f. ἐξ EX-² + ὁδός way.] **1.** The book of the O.T. which describes the departure of the Israelites out of Egypt. **2.** A going out or forth; *esp.* the departure of the Israelites from Egypt; emigration. Also *fig.* 1623. var. **E·xody.**

‖**Ex officio, ex-officio,** *advb. phr.* 1533. [L., 'arising out of (one's) duty or office' (*officium*).] In discharge of duty, in virtue of one's office; hence = OFFICIAL *a.*

Exogamy (eksǫ·gămi). 1865. [f. EXO- + Gr. γάμος marriage + -Y³; cf. contemp. ENDOGAMY.] The custom by which a man is bound to take a wife from outside his own clan or group; opp. to *endogamy.* Hence **Exoga·mic** *a.* pertaining to e. **Exo·gamous** *a.* practising, of the nature of, or pertaining to, e.

Exogen (e·ksodʒėn). 1838. [– Fr. *exogène* (de Candolle, 1813), mod.L. *exogena, -us* (after *indigena, -us*) adj., growing on the outside; see EXO-, -GEN.] *Bot.* A plant whose stem grows by deposit on the outside; opp. to ENDOGEN.

Exogenous (eksǫ·dʒĭnəs), *a.* 1830. [f. mod.L. *exogena, -us* (see prec.) + -OUS.] **a.** *Bot.* Growing by additions on the outside; of the nature of an exogen; pertaining to or characteristic of the exogens. **b.** *Path.* = EXOGENETIC. 1883. **c.** *Anat.* (Of a portion of bone) growing out from a previously ossified part; opp. to *autogenous* 1854.

Hence **Exo·genously** *adv.*

†**E·xolete,** *a.* 1611. [– L. *exoletus*, pa. pple. of *exolescere*, f. *ex-* EX-¹ + *olescere*; see OBSOLETE.] Obsolete; effete, insipid; faded –1736.

†**Exolu·tion.** Also **exsolution.** 1615. [– L. *ex(s)olutio*, f. *ex(s)olut-*, pa. ppl. stem of *ex(s)olvere*; see next, -ION.] The action of loosening or setting free; relaxation; *esp.* the emission of 'animal spirits', formerly assumed as the cause of swooning; faintness –1662.

†**Exo·lve,** *v.* 1578. [– L. *ex(s)olvere*, f. *ex-* EX-¹ + *solvere* loosen.] *trans.* To slacken; also 'to pay clear off' (Bailey). *intr.* for *refl.* To dissolve. –1657.

‖**Exomis** (eksōᵘ·mis). 1850. [Gr. ἐξωμίς, f. ἐξ EX-² + ὦμος shoulder.] A vest without sleeves, leaving the shoulders bare; worn by artisans and slaves. So **Exo·mion.** Browning.

‖**Exomologesis** (eks₁ǒ:mǫlǫgī·sis). 1592. [Gr. ἐξομολόγησις, f. ἐξομολογεῖν confess. See HOMOLOGATE.] A full or public confession.

Exomphalos (eksǫ·mfălǫs). 1754. [– Gr. ἐξόμφαλος prominent navel, f. ἐξ EX-² + ὀμφαλός navel.] A rupture or protrusion at the navel.

‖**Exon** (e·xǫn). 1767. [repr. the pronunc. (ęgzaṅ) of Fr. *exempt.* Cf. EXAUN.] Title of the four officers of the Yeomen of the Royal Guard, styled *corporals* in their commissions, and ranking below the 'Ensign'.

Exonerate (egzǫ·nĕreⁱt), *v.* 1524. [– *exonerat-*, pa. ppl. stem of L. *exonerare*, f. *ex-* EX-¹ + *onus, oner-* burden; see -ATE³.] **1.** *trans.* To take off a burden from; to relieve *of*; to unload, lighten. **2.** To discharge, get rid of 1542. **3.** To free from (a duty, obligation, payment, charge, etc.; also, from blame) 1548.

1. Success would certainly e. our finances WELLINGTON. **2.** To exonerat the blader..whan nede shall requyre BOORDE. Neither did this riuer e. itself into any sea HAKLUYT. **3.** Mr. Hastings.. offered to e. the company from that 'charge' BURKE. To e. myself of a greater crime W. IRVING.

Hence **Exo·nerate** *pple.* exonerated. **Exo:nera·tion,** the action of discharging, disburdening or relieving, or the state of being relieved from a duty, office, obligation, payment, etc.; also from blame; a formal discharge. **Exo·nerative** *a.* tending to give relief (from an obligation). **Exo·nerator.**

‖**Exoneretur** (egzǫ:nĕrī·təɹ). 1824. [L. = 'let him be discharged', 3rd. pers. sing. pres. subj. pass. of *exonerare*; see prec.] *Law.* 'An entry made upon the bail-piece upon render of a defendant to prison in discharge of his bail' (Wharton).

Exophtha·lmia. 1721. [mod.L., f. next + -IA¹.] = EXOPHTHALMUS.

Exophthalmus, -os (eks₁ǫfþæ·lmǒs, -ǫs). 1872. [mod.L. – Gr. ἐξόφθαλμος with prominent eyes, f. ἐξ EX-² + ὀφθαλμός eye.] *Path.* Protrusion of the eye-ball. Hence **Exophtha·lmic** *a.* of, pertaining to, or characterized by, e. var. **Exophtha·lmy.**

†**Exo·pt,** *v.* [– L. *exoptare*, f. *ex-* EX-¹ + *optare* wish.] To desire greatly. FORREST. So †**Exopta·tion,** earnest desire.

Exorable (e·ksŏrăb'l), *a.* Now *rare.* 1563. [– L. *exorabilis*, f. *exorare*; see next, -BLE. Cf. Fr. *exorable.*] Capable of being moved by entreaty. Hence **E·xorableness.**

†**E·xorate,** *v.* 1599. [– *exorat-*, pa. ppl. stem of L. *exorare*, f. *ex-* EX-¹ + *orare* pray; see -ATE³.] *trans.* To entreat; to prevail upon by entreaty –1654. Hence †**Exora·tion.**

Exo·rbital, *a.* 1876. [f. EX-¹ + ORBIT + AL¹.] Outside the orbit.

Exorbitance (egzǭ·ɹbităns). 1611. [f. EXORBITANT; see -ANCE.] †**1.** Aberration from the due or ordinary track; eccentricity, irregularity, anomaly. Also, aberration of mind. –1842. **2.** Transgression of law or morality; misconduct, lawlessness, criminality (*arch.*) 1611. **3.** Excessiveness; now chiefly, of demands, charges, prices, etc. 1646.

2. The Border robbers..had committed many exorbitances SCOTT. **3.** The e. of the duties on tea and tobacco MCCULLOCH. So **Exo·rbitancy.**

Exorbitant (egzǭ·ɹbitănt). 1460. [– *exorbitant-*, pr. ppl. stem of Chr.L. *exorbitare*, f. ex- EX-¹ + *orbita* ORBIT; see -ANT¹. Cf. Fr. *exorbitant.*]

A. *adj.* †**1.** Leaving a specified track –1674. **2.** Deviating from the normal track; †eccentric; anomalous; abnormal 1460. †**3.** Forsaking, or apt to forsake, the right path; erring –1716. **4.** Exceeding ordinary or proper bounds; excessive; outrageously large 1621.

2. Causes e., and such as their lawes had not provided for HOOKER. **4.** E. appetites BURTON, Impositions R. COKE, tributes GIBBON, influence 1771. Hence **Exo·rbitantly** *adv.*

†**B.** *sb.* One who or something which exceeds proper limits (*rare*) –1714.

Exorbitate (egzǭ·ɹbiteⁱt), *v.* ?*Obs.* 1600. [– *exorbitat-*, pa. ppl. stem of Chr.L. *exorbitare*; see prec., -ATE³.] *intr.* To deviate from the usual course or orbit. Hence **Exorbita·tion.**

Exorcise: see EXORCIZE.

Exorcism (e·ksǭɹsiz'm, egzǭ·ɹsiz'm). ME. [– eccl.L. *exorcismus* – eccl.Gr. ἐξορκισμός, f. ἐξορκίζειν, f. ἐξ EX-² + ὅρκος oath; see -ISM.] **1.** The action of exorcising or expelling an evil spirit by adjuration, etc. †**2.** *improp.* Conjuration; the ceremonies observed in calling up spirits –1652. **3.** A formula employed in exorcizing 1550.

Exorcist (e·ksǭɹsist, egzǭ·ɹsist). ME. [– eccl.L. *exorcista* – Gr. ἐξορκιστής; see prec., -IST.] **1.** One who drives out evil spirits by adjuration, etc.; *spec.* one of the four lesser orders in the R. C. Church. †**2.** One who calls up spirits by magical rites –1621.

1. Exorcists, that served to dispossess such as were possessed by the Devil SELDEN. **2.** *Jul. C.* II. i. 323.

Exorcize, -ise (e·ksǭɹsəiz, egzǭ·ɹsəiz), *v.* 1546. [– (O)Fr. *exorciser* or eccl.L. *exorcizare* – Gr. ἐξορκίζειν; see EXORCISM, -IZE. The better form *exorcize* is the least in use.] **1.** *trans.* To drive out (an evil spirit) by the use of a holy name; to call forth, expel. **2.** To clear of evil spirits; to purify 1645. **3.** To adjure (an evil spirit). Also, to conjure up. Now *rare.* 1584.

1. Touched him on the shoulder with his staff and exorcised the demon MRS. JAMESON. **2.** Monks huddled together..as if to e. the land of a demon LYTTON. Hence **Exorciza·tion,** the action of exorcizing. **Exorcizer,** one who exorcizes.

‖**Exordium** (egzǭ·ɹdiǒm). Pl. **-iums, -ia.** 1581. [L., f. *exordiri*, f. *ex-* EX-¹ + *ordiri* begin.] The beginning of anything; *esp.* the introductory part of a discourse, treatise, etc.

I shall consider them jointly, as in way of E. to the rest SELDEN. Hence **Exo·rdial** *a.* introductory.

†**Exo·rnate,** *v.* 1539. [– *exornat-*, pa. ppl. stem of L. *exornare*, f. *ex-* EX-¹ + *ornare* adorn; see -ATE³.] To adorn, embellish–1589. Hence †**Exorna·tion.**

†**Exo·rtion.** 1657. [f. *exort-*, pa. ppl. stem of L. *exoriri* (f. *ex-* EX-¹ + *oriri* arise) + -ION. Cf. cl.L. *exortus.*] The action of arising or emerging; point of emergence.

†**Exoscula·tion.** 1560. [– L. *exosculatio*, f. *exosculat-*, pa. ppl. stem of *exosculari*, f. *ex-* EX-¹ + *osculari* kiss; see -ION.] **1.** A hearty kiss –1652. **2.** *Anat.* Anastomosis 1634.

Exosmose (e·ksǫzmōᵘs). 1828. [– Fr. *exosmose* (Dutrochet); see next. Cf. ENDOSMOSE.] = next.

Exosmosis (eksǫzmōᵘ·sis). 1839. [mod.L. (whence Fr. *exosmose*), f. Gr. ἔξω EXO- + ὠσμός pushing + -OSIS. Cf. ENDOSMOSIS.] *Phys.*, etc. The passage of a fluid outwards through a porous septum, to mix with external fluid. Hence **Exosmo·tic** *a.*

Exossate (eks₁ǫ·seⁱt), *v.* 1721. [– *exossat-*, pa. ppl. stem of L. *exossare* to bone, f. *ex-* EX-¹ + *os, oss-* bone; see -ATE³.] *trans.* To deprive of bones; †to cause (fruits) to grow without stones. Hence **Exossa·tion.**

†**Exo·sseous,** *a.* [f. L. *exossis, exossus* (f. *ex-* EX-¹ + *os, oss-* bone) + -EOUS, after OSSEOUS.] Boneless. SIR T. BROWNE.

‖**Exostosis** (eksǫstōᵘ·sis). 1736. [mod.L. – Gr. ἐξόστωσις (Galen) outgrowth of bone, f. ἐξ EX-² + ὀστέον bone; see -OSIS.] **1.** *Path.* The formation of bone on another bone, or on some other structure in the body. Also *concr.* a bony tumour found upon a bone or cartilage. **2.** *Bot.* A diseased condition of plants, in which hard woody projections grow from the main stem or roots 1866. Hence **Exo·stosed** *ppl. a.* affected with e. **Exosto·tic** *a.* pertaining to e.; of the nature of an e.

Exostracize (eksǫ·străsəiz), *v.* 1838. [–Gr. ἐξοστρακίζειν, f. ἐξ EX-² + ὀστρακίζειν OSTRACIZE.] To banish by ostracism; also *fig.* Hence †**Exo·stracism.**

Exoteric (eksote·rik). 1655. [– L. *exotericus* – Gr. ἐξωτερικός, f. ἐξωτέρω, compar. of ἔξω outside; see EXO-, -IC.]

A. *adj.* **1.** Pertaining to the outside; external 1662. **2.** Suitable to the uninitiated. Hence, of disciples, etc.: Belonging to the outer circle. Opp. to ESOTERIC, q.v. 1655. **3.** *transf.* Current among the outside public; popular 1813.

2. Plato like Pythagoras had e. and esoteric opinions LEWES.

B. *sb.* **1.** *pl.* (After Gr. τὰ ἐξωτερικά) Exoteric doctrines or treatises 1738. **2.** One of the uninitiated; an outsider 1697.

Hence **Exote·rical** *a.*, **-ly** *adv.*

Exo·tery. 1763. [prob. a misprint.] Exoteric doctrine or instruction.

Exotic (egzǫ·tik). 1599. [– L. *exoticus* – Gr. ἐξωτικός, f. ἔξω; cf. EXOTERIC.]

A. *adj.* **1.** †Alien; introduced from abroad, not indigenous. **†b.** Drawn from outside –1727. **2.** Foreign (now *rare*); hence †outlandish, barbarous 1629.

1. An exotick and forain territory 1650. An e. plant 1660. **2.** An e. habit and demeanour SWIFT.

B. *sb.* **1.** A plant or †animal of foreign extraction; a foreign plant not acclimatized. Also *transf.* and *fig.* 1645. **2.** A foreigner (*rare*) 1651.

Hence †**Exo·tical** *a.* †**Exo·tical-ly** *adv.*, **-ness.** **Exo·ticism,** tendency to adopt what is e.; e. character; a foreign idiom or expression.

Expand (ekspæ·nd), *v.* ME. [– L. *expandere*, f. *ex-* EX-¹ + *pandere* spread.] **1.** *trans.* To spread out; to open out, unfold; to spread out smooth; also, to display, *lit.* and *fig.* **b.** To develop; to write out in full; in *Alg.* to state at length in a series 1802. **2.** *intr.* for *refl.* To spread itself out; to unfold, open out; to develop 1560. **3.** *trans.* 'To spread out every way' (J.); to cause to increase in bulk; to dilate, enlarge. Also *refl.* 1645. **4.** *intr.* for *refl.* To increase in bulk, swell; to dilate; also *fig.* 1791.

1. E. thy sails POPE. Sicily then lay expanded like a map beneath our eyes L. HUNT. **2.** Streams ..expanding..to deep green lakes TYNDALL. **3.** To e. the Spirits 1707, a volume MACAULAY, the chest 1894. **4.** When the air is warmed, it expands 1854. Hence **Expa·nder,** one who, or that which, expands.

Expanding, *ppl. a.* 1776. [f. prec. + -ING².] **1.** That opens out or is opening out. **2.** That becomes enlarged 1874.

2. *E.-alloy*, such as expands in cooling; *E. bit*, a boring-bit whose diameter is adjustable KNIGHT.

†**Expa·nse,** *a.* ME. [– L. *expansus*, pa. pple. of *expandere* EXPAND.] **1.** *Bot.* Expanded, spread out 1819. **2.** Separate; opp. to COLLECT. (See Skeat in *Chaucer's Astrolabe* (1872) Gloss.)

Expanse (ekspæ·ns), *sb.* 1667. [– mod.L. *expansum* (n. of L. *expansus*, pa. pple. of *expandere*), in Eng. contexts XVII–XVIII, used to render Heb. *rāḳîᶜa* (Vulg. *firmamentum*), f. *rāḳaᶜ* beat, stamp, beat out, spread out.] **1.** That which is expanded or spread out; a wide extent of anything; *esp.* in *The expanse*: the firmament. **2.** Enlargement, expansion. Also, the amount or distance of expansion. 1860.

1. Let there be Lights High in th' e. of Heaven MILT. *P. L.* VII. 340. The broad e. of brow SCOTT.

†**Expa·nse,** *v.* 1477. [– *expans-*, pa. ppl. stem of L. *expandere* EXPAND.] = EXPAND *v.* 1, 3. –1706.

Expansible (ekspæ·nsib'l), *a.* 1691. [f. as prec. + -IBLE. Cf. Fr. *expansible*.] That can be expanded.

Readily e...by Heat BOYLE. An e. system of theology 1850. Hence **Expa:nsibi·lity,** e. quality. **Expa·nsibleness. Expa·nsibly** *adv.*

Expansile (ekspæ·nsil, -əil), *a.* 1730. [f. as prec. + -ILE.] **1.** Capable of expansion 1776. **2.** Of, or of the nature of, expansion.

1. E. and contractile by heat and cold FORDYCE.

Expansion (ekspæ·nʃən). 1611. [– late L. *expansio*, f. as prec.; see -ION.] **1.** The action or process of expanding or spreading out; the state of being expanded or spread out 1646. **b.** Development; writing out in full; in *Alg.* the process or result of working out a contracted expression 1858. **2.** Anything that is spread out; an expanse 1611. **†3.** Extent; space to which anything is extended; also, pure space –1712. **4.** Dilatation; an instance of this 1634. **b.** *Comm.*, etc. An extension (of business transactions); also, an increase of the circulating medium 1847. **5.** The amount or degree of dilatation 1790. **6.** *concr.* An expanded portion; what (a thing) is expanded into 1860. **7.** *Steam-engine.* The increase in bulk of the steam which takes place in a partially filled cylinder after communication with the boiler is cut off 1782.

1. The easie e. of the wing of a bird GREW. **2.** All that lies Beneath the starr'd e. of the skies 1760. **4.** The love of liberty is simply the instinct in man for e. M. ARNOLD.

attrib. and *Comb.*, as *e.-theory*; **e.-coupling,** one consisting of an e.-drum of thin copper between the extremities of two pipes, which, in elongating, press the sides of the drum in, and draw them out in cooling; **-curb,** in *Horology*, a contrivance for counteracting expansion and contraction; **-drum,** an arrangement by which an occasional change of speed may be effected; **-engine,** one in which the piston is propelled, during the latter part of its course, by the expansion of the steam first introduced; **-gear,** an apparatus for cutting off steam from the cylinder at a given point of the stroke; **-joint,** 'a stuffing-box joint connecting the steam pipes, so as to allow one of them to slide within the enlarged end of the other when the length increases by expansion' (Weale); **-slide,** a slide belonging to the **e.-valve,** a valve which shuts off the steam in its passage to the cylinder.

Expansionist (ekspæ·nʃənist). 1862. [f. prec. + -IST.] One who advocates expansion. Also *attrib.*

Expansive (ekspæ·nsiv), *a.* 1651. [f. *expans-* (pa. ppl. stem of L. *expandere* EXPAND) + -IVE.] **1.** Tending or adapted to expand. **2.** Of or pertaining to expansion; depending upon the principle of expansion 1782. **3.** Having wide bounds, or a wide range; broad, extensive; comprehensive 1806.

1. E. ether 1805, utterance 1858. An e. force 1886. **2.** The said new or e. engine *Watt's Patent* No. 1321, 4. **3.** An e. intellect D'ISRAELI, forehead 1834. Hence **Expa·nsive-ly** *adv.*, **-ness. Expansi·vity** (*rare*).

†‖**Expa·nsum.** 1635. [mod.L.; see EXPANSE *sb.*] = EXPANSE *sb.* –1794.

†**Expa·nsure.** 1606. [f. as prec. + -URE.] The process of expanding; also, = EXPANSE *sb.* 1. –1611.

‖**Ex parte, ex-parte** (e:kspā·ɹti), *advb. phr.* used as *adj.* 1672. [L. EX, abl. of *pars* side, PART *sb.*] **1.** orig. *Law.* Made or executed on one side only. **2.** *gen.* Of statements, etc.: Made by or in the interest of one side only 1812.

Expatiate (ekspēⁱ·ʃi,eⁱt), *v.* 1538. [– *ex(s)patiat-*, pa. ppl. stem of L. *ex(s)patiari*, f. *ex-* EX-¹ + *spatiari* walk, f. *spatium* SPACE *sb.*; see -ATE³.] **1.** *intr.* To walk about at large, wander at will. Also *transf.* and *fig.* **2.** To speak or write at some length; to be copious in description or discussion. Const. *on, upon.* 1612. **†3.** *trans.* To enlarge, extend; to spread abroad; to magnify. Also †*refl.* and *intr.* for *refl.* –1738. **†b.** 'To allow to range' (J.). *refl.* only. –1695.

1. Winter-flies..crawl out..to e. in the sun LOWELL. **2.** Ancient orators used to e. in praise of their country BP. BERKELEY. **3.** The Jordan..expatiateth itself into the waters of Merom FULLER.

Hence **Expa·tiater, -or. Expa:tia·tion,** the action of expatiating. **Expa·tiative** *a.* expansive. **Expa·tiatory** *a.* characterized by expatiation.

Expatriate (ekspēⁱ·tri,eⁱt), *v.* 1768. [– *expatriat-*, pa. ppl. stem of med.L. *expatriare*, f. *ex-* EX-¹ + *patria* native land.] **1.** *trans.* To drive (a person) away from his native country; to banish 1817. **2.** *refl.* (rarely *intr.* for *refl.*) To withdraw from one's native country; to renounce one's allegiance 1768.

1. He apologized at length for proposing to e. the negroes 1856. Hence **Expa·triate** *ppl. a.* expatriated; *sb.* an expatriated person.

Expatriation (ekspēⁱ:tri,ēⁱ·ʃən). 1816. [f. prec.; see -ATION.] **1.** The action of banishing a person from his own country; the state of being banished. **2.** The action of withdrawing from one's country; emigration. Also, renunciation of one's allegiance. 1825.

2. The bishops and clergy sought refuge in e. 1839.

Expect (ekspe·kt), *v.* 1560. [– L. *ex(s)pectare*, f. *ex-* EX-¹ + *spectare* look.] **†1.** *intr.* To wait –1765. **†2.** *trans.* To wait for, await –1822. **3.** To look for mentally; to look forward to, regard as about to happen; to anticipate the occurrence or the coming of. Const. with simple *obj.*, *obj.* and *inf.*, or clause as *obj.*; also *absol.* 1601. **4. a.** with *can* = 'to look for with likelihood' 1650. **b.** To look for as due from another; to look for and require 1634. **5.** To suppose, surmise *that.* Now *dial.* or *colloq.* 1592.

1. *Heb.* 10:13. **2.** Prisons e. the wicked COWPER. **3.** They expected us, and we expected to come DE FOE. They did not e. she could ever recover 1726. **4. b.** England expects every man to do his duty NELSON.

Hence †**Expe·ct** *sb.* expectation. **Expe·ctable** *a.* to be expected. **Expe·ctedly** *adv.* according to expectation. **Expe·cter,** †**-or,** one who expects.

Expectance (ekspe·ktăns). 1602. [– L. *ex(s)pectantia*, f. *ex(s)pectant-*, pr. ppl. stem of *ex(s)pectare*; see prec., -ANCE.] **1.** The action or state of waiting for anything. Somewhat *arch.* 1603. **2.** The action of looking for mentally. *Obs.* or *arch.* 1631. **†b.** The condition of being expected; as, *in expectance* –1640. **†3.** Ground, reason, or warrant for expecting something –1793. **†4.** That which is expected 1684.

3. A good estate in possession; fine expectances besides RICHARDSON. So **Expe·ctancy.**

Expectancy (ekspe·ktănsi). 1598. [f. as prec.; see -ANCY.] **†1.** = EXPECTANCE 1. (*rare.*) 1649. **2.** = EXPECTANCE 2; also, an instance of this 1600. **b.** *esp.* The position of being entitled to anything at some future time, either as a remainder, or reversion, or on the death of some one 1811. **c.** That from which much is expected (*arch.*) 1602. **3.** = EXPECTANCE 2 b; also, anything in expectance 1598. **4.** The extent of reasonable expectation 1620.

2. c. Th' expectansie and Rose of the faire State *Haml.* III. i. 160.

Expectant (ekspe·ktănt). ME. [f. as prec.; see -ANT¹.]

A. *adj.* **1.** In a state of expectation; waiting, looking out; *esp.* that expects a succession, appointment, or the like. **2.** Existing in expectancy; reversionary 1628.

1. An anxious and e. eye SOUTHEY. An e. occupier 1886. **2.** A fee simple e. COKE. Hence **Expe·ctantly** *adv.*

B. *sb.* One who expects an arrival, occurrence, etc.; one who looks to receive something; *esp.* in *Law*, an *expectant heir* 1625.

Expectation (ekspektēⁱ·ʃən). 1538. [– L. *ex(s)pectatio*, f. *ex(s)pectat-*, pa. ppl. stem of *ex(s)pectare*; see EXPECT, -ION. Cf. (O)Fr. *expectation*.] **1.** The action or state of waiting, or of waiting for (something). Now only: Expectant waiting. 1550. **b.** *Med.* The method of waiting upon the efforts of nature in the treatment of a disease 1689. **2.** The action of mentally looking for something to take place; anticipation 1552. **3.** Expectancy 1538. **4.** Ground or warrant for expecting 1611; *pl.* prospects of inheritance or of testamentary gifts 1669. **5.** The condition of being expected; only in phr. *in expectation* 1657. **6.** That which is expected or looked forward to 1596. **7.** The degree of probability of the occurrence of any contingent event 1832.

2. Our expectations that others will act so and so in such circumstances BUTLER. **4.** I have what are called expectations LYTTON. **7.** Phr. *Expectation of life*: that duration which may reasonably be expected from a life of a given age.

Expectative (ekspe·ktătiv). 1488. [– med. L. *expectativus* (in phr. *gratia expectativa*), f. as prec.; see -IVE. Cf. Fr. *expectatif, -ive*, adj. and sb. (XVI).]

A. *adj.* **1.** Of or pertaining to expectation; †of prospective effect. **2.** Characterized by waiting for events 1611.

B. *sb.* **†1.** Something in expectation; an expectancy –1758. **2.** A mandate given by the pope or king conferring the expectation of a benefit; also called *expectative grace* 1563.

†**Expe·ction.** 1532. [erron. f. EXPECT, after apparent anal. of *inspect, inspection.*] = EXPECTATION. –1658. So **Expe·ctive** *a.* (*rare*) = EXPECTATIVE.

Expectorant (ekspe·ktŏrănt). 1782. [– *expectorant-*, pr. ppl. stem of L. *expectorare*; see next. -ANT¹.]

A. *adj.* That promotes expectoration 1811.

B. *sb.* An expectorant medicine.

Expectorate (ekspe·ktŏreˡt), *v.* 1601. [– *expectorat-*, pa. ppl. stem of L. *expectorare*, f. *ex-* Ex-¹ + *pectus, pector-* breast; see -ATE³.] **1.** *trans.* †To clear out from the chest or lungs –1678; to eject (phlegm, etc.) from the chest or lungs by coughing, hawking, or spitting 1666. Also *absol.* = to spit 1827. †**2.** To expel from the breast or mind –1656. Also *refl.* and *intr.* for *refl.*

Expectoration (ekspe:ktŏrēˡ·ʃən). 1672. [f. prec.; see -ATION.] **1.** The action of expectorating; discharge of phlegm from the chest by coughing, etc. **2.** *concr.* That which is expectorated, as phlegm 1817.

Expectorative (ekspe·ktŏrătiv). 1666. [f. as prec.; see -IVE.]

A. *adj.* Of or pertaining to expectoration 1883.

B. *sb.* = EXPECTORANT *sb.*

Expede (ekspī·d), *v. Sc.* 1513. [– L. *expedire*; see EXPEDITE *v.*] = EXPEDITE *v.* 4.

†**Expe·diate** *a.* [f. Fr. *expédié*, pa. pple. of *expédier* – med.L. *expediare* (= L. *expedire*).] Expeditious. EVELYN.

[**Expediate** *v.*, prob. error for EXPEDITE.]

Expedience (ekspī·diĕns). 1593. [f. as next, see -ENCE; partly f. EXPEDIENT.] †**1.** Dispatch; also, that which requires dispatch; an expedition, etc. –1606. 2. = EXPEDIENCY 1. ?*Obs.* 1619. **3.** = EXPEDIENCY 2; *pl.* interested motives, etc. 1608.

Expediency (ekspī·diĕnsi). 1612. [– late L. *expedientia* advantage (Boethius); in later use f. EXPEDIENT; see -ENCY.] **1.** The quality of being expedient; suitability to the conditions; fitness, advantage; †an advantage. **2.** The consideration of what is expedient, as a rule of action; what is politic, as dist. from what is just or right 1612. **b.** occas. in *pl.* The requirements of expediency 1843.

1. In some perplexity..about the e. of the voyage 1741. **2.** Matters of mere e., that affect neither honor, morality, or religion CHATHAM. Following his duty instead of consulting e. JANE AUSTEN.

Expedient (ekspī·diĕnt). ME. [– *expedient-*, pr. ppl. stem of L. *expedire*; see EXPEDITE *v.*, -ENT. Partly through Fr. *expédient.*]

A. *adj.* †**1.** Expeditious. SHAKS. **2.** Advantageous; fit, proper, or suitable to the circumstances of the case ME. **3.** Useful, politic, as opp. to just or right. Often *absol.* 1774.

1. *Rich. III*, I. ii. 217. **2.** Those things to know for me be full e. 1519. The most e. settlements for a trading country 1806. **3.** Too fond of the right to pursue the e. GOLDSM. Hence **Expe·diently** *adv.*

B. *sb.* †**1.** That which helps forward, or conduces to an object; a means to an end (*rare*) –1667. **2.** A device adopted in an exigency; a resource, shift 1653.

2. Finding out expedients..for shifting from one to another all personal Punishments BREVINT.

Expediential (ekspe:di,e·nʃăl), *a.* 1850. [f. EXPEDIENCY + -AL¹.] Of, pertaining to, or having regard to, what is expedient. Hence **Expedie·ntially** *adv.*

Expe·diment. 1547. [– late and med.L. *expedimentum*, f. L. *expedire*; see EXPEDITE *v.*, -MENT.] †**1.** An expedient –1677. **2.** 'The whole of a person's goods and chattels, bag and baggage' (Wharton).

Expeditate (ekspe·diteˡt), *v.* 1502. [– *expeditat-*, pa. ppl. stem of med.L. *expeditare*, f. *ex-* Ex-¹ + *pes, ped-* foot, on anal. of med.L. *excapitare* decapitate.] To cut off from (a dog) three claws or the ball of the forefoot; to law. Now *Hist.* Hence **Expedita·tion.**

†**E·xpedite,** *a.* 1545. [– L. *expeditus*, pa. pple. of *expedire*; see next, -ITE².] **1.** Free of impediments; unimpeded –1694. **2.** Of soldiers, etc.: Lightly equipped so as to move quickly –1792. **3.** Ready, prompt, expeditious –1792. Hence †**E·xpedite-ly** *adv.*, †**-ness.**

Expedite (e·kspĭdəit), *v.* 1471. [– *expedit-*, pa. ppl. stem of L. *expedire* extricate (orig. free the feet), make ready, put in order, f. *ex-* Ex-¹ + *pes, ped-* foot; see -ITE².] †**1.** *trans.* To clear of difficulties –1681. **2.** To help forward, hasten the progress of 1618. **3.** To perform quickly, dispatch 1471. **4.** To dispatch, issue officially; *transf.* to send out (an army, munitions, etc.). Now *rare.* 1606.

1. MILT. *P. L.* x. 474. **2.** To e. one's desires RALEGH, destruction FULLER, a local bill MACAULAY. **3.** To e. an order SMEATON. **4.** Though such charters be expedited of course BACON. Hence **E·xpediter.**

Expedition (ekspĭdi·ʃən). ME. [–(O)Fr. *expédition* – L. *expeditio*, f. as prec.; see -ION.] †**1.** The action of expediting; the condition of being expedited; prompt execution or supply; dispatch –1667. **2.** A sending or setting forth for some definite purpose; *esp.* a warlike enterprise ME. **3.** *concr.* What is thus sent out, e.g. a body of persons, a fleet, etc. 1693. **4.** The quality of being 'expedite'; promptness, haste, speed 1529.

1. A bill against Pluralityes is committed. Several other things in e. MARVELL. **2.** Mean while the Son On his great E. now appeer'd MILT. *P. L.* VII. 193. **3.** An e. may consist of a single ship CORY. **4.** With winged e., Swift as the lightning glance MILT.

Hence **Expedi·tionary** *a.* of, pertaining to, or sent on an e.; †*sb.* a papal officer who took care of dispatches. †**Expedi·tioner**, one who engaged in an e. **Expedi·tionist**, one who goes on an e.

Expeditious (ekspĭdi·ʃəs), *a.* 1599. [f. prec.; see -ITIOUS².] **1.** Characterized by expedition; performed with expedition 1610. **2.** Acting or moving with expedition; speedy.

1. E. measures 1832, travelling 1866. **2.** An e. set of workmen 1771. **Expedi·tious-ly** *adv.*, **-ness.**

†**Expe·ditive,** *a.* [f. EXPEDITE *v.* + -IVE. Cf. Fr. *expéditif* in same sense.] Expeditious. BACON.

Expel (ekspe·l), *v.* ME. [– L. *expellere*, f. *ex-* Ex-¹ + *pellere* drive, thrust.] **1.** *trans.* To drive out; to eject by force. Const. *from* (occas. *out of*); also with double obj. (*from* omitted). **2.** To turn out, eject from a society, etc. 1534. †**3.** To reject from consideration –1742. †**4.** To keep out. *Haml.* v. i. 239.

1. Power to expell and cast out devils 1577. He sent..two knights..to e. them the convent HUME. To e. an idea from consciousness H. SPENCER. **2.** To be expell'd the University 1648. Hence **Expe·llable** *a.* capable of being, or liable to be, expelled. **Expe·llent** *a.*, also **-ant**, that expels or tends to e.; *sb.* an expellent medicine. **Expe·ller.**

Expend (ekspe·nd), *v.* ME. [– L. *expendere*, f. *ex-* Ex-¹ + *pendere* weigh, pay. Cf. DISPEND, SPEND *v.*] **1.** *trans.* To pay away, lay out, spend (money); *esp.* for determinate objects. Const. *in, upon.* Also *absol.* Also *transf.* and *fig.* **2.** To use up (material or force) in any operation; also *refl.* 1745. **b.** *Naut.* To lose (spars, masts, etc.); to pay out (rope) 1801. †**3.** To weigh mentally –1677.

1. To e. money in beer 1867. *transf.*, etc. To e. time SHAKS., care 1728, wisdom EMERSON, blood 1854. **2.** The English archers..having expended their arrows, drew their swords 1859.

Hence **Expe·ndable** *a.* **Expe·nder.**

†**Expe·nditor.** 1499. [– med.L. *expenditor*, f. *expenditus*, irreg. pa. pple. (after *venditus* sold) of *expendere*; see prec., -OR 2.] *Law.* One who has charge of expenditure; *spec.* formerly an officer appointed to disburse the money collected by tax for the repair of sewers –1847.

Expenditure (ekspe·nditiŭɹ). 1769. [f. EXPEND, after prec.; see -URE.] **1.** The action or practice of expending; disbursement; consumption. **2.** The amount expended from time to time 1791.

1. Our e. purchased commerce and conquest BURKE. A vast e. of pains BROWNING. **2.** The Income and E. of Great Britain 1791.

Expense (ekspe·ns). ME. [–AFr. *expense*, alt. of OFr. *espense* – late L. *expensa*, fem. (sc. *pecunia* money) of pa. pple. of L. *expendere* EXPEND.] †**1.** The action of expending; the state of being expended; disbursement; consumption; loss –1797. †**2.** Money, or a sum, expended –1765. **3.** Burden of expenditure; the cost or sacrifice involved in any course of action, etc. 1632. **b.** In *pl.* esp.: 'Money out of pocket', or its reimbursement ME. **c.** An occasion of expense 1873.

1. All of them..dread a woman of expence FORDYCE. The sun is not wasted by e. of light FRANKLIN. **2.** Where a People thrive, there the income is greater than the expence PETTY. **3. b.** There's expences for thee SHAKS. **c.** His sons are an e. to him 1894.

Comb. **e.-magazine,** a magazine in which a small portion of ammunition is kept for immediate use.

Hence †**Expe·nseful** *a.* costly; also extravagant. †**Expe·nseless** *a.* without e.

Expensive (ekspe·nsiv), *a.* 1628. [f. *expens-*, pa. ppl. stem of L. *expendere*; see EXPEND, -IVE. Assoc. early with EXPENSE.] **1.** Given to expenditure; lavish; extravagant (now *rare*). **2.** Attended with expense; costly, dear. Also *transf.* 1634.

1. E. of ink BP. HALL, Health and Fortune STEELE, time 1817. Sir Oliver, likewise an e. man CARLYLE. **2.** An e. remedy EVELYN, education FROUDE.

Hence **Expe·nsively** *adv.* **Expe·nsiveness**, the quality of being e.; costliness; extravagance (now *rare*).

Expergefaction (ekspə̄:ɹ,dʒĭfæ·kʃən). Now *rare.* 1638. [– late L. *expergefactio*, f. *expergefact-*, pa. ppl. stem of L. *expergefacere*, f. *expergere* awake, arouse; see -FACTION.] The action of awakening or rousing; the state or fact of being awakened.

Experience (ekspīᵊ·riĕns), *sb.* ME. [–(O)Fr. *expérience* – L. *experientia*, f. *experiri* try; see Ex-¹, -ENCE.] †**1.** The action of putting to the test; trial –1668; an experiment –1763. †**2.** Proof by trial; demonstration –1715. **3.** The observation of facts or events, considered as a source of knowledge ME. **4.** The fact of being consciously the subject of a state or condition, or of being consciously affected by an event. Also, an instance of this. ME. **b.** A state of mind or feeling forming part of the inner religious life 1674. **5.** What has been experienced 1607. **6.** Personal knowledge 1553; †an experimental fact, maxim, rule, or device –1698. **7.** The state of having been occupied in any study or practice, in affairs, or in the intercourse of life; the duration or extent of such occupation; the qualifications thereby acquirèd 1483.

1. Make E. of my loyalty, by some service SHIRLEY. **3.** E. informs us only of what has been, but never of what must be REID. **4.** Experiens..were ynough for me To speke of wo that is in mariage CHAUCER. **b.** A repetition of Christiana's e. BUNYAN. **5.** Profound study of Indian e. MILL. **6.** Most men have the generosity to pay for their own e. 1791. **7.** His yeares but yong, but his e. old *Two Gent.* II. iv. 69.

Experience (ekspīᵊ·riĕns), *v.* 1533. [f. prec. sb.] †**1.** *trans.* To make experiment of; to test, try –1780; to prove by experience –1750. **2.** To have experience of; to feel, suffer, undergo 1588; to find by experience 1580. †**3.** To give experience to; to train (soldiers). Also in *passive*: To be taught by experience. –1654.

2. What we e. in the present world BUTLER. Phr. *To e. religion* (U.S.): to be converted. **3.** The Footmen..being experienced to run suddenly with the Horse men, leaped into the battail TOPSELL.

Hence **Expe·rienced** *ppl. a.* having experience; wise or skilful through experience; †tested; felt, suffered, undergone. **Expe·riencer,** one who experiences, or †makes experiments.

†**Expe·rient,** *a.* ME. [– *experient-*, pr. ppl. stem of L. *experiri*; see EXPERIENCE, -ENT. Cf. OFr. *experient*, adj.] Experienced –1630.

Experiential (ekspīᵊ:ri,e·nʃăl), *a.* 1816. [f. EXPERIENCE *sb.* + -IAL, after *inference, inferential*, etc.] Of, pertaining to, or derived from, experience or observation.

Phr. *E. philosophy*: the system which derives all knowledge from experience.

Hence **Experie·ntialism**, the doctrine that all knowledge is derived from experience. **Experie·ntialist**, an adherent of experientialism. **Experie·ntially** *adv.*

Experiment (ekspe·rimĕnt), *sb.* ME. [– OFr. *experiment* or L. *experimentum*, f. *experiri* try; see EXPERIENCE, -MENT.] **1.** The action of trying anything; a test, trial. Now *arch.* **2.** A procedure adopted in uncertainty whether it will answer the purpose 1594. **3.** An action or operation undertaken in order to discover something unknown, to test a hypothesis, or establish or illustrate some known truth ME. **4.** Experimentation 1678. †**5.** Experience; an instance of this. Const. *of.* –1741. †**6.** Practical proof; an example –1684.

2. It is good..not to try Experiments in States BACON. **4.** This is proved by E. 1678. **5.** I know by som experiments which I have had of you HOWELL.

Experiment (ekspe·rimĕnt), *v.* 1481. [f. prec. sb.] †**1.** *trans.* To experience –1727. †**2.** To ascertain or establish by trial –1812. †**3.** To make an experiment upon, test, try –1776. **4.** *intr.* To make an experiment or experiments. Const. *on.* 1787.

4. A person who has experimented with a reflector 1837. Hence **Expe:rimenta·tion,** the action or process of experimenting, a series of experiments. **Expe:rime·ntative** *a.* inclined to make an experiment; of the nature of an experiment. †**Expe·rimenta:tor** (*rare*), an experimenter; also, an empiric. **Expe·rimenter, -or, Expe·rimentist,** one who makes or tries experiments.

Experimental (ekspe:rime·ntal). ME. [– med.L. *experimentalis*; see EXPERIMENT *sb.*, -AL[1].]

A. *adj.* **1.** Based on or derived from experience; founded on experience only. **2.** Based on, derived from, or ascertained by experiment 1570. **3.** Tentative 1818. **4.** Relating to experiments; used in or for making experiments 1792.

2. Phr. *E. philosophy*: (*a*) the philosophy which insists on experiment as the necessary foundation of all reasoned conclusions; (*b*) Physics or 'natural philosophy' as demonstrated by means of experiments (now *rare*). So also, *e. chemistry, physics, science.* Hence *e. philosopher*, etc. Hence **Expe:rime·ntally** *adv.* by experience; by means of experiment.

B. *sb.* A trial; an experimental proof; a datum of experience; in *pl.* experimental knowledge 1628.

Hence **Expe:rime·ntalism,** the principles of the e. school in philosophy or science; e. research. **Expe:rime·ntalist,** one who experiments in some branch of science; one who is fond of trying experiments. **Expe:rime·ntalize,** *v. intr.* to make or try experiments.

†**Expe:rimenta·rian.** 1661. [f. EXPERIMENT *sb.* + -ARIAN.]

A. *adj.* Relying on experiment –1816.

B. *sb.* An experimental philosopher 1690.

Experimented (ekspe·rimĕntĕd), *ppl. a.* 1477. [f. EXPERIMENT *v.* + -ED[1].] **1.** Experienced; practised *in* (an art). Now *rare.* †**2.** Proved or known by experience –1807. †**3.** Met with in experience –1812.

†**Experre·ction.** [f. *experrect-* (pa. ppl. stem of L. *expergisci* wake up) + -ION.] The action of waking up. P. HOLLAND.

Expert (ekspə̄·ɹt), *a.*[1] ME. [– (O)Fr. *expert*, refash. of †*espert* after L. *expertus*, pa. pple. of *experiri* try. Cf. EXPERIENCE.] †**1.** Experienced (*in*), having experience (*of*) –1672. **2.** Trained by practice, skilled. Const. *at, in,* †*of, to* with *inf.* ME. †**3.** Tried, proved by experience –1612.

1. A Militia..e. in war PETTY. **2.** Maystres.. That were of lawe e. and curious CHAUCER. An e. Arithmeticien DEE. E. Mariners 1632. E. Valour 1665. **3.** His Pylot Of verie e., and approu'd Allowance *Oth.* II. i. 49. Hence **Expe·rt-ly** *adv.*, **-ness.**

†**Expe·rt,** *a.*[2] ME. [– L. *expers, expert-* lit. 'having no part in', f. *ex-* EX-[1] + *pars, part-* PART *sb.*] Devoid of, free from –1660.

Expert (e·kspə̄ɹt), *sb.* 1825. [– Fr. *expert* (the adj. used subst.); see EXPERT *a.*[1]] **1.** One who is EXPERT (sense 2) 1853. **2.** One whose special knowledge or skill causes him to be an authority; a specialist; also *attrib.* 1825.

1. An e. at hurdle-making ROGERS. **2.** My writing was well known; experts swore that the forgery was by me BESANT. *attrib.* E. evidence, witness, etc.

†**Expe·rt,** *v.* ME. [– *expert-*, pa. ppl. stem of L. *experiri*; see EXPERT *a.*[1]] To experience; to know by experience –1587.

‖**Expertise** (ekspəɹtī·z). 1869. [Fr.] Expert opinion or knowledge; also, the quality or state of being expert.

†**Expe·tible,** *a.* 1569. [– L. *expetibilis*, f. *expetere* desire, f. *ex-* EX-[1] + *petere* seek; see -BLE.] To be wished for; desirable –1679.

Expiable (e·kspiăb'l), *a.* 1570. [– Fr. *expiable* or eccl.L. *expiabilis*, f. *expiare*; see EXPIATE *v.*, -BLE.] Capable of being *expiated*; as, *an e. wrong.*

†**E·xpiate,** *ppl. a.* [– L. *expiatus*, pa. pple. of *expiare*; see next, -ATE[2].] Of an appointed time: Fully come. *Rich. III,* III. iii. 23.

Expiate (e·kspi,e[i]t), *v.* 1594. [– *expiat-*, pa. ppl. stem of L. *expiare*, f. *ex-* EX-[1] + *piare* seek to appease (by sacrifice), f. *pius* devout, PIOUS; see -ATE[3].] **1.** *trans.* To avert by religious ceremonies. *Obs.* exc. *Antiq.* 1611. †**2.** To purify with religious rites –1660. **3.** To extinguish the guilt of 1608. **4.** To pay the penalty of 1665. **5.** To make reparation for 1626. Also †*intr.* with *for.* †**6.** To extinguish by suffering to the full; to end by death –1615.

2. To Lustrate and E. a City STANLEY. **3.** An Affront that nothing but Blood can e. ADDISON. **4.** To e. the act with one's life STUBBS. **5.** To e. wrongs by benefits EMERSON. **6.** SHAKS. *Sonn.* xxii.

Hence **E·xpiatist, E·xpiator,** one who atones fully for.

Expiation (ekspi,ē[i]·ʃən). 1482. [– L. *expiatio*, f. as prec.; see -ION. Cf. (O)Fr. *expiation.*] **1.** The action of expiating or making atonement for, etc.; also, the condition of being expiated. **2.** The means by which atonement is made 1538.

1. I will found masses for his soul, in e. of my guilt SCOTT. Phr. *Fast* (or *feast*) *of Expiation*: a Jewish ceremony observed on the 10th day of Tisri, when the High Priest made e. for his own sins and those of the people. **2.** Human victims as an e. for guilt W. ROBERTSON. Hence **Expia·tional** *a.* pertaining to e.

Expiatory (e·kspiătəri), *a.* 1548. [– eccl.L. *expiatorius*, f. as prec.; see -ORY[2].] Having the attribute of expiating; serving to expiate. Const. *of.* So †**Expiato·rious** *a.*

†**E·xpilate,** *v.* [– *expilat-*, pa. ppl. stem of L. *expilare*, f. *ex-* EX-[1] + *pilare* plunder; see -ATE[3].] *trans.* To pillage, plunder. BP. HALL. Hence **Expila·tion,** the action of pillaging; *concr.* plunder. †**E·xpilator,** a pillager.

Expirant (ekspəi·rănt). *rare.* 1836. [f. EXPIRE *v.* + -ANT.] A name for a supposed vessel in plants, which assists in evaporation.

Expiration (ekspirē[i]·ʃən). 1526. [– L. *ex(s)piratio*, f. *ex(s)pirat-*, pa. ppl. stem of *ex(s)pirare*; see EXPIRE, -ION.] **1.** The action of breathing out (air, etc.); emission 1642. **2.** The action of breathing out air from the lungs. Also *transf.* of plants. 1603. †**3.** Exhalation; that which is expired; an exhalation –1667. †**4.** The action of breathing one's last; death –1807. Also †*transf.* and *fig.* **5.** The coming to an end; termination, close 1562.

1. Regular inspirations and expirations of air, by caverns and fissures MORSE. **3.** The true Cause of Cold, is an E. from the Globe of the Earth BACON. **4.** The Lord Treasurer..had notice of the Clark's e. CLARENDON. **5.** A fortnight after the e. of the treaty CLARENDON.

Expiratory (ekspəi[ə]·rătəri), *a.* 1847. [f. EXPIRAT(ION + -ORY[2].] Of or pertaining to expiration.

Expire (ekspəi[ə]·ɹ), *v.* ME. [– (O)Fr. *expirer* – L. *ex(s)pirare*, f. *ex-* EX-[1] + *spirare* breathe.] **1.** *trans.* To breathe out (air, etc.) from the lungs. Also *absol.*1590. †**2.** To give out, emit, exhale –1808. †**3.** *intr.* To pass out in, or like, breath; hence, of the winds, etc.: To rush forth –1729. †**4.** *trans.* To breathe out in the article of death –1720. **5.** *intr.* To breathe one's last, die ME. Also *transf.* **6.** To come to an end; to terminate; to become void; to become extinct 1450. †**7.** To cause to expire or cease; to put an end to –1612.

1. *absol.* [The Whales] expired with a rushing sound, the instant the blow-hole was exposed GOSSE. **2.** Ev'ry shrub expires perfume CHURCHILL. **3.** The linstocks touch, the ponderous ball expires DRYDEN. **5.** God onely knows..what becomes of a mans spirit, when he expireth HOBBES. *transf.* A lamp that was just expiring GOLDSM. **6.** Until your date e. SHAKS. A truce which expired in..1635. 1659. The title of the daughters expired on the birth of a son CRUISE. **7.** *Rom. & Jul.* I. iv. 109.

var. †**E·xpirate** (in sense 1). Hence †**Expi·re** *sb.* expiry. **Expi:ree·**, an ex-convict. **Expi·rer,** one who expires; also, an *expiree.*

Expiring (ekspəi[ə]·riŋ), *ppl. a.* 1609. [f. prec. + -ING[2].] That expires; breathing out air from the lungs, etc.; breathing his or its last, dying; coming to an end.

Thy e. breath HABINGTON. *fig.* Bubbles in e. foam RUSKIN. The e. year 1705, lease BYRON.

Expiry (ekspəi[ə]·ri). 1752. [f. EXPIRE + -Y[3].] = EXPIRATION 4, 5.

The e. of a term, a contract SMILES.

Expiscate (ekspi·ske[i]t), *v.* Chiefly *Sc.* 1611. [– *expiscat-*, pa. ppl. stem of L. *expiscare*, f. *ex-* EX-[1] + *piscare* to fish; see -ATE[3].] *trans.* To fish out; hence, to find out by scrutiny.

To e. intelligible reasons 1864. Hence **Expisca·tion,** the act of expiscating. **Expi·scator. Expi·scatory** *a.* tending to fish out (*rare*).

Explain (eksplē[i]·n), *v.* 1513. [Earliest form *explane* – L. *explanare*, f. *ex-* EX-[1] + *planus* PLAIN *a.*[1], to which the mod. sp. is assim.] †**1.** To make smooth –1650. †**2.** To open out, spread out flat. Also *refl.* and *intr.* for *refl.* –1721. **3.** To unfold; to make plain or intelligible 1513. **4.** To interpret 1608. **5.** To account for 1736. **6.** *refl.* To make oneself understood, speak plainly 1624. **7.** *intr.* **a.** To say in explanation *that* 1867. †**b.** To speak one's mind *against, upon* –1764.

2. The Horse-Chesnut is..ready to e. its leaf 1684. **3.** To e. what is meant by the nature of man BUTLER. **4.** To define fire by heat would be to e. a thing by itself BP. BERKELEY. Phr. *To e. away*: to do away with by explanation.

Hence **Explai·nable** *a.* capable of explanation. **Explai·ner.**

†**Explai·t,** *v.* Also **explat(e.** [f. EX-[1] + PLAIT *v.* Cf. EXHALE *v.*[2]] To unravel. B. JONS.

E·xplanate, *a.* 1846. [– L. *explanatus*, pa. pple. of *explanare*; see EXPLAIN, -ATE[2].] *Entom.*, etc. Spread out flat.

Explanation (eksplănē[i]·ʃən). ME. [– L. *explanatio*, f. *explanat-*, pa. ppl. stem of *explanare*; see EXPLAIN, -ION.] **1.** The action or process, or an instance, of explaining. **2.** That which explains, makes clear, or accounts for; a method of explaining 1610. **3.** A mutual declaration of the sense of spoken words, motives of actions, etc., with a view to adjust a misunderstanding and reconcile differences; hence, a mutual understanding or reconciliation 1840.

1. I pass to the E. of the following Table EVELYN. **2.** My E. of the Mystery of Godliness HY. MORE. The e. offered..proves to be erroneous SIR B. BRODIE. **3.** To come to an e. with one's father 1840.

Explanative (eksplæ·nătiv), *a.* 1750. [– late and med.L. *explanativus*, f. as prec.; see -IVE.] Explanatory.

Explana·to-, comb. f. L. *explanatus* EXPLANATE, in sense 'spread, or spreading out, in a plane'.

Explanatory (eksplæ·nătəri), *a.* 1618. [– late L. *explanatorius*, f. *explanat-*; see prec., -ORY[2].] Serving to explain, containing an explanation; having the function of explaining.

A short essay, accompanied with two e. prints HOGARTH. Hence **Expla·natorily** *adv.* **Expla·natoriness,** e. quality.

†**Explees,** obs. f. ESPLEES, *Law.*

†**Exple·te,** *v.* Also †**explea·t.** ME. [– *explet-*, pa. ppl. stem of L. *explēre*, f. *ex-* EX-[1] + *plēre* fill.] **1.** *trans.* To fill out; to complete (a period of time) –1657. **2.** To do fully –1611. Hence †**Exple·tion,** fulfilment.

Expletive (e·ksplĭtiv, eksplī·tiv). 1612. [– late L. *expletivus*, f. as prec.; see -IVE. Cf. Fr. *explétif, -ive.*]

A. *adj.* **1.** Serving to fill out; introduced merely to fill up; *occas.*, redundant 1656. **2.** Tending or seeking to supply a loss; compensative. HALLAM.

1. He uses them [oaths] as e. phrases..to plump his speech BARROW. **2.** E. justice HALLAM.

B. *sb.* **1.** An expletive word or phrase; *esp.* an oath 1612. **2.** A person or thing that merely serves to fill up space 1688.

1. Expletives he very early ejected from his verses JOHNSON. **2.** A sort of e. at the table, serving to stop gaps 1872.

Hence **Expletive-ly** *adv.*, **-ness.** So **E·xpletory** *a.* serving to fill up.

Explicable (e·ksplikăb'l), *a.* 1556. [– Fr. *explicable* or L. *explicabilis*, f. *explicare*; see next, -BLE.] That may be explained or accounted for.

Explicate (e·ksplike[i]t), *v.* 1531. [– *explicat-*, pa. ppl. stem of L. *explicare*, f. *ex-* EX-[1] + *plicare* fold; see -ATE[3].] †**1.** *trans.* To unfold; to expand; to display –1712. †**2.** To disentangle –1713. **3.** To bring out what is implicit in 1628. **4.** = EXPLAIN *v.* 3. Now *rare.* 1531. †**5.** = EXPLAIN *v.* 5. –1729.

1. The leaves..e. themselves SHARROCK. **4.** To e. obscure passages 1650. **5.** Perceptions..which..it may not be very easy at first view to e. BUTLER.

Hence †**E·xplicate** *ppl. a.* unfolded; fully stated; explained. †**E·xplicator** (*rare*).

Explication (eksplikēⁱ·ʃən). 1528. [– Fr. *explication* or L. *explicatio*, f. as prec.; see -ION.] **1.** The action or process of expanding, developing, or explaining; explanation, interpretation; †an exposition; †a paraphrase. **†2.** = EXPLANATION 3. –1745.

1. A better e. of a controverted line JOHNSON.

Explicative (e·ksplikeⁱtiv), *a.* 1627. [– Fr. *explicatif*, f. *expliquer*; see EXPLICATE, -ATIVE.] **†1.** Tending to unfold (itself) –1677. **2.** Explanatory; explicit; in *Logic*, = ESSENTIAL. 1649.

2. The new judgments..are all e. or analytic 1877. Hence **E·xplicatively** *adv.*

Explicatory (e·ksplikătəri), *a.* 1625. [f. EXPLICATE + -ORY².] Having the function of explaining.

‖**E·xplicit.** ME. [Late L.; app. short for *explicitus* (*est liber*) lit. 'the book is unrolled'. Also taken as a vb. in 3rd pers. sing., 'Here ends', with pl. *expliciunt*.] A word used to indicate the end of a book, etc. **b.** as *sb.* The last words or lines of a volume or section of a book; *fig.* conclusion, finis 1658.

Explicit (ekspli·sit), *a.* 1613. [– Fr. *explicite* or L. *explicitus*, pa. pple. of *explicare*; see EXPLICATE.] **†1.** Free from folds or intricacies –1697. **2.** Developed in detail; hence, clear, definite 1651. **3.** Of declarations, etc.: Distinctly expressing all that is meant; leaving nothing merely implied; express 1613. **4.** Of persons, etc.: Speaking out fully all that is meant; having no reserves; outspoken 1726.

1. The plot whether intricate or e. MILT. **2.** *E. faith, belief* (Theol.): acceptance of a doctrine with distinct apprehension of all that it involves; opp. to *implicit faith*. **3.** There was an e. consent and an implicit consent CROMWELL. Hence **Expli·citly** *adv.* expressly. **Expli·citness.**

Explode (eksplōᵘ·d), *v.* 1538. [– L. *explodere* drive out by clapping, hiss off the stage, f. *ex-* EX-¹ + *plaudere* clap the hands. Cf. APPLAUD, PLAUDIT.] **†1.** *trans.* To clap and hoot off the stage; hence *gen.* to drive away with expressions of disapprobation. Also *fig.* –1823. **2.** To reject with scorn; also, to discard. Still used occas. in *pass.* with sense: To be disused as obsolete. 1538. **3.** To cause to be rejected; to discredit; †to bring into disuse 1635. **†4.** To drive forth (air); to drive out with violence and sudden noise –1826. **5.** *intr.* To go off with a loud report, or to fly in pieces, under the influence of suddenly developed internal energy. Also *transf.* and *fig.* 1790. **6.** *trans.* To cause to go off with a loud noise; to blow up. Also *transf.* and *fig.* 1794. **7.** *Phonetics.* To utter with a puff of breath, as one of the stop consonants *p, b, t, d, k, g*.

1. Vertue and Wisdom..were hissed out, and exploded by the common people BURTON. **2.** But the court *una voce* exploded this reason, and said [etc.] BACON. **3.** To e. a lie 1872, a fallacy 1881. Hence **Explo·dent** (*Phonetics*) = EXPLOSIVE B. 1. **Explo·der**, one who or that which explodes; a contrivance for exploding gunpowder, etc.

Exploit (eksploi·t), *sb.* [ME. *esploit*, *exploit*, *-ployte* – OFr. *esplait* achievement, *esploit* m., *esploite* fem. (mod. *exploit*):– Gallo-Rom. **explictum*, *-*ta*, L. *explicitum*, -*ta* n. and fem. pa. pples. of *explicare* EXPLICATE.] **†1.** Advantage; furtherance. Const. *of*. –1525. **†2.** The endeavour to gain advantage or mastery over; hence, a military or naval enterprise –1755. **3.** An act or deed; a brilliant feat 1538. **†4.** *Law.* A citation or summons; a writ –1682.

2. *All's Well* IV. i. 41. **3.** For many years it was counted a great e. to pass this strait DE FOE.

Exploit (eksploi·t), *v.* [ME. *expleite* – Fr. *expleiter* accomplish, enjoy (mod. *exploiter*) :– Gallo-Rom. **explicitare*, f. L. *explicare*; see prec.] **†1.** *trans.* To achieve –1687. **†2.** To act with effect; to get on –1602. **3.** To work (a mine, etc.); to turn to account 1838. **4.** *transf.* To utilize for selfish purposes; to make capital out of 1847. **5.** *intr.* To conduct mining operations *for* 1887.

1. They knewe wel that they shold no thyng exployte of their entente CAXTON. **3.** To e. mineral resources 1865, the riches of the East 1890.

Hence **Exploi·table** *a.* capable of being exploited. **Exploi·tative** *a.* concerned with exploiting. **Exploi·ter. Exploi·ture**, the action of exploiting, †achieving, or developing.

Exploitation (eksploitēⁱ·ʃən). 1803. [– (O)Fr. *exploitation*, f. *exploiter*; see prec., -ATION.] The action of turning to account; the action of utilizing for selfish purposes.

The e. of the credulous public 1868. So **Exploi·tage.**

†Explo·rate, *v.* 1549. [– *explorat-*, pa. ppl. stem of L. *explorare*; see EXPLORE, -ATE³.] = EXPLORE –1646. Hence **Explo·rative** *a.* exploratory; inclined to make explorations. **Explo·ratively** *adv.*

Exploration (eksplorēⁱ·ʃən). 1543. [– Fr. *exploration* or L. *exploratio*, f. as prec.; see -ION.] **†1.** The action of examining; scrutiny –1655. **2.** *Med.*, etc. The examination of an organ, a wound, etc. by the use of the finger, a probe, or the like 1860. **3.** The action of exploring; an instance of this 1823.

2. E. of the Rectum 1880. **3.** E. of the sources of the Nile 1880.

Explorator (e·ksplorēⁱ:təɹ). 1450. [– L. *explorator*; see EXPLORATE, -OR 2.] One who or that which explores; †a scout; an 'electrical explorer'.

Exploratory (eksplǫ·rătəri), *a.* 1620. [– L. *exploratorius*, f. prec.; see -ORY².] Of or pertaining to exploration; serving or intended for exploration; bent on exploration.

Explore (eksplōᵊ·ɹ), *v.* 1585. [– Fr. *explorer* – L. *explorare* search out.] **1.** *trans.* To seek to find out; †to search for; to make proof of (MILT. *P. L.* II. 632). **2.** To look into closely, scrutinize; to pry into 1592; to probe (a wound) 1767. **3.** *esp.* To search into (a country, etc.); to go into or range over for the purpose of discovery 1616. **4.** *intr.* To conduct operations in search *for* 1823.

1. To e. The city's strength MASSINGER, a fit opportunity 1822. **2.** To e. a bookstall LAMB. **3.** He..recommended us to e. Wapping BOSWELL. Hence **Explo·rable** *a. rare.* **Explo·rement**, exploration.

Explorer (eksplōᵊ·rəɹ). 1684. [f. prec. + -ER¹.] One who explores (a country, etc.); that which examines or †tests; *spec.* an apparatus for exploring a wound or a cavity in a tooth.

Phr. *Electrical e.*: an apparatus for detecting a bullet or other metallic substance in the tissues.

Exploring (eksplōᵊ·riŋ), *vbl. sb.* 1841. [f. as prec. + -ING¹.] The action of EXPLORE *v.* Also *attrib.*, as in *exploring needle, trochar*, etc.

Explosible (eksplōᵘ·zib'l), *a.* 1799. [f. EXPLOS(ION + -IBLE.] Capable of being exploded.

Explosion (eksplōᵘ·ʒən). 1656. [– L. *explosio* (sense 1), f. *explos-*, pa. ppl. stem of *explodere* EXPLODE; see -ION. Senses 1 and 2 app. first in Eng.] **†1.** The action of rejecting with scorn –1796. **2.** The action of driving out, or of issuing forth, with violence and noise 1667; *spec.* explosive utterance (of a sound) 1879. **3.** The action of going off with a loud noise, or of bursting, under the influence of suddenly developed internal energy 1744; the resulting noise 1775. Also *transf.* **4.** A bursting forth into sudden activity; an outburst (of anger, laughter, etc.) 1817.

2. Frequent explosions of fire and smoke, emitted from the mountain MORSE. **3.** The e. of a bomb 1762, of a glass jar, battery, etc. IMISON, of powder 1816. **4.** A desperate conspiracy which threatened an e. 1817.

Explosive (eksplōᵘ·siv). 1667. [f. EXPLOS(ION + -IVE.]

A. *adj.* **1.** Tending to drive or burst forth with violence and noise. **2.** *spec.* Of a consonant-sound: Produced by explosion of breath; stopped 1854. **3.** Of, pertaining to, or of the nature of, an explosion 1844.

1. E. power 1667, nitre BURKE. **2.** The e. consonants *b, d, g, p, t*, and *k* 1854. **3.** E. laughs DICKENS.

B. *sb.* **1.** An explosive consonant (see A. 2) 1878. **2.** An explosive agent or compound 1874.

2. The principal explosives used in mining are gunpowder..nitroglycerin [etc.] RAYMOND.

Hence **Explo·sive-ly** *adv.*, **-ness.**

Expoliation: see EXSPOLIATION.

†Expo·lish, *v.* [f. EX-¹ + POLISH *v.*, after L. *expolire*. Cf. EXHALE *v.*², EXPLAIT.] *trans.* To polish thoroughly. HEYWOOD.

†Expo·ne, *v.* ME. [– L. *exponere*; see EXPOUND. Since XVI chiefly Sc.] **1.** *trans.* To expound –1632. **2.** To expend (effort, money) –1587. **3.** To expose –1651.

Exponent (ekspōᵘ·nĕnt). 1581. [– *exponent-*, pr. ppl. stem of L. *exponere* EXPOUND; see -ENT.]

A. *adj.* That sets forth or interprets.

B. *sb.* **1.** One who sets forth in words, expounds, or interprets. Also, that which serves to interpret. 1812. **2.** *Algebra.* A symbol denoting a power; an index. Now written at the right hand of and above the symbol of the quantity affected by it. 1706. **3.** He who or that which sets forth as a representative or index 1825.

1. This form of discontent found its e. in John Wycliffe FROUDE. **2.** Phr. †*E. of the Ratio*: the quotient which arises when the antecedent is divided by the consequent. **3.** Price is the e. of exchangeable value 1833.

Exponential (eksponeˑnʃăl). 1704. [– Fr. *exponentiel* (J. Bernouilli), f. as prec.; see -IAL.]

A. *adj.* **1.** That sets forth or exhibits (*rare*) 1730. **2.** *Math.* Involving the unknown quantity or variable as an exponent. So *e. equation, function, quantity*, etc.

2. *E. series*, the infinite series $1 + x + \frac{1}{2}x^2 + \frac{1}{6}x^3$ etc.

B. *sb. Math.* An exponential quantity or function; *spec.* the Napierian base *e* raised to the power denoted by the variable; the Napierian antilogarithm of the variable 1784.

Exponible (ekspōᵘ·nib'l). 1569. [– med.L. *exponibilis*, f. *exponere*; see EXPONE, -IBLE. Cf. OFr. *exponible*.]

A. *adj.* That admits or requires explanation; *spec.* in *Logic*, of a proposition, that requires restatement for use in a syllogism 1788.

B. *sb.* An exponible proposition.

Export (ekspōᵊ·ɹt), *v.* 1485. [– L. *exportare*, f. *ex-* EX-¹ + *portare* carry.] **†1.** *trans.* To take away, carry off. Also *fig.* –1691. **2.** *Comm.* To send out (commodities) from one country to another. Also *transf.* and *fig.* 1665.

1. They e. honour from a man and make him a returne in Enuy BACON. **2.** To e. Corn MANLEY, black cattle PETTY, olives 1841. Hence **Expo·rtable** *a.* and *sb.*

Export (e·kspoɹt), *sb.* 1690. [f. prec.] *Comm.* That which is exported; also, the action of exporting, exportation.

1. Our commerce, the imports and exports of the nation BURKE. **2.** The e. of arms to Spain 1874. *Comb.*: **e. bill**, a bill drawn against exported goods; **e. duty**, a duty paid on exported goods.

Exportation (ekspoɹtēⁱ·ʃən). 1610. [– L. *exportatio*, f. *exportat-*, pa. ppl. stem of *exportare*; see EXPORT *v.*, -ION.] **†1.** The action of carrying or sending out –1789. **2.** *Comm.* The sending out (of commodities) from one country to another 1641. **3.** quasi-*concr.* That which is exported; †*pl.* exports 1664.

Exporter (ekspōᵊ·ɹtəɹ). 1691. [f. EXPORT *v.* + -ER¹.] One who exports; an export trader.

Expose (ekspōᵘ·z), *v.* 1474. [– (O)Fr. *exposer*, based on L. *exponere*; see EXPOUND, POSE *v.*¹] **1.** *trans.* To put out; 'to cast out to chance' (J.); *esp.* to abandon (an infant) 1611. **2.** To leave without shelter or defence; †to imperil 1477. **3.** To lay open (to danger, ridicule, etc.); to render accessible or liable *to* action or influence 1474. **4.** To exhibit openly 1623; *Eccl.* to exhibit (the Host, relics, etc.) for adoration or veneration 1644. **5.** To put up *for* (or *to*) sale. Now chiefly *Sc.* 1610. **6.** To make known, disclose (secrets, etc.). Formerly: To set forth, explain. 1483. **7.** To unmask, show up 1693. **†b.** In 17–18th c.: To hold up to ridicule (what is not ridiculous) –1772. **8.** *Photog.* To subject (a plate, etc.) to the action of actinic rays 1848.

1. This practice of exposing children HUME. **2.** To e. the gunners 1885. **3.** Exposed to severe trials 1865, to inharmonious influences J. MARTINEAU. **4.** The Beggar, who exposes his Sores STEELE. To e. a card 1870, a vein of quartz RAYMOND. **6.** The whole truth is not always to be exposed BOSWELL. **7.** To e. the Follies of Men DRYDEN, an imposture MOZLEY.

Hence **Expo·sal**, exposure. **Expo·sedness. Expo·ser.**

‖**Exposé** (ekspoze). 1803. [Fr., pa. pple. of *exposer*; see prec.] **1.** A recital of facts and particulars. **2.** A showing up of something discreditable 1831. (Also written **Expose** (ékspō^u·z) *U.S.* 1715.)

Exposition (ekspozi·ʃən). ME. [(O)Fr. *exposition* or L. *expositio*; see Ex-[1], POSITION.] **1.** The action of exposing, or the condition of being exposed 1530. †**2.** = EXPOSURE 3. –1834. **3.** The action of putting out to public view; a display, show, exposure 1649; an EXHIBITION 1868. **b.** *Eccl.* in spec. use: see EXPOSE *v.* 4. **4.** The action of setting forth, or of explaining; a detailed explanation or interpretation ME. **5.** *Logic.* As tr. Gr. ἔκθεσις: the selection of some sensible object, in order to prove a general relation apprehended by the intellect 1588.

2. An Easterly E. EVELYN. **3.** An e. of the holy wafer BECKFORD. E. on the pillory 1836. The World's Columbian E. at Chicago 1891. **4.** The exposicioun of this holy praier CHAUCER. You know the Law, your e. Hath beene most sound SHAKS. The great expositions of feudal custom STUBBS.

Hence **Exposi·tional** *a.* of the nature of an e.

Expositive (ekspǫ·zitiv), *a.* 1535. [f. EXPOSITION + -IVE.] Descriptive; explanatory.

Expositor (ekspǫ·zitəɹ). ME. [– (O)Fr. *expositeur* or late L. *expositor*, f. *exposit-*, pa. ppl. stem of L. *exponere*; see EXPOSE, -OR 2.] One who, or that which, sets forth in detail, explains, or expounds.

Expository (ekspǫ·zitəri), *a.* 1628. [– late L. *expositorius* (Boethius), f. as prec.; see -ORY[2].] Of, pertaining to, or of the nature of, exposition; containing an exposition; explanatory.

A glossary or e. index to the poetical writers JOHNSON.

‖**Ex post facto** (eks pō^{u}st fæ·kto). 1649. [erron. division of late L. *ex postfacto* (Digest of Justinian) from what is done afterwards, i.e. *ex* from, out of, with abl. of *postfactum*.] From an after act or deed; = 'after the fact'. **b.** As quasi-*adj.* Done after another thing, and operating retrospectively, *esp.* in *Ex post facto law* 1789.

b. An ex-post facto law BENTHAM. They might have objected to the tax had it been *ex post facto* MCCULLOCH.

Expostulate (ekspǫ·stiŭleˈt), *v.* 1534. [– *expostulat-*, pa. ppl. stem of L. *expostulare*; see Ex-[1], POSTULATE *v.*] †**1.** *trans.* To demand –1670. †**2.** To complain of; to plead *with* a person about; to debate (a matter) as an aggrieved person –1789. †**3.** *intr.* To complain; to discourse –1773. **4.** To reason earnestly and kindly *with* (a person), *about*, *for*, *on*, or *upon* (a thing), for the purpose of reprehension or dissuasion 1574.

3. 3 *Hen. VI*, II. v. 135. **4.** He expostulated with him on the impropriety of such conduct to strangers LIVINGSTONE. Hence **Expo·stulator.**

Expostulation (ekspǫ:stiulēˈ·ʃən). 1586. [– L. *expostulatio*, f. as prec.; see -ION.] **1.** The action of expostulating; earnest and kindly protest. **2.** An uttered remonstrance, protest, or reproof 1597.

2. That pathetick E...of Ezekiel. Why will ye die! 1748.

Expostulatory (ekspǫ·stiŭlātə:ri), *a.* 1586. [f. EXPOSTULATE + -ORY[2].] Characterized by, or of the nature of, expostulation.

Mr. Jane..wrote me an e. letter WARBURTON.

†**Expo·sture.** [f. EXPOSE, after *posture*, etc.] = EXPOSURE. *Cor.* IV. i. 36.

Exposure (ekspō^u·ʒiŭɹ). 1606. [f. EXPOSE, after *enclosure*, or the like; see -URE.] **1.** The action of exposing; the fact or state of being exposed (see EXPOSE *v.*). **2.** *concr.* A surface laid open to view, or to the operation of any agency 1611. **3.** The manner or degree in which anything is exposed; *esp.* situation with regard to sun and wind; aspect 1664.

1. Our naked Frailties..That suffer in e. *Macb.* II. iii. 133. Free e. to cold 1844. The e. of a forgery 1873. *Photog.* Ten seconds of e. 1847 (cf. EXPOSE *v.* 8). **3.** The Fruits of the Northern E. ripen last of all 1710.

Expound (ekspau·nd), *v.* [ME. *expoune*, *expounde* – OFr. *espondre* (pres. stem *espon-*) :– L. *exponere* expose, publish, exhibit, explain, f. *ex-* Ex-[1] + *ponere* put, place.] **1.** *trans.* To set forth in detail. **2.** To explain; *esp.* to interpret (Scripture, religious formularies, etc.) ME. †**3.** To expose to view –1664.

1. I have..an excellent interpretation..which I will e. to you JOWETT. **2.** To e. an Ambiguyte 1511, a parable UDALL. The Pope was forced to e. himself BRAMHALL. **3.** First, he expounded both his Pockets BUTLER *Hud.* II. iii. 1087. Hence **Expou·nder**, one who or (occas.) that which expounds.

Express (ekspre·s), *a. adv.* and *sb.*[1] ME. [– (O)Fr. *exprès* – L. *expressus* distinctly or manifestly presented, pa. pple. of *exprimere* (cf. EXPRESS *v.*).]

A. *adj.* **1.** Exactly resembling, exact. Now chiefly with reminiscence of *Heb.* 1:3. 1513. †**2.** Stated –1686. **3.** Expressed and not merely implied; definite, explicit; unmistakable in import ME. Hence of persons, a state of mind, etc.: †Explicit, fixed –1778. **4.** Done, made, or sent on purpose ME.

1. Hee Created thee, in the Image of God E. MILT. *P.L.* VII. 528. **3.** E. testimony 1662, contracts, malice BLACKSTONE. Sometimes by e., more often by tacit understanding BRYCE. **4.** E. laws were made to prevent [it] PRIESTLEY.

Phrases. *E. train*: orig. = 'special train'; later, a passenger train running expressly to one particular place; now, a fast train stopping only at important stations. Hence *E. speed. E. delivery*: (in the Postal service) immediate delivery by special messenger; so *e. fee, messenger, packet, etc. E. rifle*: one with a high initial velocity and a low trajectory.

B. *adv.* †**1.** Clearly; distinctly –1712. †**2.** Directly *against*; exactly; completely –1513. **3.** Specially, on purpose; hence, with speed; now, by express messenger or train ME.

3. A piece of news worth sending e. LOWELL.

C. *sb.*[1] **1.** = *E. messenger*: see A. 4. Hence *transf.*, The message sent by an express 1642. **2.** Short for *e.-train*, *e. rifle* 1848. **3.** *U.S.* An institution or agency for the transmission of parcels 1858.

Hence **Expre·ss** *v.* to send by express. (*U.S.*) **Expre·ssage**, the sending of a parcel by express; the charge for this. **Expre·ssly** *adv.* in an e. manner. **Expre·ssness.**

†**Express** (ekspre·s), *sb.*[2] 1513. [f. the vb.] **1.** The action of expressing; an instance of this. Const. *of*. –1716. **b.** A manifestation. (Revived by Kingsley with stress *e·xpress.*) –1663. **2.** A phrase; an utterance; an injunction –1677. **3.** A graphic representation, image; also *fig.* –1646.

1. b. Making all Thy creatures to be expresses of Thy power JER. TAYLOR.

Express (ekspre·s), *v.* [– OFr. *expresser* – Rom. **expressare*, f. *ex-* Ex-[1] + *pressare* PRESS *v.*[1]; repr. in use L. *exprimere*.]

I. 1. *trans.* To press or squeeze out; hence *fig.*, to extort or elicit by pressure ME. **2.** To press out the contents of. Now *rare*. 1633.

1. E. the juice and spirit 1757. *fig.* The truth was by torture expressed HOLLAND. So affliction Expresseth virtue fully WEBSTER.

II. 1. To portray, represent. *Obs.* or *arch.* in general sense. ME. †**b.** To be an image of, resemble –1697. **2.** To represent symbolically 1649. **3.** To reveal by external tokens; to betoken. Now chiefly with reference to feelings or personal qualities. 1549. **4.** To represent in language; to set forth; to give utterance to. (The prevailing use.) ME. **b.** *refl.* To put one's thoughts into words; to state one's opinion 1601. †**5.** To mention, specify; to describe –1798. **6.** To state or mention explicitly; opp. to *imply* 1596.

1. Loggan used long strokes in expressing flesh H. WALPOLE. **b.** Man expresseth God..as the childe doeth resemble hys father or mother UDALL. **2.** A child to e. coming into the world, an old man for going out of it BP. STILLINGFL. Phr. *To e. a quantity in terms of another.* **3.** Never did tone e. indifference plainer JANE AUSTEN. **4.** A phrase they have got among them, to e. their nomeaning by VILLIERS. No words can e. too strongly the caution which should be used BUTLER. **6.** Hints and allusions expressing little, insinuating much BERKELEY. Hence †**Expre·ssedly** *adv.* statedly; expressly. **Expre·sser, -or. Expre·ssible,** †**-able** *a.*

Expression (ekspre·ʃən). 1460. [– (O)Fr. *expression* or L. *expressio*, f. *express-*, pa. ppl. stem of *exprimere* (cf. prec.); see -ION.] **1.** The action of pressing or squeezing out; †an expressed drink, juice, etc. 1594. **2.** The action of representing in words or symbols; utterance 1460. **b.** The action of manifesting by action or other external tokens 1647. **3.** quasi-*concr.* An utterance, declaration, representation; a sign, token. (Now only with *of.*) 1628. **4.** Manner or means of representation in language; diction 1628; a word, phrase, or form of speech 1646; in *Alg.* a collection of symbols together expressing a quantity 1796. **5.** Of the countenance, voice, attitude, etc.: Expressive quality 1774. **b.** Look, intonation, etc., as indicating a state of feeling 1830. **6.** *Fine Arts.* The fact or way of expressing character, sentiment, action, feeling, etc., in a work of art 1715.

1. The crushing of the coco-nut for the e. of the oil 1859. **2.** To encourage the fullest e. of public feeling FROUDE. Phr. *Beyond, past e.*; *to seek, find e.* **3.** An unguarded e. 1714. **4.** A great range of e. 1859. Ambiguous expressions FROUDE. **5.** His eyes possessing wonderful..e. MEDWIN. **6.** Raphael's feeling for e. 1816. She played with e. 1864.

Hence **Expre·ssional** *a.* of or pertaining to e., *esp.* in the fine arts. **Expre·ssionism**, the methods, style, or attitude of expressionists, esp. in artistic technique. **Expre·ssionist**, an artist whose work aims chiefly at 'expression'; now esp. in reference to artistic technique. **Expressioni·stic** *a.* **Expre·ssionless** *a.*

Expressive (ekspre·siv), *a.* ME. [– Fr. *expressif*, *-ive* or med.L. *expressivus*, f. as prec.; see -IVE.] †**1.** Tending to press out. ME. only. **2.** Concerned with expression 1747. **3.** Serving to express 1711. **4.** Full of expression; formerly also, †explicit 1690. **5.** Open in expressing (sentiments). Const. *of* (*rare*). 1601. †**6.** Expressing itself in action –1747.

2. The e. arts REID, powers 1891. **4.** The e. term of Bung, as signifying a public-house landlord 1859. E. features D. WILSON. **5.** Not enough e. of our pleasure LAMB. Hence **Expre·ssively** *adv.*, **-ness.**

Expressless (ekspre·sles), *a. arch.* 1586. [f. EXPRESS *a.* + -LESS.] That cannot be expressed.

Expressman (ekspre·smæ̆n). 1847. [f. EXPRESS *sb.*[1] 3.] A man employed in receiving and delivering parcels; *esp.* an employé of one of the U.S. express companies.

†**Expre·ssure.** 1598. [f. EXPRESS *v.* + -URE.] = EXPRESSION –1850.

An operation more diuine, Than breath or pen can giue e. (= description) to SHAKS. Th' e. (= image) that it beares: Greene let it be *Merry W.* V. v. 71.

†**E·xprobrate,** *v.* Also **exprobate** (app. after *reprobate*). 1543. [– *exprobrat-*, pa. ppl. stem of L. *exprobrare*, f. *ex-* Ex-[1] + *probrum* shameful deed.] **1.** To make (a thing) a matter of reproach. Const. *to*, *unto*, or dat. –1670. **2.** To reproach (a person). Const. *with*. –1638.

Hence **Exprobra·tion** (*arch.*), the action of upbraiding; reproachful language. †**Expro·brative,** †**Expro·bratory** *adjs.* reproachful.

‖**Ex professo** (eks profe·so). 1823. [L.] Professedly, by profession.

Expromission (ekspromi·ʃən). 1818. [f. as next, see -ION; cf. Fr. *expromission*.] *Civil Law.* The act by which a new debtor undertakes the debt of a former one, who is thereby released.

Expromissor (ekspromi·sǫɹ). 1695. [– late L. *expromissor*, f. *expromiss-*, pa. ppl. stem of L. *expromittere* (Varro) promise or agree to pay; see Ex-[1], PROMISE *v.*, -OR 2.] *Civil Law.* One who promises to pay; *spec.* one who undertakes the debt of another, thereby releasing him; dist. from a 'surety' or 'bail'.

Expropriate (ekspro^u·priˌeˈt), *v.* 1611. [– *expropriat-*, pa. ppl. stem of med.L. *expropriare*, f. *ex-* Ex-[1] + *proprium* PROPERTY; see -ATE[3].] **1.** *trans.* To dispossess of ownership; to deprive of property. (Now chiefly to deprive of property for the public use, generally with compensation.) †**2.** To put out of one's own control. BOYLE.

1. A power to e. the owner of the land required 1875. **2.** When you have..Consign'd your expropriated will to God 1660.

Expropriation (ekspro^u:priˌēˈ·ʃən). 1449. [– med.L. *expropriatio*, f. as prec.; see -ION. In mod. use directly from prec.] †**a.** The action of giving up one's whole property –1648. **b.** The action of depriving of property 1848. **c.** The action of taking (property) out

of the owner's hands, *esp.* by public authority 1878.
c. The e. of the railways 1889. So **Expro·priator.**

†**Expu·gn,** *v.* ME. [– OFr. *expugner* or L. *expugnare* take by storm, f. *ex-* Ex-¹ + *pugnare* fight.] **1.** To take by fighting; to storm –1640. **2.** To overcome or expel by force of arms; to vanquish –1699.
Hence †**Expugnable** *a.* that may be taken by force, conquered, or overcome. †**Expu·gnance,** storming, conquest. †**Expugnation,** the action of taking by storm; conquest; assault. †**Expu·gnative.** †**Expu·gnatory** *adjs.* tending to e.; offensive. †**Expu·gner.**

†**Expulse** (ekspɒ·ls), *v.* ME. [– *expuls-*, pa. ppl. stem of L. *expellere* EXPEL. Cf. (O)Fr. *expulser.*] *trans.* = EXPEL; sometimes with a stronger notion of violence –1842.
Adam our first parent was expulsed paradise STUBBES. Hence †**Expu·lser.**

Expulsion (ekspɒ·lʃən). ME. [– L. *expulsio*, f. as prec.; see -ION. Cf. (O)Fr. *expulsion.*] The action of expelling, or driving out by force. Also the fact or condition of being expelled.
The e. of the Spaniards 1659, of a member from the House of Commons 1816, of air 1851.

Expulsive (ekspɒ·lsiv), *a.* ME. [– (O)Fr. *expulsif, -ive* – late and med.L. *expulsivus*, f. as prec.; see -IVE.] **1.** Tending or having power to expel. Chiefly of the action of drugs, etc. †**2.** Subject to expulsion; hence, driven out. HAWES. †**3.** = REPELLENT –1662.
1. Of poysons most expulsyfe 1471. So **Expu·lsory** *a.* pertaining to expulsion (*rare*). †**Expu·lsure,** expulsion.

Expunction (ekspɒ·ŋkʃən). 1606. [– L. *expunctio*, f. *expunct-*, pa. ppl. stem of *expungere*; see next, -ION.] The action of expunging; an erasure; †removal.

Expunge (ekspɒ·ndʒ), *v.* 1602. [– L. *expungere* mark for deletion by points set above or below, f. *ex-* Ex-¹ + *pungere* prick. The Eng. sense is due in part to assoc. w. *sponge.*] **1.** *trans.* To strike out, blot out, erase, omit. **2.** *fig.* To wipe out, efface, destroy, put an end to 1628. **3.** To get rid of, remove (a person) 1616.
1. Having expunged the Passages which had given him offence ADDISON. **2.** To e. an offence 1638. **3.** To e. God from Science MANNING.

Expurgate (e·kspɒɹgeᶦt, ekspǝ̄·ɹgeᶦt), *v.* 1621. [– *expurgat-*, pa. ppl. stem of L. *expurgare*, f. *ex-* Ex-¹ + *purgare*; see PURGE *v.*, -ATE³.] †**1.** *trans.* To purge or clear out –1652. **2.** To purify or amend (a book, etc.) by removing what is objectionable. Also *absol.* 1678.
The best edition Expurgated by learned men BYRON. Hence **Expurgator,** one who expurgates or purifies. **Expu:rgato·rial** *a.* of or pertaining to an expurgator; tending to e. or clear of guilt. **Expu·rgatory** *a.* of or pertaining to expurgation; tending to e. or clear of impurity, guilt, etc.

Expurgation (ekspɒɹgē·ʃən). ME. [Partly – L. *expurgatio* in med.L. sense 'cleansing', 'freeing from impurities', partly f. EXPURGATE. Cf. Fr. *expurgation* (OFr. *espurgacion*).] **1.** The action of expurgating, cleansing, or amending, by removal of what is objectionable; an instance of this. †**2.** *Astr.* The reappearance of the sun after an eclipse; emersion –1362.
1. Arts and Learning want this e. SIR T. BROWNE. The e. of the History of the Quakers SOUTHEY, of those members opposed to the Fronde 1839.

Expurge (ekspǝ̄·ɹdʒ), *v.* Now *rare.* 1483. [– Fr. *expurger*, refash. f. OFr. *espurger* :– L. *expurgare* EXPURGATE.] = EXPURGATE.

†**Exqui·re,** *v.* 1607. [– L. *exquirere*; see next.] To search out, seek for –1642.

Exquisite (e·kskwizit). ME. [– L. *exquisitus*, pa. pple. of *exquirere* search out, f. *ex-* Ex-¹ + *quærere* search, seek.]
A. *adj.* **1.** Sought out, 'recherché'. †**2.** Careful, exact, minute –1757. **3.** Carefully or highly elaborated 1552. †**4.** Of a person: Consummate –1823. **5.** Such as to excite intense delight or admiration. (The prevailing sense.) **6.** Of pain, pleasure, etc.: Keen, intense 1644. **7.** Of the senses, etc.: Keenly sensitive to impressions; delicate, finely strung 1643.
1. I haue no e. reason for't, but I haue reason good enough SHAKS. With e. thanks 1650. The most e. morsels 1715, fish GIBBON. **2.** Accuracy or e. digestion of their laws BURKE. **3.** E. workmanship 1561, torments 1603, cookery HUME, ignorance and stupidity JAS. MILL. **4.** A most e. sloven DE FOE. **5.** A babe of e. beauty 1632. **7.** A person of an e. Palate STEELE.
B. *sb.* One who is over-nice in dress; a dandy, fop 1819.
Hence **E·xquisitely** *adv.* in an e. manner or degree. **E·xquisiteness. E·xquisiti:sm,** dandyism, foppishness.

†**Exqui·sitive,** *a. rare.* 1660. [f. L. *exquisit-* ppl. stem (see EXQUISITE) + -IVE.] Tending to search out; curious. Hence **Exqui·sitively** *adv.* = EXQUISITELY (*rare*). **Exqui·sitiveness** = EXQUISITENESS (Sterne).

Exsanguinate (eks,sæ·ŋgwineᶦt), *v.* 1800. [– L. *exsanguinatus*, f. *ex-* Ex-– + *sanguis* blood; see -ATE².] To drain of blood.

Exsanguine (eks,sæ·ŋgwin), *a.* 1647. [f. Ex-¹ + SANGUINE, after L. *exsanguis* bloodless, f. *ex-* Ex-¹ + *sanguis* blood.] Bloodless; anæmic. Also *fig.* So †**E:xsangui·neous** *a.* bloodless. **Exsangui·nity,** anæmia. **Exsa·nguinous, Exsa·nguious, -eous** *adjs.* bloodless.

Exscind (eksi·nd), *v.* Also *erron.* **excind.** 1662. [– L. *exscindere* cut out, f. *ex-* Ex-¹ + *scindere* cut.] To cut out, excise (*lit.* and *fig.*); †to cut off, destroy.
The exscinding. . of the Amorites BARROW.

†**Exscribe,** *v.* 1607. [– L. *exscribere* write out, copy, f. *ex-* Ex-¹ + *scribere* write.] To copy or write out; to transcribe –1716. Hence †**Exscript,** a copy, written extract †**Exscri·ption.**

†**Exscu·lp,** *v. rare.* 1578. [– L. *exsculpere*, f. *ex-* Ex-¹ + *sculpere* cut, carve.] To cut out. Hence †**Exscu·lption** (*rare*).

Exsect (ekse·kt), *v.* 1641. [– *exsect*, pa. ppl. stem of L. *exsecare*, f. *ex-* Ex-¹ + *secare* cut.] To cut out. Also *fig.* **Exse·ction,** a cutting out or away.

Exsert (eks,sǝ̄·ɹt), *v.* 1665. [– *exsert-*, pa. ppl. stem of L. *exserere*; see EXERT.] †**a.** To manifest in action, exercise. **b.** (chiefly *Biol.*) To thrust forth or out 1836. Hence **Exse·rt** *ppl. a.* exserted.

Exserted (eks,sǝ̄·ɹtėd), *ppl. a.* 1816. [f. prec. + -ED.¹] *Biol.* Stretched forth or out; thrust out from, or as from, a sheath; projecting.
Phr. *E. sting*: one that cannot be drawn within the body. Hence **Exse·rtion,** the action of exserting; the being exserted.

Exsertile (eks,sǝ̄·ɹtil), *a.* 1828. [– Fr. *exsertile*, f. *exsert* exserted + *-ile* -ILE.] Capable of being exserted.

Ex-se·rvice, *a.* 1907. [Ex-¹ 2.] Having formerly belonged to one of the fighting services.

Exsi·bilate, *v. rare.* 1601. [– *exsibilat-*, pa. ppl. stem of L. *exsibilare*, f. *ex-* Ex-¹ + *sibilare* hiss; see -ATE³.] To hiss off the stage. Hence **Exsibila·tion** (*rare*).

Exsiccant (eksi·kǎnt). 1657. [– *exsiccant-*, pres. ppl. stem of L. *exsiccare*; see next, -ANT.]
A. *adj.* Drying; having the power of drying up.
B. *sb.* An exsiccant drug or medicine 1676.

Exsiccate (e·ksikeᶦt, eksi·keᶦt), *v.* 1545. [– *exsiccat-*, pa. ppl. stem of L. *exsiccare*, f. *ex-* Ex-¹ + *siccare*, f. *siccus* dry; see -ATE³.] To dry up. *trans.* and *intr.* for *refl.*
Bodies. . that have been exsiccated into Mummy HALE. Hence **Exsicca·tion,** the action of drying what is moist; thoroughly dried condition. **E·xsiccator,** an apparatus for exsiccating.

Exsiccative (e·ksikeᶦtiv, eks,si·kǎtiv). ME. [– med.L. *exsiccativus*, f. as prec.; see -IVE.]
A. *adj.* Tending to make dry or to produce dryness.
B. *sb.* An exsiccative medicine or substance.

Exsolution: see EXOLUTION.

†**Exspolia·tion.** 1612. [– late L. *exspoliatio*, f. *exspoliat-*, pa. ppl. stem of L. *exspoliare*, f. *ex-* Ex-¹ + *spoliare* pillage, despoil; see -ION.] The action of spoiling; a stripping off or removal –1678.

Exspuition (ekspu,i·ʃən). 1650. [– L. *exspuitio*, f. *exspuere*, f. *ex-* Ex-¹ + *spuere* spit; see -ION.] The action of spitting out from the mouth. Also *transf.* and *concr.* So **Exspu·tory** *a.* that is spit out or ejected (*rare*).

†**Exsti·ll,** *v.* 1651. [– L. *exstillare*, f. *ex-* Ex-¹ + *stillare*, f. *stilla* drop.] To come or send out in drops –1819.

†**Exsti·mulate,** *v.* 1603. [– *exstimulat-*, pa. ppl. stem of L. *exstimulare*; see Ex-¹, STIMULATE.] To stimulate; to provoke; to spur on, incite –1683. Hence †**Exstimula·tion.**

Exstipulate (eks,sti·piŭlėt), *a.* 1830. [f. Ex-¹ + STIPULA, STIPULE + -ATE².] *Bot.* Having no stipules.

Exstrophy (e·kstrŏfi). Also **extrophy.** 1836. [f. Gr. ἐκ-, ἐξ- + στροφ-, στρέφειν to turn.] *Path.* A turning inside out of a part; *esp.* a congenital malformation in which the bladder appears to be turned inside out.

†**Exstru·ct,** *v.* 1534. [– *exstruct-*, pa. ppl. stem of L. *exstruere*, f. *ex-* Ex-¹ + *struere* pile up, build.] To build or pile up –1657. Hence †**Exstru·ction.** †**Exstru·ctive** *a.* (*rare*).

Exsuccous (eks,sɒ·kəs), *a.* 1646. [f. L. *exsuccus* (f. *ex-* Ex-¹ + *succus* juice) + -OUS.] Without juice, sapless. Also *fig.*

Exsuction (eksɒ·kʃən). 1660. [f. Ex-¹ + SUCTION.] The action of sucking out.

Exsudate, obs. f. EXUDATE.

Exsufflate, *v.* Now *Hist.* 1666. [– *exsufflat-*, pa. ppl. stem of late (esp. eccl.) L. *exsufflare*, f. *ex-* Ex-¹ + *sufflare* blow; see -ATE³.] To blow out or away. Hence **Exsuffla·tion** (now *Hist.*), the action of blowing out; *spec.* in *Eccl.* exorcism, or renunciation of the devil, by the action of blowing.

†**Exsu·fflicate,** *a. rare.* [app. arbitrary f. EXSUFFLATE.] ? Puffed up, inflated. *Oth.* III. iii. 182.

†**Exsu·perance.** 1603. [– Fr. †*exsupérance* – L. *exsuperantia*; see next, -ANCE.] The condition or fact of exceeding; excess –1682.

†**Exsu·perate,** *v.* 1559. [– *exsuperat-*, pa. ppl. stem of L. *exsuperare*, f. *ex-* Ex-¹ + *superare* rise above, f. *super* above; see -ATE³.] To overtop, surpass; to overcome –1708. So †**Exsu·perant** *a.* excessive.

Exsurge (eks,sǝ̄·ɹdʒ). 1578. [– L. *exsurgere*, f. *ex-* Ex-¹ + *surgere* rise.] *intr.* To rise up, start out. Hence **Exsu·rgent** *a.* rising up above the rest.

†**Exsu·scitate,** *v.* 1574. [– *exsuscitat-*, pa. ppl. stem of L. *exsuscitare*, f. *ex-* Ex-¹ + *suscitare* raise, rouse, awaken; see -ATE³.] *trans.* To rouse up, awaken. Hence †**Exsu:scita·tion.**

‖**Exta** (e·kstă). 1663. [L.] The viscera; *spec.* (*Antiq.*) the entrails of a victim from which auguries were taken by soothsayers.

Extacie, -cy, obs. ff. ECSTASY.

†**E·xtance.** [– L. *ex(s)tantia*, f. *ex(s)tant-*, pres. ppl. stem of *ex(s)tare* stand out; see EXTANT, -ANCE.] Emergence. SIR T. BROWNE.

†**E·xtancy.** 1644. [f. as prec.; see -ANCY.] The quality or state of standing out; *concr.* a protuberance –1689.

Extant (e·kstænt, ekstæ·nt). 1545. [– *ex(s)tant-*, pres. ppl. stem of L. *ex(s)tare* be prominent or visible, exist, f. *ex-* Ex-¹ + *stare* stand; see -ANT.]
A. *adj.* **1.** Standing out or above any surface; projecting, protuberant. *arch.* **2.** Standing forth to the view; conspicuous. *rare.* 1557. **3.** In existence; existing 1561; continuing to exist 1581.
1. In St. Paul's it is e. out of the wall 1766. **2.** E. to the eie 1570. **3.** In this e. moment SHAKS. None of his letters during those years are e. BOSWELL.
†**B.** *sb.* An extant copy 1592. **b.** *pl.* Remains 1659.

Extatic, obs. f. ECSTATIC.

Extemporal (ekste·mpŏrăl), *a.* Now *rare.* 1570. [– L. *extemporalis*; see EXTEMPORE, -AL¹.] Extemporary, impromptu. var. †**Exte·mporate.**

Extemporaneous (ekste:mpŏrē·niəs), *a.* 1656. [f. late L. *extemporaneus* (f. as prec.) + -OUS; see -ANEOUS.] **1.** Not premeditated, offhand, extempore. Rarely of a person. **2.** Made for the occasion 1725.
1. E. pulpiteers 1812, prayer MACAULAY. **2.** An e. supper 1872. var. †**Extempora·nean.** Hence **Extempora·neous-ly** *adv.*, **-ness.**

Extemporary (ekste·mpŏrări). 1610. [f. EXTEMPORE + -ARY¹, after *temporary.*]

A. *adj.* **1.** Unpremeditated; EXTEMPORE. Occas. of a speaker. †**2.** Arising at the moment –1758. **3.** Made for the occasion; hastily provided; makeshift 1631.

1. I have never known a truly e. preacher LD. COCKBURN. **3.** An E. Collation EVELYN.

†**B.** *sb.* An extemporary speech or action. FULLER.

Hence **Exte·mporarily** *adv.* **Exte·mporariness.**

Extempore (eks,te·mpŏri). 1553. [– L. phr. *ex tempore* on the spur of the moment, i.e. *ex* out of, *tempore*, abl. of *tempus* time.]

A. *adv.* **1.** At the moment, without preparation; off-hand. †**2.** On the instant; at once –1663.

1. Phr. *To speak, pray e.* †*To live e.*: to live from hand to mouth. **2.** I'd yeeld e. my breath 1663.

B. *adj.* **1.** Arising out of the moment; casual; sudden 1639. **2.** Made or done at the moment, without preparation. Occas. of a speaker, etc. 1637. **3.** Makeshift 1694.

1. Such a slight e. business SOUTH. **2.** E. translation into English STANLEY. An e. preacher 1886. **3.** An e. sofa 1856.

†**C.** *sb.* Extempore speech, writing, or performance; an impromptu –1815.

Extemporize (ekste·mpŏrəiz), *v.* 1717. [f. prec. + -IZE.] **1.** *intr.* To speak, compose, or perform extempore. **2.** *trans.* To compose off-hand 1817. **3.** To invent for the occasion 1858.

2. To leave half of the dialogue to be extemporised 1880. **3.** Gunners..cannot be extemporized 1858. Hence **Exte:mporiza·tion,** improvisation; an extempore performance. **Exte·mporizer.**

†**Exte·mpory,** *adv.* and *a.* Var. of EXTEMPORE –1775.

Extend (ekste·nd), *v.* ME. [– L. *extendere*, f. *ex-* EX-[1] + *tendere* stretch.]

I. 1. *trans.* To stretch, pull, or straighten out, to strain; to expand 1639. **2.** To stretch, draw in a specified direction, or for a specified distance. Also *refl.* and *intr.* for *refl.* 1481. †**b.** To tend –1605. **3.** *trans.* To lengthen; to carry further 1569. **4.** To spread out in area 1675. **b.** *Metaph.* To possess extension 1666. **c.** *intr.* To cover an area; to have a certain range or scope 1481. **5.** *trans.* To enlarge in area, range, or scope. Also *intr.* for *refl.* 1580. †**6.** To exaggerate. *Cymb.* I. i. 25.

1. To e. a vine ME., one's nerves POPE, a horse's stride 1753. Hector's Corps extended on a Bier CONGREVE. To e. shorthand notes 1826, contractions 1874. **b.** esp. *pass* and *refl.* of a horse: To exert itself to the full; to go 'all out'; hence *gen.* 1856. **3.** To e. a Sermon DONNE, a railway line 1854. **5.** To e. the bounds BARET, the law of reason HOOKER, the Sight ADDISON.

II. 1. To stretch forth, hold out; to accord 1601. †**2.** To display (malice), inflict (vengeance), issue (process) *against, upon* –1597. **b.** *Law.* To present (a protest) 1889.

1. Let there be none to e. mercy to him *Ps.* 109:12.

III. 1. To assess, value ME. **2.** *Law.* To take possession of by a writ of extent; to levy upon 1585; *transf.* to take possession of by force 1606.

Hence †**Exte·ndant** *a.* amounting *to*; *Her.* = DISPLAYED. **Exte·ndible** *a.* extensible; in *Law*, subject to seizure under a writ of extent. **Exte:ndibi·lity.** †**Exte·ndure,** extension; extent.

Extended (ekste·ndėd), *ppl. a.* 1450. [f. prec. + -ED[1].] **1.** Stretched or spread out; †strained 1552. **2.** Continued, prolonged 1450. **3.** Enlarged in area, comprehension, or scope; extensive 1700. **4.** Having extension 1666. **5.** *Law.* Valued; seized upon and held in satisfaction of a debt 1625. Hence **Exte·nded-ly** *adv.*, **-ness.**

Extender (ekste·ndəɹ). Also **-or.** ME. [f. as prec. + -ER[2], -OR 2.] **1.** One who or that which extends; †*spec.* the EXTENSOR muscle 1611. †**2.** A surveyor or valuer –15..

†**Exte·ndlessness.** App. in sense 'boundlessness'. HALE.

Exte·nse. *Obs.* or *arch.* 1614. [– OFr. *extense* or L. *extensus*, pa. pple. of *extendere* EXTEND.]

A. *adj.* Having 'extension' (HY. MORE); extensive 1644.

†**B.** *sb.* What is extended, an expanse 1614.

Extensible (ekste·nsib'l), *a.* 1611. [– Fr. *extensible* or med.L. *extensibilis*, f. *extens-*, pa. ppl. stem of L. *extendere*; see EXTEND, -IBLE.] **1.** Capable of being extended in any dimension or direction; capable of being protruded. **2.** Capable of being enlarged in scope or meaning 1654.

1. An artery is an e., elastic tube GOOCH. Hence **Exte:nsibi·lity,** e. quality. **Exte·nsibleness.**

Extensile (ekste·nsil), *a.* 1744. [f. as next + -ILE.] **1.** Capable of being stretched out. **2.** Of a tentacle, etc.: Capable of being protruded 1802.

Extension (ekste·nʃən). ME. [– late L. *extensio*, f. *extens-*, *extent-*, pa. ppl. stem of L. *extendere*; see -ION. Cf. Fr. *extension.*] **1.** The action of extending; extended state or condition. **2.** *Law.* The extending of a protest (see EXTEND II. 2b) 1889. **3.** The action or process of spreading out in area; the condition of being spread out. Also †*concr.* An expanse. 1684. †**4.** Extent –1708. **b.** *Physics* and *Metaph.* The property of being extended; spatial magnitude 1624. **c.** An extended body or space 1739. **5.** The range over which anything extends 1604. **6.** *Logic.* The range of a term as measured by the number of objects to which it applies; opp. to *intension* or *comprehension* 1725. **7.** Enlargement in length, duration, area, or scope 1590; *concr.* an extended portion 1854.

1. Extention of the Synnues 1599. You must use Extention almost to every Dislocation 1612. Fullnesse of Meat..causeth an E. of the Stomacke BACON. **4. b.** Our perceptions of the specific e. of the body—its size and shape H. SPENCER. **6.** A Bowl, in its E., includes a wooden Bowl, a brass Bowl, etc. WATTS. **7.** *University E.*: the extending of the scope and work of the universities, *e.g.* to non-resident students.

Hence **Exte·nsional** *a.* of, pertaining to, or possessed of e. **Exte·nsionist,** one who advocates the e. of anything, *e.g.* of University Teaching; also *colloq.* one who attends the meetings of the University E. Association.

Extensity (ekste·nsĭti). 1834. [f. as prec. + -ITY.] The quality of having (a certain) extension; in *Psychol.* of the breadth of sensation, as opp. to *intensity*.

Extensive (ekste·nsiv), *a.* 1605. [– Fr. *extensif, -ive* or late L. *extensivus*, f. as prec.; see -IVE.] †**1.** Extensible –1691. **2.** That enlarges in scope 1832. **3.** Having a wide extent, comprehension, or scope. Of purchases, etc.: Large in amount. 1706. **4.** Of, pertaining to, or possessed of extension; occupying space 1624. **5.** *Logic.* Denoting a large number of objects; opp. to *intensive* 1686.

1. Silver beaters chuse the finest coin, as..most e. under the hammer BOYLE. **3.** E. plantations PENNANT, markets ADAM SMITH, capital ALISON, quotation 1846. Hence **Exte·nsive-ly** *adv.*, **-ness.**

Extensor (ekste·nsəɹ). 1713. [mod.L., f. as prec. + -OR 2.] **1.** A muscle which serves to extend or straighten any part of the body; opp. to *flexor*. **2.** *attrib.* 1830.

‖**Exte·nsum.** [L., n. of pa. pple. of *extendere* EXTEND.] A body possessed of extension. CUDWORTH.

†**Exte·nsure.** 1594. [f. EXTENSION (see senses 1, 4), with substitution of -URE.] The condition of being extended; the action of extending; extent –1631.

Extent (ekste·nt), *sb.* [ME. *extente* – AFr. *extente* – med.L. *extenta*, subst. use of fem. pa. pple. of L. *extendere* EXTEND.] **1.** *Hist.* The valuation of land or other property; assessment; also, assessed value ME. **2.** *Law.* A writ to recover debts of record due to the Crown, under which the body, lands, and goods of the debtor may be seized to compel payment 1630. **b.** Seizure of lands, etc., in execution of a writ; sequestration; also, the right of seizure; also, execution 1592. †**c.** *transf.* An assault –1601. †**3.** Rents, etc., arising from extended lands –1626. **4.** 'Space or degree to which anything is extended' (J.); thus, dimensions, compass, size 1624; breadth of comprehension, scope 1594. **5.** *concr.* An extended space 1627. †**6.** The action of extending –1719.

4. The Serpent..Of huge e. MILT. *P. L.* VII. 496. The e. of the power which was to be exercised by the Sovereign MACAULAY. **6.** *Haml.* II. ii. 390.

†**Extent,** *a.* ME. [– L. *extentus*; see prec.] = EXTENDED –1664.

Extenuate (ekste·niu,eᵗt), *v.* 1529. [– *extenuat-*, pa. ppl. stem of L. *extenuare*, f. *ex-* EX-[1] + *tenuis* thin; see -ATE[3].] **1.** To make thin or lean. Somewhat *arch.* 1533. **2.** To thin out, render thinner 1559. †**3.** To lessen in size, number, amount, or degree; to weaken the force of, mitigate –1773. †**4.** To disparage –1705. **5.** To estimate or state at a low figure; to underrate. Somewhat *arch.* 1529. **6.** Hence: To lessen, or seem to lessen, the seeming magnitude of (guilt or offence) by partial excuses. Also of circumstances: To serve as an extenuation of 1570. ¶**b.** Improp.: To extenuate the guilt of 1741.

1. To e. the body by fasting SOUTHEY. **2.** To e. gold into plates HAKLUYT. To e. humours MARKHAM, the air VINCE. **4.** Just are thy ways.. Who can e. thee MILT. *P. L.* X. 645. **5.** Cuffe extenuated both the Danger and Difficulty 1625. **6.** Fortune, there, extenuates the Crime. What's Vice in me, in only Mirth in him CONGREVE.

Hence †**Exte·nuate** *ppl.a.* and *a.* extenuated. **Exte·nuative** *a.* tending to e.; *sb.* something serving to e. guilt, or to emaciate. **Exte·nuator. Exte·nuatory** *a.* characterized by extenuation.

Exte·nuating, *ppl. a.* 1607. [f. prec. + -ING[2].] That extenuates. Chiefly in *Extenuating circumstances*: circumstances that tend to diminish culpability. Hence **Exte·nuatingly** *adv.*

Extenuation (ekste:niu,eᵗ·ʃən). 1542. [– L. *extenuatio*, f. as EXTENUATE; see -ION. Cf. (O)Fr. *exténuation.*] **1.** The action of extenuating; extenuated condition. **2.** The action of lessening the guilt of (an offence) by partial excuses; a plea in mitigation of censure 1651.

2. In e. of a noble error MACKINTOSH.

Exterior (ekstīᵊ·riəɹ). 1533. [– L., compar. of *exterus* outside.]

A. *adj.* **1.** Outer; pertaining to or connected with the outside; visible on the outside 1570. **2.** Situated outside (an object); coming from without; concerned with what is without; external, extrinsic. Const. *to.* 1533. †**b.** Foreign (*rare*) 1540.

1. Not th e., nor the inward man Resembles that it was *Haml.* II. ii. 6. Phr. *E. angle* (Geom.): the angle included between any side of a triangle or polygon and the production of the adjacent side; also, an angle included between a straight line falling upon two parallel lines and either of the latter on the outside. **2.** Without e. help sustaind MILT. *P. L.* IX. 336. **b.** Other exteriour potentates 1540.

B. *sb.* (Not in Johnson.) **1.** An exterior thing (*rare*); in *pl.* = EXTERNALS 1591. **2.** The outside; outward aspect or demeanour 1695.

2. The engaging e. of urbanity HAN. MORE. The most pious e. MOZLEY.

Hence **Exte:rio·rity,** outwardness; devotion to the external instead of to the spiritual; 'the psychical act by which sensations are referred to the external world' (*Syd. Soc. Lex.*). **Exte·riorize** *v.* to attribute an external existence to (states of consciousness); hence **Exte:rioriza·tion. Exte·riorly** *adv.* on the outside or surface; as regards externals; in an e. position or direction.

Exterminate (ekstɔ̄·ɹmineᵗt), *v.* 1541. [– *exterminat-*, pa. ppl. stem of L. *exterminare* (in cl.L. only in sense 1; in Vulg. in sense 2), f. *ex-* EX-[1] + *terminus* boundary; see -ATE[3].] †**1.** *trans.* To drive, force *from, of, out of* the boundaries or limits of; to banish, put to flight –1692. **2.** To destroy utterly; to root out, extirpate 1649. †**3.** To get rid of, destroy; in *Math.*, to ELIMINATE –1827.

1. To e. rank Atheism out of the world BENTLEY. **2.** The Holy League..was to e. heresy MOTLEY. **3.** A remorse that..exterminated his peace GODWIN.

Hence **Exte·rminable** *a.* that may be exterminated; illimitable (SHELLEY) (*rare*). **Exte·rminative** *a.* tending to e. **Exte·rminator. Exte·rminatory** *a.* tending to e.; characterized by attempts at extermination.

Extermination (ekstɔ̄:ɹminēᵗ·ʃən). 1549. [– late L. *exterminatio*, f. as prec.; see -ION. Cf. (O)Fr. *extermination.*] †**1.** Expulsion from the bounds or limits of a country; banishment, excommunication –1664. **2.** Total extirpation; utter destruction 1549. †**3.** *Math.* = ELIMINATION. –1827.

2. The e. of religion 1790, of the Small-pox 1803, the Talmud 1867.

†**Exte·rmine,** *v.* 1539. [– (O)Fr. *exterminer* – L. *exterminare*; see EXTERMINATE.] = EXTERMINATE. –1637.

Extern (ekstǝ·ɹn). Also **externe.** 1533. [– Fr. *externe* or L. *externus*, f. *exter(us* that is outside.]

A. *adj.* = EXTERNAL A. 1–4.

B. *sb.* †**1.** Outward appearance, exterior (*rare*) 1600. **2.** An outsider; *esp.* a day-pupil in a school (Fr. *externe*) 1610.

External (ekstǝ·ɹnăl). 1556. [– med.L. **externalis*, f. L. *externus*; see prec., -AL[1].]

A. *adj.* (Opp. to *internal.*) **1.** Situated outside; pertaining to, connected with, or lying towards, the outside 1591. **2.** Outwardly visible or perceptible 1556. **3.** Situated outside the object under consideration (const. *to*) 1595; †foreign –1599; in *Metaph.*, belonging to the world of phenomena, as opp. to the 'ego' 1667. **4.** Arising or acting from without 1651. **5.** Having an outside or foreign, object or sphere of operation 1770.

1. Her vertues graced with externall gifts *1 Hen. VI*, v. v. 3. E. warmth 1799. The e. meatus 1878. Phr. *E. angle*: one made by producing outwardly a side of a figure. **2.** The e. worship of God BUTLER. **3.** The e. air 1801. The e. world LOTZE. **4.** Not by externall violence, but intestine disorder HOBBES. Phr. *E. evidence*: evidence derived from circumstances outside of the thing discussed. **5.** Phr. *E. perception, senses.* The e. debt of the Republic of Chili 1891. Hence **Exte·rnally** *adv.*

B. *sb.* **1.** *sing.* The outside 1792. **2.** That which is external. In *pl.* **a.** Outward aspect; bodily qualifications; outward observances 1635. **b.** External circumstances or conditions; also, non-essentials 1652.

2. a. Adam was glorious in his externals..he had a beautiful body SOUTH. The Externals of religion JORTIN. **b.** The subordination of externals to essentials 1883.

Exte·rnalism. 1856. [f. prec. + -ISM.] **1.** Excessive regard for non-essentials, *esp.* in religion. **2.** The worship of the external world 1874.

1. Pharisaic formalities and externalisms 1875. So **Exte·rnalist,** one who has undue regard for externals.

Externality (ekstǝɹnæ·lĭti). 1673. [f. as prec. + -ITY.] **1.** The quality of being EXTERNAL. **2.** *Metaph.* The quality or fact of being external to a conscious subject 1790. **3.** An external object or characteristic; *collect.* outward things in general 1839. **4.** Absorption in externals 1833.

2. While looking at a solid object they cannot help having the conception..of its e. MILL. **4.** Enchained hopelessly in the grovelling fetters of e. LAMB.

Externalize (ekstǝ·ɹnălǝiz), *v.* Also **-ise.** 1852. [f. as prec. + -IZE.] *trans.* To make external; to embody in outward form; to attribute external existence to.

The universe is the process whereby spirit externalises itself 1877. Hence **Exte:rnaliza·tion,** the action of externalizing; *concr.* an embodiment. var. **Exte·rnize** *v.*; whence **Exte:rnaliza·tion.**

‖**Externat** (ękstęrna). 1853. [Fr., f. *externe*; see EXTERN.] A day-school.

Externate (e·kstǝɹneⁱt), *v. rare.* 1890. [f. EXTERN + -ATE[3].] To embody in outward form. Hence **Externa·tion.**

Externity (ekstǝ·ɹnĭti). 1713. [f. med.L. *externare* make external + -ITY.] Outwardness; also, the external part.

†**E·xterous,** *a. rare.* 1570. [f. L. *exter* outward + -OUS.] Outside –1647.

Exterrestrial (ekstĕre·striăl), *a.* [f. EX- *pref.*[1] + TERRESTRIAL.] Originating or located outside the earth. PROCTOR.

Exterritorial (eksteritǭ·riăl), *a.* 1880. [f. EX- *pref.*[1] + TERRITORIAL, after next.] Of or pertaining to exterritoriality.

Exterritoriality (eksteritōᵊ:riˌæ·lĭti). 1836. [– Fr. *exterritorialité*; see EX-[1], TERRITORIAL, -ITY.] The privilege accorded by the *Law of Nations* to ambassadors and their families, of being considered outside the territory, and therefore the jurisdiction, of the state to which they are sent. Also EXTRATERRITORIALITY.

†**Exte·rsive,** *a. rare.* 1657. [– med.L. *extersivus*, f. *exters-*, pa. ppl. stem of L. *extergere*, f. *ex-* EX-[1] + *tergere* wipe. Cf. DETERSIVE.] Cleansing –1661.

Extill, var. EXSTILL.

Extimulate, -ation, obs. ff. EXSTIMULATE, etc.

Extinct (eksti·ŋkt). ME. [– L. *ex(s)tinctus*, pa. pple. of *ex(s)tinguere*, f. *ex-* EX-[1] + *stinguere* quench.]

A. *pple.* Extinguished. Now *rare.*

It tooke fire..but was quickly e. 1631.

B. *adj.* **1.** Of a fire, etc.: Extinguished. Of a volcano: No longer in eruption. ME. **2.** *fig.* Quenched; that has ceased to burn or shine 1494. †**3.** Of a person: Cut off; dead; vanished –1675. **4.** That has died out or come to an end 1581.

1. A sparke or two not yet e. COWPER. **2.** Young Arthurs eies are blinded and e. 1591. **3.** My dayes are e. *Job* 17:1. **4.** All the family e. DE FOE. Phr. *After possibility of issue e.*

†**Exti·nct,** *v.* 1483. [– *extinct-*, pa. ppl. stem of L. *extinguere*; see prec.] = EXTINGUISH *v.*, in various senses –1631.

‖**Extincteur** (ękstæntör, ekstiŋktöɹ). 1878. [Fr. – L. *exstinctor*; see prec., -OR 2.] An apparatus for extinguishing fire.

Extinction (eksti·ŋkʃǝn). 1494. [– L. *ex(s)tinctio*, f. as EXTINCT *v.*; see -ION. Cf. Fr. *extinction* (XVI).] **1.** The quenching, putting out (of anything); also *fig.*; the process of becoming, or fact of being, extinct. **b.** *spec.* The slaking (of lime) 1646. **2.** Suppression, abolition; the complete wiping out (of a debt) 1651. **3.** Destruction, annihilation; †utter disgrace 1542. **4.** Of a race, etc.: A coming to an end or dying out; the condition of being extinct 1602.

1. E. of heat 1672, of volcanoes 1843, of a lamp CARLYLE. **2.** The gradual e. of the national debt MCCULLOCH. **4.** The e. of the male line BRYCE. var. †**Exti·ncture,** SHAKS.

Extinctive (eksti·ŋktiv), *a.* 1600. [orig. – med.L. *extinctivus* (see prec., -IVE); in mod. use f. prec. + -IVE.] Tending, or able, to extinguish.

Extine (e·kstin, -tǝin). 1835. [f. L. *ext(imus* most outward + -INE[1].] *Bot.* The outer membrane of the pollen grain.

Extinguish (eksti·ŋgwiʃ), *v.* 1545. [irreg. f. L. *ex(s)tinguere*; see -ISH[2] and cf. DISTINGUISH.] **1.** *trans.* To put out, quench. Also *transf.* and *fig.* **2.** To put a total end to, blot out of existence 1548. †**3.** *intr.* for *refl.* in various senses: To die out –1797.

1. They would e. the very light of nature BP. BERKELEY. Extinguishing his reason, instead of putting out his eyes LAW. **2.** To e. all memory thereof MARVELL. To e. a title, right, action, instrument (*Law*). To e. a debt 1777, a bishopric 1839, the Red man 1837. **3.** His alacrity suddenly extinguishes HUME. Hence **Exti·nguishable** *a.* able to be extinguished.

Extinguisher (eksti·ŋgwiʃǝɹ). 1560. [f. prec. + -ER[1].] One who or that which extinguishes; *esp.* a hollow conical cap for extinguishing the light of a candle or lamp. Also *transf.* and *fig.*

Extinguishment (eksti·ŋgwiʃmĕnt). 1503. [f. as prec. + -MENT.] **1.** The quenching (of fire, etc.); also *transf.* and *fig.* **2.** The putting a total end to, blotting out of existence. Cf. EXTINGUISH *v.* 2, and quots. 1535.

1. An e. of love 1639. **2.** The e. of a house 1612, of Ambiguities and doubts 1648, of a contract, right, etc. (*Law*), of a debt MORSE.

Extirp (ekstǝ·ɹp), *v. Obs.* or *arch.* 1483. [– (O)Fr. *extirper* or L. *extirpare*; see next.] = EXTIRPATE *v.* Hence †**Exti·rpable** *a.* that may be extirpated. **Exti·rper.**

Extirpate (e·kstǝɹpeⁱt, ekstǝ·ɹpeⁱt), *v.* 1539. [– *ex(s)tirpat-*, pa. ppl. stem of L. *ex(s)tirpare*, f. *ex-* EX-[1] + *stirps* stem or stock of a tree; see -ATE[3].] **1.** To pull or pluck up by the roots; to root up, eradicate 1650. **2.** To root out, exterminate; to render extinct. Const. *out of, from.* 1586. **3.** *fig.* 1539.

1. E. noxious and unprofitable Herbs RAY. To e. a tumor GOOCH. **2.** The breed ought to be extirpated out of the island LOCKE (J.). To e. gangs of thieves MACAULAY. **3.** To e. superstition LATIMER, drunkenness BENTHAM, heresy SCOTT.

Hence **E·xtirpative** *a.* tending to e. **Extirpator,** one who, or that which, extirpates.

Extirpation (ekstǝɹpē·ʃǝn). 1526. [– Fr. *extirpation* or L. *extirpatio*, f. as prec.; see -ION.] The action of extirpating or rooting up or out; total destruction; extermination.

The joint e. of woods and men MORSE. The e. of heresy 1602, of the smallpox 1846, of the buffalo 1877.

‖**Extispex** (eksti·speks). Pl. **exti·spices.** 1727. [L.; f. *exta* (see EXTA) + *-spex*, f. *specere* look at.] A HARUSPEX, q.v. So †**Extispi·cious** *a.* of or pertaining to extispicy (*rare*). **Exti·spicy,** haruspicy.

Extol (ekstǫ·l), *v.* 1494. [– L. *extollere*, f. *ex-* EX-[1] + *tollere* raise.] †**1.** *trans.* To lift up, elevate –1650. †**2.** To lift up with pride, joy, etc. –1664; to raise too high; to exaggerate, boast of –1796. **3.** To praise highly; to magnify 1509.

1. A begger from the dunghill once extold, Forgets him selfe 1601. **2.** The Hors and Foot and the Sea-Souldiers..extoll'd every one their own hazards 1652. **3.** S. John extolleth charitie in his Epistle 1582. Hence **Exto·ller,** one who extols. **Exto·lment,** the action of extolling; eulogy.

Extorsive (ekstǭ·ɹsiv), *a. rare.* 1669. [– med.L. *extorsivus*, f. *extors-* (med.L. var. of *extort-*; see next) + *-ivus* -IVE. Cf. Sc. †*extorse.*] Serving or tending to extort; obtained by extortion. Hence †**Exto·rsively** *adv.*

Extort (ekstǭ·ɹt), *v.* 1529. [– *extort-*, pa. ppl. stem of L. *extorquere*, f. *ex-* EX-[1] + *torquere* twist.] **1.** *trans.* To wrest from a reluctant person by force, violence, torture, intimidation, or abuse of legal authority, or by importunity, argument, or the like. **2.** To extract forcibly (a sense or conclusion) *from* (a passage, etc.) 1601. †**3.** To practise extortion on (a person); to strain (a law) –1681.

1. To e. treasure 1529, Tribute SHAKS., taxes 1820, compassion JAS. MILL, power 1863. **2.** Do not e. thy reasons from this clause *Twel. N.* III. i. 165.

Hence †**Exto·rt** *ppl. a.* extorted; extortionate. †**Exto·rt** *sb.* extortion, torture. **Exto·rter, -or.**

Extortion (ekstǭ·ɹʃǝn). ME. [– late L. *extortio*, f. as prec.; see -ION.] **1.** The action or practice of extorting or wresting anything, *esp.* money, from a person by force or by undue exercise of authority or power; an act of illegal exaction. **b.** *Law.* The act of any officer 'unlawfully taking, by colour of his office, any money or thing of value, that is not due to him, or more than his due, or before it is due' (Blackstone) 1607. †**2.** A wresting of the sense of a word or phrase 1652; a straining (of the nerves) 1725.

Hence **Exto·rtion** *v.* to practise extortion; *trans.* to overcharge. **Exto·rtionable** *a.* extortionate (*rare*). **Exto·rtionary** *a.* given to or marked by e. **Exto·rtionate** *a.* characterized by e.; oppressive; exorbitant. **Exto·rtioner,** one who practises e. †**Exto·rtious** *a.* characterized, or gained, by e.

Extortive (ekstǭ·ɹtiv), *a.* 1646. [f. EXTORT + -IVE. Cf. med.L. *extortivus.*] Of extortion; disposed to extort.

Extra (e·kstră). 1776. [prob. short for EXTRAORDINARY, as (earlier) Fr. *extra* for *extraordinaire*; cf. G. *extra* (XVIII).]

A. *adj.* Beyond or more than the usual, agreed, or stated amount or number; additional.

Money for any e. wants 1780. E. pay 1878.

B. *adv.* Unusually; in excess of the usual or specified amount 1823.

E. strong binding. E.-special edition. Is there anything e.-special for tea? Three maps e. 1894.

C. *sb.* What is extra or additional; anything given in addition or for which an extra charge is made; the extra charge itself; an extra fee; an additional issue of a newspaper; *spec.* at cricket, a run scored otherwise than off the bat 1803.

'With extras?'..'Yes..we learned French and music' 'L. CARROLL'. Hourly extras were issued 1888. The builder hoped to recoup himself by extras 1894.

‖**Extra** (e·kstră), *prep. rare.* 1852. [L.; contr. f. *exterā*, abl. fem. of *exter.*] Outside, externally to; as, *extra* the voltaic circuit.

Extra- (e·kstră), *prefix*, forming adjs. (in L. from phrases, as *extraordinarius*, f. *extra ordinem*) with general sense 'situated outside something', 'lying outside the province or scope of'.

Extra-a·cinous, *Anat.* outside the ACINUS or racemose gland. **Extra-alime·ntary,** situated outside the alimentary canal. **Extra-analo·gical,** outside the range of analogy. **Extra-arti·stic,** out of the range of art. **Extra-atmosphe·ric,** of or pertaining to space beyond the atmosphere. **Extra-a·xillar, Extra-a·xillary,** *Bot.* growing from above or below the axils. **Extra-brita·nnic. Extra-cano·nical,** not classed among the canonical books. **Extra-ca·psular,** 'outside a capsule, having special reference to the articular capsules' (*Syd. Soc. Lex.*). **Extra-ce·llular,** *Biol.* situated or taking place outside the walls of a cell. **Extra-chri·stian,** outside the province of Christian thought. **Extra-co·nstellary,** *Astron.* not classed under any constellation. **Extra-co·rial** [L. *corium* hide], pertaining to the outside skin or epidermis. **Extra-corpo·real,** outside the body. **Extra-co·smical,** acting outside the cosmos or universe. **Extra-cuta·neous,** outside the true skin as opp. to the epidermis. **Extra-decre·tal,** not included in the Decretals. **Extra-folia·ceous,** *Bot.* external to the leaf. **Extra-gala·ctic,** *Astron.* outside the Milky Way. **Extra-governme·ntal. Extra-gramma·tical. Extra-histo·ric, -al. Extra-hu·man. Extra-hu·ndredal,** not included in any hundred. **Extra-juda·ical,** outside the conditions of the Jewish dispensation. **Extra-ju·ral,** 'outside the court' (Poste). **Extra-le·gal. Extra-li·mital** [L. *limes, limit-*], beyond the limits of a country or district. **Extra-li·mitary,** situated beyond the limit or bounds. **Extra-lo·gical,** lying outside the domain of logic; hence, **Extra-lo·gically** *adv.* †**Extra-mari·ne,** from beyond the sea. **Extra-ma·trical** [L. *matrix, matric-*], situated outside the MATRIX of a parasitical plant. **Extra-matrimo·nial. Extra-me·dial,** lying outside or beyond the middle line. **-medu·llary. Extra-meri·dional,** *Astron.* of or pertaining to deviation from the meridian. **Extra-metaphy·sical. Extra-me·trical** = HYPERMETRICAL. **Extra-na·tional,** outside the limits of a nation. **Extra-nu·clear,** placed outside the nucleus of a cell. **Extra-o·cular,** situated or occurring outside the eyes. **Extra-offi·cial,** outside the legitimate duties or emoluments of an office. **Extra-o·rbital,** *Zool.* situated outside the eye-cavity (of a crustacean). **Extra-patria·rchal,** outside the conditions of the patriarchal dispensation. **Extra-perito-ne·al,** 'outside the peritoneum' (*Syd. Soc. Lex.*). **Extra-phy·sical,** not subject to physical laws or methods. **Extra-pla·netary,** beyond the region of the planets' movements. **Extra-po·lar. Extra-profe·ssional,** outside the ranks of a profession; outside the course of professional duties. **Extra-red,** said of rays outside the visible spectrum at its red extremity. **Extra-re·gular,** outside of, or transgressing, the rule. **Extra-sacerdo·tal. Extra-sci·entific,** beyond the scope of science. **Extra-scri·ptural,** drawn from sources outside the Scriptures; hence **Extra-scriptura·lity. Extra-se·nsible, Extra-se·nsuous,** beyond the reach of sensuous perception. **Extra-spe·ctral,** lying outside the visible spectrum. **Extra-sto·machal,** taking place outside the stomach. **Extra-syllogi·stic. Extra-te·rrene. Extra-terre·strial. Extra-the·cal,** *Zool.*, etc. situated outside the theca. **Extra-to·rrid,** existing outside the torrid zone. **Extra-tro·pical. Extra-unive·rsity. Extra-u·rban. Extra-u·terine,** existing, formed, or taking place outside the uterus. **Extra-violet,** said of rays outside the visible spectrum at its violet extremity. **Extra-zodi·acal,** *Astron.* situated outside the zodiac. See also Main Words.

Extract (e·kstrækt), *sb.* 1549. [– L. *extractum*, subst. use of n. pa. pple. of *extrahere*; see next.] †**1.** *gen.* Something extracted or drawn out; *fig.* the pith –1651. **2.** 'The substance extracted' (J.); in mod. use 'applied to the tough or viscid matter obtained by treating any matter with solvents and then evaporating the solvent' (Watts). Also loosely, any preparation containing the essential principle of a substance in a concentrated form. 1590. Also *fig.* †**b.** = EXTRACTIVE B. 2. –1813. †**3.** A summary; an outline –1681. **4.** An excerpt, quotation 1666. **5.** *Law.* †**a.** = ESTREAT *sb.* **b.** *Sc. Law.* The warrant on which execution on a judicial decree may issue; also, a properly authenticated copy of a deed or other writing of record 1606. †**6.** EXTRACTION, descent –1796.

6. Every Soul, who gets to be rich, immediately enquires into his E. NORTH.

Extract (ekstræ·kt), *v.* 1489. [– *extract-*, pa. ppl. stem of L. *extrahere*, f. *ex-* EX-[1] + *trahere* draw.] **1.** *trans.* 'To draw out of any containing body or cavity' (J.) 1570. **2.** 'To take from something of which the thing taken was a part' (J.); *esp.* to copy out, make extracts from 1607. **3.** To get out by force, effort, or contrivance; to draw forth against a person's will 1599. **4.** To obtain (elements, juices, etc.) from a thing or substance by any chemical or mechanical operation. Also *fig.* 1594. †**5.** Only in *passive*: To be derived or descended –1678.

1. To put the hand in the pocket, and e. it clutch'd *Meas. for M.* III. ii. 50. **2.** To e. Falsehoods out of a Pamphlet SWIFT. **3.** To e. an arrow 1767, consent H. WALPOLE, teeth 1878. **4.** Extracting of the oiles out of the hearbes PLAT. *fig.* To e. happiness out of ills YOUNG, pleasure out of life GEO. ELIOT. Phr. *To e. the root of a number or quantity* (Math.): to obtain the root by a mathematical operation. Hence **Extra·ct** *ppl. a.* extracted. **Extra·ctable** *a.*, also **-ible. Extra·cting** *ppl. a.* that extracts; also, ?distracting (*Twel. N.* v. i. 288).

Extraction (ekstræ·kʃən). 1477. [– (O)Fr. *extraction* – late L. *extractio*, f. as prec.; see -ION.] **1.** The action or process of extracting 1530. †**2.** That which is extracted; extract –1698. **3.** *Math.* The process or method of extracting (a root) 1557. **4.** Origin, descent; †source 1477.

1. The e. of gold from mines MORSE, of corn from Sicily NELSON, of a fœtus 1799. Phr. *Spirit of the first e.*: that which comes off at the first distillation. **2.** This rare e. . hath . . power to disperse all malignant humours B. JONS. **4.** The memory of their common e. GIBBON.

Extractive (ekstræ·ktiv). 1599. [In sense 1 – med.L. *extractivus*, f. as prec.; see -ION; in later use, f. EXTRACT *v.* + -IVE.]

A. *adj.* **1.** Tending to draw out. **2.** Capable of being extracted; of the nature of an extract 1789.

1. Phr. *E. industry*: an industry (*e.g.* agriculture, mining, fisheries, etc.) that is concerned with extracting natural productions. **2.** Separating the e. acid . . from wine 1816.

B. *sb.* **1.** An extractive substance 1844. **2.** 'The brown insoluble mass of doubtful composition, left after the preparation of vegetable extracts' (Wagstaffe) 1807.

1. The separation [of the viscous liquor] into . . albumen, aqueous e., and alcoholic e. TODD.

Extractor (ekstræ·ktəɹ). 1611. [f. EXTRACT *v.* + -OR 2.] One who, or that which, extracts; *esp.* that part of a breech-loading gun which removes the cartridge.

†**Extradi·ctionary** *a. rare.* [f. L. phr. *extra dictionem* outside of the mode of expression (see EXTRA *prep.*, DICTION) + -ARY[1].] Of fallacies: Not consisting in expression; real. SIR T. BROWNE.

Extradite (e·kstrădəit), *v.* 1864. [Back-formation from next, suggested by Fr. *extrader* (XVIII).] **1.** To give up (a fugitive foreign criminal) to the proper authorities, in pursuance of a treaty. **b.** To obtain the extradition of 1883. **2.** *Psychol.* To localize (a sensation) at a distance from the centre of sensation (*rare*) 1887.

1. b. The effort of England to e. Sheridan, of the Irish World, New York 1883. Hence **Extradi·table** *a.* liable, or rendering liable, to extradition.

Extradition (ekstrădi·ʃən). 1839. [– Fr. *extradition* (Voltaire), f. L. *ex-* EX-[1] + *traditio* TRADITION.] **1.** The action of giving up a fugitive criminal or a person accused of a crime to the authorities of the state in which the crime was committed. Hence *gen.*: Surrender (of a prisoner) by one authority to another. **2.** The process of localizing a sensation at a distance from the centre of sensation 1874. **3.** *attrib.*, as in **Extradition treaty,** a treaty by which two nations mutually agree to surrender any fugitive criminal who has committed in the other's territory any of certain specified offences 1852.

Extrados (ekstrēⁱ·dǫs). 1772. [– Fr. *extrados*, f. L. *extra* outside + Fr. *dos* back. Cf. INTRADOS.] *Archit.* The upper or exterior curve of an arch; *esp.* the upper curve of the voussoirs or stones which immediately form the arch. Cf. INTRADOS. Hence **Extra·dosed** *a.* having an e. (of a certain kind); used of an arch in which the curves of the intrados and e. are concentric and parallel.

Extradotal (ekstrădōᵘ·tăl), *a.* 1827. [f. EXTRA- + DOTAL.] *Law.* Forming no part of the dowry.

Extra-foraneous (e:kstrăfǫrēⁱ·niəs), *a.* 1781. [f. EXTRA- + L. *foris* door; see -ANEOUS.] Outdoor.

†**Extrait,** *pa. pple.* [– Fr. *extrait*; see EXTRACT *v.*] Extracted; descended. CAXTON.

Extrajudicial (e:kstrăˌdʒudi·ʃal), *a.* 1630. [– med.L. *extrajudicialis*; see EXTRA-, JUDICIAL.] **1.** Forming no part of the case before the court; not delivered from the bench; informal. **2.** Outside the ordinary course of justice; unwarranted 1641.

1. The opinion of the judge. .is considered e. 1871. Hence **E:xtrajudi·cially** *adv.*

Extrality (ekstræ·lĭti). 1926. Syncopated form of EXTRATERRITORIALITY (in its extended use).

†**Extrami·ssion.** 1630. [– med.L. *extramissio* emission of a stream of particles by the eye (see EMISSION 4); see EXTRA-, MISSION.] Emission –1674.

Extramundane (ekstrămɒ·ndēⁱn), *a.* 1665. [– late L. *extramundanus*, f. phr. *extra mundum* outside the world or universe; see EXTRA-, MUNDANE.] **1.** Of or pertaining to a region outside of our world; *fig.* remote, not of this world. **2.** Of or pertaining to what is outside the universe 1706.

1. Aerolites. .were proved to be of e. origin 1879.

Extramural (ekstrămiūᵊ·răl), *a.* 1854. [f. L. phr. *extra muros* outside the walls + -AL[1]; cf. late L. *extramuranus* in same sense.] Outside the walls of a city or town; *esp.* in *extramural* interment.

Extraneity (ektrănī·ĭti). *rare.* [f. as next + -ITY. Cf. med.L. *extraneitas.*] The quality of being extraneous. ABP. THOMSON.

Extraneous (ekstrēⁱ·niəs), *a.* 1638. [f. L. *extraneus* (see STRANGE *a.*) + -OUS; see -EOUS.] **1.** Of external origin; foreign. **2.** External *to* something specified 1655.

1. E. interference BURKE, circumstances HARE, rock LYELL. **2.** Points clearly to e. religion PALEY. Persons e. to the church ROBERTSON. Hence **Extra·neous-ly** *adv.*, **-ness.**

Extraordinary (ekstrǭ·ɹdinări, ekstraˌǭ·ɹdinări). 1460. [– L. *extraordinarius*, f. phr. *extra ordinem* out of course, in an unusual manner; see EXTRA-, ORDINARY *a.*]

A. *adj.* Out of the usual course or order; often opp. to *ordinary*; in *Mus.* †ACCIDENTAL, q. v. –1731. **2.** Out of or additional to the regular staff; supernumerary. Formerly with the notion of being specially employed for a temporary purpose. 1585. **3.** Of a kind, amount, degree, or measure not usually met with; exceptional. Now with emotional sense, expressing astonishment, etc. 1572. †**5.** = EXTRA. Often following the sb. –1812.

1. E. judgements 1553, occasions FULLER, measures 1745. **2.** The first audience of the Russian E. Embassadour, at which he made his Emperour's Presents BOYLE. **3.** These signes haue markt me extraordinarie 1 *Hen. IV*, III. i. 41. The e. influence of divine Grace 1656. An e. nose 1798. **5.** A glass e. after dinner 1812. Hence **Extra-o·rdinarily** *adv.* **Extrao·rdinariness.**

†**B.** *adv.* = EXTRAORDINARILY *adv.* –1778.

C. *sb.* **1.** †That which is extraordinary –1754; in *pl.* esp. extraordinary receipts or payments (now *arch.*) 1599. **2.** = EXTRA *sb.* 1660. †**3.** An extraordinary envoy; a supernumerary official –1671.

1. Not only the king's ordinary revenues, but the extraordinaries CARLYLE. **2.** A few extraordinaries for the house PEPYS.

Extra-parochial (e·kstră părōᵘ·kiăl), *a.* 1674. [f. EXTRA- + eccl. L. *parochia* (see PARISH) + -AL[1].] Outside the parish, or parish obligations. Hence **Extra-paro·chial-ly** *adv.*, **-ness.**

Extrapolation (e:kstrăpolēⁱ·ʃən). 1878. [f. INTERPOLATION by substitution of EXTRA- for INTER-.] The action or method of finding by a calculation based on the known terms of a series, other terms, whether preceding or following. Also *transf.*

Extraprovincial (e:kstrăˌprǒvi·nʃăl), *a.* 1685. [– med.L. *extraprovincialis*, f. *extra provinciam* outside the province; see EXTRA-, PROVINCIAL.] Outside the limits of a province.

E:xtrate:rritoria·lity. 1836. [f. mod.L. phrase *extrā territōri-um* outside the territory + -AL[1] + -ITY.] = EXTERRITORIALITY; extended later to denote the right or jurisdiction of a country over all its nationals abroad. So **E:xtraterrito·rial** *a.*

†**Extrau·ght,** *pa. pple.* 1523. [var. of EXTRACT *ppl. a.*; cf. *distraught.*] **1.** Extracted, descended –1593. **2.** Distraught –1575.

1. 3 *Hen. VI*, II. ii. 142.

Extravagance (ekstræ·văgăns). 1643. [– Fr. *extravagance*; see EXTRAVAGANT, -ANCE.]

†1. A going out of the usual path; an excursion, digression –1656. 2. The quality of being extravagant or of exceeding just or prescribed limits, *esp.* those of decorum, probability, or truth; unrestrained excess; also, an instance of this 1650. 3. Excessive prodigality in expenditure, household management, etc. 1727.

2. You will accuse me of e. in this description LADY M. W. MONTAGU. The extravagances of ignorance and credulity COLERIDGE. 3. The e. of cooks 1894.

Extravagancy (ekstræ·văgănsi). 1601. [f. next; see -ANCY.] = EXTRAVAGANCE 2, 3. 1625; also †vagrancy –1669.

Extravagant (ekstræ·văgănt). ME. [– *extravagant-*, pres. ppl. stem of med.L. *extravagari*, f. *extra* EXTRA + *vagari* wander; see -ANT. The gen. sense depends on Fr. *extravagant*, It. (*e*)*stravagante*.]

A. *adj.* †1. That wanders out of bounds; vagrant; keeping no fixed place –1672. 2. *Canon Law.* Applied to certain 'stray' decrees not originally codified or collected in the decretals ME. †3. Straggling –1669. †4. Widely divergent (*from*); remote *from*, irrelevant *to* a purpose or subject –1665. †5. Unusual, abnormal; unsuitable –1701. 6. 'Roving beyond just limits or prescribed methods' (J.); excessive, irregular, fantastically absurd. Now: Astonishingly or flagrantly excessive or extreme. 1588. 7. Prodigal, wasteful 1707.

1. At his [the cock's] warning..Th' e., and erring Spirit hyes to his Confine *Haml.* I. i. 154. 3. Too thick and e. Roots EVELYN. 6. E. in their accounts of themselves BP. STILLINGFL. E. demands 1769, opinions 1809; e. whimsies about dress MACAULAY. 7. An e. interest of 20 per cent 1707. E. of time 1739. Hence **Extra·vagantly** *adv.*

B. *sb.* 1. *Canon Law.* An 'extravagant' decree; see A. 2. 1502. †2. A vagrant –1650. †3. An eccentric –1768; a spendthrift –1825. †4. An extravagancy –1700.

Extravaganza (ekstræ:vægæ·nză). 1789. [– It. *estravaganza* (usu. *stra-*), refash. after EXTRA-.] 1. A composition, literary, musical, or dramatic, of a fantastic character 1794. 2. Bombastic extravagance of language or behaviour.

Extravagate (ekstræ·vägeᶦt), *v.* 1600. [– *extravagat-*, pa. ppl. stem of med.L. *extravagari*; see EXTRAVAGANT, -ATE³.] 1. *intr.* To stray *from, into.* 2. To wander at will 1766. 3. To exceed what is proper or reasonable 1829. Hence †**Extravaga·tion.**

Extravasate (ekstræ·väseᶦt), *v.* 1669. [f. L. *extra* EXTRA- + *vas* vessel + -ATE³.] 1. To let or force out (*esp.* blood) from its proper vessel. 2. *intr.* for *refl.* To flow out; to escape 1686.

2. Blood sometimes extravasates into the arachnoid sac TODD. Hence †**Extra·vasate** *a.* extravasated; formed by extravasation. var. †**E·xtravase.**

Extravasation (ekstræ:văsēᶦ·ʃən). 1676. [f. prec.; see -ION. Cf. Fr. *extravasation.*] 1. *Path.* The escape of an organic fluid from its proper vessels; a mass or spot of extravasated blood. 2. *Geol.* Effusion (of molten rock) from a subterranean reservoir 1842.

Extravascular (ekstrăvæ·skiŭlăɹ), *a.* 1804. [f. EXTRA- + VASCULAR.] Outside the vascular system; not vascular.

†**Extrave·nate,** *v. rare.* 1650. [f. L. *extra* EXTRA- + *vena* vein + -ATE³.] To let (blood) out of the veins –1668. Hence †**Extrave·nate** *a.* extravasated. **Extravena·tion.**

†**Extrave·rsion.** *rare.* 1691. [f. EXTRA- + VERSION; cf. contemp. †*extravert* v.] A turning out; a rendering manifest –1732. So †**Extrave·rt** *v.* to turn out so as to be visible.

†**Extrea·t,** *sb.* 1489. [var. of ESTREAT, with *ex-* for *es-* after L. For sense 2 cf. OFr. *estraite* :– L. *extracta.*] 1. = ESTREAT *sb.* –1631. 2. Extraction. SPENSER *F. Q.* V. x. 1. Hence †**Extrea·t** *v.* to estreat; to eliminate.

Extreme (ekstrī·m). 1460. [– (O)Fr. *extrême* – L. *extremus*, superl. of *exterus* outward.]

A. *adj.* 1. Outermost; endmost, situated at either of the ends (opp. to *mean*) 1503. 2. Farthest, or very far advanced in any direction; utmost, uttermost 1600. 3. Last, latest. *Obs.* or *arch.*, exc. in *Extreme unction* (see quots.). 1477. 4. Going to great lengths opp. to *moderate* 1460. 5. *Mus.* Augmented; as in *extreme interval* 1876.

1. The fruitful continent's extremest bound POPE. *E. and mean ratio* (Math.): the relation of a line and its parts, when the whole is to the greater part, as the greater part is to the less. 2. The Sea's extreamest Borders ADDISON. The e. point reached 1860. 3. The e. day 1513. Phr. *Extreme unction*: in the R. C. Church, 'a sacrament in which the sick in danger of death are anointed by a priest for the health of soul and body, the anointing being accompanied by a set form of words' (*Cath. Dict.*). 4. The most e. Povertie 1460. E. necessity 1550. E. Idolaters 1634. In dress E. COWPER. E. cases JOWETT.

†**B.** *adv.* In an extreme degree; extremely –1816.

C. *sb.* 1. quasi-*sb.*, as *In* (*the*) *extreme*: extremely 1604. †2. *sb.* The extreme point or verge; an end, extremity –1808. 3. One of two things removed as far as possible from each other, in position, nature, or condition 1555. b. *Logic.* In a proposition the subject or predicate, as distinct from the copula; in a syllogism the major or minor term, as dist. from the middle 1628. c. *Math.* The first or last term of a ratio, series, or set of numbers 1571. 4. A very high degree of anything 1593; †*pl.* extremities, straits, hardships –1667. 5. An excessive degree; also, something carried to excess, an extreme measure 1588.

1. Of one..Perplex'd in the e. *Oth.* V. ii. 347. 3. Two extremes of passion, ioy and greefe *Lear* V. iii. 198. Phr. *Extremes meet.* 4. Enthusiastical to an e. 1791. 5. To go to the e. of a lock-out 1867. Hence **Extre·meless** *a.* having no extremities; infinite (*rare*). **Extre·mely** *adv.* †to the uttermost degree; in an e. degree; very much. **Extre·meness. Extre·mist,** one who goes to extremes, or who holds e. opinions or advocates e. measures; also as *adj.*; so **Extre·mism. Extremi·stic** *a.*

Extremity (ekstre·mĭti). ME. [– OFr. *extrémité* or L. *extremitas*, f. *extremus*; see prec., -ITY.] 1. The extreme point or portion of anything; the end; in *pl.* the hands and feet 1460. †2. The 'extremes' as opp. to the 'mean' –1598. 3. The extreme or utmost degree; = EXTREME *sb.* 4. 1543. †4. Extreme intensity of anything –1797. †5. Extravagance –1712. †6. Extreme severity or rigour –1639. 7. A condition of extreme urgency or need ME. 8. A person's last moments (*arch.*) 1602. 9. An extreme measure. Chiefly in *pl.* 1639. 10. Extremeness. Somewhat *rare.* 1848.

1. Antennæ thickening towards their e. STARK. 3. Extremities of Penury and Want 1638. 4. The e. of the weather BEWICK. 6. *Com. Err.* V. i. 307. 7. Phr. *To drive, reduce to* (*the last*) *e.* or *extremities.* 9. To push matters to the e. of a civil war 1862.

Extricable (e·kstrikăb'l), *a.* 1623. [f. next; see -ABLE.] That can or may be extricated, †unravelled, or got out.

Extricate (e·kstrikeᶦt), *v.* 1614. [– *extricat-* pa. ppl. stem of L. *extricare*, f. *ex-* EX-¹ + *tricæ* perplexities; see -ATE³.] 1. *trans.* To unravel; *fig.* to clear of intricacies or perplexities. Now *rare.* 2. To disentangle; to set free *from, out of* (anything that entangles, confines, or perplexes) 1631. b. *Chem.* To disengage (gas, etc.) from a state of combination 1790.

1. Some method of extricating public affairs ALISON. 2. A thicket, out of which he knows not how to e. himself 1732. b. To e. water from an acid 1838. Hence **Extrica·tion,** the action of extricating; disentanglement; disengagement (of gas, etc.) from something containing it.

Extrinsic (ekstri·nsik), *a.* 1541. [– late L. *extrinsecus* adj. outer, f. L. *extrinsecus* adv. outwardly, f. *exter* outside + *-im* as in *interim* + *secus* alongside of.] 1. †Exterior; external. 2. Pertaining to an object in its external relations. Now *rare.* 1617. 3. Lying outside the object under consideration 1666; operating from without 1613. 4. Not inherent or essential; adventitious; opp. to *intrinsic* 1622.

1. E. ornaments JOHNSON. 2. The e. muscles which serve to move the whole external ear DARWIN. 3. Things extrinsick from..the main matter 1678. E. stimuli 1878. 4. E. advantages of birth HAZLITT.

Hence **Extri·nsical** *a.* extrinsic; †*sb.* something that is e. **Extri·nsical-ly** *adv.*, **-ness. Extri·nsicate** *v.* to exhibit outwardly; to express (*rare*).

Extro-, a quasi-L. prefix, an altered form of L. *extra*, with the sense 'outwards'. Used only in compounds, by way of antithesis to *intro-*.

Extroitive (ekstrōᵘ·itiv), *rare.* [f. EXTRO- + *it-*, pa. ppl. stem of L. *ire* go + -IVE.] Directed to external objects. COLERIDGE.

†**Extromi·t,** *v.* [app. var. of *extramit*; see EXTRO-, cf. INTROMIT.] To send out. KEN. Hence †**Extromi·ssion.**

Extrorsal (ekstrǭ·ɹsăl), *a.* 1842. [f. next + -AL¹.] *Bot.* = next.

Extrorse (ekstrǭ·ɹs), *a.* 1858. [– late L. *extrorsus* in an outward direction. Cf. Fr. *extrorse.*] *Bot.* Turned or opening outwards; said of anthers that look away from the pistils.

Extroversion (ekstrovɔ̄·ɹʃən). 1656. [f. EXTRO- + VERSION.] Turning or being turned outwards; as, *extroversion* of the bladder. So **Extrove·rt** *v.* to turn outwards 1671. Hence **E·xtrovert** *sb.* one who is concerned mainly with what is external or objective: opp. to INTROVERT *sb.* 2. 1918.

Extruct, -ion, -ive: see EXSTRUCT.

Extrude (ekstrū·d), *v.* 1566. [– L. *extrudere*, f. *ex-* EX-¹ + *trudere* thrust.] *trans.* To thrust forth; to urge out; to expel; also *occas.*, to protrude out. Also *intr.* for *refl.* (*rare*).

Presbyterianism was only extruded gradually M. ARNOLD. Hence **Extru·sive** *a.* tending to e.; characterized by extrusion.

Extrusion (ekstrū·ʒən). 1540. [– med. L. *extrusio*, f. *extrus-*, pa. ppl. stem of L. *extrudere*; see prec., -ION.] The action of extruding; the fact of being extruded.

Extuberance (ekstiū·bĕrăns). ?*Obs.* 1607. [f. next; see -ANCE.] The quality of being extuberant; *concr.* a swelling, projection, protuberance. *lit.* and *fig.* So †**Extu·berancy.**

Extuberant (ekstiū·bĕrănt), *a.* Now *rare.* 1578. [– *extuberant-*, pres. ppl. stem of late L. *extuberare*; see next, -ANT.] Swelling out, protuberant.

†**Extu·berate,** *v. rare.* 1623. [– *extuberat-*, pa. ppl. stem of late L. *extuberare*, f. *ex-* EX-¹ + *tuber* swelling; see -ATE³.] To swell, or make to swell, out or up –1768. Hence †**Extubera·tion,** protuberance.

Extume·scence. 1611. [– Fr. †*extumescence*; see EX-¹, TUMESCENCE.] A swelling up or out. So †**Extume·scency** (*rare*).

Extund (ekstɒ·nd), *v.* 1610. [– L. *extundere*, f. *ex-* EX-¹ + *tundere* beat.] To beat or hammer out; only *fig.*

†**Exty·pal,** *a.* Var. of ECTYPAL. Cudworth.

Exuberance (egziū·bĕrăns). 1638. [– Fr. *exubérance* – L. *exuberantia*, f. as next; see -ANCE.] 1. The quality or condition of being EXUBERANT; abundant productiveness; luxuriance; copiousness; redundance 1664. 2. An overflowing quantity; a superabundance 1638. †3. *concr.* An overflow; an excrescence, protuberance –1825.

1. A happy e. of animal spirits SCOTT. An e. of the metaphysical imagination JOWETT. 2. An e. of life 1868. So **Exu·berancy.**

Exuberant (egziū·bĕrănt), *a.* 1503. [– Fr. *exubérant* – *exuberant-*, pres. ppl. stem of L. *exuberare*, f. *ex-* EX-¹ + *uberare* be fruitful, f. *uber* fruitful; see -ANT.] 1. Luxuriantly fertile or prolific; abundantly productive. Also *fig.* 1645. 2. Growing or produced in superabundance 1513. 3. Overflowing, as a fountain, etc. 1678. Also *fig.* 1503.

1. E. vines EVELYN, fancy 1788. 2. E branches EVELYN. An e. population BUCKLE. 3. *fig.* E. goodness BOYLE, eloquence FULLER, narrative GEO. ELIOT, charities LECKY. Hence **Exu·berantly** *adv.*

Exuberate (egziū·bĕreᶦt), *v.* 1471. [– *exuberat-*, pa. ppl. stem of L. *exuberare*; see prec., -ATE³.] 1. *intr.* To be exuberant; to abound, overflow 1623. †2. *trans. Alchem.* ?To render fruitful (mercury, the alkahest) –1671. Hence **Exubera·tion.**

Exuccous, -ction, obs. ff. EXSUCCOUS, -SUCTION.

Exucontian (eksiukǭ·ntiăn). 1844. [– eccl. Gr. ἐξουκόντιος, f. phr. ἐξ οὐκ ὄντων out of nothing, + -AN.] *Eccl.* A name for Arians as holding Christ to be 'of a substance that was not'.

†**Exudate**, *v.* 1646. [– *ex(s)udat-*, pa. ppl. stem of L. *ex(s)udare*; see next, -ATE[3].] = EXUDE *v.* –1796.

Hence **Exuda·tion**, the process of exuding; also, *erron.*, percolation; that which is exuded. **Exu·dative** *a.* of, pertaining to, or characterized by exudation. †**Exu·datory** *a.* characterized by exudation; *sb.* a means of exuding.

Exude (egziū·d, eks-), *v.* 1574. [– L *ex(s)udare*, f. *ex-* EX-[1] + *sudare* sweat.] **1.** *intr.* To ooze out like sweat; to pass off in drops through the pores, an incision or orifice. **2.** *trans.* To sweat out or give out like sweat, to discharge through the pores, etc. Also *fig.* 1798.

1. Gum, which exudes from incisions in thick viscid drops VINES. Hence **Exu·dence** (*rare*).

†**E·xul**, *sb.* 1566. [– L. *ex(s)ul.*] = EXILE *sb.*[2], q.v.

†**E·xulate**, *v. rare.* 1535. [– *ex(s)ulat-*, pa. ppl. stem of L. *ex(s)ulare* be in exile, exile, f. *ex(s)ul*; see prec., -ATE[3].] To exile or go into exile –1640.

†**Exu·lcerate**, *a.* 1545. [– L. *exulceratus*, pa. pple. of *exulcerare*; see next, -ATE[2].] Exulcerated. *lit.* and *fig.* –1684.

Exulcerate (egzʌ·lsĕreᶦt), *v. arch.* 1533. [– *exulcerat-*, pa. ppl. stem of L. *exulcerare*, f. *ex-* EX-[1] + *ulcus, ulcer-*; see ULCER, -ATE[3].] †**1.** *trans.* To cause ulcers in –1732. **2.** *fig.* To fret; to irritate; to aggravate 1594. †**3.** *intr.* To break out into ulcers –1659.

1. It [the reume] doth e. the lunges ELYOT. **2.** I must lye perpetually and e. my conscience CHILLINGW. Hence **Exu:lcera·tion**, ulceration, *esp.* in its early stage; *concr.* an ulcerated place; also *fig.* †**Exu·lcerative**, †**Exu·lceratory** *adjs.*, tending to produce ulcers.

Exult (egzʌ·lt), *v.* 1570. [– L. *ex(s)ultare*, frequent. of *exsilire*, f. *ex-* EX-[1] + *salire* leap.] †**1.** *intr.* To spring or leap up; to leap for joy –1727. **2.** To rejoice exceedingly; to be elated; to triumph. Const. *in, at, on, over*, and *inf.* 1594.

1. The whales exulted under him CHAPMAN. **2.** Who can..not e. in being born a Briton 1756. Hence **Exu·ltance, Exu·ltancy**, exultant state or condition; gladness; triumph. **Exu·ltingly** *adv.*

Exultant (egzʌ·ltănt), *a.* 1653. [– *ex(s)ultant-*, pres. ppl. stem of L. *ex(s)ultare*; see prec., -ANT.] Exulting, triumphantly joyful.

The wild e. cry 1844. Hence **Exu·ltantly** *adv.*

Exultation (egzʌltēᶦ·ʃən). ME. [– L. *ex(s)ultatio*, f. *ex(s)ultat-*, pa. ppl. stem of *ex(s)ultare*; see EXULT, -ION.] †**1.** The action of springing or leaping up 1599. **2.** The action of exulting; triumph, joyousness, rapturous delight. Also *concr.* an object exulted over. ME. **b.** *pl.* Shouts of joy. HOOKER.

2. The e. of the Court over the decision of the judges GREEN.

Exu·ndate, *v. rare.* 1721. [– *exundat-*, pa. ppl. stem of L. *exundare*, f. *ex-* EX-[1] + *unda* wave; see -ATE[3].] *intr.* To overflow. Hence **Exunda·tion**, overflow (now *rare*).

†**Exu·ngulate**, *v.* 1623. [– *exungulat-* pa. ppl. stem of late L. *exungulare* lose the hoof, f. *ex-* EX-[1] + *ungula* nail; see -ATE[3]. The mod. senses are unexpl.] To pare off the nails, the hoofs, the white part from rose-leaves, etc. –1775.

Exuperate; Exurge, -ence, -ent; Exuscitate, -ation: see EXSU-.

†**Exu·st**, *v. rare.* 1623. [– *exust-*, pa. ppl. stem of L. *exurere*, f. *ex-* EX-[1] + *urere* burn.] *trans.* To burn up. Hence †**Exu·st** *a.* burnt or dried up. †**Exu·stible** *a.* capable of being burnt up (*rare*). †**Exu·stion**, the action or process of burning or burning up.

Exuviable (egziū·viăb'l), *a.* 1839. [– Fr. *exuviable*, f. L. *exuviæ*; see next, -ABLE.] Capable of being exuviated or sloughed off. Hence **Exu:viabi·lity**, the property of being e. (In Dicts. explained as the power of casting off exuviæ.)

‖**Exuviæ** (egziū·viᶦī). 1653. [L., clothing stripped off, skins of animals, spoils, f. *exuere* divest oneself, f. *ex-* EX-[1] + **-ou-*, **-eu-* (as in *induere* put on, ENDUE.] Cast skins, shells, or coverings of animals; any parts of animals which are shed or cast off, recent or fossil. Also *transf.* and *fig.*

Hence **Exu·vial** *a.* pertaining to, or of the nature of, e.; *sb. pl.* things stripped off; spoils. †**Exu·vious** *a.* exuvial.

Exuviate (egziū·viᶦeᶦt), *v.* 1855. [f. prec. + -ATE[3].] *intr.* To cast off or shed exuviæ; *trans.* to cast off as exuviæ.

The young crayfish e. two or three times in the course of the first year HUXLEY. Hence **Exu:via·tion.**

‖**Ex-voto** (eksᶦvōᵘ·to). 1787. [L. phr. *ex voto*, i.e. *ex* out of, *voto* abl. sing. of *votum* VOW *sb.*.] An offering made in pursuance of a vow.

Ey, obs. f. AY; see also EGG.

‖**Eyalet** (ẹyā·let). 1853. [Turk., f. Arab. *'āla* be a chief over, govern.] An administrative division of the Turkish empire; now called VILAYET, q.v.

Eyas (əi·ăs). 1486. [alt. of †*nias*, †*nyas* – (O)Fr. *niais*, (orig.) bird taken from the nest, (hence now) silly person :– Rom. **nid(i)ax, -ac-*, f. L. *nidus* nest. For the change of *a nias* to *an yas* cf. ADDER; sp. with *ey-* may be due to assoc. w. *ey* EGG *sb.*] **1.** A young hawk from the nest, or one incompletely trained. **2.** *attrib.*, as *e.-hawk*; in sense 'unfledged' as *e.-thoughts, -wings.* Also **e.-musket** (see MUSKET[1]), a sprightly child. SHAKS.

2. Ere flitting Time could wag his e. wings SPENSER.

Eye (əi), *sb.*[1] [OE. *ēaǵe*, Anglian *ēǵe* = OFris. *āge*, OS. *ōga* (Du. *oog*), OHG. *ouga* (G. *auge*), ON. *auga*, Goth. *augo* :– Gmc. **auȝon*. The OE. pl. *ēaǵan* survives in north. dial. *een* and arch. *eyne* (Spenser); the pl. in *-s* dates from XIV.]

I. The organ of sight, sometimes including the surrounding parts: **a.** in man and vertebrate animals; **b.** in invertebrate animals 1665. **2.** The eye as possessing the power of vision. Often used pleonastically for emphasis. ME. **b.** *fig.*; esp. as applied to a city, country, etc. 1599. **3.** Used in *sing.* and *pl.* for: The action or function of the eyes; the sense of seeing; 'ocular knowledge' (J.); sight ME. †**b.** Range of vision, view, sight –1711. **c.** *fig.* 1602. **4.** With reference to the direction of the eye: Look, glance, gaze OE. **5.** Observation; attention, regard ME. **6.** (in *sing.* only). The faculty of perception or discrimination of visual objects 1657. **7.** *fig.* Point of view; estimation, opinion, judgement ME.

1. Youre two eyn will sle me sodenly, I may the beaute of them not sustene CHAUCER. The pyrates..bounde his handes..and iyen LD. BERNERS. **b.** The compound eye..consists essentially of a series of transparent cone-like bodies, arranged in a radiate manner against the inner surface of the cornea 1878. Phrases. *To cry one's eyes out* (colloq.). *To wipe the e. of another shooter* (Sporting): to kill game that he has missed. *All my e.* (slang): all humbug. *My eye(s!* an exclam. of astonishment, etc. **2.** I have seen him.. with my own eyes take off his seal 1776. Phr. *Half an e.*: the smallest power of vision. *To lose an e.*, freq. = to become blind of one eye. *To put out the eyes*, freq. = to deprive of sight. *The naked e.*: see NAKED. **b.** Sorrowes eie SHAKS. Athens, the e. of Greece MILT. *P. R.* IV. 240. The e. of faith 1687. **3.** Is this face Heroes? are our eies our owne *Much Ado* IV. i. 72. Thy well-study'd marbles fix our e. POPE. **c.** I see my father..In my minds e. *Haml.* IV. iv. 6. **4.** Phrases. *To see e. to e.* (*Isa.* 52:8): often misused for to be of one mind. *Eyes right, left, front* (Mil.). *The glad e.*: an amorous or festive glance (*slang*). **5.** Phrases. *To give an e. to, have an e. upon. To have an e. to. With an e. to. To be all eyes.* **6.** To have the e. of a great captain MACAULAY. Phrases. *To estimate by e. To have, get, one's e.* (*well*) *in*: to be or become able to judge distance accurately. **7.** Phr. *In the e. of* (*the*) *law, logic*, etc.

†**II.** Slight shade, tinge. (Cf. Fr. *œil.*) –1699.

III. 1. An object resembling the eye in appearance, shape, or position; as: **a.** the axillary bud on plants; the leaf-bud of a potato; **b.** the remains of the calyx on fruit; **c.** the centre of a flower; **d.** one of the spots near the end of the tail-feathers of a peacock; **e.** a small dark spot in the eggs of a fish and insects while hatching ME. **2.** The opening through which the water of a fountain wells up 1857. **3.** A central mass; the brightest spot (of light) 1864. **4.** The centre of revolution 1760. **5.** A hole or aperture: **a.** in a needle OE.; **b.** in a tool or implement, for the insertion of some other object 1554; **c.** in the upper stone of a mill, in a kiln, etc.; also for exit or ingress, as in a fox's earth, a mine, etc. 1686; **d.** in bread or cheese, etc. (now *dial.*) 1523. **6.** A loop of metal or thread in a 'hook and eye'. Also a metal ring for holding a rod or bolt, or for a rope, etc. to pass through 1599. **b.** A loop of cord or rope; *esp.* 'the circular loop of a shroud or stay, where it goes over the mast' (Smyth) 1584. **7.** *Archit.* The centre of any part, as the *eye* of a dome, etc. Also *transf.* in *Conchology.* 1727. **8.** *Typog.* †**a.** = the FACE of a type. [Fr. *œil.*] **b.** The enclosed space in the letters *d, e, o*, etc. 1676.

5. a. So much wit..As will stop the e. of Helens needle *Tr. & Cr.* II. i. 87. **d.** Bad cheese..full of Eyes, not well prest 1688.

Phrases. *Eyes of her* (Naut.): 'the foremost part of the bay, or in the bows of a ship' (Smyth). *In the wind's e.* (Naut.): in the direction of the wind. *Glass e.*: a glass imitation of the natural eye; also, *pl.* a pair of spectacles; also = BULL'S-EYE.

Comb.: **e.-baby**, the image of the spectator seen in another's e.; **-bar**, a metal bar with an e. or hole at either end, used in bridges; **-bone**, the bony circle round the e., the orbit; **-copy**, a copy made by e.; **-dotter**, a small brush used in graining wood in imitation of bird's-eye maple; **-drop**, a tear; †**-flap** = BLINKER, q.v.; **-handle** (of a spade, etc.), a handle having an eyelet or hole; **-lens**, the lens nearest the eye in an optical instrument; **-line,** (*a*) the field or range of vision, (*b*) in *pl.* the lines above and below the e. of a bird; **-memory**, 'the impressing by will on memory things which we have seen'; **-opener,** (*a*) *U.S.* a dram, *esp.* one taken in the morning, (*b*) something that throws light on what was dark or ambiguous, (*c*) something which causes keen surprise; **-pedicel, -peduncle**, *Zool.* a pedicel or peduncle supporting an e.; **-point** = EYE-SPOT; **-probe**, *Surg.* a probe having an e. or small hole at one end; **-shade**, a shade for the eyes; **-speck**, an e. consisting of a single speck, a rudimentary e.; **-stalk** = *-peduncle*; **-stone,** (*a*) a stone resembling an e., (*b*) a calcareous body which being put into the inner corner of the e. works its way out at the outward corner and brings out any strange substance with it; **-trap**, something to catch or deceive the e.; **-tube**, the tube of the e.-piece in a telescope; **-wages**, such wages as e.-service calls for; **-waiter** = EYE-SERVANT; **-wash,** (*a*) lotion for the eye 1866; (*b*) *slang*, humbug, blarney 1884; **-wise** *a.*, wise in appearance; **-worship,** adoration performed by the e.

†**Eye**, *sb.*[2] ME. [From *an eye*, for *a neye*; see NYE. Cf. EYAS.] A brood (of pheasants) –1725.

Eye (əi), *v.* 1566. [f. EYE *sb.*[1]] †**1.** To see. *lit.* and *fig.* –1779. **2.** To direct the eyes to, look at or upon, behold, observe 1566. **3.** To keep an eye on; to observe narrowly 1586. †**4.** To have or keep in view –1771. †**5.** *intr.* To look or appear to the eye 1606. **6.** *trans.* To furnish with eyes 1854.

2. They eyed the prisoners with curiosity 1797. **3.** And Saul eyed Dauid from that day 1 *Sam.* 18:9. **5.** *Ant., & Cl.* I. iii. 97. Hence **Eye·able** *a.* that may be seen by the eye; sightly.

Eye-ball (əi·bǭl). 1590. [f. EYE *sb.*[1] + BALL *sb.*[1]] **a.** The apple or pupil of the eye 1592. **b.** The eye itself.

Eye-beam (əi·bīm). 1588. [f. EYE *sb.*[1] + BEAM.] A beam or glance of the eye.

Eye-bolt (əi·bōᵘlt). 1769. [f. EYE *sb.*[1] + BOLT *sb.*[1]] A bolt or bar eyed to receive a hook, ring, etc.

Eye·-bree. Now *Sc.* and *dial.* OE. [f. EYE *sb.*[1] + BREE *sb.*[1]] = †EYE-LID, †-LASH, -BROW.

Eyebright (əi·brəit). 1533. [f. EYE *sb.*[1] + BRIGHT.]

†**A.** *adj.* Bright to the eye (*rare*) 1607.

B. *sb.* **1.** = EUPHRASY; also *attrib.* prepared from euphrasy 1533. **2.** ? 'A kind of ale in Elizabeth's time' (Latham) 1610.

2. In days of Pimlico and Eye-bright B. JONS.

Eyebrow (əi·brau). 1585. [f. EYE *sb.*[1] + BROW *sb.*[1]; repl. EYE-BREE.] **1.** The brow or arch of hair along the upper orbit of the eye. **2.** *Archit.* A moulding over a window; also, *occas.*, the fillet 1703.

Eyed (əid), *ppl. a.* ME. [f. EYE *sb.*[1] + -ED[2].] **1.** Furnished with eyes; often with *adj.* prefix, as *Argus-, blue-*, etc. **2.** Furnished with an eye, as *eyed-hooks* 1804. **3.** Marked as with eyes; spotted 1815.

Eye·-draught. 1773. [f. EYE *sb.* + DRAUGHT.] A drawing or plan made by eye, without measurement.

Eye·ful, *sb.* 1832. [f. EYE *sb.*[1] + -FUL.] As much as fills the eye. So **Eye·ful** *a.* conspicuous; observant (now *dial.*).

Eye-glass (əi·glas), *sb.* 1611. [f. EYE *sb.*[1] + GLASS.] †**1.** The crystalline lens of the eye. *Wint. T.* I. ii. 268. **2.** †**a.** A microscope. **b.** Now, a lens of glass or crystal to assist the sight. 1767. **3.** The eyepiece of any optical instrument 1664. **4.** A glass for applying lotions to the eye 1842.

Eyehole (əi·hōᵘl). 1637. [f. EYE *sb.*[1] + HOLE.] The cavity containing the orbit of the eye; a hole to look through 1856; one of the depressions in a potato from which the buds spring (*dial.*) 1884.

Eye-lash (əi·læʃ). 1752. [f. EYE *sb.*[1] + LASH *sb.*[1]] The row of hairs fringing the edge of the eyelid; also, a single one of these.

Eyeless (əi·lės), *a.* 1570. [f. EYE *sb.*[1] + -LESS.] **1.** Without eyes (in various senses). **2.** Deprived of the eyes 1592. **3.** Blind; undiscriminating 1627.

2. Ask for this great deliverer now, and find him E. in Gaza MILT. *Sams.* 38. **3.** An e. destiny MORLEY.

Eyelet (əi·lėt), *sb.* [ME. *oilet, oylette* – OFr. *oillet* (mod. *œillet*), dim. of †*oil, œil* :– L. *oculus* eye; see -ET.] **1.** A small round hole in cloth, sail-cloth, etc., worked like a button-hole, for the passage of a lace, ring, or rope, an EYELET-HOLE; also, a short metal tube, having its ends flattened for the same purpose. **2.** An aperture or loophole, usually for observation ME. **3.** A small eye. *lit.* and *fig.* 1799. **4.** *attrib.* 1864.

4. *E.-ring*, a small metal ring, inserted in an e. to prevent wearing. *E.-punch*, a device for punching e.-holes and attaching papers together. Hence **Eye·let** *v.* to make eyelets in. **Eyeletee·r,** a stabbing instrument for piercing e.-holes.

Eyelet-hole (əi·lėt,hōᵘl), *sb.* 1497. [f. EYELET *sb.* + HOLE.] = EYELET 1, 2.

Eyelid (əi·lid). ME. [f. EYE *sb.*[1] + LID.] One of the covers of the eye, dist. as *upper* and *lower*; one of the movable folds of skin with which an animal covers or uncovers the eye at pleasure.

Phr. *To hang by the eyelids*: to be in a dangerous position.

Eyepiece (əi·pīs). 1790. [f. EYE *sb.*[1] + PIECE.] *Optics.* The lens or combination of lenses at the eye-end of a telescope or other optical instrument, by which the image, formed by the mirror or object-glass, is viewed and magnified. Also *attrib.*

The principal kinds of eyepieces are (*a*) the *Huyghenian*, or so-called *negative* from the fact of its forming the image between the lenses; (*b*) the *Ramsden*, or common astronomical, called *positive* because the image is formed outside the field-glass; (*c*) the *erecting* or *terrestrial* for ordinary telescopes, which presents the object in an erect position.

attrib. E. micrometer, a graduated slip of glass introduced through slits in the eyepiece tube, so as to occupy the centre of the field.

Eye-pit. ME. [f. EYE *sb.*[1] + PIT.] The socket of the eye; also, the depression between the eye and the orbit.

Eyer (əi·əɹ), *sb. rare.* ME. [f. EYE *v.* + -ER[1].] One who eyes or observes.

Eyer, obs. f. HEIR.

Eyer(e, obs. f. AIR.

†**Ey·(e)rer.** ME. [f. *eyre*, var. of AIRE *sb.*[2] or *v.*, + -ER[1].] A brood falcon –1494.

Eye·salve. *Obs.* exc. *fig.* OE. [f. EYE *sb.*[1] + SALVE.] Eye-ointment.

Eye-servant (əi·sō̆:ɹvănt). *Arch.* 1552. [f. EYE *sb.*[1] + SERVANT.] One who serves the eye; one who does his duty only when under the eye of his master.

Eye·-se:rvice. 1526. [f. EYE *sb.*[1] + SERVICE.] **a.** The conduct of an eye-servant. †**b.** Service seen by the eye MILT. **c.** The homage of the eye 1869.

Eye·shot. 1599. [f. EYE *sb.*[1] + SHOT *sb.*[1]] **1.** The range of the eye, seeing distance, view. **2.** A 'shot' or glance from the eye, prospect 1615.

1. Phr. *To come within e. of.*

Eye·sight. ME. [f. EYE *sb.*[1] + SIGHT.] **1.** The power of seeing; sight. **2.** The action of looking; a look. *Obs.* exc. in *By, from, in* (*a person's*) *e.* ME. **3.** The range of the eye ME.

2. That in Josephus which he sets down from his own e. 1641.

Eyesore (əi·sōᵊɹ). ME. [f. EYE *sb.*[1] + SORE *sb.*[1]] †**1.** A soreness of the eyes –1562. **2.** Something offensive to the eye; a blemish; a defect 1530. **3.** A cause or object of dislike or disgust 1548.

2. Not an E. in his whole body DRYDEN. **3.** Thou shalt be a burthen, and an Eye sore to thy friends RALEGH.

Eye·-splice. 1769. [f. EYE *sb.*[1] + SPLICE *sb.*] A splice made by turning up the end of a rope, and interlacing its strands with those of the upper part.

Eye·spot. 1801. [f. EYE *sb.*[1] + SPOT *sb.*] **1. a.** A spot resembling an eye 1879. **b.** A rudimentary eye 1877. **2.** A kind of lily having a red spot in the middle of a violet leaf. Hence **Eye·spotted** *a.* having spots resembling eyes.

Eye·string. 1601. [f. EYE *sb.*[1] + STRING *sb.*] In *pl.* The strings (i.e. tendons, etc.) of the eye, *Cymb.* I. iii. 17.

Eye·-tooth. 1580. [f. EYE *sb.*[1] + TOOTH. Perh. after Du. *oogtand*, G. *augenzahn.*] A tooth immediately under or next to the eye, a canine tooth.

Phr. *To cut one's eye-teeth*: to get out of babyhood.

Eye·water (əi·wǭtəɹ). 1590. [f. EYE *sb.*[1] + WATER *sb.*] **a.** Water flowing from the eye. Rare in *pl.* **b.** A lotion for the eye 1679. **c.** The humours of the eye 1874. **d.** *Slang.* = Gin 1869.

Eye-wink. 1598. [f. EYE *sb.*[1] + WINK *sb.*] A wink or motion of the eye, a glance; an instant. So **Eye·-winker,** eyelash or eyelid.

Eye·witness. 1539. [f. EYE *sb.*[1] + WITNESS.] †**1.** One whose evidence is of what he has seen with his own eyes –1591. **2.** One who has seen a thing done or happen 1590. †**3.** The result of actual observation –1671.

2. Wee..were eye witnesses of his Maiestie 2 *Pet.* 1:16. **3.** Give us..Eye-witness of what first or last was done MILT.

Eyght(e, obs. f. AIT, EIGHT.

Eyl(e, obs. f. AIL *sb.*[2]; also of AIL *v.*

Eyne: see EYE *sb.*[1]

Eyot, more usual var. of AIT, q.v.

Eyr, obs. f. AIR; also of EAR *v.*[1]

Eyrant (ēᵊ·rănt). [f. *eire*, var. of AIRE *v.* + -ANT.] *Her.* Applied to birds in their nests.

†**Ey·rar.** 1551. [f. *eyrie* = AERIE.] A brood (of swans).

Eyre (ēᵊɹ). Now *Hist.* ME. [– OFr. *eire* :– L. *iter* journey. *In eyre* – AFr. *en eyre*, as in *justices en eyre* (cf. AFr. *justices errauntz*, legal L. *justitiæ itinerantes*).] **1.** Itineration, circuit: in *Justices in eyer* (= L. *in itinere* on a journey). **2.** The circuit court held by these officers. Also *E. of justice, Justice e., Commission of E.* ME. **b.** The record of such a court 1614.

Eyren, -ron(e, -roun, obs. pl. ff. EGG.

Eyrie, commoner spelling of AERIE.

Eyst, Eyster, obs. ff. YEAST, OYSTER.

‖**Ezan.** 1753. [Arab.] The formula chanted by the Muezzin at the hour of prayer.

E·zod, obs. var. of IZZARD, the letter Z.

F

F (ef), the sixth letter of the Roman alphabet, repr. Semitic *wāw*, which expressed the sounds of *w* (approximately) and *u*. In early Greek writing the form F (retaining the 6th place in the alphabet) came to be appropriated to the consonantal use, while V or Y served for the vowel. Later, in the classical period, both the sound *w* and its sign F (called the DIGAMMA from its form) were lost. In the Roman adoption of the Gr. alphabet, and thence in OE., the sound given to the sixth letter was the voiceless labio-dental spirant (f), or, between two vowels, the corresponding voiced spirant (v). In mod. Eng., F is always sounded (f), exc. in *of*, where it is voiced to (v) through absence of stress.

In MSS. a capital F was often written as ff. Hence, by a misunderstanding, the spelling of certain family names, *e.g.* Ffiennes, Ffoulkes, etc.

II. As a symbol. **1.** F, f, *f* signifies 6th in serial order. **2.** *Mus.* F is the 4th note of the diatonic scale of C major. Also, the scale or key which has that note for its tonic. *F clef*: the bass clef (see CLEF[1]).

III. Abbreviations. **1.** F. = Fellow in F.G.S., F.R.S., etc. **2.** F. = FATHER, as a title of R.C. priests. **3.** F. = Fahrenheit (thermometer). **4.** F.A. = Football Association; F.A.A. or f.a.a. = *free of all average*; F.O. = Foreign Office; f.o.b. = *free on board.* **5.** In Music *f* = *forte* (loud), *ff* = *fortissimo* (very loud), or occas. *più forte* (louder) with *fff* for *fortissimo.* **6.** F (on a black-lead pencil) = 'fine'; also *attrib.* **7.** *Chem. F* = fluorine. **8.** (*Photogr.*) F (*F, f*) = focal length (used in indicating the ratio between the focal length of the lens and the diameter of the stop, as in f/4.5).

Fa (fā), *sb.* ME. [– L. *fa*(*muli*); see UT.] Name of the fourth note in Guido's hexachords, retained in solmization as the 4th note of the octave. Hence as vb. SHAKS.

Fabaceous (făbēⁱ·ʃəs), *a.* 1727 [f. late L. *fabaceus* (f. L. *faba* bean) + -OUS; see -ACEOUS.] Having the nature of a bean.

‖**Fabella** (făbe·lă). *Pl.* **-æ.** 1854. [mod.L., dim. of *faba* bean.] 'A name for the sesamoid bones in the tendon of the gastrocnemius muscle of the dog and other animals' (*Syd. Soc. Lex.*).

Fabian (fēⁱ·biăn). 1598. [– L. *Fabianus.*]

A. *adj.* **1.** Of or belonging to the Roman gens Fabia 1842. **2.** Pertaining to, or after the manner of, Q. Fabius Maximus, surnamed Cunctator ('Delayer'), who, in the Second Punic War, foiled Hannibal by dilatory tactics and avoidance of direct engagements 1808.

2. *F. Society*: a society founded in 1884, of Socialists, who deprecate immediate attempts at revolutionary action.

B. *sb.* †**1.** *Flaunting Fabian* (? = L. *licens Fabius*), a swashbuckler, a roisterer –1599. **2.** One who belongs to, or holds the doctrines of, the Fabian Society 1891. Hence **Fa·bianism.**

Fabiform (fēⁱ·bifǭɹm), *a.* 1852. [f. L. *faba* bean + -FORM.] Bean-shaped.

Fable (fēⁱ·b'l), *sb.* ME. [– (O)Fr. *fable* :– L. *fabula* discourse, story, literary plot, f. *fari* speak.] **1.** A narrative or statement not founded on fact; a myth or legend (now *rare*); a foolish story; a fabrication, falsehood. **2.** A short story devised to convey some useful lesson; an apologue. (The commonest sense.) ME. **3.** The plot or story of a play or poem; occas., †a play 1678. †**4.** Talk; discourse, narration. *rare.* –1598. **5.** The subject of common talk; a byword. *arch.* 1535.

1. It seems a F., tho' the Fact I saw DRYDEN. The old f. of Seth's pillars 1756. The fables of Oates MACAULAY. Phr. *Old wives'* (*women's*) *fables* (arch.). **2.** His F. of the Belly and the Members 1796. **3.** The Intricacy and Disposition of the F. ADDISON. **5.** He..was the f. of the place THACKERAY.

Fable (fēⁱ·b'l), *v.* ME. [– OFr. *fabler* – L. *fabulari* talk, discourse, f. *fabula*; see prec.] †**1.** *intr.* To talk, converse. [A Latinism.] –1570. †**2.** To romance –1814; to talk idly –1870. **3.** To talk falsehoods, lie 1530. **4.** *trans.* To say or talk about fictitiously; to relate as in a fable; to fabricate, invent 1553.

2. Let Æsop f. in a Winters Night 3 *Hen. VI*, V. v. 25. Fabling about moods and figures 1653. **3.** To say verity, and not to f. 1612. **4.** Turn this Heav'n itself into the Hell Thou fablest MILT. Hence **Fa·bler,** one who fables.

‖**Fabliau** (fabli,o). Pl. **-aux.** 1804. [Fr. (XVI), evolved from OFr. (Picard) *fabliau*(*u*)*x*, pl. of *fablel*, dim. of *fable*; see FABLE *sb.*, -EL[2].] A metrical tale, belonging to early French poetry.

The interesting *fabliaux* of the Anglo-Norman *trouveurs* SCOTT.

Fabric (fæ·brik, fēⁱ·brik), *sb.* 1483. [– (O)Fr. *fabrique* – L. *fabrica*, f. *faber* worker in metal, etc. Cf. FORGE *sb.*] **1.** A product of skilled workmanship; as: **a.** An edifice, a building (also *fig.*); †**b.** An engine or appliance –1657; **c.** A frame, structure (also *fig.*) 1633; **d.** A manufactured material (now only a 'textile fabric') 1753. **2.** The action or process of framing or constructing (something specified) 1611. **3.** Kind or method of construction or formation; style; texture; also *fig.* 1644. **4.** Tissue, fibre (also *fig.*) 1823; occas., structural material 1849. **5.** A place where work is carried on; a factory, manufactory 1656.

1. a. The august fabriq of Christ Church EVELYN. **c.** The wonderful f. of the human body 1848. *fig.* The f. of knowledge REID. **d.** Woollen fabrics J. R. GREEN. **2.** The fabricke, raparation, or maintenance of a Church 1611. **3.** The f. of the Church is Gothic EVELYN. *fig.* He used almost always the same f. of verse JOHNSON. **4.** *fig.* The very f. of our nature 1877. Hence †**Fa·bric** *v.* to construct, fashion, frame, make.

Fabricant (fæ·brikănt). Now *rare.* 1757. [– mod.Fr. *fabricant,* pr. pple. of (O)Fr. *fabriquer* – L. *fabricare*; see next, -ANT.] A maker or manufacturer.

Fabricate (fæ·brikeⁱt), *v.* 1598. [– *fabricat-,* pa. ppl. stem of L. *fabricari, -are,* f. *fabrica*; see FABRIC, -ATE³.] **1.** *trans.* To make anything that requires skill; to construct, manufacture. Now *rare.* **2.** To 'make up'; to frame or invent (a legend, lie, etc.); to forge 1779.

1. To f. hinges PENNANT, clocks WHEWELL, silk 1872, words 1875. **2.** Numerous lies, fabricated by the priests..were already in circulation MACAULAY. Hence **Fa·bricative** *a.* tending to fabrication. **Fa·bricator,** †**Fa·bricature,** construction; method or style of construction.

Fabrication (fæbrikēⁱ·ʃən). 1602. [– L. *fabricatio,* f. as prec.; see -ION.] **1.** The action or process of fabricating; construction, manufacture. Now *rare.* **2.** The action of 'making up'; *concr.* an invention; a forgery 1790.

1. The f. of the body HALE, of a government BURKE, of implements LYELL. **2.** The common account..is a mere f. 1846.

†**Fa·brile,** *a.* 1611. [– OFr. *fabrile* – L. *fabrilis,* f. *faber* artificer; see -ILE.] Of or belonging to a craftsman or his craft –1678.

Fabular (fæ·biŭlăɹ), *a.* 1684. [– L. *fabularis,* f. *fabula* FABLE *sb.*; see -AR¹.] Fabulous.

Fabulate (fæ·biŭleⁱt), *v.* 1616. [– *fabulat-,* pa. ppl. stem of L. *fabulari*; see FABLE *v.,* -ATE.³] †**1.** *trans.* To relate as a fable; *intr.* to talk in fables –1624. **2.** *trans.* To concoct, fabricate 1856. Hence **Fa·bulator,** a story-teller.

Fabulist (fæ·biŭlist). 1593. [– Fr. *fabuliste,* f. L. *fabula*; see FABLE *sb.,* -IST.] **1.** One who relates fables; a story-teller. **2.** One who invents falsehoods 1625.

†**Fa·bulize,** *v.* 1612. [– L. *fabula* fable; see -IZE.] **a.** *intr.* To invent fables. **b.** *trans.* To concoct, invent; to dress up as a fable; also, to relate as legend *that* [etc.]. –1818.

Fabulosity (fæbiulǫ·sĭti). 1599. [– L. *fabulositas,* f. *fabulosus*; see next, -ITY, -OSITY.] **1.** The quality of being fabulous; fabulousness. †**2.** quasi-*concr.* A fabulous statement, fable –1807.

Fabulous (fæ·biŭləs), *a.* 1546. [– Fr. *fabuleux* or L. *fabulosus,* f. *fabula* FABLE *sb*; see -OUS.] **1.** Of persons: Fond of fabling, or of listening to fables. **2.** Of the nature of, or belonging to fable, full of fables, mythical, legendary, unhistorical 1555. **3.** Spoken of in fable, fabled. [So in L.] 1601. **4.** Resembling a fable (*rare*) 1561; astonishing, incredible 1609.

1. Wanton as Girls, as old Wives, F.! COWLEY. **2.** The dark and f. Ages 1712. Dragons and other f. monsters JOWETT. **4.** Houses..let at f. rents 1857.

Hence **Fa·bulous-ly** *adv.,* **-ness.**

Faburden. Now *Hist.* late ME. [Anglicization, w. assim. to BURDEN *sb.,* of Fr. *faux-bourdon* 'false hum'; the reason for the name is disputed. See FALSE *a.,* BOURDON².] *Mus.* **1.** A sort of counterpoint; 'a term for a sort of harmony consisting of thirds and sixths, added to a canto fermo' (Stainer and Barrett). **2.** The undersong 1587; the refrain 1580. **3.** A legend, motto. NASHE.

Façade (făsā·d). 1656. [– Fr. *façade,* f. *face,* after It. *facciata*; see next, -ADE.] The face or front of a building, *esp.* the principal front. Also *transf.* and *fig.*

The f. of the palace is unequalled 1839.

Face (fēⁱs), *sb.* ME. [– (O)Fr. *face* :– Rom. **facia,* alt. of L. *facies* form, appearance, visage, aspect, prob. rel. to *fax* torch, f. **fac-* appear, shine.]

I. 1. The front part of the head, from the forehead to the chin; the visage, countenance; also *transf.* **2.** With reference to its position, often without any reference to the lit. sense ME. **3.** = Sight, presence ME. **4.** The countenance as expressive of feeling or character; a countenance having a specified expression ME. Hence *colloq.* A grimace 1570. **5.** Command of countenance; *esp.* a bold face; impudence, effrontery 1537. **6.** *Lacrosse.* (Also *f.-off.*) The action of facing (see FACE *v.* I. 3b), corresponding to the bully in hockey 1900.

1. The f. of a lion, and..the f. of an eagle *Ezek.* 10:14. His f. Deep scars of Thunder had intrencht MILT. *P. L.* I. 600. *transf.* Grotesque masks or faces W. IRVING. Phr. *To have two faces. To look a person in the f.*: to confront. *To show one's f.*: to appear (*lit.* and *fig.*). *F. to f. To throw in a person's f.* (*lit.* and *fig.*). *To set one's f.*: to give a settled expression to the countenance. **2.** Phr. *To have the wind in one's f.* (*lit.* and *fig.*). *To fly in the f. of* (*lit.* and *fig.*). **3.** Thou fleddest from the f. of Esau *Gen.* 35:1. Thy very children.. curse thee to thy f. COWPER. **4.** They weare their faces to the bent of the kings lookes *Cymb.* I. i. 13. Leaue thy damnable Faces, and begin *Haml.* III. ii. 263. **5.** With what f. then..shal ye heare these wordes? *Bk. Com. Prayer.*

II. 1. External appearance, look; also semblance *of.* Now *rare,* exc. of immaterial objects. ME. ¶**b.** = PHASE. 1646. **2.** Visible state or condition; aspect; configuration (of a country) 1587. **3.** Outward show; disguise, pretence; a pretext ME.

1. A plan which has a very good f. SCOTT. The problems of the world are always putting on new faces BRYCE. **2.** The arrival of so many ships..caused a new f. of affairs 1781. **3.** Phr. *To put a good f. on* (a matter). They set a F. of civil Authority upon Tyranny S. BUTLER. Phr. *To save one's f.*: see SAVE *v.* I. 6. *To lose f.* [tr. Chinese *tiu lien*]: to lose one's credit, good name, or reputation.

III. 1. The surface or one of the surfaces of anything ME. †**b.** *Astrol.* The third part of a sign of the zodiac, extending over 10 degrees in longitude –1819. **2.** The principal side presented by an object, as: **a.** The front or slope (of a cliff, a fault, etc.) 1632; **b.** *Arch.* The façade of a building; the exposed surface of a stone in a wall; the front of an arch 1611. **3.** The side of anything usually presented outwards or upwards 1611; the obverse (of a coin or medal) 1515; the inscribed side (of a document) 1632; the dial-plate (of a clock or watch) 1787. **4.** Each of the surfaces of a solid 1625. **5.** The active, striking, or working surface or edge (of implements, tools, etc.) 1703. **6.** An even or polished surface 1881.

1. Phrases (*orig.* Hebraisms), *The f. of the earth, the deep, the waters.* **2.** The f. of a steep incline of snow TYNDALL. **b.** The Face of the Building is narrow, and the Flank deep WOTTON. **3.** The carpet's velvet f. KEATS. The f. of an old Roman coine *L. L. L.* V. ii. 617. It ought to appear on the f. of the plea that [etc.] 1817.

IV. Technical.

1. *Fortif.* **a.** The front or outward surface of a curtain wall 1489. **b.** *Faces of a work,* those parts which form a salient angle projecting towards the country 1676. **2. a.** *Mil.* Each of the sides of a battalion when formed into a square 1853. **b.** *Ordnance. Face of a gun,* the surface of metal at its muzzle 1727. **3.** *Mining.* **a.** The end of any adit, tunnel, slope, etc., at which work is progressing, or was last done 1708. **b.** 'The principal cleaving-plane at right angles to the stratification' (Raymond) 1867. **4.** In a steam-engine, the flat part of a slide-valve; also, the corresponding flat part on a cylinder, on which the slide-valve travels 1838. **5.** *Typog.* That part of a type (or punch) which has the form of the letter. Also, the printing surface of type. 1683.

Comb.: **1.** General: as *f.-sponge, -levelling, -flatterer,* etc. **2.** Special: as **f.-ache,** pain in the facial nerves; **-ague,** an acute form of face-ache, *tic douloureux*: †**-bone** = CHEEK-BONE; †**-bread,** = SHEWBREAD; **-card,** = COAT-CARD; **-cloth,** a cloth laid over the f. of a corpse; **-guard,** a contrivance for protecting the f., *esp.* in fencing, etc.; **-hammer,** one with a flat f.; **-joint,** that joint of a *voussoir* which appears on the f. of the arch; **-lathe,** one mainly used for surfacing; **-lifting,** a form of face-massage; **-mould,** a mould for drawing the proper figure of a hand-rail on both sides of the plank; **-painter,** (*a*) a painter of portraits, (*b*) one who applies rouge, etc., to the f.; **-painting** *vbl. sb.,* portrait-painting; **-plan,** the front or principal elevation; **-plate** (*Mech.*), an enlargement of the end of the mandrel (of a lathe), to which work may be attached in order to be faced; also *attrib.*; **-stone** (*Archit.*), the slab of stone forming the f. or front, *esp.* in a cornice, entablature, etc.; **-value,** the amount stated on the f. (of a note, etc.), the apparent value; also *fig.*; **-wall** (*Building*), front wall; **-wheel** (*Mech.*) = *contrate wheel* (see CONTRATE); also, a wheel whose disc-face is adapted for grinding and polishing.

Face (fēⁱs), *v.* late ME. [f. prec. sb.]

I. †**1.** *intr.* To show a bold or a false face –1601. †**2.** *trans.* To confront with assurance or impudence –1632. **3.** To meet face to face; to oppose with confidence; to stand fronting 1632. **b.** *Lacrosse.* To put (the ball) in play by placing it between the crosses of two opposing players 1867. **4.** To look steadily at 1795.

2. Phr. *To f. down, out* (a person, a matter). **3.** Facing fearful odds MACAULAY. **4.** The need for external supplies of food..must be faced 1883.

II. 1. *intr.* To look, front, in a certain direction; also *fig.* 1594. **2.** *trans.* To look or front towards 1632; of letterpress, etc.: To stand on the opposite page to 1766. **3.** *intr.* Chiefly *Mil.* To turn the face in a stated direction 1634. **4.** *trans.* (*Mil.*) To cause (soldiers) to face 1859. **5.** To turn face upwards 1674.

1. The little chapel that faced eastwards THACKERAY. *fig.* He steadfastly faced towards peace KINGLAKE. **2.** Stand facing the light JOHNSON.

III. 1. To cover a certain breadth of (a garment) with another material; to trim, turn up. Also †*transf.* and *fig.* 1561. **2.** To cover the surface with some specified material 1670. **3.** To dress the surface of 1848. **4.** To coat (tea) with some colouring substance 1850.

1. Blue cloth, trimmed and faced with white 1759. *fig.* Rebellion,..fac'd with publick Good! DRYDEN.

Faced (fēⁱst), *ppl. a.* 1500. [f. FACE *sb.* + -ED¹,².] **1.** Furnished with or having a face; often in comb., as *bare-faced,* etc. **2.** *Arch.* '*Faced work,* thin stone, otherwise called bastard ashlar, used to imitate squared stone work. In painting, the rubbing down each coat with pumice before the next is laid on. Used also of superior plastering' (*Arch. Dict.* 1892).

Facer (fēⁱ·səɹ). 1515. [f. FACE *v.* and *sb.* + -ER¹.] †**1.** One who puts on a bold face; a braggart, bully –1611. **2.** A blow in the face 1810.

2. *fig.* I've had a good many facers in my life 1872.

†**Fa·cet,** *sb.*¹ ME. [– L. *facetus* (see FACETE), used as a proper name.] The book *Facetus de Moribus,* formerly used in schools for instruction in manners –1483.

Facet (fæ·sėt), *sb.*² Also †**facette.** 1625. [– Fr. *facette,* dim. of *face* FACE *sb.*; see -ET.] **1.** A little face; *orig.* one of the small cut and polished faces of a diamond. Also in comb., as *star-f.,* etc. **2.** *Anat.* **a.** A small flat and smooth articular surface of a bone 1836. **b.** One of the segments (*ocelli*) of a compound eye 1834. Hence **Fa·ceted** (also *erron.* **facetted**) *ppl. a.* cut into, or furnished with, facets.

Facete (făsī·t), *a.* Now *rare.* 1603. [– L. *facetus* graceful, pleasant, witty.] **1.** = FACETIOUS. *arch.* †**2.** Elegant, graceful, polished –1662.

1. A man of a f. and affable countenance WOOD. Hence †**Face·te-ly** *adv.,* †**-ness.**

Facetiæ (făsī·ʃi,ī), *sb. pl.* 1529. [– L. *facetiæ,* pl. of *facetia* jest, f. *facetus*; see prec., -Æ.] Humorous sayings or writings, pleasantries, witticisms.

Facetious (făsī·ʃəs), *a.* 1592. [– Fr. *facétieux,* f. *facétie* – L. *facetia*; see prec.] †**1.** Of manners, etc.: Polished, urbane. **2.** Characterized by, or given to, pleasantry; jocose, waggish. Formerly also: witty, humorous, amusing, gay. 1599.

2. I am no way f. nor disposed for the mirth..of Company SIR T. BROWNE. A nudge..designed to be immensely f. MRS. STOWE. Hence **Face·tious-ly** *adv.,* **-ness.**

Facia (fæ·ʃⁱa). 1881. [var. FASCIA.] The tablet over a shop-front with the occupier's name, etc.

Facial (fēi·ʃiăl, -ʃăl), *a.* 1609. [– med.L. *facialis*, f. L. *facies*; see FACE *sb.*, -AL[1]. Cf. Fr. *facial*.] Of or pertaining to the face.

Phr. *F. angle*: the angle formed by two lines, one horizontal from the nostrils to the ear, the other (called the *f. line*) more or less vertical from the nostrils to the forehead. Hence **Fa·cially** *adv.* †face to face; with reference to the face.

†Fa·ciata, Fa·ciate. [– It. *facciata* FAÇADE.] A façade. EVELYN.

Facient (fēi·ʃiĕnt), *sb. rare.* 1670. [–*facient-*, pr. ppl. stem of L. *facere* do, make; see next, -ENT.] One who does anything; a doer.

-facient, formative element repr. *-facient-*, 'making', pr. ppl. stem of L. *facere*, as in *rubefacient*, etc., and in similar words not formed in L., as *absorbefacient*, etc.; also in *calorifacient*, and the like, for which the L. vbs. would have been in *-ficare*, and adjs. in *-ficus*.

‖**Facies** (fēi·si,īz). 1611. [L.; see FACE *sb.*] †**1.** *joc.* Face. **2.** *Nat. Hist.* General appearance 1727.

Facile (fæ·səil, -il), *a.* 1483. [– Fr. *facile* or L. *facilis*, f. *facere* do; see -ILE.] **1.** That can be accomplished with little effort. (Now somewhat disparaging.) **2.** Presenting few difficulties; †easy to understand or to use 1531. **3.** Moving without effort; fluent, ready 1605. **4.** †Easy of access, affable, courteous; characterized by ease of behaviour 1590; not harsh or severe 1541. **5.** Easily led or wrought upon 1511. †**6.** quasi-*adv.* Easily –1560.

1. It is facyle to scape out of the handes of the blynd CAXTON. **2.** This f. and ready course TOPSELL. To make this curious machine more useful and f. 1676. **3.** Deaths..with f. feet avenged SWINBURNE. **4.** F. and debonair in all his deeds GREENE. A Princesse most facil to forgive injuries FULLER. **5.** Adam and his facil consort Eve Lost Paradise MILT. *P. R.* I. 51. *transf.* The facil gates of hell too slightly barrd *P. L.* IV. 967. Hence **Fa·cile-ly,** *adv.*, **-ness.**

Facilitate (făsi·liteit), *v.* 1611. [– Fr. *faciliter* – It. *facilitare*, f. *facile* (– L. *facilis*), after L. *debilitare* DEBILITATE, etc.] **1.** *trans.* To render easier; to promote, help forward. ¶**2.** To lessen the labour of, assist (a person) 1646.

1. It will..f. the present negotiation 1621. To f. the animal or natural Motions ARBUTHNOT. Hence **Facilita·tion,** the action, process, or result of facilitating; help (now *rare*). **Faci·litator.**

Facility (făsi·lĭti). 1519. [– Fr. *facilité* or L. *facilitas*; see FACILE, -ITY.] **1.** The fact or condition of being easy or easily performed; freedom from difficulty, ease 1531. **2.** Opportunity for the easy or easier performance of anything; usu. in *pl.* opportunities 1519. **3.** In action, etc.: Ease, readiness; aptitude, dexterity. Of style: Fluency. 1532. †**4.** Easiness of access or converse, affability, courtesy –1793. **5.** Easiness to be led or persuaded to good or bad, pliancy. Also *transf.* of things (*rare*). 1533. **6.** Indolent ease, indifference 1615.

1. The great facilitie of their language HOOKER. The f. with which government has been overturned in France BURKE. **2.** The facilities given to the exportation of goods manufactured at home MCCULLOCH. **3.** Famous for f. in discourse 1596. **5.** The f. of Charles was such as has perhaps never been found in any man of equal sense MACAULAY.

Facing (fēi·siŋ), *vbl. sb.* 1523. [f. FACE *v.* + -ING[1].] The action of FACE *v.* †**1.** The action of boasting, swaggering, or browbeating; a defiance –1647. **2.** *Mil.* The action of turning in another direction. Also *transf.* 1635. **3.** *concr.* (chiefly in *pl.*): Something with which a garment is faced; *esp.* the cuffs and collar of a military jacket, when of a different colour from the rest of the coat. Also *transf.* and *fig.* 1566. **4.** The action of putting a new face on or of covering or protecting the face of (anything) 1549. **5.** *concr.* **a.** A superficial coating or layer; also the material of this 1586. **b.** *esp.* The external layer of stone, etc., which forms the face of a wall, bank, etc. 1823. **c.** An external cover or protection 1849. **d.** *Founding.* Powder, as charcoal, etc., applied to the face of a mould, or mixed in with sands for heavy casting, to give a fine smooth surface to the casting 1874.

2. Phr. *To put* (one) *through* (his) *facings* (*lit.* and *fig.*). **5. a.** Of Facing Timber-buildings with Bricks 1703. The 'f.' of tea 1875. **d.** *Comb.* **f.-loam, -sand,** that used to form the face of the mould.

Facinorous (făsi·nŏrəs), *a. arch.* 1548. [– L. *facinorosus*, f. *facinus*, *facinor-* (bad) deed, f. *facere* do; see -OUS.] Extremely wicked. Common in 17th c.

Hence †**Faci·norous-ly** *adv.*, **-ness.**

Faconde, -ound, var. of FACUND.

Facsimile (fæksi·mili), *sb.* Pl. **facsimiles** 1661. [mod.L., orig. written as two words, f. L. *fac*, imper. of *facere* make, + *simile*, n. of *similis* like, SIMILAR.] †**1.** Copying; imitation. FULLER. **2.** An exact copy, counterpart, or representation. Also *transf.* and *fig.* 1691. **3.** *attrib.* 1767.

2. A fac simile might easily be taken 1691. Hence **Facsi·mile** *v.* to make or (*rarely*) serve as a f. **Facsi·milist,** one who makes facsimiles.

Fact (fækt). 1539. [– L. *factum*, subst. use of n. pa. pple. of *facere* do.] **1.** A thing done or performed: †**a.** An action, deed. Also, action in general. –1815. †**b.** An exploit; a feat –1730. **c.** An evil deed, a crime. Now *obs.* exc. in *after, before the f.*, etc. 1539. †**d.** An action cognizable in law BACON. †**2.** The making, doing, or performing –1808. **3.** Something that has really occurred or is the case; hence, a datum of experience, as dist. from conclusions 1632. **4.** *loosely*, Something that is alleged to be, or might be, a 'fact' 1729. **5.** (Without *a* and *pl.*) Truth; reality 1581. **6.** *Law.* In *sing.* and *pl.* The circumstances and incidents of a case, as dist. from their legal bearing 1718.

1. a. Gracious in f. if not in word JANE AUSTEN. **b.** He who most excels in f. of Arms MILT. *P. L.* II. 124. **c.** Accessories after the f. BLACKSTONE. **2.** I caught him in the f. GOLDSM. **3.** One f. destroys this fiction THIRLWALL. The f. of resemblance MILL. **4.** The writer's facts are untrustworthy (*mod.*). **5.** Imagination is often at war with reason and f. JOWETT. Phr. *Matter of f. Inf.*: in reality. *In point of f.*: in fact. **6.** A jury.. decides all the issues of f. 1892.

Faction (fæ·kʃən), *sb.* 1509. [– (O)Fr. *faction* – L. *factio*, f. *facere*; see prec., -ION.] †**1.** A doing or making; cf. FASHION *sb.* –1689. **2.** †A class, sort, or set of persons –1606; *spec.* in *Rom. Antiq.* one of the companies of contractors for the chariot races in the circus 1606. **3.** A party in the state or in any community or association. Always with imputation of selfish or mischievous ends or unscrupulous methods. Also *transf.* and *fig.* 1509. **4.** Factious spirit or action; party strife or intrigue; dissension 1538; †an instance of this –1662.

2. I will..leaue the f. of fooles *Tr. & Cr.* II. i. 130. **3.** The public tranquillity was disturbed by a discontented f. GIBBON. **4.** F. hath no Regard to national Interests 1738. Hence †**Fa·ction** *v. intr.* to act in a factious spirit; *trans.* to form into factions. **Fa·ctional** *a.* of or belonging to a f. or factions; factious. **Fa·ctionary** *a.* active as a partisan; belonging to a f.; *sb.* a partisan. **Fa:ctionee·r,** †**Fa·ctioner, Fa·ctionist,** a partyman.

-faction, repr. L. *-factio, -on-*, forming nouns of action related to vbs. in -FY repr. L. *-facere*, Fr. *-faire*; also occas. used (instead of -FICATION) where *-fy* repr. L. *-ficare*, Fr. *-fier*, as in *petrifaction*.

Factious (fæ·kʃəs), *a.* 1532. [– Fr. *factieux* or L. *factiosus*, f. *factio*; see FACTION, -OUS.] **1.** Given to faction; inclined to form parties or to act for party purposes; seditious 1535. **2.** Pertaining to or proceeding from faction; characterized by party spirit.

1. The censure of f. and seditious persons 1624. **2.** His F. indignation at the Princes faults BOYLE. Hence **Fa·ctious-ly** *adv.*, **-ness.**

Factitious (fækti·ʃəs), *a.* 1646. [– L. *facticius*, f. *fact-*, pa. ppl. stem of *facere*; see FACT, -ITIOUS[1].] †**1.** Made by or resulting from art; artificial –1801. †**2.** Of soil, etc.: Produced by special causes –1808. **3.** Got up; not natural or spontaneous; artificial, conventional 1678.

1. Beer, Ale, or other f. drinks BOYLE. **2.** The f. soil of the Gangetic provinces 1808. **3.** F. wants created by luxury MORSE. Hence **Facti·tious-ly** *adv.*, **-ness.**

Factitive (fæ·ktitiv), *a.* 1846. [– mod.L. *factitivus*, irreg. f. L. *factitare*, frequent. of *facere* do, make; see -IVE.] *Gram.* **a.** Of a verb: Expressing the notion of making a thing to be of a certain character in deed, word, or thought; taking a complementary object. **b.** Causative.

a. *F. object, predicate, accusative*, the complementary accusative governed by a factitive verb, *e.g.* to *make* a man king, to *call* one a fool.

Factive (fæ·ktiv), *a.* 1612. [– med.L. *factivus* creative, practical, f. *fact-*; see FACT, -IVE.] †**1.** Tending or able to make; concerned with making –1649. **2.** *Gram.* = FACTITIVE. 1880.

Factor (fæ·ktəɹ). 1485. [– Fr. *facteur* or L. *factor*, f. as prec.; see -OR 2.] **1.** One who makes or does (anything). *Obs.* or *arch.* 1563. †**2.** A partisan, adherent, approver. [Cf. L. *facere cum aliquo* to side with any one.] –1715. **3.** One who acts for another; an agent, deputy. Now *rare.* 1485. **4.** *Comm.* One who buys or sells for another; a commission merchant 1491. **b.** One of the third class of the East India Company's servants. Now *Hist.* 1675. **5.** A bailiff, land-steward. *Obs.* exc. *Sc.* 1561. **6.** *U.S. Law.* = GARNISHEE. 1878. **7.** *Math.* One of the numbers, expressions, etc., which when multiplied together produce a given number, expression, etc. 1673. **8.** *transf.* One of the circumstances, facts, or influences which produce a result 1816. **b.** *Biol.* = GENE. 1907.

3. They..Authorised..the Vicechancellor, to be the common F. for the University FOXE. **4.** A F... for Norwich Hose or Stockings 1683. **8.** The first f. in the making of a nation is its religion GLADSTONE.

Hence **Fa·ctor** *v. intr.* to act as a f.; *trans.* to deal with (goods, etc.) as a f. **Fa·ctorage,** the action of a f.; his commission; factors collectively. †**Fa·ctoress,** a female f.

Factorial (fæktō·riăl), *a.*[1] and *sb.* 1816. [f. prec. + -IAL.] **A.** *adj.* **1.** *Math.* Pertaining to a factorial or factorials 1837. **2.** Of or pertaining to a factor (sense 4) 1881.

B. *sb. Math.* **a.** *gen.* The product of a series of factors in arithmetical progression. Also, in later usage: The product of a series of factors which are similar functions of a variable that changes by a constant difference in passing from any factor to the next. 1816. **b.** *spec.* The product of an integer multiplied into all the lower integers; e.g. the *factorial* of 6 (written $\lfloor 6$ or $6!$) is $6 \times 5 \times 4 \times 3 \times 2 = 720$.

Facto·rial, *a.*[2] *rare.* 1864. [f. FACTORY + -AL[1].] Pertaining to, or consisting in, a factory.

Factorize (fæ·ktŏrəiz), *v.* 1864. [f. FACTOR + -IZE.] **1.** *trans.* (*U.S. Law*) = GARNISH *v.* 7. **2.** *Math.* To break up into factors.

Factorship (fæ·ktŏɹʃip). 1599. [See -SHIP.] The office or position of FACTOR (senses 3, 4).

Factory (fæ·ktŏri). 1560. [In senses 1, 2 repr. Pg. *feitoria* (= It. *fattoria*, Sp. *factoria*, Fr. †*factorie* (XV), later *factorerie*); in senses 3, 4 ult. – late L. *factorium* (recorded in the sense 'oil-press'). **1.** An establishment for traders carrying on business in a foreign country 1582. †**2.** The body of factors in any one place –1777. †**3.** The action or process of making anything –1678. **4.** A building, or buildings, with plant for the manufacture of goods; a manufactory; works. Also *transf.* and *fig.* 1618. **6.** *attrib.* 1841.

1. Vancouver..the main f. of the Hudson's Bay Company W. IRVING. Chaplain to the British f. at St. Petersburg MME. D'ARBLAY. **4.** *fig.* Oxford is a Greek f. EMERSON. *Comb.* **f.-cotton** (*U.S.*), unbleached cotton cloth of home manufacture.

Factotum (fæktōu·tŏm). 1566. [–med.L. *factotum*, f. L. *fac*, imper. of *facere* make, do + *totum* the whole; in Eng. context first in appellatives like *Johannes Factotum* John Do-Everything.] A man of all-work; also, a servant who manages all his master's affairs. Also formerly, a busybody. Hence **Facto·tumship,** the office of a f.

Factual (fæ·ktiuăl), *a.* 1834. [f. FACT, after ACTUAL.] Concerned with facts; of the nature of fact, actual, real.

Factum (fæ·ktŏm). 1748. [– Fr. *factum*, legal use of L. (see FACT).] **1.** *Civil Law.* 'A person's act or deed; anything stated or made certain' (Wharton). **2.** A memorial, or statement of facts. [After Fr. legal use.] 1773. †**3.** *Math.* The product of two or more factors –1817. var. †**Fa·ctus** (in sense 3). NEWTON.

Facture (fæ·ktiŭɹ). Now *rare*. ME. [– (O)Fr. *facture* – L. *factura*, f. *facere* make; see FACT, -URE.] **1.** The action, manner, or style of making (a thing); also, the thing made. ‖**2.** *Comm.* = INVOICE *sb.* (Fr.; perh. never used in Eng.) 1858.

1. The f. or framing of the inward parts BACON.

‖**Facula** (fæ·kiŭlă). Chiefly *pl.* **-læ.** 1706. [L., dim. of *fax, fac-* torch; see -ULE.] *Astron.* One of the bright spots on the surface of the sun, as dist. from the dark spots or *maculæ*. Hence **Fa·cular** *a.* of or pertaining to faculæ.

Facultate (fæ·kŏlteᶦt), *v. rare.* 1648. [– med.L. *facultare* make possible, f. L. *facultas* FACULTY; see -ATE³.] To empower; to authorize.

Facultative (fæ·kŏlteᶦtiv), *a.* 1820. [– Fr. *facultatif, -ive*, f. *faculté*; see FACULTY, -ATIVE.] **1. a.** Of enactments, etc.: Conveying a faculty or permission; permissive; hence of actions, etc.: Optional. **b.** *transf.* In scientific use: That may or may not take place, or have a specified character 1874. **2.** Of or proceeding from a faculty 1866.

1. a. Creating what is called 'occasional', 'accidental' or 'facultative' contraband 1839. Hence **Fa·cultatively** *adv.* (*rare*).

Faculty (fæ·kŏlti). [ME. *faculte* – (O)Fr. *faculté* – L. *facultas*, f. *facilis* FACILE; see -TY¹.]

I. 'The power of doing anything' (J.). **1.** An ability or aptitude, whether natural or acquired, for any special kind of action; formerly also, ability in general. Occas. limited to a natural aptitude. 1490. †**b.** Disposition –1613. **c.** General executive ability. (Chiefly U.S.) 1859. †**2.** Of things: A power or capacity –1707. **3.** A physical capability or function 1500. **4.** One of the powers of the mind; *e.g.* the will, the reason, memory, etc. 1588. †**5.** Means, pecuniary resources; property –1894.

1. Excelling in Poeticall facultie CAMDEN. I devoted all my faculties to [etc.] JOHNSON. **3.** Sight and hearing, for example, I should call faculties JOWETT. **4.** The Moral F. MACKINTOSH.

II. †**1.** A department of knowledge –1757. **2.** *spec.* One of the departments of learning at a University. Hence *Dean of a F.* ME. **3.** An art, trade, occupation, profession. Now *Hist.* ME. **4.** The whole body of Masters, Doctors (and, occas., students), in any one of the studies, Theology, Law, Medicine, Arts ME. **5.** *transf.* The members of a profession regarded as one body, *e.g.* of the medical profession (called pop. 'The Faculty') 1511.

1. The greate learned clerkes in al faculties 1553. **2.** At Bonn there is a Protestant f. of theology M. ARNOLD. **4. b.** The whole teaching staff of a college or university (*U.S.*) 1829.

III. 1. Power, liberty, or right of doing something, conferred by law or favour 1534. **b.** A dispensation, licence; esp. *Eccl.* a licence granted by an eccl. superior to some one to do something which otherwise he could not legally do 1533.

1. Duncane Hath borne his Faculties so meeke *Macb.* I. vii. 17. **b.** Private rights to particular seats, conferred by a f., *i.e.* a license from the ordinary 1872.

Comb.: **f.-pew, -seat,** a pew or seat in a church appropriated to a particular person by a f.; †**-tax,** a property or income tax.

†**Fa·cund,** *sb.* [ME. *fac(o)und(e* – OFr. *faconde* – L. *facundia*, f. *facundus*; see next.] Eloquence –1483.

Facund (fæ·kɒnd, făkɒ·nd), *a. arch.* [ME. *fac(o)und(e* – OFr. *facond* – L. *facundus*, f. *fari* speak.] Eloquent; also *fig.* of beauty, etc. So †**Facu·ndious** *a.* (in same sense). †**Facu·ndity,** eloquence.

Facy (fēᶦ·si) *a.* Now *dial.* 1605. [f. FACE *sb.* + -Y¹.] Impudent. B. JONS.

Fad (fæd), *sb.* orig. *dial.* 1834. [prob. the second element of earlier *fidfad* (XVIII), shortening of FIDDLE-FADDLE.] A crotchety notion; a pet project, *esp.* of social or political reform; a craze.

Slöjd..the last new 'fad' 1884. Hence **Fa·ddish** *a.* given to fads; of the nature of a f. **Fa·ddist,** one who has a f. **Fa·ddy** *a.*

Fad (fæd), *v.* 1847. [Goes with prec. sb.] *intr.* To be busy about trifles; hence *nonce-use*, to advocate fads.

Faddle (fæ·d'l), *v.* Now *dial.* 1688. [Cf. FAD *v.* and FONDLE, etc.] **1.** *trans.* To make much of, fondle, pet. **2.** *intr.* To trifle; to play 1755. Hence **Fa·ddle** *sb.* nonsense, trifling; usu. FIDDLE-FADDLE.

Fade (fēᶦ·d), *a.* ME. [– (O)Fr. *fade*; see next.] **1.** Of colour, etc.: Dull, wan, sombre. *Obs.* exc. *arch.* †**2.** Faded, languishing –1752. ‖**3.** [Fr. *fade.*] Insipid, commonplace 1715.

3. F. and feeble sentimentality 1862.

Fade (fēᶦd), *v.* ME. [– OFr. *fader*, f. *fade* vapid, dull, faded :– Rom. **fatidus*, prob. blending of L. *fatuus* silly, FATUOUS with *vapidus* VAPID.] **1.** *intr.* To lose freshness and vigour; to droop, wither. †**2.** To grow small or weak; to decline, decay; to shrink. *lit.* and *fig.* –1585. †**3.** *trans.* To weaken; to corrupt, taint –1775. **4.** *intr.* To grow dim, faint, or pale ME. **5.** *trans.* To dim, dull, wither. Now *rare.* 1559. **6.** *intr.* To pass away gradually; vanish, die out 1590. **7.** *Cinematogr. trans.* To cause (a picture, etc.) to pass gradually *in* or *out* of view on the screen 1918. **b.** *transf.* of sound-films and broadcasting 1927. Also *intr.*

1. Elisian Flours..that never f. MILT. *P. L.* III. 360. **4.** Thy eternal summer shall not f. SHAKS. *Sonn.* xviii. **6.** Like this insubstantiall Pageant faded *Temp.* IV. i. 155. Religious animosity.. would of itself f. away MACAULAY. Hence **Fade** *sb.* (also *f.-in* or *f.-out*): cf. sense 7 above. **Fa·ded** *ppl. a.* that has lost its freshness; withered, decayed, worn out. **Fa·dedly** *adv.* **Fa·deless** *a.*, unfading. **Fa·delessly** *adv.* **Fa·ding-ly** *adv.*, **-ness.**

Fader, obs. and dial. f. FATHER.

Fadge (fædʒ), *sb.*¹ *dial.* and *techn.* 1588. [Of unkn. origin.] A bundle of leather, sticks, wool, etc.; a bale of goods.

Fadge, *sb.*² *Sc.* 1609. [Of unkn. origin.] A large flat loaf.

Fadge (fædʒ), *v.* 1573. [Of unkn. origin.] †**1.** *intr.* To fit, suit, be suitable –1711. †**2.** To put up *with* (a thing); to agree, rub on (with a person) –1678. †**3.** *trans.* To fit (the parts of) *together* 1674. **4.** *intr.* To succeed 1573. Now *dial.* **5.** To trudge (*rare* exc. *dial.*) 1658.

2. MILT. *Divorce* Pref.

†**Fa·ding, fa·dding,** *sb.* 1611. [Of unkn. origin.] The name of a dance, app. Irish. 'With a fading' was the burden of a song. –1672.

Fadme, -om, etc., obs. ff. FATHOM.

Fady (fēᶦ·di), *a.* 1730. [f. FADE *v.* + -Y¹.] Tending to fade.

Fæces (fī·sīz), *sb. pl.* Also **feces.** 1460. [– L. *fæces*, pl. of *fæx* dregs.] **1.** Sediment; dregs. **2.** Excrement 1639. Hence **Fæcal, fe-** (fī·kăl) *a.*, of the nature of or containing f.

Fæcula, fecula (fe·kiŭlă). *Pl.* **-æ.** 1684. [– L. *fæcula* crust of wine, dim. of *fæx*. Cf. Fr. *fécule* in same sense as Eng. The erron. spelling *fecula* is usual.] **1.** 'The sediment or lees which subsides from the infusion of many vegetable substances, *esp.* applied to starch' (*Syd. Soc. Lex.*). **2.** *gen.* Sediment, dregs. *sing.* and *pl.* (*rare*). 1816.

Fæculence, -ency, -ent: see FEC-.

Faerie, faery (fēᶦ,ĕri), *sb.* (*a*). *arch.* 1590. [A var. of FAIRY, first employed *arch.* by Spenser.] = FAIRY; *esp.* the imaginary world of Spenser's *Faerie Queene*. Also *attrib.*

Fa·ffle, *v. Obs.* or *dial.* 1570. [imit.] To stutter; to flap idly in the wind, as a sail.

Fag (fæg), *sb.*¹ 1780. [f. the vb.] **1.** That which causes weariness (*colloq.*). **2.** In Eng. schools, a junior who performs certain duties for a senior. Also *transf.* a drudge. 1785.

1. Not worth the f. of going and coming MRS. CARLYLE. **2.** *transf.* The diminutive f. of the studio THACKERAY.

Fag (fæg), *sb.*² 1486. [(more fully FAG-END) of unkn. origin. In sense 2, mod. abbr. of *fag-end.*] = FAG-END. **b.** A cigarette (*slang*) 1888.

Fag (fæg), *sb.*³ 1464. [Of unkn. origin.] **1.** A knot in cloth. **2.** [perh. a different word.] A sheep tick; hence, a disease of sheep 1789.

Fag (fæg), *v.* 1530. [Of unkn. origin; cf. FLAG *v.*¹] **1.** *intr.* To flag, droop (*lit.* and *fig.*). *Obs.* exc. *dial.* **2.** To do something that wearies one; to toil 1772. **3.** *trans.* To make fatigued; to tire 1826. **4.** In Eng. schools. *intr.* To be, or act as, a fag 1806; also *trans.* to make a fag of 1824. **5.** *Naut.* To untwist or wear out the end of a rope or the edge of canvas 1841.

2. All day I am fagging at business 1772. **3.** Correcting manuscript..fags me excessively SCOTT. Phr. *To f. out*: to go as fag, *esp.* in cricket, to field.

Fage, *v.* Now *dial.* ME. [Of unkn. origin.] To coax, flatter. *trans.* and *absol.* or *intr.*

Fag-end (fæ:g,e·nd). 1613. [f. FAG *sb.*² + END *sb.*] **1.** The last part of a piece of cloth; the coarser part that hangs loose; an untwisted end of rope 1721. **2.** *transf.* The last and poorest part of anything; the extreme end.

2. The fag-ends of cigars 1853.

Faggot, fagot (fæ·gĕt), *sb.* ME. [– (O)Fr. *fagot* – It. *fagotto*, dim. of Rom. **facus*, back-formation on Gr. φάκελος bundle.] **1.** A bundle of sticks, twigs, or small branches of trees bound together for use as fuel, in fascines, or the like. **2.** *fig.* The punishment of burning alive, as heretics 1555. **3.** A bundle in general; *fig.* a collection 1489. **4.** A bundle of iron or steel rods bound together 1540. **5.** A term of abuse applied to a woman (*dial.*) 1591. †**6.** A person hired to supply a deficiency at the muster; a dummy –1802. **7.** = FAGGOT-VOTE 1817.

3. My faggot of compliments H. WALPOLE.

Faggot (fæ·gɒt), *v.* 1543. [f. prec. sb. Cf. (O)Fr. *fagoter.*] **1.** *trans.* To make a faggot of; to bind up in or as in a faggot 1598. **2.** *Metall.* To fasten together bars or rods of iron to be reheated and welded 1861. **3.** To set (a person) on the faggots to be burnt alive; also *fig.* 1543. **4.** *intr.* To make or bind faggots 1874.

Fa·ggoting, *vbl. sb.* [f. prec. + -ING¹.] **1.** The action of FAGGOT *v.* **2.** *Embroidery.* The process by which a number of threads in the material are drawn out and cross threads tied together in the middle. Hence, the work done thus 1885.

‖**Fagotto** (făgǫ·tto). 1724. [It.] = BASSOON, q.v.

Faggot-vote (fæ·gɒt,vōᵘt). 1817. [app. a transf. use of FAGGOT *sb.* 6, but taken as referring to the primary sense.] A vote manufactured for party purposes, by the transfer to persons not otherwise qualified of sufficient property to qualify them as electors. Hence **Faggot-voter.**

‖**Fahlband** (fā·lband). 1880. [G.; f. *fahl* ash-coloured + *band* stripe.] *Geol.* A stratum in crystalline rocks.

‖**Fahlerz** (fā·lērts). 1796. [G.; f. as prec. + *erz* ore.] *Min.* Grey copper or copper ore, tetrahedrite. So **Fa·hlore** (in same sense).

Fahlunite (fā·lŭnəit). 1814. [f. *Fahlun* in Sweden + -ITE¹ 2b.] *Min.* A hydrous silicate of aluminium and iron, resulting from the alteration of iolite.

Fahrenheit (fæ·rənhəit, fā·rənhəit). 1753. The name of a Prussian physicist (1686–1736), inventor of the mercurial thermometer. Used *attrib.* and *ellipt.* to denote the thermometric scale introduced by him and still in use in England and U.S., which gives the freezing-point of water as 32° and the boiling-point as 212°. Often abbreviated *F.*, *Fah.*, or *Fahr.*

‖**Faience** (fa,yāns). 1714. [Fr. *faïence*, short for *poterie* or *vaisselle de Faïence*, i.e. pottery or ware of the Italian town Faenza.] A general term for all kinds of glazed earthenware and porcelain.

Faikes (fēᶦks). Also **fakes.** 1865. [Of unkn. origin.] *Geol.* 'A Scotch miner's term for fissile sandy shales, or shaly sandstones' (Page).

†**Fail,** *sb.*¹ *Sc.* 1513. [perh. – Gael. *fàl* sod.] A turf, a sod. Also turf, as a material. –1816. *Comb.* **f.-dyke,** a wall built of sods.

Fail (fēᶦl), *sb.*² ME. [– OFr. *fail(l)e*, f. *faillir*; see next.] **1.** = FAILURE 1; now only in *without f.* = certainly. †**2.** = FAILURE 2, 3. –1734. †**b.** Death. *Hen. VIII*, I. ii. 145.

Fail (fēᶦl), *v.* ME. [– (O)Fr. *faillir* be wanting :– Rom. **fallire*, for L. *fallere* deceive, and used in the sense 'disappoint expectation, be wanting or defective'.]

I. 1. *intr.* To be absent or wanting; to be insufficient. **2.** To become exhausted, come to an end, run short, die out ME. **3.** To lose power or strength; to break down ME. †**b.**

To die. *Hen. VIII*, I. ii. 184. **4.** To prove deficient on trial ME. **5.** To be wanting at need. Chiefly with *dat.* of the person, rarely with *to.* quasi-*trans.* To disappoint ME.

1. If suche heyres shulde fayle 1543. Phr. *Time would f. me to* [etc.]. **2.** Neither shall the cruse of oile faile 1 Kings 17:14. Thy yeeres shall not fayle *Heb.* 1:12. The eldest line failing 1647. **3.** My voice suddenly fail'd WESLEY. The wind failed 1833. *fig.* Her heart within her did not f. TENNYSON. **4.** In general this rewle may not fayle CHAUCER. Loop and button failing both COWPER. **5.** Here again chronology fails us FREEMAN.

II. 1. *intr.* To be wanting or deficient *in* ME. **2.** *trans.* To lack, want. Now *rare.* ME. **3.** *To fail of*: to lack; also, †to miss, escape ME.

1. Men þat failen in charite WYCLIF. The Dialogue fails in unity JOWETT. **2.** I f. words to express my utter contempt JEFFERIES. **3.** A weak prince..seldom fails of having his authority despised GOLDSM.

III. 1. *intr.* To fall short in performance or attainment; to make default; to miss the mark, err ME. **2.** *trans.* To make default in; to disappoint; to miss. *Obs.* exc. with *inf.* as object. ME. **3.** *intr.* To become insolvent or bankrupt 1682.

1. Their bull gendereth, and faileth not *Job* 21:10. Our envious Foe hath fail'd MILT. *P. L.* VII. 139. The year in which our olives fail'd TENNYSON. His action would f. 1883. **2.** To f. trust GOUGE, expectation 1699. He failed to keep his word 1885. **3.** If that Endorser f. and be insolvent 1682. Twelve capital houses have failed 1796.

†IV. *trans.* To deceive, cheat (L. *fallere*). SPENSER *F. Q.* III. xi. 46.

†Fai·lance. 1612. [– OFr. *faillance*, f. *faillir*; see prec., -ANCE.] The quality or fact of failing; failure, neglect, falling off –1686.

Failing (fēi·liŋ), *vbl. sb.* ME. [f. FAIL *v.* + -ING¹.] **1.** The action of FAIL *v.*; a failure. **2.** A defect, fault, weakness 1590.

2. E'en his failings lean'd to Virtue's side GOLDSM.

Failing (fēi·liŋ), *prep.* 1810. [The pr. pple. of FAIL *v.*, used either intr. or trans.] In default of.

F. all else, what gossip about one another CARLYLE.

Faille (fāy, fēil). 1530. [– (O)Fr. *faille* in same senses.] **†1.** A kind of head-dress –1694. **2.** A light ribbed silk 1869.

Failure (fēi·liŭɹ). 1643. [orig. *failer* – AFr. (legal) *failer*, for OFr. *faillir*, inf. used as sb. (see -ER⁴); alt. to *failor*, *-our*, *-ure* by assim. to suff. -OR, -URE. Cf. LEISURE, PLEASURE.] **1.** A failing to occur, be performed, or be produced; non-performance; default; also, †a lapse; †an infirmity. **2.** The fact of failing, becoming exhausted, giving way under trial, etc. (see FAIL *v.*) 1695. **3.** Want of success; *concr.* a thing or person that fails of success 1643. **4.** The fact of failing in business; bankruptcy, insolvency 1702.

1. A failer of full performance 1648. Failures of the press R. COKE. **2.** Utter f. of intellect 1841. **3.** Efforts ending in..f. SEELEY. Educated failures 1889.

Fain (fēin). [OE. *fæġ(e)n*, corresp. to OS. *fagan*, *-in*, ON. *feginn* :– Gmc. **faʒin-*, *-an-*, f. **faχ-*, repr. by OE. *ġefēon* rejoice. See next.]

A. *adj.* **1.** Glad, rejoiced, well-pleased; content ME.; hence: Necessitated, obliged 1513. **2.** Disposed, willing, eager (*arch.* or *dial.*) ME. **†3.** Well-disposed. ME. only.

1. Glad and faine by flight to saue themselues SHAKS. Men were faine to eate horse-flesh GOUGE. He was f. to acknowledge [etc.] 1884.

B. *adv.* Gladly, willingly, with pleasure. *Obs.* or *arch.* ME.

I would faine dye a dry death *Temp.* I. i. 72.

Hence **Fai·nly** *adv.* (*rare*).

†Fain, *v.*¹ [OE. *fæġnian* (f. *fæġen*; see prec.) = OS., OHG., Goth. *faginōn*, ON. *fagna*; for OE. var. *fagnian* see FAWN *v.*] **1.** *intr.* To be glad, rejoice –1596. **2.** *trans.* To make glad –1480. **3.** To rejoice in, enjoy –1606.

1. [She] faynes to weave false tales SPENSER.

Fain (fēin), *v.*² 1870. orig. *dial.* [var. FEN *v.*] In *fain(s) I*, etc., expressing intention to decline participation in a task, etc.

‖**Fainéant** (fęnęaṅ). 1619. [Fr.; f. *fait* he does + *néant* nothing.] **A.** *sb.* A do-nothing; an idler. **B.** *adj.* That does nothing; idle, sluggard 1855.

Hence **Fai·neance, -cy,** f. quality or condition. ‖**Faineantise,** 'do-nothing-ness'; indifference.

Faint (fēint), *sb.* ME. [f. FAINT *a.* and *v.*] **†1.** Faintness –1600. **2.** A swoon 1808.

2. The Saint, Who propped the Virgin in her f. SCOTT.

Faint (fēint), *a.* ME. [– OFr. *faint*, *feint*, feigned, sluggish, cowardly, pa. pple. of *faindre*, *feindre* FEIGN. Cf. FEINT *a.*] **†1.** Feigned –1568. **†2.** Sluggish –1680. **3.** Wanting in courage, spiritless. Now chiefly in *f. heart.* ME. **4.** Wanting in strength or vigour; languid, feeble ME. **5.** Striking the senses or the mind feebly; dim, indistinct, hardly perceptible 1552. **b.** *F. lines*, pale or indistinct lines to guide writing. **6.** Feeble through inanition, fear, or exhaustion; inclined to swoon ME. **7.** Producing faintness; sickly; oppressive 1525.

3. F. heart ne'er won fair lady 1569. **4.** Damn with f. praise POPE. **5.** F. reflections HOOKE, odours SHELLEY. Not the faintest chance 1884. **7.** The Weather was very wet, hot and f. 1712.

Hence **Fai·ntish** *a.* somewhat f., **-ness.** **Fai·ntly** *a.* and *adv.* **Fai·ntness.** **Fai·nty** *a.* faintish.

Faint (fēint), *v.* ME. [f. FAINT *a.*] **1.** *intr.* To lose heart or courage, become depressed, give way. Now only *arch.* after Biblical uses. **2.** To become faint, grow weak, decline. *Obs.* exc. *poet.* ME. **3.** To swoon. Also with *away.* ME. **b.** To droop, sink *into. lit.* and *fig.* (*rare*) 1712. **4.** To lose colour or brightness; to fade, die away. Now *rare.* ME. **5.** *trans.* To make faint, depress, weaken. Now *rare.* ME.

1. As we have received mercy, we f. not 2 *Cor.* 4:1. **2.** You f. in courage 1623. **3.** Oh, I shall f. ETHEREDGE. He fainted away GROTE. **b.** There Affectation..Faints into airs POPE. **5.** It faints me To thinke what followes *Hen. VIII*, II. iii. 103.

Faint-heart (fēi·nthāɹt). 1580. [f. FAINT *a.* + HEART *sb.*] **A.** *sb.* **†1.** The condition of having a faint heart. SIR T. NORTH. **2.** One who has a faint heart; a coward 1870.

B. *adj.* Faint-hearted, spiritless 1590.

So **Fai:nt-hea·rted** *a.* wanting energy, courage, or will to do anything; timid, cowardly. **Fai:nt-hea·rted-ly** *adv.* **-ness.**

Fainting (fēi·ntiŋ), *vbl. sb.* ME. [f. FAINT *v.* + -ING¹.] The action of FAINT *v.*; *esp.* swooning. Also *attrib.* in *f. fit.* So **Fai·ntingly** *adv.*

†Fai·ntise. ME. [– OFr. *faintise*, (also mod.) *feintise*, f. *faint*, *feint*; see FAINT *a.*] Deceit; hypocrisy; feebleness; cowardice –1485.

†Fai·ntling. 1614. [f. FAINT *a.* + -LING¹.] **A.** *sb.* One who is faint or faint-hearted. **B.** *adj.* Faint-hearted 1712.

Faints (fēints), *sb. pl.* 1743. [pl. of FAINT *a.* (quasi-*sb.*).] The impure spirit which comes over first and last in the process of distillation. Also *attrib.*

Fair (fēᵊɹ), *sb.*¹ ME. [– OFr. *feire* (mod. *foire*) :– late L. *feria*, sing. of cl. L. *feriæ* holiday.] A periodical gathering of buyers and sellers, in a place and at a time ordained by charter or statute or by ancient custom. Often specialized, as *cattle-*, *horse-*, *ram-*, etc., *f.*; *Easter-f.* Also (*fancy f.*) applied *transf.* to a bazaar or sale of fancy goods for a charitable purpose. Also *attrib.*

Phr. *A day after the f.*: too late.

Fair (fēᵊɹ), *a.* and *sb.*² [OE. *fæġer* = OS., OHG. *fagar*, ON. *fagr*, Goth. *fagrs* :– Gmc. **faʒraz.*]

A. *adj.* (No longer opp. to *foul* exc. with the sbs. *weather*, *means.*)

I. 1. Beautiful to the eye; of pleasing form or appearance. **†b.** Used as a term of address –1588. **2.** †Desirable, reputable –1676; considerable ME. **†3.** Of language, etc.: Elegant. Hence *f. speaker.* –1477. **4.** Attractive at first sight or hearing; specious, flattering OE.

1. The fairest of her Daughters Eve MILT. *P. L.* IV. 324. Tweed's f. river SCOTT. Phr. *The f. sex.* **b.** Faire sir, God saue you *L. L. L.* V. ii. 310. **2.** A f. fortune 1654, heritage 1859. **4.** A fayre speaker, and a deepe dissembler GRAFTON.

II. Of complexion, etc.: Light as opp. to dark 1551.

Are Violets not sweet, because not f. DRYDEN.

III. 1. Free from blemish or disfigurement; clean, clear. Of a line, curve, or surface: Free from irregularities; smooth, even (now chiefly *Naut.*). ME. **2.** Free from moral stain, unblemished ME. **3.** Free from bias, fraud, or injustice; equitable, legitimate ME. **4.** Tolerable; passable; average 1860.

1. A fayre white lynnen clothe 1552. A faire cleere water B. GOOGE. A very f. hand 1697. **2.** My f. fame SHELLEY. Phr. *To stand f.* **3.** A f. subject of presumption PALEY. F. game for ridicule BENTHAM. Phr. *A f. field and no favour. F. play.* **4.** A person in f. health 1875.

IV. 1. Favourable ME. **2.** 'Likely to succeed' (J.); promising, advantageous, suitable ME. **3.** Gentle, peaceable, not violent ME. **4.** Free from obstacles; unobstructed, open 1523. **5.** Clear, distinct, plainly to be seen. Now chiefly *dial.* 1577.

1. Faire weather *Matt.* 16:2. The f. season 1671. To proceed..with the first f. wind 1790. **2.** So faire an opportunitie KNOLLES. F. pretensions BURKE. **3.** By f. meanes or foul 1659. **4.** The fairest though farthest way about R. FORD. **5.** F. on the face [GOD] wrote the index of the mind P. FLETCHER.

Comb.: *Fair-haired*, etc.; **f.-curve** (*Naut.*): in delineating ships, a winding line which varies according to the part of the ship it is intended to describe; **-world**, a state of prosperity (MILT.).

B. *sb.*² [The adj. used *absol.* or *ellipt.*] **1.** That which is fair (in senses of the adj.) ME. **2.** One of the fair sex; *esp.* a beloved woman. Now *arch.* or *poet.* ME. **†3.** Beauty; also *pl.* points of beauty –1633.

1. Can we not Partition make..Twixt faire, and foule? *Cymb.* I. vi. 37. *To see f.* (colloq.): to see fair play. **2.** O happie faire! Your eyes are loadstarres *Mids. N.* I. i. 182.

Fair (fēᵊɹ), *adv.* [OE. *fæġre*, f. *fæġer* FAIR *a.*] In a fair manner or degree: beautifully; civilly (now only in *to speak* (*a person*) *f.*) OE.; clearly, legibly 1513; equitably, impartially ME.; †becomingly –1665; favourably, as in *f. befall*, etc. OE.; †gently –1804; †'due (north, etc.)' –1720; 'clean', 'full' ME.

Fair (fēᵊɹ), *v.* [ME. *feiren*, OE. *fæġrian*, f. *fæġer* FAIR *a.*] **1.** *intr.* To appear or become fair. **†2.** *trans.* To make fair –1600. **3.** *Shipbuilding.* To make fair or level; to ascertain the correctness of curvature in the parts of a ship. Also, to fit according to the curvature. 1867. Also of an aeroplane (cf. FAIRING *vbl. sb.*²).

2. Fairing the foul with art's false borrow'd face SHAKS. *Sonn.* cxxvii.

Fair and square. 1604.

A. *adj.* Honest, just, straightforward 1649.

B. *adv.* In a just or straightforward manner.

Fair-copy, *sb.* 1873. A copy of a document, etc., after final correction. Hence **Fair-copy** *v.* to write out in fair-copy 1840.

Fai·r-faced, *a.* 1588. **1.** Having a blonde, or a beautiful, countenance. **2.** Having a fair appearance; in bad sense, specious 1595.

Fairfieldite (fēᵊ·ɹfīldəit). 1879. [f. *Fairfield* County (in Connecticut) where found; see -ITE¹ 2 b.] *Min.* A hydrous phosphate of calcium, manganese, and iron.

†Fai·rhead. ME. [f. FAIR *a.* + -HEAD.] Beauty –1560. var. **†Fai·rhood.**

Fairing (fēᵊ·riŋ), (*vbl.*) *sb.*¹ 1574. [f. FAIR *sb.*¹ + -ING¹.] A complimentary gift; *orig.* one given at or brought from a fair. Also *fig.*

Fairing, *vbl. sb.*² 1867. [f. FAIR *v.* + -ING¹.] The streamlining of a vessel, vehicle, etc.; the structure added for this purpose.

Fairish (fēᵊ·riʃ). 1611. [f. FAIR *a.* and *adv.* + -ISH¹.] **A.** *adj.* Somewhat fair, passable; fairly large (*colloq.*). **B.** *adv.* In a fair manner; to a fair degree (*colloq.*) 1836.

Fair Isle (fēᵊ·rəil). 1851. Name of one of the Shetland islands used attrib. to designate woollen articles knitted in certain designs characteristic of the island.

Fair-lead (fēᵊ·ɹlīd). 1841. *Naut.* **a.** Such leading of a rope through the block or sheave aloft, that it does not cut or chafe any of the rigging or cross any other ropes 1860. **b.** (Also **Fair-leader.**) A strip of board, with holes in it, for running rigging, to lead through; also, a block or thimble for the same purpose.

Fairly (fēᵊ·ɹli), *adv.* ME. [f. FAIR *a.* + -LY².] **†1.** Beautifully; in bad sense, speciously –1870. **2.** Equitably, candidly, impartially 1676. **3.** Becomingly; proportionably 1596; legitimately, opp. to *foully* 1632.

†4. Gently –1634. **5.** Clearly, distinctly 1661. **6.** Completely, 'clean'; actually, really 1596. **7.** Moderately 1805.

1. Raiment..Most f. woven MORRIS. **2.** Treated f. 1851, f. considered 1862. **3.** His time will be f... employed 1800. **4.** I f. step aside, And hearken MILT. **6.** We were f. in the trap 1873. **7.** F. safe WORDSW.

Fai·r-mai·d. 1776. **1.** = FUMADE, q.v. 1848. **2.** In various names of plants; as **Fair maid(s of February,** the Snowdrop; etc.

Fairness (fēə·ɹnės). OE. [f. FAIR *a.* + -NESS.] The quality or condition of being fair; beauty; lightness of colour, as of the skin, etc.; fair dealing; etc.

Fa:ir-spo·ken, *a.* 1460. Of persons: Courteous; smooth-tongued; of words: Bland.

F. sword-men..whose words are softer than butter 1647.

Fai·r-tra·de. 1774. **1.** Trade carried on legally, as opp. to *contraband.* Also, in the 18th c., euphemistic for smuggling. **2.** The principle that reciprocity should be the principle of free-trade 1881.

Hence **Fair-tra·der** 1673.

Fai·rway. Also **fare-way.** 1584. [See FAIR *a.* IV. 4.] A navigable channel in a river or between rocks, sandbanks, etc. **b.** *Golf.* The smooth (trimmed) part of a golf-course between tee and putting-green (cf. ROUGH *sb.* I. 1c) 1910.

Fai·r-weather, *a.* 1736. **1.** Fit or suitable only for fair weather 1810. **2.** *fig.* 1736.

1. F. craft 1883. **2.** A f. service..of God E. IRVING.

Fairy (fēə·ri). ME. [– OFr. *faerie, faierie* (mod. *féerie*), f. *fae* (mod. *fée*); see FAY *sb.*², -ERY.]

A. *sb.* †**1.** Fairy-land; see FAERIE. –1610. †**2.** The inhabitants of fairy-land collectively –1603. †**3.** Enchantment, magic; an illusion –1533. **4.** One of a class of supernatural beings of diminutive size, popularly supposed to have magical powers, and to meddle for good or evil in the affairs of man. See ELF *sb.*, FAY *sb.*² ME. **5.** *transf.* An enchantress *Ant. & Cl.* IV. vii. 12; a small graceful woman or child 1838.

1. The Queene of Faerie B. JONS. **3.** Hit nis but fantum and feiri ME. **4.** Twilight fairies tread the circled Green COLLINS. *F. of the mine* (MILT.): a goblin supposed to inhabit mines; used later as = Ger. *kobold* or *gnome.*

B. *adj.* **1.** Of, pertaining to, or of the nature of fairies; enchanted, illusory 1640. **2.** Fairy-like; delicate, finely formed or woven 1788.

2. F. palms..f. pines TENNYSON. F. textures 1883.

Comb.: **fairies'-arrow** = ELF-SHOT 2; **f.-bird,** the Little Tern; **-cheeses,** *Malva rotundiflora* from the shape of the seeds; **-circle,** (*a*) = FAIRY-RING, (*b*) a fairy-dance, (*c*) a circle of fairies dancing; hence **-circled** *a.*; **-cups,** *Primula veris*; hence **-cupped** *a.*; **-dart** = ELF-SHOT 2; **-flax,** *Linum catharticum*; **-grass,** *Briza media*; **-lights,** small coloured lights used esp. for outside illumination; **-loaf,** a fossil sea-urchin said to be made by the fairies; **-martin,** Australian name for *Hirundo ariel*; **-money,** money given by fairies, said to crumble away rapidly; **-mushroom,** a toadstool; **-shrimp,** *Chirocephalus diaphanus,* a British freshwater crustacean; **-stone,** (*a*) a fossil sea-urchin, (*b*) a flint arrow-head; **fairies'-table,** various fungi; **-treasure, -wealth** = *fairy-money*; †**-walk** = FAIRY-RING. Hence **Fai·rily** *adv.* **Fai·rihood.**

Fairyism (fēə·ri,iz'm). 1715. [f. prec. + -ISM]. **a.** Fairy power. Hence *transf.* of a poet. **b.** The conditions of fairy existence; fairyland 1763. **c.** Belief in fairies, fairy-lore 1835.

Fairyland (fēə·rilænd). 1590. [f. as prec. + LAND *sb.*] The country of the fairies.

Fairy-ring (fēə·ri,riŋ). 1559. A circle of grass of a different colour from the grass surrounding it, a phenomenon caused by the growth of certain fungi, but popularly supposed to be produced by fairies when dancing.

Fai·ry-tale. 1750. [After Fr. *conte de fée.*] A tale about fairies. Also *transf.*

‖**Fait accompli** (fęt akonpli). 1845. [Fr. 'accomplished fact'.] A thing that is over and done with.

Faith (fēiþ), *sb.* [ME. *feþ, feiþ* – AFr. *fed,* OFr. *feid, feit* (pronounced *feiþ*) FAY *sb.*¹ :– L. *fides, fide-* f. **fid-*, var. of **fid-* in *fidus* trustworthy, *fidere* trust. Final *-th* may have been supported by *truth.* In theol. use *faith* renders eccl. L. *fides,* which translates Gr. πίστις of the N.T.]

I. 1. Confidence, reliance, trust. In early use, only with reference to religious objects. Const. *in,* †*of.* **b.** Belief proceeding from reliance on testimony or authority 1551. **2.** *Theol.* **a.** Belief in the truths of religion as contained in Holy Scripture or in the teaching of the Church. **b.** Saving or justifying faith, as a conviction operative on the character and will; opp. to *speculative faith.* **c.** The spiritual apprehension of divine truths. Often ascribed to the exercise of a special faculty in man, or to supernatural illumination. ME. **3.** That which is or should be believed ME.

1. F. in Ward's pills TUCKER, in the constancy of a law CHALMERS, in God J. H. NEWMAN. **b.** The absolute rejection of authority..the annihilation of the spirit of blind f. HUXLEY. Phr. *To pin one's f. to or upon.* **2. a.** Abraham the father of fayth EDEN. **b.** Even so f., if it hath not works, is dead, being alone *Jas.* 2:17. **c.** F...the faculty by which we realize unseen things GOULBURN. **3.** *The Christian, Jewish, Moslem* etc., *f. The f.*: the true religion; usu. = the Christian f. *Of f.*: part and parcel of the f. †*Act of the f.*: = AUTO-DA-FÉ.

II. †**1.** Power to produce belief, credit –1808. †**2.** Attestation, confirmation, assurance –1730. **3.** Assurance given, formal declaration, pledge, promise. *Obs.* exc. in *on the f. of.* ME.

3. Phr. *To give (one's) f.* On the f. of his oath they had placed themselves in his power THIRLWALL.

III. 1. The duty of fulfilling one's trust; fealty; the obligation of a promise or engagement ME. **2.** The quality of fulfilling one's trust; fidelity, loyalty ME.

1. Vpon the feyth that ye owe to me CAXTON. Phr. *To engage, pledge, plight (one's) f.*; *to perjure (one's) f.*; *to keep, break, violate (one's) f.*; *breach of f.* **2.** Confidence..in our f. and probity T. JEFFERSON. Phr. *Good f.*: fidelity, loyalty, BONA FIDES. *Bad f.*: faithlessness; intent to deceive. *Punic* (occas. *Carthaginian*) *f.* (= L. *fides Punica*): faithlessness. *In (good) f.*: in truth. *By* or *on my, thy,* etc., *f.*; *my f.* (= Fr. *ma foi!*): quasi-oaths.

Comb.: **f.-cure,** a cure wrought by means of 'the prayer of faith' (Jas. 5:15); **-healer,** one who believes in or practises f.-cure; **-healing,** healing by f.-cure.

Hence †**Faith** *v. trans.* to provide with a f.; to utter on one's f.; to give f. to, believe, trust. †**Faithed** *ppl. a.* having (feeble, etc.) f.; given on one's f.

Faithful (fēi·þfŭl). ME. [f. prec. + -FUL.]

A. *adj.* †**1.** Full of or characterized by FAITH (sense I. 2); believing –1759. **2.** Firm in fidelity or allegiance to a person to whom one is bound by any tie; constant, loyal, true. Also *transf.* of things. ME. **3.** True to one's word or profession ME.; †of a covenant, etc.: Binding –1601. **4.** Conscientious in the fulfilment of duty; *esp.* of the duty of telling unwelcome truths ME. **5.** Trustworthy, veracious; reliable ME. **6.** True to the fact or the original, accurate 1529. **7.** *absol.* Chiefly *pl.* = 'True believers'; the orthodox of any religious community 1558.

1. F. Abraham *Gal.* 3:9. **2.** F. allies DE FOE. His f. dog shall bear him company POPE. Whose hand was f. to his sword SCOTT. **3.** The faithfull God *Deut.* 7:9. **5.** Memoirs scarcely more f. than romances SCOTT. **6.** A f. report FIELDING. **7.** The faithfull which departed this life before the comming of Christ HOOKER. Phr. *Father of the f.* (after *Rom.* 4:11): Abraham. *Commander* or *Father of the F.*: Moslem titles of the Caliph.

†**B.** *adv.* = FAITHFULLY. –1651. **C.** *sb.* **a.** A true believer 1571. **b.** A trusty follower 1648. Hence **Fai·thfully** *adv.* confidingly; loyally; accurately; with binding assurances. *Yours f.*: one of the more formal phr. used in subscribing a letter, now regular in business use. **Fai·thfulness.**

Faithless (fēi·þlės), *a.* ME. [f. FAITH *sb.* + -LESS.] **1.** Without belief or trust; unbelieving. **b.** Without religious faith; without Christian faith. Also absol. *The f.*: unbelievers. Now *rare.* 1534. **2.** Destitute of good faith; false to vows, etc., perfidious, disloyal ME. **3.** Not to be trusted or relied on; unstable, treacherous, delusive 1603.

1. And bee not faithlesse, but beleeuing *John* 20:27. **2.** A man..of a..f. disposition 1678. **3.** The midnight murd'rer bursts the f. bar JOHNSON. Hence **Fai·thless-ly** *adv.*, **-ness.**

Fai·thworthy, *a.* 1535. [f. FAITH *sb.* + WORTHY *a.* II.] Worthy of belief or trust, trustworthy.

Faitour (fēi·təɹ). Now *arch.* ME. [– AFr. *faitour* impostor, OFr. *faitor* doer, maker :– L. *factor* FACTOR; see -OUR. The special sense 'impostor' seems to be peculiarly AFr.] An impostor, cheat; *esp.* a vagrant who shams illness or pretends to tell fortunes.

These faytours that ben called sothe sayers 1496.

Fake (fēik), *sb.*¹ 1627. [See FAKE *v.*¹] *Naut.* One of the circles or windings of a cable or hawser, as it lies in a coil.

Fake (fēik), *sb.*² *slang.* 1827. [f. FAKE *v.*²] **1.** An act of faking; a trick, invention; a faked or cooked report. **2.** That which is used for faking 1866.

Fake (fēik), *v.*¹ ME. [app. f. FAKE *sb.*¹ which, however, appears much later. Cf. Sc. *faik* (XVI) fold.] *Naut.* To lay a rope in fakes; to coil.

Fake (fēik), *v.*² *slang.* 1812. [Later form of †*feak,* †FEAGUE beat, thrash – G. *fegen* polish, furbish, sweep, (slang) thrash, scold.] **1.** *trans.* In thieves' language: To perform any operation upon; to 'do', 'do for'; to plunder, wound, kill; to do up; to tamper with, for the purpose of deception. **2.** *absol.* or *intr.* To steal 1812.

1. A horse faked up for sale 1874. Faked diamonds 1887. A faked report (*mod.*). Hence **Fa·kement** (*slang*), a piece of manipulation, dodge; vaguely, a thing, 'concern'; a trimming. **Fa·ker.**

‖**Faki.** 1872. [Arab. *faḳīh* one learned in the law.] A title given in Africa to schoolmasters.

Fakir (fǎkīə·ɹ, fēi·kiəɹ). Also **faquir, fakeer,** etc. 1609. [– (partly through Fr. *faquir*) Arab. *faḳīr* poor, poor man.] A poor man; *spec.* a Moslem religious mendicant; applied loosely to Hindu devotees and naked ascetics. **b.** (fēi·kəɹ). Erron. f. *faker* (*U.S.*) 1902.

Fa-la (fālā). 1595. Used as a refrain. Also, a sort of madrigal or ballet in vogue in the 16th and 17th c.

‖**Falbala** (fæ·lbǎlǎ). 1704. [– Fr. *falbala* (XVII), of unkn. origin. See FURBELOW *sb.*] A trimming for women's petticoats, scarves, etc.; a flounce.

Falcade (fælkā·d). 1730. [– Fr. *falcade* – It. *falcata,* f. *falcare* bend.] *Manège.* The action of a horse when the haunches and the legs bend very low, as in curvets. (Dicts.)

Falcate (fæ·lkeit), *a.* 1826. [– L. *falcatus,* f. *falx, falc-* sickle; see -ATE².] *Anat.,* etc. Bent or curved like a sickle. So **Fa·lcated** *a.* †**Falca·tion,** the condition of being f.; *concr.* that which is f.

Falchion (fǭ·lʃiǭn), *sb.* [ME. *fauchoun* – OFr. *fauchon* :– Rom. **falcio, -iōn-,* f. L. *falx, falc-* sickle. Latinized sp. with *l* XVI.] **1.** A broad sword more or less curved with the edge on the convex side. Later: A sword of any kind. †**2.** = BILL *sb.*¹ 4 or BILL-HOOK. –1664.

1. Phr. *Single, double f., case of falchions*: obs. species of sword-play.

Falcidian (fælsi·diǎn), *a.* 1656. [f. *Falcidius* + -AN.] In *F. law* (*Lex Falcidia*), a law carried by P. Falcidius, by which a Roman citizen was obliged to leave at least a fourth part of his estate to his legal heirs. Hence *F. portion.*

Falciform (fæ·lsifǭɹm), *a.* 1766. [f. L. *falx, falc-* sickle + -FORM.] Sickle-shaped, curved, hooked. Freq. in *Anat.,* as in *f. cartilage, ligament, process,* etc.

Falcon (fǭ·kən, fǭ·lkən). [ME. *faucon* – (O)Fr. *faucon,* obl. case of *fauc* :– late L. *falco, falcōn-,* expl. by Festus as f. *falx* scythe, from the bird's sickle-like claws, but perh. – Gmc. **falkon,* repr. by OE. personal name *Falca* = OS., OHG. *falco* (Du. *valk,* G. *falke*). Spelling refash. XV after L.] **1.** *Ornith.* One of a family of the smaller diurnal birds of prey, characterized by a short hooked beak, strong claws, and great destructive power; *esp.* one trained to the pursuit of other birds or game, usually the Peregrine Falcon. In *Falconry,* applied only to the female, the male being called the *tercel* or *tiercel.* **2.** An ancient kind of light cannon 1496.

1. A Faulcon towring in her pride of place *Macb.* II. iv. 12. *Comb.*, chiefly *attrib.*, as (sense 1) *f.-face*; *-eyed*, a.; (sense 2) *-shot*.

Falconer (fǭ·kənəɹ, fǭ·lkənəɹ). [ME. *fauconer* – AFr. *fauconer*, OFr. *-ier* (mod. *fauconnier*); see prec., -ER[2] 2.] **1.** One who hunts with falcons. **2.** A keeper and trainer of hawks ME.

1. Thise ffauconers..with hir haukes han the heron slayn CHAUCER.

Falconet (fǭ·kŏnėt). 1559. [In sense 1 – It. *falconetto*, dim. of *falcone*; in sense 2 f. FALCON + -ET.] **1.** A light cannon used in the 16th and 17th c. **2.** A species of Shrike (order *Passerinæ*) 1851.

Fa·lcon-ge·ntle. ME. [After Fr. *faucon gentil*, in med.L. *falco gentilis*.] The female or young of the Goshawk (*Astur palumbarius*).

Falconine (fæ·lkŏnəin), *a.* [f. FALCON + -INE[1].] Like a falcon or hawk, belonging to the *Falconidæ*. (Dicts.)

Falconry (fǭ·kənri). 1575. [– Fr. *fauconnerie*; see FALCON, -RY.] The art of breeding and training hawks; also, *occas.*, the practice of hawking.

Falculate (fæ·lkiŭleᶦt), *a.* 1847. [f. L. *falcula*, dim. of *falx*, *falc-* sickle; see -ULE, -ATE[2].] Of the form of a little sickle, small and curved.

Faldage (fæ·ldėdʒ). 1692. [– AL. *faldagium*, f. OE. *fald* FOLD *sb.*[1] + *-agium*; see -AGE. In XVI anglicized as FOLDAGE.] *Law.* An old privilege by which a lord of the manor could set up folds in any fields within the manor, in which his tenants were obliged to put their sheep, to manure the land.

Falderal, falderol (fæ:ldəræ·l, fǫ:ldərǫ·l). [Obscurely related to FAL-LAL.] **1.** As a refrain in songs 1701. **2.** A gewgaw, trifle; a flimsy thing 1820.

‖**Faldetta** (falde·tă). 1834. [It. dim. of *falda* fold of cloth, skirt.] A combined hood and cape, worn by women in Malta.

†**Fa·ldfee.** *rare.* [app. f. OE. *fald*, FOLD *sb.*[1] + *feoh* (see FEE).] *Law.* Some kind of manorial dues. BLOUNT. (Possibly an error.)

†**Fa·lding.** ME. [Cf. OIr. *feld-r* cloak.] A kind of frieze, or a garment of the same –1526.

†**Faldi·story.** 1675. [– med.L. *faldistorium*, var. of *faldistolium*; see FALDSTOOL.] The seat or throne of a bishop within the chancel –1768.

Faldstool (fǭ·ldstūl). OE. [– med.L. *faldistolium* – WGmc. **faldistōl* = late OE. *fældestol*, *fyld(e)stōl* :– Gmc. **falþistōlaz*, f. **falþan* FOLD *v.*[1] + **stōlaz* STOOL *sb.*] **1.** *Eccl.* An armless chair used by bishops and other prelates when they do not occupy the throne or when officiating in any but their own church. **2.** A movable folding-stool or desk at which worshippers kneel; *esp.* one used by the sovereign at the coronation 1603. **3.** A small desk at which the Litany is said or sung 1626.

Falern(e (fălə̄·rn), *a.* and *sb. poet.* 1601. [– L. (*vinum*) *Falernum*.] = next.

Falernian (fălə̄·ɹniăn), *a.* 1726. [f. as prec. + -IAN.] Of or pertaining to the *ager Falernus* in Campania, celebrated for its wine. Also *absol.* Falernian wine.

Falk (fǭk), *sb.* 1698. [Of unkn. origin.] A name applied dial. to the Razor-bill.

Fall (fǭl), *sb.*[1] [ME. *fal(l)*, partly – ON. *fall* fall, death in battle, sin, downfall; partly a new formation on the verb.] An act or instance of falling.

I. 1. A dropping down by the force of gravity; also *fig.* ME.; *concr.* that which falls; also *pl.* 1742. **2.** (Earlier †*F. of the leaf.*) The season when leaves fall from the trees; autumn. Chiefly Amer. Now *rare* in Eng. literary use. 1545. **3.** The manner in which anything falls 1535. **4.** Birth or production by dropping from the parent; the quantity born or produced 1796.

1. A green plum that..falls..before the f. should be SHAKS. *fig.* The f. of the Stuarts HALLAM. *concr.* A large aërolitic f. LOCKYER. **2.** In the spring and f. he was alwaies disturbed 1714. **3.** The f. of the cards 1885. **4.** The principal f. of lambs HOWITT.

II. 1. A sinking down, subsidence; also *fig.* decline, decay 1571. **2.** The discharge or disemboguement of a river; †the place of this; the mouth 1577. **3.** The falling of a stream of water down a declivity; hence, a cascade, cataract, waterfall. Freq. in *pl.* 1579. **4.** Downward direction of a surface or outline; a slope or declivity 1565. **5.** The distance through which anything falls; the difference in the levels (of ground, water, etc.) 1686. **6.** The sinking down of the fluid in a meteorological instrument; hence, of temperature, and of the instrument 1806. **7.** *Mus.* A lowering of the note or voice; cadence 1601. **8.** A sinking down in price, value, etc.; depreciation 1555.

1. The rise and f. of the spring-tides LYELL. *fig.* The f. of Venice OTWAY, of day 1712. **2.** The Po..before its F. into the Gulf ADDISON. **3.** The falls of Clyde 1806. **4.** The f. of the hills SCOTT, of the shoulders 1847. **5.** Hart's Weir..has a f. of 3 ft. 1881. **7.** That straine agen, it had a dying f. *Twel. N.* I. i. 4. **8.** The f. of the market BP. HALL, of Interest PETTY, of rents MACAULAY.

III. 1. A falling to the ground; also *fig.* of an institution ME. **2.** *Wrestling.* The fact of being thrown by one's opponent; hence, a bout at wrestling 1553. **3.** A felling of trees; *concr.* the timber felled at one time 1572. **4.** The capture or surrender of a city, fortress, etc. 1586. **5.** *fig.* A succumbing to temptation; moral ruin ME. **6.** Death, destruction, overthrow ME.

1. [The house] fell: and great was the f. of it *Matt.* 7: 27. The hero's f. W. IRVING. **2.** You shall trie but one f. *A. Y. L.* I. ii. 216. **4.** The f. of Londonderry MACAULAY. **5.** Phr. *The f.*, *the f. of man* (Theol): the sudden lapse into a sinful state produced by Adam's transgression. **6.** Now happened the f. of..Oliver Cromwell 1659.

IV. As a measure (orig. = *perch, pole, rod*), the 40th part of a furlong 1597.

†**V.** What befalls a person –1853.

Black be your fa! BURNS.

VI. 1. a. A band or collar worn falling flat round the neck 1599. **b.** A kind of veil worn by women 1611. **2.** *Mech.* The loose end of the tackle, to which the power is applied in hoisting 1644; an apparatus for lowering bales, etc.; also *Naut.* in *pl.* 1832.

Comb.: **f.-board,** a shutter hinged at the bottom; **-trap** = FALL *sb.*[2]

Fall (fǭl), *sb.*[2] [OE. *fealle* in *mūsfealle* mouse-trap, surviving in PITFALL, and in Sc. *mouse-faw*, *ratton-faw*.] Something that falls; a trap-door, trap. Cf. PITFALL.

Fall (fǭl), *sb.*[3] 1694. [Local Sc. pronunc. of *whale* (in Aberdeenshire *wh* is pronounced f).] **a.** The cry given when a whale is sighted or harpooned. **b.** The chase of a whale or school of whales 1820.

Fall (fǭl), *v.* Pa. t. **fell** (fel); pa. pple. **fallen** (fǭ·l'n). [OE. *feallan*, *fallan* = OFris., ON. *falla*, OS., OHG. *fallan* (Du. *vallen*, G. *fallen*) :– Gmc. reduplicating str. vb. **fallan*, pa. t. **fefell-*. Cf. FELL *v.*]

I. 1. *intr.* To descend (primarily by gravity); to drop from a high or relatively high position; also *fig.* **2.** To become detached and drop off; also *fig.* ME. **3.** Of the young of animals: To be dropped or born ME. **4.** Of speech, etc.: To issue or proceed *from* 1605.

1. The Priest let f. the booke *Tam. Shr.* III. ii. 163. What if heaven f., say you BP. HALL. *fig.* Falne from his first perfection BURTON. Most fiercely fell their fury on the Dutch FULLER. The evening fell SCOTT. Provb. *F. back, f. edge*: come what may. **2.** *fig.* My fevered mood fell from me 1890. **3.** The lambs should f. in May 1864. **4.** Wisdom falling from his Tongue 1770.

II. 1. To descend, sink *into*, *to*; to decline ME. **2.** Of land: To slope 1573. **3.** Of a river, etc.: To discharge itself, issue *into*. Also *transf.* of a road. ME. **4.** To subside; also *fig.* ME. **5.** Of the countenance: To lose animation; to assume a look of dismay or disappointment. [Orig. a Hebraism.] ME. **6.** To be lowered in direction 1586. †**7.** To shrink; to become lean –17... **8.** To sink to a lower point, as the mercury in a barometer; to be reduced, as temperature 1658. **9.** *Mus.* To sound a lower note 1597. **10.** To decrease; to be diminished in price or value 1580.

1. The obsequious billows f. OTWAY. We f. below our position TRENCH. **3.** Rivers that f. into Lake Huron 1825. **4.** It fell calm 1670. *fig.* What though..wit, like ocean, rose and fell SHELLEY. **5.** Cain was very wroth, and his countenance fell *Gen.* 4: 5. **6.** His eyes fell 1889. **7.** A good leg will f. SHAKS. **10.** The Rents of Land are generally fall'n PETTY. The exchange fell below par 1812.

III. 1. *intr.* To lose the erect position; to become suddenly prostrate; also *fig.* ME. **2.** To prostrate oneself. [Heb. idiom.] OE. **3.** To yield to temptation; *esp.* of a woman: To surrender her chastity ME. **4.** To drop down wounded or dead; to die by violence; *rarely*, by disease; also *fig.* ME. **5.** Of a building, etc.: To come down in fragments ME.

1. Starting aside I slipped and fell DICKENS. *fig.* When proud Granada fell BYRON. The proposition fell to the ground MACAULAY. **2.** I fell at his feete to worship him *Rev.* 19:10. **3.** It is their Husbands faults If wiues do f. *Oth.* IV. iii. 88. **4.** Sheo fallethe dede as any stoone CHAUCER. Seven lions fell to his rifle in one day 1892. Phr. *To f. a prey, sacrifice, victim to. To f. in a snare, into danger, error*, etc. **5.** Babylon is fallen, is fallen *Isa.* 21: 9. Phr. *To f. in* or *to pieces, powder. To f. in two, asunder.*

IV. To move precipitately or with violence; to rush ME.

His master fell about his ears and beat him PEPYS.

V. 1. To have or take its direction; to be directed; to settle or impinge 1570. **2.** Of a lot, etc.: To light *upon* a particular object ME. **3.** To come as a lot, portion, or possession; rarely *impers.* ME. **4.** To come as a burden or duty 1599. †**5.** To appertain or belong; also *impers.* –1563.

1. The rays falling on the pupil BP. BERKELEY. His eye fell..upon Cissy 1886. **2.** The lot fell vpon Matthias *Acts* 1: 26. **3.** The whole fighting fell to Sir Horace CARLYLE. **4.** The expense..must f. upon the purchaser 1885.

VI. 1. To come by chance or casually ME. **2.** To come naturally ME.; to be naturally divisible *into* 1641.

1. As for riches, if they f. in my way, I refuse them not BP. HALL. You f. 'mongst Friends SHAKS. The degenerate days on which he had fallen DISRAELI. **2.** The subject..falls into four divisions 1862.

VII. 1. To pass (suddenly) †*in*, *into*, †*to* some specified condition or relation ME. **2.** With compl.: To become (what the complement signifies) ME. **3.** To lapse, as a benefice, etc.; †to become vacant, as a living 1530. †**4.** To change *to*, *into* (something worse) –1586.

1. To f. into the travaile of childe birthe LAMBARDE. My way of life is falne into the Seare, the yellow Leafe *Macb.* V. iii. 23. Phr. *To f. in love.* **2.** His horse fell lame SOUTHEY. To f. heir to an estate 1891. **3.** When the living fell, it was given elsewhere JANE AUSTEN.

VIII. To occur, come to pass, befall, result ME.

The xiij day of March fil vp-on a Saterday CHAUCER. Oft..sorrows f. GOLDSM. *impers.* As it fell..an elder 'gan to tell The story MORRIS. Phr. *Fair f.*, *Foul f.*: may good *or* evil befall.

IX. Transitive senses. **1.** To let fall, drop. *Obs.* exc. in *Bellringing.* 1475. †**2.** To lower –1795. †**3.** To bring or throw to the ground. *lit.* and *fig.* –1625; to cut down (trees). *Obs.* exc. *dial.* or *U.S.* ME. †**4.** To direct (*upon*) GOLDSM. †**5.** = 'To fall from' SIR T. HERBERT. **6.** To have as one's share, come in for, obtain. Now *dial.* ME.

1. To f. an axe SHAKS., an argument DRYDEN, a drawbridge 1808. **2.** To f. a Gun 1692, the voice 1748, the value of land BURKE. **3.** To f. the vnder wode 1523. **5.** To f. the precipice 1665.

Special Combs. **1.** With prep. (and prepositional phrases).

F. a-. To set about, begin. Now only *arch.* with vbl. sbs. in *-ing*. **F. across** —. To come upon by chance. **F. behind** —. To be outstripped or left behind by. **F. down** —. **a.** See DOWN *prep.* **b.** To drop down (a river, etc.). **F. for** —. To be captivated or carried away by; to yield to the attractions of (orig. *U.S. slang*). **F. from** —. **a.** See simple senses. †**b.** To disagree with. †**c.** To drop away from, forsake; to renounce one's allegiance to. †**d.** To drop out of, give up (a practice, etc.); to break (a commandment). **F. in** (= *into*) —. **a.** = *F. into.* †**b.** *To f. in hand to, with*: to set about. **F. into** —. †**a.** To drop into. †**b.** To make a hostile inroad upon. **c.** To take (one's place), take one's place in (*lit.* and *fig.*). **d.** To enter upon (*esp.* talk), to begin the discussion of. †**e.** To come within (the range of). †**f.** To be included among. **g.** To take up with, accommodate oneself to. **h.** To drop into (a habit, etc.). **To f. off**—. **a.** Of an animal: To lose appetite for; to refuse. **b.** Of a vessel: To deviate from (her course). **F. on** —. †**a.** To break out into, set about (an action or state). **b.** *Mil.* To make a descent or attack upon; to rush upon, assault. **c.** To come across; †to hit upon (an expedient). **d.** To have recourse to. **e.** *To f. on one's feet*: *fig.* to fare fortunately. **F. to** —. †**a.** To attach oneself to; also, to make one's peace with. †**b.** To agree with, accede to (a proposal, etc.). **c.** To apply or betake oneself to; to begin. **F. under** —. **a.** To come or be classed under. **b.** To be subjected to. **F. unto** —. = *F. to*, in various senses. **F. upon** —. **a.** = *F. on* †a, b, c. †**b.** To begin upon, set about. **c.** To come (casually) to, take up with. **d.** *Geom.* Of a line, point, etc.: To cover, come exactly upon. †**e.** To become chargeable to (the parish). †**F. with** —. To come upon in due course; esp. *Naut.* to make (land). **F. within** —. To be included in; to come within the operation or scope of.

2. With adverbs.

F. aboard. a. To strike or encounter; see ABOARD. †**b.** To make a beginning. **F. astern.** See VI. 2, and ASTERN. **F. away. a.** See simple senses and AWAY. **b.** To draw off, desert, revolt. **c.** To become a backslider, to apostatize (*from*). †**d.** To lose flesh. **e.** To decay, pine away, perish, vanish. **F. back. a.** See simple senses and BACK. **b.** To step back, give way; to retreat. †**c.** To fall into arrear (in payments, etc.). **F. back on, upon. a.** *Mil.* To retire to. **b.** *fig.* To have recourse to (something) when other things fail. **F. down. a.** See simple senses and DOWN. **b.** Of a ship, etc.: To drop down towards the sea. †**c.** To swoop down. †**d.** To sicken. **F. foul. a.** To come into collision. **b.** *fig.* To clash, come into conflict (with); to quarrel. **c.** To make an attack. **F. in. a.** See simple senses and IN. **b.** To drop to pieces inwardly, as a building; also *transf.* of a cliff. †**c.** To make one's way in. Of a ship: To take a course (to land). **d.** To happen, occur, take place. Now *rare.* **e.** *Mil.* To get into line, take one's place in the ranks. **f.** To form (troops) in line; to parade. **g.** To agree, fit in. †**h.** To make up a quarrel. Cf. *F. out.* †**i.** To give way. **j.** To come to an end, terminate; to become due, as a debt; to become available. **To f. in with. a.** To come upon by chance, meet with. Also †To arrive at (land). **b.** To drop into the views of, agree with; to make common cause with. **c.** To accede to (a proposal), join in (a project). **d.** To harmonize, match. Of a point, etc., of time: To coincide with. **e.** To concur with; to conform to; to humour. **F. off. a.** See simple senses and OFF. **b.** To drop off in position; to step aside or back, withdraw. **c.** *Naut.* Of a vessel: To fail to keep her head to the wind. **d.** *Naut.* To part company; to move away. Of a coast-line: To trend away. **e.** To become estranged, draw off; to revolt. **f.** To decrease in amount, intensity, or number. **g.** To decline; to degenerate. **F. on.** †**a.** To come on, as night. **b.** To make an attack, join battle. **c.** To set to work, begin. Now *rare.* **F. out. a.** *intr.* See simple senses and OUT. **b.** *Mil.* To drop out of the ranks; to drop behind. **c.** To disagree, quarrel. Also with *with.* **d.** To come about by chance (*rare*). **e.** To happen, occur, arise. Now chiefly *impers.* **f.** To prove to be, turn out. **F. out of. a.** See simple senses and OUT. **b.** *Mil.* To drop out of the ranks. **F. over a.** See simple senses and OVER. †**b.** To go over *to* (the enemy). **F. short. a.** To give out, fail. **b.** Of a shot, etc.: Not to reach the mark. **F. short of. a.** To fail to obtain; to fail in performing. **b.** To fail of attaining to; not to reach the same amount, degree, etc. as. **F. through.** To break down, come to naught, miscarry. **F. to. a.** Of a gate, etc.: To shut automatically. **b.** To set to work, begin; *esp.* to begin eating; also, to come to blows. †**F. together. a.** Of the eyes: To close. **b.** To collapse, contract. **c.** †*F. together by the ears*: To quarrel.

†**Falla·ce.** ME. [– (O)Fr. *fallace* – L. *fallacia*; see FALLACY.] = FALLACY 1–3. –1634.

Fallacious (fălēⁱ·ʃəs), *a.* 1509. [– (O)Fr. *fallacieux* – L. *fallaciosus*, f. *fallacia*; see next, -ACIOUS.] **1.** Containing a fallacy. **2.** †Deceitful –1769; deceptive, misleading 1651. **3.** Disappointing expectation, delusive 1667.

1. F. syllogisms REID. **2.** F. Muse COWLEY, evidence FROUDE. **3.** That f. Fruit MILT. *P. L.* IX. 1046.

Hence **Falla·cious-ly** *adv.*, **-ness.**

Fallacy (fæ·lăsi). 1481. [– L. *fallacia*, f. *fallax, -ac-*, f. *fallere* deceive; see -ACY.] †**1.** Deception, trickery; a deception; a lie –1749. **2.** †Deceitfulness 1641; deceptiveness, unreliability 1654. **3.** A deceptive argument, a sophism. In Logic *esp.* a flaw which vitiates a syllogism; any of the types of such flaws. Also, sophistry. 1562. **4.** An error, *esp.* one founded on false reasoning. Also, error. 1590. **5.** Unsoundness (of arguments); delusiveness (of opinions, etc.); †fallibility (*rare*) 1651.

1. Winning by Conquest what the first man lost By f. surprized MILT. *P. R.* I. 155. **2.** The f. of human friendship K. WHITE. **4.** Absurd and mischievous fallacies SYD. SMITH. **5.** The f. of expectations 1850. vars. †**Fa·llax.** †**Falla·xity.**

Fal-lal (fæ:lˌlæ·l). 1706. [perh. suggested by FALBALA.] **A.** *sb.* **1.** A piece of finery or frippery. Chiefly *pl.* **2.** = FA-LA. 1864.

†**B.** *adj.* Affected, finicking, foppish –1818. Hence **Falla·lery,** tawdry finery.

†**Falla·tion** [perh. f. FALLACIOUS, on the analogy of *suspicious, suspicion.*] = FALLACY 3. ASCHAM.

Fallen (fǭ·l'n), *ppl. a.* ME. [See FALL *v.*] **1.** That has come or dropped down. **2.** Of the sun: Having set. TENNYSON. **3.** Shrunken, emaciated, as flesh 1722. **4.** Laid low, or brought to the ground (*lit.* and *fig.*) 1631. **b.** *absol.* with *the*: Those who have died in battle 1914. **5.** *fig.* **a.** Morally ruined. **b.** That has come down in fortune. 1628.

4. Midst f. palaces 1835. The f. king FREEMAN.

†**Fallency.** 1603. [– med.L. *fallentia* in same sense, f. L. *fallere* deceive; see -ENCY.] An instance of the failure of a rule; an exception –1660.

Faller (fǭ·ləɹ). ME. [f. FALL *v.* + -ER¹.] One who or that which falls; *esp.* any of various appliances in spinning machines.

Fallible (fæ·lib'l), *a.* ME. [– med.L. *fallibilis*, f. L. *fallere* deceive; see -IBLE.] **1.** Liable to be deceived or to err. **2.** Liable to be erroneous, unreliable ME.

1. A f. being will fail somewhere JOHNSON. **2.** Hopes that are f. *Meas. for M.* III. i. 170. Hence **Fallibi·lity,** liability to err or †to mislead. **Fa·llibly** *adv.*

Falling (fǭ·liŋ), *vbl. sb.* ME. [f. FALL *v.* + -ING¹.] **1.** The action of FALL *v.* **2.** *Path.* In *F. of the womb*: a pop. term for *prolapsus uteri* (*Syd. Soc. Lex.*). †**3.** A depression; a hollow, declivity –1712. **4.** *concr.* That which falls or has fallen; also *fig.* ME.

Comb., as *f. off*, decadence, defection, diminution; *f. out*, disagreement, quarrel; †ending.

Falling (fǭ·liŋ), *ppl. a.* ME. [f. as prec. + -ING².] That falls, in various senses of the vb.

Comb. **a.** *F.-†disease, †-evil, †-ill, -sickness* (now *rare*) = EPILEPSY. **b. f.-band** = FALL *sb.*¹ VI. 1a; †**-door** = *folding-door*; †**-hinge,** one by which a door, etc., rises vertically when opened; **-moulds** (*Arch.*), 'the two moulds applied to the vertical sides of the railpiece,..in order to form the back and under surface of the rail and finish the squaring' (Gwilt); **-sluice,** a flood-gate which opens automatically in the event of a flood; **-star,** a meteor; a shooting star.

Fallopian (fălōᵘ·piăn), *a.* 1706. [f. *Fallopius*, latinized form of the name of Gabriello *Fallopio* (1523–62), It. anatomist. See -AN.] *Anat.* Discovered by, or named after, Fallopius; as *F. tubes*, 'two canals inclosed in the peritoneum..communicating from the sides of the *Fundus Uteri* to the ovaries' (MAYNE); *F. canal*; etc.

Fallow (fæ·loᵘ), *sb.* ME. [OE. *fealh, fealg-* = MLG. *valge* (G. *felge*).] †**1.** A piece of ploughed land; also *collect.* –1713. **2.** Ground ploughed and harrowed, but left uncropped for a year or more 1523. **3.** The state, or interval, of being fallow; also *fig.* 1523. **4.** *attrib.* 1678.

1. All our Vineyards, Fallowes, Meades, and Hedges..grow to wildnesse *Hen. V*, V. ii. 54. **2.** Phr. *Summer f.*: so called because summer is chosen for the sake of killing the weeds. *Green, cropped*, or *bastard f.*: one from which a green crop is taken. **3.** *fig.* Your f. adds to your fertility BURKE. **4.** *F.-chat, -finch*, the Wheatear (*Saxicola œnanthe*).

Fallow (fæ·loᵘ), *a.*¹ [OE. *falu* (*fealu*); obl. *fealwe*, etc. = OS. *falu* (Du. *vaal*), OHG. *falo* (G. *fahl, falb*), ON. *fǫlr* :– Gmc. **falwaz*.] **1.** Pale brownish or reddish yellow. Now chiefly in FALLOW-DEER. **2.** *absol.* Name of a colour 1741.

1. Many a dere both rede and falowe FABYAN.

Fallow (fæ·loᵘ), *a.*² 1460. [attrib. use of FALLOW *sb.*] Of land: **a.** That is uncropped for the current year. **b.** Uncultivated. †**c.** Ploughed ready for sowing. Also *transf.* and *fig.*

a. Her f. Leas SHAKS. **b.** Breake vp your f. ground *Jer.* 4:3. Hence **Fa·llowness,** f. condition; idleness.

†**Fa·llow,** *v.*¹ [OE. *fealuwian*, f. *fealu*; see FALLOW *a.*¹] To become pale or yellow; hence, to wither. Of the face: To blanch, grow pale. –1584.

Fallow (fæ·loᵘ), *v.*² [OE. *fealgian*, f. *fealg-* FALLOW *sb.* Cf. LG. *falgen*, MHG. *valgen, velgen.*] **1.** *trans.* To plough or break up; to prepare for sowing. **2.** To lay fallow, for the purpose of destroying weeds, and for mellowing the soil; also *fig.* ME.

2. Scarce any f., a few sow clover A. YOUNG. Hence **Fa·llowist** (*nonce-wd.*), one who favours the practice of fallowing land.

Fallow-deer (fæ·loᵘˌdīᵊɹ). 1500. [f. FALLOW *a.*¹ + DEER.] A species of deer (*Cervus dama* or *Dama vulgaris*) smaller than the stag or *red* deer. So called from its colour.

†**Fa·lsary.** ME. [– L. *falsarius* forger, f. *falsus*; see next, -ARY¹.] **1.** One who falsifies (a document) –1828; a forger –1697. **2.** A deceitful person –1652.

1. The ground for our f. to forge this Epistle BENTLEY.

False (fǭls, fǫls). [OE. *fals* adj. and sb. – L. *falsus* adj. and *falsum* sb., prop. pa. pple. of *fallere* deceive. In ME. reinforced by or newly – OFr. *fals, faus*, fem. *false* (mod. *faux, fausse*) :– L. *falsus, -a.*]

A. *adj.* **I. 1.** Erroneous. **2.** Not according to rule, principle, or law; wrong ME. **3.** Incorrect; unfair ME. **4.** Defective 1523.

2. Phr. *F. concord* (Gram.): a breach of any rule for the agreement of words in a sentence. *F. cadence* (Mus.): an interrupted or deceptive cadence. *F. relation* (Mus.): the separation of a chromatic semitone between two parts. *F. imprisonment* (Law): the trespass committed against a person by imprisoning him contrary to law. **b.** *Mus.* Inaccurate in pitch; out of tune 1597. **c.** *Her.* Voided 1864. **3.** F. dice 1551. A f. ballance *Prov.* 20:23. F. play DONNE. A f. step (= Fr. *faux pas*) 1700. *F. start* (in a race): a wrong start; often *transf.* and *fig.* **4.** *F. bearing* (Arch.): 'any bearing which is not directly upon a vertical support' (Webster).

II. 1. Purposely untrue; mendacious ME. **2.** Deceitful, treacherous. Formerly often pleonastically, as in *f. traitor*, etc. ME. **3.** Fallacious, deceptive; distorting 1531.

1. And they said, It is f. 2 *Kings* 9:12. F. Accusation SHAKS., Prophets BP. STILLINGFL. **2.** F. as hell, and cruel as the grave SOUTH. The Ground is f. under us 1692. **3.** The Devill makes us f. spectacles 1641. Looking..through a f. medium MACAULAY. Phr. †*F. door, postern.*

III. 1. Counterfeit, sham OE.; pretended ME.; artificial 1591; suprious 1600. **2.** *Nav.* and *Mil.* Counterfeited to deceive an enemy; feigned ME. **3.** Improperly so called 1578. **4.** In *f. dyes, colours* (= Fr. *teint faux*): fugitive dyes. **5.** (Chiefly *Mech.*) Subsidiary, supplementary 1552.

1. F. charter parties 1558, wreits 1609; f. prophets HULOET; f. learning POPE. Phr. *F. key*: a skeleton key. **2.** Phr. *Under f. colours. To hang out f. colours. F. alarm*: an alarm without foundation. *F. attack*; a feigned movement, intended to divert the attention of the enemy from the real attack. *F. fire*: †(*a*) a blank discharge of firearms; (*b*) a fire made to deceive an enemy, or as a signal by night. **3.** *F. ribs*: the five inferior ribs on each side. F. topaz, *i.e.* Yellow Quartz 1776. F. acacia 1861. **5.** Phr. *F. bottom*: a horizontal partition in a vessel. *F. keel, keelson, post, rail, stay, stem, stern, stern-post* (Shipbuilding). *F. deck*: a grating or the like supported above the main deck by the 'close fights'. *F. pillar, roof* (Arch.). Hence **Fa·lsely** *adv.* **Fa·lseness.**

B. *adv.* †**1.** Untruly –1621. **2.** Improperly; in the wrong direction; incorrectly 1591. **3.** Faithlessly, perfidiously; chiefly in *To play (a person) f.* 1590.

1. *Hen. VIII*, II. iv. 136. **2.** The Musitian.. plaies f. *Two Gent.* IV. ii. 59. **3.** His mother plaid f. with a Smyth *Merch. V.* I. ii. 48.

C. *sb.* †**1.** Fraud, falsehood, treachery –ME. **2.** One who or that which is false ME. †**3.** *Fencing.* = FEINT 1637.

2. My f., ore-weighs your true SHAKS.

Comb. **1.** Of the adj., as *f.-coiner*, etc.; *f.-faced, -hearted* (whence *-heartedness*), etc. **2.** Of the adv., as *f.-boding, -promising*, etc.; *f.-derived, -imagined*, etc.; *f.-colour, -play* vbs., etc.

†**False,** *v.* ME. [– OFr. *falser* (mod. *fausser*) :– late L. *falsare*, f. *falsus* FALSE *a.*] **1.** To fail, or cause to fail, or give way. Only in ME. **2.** *trans.* To counterfeit (money); to forge (a document) –1553. **3.** To falsify; to corrupt –1598. **4.** To be or prove false to. Also *absol.* –1624. **5.** To maintain to be false, impugn –1708.

2. All that falsen the popes lettres 1450. **4.** He.. hath his trouthe falsed CHAUCER. *absol.* All that falsen or use false measures 1450. **5.** To f. a principle ME. Hence †**Fa·lser.** So †**Fa·lsery,** falsification, deception.

Falsehood (fǭ·lshud). late ME.; earlier **-head.** [f. FALSE *a.* + -HEAD, -HOOD.] †**1.** Falseness, deceitfulness, mendacity, faithlessness –1534. **2.** Want of conformity to fact or truth; (intentional) falsity; an untrue proposition, doctrine, etc.; untrue propositions, etc. generally ME. **3.** Deception, falsification, imposture; a forgery, counterfeit (*Obs.* or *arch.*) ME. **4.** Intentional assertion of what is false; lying 1662. **5.** A lie. Also, lies in general ME.

2. In your answeres there remaineth falshood *Job* 21:34. Each age has to fight with its own falsehoods HELPS. **3.** No falshood can endure Touch of Celestial temper MILT. *P. L.* IV. 122. **4.** Herodotus was..suspected of falshood BP. STILLINGFL. **5.** To tell a f. RUSKIN. An edifice of f. 1856.

‖**Falsetto** (fǭlse·to). 1774. [It., dim. of *falso* FALSE; cf. Fr. *fausset.*] **1.** A forced voice of a register above the natural; the head voice; also *fig.* **2.** One who sings with a falsetto voice 1789. **3.** *attrib.* 1826.

1. *fig.* The mock heroick f. of stupid tragedy BURKE. var. (anglicized) †**Falset.**

Falsification (fǭ:lsifikēi·ʃən). 1565. [– med.L. *falsificatio* in same senses, f. *falsificare*; see FALSIFY, -ATION. Cf. (O)Fr. *falsification.*] **1.** The action of making (something) false: fraudulent alteration; perversion (of facts); counterfeiting. **2.** The showing (something) to be groundless or wrong, as assurances, an item of charge in an account, etc. 1845.

1. By f. of the wordes, wittingly to endeuour that anything may seeme diuine which is not HOOKER. Their..manifest falsifications both of manners and history 1799.

Falsificator (fǭ·lsifikēi:təɹ). 1609. [f. *falsificat-*, pa. ppl. stem of med.L. *falsificare*; see next, -ATOR.] One who deals in falsification; a falsifier.

Falsify (fǭ·lsifəi, fǫ·-), *v.* 1449. [– (O)Fr. *falsifier* or med.L. *falsificare*, f. L. *falsificus* making false, f. *falsus* FALSE *a.*; see -FY.] **1.** *trans.* To make false or incorrect 1502. †**2.** To counterfeit –1699. **3.** To declare or prove to be false; *esp.* in *Law* 1449. **b.** To fail in fulfilling, or prevent the fulfilment of (a prediction, expectation, etc.) 1596. †**4.** *intr.* To deal in falsehoods –1777. †**5.** *trans.* To prove false to (one's faith, word, etc.) –1670; †*intr.* to give way (PEPYS). †**6.** *Fencing.* To feign (a blow); to make (a blow) under cover of a feint. Also *absol.* –1680.

1. To falsifie the Scriptures HOBBES, facts and dates EMERSON, our standards 1848, the relation between parties M. PATTISON. **3.** No man can f. any material fact here stated T. JEFFERSON. Conclusive evidence to f. the warranty 1817. **b.** By so much shall I falsifie mens hopes 1 *Hen. IV*, I. ii. 235. **6.** As th' are wont to f. a Blow BUTLER.

Hence **Fa·lsifiable** *a.* that may be falsified. **Fa·lsifier,** one who falsifies. †**Fa·lsify** *sb.* a feint (in *Fencing*).

Falsism (fǭ·lsiz'm, fǫ·-). 1840. [f. FALSE *a.* + -ISM.] **a.** A statement which is evidently false. **b.** A platitude which is not even true. (Opp. to *truism* in both senses.)

Falsity (fǭ·lsĭti, fǫ·-). ME. [– L. *falsitas*, f. *falsus*; see FALSE *a.*, -ITY. Cf. ME. *fals(e)te* treachery, fraud – OFr. *falseté* (mod. *fausseté*).] **1.** The quality or condition of being false: **a.** Contrariety or want of conformity to truth or fact 1576; **b.** Deceitfulness, insincerity 1603. **2.** That which is false 1557. **3.** False conduct; treachery, fraud –1581.

1. a. Between veritie & falsitie there is no meane FULKE. **b.** Cressids falsitie 1603. **2.** Every f. that could be devised MARRYAT.

Falstaffian (fǫlstæ·fiăn), *a.* 1808. Characteristic of or resembling Falstaff in Shaks. *Hen. IV*, *Hen. V*, and *Merry Wives*; fat, jovial, humorous. Also, resembling his 'ragged regiment' (*Hen. VI*, III. ii).

Falter (fǭ·ltəɹ, fǫ·-), *v.*[1] ME. [perh. f. ME. *falde* FOLD *v.*[1] (which was used esp. of the faltering of the legs and the tongue) + *-ter*, as in TOTTER.] **1.** To stumble, stagger; of the limbs, to give way ME; of the tongue, to speak unsteadily 1533. **2.** To stumble in one's speech; to stammer. Of the voice, etc.: To come forth incoherently. Also *trans.*, with quoted words as obj. ME. **3.** To waver; to flinch, hesitate in action; to give way 1521. Also *transf.* of inanimate things (U.S.) 1745.

1. Which [mare] now suddenly faultring under him KNOLLES. Wee find the tongue more apt to f. 1671. **2.** Her speach falters MARSTON. Even in the middle of his song He falter'd TENNYSON. *trans.* Faltering, 'I am thine' TENNYSON. The Dean faltered out that he meant no harm MILMAN. **3.** A part of the army faultered considerably JAS. MILL. His hopes began to f. 1802. Hence **Fa·lter** *sb.* a faltering; a faltering sound. **Fa·lteringly** *adv.*

Falter (fǭ·ltəɹ), *v.*[2] 1601. [perh. – OFr. **faltrer*, recorded as *fautrer* strike, beat.] *trans.* To thrash (corn) clean; hence, to cleanse.

‖**Falun** (falön). Usu. in *pl.* 1833. [Fr.] *Geol.* 'A French provincial term for the shelly Tertiary strata of Touraine and the Loire' (Page). Hence **Falu·nian** *a.* Upper Miocene.

‖**Falx** (fælks). Pl. **falces.** 1706. [L.; = 'sickle'.] *Anat.* A process of the *dura mater*, sometimes called *F. cerebri.*

Famatinite (fămæ·tinəit). 1875. [Named from the *Famatina* mountains in the Argentine Republic; see -ITE[1] 2 b.] *Min.* An antimonial variety of enargite.

Famble (fæ·mb'l), *sb. slang.* 1567. [perh. f. FAMBLE *v.* in its (prob.) orig. sense 'grope, fumble'.] **1.** A hand. †**2.** A ring –1691. Hence †**Fa·mbler,** a glove; also, one who goes about selling counterfeit rings.

Fa·mble, *v.* ME. [The word may orig. have had the sense 'grope, FUMBLE'; cf. Sw. *famla*, Da. *famle* grope, metath. f. ON. *falma.*] **1.** *intr.* To stammer. Now *dial.* **2.** To eat without an appetite (*dial.*) 1877.

Fa·mble-cro:p. *dial.* 1825. [Cf. FAMBLE *v.* 2.] The first stomach in ruminating animals.

Fame (fēim), *sb.*[1] ME. [– OFr. *fame* – L. *fama.*] **1.** That which people say; public report, common talk; a rumour. **2.** Reputation. Usu. in good sense. ME. **3.** The condition of being much talked about. Chiefly in good sense: Celebrity, honour, renown ME. †**4.** Evil repute –1592.

1. As the f. runneth MORE. A mischefe F...That mouing growes, and flitting gathers force SURREY. **2.** His virtues passed his f. TREVISA. Phr. *House of ill f.*: see HOUSE. **3.** The f. of Achilles EDEN, of English valour MACAULAY. Hence **Fa·meful** *a.* renowned. **Fa·meless** *a.* undistinguished; **-ly** *adv.*

†**Fame,** *sb.*[2] [– (O)Fr. *faim* :– L. *fames* hunger.] Hunger. LD. BERNERS.

Fame (fēim), *v.* Now *rare.* ME. [– OFr. *famer*, f. *fame* FAME *sb.*[1] Cf. med.L. *famare.*] **1.** *trans.* To tell abroad, report. **2.** To make famous ME. **3.** Short for DEFAME, DIFFAME. ME.

1. His prayse to f. ABP. PARKER. Thou art famed..To have wrought..wonders with an ass's jaw MILT. *Sams.* 1094. **2.** His name on every shore Is famed and feared BYRON.

†**Fame·lic,** *a.* 1614. [– L. *famelicus* hungry, f. *fames* hunger; see -IC. Cf. Fr. *famélique.*] Pertaining to hunger; appetizing –1653.

Familiar (fămi·liăɹ, -lyăr). ME. [Early forms *familier*, *famuler* – (O)Fr. *familier*, †*famulier*; forms in *-iar(e* (also early) reflect the original L. *familiaris*, f. *familia* family. See -AR[1].]

A. *adj.* **1.** Of or pertaining to a family or household; domestic. Now *rare.* **2.** On a family footing; intimate; in bad sense, unduly intimate. Const. *with.* ME. **3.** Of animals: Domesticated; also *fig.* 1483. †**4.** Of food, etc.: Suitable –1661. **5.** Well or habitually acquainted. Const. *with.* 1508. **6.** Known from constant association; well known 1490; common, current, usual. Const. *to.* 1599. †**7.** Affable; courteous, sociable –1751. **8.** Free, unceremonious *with*; *occas.*, too free ME.

1. Nothyng is werse..than..a famyliar enemye ME. **2.** A f. and privileged guest 1847. Phr. *F.* †*devil, spirit*: a demon supposed to attend at a call. **3.** *fig.* Good wine, is a good familiar Creature, if it be well vs'd *Oth.* II. iii. 313. **5.** Men f. with all ancient and modern learning MACAULAY. **6.** An experiment f. to nurses 1756. An article of general and f. supply ROGERS. **7.** Be thou f.; but by no means vulgar *Haml.* I. iii. 61. Hence **Fami·liarly** *adv.* **Fami·liarness.**

B. *sb.* **1.** A member of a person's family or household (*Obs.* in gen. sense); in *R. C. Ch.*, a person who belongs to the household of the Pope or a bishop, and renders domestic services 1460; an officer of the Inquisition, chiefly employed in arresting and imprisoning the accused 1560. **2.** An intimate friend or associate ME. **3.** A familiar spirit (see A. 2, quot.) 1584. Also *transf.* and *fig.*

2. Hugh Capet..was his famulyer and chief counceler FABYAN. **3.** A flie, otherwise called a divell or f. 1584. Hence †**Fami·liarist,** an authority on f. spirits DE FOE.

Familiarity (fămiliæ·rĭti). ME. [– (O)Fr. *familiarité* – L. *familiaritas*, f. *familiaris*; see prec., -ITY.] †**1.** The quality proper to a member of a family; hence, devotion, fidelity –1576. †**2.** Suitableness (of food, etc.) –1646. **3.** The state of being familiar; intimacy 1450; undue intimacy ME. †**b.** *concr.* A familiar person or persons. Also *collect.* –1665. **4.** Close or habitual acquaintance *with* (a thing); habituation 1601. **5.** Absence of ceremony, free intercourse, *esp.* with inferiors ME. **b.** Something allowed or justified only by intimacy. Usu. in *pl.* 1641. **6.** *Astrol.* An aspect 1819.

3. The old f. and kindness between the two kings MARVELL. **b.** The leaving of Parents, or other f. whatsoever MILT. **5.** Familiaritie bringeth contempt UDALL. **b.** Guilty of a f. 1875.

Familiarize (fămi·liărəiz), *v.* 1608. [– Fr. *familiariser*, f. *familiaire* FAMILIAR + *-iser* -IZE.] **1.** *trans.* To make (a thing, *rarely* a person) familiar or well known. **2. a.** To put (a person) on a footing of intimacy 1754. **b.** *refl.* (and *intr.* for *refl.*) To adopt a familiar demeanour; also, 'to make oneself cheap'. Now *rare.* 1685. **3.** To accustom (*to*, †*into*, *to do*). Now *rare.* 1646. **b.** To make well acquainted, at home *with* 1687. †**4.** To domesticate (an animal) –1682.

1. Shakespeare..familiarizes the wonderful JOHNSON. **3. b.** Familiarized with Hardships and Hazards PETTY. Hence **Fami:liariza·tion,** the action of familiarizing; an instance of this. **Fami·liarizer. Fami·liari:zingly** *adv.*

†**Fami·liary,** *a.* [– med.L. *familiarius*, f. *familia* FAMILY; see -ARY[1].] Pertaining to the control of a family; domestic. MILT.

†**Fami·lic,** *a.* 1660. [– med.L. *famelicus* domestic, with assim. to L. *familia* FAMILY; see -IC.] Pertaining to a family; also, domestic, familiar –1684.

Familism (fæ·miliz'm). 1642. [f. FAMILY 7 + -ISM.] **1.** The doctrine and practice of the Familists. **2.** In Fourier: The tendency to form a group existing among members of a family 1848.

Familist (fæ·milist). 1592. [f. as prec. + -IST.] †**1.** The head of a family, a familyman –1658. †**2.** One of the same household –1638. **3.** A member of the sect called the *Family of Love*; see FAMILY 7. 1592. Hence †**Famili·stic, -al** *a.*, pertaining to the Familists or Familism, or to a family.

Familistery (fæmili·stĕri). *rare.* 1865. [– Fr. *familistère*, formed by substituting *famil-* (L. *familia*) for the first element of *phalanstère*; see PHALANSTERY.] The abode of a community living together as one family.

Family (fæ·mĭli), *sb.* ME. [– L. *familia* household, f. *famulus* servant; see -Y[3].] **1.** The servants of a house; the household. *Obs.* exc. in *f. of servants.* –1794. **b.** The staff of a military officer, or (in India) state official 1808. **2.** The body of persons who live in one house or under one head, including parents, children, servants, etc. 1545. **3.** The group consisting of parents and their children, whether living together or not; in wider sense, all those who are nearly connected by blood or affinity 1667. **b.** A person's children regarded collectively 1732. **4.** Those descended or claiming descent from a common ancestor; a house, kindred, lineage ME.; a race; a people or group of peoples 1583. **5.** *transf.* and *fig.* (with mixed notion of 3 and 4) 1611. **6.** A group of objects, connected together and distinguished by the possession of some common features or properties 1626. **b.** In scientific classification: A group of allied genera. (Usually, a 'family' is a subdivision of an 'order'; but in botany 'family' is synonymous with 'order'.) 1753. **7.** *F. of*

Love: a sect which originated in Holland, and found a footing in England about 1580; they held that religion consisted chiefly in love, and that absolute obedience was due to all established governments 1579. **8.** *attrib.*, as in *f. life, butcher, plate*, etc. 1602.

1. b. The Staff Officers of Sir John Moore's f. 1809. **2.** Phr. *Happy F.*: a collection of birds and animals of different natures living together peaceably in one cage. **3.** We pass..through the love of our f...to love Mankind 1796. Phr. *The Holy F.*: a group usually consisting of Joseph, Mary, and the child Jesus. **4.** Let vs assayle the Family of Yorke 3 *Hen. VI*, II. ii. 129. People of no family BENTHAM. The great Teutonic f. MACAULAY. **5.** Of all the Familys and Societys of Christians, they are most hated 1650. **6.** The classification of simple minerals into families 1813. Phr. *F. of curves*: a group of curves of different kinds, all defined by the same equation of an indeterminate degree.

Phrases. **a.** *In a f. way*: without ceremony. **b.** (*To be*) *in the f. way*: pregnant.

Comb.: **f. Bible,** a large Bible for use at f. prayers (often containing on its fly-leaves a f. record or register of births, etc.); **f.-compact,** a treaty made in the 18th c. between the Bourbon dynasties of France, Spain, and the Two Sicilies for common action, *esp.* against England and Austria; **-tree,** a genealogical tree.

Famine (fæ·min). ME. [– (O)Fr. *famine*, f. *faim* hunger :– L. *fames*.] **1.** Extreme and general scarcity of food; an instance of this. Also *transf.* **2.** Hunger; hence, starvation ME. Also *fig.*

1. By reason whereof ensued a great famyne FABYAN. *transf.* The threatened water f. 1888. **2.** To die of f. 1773. *Comb.* **f.-fever,** (*a*) typhus; (*b*) relapsing fever. Hence †**Fa·mine** *v.* to starve.

Famish (fæ·miʃ), *v.* ME. [Extended form (after vbs. in -ISH²) of ME. *fame* v. (XIV), aphetic – OFr. *afamer* (mod. *affamer*) :– Rom. **affamare*, f. L. *ad* AF- + *fames* hunger; cf. *distinguish, extinguish*.] **1.** *trans.* To reduce to the extremities of hunger; to starve; also *fig.* **2.** To kill with hunger, starve to death ME. †**b.** To deprive *of* anything necessary to life. MILT. **3.** *intr.* To suffer the extremity of want of food; to be intensely hungry. Const. *for.* 1535. †**b.** To perish from want of food –1796.

1. Till Paris was besieg'd, famisht, and lost SHAKS. *fig.* To f. affection HOWELL. **2. b.** MILT. *P. L.* XII. 78. **3.** Resolu'd rather to dy then to f. *Cor.* I. i. 5. **b.** Now none f. who deserve to eat DRYDEN.

Hence **Fa·mishment** (now *rare*), the state, condition, or process of being famished; general dearth.

†**Famo·se,** *a.* ME. [– L. *famosus*, f. *fama* fame; see -OSE¹.] = FAMOUS –1625.

Famo·se, *v. Obs.* exc. *arch.* 1590. [f. prec.] To make famous.

Famous (fēⁱ·məs), *a.* ME. [– AFr. *famous*, OFr. *fameus* (mod. *-eux*) – L. *famosus*; see FAMOSE *a.*, -OUS.] **1.** Celebrated in fame or public report; much talked about, renowned. Const. *for.* **2.** In bad or neutral sense: Notorious. *Obs.* exc. *arch.* ME. †**3.** Common, ordinary –1744. **4.** As a strong expression of approval (chiefly *colloq.*): Excellent, 'capital' 1798.

1. His..fadre of famouse memorye 1512. Of f. London town COWPER. **2.** That f. infamous English Rebel Stuckley 1680. **4.** 'Twas a f. victory SOUTHEY. Hence †**Fa·mous** *v.* to make f. **Fa·mously** *adv.* †openly; †notoriously; excellently, capitally (*colloq.*). **Fa·mousness,** the state of being f.

Famp (fæmp). 1836. [Of unkn. etym.; orig. *n. dial.*] *Geol.* 'An indurated wavy calcareous shale' (Phillips) found among limestone rocks. Also *attrib.*

Famulary (fæ·miŭlări), *a. rare.* 1840. [– L. *famularis*, f. *famulus* servant; see -ARY².] Of or belonging to servants.

†**Fa·mulative,** *a.* [– med.L. *famulativus* due from a servant, f. *famulat-*, pa. ppl. stem of L. *famulari* be a servant; see -IVE, -ATIVE.] Having the attribute of serving. CUDWORTH.

‖**Famulus** (fæ·miŭlŭs). *Pl.* **-li.** 1837. [L.; = 'servant'.] An attendant; *esp.* on a scholar or a magician.

Fan (fæn), *sb.*¹ [OE. *fann* – L. *vannus*.] **1.** An instrument for winnowing grain; *orig.* a basket of special form (also, earlier, a wooden shovel) used for separating the corn from the chaff by throwing it into the air; *now*, a fanning-machine 1669. Also *transf.* and *fig.* (occ. with allusion to *Matt.* 3:12) 1559. †**b.** A quintain. CHAUCER. **2.** An instrument for agitating the air, to cool the face, etc. with an artificial breeze; *esp.* one constructed so as to fold up in small compass and to take, when expanded, the form of a sector of a circle 1555. **3.** *poet.* A wing [? After It. *vanni*.] 1640. **4.** Anything spread out in the shape of a fan (sense 2); *e.g.* a leaf, the tail of a bird, a window, etc. 1599. **5.** A rotating apparatus, usu. consisting of an axle or spindle, with arms bearing flat or curved blades: **a.** for producing a current of air for ventilation, etc. 1835; **b.** for regulating the throttle-valve of a steam-engine 1887; **c.** in a windmill 1825; etc. **6. a.** The flukes of the whale's tail. **b.** *Naut.* The screw (or a blade of the screw) of a propeller. **c.** *Angling.* A similar device on spinning-bait. 1785. †**7.** Confused with FANE *sb.*¹ –1650. **8.** [f. the vb.] The action or result of fanning. *Tr. & Cr.* V. iii. 41.

1. The oxen..shall eat clean provender, which hath been winnowed with the shovel and with the f. *Isa.* 30:24. *fig.* The fire and f. of iudgment and discretion LAMBARDE. **3.** The fans Of careless butterflies KEATS.

Combs. **1.** General: as *f. -stick, -shell, -painter, -shaped*, etc. **2.** Special: **f.-fly** (*Mech.*), an instrument to decrease speed by its action on the air; **-governor** = FAN 5 b; **-groining** (*Arch.*) = *fan-tracery*; **-mount** [= Fr. *monture d'éventail*], the frame upon which a f. is mounted; **-palm,** any palm having f.-shaped leaves; **-plant,** the palmetto; **-tracery** (*Arch.*), a kind of vaulting composed of pendent semi-cones covered with foliated panel-work; **-vaulting** = *fan-tracery*; **-window,** 'a semicircular window with radial sash' (Knight); **-work** = *fan-tracery*.

Fan (fæn), *sb.*² orig. *U.S.* 1889. (In earlier use *fann*, 1682.) [abbrev. of FANATIC.] An enthusiast (orig. a keen spectator of a sport, in early use esp. baseball).

Fan (fæn), *v.* [OE. *fannian*, f. FAN *sb.*¹] **1.** *trans.* To winnow (corn, etc.); to drive away by or as by the action of a fan ME. **2.** *intr.* †To make a fan-like movement; to flap. Of the wind: To blow. Now *rare.* ME. **3.** *trans.* To move or drive with or as with a fan ME. **4.** To drive a current of air upon, with, or as with a fan 1607. **5.** To blow or breathe gently upon 1590. **6.** To spread out like a fan. Also, *To f. out.* 1592.

1. To f. corne GOUGE. As chaff, which, fanned, The wind drives MILT. **2.** Fanning in his face with a Peacocks feather *Hen. V*, IV. i. 212. **3.** Fanning their joyous leaves to thy soft lays MILT. *Lycidas* 40. **4. a.** Fanned into Slumbers STEELE. By slow Degrees he fans the gentle Fire 1709. **5.** High Taurus snow, Fan'd with the Easterne wind *Mids. N.* III. ii. 142.

Fanal (fē·năl). *Obs.* exc. *arch.* 1471. [– Fr. *fanal* – It. *fanale*.] A beacon, a lighthouse; a ship's lantern.

‖**Fanam** (fənā·m). 1555. [Corrupt f. Malayālam *paṇam*, f. Skr. *paṇa* wealth.] A small coin, formerly the usual money of account in South India.

Fanatic (fănæ·tik). 1533. [– Fr. *fanatique* (Rabelais) or L. *fanaticus* pertaining to a temple, inspired by a deity, frenzied, f. *fanum* temple; see FANE *sb.*², -ATIC.]

A. *adj.* †**1.** Of an action or speech: Such as might result from possession by a deity or demon; frantic. Of a person: Frenzied. –1660. **2.** Of persons, etc.: Affected by excessive and mistaken enthusiasm, *esp.* in religious matters 1647.

1. Persons Divinely inspired, and Fanatick STANLEY. **2.** All our lunatic f. Sects BUTLER.

B. *sb.* †**1.** A (religious) maniac –1806. **2.** A fanatic person; an unreasoning enthusiast; applied about 1650 to Nonconformists. Also with *of.* 1644.

2. A new word coined, within few months, called fanatics..seemeth well..proportioned to signify ..the sectaries of our age FULLER.

Fanatical (fănæ·tikăl), *a.* 1550. [f. prec. + -AL¹; see -ICAL.] †**1.** Possessed by a deity or by a devil; frantic, mad –1633. **2.** = FANATIC *a.* 2. 1550. †**b.** Extravagant. *L. L. L.* V. i. 20. †**3.** Of or pertaining to the Nonconformists –1703.

Hence **Fana·tical-ly** *adv.*, **-ness.**

Fanaticism (fanæ·tisiz'm). 1652. [f. FANATIC + -ISM.] †**1.** The condition of being possessed. SHAFTESB. **2.** Excessive enthusiasm, *esp.* in religious matters, frenzy; an instance or form of this 1652.

2. Dark F. rent Altar, and screen, and ornament SCOTT.

Fanaticize (fănæ·tisəiz), *v.* Also **-ise.** 1715. [f. as prec. + -IZE.] To make, or become, fanatical.

†**Fa·natism.** 1680. [– Fr. *fanatisme*.] = FANATICISM –1800.

Fancied (fæ·nsid), *ppl. a.* 1568. [f. FANCY *v.* + -ED¹.] **1.** Formed or portrayed by the fancy; imaginary. †**2.** Artistically designed –1782. **3.** Favourite 1589.

2. The prettiest f. [buckles] I ever saw 1782.

Fancier (fæ·nsiəɹ). 1765. [f. as prec. + -ER¹.] **1.** One who fancies; a dreamer 1828. **2.** One who makes artistic designs 1856. **3.** One who fancies, and has a critical knowledge of, some class of curiosities, plants, animals, etc.; as in *dog-, flower-, pigeon-f.* 1765.

Fanciful (fæ·nsifŭl), *a.* 1627. [f. FANCY *sb.* + -FUL.] **1. a.** Endowed with fancy (*rare*). **b.** Disposed to indulge in fancies; whimsical. 1695. **2.** Displaying fancy in design; fantastic, odd 1627. **3.** Imaginary, unreal 1697.

1. a. A careful and f. pattern-drawer POPE. **b.** Cowley [had] a very f. mind COLERIDGE. **2.** A petticoat of a f. pattern SCOTT. **3.** F. claims 1868. Hence **Fa·nciful-ly** *adv.*, **-ness.**

Fanciless (fæ·nsilės), *a.* 1753. [f. FANCY *sb.* + -LESS.] Destitute of fancy; as, *f. compositions.*

Fancy (fæ·nsi). 1465. [Early forms *fantsy, fansey* (Paston Letters), contr. of FANTASY.]

A. *sb.* †**1.** = FANTASY *sb.* 1. –1722. †**2.** = FANTASY *sb.* 2. –1659. **3.** Delusive imagination; an instance of this 1597. **4.** In early use = IMAGINATION (see FANTASY 4). In later use, *fancy* signifies aptitude for the invention of illustrative or decorative imagery, while *imagination* is the power of giving the consistency of reality to ideal creations. Often *personified.* 1581. **b.** A mental image 1663. **5.** Inventive design; an invention 1665; †*esp.* in *Music*, a composition in an impromptu style –1789. **6.** An arbitrary notion 1471. **7.** Caprice; a caprice, a whim; a whimsical thing 1579; †fantasticalness –1823. **8.** Capricious preference; an inclination 1465; †*spec.* amorous inclination, love –1712. **9.** Taste, critical judgement in matters of art or elegance 1665. †**10.** 'Something that pleases or entertains' (J.) –1721. **11.** *The fancy*: all who fancy a particular amusement or pursuit; *esp.* the prize-ring or its frequenters 1811; also, pugilism; sporting in general 1820. **12.** The art or practice of breeding animals so as to develop particular points; also, one of these points; also *attrib.* 1862.

3. Phancies of a deluded mind 1693. **4.** Pleasures of the Imagination or F. (which I shall use promiscuously) ADDISON. The f. sees the outside.. The imagination sees the heart and inner nature, and makes them felt RUSKIN. **6.** As wild a f. as [etc.] COLERIDGE. **7.** The fancies of patients 1860. **8.** The tune..caught the f. of the nation MACAULAY. Phr. *To have, take a f. for, to. spec.* Tell me where is fancie bred *Merch. V.* III. ii. 63. **9.** They possess..f. for form RUSKIN. **10.** London-Pride is a pretty F. for borders 1712. **11.** A great book sale..had congregated all the *F.* DE QUINCEY.

Comb.: **f.-free,** free from the power of love; **-sick** *a.*, love-sick; **-woman,** a kept mistress.

B. *adj.* [The sb. used attrib.; rarely predicative.] **1.** Fine, ornamental; opp. to *plain* 1761. **b.** Of flowers, etc.: Parti-coloured 1793. **c.** *ellipt.* That deals in fancy goods 1821. **2.** Added for ornament or extraordinary use 1794. **3.** Calling forth or resulting from the exercise of fancy or caprice 1646. **4.** Based upon conceptions of the FANCY (*sb.* 3) 1800.

1. F. breads 1853, stitches 1866, types 1888. **b.** Webbs' F. Pansy 1893. **c.** *F. fair*: see FAIR *sb.*¹ *F. ball* = *F.-dress ball* (see FANCY DRESS). **2.** F. stops [in an organ] 1874. Phr. *F. roller* (in Cotton Spinning): a roller that overruns the periphery of the cylinder, and thereby admits heavy carding. **3.** F. shooting DICKENS, prices MACAULAY, pigeons 1881. Phr. *F. franchise*; one based on an arbitrary qualification. *F. stocks*: stocks estimated by caprice. **4.** A f. portrait 1873.

Fancy (fæ·nsi), *v.* 1545. [f. prec. sb., or partly contr. of FANTASY *v.*] **1.** *trans.* To frame in fancy; to portray in the mind; to conceive, imagine. Also, to suppose oneself to perceive. 1646. **2.** To believe without being able to prove; to have an idea *that* 1672. †**3.**

To contrive, devise, design, plan –1759. **4.** To have a good conceit of (oneself, etc.). *colloq.* 1866. **5.** To take a fancy to; to like 1545. **b.** To breed (animals or birds), to grow (plants) so as to develop in them particular points 1851.

1. She fancies musick in his tongue SWIFT. We read Bingham, and f. we are studying ecclesiastical history M. PATTISON. F., now! 1881. **2.** The estate is, I f., theirs yet COBBETT. **4.** I..fancied my game at whist 1886. **5.** I neuer yet beheld that speciall face, Which I could fancie *Tam. Shr.* II. i. 12. The patient may eat anything that he fancies 1894.

Fancy dress. 1770. A costume arranged fancifully, usually representing some fictitious or historical character. *attrib.*, in *f.-d. ball.*

Fancy man. a. A man who is fancied; a sweetheart 1835. **b.** *pl.* = *The fancy* (see FANCY *sb.* 11) 1847. **c.** *slang.* A man who lives on the earnings of a prostitute 1821.

Fa·ncy work. 1842. Ornamental, as opp. to plain, work, *esp.* in needlework, etc.; *rarely*, a piece of such work.

Fanda·ngle. *colloq.* 1880. [perh. alt. of next, after *newfangle.*] Fantastic ornament; tomfoolery. Also as *adj.*

Fandango (fændæ·ngo). 17... [– Sp. *fandango*; perh. of Negro origin.] **1.** A lively dance in ¾ time; also, the tune for this. **2.** A social assembly for dancing; a ball. Now *U.S.* 1760.

†**Fane,** *sb.*[1] [OE. *fana* = OFris. *fana*, OS., OHG. *fano* (G. *fahne*), ON. *fani*, Goth. *fana* :– Gmc. **fanon*, rel. to L. *pannus* (piece of) cloth.] **1.** A flag, banner; pennant –1806. **2.** A weathercock. See VANE. –1773.

Fane (fēⁱn), *sb.*[2] *poet.* ME. [– L. *fanum* temple.] A temple. Also *transf.* and *fig.*

Old Iona's holy f. SCOTT.

‖**Fanega** (fanē·gă). 1502. [Sp. *fanega*, also *hanega.*] A Spanish dry measure, usually equal to a bushel or a bushel and a half.

‖**Fanfare** (fænfēᵊ·ɹ, fañfār). 1605. [– Fr. *fanfare*, of imit. origin.] A flourish, call, or short tune, sounded by trumpets, bugles, or hunting-horns. Also *transf.* and *fig.*

fig. After all his Fanfares about a separate Peace TEMPLE.

‖**Fanfaron** (fæ·nfărǫn), *sb.* (*a.*) 1622. [Fr.; see prec., -OON.] **1.** A blusterer, boaster, braggart; *attrib.* or *adj.* braggart 1670. ¶**2.** = FANFARE. 1848.

1. An excellent f., a Major Washington H. WALPOLE.

Fanfaronade (fæ:nfărǫnēⁱ·d, fañfaronād), *sb.* 1652. [– Fr. *fanfaronnade*, f. *fanfaron*. Cf. Sp. *fanfarronada.*] **1.** Boisterous or arrogant language, brag; ostentation; an instance of this. ¶**2.** = FANFARE. 1812.

1. The Gasconads of France, Rodomontads of Spain, Fanfaronads of Italy URQUHART. Hence **Fa:nfarona·de** *v.* to bluster, swagger.

Fang (fæŋ), *sb.* [Late OE. *fang* – ON. *fang* capture, grasp, embrace = OFris., OS., OHG. *fang*, f. Gmc. **faŋʒ-*, **faŋχ-*, repr. by OE. *fōn*; see FANG *v.*[1] The development of sense II 2 is obscure.]

I. †**1.** A capture, catch; also, a grip –1600. **2.** *concr.* That which is caught or taken; plunder, spoils. (*Obs.* exc. *Sc.*) OE.

1. The Icie phange..of the winters winds SHAKS.

II. An instrument for catching or holding. †**1.** A noose, trap; also *fig.* –1794. **2.** A canine tooth, a tusk. In *pl.* teeth (of dogs, etc.). Also *fig.* and *transf.* 1555. **b.** The venom-tooth of a serpent; also the claws, provided with poison-ducts, which terminate the chelicerae of a spider 1800. †**3.** A claw or talon (Dicts.); in *Bot.*, the shoots or tendrils by which hold is taken 1768. **4. a.** A spike; the tang of a tool 1769. **b.** The root of a tooth, or one of its prongs 1666. †**c.** A prong of a divided root –1727.

2. The fatal F. drove deep within his Thigh DRYDEN. *fig.* The verie phangs of malice *Twel. N.* I. v. 196. *transf.* Fangs of broken ice KANE. **b.** Each horn is tubular, like an adder's f. DARWIN.

III. Technical. **1.** *Naut.* **a.** = VANG. 1513. **b.** *pl.* The valves of a pump-box 1769. **2.** *Mining.* An air-channel 1661.

Fang (fæŋ), *v.*[1] Now *arch.* or *dial.* [ME. *fang* (XIII), f. *fangen*, pa. pple. of OE. *fōn* capture, which it gradually superseded; cf. OFris. *fā*, OS., OHG. *fahan*, ON. *fá*, Goth. *fāhan*, rel. to L. *pangere* fix. See prec.] **1.** *trans.* To lay hold of, grasp, hold, seize; to clasp. *Obs.* exc. *arch.* **2.** To receive, accept. *Obs.* exc. *dial.* OE. **3.** = TAKE in various uses; *esp.* with obj. *arms, counsel, leave, a name, one's way* OE. **4.** *intr.* To seize, lay hold *on*; to take *to*; to set upon OE. **5.** To begin *on* OE. †**6.** *intr.* To take one's way, go; also, to swerve *from* –1536.

1. Hee's in the lawes clutches, you see hee's fanged DEKKER & WEBSTER. **2.** Phr. *To f. cristendom*: to receive baptism, become Christian.

Fang (fæŋ), *v.*[2] 1808. [f. FANG *sb.*] **1.** *trans.* To strike one's fang or fangs into (*rare*). **2.** *To f. a pump*: to give it a grip of the water; to prime 1819.

Fanged (fæŋd), *a.* 1602. [f. FANG *sb.* + -ED[2].] Furnished with fangs.

Whom I wil trust as I will adders fang'd SHAKS.

†**Fa·nger.** ME. [f. FANG *v.*[1] + -ER[1].] One who takes another under his protection, a guardian; one who catches or captures; that with which one catches hold (*e.g.* a tooth) –1763.

Fanging (fæ·ŋiŋ), *vbl. sb.* 1493. [f. as prec. + -ING[1].] **1.** The action of FANG *v.* **2.** *Mining.* (A main of) air-pipes used for ventilation in mines 1747.

Fangle (fæ·ŋg'l), *sb.* 1548. [erron. f. NEW-FANGLED, later form of *newfangle* 'eager for novelty'.] **1.** *New fangle*: a new fashion or crotchet; a novelty. (Always contemptuous.) Now *rare.* †**2.** A fantastic, foppish, or silly contrivance; a piece of finery; foppery, fuss –1695. So **Fa·ngle** *v.* to fashion, fabricate; to trick out. *Obs.* exc. *dial.* **Fa·nglement,** the action of fangling; hence, a contrivance.

†**Fa·ngled,** *ppl. a.* 1587. [f. prec. + -ED[2].] Characterized by fopperies –1611.

Our f. world *Cymb.* V. iv. 134.

Fangless (fæ·ŋlės), *a.* 1597. [f. FANG *sb.* + -LESS.] Without a fang or fangs.

Like to a Fanglesse Lion SHAKS.

Fangot (fæ·ŋgǫt). 1673. [– It. *fangotto*, var. of *fagotto* FAGGOT.] A quantity of wares, *esp.* raw silk, from 1 to 3 cwt.

Fanion (fæ·nyǫn). 1706. [– Fr. *fanion*, prob. for **fanillon*, dim. of *fanon* FANON.] A banner carried at the head of the baggage of horse brigades; also, a small flag used in surveying stations, named after these.

Fa·n-light. 1819. A fan-shaped, or (*loosely*) any, window over a door.

Fannell (fæ·nĕl). Now *Hist.* 1530. [– med.L. *fanula* or *fanonellus*, dim. of *fano* (see FANON).] = FANON.

Fanner (fæ·nəɹ). 1515. [f. FAN *sb.* or *v.*] **1.** One who fans. **2.** Any kind of contrivance to blow away the chaff (*lit.* and *fig.*) 1788. **3.** A ventilating or cooling apparatus 1874. **4.** A kind of hawk so called from the motion of its wings. Also *vanner-hawk.* 1875.

Fanning (fæ·niŋ), *vbl. sb.* 1577. [f. FAN *v.* + -ING[1].] **1.** The action of FAN *v.* in various senses. **2.** = FAN-*tracery.* RUSKIN. Comb.: *f.-machine. -mill* (= FANNER 2).

Fanon (fæ·nǫn). ME. [– (O)Fr. *fanon* – Frankish **fano* cloth = OS., OHG *fano*; see FANE *sb.*[1] Cf. GONFANON.] **1.** A maniple. **2.** A veil of four colours in stripes, worn by the Pope; formerly called the 'orale' 1844.

Fan-tail (fæ·ntēⁱl), *sb.* 1728. [f. FAN *sb.*[1] + TAIL *sb.*[1]] **1.** A tail or lower end in the shape of a fan. **2.** A variety of the domestic pigeon, so called from the shape of its tail 1735. **3.** A genus (*Rhipidura*) of Birds found in Australia 1848. **4.** *Mech.* A kind of joint. Cf. *dove-tail.* 1858. **5.** 'A form of gas-burner in which the burning jet has an arched form' (Knight). **6.** *attrib.*, as *fan-tail hat*, also *fantail*, a sou'-wester 1850. Hence **Fan-tail** *v.* to work its tail like a fan: said of a whale. **Fan-tailed** *a.*

Fan-tan (fæ·ntæn). 1878. [Chinese *fan t'an* repeated divisions.] A Chinese gambling game, in which the number of coins, etc. placed in a bowl has to be guessed after a large handful has been counted off in fours; also, a gambling game of cards.

Fantasia (fantazī·a, fæntā·ziă). 1724. [– It. *fantasia* (see FANTASY).] **1.** *Mus.* 'A composition in a style in which form is subservient to fancy' (Stainer and Barrett). ‖**2.** In the Levant and N. Africa: **a.** Pomp, self-importance; **b.** An Arab dance; also, a set of evolutions on horseback by a troop of Arabs. 1838.

Fantasied, phantasied (fæ·ntasid), *ppl. a. arch.* 1561. [f. FANTASY *sb.* and *v.* + -ED.] Framed by the fancy; full of (strange, new) fancies; imaginative; whimsical.

I finde the people strangely f. *John* IV. ii. 144.

Fantasm(a, etc.: see PHANTASM(A, etc.

Fantasque (fæntæ·sk). 1698. [– Fr. *fantasque* (XVI), popularized form of *fantastique.*] **A.** *adj.* Fanciful, fantastic (*rare*) 1701. †**B.** *sb.* Fancy, whim –1703.

Fantassin (fæ·ntæsin). 1835. [– Fr. *fantassin* – It. *fantaccino*, augment. and pejorative f. *fante* foot-soldier. Cf. INFANTRY.] A foot-soldier.

Fantast, phantast (fæ·ntæst). 1588. [In XVI, *phantast* – med.L. *phantasta* – Gr. φανταστής (prop. 'boaster'), whence G. *fantast* (Luther), the source of the mod. Eng. use.] **1.** A visionary; a flighty, impulsive person. **2.** A fantastic writer 1873.

Fantastic (fæntæ·stik). ME. [– (O)Fr. *fantastique* – med.L. *fantasticus*, late L. *phantasticus* – Gr. φανταστικός, f. φαντάζειν make visible, -εσθαι have visions, imagine. See FANTASY, -IC.]

A. *adj.* **1.** Existing only in imagination, unreal (*Obs.*); perversely or irrationally imagined. †**2.** Of the nature of a phantasm –1716. †**3.** Of or pertaining to phantasy (see FANTASY *sb.* 1, 4); imaginative –1793. **4.** Of persons, etc.: †Imaginative –1847; fanciful, capricious; foppish in dress –1702. Now: Extravagantly fanciful, odd in behaviour. **5.** Arbitrarily devised. Now *rare.* 1658. **6.** Eccentric, quaint, or grotesque in design or conception 1616. **b.** Making fantastic movements (in the dance). An arbitrary sense. 1632.

B. *sb.* **1.** One who has fanciful or wild ideas. *Obs.* exc. *arch.* 1598. †**2.** A fop –1680.

1. A F., whose brain was turned with monkish fancies 1882. Hence **Fanta·stical** *a.* and †*sb.* (in same senses). **Fanta:stica·lity,** fantasticalness; *concr.* a whim, crotchet. **Fanta·stically** *adv.* **Fanta·sticalness,** the condition or fact of being fantastical; whimsicality. **Fanta·sticate** *v.* †*trans.* to fancy; *intr.* to frame fantastic notions (*rare*). **Fanta·sticism,** †subjectivism (CUDWORTH); the following of caprice in art or speculation. †**Fanta·sticly** *adv.* **Fanta·sticness** (now *rare*). †**Fanta·stico,** an absurd or irrational person.

†**Fa·ntastry.** 1656. [f. as FANTAST + -RY, with ref. to the meaning of the Gr. φανταστής 'ostentatious person, boaster'.] **a.** Fantastic display or show; showy trappings. **b.** Visionary delusion. **c.** Deceptiveness. –1710.

c. The Phantastry of Sense CUDWORTH.

Fantasy, phantasy (fæ·ntăsi), *sb.* ME. [– OFr. *fantasie* (mod. *fantaisie*) = It. *fantasia* – L. *phantasia* – Gr. φαντασία appearance (later, phantom), faculty of imagination, etc.; see FANTASTIC, -Y[3]. Cf. FANCY.] †**1.** Mental apprehension of an object of perception –1669. †**2.** A phantom; an illusory appearance –1583. **3.** Delusive imagination, hallucination. ? *Obs.* ME. **4.** Imagination; the process, the faculty, or the result of forming representations of things not actually present. (Cf. FANCY *sb.* 4.) Also *personified.* Now usually: Visionary fancy. 1553. **b.** *esp.* in *Music*; a fantasia 1597. **5.** A supposition resting on no solid grounds. (Now emphatically contemptuous.) ME. **6.** Caprice; a caprice, a whim 1450. †**7.** Inclination, liking, desire –1618.

2. All is but fantesey and enchauntementes LD. BERNERS. **3.** You tremble and look pale: Is not this something more then Fantasie *Haml.* I. i. 54. **4.** By the power of phantasy we see Colours in a Dream NEWTON. A monstrous f. of rusty iron DICKENS. **5.** Less than fancy—mere f. 1876.

Fantasy, phantasy (fæ·ntăzi, -ăsi), *v.* ME. [– OFr. *fantasier*, f. *fantasie* (see prec.).] **1.** *trans.* = FANCY *v.* 1. Now *arch.* with sense: To imagine in a visionary manner. Also *absol.* †**2.** To take a fancy or liking to. Also with *inf.*, to 'take it into one's head'. –1641. **3.** *intr.* To play fantasias. CARLYLE.

Fantee (fæ·ntī). 1819. Also **Fanti.** A member, or the language, of a Negro tribe inhabiting the Gold Coast. **b.** Phr. *To go f.*: to join the natives of a district and conform to their habits 1886.

†**Fa·nterie.** 1577. [– OFr. *fanterie* – It. *fanteria*, f. *fante* foot-soldier; see -ERY, INFANTRY.] Infantry –1601.

‖**Fantoccini** (fæntǫtʃī·ni). 1771. [It., pl. of *fantoccino*, dim of *fantoccio* puppet, f. *fante* boy; see prec.] **1.** *pl.* Puppets (see PUPPET *sb.* 3) 1791. **2.** A puppet show.

Fantom, Faquir; see PHANTOM, FAKIR.

†‖**Far,** *sb.* ME. [L.] A coarse kind of wheat; spelt –1624.

Far (fāɹ), *adv.* [OE. *feor(r)* = OFris. *fēr, fīr*, OS. *fer, ferro* (Du. *ver*), OHG. *fer, ferro*, ON. *fjarri*, Goth. *fairra* :– Gmc. **ferrō*, compar. formation on **fer-* :– IE. **per-*, repr. by Skr. *pára*, Gr. πέρα further.] **1.** At a great distance: **a.** in space; **b.** in past time ME. Also *fig.* **2.** To a great distance; widely OE. **3.** To or at an advanced point of progress: **a.** in space; also *fig.* ME ; **b.** in time ME **4.** By a great interval, widely OE. **5.** Preceded by *as, how, so, thus*, with the notion of *definite* quantity ME. **6.** quasi-*sb.* ME.

1. a. Sum ferrer and sum nerrer WYCLIF. Things near seem further off; farst off, the nearst at hand HY. MORE. Phr. *F. and near* or *nigh*; *f. or near. fig.* In a f. from unfriendly fashion W. BLACK. **2.** He..remov'd his Tents farr off MILT. *P. L.* XI. 727. **3. a.** We travell'd fast and f. SOUTHEY. *fig.* This was going too f. CRUISE. **b.** With genitive: It is f. nights (= Gr. πόρρω τῆς νυκτός) HOLINSHED. But the day is farre spent 1602. **4.** Following not f. after himself KNOLLES. They were not f. wrong JOWETT. Phr. *F. (and) away*; *f. other.* **5.** Thus f. Josephus CRUISE. To decide how f. he deserved it THIRLWALL **6.** *From f.*: at a distance. *By f.*: by a great interval. *In so f.*: to such an extent.

Comb., as *f.-beaming*; *-withdrawal*; **-back** *a.*, ancient; **-eastern** *a.*, belonging to the extreme east; **-gone** *a.*, advanced to a great extent; **-northern** *a.*, lying in the extreme north; **-seeing** *a.*, far-sighted; **-seen** *a.*, seen at a distance; **-southern** *a.*, at the extreme south; so **-western** *a.*

Far (fāɹ), *a.* [OE. *feorr* = OFris. *fēr, fīr*, OS. *fer*, OHG. *fer* :– WGmc. **ferro-*. As the adj. does not occur in Goth. or ON., it is prob. derived from the adv.] **1.** Remote: **a.** in space; **b.** *fig.* 1531. **2.** Extending to a distance, long ME. **3.** The remoter of two; in early use also in the comparative ME.

1. a. Folke cam..from ferre ways for to seke hym CAXTON. A f. whisper SHELLEY. Phr. *The F. West*: now *esp.* the western parts of U.S. or of N. America. **b.** A vice..farrest from humanitee ELYOT. His own f. blood TENNYSON. F. landmarks of time HAWTHORNE. **2.** Her grete & ferre Journey FISHER. As one farre in elde SPENSER. **3.** The farre ende of high holborn 1540.

Far, *v.* Now *dial.* [OE. *feorran, fyrran* = OHG. *firren*, ON. *firra* :– Gmc. **ferrjan*, f. **ferro-*; see FAR *adv.*] *trans.* To put far off, remove.

Pooh, wench! latter days be farred! MRS. GASKELL.

Far, obs. var. of FARROW, young pig.

Fa·r-abou·t.

A. *adv.* †To a great distance around; †at a great distance; †far astray; by far, very much (*dial.*) ME.

†**B.** *sb.* A digression, wandering 1639.

Farad (fæ·răd). 1881. [f. name of Michael *Faraday*, English electrician (1791–1867), with assim. to -AD.] *Electr.* The capacity of a conductor in which the electrical pressure is raised one volt by the addition of one coulomb.

Faradaic (færădē¹·ik), *a.* 1875. [f. *Faraday* (see prec.) + -IC.] Distinctive epithet of inductive electricity and of the phenomena pertaining to it. var. **Fara·dic.**

Faradism (fæ·rădiz'm). 1876. [– Fr. *faradisme*, f. as prec.; see -ISM.] Inductive electricity; also, its therapeutic application. var. **Fa·radaism.**

Faradization (fæ:rădəizē¹·ʃən). 1867. [– Fr. *faradisation* (Duchenne), f. as prec.; see -ATION.] The application of induced currents of electricity to the body.

Faradize (fæ·rădəiz), *v.* 1864. [– Fr. *faradiser* (Duchenne), f. as prec.; see -IZE.] *trans.* To stimulate by means of faradaic currents. Hence **Faradi·zer.**

Farand, etc.: see FARRAND.

†**Fa·randine.** 1663. [– Fr. *ferrandine*, said to be f. the name of the inventor, *Ferrand*, of Lyon (*c.* 1630).] A fabric of silk, wool, and hair; also, a dress made of this. Also *attrib.* –1673.

‖**Farandole** (farañdol). 1863. [Fr. – mod. Pr. *farandoula.*] A Provençal dance in ⁶⁄₈ time.

Far-away (fār,āwē¹·, fā·r,āwē¹). ME. [f. FAR *adv.* and AWAY.] **A.** *adj.* **1.** Remote in space, time, or relationship 1816. **2.** Of a look, etc.: Absent, dreamy 1881.

1. 'Pate's a far-awa cousin o' mine' SCOTT.

B. *adv.* A long way off ME.

C. *sb.* What is far away; the distance 1823.

Fa·r-betwee·n, *a.* 1743. Occurring at long intervals.

Like angel-visits, few and far between CAMPBELL.

†**Farce,** *sb.*[1] ME. [– OFr. *farce* stuffing, f. *farcir, farsir*; see FARCE *v.*] Force-meat, stuffing –1823.

Farce (fāɹs), *sb.*[2] 1530. [– Fr. *farce* (XVI), specific application of prec.] **1.** A dramatic work (usually short) intended only to excite laughter; the species of the drama constituted by these. **2.** Anything fit only to laugh at; a hollow pretence, a mockery 1696.

1. Suche as writte farcis and contrefait the vulgare speche PALSGR. Those Nauseous Harlequins in F. may pass DRYDEN. **2.** The f. of fashion W. IRVING.

Farce (fāɹs), *v. Obs.* or *arch.* ME. [– OFr. *farsir* (mod. *farcir*) :– L. *farcire* stuff.] To stuff. Const. *with.* †**1.** *trans.* To stuff with forcemeat, herbs, spices, etc. –1736. †**2.** To cram with food; also, to fill out –1669. †**3.** *gen.* To cram *full of*; also, to overlay thickly –1634. **4.** *fig.*; *esp.* to season, spice (a speech, etc.) ME.

1. To f. Cucumbers 1736. **2.** If thou would'st f. thy leane ribbes with it too B. JONS. **3.** A Helmet ..full farsed with Mayle SPEED. **4.** Stale apothegmes..to f. their Scenes withall B. JONS. Hence †**Fa·rcement,** stuffing. **Fa·rcer,** one who writes or acts a farce.

‖**Farceur** (fārsör). 1828. [Fr., f. *farcer* act farces.] A joker, wag.

Farcical (fā·ɹsikăl), *a.*[1] 1716. [f. FARCE *sb.*[2] + -ICAL.] **1.** Of, belonging to, or of the nature of farce. **2.** That is fit only to be laughed at; extremely ludicrous or futile 1739.

1. The Comedy of Errors is Shakespere's one f. play DOWDEN. Hence **Fa·rcical-ly** *adv.*, **-ness. Farcica·lity,** f. quality.

Farcical (fā·ɹsikal), *a.*[2] 1762. [f. FARCY + -ICAL.] Pertaining to the farcy. STERNE.

†**Fa·rcilite.** 1799. [f. FARCE *sb.*[1] + -LITE.] *Min.* Pudding-stone –1811.

Fa·rcin. Now *dial.* ME. [–(O)Fr. *farcin* :– late L. *farciminum* (Vegetius), beside *farcimen*, f. *farcire* FARCE *v.*, so named from the purulent eruptions with which the affected animal is 'stuffed'. See FARCY.] = FARCY 1.

Farcing (fā·ɹsiŋ), *vbl. sb.* 1532. [f. FARCE *v.* + -ING[1].] **1.** The action of FARCE *v.* 1540. **2.** *concr.* Forcemeat.

Farctate (fā·ɹktēt), *a.* 1832. [f. L. *farctus*, pa. pple. of *farcire* FARCE *v.* + -ATE[2].] *Bot.* 'Stuffed, crammed or full; without vacuities' (Webster).

Farcy (fā·ɹsi), *sb.* 1481. [Later var. of FARCIN. For loss of *n* cf. BOOTY.] **1.** A disease, *esp.* of horses, closely allied to glanders. **2.** The same disease as communicated to man 1762.

Comb.: **f. bud,** one of the small tumours which occur during the progress of f.; **f. button** = *f. bud.*

Fard (fāɹd), *sb. Obs.* exc. *arch.* 1540. [– (O)Fr. *fard*, f. *farder* paint (the face), f. OFr. *farde.*] Paint (esp. white paint) for the face. Also *fig.*

Rouge and f. 1766. *fig.* The f. of Eloquence 1663.

†**Fard** (fāɹd), *v.* 1450. [– (O)Fr. *farder*; see prec.] *trans.* To paint (the face) with fard; *transf.* and *fig.* to embellish or gloss over anything –1816.

†**Fa·rdage.** 1578. [–(O)Fr. *fardage* impedimenta, etc., f. *farder* load, f. *farde* burden; in sense 2 – mod.Fr. in same sense. Cf. next.] **1.** Impedimenta, baggage –1600. **2.** = DUNNAGE –1860.

Fardel (fā·ɹdĕl), *sb.*[1] ME. [– OFr. *fardel* (mod. *fardeau*) burden, load :– dim of Rom. **fardum* – Arab. *fard, farda* camel-load; see -EL[2].] **1.** A bundle, a little pack. Also *collect.* **2.** *fig.*; *esp.* a burden of sin, sorrow, etc. ME. †**3.** A wrapping –1649.

2. None sees the f. of his faults behind HERRICK.

†**Fa·rdel,** *sb.*[2]. Also *Sc.* FARL. ME. [repr. OE. *fēorða dǣl* fourth part.] A fourth part of anything. Also in *pl.* Fragments. –1883.

†**Fa·rdel,** *sb.*[3] 1523. [– Du. *voordeel* advantage.] Profit –1569.

†**Fa·rdel,** *v.* 1582. [f. FARDEL *sb*[1].; cf. OFr. *fardeler* in same sense. In sense 2, contemp. *furl* has been assoc. w. *fardel*; see FURL *v.*] **1.** *trans.* To make into a bundle –1701. **2.** *Naut.* = FURL *v.* –1704.

Fare (fēᵊɹ), *sb.*[1] [orig. two wds.: OE. *fær* str. neut., and OE. *faru* str. fem.; both f. root of FARE *v*[1].] †**1.** A going, journeying; way; voyage –1751; an expedition, as in *herring-f.* –1530. **2.** †A road, track; *esp.* the track of a hare or rabbit (now *dial.*) 1509. †**3.** A number of persons prepared for a journey; also *transf.* –1634. **4.** †A passage for which a price is paid; hence, cost of conveyance (now only of persons) ME. Also *transf.* of the person or (now *rarely*) persons conveyed 1562. **b.** A load or catch of fish. *U.S.* †**5.** Bearing; aspect –1540; doings –1548; display; commotion –1475. †**6.** Condition; state of things, success –1611. **7.** Food; supply of food; also *fig.* ME.

1. Nought the morrow next mote stay his f. SPENSER *F. Q.* V. x. 16. **4.** Making the whole f. (or passage) worth foure shillings LAMBARDE. What's your f. FOOTE. *transf.* The f. was taken up in Grivell-Street 1696. **6.** Phr. *What f.* (cf. *What cheer?*); How now faire Lords? What faire? What newes abroad SHAKS. **7.** After such delicious f. MILT. *P. L.* IX. 1028. *Bill of f.*: see BILL. *Comb.*: **f. indicator,** a device for registering fares paid in a public conveyance.

Fare (fēᵊɹ), *sb.*[2] Now *dial.* 1557. [f. FARE *v.*[2]; see FARROW *sb.*] A litter of pigs.

†**Fare,** *sb.*[3] 1628. [– It. *faro* – L. *pharus*, Gr. φάρος PHAROS.] A promontory (marked by a lighthouse) at the entrance of the Strait of Messina. Hence, the strait itself. –1739.

Fare (fēᵊɹ), *v.*[1] Pa. t. and pple. **fared.** [OE. *faran* = OFris., ON. *fara*, OS., OHG., Goth. *faran* (Du. *varen*, G. *fahren*) :– Gmc. **faran*, f. **far-* :– IE. **por-*.] **1.** *intr.* To make one's way, travel. Now *arch.* or *poet.* **2.** In wider sense = GO. OE. **3.** rarely *trans.* Of a horse: To take along. CARLYLE. **4.** †To 'go on', act –1697; to bid fair (*dial.*) 1849. **5.** *impers.* To 'go'; to turn out ME. **6.** To 'get on' OE. **7.** *spec.* To 'get on' in respect of food; to feed (*well, ill*, etc.) ME. **8.** Used in imperative with *well*: **a.** with the person as *subj.*; **b.** *impers.*; = FAREWELL *interj.* (*arch.*) ME.

1. Sadly they fared along the sea-beat shore POPE. **2.** One..in would f. SPENSER. Phr. *To f. astray.* **3.** The good pony 'Larry' faring us 1867. **4.** He fared as one out of his wits FOXE. To f. angerly with anyone RALEGH. **5.** How fares it with the happy dead TENNYSON. **6.** Ill fares the traveller now COWPER. Phr. *To go farther and f. worse.* **7.** A certaine rich man..fared sumptuously every day *Luke* 16:19. **8. a.** F. ye well *Acts* 15:29. **b.** For ever, f. thee well BYRON.

†**Fare,** *v.*[2] [var. of FARROW *v.*] *intr.* Of a sow: To litter. TUSSER.

Farewell (fēᵊɹwe·l), *interj.* Also *sb.* (*a.*) and *adv.* ME. [*Fare* (see FARE *v.* 8) + *well*, as one word.]

A. *interj.* **1.** An expression of good wishes at parting, originally addressed to the one setting forth, but now = Good-bye! Adieu! *poet.* or *rhet.* ME. **2.** *fig.* = Good-bye to, no more of (anything) ME.

1. And now farewel DRYDEN. **2.** Farewel my book and my devocioun CHAUCER.

B. *sb.* **1. a.** The *interj.* used subst., as a name for itself. So now in *To bid f.*, where *farewell* was orig. the *infinitive.* **b.** An utterance of the word 'farewell'; a parting salutation, adieu. ME. †**2.** A payment on quitting a tenancy. 1523. **3.** *attrib.* or *adj.* Pertaining to or signifying a farewell. (In this use commonly stressed *fa·rewell.*) 1711.

1. a. I take my farewel of this subject ADDISON. **b.** I cannot think the thing f. TENNYSON. **3.** A few final or f. farewells DE QUINCEY.

†**C.** *adv. To go f.*: to go away. CHAUCER.

Farewell (fēᵊɹwe·l), *v.* 1580. [f. prec.] To bid or say good-bye to; also *intr.*

Far-famed (fā·ɹ,fē¹·md), *a.* 1624. [f. FAR *adv.* + pa. pple. of FAME *v.* 2.] Famed to a great distance; well known, celebrated.

†**Fa·r-fet,** *a.* 1533. [f. FAR *adv.* + *fet*, pa. pple. of FET *v.*] **1.** = FAR-FETCHED –1680. **2.** as *sb.* The figure *Metalepsis* (*rare*) 1589.

†**Far-fetch,** *sb.* 1562. [Back-formation from FAR-FETCHED.] **1.** A deeply-laid stratagem –1678. **2.** Fondness for far-fetched ideas 1813. So †**Far-fetch** *v.* to derive in a far-fetched manner (*rare*).

Far-fetched (fā·ɹ₁fetʃt, fāɹ₁fe·tʃt), *ppl. a.* 1583. [f. FAR *adv.* + pa. pple. of FETCH *v.*] **1.** Brought from far. *Obs.* exc. *arch.* **2.** Studiously sought out; not easily or naturally introduced; strained 1607.

1. A far fetch'd Pedigree, through so many hundred years CLARENDON. **2.** Some far-fetched conceit 1844.

Far-forth, *adv.* Now usu. as two wds. ME. [See FAR and FORTH.] †**1.** Far, far on –1590. **2.** To a definite degree or distance. *Obs.* exc. in *So far forth*. ME.

1. The humid night was farforth spent SPENSER. **2.** Soffre ye thus farre forthe TINDALE *Luke* 22:51. Know thus far forth SHAKS. Hence **Far-fo·rthly** *adv.* to a great or definite extent; entirely.

Fargite (fā·ɹgəit). 1868. [f. (Glen) *Farg* in Fifeshire + -ITE[1] 2 b.] *Min.* A red natrolite, containing about 4 p.c. of lime. DANA

Farina (fărəi·nă, fărī·nă). 1707. [– L. *farina*, f. *far* corn.] **1.** The flour or meal of any species of corn, nut, or starchy root 1800; a powdery substance, dust 1707. **b.** A preparation of maize used for puddings (*mod.*). **2. a.** *Bot.* = Pollen 1721. **b.** *Chem.* Starch 1813. **c.** *Entom.* A mealy powder found on some insects 1828. **d.** *Fossil f.*: 'a white infusorial or microphytal earth—the Bergmahl of the Swedes and Laplanders' (Page) 1816.

Farinaceous (færinēi·ʃəs), *a.* 1656. [– late L. *farinaceus*, f. *farina* (see prec.) + -OUS; see -ACEOUS.] **1.** Consisting or made of flour or meal. **2.** Yielding flour or starch; starchy 1667. **3.** Of a mealy nature 1664. **4.** Having a mealy appearance 1646.

1. A mild f. diet 1807. **2.** F. vegetables 1732, seeds 1873. **3.** Cotyledons thick, fleshy or f. SIR W. HOOKER. **4.** All f. or mealy winged animals, as Butter-Flies, and Moths SIR T. BROWNE. **Farina·ceously** *adv.*

‖**Farinha** (farī·nʸă). 1726. [Pg. :– L. *farina*.] = CASSAVA 2.

Farinose (fæ:rinōᵘ·s). 1727. [– late L. *farinosus*, f. *farina*; see FARINA, -OSE[1].] **A.** *adj.* Mealy; *spec.* in *Bot.*, *Zool.*, etc. (see FARINA). **B.** *sb. Chem.* One of the constituents of a starch grain 1882.

‖**Fario** (fēᵊ·ri₁o). 1753. [Late L. (Ausonius) = salmon trout.] A salmon when about half-grown.

Farl (fāɹl), *sb. Sc.* 1724. [contr. f. FARDEL *sb.*[2]] A thin cake made of flour or oatmeal; *orig.*, the fourth part of such a cake.

†**Farl,** *v.* 1622. [contr. f. FARDEL *v.*] = FARDEL *v.*

Farleu (fā·ɹliu). 1670. [Of unkn. origin.] *Law.* A money payment in lieu of a heriot; also, 'the best good' as dist. from 'the best beast'.

Farley, -i(e, -ik, -y(e: see FERLY.

†**Farm,** *sb.*[1] [OE. *feorm*, of unkn. origin.] Food, provision; hence, a banquet –1500.

Farm (fāɹm), *sb.*[2] [ME. *ferme* – (O)Fr. *ferme* :– med.L. *firma* fixed payment, f. L. *firmare* fix, settle, confirm, in med.L. contract for, f. L. *firmus* FIRM *a.*] †**1.** A fixed yearly amount (whether in money or in kind) payable as rent, tax, or the like. Also *Rent and f.* –1767. **2.** A fixed yearly sum accepted as a composition for taxes or other moneys to be collected; also, a fixed charge imposed on a town, county, etc. to be collected as taxes within its limits. Now *Hist.* ME. **b.** The letting-out of a tax or taxes to a 'farmer'; the privilege thus conferred. Now *Hist.* 1667. **3.** Hence: The condition of being 'farmed out' ME. †**4.** A lease –1647. **5.** A tract of land held (orig. on lease) for the purpose of cultivation; sometimes specialized as *dairy-*, *grass-*, *poultry-f.* 1523. Also a tract of water used as a preserve, as *fish-*, *oyster-f.*, etc. 1865. **6.** A farm-house 1596. **7.** A place where children are 'farmed' 1869.

1. The usual. .feorm or rent BLACKSTONE. **2. b.** The first f. of postal income was made in 1672. 1885. **3.** Districts which were in a condition to be let to f. BURKE. **4.** To refuse to make any longer farmes unto. .Tenants SPENSER. **5.** The pleasant Villages and Farmes MILT. *P. L.* IX. 448. **6.** A ferme or mannor house P. HOLLAND.

Comb.: **f.-crossing,** a railway-crossing from one part of a f. to another; **-hand,** any person that works on a f.; **-stock,** the cattle, etc., implements, and produce of a f.; **-store,** farm-produce.

Farm, *v.*[1] Now *dial.* [OE. *feormian*; etym. unkn.] To cleanse, empty.

Farm (fāɹm), *v.*[2] ME. [f. FARM *sb.*[2]] **1.** *trans.* To take or hold for a term at a fixed payment. **2.** To let to another for a fixed payment; as, land to a tenant (now *rare*) 1593; the proceeds of customs, taxes, tithes, etc. 1602; labour 1607. **3.** To contract for the maintenance and care of (persons, an institution, etc.) at a stipulated price. Also *To f. out.* 1666. **4.** To cultivate, till 1806. **5.** *intr.* To be a farmer; to till the soil 1719.

1. Abram. .farmed. .some ground on them BP. PATRICK. To f. a lottery JOHNSON, tin-mines M. PATTISON. **2.** We are inforc'd to farme our royall Realme SHAKS. If I be minded to f. out my Tythes 1704. They farmed out the Indians W. ROBERTSON. **5.** I farmed upon my own land DE FOE. Hence †**Fa·rmage,** the system of farming; leasehold tenure; the profits from a farm; cost of cultivation.

Farmer (fā·ɹməɹ). [ME. *fermour* – AFr. *fermer*, (O)Fr. *fermier*, which combined the uses of med.L. *firmarius* and *firmator*; in the more mod. uses apprehended as f. FARM *v.* + -ER[1].] **1.** One who undertakes the collection of taxes, revenues, etc., paying a fixed sum for the proceeds. **b.** *Mining.* The lessee of 'the lot and cope of the king' (see COPE *sb.*[3]) 1653. †**2.** *gen.* One who has a lease of anything 1523. **3.** *spec.* One who rents land for the purpose of cultivation 1487. **4.** One who 'farms' land, whether as tenant or owner 1599. **5.** One who undertakes to perform (a work or service) at a fixed price 1838. †**6.** A farm-bailiff –1580.

1. Speculators, farmers of revenues, and others 1864. **4.** I eat like a f. 1771. **5.** The f. of infants 1838.

Fa·rmeress. 1672. [See -ESS[1].] A woman who farms land; also, a farmer's wife.

Farmer-general. 1711. [tr. Fr. *fermier général*.] One who, under the old French monarchy, farmed the taxes of a district.

†**Fa·rmerly,** *a.* 1674. [f. FARMER + -LY[1].] Like a farmer –1793.

†**Fa·rmership.** 1551. [f. as prec. + -SHIP.] The state or occupation of being a farmer; stewardship –1624.

Farmery (fā·ɹməri), *sb.* 1656. [f. FARM *sb.* + -ERY.] The buildings, yards, etc., belonging to a farm.

Farmhold (fā·ɹmhoᵘld). 1449. [f. FARM *sb.*[2] + HOLD *sb.*] A quantity of land held as a farm.

Fa:rm-hou·se. 1598. [f. FARM *sb.*[2] + HOUSE.] The chief dwelling-house attached to a farm.

Farming (fā·ɹmiŋ), *vbl. sb.* 1591. [f. FARM *v.*[2] + -ING[1].] **1.** The action or system of farming (out) or letting out to farm (the revenue, etc.). **2.** The business of cultivating land, raising stock, etc. 1733. **3.** *attrib.* 1764.

2. When I am told that f. answers to gentlemen .I never believe it A. YOUNG.

†**Fa·rmost,** *a.* 1618. [f. FAR + -MOST.] Irreg. superl. of FAR –1700.

Farm-stead (fā·ɹm₁sted). 1807. [f. FARM *sb.*[2] + STEAD.] A farm with the buildings upon it, a homestead. So **Fa·rm-stea:ding.**

Fa:rm-ya·rd. 1748. The yard or enclosure attached to a farm-house or surrounded by farm-buildings. Also *attrib.*

Farness (fā·ɹnės). ME. [See -NESS.] The state of being far (or, *occas.*, far-reaching); *concr.* distant parts.

F. of sight and fixedness of purpose BANCROFT.

Faro (fēᵊ·ro). 1713 (**farroon**). [– Fr. *pharaon* PHARAOH; the title is said to have been applied orig. to the king of hearts in the game.] A gambling game at cards, in which the players bet on the order in which certain cards will appear when taken singly from the top of the pack.

Comb. **f. bank,** (*a*) a gambling-house where f. is played; (*b*) the money staked by the banker against the other players.

Faröelite (fā·ro₁ėləit). 1858. [f. *Faröe* + -LITE.] *Min.* A variety of Thomsonite occurring 'in spherical concretions, consisting of lamellar radiated individuals, pearly in cleavage' (Dana).

Far-off (fā·ɹ₁ǫ·f), *a.* 1590. [f. FAR *adv.* + OFF *adv.*, orig. as two words.] Far distant, remote.

The far-off Curfeu MILT. Those far-off days 1877.

‖**Farouche** (faruʃ). 1765. [Fr., alt. of OFr. *faroche*, *forache* :– med.L. *forasticus*, f. L. *foras* out-of-doors.] Sullen, shy and repellent in manner.

Farraginous (fărēi·dʒinəs), *a.* 1615. [f. L. *farrago*, *-gin-* (see next) + -OUS.] Hotchpotch.

A f. concurrence of all conditions, tempers, sex, and ages SIR T. BROWNE.

Farrago (fărēi·go). 1632. [– L. *farrago* mixed fodder for cattle, hence *fig.* a medley, f. *far* spelt, corn.] A confused group; a medley, mixture, hotchpotch.

This f. of cowardice, cunning, and cant CANNING.

Fa·rrand, farrant, *a. Sc.* and *n. dial.* ME. [perh. an application of *farande*, north. pr. pple. of FARE *v.*[1]] †**1.** Of a person: well favoured, comely; of things: Becoming. Only in ME. **2.** Having a specified appearance, disposition, or temperament; as, *auld-*, *fighting-*, *foul-f.* Hence **Fa·rrandly, farrantly** *adv.*

Farreation (færi₁ēi·ʃən). 1656. [– late L. *farreatio* for L. *confarreatio*; see CONFARREATION.] = CONFARREATION.

Farrier (fæ·riəɹ), *sb.* 1562. [– OFr. *ferrier* :– L. *ferrarius*, f. *ferrum* horseshoe, prop. iron; see -IER.] **1.** One who shoes horses; a shoeing smith; hence, one who treats the ailments of horses. **2.** An official who has care of the horses in a cavalry regiment 1832.

Hence **Fa·rrier** *v.* (*rare*), to treat (an animal) as a f. does; *intr.* to practise farriery. **Fa·rriery,** the art of the f.; now = veterinary surgery.

Farrow (fæ·roᵘ), *sb.* [OE. *færh* (*fearh*) = OS. **farh*, OHG. *farah* :– WGmc. **farχa* :– IE. **porkos*, whence L. *porcus*, Gr. πόρκος; see PORK.] †**1.** A young pig –ME. **2.** An act of farrowing. [Prop. f. the vb.] 1601. **3.** Hence *concr.* A litter of pigs; occas. in sing. with numeral (after Shaks.) 1577.

2. That hath eaten Her nine F. *Macb.* IV. i. 65.

Farrow (fæ·roᵘ), *a.* Chiefly *Sc.* 1494. [– Flem. *verwe*, *varwe*, in *vervekoe*, *varwekoe*, †*verrekoe* cow that has become barren.] Of a cow: That is not with calf. Also in *To be*, *go*, or *run f.*

Farrow (fæ·roᵘ), *v.* ME. [f. FARROW *sb.*] **1.** *trans.* Of a sow: To bring forth (young). **2.** *intr.* To produce a litter ME.

‖**Farsang** (fā·ɹsæŋ). 1613. [Pers.; see PARASANG.] 'A Persian measure of distance—the *Parasang* of the ancients—about four miles' (H. H. Wilson).

Farse (fāɹs), *sb.* 1842. [A mod. adaptation of med.L. *farsa*; see FARCE *sb.*[2]] *Eccl. Antiq.* An amplification inserted into a liturgical formula; also, each of the hortatory or other passages in the vernacular interpolated between the Latin sentences in chanting the lesson or epistle. So **Farse** *v.* to amplify by the insertion of certain words; to provide (an epistle) with a f. Also *transf.*

Far-sighted (fāɹ₁səitėd), *a.* 1641. [f. FAR *adv.* + SIGHT + -ED[2].] **1.** *fig.* Looking far before one; forecasting, shrewd. **2.** *lit.* Hypermetropic 1878.

1. The fair and far-sighted eye of his natural discerning MILT. Hence **Far-sighted-ly** *adv.*, **-ness.** So **Far-sight,** ability to see far; also *attrib.*

Fart (fāɹt), *sb.* Not in decent use. ME. [f. the vb.] A breaking wind.

Fart (fāɹt), *v.* Not in decent use. [OE. **feortan* (in *feorting* vbl. sb., ME. *uerten*, corresp. to MLG. *verten*, OHG. *ferzan*, MHG. *verzen*, *vurzen* (G. *farzen*, *furzen*), ON. (with metathesis) *freta* :– Gmc. **fertan*, **fartan*, **furtan*.] **1.** *intr.* To break wind. **2.** *trans.* To send forth as wind from the anus 1632.

Farther (fā·ɹðəɹ). [ME. *ferþer* (whence *farther*) is a mere var. of FURTHER. The primary sense of these, 'more forward, more onward', being coincident with that of the comparative of *far*, the forms *further*, *farther*, ultimately displaced the regular comparative *farrer*. The form *farther* is now preferred as the comparative of *far*, while *further* is used where the notion of *far* is absent.]

A. *adv.* **1.** More forward; to or at a more advanced point: **a.** in space, a course of procedure, etc.; **b.** in time 1548. **2.** To a greater extent 1513. **3.** In addition ME. **4.** To or at a greater distance; by a greater interval ME.

1. a. To walk f. 1460. **b.** To argue f. MAR. EDGEWORTH. **2.** To know f. *Temp.* I. ii. 33. **3.** Nay f., [etc.] DE FOE. **4.** Phr. *To wish any one f.*

B. *adj.* †**1.** = FURTHER *a.* 1. –1534. **2.** More extended, additional, more 1520. **3.** More distant 1568.

2. Down he sat without f. bidding DICKENS. **3.** The f. syde of London GRAFTON.

Farther (fā·ɹðəɹ), *v.* Now *rare.* [The regular phonetic descendant in standard English of ME. *ferþren*; see FURTHER *v.*] *trans.* = FURTHER *v.*

†**Fa·rtherance.** *rare.* 1785. [f. prec. + -ANCE.] = FURTHERANCE.

†**Fa·rtherer.** 1494. [f. as prec. + -ER[1].] = FURTHERER –1655.

†**Fa·rthermore.** ME. [var. of FURTHERMORE.] **A.** *adv.* = FURTHERMORE –1535. **B.** *adj.* More remote 1610.

Farthermost (fā·ɹðəɹmōᵘst), *a.* 1618. [var. of FURTHERMOST.] Farthest, most remote or distant.

Farthest (fā·ɹðėst). ME. [var. of FURTHEST; used as superl. of FAR; see FARTHER.]

A. *adj.* **1.** Most distant or remote. Also with *off.* **2.** Longest 1633. **3.** *absol.* of space, future time, or degree 1596.

3. At the f. by flue of the clocke *Merch. V.* II. ii. 122.

B. *adv.* To or at the greatest distance. Also with *off.* 1598.

Farthing (fā·ɹðiŋ), *sb.* [OE. *fēorþing, -ung*, f. *fēorþa* FOURTH, perh. after ON. *fjórðungr* quarter; see -ING[3].] **1.** The fourth part of a penny; the coin of this value. In N.T. used for the two Roman coins *as* and *quadrans.* **2.** *transf.* and *fig.* A very little, a bit ME. †**3.** The fourth **a.** of an acre; **b.** of a hide –1630.

2. In hire cuppe was no ferthing sene Of grees CHAUCER. *Comb.* **f.-land,** 'commonly thirtie acres' (Carew); 'the fourth part of an Acre' (Worlidge).

Farthingale (fā·ɹðiŋ,gēⁱl). 1552. [Early forms *vard-, verd-, fard-* – OFr. *verdugale, vertugalle*, altered – Sp. *verdugado*, f. *verdugo* rod, stick, f. *verde* green.] A frame-work of hoops, usually of whalebone, formerly used for extending the skirts of women's dresses; a hooped petticoat.

The Women wear great Vardingales, standing.. far out at each side RAY.

†**Fa·rthingdeal.** ME. [repr. OE. *fēorþan dǣl*, accus. of *fēorþa dǣl*; see FOURTH, DEAL *sb.*[1]] **1.** *gen.* A fourth part. ME. only. **2.** *spec.* The fourth part of an acre; a rood –1607. **b.** A quarter of a yard of land 1640. var. **Far(r)undell.**

‖**Fasces** (fæ·siz), *sb. pl.* 1598. [L., pl. of *fascis* bundle.] **1.** A bundle of rods bound up with an axe in the middle, its blade projecting. **2.** *transf.* and *fig.* The ensigns of authority or power; hence, authority 1619.

The sen[r] proctor..laid down the f. of his authority WOOD.

Fascet (fæ·sėt). 1662. [Of unkn. origin.] A tool used to introduce glass bottles into the annealing oven.

Fascia (fæ·ʃiă). *Pl.* **-iæ**; in *Arch.* **-as.** 1563. [– L. *fascia* band, fillet, casing of a door, etc., rel. to FASCES.] †**1.** in *Lat.* sense: A band, fillet –1606. **2.** *Arch.* Any long flat surface of wood, stone, or marble, *esp.* in the Ionic and Corinthian orders, each of the three surfaces which make up the architrave. (Cf. FACIA.) 1563. **3.** *Anat.* A thin sheath of fibrous tissue investing a muscle or some special tissue or organ; an aponeurosis 1788. **4.** Anything resembling a band or stripe: **a.** *Astron.* The belt of a planet 1704; **b.** *Conchol.* A row of perforations 1877; **c.** *Bot., Zool.*, etc. A band of colour 1752; **d.** *Her.* = FESSE. 1880.

Fascial (fæ·ʃiăl), *a.*[1] *rare.* 1832. [f. FASCES + -IAL.] Of or pertaining to the (Roman) fasces.

Fascial (fæ·ʃiăl), *a.*[2] [f. FASCIA + -AL[1].] *Anat.* Of or pertaining to the fasciæ; aponeurotic.

Fasciate (fæ·ʃiĕt), *a.* [f. FASCIA 4 c + -ATE[2].] *Bot.* = FASCIATED.

Fasciate (fæ·ʃi,eⁱt), *v.* 1658. [– *fasciat-*, pa. ppl. stem of L. *fasciare* swathe, f. *fascia*; see FASCIA, -ATE[3].] To bind with or as with a fascia.

Fasciated (fæ·ʃi,eⁱtėd), *ppl. a.* 1715. [f. FASCIA + -ATE[2] + -ED[1]. Cf. Fr. *fascié.*] **1.** *Bot.*, etc. Compressed or massed together 1811. †**2.** Of a roof: Coved on two opposite sides only 1715. **3.** Marked with bands or stripes 1752.

Fasciation (fæsi,ēⁱ·ʃən). 1650. [– *fasciat-* (see FASCIATE *v.*) + -ION.] **1.** The binding up of a limb, etc., with bandages; †a bandage –1658. **2.** The process of becoming fasciated; also, fasciated condition (see FASCIATED 1) 1677.

Fascicle (fæ·sik'l). 1622. [– L. *fasciculus*, dim of *fascis*; see FASCES, -CULE.] **1.** A bunch, bundle. Now only in scientific use. **b.** *Bot.* A number of leaves, flowers, roots, etc. growing or occurring in a bunch, bundle, or tuft 1794. **c.** *Anat.* A bundle of fibres, chiefly applied to nerve structures 1738. **2.** A part, number, instalment (of a printed work) 1647. Hence **Fa·scicled** *ppl. a.* (*Bot.*), growing in a f.

Fascicular (făsi·kiŭlăɹ), *a.* 1656. [f. FASCICULUS + -AR[1].] †**1.** Belonging to a bundle. (Dicts.) **2.** Pertaining to, or of the nature of, a FASCICLE, as, *f. tissue, fibres* 1805. Hence **Fasci·cularly** *adv.*

Fasciculate (făsi·kiŭlĕt), *a.* 1794. [f. as prec. + -ATE[2].] Arranged in a FASCICLE; fascicle-like. So **Fasci·culated** *ppl. a.*

Fasciculation (făsi:kiulēⁱ·ʃən). [f. as prec.; see -ATION.] The state of being fasciculate; that which is fasciculated.

Fascicule (fæ·sikiŭl). 1609. [– L. *fasciculus*, after Fr. *fascicule*; cf. FASCICLE, FASCICULUS.] †**1.** A handful. EVELYN. **2.** = FASCICLE 2. 1880. **3.** = FASCICLE 1 c. 1745.

Fasciculite (făsi·kiŭləit). 1823. [f. prec. + -ITE[1] 2 b.] *Min.* Tufted fibrous hornblende.

‖**Fasciculus** (făsi·kiŭlŏs). *Pl.* **-li.** 1713. [L., dim. of *fascis*; see FASCES, -CULE.] **1.** = FASCICLE 1; chiefly in scientific use. **2.** = FASCICLE 2. 1844.

Fascinate (fæ·sineⁱt), *v.* 1598. [– *fascinat-*, pa. ppl. stem of L. *fascinare*, f. *fascinum* spell, witchcraft; see -ATE[3].] †**1.** *trans.* To affect by witchcraft; to enchant, lay under a spell –1657. **2.** To cast a spell over by a look (said *esp.* of serpents); to render unable to move or resist 1641. **3.** *fig.* To attract and hold the attention of by an irresistible influence 1651.

1. To f. and cure stinking breaths 1657. **2.** The serpent fascinates its prey, apparently by the power of its eyes 1845. **3.** A wit that would f. sages MOORE. The eye of the Ancient Mariner fascinated the wedding guest BURTON. Hence **Fa·scinating** *ppl. a.* irresistibly attractive, charming. **Fa·scinatingly** *adv.* **Fa·scinative** *a.* tending to f. **Fa·scinator.**

Fascination (fæsinēⁱ·ʃən). 1605. [– L. *fascinatio*, f. as prec.; see -ION. Cf. Fr. *fascination.*] **1.** The casting of a spell; sorcery, enchantment; an instance of this. *Obs.* exc. *Hist.* †**b.** The state of being under a spell –1767. **2.** The action or faculty of fascinating, as serpents are said to do 1796. **3.** Fascinating quality, irresistibly attractive influence; an instance or mode of this 1697.

2. The f. of the serpent on the bird held her mute and frozen LYTTON. **3.** That perilous f. which haunts the brow of precipices HAWTHORNE.

Fascine (fæsī·n), *sb.* 1688. [– Fr. *fascine* – L. *fascina*, f. *fascis* bundle.] **1.** *Mil.* A long cylindrical faggot of brushwood or the like, firmly bound together, used in filling up ditches, constructing batteries, etc. Usu. in *pl.* **2.** *transf.* in non-military uses 1712.

2. A large Dike or Peer made of Fachines and Earth 1723. *Comb.* **f.-dwelling,** a lacustrine habitation supported on fascines. Hence **Fasci·ne** *v.* to fill up with fascines.

Fascist (fæ·ʃist). 1921. [– It. *fascista*, f. *fascio* bundle, sheaf, assemblage, association (of forces) :– L. *fascis*; see FASCES, -IST.] One of a body of Italian nationalists organized in 1919 under Benito Mussolini to oppose Bolshevism. Hence **Fa·scism,** their principle and organization.

Fash (fæʃ), *sb. Sc.* and *n. dial.* 1794. [f. the vb.] Trouble, vexation; bother. So **Fa·shery** (in the same senses).

Fash (fæʃ), *v.* Chiefly *Sc.* and *n. dial.* 1533. [– early mod.Fr. *fascher* (now *fâcher*) :– Rom. **fastidicare*, f. L. *fastus* disdain.] **1.** *trans.* To trouble, vex, bother, weary. **2.** *intr.* for *refl.* To weary; to bother oneself; to take trouble 1585.

1. Never f. yoursel' wi' me..but look to yoursel' SCOTT.

Fashion (fæ·ʃən), *sb.* [ME. *faciun, fas(s)oun* – AFr. *fasun*, (O)Fr. *façon* :– L. *factio, -ōn-*, f. *fact-*, pa. ppl. stem of *facere* make, do; see -ION.] †**1.** The action or process of making –1762. **2.** Make, build, shape; hence, appearance (*arch.*) ME. †**b.** Form as opp. to matter –1614. **3.** A particular make, shape, cut, etc. ME. **4.** Kind, sort. Now *rare.* 1562. **5.** Manner, mode, way (*rare* in *pl.*) ME. **6.** Mode of action, behaviour, demeanour, air (now *rare*) ME.; *pl.* actions, gestures, ways (now *rare*) 1569. †**7.** Outward action; pretence –1816. **8.** A current usage 1489; †in *pl.* often = 'manners and customs', ways –1721. **9.** Conventional usage in dress, mode of life, etc., *esp.* as observed in the upper circles of society; conformity to this. Often *personified.* 1602. **b.** Fashionable people 1807.

1. They judge the f. to be worth about 5*s.* per oz. more PEPYS. **2.** The f. of his countenance was altered *Luke* 9:29. **3.** I do not like the f. of your garments *Lear* III. vi. 84. **4.** Phr. *In f. to*: of a sort to (*Merch. V.* I. ii. 23). **5.** After quite another f. DE FOE. Phr. *After, in, a* or *some f.*: not too well. **6.** With such a grace, with such a f. THACKERAY. **8.** The mind still turns where shifting f. draws GOLDSM. Dressed in country f. 1859. **9.** The glasse of F., and the mould of Forme *Haml.* III. i. 161.

Phrases. *The f.* **a.** The mode of dress, etiquette, style of speech, etc., adopted in society for the time being. **b.** The person or thing that is fashionable to admire or discuss. *In, out of (the) f.*: in, out of, vogue; according or contrary to the customary rule. (*Man, woman*) *of f.*: †**a.** Of high quality, breeding, or repute. **b.** *Now*, That moves in good society, and conforms to its rules.

Comb.: **f. paper,** a journal of the fashions or of fashionable life; **f.-piece** (*Naut.*), one of the 'two Timbers which describe the breadth of the Ship at the Stern' (Harris); **f.-plate,** 'a pictorial design showing the prevailing style or new style of dress' (W.).

Hence **Fa·shionless** *a.* without f. or shape.

Fashion (fæ·ʃən), *v.* ME. [f. prec. sb., after (O)Fr. *façonner.*] **1.** *trans.* To give fashion or shape to; to form, mould, shape. Also with *out.* **2. a.** To frame, make (*rare*) 1549. †**b.** To contrive, manage 1604. †**3.** To change the fashion of; to transform –1753; †to counterfeit, pervert SHAKS. **4.** To accommodate, adapt *to.* Also *refl.* and *intr.* for *refl.* Now *rare.* 1526.

1. Did not one f. vs in the wombe *Job* 31:15. A smith to f. his steel into picks and awls ROGERS. **2. b.** His going thence, which I will f. to fall out betweene twelue and one *Oth.* IV. ii. 242. **3.** F. thyself to Paul 1592. *Much Ado* I. iii. 31. **4.** Doctrines fashioned to the varying hour GOLDSM.

Fashionable (fæ·ʃənăb'l). 1606. [f. FASHION *v.* and *sb.* + -ABLE.]

A. *adj.* †**1.** Capable of being fashioned, shaped, or moulded –1656. †**2.** Pertaining to the outward form; merely formal –1616. †**3.** Of a good fashion or appearance; stylish –1720. **4. a.** Of persons: Observant of or conforming to the fashion 1606. **b.** Of things: Conformable to fashion; in accordance with prevailing usage; current (now in depreciatory sense) 1608. **5.** Of, pertaining to, or characteristic of the world of fashion; patronized by people of fashion 1712.

4. Like a f. Hoste, That slightly shakes his parting Guest by th' hand *Tr. & Cr.* III. iii. 165. **b.** His..attire more f. FULLER. **5.** In f. or political saloons EMERSON.

B. *sb.* A fashionable person. Usu. in *pl.* 1800.

Our fair fashionables 1800.

Hence **Fa·shionableness,** f. quality. **Fa·shionably** *adv.* in a f. manner.

†**Fa·shional,** *a.* 1617. [f. FASHION *sb.* + -AL[1].] = FASHIONABLE *a.* 2, 3. –1629.

Fashioned (fæ·ʃənd), *ppl. a.* 1577. [f. FASHION *sb.* + -ED[2].] Having a fashion of a specified kind, as *old-f.*, etc.

Fashioner (fæ·ʃənəɹ). 1548. [f. FASHION *v.* + -ER[1].] One that fashions; *esp.* a tailor, costumier, modiste (now *arch.*).
A f. of doublets SCOTT.

Fashionist (fæ·ʃənist). 1616. [f. FASHION *sb.* + -IST.] **1.** A follower of the fashions. **2.** One who sets the fashions. MILMAN.

Fa·shion-monger. 1599. [f. FASHION + MONGER.] One who studies and follows the fashions. Hence †**Fashion-monging** *ppl. a.*

Fashious (fæ·ʃəs), *a. Sc.* and *n. dial.* 1536. [– Fr. †*fascheux* (now *fâcheux*), f. *fascher* (*fâcher*); see FASH *v.*, -IOUS.] Causing anxiety or trouble; tiresome, vexatious.

Fassaite (fæ·seˌəit). 1814. [f. *Fassa* (in the Tyrol) + -ITE[1] 2 b.] *Min.* †**a.** Foliated zeolite. **b.** A variety of pyroxene, containing a little alumina.

Fast (fɑst), *sb.*[1] [Early ME. *faste* – ON. *fasta* = OS., OHG. *fasta*, f. Gmc. **fastējan*; see FAST *v.*[2]] **1.** An act of fasting; **a.** as a religious observance, or as an expression of grief; **b.** in general ME; †**c.** Abstinence from food; also *personified* –1795. **2.** A day or season appointed for fasting ME.
1. b. *To break (one's) f.*: see BREAK *v.* **c.** Surfet is the father of much f. *Meas. for M.* I. ii. 130. **2.** The people of Nineueh..proclaimed a f. *Jonah* 3:5.
Comb.: **f.-day,** a day to be observed as a f.; **-mass,** Shrovetide.

Fast (fɑst), *sb.*[2] [Late ME. *fest* – ON. *festr* rope for mooring a ship to the shore, f. *festa* fasten, f. *fastr* FAST *a.* In mod. Eng. assim. to the adj.] *Naut.* A rope, etc. by which a ship or boat is fastened to a wharf.

Fast (fɑst), *sb.*[3] 1836. [The adj. used *absol.*] That which is fast or fixed; *esp.* shore or land ice.

†**Fast,** *sb.*[4] [– Fr. *faste* – L. *fastus.*] Arrogance, pompousness. H. WALPOLE.

Fast (fɑst), *a.* [OE. *fæst* = OFris. *fest*, OS. *fast* (Du. *vast*), OHG. *festi* (G. *fest*), ON. *fastr*; prob. orig. :– Gmc. **fastuz*; see FAST *v.*[2]]
I. Firm. **1.** Firmly fixed; not easily moved or shaken; settled, stable. *Obs.* or *arch.*, exc. as in sense 4. **b.** Not easily turned aside, constant, steadfast. Now only in *f. foe* (arch.), *f. friend.* OE. **c.** Of sleep: Deep, sound, unbroken. *Obs.* exc. *dial.* 1592. **d.** Of a colour: Permanent 1658. **2.** Firmly or closely knit together, compact, dense, solid. *Obs.* exc. *dial.* OE. †**3.** Strong; secure against attack or access. Cf. FASTNESS. –1633. **4.** Firmly attached to something else; that cannot easily escape or be extricated; fixed to the spot. *lit.* and *fig.* ME. **b.** Of a knot, band, etc.: Not easily loosed. Also *fig.* 1553. **5.** Of a door, etc.: Close shut, bolted, or locked ME. **6.** Tenacious. *Obs.* exc. in *f. hold of.* –1724.
1. b. England must be the f. friend, or the determined enemy, of France BURKE. **c.** All this while in a most f. sleepe *Macb.* v. i. 9. Phr. *F. aground, ashore, asleep*: fixed on the ground, the shore, in sleep. **2.** In close array and f. SCOTT. **4.** F. in preson 1535. F. with the gout SCOTT. Phr. *To make f.*: to connect or fix firmly; also *absol.* (Naut.). **6.** Roses Damask & Red are f. Flowers of their Smels BACON.
II. Rapid. [app. a sense developed first in the adv.] **1.** Of action, motion, etc.: Quick, swift. Hence of an agent: Moving, or causing to move, rapidly. ME. **b.** Coming in quick succession. SHELLEY. **c.** Of a watch, etc.: Ahead of the true time 1840; also of scales: indicating more than the actual weight 1908. **2.** Adapted to, or productive of, quick movement; *spec.* in *Cricket, Football,* and *Billiards* 1857. **3.** Living too fast; dissipated; dissolute. Often applied to women in milder sense: Disregardful of restraint. Also *transf.* 1745.
1. Idle Weeds are f. in growth *Rich. III*, III. i. 103. A good f. bowler 1886. **2.** A f. line of railway 1895. The ground [at a football match] was very f. 1891. **3.** All the f. men were anxious to make their acquaintance 1841. Lucknow is a f. place L. OLIPHANT.
Comb.: **f.-pulley,** also in *f. and loose pulley*, a contrivance for disengaging and re-engaging machinery, consisting of two pulleys, one fixed on an axle, the other, having a bush, loose, so that the band conveying the motion may be shifted from one pulley to the other at pleasure; **f.-shot,** in *Mining*, a shot that has discharged without disturbing the coal.

Fast (fɑst), *adv.* [OE. *fæste* = OS. *fasto* (Du. *vast*), OHG. *fasto* (G. *fast* almost), ON. *fast* :– Gmc. **fastō*, f. **fastuz* (prec.).] **1.** In a fast manner, so as not to be moved or shaken; *lit.* and *fig.*; firmly, fixedly. **2.** With firm grasp, attachment, or adhesion; tightly, securely. *lit.* and *fig.* OE. **3.** In a close-fitting manner; so as to leave no opening ME. **4.** Of proximity: Close, hard; very near. Now only in *f. beside, f. by* (arch. or poet.). ME. †**5.** Closely, at once –1782. **6.** Quickly, rapidly, swiftly ME.; in quick succession 1591.
1. Stand f. in the faith 1 *Cor.* 16:13. Phr. *To sleep fast*, i.e. soundly. **2.** F. binde, f. finde *Merch.V.* II. v. 53. Phr. *To stick f.*: often *fig.* to be nonplussed. **3.** Substantial dores, Cross-barrd and bolted f. MILT. *P. L.* IV. 190. **4.** F. by Hell Gate MILT. *P. L.* II. 725. **6.** His health was breaking f. TREVELYAN. My thoughts come f. SHELLEY. Phr. *To live f.*: **a.** to expend quickly one's vital energy; **b.** to live a dissipated life.

†**Fast,** *v.*[1] [OE. *fæstan* = OFris. *festia*, OS. *festian* (Du. *vesten*), OHG. *festen*, ON. *festa*; :– Gmc. **fastjan*, f. **fastuz* (prec.).] **1.** To make fast to something; to bind together. Also *refl.* and *intr.* for *refl.* –1665. **2.** To fix in something else; to fix firmly –1664. **3.** To confirm (a covenant); to pledge (faith, etc.) –1470.

Fast (fɑst), *v.*[2] [OE. *fæstan* = OFris. *festia*, (M)Du. *vasten*, OHG. *fastēn* (G. *fasten*), ON. *fasta*, Goth. *fastan* :– Gmc. **fastējan*, f. **fastuz*; see FAST *a.*] **1.** *intr.* To abstain from food, or to 'eat meagre', either as a religious observance or as an expression of grief. **2.** *gen.* To go without food (or drink). Const. *from.* Also *transf.* OE. †**3.** *trans.* To pass (time) fasting –1681.
1. We f. by way of penitence J. H. NEWMAN. *fig.* To f. from sinne SIR. T. HERBERT. **2.** Fasting he went to sleep, and fasting wak'd MILT. *P. R.* II. 284. Phr. *To f. against, upon* (a person) (*Irish Antiq.*): to sit without food or drink at the door of a debtor, or any person who refused to satisfy a lawful demand.

Fast and (†or) loose. 1557. **a.** An old cheating game played with a stick and a belt or string 1578. **b.** *fig.* Slippery or inconstant, as in *To play (at) fast and loose* 1557. **c.** Shiftiness 1648.

Fa·sten, *sb. Obs.* exc. in *Comb.* [OE. *fæsten* :– Gmc. **fastunjam*, f. **fastējan* FAST *v.*[2]; rel. to OS. *fastunnia*, Goth. *fastubni.*] = FAST *sb.*[1] 1, 2.

Fasten (fɑ·s'n), *v.* [OE. *fæstnian* = OFris. *festna*, OS. *fastnon*, OHG. *fastinōn*, *fest-* :– WGmc. **fastinōjan*, f. **fastuz* FAST *a.*, see -EN[5].] To make FAST. †**1.** *trans.* To make firm or stable; to confirm –1643. †**2.** To make firm or solid; to strengthen –1557; *intr.* to set –1730. †**3.** To make fast (in fetters). Also *intr.* –1632. **4.** *trans.* To make fast to something else; to attach by a tie or bond. Also *absol.* or *intr.* ME. **5.** To make fast, secure. Also †*intr.* ME. †**6.** To close (the hands, teeth) with a grip –1607. †**7.** To deliver effectively (a blow) –1697. **8.** *fig.* in senses 4, 5: To fix (something) *upon* a person ME. **9.** intr. *To f. on, upon*: †**a.** To obtain a firm hold upon; **b.** to seize on, lay hold of. ME.
2. *intr.* Buildings..are taken with the Frost.. before ever they have fasten'd 1726. **4.** My wife and I, Fastned our selues at eyther end the mast SHAKS. **5.** Breeches fasten'd with Buttons 1696. To f. the door FIELDING. Sit at the helm—f. this sheet SHELLEY. **7.** Wee could never come once to f. a blow on him 1632. **8.** If I can f. but one Cup vpon him *Oth.* II. iii. 50. The eyes of all..were fastened on him *Luke* 4:20. Phr. *To f. a quarrel upon.*

Fastener (fɑ·s'nəɹ). 1628. [f. prec. + -ER[1].] **1.** One who or that which fastens 1755. †**2.** *slang.* A warrant for arrest –1785.

Fastening (fɑ·s'niŋ), *vbl. sb.* ME. [f. as prec. + -ING[1].] **1.** The action of FASTEN *v.* †**2.** The condition of being fastened. Only in ME. **3.** *concr.* That which fastens or makes secure ME.
3. Sash Fastenings 1769. The fastenings of a cuirass 1850.

Fastens. 1616. Short for next.

Fastens-een, -eve, -even. *Sc.* and *n. dial.* ME. [f. OE. *fæstenes*, genitive of *fæsten* FASTEN *sb.*, + EVEN, EVE.] The eve of or day before the fast (of Lent); SHROVE-TUESDAY.

Faster (fɑ·stəɹ). ME. [f. FAST *v.* + -ER[1].] One who fasts or abstains from food.

‖**Fasti** (fæ·stəi). 1611. [L., pl. of *fastus* (*dies*) a lawful day, a day on which the courts sat.] **a.** *Rom. Antiq.* A calendar or calendars, indicating the lawful days for legal business, and also the festivals, games, anniversaries, etc., connected with each day of the year. **b.** *transf.* A chronological register of events.

Fastidio·sity. [f. next + -ITY; see -OSITY.] Fastidiousness. SWIFT.

Fastidious (fæ̆sti·diəs), *a.* ME. [– L. *fastidiosus*, f. *fastidium* loathing; see -IOUS. Cf. Fr. *fastidieux.*] †**1.** That creates disgust –1734. †**2.** That feels disgust –1678; full of pride; disdainful –1796. **3.** Easily disgusted, squeamish; over-nice 1612.
1. Folly is..f. to society BARROW. **2.** Proud youth! f. of the lower world YOUNG. **3.** A f. age.. and one of false refinement TRENCH. Hence **Fasti·dious-ly** *adv.*, **-ness.**

Fastidium (fæ̆sti·diŏm). *rare.* 1734. [– L. *fastidium*, f. *fastus* FAST *sb.*[4]] Disgust; ennui.

Fastigiate (fæsti·dʒiˌĕt), *a.* 1662. [f. L. *fastigium* summit of a gable, top, vertex + -ATE[2].] **1.** Sloping up to a point like a cone or pyramid; in *Bot.* having flowers or branches whose extremities form a cone-like outline. **2.** †**a.** *Bot.* Formerly (after Fr. *fastigié*): Having a horizontal surface at the top, as in an umbel or corymb –1794. **b.** Hence, of a zoophyte: = CORYMBED 1846.

Fastigiate (fæsti·dʒiˌeⁱt), *v.* 1647. [f. as prec. + -ATE[3].] *trans.* To make pointed at the top like a gable; *intr.* to taper to a point. Hence **Fasti·giated** *ppl. a.* 'roofed, narrowed up to the top' (J.).

†**Fasti·gious,** *a.* 1670. [f. next + -OUS; the fig. sense is – med.L. *fastigiosus* sumptuous.] With gables; *fig.* pretentious –1697.

‖**Fastigium** (fæsti·dʒiŏm). 1677. [L.] **1.** Apex, summit; in *Arch.* the ridge of a house. **2.** The gable end (of a roof); a pediment 1849. **3.** The acme of intensity (of a disease) 1876.

Fasting (fɑ·stiŋ), *vbl. sb.* ME. [f. FAST *v.*[2] + -ING[1].] **1.** The action of FAST *v.*[2] †**2.** A season of abstinence from food –1656. **3.** *attrib.*, as in **f.-spittle,** the saliva that is in the mouth before one's fast is broken 1460. Hence **Fa·sting-day** = FAST-DAY.

Fastish (fɑ·stiʃ), *a.* 1854. [f. FAST *a.* + -ISH[1].] Somewhat fast.

Fa·stland. 1883. [f. FAST *a.* + LAND; after G. *festland.*] The mainland, as dist. from the islands; the continent.

Fastly (fɑ·stli), *adv. arch.* OE. [f. FAST *a.* + -LY[2]. Now repl. by FAST *adv.*] †**1.** = FAST *adv.* –1817. **2.** Rapidly; hence, readily. Now *rare.* ME.

Fastness (fɑ·stnės). [OE. *fæstnes*, f. FAST *a.* + -NESS; for the concr. use of *-ness* cf. *wilderness.*] **1.** The quality or state of being FAST, in various senses. †**2.** Of style: Conciseness, pithiness. ASCHAM. †**3.** That which fastens or keeps fast –1676. **4.** A place not easily forced; a stronghold OE.
4. They would rather tempt us to attempt them in their f. CROMWELL.

Fastuous (fæ·stiuˌəs), *a.* Now *rare.* 1638. [– late L. *fastuosus*, in cl.L. *fastosus*, f. *fastus* FAST *sb.*[4]; see -OUS, -UOUS.] Haughty, arrogant, pretentious, ostentatious. Hence †**Fastuo·sity,** f. quality. **Fa·stuous-ly** *adv.*, **-ness.**

†**Fat** (fæt), *sb.*[1] [obs. form of VAT.] **1.** A vessel; *esp.* a large vessel for liquids –1755. **3.** A cask or barrel to contain dry things –1812. **4.** A measure of capacity –1706.
1. In thy Fattes our Cares be drown'd SHAKS.

Fat (fæt), *a.* and *sb.*[2] [OE. *fǣt(t)* = OFris. *fatt, fett*, MDu., MLG. *vett* (Du. *vet*), OHG. *feizzit* (G. *feist*) :– WGmc. **faitiða*, pa. ppl. formation on Gmc. **faitjan* fatten, f. **faitaz* adj. fat.]
A. *adj.* **I. 1.** Of an animal used for food: Fatted, ready to kill. **2.** In well-fed condition, plump; well supplied with fat; in bad sense, corpulent, obese. Also *fig.* OE. **3.**

transf. Of things: Thick, full-bodied; *spec.* of printing types ME.

1. A feste of fatte bestes WYCLIF *Isa.* 25:6. 2. A f. baby 1864. So f. a man one rarely sees 1856. 3. *F. letter* is a letter with a broad stem 1841.

II. 1. Containing much fat; greasy, oily, unctuous OE. Of wood, etc.: Resinous (*U.S.*) 1831. Of coal: Bituminous 1883. **2.** Of mould, clay, etc.: Containing much plastic matter; sticky. Of limestone: Pure. 1502. **3.** Of fluids: Charged with solid or extraneous particles ME.

1. Cloid with F. Meate SHAKS. F. Amber DRYDEN. 2. A f. Earth full of Allom MOXON. 3. F. standing water 1587. A f. mist 1659. F. ale SCOTT.

III. 1. Yielding rich returns ME. **2.** Well supplied with what is needful or desirable 1563.

1. The broad f. fields of Kent 1851. A f. Lawsuit 1854. F. jobs 1883, livings 1895. 2. In a f. pasture *Ezek.* 34:14. A f. Cit 1764. Phr. *F. work* (Typog.), work especially paying to the compositor who works by the piece. *F. page*: one having many blanks. *A f. lot* (colloq.): a great deal (often *iron*)..

IV. Like a fat animal; slow-witted, inert, self-complacent 1588.

Make the heart of this people f. *Isa.* 6:10.

Comb.: **f.-bird,** (*a*) the Pectoral Sandpiper (*U.S.*); (*b*) the Guacharo; **-trained** (sense I. 2 or IV); **-headed** *a.*, having a f. head; dull, stupid; **-lute,** a mixture of pipeclay and linseed oil for filling joints.

Hence **Fa·tly** *adv.* †greasily; largely; clumsily. **Fa·ttish** *a.* somewhat f. †somewhat greasy.

B. *sb.*[2] **1.** The adj. used *absol.* The fat part of anything ME. **b.** *transf.* The richest part of anything. Hence, Plenty, superabundance. *Obs.* exc. in *The f. of the land.* 1570. **2. a.** The oily concrete substance of which the fat parts of animal bodies are chiefly composed. Often specialized as *beef-*, *mutton-*, etc. *f.* **b.** *Chem.* Any of a class of organic compounds of which animal fat is the type. 1539. **3.** Corpulence, obesity 1726. **4.** In various trades, etc., applied to especially paying kinds of work 1700.

4. *Fat* among printers means void spaces GROSE. A piece of 'fat' (that is, a good piece of exclusive news) 1890. Phr. (*All*) *the f. is in the fire*: in early use, the design has irremediably failed; now used when something has been said or done which is sure to provoke an explosion of anger.

Fat (fæt), *v.* [OE. *fǣttian*, f. *fǣt(t)* FAT *a.*] **†1.** *trans.* As tr. Heb. *diššen*: To anoint (the head); to load (an altar) with fat –1698. **2.** *intr.* To become fat. Also *fig.* ME. **3.** *trans.* To make fat, fatten; to fertilize (the soil) ME.

2. The hogs which have been fatting 1704. 3. Numbers of black cattle are fatted here GRAY. This..fatted the sheep 1829. Which with the ashes left after the burning fatteth the ground GAGE.

Fatal (fē̆ⁱ·tăl), *a.* ME. [– (O)Fr. *fatal* or L. *fatalis*, f. *fatum* FATE; see -AL[1].] **†1.** Allotted or decreed by fate; destined, fated –1713. **†2.** Doomed *to* –1668. **3.** Of the nature of fate; inevitable, necessary 1605. **4.** Concerned or dealing with destiny ME.; †prophetic –1635; †ominous –1658. **5.** Fateful ME **6.** Deadly, destructive, ruinous. Const. *to.* 1514. **7.** Hence, in a weakened sense: Disastrous, gravely mischievous 1681.

3. Nature is a blind and f. Agent 1663. 4. The Parcæ (or fatall Goddesses) are three 1624. The f. thread of life 1704. 5. The f. spot SCOTT. 6. A f. instrument GOLDSM., stroke COWPER, disease 1803, error H. SPENCER, accident 1895. 7. Wars had also a f. influence on population 1794. Hence **Fa·tally** *adv.*

Fatalism (fē̆ⁱ·tăliz'm). 1678. [f. prec. + -ISM, perh. – Fr. *fatalisme.*] **1.** The doctrine that all things are determined or arbitrarily decreed by fate. (In early use not distinguished from 'necessitarianism'.) **2.** Submission to the decree of fate 1734.

Fatalist (fē̆ⁱ·tălist). 1650. [f. as prec. + -IST, perh. – Fr. *fataliste.*] **1.** One who holds the doctrine of fatalism **2.** One whose conduct is regulated by fatalism 1734. **3.** *attrib.* or *adj.* = next 1843.

Fatalistic (fē̆ⁱtăli·stik), *a.* 1832. [f. prec. + -IC.] Of, pertaining to, or of the nature of fatalism.

Fatality (fĕtæ·lĭti). 1490. [– Fr. *fatalité* or late L. *fatalitas*, f. L. *fatalis*; see FATAL, -ITY.] **1.** The condition of being predetermined by or subject to fate or destiny; the agency of fate or necessity; also *fig.* 1631. **b.** That which a person or thing is fated to 1589. **2.** Predestined liability to disaster 1654. **3.** Fatalness; a fatal influence 1490. **4.** A calamity 1648; a disaster resulting in death 1840.

1. The blind impulses of F. and Fortune BENTLEY. 2. The f. attending an accursed house SYMONDS. 3. The insidious f. of hot countries KANE. 4. Fatalities to which the human race is liable 1815.

Fatalness (fē̆ⁱ·tălnės). 1651. [f. FATAL + -NESS.] **1.** 'Invincible necessity' (J. and mod. Dicts.). **2.** Disastrous nature; deadly quality.

‖**Fata Morgana** (fā·tă mǫɹgā·nă). 1818. [It. *fata* a fairy; *Morgana*, sister of the legendary Arthur, app. located in Calabria by Norman settlers.] A kind of mirage most frequently seen in the Strait of Messina, attributed formerly to fairy agency. Also *fig.*

attrib. Cloud mountains, and fatamorgana cities CARLYLE.

Fate (fē̆ⁱt), *sb.* ME. [orig. – It. *fato*, later – its source, L. *fatum* lit. 'that which has been spoken', pa. pple. neut. of *fari*. The L. sense was, primarily, a sentence of the gods (= Gr. θέσφατον); subseq., 'lot' or 'portion' (= Gr. μοῖρα), and hence as in sense 1. See also FAY. *sb.*[2]] **1.** The principle, power, or agency by which events are unalterably predetermined from eternity. Often *personified.* **2.** *Mythol.* **a.** The goddess of Fate; in Homer Μοῖρα. **b.** *pl.* In Gr. and Rom. mythol., the three goddesses, Clotho, Lachesis, and Atropos, supposed to determine the course of human life (Gr. Μοῖραι, L. *Parcæ*, *Fata*) 1590. **3.** That which is fated to happen; in *pl.* Predestined events 1667. **b.** An oracle. MRS. BROWNING. **4.** What will become of, or has become of (a person or thing); ultimate condition, destiny 1768. **b.** Death, destruction, ruin ME. **c.** An instrument of death or destruction (*poet.*) 1700.

1. F. was something that even the gods often endeavoured..to resist PRIESTLEY. 2. We three Sat muffled like the Fates TENNYSON. 3. What I will is F. So spake th' Almightie MILT. He deserves a better f. 1668. 4. Anxiety for the f. of the Edystone SMEATON. The f. of a minister who.. had thwarted the popular will FROUDE. Phr. *To decide, fix, seal one's f.* c. Hissing fly the feather'd fates POPE.

Fated (fē̆ⁱ·tėd), *ppl. a.* 1601. [f. prec. + -ED[2].] **1.** Appointed by fate 1715. **2.** Doomed to destruction 1817. **3.** Fateful. SHAKS. **4.** Guided or driven on by fate 1801. **¶5.** Of armour: Made proof by spells. DRYDEN.

2. Cavalry..were fast approaching the f. city MACAULAY.

Fateful (fē̆ⁱ·tfŭl), *a.* 1715. [f. as prec. + -FUL.] **1.** Prophetic of destiny. **2.** Fraught with destiny; decisive 1800. **3.** Controlled as if by fate 1876. **4.** = FATAL 6. 1764. **5.** Of eventful history 1886.

1. That f. Hebrew Prophecy CARLYLE. 2. Each minute seemed f. to her 1861. 4. The soldier's f. steel 1808. Hence **Fa·teful-ly** *adv.*, **-ness.**

Fat-faced, *a.* 1632. [f. FAT *a.* + FACE *sb.* + -ED[2].] Having a fat face; *spec.* in *Printing*, as *fat-faced Egyptian.*

Fat-head. 1842. [f. FAT *a.* + HEAD.] **1.** A stupid dolt. **2. a.** A labroid fish, *Semicossyphus* or *Pimelometopon pulcher.* **b.** The Blackheaded Minnow, *Pimephales promelas.*

Fat-hen (fæ·tˌheːn). 1795. A name for certain plants of the Goosefoot tribe, *Chenopodium bonus-henricus* and *Atriplex patula.*

Father (fā·ðəɹ), *sb.* [OE. *fæder* = OFris. *feder*, OS. *fadar* (Du. *vader*), OHG. *fater* (G. *vater*), ON. *faðir*, Goth. *fadar* :– Gmc. **fađēr* :– IE. **pətḗr*, repr. also by L. *pater*, Gr. πατήρ, Skr. *pitar-*. For the change of d to ð cf. *brother*, *mother*, *gather*, *hither*, *together*, *whether.*] **1.** One who has begotten a child, a male parent, the nearest male ancestor. Also *fig.* and *transf.* **2.** A male ancestor more remote than a parent, *esp.* the founder of a race or family, a progenitor. In *pl.* ancestors. Also loosely for 'a man of old', 'a patriarch'. OE. **3.** One who institutes, originates, calls into being; a designer, framer, originator. Also, the first or a distinguished example of (an immaterial thing). ME. **4.** One who performs the offices of a father by protecting care, etc.; one to whom filial reverence and obedience are due OE. **5. a.** Applied to God, expressing His relation to Jesus, to mankind in general, or to Christians (as His children by regeneration or adoption) OE. **b.** Theol. *The F.*; the First Person of the Trinity OE. **6.** *Eccles.* **a.** A confessor or spiritual director ME. **b.** A priest; a superior of a monastic house 1571. **c.** Applied to bishops 1508. **d.** *The Holy F.*: the Pope ME. **e.** Prefixed to the name of a priest. Also abbrev. (chiefly in R.C. use) F., Fr. 1529. **7.** A respectful title given to an old man; also in personifications, as *F. Christmas*, *F. Thames*, *F. Time* (cf. TIME *sb.* III. 2) 1559. **8.** The oldest member of a society, etc. 1705; the leading individual of a number 1600. **9.** *pl.* The leading men or elders of a city or an assembly 1590.

1. His Fathers own Son 1670. *fig.* Thy wish was F. (Harry) to that thought 2 *Hen. IV*, I. i. 8. The child is f. of the man WORDSW. 2. One man alone, the f. of us all, Drew not his life from woman COWPER. Phr. *To be gathered to* or *sleep with one's fathers.* 3. Abraham the f. of fayth EDEN. The F. of Lies himself (cf. *John* 8:44) 1826. Plato as the f. of Idealism JOWETT. Phr. *F. of Lights*, etc.: God. *The Fathers* (*of the Church*): the early Christian writers. *The Fathers* (U.S.): the framers of the constitution. 4. A F. of the Common-weale 1 *Hen. VI*, III. i. 98. I will be a f. to thee MASSINGER. 6. a. Penance, f., will I none SCOTT. b. A F. of a Convent ADDISON. 7. In vain on f. Thames she calls for aid POPE. 8. The F. of the City HEARNE. The F. of Waters JOHNSON. 9. The fathers of the council GIBBON.

Comb.: **f.-dust** = POLLEN; **-general,** the chief of the Society of Jesus; †**-queller,** a parricide.

Father (fā·ðəɹ), *v.* ME. [f. prec. sb.] **1.** *trans.* To be or become the father of; to beget. Also *fig.* 1483. **2.** To appear or acknowledge oneself as the father (or, hence, as the author) of; to adopt, take the responsibility of ME. **3.** To act as a father to, look after 1577. **4.** To provide with a father; to fix the paternity of *on* or *upon.* Also *fig.* 1542.

1. Cowards f. Cowards, & Base things Syre Bace SHAKS. *fig.* Shall Error..still f. Truth TENNYSON. 2. Men of wit, Who often father'd what he writ SWIFT. 4. The Lady fathers her selfe SHAKS. *fig.* This saiying..is fathered on Socrates UDALL.

Phr. *To f.* (a thing) *upon* (something else): to trace to (something) as a source or origin.

Fatherhood (fā·ðəɹˌhud); also †**-head.** ME. [f. FATHER *sb.* + -HOOD, -HEAD.] **1.** The relation of a father to a child; paternity. Also *fig.* **†2.** Authority of or as of a father –1690. **†3.** The personality of a father, as a form of address –1682.

Father-in-law (fā·ðərinlǭ). ME. [After AFr. *en ley*, OFr. *en loi* (*de mariage*) 'in law (of marriage)'.] **1.** The father of one's husband or wife. **2.** = STEPFATHER. (A misuse.) 1552. **3.** as *vb.* FIELDING.

1. Gerard..called to hym his father in law, his wyfes f. LD. BERNERS.

†**Fa·therkin.** [OE. *fæder cyn*, f. *fæder* genitive + *cyn* KIN.] Descent by the father's side –1556.

Fatherland (fā·ðəɹlæ̆nd). 1623. [f. FATHER *sb.* + LAND.] **1.** The land of one's birth. **2.** The land of one's fathers; mother-country 1822.

1. *The F.*: now usually = Germany.

Fa·ther-la·sher. 1674. The name of two species of sea-fish, *Cottus bubalis* and *scorpius.*

Fatherless (fā·ðəɹlės), *a.* ME. [See -LESS.] **1.** Having no father. **2.** Of a book, etc.: Without a known author 1611.

1. A father of the f. *Ps.* 68:5. 2. F. essays 1803.

Fatherlike (fā·ðəɹləik). ME. [See -LIKE.] **A.** *adj.* **1.** †Like one's father –1614. **2.** Like a father; fatherly 1570. **B.** *adv.* In a fatherly manner, as a father 1604.

Father-long-legs. 1796. = *DADDY-LONG-LEGS.

Fatherly (fā·ðəɹli), *a.* [OE. *fæderlić*, f. *fæder* father + *-lić*; see -LY[1].] **†1.** Paternal –1633; ancestral; also, venerable –1634. **2.** Resembling a father 1577. **3.** Such as is proper in or from a father ME.

3. With my fatherlie blessing JAS. I. Hence **Fatherliness.** So **Fa·therly** *adv.* in a f. manner.

Fathership (fā·ðəɹʃip). 1583. [See -SHIP.] The position of a father; paternity, fatherhood.

Fathom (fæ·ðəm), *sb.* [OE. *fæþm*, corresp. to OFris. *fethem*, OS. *faðmos* pl. two arms outstretched (Du. *vadem, vaam* 6 feet), OHG. *fadum* cubit (G. *faden* 6 feet), ON. *faðmr* embrace, bosom :– Gmc. **faþmaz*, f. base **faþ-*.] †**1.** In *pl.* The embracing arms (OE. only); †*fig.* grasp, power –1622. **2.** †**a.** A stretching of the arms in a straight line to their full length –1785. **b.** *fig.* Breadth of comprehension, grasp; ability (*arch.*) 1604. **3.** A measure of length: †**a.** A CUBIT –ME.; **b.** The length of the outstretched arms; hence, 6 feet; now chiefly used in taking soundings OE. **4.** In *Mining*, 6 feet square by the whole thickness of the vein 1778. **5.** A quantity of wood 6 ft. square in section 1577.

2. b. Another of his Fadome, they haue none *Oth.* I. i. 153. **3. b.** Full fadom fiue thy Father lies SHAKS.

Fathom (fæ·ðəm), *v.* [OE. *fæþmian*, f. *fæþm* FATHOM *sb.*] **1.** *trans.* To encircle (and, hence, to measure) with extended arms. Also *transf.* and *fig.* ME. **2.** To measure with a fathom-line; to sound; also *fig.* 1613. **b.** To get to the bottom of, thoroughly understand 1625. **3.** *intr.* To take soundings (*lit.* and *fig.*) 1607.

1. Stocks of Vines..as big in bulk as two men can f. HEYLIN. *fig.* Cæsar..in his arms Fathoming the earth MASSINGER. **2.** *fig.* O God, who can fadome thy eternity 1642. **b.** [His] character I am..unable to f. MME. D'ARBLAY.

Hence **Fa·thomable** *a.* **Fa·thomer,** one who fathoms; an instrument for taking soundings.

Fathomless (fæ·ðəmlės), *a.* 1606. [f. prec. + -LESS.] **1.** That cannot be measured or fathomed. **2.** *fig.* That cannot be penetrated; incomprehensible 1645.

1. F. and unquiet deeps MILT. **2.** The f. mystery of the universe 1883. Hence **Fa·thomlessly** *adv.*

Fatidic, -al (feⁱti·dik, -ăl), *a.* 1607. [– L. *fatidicus*, f. *fatum* FATE + *-dicus*, f. weak var. of base of *dīcere* say; see -IC, -ICAL.] Of or concerned with predicting fates; gifted with the power of prophecy; prophetic.

The Ancients write of some Trees, that they are Fatidical HOWELL. Hence **Fati·dically** *adv.*

Fa·tigable, Fati·guable, *a.* 1608. [– OFr. *fatigable* – late L. *fatigabilis*, f. L. *fatigare*; see FATIGUE *v.*, -ABLE.] Capable of being fatigued; easily tired. Hence **Fa·tigableness, Fati·guableness.**

†**Fa·tigate,** *pa. pple.* 1471. [– L. *fatigatus*, pa. pple. of *fatigare* FATIGUE *v.*; see -ATE².] Fatigued –1607.

His doubled spirit Requickened what in flesh was f. *Cor.* II. ii. 121.

†**Fa·tigate,** *v.* 1535. [– *fatigat-*, pa. ppl. stem of L. *fatigare* FATIGUE *v.*; see -ATE³.] Hence **Fatiga·tion,** the action of fatiguing; weariness.

Fatigue (fătī·g), *sb.* 1669. [– Fr. *fatigue*, f. (O)Fr. *fatiguer*; see next.] **1.** Weariness resulting from bodily or mental exertion 1719. **2.** *transf.* The condition of weakness in metals caused by repeated blows or continued strain 1854. **3.** That which causes weariness; labour, toil 1669. **4.** The extra-professional duties of a soldier 1776. **b.** Short for *f.-party* 1876.

1. Extremities of famine and f. PRESCOTT. **3.** The fatigues of the election are over BURKE.

Comb.: **f.-call,** the call to f.-duty; **-dress,** the dress worn on f.-duty; **-duty** = FATIGUE *sb.* 4; **-party,** a party of soldiers on f.-duty.

Hence **Fati·gueless** *a.* **Fati·guesome** *a.* wearisome.

Fatigue (fătī·g), *v.* 1693. [– (O)Fr. *fatiguer* – L. *fatigare* exhaust as with riding or working, weary, harass, f. **fatis* in *ad fatim, affatim* to satiety, prop. 'to bursting' (cf. *fatiscare, -ari* burst open, gape open).] **1.** *trans.* 'To tire, weary; to harass with toil; to exhaust with labour' (J.). **2.** To weaken by straining 1794.

Fatiloquent (feⁱti·lŏkwĕnt), *a.* 1656. [f. L. *fatiloquus*, f. *fati-*, comb. form of *fatum* FATE + *-loquus*, f. *loqui* speak, after *eloquent*, etc.] Declaring fate; prophetic. So †**Fati·loquency** (*rare*). †**Fati·loquist,** a fortune-teller.

Fatiscent (făti·sĕnt), *a.* 1807. [– *fatiscent-*, pres. ppl. stem of L. *fatiscere* yawn; see -ENT.] Having chinks or clefts; cracked. Hence **Fati·scence** (*Geol.*), the condition of being f.

Fatling (fæ·tliŋ), *sb.* 1526. [f. FAT *v.* + -LING¹; cf. *nursling.*] A calf, lamb, or other young animal fatted for slaughter.

Fatling (fæ·tliŋ), *a.* [dim. of FAT *a.*, after prec.; see -LING¹.] Small and fat. TENNYSON.

Fatness (fæ·tnės). OE. [f. as prec. + -NESS.] **1.** The quality or state of being fat; fullness of flesh, corpulence. †Of a tree: Oiliness, juiciness. Of soil: Unctuous nature; hence fertility. †**2.** That which makes fertile –1738. †**3.** *concr.* Fat –1697. †**4.** The richest or best part of anything –1665.

1. God giue thee the dew of heauen, and the fatnesse of the earth *Gen.* 27:28. **2.** Thy paths drop fatnesse *Ps.* 65:11. **4.** Cities, which..devoured the f. of the whole Kingdom 1644.

Fatted (fæ·tėd), *ppl. a. arch.* 1552. [pa. pple. of FAT *v.*] Made or grown fat, fattened. Now only in *to kill the f. calf*, after Luke 25.

Fatten (fæ·t'n), *v.* 1552. [f. FAT *a.* + -EN⁵.] **1.** *trans.* To make fat or plump; usually, to make fit to kill. Also *transf.* and *fig.* **2.** *intr.* To become fat; also *fig.* 1638. **3.** *trans.* To enrich (the soil); to fertilize. Also *transf.* and *fig.* 1563.

1. To f. turkeys..give them mashed potatoes [etc.] SOYER. **2.** *fig.* Persons, who f. on the calamities of their country HUME. **3.** The river Nilus, whose overflowings doe marveylously f. the earth FULKE. Hence **Fa·ttener,** one who or that which fattens.

Fattrels (fæ·trėlz), *sb. pl. Sc.* [– Fr. †*fatraille* trash (COTGR.).] Ribbon-ends. BURNS.

Fatty (fæ·ti), *a.* ME. [f. FAT + -Y¹.] **1.** Resembling, or of the nature of, fat, oleaginous, greasy. **2.** Consisting of or containing fat 1615. **3.** Marked by morbid deposition of fat 1866.

1. F. ink 1879. **2.** A *F. tumour* is a mass of soft yellow fat, generally enclosed in a..thin fibrous capsule *Syd. Soc. Lex.* **3.** *F. degeneration*, that condition in which a part or the whole of any tissue or organ is replaced by fat *Syd. Soc. Lex.* *F. heart* or *kidney* = f. degeneration of the heart or kidney.

Phrases. *F. oil* = fixed oil. *F. acids*, a group of acids extracted from fats and fixed oils in saponification. *F. acid series* = *acetic series of acids*.

Hence **Fa·ttily** *adv.*, only in *fattily-degenerated*. **Fa·ttiness,** f. condition or quality.

†**Fa·tuate,** *ppl. a.* [– late L. *fatuatus*, pa. pple. of *fatuari*, f. *fatuus*; see FATUOUS, -ATE².] Rendered fatuous. B. JONS.

Fatuitous (fătiū·itəs), *a.* 1734. [f. next + -OUS.] Characterized by fatuity.

Fatuity (fătiū·ĭti). 1538. [– Fr. *fatuité* or L. *fatuitas*, f. *fatuus*; see -ITY.] **1.** Folly. Now chiefly: Idiotic folly; mental blindness caused by infatuation. Also, that which is fatuous. **2.** Idiocy, dementia. Now *rare*. 1621.

1. O strange f. of youth THACKERAY. var. **Fa·tuism** (in sense 2).

Fatuous (fæ·tiuəs), *a.* 1608. [f. L. *fatuus* foolish, silly, insipid + -OUS.] **1.** Foolish, vacantly silly, stupid, besotted 1633. **2.** That is imbecile; idiotic. Now *rare* exc. in *Sc. Law*. 1773. †**3.** In L. sense: Insipid, vapid –1624.

1. F. commonplaces MORLEY, disregard for intellect 1878. Phr. *F. fire* = IGNIS FATUUS. So *f. light, vapour*, etc. Hence **Fa·tuous-ly** *adv.*, **-ness.**

Fat-witted, *a.* 1596. [f. FAT *a.* + WIT + -ED².] Dull, slow, thick-headed.

Faubourg (fōbur). [Late ME. *fabo(u)r, faubourgh* – Fr. *faubourg*, †*faulbourg*, †*fauxbourg* (XV), the earlier existence of which is vouched for by med.L. *falsus burgus* (XIV) 'false city', i.e. not the city proper.] A portion of a town or city lying outside the gates; a suburb. (In Paris still applied to parts of the city now included within the walls.)

Faucal (fǭ·kăl). 1864. [f. next + -AL¹.]

A. *adj.* Of or pertaining to the fauces or throat. Applied chiefly to certain deep guttural sounds, *esp.* in the Semitic languages.

B. *sb.* A faucal sound 1883.

‖**Fauces** (fǭ·sīz), *sb. pl.* 1541. [L., = throat.] **1.** *Anat.* The cavity at the back of the mouth, from which the larynx and the pharynx open out. **2.** *Bot.* The throat of a calyx, corolla, etc. 1840. **3.** *Conch.* That portion of the chamber of a shell which can be seen from the aperture.

Hence **Fau·cial** *a.* of, pertaining to, or proceeding from, the f.

Faucet (fǭ·sėt), *sb.*¹ ME. [– (O)Fr. *fausset* – Pr. *falset*, f. *falsar* bore (= (O)Fr. *fausser* damage, break into).] †**1.** A peg or spigot to stop the vent-hole in a cask or in a tap; a vent-peg –1741. **2.** A tap for drawing liquor from a barrel, etc. Now *dial.* and *U.S.* ME. †**b.** A tapster. B. JONS. **3.** *U.S.* 'The enlarged end of a pipe to receive the spigot end of the next section' (Knight).

†**Fau·cet, Fau·set,** *sb.*² 1684. [Corrupt f. FACET.] = FACET. Also used of a faceted stone. –1712.

Faucitis (fǭsəi·tis). 1875. [f. FAUCES + -ITIS.] *Path.* Inflammation of the fauces.

†**Fau·fel(l.** 1594. [– Arab. *fawfal, fūfal.*] = ARECA –1693.

Faugh (fǭ), *interj.* 1542. An exclam. of abhorrence or disgust.

Fough, he smells all lamp-oyle B. JONS.

Fauld, Sc. and dial. var. of FOLD.

Fauld (fǭld). 1874. [perh. = prec.] *Min.* 'The tymp-arch or working arch of a furnace' (Knight).

Fault (fǭlt, fǫlt), *sb.* [ME. *faut(e* – (O)Fr. *faute* and *faut* :– Rom. **fallita*, **fallitum*, subst. use of fem. and n. of **fallitus*, pa. pple. of L. *fallere* FAIL *v.* The sp. with *l*, following Fr. †*faulte* (XIV), finally influenced the pronunc., but the orig. pronunc. (fǭt) survives in many dialects.] †**1.** Deficiency, want *of* (something specified). Also *absol.* –1591. †**2.** Default, failing, neglect –1587. **3.** A defect, imperfection. (In *Morals*, something less serious than a *vice*.) ME. †**4.** A flaw, crack; *Mil.* a gap in the ranks –1698. **5.** Something wrongly done: **a.** A misdeed, transgression, offence ME.: **b.** A slip, error, mistake 1523. **6.** *spec.* in *Tennis* and *Rackets*. A stroke which fails to make the ball fall within the prescribed limits 1599. **7.** Responsibility for an untoward occurrence; also, the defect in things, conditions, etc., to which such an occurrence is attributable ME. **8.** *Hunting*. Loss of scent; a check caused by this 1592. **b.** *fig.* *At f.*: at a loss 1833. **9.** *Geol.*, etc. A break in continuity of the strata or vein. In coal-seams, coal rendered worthless by its condition in the seams, as *slate-f., dirt-f.*, etc. 1881. **10.** *Telegr.* An imperfect insulation; a leakage 1863.

2. Phr. *Without f.*, (= Fr. *sans faute*): without fail. **3.** Great men too often have greater faults than little men can find room for LANDOR. An essential f. of the Pythagorean theory 1884. Phr. *To a f.* (qualifying an adj.): so much so that it becomes a f.; excessively. *With all faults* (occas. abbrev. 'A.F.'): with all defects, *i.e.* the seller will not make them good. **4.** *John* IV. ii. 33. **5. a.** The f. of telling a lie JOWETT. **b.** A f. in the deduction WATTS. **7.** Lay the f. on me DE FOE. Phr. *To be in f.*: to be to blame. Voiceless through the f. of birth TENNYSON. **8.** Bad hounds never *hit off a f.* (= recover a lost scent) themselves FIELDING. The wisest antiquarians were at f. 1886.

Phrases. *To find (a) f.*: to discover or perceive a f. (senses 3–5) *in* a person or thing. Hence, idiomatically, *To find f.* (*with*, †*at*): to express dissatisfaction (with), censure.

Comb.: **f.-finder** *sb.*; **f.-reader,** one who can trace the correspondence of strata interrupted by a f.; **-rock, -stuff,** the fragmentary rock, formed into a belt or wall-like mass, which marks the line of fracture; **-slip,** the smooth surface of the fractured rocks in some types of faults.

Fault (fǭlt, fǫlt), *v.* ME. [f. prec. sb.; cf. OFr. *faulter*, which may be the source in the older senses.] †**1.** *intr.* To be wanting or absent –1525. †**2.** To be lacking *in* –1606. †**3.** *trans.* To stand in need of –1475. †**4.** *intr.* To come short of a standard; to make default, fail –1677. **5.** *intr.* To do or go wrong; hence, sometimes, to sin. *Obs.* exc. *arch.* ME. †**6.** To make a mistake, err, blunder –1765. **7.** *trans.* To find fault with, to blame or censure (*rare*) 1559; to impugn or mark as faulty (*rare*) 1585. **8.** *Hunting*. To put (a hound) at fault; to throw off the scent (*rare*) 1873. **9.** *Geol.*, etc. To cause a fault in, dislocate (chiefly *pass.*) 1849.

2. He faulted in common civilitie P. HOLLAND. **5.** Had I died for thee I had faulted more BROWNING. **9.** Phr. *To f. down* or *through*: to cause a fault by driving (part of a stratum) *through* (another).

†**Fau·lter.** 1535. [f. prec. + -ER¹.] One who commits a fault –1840.

Faultful (fǭ·lt-, fǫ·ltful), *a.* 1591. [f. FAULT *sb.* + -FUL.] Faulty, culpable. Hence **Fau·ltfully** *adv.*

Faulting (fǭ·lt-, fǫ·ltiŋ), *vbl. sb.* 1450. [f. FAULT *v.* + -ING¹.] †**1.** The action of FAULT *v.*

–1679. **2.** *Geol.* Dislocation of strata; an instance of this 1849.

Faultless (fǭ·lt-, fǫ·ltlės), *a.* ME. [f. FAULT *sb.* + -LESS.] **1.** Without defect. **2.** That has committed no fault 1513; *transf.* not caused by any fault –1752.

1. A f. piece POPE. The f. model of a rule FREEMAN. **2.** For our sinnes he faultlesse suffered paine FAIRFAX. **b.** *F. pardon*, a pardon for an alleged offence never committed. Hence **Fau·ltless-ly** *adv.*, **-ness.**

Faulty (fǭ·lti, fǫ·lti), *a.* ME. [f. as prec. + -Y¹; partly after Fr. *fautif.*] **1.** Containing faults; defective, imperfect, unsound. **2.** Of persons, etc.: Having imperfections; apt to come short of duty 1574. †**3.** That has committed a fault; also, that is in fault or to blame –1614. **4.** Of the nature of a fault; censurable 1548.

1. He [the colt] came of a f. Mare DRYDEN. A f. digestion BP. BERKELEY. **2.** F. morals RICHARDSON. **4.** A f. habit of mind GOULBURN.

Hence **Fau·ltily** *adv.*, **Fau·ltiness.**

Faun (fǭn). ME. [– (O)Fr. *faune* or L. *Faunus* god or demigod worshipped by shepherds and farmers and identified with Gr. *Πάν* (see PAN *sb.*²).] *Myth.* One of a class of rural deities; represented as men with horns and the tail of a goat, and, later, with goats' legs, and lustful, like the Satyrs.

The reeling F., the sensual feast TENNYSON.

Fauna (fǭ·nă). Pl. **-æ**; also **-as.** 1771. [mod.L. application of the proper name *Fauna* of a rural goddess, sister of *Faunus* (see prec.). Cf. FLORA.] **1.** A collective name for the animals or animal life of any particular region or epoch. **2.** A treatise upon these animals 1885.

1. The f. of tropical America 1846. The carboniferous f. 1851. Hence **Fau·nal** *a.* of or pertaining to the f. of a country. **Fau·nist,** one who studies or treats of the f. of a district. **Fauni·stic, -al** *a.* of or pertaining to a faunist; hence, relating to a f. **Fauno·logy,** that branch of zoology which treats of the geographical distribution of animals; hence, **Faunolo·gical** *a.*

Faurd, Sc. pronunc. of *favoured*, as in *well-f.*

Fause, Sc. and dial. f. FALSE *a.*

Fau·se-house. *Sc.* [f. prec. + HOUSE.] A hollow made in a corn-stack, with an opening on the most windy side, for the purpose of drying the corn. BURNS.

Fau·sen. 1547. [Of unkn. origin.] A kind of eel; variously applied. Now *dial.*

Faussebraie, -braye (fos₁brę̄). 1489. [– Fr. *fausse-braie*, f. *fausse*, fem. of *faux* false + *braie* BRAYE.] *Fortif.* An artificial mound or wall thrown up in front of the main rampart. In early use, a covered way.

Fauterer (fǭ·tərəɹ). 1662. [Extended f. *fauter* for FAUTOR, as e.g. *caterer*; see -ER¹.] = FAUTOR.

‖**Fauteuil** (fōtö̆y). 1744. [Fr. :– OFr. *faudestuel, faldestoel*; see FALDSTOOL.] An armchair. **b.** pop. (fōᵘ·til). A seat in a theatre, omnibus, etc. designed to resemble an armchair 1901.

Fautor (fǭ·tǒɹ, -əɹ). [ME. *fautour* – (O)Fr. *fauteur* – L. *fautor*, f. *favēre* FAVOUR *v.*; see -OUR, -OR 2.] **1.** A partisan, abettor. †**2.** A patron –1691.

1. Apologists and fautors of tyranny AUSTIN. So †**Fau·tress,** †**Fau·trix,** a female f.

‖**Fauvette** (fove·t). 1797. [Fr., f. *fauve* fallow.] A warbler, *esp.* the garden warbler.

‖**Faux** (fǭks). *rare.* 1828. [Assumed nom. sing. to L. *fauces.*] = FAUCES.

‖**Faux pas** (fo₁pā). 1676. [Fr. *faux* false + *pas* step.] A false step (*fig.*); a slip, a trip; *esp.* a woman's lapse from virtue.

†**Fava·ginous,** *a.* 1658. [irreg. f. L. *favus* honey-comb, after *fabaginus, oleaginus.*] Resembling a honeycomb –1686.

†**Fa·vel.** ME. [– OFr. *fauvel*, f. *fauve* fallow-coloured; see -EL².]

A. *adj.* Of a horse: = FALLOW *a.*¹ 1489.

B. *sb.* **1.** As the proper name of a horse. Only ME. **2.** The fallow horse proverbial as the type of cunning or duplicity. Only in *To curry F.*: see CURRY *v.* **3.** Hence, a personification of duplicity –1576.

‖**Favella** (fǎve·lǎ). *Pl.* **-æ.** 1857. [mod.L.; prob. an incorrect dim. of L. *faba* bean, infl. by Fr. *fève.*] *Bot.* See quot.

F., a form of the conceptacular fruit of florideous Algæ in which the spores are collected into spherical masses which lie on the outer surface of the frond *Syd. Soc. Lex.* Hence **Favelli·dium,** a compound f.

Faveolate (fǎvī·oleⁱt), *a.* 1866. [f. mod.L. *faveolus* (cf. Fr. *favéole*), dim. of L. *favus* honeycomb + -ATE². Cf. Fr. *favéolé.*] Honeycombed, cellular.

Faverel (fæ·vĕrĕl). 1597. [var. of next.] **a.** An onion. **b.** Whitlow-grass 1770. **c.** *Veronica anagallis* 1884.

†**Faverole.** ME. [– OFr. *faverole* (mod. *fèverole* horse-bean, w. assim. to *fève*), dim. of *fève* bean.] A name of various plants; esp. Water Dragons.

†**Faviform** (fēⁱ·vifǭɹm), *a.* 1753. [f. L. *favus* honeycomb + -FORM.] Formed like a honeycomb; *spec.* in *Surg.* of certain ulcers.

Favillous (fǎvi·ləs), *a.* [f. L. *favilla* hot ashes + -OUS. Cf. med.L. *favillosus.*] Consisting of or resembling ashes. SIR T. BROWNE.

Favonian (fǎvōᵘ·niǎn), *a.* 1656. [– L. *favonianus*, f. *Favonius* the west wind; see -IAN.] Of or pertaining to the west wind; hence, gentle, propitious.

Favosites (fævosəi·tīz). Also in Eng. form **fa·vosite.** 1832. [mod.L. (Lamarck), f. L. *favus* honeycomb + *-osus* -OSE¹ + *-ites* -ITE¹ 2 a.] *Geol.* A genus of fossil zoophytes, resembling a honeycomb.

Favour, favor (fēⁱ·vəɹ), *sb.* ME. [– OFr. *favour, -or* (mod. *faveur*) – L. *favor, -ōr-*, f. *favēre* regard with goodwill, rel. to *fovēre* cherish.] **1.** Propitious or friendly regard, goodwill, *esp.* on the part of a superior or a multitude; approving disposition towards a thing 1827. †**b.** The object of favour –1667. **2.** Exceptional kindness; an instance of this ME. **b.** *Comm.*, etc. Communication, letter 1645. **3.** Kind indulgence: **a.** Leave, permission, pardon 1580; †**b.** 'Lenity, mitigation of punishment' (J.); a lenient act –1780; †**c.** An indulgence, privilege –1737. **4.** Partiality, bias ME. **5.** Aid, support, furtherance ME. **6.** (*concr.* of 1.) Something given as a mark of favour; *esp.* a knot of ribbons, a glove, a ribbon, cockade, etc. 1588. **7.** That which wins goodwill; attractiveness, comeliness; an attraction, charm. *Obs.* exc. *arch.* ME. **8.** Appearance, aspect, look (now *arch.* or *dial.*) 1450; countenance, face (now *arch.*) 1525; †a feature –1655.

1. Is he inconstant, sir, in his fauours *Twel. N.* I. iv. 7. To look with f. on an enterprise 1884. Phr. *To curry f.*: corruption of *to curry Favel*; see CURRY *v.*¹ and FAVEL *sb.* **b.** Man, His chief delight and f. MILT. *P. L.* III. 664. **2.** I have a friend..who will..do me so much f. SCOTT. I came to ask a f. of you TENNYSON. **b.** Your favor of June the 14th T. JEFFERSON. **3. a.** Phr. *By, with* (your, etc.) *f.* Under f., I say it's an Anapæst BENTLEY. **4.** Withoute fauour iuge the trouthe LYDG. Phr. *Challenge to the f.* (Law): see CHALLENGE *sb.* **5.** Under favor of the night, to surprise the Bellerophon 1854. **6.** This f. shalt thou wear *L. L. L.* v. ii. 130. A f. of blue, green, and white ribbons 1859. **7.** Thine eye desireth fauour and beautie *Ecclus.* 40:22. **8.** In thy Face, one F. from the rest I singled forth DRAYTON.

Phr. **In f. of** (= Fr. *en faveur de*), used as a prep. with senses: **a.** On the side of; **b.** To the advantage of; in *Comm.* so as to be payable to; **c.** Out of a preference for.

Hence †**Fa·vourize** *v.* = next. †**Fa·vourless** *a.* without bias or beauty. †**Fa·vourous** *a.* obliging, pleasing. †**Fa·voursome** *a.* acceptable.

Favour, favor (fēⁱ·vəɹ), *v.* ME. [– OFr. *favorer* – med.L. *favorare*, f. L. *favor*; see prec.] **1.** *trans.* To regard with favour or kindness; to approve. **2.** To countenance, encourage; to oblige (a person) *with* something ME. **3.** To treat with partiality; also, to side with ME.; in *Comm.* to be at prices favourable to 1890. **4.** To aid, support; to point in the direction of 1526. **5.** To prove advantageous to; to facilitate 1634. **6.** To deal gently with; to ease, save, spare. Now *colloq.* and *dial.* 1526. **7.** To resemble in features. Now *colloq.* 1609.

1. Men fauour Wonders BACON. **2.** To f. a deceit BUTLER. **3.** Oats favoured buyers 1890. **4.** If Providence should..f. the allied arms BURKE. To f. a Suspicion STEELE. **5.** The Wind favours them 1699. **6.** Walking in the dark, in the garden, to f. my eyes PEPYS. **7.** He favours you in the face 1690.

Hence **Fa·vourer,** one who favours. †**Fa·vouress** (*rare*). **Fa·vouringly** *adv.*

Favourable, favorable (fēⁱ·vŏrǎb'l), *a.* ME. [– (O)Fr. *favorable* – L. *favorabilis*, f. *favor*; see FAVOUR *sb.*, -ABLE.] †**1.** Winning favour; hence, pleasing, comely –1590. **2.** Well-disposed, propitious ME.; gracious (now *arch.*) 1502. †**3.** Partial –1460. **4.** Approving, commendatory 1655; †palliative –1772. **5.** Of an answer, etc.: That concedes what is desired. Of appearances: Promising. 1734. **6.** Facilitating one's purpose or wishes 1460.

2. Bee fauourable to thy people 1548. **4.** Giving a f. account of the place DE FOE. F. circumstances..may justify a doubt [etc.] 'JUNIUS'. **5.** A f. oracle GIBBON, aspect SCOTT. **6.** A f. breeze 1774.

Hence **Fa·vourableness. Fa·vourably, fa·vorably** *adv.*

Favoured (fēⁱ·vəɹd), *ppl. a.*¹ 1725. [f. FAVOUR *v.* + -ED¹.] In senses of the vb.

Most f. nation: that to which the greatest privileges are granted by the terms of a treaty.

Favoured (fēⁱ·vəɹd), *ppl. a.*² [f. FAVOUR *sb.* + -ED².] **1.** Having an appearance or features of a specified kind; as, *evil-, hard-, ill-, well-*, etc. *f.* **2.** Provided with rosettes, or the like. Only in *comb.* 1850. Hence **Fa·voured-ly** *adv.*, **-ness.**

Favourite, favorite. 1583. [– Fr. †*favorit* (mod. *favori*, fem. *-ite*) – It. *favorito*, pa. pple. of *favorire*, f. *favore* FAVOUR *v.*]

A. *sb.* **1.** A person or thing regarded with peculiar favour, one preferred above others 1583; in *Racing*, etc. the competitor or competing animal 'fancied', as being most likely to win 1813. **2.** One who stands unduly high in the favour of a prince, etc. 1599. **3.** A curl or lock of hair hanging loose upon the temple: worn in the 17th and 18th centuries. [Cf. F. *favoris* whiskers.] 1690. †**4.** = FAVOURER –1591.

1. This new Favorite Of Heav'n, this Man of Clay MILT. *P. L.* IX. 175. **2.** Like fauourites, Made proud by Princes *Much Ado* III. i. 9.

B. *adj.* Regarded with especial favour, liking, or preference 1711.

[Fortune's] spoiled and favorite child BYRON.

Phr. *Favorite son* (U.S.): a politician admired in his own State, but little regarded beyond it.

Favouritism (fēⁱ·vŏritiz'm). 1763. [f. prec. + -ISM.] **1.** A disposition to show, or the practice of showing, undue partially to an individual or class. **2.** The condition of being a favourite; favour 1808.

1. We conduct war upon the principles of f. BURKE.

‖**Favus** (fēⁱ·vŏs). 1706. [L., = honeycomb.] *Path.* A contagious disease of the skin, characterized by pustules, so called as resembling a honeycomb. Also *attrib.* Hence **Fa·vous** *a.* resembling a honeycomb, or this disease.

Fawe(n, -er, obs. ff. FAIN, FAVOUR.

Fawkener(e, obs. f. FALCONER.

Fawn (fǭn), *sb.*¹ ME. [– (O)Fr. *faon*, †*foun*, †*feon* :– Rom. **feto*, **fetōn-*, f. *fetus* offspring, FŒTUS. For sp. and pronunc. cf. LAWN *sb.*¹] †**1.** A young animal, cub –1603. **2.** A young fallow deer, a buck or doe of the first year ME. **3.** Short for *f.-colour* 1892.

1. The Fawne [of a seal] at the first is white 1603. *Comb.* **f.-colour,** a light yellowish brown (hence *f.-coloured* adj.).

†**Fawn,** *sb.*² 1590. [f. FAWN *v.*¹] An act of fawning; a servile cringe, a wheedling courtesy –1744.

Fawn (fǭn), *v.* [ME. *vawene, fau(h)ne*, repr. OE. *fagnian*; var. of *fæġnian* rejoice, f. *fæġen*, also *fagen* FAIN *a.*] **1.** *intr.* To show delight or fondness (by wagging the tail, whining, etc.) as a dog does. Often with *on, upon.* **2.** To affect a servile fondness ME.

1. He can both fawne like a Spaniell, and bite like a Mastiue DEKKER. A puppy fawns upon its dam 1776. **2.** How the knave fawned when I was of service to him LAMB. Hence **Faw·ner,** a toady. **Faw·ning-ly** *adv.*, **-ness.**

†**Fax,** *sb.* [OE. *feax* = OFris. *fax*, OS., OHG. *fahs*, ON. (and mod. Norw.) *fax*. The word occurs in the proper names *Fairfax, Halifax.*] The hair of the head –1606. Hence †**Faxed** *a.* having hair, as *f. star*, a comet.

Fay (fēⁱ), *sb.*¹ *Obs.* or *arch.* ME. [– OFr. *fei* (mod. *foi*), earlier *feit, feid*; see FAITH.] = FAITH, in various senses. Used esp. in asseverative phrases and quasi-oaths; as, *By my f.*, etc.

Fay (fēi), *sb.*[2] Also formerly in Fr. form **fée.** ME. [– OFr. *faie, fae* (mod. *fée*) :– L. *fata* the Fates (pl. of *fatum* FATE), taken as fem. sing. in Rom.] = FAIRY *sb.* 4.

Fay (fēi), *sb.*[3] 1747. [f. FAY *v.*[2]] The clearings from the surface; the dross of metals, the surface soil.

Fay (fēi), *v.*[1] [OE. *fēġan* = OS. *fōgian* (Du. *voegen*), OHG. *fuogen* (G. *fügen*) :– WGmc. **fōgjan* fit, adapt, join.] †**1.** *trans.* To fit, adapt, or join; to put together; to fix in position –ME. **2.** *intr.* Of a coat: To fit. *U.S.* 1866. **3.** To suit, do. Now *dial.* ME. **4.** *Ship-building.* **a.** *trans.* To fit closely and exactly *to* 1754. **b.** *intr.* To fit close 1794.

Fay, feigh (fēi), *v.*[2] [ME. *fæȝen, feȝen* – ON. *fægja* cleanse, polish.] *trans.* To cleanse, polish; to clear away. Now only *dial.*

Fay, obs. var. of FEY *a.*

Fayalite (fēi·ăləit). 1844. [f. *Fayal*, one of the Azores; see -ITE[1] 2 b.] *Min.* A silicate of iron and other bases.

Fayence, var. of **Faience.**

†**Fayles.** ME. [Said to be connected with FAIL *v.*] An obs. form of Backgammon –1598.

Fayto(u)r: see **Fait-.**

Faze (fēiz), *v.* 1890. [var. of FEEZE *v.*[1]] *U.S. trans.* To discompose.

‖**Fazenda** (faze·ndă). 1825. [Pg., = Sp. HACIENDA.] An estate or large farm. Also the homestead belonging to it.

Feaberry (fī·bĕri, fē·bĕri). *dial.* 1597. [perh. for **theve-berry*, f. ME. *theve* repr. OE. *þēfe* prickly shrub.] A gooseberry. Also *attrib.*

†**Feague,** *v.* 1589. [See FAKE *v.*[2]] **1.** *trans.* To beat, whip. Also *fig.* –1691. **2.** = FAKE *v.*[2] –1690.

Feal (fīl), *a. arch.* 1568. [– OFr. *feal*, alt. f. *feeil* :– L. *fidelis*; see next.] Faithful, constant, loyal.

Fealty (fī·ălti). ME. [– OFr. *feau(l)te, fealte* (mod. *féauté*) :– L. *fidelitas, -tat-*, f. *fidelis* faithful, f. *fides* FAITH; see -TY[1].] **1.** The obligation of fidelity on the part of a feudal tenant or vassal to his lord. **2.** The recognition of this obligation by taking an oath upon a book. Also *pl.* ME. **3.** *transf.* and *fig.* 1530.

2. Phr. *To do, make, receive, swear*, etc. *f.* **3.** We all to him [God] owe f. and service 1530.

Fear (fīᵊɹ), *sb.* [ME. *fēr-e*, repr. OE. *fǣr* sudden calamity, danger, corresp. to OS. *vār* ambush, MDu. *vare* fear (cf. Du. *gevaar* danger), OHG. *fāra* ambush, stratagem, danger, deceit (G. *gefahr* danger) :– Gmc. **fǣraz, -am, -ō*.] †**1.** In OE.: A peril. **2.** The emotion of pain or uneasiness caused by the sense of impending danger, or by the apprehension of evil. In early use applied to the more violent extremes of the emotion. Often *personified.* ME. **b.** A state of alarm or dread ME. **3.** The state of fearing (something); *esp.* a mingled feeling of dread and reverence towards God (or, formerly, any rightful authority) ME. **4.** Solicitude, anxiety for the safety of a person or thing 1490. **5.** In objective senses: **a.** Ground for alarm 1535; †**b.** Capability of inspiring fear –1654; †**c.** Something that is, or is to be, feared –1667.

2. Feare and dread shall fall vpon them *Ex.* 15:16. Needless Fears DE FOE. **b.** In f. and trembling 1771. **3.** Phr. *For f.*, where in mod. use the sense of the sb. is often weakened; thus *for f. that* or *lest* = 'lest'. The feare of the Lord is the beginning of wisedome *Ps.* 111:10. **4.** Phr. *For, in, f. of one's life.* **5. a.** They are afrayed, where no feare is COVERDALE *Ps.* 52[53]:5. **b.** *Jul. C.* II. i. 190. **c.** I wil mocke when your feare cometh *Prov.* 1:26.

Fear (fīᵊɹ), *v.* [OE. *fǣran* = OS. *fāron* lie in wait (MDu. *vaeren* fear), OHG. *fārēn* plot against, lie in wait, ON. *fǽra* taunt, slight; cf. Goth. *ferjans* pl. liers-in-wait.]

I. 1. *trans.* To inspire with fear; to frighten. Now *arch.* or *vulgar.* †**2.** To frighten away, deter *from* –1632.

1. Warwicke was a Bugge that fear'd vs all SHAKS. **2.** A scar-crow..to feare the birds of prey SHAKS.

II. 1. *intr.* (and *refl.*) To feel fear, be afraid ME. **2.** *trans.* To regard with fear, be afraid of 1460; also with *inf.* (*vbl. sb.*, etc.) as object 1603. **3.** To regard with reverence and awe ME. **4.** To have an uneasy sense of the probability of; to apprehend (opp. to *hope for*) 1597. **b.** with *subord. clause.* To be afraid *that* (in neg. sentences *but* or *but that* = that..not) 1526. **5.** To be apprehensive about, to fear something happening to. †*trans.* and *intr.* with *for*, †*of.* 1526. †**6.** To doubt or distrust –1607.

1. Phr. (colloq.) *Never f. I f. me* (arch.). I feared lest I should drop down 1823. **2.** Nor Fate I f. DRYDEN. Dorothee..feared to obey 1794. **3.** Who .feared nought but God 1827. **4.** I feared it would be..two hundred Pounds 1726. **5.** Let the greedy merchant f. For his ill-gotten gain DRYDEN.

Hence **Feared** *ppl. a.* (esp. in senses II. 2, 4). †**Fea·redness. Fea·rer,** one who fears.

†**Fear-babe.** 1580. [f. FEAR *v.* + BABE.] A thing fit only to scare a baby –1621.

Fear(e, var. of FERE. *Sc.*

Fearful (fīᵊ·ɹful), *a.* ME. [f. FEAR *v.* + -FUL.] **1.** Causing fear; dreadful, terrible, awful; often *hyperbolical.* **2.** Frightened, timid, apprehensive. Now usually with *of*, or with *lest* or *that.* ME. †**b.** Anxious, concerned; with *about, of* –1593. **3.** Of looks, words, etc.: Indicating fear or terror 1535. †**4.** Cautious, wary –1791. **5.** Full of awe or reverence 1567.

1. Death is a fearefull thing SHAKS. He complained of f. thirst TYNDALL. **2.** Chubs..be a very f. fish WALTON. F. to offend POPE. A f. joy KEBLE. **3.** Cold fearefull drops stand on my trembling flesh SHAKS. Hence **Fea·rful-ly** *adv.*, **-ness.**

Fearless (fīᵊ·ɹlės), *a.* ME. [f. FEAR *sb.* + -LESS.] **1.** Without fear. †**2.** Not feared; free from danger –1745.

1. A man .fearless of what's past, present, or to come SHAKS. Hence **Fea·rless-ly** *adv.*, **-ness.**

Fearnought (fīᵊ·ɹnǭt). 1772. [FEAR *v.* (in imper.) + NOUGHT.] **1.** A stout, thick woollen cloth, used chiefly for seamen's coats, also as a covering for portholes, the doors of powder magazines, etc. Cf. DREADNOUGHT. **2.** A drink to keep up the spirits 1880.

Fearsome (fīᵊ·ɹsŏm), *a.* 1768. [f. FEAR *v.* or *sb.* + -SOME[1].] **1.** Fear-inspiring; dreadful. ¶**2.** ? *erron.* Timid, apprehensive 1863.

1. War's a f. thing SCOTT. **2.** I'm but a silly f. thing 1871. Hence **Fea·rsome-ly** *adv.*, **-ness.**

†**Fea·sance.** 1538. [– AFr. *fesa(u)nce*, (O)Fr. *faisance*, f. *fais-*, pres. stem of *faire* do; see -ANCE. Cf. MALFEASANCE.] The execution of a condition, obligation, etc. –1741.

†**Fea·straw.** 1595. [Perversion of *festue* FESCUE, infl. by *straw.*] = FESCUE –1660.

Feasible (fī·zib'l), *a.* 1460. [Early forms also *fesable, faisable* – (O)Fr. *faisable*, †*faisible*, f. *fais-*, pres. stem of *faire* do; see -BLE.] **1.** Capable of being done, carried out, or dealt with successfully in any way; possible, practicable. **2.** Of a proposition, theory, story, etc.: Likely, probable 1656.

1. To an infinite power all things are equally faisable 1647. I know all Lands are not so Fecible as others are BLITH. **2.** The only f. theory..proposed LYELL. Hence **Fea·sibi·lity,** the quality or fact of being f. **Fea·sibly** *adv.*, **Fea·sibleness.**

Feast (fīst), *sb.* [ME. *feste* – OFr. *feste* (mod. *fête*) :– L. *festa* n. pl. (taken as fem. sing. in Rom.) of *festus* festal, joyous.] **1.** A religious anniversary appointed to be observed with rejoicing (hence opp. to a *fast*). **b.** A village festival held annually on the feast of the saint to whom the parish church is dedicated 1559. **2.** A sumptuous meal or entertainment for many guests; a banquet, *esp.* one of a more or less public nature ME. **3.** An unusually abundant and delicious meal; something delicious to feed upon; a treat. Also *fig.* ME. †**4.** Rejoicing, festivity –1667.

1. You shall keepe it a f. by an ordinance for euer *Ex.* 12:14. Phr. *Movable feasts*: those of which the date varies from year to year; opp. to *immovable feasts*, as *Christmas*, etc. **2.** The nexte day she made them a great feest at dyner LD. BERNERS. **3.** This makes thy morsell a perpetuall F. QUARLES. Enough's a F. POPE. How little of a f. for the senses M. ARNOLD. **4.** Ministring Spirits, traind up in F. and Song MILT. *P. L.* vi. 167.

Phrase. *To make f.* (= Fr. *faire fête*): **a.** To make merry, rejoice; later, to feast (*arch.*). †**b.** To make much of (a person).

Comb. **f.-day,** a day on which a f. (senses 1, 2) is held.

Feast (fīst), *v.* [ME. *fest(e)* – OFr. *fester* (mod. *fêter*), f. *feste*; see prec.] **1.** *intr.* To make or partake of a feast, regale oneself. Also *fig.* ME. **2.** *trans.* To provide a feast for, regale. Also *refl.* Also *fig.* ME. **3.** To entertain hospitably and sumptuously 1490.

1. There festen they, there dauncen they and synge CHAUCER. *fig.* With my love's picture then my eye doth f. SHAKS. *Sonn.* xlvii. **2.** The Lorde Bartholomew..magnificently feasted there the Queene LAMBARDE. *fig.* F. your eares with the Musicke awhile SHAKS. Hence **Fea·ster,** one who provides, or one who partakes of, a feast; a luxurious liver.

Feastful (fī·stful), *a. arch.* ME. [f. prec. + -FUL.] **1.** Occupied in or given to feasting; of the nature of feasting; festive. **2.** Filled with feasting. LAMB.

1. The Bridegroom and his f. friends MILT.

†**Fea·stly,** *a.* [f. FEAST *sb.* + -LY[1].] Festive, jolly. CHAUCER.

Feat (fīt), *sb.* [ME. *fete*, later *fayte* – OFr. *fet*, (also mod.) *fait* :– L. *factum*, subst. use of n. sing. of *factus*, pa. pple. of *facere* do.] †**1.** = FACT 1 a –1732. **2.** An exceptional act or achievement; *esp.* a deed of valour. Now somewhat *arch.* ME. **3.** A surprising trick, a 'tour de force' 1564. †**4.** A kind, or department, of action –1652. †**5.** The art or knack of doing anything –1681. †**6.** Fact, actuality –1500.

2. Wonderfull in feates of warre *Judith* 11:8. **3.** Feats of balancing IMISON. A wonderful f. of architectural skill 1867. **4.** *The f. of merchandise*: mercantile business. (*The*) *f. of war*: warfare. *Feats of war*: military duties or exercises.

Feat (fīt), *a.* and *adv.* Now *arch.* or *dial.* [ME. *fete* – OFr. *fet* (mod. *fait*) :– L. *factus* (see prec.); lit. 'made (for something)'.]

A. *adj.* **1.** Fitting (*for, to*). **2.** Apt; adroit; dexterous 1519. **3.** Neat, elegant; hence, neatly attired ME. **4.** Affected, finikin 1540.

2. Neuer Master had A Page..So feate *Cymb.* V. v. 88. **3.** Looke how well my Garments sit vpon me, Much feater than before *Temp.* II. i. 273. **4.** I hold such to be but f. boldness 1647.

B. *adv.* In a feat manner 1455.

†**Feat,** *v.* ME. [f. prec. adj.] **1.** *trans.* To equip, make fit –1613. **2.** *Falconry.* To wipe (the beak) –1575. **3.** ? To constrain to propriety. *Cymb.* I. i. 49.

Feateous, obs. var. of FEATOUS *a.*

Feather (fe·ðəɹ), *sb.* [OE. *feþer* = OFris. *fethere*, OS. *fethara* (Du. *veer*), OHG. *fedara* (G. *feder*), ON. *fjǫðr* :– Gmc. **feþrō* :– IE. **petra*, f. **pet- *pt-*, repr. also by Skr. *pátram* wing, Gr. πτερόν, πτέρυξ wing, L. *penna* PEN *sb.*[2]]

I. 1. One of the epidermal appendages of a bird, usually a central shaft or midrib, of a horny nature, in part tubular, for the rest square in section and solid, fringed on either side with a 'vane', *i.e.* a row of thin narrow plates mutually adpressed (the 'barbs'), which form a rounded outline at the end. Often specialized as *contour-, covert-, pin-, quill-*, etc. *f.* **2.** *collect.* Plumage; also *transf.* (of plants); and *fig.*: Attire, 'get-up' ME. **b.** Description of plumage; species (of bird). Often *transf.* 1581. †**3.** *pl.* Wings –1614. **4.** A feathered animal. Also *collect.* Feathered game. 1601.

1. She proyneth & setteth her feders in ordre FISHER. Phr. *To smooth one's rumpled feathers*: to recover one's equanimity. *To mount, show the white f.*: to perceive, show signs of cowardice (a white feather in a game-bird's tail being a mark of inferior breeding). *Fine feathers make fine birds.* **2.** In full clerical f. THACKERAY. Phr. *In fine, good, high*, etc. *f.*: in good health, spirits, etc. **b.** I am not of that F., to shake off My Friend when he must neede me *Timon* I. i. 100. Provb. *Birds of a f. flock together.* **3.** Set feathers to thy heeles *John* IV. ii. 174. **4.** Like the Haggard, checke at euery F. *Twel. N.* III. i. 71.

II. 1. Simply; or *pl.* as a commodity OE. **2.** A portion, or (*sing.* and *pl.*) portions, of a feather attached to the base of an arrow. Also *collect.* 1631. **3.** A plume, *esp.* in *ostrich-f.* 1473. **4.** As a type of an object weighing little, and easily moved; hence, a trifle 1562. **b.** = FEATHERWEIGHT 1760.

3. Phr. *A f. in the cap, hat*: a mark of honour (*lit.* and *fig.*). *Prince of Wales's feathers*, also *The f.*:

the plume of three ostrich feathers, first adopted as a crest by the Black Prince. **4.** I am a F. for each Wind that blows *Wint. T.* II. iii. 154.

III. Something resembling a feather. **1.** A tuft or ridge of hair standing more or less upright: **a.** on human beings 1530; **b.** on horses 1580. **2.** A flaw having a feather-like appearance in a precious stone 1866. **3.** In techn. uses: **a.** A longitudinal rib added to a shaft, etc. to increase its strength 1823. **b.** *Mining*, etc. One of two slightly curved pieces of iron, placed in a hole drilled in a stone, with the concave surfaces towards each other, which are forced apart with an iron punch, and thus break the stone asunder 1865. **c.** A projection on a board, implement, or piece of machinery; *esp.* one intended to fit into some other part 1765.

IV. [f. the vb.] *Rowing.* The action of feathering 1865.

attrib. and *Comb.* **1.** General, as *f.-bolster, -beater, -tasselled, -legged, -nerved, -wise* adv., etc. **2.** Special: **f.-alum,** see ALUM; **-brain,** a person with a light or weak brain, whence **-brained** *a.*; **-cloth,** a mixture of cloth and feathers woven together; †**-driver,** (*a*) = QUILL-DRIVER, (*b*) 'one who cleanses feathers by whisking them about' (J.); **-duster,** a brush made of feathers, for dusting; **-heeled** *a.* = -FOOTED; **-joint,** 'a mode of joining the edges of boards by a fin or f. let into opposite mortises on the edges of the boards' (Knight); **-mail,** the dress of feathers resembling a coat of mail formerly worn by the Indians of Mexico; †**-maker,** one who dresses or deals in feathers; **-man,** one who deals in feathers; **-ore,** the capillary form of native sulphantimonite of lead; **-pated** *a.* = *feather-brained*; **-poke,** (*a*) a bag of feathers, (*b*) a name of the Willow Warbler, the Long-tailed Titmouse, and the Wren, perh. from the appearance of their nests; **-pulp,** the pulp or matrix from which the f. is formed; **-shot copper,** that made by pouring melted copper into cold water; **-spray,** that thrown off, like a pair of wing feathers, by the cut-water of fast steamers; **-spring,** the spring in a gun-lock which causes the *sear* to catch in the notch of the tumbler; **-star,** a starfish (*Comatula rosacea*); **-top,** nickname of a parrot (also *attrib.* = next); **-topped** *a.*, (of a wig) frizzed at the top; **-tuft,** an edible mushroom, *Clavaria cristata.*

b. In plant-names, as **F.-bow** = FEVERFEW; **-fern,** *Spiræa japonica*; **-grass,** a perennial feathery grass (*Stipa pennata*); **-top grass,** *Calamagrostis epigejos*; etc.

Feather (fe·ðəɹ), *v.* [OE. *gefiðrian*; from XIII (in pa. pple.) a new formation on the sb.] †**1.** *trans.* To give wings to. *lit.* and *fig.* –1825. **2.** To fit, clothe, or provide with or as with a feather or feathers, as an arrow, a hat, etc. ME. Also *refl.* and *intr.* for *refl.* (now *dial.*) 1450. **3.** To cover with feathers: **a.** internally, in phr. *To f. one's nest*: to enrich oneself 1583; **b.** externally, in phr. *To tar and f.* 1774. †**4.** Of a cock: To cover with outspread feathers; to tread –1700. **5.** *intr.* To move, grow, extend, etc. in a feathery form 1770. **b.** *U.S.* Of cream: To rise upon the surface of tea, etc. like small flakes or feathers 1860. **6.** To be marked with feather-like lines, as tulips, etc. 1833. **7.** *trans.* To cut (wood, etc.) down gradually to a thin edge 1782. **8.** To turn (an oar) as it leaves the water so that it may cut the air edgeways 1740. **9.** *Shooting.* To knock a few feathers from (a bird) without killing 1890. **10.** *Hunting.* **a.** Of a hound: To make a quivering movement with the tail and body, while searching for the trail 1803. **b.** Of the huntsman: To set the hounds direct on the trail 1884.

2. An arrow feathered with his own wing ARBUTHNOT. A craggy hill, feathered with birch SOUTHEY. **5.** The snow came feathering down G. COLMAN. The ripple feathering from her bows TENNYSON. **9. a.** See that old bitch how she feathers—how her stern vibrates with the quickened action of her pulses 1839.

Fea·ther-be·d. OE. **1.** A bed stuffed with feathers. Also *fig.* **2.** The Willow Warbler; also the Whitethroat 1854.

Feathered (fe·ðəɹd), *ppl. a.* OE. [f. FEATHER *sb.* and *v.* + -ED.] **1.** Provided with feathers. Also in comb., as *black-, well-*, etc. *f.* ME. **2.** Winged, fleet 1587. **3.** Of an arrow: Fitted with a feather. Of a wound: Inflicted by an arrow. OE. **4.** Adorned with a feather or plume of feathers 1624. **5.** Furnished with something feather-like 1686. **6.** Of an oar: That is or has been turned so as to feather 1812.

1. A f. wanderer SMILES. **2.** I saw young Harry.. Rise from the ground like f. Mercury 1 *Hen. IV*, IV. i. 106. **3.** Across the shoulders came the feather'd wound DRYDEN. **5.** The f. grass KEATS. The arch ..is richly feathered (cf. FEATHERING *vbl. sb.*) RICKMAN.

Fea·ther-e·dge, *sb.* 1785. [f. as prec. + EDGE.] The fine edge of a board, etc. that thins off to one side, so as to resemble a wedge in section. Hence **Fea·ther-e·dge** *v.* to cut to a feather-edge. Also *transf.* to turn (oneself) sideways. **Fea·ther-e·dged** *ppl. a.*

Fea·therfew. ME. [Corrupt var. of FEVERFEW.] = FEVERFEW.

Fea·ther-foo·ted, *a.* 1565. [See -ED[2].] Having feet covered with feathers 1580. **b.** *fig.* Moving silently and swiftly.

Fea·ther-head. 1831. An empty or light head; an empty-headed person. Hence **Fea·ther-hea·ded** *a.*

Featheriness (fe·ðərinės). 1689. [f. FEATHERY + -NESS.] Feathery state or condition; *fig.* lightness, fickleness.

Feathering (fe·ðəriŋ), *vbl. sb.* 1530. [f. FEATHER *v.* + -ING[1].] **1.** The action of FEATHER *v.* 1640. **2.** *concr.* The plumage of birds; the feather of an arrow; feather-like structure or marking 1530; *Arch.* tracery consisting chiefly of small arcs and foils 1816.

Feathering (fe·ðəriŋ), *ppl. a.* 1740. [f. as prec. + -ING[2].] That feathers; in senses of the vb. 1789. **b.** Of an oar, paddle-wheel, float, etc.: see FEATHER *v.* 8.

b. *F. Paddle-wheel*, a wheel whose floats have a motion on an axis, so as to descend nearly vertically into the water and ascend the same way, avoiding beating on the water in the descent and lifting water in the ascent KNIGHT.

Featherless (fe·ðərlės), *a.* ME. [See -LESS.] Without feathers, in various senses.

Fea·ther-stitch. 1882. A kind of stitch in needlework, producing an ornamental zigzag line. Hence as vb.

Fea·ther-weight. 1812. **1.** A weight no greater than that of a feather; hence, a very small thing 1838. **2.** *Racing.* The lightest weight a horse may carry in a handicap; a jockey not over 4st. 7. 1812. **3.** *Boxing.* A boxer whose weight is from 9st. to 8st. 6, as dist. from a *heavy-, middle*, or *light-weight* 1889.

Fea·ther-work. 1665. [f. FEATHER *sb.* + WORK *sb.*] The art of working in feathers; also *concr.*; also = FEATHERSTITCH.

Feathery (fe·ðəri), *a.* 1580. [f. as prec. + -Y[1].] **1.** Of birds: Feathered 1634. **2.** Fringed, tipped, or flecked with something feather-like 1792. **3.** Resembling feathers or plumes 1580.

1. His [the cock's] f. dames MILT. **2.** The f. canes 1826, pine-branches 1876. **3.** The f. snows COWPER.

Featly (fī·tli), *adv.* (*a.*) *arch.* ME. [f. FEAT *a.* + -LY[2].] **1.** Fitly; neatly; †exactly. **2.** Cleverly, deftly; nimbly ME. **3.** *adj.* Graceful; neat 1801.

2. She dances f. *Wint. T.* IV. iv. 176. **3.** In f. cloak 1822. So **Fea·tness,** elegance, trimness.

†**Fea·tous** *a.* [ME. *fetys* – OFr. *fetis, feitis, faictis*, f. L. *factitius*; see FACTITIOUS. In XVI–XVII apprehended as a deriv. of FEAT *a.*, and variously ended *-ish, -ous, -eous, -uous.*] **1.** Well-formed, handsome, becoming. Often of dress: Artistically fashioned. –1648. **2.** 'Dexterous' (J.).

1. Ye think it fine and f. to be called roses..and Lilies 1570. Hence †**Fea·tously** *adv.*

Feature (fī·tiŭɹ), *sb.* ME. [– OFr. *feture, faiture* form :– L. *factura* formation, creature, f. *fact-*, pa. ppl. stem of *facere* do; see -URE. Cf. FACTURE.] **1.** Make, form, fashion, shape; proportions. Now *arch.* †**b.** Good form or shape; comeliness –1594. †**c.** *concr.* Something formed or shaped. Cf. CREATURE. –1667. †**2.** In *pl.* and distributively: The build or make of the various parts of the body. **b.** *concr.* A part of the body; a limb. –1752. **3. a.** In *pl.* and in *sing.* with distrib. adj.: The lineaments of the face, the form or mould of its parts. Also *collect.* in *sing.* ME. **b.** *concr.* Any one part of the face 1828. **4.** *transf.* A distinctive part of anything 1692.

1. Horses of fine f. 1600. An image, huge of f. as a cloud KEATS. **b.** Cheated of F. by dissembling Nature SHAKS. **c.** So sented the grim F., and upturn'd His Nostril wide MILT. *P. L.* X. 279. **3.** Under such simple and homly f., lay..a most subtil..wit KNOLLES. *fig.* The Features of the Mind BUTLER. **4.** Anything exhibited or advertised as particularly attractive; *spec.* the principal attraction in a cinema programme; a prominent article, etc. in a newspaper.

Feature (fī·tiŭɹ), *v.* 1755. [f. prec. sb.] **1.** *trans.* = FAVOUR *v.* 7. **2.** To affect or mould the features of; to stand as a feature upon 1810. **3.** To sketch the features of 1791. **4.** To make a special feature of; *spec.* to exhibit as a prominent feature in a dramatic piece 1888.

Featured (fī·tiŭɹd), *ppl. a.* 1500. [f. FEATURE *sb.* and *v.* + -ED.] †**1.** Fashioned, formed, shaped; well-formed; comely –1774. **2.** Shaped into or expressed by features 1742. **3.** Furnished with features of a specified cast 1790.

3. That hard-f.. old forester 1861.

Featureless (fī·tiŭɹlės), *a.* 1600. [See -LESS.] Without (good) features; having no marked feature. Of business: Uneventful.

Featurely (fī·tiŭɹli), *a.* 1819. [See -LY[1].] Having marked features; characteristic.

Feaze (fīz), *v.* *Obs.* exc. *Naut.* 1568. [prob., as naut. term, of LDu. origin; cf. MLG., MDu. *vēse* fringe, frayed edge; rel. to †*fas* border, fringe, OE. *fæs, fas*, OHG. *faso, fasa* (G. *faser* fibre, filament, *fasern* fray out).] *trans.* To unravel (a rope, etc.); *intr.* of a rope or thread: To unravel at the end. Hence **Fea·zings** *vbl. sb. pl.* the fagging out of an unwhipped rope.

Feaze, var. of FEEZE *sb.* and *v.*

Febricitant (fībri·sitănt). Now *rare.* 1541. [– *febricitant-*, pres. ppl. stem of L. *febricitare* have a fever, f. *febris* fever; see -ANT. Cf. Fr. *fébricitant* (XV), which may be partly the source.] **A.** *adj.* Affected with fever; feverish 1599. †**B.** *sb.* One affected with fever –1650.

†**Febri:cita·tion.** 1584. [f. *febricitat-*, pa. ppl. stem of L. *febricitare*; see prec., -ION.] The state of being in a fever, feverishness. So **Febri·city.** BROWNING.

Febricula (fībri·kiŭlă). 1746. [– L. *febricula*, dim. of *febris* fever; see -CULE.] A slight fever, soon over. Hence **Febri·culose,** †**Febri·culous** *adjs.* having a slight fever. **Febriculo·sity,** feverishness.

Febrifacient (fībrifē[i]·ʃ[i]ĕnt). 1803. [f. L. *febris* fever + -FACIENT.] **A.** *adj.* Fever-producing. **B.** *sb.* Something that produces fever.

Febriferous (fībri·fĕrəs), *a.* 1874. [f. as prec. + -FEROUS.] Producing fever, as a *f. locality.*

Febrific (fībri·fik), *a.* 1710. [– Fr. †*fébrifique* (COTGR.), f. L. *febris* fever; see -FIC.] Producing fever; also, FEVERISH.

Febrifuge (fe·brifiŭdʒ). 1686. [– Fr. *fébrifuge*, f. as prec.; see -FUGE.]

A. *adj.* Anti-febrile 1707.

B. *sb.* An anti-febrile medicine; hence, a cooling drink. Also *transf.* and *fig.* Hence **Febri·fugal, febrifu·gal** *a.* †**Febrifugous** *a.*

Febrile (fī·bril, fe·bril), *a.* 1651. [– Fr. *fébrile* or med.L. *febrilis*, f. as prec.; see -ILE.] Of or pertaining to fever; produced by or indicative of fever. †Of a person: Suffering from fever.

F. heat 1666, irritation KINGLAKE. Hence **Febri·lity,** feverishness.

Febronian (febrō[u]·niăn), *a.* 1856. [f. *Febronius* + -AN.] Of or pertaining to (Justinus) Febronius; a pseudonym of J. N. von Hontheim of Treves (18th c.), who wrote maintaining the independence of national churches. Hence **Febro·nianism,** the doctrine itself.

February (fe·bruări). Also abbrev. *Feb.* [ME. *feverer* – OFr. *feverier* (mod. *février*) :– late L. (Rom.) *febrarius*, for L. *februarius*, f. *februa* n. pl. Roman festival of purification held on 15 February.] **1.** The second month of the year, containing twenty-eight days, except in bissextile or leap-year, when it has twenty-nine. **2.** *attrib.* 1599.

2. You have such a Februarie face SHAKS.

Februa·tion. Now *rare.* 1652. [– L. *februatio*, f. *februare* purify; see prec., -ATION.] A ceremonial purification.

Fecal, feces, etc.: see FÆCAL, etc.

Fecial, var. of FETIAL.

Fecifork (fī·sifǭɹk). 1826. [f. L. *fæci-* comb. f. FÆCES + FORK.] *Entom.* The anal fork on which the larvæ of *Cassida*, etc., carry their fæces.

Feck (fek). *Sc.* and *n. dial.* 1470. [Aphetic f. *effeck*, Sc. var. of EFFECT *sb.*] †**1.** Effect, tenor, substance –1600. **2.** Efficacy, value; hence, vigour, energy 1535. **3.** Amount, quantity. *The (most) f.*: the bulk, the greatest part.

Hence **Fe·ckful** *a.* efficient, powerful. **Fe·ckfully** *adv.* **Feckless** *a.* ineffective, futile, weak. **Fe·ckless-ly** *adv.*, **-ness.** **Fe·ckly** *adv.* mostly; almost.

Fecket (fe·kėt). *Sc.* [Of unkn. origin.] An under waistcoat. BURNS.

Fecula: see FÆCULA.

Feculence (fe·kiŭlĕns). 1648. [– (O)Fr. *féculence* or late L. *fæculentia*, f. *fæculentus*; see next, -ENCE.] **1.** The quality or state of being feculent; foulness 1860. **2.** *concr.* Feculent matter; dregs, dross, scum. Now chiefly, filth. So †**Fe·culency** 1607.

Feculent (fe·kiŭlĕnt), *a.* 1471. [– Fr. *féculent* or L. *fæculentus*, f. *fæc-*; see FÆCES, -ULENT.] **1.** Containing or of the nature of fæces or dregs; abounding with sediment or impurities; thick, turbid. Now usually: Foul, fetid. Also *fig.* †**2.** Covered with fæces. SPENSER *F. Q.* II. vii. 61.

1. *fig.* Every word here is f. and stinks NORTH.

Fecund (fe·kɒnd, fī·kɒnd), *a.* ME. [– Fr. *fécond* or L. *fecundus.*] **1.** Fruitful in offspring or vegetable growth; prolific, fertile. Now chiefly *transf.* and *fig.* **2.** Fertilizing 1686.

1. This is..f. of other fault and misfortune RUSKIN. var. †**Fecu·ndous.**

Fecundate (fe-, fī·kŏndeᶦt), *v.* 1631. [– *fecundat-*, pa. ppl. stem of L. *fecundare*, f. *fecundus*; see prec., -ATE³.] *trans.* To render fruitful or productive; *esp.* to make the female (individual or organ) fruitful by the introduction of the male element; to impregnate.

Nature has something more in view than that its own proper males should f. each blossom DARWIN.

Fecundation (fe-, fīkŏndēᶦ·ʃən). 1541. [f. as prec. + -ION.] The process of fecundating; fertilization, impregnation.

†**Fecu·ndify,** *v. rare.* 1730. [f. FECUND + -FY.] = FECUNDATE.

Fecundity (fīkɒ·ndĭti). ME. [– Fr. *fécondité* or L. *fecunditas*, f. *fecundus*; see FECUND, -ITY.] **1.** The faculty of reproduction, the capacity for bringing forth young; productiveness. **2.** *Bot.* The power of germinating 1691. **3.** The quality of producing abundantly; fertility ME. **4.** Productiveness in general 1555. **5.** Fertilizing power 1642.

4. The extreme f. of the press W. IRVING. **5.** The River Nilus is famous for its..Fœcundity 1680.

Fed (fed), *ppl. a.* 1483. [pa. pple. of FEED *v.*] **a.** Supplied with food, nourished. **b.** *F. up*: surfeited, disgusted, bored (*slang*) 1900.

†**Fe·darie.** 1603. [var. of *feodary* FEUDARY, q.v.] A confederate –1611.

Camillo is A Federarie [perh. a misprint or correction] with her *Wint. T.* II. i. 90.

‖**Feddan** (fedā·n). Also **fedan.** 1817. [Arab. *faddān* a yoke of oxen, an acre.] An Egyptian measure of land, rather more than an English acre.

Federacy (fe·dĕrăsi). 1647. [f. FEDERATE *a.* (see -ACY), or shortened f. CONFEDERACY.] **1.** The state of being joined by a treaty; an alliance. **2.** A CONFEDERACY 1803.

Federal (fe·dĕrăl). 1645. [– mod.L. **fœderalis*, f. *fœdus, fœder-* covenant; see -AL¹. Cf. Fr. *fédéral* (XVIII).]

A. *adj.* **1.** Of or pertaining to a covenant, compact, or treaty; *spec.* (*Theol.*) pertaining to the Covenant of Works or Covenant of Grace. **2.** Of or pertaining to, or of the nature of, that form of government in which two or more states constitute a political unity while remaining independent as to their internal affairs; of or pertaining to the political unity so constituted 1777. **3.** *U.S. Hist.* **a.** Favouring a strong federal, i.e. central, government 1788. **b.** Of or pertaining to the Northern or Union party in the American Civil War of 1861–65. 1861. **4.** United in a league, allied 1867.

1. *F. theology*: the system based on the doctrine of covenants made by God with Adam as repr. mankind, and with Christ as repr. the Church. **2.** There was not..any f. bond among the several tribes STUBBS. A F. coinage 1876. **3. a.** He [Hamilton] is the..impersonation of the national or F. School CALHOUN.

B. *sb.* Chiefly *pl.* One on the side of the Union in the American Civil War 1867.

Hence **Fe·derally** *adv.* on the basis of a covenant; after the manner of a federation.

Federalism (fe·dĕrăliz'm). 1793. [– Fr. *fédéralisme*, f. *fédéral*; see prec., -ISM.] The federal principle or system of political organization (see FEDERAL *a.* 2); advocacy of this principle. In *U.S. Hist.* the principles of the Federal party (see FEDERAL *a.* 3).

Federalist (fe·dĕrălist), *sb.* 1787. [– Fr. *fédéraliste*, f. *fédéral*; see FEDERAL, -IST.] **1.** One who advocates federalism or federal union 1792. **2.** *U.S. Hist.* A member of the Federal party 1787. **3.** *attrib.* 1801.

2. The advocates of a central national authority had begun to receive the name of Federalists BRYCE. Hence **Federali·stic** *a.* inclined to federalism.

Federalize (fe·dĕrăləiz), *v.* 1801. [– Fr. *fédéraliser*, f. *fédéral*; see FEDERAL, -IZE.] **a.** *trans.* To unite in federal union. **b.** To decentralize; to take from the central authority and hand over to federal bodies in the state or states in a union. Hence **Fe:deraliza·tion,** the action of federalizing or the state of being federalized.

Federarie; see FEDARIE.

Federate (fe·dĕrĕt). 1671. [– L. *fœderatus*, pa. ppl. formation on *fœdus, fœder-* covenant, + *-atus* -ATE². Cf. Fr. *fédéré.*] **A.** *adj.* Federated, confederate, allied, in league 1710.

In a f. Alliance, the two Societies still subsist intire WARBURTON.

B. *sb.* **1.** One of the parties to a covenant 1671. **2.** *French Hist.* Used as tr. Fr. *fédéré* 1792.

2. They invited armed federates, as they were called, in July 1791, to Paris 1792.

Federate (fe·dĕreᶦt), *v.* 1814. [– *fœderat-*, pa. ppl. stem of late L. *fœderare*, f. as prec.; see -ATE³.] **1.** *intr.* To enter into a league for a common object 1837. **2.** *trans.* To band together as a league; to organize on a federal basis.

1. Thus, at Lyons..we behold..sixty thousand, met to f. CARLYLE. **2.** To f. the Continent against England 1885. Hence **Fe·deratist** = FEDERATIONIST.

Federation (fedĕrēᶦ·ʃən). 1721. [– Fr. *fédération* – late L. *fœderatio*, f. as prec.; see -ION.] **1.** The action of uniting in a league or covenant. Now chiefly *spec.* the union of several states, etc. under a federal government, each retaining control of its own internal affairs. **2.** A society; a league; a federated body 1791.

1. *F. of the (British) Empire, Imperial F.*: a project under which the colonies were to form one state with the mother country in relation to all that concerned the safety and well-being of the empire as a whole. **2.** The Miners' F., the Shipping F. 1895. Hence **Federa·tionist,** an advocate of f.

Federative (fe·dĕrĕtiv), *a.* 1690. [f. L. *fœderat-* (see FEDERATE *v.*) + -IVE; perh. partly – Fr. *fédératif.*] **1.** Of or pertaining to the formation of a covenant, league, or alliance. Now *Hist.* **2.** Pertaining to, or forming part of, a federation; of the nature of a federation 1781. **3.** Inclined to form federations 1885.

2. Argos, with the f. cities attached to her GROTE.

†**Fe·dity.** 1539. [– L. *fœditas, -tat-*, f. *fœdus* foul; see -ITY.] **1.** Foulness, moral or physical –1657. **2.** *pl.* Loathsome practices –1755.

†**Fee,** *sb.*¹ [OE. *feoh, fioh, fēo* = OFris. *fia*, OS. *fehu* cattle, property (Du. *vee* cattle), OHG. *fihu, fehu* cattle, property, money (G. *vieh* cattle), ON. *fé* cattle, property, money, Goth. *faihu* :– Gmc. **fehu* :– IE. **peku-*, repr. by Skr. *paçu*, L. *pecu* cattle (cf. L. *pecunia* money).] **1.** Livestock, cattle –1535. **2.** Movable property –1596. **3.** Money –1677.

Fee (fī), *sb.*² ME. [– AFr. *fee* = OFr. *feu, fiu, fieu*, (also mod.) *fief*, pl. *fiez* :– Rom. **feudum*, med.L. *feodum, feudum* (IX), which has been derived from Frankish **fehu-ōd* 'cattle-property', rel. to OHG. *fehu*, OE. *fēo*, etc.; see prec.] **1.** *Feudal Law.* An estate in land (in England always a heritable estate) held on condition of homage and service to a superior lord; a fief, feudal benefice. Now *Hist.* **2.** *Common Law.* An estate of inheritance in land. (In Eng. Law understood to be held feudally of the Crown, and thus = sense 1. In U.S. the holder of the fee is the absolute owner of the land.) 1535. **3.** A territory held in fee; a lordship ME. †**4.** The heritable right to an office of profit, held feudally, or to a pension or revenue –1823. †**5.** Employment, service –1596.

1. Phr. *Ecclesiastical f.*: one held by an eccl. person or corporation, owing only spiritual service. *Knight's f., lay f.*: see KNIGHT'S FEE, LAY-FEE. **2.** Phr. FEE-SIMPLE, -TAIL. *In f.*, usu. = 'in fee simple'. *Base f.*: see BASE *a.* *To hold in f.* (fig.): to hold as one's absolute and rightful possession; Once did she hold the gorgeous East in f. WORDSW. *At a pin's f.*: at the value of a pin. **5.** Venus Damzels, all within her f. SPENSER *F.Q.* VI. x. 21.

II. †**1.** A tribute to a superior –1602. **2.** Payment to a public officer (? orig. one who held his office 'in fee') for the execution of his functions 1450; hence, professional or other remuneration 1583; charge, pay ME. †**3.** A perquisite; any allotted portion –1736. **4.** A fixed salary or wage. Also *pl.* Wages. Now *Sc.* or *Hist.* ME. **5.** †A reward –1633; a gratuity 1592; †in bad sense, a bribe –1643.

2. To the Auditor for his F. xiiij *s.* 1546. What f., doctor MAR. EDGEWORTH. **3.** I, heere's a Deere, whose skins a Keepers F. 3 *Hen. VI*, III. i. 23. **5.** Unstain'd with gold or f. MILT.

Comb.: **f.-estate,** lands or tenements for which some service is paid to the chief lord; **-expectant** (see EXPECTANT *a.* 2.); **-fund** (*Sc. Law*), certain dues of Court out of which the officers of the Court are paid.

Fee (fī), *v.* ME. [f. prec.] †**1.** *trans.* ? To invest with a fief 1483. **2.** *trans.* To give a fee to 1529. **3.** To engage for a fee; *Sc.* to hire (servants, etc.); †in bad sense, to bribe ME.

2. The writings drawn, the lawyer fee'd SWIFT. **3.** Without Feeing the Journalists DE FOE.

Feeble (fī·b'l). ME. [– AFr., OFr. *feble*, var. of *fieble* (mod. *faible*), later forms of *fleible* :– L. *flebilis* that is to be wept over, (hence in Rom.) weak, f. *flēre* weep; see -BLE.]

A. *adj.* **1.** Lacking strength; weak; infirm; having little power of resistance. **2.** Lacking moral or intellectual strength ME. **3.** Wanting in energy, force, or effect ME. **4.** Of a phenomenon, etc.: Faintly perceived 1860.

1. His heed maye be harde, but feble his brayne SKELTON. Bunches lateral..stem f. WITHERING. F. folk EMERSON. **2.** F. and without volition CARLYLE. F. minds MACAULAY. **3.** The old, f., and day-wearied Sunne *John* V. iv. 35. My f. Reason HOBBES. F. conduct 1862. *Comb.* **f.-minded** *a.* (whence **-mindedness**). Hence **Fee·bleness. Fee·bling** [-LING¹], a f. person. **Fee·blish** *a.* somewhat f. **Fee·bly** *adv.*

B. *sb.* †**1.** A feeble person –1826. **2.** = FOIBLE *sb.* 1. 1678. **3.** *Fencing.* = FOIBLE *sb.* 2. 1645.

1. The most forcible of feebles DISRAELI. **2.** Modesty's my forte, And pride my f. BYRON.

Feeble (fī·b'l), *v.* ME. [f. the adj.] †**1.** *intr.* To become feeble –1496. **2.** *trans.* To enfeeble. Now *arch.* ME. var. (in sense 2) †**Fee·blish.**

Feebless. *arch.* [ME. *feblesse* – OFr. *feblesse* (mod. *faiblesse*), f. *feble* FEEBLE *a.*; see -ESS².] Feebleness; infirm health.

Feed (fīd), *sb.* 1573. [f. the vb.] **1.** The action of feeding; also, the giving of food 1576. **2.** †Feeding-ground; pasturage, pasture; green crops 1573. **3.** Food (for cattle); fodder, provender 1588; also, an allowance or meal given to a horse, etc. 1735. **4.** *colloq.* A meal; a feast 1808. **5.** The action or process of feeding a machine, or supplying material to be operated upon; also, the material, or the amount, supplied; the charge of a gun 1839. **b.** Short for *f.-gear, -pump*, etc.; a feeder 1839.

1. Birds coming late from F. 1686. Phr. *To be off one's f.* (of animals, and *colloq.* of persons); to have lost one's appetite. *On the f.* (said of fish): on the look-out for food; eating. **2.** For such pleasure till that hour At F. or Fountain never had I found MILT. *P.L.* IX. 597. **3.** One f. of oats in the nose-bag 1859.

Comb. **1.** General: as *f.-bag, -pipe, -pump, -cutter,* etc. **2.** Special: **f.-apron** = *feed-cloth*; **-cloth,** a revolving cloth which carries the cotton, etc., into a spinning, carding, or other machine; **-door,** the door through which a furnace is supplied with fuel; **-head,** (*a*) a cistern of water for supplying the boiler from above; (*b*) *Founding*, 'the metal above and exterior to the mold which flows into the latter as the casting contracts' (Knight); **-motion,** a contrivance for giving a forward motion to material in a machine; **-screw** (*Lathe*), 'a long screw employed to impart a regular motion to a tool-rest or to the work' (Knight); **-trough,** a trough containing a supply of water for a locomotive; **-water,** a supply of water for a steam boiler, etc.; **-wheel,** a revolving wheel or disc which carries forward an object or material.

Feed (fīd), *v.* Pa. t. and pple. **fed.** [OE. *fēdan* = OFris. *fēda*, OS. *fōdean* (Du. *voeden*), OHG. *fuoten*, ON. *fœða*, Goth. *fōdjan* :– Gmc. **fōdjan*, f. **fōðon* FOOD.] **1.** *trans.* To give food to; to supply with food; to put food into the mouth of; to suckle (young). **2.** *fig.* To gratify, minister to the demands of, any sense, passion, feeling, hope, desire, or the like OE. **3.** *intr.* To take food, eat. Of persons now only *colloq.* Also *fig.* ME. **4.** *trans.* To yield, be, or serve as, food for (*lit.* and *fig.*) ME. **5.** To nourish, cause to grow, support, sustain OE. **6.** To fill with food, to pamper, to fatten; occas. of the food (*dial.*) 1552; *intr.* to grow fat (*dial.*) 1727. Also *fig.* **7.** *trans.* To keep supplied 1582. **b.** To supply (a machine, a workman) continuously with material to work upon. Also *intr.* of the material. 1669. **8.** To cause to be eaten by cattle; to use (land) as pasture. Often *to f. bare, close, down, off.* 1651. Also *transf.* To supply continuously (material to be consumed, etc.) 1860. **b.** To deal out (food) to animals, etc. (*U.S.*) 1883. **9.** Of cattle: To eat, eat off, feed upon 1725.

1. Fede your hawke and sey not geve here mete 1450. Pelias..was fed by a mare 1821. He is too weak to f. himself (*mod.*). **2.** Þe soule is fedde wiþ charite WYCLIF. To f. my humor *Rich. III*, IV. i. 65. Phr. *To f. the eyes, sight, ear.* **3.** *fig.* Cholera feeds upon impurities of every sort 1883. **4.** Phr. *To f. the fishes* (slang): to be drowned. **5.** A mountain-spring that feeds a dale SHAKS. **6.** *Sports.* To pass the ball, etc., to a player. *Theatr.* To supply an actor with a cue. Phr. *To f. off*: to fatten for sale or slaughter. **7.** The warm springs that f. the.. Baths ADDISON. **b.** She..fed The turning spindle with the twisting thread 1808. **8. b.** Mangel-wurzel..is fed to the cows in winter 1883. **9.** The sheep have fed it too close for a grip of the hand JEFFERIES.

Feed (fīd), *ppl. a.* 1460. [f. FEE *v.* + -ED[1].] †**1.** Bound to feudal service. Only in *f. man*; see FEEDMAN. **2.** Paid by fees; hired; bribed; *Sc.* employed for wages 1579.

Feeder (fī·dəɹ). ME. [f. FEED *v.* + -ER[1].] **1.** One who feeds or supplies food to; †one who maintains (a parasite, etc.). Also *transf.* and *fig.* 1579. **2.** One who or that which eats or takes food; also *transf.* of a plant, a flame 1562; *pl.* cattle for fattening 1796. **3.** An organ or appliance for feeding (senses 1 and 2); *spec.* in *Entom.* 1811. **4.** One who feeds up cattle for slaughter ME. **5.** A stream which flows into another body of water; a tributary; also *transf.* and *fig.* 1795. **b.** *spec.* 'A water course which supplies a canal or reservoir by gravitation or natural flow' (W.) 1825. **6.** *Mining.* **a.** A smaller lode falling into the main lode or vein 1728. **b.** An underground spring 1702. **c.** A stream of gas escaping from a fissure in the ground; a blower 1881. **7.** One who or that which supplies material for consumption or elaboration; *esp.* one who or that which supplies material to a machine 1669. **8.** *Electr. Engin.* A wire bearing a subsidiary current; a branch-wire to supply a house, etc. 1892.

1. The horsse remembers..his f. 1616. *fig.* The Tutor and the F. of my Riots SHAKS. **2.** He [the barbel] is a curious f. WALTON. **5.** The Kennet.. is one of the main feeders of the Thames 1878.

Feeding (fī·diŋ), *vbl. sb.* OE. [f. as prec. + -ING[1].] **1.** The action of FEED *v.* **2.** *concr.* That which is eaten; food. Now *rare.* ME. **3.** Grazing-ground; pasturage. Now *dial.* ME.

1. The f. of singing-birds RAY. **2.** His [the Pike's] f. is usually fish or frogs WALTON. **3.** Lands or feedings, apt for milch kine 1554.

Comb.: **f.-bottle,** a bottle for supplying milk or the like to infants; also *attrib.* in fig. sense; **-cloth** = FEED-*cloth*; **-tube,** 'an elastic tube.. which is passed into the stomach' (*Syd. Soc. Lex.*)

†**Fee·dman.** 1460. [f. FEED *ppl. a.* + MAN *sb.*] **1.** One holding a FEE (*sb.*[2]); a vassal–1565. **2.** A soldier serving for pay –1722.

Fee-farm (fī·fāɹm). ME. [– AFr. *fee-ferme*, OFr. *feuferme, fiofferme*; see FEE *sb.*[2] and FARM *sb.*[2]).] *Law.* **1.** The tenure by which land is held in fee-simple subject to a perpetual fixed rent, without other services; the estate of the tenant in land so held; *rarely*, the land itself. Also *fig.* 1460. **2.** The rent paid for an estate so held ME. **3.** *attrib.*, esp. in *fee-farm-rent* 1638. Hence **Fee-farmer.**

Fee-faw-fum (fī fǭ fʊm). 1605. **1.** Doggerel spoken by the giant in 'Jack the giant killer' upon discovering the presence of Jack. **2. a.** An exclam. indicating a murderous intention 1690. **b.** Nonsense, fit only to scare children. Also *attrib.* 1811. **3.** A term for 'a blood-thirsty person' 1678.

1. *Lear* III. iv. 188. **2. b.** This is all fee-faw-fum 1890.

Feel (fīl), *sb.* ME. [f. next.] **1.** The action of feeling (see FEEL *v.*); an instance of this 1461. **2.** The sense of touch. Now only in *to the f.* ME. **3.** A feeling or sensation, mental or physical 1737. **4.** Ascribed as a quality to a material object: The kind of sensation which it produces 1739.

2. A rough texture to the f. 1874. **3.** With all sorts of queer feels about me H. WALPOLE. **4.** The general f. of the air is very mild MRS. PIOZZI.

Feel (fīl), *v. Pa. t.* and *pple.* **felt** (felt). [OE. *fēlan* = OFris. *fēla*, OS. *gifōlian* (Du. *voelen*), OHG. *fuolen* (G. *fühlen*), :– WGmc. **fōljan*.]

I. 1. *trans.* To handle in order to experience a tactual sensation; to examine by touching. Hence, to try by touching 1833. **2.** *absol.* and *intr.* **a.** To touch with the hand or finger. Const. *at, of* (now *dial.* and *U.S.*), †*to*. 1599. **b.** To search, try to ascertain, by handling or touch; to grope. Const. *after, for.* Also †*fig.* ME. **3.** *Mil. trans.* To examine by cautious trial the nature of (ground), the strength of (an enemy) 1793. Also *intr.* with *for*: To try to locate (the enemy) 1839.

1. Suffer mee, that I may feele the pillars *Judg.* 16:26. To f. the bit gently with the bridle-hand 1833. Phr. *To f. one's way*: to find it by groping; also *fig.* **2. b.** If haply they might feele after him, and finde him *Acts* 17:27. Come neere.. that I may feele thee..whether thou bee my very sonne Esau, or not *Gen.* 27:21.

II. 1. *trans.* To perceive by the sense of touch ME.; more widely, to perceive through those senses which are not referred to any special organ; to have a sensation of (heat or cold, a blow, a wound, etc.) OE. **b.** *absol.* and *intr.* To have sensations of touch, etc. ME. **2.** To perceive by smell or taste (now *dial.*) ME. †**3.** To perceive mentally –1483. **4.** To be conscious of; to experience ME. **b.** *intr.* (for earlier *refl.*) with *complement.* To be consciously; to regard oneself as 1816. **5.** To undergo consciously. †Also *intr.* const. *of.* ME. **6.** To be sensibly affected by. Also *transf.* and *fig.* of inanimate objects. ME. **7.** *intr.* To have sympathy *with*, compassion *for*, or the like 1605. **8.** †**a.** To think, hold as an opinion (after L. *sentire*) –1544. **b.** To believe on grounds not distinctly perceived; to have a conviction of (a fact) 1613.

1. The lawyer can not vnderstond the matter tyl he fele his mony 1545. We..felt not the cold 1662. Phr. *To f. one's legs.* **b.** The meanest thing that feels WORDSW. **4.** He best can paint 'em [woes] who shall f. 'em most POPE. **b.** I don't f. myself MRS. H. WOOD. Phr. *To f. up to* (one's work, etc.): see UP *adv.*[2] *To f. like* (doing something); to have an inclination for (? orig. *U.S.*: now common). **5.** To f. inconvenience from heat 1767. **6.** I was too young to f. my loss 1726. Phr. *To f. the helm*, said of a ship when she begins to obey the helm. **7.** No man can see his army perish by want without feeling for them WELLINGTON. **8. b.** Legislation felt to be inexpedient 1895.

III. In quasi-passive sense with complement: To be felt as having a specified quality; to seem 1581.

The air felt chilly 1825.

Hence **Fee·lable** *a.* that may or can be felt.

Feeler (fī·ləɹ). 1526. [f. FEEL *v.* + -ER[1].] **1.** One who or that which feels. **2.** *Biol.* One of the organs with which certain animals are furnished, for trying objects by the touch or for searching for food; a palp 1665. Also *transf.* and *fig.* **3.** One sent out to feel the enemy; *transf.* a proposal or hint put forth or thrown out in order to ascertain the opinions of others 1830.

2. Her ships were the feelers with which she touched on Greece and Italy MERIVALE.

Feeling (fī·liŋ), *vbl. sb.* ME. [f. FEEL *v.* + -ING[1].] **1.** The action of FEEL *v.* in various senses. Chiefly *gerundial.* **2.** The faculty or power by which one feels (in sense II. 1. of the vb.); the general sensibility of the body, as dist. from the special senses ME.; a physical sensation or perception due to this ME. **3.** The condition of being emotionally affected; an emotion ME.; *pl.* emotions, susceptibilities, sympathies 1771. **4.** Capacity or readiness to feel; susceptibility to the higher emotions; *esp.* tenderness for the sufferings of others 1588. **5.** Pleasurable or painful consciousness ME. **6.** What one feels in regard to something; also, the objective quality occasioning this. Also *transf.* of a language. 1449. **7.** *Psychol.* **a.** 'A fact or state of consciousness' (J. S. Mill and others). **b.** As a generic term comprising sensation, desire, and emotion only. **c.** (After Kant's *gefühl*) The element of pleasure or pain in any state. **d.** An intuitive cognition or belief. 1739. **8.** In *Fine Art*; cf. senses 3–5. **a.** *Painting.* That 'quality in a work of art which..depicts the mental emotion of the painter' 1854. **b.** *Arch.* The general tone of a building or style of architecture; the impression produced on a spectator 1859.

1. The first f. of a febrile attack 1805. **2.** There is not a living creature..but hath the sence of f., although it have none else P. HOLLAND. **3.** All classes..were agreed in one common f. of displeasure FROUDE. **4.** She has..not one grain of F. SWIFT. **6.** The apprehension of the good, Giues but the greater f. to the worse *Rich. II*, I. iii. 301.

Feeling (fī·liŋ), *ppl. a.* ME. [f. as prec. + -ING[2].] That feels. **1.** Sentient; capable of sensation. **2.** Accessible to emotion; sympathetic, compassionate 1618; of language: Indicating emotion 1586. **3.** That is deeply or sensibly felt or realized, heart-felt, vivid 1530.

2. His f. wordes SPENSER. **3.** A f. sense Of all your royal favours 1721. Hence **Fee·lingly** *adv.*

Feer(e, var. of FERE *sb.*[1]; also obs. f. FEAR.

Fee:-si·mple. 1463. [– AFr. *fee-simple*; see FEE *sb.*[2], SIMPLE.] *Law.* An estate in land, etc., belonging to the owner and his heirs for ever, without limitation to any class of heirs. *In fee-simple*: in absolute possession. Also *transf.* and *fig.*

fig. He will sell the fee-simple of his saluation *All's Well* IV. iii. 311.

Feet, *pl.* of FOOT.

Fee:-tai·l. 1495. [– AFr. *fee tailé* = AL. *feudum talliatum*; see FEE *sb.*[2], TAIL *a.*] *Law.* An estate of inheritance entailed or limited to some particular class of heirs; a limited fee. *Fee-tail expectant*: see EXPECTANT *a.* 2.

Feetless (fī·tlės), *a.* 1605. [See -LESS.] Without feet.

Feeze (fīz), *sb.* ME. [f. next.] **1.** A rush; hence, a violent impact. Also, a rub. Now *dial.* and *U.S.* **2.** *U.S. colloq.* A state of perturbation 1846.

1. Phr. *To fetch* or *take* (*one's*) *f.*: to take a short run before leaping.

Feeze (fīz), *v.*[1] Now *dial.* [OE. *fēsian*, of unkn. origin. Cf. FAZE.] †**1.** *trans.* To drive; to drive off or away –1689. **2.** To frighten ME. **3. a.** *vaguely*, To 'do for' (a person) 1596. **b.** To beat, flog 1610.

3. a. Ile pheeze you infaith *Tam. Shr.* Induct. i. 1.

Feeze (fīz), *v.*[2] *dial.* 17.. [Of unkn. origin.] **1.** *trans.* To turn, as a screw; also *fig.* 1806. **2.** *intr.* for *refl.* To wind in and out; to hang off and on.

Feff, Feffment: see FEOFF.

Fegary (fīgē·ri). 1600. A corruption of VAGARY, q.v.

Fegs (fegz). Now *Sc.* and *dial.* 1598. [Distortion of FAY *sb.*[1], FAITH, perh. + -KIN(S.] An exclam., expressing asseveration or astonishment. Also as an (unmeaning) sb.

Feign (fēⁱn), *v.* [ME. *feigne, feine, fene* – (O)Fr. *feign-*, pres. stem of *feindre* :– L.

fingere form, mould, conceive, contrive.] **1.** *trans.* To fashion, form, shape. Now only after L. **2.** To invent; to forge ME. **3.** To relate in fiction; to fable. Now *rare.* ME. **†b.** *absol.* and *intr.* To indulge in fiction –1636. **4.** To suppose arbitrarily or erroneously. Now *rare.* ME. **5.** *trans.* To assert or maintain fictitiously; to pretend ME. **†6.** To practise dissimulation, dissemble (*refl.* and *intr.* for *refl.*) –1559. Also *trans.* To conceal SPENSER. **7.** *trans.* To make a show of, pretend, simulate, sham; also *absol.* ME. **8.** *refl.* and *intr.* To pretend, make oneself appear ME. **9.** To counterfeit 1484. **†10.** To make a feint –1632. **†11.** *Mus.* To sing softly; also, to sing with due regard to the 'accidentals' –1553. **†12.** To shirk (*trans.* and *intr.*) –1535.

2. Thou hast feigned This tale GOWER. 3. Things..worse Than Fables yet have feign'd MILT. *P. L.* XI. 627. 4. The Straights, where they fained Hercules his pillars to be BP. STILLINGFL. 7. Escaped death, onely by feigning it 1741. *absol.* She cannot f. C. BRONTË. 8. Faine thy selfe to be a mourner 2 *Sam.* 14:2. 12. There they made a great assaut. The Englysshmen fayned nat LD. BERNERS. **Feigned** *ppl. a.* **Fei·gned-ly** *adv.*, **-ness. Fei·gner. Fei·gningly** *adv.*

Feint (fēⁱnt), *sb.* 1679. [– (O)Fr. *feinte*, subst. use of fem. of pa. pple. of *feindre* FEIGN.] **1.** A feigned or false attack; *esp.* in *Mil.* a movement made with the object of deceiving an enemy as to a general's real plans 1683. **2.** *transf.* and *fig.* An assumed appearance; a pretence, stratagem 1679.

1. A f. at the head BAKER. An attack on India by way of f. G. DUFF.

Feint (fēⁱnt), *a.* ME. [– (O)Fr. *feint*, pa. pple. of *feindre* FEIGN.] Feigned, false, or counterfeit; sham. Now *rare.* **b.** In commercial use: = FAINT *a.* 5b.

The Major..made a f. Retreat 1702.

Feint, *v.* ME. [In sense 1 f. Fr. *feint* (see prec.); in sense 2 f. FEINT *sb.*] **†1.** To deceive. ME. only. **2.** *Mil.*, etc. **a** *intr.* To make a feint or sham attack. **b.** *trans.* To pretend to make (a pass or cut). 1833.

†Fei·rie, *a. Sc.* ME. [perh. repr. OE. **fēriġ*, f. *fōr* action of going + *-iġ* -Y¹; cf. synon. FERE *a.*] Fit to travel; hence, nimble, vigorous. –1794.

Felanders, obs. f. FILANDERS.

Fela·pton. 1551. *Logic.* A mnemonic word representing the fourth mood in the third syllogistic figure, in which a universal negative major premiss and a universal affirmative minor yield a particular negative conclusion.

Feldspar, felspar (fe·ldspaɹ, fe·lspaɹ). 1757. [alt. of G. *feldspat(h)*, f. *feld* field + *spat(h)* spar. Cf. SPAR *sb.*³ The common sp. *fels-* is due to false deriv. from G. *fels* rock. The current G. form is *feldspat.*] *Min.* Name of a group of minerals, usually white or flesh-red in colour, occurring in crystals or in crystalline masses. They consist of a silicate of alumina with soda, potash, lime, etc. Also *attrib.* Hence **Fe·ldsparite** = FELDSPAR.

Feldspathic, felspathic (feld-, felspæ·þik), *a.* 1832. [f. *fel(d)spath* (see prec.) + -IC.] Of the nature of or containing feldspar. var. **Fe:l(d)spatho·se.**

†Fele. [OE. (WS.) *feola, fela* = OFris. *felo*, OS. *filo, filu* (Du. *veel*), *filo* (G. *viel*), ON. *fiǫl*, Goth. *filu* :– Gmc. **felu* :– IE. **pélu*; cf. Gr. πολύς.]

A. *adv.* (and quasi-*sb.*) Much –1598.

B. *adj.* (Indeclinable) **1.** With *sb.* in *pl.* Many –1598. **b.** With *sb.* in *sing.* Much –1535. **2.** In predicative use: Much, many. Also in compar.: more in number. Only ME. **3.** *absol.* in *pl.* Many persons –1450 Hence **†Fe·lefold** *a.* (*adv.*) = MANIFOLD. Chaucer.

Felicific (fīlisi·fik), *a.* 1865. [f. L. *felix, felic-* happy + -FIC.] Making happy; productive of happiness.

†Feli·cify, *v. rare.* 1683. [f. L. *felix, felic-* + -FY.] To render happy; also *absol.* –1698.

†Feli·citate, *pa. pple.* [– late L. *felicitatus*, pa. pple. of *felicitare*; see next, -ATE².] Made happy. *Lear* I. i. 77.

Felicitate (fīli·siteⁱt). *v.* 1628. [– *felicitat-*, pa. ppl. stem of late L. *felicitare* make very happy, f. *felix* happy; see -ATE³.] **1.** To make happy; also *absol.* Now *rare.* **2.** To reckon or pronounce happy; to congratulate (now only a person). Const. *on, upon.* 1634. **†3.** To offer congratulations on 1684.

1. Since I cannot make myself happy, I will have the glory to f. another DRYDEN. 2. A great poet felicitated himself that poetry was not the business of his life D'ISRAELI. 3. To f. his Majesties happy return 1684. Hence **Feli:cita·tion,** the action of congratulating; a congratulatory speech or message; also *attrib.* **Feli·citator.**

Felicitous (fīli·sitəs), *a.* 1735. [f. FELICITY + -OUS.] **1.** Characterized by felicity, blissful (*rare*) 1824; †prosperous, successful 1735. **2.** Strikingly apt; of persons: Happy in expression, manner, or style 1789.

2. A f. adaption of the organ to the object PALEY. F. in jests upon his own figure LAMB. Hence **Feli·citous-ly** *adv.*, **-ness** (Dicts.).

Felicity (fīli·siti). ME. [– (O)Fr. *félicité* – L. *felicitas*, f. *felix, felic-* happy; see -ITY.] **1.** The state of being happy; happiness (in mod. use, intense happiness, bliss). **2.** That which causes happiness; a source of happiness, a blessing ME. **3.** Prosperity (now *rare*) ME.; †*pl.* prosperous circumstances; successes –1731; a fortunate trait 1761. **4.** A happy faculty in art or speech 1605; a strikingly apt expression 1665. **†5.** Of a planet: A favourable aspect. Only ME.

1. Absent thee from felicitie awhile *Haml* V. ii. 358. 2, His coine..is his only hope and felicitie 1597. 3. The felicities of Salomon BACON. 4. Those felicities which cannot be produced at will by wit and labour JOHNSON.

Felid (fī·lid). [– mod.L. *felidæ*, f. *feles* cat; see -ID³.] One of the *Felidæ* or cat-tribe.

Feliform (fī·lifǭɹm), *a.* [f. L. *feles* cat + -FORM.] Having the form of a cat.

Feline (fī·ləin, -lin). 1681. [– L. *felinus*, f. *feles* cat; see -INE¹.]

A. *adj.* **1.** Of or pertaining to cats or their species, cat-like in form or structure. **2.** Resembling a cat in character or quality 1843.

1. The f. quadrupeds 1833. 2. The f. care with which he stepped aside from any patches of mire LYTTON.

B. *sb.* An animal of the cat tribe 1861.

Hence **Fe·line-ly** *adv.*, **-ness. Feli·nity,** f. quality; a cat-like disposition; the typical qualities of the cat tribe.

Fell (fel), *sb.*¹ [OE. *fel(l* = OFris., OS. *fel* (Du. *vel*), OHG. *fel* (G. *fell*), ON. *ber-fjall* bear-skin, Goth. *pruts-fill* 'swelling-skin' :– Gmc. **fellam* :– IE. **pello-*, repr. also by L. *pellis*, Gr. πέλλα skin.] **1.** The skin or hide of an animal, usu. with the hair, wool, etc. Also *transf.* of the human skin OE. **2.** A covering of hair, wool, etc., *esp.* when thick or matted; a fleece 1600.

1. They carie furth..purple died felles 1551. A light brown f. stood out very clearly H. STANLEY. 2. We are still handling our Ewes and their Fels you know are greasie SHAKS. My F. of haire SHAKS.

Fell (fel), *sb.*² ME. [– ON. *fjall* and *fell* hill, mountain, presumably rel. to OS. *felis*, OHG. *felis, felisa* (G. *fels*) rock.] **1.** A hill, mountain. *Obs.* exc. in *Bowfell, Scafell*, etc. **2.** A moorland ridge, down. Now chiefly *north.* and *Sc.* ME. **¶b.** In 16–17th c.: A marsh, fen 1514.

†Fell, *sb.*³ [– L. *fel* (*fell-*) gall.] Gall; hence, rancour. SPENSER.

Fell (fel), *sb.*⁴ 1625. [f. FELL *v.*; see FALL *sb.*¹] **1.** The action of FELL *v.*: **a.** A knock-down blow (*dial.*) 1877. **b.** A cutting down of timber; also *concr.* 1650. **c.** The sewing down (a fold, etc.) level with the cloth; *concr.* a felled seam 1874. **d.** A fall of lambs B. JONS. **2.** The line of termination of a web, formed by the last weft-thread 1874.

Fell (fel), *sb.*⁵ 1653. *Mining.* Lead ore in its rough state; also, lead ore siftings.

Fell (fel), *a.* and *adv.* ME. [– OFr. *fel* :– Rom. **fel(l)o*, the obl. form of which is repr. by FELON.]

A. *adj.* **1.** Fierce, savage; cruel, ruthless; terrible. Now *poet.* or *rhet.* **2.** Dire, intensely painful or destructive. Now *poet.* or *rhet.*; also *dial.* ME. **†3.** Hot, virulent –1590. **4.** Full of spirit, doughty (now *dial.*) ME.; eager (*for, on, †to*); intent *upon* 1666. **†5.** Shrewd; clever, cunning –1725. **6.** 'Mighty'. *Obs.* exc. *Sc.* 1515.

1. My f. hate DEKKER. The..Ban-dog..is fierce, is f. 1688. 2. Despair and f. Disease GRAY. Biting Boreas, f. and doure BURNS. 3. *Mids. N.* II. i. 20. 4. I am so f. to my business that I..will not go PEPYS. 6. A f. time 1586.

B. *adv.* In a fell manner; †cruelly, fiercely; eagerly, vigorously, excessively (now *dial.*) ME.

Fell (fel), *v.*. *Pa. t.* and *pple.* **felled** (feld). [OE. (Anglian) *fellan*, (WS.) *fyllan*, **fiellan* = OFris. *falla, fella*, OS. *fellian* (Du. *vellen*), OHG. *fellen* (G. *fällen*), ON. *fella* :– Gmc. **falljan*, causative of **fallan* FALL *v.*] **1.** To cause to fall; to knock or bring down. †To kill –1681. †Also *fig.* **2.** To cut down (a tree) OE. **†3.** To bring or let down, lower –1620. **4.** To stitch down (the wider of the two edges left projecting by a seam) so that it lies flat and smooth on the under-side of the seam. Also, *to f. a seam.* 1758.

1. Oak or Firr..in Wood or Mountain fell'd MILT. *P.L.* VI. 575. Hence **Fe·llable** *a.* **Fe·ller,** one who or that which fells; a wood-cutter; an attachment to a sewing machine for felling.

Fellah (fe·lā). *Pl.* **fellaheen, fellahs.** 1743. [– Arab. *fallāḥ* husbandman, f. *falaḥa* split, till the soil.] A peasant in Arabic-speaking countries; in *Eng.* used *esp.* of those of Egypt.

Fell-fare, var. of FIELDFARE.

Fellic (fe·lik), *a.* 1884. [f. L. *fel, fell-* gall + -IC.] Only in *Fellic acid*; an acid, $C_{23}H_{40}O_4$, said to accompany cholic acid in human bile.

Fellifluous (feli·fluəs), *a.* 1656. [– late L. *fellifluus* (f. L. *fel* gall + *fluere* flow) + -OUS.] Flowing with gall.

Fellinic (feli·nik), *a.* 1845. [f. L. *fel, fell-* + -IN¹ + -IC.] *Chem.* In *Fellinic acid*: **a.** an acid, $C_{50}H_{36}O_8 4HO$, obtained by treating bile with hydrochloric acid (Berzelius); **b.** a new acid discovered by Schotten in human bile.

Fe·llmo:nger. 1530. [f. FELL *sb.*¹ + MONGER.] A dealer in skins or hides, *esp.* sheep-skins; now, an operative who works skins.

Fellness (fe·lnės). ME. [See -NESS.] **1.** The quality of being fell; fierceness, cruelty; †sternness; keenness (of wind). **†2.** Shrewdness, wisdom. WYCLIF.

Felloe (fe·loᵘ), **felly** (fe·li). [OE. *felg*, pl. *felga*, corresp. to MLG., MDu. *velge* (Du. *velg*), OHG. *felga* (G. *felge*), of unkn. origin. For the twofold development cf. *bellows, belly.* In Eng., both forms are in use; in U.S., *felly* is preferred.] The exterior rim, or a part of the rim, of a wheel, supported by the spokes. In *pl.* the curved pieces of wood, which, joined together, form the rim.

Breake all the Spokes and Fallies from her wheele *Haml.* II. ii. 517.

Fellon(e, obs. ff. FELON.

Fellow (fe·loᵘ), *sb.* [Late OE. *fēolaga* – ON. *félagi*, f. *fé* (= OE. *feoh* FEE *sb.*¹) + **laȝ-*, base of LAY *v.*; primarily, one who lays down money in a joint undertaking (cf. ON. *félag* business partnership).] **†1.** One who shares with another in anything; a partner, colleague, co-worker –1626; in bad sense: An accomplice –1848. Also with *of* –1667. **2.** More vaguely: A companion, associate, comrade. †Also *fig.* and *transf.* ME. †Occas. of women –1611. **3.** One of a pair; the mate, 'marrow'; a counterpart, match ME. **4.** An equal: **a.** in rank (now chiefly *pl.*) ME.; **b.** in ability, etc. ME.; **c.** in kind 1477; **d.** in date (chiefly *pl.*) 1874. **5.** A member of a company or party with common interests ME. **6.** In college or university use: **a.** *orig.* One of the company or corporation who, with their head, constitute a college, and receive emoluments from the corporate revenues 1449. Hence **b.** One of the holders of certain stipendiary positions (called 'Fellowships') tenable for a limited period, on condition of pursuing some specified branch of study 1888. **c.** A member of the governing body, e.g. in the University of London 1837. **7.** A member, or one of certain privileged members, of various learned societies, e.g. the Royal Society, etc. 1664. **8.** Familiar for: man, male person ME. **9.** A term of address: **†a.** orig. = 'comrade' –1594; **b.** *contemptuously* ME.

1. The fellows of his crime MILT. *P. L.* I. 606. 2. Fellows in arms 1653. Phr. *Good* or *jolly f.* = 'boon companion'. *To be* (*hail*) *f. well met*: to be on free and easy terms *with* (a person). 3. Giue

me thy Gloue Souldier; Looke, heere is the f. of it *Hen. V*, IV. viii. 42. **4. a.** His fellowes late, shall be his subjects now 1600. **b.** In reasonynge..he hadde few fellowes 1551. **8.** A worthy F. *Timon* I. i. 229. Phr. *Poor f.*: an exclam. of pity. *My dear f., my good f.* (implying a tone of remonstrance), *old f.* *A f.*: often = 'one', 'anybody' (e.g. the speaker himself). **9. b.** You..have so disdainfully called him f. FIELDING.

attrib. and *Comb.*, as *f.-apostle, -Christian, -communicant, -man, -traveller, tribesman*, etc.; also, **f.-ci·tizen,** a citizen of the same city or polity as another; **-cou·ntryman; -craftsman,** one of the same craft; **-subject,** a subject of the same sovereign.

Fellow (fe·lo^u), *v.* ME. [f. prec. sb.] **1.** *trans.* †To join in partnership or companionship *with, to* –1594; to make an equal *with, to* 1450. †**2.** To be associated with; to be a partner in –1639. **3.** To match 1656. **4.** *nonce-use.* To address as 'fellow'. FIELDING.

4. Don't f. me FIELDING.

Fe:llow-co·mmoner. 1591. [f. FELLOW *sb.*] †1. A joint-partaker with others; *esp.* one who eats at the same table; see COMMONER *sb.* –1642. **2.** A class of undergraduates in Oxford, Cambridge, and Dublin, who dine at the Fellow's table. (Practically *Obs.*) 1637. **3.** One who has a right of common with others. LOCKE.

Fe:llow-crea·ture. 1648. [f. as prec.] A production of the same Creator; now used only of human beings and (occas.) animals.

Yon worm, man's fellow-creature BROWNING.

†**Fe:llow-fee·l,** *v.* 1612. [Back-formation from next.] **1.** *intr.* To share the feelings of others; to sympathize *with* –1641. **2.** *trans.* To share the feeling of. ROGERS.

Fe:llow-fee·ling, *vbl. sb.* 1613. [tr. L. *compassio*, Gr. συμπάθεια SYMPATHY.] **1.** Sympathy. **2.** Sense of community of interest 1712.

2. A fellow-feeling makes us wond'rous kind BYRON.

Fe:llow-hei·r. 1585. A joint heir.

Fellowless (fe·lo^ulės), *a.* ME. [f. FELLOW *sb.* + -LESS.] Without a fellow; †solitary; peerless (*poet.*).

†**Fe·llowlike.** 1526. [f. as prec. + -LIKE.] **A.** *adj.* Like a companion or mate; companionable –1633. **B.** *adv.* Like one's fellows; similarly –1569; sociably –1678.

Fe·llowly. ME (Revived in poet. and rhet. use.) [f. as prec. + -LY¹.] **A.** *adj.* **1.** Like or pertaining to a fellow; social –1578. **2.** Companionable –1688.

2. Mine eyes ev'n sociable to the shew of thine Fall f. drops *Temp.* v. i. 64.

B. *adv.* On equal terms; sociably; hence, familiarly –1631.

†**Fe·llowred.** Only ME. [f. as prec. + -RED.] **1.** Company, fellowship. **2.** Intercourse. **3.** A company of fellows.

Fellowship (fe·lo^uʃip), *sb.* ME. [f. FELLOW *sb.* + -SHIP.] **1.** †Partnership –1623; participation, community of interest, sentiment, nature, etc. ME. **2.** Companionship, company, society ME. **3.** †Dealing –1613; intercourse, *esp.* spiritual ME. **4.** = COMMUNION 3. ME. **5.** The spirit of comradeship ME. **6.** A body of fellows or equals; a company. Now *arch.* ME. **7.** A guild, corporation, company; also †*collect.* ME.; an association of any kind 1541. **8.** The position, or the emoluments, of a fellow in a college, university, learned society, etc. 1536; †*collect.* the body of fellows in a college, etc.; the society constituted by them –1796. **9.** *Arith.* The process by which gain or loss is divided among partners 1561. **10.** *pl.* = *Fellowship porters* (see *Comb.*) DICKENS.

1. A F. in a crie of Players *Haml.* III. ii. 289. I feel by proof That f. in pain divides not smart MILT. *P. R.* I. 401. **2.** To renounce f. with anyone MACAULAY. **3.** F. with the Saints A. V. *Transl. Pref.* 3. **4.** Phr. *To give the right hand of f.* (after Gal. 2:9): to acknowledge as entitled to communion (a literal giving 'the right hand of f.' being in some Protestant denominations a part of the ceremony); also *transf.* **5.** A point of good f. JAS. I. **6.** The goodly felowship [L. *numerus*] of the Prophetes *Bk. Com. Prayer* 1549. **7.** Land is sometimes leased to a small f. JOHNSON. *Comb.* **F. porter,** a member of the f. of the Porters of Billingsgate, a guild having certain monopolies in the City of London.

Fellowship (fe·lo^uʃip), *v.* ME. [f. prec. sb.] †**1.** *trans.* To unite in fellowship. Also *refl.* –1561. †**2.** To accompany –1483. **3.** To admit to fellowship. Now only in religious use. ME. **4.** *intr.* To join in (religious) fellowship. Chiefly U.S. ME.

Fe:llow-so·ldier. 1526. A companion-in-arms.

Felly (fe·li), *adv.* ME. [f. FELL *a.* + -LY².] In a fell manner; fiercely, cruelly, malignantly; †terribly, hence (*dial.*) exceedingly –1807; †craftily, cunningly –1530.

Felly: see FELLOE.

‖**Felo-de-se** (fe:lo di sī·). *Pl.* **felones-, felos-de-se.** 1651. [Anglo-L. *felo* FELON, *de se* of himself.] **1.** One who 'deliberately puts an end to his own existence, or commits any unlawful malicious act, the consequence of which is his own death' (Blackstone). Also *fig.* **2.** Hence, Self-murder, suicide 1771.

Felon (fe·lǫn), *a.* and *sb.*¹ ME. [– (O)Fr. *felon* (OFr. nom. *fel*: see FELL *a.*) = Pr. *felon* (*fel*) :– med.L. *fel(l)o, fel(l)ōn-*, of unkn. origin.]

A. *adj.* **1.** Cruel, fierce, terrible; wicked, base. Now *poet.* Also *transf.* of things and places. †**2.** Courageous –1596. †**3.** 'Terribly' great. *Sc.* –1605. †**4.** Stolen. FULLER.

1. Courtesies..No gratitude in f. minds beget DRYDEN. *transf.* The f. winds MILT. *Lycidas* 91.

B. *sb.*¹ †**1.** A vile or wicked person. Sometimes applied to the Devil. –1814. **2.** *Law.* One who has committed felony. Also *attrib.* as *f. blow.* ME. †**3.** Villany, baseness; perfidy. ME. only.

1. He, the King of Heav'n..Down to the deep abyss the flaming F. strook DRYDEN.

Hence **Fe·loness,** a female f. BROWNING. †**Fe·lonly** *adv.* in a f. manner. **Fe·lonry,** the whole class of felons. (Applied orig. to the convict population of Australia.)

Felon (fe·lǫn). *sb.*² ME. [app. a specific application of prec.; cf. med.L. *fel(l)o* in same sense.] **1.** A small abscess or boil, an inflamed sore; *esp.* a whitlow under or near the nail of a finger or toe. **2.** *attrib.* in names of plants, herbs, etc., as **F.-wort,** (*a*) *Solanum dulcamara*; (*b*) *Chelidonium majus*; (*c*) *Geranium robertianum.* 1715.

Felonious (felō^u·niəs), *a.* 1575. [f. FELONY + -OUS.] **1.** Wicked, atrociously criminal. Now chiefly *poet.* **2.** *Law.* Of or pertaining to, or of the nature of, felony. Hence *pop.*: Thievish. 1634. Of a person: That has committed felony 1857.

1. F. outrages P. HOLLAND. **2.** O thievish night! Why should'st thou, but for some f. end, In thy dark lantern thus close up the stars? MILT. *Comus* 196.

Hence **Felo·nious-ly** *adv.*, **-ness.**

†**Fe·lonous,** *a.* ME. [f. FELON + -OUS.] Of the nature of a felon; like a felon –1596. Hence †**Fe·lonously** *adv.*

Felony (fe·lǫni). ME. [– (O)Fr. *felonie*, f. *felon*; see -Y³.] †**1.** Wickedness, baseness –1489; wrath (after OFr.) –1523. †**2.** Guile, perfidy –1533. †**3.** A crime, misdeed, sin –1523. **4.** *Feudal Law.* An act on the part of a vassal which involved the forfeiture of his fee ME. **5.** *Common and Statute Law.* Any of a class of crimes regarded by the law as of a graver character than misdemeanours. (Including, besides statutable offences, those which formerly involved forfeiture of lands and goods, and corruption of blood; sometimes also, misprision of treason, which is a misdemeanour.) ME.

Felsite (fe·lsəit). 1794. [f. FELS(PAR) + -ITE¹ 2b.] *Min.* = FELSTONE; also *attrib.* Hence **Felsi·tic** *a.* consisting of or containing f.

Felspar, Felspath-: see FELDS-.

Felstone (fe·lstǫn). 1858. [– G. *felsstein*, f. *fels* rock + *stein* stone. First used vaguely for amorphous rocks; now = FELSITE.] *Min.* A designation of compact feldspar occurring in amorphous rock-masses.

Felt (felt), *sb.*¹ [OE. *felt*, corresp. to OS. *filt* (Du. *vilt*), (O)HG. *filz* :– WGmc. **felta*, **felti*. Cf. FILTER *sb.*] **1.** A kind of cloth or stuff made of wool, or of wool and fur or hair, fulled or wrought into a compact substance by rolling and pressure, with lees or size. Also *pl.* **2.** A piece of this; something made of this, *esp.* a felt hat (whence †*transf.* a hat of any material) 1450. **3.** A thickly matted mass of hair or other fibrous substance ME.

1. Mute Silence with her feet in f. WOLCOT. **2.** The bed Of rugs and felts M. ARNOLD. *Comb.* **f.-grain,** 'the grain of wood whose direction is from the pith to the bark; the direction of the medullary rays in oak and some other timber' (KNIGHT).

Felt (felt), *sb.*² *dial.* 1708. [perh. a confusion of FELL *sb.*¹, FELT *sb.*¹, PELT *sb.*] A skin or hide.

Felt (felt), pa. pple. of FEEL *v.*

Felt (felt), *v.* ME. [f. FELT *sb.*¹] **1.** *trans.* To make into felt; to mat or press together into a felt-like consistence 1513; to make of felt ME. **2.** *intr.* for *refl.* To form into felt-like masses, to become matted together 1791. **3.** To cover with felt 1883.

1. They fal to beat, to f., and thicken it close with their feet HOLLAND. **3.** To f. the cylinder of a steam-engine 1895.

Fe·lter, *v.* Now *dial.* ME. [– OFr. *feltrer* (mod. *feutrer*) f. *feltre* (mod. *feutre*) :– med.L. *feltrum, filtrum*; see FILTER *sb.*] **1.** *trans.* To tangle; to mat together. **2.** To entangle 1567. †**3.** = FILTER *v.* B. JONS.

Felting (fe·ltiŋ), *vbl. sb.* 1686. [f. FELT *v.* + -ING¹.] **1.** The action or process of making felt. **2.** *concr.* Felted cloth 1849. **3.** *attrib.* 1805.

Felucca (felɒ·kă). 1628. [– It. *feluc(c)a* – Sp. †*faluca* – Arab. *fulk* (now repl. by romanized *falūkah*), perh. – Gr. ἐφόλκιον sloop.] A small coasting vessel propelled by oars or lateen sails, or both, used chiefly in the Mediterranean.

Brancaccio..fled in a f. [a boat about as big as a Gravesend barge] 1662. Hence **Felu·cca** *v.* to put on board a f. DE FOE.

Felwort (fe·lwɒɹt). [OE. *feldwyrt*, f. *feld* field + *wyrt* root.] **a.** *Gentiana lutea*, and other species of gentian. **b.** *Swertia perennis.*

Female (fī·mē^il). [ME. *femelle, female* – (O)Fr. *femelle* :– L. *femella*, dim. of *femina* woman. The present form is due to assoc. w. *male.*]

A. *adj.* **1.** Belonging to the sex which bears offspring. **2.** *Bot.* **a.** Of the parts of a plant: Fruit-bearing; resulting in a new individual 1791. **b.** Of a blossom or flower: Having a pistil and no stamens; pistillate; fruit-bearing 1796. **c.** Of plants, trees: Applied arbitrarily, *esp.* in **Female hemp** = *fimble-hemp* (see FIMBLE *sb.*) 1548. **3.** Consisting of females 1552. **4.** Of or pertaining to a woman or women 1635. **5.** Characteristic of womankind 1632. †**6.** Womanish –1771. **7.** Epithet of various material and immaterial things, denoting simplicity, inferiority, weakness, or the like ME. **8.** Applied, *esp.* in *Mech.*, to that part of an instrument or contrivance which receives the corresponding or male part 1669.

1. Who is this, what thing of Sea or Land? Femal of sex it seems MILT. *Sams.* 711. The Femal Bee— *P. L.* VII. 490. **2. c.** The male [pympernel] hath a crimsin floure, and the f. hath a blewe TURNER. The f. Iuy so Enrings the barky fingers of the Elme *Mids. N.* IV. i. 48. **3.** Heifars from his F. Store he took DRYDEN. **4.** The force of f. lungs POPE. A f. reign GIBBON. **5.** Femal charm MILT. *P. L.* IX. 999. **7.** The ancients called sapphires male and f...the pale blue, approaching the white, [was] the f. EMANUEL. *F. rime*: = *feminine rime*: see FEMININE. **8.** *F. screw, socket*, a circular hole or socket having a spiral thread adapted to receive the thread of the male screw.

B. *sb.* **1.** A female animal ME. **2.** A female person; as a synonym for 'woman' now only contemptuous ME. **3.** *attrib.* 1599.

1. Conception and Parturition, in the Human f. CARPENTER. **2.** The females..incapable of performing any military service CRUISE. They are no ladies. The only word good enough for them is the word of opprobrium—females 1889. **3.** A f. foe HOWELL.

†**Femalist.** [f. prec. + -IST.] One devoted to the female sex. MARSTON.

Femality (fīmæ·lĭti). 16.. [f. FEMALE *a.* + -ITY. Cf. OFr. *femeleté.*] **1.** Female nature; *pl.* females 1754. **2.** Unmanliness.

Femalize (fī·măləiz), *v.* 1674. [f. as prec. + -IZE.] †**1.** *intr.* To become effeminate. **2.** *trans.* To give a feminine ending to 1709.

2. The following femalized Christian names: Alexandrina, Andrewina..and Williamina 1887.

Feme (fem). Also (exc. techn.) **femme.** ME. [– AFr., OFr. *feme* (mod. *femme*) :– L. *femina.*] **1.** *Law.* (Chiefly conjoined with *baron.*) Wife. †2. In 16th c. often playfully for: Woman –1653.

1. The feme is entitled to dower BACON.

Phr. *Law.* **Feme covert** (fe·m kɒ·vəɹt), a woman under cover or protection of her husband; a married woman. **Feme sole** (fe·m sōᵘ·l), an unmarried woman, a spinster; a widow. Also, a married woman who with respect to property is as if she were unmarried. Also *attrib.*, as *feme-sole merchant, trader.*

Femerell (fe·mĕrĕl). late ME. [In XV *fomerel(l, fumrell, fumerill, femerell* – OFr. *fumeril* louvre (in med.L. *fumerillum, -ellum*), of obscure formation.] A lantern, louvre, or covering placed on the roof of a kitchen, hall, etc., for ventilation or escape of smoke.

Femicide (fe·misəid). 1801. [irreg. f. L. *femina* woman + -CIDE 2, after *homicide.*] The killing of a woman.

†**Fe·minal,** *a.* ME. [– med.L. *feminalis*, f. *femina* woman; see -AL[1]. Cf. OFr. *feminal.*] Of or pertaining to a woman –17..

Feminality (feminæ·lĭti). 1646. [f. prec. + -ITY.] **1.** The quality of a female; female nature. Now *rare.* **2.** *pl.* only *concr.* or quasi-*concr.* A female trait or peculiarity; also, a knick-knack such as women like 1825.

†**Fe·minate,** *a. rare.* 1533. [– L. *feminatus*, f. *femina* woman; see -ATE[2].] Effeminate; femine –1633.

Femineity (feminī·ĭti). 1820. [f. L. *femineus* womanish (f. *femina* woman) + -ITY.] Womanliness; womanishness. So **Femini·lity.**

Feminie (fe·mini). *arch.* ME. [– OFr. *femenie*, f. L. *femina* woman + *-ie* -Y[3].] Womankind; a set of women, *esp.* the Amazons.

He conquered all the regne of F. CHAUCER.

Feminine (fe·minin). ME. [– (O)Fr. *féminin, -ine* or L. *femininus, -ina*, f. *femina* woman; see -INE[1].]

A. *adj.* **1.** Belonging to the female sex; female. Now *rare.* **2.** Hence *transf.* of objects to which sex is attributed 1601. **3.** Of or pertaining to a woman or to women; carried on by women 1489. **4.** Characteristic of women; womanlike, womanly ME. **5.** Depreciatively: Womanish, effeminate. ?*Obs.* ME. **6.** *Gram.* Of the gender to which appellations of females belong ME.

1. Those Male, These F. MILT. *P. L.* I. 423. **2.** They say that the Moone is a planet Fœminine P. HOLLAND. **3.** F. society DISRAELI, discussion 1865. **4.** Of a fœminine and delicate body P. HOLLAND. **5.** He was of so unhappy a f. temper, that he was always in a terrible fright CLARENDON. **6.** Every noun denoting a female animal is f. 1845. Phr. *F. rime*: in French verse, one ending in a mute *e* (as being the feminine suffix); hence, a rime of two syllables of which the second is unstressed. So *f. ending*; *f. cæsura*, one which does not immediately follow the ictus.

B. *sb.* **1.** The adj. used absol. ME. **2.** *Gram.* A word of the feminine gender 1607.

1. The fond F. GLANVILLE. The eternal f. 1892. **2.** Seamstress and songstress are double feminines 1885.

Hence **Fe·minine-ly** *adv.*, **-ness. Fe·mininism,** the state of being f.; a woman's expression.

Femininity (femini·nĭti). ME. [f. prec. + -ITY. Superseded FEMINITY.] **1.** Feminine quality; in early use also, female nature. **2.** Womanishness 1863. **3.** *concr.* Womankind 1865.

1. O serpent under femynynytee CHAUCER.

Feminism (fe·miniz'm). 1851. [– L. *femina* woman + -ISM; in sense 2 – Fr. *féminisme* (Fourier, 1837).] **1.** The qualities of women (*rare*). **2.** Advocacy of the claims and rights of women 1895. So **Fe·minist.**

Feminity (fĭmi·nĭti). ME. [In XV *feminitie*, – (O)Fr. *féminité* – med.L. *feminitas*, f. L. *femina* woman; see -ITY.] = FEMININITY.

The mirrhor of feminitie SPENSER.

Feminize (fe·minəiz), *v.* 1652. [f. L. *femina* + -IZE. Cf. Fr. *féminiser* (XVI).] To make or become feminine.

‖**Femme de chambre** (fam də ʃãñbr). 1762. [Fr.] **1.** A lady's maid. **2.** A chambermaid 1890.

Femoral (fe·mŏrăl). 1782. [f. L. *femur, femor-* thigh + -AL[1].] **A.** *adj.* Of or pertaining to the femur or thigh. Chiefly *Anat.*, as *f. artery*, etc. **B.** *sb.* [sc. *artery*] 1859.

Femur (fī·mɒɹ). *Pl.* **femurs** (fī·mɒɹz), **femora** (fe·mŏră). 1563. [– L. *femur*; see prec.] **1.** *Anat.* The thigh bone in vertebrata 1799. **2.** *Entom.* The analogous part in an insect; the third articulation of the foot 1834. **3.** *Arch.* 'The space between the channels [of the Triglyph]' (Gwilt) 1563.

Fen (fen), *sb.*[1] 1731. [OE. *fen(n)* = OFris. *fen(n)e*, OS. *fen(n)i* (Du. *veen*), OHG. *fenna, fenni* (G. *fenn*), ON. *fen*, Goth. *fani* :– Gmc. **fanjam, -jaz, -jō.*] **1.** Low land covered wholly or partially with shallow water, or frequently inundated; a tract of such land, a marsh. †**2.** Mud, clay, mire, filth –1535.

1. The margin of the broad reedy f. STEVENSON. *The fens*: certain low-lying districts in Cambridgeshire, Lincolnshire, and adjoining counties. *attrib.* and *Comb.*, as *f.-boat, -duck, -fowl, -grass, -land* (whence *-lander*), etc.; also **f.-berry,** the cranberry (*Vaccinium oxycoccus*); **-cricket,** the mole cricket (*Gryllotalpa vulgaris*); **-fire** = IGNIS FATUUS; **-goose,** usually the Gray-Lag Goose (*Anser cinereus*); **-man,** an inhabitant of the fens; **-reeve,** an officer having charge of f. lands; etc.

Fen (fen), *sb.*[2] *dial.* 1731. [OE. *fyne* mildew; the mod. form (with *e* for OE. *y*) is Kentish; cf. FENNY *a.*[2], FINEW *v.*] A mould that attacks the hop-plant.

‖**Fen,** *sb.*[3] ME. [– Arab. *fann* species, class.] A section in Avicenna's Canon. CHAUCER.

Fen (fen), *v.* 1823. [Usually taken to be a corruption of FEND *v.*] *trans.* To forbid. Used chiefly by boys at marbles, etc.

'I'm fly,' says Jo. 'But f. larks, you know!' DICKENS.

Fence, *sb.* [ME. *fens*, aphetic of *defens*, DEFENCE.] †**1.** = DEFENCE –1664. **2.** The action, practice, or art of fencing, or use of the sword. Also *transf.* 1533. †**3.** Means or method of defence; protection, security –1756. **4.** *concr.* That which serves as a defence; a bulwark, defence. (*arch.*) ME. **5.** An enclosure or barrier (*e.g.* a hedge, wall, railing, etc.) along the boundary of any place which it is desired to defend from intruders. Often qualified, as *gun-f.*, RING-FENCE, *wire*, etc. *f.* Also *transf.* and *fig.* 1512. **6.** *Mech.* A guard, guide, or gauge designed to regulate the movements of a tool or machine 1703. **7.** A state of prohibition (cf. L. *in defenso*). STUBBS. **8.** *Thieves' slang.* A receiver of stolen goods; a house where they are received 1700.

1. *Cap of f.*: see CAP *sb.*[1] 1. **2.** The wager at f. with Laertes 1863. *transf.* The Sophists were cunning masters of f. BLACKIE. **4.** Deer-hides..made a rude f. against the blast SCOTT. **5.** The famished lion..O'erleaps the fences of the nightly fold DRYDEN. *fig.* The strong fences of shame and awkwardness LAMB. Phr. *Sunk f.*: one placed along the bottom of a depression in the ground; also, a ditch. *To be on the f.* (U.S.): to be undecided in opinion, or neutral in action. *To make a Virginia f.* (U.S.): to walk like a drunken man.

Comb.: **f.-lizard,** the common small lizard or swift of the United States; †**-man,** a gladiator; **-month,** (*a*) orig. the fawning-time of deer, a period of about 30 days, during which hunting was forbidden; (*b*) the close season for fishing, etc., not restricted to one month; **-play,** †a gladiatorial combat; *transf.* discussion; †**-roof,** a roof for defence (= L. *testudo*); **-season, -time,** a close season or time for fish, swans, etc.; **-shop,** a shop at which stolen goods are sold.

Hence **Fe·nceful** *a.* affording defence. **Fe·nceless** *a.* unenclosed; defenceless.

Fence (fens), *v.* ME. [f. the sb.] **1.** *intr.* To practise the use of the foil or sword; to use the sword scientifically. Also *fig.* of a witness, etc. 1598. **2.** *trans.* To screen, shield, protect. Const. *against, from.* 1510. †**3.** *intr.* To provide protection *against* –1759. **4.** *trans.* To keep out, ward off, repel (*arch.*) 1592. **5.** To surround with or as with a fence; to enclose, fortify. Also *fig.* ME **6.** *intr.* Of a horse: To leap a fence 1884. **7.** *trans.* To close for hunting or fishing. BLACKSTONE. **8.** *slang.* To purchase or sell with guilty knowledge (stolen goods). Also *absol.* 1610.

1. Alas sir, I cannot f. *Merry W.* II. iii. 14. *fig.* For several months..diplomatists fenced among themselves MOTLEY. **2.** A place well fenced from the wind HAKLUYT. He fenced his royal promise with an *if* TENNYSON. **3.** To f. against the infirmities of ill health STERNE. **4.** A cup of sack shall f. the cold SCOTT. **5.** Well fenced either with hedge or pale DE FOE. Fenced round by trees 'B. CORNWALL'. *fig.* Fenced by etiquette EMERSON.

Phr. *To f. the tables* (in Sc. Presbyterian Churches): to deliver an exhortation calculated to deter unworthy persons from communicating.

Hence **Fe·ncer,** one who fences; a swordsman; a horse that jumps fences; a receiver of stolen goods (*slang.*)

Fencible (fe·nsib'l). ME. [aphet. f. *defensable*, DEFENSIBLE.]

A. *adj.* **1.** Fit and liable for defensive military service. Chiefly *Sc.* **2.** Capable of being defended 1590. **3.** The sb. used *attrib.*: Belonging to the *Fencibles* 1795.

1. Let f. men..keep watch and ward CARLYLE. **2.** Houses..fensible against the Arabs LITHGOW.

B. *sb.* A soldier liable only for service at home. Also *land-, river-, sea-f.* 1796.

Fencing (fe·nsiŋ), *vbl. sb.* 1489. [f. FENCE *v.* + -ING[1].] **1.** The action or art of using the sword scientifically; the practice of this art with a blunted sword, foil, or stick. Also *fig.* 1581. **2.** The action of protecting, or of setting up a defence *against* 1489. **3.** The action of putting up fences or enclosing with a fence 1628; *concr.* an enclosure or railing; fences collectively; also (U.S.) the materials for these 1585. **4.** The action of leaping a fence 1827. **5.** *slang.* The receiving of stolen goods 1851.

1. F. is warre without anger FULLER. *fig.* A piece of diplomatic f. FREEMAN.

Fend (fend), *sb. Sc.* and *dial.* 1658. [f. next vb.] **1.** A shift or venture 1724. **2.** Fare 1804. †**3.** *Naut.* = FENDER.

Fend (fend), *v.* ME. [aphet. f. DEFEND.] **1.** *trans.* = DEFEND *v.* (*arch.* or *poet.*) Also *refl.* and *intr.* for *refl.* **2.** *intr.* In *To f. and prove*: To argue 1575. **3.** *trans.* To ward or keep off; *esp.* with *off* ME. **4.** *intr.* To make a shift (*Sc.* and *dial.*) 15.. **b.** = FARE *v.*[1] (*dial.*) 1781.

1. Freedom..shall..f. you with his wing EMERSON. **3.** To f. off the weather SCOTT.

Fend(e, obs. f. FIEND.

Fender (fe·ndəɹ). ME. [f. FEND *v.* + -ER[1].] **1.** = DEFENDER. Now *dial.* **2.** Something that fends or wards off something else 1615: *spec.* **a.** *Naut.* A piece of old cable, or other device, hung over or fixed on a vessel's side to preserve it from damage, e.g. by collision with another vessel or with a wharf 1626. **b.** A large piece of timber placed as a guard in front of a pier, dock-wall, etc. 1739. **c.** A mudguard on a carriage-step 1884. **3.** A metal frame placed in front of a fire to keep falling coals from rolling into the room 1688. **4.** A sluice-gate; *occas.*, the whole sluice 1847.

Comb.: **f.-beam,** (*a*) a beam suspended over a vessel's side to ward off ice, etc.; (*b*) = *f.-stop*; **-pile** = FENDER 2 b; **-stop,** the beams fixed at the end of a line of rails to stop the carriages and prevent their running off.

Fe·ndy, *a. dial.* 1782. [f. FEND *v.* + -Y[1].] Resourceful; managing.

†**Fe·nerate,** *v.* 1623. [– *fænerat-*, pa. ppl. stem of L. *fænerare, -ari*, f. *fænus, fænor-* interest; see -ATE[3].] To lend on interest. (Dicts.) Hence †**Fenera·tion,** the action or practice of fenerating; usury.

Fenestella (fenėste·lă). 1797. [– L., dim. of *fenestra* window; see -EL[2].] **1.** *Arch.* A small windowlike niche on the south side of the altar, containing the piscina and often the credence. **b.** A small window 1848. **2.** *Zool.* 'A polyzoon; known by many fossil remains in Devonian limestones and other rocks' (Rossiter) 1849.

Fenestellid (fenėste·lid). 1882. [f. L. *fenestella* (prec.) + -ID[3].] *Palæont.* One of the *Fenestellidæ*, a family of palæozoic polyzoans.

†**Fene·ster.** ME. [– OFr. *fenestre* (mod. *fenêtre*) :– L. *fenestra*; see next.] A window –1548.

‖**Fenestra** (fĭne·stră). *Pl.* **-træ.** 1828. [L. *fenestra* window, etc.] **1.** *Anat.* A small hole or opening in a bone, etc. **2.** *Bot.* A small mark or scar, indicating the part at which the seed has separated from the ovary (Stark) 1828. Also, 'an opening through a membrane' 1866.

1. The f. ovalis or opening into the vestibule [of the ear] and the f. rotunda or opening into the cochlea 1884.

†**Fene·stral**, *sb.* ME. [– OFr. *fenestral* or med.L. *fenestrale*; see FENESTER, -AL[1].] A window-frame or lattice, often fitted with cloth or paper instead of glass; *rarely*, a window-pane –1530.

Fenestral (fĭne·străl), *a.* 1674. [f. L. *fenestra* window, etc., + -AL[1].] **1.** Of or pertaining to a window. **2.** *Anat.*, etc. 'Having small openings like windows' (Wagstaffe).

Fenestrate (fĭne·strĕt), *a.* 1835. [– L. *fenestratus*, pa. pple. of *fenestrare* furnish with openings or windows; see FENESTRA, -ATE[2].] **1.** Having small window-like openings or perforations. Chiefly *Bot.* and *Zool.* **2.** *Entom.* = FENESTRATED 3. 1842.

Fenestrated (fĭne·streⁱtėd), *ppl. a.* 1826. [f. L. *fenestratus* (see prec.) + -ED[1].] **1.** *Arch.* Furnished with windows 1849. **2.** = FENESTRATE 1. 1849. **3.** *Entom.* Having transparent spots 1826.

Fenestration (fenėstrēⁱ·ʃən). 1846. [f. *fenestrate* v.; see prec., -ATION. In sense 1 perh. after Fr. *fénestration* in same sense.] **1.** *Arch.* The arrangement of windows in a building. **2.** *Anat.* The becoming, or the being, fenestrated 1870.

Fenestrule (fĭne·strul). 1872. [– L. *fenestrula*, dim. of *fenestra* window; see -ULE.] *Zool.* One of the openings in the zoarium of Fenestella, Polypora, and allied species.

Fenian (fī·niăn). 1816. [f. OIr. *féne* 'one of the names of the ancient population of Ireland' (Windisch), confused in mod. times with *fiann* fem. collect., a body of warriors who defended Ireland in the time of Finn, a legendary Irish king. See -IAN.]

A. *sb.* **1.** Applied to mercenary tribes acting as a permanent force for the support of the Ard Rig, or king of Eire. **2.** One of a 'brotherhood' form among the U.S. Irish for the overthrow of English rule in Ireland 1864.

B. *adj.* Of or pertaining to the Fenians or to Fenianism 1861.

Hence **Fe·nianism**, the principles, purposes, and methods of the Fenians.

Fenks (fenks), *pl.* 1820. [Of unkn. origin.] The fibrous parts of the blubber of a whale, which contain the oil; the refuse of the blubber when melted.

‖**Fennec** (fe·nėk). 1790. [Arab. *fanak*.] *Zool.* A small African fox-like animal (*Canis zerda*) having very long ears.

Fennel (fe·nĕl). [OE. *finugl*, *finule* fem., *fenol*, *finul* masc., – pop. forms **fenuclum*, *-oclum*, of L. *feniculum*, dim. of *fenum* hay.] *Bot.* **1.** A fragrant perennial umbellifer (*Fœniculum vulgare*) having yellow flowers, made use of in sauces, etc. **2.** Applied to plants resembling fennel 1523.

1. There's F. for you *Haml.* IV. v. 180. **Sweet F.**, *Fœniculum dulce* or *officinale*, grown in kitchen gardens for the sake of its leaves. **2. Dog** or **Dog's F.**, *Anthemis cotula*. **Hog's F.**, *Peucedanum officinale*. **F.-flower**, a herb of the genus *Nigella*. **F.-giant**, a plant of the genus *Ferula* = *Giant-f.* *Comb.*: **f. oil**, 'the oil of common fennel containing anethol and a terpene' (Watts); **f. water**, a spirituous liquor prepared from fennel seed.

Fennish (fe·niʃ), *a.* 1574. [f. FEN *sb.*[1] + -ISH[1].] **1.** = FENNY *a.*[1] 1. 1577. **2.** Belonging to or produced from a fen 1574.

Fenny (fe·ni), *a.*[1] [OE. *fennig*, f. *fenn* FEN *sb.*[1]; see -Y[1].] **1.** Of the nature of fen; boggy, swampy. **2.** = FENNISH 2. 1543. †**3.** Muddy, dirty –1635.

2. Fillet of a f. snake SHAKS. F. rushes KEATS.

Fe·nny, *a.*[2] Now *dial.* [OE. *fynig*, f. *fyne* FEN *sb.*[2]; see -Y[1].] Mouldy.

†**Fenouille·tte.** 1706. [– Fr., f. *fenouil* FENNEL.] Fennel water –1758.

†**Fe·nsive**, shortened f. DEFENSIVE.

Fent (fent), *sb.* ME. [– (O)Fr. *fente* slit :– Rom. **findita* (repl. L. *fissa*), subst. use of fem. pa. pple. of L. *findere* cleave, split. See VENT *sb.*[1]] **1.** A short slit or opening in a robe. Also a placket-hole. Now chiefly *dial.* **2.** A remnant (of cloth) 1847.

Fenugreek (fe·niugrīk). [OE. *fenogrecum*, superseded in ME. by adoption of (O)Fr. *fenugrec* – L. *fenugræcum*, for *fenum græcum* 'Greek hay'; the Romans used the dried plant for fodder.] A leguminous plant (*Trigonella fœnum græcum*), the seeds of which are used by farriers. Also *attrib.*

Feodary, Feodatory: see FEU-.

Feoff, var. of FIEF *sb.*

Feoff (fef), *v. P. t.* and *pple.* **feoffed.** ME. [– AFr. *feoffer*, OFr. *fieuffer*, *fieffer*, f. *fief* FIEF *sb.* See FEE *sb.*[2]] **1.** *Law.* = ENFEOFF *v.* 1. ? *Obs.* †Also *fig.* –1656. †**2.** To confer (a heritable possession) *upon*. Chiefly *fig.* –1649.

Feoffee (fefī·). ME. [– AFr. *feoffé*, pa. pple. of *feoffer*; see prec., -EE[1].] *Law.* **1.** The person to whom a feoffment is made 1542. **2.** *spec.* One of a board of trustees holding land for charitable or other public purposes.

Feoffment (fe·fmĕnt). ME. [– AFr. *feoffement*; see FEOFF *v.*, -MENT.] *Law.* **1.** The action of investing with a fief or fee. Applied *esp.* to conveyance by livery of seisin (at common law usually evidenced by a deed). †**2.** The deed or instrument by which corporeal hereditaments are conveyed –1672. **3.** The fief conferred ME.

1. Phr. *F. in, of, upon trust, f. to uses*: a grant of land in trust for another, or for certain uses.

Feoffor, feoffer (fe·fəɹ). ME. [– AFr. *feoffour*, f. *feoffer* FEOFF *v.*; see -OUR, -ER[2].] **1.** One who makes a feoffment to another. ¶**2.** Misused for FEOFFEE. –1603.

†**Fer**, *v.* App. meaningless. See context of *Hen. V.* IV, iv. 29.

Fer, *obs.* f. FAR; FEAR *sb.*; FIRE.

Feracious (fĕrēⁱ·ʃəs), *a.* 1637. [f. L. *ferax*, *ferac-* f. *ferre* (bear) + -OUS. See -ACIOUS.] Bearing abundantly; fruitful.

Feracity (fĕræ·sĭti). *rare.* ME. [– L. *feracitas*, f. *ferax*; see prec., -ITY.] The quality of being feracious.

Feral (fīᵊ·răl), *a.*[1] 1621. [– L. *feralis* pertaining to funeral rites or to the dead.] **1.** Deadly, fatal. Freq. in *Astrol.* **2.** Funereal, gloomy 1640.

1. F. diseases BURTON, Signes 1647. **2.** Ferall Birds that love Darknesse GAUDEN.

Feral (fīᵊ·răl), *a.*[2] 1604. [f. L. *ferus* (fem. sb. *fera*, sc. *bestia*, wild animal) + -AL[1].] **1.** Wild, untamed; uncultivated. Often of animals and plants that have run wild. 1659. **2.** Of, pertaining to, or resembling a wild beast; brutal, savage.

‖**Ferash** (fera·ʃ). *Anglo-Ind.* 1600. [Urdu *farrāš* from Arab. *farrāš* carpet spreader.] A menial servant who spreads carpets, pitches tents, etc.

Ferberite (fɔ̄·ɹbĕrəit). 1811. [f. *Ferber* proper name + -ITE[1] 2b.] †**1.** (After J. J. Ferber.) A variety of gneiss. **2.** (After R. Ferber.) A variety of wolfram from Southern Spain 1868.

Ferd, obs. f. FEARED *ppl. a.*

‖**Fer-de-lance** (fęr də lāns, fēᵊɹ də lɑns). 1880. [Fr., lance-head ('-iron').] **1.** *Her.* A lance-head used as a charge 1892. **2.** A venomous serpent (*Trigonocephalus lanceolatus*) of Brazil 1880.

Fer-de-moline (fēᵊɹ də mǫ·lin). 1741. [– Fr. *fer de moulin* 'iron of a mill'.] *Her.* A bearing: The iron support for the moving mill-stone.

Fere, *sb.*[1] Now *arch.* [ME. *fere*, aphet. f. OE. *ġefēra* :– **ʒifōrjon*, f. **ʒi-* Y- + **fōrā* going, way (see FORE *sb.*), f. ablaut root of *faran* FARE *v.*[1]; cf. YFERE.] **1.** A companion, mate; whether male or female. **2.** A husband or wife ME. **3.** An equal ME.

2. The nuptial f. Of famous Vulcan CHAPMAN.

†**Fere**, *sb.*[2]. ME. [aphet. f. OE. *ġefēr* n. (:– **ʒifōrja(m)*), f. as prec.] Companionship; chiefly *concr.* a company. Only ME.

Phr. *In f.*, *i f.* (often written *yfere*): together; in common.

†**Fere**, *a.* Now *Sc.* ME. [– ON. *fœrr* :– (ult.) Gmc. **fōrā* (see FORE *sb.*) f. ablaut stem of OE. *faran* FARE *v.*[1]] Able to go, in health; hence *gen.* able; sound, whole.

I trust to find ye baith haill and f. SCOTT.

†**Fere**, *v.*[1] [OE. *fēran* weak vb., corresp. to OS. *fōrian* (Du. *voeren*) carry, OHG. *fuoren* (G. *führen*) lead, bring, ON. *fœra* (Sw. *föra*, Da, *føre*) bring; :– Gmc. **fōrjan*, causative of **faran* FARE *v.*[1]] *intr.* = FARE *v.*[1] (exc. in senses 3, 5) –1483.

†**Fere**, *v.*[2] ME. [aphet. f. AFFEIR, EFFEIR]. *intr.* To fall by right, appertain, become. Chiefly *impers.* –1513.

Fere, obs. f. FAR, FEAR, FIRE.

Feretory (fe·rĭtŏri). [ME. *fertre* – OFr. *fiertre* :– L. *feretrum* – Gr. φέρετρον bier, f. φέρειν bear, with instr. suffix; altered to *fertour* and thence to *feretory* by assim. to words in *-tory*.] **1.** A portable or stationary shrine, often richly adorned, in which were kept the relics of saints; a tomb. **2.** A bier ME. **3.** The part of an abbey or a church in which shrines were deposited 1449.

1. Porphyry stones for Edward the Confessor's f. H. WALPOLE. var. ‖**Fe·retrum** (in sense 1).

Ferforth, obs. f. FAR-FORTH.

Fergusonite (fɔ̄·ɹgəsənəit). 1827. [f. *Ferguson* (of Raith) + -ITE[1] 2b.] *Min.* 'A metaniobate (and tantalate) of yttrium with erbium, cerium, uranium, iron, calcium, etc.' (Dana).

‖**Feria** (fīᵊ·riă). 1853. [L. *feria* holiday; see FAIR *sb.*[1]] *Eccl.* A week-day, *esp.* an ordinary week-day as opp. to a festival.

Ferial (fīᵊ·riăl). ME. [– (O)Fr. *férial*, or its source med.L. *ferialis*, f. L. *feriæ* FAIR *sb.*[1]]

A. *adj.* **1.** Pertaining to the days of the week, or to a week-day as dist. from a festival. **2.** Pertaining to a holiday 1500.

Phr. *F. day, time* (Sc. Law): in which the courts were closed and legal process was invalid.

B. *sb.* A week-day not a feast or festival 1877.

†**Feria·tion.** 1612. [– med.L. *feriatio*, f. *feriat-*, pa. ppl. stem of L. *feriari* make holiday, f. *feria*; see FERIA, -ION.] Holiday keeping; cessation of work –1822.

†**Fe·rie**, *sb.* ME. [– (O)Fr. *férie* – L. *feria*.] **1.** A festival, holiday. Also *attrib.* –1616. **2.** = FERIA. –1588.

Ferine (fīᵊ·rəin). 1640. [– L. *ferinus*, f. *fera* wild beast; see FERAL *a.*[2], -INE[1].]

A. *adj.* **1.** Pertaining to, or of the nature of, wild animals; wild, untamed 1677. **2.** Of human beings, etc.: Bestial, beast-like 1640. **3.** Of a disease; Malignant (*rare*) 1666.

1. Some in f. Venation take delight MOTTEUX.

B. *sb.* A wild beast. (Dicts.)

Hence **Fe·rine-ly** *adv.*, **-ness.**

Feringhee (fĕri·ŋgi). 1634. [Oriental adoption of FRANK, with Arab. ethnic suffix *-i*; in Arab. *faranji*, in Pers. *farangī*.] Formerly, the Indian term for a European; now used chiefly of the Indian-born Portuguese, and contemptuously of other Europeans.

Ferio (fe·ri,o). 1551. *Logic.* A mnemonic word representing the fourth mood of the first syllogistic figure, in which a universal negative major premiss and a particular affirmative minor yield a particular negative conclusion.

Ferison (ferəi·sǫn). 1509. *Logic.* A mnemonic word representing the sixth mood of the third syllogistic figure, in which a universal negative major premiss and a particular affirmative minor yield a particular negative conclusion.

Ferity (fe·rĭti). 1534. [– OFr. *ferite* or L. *feritas*, *-tat-*, f. *ferus* wild; see -ITY.] **1.** The quality of being wild or savage. **2.** Savage or barbarous condition 1646. †**3.** Barbarity, savage cruelty –1718.

2. The ancient Rudeness and F. of our Country STANHOPE.

Fe·rling. Now *Hist.* [OE. *fērþling*, f. *fēorþa* FOURTH + -LING[1].] = FARTHING.

Ferly (fɔ̄·ɹli). [OE. *fǣrlić*, f. *fǣr* FEAR *sb.* + *-lić* -LY[1].]

†**A.** *adj.* **1.** Sudden – ME. **2.** Terrible –1577. **3.** Strange, wonderful –1650; wonderfully great –1450.

2. Furres of f. bestes 1460. Hence †**Fe·rly** *adv.*

B. *sb.* Now *Sc.* and *dial.* **1.** A marvel ME. **2.** Wonder, astonishment ME.

Fermacy, obs. f. PHARMACY.

Fermage, Ferm(e, etc., var. of FARMAGE, FARM, etc.

Fermail (fɔ̄·ɹmeⁱl). 1480. [– (O)Fr. *fermail* (OFr. also *-aille*) :– med.L. *firm-*, *fermaculum* clasp, brooch, buckle, f. L. *firmare* fix; see FIRM *v.*, -AL[1].] *Her.*, etc. A buckle or clasp; a setting.

Ferment (fɔ̄·ɹmĕnt), *sb.* ME. [– (O)Fr. *ferment* or L. *fermentum*, f. *fervēre* boil; see -MENT.] **1.** *orig.* Leaven or yeast; hence *gen.* that which causes fermentation. Also *fig.* **2.** = FERMENTATION 1. 1605. **3.** *fig.* Agitation, tumult 1672.

1. Pasteur..proved the real 'ferments'..to be organised beings TYNDALL. *fig.* This hypothesis lays a f. for frequent rebellion LOCKE. 2. The first f. of new wine 1744. 3. To allay the general f. 1781.

Ferment (fəɹme·nt), *v.* ME. [– (O)Fr. *fermenter* – L. *fermentare*, f. *fermentum*; see prec.] **1.** *intr.* To undergo the action of a ferment; to suffer fermentation; to 'work'. (In early use primarily of dough or saccharine fluids.) Also *fig.* **2.** *trans.* To subject to fermentation; to cause fermentation in 1672. **3.** *transf.* and *fig.* To work up into an agitation; to excite, stir up 1660.

1. *fig.* My griefs..f. and rage MILT. *Sams.* 619. 2. *fig.* Fanaticism..fermented with the leaven of earthly avarice 1759. 3. Ye vig'rous swains, while youth ferments your blood POPE.

Hence **Ferme·ntable** *a.* capable of fermentation. **Fermente·scible**, (also *erron.* **-iscible**), *a.* capable of causing or of undergoing fermentation.

†**Ferme·ntal,** *a.* 1650. [f. FERMENT *sb.* + -AL[1].] Pertaining to, or of the nature of, a ferment or fermentation –1694.

Fermentarian (fɔ̄ɹmĕntēᵊ·riăn). 1775. [f. med.L. *fermentarius* sb., in same sense, f. late L. *fermentarius* adj., f. L. *fermentum* FERMENT *sb.*; see -ARY[1], -ARIAN.] A term of reproach applied by Latin to Greek Christians, as using fermented bread in the Eucharist.

†**Fe·rmentate,** *v.* 1599. [– *fermentat-*, pa. ppl. stem of L. *fermentare* FERMENT *v.*; see -ATE[3].] *trans.* To cause to ferment; to leaven –1670.

Fermentation (fɔ̄ɹmĕntēⁱ·ʃən). ME. [– late L. *fermentatio*, f. as prec.; see -ION. Cf. Fr. *fermentation*.] The action or process of fermenting. **1.** A process of the nature of that resulting from the operation of leaven on dough or on saccharine liquids.

The features of the process are an effervescence, with evolution of heat, in the substance operated on, and a resulting alteration of its properties. In early use, the term was applied to all chemical changes exhibiting these characters. In modern science it is restricted to a definite class of chemical changes peculiar to organic compounds, and produced in them by a 'ferment' (see FERMENT *sb.* 1), and variously qualified as *acetous*, *lactic*, *putrefactive*, etc. (see these words). In popular language the term usually conveys the notion of a sensible 'working', which is not involved in the chemical sense, but its application is now similarly restricted.

2. *fig.* The state of being excited by emotion or passion; agitation; working (sometimes towards a better condition of things) 1660.

2. Predicting..the happy future State of our Country; and that the then F. would be perfective to it 1682. The intellectual f. of Germany MILL.

Fermentative (fɔ̄ɹme·ntătiv), *a.* 1661. [f. as prec. + -IVE. Cf. Fr. *fermentatif*, *-ive*.] **1.** of, pertaining to, or of the nature of fermentation; developed by fermentation 1665. **2.** Tending to cause or undergo fermentation.

1. F. changes 1869. Hence **Ferme·ntative-ly** *adv.*, **-ness.** So **Ferme·ntatory** (in sense 1).

Fermentive (fəɹme·ntiv), *a.* 1656. [f. FERMENT *sb.* or *v.* + -IVE.] Tending to produce fermentation.

†**Fe·rmerer.** ME. [aphet. f. AFr. *enfermerer*, OFr. *-ier*, f. *enfermerie*; see next, -ER[2]. Cf. med.L. *firmarius*, beside *infirmarius* INFIRMARER.] The superintendent of a (monastic) infirmary. CHAUCER.

Fe·rmery, fa·rmery. Now *Hist.* ME. [aphet. f. OFr. *enfermerie* – med.L. *infirmaria*; see INFIRMARY, -ERY. Cf. med.L. aphet. forms *firmaria*, *-arium*, *fermaria*, *-arium*.] = INFIRMARY.

†**Fe·rmillet.** 1475. [– OFr. *fermillet*, *fermaillet*, dim. of *fermail* FERMAIL.] A clasp, buckle, or setting –1633.

†**Fern,** *a.* and *adv.* [OE. *fyrn*, cogn. w. OS. *furn*, *forn* formerly, OHG. *forn* formerly, ON. *forn* adj. ancient.]

A. *adj.* Former, ancient, of old –1571.

B. *adv.* Long ago, formerly –ME.

Fern (fɔ̄ɹn), *sb.* [OE. *fearn* = MDu. *væren* (Du. *varen*), OHG. *farn* (G. *farn*):– WGmc. **farno*.] *Bot.* One of a large group of vascular cryptogamous plants constituting the N.O. *Filices*; a single plant or frond; also *collect.* in *sing.*

Flowering or **Royal F.**: *Osmunda regalis*; see OSMUND[2]. **Hard f.** = *Blechnum.* **Lady f.** = *Athyrium filix-femina.* **Male f.** = *Lastrea filix-mas.* **Prickly f.** = *Polystichum aculeatum.* See also *bladder-*, *buckler-*, etc. *f.*

Comb.: **f.-bracken** = BRACKEN[1]; **-brake** = prec.; also, a thicket of f.; **-chafer**, a beetle (*Scarabæus* or *Amphimalla solstitialis*); **-gale**, the Sweet F. (*Myrica comptonia*); **-tree** = *tree f.*; **-web**, a beetle (*Scarabæus* or *Melorontha horticola*).

†**Ferna·mbuck.** 1595. [Corruptly f. *Pernambuco*.] = BRAZIL *sb.* 1. Also *attrib.* –1722.

Fernery (fɔ̄·ɹnĕri). 1840. [f. FERN *sb.* + -ERY.] A place or a glass case in which ferns are grown.

Fe·rn-owl. 1678; [f. FERN *sb.* + OWL.] **a.** The Nightjar or Goatsucker. **b.** The Short-eared owl 1885.

Fe·rn-seed. 1596. [f. as prec. + SEED *sb.*] The seed of the fern; once popularly supposed to be an invisible seed and to confer invisibility upon its possessor.

1 *Hen. IV*, II. i. 96.

Ferntickle (fɔ̄·ɹntik'l). Now *dial.* 1483. [Of unkn. origin.] 'A freckle on the skin, resembling the seed of fern' (Webst.).

Ferny (fɔ̄·ɹni), *a.* 1523. [f. FERN *sb.* + -Y[1].] **1.** Abounding in fern. **2.** Of, pertaining to, or consisting of fern 1710. **3.** Resembling fern 1791.

†**Fe·rnyear, fern year.** [OE. *fyrnġear*; see FERN *a.*, YEAR.]

A. *sb.* **1.** A past year –1562. **2.** Last year –1737.

2. Farwel al the snowgh of ferne yere CHAUCER.

B. *adv.* In past years; in the course of last year –1806.

Ferocious (fĕrōᵘ·ʃəs), *a.* 1646. [f. L. *ferox*, *feroc-*: see -IOUS.] **1.** Fierce, savage; savagely cruel or destructive. **2.** Indicating ferocity 1728.

1. The Lyon a..f. animall SIR T. BROWNE. 2. F. eyes 1826. Hence **Fero·cious-ly** *adv.*, **-ness.**

Ferocity (fĕrǫ·sĭti). 1606. [–(O)Fr. *férocité* or L. *ferocitas*, f. as prec.; see -ITY.] The quality or state of being ferocious; habitual fierceness or savageness.

It [fear] is always joined with f. RUSKIN.

†**Fe·rous,** *a. rare.* 1653. [f. L. *ferus* wild + -OUS.] Wild, savage.

-ferous, in use always **-iferous** (i·fĕrəs), an adjectival suffix f. L. *-fer* producing (f. *ferre* to bear) + -OUS; as, *auriferous*, *frugiferous*, *luciferous*, etc.

Ferox (fe·rǫks). 1867. [– L. (*salmo*) *ferox*, lit. 'fierce salmon', the scientific name.] A fish (*Salmo ferox*), the great Lake Trout.

†**Fe·rrament.** ME. [– OFr. *ferrement* – L. *ferramentum* implement of iron, f. *ferrum* iron; see -MENT.] *pl.* Articles of iron; *e.g.* instruments, tools, irons, shackles, fittings, etc. –1660.

Ferrandin, var. of †FARANDINE.

Ferra·ra, *rare.* 1762. A broadsword; an 'Andrea Ferrara'. Cf. ANDREW 1. –1785.

†**Fe·rrary.** 1609. [– L. *ferraria* iron mine, iron works, subst. use of fem. of *ferrarius* occupied with iron, f. *ferrum* iron; see -ARY[1].] The smith's art –1611.

Ferrate (fe·reⁱt). 1854. [f. L. *ferrum* iron + -ATE[4].] *Chem.* A salt of ferric acid.

Ferrateen. *rare.* Cf. FERRETING *sb.* SCOTT.

Ferr(e, obs. of FAR *adv.*, *a.*, and *v.*

†**Fe·rren,** *adv.* and *a.* [OE. *feorran*, *feorrane*, corresp. to OS. *ferran*, *-ana*, OHG. *ferrana*, *-ano*, f. Gmc. **ferrō*; see FAR *adv.*]

A. *adv.* **1.** From far –ME. **2.** Afar –ME. **3.** With preps. *of*, *on* (*o*), *from ferren*: from or at a distance –1470.

B. *adj.* Distant, far –1548.

Ferreous (fe·rĭ,əs), *a.* 1646. [f. L. *ferreus* (f. *ferrum* iron) + -OUS; see -EOUS.] **1.** Pertaining to, consisting of, or containing iron. **2.** Like iron: **a.** in hardness 1822; **b.** in colour 1889.

†**Fe·rrer, fe·rrour.** ME. [– OFr. *fereor*, *ferour* (mod. *ferreur*) :– med.L. *ferrator*, f. *ferrare* shoe horses, f. L. *ferrum* iron, in med.L. horseshoe; see -OUR, -ER[2].] **1.** A worker in iron –1609. **2.** = FARRIER 1. –1798.

Ferret (fe·rĕt), *sb.*[1] [Late ME. *fyrette*, *forette*, *firette* – OFr. *fuiret*, (also mod.) *furet*, by suffix-substitution from OFr. *fuiron* (:– Rom. **furione*), beside *furon* :– late L. *furo*, *furōn-* thief, ferret, f. L. *fur* thief.] A half-tamed variety of the common polecat, (*Putorius fœtidus*), kept for driving rabbits from their burrows, destroying rats, etc. Also *transf.* and *fig.*

Comb. **f.-eye,** 'the spur-winged goose, so called from the red circle around the eyes' (Webst.).

Hence **Fe·rrety** *a.* like a f. or a ferret's.

Ferret (fe·rĕt), *sb.*[2] 1576. [prob. – It. *fioretti* floss-silk, pl. of *fioretto*, dim. of *fiore* FLOWER *sb.*] †**1.** attrib. *F.-silk* = floss-silk –1612. **2.** A stout cotton (or silk) tape. Also *attrib.* 1649.

†**Fe·rret,** *sb.*[3] *rare.* 1662. [– Fr. *ferret*, f. *fer* iron; see -ET.] *Glass-making.* An iron used for trying whether the melted glass is fit to work; also, an iron for forming the ring at the mouth of bottles. (Now only in Dicts.)

Ferret (fe·rĕt), *v.* 1450. [f. FERRET *sb.*[1]; cf. Fr. *fureter*.] **1.** *intr.* To hunt with ferrets; *trans.* to clear out by means of a ferret. **2.** *trans.* To take (rabbits, etc.) with ferrets. Also, to drive forth by means of a ferret. 1577. **3.** To hunt after, to worry 1599; to drive *from*, *off*, *out of* 1601; to search (a place) 1583. **4.** *intr.* To rummage, search about 1580. **5.** *trans.* With *out*, *up*: To search out, bring to light 1577.

3. And..vow'd He'd f. him, lurk where he wou'd BUTLER *Hud.* I. iii. 236. To f. this vermin brood out of the colonies W. IRVING. 5. I have ferreted out evidence, got up cases DICKENS. Hence **Fe·rreter.**

Ferreting (fe·rĕtiŋ), *sb.* 1670. [f. FERRET *sb.*[2] + -ING[1].] = FERRET *sb.*[2]

Ferretto (fere·to). Also **feretto.** 1662. [– It. *ferretto* (*di Spagna*), dim. of *ferro* iron :– L. *ferrum*.] Copper calcined with brimstone or white vitriol, used to colour glass.

Ferri- (fe·ri), formerly **ferrid-,** comb. f., indicating the presence of iron in the 'ferric' state (cf. FERRO-). **Ferricyanhy·dric** or **Ferricya·nic acid,** an acid, H_4FeCy_6, procured from various ferricyanides, and crystallizing in lustrous brownish-green needles. **Ferricy·anide,** a salt of ferricyanhydric acid, e.g. *potassium ferricyanide*, red prussiate of potash; *ferrous ferricyanide*, Turnbull's blue. **Ferricya·nogen,** the hypothetical radical $FeCy_2$ supposed to exist in ferricyanhydric acid.

Ferriage (fe·ri,ėdʒ). ME. [f. FERRY *sb.* and *v.* + -AGE.] **1.** The action or business of ferrying; conveyance over a ferry 1450. **2.** The fare or price paid for the use of a ferry.

1. We were detained..waiting f. 1880.

Ferric (fe·rik), *a.* 1799. [f. L. *ferrum* iron + -IC. Cf. Fr. *ferrique*.] **1.** Of, pertaining to, or extracted from iron. **2.** *Chem.* Applied to compounds in which iron exists in its higher valency, as *ferric acid*, a hypothetical acid N_2FeO, assumed to exist in the salts called ferrates.

Ferrier (fe·ri,əɹ). ME. [f. FERRY *v.* + -ER.[1]] = FERRYMAN.

Ferriferous (feri·fĕrəs), *a.* 1811. [f. L. *ferrum* iron + -FEROUS.] Producing iron, as *f. rocks.*

Ferris (fe·ris). 1893. [f. the name of G. W. G. *Ferris*, U.S. engineer.] *F. wheel*, an amusement device consisting of an enormous revolving vertical wheel supporting passenger cars on its periphery.

Ferrite (fe·rəit). 1879. [f. L. *ferrum* iron + -ITE[1] 2b, 4b.] **1.** *Min.* Amorphous hydroxide of iron of undetermined composition. **2.** *Chem.* 'A combination of ferric oxide with a metallic oxide more basic than itself, as *barium ferrite*, $BaFe_2O_4$; etc.' (Muir).

Ferro- (fero). **1.** Used as comb. f. of L. *ferrum* iron, chiefly *Min.* in the names of species containing iron, as **ferro-calcite,** a variety of calcite which contains carbonate of iron and turns brown on exposure; **ferromagne·tic** *a.*, = PARAMAGNETIC; **ferromagnetism,** = PARAMAGNETISM; **ferromanganese,** an alloy of iron and manganese (containing 15 per cent. and upward of manganese); **ferro-tungsten,** iron containing a certain percentage of tungsten.

2. *Chem.* Now applied to designate 'ferrous' as opp. to 'ferric' compounds of iron (cf. FERRI-). **Ferrocyanhy·dric** or **ferrocya·nic acid**, a tetrabasic acid, H_4FeCy_6, forming a white crystalline powder. **Ferrocy·anide**, a salt of ferrocyanhydric acid, as *potassium ferrocyanide*, popularly yellow prussiate of potash. **Ferrocya·nogen**, the hypothetical radical $FeCy_6$ supposed to exist in ferrocyanides. †**Ferropru·ssiate** = *Ferrocyanide.* †**Ferropru·ssic acid** = *Ferrocyanhydric acid.*

Fe:rro-co·ncrete. 1900. = REINFORCED *c.*

Ferroso- (ferōᵘ·so), comb. f. of mod.L. *ferrosus* FERROUS, in *ferroso-ferric oxide*, Fe_3O_4.

Ferrotype (fe·rŏtəip). 1879. [f. FERRO- + -TYPE.] A process by which positive photographs are taken on thin iron plates; a photograph so taken. Also *attrib.*

Ferrous (fe·rəs), *a.* 1865. [f. L. *ferrum* iron + -OUS.] *Chem.* A term applied to compounds in which iron combines as a divalent, e.g. *ferrous oxide*, FeO.

Ferruginate (fĕrū·dʒineᵗt), *v.* [f. L. *ferrugo, -gin-* (see FERRUGINOUS) + -ATE³.] To give the colour or properties of iron rust to. Hence **Ferru·ginated** *ppl. a.* (Dicts.)

Ferrugineous (ferudʒi·nĭəs), *a.* 1663. [f. L. *ferrugineus* (see next) + -OUS; see -EOUS.] = next.

Ferruginous (fĕrū·dʒinəs), *a.* 1656. [f. L. *ferrugo, -gin-* iron rust, dark red (f. *ferrum* iron) + -OUS. Cf. Fr. *ferrugineux.*] **1.** *orig.* Of the nature of, or containing, iron rust; *now*, Of the nature of iron; containing iron 1661. **2.** Of the colour of iron rust; reddish brown.

Ferrule, ferrel (fe·rəl), *sb.* 1611. [alt. (prob. by assim. to L. *ferrum* iron, and -ULE) of *verrel, -il* (XVII), later from of *vyrelle, -ille, -ol* (XV) – OFr. *virelle, virol(e)*, mod. *virole* – L. *viriola, -olæ*, f. *viriæ* bracelet.] **1.** A ring or cap of metal put round the end of a stick, tube, etc., to strengthen it, or prevent splitting and wearing. **2.** A ring or band for strengthening anything, or holding the parts of anything together 1632. **3.** *Steam-Engine*, 'A bushing for expanding the end of a flue' (Webst.).

Hence **Fe·rrule, fe·rrel** *v.* to fit or furnish with a f. 1496. **Fe·rruled** *ppl. a.* provided with a f.

Ferruminate (fĕrū·mineᵗt), *v.* ? *Obs.* 1623. [– *ferruminat-*, pa. ppl. stem of L. *ferruminare*, f. *ferrumen, -min-* cement, f. *ferrum* iron; see -ATE³.] To cement, solder, unite. Hence **Ferru:mina·tion.**

Ferry (fe·ri), *sb.* ME. [– ON. *ferja* ferry-boat, or *ferju-*, as in *ferjukarl, -maðr* ferryman, *ferjuskip* ferryboat = MDu. **vēre* (Du. *veer*), MHG. *vër(e)* (G. *fähre*) :– Gmc. **farjōn*, f. **far-* go; see FARE *sb.*¹] †**1.** A passage or crossing. ME. only. **2.** *esp.* A place where boats pass over a river, etc., to transport passengers and goods ME **3.** Provision for conveyance by boat from one shore to the other 1489. †**b.** = FERRY-BOAT –1798. **4.** *Law.* The right of ferrying men and animals across a river, etc., and of levying toll for so doing 1721.

3. A f. was established where London Bridge now stands 1892. **b.** The French had sunk divers Ferries and other Boats in the River 1701.

Comb.: **f.-bridge**, a form of ferry-boat in which a railway train is transported across a river or bay; **-railway**, 'one whose track is on the bottom of the watercourse and whose carriage has an elevated deck which supports the train' (Knight).

Ferry (fe·ri), *v.* [– ON. *ferja* ferry = OS., OE. *ferian* carry, transport (which survived in ME. *ferie*), OHG. *ferren* (MHG. *vern*), Goth. *farjan* :– Gmc. **farjan*, f. **far-* go.] †**1.** *trans.* To convey from one place to another –1583. **2.** *esp.* To transport over water (formerly including the sea) in a boat or ship, etc. OE. **b.** To work (a boat, etc.) *across* or *over* 1771. **3.** *intr.* for *refl.* To go; now only, to pass over water in a boat or by a ferry; of a boat: To pass to and fro OE.

2. Charon is tyr'd, with ferring soules to hell HEYWOOD. **3.** Crist seide to hem verie we over þe water WYCLIF. Upon these waters doe f. fiftie thousand Boats 1630.

Fe·rry-boat. ME. [f. FERRY *sb.* + BOAT *sb.*] A boat for conveying passengers, etc., across a ferry.

Fe·rryman. 1464. [f. FERRY *sb.* + MAN *sb.*] One who keeps or looks after a ferry.

†**Fers.** ME. [– OFr. *fierce, fierche*, etc., – (ult.) Pers. *farzān* 'wise man', 'counsellor'.] *Chess.* **1.** The queen –1676. **2.** A pawn which has passed to the eighth square. CAXTON.

Phr. *The ferses twelve*: all the men exc. the king (Skeat).

Fers, obs. f. FIERCE *a.*, VERSE *sb.*

Fe·rter, *v.* ME. [f. ME. *fertre*; see FERETORY.] To put in a shrine.

Ferth, obs. f. FOURTH.

Ferther, obs. f. FURTHER *v.*

Fertile (fɔ̄·ɹtil, -təil), *a.* 1460. [– Fr. *fertile* – L. *fertilis*; see -ILE.] **1.** Producing in abundance; fruitful, prolific. Also *transf.* and *fig.* **2.** Causing or promoting fertility 1597. †**3.** Copiously produced, abundant –1667.

1. A soil..f. of..weeds 1785. F. plains C. BRONTË. *fig.* F. in resources T. JEFFERSON. A land f. in warriors FREEMAN. **2.** F. slime EMERSON. **3.** With adorations, fertill teares *Twel. N.* I. v. 274. Hence **Fe·rtilely** *adv.* **Fe·rtileness** = FERTILITY (*rare*).

†**Ferti·litate,** *v.* 1634. [f. next + -ATE³, after *debilitate.*] To render fertile, fertilize –1650.

Fertility (fəɹti·lĭti). 1490. [– Fr. *fertilité* – L. *fertilitas, -tat-*, f. *fertilis*; see FERTILE, -ITY.] The quality of being FERTILE; fecundity, fruitfulness, productiveness; *pl.* productive powers. Also *transf.* and *fig.*

Thy waste More rich than other climes' f. BYRON. The f. of this clover absolutely depends [etc.] DARWIN. *fig.* I found some f. of fancy JOHNSON. F. of invention PLAYFAIR, thought MACAULAY, resource 1878.

Fertilization (fɔ̄:rtiləizē·ʃən). Also **-isation.** 1857. [f. FERTILIZE + -ATION. Cf. Fr. *fertilisation.*] The action or process of rendering fertile; *spec.* in *Biol.* fecundation (see FERTILIZE 2).

These species..require the aid of insects for their f. DARWIN.

Fertilize (fɔ̄·ɹtiləiz), *v.* 1648. [f. FERTILE + -IZE. Cf. Fr. *fertiliser.*] **1.** *trans.* To make fertile; to enrich (the soil). **b.** *gen.* To render productive. (*lit.* and *fig.*) 1828. **2.** *Biol.* To make (an ovum, an oospore, a female individual or organ) fruitful by the introduction of the male element; to fecundate. Chiefly *Bot.* 1859.

1. He fertilised bogs, and cultivated barren sands 1760. Intense religious conviction fertilizes intellect 1866. **3.** I have not found a single terrestrial animal which can f. itself DARWIN.

Hence **Fe·rtili:zable** (also **-isable**), *a.* that can be fertilized or fecundated.

Fertilizer (fɔ̄·ɹtiləizəɹ). 1661. [f. prec. + -ER¹.] **1.** One who or that which fertilizes land; said *esp.* of manures. **2.** An agent of fertilization in plants 1844.

2. Flies are good fertilizers DARWIN.

Ferula (fe·rŭlă). ME. [– L. *ferula* giant fennel, rod.] **1.** *Bot.* The giant fennel. **2.** A rod, cane, or other instrument of punishment, *esp.* a flat ruler; *fig.* school discipline 1580. **3.** *Surg.* A long splint 1688.

Hence **Ferula·ceous** *a.* resembling a f.; having a stalk like a f.

Ferula·ic, fe·rulic, *a.* 1876. [f. FERULA + -IC.] *Chem.* In *Ferul(a)ic acid*: $C_{10}H_{10}O_4$, contained in Asafœtida.

†**Fe·rular.** 1594. [f. FERULA, FERULE (in sense 2) + -AR¹.] = FERULA 2. –1688.

Ferule (fe·riul), *sb.* ME. [– L. *ferula* FERULA. Cf. Fr. *férule* (XV).] **1.** = FERULA 1. **2.** = FERULA 2. 1599. Hence **Fe·rule** *v.* to beat, strike with a f.

†**Fe·rvence.** ME. [– OFr. *fervence* or its source, late and med.L. *ferventia*, in same senses, f. *fervent-*, pres. ppl. stem of *fervēre*; see FERVENT, -ENCE.] **1.** Boiling or glowing heat. Also, Violent ebullition. –1634. **2.** *fig.* Warmth of the emotions, fervency –1591.

2. My f. of love HEN. VIII.

Fervency (fɔ̄·ɹvĕnsi). 1554. [f. as prec.; see -ENCY.] **1.** The state or quality of being FERVENT; intensity of heat. Now *rare.* 1598. **2.** *fig.* Heat of mind; warmth of devotion, zeal, ardour, eagerness.

2. Peter in a feruencie first left his bote KNOX.

Fervent (fɔ̄·ɹvĕnt), *a.* ME. [– OFr. *fervent* – L. *fervens, -ent-*, pres. pple. of *fervēre* boil, glow; see -ENT.] **1.** Hot, burning, glowing, boiling. †**b.** Of cold: Intense –1634. **2.** Of persons, etc.: Ardent, intensely earnest ME. **b.** Of conflict, uproar, etc.: Hot, fierce, raging. Now *rare.* 1465.

1. The Elements shall melt with feruent heat 2 *Pet.* 3.10. **b.** The f. frost so bitter wes 1535. **2.** Feruent to fight ME. My Heart in f. Wishes burns WESLEY. **b.** A moment ends the f. din WORDSW. Hence **Fe·rvent-ly** *adv.*, **-ness.**

Fervescent (fəɹve·sĕnt), *a.* 1683. [– *fervescent-*, pres. ppl. stem of L. *fervescere*, inceptive verb f. *fervēre*; see prec., -ESCENT.] Growing hot.

Fervid (fɔ̄·ɹvid), *a.* 1599. [– L. *fervidus*, f. *fervēre*; see FERVENT, -ID¹.] **1.** Burning, glowing, hot. Now *poet.* or *rhet.* **2.** *fig.* Glowing, impassioned 1656.

1. The mounted Sun Shot down direct his f. Raies MILT. *P. L.* v. 301. **2.** He is warm rather than f. JOHNSON. F. loyalty MACAULAY. A f. preacher 1872.

Hence **Fervi·dity**, intense heat (*lit.* and *fig.*). **Fe·rvid-ly** *adv.*, **-ness.**

Fervour, fervor (fɔ̄·ɹvəɹ). ME. [– OFr. *fervo(u)r* (mod. *ferveur*) – L. *fervor*, f. *fervēre*; see FERVENT, -OR 1. In U.S. *fervor* is usual, in Eng. *fervour.*] **1.** Glowing condition, intense heat. **2.** Warmth or glow of feeling, passion, vehemence, zeal ME.

1. The f. of an African climate 1794. **2.** She..had more feruor of deuocion CAXTON.

Fesapo. *Logic.* A mnemonic word representing the fourth mood of the fourth syllogistic figure, in which a universal negative major premiss and a universal affirmative minor yield a particular negative conclusion.

Fescennine (fe·senəi:n). 1601. [– L. *Fescenninus* pertaining to *Fescennia* in Etruria, famous for scurrilous dialogues in verse. see -INE¹.]

A. *adj.* Pertaining to Fescennia; usually, licentious, obscene, scurrilous.

†**B.** *sb.* A song or verses of a licentious or scurrilous character –1660.

Fescue (fe·skiu), *sb.* [Late ME. *festu(e)* – OFr. *festu* (mod. *fétu*) :– Rom. **festucum*, for L. *festuca* stalk, stem, straw. The dissimilative change from *festue* to *fescue* appears XVI.] †**1.** A straw, rush, twig; hence, a thing of little importance –1610. **2.** A small stick, pin, etc., used as a pointer in teaching children their letters 1513. †**3.** *transf.* **a.** The shadow on a sundial 1607. **b.** A plectrum for use with the harp 1616. **4.** More fully *Fescue-grass*: A genus (*Festuca*) of grasses. *Hard, Sheep's Meadow F.*: tr. *F. duriuscula, ovina, pratensis*, botanical names of species. 1794.

1. Thin strawes and fescues small P. HOLLAND. **2.** Play schoolmaster, point as with a f. BROWNING. Hence †**Fescue** *v.* to direct or assist in reading with a f.

Fesse¹ (fes). 1486. [– OFr. *fesse*, var. of *faisse* :– L. *fascia* band; see FASCIA.] *Her.* An ordinary formed by two horizontal lines drawn across the middle of the field, and containing between them one third of it.

Phr. *Party per f.*: (of the shield) divided by a horizontal line through the middle. *Comb.*: **f.-point,** the exact centre of the escutcheon; **-ways, -wise** *adv.* horizontally.

Fesse². Now *dial.* 1577. [Of unkn. origin.] A pale blue colour.

Fest, fest-, obs. ff. FAST, FAST-, FEAST, FIST.

‖**Festa** (fe·stă). 1818. [It. :– L. *festa* (see FEAST *sb.*).] A feast, festival, holy day.

Festal (fe·stăl), *a.* (*sb.*) 1479. [– OFr. *festal* – late L. *festalis*, f. *festum* FEAST *sb.*; see -AL¹.] **1.** Of or pertaining to a feast or festivity; festive, joyous. **2.** Befitting a feast 1747. **3.** *sb.* A feast, festivity 1818.

1. A f. Day 1740, dress 1838. F. people HAWTHORNE. **2.** F. mirth 1749. Hence **Fe·stally** *adv.*

Fester (fe·stəɹ), *sb.* ME. [– OFr. *festre* :– L. FISTULA, with *-re* repl. *-le* as in Fr. *chapitre* CHAPTER, *épître* EPISTLE.] **1.** *orig.* = FISTULA; *later*, a rankling sore, an ulcer. In mod. use: 'A superficial suppuration resulting from irritation of the skin' (Quain). †**2.** A scar –1541. **3.** [from the vb.] The action or process of causing a fester 1860.

3. Used to the f. of the chain upon their necks I. TAYLOR.

Fester (fe·stəɹ), *v.* ME. [f. prec. sb., or OFr. *festrir.*] **1.** *intr.* Of a wound or sore: To become a fester, to gather or generate pus, to ulcerate. Of an arrow, poison, etc.: To envenom the surrounding parts; to rankle. Hence *fig.* of grief, etc. **2.** To putrefy, rot 1540. **3.** *trans.* To cause festering in (*lit.* and *fig.*); to allow to rankle 1579. †**4.** = CICATRIZE 1. –1541.

1. A prick or cut that festers WESLEY. The troubles of Saxony..were already festering in silence FREEMAN. **2.** Lillies that f. smell far worse then weedes SHAKS. **3.** That will heal, instead of festering, the wounds of our minds MRS. SHELLEY. Hence **Fe·sterment**, the process or state of festering: *dial.* a rotting mass.

Festilogy (festi·lŏdʒi). Also **festo-**. 1845. [– med.L. *festilogium*, f. L. *festum* feast, after *martilogium*, contracted form of *martyrologium*; the word was a translation of MIr. *félire*; see -LOGY.] A treatise on ecclesiastical festivals.

†**Fe·stinate,** *a. rare.* 1605. [– L. *festinatus*, pa. pple. of *festinare*; see next, -ATE².] Hasty, hurried –1822.

Lear III. vii. 10. Hence **Fe·stinately** *adv.*

Festinate (fe·stineˈt), *v.* 1652. [– *festinat-*, pa. ppl. stem of L. *festinare* hasten; see -ATE³.] To hasten (*trans.* and †*intr.*). Hence **Festina·tion**, haste, speed. ? *Obs.*

†**Festi·n(e.** 1520. [– Fr., Sp. *festin* and It. *festino*; see next.] = next –1819.

†**Festino** (festi·no). 1741. [– It. *festino*, dim. of *festa* FEAST *sb.* Hence Fr. and Sp. *festin.*] An entertainment or feast –1865.

How..obliging to go to Madame Grifoni's f. H. WALPOLE.

Festino (festəi·no). 1551. *Logic.* A mnemonic word, representing the third mood of the second syllogistic figure, in which a universal negative major premiss and a particular affirmative minor yield a particular negative conclusion.

Festival (fe·stivăl). ME. [– OFr. *festival* – med.L. *festivalis*, f. L. *festivus*; see next, -AL¹.]

A. *adj.* **1.** Of or pertaining to a feast, befitting a feast-day. (Now felt as the sb. used *attrib.*) †**2.** Glad, joyful, merry –1686.

1. Such dayes are festiuall to those Saincts, that [etc.] FULKE. **2.** Our most f. and freeer joys JER. TAYLOR.

B. *sb.* A time of festive celebration, a festal day; also, *occas.* a merrymaking 1589. **b.** A musical performance, or series of performances, at recurring periods, e.g. the *Handel Festival*; also in extended use, e.g. a *Shakespeare F.*

The morning trumpets f. proclam'd Through each high street MILT. *Sams.* 1598.

Hence †**Fe·stivally** *adv.* joyously, gaily; in a f. or holiday manner.

Festive (fe·stiv), *a.* 1651. [– L. *festivus*, f. *festum* FEAST; see -IVE.] **1.** Pertaining to, or befitting, a feast; mirthful, glad, cheerful. **2.** Convivial, jovial; devoted to feasting 1735.

1. The glad Circle..yield their Souls To f. mirth THOMSON. The f. board 1839. **2.** *The f. season*: = 'Christmas-tide'. Hence **Fe·stively** *adv.* So **Fe·stivous** *a.* (in all senses).

Festivity (festi·vĭti). ME. [– (O)Fr. *festivité* or L. *festivitas*, f. *festivus*; see prec., -ITY.] **1.** †Festive quality, condition, or nature; (of writing, etc.) agreeable elegance –1681; rejoicing, mirth, gaiety 1756. **2.** A festive celebration, an occasion of feasting. *pl.* Festive proceedings. ME.

1. The f. of his poems FULLER. A time of general f. 1756. **2.** To share in the festivities of the day LYTTON.

Festoon (festū·n), *sb.* 1676. [– Fr. *feston* – It. *festone* prop. 'festal ornament', f. *festa* FEAST *sb.*; see -OON.] **1.** A chain or garland of flowers, leaves, etc., hanging in a curve between two points. Also *transf.* 1686. **2.** *Arch.* A carved or moulded ornament representing this 1676. **3.** *Ornith.* A lobe on the cutting edge of a hawk's beak 1855.

1. Here..see..vines, trained in festoons, from tree to tree A. YOUNG. **2.** Flora and boys in alto-relievo supporting festoons H. WALPOLE. Hence **Festoo·nery**, a group of objects arranged in festoons. **Festoo·ny** *a.*, of, pertaining to, or like a f. (*rare*).

Festoon (festū·n), *v.* 1789. [f. prec.] †**1.** *intr.* To hang in festoons. **2.** *trans.* To adorn with or as with festoons 1800. **3.** To form into festoons. Also with *up.* 1801. **4.** To connect by festoons 1832.

4. Growths of jasmine turn Their humid arms festooning tree to tree TENNYSON.

Festucine (fe·stiŭsəin), *a.* 1646. [f. L. *festuca* stalk + -INE¹.] **1.** Straw-coloured. **2.** *Min.* Epithet for a splintery fracture 1823.

1. A little insect of a f. or pale green SIR T. BROWNE.

†**Festu·cous,** *a.* [f. as prec + -OUS.] Straw-like. SIR T. BROWNE.

†**Fe·sty,** *v.* ME. [– OFr. *festier, festeier* (mod. *festoyer*), f. *feste* FEAST *sb.* Cf. It. *festeggiare.*] = FEAST *v.* in various senses –1500.

Fet, *v.* Now *dial.* [ME. *fette, fete*, repr. OE. *fetian;* see FETCH *v.*] A synonym of FETCH *v.* in various senses.

Dauid sent, and fet her to his house 2 *Sam.* 11 : 27.

Fet, obs. f. FAT.

Fetch (fetʃ), *sb.*¹ 1530. [f. FETCH *v.*] **1.** The action of fetching (*lit.* and *fig.*); a long stretch, a far-reaching effort 1549. **2.** A contrivance, dodge, trick 1530. **3.** *Naut.* **a.** An act of tacking 1555. **b.** The line of continuous extent from point to point, *e.g.* of a bay or of open sea 1867. **4.** *dial.* An indrawn breath; also, a difficulty in breathing 1832.

2. The crafty fetches of the wilie Prince 1635.

Fetch (fetʃ), *sb.*² 1787. [Of unkn. origin.] The apparition, double, or wraith of a living person.

Fetch, obs. f. VETCH.

Fetch (fetʃ), *v.* [Late OE. *feććan*, alteration of *fetian* (surviving in dial. FET *v.*) by combination of t and j (consonantal i) to produce tʃ (as in *ortğeard* ORCHARD); prob. rel. to OE. *fatian*, OFris. *fatia*, OHG. *fazzōn* (G. *fassen*) grasp, perh. orig. 'put in a vessel' (*fat*, VAT).] **1.** *trans.* To go in quest of, and bring back. **2.** To cause to come; to succeed in bringing; to draw forth, elicit. Now *rare.* ME. †**b.** To restore to consciousness –1744. **3.** Of a commodity: To bring in, sell for. †Also *rarely* of money: To purchase. 1605. **4.** To move to interest, attract irresistibly. Also *absol.* Not in dignified use. 1605. †**5.** To go and receive; to get, 'come by' –1656. **6.** To draw from a (remote) source (now *rare*) 1552; †to derive as from a cause or origin; to infer –1691. **7.** To draw (breath): hence, to heave (a sigh); to utter (a groan); to drain (a draught) 1552. **8.** To deal (a blow); to make (a stroke). Now *colloq.* ME. †**b.** Hence, To 'have at', reach (a person) –1625. **9.** To make or perform (a movement, etc.). Now *arch.* 1530. **10.** *Naut.* **a.** To arrive at, reach; to come up with 1556. **b.** to get into (? *Obs.*) 1630. **c.** *intr.* To take a course; to bring one's vessel up 1586.

1. Ile goe f. thy sonnes To backe thy quarrell *Tit A.* II. iii. 53. Goe f. me Wine LITHGOW. Phr. *To f. and carry*: *lit.* chiefly of dogs; *fig.* to run to and fro with news, tales, etc. **2.** Thy hounds shall ..f. shrill ecchoes from the hollow earth *Tam. Shr.* Induct. ii. 48. To f. butter in a churn 1844. Phr. *To f. the water*, and (hence) *to f. the pump*: to obtain a flow of water by 'priming'. **b.** She.. then fainted agaïne, and agaïne they fetched her 1621. **3.** The Guido, what did that f. FOOTE. **6.** To f. a fashion from the French 1631, a parallel case out of Roman history 1806. **7.** Fetching such dreadful Groans 1707. **8.** His hand fetcheth a stroke with the axe *Deut.* 19 : 5. **9.** Colts, Fetching mad bounds *Merch. V.* v. i. 73. Phr. *To f. a compass*: see COMPASS *sb.*¹ 10. **10. a.** To f. the bridges 1835. **b.** To f. the wind 1630, the wake of a vessel STURMY. Phr. *To f. headway* or *sternway*: to gather motion ahead or astern. *To f. way*: to break loose. **c.** To f. to windward 1836.

Comb. with advs. **F. away.** *intr.* To get loose. **F. down.** *trans.* = *bring down* (see BRING *v.*). **F. off.** †**a.** To bring out of a difficulty. †**b.** To do or do for; to make an end of. †**c.** To drink off. **F. out.** To draw forth; to develop and display. **F. up.** †**a.** To raise. **b.** To vomit or promote expectoration of. **c.** To recall. **d.** To make up (lee-way, lost ground, time, etc.). †**e.** To come up with. **f.** *Naut.* To come or get to (a place). **g.** *intr.* for *refl.* To 'pull up'; to stop.

Fetch-, the vb.-stem in *comb.*, as in *f.-water*, a water-carrier, etc.

Fetch-candle. = FETCH-LIGHT. (Dicts.)

Fetcher (fe·tʃəɹ). 1552. [f. FETCH *v.* + -ER¹.] One who or that which fetches.

Fetching (fe·tʃiŋ), *ppl. a.* 1581. [f. as prec. + -ING².] †**1.** That contrives; crafty, designing –1583. **2.** Fascinating, 'taking' 1880.

Fetch-light. 1692. [perh. f. FETCH *sb.*², or f. FETCH *v.*] A name for the 'corpse-candle' supposed to be seen before a person's death travelling from his house to his grave.

Fête (fęt, fēˈt), *sb.* 1754. [– Fr. *fête*, mod. form of *feste* FEAST *sb.*] **1.** A festival, an entertainment on a large scale. **2.** The festival of the saint after whom a person is named; in R.C. countries observed as a birthday is in England 1840. Also *attrib.*, as *f.-day.*

Fête (fēˈt), *v.* 1819. [f. prec. sb., after Fr. *fêter.*] *trans.* To entertain at a fête; to feast; to give a fête in honour of.

Fete, obs. f. FEAT, FEET.

‖**Fête-champêtre.** 1774. [Fr., f. *fête* FÊTE *sb.* + *champêtre* rural.] An outdoor entertainment, a rural festival.

Fetial, fecial (fī·ʃăl). 1533. [– L. *fetialis* (erron. *fec-*): origin unkn.]

A. *adj.* Of or pertaining to the *fetiales* (see B.); heraldic, ambassadorial 1553.

B. *sb.* One of the *fetiales*, a Roman college of priests or heralds, who performed the rites connected with the declaration of war and the conclusion of peace.

Feticide: see FŒ-.

Fetid, fœtid (fe·tid, fī·tid). 1599. [– L. *fetidus* (often miswritten *foetidus*), f. *fetēre* stink; see -ID¹.]

A. *adj.* Having an offensive smell, stinking.

†**B.** *sb. pl.* Fetid drugs –1748. Hence **Feti·dity,** f. quality, state, or condition; foulness, offensiveness. **Fe·tid-ly** *adv.*, **-ness.**

Fetis(e, obs. var. of FEATOUS *a.*

Fetish, fetich(e (fe·tiʃ, fī·tiʃ). 1613. [– Fr. *fétiche* – Pg. *feitiço* charm, sorcery, subst. use of the adj. meaning 'made by art' :– L. *factitius* FACTITIOUS.] **1. a.** *orig.* Any object used by the Negroes of the Guinea coast and neighbourhood as an amulet or means of enchantment, or regarded by them with dread. **b.** *Anthropol.* An inanimate object worshipped by savages as having magical powers or as being animated by a spirit. **c.** *fig.* Something irrationally reverenced 1837. †**2.** Incantation; a magical or religious rite or observance; an oath –1828.

1. a. The chief fetiche is the snake 1761. **c.** Public opinion, the fetish even of the nineteenth century LOWELL. *Comb.* **f.-man, -woman,** (*a*) one who claims to have power over fetishes: (*b*) a fetish-worshipper.

Hence †**Fe·tish** *v.* to provide or adorn with a f.; *intr.* for *refl.* to dress up. **Fetishee·r, fe·tisher,** a medicine-man; a priest; also = FETISH *sb.* 1. **Fe·tishism, fetichism,** the worship of fetishes, or the superstition of which this is the feature. **Fe·tishist, fetichist,** one who worships a f.; also quasi-*adj.* **Fetishi·stic, fetichistic** *a.* of, pertaining to, characterized by, or resembling fetishism.

Fetlock (fe·tlǫk), *sb.* [ME. *fete-, feetlak, fetlok*, corresp. to MHG. *vizzeloch, -lach* (G. *fissloch*), rel. to G. *fessel* fetlock, deriv. of Gmc. **fet-* (:– IE. **ped-*), var. of the base of FOOT.] **1.** That part of a horse's leg where the tuft of hair grows behind the pastern-joint; the tuft itself. **2.** = FETTERLOCK 2. 1695.

1. Fetlocks shag, and long SHAKS. Steeds..fetlocke deepe in gore *Hen. V*, IV. vii. 82. Hence **Fe·tlocked** *a.* having a f.; hobbled by the f., hampered, shackled.

Fetor, fœtor (fī·təɹ). 1450. [– L. *fetor* (incorrectly *fœtor*), f. *fetēre* stink; see -OR 1. Cf. FETID.] An offensive smell; a stench.

Fetter (fe·təɹ), *sb.* [OE. *feter*, corresp. to OS. pl. *feteros* (Du. *veter* lace), OHG. *fezzera* (early mod. G. *fesser*), ON. *fjǫturr* :– Gmc. **feterō*, **feteraz*, f. **fet-* :– IE. **ped-* FOOT, as in synon. L. *pedica*, Gr. πέδη.] **1.** A chain or shackle for the feet of a man or animal; hence *gen.* a bond, shackle (rare in *sing.*). In *pl.* = Captivity 1704. **2.** *transf.* and *fig.* Anything that confines or impedes; a check, restraint OE.

1. His feters that were on his fete CAXTON. To escape fetters and the sword ADDISON. **2.** Passion's too fierce to be in Fetters bound DRYDEN. Hence **Fe·tterless** *a.* that is not or cannot be fettered.

Fetter (fe·təɹ), *v.* ME. [f. prec. sb., or orig. – ON. Cf. OFris. *fiteria*, ON. *fjǫtra.*] **1.** *trans.* To bind with or as with fetters; to chain, fasten, shackle. **2.** *transf.* and *fig.* To impose restraint upon; to confine, impede 1526.

1. Elles had I dweld..I-fetered in his prisoun for evere moo CHAUCER. 2. The generality of the World are fettered by Rules STEELE. Fettered by superstition 1788. Hence **Fe·ttered** *ppl. a.* in senses of the vb.; *spec.* in *Biol.* 'applied to the limbs of animals when, by their retention within the integuments, or by their backward stretched position, they are unfit for walking (*Syd. Soc. Lex.*). **Fe·tterer.**

Fetterlock (fe·təɹlǫk). ME. [f. FETTER *sb.* + LOCK. *sb*[2]] **1.** As a corruption of FETLOCK (sense 1) 1587. **2.** An apparatus fixed to the foot of a horse to prevent his running away ME. **b.** *Her.* A representation of this 1605.

Fettle (fe·t'l), *sb.* 1750. [f. next vb.] **1.** Condition. **2.** The material used for fettling a furnace 1894.

1. A Shetland pony in good f. E. WAUGH.

Fettle (fe·t'l), *v.* ME. [f. (dial.) *fettle* sb., OE. *fetel* girdle, OHG. *fezzil* (G. *fessel*) chain, band, ON. *fetill* bandage, strap :- Gmc. **fatilaz*, f. **fat-* hold; cf. FETCH *v.*] **1.** *trans.* To make ready, put in order. Now only *dial.* **b.** *techn.* To line (a puddling furnace, etc.); to scour (rough castings) 1881. **†2.** *refl.* and *intr.* for *refl.* To get (oneself) ready; to address oneself to battle –1674. **b.** To busy oneself 1745. Hence **Fe·ttler.** *dial.* and *techn.*

‖**Fettstein** (fe·tstəin). 1815. [G., f. *fett* fat + *stein* stone.] *Min.* = ELÆOLITE.

Fetus: see FŒTUS.

‖**Fetwa** (fe·twă). 1625. [Arab. *fatwā*, pronounced by the Turks *fetva.*] A decision given (usually in writing) by a Mufti.

Feu (fiū), *sb.* 1497. [– OFr. *feu*; see FEE *sb.*[2]] *Sc. Law.* **1.** = FEE *sb.*[2] 1; also a tract of land held in fee 1609. **2.** A feudal tenure of land in which the vassal makes a return of grain or money (opp. to WARD *sb.* III, 2 and BLANCH *a.* 3); a grant of land on these conditions; in mod. use, = FEU-FARM 1497. **b.** A piece of land held in f. 1791. Hence **Feu** *v.* to grant upon f. **Feu·ar,** one who holds land upon f.

†Feu·age. *rare.* 1618. [– OFr. *feuage*, f. *feu* fire; see -AGE. In med.L. *focagium.*] A tax upon chimneys or hearths –1706.

Feud[1] (fiūd). [ME. *fede* – OFr. *fede, feide* – MLG., MDu. *vēde*, MLG. *veide*, corresp. to OHG. *fēhida* (G. *fehde*) = OE. *fǣhþu* enmity, OFris. *fāithe, fēithe* :- Gmc. **faixiþō*, f. **faix-*; see FOE, -TH[1].] **†1.** Active hatred, hostility, ill will –1787. **2.** A state of bitter and lasting mutual hostility; *esp.* such a state existing between two families, tribes, or individuals, marked by murderous assaults in revenge for some previous insult or wrong ME. More fully *deadly f.* 1568. **3.** A quarrel, contention, bickering 1565.

2. He [Argyle] was at F. with all his Superiors in Scotland 1661. A tribe which was at deadly f. with the Joasmis H. H. WILSON. *Comb.* **f.-bote** [– OE. *fǣhþ-bōt*], a recompense for engaging in a feud, a compensation for homicide.

Feud[2], **feod** (fiūd). 1614. [– med.L. *feudum, feodum* (IX), usu. taken to be of Gmc. origin, but no evidence can be adduced.] = FEE *sb.*[2] 1, 3.

His Majesty conferred on him the title of Duke of Bronte, annexing to it the f. of that name 1806.

Feudal (fiū·dăl), *a.*[1] †Also **feodal.** 1614. [– med.L. *feudalis, feodalis*, f. *feudum, feodum*; see prec., -AL[1]. Cf. Fr. *féodal* (XV).] **1.** Of, pertaining to, or of the nature of, a feud or fief. **2.** Of or pertaining to the holding of land in feud 1639. **3.** Of or pertaining to the feudal system; existing or such as existed under that system 1665.

1. The conversion of allodial into f. estates 1861. 2. The feodal polity BLACKSTONE. F. tenures GIBBON. Phr. *F. system*: the system of polity which prevailed in Europe during the Middle Ages, based on the relation of lord and vassal arising out of the holding of lands in feud. 3. Two ancient f. castles 1840. Hence **Feu·dally** *adv.* in a f. manner or under f. conditions. **Feu·dalism,** the f. system or its principles. **Feu·dalist,** a representative, or an adherent, of the f. system. **Feudali·stic** *a.* of the nature of feudalism; inclined to feudalism.

Feudal (fiū·dăl), *a.*[2] *rare.* [f. FEUD[1] + -AL[1].] Of or pertaining to (a deadly) feud. SCOTT.

Feudality (fiūdæ·lĭti), *a.* 1701. [– Fr. *feudalité* (COTGR.), *féodalité*, f. *feudal* (COTGR.) *féodal*; see FEUDAL *a.*[1], -ITY. In med.L. *feudalitas.*] **1.** Feudal quality or state; the principles and practice of the feudal system; *pl.* feudal principles 1790. **2.** A feudal regime; a feudal-like power; a fief 1800. **†3.** *Law.* Fealty. (Dicts.)

2. Capital in Great Britain has become a f. 1821.

Feudalize (fiū·dăləiz), *v.* 1828. [f. FEUDAL *a.*[1] + -IZE.] *trans.* To bring under the feudal system; to convert (lands) into feudal holdings; also, to reduce (persons) to the condition of feudal vassals. Hence **Feu:daliza·tion.**

Feu·dary, feo·dary. Now *arch.* ME. [– med.L. *feodarius*, f. *feodum, feudum* FEUD[2]; see -ARY[1].]

A. *sb.* **1.** One who holds lands of an overlord on condition of homage and service; a feudal tenant, a vassal. **b.** A subject, dependant, servant 1620. **†2.** An officer of the ancient Court of Wards, who received the rents of the wards' lands –1736. **¶3.** A confederate. (See FEDARIE.)

B. *adj.* Feudally subject. Const. *to.* 1577.

†Feu·datary. 1586. [– med.L. *feudatarius*, f. *feudat-*, pa. ppl. stem of *feudare* enfeoff; see -ATE[3], -ARY[1].]

A. *adj.* = FEUDATORY A. 1. –1674.

B. *sb.* = FEUDATORY B. –1818.

Feudatory (fiū·dătəri). Also **†Feodatory.** 1592. [– med.L. *feudatorius*, f. as prec.; see -ORY[2].]

A. *adj.* **1.** Owing feudal allegiance *to*; subject. **2.** Of or pertaining to vassals or retainers 1861.

1. He is F. to the Pope 1680.

B. *sb.* **1.** One who holds his lands by feudal tenure; a feudal vassal 1765. **2.** A feud, fief, fee; a dependent lordship 1644.

‖**Feu de joie** (fö də ʒwa). 1609. [Fr.; = 'fire of joy'.] **†1.** A bonfire; also *fig.* –1771. **2.** A salute fired by musketry on occasions of public rejoicing, so that it passes from man to man rapidly and steadily, giving one continuous sound 1801.

Feudist[1] (fiū·dist). 1607. [– Fr. *feudiste* or mod.L. *feudista*; see FEUD[2], -IST.] **1.** A writer on feuds; one versed in feudal law. **†2.** One living under the feudal system. BLACKSTONE.

Feu·dist[2]. *U.S.* 1901. [f. FEUD[1] + -IST.] A person who has a feud with another.

Feu-farm (fiū·fāɹm). ME. [– OFr. *feu-ferme*; see FEE-FARM.] *Sc. Law.* That kind of tenure by which land is held of a superior on payment of an annual rent. Hence, the annual rent itself.

†Feuille (föy). [– Fr. *feuille* leaf.] A thin plate, a leaf. PETTY.

‖**Feuillemorte** (föymort), *a.* 1690. [– Fr.; = 'dead leaf'. See FILEMOT.] Of the colour of a dead leaf, brown or yellowish brown.

†Feuillet[1]. [– Fr. *feuillette* :– med.L. *folietta* a measure of wine.] A half-hogshead. BURKE.

‖**Feuillet**[2] (föyę). 1874. [Fr., dim. of *feuille* leaf.] *Diamond-cutting.* 'The projecting points of the triangular facets in a rose-cut diamond, whose bases join those of the triangles of the central pyramid' (Knight).

‖**Feuilleton** (föytoṅ). 1845. [Fr., f. *feuillet*, dim. of *feuille* leaf; see -ET, -OON.] In French (and other) newspapers, the part of one or more pages (usually at the bottom) appropriated to light literature, criticism, etc.; an article or work printed in that part.

Hence **Feui·lletonist,** a writer of feuilletons.

†Feute, fewte. ME. [– OFr. *fuite*, f. *fuir* :– L. *fugere* flee.] The traces or track (of an animal) –1485.

Feuterer: see FEWT-.

Fever (fī·vəɹ), *sb.* [OE. *fēfor* – L. *febris*; reinforced in ME. from AFr. *fevre*, (O)Fr. *fièvre* :– L. *febris.*] **1.** *Path.* A morbid condition of the system, characterized by increased heat, and excessive change and destruction of the tissues. Often specialized as *intermittent, puerperal, scarlet, typhoid, yellow*, etc. *f.* (see these words). **†2.** In *pl.* with sing. sense –1605. **3.** A state of intense nervous excitement, agitation, heat 1586.

1. Have a care of coming neare those that have the feavour 1678. 3. An enuious Feauer Of pale and bloodless Emulation *Tr. & Cr.* I. iii. 133. A mode of life free from..f. of mind J. H. NEWMAN.

Comb.: **f.-blister,** the herpes of the lips often produced by f. or catarrh; **-bush,** the *Benzoin odoriferum*; also the *Prinos verticillātus*; **-fly,** the *Dilophus vulgaris*; **-heat,** the high temperature of the body in f.; also *fig.*; **-nut,** the seeds of *Cæsalpina bonducella*; **-root,** the *Pterospora andromedea*; also the *Triosteum perfoliatum*; **-sore,** name of a species of caries or necrosis; **-tree,** the *Eucalyptus globulus*; also the *Pinckneya pubens*; **-twig,** the *Celastrus scandens*; **-weed,** a plant of the genus *Eryngium*; **-wort,** the *Triosteum perfoliatum.*

Fever (fī·vəɹ), *v.* 1606. [f. prec. sb.] **1.** *trans.* To throw into a fever; also *fig.* **2.** *intr.* To be seized with a fever; also *fig.* 1754.

1. The white hand of a Lady Feauer thee *Ant. & Cl.* III. xiii. 138. 2. She fevered and died 1754.

Feveret (fī·verėt). 1712. [f. as prec. + -ET.] A slight fever.

Feverfew (fī·vəɹfiū, fe·v-). [OE. *feferfuge* – L. *febrifuga, -fugia*, f. L. *febris* FEVER *sb.* + *fugare* drive away; but the mod. form descends from an adoption of AFr. **fevrefue, feiverfue* (XIII).] *Bot.* **a.** The plant *Pyrethrum parthenium.* **b.** *dial.* The *Erythræa centaurium.*

Feverish (fī·vəriʃ), *a.* ME. [f. FEVER *sb.* + -ISH[1].] **1.** Having the symptoms constituting fever; †ill of a fever 1647. **2.** *fig.* Excited, fitful, restless 1634. **3.** Of the nature of fever; pertaining to or resembling fever ME. **4.** Apt to cause fever. Of a country: Infested by fever. 1669.

1. [I] have had a restless f. night PENN. 2. Men..Strive to keep up a frail and f. being MILT. *Comus* 8. 3. F. Thirst 1695, Rigors 1732, exacerbations 1802. 4. The f. shore of St. Domingo 1803. Hence **Fe·verish-ly** *adv.*, **-ness.**

Feverous (fī·vərəs), *a.* ME. [f. as prec. + -OUS.] **1.** = FEVERISH †1, 2, 3. **2.** Apt to cause fever 1626. Hence **Fe·verously** *adv.*

†Fe·very *a.* [f. as prec. + -Y[1].] Affected by fever. B. JONS.

Few (fiū), *a.* *compar.* **Fewer.** *superl.* **Fewest.** [OE. *fēawe, fēawa*, contr. *fēa*, corresp. to OFris. *fē*, OS. *fa(o)*, OHG. *fao, fō*, ON. *fár* (whence ME. *fā, fō*), Goth. pl. *fawai*; repr. Gmc. **faw-* :– IE. **pau-*, as in L. *paucus*, Gr. παῦρος small.] **1.** Not many; amounting to a small number. (In *a few, some few*, opp. to 'none at all'.) *absol.* = *few persons.* OE. **b.** Followed by a partitive genitive, and later by *of* OE. **2.** Used with a pl. sb. to form a virtual collective noun, preceded by *a, every*, (rarely) *that*, but construed with pl. verb ME. **†3.** Of a company or number: Small –1828. **4.** Of quantity: Not much ME.

1. Man that is borne of a woman, is of f. dayes *Job* 14:1. F. espied him HALL. **b.** Ye were the fewest of all people *Deut.* 7:7. Phr. *Some f.*: an inconsiderable number of. Also *ellipt., absol.*, and with *of. The f.*: a specified company small in number. Now often = 'the minority': opp. to *the many.* †*In f.*; in few words, in short. 2. Thieves, of which, it seems, there were not a f. DE FOE. Phr. *A faithful, select* etc. *f. A good f.*: a fair number. *Every f.* (*hours, miles*, etc.). 3. So f. company, that [etc.] SWIFT. 4. *A f. broth, gruel, porridge* (now *dial.*). *A f.*: 'a good bit' (*colloq.* or *slang*).

Hence **Few·ness,** the quality of fact of being f.

Fewmets: see **Fu-.**

†Few·terer. [ME. *vewter*, early mod. Eng. *fewterer*, app. – AFr. *veutrier* (= AL. *veltrarius*, etc.) in same sense, f. OFr. *veutre, v(e)autre, veltre* (mod. *vautre*) – Rom. **veltrus*, contracted and dissim. form of L. *vertragus* (Martial) greyhound, of Gaulish origin.] A keeper of greyhounds; hence, an attendant –1801.

Fewtrils (fiū·trilz), *sb. pl. dial.* 1750. [Cf. FATTRELS.] Little things, trifles.

Fey (fē[i]), *a.* Chiefly *Sc.* [OE. *fǣge* = OS. *fēgi* (Du. *veeg*), OHG. *feigi* (G. *feige* cowardly), ON. *feigr* :– Gmc. **faigjaz.* After c1400 chiefly *Sc.*] **1.** Fated to die, doomed; also, dying. **†2.** Presaging death –1799. **†3.** Accursed, unlucky –1513. **†4.** Feeble, timid; weak –1513.

Fey, Feyn(e(n, FAY, vars of FEIGN *v.*

Fez (fez). 1802. [– Turk. *fez*, perh. through Fr.; said to be named after the town of *Fez*, capital of Morocco and chief place of its manufacture.] A skull-cap in the form of a truncated cone, of a dull crimson colour, with a black tassel; the national head-dress of the Turks.

ff. = and the following, *et seq.*; also abbrev. of FORTISSIMO.

‖**Fiacre** (fiakr). 1699. [Fr.; named after the Hôtel de St. *Fiacre*, rue St. Antoine, Paris, where these carriages were first stationed.] A small four-wheeled carriage for hire, a French hackney-coach.

†**Fiançailles,** *sb. pl.* 1477. [– Fr. *fiançailles* sb. pl., f. *fiancer* (see next).] A betrothal –1655.

†**Fi·ance,** *v.* 1450. [– (O)Fr. *fiancer*, f. OFr. *fiance* promise]. **1. a.** = AFFIANCE *v.* –1618. **b.** To take as one's betrothed –1587. **2.** To put on one's parole 1592.

‖**Fiancé** *masc.*, **Fiancée** *fem.* (fiãnse). 1853. [Fr., pa. pple. of *fiancer* betroth; see prec.] A betrothed person.

Fiant (fəi·ant). 1534. [L.; the first word in the formula *fiant literæ patentes* 'let letters patent be made out'.] A warrant addressed to the Irish Chancery for a grant under the Great Seal.

†**Fi·ants,** *sb.* 1576. [– OFr. *fient*, (also mod.) *fiente* dung, repr. pop. L. **femitum*, **femita* – (ult.) **femus*, for L. *fimus* dung. The specialization of sense seems to be English.] The dung of certain animals, *e.g.* the badger, fox, etc. –1741.

Fiar (fī·ăɹ), *sb. Sc.* 1597. [app. f. FEE *sb.*[2] + -AR[2], -ER[2].] The owner of the fee-simple of a property, as opp. to the life-renter.

Fiasco (fi,æ·sko). 1855. [– It. *fiasco*, in phr. *far fiasco* lit. 'to make a bottle', which involves an unexplained allusion. See FLASK *sb.*[1]] ‖**1.** A bottle, flask 1887. **2.** A failure or breakdown, *esp.* in a dramatic or musical performance.

Fiat (fəi·æ̆t). 1631. [– L.; = 'let it be done'. 'let there be made'; 3rd pers. sing. pres. subj. of *fieri*.] **1.** *orig.* The word 'fiat', alone or in a formula, by which a competent authority sanctioned the doing of something; hence, an authorization 1636. **b.** *gen.* An authoritative pronouncement 1750. **2.** With reference to '*Fiat lux*' (let there be light) Gen. 1:3 in the Vulgate: A command having for its object the creation of something 1631.

1. Nothing can be concluded without the King's F. 1647. **b.** Whose f. in matters of fashion was law 1883. **2.** If it be a Spirit that immediately produces every effect by a *fiat* or act of his will BP. BERKELEY. *Comb.* **f.-money,** *U.S.* money (such as an inconvertible paper currency) which is made legal tender by a f. of the government. **Fi·at** *v.* to attach a f. to; to sanction (*rare*). **Fi·atist** *U.S.*, an advocate of f.-money.

Fiaunt, obs. var. of FIANT.

Fib (fib), *sb.*[1] *colloq.* 1568. [prob. short for FIBLE-FABLE.] **1.** A trivial falsehood; often *euphem.* for 'a lie' 1611. **2.** A fibber.

1. No one was used to..telling polite fibs H. JAMES.

Fib (fib), *sb.*[2] 1814. [f. FIB *v.*[2]] A blow.

Fib (fib), *v.*[1] 1690. [f. FIB *sb.*[1]] *intr.* To tell a fib; to lie.

I do not say he lyes but his Lordship fibbs most abominably DRYDEN. Hence **Fi·bber.**

Fib (fib), *v.*[2] *slang.* 1665. [Of unkn. origin.] *trans.* To deliver blows in quick succession upon, as in pugilism. Also *absol.* or *intr.*

fig. I have fibbed the Edinburgh (as the 'fancy' say) most completely SOUTHEY.

Fi·ble-fa·ble. Now *dial.* 1581. [Redupl. f. FABLE.] Nonsense.

†‖**Fibra.** Pl. **-ræ, -ra's.** 1641. [L.; see next.] A fibre, filament –1661.

Fibre (fəi·bəɹ), *sb.* ME. [– (O)Fr. *fibre* – L. *fibra*. Formerly spelt *fiber* in England, as still in U.S.] †**1.** After L.: **a.** A lobe or portion of the liver. **b.** *pl.* The entrails. –1601. **2.** *Phys.* One of the thread-like bodies or filaments, that in part compose animal and vegetable tissue 1607. **3.** One of the thread-like filaments which form a textile or other material substance 1827. **4.** *collect.* A substance consisting of fibres. Also, Fibrous structure. 1810. **5.** A subdivision of a root; occas. of a twig 1656.

2. The optic nerve..might contain as many as a million of fibres BAIN. The fibres of the cocoanut LUBBOCK. *Fibres of Corti*: see CORTIAN *a.* *fig.* Every f. of him is Philistine CARLYLE. **3.** A silk f. FARADAY. Fibres of glass 1832. **4.** Bone and f. EMERSON. *fig.* There is an improvement in our f.—moral if not political BAGEHOT.

Comb. **f.-gun,** 'a device for disintegrating vegetable fiber' (Knight).

Hence **Fi·bred** *ppl. a.* furnished with fibres; chiefly in comb. **Fi·breless** *a.* without fibres or strength. **Fi·briform, Fi·brine,** *adjs.* f.-like.

Fibril (fəi·bril). 1664. [– mod.L. *fibrilla*; see next.] **1.** *Phys.* A small fibre; the subdivision of a FIBRE in a nerve, muscle, etc. 1681. **2.** *Bot.* The ultimate subdivision of a root.

Fibrilla (fəibri·lă). *Pl.* **-læ** (-lī). 1665. [mod.L. *fibrilla*, dim. of L. *fibra* FIBRE.] = prec.

The ultimate fibrillæ of muscles 1854. Hence **Fi·brillar** *a.* of, pertaining to, composed of, or characteristic of, a f. or fibrillae. **Fi·brillary** *a.* fibrillar. **Fi·brillate** *v. intr.* (of the blood) to turn into fibrillæ. **Fi·brillated** *ppl. a.* having a fibrillar structure. **Fibrilla·tion,** the becoming, or the being, fibrillated; *concr.* a fibrillated mass. **Fibri·lliform** *a.* **Fi:brillo·se** *a.* supplied with, or composed of, fibrils; finely striate. †**Fi·brillous** *a.* full of fibrils; pertaining to a f.

Fibrin (fəi·brin). Formerly also **fibrine, fibrina.** 1800. [f. FIBRE + -IN[1].] An albuminoid or protein compound substance found in animal matter; coagulable lymph. Also, a similar substance found in vegetable matter.

The f. of flesh appears to differ from that of blood ROSCOE. Hence **Fibrina·tion,** the action or process of adding f. to the blood. **Fi·brinous** *a.* composed of, pertaining to, or of the nature of, f.

Fibrino- (fəi·brino), comb. form of FIBRIN, as in:

Fi:brino-albu·minous *a.*, consisting of fibrin and albumen. **Fi·brinogen** [see -GEN], a proteid substance, entering into the composition of fibrin. **Fi:brinogene·tic, -ge·nic, Fibrino·genous** *adjs.*, producing fibrin. **Fi:brino-pla·stic** *a.*, concerned in the formation of fibrin. **Fi:brino-pla·stin** = GLOBULIN. **Fi:brino-pu·rulent** *a.*, containing a mixture of fibrin and pus.

Fibro- (fəi·bro), comb. form of FIBRE, indicating a fibrous condition.

Fi:bro-are·olar *a.*, consisting of fibrous and areolar or connective tissue. **Fi·brobla:st** [see -BLAST], one of the cells in which fibrous tissue is immediately formed. **Fi:bro-calca·reous** *a.*, consisting of fibrous tissue and containing calcareous bodies. **Fi:bro-ca·rtilage,** a firm elastic material partaking of the structure and character of fibrous tissue and cartilage; hence **Fi:bro-cartila·ginous** *a.* **Fi:bro-ce·llular** *a.*, composed of fibrous and cellular tissue. **Fi:bro-chondri·tis** 'inflammation of a fibro-cartilage' (*Syd. Soc. Lex.*) **Fi:bro-cy·stic** *a.*, consisting of fibrous tissue and cysts. **Fi:bro-cysto·ma,** a tumour containing fibrous tissue and cysts. **Fi:bro-fe·rrite,** *Min.* ferric sulphate occurring in fibrous silky tufts and masses of a yellow colour. **Fi:bro-inte·stinal** *a.*, in '*fibro-intestinal layer*, the innermost of the two layers into which the mesoderm of some Invertebrata divides' (*Syd. Soc. Lex.*). **Fi:bro-myo·ma,** 'a myoma in which the tumour contains a large proportion of fibrous connective tissue' (*Syd. Soc. Lex.*); hence **Fi:bro-myo·matous** *a.* **Fi:bro-neuro·ma,** 'the form of neuroma which consists chiefly of fibrous connective tissue' (*Syd. Soc. Lex.*). **Fi:bro-nu·cleated** *a.*, composed of fibrous tissue mixed with elongated nuclei. **Fi:bro-pla·stic** *a.*, fibre-forming; said *esp.* of a tissue organized from the lymph exuded on wounds. **Fi:bro-sarco·ma,** a tumour intermediate between a fibroma and a sarcoma. **Fi:bro·se-rous** *a.*, possessing the nature of both fibrous and serous membranes. **Fi:bro-va·scular** *a.*, *Bot.* composed of a mixture of fibrous tissue and vascular tissue.

Fibroid (fəi·broid). 1852. [f. FIBRE + -OID.] **A.** *adj.* Resembling fibre or fibrous tissue; *f. change, degeneration*, a morbid change into fibre or fibrous tissue.

B. *sb. Path.* A fibroid tumour 1872.

Fibroin (fəi·broᵘin). 1861. [f. FIBRO- + -IN[1].] A chemical substance which is the chief constituent of silk, cobwebs, and the horny skeleton of sponges.

Fibrolite (fəi·brŏləit). 1802. [f. FIBRO- + -LITE.] A fibrous mineral consisting chiefly of aluminium silicate. Hence **Fibroli·tic** *a.*

Fibroma (fəibrōᵘ·mă). Pl. **-mata** (-mătă). 1847. [mod. L., f. L. *fibra* FIBRE + -OMA.] A fibrous tumour. var. **Fi·brome.**

Fibrosis (fəibrōᵘ·sis). 1873. [mod.L., f. as prec. + -OSIS.] *Path.* Fibroid degeneration. Hence **Fibro·tic** *a.*

Fibrous (fəi·brəs), *a.* 1626. [f. FIBRE + -OUS. Cf. Fr. *fibreux*.] **1.** Full of fibres; formed of fibres. **2.** Fibre-like 1707.

1. F. flesh 1657, gypsum 1813, bark 1846. Hence **Fi·brous-ly** *adv.*, **-ness** var. †**Fibro·se** *a.*

Fibster (fi·bstəɹ). 1848. [f. FIB *v.*[1] + -STER.] One who fibs.

Fibula (fi·biŭlă). *Pl.* **-læ, -las.** 1673. [– L. *fibula*, perh. f. base of *figere* fix.] ‖**1.** *Antiq.* A clasp, buckle, or brooch. **2.** *Anat.* The long or splint bone on the outer side of the leg (app. as resembling the tongue of a clasp) 1706.

1. The F., whose shape..Still in the Highland broach is seen WORDSW. Hence **Fi·bular** *a.* of, pertaining to, or †resembling the f.

-fic, *suffix*, repr. L. *-ficus* '-making, -doing' (f. weakened root of *facere*), forming adjs. (1) from sbs., with sense 'making, causing, producing', as in *pacificus*; or 'performing', as *sacrificus*; (2) from adjs., with sense 'performing actions of a specified kind', as *magnificus*, also, later, 'bringing into a specified state', as *beatificus*; (3) from vbs., with sense 'causing to', as *horrificus*; (4) from advs., only in *beneficus, maleficus*, from the phrases *bene, male facere*.

-fication (fikēⁱ·ʃən), *suffix*, repr. L. *-ficationem*, the regular formative of nouns of action from vbs. in *-ficare*: see -FY. In scientific language the suffix forms many sbs., some of which have no corresponding vb.; as, *acetification, dentification*, etc.

Ficelle (fise·l). 1882. [– Fr. *ficelle* packthread.] Only in comb., as *f.-lace*, string-coloured lace.

Fichu (fiʃü, fi·ʃiu). 1803. [– Fr. *fichu*, of unexpl. form and origin.] A triangular piece of muslin, lace, or the like, worn by ladies to cover the neck, throat, and shoulders, formerly also the head.

Fickle (fi·k'l), *a.* [OE. *ficol*, rel. to *ġefic* deceit, *befician* deceive (Gmc. **fik-*), and further to *fǣcne* deceitful, *fācen* deceit, -ful (Gmc. **faik-*), corresp. to OS. *fēkan*, OHG. *feihhan*, ON. *feikn* portent.] †**1.** False, deceitful, –1533. **2.** Changeable, changeful, inconstant, uncertain, unreliable ME.

2. O Fortune, Fortune, all men call thee f. *Rom. & Jul.* III. v. 60. The f. heart of man SCOTT. F. health URE. Hence **Fi·ckleness. Fi·ckly** *adv.* (now *rare*), in a f. manner, †deceitfully.

‖**Fico** (fī·ko). 1577. [It. :– L. *ficus* FIG *sb.*[1] Cf. FIGO.] †**1.** = FIG *sb.*[1] 2. –1630. **2.** = FIG *sb.*[1] 4. *arch.* 1598. †**3.** = FIG *sb.*[2] –1602.

2. A f. for the phrase *Merry W.* I. iii. 33.

Ficoid (fəi·koid). 1741. [– mod.L. *ficoïdes*, f. L. *ficus* fig; see -OID. Cf. Fr. *ficoïde*.] **A.** *adj.* Related to or resembling the genus *Ficus*; also, fig-like 1884.

B. *sb.* A plant of the N. O. *Mesembriaceæ*.

Ficoidal (fikoi·dăl). 1846. [f. as prec. + -AL[1].]

A. *adj.* **1.** Related to or resembling the genus *Ficus* 1884. **2.** Pertaining to, or of the nature of, the N. O. *Ficoideæ* or *Mesembriaceæ* 1846.

2. *F. alliance*: a group containing the Mesembriaceæ and three other orders. (Lindley.)

B. *sb.* A plant belonging to the *Ficoidal Alliance* 1846.

‖**Ficoides** (fikoi·dīz). 1753. [mod.L. *ficoïdes*; see FICOID.] A botanical name applied to various plants, e.g. the Ice-plant (*Mesembrianthemum crystallinum*).

Fictile (fi·ktil), *a.* 1626. [– L. *fictilis*, f. *fict-*, pa. ppl. stem of *fingere* fashion; see -ILE.] **1.** Capable of being moulded. Now *rare*. 1675. **2.** Moulded into form by art; made of earth, clay, etc., by a potter 1626. **3.** Having to do with pottery 1854.

1. The several F. clays EVELYN. **2.** A f. deity 1655. F. coffins 1825. **3.** F. Craft 1888. Hence **Fi·ctileness. Ficti·lity.** f. quality; *concr.* an article of f. ware.

Fiction (fi·kʃən). ME. [– (O)Fr. *fiction* – L. *fictio*, f. as prec.; see -ION.] †**1.** The action or product of fashioning or imitating –1790. †**2.** Feigning; deceit, dissimulation, pretence –1609. **3.** The action of feigning or inventing imaginary existences, events, states of things, etc. 1605. **b.** That which is feigned or invented; invention as opposed to fact ME. **c.** A statement proceeding from mere invention; such statements collectively 1611. **4.** Fictitious composition. Now usually, prose novels and stories collectively, or the composition of such works. 1599. **5.** A supposition known to be at variance with fact, but conventionally accepted: **a.** in *Law* 1590; **b.** *gen.* (chiefly *transf.*) 1828.

1. *concr.* The unscented fictions of the loom COWPER. **3.** To be pleased in the f. of that, which would please a man if it were reall, is a Passion.. adhærent to the Nature..of man HOBBES. F. and Fraud HARTLEY. **b.** The fictions of the Virgilian age GLADSTONE. **c.** Let us cast away all f. 1655. **4.** Old people like history better than f. LYTTON. **5. a.** A..f. of our law that all real property was originally granted by the king CRUISE. **b.** To reduce debt by borrowing..is a manifest f. in finance 1828.

Hence **Fi·ctional** *a.* pertaining to, or of the nature of f. **Fi·ctionally** *adv.* by means of a work of f. **Fictionee·r, Fi·ctioner, Fi·ctionist,** a writer of f.

†**Fi·ctious,** *a.* 1641. [f. as prec. + -OUS; see -IOUS.] **1.** = FICTITIOUS. –1813. **2.** Characterized by fiction –1813.

Fictitious (fikti·ʃəs). *a.* 1615. [f. L. *ficticius* (f. as prec.) + -OUS; see -ITIOUS.] **1.** †Artificial; counterfeit, sham, not genuine. **2.** Feigned, assumed; not real 1633. **3.** Feigned to exist; imaginary 1621. **4.** Of the nature of fiction 1733. **5.** Created by a fiction (legal or conventional) 1837.

1. By shedding f. tears 1734. **2.** A f. character SCOTT, name DICKENS. **3.** A company of f. Saints BURTON. **4.** A f. narrative THIRLWALL. **5.** Adoption, as a method of obtaining a f. son MAINE.

Hence **Ficti·tious-ly** *adv.*, **-ness.**

Fictive (fi·ktiv), *a.* 1491. [– Fr. *fictif, -ive* or med.L. *fictivus*, f. as prec.; see -IVE.] **1.** †Given to feigning 1491; imaginatively creative 1865. **2.** Fictitious, feigned, sham 1612.

2. Dabbling in the fount of f. tears TENNYSON.

†**Fictor** (fi·ktəɹ, -ɔɹ). 1665. [– L. *fictor*, f. as prec.; see -OR 2.] One who frames or fashions; *esp.* an artist or modeller in clay, etc. –1677.

Ficus (fəi·kɒ̆s). ME. [– L. *ficus* fig-tree, fig.] *Path.* 'A fleshy substance or kind of Condyloma resembling a fig' (Mayne).

Fid (fid), *sb.* chiefly *Naut.* 1615. [Of unkn. origin.] **1.** A conical pin of hard wood, used to open the strands of a rope in splicing. **2.** A square bar of wood or iron, with a shoulder at one end, used to support the weight of the topmast 1644. **3.** A plug of oakum for the vent of a gun; also (? *transf.*) a plug or quid of tobacco 1626. **4.** *dial.* A small thick piece of anything 1838. **5.** 'A wooden or metal bar or pin, used to support or steady anything' (Webster) 1851. Hence **Fid** *v.* to fix (a topmast, etc.) with a f.

‖**Fidalgo** (fidæ·lgo). 1638. [Pg., contr. for *filho de algo* son of something. Cf. HIDALGO.] A Portuguese noble.

Fiddle (fi·d'l), *sb.* [OE. *fiþele* = (M)Du. *vedel* (*veel*), OHG. *fidula* (G. *fiedel*), ON. *fiðla* :– Gmc. **fiþula* – Rom. **vitula*, f. L. *vitulari* celebrate a festival, be joyful (cf. *Vitula* goddess of victory and jubilation).] **1.** A stringed musical instrument of the viol kind; usu. a violin. **2.** One who plays the fiddle; a fiddler; hence *transf.* a mirth-maker, jester 1600. **3.** Something resembling a fiddle: **a.** *Naut.* A rack or frame to prevent things from rolling off the table in bad weather 1865; **b.** *Agric.* A long wooden bar, attached by ropes at its ends to the traces of a horse, and used to drag loose straw or hay on the ground, [etc.] 1874. **4.** *slang.* **a.** A writ to arrest 1700. **b.** *Scotch* (†*Welsh*) *f.*: the itch 1700. **c.** *Stock Exch.* A sixteenth (of a pound) 1825. **5.** As an exclam. = FIDDLESTICK 3. 1695.

3. a. A heavy sea, which..caused the production of 'fiddles' on the saloon tables at lunch time 1865. **4. c.** To do business with me at a f. 1825.

Phrases. *As fit as a f.*: in good form. *To play first* (or *second*) *f.*: to take a leading (or inferior) position; so *to play third f.*

Comb.: **f.-back** a back (of a chair) shaped like a f., also *attrib.*; **-block** *Naut.* a block with two sheaves, one over the other, the smaller one underneath; **-bow** = FIDDLESTICK 1.; **-dock,** the *Rumex pulcher* of Linnæus; **-fish,** (*a*) the Angel-fish or Monk-fish; (*b*) the king-crab (*Limulus polyphemus*); **-pattern,** the pattern of f.-headed spoons and forks; **-patterned** *a.* = FIDDLE-HEADED b.; **-wood,** (*a*) the *Citharexylon*; (*b*) *Scrophularia aquatica.*

Fiddle (fi·d'l), *v.* ME. [f. prec. sb.] **1.** *intr.* To play the fiddle; now *familiar* or *contemptuous.* Also *fig.* **b.** quasi-*trans.* ME. **2.** To make aimless or frivolous movements; to act idly or frivolously. Also with *about.* 1530. **3.** *trans.* To cheat. Now only *slang.* 1604.

1. Others..Teach Kings to f., and make Senates dance POPE. **2.** He took a pipe in his hand, and fiddled with it till he broke it SWIFT. Fiddling with Franchise Bills 1884.

Fiddlededee (fi:d'ldidī·). 1784. [f. FIDDLE *sb.* or *v.* with a nonsensical addition.] **A.** *interj.* Nonsense! **B.** *sb.* Nonsense (*mod.*).

Fiddle-faddle (fi·d'lˌfæ·d'l). 1577. [Redupl. f. FIDDLE.]

A. *sb.* **1.** Trifling talk or action; in *pl.* trivial matters. **2.** A trifler; a chatterbox 1602. **B.** *adj.* Trifling, fussy 1617. **C.** *interj.* Nonsense! Bosh! 1671. Hence **Fi·ddle-fa·ddle** *v. intr.* to fuss, mess about.

Fi·ddle-head. 1799. [f. FIDDLE *sb.* + HEAD *sb.*] **1.** *Naut.* The ornamental carving at the bows of a vessel, which ends in a scroll turning inward like the head of a violin. **2.** A head as empty as a fiddle 1887. Hence **Fi·ddle-hea·ded** *a.* **a.** *Naut.* Having a fiddle-head. **b.** Having the handle made after the pattern of a fiddle, as a fork, spoon. **c.** Empty-headed.

Fiddler (fi·dləɹ). [OE. *fiþlere* = ON. *fiðlari*; see -ER[1].] **1.** One who plays on the fiddle, *esp.* for hire. †**2.** A trifler –1735. **3.** *slang.* A sixpence 1885. **4. a.** A fly resembling a cockroach 1750. **b.** The angel or shark-ray 1887. **c.** The sandpiper (*local*) 1885. **d.** A small crab of the genus *Gelasimus*; also called *fiddler-crab* 1714.

1. *Fiddler's Green* (Naut.): 'a sailor's elysium, in which wine, women, and song figure prominently' (Farmer). **4. d.** A 'Fidler-Crab' (as it is sometimes called from the rapidity with which it works its elbows) 1867.

Fiddlestick (fi·d'lstik), *sb.* ME. [f. FIDDLE *sb.* + STICK *sb.*[1]] **1.** The bow strung with horsehair with which the fiddle is played. **2.** *joc.* Something insignificant or absurd. Often substituted for another word in derision. 1621. **3.** As *interj.* Nonsense ! Often in *pl.* 1600.

Fi·ddle-string. 1728. [f. as prec. + STRING *sb.*] One of the strings on a fiddle. Also *fig.*

I do but..fret myself to fiddlestrings MRS. CARLYLE.

Fiddling (fi·dliŋ), *ppl. a.* 1580. [f. FIDDLE *v.* + -ING[2].] **1.** That plays the fiddle. **2.** Of persons: Busy about trifles. Of things: Petty, futile. 1652.

Fidei-commissum (fəi:diˌəiˌkǫmi·sǒm). 1727. [– L. *fidei-commissum*, n. pa. pple. of *fidei-committere* entrust a thing to a person's good faith, f. *fidei*, dat. of *fides* faith + *committere* entrust, commit.] *Rom. Law.* A bequest which a person made by begging his heir or legatee to transfer something to a third person.

Fideism (fəi·diˌiz'm). 1885. [f. L. *fides* faith + -ISM.] A mode of thought according to which knowledge is based on a fundamental act of faith.

Fidejussor (fəidiˌdʒɒ·səɹ, -ɔɹ). 1539. [– L. *fidejussor*, f. *fide-jubēre*, f. *fide*, abl. of *fides* faith, + *jubēre* order; see -OR 2.] *Civil Law.* One who authorizes the bail of or goes bail for another; a surety. So **Fideju·ssion. Fideju·ssory** *a.*

Fidelity (fəi-, fide·liti). 1494. [– Fr. *fidélité* or L. *fidelitas*, f. *fidelis* faithful, f. *fides* faith; see -ITY.] **1.** The quality of being faithful; faithfulness, loyalty to a person, party, etc. 1508. **b.** Conjugal faithfulness 1694. †**c.** Word of honour –1598. **2.** Strict conformity to truth or fact; †veracity; exact correspondence 1534.

1. F. to engagements BENTHAM. †*To make f.*: to take an oath of fealty 1494. **c.** By my f. this is not well *Merry W.* IV. ii. 160. **2.** The principall thing required in a witnesse is fidelitie HOOKER. The F. of the Translation POPE.

Fidepromissor (fəi:diˌpromi·sɔɹ). 1875. [– L. *fidepromissor*, f. *fidepromittere*, f. *fides* faith + *promittere* promise; see -OR 2.] *Rom. Law.* One who pledges himself as security for another; a bail, surety.

Fidge (fidʒ), *sb. colloq.* or *dial.* 1731. [f. next vb.] **1.** The action or habit of fidgeting; the state of being fidgety; also, a commotion, fuss. **2.** A restless person 1884.

Fidge (fidʒ), *v.* Now *dial.* 1575. [prob. symbolic; cf. FIG *v.*[3], FIKE *v.*, n. dial. *fitch* (XVII).] *intr.* and *trans.* To fidget; to twitch.

Fidget (fi·dʒėt), *sb.* 1674. [prob. f. FIDGE *v.*] **1.** A condition of vague physical uneasiness, seeking relief in irregular bodily movements. App. first used in *the fidget(s* (now always pl.) as if the name of a malady. Hence *transf.* uneasiness, restlessness. **2.** [From the vb.] One who fidgets, or who gives others the fidgets 1837. **3.** [From the vb.] The act of fidgeting 1860.

Fidget (fi·dʒėt), *v.* 1754. [f. prec. sb.] **1.** *intr.* To move restlessly, impatiently, or uneasily to and fro; also, to worry. **2.** *trans.* To cause to fidget; to trouble, worry 1785.

2. She says I f. her to death JANE AUSTEN.

Fidgety (fi·dʒėti), *a.* 1730. [f. FIDGET + -Y[1].] Inclined to fidget; uneasy, restless. Hence **Fi·dgetily** *adv.* **Fi·dgetiness.**

Fidibus (fi·dibǒs). 1829. [– G. *fidibus* (XVII) of undetermined origin.] A paper spill for lighting a pipe, etc.

†**Fidi·cinal,** *a.* [f. L. *fidicen, fidicin-* lute-player + -AL[1].] Of or pertaining to a player on stringed instruments. SIR J. HAWKINS.

Fiducial (fəidiū·ʃ'ăl, fidiū·ʃăl), *a.* 1571. [– late L. *fiducialis*, f. *fiducia* trust, f. *fidēre* trust; see -AL[1], -IAL.] **1.** *Theol.* Of or pertaining to, or of the nature of, trust or reliance 1624. †**2.** Trusted, trusty. HY. MORE. **3.** In *Surveying, Astron.* etc. Of a line, point, etc.: Assumed as a fixed basis of comparison 1571. **4.** = FIDUCIARY (Webster).

1. Faith..a fiduciall assent to diuine Promises 1624. Hence **Fidu·cially** *adv.*

Fiduciary (fəidiū·ʃ'ări). 1593. [– L. *fiduciarius*, f. as prec.; see -ARY[1]. In sense A. 3 after Fr. *fiduciaire.*]

A. *adj.* **1. a.** Of a person: Holding something in trust. *Obs.* exc. in *Rom. Law.* 1647. **b.** Of or pertaining to a trustee or a trusteeship 1795. **2.** Of a thing: Held or given in trust 1641. **3.** Of the nature of, proceeding from, or founded on trust or confidence 1640.

2. Uses of land..were considered as f. deposits BLACKSTONE. **3.** The f. currency of the United States 1892.

B. *sb.* **1.** One who holds anything in trust; a trustee 1631. †**2.** One who identifies justifying faiths with assurance of one's own salvation –1684. †**3.** Credentials. ABP. BANCROFT.

1. Persuade..Sir Hugh to make me his..f. in this SCOTT. Hence **Fidu·ciarily** *adv.*

Fie (fəi), *interj.* [ME. *fi, fy* – (O)Fr. *fi* :– L. *fi*; cf. ON. *fý*, which may have contributed to the ME. currency.] **1.** An exclam. expressing disgust or reproach. Now in dignified use. **2.** quasi-*sb.* or *sb.* 1550.

Fief (fīf), *sb.* 1611. [– (O)Fr. *fief*; see FEE *sb.*[2] Cf. FEOFF *v.*] = FEE *sb.*[2] 1. Also *transf.* and *fig.*

Male f., f. masculine: one that could be held by males only. Hence †**Fief** *v.* to grant as a f.

†**Fiel,** *a. Sc.* [perh. a survival of ME. *fele* (OE. *fǣle*) proper, good.] Comfortable BURNS.

Field (fīld), *sb.* [OE. *feld*, corresp. to OFris., OS. *feld* (Du. *veld*), OHG., G. *feld* :– WGmc. **felþu.*]

I. Ground. †**1.** Open land as opp. to woodland; a plain –1697. **2.** The country as opp. to a town or village. *Obs.* exc. *arch.* ME. **3.** Land or a piece of land appropriated to pasture or tillage OE. **4.** A piece of ground put to a particular use; as, a *bleach field* (cf. BLEACH *v.*[1]). **5.** An extent of ground containing some special natural production; as *coal, oil,* etc. *fields* 1859. **6.** The ground on which a battle is fought; a battlefield. Also *fig.* ME. **7.** More widely: The scene of military operations 1612. **8.** A battle; as *a hard-fought field* ME.; †order of battle –1678. **9.** The ground on which some outdoor games are played 1788; in *Baseball*, the ground in which the fielders stand 1875. **10.** *collect.* Those who take part in any outdoor contest or sport. **a.** *Sporting.* All the competitors except the favourite 1771. **b.** *Cricket.* The side who are in the field; also the players on both sides 1850. **11.** *Cricket* and *Baseball.* = FIELDSMAN. 1830.

2. *Mids. N.* II. i. 238. **3.** The fields !..All spring and summer is in them RUSKIN. COMMON *f.*, OPEN

FIELD: see these words. 6. They haue vs'd Their deerest action, in the Tented F. *Oth.* I. iii. 85. *fig.* To drive the sophists from the field 1848. Phr. *To keep, maintain the f.*: to continue the fight. *To hold the f.*: to hold its ground; to remain in possession. 7. Esmond..took the field. under Webb's orders THACKERAY. 8. Phr. *To pitch, set a f.*: to choose one's battleground, order one's men for fighting. 10. a. Phr. *To bet, back, lay against the f.*

II. An extended surface. **1.** A large stretch; an expanse 1577. **2. a.** *Her.* The surface of a shield, or of one of its divisions ME. **b.** The groundwork of a picture, etc. 1634. **c.** *Numism.* The plain part of a coin 1876. **d.** Of a flag: The ground of each division 1867.

1. Yon f. of stars *Per.* I. i. 37. Fields of Air DRYDEN, of ice 1813. The whole f. of English history 1867. 2. a. Sir Lancelot's azure lions.. Ramp in the f. TENNYSON.

III. 1. An area or sphere of action, operation, or investigation ME. **2.** *Physics.* The area or space under the influence of, or within the range of, some agent 1863.

1. As for the increase of Vertue generally..it is a large F. BACON. [A] wide f. for trade 1750. The f. of a telescope 1765. Phr. *F. of view*: the space to which observation is limited. 2. *Magnetic f.*: any space possessing magnetic properties, either on account of magnets in its vicinity or on account of currents of electricity passing through or round it.

Comb. 1. General: as *f.-dew, -dweller, -fortification, -husbandry, -movements, -service*, etc.

2. Special: **a** Prefixed to names of animals, birds, insects, etc., often with sense 'wild', and opp. to *house* or *town*, as *f.-cricket, -mouse, -spider*; **f.-duck,** the little bustard (*Otis tetrax*); **-lark** (*Alauda arvensis*); **-martin** (*Tyrannus carolinensis*); **-plover** (*U.S.*), a name for two species of plover, and for a sandpiper (*Bartramia longicauda*); **-sparrow** (U.S.) (*Spizella pusilla* or *S. agrestis*); **-titling,** the Tree Pipit (*Anthus arboreus*); **-vole** (*Arvicola arvensis*).

b. In names of plants growing in the fields, as **f.-ash** (*Pyrus aucuparia*); **-basil:** see BASIL[1]; **-madder,** †(*a*) rosemary, (*b*) book-name for *Sherardia arvensis*; **-southernwood** (*Artemisia campestris*).

c. f.-allowance, an allowance to officers and (formerly) privates, when in the field, to meet extra expenses; **-artillery,** light ordnance fitted for travel and use in active operations; **-battery,** a battery of f.-guns; **-carriage,** the carriage for a f.-gun, its ammunition, etc.; **-club,** a society for the outdoor study of Natural History; **-colours** (*Mil.*), small flags for marking out the ground for the squadrons and battalions; also the colours used by an army when in the field; **-cornet,** 'the magistrate of a township in Cape Colony' (Simmonds); **-driver** (U.S.), a civil officer whose duty it is to take up and impound stray cattle; **-events,** athletic events, such as weight-putting, etc., as distinguished from events on the running track; **-gun** = *f.-piece*; **-hand** (*a*) a slave who works on a plantation; (*b*) a farm-labourer; **-hospital,** (*a*) an ambulance; (*b*) a temporary hospital erected near a field of battle; **-ice,** ice that floats in large tracts; **-lens** = FIELD-GLASS 3; **-magnet,** part of a dynamo, 'usually a massive stationary structure of iron surrounded by coils of insulated copper wire', the function of which is to provide the *magnetic field*; **-naturalist,** one who studies out of doors; **-park,** 'the spare carriages, reserved supplies of ammunition, tools, etc., for the service of an army in the field' (Wilhelm); **-piece,** a light cannon for use on a field of battle; **-practice,** 'military practice in the open field' (Ogilvie); **-show** = *f.-trial*; **-sports,** outdoor sports, *esp.* hunting; **-telegraph,** one used in military operations; **-train,** a body of men consisting chiefly of commissaries and conductors of stores, which belong to the Royal Artillery; **-trial,** a trial in the open field, *esp.* of hunting-dogs.

Field (fīld), *v.* 1529. [f. prec. sb.] **1.** *intr.* To go into the FIELD (sense I. 2.) 1868. **2.** *trans.* To expose (corn, malt, etc.) to the action of the air 1844. †**3.** *intr.* To take the field (see FIELD *sb.* I. 7) –1590. **4.** *intr.* To back the field against the favourite 1886. **5.** *intr.* To act as fielder in cricket, etc.; *trans.* to stop and return the ball. 1824. **6.** *Sports.* To put into the field 1922.

3. Who, soone prepard to f., his sword forth drew SPENSER.

Fie·ld-bed. 1580. **1.** A bedstead for use in the field. **2.** A bed upon the ground 1592.

Fie·ld-book. 1616. A book for use in the field, as by a land-surveyor for taking notes, or by a naturalist for preserving collected specimens.

Fie:ld-conve·nticle. 1678. An open-air religious meeting.

Fie·ld-day. 1747. **1.** *Mil.* A day on which troops are drawn up for exercise in field evolutions; a military review; hence *transf.* and *fig.* a day occupied with brilliant or exciting events. **2.** A day spent in the field, e.g. by the hunt, or by field-naturalists, etc. 1823.

Fielded (fī·ldėd), *ppl. a.* 1607. [f. FIELD *v.* + -ED[1].] **1.** Engaged in a field of battle. *Cor.* I. iv. 12. **2.** Of a ball, in *Cricket*: Stopped and returned 1884.

†**Fie·lden.** 1604. [f. FIELD *sb.* + -EN[4].] **A.** *adj.* Open; consisting of fields; rural, rustic –1669. **B.** *sb.* Field land –1712.

Fielder (fī·ldəɹ). ME. [f. FIELD *sb.* and *v.* + -ER[1].] †**1.** One who works in the field. ME. only. **2.** FIELDSMAN. 1853.

Fieldfare. (fī·ldfēᵊɹ). [Late OE. *feldefare*, ME. *feldefare* (4 syll.), perh. f. *feld* FIELD + stem of FARE *v.*[1], but the medial *e* in early forms is not accounted for.] A species of Thrush (*Turdus pilaris*), which spends the winter in the British Islands.

Hollies with scarlet berries gemm'd, the fell-fare's food M. ARNOLD.

Fie·ld-glass. 1831. [f. FIELD *sb.* + GLASS.] **1.** A binocular telescope for use in the field 1836. **2.** 'A small achromatic telescope, usually from 20 to 24 inches long, and having from three to six joints' (Ogilvie). **3.** That one of the two lenses forming the eye-piece of an astronomical telescope or compound microscope, which is the nearer to the object glass 1831.

Fie·ld-ma·rshal. 1614. [transl. G. *feldmarschall*, Fr. *maréchal de camp*.] The title of a military officer of the highest rank in German-speaking and other armies. (First conferred in the British army in 1736.)

Fie·ld-meeting. 1603. [f. FIELD *sb.* + MEETING.] **1.** A duel. **2.** *Hist.* A religious meeting in the open air 1649.

Field officer. 1656. 'An officer above the rank of captain, and under that of general' (Stocqueler).

Fie:ld-prea·ching. 1739. [f. FIELD *sb.* + PREACHING.] The practice of preaching in the open air.

Fieldsman (fī·ldzmǣn). 1823. [f. FIELD *sb.* + MAN.] **a.** *Cricket.* One of the side which is fielding; a fielder 1824. **b.** *Sporting.* One who habitually backs the field.

Fie·ld-work. 1777. [f. FIELD *sb.* + WORK.] **1.** Work done in the field, or in the fields. **2.** *Mil.* A temporary fortification thrown up by troops operating in the field 1819.

†**Fie·ldy,** *a.* ME. (f. FIELD *sb.* + -Y[1].] Level, open; exposed; that grows in the fields –1598.

Fiend (fīnd). [OE. *fēond* = OFris. *fīand*, OS. *fīond* (Du. *fijand*), OHG. *fīant* (G. *feind*), ON. *fjándi*, Goth. *fijands* :– Gmc. pres. pple. of **fijējan* (OE. *fēoġan*, ON. *fía*, Goth. *fijan* hate). Cf. FRIEND.] †**1.** An enemy, foe. –ME. **2.** *spec.* The arch-enemy of mankind; the devil OE. **3.** An evil spirit generally; a demon, devil OE. **4.** *transf.* A person of superhuman wickedness or cruelty ME. **b.** †A grisly monster (e.g. a dragon). Also applied to baleful agencies personified, or hyperbolically. ME. **c.** With qualifying word: A devotee or addict, esp. to something injurious, as *dope f.*, *opium f.* (orig. *U.S. slang*) 1889.

2. The Gates..belching outrageous flame since the F. pass'd through MILT. *P.L.* x. 233. 3. Goethe's scoffing f. MACAULAY. 4. Where human fiends on midnight errands walk CAMPBELL. c. The botany-f., cyclist-f., interviewer-f. (*mod.*).

Hence †**Fie·ndful** *a.* wrought by fiends (*rare*). **Fie·ndlike** *a.* resembling, or characteristic of, a f. **Fie·ndly** *a.* †hostile; fiendish.

Fiendish (fī·ndiʃ), *a.* 1529. [f. prec. + -ISH[1].] Resembling, or characteristic of, a fiend; superhumanly cruel or malignant.

F. brualities FREEMAN. **Fie·ndish-ly** *adv.*, **-ness.**

Fierce (fīᵊɹs), *a.* ME. [– AFr. *fers*, OFr. *fiers*, nom. of *fer, fier* (mod. *fier* proud) :– L. *ferus* wild, untamed.] **1.** Violent and intractable in temper; vehement and merciless in anger or hostility. (Less emphatic than FEROCIOUS, q.v.) †**2.** High-spirited, valiant –1533. †**3.** Proud, haughty –1593. **4.** Of natural agents, disease, passions, etc.: Vehemently raging ME. **5.** Ardent; furiously zealous or active ME. **6.** quasi-*adv.* Fiercely ME.

1. Moloc..the fiercest Spirit That fought in Heav'n; now fiercer by despair MILT. *P.L.* ii. 44. F. Tigers couched around DRYDEN. 4. The f. anger of the Lord *Jer.* 25:37. F. cold 1863; discussion 1874. 5. Vengeful slaughter, f. for human blood POPE.

Hence **Fie·rce-ly** *adv.*, **-ness.**

Fie·rding. *pseudo-arch.* 1768. [– Sw. *fjerding* :– ON. *fjórðungr*; see FARTHING.] An alleged name for a quarter of a hundred or a shire.

‖**Fieri** (fəi·ĕrəi). 1640. [L. inf.: = 'to be made, come into being'. Cf. ESSE, POSSE.] In med.L. phr. *in fieri*: in process of being made or coming into being.

The contract is still *in fieri* 1832.

‖**Fieri facias** (fəi·ĕrəi, fēⁱ·ʃiæs). 1463. [L.; = 'cause to be made', f. *fieri* (see prec.) + *facias*, 2nd pers. sing. pres. subj. of *facere* do, make.] *Law.* 'A writ wherein the sheriff is commanded that he cause to be made out of the goods and chattels of the defendant, the sum for which judgement was given' (Blackstone); the common process for executing a judgement. Often abbrev. *Fi. fa.* (fəi·fēⁱ·).

‖**Fierté** (fyęrte). 1673. [Fr. *fierté*, f. *fier*; see FIERCE, -TY[1].] Haughtiness; high spirit.

Fiery (fəiᵊ·ri), *a.* ME. [f. FIRE *sb.* + -Y[1].] **1.** Consisting of or containing fire; fire-bearing. **2.** Wrought, tested, or performed by the agency of fire; in *f. trial* with reference to the testing of metals ME. **3.** Resembling fire; glowing, of a blazing red ME. **4.** Hot as fire; red hot, burning ME.; acting like fire 1535. **5.** Of persons, etc.: Ardent, eager, fierce, spirited ME.; fiercely irritable 1590. Also *transf.* of a horse 1593. **6.** Of a vapour: Liable to take fire. Hence of a mine, etc.: Containing inflammable gas. 1751.

1. Where no volcano pours his f. flood COWPER. 2. The f. trial which England went through FREEMAN. 3. Purple or f. clouds MORLEY. 4. The f. Suns too fiercely Play DRYDEN. A red f. tumour 1758. 5. A f. Soul, which working out its way, Fretted the Pigmy-Body to decay DRYDEN. The f. Courser DRYDEN. 6. The seam of coal was known to be f. 1868. Hence **Fie·rily** *adv.*, **Fie·riness.**

Fiery-cross; see FIRE-CROSS. Also *fig.*

Fife (fəif), *sb.* 1548. [– G. *pfeife* PIPE *sb.*[1] or Fr. *fifre* – Swiss G. *pfifre* (G. *pfeifer* PIPER).] **1.** *Mus.* A small shrill-toned instrument of the flute kind, used chiefly to accompany the drum in military music 1555; also, its sound 1627. **2.** A fifer 1548.

1. Their step was regulated by the f. GROTE.

Comb.: **f.-major** (*Mil.*), a non-commissioned officer who superintends the fifers of a regiment.

Fife (fəif), *v.* 1817. [f. prec. sb.] *intr.* To play on a fife; *trans.* to play (a tune) on or as on a fife. Hence **Fi·fer.**

Fife-rail (fəif,rēⁱ·l). 1721. [Of unkn. origin.] †**a.** 'Rails forming the upper fence of the bulwarks on each side of the quarter-deck and poop in men-of-war' (Smyth). **b.** The rail round the main-mast, furnished with belaying pins for the running rigging.

Fifish (fəi·fiʃ), *a. Sc.* [f. the county of *Fife* + -ISH[1]; applied orig. to people from that county.] Somewhat deranged. SCOTT.

Fifteen (fiftī·n, fi·ftīn). [OE. *fīftēne* (*-tiene*) = OFris. *fīftīne*, OS. *fīftein* (Du. *vijftien*), OHG. *fimfzehan* (G. *fünfzehn*), ON. *fimtán*, Goth. *fimftaihun*.] The cardinal number made up of ten and five; symbols 15, XV.

A. as *adj.* **1.** with *sb.* (*a*) expressed, or (*b*) omitted. †**2.** = Fifteenth *a.* –1623.

1. *The F.*: the Court of Session (formerly) consisting of fifteen Judges. Also, the Jacobite rising in 1715.

B. as *sb.* †**1.** *Eng. Hist.* = FIFTEENTH *sb.* 1. –1643. **2.** A set of fifteen persons or things 1674.

Fifteenth (fiftī·nþ, fi·ftīnþ). [Late OE. *fīftēnþa* (XI), ult. superseding OE. *fīftēoþa*, ME. *fiftethe*. The ending -TH dates from the XIV only.] The ordinal belonging to the cardinal fifteen.

A. *adj.* With sb. (*a*) expressed, or (*b*) omitted.

F. part: one of fifteen equal parts of any quantity.
B. *sb.* **1.** A fifteenth part; *esp.* in *Eng. Hist.* A tax of one-fifteenth formerly imposed on personal property ME. **2.** *Mus.* The interval of a double octave 1597. Also, a stop in an organ sounding two octaves above the Open diapason 1613.

Fifth (fifþ). [OE. *fīfta* = OFris. *fīfta*, OS. *fīfto* (Du. *vijfde*), OHG. *fimfto* (G. *fünfte*), ON. *fimti* :- Gmc. **fimftōn* :- IE. **peŋqto-* (cf. Gr. πέμπτος, L. *quintus*), f. **peŋqwe* FIVE. The normal *fift* survives dial.; the standard form (XIV) has *-th* after *fourth*.] The ordinal belonging to the cardinal five.
A. *adj.* With *sb.* (*a*) expressed, or (*b*) omitted.
F. part: one of five equal parts of any quantity. *The f. wheel of a coach*, etc.: used to describe something superfluous.
B. *sb.* **1.** = *fifth part.* Also, a fifth part of movable goods granted to the king. 1557. **2.** *Mus.* The interval of three tones and a semitone, embracing five diatonic degrees of the scale 1597. **b.** The concord of two notes separated by this interval 1656. **3.** *pl.* Articles of the fifth degree in quality 1881.
Comb.: **f.-wheel,** 'a wheel or segment above the fore-axle of a carriage and beneath the bed.. [forming] an extended support to prevent the careening of the carriage bed' (Knight).

Fifth monarchy. 1657. The last of the five great empires referred to in the prophecy of Daniel (Dan. 2:44), in the 17th c. identified with the millennial reign of Christ predicted in the Apocalypse. Also *attrib.*, *esp.* in **Fifth-monarchy man,** one of those in the 17th c. who believed that the second coming of Christ was near at hand, and that it was their duty to establish his reign by force.

Fiftieth (fi·ftiėþ), *a.* (*sb.*) [OE. *fīftigeoþa*, corresp. to ON. *fimmtugandi*; f. FIFTY on the anal. of TENTH. See -TH[2].] The ordinal belonging to the cardinal fifty.
F. part: one of fifty equal parts of any quantity.

Fifty (fi·fti). [OE. *fīftig* = OFris., OS. *fīftich* (Du. *vijftig*), OHG. *fimzug* (G. *fünfzig*), ON. *fimmtigr*, Goth. *fimftigjus*; see FIVE, -TY[2].]
A. *adj.* The cardinal number equal to five tens; symbols 50, l. Also with sb. omitted. **b.** A large number 1818.
B. *sb.* A set of fifty persons or things OE. **2.** The age of fifty years 1714. **b.** *The fifties*: The years between fifty and sixty in a century or in one's life 1880. †**3.** A fifty-gun ship –1799.
Fifty-fifty *adv.*, on a basis of fifty per cent. each; equally; *a.*, equal, shared equally, half-and-half (*colloq.*, orig. *U.S.*) 1913.

Fig (fig), *sb.*[1] ME. [– (O)Fr. *figue* – Pr. *fig(u)a* :- Rom. **fica*, for L. *ficus* fig-tree, fig.] **1.** The fruit of the fig-tree or *Ficus*, esp. of *F. carica*. **b.** = FIG-TREE. ME. **c.** In the E. and W. Indies applied to the Banana, also to the Cochineal Cactus 1582. †**2.** = A poisoned fig; often *F. of Spain, Italian f.* –1691. **3.** As the name of a disease, from the resemblance in shape. †**a.** The disease *Ficus* or the piles. Also *pl.* –1550. **b.** *Farriery*. An excrescence on the frog of a horse's foot 1607. **4.** As a type: Anything small, valueless, or contemptible ME. **5.** A small piece (of tobacco). *U.S.* 1837.
1. The F. which..gave our first Parents Cloaths CHURCHILL. **b.** *Indian F.*: the Banyan (*F. indica*), or the Pipal (*F. religiosa*). **2.** Tamberlaine..did cause a F. to be given him, and after his death married his widow NORTH. **4.** And so a f. for Miss Edgeworth THACKERAY. Phr. *To care, give a f., or fig's end for, to value (a person or thing) a f.*, etc.
Comb.: **f.-apple,** a kind of apple without a core; **-bird,** (*a*) = BECCAFICO; (*b*) the chiff-chaff (*local*); **-cake,** a round cake made of figs and almonds worked up into a hard paste; **-dust** finely ground oatmeal, used as food for caged birds (*Cent. Dict.*); **-eater,** (*a*) one who eats figs; (*b*) = BECCAFICO; **-fauns** = L. *fauni ficarii* (see Forcellini s.v. *ficarius*); **-finch** = BECCAFICO; **-gnat,** a gnat, *Culex ficarius*, injurious to the f.; **-marigold,** a name of species of *Mesembrianthemum*; **-pecker** = BECCAFICO; **-shell,** a shell somewhat resembling a f.

†**Fig** (fig), *sb.*[2] 1579. [– Fr. *figue* (in phr. *faire la figue*), – It. *fica*.] A contemptuous gesture in which the thumb is thrust between two of the closed fingers or into the mouth. Also *f. of Spain.* –1600.
Hen. V, III. vi. 62.

Fig (fig), *sb.*[3] 1841. [f. FIG *v.*[4] 2.] **1.** Dress, equipment, only in phr. *in full f.* **2.** Condition, form 1883.

†**Fig,** *v.*[1] *rare.* 1609. [f. FIG *sb.*[1]] *trans.* Only in †*To f. away* (a person): To get rid of by means of a poisoned fig.

†**Fig,** *v.*[2] [f. FIG *sb.*[2]] *trans.* To insult by giving the fig to. 2 *Hen. IV*, V. iii. 123.

†**Fig,** *v.*[3] 1595. [var. of FIKE *v.*[1]; cf. FIDGE *v.*] *intr.* To move briskly to and fro.

Fig. (fig), *v.*[4] 1692. [var. of FEAGUE.] **1.** *trans.* = FEAGUE *v.* 2. 1810. **2.** *To f. out*: to dress, get up. Also with *up*. 1837. †**3.** ? To stuff. R. L'ESTRANGE.

Figary, var. f. FEGARY.

†**Fi·gent,** *a.* 1598. [app. f. FIDGE *v.* + -ENT.] Fidgety, restless –1627.
A wrangling advocate, Such a f. little thing 1616.

Fi·ggery, *sb.* [f. FIG *sb.*[3] or *v.*[4] + -ERY.] Dressy ornament. THACKERAY.

†**Figgum.** ? Juggler's tricks. B. JONS.

Fight (fəit), *sb.* [OE. *feohte*, *feoht*, *ġefeoht*, f. base of the verb. Cf. OFris. *fiuht*, OS., OHG. *fehta* (Du. *gevecht*), OHG. *gifeht* (G. *gefecht*).] **1.** The action of fighting. Now only *arch.* **2.** A combat, battle: **a.** = BATTLE *sb.* 1. Now *arch.* or *rhet.* OE. **b.** A combat between two or more persons or animals. Not now applied (exc. *rhet.*) to a duel. ME. **3.** *fig.* Strife, conflict, struggle for victory OE. **4.** Strength or inclination for fighting; pugnacity 1812. †**5.** A kind of screen to conceal and protect combatants on shipboard. Usu. in *pl.* –1678.
1. Fall'n in f. TENNYSON. **2. a.** This was the issue of Hornsby F. LD. FAIRFAX. **b.** An Eagle and a Serpent wreathed in f. SHELLEY. Phr. *Running f.*: one kept up while one party flees and the other pursues. *Sham f.*: a mimic battle (to exercise troops, or for display). **3.** Fight the good f. of faith 1 *Tim.* 6:12. **4.** Their country had f. enough in her yet 1886. Phr. *To show f.* **5.** Vp with your fights Giue fire *Merry W.* II. ii. 142.

Fight (fəit), *v.* *Pa. t.* and *pple.* **fought** (fǭt). [OE. *feohtan* = OFris. *fiuhta*, OS. *fehtan* (Du. *vechten*), OHG. *fehtan* (G. *fechten*) :- WGmc. **fextan*.] **1.** *intr.* To contend in battle or single combat. Const. *against*, *with* (a person); hence, *to f. together*. OE. **2.** *transf.* and *fig.* To contend, strive for victory, engage in conflict OE. **3.** quasi-*trans.* with cogn. object ME.; also to maintain (a cause, etc.) by fighting 1600; to make (one's way) by fighting 1859. **4.** *trans.* To engage or oppose in battle; to war against. Also *transf.* and *fig.* 1697. **5.** To contend for (a prize) 1826. **6.** To cause to fight 1680. **7.** To manage, or manœuvre (troops, a ship, guns, etc.) in battle 1779.
1. We..fought a long houre by Shrewsburie clocke 1 *Hen. IV*, V. iv. 151. To f. for a principle 1847. Phr. *To f. with one's own shadow*: to struggle vainly; to talk at random. *To f. (for) one's own hand, to f. tooth and nail*: see HAND, TOOTH. **2.** For Modes of Faith let graceless zealots f. POPE. **3.** F. the good fight of faith 1 *Tim.* 6:12. To f. a business 1784, an action (at law) 1893. **6.** To f. cocks SCOTT, dogs DICKENS.
Phrases. *To f. down*: to overcome. *To f. off*: *trans.* to repel; *intr.* to try to back out of. *To f. out*: to settle by fighting, to fight to the end; often *to f. it out*. *To f. shy*: to avoid intercourse with a person, evade an undertaking, etc.

Fighter (fəi·təɹ). ME. [f. FIGHT *v.* + -ER[1]; cf. OE. *feohtere*, OHG. *fehtāri*.] **1.** One who fights; *occas.* a combatant, a warrior. †**2.** A pugnacious person; a brawler –1557.

Fighting (fəi·tiŋ), *vbl. sb.* ME. [f. FIGHT *v.* + -ING[1].] The action of FIGHT *v.*, in various senses.
Warres and fightinge COVERDALE. The rewards of their fightings FREEMAN.
Comb.: **f.-cock,** see COCK *sb.*[1]; **-field** = BATTLE-FIELD.

Fighting (fəi·tiŋ), *ppl. a.* ME. [f. as prec. + -ING[2].] That fights, able and ready to fight, bearing arms, warlike.
xx[ti] thousand fyghtyng men 1500. Phr. *A f. chance*: a chance of gaining something by fighting.
Comb.: **f. crab,** *Gelasimus bellator*; **f. fish,** a Siamese fish (*Betta pugnax*); **f. sandpiper,** the ruff. Hence **Fi·ghtingly** *adv.* pugnaciously.

Fi·g-leaf. 1535. [f. FIG *sb.*[1] + LEAF.] The leaf of a fig-tree; chiefy with reference to Gen. 3:7. Also *fig.*
They sewed fig leaves together *Gen.* 3:7. *fig.* The fig-leaves of decent reticence KINGSLEY.

Figment (fi·gměnt). ME. [– L. *figmentum*, f. **fig-*, base of *fingere* fashion; see -MENT.] †**1.** Something moulded or fashioned, e.g. an image –1664. **2.** A product of invention; a fiction ME.; an arbitrarily framed notion of the mind 1624.
2. To defend [God's] justice with false tales and figments 1639. Beauty, virtue, and such like are not figments of the mind BP. BERKELEY.
Hence **Figme·ntal** *a.* of the nature of a f.

†**Fi·go.** 1599. [– OSp. and Pg. *figo*.] = FICO. –1640.

Fi·g-tree. ME. [f. FIG *sb.*[1] + TREE.] A tree of the genus *Ficus*, esp. *F. carica*.

Figuline (fi·giŭlin, -əin). 1657. [– L. *figulinus*, f. *figulus* potter; see -INE[1].]
A. *adj.* Made of earthenware.
B. *sb.* **1.** An earthen vessel; in *pl.* pottery 1878. **2.** Potter's clay 1859.

Figurable (fi·giŭrăb'l), *a.* 1605. [– (O)Fr. *figurable*, f. *figurer*; see FIGURE *v.*, -ABLE.] Capable of receiving a definite figure or form, or of being represented figuratively.
Lead is f., but not water JOHNSON. Hence **Fi·gurabi·lity.**

Fi·gural, *a.* 1450. [– OFr. *figural* or late and med.L. *figuralis*, f. *figura*; see FIGURE *sb.*, -AL[1].] †**1.** = FIGURATIVE 1, 3. –1621. †**2.** *Arith.* Of numbers: Representing some geometrical figure, as a square, cube, etc.; consisting of factors –1674. **3.** Pertaining to †figure, or figures (*rare*) 1650. **4.** *Mus.* = FIGURATE *a.* 4. (Dicts.) Hence †**Fi·gurally** *adv.*

‖**Figurant** (figüraṅ) *masc.*, **Figurante** (figüräṅt) *fem.* 1775. [Fr. *figurant*, *-ante*, pres. pple. of *figurer* FIGURE *v.*; see -ANT.] **1.** A ballet-dancer 1790. **2.** One who figures on the stage but has little or nothing to do or say.

‖**Figurante** (figura·nte). *Pl.* **-ti,** *occas.* **-tes.** 1782. [It.; cf. prec.] = prec. 1. Also *transf.*

Figurate (fi·giŭrẽ[i]t). 1530. [– L. *figuratus*, pa. pple. of *figurare* form, fashion, f. *figura* FIGURE; see -ATE[2].]
A. *ppl. a.* †**1.** Based on, or involving the use of figures or metaphors; metaphorical –1728. **2.** Having definite form or shape. Now only *Med.* 1626. **3.** *Math.* †**a.** = FIGURAL 2. –1674. **b.** *F. numbers*: numbers, or series of numbers, formed from any arithmetical progression in which the first term is a unit, and the difference a whole number, by taking the first term, and the sums of the first two, first three, first four, etc., terms as the successive terms of a new series, from which a third series may be formed in the same manner, and so on. So *F. arithmetic*, the science of such numbers.
Thus from the series 1, 2, 3, 4, etc., a second series 1, 3, 6, 10, etc. ('triangular' numbers) may be formed; and from this a third series, 1, 4, 10, 20 ('pyramidal' numbers).
4. *Mus.* **a.** Involving passing discords by the freer melodic movement of one or more voice parts. **b.** = FLORID 3 a. 1708.
B. *sb.* That which is figurate; *esp.* a figurate number 1610.
Hence †**Fi·gurately** *adv.* in a f. manner.

†**Fi·gurate,** *v.* 1533. [– *figurat-*, pa. ppl. stem of L. *figurare*; see prec., -ATE[3].] **1.** *trans.* To give shape to –1623. **2.** To represent by a figure –1654; to treat as figurative 1806.

Figuration (figiŭrẽ[i]·ʃən). ME. [– (O)Fr. *figuration* or L. *figuratio*, f. as prec.; see -ION.] **1.** The action or process of giving shape to; determination to a certain form; also quasi-*concr.* the resulting form or shape. **2.** *Mus.* Employment of florid counterpoint; alteration by the introduction of passing-notes, rapid figures, etc. 1597.

Figurative (fi·giŭrătiv), *a.* ME [– late L. *figurativus*, f. as prec.; see -IVE, -ATIVE. Cf. (O)Fr. *figuratif*, *-ive*.] **1.** Representing by a figure or emblem; symbolic, typical. **2.** Pertaining to, or of the nature of, pictorial or plastic representation 1607. **3.** Of speech: Based on figures or metaphors; metaphorical, not literal ME. **b.** Metaphorically so called ME. **4.** Abounding in figures of speech 1589. †**5.** *Mus.* = FIGURATE *a.* 4. 1744.
1. F. and mystic ceremonial 1853. **2.** Both geometric as well as animal and f. decorated forms 1889. **3.** By a f. and borrowed speech he declareth the horror..of the damned COVERDALE. **b.** To

confound real with f. sovereignty 1832. **4.** F. expressions DRYDEN, authors 1740. Hence **Fi·gurative-ly** *adv.*, **-ness.**

Figure (fi·gəɹ, -iŭɹ), *sb.* ME. [– (O)Fr. *figure* – L. *figura*, f. **fig-*, base of *fingere* fashion; see -URE.]

I. Form, shape. **1.** The form of anything as determined by the outline; shape generally ME.; hence, †posture –1684. **2.** *Geom.* A definite form constituted by a line or lines so arranged as to enclose a superficial space, or by a surface or surfaces enclosing a space of three dimensions; any of the classes of such forms, as the triangle, cube, sphere, etc. ME. **3.** Of persons, etc.: Bodily shape; the bodily frame ME. **4.** A person as seen or (*transf.*) thought of ME. **5.** Conspicuous appearance 1691. **6.** Importance, mark (now only in *man, woman of f.*) 1692. **b.** Style of living. *arch.* 1602.

1. The F. of a Bell partaketh of the Pyramis BACON. Solidity and Extension, and the Termination of it, F. LOCKE. **3.** Wise Nestor then his reverend f. rear'd POPE. **4.** What a f. of a man is there! DRYDEN. Phr. *F. of fun* (colloq.): an oddity. The disappearance of this brilliant f. [Hamilton] BRYCE. **5.** Phr. *To make* (colloq. *cut*) *a f.* **6. b.** He obliged her not to increase her f., but to live private DE FOE.

II. Represented form. **1.** The image, likeness, or representation *of* something; *esp.* of the human form in sculpture, painting, etc. ME. †**2.** Represented character; part; hence, position, capacity –1721. **3.** An emblem, type ME.

1. A..playne f. of idlenesse ELYOT. Carued figures of Cherubims 1 *Kings* 6:29. Pourtraitures and Figures of those who had been Travellers 1676. **2.** Brauely the f. of this Harpie, hast thou Perform'd *Temp.* III. iii. 83. **3.** The Rock..was a Type and F. of Christ 1651.

III. Devised form. **1.** A diagram, an illustration. *Abbrev.* fig. ME. **2.** *Astrol.* A diagram of the aspects of the astrological houses; a horoscope ME. **3.** An arrangement of lines, etc., forming an ornamental device; one of the devices combined into a decorative pattern; also *transf.* of natural markings. Also *collect.* 1597. **4.** *Dancing.* Any of the evolutions or movements of a dance or dancer; also, a set of evolutions 1636. **5.** *Skating.* 'A movement, or series of movements, beginning and ending at the centre' (*Badm. Libr.*) 1869.

1. For the more declaracioun, lo here the f. CHAUCER. **2.** Phr. *To cast, erect, set a f.*: to calculate astrologically. **3.** His bonnet sedge, Inwrought with figures dim MILT.

IV. †**1.** A written character; e.g. a letter, etc. –1660. **2.** A character or symbol representing a number ME. **3.** Hence, An amount, number, sum of money expressed in figures 1842.

2. Phr. *Two* (or *double*), *three, four*, etc. *figures*: ten or more, a hundred or more, a thousand or more, etc., a sum of money so expressed. *F. of eight*: see EIGHT *sb.* 3. **3.** An uncommonly stiff f. THACKERAY.

V. Repr. Gr. σχῆμα. **1.** *Rhet.* Any form of expression which deviates from the normal; e.g. Aposiopesis, Hyperbole, Metaphor, etc. ME. **b.** Less widely: A metaphor or metaphorical expression ME. **2.** *Grammar.* Any permitted deviation from the normal form of words (e.g. Aphæresis, Syncope, Elision), or from the ordinary rules of construction (e.g. Ellipsis) 1669. **3.** *Logic.* The form of a syllogism as determined by the position of the middle term in the premisses 1551. **4.** *Mus.* 'Any short succession of notes, either as a melody or a group of chords, which produces a single, complete, and distinct impression' (Grove).

1. Your termes, your coloures, and your figures, kepe hem in store, til [etc.] CHAUCER. **b.** That.. destroyer of fine figures..common sense POPE.

Comb. **1.** General: as, *f.-painting, -training, -weaving*, etc.

2. Special: **f.-servant,** *nonce-wd.*, a commercial clerk; **-skating,** the art or practice of skating in figures (see sense III. 5); **-stone** (*Min.*) = AGALMATOLITE. See also Main Words.

Figure (fi·gəɹ, -iŭɹ), *v.* ME. [– (O)Fr. *figurer* – L. *figurare*, f. *figura* FIGURE *sb.*] †**1.** *trans.* To give figure to; to shape –1790. **2.** To represent in a diagram or picture ME. **3.** To picture in the mind, imagine 1603. **4.** To represent by speech or action 1475. **5.** 'To prefigure, foreshow' (J.) 3 *Hen. VI*, II. i. 32. **6.** To represent typically ME. †**7.** To resemble in form –1779. †**8.** To represent as resembling –1523. **9.** To express by a metaphor or image ME. **10.** To adorn or mark with figures 1480. **11. a.** *trans.* To mark with (numerical) figures 1683. **b.** *intr.* To use figures in arithmetic 1854. **c.** *trans.* (*Mus.*) To write figures over or under (the bass) in order to indicate the intended harmony 1674. **12.** *intr.* (*Dancing*). To perform a figure or set of evolutions 1744. **13.** *intr.* To appear; often with *as* 1602; also to make a distinguished appearance 1736. **14.** *U.S.* To reckon, calculate 1865.

2. The sacred Cross; and figured there The five dear wounds our Lord did bear WORDSW. **3.** You cannot f. a duller season H. WALPOLE. **4.** *Rich. III*, I. ii. 194. **6.** Soft Peace they [olives] f. DRYDEN. **10.** Blue velvet figured with tawny 1480. **11. a.** Your draft is worded for twenty pounds, and figured for twenty-one COWPER. **b.** Phr. *To f. up*: to reckon with figures. *To f. out*: to work out by means of figures; also, more widely, to estimate or calculate (chiefly *U.S.*). **13.** Persons who figured..in the rebellion 1736.

Fi·gure-ca:ster. 1584. †**1.** One who casts figures (see FIGURE *sb.* III. 2 and CAST *v.* VI); 'a pretender to astrology' (J.) –1642. **2.** One who casts up figures 1831. So **Fi·gure-ca:sting** *vbl. sb.*

Figured (fi·gəɹ'd, -iŭɹd), *ppl. a.* ME. [f. FIGURE *v.* and *sb.* + -ED.] **1.** In senses of the vb. 1552. **2.** Having a particular shape ME. †**3.** Having definite shape; also, formed into patterns –1789. **4.** Adorned with patterns or designs 1489. **5.** Adorned with rhetorical figures; figurative 1500. **6.** *Mus.* **a.** = FIGURATE *a.* 4a. **b.** *F. bass* = THOROUGH-BASS 1879.

3. Geese and cranes..move in f. flights G. WHITE. **4.** F. Satin 1611. *F. card* = COURT CARD. **5.** The f. language of which he is a master M. ARNOLD.

Fi·gure-fli:nger. 1587. Contemptuous for FIGURE-CASTER 1.

Fi·gure-hea·d. 1765. **1.** A piece of carving, usually a bust or figure, placed over the cut-water of a ship. **2.** Said depreciatingly of one who is the nominal but not the real head of an enterprise, etc. Also *attrib.* 1883. **3.** *Arch.* A corbel-head 1874.

Figurine (figiŭrī·n). 1854. [– Fr. *figurine* – It. *figurina*, dim. of *figura* FIGURE *sb.*; see -INE.] A small carved or sculptured figure.

Figuring (fi·gəriŋ, -iŭriŋ), *vbl. sb.* ME. [f. FIGURE *v.* + -ING¹.] **1.** The action of FIGURE *v.* Also with *out.* 1534. †**2.** ? Configuration, form (or perh. emblematic significance). CHAUCER.

†**Fi·gurist.** 1585. [f. as prec. + -IST.] One who explains something as figurative (e.g. the presence of Christ in the Eucharist) –1737.

Fi·g-wort. 1548. [See FIG. *sb.*¹ 3a.] The name of plants reputed to cure the 'fig'. **a.** The pilewort. **b.** The genus *Scrophularia.* 1597.

Fike (fəik), *sb. Sc.* 1605. [f. FIKE *v.*] †**1.** The itch, or anything that causes one to fidget. Also, *the fikes* = the fidgets. –1758. **2.** Anxiety about trifles, fuss, trouble 1719. **3.** Flirtation 1808.

Fike (fəik), *v. Sc.* and *n. dial.* ME. [– ON. (MSw.) *fikja* move briskly, be restless or eager. See FIG *v.*³] **1.** *intr.* To move restlessly, fidget; also *fig.* Also, to flinch. **b.** To flirt 1804. **2.** *trans.* To vex, trouble 1572. Hence **Fi·kery,** fidgetiness; fuss.

†**Filace.** ME. [– AFr. *filaz* file of documents – med.L. *filacium*, either f. L. *filum* thread, FILE *sb.*², or shortening of late L. *chartophylacium* chest for papers – Gr. χαρτοφυλάκιον, f. χάρτης paper, CHART + φυλακ- (φυλάσσειν) keep, guard.] *Law.* = FILE *sb.*² I. 3b. –1537. var. **Filaze.**

†**Fila·ceous,** *a.* 1626. [f. med.L. *filacius* (-*eus*), f. L. *filum* thread + -OUS; see -ACEOUS.] Consisting of thread-like parts –1694.

Filacer, Filazer (fi·lăsəɹ, -zəɹ). 1512. [– Law Fr. *filacer* (-ER²), f. AFr. *filaz*; see FILACE.] *Law.* A former officer of the superior courts at Westminster, who filed original writs, etc., and issued processes thereon.

Filament (fi·lăment). 1594. [– Fr. *filament* or mod. L. *filamentum*, f. late L. *filare* spin, f. L. *filum* thread; see -MENT.] **1.** A tenuous thread or thread-like body; a minute fibre; also *transf.* **b.** *spec.* The infusible conductor placed in the glass bulb of an incandescent electric lamp 1881. **2.** *Bot.* That part of the stamen which supports the anther 1756.

1. *transf.* Slender as a f. of air DE QUINCEY.

Hence **Filame·ntary** *a.* of, pertaining to, or of the nature of a f. or filaments. **Fi:lamenti·ferous** *a.* provided with filaments. **Filame·ntoid** *a.* like a f. **Fi:lamento·se, Filame·ntous** *adjs.* composed of or containing filaments; thread-like; bearing filaments. **Filame·ntule,** a small f. (*rare*).

Filander¹ (filæ·ndəɹ). Chiefly *pl.* 1486. [– (O)Fr. *filandre*, rel. to OFr. *filandrier*, -*iere*, (mod. *filandière* fem.) spinner, ult. f. *filer* spin; cf. prec.] In *pl.* Thread-like intestinal worms causing a disease in hawks; also, the disease.

†**Fila·nder.**² 1737. [Of unkn. origin.] A name given to a species of *Macropus* (*M. brunii*). Also *F. Kangaroo.*

Filander, *v.*: see PHILANDER.

Filar (fəi·lăɹ), *a.* 1874. [f. L. *filum* thread + -AR¹.] Of or pertaining to a thread; *esp.* in *f. micrometer, microscope*, one having threads across its field of view.

Filarial (filēᵊ·riăl), *a.* 1881. [f. mod.L. *filaria*, f. as prec. + -AL¹.] Of or pertaining to the genus *Filaria* of parasitic worms. Hence **Fila·riform** *a.* of the form of **Filaria. Fila·rious** *a.* infected with *Filaria.*

Filate (fəi·lĕt), *a.* 1826. [f. L. *filum* thread + -ATE².] *Entom.* Of inversatile antennæ; Having neither a terminal nor a lateral bristle.

Filatory (fi·lătəri). [f. *filat-*, pa. ppl. stem of late L. *filare* spin, after *lavatory*, etc.; see -ORY¹.] A machine for forming or spinning threads. Tooke.

Filature (fi·lătiŭɹ). 1759. [– Fr. *filature* – It. *filatura*, f. *filare* spin; see -URE.] **1.** The action of spinning into threads; the reeling of silk from cocoons 1783. **2.** An establishment for reeling silk.

1. Buying up the cocoons for the Italian f. BURKE.

Filaze, Filazer: see FILACE, FILACER.

Filbert (fi·lbəɹt). ME. [Earliest forms *philliberd, fylberde* – AFr. *philbert*, short for **noix de Philibert* (cf. Norman dial. *noix de filbert*) St. Philibert's nut, so named from its ripening about his day, 22 Aug. (O.S.).] **1.** The fruit or nut of the cultivated hazel (*Corylus avellana*). **2.** The tree bearing the nut ME.

1. Something bigger, and more oval than a Fillbeard 1712. *attrib.* F. nails TROLLOPE.

Filch (filʃ, filtʃ), *sb.* 1622. [Belongs to next vb.] †**1.** A staff with a hook at one end, used to steal things from hedges, open windows, etc. –1700. **2.** That which is filched 1627. †**3.** A filcher –1810.

Filch (filʃ, filtʃ), *v.* 1561. [orig. thieves' slang, of unkn. origin.] **1.** *trans.* To steal, *esp.* things of small value; to pilfer; *occas.*, to carry off furtively. **2.** To rob (*of* something) 1567.

1. Or els filtch Poultry, carying them to the Alehouse 1561. To f. a book out of a Library PALEY. Hence **Fi·lcher,** a petty thief. †**Fi·lchingly,** stealthily, surreptitiously.

File (fəil), *sb.*¹ [OE. (Anglian) *fīl* = OS. *fila* (Du. *vijl*), OHG. *fihala, fila* (G. *feile*) :– WGmc. **fiχalā.*] **1.** A metal (usually steel) instrument, having one or more of its faces covered with small cutting edges or teeth, for abrading, reducing, or smoothing surfaces. Also *fig.* OE. **2.** *slang.* An artful or shrewd person. Also, a 'cove'. 1812.

1. She [the serpent] fond a fyle whiche she beganne to gnawe with her teethe CAXTON. *fig.* The critic's f. AKENSIDE. **2.** Old Blow-hard was a dry old f. HUGHES.

Combs. **1.** General: as *f.-chisel, -cleaner, -cutter, -cutting, -grinder, -grinding*, etc.

2. Special: as **f.-blank,** a piece of soft steel, ready for cutting, to form a f.; also *attrib.*; **-shell,** a species of *Pholas*, so named from the roughness of its shell.

File (fəil), *sb.*² 1525. [– (O)Fr. *fil* :– L. *filum* thread.]

I. Senses repr. Fr. *fil.* †**1.** A thread; also *fig.* and *transf.* –1607. †**2.** The thread, course, or tenor (of a story, etc.) –1647. **3.** A string, wire, or other contrivance, on which papers are placed for preservation and reference 1525. **b.** *esp.* one in a court of law to hold proceedings or documents in a cause, etc.; the list of documents, etc., in a cause 1607. †**c.** A list or roll –1795. **4.** A collection of papers placed on a file, or merely arranged in order of date or subject for reference 1626. **5.** *Her.* = LABEL *sb.* 5. 1562.

2. Let me resume the F. of my Relation WOTTON. **3.** Keep the tradesmen's notes upon a f. 1732. **b.** Causes unjudg'd disgrace the loaded f. PRIOR. **c.** Our present Musters grow vpon the f. SHAKS. **4.** A f. of the *Times* LD. HOUGHTON.

II. Senses repr. Fr. *file.* **1.** *Mil.* The number of men (in the mod. Eng. formation of infantry now only two) constituting the depth of a formation in line. Also *transf.* and *fig.* 1598. **b.** A small body of men, formerly from two to twelve or more, but now usually two. Also, when 'marching in files', two soldiers abreast. 1616. **2.** A row of persons, animals, or things placed one behind another 1603. **3.** *Chess.* One of the eight lines of squares extending from player to player 1614. **4.** The run or track of a hare 1815.

1. Phr. *In f.*: one behind the other. INDIAN, SINGLE *f.* (see adjs.). *Rank and f.*: see RANK *sb.* *To close files*: see CLOSE *v.* III. 1. **b.** I shall send a sergeant and a f. of marines to fetch you MARRYAT. **2.** Phr. *The common f.* = 'the common herd'. *Cor.* I. vi. 43. *Attrib.* and *Comb.*, as *f.-leader*, the soldier at the front of a f. Also, **f.-fire, -firing,** firing by files, now called independent (opp. to volley-) firing; **-marching,** marching in files, by turning from a formation in line to the right or left, so that the line becomes a series of files facing to the right or left flank.

†**File** (fəil), *sb.*[3] *slang.* 1673. [Of unkn. origin.] A pick-pocket –1743. So †**File** *v.*[4]

File (fəil), *v.*[1] ME. [f. FILE *sb.*[1]] **1.** *trans.* To rub smooth, reduce the surface of, with a file; (contextually) to sharpen. **2.** *fig.* To smooth or polish, as with a file ME.

1. To f. the edges of new shillings 1696. **2.** Precious phrase by all the Muses fil'd SHAKS. And f. your tongue to a little more courtesy SCOTT.

File (fəil), *v.*[2] [OE *fȳlan* = MLG. *vūlen*, MHG. *viulen* :– WGmc. **fūljan*, f. Gmc. **fūlaz* FOUL *a.*] **1.** *trans.* To render foul; to DEFILE. ME. †**2.** To charge with a crime, accuse –1759.

1. For Banquo's Issue haue I fil'd my Minde *Macb.* III. i. 65. To f. my hands in villain's blood 1611.

File (fəil), *v.*[3] 1450. [f. FILE *sb.*[2]] **1.** *trans.* †To string upon a thread; to place on a file; to place in consecutive order for preservation and reference. Also *transf.* and *fig.* 1581. **b.** *spec.* To place in due manner among the records of a court or public office 1511. †**2.** To arrange in consecutive order –1676. †**3.** To arrange (men, etc.) in a file or files –1643. **4.** *intr.* To march or move in file. Also with *away*, etc. 1616. **5.** *trans.* To cause to file off 1831.

1. Miss Abbey filed her receipts DICKENS. *fig.* Dan Chaucer. . On fames eternall beadroll worthie to be fyled SPENSER. **b.** Phr. *To f. a bill* (*in Chancery*), *an information.* **2.** I would have my several courses and my dishes well filed BEAUM. & FL. **4.** Phr. *To f. off*: 'to wheel off by files from moving on a spacious front, and march in length' (Stocqueler). The Enemy filed off. towards the Thickets 1708. †*To f. with*: to march in line *with*

File-fish. 1774. [f. FILE *sb.*[1] + FISH *sb.*[1]] A fish of the genus *Balistes*, having its skin granulated like a file.

Filemot (fi·lĭmǫt). 1647. [alt. of FEUILLEMORTE.] **A.** *adj.* = FEUILLEMORTE *a.* **B.** *sb.* The name of a colour, viz. that of a dead or faded leaf 1655.

Filer (fəi·ləɹ). 1598. [f. FILE *v.*[1], [3] + -ER[1].] One who files or works with a file.

Filet (fi·lėt). 1904. [– Fr. *filet* thread, lace.] A kind of net or lace with a square mesh. Also *attrib.*

Filial (fi·liăl), *a.* ME. [– (O)Fr. *filial* or Chr. L. *filialis*, f. L. *filius* son, *filia* daughter.] **1.** Of or pertaining to a son or daughter; due from a child to a parent. **2.** 'Bearing the character or relation of a son or daughter' (J.). Now only *transf.* and *fig.* of a thing: That is the offspring of something else. 1667.

1. F. respect 1759. **2.** Thus the f. Godhead answering spake MILT. *P. L.* vi. 722. Hence **Filia·lity,** f. quality or relation. **Fi·lial-ly** *adv.*, **-ness.**

Filiate (fi·li,eⁱt), *v.* 1791. [– *filiat-*, pa. ppl. stem of med.L. *filiare* acknowledge as a son, f. L. *filius* son; see -ATE[3].] *trans.* = AFFILIATE *v.*

Filiation (fili,ēⁱ·ʃən). 1529. [– (O)Fr. *filiation* – Chr. and med.L. *filiatio* sonship, f. L. *filius* son; see -ATION.] **1.** *Theol.* The becoming, or the being, a son. **2.** Sonship 1659. **3.** A person's parentage, 'whose son one is' 1611. **4.** Descent, transmission *from* 1799. **5.** Genealogical relationship 1794. **6.** Formation of branches or offshoots; chiefly *concr.* an offshoot of a society or language 1777. **7.** = AFFILIATION 3. 1561.

3. Mr. Cust's reasoning, with respect to the f. of Richard Savage 1799. **5.** The true f. of the sciences H. SPENCER. **7.** *fig.* The f. of a literary performance is difficult of proof BOSWELL.

Filibeg (fi·libeg). *Sc.* 1746. [– Gael. *feileadh-beag*, f. *feileadh* a fold + *beag* little, as dist. from *feileadh-mor* the large kilt of primitive form.] A kilt.

Filibuster (fi·libɒstəɹ), *sb.* 1587. [The ult. source is Du. *vrijbuiter* FREEBOOTER, of which the earliest examples are obvious alterations; the present use begins with the adoption (XVIII) of Fr. *flibustier* (XVII); this was succeeded (XIX) by the present form, – Sp. *filibustero*, which itself is from Fr.] †**1.** *gen.* = FREEBOOTER (*rare*). 1587. **2.** *spec.* One of a class of piratical adventurers who pillaged the Spanish colonies in the West Indies in the 17th c. 1792. **b.** Applied to the lawless adventurers from the United States who between 1850 and 1860 followed Lopez in his expedition to Cuba, and Walker in his expedition to Nicaragua 1854. **3.** Hence, One who engages in unauthorized and irregular war against foreign states 1860. **4.** *nonce-use.* A pirate craft. MOTLEY. **5.** *U.S.* One who practises obstruction in a legislative assembly 1889.

Filibuster (fi·libɒ:stəɹ), *v.* 1853. [f. prec. *sb.*] **1.** *intr.* To act as a filibuster. Also *trans.* To subject to the methods of a filibuster 1862. **2.** *U.S.* To obstruct progress in a legislative assembly 1882.

2. The objectionable practices of 'filibustering' and 'stone-walling' 1882.

Filibusterism (filibɒ·stəriz'm). 1862. [f. prec. + -ISM.] The practice of filibustering; inclination to filibustering.

Filical (fi·likăl), *a.* 1835. [f. L. *filix, filic-* fern + -AL[1].] Of or pertaining to ferns.

Filicide[1] (fi·lisəid). 1823. [f. L. *filius, filia*; see -CIDE 1.] One who kills a son or a daughter.

Filicide[2] (fi·lisəid). 1665. [f. as prec.; see -CIDE 2.] The action of killing a son or a daughter.

Filiciform (fili·sifǭɹm), *a.* 1846. [f. as FILICAL + -FORM.] Fern-shaped.

Filicoid (fi·likoid). 1847. [f. as prec. + -OID.] **A.** *adj.* Resembling a fern. **B.** *sb.* A fern-like plant 1847.

Filiety (filəi·ėti). [– late L. *filietas* sonship (tr. Gr. υἱότης), f. L. *filius* son; see -ITY.] = FILIATION 2. J. S. MILL.

Filiferous (fəili·fĕrəs), *a.* 1841. [f. L. *filum* thread + -FEROUS.] Having thread-like parts.

Filiform (fəi·lifǭɹm), *a.* 1757. [f. as prec. + -FORM; cf. Fr. *filiforme.*] Having the form of a thread.

F. crystals of felspar 1811.

Filigrane (fi·ligrēⁱn), *sb.* 1668. [– Fr. *filigrane* – It. *filigrana*, f. L. *filum* thread + *granum* seed.] **1.** = FILIGREE *sb.* 1. Also *transf.* of architectural ornament, etc. **2.** *attrib.* = FILIGREE 2. 1680.

1. For airy towers of almost filigraine we have none to be compared with those of Rheims H. WALPOLE. Hence †**Fi·ligraned** *ppl. a.* made of f.

Filigree, filagree (fi·ligri, -ăgri), *sb.* 1693. [alt. of *filigreen*, var. of prec.] **1.** 'Jewel work of a delicate kind made with threads and beads, usually of gold and silver' (*Encycl. Brit.*). **2.** *attrib.* Made of, or worked in, filigree 1747.

2. Gold f. baskets containing flowers 1886. Hence **Fi·ligreed** *ppl. a.* ornamented with, or worked in, f.

Filing (fəi·liŋ), *vbl. sb.* ME. [f. FILE *v.*[1] + -ING[1].] **1.** The action of FILE *v.*[1] **2.** *concr.* usu. *pl.* One of the particles rubbed off by the action of the file, as *iron filings* ME.

‖**Filioque** (fili,ōᵘ·kwi). 1876. [L.; = 'and from the Son'.] The word inserted in the Western version of the Nicene Creed to assert the doctrine of the procession of the Holy Ghost from the Son as well as from the Father. Also *attrib.*, as *filioque clause*, etc.

‖**Filipendula** (filipe·ndiulă). *Obs.* exc. *Bot.* 1540. [– med.L. *filipendula*, fem. of *filipendulus* hanging by a thread, f. L. *filum* thread + *pendulus* hanging (down). Cf. Fr. *filipendule.*] The drop-wort (*Spiræa filipendula*). So **Filipe·ndulous** *a.* hanging by or as by a thread.

Fill (fil), *sb.*[1] [OE. *fyllu* = OHG. *fulli* (G. *fülle*), ON. *fyllr*, Goth. *ufarfullei* :– Gmc. **fullīn*, f. **fullaz* FULL *a.* In senses 2 and 3 f. the verb.] **1.** A full supply; enough to satisfy want. **2.** A filling, charge. *lit.* and *fig.* 1555. †**3.** Of a river: The headwaters; opp. to *fall.* DRAYTON.

1. Thou mayest eate grapes thy f. *Deut.* 23:24. Talk your f. to me GRAY. **2.** A f. of tobacco STEVENSON.

Fill (fil), *sb.*[2] Now *dial.* 1596. [dial. var. of THILL[1].] **1.** *pl.* = THILLS. *Sing.* 'The space between the shafts' (J.). *Comb.* **f.-horse** = shaft-horse.

Fill (fil), *v.* *Pa. t.* and *pple.* **filled** (fild). [OE. *fyllan* = OFris. *fullia*, OS. *fullian* (Du. *vullen*), OHG. *fullen* (G. *füllen*), ON. *fylla*, Goth. *fulljan* :– Gmc. **fulljan*; f. **fullaz* FULL *a.*]

I. To make full. **1.** To supply with as much as can be held or contained; to put or pour into till no more can be received. †**2.** To impregnate –1645. **3.** *intr.* To become full. Of the bosom: = *fill out.* 1607. **4.** *Naut.* **a.** *trans.* Of the wind: To distend (the sails) 1610. **b.** *intr.* Of a sail: To become full of wind 1835. Also *absol.* **5.** To stock abundantly OE. **6.** To make up with some foreign material; to adulterate 1887.

1. A vessel filled to the lip 1645. Ely's Sons, who fill'd with lust and violence the house of God MILT. **3.** In a few weeks, when the town fills 1713. **4. a.** South winds filling the sails BOWEN. Phr. *To f. the sails*: 'to brace the yards so that the wind strikes the after side of the sails' (Smyth). **5.** Be fruitful, and multiply, and f. the waters of the seas *Gen.* 1:22.

II. 1. To occupy the whole capacity or extent of; also, to pervade ME. **2.** To hold or occupy; to discharge the duties of ME. **3.** To put a person or thing into (a vacant place) 1593.

1. Glaciers which once filled the valley TYNDALL. Their fame filled Europe 1848. Phr. *To f. the bill* (slang): (*a*) *Theatr.*: 'To excel in conspicuousness, as a star actor whose name is "billed" to the exclusion of the rest of the company' (Farmer). (*b*) *U.S.* To meet all the requirements of the case. **2.** I f. a place, I know't *All's Well*, I. ii. 69. †*To f. the time*: to meet the needs of the moment *Ibid.* III. vii. 33. **3.** To f. an episcopal chair FREEMAN.

III. 1. To produce a sense of fullness in; to satisfy ME. Also †*intr.* **2.** To execute, perform; to fulfil (a prophecy, engagement, etc.); to complete (a period of time, etc.) OE.

1. To see meate f. Knaues, and Wine heat fooles *Timon* I. i. 271. **2.** To f. an order 1866. An olde man, that hath not filled his dayes *Isa.* 65:20.

IV. 1. To put into a vessel to fill it; hence, to pour out. *Obs.* exc. *arch.* 1450. Also *absol.* **2.** To fill a receptacle with; to put or take a load of on board a ship ME.

1. *absol.* In the cup which she hath filled f. to her double *Rev.* 18:6. **2.** Here we filled water, and after set saile 1557.

Combs. **1.** With advs. **F. in. a.** *trans.* To complete (an outline). **b.** To put in what will fill a vacancy or blank space. **F. out. a.** *trans.* To enlarge or extend to the desired limit. **b.** *intr.* To become distended or rounded in outline. **c.** *trans.* To pour out. **F. up. a.** *trans.* To fill to repletion. **b.** To complete the filling of. **c.** To supply (a deficiency, a vacancy). **d.** = *fill in* b. **e.** To stop up; to do away with by filling. **f.** *intr.* 'To grow full' (J.). **2.** Special. Prefixed to sbs., with sense 'he who or that which fills something', as **f.-basket,** a name of certain large or prolific kinds of peas, etc.; **-belly,** a glutton; **-(the)-dike** *a.* epithet of February; etc.

Filler[1] (fi·ləɹ). 1496. [f. FILL *v.* + -ER[1].] **1.** One who or that which fills (see FILL *v.*). **2.** Something used for filling 1591.

2. It [an epithet] is a mere f., to stop a vacancy in the Hexameter DRYDEN.

Filler[2] (fi·ləɹ). 1695. [f. FILL *sb.*[2] + -ER[1].] A thill- or shaft-horse. Also *attrib.*, as **f.-horse.**

Fillet (fi·lėt), *sb.* [ME. *filet* – (O)Fr. *filet* :– Rom. dim. of L. *filum* thread; see FILE *sb.*[2], -ET.] **1.** A head-band of any material, used for binding the hair, for keeping the head-dress in position, or for ornament. Also *fig.* with reference to the *vitta* with which in antiquity the heads of sacrificial victims were adorned. **2.** A strip of any material suitable for binding; a band or bandage 1601. **3.** A thin narrow strip of any material; e.g. of metal in *Coining*, of card-clothing in the *Carding-engine*; a curb to confine the curds in making cheese; etc. 1663. †**4.** (after Fr. *filet*): A thread or string. *lit.* and *fig.* –1735. **5.** A band of fibre; a flap of flesh: †**a.** A muscle –1543; **b.** 'A tract of obliquely-curved white nerve-fibres seen on the surface of the pons Varolii' (*Syd. Soc. Lex.*); †**c.** A lobe of the liver –1692; **d.** *pl.* The loins (of an animal, *rarely* of a man) ME. **6.** *Cookery.* **a.** A fleshy portion of meat, easily detachable; *esp.* the undercut of a sirloin; one of the thick slices into which a fish is easily divided ME. **b.** The middle part of a leg of veal, boned, rolled, and tied with a string or 'fillet'; a piece of beef, fish, etc. similarly treated 1700. **7.** Any object resembling a fillet or band 1611. **8.** *Arch.* **a.** A narrow flat band separating two mouldings; a fascia. **b.** A small band between the flutes of a column. 1473. **9.** *Her.* A horizontal division of a shield, one-third or one-fourth of the depth of a CHIEF *sb.* 1572. **10.** *Entom.* and *Ornith.* **a.** A coloured band or stripe. **b.** In a spider: The space between the eyes and the base of the mandibles or cheliceræ. 1668. **11.** In techn. uses: **a.** A raised rim or ridge on any surface, *esp.* 'a ring on the muzzle and cascabel of a gun' (Smyth); also, the thread of a screw 1703. **b.** *Carpentry.* A narrow strip of wood fastened upon any surface to serve as a support, etc., or to strengthen an angle formed by two surfaces 1779. **c.** *Bookbinding.* A plain line impressed upon the cover of a book. Also, a tool for doing this. 1641.

Fillet (fi·lėt), *v.* *Pples.* **filleted, filleting.** 1604. [f. FILLET *sb.*] **1.** *trans.* To bind with or as with a fillet. **2.** *Cookery.* To divide into fillets 1846. **3.** To mark or ornament with fillets; now chiefly in *Bookbinding* 1621.

Filleting (fi·lėtiŋ), *vbl. sb.* 1598. [f. prec. + -ING[1].] **1.** The action of FILLET *v.* **2.** *concr.* **a.** Tape for binding; a band or bandage 1639. **b.** A head-band 1648. **c.** Fillets or ornamental lines 1747.

2. b. Put on thy holy fillitings HERRICK.

Filli-: see also FILI-.

Filling (fi·liŋ), *vbl. sb.* ME. [f. FILL *v.* + ING[1].] **1.** The action of FILL *v.* **2.** *concr.* Also *pl.* That which fills or is used to fill a cavity or vacant space, to stop a hole, to make up a bank or road, the interior of a wall, etc. ME. **b.** Something of inferior quality put in to occupy space 1640. **3.** *Brewing.* In *pl.*: Prepared wort, added to casks of ale to cleanse it 1858.

Fillip (fi·lip), *sb.* 1530. [imit.] **1.** A movement made by bending the last joint of a finger against the thumb and suddenly releasing it; a smart stroke or tap given by this means. **b.** A trifle; a moment 1621. **2.** A smart blow (with the fist, etc.). Now *rare.* 1543. **3.** That which serves as a stimulus 1700.

1. The Prince..by a f., made some of it [wine] fly in Oglethorpe's face BOSWELL. **b.** Not worth a f. BYRON. 3. The filip of a little scandal 1847.

Fillip (fi·lip), *v.* 1535. [See prec. sb.] **1.** *trans.* To put into motion by a fillip; hence, to stimulate. **2.** To strike with a fillip 1580. **3.** *gen.* To strike smartly 1577. **4.** *intr.* To make a fillip with the fingers 1577.

1. To f. off crumbs from a muff MME. D'ARBLAY. 2. If you f. a Lute-string, it sheweth double or Treble BACON. 3. If I do, fillop me with a three-man-Beetle 2 *Hen. IV*, I. ii. 255.

Fillipeen, var. of PHILIPPINA.

Fillister (fi·listəɹ). 1819. [perh. based on synon. Fr. *feuilleret*; for the repr. of Fr. *feuill-* by *fil-* cf. FILEMOT.] A rabbeting plane used in making window-sashes, etc.; also, 'the rabbet on the outer edge of a sash-bar, to hold the glass and the putty' (Knight).

Filly (fi·li), *sb.* [Late ME. but prob. much older if – ON. *fylja* :– **fuljōn*, parallel to OHG. *fuli(n)* (also *fulihha*, MHG. *fülhe*), f. Gmc. **ful-* FOAL.] **1.** A young mare, a female foal. **2.** *transf.* A young lively girl 1616. **3.** *attrib.* 1523.

2. I believe nobody will be very fond of a Hide-park f. for a wife SEDLEY. Hence †**Fi·lly** *v.* to give birth to a f.

Film (film), *sb.* [OE. *filmen* membrane = OFris. *filmene* skin :– WGmc. **filminja*, ult. f. **fellam* FELL *sb.*[1]] †**1.** A membrane –1764. **2.** A thin pellicle or lamina of any material 1577. **3.** *Photogr.* A thin pellicle or coating of collodion, gelatin, etc., spread on photographic paper or plates, or used by itself instead of a plate 1845. **4.** A morbid growth upon the eye. Also *fig.* 1601. **b.** A celluloid roll of film used for a cinema picture 1897. **c.** A cinema performance; *pl.* the cinema 1911. **5.** *transf.* A slight veil of haze, mist, or the like. *lit.* and *fig.* 1833. **6.** A fine thread or filament 1592. **7.** Comb., as *f. actress, -camera, star.*

2. An icy gale..o'er the pool Breathes a blue f. THOMSON. 4. He from thick films shall purge the visual ray POPE. Phr. *The f. of death.* 6. When.. floating films envelope every thorn COWPER.

Film (film), *v.* 1602. [f. prec. sb.] **1.** *trans.* To cover with or as with a film. **2.** *intr.* for *refl.* To become covered with a film; to grow dim as if covered with a film 1844. **3.** *trans.* To make a cinema film of, put on the films 1915.

1. It will but skin and filme the Vlcerous place SHAKS.

Filmy (fi·lmi), *a.* 1604. [f. FILM *sb.* + -Y[1].] †**1.** Of membranous structure –1665. **2.** Forming a thin pellicle or coating 1628. **3.** Gauze- or gossamer-like 1604. **4.** Covered with or as with a film 1825.

2. The area of f. ice KANE. 3. A veil of f. lawn SCOTT. 4. The f. orb of the moon HT. MARTINEAU. Hence **Fi·lmily** *adv.* **Fi·lminess.**

Filoplume (fəi·lŏplūm). 1884. [– mod.L. *filopluma*, f. L. *filum* thread + *pluma* feather; see -O-.] *Ornith.* A thread-feather; the nearest approach to hairs that birds have. Hence **Fi:lopluma·ceous** *a.*

Filose (fəilōᵘ·s), *a.* 1823. [f. L. *filum* thread + -OSE[1].] *Bot.* and *Zool.* Having a thread-like termination.

Filoselle (fi·lŏsel). 1612. [– Fr. *filoselle.*] A silk thread less glossy than floss silk.

Filosofe, -phie, obs. ff. PHILOSOPH, -Y.

Filter (fi·ltəɹ), *sb.* [Late ME. *filtre* – OFr. *filtre*, var. of *feltre* (mod. *feutre* felt) :– med.L. *filtrum* – WGmc. **filtir* FELT *sb.*[1]] †**1.** = FELT *sb.*[1] **2.** A piece of felt, woollen cloth, paper, or other porous substance, through which liquids are passed to free them from matter held in suspension. Now only *Chem.* 1563. **b.** Any contrivance for freeing liquids from suspended impurities; *esp.* a vessel in which the liquid is made to pass through sand, charcoal, or some porous substance. Also *transf.* and *fig.* 1605. **3.** A material for filtering. *rare.* 1823.

2. *Capillary f.*: 'a mode of freeing water of its larger impurities by means of a cord of loose fiber' (Knight).

Comb.: **f.-bed** a pond or tank with a false bottom covered with sand or gravel, serving as a large filter; also *fig.*: **-faucet,** 'one having a chamber containing sand, sponge, or other material to arrest impurities' (Knight); **-paper,** porous paper for filtering; **-press,** (*a*) a filter in which the liquid is forced through by pressure; (*b*) a machine for extracting oil from fish.

Filter (fi·ltəɹ), *v.* 1576. [f. the sb.; cf. Fr. *filtrer* (XVI).] **1.** *trans.* To pass (a liquid) through a filter in order to free it from impurities. Also *absol.* Also *transf.* and *fig.* **b.** Said of the filtering material 1854. **2.** To cause to percolate through a porous medium (now only in *pass.*) 1583. **3.** *intr.* To pass as through a filter; to percolate 1798. **4.** To obtain by filtering. Also *transf. rare.* 1794.

3. *transf.* Filtration. When you are held up at a road junction by a person regulating traffic, do not turn to the left—that is, filter—unless [etc.] *Highway Code* (Ministry of Transport) § 85. 1935.

Filter, var. of PHILTRE.

Filtering (fi·ltəriŋ), *vbl. sb.* 1830. [f. FILTER *v.* + -ING[1].] The action of FILTER *v.*

Comb.: **f.-basin,** the chamber in which water from the reservoir is received and filtered before entering the mains; **-cup,** a cup of porous wood used to illustrate the pressure of the atmosphere; **-press** = *filter-press*; **-stone,** any porous stone used in filtering water; **-tank** = *f.-basin.*

Filth (filþ). [OE. *fȳlþ* = OS. *fūlitha* (Du. *vuilte*), OHG. *fūlida*; f. Gmc. **fulaz* FOUL *a.*; see -TH[1].] †**1.** The quality or state of being foul; in *pl.* indignities –1579. **2.** *concr.* Foul matter; †rottenness –1526; †pus –1696; dirt. Now only: Loathsome dirt. Rarely in *pl.* ME. **3.** *fig.* Moral defilement; corruption; pollution; obscenity OE. **4.** Said of a person: A vile creature; a scoundrel; a drab. *Obs.* exc. *dial.* ME.

4. *Lear* (Qo. 1) IV. ii. 39.

Filthy (fi·lþi), *a.* ME. [f. FILTH + -Y[1].] **1.** Full of filth; besmeared with filth; dirty, foul, nasty, unclean. Now *rare* in polite speech. **2.** Fond of filth 1526. **3.** Morally foul; obscene 1535. †**4.** Low, mean, scurvy, disgusting –1828. **5.** quasi-*adv.* 1616.

1. Stinking streates and f. lanes 1581. The fogge and filthie ayre *Macb.* I. i. 12. He which is f., let him be f. still: and hee that is righteous, let him bee righteous still *Rev.* 22:11. 4. Doulas, f. Doulas 1 *Hen. IV*, III. iii. 79. Phr. *F. lucre*: dishonourable gain = Gr. αἰσχρὸν κέρδος (Tit. 1:11). Also *joc.* for 'money'.

Hence **Fi·lthify** *v.* to make f. (*lit.* and *fig.*). **Fi·lthily** *adv.* **Fi·lthiness.**

Filtrate (fi·ltrēⁱt), *sb.* 1845. [f. as next; see -ATE[1].] The liquor which has been passed through a filter.

Filtrate (fi·ltrēⁱt), *v.* 1612. [– *filtrat-*, pa. ppl. stem of mod.L. *filtrare*; see FILTER *sb.*, -ATE[3].] **1.** *trans.* = FILTER *v.* 1. **2.** = FILTER *v.* 2. 1661. **3.** *intr.* = FILTER *v.* 3. 1725.

Filtration (filtrēⁱ·ʃən). 1605. [– Fr. *filtration* (XVII), *f. filtrer*; see FILTER *v.*, -ATION.] **1.** The action or process of filtering. Also *fig.* **2.** Percolation 1664.

1. *transf.* See s.v. FILTER *v.* quot.

Fimble (fi·mb'l). 1484. [Earlier *fem(b)le* – Du. *femel*, LG. *fimel* – Fr. (*chanvre*) *femelle* 'female (hemp)', this name being pop. applied to what modern botanists call the male plant.] **1.** The male plant of hemp. More fully *f. hemp.* **2.** *attrib.* 1519.

‖**Fimbria** (fi·mbriă). 1752. [Late L. *fimbria* (earlier only in pl. *fimbriæ*) border, fringe.] A fringe: *spec.* **a.** *Anat.* the fringed end of the Fallopian tube; **b.** *Bot.* the fringe-like ring of the operculum of mosses. Hence **Fi·mbrial** *a.* (Dicts.)

Fimbriate (fi·mbri,ēⁱt), *a.* 1829. [– L. *fimbriatus*; see prec., -ATE[2].] **a.** *Her.* = FIMBRIATED. **b.** *Bot.* and *Zool.* Fringed.

Fimbriate (fi·mbri,ēⁱt), *v.* 1486. [f. as prec.; see -ATE[3] and cf. next.] *trans.* To finish with a border of any kind.

Fimbriated (fi·mbri,ēⁱtėd), *ppl. a.* 1486. [f. as prec. + -ED[1], perh. after med.L. *fimbriatus* in same sense.] **a.** *Her.* Of a bearing: Bordered with a narrow band or edge. **b.** *gen.* Having a fringe; fringed 1698.

Fimbriation (fimbri,ēⁱ·ʃən). 1864. [f. as prec.; see -ATION.] The condition or fact of being fimbriated; *concr.* a fringe or border.

Fi·mbricate *a.*, erron. var. of FIMBRIATE *a.*

Fimetarious (fimitēᵊ·riəs), *a.* 1866. [f. L. *fimetum* dunghill + -ARIOUS.] Growing on or amidst dung. So **Fime·tic** *a.* pertaining to or concerned with dung. RUSKIN.

Fin (fin), *sb.* [OE. *fin(n)* = MLG. *finne*, MDu. *vinne* (Du. *vin*); a word of the North Sea area, prob. ult. rel. to L. *pinna* feather, wing.] **1.** An organ attached to various parts of the body in fishes and cetaceans, which serves for propelling and steering in the water. Qualified as *anal, caudal, dorsal, pectoral, ventral*, etc., according to position. Applied also to analogous organs in other animals, as seals, penguins, etc. **2.** Something resembling a fish's fin: **a.** *joc.* The arm and hand (of a man), or simply the hand 1785. †**b.** The lid (of the eye) –1623. **c.** The baleen of a whale; hence, a strip of whalebone 1634. **3.** A projecting part: †**a.** A lobe of the liver or lungs 1615. **b.** A lateral projection on the coulter of a plough 1653. **c.** *Mech.* 'A slip inserted longitudinally into a shaft or arbor, and left projecting' (Knight). Also, 'a tongue on the edge of a board' (Knight). **d.** An additional keel-surface in aircraft 1836. **4.** *dial.* The herb rest-harrow. Also *fin-weed.* 1649.

1. All fish..of shell or f. MILT. Fish of every f. (= of every species) POPE. **2. a.** Tip us your f. (*slang*) 1896.

Comb.: **f.-back** = FINNER; also *attrib.*; **-fish** = FINNER; **-foot,** (*a*) a swimming foot; a pleiopod; (*b*) a name for birds of the genera *Heliornis* or *Podica*; **-footed** *a. Ornith.*, (*a*) web-footed; (*b*) lobate-footed; (*c*) 'in Mollusca, pteropod' (*Cent. Dict.*); **-keel,** a keel shaped like a dorsal f. inverted; **-ray,** one of the processes which support the skin of the fins; **-spine,** a spine or spiny ray of a fish's f.; **-spined** *a.*, acanthopterygious; **-toed** *a.* = *-footed*; **-weed** (see sense 4); **-whale** FINNER.

Fin (fin), *v.* 1513. [f. prec.] To cut off the fins from (a fish); to cut up (a chub).

Fin, obs. f. FINE *sb.*[1] and *a.*

Finable, fineable (fəi·năb'l), *a.*[1] 1485. [f. FINE *v.*[2] + -ABLE.] **1.** Liable to a fine. **2.** Of a tenure: Subject to a fine on renewal 1600.

1. A f. offence 1860, offender 1896. **2.** F. Copyhold 1641.

Finable (fəi·năb'l), *a.*[2] [f. FINE *v.*[3] + -ABLE.] That can be clarified, refined, or purified. (Mod. Dicts.)

Final (fəi·năl), *a.* ME. [– (O)Fr. *final* or L. *finalis*, f. *finis* end; see FINE *sb.*[1], -AL[1].]

A. *adj.* **1.** Coming at the end; marking the last stage; ultimate. **2.** Putting an end to something; conclusive ME. **3.** Having regard to end or purpose; chiefly in *Final Cause* (see CAUSE *sb.* I. 4.) ME.

1. The f. debt to Nature MILT., chapter 1865. Phr. *F. process* (*Law*): process of execution; opp. to *mesne process.* **2.** Examples, where Sea-Fights have been Finall to the warre BACON.

B. *sb.* **1.** The adj. used *absol.* Completion, end, finish. Now *rare.* 1582. **2.** The adj. used *ellipt.*: e.g. **a.** The final letter of a word 1627. **b.** *Athletics.* The deciding game, heat, or trial 1830. **c.** The last of a series of examinations; also *pl.* (Oxford *colloq.*) 1894.

Hence **Fi·nalism,** the belief that the end has been reached. **Fi·nalist,** one who holds this belief; also, a competitor left in for the final contest.

‖**Finale** (finā·le). 1783. [It. *finale* adj. (used subst.).] **1.** *Mus.* **a.** 'The last movement of a symphony, sonata, concerto, or other instrumental composition'. **b.** 'The piece of music with which any of the acts of an opera are brought to a close' (Grove). **2.** The closing part of a drama or any other public entertainment 1814. **3.** The end; the final catastrophe 1785.

3. In the real battle..we are most pleased with the *finale* 1816.

Finality (fəinæ·lĭti). 1541. [– Fr. *finalité* – late L. *finalitas*, f. L. *finalis*; see FINAL, -ITY.] †**1.** An end in view. *rare.* 1541. **2.** The relation of being an end or final cause; the principle of final cause viewed as operative in the universe 1859. **3.** The quality, condition, or fact of being final; also, the belief that something is final (first used in this sense of the Reform Bill of 1832) 1833; *concr.* something that is final 1833. **4.** *attrib.* 1839.

3. Althorp's explanations as to the f...of the Bill CROKER. **4.** John Russell..He is our own F. John 1839.

Finally (fəi·năli), *adv.* ME. [f. FINAL + -LY[2], after OFr. *final(e)ment*, late L. *finaliter.*] **1.** In the end, lastly, at last, ultimately. **2.** So as to make an end; decisively, conclusively ME.

1. Evil prevailing f. over good BUTLER. **2.** Many men are f. lost SOUTH.

Finance (fi-, fəinæ·ns), *sb.*[1] ME. [– (O)Fr. *finance* †end, †payment, money (cf. AL. *financia* payment XIV), f. *finer* make an end, settle, etc., f. *fin* end; see FINE *sb.*[1] The senses now current are from mod. Fr. usage.] †**1.** Ending. *rare.* –1616. †**2.** Payment of a debt, or of compensation; *esp.* a ransom –1597. †**3.** Supply (of goods); stock of money; substance –1502. †**4.** Borrowing of money at interest –1721. †**5.** A tax; taxation; crown or state revenues –1670. **6.** *pl.* The pecuniary resources of a sovereign or state; hence, of a company or individual 1739. **7.** The management of money; *esp.* the science of levying and applying revenue in a state, corporation, etc. 1770. **8.** *attrib.*, as *f. committee*, etc. 1467.

5. All the finances or revenues of the imperial crown..be either extraordinary or ordinary LAMBARDE. **7.** No scheme of f. can be bottomed on sound principles which [etc.] MCCULLOCH. Hence †**Fina·ncer.**

†**Finance,** *sb.*[2] *Sc.* 1473. [perh. – AFr. **finance*, f. **finer* refine (see FINE *v.*[3]), f. *fin* FINE *a.* Cf. med.L. *finare* refine (XIII), also *finire* (XIV), *finitio* refining.] Fineness (of gold, etc.) –1555.

Finance (fi-, fəinæ·ns), *v.* 1478. [f. FINANCE *sb.*[1]] †**1.** *trans.* To put to ransom; *intr.* to pay ransom –1494. **2.** *trans.* To furnish with finances; to find capital for 1866. **3.** *intr.* To engage in financial operations; to provide oneself with capital 1827.

Financial (finæ·nʃăl), *a.* 1769. [f. FINANCE *sb.*[1] + -IAL.] Of or pertaining to finance or money matters.

Phr. *F. year*: the annual period for which accounts are made up. Hence **Fina·ncially** *adv.* from a f. point of view.

Financier (finæ·nsiəɹ). 1618. [– Fr. *financier*, f. *finance*; see FINANCE *sb.*[1], -IER.] †**1.** *Fr. Hist.* An administrator, collector, or farmer of taxes before the Revolution –1755. **2.** One who is skilled in levying and managing public money 1618. **3.** A capitalist concerned in financial operations 1867.

2. The objects of a f. are..to secure an ample revenue; to impose it with judgment..to employ it economically [etc.] BURKE.

Finary, obs. f. FINERY[2] a puddling furnace.

Finch (finʃ). [OE. *finć* = MDu. *vinke* (Du. *vink*), OHG. *finc(h)o* (G. *fink*) :– WGmc. **finki*, **finkjo(n)*.] A name for many birds of the order *Passeres*, esp. those of the genus *Fringilla* or family *Fringillidæ*.

Phr. †*To pull a f.* = 'to pluck a pigeon'. CHAUCER. *Comb.* †**f.-egg,** a contemptuous epithet. SHAKS.

Fi·nch-backed, *a.* ? *Obs.* 1796. = next.

Finched (finʃt), *ppl. a.* 1786. [Of unkn. origin.] Of cattle: Streaked with white along the back.

Find (fəind), *sb.* 1825. [f. next vb.] **1.** An act or instance of finding; e.g. the finding of a fox, or minerals, treasure, etc. Somewhat *colloq.* **2.** *concr.* That which is found 1847.

1. Phr. *A sure f.*: in *Sporting*, a place where a f. is sure to be made; *colloq.* one who is sure to be found.

Find (fəind), *v. Pa. t.* and *pple.* **found** (faund). [OE. *findan* = OFris. *finda*, OS. *findan, fiþan* (Du. *vinden*), OHG. *findan* (G. *finden*), ON. *finna*, Goth. *finþan* :– Gmc. **finþan.*]

I. 1. *trans.* To come across, fall in with, light upon. Primarily of persons; hence of things viewed as agents. **2.** To discover the whereabouts of (something hidden or not previously observed) ME. **3.** To come to have, receive, get OE. **4.** To gain or recover the use of 1535. **5.** To discover on inspection or consideration (cf. Fr. *trouver*). Also *refl.* ME. **6.** To learn by experience or trial; also to feel to be (cf. Fr. *trouver*) ME.

1. Which impels the water it findes in its way BOYLE. Affliction never leaves us as it finds us BP. HALL. **2.** A curse on him who found the Oare COWLEY. **3.** Phr. *To f. favour*, (see FAVOUR *sb.*). *To f. one's account in*: to experience to be profitable. **4.** Phr. *To find one's feet*: lit. of a child: To be able to stand; *fig.* to develop or feel one's powers. **5.** Phr. *To f. fault* (see FAULT *sb.*). I f. no sense..in what you say BP. BERKELEY. *refl.* To f. oneself perplexed 1633. Pray, Sir, How d'ye F. your self 1692. **6.** *Dan.* 5:27. Phr. *To f. it impossible*, etc., *to do so and so.*

II. 1. To discover or attain by search or effort OE.; also *refl.* 1647. **2.** To succeed in obtaining ME. **3.** Of things: To obtain as if by effort 1810; to arrive at ME ; to come home to the understanding or conscience of 1834. †**4.** To contrive, devise, invent; to discover –1660. **5.** *Law.* To determine and declare to be ME.; to agree upon and bring in (a verdict) 1574; to ascertain the validity of (an instrument) 1512.

1. To f. a hole in a Lease 1553, the centre of a circle WHISTON. *refl.* Browning may be said almost to have found himself in [etc.] 1889. **2.** To f. Security for Expenses 1868, time to read a book 1868, courage to speak (*mod.*). Phr. *To f. in one's heart*: to be inclined; now usu., to be hard-hearted enough. **3.** Phr. *To f. expression, ingress, outlet, place*, etc. Whatever *finds* me, bears witness for itself that it has proceeded from a Holy Spirit COLERIDGE. *To f. one's way*: to go or be brought to a place in spite of difficulties, or not quite as a matter of course. **5.** The Crowner.. finds it Christian buriall SHAKS. Is he found guilty SHAKS. The jury..found a verdict of guilty MACAULAY. Phr. *To f. a (true) bill*: see BILL *sb.*[3]

III. 1. To supply ME. **2.** To support, provide for (a person) ME.

1. The hotels do not f. breakfast 1814. Wages £18, *all found* but beer 1884. **2.** Phr. *To f. in*: to supply with. *To f. oneself*: to provide for one's own living or needs. †Also *transf.* of a war. The war in continuance will finde it selfe BACON.

Comb. with adv. **F. out. a.** To discover; to invent; to unriddle, solve. **b.** To come upon by searching. **c.** To detect; to penetrate the disguise of.

Hence **Fi·ndable** *a.* that may be found. **Fi·nd-fault** (*dial.*), a censorious person.

Finder (fəi·ndəɹ). ME. [f. FIND *v.* + -ER[1].] **1.** One who or that which finds. **2.** *spec.* A small telescope attached to the large one for the purpose of finding an object more readily 1784. **b.** A microscopic slide divided by crossed lines, so that any point in the field can be identified readily 1867. **c.** *Photogr.* A supplementary lens attached to a camera, to locate the object in the field of view 1894.

‖**Fin de siècle** (fæn də syękl'). 1890. [Fr.] A phrase used as an adj.: Characteristic of the end of the (nineteenth) century; advanced, modern; also, decadent.

Findhorn: see FINNAN.

Finding (fəi·ndiŋ), *vbl. sb.* ME. [f. FIND *v.* + -ING[1].] **1.** The action of FIND *v.*; that which is found; also, a find. **2.** The action of maintaining or supporting ME; †keep, provision, support –1573. **b.** in *pl.* Tools, materials, accessories, etc., used by shoemakers, dressmakers, and jewellers 1846. **3.** The result of a judicial enquiry; the verdict of a jury 1859.

1. When a man..in the deep mines of knowledge, hath furnisht out his findings MILT. **3.** The court-martial still adheres to its f. of murder 1859.

Findon: see FINNAN.

†**Fi·ndy** *a.* [ME. *findiȝ*; cf. OE. *ġefyndiġ* capable, Da. *fyndig* powerful, solid, f. *fynd* strength, substance. See -Y[1].] Firm, solid, weighty –1677.

A May cold and windie maketh the barn full and fyndie 1677.

Fine (fəin), *sb.*[1] [– (O)Fr. *fin* :– L. *finis* end, in med.L. sum to be paid on concluding a lawsuit.]

I. End. (*Obs.* exc. in *in fine.*) †**1.** Cessation, end, conclusion –1839. †**2.** End of life, death –1556. †**3.** End in view, aim –1603. †**4.** Final issue, result –1605.

1. Still the fine's the Crowne *All's Well* IV. iv. 35. Phr. *In f.*: †(*a*) at last; (*b*) to conclude; also, in short. **3.** To what f. is soche loue, I can not seen CHAUCER.

II. *Law.* A 'final agreement'; 'an amicable composition or agreement of a suit, either actual or fictitious, by leave of the king or his justices' (Blackstone) ME. **b.** *spec.* The compromise of a fictitious or collusive suit for the possession of lands; formerly in use as a mode of conveyance 1483. †**c.** Hence *gen.* A contract, agreement. ME only.

b. The cognizor (= the defendant who acknowledged the right of the plaintiff to the land) was said to *acknowledge* or *levy a fine.* Also *to sue a fine* O.E.D.

III. A composition paid. **1. a.** *Feudal Law.* A fee (as dist. from rent) paid by the tenant or vassal to the lord on the transfer or alienation of the tenant-right, etc. ME. **b.** *Mod. Law.* A sum of money paid by the tenant on the commencement of his tenancy in order that his rent may be small or nominal 1523. **2.** A sum of money paid to make one's peace, settle a matter, obtain one's release, etc. ME. **b.** A certain sum of money imposed as the penalty for an offence; hence, a penalty of any kind (*arch.*) 1503. †**3.** A fee paid for any privilege; probate duty on a will –1744.

2. b. Fines to the amount of £85,000..were imposed on the Covenanters HALLAM.

Comb. **f.-rolls** (= *rotuli oblatorum* or *finium*): the Rolls on which were entered the sums of money, etc., offered to the king by way of oblation or fine for the passing of charters or grants, etc.

||**Fine** (fi·nĭ), *sb.*[3] 1873. [Irish.] An Old Irish family or sept.

Fine (fəin), *a.* ME. [– (O)Fr. *fin* :– Rom. **finus*, f. L. *finire* to FINISH, after such pairs as *grossus, grossire*.]

I. 1. Of superior quality. **2.** Free from dross or impurity; clear, pure, refined ME. Of gold or silver: Containing so many 'carats' (see CARAT) or 'ounces' (*sc.* per lb. troy) of pure metal 1594. †**3.** Pure, sheer, absolute; perfect –1706. †**4.** Consummate –1604. **5.** Admirably skilful ME.

1. With pelure þe finest vpon erthe LANGL. **2.** The air subtle and f. 1567. Two vessels of f. copper, precious as gold *Ezra* 8:27. The purest gold, 24 carats f. 1862. **5.** Pope was a really f. judge of literature STEPHEN.

II. 1. Exquisitely fashioned; delicate ME. **2.** Not COARSE; delicate in structure or texture ME.; comminuted 1535; attenuated, subtle, rare 1626; very thin or slender ME.; in *Athletics*, reduced in fat to the proper point by training 1815. **3.** Sharp-pointed, keen-edged, as a weapon, etc. ME. **4.** Of reasoning, etc.: Subtle, refined. Of senses, instruments, etc.; Capable of delicate discrimination; sensitive 1567. †**5.** Ingenious. In bad sense, cunning, artful –1766.

1. They..with f. fingers cropt..The tender stalks SPENSER. A moment of finer joy 1797. **2.** F. linen 1721. F. feathery snow SHELLEY. The exudation of a f. fluid 1783. Long f. lashes SHELLEY. *fig.* F. margins of profit 1884. Trained too f. R. L. STEVENSON. **4.** F. Raillery DRYDEN. A f. balance 1879. **5.** Some of the finer Iesuits 1610.

III. Eng. senses (chiefly = Fr. *beau*). **1.** Excellent; admirable. Often *ironical.* ME. **2.** Handsome ME.; of the features, etc.: 'Beautiful with dignity' (J.) 1801. **3.** Of handsome size 1590. **4.** Of the weather, a day, etc.: Bright or cloudless. Often merely: Free from rain. 1704. **5.** Of dress: Smart. Hence of persons: Smartly dressed. 1526. **6.** Polished, refined, fastidious, etc. 1546. **7.** Of speech, writing, etc.: Affectedly ornate or elegant 1773; complimentary 1848.

1. Saying f. Things STEELE. F. lessons CHATHAM, times KINGSLEY. Your f. goings-on 1890. **2.** A monstrous f. woman 1867. A man of f. presence 1878. **3.** A f. slice of bread 1833. A f. child 1870. **4.** Was ever a May so f. TENNYSON. Phr. *One of these f. days* (= Fr. *un de ces beaux jours*): often *playful* or *derisive*. **5.** F. feathers make f. birds *Prov*. F. as a col'nel of the guards SWIFT. **6.** Soft Adonis, so perfum'd and f. POPE. **7.** A f. name for self-indulgence MORLEY.

B. *sb.* (The adj. used absol.) That which is fine; e.g. fine weather, etc. 1607.

C. *adv.* = Finely ME.

Combs.: **1.** General: *f.-looking, -featured, -grained, -spirited, -timbered, -woolled*, etc.

2. Special: **f.-arch,** 'the smaller fritting-furnace of a glass-house' (Knight); **-boring** *vbl. sb.*, the process of giving a f. bore to a gun; **-cut** *a.*, (*a*) delicately chiselled; (*b*) cut so as to be f., as tobacco, etc.; **-stuff,** finely sifted lime and sand mixed with hair, to form the second coat of plaster for a room; **-world** = BEAU-MONDE.

†**Fine,** *v.*[1] ME. [– OFr. *finer* :– Rom. **finare*, f. L. *finis* end.] To come or bring to an end; to finish –1593.

Time's office is to f. the hate of foes SHAKS.

Fine (fəin), *v.*[2] ME. [f. FINE *sb.*[1]] †**1.** *trans.* To pay as a fine or composition –1599. **2.** *intr.* To pay a fine or sum of money ME. **3.** *trans.* To punish by a fine; to mulct. Hence simply, †to punish. 1559.

2. Mr. Crow..hath fined for (i.e. to escape the duties of) Alderman PEPYS. In England, women ..fined to the crown for leave to marry whom they would HALLAM. **3.** He was..fined five talents 1662, fined in 400 Pound BP. BURNET.

Phrase. *To f. down* or *off*: to arrange for a reduction of (rent) upon payment of a fine.

Fine (fəin), *v.*[3] ME. [f. FINE *a.* Cf. Fr. *finer*, med.L. *finare* refine; also FINANCE *sb.*[2]] To make or become fine. **1.** To make fine or pure; to clarify, refine. Now only of beer. Also with *down*. **2.** *intr.* To grow or become fine. *lit.* and *fig.* Also with *down.* 1552. †**3.** To make beautiful or handsome –1664. **4.** To make small, thin, or slender 1548. **5.** *intr.* To become fine, thin, etc.; esp. with *away, down, off* 1858.

1. To f. and thin the blood 1797. To 'f. down' Spirits 1823. **2.** [The ale] hadn't had quite time to f. down HUGHES.

Fine art. 1767. (orig. in *pl.* as tr. Fr. *beaux-arts*; cf. FINE *a.* III.] **1.** In *pl.* The arts which are concerned with 'the beautiful', or which appeal to taste. Often restricted to the arts of design, as painting, sculpture, architecture. Hence in *sing.* one of these arts; also *transf.*, e.g. of poaching, parliamentary obstruction, etc. **2.** *Collect. sing.* The fine arts as a department of study or practice (*mod.*).

Fine-draw, *v.* 1755. [f. FINE *a.* and *adv.* + DRAW *v.*] **1.** *trans.* To draw and sew together so finely that the join is not noticed; to mend neatly. **2.** To draw out to minute fineness. *lit.* and *fig. rare.* 1761. Hence **Fine-draw·n** *ppl. a.* drawn fine; drawn out to extreme fineness. Also in *Sporting*: Reduced in weight or fat by exercise or training.

†**Finee·r,** *v.*[1] 1708. [Early form of VENEER.] = VENEER *v.* –1832.

†**Fineer,** *v.*[2] [app. – Du. *fineeren, fijneren* to collect riches, – OFr. *finer*; cf. FINE *v.*[2]] To run into debt by getting goods made up in such a fashion as to be unfit for every other purchaser, and then refusing to take them except upon credit. GOLDSM.

Fineless (fəi·nlės), *a. rare.* 1604. [f. FINE *sb.*[1] + -LESS.] Boundless, infinite. *Oth.* III. iii. 173.

Finely (fəi·nli), *adv.* ME. [f. FINE *a.* + -LY[2].] In a fine manner (see senses of the adj.).

Wee'll betray him f. *Merry W.* v. iii. 22.

Fineness (fəi·n,nės). ME. [f. FINE *a.* + -NESS.] **1.** The quality or state of being FINE. **2.** In metals: Comparative freedom from alloy 1487.

Finer (fəi·nəɹ). 1489. [f. FINE *v.*[3] + -ER[1].] One who or that which fines or refines, a refiner.

Finery[1] (fəi·nĕri). 1680. [f. FINE *a.* + -ERY, after BRAVERY 3.] **1.** Smartness, ostentatious elegance or splendour 1729. **2.** *concr.* Gaudy decoration; showy dress. Also in *pl.* 1680. †**3.** *pl.* Things which are finely wrought. DERHAM.

2. My sisters envied my new f. JOHNSON.

Finery[2] (fəi·nĕri). 1607. [– Fr. *finerie*, f. *finer* refine, FINE *v.*[3]; see -ERY.] A hearth where cast iron is made malleable, or in which steel is made from pig-iron. Also, the action of refining iron (*rare*).

Fi·ne-spu·n, *a.* 1647. [f. FINE *adv.* + SPUN *ppl. a.*] Spun or drawn out to extreme tenuity; flimsy. *lit.* and *fig.*

Fine-spun theories EMERSON.

Finesse (fine·s), *sb.* 1528. [– Fr. *finesse* :– Rom. **finitia*, f. **finus* FINE *a.*; see -ESS[2].] †**1.** = FINENESS in various senses –1701. **2.** Delicacy of manipulation or discrimination; refinement, refined grace. (Now *rare*, exc. as Fr.) 1564. **3.** Artfulness, subtle strategy 1530. **4.** An artifice, stratagem 1562. **5.** *Whist.* An attempt, by the second or third player, to get or keep the command of a suit by heading a trick with an inferior card, though holding a higher one of the suit not in sequence 1862.

1. Copwebs of learning, admirable for the f. of thread and worke BACON. **2.** The f. of her smile 1791. **3.** The f. of love JANE AUSTEN.

Finesse (fine·s), *v.* 1746. [f. prec. sb.] **1.** *intr.* To use finesse, artifice, or stratagem 1778; *trans.* to bring by artifice *into* (a specified state). Also with *away.* 1814. **2.** *Whist. intr.* To attempt to take a trick by finesse 1746; also *trans.* To play (a card) for the purpose of finessing 1837.

1. But our author can hector as well as f. 1803.

Fine-still, *sb.* 1731. [f. FINE *a.* + STILL *sb.*[1]] A vessel used in distilling spirit from treacle. Hence **Fine-still** *v.* to distil spirit from treacle, etc. **Fine-stiller.**

Fi·new, *sb.* Now *dial.* 1556. [f. next.] Mouldiness, mould.

Fi·new, *v.* Now *dial.* [OE. *fynegian*, f. *fyniġ* mouldy, f. *fyne* mould; see FEN *sb.*[2]] To become or cause to become mouldy or musty. Hence †**Fi·newed** *a.*

||**Fingan, Finjan** (fingā·n, -dʒā·n). 1609. [Arab. *finjān* – Pers. *finjān* cup, in Egypt *fingān*.] A small porcelain coffee cup, used in the Levant.

Finger (fi·ŋgəɹ). [OE. *finger* = OFris. *finger*, OS., OHG. *fingar* (Du. *vinger*, G. *finger*), ON. *fingr*, Goth. *figgrs* :– Gmc. **fiŋʒraz*.]

I. 1. One of the five terminal members of the hand; *esp.*, one of the four excluding the thumb. **2.** *transf.* and *fig.* 1612. **3.** One of the divisions of the foot in reptiles, or of the articulations of a bat's wing; also, one of the two parts forming a chelate or forceps-joint 1607. **4.** As a measure. **a.** The breadth of a finger; ¾ inch ME. **b.** *U.S. slang.* A 'nip' of liquor. [So Fr. *doigt*.] 1888. **c.** In U.S., the length of a finger (about 4½ inches). **5.** The part of a glove which receives a finger 1565. **6.** Skill in fingering (a musical instrument); touch 1741.

1. The fingers are 5 in number in each hand; they are named thumb, index, middle, ring, and little f. 1861. *Fore-f.*: the index f. **2.** This is the f. (= 'instrument of work') of God *Exod.* 8:19. Phrases. **a.** *To lay* or *put one's f. upon*: to indicate with precision. *To twist* (a person) *round one's* (*little*) *f.*: to make him do anything. **b.** *His fingers are all thumbs*: he is extremely clumsy. *With a wet f.*: with perfect ease. **c.** *To burn one's fingers*: see BURN *v. To have a f. in*: to take some part in; so *to have a f. in the pie*. See also FINGER-END. **6.** An admirable f. upon the harpsichord RICHARDSON.

II. 1. A finger-like projection 1702. **2.** A short and narrow piece of anything; also, short for *f.-biscuit* 1846. **3.** Something that does the work of a finger: the 'hand' of a clock (now *dial.*); in *Mech.*, any small projecting rod, wire, or piece which is brought into contact with an object to initiate, direct, or arrest motion, or to separate materials 1496. **4.** *Printing.* A gripper to hold the paper in a printing-machine 1869. **5.** In a reaping machine, the pointed sheaths through which the knife passes in cutting laid corn 1860.

1. Our fig tree..has furled Her five fingers BROWNING. **2.** Fingers of toast 1865. **3.** Fancy, like the f. of a clock, Runs the great circuit COWPER.

Combs. **1.** General: as *f.-ring, -tip*, etc.; *-biscuit, prayer-book*; *-shaped*, adj.

2. Special: **f.-alphabet** (cf. *dactylology*); **-bar,** = CUTTER-BAR (*b*); **-board,** (*a*) 'the flat or slightly rounded piece of wood attached to the neck of instruments of the violin and guitar class, on to which the strings are pressed when stopped by the fingers' (Stainer and Barrett); (*b*) a keyboard, manual; **-bowl** = *f.-glass*; **-breadth** (also *finger's breadth*), = FINGER I. 4a; **-brush,** a brush of stiff hairs cut square at the ends, which bookbinders draw across the fingers, so as to jerk colour off it in spots; **-coral,** a millepore (*Millepora alicornis*); **-cymbals,** castanets; **-fern,** a kind of Spleenwort (*Asplenium ceterach*); **-fish,** the star-fish; **-flower,** the foxglove; **-glass,** a glass vessel to hold water, for rinsing the fingers after dessert; **-grass,** grass of the genus *Digitaria* (N.O. *Gramineæ*); **-guard,** the quillons of a sword recurved towards the pommel as a protection to the fingers; **-hole,** (*a*) one of a series of holes in a wind-instrument, which are opened and closed by the fingers in playing; (*b*) *Bowls.* either of two holes in a bowling ball, to give players a hold; (*c*) any of the small holes in the disc of a dial telephone; **-mark,** the mark left upon a surface where a f. has touched it; **-mark** *v.*, to mark with a (dirty) f.; **-mirror,** a dentist's mouth-mirror fitted with an attachment to the f.; **-nut** (cf. *f.-screw*); **-orchis,** *Palma christi*; **-parted** *a.*, *Bot.* divided into finger-like lobes; **-plate,** a plate of metal or porcelain on a door, above and below the handle, to prevent f.-marks; **-print** = *f.-mark*, also *fig.*; with specific reference to the recording by the police of impressions taken from the finger-tips of criminals, suspects, etc.; also *attrib.*; hence **-print** *v. trans.*, to take the finger-prints of; **fingers-and-thumbs,** *Lotus corniculatus*; **fingers-and-toes,** (*a*) = prec.; (*b*) = ANBURY 2; **-screw,** one made with wings so that it may be turned with the fingers; a thumb-screw; **-shield,** *Needlew.* a silver appliance worn on the first f. of the left hand, to protect it from the needle; **-sponge,** one with finger-shaped branches; **-steel,** a steel for whetting a currier's knife; **-watch,** a watch that can be set forwards or backwards by the f. See also Main Words.

Finger (fi·ŋgəɹ), *v.* 1450. [f. prec. sb.] **1.** *trans.* To point at with the finger –1483. **2.** To hold or turn about in one's fingers; also, to do this repeatedly 1590; to receive or handle (money) with unworthy motives

1581. **3.** *intr.* To make restless or trifling movements with the fingers 1655. **4.** *trans.* To touch thievishly; to pilfer, filch. Also with *from*. 1530. **5.** To play upon (an instrument) with the fingers 1515. **b.** To mark (a piece of music) with figures indicating the fingers with which the notes are to be played 1816. **6.** *fig.* To elaborate. *rare.* 1816.

2. To f. the fine needle and nyce thread SPENSER. The Cardinals have finger'd Henry's gold TENNYSON. Hence **Fi·ngerer**, one who fingers; *esp.* a thief.

Fingered (fi·ŋgəɹd), *a.* 1529. [f. FINGER *sb.* + -ED².] **1.** Having or provided with fingers; as *light-*, *rosy-*, *three-f.* **2.** *Bot.* Of a leaf or plant: Digitate. Of the fruit or root: Shaped like a finger. 1668.

Finger-e·nd, finger's e·nd. *Pl.* **finger-ends, fingers' ends.** ME. The end or tip of the fingers.

Phr. *At one's finger(s' ends*: ready at hand. *To have at one's finger(s' ends* or *tips*: to be thoroughly familiar with.

Fingering (fi·ŋgəriŋ), *sb.* 1681. [Earliest forms *fingram*, *fingrine*; perh. alt. of OFr. *fin grain* 'fine grain' (cf. GROGRAM).] **1.** A kind of wool or yarn used chiefly in knitting stockings. †**2.** A kind of woollen cloth. *Sc.* –1733.

Fingering (fi·ŋgəriŋ), *vbl. sb.* ME. [f. FINGER *v.* + -ING¹.] **1.** The action of FINGER *v.* **2.** *Mus.* **a.** The action or method of using the fingers in playing upon an instrument ME. **b.** The indication, by figures set against the notes of a piece of music, of the fingers to be used in playing them 1879. **3.** *attrib.* 1603.

1. The Directors. .had expected the f. of the money JAS. MILL.

Fingerling (fi·ŋgəɹliŋ). ME. [f. FINGER *sb.* + -LING¹.] †**1.** A finger-stall –1580. **2.** A name for the parr (*Salmo salmulus*) 1705.

Fi·nger-post. 1785. A post set up at the parting of roads, often with a pointing finger, to indicate the directions of the roads. Also *transf.* and *fig.*

F. post (slang): a parson, so called, because like the finger post, he points out a way he. probably will never go, i.e. the way to heaven GROSE.

Fi·nger-stall. 1483. A cover or protection for the finger, usually of leather, used when the finger is hurt, in dissections, etc.

Fi·nger-stone. 1773. A cylindrical stone, convexly tapering to a point; a belemnite.

†**Fingle-fangle.** 1652. [redupl. of FANGLE. Cf. FIDDLE-FADDLE.] A trifle; something whimsical. Also *attrib.* –1710.

Fingram, obs. var. of FINGERING *sb.*

Fingrigo (fi·ŋgrigo). 1707. [Jamaican name.] A prickly climbing shrub, *Pisonia aculeata*.

Finial (fi·niăl). ME. [– AFr. **finial* or AL. **finialis*, f. (O)Fr. *fin*, L. *finis* end; see FINE *sb.*¹, -AL¹.]

A. *adj.* †**1.** = FINAL –1486. **2.** Crowning. *rare.* 1888.

B. *sb.* *Arch.* An ornament placed upon the apex of a roof, pediment, or gable, or upon each corner of a tower, etc. Also *fig.* 1448.

fig. The absolute perfection and finiall of many noble and excellent Actions P. HOLLAND.

Finical (fi·nikăl), *a.* 1592. [prob. orig. academic slang, f. FINE *a.* + -ICAL; poss. suggested by MDu. *fijnkens* accurately, neatly, prettily (Kilian).] Over-nice or particular, affectedly fastidious or precise; of things, over-scrupulously finished.

F. Style. .consists of the most curious, affected, mincing metaphors POPE. Such a pretty, little, delicate, ladylike, f. gentleman MISS MITFORD. Hence **Fi·nically** *adv.* **Fi·nicalness,** f. quality; also, a f. thing. **Finica·lity,** finicalness.

Finicking, Finikin (fi·nikiŋ, -in). 1661. [f. prec., with substitution of suffix -ING².]

A. *adj.* Finical; dainty, fastidious, mincing; excessively precise in trifles; of things, over-delicately finished; also, trifling. var. **Fi·nicky.** *dial.* and *U.S.*

†**B.** *sb.* **1.** A finicking person 1744. **2.** A variety of pigeon –1867.

Finific (fəini·fik), *a.* [f. L. *finis* end, limit + -FIC.] Putting a limit to. COLERIDGE.

†**Fi·nify,** *v.* 1586. [f. FINE *a.* + -FY.] *trans.* To make fine; to trick up –1708.

Finikin, var. of FINICKING.

Fining (fəi·niŋ), *vbl. sb.* 1502. [f. FINE *v.*³ + -ING¹.] **1.** The operation or process of refining (metals); *esp.* that of converting cast iron into wrought iron by heating it in contact with charcoal. **2.** The operation or process of clarifying (a liquid; *esp.* beer, wine, etc.) 1607; *concr.* anything used for this purpose (usu. *pl.*) 1772.

Comb. **f.-pot,** a crucible in which metals are refined.

Finis (fəi·nis). 1460. [L.] The L. word for 'end', often placed at the end of a book. Hence, end of life, death 1682.

Finish (fi·niʃ), *sb.* 1790. [f. next vb.] **1.** The conclusion, end; *ellipt.* in *Sporting*. **2.** That which finishes, completes, or perfects 1793; in *Building*, the last coat of paint or plaster 1823. **3.** Finished condition or quality 1805. **4.** *slang.* A house of entertainment, where the night is finished. THACKERAY.

1. Phr. *To be in at the f.* (i.e. the death of the fox). **2.** To put an American f. to her education 1890. **3.** A want of f. in the manufacture 1805.

Finish (fi·niʃ), *v.* [ME. *fenisshe* – OFr. *feniss-* (mod. *finiss-*), lengthened stem of *fenir* (altered to *finir*) :– L. *finire*, f. *finis* end; see FINE *sb.*¹, -ISH².] **1.** *trans.* To bring to an end; to go through the last stage of. Often: To make an end of, cease (doing something). **2.** To bring to completion; to complete ME. **3.** To deal with or dispose of the whole or the remainder of 1526; to dispatch, kill; also, to complete the discomfiture of; to reduce to exhaustion (now chiefly *colloq.*) 1611. **4.** To perfect finally or in detail 1551. **5.** *intr.* To come to an end; to cease, leave off 1450; †to die *Cymb.* V. v. 36.

1. His Griefs with Day begun, Nor were they finish'd with the setting Sun DRYDEN. **2.** F. sowing greenhouse plants 1816. **3.** Five Germans, who were resolved to f. me 1755. **4.** To f. the plastering 1703, a pretty woman JANE AUSTEN **5.** Exeter doth wish His dayes may f., ere the haplesse time SHAKS.

Finished (fi·niʃt), *ppl. a.* 1583. [f. prec. + -ED¹.] **1.** In senses of the vb. **2.** Consummate, perfect, accomplished 1709.

2. A f. naturalist HENSLOW, gentleman DISRAELI.

Finisher (fi·niʃəɹ). 1526. [f. as prec. + -ER¹.] **1.** One who or that which finishes (see the vb.). **2. a.** In various trades: The workman, or machine, that performs the final operation in manufacture 1691. **b.** *colloq.* Something that 'does for' any one; 'a settler'; in *Pugilism*, a blow that ends a fight; also one who gives this.

1. O Prophet of glad tidings, f. Of utmost hope MILT. **2.** Phr. *F. of the law* (joc.): the hangman.

Finishing (fi·niʃiŋ), *vbl. sb.* 1535. [f. as prec. + -ING¹.] **1.** The action of FINISH *v.* **2.** *concr.* That which completes or gives a finish to anything 1663.

attrib. and *Comb.*, as *f. governess*, etc.; also **f. cloth,** calico prepared for f.; **-coat,** in *Building*, the last coat of plaster; **-press,** in *Bookbinding*, a small press used in 'finishing'; **-rolls,** i.e. in a rolling-mill; **-school,** a school where young ladies are 'finished'.

Fi·nishing, *ppl. a.* 1705. [f. as prec. + -ING².] That finishes; *esp.* in *the f. stroke* or *touch*.

Finite (fəi·nəit). 1493. [– L. *finitus*, pa. pple. of *finire* FINISH *v.*]

A. *adj.* †**1.** Fixed, definite –1680. **2.** Having bounds, ends, or limits; bounded, limited; opp. to *infinite* 1587. **3.** *Math.* Of a line: Terminated. Of a quantity, number, distance: Limited. Of a solution: Resulting in a finite quantity. 1570. **4.** *Gram.* Of a verb: Limited by number and person 1795.

2. Whatsoever we imagine, is F. HOBBES. F. Duration BENTLEY. A f. nature JOWETT.

B. quasi-*sb.* **1.** The adj. used absol. 1687. **2.** A finite thing; a finite being 1619.

Hence **Fi·nite** *v.* to make f.; to subject to limitations. **Fi·nite-ly** *adv.*, **-ness.**

Finiteless: a spurious Dict. wd.; a misreading of 'fruitlesse' in SIR T. BROWNE.

Finitesimal (fəinite·simăl), *a.* 1861. [f. FINITE *a.*, after *millesimal*, etc.] *Math.* Denoted by the ordinal of a finite number.

Finitude (fi·nitiūd). 1644. [f. FINITE *a.* + -TUDE.] Finiteness.

Finless (fi·nlės), *a.* 1596. [f. FIN *sb.* + -LESS.] Without fins.

Finlet (fi·nlėt). 1874. [f. FIN *sb.* + -LET.] A small fin.

Finn (fin). [OE. *Finnas* pl., corresp. to G. *Finne*, ON. *Finnr*; recorded as L. *Fenni* (Tacitus), Gr. *Φίννοι* (Ptolemy).] Germanic name of a people of North-Eastern Europe and Scandinavia calling their country Suomi and speaking a Ural-Altaic language; applied also to peoples allied thereto.

Finnan (fi·năn). Also **findhorn, findon, finnon.** 1774. [Earlier forms also *findon*, *findram*, *fintrum*, *findhorn*; name of the river *Findhorn*, confused with *Findon*, a village in Kincardineshire.] A haddock cured with the smoke of green wood, turf, or peat earth. More fully *f. haddock* (*haddie*).

Finned (find), *a.* ME. [f. FIN *sb.* + -ED².] Having a fin or fins; as *prickly-f.*, etc.

Finner (fi·nəɹ). 1793. [f. FIN *sb.* + -ER¹.] **1.** A whale of the genus *Balænoptera*, esp. the Rorqual, so named as having a dorsal fin. **2.** A white trout, called also *finnoc*. 1803.

Finnic (fi·nik), *a.* 1668. [f. FINN + -IC.] Pertaining to the Finns, or to the group of peoples ethnically allied to the Finns; Finnish. Also **Finno-,** as in *Finno*-UGRIAN.

Finnicking, Finnikin; see FINICKING.

Finnish (fi·niʃ), *a.* 1789. [f. FINN + -ISH¹.] Pertaining to the Finns, or (*rarely*) to the Finnish group. Also *absol.* the Finnish language.

Finny (fi·ni), *a.*¹ 1590. [f. FIN *sb.* + -Y¹.] **1.** Having fins. **2.** Of the nature of a fin; fin-like 1648. **3.** Of or pertaining to fish; also, teeming with fish 1764.

3. He. .With patient angle, trolls the f. deep GOLDSM.

‖**Finochio** (finǫ·kio). 1723. [It. *finocchio* :– pop. L. **fenoclum*; see FENNEL.] The sweet fennel (*Fœniculum dulce*); also called the dwarf or French fennel.

Fiord, fjord (fyōᵊɹd). 1674. [– Norw. *fiord* :– ON. *fjǫrðr* :– **ferþuz*. Cf. FIRTH², FORD.] A long narrow arm of the sea, running up between high banks or cliffs, as on the coast of Norway.

Fiorin (fəi·ŏrin). 1809. [app. – Ir. *fiorthán* long coarse grass.] A species of grass (*Agrostis alba*). Also *f.-grass*.

Fiorite (fiōᵊ·rəit). 1808. [f. *Santa Fiora*, its locality; see -ITE¹ 2b.] *Min.* An incrustation formed from the decomposition of the siliceous minerals of volcanic rocks about fumaroles, or from the siliceous waters of hot springs.

‖**Fioritura** (fiǫritū·rā). *Pl.* **-re.** 1841. [It., f. *fiorire* to flower.] A florid ornament or embellishment in music. Usu. *pl.*

Fip (fip). U.S. 1860. [Short for *fippenny bit*.] See quot.

Fippenny Bit, or contracted, *Fip*, fivepence. In Pennsylvania. .the vulgar name for the Spanish half-real BARTLETT. Hence **Fi·psworth** 1844.

Fi·ppence. 1607. [colloq. f. *five pence*.] = Fivepence. *colloq.*

Fipple (fi·p'l). 1626. [Cf. Icel. *flipi* lip of a horse.] The plug at the mouth of some wind-instruments, diverting the flow of air toward the sounding edge.

Fir (fəɹ). [ME. *firr*, *fyrre*, w.midl. *ve(e)r*, *vyrre*; prob. – ON. *fyri-* (in *fyriskógr* fir-wood, etc.) :– Gmc. **furχōn*, f. **furχō*, whence OE. *furhwudu* fir-wood, OHG. *forha* (G. *föhre*), ON. *fura*.] **1.** The name given to a number of coniferous trees, of different genera. **Scotch F.** (*Pinus sylvestris*), a native of arctic Europe and Asia; called also *Scotch Pine*. **Silver F.** (*Abies pectinata*), a native of middle and southern Europe. *Silver F. of Canada* (*Abies balsamea*), a small tree which furnishes 'Canada balsam'. **Spruce F.** (*Picea excelsa*); called also *Norway Spruce*. **2.** The wood of any of these trees ME.

2. Phr. *F.-in-bond*: a name given to all timbers built in walls.

Fire (fəiᵊɹ), *sb.* [OE. *fȳr* = OFris., OS. *fiur* (Du. *vuur*), OHG. *fiur*, *fūir* (G. *feuer*) :– WGmc. **fūir*, corresp. to Gr. *πῦρ*.] **1.** The active principle operative in combustion; popularly conceived as a substance visible in the form of flame or of ruddy glow or incandescence. **b.** as one of the four elements ME. **c.** Volcanic heat, flame, or glowing lava 1582. †**d.** *Farriery.* = Cautery –1737. **2.** State of ignition or combustion ME. **3.** Fuel in a state of combustion, e.g. on a hearth or altar, in a furnace, etc. Also *transf.* and *fig.* OE. †**4.** The means of lighting a fire; fuel –1793. **5.** Destructive burning, *esp.* of a building, forest, etc.; a conflagration. Also *fig.* ME. **b.** As an exclam. 1682. **6.** Torture or death by burning 1646. **7.** Lightning; a thunderbolt OE. **8.** A combustible composition for producing a conflagration; a firework 1602. **9.** *Coal Mining.* = FIREDAMP 1883. **10.** Luminosity, fire-like glow 1591. **11.** Heating quality (in liquors) 1737. **12.** Fever, inflammation; disease as a consuming agency ME. **13.** *fig.* (sense 1). **a.** Ardour of passion, *esp.* of love or rage ME. **b.** Ardour of temperament; courage, zeal, enthusiasm, spirit 1601. **c.** Glowing imagination, brightness of fancy; genius; inspiration 1656. **14.** The action of firing guns, etc. 1590.

1. As red as þe fuyr ME. **b.** The force of f. ascended first. Then air succeeds DRYDEN. Phr. †*F. of Hell* (Alchem.) = ALKAHEST. *To set f. to*: to apply f. to, ignite. *There is no smoke without f.*: there is no strong rumour without some ground for it. **2.** Phr. *On f.*: ignited, burning; also *fig. To set the Thames on f.*: to make a brilliant reputation. *To catch, take f.* (see the vbs.). **3.** Cold weather; forced to have a f. BP. BERKELEY. *A burnt child dreads the f.* Provb. *The fat is in the f.*: see FAT *sb.*[2] **5.** A narrative of the late dreadful f. in London 1667. Phr. *F. and sword. To go through f. and water*: to face the greatest dangers. **6.** *F. and faggot*: see FAGGOT. **8.** *Greek f.*: a combustible composition first used in warfare by the Greeks of Constantinople. *Wild f.*: see WILDFIRE. **10.** Starres, hide your fires *Macb.* I. iv. 51. *Fires of St. Elmo*: see CORPOSANT. *Fires of heaven*: (*poet.*) the stars. **12.** *St. Anthony's f.*: erysipelas. **13 a.** The wicked f. of lust *Merry W.* II. i. 68. **b.** Full of f. and courage 1814. **c.** Corneille's noble f. POPE. **14.** Phr. *To open f.*: to begin firing. *Between two fires*: lit. and fig. *Under f.*: within the range of an enemy's guns. *False f., Running f.* (see the adjs.). *Kentish f.*: see KENTISH.

Fire- in Comb.

1. General: as, *f.-ordeal*, etc.; *-beacon, -signal*, etc.; *-basket*, a portable grate; *-bellows, -cheek, -grate, -stove*, etc.; *-bell, -main*, etc.; *-darting*, etc.; *-kindler*, etc.; *-extinguisher, -extinguishing*, etc.; *-baptism*; *-crowned, -lit, -scarred, -seamed*, etc.; *-hollowing*, etc.

2. Special: **f.-action,** the action of firing, *esp.* skirmishing in line; **-alarm,** an automatic arrangement by which notice of f. is given; also *attrib.*; **-ant,** one of certain small ants, whose bite is painful; **-back,** a pheasant of the genus *Euplocamus* (*E. ignitus*); **-balloon,** one whose buoyancy is derived from a flaming combustible suspended at its mouth; **-bar,** a bar of a grate or of a boiler furnace; **-barrel,** a cylinder filled with combustibles, used in f.-ships; **-blast,** a disease of certain plants, giving them a scorched appearance; **-blight,** a disease of hops; **-board,** a board used to close up a fireplace in summer, a chimney-board; **-boat** = FIRE-SHIP 1; **-boom** (*Naut.*), one of the long spars swung out from a ship's side to prevent the approach of f.-ships, or of vessels on f.; **-brick,** one capable of resisting great heat without fusion; **-bridge,** a 'plate or wall at the back of the furnace to prevent the fuel being carried over' (Knight); **-brigade,** an organized body of firemen; **-clay,** a clay capable of resisting great heat, used for f.-bricks, etc.; **-company,** (*a*) a f.-brigade; (*b*) a f. insurance company; **-dog** = ANDIRON; **-drill,** (*a*) drill practised by firemen and others in view of fires; (*b*) a primitive contrivance, consisting of an obtuse-pointed stick which is twirled between the hands with the point in a hole in a flat piece of soft wood till f. is produced; **-escape,** an apparatus for facilitating escape from burning buildings; **-flag,** (*a*) a meteoric flame; (*b*) a flag of distress, when a ship is on f.; **-flair,** the sting-ray, *Trygon pastinaca*; **-guard,** a wire frame, or the like, put in front of a fireplace for the protection of children or others; also a grating to keep the coals from coming out of the bars of a f.; **-hose,** a hose-pipe for conveying water to a f.; **-insurance,** insurance against losses by f.; also *attrib.*; **-office,** an office for issuing f.-policies; a f. insurance company; **-opal,** a variety of opal showing flame-coloured internal reflections; **-piece,** (*a*) = FIRE-ARM; (*b*) a picture of a conflagration; **-plug,** a contrivance for connecting a hose with a water-main, in case of f.; **-policy,** the instrument received from an insurance office, guaranteeing the insurer against loss by f.; **-raft,** a raft for setting an enemy's shipping on f.; **-roll** (*Naut.*), a peculiar beat of the drum on an alarm of f.; **-setting,** the softening or cracking of the working-face of a lode, to facilitate excavation, by exposing it to the action of f.; **-shovel,** a shovel for placing coals on a f., etc.; **-stick,** (*a*) a burning brand; (*b*) = *f.-drill*, (*b*); **-stink** (*Mining*), the stench from decomposing iron pyrites, caused by the formation of sulphuretted hydrogen; **-swab** (*Naut.*), the wet bunch of rope-yarn used to cool a gun in action and swab up any grains of powder; **-teazer,** a stoker; **-trap,** a place difficult to get out of in case of f.; **-tree,** (*a*) a kind of firework; (*b*) = *flame-tree*; (*c*) in New Zealand the *Metrosideros tomentosa*; **-tube,** a pipe-flue; **-water,** (*a*) = ALKAHEST; (*b*) ardent spirits; **-wood,** wood for burning; fuel; **-worship,** the adoration of f.; hence **-worshipper.**

b. In various plant-names, as **f.-bush,** *Embothrium coccineum*, etc.; and in local names of birds and insects, as **f.-crest,** the golden-crested wren; **-tail,** (*a*) the redstart; (*b*) one of the insects termed *Chrysididæ*; etc.

Fire (fəiᵊɹ), *v.* [OE. *fȳrian*, f. FIRE *sb.*] †**1.** *trans.* To supply with firing. OE. only. **2.** *trans.* To set on fire, so as to destroy; to ignite, kindle. Also *transf.* ME. **3.** *fig.* To inflame, heat, kindle (a person; also a passion, etc.) ME. **4.** *intr.* To catch fire, to be kindled or ignited; also *fig.* and *transf.* 1568. **5.** To drive *out, out of, from*, etc., by fire. Also *fig. rare.* 1530. **6.** To subject to the action of fire, as pottery, bricks, etc. 1662. **7.** *Farriery.* To cauterize 1607. **8.** To supply with fuel; to attend to the fire of; also *absol.* 1760. **9.** To apply fire to, so as to explode; to let off 1530. **10.** *intr.* or *absol.* To discharge a gun or other fire-arm 1645. **11.** *intr.* Of a gun, etc.: To go off. Also *fig.* 1668. **12.** To propel (a missile) from, or as from, a gun. Also *fig.* 1588. **13.** orig. *U.S. slang.* To eject, expel, or dismiss peremptorily. Often with *out.* 1873.

2. He fired his camp THIRLWALL. **3.** They..firen lecherie HOCCLEVE. Fired was each eye SCOTT. **4.** *fig.* Women are flax, and will f. in a moment MARSTON. Phr. *To f. up*: to show sudden heat. *transf.* [The sun] fires the prowd tops of the Easterne Pines SHAKS. **5.** *Lear* V. iii. 23. **8.** Phr. *To f. up*: to light up the fire of a furnace; hence *colloq.* to light one's pipe. **9.** *To f. a broadside*: to f. all the guns on one side of a ship; also *fig.* **10.** He fired, and hit two DE FOE. Phr. *To f. away* (fig.): to go ahead. *colloq.*

Fi·re-arm. Usu. *pl.* 1646. [f. FIRE *sb.* + ARM *sb.*[2]] A weapon from which missiles are propelled by an explosive, e.g. gunpowder. (The sing. is late and rare.)

Fi·re-ball. 1555. [f. FIRE *sb.* + BALL *sb.*[1]] **1.** A ball of fire or flame; *esp.* a large luminous meteor, or lightning in a globular form. **2.** *Mil.* A ball filled with combustibles or explosives, used as a projectile, to damage an enemy or set fire to his works 1595. **3.** *Her.* A ball represented with fire issuing from the top 1830. **4.** A ball of coal-dust and clay, used for kindling fires.

Fi·re-bird. 1824. The Baltimore oriole, *Icterus galbula*.

Fi·re-boot, -bote. Now *Hist.* 1484. [f. FIRE *sb.* + BOOT *sb.*[1]] *Law.* The mending of a fire; wood used for this purpose; the right of a tenant to take fire-wood from the landlord's estate.

Fi·re-box. 1555. [BOX *sb.*[2]] †**1.** A tinder-box –1840. **2.** The chamber of a steam-boiler in which the fuel is burnt 1830.

Fi·re-brand. ME. [f. FIRE *sb.* + BRAND *sb.*] **1.** A piece of wood kindled at the fire. **2.** *fig.* One who, or that which, kindles strife or mischief, inflames the passions, etc. ME. †**3.** = BRAND-MARK –1704.

Fi·re-cross, fi:ery-cro·ss. 1547. A cross or piece of wood burnt at one end and dipped in blood at the other—symbolical of fire and sword—used anciently in Scotland to summon the clans for war.

Fi·re-damp. 1677. [See DAMP *sb.*1.] Carburetted hydrogen or marsh-gas, which is given off by coal and is explosive when mixed in certain proportions with air.

Fi·re-drake. [OE. *fȳr-draca* fire-dragon.] **1.** A 'fiery dragon'; a creature of Germanic mythology. †**2.** A fiery meteor; also, a will-o'-the-wisp –1851. †**3.** A kind of firework –1634. †**4.** *transf.* **a.** An alchemist's assistant B. JONS. **b.** A man with a fiery nose SHAKS. **c.** = FIRE-EATER 2. 1626.

Fi·re-ea:ter. 1672. **1.** A juggler who eats fire. **2.** One who is fond of fighting; a duellist; one who seeks occasion to fight 1804.

Fi·re-engine. 1680. [f. FIRE *sb.* + ENGINE *sb.*] **1.** A machine for throwing water to extinguish fires. **2.** A steam-engine. *Obs.* exc. *local.* 1722.

Fi·re-eyed, *a.* 1596. Having eyes glowing as with fire.

The fire-ey'd Maid of smoakie Warre SHAKS.

Fi·re-fang, *v.* Now *dial.* 1513. [f. FIRE *sb.* + FANG *v.*[1]] *trans.* To lay hold of with fire; to singe, scorch. Hence **Fi·re-fanged** *ppl. a.*, †(*a*) caught by the fire, singed, scorched; (*b*) *spec.* of barley, etc.; also of cheese: Having a scorched or singed appearance, smell, or taste, as if overheated.

Fi·re-flaught. Orig. *Sc.* ME. [f. FIRE *sb.* + FLAUGHT.] Lightning; a flash of lightning; hence *transf.* a sudden burst or rush.

Fi·re-fly. 1658. [f. FIRE *sb.*] A lampyrid or elaterid insect which has the property of emitting phosphorescent light. Also *attrib.*

Fi·re-hook. 1467. [f. as prec.] A hook used in pulling down burning buildings; also, one used for raking and stirring the furnace fire.

†**Fi·re-ho·t,** *a.* OE. [f. as prec.] Hot as fire; also *fig.* –1678.

Fi·re-iron. ME. †**1.** An iron (or steel) for striking a light –1530. **2.** *pl.* Implements for tending the fire, usu. shovel, tongs and poker 1812.

Fireless (fəiᵊ·ɹlės), *a.* 1598. [f. FIRE *sb.* + -LESS.] †**1.** Unlit 1649. **2.** Devoid of fire; without a fire; also *fig.* 1598.

Fi·re-light. OE. The light given by a fire; †lightning.

Fi·relock. 1547. [See LOCK *sb.*[2]] **1.** A gunlock in which sparks were produced to ignite the priming; orig. the WHEEL-*lock*, later the FLINT-*lock*. **2.** A musket having such a lock 1590. **3.** A soldier armed with this 1645. **4.** *attrib.*, as *f. musket*, etc. 1577.

Fireman (fəiᵊ·ɹmăn). 1626. †**1.** One who uses fire-arms –1727. **2.** One who attends to the fire of a steam-engine, etc.; a stoker 1657. **3.** One who is employed to extinguish fires 1714. **4.** One who examines the workings of a mine for fire-damp, attends to the blasting, etc. 1866.

†**Fi·re-master.** 1622. An officer of artillery who superintended the manufacture of explosives or fireworks –1824.

Fi·re-new, *a. arch.* 1594. [Cf. BRAND-NEW and G. *feuerneu.*] †Fresh from the fire or furnace; hence, brand-new.

Your f. stampe of Honor is scarce currant SHAKS.

Fi·re-pan. [OE. *fȳrpanne*, f. *fȳr* FIRE *sb.* + *panne* PAN *sb.*[1]] **1.** A pan for holding or carrying fire, e.g. a portable grate. †**2.** The pan which held the priming of a flint-lock gun 1613. **3.** *Mining.* A kind of fire-lamp 1883.

Fi·re-place. 1702. A place for a fire, *esp.* the open recess at the base of the chimney appropriated to the fire; a hearth.

Fi·re-pot. 1627. **a.** *Hist.* An earthen pot filled with combustibles used as a missile. **b.** The receptacle for the fire in a furnace, etc. 1871. **c.** A crucible 1874.

Fi·re-proof, *a.* 1638. [f. FIRE *sb.* + PROOF *a.*] Proof against fire; incombustible. Hence **Fire-proofing** *vbl. sb.* the process of rendering f.; also, material for use in making anything f.; also *attrib.*

Firer (feiᵊ·rəɹ). 1602. [f. FIRE *v.* + -ER[1].] One who, or that which, FIRES: an incendiary (now only with *of*) 1602; one who fires a gun; also the gun itself, usu. in *comb.*, as *quick-f.* 1868.

Fi·re-rai:sing, *vbl. sb.* Orig. techn. in *Sc. Law.* 1685. [f. FIRE *sb.* + RAISING *vbl. sb.*] Arson, incendiarism.

Fi·re-screen. 1758. **1.** A screen to intercept the heat of the fire. **2.** A fire-guard 1874. **3.** *Naut.* A piece of fearnought used as a screen where it is necessary to pass the powder 1815.

Fi·re-ship. 1588. **1.** A vessel filled with combustibles, and sent adrift among ships, etc., to destroy them. **2.** *slang.* One suffering from venereal disease 1672.

Fireside (fəiᵊɹsəi·d, *attrib.* fəiᵊ·ɹsəid). 1563. [f. FIRE *sb.* + SIDE *sb.*[1].] The side of a fireplace; hence, the space about the fire; the hearth. **2.** *transf.* Home, home-life 1848; †one's household –1785. **3.** *attrib.* 1740.

Fi·re-stone. [OE. *fȳrstān*, f. *fȳr* FIRE *sb.* + *stān* STONE *sb.*] †**1.** Iron pyrites, formerly used in striking fire; also, a flint –1865. **2.** A stone that resists the action of fire; one used for lining furnaces and ovens 1475. **b.** A local name for the soft calcareous sandstone sold under the name of hearthstone 1707.

Fi·re-work, fi·rework. 1560. †**1.** Work done by, in, or with fire –1686. †**2.** An apparatus for working with fire, a furnace –1674. **3.** †A combustible or explosive composition for use in war; a projectile or the like charged with this 1560. **4.** Any contrivance for producing with fire a pleasing or scenic effect 1575; *esp.* a rocket, squib, etc. 1611; *pl.* (formerly also *sing.*) a pyrotechnic display 1588. Also *fig.* **5.** *attrib.* 1885.

3. The construction of all fireworks is understood at the ordnance-office BURKE. **4.** *fig.* He has neither squibs nor fireworks..the curs'd carrier lost his best book of phrases 1670.

Fi·re-wo:rker. 1626. †**1.** An artillery officer, or other person, who has to do with explosives in war –1800. **2.** A pyrotechnist 1772.

Firing (fəiᵊ·riŋ), *vbl. sb.* 1485. [f. FIRE *v.* + -ING[1].] **1.** The action of setting or of becoming on fire 1548. **2.** The action of subjecting to the operation of fire 1782. **3.** *Farriery.* Cauterizing 1644. **4.** Name of a disease in tobacco and in flax 1688. **5.** The feeding and tending of a fire or furnace 1892. **6.** The discharging of fire-arms, a mine, etc. 1603. **7.** *concr.* Fuel 1555; †a quantity of burning fuel 1485.

2. The glazing and f. of pottery 1885. The.. 'firing' of tea is a kind of roasting 1888. **6.** Night coming on, the f. on both sides ceased 1790.

Combs., as *f.-line, -party*, etc.; also **f.-point,** the temperature at which an inflammable oil is liable to spontaneous combustion.

†**Firk, ferk,** *sb.* 1611. [f. next vb.] **1.** A flick, flip –1679. **2.** A trick, dodge; also, a prank –1682.

Firk, ferk (fɔ̄ɹk), *v.* [OE. *fercian, færcian*, prob. f. *fær* (see FARE *sb.*[1]).] †**1.** *trans.* To bring, conduct –ME. **2.** To drive, force, or move sharply and suddenly *off, out, up* ME. †**b.** To contrive to get; also, to cheat, rob (any one) –1709. †**3.** *refl.* and *intr.* To move quickly, hasten; also (*intr.*) to move about briskly –1679. **4.** *trans.* To beat, trounce, drub 1567.

2. b. As from poor clients lawyers f. money DEKKER. **3.** How would he f...Up and about B. JONS. **4.** M.Fer: Ile fer him, and firke him *Hen. V*, IV. iv. 29.

Firkin (fɔ̄·ɹkin), *sb.* ME. [In XV *ferdekyn*, prob. – MDu. **vierdekijn*, dim. of *vierde* fourth part; see -KIN.] **1.** A small cask for liquids, fish, butter, etc., orig. holding a quarter of a barrel. Also applied joc. to a person. **2.** As a measure of capacity: Half a kilderkin (varying according to the commodity) 1465. *Comb.* **ale-f.:** see ALE.

Firlot (fɔ̄·ɹlǫt). *Sc.* ME. [Found in AL. *firlota, ferlota, ferthelota* (XIII) prob. – ON. *fjórði hlotr* fourth part (LOT).] **1.** A measure of capacity for corn, etc., the fourth part of a boll; also, a great quantity. **2.** A vessel used to measure a firlot 1573.

2. The old castle, where the family lived, in their decadence, as a mouse lives under a f. SCOTT.

Firm (fɔ̄ɹm), *sb.* 1574. [In earliest use – Sp. *firma*, later – It. *firma*, of the same origin, med. L. *firma* (cf. FARM *sb.*[2]), f. L. *firmare* strengthen, in late L. confirm by one's signature, f. *firmus* FIRM *a.*] †**1.** Signature –1755. **2.** The style or name under which a commercial house transacts business; hence, a partnership of two or more persons for carrying on a business. Also *transf.* (chiefly in sarcastic use). 1744.

1. The Grand Signior's F. or Name 1688. **2.** Trading under the f. of 'Grant & Co.' 1864. A f. of solicitors 1882.

Firm (fɔ̄ɹm), *a.* and *adv.* [ME. *ferm(e)* – (O)Fr. *ferme* :– L. *firmus*. Conformed XVI to L. sp.]

A. *adj.* **1.** Having a close consistence; solid; not readily yielding to pressure or impact 1611. **2.** Securely fixed, not easily moved, stable 1597. **3.** Steady in motion or action; not relaxed or nerveless 1593. **4.** Healthy; sound. ? *Obs.* 1577. **5.** Fixed, settled, established; immutable; †secure; †sure; well-founded ME. **6.** Constant, steadfast; unwavering; resolute ME.; indicating steadfastness 1802. **7.** *Comm.* Of prices: Not drooping. Of commodities: Not depressed in market value. Also *transf.* of the market, season, etc. 1883.

1. Down they light On the f. brimstone MILT. **2.** As possitiue, as the earth is firme SHAKS. **3.** Moving nigh, in slow But f. Battalion MILT. So f. a touch [on the piano] 1834. **5.** Firme and irreuocable is my doombe *A.Y.L.* I. iii. 85. **6.** F. Roman Catholicks 1659. A f. friendship 1751, belief 1873. F. eyes 1878. **7.** Phr. *A f. offer*: one which the offerer will not improve upon.

Phr. †**F.land, f.-land:** dry land, solid earth; the mainland (opp. to an island).

B. *adv.* and quasi-*adv.* Chiefly in phr. *to stand f.* (lit. and fig.), and *to hold f.* (*to*) ME.

Firm (fɔ̄ɹm), *v.* Now *rare* exc. techn. ME. [Partly – (either through Fr. *fermer* or directly) L. *firmare* (see FIRM *sb.*); partly a new formation on the adj.] **1.** *trans.* To make firm or solid; †to establish, confirm –1703; †to make (a title, etc.) secure –1669. †**2.** To make (a document) valid by seal, signature, or the like –1690; to affix (one's name) to a document –1620. **3.** *intr.* To become firm 1882.

1. As pilot..Upon his card and compas firmes his eye SPENSER. Jove has firm'd it with an Awfull Nod DRYDEN. **2.** He..firmed therevnto his name 1582.

Firmament (fɔ̄·ɹmămĕnt). ME. [– (O)Fr. *firmament* – L. *firmamentum*, f. *firmare* strengthen, f. *firmus* FIRM *a.*; see -MENT. The L. word was adopted in Vulg., in imitation of LXX Gr. *στερέωμα* (f. *στερεός* firm), as the rendering of a Heb. word probably meaning 'expanse'.]

1. The arch or vault of heaven; the sky. Now only *poet.* or *rhet.* Also *transf.* and *fig.* †**2.** *Old Astron.* The sphere containing the fixed stars; the eighth heaven of the Ptolemaic system –1665. †**b.** Hence, *occas.*, any of the other spheres –1551. †**3.** A substratum, a firm support or foundation. *lit.* and *fig.* –1701.

1. Bright was the day, and bliew the f. CHAUCER. Praise him in the f. of his power *Ps.* 150 : 1. *transf.* This F. Of Hell MILT. **2. b.** *First f.*: the *Primum mobile*. CHAUCER. **3.** This duty to parents is the very f. and bond of commonwealths JER. TAYLOR.

Hence **Firmame·ntal,** †**Firmame·ntary** *adjs.* pertaining to the f.; of the nature of a permanent substratum.

Firman (fɔ̄·ɹmăn, ‖fermā·n). 1616. [– Pers. *firmān* = Skr. *pramāṇam* (right) measure, standard, authority.] An edict or order issued by an Oriental sovereign, *esp.* the Sultan of Turkey; a grant, licence, passport, permit.

†**Firma·tion.** 1646. [– med.L. *firmatio*, f. *firmat-*, pa. ppl. stem of L. *firmare* make firm; see FIRM *v.*, -ION.] A making firm.

Firmer (fɔ̄·ɹməɹ). 1823. [– Fr. *fermoir* chisel for making mortices, altered f. *formoir*, anglicized as FORMER *sb.*[2].] In *f.-chisel*: a broad thin chisel, with the sides parallel to a certain length, and then tapering; used in making the sides of mortices. *F.-tools* are the ordinary short chisels and gouges of wood-workers; opp. to *paring* tools.

†**Fi·rmitude.** 1541. [– L. *firmitudo*, f. *firmus* FIRM *a.*; see -TUDE.] The quality or state of being FIRM; strength; resolution –1701.

†**Fi·rmity.** 1450. [Earlier *fermete* – (O)Fr. *fermeté*, f. *ferme* FIRM *a.*; see -ITY. Refash. after L. *firmitas*.] Firmness, solidity, stability. Also *fig.* –1729.

†**Firmless** (fɔ̄·ɹmlės), *a.* 1598. [f. FIRM *v.*; see -LESS.] Shifting –1744.

Does passion still the f. mind control POPE.

Firmly (fɔ̄·ɹmli), *adv.* ME. [f. FIRM *a.* + -LY[2].] In a firm manner.

Firmness (fɔ̄·ɹmnės). 1561. [f. as prec. + -NESS.] **1.** The state or quality of being FIRM. **2.** *Comm.* Steadiness in price or of prices 1880.

1. Constauncye and firmnes of minde 1561. Fluidity and F. BOYLE. By f. I mean not only strength but stability PALEY.

‖**Firn** (firn). 1853. [G. *firn, firne*, lit. 'last year's' (snow); see FERN *a.*] The imperfectly consolidated granular snow of the glaciers.

Firring: see FURRING.

Firry (fɔ̄·ri), *a.* 1833. [f. FIR + -Y[1].] Of or pertaining to the fir; abounding in firs.

The tender dove In f. woodlands making moan TENNYSON.

First (fɔ̄ɹst). [OE. *fyr(e)st* = OFris. *ferost, -est, ferst*, OS. **furist*, OHG. *furist* (*furisto* prince, whence G. *fürst*), ON. *fyrstr* :– Gmc. **furistaz*, superl. formation on **fur- *for-* :– IE. **pr̥-*, whence L. *primus*, Gr. *πρῶτος*, Skr. *prathamás*.]

A. *adj.* **I. 1.** That is before all others in time; earliest. Hence used as the ordinal of ONE. **2.** Preceding all others in serial order OE. **3.** Foremost in position ME. **4.** Foremost in rank, importance, or excellence ME.

1. Oure f. father DUNBAR. The f. writer of History 1662. The f. to find fault (*mod.*). Phr. *At f. sight, at (the) f. blush. (The) f. thing*: = as the f. thing that is done; The f. thing in the morning DICKENS. **2.** The f. blow is half the battle GOLDSM. The f. turning on the right (*mod.*). Phr. *The F.* (sc. *day*), spec. the f. of September (when partridge-shooting begins). *The f. two (three*, etc.); also, earlier, *the two (three*, etc.) *f.* (= Fr. *les deux premiers*). **3.** Taking a plunge head f. 1877. The f. row of seats (*mod.*). **4.** *The F. Lord of the Admiralty*. (*Mus.*) Highest or most prominent in carrying the melody, among several voices or instruments of the same class; as *f. violin*.

II. *absol.* (quasi-*sb.*) **1.** *The f.*: **a.** the person or thing first mentioned 1562; **b.** the beginning, as *the f. of the ebb*, etc. 1586. **2.** *From the f.*: from the beginning. *From f. to last*: from beginning to end. 1611. *At f.*: at the beginning or first stage 1577. **3.** *ellipt.* Anything that is first; e.g. a place in the first class; a man who has taken such a place; the best quality of butter, etc.; in *Mus.* the upper part of a duet, trio, etc. 1587. *F. of Exchange*: the f. of a set of bills of exchange of even tenor and date.

B. *adv.* [OE. *fyrst*, accus. neut. of the *adj.*] **1.** Before any other person or thing in time, serial order, position, rank, etc. OE. **2.** For the first time ME.

1. Who f. offend will f. complain PRIOR. I wounded one who f. assaulted me GOLDSM. Phr. *F. and last*: reckoned altogether, in all. *F. or last*: sooner or later. **2.** Whan seyntes felle fryst from hevene 1461.

Combs. **1.** General, chiefly of *adv.* with ppl. adjs.: as *f.-begotten, mentioned, -named*, etc.; *-comer*, etc. Also **f.-movable, -moved, -mover, moving:** = *primum mobile*.

2. Special: as *f.-chop, -cousin*, etc. (see the sbs.). Also **f.-aid,** assistance given in the case of street-accidents, etc., pending the arrival of a doctor; **-birth,** a f.-born child; also *fig.*; **f.-coat,** the f. layer of plaster or paint; **-cost,** prime cost; also *attrib.*; **-foot** (*north.*), the f. person to enter a house in the new year; hence *-footing*; **f. form,** the lowest form in a school; **f. night,** the night on which a play is f. produced on the stage; also *attrib.*; hence *f.-nighter, -nighting*; **f. storey** = FIRST FLOOR. See also Main Words.

†**First:** see FRIST *sb.* and *v.*

Fi·rst-born, *a.* ME. [f. FIRST *adv.* + BORN *a.*] That is born first, eldest. Also *absol.*

The first borne sonne *Deut.* 21 : 15. Her first-born MILT. *P.L.* I. 489.

Fi·rst class, first-class.

A. (as two wds.) The first (and usually the most important) of a series of classes in which things or persons are grouped. Also *ellipt.* A place in the first class of an examination list; one who has taken such a place. 1807.

B. *attrib.* or *adj.* (with the hyphen). **1.** Of or belonging to the first class 1846. **b.** In *U.S.* occas. used of the lowest grade; as a first-class clerk. **2.** *gen.* Of the highest grade; of the first or best quality 1858. *colloq.* Extremely good 1879. **3.** quasi-*adv.* 1895.

1. An Oxford first-class man 1860. A first-class carriage 1846. **2.** A question of first-class importance 1885. **3.** To look, travel, get on first-class (*mod.*).

First-day. 1690. Sunday; so called by the Quakers.

First-floor. 1663. **1.** The floor next above the ground floor 1865. **2.** The ground-floor. Now only *U.S.*

Fi·rst-fruit. Chiefly *pl.* ME. [orig. as two wds.; = L. *primitiæ*.] **1.** The earliest products of the soil; hence *transf.* and *fig.* of anything; e.g. of a man's work. **2.** *Eccl.* and *Feudal Law.* The first year's income or profits, formerly paid by each new holder of a benefice, or any office of profit, to some superior ME.

1. The first-fruits to the gods he gave POPE. One of the first-fruits of the great national re-action FREEMAN.

First hand. 1732. **1.** adv. phr. *At first hand*: From the first source or origin; direct from the maker, etc. Also without *at*. **2.** *adj.* (*first-hand*). Of or belonging to the first source, original 1748.

1. Matters we cannot well know at first hand M. ARNOLD. **2.** First-hand information 1890.

Firstling (fɔ̄·ɹstliŋ). 1535. [See -LING[1].] The first of its kind to be produced, or appear. Usu. *pl.*, like *first-fruits.* **b.** *esp.* The first offspring of an animal, the first-born of the season 1593. Also *attrib.*

Lord Chancellor Bacon..procured the firstlings of the species [plane] from Sicily 1830. **b.** The Firstlings of my Woolly breed DRYDEN. *attrib.* The f. males *Deut.* 15:19.

Firstly (fɔ̄·ɹstli), *adv.* 1532. [f. FIRST *a.* + -LY[2].] **1.** In the first place, before anything else, first. (Used only in enumerating heads, etc., of discourse. Many prefer *first.*) **2.** quasi-*sb.* The word *firstly* 1698.

1. First (for I detest your..pedantic neologism of *firstly*) DE QUINCEY.

First rate, first-rate. 1666.

A. As *phr.* and *adj.* **1.** *First rate*: the highest of the rates (see RATE *sb.*[1]) by which vessels of war are distinguished. **2.** *attrib.* *First-rate*: of the first rate (said of vessels); hence *gen.* Of the highest class 1671. **3.** Hence, Extremely good 1812. **4.** quasi-*adv.* (*colloq.*) Excellently, very well 1844.

2. A question of first-rate importance 1853. A first-rate power G. DUFF.

B. *sb.* **1.** *Naut.* A war vessel of the first rate 1708. **2.** *transf.* A person or thing of the highest class 1683. Hence **First-rater.**

Firth[1] (fɔ̄ɹþ). Chiefly *north.* ? *Obs.* ME. [Metathesis of FRITH *sb.*[2]] = FRITH *sb.*[2], q.v.

Firth[2] (fɔ̄ɹþ). Orig. *Sc.* ME. [– ON. *fjǫrðr* FIORD.] An arm of the sea: an estuary of a river.

Fi·r-tree. ME. [f. FIR + TREE.] = FIR 1.

Firy, obs. f. FIERY.

Fisc, fisk (fisk). 1598. [– Fr. *fisc* or its source L. *fiscus* rush-basket, purse, treasury. The current sp. in Sc. Law is *fisk*, in other uses *fisc.*] **1.** *Antiq.* The public treasury of Rome; the imperial treasury or privy purse of the Emperor. **b.** An exchequer. Now *rare.* 1599. **2.** *Sc. Law.* The public treasury or 'Crown' to which estates lapse by escheat. †Hence incorrectly: The right of the Crown to the estate of a rebel. 1680. **3.** [After It. *fisco.*] = FISCAL *sb.* 2b. BROWNING.

Fiscal (fi·skăl). 1539. [– Fr. *fiscal* or L. *fiscalis*, f. *fiscus* treasury. See prec.]

A. *adj.* **1.** Of or pertaining to the treasury of a state or prince 1563. **2.** Of or pertaining to financial matters. (Chiefly *U.S.*) 1865.

1. The king's f. prerogatives, or such as regard his revenue BLACKSTONE. **2.** The work of the past f. year 1880.

B. *sb.* †**1.** = FISC 1. b. 1590. **2.** †**a.** A treasurer –1676. **b.** In Italy, Spain, etc., a legal official, having the function of public prosecutor; under the Holy Roman Empire, the highest law officer of the crown 1539. **c.** In Holland, etc.: A magistrate who takes cognizance of offences against the revenue 1653. **d.** *Sc.* Short for PROCURATOR-FISCAL. 1681. **3.** In Cape Colony, the name of a shrike (*Lanius collaris*) 1822.

Hence **Fisca·lity,** exclusive regard to f. considerations. **Fi·scally** *adv.*

‖**Fiscus** (fi·skɒ̆s). 1650. [L.; see FISC.] = FISC 1.

Fish (fiʃ), *sb.*[1] [OE. *fisċ* = OFris. *fisk*, OS., OHG. *fisc* (Du. *visch*, G. *fisch*), ON. *fiskr*, Goth. *fisks* :– Gmc. **fiskaz* :– IE. **piskos*, rel. to L. *piscis.*] **1.** In pop. language, any animal living exclusively in the water, including cetaceans, crustaceans, molluscs, etc. In scientific language any vertebrate animal provided with gills throughout life, and cold-blooded; the limbs, if present, being modified into fins. (The collect. *sing.* is often used as *pl.*) OE. **2.** *fig.* 1722. **3.** The flesh of fish, *esp.* as used for food; opp. to *flesh* (i.e. of land-animals) and *fowl* ME. **4.** *Astron. The F.* or *Fishes* (L. *Pisces*), a zodiacal constellation, between Aquarius and Aries ME.

1. The whale, the limpet, the tortoise, and the oyster..as men have been willing to give them all the name of fishes, it is wisest for us to conform GOLDSM. Phr. *A pretty kettle of f.* (colloq.): a fine muddle. *To feel like a f. out of water*: to feel out of one's element. *To drink like a f.*: to be always drinking. *All is f. that comes to* (*his*) *net*: he turns everything to account. *Royal F.*: whale and sturgeon. **2.** The f. [a rich young booby] is hook'd FOOTE. He was an odd-f. FRANKLIN. **3.** Phr. *Neither f. nor flesh* (*nor good red herring*), also *neither f., flesh, nor fowl*: neither one thing nor another. *To have other f. to fry*: to have other things in hand.

attrib. and Comb. **1.** General: as *f.-bone*; *-ball*; *-curer*; *-dinner*; *-market*; *-woman*, etc.

2. Special: **f.-backed** *a.*, swelling upwards, like a fish's back; **-bed,** a deposit containing the fossil remains of fishes; **-bellied,** curved underneath, like a fish's belly; **-carver,** a carving knife for f.; *pl.* a carving knife and fork for f.; **-crow** (*U.S.*), a crow (*Corvus ossifragus*) that feeds mainly on f.; **-culture,** the artificial breeding of f.; hence, **-cultural** *a.*, **-culturist; -eagle,** an eagle that preys upon f.; †**-ears,** gills; **-eater,** (*a*) one who lives chiefly on f.; (*b*) *pl.* a knife and fork to eat f. with; **-fag,** a fishwife; **-farm,** a place where f.-culture is carried on; hence **-farmer, -farming; -flour,** (*a*) = *f.-meal*; (*b*) a dry inodorous fertilizer made from fishes; **-gaff,** a pole with an iron hook at the end for securing heavy f. when caught with a line; **-globe,** a spherical glass vessel in which f. are kept; **-glue,** glue obtained from the bladders and sounds of f., isinglass; **-guano** = *f.-manure*; **-hawk,** the osprey, or bald buzzard (*Pandion haliaëtus*); **-kettle,** a long oval vessel for boiling f.; **-knife,** a broad knife for carving f. at table; also, a knife for eating f. with; **-ladder,** a series of steps to enable f. to ascend a fall or dam; **-liquor,** the liquid in which a fish has been boiled; **-lock** = *f.-weir*; **-louse,** any crustacean parasitic on fishes; **-manure,** a fertilizer composed of f.; **-maw,** the sound or air-bladder of a f.; **-meal,** dried f. ground to a meal; **-oil,** oil obtained from fishes and marine animals, *spec.* cod-liver oil and whale oil; **-owl,** an eared fishing owl, of the genus *Ketupa*, with rough feet; **-pass** = *f.way*; **-pearl,** an artificial pearl, manufactured in Germany; **-pomace,** the refuse of f., used as a fertilizer; **-pool,** a fishpond; **-pot,** a wicker basket for catching f., *esp.* eels, crabs, lobsters, etc.; **-room,** a place parted off in the after-hold of a man-of-war, formerly used for stowing salt fish; **-sauce,** a sauce to be eaten with fish; **-scrap** = *f.-pomace*; **-slice,** a f.-carving knife; also, an instrument for turning f. in the pan; **-slide,** 'a f.-trap for shallow rivers and low waterfalls' (*Cent. Dict.*); **-sound,** the swimming-bladder of a f.; **-story,** an incredible 'yarn'; **-strainer,** (*a*) 'a metal cullender with handles for taking f. from a boiler'; (*b*) 'an earthenware slab with holes, placed at the bottom of a dish to drain the water from cooked fish' (Simmonds); **-tongue,** an instrument occas. used by dentists for removing wisdom-teeth; so named from its shape; **-torpedo,** a f.-shaped torpedo, having an automatic swimming action; **-trowel,** a trowel-shaped f.-carver; **-way,** an arrangement for enabling f. to ascend a fall or dam; **-weir,** a weir on a river for taking or preserving fishes; **-wood,** (*a*) *Piscidia erythrina*, used to intoxicate f.; (*b*) *Euonymus americanus*; **-works,** (*a*) 'the appliances and contrivances used in f.-culture'; (*b*) 'a place where the products of the fisheries are utilized, a f.-factory' (*Cent. Dict.*); **-yard** = *fish-weir.*

Fish (fiʃ), *sb.*[2] 1666. [f. FISH *v.*[2], after Fr. *fiche.*] **1.** *Naut.* 'A long piece of hard wood, convex on one side and concave on the other' (Smyth), used to strengthen a mast or yard; a fish-piece. **2.** A flat piece of iron, wood, etc., laid upon a beam, rail, etc., or across a joint, to protect or strengthen it; in railway work = *fish-plate* 1847.

Comb.: **f-bar,** 'the splice bar which breaks the joint of two meeting objects, as of railroad rails' (Knight); **-beam,** 'a composite beam, where an iron plate is sandwiched between two beams'; **-bolt,** a bolt for fastening f.-plates and rails together; **-joint,** a joint or splice made with fish-plates; hence **-joint** *v.*; **-front, -paunch** = sense 1; **-piece** = 1, 2; **-plate,** one of two pieces bolted together through the ends of two rails on either side of their meeting-point to cover and strengthen the joint; hence **f.-plating.**

Fish (fiʃ), *sb.*[3] 1728. [– Fr. *fiche*, f. *ficher* (see FISH *v.*[2]), assoc. w. FISH *sb.*[1] because of the shape.] A small flat piece of bone or ivory, sometimes fish-shaped; used as a counter in games. (Pop. confused with FISH *sb.*[1]; hence the collect. *sing.* is used for *pl.*)

Fish (fiʃ), *sb.*[4] 1825. [f. FISH *v.*[1]] **1.** An act of fishing (*colloq.*) 1880. **2.** The purchase used in 'fishing' an anchor 1825.

Comb. (chiefly *Naut.*): **f.-back,** a rope attached to the hook of the f.-block, and used to assist in fishing the anchor; **-block,** the block of a f.-tackle.; **-davit,** a davit for fishing the anchor; **-fall,** the tackle depending from the f.-davit; **-tackle,** that used for fishing the anchor. Also FISH-HOOK 2.

Fish (fiʃ), *v.*[1] *Pa. t.* and *pple.* **fished** (fiʃt). [OE. *fisċian* = OFris. *fiskia*, OS. *fiskon* (Du. *visschen*), OHG. *fiskōn* (G. *fischen*), ON. *fiska*, Goth. *fiskōn* :– Gmc. **fiskōjan*, f. **fiskaz* FISH *sb.*[1]]

I. *intr.* **1.** To catch or try to catch fish; to use nets, etc., for taking fish. **2.** *transf.* 1655. **3.** To use artifice to obtain a thing, elicit information, etc. Const. *after, for.* 1563.

2. To f. for silver at a wreck 1690. Phr. *To f. in troubled waters*: to seek one's account in other people's troubles. **3.** The first woman who fishes for him, hooks him 1848. To f. for compliments (*mod.*).

II. *trans.* **1.** To catch or try to catch (fish); to take as fish are taken; to collect (corals, pearls, etc.) from the bottom of the sea 1585. **2.** *transf.* To draw or pull *out, up, out of* 1632. **3.** To try catch fish in ME.; *transf.* to search through *for* 1727. **4.** Chiefly with *out*: To get by artifice or patient effort ME.

2. Phr. *To f. the anchor* (Naut.): to draw up the flukes to the gunwale. **3.** To f. a stream 1838. **4.** I could not f. from him.. what was the matter PEPYS.

III. [f. *sb.*[1]] *trans.* To dress (land) with fish-refuse. *U.S.* 1651.

Fish (fiʃ), *v.*[2] 1626. [– (O)Fr. *ficher* fix :– Rom. **figicare*, intensive of L. *figere* fix.] **1.** *trans.* To fasten a fish upon (a beam, mast, etc.) so as to strengthen it; to mend with a fish or fishes. Also *To f. together.* **2.** To join (the rails) with a fish-joint 1850.

Fi·sh-day. ME. [f. FISH *sb.*[1] + DAY *sb.*] A day on which fish is eaten; a fast-day.

Fisher (fi·ʃəɹ). [OE. *fisċere* = OFris. *fisker*, OS. *fiskari* (Du. *visscher*), OHG. *fiscāri* (G. *fischer*), ON. *fiskari* :– Gmc. **fiskarjaz*, f. **fiskaz*; see FISH *sb.*[1], -ER[1].] **1.** = FISHERMAN 1. Also *transf.* and *fig.* Now *arch.* **2.** An animal that catches fish 1562; *spec.* the pekan or Pennant's marten (*Mustela pennanti*) of N. America; also its fur 1796. **3.** A fishing-boat 1864. **4.** *attrib.* (*esp.* in sense 'that is a fisher'), as *f.-boat*, *-boy*, *-folk*, *-girl*, *-woman*, etc. 1525.

Fisherman (fi·ʃəɹmæ̆n). 1526. [f. prec. + MAN.] **1.** One whose occupation is to catch fish. **2.** An animal that catches fish 1634. **3.** A fishing-boat 1604. *Comb.* **Fisherman's ring,** the Pope's ring of investiture, 'wherein is represented St. Peter, drawing his net full of fishes' (Chambers).

Fishery (fi·ʃĕri). 1528. [f. FISH *v.*[1] + -ERY, or f. FISHER + -Y[3].] **1.** The business of catching fish, or of taking other products of the sea or rivers from the water. Often specialized as *bank-*, *bay-*, *cod-*, *pearl-*, etc., *f.* **2.** A fishing-ground 1699. **3.** A fishing establishment 1710. **4.** *Law.* The right of fishing in certain waters 1748. **5.** *attrib.*, as *fisheries school*, etc. 1528.

4. Phr. *Free f.*, an exclusive right of fishing in public water, derived from royal grant; *several f.*, an exclusive right to fish derived from ownership of the soil; *common of f.*, the right of fishing in another man's water; *common f.*, the right of all to fish in public waters.

Fishful (fi·ʃful), *a.* 1550. [f. FISH *sb.*[1] + -FUL.] Abounding in fish.

Not far from a F. Lake HEYLIN.

Fi·sh-gig. 1642. [var. of FIZGIG.] = FIZGIG 4.

Fi·sh-hook. ME. [f. FISH *sb.*[1] and *v.*[1] + HOOK *sb.*] **1.** A hook for catching fish. **2.** *Naut.* An iron hook forming part of the tackle used to fish the anchor 1627.

Fishify (fi·ʃifəi), *v.* 1592. [f. FISH *sb.*[1] + -FY.] *trans.* To turn (flesh) into fish.

Fishing (fi·ʃiŋ), *vbl. sb.*[1] ME. [f. FISH *v.*[1] + -ING[1].] **1.** The action, art, or practice of catching fish. **2.** = FISHERY 2, 4. 1495.

Comb.: **f.-float** (*U.S.*), 'a scow used in seine-fishing, from which an apron is let down to the bed of a river for the more convenient handling of the seine; **-rod,** a long slender tapering rod to which a line is attached for angling; **-room,** a portion of the shore set apart for the curing and storing of fish; **-tube** (*Microscopy*), an open-ended glass tube for selecting a microscopic object in a fluid.

Fi·shing, *vbl. sb.*² 1798. [f. FISH *v.*² + -ING¹.] The action of strengthening or supporting with a fish.

Fishing (fi·ʃiŋ), *ppl. a.* 1688. [f. FISH *v.*¹ + -ING².] **1.** That catches fish. **2.** Of an accusation, inquiry, etc.: Preferred in order to elicit information which cannot be gained directly 1831.

2. Colourable and f. Articles of accusation 1863.

Fishmonger (fi·ʃmɒŋgəɹ). 1464. [f. FISH *sb.*¹ + MONGER.] One who deals in fish.

Fishpond (fi·ʃpǫnd). ME. [f. as prec. + POND.] **1.** A pond in which fish are kept; also *joc.* the sea (cf. *herring-pond*). **2.** A depression in a card-table to hold counters (see FISH *sb.*³). COWPER.

Fi·sh-scale. 1661. [f. as prec. + SCALE *sb.*²] One of the scales of a fish's skin. Chiefly *attrib.*

Fish-skin (fi·ʃ,skin). 1651. [f. as prec. + SKIN *sb.*] The skin of a fish.

attrib. and *Comb.*: **fish-skin disease,** ichthyosis; **fish-skin grain,** grain (in leather) resembling a fish's skin.

Fi·sh-tail. 1840. [f. as prec. + TAIL *sb.*¹] The tail of a fish. Chiefly *attrib.*, as in *fish-tail burner* (also *fish-tail*), a kind of gas-burner with a spreading flame; **fish-tail wind,** a shifting breeze, blowing now on this side, now on that, of its main direction.

Fishwife (fi·ʃwəif). 1523. [f. as prec. + WIFE.] A woman who sells fish.

Fishy (fi·ʃi), *a.* 1547. [f. as prec. + -Y¹.] **1.** Abounding in fish. Now *poet.* or *joc.* 1552. **2.** Fish-like; (of the eye) dull, vacant 1611. **3.** Proceeding from fish 1616. **4.** Having the savour, smell, or taint of fish 1547. **5.** Consisting of, or produced from, fish 1699. **6.** *colloq.* or *slang.* **a.** Of dubious quality, questionable, 'shady'. **b.** Having fishy eyes; hence, languid or 'seedy'. 1844.

1. The f. flood POPE. **2.** A pallid young man with a f. eye SALA. **6.** F. about money matters 1882.

Hence **Fi·shily** *adv.* **Fishiness.**

Fisk: see FISC.

†**Fisk,** *v.* ME. [poss. a frequent. (with *-k* suffix as in *walk, talk*) of OE. *fȳsan* hurry, or of *fēsian, fȳsian* FEEZE *v.*¹ Cf. synon. Sw. *fjäska*, frequent. of *fjäsa* bustle, make a fuss.] To move briskly, frisk, whisk –1700.

Than he is busi. .then he fyskes a brode LATIMER.

Fissi-, less correctly **fisso-,** comb. f. L. *fissus, findere* to split, used to indicate the condition of being cleft.

Fi:ssigemma·tion, a mode of reproduction intermediate between fission and gemmation. **Fi:ssili·ngual** *a.* [L. *lingua*], having the tongue cleft; said of a sub-order of saurian reptiles, the *Fissilinguia.* **Fi:ssipa·lmate** *a.* [see PALMATE], partially web-footed; semi-palmate. Hence **Fi:ssipalma·tion,** partial palmation. **Fi:ssiro·stral** *a.* [L. *rostrum*], having a deeply cleft beak; belonging to the *Fissirostres.* **Fi:ssiro·strate** *a.* = prec.

Fissile (fi·sil), *a.* 1661. [– L. *fissilis*, f. *fiss-*, pa. ppl. stem of *findere* cleave; see -ILE.] Capable of being split; cleavable; inclined or tending to split. Hence **Fissi·lity,** f. quality.

Fission (fi·ʃən). 1841. [– L. *fissio*, f. as prec.; see -ION.] **1.** The action of splitting or dividing into pieces 1865. **2.** *Biol.* The division of a cell or organism into new cells or organisms, as a mode of reproduction.

Fissiparous (fisi·pǎrəs). 1835. [irreg. f. FISSI- + -PAROUS, after *viviparous*, etc.] Producing new individuals by fission; relating to reproduction by fission.

Hence **Fi:ssipa·tion, Fissi·parism,** the process of f. reproduction. **Fi:ssipa·rity,** the attribute of being f.

Fissiped, fissipede (fi·siped, -pīd). 1646. [– late L. *fissipes, -ped-*, f. *fissi-* FISSI- + *pes, ped-* foot.]

A. *adj.* Having the toes separated 1656.

B. *sb.* An animal having its toes divided.

Hence **Fissi·pedal** *a.*, **Fissi·pedate** *a.* = FISSIPED *a.*

Fissive (fi·siv), *a.* 1875. [f. *fiss-* in FISSION + -IVE.] Pertaining to, or of the nature of, fission.

Fissuration (fiʃiurē¹·ʃən). 1864. [– Fr. *fissuration*, f. *fissurer*, f. *fissure*; see next, -ATION.] **1.** The action of fissuring; the being fissured. **2.** *Biol.* = FISSION. 1867.

Fissure (fi·ʃiŭɹ), *sb.* ME. [– (O)Fr. *fissure* or L. *fissura*, f. *fiss-*; see FISSILE, -URE.] **1.** A cleft or opening (usu. long and narrow) made by splitting, cleaving, or separation of parts; 'a narrow chasm where a breach has been made' (J.) 1606. Also *fig.* **2.** *spec.* **a.** *Path.* A narrow solution of continuity produced by injury or ulceration; also, an incomplete fracture of a bone, without separation of parts ME. **b.** *Anat.*, *Bot.*, etc. A natural cleft in an organ or part; e.g. one of the *sulci* which separate the convolutions of the brain 1656. **c.** *Her.* A diminutive of the bend sinister 1486. **3.** = FISSURATION 1. 1633.

1. The gaping fissures to receive the rain THOMSON.

Comb.: **f.-needle,** a spiral needle for catching together the gaping lips of wounds; **f.-vein,** a f. in the earth's crust filled with mineral (RAYMOND).

Hence **Fi·ssural** *a.* of or pertaining to a f.; inclined to form fissures.

Fissure (fi·ʃiŭɹ), *v.* 1656. [f. prec. sb.] **1.** To make a fissure or fissures in; to cleave, split. **2.** *intr.* To become cleft or split.

Fist (fist), *sb.* [OE. *fȳst* = OFris. *fest*, MLG. *fūst* (Du. *vuist*), OHG. *fūst* (G. *faust*) :– WGmc. **fūsti.*] **1.** The hand clenched or closed tightly, with the fingers doubled into the palm, *esp.* for the purpose of striking a blow. **b.** Hence, grasp, grip, clutches. Now chiefly *joc.* ME. **2.** The hand. *Obs.* exc. *joc.* ME. **b.** *Printer's slang.* An index mark 1488. **3.** Handwriting. Now only *joc.* 1553.

1. The Queen. .brake the glasse windowes with her fiste 1626. **b.** More light then Culver in the Faulcons f. SPENSER *F.Q.* II. vii. 34. Phr. *Hand over f.*: = HAND OVER HAND. **2.** Give us your f., old fellow (*colloq.*) 1896. **3.** To write a tolerable f. 1864.

Hence **Fi·sted** *ppl. a.*, having fists, as *close-f.*, etc. **Fi·stful** *sb.*, a handful. **Fistia·na** (*joc.*), matters relating to boxing. **Fi·stic** *a.* (*vulgar*), pugilistic.

Fist (fist), *v.* ME. [f. FIST *sb.*¹] †**1.** *intr.* To fight with the fists –1705. **2.** *trans.* To strike with the fist 1597. **3.** To grasp with the fist; to handle. Now *esp. Naut.* 1607.

2. To the choleric fisting of every rogue Thy ear is liable *Per.* IV.vi.177.

†**Fi·stic,** *sb.* 1548. [– (through med.L.) Arab. *fustuḳ, fistuḳ* – Pers. *pistah*, whence (ult.) PISTACHIO.] = PISTACHIO. –1708. Also *f. nut.*

Fisticuff (fi·stikɒf), *sb.* Also **fisty-.** 1605. [prob. f. *fisty* (XVII) adj. + CUFF *sb.*²] In *pl.* Blows or fighting with the fists. Also *attrib.* Hence **Fi·sticuff** *v. trans.* to cuff with the fists (also *fig.*); *intr.* to fight or spar with the fists.

†**Fi·stinut.** 1676. [Corrupt f. *fistic nut*: see FISTIC *sb.*] –1775.

‖**Fistula** (fi·stiŭlă), *sb.* 1481. [L.; = 'pipe, flute'; in OFr. *festre* FESTER *sb.*] **1.** *Path.* — long, narrow, suppurating canal of morbid origin in some part of the body; a long, sinuous, pipe-like ulcer with a narrow orifice. Also *fig.* and *transf.* **2.** A natural pipe or spout in cetaceous animals, insects, etc. 1646. **3.** *Eccl.* A tube through which in early times communicants received the consecrated wine; now used by the Pope only 1670. ‖**4.** *Mus.* A reed instrument or pipe of the ancient Romans 1717.

1. Henry, notwithstanding his f. and his fever, was able to sit on horseback J.R. GREEN. **2.** The f. or spout [of the Whale] SIR T. BROWNE.

Hence **Fi·stular** *a. Bot.* hollow or cylindrical like a pipe or reed: *Path.* pertaining to, or of the nature of, a f. So †**Fi·stulary** *a.* **Fi·stuliform** *a.* of the form of a reed or tube. **Fistulo·se, Fi·stulous** *adjs.* fistular; resembling a pipe or tube in form.

†**Fi·stulate,** *v.* 1607. [– *fistulat-*, pa. ppl. stem of med.L. *fistulari* fester, f. FISTULA; see -ATE³.] **1.** *intr.* To form or grow to a fistula. **2.** *trans.* To make tubular 1751.

Fit, fytte (fit), *sb.*¹ *Obs.* exc. *arch.* [OE. *fitt* = OS. **fittia*; identified by some with OHG. *fizza* list of cloth (G. *fitze* skein of yarn, †thread with which weavers mark off a day's work) and ON. *fit* hem; but cf. next.] **1.** A part or section of a poem or song; a canto. **2.** A strain of music, stave 1500.

1. Lo, lordes, heer is a fyt CHAUCER.

Fit (fit), *sb.*² [OE. *fitt* (once) prob. 'conflict', original meaning perh. 'juncture', 'meeting', 'match', which might relate this word to or identify it with prec. Cf. FIT *a.*, *v.*¹] †**1.** Conflict. Only in OE. †**2.** A position of hardship or danger; an exciting experience; in 16th c. occas., a mortal crisis –1601. **3. a.** A paroxysm; also, later, a sudden and severe but transitory attack (of illness) 1547. †**b.** *spec.* A paroxysm of lunacy –1722. **c.** A sudden seizure, such as fainting, hysteria, apoplexy, paralysis, or epilepsy; in recent use, *esp.* an epileptic or convulsive fit 1621. **4.** Hence *transf.* **a.** A sudden and transitory state of activity, inaction, etc. 1586. **b.** A spell, a short period. *Obs.* exc. *dial.* 1583. **c.** A mood, humour 1680. **d.** A violent access of laughter, rage, etc. 1654.

2. Feeling the f. that him forewarnd to die 1591. **3.** He had a Feauer. .And when the F. was on him, I did marke How he did shake *Jul. C.* I. ii. 120. A f. of rheumatism or gout BAIN. **b.** *Tit. A.* IV. i. 17. **c.** Fits are a mighty help in the Government of a good-natured Man STEELE. Phr. *To beat into fits* (colloq.): to 'beat hollow'. *To give* (a person) *fits*: to inflict humiliating defeat on; also, to scold vigorously. **4. a.** We have our hot and cold fits alternately FLAVEL. Phr. *By fits (and starts)*: fitfully, spasmodically. **d.** A prolonged f. of grumbling 1874.

Fit (fit), *sb.*³ 1688. [f. FIT *v.*¹] **1.** The process of fitting or rendering fit. **2.** A fitting or adaptation of one thing to another, e.g. the adjustment of dress to the body; *concr.* a garment that fits 1823. **3.** *Soap-making.* The condition of the liquid soap in the operation of fitting (see FIT *v.*¹) 1885.

1. Phr. †*Out of f.*: fitted out, settled in life; Till my children are out of F. BUNYAN. **2.** *concr.* It's rather a tight f. 1831. *Comb.* **f.-rod,** a small iron rod with a hook at the end, used in *Shipbuilding* to ascertain the length of the bolts or treenails to be driven in.

Fit (fit), *a.* ME. [Of unkn. origin.] **1.** Suited to the circumstances of the case, answering the purpose, proper or appropriate. Const. *for*, or *to* with *inf.* Also *absol.* **2.** Becoming, convenient, proper, right. Now only in predicative use. ME. †**3.** Of the right measure or size –1703. **4.** Properly qualified 1573. **5.** In a suitable condition; prepared, ready. Const. *for* or *to* with *inf.*; otherwise *Obs.* exc. *dial.* 1568. **b.** Inclined, disposed. Now chiefly *colloq.* and *dial.*: Angry enough *to*; ready *to*. 1580. **6.** *Sport.* In good form or condition; hence *colloq.* perfectly well 1869. **7.** quasi-*adv.* = FITLY. ME.

1. Prethee call Gardiner to me, my new Secretary. I find him a f. fellow *Hen. VIII*, II. ii. 117. A f. opportunity 1852. *absol.* Survival of the fittest 1867. **2.** What is setled by Custome, though it be not good, yet at least it is f. BACON. Phr. *To think, see f.* **4.** F. to command TEMPLE. Phr. *F. to hold a candle to*: see CANDLE. **5.** F. for treasons SHAKS., for service 1823. **b.** Standing till you are f. to sink J. H. NEWMAN. **6.** Phr. *As f. as a fiddle*: see FIDDLE *sb.*

Fit (fit), *v.*¹ ME. [exc. in sense 1, which is of unkn. etym., app. f. FIT *a.*]

†**I.** *trans.* To array, marshal (soldiers). ME. only.

II. †**1.** *intr.* To be fit, or suitable. Chiefly *impers.* –1725. **b.** To harmonize *with* –1594. **2.** *trans.* To befit. Chiefly *impers.* 1586. †**3.** To answer, suit –1749. **4.** To be correctly shaped or adjusted to. Said *esp.* of dress; also *fig.* Often *absol.* 1581. **b.** *intr.* with *in* (adv. and prep.), *into, in with* 1694.

1. b. Why dost thou laugh? it fits not with this houre SHAKS. **2.** This insolence other kind of answer fits MILT. **3.** Phr. †*To f.* (= serve) *one's turn.* **4.** Euerie true mans apparrell fits your Theefe SHAKS. Phr. *The cap fits*: see CAP *sb.*¹ *To f. to a T*: see T. *intr.* A statement which curiously fits in with our story FREEMAN.

III. *trans.* **1.** To make fit or suitable; to adapt to the object in view; to qualify; to make ready. Const. *for, to* with *sb.* or *inf.*; otherwise *dial.* only. 1597. **2.** To arrange so as to conform or correspond

1580. **3.** To fix, apply, adjust, or insert exactly 1611. **4.** *Soap-making.* To bring (fluid soap) into such a condition that it will separate into two strata, the upper purer than the lower 1866.

1. The vessels of wrath fitted to destruction *Rom.* 9:22. To f. a man for a particular calling 1647. **2.** To f. words to a thought BOYLE. **3.** Let each..F. well his Helme MILT. *P.L.* vi. 543. Phr. *To f. on*: to try on (a garment, etc.). *To f. the cap on*: to take an allusion as applying to oneself.

IV. 1. To supply *with* what is fit or suitable 1591. **2.** To visit with a fit penalty; to punish. *Obs.* exc. *Australian.* 1625.

1. I wil f. him to morrow with a Trout for his breakfast WALTON. Phr. *To f. out*: to equip, rig out. *Obs.* exc. *Naut.* or *transf. To f. up*: to supply with necessary fitting or stores. **2.** With a look that implied—I'll f. you for this MISS BURNEY.

†**Fit,** *v.*[2] [f. FIT *sb.*[2]] To force by fits or paroxysms *out of* (the usual place) SHAKS. *Sonn.* cxix.

Fitch (fitʃ), *sb.*[1] Now *dial.* ME. [var. of VETCH.] = VETCH; the plant *Vicia sativa*, or its seed. Also *attrib.*

Fitch (fitʃ), *sb.*[2] 1502. [– early Du. *fisse, visse, vitsche*; see FITCHEW.] **1.** = FITCHEW. 1550. **2.** The fur of a polecat 1502. **3.** A brush made of the hair of a polecat; also, a small hog's-hair brush 1873.

Fitché, -ée (fi·tʃe), *a.* Also **Fitchy.** 1572. [– Fr. *fiché, fichée*, pa. pple. of *ficher* fix; see FISH *v.*[2], -EE[1].] *Her.* Fixed; applied to a cross, the lower extremity of which is sharpened to a point. Also **Fitched** *a.*

Fitchet (fi·tʃét). 1535. [dim of FITCH *sb.*[2]; see -ET.] **1.** = FITCHEW 1, 2. **2.** *erron.*: The weasel. *Obs.* exc. *dial.* 1693.

Fitchew (fi·tʃū). ME. [– OFr. *ficheau*, dial. var. of *fissel* (pl. *fissiaulx*), later *fissau*, dim. of a word appearing in early Du. as *fisse, visse, vitsche*, whence ult. also synon. FITCH *sb.*[2]] **1.** A foumart, polecat. **2.** The fur of the polecat ME. var. †**Fi·tchock.**

†**Fi·tchy,** *a.*[1] 1610. [f. FITCH *sb.*[1] + -Y[1].] Resembling a vetch.

Fitchy (fi·tʃi), *a.*[2] 1650. [f. as *fiché, -ée*; see -Y[5].] *Her.* FITCHÉ, q.v.

Fitful (fi·tful), *a.* 1605. [f. FIT *sb.*[2] + -FUL. A word used once by Shaks.; popularized since 1800.] **1.** Characterized by paroxysms. *Obs.* exc. in Shaks. **2.** Coming and going by fits and starts; irregularly changeable; spasmodic, shifting, capricious 1810.

1. Lifes fitfull Feuer *Macb.* III. ii. 23. **2.** The f. breeze SCOTT. Hence **Fi·tful-ly** *adv.*, **-ness.**

Fitly (fi·tli), *adv.* 1550. [f. FIT *a.* + -LY[2].] In a way that is fit; properly, becomingly, suitably; †opportunely.

A word f. spoken *Prov.* 25:11.

Fitment (fi·tmĕnt). 1608. [f. FIT *v.*[1] + -MENT.] †**1.** A making fit. *Cymb.* v. v. 409. †**2.** That which is fitting. *Per.* IV. vi. 6. **3.** A piece of furniture. Usu. *pl.* Fittings. 1851.

Fitness (fi·tnės). 1580. [f. FIT *a.* + -NESS.] **1.** The quality or state of being fit, or of being fitted. †**2.** The quality of fitting exactly –1793. †**3.** Readiness. *Haml.* v. ii. 209.

1. Haue you, I say, an answere of such f. for all questions SHAKS. To insist..on a mere moral f. 1858. Phr. *The (eternal) f. of things*: 'fitness' or conformity to the relations inherent in the nature of things: an 18th c. phrase referring to Clarke's ethical theory. Hence pop.: What is fitting or appropriate.

Fitted (fi·tėd), *ppl. a.* 1736. [f. FIT *v.*[1] + -ED[1].] In the senses of the vb.; also *fitted-up*. Often predicatively: Adapted, calculated, likely. Const. *to* with *inf.*

Circumstances..f. to be, to them, a state of discipline 1736. Hence **Fi·ttedness.**

†**Fi·tten,** *sb.* ME. [Of unkn. origin.] An untruth, an invention –1825. Hence †**Fi·tten** *v. intr.* to fib, tell lies.

Fitter (fi·təɹ), *sb.*[1] 1660. [f. FIT *v.*[1] + -ER[1].] **1.** One who or that which fits (see the vb.). **2.** *spec.* in various trades. Also in *Comb.*, as *gas-, hot-water-*, etc., *f.* 1858.

Fitter (fi·təɹ), *sb.*[2] *local.* 1678. [f. dial. *fitt* vend and load (coals); of unkn. origin; see -ER[1].] A coal-broker who vends and loads coals.

Fi·tters, *sb. pl.* Now *dial.* 1532. [f. †*fitter*, break into small fragments; of unkn. origin.] Fragments, pieces.

Which Image..was with Fire from Heaven broken into f. RALEGH.

Fitting (fi·tiŋ), *vbl. sb.* 1607. [f. FIT *v.*[1] + -ING[1].] **1.** The action of FIT *v.*[1] **2.** *concr.* Anything used in fitting. Usu. in *pl.*: Fixtures, apparatus, furniture. 1823. **3.** *Mech. Engin.* The bringing together and adjusting of the parts of engines, machines, etc. 1878.

2. All the roofs, floors, and fittings were burned FREEMAN.

Fitting (fi·tiŋ), *ppl. a.* 1535. [f. as prec. + -ING[2].] That fits; becoming, proper, suitable; that fits exactly. Hence **Fi·tting-ly** *adv.*, **-ness.**

‖**Fitz** (fits). ME. [AFr. spelling of OFr. *fiz* (pron. fits), earlier *filz* (mod. *fils*) :– L. *filius* son.] The AFr. word for 'son'; chiefly *Hist.* in patronymic designations, e.g. *Fitzherbert, Fitzwilliam*, etc., which survive as surnames. In later times new surnames of the kind have been given to the illegitimate sons of princes. Used by Macaulay to designate an Irishman of Anglo-Norman extraction.

‖**Fiumara** (fiūmā·ra). 1820. [It.] A mountain torrent; also the dry bed left by it.

Five (fəiv). [OE. *fīf* = OFris., OS. *fīf* (Du. *vijf*), OHG. *fimf, finf* (G. *fünf*), ON. *fimm*, Goth. *fimf* :– Gmc. **fimfi* :– IE. **pempe*, alt. f. **peŋqwe*, whence Skr. *pañca*, Gr. πέντε, πέμπε, L. *quinque*.] The cardinal number next after four; symbols 5, V.

A. as *adj.* **1.** With sb. expressed. **2.** With ellipsis of sb. OE.

1. Lord Warden of the fiue (= Cinque) ports 1631. Phr. *The five senses, wits*: see the sbs. *F. Nations* (Amer. Hist.), the five confederated tribes of Indians. **2.** Ffiue of the clocke, *hora quinta* HULOET. Let me haue Claudios head sent me by fiue SHAKS.

B. as *sb.* **1.** The abstract number five ME. **2.** A set of five things 1674. **3.** *pl.* **a.** The five fingers 1825. **b.** Gloves, shoes, etc., of the fifth size 16.. **c.** Short for *five-pound note* 1837. **d.** Short for *five-per-cents* 1848. **e.** (See FIVES[2].)

2. (*Cards*) A f. of spades 1870. (*Cricket*) To hit a ball for f. 1859. **3. c.** Ten to one in fives 1860.

Combs. **1.** General: as *f.-act, -guinea, -year-old*, etc.; *-barred, -foiled, -lobed, -rayed*, etc.; *-cleft*.

2. Special: as **f.-acre,** a plot consisting of five acres; **-finger exercise,** a piece of music to practise the fingers in pianoforte playing; **-lined** *a.*, consisting of or marked with five lines, *esp.* of an urgent parliamentary whip; **-mile Act,** an act passed in 1665 forbidding Non-conformist teachers who refused to take the non-resistance oath to come within five miles of any town, etc.; **-per-cents,** stock or shares paying five per cent on their nominal value; **-stroke** (*Billiards*), a stroke by which five points are scored. Also, **f.-o'clock** (see A. 2, quots.), used *attrib.* in **f.-o'clock tea** (colloq. *a f.-o'clock*).

Fi·ve-fi:nger. [OE. *fīfingre*, f. *fīf* FIVE + FINGER.] **1.** A name of plants: **a.** The cinquefoil (*Potentilla reptans*, etc.). **b.** The oxlip (*Primula elatior*). **c.** *Lotus corniculatus.* **2.** A species of star-fish 1678. †**3.** *Cards.* The five of trumps –1674. *Comb.* **five-finger-grass** = 1 a.

Fivefold (fəi·vfōᵘld). [OE. *fīffeald*, f. *fīf* FIVE + *-feald* -FOLD.]

A. *adj.* **1.** Consisting of five together. **2.** Five times as great or numerous; quintuple 1557.

1. Thy tongue, thy face, thy limbes, actions, and spirit, Do giue thee fiue-fold blazon *Twel. N.* I. v. 312.

B. *adv.* In fivefold proportion 1571.

Fi·ve-leaf. [OE. *fīflēafe*, f. *fīf* FIVE + *lēaf* LEAF.] The plant cinquefoil (*Potentilla reptans*).

Fiveling (fəi·vliŋ). [f. FIVE + -LING[1].] 'A twin crystal consisting of five individuals' (*Cent. Dict.*).

Fivepence (fəi·vˌpĕns). Also *colloq.* FIPPENCE. [f. FIVE + PENCE.] The value of five pennies. In U.S. the value of 5 cents or $2\frac{1}{2}d$.

Fivepenny (fəi·vpəni), *a. mod.* [f. FIVE *a.* + PENNY.] Valued at fivepence. *A fivepenny rate*: one at fivepence in the pound.

Fiver (fəi·vəɹ). *colloq.* 1853. [f. FIVE + -ER[1].] **1.** A five-pound note. In U.S. a five-dollar note. **2.** Anything that counts as five, as a hit for five at cricket.

†**Fives**[1]. 1596. [alt. f. AVIVES.] The strangles. *Tam. Shr.* III. ii. 54.

Fives[2] (fəivz). 1636. [pl. of FIVE *sb.*, used as *sing.* The reason for the name is obscure.] A game in which a ball is struck by the hand against a wall of a prepared court. The number of 'points' in the game is variously 11, 15, 20, or 25.

Comb. **f.-court,** a prepared court where fives is played.

Fi:ve-twe·nty. *U.S.* Used *attrib.* in *Five-twenty bonds* (or *five-twenties*), certain bonds issued by the U.S. government in 1862, 1864, and 1865; so called from being redeemable at any time after *five* years from date of issue and payable in full at the end of *twenty* years.

Fix (fiks), *sb.* 1839. [f. the vb.] **1.** orig. *U.S.* A position from which it is difficult to move, a 'tight place'; a predicament. **2.** The material used for lining a puddling-furnace 1871.

†**Fix,** *a.* ME. [See next.] = FIXED in various senses –1673.

Fix (fiks), *v. Pa.t.* and *pple.* **fixed** (fikst). ME. [Partly f. pa. pple. †*fix* (see prec.) – OFr. *fix* (mod. *fixe*) or its source L. *fixus*, pa. pple. of *figere* fix, fasten; partly – med. L. *fixare*, f. L. *fixus*.]

I. 1. *trans.* To fasten, make firm or stable; to set or place and secure against displacement. In immaterial sense: To attach firmly; to implant securely (principles, etc.) 1533. **2.** To give stability or constancy to 1604. **3.** To direct steadily and unwaveringly, fasten, set (one's eyes, attention, etc.) *on, upon,* †*to* ME. Also *absol.*, and *intr.* for *refl.* **b.** Of an object of vision or thought: To rivet (the eye, the attention, etc.) 1752. **c.** To make immobile or rigid. Also *intr.* for *refl.* 1664. **4.** *trans.* To deprive of volatility or fluidity. Also *intr.* for *refl.* 1460. **5.** *trans.* To make (a colour, a drawing, etc.) fast or permanent 1665. **6.** To 'corner' 1736; to hold (a person) occupied 1668.

1. His head to be fixed on a poole HALL. I resolved..to f. his Face in my Memory BUDGELL. To f. an imputation on a person BP. BERKELEY. **2.** To f. fluctuating opinions 1793. **3.** Why are thine eyes fixt to the sullen earth? SHAKS. To f. the mind upon Heaven 1665. *absol.* Nothing on which attention can f. JOHNSON. **c.** Ere death her charms should f. 1842.

II. 1. To place definitely and permanently 1568; to establish, to locate 1638. **2.** *intr.* for *refl.* To settle permanently 1638. **3.** To take up one's position mentally (? *Obs.*) 1623; to decide, determine *to* 1788. **4.** To determine the place, time, incidence, etc., of 1662. **5.** To settle or assign definitely; to determine 1660. **6.** To give a permanent form to 1712. **7.** To adjust, make ready for use 1663. **8.** To line with a fix (see FIX *sb.* 2) 1881.

1. Phr. *To fix a person up* (colloq.): to provide him with quarters. We are fixed here for some time SOUTHEY. **2.** I had..thoughts of fixing in town JANE AUSTEN. **3.** Phr. *To f. on* or *upon*: to decide upon, choose. **4.** Here will I f. the limits of transgression JOHNSON. Phr. *To f.* (a person) *with costs, liability*, etc.: to put upon him the obligation of meeting them. **5.** The opening of the session..is fixed for next Tuesday FRANKLIN. **6.** It [Wycliffe's Translation of the Bible] has fixed the language MAURICE. **7.** To f. the press for copying WASHINGTON.

Hence **Fi·xable** *a.* **Fixer,** one who or that which fixes.

Fixation (fiksēⁱ·ʃən). ME. [– med.L. *fixatio* (*Alch.*), f. *fixat-*, pa. ppl. stem of *fixare*; see prec., -ION. Cf. Fr. *fixation.*] **1.** The action of fixing (see FIX *v.*) 1652; the fact or condition of being fixed 1631; a fixed †location, proportion or standard 1614. **2.** *esp.* in scientific uses: The action of depriving of volatility or fluidity. In mod. use: The process of rendering solid a liquid or semi-liquid substance; also, the process of causing (a gas) to combine with a solid. ME. †**b.** The condition of being non-volatile or able to resist the action of fire –1721.

1. The f. of the Popes in the Metropolis HEYLIN. The F. of Colours 1671. The f. of the punishment BENTHAM, of Thought 1864. On locomotion and f. in plants and animals 1894.

Fixative (fi·ksătiv). 1644. [f. FIX *v.* + -ATIVE. Cf. Fr. *fixatif.*]

A. *adj.* Tending to fix.

B. *sb.* That which serves to set or fix colours, charcoal drawings, etc. 1870.

Fixature (fi·ksătiŭɹ). 1860. [f. as prec., after *curvature*, etc.] A gummy preparation for fixing the hair.

A stick of f. for the mustachios 1860.

Fixed (fikst), *ppl. a.* ME. [f. FIX *v.* + -ED¹.] **1.** Placed or attached firmly 1577. **b.** *Her.* Of a cross: extending to each side of the shield. 1688. **2.** In immaterial sense: Firmly attached or implanted. Now rarely of persons: Firmly resolved; constant. 1552. **3.** Made rigid or immobile 1608. **4. a.** Deprived of volatility 1766. **b.** Not easily volatilized 1641. **c.** Of acids and oils: That cannot be evaporated or distilled without decomposition 1800. **5.** Fast, permanent, as a colour, etc. 1791. **6.** Stationary or unchanging in relative position ME. **7.** Not fluctuating; definite, permanent 1698. **8.** Prepared, put in order 1638.

1. Where the firm or f. Ice lies 1694. **2.** *Fixed idea*: an idea unduly dominant in the brain [Fr. *idée fixe*]. *Fixed fact*: a well-established fact (*U.S.*). A man of no fixt Resolution HEARNE. **3.** Her eyes..were f. and staring W. BLACK. **4. a.** †*Fixed air*: Black's name for *carbonic dioxide* (*carbonic acid*); see AIR *sb.* I.2. **6.** *Fixed point*: a place where a policeman is permanently stationed. *Fixed star*: star which appears always to occupy the same position in the heavens (cf. *planet*). *Fixed capital*: see CAPITAL *sb.*² **7.** One loves f. Laws, and the other arbitrary Power SIR W. TEMPLE. **8.** '*Fixed ammunition*: a charge of powder and shot enclosed together in a wrapper or case ready for loading' (Knight).

Hence **Fi·xedly** *adv.* **Fi·xedness**, the quality or condition of being f.; †the quality of being non-volatile.

Fixidity (fiksi·dĭti). Now *rare.* 1762. [Badly f. FIX *a.* or FIXED *ppl. a.*, after *fluidity.*] = FIXITY.

Fixing (fi·ksiŋ), *vbl. sb.* 1605. [f. FIX *v.* + -ING¹.] **1.** The action of FIX *v.* in various senses; *concr.* that which fixes. **2.** *concr.* In *pl.* (orig. *U.S.*) Apparatus, equipment; trimmings; garnishing 1827. **b.** = FIX *sb.* 2. 1874. *Comb.* **f.-bath** (*Photogr.*), the bath in which a developed negative or positive is plunged in order to fix it.

†Fi·xion. 1555. [– med.L. *fixio* in same sense, f. *fixare*; see FIX *v.*, -ION.] = FIXATION 2. –1631.

Fixity (fi·ksĭti). 1666. [f. FIX *a.* + -ITY. Later (XVIII) partly through Fr. *fixité.*] **1.** Orig. *spec.*: The property of enduring heat without volatilization or loss of weight. **2.** *gen.* The quality or condition of being fixed (see FIXED) 1791.

2. *Fixity of Tenure*: the condition of having a permanent tenure.

Fixive (fi·ksiv), *a. rare.* [f. FIX *v.* + -IVE, after *active.*] Adapted or tending to fix. COLERIDGE.

Fixture (fi·kstiŭɹ). 1598. [Altered f. FIXURE, after *mixture.*] **1.** The action of fixing; the process of becoming fixed; fixedness. **2.** Anything fixed, or made firm, stable, or immobile; *U.S.* in *pl.* 'fixings' 1812. **3.** *Law.* In *pl.*, 'Things of an accessory character annexed to houses or lands, which become, immediately on annexation, part of the realty itself' (Wharton) 1758. **4.** A person or thing permanently established in a particular place or position 1788. **5.** *Sports*, rarely *Comm.* An appointment or date for a meet, race, etc.; hence, the meet, race, etc., itself. 1825.

1. The firm f. of thy foote *Merry W.* III. iii. 67. **2.** There are no fixtures in nature. The universe is fluid and volatile. EMERSON. **4.** Miss Goldsworthy was a f. at her side MME. D'ARBLAY. **5.** Fixtures of the principal..yachting clubs 1869.

Fixure (fi·ksiŭɹ). *Obs.* or *arch.* See prec. 1603. [– late L. *fixura*, f. *figere* to FIX; see -URE.] Fixed condition, position, or attitude; fixedness, stability.

Fizgig, fisgig (fi·zgig). 1529. [In senses 1–2 the first element may be †*fise* breaking wind, or FIZZ *v.*; the second is GIG *sb.*¹; sense 3 is app. – FIZZ only; for sense 4 cf. Sp. *fisga* harpoon.] **1.** A frivolous gadabout woman; = GIG *sb.*¹ II. 1. **2.** A whipping-top 1656. **3.** A kind of firework; a squib 1644. **4.** A kind of harpoon. Also FISH-GIG. 1565. **5.** A gimcrack; a crotchet 1822.

Fizz, fiz (fiz), *sb. colloq.* 1734. [f. next vb.] **1.** A hissing sound 1842. **2.** A fuss 1734; 'go' 1856. **3.** Something that fizzes; *esp.* champagne 1864.

Fizz, fiz (fiz), *v.* 1665. [imit.] To make a hissing or sputtering sound; to move with a hissing sound. Hence **Fi·zzy** *a.*, effervescent.

Fizzle (fi·z'l), *sb.* 1598. [f. next vb.] **1.** The action of breaking wind quietly; the action of hissing or sputtering. **2.** A failure or fiasco 1846.

Fizzle (fi·z'l), *v.* 1532. [app. f. FIZZ *v.* (but this is recorded later) + -LE.] **†1.** *intr.* To break wind quietly –1739. **2.** *intr.* To hiss or sputter 1859. **3.** *fig.* (chiefly *U.S. colloq.*) To fail, make a fiasco 1847.

2. The black oil fizzles 1859.

‖**Fjeld** (fyeld). 1860. [– Norw. *field* :– ON. *fiall*; see FELL *sb.*²] An elevated rocky plateau, almost bare.

Fjord, var. of FIORD.

Flabbergast (flæ·bəɹgast), *v. colloq.* 1772. [perh. an arbitrary formation on FLABBY and AGHAST.] *trans.* To put to confusion and embarrassment; to astonish utterly, confound. Hence **Fla·bbergast** *sb.*, gasconade (*rare*).

Flabby (flæ·bi), *a.* 1697. [Expressive alt. of *flappy* (XVI), f. FLAP *v.* + -Y¹.] **1.** Hanging loose by its own weight, yielding to the touch and easily moved or shaken, flaccid, limp. **2.** Weak, wanting 'back-bone'; nerveless 1791. **3.** Clammy 1780.

1. His f. Flanks decrease DRYDEN. **2.** An indolent f. kind of creature CARLYLE. **3.** F. weather 1780.

Hence **Fla·bbily** *adv.* **Fla·bbiness.**

†Fla·bel. 1552. [– L. *flabellum* small fan.] A fan –1681.

Flabellate (flăbe·lĕt), *a.* 1819. [f. L. *flabellum* (see prec.) + -ATE².] *Bot.* and *Zool.* Fan-shaped.

Flabellation (flæbĕlēⁱ·ʃən). 1658. [– Fr. *flabellation* – med. L. *flabellatio*, f. *flabellat-*, pa. ppl. stem of late L. *flabellare*, f. FLABELLUM; see -ION.] *Surg.* The action of fanning.

Flabe·lli-, comb. f. L. *flabellum* fan, indicating a fan-like form or arrangement, as in *flabellifoliate, flabellinerved* adjs.

Flabelliform (flăbe·lifǫɹm), *a.* 1777. [f. L. *flabellum* + -FORM.] Fan-like.

‖**Flabellum** (flăbe·lŏm). Pl. **-la** (erron. **-i**). 1867. [L. ; see FLABEL.] **1.** A fan; *esp.* used of a fan carried in religious ceremonies 1875. **2.** *Science.* A fan-shaped part of anything.

†Fla·bile, *a. rare.* 1727. [– (later senses of) L. *flabilis* airy, f. *flare* blow; see -ILE.] Of musical instruments: Wind-. Also *transf.*

Flaccid (flæ·ksid), *a.* 1620. [– Fr. *flaccide* or L. *flaccidus*, f. *flaccus* flabby; see -ID¹.] **1.** Wanting in stiffness, hanging or lying loose in wrinkles; limp; flabby; relaxed. Chiefly of flesh. **2.** Wanting vigour and energy, limp, feeble 1647.

1. His double chin over his f. whitey-brown shirt collar THACKERAY. **2.** A scheme that had left us f. and drain'd TENNYSON. Hence **Fla·ccid-ly** *adv.*, **-ness.**

Flaccidity (flæksi·dĭti). 1676. [f. prec. + -ITY.] **1.** The quality or condition of being flaccid. **2.** A disease of silkworms [tr. It. *flaccidezza*, Fr. *flacherie.*] 18...

‖**Flacherie** (flaʃərī). 1885. [Fr.] = FLACCIDITY 2.

Flacian (flēⁱ·ʃiăn). 1565. [f. *Flacius* + -AN.]

A. *adj.* Of or pertaining to Flacius Illyricus, a Protestant divine of the 16th c., who opposed the adiaphorist views of Melanchthon.

B. *sb.* A follower of Flacius Illyricus; an anti-Adiaphorist. Hence **Fla·cianism,** the doctrine of the Flacians.

Flacker (flæ·kəɹ), *v.* Now *dial.* [ME. *flakere*, prob. repr. an OE. **flacorian*, f. *flacor* (of arrows) flying, f. imit. base **flak-*, repr. also in MHG. *vlackern* flicker (G. *flackern*), ON. *flǫkra, flǫkta* flutter. See FLICKER *v.*] *intr.* To flap, flutter, throb. Also *trans.* To flap (the wings). ME.

Flacket (flæ·kĕt). Now *dial.* ME. [– ONFr **flaquet, flasquet* (= Central OFr. *flaschet, flachet*), dim. of *flasque* (*flasche, flache*); see FLASK *sb.*¹, -ET.] A flask, or bottle; now, a barrel-shaped vessel for holding liquor.

‖**Flacon** (flakoṅ). 1824. [Fr.; see FLAGON.] A small stoppered bottle; *esp.* a smelling-bottle.

Flag (flæg), *sb.*¹ ME. [Related in some way to (i) Du. *flag*, occurring in Bible of 1637, Job 8:11 margin (where A.V. has the same word) and to (ii) Da. *flæg* yellow iris.] **1.** One of various endogenous plants, with a bladed or ensiform leaf, mostly growing in moist places. Now properly, a member of the genus *Iris* (esp. *I. pseudacorus*). **b.** In *pl.* or *collect. sing.* A kind of coarse grass 1577. **2.** The blade of a plant, e.g. of *Iris* and of cereals 1578.

1. The greene flagge [will] smoke in the flame LD. BERNERS. **2.** The wheat was then showing a beautiful f. JEFFERIES.

Comb.: **f.-basket** (*dial.*), a basket made of reeds; **-broom**, a broom commonly made of birch-twigs, or of the leaves of the dwarf palm; **-leaf**, an iris; **-worm**, a worm found in the roots of flags and used by anglers.

Flag (flæg), *sb.*² ME. [prob. of Scand. origin; cf. Icel. *flag* spot where a turf has been cut out, ON. *flaga* slab of stone. Cf. FLAKE *sb.*²] **1.** A turf, sod. Also *collect.* Now *dial.* **2.** A flat slab of any fine-grained rock which may be split into flagstones; a flagstone 1604. In *pl.* A flagged foot-pavement. 1802.

Flag (flæg), *sb.*³ 1575. [Cf. 'the flagg or the fag federis' of a hawk's wing (*Bk. of St. Albans*); see FAG *sb.*²] **a.** *pl.* The quill-feathers of a bird's wing. **b.** The crural feathers of a hawk 1890.

Flag (flæg), *sb.*⁴ 1530. [perh. orig. an application of next.] **1.** A piece of stuff (usually bunting), varying in size, colour, and device, but usu. oblong or square, attached by one edge to a staff or to a halyard, used as a standard, ensign, or signal, and also for display. Also *transf.* and *fig.* **2.** *Naut.* A flag carried by a flagship, as an admiral's emblem of rank afloat 1695. **b.** A flagship 1652. **c.** Applied to the admiral 1665. **3.** *slang.* An apron 1851. **4.** *Sporting.* The tail of a setter or Newfoundland dog. Also occas. of a horse. 1859. **5.** *Printing.* A mark indicating an omission by the compositor; an 'out'.

1. *Black, red, white, yellow f.*, see BLACK FLAG, and the adjs. *fig.* Beauties ensigne yet Is Crymson in thy lips..And Deaths pale f. is not aduanced there *Rom. & Jul.* V. iii. 96. Phr. *F.* (*of truce*): a white flag, carried or displayed by an enemy, to express a wish for a parley. Hence, the person or the ship dispatched with it. *To lower* or *strike one's f.*: to take it down, *esp.* in token of respect, submission, or surrender. **2.** *To hoist* or *strike one's f.*: (of the admiral) to enter upon or relinquish command.

Comb.: **f.-boat,** a mark-boat in sailing or rowing matches; **-captain,** the captain of a flagship; **-day,** a day on which money is raised for a cause by the sale of small flags or other tokens as evidence of having given; **-lieutenant,** an officer acting as aide-de-camp to an admiral; **-list,** the roll of flag-officers or admirals; **-pay,** the pay of a flag-officer or admiral; **-rank,** the rank of admiral; **-share,** an admiral's share (one-eighth) of prize-money; **-station** (*Railways*), a place where trains stop only when signalled to do so; **-wagging** (*Mil. slang*), signalling with flags held in the hand.

†Flag, *a.* 1591. [Of unkn. origin.] Hanging down, drooping, pendulous –1765.

Flag (flæg), *v.*¹ 1545. [rel. to prec.] **1.** *intr.* To hang down; to flap about loosely. **†b.** *trans.* To allow to droop; to drop –1757. **2.** *intr.* To become flaccid. Now only of plants: To droop, fade. 1611. **†3.** *intr.* Of wings: To move feebly or ineffectually. Of a bird: To move its wings feebly. Also *fig.* –1764. **4.** *transf.* To lag through fatigue; to lose vigour or energy 1639. **b.** Of an author, a game, conversation, etc.: To grow dull or languid 1678. **†5.** *trans.* **a.** *lit.* Of a bird, etc.: To cease to ply vigorously (its wings) from fatigue. Of conditions, etc.: To clog, impede –1715. **b.** Hence To depress, enfeeble –1757.

1. Its sails were flagging in the breathless noon

SHELLEY. **2.** The white crops f., and the turnip-leaves turn yellow 1846. **3.** The Wings of Time flagg'd dully after it COWLEY.

Flag (flæg), *v.*[2] 1685. [f. FLAG *sb.*[1]] †**1.** *trans.* To plant *about* with reeds. EVELYN. **2.** To tighten (the seams of a barrel) with rushes 1757. **3.** To cut off the blade of (wheat) 1846.

Flag (flæg), *v.*[3] 1615. [f. FLAG *sb.*[2]] *trans.* To pave with or as with flagstones.

Flag (flæg), *v.*[4] 1875. [f. FLAG *sb.*[4]] **1.** To place a flag over or upon; to decorate with flags. **2. a.** To inform, communicate, or warn by flag-signals 1886. **b.** To decoy (game, *esp.* deer) by waving a flag or the like 1884.

Flagellant (flădʒe·lănt), flæ·dʒĕlănt). 1563. [– *flagellant-*, *pres. ppl.* stem of L. *flagellare* whip, f. *flagellum*, dim. of *flagrum* scourge; see -ANT.]

A. *sb.* **1.** One of a 13th c. sect of fanatics (L. *flagellantes*) who scourged themselves by way of religious discipline or penance. Usu. *pl.* **2.** *transf.* One who flagellates (himself or others). Also *fig.* 1785.

B. *adj.* Given to flagellation. Also *fig.* 1880. The f. head-master of Eton SWINBURNE.

Hence **Flage·llantism.**

Flagellate (flæ·dʒĕlĕt), *a.* 1877. [f. FLAGELLUM + -ATE[2].] **1.** *Biol.* Furnished with vibratile flagella; also, = FLAGELLIFORM. **2.** *Bot.* Having runners or runner-like branches 1882.

Flagellate (flæ·dʒĕleᶦt), *v.* 1623. [– *flagellat-*, *pa. ppl.* stem of L. *flagellare*; see FLAGELLANT, -ATE[3].] *trans.* To scourge, whip. Also *fig.*

[That] the angels were created only to f. and burn us LANDOR.

Flagellated (flæ·dʒĕleᶦtĕd), *a.* 1887. [f. FLAGELLATE *a.* + -ED[1].] *Zool.* and *Biol.* Provided with flagella

Flagellation (flæ:dʒĕlēᶦ·ʃən). ME. [– eccl. L. *flagellatio*, f. as FLAGELLATE *v.*; see -ION.] The action of scourging; *esp.* the scourging of Christ, or a picture of this.

Flagellator (flæ·dʒĕleᶦtəɹ). 1691. [– late L. *flagellator*, f. as prec.; see -OR 2.] One who scourges or flogs; a FLAGELLANT. Hence **Fla·gellato:ry** *a.* pertaining to flagellation.

Flagelliform (flădʒe·lifǫrm), *a.* 1826. [f. FLAGELLUM + -FORM.] *Zool.* and *Bot.* Having the form of a FLAGELLUM.

‖**Flagellum** (flădʒe·lŏm). *Pl.* **-la.** 1807. [L.; see FLAGELLANT.] **1.** *joc.* A whip, scourge. **2.** *Bot.* A runner 1887; *Zool.* and *Biol.* a lash-like appendage 1852.

Flageolet[1] (flædʒŏle·t, flæ·dʒŏlĕt). 1659. [– Fr. *flageolet*, dim. of OFr. *flag(e)ol*, *flajol* – Pr. *flajol*, of unkn. origin; see -ET.] **1.** A small wind instrument, having a mouth-piece at one end, six principal holes, and sometimes keys. **2.** An organ-stop with the tone of a flageolet 1852.

Phr. *F. tones*, the natural harmonics of stringed instruments, so called from the quality of their tone.

‖**Flageolet**[2] (flædʒole·t, flaʒole). 1885. [Fr.] A species of kidney-bean.

Flagging (flæ·giŋ), *vbl. sb.*[1] 1611. [f. FLAG *v.*[1] + -ING[1].] The action of FLAG *v.*[1]

Fla·gging, *vbl. sb.*[2] 1622. [f. FLAG *v.*[3] + -ING[1].] **1.** The action of paving with flagstones 1656. **2.** *concr.* The material used in paving; hence, the pavement.

Flagging (flæ·giŋ), *ppl. a.* 1545. [f. FLAG *v.*[1] + -ING[2].] That flags; drooping; failing. Hence **Fla·ggingly** *adv.*

Flaggy (flæ·gi), *a.*[1] ME. [f. FLAG *sb.*[1] + -Y[1].] **1.** Abounding in flags or reeds; made of flags or reeds; flag-like. **2.** Of corn, straw, etc.: Having a large FLAG 1842.

1. Old Chamus f. banks G. FLETCHER.

Flaggy (flæ·gi), *a.*[2] Now *dial.* 1565. [f. FLAG *v.*[1] + -Y[1].] **1.** Hanging down limply, drooping 1576. **2.** Flaccid, flabby.

1. His f. winges when forth he did display, Were like two sayles SPENSER. Hence **Fla·gginess.**

Flaggy (flæ·gi), *a.*[3] 1847. [f. FLAG *sb.*[2] + -Y[1].] Readily split into flags, laminate.

Flagitate (flæ·dʒiteᶦt), *v.* 1623. [– *flagitat-*, pa. ppl. stem of L. *flagitare* demand earnestly; see -ATE[3].] *trans.* To entreat earnestly; to importune (*rare*).

Carteret himself shall go and f. the Dutch CARLYLE. Hence **Flagita·tion,** earnest or passionate importunity.

Flagitious (flădʒi·ʃəs), *a.* ME. [– L. *flagitiosus*, f. *flagitium* importunity, shameful crime, f. *flagitare*; see prec., -IOUS.] **1.** Of persons: Guilty of or addicted to atrocious crimes; *loosely*, infamous. **2.** Of actions, character etc.: Extremely wicked; heinous, villainous 1550.

1. Crimes shall..whelm in ruin yon f. town POPE. **2.** The f. life of the Pontiff BRYCE.

Hence **Flagi·tiously** *adv.* **Flagi·tiousness.**

Flag-man. 1666. [f. FLAG *sb.*[4] + MAN.] †**1.** An admiral, a flag-officer –1713. **2.** One who carries or signals with a flag 1832.

Flag-officer. 1665. [f. FLAG *sb.*[4] + OFFICER.] *Naut.* An officer who carries a flag. **a.** An admiral, vice-admiral, or rear-admiral. **b.** In *U.S.* navy 1857–1862, an officer in actual command of a squadron.

Flagon (flæ·gǫn). [Late ME. *flakon*, *flagan* – AFr. **flagon*, (O)Fr. *flacon*, earlier **flascon* :– late L. *flasco*, *-ōn-* FLASK *sb*[1]. For the change of inter-sonant *k* to *g* cf. SEXTON, SUGAR.] **1.** A large bottle for holding wine or other liquors; now often, a glass bottle of flattened globular shape with a neck. **2.** A large vessel containing a supply of drink for use at table; now *esp.* one with a handle and spout 1512. **3.** As much as a flagon will hold; also, a flagon and its contents 1602.

2. He set the f. on the table, and sat down SCOTT. **3.** He had..drank many a flaggon JOHNSON.

Flagrance (flēᶦ·grăns). *rare.* 1612. [orig. – OFr. *flagrance* or its source L. *flagrantia*; see next, -ANCE. In mod. use f. FLAGRANT.] = next.

Flagrancy (flēᶦ·grănsi). 1599. [– L. *flagrantia*, f. *flagrant-*; see next, -ANCY.] **1.** *lit.* Glowing or blazing condition. *Obs.* or *arch.* Also *fig.* **2.** Of an offence, evil, etc.: Heinousness, enormity 1714.

1. Lust causeth a Flagrancie in the Eyes BACON. **2.** The f. of the provocation H. WALPOLE.

Flagrant (flēᶦ·grănt), *a.* 1450. [– Fr. *flagrant* or *flagrant-*, pres. ppl. stem of L. *flagrare* burn, blaze, be enflamed; see -ANT.] **1.** *lit.* Blazing, glowing. *arch.* Also *fig.* 1513. **2.** Actually in progress. *rare.* 1818. †**3.** Of feelings, etc. (*rarely* of persons): Ardent, burning –1784. **4.** †Resplendent 1500; †burning (from the lash) –1838; flaring 1858. **5.** Of an offence, etc.: Glaring, scandalous, 'flaming into notice' (J.) 1706. †**6.** = FRAGRANT. –1611.

1. Forthwith burst The f. lightnings T. AIRD. **2.** In moments of f. civil war HALLAM. Phr. *In f. delict* (= L. *flagrante delicto*): in the act. **3.** F. Rage 1708, zeal COWPER. **4.** T[utchin] f. from the lash POPE. **5.** A f. violation of religion THIRLWALL.

Hence **Fla·grantly** *adv.*

†**Fla·grate,** *v.* 1705. [– *flagrat-*, pa. ppl. stem of L. *flagrare*; see prec., -ATE[3].] To burn; also (*intr.*) to DEFLAGRATE. –1756. Hence †**Flagra·tion,** burning; a conflagration.

Fla·g-root. *U.S.* 1851. [f. FLAG *sb.*[1]] The root of the sweet flag (*Acorus calamus*); also the plant.

Fla·g-ship, fla·gship. 1672. [f. FLAG *sb.*[4] + SHIP *sb.*[1]] A ship bearing an admiral's flag.

Fla·g-staff, fla·gstaff. *Pl.* **-staffs.** 1613. [f. FLAG *sb.*[4] + STAFF *sb*[1].] A staff on which a flag is hung.

Fla·g-stone, fla·gstone. 1730. [f. FLAG *sb.*[2] + STONE *sb.*] **1.** A flag suitable for paving, etc.; hence often in *pl.* = pavement. **2.** Sandstone capable of being split up into flags 1812.

Flail (flēᶦl), *sb.* [OE. **fleġil*, in ME. *fleȝȝl* (ORM), *fleil*, *fleyl* = OS. *flegil*, (M)Du. *vlegel*, (O)HG. *flegel* :– WGmc. **flagil-* prob. – L. *flagellum* scourge, (in Vulg.) flail. In ME. prob. – OFr. *flaiel*, MDu. *vlegel.*] **1.** An instrument for threshing corn by hand, consisting of a wooden staff or handle, at the end of which a stouter and shorter pole or club, called a swingle or swipple, is so hung as to swing freely. Also *fig.* **2.** A military weapon resembling a threshing-flail, but usually of iron, and often having the striking part armed with spikes 1475. Also *transf.* 1450.

1. Nor did great Gideon his old F. disdain, After won Fields COWLEY. **2.** *Protestant f.* (Eng. Hist.): a short staff, loaded with lead, carried by Protestants at the time of the 'Popish Plot' (1678–81).

Comb. **f.-stone,** an elongated stone with a hole at one end, for use as a flail-swingle.

Hence †**Flai·ly** *a.* acting like a f. (*rare*).

Flail (flēᶦl), *v.* ?ME. [f. prec. sb.] **1.** *trans.* To scourge, whip; to thrash. **2.** To strike with or as with a flail 1583. **3.** To thresh (corn) with a flail 1821.

Flain, obs. pa. pple. of FLAY.

Flair[1] (flēəɹ). ME. [– (O)Fr. *flair*, f. *flairer* smell :– Rom. **flagrare*, for L. *fragrare*; see FRAGRANT.] †**1.** An odour, a smell. ME. only. ‖**2.** [mod. Fr.] Power of 'scent', instinctive discernment 1881.

Flair[2] (flēəɹ). Also **flare.** 1668. [– OFr. *flair* some kind of flat fish.] The ray or skate.

Flair, var. of FLARE.

Flake (flēᶦk), *sb.*[1] ME. [perh. – ON. *flaki*, *fleki* wicker shield (Da. *flage* hurdle).] **1.** A (wattled) hurdle; sometimes used as a temporary gate. Now *dial.* **2.** A frame or rack for storing provisions ME.; a frame for drying fish, etc. 1623. **3.** *Naut.* 'A small shifting stage, hung over a ship's side to caulk or repair a breach' (Smyth) 1867. **4.** *Mining.* A framework of boards, used as a shelter against wind and rain 1653.

2. Flakes whereon men yeerely dry their fish 1623.

Flake (flēᶦk), *sb.*[2] ME. [Immediate source unkn.; the several senses may represent derivatives of different origin; comparable forms in Scand. langs. are Norw. *flak*, *flāk*, patch, flake, *flake* form into flakes, Sw. *isflak* ice-floe, ON. *flakna* flake off, split. Cf. FLAW *sb.*[1], FLAUGHT.] **1.** A light fleecy tuft or mass; a flock; a fleecy streak. **2.** A portion of ignited matter thrown off by a burning or incandescent body; a flash ME. **3.** A scale 1500. **4.** A thin broad piece peeled, split, or torn off from something 1591. **5.** A stratum, lamina, or layer; a floe 1555. **6.** A bundle of parallel threads or fibres; a lock or band of hair. *arch.* 1592. **7.** A kind of carnation with striped petals 1727. **8.** *attrib.*, as in *f.-tobacco*, etc. 1886.

1. As flakes fallen in great snowes CHAUCER. Flying flakes of foam KINGSLEY. **2.** Huge flakes of Flames DRYDEN. **3.** Little Flakes of Scurfe ADDISON. **4.** The shells..scaling off in flakes DARWIN. Flint Flakes having a fine cutting edge LYELL. Flakes of flesh 1894. **5.** Flakes of ice 1820, of Salmon 1892.

Comb.: **f.-knife,** a chip of hard stone used in prehistoric times as a cutting instrument; **-stand,** the cooling tub of a still-worm; **-white,** a pigment made from the purest white lead in the form of flakes or scales.

Flake (flēᶦk), *v.* ME. [f. prec. sb.] **1.** *intr.* To fall †in or as in flakes. **2.** *trans.* To cover with or as with flakes; to fleck 1602. **3.** To chip; to break *away*, or take *off* in flakes or layers 1627. **4.** *intr.* for *refl.* To come *away* or *off* in flakes 1759. **5.** *trans.* To mark with streaks 1615.

4. Its stuccoed cupola was flaking off piecemeal 1877. **Flaked** *ppl. a.* arranged in or formed into flakes or layers; marked with streaks. **Fla·king** *vbl. sb.*

Flaker (flēᶦ·kəɹ). 1879. [f. prec. + -ER[1].] **1.** One who flakes flint for gun-flints. **2.** An instrument for flaking flint 1891.

Flaky (flēᶦ·ki), *a.* 1580. [f. FLAKE *sb.*[2] + -Y[1].] **1.** Consisting of flakes, or of what resembles flakes. **2.** Separating easily into flakes; flakelike 1672.

1. A snow, moist and f. KANE. **2.** A flat, luscious and f. Fish like the Salmon 1758. Hence **Fla·kiness,** f. quality or condition.

Flam (flæm), *sb.*[1] and *a.* 1625. [See FLAM *v.*] †**1.** A caprice, whim –1672. †**2.** A conceit –1755. **3.** A fabrication, falsehood; a piece of deception, a trick 1632; humbug; 'blarney' 1692.

2. Philips writes little flams..on Miss Carteret SWIFT. **3.** The letter's a f. 1888.

†**B.** *adj.* Counterfeit, fictitious, sham –1692.

Flam (flæm), *sb.*[2] 1796. [prob. imit.] A signal by beat of drum.

Flam (flæm), *v.* 1500. [Belongs to FLAM *sb.*[1]; perh. short for FLIM-FLAM.] †**1.** *trans.* ?To counterfeit, mock. **2.** To deceive by a lie or trick, or by flattery; also with *off*, *up.* Now *dial.* or *U.S.* 1637.

2. A God, who is not to be flamm'd off with Lyes SOUTH.

Flamb(e, obs. ff. FLAME.

Flambeau (flæ·mbō^{u}). *Pl.* **-eaus, -eaux,** etc. 1632. [– (O)Fr. *flambeau*, dim. of *flambe*, †*flamble* :– L. *flammula*, dim. of *flamma* FLAME.] A torch; *esp.* one made of several thick wicks dipped in wax; a lighted torch.

An open grave, with four tall flambeaus..placed at the corners SCOTT.

Flamboyant (flæmboi·ănt). 1832. [–Fr. *flamboyant*, pres. pple. of *flamboyer*, f. *flambe*; see prec.]

A. *adj.* **1.** *Arch.* Characterized by waved lines of contrary flexure in flame-like forms (Gwilt): of the style prevalent in France in the 15th and early 16th c. Also *absol.* (quasi-*sb.*). Hence, *loosely*, Florid, floridly decorated 1879. **2.** Of wavy form, like the outline of a flame. Said chiefly of a sword. 1876. **3.** Flamingly or gorgeously coloured 1851.

1. Etchingham church, with its..curious f. window 1883. F. perorations 1883. **2.** With massive face, f. hair GEO. ELIOT.

B. *sb.* A name of plants with flame-coloured flowers; e.g. *Poinciana regia* 1879.

Flame (flē^{i}m), *sb.* [ME. *flaume, flamme, flame* – AFr. **flaume*, OFr. *flame*, (also mod.) *flamme* :– L. *flamma*. For the pronunc. cf. *angel, chamber, strange*.] **1.** Vapour heated to the point of combustion; ignited gas. Also *fig.* **b.** *pl.* (with *the*) = fire 1483. **2.** The condition of visible combustion. Also *transf.* of a wound, etc., inflamed; and *fig.* 1490. **3.** *transf.* A bright beam or ray of light ME. **4.** *fig.* Brilliance, brilliant colouring 1781. **5.** Something resembling a flame of fire 1602. **6.** *fig.* (of sense 1): **a.** A burning feeling or passion, *esp.* of love ME. **b.** quasi-*concr.* The object of one's love. Now only *joc.* 1647. †**c.** Brightness of fancy, power in writing –1702. **7.** A name of certain British moths, e.g. *Geometra rubidata*, etc. 1819.

1. The flames ascended above my head SEWEL. Flame consists of particles of carbon brought to a white heat,—an opinion of Sir Humphry Davy's BREWSTER. *fig.* Let me not liue..After my f. lackes oyle SHAKS. **2.** [My heart] 'tis all on f. COWLEY. His face was all over in a f. 1790. **4.** That jewel of the purest f. COWPER. **5.** A f. of colour 1888. **6. a.** So true a f. of liking SHAKS. **b.** Euphelia serves to grace my Measure; But Cloe is my real F. PRIOR.

attrib. and *Comb.*

1. General: as *f.-banner*; *-breathing*; *-bred, -robed, -uplifted, -winged*; *-shaped*; *-proof*; etc.

2. Special: **f.-bearer,** a humming-bird of the genus *Selasphorus*; **-bed** (*Steam-engine*), the fire-brick floor of a f.-chamber; **-bridge,** 'a wall rising from the floor of a furnace to cause the flame to impinge upon the bottom of the boiler' (Knight); **-chamber** (*Steam-engine*), 'the space immediately behind the bridge in which the combustion of the inflammable gases that pass over the bridge is..completed' (Rankine); **-engine,** an early name for the gas-engine; **-furnace,** one in which the ore or metal is exposed to the action of flame, but is not in contact with the fuel; **-kiln** (cf. *f.-furnace*). **b.** in names of plants with vivid scarlet or crimson flowers: **f.-flower,** a species of *Kniphofia* (*Tritoma*); **-tree,** (*a*) the *Sterculia acerifolia* of N. S. W.; (*b*) the *Nuytsia floribunda* of W. Australia; (*c*) the *Butea frondosa* or palash tree.

Hence **Fla·meless** *a.* devoid of f.; burning without f. **Fla·melet,** a small f.

Flame (flē^{i}m), *v.* ME. [– OFr. *flamer, flammer* (mod. *flamber* XVI), f. *flam(m)e* FLAME *sb.*] **1.** *intr.* To burn with a flame or with flames; to emit flames; to blaze. Also *fig.* **2.** *fig.* Of the passions, etc.: To burn like flames. Of persons: To burn; to look angrily or passionately *upon*. Also with *out, up*. 1548. **3.** *transf.* To glow like flame or as with flames ME. **4.** *intr.* To move as or like flame 1633; *trans.* to convey by flaming ME. †**5.** To burn, set on fire –1737. †**6.** To kindle, inflame, excite, animate –1640. **7.** To subject to the action of flame. 1875.

1. His left Hand which did f...Like twentie Torches *Jul. C.* I. iii. 16. *fig.* The Republic..flames out..with Civil War 1793. **2.** He flamed with indignation MACAULAY. **3.** The rising sun Flames on the ruins DYER. **4.** *trans.* In euery Cabyn, I flam'd amazement *Temp.* I. ii. 200. **6.** Flam'd with zeal of vengeance inwardly, He ask'd [etc.] SPENSER, *F.Q.* V. i. 14.

Fla·me-co:lour. 1608. The colour of flame; a bright reddish yellow or orange. Hence **Fla·me-coloured** *a.*

Flamen (flē^{i}·men). ME. [– L. *flamen*.] **1.** *Rom. Antiq.* A priest devoted to the service of a particular deity. Hence *transf.* of other priests. **2.** The L. *flamen* and *archiflamen* (see ARCH-FLAMEN) were used by Geoffrey of Monmouth to denote two grades of priests in heathen Britain, who were alleged to have been replaced on the conversion of the island by bishops and archbishops. Hence pseudo-*Hist.* ME.

1. No person is elected to the office of one of the greater flamens, i.e. a f. of Jupiter, Mars, or Quirinus..unless [etc.] 1880. *transf.* Let the poor guardless natives never feel The flamen's fraud 1808.

Flaming (flē^{i}·miŋ), *ppl. a.* ME. [f. FLAME *v.* + -ING[2].] **1.** That flames; in flames or on fire. Also *fig.* **2.** Burning hot, inflamed 1697. **3.** *transf.* Flashing, glowing, brilliant; very bright or vivid ME. **4.** *fig.* Highflown; startling; flagrant 1606. **5.** Flamboyant ME.

1. A f. sword *Gen.* 3:24. **2.** Under a f. sun 1871. **3.** †*F. fly* = FIREFLY. F. poppies 1863. **4.** A f. attack against some poor man HELPS. Hence **Fla·mingly** *adv.*

Flamingo (flămi·ŋgo), 1565. [Early forms *flemengo, -ingo* – Pg. *flamengo* – Pr. *flamenc*, f. *flama* FLAME *sb.* + Gmc. suffix *-ing-* -ING[3]; so named because of its bright plumage.] A bird of the genus *Phœnicopterus*, with bright scarlet plumage, long and slender legs and neck, and a heavy bent bill. Also *attrib.* in **f. flower** or **plant,** a name for *Anthurium scherzerianum*.

†**Flami·nical,** *a.* [f. L. *flamen, flamin-* + -ICAL.] Of or pertaining to a flamen. MILTON.

Flammable (flæ·măb'l), *a.* 1813. [f. L. *flammare*, f. *flamma* flame; see -ABLE.] = INFLAMMABLE. Hence †**Flammabi·lity.**

†**Flamma·tion.** [– med.L. *flammatio*, f. *flammat-*, pa. ppl. stem of L. *flammare*; see prec., -ION.] Exposure to fire. SIR T. BROWNE.

Flammeous (flæ·mĭəs), *a.* Now *rare.* 1646. [f. L. *flammeus* (f. *flamma* flame) + -OUS; see -EOUS.] **1.** Of the nature of flame 1664. **2.** Flame-like; hence, shining, resplendent 1646. **3.** Flame-coloured 1656.

Flammi·gerous, *a. rare.* 1592. [f. L. *flammiger* flame-bearing + -OUS; see -GEROUS.] Bearing flame. Usu. *fig.*

Flammi·vomous, *a. rare.* 1663. [– late L. *flammivomus* (f. *flamma* flame + *-vomus* vomiting) + -OUS.] Vomiting out flame.

Flamy (flē^{i}·mi), *a.* 1494. [f. FLAME *sb.* + -Y[1].] **1.** Of or pertaining to flame or flames; consisting of, or beset with, flames. **2.** Flame-like 1626. †**3.** Effected by flame –1635.

Flan (flæn). 1868. [– Fr. *flan*, orig. a round cake; see FLAWN.] *Coining.* A disc of metal before stamping; a blank. **b.** (Also ‖flaṅ) An open tart containing fruit, etc. (cf. FLAWN) 1846.

Flanch (flanʃ), *sb.*[1] Also **flanque.** 1562. [perh. – OFr. *flanche* fem., = *flanc* masc., FLANK.] *Her.* A sub-ordinary formed on each side of the shield by a line convex towards the centre, always borne double. Hence **Fla·nched** *ppl. a.*

Flanch (flanʃ), *sb.*[2] Also **flaunch.** 1726. [This and its var. FLANGE are prob. f. FLANCH, FLANGE *vbs.*] = FLANGE *sb.* 2.

Flanch (flanʃ), *v.* Also **flaunch.** 1776. [*flanch* and *flange* vbs. may be – OFr. *flanchir* (presumably f. *flanche*, var. of *flanc* FLANK) and *flangir*, which are used as synonyms of *fléchir* bend, but the chronological evidence does not favour this.] *intr.* To spread, widen out; to slope outwards towards the top. Also with *out, off.*

Flanconade (flæ·ŋkŏnē^{i}:d). 1664. [–Fr. *flanconade*, f. *flanc* FLANK; see -ADE.] *Fencing* A thrust in the side.

†**Fla·nderkin.** 1694. [f. next + -KIN.] A Fleming. Also *attrib.* = Flemish. –1821.

Flanders (fla·ndəɹz). 1460. [– Du. *Vlaanderen* pl.; an ancient countship now broken up.] †Short for: **a.** *Flanders-lace*; **b.** *Flanders-horse.* –1718. **2.** *Attrib.* 1460.

‖**Flâneur** (flanör). 1872. [Fr., f. *flâner* lounge.] A lounger or saunterer, an idle man about town. Hence ‖**Flânerie** (flan'ri), the disposition or practice of a f.

Flang (flæŋ). 1858. [Of unkn. origin.] A miner's two-pointed pick.

Flange (flændʒ), *sb.* 1688. [prob. f. next; see FLANCH *sb.*[2]] **1.** A widening or branching out, as of a vein of ore; the part that widens out. **2.** A projecting flat rim, collar, or rib, used to strengthen an object, to guide it, to keep it in place, to facilitate its attachment to another object, etc. 1735. **3.** Hence, any rim or projecting surface; also, a flattened-out disc for covering the end of a pipe or cylinder. Also *blank-f.* 1876.

attrib. and *Comb.*, as **f.-joint,** a joint in pipes, etc., made by two flanges bolted together; **-pipe** (*U.S.*), pipe in sections with flanges for fixing together; **-rail,** (*a*) *U.S.* a rail having on one side a flange to keep wheels, etc., from running off; (*b*) a rail with a flanged base.

Flange (flændʒ), *v.* 1820. [perh. – OFr. *flangir*; see FLANCH *v.*] **1.** *intr.* To widen out. Also with *out.* **2.** *trans.* To supply with a flange, form a flange upon 1873. Hence **Flanged** *ppl. a.* made or fitted with a flange.

Flank (flæŋk), *sb.* ME. [– (O)Fr. *flanc* :– Frankish **hlanca* side.] **1.** The fleshy or muscular part of the side of an animal or a man between the ribs and the hip. †**2.** The belly; the womb –1481. **3.** *Farriery. pl.* A wrench or other grief in the back of a horse 1706. **4.** The side or lateral part of anything, e.g. of a building, etc. 1624. **5.** *Mil.* The extreme left or right side of an army or body of men in military formation; a wing 1548. **6.** *Fortif.* Any part of a work so disposed as to defend another by a flanking fire; *esp.* the part of a bastion reaching from the curtain to the face and defending the opposite face 1590. **7.** *Mech.* The straight part of the tooth of a wheel which receives the impulse 1842.

1. Marking-irons to brand the flanks of colts and cattle ROGERS. **4.** Mountains..With cities on their flanks TENNYSON. **5.** He scarce Had ended, when to Right and Left the Front Divided, and to either F. retird MILT. Phr. *To turn the f. of*: see TURN.

attrib. and *Comb.* (senses 5, 6), as *f. attack, company, defence, file, fire, march, movement*, etc.; *f.-wise* adv. Also, **f.-bone,** the ilium; **-wall,** a side wall.

Flank (flæŋk), *v.* 1548. [f. prec. sb. Cf. Fr. *flanquer*.] †**1.** *intr.* To shoot on the flank or sideways. **2.** *trans.* To strengthen or protect on the flank. Also *fig.* 1596. **3.** To menace or attack the flank of; to take in flank 1599. **4.** To be placed or situated at the flank of. Also *pass.* *To be flanked by* or *with*: to have on the flanks. 1651. †**b.** *intr.* To border *on* or *upon* –1828. **5.** *trans.* To march past or go round the flank of; *U.S. slang*, to dodge, etc. 1872. **6.** Of a ship: To present the broadside to (a gale) 1762.

2. A strong intrenchment, flanked with bastions 1783. **3.** The ball [of one of our guns] flanked our own trenches 1782. **4.** A mountain, flanked by real precipices L. STEPHEN.

Flanker (flæ·ŋkəɹ), *sb.* 1550. [f. FLANK *v.* + -ER[1].] **1.** Anything which flanks; *esp.* a fortification placed so as to command the flank of an enemy. **2.** One posted on either flank; esp. *Mil.* one of a body of skirmishers thrown out upon the flanks of an army, to guard the line of march 1586.

2. Their services as scouts and flankers proved invaluable 1863.

Flanker (flæ·ŋkəɹ), *v.* 1598. [f. prec.; cf., however, Du. *flankeren* – Fr. *flanquer* FLANK *v.*] **1.** *trans.* To support or protect on the flanks; to defend or command from a flanker; to strengthen with flankers. **2.** *intr.* To make an attack on the flank 1603.

Flannel (flæ·nĕl), *sb.* 1503. [Early forms *flan(n)en, flan(n)ing* – W. *gwlanen* woollen article, f. *gwlân* wool.] **1.** An open woollen stuff, of loose texture, usually without a nap. **b.** *joc.* A Welshman. *Merry W.* V. v. 172. **2.** *pl.* Underclothing, bandages, or garments of flannel 1722. **3.** *attrib.* Made of, or resembling, flannel 1585.

2. Phr. *To get* or *receive one's flannels* (Harrow slang); to get into the school cricket or football eleven. *Comb. f.-cake*, a thin griddle-cake.

Hence **Flannele·tte,** †(*a*) a very soft flannel measuring 28 inches in width; (*b*) an imitation flannel made of cotton. **Fla·nnelly** *a.* f.-like; also *fig.*

Flannel (flæ·nĕl), *v.* 1836. [f. prec. sb.] *trans.* To wrap in flannel; to rub with flannel. Hence **Fla·nnelled** *ppl. a.* 1784.

Flanning (flæ·niŋ). 1849. [f. dial. *flan* splay or bevel internally + -ING[1].] The internal flare or splay of a window-jamb or fireplace.

Flap (flæp), *sb.* ME. [f. next vb.; cf. Du. *flap* blow, lid of a can, etc.] **1.** The action of FLAP *v.*; *esp.* the motion of something broad and loose, or a blow given with it; also the resulting noise. †**2.** Something broad to strike with; e.g. a fly-flapper –1726. **3.** 'Anything that hangs broad and loose, fastened only on one side' (J.) 1522. **4.** Something broad and flat, hanging or working (vertically) on or as on a hinge; e.g. a valve 1565. **b.** *Anat.* †(*a*) The epiglottis –1802; (*b*) in fishes: The operculum or gill-cover 1881. **5.** A broad and loose piece of anything 1603. **6.** *Surg.* A portion of skin or flesh, separated from the underlying part, but remaining attached at the base 1807. **7.** *pl. Farriery.* A disease in the mouth of horses 1587.

1. The f. of a swan's wing would break a man's leg GOLDSM. Slang phr. *In a flap*: in a state of agitation. **3.** Thou greene Sarcenet f. for a sore eye *Tr. & Cr.* v. i. 36. The flaps of a hat 1892. **4.** One Table, the F. broken 1754. *Tide f.*: a valve used to shut off the water from a sewer. **5.** The damn'd flat flaps of shoulders of mutton FOOTE.

Comb.: **f.-fracture** = *compound fracture*; **-mouth**, one with broad hanging lips; **-sight**, in a rifle, one that turns up or down on a hinge.

Flap (flæp), *v.* ME. [prob. imit., like *clap*, *slap*, *rap*, *tap*; cf. Du. *flappen* strike, clap.] **1.** *trans.* To strike with a sudden blow. *Obs.* exc. *dial.* **2.** To strike with something flexible and broad ME. **b.** *intr.* To make a flap or stroke 1581. **3.** *trans.* To toss smartly (now *dial.*) ME.; *intr.* to flop *down* (colloq.) 1660. **4.** *intr.* To swing or sway about loosely; to flutter 1529. **b.** *trans.* (*causal*) To cause to flap 1565. **5.** *intr.* Of a hat: To have the flaps swaying up and down 1679; *trans.* to pull down the flaps of 1751. **6.** *trans.* To move up and down, beat (the wings) 1567. Also *absol.* and *intr.* Also of wings. **7.** *intr.* (with adv.) To make way by flapping 1775.

1. †*To f. in the mouth* (*with a lie*): to tell a bare-faced falsehood to. **2.** They flapp'd my light out as I read TENNYSON. **4.** The cheery deep-red curtains flapped and fluttered idly in the wind DICKENS. **5.** *trans.* They had flapped their hats over their eyes SMOLLETT. **7.** A slate-blue heron flapped fifty yards up the creek KINGSLEY.

Flapdoodle (flæpdū·d'l), *sb. colloq.* 1833. [Arbitrary.] **1.** 'The stuff they feed fools on'. MARRYAT. **2.** Nonsense; 'bosh'; also, a gewgaw 1878. Hence **Flapdoo·dle** *v. intr.* to talk nonsense.

†**Flap-dragon** (flæ·pdræ:gǫn), *sb.* 1588. [f. FLAP *v.* + DRAGON.] 'A play in which they catch raisins out of burning brandy and, extinguishing them by closing the mouth, eat them' (J.). Also, that which is thus caught and eaten. –1622.

Thou art easier swallowed then a f. SHAKS. Hence **Fla·pdragon** *v.* to swallow, as a f. SHAKS.

Flapjack (flæ·pˌdʒæk). Now *dial.* or *U.S.* 1600. [f. FLAP *v.* (sense 3) + JACK *sb.*[1]] **1.** A pancake; also, an apple turnover. **2.** *dial.* The lapwing 1847.

Flapper (flæ·pəɹ), *sb.* 1570. [f. FLAP *v.* + -ER[1].] **1.** One who flaps or strikes another. Hence (after Swift): One who arouses the attention or jogs the memory; a remembrancer. Also, a reminder. 1726. **2.** That which flaps 1570. **3.** A young wild duck 1773. **4.** A broad fin or flipper; the tail of a crustacean 1836. **5.** Applied to young girls who have not yet 'put their hair up': sometimes with implication of flightiness or lack of decorum (*slang* or *colloq.*) 1903.

1. [The absent-minded philosophers of Laputa] always keep a *F*...in their family..And the Business of this Officer is..gently to strike with his Bladder the mouth of him who is to speak, and the Right Ear of him..to whom the Speaker addresseth himself SWIFT, *Gulliver*, III. ii. 17.

Comb. **f.-skate**, *Raia intermedia*.

Flare (flēᵊɹ), *sb.*[1] Also (in sense 4) **flair.** 1814. [f. FLARE *v.*] **1.** A dazzling but unsteady light; a sudden outburst of flame. Also *fig.* Ostentation. **2.** *Naut.* = FLARE-UP 3. Also *transf.* 1883. **3.** *Photogr.* An indistinct image of the diaphragm in the camera 1868. **4.** *Shipbuilding.* Gradual swelling or bulging outwards and upwards 1833; *transf.* of a skirt, etc.

Flare (flēᵊɹ), *sb.*[2] *dial.* 1847. [Of unkn. origin.] The fat about a pig's kidney. Also *attrib.*

Flare (flēᵊɹ), *v.* 1550. [Of unkn. origin (perh. Scand.).] **1.** *trans.* To spread out, display. Hence, To wave to and fro. 1550. †**2.** *intr.* To spread out conspicuously –1837. **3.** To spread or cause to spread gradually outwards 1644. **4.** *intr.* To burn with a spreading, unsteady flame; to shine as such a flame does; to glow with or as with flame. Also *transf.* and *fig.* 1632. **b.** *trans.* To light up with a flare 1745.

2. *Merry W.* IV. vi. 42. **3.** Their gunwales f. outwards W. IRVING. A skirt slightly flared about the hem 1930. **4.** Phr. *To f. up*: to burst into a sudden blaze; hence, to break out into sudden anger.

Flare-up (flēᵊrˌɒp). 1837. [f. the phr.; see prec. Usu. stressed on first syll.] **1.** A sudden breaking out into flame 1859. **2.** *fig.* A violent commotion 1837. **3.** *Naut.* A night-signal made by burning something highly inflammable 1858.

2. Some of our young citizens..got into a flare-up with a party of boatmen..a desperate row it was too HALIBURTON.

Flaring (flēᵊ·riŋ), *ppl. a.* 1593. [f. FLARE *v.* + -ING[2].] **1.** That flares; †spreading out conspicuously –1641; glaring, showy, gaudy 1610. **2.** Of a vessel, etc.: That has its sides curving gradually outwards from the base 1627. **3.** Blazing irregularly; shining brightly and fitfully 1632.

3. F. tapers brightening as they waste GOLDSM. Hence **Fla·ringly** *adv.* (Dicts.).

Flash (flæʃ), *sb.*[1] ME. [– (O)Fr. *flache* in same sense, Central Fr. form of Picard and Norman dial. *flaque* – MDu. *vlacke*.] A pool, a marshy place. Now *local.*

Flash (flæʃ), *sb.*[2] 1566. [f. FLASH *v.*]

I. 1. A sudden outburst of flame or light; a sudden, quick, transitory blaze. **2.** *transf.* The brief period during which a flash is visible 1625. **3.** A brief outburst of something regarded as resembling a flash 1602. **4.** Superficial brilliancy; ostentation 1605. †**5.** A brilliant or showy person; usually, a coxcomb, fop –1808. **6.** A preparation of cayenne pepper or capsicum with burnt sugar, for colouring spirits 1820. **7.** *U.S.* A brief telegraphic news dispatch.

1. Three flashes of blue Light'ning DRYDEN. Phr. *F. in the pan*: *lit.* an explosion of gunpowder without any communication beyond the touch-hole: *fig.* an abortive effort or outburst. **2.** *In a f.*: instantaneously. **3.** Flashes of Merriment *Haml.* v. i. 210.

II. (cf. FLASH *v.* I.) **1.**† A sudden movement of water; a splash; a breaker –1713. **b.** A sudden rush of water, let down from a weir, to take a boat over shallow places 1677. †**2.** *transf.* A sudden burst of rain, wind, etc. –1808. **3.** A contrivance for producing a 'Flash' (senses II. 1, 1b.) 1768.

Comb.: **f.-flue**, the flue underneath an egg-end or similar externally fired boiler; **-lamp**, (*a*) *Photogr.* a lamp used to give a f.-light; (*b*) an electric torch (see TORCH *sb.*); **-light**, (*a*) a light so arranged as to give forth sudden flashes, used for signals and in lighthouses; (*b*) Photogr. a sudden light, usually made by blowing magnesium powder through a small flame; **-pan**, (*a*) the pan for holding the priming in an old flint-lock; (*b*) a pan in which powder is flashed as a signal; **-point** = *flashing-point*; **-test**, a test to determine the flashing-point of kerosene, etc.; **-wheel**, a sort of paddle-wheel revolving in a chase or curved water-way, by which the water is raised from the lower to the higher level.

Flash (flæʃ), *a.* Chiefly *colloq.* 1700. [f. FLASH *sb.*[2]] **1.** Gaudy, showy; 'swell' 1785. **2.** Counterfeit, sham 1812. **3.** *slang.* Knowing, wide-awake, 'fly' 1812. **4.** Connected with or pertaining to the class of sporting men, or that of thieves, tramps, and prostitutes 1700. **b.** Thieves' cant, slang 1746.

1. F. fellows, who live nobody knows where 1785. Meurice's f. hotel 1841. **2.** F. notes 1821. **4.** Poor Tom was..Full f., all fancy BYRON. A f. crib 1839.

Flash (flæʃ), *v.* ME. [app. echoic; cf. *plash*, *dash*, *splash*, *slash*.]

I. 1. *intr.* Of the sea, waves, etc.: To rush along the surface; to rise and dash. Also with *up*. †**2.** *trans.* To dash or splash (water) *about*, *abroad*, *upon* –1813. **3.** To send a flash or rush of water down (a river); also *absol.* Also, to send (a boat) down by a flash. 1791.

1. The Tivy..flashed in a sheet of foam through the chasm MEDWIN.

†**II.** *trans.* To slash; also, to dash –1548.

III. [app. transf. from sense I. 1.] **1.** *intr.* Of fire or light: To break forth suddenly. Of lightning: To play. ME. **b.** Of a hydro-carbon: To give forth vapour at igniting temperature 1890. **2.** To emit or reflect light suddenly or intermittently; to gleam 1791. **3.** *trans.* To emit or convey (light, fire, etc.). in a sudden flash or flashes. Also *transf.* and *fig.* 1589. **4.** *intr.* To come, move, or pass, like a flash of light 1590. **5.** To break out *into* sudden action; to pass abruptly *into* a specified state 1605. **6.** *trans.* To cause to flash; to kindle or illuminate with a flash 1632. **7.** To express or communicate by a flash or flashes 1789. **8.** *intr.* To make a display, show off. Now *colloq.* or *slang.* 1607. **9. a.** *Glass-making. trans.* and *intr.* To expand into a sheet. Also *trans.* To cover (colourless glass) with a film of coloured glass. 1839. **b.** *Electr.* To make (a carbon filament) uniform in thickness, by plunging it when heated into a heavy hydro-carbon gas 1888.

1. Lightning flashed about the summits of the Jungfrau TYNDALL. Phr. *To f. in the pan*: *lit.* said of a gun, when the priming is kindled without igniting the charge; *fig.* to fail after a showy effort. **2.** Flash'd all their sabres bare TENNYSON. Her eyes flashed 1857. **3.** His eyes flashed fire 1854. **4.** Ever and anone the rosy red Flasht through her face SPENSER *F. Q.* III. ii. 5. **5.** Phr. *To f. up*: to burst into sudden passion or anger. **7.** The intelligence was flashed next day all over England BURGON.

Fla·sh-board. 1768. [f. FLASH *v.* + BOARD *sb.*] A board set up on edge on a mill-dam, when the water is low, to throw more water into the mill-race.

Flasher (flæ·ʃəɹ). 1611. [f. FLASH *v.* + -ER[1].] **1.** One who or that which flashes. †**2.** A person of brilliant appearance or accomplishment –1780. **3. a.** 'A name of the lesser butcher-bird: see *Flusher*' (Ogilvie). **b.** A fish (*Lobotes surinamensis*). 1882.

Flash-house. 1816. [f. FLASH *a.*4 + HOUSE *sb.*[1]] A resort of thieves; also, a brothel.

Flashily (flæ·ʃili), *adv.* 1730. [f. FLASHY + -LY[2].] In a flashy manner.

Flashiness (flæ·ʃinės). 1603. [f. as prec. + -NESS.] The quality of being flashy.

Flashing (flæ·ʃiŋ), *vbl. sb.* 1573. [f. FLASH *v.* + -ING[1].] **1.** The action of FLASH *v.* **2.** The process of letting down a flash of water to carry a boat over shallow places 1791. **3.** *techn.* **a.** *Glass-making.* (See FLASH *v.* III. 9 a.) 1832. **b.** *Electr.* (See FLASH *v.* III. 9 b.) 1892.

attrib. and *Comb.*, as *f.-furnace* (sense 3 a); **f.-point**, the temperature at which the vapour given off from an oil or hydrocarbon will flash or ignite.

Flash-man. (Also as two wds.) 1789. [f. FLASH *a.*] **a.** One who is flash; a companion of thieves; a fancy-man. **b.** A patron of the ring; a 'swell' 1812.

Flashy (flæ·ʃi), *a.* 1583. [f. FLASH *sb.*[2] and *v.* + -Y[1].] †**1.** Splashing –1611. †**2.** Watery, frothy –1771; †insipid –1847; †*fig.* trifling; void of meaning, trashy –1745. **3.** Giving off flashes; sparkling, brilliant. *lit.* and *fig.* Also, lasting only for a flash. 1609. **b.** Showy, but shallow; cheaply attractive 1690. †**4.** Excited –1781. **5.** Showy; gaudy, glaring 1801. **6.** Of persons: Fond of cutting a dash 1687.

3. A fine, f., disagreeable day SCOTT. **b.** A f. rhetorician DE QUINCEY. **6.** Veteran topers, f. young men,, visitors from the country HAWTHORNE.

Flask (flask), *sb.*[1] OE. [In sense 2 – Fr. *flasque* (XVI); in sense 3 prob. – It. *fiasco*; the Fr. form (OFr. *flasche*, *flaske*) represents med.L. *flasca* (Isidore), the It. form med.L. *flasco*, *flascōn* (see FLAGON); ult. origin dubious.] †**1.** In OE.: A vessel for carrying liquor. **2.** A case of leather or metal (or formerly of horn) to carry gunpowder in. Now *powder-f.* 1549. **3.** A bottle, usually of glass, of bulbous shape, with a long narrow neck; often covered with wicker-work or plaited grass, etc., for protection, as in *Florence flasks*, in which wines, oil, etc., are exported from Italy. In verse occas. = bottle. Also, the contents of a flask. 1693. **b.** A flat bottle of glass or metal for the pocket; used to carry wine or spirits for a journey 1814. **c.** *Mining.* An iron bottle, of 76½ pounds capacity, in which quicksilver is sent to market 1872. **4.** *Founding.* A frame or box used to hold a portion of the mould for casting. [? a distinct wd.] 1697.

Comb.: **f.-leather,** a fastening for a powder-f.; **-shell,** a mollusc whose shell is f.-shaped.

†**Flask,** *sb.*[2] 1578. [– Fr. *flasque*, var. of *flaque* plank, – Du. *vlak* (flat) surface.] The bed of a gun-carriage –1800.

Flask (flask), *v.* [f. FLASK *sb.*[1]] *trans.* To put into a flask. BROWNING.

Flasket (fla·skėt). 1460. [– ONFr. *flasquet*; see FLACKET. Sense 1 appears to be unkn. in French.] **1.** 'A long shallow basket' (J.); also, a similar article made of metal. **b.** *dial.* A shallow washing tub 1814. **2.** A small flask 1577.

1. They gathered flowers to fill their f. SPENSER. The silver stands with golden flaskets grac'd POPE.

Flat (flæt), *sb.*[1] 1801. [alt. by assoc. w. FLAT *a.* of Sc. *flet* inner part of a house (OE. *flet* floor, dwelling = ON. *flet*, etc. :– Gmc. **flatjam*, f. **flataz* FLAT *a.*).] **1.** A floor or storey in a house. **2.** A suite of rooms on one floor, forming a complete residence 1824.

2. The rents of these flats seem to be extortionate 1887.

Flat (flæt), *a.*, *adv.*, and *sb.*[2] ME. [– ON. *flatr* = OHG. *flaz* :– Gmc. **flataz*, of uncertain relationship.]

A. *adj.* **I.** Lit. senses. **1.** Horizontally level; without inclination. Of a seam of coal: Not tilted. **2.** Spread out, stretched or lying at full length (*esp.* on the ground); usu. predicative (often quasi-advb.) with *fall, fling, lie,* etc. ME.; levelled, overthrown 1560; lying in close apposition 1559. **b.** *Paper-making.* Packed without folding 1890. **3.** Without curvature, indentation, or projection of surface; plane; level ME. **4.** *transf.* in *Painting.* Without relief or projection 1755. **5.** Broad and thin; of a vessel, wide and shallow ME.

1. Houses..f. a-top SIR T. HERBERT. *F. arch* (Arch.): 'an arch in which the sides of the voussoirs are cut so as to support each other, but their ends form a straight line top and bottom' (Shipley). **2.** What ruins kingdoms and lays cities f. MILT. *P. R.* IV. 363. **3.** Thy..f. Medes *Temp.* IV. i. 63. *Chest, flat.* A chest which has lost its rounded front *Syd. Soc. Lex.* **4.** *F. tint*: one of uniform shade. **5.** Her feet are f. like a Ducks Feet 1697.

II. Senses of fig. origin. **1.** Absolute, downright, unqualified, plain; peremptory. Now chiefly of a denial, contradiction, etc. 1551. **2.** Prosaic, dull, uninteresting, lifeless, monotonous, insipid 1573. **3.** Deficient in sense or vigour; stupid, dull, slow-witted 1599. **4.** Wanting in spirit; dull. Also, out of spirits, depressed. 1602. **b.** Of trade, etc.: Dull, inactive 1831. **5.** Of drink, etc.: Dead, insipid, stale 1607. **6.** Of sound, etc.: Not clear and sharp; dead, dull 1626. **b.** *Mus.* Of a note or singer: Relatively low in pitch; below the true pitch. Of an interval or scale: = MINOR. 1591. **7.** *Gram.* †**a.** Of an accent, a syllable: Unstressed –1612. **b.** Of a consonant: Voiced 1874. **8.** *Comm.* Unvarying, fixed 1898.

1. That in the Captaine's but a chollericke word, Which in the souldier is f. blasphemie SHAKS. A f. calm 1880. F. disobedience 1891. Phr. *That's f.*: an expression of one's final resolve. **2.** How weary, stale, f., and vnprofitable Seemes to me all the vses of this world SHAKS. A dull, f. Presbiter preached PEPYS. My news falls f. DICKENS. **4.b.** A f. market for maize 1894. **5.** A scent of f. ale GEO. ELIOT. **6.** Arions Harpe, Now delicately f., now sweetly sharp DRUMM. OF HAWTH. *B, D, E,* etc. *flat*: a semitone lower than B, D, E, etc. **8.** The f. cost, a f. fare, a f. rate 1898.

Comb.: **f. arch** (see I. 1, quot.); **-bedded** *a.* (*Geol.*), having a naturally plane cleavage; **-bill,** a bird having a broad flat bill, *e.g.* one of the genus *Platyrhynchus*; **-car** (*U.S.*), a railroad car consisting of a platform without sides or top; **f. chisel,** a smoothing chisel; **f. impression** (*Printing*), see *flat pull*; **f. nail,** a small sharp-pointed nail, with a flat thin head; **f. pull** (*Printing*), 'a simple proof without under or over-laying' (Jacobi); **f. race,** a race over clear and level ground; **-rail,** 'a railroad rail consisting of a simple flat bar spiked to a longitudinal sleeper' (Knight); **f. rod** (*Mining*), one of a series of rods for communicating motion from the engine, horizontally, to the pumps or other machinery in a distant shaft; **f. rope** (for mining shafts), one made by sewing together a number of ropes, making a wide flat band; **-sheets** *pl.* (*Geol.* and *Mining*), 'thin beds, flat veins, or blanket veins or deposits of some mineral usually different from the adjacent layers; often contact-deposits' (*Standard Dict.*); **-tool,** (*a*) 'a turning chisel which cuts on both sides and on the end, which is square' (Knight); (*b*) an elongated conical tool used in flat chasing; **-ware,** plates, dishes, saucers and the like, collectively, as distinguished from hollow ware. See also Main Words.

B. *adv.* †**1.** By horizontal measurement 1663. **2.** Downright, absolutely, positively, plainly; entirely, fully, quite. Now *rare.* 1577. †**3.** Directly, exactly –1654.

2. Sir Harry contradicted him f. 1770.

C. *absol.* and *sb.*[2] **1.** *absol.* (quasi-*sb.*) That which is flat; e.g. the flat surface of a sword, etc. ME. **b.** Level ground. Also, A racecourse without hedges or ditches. 1836. **2.** A horizontal plane; a level as opp. to a slope 1605. †**b.** A geometrical plane; an even surface –1674. **3.** *Building.* The horizontal part of a roof, usually covered with lead 1842. **4.** *Mining.* A horizontal bed or stratum of coal, stone, etc.; a horizontal vein or portion of a vein of metal 1747. **5.** A piece of level ground; a plain; also *fig.* ME.; a swamp 1610. **6.** Usu. *pl.* A nearly level tract, over which the tide flows; a shallow, shoal 1550. **7.** Something broad and thin (see quots.) 1545. **8.** Something broad and shallow (see quots.) 1640. **9.** *Ship-building.* **a.** *pl.* 'All the floor-timbers that have no bevellings in mid-ships' (Smyth) 1815. **b.** The partial deck or floor of a particular compartment 1869. **10.** *Theatr.* A part of a scene mounted on a wooden frame which is pushed horizontally or lowered on to the stage 1807. **11.** *House-Painting.* A surface painted so as to appear dead (see DEAD *a.* V. 1.). Also, the pigment employed for this. 1823. **12.** *slang.* A person who is 'only half sharp'; a simpleton 1732. **13.** *Mus.* **a.** A note lowered half a tone below the natural pitch. **b.** The sign ♭ which indicates this lowering of the note. 1589.

1. The f. of the hand SCOTT, of the back DICKENS. **b.** In steeple-chases, hurdle races, and on the f. 1886. **5.** The Cambridgeshire flats or marshes 1859. **6.** The boat grounded on the flats a little to the east of the pier 1813. **7.** *Flats,* a cant name for playing cards J. H. VAUX. Small drawings.. greatly injured by the..deep gold flats brought close up to them 1886. **8. a.** A broad flat-bottomed boat 1749. **b.** A broad shallow basket for packing produce for market 1640. **c.** *U.S.* = *flat-car* (see A. *Comb.*) 1864. **d.** *U.S.* A low-crowned hat 1859. **13.** Phr. *Sharps and flats*: the black keys of the keyboard of a piano; also punningly, sharpers and their victims.

Flat (flæt), *v.* 1607. [f. FLAT *a.*] †**1.** *trans.* To lay flat, raze, overthrow –1637. **2.** *Naut.* To force (the sail) flat against the mast 1642. **3.** *trans.* To make flat in shape. Now ordinarily FLATTEN. 1613. †**4.** *intr.* To become flattened –1725. †**5.** *trans.* To make dull, insipid, or spiritless –1710; *intr.* to become dull, depressed or feeble –1718. †**6.** *Mus.* To lower by one semitone –1685. **7.** To cover (a surface) with lustreless paint; in *Carriage-building,* to remove the gloss from (a surface) 1842. **8.** *U.S.* To reject (a lover) 1859.

4. U.S. *To f. out*: to become gradually thinner. Hence *fig.* to prove a failure, to collapse, etc. **5.** *intr.* Their loyalty flatteth and deadeth by degrees FULLER.

Hence **Fla·tted** *ppl. a.*

Fla·t-boat. (Also as two wds.) 1660. **1.** A flat-bottomed boat, used for transport, *esp.* in shallow waters. **b.** *U.S.* A large roughly-made boat formerly much used for floating goods, etc., down western rivers 1837.

Fla·t-bottom, *sb.* 1579. A boat with a flat bottom. Also *attrib.*

Fla·t-bo·ttomed, *a.* 1582. Having a flat bottom: chiefly of a boat.

Fla·t-cap. 1598. †**1.** A round cap with a low, flat crown, worn in 16–17th c. by London citizens –1891. †**2.** One who wears a flat-cap; *esp.* a London citizen or 'prentice –1822. **3.** A size of writing paper, 14 × 17 inches 1875.

Flated (flēⁱ·tėd), *a.* 1887. [f. *flat-*, pa. ppl. stem of L. *flare* blow + -ED[1].] *Phonetics.* Of consonant-sounds: Produced by *flatus,* i.e. by breath without vibration of the vocal chords.

Flat fish, fla·t-fish. 1710. Fish of the family *Pleuronectidæ*, which includes the sole, turbot, plaice, etc.

Fla·t-foot. 1870. A condition of the foot in which the tarsus possesses little or no arch.

Fla·t-foo·ted, *a.* 1601. [Stress variable.] **1.** Having flat feet (see prec.); splay-footed. **2.** *U.S. colloq.* Downright, plain and positive 1846.

Fla·t-head. 1832. **1.** One who has a flat head; *spec.* a member of a tribe of N. American Indians erroneously supposed to flatten their children's heads artificially 1837. **2.** *Australia.* A fish of the genus *Ceratodus* 1832. **3.** *U.S.* 'A snake which flattens its head, as a species of Heterodon' (*Cent. Dict.*) 1888. **4.** *Arch.* An ornament of an archivolt with a flat uncarved surface 1883. Hence **Fla·t-hea·ded** *a.*

Fla·t-iron, *sb.* 1810. An iron with a flat face for smoothing linen, etc. Also *attrib.* Hence **Fla·t-iron** *v.* to smooth with a flat-iron.

†**Fla·tive,** *a.* 1599. [f. *flat-*, pa. ppl. stem of L. *flare* blow + -IVE; perh. after contemp. *inflative*, med.L. *inflativus*, in same sense.] Flatulent –1607.

Fla·tland. 1884. An imaginary land in space of two dimensions.

Fla·tling(s. Now *arch.* or *dial.* ME. [f. FLAT *a.* + -LING(S[2].]

A. *adv.* **1.** At full length, flat. **2.** With the flat side 1470. **3.** Of motion: Horizontally 1598. **4.** *dial.* Plainly, peremptorily 1847.

2. So that the blade struck me flatlings SCOTT.

B. *adj.* (*flatling.*) Of a blow: Dealt with the flat side of a weapon –1609.

†**Fla·tlong,** *adv.* 1570. [f. as prec. + -LONG.] **1.** In or into a prostrate position –1632. **2.** With the flat side; with the flat sides in contact –1648.

Flatly (flæ·tli), *adv.* ME. [f. FLAT *a.* + -LY[2].] **1.** In a prostrate position. ? *Obs.* **2. a.** with small curvature 1797. **b.** Without relief 1883. **3.** Plainly, bluntly; decisively 1562; absolutely, completely 1577. **4.** Spiritlessly; without zest 1644.

3. F. against Scripture MILT. **4.** We shall but f. relish the most poinant meates DIGBY.

Flatness (flæ·tnės). ME. [f. FLAT *a.* + -NESS.] **1.** The quality or condition of being flat. **2.** The quality of having a small curvature 1683. **3.** 'Want of relief or prominence' (J.) 1702. **4.** Plainness (of speech) 1887; absoluteness 1611. **5.** Want of interest or incident 1882. **6.** Deadness 1626. **7.** Want of spirit or energy 1641. **8.** Of an author, etc.: Prosaic dullness 1649.

2. The f. of the Earth at the Poles 1796. **4.** The flatnesse of my miserie *Wint. T.* III. ii. 123. **6.** Flatnesse of Sound BACON. F. in Cyder 1707. **7.** The f. of being content with common reasons PALEY.

Fla·t-nose. 1636. **A.** *sb.* One who has a flat nose. **B.** *adj.* = **Fla·t-nosed** *a.* (1530) having a flat nose.

Flatten (flæ·t'n), *v.* 1630. [f. FLAT *a.* + -EN[5].] †**1.** *trans.* To lay flat on the ground. *rare.* 1712. **2.** = FLAT *v.* 3. 1630. **3.** *intr.* (for *refl.*) To become flat or more flat. Also with *out.* 1721. Of a wind or storm: To decrease in force 1748. **4.** = FLAT *v.* 5. 1631. **5.** To lower (a note) in pitch; also *absol.* 1824. **6.** To deprive (paint) of its lustre. 1823. **7.** *Aviation. To f. out* (intr.), to bring an aeroplane into a position parallel with the ground; also, of the aeroplane, to assume such a position 1913.

Phr. *To f. in a sail* (Naut.): to extend it more nearly fore-and-aft of the vessel.

Hence **Fla·ttener,** one who flattens; something used for flattening.

Fla·ttening, *vbl. sb.* 1726. [f. prec. + -ING[1].] The action or process of making, or of becoming, flat. In *Glass-making,* the process of laying out (sheet-glass) flat. 1879. **b.** Flattened condition.

attrib. and *Comb.* (chiefly in *Glass-making*), as *f. arch, furnace, iron, kiln, oven, stone, tool.*

Flatter (flæ·təɹ), *sb.* 1714. [f. FLAT *v.* + -ER[1].] **1.** A workman who makes something flat. **2.** A tool used in making things flat, e.g. a very broad-faced hammer used by smiths 1874.

Flatter (flæ·təɹ), *v.*[1] [ME. *flattere*, of unkn. origin; perh. back-formation from FLATTERY.] †**1.** *intr.* To show delight or fondness, e.g. as a dog does by wagging its tail –1607. **2.** *trans.* To try to please or win the favour of by obsequiousness; to court, fawn upon ME. **3.** To praise or compliment unduly or insincerely. Also *absol.* ME. **4.** To gratify the vanity or self-esteem of; to cause to feel honoured ME. **5.** To play upon the vanity of; to beguile with artful blandishments; to coax, wheedle 1500. **6.** To beguile (sorrow, etc.); also with *to.* Now *arch.* 1580. **7.** To inspire with hope, usually on insufficient grounds. Also, To foster (hopes). ME. **b.** To please with the idea *that.* Now chiefly *refl.* 1592. **8.** To gratify (the eye, ear, etc.) 1695. **9.** To represent too favourably; to exaggerate the good points of. Also *absol.* 1581.

1. Lyk to the scorpioun..That flaterest with thin heed whan thou wilt stynge CHAUCER. **2.** To f. kings, or court the great GOLDSM. **4.** When I tell him, he hates Flatterers, He says, he does; being then most flattered SHAKS. **5.** Priests and women must be flattered 1591. **6.** F. my sorrows with report of it SHAKS. **7.** Hope..doth f. thee in thoughts vnlikely SHAKS. **9.** Yet the Painter flatter'd her a little SHAKS. Hence **Fla·tterer,** one who flatters; *esp.* one who employs false praise to serve his own purposes.

†**Fla·tter,** *v.*[2] ME. [Of imit. origin; cf. *flacker, flutter, flitter.*] *intr.* To float, flutter –1803.

Fla·ttering, *ppl. a.* ME. [f. FLATTER *v.*[1] + -ING[2].] That flatters, in senses of the vb.

That f. tongue of yours wonne me *A.Y.L.* IV. i. 188. A flatt'ring dreame SHAKS. Opinions..f. to national vanity BURKE. A f. painter GOLDSM. Hence **Fla·tteringly** *adv.*

Flattery (flæ·těri). ME. [– OFr. *flaterie* (mod. *flatterie*), f. *flater* vb. 'flatter (which would normally have given *flat* in Eng.), prob. f. Gmc. **flat-* FLAT *a.*, and orig. meaning 'pat, smooth, caress'.] **1.** The action or practice of flattering; false or insincere praise; adulation; blandishment. **2.** *fig.* Gratifying delusion 1600.

1. F. is the destruction of all good fellowship DISRAELI. **2.** My friend and I are one: Sweet f. SHAKS.

Flatting (flæ·tiŋ), *vbl. sb.* 1611. [f. FLAT *v.* + -ING[1].] **1.** The action or process of making flat, *spec.* the process of rolling metal into plates; in *Glass-making*, the process of flattening a split glass cylinder. †**2.** The process of becoming flat –1675. **3.** *Gilding* and *House-painting.* The action of FLAT *v.* 7. Also *concr.* The overlaid coat. 1823.

attrib. and *Comb.*, as *f. furnace, hammer, hearth, stone, tool* (chiefly in *Glass-making*: see 1); *f. coat, colour, white* (sense 3); **f.-mill,** a mill for flattening, *esp.* one for rolling metal into sheets and forming the ribbon from which the planchets are cut in coining.

Flattish (flæ·tiʃ), *a.* 1611. [f. FLAT *a.* + -ISH[1].] Somewhat flat.

Flatulence (flæ·tiŭlěns). 1711. [f. next; see -ENCE. Cf. *flatulency* (XVII).] **1.** The condition of being charged with gas 1816. **2.** The state of having the alimentary canal charged with gas; also, the tendency in foods to produce this state 1858. **3.** *fig.* Windiness, vanity; pomposity 1711. So **Fla·tulency** (in senses 2, 3).

Flatulent (flæ·tiŭlěnt), *a.* 1599. [– Fr. *flatulent* (Paré) – mod. L. *flatulentus*, f. L. *flatus* blowing, blast, f. *flare* blow; see -ULENT.] †**1.** Of a windy nature. Of a tumour: Turgid with air. –1745. **2.** Generating or apt to generate gas in the alimentary canal 1599. **3.** Attended with or caused by the accumulation of gases in the alimentary canal. Of persons: Troubled with flatulence. 1655. **4.** *fig.* Puffed up, windy; empty, vain, pretentious 1658.

2. Pease and Beans are f. meat BLOUNT. **3.** A f. Asthma 1655. **4.** F. with fumes of self-applause YOUNG. Hence **Fla·tulent-ly** *adv.*, **-ness.**

†**Flatuosity** (flæ:tiu,ǫ·sĭti). 1597. [f. next + -ITY. Cf. Fr. *flatuosité.*] **1.** = FLATULENCE 2. –1727. **2.** *concr.* A quantity of wind, air, or gas –1601.

†**Fla·tuous,** *a.* 1580. [f. med.L. *flatuosus*, f. L. *flatus* (see next) + -OUS. Cf. Fr. *flatueux.*] **1.** = FLATULENT –1720. **2.** Caused by inflation. SIR T. BROWNE. Hence †**Fla·tuousness.**

Flatus (flē̆ⁱ·tɒ̆s). *Pl.* **flatuses.** 1669. [– L. *flatus* blowing, etc., f. *flare* blow.] ‖**1.** A blowing; a breath, a puff of wind 1692. **2.** *Path.* Wind accumulated or developed in the stomach or bowels 1669. **3.** A morbid inflation. *lit.* and *fig.* 1702.

Flat-ways, -wise (flæ·twēⁱz, wəiz). 1601. [f. FLAT *a.* + -WAYS, WISE *sb.*[1]] With the flat side uppermost, foremost, or applied to another surface; not EDGE-WAYS.

Flaught (flǭt, *Sc.* flaχt), *sb.* Chiefly *Sc.* [ME. *flaȝt*, prob. repr. either OE. **fleaht* or ON. **flahtr*, :– Gmc. **flaχtuz*, f. either of the parallel roots **flaχ-*, **flak-* whence FLAW *sb.*[1] and FLAKE *sb.*[2]] **1.** = FLAKE *sb.*[2] 1, 2. **2.** A sudden blast. *Sc.* 1802.

1. When your eyes Wax red and dark, with flaughts of fire between SWINBURNE.

Flaunt (flǭnt), *sb.* Now *rare.* 1590. [f. FLAUNT *v.*] **1.** The action or habit of making a display 1625. †**2.** Showy dress, finery –1611.

2. In these my borrowed Flaunts *Wint. T.* IV. iv. 23.

Flaunt (flǭnt), *v.* 1566. [Of unkn. origin.] **1.** *intr.* Of plumes, etc.: To wave gaily 1576. **2.** Of persons: To move about or display oneself ostentatiously, impudently, or defiantly. Of things: To be extravagantly gaudy or conspicuous. 1566. **3.** *trans.* To parade, show off 1827.

1. Orange and lemon trees f. over the walls 1789. **2.** One flaunts in rags, one flutters in brocade POPE. **3.** [The pirates] flaunted their sails in front of Ostia itself FROUDE. Hence **Flau·nting** *ppl. a.* waving gaily or proudly; making an obtrusive display. **Flau·ntingly** *adv.*

‖**Flautino** (flautī·no). 1724. [It.; dim. of *flauto* flute.] *Mus.* **a.** A small flute, piccolo, or flageolet. **b.** A small accordion 1876. **c.** An organ flute-stop 1852.

Flautist (flǭ·tist). 1860. [– It. *flautista*, f. *flauto* FLUTE *sb.*[1]; see -IST.] One who plays the flute; a flutist.

‖**Flauto** (flau·to). 1724. [It., = flute.] A flute; also, a name for several organ-stops.

F. piccolo, an octave flute. *F. traverso*, a traverse, or German flute. DANNELEY.

Flavaniline (flēⁱvæ·niləin). 1882. [f. L. *flavus* yellow + ANILINE.] *Chem.* A yellow colouring matter, $C_6H_{14}N_2ClH$, obtained by heating acetanilide with zinc chloride for several hours to 250–260°.

Flavescent (fleⁱve·sěnt), *a.* 1853. [– *flavescent-*, pres. ppl. stem of L. *flavescere*. f. *flavus* yellow; see -ESCENT.] Turning a pale yellow; yellowish.

Flavin (flē̆ⁱ·vin). Formerly also *flavine.* 1853. [f. L. *flavus* yellow + -IN[1].] *Chem.* A yellow dye-stuff prepared from quercitron bark.

Flavo- (flē̆ⁱvo), comb. f. L. *flavus*, indicating a yellow tint.

Flavorous (flē̆ⁱ·vərəs), *a.* Also **flavourous.** 1697. [f. next + -OUS.] **1.** Full of flavour; 'fragrant, odorous' (J.). **2.** *fig.* Having a flavour *of* (*rare*) 1885.

Flavour, flavor (flē̆ⁱ·vəɹ), *sb.* ME. [– OFr. *flaor*, infl. by *savour*; the OFr. word, if cogn. with It. †*flatore*, repr. Rom. **flator*, blend of L. *flatus* blowing, breath, and *fœtor* stench.] **1.** A smell, odour. In mod. use: A trace of a particular odour. **2.** The element in the taste of a substance which depends on the co-operation of the sense of smell; a slight peculiarity of taste distinguishing a substance from others; a trace of a particular kind of taste; a savour 1697. **3.** *fig.* **a.** An undefinable characteristic quality instinctively apprehended. **b.** Piquancy, zest. 1699.

1. An earthy f. DICKENS. **2.** The Flavor of Canary 1745. Oak..smoke gives the peculiar f. to that bacon MRS. PIOZZI. **3.** The f. of Socratic irony JOWETT. Hence **Fla·vourless** *a.*

Flavour (flē̆ⁱ·vəɹ), *v.* ME. [f. prec. sb.] †**1.** *intr.* To be odorous, savour, smell. ME. only. **2.** To give flavour, taste, or scent to; to season 1542. **3.** To try the flavour of. LAMB.

Flavoured (flē̆ⁱ·vəɹd), *ppl. a.* 1740. [f. FLAVOUR *sb.* and *v.* + -ED.] **a.** Mixed with something to impart a flavour 1764. **b.** Having (a specified) flavour 1740.

a. Herbs, or flavour'd fruits DODSLEY. **b.** Nicely-flavoured mince-meat 1867.

Flavouring (flē̆ⁱ·vəriŋ), *vbl. sb.* 1845. [f. FLAVOUR *v.* + -ING[1].] **1.** The action of FLAVOUR *v.*; also *attrib.* **2.** *concr.* Something used to impart flavour 1845.

Flavous (flē̆ⁱ·vəs), *a.* 1666. [f. L. *flavus* yellow + -OUS.] Yellow.

Flaw (flǭ), *sb.*[1] ME. [perh. – ON. *flaga* slab of stone, prob. :– Gmc. **flaχ-*, **flaʒ-*, parallel and synon. with **flak-*, whence FLAKE *sb.*[2], which *flaw* closely resembles in sense.]

I. †**1.** A flake (of snow); a flake or spark (of fire) –1597. **2.** A fragment. *Obs.* exc. *Sc.* 1605. **3. a.** A turf, or *collect.* turf 1811. †**b.** A slab of stone 1570.

1. 2 *Hen. IV*, IV. iv. 35. **2.** But this heart shal break into a hundred thousand flawes *Lear* II. iv. 288.

II. 1. A crack, breach, fissure, rent, rift. Also *fig.* 1606. **2.** A defect, fault 1586. **b.** *esp.* An invalidating defect in a legal document or procedure, a title, etc. 1616.

1. Or some frail China-jar receive a F. POPE. **2.** Thou hast a Crack, F., soft Place in thy Skull S. BUTLER. Health without a f. C. BRONTË. **b.** A f. in the indictment 1883.

Hence **Flaw·less** *a.* **Flaw·less-ly** *adv.*, **-ness.**

Flaw (flǭ), *sb.*[2] 1513. [prob. – MLG. *vlāge*, MDu. *vlāghe* (Du. *vlaag*), the primary sense of which may be 'stroke'.] **1.** A sudden blast or gust, usually of short duration. Also *fig.* **b.** A short spell of rough weather 1791. †**2.** *fig.* A sudden onset; a burst of feeling or passion; a sudden uproar or tumult –1676.

1. It blew..not only by squalls and flaws but a settled terrible tempest DE FOE. **2.** O, these flawes and starts..would well become A woman's story *Macb.* III. iv. 63.

Flaw (flǭ), *v.*[1] 1613. [f. FLAW *sb.*[1]] **1.** *trans.* To make a flaw in; to crack. Also *fig.* **2.** *intr.* To become cracked. †Also, to break *off* in flakes. 1648.

1. The Brazen Cauldrons with the Frost are flaw'd DRYDEN. *fig.* France hath flaw'd the League SHAKS.

Flaw (flǭ), *v.*[2] 1805. [f. FLAW *sb.*[2]] *intr.* To blow in gusts; *trans.* to ruffle as a flaw of wind does. *rare.*

Flaw, obs. f. FLAY.

Flawn (flǭn). *arch.* ME. [– OFr. *flaon* (mod. *flan* FLAN) :– med.L. *flado, fladon-* (x) –Frankish **flado* flat cake (Du. *vlade, vla* pancake) :– WGmc. **flaþō*.] A kind of custard or cheese-cake. Also, a pancake.

Flawy (flǭ·i), *a.* 1712. [f. FLAW *sb.*[1] and [2] + -Y[1].] **1.** Full of defects. **2.** Gusty 1828.

Flax (flæks), *sb.* [OE. *flæx* (*fleax*) = OFris. *flax*, (M)Du. *vlas*, OHG. *flahs* (G. *flachs*) :– WGmc. **flaχsa*, prob. to be referred to Gmc. **flaχ-* **fleχ-* :– IE. **plok-* **plek-* in Gr. πλέκειν, L. *plectere*, G. *flechten* plait.] **1.** The plant *Linum usitatissimum* bearing blue flowers which are succeeded by pods containing the seeds known as linseed. It is cultivated for its textile fibre and for its seed. **2.** The fibres of the plant whether dressed or undressed. Also *transf.* ME. †**3.** As a material of which a candle or lamp wick is made; the wick itself –1632. **4.** Cloth made of flax; linen OE.

1. F...is called of the Northen men lynt TURNER. **Mountain F.,** (1) *Linum catharticum*; (2) *Erythræa centaurium.* **New Zealand F.,** *Phormium tenax* (also called *f.-bush, -lily, -plant*), a native of New Zealand, the leaves of which yield a textile fibre. **3.** The smoking f. shall he not quench *Isa.* 42:3.

attrib. and *Comb.* **1.** General: as in *f.-culture, -fibre, -mill, -sandal, -thread*, etc. **2.** Special: as **f.-brake,** a toothed instrument for bruising f.-stalks; **-comb,** a f.-hackle; **-cotton,** cottonized flax; **-hackle,** an instrument for hackling or straightening the fibres of the flax; **-wench, -wife, -woman,** a female f. worker.

b. In plant-names, as **f.-weed,** *Linaria vulgaris*, toad-flax; etc.

Flaxen (flæ·ksěn, flæ·ks'n). 1520. [f. FLAX *sb.* + -EN[4].]

A. *adj.* **1.** Made of flax 1521. **2.** Of the colour of dressed flax 1523. **3.** Of or pertaining to flax 1707.

1. A f. thread 1825. **2.** All F. was his Pole *Haml.*

IV. v. 196. **3.** The f. trades of the United Kingdom 1875.

†**B.** *sb.* Material made of flax; linen; a linen cloth –1696.

Fla·x-seed, fla·xseed. 1562. The seed of flax, linseed. **b.** The plant *Radiola millegrana* 1848.

Flaxy (flæ·ksi), *a.* 1634. [f. FLAX *sb.* + -Y[1].] Like flax; made of flax.

Flay (flēⁱ), *v. Pa. t.* and *pple.* **flayed.** [OE. *flēan* = MDu. *vlae(gh)en* (Du. *vlaen*), ON. *flá* :- Gmc. **flaχan*, of unkn. origin.] **1.** *trans.* To strip off the skin of; to skin. **b.** To excoriate ME. **2.** *fig.* and *transf.* 1584. **3.** To strip or peel off (skin); also *transf.* ME.

1. No doubt, they would have flea'd me alive CONGREVE. **b.** With a back flayed and an eye knocked out MACAULAY. **2.** To f. the people with requisitions FROUDE. To f. an author 1884. **3.** It [the frost] flaw'd the very skin of my face EVELYN.

Hence **Flay·er**, one who flays or fleeces. **Flay·-flint,** a skinflint.

Flea (flī), *sb.* [OE. *flēa(h)*, corresp. to MLG., MDu. *vlō* (Du. *vloo*), OHG. *flōh* (G. *floh*), ON. *fló*; repr. Gmc. base **flauχ-* or perh. **þlauχ-* (cf. FLEE *v.*).] A small wingless insect (or genus of insects, *Pulex*, the common flea being *P. irritans*), well known for its biting propensities and its agility in leaping; it feeds on the blood of man and of other animals. **b.** = *flea-beetle* (see *Comb.*) 1805. **c.** *transf.* of small crustaceans which leap like a flea 1888.

A f. Hath smaller fleas that on him prey; And these have smaller still to bite 'em SWIFT. **c.** SAND-F., WATER-F. (see the sbs.).

Phr. *A f. in one's ear*: a stinging or mortifying reproof, rebuff, or repulse: chiefly in phr. *to go* (*send*, etc.) *away with a f. in one's ear.*

Comb.: **f.-beetle,** a small leaping beetle of the genus *Haltica*, destructive to hops, grape-vines, turnips, etc.; **-louse,** a leaping plant-louse of the genus *Psyllidæ*; †**-seed,** *Plantago psyllium*; **-wood,** bog myrtle, *Myrica gale.*

Flea (flī), *v.* Also *dial.* **fleck.** 1610. [f. prec.] To rid of fleas.

Flea·-bane. 1548. [See BANE *sb.*] A name of plants: *esp.* **a.** the genus *Inula* (or *Pulicaria*); **b.** the genus *Erigeron* 1813; **c.** *Plantago psyllium* (from the appearance of the seed) 1578.

Flea·-bite. 1570. [f. FLEA *sb.* + BITE *sb.*] **1.** The bite of a flea, or the red spot caused by it. **2.** *fig.* A trifling inconvenience or discomfort 1582.

Flea-bitten, *a.* 1570. [f. as prec. + BITTEN *ppl. a.*] **1.** Bitten by (or full of) fleas 1621. **2.** Of the colour of a horse, etc.: Having bay or sorrel spots or streaks, upon a lighter ground.

2. [Pointers] of a flea-bitten blue or grey E. JESSE.

Fleak(e, obs. or dial. f. FLAKE.

Fleam, obs. and dial. var. of PHLEGM.

Fleam (flīm), *sb.* 1552. [– OFr. *flieme* (mod. *flamme*):– Rom. **fleutomum* (med.L. *fledomum, fletoma*), for late L. *phlebotomus* – Gr. φλεβοτόμον, subst. use of n. of adj. (see PHLEBOTOMY).] **1.** A surgical instrument for letting blood or for lancing the gums; a lancet. *Obs.* or *arch.* exc. in *U.S.* **2.** A lancet for bleeding horses 1616.

Comb. **f.-tooth,** a fleam-shaped tooth of a saw.

Fleamy, obs. and dial. var. of PHLEGMY.

Flear, obs. f. FLEER.

Fleawort (flī·wɒɹt). [OE. *flēawyrt*, f. FLEA *sb.* + WORT[1].] A name of plants: *esp.* **a.** *Inula conyza*, and some species of *Cineraria* and *Erigeron*, supposed to destroy fleas; **b.** *Plantago psyllium*, the seeds of which resemble fleas. Cf. FLEABANE.

Flebotomy: see PHLE-.

‖**Flèche** (fleʃ). 1710. [Fr., primarily 'arrow'.] **1.** *Fortif.* = ARROW 7. **2.** *Arch.* A slender spire 1848.

Fleck (flek), *sb.*[1] 1598. [Proximate source may be ON. *flekkr* sb., *flekka* vb., or MLG., MDu. *vlecke* (Du. *vlek*) = OHG. *flec, fleccho* (G. *fleck, flecken*), of unkn. origin.] **1.** A blemish, freckle, spot. Also *fig.* **2.** A flake, speck 1750.

1. *fig.* Flecks of sin TENNYSON. **2.** Flecks and scraps of snow EMERSON.

Hence **Fle·ckless** *a.* without spot or blemish.

Fleck, *sb.*[2] Now *dial.* 1575. = FLARE *sb.*[2]

Fleck (flek), *v.*[1] ME. [See FLECK *sb.*[1], which occurs much later.] To spot, streak, or stripe; to dapple, variegate.

Two Kids Both fleck'd with white DRYDEN.

Fleck, *v.*[2] Now *dial.* 1565. [perh. var. of FLAG *v.*[1]] *intr.* To fly low; to flit, flutter about. Also *transf.* and *fig.*

Flecker (fle·kəɹ), *v.* 1828. [f. FLECK *v.*[1] + -ER[5].] To mark with flecks; to scatter like flakes.

†**Flect,** *v. rare.* 1548. [– L. *flectere* bend.] *trans.* To bend. *lit.* and *fig.* –1578.

Flection, -al, -less: see FLEXION.

Flector, (fle·ktǒɹ, -əɹ). 1666. [f. FLECT *v.* + -OR 2.] = FLEXOR.

Fled (fled), *ppl. a.* 1621. [pa. pple. of FLEE *v.*] In senses of the vb.

Fledge, *a.* Now *dial.* [repr. var. **flečġe* of OE. **flyċġe* recorded only in *unfligge* (x), glossing L. *implumes*; corresp. to MDu. *vlugghe* (Du. *vlug*), OHG. *flucchi* (G. *flügge* is from LG.) :- WGmc. **fluȝȝja*, f. **fluȝ-*, weak base of **fleuȝan* FLY *v.*[1]] **1.** Fit to fly; having the feathers developed, fledged ME. **2.** Furnished for flight. Const. *with.* Also *fig.* 1631.

2. All the fond hopes, which forward Youth and Vanitie are f. with MILT. Hence **Fle·dgeless** *a.*

Fledge (fledʒ), *v.* 1566. [f. prec.] **1.** *intr.* Of a young bird: To become fully plumed. Also *fig.* **2.** *trans.* To bring up (a young bird) until its feathers are grown. Also *fig.* 1589. **3.** To furnish or adorn with or as with feathers or down 1597. **4.** To feather (an arrow) 1796.

2. Shylocke..knew the bird was fledg'd *Merch. V.* III. i. 32. **3.** The Iuuenall whose Chin is not yet fledg'd 2 *Hen. IV*, I. ii. 23. *fig.* Lightlier move The minutes fledged with music TENNYSON.

Fledgeling, fledgling (fle·dʒliŋ). 1830. [f. FLEDGE *a.* + -LING[1], after *nestling.*] **1.** A young bird just fledged. Also *fig.* 1846. **2.** *attrib.*, as *f. poets.*

Fledgy (fle·dʒi), *a.* [f. as prec. + -Y[1].] Covered with feathers. KEATS.

Flee (flī), *v. Pa. t.* and *pple.* **fled** (fled). [OE. *flēon* = OFris. *flīa*, OS. *fliohan* (MDu. *vlīen*, Du. *vlieden*), OHG. *fliohan* (G. *fliehen*), ON. *flý(j)a*, Goth. *þliuhan* :- Gmc. **þleuχan*. Already in OE. confused with FLY *v.*[1]]

I. *intr.* **1.** To run away from or as from danger; to take flight. **2.** To withdraw hastily, take oneself off, go away. Const. *from, out of.* OE. **3.** To make one's escape ME. **4.** To disappear, vanish. Also with *away.* ME. **5.** Occas. used for FLY (= L. *volare*) OE.

1. The Rogue fled from me like Quick-siluer SHAKS. In vain for Life He to the Altar fled PRIOR. **2.** Two years later he fled from society 1848. **4.** As I approached, the morning's golden mist..fled SHELLEY. **5.** Loues golden arrow at him should haue fled SHAKS.

II. *trans.* **1.** To run away from; to avoid, shun OE. **2.** To contrive to avoid, escape from, evade. Now *rare.* ME.

1. So fled his Enemies my Warlike Father SHAKS. F. fornication 1 *Cor.* 6:18.

Fleece (flīs), *sb.* [OE. *flēos* = Du. *vlies*, MHG. *vlies* (G. *vlies*) :- WGmc. **fleusa*, and OE. *flēs* (WS. *flīes*) :- WGmc. **fleusi*; prob. ult. rel. to the base of L. *pluma* feather.] **1.** The woolly covering of a sheep or similar animal. **2.** The quantity of wool shorn from a sheep at one time 1460. **3.** Anything resembling a fleece 1513. **4.** *spec.* The thin sheet of cotton or wool fibre that is taken from the breaking-card 1853.

1. Its [the Alpaca's] f. is superior to that of the sheep in length and softness SIMMONDS. *Order of the Golden F.*: an order of knighthood instituted at Bruges in 1430 by Philip the Good, duke of Burgundy. **3.** Witnesse this snow-white f. vpon my head 1600. Soft as the fleeces of descending snows POPE.

Comb. **f.-wool,** that shorn from the living animal.

Hence **Flee·ced** *ppl. a.* furnished with a f. **Flee·celess** *a.*

Fleece (flīs), *v.* 1537. [f. prec. sb.] **1.** *trans.* To strip of the fleece; to clip off the wool from. *lit.* and *fig.* 1628. **2.** To pluck or shear (the wool) *from* a sheep. Hence *fig.* Now *rare.* 1537. **3.** To strip completely of money, property, etc.; to exact money from; to rob heartlessly; to victimize 1572. **4.** To overspread as with a fleece or with fleeces 1730.

1. A Clergy, that shall more desire to f., Then feed the flock WITHER. **3.** In bad inns you are fleeced and starved GOLDSM. **4.** Stones..fleeced with moss WORDSW.

Fleecy (flī·si), *a.* 1567. [f. FLEECE *sb.* + -Y[1].] **1.** Fleeced, wool-bearing; having a fleece-like nap 1590. **2.** Consisting of or derived from fleeces; resembling a fleece; woolly 1567.

1. *F. star* = Aries; The fleecie Starr that bears Andromeda MILT. *P. L.* III. 558. **2.** F. wealth MILT., skies, snows DRYDEN, waves LONGF.

Fleer (flī·əɹ), *sb.*[1] Now *rare.* ME. [f. FLEE *v.* + -ER[1].] One who flees.

Fleer (flīᵊɹ), *sb.*[2] 1604. [f. FLEER *v.*] **1.** A mocking look or speech. †**2.** 'A deceitful grin of civility' (J.) –1727.

1. Marke the Fleeres, the Gybes *Oth.* IV. i. 83. **2.** Such a sly, treacherous f. upon their face SOUTH.

Fleer (flīᵊɹ), *v.* ME. [prob. of Scand. origin; cf. Norw. and Sw. dial. *flira*, Da. dial. *flire* grin, laugh unbecomingly.] †**1.** *intr.* To make a wry face; to grin, grimace –1790. **2.** To laugh coarsely 1553. †**3.** To smile obsequiously *on, upon* –1673. **4.** To smile or grin contemptuously; hence, to gibe, jeer, sneer ME. **5.** *trans.* To laugh in derision at 1622.

1. Let her fleere, and looke a scew B. JONS. **2.** He whispered to me..'This is a Tythe-goose'; and then fleer'd 1747. Hence **Flee·rer. Flee·ringly** *adv.*

Fleet (flīt), *sb.*[1] [OE. *flēot* (once) ship or ships collect., f. *flēotan* float, swim; see FLEET *v.*[1]] **1.** A sea force, or naval armament; in mod. use, a number of ships under the orders of the admiral in chief, or of the flag-officer in command of a division. **b.** A number of ships or boats sailing in company 1697. **c.** *transf.* of persons, birds, or other objects (now *rare*) ME.; a number of vehicles or aircraft forming a definite group or unit 1889. **2.** *Fisheries.* A row of herring nets fastened together end to end 1879.

1. Phr. *To go round* or *through the f.*: to be flogged on board each vessel in the fleet.

Fleet (flīt), *sb.*[2] Now *local.* [OE. *flēot* (also *flēote* or *-a*), corresp. to OFris. *flēt*, (M)Du. *vliet*, MHG. *vliez*, ON. *fljót*, f. Gmc. **fleut-* FLEET *v.*[1]] A place where water flows; a creek, inlet, run of water.

The Fleet: a run of water flowing into the Thames between Ludgate Hill and Fleet Street, now a covered sewer; hence, the prison which stood near it. attrib.: *F. books*, the records of Fleet marriages. *F. marriage*, one performed clandestinely by a Fleet parson in the Fleet; also *Fleet-Street marriage. F. parson*, one of the disreputable clergymen who were to be found about the Fleet ready to perform clandestine marriages. *F. register* = *Fleet book.*

Fleet (flīt), *a.*[1] 1529. [prob. much older, if – ON. *fljótr*, **flīotr*, f. Gmc. **fleut-* (see prec.).] **1.** Swift in onward movement; nimble. Said primarily of living beings, their movements, etc.; hence of things viewed as self-moving, thoughts, etc. Not in colloq. use. **2.** Evanescent, shifting; not lasting. *poet.* 1812.

1. Their conceites haue winges, Fleeter then arrowes, bullets, wind *L. L. L.* V. ii. 261. Thir horses..f. and strong MILT. *Comb.* **f.-foot** *a. poet.* f. of foot; also *fig.* Hence **Flee·tly** *adv.* **Flee·tness,** swiftness, transitoriness.

Fleet (flīt), *a.*[2] *dial.* and *Agric.* 1621. [perh. repr. OE. **flēat*, corresp. to Du. *vloot* shallow, f. base of FLEET *v.*[1]] Shallow.

Fleet (flīt), *v.*[1] [OE. *flēotan* float, swim = OFris. *fliata*, OS. *fliotan* (Du. *vlieten*), OHG. *fliozan* (G. *fliessen*), ON. *fljóta* float, flow :- Gmc. **fleutan.*]

I. 1. *intr.* To float; †to sail. †**2.** To drift. Also *transf.* –1744. †**3.** To swim –1600. †**4.** Of a person: To be afloat; to travel by water; to sail –1725. †**5.** To fluctuate, waver –1638.

1. Oil doth naturally f. above FRENCH.

II. †**1.** To flow –1630. †**2.** To overflow, abound –1526. **3.** †**a.** To waste *away*; to fall to pieces –1661. **b.** To fade or die out. *Obs.* or *arch.* 1576. **4.** To glide away like a stream; to slip away; hence, to flit, migrate, remove, vanish ME. **b.** *trans.* To pass, while away (time). *rare.* 1600. **5.** *intr.* To move swiftly, to flit, fly ME.

1. Still gliding forth, altho' it f. full slow 1630. **3. b.** How all the other passions f. to ayre SHAKS. **4.** Our souls are fleeting hence MARLOWE. **b.** Many yong Gentlemen..f. the time carelesly SHAKS.

III. *Naut. trans.* To change the position of, shift (a block, rope, etc.). Also *absol.* 1769.

Fleet (flīt), *v.*[2] ME. [prob. f. OE. *flēt* cream, f. root of *flēotan* FLEET *v.*[1]; or perh. a use of FLEET *v.*[1]] *trans.* To take off that which floats upon the surface of a liquid; *esp.* to skim (milk, the cream from milk). Also *transf.* and *fig.*

Flee·ten, *a.* 1618. [Altered f. FLOTTEN, assim. to FLEET *v.*[2]] **1.** (See FLOTTEN.) **2.** Of the colour of skimmed milk 1618. **3.** quasi-*sb.* Skimmed milk. WEBSTER.

Fleeting (flī·tiŋ), *vbl. sb.* Now *dial.* ME. [f. FLEET *v.*[2] + -ING[1].] The action of skimming a liquid, *esp.* milk. **b.** *concr.* in *pl.* Skimmings, curds 1611. *Comb.* **f.-milk,** skim-milk.

Fleeting (flī·tiŋ), *ppl. a.* OE. [f. FLEET *v.*[1] + -ING[2].] That fleets; †shifting, unstable; changeable, inconstant –1650; passing swiftly by 1600; gliding swiftly away 1697; transitory 1563.

The f. Moone No Planet is of mine *Ant. & Cl.* v. ii. 240. The f. yeare SHAKS. Pleasure the most f. of all things JOWETT. Hence **Flee·ting-ly** *adv.*, **-ness.**

Flegm, Flegm-: see **Phlegm, Phlegm-.**

†**Fleme,** *v.* [OE. *flīeman*, f. *flēām* flight :– Gmc. **plauχmon*, f. ablaut var. of **pleuχ-* FLEE *v.*] **1.** *trans.* To cause to flee; hence, to banish, exile –1814. **2.** *intr.* To flee, run away. *rare.* ME. only.

1. Lawe is nye flemede out of this contree HOCCLEVE. Hence †**Fle·mer,** one who puts to flight.

Fleming (fle·miŋ). [Late OE. *Flæmingi* – ON. *Flæmingi*, later reinforced by MDu. *Vlāming* (whence ON.), f. *Vlām-*, whence *Vlaanderen* Flanders; see -ING[3].] **1.** A native or inhabitant of Flanders. †**2.** A Flemish vessel. DRAKE.

Flemish (fle·miʃ), *a.* 1488. [– MDu. *Vlāmisch* (Du. *Vlaamsch*), = OFris. *Flamsk*, assim. to FLEMING; see -ISH[1].] **1.** Of or belonging to Flanders or the Flemings. *absol.* The Flemish language 1727. **2.** Resembling a Fleming 1598.

2. This F. drunkard *Merry W.* II. i. 23.

Comb.: **F. account,** one showing a deficit; **F. bond** (see BOND *sb.*[1]); **F. brick,** a hard yellowish brick, used for paving; **F. eye** (*Naut.*), 'a kind of eye-splice in which the ends are scraped down, tapered, passed oppositely, marled, and served over with spun yarn' (Smyth); **F. horse** (*Naut.*), a foot-rope at the yard-arms of topsail yards; **F. point,** 'a Guipure Lace, also known as Point de Brabant' (Caulfield); **F. stitch,** 'one of the Fillings in Honiton Lace' (*Ibid.*).

Flench, flinch, flense (flenʃ, flinʃ, flens), *v.* 1814. [– Da. *flense* = Norw. *flinsa, flunsa* flay.] **1.** *trans.* To cut up and slice the fat from (a whale or seal). **2.** To flay or skin (a seal) 1874.

Flesh (fleʃ), *sb.* [OE. *flǣsc* = OFris. *flask*, OS. *flēsk* (Du. *vleesch*), OHG. *fleisc* (G. *fleisch*), ON. *flesk* swine's flesh, pork, bacon :– Gmc. **flaiskaz, -iz.*]

I. 1. The soft substance, *esp.* the muscular parts, of an animal body; that which covers the framework of bones. **2.** *transf.* The soft pulpy substance of fruit, or a plant; that part which encloses the core or kernel, *esp.* when eatable. So Gr. σάρξ, L. *caro*, Fr. *chair.* 1572. **3.** Put for: Quantity or excess of flesh; hence, embonpoint 1548. **4.** Animal food; in recent use, butcher's meat, to the exclusion of poultry, etc., as well as of *fish* (see FISH *sb.*[1]). Somewhat *arch.* OE. **5.** The visible surface of the body 1606.

1. Phr. *Raw f.*: that exposed by removal of the skin. *F. and fell*: the whole substance of the body; hence, as quasi-*advb.* phr.: entirely. *Proud f.*: the overgrowth of the granulations which spring up on a wound; also *fig.* *To go after* or *follow strange f.*: a Biblical expression referring to unnatural crime. **3.** A beautefull Prince, beginninge a littel to growe in f. HALL. **4.** No maner of person shall eate any Fleshe on the same [Fishe] daye 1562. **5.** Although my f. be tawny 1657.

II. Fig., etc. uses (chiefly Biblical). **1.** That which has corporeal life OE. **2.** The physical frame of man; the body OE. **b.** The body (of Christ), as spiritually eaten by believers; also, the bread in the sacrament of the Lord's Supper OE. **3.** Human nature with its corporeal necessities and limitations OE. **4.** The sensual appetites and inclinations. In theol. language, the depraved nature of man in its conflict with the promptings of the Spirit. ME.

1. What f., what person could be saued PRYNNE. Phr. *All f.* (*omnis caro*, Vulg. = Hebraistic Gr. πᾶσα σάρξ): all animals; in narrower sense, all mankind. **2.** In my fleysch y schal se god ME. Phr. *In (the) f.*: in a bodily form; also, in life, living. *After the f.*: in bodily likeness. **3.** The thousand Naturall shockes That F. is heyre too *Haml.* III. i. 63. **4.** I know what F. will object FULLER. *Sins of the f.*: esp. those of unchastity.

Phr. *One's (own) f.*: one's near kindred or descendants. Now *rare* exc. in FLESH AND BLOOD. *One f.*: said (after *Gen.* 2:24) of husband and wife to express the closeness of the marriage tie.

attrib. and *Comb.* **1.** General: as *f.-diet*, †*-market*, *-tint*; *-eater*, *-former*; *-gorged*; *-pink*, *-red*; etc. **2.** Special: **f.-bird,** a carnivorous bird; **-brush,** a brush used for rubbing the body, in order to excite the circulation; **-flea,** the chigoe, *Sarcopsylla penetrans*; **-glove,** a glove used to stimulate the circulation by rubbing the f.; **-hook,** a hook for removing meat from the pot; **-juice,** 'the reddish acid liquid which is contained in dead muscle' (*Syd. Soc. Lex.*); **-knife** = *fleshing-knife*; **-meat,** flesh as an article of food; **-quake** [after EARTHQUAKE], a trembling of the body; **f. side,** the side of a skin that was nearest the f., opp. to *grain side*; **-taster,** an officer who tests the wholesomeness of meat; **-traffic,** 'the slave trade' (Smyth); **-worm,** a worm that feeds on f.; also the *Trichina spiralis*; **-wound,** a wound that does not extend beyond the f.

Flesh (fleʃ), *v.* 1530. [f. prec. sb.] **1.** *trans.* To give a taste of the flesh of the game killed to (a hawk or hound), in order to incite it to the chase. Hence, to render (an animal) eager for prey by the taste of blood. **2.** *transf.* and *fig.* To initiate in or inure to bloodshed or warfare; to render inveterate, harden 1530; to incite, animate (? *Obs.*) 1573. **3.** To plunge (a weapon) in the flesh, esp. for the first time. Also *transf.* and *fig.* 1592. **4.** To clothe with flesh (chiefly *fig.*) 1661; †to fatten –1682. **5.** *Leather-manuf.* To remove the adhering flesh from (a skin or hide) 1777.

1. An old bitten cur..fleshed to the game T. ADAMS. **2.** Flesht and blooded in the slaughter of many thousands of the English nation 1646. Fleshing men in leudness and wickedness HY. MORE. **3.** Impatient strait to f. his virgin-sword POPE.

Flesh and blood. OE. [See prec. and BLOOD.] **1.** The body. **b.** Mankind, an individual man or men OE. **c.** Humanity 1450. **2.** (One's) near kindred ME. **3.** The plant *Potentilla tormentilla* 1853.

1. *In flesh and blood*: in a bodily form. *To take flesh and blood*: to become incarnate. **b.** *To be flesh and blood*: to have human feelings and weaknesses. **c.** Things which flesh and blood cannot bear DICKENS.

Fle·sh-colour. 1611. [f. FLESH *sb.* + COLOUR.] The colour of the flesh (of a 'white' human being) as seen through the skin; 'a light pink with a little yellow'. Hence **Fle·sh-coloured** *a.*

Fleshed (fleʃt), *ppl. a.* ME. [f. FLESH *sb.* and *v.* + -ED.] **1.** Clothed or furnished with flesh. **2.** [Cf. Fr. *acharné.*] Inured to bloodshed; initiated; animated by hatred 1591.

2. Flesht Villaines, bloody Dogges *Rich. III*, IV. iii. 6.

Flesher (fle·ʃəɹ). Chiefly *Sc.* ME. [f. FLESH *sb.* + -ER[1].] **1.** A butcher. **2.** *U.S.* A fleshing-knife 1885.

Fle·sh-fly. ME. [f. FLESH *sb.* + FLY *sb.*[1]] **1.** A fly which deposits its eggs (or larvæ) in dead flesh; a blow-fly. **2.** *fig.* of persons 1532.

2. These flesh-flies of the land, Who fasten without mercy on the fair COWPER.

Fle·shhood. *arch.* ME. [f. FLESH *sb.* + -HOOD.] The condition of being in the flesh; incarnation.

God..who hast thyself Endured this f. E.B. BROWNING.

Fleshiness (fle·ʃinės). ME. [f. FLESHY *a.* + -NESS.] The state of being fleshy; fullness of flesh; *concr.* a fleshy growth.

Fleshing (fle·ʃiŋ), *vbl. sb.* 1576. [f. FLESH *v.* and *sb.* + -ING[1].] **1.** The action of FLESH *v.* (sense 1). **2.** *Leather-manuf.* The action of scraping off the adhering flesh from a skin; also *pl.* that which is scraped off 1777. **3.** *pl.* Flesh-coloured tights, as worn upon the stage 1838.

Comb. **f.-knife,** a large two-handled implement with a blunt edge, used in fleshing skins.

Fleshless (fle·ʃlės), *a.* 1586. [f. FLESH *sb.* + -LESS.] Without flesh; lean.

Fleshliness (fle·ʃlinės). [OE. *flǣsclīcness*; see FLESHLY and -NESS.] **1.** †**a.** In OE.: Incarnate condition. **b.** Carnality ME. †**2.** Fleshiness –1611.

†**Fle·shling.** *rare.* 1548. [f. FLESH *sb.* + -LING[1]. Cf. *worldling.*] A fleshly-minded person.

Fleshly (fle·ʃli). [OE. *flǣsclīc*; see FLESH *sb.*, -LY[1].]

A. *adj.* **1.** Of or pertaining to the flesh, i.e. the body; = CARNAL. **2.** = FLESHY 1, 2. ME. †**3.** Of a hound: Fond of flesh. *rare.* 1576.

1. The fleschely arm WYCLIF. F. fansey 1550, lethargie 1602, reasonings CROMWELL. **2.** To fatt and fleshlye 1562. The f. heart of man MARLOWE. F. integuments KANE.

†**B.** *adv.* **1.** Corporeally; materially as opp. to spiritually –1635. **2.** Carnally, sensually –1612.

Fleshment (fle·ʃmĕnt). [f. FLESH *v.* + -MENT.] The action of 'fleshing'; hence, the excitement resulting from a first success. *Lear*, II. ii. 130.

†**Fle·shmonger.** OE. [See MONGER.] **1.** A butcher –1597. **2.** A fornicator, a pander –1624.

Fle·sh-pot. 1535. A pot in which flesh is boiled. Hence *pl.* Luxuries or advantages regarded with regret or envy.

Whan we sat by yͤ flesh pottes, and had bred ynough to eate COVERDALE *Exod.* 16:3.

Fleshy (fle·ʃi), *a.* ME. [f. FLESH *sb.* + -Y[1].] **1.** Well furnished with flesh; fat, plump. **2.** Of, pertaining to, or consisting of flesh; without bone ME. **b.** Of a plant, leaf, fruit, etc.: Pulpy, not fibrous 1577. †**3.** = CARNAL 1, 3. –1668. **4.** Resembling flesh 1555.

1. A fine, f., comfortable dame W. IRVING. **2.** F. morsels DRYDEN. The f. tabernacle HAWTHORNE. **b.** The whole body of the Figge is fleshie 1577. **3.** F. desires 1668. **4.** A fleshie taste 1665.

Fletch (fletʃ), *v.* 1635. [alt. of FLEDGE *v.* 4, which, however, is recorded much later.] *trans.* To fit (an arrow) with a feather. Also *fig.*

He..fletches them [his curses] with a prophane classical parody WARBURTON.

Fletcher (fle·tʃəɹ). ME. [– OFr. *flech(i)er*, f. *fleche* arrow, of unkn. origin; see -ER[2].] **1.** One who makes or deals in (bows and) arrows. *Obs.* exc. *Hist.* or *arch.* †**2.** A bowman MORE.

‖**Fleur** (flör). 1841. [Fr.] An ornamental flower. Hence **Fleured** *ppl. a.* adorned with a f. or fleurs.

Fleur-de-lis (flör də lī, līs), **flower-de-luce** (flauᵊ:ɹ dĭ lū·s). *Pl.* **fleurs-de-lis, -luce, flower de luces.** [Late ME. *flour de lys* – OFr. *flour de lys*, i.e. *flour* FLOWER, *de* of, *lis* (L. *lilium* lily); late ME. and early mod.E. *flower de lice* or *delice* (cf. AFr. pl. *fleurs delices* XIII) was assoc. w. a fanciful L. *flos deliciæ* 'flower of delight'. The Fr. form (= 'lily-flower') is scarcely found in Eng. before XIX. The form *flower-de-luce* now survives only as a poetical archaism and in *U.S.* It is prob. of fanciful origin.] **1.** The flower of a plant of the genus *Iris* (esp. *I. pseudacorus*); also, the plant. **2.** The heraldic lily; a device supposed by some to have represented an iris, by others the top of a sceptre, or that of a battle-axe, or other weapon ME. **b.** The royal arms of France; hence the French royal family, the French flag (before 1789), the French nation or government ME. **3.** The representation of a heraldic fleur-de-lis on any article. Also (*Fr. Hist.*) a brand-mark on a criminal 1475.

Fleuret[1] (flūᵊ·rėt), ‖**fleurette** (flöre·t). 1811. [– Fr. *fleurette*, dim. of *fleur* flower; see -ET.] An ornament like a small flower.

Fleuret[2]. 1648. [– Fr. *fleuret* (XVI) – It. *fioretto* in same sense, dim. of *fiore* flower.] *Fencing.* A fencing-foil.

‖**Fleuron** (flöroṅ). [In XIV *floroun* (Chaucer) – OFr. *floron* (mod. *fleuron*), f. *fleur* flower.] **1.** A flower-shaped ornament, used *esp.* in architecture or printing, on coins, etc. **2.** Puffs of pastry-work for garnishing 1724. Hence **Fleuronée** *a.* = BOTONÉ.

Fleury (flūᵊ·ri), **flory** (flōᵊ·ri), *a.* ME. [– OFr. *floré, flouré* (mod. *fleuré*), f. *fleur* flower; see -Y[5].] *Her.* Decorated with fleurs-de-lis; *esp.* of a cross: Having its arms tipped with fleurs-de-lis.

Flew (flū). 1575. [Of unkn. origin.] Usu. *pl.* The large chaps of a deep-mouthed hound (e.g. the bloodhound). Hence **Flewed** *ppl. a.* having flews (of a stated kind).

Flew, pa. t. of FLY *v.*

Flex (fleks), *sb.* 1907. [abbrev. of FLEXIBLE.] Flexible insulated wire.

Flex (fleks), *v.* 1521. [– *flex-*, pa. ppl. stem of L. *flectere* bend.] *trans.* To bend. Now *scientific.*

A single muscle..flexes the thigh 1845. Hence **Flexed** (flekst) *ppl. a.* bent; now only *Her.* and in scientific use.

Flex(e, obs. form of FLAX.

†**Flexa·nimous,** *a.* 1621. [f. L. *flexanimus*, f. *flex-* (see FLEX *v.*) + *animus* mind; see -OUS.] Having power to bend or influence the mind –1672.

Flexibility (fleksibi·lĭti). 1616. [– Fr. *flexibilité* or late L. *flexibilitas*, f. L. *flexibilis*; see next, -ITY.] **1.** The quality of being flexible; pliancy 1616; adaptability; freedom from stiffness or rigidity 1783. **2.** Of the voice or fingers: Capacity for rapid and varied execution or delivery. Also *pl.* 1795.

1. The f. and instability of that gentleman's nature CLARENDON. F. of limb 1859, of intelligence 1865. **2.** F. of throat 1795.

Flexible (fle·ksib'l), *a.* ME. [– (O)Fr. *flexible* or L. *flexibilis*, f. as prec.; see -IBLE.] **1.** Capable of being bent, admitting of change in figure without breaking; yielding to pressure, pliable, pliant 1548. **2.** Willing or disposed to yield to influence or persuasion; easily led, tractable ME. **3.** Capable of modification or adaptation; pliant, supple 1643.

1. When the splitting winde Makes f. the knees of knotted Oakes SHAKS. **2.** Our judge, therefore, must not be partial, f., nor ignorant 1533. The tender and f. age of her son 1642. **3.** A more f. rule of judgement 1841. F. politics SYD. SMITH. Hence **Fle·xibleness,** flexibility. **Fle·xibly** *adv.*

Flexile (fle·ksil), *a.* Now *rare.* 1633. [– L. *flexilis*, f. as prec.; see -ILE.] **1.** Easily bending or bent, pliant, supple, flexible. Of the features: Mobile. **2.** *transf.* and *fig.* **a.** Yielding, tractable 1651. **b.** Versatile 1744.

Flexion, flection (fle·kʃən). 1603. [– L. *flexio*, f. *flex-*; see prec., -ION. The sp. *flection* (XVIII) is on the anal. of words like *direction*, etc.] **1.** The action of bending, curvature; bent condition; an instance of this 1656. **b.** *esp.* The bending of a limb or joint by the action of the flexor muscles. Cf. EXTENSION. 1615. **2.** †Alteration, change, modification –1655; inflexion 1758. **3.** *concr.* A bend, curve. Also, a joint. 1670. **4.** *Gram.* Modification of the form of a word; = INFLEXION 4. 1605.

2. Flections and intonations of the voice GROTE. **4.** The f. or conjugation of the verb DE FOE.

Hence **Fle·xional, flect-** *a.* of, pertaining to, or of the nature of f., *esp.* in *Grammar.* Also, of a language: Possessed of, or based upon flexions. **Fle·xionless, flect-** *a.* devoid of f. or flexions; only in grammatical sense.

†**Fle·xive,** *a.* 1629. [f. L. *flex-*; see prec., -IVE.] Tending to bend, flexible –1791.

Flexor (fle·ksəɹ). 1615. [– mod.L. *flexor*, f. as prec. + -OR 2.] A muscle whose function it is to produce flexion in any part of the body; as, the *flexors* of the abdomen. Opp. to *extensor.*

Flexuose (fleksiu,ōᵘ·s), *a.* 1727. [– L. *flexuosus*, f. *flexus* a bending, f. as prec.; see -OSE[1].] *Bot.* Winding in and out, undulating, crooked. Hence **Flexuo·sity,** f. quality; a winding.

Flexuoso-, comb. form of FLEXUOSE or FLEXUOUS, indicating a flexuous form or arrangement.

Flexuous (fle·ksiu,əs), *a.* 1605. [f. as FLEXUOSE + -OUS; see -UOUS.] **1.** Full of bends or curves; winding, sinuous. Now chiefly of animal and vegetable structures. **2.** Moving in bends or waves. *rare.* 1626.

2. The F. Burning of Flames BACON.

Flexure (fle·ksiŭɹ). 1592. [– L. *flexura*, f. *flex-*; see prec., -URE.] **1.** The action of flexing or bending; curvature; an instance of this. **2.** Flexed or bent condition; bent figure or posture; bending, or winding form 1628. **3.** Flexibility 1651. **4.** *concr.* Anything of bent shape; a bend, curve, turn, winding 1607. **5.** *Math.* The bending or curvature of a line, surface, or solid 1672. **6.** *Geol.* A bending of strata under pressure 1833.

1. There's those are made For f., let them stoope 1592. **2.** The details..of giving f. to the rivers, [etc.] 1826. **4.** Now the last f. of our way we reach'd CARY. **5.** *F. of a curve*: its bending towards or from a straight line. Hence **Fle·xural** *a.* of or relating to f.

Flibbertigibbet (fli·bəɹti,dʒi:bėt). 1549. [orig. *flibbergib*; prob. imit. of unmeaning chatter.] **1.** A gossip; a flighty woman. **2.** The name of a fiend (*Lear* III. iv. 120); applied in Scott's *Kenilworth* to a mischievous and flighty urchin 1603.

Flibustier, var. of FILIBUSTER *sb.*

‖**Flicflac.** [Fr.; imit. of a succession of sharp sounds.] A kind of step in dancing. THACKERAY.

Flick (flik), *sb.*[1] ME. [imit.] **1.** A light blow, e.g. one given with a whip; also, a jerk. **2.** The sound of this; hence, any slight, sharp sound 1844. **3.** *concr.* Something thrown off with a jerk; a dash, splash 1848. **4.** *pl.* The cinema (*slang*) 1926.

Flick, *sb.*[2] *dial.* = FLECK *sb.*[2]

Flick (flik), *v.*[1] *Cant.* 1677. [prob. a dial var. of FLITCH *v.*] To cut.

Flick (flik), *v.*[2] 1816. [f. FLICK *sb.*[1]] **1.** *trans.* To strike lightly with something flexible, as a whip 1838. **2.** To remove with a smart stroke of something flexible 1847. **b.** To jerk (*off*, etc.) 1816. **3.** *intr.* To move with quick vibrations; to flutter 1853. **4.** *trans.* To move or shake with a flick 1844.

1. Flicking each other with our towels 1875. **2. b.** Spots of ink flicked at random out of a pen PEACOCK. **4.** I was afraid of flicking my line into my host's eye 1877.

Flicker (fli·kəɹ), *sb.*[1] 1849. [f. FLICKER *v.*] **1.** A flickering movement 1857. **2.** A wavering unsteady light or flame. Also *fig.*

2. The last cold f. of twilight 1862. *fig.* This little f. of enthusiasm KANE.

Flicker (fli·kəɹ), *sb.*[2] *U.S.* 1849. [imit. of the bird's note.] A name of various species of woodpecker; *esp.* the yellow-shafted woodpecker (*Colaptes auratus*).

The flicker's cackle is heard in the clearing THOREAU.

Flicker (fli·kəɹ), *v.* [OE. *flicorian, flycerian* (cf. LG. *flickern*, Du. *flikkeren*), synon. in its earliest use with ME. *flakere*, dial. *flacker*; see FLACKER *v.*] **1.** *intr.* Of a bird: To flutter or hover; *occas.*, to flap the wings. †**2.** To caress; hence, to dally, hanker, look longingly (after) –1806. **3.** To wave to and fro; to flutter; to quiver, vibrate, undulate 1450. **4.** To flash up and die away by turns. Of a flame: To burn fitfully. (The prevailing sense.) Also *transf.* and *fig.* 1605.

1. Above hir heed her dowves flikeringe CHAUCER. **3.** The high masts flicker'd as they lay afloat TENNYSON. **4.** Sheet lightning, flickering harmlessly in the distance FROUDE. The fire.. flickers low 1871. Hence **Fli·ckeringly** *adv.*

†**Fli·ckermouse.** 1630. [alt. f. FLITTERMOUSE.] A bat –1708.

Flidge, obs. f. FLEDGE.

Flier, alternative f. FLYER.

Flight (fləit), *sb.*[1] [OE. *flyht*, corresp. to OS. *fluht*, (M)Du. *vlucht* :– WGmc. **fluχti*, f. weak grade of Gmc. **fleuʒan* FLY *v.*[1]] **1.** The action or manner of flying or moving through the air with or as with wings. **b.** *Falconry.* Pursuit of game, etc. by a hawk; also, the quarry flown at 1530. **2.** Swift movement, e.g. of a projectile ME. **3.** *fig.* A mounting or soaring; an excursion or sally (of the imagination, wit, ambition, caprice, etc.) 1668. **4.** The flight feathers 1735. **5.** The distance which a bird can or does fly; also *fig.* and *transf.* 1600. **6.** The series of stairs between any two landings; also *transf.* of terraces, locks, etc. 1703. **7.** A number of beings or things flying in or passing through the air together ME. **8.** The young birds that take wing at one time 1577. **9.** A flight-arrow (see *Comb.*) 1464; also = FLIGHT-SHOOTING 1557. **10.** The husk or glume of oats 1831. **11.** *Naut.* = FLY-BOAT. 1769. **12.** *Angling.* The set of fish-hooks in a spinning-trace 1865.

1. c. A Royal Air Force unit consisting of about five or six machines 1914. **2.** The f. of a Javelin POPE, of years YOUNG, of ships SHELLEY, of clouds RUSKIN. **3.** Old Pindar's flights DENHAM. Speculative flights LAW. **5.** Within an eagle's f. S. ROGERS. Phr. *F. of a shot*: 'the trajectory formed between the muzzle of a gun and the first graze' (Smyth). **7.** A f. of flies 1556, of angels HAWTHORNE, of arrows TENNYSON. Phr. *In the first f.* (colloq.): in the van. **8.** The March f. of pigeons 1897. **9.** *Much Ado* I. i. 40.

Comb.: In titles of officers of various ranks in the Royal Air Force, as *F. Commander, F. Lieutenant*; **f.-arrow,** a light and well-feathered arrow for long-distance shooting; **-feather,** one of the wing-feathers on which power of f. depends.

Flight (fləit), *sb.*[2] [OE. **flyht* = OFris. *flecht*, OS., OHG. *fluht* (Du. *vlucht*, G. *flucht*), ON. *flótti* :– Gmc. **pluχtiz*, f. weak grade of **pleuχan* FLEE.] The action of fleeing or running away from or as from danger, etc.; hasty departure ME.

Pray ye that your f. be not in the winter *Matt.* 24:20. To seek safety in f. 1760. Phr. *To put to f.*

†**Flight,** *a.* 1581. [f. FLIGHT *sb.*[1]] Swift, fleet –1642.

Flight (fləit), *v.* 1571. [f. FLIGHT *sb.*[1], [2].] **1.** *trans.* To put to flight; hence, to frighten. **2.** †To migrate; = FLIT –1752; also, to fly in flights 1879. **3.** To feather (an arrow) 1869.

Flighted (fləi·tėd), *ppl. a.* 1634. [f. FLIGHT *sb.*[1] + -ED[2].] **1.** Having a certain flight. Only in *drowsy-f.* MILT. **2.** Feathered 1735.

Flighter (fləi·təɹ). 1825. [Earliest form *flichters* (Jamieson), perh. rel. to Sc. dial. *flichter* flutter, move through the air.] *Brewing.* 'A horizontal vane revolving over the surface of wort in a cooler, to produce a circular current in the liquor' (Knight).

Fli·ght-shooting, *vbl. sb.* 1801. [f. FLIGHT *sb.*[1] + SHOOTING *vbl. sb.*] **1.** *Archery.* Distance-shooting with flight-arrows. **2.** Shooting wild-fowl as they fly over 1840.

Fli·ght-shot. 1455. [f. FLIGHT *sb.*[1] + SHOT *sb.*] **1.** The distance to which a flight-arrow is shot, a bow-shot. **2.** A shot taken at wild-fowl in flight 1887.

1. Some two flight-shoot to th' Alehouse J. TAYLOR.

Flighty (fləi·ti), *a.* 1552. [f. FLIGHT *sb.*[1] + -Y[1].] **1.** Swift, fleet. *rare.* **2.** Given to flights of imagination, humour, caprice, etc.; guided by whim or fancy; fickle, frivolous. Of a horse: Skittish. 1768. **3.** Light-headed. Also *absol.* 1802.

1. The f. purpose neuer is o're-tooke Vnlesse the deed go with it *Macb.* IV. i. 145. **2.** A f. gossiping damsel 1878. Hence **Fli·ghtily** *adv.* **Fli·ghtiness.**

Flim-flam (fli·mflæm). 1538. [Symbolic redupl. formation with vowel variation; cf. WHIM-WHAM.]

A. *sb.* **1.** A piece of nonsense 1546. **2.** A paltry trick or pretence 1538. **3.** *collect.* Nonsense; humbug, deception 1570.

3. I tell thee 'tis all flim-flam FIELDING.

B. *adj.* Frivolous, nonsensical; also deceptive, sham 1577.

Flimsy (fli·mzi). 1702. [prob. based on FLIM-FLAM; see -SY.]

A. *adj.* **1.** Without strength or solidity; easily destroyed; slight, unsubstantial. †Of persons, etc.: Frail, delicate –1753. **2.** Without solid value, slight, trivial; frivolous, trifling, superficial 1827.

1. As fine As bloated spiders draw the f. line COWPER. I have a very f. constitution H. WALPOLE. **2.** A f. hypothesis learnt from Bolingbroke L. STEPHEN.

B. *sb.* **1.** *slang.* A bank-note 1824. **2.** Thin or transfer paper; hence, reporters' copy 1859. Hence **Fli·msily** *adv.* **Fli·msiness.**

Flinch (flinʃ), *v.* Also †**flench.** 1563. [– OFr. *flenchir, flainchir* turn aside – WGmc. **χlaŋkjan*, whence (M)HG. *lenken* bend, turn.] **1.** *intr.* To give way, draw back, yield ground. In later use: To shrink *from* something as dangerous, painful, or difficult 1579. †**2.** To slink, sneak off –1622. **3.** To shrink under pain; to wince 1677; to BLENCH 1883. **4.** quasi-*trans.* To withdraw from, lose (one's ground) 1674.

1. The peasants withstood without flinching several attacks in front ALISON. **3.** A child.. may..be accustom'd to bear very..rough usage without flinching LOCKE. Hence **Flinch** *sb.* the action of flinching. **Fli·ncher,** one who flinches or shrinks *from* (an undertaking, etc.); one who passes the bottle. **Fli·nchingly** *adv.*

Flinder-mouse (fli·ndəɹ,mous). Now *dial.* 1481. [f. ME. *vlindre* (= mod. Du. *vlinder*, butterfly) + MOUSE.] A bat. Cf. FLITTER-MOUSE.

Flinders (fli·ndəɹz), *sb. pl.* rarely *sing.* 1450. [prob. of Scand. origin; cf. Norw. *flindra* thin chip or splinter.] Fragments, pieces, splinters. Chiefly in phrases, as *to break* or *fly in(to flinders.*

Fling (fliŋ), *sb.* 1550. [f. next vb.] **1.** An act of flinging; a cast, throw 1589. **2.** *fig.* A passing attempt at or attack upon something; also, a gibe, scoff 1550. **3.** A hasty, reckless, or wanton movement; a rush. *lit.* and *fig.* Now *rare.* 1556. **4.** A flinging about of the body or limbs; *esp.* in the dance called *the Highland f.* 1806. **b.** A plunge; of a horse: A kicking out 1568. **5.** A fit or spell of unrestrained indulgence of one's impulses 1827. †**6.** 'A thing of nought.' FULLER.

2. A f. at the Ægyptian crowne GREENE, at the clergy 1760. **4.** Highlanders..dancing the f. to the music of the bagpipe 1806. **5.** I should like to have my f. out before I marry THACKERAY.

Fling (fliŋ), *v. Pa. t.* and *pple.* **flung** (flɒŋ). ME. [perh. – unrecorded ON. **flinga*, rel. to *flengja* (Sw. *flänga*, Da. *flænge*) flog, but the sense is remote.]

I. *intr.* **1.** To move with haste or violence from or towards an object; to dash, rush. **2.** Of a horse, etc.: To kick and plunge violently, to be unruly or restive ME. **b.** Similarly of persons. Also, *to f. out*: to break out into invective or complaint. 1531. **3.** *Sc.* To caper, dance 1528.

1. He flung from me like a whirlwind GALT. As sword that, after battle, flings to sheath MRS. BROWNING. **2.** A Colt, giue him the bridle, he flinges about GOSSON.

II. *trans.* **1.** To throw, cast, toss, hurl; *esp.* to throw with violence or hostile intent ME. Also *absol.* **2.** *refl.* = sense I. 1. Also *fig.* 1700. **3.** To extend (one's arms) with a sudden movement; *transf.* of a plant, etc. Also, to kick *up* (one's heels), *etc.* 1657. **4.** To cast scornfully (one's eyes, etc.) in a certain direction 1654. **5.** To emit, send forth, give out, diffuse 1632. **6.** To throw down; *spec.* in wrestling. Of a horse: To throw off (his rider). Also *fig.* To give a fall to. 1790.

1. Who loues the King..F. vp his cap SHAKS. F. dirt enough and some will stick 1706. **3.** The young colt..flung up her heels TENNYSON. **5.** West winds..About the cedarn allies f. Nard and casia's balmy smells MILT. *Comus* 989. **6.** His horse started, flung him, and fell upon him H. WALPOLE.

Phrases. *To f. aside*, to disregard, reject. *To f. away*, to discard, dismiss; to throw away, squander. *To f. down*, to throw on the ground, overthrow, demolish. *To f. off*, to abandon, disown; to throw off the scent. *To f. up*, to throw up (an earthwork); to give up, abandon; also (*dial.*) to rake up and utter as a reproach. *To f. in one's teeth*: see CAST *v.* *To f. open*, to open suddenly and violently; similarly, *to f. to*, to shut suddenly or forcibly.

Comb. **f.-dust, -stink,** a street-walker, a harlot. Hence **Fli·nger,** one who flings; (*intr.*) a dancer; (of a horse) a kicker; (*trans.*) one who throws.

Flint (flint), *sb.* [OE. *flint* = MDu. *vlint*, rel. to OHG. (G. dial.) *flins* and perh. to Gr. πλίνθος, tile (see PLINTH).] **1.** A hard stone, most commonly of a steely grey colour, found in roundish nodules, usually covered with a white incrustation. It is one of the purest native forms of silica. In early use, any hard stone. Also *transf.* OE. **b.** As a type of anything hard and unyielding ME. **2.** A piece of this stone, as giving off sparks when struck with iron or steel OE. **3.** A nodule or pebble of flint ME.

1. Arrow-heads of f. LONGF. **b.** Callum, f. to other considerations, was penetrable to superstition SCOTT. **2.** Sparks struck from a Flint and a Steel 1665. The F. of the Pistol failed 1679.

Phr. *To skin a f.*, a hyperbolical exemplification of avarice.

Comb.: **f.-flake,** a flake or chip of f. used in prehistoric times as a cutting instrument; **-gravel,** gravel containing flints; **-gun,** a gun with a flint-lock; **-head,** an arrow-head made of f.; †**-heart** *a.* = next; **-hearted** *a.*, hard-hearted; **-mill,** (*a*) *Pottery*, a mill in which flints are ground to powder for mixing with clay; (*b*) *Mining*, 'a mode formerly adopted for lighting mines, in which flints studded on the surface of a wheel were made to strike against a steel and give a quick succession of sparks' (Knight); **-rope,** the stem of the sponge *Hyalonema sieboldii* (Cass.); **-skinning,** *fig.* parsimonious saving; **-wall,** 'a wall made of broken flints set in mortar, and with quoins of masonry' (Knight); **-ware,** U.S. name for STONEWARE, q.v.; **-wood,** a name in N.S. Wales for *Eucalyptus pilularis*; †**-wort,** a name for aconite, as growing on bare rocks (*nudis cautibus*), according to Pliny.

Flint (flint), *v.* 1803. [f. prec. sb.] To provide with a flint or flints; also, to pave with flints.

Flint-glass. 1675. **1.** A pure lustrous glass, now made from a composition of lead oxide, sand, and alkali; originally made with ground flint or pebble as the siliceous ingredient 1683. †**2.** An article made of this glass –1766. **3.** *attrib.* 1683.

1. A Pipe made of Chrystal, or Flint-Glass 1683.

Fli·nt-lock. 1683. [See LOCK *sb.*[2] I. 5.] **a.** A gunlock in which a flint, screwed to the cock, is struck against the hammer and produces sparks which ignite the priming. Also *attrib.* **b.** A gun fitted with this lock.

Fli·ntstone. ME. [f. FLINT *sb.* + STONE.] = FLINT *sb.*

Flinty (fli·nti), *a.* 1542. [f. FLINT *sb.* + -Y[1].] **1.** Of, consisting of, or derived from flint; containing flint-stones 1591. **2.** Resembling flint 1542. **3.** *fig.* Obdurate, harsh 1536.

1. F. bulwarkes SHAKS., gravel BACON. **3.** The f. heart of base self-interest BURKE. Hence **Fli·ntily** *adv.* **Fli·ntiness. Fli·nty-hearted** *a.* having a hard heart or core.

Flip (flip), *sb.*[1] 1682. [perh. f. FLIP *v.* with the notion of 'whipping up' into froth.] †**1.** The slimy scum rising to the surface of salt-pans. **2.** A mixture of beer and spirit sweetened with sugar and heated with a hot iron. (Cf. *egg-flip*.) 1695.

Comb. **f.-dog,** an iron heated to warm f.

Flip (flip), *sb.*[2] 1692. [f. FLIP *v.*] **1.** A smart stroke or blow. Also *fig.* **2.** A sudden jerk or movement 1821. **3.** A flight in aircraft (*colloq.* or *slang*) 1914.

Flip (flip), *v.* 1594. [prob. contr. of FILLIP *v.*; but cf. FLIP-FLAP.] **1.** To put into motion with a flip; to toss (a coin) 1616. **2.** To move with a flip or jerk. *trans.* and *intr.* 1712. **3.** *trans.* and *intr.* To strike smartly and lightly (*at*) 1861.

1. Flipping the ash from his cigarette 1885.

Flipe (fləip), *v.* Chiefly *Sc.* ME. [Cf. MDa. *flippe* vb. skin; also north. dial. *flipe* sb. fold or flap, thin piece.] **1.** *trans.* To peel, flay. Now *dial.* †**2.** To turn up or down, fold back; also, to turn inside out –1788.

Flip-flap (fli·pflæp). 1529. [redupl. formation on FLAP.] **A.** *adv.* With a repeated flapping movement 1583.

B. *sb.* †**1.** Something that 'goes flip-flap', e.g. a hanging piece of cloth, a fan –1611. **2.** *slang.* **a.** A kind of somersault; also, a costers' dance 1676. **b.** *Fireworks.* A cracker 1885. **c.** In a place of amusement, a machine with passenger cars hung at the ends of horizontal rotating arms 1908. **3.** *U.S.* A kind of tea-cake 1876.

3. Dough-nuts and flipflaps 1876.

C. *adj.* That 'goes flip-flap' 1841.

Flippancy (fli·pănsi). 1746. [f. next; see -ANCY.] The quality of being FLIPPANT.

Flippant (fli·pănt), *a.* 1605. [f. FLIP *v.* 2 + -ANT, perh. in imitation of heraldic adjs., as *couchant*, etc.] †**1.** Moving lightly or alertly; pliant, flexible, limber –1677.† **2.** Of the tongue: Nimble, voluble. Hence of persons and of conversation: Fluent, voluble. –1794. †**3.** Sportive, playful –1784. **4.** Displaying unbecoming levity 1724. **5.** *absol.* A flippant person 1791.

1. A bird of the flippantst wing 1622. **2.** She was wise, a most f. tongue she had CHAPMAN. **3.** The squirrel, f., pert, and full of play COWPER. **4.** Sherlock's f. but entertaining letters MME. D'ARBLAY.

Hence **Fli·ppant-ly** *adv.*, **-ness.**

Flipper (fli·pəɹ), *sb.* 1822. [f. FLIP *v.* + -ER[1].] **1.** A limb used to swim with; e.g. any limb in a turtle, a seal, or a walrus; the fore-limb of a cetacean; the wing of a penguin; the fin of a fish. **2.** *transf.* The hand 1832. **3.** *Theat.* 'Part of a scene, hinged and painted on both sides, used in trick changes' (Farmer).

Flirt (flɜ̄ɹt), *sb.* 1549. [app. an imit. formation; cf. *flick, flip,* and *spurt, squirt.* So the verb.] **1.** A rap, fillip. Now *dial.* 1577. **2.** A sudden jerk, a quick throw or cast, a darting motion 1590. †**3.** A jest; a gibe –1726. †**4.** 'A pert young hussey' (J.) –1774. **5.** One who FLIRTS (sense 6); also, a person to flirt with 1732. **6.** *Watchmaking.* 'A lever or other device for causing sudden movement of mechanism' (Britten) 1786.

2. Hedge-sparrows have a remarkable f. with their wings G. WHITE. **4.** My aunt told me she was a forward f. JOHNSON. **5.** A f. too, in the worst and meanest degree of flirtation JANE AUSTEN. General Tufto is a great f. of mine THACKERAY.

Flirt (flɜ̄ɹt), *v.* 1553. [Goes with FLIRT *sb.*] **1.** *trans.* To throw or propel with a jerk or sudden movement. Cf. FILLIP *v.* 1583. †**2.** To rap, fillip –1631. **3.** To give a brisk, sudden motion to; to flick 1665. †**4. a.** *intr.* To turn up one's nose; hence, to sneer, gibe, scoff *at* –1734. †Also *trans.* –1686. **5.** *intr.* To move with a jerk or spring; to spring, dart 1583. †Also *fig.* **6.** To play at courtship; practise coquetry. Often *to f. with* (a person). 1777. **b.** To play, trifle *with* (something) 1859.

1. To f. inke in everie mans face DEKKER. **3.** Those birds which have a habit of flirting up the tail 1834. *To f. a fan*: to open and shut it with a jerk, to wave it smartly. **6.** Every man likes to f. with a pretty girl, and every pretty girl likes to be flirted with GEO. ELIOT. Hence **Fli·rter. Fli·rtingly** *adv.*

Flirtation (flɜɹtēi·ʃən). 1718. [f. prec. + -ATION.] †**1.** 'A quick, sprightly motion. A cant word among women.' (J.) 1737. **2.** The action or behaviour of a flirt; †frivolity; playing at courtship. Also *transf.* and *fig.* 1718.

2. The great art of f. 1876. *transf.* The flirtations ..between Mr. Pitt and Ld. Loughborough 1792.

Flirtatious (flɜɹtēi·ʃəs), *a.* 1834. [irreg. f. prec. + -OUS, on anal. of *ambition, ambitious*; see -TIOUS.] Given to flirtation; of the nature of flirtation.

Hence **Flirta·tious-ly** *adv.*, **-ness.**

†**Flirt-gill** (-dʒil). Also **-gillian.** 1592. [f. FLIRT *sb.* or *v.* + GILL nickname for *Juliana.*] A woman of light behaviour. Cf. GILL-FLIRT.

I am none of his flurt-gils *Rom. & Jul.* II. iv. 162.

Flirtigig, -gigs (flɜ̄·ɹtigig(z). *dial.* 1683. [f. FLIRT *v.* + GIG *sb.*[1]; cf. *whirligig.*] A giddy, flighty girl.

Flisk (flisk), *sb. dial.* 1818. [f. next.] **1.** A whim, a freak. *Sc.* **2.** A fillip with the finger 1891.

Flisk (flisk), *v.* Now *dial.* 1596. [imit.; cf. *whisk.*] **1.** To frisk, caper. **2.** *trans.* To put out, displease 1792. **3.** To flick 1847.

1. To flit away the flisking flies GOSSON. Hence **Fli·sky** *a.* frolicsome; skittish.

Flit (flit), *sb.* 1835. [f. FLIT *v.*] **a.** A removal. **b.** A flutter; a light touch 1873.

†**Flit,** *a. poet.* 1590. [var. of FLEET *a.*, influenced by FLIT *v.* Cf. also FLIGHT *a.*] **a.** Swift, quickly-moving –1600. **b.** Fleeting; airy, unsubstantial –1633.

a. Now, like a stag; now, like a faulcon f. SPENSER.

Flit (flit), *v.* [ME. *flitte(n)*, *flutte(n)* – ON. *flytja*, f. **flut-*, weak grade of the base of *fljóta*; see FLEET *v.*[1]] **1.** *trans.* To remove to another place. †**2.** To get rid of; to drive *away* –1596. **3.** *intr.* To shift one's position; to be gone, depart, pass away ME. **4.** *intr.* To remove from one habitation to another. Chiefly *north.* or *Sc.* 1504. †**5.** To change; to alter, shift about, give way –1816. **b.** Of a flame: To die down 1839. **6.** To move along, pass, proceed; to fly or pass lightly and swiftly. Also, to flutter. ME.

2. Fannes..To f. away the flisking flies GOSSON. **3.** To f. owt of this lyfe 1619. **5.** God..that may not chaunge and flitte CHAUCER. **b.** Like a candle..flitting and flaring alternately MARRYAT. **6.** Postmen..f. to and fro DICKENS. A shadow flits before me TENNYSON. So smoothly o'er our heads the days did f. MORRIS.

Hence †**Flit,** †**Fli·tten** *ppl. a.* that has gone away. **Fli·tting-ly** *adv.*

Flitch (flitʃ), *sb.* [OE. *flićće*, corresp. to MLG. *vli(c)ke*, ON. *flikki* (whence dial. *flick* from XV) :– Gmc. **flikkjam*, f. **flīk-*, as in ON. *flik* rag.] **1.** The side of an animal, now only of a hog, salted and cured; a 'side' of bacon. **2. a.** A square piece of blubber from a whale 1787. **b.** A steak cut from a halibut 1884. **3.** A slice, cut lengthways from the trunk of a tree 1823. **b.** One of several planks fastened side by side to form a compound beam 1874.

Comb. **f.-beam,** 'a beam made in layers of material pinned together' (Knight).

Flitch (flitʃ), *v.* 1875. [f. prec.] *trans.* To cut into flitches; to cut as a flitch is cut.

Flite, flyte (fləit), *v.* Now *dial.* [OE. *flītan* = OS. *andflītan* contend, OHG. *flīʒ(ʒ)an* strive (G. *sich befleissen* busy oneself).] †**1.** *intr.* To contend, strive; to wrangle –1725. **2.** To scold. Const. *at.* 1500. Also *trans.* **3.** *intr.* To debate ME. †**4.** To complain –1585.

Flitter (fli·təɹ), *sb.*[1] 1820. [f. FLITTER *v.*] A flittering motion. *Comb.* **f.-winged** *a.* having wings that flutter.

Flitter (fli·təɹ), *sb.*[2] 18... [– G. *flitter.*] A minute square of thin metal, used in decoration. Also *collect.*

Flitter (fli·təɹ), *v.* 1542. [f. FLIT *v.* + -ER[5].] **1.** *intr.* Of birds, etc.: To flit about; to flutter 1563. †**2.** Of a flower: To fade, wither –1847. †**3.** To fly all about –1677. **4.** *trans.* To make to flit; to shuffle (cards). *rare.* 1864.

Flitter-mouse (fli·təɹmaus). 1547. [f. FLITTER *v.* + MOUSE, after Du. *vledermuis* or G. *fledermaus.* Cf. FLICKER-, FLINDERMOUSE.] A bat.

Fli·ttern. 1682. [app. rel. to next.] A young oak tree; †also, a strip of its wood. *Comb.*: **f.-bark,** the bark of young oak trees.

Fli·tters, *sb. pl.* Now *dial.* 1620. [alt. f. FITTERS, assoc. w. FLITTER *v.*] Fragments; splinters, tatters.

Flitting (fli·tiŋ), *vbl. sb.* ME. [f. FLIT *v.* + -ING[1].] **1.** The action of FLIT *v.* **2.** *esp.* A removal from one abode to another. Chiefly *north*, and *Sc.* ME.

2. Phr. *Moonlight f.*: removal by moonlight, i.e. by night or by stealth.

†**Fli·tty,** *a.* [f. FLIT *v.* + -Y[1].] Unstable, flighty. HENRY MORE.

Flivver (fli·vəɹ). orig. *U.S. slang.* 1920. [Of unkn. origin.] A cheap motor car or aeroplane.

Flix (fliks). 1666. [Of unkn. origin.] Fur; the down of a beaver.

Flix, obs. f. FLUX.

†**Flo.** *Pl.* **flon.** [OE. *flā*, rel. to *flān* (= ON. *fleinn*), whence Sc. †*flane.*] An arrow –1450.

Float (flōᵘt), *sb.* [(1) OE. *flot* floating = ON. *flot*; (2) OE. *flota* ship, fleet = ON. *floti*; various mod. uses are f. the vb.]

I. 1. The action or condition of floating; *esp.* in phr. *on* (rarely *at*) *f.* = AFLOAT. Now *rare.* †**2.** The flux of the tide. *lit.* and *fig.* –1797. †**3.** A wave, billow. *lit* and *fig.* Also, the sea. –1655. †**4.** An overflow; a flood. *lit.* and *fig.* –1763.

1. And now the sharp keel of his little boat Comes up with ripple and with easy f. KEATS. **2.** Hee being now in F. (= at high water) for Treasure BACON. **3.** *Temp.* I. ii. 234.

II. A floating object. **1.** A mass of weeds, ice, etc. floating on the water 1600. **2.** A raft or raft-like construction 1535; a flat-bottomed boat 1557. **3.** Any floating appliance for supporting something in the water; e.g. the cork or quill attached to a fishing-line to show by its movement when a fish bites ME.; the cork used to support a fishing net, etc. in the water 1577; a hollow or inflated part or organ that supports an animal in the water 1832; an inflated bag or pillow to sustain a person in the water 1874; a structure fitted to a flying machine to enable it to float on water 1897. **4.** A hollow metallic ball, or the like, used to regulate the water-level in a boiler or tank 1752. **5.** *Theatr. pl.* The footlights; *sing.* a row of footlights 1862. **6.** A float-board (see *Comb.*) 1611.

III. 1. Something broad, level, and shallow; *esp.* a low-bodied cart for carrying heavy articles, live stock, etc. 1866. †**2.** A unit of measurement for embanking work 1707.

2. [Banks] are measured by the F. or Floor, which is eighteen foot square, and one deep MORTIMER.

IV. 1. A tool for floating or making level; e.g. in *Plastering*, a trowel or rule for giving a plane surface to the plaster 1703; a single-cut file 1750; a **polishing-block** used in marble-working; the serrated plate used by shoemakers for rasping off the ends of the pegs inside the boot or shoe 1874. **2.** A dock or place where vessels may float 1840. **3.** One of the trenches used in 'floating' land 1785. **4.** *Geol.* and *Mining.* Loose rock brought down by water from its original formation. Also short for *f.-ore* (see *Comb.*). Chiefly *U.S.* 1814. **5.** *Weaving.* The passing of weft-threads over a portion of the warp without being interwoven with it; also, the mass of thread so passed 1863.

Comb.: **f.-ball,** the ball of a ball-cock; **-board,** one of the boards of an undershot water-wheel, one of the paddles of a paddle-wheel; **-case,** a CAISSON or CAMEL; **-copper** (see *float-mineral*); **-file,** a single-cut file; **-gauge,** a water gauge, where the height of water in a steam-boiler is registered by means of a f.; **-gold** (see *float-mineral*); **-ironed** *a.*, ironed by a machine having springs and resilient padding to the rollers; **-mineral,** fragments of ore detached and carried away by the action of water or by erosion; also, fine particles of metal which are detached in the process of stamping and do not readily settle in water; **-ore, -quartz** (see *f.-mineral*); **-valve,** a valve actuated by a f.

Float (flōᵘt), *v. Pa. t.* and *pple.* **floated.** [Late OE. *flotian* = OS. *floton* (MDu. *vlōten*), ON. *flota* :- Gmc. **flotojan*, f. **flot-*, weak grade of base of FLEET *v.*[1] Reinforced in ME. by, if not entirely due to, OFr. *floter* (mod. *flotter*) :- Rom. **flottare*, prob. – Gmc. **flot-*.]

I. *intr.* **1.** To rest on the surface of any liquid; to be buoyed up; to be or become buoyant. **2.** To move quietly and gently on the surface of a liquid, participating in its motion ME. **3.** To be suspended *in* a liquid with freedom to move; to swim 1596. **4.** To move freely and gently in or through the air, as if buoyed up or carried along by it. Also *fig.* 1634. **5.** *Weaving.* Of a thread: To pass over or under several threads either of the warp or weft, instead of being interwoven with them 1878. **6.** *Comm.* Of an acceptance: To be in circulation 1778. **b.** Of a company, etc.: To get floated (see III. 3) 1884.

1. Her timbers yet are sound, And she may f. again COWPER. **2.** The boat floating near to him, he seized hold of it W. IRVING. *fig.* The vulgar f. as passion drives YOUNG. **4.** The clouds that flit, or slowly f. away COWPER. *fig.* Here floated the latest anecdote of Bolivar DISRAELI.

II. *trans.* **1.** To cover or flood with a liquid; also *transf.* and *fig.* 1586. **2.** To cause to float; to cause to rest or move on the surface of a fluid; also *fig.* 1606. **3.** To get (a company, scheme, etc.) afloat or fully started; to procure public support for 1883. **4.** To convey by or along the surface of water 1739. **5.** *techn.* **a.** To levigate (pigments) by causing them to float in a stream of water 1883. **b.** *Electrotyping* and *Stereotyping.* To cover (a forme, a page of type) with fluid plaster of Paris, either to fill up spaces, or to form a plaster mould 1880. **6.** To render smooth and level. **a.** *Plastering.* To level (the surface of plaster) with a float 1703. **b.** *Farriery.* To file the teeth of (a horse) 1886. **7.** *Weaving.* To form (a figure) with floating threads (see I. 5) 1894.

1. The field was floated with blood JAS. MILL. To f. meadows at five pounds an acre 1833. **2.** For want of water to f. them over some flats in the Lagunes DAMPIER. **3.** To f. loans 1872, rumours 1883. **4.** The treasures of Africa were floated on rafts to the mouth of the Euphrates GIBBON.

Hence **Floa·table** *a.* that can f., or (*U.S.*) be floated on; *absol.* something that floats.

Floatage (flōᵘ·tėdʒ). 1626. [f. FLOAT *sb.* + -AGE. Cf. Fr. *flottage.*] **1.** The action or state of floating. **2.** *concr.* Anything that floats; e.g. FLOTSAM; also the right to flotsam 1672. **3.** Buoyancy 1877. **4.** The part of a ship above the water-line 1839.

Floatation, flotation (flotēⁱ·ʃən). 1806. [f. FLOAT *v.* + -ATION, after Fr. *flottaison.* The sp. with *flot-* has been adopted to make the word conform to *flotilla* and *rotation.*] **1.** The action, fact, or process of floating; the condition of keeping afloat. **2.** The action of floating a company, etc. 1889.

1. *Centre of f.*: the centre of gravity in a floating body. *Plane* or *line f.* = Fr. *flottaison, ligne de flottaison*, the plane or line in which the horizontal surface of a fluid cuts a body floating in it. *Stable f.*: the position of equilibrium in a floating body.

Floa·t-boat. ME. [f. FLOAT *sb.* or *v.* + BOAT; so called because it was towed astern.] †A ship's long-boat –1659. **b.** A raft 1600.

Floater (flōᵘ·təɹ). 1717. [f. FLOAT *v.* + -ER[1].] **1.** One who or that which floats; *esp.* 'a contrivance indicating the height of level of a fluid in a vessel, whose depth we cannot at the time directly examine' (Nichol). **2.** *Stock-Exch.* A government stock certificate, a railway-bond, etc. accepted as a recognized security 1871. **3.** *U.S. Politics.* A voter who is not attached to any political party 1883.

Floating (flōᵘ·tiŋ), *vbl. sb.* 1562. [f. FLOAT *v.* + -ING[1].] **1.** The action of FLOAT *v.* **2.** *concr.* in *Plastering.* 'The second coat in three-coat work' (P. Nicholson) 1823.

Floating (flōᵘ·tiŋ), *ppl. a.* 1578. [f. as prec. + -ING[2].] **1.** That floats (see the vb.). **2.** *Comm.* Of a cargo: At sea. Of trades, rates, etc.: Of or pertaining to cargoes at sea. 1848. **3.** Having less than the usual attachment 1806. **4.** Fluctuating 1594. **5.** *Finance.* Not fixed or permanently invested; unfunded 1816. **b.** Of an insurance policy: Variable 1839.

1. The sun-beams trembling on the f. tides POPE. **3.** *F. Ribs*, 'the last two of the false ribs, whose anterior extremities are not connected to the rest or to each other' MAYNE. F. kidney 1889. **4.** The f. population of the city 1876. **5.** Variations in the amount of f. capital MCCULLOCH. The f. debt 1893.

Comb.: **f.-anchor,** 'a frame of spars and sails dragging overboard, to lessen the drift of a ship to leeward in a gale' (Knight); **f. battery,** a vessel fitted up and used as a battery; **f. dock,** a large (usually rectangular) vessel made with water-tight compartments, and used as a graving-dock; **f. harbour,** 'a breakwater composed of large masses of timber, anchored and chained together ..which rise and fall with the tide' (Brees); **f. lever** (*Railway*), a name applied to the horizontal brake-levers beneath the car-body; **f. pier,** a landing-stage which rises and falls with the tide; **f. plate** (*Stereotyping*), a flat cast-iron plate, upon which the mould is laid, with the impression downwards.

Floating bridge. 1706. [f. FLOATING *ppl. a.*] **a.** A bridge in the form of a redoubt, consisting of two boats covered with planks. **b.** One made of two small bridges, laid one over the other in such a manner that the uppermost can be run out by the help of cords and pulleys placed along the sides of the under-bridge 1727. **c.** A collection of beams of timber, floating on the surface of a river, and reaching across it. **d.** A flat-bottomed ferry steamboat in harbours or rivers, running on chains laid across the bottom 1858. **e.** A passage formed across a river or creek by means of bridges of boats 1867.

Floating island. 1638. [f. as prec.] **1.** An island that floats. **2.** *Cookery.* (*U.S.*) A custard with floating masses of whipped cream or white of eggs 1771.

Floating light. 1793. [f. as prec.] **a.** A lightship. **b.** A life-buoy with a lantern, for use at night.

Floatingly (flōᵘ·tiŋli), *adv.* 1660. [f. as prec. + -LY[2].] In a floating manner.

Floa·t-stone. 1703. [f. FLOAT *v.* + STONE.] **1.** A rubbing-stone upon which bricks with curved surfaces are rubbed. **2.** A stone so light as to float upon water, e.g. a spongy variety of opal 1805.

Floaty (flōᵘ·ti), *a.* ME. [f. FLOAT *sb.* or *v.* + -Y[1].] †**1.** Watery. ME. only. **2.** Capable of floating; hence, of a ship: Drawing little water 1608.

Floccillation (flǫksilēⁱ·ʃən). 1842. [f. mod.L. *floccillus*, dim. of L. *floccus* FLOCK *sb.*[2] + -ATION.] = CARPHOLOGY.

Flo:cci-nau:ci-ni:hili-pi:li-fica·tion. *joc.* 1741. [f. L. *flocci, nauci, nihili, pili* words signifying 'at little' or 'at nothing' (see Eton Latin Grammar) + -FICATION.] The action or habit of estimating as worthless.

Floccose (flǫ·kōᵘs, flǫkōᵘ·s), *a.* 1752. [– late L. *floccosus*, f. *floccus* FLOCK *sb.*[2]; see -OSE[1].] **1.** Furnished with a tuft or tufts of woolly hair. **2.** *Bot.* Covered with or composed of flocci 1830.

Floccular (flǫ·kiŭlăɹ), *a.* 1870. [f. FLOCCULUS + -AR[1].] *Anat.* Of or pertaining to the flocculus of the cerebellum.

Flocculate (flǫ·kiŭlět), *a.* 1826. [f. FLOCCULUS + -ATE².] *Entom.* Furnished with a curling lock of hair.

Flocculate (flǫ·kiŭleⁱt), *v.* 1877. [f. as prec. + -ATE³.] *trans.* To aggregate into flocculent masses. Hence **Floccula·tion,** the process of flocculating.

Flocculence (flǫ·kiŭlĕns). 1847. [f. FLOCCULENT; see -ENCE.] The condition of being flocculent. So **Flo·cculency.**

Flocculent (flǫ·kiŭlĕnt), *a.* 1800. [f. L. *floccus* FLOCK *sb.*² + -ULENT.] **1.** Resembling flocks or tufts of wool; woolly. **2.** Of the atmosphere: Holding particles of aqueous vapour in suspension 1878. **3.** Downy 1870.

‖**Flocculus** (flǫ·kiŭlŏs). *Pl.* **-li.** 1799. [mod. L., dim. of L. *floccus* FLOCK *sb.*²] A small flock or tuft. **1.** A small quantity of loosely-aggregated matter resembling a flock of wool, held in suspension in, or precipitated from, a fluid. **2.** *Anat.* A small lobe in the under surface of the cerebellum; the sub-peduncular lobe 1840.

‖**Floccus** (flǫ·kŏs). *Pl.* **-i.** 1842. [L., = FLOCK *sb.*²] Something resembling a flock of wool. **a.** *Bot.* A tuft of woolly hairs; also *pl.* the *hyphæ*, or thread-like cells, which form the mycelium of a fungus. **b.** *Zool.* The tuft of hairs which terminate the tail in mammals 1842. **c.** 'A tuft of feathers on the head of young birds' (Webster). **d.** 'The down of unfledged birds' (Worcester).

Flock (flǫk), *sb.*¹ [OE. *flocc* = MLG. *vlocke*, ON. *flokkr*; of unkn. origin.] **1.** A band, body, or company (of persons). Now only as *transf.* from 2 or 3. **2.** A number of animals of one kind, feeding or travelling in company. Now chiefly of birds (*esp.* geese) or as in sense 3. Also *transf.* ME. **3.** *esp.* A number of sheep or goats kept together under the charge of one or more persons. Also *transf.* and *fig.* ME. **4.** *fig.* A body, or the whole body of Christians, in relation to Christ; a congregation in relation to its pastor ME.; a family of children in relation to their parents.

1. A flocke of men of armes LD. BERNERS. **2.** Sixteene Elephants together in one flocke RALEGH. **3.** A goat, the patriarch of the f. SCOTT. **4.** Feede the flocke of God which is among you 1 *Pet.* 5:2.

Comb. **f.-duck** (*U.S.*), a scaup-duck.

Flock (flǫk), *sb.*² ME. [– (O)Fr. *floc* :– L. *floccus.*] **1.** A lock, tuft, particle (of wool, cotton, etc.); †hence, anything of no account. **2.** *pl.* A material consisting of the coarse tufts and refuse of wool or cotton, or of cloth torn to pieces by machinery, used for stuffing beds, cushions, mattresses, etc. ME. **3.** *pl.* (later *collect. sing.*) Powdered wool or cloth, or cloth-shearings, used formerly for thickening cloth and now in making flock-paper 1483. **4.** *pl.* Of chemical precipitates, etc.: Light and loose masses, resembling tufts of wool 1592.

1. I will never care three flocks for his ambition LYLY. **2.** Their fleece [is] for flockes, not cloath 1589.

Comb.: **f.-bed,** one stuffed with f.; **-paper,** 'paper prepared for walls by being sized in the first instance..and then powdering over it f... which has been previously dyed' (Brande); **-powder** = sense 3.

Flock (flǫk), *v.*¹ ME. [f. FLOCK *sb.*¹] †**1.** *trans.* To gather together into a company –1586. †**2.** To lead *away* in a flock –1672. **3.** *intr.* To gather in a company or crowd; to come or go in great numbers, to troop ME. †**4.** *trans.* To crowd upon 1609.

3. Many yong Gentlemen flocke to him euery day SHAKS. **4.** Good fellowes trooping, flock'd me so 1609.

Flock (flǫk), *v.*² 1530. [f. FLOCK *sb.*²] **1.** *trans.* **a.** To stuff with flocks. **b.** To cover with flock or wool-dust (see FLOCK *sb.*² 3) 18... †**2.** To treat with contempt; also *absol.* –1575. †**Flo·ckling.** [See -LING¹.] One of a flock. BROME.

†**Flo·ck-meal,** *adv.* [OE. *floccmælum*; see FLOCK *sb.*¹, -MEAL.] By companies, troops, or heaps –1611.

Flocky (flǫ·ki), *a.* 1597. [f. FLOCK *sb.*² + -Y¹.] **a.** Flock-like. **b.** Floccose.

Floe (flōᵘ). 1817. [prob. – Norw. *flo* layer, level piece :– ON. *fló* layer, stratum. Cf. FLAW *sb.*¹ The earlier word was FLAKE *sb.*²] A sheet of floating ice; a detached portion of a field of ice. Also *ice-f.*

Comb.: **floeberg,** a berg of f.-ice; **f.-flat,** a seal = *floe rat*; **-ice,** undulating ice forming a vast plain; **f. rat,** the small ringed seal (*Phoca hispida*).

Flog (flǫg), *v.* 1676. [Recorded as a cant word by Coles. Prob. of imit. origin, like *flack, flap*; perh. suggested by L. *flagellare* FLAGELLATE *v.*] **1.** To beat, whip; to chastise with repeated blows of a rod or whip. **2.** *gen.* To beat, lash, strike. *Fishing.* To cast the fly-line over (a stream) repeatedly. *Cricket.* To punish (bowling). 1801. **b.** *intr.* Of a sail: To flap heavily 1839.

2. A salmon bullied into rising by a customer who..kept flogging on 1867. Hence **Flo·gger,** one who or that which flogs; also, a kind of tool, a bung-starter.

Flogging (flǫ·giŋ), *vbl. sb.* 1758. [f. prec. + -ING¹.] The action of FLOG *v.*

Comb.: **f.-chisel,** a large cold chisel used in chipping castings; **-hammer,** a small sledge-hammer used for striking a f.-chisel.

Flon, flone, vars. of †*flane*, arrow.

Flong, obs. pa. t. and pple. of FLING *v.*

Flood (flɒd), *sb.* [OE. *flōd*, corresp. to OFris., OS. *flōd* (Du. *vloed*), OHG. *fluot* (G. *flut*), ON. *flóð*, Goth. *flōdus* :– Gmc. **flōðuz*, *-am*, f. **flō-* :– IE. **plō-* (as in Gr. πλώειν swim, πλωτός navigable). For the pronunc. cf. *blood.*] **1.** The flowing in of the tide; as in *ebb and f.*, etc. Also *fig.* **2.** A body of flowing water; a river, stream, usually a large river. Now only *poet.* OE. **3.** Water as opp. to land, often contrasted with *field* and *fire.* Also *pl.* Now *poet.* or *rhet.* OE. **4.** An overflowing or irruption of a great body of water over land not usually submerged; an inundation, a deluge OE. **5.** A profuse and violent outpouring of water; a swollen stream; a violent downpour of rain. ME. Also *fig.* ME. **b.** *transf.* of tears, flame, light, lava, a concourse or influx of persons, etc. 1589. †**6.** *pl.* = FLOODING 2. (Dicts.)

1. *fig.* There is a Tide in the affayres of men, which taken at the F., leades on to Fortune SHAKS. **2.** The water of the f. Iordan 1605. **3.** Through f., through fire, I do wander euerie where SHAKS. The accidents of f. and field [cf. *Oth.* I. iii. 135] 1857. **4.** *The F.*: the deluge in the time of Noah; hence often *Noah's f.* Shipwreck..fire, and f. COWPER. *transf.* His eyes in f. with laughter SHAKS.

Comb.: **f.-anchor,** 'that which the ship rides by during the flood-tide' (Smyth); **-flanking** (*Hydraulic Engin.*), a mode of embanking with stiff moist clay; **-light,** artificial light projected from different directions so that shadows are eliminated; hence as vb.; so **f.-lit** *a.*; **-loam** = ALLUVIUM; **-mark,** the high-water mark.

Flood (flɒd), *v.* ME. [f. prec. sb.] **1.** *trans.* To cover with a flood; to inundate. **2.** To cover or fill with water. Of rain, etc.: To fill (a river) to overflowing. 1881. **3.** To pour in a flood. *rare.* 1829. **4.** *intr.* To come in a flood or floods. *lit.* and *fig.* 1755. **5.** To suffer from uterine hæmorrhage 1770.

1. The streets in Oxon were all flouded with water WOOD. **2.** To f. grass lands LOUDON, a colliery 1883. **4.** Far back, through creeks and inlets making, Comes silent, flooding in, the main CLOUGH. Hence **Floo·der.**

Floo·d-ga:te, floo·dgate. ME. [f. FLOOD *sb.* + GATE *sb.*¹] **1.** *sing.* and *pl.* A gate or gates that may be opened or closed, to admit or exclude water, *esp.* the water of a flood; *spec.* the lower gates of a lock. **b.** *transf.* and *fig.* ME. **2.** A sluice 1559. †**3.** The stream that is closed by or passes through a flood-gate; a strong stream, a torrent. Also *transf.* and *fig.* –1651.

1. b. The floodgates were opened, and mother and daughter wept THACKERAY. **3.** Of her gored wound..He..did the floudgate stop With his faire garment SPENSER.

Flood-hatch. 1587. [See HATCH.] A framework of boards sliding in grooves, to be raised in time of flood; a sluice, floodgate. *lit.* and *fig.*

Flooding (flɒ·diŋ), *vbl. sb.* 1674. [f. FLOOD *v.* + -ING¹.] **1.** The action of FLOOD *v.*; *pl.* floods; *fig.* fullness. **2.** Uterine hæmorrhage, *esp.* in connection with parturition 1710.

Floo·d-ti·de. 1719. [f. FLOOD *sb.* + TIDE.] = FLOOD *sb.* 1.

Flook: see FLUKE.

Flookan, flooking (flu·kăn, -iŋ). 1728. [Of unkn. origin.] *Mining.* A cross-course or transverse vein composed of clay; also, a sort of clayey substance, often found against the walls of a quartz reef, and accompanying cross-spurs and slides.

Floor (flōᵊɹ), *sb.* [OE. *flōr*, corresp. to (M)Du. *vloer*, MHG. *vluor* (G. *flur*), ON. *flór* :– Gmc. **flōruz.*]

I. 1. The layer of boards, brick, stone, etc. in an apartment, on which people tread; the under surface of the interior of a room. Hence, any analogous surface. **2.** The structure of joists, etc. supporting the flooring of a room 1703. Hence, the ceiling of a room. Also *transf.* of the sky. 1596. **3.** *Naut.* **a.** 'The bottom of a vessel on each side of the kelson' (Smyth). †**b.** The deck –1683. **c.** *pl.* = *floor-timbers* 1805. **4.** In legislative assemblies, the part of the house where the members sit, and from which they speak. Hence *fig.* The right of speaking. 1774. **5.** A set of rooms and landings in a house on the same level; a story. See FIRST-FLOOR. 1585.

2. The floore of heauen SHAKS. **4.** Phr. *To take the f.*: to get up to address a meeting; to take part in a debate; said also of taking part in a dance. Chiefly *U.S.* **5.** Old footsteps trod the upper floors TENNYSON.

II. 1. An artificial platform or levelled space, for the carrying on of some industry, *esp.* threshing OE. **2.** A naturally level surface. Also = the ground (now *dial.*). ME.

2. Sunk though he be beneath the watery f. MILT.

III. 1. A foundation. ? *Obs.* 1556. **2.** The stratum on which a seam of coal, etc. immediately lies 1869.

IV. 1. A layer, a stratum; a horizontal course 1692. **2.** A unit of measurement used for embankment work (= 400 cubic feet) 1707. **3.** = FLOAT *sb.* III. 2, q.v. 1707.

Comb.: **f.-arch,** an arch with a flat extrados; **-frame,** (*a*) the framework of the f. in a vessel; (*b*) *U.S.* the main frame of the body of a railway-carriage underneath the f.; **-head,** (*a*) the upper end of one of the f.-timbers in a vessel; (*b*) 'the third diagonal, terminating the length of the floors near the bilge of the ship' (Smyth); **-hollow,** 'the inflected curve that terminates the f. next the keel, and to which the f.-hollow mould is made'; **-light,** a frame with glass panes in a f.; **-plan,** (*a*) *Ship-building*, 'a longitudinal section, whereon are represented the water-lines and ribband-lines' (Smyth); (*b*) *Arch.*, a horizontal section, showing the thickness of the walls and partitions, the arrangement of the passages, apartments, and openings at the level of the principal f. of the house; **-riband,** the riband next below the f.-heads which supports the floors; **-timber(s,** those parts of the ship's timbers which are placed immediately across the keel; **-walker,** *U.S.* = SHOP-WALKER.

Floor (flōᵊɹ), *v.* ME. [f. prec.] **1.** *trans.* To cover or furnish with a floor or floors; to form the floor of. **2.** To bring to the floor or ground; to knock down 1642. **3.** *fig.* (*colloq.*) **a.** To nonplus 1840. **b.** To overcome in any way 1827. **c.** To do thoroughly; to finish 1836. **d.** *intr.* ? To get a fall. J. H. NEWMAN. **4.** To place *upon* (something) as a floor 1871.

1. Forests, floored with bright-green moss B. TAYLOR. **2.** Crib. floored him with a blow of great strength 1812. **3. b.** I was the only man who could f. O'Connell LD. BEACONSFIELD. **c.** To f. a paper 1852, a bottle 1861.

Floorage (flōᵊ·rėdʒ). *rare.* 1734. [f. as prec. + -AGE.] Floors collectively, amount of flooring.

Floor-cloth, floo·rcloth. 1746. [f. as prec. + CLOTH.] **1.** A fabric for covering floors; e.g. oilcloth, linoleum, etc. **2.** A housemaid's cloth for washing floors 1851.

Floorer (flōᵊ·rəɹ). 1795. [f. FLOOR *v.* + -ER¹.] One who or that which floors (*lit.* and *fig.*); e.g. a knock-down blow, a piece of bad news, a decisive argument or retort. Also in university slang, a question or paper too hard to be mastered.

Flooring (flōᵊ·riŋ), *vbl. sb.* 1624. [f. as prec. + -ING¹.] **1.** The action of FLOOR *v.* 1632. **2.** *concr.* The floor of a room, etc.; also, the materials of which it is made 1624; a natural floor 1697. **3.** *Malting.* The operation of spreading the grain on the malt-floor, and treating it 1839. *Comb.* **f.-clamp,** an implement for closing up the joints of flooring boards.

Floorless (flōᵊ·ɹlės), *a.* 1847. [f. FLOOR *sb.* + -LESS.] Having no floor.

Flop (flǫp), *sb. colloq.* and *dial.* 1662. [See the vb.] **1.** An act of flopping; the resulting sound 1823. †**2.** = FLAP *sb.* 1 b. 1662.

Flop (flǫp), *adv.* and *interj. colloq.* 1728. [The vb. stem.] With a flop, or flopping noise.

Flop (flǫp), *v. colloq.* and *dial.* 1602. [var. of FLAP *v.*, indicating a duller or heavier sound.] **1.** *intr.* To swing or sway about heavily and loosely; to FLAP. **2.** To move clumsily and heavily; to move with a sudden bump or thud 1692. **3.** *trans.* To throw suddenly, usually with a flop 1823. **4.** To move (wings) heavily and loosely up and down 1859.

2. A..grey sea flopping up on our weather bow 1887.

Floppy (flǫ·pi), *a. colloq.* 1858. [f. FLOP *v.* + -Y¹.] Having a tendency to flop about.

Flora (flōᵊ·ră). *Pl.* **-æ;** also **-as.** 1508. [– L. *Flora* the goddess of flowers, f. *flos, flor-* flower.] **1.** In Latin mythology, the goddess of flowers; hence, the personification of nature's power in producing flowers. **2.** A descriptive catalogue of the plants of any area, period, etc. 1777. **3.** The plants or plant life of a region or epoch 1778.

1. With voice Milde, as when Zephyrus or F. breathes MILT.

Floral (flōᵊ·răl), *a.* 1647. [– L. *floralis* or directly f. L. *flor-* (see prec.); see -AL¹.] **1.** *Hist.* Pertaining to or in honour of Flora. **2.** Pertaining to a flora or floras 1870. **3.** [f. L. *flos, flor-*.] Of or pertaining to a flower or flowers 1753.

1. Phr. *F. shows* = L. *Floralia*. **2.** Phr. *F. zone*: one of the tracts into which the earth's surface may be divided with reference to vegetable life. **3.** *F. Leaf* expresses one found near the flower, and which never appears but with the flower E. CHAMBERS. *F. envelope* (see ENVELOPE *sb.*). Hence **Flo·rally** *adv.* in the manner of a flower.

†**Flo·ramour.** Also **-amor.** 1548. [– OFr. **flor amour* (in COTGR., *fleur d'amour*) lit. 'flower of love'. Cf. G. *floramor* (XVI).] A name given to various species of *Amaranthus* –1676.

‖**Floreal** (flōᵊ·riăl), *sb.* 1827. [Fr. *Floréal*, f. L. *floreus* of flowers, f. *flos, flor-* flower; see -AL¹.] The eighth month of the year in the French Republican calendar, extending from April 20 to May 19.

Florence (flǫ·rĕns). ME. [–(O)Fr. *Florence*, name of the chief city of Tuscany, = early It. *Fiorenze*, now *Firenze* :– L. *Florentia*.] †**1.** A gold florin –1598. **2.** A woven fabric: **a.** of wool (*Obs.* exc. *Hist.*) 1483; **b.** of silk 1882. †**3.** A kind of wine brought from Florence –1757.

Comb.: **F.-flask** (see FLASK *sb.*¹3); **-oil,** a superior kind of olive oil.

Florentine (flǫ·rĕntəin). 1545. [– Fr. *Florentin,-ine* or L. *Florentinus*, f. *Florentia*; see prec., -INE¹.]

A. *adj.* Of or pertaining to Florence; *esp.* in **F. mosaic,** a kind of mosaic made by inlaying precious stones in marble or the like 1603.

B. *sb.* **1.** A native or inhabitant of Florence 1591. **2.** A textile fabric of silk or †wool 1545. **3.** A kind of pie or tart; *esp.* a meat pie 1567. **4.** The Florentine dialect of Italian. MILMAN.

3. A Florendine of a kidney of Veal 1750.

‖**Flores** (flō·res). 1858. [Sp.; pl. of *flor* FLOWER.] The best quality of indigo dye.

Florescence (flore·sĕns). 1793. [– mod.L. *florescentia*, f. *florescent-*; see next, -ENCE.] The process of bursting into flower; the period or state of flowering; *concr.* flowers collectively.

Florescent (flore·sĕnt), *a.* 1821. [– *florescent-*, pr. ppl. stem of L. *florescere*, inceptive of *florēre*; see -ESCENT.] Bursting into flower, flowering. *lit.* and *fig.*

Floret (flōᵊ·rĕt). 1671. [f. L. *flos, flor-* flower + -ET.] **1.** *Bot.* One of the little flowers that make up a composite flower or the spikelet in grasses. **2.** A floweret 1791.

1. The *florets of the disk*..occupy the centre of the head of a composite; while *florets of the ray* occupy the circumference 1866.

Floret, obs. var. of FLEURET².

†**Flo·riage.** 1782. [irreg. f. L. *flos, flor-* flower, after *foliage*.] **1.** Bloom, blossom. **2.** 'The leaves of flowers' (Webster).

Floriated (flōᵊ·ri,eⁱtĕd), *ppl. a.* [irreg. f. as prec. + -ATE³ + -ED¹. See -I-.] Decorated with floral ornaments; as, a *floriated coronet*. var. **Flo·reated.**

Floricomous (flori·kŏməs), *a. rare.* 1727. [f. late L. *floricomus*, (f. *flori-*, comb. form of *flos* flower + *coma* hair) + -OUS.] †**1.** Having the top adorned with flowers. **2.** *Zool.* Epithet of certain sponges, the rays of which end in a bunch of curved branches.

Floriculture (flǫ·-, flōᵊ·rikɒltiŭr). 1822. [f. *flori-*, comb. form of L. *flos* flower + CULTURE, after *horticulture*.] The cultivation of flowering plants. Hence **Floricu·ltural** *a.* **Floricu·lturist,** one devoted to or skilled in f.

Florid (flǫ·rid), *a.* 1642. [– Fr. *floride* or L. *floridus*, f. *flos, flor-*, flower; see -ID¹.] †**1.** Abounding in or covered with flowers; flowery –1682. **2.** *fig.* Profusely adorned as with flowers; elaborately, or excessively ornate 1656. **3. a.** *Mus.* Running in rapid figures, divisions, or passages; also, = FIGURATE *a.* 4 a. 1879. **b.** *Arch.* Enriched with decorative details 1704. †**4.** Of blooming appearance; brilliant. Of colour: Bright. –1770. **5.** Of the complexion, etc.: Rosy, flushed with red 1650. †Of the blood: Bright red (i.e. arterial) –1797. **6.** In the bloom of health. Now *rare.* 1656.

1. This f. Earth MILT. The f. glories of the Spring VAUGHAN. **2.** A f. speech 1658. In f. impotence he speaks POPE. A f. apparel THACKERAY. **3.** A f. style of Jacobean architecture 1886. **5.** A f. face 1865. **6.** Vigorous and f. Health HUME. Hence **Flori·dity,** f. quality or state. **Flor·id-ly** *adv.*, **-ness.**

Florida (flǫ·ridă). The name of a State in the extreme south-east of the United States, used *attrib.*, as in **F.-water,** a perfume similar to eau-de-Cologne, largely used in the United States; etc.

Florideous (flori·dīəs), *a.* 1884. [f. mod.L. *Florideæ* (f. L. *floridus* FLORID) + -OUS.] *Bot.* Belonging to the *Florideæ*, an order of Algæ, or having the characters of that group.

Floriferous (florifĕrəs), *a.* 1656. [f. L. *florifer* (f. *flori-*, comb. form of *flos* flower) + -OUS; see -FEROUS.] Producing flowers.

Florification (flōᵊ:rifikēⁱ·ʃən). 1796. [– Fr. *florification*, f. *flori-* (see prec.); see -FICATION.] The action or process of flowering.

Floriform (flōᵊ·rifǭəm), *a.* 1805. [f. *flori-* (see prec.) + -FORM.] Having the form of a flower.

Florikan, floriken (flōᵊ·rikăn, -kĕn). Also **-can, -kin.** 1780. [Of unkn. origin.] Either of two species of small bustard, the Bengal Florikan (*Sypheotides bengalensis*), or the Lesser Florikan (*S. auritus*).

†**Flo·rilege.** 1651. [– Fr. *florilège*, or direct – next.] = next –1665.

Florilegium (flōᵊrilī·dʒiŏm). 1647. [mod.L. (L. *flos, flor-* flower, *legere* gather), tr. Gr. ἀνθολόγιον ANTHOLOGY.] *lit.* A collection or selection of flowers; hence *transf.* an anthology.

Florin (flǫ·rin). ME. [– (O)Fr. *florin* – It. *fiorino*, f. *fiore* flower; the coin orig. so named bore the figure of a lily on the obverse and on the reverse the Latin name of the city, *Florentia*, whence the use of OFr. and ME. (to early mod. Eng.) *florence* for the coin.] **1.** The English name of a gold coin weighing about 54 grs., first issued at Florence in 1252. **2.** An English gold coin of the value of six shillings and eightpence, issued by Edward III. Now *Hist.* 1480. **3.** The English name of various continental coins 1611. **4.** An English silver coin of the value of two shillings, first minted in 1849.

Florist (flǫ·-, flōᵊ·rist). 1623. [f. L. *flos, flor-* flower + -IST, after Fr. *fleuriste* or It. *fiorista*.] One who cultivates flowers; one skilled in knowledge of flowering plants; also, one who deals in flowers.

Floroun, var. of FLEURON.

‖**Floruit** (flōᵊ·riu,it). 1843. [L., 3rd sing. pf. ind. of *florēre* flourish. Cf. *habitat*.] Used for: The period during which a person 'flourished'.

Florula (flōᵊ·riŭlă). 1847. [app. dim. of FLORA; see -ULE.] A small flora or collection of plants.

Florulent (flōᵊ·-, flǫ·rⁱŭlĕnt), *a.* 1592. [– L. *florulentus*, f. *flos, flor-* flower; see -ULENT.] Abounding in flowers, flowery.

Flory, *a. Her.* = FLEURY.

Floscular (flǫ·skiŭlăɹ), *a.* 1793. [f. L. *flosculus* (see next) + -AR¹.] Composed of floscules or flowerets.

Floscule (flǫ·skiul). 1669. [– Fr. *floscule* or L. *flosculus*, f. *flos* flower; see -CULE.] *Bot.* A floret. Also *fig.*

†**Flo·sculet.** [f. L. *flosculus* (see prec.) + -ET.] A little flower. HERRICK.

Flosculous (flǫ·skiŭləs), *a.* 1646. [f. as prec. + -OUS. With sense 2 cf. Fr. *flosculeux* (XVIII).] †**1.** Of the nature, or having the savour, of flowers –1682. **2.** *Bot.* Composed of floscules or florets. Of a floret: Tubular. 1830. So **Flosculo·se** *a.* (Dicts.)

‖**Flos-ferri** (flǫ·sfe·rəi). 1748. [L.; = 'flower of iron'.] *Min.* A coralloid variety of aragonite, often found with iron ore.

Flosh (flǫʃ), *sb.* 1874. [Of unkn. origin.] *Metallurgy.* 'A hopper-shaped box in which ore is placed for the action of the stamps' (Knight).

Floss¹ (flǫs). 1759. [Early forms also *flosh, flox* – Fr. *floche*, as in *soie floche* floss-silk, OFr. *flosche* down, pile of velvet; of unkn. origin.] **1.** The rough silk which envelops the cocoon of the silk-worm 1759; *transf.* the silk of maize and other plants 1846. **2.** = FLOSS-SILK. 1871. **3.** A flossy surface; also, fluff 1784. **4.** *attrib.*, as in *f. thread*, etc. 1864. Hence **Flo·ssy** *a.* floss-like.

Floss² (flǫs). 1839. [– G. *floss* in same sense, cogn. w. FLOAT *sb.*] *Metallurgy.* **1.** The fluid glass floating upon the iron in the puddling furnace produced by the vitrification of the oxides and earths which are present. **2.** White cast iron, as employed for the manufacture of steel 1839.

Comb. **f.-hole,** (*a*) a hole at the back of a puddling furnace, at which the slags of the iron pass out; (*b*) 'the tap-hole of a melting-furnace' (Knight).

Floss³ (flǫs). [Cf. G. *floss* in same sense. (In *The Mill on the Floss* the word *Floss* is a proper name.)] A stream. CARLYLE.

Floss-silk. Also **flox-, flosh-silk.** 1759. [f. FLOSS¹.] **a.** The rough silk broken off in the winding of cocoons. **b.** Untwisted filaments of silk used in embroidery and crewel-work 1863.

Flota (flōᵘ·tă). 1690. [– Sp. *flota* fleet.] The name given to the Spanish fleet which used to bring back to Spain the products of America and the W. Indies.

Flotage, Flotation, etc.: see FLOAT-.

Flotant (flōᵘ·tănt), *a.* 1610. [– Fr. *flottant*, pres. pple. of *flotter* FLOAT *v.*; see -ANT.] *Her.* A term applied to anything flying in the air, or displayed, or swimming.

†**Flote,** *sb.*¹ [OE. *flota* = MDu. *vlote*, ON. *flote*; see FLOAT *sb.*] A fleet or flotilla –1577. **2.** = FLOTA. 1673.

†**Flote,** *sb.*² ME. [– OFr. *flote* company of persons, multitude, orig. (XII) fleet of ships (mod. *flotte*), ult. – OE. *flota*; see FLOAT *sb.*] A company, troop; also, a herd (of cattle), a shoal (of fish) –1647.

†**Flote,** *v.* 1573. [Either f. *flot* scum or back-formation from *floten* FLOTTEN.] *trans.* = FLEET *v.*² 1. –1669.

Floter, obs. f. FLUTTER.

Flotilla (floti·lă). 1711. [– Sp. *flotilla*, dim. of *flota* = Pr. *flota*, OFr. *flote* (mod. *flotte*) fleet; see FLOTE *sb.*²] A small fleet; a fleet of boats or small vessels.

Flotsam (flǫ·tsăm). 1607. [Early forms also *flotsen, -son* – AFr. *floteson*, f. *floter* FLOAT *v.* For the form cf. JETSAM.] **1.** *Law.* Wreckage found floating on the surface of the sea. Usually assoc. w. JETSAM. Also *transf.* and *fig.* **2.** Newly ejected oyster-spawn 1879.

†**Flo·tten,** *ppl. a.* Also *floten.* 1600. [pa. pple. of FLEET *v.*¹ and ².] **1.** Flooded with water 1601. **2.** Skimmed. *F. milk*, skim-milk. –1661.

Flounce (flauns), *sb.*¹ 1583. [f. FLOUNCE *v.*¹] The action of flouncing; a sudden fling or jerk; a plunging or flopping movement; occas. expressing impatience or disdain.

Flounce (flauns), *sb.*² 1713. [alt., prob. by assim. to FLOUNCE *v.*¹, of earlier FROUNCE *sb.*¹] **1.** A strip gathered and sewed on by its upper edge around the skirt of a lady's dress, and left hanging and waving. **2.** *Mil.* The leather flap closing the holster-pipe 1833.

Flounce (flauns), *v.*¹ 1542. [Of obscure origin (like *bounce, pounce, trounce*); connection with Norw. *flunsa* hurry, Sw. dial. *flunsa* fall with a splash, cannot be asserted.] **1.** *intr.* To dash, flop, plunge, rush. **2.** To make abrupt and jerky movements with the limbs or body; to throw the body about; to plunge, flounder, struggle. Usu. said of bulls, horses, or aquatic animals. 1609. †**3.** To express displeasure by agitated movements –1756. †**4.** *trans.* To dash or drive with violence –1794.

1. He flounced from the water like a carp 1784. **2.** When one hath struck a great fish, he plungeth and flounceth 1641. **3.** If you f., I fly FOOTE.

Flounce (flauns), *v.*² 1672. [alt. f. FROUNCE *v.*; see FLOUNCE *sb.*²] †**1.** *trans.* To curl, frizz. **2.** To adorn or trim with a flounce or flounces; also *transf.* 1711.

2. Flounced and furbelowed from Head to Foot ADDISON.

Flouncing (flau·nsiŋ), *vbl. sb.* 1766. [f. FLOUNCE *v.*² + -ING¹.] **a.** The action of the vb. **b.** *concr.* A flounce; also, material for flouncing.

Flounder (flau·ndəɹ), *sb.*¹ 1450. [– AFr. *floundre* (in AL. *flundra* XIII), OFr. (and mod. Norman dial.) *flondre*, prob. of Scand. orig. (cf. OSw. *flundra*, Da. *flynder*, ON. *flyðra* :– **flunþriōn*).] **1.** A small flat-fish, *Pleuronectes flesus*. In U.S. applied to other species of flat-fish. **2. a.** *dial.* = FLUKE 2. 1853. **b.** *Bootmaking.* A tool used 'to stretch leather for a boot front in a blocking or crimping board' (Knight) 1874.

Flounder (flau·ndəɹ), *sb.*² 1867. [f. next vb.] The action of FLOUNDER *v.*

Flounder (flau·ndəɹ), *v.* 1592. [prob. blending of FOUNDER *v.* and BLUNDER, assisted by the frequency of *fl-* in words expressing impetuous, clumsy, or rough movement, e.g. *fling, flounce.*] **1.** *intr.* In early use, to stumble; later, to struggle violently and clumsily; to plunge, to roll and tumble about in or as in mire. Also with *on, along*, etc. Also *transf.* and *fig.* †**2.** *trans.* To cause to flounder; to confound –1685.

1. You f. in mud at every step THACKERAY. *fig.* They f. about between fustian in expression, and bathos in sentiment HAZLITT.

Flour (flauᵊɹ), *sb.* ME. [Differentiated sp. of FLOWER (ME. *flour of huete*; cf. Fr. *fleur de farine* pure wheaten flour); the sp. *flower* continued till early XIX.] **1.** Orig., the finest quality of meal; hence, the finer portion of meal (wheat or other) which is separated by bolting. Also, in mod. use, the meal of wheat as opp. to that from other grain. **2.** Hence, the fine soft powder of any substance ME. **3.** *attrib.*, as *f.-dredge, -mill*, etc. 1806.

2. F. of mustard 1855, of sulphur 1894.

Comb.: **f.-beetle**, a beetle (*Tenebrio molitor*) which feeds on f.; **-bolt, -bolter**, a flour-sieve; **-dresser**, a cylinder for dressing f., instead of passing it through bolting cloths; **-emery**, emery reduced to a fine powder; **-gold**, the finest alluvial drift-gold; **-mite**, one of several acarids which are found in f.; **-moth**, a moth which feeds on f., esp. *Pyralis farinalis*.

Flour (flauᵊɹ), *v.* 1651. [f. prec. sb.] **1.** *trans.* To sprinkle with flour; to powder (a wig). **2.** *U.S.* To grind (grain) into flour 1828. **3.** *intr. Mining.* Of mercury: To break up into dull particles coated with some sulphide and incapable of coalescing with other metals 1882. Hence **Floured** *ppl. a.* (in senses 1, 3).

Flourish (flɒ·riʃ), *sb.* 1500. [f. next vb.] **1.** The blossom on a fruit-tree. *Sc.* and *n. dial.* **2.** †The condition of being in blossom –1818; *fig.* prosperity, vigour; perfection, prime (now *rare*) 1597. †**3.** Ostentatious embellishment; gloss –1632. **4.** *Penmanship.* A decoration executed with a sweep of the pen 1652. **5.** Literary or rhetorical embellishment; parade of fine words or phrases; a florid expression 1603. †**b.** A boast, brag –1706. **6.** An ostentatious waving about of a weapon or anything else; a showy movement 1601. **7.** *Mus.* **a.** A fanfare (of horns, trumpets, etc.) 1594. **b.** A florid passage; a florid style of composition; a decorative addition introduced by player or singer 1646.

2. *fig.* The *Court Circular* remains in full f. THACKERAY. **3.** Time doth transfixe the florish set on youth SHAKS. **5.** He commenced with a f. about his sufferings for the Plot SCOTT. **6.** Like seeming Fencers we are meeter for a f., then defence 1601. **7. a.** They..received him [Waverley] with a triumphant f. upon the bagpipes SCOTT.

Flourish (flɒ·riʃ), *v. Pa. t.* and *pple.* **flourished.** ME. [– (O)Fr. *floriss-*, lengthened stem (see -ISH²) of *florir* (mod. *fleurir*) :– Rom. **florire*, for L. *florēre*, f. *flos, flor-* FLOWER.]

I. *intr.* **1.** Of a plant or tree: †To blossom –1578; to grow vigorously and luxuriantly; to thrive ME. **2.** *gen.* To thrive ME. Of things: To attain full development; to be prosperous or successful, be in vogue ME. **3.** To be at the height of fame or excellence; to be in one's prime. Also used in pa. t. of a person to indicate the date of his activity (cf. FLORUIT). ME.

1. To smelle the sote savour of the vyne whanne it florissheth CHAUCER. I the Lord. have made the dry tree to f. *Ezek.* 17:24. **2.** The poor law system..has flourished for over three centuries 1885. **3.** Spenser and Fairfax both flourished in the reign of Queen Elizabeth DRYDEN.

II. †**1.** *trans.* To adorn with flowers or verdure; to cause to thrive –1614. †**2.** *gen.* To adorn, embellish, ornament –1716; to embellish with flourishes (see FLOURISH *sb.* 4 –1660. **3.** †To embellish with flowers of speech –1691; *intr.* to use florid language 1700. †**4.** *trans.* To work up ornamentally. BACON.

3. You have..wanted no art to f. your warm passion SHIRLEY.

III. 1. To brandish (a weapon, etc.); to wave about by way of show or triumph. Also *intr.* of the weapon, etc. ME. Also †*absol.* **2. a.** *trans.* To display ME. **b.** *intr.* 'To boast, brag' (J.); to 'show off' 1674. †**3.** To move with a flourish –1735. †**4.** *Mus.* and *Fencing.* To give a short fanciful exhibition by way of exercise before the real performance. To play, with a flourish. Of trumpets: To sound a flourish. –1810.

1. Old Mountague..flourishes his Blade in spight of me SHAKS. **2. a.** He..florisht his colours in signe of victory 1638. **4.** Why do the Emperors trumpets f. thus SHAKS.

Hence **Flou·risher**, one who or that which flourishes. **Flou·rishingly** *adv.* in a flourishing manner; †ostentatiously.

Floury (flauᵊ·ri), *a.* 1591. [f. FLOUR *sb.* + -Y¹.] Of or resembling flour; yielding flour; covered with flour or powder.

Flout (flaut), *sb.* 1570. [f. FLOUT *v.*] A mocking speech or action.

Flout (flaut), *v.* 1551. [perh. – Du. *fluiten* whistle, play the flute, hiss (*uitfluiten*); cf. synon. G. colloq. *pfeifen auf* 'pipe at'.] **1.** *trans.* To mock, jeer, insult; to express contempt for. †**b.** To quote mockingly. *Much Ado* I. i. 290. **2.** *intr.* To behave with contumely, to mock, jeer, scoff; to express contempt by action or speech. Const. *at.* 1575.

1. Where the Norweyan Banners flowt the Skie *Macb.* I. ii. 49. Phillida flouts me WALTON. **2.** Ah, you may f. and turn up your faces BROWNING.

Hence †**Flou·tage**, mockery B. JONS. **Flou·ter. Flou·tingly** *adv.* in a flouting manner. †**Flou·ting-stock**, (*a*) a butt for flouting; (*b*) = FLOUT *sb.* (*Merry W.* IV. v. 83.)

Flow (flōᵘ), *sb.*¹ 1450. [f. FLOW *v.*] **1.** The action or fact of flowing; an instance or mode of this. Orig. said of liquids, now of air, electricity, etc. Also 'The course or direction of running waters' (Smyth). **b.** The quantity that flows 1807. **c.** *concr.* That which flows 1802. **2.** *transf.* and *fig.* Any movement resembling the flow of a river and connoting a copious supply; an outpouring or stream; *esp.* of speech. Hence, of dress, outlines, etc. 1641. **3.** The incoming of the tide; opp. to *ebb* 1583. Also *fig.* **4.** †A deluge, flood –1571; an overflowing 1606. **5.** *Porcelain Manuf.* A flux for causing the colours to flow or blend in firing 1878. †**6.** A full-bottomed wig –1756.

1. The f. of a brook 1856, of a current of air TYNDALL. **c.** The f. Of Iser, rolling rapidly CAMPBELL. Flows of lava LYELL. **2.** The Feast of Reason and the F. of Soul POPE. A f. of callers 1812, of talk 1873. Phr. *F. of spirits*: in early use, a sudden access of exhilaration; now, a state of habitual cheerfulness. **3.** Ocean's ebb, and ocean's f. BURNS.

Flow (flōᵘ), *sb.*² Also **flo(w)e.** 16... [perh. – ON. **flówe* (Icel. *flói*) of same meaning, rel. to *flóa* FLOW *v.*] **1.** 'A watery moss, a morass' (Jam.). Also, a low-lying piece of watery land. **2.** A quicksand 1818. **3.** *attrib.* as in *f.-bog* or *f. moss*, a peat bog, the surface of which rises and falls with every increase or diminution of the water 1831.

Flow (flōᵘ), *v. Pa. t.* and *pple.* **flowed** (flōᵘd). [OE. *flōwan*, f. Gmc. **flō-*, whence also ON. *flóa* flood, MLG. *vlōien*, Du. *vloeien* flow and FLOOD. The sense-development has been infl. by unrelated L. *fluere.*]

I. 1. *intr.* Of fluids, a stream, etc.: To move with a continual change of place among the particles or parts; to move along in a current; to circulate. †**2.** To become liquid; to melt. *lit.* and *fig.* –1737. **b.** *Ceram.* To work or blend freely: said of a glaze (*Cent. Dict.*). **c.** Of a metal: To change its form under impact or tensile or compressive strain 1888. **3.** To come, go, move or pass as a stream ME. **4.** Of a garment, hair, etc.: To hang loose and waving 1606. **5.** *Math.* To increase or diminish continuously by infinitesimal quantities. See FLUENT. 1715. †**6.** *trans.* To make to flow –1579.

1. Siloa's Brook that flow'd Fast by the Oracle of God MILT. *P. L.* I. 11. Trade, which like blood should circularly f. DRYDEN. **2.** Oh that..the mountains might f. down at thy presence *Isa.* 64:1. **3.** As fast years f. away SHELLEY. Conversation flowed freely 1870. **4.** Her bright hayre loose flowing B. JONS.

II. 1. To stream forth OE.; to issue or proceed *from, out of.* Also *transf.* and *fig.* ME. **2.** Of the menstrual discharge. Said also of the person. 1754.

1. Endless tears f. down in streams SWIFT. *fig.* This rule flows..from the nature of a remainder CRUISE.

III. 1. Of the sea, etc.: To rise and advance. OE. †**2.** To rise and overflow. Also *fig.* –1625. (The obs. pa. pple. *flown* was orig. used in this sense.) †**3.** Of the eyes: To become overfull –1710. **4.** Of wine, etc.: To be poured out abundantly; also *fig.* OE. **5.** *trans.* To flood ME.; hence, to cover with varnish, glaze, or the like, by allowing it to flow over the surface 1864.

1. Thys yere the Thamys did flowe three times in one daye 1568. *fig.* Doth it [pride] not f. as hugely as the Sea SHAKS. **2.** Let Nylus f. BEAUM. & FL. *fig.* The Sons of Belial, flown with insolence and wine MILT. *P. L.* I. 501.

Hence **Flow·age**, the act of flowing; flooded state.

Flowe(n, obs. pa. t. and pple. of FLY *v.*¹

Flower (flauᵊɹ, flau·əɹ), *sb.* [ME. *flur, flour* – AFr. *flur*, OFr. *flor, flour* (mod. *fleur*) :– L. *flos, flor-*.] **1.** A complex organ in phenogamous plants, comprising a group of reproductive organs and its envelopes. In pop. use, the characteristic feature of a *flower* is the coloured (not green) envelope; in botanical use, a flower consists normally of one or more stamens or pistils (or both), a corolla, and a calyx. **b.** In *Bryology*, the growth comprising the reproductive organs in mosses. **2.** *transf.* **a.** The down of the dandelion and thistle. ? *Obs.* 1530. †**b.** *pl.* = CATAMENIA. [After Fr. *fleurs.*] –1741. **c.** *Anc. Chem.* (*pl.*, earlier *sing.*): The pulverulent form of any substance, *esp.* as condensed after sublimation ME. **d.** Applied to various fungoid growths; a scum formed on wine, vinegar, etc., in fermentation 1548. **3.** A blossom considered independently of the plant; also *fig.* ME. **4.** A flowering plant 1500. **5.** The representation of a flower; *esp.* the FLEUR-DE-LIS (senses 2, 3) ME. **6.** An adornment or ornament; *esp.* an ornament of speech (*rare* in *sing.*) 1508. **7.** 'The pick' of a number of persons or things ME. **8.** The best, choicest, most attractive part of anything; also the gist (of a matter) 1568. **9.** The brightest example of any quality ME. **10.** The condition of being in bloom 1697. **11.** The period or state of bloom, vigour, or prosperity ME.

1. *fig.* This bud of Loue..May proue a beautious F. when next we meete SHAKS. **3.** *fig.* Nay hee's a f., in faith a very f. SHAKS. **5.** Flowers were the first Ornaments that were used at the head of.. Pages 1771. Phr. *F. of the winds* (Naut.): 'the mariner's compass on maps and charts' (Smyth). **6.** That's Æneas..hee's one of the flowers of Troy SHAKS. **7.** The flowre..of the Elect TOMSON. **8.** Thrice-happy days! The f. of each, those moments when we met TENNYSON. **9.** He is not the f. of curtesie SHAKS. **10.** An Orchard in F. ADDISON. **11.** A man in the f. of life, about thirty SCOTT.

Comb.: **f.-animals,** the Anthozoa; **-cup,** (*a*) the calyx; (*b*) the cup-shaped receptacle formed by a f.; **-fence,** the plant *Poinciana pulcherrima*; **-head,** an inflorescence consisting of a close cluster of sessile florets; **-pecker,** (*a*) any bird of the family *Dicæidæ*; (*b*) an American honey-creeper or guitguit; **-piece,** (*a*) a picture with flowers for its subject; (*b*) an arrangement of flowers; **-stalk,** the peduncle supporting the flower-head.

Flower (flau·əɹ), *v.* ME. [f. the sb., prob. after OFr. *florir, flourir* FLOURISH *v.*] **1.** *intr.* To bloom or blossom; to produce flowers. Of a flower: To expand. Also *fig.* **b.** *trans.* To bring into flower 1850. †**2.** *transf.* Of beer, etc.: To froth, mantle –1750. †**3.** *intr.* To FLOURISH (I. 2, 3) –1531. †**4.** *trans.* To adorn or cover with or as with flowers or a flower –1791. **5.** To embellish with figures of flowers 16..

1. A rose, þat flowred and fayled ME. *fig.* Whose drooping phansie never flowred out HY. MORE. **2.** It makes beer to mantle, f., and smile at you 1694. **5.** The waistcoat I am flowering RICHARDSON.

Hence **Flow·ered** *ppl. a.* covered or adorned with flowers; bearing flowers (of a specified kind or number). **Flow·erer,** a person or thing that flowers.

Flowerage (flauᵊ·rėdʒ). 1831. [f. FLOWER *sb.* and *v.* + -AGE.] **a.** Flowers collectively, blossom; a display of flowers; floral decoration. *lit.* and *fig.* **b.** The process or result of flowering. *lit.* and *fig.*

Floweret (flauᵊ·rėt). Chiefly *poet.* ME. [f. FLOWER *sb.* + -ET.] A small flower.

Flowerful (flauᵊ·ɹfŭl), *a.* 1848. [See -FUL.] Abounding in or filled with flowers.

†**Flow·er-ge·ntle.** 1561. [f. FLOWER *sb.* + GENTLE *a.*; app. after Fr. *fleur noble.*] = FLORAMOUR. –1783.

Flow·ering, *vbl. sb.* ME. [f. FLOWER *v.* + -ING¹.] **1.** The action of FLOWER *v.* in various senses. **2.** In *pl.* Figures of flowers 1864.

Flowering (flauᵊ·riŋ), *ppl. a.* ME. [f. as prec. + -ING².] **1.** That flowers; often in plant-names, as *flowering ash, box, fern,* etc. (see the sbs.) 1592. †**2.** Flourishing –1621. **3.** = FLOWERY. Also, pertaining to or issuing from flowers. 1593.

3. Groves of Myrrhe, And flouring Odours MILT.

Flowerless (flauᵊ·ɹlės), *a.* 1500. [-LESS.] Without flower or bloom; *spec.* in *Bot., f. plant* = CRYPTOGAM. Hence **Flow·erlessness.**

Flower-pot, flowerpot (flauᵊ·ɹpǫt). 1598. **1.** A vessel, commonly of red earthenware, for soil in which flowers are grown. **2.** A kind of fire-work 1842.

Flowery (flauᵊ·ri), *a.* ME. [f. FLOWER *sb.* + -Y¹.] **1.** Abounding in, covered with, or producing flowers. **2.** Composed of flowers; proceeding from or characteristic of flowers 1635. **3.** Ornamented with flowers or figures of flowers 1667. **4.** Abounding in flowers of speech; florid 1603. **5.** *Her.* = FLEURY. 1681.

4. A man of f. tongue 1879.

Flowing (flōᵘ·iŋ), *vbl. sb.* OE. [f. FLOW *v.* + -ING¹.] **1.** The action of FLOW *v.* in various senses. **2.** *concr.* That which flows, a stream, a wave (now *rare*) ME.; †an overflowing; a flood –1663.

Flowing (flōᵘ·iŋ), *ppl. a.* OE. [f. as prec. + -ING².] **1.** That flows (see FLOW *v.*) †**b.** *Math.* = FLUENT. –1842. **2.** Of lines, curves, etc.: Smoothly continuous and free from stiffness 1709. **3.** Of hair, garments, etc.: Waving, unconfined, streaming 1606. **4.** Rising like the tide; brimming, copious 1526.

1. Phr. *F. Metals*: see FLOW *v.* I. 2 c. F. eloquence 1627, numbers COWPER, urbanity 1766. **2.** Phr. *F. tracery* (Arch.): tracery where the lines branch out into leaves, arches, etc. 1815. **3.** A ship is therefore said to have a *flowing sheet* when the wind crosses the line of her course nearly at right angles FALCONER. **4.** Fat contentions and f. fees MILT.

Hence **Flow·ing-ly** *adv.*, **-ness.**

Flowk, obs. Sc. f. FLUKE.

Flown (flōᵘn), *ppl. a.* 1608. [pa. pple. of FLY *v.*¹] Used adjectively in senses of FLY *v.*¹ Also with *out,* and as in *far-, new-flown.*

Floyt(e, var. of FLUTE *sb.*¹

Flu: see FLUE *sb.*⁵

Fluate (flū·eⁱt), *sb.* 1794. [– Fr. *fluate,* early name for compounds of fluorine, esp. the fluorides, f. *fluor* fluorine + *-ate*; see -ATE⁴.] **1.** *Chem.* Now called FLUORIDE, q.v. **2.** A hydrofluosilicate applied to building-stone to harden it 1887.

Fluc(c)an: = FLOOKAN, q.v.

Flucti-, comb. f. L. *fluctus* wave, in **flucti·ferous** *a.*, bearing or producing waves; **flucti·sonous** *a.*, sounding with waves; etc. (Dicts.)

Fluctuable (flɒ·ktiuăb'l), *a. rare.* 1882. [f. FLUCTUATE + -ABLE.] Capable of fluctuating. (Dicts.) Hence **Fluctuabi·lity,** the quality of being f. H. WALPOLE.

Fluctuant (flɒ·ktiuănt), *a.* 1560. [– (O)Fr. *fluctuant,* pr. pple. of OFr. *fluctuer* – L. *fluctuare*; see next, -ANT.] **1.** Moving like the waves. Chiefly *fig.* **2.** Floating on the waves 1605.

1. His genius is f. and moonstruck SWINBURNE. **2.** Whether it be f. as the ark of Noah [etc.] BACON.

Fluctuate (flɒ·ktiu,eⁱt), *v.* 1634. [– *fluctuat-*, pa. ppl. stem of L. *fluctuare,* f. *fluctus* current, flow, wave, f. *fluct-*, pa. ppl. stem of *fluere* flow; see -ATE³.] **1.** *intr.* To move like a wave or waves, rise and fall in or as in waves; to be tossed up and down on the waves. Now *rare.* 1656. **2.** *fig.* To vary irregularly, undergo alternating changes; to be unstable; to vacillate, waver 1634. **3.** *trans.* To unsettle 1788; to throw into a wave-like motion 1850.

1. So sounds, so fluctuates, the troubled sea 1711. **2.** Fluctuating..betuix love and feare 1634. Money fluctuates in price CRUMP. **3.** A breeze began to..f. all the still perfume TENNYSON.

Fluctuation (flɒktiu,ē¹·ʃən). 1450. [–(O)Fr. *fluctuation* or L. *fluctuatio,* f. as prec.; see -ION.] **1.** A motion like that of the waves, an alternate rise and fall. Now *rare* in physical sense. 1646. **b.** *Path.* The undulation of a fluid in any cavity or tumour of the body 1620. **2.** The action or condition of fluctuating; repeated variation, vicissitude. In *pl.* 'ups and downs'. 1609. **3.** Vacillation, wavering 1450.

1. This f. of the sea GOLDSM. **2.** Changes and fluctuations of government 1712. F. of temperature and season PALEY. **3.** Fluctuations of the Mind 1717.

Flue, flew (flū), *sb.*¹ ME. [– MDu. *vluwe* fishing-net (Du. *flouw* snipe-net).] A fishing-net; **a.** a drag-net; **b.** a fixed net. Also *flue-net.*

Flue (flū), *sb.*² 1589. [app. – Flem. *vluwe* of same meaning; see FLUFF *sb.*¹] Down, nap; fluff. Also *pl.* bits of down.

Flue (flū), *sb.*³ 1582. [Of unkn. origin; the primary meaning is uncertain.] **1.** In early use = CHIMNEY; subseq. a smoke-duct in a chimney. Hence applied to a hot-air passage in a wall; a pipe or tube for conveying heat to water in some steam-boilers; and the like. **2.** *Organ-building.* The fissure or wind-way of mouth-pipes (hence also called flue-pipes) 1879. **3.** *slang.* = SPOUT *sb.* 4. 1821.

3. *In f.*: in pawn. *Up the f.*: (*a*) pawned; (*b*) dead.

Comb.: **f.-boiler,** 'a steam-boiler whose water space is traversed by flues' (Knight); **-bridge,** a wall of fire-brick in a reverberatory furnace, between the hearth and the f.; **-pipe,** an organ-pipe with a f. (see 2), a mouth-pipe, as opp. to a reed-pipe; **-plate,** 'a plate into which the ends of the flue are set' (Knight); **-stop,** an organ-stop made up of f.-pipes, or for a f. opening; **-work,** the f.-stops of an organ collectively as dist. from the reed-stops.

Flue (flū), *sb.*⁴ 1860. [Of unkn. origin.] *Naut.* The FLUKE of an anchor, or that of a harpoon.

Flue (flū), *sb.*⁵ Also **flu.** *colloq.* 1839. Short for INFLUENZA.

†**Flu·ence.** 1607. [f. as next; see -ENCE. Cf. Fr. *fluence.*] **1.** A flowing, a stream. CHAPMAN. **2.** = FLUENCY 2. –1691.

Fluency (flū·ĕnsi). 1623. [f. next; see -ENCY.] †**1.** Affluence, copiousness –1726. **2.** Readiness, smoothness; ease; used *esp.* of speech 1636.

1. F. in teares 1657. **2.** He indulged his satirical f. on the scientific collectors 1814.

Fluent (flū·ĕnt). 1589. [– *fluent-*, pr. ppl. stem of L. *fluere* flow; see -ENT.]

A. *adj.* **1.** That flows, flowing. Also *transf.* and *fig.* 1607. **2.** Capable of flowing easily; fluid, liquid 1601. **b.** *fig.* Fluid, liable to change 1648. †**3.** Flowing freely or abundantly –1682. **4.** Of speech, style, etc.: Flowing easily and readily 1625. **b.** Of a speaker, etc.: Ready in the use of words 1589. **5.** *Math.* In the doctrine of fluxions: Continuously increasing or decreasing by an infinitesimal quantity 1734.

2. b. The general body of opinion is very f. HELPS. **4.** Their f. praying and preaching WOOD. **b.** Fluent Shakespear scarce effac'd a line POPE.

Hence **Flu·ent-ly** *adv.*, †**-ness.**

B. *sb.* †**1.** A stream, a current of water –1705. **2.** *Math.* The variable quantity in fluxions which is continually increasing or decreasing 1706. Hence †**Flue·ntial** *a.* of or pertaining to fluents.

Fluey (flū·i), *a.* 1861. [f. FLUE *sb.*² + -Y¹.] Covered with flue.

Fluff (flɒf), *sb.*¹ 1790. [prob. of dial. origin and an alt. f. FLUE *sb.*², the *f* being symbolic of puffing away some light substance; cf. Flem. *vluwe* of same meaning, Du. *fluweel* velvet.] **1.** Anything light, feathery, and flocculent. **2.** A soft, downy mass or bunch 1862. **b.** *Bit of fluff* (slang): a young woman 1903.

Fluff (flɒf), *sb.*² *Sc.* and *n. dial.* 1818. [Goes with Sc. (XVIII) *fluff v.* puff, pant, of imit. origin.] A puff; a whiff; a slight explosion. *lit.* and *fig.*

Comb.: **f.-gib,** a squib. SCOTT.

Fluff (flɒf), *v.* 1859. [f. FLUFF *sb.*¹] **1.** *trans.* *Leather-manuf.* To whiten the flesh side of a skin 1882. **2.** To pick into oakum 1892. **3.** To shake *out* or *up* into a soft mass like fluff 1885. **4.** *intr.* To move or float softly like fluff; to settle *down* like a ball of fluff 1872. **5.** *slang.* In *Fluff it!* = 'take it away, I don't want it' 1859.

3. The 'Johnny Crows'..f. and plume and dust themselves without cessation LADY BRASSEY.

Fluffy (flɒ·fi), *a.* 1825. [f. FLUFF *sb.*¹ + -Y¹.] **1.** Consisting of or resembling fluff; soft and downy. **2.** Covered with fluff, down, fur, or the like; downy 1848.

1. F. whiskers THACKERAY. **2.** The f. yellow chickens 1879.

Hence **Flu·ffiness,** f. quality.

Flugelman: see FUGLEMAN.

Fluid (flū·id). 1603. [– (O)Fr. *fluide* or L. *fluidus,* f. *fluere* flow; see -ID¹.]

A. *adj.* **1.** Having the property of flowing; consisting of particles that move freely among themselves, so as to give way before the slightest pressure. (A general term including both *gaseous* and *liquid* substances.) Also *fig.* and of non-physical things. **2.** Flowing easily and clearly; fluent; as speech, etc. 1691.

1. The language of the Bible is f., passing, and literary, not rigid, fixed, and scientific M. ARNOLD.

B. *sb.* **1.** A fluid substance 1661.

Fluids are divided into liquids, which are incompletely elastic, and gases, which are completely so.

2. One of several subtle, imponderable, all-pervading substances, whose existence has been assumed to account for the phenomena of heat, magnetism, and electricity 1750.

1. The air being a f. BOYLE. Moderate exercise will enrich the Fluids 1704. **2.** The particles of the electrical f. FRANKLIN.

Comb.: **f.-compass,** 'that in which the card revolves in its bowl floated by alcohol' (Adm. Smyth); **-lens,** one in which a liquid is imprisoned between circular glass discs of the required curvature.

Hence **Flu·idal** *a.* (*Geol.*) of or resembling a f., as the *fluidal* structure of vitreous rocks. **Flui·dic** *a.* of the nature of a f.; in *Spiritualism,* of or belonging to a supposed inner 'double' (of fluid or ethereal consistence) possessed by every being. **Flui·dify** *v.* to make f. **Fluidifica·tion.**

Fluidism (flū·idiz'm). 1835. [f. prec. + -ISM.] **1.** The theory which refers all diseases to the state of the fluids in the body. **2.**

Spiritualism. The hypothesis of the existence of supersensible fluidic bodies (see FLUIDIC). So **Flu·idist,** one who supports f. (in either sense).

Fluidity (flu,i·dĭti). 1603. [f. FLUID *a.* + -ITY. Cf. Fr. *fluidité* (XVI).] **1.** The quality or condition of being FLUID 1605. **2.** Of speech, etc.: The quality of flowing easily and clearly.

1. *fig.* The f. of Radicalism 1886. **2.** There is the same comparative tenuity and f. of verse SWINBURNE.

†**Flu·idness.** 1626. [-NESS.] = FLUIDITY. –1670.

Fluke (flūk), *sb.*[1] [OE. *flōc*, corresp. to ON. *flóki*, rel. by gradation to MLG., MDu. *flac*, OHG. *flah* (G. *flach*) flat.] **1.** A flat fish, *esp.* the common flounder, *Pleuronectes flesus*. **2.** A parasitic trematode worm, of several species, found *esp.* in the livers of sheep, so called from its shape 1668. **3.** A variety of kidney potato 1868.

1. Wry-mouthed Flooke CAREW. Hence **Flu·ky** *a.*[1] infested with flukes.

Fluke (flūk), *sb.*[2] 1561. [perh. transf. use of FLUKE *sb.*[1], from the shape.] **1.** One of the broad triangular plates of iron on each arm of the anchor, which enter the ground and hold the ship. **b.** Anything resembling the prec. in shape; esp. *U.S.* 'one of the barbs of a harpoon or toggle-iron; a flue' (*Cent. Dict.*) 1605. **2.** *pl.* 'The two parts which constitute the large triangular tail of the whale' (Smyth) 1725.

1. Her owne anker, which by one of the floukes tooke fast hold P. HOLLAND. **b.** The f. of a lance 1613, of an arrow 1841. '*Fluke*, in mining..an instrument used for cleansing the hole previous to blasting' (Weale). **2.** Phr. *To turn* or *peak the ukes*: of a whale, to go under; hence (*Naut. slang*) to go to bed.

Fluke (flūk), *sb.*[3] *colloq.* 1857. [perh. of dial. origin (cf. dial. *fluke* guess, miss in fishing); or perh. a pun on FLUKE *sb.*[1] with allusion to its synon. FLOUNDER *sb.*[1]] In *Billiards*, A successful stroke made by accident or chance. Hence *gen.* an unexpected success; a piece of good luck. *A f. of wind*: a chance breeze. Hence **Flu·ky** *a.*[2] of the nature of a f.; uncertain. **Flu·kily** *adv.*

Fluke (flūk), *v.*[1] 1840. [f. FLUKE *sb.*[2]] **1.** *intr.* Of a whale: To use the flukes in swimming 1840. **2.** *trans.* **a.** To disable the flukes of (a whale) by spading. **b.** To fasten (a whale) by means of a chain or rope (*Cent. Dict.*).

Fluke (flūk), *v.*[2] 1881. [f. FLUKE *sb.*[3]] **1.** *Billiards. trans.* To hit or pocket (a ball) by a fluke; to make (a stroke) by a fluke. **2.** *transf.* To get (*in*) or obtain by a fluke 1885.

Flume (flūm), *sb.* [ME. *flum, flun* – OFr. *flum, flun* :- L. *flumen* river, f. *fluere* flow.] †**1.** A stream, a river; also, water –1652. **2.** A mill-tail 1855. **3.** *U.S.*, etc. An artificial channel for a stream of water to be applied to some industrial use 1784. **b.** A deep narrow channel or ravine with a stream running through it 1792.

Flummery (flɒ·məri). 1618. [– Welsh *llymru*, of unkn. etym.; the *fl-* is for Welsh *ll-*.] **1.** 'A kind of food made by coagulation of wheatmeal or oatmeal' (J.). In *Mod. Cookery*, any of various sweet dishes made with milk, flour, eggs, etc. **2.** *fig.* Mere compliment; nonsense, humbug, empty trifling 1749. Also *attrib.*

2. A fine f. about the..eminent genius of the person whom they are addressing THACKERAY. Hence †**Flu·mmer** *v.* to humbug.

Flummox (flɒ·məks), *v. colloq.* or *vulgar.* 1837. [prob. of dial. origin; cf. dial. *flummock* confuse, *flummox* maul, mangle, *flummocky* slovenly, beside *slummock* slattern; imit. or symbolic formations.] **1.** *trans.* To bring to confusion; to 'do for'; to bewilder, nonplus. **2.** *intr. U.S.* To give up, collapse 1847. Hence **Flu·mmox** *sb.* any failure.

Flump (flɒmp), *v. colloq.* 1790. [imit.; cf. *dump, plump, slump*.] **1.** *intr.* To fall or move heavily with a dull noise 1816. **2.** *trans.* To set or throw *down* with a dump 1830. **3.** Used advb. With a flump 1790. Hence **Flump** *sb.* the action or sound of flumping.

Flung (flɒŋ), pa. pple. of FLING *v.*

Flunk (flɒŋk), *v. U.S.* 1823. [Cf. FUNK *v.*[2], and †*flink* (*U.S.*) behave in a cowardly manner.] **1.** *intr.* To give up, back out, fail utterly. Also quasi-*trans.* To shirk (a recitation). **2.** *trans.* To cause to flunk; to pluck. Hence **Flunk** *sb.* a total failure, *esp.* in a college examination.

Flunkey (flɒ·ŋki), *sb.*[1] 1782. [orig. Sc.; poss. f. FLANKER 'one who stands at a person's flank'; see -Y[6].] **1.** A male servant, usu. in livery, *esp.* a footman, lackey; often *contempt.* Hence **2.** One who behaves obsequiously to his superiors in rank or position; a toady, snob 1855. Hence **Flu·nkeydom,** the domain of flunkeys; flunkeys collectively; the spirit of a f. **Flu·nkeyism,** the manners, speech, etc., of a f.

Flunkey (flɒ·ŋki), *sb.*[2] *U.S.* 1841. [f. FLUNK *v.* or *sb.* + -Y[6].] One who 'flunks' or fails; *esp.* an ignorant person who dabbles in financial speculation.

Fluo- (flū·o). *Chem.* and *Min.* Abbrev. of FLUOR, used as comb. form in compounds containing fluorine.

Flu:obo·rate, a salt of fluoboric acid. **Flu:o-bo·ric acid,** orig. the gas terfluoride of boron (BF_3), now applied to the compound ($H_2B_2O_4$. 6HF) obtained by saturating water with this. **Flu:oce·rine, Flu:o-ce·rite,** a native fluoride of cerium and the allied metals. **Flu:o-hy·dric** (acid) = *Fluorhydric*. Also in the names of other acids of which fluorine is a component, and in the names of salts as **Flu:o-pho·sphate, -si·licate,** etc.

Fluor (flū·ǫɹ), *sb.* 1621. [– L. *fluor*, f. *fluere* flow; see -OR 1. In sense 4, after G. Agricola (1546) *fluores* pl., tr. G. *flüsse*; cf. Fr. †*flueur*.] †**1.** A flow or flowing; a flux, stream –1671. **2.** *spec.* in *Path.* †**a.** *pl.* = FLOWER 2.b. 1621. ‖**b. Fluor albus** = LEUCORRHŒA. 1754. †**3.** A fluid state; *concr.* a fluid mass; in *pl.* the humours (of the body) –1721. **4.** *Min.* †**a.** A generic name for a class of minerals resembling gems, but readily fusible, and useful as fluxes in smelting –1692. **b.** Since 1771 applied *spec.* to such of these minerals as contain fluorine, chiefly (now only) to calcium fluoride or FLUOR-SPAR. **5.** *attrib.* †**f. acid,** hydrofluoric acid –1828.

Fluor- (flū·or), comb. f. FLUORINE bef. vowels. **Fluorhydric** [+ HYDR(-OGEN + -IC] **acid,** *Chem.* hydrofluoric acid (HF).

Fluorated (flū·ŏre[i]tĕd), *ppl. a.* 1796. [f. FLUOR- + -ATE[4] + -ED[1].] Combined with hydrofluoric acid.

Fluorene (flū·ŏrīn). 1883. [f. FLUOR + -ENE.] *Chem.* A hydro-carbon extracted from coal-tar ($C_{13}H_{10}$); when impure it is fluorescent, whence the name.

Fluoresce (fluŏre·s), *v.* 1874. [Back-formation from FLUORESCENCE.] To be or become fluorescent.

Fluorescein (fluŏre·si,in). 1876. [f. prec. + -IN[1].] *Chem.* A product fluorescent in solution obtained by heating phthalic anhydride with resorcin.

Fluorescence (fluŏre·sĕns). 1852. [f. FLUOR-SPAR (by G. G. Stokes, 1819–1903), after *opalescence*; see -ESCENT.] The coloured luminosity produced to some transparent bodies by the direct action of light, esp. of the violet and ultra-violet rays; the property, in certain substances, of rendering the ultra-violet rays visible, so as to produce this phenomenon.

Fluorescent (fluŏre·sĕnt), *a.* 1853. [f. as prec.; see -ESCENT.] Possessing or proceeding from fluorescence.

Fluoric (fluǫ·rik), *a.* 1790. [– Fr. †*fluorique*, f. *fluor*; see FLUOR, -IC.] Pertaining to or obtained from fluor or fluor-spar.

Fluoride (flū·ŏrid, -əid). Also **-id.** 1826. [f. FLUOR(INE + -IDE.] *Chem.* A binary compound of fluorine with another element.

Fluorine (flū·ŏrin, -əin). 1813. [– Fr. *fluorine* (suggested to Sir H. Davy by Ampère, 1813), f. *fluor* FLUOR 4 b + *-ine* -INE[5].] *Chem.* A non-metallic element (symbol F), forming, with bromine, chlorine, and iodine, the halogen group.

Fluorite (flū·ŏrəit). 1868. [– It. *fluorite* fluor-spar; see FLUOR, -ITE[1] 2 b.] *Min.* = FLUOR-SPAR.

Fluoroid (flū·ŏroid). [f. FLUOR + -OID.] *Crystallogr.* A solid bounded by twenty-four triangular planes; occurring frequently in fluor-spar.

Fluor-spar (flū·ǫɹ,spāɹ). 1794. [f. FLUOR + SPAR *sb.*[2]] *Min.* Native fluoride of calcium (CaF_2); found abundantly in Derbyshire, and often called *Derbyshire spar*.

Flurry (flɒ·ri), *sb.* 1698. [f. †*flurr* scatter, ruffle, fly up with a whirr, prob. after *hurry*.] **1.** A sudden agitation of the air, a gust or squall. **b.** Chiefly *U.S.* A sharp and sudden shower; a sudden rush (of birds) 1828. **2.** A sudden commotion; nervous agitation, flutter, hurry 1710. **b.** The death-throes of a whale 1823.

1. Flurries from the Hills 1698. **b.** Flurries of snow W. IRVING. **2.** In a fright and a f. TUCKER.

Flurry (flɒ·ri), *v.* 1757. [f. prec. sb.] **1.** *trans.* To agitate, 'put out'. **2.** *intr.* To flutter down in sudden or gusty showers. ?*U.S.* 1883. Hence **Flu·rried** *ppl. a.*; **-ly** *adv.*

Flurt, obs. f. FLIRT.

Flush (flɒʃ), *sb.*[1] 1596. [f. FLUSH *v.*[1]] A flight of birds suddenly started up.

Flush (flɒʃ), *sb.*[2] ME. [f. FLUSH *v.*[2]] †**1.** A pool or puddle –1513. **2.** A sudden flow; a rush of water coming or let down suddenly 1529. **b.** A sudden abundance of anything 1592. **3.** A rush of emotion or passion; elation or excitement arising from this, or from success, etc. 1614. **4.** A fresh growth (of grass, leaves, or flowers) 1773. **5.** The act of cleansing a drain by flushing 1883. **6.** A glow of light or colour, *esp* the reddening in the face caused by a rush of blood; the rush of blood itself 1630. **7.** Glow, freshness, vigour (of beauty, health, life) 1735.

2. b. The great f. of gold BACON. **3.** Unreasonable flushes of proud and vaine joy RALEGH. Phr. *In the (first, full) f.* **4.** The young shoots, now in full 'f.' after a heavy shower 1893. **6.** Hectic flushes 1803.

Flush (flɒʃ), *sb.*[3] 1529. [– Fr. †*flus*, (also mod.) *flux* XV (whence Flem. *fluys* and Sp. *flux*, It. †*flusso*) – L. *fluxus* FLUX.] *Cards.* A hand consisting of cards all of one suit.

Flush (flɒʃ), *a.*[1] 1594. [prob. f. FLUSH *v.*[2]] **1.** Abundantly full; in flood 1607. **2.** Full of life or spirit. Hence, Self-confident. Now *rare.* 1604. **3.** Plentifully supplied (*esp.* with money). Const. *of.* Of money: Plentiful. 1603. **4.** Of a high colour; blushing; flushed 1594. **5.** Even, level, in the same plane (*with*) 1626; even or level with the adjacent surface 1823.

1. In the f. moment of joy DISRAELI. **2.** F. youth reuolt SHAKS. **3.** Tom is always very f. or very hard up 1871. **4.** Thy Cheeke, now f. with Roses DRAYTON. Hence **Flu·shness,** f. condition.

Flush (flɒʃ), *a.*[2] 1591. [f. FLUSH *sb.*[3]] *Cards.* †Holding a flush. Of a hand or sequence: Forming or including a flush.

Flush (flɒʃ), *v.*[1] ME. [First in pa.t. forms *fliste, fluste*, the vocalism of which suggests an OE. **flysćian*, of imit. origin.] **1.** *intr.* To fly up quickly and suddenly; to take wing. †Also, to fly with a whirr. †Also *fig.* of persons –1642. **2.** *trans.* To cause to fly or take wing; to put up 1450.

2. Lete the spanyell flusch up the covey 1450.

Flush (flɒʃ), *v.*[2] 1548. [orig. identical with FLUSH *v.*[1], the notion of sudden movement being common to the two verbs; the range of meaning is similar to that of FLASH *v.*] **I.** Expressing sudden movement. **1.** *intr.* To rush out suddenly and copiously; to flow with force. Also *fig.* **2.** *trans.* To cause (water) to flow; to draw off water from 1594. **3.** To cleanse (a drain, etc.) by means of a rush of water 1789; to inundate (a meadow) 1861. **4.** *intr.* Of a plant: To shoot. Also *trans.* to cause to shoot. 1810. **5.** *intr.* 'To become fluxed or fluid' (*Cent. Dict.*) 1885.

1. The..Well-head, whence first flushed forth this muddy Nylus 1624. **2.** To f. a pond 1594. **3.** Sewer pipes should be flushed from time to time 1871. *fig.* F. out your sins with tears 1884.

II. With reference to light or colour. **1.** *intr.* To glow with sudden brilliance. Cf. FLASH *v.* III.2. 1809. **2.** Of the blood, etc.: To come with a rush, produce a heightened colour 1667. **3.** Of the face, etc.: To become suddenly red or hot 1709. **4.** *trans.* To make red or ruddy 1697; to suffuse or adorn with glowing colour 1746. **5.** To animate 1633.

1. As I have seen the rosy red flushing in the northern night TENNYSON. **2.** In her Cheek distemper flushing glowd MILT. *P.L.* IX. 886. **4.** How faintly-flush'd, how phantom-fair Was Monte Rosa TENNYSON. **5.** Armies flush'd with conquest ADDISON.

Flush (flɒʃ), *v.*³ 1842. [f. FLUSH *a.*¹ 5.] **1.** *trans.* To make flush; to fill in (a joint) level with the surface; to point. **2.** *Weaving.* To throw (a thread) on the surface over several threads without intersection. Also *intr.* of the thread. 1878.

†**Flush** (flɒʃ), *adv.* [f. FLUSH *a.*¹] Directly, straight. FARQUHAR.

Flusher (flɒ·ʃəɹ). *dial.* Also **flasher.** 1674. [perh. f. FLUSH *v.*², in allusion to the red colour.] The Red-backed Shrike, *Lanius collurio.*

Flushing (flɒ·ʃiŋ), *sb.* 1833. [f. name of *Flushing* (Du. *Vlissingen*), a port in Holland.] A kind of rough and thick woollen cloth, first made at Flushing.

Flu·shing, *vbl. sb.* 1573. [f. FLUSH *v.*² + -ING¹.] The action of FLUSH *v.*² in various senses; *esp.* the cleansing (of a sewer, etc.) by a rush of water.

Fluster (flɒ·stəɹ), *sb.* 1676. [See next vb.] **1.** †**a.** Heat from drinking 1710. **b.** A confused or agitated state of mind; a flurry, flutter 1728. †**2.** ? Pomp, splendour –1716.

Fluster (flɒ·stəɹ), *v.* ME. [Of unkn. origin, but resembling in sense Icel. *flaustr* hurry, *flaustra* to bustle.] †**1.** ? To excite, stimulate. ME. only. **2.** *trans.* To flush or excite with drink 1604. **3.** *intr.* To be excited or eager; to bustle 1613. **4.** *trans.* To flurry, confuse 1724.

2. His head is flustered with burgundy THACKERAY. **3.** The Dutch gunboat came flustering up KIPLING. Hence **Flu·stered** *ppl. a.* half-tipsy; confused, flurried.

Flustrate (flɒ·streⁱt), *v. vulgar.* 1712. [f. FLUSTER *v.* + -ATE³.] = FLUSTER *v.* 2 and 4. Hence **Flustra·tion,** fluster, agitation.

Flute (flūt), *sb.*¹ late ME. [Earliest forms *flowte, floite* (XIV), in XVI-XVII often *fluit* (cf. Du. *fluit*) – OFr. *flahute, fleute, flaüte* (mod. *flûte*), prob. – Pr. *flaüt.*] **1.** A musical wind instrument, consisting of a hollow cylinder or pipe, with holes along its length, stopped by the fingers, or by keys which are opened by the fingers.

The flute of the ancients was blown through a mouthpiece at the end. The modern flute, which is the *transverse* or *German flute*, is blown through an orifice at the side near the upper end.

2. A flute-player 1542. **3.** An organ-stop having a flute-like tone; also *f.-stop* 1613. **4.** Anything resembling a flute in shape; e.g. a long thin French breakfast-roll; †a tall, slender wine-glass; etc. 1649. **5.** *Arch.* A channel or furrow in a pillar, resembling the half of a flute split lengthwise, with the concave side outwards 1660. **6.** Hence any similar groove or channel 1727.

1. Indians met vs on the way, playing vpon Flutes; which is a token that they come in peace PURCHAS.

Comb.: **f.-bird** (*Australia*), the piping crow (*Gymnorhina tibicen*); **-bit,** a boring tool, used in boring hard woods; **-glass,** see sense 4 above; **-stop** = sense 3 above.

Flute (flūt), *sb.*² 1567. [– Fr. *flûte* – Du. *fluit*, a transf. use of *fluit* flute – Fr.; see prec.] *Naut.* **1.** 'A pink-rigged fly-boat, the after part of which is round-ribbed' (Smyth). **2.** A vessel of war, carrying only part of her armament, to serve as a transport 1666. Hence *Armed en f.* (Fr. *armé en flûte*), said of such a vessel.

Flute (flūt), *v.* ME. [– OFr. *fleuter* (mod. *flûter*), f. *flûte* FLUTE *sb.*¹] **1.** *intr.* To play upon a flute or pipe; also, to whistle or sing in flute-like tones. **2.** *trans.* To play (an air, etc.) on a flute; to sing in flute-like notes 1842. **3.** To form flutes (see FLUTE *sb.*¹ 5, 6) in; to arrange a dress, etc., in flutes 1578.

1. quasi-*trans.* And f. his friend, like Orpheus from the dead M. ARNOLD. **2.** Some..swan.. fluting a wild carol ere her death TENNYSON. The redwing flutes his o-ka-lee EMERSON.

Fluted (flū·tėd), *ppl. a.* 1611. [f. FLUTE *sb.*¹ and *v.* + -ED.] **1.** Having, furnished, or ornamented with flutes. **2.** *Mus.* Of a thin and flute-like tone 1787.

1. *F. spectrum*, one in which the spectrum lines appear to be grouped in flutes. F. pillars BP. BERKELEY. **2.** A f. falsetto P. BECKFORD.

‖**Flute-douce** (flūt,dus). 1676. [Fr. *flûte douce* lit. 'sweet flute'.] †**1.** The highest-pitched variety of the old flute with a mouth-piece –1747. **2.** An organ-stop so named 1876.

Fluter (flū·təɹ). ME. [f. FLUTE *v.* + -ER¹.] **1.** A flute-player. Now *rare*; repl. by FLUTIST or FLAUTIST. **2.** One who makes flutings 1858.

Fluting (flū·tiŋ), *vbl. sb.* 1481. [f. FLUTE *v.* + -ING¹.] **1.** The action of FLUTE *v.*; *esp.* the action of making flutes in columns, frills, etc.; ornamentation with flutes; fluted work. Also *attrib.*, as *f.-lathe, -plane,* etc. **2.** = FLUTE *sb.*¹ 5, 6. Also *collect.* 1611.

1. The earliest flutings of the lark 1874. **2.** She ran her fingers through the flutings of her frills 1880.

Flutist (flū·tist). 1603. [f. FLUTE *sb.*¹ + -IST.] A player on the flute.

Flutter (flɒ·təɹ), *sb.* 1641. [f. next vb.] **1.** A fluttering; the action or condition of fluttering. **b.** *colloq.* A run, a burst 1857. **2.** An agitated or disordered condition 1748. †**3.** Ostentatious display, fuss, sensation, stir –1822. **4.** *slang.* A venture, e.g. at betting, cards, etc. 1874.

1. The f. of a Fan ADDISON. **2.** Phr. *To be in, fall, put,* etc., *into a f.* **3.** All f., pride, and talk POPE.

Comb. **f.-wheel,** a water-wheel placed at the bottom of a chute so as to receive the impact of the water in the chute and penstock.

Flutter (flɒ·təɹ), *v.* [OE. *floterian, -orian* frequent. of Gmc. **flut-*; see FLEET *v.*¹, -ER⁵, and cf. synon. G. *flattern,* †*flotteren,* †*flutteren.*] †**1.** *intr.* To float to and fro. Also *fig.* –1800. **2.** Of birds: To move or flap the wings rapidly without flying or with short flights. Also *transf.* and *fig.* OE. **3.** *transf.* To move about aimlessly, restlessly, sportively, or ostentatiously 1694. **4.** To move with quick vibrations or undulations 1561. **5.** To tremble with excitement; to be in agitation 1668. **6.** *trans.* (*causatively*). To cause to flutter; to move (a thing) in quick irregular motions 1621; *fig.* to throw (a person) into confusion, agitation, or tremulous excitement 1664.

2. Like as byrdes flotre aboute their nestes COVERDALE *Isa.* 31:5. **3.** One flaunts in rags, one flutters in brocade POPE. **4.** Teach..little hearts to f. at a Beau POPE. It [the pulse] paused —it fluttered SHELLEY. **5.** Fluttering with her own audacity THACKERAY. **6.** All unawares, Fluttering his pennons vain MILT. *fig.* Like an Eagle in a Dove-coat, I Flutter'd your Volcians in Coriolus *Cor.* (Fo. 3) V. vi. 116.

Hence **Flu·tterer,** one who or that which flutters (*lit.* and *fig.*). **Flu·tteringly** *adv.*

Fluty (flū·ti), *a.* 1823. [f. FLUTE *sb.*¹ + -Y¹.] Flute-like in tone, soft and clear.

Fluvial (flū·viăl), *a.* ME. [– L. *fluvialis,* f. *fluvius* river, f. *fluere* flow; see -AL¹.] Of or pertaining to a river or rivers; found or living in a river. Hence **Flu·vialist,** one who explains certain geological phenomena by the action of streams.

Fluviatile (flū·viătil), *a.* 1599. [– Fr. *fluviatile* – L. *fluviatilis*, f. *fluviatus* moistened, wet, f. *fluvius* (prec.); see -ILE.] Of or pertaining to a river or rivers; found, growing, or living in rivers; formed or produced by the action of rivers.

F. Fishes 1681, mud 1823, denudation HUXLEY.

†**Fluvia·tion.** [f. L. *fluviatus* (see prec.) + -ION.] The process of steeping (flax) in water. SIR T. BROWNE.

Fluvio- (flū·vio), comb. f. L. *fluvius* river, as in **flu·vio-marine** *a.*, an epithet of deposits formed by river-currents at the bottom of the sea; etc.

Flux (flɒks), *sb.* ME. [– (O)Fr. *flux* or L. *fluxus*, f. *fluere* flow.]

I. *spec.* **1.** An abnormally copious flowing of blood, excrement, etc., from the bowels or other organs. *spec.* An early name for dysentery. **2.** A flowing out, issue, discharge (of humours, etc.) 1447; †also, that which flows or is discharged –1654.

1. Phr. *Bloody f.* (cf. BLOODY); Rendered unfit for action by a bloody f. 1777. **2.** *A.Y.L.* III. ii. 70.

II. *gen.* **1.** The action of flowing. Now usu. *fig.* 1600. **2.** The flowing in of the tide. Often in phr. *flux and reflux.* 1612. **3.** A flowing stream, a flood. Also *transf.* and *fig.* 1600. †**4.** The passing away (of life, time, etc.) –1759. **5.** A continuous succession of changes 1625. **6.** *Math.* A continued motion (of a point) 1656. **7.** *Physics.* The rate of flow of any fluid across a given area; the amount which crosses an area in a given time 1863.

1. Fire to subsist requires a F. of Air 1748. **2.** A..f. and reflux of fears and hopes DE FOE. **3.** *transf.* The Fluxe of companie *A.Y.L.* II. i. 52. *fig.* This f. of guesses M. ARNOLD. **5.** The bodies of all animals are in a constant f. BUTLER.

III. †**1.** Liquefaction or fusion –1799. **2.** *Metall.* Any substance that is mixed with a metal, etc., to facilitate its fusion; also a substance used to render colours fusible in enamelling and the colouring of porcelain and glass 1704.

2. The *black f.* is formed, by setting fire to a mixture of one part of nitrate of potassa, and two of bi-tartrate of potassa.. *White f.* is obtained by projecting into a red-hot crucible equal parts of the same salts 1826.

†**Flux** (flɒks), *a.* 1677. [– L. *fluxus,* ppl. a., f. *fluere* flow.] That is in a state of flux; fluctuating, ever-changing –1797.

Flux (flɒks), *v.* 1477. [f. FLUX *sb.*] †**1.** *trans.* To treat by subjecting to a flux; also, to produce a flux in (a person); †also *fig.* –1785. †**b.** *intr.* –1755. **2.** *intr.* †**a.** To bleed copiously 1638. **b.** To flow copiously 1823. **3.** *trans.* To make fluid, fuse 1477. **4.** To treat with a flux (see FLUX *sb.* III. 2) 1781. **5.** *intr.* To become fluid; to melt 1669.

1. *fig.* Praying for the Dead, which doth so f. the pocket 1660. **2. b.** Once fix the seat of your disorder, and your fancies f. into it LAMB. Hence †**Fluxa·tion,** treatment by fluxing; flowing on.

Fluxible (flɒ·ksib'l), *a. Obs.* or *arch.* 1471. [– OFr. *fluxible* or late L. *fluxibilis* liquid, f. *flux-*, pa. ppl. stem of *fluere* flow; see -IBLE.] **1.** Apt to flow, fluid 1551. **2.** Capable of being melted 1471. **3.** Liable to flux or change 1561. Hence **Flu·xibly** *adv.* **Fluxibi·lity. Flu·xibleness,** f. quality.

Fluxile (flɒ·ksil), *a. Obs.* or *arch.* 1605. [– late L. *fluxilis*, f. as prec.; see -ILE.] = FLUXIBLE 1, 3. Hence **Fluxi·lity,** f. quality.

Fluxion (flɒ·kʃən). 1541. [– (O)Fr. *fluxion*, or f. as prec.; see -ION.] **1.** The action of flowing; a flowing forth. Also continuous or progressive change. Now *rare.* 1599. †**b.** = EFFLUVIUM 2 a. –1748. **2.** An excessive flow of blood, serum, etc., to any organ or part of the body. Also *concr.*, that which flows. 1541. **3.** = FLUX *sb.* I. 1. 1563. **4.** *Math.* [mod.L. *fluxio.*] In the Newtonian form of the infinitesimal calculus: 'The rate or proportion at which a flowing or varying quantity increases its magnitude' (Hutton). (But used by 18th c. writers for what Newton called the 'moment' of a fluent, and modern analysts call the 'differential'.) 1704. **b.** Hence *Fluxions* is used as a name for the Newtonian calculus 1702. ¶ **c.** *loosely.* An infinitesimal quantity. DE QUINCEY.

Comb. **f.-structure** (*Geol.*), 'an arrangement of the crystallites, crystals, or particles of a rock in streaky lines..indicative of the internal movement of the mass previous to its consolidation.' Called also *flow-structure.*

Hence **Flu·xional** *a. Math.* of or pertaining to a f. or the method of fluxions; pertaining to flowing, fluxible. **Flu·xionary** *a. Math.* fluxional; of the nature of, or subject to continuous change. **Flu·xionist,** one who uses or is skilled in mathematical fluxions.

†**Flu·xive,** *a.* 1597. [– med. L. *fluxivus* fleeting, transitory, f. as prec.; see -IVE.] Apt to flow, fluid (*lit.* and *fig.*). Also fluctuating, variable. –1716.

†**Flu·xure** (flɒ·ksiŭɹ). 1596. [– L. *fluxura* flowing, f. as prec.; see -URE.] **a.** The quality of being fluid 1599. **b.** That which flows –1622.

Fly (fləi). *sb.*¹ *Pl.* **flies** (fləiz). [OE. *flȳġe, flēoġe* = OS., OHG. *flioga* (Du. *vlieg*, G. *fliege*) :– WGmc. **fleuʒ(j)ō*, f. Gmc. **fleuʒan* (see next); cf. ON. *fluga.*] **1.** †Any winged insect; as the bee, gnat, locust, moth, etc.; cf. BUTTERFLY –1774. **b.** Any dipterous or two-winged insect OE. **2.** In farmers' and gardeners' language, the insect parasite chiefly injurious to a particular crop or animal; hop-fly, potato-fly, sheep-fly. Hence *collect.* in *sing.* the corresponding disease. 1704. **3.** *Angling.* **a.** An insect attached to a hook as a lure in fly-fishing 1653. **b.** An artificial fly, i.e. a fish-hook dressed to resemble some insect 1589. †**4. a.** A familiar demon. **b.** *transf.* A spy (cf. Fr. *mouche*). **c.** A parasite (cf. L. *musca*). –1649. **4.** *Printing.* The person who takes the sheets from the press; also, that part of a printing machine which usually does this now. 1732.

1. Phr. *F. in amber*: cf. AMBER *sb.*[1] 3. *To break, crush, a f. upon the wheel* (fig.): to spend great energy and labour on something not worth it. *A f. in the ointment* [after Eccles. 10:1]: a trifling circumstance which spoils the enjoyment of a thing. *There are no flies on*: there is no fault to be found with; there is nothing 'shady' about (orig. *Colonial* and *U.S. slang*). **Black f.,** *U.S.* any one of the species of the genus *Simulium*, some of which cause great suffering by their bites. **Hessian f., Spanish f., Tsetse-f.,** etc.: see HESSIAN, etc. **3.** Or with a Flie, either a natural or an artificial Flie WALTON.

Combs.

1. General: as *f.-belt, -country, -maggot, -maker, -tackle, -taker*, etc.

2. Special: **f.-bird,** a humming-bird (cf. Fr. *oiseau-mouche*); **-blister,** a plaster made of *Cantharides*; **-book,** a case in the form of a book for artificial flies; †**-cap,** a kind of head-dress formerly worn by women; **-case,** the covering of an insect; *spec.* the elytron of beetles; **-hook,** a hook baited with a f.; **-line,** a line for f.-fishing; **-nut,** 'a nut with wings, to be twisted by the hand' (Knight); **-paper,** paper prepared to catch or poison flies; **-powder,** a powder used to kill flies; **-rod,** a rod for f.-fishing; **-snapper,** *U.S.*, a name of certain f.-catching birds, (*a*) the genus *Myiagra*; (*b*) *Phainopepla nitens*; **-speck, -spot,** a stain produced by the excrement of an insect; **-water,** a solution of arsenic, or decoction of quassia-bark, for killing flies; **-weevil,** *U.S.*, the common grain-moth (*Gelechia cerealella*); **-weight,** a boxer whose weight is 8 st.

b. In plant-names, as **f.-agaric,** *Agaricus muscarius*, called also FLY-BANE; **-honeysuckle,** (*a*) a variety of honeysuckle (*Lonicera xylosteum*); (*b*) a species of Halleria; **-orchid, -orchis,** a name for *Ophrys muscifera.*

Fly (fləi), *sb.*[2] *Pl.* **flies.** OE. [f. FLY *v.*[1]]

I. 1. †The action, or (*rec.*) an act of flying. **2.** *On the f.*: orig. on the wing; hence, in motion; in *Base-ball*, the course of a ball that has been struck, until it touches the ground. 1851.

II. 1. A quick-travelling carriage; *esp.* a light vehicle, introduced at Brighton in 1816, and originally drawn by men; subseq. extended to any one-horse covered carriage, as a cab or hansom, let out on hire 1708. **2.** Something attached by the edge (cf. FLAP *sb.*); as **a.** A strip or lap on a garment, to contain or cover the button-holes 1844; **b.** The sloping part of the canvas of a tent; also, the flap at the entrance, forming a door 1810; **c.** The breadth from the staff of a flag to the end; also, the part of a flag farthest from the staff 1841; **d.** *pl. Theatr.* The space over the proscenium 1805. **3.** *techn.*

a. *Naut.* A compass card 1571. **b.** A speed-regulating device, usually consisting of vanes on a rotating shaft, used in the striking parts of clock-machinery, etc. 1599. **c.** A fly-wheel, a pair of weighted arms, or other similar device, used to regulate the speed of machinery 1648. **d.** = FANNER 2. 1807. **e.** One of the cylinders of a carding machine 1842. **f.** In *Knitting* (*machine*), another name for the Latch; in *Spinning*, the arms which revolve around the bobbin in a spinning-frame, to twist the yarn; in *Weaving*, a shuttle driven through the shed by a blow or jerk (Knight). Also in *Hand-spinning*: the spindle 1851. **g.** In the pianoforte, a hinged board which covers the keys when not in use. **4.** Waste cotton 1879.

Comb. **f.-ball** (*Base-ball*), a ball that may be caught 'on the f.'; **-bill,** a handbill to be scattered broadcast, also *attrib.*; **-block** (*Naut.*), 'the block spliced into the topsail-tye' (Smyth); **-bridge** = FLYING BRIDGE; **-coach** = FLY *sb.*[2] II. 1; **-governor** = FLY *sb.*[2] II. 3 c; **-press,** a screw press worked by a f. (see FLY *sb.*[2] II. 3 c); **-punching-press,** a press for cutting teeth on saws, and the like; **-rail,** that part of a table which turns out to support the leaf; **-table,** a table with flaps; **-title,** the half-title in front of the general title, or which divides sections of a work.

Fly (fləi), *a. slang.* 1811. [Has been (doubtfully) referred to FLY *v.*[1]] **1.** Knowing, wide-awake. **2.** Of the fingers: Nimble, skilful 1834.

Fly (fləi), *v.*[1] Pa. t. **flew** (flū); pa. pple. **flown** (flōᵘn). [OE. *flēogan* = OFris. *fliāga*, OS. **fliogan* (Du. *vliegen*), OHG. *fliogan* (G. *fliegen*), ON. *fljúga* :– Gmc. **fleuȝan*.]

I. 1. *intr.* To move through the air with wings OE. Also *fig.*; *esp.* of fame, a report, etc. ME. **b.** Occas. = 'fly away' 1480. **c.** *intr.* and *trans.* To travel or traverse by aircraft; to pilot aircraft 1884. **2.** *trans.* (*causatively*). To set (birds) flying 1607. **3.** *Hawking.* **a.** Of the hawk: To gain by flying a position of attack. Const. *at.* 1674. **b.** Of the falconer: To cause to attack by flying 1591. **c.** To chase with a hawk. Also of the hawk. 1590. **4.** *intr.* To pass or rise quickly in or through the air OE. **b.** Of stairs: To descend or ascend without change of direction 1685. **5.** *trans.* (*causatively*). To cause to fly 1739. **6.** *intr.* To float loosely, to flutter, wave 1659. **b.** *trans.* To set flying; to carry at the mast-head; to hoist; occas. with *out* 1655. **7.** *intr.* To move or travel swiftly; *esp.* of time ME. **8.** To move with a start or rush 1590. **9.** Of things: To be forced or driven off suddenly or with a jerk ME. Of money: To 'go' rapidly 1632. **b.** To break up suddenly, shiver, split up 1470. **c.** *Naut.* Of the wind: To shift or veer suddenly 1699.

1. Phr. *As the crow flies*: see CROW *sb.*[1] *fig. To f. high, low*: to aim at, avoid, distinction, notoriety, etc. **b.** The black bat, night, has flown TENNYSON. **2.** Ile flie my Hawke with yours 1607. **4.** You leaden messengers..F. with false ayme SHAKS. To f. over a gate 1791. **5.** O Madam, You f. your thoughts like kites TENNYSON. *To f. a kite* (colloq. or slang): to raise money by an accommodation bill; hence *to f. a bill.* **6.** To. march with drums beating and colours flying 1659. **b.** The steamship..flying signals of distress 1885. **7.** The velocity with which the earth flies through space TYNDALL. **8.** In a violent commotion, they had flown to arms 1847. She flew up-stairs 1854. Phr. *To f. in the face of*: see FACE *sb. To f. at, on, upon*: to spring with violence upon, attack with fury, rush upon; *lit.* and *fig. To f. in* or *into* (a passion, etc.); to pass suddenly into. *To f. off*: *lit.* to start away; to revolt; *fig.* to take another course; to break away (from an agreement, etc.). *To f. out*: (*a*) to rush out; (*b*) to explode or burst out into violent action, language, or temper. **9.** From the could stone sparkes of fire doe flie SHAKS. I shall certainly make his money f. LADY C. BURY. Phr. *To f. open, to, up.* **b.** The crackling faggot flies GOLDSM. **c.** The Winds f. in a moment quite round the Compass DAMPIER. *To f. up in the wind*, is when a ship's head comes suddenly to windward, by carelessness of the helmsman SMYTH.

Phrase. *To let f.* **a.** To discharge (missiles); *absol.* to fire, shoot. Also *fig.* **b.** *Naut.* To allow (a sail or sheet) to f. loose; rarely to set (a sail), to carry, hoist (colours).

II. In senses of FLEE (exc. II. 2) OE.

I'll make him f. the land B. JONS. Unless..one f. into the Ports for shelter 1653. He [Hermes] grasps the wand that causes sleep to f. POPE. True pity..flies the rich 1839.

Fly (fləi), *v.*[2] Pa. t. and pple. **flied, flyed.** 1836. [f. FLY *sb.*[1] and [2].] To travel by, or convey in, a fly.

Fly-away. 1775. [f. vbl. phr.; see FLY *v.*[1]] **A.** *adj.* Ready or apt to fly away. Of articles of dress: Streaming, loose. Of persons: Flighty, extravagant.

Servant-girls with flyaway caps on their heads 1871.

B. *sb.* One that flies away. Cf. *runaway.* 1838. **b.** *Naut.* A delusive appearance of land, a mirage. Also *quasi*-proper name, *Cape Flyaway.* 1867.

a. Truth is such a flyaway EMERSON.

Fly-bane. 1597. [f. FLY *sb.*[1] + BANE.] **1.** A pop. name of plants: (*a*) = CATCHFLY; (*b*) the ploughman's spikenard (*Inula conyza*); (*c*) *Agaricus muscarius.* **2.** Poison for flies. SWIFT.

Fly·-bi·tten, *ppl. a.* 1597. [f. as prec. + BITTEN.] Bitten by flies: †**a.** Fly-specked; †**b.** FLY-BLOWN 1598; **c.** Stung by flies 1884.

a. These Fly-bitten Tapistries 2 *Hen. IV*, II. i. 159.

Fly·-blow, *sb.* 1556. [f. FLY *sb.*[1] + BLOW *sb.*[2]] The egg or young larva of a blow-fly. Also *collect.*

Fly·-blow, *v.* 1603. [f. FLY *sb.*[1] + BLOW *v.*[1]] **1.** *trans.* Of the fly: To deposit eggs in (meat, etc.); hence, to corrupt secretly, taint. Chiefly *fig.* **2.** *intr.* Of flies: To deposit their eggs. POPE.

Fly-blown (fləi·blōᵘn), *ppl. a.* 1529. [f. as prec. + BLOWN *ppl. a.*[1]] **1.** Full of fly-blows; tainted, putrid, impure. Also *fig.* **2.** *slang.* Drunk 1877.

Fly-boat (fləi·bōᵘt). 1577. [– Du. *vlieboot* boat used orig. on the *Vlie*, a channel leading out of the Zuyder Zee; later assoc. with FLY *sb.*[1]] **1.** A fast-sailing vessel used: **a.** *esp.* in the coasting trade (*Obs.* exc. *spec.* a Dutch flat-bottomed boat) –1769; **b.** for warlike purposes, voyages of discovery, etc. (*Obs.* exc. *Hist.*) 1590. †**2.** A small boat, *esp.* a ship's boat –1820. †**3.** A Shetland herring buss –1794. **4.** A swift passage boat used on canals 1841.

Fly·-catcher. 1600. [f. FLY *sb.*[1] + CATCHER.] **1.** One who, or that which, catches flies. **2.** A bird that catches flies; in England, esp. *Muscicapa grisola*; in America, esp. *Tyrannus carolinensis* or *T. pipiri* 1678. **3. a.** A spider that catches flies 1750. **b.** = FLY-TRAP 2. 1863.

1. 'The fly-catcher', as he [Darwin] was known to the crew, was a prime favourite 1887.

Fly·-dung, *v.* 1860. [f. FLY *sb.*[1] + DUNG *v.*] *Dyeing.* In the process of dyeing with madder: To subject for the first time to the process of dunging (see DUNG *v.* 3.).

Flyer, flier. ME. [f. FLY *v.*[1] + -ER[1]. Both forms are in good mod. use.] **1.** That which flies or is carried by the air. **b.** An airman. **2.** One who or that which moves with exceptional speed, e.g. a fish, horse, ship, etc. 1795. **3.** Applied to parts of a machine that have a quick revolution; e.g. an appliance for regulating the motion of a roasting-jack; a sail of a windmill; that part of a spinning machine which twists the thread as it conducts it to and winds it upon the bobbin; etc. 1674. **4. a.** *pl.* Steps forming a straight flight; opp. to *winders* 1667. **b.** *U.S.* A small handbill or fly-sheet 1889. **c.** *Printing.* 'A vibratory rod with fingers which take the sheet of paper from the tapes and carry it to the delivery table' (Knight). **5.** A flying jump or leap 1883. **b.** Hence, *U.S.*, A speculative purchase of stock by one not a regular buyer, in hope of immediate profit 1886. **6.** = FLEER *sb.*[1] 1460.

Fly-fish, *v.* 1755. [Back-formation from FLY-FISHING *vbl. sb.*] *intr.* To fish with a fly as bait. Hence **Fly·-fisher.**

Fly·-fishing, *vbl. sb.* 1653. [f. FLY *sb.*[1]] Fishing with a fly.

Fly·-flap. ME. [f. FLY *sb.*[1] + FLAP *sb.*] **1.** An instrument for driving away flies. †**2.** A stroke with a fly-flap 1735. Hence **Fly·-flap** *v.* to strike with a fly-flap; to beat, whip. **Fly·-flapper,** one who drives away flies with a fly-flap; a FLY-FLAP (sense 1).

Flying (fləi·iŋ), *vbl. sb.* 1548. [f. FLY *v.*[1] + -ING[1].] **1.** The action of FLY *v.*[1] **2.** *attrib.*, as *f.-machine*; also **f. country, county** (*Hunting*), one that affords long unbroken runs; **f. fence,** one to be taken at a flying leap; **f. time,** the time when a hawk is in condition to be flown.

Flying (fləi·iŋ), *ppl. a.* OE. [f. FLY *v.*[1] + -ING[2].] **1.** That moves through the air with wings. **b.** In names of insects, as *f.-glow-worm.* Also of fish, reptiles, quadrupeds, etc., which by means of special appendages make movements resembling flight; as *f.-frog, -gurnard, -herring, -lemur, -lizard, -phalanger, -squid.* Also **f.-dog,** a kind of vampire-bat; **f. hart, stag** = Fr. *cerf-volant*, a stag-beetle. 1626. **2.** That passes (quickly) through the air 1535. **3.** Floating loosely, fluttering; hanging loose 1607. **4.** That passes or travels swiftly; rapid 1658. †**b.** *esp.* in *f. post*, a post travelling by relays of horses –1705. **c.** Passing; hasty, transient. Also, Rapidly constructed, temporary. 1665. **5.** That flies about; used *esp.* of a tale, rumour, etc., circulating without definite authority ME. **6.** That flees 1594.

1. So seem'd Farr off the f. Fiend MILT. Phr. †*F. pension* (fig.): a pension to commence if the pensioner lost his place H. WALPOLE. **2.** A f., shuting or falling star 1563. **3.** Phr. *F. jib*, 'a light sail set before the jib, on the *flying jib-boom*'. *With f. colours* (fig.): with outward signs of success. †*Under* or *with f. seal*: said of a letter with seal attached but not closed; I enclose the letter which I have written to the Prince Regent under a f. seal WELLINGTON. **4.** The f. Hours ROWE. Phr. *F. leap*: a running jump. *F. handicap, mile*: one in which the starting post is passed at full speed. **c.** A f. trip to London 1806. To lay down a f. line to Lucknow 1857. Phr. (*Mil.* and *Naval*) *F. brigade, column, hospital, party, squadron. F. artillery*: a corps trained to rapid evolutions. *F. camp*: see CAMP *sb.*[2] *F. sap*: a sap formed by placing and filling several gabions at the same time. **5.** *F. sheet* a leaflet printed for distribution broadcast. F. pains 1805. **6.** To persecute from far the f. Doe DRYDEN.

Fly·ing bri·dge. 1489. [f. FLYING *ppl. a.*] †**a.** As tr. Fr. *pont-levis* (drawbridge) CAXTON. †**b.** = FLOATING BRIDGE. –1726. **c.** A temporary bridge for military purposes 1876.

Fly·ing bu·ttress. 1669. A prop or stay (usually carried by a segment of an arch), springing from a pier or other support, and abutting against a structure, for the purpose of resisting thrust.

Fly·ing fish. 1511. [f. FLYING *ppl. a.* + FISH *sb.*[1]] Either of two kinds of fish (*Dactylopterus* and *Exocœtus*), which are able to rise in the air by means of enlarged wing-like pectoral fins. **b.** A constellation 1868.

Fly·ing fo·x. 1759. [f. as prec. + FOX.] A family of fruit-eating bats (*Pteropidæ*), found in the tropical East and in Australia.

Fly·ing machi·ne. 1736. [f. FLYING *vbl. sb.* + MACHINE *sb.*] **1.** A kind of trapeze. **2.** A machine capable of being controlled in the air; usu. a heavier-than-air machine dependent on motor power 1848.

Fly·ing squi·rrel. 1624. [f. FLYING *ppl. a.* + SQUIRREL.] A name for two genera (*Pteromys* and *Sciuropterus*) of *Sciuridæ*, which can float through the air by means of an extension of the skin connecting their fore and hind limbs.

Fly·-leaf. 1850. [FLY *sb.*[2]] A blank leaf at the beginning or end, but *esp.* at the beginning, of a book; the blank leaf of a circular, etc.

Fly·man. 1845. [f. FLY *sb.*[2] + MAN *sb.*] **1.** One who drives a fly. **2.** *Theatr.* A man stationed in the flies, to work the ropes, etc. 1883.

Fly·-net. [f. FLY *sb.*[1] OE. *flēohnet.*] A net to keep away flies.

Flysch (fliʃ). 1853. [Swiss dial.] *Geol.* An Alpine series of tertiary strata, consisting of slates, marls, and fucoidal sandstones.

Fly·-sheet. 1875. [f. FLY *v.*[1]] = *flying sheet*: see FLYING *ppl. a.*

Fly·-trap. 1774. [f. FLY *sb.*[1] + TRAP *sb.*[1]] **1.** A trap for flies 1855. **2.** A fly-catching plant, esp. *Apocynum androsæmifolium*. Venus's flytrap = *Dionæa muscipula*.

Fly·-wheel. 1784. [f. FLY *sb.*[2] + WHEEL.] A wheel with a heavy rim, attached to a revolving shaft, in order either to regulate the motion of the machinery, or to accumulate power.

†**Fnese,** *v.* [OE. **fnēosan*, *ġefnēsan*, cogn. w. Du. *fniesen*, ON. *fnýsa* (Sw. *fnysa*, Da. *fnyse* snort). See SNEEZE.] *intr.* To sneeze; also, to puff, snort –ME.

Foal (fōᵘl), *sb.* [OE. *fola* = OFris. *fola*, OS. *folo*, MDu. *volen*, (also mod.) *veulen* OHG. *folo* (G. *fohlen* n.), ON. *foli*, Goth. *fula* :– Gmc. **folon*, rel. to synon. L. *pullus*, Gr. πῶλος, Arm. *ul.* Cf. FILLY.] **1.** The young of the equine genus of quadrupeds; *properly*, a colt; but also, a filly. **2.** *attrib.*, as **f.-teeth,** the first teeth of a horse 1696.

Phr. *In f.*, *with f.*, (of a mare) pregnant.

Foal (fōᵘl), *v.* ME. [f. prec. sb.] **1.** *trans.* To bring forth (a foal); said of a mare, she-ass, etc. **2.** *absol.* or *intr.* 1521.

Foalfoot (fōᵘ·lfut). Also **foal's foot.** ME. [Named from the shape of the leaves.] = COLTSFOOT.

Foam (fōᵘm), *sb.* [OE. *fām* = (O)HG. *feim* :– WGmc. **faim-* :– IE. **poimo-*, rel. to L. *pumex* PUMICE and *spuma* SPUME *sb.*] **1.** The aggregation of minute bubbles formed in water or other liquid by agitation, fermentation, effervescence, etc. **b.** *spec.* The foaming saliva issuing from the mouth in epilepsy, rabies, etc. OE. Also *fig.* **2.** Foaming water, the sea. *arch.* OE. **3.** *Min.* = APHRITE.

Comb.: **f.-bow,** a bow similar to a rainbow, formed by sunlight upon f.; **-cock** (*Steam-engine*), a cock at the water level, to blow off scum; **-spar, -stone,** see APHRITE and APHRODITE *sb.*[2]

Foam (fōᵘm), *v.* OE. [New formation on FOAM *sb.*, superseding OE. *fǣman* (ME. *feme*) = OHG. *feimen* :– WGmc. **faimjan.*] **1.** *intr.* To emit foam; *esp.* to froth at the mouth. Often used hyperbolically. Of a horse, etc.: To be covered with foam. **2.** To froth, gather foam. Also fig. ME. **3.a.** *intr.* Of a goblet, etc.: To be filled with foaming liquor. **b.** *trans.* To fill or brim with foaming liquor. 1725. **4.** *trans.* To send forth or emit in or like foam. Chiefly *fig.* ME. **5.** *nonce-use.* To draw (a chariot) *along* amid foam. KEATS.

1. He [Cæsar]..foam'd at mouth, and was speechlesse SHAKS. **2.** The anger'd Ocean fomes *Ant. & Cl.* II. vi. 21. **4.** Foaming out their own disgrace COWPER. Hence **Foa·mingly** *adv.*

Foamless (fōᵘ·mlės), *a.* 1821. [See -LESS.] Free from foam.

Foamy (fōᵘ·mi), *a.* [OE. *fāmiġ*, *fǣmiġ*, f. *fām* FOAM *sb.*; see -Y[1].] **1.** Covered with foam, frothy. **2.** Consisting of, pertaining to, or resembling foam ME.

2. The f. surf COWPER. F. lilac-blossom MALLOCK.

Fob (fǫb), *sb.*[1] ME. [f. FOB *v.*[1]] †**1.** A cheat, impostor. ME. only. **2.** A trick, an artifice. Now only *slang.* 1622.

Fob (fǫb), *sb.*[2] 1653. [orig. cant term; prob. of G. origin (cf. G. dial. *fuppe* pocket, *fuppen* vb.).] **1.** A small pocket formerly made in the waistband of the breeches and used for carrying a watch, money, etc. **2.** U.S. = *fob-chain* 1889. **3.** *attrib.*, as **f.-chain,** the chain attached to a watch carried in the fob.

Fob (fǫb), *v.*[1] 1583. [Parallel to FOP *v.* 2 and G. *foppen* quiz, banter.] **1.** *trans.* To cheat, deceive, 'take in'. **2.** To procure, or promote by trickery. Also with *in, into, upon.* ? *Obs.* 1653. **3. Fob off.** To put off deceitfully; to baffle, cajole; to put off *with* something inferior 1597. †**b.** To put off or get rid of by a trick –1641.

1. While every one else he is fobbing, He still may be honest to me FIELDING.

Fob (fǫb), *v.*[2] 1818. [f. FOB *sb.*[2]] To put into one's fob, to pocket.

Focal (fōᵘ·kăl), *a.* 1693. [– mod.L. *focalis*, f. FOCUS; see -AL[1].] Of or pertaining to a focus; collected or situated at a focus. Also *fig.*

Phr. *F. distance* or *length* (of a lens or mirror): the distance between the centre and the focus. *F. plane*: the locus of the foci of different systems of parallel rays refracted through a lens. *F. plane shutter* (Photogr.): a blind with (usu. adjustable) slit that moves across the front of the plate or film. *F. point*: the intersection of a f. plane with the axis of the lens. Hence **Fo·cally** *adv.* at a focus.

Focalize (fōᵘ·kăləiz), *v.* 1845. [f. FOCAL *a.* + -IZE.] **1.** *trans.* To bring to a focal point; to focus. Also *fig.* **2.** To adjust the focus of (the eye); also *absol.* (of the eye) 1878.

1. Light is focalized in the eye, sound in the ear DE QUINCEY. Hence **Focaliza·tion.**

Focimeter (fosi·mĭtəɹ). Also **foco-.** 1853. [f. FOCUS + -METER.] *Photogr.* An instrument for finding the chemical focus of a lens which has not been properly achromatized.

Focimetry (fosi·mėtri). Also **foco-.** 1881. [f. as prec. + -METRY.] Measurement of focal distance.

Fo'c'sle: see FORECASTLE.

Focus (fōᵘ·kɒ̆s), *sb.* Pl. **foci;** also **focuses,** irreg. **focusses.** 1644. [– L. *focus* fireplace, domestic hearth.] **1.** *Geom.* **a.** In plane geometry: One of the points from which the distances to any point of a given curve are connected by a linear relation 1656. **b.** In solid geometry (see quot.) 1874. **2.** *Optics, Heat,* etc. The point at which rays meet after being reflected or refracted; also, the point from which the rays appear to proceed (= *virtual f.*) 1685. Also *transf.* and *fig.* **b.** That point or position at which an object must be situated, in order that the image produced by the lens may be clear and well-defined. Hence *in,* or *out of f.* (lit. and fig.). 1713. **c.** The focal length (of a lens); also, the adjustment (of the eye, or an eyeglass) necessary to produce a clear image 1693. **3.** *Acoustics.* The point or space towards which the sound waves converge 1644. **4.** Of a disease: The, or a, principal seat 1684. **5.** The centre of activity, or area of greatest energy, of a storm, eruption, etc. Also *fig.* 1796.

1. The ellipse and hyperbola have each two foci; but the parabola only one HUTTON. **b.** A point through which can be drawn two lines, each touching the surface and the imaginary circle at infinity and such that the tangent plane to the surface through either also touches the circle at infinity SALMON. **2.** *Conjugate foci*: see CONJUGATE *a. Principal f.*: the point at which parallel rays meet after passing through a convergent lens. *Solar f.* = prec. *Actinic* or *chemical f.* (of a lens), the point to which the actinic rays converge. **b.** *fig.* The bringing all these scattered counsels into a f. FRANKLIN. **5.** The centre or f. of the West Indian hurricanes 1875. *fig.* The principal f. of scientific activity HUXLEY.

Focus (fōᵘ·kɒ̆s), *v.* Pples. **focused, -ing;** irreg. **focussed, -ing.** 1775. [f. prec. sb.] **1.** *trans.* To cause to converge to or as to a focus 1807. Also *intr.* for *refl.* **2.** To adjust the focus of (the eye, a lens, etc.) 1814. **3.** To bring into focus 1775.

3. The image..is focussed..by..adjusting the lens 1865.

Fodder (fǫ·dəɹ), *sb.* [OE. *fōdor* = MLG. *vōder*, (M)Du. *voeder*, OHG. *fuotar* (G. *futter*), ON. *fóðr* :– Gmc. **fōðram*, f. **fōð-*; see FOOD.] †**1.** Food in general –1634. **2.** Food for cattle; now only dried food, as hay, straw, etc., for stall-feeding OE.

Fodder (fǫ·dəɹ), *v.* ME. [f. prec. sb.] *trans.* To give fodder to (cattle); to feed *with* (something) as fodder. Also *transf.* and *fig.* Hence **Fo·dderer,** one who fodders or feeds (cattle).

Fodient (fōᵘ·diĕnt). 1676. [– *fodient-*, pr. ppl. stem of L. *fodere* dig; see -ENT.]

A. *adj.* Digging; burrowing.

B. *sb.* [*sc.* animal.] 1879.

Foe (fōᵘ), *a.* and *sb.* [repr. two distinct OE words: (1) *fāh* adj. (= OFris. *fāch*) :– WGmc. **faiχa*; (2) *ġefā* sb., orig. subst. use of **ġefāh* adj. at feud (with) = OHG. *gifēh* at feud, odious :– WGmc. **ʒafaiχa*, f. *ʒa-* Y- + **faiχ-*. The prefix *ġe-* fell away in early ME., so that the simple adj. and the orig. compound sb. became coincident.]

†**A.** *adj.* **1.** At feud *with*; inimical (*to*) –1603. **2.** Hindering progress, rough. ME. only.

1. An enemie-country and f.-land FLORIO.

B. *sb.* (Now usu. repl. by ENEMY, exc. *rhet.*) **1.** In early use, an adversary in deadly feud or mortal combat; now, one who hates and seeks to injure another OE. Also *transf.* and *fig.* **2.** One belonging to a hostile army or nation, an enemy in battle or war ME. **3.** *collect.* A hostile force 1593.

1. He makes no friend who never made a f. TENNYSON. *transf.* and *fig.* A F. to th' publike Weale SHAKS. Grief is a f. CRABBE. **2.** Give thy brave foes their due ADDISON. **3.** Whispering with white lips—'The f.! they come! they come!' BYRON.

Hence †**Foe** *v.* to set at enmity; to make or treat as an enemy. †**Foe·hood,** enmity; a state of mutual hostility.

Fœderal, -ly, Fœdity: see FED-.

Foeman (fōᵘ·măn). *arch.* and *poet.* [OE. *fāhman*, f. *fāh* FOE *a.* + MAN.] An enemy in war.

Fœtal, fetal (fī·tăl), *a.* 1811. [f. FŒTUS + -AL[1].] Of or pertaining to or of the nature of a fœtus; in the condition of a fœtus.

Fœta·tion, feta·tion. 1669. [– *fetal-*, pa. ppl. stem of L. *fetare* (*foet-*) bring forth, breed; see -ION.] The formation of a fœtus or embryo.

Fœticide, feticide (fī·tisəid). 1844. [f. FŒTUS; see -CIDE 2.] The action of destroying a fœtus or causing abortion.
Hence **Fœtici·dal** *a.* of or pertaining to f.

Fœtid, Fœtor, var. ff. FETID, FETOR.

Fœtus, fetus (fī·tǒs). ME. [– L. *fetus* (often miswritten *foetus*) pregnancy, giving birth, young offspring, abstract sb. parallel to adj. *fetus* pregnant, productive. The better form with *e* is rare exc. in U.S.] The young of viviparous animals in the womb, and of oviparous animals in the egg, when fully developed.

Fog (fǫg), *sb.*[1] ME. [Of unkn. origin; see next.] **1. a.** The aftermath. **b.** The long grass left standing through the winter; rank grass. **2.** *Sc.* and *north.* = Moss 1450.
1. b. (*To leave*) *under f.*: with the long grass standing.

Fog (fǫg), *sb.*[2] 1544. [Identical in form with prec., whence FOGGY *a.*, whence perh. (by back-formation) *fog* thick mist, but the sense-development is not clear. See FOGGAGE.]
†**I.** Flabby substance (in the body), unwholesome fat; waste flesh 1586.
II. 1. Thick mist or watery vapour suspended in the atmosphere at or near the earth's surface; an obscured condition of the atmosphere due to this 1544. **2.** *transf.* and *fig.* 1601. **3.** *Photogr.* A cloud or coating obscuring a developed plate 1858.
1. Drooping fogge as blacke as Acheron SHAKS. **2.** Phr. *In a f.*: at a loss to know what to do. More puzel'd then the Ægyptians in their fogge SHAKS.
Combs. **1.** General: esp. in the names of instruments used for giving warning in foggy weather, as *f.-alarm, -bell, -gun, -horn, -trumpet, -whistle.* Also F.-SIGNAL.
2. Special: **f.-bow,** a bow, similar to the rainbow, produced by the action of light on the particles of f.; **-circle** = prec.; **-ring,** a bank of f. arranged in a circular form.

Fog (fǫg), *v.*[1] 1715. [f. FOG *sb.*[1]] **1.** *intr.* To become overgrown with moss. *Sc.* **2.** *Agric. trans.* **a.** To leave land under fog (see FOG *sb.*[1] 1) 1814. **b.** To feed (cattle) on fog 1828.

Fog (fǫg), *v.*[2] 1599. [f. FOG *sb.*[2]] **1.** *trans.* To envelop with or as with fog; to stifle with fog. Also *fig.* **2.** *intr.* To become covered or filled with fog. (Dicts.) **3.** *Photogr. trans.* To cloud or cover with an obscuring coating 1854.
Phr. *To f. off*: to perish from damp, as cuttings.

†**Fog,** *v.*[3] *rare.* 1588. [perh. back-formation from FOGGER[1].] *intr.* To act in a pettifogging manner –1641.
Where would'st thou f. to get a fee 1628.

Fog-bank. 1659. [f. FOG *sb.*[2] + BANK *sb.*[1]] 'A dense haze, presenting the appearance of a thick cloud resting upon the horizon' (Smyth).

Foge (fōᵘdʒ). *Cornwall.* 1778. [perh. local pronunc. of FORGE *sb.*] *Min.* A forge or blowing-house for smelting tin.

Foggage (fǫ·gėdʒ). *Sc.* 1500. [– Sc. Law-Latin *fogagium* (c1200), f. FOG *sb.*[1]; see -AGE.] **1.** *Law.* The pasturing of cattle on fog; the privilege of doing this. **2.** = FOG *sb.*[1] 2. 1786.

Fogger[1] (fǫ·gəɹ). 1576. [prob. f. *Fugger*, surname of the Augsburg family of merchants and financiers in the 15th and 16th cc.] †**1.** A person given to underhand practices for the sake of gain; esp. a low-class lawyer. Usually preceded by *petty.* –1600. **2.** *dial.* A huckster 1800. **3.** A middleman in the nail and chain trade 1868.

Fogger[2] (fǫ·gəɹ). *dial.* 1851. [f. FOG *v.*[1] + -ER[1].] A farm-hand chiefly engaged in feeding cattle.

Foggy (fǫ·gi), *a.* 1529. [f. FOG *sb.*[1] + -Y[1]. See FOG *sb.*[2]] **1.** Resembling, consisting of, or covered with fog 1635. †**2.** Boggy, marshy –1661. †**3.** Of flesh, etc.: Flabby or spongy in consistency; = BOGGY *a.* Hence of persons or animals: Unwholesomely bloated, puffy. –1828. **4.** [Cf. L. *pinguis aer.*] Of air, mist, cloud, etc.: Thick, murky. Hence (through FOG *sb.*[2]): Of the nature of, or resembling, fog or thick mist; full of fog. 1544. **b.** *fig.* Obscure, dull, bemuddled 1603. **5.** Beclouded, dim, indistinct 1840. **6.** *Photogr.* Fogged, indistinct 1859.
4. The . . f. asthmatic town of Glasgow 1812. Hence **Fo·ggily** *adv.* **Fo·gginess.**

Fogle (fōᵘ·g'l). *slang.* 1811. [Of unkn. origin.] A (silk) handkerchief.

Fogless (fǫ·glės), *a.* 1853. [f. FOG *sb.*[2] + -LESS.] Without fog, clear.

Fog-signal. 1759. [f. FOG *sb.*[2] + SIGNAL *sb.*] **1.** *Naut.* Any sound made in fogs as a warning to other vessels. **2.** *Railways.* A detonator placed on the metals in foggy weather to guide drivers of trains 1856.

Fogy, fogey (fōᵘ·gi). 1780. [rel. to slang *fogram* (XVIII) antiquated, old-fashioned (person), of unkn. origin.] **1.** *Sc.* An invalid or garrison soldier 1785. **2.** (Orig. *Sc.*) A man advanced in life; *esp.* one with antiquated notions, an old-fashioned fellow. Usu. preceded by *old.* 1780.
2. The honest rosy old fogies THACKERAY.
Hence **Fo·gydom, fo·geydom,** the state or condition of a f.; fogies as a class. **Fo·gyish** *a.* somewhat antiquated. **Fo·gyism,** the state of being a **f.**; the characteristic behaviour of fogies.

Foh, var. of FAUGH.

‖**Föhn** (fōn). 1865. [G., in OHG. *phōnno*, MHG. *fœnne*, ult. :– L. (ventus) *Favonius* mild west wind.] A warm dry south wind which blows down the valleys on the north side of the Alps.

Foible (foi·b'l). 1648. [– Fr. *foible*, obs. f. *faible*; see FEEBLE.]
†**A.** *adj.* Weak –1741.
B. *sb.* **1.** A weak point; a failing or moral weakness 1673. **2.** *Fencing.* The portion of a sword from the middle to the point. 1648.
1. A f. of Mr. Holt's . . was omniscience THACKERAY.

‖**Foiblesse.** ? *Obs.* 1685. [Fr., obs. sp. of *faiblesse*; see prec., -ESS[2].] A failing; a weakness *for* (something).

Foil (foil), *sb.*[1] ME. [(1) – OFr. *foil* masc. :– L. *folium* leaf; (2) – OFr. *foille* fem. (mod. *feuille*) :– L. *folia*, pl. of *folium* (n. pl. taken as fem. sing.).] †**1.** A leaf –1450. **2.** The representation of a leaf: **a.** *Her.* 1562; **b.** *Arch.* One of the small arcs or spaces between the cusps of a window 1835. †**3.** Anything flat and thin; as a layer, a paring, a counterfoil –1738. **4.** Metal hammered or rolled into a thin sheet; as *gold-, silver-, tin-f.* ME. **b.** An amalgam of tinfoil and mercury placed behind the glass of a mirror, to produce a reflection 1583. **c.** A backing 1684. **5.** A thin leaf of some metal placed under a precious stone to increase its brilliancy or under some transparent substance to make it appear to be a precious stone 1592. †**b.** The setting (of a jewel) –1650. **6.** Anything that serves by contrast of colour or quality to adorn or set off another thing 1581.
5. b. A foyle wherein thou art to set The precious Iewel of thy home returne SHAKS. **6.** I need no foile, nor shall I think I'me white only between two Moores 1639. *Comb.* **f.-stone,** an imitation jewel.

Foil (foil), *sb.*[2] 1478. [f. FOIL *v.*[1] II. 1.] †**1.** *Wrestling.* A throw which is almost a fall –1687. **2.** A repulse, defeat; a baffling check. *arch.* 1478.
2. It may give a man many a . . f. and many a disheartening blow SOUTH.

Foil (foil), *sb.*[3] 1576. [f. FOIL *v.*[1] I. 2. Cf. OFr. *foulis*, (O)Fr. *foulée* in same sense, f. *fouler* FOIL *v.*[1]] The track of a hunted animal. Also *transf.* and *fig.*
Phr. *To run* (*upon*) *the f.*: to run over the same track a second time (thus baffling the hounds).

Foil (foil), *sb.*[4] 1594. [Of unkn. origin.] **1.** A light weapon used in fencing; a kind of small-sword with a blunt edge and a button at the point. **2.** *pl.* The exercise of fencing with foils 1600.
1. They would have most willingly taken the buttons off the foils DRUMM. OF HAWTH.

Foil (foil), *v.*[1] ME. [perh. – AFr. *fuler, var. of (O)Fr. *fouler* :– Rom. *fullare, f. L. *fullo* FULLER *sb.*[1]]
I. In sense of Fr. *fouler.* †**1.** *trans.* To tread under foot, trample down –1603. **2.** *Hunting.* Of animals: To run over or cross (the ground, scent, or track) with the effect of baffling the hounds 1651.
II. 1. To overthrow, defeat; to beat off, repulse, discomfit. †In *Wrestling*: To inflict a foil upon: see FOIL *sb.*[2] 1. Also *fig.* 1548. **2.** To frustrate, render nugatory; to baulk; to baffle 1564.
1. The Wrastler That did but lately foile the synowie Charles SHAKS. Those Armies bright, which but th' Omnipotent none could have foyld MILT. **2.** Faith shall be easily shaken, hope quickly foyled 1612.
III. Influenced by FOUL *a.* and *v.*[1] **1.** To foul, defile, pollute. Now *dial.* ME. †**2.** To dishonour; to violate –1592.
Hence **Foi·ler,** one who foils.

†**Foil,** *v.*[2] 1616. [perh. – Fr. *fouiller* grub up; cf. *fouilleuse, fouilleur* kind of light plough.] *trans.* To subject (land) to the third ploughing in preparing it for sowing –1669.

Foil (foil), *v.*[3] 1611. [f. FOIL *sb.*[1]] *trans.* To apply foil or a foil to.

Foiling (foi·liŋ), *vbl. sb.*[1] 1533. [f. FOIL *v.*[1] + -ING[1].] The action of FOIL *v.*[1]; *esp.* the treading of a deer or other animal. Hence the slot or trail 1576.

Foiling (foi·liŋ), *vbl. sb.*[2] 1583. [f. FOIL *v.*[3] + -ING[1].] **a.** The action or process of backing (glass) with foil. **b.** *Arch.* Ornamentation by foils; a foil ornament 1849.

†**Foin,** *sb.*[1] ME. [– OFr. *foïne* (mod. *fouine*), *faïne*, Walloon *fawine* :– Rom. (*meles*) *faguina, f. L. *fagus* beech.] The beech-marten (*Mustela foina*), or its fur –1718.

Foin (foin), *sb.*[2] 1450. [f. FOIN *v.*] **1.** A thrust or push with a pointed weapon. *Obs.* or *arch.* Also *fig.* †**2.** = FOIL *sb.*[4] –1701.

Foin (foin), *v.* ME. [f. OFr. *foine, foisne*, trident (mod. *fouine*) prob. three-pronged fish-spear :– L. *fuscina.*] **1.** *intr.* To make a thrust with a pointed weapon; to lunge, push. Also *transf.* and *fig.* †**2.** *trans.* To thrust at, pierce, prick –1548.
1. Ye foine only at your owne shadow JEWEL. *transf.* The boare continually foining at him with his great tuskes 1562. Hence †**Foi·nery,** thrusting with the foin, fencing with the point. **Foi·ningly** *adv.*

Foison (foi·z'n), *sb.* ME. [– (O)Fr. *foison* :– Rom. *fūsio, -ōn-, for L. *fūsio, -ōn-* outpouring; see FUSION, PROFUSION.] **1.** Plenty; a great quantity or number. *arch.* **b.** Plentiful crop or harvest 1587. **2.** Inherent vitality; power, strength, capacity. *pl.* Resources. Now chiefly *Sc.* ME.
1. b. Earths increase, foyzon plentie, Barnes and Garners neuer empty SHAKS. Hence **Foi·sonless** *a.* (chiefly *Sc.*), wanting substance, strength, or sap.

†**Foist, fust,** *sb.*[1] 1485. [– (O)Fr. *fuste* – It. †*fusta*, f. *fusto* stem, trunk, etc. or – L. *fustis* cudgel.] **1.** A light galley propelled by oars and sails –1777. **2.** A barge –1616.

Foist, *sb.*[2] 1533. [– OFr. *fuste* (mod. *fût*) wine-cask (= It. *fusto* cask) :– L. *fustis* cudgel.] †**1.** A cask for wine. **2.** Hence, fustiness 1819.

†**Foist,** *sb.*[3] 1591. [f. FOIST *v.*[1]] **1.** A cheat, a rogue; a pickpocket –1700. **2.** A piece of roguery –1677. **3.** Something foisted in. NORTH.

Foist (foist), *v.*[1] 1545. [– Du. dial. *vuisten*, f. *vuist* FIST *sb.*] †**1.** *Dicing. trans.* To palm (a 'flat' or false die), so as to be able to introduce it when required. Also *intr.* to cheat by this means. –1565. †**2.** *intr.* To cheat. Cf. COG *v.*[3] –1611. **3.**† To put forth fraudulently –1678. **b.** To introduce surreptitiously or unwarrantably *into*; also with *in* adv. 1563. **c.** To palm off; to fix stealthily or unwarrantably *on* or *upon* 1599.
1. Through Foisting and Cogging their Die, and other false play 1565. Phr. *To f. in*: to introduce (the flat) surreptitiously when palmed. **3. b.** Interpolations . . foisted into the Odyssey LYTTON. **c.** To attempt to f. himself upon a borough with which he had no connexion 1841. Hence †**Foi·ster.**

Foist (foist), *v.*[2] 1583. *Obs.* exc. *dial.* [f. FOIST *sb.*[2]] *intr.* To smell or grow musty.

Foisty (foi·sti), *a.* See also FUSTY. 1519. [f. FOIST *sb.*[2] + -Y[1].] Fusty, musty, mouldy. *lit.* and *fig.* So **Foi·stied** *ppl. a.* become f. **Foi·stiness,** f. quality or condition.

Fokker (fǫ·kəɹ). 1913. [f. the name of A. H. G. *Fokker*, Dutch inventor.] A German tractor monoplane.

Fold (fōuld), *sb.*[1] [OE. *fald*, contr. of *falæd*, *falod*, *-ud*, corresp. to OS. *faled*, MLG. *valt*, Du. *vaalt*.] A pen or enclosure for domestic animals. **b.** The sheep in a fold 1669.

The lee-lang night we watch'd the fauld BURNS. *fig.* There shall be one f. and one shepherd *John* 10: 16. **b.** The bleating F. DRYDEN.

Comb. **f.-garth, -yard,** farm-yard.

Fold (fōuld), *sb.*[2] [ME. *fald*, f. FOLD *v.*[1]] **1.** A bend or ply in or as in anything flexible; either, or both together, of the parts brought together in folding. Also *fig.* and *transf.* **2.** Something that is or may be folded; e.g. one of the leaves of a folding door ME. **3.** The action of folding; †a clasp 1606. **4.** The mark made by folding 1840. **5.** By an erron. analysis *manifold*, *threefold*, etc. (see -FOLD *suffix*): Times, repetitions ME.

1. The f. of a mantle SCOTT. *fig.* The folds and doubles of Sylla's disposition DRYDEN. *transf.* The folds (= coils) of an adder SHAKS., of the mountains W. IRVING, of the alimentary canal 1841.

Fold (fōuld), *v.*[1] Pa. t. and pple. **folded** (fōu·ldėd). [OE. *faldan*, *fealdan* = MDu. *vouden* (*vouwen*), OHG. *faltan* (G. *falten*), ON. *falda*, Goth. *falþan* :- Gmc. redupl. str. vb. **falþan*.] **1.** *trans.* To arrange (a piece of cloth, etc.) so that one part lies reversed over or alongside another; to bend over upon itself. Also with *in*, *over*, *together*. Also *intr.* for *refl.* 1857. **2.** *trans.* To coil, wind (*about*, *round*, etc.). Also *intr.* for refl. 1579. †**3.** *intr.* To give way; to fail, falter -1596. **4.** *trans.* To lay (the arms, etc.) together, so as to overlap; to clasp (the hands) together. Also *intr.* for *refl.* OE. **5.** To enclose in or as in a fold or folds; to wrap up; to swathe, envelop. Now only with *in*. ME. **6.** To clasp (*in one's arms*, *to one's breast*), embrace ME.

1. *fig.* When death hath foulded up thy dayes 1633. **2.** When I feel about my feet The berried briony f. TENNYSON. **3.** I..feele my wits to faile, and tongue to f. SPENSER. **4.** Folde thine handes together yet a litle, that thou mayest slepe COVERDALE *Prov.* 6: 10. **6.** The mountain isles..Folded in shadows gray B. TAYLOR.

Fold (fōuld), *v.*[2] [OE. *faldian*; f. FOLD *sb.*[1]] **1.** *trans.* To shut up (sheep, etc.) in a fold; also *absol.* Also *fig.* **2.** To place sheep in a fold upon (ground) for the purpose of manuring it 1671.

1. The star that bids the shepherd f. MILT. *Comus* 93. Hence **Fo·lder,** a shepherd.

-fold, *suffix* (OE. *-fald*, (*-feald*) = OFris., OS. *-fald* (Du. *-voud*), (O)HG. *-falt*, ON. *-faldr*, Goth. *-falþs*), a Com. Gmc. terminal element, cogn. w. FOLD *v.*[1], and with the Gr. -παλτος, -πλασιος, also with πλο- in ἁπλός, and prob. with the L. (*sim-*)*plex*. Appended to cardinal numerals (and adjs. meaning 'many'), forming adjs. which serve chiefly as arithmetical multiplicatives. In educated use this multiplicative sense survives chiefly in the adv. and quasi-sb.; the adjs. express rather a plurality of things more or less different, as in 'a twofold charm'.

†**Foldage** (fou·ldėdʒ). 1533. [Later (anglicized) form of FALDAGE; cf. AL. *foldagium* (XVI).] **a.** = FALDAGE -1628. **b.** The practice of feeding sheep in movable folds -1657.

Folder (fōu·ldəɹ), *sb.* 1552. [f. FOLD *v.*[1] + -ER[1].] One who or that which folds; *esp.* an instrument for folding paper, etc.; *U.S.* a small folded but unstitched pamphlet. **b.** A folding cover for loose papers 1922.

Folderol, *v.* 1847. To sing folderol.

Folding (fōu·ldiŋ), *ppl. a.* 1611. [f. FOLD *v.*[1] + -ING[2].] That folds; that is or can be folded; as *f.-bed*, *-boat*, *-screen*, *-table*, etc.

Fo·lding doo·r. 1611. [f. prec. + DOOR.] A door consisting of two parts hung on opposite jambs, so that their edges come into contact when the door is closed. Now usu. *pl.*

Foldless (fōu·ldlės), *a.*[1] 1822. [f. FOLD *sb.*[1] + -LESS.] Having no fold or pen.

Foldless (fōu·ldlės), *a.*[2] 1845. [f. FOLD *sb.*[2] + -LESS.] Without a fold or crease.

†**Foleye·,** *v.* [- OFr. *foleier*, f. *fol* (mod. *fol*, *fou*) foolish.] *intr.* To play the fool. CHAUCER.

‖**Folia** (fōu·liă), *sb. pl.* 1730. [L., pl. of *folium* leaf.] **1.** *Bot.* Leaves (of a plant). **2.** Laminæ 1796.

Foliaceous (fōuliₗē·ʃəs), *a.* 1658. [f. L. *foliaceus* leafy, f. *folium*; see -ACEOUS.] **1.** Having the appearance or nature of a leaf. Of cryptogamous plants: Having organs resembling leaves. **b.** Of or pertaining to a leaf or leaves 1816. **2.** Consisting of or having the character of thin leaf-like plates or laminæ 1728. **3.** *Zool.* & *Entom.* Shaped or arranged like leaves 1828.

1. Teeth of the calyx f. 1806. **b.** A f. or farinaceous diet 1816. **2.** A..f. spar 1728. **3.** Valves f. 1854.

Foliage (fōu·liₗėdʒ), *sb.* 1598. [Early forms *foillage*, *fuellage* (assim. to L. *folium*) - (O)Fr. *feuillage*, †*foillage*, f. *feuille* leaf; see FOIL *sb.*[1], -AGE.] **1.** Leaves (of a plant or tree) collectively; leafage 1601. **2.** In *Art*: The representation of leaves, or of a cluster of leaves, sprays, or branches, used for decoration or ornament.

1. These naked shoots..Shall put their graceful f. on again COWPER.

Comb.: **f. leaf,** a leaf in the restricted sense of the word, excluding petals and other modified leaves; **f. plant,** one cultivated for its f., and not for its blossom.

Hence **Fo·liage** *v.* to adorn with f. or with a representation of leaves and flowers.

Foliaged (fōu·liₗėdʒd), *ppl. a.* 1754. [f. FOLIAGE *sb.* and *v.* + -ED.] **1.** Decorated or ornamented with the representation of foliage. **2.** Covered or furnished with (natural) foliage 1815.

1. F. velvet SHENSTONE. **2.** A f. lattice SHELLEY.

Foliar (fōu·liăɹ), *a.* 1875. [- mod.L. *foliaris*, f. L. *folium* leaf; see -AR[1]. Cf. Fr. *foliaire*.] Of, pertaining to, or of the nature of a leaf.

In many Ferns the original axile bundle widens out..into a tube, which..has..a relatively small slit or *foliar gap*..from the margin of which one or several bundles pass into the leaf 1884. So **Fo·lial** *a.* in same sense.

Foliate (fōu·liĕt), *a.* 1626. [- L. *foliatus* leaved, leafy, f. *folium* leaf; see -ATE[2]. In sense 1 f. FOLIATE *v.*] †**1.** Beaten out into a thin sheet or foil -1819. **2.** Leaf-like 1658. **3.** *Bot.* **a.** Furnished with leaves 1677. **b.** Having (so many) leaflets 1840.

2. Phr. *F. curve* (Geom.): a curve of the 2[d] order..consisting of two infinite legs crossing each other, forming a kind of leaf HUTTON. **3. b.** 10-f. 1840.

Foliate (fōu·liₗeit), *v.* 1665. [f. L. *folium* leaf + -ATE[3]. With sense 1 cf. med.L. *foliare* beat (metal) into foil.] **1.** †*trans.* To beat to a leaf or foil 1721; *intr.* to split into leaves or laminæ 1798. **2.** *trans.* To foil (glass) 1665. **3.** *intr.* To put forth leaves 1775. **4.** *trans.* To decorate with foils (see FOIL *sb.*[1] 2 b) 1812. **5.** *trans.* To mark the folios or leaves of (a volume, etc.) with consecutive numbers 1846.

4. The Arabs pointed and foliated the arch RUSKIN.

Foliated (fōu·liₗeitėd), *ppl. a.* 1650. [f. FOLIATE *a.* and *v.* + -ED.] **1.**† = FOLIATE *a.* 1. BOYLE. **b.** Silvered 1665. **2.** Composed of laminæ. Chiefly *Geol.* and *Min.* 1650. **3.** Shaped like a leaf or leaves 1846. **4.** *Arch.*, etc. **a.** Ornamented with foils 1840. **b.** Consisting of or ornamented with leaf-work 1849. **5.** Furnished with or consisting of leaves 1721.

2. Mica schist and gneiss f. 1866. **4. a.** *F. Arch*, an arch with a trefoil, cinquefoil, or multifoil under it PARKER.

Foliation (fouliₗē·ʃən). 1623. [f. FOLIATE *a.* and *v.*; see -ATION.] **1.** The leafing (of a plant); the state of being in leaf. †**b.** *concr.* Something resembling a leaf 1658. **2.** *Bot.* †**a.** The assemblage of leaves or petals forming a corolla -1747. **b.** = VERNATION 1794. **3.** The action of beating (metal) into foil 1755. **4.** *Geol.* The process and the property of splitting up into leaf-like layers; also the laminæ or plates into which crystalline rocks are divided 1851. **5.** *Arch.* Tracery consisting chiefly of small arcs or foils 1816. **6.** The consecutive numbering of the folios (or leaves) of a book or MS. 1846. **7.** The application of foil to glass. (Dicts.)

2. a. The f. of a tulip HERVEY. **b.** Flowers regular, with..gyrate f. LINDLEY. **5.** Foliations hanging free like lace-work FREEMAN.

Folia·to-, comb. f. L. *foliatus*, in sense 'formed like a leaf'.

Fo·liator. 1848. [f. FOLIATE *v.* + -OR 2.] One who foliates the leaves of a book.

Foliature (fōu·liatiŭɹ). 1676. [- L. *foliatura* leaf-work, f. *foliatus* FOLIATE *a.*; see -URE.] **1.** A cluster of leaves; also, leaf-ornamentation. **2.** 'The state of being hammered into leaves' (J.).

Foliicolous (fōu:liₗi·kŏləs), *a.* 1874. [f. L. *folii-* comb. f. *folium* leaf + *col-* (stem of *colere* inhabit) + -OUS.] Growing parasitically on leaves. So **Fo:lii·ferous** *a.*, also *erron.* **foliferous,** bearing leaves. **Fo·liifo:rm** *a.* leaf-shaped. **Fo:lii·parous** *a.* 'producing leaves only' (*Treas. Bot.*).

Folily, cf. FOLLIFUL, FOLIFUL *a.*

Folio (fōu·lio). 1533. [In I, a generalization of the med.L. use of the abl. of L. *folium* leaf, in references 'at leaf so-and-so', or a latinization of It. *foglio*; in II 1, *in folio* - It. *in foglio*.]

A. *sb.* **I.** With reference to pagination. **1.** A leaf of paper, parchment, etc., which is numbered only on the front. **2.** *Book-keeping.* The two opposite pages of an account-book when used concurrently; also one page when used for both sides of an account 1588. **3.** *Printing.* The page-number of a printed book 1683. **4.** *Law.* A certain number of words (in England 72 or 90, in U.S. generally 100) taken as a unit in reckoning the length of a document 1836.

II. With reference to size. **1.** *In folio*, i.e. 'in the form of a full-sized sheet folded once'. Also *transf.* and *fig.* 1582. **2.** A sheet of paper when folded once 1616. **3.** A volume made up of sheets of paper folded once; a volume of the largest size 1628. Also *attrib.*

1. I am for whoie volumes in f. *L.L.L.* I. ii. 192. **2.** Severall folios of dried plants EVELYN.

B. *adj.* Formed of sheets or a sheet folded once; folio-sized. Often following the sb. 1597.

A history in ten volumes f. (*mod.*).

Folio (fōu·lio), *v.* [f. prec. sb.] = FOLIATE *v.* 5.

Foliolate (fōu·liŏleit), *a.* 1866. [f. FOLIOLE + -ATE[2].] Of, pertaining to, or consisting of folios or leaflets; as in '3-foliolate', etc.

Foliole (fōu·lioul). 1794. [- Fr. *foliole* - late L. *foliolum*, dim. of L. *folium* leaf.] **1.** *Bot.* One of the divisions of a compound leaf; a leaflet. **2.** *Zool.* A small leaf-like appendage 1849.

Foliose (fouliōu·s), *a.* 1727. [- L. *foliosus* leafy, f. *folium* leaf; see -OSE[1].] Having, or abounding in, leaves; leafy. Hence **Folio·sity,** f. condition.

Folious (fōu·liəs), *a.* 1658. [f. L. *foliosus* (see prec.), + -OUS.] Abounding in, or of the nature of, leaves; foliose.

‖**Folium** (fōu·liŏm). 1848. [L., = leaf.] **1.** = FOLIO *sb.* II. 2. 1886. **2.** *Geom.* **a.** A finite loop of a nodal curve terminated at both ends by the same node. **b.** *F. of Descartes*, a plane nodal cubic curve with real nodal tangents, and one real inflexion at infinity. 1848.

Folk (fōuk). [OE. *folc* = OFris. *folk*, OS., OHG. *folc* (Du., G. *volk*), ON. *folk* people, army, detachment :- Gmc. **folkam*, the original meaning of which is perh. best preserved in ON.] **1.** A people, nation, race, tribe. Now *arch.* **b.** *transf.* of animals (After Heb.) ME. **2.** An aggregation of people in relation to a superior, e.g. God, a king or priest; the mass; the people; the vulgar. *Obs.* exc. *arch.* OE. **3.** Men, people indefinitely; often qualified by an adj. or phr. (Now chiefly *colloq.*) OE. **4.** *pl.* The people of one's family, parents, children, relatives 1715.

1. b. The conies are but a feeble f. *Prov.* 30: 26. **2.** The said hoost of the Hebreux..were al folke of god CAXTON. **3.** Upon the steedes..Ther seeten f. CHAUCER. I have heard wise folks say [etc.] SWIFT. Unkind to the poor f. 1845. **4.** Your young folks are flourishing HT. MARTINEAU.

attrib. and *Comb.* **1.** General: *esp.* with the sense 'of, pertaining to, current or existing among, the people'; as *f.-belief, -custom, -dance, -laws, -literature, -name, -play, -song, -speech, -tale*, etc.
2. Special: **f.-etymology,** usu. the popular perversion of the form of words in order to give it a meaning; **-free** *a.*, having the rights of a freeman; **-leasing** (OE. *Law*), public lying, slander.

Fo·lkland. *Obs.* exc. *Hist.* A term of OE. law, designating land held by a certain kind of tenure; opp. to BOOKLAND.
The prevailing view of the antithesis has been that *folkland* was land belonging to the state, which the king or the witan might grant to a person for his life, but which did not descend to heirs, while *bookland* was land held by charter or deed. Another view is that *folkland* was land heritable by *folkright* or common law, while the estate in *bookland* was conferred by deed, and could be alienated freely. See *Eng. Hist. Rev.* VIII. (1893).

Folk-lore (fōᵘ·kˌlōᵊɹ). 1846. [f. FOLK + LORE *sb.*[1]] The beliefs, legends, and customs, current among the common people; the study of these.

Fo·lkmoot, folkmote. *Obs.* exc. *Hist.* [OE. *folc-mōt, -ġemōt*, f. *folc* FOLK + *mōt, ġemōt* meeting. See MOOT *sb.*] A general assembly of the people of a town, city, or shire. Hence †**Fo·lk-mooter,** ? a parochial politician. MILT.

Fo·lkright. *Obs.* exc. *Hist.* [OE. *folcriht*, f. *folc* FOLK + *riht* RIGHT *sb.*[1]] 'Common law, public right, the understood compact by which every freeman enjoys his rights as a freeman' (Bosw.).

Follicle (fǫlik'l). 1646. [– L. *folliculus* little bag, dim. of *follis* bellows.] **1.** *Anat.* A small sac. Chiefly, 'a simple lymphatic gland, consisting of lymphoid tissue arranged in the form of a sac' (*Syd. Soc. Lex.*). **2.** *Bot.* 'A kind of fruit, consisting of a single carpel, dehiscing by the ventral suture only' (Lindley); formerly, any capsular fruit 1706. **b.** A small bag or vesicle distended with air 1793. **3.** *Entom.* A cocoon 1856.
Hence **Folli·cular** *a.* of the nature of, or resembling, a f.; composed or consisting of follicles; *Path.* affecting the follicles of a particular organ. **Folli·culated** *ppl. a.* provided with a f. or follicles; contained in a cocoon. **Folli:culi·tis,** *Path.* inflammation of a f. or follicles. **Folli:culo·se, Folli·culous** *adjs.* full of or containing follicles; of the nature or appearance of a f.

†**Fo·lliful,** *a.* Also **foliful.** 1549. [f. FOLLY *sb.* + -FUL.] Full of foolishness –1763.

Follow (fǫ·lōᵘ), *sb.* 1870. [f. next vb.] **1.** The action of FOLLOW *v.* **2.** *Billiards.* A stroke which causes the player's ball to follow the object-ball after impact. Also, the impulse given to the ball by this stroke 1873. **3.** *Cricket* (also **follow-on**) 1881; *Golf*, etc. (**follow-through**) 1897: see FOLLOW *v.*

Follow (fǫ·lōᵘ), *v.* [OE. *folgian*, corresp. to OFris. *fol(g)ia, fulgia*, OS. *folgon* (Du. *volgen*), OHG. *folgēn* (G. *folgen*), beside OE. *fylgan*, ON. *fylgja* accompany, help, lead, follow, pursue; f. Gmc. **fulʒ-*, of unkn. origin.]
I. *trans.* **1.** To go or come after; to move behind in the same direction. **b.** To go forward along, keep in (a path, track, etc.) *lit.* and *fig.* ME. **2.** *fig.* To come after in sequence or series, order of time, etc.; to succeed ME. **3.** To go after as an attendant, or as an admirer, auditor, or the like OE. **4.** *fig.* To go with; to be consequent upon OE. **5.** To go in pursuit of, try to come up with; to pursue, chase OE. †**b.** *fig.* To follow up, prosecute; to enforce (law) –1693. **6.** *fig.* (Cf. sense 3). To treat or take as a guide, leader, or master; to accept the authority or example of; to espouse the opinions or cause of OE. **7.** To act upon or in accordance with (advice, example, etc.); to take as a model, 'walk after' OE. **8.** To walk in, pursue, or practise (a way of life, etc.); *esp.* to practise (a calling) for a livelihood OE. **9.** To watch the progress or course of (a moving object, etc.); to keep up with (an argument, train of thought, etc.; also a person as he reasons or recounts) 1697.
1. As any kyde or calf folwynge his dame CHAUCER. **b.** To f. the turnpike road COBBETT. Phr. *To f. the drum*: to be a soldier. *To f. the hounds*: to hunt with dogs. **2.** One misfortune followes another 1659. Punishment must f. conviction 1817. **3.** Thou for wages followest thy master SHAKS. **4.** Surely goodnes and mercie shall followe me all the daies of my life *Ps.* 23:6. **5.** To f. pleasure CHATHAM, knowledge TENNYSON. **b.** Since I haue euer followed thee with hate SHAKS. **6.** With pure harte and mynde to folowe thee *Bk. Com. Prayer.* **7.** Most men admire Virtue, who f. not her lore MILT. *P.R.* I. 483. **8.** Phr. *To f. the sea*: to practise the calling of a sailor. **9.** The argument is too difficult for them to f. JOWETT.
II. *intr.* **1.** To go or come after a person or thing; also, to go as an attendant, etc. Const. *after*. Also *fig.* ME. **2.** To result; to be, or occur as, a consequent. Const. *from*. ME. **3.** To go in pursuit. Const. *after*. Also *fig.* of things. ME.
1. For still temptation follows where thou art SHAKS. Phr. *As follows*: a prefatory formula, *impers.* in const., and therefore to be always used in the sing. *F.-my-leader*, game in which each player must do as the leader does. **3.** Vp, f. after the men *Gen.* 44:4. Phr. *To f. after*: to strive to compass; *Ps.* 119:150.
Combs. (with advbs.). **F. on. a.** *intr.* To continue following. **b.** *intr.* Of a side at *Cricket*: To go in again at once after the first innings, in consequence of having made a prescribed number of runs less than the other side in the first innings. **F. through** *Golf*, etc. (*intr.*): to carry the stroke through to the full extent after striking the ball; **F. up.** *trans.* **a.** To go after or pursue closely. **b.** To prosecute with energy.

Follower (fǫ·lōᵘˌəɹ). [OE. *folgere*, f. as prec. + -ER[1].] **1.** One who follows; a pursuer 1593; an attendant, or servant OE.; an adherent or disciple ME. **b.** *colloq.* One who courts a maidservant 1838. **2.** Something that succeeds something else 1450. **3.** *Sc.* and *n. dial.* The young of cattle 1584. **4.** *Mech.*
a. In various kinds of presses: The plate or block by which the pressure is applied 1676. **b.** *Steam-engine.* The cover or plug of a stuffing-box, which rests upon and compresses the packing; a gland 1874. **5.** *Stationery.* 'A sheet of parchment, which is added to the first or indenture, etc. sheet' 1858.

Following (fǫ·lōᵘˌiŋ), *vbl. sb.* ME. [f. as prec. + -ING[1].] **1.** The action of FOLLOW *v.* **2.** *concr.* A body of followers; followers collectively 1450.

Fo·llowing, *ppl. a.* ME. [f. as prec. + -ING[2].] **1.** That follows 1626. **2.** That comes next or after; succeeding, ensuing ME. Also *absol.* (*the f.*). ME. **3.** Of wind or tide: ? Moving in the direction of the ship's course 1807. **4.** *Billiards*, etc. *F. stroke* = FOLLOW *sb.* 2. 1867.

Folly (fǫ·li), *sb.* Pl. **follies.** [ME. *foly(e*, – (O)Fr. *folie*, f. *fol* foolish, FOOL; see -Y[3].] **1.** The quality or state of being foolish; want of good sense, weakness or derangement of mind; also, unwise conduct. **b.** With *a* and *pl.* ME. †**2.** Wickedness, evils, mischief, harm. Also with *a* and *pl.* –1535. †**3.** Lewdness, wantonness. Also with *a* and *pl.* –1634. †**4.** Madness, mania (= Fr. *folie*); hence, rage –1670. **5.** A name given to any costly structure considered to have shown folly in the builder. (But cf. Fr. *folie*, 'delight', 'favourite abode'.) 1654.
1. Where ignorance is bliss, 'Tis f. to be wise GRAY. **b.** The follies of the town GOLDSM. **2.** Because he hath..committed folye in Israel COVERDALE *Josh.* 7:15. **3.** *Oth.* V. ii. 132. Hence **Fo·lly** *v.* to commit f.

‖**Fomalhaut** (fōᵘ·mălˌhǫ:t). 1594. [– Arab. *fam al-ḥūt* mouth of the fish.] *Astron.* A star of the first magnitude in the constellation Southern Fish (*Piscis Australis*).

Fo·ment, *sb.* Now *rare.* 1540. [– L. *fomentum*; see next.] **1.** = FOMENTATION 1 b. †**2.** *fig.* Fomentation, encouragement; also, stimulus –1704.

Foment (fome·nt), *v.* 1611. [–(O)Fr. *fomenter* – late L. *fomentare*, f. L. *fomentum* lotion, poultice, lenitive, f. *fovēre* heat, cherish.] **1.** *trans.* To bathe with warm or medicated lotions; to apply fomentations to. †**2.** 'To cherish with heat, to warm' (J.) –1667. †**3.** To rouse or stir up; to excite, irritate. Also *intr.* for *refl.* –1724. **4.** To promote the growth or spread of; to cherish; to stimulate, encourage, instigate; *esp.* in a bad sense 1622.
2. All things ..these soft fires..f. and warme MILT. *P.L.* iv. 669. **4.** That humour which foments thy malady QUARLES. To f. extravagance M. PATTISON. var. †**Fo·mentate** *v.* (in sense 1). Hence **Fome·nter.**

Fomentation (fōᵘmĕntēⁱ·ʃən). ME. [–(O)Fr. *fomentation* or late L. *fomentatio*, f. *fomentat-*, pa. ppl. stem of *fomentare*; see prec., -ION.] **1.** *Med.* The application to the surface of the body of flannels, etc. soaked in hot water, whether simple or medicated, or of any other warm, soft, medicinal substance. **b.** *concr.* That which is so applied 1546. **2.** *fig.* Encouragement, instigation; a stimulus 1612.
2. The f. of Hungarian discontent 1861.

‖**Fomes** (fōᵘ·mīz). *pl.* **fomites** (fōᵘ·mitīz) 1658. [L., = 'tinder'.] †**a.** The morbific matter (of a disease). **b.** 'Any porous substance capable of absorbing and retaining contagious effluvia' (Mayne). Also *fig.* 1803.
The most important fomites are bed-clothes, bedding, woollen garments, carpets, curtains, letters, etc. 1882.

†**Fon.** ME. [Obscurely rel. to FON *v.*] **A.** *sb.* A fool –1595. **B.** *adj.* Foolish, silly –1538.

†**Fon,** *v.* ME. [Occurs earlier as *fonned*; see FOND *a.* See also FUN *v.*] **1.** *intr.* To lose savour. Only in pa. pple.; see FOND *a.* **2.** To be or become foolish or infatuated –1570. **3.** *trans.* To befool –1460.

Fond, *sb.*[1] †Also **fonds.** Now only as Fr., pronounced (foṅ). 1664. [– Fr. *fond, fonds*) :– OFr. *fonz, fons* :– (ult.) L. *fundus.* In XVIII repl. by FUND, exc. as Fr.] **1.** Foundation, ground, groundwork. (In Fr. now *fond.*) **2.** A source of supply. (In Fr. now *fonds.*) 1685. †**3.** A stock of money; pecuniary means, revenues. (In Fr. now *fonds.*) –1691. †**4.** A sum of money, stock of goods, or the like, serving as a security for specified payments. (In Fr. now *fonds.*) –1714. †**5.** *Printing* = FOUNT. 1678.
1. The present Prizes..being a better fond of credit 1665.

Fond (fǫnd), *a.* and *sb.*[2] [In ME. *fonned, -yd*, having the form of a pa. pple. of FON *v.* (recorded later, XIV). But the chronology of the words as known suggests that ME. *fonned* was directly f. FON *sb.* + -ED[2] (cf. the etym. of *wicked, wretched*).]
A. *adj.* **1.** That has lost its savour; insipid. *Obs.* exc. *dial.* **2.** Infatuated, foolish; now, foolishly credulous or sanguine ME. **3.** Idiotic, imbecile; also dazed. Now *dial.* ME. †**4.** Of things: Valued only by fools –1645. **5. a.** Of persons, their actions, etc.: Foolishly tender; doting. Now in good sense: Affectionate, loving. Also with *of*, †*on* 1579. **b.** Of opinions, etc.: Cherished with unreasoning affection 1635. **6.** †Eager for, desirous of (const. *of*) –1779; also with *to* and *inf.* 1546.
2. His own f. ineptitude CARLYLE. **4.** Not with f. Sickles of the tested gold SHAKS. **5. a.** I called up the many f. things I had to say GOLDSM. F. of the sports of the field STRUTT. **b.** Edward's..f. opinion of his own capacity CARTE.
†**B.** *absol.* and *sb.* A foolish person –1575.

†**Fond,** *v.*[1] [OE. *fandian*, corresp. in form to OFris. *fandia*, OS. *fandon*, OHG. *fantōn.*] To attempt, try, endeavour, tempt.

†**Fond,** *v.*[2] 1530. [f. FOND *a.*] **1.** *intr.* To play the fool –1541. **2.** To dote. Const. *on, over, upon.* –1601. **3.** *trans.* To make a fool of –1567. **4.** To fondle; also, to beguile –1697.
4. The Tyrian hugs, and fonds thee on her breast DRYDEN.

Fond, obs. pa. t. FIND: obs. f. FOUND *v.*[1]

‖**Fondaco** (fǫ·ndako). 1632. [It. – Arab.] An inn.

Fondant (fo·ndănt). 1877. [– Fr. *fondant* subst. use of pr. pple. of *fondre* melt.] A name for sweetmeats that melt in the mouth.

Fondle (fǫ·nd'l), *v.* 1694. [Back-formation from FONDLING *sb.* Cf. *sidle, suckle.*] †**1.** *trans.* To cocker, pamper –1789. **2.** To handle or treat with fondness. Also, to press fondly *to* (the heart). 1796. **3.** *intr.* To behave fondly; to toy 1720.
2. The prince fondled it [the bird] to his heart W. IRVING. Hence **Fo·ndler,** one who fondles. **Fo·ndle** *sb.* an act of fondling.

Fondling (fǫ·ndliŋ), *vbl. sb.* 1714. [f. prec. + -ING[1].] Affectionate handling; a fond gesture.

Fondling (fǫ·ndliŋ), *sb.* ME. [f. FOND *a.* + -LING[1].] †**1.** A fond or foolish person. Also *transf.* of animals. –1781. **2.** One who is much fondled or caressed; a pet. Also *fig.* Now *rare.* 1640.

Fondly (fǫ·ndli), *adv.* ME. [f. FOND *a.* + -LY².] †**1.** Foolishly –1648. **2.** With fond credulity 1762. **3.** Affectionately, lovingly, tenderly. Also, caressingly. 1593.

2. You would f. persuade me that [etc.] GOLDSM. **3.** My heart untravell'd f. turns to thee GOLDSM.

Fondness (fǫ·ndnės). ME. [f. FOND *a.* + -NESS.] **1.** Foolishness; 'weakness; want of sense of judgement' (J.). Now *dial.* **2.** Foolish affection; unreasoning tenderness 1579. **3.** Affectionateness, tenderness 1603. **4.** Instinctive liking 1654.

1. The fondnesse of this opinion 1609. **3.** A mother's f. reigns Without a rival HAN. MORE. **4.** The f. of the negro races..for..fables 1885.

Fondon. 1881. [Of unkn. origin.] *Mining.* A large copper vessel, in which amalgamation is practised. RAYMOND.

Fondu (foṅdü). Also **-us.** 1848. [– Fr. *fondu*, pa. pple. of *fondre* melt.] That kind of painting on calico in which the colours melt into each other.

‖**Fondue** (foṅdü). 1878. [Fr., pa. pple. fem. of *fondre* melt.] A dish of melted cheese with eggs, etc.

Fone, obs. pl. of FOE.

Font (fǫnt), *sb.*¹ [Late OE. *font*, var. of *fant* – OIr. *fant, font* – L. *fons, font-* spring, fountain, in spec. eccl. use, *fons* or *fontes baptismi* water(s) of baptism. ME. *funt* (XII–XVI, a regular Sc. form), *fount* (XIV–XVII) are – AFr. *funz* (OFr. *fonz*), from the same L. source.] **1.** A receptacle, usu. of stone, for the water used in baptism. **2.** *transf.* **a.** A receptacle for holy water 1542. **b.** The reservoir for oil in a lamp 1891. **3.** = FOUNT¹. *poet.* 1611.

1. Crystnyd I was in a funt of stoon BOKENHAM. **3.** Near f. or stream SHENSTONE.

Font (fǫnt), *sb.*² 1578. [– Fr. *fonte*, f. *fondre* melt. Sense 2 now usually FOUNT².] **1.** The process of casting or founding. *rare.* **2.** *Printing.* = FOUNT².

Fontal (fǫ·ntăl). 1656. [– OFr. *fontal* or med. L. *fontalis* in same senses, f. L. *fons, font-* spring; see -AL¹.]

A. *adj.* **1.** Of or pertaining to a fountain, spring, or source; original, primary. **2.** Baptismal 1797.

1. Godhead F. and Deriv'd KEN.

B. *sb.* †**1.** Source, well-spring (*fig.*) 1711. **2.** *Her.* A water-pot 'from whence issues water all proper' 1688.

Fontanelle, fontanel (fǫntăne·l). 1541. [– Fr. *fontanelle* – mod. L. *fontanella*, latinization of OFr. *fontenelle*, dim. of *fontaine* FOUNTAIN; see -EL.] **1.** *Anat.* †**a.** The hollow between two muscles. R. COPLAND. **b.** One of several membranous spaces in the head of an infant which lie at the adjacent angles of the parietal bones 1741. †**2.** *Med.* An artificial ulcer or a natural issue for the discharge of humours from the body –1779. **b.** Hence, Any outlet 1649.

2. b. This narrow fontanel of perforated rock 1848.

‖**Fontange** (foṅtaṅʒ). 1689. [Fr., f. *Fontanges* the territorial title of a mistress of Louis XIV.] A tall head-dress formerly worn.

Food (fūd), *sb.* [Late OE. *fōda* :–*fōđon, a unique formation; see FEED, FODDER.] **1.** What one takes into the system to maintain life and growth, and to supply waste; aliment, nourishment, victuals. **b.** What one eats, as opp. to 'drink' 1610. **c.** An article, or kind of food ME. **2.** With ref. to plants: That which they absorb from the earth and air; nutriment 1759. **3.** *fig.*; *esp.* in sense: Matter to discuss or dwell upon OE.

1. Phr. *To be f. for fishes*: to be drowned. *F. for powder*: fit only to be shot at or to die in battle. **3.** Chewing the f. of sweet and bitter fancie SHAKS. F. for thought SOUTHEY.

Comb.: **f.-rent**, rent in kind; **-yolk**, the non-germinative part of the yolk of an egg, which nourishes the embryo. Hence †**Food** *v.* to supply f. to; to feed, support.

Foodful (fū·dful), *a.* Chiefly *poet.* 1638. [see -FUL.] Abounding with or supplying food or nutriment.

The f. Earth 1638. *fig.* The f. nurse of ambition BURKE.

Foodless (fū·dlės), *a.* ME. [see -LESS.] Without food; (of a country, etc.) barren.

Foody (fū·di), *a.* [see -Y¹.] Full of, or supplying food CHAPMAN.

Fool (fūl), *sb.*¹ and *a.* [ME. *fol* sb. and adj. – OFr. *fol* (mod. *fol, fou* mad) :– L. *follis* bellows, inflated ball (later, fig.) 'wind-bag', empty-headed person.]

A. *sb.* **1.** One deficient in judgement or sense, a silly person, a simpleton. (In Biblical use applied to vicious or impious persons.) **2.** One who professionally counterfeits folly for the entertainment of others, a jester, clown ME. **3.** One who is made to appear a fool; a dupe. Now somewhat *arch.* ME. **4.** One who has little or no reason or intellect; a weak-minded or idiotic person. *Obs.* exc. in *natural* or *born f.* 1540.

1. There ben more fooles than Wysemen CAXTON. The f. hath said in his heart, There is no God *Ps.* 14:1. Phr. *To be a f. to*: to be as nothing compared to. **2.** Phr. *To play the f.*: to act the part of a jester; hence *gen.* to act like a f. (sense 1). **3.** Phr. *To make a f. of. To be a f. for one's pains*, to have one's labour for nothing.

Comb.: **f.-begged** *a.*, ? foolish, idiotic (cf. BEG); **-born**, begotten by a f.; **-duck** (*U.S.*) the ruddy duck, *Erismatura rubida*; **-fish** (*U.S.*) a pop. name for *Manocanthus broccus*, also for *Pleuronectes glaber*; †**-happy** *a.*, lucky without contrivance; **-hen** (*U.S.*), grouse, *esp.* young grouse, in the early part of the season.

b. Comb. with genitive *fool's*: **fool's errand,** a profitless undertaking; †**fool's gold,** iron pyrites; **fool's paradise,** a state of illusory happiness or good fortune; **fool's parsley,** a poisonous weed, the Lesser Hemlock (*Æthusa cynapium*); hence, a book name of the genus *Æthusa*.

B. *adj.* Foolish, silly. *Obs.* exc. *Sc.* and *dial.* and *vulgar*; frequent since *c*1800 in U.S. Fighting is a f. thing COLVIL.

Fool (fūl), *sb.*² 1598. [perh. transf. use of prec. suggested by *trifle*; see quot.] †**1.** (See quot.) –1688. **2.** A dish of fruit stewed, crushed, and mixed with milk, cream, or custard 1747.

1. *Mantiglia*, a kinde of clouted creame called a foole or a trifle in English FLORIO.

Fool (fūl), *v.* ME. [f. FOOL *sb.*¹] †**1.** *intr.* To be or become foolish or insane –1489. **2.** To play the fool, trifle, idle 1593; †to play the buffoon –1641. Also quasi-*trans. Twel. N.* V. i. 44. **3.** *trans.* To make a fool of; to dupe. Also, to balk. 1596. †**4.** To make foolish; to infatuate –1641.

2. While I stand fooling heere SHAKS. **3.** That you are fool'd, discarded, and shook off By him, for whom these shames ye underwent SHAKS. **4.** *Lear* II. iv. 278.

Phr. *To f. away* (also simply): to throw away or part with foolishly.

Foolery (fū·lėri). 1552. [f. FOOL *sb.*¹ + -ERY.] **1.** The practice of fooling or acting foolishly 1579. **2.** A ridiculous action, performance, or thing 1552. **3.** Fools as a class. SYD. SMITH.

1. But sike fansies weren foolerie SPENSER. **2.** The pleasing levities, and agreeable fooleries of a girl 1772.

Foo·lha:rdiness. ME. [f. FOOLHARDY + -NESS.] The quality of being foolhardy. So †**Foolhardice,** †**Foo:lha·rdiment.**

Foolhardy (fū·lhā:ɹdi), *a.* ME. [– OFr. *folhardi* 'foolish-bold', i.e. *fol* foolish, FOOL *sb.*¹ and *a.* + *hardi* HARDY *a.*] Daring without judgement, foolishly adventurous or bold. Hence **Foo·lha:rdily** *adv.* Also **Foo·lha:rdihood,** foolhardiness.

†**Fool-hasty,** *a.* ME. [– OFr. *fol hastif*, f. as prec. + *hastif* HASTY.] Foolishly hasty, precipitate –1600.

†**Foo·lify,** *v.* 1581. [f. FOOL *sb.*¹ + -FY.] To make a fool of, render foolish –1641.

Fooling (fū·liŋ), *vbl. sb.* 1601. [f. FOOL *v.* + -ING¹.] The action of FOOL *v.* 1609. **b.** Preceded by an adj. = Condition or humour for fooling.

b. Put me into good f. *Twel. N.* I. v. 36.

Foolish (fū·liʃ), *a.* ME. [f. FOOL *sb.*¹ + -ISH¹.] **1.** Fool-like, wanting in sense or judgement. **2.** Befitting a fool; proceeding from, or indicative of folly ME. **3.** Ridiculous 1514. **4.** Humble, paltry, poor, mean, trifling. *arch.* or *dial.* 1592.

1. Women are so very f., Mr. Squeers DICKENS. **2.** Where Wits..wonder with a f. face of praise POPE. **3.** A f. figure He must make PRIOR. **4.** We haue a trifling f. Banquet towards SHAKS. Hence **Foo·lishly** *adv.*

Foolishness (fū·liʃnės). 1470. [f. prec. + -NESS.] **1.** The quality or condition of being foolish. **2.** A foolish act or thing 1535.

2. They deuysed another foolishnes COVERDALE *Wisd.* 19:3.

†**Fool-large.** ME. [– OFr. *follarge*, f. *fol-* FOOL *a.* + *large* liberal; see LARGE.] **A.** *adj.* Foolishly liberal, prodigal –1603. **B.** *sb.* **1.** A spendthrift –late ME. **2.** Prodigality CAXTON.

A. In spenynge he was fol large R. GLOUC.

Fool-proof (fū·lprūf), *a.* orig. *U.S.* 1902. [PROOF *a.* 1 b]. Proof against even the incompetence of a fool; safeguarded against all accidents.

Foo·l's-cap, foo·lscap. 1632. **1.** A cap, usually garnished with bells, formerly worn by fools or jesters. **2.** The device of a fool's cap used as a watermark for paper 1795. **3.** A long folio writing- or printing-paper, 16¾ to 17 inches by 13½ inches in size 1700.

attrib., as **foolscap folio, octavo, quarto,** said of a volume consisting of sheets of foolscap size folded in the manner specified.

Fool's coat. 1589. **1.** The motley coat of a buffoon. Also *transf.* and *fig.* **2.** A name for the goldfinch 1682. **3.** A bivalve mollusc, *Isocardia cor* (*Cent. Dict.*).

Foot (fut), *sb.* *Pl.* **feet** (fīt). [OE. *fōt*, pl. *fēt* = OFris. *fōt*, OS. *fōt, fuot* (Du. *voet*), OHG. *fuoz* (G. *fuss*), ON. *fótr*, Goth. *fōtus* :– Gmc. **fōt-* :– IE. **pōd-* **ped-* **pod-*, repr. by Skr. *pādas* foot, Gr. πούς, ποδ-, L. *pēs, ped-*.]

I. 1. The lowest part of the leg beyond the ankle-joint. †**b.** The whole limb from the hip-joint to the toes. Also *great f.* –1661. **2.** Viewed as the organ of locomotion OE. **b.** Hence, a person as walking. *Obs.* exc. *dial.* in *first f.* ME. **3.** *ellipt.* Foot-soldiers 1568. **4.** The end of a bed, a grave, etc. towards which the feet are placed. Formerly often *pl.* ME. **b.** The part of a stocking, etc. which covers the foot 1577.

1. The fote to go, and hand to hold and rech 1538. **2.** Death, Which I did thinke, with slower f. came on SHAKS. *fig.* Unless..I lame the f. Of our design *Cor.* IV. vii. 7. **3.** The Forty-Fourth Foot 1878. **4.** In a cofre at my beddes feet HOCCLEVE.

II. *Pros.* [tr. of L. *pes*, Gr. πούς; said to be with reference to the movement of the foot in beating time.] A division of a verse, consisting of a number of syllables one of which has the ictus or principal stress OE.

III. 1. A lineal measure originally based on the length of a man's foot. (The English foot consists of 12 inches. Hence *square* or *cubic f.*, equal to the content respectively of a square and a cube the side of which measures one foot. Often in *sing.* when preceded by numerals. OE. **2.** (See quot.) 1602.

1. A doore in brede iiij foote standard 1459. Ile starue ere I rob a foote further SHAKS. Phr. †*Every f.* (*and anon.*): incessantly. **2.** *Foot*, an ancient measure for black Tin, two gallons; now a nominal measure, but in weight 60 lb. 1778.

IV. Analogous uses. **1.** The lower part, on which an object rests; the base ME. **2. a.** *Zool.* Applied to various organs of locomotion or attachment in invertebrate animals 1835. **b.** *Bot.* The part (of a petal) by which it is attached; the part (of a hair) below the epidermis; etc. 1671. **3.** The extremity of the leg (of a pair of compasses, a chair, etc.) 1551. **4.** *pl.* The commercial name for the small plates of tortoise-shell which line the carapace.

1. A Lauer of brasse, and his foote also of brasse *Exod.* 30:18.

V. 1. The lowest part or bottom, as of an eminence, a wall, ladder, staircase, etc. ME. **b.** The beginning or end of the slope (of a bridge) 1450. **2.** The lower end, bottom (of a page, a list, a table, etc.) 1669. †**3.** What is written at the foot; as, the sum (of an account) –1712; the refrain (of a song) –1621. **4.** (Pl. *foots.*) Bottoms, dregs, as of oil, sugar, etc. 1560.

1. At þe f. of the hille Mount Olympus TREVISA. The F. of a Mast 1815. **2.** *At f.*: at the bottom (of a page); Placing the..correction at f. 1855.

Phr. *F. of a fine* (Law): that one of the parts of a tripartite indenture recording the particulars of a fine (see FINE *sb.*¹), which remained with the court. It was actually at the foot of the undivided sheet, and had its indentation at the top.

VI. †**1.** Standing-ground –1662. †**2.** =

FOOTING *vbl. sb.* 6.–1827. †**3.** Standard rate of calculation or value –1734.

2. I wish all correspondence was on the f. of writing and answering when one can FRANKLIN. **3.** †*Under f.*: below standard value; Not deem'd a pen'worth under f. QUARLES.

Phrases.

a. *To have one f. in the grave*: to be near death. **b.** *F. to f.*: in close combat. *Feet foremost*: lit., hence also 'as a corpse'. **c.** *To find* or *know the length of* (a person's) *f.*: to discover or know his weaknesses. **d.** *To set* (a person) *on his feet*: to make his position or means of living secure. *To drop* or *fall on one's feet*: see FALL *v.* *To keep one's feet*: to stand or walk upright. **e.** *To put one's f. down*: to take up a firm position. *To put one's f. in* or *into it*: to get into difficulties; to blunder (*colloq.*). **f.** *To take to one's feet*: to walk. **g.** *To put* (or *set*) *the* (or *one's*) *best f. foremost*: see BEST *a.* **h.** *At* (a person's) *feet*: low on the ground close to him; also, *fig.* in the attitude of supplication, homage, subjection or discipleship. **i. On foot:** walking or running; astir; in active existence, employment, or operation. **j. Under foot:** beneath one's feet; *Naut.* 'Under the ship's bottom; said of an anchor which is dropped while she has headway' (Adm. Smyth); also of the movement of the tide, etc.

Combs.: **1.** General: as *f.-gear*, etc.; *-party*, etc.; *-company*, *-drill*, etc.; *-passage*, *-road*, *-track*, etc.; *-bellows*, *-lathe*, *-press*, etc.; *-feathered*, *-gilt*, etc.

2. Special: †**f.-and-half-f.** *a.*, sesquipedalian; **-and-mouth-disease,** a febrile affection of horned cattle, etc., communicable also to man; **-bank** (*Fortif.*) = BANQUETTE; **-base** (*Arch.*) the moulding above a plinth; **-bath,** (*a*) the act of bathing the feet; (*b*) a vessel for this purpose; **-bone,** the tarsus; **-bridge,** (*a*) a bridge for f.-passengers only; (*b*) an arched bridge which carries a footstep bearing; **-cushion,** *spec.* (*Entom.*) a pulvillus; **-fault** (*Lawn Tennis*), a fault made by overstepping the base-line, or by failure to maintain contact with the ground, while serving; hence as vb.; **-halt,** a disease which attacks the feet of sheep; **-hill,** a hill lying at the base of a mountain; **-hole,** a hole in which to place the f. (in climbing); **-iron,** (*a*) an iron fastened to the f.; (*b*) a step for a carriage; **-jaw,** one of the anterior limbs of crustacea, etc., which are modified so as to assist in mastication; **-key,** an organ pedal; **-level,** an instrument which serves as a level, a square, and a foot-rule; **-licker,** a toady; **-line,** (*a*) *Printing*, the bottom line in a page; (*b*) *Fishing*, 'the lead-line or lower line of a net or seine' (*Cent. Dict.*); **-pad,** *spec.* (*Entom.*) = *f.-cushion*; **-page,** a boy attendant or servant; **-plate,** (*a*) a carriage step; (*b*) the platform on a locomotive engine for the driver and fireman; **-post,** a postman or messenger who travels on f.; postal delivery by their means; **-pound,** (*Mech.*), the quantity of energy required to raise a pound weight one foot; **-poundal,** a unit consisting of the energy of a pound weight moving at the rate of one foot per second; **-race,** a race run by persons on f.; **-rail,** (*a*) a rail (e. g. of a table or seat) upon which the feet are rested; (*b*) a railroad rail having wide-spreading foot flanges; (*c*) a narrow moulding raised on a vessel's stern; **-rope,** (*Naut.*), (*a*) the bolt-rope to which the lower edge of a sail is sewed; (*b*) a rope extended beneath a yard upon which the sailors stand when furling or reefing; **-rot,** an inflammatory disease of the foot of cattle and sheep; whence *f.-rotting* (vbl. sb.), treating sheep that have the f.-rot; **-rule,** a measuring rule one foot long; **-screw,** a supporting foot, for giving a machine or table a level standing on an uneven floor; **-space-rail** (*Naut.*), the rail that terminates the foot of the balcony, and in which balusters step; **-stick,** (*Printing*), a bevelled stick put at the bottom of a page or pages to quoin up against; **-stove,** a stove to warm the feet; **-sugar** = *foots*: see FOOT *sb.* V. 4; **-ton,** the amount of energy capable of raising a ton weight one foot; **-trench,** a shallow trench; **-tubercle,** one of the lateral processes on each segment of some of the Annelida; also called *Parapodia*; **-valve** (in a steam-engine), the valve between the air-pump and the condenser; **-waling** (*Naut.*), the inside planking or lining of a ship over the floor-timbers; **-wall** (*Mining*), the wall or side of rock which is under a vein or lode; **-washing,** the washing of another's feet, *esp.* as a religious observance; **-work,** (*a*) a work to protect the foot of a structure; (*b*) *Football*, dribbling, etc.; **-worn** *a.*, (*a*) worn by the feet; (*b*) footsore.

Foot (fut), *v.* ME. [f. prec. sb.] **1.** *intr.* To step or tread to measure or music; to dance. Esp. in *to f. it*. Also quasi-*trans.* with cogn. object. **2.** To move the feet as in walking; to go on foot. Now *rare.* 1570. **3.** *trans.* To set foot on; to tread; to walk over 1557. **4.** To settle, establish. Chiefly *refl.* and in *pass.* = to have or get a foothold *in*. 1599. †**5.** *trans.* To strike with the foot; to kick; *fig.* to spurn –1808. **b.** *intr.* or *absol.* To do foot-work. *colloq.* (*Football*). 1852. **6.** *trans.* Of a hawk, etc.: To clutch with the talons. Also *fig.* 1575. **7.** To make or add a foot to 1465. **8.** To sum up at the foot of (a bill, etc.). Now usu. with *up*. Chiefly *colloq.* 1490. **b.** To pay (a bill). *colloq.* 1848. **c.** *intr.* To total *up* to. Const. with or without *to*. 1867.

1. F. it featly here and there SHAKS. To f. a hornpipe 1842. **2.** Theeues doe f. by night SHAKS. **3.** Lucil..vsed to fote the streates of Rome SIR T. NORTH. **5.** *Merch. V.* I. iii. 119. **6.** The holy eagle Stoop'd, as to f. us SHAKS. **8. c.** His total losses footed up to £5,000. 1893.

Football, foot-ball (fu·tbǫl). ME. [f. FOOT *sb.* + BALL *sb.*[1]] **1.** An inflated ball used in the game (see 2). It consists of an inflated bag or bladder enclosed in a leather case. 1486. **2.** An open-air game played with this ball by two sides, each of which endeavours to kick or carry the ball to the goal of the other side ME. **3.** *fig.* 1532.

2. Foote balle, wherein is nothinge but beastlie furie and exstreme violence ELYOT. **3.** The.. institutions of the mistress of the world had become the f. of ruffians FROUDE. Hence **Foo·tball** *v.* to kick like a f.; also *fig.*

Footboard (fu·tbōᵊɹd). 1766. [f. FOOT *sb.* + BOARD.] **1.** A board to support the foot or feet; a board to stand on; e.g. a small platform at the back of a carriage on which the footman stands; the foot-rest of a driving-box; in *U.S.* the foot-plate of a locomotive engine. **b.** A treadle 1874. **2.** An upright board set across the foot of a bedstead 1843.

Foo·tboy. 1590. †**a.** A boy-attendant. **b.** A page-boy.

Foo·t-breadth, †-brede. ME. [See BREADTH and BREDE *sb.*[2]] The breadth of a foot (as a measure).

No, not so much as a foot breadth [of their land] *Deut.* 2:5.

Foo·t-cloth. 1480. †**1.** A large richly-ornamented cloth laid over the back of a horse and hanging down to the ground on either side –1805. **2.** A cloth to set the feet upon, a carpet 1639.

2. A foot-cloth for your majesty's chief room of state SWIFT.

Footed (fu·tėd), *ppl. a.* 1453. [f. FOOT *sb.* and *v.* + -ED.] Furnished with or having feet (*rarely* a foot). **1.** Furnished with feet; having feet *like* (a dog, etc.) 1529. **2.** Having, or provided with, a foot or feet; also, mended with a (new) foot 1453. **3.** *Archery.* Of an arrow: Having a different and harder wood dovetailed on at the pile end 1856.

1. An animal..f. like a goat 1727. *Brazen-*, *cat-*, *claw-f.*: cf. those words. **2.** New-f. boots and shoes 1844.

Footer (fu·təɹ), *sb.*[1] 1608. [f. FOOT *sb.* or *v.* + -ER[1].] **1.** One who goes on foot. *rare.* **2.** *Falconry.* Of the hawk: One good at seizing the quarry with its talons 1879. **3.** With a numeral prefixed: A person or thing of that number of feet in height or length; as *six-f.*, etc. 1844.

Footer (fū·təɹ), *sb.*[2] *dial.* or *slang.* 1753. [transf. use of FOUTRE.] One who potters about.

Footer, *sb.*[3]: see -ER[6].

Foo·tfall, foo·t-fall. 1610. The fall of the foot on the ground in walking; a footstep, tread.

Her footfall was so light 1873.

Foo·t-guards, foo·tguards. 1675. A body of picked foot-soldiers for special service as a guard. Now the proper name of five infantry regiments, the Grenadier, Coldstream, Scots, Irish, and Welsh Fusilier Guards.

Foothold (fu·t₁hōᵘld). 1625. [See HOLD *sb.*[1]] A hold or support for the feet; a surface (secure or otherwise) for standing or walking on; stable position of the feet. Also *transf.* and *fig.*

Foo:t-ho·t, *adv.* ? *Obs.* ME. [f. FOOT *sb.* + HOT *a.* or *adv.*; cf. *footsore*.] **a.** In hot haste, without pause. **b.** Occas. = 'closely', as in *to follow foot-hot*.

Footing (fu·tiŋ), *vbl. sb.* ME. [f. FOOT *v.* + -ING[1].] **1.** The act of walking; a step or tread. Now *rare.* 1583. **b.** Dancing 1561. **2.** A footprint, or footprints collectively; a trace, trail. Also *fig.* Now *rare.* 1572. **3.** The action of placing the feet securely; stable position of the feet, foothold ME. **4.** Surface for walking or standing upon 1596. **5.** *fig.* Firm or secure position; established place; foothold, establishment 1586. **6.** The agreed or understood basis, conditions or arrangements on which a matter is established; the position assigned to a person, etc. in estimation or treatment 1657. **b.** Relative status (as an equal, etc.) 1742. **7.** Entrance on a new position, etc.; hence, a fee demanded on the occasion of such entrance, etc. 1710. **8.** The action of putting a foot to anything 1805; also *concr.* that with which something is footed 1591. **9.** *Arch.* A projecting course or courses at the foundation of a wall, etc. 1703. **10.** *Whale-fishing.* The refuse whale blubber, not wholly deprived of oil 1820.

3. Stande sure, and take good fotyng SKELTON. **4.** Where scarce was f. for the goat SCOTT. **5.** In former times, when England had a f. in France 1586. **6. b.** I was admitted to his table upon the f. of half friend, half underling GOLDSM. *Comb.*: **f. beam, f. dormant,** the tie-beam of a roof.

Footle (fū·t'l), *v. slang.* 1892. [perh. alt., by assoc. with -LE, of (dial.) *footer* bungle, idle or potter about, presumably rel. to FOOTER *sb.*[2]] *intr.* To talk or act foolishly. Hence **Foo·tle** *sb.*, twaddle. **Foo·tling** *ppl. a.*, 'drivelling', 'blithering'.

Footless (fu·tlės), *a.* ME. [-LESS.] Having no foot or feet. Also *transf.* and *fig.*

Footlights (fu·tləits), *sb. pl.* 1836. A row of lights placed in front of the stage of a theatre, on a level with the feet of the actors. Often *transf.* = 'the stage'.

Footman (fu·tmǣn). ME. [f. FOOT *sb.* + MAN *sb.*] **1.** One who goes on foot, a pedestrian. Now chiefly *dial.* †**b.** A footpad –1666. **2.** A foot-soldier. ME. †**3.** An attendant or footservant; formerly, a servant who ran before his master's carriage –1818. **4.** A man-servant in livery employed chiefly to attend the carriage and wait at table 1706. Also *fig.* **5.** A stand to support a kettle, etc., before the fire 1767. **6.** A moth of the family *Lithosiidæ* 1819.

4. *fig.* The Whigs, who..submitted to be the footmen of the Duke of Newcastle MACAULAY.

Footmanship (fu·tmǣnʃip). 1562. [f. prec. + -SHIP.] **1.** The action of, or skill in, running or walking. ? *Obs.* **2.** The office of a footman 1833.

†**Foo·t-mantle.** ME. **a.** ? An over-garment worn by women when riding. **b.** = FOOTCLOTH 1. –1818.

Foot-mark, footmark (fu·tmāɹk). 1641. A mark on, or made by, the foot; a footprint.

Foo·t-note (fu·t₁nōᵘt). 1841. A note or comment added at the foot of the text.

Foot-pace (fu·tpeⁱs). 1538. [See PACE *sb.*] **1.** A walking-pace. **2.** Something on which to set the feet: †**a.** a carpet or mat –1653; **b.** a raised portion of a floor: e.g. the step on which an altar stands 1580; **c.** a hearth-stone 1652; **d.** a half-landing on a staircase, etc. 1703.

Footpad (fu·tpæd). *Obs.* exc. *Hist.* 1683. [See PAD *sb.*[2]] A highwayman who robs on foot.

Foot-path, footpath (fu·tpɑþ). 1526. **1.** A path for foot-passengers only. †**2.** ? A pedestal 1580. **3.** *attrib.* 1611.

1. Horseway, and foot-path *Lear* IV. i. 58. **3.** Jog-on, Jog-on, the foot-path way *Wint. T.* IV. iii. 132.

Footprint (fu·tprint). 1552. The impression left by the foot; *spec.* in *Geol.* Also *fig.*

Certain fossil foot-prints of a reptile..found in strata of the ancient coal-formation LYELL.

Footrill (fu·tril). Also **footrail, futteril.** 1686. [Of unkn. origin.] *Coal-mining.* The entrance to a mine by means of a tunnel driven into a hill-side.

Foot-slog (fu·tslǫg), *v.* 1906. [SLOG *v.* 2.] *intr.* To tramp, march. Hence **Foo·t-slog** *sb.* **Foo·t-slo:gger,** an infantryman, a pedestrian.

Foo·t-sore. 1719. **A.** *adj.* Sore as to the feet. **B.** *sb.* A complaint of the foot 1874.

Footstalk (fu·tstǭk). 1562. [f. FOOT *sb.* + STALK *sb.*[1]] A slender stem or support fitted into a foot or base. **a.** *Bot.* The stalk or petiole of a leaf; the peduncle of a flower. **b.** *Zool.* A process resembling a petiole; e.g.

the muscular attachment of a barnacle, the stalk of a crinoid, etc. 1826. **c.** *gen.* 1831.

Footstall (fu·tˌstǫl). 1585. [f. FOOT *sb.* + STALL *sb.*[1]] **1.** The base or pedestal of a pillar, etc. **2.** 'A woman's stirrup' (J.).

Footstep (fu·tstep). ME. [See STEP.] **1.** A step of the foot; a footfall; also, the distance traversed by the foot in stepping 1535. **2.** A footprint ME. Also *fig.* †**3.** *fig.* A mark, token, or indication left by anything –1785. **4.** A step or raised structure on which to put the foot 1549. **b.** A bearing to sustain the foot of a vertical shaft or spindle 1683.

1. Hold up my goings in thy paths, that my footsteps slip not *Ps.* 17:5. **2.** *fig.* Phr. *To follow* or *walk in a person's footsteps.* **4.** At the footestep of the Altar SIR T. BROWNE.

Foo·tstool. 1530. **1.** A stool upon which to rest the foot or feet. **b.** *U.S.* The earth 1821. †**2.** A stool to step upon in mounting –1702.

1. *fig.* Sit thou at my right hand, until I make thine enemies thy f. *Ps.* 110:1.

Footway (fu·twe[i]). 1526. [f. FOOT *sb.* + WAY *sb.*] **1.** = FOOT-PATH 1. **2.** *Mining.* 'The series of ladders and sollars by which men enter or leave a mine' (Raymond) 1778.

Footy (fū·ti), *a.*[1] 1752. [var. of dial. *foughty* musty.] Paltry, mean; insignificant. *dial.* and *colloq.*

Footy (fu·ti), *a.*[2] 1864. [f. FOOT *sb.* + -Y[1].] Having foots or dregs. (Dicts.)

Foozle (fū·z'l), *sb.* 1860. [Cf. next vb.] **1.** A fogy; (*U.S.*) a fool. **2.** *Golf.* A foozling stroke 1890.

Foozle (fū·z'l), *v.* 1857. [– G. (Bavarian dial.) *fuseln* work hurriedly and badly; cf. FUSEL.] **1.** *intr.* To fool. **2.** *trans.* To make a mess of, bungle. *Golf* and *slang.* Also *absol.* 1892.

2. To f. one's tee shot 1892. Hence **Foo·zler.**

Fop (fǫp), *sb.* ME. [Connection with next cannot be maintained in view of the difference in sense.] †**1.** A fool –1716. **2.** One who is foolishly attentive to his appearance, dress, or manners; a dandy, an exquisite 1672.

2. His tightened waist, his stiff stock [etc.].. denoted the military f. DISRAELI. Hence **Fo·pling**, a petty f.

†**Fop,** *v.* 1529. [app. – G. *foppen* (XIV) cheat, deceive; prob. orig. thieves' cant. Cf. FOB *v.*[1]] **1.** *intr.* To play the fool. **2.** *trans.* = FOB *v.*[1] –1694.

†**Fopdoodle.** 16... [f. FOP *sb.* + DOODLE *sb.*] A fop, fool, or simpleton –1664.

Foppery (fǫ·pĕri). 1546. [f. FOP *sb.* and *v.* + -ERY.] †**1.** Foolishness, imbecility; a foolish action, etc.; something foolishly esteemed –1758. **2.** The characteristics of a fop; coxcombry, dandyism 1697. **b.** *concr.* Foppish finery 1711.

2. Modern politeness..runs often into affectation and f. HUME.

Foppish (fǫ·piʃ), *a.* 1605. [f. FOP *sb.* + -ISH[1].] †**1.** Foolish, silly –1720. **2.** Resembling or befitting a fop or dandy 1699.

1. Wisemen are growne f. SHAKS. **2.** A vain, f. young man EVELYN. **Fo·ppish-ly** *adv.*, **-ness.**

For (fǭr, fǫɹ, fəɹ), *prep.* and *conj.* [OE. *for* = OFris., OS. *for*, Goth. *faur*, prob. reduction of Gmc. *fora before (of place and time), repr. by OE. *fore* = OFris., OS., OHG. *fora*, beside OS., OHG. forms with *-i*, viz. *furi* (G. *für*) and ON. *fyrir*; see FORE *adv.* and *prep.*]

A. *prep.* †**I.** = BEFORE in various uses. **1. a.** In front of –1601. **b.** In asseveration. (Cf. Gr. πρός.) In later use repl. by FORE. –ME. **2.** Of time –ME. **3.** In preference to, above –1504.

1. a. F. whose throne 'tis needfull..to kneele SHAKS.

II. 1. Representing, as representative of OE. **2.** In place of, instead of OE. **3.** In exchange for; as the price of OE; in requital of OE.

1. Walker returned thanks f. his lady 1843. Phr. *Once f. all.* **2.** Will he f. a fish giue him a serpent *Luke* 11:11. They will employ somebody to do the business f. them 1895. **3.** Men gaf flueten schillynges f. a goos or a heen ME. Punishment f. his misdeeds 1818.

III. In defence or support of; in favour of, on the side of. Opp. to *against.* OE. **b.** In honour of. Also *To name a child for* (= after) a person (now *Sc.* and *U.S.*) 1800.

Take my Word f. it she is no Fool STEELE. You argue f. it in vain HELPS. Hence quasi-*sb.* *Fors and againsts*: 'pros and cons'.

IV. 1. With the object or purpose of OE. **b.** For the purpose of being or becoming 1489. **c.** Conducive to 1553. **2.** In order to obtain ME. **3.** Indicating the object to which the activity of the faculties or feelings is directed 1592. **4.** Before an *inf.*, usu. *for to* = 'in order (to)'. Hence *for to* merely for *to.* Now *arch.* or *vulgar.* ME. **5.** Indicating destination. **a.** With the purpose of going to. Now chiefly after *to depart, start, sail, leave, steer, make*; also after the pple. *bound.* 1489. **b.** *transf.* of time 1885. **c.** Introducing the intended recipient, or the thing to which something is intended to belong, or the like ME. **6. a.** Following a vb., adj., or noun of quality, denoting appointment, appropriation, fitness, etc. ME. **b.** Following a sb., or predicatively = Appointed, adapted, or suitable for ME. **7.** Of result or effect; used after *cause, ground, motive, reason*, etc. (Cf. REASON *sb.* II.) **8.** Designating an amount to be received or paid. Also in *Cricket*: With the result of (so many runs), at the cost of (so many wickets). 1776.

1. An order..f. the payment of the balance to the plaintiff 1891. To go out f. a walk (*mod.*). Phr. *For company*: see COMPANY *sb.* **b.** To go f. a soldier 1741. **c.** It is f. the general good 1664. **2.** The drawers..struck work f. an advance of wages 1883. Phr. *I would not f. anything, f. a great deal, f. the world*, etc. Hence also, *To play f. a certain stake. To try a man f. his life. F. (one's) life*: in order to save one's life; also hyperbolically, with one's utmost efforts. **3.** O f. a Falkners voice, To lure this Tassell gentle back againe SHAKS. **4.** What went ye out f. to see *Luke* 7:25. **5. a.** We sailed from hence directly f. Genoa ADDISON. **b.** It is getting on f. four (*mod.*). **c.** Madam, they are f. you SHAKS. A fireproof chamber f. the muniments M. PATTISON. **6. a.** Very fit f. a wife JANE AUSTEN. Important enough f. separate treatment (*mod.*). **b.** By no means a match f. his enemies ADDISON. **8.** The signature was good f. more than that STEVENSON. The score stood at 150 for 6 wickets (*mod.*).

V. 1. With the purpose or result of benefiting or gratifying; as a service to OE. Also *ironically.* **2.** As affecting the interests or condition of (a person or thing) 1537. **3.** Governing a sb. or pers. pron. followed by an inf., with sense '*that he*, etc. *may, might, should*', etc. 1508.

1. Dangers..Which he f. us did freely undergo MILT. To shift f. my selfe 1631. **2.** This..bodes ill f. the peace of Europe 1883. **3.** What a condition f. me to come to 1843.

VI. Of attributed or assumed character; = as. OE.

Know f. trouth that..god loueth fayth LD. BERNERS. I know f. a fact that [etc.] 1843. Phr. *To take f. granted, to leave f. dead*, etc. *F. certain, sure*, see these adjs. (*I*, etc.) *f. one. F. the first, second*, etc. *time. F. good (and all)*: see GOOD *sb.*

VII. 1. By reason of (a feeling, etc.) OE. **2.** On account of OE. **b.** In adjurations = *for the sake of.* Also in exclams. OE. **3.** Of an operative cause: As the effect of. (Now chiefly after comparatives.) ME. **4.** Of a preventive cause or obstacle. **a.** In spite of, notwithstanding OE. **b.** Indicating the presence or operation of an obstacle. In neg. sentences; also after *if it were not, were it not*; occas. = for fear of. OE. †**c.** Against –1728.

1. Our men raised a shout f. joy DE FOE. Phr. *F. fear of, that*, etc.: see FEAR *sb.* **2.** Notorious both f. covetousness and f. parsimony MACAULAY. Phr. *F. cause*: see CAUSE *sb.* **b.** Alas! f. my master 1460. F. shame! BYRON. †*For because*: see BECAUSE. **3.** To die f. thirst standyng in the river HALL. The worse f. liquor (*mod.*). Phr. *F. want of*: see WANT *sb.* **4. a.** This Alexander the Great f. all his greatness died HY. MORE. F. all her feelings are so fine 1786. **b.** Uninhabitable f. heat RAY. Spare not f. spoiling of thy steed SCOTT.

VIII. Of correspondence or correlation. **1.** Prefixed to a number or quantity to which another corresponds in some different relation ME. **2.** Preceded and followed by the same sb. (without article or defining word), in idiomatic expressions indicating equality in number or quantity between objects compared or contrasted ME.

1. It contains..f. one inch of lean four or five of stringy fat 1806. **2.** Bulk f. bulk heavier than a Fluid BENTLEY.

IX. 1. As regards ME. **2.** In proportion to, considering; considering the nature or capacity of 1631.

1. The king's condition f. money PEPYS. Phr. †*F. me* = as f. me; *f. my, his*, etc. *part*: see PART; *f. the rest* (= Fr. *du reste*): see REST *sb.*[2] *As f.*: see AS. *F. all* or *aught I know*, I know nothing to the contrary. (*He may do it*) *f. me*, i.e. with no opposition from me. *F. all the world*: used to emphasize assertions of likeness. **2.** A man of an excellent character f. a Lawyer RICHARDSON.

X. 1. Marking actual or intended duration; e.g. *f. long, f. the time, f. life, f. ay, ever* 1450. *F. once, f. the nonce*: see ONCE, NONCE.

B. *conj.* **1.** Because. *Obs.* exc. *arch.* ME. **2.** Introducing the ground or reason for something previously said: Seeing that, since OE. †**3.** In order that –1593. †**4.** *F. and*: = 'and moreover' –1617.

1. They are..iealious for they're iealious SHAKS. **2.** Nowe is good tyme F. al Englond praith f. vs CAXTON. **3.** 3 *Hen. VI*, III. i. 9. **4.** A Spade f. and a shrowding-Sheete *Haml.* V. i. 103.

For-, *pref.*[1] [OE. *for-, fær-* = OFris. *for-, fir-*, OS. *for-*, OHG. *fir-, far-* (Du., G. *ver-*), Goth. *fair-, faur-*, corresp. to Gr. περι-, παρα-, L. *per-, por-*, Skr. *pári, purā*; IE. prefix with variation of form and wide extent of meaning, but esp. implying (1) rejection, exclusion, prohibition, (2) destruction, (3) exhaustion.] A prefix used to form vbs. and adjs.; now entirely obsolete as a living formation.

I. Forming vbs. **1.** Prefixed to vbs. with sense 'away', 'off', as in **forcast** –ME. **2.** With sense of prohibition, exclusion, or warding off, as in FORBID; †**forsay,** to renounce, exclude by command –1579. **3.** With the notion of passing by, abstaining from, or neglecting, as in FORBEAR, FORGO –ME. **4.** Implying destructive, painful, or prejudicial effect, as in **fordeem,** FORDO. **b.** With sense of 'asunder, in pieces', as in **forhale,** *fig.* to distract. **5.** Expressing the notion of something done in excess, or so as to overwhelm or overpower; in pa. pples.; as **forfrighted,** greatly terrified; etc. –1603. **b.** Prefixed to intr. vbs., with sense 'to weary or exhaust (oneself) by' doing what the vb. denotes, as in FORWANDER, FORWEEP. Also in pa. pples. and ppl. adjs.: **forsung (-songen); forwake, -waked,** wearied with waking or watching. **6.** With sense 'all over', 'through and through', as in **forcratch,** to scratch all over. **7.** Prefixed to transitive vbs. with intensive force, or, occas., without modifying the sense, as in **fordread. 8.** Forming factitive vbs. from adjs. or sbs. of quality; as in **formeagre,** to make lean; **forfatted** pa. pple., fattened.

II. In adjs. [Cf. L. *per-*, Gr. περι-.] Giving to an adj. the sense of an absolute superlative, 'very', 'extremely'; as *for-black, -dry, -hoar, -old, -weary.*

For-, *pref.*[2], OE. *for-*; freq. in OE. and ME. as a var. of FORE-; cf. ME. *forganger* and FOREGANGER.

For-, *pref.*[3], occurring only in wds. adopted from Fr., as FORFEIT; repr. OFr. *for-, fors-*, identical with *fors* adv. (mod.Fr. *hors*):– L. *foris, foras.*

Forage (fo·rėdʒ), *sb.* ME. [– (O)Fr. *fourrage*, f. OFr. *fuerre* (mod. *feurre* straw) – Frankish *fōder fodder; see -AGE.] **1.** Food for horses and cattle; in early use, *esp.* dry winter food, as opp. to grass. Also *transf.* and *fig.* **2.** The act of foraging or providing forage 1481. †**3.** In *pl.* Foragers –1603.

2. A detachment for f. LYTTON. *transf.* And he [the lion] from forrage will incline to play *L.L.L.* IV. i. 93.

Comb. **f.-cap,** the undress Glengarry cap worn by infantry soldiers.

Forage (fǫ·rėdʒ), *v.* ME. [– (O)Fr. *fourrag(i)er*, f. *fourrage*; see prec.] **1.** *trans.* To collect forage from; to overrun (a country) for the purpose of obtaining or destroying supplies. Also, to plunder, ravage. **2.** *intr.* To rove in search of forage or provisions; also, to raid 1530. **3.** To make a roving search *for*; to rummage 1768. †**4.** To raven.

lit. and *fig.* –1698. **5.** *trans.* To supply with forage or food 1552. **6.** To obtain by foraging 1656.

1. To F. whole Countries 1700. **2.** Oxen and bulls..taken in foraginge ELYOT. **3.** Foraging among the old manuscripts W. IRVING. **4.** Whiles his..Father..Stood smiling, to behold his Lyons Whelpe F. in blood of French Nobilitie SHAKS.

Forager (fǫ·rėdʒəɹ). ME. [– OFr. *forragier*, f. *forrage* FORAGE *sb.*; also OFr. *forrageour* (mod. *fourrageur*), f. *forragier* FORAGE *v.*; see -ER².] †**1.** A harbinger –1616. **2.** One who forages 1489. **b.** A foraging ant (*Eciton*) 1863.

Foralite (fōᵊ·rălait). 1859. [f. L. *forare* to bore + -LITE.] *Geol.* A name for certain tube-like markings which occur in sandstones, etc.

‖**Foramen** (forēⁱ·mėn). *Pl.* **foramina** (foræ·mină). 1671. [– L. *foramen*, *-min-*, f. *forare* BORE *v.*¹] An opening or orifice, a hole or short passage. Applied variously in *Anat.*, *Zool.*, etc.

The *f. of an ovule* is an aperture through the integuments, allowing the passage of the pollen tubes to the nucleus *Treas. Bot.* s.v.

Foraminate (foræ·minėt), *a.* [Back-formation from FORAMINATED, or f. L. *foramen* (see prec.) + -ATE².] = FORAMINATED.

Foraminate (foræ·mineⁱt), *v.* 1599. [f. L. *foramen* FORAMEN + -ATE³.] To bore, pierce, perforate.

Foraminated (foræ·mineⁱtėd), *ppl. a.* 1599. [f. prec. + -ED¹.] Bored, pierced, perforated.

Foraminifer (forămi·nifəɹ). 1841. [f. L. *foramin-* FORAMEN + *-fer* bearing.] A rhizopod of the order *Foraminifera*.

‖**Foraminifera** (foræ:mini·fĕră), *sb. pl.* 1835. [mod. L. neut. pl. of prec.] *Zool.* An order of *Rhizopoda*, furnished with a shell or test, usually perforated by pores (*foramina*). So **Fora:mini·feral** *a.* pertaining to the *Foraminifera*; consisting of or containing foraminifera. **Fora:mini·ferous** *a.* furnished with foramina; said of the *Foraminifera* and their shells; also (less correctly), consisting of or containing foraminifera. †**Fora·minous** *a.* full of holes, perforated, porous.

Forasmuch (fǫrăzmʊ·tʃ), *adv.* ME. [orig. *for as much*, tr. OFr. *por tant que* for so much as; north. *for as mekill*, Sc. also *forasmekle*.] Only in *Forasmuch as*: **a.** In consideration that, seeing that. Now *formal* or *arch.* †**b.** Occas.: So far as –1654.

Foray (fǫ·reⁱ), *sb.* ME. [prob. f. next.] **1.** A hostile or predatory incursion, a raid. Also *transf.* and *fig.* †**2.** Booty taken in a foray –1598. †**3.** The advance-guard of an army –1587.

1. Red hand in the f., How sound is thy slumber SCOTT.

Foray (fǫ·reⁱ), *v.* ME. [Back-formation from FORAYER.] **1.** *trans.* To scour or ravage in search of forage or booty; to pillage. (Revived by Sir W. Scott.) **2.** *intr.* To make a raid; to pillage ME.

1. When Roderick foray'd Devanside SCOTT.

Forayer (fǫ·reⁱəɹ). [ME. *forayer* – OFr. *forrier* forager (mod. *fourrier* quartermaster) :– Rom. **fodrarius*, f. **fodro* FODDER. Cf. FORAGE *sb.*] **1.** One who forays; a forager, a raider. †**2.** A foregoer, harbinger, or courier –1549.

1. Sending with forreiars certaine guides P. HOLLAND.

†**Forba·r, foreba·r**, *v.* ME. [– AFr., OFr. *forbarrer*, f. *for-* FOR- *pref.*³ + *barrer* BAR *v.*] **1.** *trans.* To hinder –1450. **2.** To shut out; to bar, deprive, or exclude (a person); *esp.* in *Law* –1671.

Forbear, forebear (foɹbēᵊɹ, fōᵊ·ɹbēᵊɹ), *sb.* Orig. *Sc.* 1470. [f. *for-* FORE- + *bear, beer*, agent-noun of BE; see BEER *sb.*²] An ancestor, progenitor (usu. more remote than a grandfather).

Forbear (fǭɹbēᵊ·ɹ), *v.* Pa. t. **-bore** (-bōᵊ·ɹ), pa. pple. **-borne** (-bōᵊ·ɹn). [OE. *forberan* = OHG. *farberan* restrain, abstain, Goth. *frabairan* endure; f. FOR- *pref.*¹ + BEAR *v.*¹] †**1.** *trans.* To bear; to tolerate, endure –1742. †**2.** To bear up against, control. Also *refl.* and *intr.* for *refl.* –ME. †**3.** To do without, spare –1667; †to part with or from –1590: †to avoid, shun; to leave alone –1673. **4.** To abstain or desist from ME. **5.** *absol.* and *intr.* To abstain, refrain. Const. *to* with *inf.*, also *from*. ME. **6.** *trans.* To withhold, keep back ME; *refl.* to refrain (*rare*) 1535. **7.** To spare, show mercy or indulgence to. Now *rare*. OE. **b.** *intr.* To show forbearance. Const. *with*. 1591. **8.** *trans.* To abstain from enforcing (what is due), *esp.* the payment of (a debt). Now *rare*. 1570.

3. MILT. *P. L.* ix. 747. **4.** I forbore pressing them further 1655. **5.** The lovers of Hampden cannot f. to extol him at Falkland's expense M. ARNOLD. **6.** F. thy bloody hand MARLOWE. *refl.* Forbeare thee from medling with God. 2 *Chron.* 35:21. **7.** The quycke fire doth not forbeare the wod be it wette or drye LD. BERNERS. Phr. *To bear and f.* (now *intr.* but orig. *trans.*). **8.** Money lent, or forborn HUTTON. Hence **Forbea·rant** *a.* forbearing. **Forbea·rer,** one who or that which forbears. **Forbea·ring-ly** *adv.*, **-ness.**

Forbearance (fǭɹbēᵊ·răns). 1576. [f. prec. + -ANCE; orig. (like *abearance*) legal.] **1.** The action or habit of forbearing. Const. *to, from, to* with *inf.* 1591. **2.** Forbearing conduct or spirit; long-suffering; lenity 1599. **3.** Abstinence from enforcing what is due, *esp.* the payment of a debt 1576.

1. True Noblenesse would Learne him f. from so foul a Wrong SHAKS. **2.** The vertue of patience or f. 1599. **3.** F. is no quittance *Prov.* He..soon shall find F. no acquittance MILT.

Forbecause: see BECAUSE A. 1 and B. 1.

†**Forbi·d**, *sb.* 1602. [f. next vb.] A forbidding –1740.

Forbid (fǭɹbi·d), *v.* Pa. t. **forbad, -bade** (-bæ·d); pa. pple. **for·bidden** (-bi·d'n). [OE. *forbēodan* = OFris. *forbiāda*, Du. *verbieden*, OHG. *farbiotan* (G. *verbieten*), Goth. *faurbiudan*; see FOR- *pref.*¹ + BID.] **1.** *trans.* To command not to; to prohibit. Also *absol.* **2. a.** *fig.* To exclude, keep back, hinder, restrain. Now chiefly: To render impossible or undesirable. OE. †**b.** To defy, challenge. BP. ANDREWES. †**c.** To lay under a ban –1819.

1. Forbeed us thing, and that desire we CHAUCER. F. the Sea for to obey the Moone SHAKS. The governor of the Castle forbad the Church Service to be performed 1865. **2.** For bede þi tonge fra ill HAMPOLE. Th' Applause of list'ning Senates to command..Their Lot forbad GRAY. *God, Heaven, the Lord f.*, a deprecatory phr.; also *absol.* as an exclam. **c.** He shall liue a man forbid *Macb.* I. iii. 21.

Hence †**Forbi·d** *ppl. a.* forbidden. **Forbi·ddance,** the action of forbidding; prohibition, interdiction. **Forbi·dder.**

Forbidden (fǭɹbi·d'n), *ppl. a.* ME. [pa. pple. of prec.] In senses of the vb.

Phr. *F. degrees*, certain degrees of relationship within which people are forbidden to marry. *F. fruit*, (*a*) that forbidden to Adam (*Gen.* 2:17), also *fig.*; (*b*) hence, a name for varieties of *Citrus*, esp. *C. decumana*.

Hence **Forbi·dden-ly** *adv.*, **-ness.**

Forbidding (fǭɹbi·diŋ), *ppl. a.* 1573. [see -ING².] **1.** That forbids (see the vb.). **2.** *esp.* Repellent, repulsive, uninviting 1712.

2. An elderly man of remarkably hard features and f. aspect DICKENS. The morning looked f. enough HARDY. Hence **Forbi·dding-ly** *adv.*, **-ness.**

Forblack; see FOR- *pref.*¹ II.

†**Forbo·de**, *sb. Obs.* exc. *arch.* [OE. *forbod*, f. *forbēodan* FORBID; = Du. *verbod*, (MH)G. *verbot*, ON. *forboð*.] A forbidding; a prohibition. Hence †**Forbo·de** *v.* to forbid.

†**Forbrui·se**, *v.* ME. [f. FOR- *pref.*¹ + BRUISE.] To bruise severely; to break to pieces –1450.

Forby(e (fǭɹbəi·). ME. [f. FOR-¹ + BY. Cf. G. *vorbei*.]

A. *prep.* **1.** Of position: Hard by. *Obs.* exc. *Sc.* 1596. **2.** Of motion: Close by; past. *Obs.* exc. *arch.* ME. **3.** Besides: not to mention. Only *north.* or *arch.* 1536.

2. They passed foreby the frenchmens busshment LD. BERNERS.

B. *adv.* **1.** Of motion: Aside ME.; along, past (now *rare*) ME. **2.** Besides, in addition 1590.

1. He salutyd them in passynge forby LD. BERNERS.

†**Forca·rve**, *v.* [OE. *forceorfan*, f. FOR- *pref.*¹ + *ceorfan* CARVE.] *trans.* To carve or cut asunder, down, out, through; to cut in two, to pieces –1460.

Force (fōᵊɹs), *sb.*¹ ME. [– (O)Fr. *force* :– Rom. **fortia*, f. L. *fortis* strong.]

I. †**1.** Physical strength. Rarely in *pl.* (= Fr. *forces*). –1816. **2.** Strength, impetus, violence, or intensity of effect ME. **3.** Power or might; *esp.* military power ME. **b.** In early use, the strength (of a defensive work, etc.). Subseq., the fighting strength (of a ship). 1577. **4.** A body of armed men, an army. In *pl.* the troops or soldiers composing the fighting strength of a kingdom or of a commander ME. **b.** A body of police; often absol. *the force* = policemen collectively 1851. **5.** Physical strength or power exerted upon an object; *esp.* violence or physical coercion ME. **b.** *spec.* in *Law*: Unlawful violence offered to persons or things 1480. **6.** Mental or moral strength. Now only, power of effective action, or of overcoming resistance. ME. **7.** Of things: Power to influence, affect, or control 1582; virtue, efficacy 1551. **8.** Of a law, etc.: Binding power, validity 1594. **9.** The real import or significance (of a document, word, sentence, symbol, etc.) 1555. **10.** †**a.** (Without article prefixed): A large quantity or number; const. *of* –1570. **b.** *A force*: a large number or quantity. *The f.*: the majority. *Obs.* exc. *dial.* 1722. **11.** *Physics*, etc. (Cf. mod. scientific uses of L. *vis*.) **a.** (= Newton's *vis impressa*: cf. sense 5). An influence operating on a body so as to produce an alteration or tendency to alteration in its state of rest or of uniform motion in a straight line; the intensity of such an influence as a measurable quantity. (Now merely the name for a measure of change of motion.) 1665. **b.** Formerly used for kinetic (often including potential) energy: see ENERGY. 1841. **c.** The cause of motion, heat, electricity, etc., conceived as consisting in principle or power inherent in, or coexisting with, matter; such principles or powers viewed generically. (This sense is no longer recognized. *Force* is now generic.) 1842. **d.** *transf.* and *fig.* An agency, influence, or source of power likened to a physical force 1785.

1. His eye was not dimme, nor his naturall f. abated *Deut.* 34:7. Phr. *With all one's f.* **2.** They break the f. of the fall GOLDSM. **3.** Inferior in fighting f. 1888. **b.** Ships of good f. DAMPIER. **4.** The valour and atchievements of our forces by sea and land SWIFT. **5.** F. can accomplish many things which would be beyond the reach of cunning BENTHAM. Phr. *By force* = by employing violence, also †under compulsion. **b.** *By f. and arms*: tr. Law L. *vi et armis*. It seems I broke a close with f. and arms TENNYSON. *A f.*: an act of unlawful violence. **6.** A Task which is infinitely above his F. DENNIS. **7.** It [learning] teacheth men the f. of circumstances BACON. Beauty loses its f., if not accompanied with modesty STEELE. In..these two reasons there is f. GROTE. **8.** Hath not his edict the f. of a law HOOKER. Phr. †*Of force*: of binding power: For a Testament is of f. after men are dead *Heb.* 9:17. *In f.*: operative at the time. So *to put in f.*: *to come into f.* **9.** The f. of a Sacrament 1555, of the Particle *For* STEELE, of a fine BLACKSTONE. **10. a.** With f. hawberks, swerdes and knyvys ME. **11. a.** The f. of gravity 1871. **b.** Phr. *Conservation of f.*: see CONSERVATION. **d.** To be a f. in the Legal Profession 1891.

II. Senses derived from FORCE *v.*¹ †**1.** The plunger of a force-pump –1747. **2.** The upper die in a metal-stamping machine 1879. **3.** *Cards.* An act of forcing 1862. **4.** *Billiards.* A screw-back. *U.S.* 1881.

Phrases. **a.** *By force of*: by dint of, by virtue of. Also (later), *by the f. of*. **b.** *In f.*: (*a*) *Mil.* Of a host, enemy, etc.: (Collected) in numbers and strength; (*b*) of persons: In full command of one's powers, energies, or abilities. †**c.** *Of f.*: with *inf.*, powerful enough *to* do something. †**d.** *Of* (or *on*) *f.*: of necessity, perforce. †**e.** *It is f.*: it is of consequence; usu. neg. †**f.** *To hunt*, (etc.) *at f.* (also *of* or *by f.*): to run (the game) down with dogs.

Comb.: **f.-bill,** a bill of a coercive nature, esp. one authorizing the use of troops to secure its enforcement; **-pipe,** the pipe of a FORCE-PUMP in which the piston works.

Force (fōᵊɹs), *sb.*² *north.* Also **foss.** 1600. [– ON. *fors*, OWScand. *foss* (Sw. *fors*, Da. *fos*), without cognates elsewhere in Gmc.] A waterfall or cascade.

Force (fōᵊɹs), *v.*¹ ME. [– (O)Fr. *forcer*, f. *force* FORCE *sb.*¹]

I. 1. *trans.* To use violence to; to violate (a woman). **2.** To constrain by force (whether physical or moral); to compel ME.; to put a strained sense upon (words) 1662. **b.** *Whist.* To compel (a player) to trump a trick, by leading a suit of which he has none 1746. **3.** To compel or constrain (a person, oneself, etc.) *to do* a thing (†occas. with *to* omitted) ME. **4.** To urge, compel to violent effort; †to exert (one's strength) to the utmost. Also †*refl.* and *intr.* ME. **5.** To overpower by force; to enter, take, or pass through, by force; to storm (a stronghold); to board (a ship) 1581. **b.** To break open (a gate, etc.); to break (a lock). Also *to f. open* 1623. †**c.** To overpower (troops, a guard) –1781. **6.** To drive by force, impel. Chiefly const. with prep., or with advbs. 1582. **7.** *intr.* To make one's way by force. Now *rare.* 1653. †**8.** To lay stress upon, press home, urge. Also, To enforce (a law, etc.) –1607. **9.** To bring about by force or effort; to effect. *lit.* and *fig.* 1551. **10.** To obtain or take by force; to win by violence; to extort, elicit 1602. **11.** To hasten by artificial means the maturity of. Also *intr.* for *refl.* 1719.

1. To f. a maide 1620. **2.** Art thou King, and wilt be forc't SHAKS. Phr. *To f. one's hand*: to compel one to act prematurely or the like. **3.** To f. a person to resign 'JUNIUS'. **4.** High on a Mounting Wave, my head I bore, Forcing my Strength, and gath'ring to the Shore DRYDEN. Phr. *To f. the pace* or *the running* (in a race). *To f. the bidding* (at a sale by auction). *To f. one's voice. To f. the game* in *Cricket*: to take risks in order to score rapidly. **5.** At length the Citie..was forced by assault GOLDING. **6.** We were forc'd by contrary Winds into St. Remo ADDISON. **7.** We gradually f. ahead, breasting aside the floes KANE. **9.** I don't f. appetite CONGREVE. Phr. *To f. a passage, one's way.* **10.** It stuck so fast..That scarce the Victor forc'd the Steel away DRYDEN.

II. †**1.** To strengthen, reinforce; also, to garrison, to man –1810. †**2.** Chiefly in neg. sentences: To attach force to; to care for, regard –1614; with *inf.* as *obj.*: To care *to* –1591. †**b.** *intr.* To care. Const. *for, of,* occas. *on.* –1605. †**3.** *impers.* To be of force; to matter, signify –1603.

1. *Macb.* V. v. 5. **2.** I f. not argument a straw SHAKS. *Lucr.* 1021. Your oath once broke, you f. not to forsweare *L.L.L.* V. ii. 440.

†**Force,** *v.*[2] ME. [Altered f. FARCE *v.*, by confusion with prec.] = FARCE *v.* 1, 2. Also *fig.* –1793.

fig. Wit..larded with malice and malice forced with wit *Tr. & Cr.* V. i. 64.

Forced (fōᵊɹst), *ppl. a.* 1548. [f. FORCE *v.*[1] + -ED[1].] **1.** Subjected to violence 1621. **2.** Enforced, compulsory; not spontaneous or optional 1576. **3.** Produced or maintained with effort 1596. **b.** In literary use: Strained, distorted 1583. **c.** Artificial, constrained, unnatural 1621. †**4.** Artificially made; opp. to *natural.* Chiefly of soils. –1688. **5.** Of plants, etc.: Made to bear, or produced, out of the proper season 1695. †**6.** Fortified –1602.

2. A f. peace 1734. Phr. *F. move* (in a game). **3.** Phr. *F. march.* **b.** Forc'd interpretations 1724. **c.** Her forc'd civilities DRYDEN. Hence **Fo·rced-ly** *adv.*, **-ness.**

Forceful (fōᵊ·ɹsful), *a.* 1571. [f. FORCE *sb.*[1] + -FUL.] **1.** Full of force; powerful; cogent. **2.** Acting with force or violence 1592. **3.** quasi-*adv.* Forcefully 1718.

1. A f. minister BRYCE, argument 1870. **2.** Against the Steed he threw His f. Spear DRYDEN. Hence **Fo·rceful-ly** *adv.*, **-ness.**

Forceless (fōᵊ·ɹslės), *a.* 1532. [f. as prec. + -LESS.] Without force; feeble.

Feeble heart and f. hand SCOTT.

Force-meat (fōᵊ·ɹsˌmīt). 1688. [f. FORCE *v.*[2] + MEAT.] Meat chopped fine, spiced, and highly seasoned, chiefly used as stuffing or as a garnish. Also *attrib.*

Forcement (fōᵊ·ɹsmĕnt). ME. [– (O)Fr. *forcement*, f. *forcer*; see FORCE *v.*[1] + -MENT.] †**1.** Strengthening; a fortification –1533. †**2.** Compulsion –1634. **3.** *Gunnery.* Excess of diameter of the projectile over that of the bore 1892.

Forceps (fǭ·ɹseps). *sing.* and *pl.* 1634. [– L. *forceps.*] **1.** An instrument of the pincers kind, used for seizing and holding objects, *esp.* in surgical and obstetric operations. **2.** *Anat., Entom.,* and *Zool.* Some organ or part of the body that has the shape of, or may be used as, a forceps. †Also, one of the two branches of this. 1661. Also *attrib.*

Fo·rce-pump. 1659. [f. FORCE *sb.* or *v.* + PUMP *sb.*[1]] **1.** A pump employed to force water, etc. beyond the range of atmospheric pressure. **2.** The plunger-pump for supplying the boiler of a locomotive engine 1858.

Forcer (fōᵊ·ɹsəɹ). 1556. [f. FORCE *v.*[1] + -ER[1].] **1.** One who or that which forces. **2.** An instrument or means of forcing; e.g. the plunger or piston of a force-pump 1634; a force-pump 1731; †a contrivance for propelling water –1736.

Forcible (fōᵊ·ɹsib'l), *a.* ME. [– legal AFr., OFr. *forcible*, f. *forcer*; see FORCE *v.*[1], -IBLE.] **1.** Done by force; involving the use of force; *esp.* in Law, *Forcible detainer, entry.* **2.** Possessing force; †strong, powerful –1802. telling; convincing 1570. †**3.** Unavoidable –1574. †**4.** 'Valid, binding, obligatory' (J.) 1584. **5.** quasi-*adv.* Forcibly 1582.

1. A f. entry or detainer; which is committed by violently taking or keeping possession, with menaces, force, and arms, of lands and tenements, without the authority of law BLACKSTONE. **2.** He prepared a f. armie to attend him RALEGH. A f. argument 1594. F. reasons BURKE. Hence **Fo·rcibleness. Fo·rcibly** *adv.*

Fo·rcible fee·ble. 1844. [After SHAKS. 2 *Hen. IV*, III. ii. 179.] A feeble person who makes great pretence of vigour. Also *attrib.* or as *adj.*

Italics, that last resource of the Forcible Feebles DISRAELI.

Forcing (fōᵊ·ɹsiŋ), *vbl. sb.* ME. [see -ING[1].] **1.** The action of FORCE *v.*[1] †**2.** *concr.* A material used in forcing wine –1743.

2. The Victualler puts..with it the usual Forcing or Fining 1743.

Comb.: **f.-engine,** a fire-engine; **-hazard** (*Billiards*), a stroke requiring more than usual force. Also in reference to the forcing of flowers, etc., as *f.-bed, -frame, -glass, -house, -pit,* etc.; and quasi-*adj.* with sense 'suitable for forcing', as in *f. rose, variety.*

Fo·rcing-pump. 1727. = FORCE-PUMP.

†**Fo·rcipal,** *a.* [f. L. *forceps, -cip-* FORCEPS + -AL[1].] Of the nature of a forceps SIR T. BROWNE.

Forcipate (fǭ·ɹsipeˈt), *a.* 1668. [f. as prec. + -ATE[2].] *Bot.* and *Zool.* Formed like a forceps. So **Fo·rcipated** *a.*

Forcipa·tion. [f. as prec. + -ATION.] †**1.** Torture by nipping with forceps. BACON. **2.** *Zool.* The state of being forcipated (*Cent. Dict.*).

Forcite (fōᵊ·ɹsəit). Also **forsite.** 1883. [f. FORCE *sb.*[1] + -ITE[1] 4 a.] A variety of dynamite.

Forclose: see FORECLOSE.

†**Forcu·t,** *v.* ME. [f. FOR- *pref.*[1] + CUT *v.*] To cut into, cut in pieces. CHAUCER.

Ford (fōᵊɹd), *sb.* [OE. *ford* = OFris. *forda*, OS. *-ford* in place-names (Du. *voorde*), (O)HG. *furt* :– WGmc. *furdu* (cf. ON. *fjọrðr* FIORD :– **ferþuz*), f. Gmc. **fer- *far- *fur-*; see FARE *v.*[1]] **1.** A shallow place in a river or other water, where a man or beast may cross by wading. †**2. a.** A tract of shallow water. **b.** *poet.* A stream, current. –1780.

1. Drown'd in passing thro' the f. TENNYSON. **2. b.** With water of the f. Or of the clouds, to moisten their roots dry SPENSER. Hence **Fo·rdless** *a.* without a f.; that cannot be forded.

Ford (fōᵊɹd), *v.* 1614. [f. prec. sb.] **1.** *trans.* To cross (water) by means of a ford; to wade through. Also *fig.* and *causatively.* **2.** *intr.* To cross (*over*) by means of a ford 1675.

1. *fig.* His last Section which is no deepe one, remains only to be foarded MILT. Hence **Fo·rdable** *a.* that may be forded. **Fo·rdableness.**

Fordo, foredo (fǭɹ-, foᵊɹdū·), *v.* Pa. t. **-did** (-di·d). Pa. pple. **-done** (-dʊ·n). [OE. *fordōn* = OS. *fardōn* (Du. *verdoen*), OHG. *fartuon* (G. *vertun*); see FOR- *pref.*[1], DO *v.*] **1.** *trans.* To put an end to. *Obs.* exc. *arch.* OE. **2.** To destroy, ruin, lay waste. *arch.* OE. †**3.** To undo (a person) –1647. **4.** To do away with ME. **5.** Pa. pple. only: Exhausted, worn out. *arch.* 1547.

1. She for dispayr fordede hyre self CHAUCER. Its rites foredone, its guardians dead 1833. **4.** To wipe away and foredoe the shamefull blot P. HOLLAND. **5.** With Indian heats at last fordone M. ARNOLD. Hence **Fordo·ne** *ppl. a.* exhausted, overcome, tired out.

†**Fordri·ve,** *v.* [OE. *fordrīfan*, f. FOR- *pref.*[1] + *drīfan* DRIVE *v.*; = OHG. *fartrīban* (G. *vertreiben*).] *trans.* To drive forth, drive about –1513.

†**Fordru·nken,** *ppl. a.* [OE. *fordruncen*, f. FOR-*pref.*[1] + DRUNKEN; = MLG. *verdrunken.*] Drunk, overcome with drink –1513.

†**Fordry·,** *v.* [OE. *fordrūgian* (intr.), f. FOR- *pref.*[1] + *drūgian* DRY *v.*] *intr.* To dry up –1494.

†**Fordwi·ne,** *v.* OE. [f. FOR- *pref.*[1] + DWINE; = MDu. *verdwijnen.*] *intr.* To fade away, wither; to vanish –ME.

†**Fore,** *sb.* [OE. *fōr* = OHG. *fuora* (G. *fuhre*), :– Gmc. **fōrō*, f. **for-*, grade var. of **far-*; see FARE *v.*[1]] **1.** A journey, expedition. Also, an expeditionary force. –ME. **2.** A track, trace –ME.

2. Who folweth Cristes gospel and his f. CHAUCER.

Fore (fōᵊɹ), *a.* 1490. [Evolved from analysis of combs. of FORE- *prefix*, e.g. *forehead, foreland, forepart.*]

I. As adj. *in concord.* **1.** Situated or appearing in front, or in front of something else; usually opp. to *back, hind-* 1500. †**2.** Anterior, previous, former –1718.

1. The alimentary canal may therefore be distinguished into a f. and a hind gut HUXLEY.

II. quasi-*sb.* or *ellipt.* The fore part of anything, e.g. the bow of a ship 1888. **b.** *Naut.* (see quot.) 1860.

b. *At the f.*, means at the fore-royal mast-head W. C. RUSSELL.

Phr. **To the f. a.** Of a person: On the spot, within call. **b.** Alive. **c.** Of money, etc.: Forthcoming; available. **d.** In view, conspicuous. So *to come to the f.*, to come to the front, or into view.

Fore (fōᵊɹ), *adv.* and *prep.* [OE. *fore* = OFris. *for(e), fara*, OS., OHG. *fora* (Du. *voor*, G. *vor*), Goth. *faura* :– Gmc. **for-*, rel. to Skr. *purā́*, Gr. πρό, παρά, L. *pro, præ, per.* From XVI often regarded as abbr. of *before* and written *'fore.* Now only in FORE AND AFT.]

†**A.** *adv.* **1.** Before, previously –1600. **2.** In advance –1500.

1. The eyes (f. dutious) now..looke an other way SHAKS.

B. *prep.* = FOR *prep.* in various uses OE.

F. these witnesses *Wint. T.* IV. iv. 401. F. God I thinke so SHAKS. Prizest him 'fore me SHAKS.

Fore (fōᵊɹ), *int.* 1878. [prob. aphet. f. BEFORE or AFORE.] *Golf.* A warning cry to people in front of the stroke.

Fore-, *prefix.* [Identical with FORE *adv.* and *prep.*] In OE. used as a prefix (1) to verbs, adding the sense of 'before' (in either time, position, order, or rank), and (2) to sbs., either forming designations of objects or parts occupying a front position, or expressing anteriority of time. For occasional or self-explanatory combinations see O.E.D.

Combs.:

a. With reference to place: **f.-action,** the movement of a horse's front legs; †**-beak,** the prow of a vessel; †**-buttock** (joc.), the breast (of a woman) SWIFT; **-flank,** (*a*) the front part of the flank; (*b*) a projection of fat, upon the ribs, immediately behind the shoulder; **-hearth,** a projecting bay in the front of a blast-furnace hearth; **-hooks** (*Naut.*) = *breast-hooks*; **-page,** the first page (in a printed work); **-piece** (*Saddlery*), the flap attached to the fore-part of a side-saddle, to guard the rider's dress; **-step,** (*a*) a step forward; (*b*) *pl.* steps in front, tracks; **-thwart,** the seat of the bowman in a boat; **-winning** (*Mining*), advanced workings.

b. With reference to time: †**f.-eatage,** the opportunity of pasturing one's cattle before others; †**-title,** prescriptive title.

Forea·ct, *v.* 1618. [f. FORE- + ACT *v.*] *trans.* and *intr.* To act beforehand (see ACT *v.*).

Fore-adapt, -advise, etc.: see FORE- and the simple vbs.

†**Fo:re-alle·ged,** *ppl. a.* 1587. [f. FORE- + *alleged* (ALLEGE *v.*[2]).] Previously alleged or quoted –1701.

Fore and aft. 1618. [Not continuous with OE. and ME. *fore* (see FORE *adv.* and *prep.*); perh. of LG. origin; cf. Du. *van voren en van achteren.*] *Naut.*

A. *adv.* **1.** Of position: In or at both bow and stern; hence, along the length of or all over the ship 1627. **2.** Of motion or direction: Alternately towards the bow and stern, backwards and forwards 1726. **3.** From stem to stern 1618.

3. He..raked her fore and aft with his Cannon 1709.

B. *adj.* (usu. with hyphens). Placed or directed in the line of the vessel's length. Of sails: Applied to all sails which are not set to yards. 1820.

Fo:re-appoi·nt, *v. arch.* 1561. [See FORE-.] To appoint beforehand. Hence **Fore-appoi·ntment,** previous appointment, preordination.

Forearm (fōᵊ·ɹ,ā̆ɹm), *sb.* 1741. [f. FORE- + ARM *sb.*[1]] The part of the arm between the elbow and the wrist. Also *transf.*

Forearm (foᵊrā·ɹm), *v.* 1592. [f. as prec. + ARM *v.*[1]] *trans.* To arm beforehand. *lit.* and *fig.*

Forewarned, forearmed GREENE.

Fore-axle, -beam: see FORE- and AXLE, BEAM.

Forebode (foᵊɹbōᵘ·d), *v.* 1603. [f. FORE- + BODE *v.*] **1.** *trans.* To announce beforehand 1664; of things, to betoken, portend 1656. **2.** To have a presentiment of (*usually* evil); to anticipate, to apprehend beforehand 1603. **b.** *intr.* or *absol.* To forecast 1711.

1. Old men foreboded evil days to come 1879. Long flights f. a fall COWPER. 2. I foreboded mischief the moment I heard [etc.] 1793. b. If I f. aright HAWTHORNE. Hence †**Forebode** *sb.*, **Forebo·dement,** a foreboding. **Forebo·der,** one who or that which forebodes. **Forebo·dingly** *adv.*

Foreboding (foᵊɹbōᵘ·diŋ), *vbl. sb.* ME. [f. prec. + -ING[1].] **1.** The action of FOREBODE *v.*; hence, a prediction, a presage. Now only of evil. **b.** A portent, omen ME. **2.** A presentiment of coming evil 1603.

Fore-body (fōᵊ·ɹbǫ:di). 1830. [f. FORE-.] *Naut.* That part of a ship before the dead-flat.

Fo·re-cabin. 1816. [f. FORE- + CABIN *sb.*] A cabin in the fore-part of the vessel; *spec.* one for second-class passengers, with inferior accommodation.

Forecast (fōᵊ·ɹkɑst), *sb.* 1535. [f. next vb.] **1.** The action, habit, or faculty of forecasting; foresight of consequences and provision against them. Now *rare.* 1541. **b.** A forecasting or anticipation, *esp.* with regard to the weather 1673. †**2.** A plan, scheme, or device made beforehand –1754.

1. Evils which no f. could avert PRESCOTT. b. The 'wet or dry' part of our forecasts *Times.* 2. That f. or decree by the power of which the world was 1674.

Forecast (foᵊɹkɑ·st), *v.* Pa. t. and pple. **-cast, -casted.** ME. [f. FORE- + CAST *v.*] **1.** *trans.* To contrive or plan beforehand; to foreordain, predestine. **b.** To consider beforehand 1534. **2.** To estimate, or conjecture beforehand 1494. **3.** (? from the *sb.*) To take a forecast of; to foreshadow 1883.

1. At the first sight the thing which was forecast by good order, seemeth to happen by adventure GOLDING. 2. Quene Margaret..ever forcastyng and doubtyng, the chaunce that might happen HALL. *absol.* If it happen as I did f. MILT. Hence **Foreca·ster,** one who forecasts.

Fo·recastle. Also **fo'c'sle,** after sailors' pronunc. (fōᵘ·ks'l). ME. [f. FORE- + CASTLE.] **1.** *Naut.* A short raised deck forward; in early use raised like a castle to command the enemy's decks. Now *arch.* or *Hist.* **2.** The fore-part of a ship 1490. **3.** In merchant vessels, the forward part, under the deck, where the sailors live 1840. **4.** *attrib.*, as *f.-deck*, etc. 1726.

†**Forechoo·se,** *v.* ME. [see FORE-.] *trans.* To choose beforehand, pre-elect –1587. Hence **Forecho·sen** *ppl. a.*

Fo:re-ci·ted, *ppl. a.* 1576. [f. FORE- + *cited* (CITE *v.*).] Previously cited.

Foreclose (foᵊɹklōᵘ·z), *v.* ME. [– *forclos*, pa. pple. of (O)Fr. *forclore*, f. *for-* FOR- *pref.*[3] + *clore* CLOSE *v.*; there has been assoc. with FOR- *pref.*[1] or with FOR- *pref.*[2], FORE-.] **1.** *trans.* To bar, shut out completely. †**2.** To close fast, stop up (an opening, way, etc.) –1751. **3.** To hinder the action, working, or activity of 1536. **4.** *Law of Mortgage.* To bar or exclude (the person entitled to redeem) upon non-payment of money due; to deprive of the equity of redemption. Const. *from.* 1728. **b.** To bar (a right of redemption); to take away the power of redeeming 1704. **5.** To close or settle by anticipation 1722. **6.** To establish an exclusive claim to 1599.

1. The Puritans being thus foreclosed and shut out of the Church NEAL. 3. The Imbargo with Spaine..foreclosed this trade CAREW. 4. To f. the mortgage W. IRVING. 6. Finding ..even virtue and truth foreclosed and monopolized EMERSON.

Foreclosure (foᵊɹklōᵘ·ʒ[i]uɹ). 1728. [f. prec. + -URE.] The action of foreclosing (a mortgage); a proceeding to bar the right of redeeming mortgaged property.

†**Fo:reconcei·ve,** *v.* 1553. [f. FORE-.] *trans.* To conceive beforehand, to preconceive –1662.

Fore-court (fōᵊ·ɹkoᵊɹt). 1535. [f. FORE- + COURT *sb.*[1]] The court or enclosed space in front of a building, the outer court.

Fore-dated, -day: see FORE- and DATE *v.*, DAY *sb.*

†**Fo·re-deck.** 1565. [f. FORE- + DECK *sb.*] The deck at the fore-part of a ship; the fore-part of the deck –1747.

†**Fo:redee·m,** *v.* 1542. [f. FORE- + DEEM.] **1.** *trans.* To judge beforehand; to forecast. Also *intr.* with *of.* –1660. **2.** To deem in advance 1612.

1. To foredeme the wurste UDALL.

Forede·stine, *v.* ME. [f. FORE- + DESTINE *v.*] To destine beforehand, predestine. So **Forede·stiny,** †prediction; destiny.

Foredoom (fōᵊ·,dūɹm), *sb.* 1563. [f. FORE- + DOOM *sb.*] A judgement pronounced beforehand; destiny.

Foredoom (fōᵊ·ɹ,dūm), *v.* 1592. [f. FORE- + DOOM *v.*] **1.** *trans.* To doom beforehand (*to* or *to do*); to foreordain (a thing) 1608. **2.** To forecast, foreshadow 1592.

1. Efforts..foredoomed to failure 1878. Foredooming that which is to be N. FAIRFAX.

Fore-edge (fōᵊ·r,edʒ). 1665. [f. as prec. + EDGE *sb.*] The front or outer edge; *esp.* of a book, or of a leaf in a book.

Fore-elders (fōᵊ·r,eldəɹz), *pl.* Chiefly *north.* ME. [f. FORE- + ELDER(S. Cf. ON. *foreldran* in same sense.] Ancestors, progenitors.

Fore-end (fōᵊ·r,end). ME. [f. as prec. + END *sb.*] **1.** Of place: The fore-part, front. Now chiefly *Naut.* **b.** The fore-part of the stock of a gun 1881. **2.** Of time: The beginning. Now *dial.*; chiefly = *spring* 1611.

2. In all The fore-end of my time *Cymb.* III. iii. 73.

Forefather (fōᵊ·ɹfāðəɹ). ME. [– ON. *forfaðir*; superseded OE. *forþfæder*, early ME. *forþfader*; cf. Du. *voorfader.*] An ancestor, a progenitor. Chiefly *pl.*

The rude Forefathers of the Hamlet GRAY. Phr. *Forefathers' day* (U.S.): the anniversary of the day on which the first settlers landed at Plymouth, Mass.

Forefeel (foᵊɹfī·l), *v.* 1580. [f. FORE- + FEEL *v.*] To feel beforehand, have a presentiment of.

With unwieldy waves the great sea forefeels winds That both ways murmur CHAPMAN. Hence **Fo·refeel,** *sb.* **Fo·refeeling** *vbl. sb.* a presentiment.

†**Fo·refence,** *sb.* 1609. [f. as prec. + FENCE *sb.*] A first or front defence; a bulwark –1677.

Forefend: see FORFEND.

Forefield (fōᵊ·ɹfīld). 1681. [f. FORE- + FIELD *sb.*] *Mining.* The face of the workings.

Forefinger (fōᵊ·ɹfiŋgəɹ). 1450. [f. FORE- + FINGER, perh. after Du. *voorvinger.*] The finger next the thumb; the *first* or *index finger.*

[**Foreflow** *v.*, 'to flow before', *Dryden*, in Dicts. is a mistake for *foreslow.*]

Fore-foot (fōᵊ·ɹfut), *sb.* 1481. [f. FORE- + FOOT, perh. after Du. *voorvoet* (cf. G. *vorderfuss*).] **1.** One of the front feet of a quadruped. †**b.** *joc.* The hand. *Hen. V*, II. i. 71. **2.** *Naut.* 'A timber which terminates the keel at the forward extremity, and forms a rest for the stem's lower end' (Adm. Smyth) 1770.

Forefront (fōᵊ·ɹfrɒnt). 1470. [f. FORE- + FRONT.] **1.** The principal face or foremost part. Now *rare.* Now usually *fig.* **2.** The front of the body as opp. to the 'back' 1880.

1. Set ye Uriah in the f. of the hottest battle 2 *Sam.* 11:15. Hence **Fo·refront** *v.* to build a (new) f. to STERNE.

Fo·re-game. 1594. [f. FORE-.] A preliminary game.

Foreganger (fōᵊ·ɹgæŋəɹ). ME. [f. FORE- + GANGER *sb.*[1]] †**1.** A fore-runner; also, a predecessor –1460. **2.** *Naut.* 'A short piece of rope immediately connecting the line with the shank of the harpoon, when spanned for killing' (Adm. Smyth) 1794.

Foregate (fōᵊ·ɹgē[i]t). 1503. [f. FORE- + GATE *sb.*[1]] The front or principal entrance.

Foregather: see FORGATHER.

Foregift (fōᵊ·ɹgift). 1744. [f. FORE- + GIFT *sb.*] *Law.* 'A premium for a lease' (Wharton).

Forego (foᵊɹgōᵘ·), *v.* Pa. t. **forewent;** pa. pple. **foregone.** [OE. *foregān*, f. FORE + *gān* GO.] *trans.* To go before, precede, in place or time. Also *intr.* Also quasi-*trans.* with cognate obj. OE. See also FORGO.

The cause doth alwayes his effect fore-goe 1619. *intr.* And now they bene to heauen forewent SPENSER. Hence **Forego·ing** *ppl. a.* preceding (in place or time); also *absol.* (quasi-*sb.*).

Foregoer (foᵊɹgōᵘ·əɹ). ME. [f. FORE- + GOER.] †**1.** A forerunner, a harbinger; *spec.* a purveyor –1745. **2.** One who or that which goes in front; a leader; hence, an example, pattern ME. **3.** A predecessor 1553. **4.** *Naut.* = FOREGANGER 2. 1694.

3. He..in knowledge clerely exceded all his foregoers 1553.

Foregone (foᵊɹgǫ·n), *ppl. a.* 1600. [pa. pple. of FOREGO *v.*] That has gone before or gone by; (of time) past.

Foregone conclusion: a Shakespearian phrase, variously interpreted. Now used for: A decision or opinion formed before the case is argued or the full evidence known; also, a result that might have been foreseen as inevitable.

Foreground (fōᵊ·ɹgraund). 1695. [– Du. *voorgrond*; cf. G. *vordergrund.*] **1.** That part of a view which is in front and nearest the spectator; *esp.* as represented in a picture. **2.** *fig.* The most conspicuous position 1816. **3.** *attrib.* 1827.

1. White can subsist on the f. of the Picture DRYDEN. 3. F. studies in colour RUSKIN.

Foreguess (fōᵊɹge·s), *v.* ME. [f. FORE- + GUESS.] *trans.* To forecast, conjecture.

Fo·re-ha:mmer. *Sc.* and *n. dial.* 1543. [f. as prec. + HAMMER. Cf. Du. *voorhamer.*] The large hammer which strikes first; a sledge-hammer.

Forehand (fōᵊ·ɹ,hænd). 1545. [f. FORE- + HAND *sb.*]

A. *adj.* †**1.** *Archery. F.* (*shaft*): an arrow for shooting straight before one. Opp. to *under-hand.* –1597. **2.** Done or given at some earlier time. Of payments, etc.: Made in advance. ? *Obs.* exc. *dial.* 1599. **3.** Foremost 1644. **4.** *Lawn Tennis*, etc. Of a stroke or court: Not backhanded (cf. BACK-HAND *sb.*) 1889.

2. F. notice of a trial 1678. To pay a f. rent 1790. 3. Our auld f. ox SCOTT.

B. *sb.* **1.** The position in front or above 1557. **b.** That which holds the front position; the vanguard, hence the mainstay. *Tr. & Cr.* I. iii. 143. **2.** That part of a horse which is in front of the saddle 1617.

1. But for Ceremonie, such a Wretch..Had the f. and vantage of a King *Hen. V*, IV. i. 297.

Fo·re-ha:nded. 1591. [f. as prec. + -ED[2].] †**1.** Having a forehand; 'formed in the foreparts' (J.). Said of horses, and *transf.* –1680. **2.** Looking to the forehand; prudent, thrifty; hence, well-to-do. Now only *U.S.* 1650. **3.** *Lawn Tennis*, etc. Played forehand 1889.

2. An early and f. care JER. TAYLOR. The wives of f. farmers..were apt to be somewhat exalted 1883.

Forehead (fǫ·rėd). [OE. *forhēafod*, f. FOR-[2], FORE- + *hēafod* head. Cf. OFris. *forhāfd*, MLG. *vorhōved*, Du. *voorhoofd*, G. *vor-*, *vorderhaupt.*] **1.** That part of the face between the eyebrows and the natural line of the hair. Also *transf.* and *fig.* 1602. †**2.** (Cf. L. *frons.*) **a.** Capacity of blushing; modesty. **b.** Command of countenance; assurance. –1775. **3.** The front part, forefront; *spec.* in *Mining*, = FOREFIELD. 1525. †**4.** A leader –1641.

1. *fig.* The forhead of the morning *Cor.* II. i. 57. 2. b. With what f. Darest thou call me so DRYDEN. 4. Pretending to be a f. of Divinity SIR E. DERING.

Hence **Fo·reheadless** *a.* †without sense of shame; destitute of confidence.

Forehea·r, *v.* 1599. [f. FORE- + HEAR *v.*] To hear beforehand. *trans.* and *intr.*

Fore-hearth, etc.; see FORE- *pref.*

†Forehe·nt, *v.* [f. FORE- + HENT.] *trans.* To seize beforehand, cut off (in flight). SPENSER.

†Forehew, *v.* erron. f. obs. *forhew,* to hew in pieces. (Dicts.)

Forehold (fōᵊɹ·ˌhōᵘld). 1641. [f. FORE- + HOLD *sbs.*[1] and [2].] †**1.** Advance. **2.** *Naut.* 'The part of the hold before the fore hatchway' (Adm. Smyth) 1790.

[**Foreholdings,** quoted by Johnson from L'Estrange, is a mistake for *Forebodings.*]

Fo·re-horse. 1480. [f. FORE- + HORSE.] The foremost horse in a team, leader. Also *transf.* and *fig.*

Foreign (fǫ·rĕn). [ME. *forein(e* – OFr. *forein, forain* :– Rom. **foranus,* f. L. *foras* acc. pl., *foris* locative pl. of **fora,* var. of *fores* door. See FOR- *pref.*[3] For the sp. with *-eign* cf. *sovereign.*]

A. *adj.* †**1.** Out of doors; outside –1619. †**b.** ?Excluded (from court, etc.) 1613. **2.** Not one's own; = L. *alienus.* Now *rare.* ME. **3.** Proceeding from other persons or things ME. **4.** Alien in character; irrelevant, dissimilar, inappropriate. Now only with *from, to.* ME. **5.** Introduced from outside; *esp.* in surgical use, of substances embedded in tissues of the body 1621. **6.** Situated outside an estate, district, province, etc. 1495; belonging to or coming from another district, society, etc. 1460. **7.** Not in one's own land ME. **8.** Not domestic or native ME. **9.** Carried on or taking place abroad, into or with other countries 1548. **10.** Dealing with matters concerning other countries. Also, intended for use in transactions, etc., with other countries, as in *foreign bill,* etc. 1655. †¶**11.** Used as tr. L. *forensis*: Made in open court. CHAUCER.

1. [The steward] is to see into all offices, soe well foraine, as at home 1605. **b.** *Hen. VIII,* II. ii. 129. **3.** Foreyne helpe CHAUCER. A f. impulse 1712, cause 1834. **4.** F. from people's thoughts SWIFT, to the argument BP. BERKELEY. A purpose f. from his pursuits HELPS. **7.** Forain universities 1700. They [in U.S.] usually talk of corporations belonging to other States as 'foreign' BRYCE. **9.** F. Missions 1796. F. trade 1840. **10.** The f. policy of England EMERSON. *Foreign Office*: the department of the 'Secretary of State for F. Affairs'; also, the buildings.

Phrases *F. attachment*: see ATTACHMENT. †*F. intent*: a constructive sense not implied in the wording of the instrument; opp. to *common intent.*

Comb. Chiefly locative and parasynthetic, as *f.-built, -going, -looking, -made, -manned, -owned,* adjs.

B. *sb.* †**1.** = FOREIGNER 1. Also, a foreign vessel. –1643. †**2.** Short for *chambre foreine,* i.e. a privy. CHAUCER. **3.** That part of a town which lies outside the parish proper. Now *local.* 1668. **b.** *pl.* The outer court of a monastery 1668.

Hence **Fo·reignism,** the imitation of what is foreign; a f. idiom, phrase, or term. **Fo·reignize** *v.* to become, or render, f. **Fo·reignness.**

Foreigner (fǫ·rĕnəɹ). ME. [f. FOREIGN *a.* + -ER[1], after *stranger,* which it superseded in the sense 'one belonging to another country', for which †*foreign* was also used.] **1.** A person born in another country; an alien. (Chiefly applied to those whose native language is a foreign one.) **b.** *transf.* Some thing produced or brought from abroad; *esp.* a foreign vessel 1677. **2.** One of another country, parish, etc.; an outsider. Now *dial.* †Also *fig.* ME.

1. Horse and Foot..as well English as Foreigners 1703. **2.** No F., as men of Bolton, Blackburne, or any other places 1565. *fig.* Joy is such a forrainer, So meere a stranger to my thoughts DENHAM.

Fo:re-inte·nd, *v.* 1580. [f. FORE-.] To intend beforehand.

Forejudge (fōᵊɹˌdʒɒ·dʒ), *v.* 1561. [f. FORE- + JUDGE *v.* after Fr. *préjuger,* L. *præjudicare* PREJUDGE.] **1.** *trans.* To determine beforehand or without a fair trial; to prejudge. Also *absol.* †**2.** To form an opinion of beforehand. Also *intr.* with *of.* –1792. So **Foreju·dgement,** judgement formed beforehand; †a judicial precedent.

Foreknow (foᵊɹnōᵘ·), *v.* 1450. [f. FORE- + KNOW *v.*] **1.** *trans.* To know beforehand, have previous knowledge of. **2.** *intr.* To have previous knowledge *of* 1703.

1. St. Paul..fore-knew there would be Heresies among them 1680.

Hence **Foreknow·ingly** *adv.* Also †**Foreknow·able** *a.* that may be foreknown. †**Foreknow·er.**

Foreknowledge (foᵊɹnǫ·lėdʒ). 1535. [f. FORE-.] Knowledge of an event, etc., before it exists or happens; prescience.

If I foreknew, F. had no influence on their fault MILT. *P. L.* III. 118.

Forel, forrel (fǫ·rĕl). ME. [– OFr. *forel* (mod. *fourreau*) sheath, f. *fuerre* – Frank. **fōder* = OHG. *fōtar, fuotar* case, cover (G. *futter* lining), Goth. *fōdr* sheath :– Gmc. **fōðram,* rel. to Skr. *pātram* receptacle, f. *pāti* protects.] **1.** †A sheath. ME. only. **b.** A case or covering for a book or manuscript. Now *dial.* ME. **2.** A kind of parchment resembling vellum, used for covering (account-) books 1549. **3.** A selvedge or border 1691. Hence †**Fo·rel, fo·rrel** *v.* to cover with f. or a f.

Foreland (fōᵊ·ɹlănd). ME. [f. FORE- + LAND. Cf. ON. *forlendi* land between hills and sea, Du. *voorland.*] **1.** A cape, headland, or promontory. **2.** A strip of land in front of something; e.g. 'a space left between the base of a canal bank, and an adjacent drainage cut or river, so as to favour the stability of the bank' 1867. **b.** *Fortif.* = BERM 1. 1704. **3.** Land or territory lying in front 1851.

1. Unum foreland vocat. le Holyhede BOTONER.

Forelay (foᵊɹlēⁱ·), *v.* 1548. [f. FORE- + LAY *v.*] **1.** *trans.* To lie in wait for, waylay. *Obs.* exc. *dial.* **b.** *fig.* To lay obstacles in the way of. Now *rare.* 1571. **2.** To lay down or plan beforehand. *Obs.* exc. *dial.* 1605.

1. b. The Lord..forlayeth their craftynesse GOLDING. **2.** I levell at no man with a forelayd designe 1640.

†**Foreleader.** ME. [f. FORE- + LEADER.] One who leads the advance; a chief leader –1648.

Foreleg (fōᵊ·ɹleg). 1483. [f. FORE- + LEG *sb.*] One of the front legs of a quadruped.

Fore-lie, -lift, etc.: see FORE- and LIE, LIFT, etc.

Forelive (foᵊɹli·v), *v.* 1599. [f. FORE- + LIVE *v.*] To live before another.

Forelock (fōᵊ·ɹlǫk), *sb.*[1] 1467. [f. FORE- + LOCK *sb.*[2]] †**1. a.** ? Some piece of horse-harness. **b.** In mediæval armour, a clasp or catch to hold the helm (*Cent. Dict.*). **2.** A wedge (usu. of iron) thrust through a hole in the end of a bolt in order to keep it in its place. Now chiefly *Naut.* 1514.

Comb.: **f.-bolt,** a bolt fitted to receive a f.; **-hook** (*Rope-making*), a winch in the tackle-block by which a bunch of three yarns is twisted into a strand.

Hence **Fo·relock** *v. trans.* to fasten with a f.

Forelock (fōᵊ·ɹlǫk), *sb.*[2] OE. [f. FORE- + LOCK *sb.*[1]] **1.** A lock of hair growing from the fore-part of the head. **2.** *fig.* 1589.

2. Phr. *To take time, opportunity,* etc. *by the f.* (Suggested by Phædrus *Fab.* V. viii.). The occasion..was bald behind, and must be grasped by the f. MOTLEY.

Forelook (fōᵊ·ɹluk), *sb.* ME. [f. as prec. + LOOK *sb.*] **a.** A look forward (*Obs.* exc. *U.S.*). †**b.** Foresight, providence.

Forelook (foᵊɹlu·k), *v.* Also **for-.** ME. [f. as prec. + LOOK *v.*] **1.** *trans.* To look at or see beforehand. **2.** *intr.* To look ahead or forward 1494. †**3.** To bewitch –1611. Hence **Foreloo·ker.**

Forelooper, -loper (fōᵊɹlū·pəɹ, -lōᵘ·pəɹ). *S. Afr.* 1863. [– Du. *voorloper,* f. *voor-* FORE- + *loper,* f. *lopen* walk, run.] A boy who walks with the foremost pair of a team of oxen.

Foreman (fōᵊ·ɹmăn). *Pl.* **foremen.** ME. [f. FORE- + MAN, perh. after ON. *formaðr* leader, or immed. – Du. *voorman* (cf. G. *vormann*).] †**1.** One who goes in front –1674. **2.** The principal juror who acts as spokesman of the jury, and communicates their verdict to the court 1538. **3.** One who takes the most prominent part. *Obs.* exc. *locally* in municipal use. 1603. **4.** The principal workman; *spec.* one who has charge of a department of work 1574. ¶**5.** As tr. Du. *voerman* carrier 1641.

2. I will looke grauely..like the fore-man of a Jury DEKKER. **3.** The f. of the Apostles, Peter PORSON. **4.** *Working f.*: one who both supervises others working, and works himself.

Foremast (fōᵊ·ɹmɑst). 1582. [f. FORE- (and FORE *prep.*) + MAST *sb.*[1]] **1.** The forward lower-mast in all vessels. **2.** ? The station of being 'before the mast'; hence, quasi-*adj.* characteristic of a foremast man 1626.

2. Foremast man, seaman, a sailor below the rank of petty officer. His f. air, and somewhat rolling gait BYRON.

Fore-mean: see FORE- and MEAN *v.*[1]

Fo:re-me·ntion, *v.* 1660. [f. FORE- + MENTION.] To mention beforehand. Hence **Fo:re-me·ntioned** *ppl. a.*; also *ellipt.* 1587.

Foremost (fōᵊ·ɹmoᵘst, -məst). [Alteration (XVI), by assoc. with FORE-, of *formost,* itself an alt., by assoc. with -MOST, of *formest* (XII), f. *forme,* OE. *forma* first + -EST, the result being a double superlative. Cf. FORMER *a.*]

A. *adj.* **1.** First †in time –1587, †in serial order –1542, or position ME. **2.** Most notable or prominent, best, chief OE.

1. Our formest fader adam CAXTON. The f. fynger 1542. Formost to stand against the Thunderers aime MILT. *P. L.* II. 28. **2.** Men ever famous, and formost in the achievements of liberty MILT.

B. *adv.* First in position or rank; †formerly also, in time, serial order, etc. Also in *first and f.* OE.

Hence †**Fo·remostly** *adv.* in front.

Foremother (fōᵊ·ɹmɒðəɹ). 1582. [f. FORE- + MOTHER *sb.*[1], after *forefather.*] A female ancestor.

Forename (fōᵊ·ɹnēⁱm), *sb.* 1533. [f. FORE- + NAME *sb.,* after Fr. *prénom,* L. *prænomen,* Du. *voornam,* etc.] First or Christian name; in *Rom. Antiq.* = PRÆNOMEN.

†**Fo·rename,** *v.* 1490. [f. FORE- + NAME *v.*] *trans.* To name beforehand –1633. Hence **Fo·renamed** *ppl. a.* named or mentioned before.

Forenight (fōᵊ·ɹnəit). 1513. [f. FORE- and FORE *prep.*] †**1.** The previous night 1583. **2.** *Sc.* The interval between twilight and bed-time.

Forenoon (fōᵊ·ɹnū·n). 1506. [f. as prec. + NOON.] The part of the day before noon. Also *attrib.*

Fore-notice: see FORE- and NOTICE *sb.*

†**Fore·nsal,** *a.* [f. as next + -AL[1].] = next. HY. MORE.

Forensic (fǫre·nsik). 1659. [f. L. *forensis,* f. *forum*; see FORUM, -IC.]

A. *adj.* Pertaining to, connected with, or used in courts of law; suitable or analogous to pleadings in court.

A f. term LOCKE, manner DICKENS. *F. medicine*: medicine in its relation to law; medical jurisprudence.

B. *sb. U.S.* A speech or written thesis maintaining one side or the other of a given question 1830. Hence †**Fore·nsical** *a.*, **-ly** *adv.*

Foreordain (foᵊ·rˌǫɹdēⁱ·n), *v.* ME. [f. FORE + ORDAIN.] *trans.* To ordain or appoint beforehand; to predestinate.

Fo:reo·rdinate, *v.* 1858. [f. FORE- + ORDINATE *v.*] *trans.* To foreordain. Hence **Fo:reordina·tion,** previous ordination or appointment, predestination.

Fore-part, forepart (fōᵊ·ɹpaɹt). ME. [f. FORE- + PART *sb.*] **1.** The foremost, first, or most advanced part; the front. †**2.** A stomacher –1640. **3.** The earlier part 1614.

Forepassed, -past (foɹpɑ·st), *ppl. a.* 1557. [f. FORE- + *passed,* PAST.] That has previously passed, or been passed. Now only of time.

Fo·repeak. 1693. [f. FORE- + PEAK *sb.*[2] Cf. Du. *voorpiek.*] *Naut.* The extreme end of the forehold in the angle of the bows.

Fore-piece (fōᵊ·ɹpīs). 1788. [f. FORE- + PIECE.] The foremost, first, or front piece. **b.** *Theatr.* A 'curtain-raiser' 1814. **c.** *Saddlery.* The flap attached to the fore-part of a side-saddle, to guard the rider's dress 1874.

†**Fo:re-posse·ss,** *v.* 1579. [f. FORE- + POSSESS.] *trans.* To possess beforehand *with* –1635.

†**Forepri·se, -prize,** *v.* 1577. [f. FORE- + PRIZE *v.*[2]] *trans.* To take beforehand; to take

for granted; to allow for; to forestall, anticipate –1693.

Fo·re-purpose, *sb.* 1551. [f. FORE- + PURPOSE.] A purpose settled beforehand. Hence **Forepu·rpose** *v.*

†**Fore-quote,** *v.* 1598. [f. FORE- + QUOTE.] *trans.* To quote or cite beforehand –1670.

Fore-rank, etc.: see FORE- and RANK, etc.

Fo:re-rea·ch, *v.* 1644. [f. FORE- + REACH *v.*[1]] Chiefly *Naut.* **1.** *intr.* To shoot ahead. **2.** *trans.* To reach beyond, pass. Also *fig.* 1803. **3.** To anticipate 1874.

2. *fig.* The general, coming back by a different route, had fore-reached them in such a scheme NAPIER.

†**Fore-rea·d,** *v.* 1591. [f. FORE- + READ.] *trans.* To read beforehand 1620; to signify beforehand –1612; to predestine 1636.

Fore-recited, etc.: see FORE-.

Fore-rider (fōᵊ·ɹ,rəidəɹ). 1470. [f. FORE- + RIDER. Cf. Du. *voor-rijder.*) One who rides in front; *esp.* †a scout; an outrider; †a harbinger.

Foreright (fōᵊ:ɹ,rəi·t), rarely **-rights.** ME. [f. FORE *adv.* + -RIGHT.]

†**A.** *adv.* Directly forward, straight ahead –1796.

No less fore-right the rapid chace they held POPE.

B. *prep.* †**1.** Straight along. FULLER. **2.** Opposite. *dial.* 1858.

C. *adj.* †**1.** Straight forward –1748. **2.** Of a branch, etc.: Shooting straight out 1741. **3.** *dial.* Of persons: Headstrong; straightforward; plain-spoken 1736.

1. His sayle Being fill'd and prosper'd with a fore-right Gale QUARLES.

D. *sb.* [The *adj.* used *absol.*] Something that is foreright 1754.

Fore-run (foᵊɹ,rʊ·n), *v.* OE. [f. FORE- + RUN *v.*] **1.** *intr.* To run on in front. OE. only. **2.** *trans.* To outrun. *Obs.* exc. *fig.* 1513. †**3.** To run in front of; hence, to act as harbinger of. Also *transf.* to precede. –1750. **4.** To be the precursor of 1590. **5.** To forestall 1591.

4. These signes f. the death of Kings SHAKS. **5.** By anticipating and forerunning false reports RALEGH.

Forerunner (fōᵊ·ɹrʊ:nəɹ). ME. [f. prec. + -ER[1].] **1.** One who runs before, *esp.* one sent to prepare the way and herald a great man's approach, a harbinger; also, a guide. Also *transf.* and *fig.* **2.** A predecessor; also, an ancestor 1595. **3.** A prognostic or sign of something to follow 1589. **4.** *Naut.* **a.** = FOREGANGER. 1694. **b.** A piece of rag, terminating the stray-line of the log line 1815.

1. John the baptist, whych was the fore runner of. .Christ COVERDALE. Death our Fore-runner is, and guides To Sion KEN. **2.** Arthur, that great fore-runner of thy bloud *John* II. i. 2.

†**Foresaid** (fōᵊ·ɹsed), *a.* OE. [f. FORE- + SAID.] = *Aforesaid* (see AFORE).

Fore-sail (fōᵊ·ɹsēⁱl). 1481. [f. FORE- + SAIL *sb.*[1] Cf. Du. *voorzeil.*] The principal sail set on the foremast; in square-rigged vessels, the lowest square sail on the foremast; in fore-and-aft rigged, the triangular sail before the mast.

Fore-say (foᵊɹsēⁱ·), *v.* [OE. *foresecġan*; f. FORE- + *secġan* SAY *v.*[1]] *trans.* To foretell, predict. Now *rare.*

Foresee (foᵊɹsī·), *v.* [OE. *foresēon*, f. FORE- + *sēon* to SEE. In XVI perh. partly a new formation.] **1.** *trans.* To see beforehand, have prescience of. †**2.** To provide –1637; to see to beforehand –1626. †**3.** *intr.* To exercise foresight, make provision –1626.

1. A prudent man foreseeth the euil, and hideth himselfe *Prov.* 27:12. **3.** He plots, complots, forsees, prevents, directs QUARLES.

Phr. (*Alway*) *foreseen* or *foreseeing that*: provided that; Forseen alwey, that yf .my doughtres dye [etc.] ME. Hence **Foresee·able** *a.* **Foresee·r. Foresee·ingly** *adv.*

Foreshadow (fōᵊ·ɹʃæ:doᵘ), *sb.* 1831. [f. FORE- + SHADOW *sb.*; suggested by the verb.] *fig.* A shadow cast before; an indication of something to come.

Foreshadow (foᵊɹ,ʃæ·doᵘ), *v.* 1577. [f. FORE- + SHADOW *v.*] *trans.* To serve as the shadow thrown before (an object); hence, to represent imperfectly beforehand, prefigure. Occas. (of a person), to have a foreboding of. Hence **Foresha·dower.**

Fore-sheet (fōᵊ·ɹʃīt). 1667. [f. FORE- + SHEET *sb.*[2]] *Naut.* **1.** The rope by which the lee corner of the fore-sail is kept in place. **2.** *pl.* The inner part of the bows of a boat, fitted with gratings upon which the bow-man stands (Adm. Smyth) 1719.

Foreship (fōᵊ·ɹʃip). [OE. *forsċip*, f. FOR- *pref.*[2], FORE- + *sċip*, SHIP.] The fore-part of a ship; the prow.

Foreshore (fōᵊ·ɹʃōᵊɹ). 1764. [f. FORE- + SHORE *sb.*[1]] **1.** The fore-part of the shore; that part which lies between the high- and low-water marks. Also *transf.* **2.** *Hydraulic Engin.* **a.** A bank a little distance from a sea-wall to break the force of the surf. **b.** The seaward-projecting, slightly inclined portion of a breakwater. 1841.

Foreshorten (foᵊɹ,ʃǭ·ɹt'n), *v.* 1606. [prob. – Du. *verkorten*; cf. G. *verkürzen* and Fr. *raccourcir*, It. *scorciare.*] *trans.* To cause to be apparently shortened in the directions not lying in a plane perpendicular to the line of sight. Also, to delineate so as to represent this effect. Also *transf.* and *fig.*

fig. Lives, that lie Fore-shorten'd in the tract of time TENNYSON.

Foreshot (fōᵊ·ɹʃǫt). 1839. [f. FORE- + SHOT.] **1.** A projecting part of a building. **2.** In distilling: The spirits which first come over 1893.

Foreshow (foᵊɹʃōᵘ·), *v.* [XVI f. FORE- + SHOW; in sense 1, OE. *foresċēawian.*] †**1.** *trans.* To look out for; to provide. OE. and early ME. only. **2.** To show beforehand; to foretell; to pre-figure 1561. †**3.** To show forth –1608.

2. Astrologers, that future fates foreshew POPE. The falling of the mercury foreshews thunder IMISON. **3.** Your lookes fore-shew You haue a gentle heart SHAKS. Hence †**Fo·reshow** *sb.* a manifestation beforehand. **Foresho·wer.**

Foreside (fōᵊ·ɹ,səid). ME. [f. FORE- + SIDE.] **1.** The fore-part; the front or upper side. Now *rare* exc. *techn.* **2.** The front side or edge 1703.

Foresight (fōᵊ·ɹsəit). ME. [prob. after ON. *forsjá*, *-sjó*, and later felt as etymol. rendering of (O)Fr. *providence*, L. *providentia*; cf. OHG. *forasiht.*] **1.** The action or faculty of foreseeing; prevision. **2.** The action of looking forward (*lit.* and *fig.*) 1591; perception gained by looking forward; prospect ME. **3.** Care or provision for the future ME. **4.** *Surveying.* 'Any reading of the leveling-rod, after the first, taken at a given station'. ? U.S. only. 1855. **5.** The muzzle-sight of a gun 1859.

1. Want of f. makes thee more merry BP. HALL. **2.** Let Eve. .Here sleep below, while thou to f. wak'st MILT. **3.** Shapd in the glass of the divine F. COWLEY. Hence **Fo·resighted** *ppl. a.* having f.; characterized or controlled by f. **Fo·resightful** *a.* full of f.

Foresignify (foᵊɹsi·gnifəi), *v.* 1565. [f. FORE- + SIGNIFY *v.*] *trans.* To signify beforehand; to prefigure; †to foretell. Hence **Foresignifica·tion,** a premonition (*rare*).

Foreskin (fōᵊ·ɹskin). 1535. [After G. *vorhaut* (Luther), based on L. *præputium* PREPUCE.] The prepuce.

Fore-skirt: see FORE- and SKIRT *sb.*

Foreslack: see FORSLACK.

Foresleeve (fōᵊ·ɹ,slīv). ME. [f. FORE- + SLEEVE *sb.*] **a.** The fore part of a sleeve. **b.** That part of a dress-sleeve which covers the fore-arm.

Foreslow: see FORSLOW.

Forespeak (foᵊɹ,spī·k), *v.* Also **for-.** ME. [f. FORE- + SPEAK *v.*] **1.** *trans.* To speak or speak of beforehand; to foretell, predict. Now *rare.* †**2.** *intr.* To speak beforehand; to prophesy –1656. †**3.** *trans.* To speak forth or out –1547. **4.** To speak for in advance 1659.

1. To f. fair weather 1654. **2.** These are the days fore-spoken of 1646. **4.** To f. impunity for so strange boldness L'ESTRANGE. Hence **Forespea·king** *vbl. sb.* †a preface; †*a* prediction.

Forespeak: see FORSPEAK, to bewitch, etc.

†**Fo·respeech.** [f. FORE- + SPEECH; in OE. *foresprǣċ*, *-spǣċ.*] An introductory speech, a preface –1688.

†**Forespe·nt,** *ppl. a.* 1578. [f. FORE- + SPENT, pa. pple. of SPEND.] Spent previously –1641.

Forest (fǫ·rėst), *sb.* ME. [– OFr. *forest* (mod. *forêt*) – late L. *forestis* (*silva*) 'outside wood', royal forest reserved for hunting, obscurely f. *foris* out of doors, outside; in AL. *foresta*, *forestum.*] **1.** An extensive tract of land covered with trees and undergrowth sometimes intermingled with pasture. Also *transf.* and *fig.* **b.** In Great Britain, the name of districts formerly covered with trees, as *Ashdown*, *Ettrick*, *Sherwood*, *Wychwood F.* **2.** *Law.* A woodland district, usually belonging to the king, set apart for hunting wild beasts and game, etc., having its own laws and officers ME. †**3.** A wild, uncultivated waste –1659.

attrib. and *Comb.*:

1. General: as *f.-alley*, etc.; and *esp.* with sense 'haunting or inhabiting a f.', as *f.-bear*, *-boar*, *-dove.*

2. Special: **f.-bed** (*Geol.*), a stratum originating from a primeval f.; **-fly,** a fly of the genus *Hippobosca*, esp. *H. equina*; **-laws,** laws relating to royal forests, enacted by the Norman kings; **-marble,** an argillaceous laminated shelly limestone, forming one of the upper portions of the Lower Oolite; **-tree,** any tree of large growth, fitted to belong to a f.; **-wards** *adv.* towards the f.

Hence **Fo·restage,** duty paid by foresters to the king; duty paid to the king's foresters; *collect.* tree-growth. **Fo·restal** *a.* of or pertaining to a f.

Forest (fǫ·rėst), *v.* 1818. [f. prec.] *trans.* **a.** To place in a forest. KEATS. **b.** To plant with trees 1865.

a. O Haunter. .of. .woods. .Where. .Art thou now forested KEATS.

†**Fo·re-staff.** 1669. [f. FORE- + STAFF.] *Naut.* = CROSS-STAFF 2. –1769.

†**Fo·re-stage.** ME. [f. FORE- + STAGE.] *Naut.* = FORECASTLE 1; hence a ship with a forecastle –1481.

Forestall (fōᵊ·ɹ,stǭl), *sb.* [In sense 1, OE. *for(e)steall*, f. FORE- + *steall*, (app.) 'position taken up'. In sense 2 f. FORE- + STALL *sb.*[1], in AL. *forstallum* piece of land in front of building (Kent, XIII).] †**1.** In OE.: An ambush, plot. Hence in *Law*, 'waylaying' or 'intercepting in the highway'; also the jurisdiction in respect of this offence. –1610. **2.** Something situated in front 1556; *esp.* the space in front of a farm-house, or the way leading to it. *dial.* 1661. **3.** A (horse's) frontlet. Cf. *headstall.* 1519.

Forestall (foᵊɹ,stǭ·l), *v.* late ME. [Implied earlier in AL. *for(e)stallare* forestall the market, waylay (XIII), *forstallatio* waylaying (XII), AFr. *forstallour* forestaller of markets (XIII), f. OE. *for(e)steall* interception, waylaying, ambush (see prec.).] †**1.** To lie in wait for, intercept, cut off –1741. **2.** To intercept (goods, etc.) before they reach the public markets; to buy (them) up privately with a view to enhance the price. (Formerly an indictable offence.) ME. **b.** To anticipate or prevent sales at (a market, etc.) by buying up or selling goods beforehand or by dissuading persons from bringing them in ME. †**3.** To beset, obstruct by armed force (a way, etc.) –1611. **4.** Hence *gen.* To hinder, obstruct, or prevent by anticipation. Now *rare.* 1579. †**b.** To bar or deprive by previous action *from*, *of*, *out of* –1660. †**5.** To preoccupy, secure beforehand –1685. **6.** To be beforehand with in action; to anticipate. (The chief current sense.) 1585.

2. Suffer not these riche men to bie up al, to ingrosse and forstalle 1551. **b.** *fig.* To f. the market of honour FULLER. **4. b.** May This night f. him of the comming day *Cymb.* III. v. 69. **6.** What need a man f. his date of grief MILT. *Comus.* 362. And this he did to forestal any tidings BUNYAN. Hence **Foresta·ller,** one who forestalls; *esp.* one who forestalls the market. **Foresta·lment.**

Forestalling (foᵊɹ,stǭ·liŋ), *vbl. sb.* ME. [f. prec. + -ING[1].] †**1.** The action of obstructing a person in the highway or a deer on its way back to the forest –1594. **2.** The buying up of goods beforehand, etc. 1548. **3.** The action of anticipating 1642. †**4.** The action of appropriating beforehand. FULLER.

2. Usury is. .a f. of money 1800.

Fore-stay (fōᵊ·ɹ,stēⁱ). ME. [f. FORE- + STAY *sb.*[1]] **1.** *Naut.* A stay or strong rope reaching from the foremast-head towards the bowsprit end; also, a sail hoisted on the fore-stay. **2.** *Printing. F. of press*, the leg which supports the frame or ribs of a hand-press 1833.

Forester (fǫ·restəɹ). ME. [– (O)Fr. *forestier*, f. *forest* FOREST; in AL. *forestarius* (XI).] **1.** An officer having charge of a forest (see quot.); also, one who looks after the growing timber on an estate. Occas. (*poet.*), a huntsman. **2.** One who lives in a forest 1513. **b.** A bird or beast of the forest 1630. **c.** A name of some moths of the family *Zygænidæ* 1819. **d.** = *forest-tree* 1664. **4.** A member of the 'friendly society' called the 'Ancient Order of Foresters' 1851.

1. A Forester is an officier of a forest of the King (or of an other man) that is sworne to preserue the Vert and Venison of the same forest, and to attend vpon the wild beasts within his Bailiwick, and to attach offendors there..and the same to present at the courts of the said forest MANWOOD. **2.** Above the loftiest ridge..Where foresters and shepherds dwell WORDSW. Hence **Fo·restership.**

Fore-stick (fōᵊ·ɹ,stik). *U.S.* 1872. [f. FORE-.] The front stick lying on the andirons in a wood fire.

Forestry (fǫ·restri). 1823. [f. FOREST *sb.* + -RY.] **1.** Wooded country; a vast extent of trees. **2.** The science and art of forming and cultivating forests, management of growing timber 1859.

1. *transf.* Lost amid the f. Of masts BYRON.

Foret, obs. f. FERRET *sb.*[1] and [2].

Fore-tack (fōᵊ·ɹtæk). 1669. [f. FORE- + TACK *sb.*[1]] *Naut.* The rope by which the weather corner of the fore-sail is kept in place.

Foretaste (fōᵊ·ɹ,tēⁱst), *sb.* ME. [f. FORE- + TASTE *sb.*[1]] A taste beforehand; an anticipation, partial enjoyment in advance.

Foretaste (foᵊɹ,tēⁱ·st), *v.* 1450. [f. FORE- + TASTE *v.*] **1.** *trans.* To taste beforehand, have a foretaste of. **2.** 'To taste before another' (J.) 1667.

2. Foretasted Fruit Profan'd first by the Serpent MILT. *P.L.* IX. 929. Hence **Foreta·ster.**

†**Foretea·ch,** *v.* 1591. [f. FORE- + TEACH *v.*] *trans.* To teach beforehand –1661.

Foretell (foᵊɹte·l), *v.* ME. [f. FORE- + TELL *v.*; superseding FORE-SAY.] **1.** To tell of beforehand; to predict, prophesy; to foreshow. †**2.** To inform or enjoin beforehand –1679. †**3.** *intr.* To prophesy *of* –1667.

1. These Magi..foretold things to come DE FOE. **3.** One greater, of whose day he shall f. MILT. *P. L.* XII. 242. Hence **Forete·ller.**

Forethink (foᵊɹþi·ŋk), *v.* [OE. *foreþenćan*, f. FORE- + *þenćan* THINK *v.*[2]] †**1.** *trans.* To think out beforehand, contrive, plan –1715. **2.** To contemplate beforehand; to presage (evil). Now *rare.* 1547. †Also *intr.* with *of.* –1701.

2. Rather of a friend [to] hope the best, then forethinke the worst 1547.

Forethought (fōᵊ·ɹþǭt), *sb.* ME. [f. FORE- + THOUGHT *sb.*, parallel to prec.; repl. OE. *foreþanc* consideration, forethought, providence.] **1.** A thinking out or contriving beforehand; previous consideration; anticipation. †**2.** A pre-conceived idea or design, an anticipation –1729. **3.** Thought for the future 1719.

1. (*Crime, evil*, etc.) *of f.*: premeditated; we urge no crimes, that were not crimes of f. BURKE. **3.** Just so much f. as is necessary to provide for the morrow JOWETT. Hence **Forethou·ghtful** *a.* having f.

Forethought (fōᵊ·ɹþǭt), *ppl. a.* ME. [pa. pple. of FORETHINK *v.*] **1.** Thought out or contrived beforehand; premeditated. Cf. AFORETHOUGHT. †**2.** Anticipated 1666.

1. Slaine..with malice prepensed or f. COKE.

Foretime (fōᵊ·ɹtəim), *sb.* 1540. [f. FORE- + TIME *sb.*] Former time; a former time; the past. Also *attrib.* and †as *adv.*

It was called in f. Norton Dany P. HOLLAND.

Foretoken (fōᵊ·ɹtōᵘk'n), *sb.* [OE. *foretācn*, f. FORE- + *tācn* TOKEN.] A premonitory token; a prognostic.

Foretoken (foᵊɹtōᵘ·k'n), *v.* 1598. [f. prec. sb.] *trans.* To be a foretoken of; to betoken beforehand.

A dolefull chance, but yet..foretokening good luck 1598.

Fore-tooth (fōᵊ·ɹ,tūþ). OE. [f. FORE- + TOOTH *sb.*] **1.** One of the front teeth. *rare* in *sing.* †**2.** *pl.* The first or milk-teeth –1651.

Foretop (fōᵊ·ɹtǫp). ME. [f. FORE- + TOP *sb.*[1]] †**1.** The fore-part of the crown of the head; *loosely*, the top of the head –1781. †**2.** The lock of hair upon the fore-part of the head; the similar part of a wig –1814. **3.** The tuft of hair hanging between the ears of a horse, etc. 1607. **4.** The TOP of a foremast 1509. **b.** Short for *fore-topgallant-mast-head* 1800. **5.** *U.S.* The front seat on the top of a vehicle 1850.

4. *Military f.*: an armed f. of a war vessel.

Fore-topgallant (fōᵊɹ,tǫpgæ·lănt), *a.* 1627. [f. FORE- + TOPGALLANT.] *Naut.* In **fore-topgallant-mast,** the mast above the fore-topmast; hence with sense 'of or belonging to the fore-topgallant-mast', as *f.-sail*, etc.

Fore-topmast (fōᵊɹ,tǫ·pmɑst). 1626. [f. FORE- + TOPMAST.] *Naut.* The mast above the foremast; also *attrib.*

Fore-topsail (fōᵊɹtǫ·pseⁱl, -s'l). 1582. [f. FORE- + TOPSAIL.] *Naut.* The sail above the fore-sail; also *attrib.*

Forever (fǫre·vəɹ), *adv.* Now chiefly *U.S.* 1670. **1.** *For ever* (see EVER *adv.*), written as one word. **2.** quasi-*sb.* Eternity 1858.

2. Life, death, and that vast for-ever KINGSLEY. So **Fore·vermore** *adv.*: see EVERMORE 1.

Fore-vouched: see FORE- and VOUCH.

†**Fo·reward.** ME. [f. FORE- + WARD *sb.*] **1.** The first line of an army, vanguard, front –1664. **2.** The command of, or a position in, the van –1576.

Forewarn (foᵊɹwǭ·ɹn), *v.* ME. [f. FORE- + WARN *v.*[1]] *trans.* To warn, caution, or admonish beforehand; also, to give previous notice to.

We were fore-warned of your comming SHAKS.

†**Fo·re-wind.** 1561. [f. FORE- + WIND *sb.*[1]] A wind that blows a ship forward on her course –1682.

†**Fo·re-wit,** *sb.* ME. [f. FORE- + WIT.] **1.** Foresight, prudence –1631. **2.** A leading wit, a leader in matters of taste and literature. B. JONS.

1. Yet is one good f. woorth two after wits 1546.

†**Fore-wit,** *v.* Pres. 1st, 3rd sing. **-wot.** [OE. *forewitan*, f. FORE- + *witan* WIT *v.*[1]] *trans.* To know beforehand –ME. Hence **Fore-wi·tter.**

Forewoman (fōᵊ·ɹwumăn), pl. **-women** (-wimėn). 1709. [f. FORE- + WOMAN.] A woman who acts as chief: **a.** in a jury of matrons; **b.** in a shop or department.

Foreword (fōᵊ·ɹwɒɹd). 1842. [f. FORE- + WORD *sb.*, tr. G. *vorwort.*] A word said before something else; hence, a preface.

Fore-yard[1] (fōᵊ·ɹ,yaɹd). ME. [f. FORE- + YARD *sb*[1].] The yard or court in front of a building.

Fore-yard[2] (fōᵊ·ɹ,yaɹd). 1627. [f. FORE- + YARD *sb*[2].] *Naut.* The lowest yard on the foremast.

Forfalt, -fault, -faute: see FORFEIT.

†**Forfear,** *v.* ME. only. [f. FOR- *pref.*[1] + FEAR *v.*] To terrify. Only in pa. pple.

Forfeit (fǭ·ɹfit), *sb.* [ME. *forfet* – OFr. *forfet* crime, (also mod.) *forfait*, f. *for(s)faire* transgress, etc. (med.L. *forisfacere*), f. *for(s)-* beyond, outside, sc. what is right (:–L. *foris* outside; cf. FOREST) + *faire* do.] †**1.** A misdeed, crime, transgression; hence, wilful injury. Also with *of*: Breach or violation *of*, –1668. **2.** Something to which the right is lost by the commission of a crime or fault; hence, a penal fine, a penalty 1450. **b.** *transf.* of a person. *Meas. for M.* IV. ii. 167. **3.** A trivial mulct or fine for breach of a rule or by-law, or the like. Also, in certain games, an article given up by a player for making some mistake, and afterwards redeemed by performing some ludicrous task. 1603. **4.** [f. the vb.] = FORFEITURE 2. ME.

1. The Censure..dayly toke hede to the forfaytes done 1533. **2.** I craue the Law, The penaltie, and forfeite of my bond SHAKS. **3.** And here I took pleasure to take forfeits of the ladies PEPYS. **4.** Debts they could clear no other way but by the f. of their honour 1716.

Forfeit (fǫ·ɹfit), *a.* [ME. *forfet, forfait* – OFr. *forfet, -fait*, pa. pple. of *forfaire*; see prec.] Lost or to be given up as the penalty of a crime or fault or breach of an engagement. Const. *to, unto.*

His braines are forfeite to the next tile that fals SHAKS. The wish To tread the f. Paradise EMERSON.

Forfeit (fǭ·ɹfit), *v.* ME. [f. FORFEIT *sb.*] †**1.** *intr.* To do amiss, sin, transgress –1530. **2.** *trans.* To lose, lose the right to; to render oneself liable to be deprived of; also, to have to pay in consequence of a crime, offence, breach of duty, or engagement. Const. *to.* 1466. **b.** *gen.* To lose by misconduct ME. **c.** To lose or give up, as a necessary consequence ME. **d.** *absol.* 1727. **3.** To subject to forfeiture; to confiscate. *Obs.* exc. *Hist.* ME. †**4.** To exact a forfeit from –1736. †**5.** To cause the forfeiture, loss, or ruin of –1705.

2. My life and effects were all forfeited to the English government DE FOE. **b.** He had done nothing to f. her love TROLLOPE. **c.** The moral sentiment..never forfeits its supremacy EMERSON. **3.** All his substance should be forfeited *Ezra* 10:8. **5.** Such another forgetfulness Forfeits your life 1611. Hence **Fo·rfeitable** *a.* subject to forfeiture. **Fo·rfeiter,** †an evil-doer; one who forfeits or incurs forfeiture.

Forfeiture (fǭ·ɹfitiūɹ). ME. [– OFr. *forfaiture*, f. *forfet* FORFEIT *sb.*; see -URE.] †**1.** Transgression or violation of a law; crime, sin –1628. **2.** The fact of losing or becoming liable to lose (an estate, goods, life, an office, right, etc.) in consequence of a crime, offence, or breach of engagement. Const. *of*, †*on.* ME. †**b.** The penalty of the transgression –1667. **3.** *concr.* That which is forefeited; a penalty, a fine. ? *Obs.* ME.

2. Vppon peyne of forfetor of xl[s] 1467. **b.** MILT. *P. L.* III. 221. **3.** A f., part of which went to the informer COBBETT.

Forfend, forefend (fǭɹfe·nd, foᵊɹfe·nd), *v.* ME. [f. FOR- *pref.*[1] + FEND *v.*] †**1.** *trans.* To forbid, prohibit –1823. **2.** To avert; *esp.* in *God* (etc.) *forfend*; also *absol.* as an exclam. *arch.* ME. **3.** To secure or protect by precautionary measures. Now chiefly *U.S.* 1592.

2. F. the sight FIELDING.

Forfex (fǭ·ɹfeks). 1712. [– L. *forfex.*] **1.** A pair of scissors. **2.** *Entom.* A pair of anal organs, which open or shut transversely, and cross each other 1826. So **Fo·rficate** *a.* shaped like a pair of scissors.

Forficulate (fǭɹfi·kūleⁱt), *v.* [f. mod. L. *forficula* (whence Fr. *forficule*) earwig (dim. of L. *forfex*; see prec., -CULE) + -ATE[3].] *intr.* To 'creep', as if a *forficula* or earwig were crawling on one's skin. LYTTON.

Forfou·ghten, *pple.* and *ppl. a. Obs.* exc. *Sc.* ME. [f. FOR- *pref.*[1] + *foughten* FOUGHT.] Worn-out with fighting. Also *transf.*

We are f., & moche blood haue we loste MALORY.

Forgather, foregather (fǭɹgæ·ðəɹ), *v.* Chiefly *Sc.* 1513. [– Du. *vergaderen* meet, assemble (= G. *vergattern*), with accommodation to FOR- *pref.*[1], GATHER *v.*] **1.** *intr.* To gather together. **2.** To encounter, meet (accidentally); *esp.* to meet *with* 1600. **b.** To associate *with* 1782.

1. The Scottis all forgadderit in Argyle 1535. **2.** Twa dogs..Forgather'd ance upon a time BURNS.

Forge (fōᵊɹdʒ), *sb.* ME. [– (O)Fr. *forge* :– Rom. **faurga* :– L. *fabrica* trade, manufactured object, workshop, forge.] †**1.** Manufacture, construction; make, workmanship –1691. **2.** A smithy. Also *transf.* and *fig.* ME. **3.** An open hearth or fireplace with a bellows attached, used by blacksmiths for heating iron to render it malleable; a similar apparatus on wheels for military use. Also *transf.* and *fig.* 1481. **4.** A hearth or furnace for melting or refining metals. Also, the workshop, etc., where this work is carried on. 1601. **5.** *Comm.* Short for *forge iron* 1890.

1. In the greater Bodies the F. was easie, the Matter being ductile and sequacious RAY. **2.** *fig.* The brain..is the f. in which all the speculations of the understanding..are hammered-out COLLIER. **3.** *fig.* Come to the F. with it, then shape it: I would not haue things coole *Merry W.* IV. ii. 239.

Comb.: **f.-cart** (*Mil.*), a travelling f. for service in the field; **-cinder,** the slag from a f. or bloomery; **-fire,** (*a*) a smith's fire; (*b*) a puddling furnace; **-man,** a forger or smith; *spec.* a superior class of coach-smith, having a hammer-man under him; **-pig,** a pig of forge-iron, also *collect.*; **-rolls,** the train of rolls by which the slab or bloom is converted into puddled bars; **-wagon**

= *forge-cart*; **-water,** water in which heated irons have been dipped, formerly in use as a medicine.

Forge (fōᵊɹdʒ), *v.*¹ ME. [– (O)Fr. *forger* :– L. *fabricare* FABRICATE.] **1.** *trans.* = FABRICATE *v.* 1. Now only as *transf.* use of 2. **2.** To shape by heating in a forge and hammering; to beat into shape; †to coin (money). Also fig. ME. **b.** *absol.* or *intr.* To work at the forge ME. †**3.** To frame or fashion –1562; †to coin (a word, etc.) –1690. **4.** *esp.* To fabricate, invent (a false story, lie, etc.); to devise (evil). Also, to fable. ME. **5.** To make (something) in fraudulent imitation of something else; to make or devise in order to pass off as genuine ME.; to counterfeit 1535. **6.** *intr.* To commit forgery 1591.

1. Of wexe he forged an ymage GOWER. **2.** Cursyd be he..that forgyd thy sword LD. BERNERS. Phr. †*To f. and file*: to fashion completely, make ready. **3.** To f. newe English wordes 1571. **4.** In which delit they wol f. a long tale CHAUCER. **5.** To f. a will 1605, the University seal WOOD. **6.** But Pens can f., my Friend, that cannot write POPE.

Forge (fōᵊɹdʒ), *v.*² 1796. [perh. aberrant pronunc. of FORCE *v.*¹, similarly used from XVII.] *intr.* Of a vessel: To make way, 'shoot ahead' (Adm. Smyth), *esp.* by mere momentum, or the pressure of tide.

She forged on without any sail T. FORREST.

Forger (fōᵊ·ɹdʒəɹ). ME. [f. FORGE *v.*¹ + -ER¹.] **1.** One who forges, makes, or frames; now only, a fabricator (of false stories, etc.). **2.** One who forges (metal) or works at a forge; a smith; †a coiner of money ME. **3.** One who makes fraudulent imitations (of documents, coins, etc.) 1552.

Forgery (fōᵊ·ɹdʒĕri). 1574. [f. FORGE *v.*¹ + -ERY.] †**1.** The action or craft of forging metal –1671. **2.** Invention; fictitious invention, fiction. Now only *poet.* 1583. **3.** The making of a thing in fraudulent imitation of something; *esp.* the forging, counterfeiting, or falsifying of a document 1593. **b.** The being forged. *rare.* 1665. **c.** *concr.* That which is forged, counterfeited, or fabricated 1574.

1. Useless the f. Of brazen shield and spear MILT. **2.** I in f. of shapes and trickes, Come short of what he did SHAKS. **3.** F. or the *crimen falsi*.. 'the fraudulent making or alteration of a writing to the prejudice of another man's right' BLACKSTONE. **c.** A manifest f. GIBBON.

Forget (fǫ̆ɹge·t), *v.* Pa. t. **forgot** (-gǫ·t), *arch.* **forgat** (-gæ·t). Pa. pple. **forgotten** (-gǫ·t'n), *arch.* and *poet.* **forgot** (-gǫ·t). [OE. *forġietan* = OFris. *forjeta*, OS. *fargetan* (Du. *vergeten*), OHG. *firgezzan* (G. *vergessen*); WGmc. vb. f. **fer*- FOR- *pref.*¹ 3 + **ȝetan* take hold of, GET.] **1.** *trans.* To lose remembrance of; to cease to retain in one's memory; to fail to recall to mind 1787. Also *absol.* **2.** To omit or neglect through inadvertence. Chiefly with *infinitive* as obj. In poetry occas. *fig.* of things. OE. **3.** To cease or omit to think of OE. **4.** To neglect wilfully, disregard, overlook, slight ME.

1. And a fourth whose name I have forgot 1676. *absol.* Hee hath said in his heart, God hath forgotten *Ps.* 10:11. **2.** The winds f. to roar POPE. **3.** The world forgetting, by the world forgot POPE. **4.** Men wallow in wealth, and f. God 1703.

Phr. *To f. oneself*: to omit care for oneself; to behave unbecomingly; to lose consciousness.

Hence **Forge·ttable** *a.* that may be forgotten. **Forge·tter**, one who forgets. **Forge·ttingly** *adv.* forgetfully.

Forgetful (fǫ̆ɹge·tful), *a.* ME. [f. prec. + -FUL.] **1.** Apt to forget; having a bad memory. Also, that forgets. **2.** Heedless, neglectful 1526. **3.** That causes to forget. Chiefly *poet.* 1557.

1. F. of the glory of the past TYNDALL. **2.** Be not f. to entertain strangers *Heb.* 13:2. **3.** The sound of that f. shore TENNYSON. Hence **Forge·tfully** *adv.*

Forgetfulness (fǫ̆ɹge·tfulnės). ME. [f. prec. + -NESS.] **1.** The quality of being apt to forget, the state of forgetting 1477. **2.** The condition of forgetting everything ME. **3.** The state of being forgotten, oblivion. ? *Obs.* 1561. **4.** Disregard, inattention, neglect 1576.

1. A sweet f. of human cares POPE. **2.** Euer with deth cometh forgetfulnes ME. **4.** F. of social duties JOHNSON.

Forgetive (fōᵊ·ɹdʒėtiv), *a.* 1597. [Commonly taken as a deriv. of FORGE *v.*¹] Now used for: Apt at forging, inventive, creative. The orig. meaning is uncertain. See 2 *Hen. IV*, IV. iii. 107.

Forge·t-me-no:t. 1532. [In sense 1 tr. OFr. *ne m'oubliez mie* do-not-forget-me, whence MHG. *vergiz mīn niht* (G. *vergissmeinnicht*). In the 15th c. the flower was supposed to ensure that those wearing it should never be forgotten by their lovers.] **1.** The name of various kinds of *Myosotis*, esp. *M. palustris*, a plant having bright blue flowers with a yellow eye. **2.** The Germander Speedwell (*Veronica chamædrys*) 1853. †**3.** The Ground Pine (*Ajuga chamæpitys*) –1597.

1. Eyes.. Blue as the blue forget-me-not TENNYSON.

Forging (fōᵊ·ɹdʒiŋ), *vbl. sb.* ME. [f. FORGE *v.*¹ + -ING¹.] **1.** The action of FORGE *v.*¹; an instance of the same. **b.** *concr.* A forged mass (of iron, etc.) 1858. **2.** *attrib.*, as *f.-hammer*, etc. 1874.

Forgivable (fǫ̆ɹgi·văb'l), *a.* Also **-eable.** 1550. [f. next + -ABLE.] That may be forgiven, pardonable.

Forgive (fǫ̆ɹgi·v), *v.* Pa. t. **forgave** (fǫ̆ɹgēⁱ·v). Pa. pple. **forgiven** (fǫ̆ɹgi·v'n). [OE. *forġiefan*, f. FOR- *pref.*¹ + *ġiefan* GIVE; corresp. to OS., OHG. *fargeban* (Du. *vergeven*, G. *vergeben*), ON. *fyrirgefa* forgive, Goth. *fragiban* grant; Gmc. tr. of med.L. *perdonare*.] †**1.** *trans.* To give, grant –1483. †**2.** To give up, cease to harbour (resentment, etc.) –1533. **3.** To remit (a debt); to give up claim to requital for, pardon (an offence). Const. with simple obj.; also with thing in the accus. and person in the dat. OE. **4.** To give up resentment against, pardon (an offender). Also (now *rarely*) to abandon one's claim against a debtor. OE. **5.** *absol.* (of 3 and 4) OE. **6.** To make excuse for, regard indulgently. Now only in *imper.* as an entreaty. 1667. †**7.** = MISGIVE. P. HOLLAND.

2. Oberon..forgaue all the yll wyll that he had to Huon LD. BERNERS. **3.** Forgiue a moytie o the principall SHAKS. The people that dwel therein shalbe forgiuen their iniquitie *Isa.* 33:24. **4.** F. me if I remind you, that [etc.] SCOTT. **5.** To err is human, to f., divine POPE. **6.** Thy frailtie and infirmer Sex forgiv'n MILT. *P. L.* x. 956. F. these wild and wandering cries TENNYSON.

Hence **Forgi·ver. Forgi·ving** *ppl. a.* that forgives; inclined to f.; indicating forgiveness. **Forgi·ving-ly** *adv.*, **-ness.**

Forgiveness (fǫ̆ɹgi·vnės). [OE. *forġief(e)nes*; see prec., -NESS.] **1.** The action of forgiving; the condition or fact of being forgiven. **2.** Disposition or willingness to forgive ME. **b.** in *pl.* (A Hebraism.) 1611.

1. In whom we have..the f. of sins *Eph.* 1:7. The f. of injuries BUTLER. **2.** But there is f. with thee, that thou mayest be feared *Ps.* 130:4. **b.** To the Lord our God belong mercies and forgiuenesses *Dan.* 9:9.

Forgo, forego (fǫ̆ɹ-, foᵊɹgōᵘ·), *v.* Pa. t. **for-, forewent.** Pa. pple. **for-, foregone.** [OE. *forgān*; see FOR- *pref.*¹, GO *v.*] †**1.** *intr.* To go past, pass away –1563. †**2.** *trans.* To go by, pass over (*lit.* and *fig.*). Hence, to neglect, overlook, slight. *Obs.* exc. *arch.* OE. **3.** To go from, forsake, leave. *Obs.* exc. *arch.* ME. **4.** To abstain from; to let go or pass; to give up OE. †**5.** Only in pa. pple.: Exhausted with going, wearied; faint –1597.

3. Their altars they f., their homes they quit WORDSW. **4.** I am vnarm'd, forgoe this vantage, Greeke *Tr. & Cr.* V. viii. 9. He had foregone to be a Christian HAWTHORNE. Hence **Forgo·er.**

Forgotten: see FORGET *v.*

Forhale: see FOR- *pref.*¹ I.4.

†**Fori·nsecal,** *a.* 1539. [f. L. *forinsecus* (adv.) out of doors + -AL¹.] = FOREIGN *a.* in various senses –1732.

Forisfamiliate (foᵊ:risˌfămi·liˌeⁱt), *v.* Pa. pple. *Sc.* **-at, -ate.** 1609. [– *forisfamiliat-*, pa. ppl. stem of med.L. *forisfamiliare*, f. *foris* outside + *familia* family; see -ATE³.] *Civil* and *Sc. Law.* To emancipate (a son) by assigning to him part of the heritage and giving him seisin thereof. Hence **Fo:risfami:lia·tion**, the action of forisfamiliating (a son); also *transf.*

Forjudge, forejudge (fǫ̆ɹdʒʊ·dʒ), *v.* ME. [– OFr. *forjugier* in same senses, f. *for*- FOR- *pref.*³ + *jugier* (mod. *juger*) JUDGE *v.*; in med.L. *forisjudicare* (XII), *forjudicare* (XIV) dispossess.] **1.** To exclude, oust, or dispossess by a judgement. *Obs.* exc. in *Law.* 1470. †**2.** To condemn judicially (*to* a penalty) –1752.

1. To be forejudged of life and limb BLACKSTONE. Hence †**Forjudgement.**

Fork (fǭɹk), *sb.* [OE. *forca*, *force*, corresp. to OFris. *forke*, OS. *furka*, OHG. *furcha* (Du. *vork*, G. *furke*), ON. *forkr*; Gmc. – L. *furca* pitchfork, forked stake, whence (O)Fr. *fourche*, ONFr. *fourque* (which reinforced the word in ME.).]

I. 1. An instrument consisting of a long straight handle, furnished at the end with two or more prongs or tines, and used for carrying, digging, lifting, or throwing; often specialized as *dung-*, *hay-*, etc. *f.* †**b.** The forked tongue of a snake. SHAKS. **2.** An instrument with two, three, or four prongs, used at table, in cooking, etc. 1463. **3.** *pl.* The prongs of a fork. Also *transf.* 1674. **4.** A steel instrument with two prongs which, when set in vibration, gives a musical note; a *tuning-fork* 1799.

1. b. Thou dost feare the soft and tender forke Of a poore worme SHAKS. **3.** *transf.* A thunderbolt with three forks ADDISON.

II. An object having two (or more) branches. †**1.** A gallows –1680. **2.** A stake, staff, or stick with a forked end; used as a prop, a rest, or the like ME. **b.** A divining-rod 1886. †**3.** The barbed head of an arrow. *Lear* I. i. 146. **4.** *techn.* **a.** A piece of steel fitting into the chuck of a lathe, used for carrying round the piece to be turned 1858. **b.** The front or back projection of a saddle 1833. **5.** *Mining.* The bottom of the sump 1778. **6.** [f. the vb.] A forking, bifurcation, or division into branches; the point at which anything forks. Hence, each of the branches. (See quots.) ME.

5. When a mine is in fork the bottom of the engine-shaft is clear of water 1869. **6.** The thigh, and entire leg from the f. to the ankle BAKER. A f. in the road W. IRVING, of a tree 1843, of flame 1871, of a river, 1877.

Comb.: **f.-beam** (*Naut.*) 'a forked piece of timber.., scarphed, tabled, and bolted, for additional security to the sides of beams athwart large openings in the decks' (Weale); **-beard,** any of various fishes of the genus *Phycis*; **-chuck** (*Wood-turning*), a chuck with two or more teeth; **-moss,** *Dicranum bryoïdes*; **-wrench,** a spanner with two jaws which embrace a nut or square on a coupling.

Fork (fǭɹk), *v.* ME. [f. prec.] **1.** *intr.* To form a fork; to divide into branches. Of corn: To sprout 1707. †Also *fig.* **2.** *trans.* To make fork-shaped 1640. **3.** To raise or move with or as with a fork; to dig, take, or throw *in*, *out*, *up*, etc., with a fork 1647. **4.** *Mining.* To pump (a mine) dry; to remove (water) by pumping 1702.

1. The lightning forked and flashed 1851. Here the road forked 1853. **3.** To f. hay 1802. Phr. *To f. out, over,* or *up*: to give up, hand over, pay; F. out your balance in hand DICKENS. **4.** The mine has been 'forked' 1893.

Forked (fǭɹkt), *ppl. a.* ME. [f. FORK *sb.* + -ED².] **1.** Having a fork; shaped like a fork, bifurcate, branching. **b.** Having (so many) forks or prongs, as *three-f.* 1535. †**c.** Of an arrow: Barbed –1673. **2.** Two-legged. *Lear* III. iv. 113. **3.** Horned 1586. †**4.** Of an argument, etc.: That points more than one way; containing a dilemma; equivocal –1681. **5.** *ellipt.* for *f.-headed* or *-tailed* 1674.

1. Like a f. Radish, with a Head fantastically caru'd vpon it SHAKS. F. Light'nings 1729. Yon f...hill SHELLEY. A three-f. flickering tongue BOWEN. **4.** Giue f. counsel; take prouoking gold On eyther hand, and put it vp B. JONS. **Fo·rkedly** *adv.*, **-ness.**

Fo·rk-head. 1590. †**1.** An arrow with barbed head. SPENSER. **2.** *Mech.* 'The double head of a rod which divides in order to form a connection by means of a pin' (Knight) 1874. **b.** = CROSS-TAIL. 1839.

Fork-tail. 1611.

†**A.** *adj.* = *forked-tail(ed).*

B. *sb.* **1.** A salmon in the fourth year of its growth 1753. **2.** Formerly applied in England to the Kite; now in India to birds of the genus *Henicurus*. Hence **Fork-tailed** *a.* having a forked tail.

Forky (fǭ·ɹki), *a.* 1697. [f. FORK *sb.* + -Y[1].] Shaped like a fork, forked. Also *fig.* and *allusively*.

A meagre man with a..black f. beard SWIFT. Hence **Fo·rkiness,** the condition of being f.

Forlay, var. of FORELAY.

†**Forlea·ve,** *v.* ME. only. [f. FOR- *pref.*[1] + LEAVE *v.*[1]] *trans.* To leave behind, give up, abandon.

†**Forle·se,** *v.* Pa. pple. **forloren, forlorn.** [OE. *forlēosan* = OFris. *forliāsa*, OS. *far-, forliosan* (Du. *verliezen*), OHG. *firliosan* (G. *verlieren*), Goth. *fraliusan*; Gmc., f. **fer-* **fra-* FOR- *pref.*[1] + **leusan* LOSE *v.*[1] From XV only in pa. pple.] **1.** *trans.* To LOSE, in various senses –1663. **2.** To destroy, cause to perish –1664. **3.** To leave, forsake –1600.

†**Forle·t,** *v.* [OE. *forlǣtan*; see FOR- *pref.*[1], LET *v.*[1]] **1.** *trans.* To allow –ME. **2.** To leave, forsake; to abandon –1610. **3.** To omit; to cease from –ME. **4.** To let go –ME.

Forlore: pa. t. and pple. of FORLESE.

Forlorn (fǭɹlǭ·ɹn). OE. [pa. pple. of FORLESE.]

A. *adj.* †**1.** Lost, not to be found 1577. †**2.** Morally lost; depraved –1683. **3.** †Lost, doomed to destruction –1719; desperate, hopeless 1603. **4.** Abandoned, forsaken; desolate OE. **5.** In pitiful condition, wretched 1582.

3. †*F. fort*: one held at extreme risk. [We] sit down in a f. Scepticism BP. BERKELEY. **4.** Yon dreary Plain, f. and wilde MILT. *P. L.* I. 180. Like one that..is of sense f. COLERIDGE. **5.** His f. appearance GIBBON.

†**B.** *sb.* **1.** A forlorn person –1814. **2.** Short for FORLORN HOPE. Also *pl.*, the men forming a forlorn hope. Also *transf.* and *fig.* 1645.

1. Forc'd to liue in Scotland a Forlorne SHAKS. **2.** Captain Ireton with a f. of Colonel Rich's regiment CROMWELL. *fig.* Criticks..Who..still charge first, the true f. of wit DRYDEN.

Hence **Forlo·rn-ly** *adv.*, **-ness.**

Forlo·rn ho·pe. 1539. [– Du. *verloren hoop* 'lost troop', i.e. *verloren*, pa. pple. of *verliezen* (see FORLESE), *hoop* company (HEAP).] **1.** Orig., a picked body of men, detached to the front to begin the attack. Now usually, a storming-party. Also *transf.* and *fig.* 1572. **b.** *pl.* Reckless bravos 1539. **c.** A desperate enterprise 1768. **2.** With wordplay: A faint hope, a 'hope against hope' 1641.

1. c. The wary..never went upon a forlorn hope 'JUNIUS'. **2.** She had had a forlorn hope of a letter 1885.

Form (fǭɹm), *sb.* ME. [– (O)Fr. *forme* :–L. *forma* mould, shape, beauty.] **1.** The visible aspect of a thing; now usu., shape, configuration; *occas.*, the figure of the body as dist. from the face ME. **b.** *pl.* The shape of the different parts of the body 1837. **c.** *Crystallogr.* 'A set of faces symmetrically related' 1878. †**d.** Beauty, comeliness –1632. †**2.** An image, likeness, or representation (of a body). Also *fig.* –1610. **3.** A body considered in respect to its outward shape; *esp.* that of a person ME. **4.** *Philos.* **a.** In the Scholastic philosophy: The essential determinant principle of a thing; that which makes anything (*matter*) a determinate species or kind of being; the essential creative quality ME. **b.** In Bacon's usage: The objective conditions on which a sensible quality or body depends for its existence 1605. **c.** In Kant: That (subjective) factor of knowledge which gives reality and objectivity to the thing known 1803. **5.** The particular mode in which a thing exists or manifests itself ME.; a species, kind, variety 1542. **b.** *Gram.* (*a*) One of the various modes of pronunciation, spelling, or inflexion under which a word may appear. (*b*) The external characteristics of words, as dist. from their signification. 1861. **6.** †**a.** *gen.* A grade or degree of rank, quality, excellence, or eminence –1710. **b.** *spec.* One of the numbered classes into which the pupils of a school are divided according to proficiency 1560. †**7.** A model, type, or pattern –1690. **8.** Due shape; regularity, good order; also, military formation 1595. **9.** Style of expressing the thoughts and ideas in composition, including the arrangement and order of the parts. Also, good or just order (of ideas, etc.) †logical sequence. 1551. †**10.** Manner, method, way (of doing anything) –1641. **11.** Formal procedure (*e.g.* at law) ME. **12.** A set or fixed order of words ME. **13.** A set method of outward behaviour or procedure; a ceremony or formality. (Often *slightingly*.) 1612. †**b.** A way of behaving oneself; in *pl.* = manners –1639. **14.** Observance of etiquette, ceremony, or decorum. Often *depreciatively*: Mere outward ceremony or formality. ME. **15.** *Sporting.* Of a horse: Condition in regard to health and training; fitness; style and speed in running. Said also of athletes and players generally. 1760. **b.** *transf.* Liveliness, high spirits, conversational powers, or the like. *colloq.* 1877.

1. Her face was expressive: her f. wanted no feminine charm MACAULAY. In the f. of a globe 1875. In painting, colour is subordinate to f. 1879. **d.** Hee hath no forme nor comelinesse *Isa.* 53 : 2. **3.** To forget the f. I loved COLERIDGE. **5.** For Forms of Government let fools contest POPE. A f. of cold BAIN. **6. a.** A Physician of the first f. 1710. **8.** In goodly f. comes on the enemy SHAKS. **9.** *Haml.* III. i. 171. *spec.* (*Mus.*) the shape and order in which musical ideas are presented 1876. **10.** Phr. *In like f.*: in like manner. **11.** A paper..sent to me as a matter of f. 1787. Phr. *In f.* (now usu. *in due* or *proper f.*). **12.** Any set f. of common prayer HOOKER. The f. of this fine is [etc.] CRUISE. **13.** The Forms and Civilities of the last Age ETHEREGE. It doth much adde to a Mans Reputation..to have good Formes BACON. **14.** The glass of fashion and the mould of f. SHAKS. Phr. *In* (*full, great*) *f. Good* (or *bad*) *f.*: (good or bad) manners. **15.** Phr. *In f.*: in condition; so *out of f.*

II. 1. A long seat without a back. [So OFr. *forme*, med.L. *forma*.] ME. **2.** *Mech.* A mould, shape, or implement on which anything is fashioned 1653. **3.** *Printing.* A body of type, secured in a chase, for printing at one impression. (Often *forme.*) 1481. **4.** The nest or lair in which a hare crouches. Also *rarely*, of a deer. Also *transf.* ME.

4. *transf.* Some Fames are most difficult to trace home to their f. FULLER.

Comb. **f.-word** (*Gram.*), a word serving the function of an inflexion.

Form (fǭɹm), *v.*[1] ME. [– OFr. *fourmer*, (also mod.) *former* – L. *formare*, f. *forma* FORM *sb.*] **1.** *trans.* To give form or shape to; to fashion, mould ME. **b.** To give a specified form to; to mould or fashion *into, after, by, from, upon*; to conform *to* ME. **2.** To mould by discipline or education; to train, instruct. Also *refl.* ME. **3.** To place in order, arrange. Also, to embody, organize *into* ME. Also *intr.* for *refl.* **4.** To construct, frame; to bring into existence, produce. Const. *from, of, out of.* Also, to articulate (a word, etc.). ME. **b.** To frame in the mind, conceive; †to imagine 1595. **c.** *refl.* and *intr.* for *refl.* 1801. **5.** To develop in oneself (habits); to enter into, contract (an alliance, friendship, etc.) 1736. **6.** To go to make up, to compose ME.; to serve for; to make *one* or *part of* 1821. **7.** *Gram.* To construct by derivation, composition, etc. 1824. **8.** *Mil.* and *Naval.* To draw up (troops, etc.) in order 1816. Also *refl.* and *intr.* 1722.

1. The Rib he formd and fashond with his hands MILT. **b.** A state formed after the model of Crete JOWETT. **2.** Van Helmont..was formed in the school of Alchěmy SIR H. DAVY. Men formed for command (*mod.*). **4.** The sound of man's voice was not yet formed 2 *Esd.* 6:39. **b.** To f. an estimate BURKE, a notion 1861, a judgment MARTINEAU. **5.** Active habits are to be formed by exercise BUTLER. To f. a junction 1781, connexions COWPER. **6.** Letters four do f. his name COLERIDGE. **8.** *intr.* Riflemen f. TENNYSON. Phr. *To f. the siege* (*of* a place): to commence active siege-operations against it.

Form (fǭɹm), *v.*[2] 1575. [f. the sb.: see FORM *sb.* II. 4.] *intr.* Of a hare: To take to her form; to seat.

First think which way shee fourmeth, on what wind B. JONS.

Form- (fǭɹm), in *Chem.*, combining form of FORMIC or FORMYL, as in **Fo·rmamide,** the amide of formic acid. (Cf. the termination of *chloro-form*).

-form (fǭɹm), repr. Fr. *-forme*, L. *-formis*, f. *forma* FORM *sb.*, a termination used to form adjs. (1) with the sense 'having the form of', as in *cruciform*, etc.; (2) referring to number of forms, as *uniform*, etc. The termination is always preceded by *-i-*.

Formal (fǭ·ɹmăl). ME. [– L. *formalis*, f. *forma*; see FORM *sb.*, -AL[1]. Cf. (O)Fr. *formel*.] **A.** *adj.* **1.** Pertaining to FORM. **a.** *Metaph.* Pertaining to the constitutive essence of a thing. Opp. to *material*. So *formal cause* (see CAUSE *sb.*). ME. **b.** Pertaining to the visible form, arrangement, or external qualities of a thing 1639. **c.** *Logic.* Concerned with the form, as dist. from the matter, of reasoning 1856. **d.** Of or pertaining to conventionality. POPE. **2.** That is (so and so) in respect of form 1563. **3.** That is according to form or rule ME. †**b.** Of a story, etc.: Circumstantial –1708. †**4. a.** Regular, methodical –1701. **b.** Of feature, stature, etc.: Regular –1576. **c.** Normal in intellect, sane 1590. **5.** Done or made with the forms that ensure validity; explicit and definite 1547. **6.** Ceremonial, 'state' 1602. **7.** That is merely matter of form 1648. **8.** Of persons, their manners and actions: Rigorously observant of forms; precise; prim in attire; ceremonious. Usually *reproachful*. 1514. **9.** Marked by excessive regularity or symmetry; wanting in ease or freedom 1597.

1. a. For deceit is the f., constituent reason of hypocrisy SOUTH. **d.** Still in constraint your suff'ring Sex remains, Or bound in f., or in real chains POPE. **2.** *F. sin* (Theol.): one which is such not merely in the outward act, but in the constitutive circumstances, e.g. intention. So *f. schism, schismatic*, etc. †*F. Protestants*, i.e. those who are such merely in outward form. **3.** A f. sylogysme MORE, siege DE FOE, courtship FIELDING. **4. c.** With wholsome sirrups, drugges, and holy prayers To make of him a formall man againe *Com. Err.* V. i. 105. **5.** A f. decision 'JUNIUS', inhibition FROUDE. **6.** A f. call 1875. **7.** A f. preachment MILTON, act CRUISE. **8.** F. bows PRIOR. **9.** The old f. school of gardening 1874.

B. *sb.* In *pl.* Things that are formal 1605.

Forma·ldehyde. 1873. [See FORM-.] Formic aldehyde, used in solution as a disinfectant. Hence **Fo·rmalin** [-IN[1]] 1893.

Formalism (fǭ·ɹmăliz'm). 1840. [f. FORMAL *a.* + -ISM.] **1.** Strict or excessive adherence to prescribed forms; an instance of this. **2.** The disposition to exalt what is formal or outward, *esp.* in matters of religion 1856.

1. The constitutional f. of three reigns STUBBS. **2.** The family devotions were long, but there was no f. FROUDE.

Formalist (fǭ·ɹmălist). 1607. [– Fr. *formaliste* (XVI) or med.L. *formalista*; see FORMAL, -IST.] †**1.** A solemn pretender to wisdom. BACON. †**2.** A time-server in religion –1632. **3.** A stickler for forms, etiquette, routine, or ceremonial 1637.

3. Though the f. will say, what no decency in Gods worship MILTON. Hence **Formali·stic** *a.*

Formality (fǭɹmæ·lĭti). 1531. [– Fr. *formalité* or med.L. *formalitas*, f. *formalis*; see FORMAL, -ITY.] †**1.** Formal or essential nature –1737. †**b.** Formal aspect or category –1668. †**2.** That which pertains to outward form –1649. †**3.** Method, regularity; uniform practice –1655. †**4.** Literary or artistic form –1677. **5.** Conformity to rule; customary propriety. Often *depreciatively*. 1597. **6.** Ceremony, elaborate procedure 1666. **7.** A ceremony; a formal act or observance 1674. **8.** Something required to be done for form's sake (often *depreciatively*) 1647; †ceremonious attention –1726. **9.** *pl.* or *collect. sing.* Robes or insignia of office or dignity. *Obs.* exc. *Hist.* 1575. **10.** The attribute of being formal; precision; excessive regularity or stiffness 1599.

1. Motion is the F. of Wind 1686. **3.** Such judges (whose f. was first to Imprison, and after, at their leisure, to Examine) CLARENDON. **5.** The attyre..being a matter of meere formalitie HOOKER. **6.** To Gresham College; where a great deal of do and f. in choosing of the Council PEPYS. **8.** Fasts, vigils, formalities and mass-work CARLYLE. **10.** The frozen f...of Charles occasioned extreme disgust 1789.

Formalize (fǭ·ɹmăləiz), *v.* 1597. [f. FORMAL *a.* + -IZE, partly through Fr. *formaliser* (XVI).] †**1.** *trans.* To give formal being to; to 'inform' –1678. **2.** To give definite shape to 1646. **3.** To render formal 1855. **4.** *intr.* To act with formality 1656. †**5.** To cavil at, or (*intr.*) to cavil; also (*intr.*) to affect scruples –1797. Hence **Fo:rmaliza·tion.**

Formally (fǭ·ɹmăli), *adv.* ME. [f. FORMAL *a.* + -LY[2].] **1.** In formal respects 1570. †**2.** In good form –1548. †**3.** According to the principles of art or science –1597. †**4.** Regularly –1674. **5.** Explicitly 1526. **6.** In prescribed or customary form; statedly 1564. **7.** Ceremoniously 1611. **8.** As a matter of form 1870.

1. Hence what is f. correct may be materially false 1864. **5.** You and your followers do stand f. divided against the authorised guides of the church HOOKER. **6.** Waller..has f. refused H. WALPOLE.

‖**Format** (fǭ·ɹmæt, fǭ·ɹmā, ‖forma). 1840. [– Fr. *format* (XVIII) – G. *format* (XVII) – L. *formatus* (sc. *liber* book), pa. pple. of *formare* FORM *v.*[1]] The shape and size of a book, e.g. folio, quarto, octavo.

Formate (fǭ·ɹmĕt), *sb.* Also (less well) **formiate.** 1807. [f. FORM(IC) + -ATE[4].] *Chem.* A salt of formic acid.

Formation (fǭɹmē[i]·ʃən). 1450. [– (O)Fr. *formation* or L. *formatio*, f. *format-*, pa. ppl. stem of *formare*; see FORM *v.*[1], -ION.] **1.** A putting or coming into form; creation, production. **2.** *concr.* The thing formed 1646. **3.** The manner in which a thing is formed; formal structure, conformation 1774. **4.** *Mil.* An arrangement or disposition of troops 1796. **5.** *Geol.* 'Any assemblage of rocks, which have some character in common, whether of origin, age, or composition' (Lyell) 1815.

1. The F. of the Body in the Womb COWLEY. **3.** Remarks..as to the f. of clouds 1808. **4.** The usual Roman f. in battle was in triple line FROUDE.

Formative (fǭ·ɹmătiv), *a.* (*sb.*) 1490. [– OFr. *formatif, -ive*, or med.L. *formativus*, f. as prec.; see -IVE.] **1.** Having the faculty of forming or fashioning. **2.** Of or pertaining to formation or moulding 1850. **3.** *Biol.* and *Path.* Producing, or attended with the production of, new tissue 1877. **4.** *Gram.* Serving to form words 1711.

1. The f. Word of God GAUDEN. **4.** To get at the root of a word we must remove all the f. elements 1872.

B. *sb. Gram.* **a.** A formative element (see A. 4) 1816. **b.** 'A word formed in accordance with some rule or usage, as from a root' (Webster).

Hence **Fo·rmative-ly** *adv.*, **-ness.**

†**Fo·rme,** *a.* [ME. *forme*, repr. OE. *forma*; see FOREMOST, FORMER.] **1.** First; also, former –1450. **2.** Foremost –1523.

quasi-*Comb.*, in **f.-fader,** (*a*) (our) first father, Adam; (*b*) = FOREFATHER; **-moder,** (our) first mother, Eve; **-mete,** breakfast; **-ward,** vanguard.

Forme (*Printing*): see FORM *sb.* II. 3.

Formé, -ée (fǭ·ɹme), *a.* Also **Formy.** 1610. [Fr., pa. pple. of *former*, FORM *v.*[1]] *Her.* = PATTÉE.

Formed (fǭɹmd), *ppl. a.* ME. [f. FORM *v.* + -ED[1].] **1.** In senses of FORM *v.* **2.** *esp.* †**a.** Drawn up according to rule; formal, set –1725. **b.** Decided, definite, settled 1605. **c.** Perfected by training or discipline; matured 1833. **3.** *Her.* = FORMÉ, -ÉE. 1592.

2. b. Without any f. intention of mendacity JAS. MILL.

†**Formedon** (fǭ·ɹmĕdǫn). *Obs.* exc. *Hist.* 1485. [– AFr. *formedon* – AL. *forma doni, f. donationis* (XIII) 'form of gift'.] *Law.* A writ of right formerly used for claiming entailed property.

†**Fo·rmel, formal,** *sb.* ME. [– (O)Fr. *formel* (see FORMAL) in *faucon formel* (whence med.L. *formelus*), an epithet applied to hawks, perh. in the sense 'regular', 'proper', the female being better for sport.] The female of the eagle or the hawk. Also *attrib.* –1688.

Formene (fǭ·ɹmīn). 1884. [f. FORM(IC + -ENE.] Methane or marsh-gas.

Former (fǭ·ɹməɹ), *sb.*[1] ME. [f. FORM *v.* + -ER[1].] **1.** One who forms; a maker, creator, fashioner. **2.** A tool or instrument used in forming articles; e.g. a templet, pattern, or gauge by which pottery, etc. is shaped; a cutter by which patterns, etc. are cut; etc. 1644.

†**Fo·rmer,** *sb.*[2] 1530. [– OFr. *formoir* chisel (now *fermoir*); see -ER[2] 3.] A kind of chisel or gouge; said to be used before the paring chisel in all works –1751.

Former (fǭ·ɹməɹ), *a.* ME. [f. ME. *forme* (OE. *forma*; see FOREMOST) + -ER[3].] **1.** Earlier in time. Now chiefly: Pertaining to the past, or to a period anterior to that in question. †**b.** *Occas.* = FORME, first, primeval –1529. **c.** Formerly possessed, occupied, etc. ME. **2.** *The former* (often *absol.*): **a.** The first in order of two. †Also the (immediately) preceding. 1588. **b.** The first mentioned of two; opp. to *latter* 1597. †**3.** Front, fore –1678.

1. He shall come vnto vs.. as the latter and f. raine *Hos.* 6:3. More like her f. self 1852. **b.** A Blysful lyf...Ledden the peoples in the f. age CHAUCER. **d.** *U.S.* Used to designate a former holder of an office; = English *ex-* 1905.

Formeret (fǭ·ɹmĕrĕt). 1872. [– Fr. *formeret*, f. *forme* FORM *sb.*] *Arch.* Rib moulding placed at the junction of a vault with the vertical wall.

Formerly (fǭ·ɹməɹli), *adv.* 1590. [f. FORMER *a.* + -LY[2].] †**1.** Before another or something else; first –1645. **2.** At some past time 1599. †**3.** Just now –1766.

3. *Merch. V*, IV. i. 362. So †**Fo·rmerness.**

Formful (fǭ·ɹmfŭl), *a.* 1727. [f. FORM *sb.* + -FUL.] Full of form or forms; shapely; imaginative.

Formic (fǭ·ɹmik), *a.* 1791. [f. L. *formica* ant; see FORM-, -IC.] **1.** *Chem.* In *F. acid*: a colourless irritant volatile acid contained in a fluid emitted by ants. **2.** Of or pertaining to ants. *rare.* 1816.

Phr. *F. ethers*, ethers obtained by substituting alcoholic radicals for the basic hydrogen of f. acid.

‖**Formica** (fǭɹməi·kă). ME. [L.; = 'ant'.] **1.** *Entom.* The typical genus of the family *Formicidæ*, the ant 1865. **2.** A kind of ulcer, abscess, or excrescence, occurring *esp.* in a hawk's bill or a dog's ears ME.

Formicarioid (fǭɹmikē[ə]·ri,oid), *a.* 1874. [– mod.L. *Formicarioidiæ*, f. med.L. *formicarium* ant-hill, f. *formica* ant; see -ARY[1], -OID.] Of or belonging to the *Formicarioideæ* or ant-thrushes. Also *sb.*, one of this family.

Formicary (fǭ·ɹmikări). 1816. [– med.L. *formicarium* ant-hill; see prec.] An ants' nest, ant-hill.

Formicate (fǭ·ɹmike[i]t), *v.* 1684. [– *formicat-*, pa. ppl. stem of L. *formicare* crawl like ants (said of the pulse or skin), f. *formica* ant; see -ATE[3].] *intr.* To crawl like ants; *transf.* to swarm *with* moving beings.

Formication (fǭɹmikē[i]·ʃən). 1707. [– L. *formicatio*, f. as prec.; see -ION.] *Path.* A sensation as of ants creeping over the skin.

Formicid (fǭ·ɹmisid). Also **-cide.** 1878. – mod.L. *Formicidæ* f. L. *formica* ant; see -ID[3].]

A. *sb.* A member of the family *Formicidæ* or ants.

B. *adj.* Of or belonging to this family.

Formidable (fǭ·ɹmidăb'l), *a.* 1508. [– Fr. *formidable* or L. *formidabilis*, f. *formidare* to fear; see -ABLE.] That gives cause for fear or alarm; fit to inspire apprehension. Now usually: Likely to be difficult to deal with; giving cause for apprehension of defeat or failure. Often used playfully.

Barbarossa, that f. pirat 1678. Swords of f. dimensions 1834. Hence **Fo:rmidabi·lity, Fo·rmidableness,** the quality of being f. **F·ormidably** *adv.*

†**Formi·dolous,** *a.* 1656. [– L. *formidolosus*, f. *formido* sb. dread; see -OUS.] Fearful, terrible; also, timorous –1773.

Forming (fǭ·ɹmiŋ), *vbl. sb.* ME. [f. FORM *v.*[1] + -ING[1].] The action of FORM *v.*[1]; the fact or process of being formed.

The f. of mens wils to the observation of the Law HOBBES.

Formless (fǭ·ɹmlės), *a.* 1591. [f. FORM *sb.* + -LESS.] Devoid of, or wanting in, form; shapeless; having no determinate or regular form.

The rising world of waters..won from the void and f. infinite MILT. **Fo·rmless-ly** *adv.*, **-ness.**

Formo- (fǭ·ɹmo). 1834. *Chem.* Comb. f. FORMIC.

Formula (fǭ·ɹmiŭlă). *Pl.* **-æ, -as.** 1638. [– L. *formula*, dim. of *forma* FORM sb.; see -ULE.] **1.** A set form of words in which something is defined, stated, or declared, or which is prescribed by custom or authority for use on ceremonial occasions. In recent use, after Carlyle, often applied disparagingly. **2.** A prescription or detailed statement of ingredients; a recipe 1706. **3.** *Math.* A rule or principle expressed in algebraic symbols 1796. **4.** *Chem.* An expression of the constituents of a compound by means of symbols and figures 1846. **5.** In general scientific use, a group of symbols and figures condensing a set of facts 1855.

1. The excellent scholastic f. *Transeat*, meaning either 'Not proven', or 'Nothing to the purpose' 1892. Man lives not except with formulas; with customs, ways of doing and living CARLYLE. **5.** *Dental f.*: see DENTAL.

Formular (fǭ·ɹmiŭlăɹ). 1563. [as adj., f. prec. + -AR[2]; as sb., var. of FORMULARY *sb.*; see -AR[2].]

A. *adj.* **1.** Formal, correct in form 1773. **2.** Pertaining to formulæ; formulary 1880.

B. *sb.* A prescribed or set form, formulary; hence, a pattern, type. ? *Obs.* 1563.

Hence **Fo:rmulari·stic** *a.* pertaining to or exhibiting formularization. **Fo·rmularize** *v.* to express in a formula; to formulate. **Fo:rmulariza·tion,** the action of formularizing.

Formulary (fǭ·ɹmiŭ.lări). 1541. [As sb., – Fr. *formulaire* or med.L. *formularius* (sc. *liber* book), f. *formula*; see FORMULA, -ARY[1], and cf. late L. *formularia* (sc. *scientia*) science of legal formulæ. As adj., f. FORMULA + -AR[2]; cf. prec.]

A. *sb.* A collection or system of formulas; a statement drawn up in formulas; a document containing the set form or forms according to which something is to be done. **b.** ? A formula 1782.

A committee of council to settle the f. of the coronation NORTH.

B. *adj.* Of the nature of a formula; of or relating to formulas 1728. Of a person: Adhering to formulas. CARLYLE.

Formulate (fǭ·ɹmiŭle[i]t), *v.* 1860. [f. FORMULA + -ATE[3], after (O)Fr. *formuler*, f. med.L. *formulare*, f. FORMULA.] To reduce to, or express in (or as in), a formula; to set forth in a definite and systematic statement. Hence **Formula·tion.**

†**Fo·rmule,** *sb.* 1677. [– (O)Fr. *formule* – L. *formula* FORMULA.] = FORMULA. –1773.

Formulism (fǭ·ɹmiŭliz'm). 1840. [f. FORMULA + -ISM.] Adherence to or dependence on formulas; also, a system of formulas. So **Fo·rmulist,** one fond of formulas. **Formuli·stic** *a.* displaying fondness for formulas.

Formulize (fǭ·ɹmiŭləiz), *v.* 1851. [f. FORMULA + -IZE.] To reduce to or express in a formula. Hence **Formuliza·tion.**

Formyl (fǭ·ɹmil). 1879. [f. FORM- + -YL.] *Chem.* The hypothetical radical (CHO) of formic acid.

Fornical (fǭ·ɹnikăl), *a.* [f. L. *fornix, fornic-* arch + -AL[1].] Pertaining to the fornix.

Fornicate (fǭ·ɹnike[i]t), *v.* 1552. [– *fornicat-*, pa. ppl. stem of eccl. L. *fornicari*, f. *fornix, fornic-* brothel, orig. arch, vaulted chamber; see -ATE[3].] *intr.* To commit fornication.

Fornicate (fǭ·ɹnikĕt), *a.* 1828. [– L. *fornicatus* vaulted, arched, f. *fornix* arch, vault; see prec., -ATE[2].] = next.

Fornicated (fǭ·ɹnike[i]tĕd), *ppl. a.* [f. as prec. + -ED[1].] Arched, bending over; *esp.* in *Bot.* of a leaf, etc.

Fornication[1] (fǭɹnikē[i]·ʃən). ME. [– (O)Fr. *fornication* – eccl. L. *fornicatio*, f. *fornicat-*; see FORNICATE *v.*, -ION.] Voluntary sexual intercourse between a man (strictly, an unmarried man) and an unmarried woman. In Scripture extended to adultery. **b.** *fig.* The forsaking of God for idols, idolatry ME.

Fornication[2] (fǭɹnikē[i]·ʃən). 1703. [– L. *fornicatio*, f. *fornicatus* FORNICATE *a.*; see -ION.] *Arch.* An arching or vaulting.

Fornicator (fǭ·ɹnike[i]təɹ). ME. [– eccl. L. *fornicator*, f. as FORNICATION[1]; see -OR 2.] One who commits fornication. So **Fo·rnicatress,** a woman given to or guilty of fornication.

Fornix (fǭ·ɹniks). 1681. [– L. *fornix* arch, vault.] Something resembling an arch. **a.** *Anat.* An arched formation of the brain. **b.** *Bot.* A small elongation of the corolla

1823. **c.** *Conchol.* The excavated part of a shell, situated under the umbo 1848.

Forpa·ss, *v.* ME. [– OFr. *for-, fourpasser,* f. *fors,* FOR- *pref.*[3] + *passer* to PASS; in Spenser the prefix is app. taken as FORE-.] **1.** *trans.* To go beyond –1579. **2.** *intr.* To pass beyond. In Spenser: To go past. –1591.
As he forpassed by the plaine With weary pace SPENSER.

Forpi·ne, *v. Obs.* exc. *arch.* ME. [f. FOR- *pref.*[1] + PINE *v.*] *trans.* To cause to pine.
Pale as a for-pyned goost CHAUCER.

Forrader (fǫ·rədəɹ), *adv.* 1898. Colloq. pronunc. of *forwarder* 'more or further forward', as in *no f.*

Forra(y, obs. f. FORAY.

Forsake (fǫ̆ɹsēⁱ·k), *v.* Pa. t. **forsook** (fǫ̆ɹsu·k). Pa. pple. **forsaken** (fǫ̆ɹsēⁱ·k'n). [OE. *forsacan* = OS. *forsakan* (Du. *verzaken*), OHG. *firsahhan*; WGmc., f. FOR-[1] + *sakan* quarrel, accuse. See SAKE.] †**1.** *trans.* To deny –1537. †**2.** To decline or refuse –1605. **3.** To give up, surrender OE.; to break off from, renounce ME. **4.** To abandon, leave entirely, withdraw from; to desert ME.
2. He..forsooke a right worshipful roome when it was offered to him CAMDEN. **3.** Forsaking country, kindred, friends COWPER. To f. idolatry 1894. **4.** Thou hast forsook Thy Juba's cause ADDISON. Larks..f. that climate in winter GOLDSM. *absol.* He'll learn to flatter and f. PRAED.
Hence **Forsa·ken,** †**forsake** *ppl. a.* deserted, left solitary or desolate; †morally abandoned. **Forsa·ken-ly** *adv.,* **-ness. Forsa·ker** (now *rare*).

†**Forsay, Forseek,** etc.: see FOR- *pref.*[1]

†**Forsha·pe,** *v.* [OE. *forsćeppan*; see FOR- *pref.*[1], SHAPE *v.*] *trans.* To metamorphose; to misshape, disfigure –1532.

†**Forsla·ck, foreslack,** *v.* ME. [f. FOR- *pref.*[1] + SLACK *v.*] **1.** *intr.* To be or grow slack. *rare.* –1579. **2.** *trans.* To neglect; to lose or spoil by slackness –1660.

†**Forslo·th,** *v.* ME. [f. FOR- *pref.*[1] + SLOTH *v.*] *trans.* To lose, neglect, spoil, or waste through sloth –1557.

Forslow·, foreslow·, *v.* [OE. *forslāwian,* f. FOR- *pref.*[1] *slāwian* be slow, f. *slāw* SLOW *a.*] **1.** *trans.* To be slow about; to lose or spoil by sloth; to put off. *Obs.* exc. *arch.* **2.** *intr.* To make slow, hinder, obstruct. *Obs.* exc. *arch.* 1563. †**3.** *intr.* To be slow or dilatory –1593.
3. Foreslow no longer, make we hence amaine SHAKS.

Forsooth (fǫ̆ɹsū·þ), *adv.* [OE. *forsōð*; see FOR *prep.* and SOOTH *sb.*] **1.** In truth, truly. Now only parenthetically with an ironical or derisive statement. **2.** quasi-*sb.* 1712.
1. For sute, madam, I lost all that I payd for him 1481. She has no Secrets, f. STEELE. **2.** Her innocent *forsooths* STEELE. Hence **Forsoo·th** *v.* to say f. to, treat ceremoniously PEPYS. **Forsoo·th** *sb.* one who says 'forsooth' freq., an affected speaker. B. JONS.

Forspeak (fǫ̆ɹspī·k), *v.* Also **fore-.** ME. [f. FOR- *pref.*[1] + SPEAK.] **1.** To bewitch. Now *Sc.* †**2.** To forbid, renounce –1579. †**3.** To speak against –1611.
3. *Ant. & Cl.* III. vii. 3.

Forspend, forespend (fǫ̆ɹspe·nd), *v.* [OE. *forspendan*; see FOR- *pref.*[1] and SPEND *v.*] *trans.* To spend completely; to wear out; *rare* exc. in pa. pple. and ppl. adj. 1571.

Forstall: see FORESTALL.

†**Forstrau·ght,** *pa. pple.* ME. [f. FOR- *pref.*[1] + *straught* in DISTRAUGHT.] Distracted. CHAUCER.

†**Forswa·t,** *ppl. a.* ME. [pa. pple. of **forsweat,* f. FOR- *pref.*[1] + SWEAT *v.*] Covered with sweat –1580.

Forswear (fǫ̆ɹswēᵊ·ɹ), *v.* Pa. t. **forswore** (-swōᵊ·ɹ). Pa. pple. *forsworn* (-swǭ·ɹn). [OE. *forswerian*; see FOR- *pref.*[1] and SWEAR *v.*] **1.** *trans.* = ABJURE. **2.** To deny or repudiate on oath or with strong asseveration ME. **3.** *intr.* To swear falsely, commit perjury OE. Also *refl.* Also *pass.* to be guilty of perjury. **4.** *trans.* To swear (something) falsely; to break (an oath); to forsake (sworn allegiance) 1580.
1. I shall f. your company SHERIDAN. **2.** If thou durst, [thou] would'st f. thy own hand and seal ARBUTHNOT. **3.** Thou shalt not forswere WYCLIF *Matt.* 5:33. He sware by his fathers soule, wherby he was neuer forsworne LD. BERNERS. Hence **Forswea·rer,** a perjurer. **Forswo·rn,** †**forswore** *ppl. a.* perjured; falsely sworn. **Forswo·rnness,** perjury.

Forsythia (fǫɹsəi·þiă). 1814. [mod.L., f. the name of William *Forsyth* (1737–1804), English botanist: see -IA[1].] Any plant of the genus of spring-flowering shrubs so named, having bright-yellow bell-shaped flowers.

Fort (fōᵊɹt), *sb.* 1557. [– (O)Fr. *fort* or It. *forte,* subst. uses of *fort, forte* strong :– L. *fortis.*] **1.** *Mil.* A fortified place; a position fortified for defensive or protective purposes, usually surrounded with a ditch, rampart, and parapet, and garrisoned with troops; a fortress. **b.** In British N. Amer. and U.S.: A trading station (orig. fortified) 1776. **2.** Now = FORTE, q.v.
1. *fig.* If there were sought in knowledge..a f. or commanding ground for strife BACON.

Fort (fōᵊɹt), *v.* ? *Obs.* 1559. [f. FORT *sb.*] *trans.* To defend or protect with a fort; to fortify; to enclose in a fort; also with *in.*
It deserues..A forted residence, 'gainst the tooth of time *Meas. for M.* V. i. 12.

Fortalice (fǭ·ɹtălis). †Also **fortilage, fortiless,** etc. ME. [– med.L. *fortalitia, -itium,* f. L. *fortis* strong.] In early use = FORTRESS; now chiefly used for: A small fort. Also *transf.* and *fig.*
Nought feard their force, that fortilage to win SPENSER.

Forte (fǭɹt), *sb.* 1648. [– Fr. *fort,* subst. use of *fort* (see FORT *sb.*); the Fr. fem. form was substituted for the masc. in Engl., as in *locale, morale.*] **1.** The strong point, that in which one excels 1682. **2.** *Fencing.* The strongest part of a sword-blade. Also *fig.* 1648.
1. Those things are not our f. at Covent Garden GOLDSM. **2.** *fig.* Acquainted..with his 'forte' and his 'foible' DE QUINCEY.

‖**Forte** (fǭ·ɹte). 1724. [It. = 'strong, loud' :– L. *fortis.*] *Mus.*
A. *adj.* (*adv.*) A direction: Strong, loud. Also *forte forte* very loud. (Abbrev. *f., ff.*)
B. *sb.* 'Forte' tone; a 'forte' passage 1759.

Forte-piano (fǭ·ɹtepiā·no). 1769. [It., original name of the PIANOFORTE.]
A. *adj.* (*adv.*) *Mus.* A direction: Loud, then suddenly soft. (Abbrev. *fp.*)
B. *sb.* The original name of the PIANOFORTE.

Forth (fōᵊɹþ). [OE. *forþ* = OFris., OS. *forth* (Du. *voort*), MHG. *vort* (G. *fort*) :– Gmc. **furþa* (cf. Goth. *faurþis* further) :– IE. **prto,* f. base repr. in FORE-.]
A. *adv.* **1.** Forwards; opp. to backwards. †Also with ellipsis of *go.* †**2.** Onwards from a specified point –1535. †**b** In ME. *forth mid, with* = 'along with'. **3.** Onwards in time. Now only in *from this time* (*day,* etc.) *f.* (somewhat *arch.*) OE. †**b.** Joined to a vb., with sense 'to go on doing' what the vb. denotes. Cf. *on.* –1808. †**4.** At or to an advanced point –1485. **5.** Forward, into view. Only with *bring, come, show,* and the like. Now often repl. by *out.* OE. **6.** Away or out from a place of origin, residence, or sojourn. Also with ellipsis of *go* (now *arch.*). Now often repl. by *out.* OE. †**7.** Abroad –1607.
1. Then f., deare Countreymen *Hen. V,* II. ii. 189. **2.** *Right f.* (see RIGHT *a.*). **5.** Stretch f. your Hand 1692. **6.** In form of Battel drawn, they issue f. DRYDEN. Maternity must f. to the streets CARLYLE. **7.** Say he dines f. SHAKS.
Phrases. **F. of.** = *out of* in various senses. Now only *poet.* or *rhet.* **And so f.** †(*a*) And then in regular sequence. †(*b*) And similarly. (*c*) Now only (like *and so on*): And the like, etcetera. †**As** or **so f.:** as or so far (*as, that*).
B. *prep.* †**1.** Forward to, up to. Chiefly with *even.* Also in *F. that*: until. –1449. **2.** Forward, out or away from; out of, from out of. Now *rare.* 1566.
2. See 'em f. the gates OTWAY. Poor Troy.. From f. her ashes shall advance her head 1592.
†**C.** *sb.* In *To have one's f.*: to have outlet; *fig.* to have free course, to have one's fling –1611.
D. Forth- in composition. In mod. Eng. *forth-* is often used as a prefix in the formation of nouns of agent and action, and ppl. adjs. corresponding to the verbal phrases in which the adv. follows the vb. Compound vbs. formed with *forth-* are rare. See Main Words.

Forth(e, obs. f. FORD.

For that, *conj.* ME. [See FOR *prep.* VII. 2.] **1.** For the reason that, because. *arch.* ¶Distinguish the mod. use of *for that* in reported speech (where both words are conjs.). †**2.** For the purpose that; in order that –1572.
1. For that I love your daughter..I must advance the colours of my love *Merry W.* III. iv. 82. ¶He had told them to go to supper..for that nothing more would be done that day MACAULAY.

†**Forthby,** *adv.* ME. = FORBY *adv.* 1. –1489.

Forthcome (fōᵊɹþkɒ·m), *v.* OE. [f. FORTH *adv.* + COME *v.*] *intr.* To come forth. Now only as a back-formation from the *ppl. a.*

Forthcoming (fōᵊɹþkɒ·miŋ), *ppl. a.* 1521. [f. phr. *come forth*; see -ING[2].] **1.** About or likely to come forth; also *simply,* coming or approaching (in time); *esp.* ready to appear or be produced when required. **2.** Ready to make or meet advances 1835.
1. Possible but never f. claimants 1893.

†**Forthgo·,** *v.* [OE. *forþgān,* f. FORTH *adv.* + *gān* GO.] **1.** *intr.* To go forth. Occas. w. cogn. obj. Of day, night, etc.: To pass away, pass. –1600. **2.** To come forth as from a source –ME.

Forthgoing (fōᵊɹþgōᵘ·iŋ), *vbl. sb.* ME. [f. FORTH *adv.* + GOING *vbl. sb.*] A going forth.

Forthgoing (fōᵊɹþgōᵘ·iŋ), *ppl. a. rare.* 1851. [f. as prec. + GOING *ppl. a.*] That goes forth; *esp.* disposed to make advances; enthusiastic.

†**Forthi·nk,** *v.* [repr. two distinct words: **a.** OE. *forþenćan* (f. FOR- *pref.*[1] + *þenćan* THINK) = OHG. *fordenchen* (G. *verdenken*); **b.** f. FOR- *pref.*[1] + OE. *þynćan* seem. Cf. MHG. *verdunken* and ON. *forðykkja* displease.]
I. f. OE. *þynćan.* **1.** *trans.* To displease –1535. **2.** *impers.* and quasi-*impers.* (*It*) *forthinks* (*me, him,* etc.): I, etc., feel regret, repent. Const. *of, for,* or *that.* –1588.
1. A thing that myght the forthenke CHAUCER. **2.** It forthinkes me sore that I haue sinned 1588.
II. f. OE. *þenćan.* **1. a.** *trans.* To despise or neglect. OE. only. **b.** *intr.* To be reluctant -ME. **2.** *trans.* To think upon with pain; to regret –1704. **3.** *refl.* To change one's mind; to repent, be sorry. Also. *intr.* for *refl.* –1599.

Forthputting (fōᵊɹþpu·tiŋ), *vbl. sb.* 1640. [f. FORTH *adv.* + PUTTING *vbl. sb.*] **1.** The action of putting forth. **2.** *U.S.* Obtrusive behaviour 1861.

Forthputting (fōᵊɹþpu·tiŋ), *ppl. a.* 1570. [f. FORTH *adv.* + PUTTING, pr. pple. of PUT *v.*] That puts forth; *esp.* that puts oneself forward; forward, obtrusive. (Now chiefly *U.S.*)

Forthright (fōᵊɹþ˛rəi·t, fōᵊ·ɹþ˛rəit), rarely **-rights.** OE. [f. FORTH *adv.* + -RIGHT.]
A. *adv.* **1.** Directly forward. **2.** Straightway ME.
2. F. upon his steed [he] Leapt SWINBURNE.
B. *adj.* **1.** Proceeding in a straight course, straight forward OE. **2.** *fig.* Going straight to the point; also, unhesitating 1855.
2. The home-thrust of a f. word LOWELL.
C. *sb.* A straight course or path (*lit.* and *fig.*). Chiefly after Shakespeare.
Here's a maze trod indeede Through fourth rights and meanders *Temp.* III. iii. 3.
Hence **Fo·rthrightness,** straightforwardness.

Fo·rthward, -wards. *Obs.* exc. *arch.* [OE. *forþweard,* f. FORTH *adv.* + -WARD; see -WARDS.]
A. *adv.* **1.** Of place: Onward(s, forward ME. **2.** Of time: †**a.** Continually, prospectively. OE. only. **b.** For the future onwards OE.
B. *adj.* = FORWARD *a.* 1470.

Forthwith (fōᵊ:ɹþwi·þ, -wi·ð), *adv.* 1450 [Partly short for earlier *forthwithal* (XI), but partly repl. ME. *forth mid* along with, at the same time, used absol.] Immediately, at once, without delay or interval.
When a defendant is ordered to plead f., he must plead within twenty-four hours WHARTON. So †**Fo·rthwithal** *adv.* (in same sense).

†**For-thy·,** *conj.* [OE. *forþī, forþȳ,* f. FOR *prep.* + *þȳ,* instr. of THE; see THE *adv.*] For this reason, therefore –1647. Hence **F. that,** earlier **f. the,** because.

Fortieth (fǭ·ɹtiėþ), *a.* (*sb.*) [OE. *fēowertigoþa*, f. FORTY on the anal. of TENTH.] The ordinal numeral belonging to the cardinal forty.

Phr. *The f. man*: one man in forty. *F. part*: one of forty equal parts of anything. Also *absol.* and quasi-*sb.*

Fortifiable (fǭ·ɹtifəiăb'l), *a.* 1609. [f. FORTIFY *v.* + -ABLE.] That may be fortified.

Fortification (fǭ:ɹtifikēⁱ·ʃən). 1489. [– Fr. *fortification* – late L. *fortificatio*, f. *fortificat-*, pa. ppl. stem of *fortificare*; see FORTIFY, -ION.] **1.** The action of fortifying in senses of the vb. 1530. **2.** *Mil.* A defensive work; a wall, earthwork, tower, etc. Chiefly *collect. pl.* 1489. **b.** *transf.* and *fig.* A means of defence 1586.

2. To make Bulwerkes, Brayes..and al other fortificacions 1512. *Comb.* **f.-agate,** a variety of agate showing, when polished, markings well described by the name.

Fortifier (fǭ·ɹtifəiˌəɹ). 1552. [f. next + -ER¹.] One who or that which fortifies; one who constructs fortifications; a supporter, upholder.

Fortify (fǭ·ɹtifəi), *v.* ME. [– (O)Fr. *fortifier* – late L. *fortificare*, f. L. *fortis* strong; see -FY.]

I. 1. *trans.* To strengthen structurally 1450; to impart strength or vigour to ME. †**2.** To render more powerful or effective –1725. **3.** To strengthen mentally or morally 1477; to confirm, add support to ME. †**4.** *intr.* To grow strong –1660.

1. To f. a Fabrick with Pitch 1697, a ship with additional timbers 1820. To f. the stomach 1849. **2.** He fortified Burdeaux with Englishmen and victayle HALL. **3.** Timidity was fortified by pride GIBBON. A charge..fortified by particulars HT. MARTINEAU.

II. To strengthen against attack. **1.** *trans.* To provide with defensive works ME. Also *transf.* **2.** To put in a position of defence 1548. **3.** *intr.* To establish a position of defence. Also *transf.* and *fig.* 1570.

1. The houses haue yee broken downe to fortifie the wall *Isa.* 22:10. **3.** For such a time do I now fortifie Against confounding Ages cruell knife SHAKS.

Fortilage, fortiless, obs. ff. FORTALICE.

†**Fo·rtin.** 1706. [– Fr. *fortin* – It. *fortino*, f. *forte*; see FORT *sb.*] A small fort; a field-fort –1744.

‖**Forti·ssimo,** *adv.* 1724. [It., superl. of *forte*; see FORTE.] *Mus.* Very loud. (Abbrev. *ff.*, *ffor.*, or *fortiss.*) Also quasi-*adj.* and as *sb.*

[**Fortition,** a spurious word: see SORTITION.]

Fortitude (fǭ·ɹtitiud). 1500. [– (O)Fr. *fortitude* – L. *fortitudo*, f. *fortis* strong; see -TUDE.] †**1.** Physical or structural strength –1703. **2.** Moral strength or courage. Now only in passive sense: Firmness in the endurance of pain or adversity. (One of the cardinal virtues.) 1500.

1. The F. of the place is best knowne to you *Oth.* I. iii. 222. **2.** She could bear the disappointments of other people with tolerable f. DICKENS. So **Fortitu·dinous** *a.* endowed with or characterized by f.

Fortlet (fǭ·ɹtlėt). ME. [f. FORT *sb.* + -LET.] A small fort.

Fortnight (fǭ·ɹtnəit). [OE. *fēowertīene niht*, ME. *fourten(n)iht* fourteen nights (in which the ancient Gmc. reckoning by nights is preserved); cf. SENNIGHT.] A period of fourteen nights; two weeks.

Phr. *This day, Monday,* †*Monday was* (*a*), etc. *f.*: a fortnight from (this day, etc.).

Fortnightly (fǭ·ɹtnəitli). 1800. [f. prec. + -LY¹·².]

A. *adj.* Happening or appearing once in a fortnight.

B. *adv.* Once in a fortnight.

†**Fortrea·d,** *v.* [OE. *fortredan*; see FOR- *pref.*¹ and TREAD *v.*] *trans.* To tread down; to destroy by trampling –1450.

In helle schulle þay be al fortrode of deueles CHAUCER.

Fortress (fǭ·ɹtrės), *sb.* ME. [– (O)Fr. *forteresse* strong place :– Rom. **fortaritia* (cf. Gallo-Rom. *vaccaritia* cow-stall, f. *vacca*), f. L. *fortis* strong. Cf. FORT *sb.*] A military stronghold, fortified place; now chiefly, one capable of receiving a large force; often applied to a strongly fortified town. Also *transf.* and *fig.*

Fortress (fǭ·ɹtrės), *v.* 1542. [f. prec. sb.] To furnish with a fortress or fortifications; to protect with or as with a fortress. Chiefly *transf.* and *fig.*

Fortuitous (fǫɹtiū·itəs), *a.* 1653. [f. L. *fortuitus*, f. *forte* by chance, f. *fors* + -OUS.] That happens or is produced by fortune or chance; accidental, casual.

A f. rencontre SCOTT. Phr. *F. concourse of atoms*: see CONCOURSE. *F. event* (Law): 'a term in the civil law applied to denote that which happens by a cause which cannot be resisted..Or it is that which neither of the parties has occasioned or could prevent' BOUVIER.

Hence **Fortu·itous-ly** *adv.*, **-ness.**

Fortuity (fǫɹtiū·iti). 1747. [irreg. f. L. *fortuitus*; see prec. and -ITY.] Fortuitous character; accident, chance; an accidental occurrence.

Fortunate (fǭ·ɹtiŭnėt), *a.* (*sb.*) ME. [– L. *fortunatus*, f. *fortuna*; see FORTUNE, -ATE².] **1.** Favoured by fortune; possessed of or receiving good fortune; lucky, prosperous. Const. *to* and *inf.* **2.** Bringing or presaging good fortune; auspicious, favourable, lucky ME. **3.** *absol.* or *sb.* A fortunate person or thing; *esp.* in *Astrol.* a fortunate planet, sign, etc. 1614.

1. Burleigh (f...to serve the best of Queens) 1705. *Fortunate Islands* (= L. *Fortunatæ Insulæ*), fabulous isles of the Western Ocean, the abode of the blessed dead. Also *fig.* **2.** A f. omen 1741, day 1841, circumstance 1849. **3.** The f. are satisfied with the possession of this world GIBBON. Hence **Fo·rtunate-ly** *adv.*, **-ness.**

†**Fo·rtunate,** *v.* ME. [– *fortunat-*, pa. ppl. stem of L. *fortunare*, f. *fortuna*; see next, -ATE³.] *trans.* To make fortunate, prosper. Also *absol.* –1792.

Fortune (fǭ·ɹtiŭn), *sb.* ME. [– (O)Fr. *fortune* – L. *fortuna* chance as a divinity, luck, esp. good luck.] **1.** Chance, hap, or luck, regarded as a cause of events and changes in men's affairs. Often (after L.) personified as a goddess, having for emblem a wheel, betokening vicissitude. †**2.** A chance, hap, accident, an adventure –1726; a mishap, disaster –1627. **3.** The chance or luck (good or bad) which falls or is to fall to any one. Also in *pl.* ME. **b.** Attributed to things, purposes, undertakings 1665. **4.** *absol.* (= good fortune) ME. **5.** One's condition or standing in life; often *absol.* a prosperous condition. Also *pl.* 1600. **6.** Amount of wealth; *concr.* wealth, substance; †formerly also *pl.* Also (with *a* and *pl.*) an ample stock of wealth. 1596. †**7.** Short for: A woman of fortune; an heiress –1823. **8.** *Astrol.* A name for the planets Jupiter and Venus 1671.

1. The chaunces of the worlde also, That we f. clepen so GOWER. You have f. on your side JUNIUS. Phr. *The f. of war. Soldier of f.*: one who fought for pay in any country or state that would employ him; also, one who has risen from the ranks by merit. **3.** Chieflie the mould of a Mans f. is in himself BACON. Phr. *To try one's f. To tell a person his f. To tell fortunes.* **4.** Your F., and Merit both, haue been Eminent BACON. **5.** My pride fell with my fortunes *A.Y.L.* I. ii. 263. Phr. *To make one's f.* **6.** He paid much too dear for his Wife's F., by taking her Person into the bargain CLARENDON. Phr. *To make a, one's f.* Men of rank and f. BERKELEY.

Comb.: **f.-book,** 'a book consulted to know f. or future events' (J.); **-hunter,** one who seeks to win a f., *esp.* by marriage; **-tell** *v.*, to tell fortunes; **-teller,** one who tells fortunes; **-telling** *vbl. sb.*, the practice of telling fortunes.

Fortune (fǭ·ɹtiŭn), *v.* ME. [– OFr. *fortuner* – L. *fortunare* make fortunate, f. *fortuna*; see prec.] †**1.** *trans.* To assign a (certain) fortune to –1606. **2.** To endow with a fortune; to dower. *rare.* 1748. †**3.** *intr.* Of events, etc.: To happen, chance, occur –1739. **b.** *impers.* 1462. †**4.** With person or thing as subject: To happen or chance *to be* or *to do* (something) –1798.

3. b. It so fortuned, that he was taken by pirates at sea BACON. Hence †**Fo·rtune** *adv.* haply, perchance.

Fortuned (fǭ·ɹtiŭnd), *ppl. a.* Now *rare.* ME. [f. FORTUNE *sb.* and *v.* + -ED. Cf. (O)Fr. *fortuné.*] Having fortune (of a specified kind); also, possessed of a fortune.

The full-Fortun'd Cæsar *Ant. & Cl.* IV. xv. 24.

Fo·rtuneless, *a.* 1596. [See -LESS.] Without (good) fortune, luckless. Also destitute of a fortune.

†**Fo·rtunize,** *v. rare.* 1596. [f. FORTUNE *sb.* + -IZE.] *trans.* To regulate the fortunes of; to make fortunate –1652.

†**Fortunous,** *a.* ME. [– OFr. *fortuneus*; see FORTUNE *sb.*, -OUS.] **1.** Fortuitous. CHAUCER. **2.** Successful 1470.

Forty (fǭ·ɹti). [OE. *fēowertiġ* = OFris. *fiuwertich*, OS. *fiwartig* (Du. *veertig*), OHG. *fiorzug* (G. *vierzig*), ON. *fjórir tigir*, Goth. *fidwor tigjus*; see FOUR, -TY².]

A. *adj.* The cardinal number equal to four tens. Symbols 40, xl, or XL. Also used indefinitely to express a large number.

On fairie ground I could beat fortie of them SHAKS.

B. *sb.* **1.** The age of 40 years 1732. **2.** A yacht of forty tons burden 1894.

Phrases. *The forties*: the years between forty and fifty of a century or of one's life. *The forty*: a designation applied to certain bodies from the number of their members; e.g. to several courts of justice in the Venetian republic; to the French Academy, and (occas.) to the Royal Academy of Arts in London. *The roaring forties*: the part of the South Atlantic, Pacific, and Indian Oceans between 40° and 50° south latitude, characterized by exceptionally boisterous westerly winds.

Comb.: **f.-spot,** the Tasmanian name for a bird, *Pardalotus quadragintus* (Gould); **-tonner** = B. 2.

Forty-five. *The Forty-five*: the year 1745, and the Jacobite rebellion of that year.

Forum (fōᵊ·ɹŏm). 1460. [– L. *forum*, rel. to *fores* (outside) door; orig. enclosure surrounding a house.] **1.** The public place or market-place of a city. In ancient Rome the place of assembly for judicial and other public business. Also *fig.* **2.** A court, tribunal 1848. Also *transf.* and *fig.* 1690.

1. Rienzi..The forum's champion, and the people's chief BYRON. **2.** Phr. *Law of the f.*: the legal rules of a particular court or jurisdiction; Limitation and prescription are applied only according to the law of the f. PARSONS. *fig.* In the f. of conscience (= L. *in foro conscientiæ*) 1874.

Forwake(d: see FOR- *pref.*¹ 5 b.

Forwa·nder, *v.* Now *arch.* or *Sc.* ME. [f. FOR- *pref.*¹ + WANDER.] To weary oneself with wandering; to wander far and wide.

Forward (fǭ·ɹwəɹd). [OE. *forweard* adv., var. of *forþweard*; see FORTHWARD. The adj. is developed from the adv., whence, in absol. use, the sb.]

A. *adj.* †**1.** In OE. The front, first, or earliest party of (anything). **2.** Near, at, or belonging to the fore-part 1601; that lies in front 1643. **3.** Onward; also 'outward' as opp. to 'return' 1603. **4.** *Comm.* Prospective, relating to future produce 1883. **5.** That is in an advanced state or condition; early. Chiefly *predicative.* 1526. **6.** Ready, prompt, eager; *esp.* with const. *to* 1523. **b.** *transf.* and *fig.* of things. ? *Obs.* 1605. **7.** Precocious 1591. **8.** In bad sense: Presumptuous; bold, immodest 1561. **9.** Of persons: Advanced, extreme; in mod. use, aggressive 1608.

2. Let's take the instant by the f. top SHAKS. The f. horizon KINGLAKE. The f. sight of a gun 1876. **3.** The f. path CARY. *F. play* (in *Cricket*): the method of playing f.: see the *adv.* 3 (quot.). **5.** As the most f. Bud Is eaten by the Canker ere it blow SHAKS. **6.** How fondly do'st thou spurre a f. Horse SHAKS. F. to give C. MATHER. A wood very f. to grow DE FOE. **7.** It will be a f. cock that croweth in the shell LYLY. **8.** A f. prating coxcomb T. BROWN. **9.** Outrage and dynamite, and what are generally known as 'f.' measures 1887.

B. *adv.* **1.** Towards the future. Now only in phrases *from this day* (*time*, etc.) *f.* OE. **b.** *Comm.* For future delivery or payment 1882. †**2.** Onward or farther in a series –1663. **3.** Towards the front 1513. **4.** Towards what is in front; (moving) onwards, on. Also with ellipsis of some part of the vb. *go.* ME. **b.** Ahead 1838. **5.** To the front or to a prominent position, into view 1611. **6.** At a point or position which is beyond or farther than another 1523. Of time: In advance 1571. **7.** *Naut.* At or towards the fore-part of a vessel 1630. **8.** *fig.* Onward, so as to progress or advance 1513.

1. Phr. *To look f.* **b.** Maize still..dear, but cheaper f. 1894. **2.** Phr. *And so f.* = and so forth, et cetera. **3.** Phr. *To play f.* (in *Cricket*): to reach f. so as to play short-pitched balls. **5.** Phr. *To bring f. To come f. To put f.* **8.** Now f. with your tale *Temp.* III. ii. 91. Phr. *To go f.*: to be going on.

C. *sb.* [The *adj.* used *absol.*] †1. The fore, front, or first part -ME. †2. *Wrestling.* A throw which causes the opponent to fall forward –1612. 3. *Football, Hockey,* etc. One who plays in the front line 1879.

Hence **Fo·rward-ly** *adv.* (and *a.*), **-ness.**

Forward (fǭ·ɹwəɹd), *v.* 1596. [f. FORWARD *adv.*] 1. *trans.* To help forward; to advance, hasten, promote, urge on. Also, †to set on foot (*rare*). 2. To accelerate the growth of (plants) 1626. 3. To send to an ulterior destination. In *Comm.* often loosely, to dispatch. 1757. 4. *Bookbinding.* To get (a sewed book) ready for the finisher by putting a plain cover on 1870.

1. To f. its interests FREEMAN. 2. Of..Efficacy to f. the Flowers 1707. 3. Forwarded this day to your address per S.W.R. three boxes marked [etc.] 1897.

Hence **Fo·rwarder,** one who or that which forwards; *spec.* in sense 4.

Fo·rwarding, *vbl. sb.* 1635. [f. prec. + -ING[1].] 1. The action of FORWARD *v.* in various senses. 2. *Bookbinding.* The operation of putting a plain cover on a book previously sewn, and preparing it for the 'finisher' 1893. 3. *attrib.*, as *f. room,* etc.; **f. agent, merchant,** one whose business is the receiving and shipment or transmission of goods.

Forwards (fǭ·ɹwəɹdz). ME. [f. FORWARD *adv.*; see -S, -WARDS. Cf. OE. *forþweardes* and Du. *voorwaarts.*]

A. *adv.* = FORWARD *adv.* (As dist. from *forward,* the form *forwards* expresses a definite direction in contrast with other directions. But in some contexts either form may be used.)

He was backwards and f. constantly DICKENS.

†B. *adj.* = FORWARD *a. rare.* –1626.

†**Forwa·rn, forewa·rn,** *v.* [OE. *forwiernan,* f. FOR- *pref.*[1] + *wiernan* forbid; see WARN *v.*[2]] *trans.* To prohibit, forbid –1820.

He did not know that the thing had been forewarned LAMB.

†**Forwa·ste,** *v.* 1563. [f. FOR- *pref.*[1] + WASTE *v.*] = WASTE *v.* –1630.

Forweary (fǭɹwi^ə·ri), *v. Obs.* or *arch.* Also **fore-.** ME. [f. FOR- *pref.*[1] + WEARY *v.*] *trans.* To weary, tire out.

†**Forwee·p,** *v.* ME. [f. FOR- *pref.*[1] + WEEP *v.*] *intr.* To exhaust oneself with weeping. Of a vine: To bleed excessively. –1500.

†**Forwe·lk,** *v.* ME. [f. FOR- *pref.*[1] + WELK *v.*] *trans.* To wither –1616.

†**Forwhy·.** [OE. *for-hwī,* f. FOR *prep.* + *hwī,* WHY, instr. of *hwæt,* neut. of *hwā* WHO.]

A. *adv.* 1. For what reason, why. 2. With connective force: For which cause, wherefore ME.

B. *conj.* 1. Because; = FOR *conj.* 1. ME. 2. = FOR *conj.* 2. ME.

Forworn (fǭɹwǭ·ɹn), *ppl. a.* 1508. [pa. pple. of †*forwear* (XIII); see FOR- *pref.*[1], WEAR *v.*[1]] Worn out, decayed, grown old.

A silly man, in simple weedes forworne SPENSER.

†**Forwra·p,** *v.* ME. [f. FOR- *pref.*[1] + WRAP *v.*] *trans.* To wrap up. Also *fig.* –1571.

Al moot be seyd, and no thyng excused, ne forwrapped CHAUCER.

†**Foryie·ld,** *v.* [OE. *forġieldan* = OHG. *fargeltan* (G. *vergelten*); see FOR- *pref.*[1], YIELD *v.*] *trans.* To repay, recompense, requite. Also *intr.* with *of.* Phr. *God,* etc. *foryield* (it) –1560.

‖**Forzando** (fǫrtsa·ndo), *adv.* 1828. [It., f. *forzare* to force.] *Mus.* = SFORZANDO.

‖**Fossa** (fǫ·să). *Pl.* **fossæ.** 1830. [L., = ditch. See FOSSE.] *Anat.* A shallow depression, pit, or cavity.

Fossane (fǫ·sēⁱn). 1781. [– Fr.; the native name is given as *foussa.*] A species of weasel or genet, found in Madagascar, etc.

Fosse (fǫs). ME. [– (O)Fr. *fosse* :– L. *fossa,* fem. pa. pple. of *fodere* dig.] 1. An excavation narrow in proportion to its length; a canal, ditch, or trench; in *Fortif.,* etc., a moat. †2. A pit –1855. 3. *Anat.* = FOSSA. 1730.

Hence **Fossed** *a.* encircled with or as with a f.

‖**Fossé** (fo·se). 1708. [Fr. :– late L. *fossatum,* n. pa. pple. of L. *fossare,* freq. of *fodere* dig.] A fosse, ditch, or sunk fence.

Fosset, obs. f. FACET, FAUCET.

Fossette (fǫse·t). 1848. [– Fr. *fossette* (OFr. *fossete*), dim. of *fosse*; see FOSSE, -ETTE.] A little hollow, depression, or dimple. **a.** *Zool.* 1856. **b.** *Path.* 'A small ulcer of the transparent cornea, the centre of which is deep' (Ogilvie).

Fossick (fǫ·sik), *v. Austral.* 1852. [Of unkn. origin; cf. dial *fossick* troublesome person, *fossicking* troublesome, *fossick* make a fuss, bustle about.] 1. *intr.* in *Mining.* To search for gold by digging out crevices with knife or pick, or by working in washing-places and abandoned workings. 2. *gen.* To rummage or hunt about 1887. 3. *trans.* To dig *out,* to hunt *up* 1870. Hence **Fo·ssicker,** one who fossicks, *esp.* a pocket-miner or a prospector for gold.

Fossil (fǫ·sil). 1569. [– Fr. *fossile* – L. *fossilis,* f. *foss-,* pa. ppl. stem of *fodere* dig; see FOSSE, -ILE.]

A. *adj.* 1. Obtained by digging; found buried in the earth 1654. 2. Now applied to the remains of animals and plants, belonging to past ages, and found embedded in the strata of the earth. (Commonly taken as the *sb.* used attrib.) Also *fig.* 1665. **b.** Used in names of certain mineral substances supposed to resemble organic products, as *f. copal, cork, farina* (see the sbs.); *f. flax, paper, wood, wool,* varieties of asbestos; etc. 3. Belonging to the past, out of date; 'petrified' 1859.

1. F. coal, and..bitumen 1816. 2. The fossill Bones of an Alligator found..near Whitby 1758. *fig.* Language is f. poetry EMERSON. 3. F. politicians 1894.

B. *sb.* †1. Any rock, mineral, or mineral substance dug out of the earth –1814. 2. Now only: The remains of a plant or animal of a former geological period found in the strata of the earth 1736. 3. *fig.* Something 'petrified', or incapable of growth or progress 1844.

3. When a man endures what ought to be unendurable, he is a f. C. BRONTË.

Comb. **f.-ore,** fossiliferous red hematite.

Hence **Fossili·ferous** *a.* bearing or containing fossils or organic remains. **Fo·ssilism,** the scientific study of fossils (*rare*); also, the state of being a f. **Fo·ssilist** (now *rare*), an authority on fossils, a palæontologist.

Fossilize (fǫ·siləiz), *v.* 1794. [f. FOSSIL *sb.* + -IZE.] 1. To turn into a fossil. *trans.* and *intr.* 2. *fig.* To cause to become antiquated, rigid, or fixed; *rarely,* to preserve as if in fossil form. Also *intr.* for *refl.* 1856. 3. *intr.* To search for fossils. LYELL.

1. 'Petrifying wells' do not..f. the things put into them 1854. 2. Ten layers of birthdays on a woman's head Are apt to f. her girlish mirth MRS. BROWNING. Hence **Fossiliza·tion.**

†**Fossi·logy.** 1776. [irreg. f. FOSSIL + -LOGY.] That branch of science which treats of fossils; palæontology; also, a treatise on this –1812. So †**Fossi·logist,** one who studies f. vars. **Fossilo·logy** (*rare*), **Fossilolo·gical** *a.*, **Fossilo·logist.**

‖**Fossor** (fǫ·sǫɹ). 1854. [L., = digger, miner; in late L., grave-digger; f. *foss-*; see FOSSE, -OR 2 b.] An officer of the early Church charged with the burial of the dead.

Fossorial (fǫsō^ə·riăl). 1836. [f. med.L. *fossorius,* adapted for digging (f. *fossor*; see prec.) + -IAL; see -ORIAL.]

A. *adj.* 1. Having a faculty of digging, burrowing, fodient. 2. Of or pertaining to fodient animals, adapted for burrowing 1845.

1. *F. Hymenoptera,* a family of insects called *Fossores.*

B. *sb.* A fossorial animal 1855.

var. **Fosso·rious** *a.*

‖**Fossula** (fǫ·siŭlă). 1843. [L., dim. of *fossa*; see FOSSA, -ULE.] A small fossa; *spec.* in *Anat.* and *Zool.* (see next).

Fossulate (fǫ·siŭlĕt), *a.* 1839. [f. L. *fossula* (see prec.) + -ATE[2].] *Anat.* and *Zool.* Having one or more long narrow grooves or depressions.

Foster (fǫ·stəɹ), *sb.*[1] *Obs.* exc. in *Comb.* [OE. *fōster* food, f. **fōð-* FOOD + instr. suffix **-trom.*] 1. Food, nourishment –1670. 2. Guardianship, keeping. *At f.,* at nurse (with a foster-parent). –1861. 3. Offspring –1513; also, a foster-child, nursling –1585. 4. *attrib.* and *Comb.*, as F.-BROTHER, -SISTER; -CHILD, -SON. Also F.-FATHER, -MOTHER; hence, *f.-city, -earth.* 1582.

Fo·ster, *sb.*[2] *Obs.* exc. *arch.* [f. prec., used as comb. form in OE. *fōsterbearn, -ċild, -brōþor,* etc.] A foster-parent, nurse.

†**Fo·ster,** *sb.*[3] ME. [contr. f. FORESTER.] ≙ FORESTER. –1607.

Foster (fǫ·stəɹ), *v.* [OE. *fōstrian* (= ON. *fóstra*), f. *fōster* FOSTER *sb.*[1]] †1. *trans.* To supply with food; to nourish, feed, support –1719. Also *fig.* †2. To bring up with parental care; often, to be a foster-parent to –1697. 3. To nurse, tend with care; to cherish ME. 4. To encourage, help to grow; to promote the development of ME.

1. One, bred but of Almes, and foster'd with cold dishes *Cymb.* II. iii. 119. 2. Some say, that Rauens f. forlorne children SHAKS. 3. Hir olde poore fader fostred she CHAUCER. 4. To f. a system of concealment BURKE, an insurrection 1844, enmities DISRAELI, superstitions 1885.

Hence **Fo·sterage,** the action, also the office or charge, of fostering (another's child); the condition of being a foster-child; the custom of putting (a child) under a foster-mother; the action of encouraging. **Fo·sterer,** a nurse, foster-parent; one who cherishes, favours, or promotes the growth of (anything); in *Anglo-Irish,* a foster-brother. **Fo·steringly** *adv.* †**Fo·sterment,** food, nourishment, subsistence.

Fo·ster-brother. [OE. *fōster-brōþor*; see FOSTER *sb.*[1]] A male child nursed at the same breast as, or reared with, another of different parentage.

Foster-child. [OE. *fōsterċild*; cf. prec.] A nurseling.

Fo·ster-father. [OE. *fōsterfæder*; cf. prec.] **a.** One who performs the duty of a father to another's child. **b.** The husband of a nurse.

Fosterling (fǫ·stəɹliŋ). [OE. *fōsterling*; see prec., -LING[1].] A foster-child.

Fo·ster-mother. [OE. *fōstermōdor*; cf. prec.] A woman who nurses and brings up another's child, either as an adoptive mother or as a nurse.

Fo·ster-nurse. 1607. [f. FOSTER *sb.*[1]; cf. prec.] A nurse who brings up another's child as her own.

Fo·ster-sister. 1649. [f. as prec.] A female child nursed at the same breast as, or reared with, another of different parentage.

Fo·ster-son. 1450. [f. as prec.]. One brought up as a son though not a son by birth.

Fostress (fǫ·strĕs). 1603. [fem. of *fosterer*; see FOSTER *v.*, -ESS[1].] A female who fosters (see FOSTER *v.*).

Fother (fǫ·ðəɹ), *sb.* [OE. *fōþer* = OS. *fōthar* (Du. *voer*), OHG. *fuodar* (G. *fuder*) :– WGmc. **fōþra,* prob. f. gradation-var. of the base **faþ-* stretch out, as in FATHOM.] 1. A load; a cart-load; hence, a mass, a lot. 2. *spec.* A definite weight: **a.** of lead, = $19\frac{1}{2}$ cwt. ME.; **b.** of coals, = $17\frac{3}{8}$ cwt. 1607.

Fother (fǫ·ðəɹ), *v.* Also **fodder.** 1789. [prob. – Du. *voederen* (now *voeren*), or LG. *fodern* = G. *füttern* to line.] *Naut.* 1. *trans.* To cover (a sail) thickly with oakum, rope-yarn, or the like, with the view of getting some of it sucked into a leak, over which the sail is drawn. 2. To stop a leak by this method 1800. Hence **Fo·ther** (fodder) *sb.* the material used for fothering.

†**Fo·tive** *a.* [f. *fot-,* pa. ppl. stem of L. *fovēre* cherish + -IVE.] Cherishing, warming. T. CAREW.

†**Fo·tmal.** ME. only. [app. a use of OE. *fōtmǣl* foot-measure (see FOOT, MEAL *sb.*[2]), in med.L. *fotmellum, -mallus* (XIII), also *pes* (foot) in same sense. The reason for the name is obscure.] A weight used for lead, app. about 70 lb.

Fou (*fū*), *a. Sc.* 1535. [var. of FULL *a.*] Drunk.

Foudroyant (fudroi·ănt, Fr. fudrwayaṅ), *a.* 1840. [– Fr. *foudroyant,* pr. pple. of *foudroyer* strike with or as with lightning, f. *foudre* :– L. *fulgur* lightning; see -ANT, and cf. FOULDER *v.*] 1. Thundering, stunning; also, dazzling. 2. *spec.* in *Path.* of a disease: Beginning suddenly in a very severe form.

†**Fouga·de.** 1643. [– Fr. *fougade* – It.

fogata, f. †*fogare* speed, fly, flee; see -ADE. Cf. FOUGUE.] = FOUGASSE; also *fig.* –1827.

Fougasse (fuga·s). 1832. [– Fr. *fougasse*, alt. f. *fougade*; see prec.] 'A small mine from 6 to 12 feet underground, charged either with powder or loaded shells' (Voyle).

Fought (fǫt), *ppl. a.* 1550. [pa. pple. of FIGHT *v.*] In senses of the vb. In attrib. use usually with advs., as *well-f.* var. **Fou·ghten.** *arch.*

† ||**Fougue** (fūg). Also †**fogue.** 1660. [– Fr. *fougue* – It. *foga* impetus, ardour, f. *fogare*. See FOUGADE.] Fury; ardour, impetuosity –1683.

Foul (faul). [OE. *fūl* = OFris., OS., OHG. *fūl* (Du. *vuil* dirty, G. *faul* rotten, lazy), ON. *fúll*, Goth. *fuls* stinking :– Gmc. **fūlaz*, f. **fū-* :– IE. **pŭ*, as in L. *pus* PUS, *putēre* stink, Gr. πύον, πύος, πῦαρ pus.]

A. *adj.* **I.** Grossly offensive to the senses, physically loathsome. **b.** Charged with offensive matter; (of a carcase) tainted with disease ME.

Thy..place of doom obscure and foule MILT.

†*The f. disease* or *evil*: (*a*) epilepsy, (*b*) syphilis.

II. Opp. to CLEAN *a.* II. **1.** Dirty, soiled; covered with or full of dirt or mire. Now chiefly: Disgustingly dirty, filthy. OE. **2.** †Of handwriting: Blotted, illegible. *F. copy*: a first copy, defaced by corrections (now *rare*). *F. proof*: one marked with many faults. 1467. **3.** Charged with defiling or noxious matter; discoloured 1535. **4.** Of food: Coarse, gross, rank; unclean, putrid. Hence applied to the eating, or the eaters, of such food. 1713. **5.** Clogged, choked, or encumbered with something foreign 1470. **b.** *Path.* Of the tongue: Furred 1800. **6.** Morally or spiritually polluted; abominable, wicked OE. **7.** Of speech: Obscene; also, disgustingly abusive OE. **8.** Applied to fish immediately after spawning 1870.

1. Þe way was foule 1450. **2.** By cause of the foule wrytyng and interlynyeng 1467. *F. bill of health*: see BILL *sb.*[3] **3.** The Seine is f. and turbid as the Avon 1756. Workings charged with f. gas 1885. **5.** *F. bottom* (Naut.), the bottom of the sea if rocky, or unsafe from wrecks. Also of a ship: Having the bottom overgrown with seaweed, shell-fish, etc. *F. coast*, one beset by reefs and breakers. *F. ground*, synonymous with *f. bottom.* **6.** Babylon the great..is become..the hold of every f. spirit *Rev.* 18:2. A court f. with all the vices of the Restoration MACAULAY. *F. fiend*, see FIEND. *F. thief*: the devil. **7.** Foule speech deserues a double hate 1530. F. songs 1833. A f. mouth 1834, tongue 1852.

III. Opp. to FAIR *a.* **1.** Ugly. Now *rare* in literary use. ME. **2.** Disgraceful, ignominious, shameful ME. **3.** *Sporting* and *Games.* Contrary to rule, irregular, unfair; said also of the player. **4.** Of the weather, etc.: Unfavourable; wet and stormy ME. **5.** Of the wind: Contrary 1726. **6.** Of a means or procedure, language, etc.: Harsh, rough, violent ME. **7.** *Naut.* (opp. to *clear*): 'Entangled, embarrassed, or contrary to' (Adm. Smyth). Const. *of*, †*on.* 1627.

1. My face is fowle with weeping *Job* 16:16. A foule noyse HOLLAND. **2.** A f. charge 1756, deed SCOTT. **3.** A f. blow 1797. F. riding 1892. Phr. *F. ball* (Baseball): a ball that falls outside the lines drawn from the home base through the first and third bases. *F. play*: unfair conduct in a game; *transf.* unfair or treacherous (and often violent) dealing. **4.** In foule wether at my booke to sit WYATT. **5.** In the teeth of a f. wind 1883. **6.** War is a f. game EMERSON. **7.** Phr. *To fall, run f. of*: see the vbs. *F. berth*, 'when a ship anchors in the hawse of another she gives the latter a f. berth' SMYTH. *F. anchor*, the anchor when it hooks some other anchor, wreck, or cable, or when the slack cable is entangled about the upper fluke of it. Also, the badge of the British Admiralty.

B. *sb.* [The adj. used *absol.* or *ellipt.*] **1.** That which is foul; something foul OE. **2.** A disease in the feet of cattle and sheep. Also, in dogs. 1523. **3.** (Partly f. FOUL *v.*) A collision or entanglement, *esp.* in riding, rowing, running, etc. In *Baseball*: A foul hit. 1754.

1. *F. befall* (see FAIR *sb.*[2]). **3.** *To claim a f.*: to allege unfair action on the part of an opponent, and claim the penalty.

C. *adv.* In a foul manner, in various senses (see the adj.) ME.

Foul (faul), *v.*[1] [In form repr. OE. *fūlian* intr. In the trans. use, prob. a new formation.] **1.** *intr.* To be or become foul. **2.** *trans.* To render filthy or dirty; to defile ME. **3.** *fig.* To pollute (with guilt); to dishonour, disgrace ME. **4.** To make ugly; to deface, disfigure ME. **5.** Chiefly *Naut.* To cause to become entangled. Also, to jam or block; to make (a sea bottom) foul or obstructed. 1726. **b.** *intr.* To get foul 1857. **c.** *trans.* To run foul of 1859. **6.** *Sporting* and *Games.* To handle or strike an opponent in a foul manner. *Baseball.* To hit a foul ball.

1. Prince's breech-loader fouls in the proportion [etc.] 1858. **2.** To f. a smock SWIFT. **3.** With hands not fouled with confiscation BURKE. **5.** A ship..fouled her propeller 1892. **b.** The chain fouled on the windlass 1860. **c.** She fouled the pier 1859.

†**Foul, fowle,** *v.*[2] ME. [– (O)Fr. *fouler*; see FULL *v.*[2], FOIL *v.*[1]] *trans.* To trample, tread, tread down –1643.

Foulard (fu·lar, fulā·ɹd). 1864. [– Fr. *foulard*, of unkn. origin.] **1.** A thin flexible material of silk, or of silk and cotton. **2.** A handkerchief of this 1879.

†**Fou·lder,** *v.* 1559. [– OFr. *fou(l)drer*, f. *fou(l)dre* (mod. *foudre*); cf. FOUDROYANT.] *trans.* To flash or thunder forth. Also *absol.* –1594.

Foully (fau·l,li), *adv.* OE. [f. FOUL *a.* + -LY[2]; in OE. *fūllīċe.*] In a foul manner; filthily ME.; hideously ME.; abominably, cruelly, treacherously ME.; obscenely OE.; insultingly ME.; †grievously –1655.

F. murdered MISS BRADDON, slandered MACAULAY.

Foul-mouthed (fau·l,mauːðd), *a.* 1596. [f. Foul *a.* + MOUTH *sb.* + -ED[2].] Using obscene, profane, or scurrilous language. Hence **Fou·lmou:thedness.**

Foulness (fau·lnės). ME. [f. FOUL *a.* + -NESS.] The quality or condition of being foul (see FOUL *a.*). Also *concr.* Foul matter.

The f. of the linen PEPYS, of the Ways and Weather PENN. *concr.* Foulnesses without number 1790.

Foumart (fū·măɹt). ME. [Early forms *folmarde, fulmert, fullimart*, f. *fūl* FOUL (i.e. stinking) + *mart* (see MARTEN).] **1.** The polecat (*Putorius fœtidus*) ME. **2.** *attrib.*, as *f.-skin*; **f.-dog,** a dog used for hunting the f.

Found (faund), *sb.* 1540. [f. FOUND *v.*[2]] The process of founding (metal, etc.).

†*Of f.* (Sc.) = of cast metal; Cross-bows, hagbuts of f. SCOTT.

Found: pa. pple. of FIND *v.*

Found (faund), *v.*[1] Pa. t. and pple. **founded.** ME. [– (O)Fr. *fonder* :– L. *fundare*, f. *fundus* bottom, foundation.] **1.** *trans.* To lay the base or substructure of; to set *on* a firm ground or base; to base, ground. Also *refl.* and *intr.* (for *refl.*) **b.** To serve as the base of 1690. **2.** To begin the building of, be the first builder of ME. **3.** *fig.* To originate, create, initiate ME. †**b.** To endow –1612. †**4.** To fasten or attach *to*. Also *fig.* –1641.

1. It fell not, for it was founded upon a rock *Matt.* 7:25. Our understanding cannot in this body f. itself but on sensible things MILT. I f. upon the evidence of my senses 1882. **b.** A folio Common-place Founds the whole pile, of all his works the base POPE. **2.** I founded palaces, and planted bowers PRIOR. **3.** To f. a school of novelists L. STEPHEN.

Found (faund), *v.*[2] ME. [– (O)Fr. *fondre* :– L. *fundere* pour, melt.] †**1.** *trans.* To mix *together*. **2.** To melt (metal) and run it into a mould; to form (an article) by running molten metal into a mould; to cast 1562. **b.** To melt or fuse (the materials for making glass); to make (glass) by melting the materials in a furnace 1782.

2. Veins..of mineral..Whereof to f...their balls Of missive ruin MILT. Hence **Fou·nding** *vbl. sb.*

Foundation (faundēⁱ·ʃən). ME. [– (O)Fr. *fondation* – L. *fundatio*. f. *fundat-*, pa. ppl. stem of *fundare*; see FOUND *v.*[1], -ION.] **1.** The action of founding or building upon a firm substructure; the state or fact of being founded. Also *fig.* **2.** *esp.* The establishing of an institution, together with provision for its perpetual maintenance ME. †**b.** The charter of establishment or incorporation –1546. **3.** That which is founded or established by endowment; an endowed institution (e.g. a monastery, college, or hospital) 1513. **b.** The endowment ME. **4.** The solid ground, basis, or principle, on which anything (material or immaterial) is founded ME. **5.** *transf.* That upon which any structure is built up; e.g. in *Dress-making*, an underskirt over which the outer skirt is hung or draped; stiffening for a garment; etc. 1874.

1. The f. of the world *John* 17:24, of the Empire of Baghdad LANE. **2.** The f. of religious houses 1859. **3.** Corpus is a very small establishment,—twenty fellows and twenty scholars, with four exhibitioners, form the f. COLERIDGE. Phr. *On the f.*: said of the members of an endowed college, etc.

Comb.: **f. -school,** an endowed school; **-stone,** one of the stones forming the f. of a building; also, a stone laid to celebrate the founding of the edifice; also *fig.*; **f. stop,** (*a*) an organ-stop whose pipes are in unison with, or one or more octaves higher or lower than, the piano strings sounded by the corresponding keys: opp. to *mutation stop*; (*b*) any one of the fundamental flue stops, as contrasted with the reed stops, etc.

Hence **Founda·tional** *a.* of, pertaining to, or of the nature of a f.; fundamental. **Founda·tioner,** one who is on the f. of an endowed school or college. **Founda·tionless** *a.* without f., baseless.

Founded (fau·ndėd), *ppl. a.* 1605. [f. FOUND *v.*[1] + -ED[1].] Based, having a (specified) base (with qualifying adv.). †Also without adv. = 'well founded', etc.

Macb. III. iv. 22. Thy hopes are not ill founded MILT. *Sams.* 1504.

Founder (fau·ndəɹ), *sb.*[1] ME. [f. FOUND *v.*[1] + -ER[1].] **1.** 'One who raises an edifice; one who presides at the erection of a city' (J.). **2.** One who institutes for the first time; †an originator (of a custom, etc.) ME. **3.** One who founds and endows (an institution) ME. †**4.** One who maintains another –1613.

Phr. **Founders'-shares, (-parts)** *pl.*, shares issued to the so-called founders of a public company, as part of the consideration for the concession, scheme, etc., which is taken over, and not forming a part of the ordinary capital. Founders' shares are now somewhat discredited. Hence **Fou·ndress,** a female f.

Founder (fau·ndəɹ), *sb.*[2] ME. [f. FOUND *v.*[2], perh. after (O)Fr. *fondeur.*] **1.** One who casts metal, or makes articles of cast metal. Often specialized as *bell-, iron-, type-f.* **2.** One who founds glass 1853

Comb.: **founder's dust,** charcoal powder and coke and coal dust ground fine and sifted for casting purposes; **founder's sand,** a species of sand obtained from Lewisham, Kent, and elsewhere, for making foundry moulds.

Founder (fau·ndəɹ), *sb.*[3] 1577. [prob. f. *found*, pa. pple. of FIND *v.* + -ER[1].] †**1.** = FINDER. **2.** *Lead-mining.* (*Derbysh.*) The first finder of a vein; hence, a miner 1601. **3.** That portion of a lead-mine which is given to the first finder of a vein; hence, the part first worked 1653.

Founder (fau·ndəɹ), *sb.*[4] 1547. [f. FOUNDER *v.*] **1.** Inflammation of the laminar structures of a horse's foot, usually caused by overwork; a similar disease in dogs. **2.** A rheumatic affection of the muscles of the chest in horses. Called also *body-, chest-f.* 1737.

Founder (fau·ndəɹ), *v.* ME. [– OFr. *fondrer* send to the bottom, submerge, but for the most part aphetic of †*afounder* (XIV) †*enfounder* (XV) – OFr. **afondrer, esfondrer, enfondrer*, mod. *effondrer* :– Rom. **ex-, infundorare* (cf. med.L. *infunderare*), f. *ex-* EX-[1], IN-[2] + **fundor-*, taken as stem of L. *fundus* bottom.] †**1.** *trans.* To burst or smash in. ME. only. †**2.** To send to the bottom –1490. **3.** *intr.* Of earth, a building, etc.: To fall down, give way 1489. †Also *causal.* –1656. **4.** *intr.* To stumble violently, collapse; to fall lame; *occas.*, to sink or stick fast (in mire or bog). (Chiefly of a horse or its rider.) ME. **5.** *trans.* To cause to break down or go lame; *esp.* to cause to have the founder; also *fig.* 1589. **6.** *intr.* Of a vessel: To fill with water and sink 1600. Also *fig.* **7.** *trans.* To cause to fill with water and sink 1659. ¶**8.** *erron.* = F. *fondre*: To burst (into tears) 1477.

4. For which his hors for feere gan to turne, And leep asyde, and foundred as he leep CHAUCER. To f. in a quicksand 1875. **5.** O stumbling jade.. Plague f. thee 1608. **6.** *fig.* But in this point All his tricks f. SHAKS.

Founderous (fau·ndərəs), *a.* 1767. [f. FOUNDER *v.* + -OUS.] Causing or likely to cause to founder; full of ruts and holes.

Foundling (fau·ndliŋ). [ME. *fundling*, perh. alt. of contemp. and synon. †*funding* (f. *fund-*, pa. ppl. stem of FIND + -ING[3]) by substitution of -LING[1]; perh. after (M)Du. *vondeling.*] A deserted infant; a child whom there is no one to claim. Also *transf.* and *fig.*

Comb.: **f.-hospital, †-house,** an institution for the reception of foundlings; **-stone,** an erratic boulder.

Foundry (fau·ndri). 1601. [f. FOUND *v.*[2] + -RY, perh. after (O)Fr. *fonderie.*] **1.** The art or business of casting metal; *concr.* castings. **2.** An establishment in which founding of metal or glass is carried on. Also *fig.* 1645.

Comb.: **f.-iron,** iron containing sufficient carbon to make it suitable for castings; **-proof,** the final proof before stereotyping or electrotyping.

Fount[1] (faunt). Chiefly *poet.* 1593. [prob. back-formation from FOUNTAIN, after *mount, mountain.*] A spring, source, FOUNTAIN.

As cleere as Founts in Iuly SHAKS. Hence **Fou·nting** *ppl. a.* welling up like a spring. HOOD.

Fount[2] (faunt), **fo̍nt** (fǫnt). Also **found;** cf. FUND. 1683. [Alteration of FONT *sb.*[2] (which remains an alternative form) – Fr. *fonte*, f. *fondre* FOUND *v.*[2]] *Printing.* A complete set of type of a particular face and size. Also fully, *f. of letter* or *type.*

Fountain (fau·ntėn). late ME. [– (O)Fr. *fontaine* :– late L. *fontana*, subst. use (sc. *aqua* water) of *fontanus*, f. *fons, font-* spring, fountain.] **1.** A spring of water issuing from the earth; also, the head-spring or source *of* a stream or river. Now *arch.* or *poet.* 1450. **b.** *fig.* A spring, source, well. (Often in *pl.*) ME. **2.** A jet or stream of water made to rise or spout up artificially; the structure built for such a jet or stream to rise and fall in; also, an erection in a public place for a constant supply of water for drinking 1509. **b.** A metal vessel or box for aerated water (cf. *soda-f.*) 1873. **3.** *Her.* A roundel, barry wavy of six, argent and azure 1610. **4.** A reservoir or compartment for holding oil, ink, etc., in a printing press, an Argand lamp, etc. **5.** *attrib.*, as in *f. light*, etc. 1645.

1. Making Rivers to ascend to their Fountains RAY. **b.** The Crown is the f. of honour LD. BROUGHAM. **2.** Like a Fountaine, with an hundred spouts SHAKS. Modern drinking fountains 1882.

Comb.: **f.-fish,** a ctenophoran; **-pen,** a pen furnished with an ink-reservoir; **-pipe,** one which supplies a f. with water; **-tree,** the deodar; also, 'a tree in the Canary Isles which distills water from its leaves' (W.); **†-water,** spring-water.

Hence **Fou·ntained** *ppl. a.* having a f. or fountains. **Fou·ntainless** *a.* without fountains. **Fou·ntainlet,** a little f. FULLER. **Fou·ntainous** *a.* of the nature of a f. (*lit.* and *fig.*); containing springs of water.

Fou·ntain-head. 1585. [See HEAD *sb.* 9.] **1.** The head-spring or source of a stream. **2.** *fig.* The chief or prime source of anything; *esp.* of information, news, etc. 1606.

2. To trace an error to its fountain-head is to refute it BENTHAM.

Fountful (fau·ntful), *a. poet.* 1611. [f. FOUNT[1] + -FUL.] Full of founts or springs.

Four (fōᵊɹ). [OE. *fēower* = OFris. *fiūwer, fiōr*, OS. *fiwar, fiuwar, fiori*, OHG. *fior, fier* (Du., G. *vier*), ON. *fjórir*, Goth. *fidwōr* :– Gmc. **petwor-* :– IE. **quetwōr-*, whence Skr. *catwāras, catúr-*, Gr. τέσσαρες, L. *quatuor.*] The cardinal number next after *three.* Symbols 4, iv or IV.

A. as *adj.* **1.** In concord with the sb. expressed. **2.** With ellipsis of sb. ME.

1. Phr. *Within the f. seas*: within the boundaries of Great Britain. *The f. corners* (*of the earth*, etc.): the uttermost parts. **2.** Be sure to come at f. (*sc.* hours of the clock) SWIFT. A barouche and f. (*sc.* horses) 1858. Phr. †*On* (*upon*, etc.) *all f.* (*sc.* feet); now *on* ALL-FOURS.

B. as *sb.* **1.** The abstract number four ME. **2.** A set of four persons or things; e.g. a four-oared boat or a crew of four oarsmen (whence *Fours*, races for four-oared boats); (*Cricket*) a hit for which four runs are scored; etc. 1599.

2. Phr. *In fours*: arranged in groups of f.; *spec.* in *Bibliography*, the number of leaves in a sheet or gathering.

Comb.: **f.-ale,** ale sold at fourpence a quart; **-centred arch** (*Arch.*), one described from f. centres; **†-corner, -cornered** *adjs.*, square; **-course** (*Agric.*), a f. years' series of crops in rotation; **-dimensional** *a.* (*Math.*), of or belonging to a fourth dimension; **-dimensioned** *a.*, having f. dimensions; **-field course** (*Agric.*), a series of crops grown in f. fields in rotation; **f. figures,** one thousand pounds or over; **-foot (way),** the space (really 4 ft. 8½ in.) between the rails on which the train runs; **f. hundred** (*U.S.*) the exclusive social set of any place; **f. -inch** *a.*, that measures f. inches, also *ellipt.* = four inch rope; **-oar,** a boat rowed with f. oars; **-oared** *a.*, propelled by f. oars or oarsmen; **-part** *a.* (*Mus.*), composed for f. parts or voices; **-post, -posted** *adjs.*, (of a bedstead) having f. posts (to support a canopy and curtains); **-poster,** a f.-posted bedstead; **-pounder,** (*a*) a gun to carry a four-pound shot; (*b*) something weighing f. pounds, as a loaf; **-stroke** *attrib.*, (of internal combustion engines) having a cycle of four strokes, intake, compression, combustion, and exhaust; **-way(s,** the place where two roads cross or f. roads meet; **-way** *a.* (in *four-way cock* or *valve*), having communication with four pipes.

†Fourb(e, *sb.* 1654. [– Fr. *fourbe* masc. cheat, impostor, (fem. imposture), XV in thieves' cant, f. *fourber* cheat, f. *fourbe* adj., – It. *furbo* adj. astute, sb. cunning person.] **1.** A cheat, an impostor –1761. **2.** A trick, an imposture –1691.

Fourché(e (fuɹʃe), *a.* 1706. [– Fr. *fourchée* forked, f. *fourche* (pitch-)fork.] *Her.* Divided into two parts towards the extremity.

Fourchette (fuɹʃet). 1754. [– Fr. *fourchette*, dim of *fourche*; see FORK, -ETTE.] A fork; something forked or fork-like. **a.** *Anat.* The thin commissure, by which the labia majora of the pudendum unite together. **b.** *Surg.* A forked instrument formerly used to divide the frænum of the tongue when short 1854. **c.** *Ornith.* The furcula of a bird 1854.

Fourfold (fōᵉ·ɹfōᵘld). OE. [f. FOUR + -FOLD.]

A. *adj.* **1.** Consisting of four things; made up of four parts ME. **2.** Quadruple OE.

1. A f. advantage BOYLE. *Comb. f.-visaged* adj.

B. *adv.* In fourfold proportion 1535.

And he shall restore the lamb f. 2 *Sam.* 12:6.

C. *sb.* A fourfold amount ME.

I restore him foure fold *Luke* 19:8. Hence **Fou·rfold** *v.* to assess in a f. ratio. *U.S.*

Four-foot, *a. Obs.* exc. *poet.* ME. [f. FOUR *a.* + FOOT *sb.*] = next.

Fou·r-foo·ted, *a.* ME. [f. as prec. + -ED[2].] Having four feet, quadruped; pertaining to quadrupeds.

Birds and four-footed beasts BERKELEY.

‖**Fourgon** (furgoṅ). 1848. [Fr.] A baggage-wagon, a van.

Four-handed, *a.* 1774. [f. FOUR + HAND *sb.* + -ED[2].] **1.** Having four feet which resemble hands; quadrumanous. **2.** Suitable for four persons 1824.

1. The fourhanded mole TENNYSON. **2.** Four-handed cribbage 1824.

Fourierism (fūᵊ·riĕriz'm). 1841. [– Fr. *Fourierisme*, f. the name *Fourier*; see -ISM.] A system invented by the French socialist Charles *Fourier* for the reorganization of society; phalansterianism. So **Fou·rierist, Fou·rierite,** an adherent of Fourierism; also *attrib.*

Four-in-hand. 1793. **1.** A vehicle with four horses driven by one person. **2.** quasi-*adv.* With a four-in-hand 1812. **3.** *attrib.*, as *four-in-hand club*, etc. 1849; quasi-*adj.* 1799.

1. The four-in-hands of the Yorkshire squires DISRAELI. **3.** quasi-*adj.* The tobacco-smoking, four-in-hand Miss Coventry WHYTE MELVILLE.

Fou·r-leaved, *a.* 1450. [f. FOUR + LEAF + -ED[2].] Having four leaves.

Four-leaved grass: †**a.** a four-leaved variety of *Trifolium repens*; **b.** the plant *Paris quadrifolia.*

Fourling (fōᵊ·ɹliŋ). 1855. [f. FOUR *sb.* + -LING[1].] **1.** One of four children born at the same time. (Dicts.) **2.** *Min.* A twin crystal made up of four independent individuals (*Cent. Dict.*).

Fourneau. 1678. [– Fr. *fourneau* furnace, oven, stove.] *Mil.* A cavity in which powder is placed for blasting.

Four o'clock. 1756. **1.** (More fully *four o'clock flower.*) The plant *Mirabilis jalapa* or Marvel of Peru. (Its flowers open in the afternoon; hence the name.) **2.** The Australian friar-bird, *Philemon corniculatus*, so called from its cry 1848. **3.** A seed-head of the dandelion 1883. **4.** A light meal taken by workmen about four o'clock in the afternoon 1825.

Fourpence (fōᵊ·ɹpĕns). 1722. [f. FOUR *a.* + PENCE.] A sum of money or coin equal to four pennies.

Fourpence-halfpenny: app. the Irish sixpence of Elizabeth; the Irish shilling of the same period was called and valued at ninepence. The [Spanish] half real . . is called . . in New England, f. ha'penny, or simply f. BARTLETT.

Fourpenny (fōᵊ·ɹpĕni), *a.* 1481. [f. FOUR *a.* + PENNY.] **1.** That costs or is valued at fourpence; quasi-*sb.* a fourpenny piece. **2.** *F. nail*: a nail 1½ in. long, of which 4 lbs. go to the thousand (i.e. 10 nominal hundreds or 1120).

Fou·rrier. *Obs.* exc. *Hist.* 1481. [– Fr. *fourrier* quartermaster, OFr. *forrier*; see FORAYER.] **1.** = FORAYER. **2.** A quartermaster 1678.

Fourscore (fōᵊ·ɹskoᵊɹ), *a.* ME. [f. FOUR *a.* + SCORE *sb.*] Four times twenty, eighty. Now *arch.* or *rhet.*

Foursome (fōᵊ·ɹsǒm). 15 . . [f. FOUR *a.* + -SOME[2].]

A. *adj.* **1.** Four (together). Also *absol.* **2.** Performed by four persons together 1814.

2. A Scotch f. reel SCOTT.

B. *sb. Golf.* A match in which four players take part, two against two, the partners on each side playing alternately 1867.

Four-square. ME. [f. FOUR + SQUARE *a.*]

A. *adj.* Having four equal sides; square. Also *transf.* and *fig.* **b.** quasi-*adv.* In a square form or position ME.

b. That tower of strength Which stood four-square to all the winds that blew TENNYSON.

B. *sb.* A figure having four equal sides 1587.

Fourteen (fōᵊɹtī·n, fōᵊ·ɹtīn). [OE. *fēowertīene* = OFris. *fiuwertīne*, OS. *fiertein* (Du. *veertien*), OHG. *fiorzehan* (G. *vierzehn*), ON. *fjórtán*, Goth. *fidwōrtaihun*; see FOUR, -TEEN.] The cardinal number composed of ten and four. Symbols 14, xiv, or XIV.

A. as *adj.* **1.** In concord with the sb. expressed. **2.** With ellipsis of sb. 1480. **†3.** = FOURTEENTH *a.* –1553.

1. †(*A*) *f. night*: a fortnight. **2.** Shee's not fourteene SHAKS. *Comb.* **f.-gun** *a.* (a vessel) carrying f. guns.

B. as *sb.* **1.** The abstract number fourteen OE. **2.** *pl.* Candles fourteen to the pound 1883.

Hence **Fourtee·ner,** a poem of f. lines; also a line of f. syllables.

Fourteenth (foᵊɹtī·nþ, fōᵊ·ɹtīnþ). [OE. *fēowertēoþa*, ME. *fourtethe*, superseded by *fourtend* (after ON. *fjórtándi*), *-tenþe*, (from XVI) *-teenth*; see -TEEN, -TH[2].] The ordinal numeral belonging to the cardinal fourteen.

A. *adj.* in concord with sb. expressed; also *ellipt.*

F.-part: one of 14 equal parts of any whole.

B. *sb.* A fourteenth part. **b.** *Mus.* The octave or replicate of the seventh 1597.

Hence **Fourteenthly** *adv.* in the f. place.

Fourth (fōᵊɹþ). [OE. *fēo(we)rþa* = OS. *fiorðo* (Du. *vierde*), OHG. *fiordo* (G. *vierte*), ON. *fjórði* :– CGmc. **fi(ð)worþon* :– IE. **qweturto-, -twrto*, whence also L. *quartus*, Gr. τέταρτος, Skr. *caturthás.*] The ordinal numeral belonging to the cardinal four.

A. *adj.* **1.** In concord with sb. expressed. **2.** With ellipsis of sb.; *esp.* of 'day' ME.

1. *F. estate*: see ESTATE *sb.* **2.** *The f.* (*of July*) U.S., the anniversary of the Declaration of Independence; also *attrib.* Also quasi-*sb.* in *pl.*

Phr. *F. part*, †*deal*: one of four equal parts of any whole.

B. *sb.* **1.** The fraction indicated by a unit in the fourth place in any system of notation having a constant modulus 1594. **2.** = *F. part.* 1741. **3.** *Mus.* A tone four diatonic degrees above or below any given tone; the interval between any tone and a tone four degrees distant from it; the harmonic combination of two such tones 1597. **4.** *pl.* Articles of the fourth degree in quality 1832.

Hence **Fou·rthly** *adv.* in the f. place, †for the f. time.

Fou·r-wheeled, *a.* 1622. [f. FOUR *a.* + WHEEL *sb.* + -ED[2].] Having or running upon four wheels.

Four-whee·ler. 1846. [f. as prec. + -ER[1].] A vehicle with four wheels; *esp.* a four-wheeled hackney carriage.

Foutre, fouter (fū·tər). 1597. [– (O)Fr. *foutre* :– L. *futuere* (the inf. used subst.).] A term of contempt.

A footra [Q. footre] for the World, and Worldlings base SHAKS. A cowardly *foutre* MARRYAT.

Fovea (fōu·vĭă). 1849. [– L. *fovea* small pit.] *Anat., Zool., Bot.* A small depression or pit; *esp.* a depression of the retina of the eye. Hence **Fo·veal** *a.* of or pertaining to or situated in a f. (Dicts.) **Fo·veate, Fo·veated** *adjs.* marked with foveæ, pitted.

‖**Foveola** (fovī·ŏlă). 1849. [L., dim. of FOVEA.] A small fovea. Hence **Fo·veolate, Fo·veolated** *adjs.* marked with small foveæ; pitted. var. **Fo·veole.**

Fovilla (fovi·lă). 1793. [mod.L., used by Linnæus in 1766; perh. an alteration of *favilla.*] *Bot.* The substance contained in the pollen-cells.

Fowage, var. of FEUAGE.

Fowl (faul), *sb.* [OE. *fugol* = OFris. *fugel*, OS. *fugal*, OHG. *fogal* (Du. G., *vogel*), ON. *fugl*, Goth. *fugls* :– Gmc. **foȝlaz*, **fuȝlaz*, f. **fluȝ-* **fleuȝ-* FLY *v.*[1]] **1.** Any feathered vertebrate animal; = BIRD 2. Now *rare* exc. *collect.* †**2.** Winged creatures. Also *collect.* in pl. sense. –1648. **3.** A barn-door fowl, a domestic cock or hen; a bird of the genus *Gallus*. Often specialized as *barn-door-*, *game-* etc. *f.* In U.S. applied also to a domestic duck or turkey. (The prevailing sense.) 1580. **4.** The flesh of birds used for food. Now only in *fish, flesh, fowl*, etc. In narrower sense: The flesh of the domestic fowl. 1673.

1. Behold the fowls of the air..your heavenly Father feedeth them *Matt.* 6:26. *collect.* All the f. of heaven were flocking to the feast KINGSLEY. **2.** Battes, or Rear-mice and other fowle GAGE.

Comb.: **f.-cholera** = *chicken-cholera* (see CHOLERA); **-foot,** the plant *Ornithopus perpusillus*; **-grass, -meadow-grass,** *Poa trivialis*; **-run,** a place where fowls may run.

Fowl (faul), *v.* [OE. *fug(e)lian*, f. *fugol* (prec.).] *intr.* To catch, hunt, shoot, or snare wildfowl. †**b.** quasi-*trans.* To hunt over, beat (a bush). B. JONS.

Such persons as may..lawfully hunt, fish, or f. BLACKSTONE.

Fowler (fau·lər). [OE. *fug(e)lere*, f. as prec. + -ER[1].] **1.** One who hunts wild birds, whether for sport or food, *esp.* with nets. Now *rare.* †**2.** A kind of light cannon, *esp.* for use on board ship –1642.

Fowlerite (fau·lĕrəit). 1832. [Named after Dr. S. *Fowler*; see -ITE[1] 2 b.] *Min.* A flesh-red variety of rhodonite containing zinc.

Fow·ling-piece. 1596. [f. FOWL *v.* + PIECE *sb.* II. 3.] **1.** A light gun for shooting wild fowl. **2.** A picture of game 1888.

Fox (fǫks), *sb.* [OE. *fox* = OS. *vuhs* (Du. *vos*), OHG. *fuhs* (G. *fuchs*) :– WGmc. **fuxs.*] **I. 1.** An animal of the genus *Vulpes*, having an elongated pointed muzzle and long bushy tail. Usually *V. vulgaris*, preserved in England and elsewhere as a beast of the chase. **2.** *fig.* A crafty man OE. **3.** The fur of the fox 1501. **4.** The constellation *Vulpecula* 1868. **5.** Some beast or fish likened to a fox, *esp.* the gemmeous dragonet (*Callionymus lyra*), called also *f.-fish. Flying-fox, Sea-fox*: see those words. 1611.

1. The wily F. remain'd A subtle pilf'ring Foe SOMERVILLE. **2.** Go ye, and tell that f. [Herod], Behold, I cast out devils *Luke* 13:32. **3.** Furd with Foxe and Lamb-skins too *Meas. for M.* III. ii. 9.

II. Obscure senses. †**1.** A kind of sword; perhaps so called from the figure of a wolf, on certain sword-blades, being mistaken for a fox –1821. **2.** *Naut.* A sort of strand, formed by twisting several rope-yarns together, and used as a seizing, or for mats, etc. 1769. **3.** A wedge driven into a split in the end of a bolt called a *fox-bolt* 1874. **4.** *In U.S. Colleges*: A freshman. Cf. Ger. *fuchs.* 1839.

1. Put up your f., and let us be jogging SCOTT.

attrib. and *Comb.* **1.** General: as *f.-bitch, -burrow, -cover, -cub, -earth, -gin, trap*, etc.

2. Special: **f.-beagle,** a beagle used for f.-hunting; **-bolt** (see sense II. 3); **-brush,** the tail of a f.; **-chase,** = FOX-HUNT; **-colour,** a reddish-yellow colour, whence *f.-coloured* adj.; **-evil,** a disease in which the hair falls off, alopecia; **-hound,** a superior variety of hound trained and used for f.-hunting; **-key,** 'a splitcotter with a thin wedge of steel driven into the end to prevent its working back'; **-sleep,** a pretended sleep; **-terrier,** one of a breed of short-haired terriers, used for unearthing foxes, but kept chiefly as pets; **-trot,** a pace with short steps, as in changing from trotting to walking; also, an American dance; also as vb.; **-wedge,** a long wedge driven between two other wedges with their thick ends placed in the opposite direction; †**-whelp,** a cub of the f. (used also as a term of contempt); **-wood,** decayed wood, *esp.* such as emits a phosphorescent light (U.S.)

b. in names of animals, etc., more or less resembling the f.; **f.-bat** = FLYING-FOX; **-fish,** see FOX I. 5; **-lynx,** a variety of lynx; **-moth,** a greyish-brown European bombycid moth (*Lasiocampa rubi*); **-shark,** the sea-fox (*Alopias vulpes*); **-snake,** a large harmless snake of the United States (*Coluber vulpinus*); **-sparrow,** a N. Amer. sparrow (*Passerella iliaca*); **-squirrel,** a N. Amer. squirrel (*Sciurus cinereus, S. niger*, etc.). **c.** in plant names: **f.-bane,** *Aconitum vulparia*; **-berry** = BEARBERRY; **-grape,** a U.S. name for several species of wild grapes.

d. in names of games in which one of the players acts as a f.: **f. and geese,** a game played on a board with pegs, draughtsmen, or the like; **f. and hounds,** a boys' game in which the 'hounds' chase the 'fox'; †**f. in** or **to the** or **thy hole,** a boys' game in which they lift up one leg and hop on the other.

Fox (fǫks), *v.* 1567. [f. prec. sb.] **1.** †*trans.* To play the fox for; *intr.* to play the fox, sham. Now *dial.* and *slang.* 1602. **2.** *trans.* To intoxicate 1611. †Also *transf.* and *fig.* †**3.** *trans.* To pierce with a fox (see FOX *sb.* II. 1) –1589. **4.** *trans.* To discolour (the leaves of a book) 1848. **5.** *intr.* Of beer: To turn sour in fermenting; also *trans.* (causatively) 1744. **6.** To repair (boots or shoes) by renewing the upper leather 1796. **7.** *intr.* To hunt the fox. *U.S.* 1887.

2. The last of whom I did almost f. with Margate ale PEPYS. Hence **Foxed** *ppl. a.* intoxicated; repaired by foxing; discoloured by decay; stained with brownish-yellow spots; etc.

Foxery (fǫ·kseri). ME. [f. FOX *sb.* + -ERY.] The character or behaviour of a fox, wiliness, cunning.

Fox-fire. Now only *U.S.* 1483. The phosphorescent light emitted by decayed timber.

Fox-fu·r. 1599. The fur of the fox; a gown trimmed with fox-fur. Hence **Fo·x-furred** *a.* trimmed with fox-fur; wearing fox-fur, or a fox-furred gown.

Fox-glove (fǫ·ks,glɒv). [OE. *foxesglōfa*, f. gen. sing. of *fox*; the Norw. *revebjelle* 'fox-bell' shows similar unexpl. assoc. with the animal.] **1.** The popular name of *Digitalis purpurea*, a common ornamental flowering plant. **b.** Used in medicine: see DIGITALIS. 1801. **2.** Applied to plants of other genera; e.g. formerly to the Mullein 1587. **3.** *attrib.* 1811.

1. Fox-glove and nightshade, side by side, Emblems of punishment and pride SCOTT.

Fo·x-hunt. 1816. The chase of a fox with hounds. So **Fo·x-hunting** *vbl. sb.* the sport of hunting the fox. **Fo·x-hunter, -huntsman,** etc.

†**Fo·xish,** *a.* ME. [See -ISH[1].] Fox-like; also *fig.* –1699.

Foxite (fǫ·kseit). 1782. [See -ITE[1].] A political follower of Charles James Fox. Also *attrib.*

Fox-like (fǫ·ksləik), *a.* 1577. [f. FOX *sb.* + LIKE *a.*] Like a fox; esp. crafty.

†**Fo·xly.** ME. [f. as prec. + -LY[1,2].]
A. *adj.* Crafty, cunning –1594.
B. *adv.* Craftily.

Foxship (fǫ·ks,ʃip). [See -SHIP.] The character or qualities of a fox. *Cor.* IV. ii. 18.

Fo·xtail. ME. [f. FOX *sb.* + TAIL *sb.*[1]] **1.** The tail of a fox, a fox's brush. Formerly a jester's badge. **2. a.** One of various species of grass with soft brush-like spikes of flowers, esp. *Alopecurus pratensis* 1552. **b.** A club-moss (*Lycopodium clavatum*) 1866. **3.** *Metall.* The cinder obtained in the last stage of the charcoal-finery process 1873.

Comb.: **f.-saw,** a dovetail saw; **-wedging,** a method of fixing a tenon in a mortise by splitting the end of the tenon and inserting a projecting wedge, then entering the tenon into the mortise and driving it home.

Foxy (fǫ·ksi), *a.* 1528. [f. FOX *sb.* + -Y[1].] **1.** Fox-like; crafty. **2.** Fox-coloured, reddish brown or yellow 1850; in *Painting*, over-hot in colouring 1783. **3.** Used to denote various defects of colour and quality resulting from age, damp, improper treatment, etc. 1805. **4.** Of beer, wine, etc.: Turned sour, not properly fermented 1847. **5.** Of grapes: Having the coarse flavour of the fox-grape (Webster).

1. Modred's narrow f. face TENNYSON. **2.** In some of the England series there is a violent f. tone, very hot and oppressive THORNBURY *Turner* II. 342. Hence **Fo·xiness.**

†**Foy,** *sb.*[1] 1590. [– (O)Fr. *foi* see FAY *sb.*[1]]; Faith, allegiance, fealty. Also as an exclam. –1694.

Foy (foi), *sb.*[2] Now *dial.* 1496. [– Du *fooi* tip, gratuity, MDu. *foye, voye* – Fr. *voie* way, journey.] A parting entertainment, present, etc., given by or to one setting out on a journey.

He did at the Dog give me, and some other friends of his, his f., he being to set sail to-day PEPYS.

‖**Foyer** (fwaye). 1859. [Fr. = hearth, home :– Gallo-Rom. **focarium*, f. L. *focus* fire.] **1.** = FOCUS 4. 1878. **2.** Orig., the green-room in French theatres; now usually, a large room in a theatre, etc., to which the audience may retire during the intervals.

Foysen, -so(u)n, -zon, etc., obs. ff. FOISON.

Fozy (fōu·zi), *a.* *Sc.* and *dial.* 1821. [Cf. Du. *voos* spongy; also Norw. *fos* spongy, LG. *fussig* porous, spongy.] Spongy, loose-textured; also of flesh = FOGGY. Also *fig.* 'fat-witted'. Hence **Fo·ziness.**

Frab (fræb), *v.* *dial.* 1848. [Of symbolic origin; cf. CRAB *v.*[2]] *trans.* To harass, worry.

Fracas (fraka; in U.S. frēi·kăs). 1727. [– Fr. *fracas*, f. *fracasser* – It. *fracassare* make an uproar.] A disturbance, uproar, brawl.

Frache. ? *Obs.* 1662. [Of unkn. origin.] A metal tray for holding glass-ware in the annealing process.

†**Fra·cid,** *a.* 1655. [– L. *fracidus* soft, mellow (of olives); later over-ripe (ὑπέρωρος Gloss. Philox.), f. *frax*, pl. *fraces* lees of oil; see -ID[1].] Rotten from over-ripeness.

Fra·cted, *ppl. a.* 1547. [f. L. *fract-* (see next) + -ED[1].] *Her.* Having a part displaced as if broken 1828.

Fraction (fræ·kʃən), *sb.* ME. [– (O)Fr. *fraction* – Chr.L. *fractio* breaking (as of bread), f. *fract-*, pa. ppl. stem of L. *frangere* break; see -ION.] **1.** The action of breaking 1504. †**2.** The result of breaking; the state of being broken; a broken place, breach, fissure, rupture; *spec.* in *Surg.* a fracture –1798. †**3.** Discord, dissension; a rupture; brawling –1721. **4.** Something broken off; a portion; a fragment 1606. **5.** *Arith.* and *Alg.* One or more aliquot parts of a unit or whole number; an expression for a definite portion of a unit or magnitude ME.

1. Though it may be said..that he suffreth f. or breaking in the Sacrament when it is broken..yet [etc.] 1602. **4.** Crumbling into Fractions and Factions 1657. **5.** *Common* or *vulgar fractions*: those in which the numerator and denominator are represented by numbers placed the one above, the other below, a horizontal line. *Complex, compound, continued, decimal, proper, improper fractions*: see those words. Hence **Fra·ction** *v.* to break into fractions CARLYLE.

Fractional (fræ·kʃənăl), *a.* 1675. [f. prec. + -AL[1].] Of, pertaining to, or dealing with a fraction or fractions; comprising or constituting a fraction; of the nature of a fraction. Hence, Incomplete, partial, insignificant.

F. currency: a small coin, or paper notes, in circulation, of less value than the monetary unit (Webster). *F. distillation*: see DISTILLATION. Hence **Fra·ctionally** *adv.*

Fractionary (fræ·kʃənări), *a.* 1674. [f. as prec., + -ARY[1].] **a.** = prec. **b.** Dealing with or carried on by fractions or fragments 1840. **c.** Tending to divide into fractions 1867.

Fractionate (fræ·kʃəne[i]t), *v.* 1867. [f. as prec. + -ATE[3].] *trans.* To separate (a mixture) by distillation or otherwise into portions of differing properties. Hence **Fractiona·tion,** the action of fractionating.

Fractionize (fræ·kʃənəiz), *v.* 1675. [f. as prec. + -IZE.] *trans.* (and *absol.*) To break up into fractions.

Fractious (fræ·kʃəs), *a.* 1725. [f. FRACTION (sense 3) + -OUS, prob. after *faction, factious.*]

Refractory, unruly; now chiefly, cross, fretful; *esp.* of children.

A terribly peevish f. fellow W. IRVING. F. cows 1880. Hence **Fra·ctious-ly** *adv.*, **-ness.**

Fracture (fræ·ktiŭɹ), *sb.* 1525. [– (O)Fr. *fracture* or L. *fractura*, f. *fract-*; see FRACTION, -URE.] **1.** The action of breaking or fact of being broken; breakage; *spec.* in *Surg.* the breaking of a bone, etc. 1541. **2.** The result of breaking; a crack, division, split; †a *splinter* 1641. **3.** The appearance of the fresh surface in a mineral, when broken irregularly by the blow of a hammer 1794. **4.** *Phonology.* Diphthongization of a vowel before a consonant group 1891.

Fracture (fræ·ktiŭɹ), *v.* 1612. [f. prec. sb.] **1.** *trans.* To cause a fracture in, *esp.* a bone, etc.; to break; to crack. **2.** *intr.* for *refl.* To suffer fracture; to break 18..

1. To f. a rib 1803, parts of a machine 1858.

‖**Frænulum** (frī·niŭlŏm). 1706. [mod.L., dim. of FRÆNUM; see -ULE.] *Anat.* A small frænum; a frænum.

‖**Frænum, frenum** (frī·nŏm). *Pl.* **-na.** 1741. [L.; = 'a bridle'.] **1.** *Anat.* A small ligament or membranous fold which restrains the motion of the organ to which it is attached. **2.** One of two minute folds of skin, in some cirripedes, which serve, through the means of a sticky solution, to retain the eggs until they are hatched. DARWIN.

Fragile (fræ·dʒil), *a.* 1513. [– (O)Fr. *fragile* or L. *fragilis*, f. **frag-*, base of *frangere* break; see -ILE.] **1.** Liable to break or be broken; brittle; easily destroyed. Also *fig.* Of persons, etc. = FRAIL. 1607. †**2.** Liable to err or fall into sin; frail –1548.

1. Of Bodies, some are F.; and some are Tough, but not F. BACON. A single f. life FROUDE. Hence **Fra·gile-ly** *adv.*, **-ness.**

Fragility (frădʒi·lĭti). ME. [– (O)Fr. *fragilité* or L. *fragilitas*, f. *fragilis*; see prec., -ITY.] **1.** The quality of being fragile or easily broken; hence, weakness, delicacy 1474. Also *fig.* †**2.** Moral weakness, folly –1624.

1. An appearance of delicacy, and even of f., is almost essential to it [beauty] BURKE. *fig.* The f. of life, of beauty JOHNSON, of popular government MAINE. **2.** The fragylyte [of Adam and Eue] LD. BERNERS.

Fragment (fræ·gmĕnt). 1531. [– Fr. *fragment* or L. *fragmentum*, f. **frag-*, base of *frangere* break; see -MENT.] **1.** A piece broken off; a (comparatively) small portion of anything 1583. **2.** *transf.* and *fig.* A detached, isolated, or incomplete part, e.g. of a writing or composition 1531.

1. *John* 6:13. Fragments of old walles LITHGOW. **2.** Howe fragmentes or partes of a Globe are measured 1571. He conuerses much in fragments and *Desunt multa's* EARLE. The 'New Atlantis' is but a f. JOWETT.

Hence **Fragme·ntal, fra·gmental** *a.* fragmentary; *Geol.* consisting of the debris of older rocks, or of the aggregated remains of plants or animals. **Fra·gmentally** *adv.*

Fragmentary (fræ·gmĕntări), *a.* 1611. [f. prec. + -ARY[1].] Of the nature of, or composed of, fragments; not complete or entire; disconnected; in *Geol.* composed of fragments of previously-existing rocks, etc. Hence **Fra·gmentarily** *adv.* **Fra·gmentariness.** var. **Fragmenti·tious** *a. rare.*

Fragmentation (frægmĕntēⁱ·ʃən). 1881. [f. as prec. + -ATION.] A breaking or separation into fragments; in *Biol.* separation into parts which form new individuals.

Fragmented (fræ·gmĕntĕd), *pa. pple.* and *ppl. a.* 1830. [f. FRAGMENT + -ED[2].] Broken into fragments, made fragmentary.

Fragmentist (fræ·gmĕntist). 1874. [f. as prec. + -IST.] A writer of fragments or of works which survive only in fragments. So **Fra·gmentize** *v.* to break into fragments.

†**Fragor.** *rare.* 1605. [– L. *fragor*, f. **frag-*, base of *frangere* break; see -OR 1.] A loud harsh noise, a crash, a din –1702.

Fragrance (frēⁱ·grăns). 1667. [– (O)Fr. *fragrance* or L. *fragrantia*; see FRAGRANT, -ANCE.] Sweetness of smell; sweet or pleasing scent.

Eve separate he spies, Veiled in a cloud of f. MILT.

Fragrancy (frēⁱ·grănsi). Now *rare.* 1578. [f. L. *fragrantia*; see next, -ANCY.] The quality of being FRAGRANT. Also with *pl.*

The goblet crown'd Breath'd aromatic fragrancies around POPE.

Fragrant (frēⁱ·grănt), *a.* 1500. [– Fr. *fragrant* or *fragrant-*, pres. ppl. stem of L. *fragrare* smell sweet; see -ANT.] Emitting a pleasant odour; sweet-smelling.

F. the fertil earth After soft showers MILT. *P. L.* IV. 645. Hence **Fra·grant-ly** *adv.*, †**-ness.**

Frail (frēⁱl), *sb.* [ME. *fraiel* – OFr. *fraiel*, of unkn. origin. Cf. AL. *fraellus, -a, -um.*] **1.** A basket made of rushes, used for packing figs, raisins, etc.; the quantity (30 to 75 lb.) contained in this. **2.** 'A rush for weaving baskets' (J.) 1755.

Frail (frēⁱl), *a.* [ME. *frele, freel* – OFr. *fraile, frele* (mod. *frêle*) :– L. *fragilis* FRAGILE.] **1.** Liable to break or be broken; easily destroyed. Of immaterial things: Subject to casualties, transient. **2.** Weak, easily overcome ME. **3.** Morally weak; unable to resist temptation; *occas.*, that lives unchastely ME. †**4.** Tender. SPENSER.

1. In that f. bark the lovers sit 1812. A profounder but a frailer bliss J. MARTINEAU. **2.** That I may know how fraile I am *Ps.* 39:4. **3.** Our most fraile affections HOOKER. Most likely a child of the f. Abbess of Leominster FREEMAN. Hence **Frai·lly** *adv.* **Frai·lness.**

Frailty (frēⁱ·lti). ME. [– OFr. *fraileté* – L. *fragilitas*, f. *fragilis* FRAGILE; see -ITY.] **1.** Liability to be crushed or to decay; perishableness, weakness; an instance of this; †also, a flaw. Now *rare.* **2.** Moral weakness; instability of mind; liability to err or yield to temptation; also, a weakness ME.

1. The works of man inherit..Their author's f., and return to dust COWPER. **2.** No farther seek..to..draw his frailties from their dread abode GRAY.

†‖**Fraischeur.** *rare.* 1599. [Fr. (now *fraîcheur*), f. *frais, fraische* (now *fraîche*) fresh.] Freshness. –1661.

Fraise (frēⁱz), *sb.*[1] 1775. [– Fr. *fraise*, transf. use of *fraise* mesentery of a calf.] **1.** A ruff 1801. **2.** *Fortif.* A palisade, made horizontal or slightly inclining to the horizon, placed for defence round a work near the berm.

Fraise (frēⁱz), *sb.*[2] 1874. [– Fr. *fraise*, f. *fraiser*, enlarge a circular hole.] A tool for enlarging a circular hole; also, in *Watch-making*, for cutting teeth in a wheel.

Fraise (frēⁱz), *v.* 1706. [– Fr. *fraiser* (see FRAISE *sb.*[1]).] *trans.* To fence or defend with or as with a fraise.

Fraken(e, -yn(e, var. ff. FRECKEN.

Framable, frameable (frēⁱ·măb'l), *a.* 1577. [f. FRAME *v.* + -ABLE.] Capable of being framed; †conformable.

Frambœsia (fræmbī·ziă). 1803. [mod. L., f. (O)Fr. *framboise* raspberry; see next, -IA[1].] *Path.* The yaws. Hence **Frambœ·sioid** *a.* like f.

†**Framboise.** 1578. [– (O)Fr. *framboise* – Gallo-Rom. **frambosia* conflation of *fraga ambrosia* 'ambrosian strawberry'.] The raspberry (*Rubus Idæus*).

Frame (frēⁱm), *sb.* ME. [f. FRAME vb.] †**I.** Advantage, benefit. ME. only.

II. †**1.** The action of framing, fashioning, or constructing; a contrivance –1645. **2.** The manner or method of framing; construction, structure; constitution, nature 1590. **3.** An established order, plan, scheme, system, *esp.* of government 1599. †**b.** A form of words; a formula; a type of syllogism –1739. †**4.** Adapted or adjusted condition; order, regularity, shape –1810. **5.** Mental or emotional disposition or state (more explicitly *f. of mind, soul,* etc.) 1665. **6.** *F.-up* (cf. FRAME *v.* 8 e) 1907.

1. John the bastard, Whose spirits toile in f. of villanies SHAKS. **2.** We have in our inward f. various affections BUTLER. **3.** But let the f. of things disioynt, Both the worlds suffer SHAKS. **4.** Put your discourse into some f. *Haml.* III. ii. 321. **5.** I am a Fellow of a very odd F. of mind STEELE. In this thankful f. I continued DE FOE.

III. 1. A structure, fabric, or engine constructed of parts fitted together. Now *obs.* or *arch.* exc. as applied to the heaven, earth, etc., regarded as a structure, or to the animal, *esp.* the human body, with ref. to its build, etc. ME. **2.** A structure of timber, joists, etc. forming the skeleton of a building ME.; a building; in later use, one composed chiefly or entirely of wood (*Obs.* exc. *U.S.*) ME. **3.** A skeleton structure or support; e.g. the ribs or stretchers for an umbrella or parasol; (*Printing*) a desk containing type cases for the use of a compositor, or the stand supporting them; (*Naut.*) the bends of timbers, or the corresponding parts of an ironclad, constituting the shape of the ship's body; etc. 1536. **4.** That in which something, *esp.* a picture, pane of glass, etc., is set or let in, as in a border or case 1600. **5.** Hence applied to utensils of which the frame or border is an important part; as: **a.** (*Founding*) a kind of ledge enclosing a board, which being filled with sand, serves as a mould for castings 1724. **b.** (*Embroidery* and *Weaving*) †a loom; now short for *lace-, stocking-f.*, etc. 1523. **c.** (*Horticulture*) a glazed structure for protecting seeds and young plants from frost, etc. 1664.

1. The starry f. 1594. This goodly f. the Earth. SHAKS. **4.** *fig.* A grass-plat..set in the heavy f. of the forest C. BRONTE.

Comb. (sense III. 2) as *f. building, cottage, house*; **f.-breaker,** one of those who resisted with violence the introduction of frames for weaving stockings, etc.; **-bridge,** a bridge constructed of pieces of timber framed together; **-dam,** a dam formed of balks of fir wood, placed endwise against the pressure; **-level,** a mason's level; **-saw,** a saw stretched in a f. to make it rigid; **-stud** (see STUD *sb.*[1] I. 1); **-tubbing,** solid wood tubbing.

Frame (frēⁱm), *v.* [OE. *framian* be of service, make progress, f. *fram* forward (see FROM); cf. ON. *frama* further, advance. The related ON. *fremja* (= OE. *fremman, fremian*) further, advance, perform, prob. influenced the sense-development.] †**1.** *intr.* To profit, be of service –ME. †**2.** To gain ground; to get on (*with*); to succeed –1669. †**3.** To make ready for use; also, to furnish *with*. ME. only. †**4.** To prepare (timber) for use in building; to perform the carpenter's work for (a building) ME. **5.** To shape; to give shape, expression, or direction to 1543. **b.** *refl.* and *absol.* To shape one's course; to resort. *Obs.* exc. *dial.* = 'go'. 1576. **c.** *intr.* for *refl.*, now chiefly *dial.* 1602. **6.** *trans.* To adapt, adjust, fit *to* or *into* 1550. †Also *intr.* for *refl.* To conform, fit –1642. **7.** *trans.* To make, construct. Now always implying the combination and fitting together of parts, and adaption to a design. 1555. **8. a.** To contrive (a plot, etc.); to fabricate; to compose; to put into words 1514. **b.** To articulate 1609. **c.** To form in the mind 1597. †**d.** To bring to pass –1597. **e.** *To f. up* (orig. *U.S. slang*): to pre-arrange (an event) with sinister intent; to fake the result of (a race, etc.); also (*to f.*), to concoct a false charge against 1910. **9.** [f. the sb.] To enclose in or as in a frame; to serve as a frame for 1705.

2. It framed not according to expectation 1669. **5.** The Iron..is softned and framed 1678. Why I can..f. my Face to all occasions SHAKS. God knows how, after that, my life was framed CARY. **b.** The beauty of this sinful dame Made many princes thither f. SHAKS. **6.** Unto this he frames his song WORDSW. **7.** The sovran Planter, when he fram'd All things to mans delightful use MILT. The fieldfare framed her lowly nest SCOTT. **8. a.** This was a Story framed long after BP. BURNET. **d.** Which Heauen so f. SHAKS.

Fra·me-house. 1817. [f. FRAME *sb.* and *v.* + HOUSE.] A house constructed with a wooden framework covered with boards.

Framer (frēⁱ·məɹ). 1561. [f. FRAME *v.* + -ER[1].] One who frames.

The f. of the government LOCKE, of an objection 1741, of a picture 1870.

Fra·mework. 1644. [f. FRAME *sb.* + WORK *sb.*] **1.** A structure composed of parts framed together; a frame or skeleton. Also *transf.* and *fig.* **2.** (As two words or hyphened.) Work done in or with a frame 1819.

1. The f. of vertebrate animals 1885. *fig.* The outward f. of law and government FREEMAN.

Framing (frēⁱ·miŋ), *vbl. sb.* ME. [f. FRAME *v.* + -ING[1].] **1.** The action, method, or process of constructing, making, or shaping anything. **2.** *concr.* Framed work; a frame or set or system of frames 1703.

Comb. **f.-chisel**, a heavy chisel for making mortises.

Fra·mpold, *a.* Also **frample,** etc. *Obs.* exc. *dial.* 1598. [Of unkn. origin.] **1.** Sour-tempered, disagreeable, peevish. **2.** Of a horse: Fiery, mettlesome 1603.

1. She leads a very f. life with him *Merry W.* II. ii. 94. **2.** Good phrampell iades MIDDLETON & DEKKER.

Franc (fræŋk). ME. [– (O)Fr. *franc*, derived from the legend *Francorum rex* king of the Franks, on gold coins first struck in the reign of Jean le Bon (1350–64).] The name of a French coin or money of account. **a.** A gold coin, in the 14th c., weighing about 60 grs. **b.** A silver coin, first struck in 1575, valued in the 18th c. at 9*d.* or 10*d.* **c.** Since 1795, a silver coin, the monetary unit of the decimal system, worth nearly 10*d.*

‖**Franc-archer** (frańkarʃe). Pl. **franc(s-)-archers.** 1675. [Fr.; *franc* free + *archer* archer.] *Fr. Hist.* One of a body of archers established by Charles VII, and exempted from taxes in consideration of their service.

Franchise (fra·ntʃiz, -tʃəiz), *sb.* ME. [– (O)Fr. *franchise*, f. *franc*, fem. *franche* free, FRANK *a.*[2] + *-ise*, repr. L. *-itia* -ESS[2].] **I.** †**1.** Freedom; exemption from servitude or subjection –1648. **2. a.** A legal immunity or exemption from a particular burden, or from the jurisdiction of a particular tribunal, granted to an individual, a corporation, etc. In early use also *collect.* or in generalized sense: The immunities, etc., belonging to a municipality, etc. ME. **b.** More widely: A privilege granted by the sovereign power to any person or body of persons. In England now chiefly *Hist.*; in U.S. applied *esp.* to the powers conferred on a company for some purpose of public utility. ME. †**3.** Freedom from arrest, secured to fugitives in certain privileged places; right of asylum or sanctuary. Hence *concr.* an asylum, sanctuary. –1601. **4.** The freedom of a body corporate or politic; citizenship 1579. †**5.** The district over which a particular privilege extends –1774. **6.** The right of voting at public elections, *esp.* for members of the legislative body. (The prevailing sense.) 1790. **b.** In recent use: One of the various qualifications for the elective franchise. *Fancy f.*: see FANCY. 1884.

2. a. All franchises and liberties of the bisshopperricks..deryvid from the crowne 1559. **b.** The f. of waife and stray COKE. Fairs, Markets, and other franchises 16.. The form which corruption takes in the populous cities [of the U.S.] is the sale of 'franchises' (especially monopolies in the use of public thoroughfares) BRYCE. **5.** Phr. †*To go* or *ride the franchises*: to beat the bounds.

†**II. 1.** Nobility of mind; liberality, magnanimity –1658. **2.** Freedom or licence of speech or manners 1567.

†**Fra·nchise,** *v.* ME. [– *franchiss-*, lengthened stem of (O)Fr. *franchir*, f. *franc*, fem. *franche* free; see FRANK *a.*[2], and cf. AFFRANCHISE, ENFRANCHISE.] = ENFRANCHISE *v.* Const. *from, of.* –1793. Hence †**Fra·nchisement** = ENFRANCHISEMENT.

Francic (fræ·nsik), *a.* ?*Obs.* 1698. [– med.L. *Francicus*, f. *Francus* FRANK *sb.*[1]] = FRANKISH.

Francisc (fransi·sk). Also **-esque, -isque.** 1801. [– med.L. *francisca*, or its adopted form in Fr.] A kind of battle-axe used by the Franks.

Franciscan (fransi·skăn). 1592. [– Fr. *franciscain* – mod.L. *Franciscanus*, f. *Franciscus* Francis; see -AN.]

A. *adj.* Of or belonging to the order of St. Francis; pertaining to the Franciscans.

The long F. controversy about poverty PUSEY.

B. *sb.* A friar of the order founded by St. Francis of Assisi in 1209.

Francize (fra·nsəiz), *v.* 1661. [– Fr. *franciser*, f. *français* French.] *trans.* To make French. Hence **Franciza·tion,** the making French; the status thus conferred.

Franco- (fræ·ŋko), comb. f. med.L. *Francus* FRANK *sb.*[1], meaning 'Frankish or French and..'; chiefly in combs., as *F.-American*, etc.; see -O-.

Francolin (fræ·ŋkŏlin). 1653. [– Fr. *francolin* – It. *francolino*, of unkn. origin.] A bird of the genus *Francolinus* (subfamily *Perdicinæ* or Partridges), somewhat resembling a pheasant. Also *f. partridge.*

Francolite (fræ·ŋkŏləit). 1850. [f. *Franco* + -LITE.] *Min.* A variety of apatite found at Wheal *Franco* in Devonshire in stalactitic masses.

Francophil(e (fræ·ŋkŏfil). 1889. [f. FRANCO- + -PHIL. A newspaper word.]

A. *adj.* Characterized by partiality to the French.

B. *sb.* One who is so affected.

‖**Franc-tireur** (frańtirōr). 1870. [Fr., i.e. *franc* free (see FRANK *a.*[2]) + *tireur* shooter, f. *tirer* shoot, of unkn. origin.] One of a corps of light infantry, originating in the wars of the French Revolution, and having an organization distinct from that of the regular army.

Frangent (fræ·ndʒĕnt), *a.* [– *frangent-*, pres. ppl. stem of L. *frangere* break; see -ENT.] Causing fractures. H. WALPOLE.

Frangible (fræ·ndʒib'l), *a.* 1440. [– OFr. *frangible* or med.L. *frangibilis*, f. *frangere* break; see -IBLE.] Capable of being broken. Hence **Frangibi·lity,** f. quality.

Frangipane (fræ·ndʒipe[i]n). 1676. [– Fr. *frangipane*, f. *Frangipani*, name of an Italian marquis who invented a perfume for scenting gloves.] **1.** A perfume prepared from, or imitating the odour of, the flower of the red jasmine. **2.** The red jasmine tree (*Plumiera rubra*) 1866. **3.** A kind of pastry, containing cream, almonds, spice, etc. 1858. var. **Frangipan(n)i** (in sense 1).

Frangulin (fræ·ŋgiŭlin). 1864. [f. the name of the tree (*Rhamnus*) *Frangula* + -IN[1].] *Chem.* 'A yellow crystallisable colouring matter, contained in the bark of the berry-bearing alder' (Watts). Hence **Frangu·lic (acid)** *a.*

†**Fra·nion.** 1571. [Of unkn. origin.] A gallant, paramour. Also, in Spenser, a loose woman. –1810.

Frank (fræŋk), *sb.*[1] and *a.*[1] [OE. *Franca* = OHG. *Franko*; supposed to be named from their national weapon, OE. *franca* javelin (cf. SAXON). Reinforced in ME. by med.L. *Francus* (VIII), (O)Fr. *Franc* (X) – Gmc.] **A.** *sb.* **1.** A person belonging to the Germanic nation, or coalition of nations, that conquered Gaul in the 6th c., and from whom the country received the name of France. **2.** A name given in the Levant to an individual of Western nationality. Cf. FERINGHEE. 1687. †**3.** With ellipsis of 'language'. A *lingua franca* or mixed tongue. NEVILE.

†**B.** *adj.* Belonging to, characteristic of, or customary among the Western nations of Europe –1688.

†**Frank,** *sb.*[2] ME. [– OFr. *franc* sty, from Gmc.] An enclosure, *esp.* a sty. Also, the process of fattening animals. –1736. Hence **f.-fed** *a.* fed in a f.; fatted.

†**Frank,** *sb.*[3] 1578. [f. FRANK *v.*[1]] A name given to the plant Spurry, from its property of fattening cattle; also *f. spurry* –1659.

Frank (fræŋk), *sb.*[4] 1713. [f. FRANK *v.*[2]] **1.** The signature of a person entitled to send letters post free. **2.** A letter or envelope bearing such a signature 1755.

1. I must..send this scrawl into town to get a f..it is not worthy of postage SCOTT.

Frank (fræŋk), *sb.*[5] *dial.* 1823. [From its note.] A heron.

Frank, *a.*[1]: see after FRANK *sb.*[1]

Frank (fræŋk), *a.*[2] ME. [– (O)Fr. *franc* :- med.L. *francus* free; orig. identical with the ethnic name *Francus* (see FRANK *sb.*[1]).] **1.** = FREE in various applications (see quots.). **2.** Liberal, bounteous, generous, lavish 1484. **3.** Not practising concealment; ingenuous, open 1555; unreserved, outspoken 1548; avowed; downright 1752. †**4.** Of plants, trees, etc.: Of superior quality; producing good and abundant fruit or the like. Of drugs, etc.: Of high quality. Cf. FRANKINCENSE. –1648. †**5.** Lusty, vigorous –1626.

1. F. and free borne in a free cytye 1470. He shulde goo f. and quite 1475. Desyrouse of f. lyberty 1538. Landes..franke and free simpliciter and wythout anye condicion MORE. It is of franke gift SPENSER. **2.** In such f. style the people lived FROUDE. **3.** In their conversation f. and open BURKE. To be f. with anyone 1870. **5.** The Sap is not so f. as to rise all to the Boughs BACON.

†**Frank,** *v.*[1] ME. [f. FRANK *sb.*[2]] **1.** *trans.* To shut up and feed in a frank –1600. **2.** To feed high; to cram –1633. Also *fig.* Hence †**Franked** *ppl. a.* fattened in a frank or pen.

Frank (fræŋk), *v.*[2] 1708. [f. FRANK *a.*[2]] **1.** *trans.* To sign (a letter, etc.), so as to ensure its being sent free of charge; to send or cause to be sent free of charge. *Obs.* exc. *Hist.* **b.** *fig.* To facilitate the coming and going of (a person) 1801. **2.** To convey gratuitously 1809. **3.** To exempt. Const. *against, from.* 1876.

2. He got an opportunity of being franked to Poland R. F. BURTON.

Frank-almoign, -almoin. [– AFr. *fraunke almoigne*; see FRANK *a.*[2] and ALMOIGN.] *Law.* See ALMOIGN 2.

Fra·nk chase. 1587. [f. FRANK *a.*[2] + CHASE *sb.*[1]] *Law.* Free chase.

None but the King can have a forest; If he chance to passe one over to a Subject, 'tis no more Forest, but frank Chase HOWELL.

Fra·nk-fee. 1531. [f. FRANK *a.*[2] + FEE *sb.*[2] Cf. AL. *feudum francum.*] A tenure of lands in fee-simple, *esp.* as opp. to *ancient demesne*; also, land so held.

†**Frank-ferm.** [– AFr. *franke ferme*; see FRANK *a.*[2] and FARM *sb.*[2] Cf. AL. *firma franca.*] *Law.* Freehold tenure at a fixed rent. BLACKSTONE.

Fra·nkfold. 1609. [f. FRANK *a.*[2] + FOLD *v.*[2]] *Law.* = FALDAGE.

Frankfort (fræ·ŋkfŏɹt). 1823. The Eng. form of the name of the German city of *Frankfurt* (cf. Fr. *Francfort*). **Frankfort black,** a fine black pigment used in copperplate engraving.

Frankincense (fræ·ŋkinsens). ME. [– OFr. *franc encens*; see FRANK *a.*[2] 4 and INCENSE.] **1.** An aromatic gum resin, yielded by trees of the genus *Boswellia*, used for burning as incense: olibanum; *occas.*, the smoke from the same. **2.** Resin resembling this, obtained from firs and pines. Also, the tree itself. 1577.

1. Curling f. ascends to Baal PRIOR.

Frankish (fræ·ŋkiʃ), *a.* (*sb.*) 1594. [f. FRANK *sb.*[1] + -ISH[1].] **1.** Of or pertaining to the Franks 1802. **2.** Of or pertaining to the Western nations 1594. **3.** *sb.* The language of the Franks 1863.

†**Frank-law.** 1607. [f. FRANK *a.*[2] + LAW.] *Law.* The condition of a full freeman (*liber et legalis homo*), esp. the liberty of being sworn in courts, as a juror or witness –1641.

Franklin (fræ·ŋklin). [ME. *francoleyn, frankeleyn* (3 syll.) – AL. *francalanus*, f. *francalis* (as in *feudum francale* FRANK-FEE; *francalia* n. pl. territory held without dues), f. *francus* free; see FRANK *a.*[2], -AL[1], -AN.] †**1.** A freeman. ME. only. **2.** A freeholder; in 14–15th c. the designation of a class of landowners ranking next below the gentry ME. †**3.** Applied to: A liberal host –1727.

2. Ful wel biloved and famulier was he With frankeleyns over al in his cuntre CHAUCER.

Franklinian (frænkli·niăn). 1767. [f. *Franklin* proper name + -IAN.]

A. *adj.* Of or pertaining to Benjamin Franklin; following Franklin (in politics).

B. *sb.* A follower of Franklin 1794.

So **Frankli·nic** *a.*, an epithet applied to electricity produced by friction; **Fra·nklinism,** frictional electricity; **Fra·nklinist,** one who follows Franklin in his theory of electricity.

Franklinite (fræ·nklinəit). 1820. [f. *Franklin*, New Jersey + -ITE[1] 2 b.] *Min.* A compound of oxides of iron, manganese, and zinc, found in brilliant black crystals.

Frankly (fræ·ŋkli), *adv.* 1540. [f. FRANK *a.*[2] + -LY[2].] In a frank manner; freely.

Kindness so f. offered C. BRONTË.

†**Fra·nk-ma·rriage.** OE. [– AFr. *franc mariage*; see FRANK *a.*[2] and MARRIAGE. Cf. AL. *maritagium francum.*] *Law.* A

tenure in virtue of which a man and his wife held lands granted to them by the father or other near relative of the wife, the estate being heritable to the fourth generation of heirs of their bodies, without any service other than fealty.

Frankness (fræ·nknės). 1553. [f. FRANK *a.*[2] + -NESS.] The quality of being FRANK; †liberality –1771; candour, ingenuousness, openness, *esp.* in speech 1553; freedom of artistic treatment 1784.

2. That happy union of f. and reserve HELPS. Military f. GIBBON.

Fra·nk-pledge. *Obs.* exc. *Hist.* 1502. [– law L. *franciplegium*, latinization of AFr. *frauncplege*, f. *fraunc* FRANK *a.*[2] + *plege* PLEDGE, mistranslation of OE. *friþborh* peace-pledge, through the corrupt forms *freoborh, friborh*, in which the first element was identified with *free*.] *OE.Law.* **1.** The system by which every member of a tithing was answerable for the good conduct of, or the damage done by, any one of the other members 16.. **2.** One of the mutually responsible members of a tithing, etc. *Occas.*, the tithing itself.

1. *transf.* The servants of the Crown were not, as now, bound in f. for each other MACAULAY. Phr. †*View of frankpledge*: a court held periodically for the production of the members of a tithing, later of a hundred or manor. Cf. COURT-LEET. ME.

Fra·nk-te:nement. 1523. [– AFr. *fraunc tenement*; see FRANK *a.*[2] and TENEMENT.] *Law.* = FREEHOLD. So **Fra·nk-te·nure.**

Frantic (fræ·ntik). [ME. *frentik, frantik* – (O)Fr. *frénétique* – L. *phreneticus* PHRENETIC. The early change from *-e-* to *-a-* is unaccounted for.]

A. *adj.* **1.** Affected with mental disease, lunatic, insane; in later use, ragingly mad. Now *rare.* **b.** *transf.* and *fig.* 1547. **2.** †Attended by frenzy –1594; delirious, wild, insanely foolish 1533. †**3.** quasi-*adv.* Frantically. *rare.* –1652.

1. I haue obserued..in phrenticke persons the strength doubled vpon them 1586. **b.** *fig.* A heart..Raging more wilde then is this franticke sea MARSTON. **2.** She displayed a f. and impotent rage GIBBON. Hence **Fra·ntically, Fra·nticly** *advs.* in a f. manner. **Fra·nticness,** f. state or condition.

†**B.** *sb.* One who is frantic; a lunatic, a delirious patient –1758.

Frap (fræp), *v.* ME. [In sense 1 perh. repr. OE. (*ġe*)*fræpġiġa*, which may contain the base of the Rom. word; in 2 – OFr. *fraper* (mod. *frapper*).] **1.** *trans.* and †*intr.* To strike; to beat. **2.** *Naut.* To bind tightly. [So in Fr.] 1548. **b.** To brace the cords of a drum by pulling them together 1874.

†**Fra·pe.** ME. [app. – OFr. *frap* multitude, of unkn. origin.] **1.** A crowd; a mob, the rabble –1710. **2.** ? Tumult. R. BRUNNE.

†**Fra·ple,** *v.* 1595. [perh. – OFr. *frapillier* grow angry, indignant.] *intr.* To dispute, wrangle, bluster –1609. Hence **Fra·pler** *sb. arch.* a blusterer.

‖**Frappé** (frape), *a.* 1848. [Fr. pa. pple. of *frapper* strike, in sense of 'ice (drinks)'.] Iced, cooled.

Frass (fræs). 1854. [– G. *frass*, f. *fressen* devour (see FRET *v.*[1]).] The excrement of larvæ; also, the refuse left behind by boring insects.

‖**Frate** (frā·te). *Pl.* **-ti** (-*ti*). 1722. [It.; lit. 'brother'.] A friar.

Frater[1] (frē[i]·tə.ɪ). Now *Hist.* [ME. *freitore, freit*(*o*)*ur* – OFr. *fraitur*, aphet. f. *refreitor* – med.L. *refectorium* REFECTORY.] The eating room of a monastery; a refectory.

‖**Frater**[2] (frē[i]·tə.ɪ). 1561. [L.; = 'brother'.] †**1.** A friar –1639. †**2.** *Cant.* = ABRAM-MAN. –1673. **3.** A brother, comrade. Also *attrib.* 1794.

Fraternal (frătə̄·ɹnăl), *a.* 1494. [– med.L. *fraternalis*, f. L. *fraternus*, f. *frater* brother; cf. (O)Fr. *fraternel* and see -AL[1].] Of or pertaining to brothers or a brother; brotherly.

The old F. quarrel of thy Race COWLEY. A f. affection for Addison L. STEPHEN. **Frate·rnally** *adv.*

Fra·ternate, *v. U.S. rare.* 1846. [f. *fraternize* by substitution of -ATE[3].] To fraternize. Hence **Fraterna·tion** (*U.S. rare*), fraternization. So **Fra·ternism** (*U.S. rare*), in same sense.

Fraternity (frătə̄·ɹnĭti). ME. [– (O)Fr. *fraternité* – L. *fraternitas*, f. *fraternus*; see FRATERNAL, -ITY.] **1.** The relation of a brother or brothers; brotherhood. **2.** The state or quality of being fraternal; brotherliness 1470. †**3.** A family of brothers. *rare.* 1635. **4.** A body or order of men organized for religious or devout purposes ME. **5.** A body of men associated by some common interest; a company, guild ME. **6.** A body of men of the same class, occupation, pursuits, etc. 1561.

2. To substitute the principles of f. in the room of that salutary prejudice called our country BURKE. **5.** I William Caxton..of the fraternyte and felauship of the mercerye CAXTON. **7.** *U.S.* A literary or social association of the alumni of a college or university; a 'Greek-Letter' Society 1777.

Fraternization (fræ:təɹnəizē[i]·ʃən). 1792. [– Fr. *fraternisation*; see next, -ATION.] The action of fraternizing or uniting as brothers, fraternal association.

They..give the kiss of f. to negroes 1792.

Fraternize (fræ·təɹnəiz, frē[i]·tə.ɪ-), *v.* 1611. [– Fr. *fraterniser*, med.L. *fraternizare*, f. *fraternus*; see FRATERNAL, -IZE.] **1.** *intr.* To associate or sympathize *with* as a brother or as brothers; to form a fraternal friendship. **2.** *trans.* To bring into fraternal association or sympathy. Now *rare.* 1656.

1. We fraternised on the spot BAKER. **2.** A regular correspondence for fraternizing the two nations BURKE. Hence **Fraterni·zer,** one who fraternizes.

Fratriage (frē[i]·tri,ėdʒ). Also **fratrage.** 1730. [– med.L. *fratriagium*, f. L. *fratr-*; see -AGE.] *Law.* A younger brother's inheritance.

Fratricide[1] (frē[i]·trisəid, fræ·tri-). 1450. [– Fr. *fratricide* or L. *fratricida*, f. *frater* brother; see -CIDE 1.] One who kills his (or her) brother. Hence **Fra·trici:dal** *a.* that kills or has killed his brother; concerned with the slaughter of brothers.

Fratricide[2] (frē[i]·trisəid, fræ·tri-). 1568. [– (O)Fr. *fratricide* or late L. *fratricidium*; see prec., -CIDE 2.] The action of killing one's brother. (In *Law* also the killing of one's sister.)

Fratry[1], **fratery** (frē[i]·tri, -tėri). 1538. [app. f. FRATER[1] + -Y[3].] = FRATER[1].

Fra·try[2]. 1532. [– med.L. *fratria, fratreia* fraternity, app. infl. by Gr. φρατρία.] **a.** A fraternity. **b.** A convent of friars.

Frau, var. of FROW.

Fraud (frǭd), *sb.* ME. [– (O)Fr. *fraude* – L. *fraus, fraud-*.] **1.** The quality of being deceitful. Now *rare.* **2.** Criminal deception; the using of false representations to obtain an unjust advantage or to injure the rights or interests of another ME. **3.** An act or instance of deception, a dishonest trick ME. **4.** A fraudulent contrivance; in mod. colloq. use, a spurious or deceptive thing 1658. **b.** *colloq.* of a person: An impostor, a humbug 1850. †**5.** State of being defrauded or deluded. MILT.

2. They look upon f. as a greater crime than theft SWIFT. *In fraud of, to the fraud of* (Law): so as to defraud; to the detriment or hindrance of. **3.** *Statute of Frauds* (Law): the statute 29 Chas. II, c. 3, by which written memoranda were in many cases required to give validity to a contract. Phr. *Pious fraud*: a deceit practised for the advancement of religion, or the like. **6.** *Comb.* **f. order** *U.S.*, an official order prohibiting the use of the mails to a person suspected of using them fraudulently.

Hence **Frau·dful** *a.* full of f., treacherous; **-ly** *adv.* **Frau·dless** *a.* free from f.; **-ly** *adv.*, **-ness.**

Fraudulence (frǭ·diŭlėns). 1610. [– OFr. *fraudulence* or eccl.L. *fraudulentia*; see next, -ENCE.] The quality or fact of being fraudulent. So **Frau·dulency.**

Fraudulent (frǭ·diŭlėnt), *a.* ME. [– OFr. *fraudulent* or L. *fraudulentus*; see FRAUD *sb.*, -ULENT.] **1.** Guilty of or addicted to fraud; deceitful, dishonest. **2.** Characterized by, or of the nature of, fraud; serving the purpose of, or accomplished by means of, fraud ME. †**3.** *Path.* (After the L. transl. of Avicenna.) Deceptive –1615.

1. Agayne is the seruaunt fals and fraudelent BARCLAY. **2.** A f. balance 1833, prospectus 1891. F. misrepresentation SIR J. W. CHITTY. Hence **Frau·dulently** *adv.*

Fraught (frǭt), *sb. Obs.* exc. *Sc.* ME. [– MDu., MLG. *vracht* (whence G. *fracht*) beside *vrecht* FREIGHT *sb.*] = FREIGHT *sb.* 1, 2.

Fraught (frǭt), *v. Obs.* exc. in pa. pple. ME. [– MDu. *vrachten* load (a ship), f. *vracht* (see prec.).] = FREIGHT *v.* 1, 2.

Fraught (frǭt), *pple.* and *ppl. a.* ME. [pa. pple. of FRAUGHT *v.*] **1.** Of a vessel: Laden. Also *full f.* **2.** *transf.* Stored, furnished, filled, equipped *with* ME.

1. Ships..wyth riches full yfraught GASCOIGNE. **2.** Wisedome (whereof I know you are f.) *Lear* I. iv. 241.

Phr. *Fraught with*: **a.** attended with; **b.** destined to produce.

Fraughtage (frǭ·tėdʒ). *arch.* ME. [f. FRAUGHT *v.* + -AGE.] = FREIGHTAGE †1, 2.

Fraxin (fræ·ksin). 1864. [f. L. *frax*(*inus*) ash + -IN[1].] *Chem.* A substance, $C_{16}H_{18}O_{10}$, occurring in the bark of the common ash, and also, together with æsculin, in the bark of the horse-chestnut.

Fraxine·lla. 1664. [mod.L., dim of L. *fraxinus* ash.] A name for cultivated species of dittany, esp. *Dictamnus fraxinella.*

Fray (frē[i]), *sb.*[1] ME. [f. FRAY *v.*[1]] **1.** A feeling of fear; fright, terror. †**2.** An assault, attack –1575. **3.** A disturbance; a brawl; a fight ME.

3. Fleete-street fraies, when Prentices with Clubs did knocke thee downe 1609.

Fray, *sb.*[2] 1630. [f. FRAY *v.*[2]] A frayed place.

Fray (frē[i]), *v.*[1] ME. [aphet. f. AFFRAY, EFFRAY *v.*] **1.** *trans.* To make afraid, frighten. **2.** To frighten or drive away. *Obs.* exc. *arch.* 1526. †**3.** To assault, attack –1575. **4.** *intr.* To quarrel or fight. *Obs.* exc. *arch.* 1460.

1. A Puritan is a Protestant fray'd out of his Wits 1604. **2.** Can he f. off the vulture from his breast SOUTH.

Fray (frē[i]), *v.*[2] 1450. [– Fr. *frayer*, earlier *freiier :– L. *fricare* rub.] **1.** *intr.* Of deer: To rub (against trees). Also *trans.* in *to f. their heads.* 1576. **2.** *trans.* To rub away; to ravel *out* the edge or end of; *occas.*, to chafe by friction 1710. **b.** *intr.* Of material: To become frayed, to ravel out 1721. †**3.** *trans.* To deflower 1565. †**4.** *intr.* To clash –1483. **5.** [from Fr.] *trans.* To clear, force (a path, way) 1849.

2. The bell-rope..was frayed into a fringe DICKENS. A suit of fray'd magnificence TENNYSON. **5.** Paths, frayed by the elephant and rhinoceros 1849. Hence **Fray·ing** *vbl. sb.*

†**Fray,** *v.*[3] *rare.* 1450. = DEFRAY *v.* –1631.

Frazzle (fræ·z'l), *v.* orig. *dial.* and *U.S.* 1825. [perh. a blend of FRAY *v.*[2] and dial. *fazzle* tangle.] *trans.* To fray, wear out. Hence **Frazzle** *sb.*, esp. in phr. *to a f.*, to a condition of exhaustion 1865.

Freak (frīk), *sb.*[1] 1563. [prob. of dial. origin.] **1.** A sudden causeless change or turn of the mind; a capricious humour, notion, whim, or vagary. **2.** Capriciousness 1678. **3.** A prank, a caper 1648. **4.** A product of irregular fancy 1784. **b.** (more fully *f. of nature* = *lusus naturæ*): A monstrosity of any species; in recent use, a living curiosity exhibited in a show 1847. **5.** quasi-*adj.* denoting something abnormal or capriciously irregular 1898.

Freak (frīk), *sb.*[2] 1870. [f. FREAK *v.*] A fleck or streak of colour.

Freak (frīk), *v.* 1637. [Sense 1 (only as pa. pple. *freaked*), perh. alt., by assoc. with *streak*, of *freckt* (see FRECK *v.*). Sense 2 f. FREAK *sb.*[1]] **1.** *trans.* To fleck or streak capriciously; to variegate. **2.** *intr.* To practise freaks; to frolic 1663.

1. The pansy freaked with jet MILT. *Lycidas* 144.

Freakish (frī·kiʃ), *a.* 1653. [f. FREAK *sb.*[1] + ISH[1].] **1.** Full of, or characterized by freaks, capricious, whimsical. **2.** Of the nature of a freak, curious 1805.

1. An ill-contrived, ugly, f. fool WYCHERLEY. Our f. climate LOWELL. **Frea·kish-ly** *adv.*, **-ness.**

Freck, frack (frek, fræk), *a. Obs.* exc. *Sc.* [OE. *frec, fric, fræc* = OHG. *freh* covetous, greedy (G. *frech* bold, insolent),

ON. *frekr* greedy, Goth. *faihufriks* avaricious.] **1.** Desirous, eager, quick, ready. **2.** Lusty, strong, vigorous 1500. Hence †**Fre·ckly, fra·ckly,** *adv.*

Freck (frek), *v.* 1621. [In pa. pple. *freckt*, shortened f. *freckled*; see FREAK *v.*] *trans.* To mark with spots or freckles; to dimple.

Fre·cken. Now *dial.* ME. [– ON. *freknur* pl.; see next.] A freckle.

A fewe freknes in his face y-spreynd CHAUCER.

Freckle (fre·k'l), *sb.* ME. [Early forms *fracel, frakel*; alt. of (dial.) *freken, fraken* (Chaucer) – ON. *freknur* pl. (Sw. *fräkne*, Da. *fregne*).] **1.** A yellowish or lightish-brown spot in the skin. **2.** Any small spot or discoloration 1547.

Freckle (fre·k'l), *v.* 1613. [f. the sb.] **1.** *trans.* To cover with freckles or spots; *intr.* to appear in spots or patches. **2.** *intr.* To become marked with freckles 1842. Hence **Fre·ckling** *vbl. sb.* a mark like a freckle; a marking with freckles.

Freckled (fre·k'ld), *ppl. a.* ME. [f. FRECKLE *sb.* + -ED[2].] **1.** Marked with freckles. **2.** Spotted ME. †**3.** Resembling a freckle. *Lev.* 13:39.

1. A f. face MARSTON. **2.** F. trout 1614, cowslips 1821.

Fred-stole: see FRITH-STOOL.

Free (frī), *a.* [OE. *frēo* = OFris., OS., OHG. *frī* (Du. *vrij*, G. *frei*), ON. **frīr*, Goth. *freis* :- Gmc. **frijaz* :- IE. **prijos*, repr. by Skr. *priyás* dear, f. **prī* to love. The primary sense of the adj. is 'dear'.]

I. 1. Not subject as a slave is to his master; enjoying personal rights and liberty of action. Also *fig.* **2.** Of a state, its citizens, institutions, etc.: Enjoying civil liberty; existing under a government which is not arbitrary or despotic, and does not encroach upon individual rights. Also, not subject to foreign dominion. ME. †**3.** Noble, honorable, of gentle birth and breeding. In ME. an epithet of courtesy. –1632. †**4.** Hence: Noble, honourable, generous, magnanimous –1604.

1. Delicate Ariel, I'll set thee f. for this SHAKS. **2.** Till the iniurious Romans did extort This Tribute from vs, we were f. *Cymb.* III. i. 49. **3.** Mirthe, that is so fair and f. CHAUCER. **4.** *Oth.* III. iii. 199.

II. 1. At liberty; allowed to go anywhere; not kept in confinement. Also, liberated. 1483. **2.** Released from ties, obligations, etc. 1596; exempt from work or duty 1697. **3.** Guiltless, innocent, acquitted. Const. *from, of.* ? *Obs.* 1602. **4.** Unimpeded, unrestricted, unhampered ME. **b.** with *to* and *inf.*: At liberty, †feeling it right, *to do* something ME. **5.** Of composition, etc.: Not observing strict laws of form; (of a translation, etc.) not adhering strictly to the original 1813. **6.** Allowable or allowed (*to* or *for* a person *to do*); open *to* 1576; open *for* all 1870. **7.** Clear, unobstructed ME. **8.** Clear *of* or *from* ME. **9.** *Naut.* Of the wind: Not adverse 1840. **10.** Not fixed or fastened 1590. **11.** Disengaged from contact or connection with anything else; relieved from the pressure of anything adjacent or superincumbent. In *Bot.* not adnate to other organs. 1715. **12.** *Chem.*, etc. Uncombined 1800. **13.** Of power or energy: Disengaged 1825. **14.** Of a material: Easily worked, loose and soft in structure 1573.

1. We would let them go f. DE FOE. Deer, as f. as in an American forest MACAULAY. **2.** A fortnight hence I shall be f. as air SIR R. PEEL. **3.** My hands are guilty, but my heart is f. DRYDEN & LEE. **4.** F. admission of the light of Heaven RUSKIN. Phr. (*To have* or *give*) *a f. hand*: complete liberty of action. **b.** I made him..Sufficient to have stood, though f. to fall MILT. **5.** The limits between f. translation and paraphrases 1813. **6.** What God..commands to some, leaves f. to all MILT. *A f. fight*: one in which all and sundry engage. **7.** Are not the streets as f. For me as for you SHAKS. **8.** Ice..f. from air-bubbles TYNDALL. **10.** Phr. *To get f.*: to get loose, to extricate.

III. 1. Acting of one's own will or choice; not determined from without. (See also FREE WILL.). OE. **2.** Ready; acting willingly or spontaneously; (of an act) spontaneous; (of an offer, assent, etc.) readily given or made ME. Of a horse: willing 1477. **3.** Ready in giving, liberal. Const. *of.* Said also of the gift. ME. **4.** Acting without restriction or limitation 1578. **b.** Abundant, copious 1635. **5.** Frank and open, ingenuous, unreserved; also, in bad sense = forward, ready to 'take liberties' 1635. **6.** Of speech: Frank, plain-spoken 1611; licentious 1852.

1. A man is said to be f., so far forth as he can do what he will BP. BERKELEY. F. choice FREEMAN. **2.** His noble f. offers left us nothing to ask BACON. F. to confess BYRON. Horses that be f. Do need no spurs GREENE. **3.** I was not very f. of it, for my Store was not great DE FOE. A f. gift 1791. **4.** Too f. feeding hath occasioned you this dreame 1632. How f. the present age is in laying taxes on the next POPE. **b.** A f. bloomer 1887. **5.** His Grace is very f. and open 1693. Not so f., fellow SHERIDAN. Phr. *To make* (or *be*) *f. with*: to treat unceremoniously: also *Naut.* to approach boldly. **6.** Where she..listened to much f. talk THACKERAY.

IV. 1. Exempt from, not subject or liable to OE. **2. a.** Exempt from, or not subject to, some particular jurisdiction or lordship. **b.** Possessed of certain exclusive rights or privileges. ME. **3.** Of land: Held without obligation of rent or service ME. **4.** Invested with the rights or immunities *of*, admitted to the privileges *of* (a corporation, city, etc.). Used with *of*, also simply. 1496. **b.** Hence: Allowed the enjoyment *of* 1687. **5.** Said of non-unionist workmen and their labour 1890. **6.** Exempt from restrictions in regard to trade; open to all traders; also, not subject to tax, toll, or duty 1631. **7.** Without payment, gratuitous 1585.

1. F. from all tax and imposition 1630, from pulmonary consumption 1885, from real difficulty 1895. **2. a.** The f. towns of Lübeck, Brehmen and Hamburg M. PATTISON. **b.** *F. chapel* (see CHAPEL *sb.*). *F. chase* = FRANK CHASE. *F. fishery* (see FISHERY). *F. marriage* = FRANK-MARRIAGE. *F. warren* (see WARREN). **4.** F. of the Grocers B. JONS., of the city 1766. **b.** F. of the house DICKENS. **6.** F. markets 1631. A f.-port SHAFTESB. **7.** F. tickets 1830, seats MACAULAY. A f. pass over a line of railway 1894. Phr. *Free school*: 'a school in which learning is given without pay' (J.). (This meaning has been denied, but on inconclusive grounds. See O.E.D.) 1494.

†**B.** *sb.* **1.** The adj. used *absol.* ME. only. **2.** A person of noble birth or breeding; a knight or lady –1549.

C. *adv.* In a free manner, freely. Now only *techn.* or *arch.* 1559. **b.** Without cost or payment. Often with *gratis*. *Scot free*: see SCOT-FREE 1568. **c.** Naut. (*To sail, go*, etc.) *f.*: i.e. with bow-lines slackened and sheets eased; opp. to *close-hauled* 1812.

Comb. **a.** in derivative combs. based upon some phrase in which the adj. is used, as *f.-agency*, *-citizenship*, etc. (after *f. agent, citizen*, etc.).

b. in comb. with a verbal or agent noun (where *free* seems partly adverbial), as F.-LIVER, -THINKER, etc.

c. In spec. phrases, etc.: †**f. alms** = *frank-almoign* (see ALMOIGN); **f. companion,** a mercenary belonging to no particular nation, but attached for the time to any prince who paid him: so **f. company; f. grace,** the unmerited favour of God; **f. love,** the doctrine of the right of free choice in sexual relations without the restraint of marriage or other legal obligation; **f.-milling** *a.* (*Mining*), (of ores) easily reducible; **f.-stuff** (*Building*), timber which is quite clean or without knots; †**f. suitor,** one of the tenants entitled to attend a manorial court; **f. ward,** detention not involving close or ignominious restraint; **f. wheel,** the driving-wheel of a bicycle able to rotate while the pedals are at rest; also as vb.

Free (frī), *v.* Pa. t. and pple. **freed.** [OE. *frēon, frēoġ(e)an* = ON. *fría, friá* :- Gmc. **frijējan*, f. **frijaz* FREE *a.*] **1.** *trans.* To make free; to set at liberty; to release from bondage or constraint. **2.** To relieve; to deliver, or exempt *from*, rid or ease *of*; to confer immunity upon OE. **3.** To clear, disengage, or disentangle (a thing) from some obstruction or encumbrance. Const. *from, of.* 1613. Also *refl.* †**b.** To open so as to allow free passage –1700. †**4.** To remove so as to leave the place clear, get rid of –1638. †**5.** To frank (a letter) –1823. **6.** *Lead-mining.* To register (a new mine, vein, etc.) by making the proper payment to the barmaster 1601.

1. They. freed the citie, and vpheld the lawes 2 *Macc.* 2:22. Freed from the restraints of fear BUTLER. **2.** Freed from feudal services CRUISE, from stamp duty CRUMP. **3.** *refl.* To f. oneself from one's difficulties 1852. **4.** F. thine owne torment DANIEL.

Free and easy. 1699.

A. *adjectival phr.* Unconstrained, natural; also, careless, slipshod. Also quasi-*adv.*

A free-and-easy way of carrying things on NEWMAN.

B. *sb.* A convivial gathering for singing, at which one may drink, smoke, etc. 1823.

Free bench. 1670. [Cf. AL. *bancus francus* (XIII).] *Law.* 'That estate in Copyhold Lands which the Wife, being espoused a Virgin, hath, after the death of her Husband, for her Dower, according to the custom of the Mannor' (Blount, *Law Dict.*).

Free-board (frī·bōᵊɹd). 1676. [tr. AFr. *franc bord*, in AL. *francum bordum*; see FRANK *a.*[2], BOARD *sb.*] **1.** *Law.* The right of claiming a certain quantity of land outside the fence of a park or forest; also, the land thus claimed. **2.** *Naut.* The space between the plank-sheer and the line of flotation 1726.

Free-boot, *v.* 1592. [Back-formation from next.] *intr.* To act as a freebooter, plunder. Hence **Free·-booting** *vbl. sb.* and *ppl. a.*

Freebooter (frī·bū:təɹ). 1570. [– Du. *vrijbuiter*, f. the equivalents of FREE *a.*, BOOTY or BOOT *sb.*[2], -ER[1]. See also FILIBUSTER.] One who goes about in search of plunder; *esp.* a pirate or piratical adventurer. Also *transf.* and *fig.*

The Danites were..Free-booters..and did all by force 1659. Hence **Free·-boo:tery,** the practice of freebooters.

†**Free·-booty.** 1623. [f. FREE *a.* + BOOTY, after prec.] Spoil (to be) taken by force –1749.

Free·-born, *a.* ME. [f. FREE *a.* + BORN *ppl. a.*] **1.** Born free, born to the conditions and privileges of citizenship, inheriting liberty. **2.** Of or befitting a free-born man 1510.

2. The f. and martial virtues of the desert GIBBON.

Free Church. 1843. **1.** *gen.* A church free from state control. In *pl.* a Nonconformist name for the Congregationalists, Baptists, etc., as dist. from the Established Church. 1869. Hence **Freechu·rchman. 2.** *The Free Church of Scotland*: the organization formed by the ministers who seceded from the established Presbyterian Church in 1843.

Free cost. 1563. In phr. *at, of, on, upon free cost* = cost-free, gratis –1764. Also as advb. phr. without prep. –1720.

Nothing comes free-cost here HERRICK.

†**Free-de·nizen,** *sb.* 1576. = DENIZEN 2. –1653. So †**Free-de·nizen** *v.* = DENIZEN *v.* 1.

Free·dman. 1601. [f. *freed* pa. pple. of FREE *v.* + MAN *sb.*] A man who has been a slave and is manumitted or emancipated.

Freedom (frī·dəm). [OE. *frēodōm*; see FREE *a.* and -DOM.] **1.** Exemption or release from slavery or imprisonment; personal liberty ME. **2.** Exemption from arbitrary control; independence; civil liberty ME. **3.** The state of being FREE; †generosity, liberality –1530; liberty of action ME. **4.** The quality of being free from the control of fate or necessity; the power of self-determination OE. †**5.** Readiness –1697. **6.** Frankness, openness, familiarity; outspokenness 1699; undue familiarity 1618. **7.** Ease, facility 1613. **8.** Boldness of conception or execution 1643. **9.** *Physics.* Capability of motion 1879. **10.** An immunity, privilege ME.; a franchise (cf. FRANCHISE *sb.* 2 a) 1596. **11.** The right of participating in the privileges of: **a.** membership *of* a company or trade 1744; **b.** citizenship *of* a town or city 1579; often conferred *honoris causa* upon eminent persons. Also the diploma conferring such freedom. **c.** The liberty or right to practise a trade; also, the 'fine' paid for this 1712. **d.** *transf.* Unrestricted use *of* 1652.

2. They died for the Libertie and Free-dome of their Cittie HOLLAND. F. of the press BYRON. **3.** He was of Knyghthod and of fredam flour

CHAUCER. F. of Thought is like F. in Actions 1718. **6.** Those innocent Freedoms I allow her OTWAY. **10.** F. from Tallage 1711, from arrest KEIGHTLEY. **11. b.** They presented me with the f. of the city WESLEY. **d.** The f. of the library BURTON.

Comb. **f.-fine,** a payment made on being admitted to the f. of a city, guild, or corporation.

Freedstool: see FRITH-STOOL.

Free-hand (frī·hænd), *a.* 1862. Of drawing: Done with a free hand, i.e. without measurements or artificial aid. Also *absol.* or quasi-*sb.*

Free-ha·nded, *a.* 1656. [f. FREE *a.* + HAND *sb.* + -ED².] Open-handed, generous.

Free-hea·rted, *a.* ME. [f. FREE *a.* + HEART + -ED².] Having a free heart; frank, open, unreserved; impulsive; generous, liberal.

The bond of freeharted and willing love GOLDING. Hence **Free-hea·rted-ly** *adv.*, **-ness.**

Freehold (frī·hōᵘld). 1467. [tr. AFr. *fraunc tenement* 'free holding'; cf. FRANK TENEMENT. In AL. *tenementum liberum.*] **1.** A tenure by which an estate (or office or dignity) is held in fee-simple, fee-tail, or for term of life 1523. **2.** An estate or office held by this tenure 1467. **3.** *attrib.* or *adj.* Held by, relating to, or of the nature of, freehold 1527.

Freeholder (frī·hoᵘldəɹ). ME. [tr. AFr. *fraunc tenaunt* 'free tenant'; in AL. *francus tenens.*] One who possesses a freehold estate.

Free lance. 1820. A term used by recent writers to denote one of those military adventurers who in the Middle Ages offered their services as mercenaries, or with a view to plunder, to belligerent states; a condottiere, a free companion. Hence *fig.* of politicians, etc.

Free-liver. 1711. One who gives free indulgence to his appetites. So **Free-li·ving** *a.*

Freely (frī·li), *adv.* [OE. *frēolīċe*; see FREE *a.*, -LY².] **1.** In a free manner; unreservedly; readily, spontaneously. **2.** Frankly, openly, plainly 1596. **3.** Without let, hindrance, or interference ME. **b.** Loosely 1869. **4.** Without stint ME. †**5.** In freedom; with absolute possession –1647. †**6.** Nobly; excellently. ME. only. †**7.** = FREE *adv.* –1759.

1. Graces..gyuen to us frely 1526. F. we serve, Because we f. love, as in our will To love or not MILT. **2.** To speak one's mind f. BERKELEY. **3.** To breathe more f. 1695. **4.** Of euery tree of the garden thou mayest f. eate *Gen.* 2:16.

Freeman (frī·mæ̆n). [OE. *frēoman*; see FREE *a.* and MAN *sb.*] **1.** One who is not a slave or serf; also later, one who is politically free. **2.** One who possesses the freedom of a city, borough, company, etc. ME.

1. A coloured free-man LYELL. The electors are citizens, burgesses, or freemen H. COX.

Freemartin (frī·mā:ɹtin). 1681. [Of unkn. origin; cf. Ir., Gael. *mart* cow (fattened for the market).] An imperfect female of the ox kind, twin-born with a male.

Freemason (frī·mēˈsən, -s'n). ME. [f. FREE *a.* + MASON.] †**1.** A member of a certain class of skilled workers in stone, who travelled from place to place, working wherever any great building was being erected, and recognizing each other by a system of secret signs and passwords. In later use (16–18th c.) a term used merely as a more complimentary synonym of 'mason'. –1723. **2.** A member of the fraternity called *Free and Accepted Masons* 1646.

Early in the 17th c., the societies of freemasons (sense 1) began to admit honorary members, who were instructed in the secret signs and in the legendary history of the craft. These were called *accepted masons*, and the distinction of being an 'accepted mason' became a fashionable object of ambition. In 1717 four of these societies or 'lodges' in London united to form a 'grand lodge', with a new constitution and ritual, and a system of secret signs; the object of the society as reconstituted being mutual help and the promotion of brotherly feeling among its members. The London 'grand lodge' has been the parent of other lodges in Great Britain and in most parts of the world.

3. *attrib.* (of or pertaining to freemasons, as *f. knock*, etc.) 1807.

Freemasonry (frī·mēˈs'nri). ME. [see -RY.] †**1.** The craft or occupation of a freemason. ME. only. **2.** The principles, practices, and institutions of freemasons 1802. **3.** *fig.* Secret or tacit brotherhood, instinctive sympathy 1810.

3. The wonderful f. of childhood 1886.

Freeness (frī·nės). Now *rare.* ME. [f. FREE *a.* + -NESS.] The quality or state of being FREE; freedom; readiness; liberality; openness, frankness.

Free-qua·rter. *Hist.* 1648. The obligation of having to provide free board and lodging for troops; also, the right to be billeted in free quarters.

Freer (frī·əɹ). 1610. [f. FREE *v.* + -ER¹.] One who frees or sets free.

Freesia (frī·ziă). 1882. [mod.L., f. name of Friedrich H. T. *Freese*, a physician of Kiel, Germany; see -IA¹.] *Bot.* A genus of iridaceous bulbous plants of the Cape of Good Hope, allied to *Gladiolus.*

Free soil. *U.S.* 1848. **A.** *sb.* Territory in which slaveholding was prohibited 1850.

B. *adj.* Epithet of a political party in 1846–56, which opposed the extension of slavery into its territories; pertaining to this party or its principles.

I went to a free soil meetin' once LOWELL. Hence **Free-soiler, Free-soilism.**

Free-spoken, *a.* 1625. [Cf. *plain-spoken.*] Accustomed to speak plainly and openly. Hence **Free-spokenness.**

Free state. 1646. **1.** Occas. = REPUBLIC. Now *rare.* **2.** *U.S.* Before the Civil War of 1861–5, a state of the Union in which slavery did not exist 1861. **3.** *Irish F. S.*, the part of Ireland separated from the U.K. and established as a Dominion 1922.

Free·-stone, freestone¹. ME. [tr. OFr. *franche pere*, AL. *lapis liber* (c1200), the adj. meaning 'of superior quality'; see FRANK *a.*² 4.] Any fine-grained sandstone or limestone that can be cut or sawn easily; a slab of such stone. Also *attrib.*

Free·-stone². 1866. A variety of the peach (or nectarine) in which the flesh parts freely from the stone when ripe. Also *f. peach.*

Free-thinker (frī·þi:ŋkəɹ). 1692. [Cf. Du. *vrijdenker*, Fr. *libre penseur* (XVII).] One who refuses to submit his reason to the control of authority in matters of religious belief; a designation claimed *esp.* by the deistic and other rejectors of Christianity in the early 18th c. Also *transf.* So **Free-thi·nking** *vbl. sb.* the principles or practice of a free-thinker; *ppl. a.* holding the principles of a free-thinker; pertaining to free-thinkers or free-thought. **Free-thought** = *Free-thinking* vbl. sb.

Free trade, free-trade. 1606. **1.** An open and unrestricted trade. **2.** Trade or commerce left to follow its natural course, i.e. without the interference of customs duties or of bounties. Also, the principles of those who advocate this state of things. Also *transf.* 1823. **3.** Smuggling 1824. **4.** *attrib.* 1829.

2. To 'inculcate in the mind of the Bourbons wise principles of free trade' COBBETT.

Free-tra·der. 1698. **1.** One allowed to trade without restriction. **2.** A smuggler; also, a smuggling vessel 1815. **3.** An advocate of free trade 1849.

Free will, free:-wi·ll, free:wi·ll. ME. [tr. late (eccl.) L. *liberum arbitrium*, whence Fr. *libre arbitre.*] **1.** (Best as two words.) Spontaneous will, unconstrained choice (to do or act). **2.** 'The power of directing our actions without constraint by necessity or fate' (J.) ME. **3.** *attrib.* (in *free-will offering*) = given spontaneously 1535.

1. To wander at their own free will JOWETT. **2.** The third way of bringing things to pass, distinct from necessity and chance, namely, free-will HOBBES. Hence **Free-wi·ller,** a contemptuous term for one who believes in the doctrine of free will, an Arminian.

Freeze (frīz), *sb.* ME. [f. FREEZE *v.*] The action of FREEZE *v.* (*lit.* and *fig.*).

Freeze (frīz), *v.* Pa. t. **froze** (frōᵘz). Pa. pple. **frozen** (frōᵘ·z'n). [OE. *frēosan* = MLG., MDu. *vrēsen* (Du. *vriezen*), OHG. *frīosan* (G. *frieren*), ON. *frjósa*, Goth. **friusan* :– Gmc. **freusan*, f. **freus-* **fraus-* **frus-* :– IE. **preus-* **prous-* **prus-*, repr. by L. *pruina* hoarfrost, Skt. *pruṣvā*.]

I. intr. uses. **1.** *impers. It freezes*: the cold is such that water becomes ice. **2.** To be converted into, or covered with, ice ME.; to become hard or rigid as the result of cold ME. **3.** To become fixed *to* (something) or *together* by the action of frost 1460. **4.** To feel very chill; to die by frost ME.; to be utterly devoid of heat 1613. Also *fig.*

1. Still it frised HALL. **2.** Port wine froze solid 1748. Our ropes were now froze 1748. *fig.* The smile on his lips froze C. BRONTË. **3.** Phr. *To f.* (*on*) *to* (U.S. and Austral.): to hold on *to*; also, to 'take to'. **4.** The north-west, where Davies freezed to his rest COLVIL. *fig.* To f. with fears POPE.

II. trans. uses. **1.** To change to a solid form by the action of cold; to congeal; to form ice on the surface of (a river, etc.). Also causatively. 1494. **b.** To congeal as if by frost ME. **c.** *fig.* To chill (feelings, etc.); to paralyse (powers, etc.) 1595. **2.** To affect with frost; to stiffen, harden, injure, kill, etc. by chilling 1596. **3.** *To f. out*: **a.** *lit.*: see FROZEN. **b.** *fig.* To exclude from business, society, etc. by chilling behaviour, severe competition, etc. (*U.S.*) 1890.

1. A froste that..frose yᵉ Thamys FABYAN. Phr. *To f. over*: to cover with ice. *To f. in, up.* **b.** A Tale..whose lightest word Would..f. thy young blood *Haml.* I. v. 16. **c.** Chill Penury..froze the genial current of the soul GRAY. Hence **Free·zer,** one who or that which freezes, or keeps extremely cold.

Freeze, obs. f. FRIEZE.

Freezing (frī·ziŋ), *vbl. sb.* ME. [f. prec. + -ING¹.] The action of FREEZE *v.* *At. f.* = at *freezing-point.*

Comb.: **f.-mixture,** a mixture, e.g. of salt and snow, which, while remaining liquid, is cold enough to f. some other liquid within its influence; **-point,** the point on the thermometer, viz. 32° Fahrenheit, 0° Centigrade, marking the temperature at which a liquid, *esp.* water, freezes.

Freezing (frī·ziŋ), *ppl. a.* 1611. [f. as prec. + -ING².] **1.** That freezes (see the vb.). **2.** *fig.*; *esp.* of manners: Chilling 1813.

2. The f. reason's colder part TENNYSON. **Free·zingly,** *adv.*

Freiesle·benite. 1850. [f. *Freiesleben* proper name + -ITE¹ 2 b.] *Min.* A sulphantimonide of lead and silver, which crystallizes in striated prisms.

Freight (frēˈt), *sb.* 1463. [– MLG., MDu. *vrecht*, var. of *vracht*; see FRAUGHT *sb.*] **1.** Hire of a vessel for the transport of goods; the service of transporting goods (orig., by water; now, esp. in *U.S.*, by land also); the sum paid for this. †Formerly also: Passage-money. **2.** The cargo or lading (of a ship); a ship-load. In *U.S.*: Anything carried by sea or land. Also *transf.* and *fig.* 1502.

1. Phr. †*To take f.*: to take passage DE FOE. **2.** A f. of sea-coals 1789. **b.** *U.S.* = *f. train* (see below). *attrib.* and *Comb.* (esp. *U.S.*), as *f. car* (= goods truck or van), *f. train* (= goods train); *f.-handler*, etc.

Freight (frēˈt), *v.* 1485. [f. prec. sb.; cf. FRAUGHT *v.*] **1.** *trans.* To furnish or load (a vessel) with a cargo; to hire or let out (a vessel) for the carriage of goods and passengers. Also *transf.* **2.** To carry as freight 1540.

1. Donco, where the marchauntes..fraight theyr shyppes 1555.

†**Freight,** *pple.* and *ppl. a.* 1494. [Contracted f. pa. pple. (*freighted*) of prec.; cf. FRAUGHT pple.] **1.** Freighted, laden –1649. Also *transf.* and *fig.* –1711. **2.** Fraught, abounding *with* –1623.

Freightage (frēˈ·tėdʒ). 1694. [f. FREIGHT *v.* + -AGE.] **1.** Hire of a vessel for the transport of goods; cost of conveyance of goods. **2.** Freight, cargo; quantity of cargo conveyed; also *transf.* and *fig.* 1803. **3.** Transport of goods. *U.S.* 1886.

Freighter (frēˈ·təɹ). 1622. [f. as prec. + -ER¹.] **1.** 'One who loads a ship, or one who charters and loads a ship' (W.). **b.** One who consigns goods for carriage inland 1872. **2.** One whose business it is to receive and forward freight 1714. **3.** A cargo vessel 1878.

Freightless, *a. rare.* 1791. [f. FREIGHT *sb.* + -LESS.] Without freight or load.

Fremd (fremd), *a.* *Obs.* exc. *Sc.* and *n.* [OE. *frem(e)de* = OFris. *fremethe*, OS. *fremithi* (Du. *vreemd*), OHG. *fremidi* (G. *fremd*), Goth. *framaþeis* strange :– Gmc. **framaþja*, f. **fram-*; see FROM.] **1.** Foreign. **2.** Strange OE; wild, as opp. to *tame* ME. **3.** Unfriendly OE. **4.** Not related; opp. to *sib* or *kin* ME.

Fremescent (frėme·sěnt), *a.* *rare.* 1837. [f. L. *fremere* roar + -ESCENT.] Murmuring, growing noisy. CARLYLE. Hence **Freme·scence** (*rare*), an incipient roaring.

‖**Fremitus** (fre·mitʊ̆s). 1820. [L., f. *fremere* roar.] A dull roaring noise; in *Path.*, a palpable vibration, e.g. of the walls of the chest.

Fren: see FRENNE.

French (frenʃ). [Late OE. *frenċisċ* :– Gmc. **fraŋkiskaz* (whence medL. *Franciscus*, the source of OFr. *franceis*), f. **Fraŋkon* FRANK *sb.*[1]; see -ISH[1]. Cf. WELSH, SCOTCH.]

A. *adj.* **1.** Of or pertaining to France or its inhabitants. **2.** French-like ME.

Phrases, etc. **a.** In names of things of (attributed) French origin, as **F. barley** (see BARLEY); **F.-blue**, artificial ultramarine; **F. bread**, a kind of fancy bread; **F. casements**, windows turning upon two vertical edges attached to the jambs; **F. chalk**, a variety of steatite, used for making marks on cloth, etc.; **F. drain**, a rubble drain; †**F. eaves**, eaves provided with a gutter to carry off the water; **F. fake**, a variety of the Flemish fake; **F.-grey**, a tint composed of white with ivory black, Indian red and Chinese blue; **F. hem**, a kind of hem employed for the finishing of flounces; **F. horn**, a metal wind-instrument (see HORN); **F. paste**, a kind of glass into which a certain quantity of oxide of lead is introduced; **F. purple**, a beautiful dye prepared from lichens; **F. red** or **rouge**, genuine carmine; **F. rice** = AMELCORN; **F. roll** (see ROLL); **F.-roof**, a mansard roof; **F. tub**, a mixture used by dyers, of the protochloride of tin and logwood; **F. window**, a long window opening like a folding door, and serving for exit and entrance.

b. In names of trees and plants; as **F.-bean** (see BEAN); **F. berry** = AVIGNON BERRY; **F. cowslip** (see COWSLIP); **F. plum**, the fruit of a variety of *Prunus domestica*, dried and exported from France.

c. In names of venereal diseases; as *F. disease*, etc.

B. *absol.* and *sb.* **1.** The French language ME. **2.** *The French* (pl.): the French people. Also (rarely) without article = French persons 1595.

1. For Frensh of Paris was to hir unknowe CHAUCER. Phr. *Pedlar's F.*: cant, thieves' slang. **2.** Phr. *F. and English*: a children's game.

French (frenʃ), *v.* *rare.* 1639. [f. prec. adj.] **1.** *To French it*: to speak French. FULLER. **2.** To render into French or give a French form to 1887.

†**French crown.** 1599. The English name for the French coin called ECU, †*escu* –1608. **b.** *Punningly*, with reference to the baldness produced by the 'French disease'. *Mids. N.* I. ii. 99.

Frenchify (fre·nʃifəi), *v.* 1592. [f. FRENCH *a.* + -FY.] **1.** *trans.* To make French, imbue with French qualities. **2.** *intr.* To become French in ideas, manners, etc.; to have French sympathies 1775.

1. F. our English solidity into Froth and Whip-syllabub 1741. Hence **Fre·nchified** *ppl. a.* French-like (*contemptuous*); having the 'French disease'.

Frenchism (fre·nʃiz'm). 1750. [f. as prec. + -ISM.] A French custom, idiom, or characteristic; a Gallicism.

French leave. 1771. Originally, the custom (in the 18th c. prevalent in France) of going away from a reception, etc. without taking leave of the host or hostess. Hence, joc., *to take French leave*: to go away, or do anything, without permission or notice.

French-like. 1550. [f. FRENCH *sb.* + -LIKE.]

A. *adv.* After the manner of the French; in French fashion.

B. *adj.* Like the French 1848.

Frenchman (fre·nʃmæ̆n). OE. [f. FRENCH *a.* + MAN; orig. two words.] **1.** A man of French birth or nationality. **2.** A good, etc.) French scholar. *colloq.* 1670. **3.** A French ship 1889. Hence **Fre·nchmanlike** *a.* and *adv.*

French polish. 1819. **1.** A polish for wood-work; a solution of resin or gum resin in alcohol or wood naphtha. **2.** The smooth glossy surface produced on wood-work by the application of this. Also *punningly*. Hence **French-polish** *v. trans.* to make smooth and glossy with French-polish (*lit.* and *fig.*). **French-polisher.**

Frenetic, etc.: see PHRENETIC, etc.

†**Frenne, fren.** 1553. [Corrupt var. of *frend* FREMD, infl. by *forenne* FOREIGN.]

A. *adj.* Strange, not related. *rare.*

B. *sb.* A foreigner, stranger, enemy –1614.

Frenum: see FRÆNUM.

†**Fre·nzic, -al,** *a.* 1547. [f. FRENZY *sb.* + -IC, + -AL[1].] Affected with frenzy; crazy, mad; wildly enthusiastic –1748.

Frenzied (fre·nzid), *ppl. a.* 1796. [f. FRENZY *v.* + -ED[1].] Affected with frenzy; crazy; distracted, frantic; wildly enthusiastic.

F. dreams SCOTT, enthusiasts L. STEPHEN. Hence **Fre·nziedly** *adv.*

Frenzy, phrenzy (fre·nzi). [ME. *frenesie* – (O)Fr. *frénésie* – med.L. *phrenesia*, for L. *phrenesis*, f. Gr. φρήν, φρεν- mind; cf. FRANTIC, PHRENETIC, and see -Y[3].]

A. *sb.* **1.** Mental derangement; delirium, or temporary insanity; now chiefly, the rage or excitement of a paroxysm of mania. Now *rare* in lit. sense. Also *fig.* **2.** A wild idea; also, a craze (*for* something) 1632.

1. Demoniac f., moping melancholy, And moonstruck madness MILT. *fig.* The Poets eye in a fine f. rolling SHAKS. **a.** The Frensy of Travelling 1707.

B. *adj.* [? sb. used attrib.] †**1.** Mad, insane crazy –1647. **2.** *dial.* Angry; passionate 1859.

Hence **Fre·nzy** *v.* to drive to f., infuriate.

Frequence (frī·kwěns). 1535. [– (O)Fr. *fréquence* – L. *frequentia*; see next, -ENCE.] **1.** An assembling in large numbers; a crowded state or condition; also *concr.* concourse, crowd. Now *arch.* †**2.** Constant use of (something); familiarity –1624. **3.** Frequent occurrence or repetition 1603.

1. The Most High, who, in full f. bright Of angels..spake MILT.

Frequency (frī·kwěnsi). 1553. [– L. *frequentia*, f. *frequent-*; see next, -ENCY.] †**1.** The state or condition of being crowded; also *concr.* a concourse –1723. †**2.** The constant use or repetition *of* –1785; familiarity *with* –1680. **3.** The fact of occurring often or being repeated at short intervals 1641. **b.** *Physics*, etc. Rate of recurrence, e.g. of a vibration 1831; *Electr.* The number of complete cycles per second of an alternating current 1891. **c.** *Statistics.* The ratio of the actual to the number of possible occurrences of an event 1897.

3. The Strength and F. of the Pulse ARBUTHNOT. The diminished f. of wars 1836. **b.** Alternating currents of high f. 1893.

Frequent (frī·kwěnt), *a.* 1531. [– (O)Fr. *fréquent* or L. *frequens, -ent-* crowded, frequent, of unkn. origin; see -ENT.] †**1.** Crowded, full –1746. **2.** Found at short distances apart; numerous. Somewhat *arch.* 1605. **3.** Commonly used or practised, well known. Now *rare.* 1531. †Of a report, etc.: Widely current –1631. **4.** Happening at short intervals; often recurring. Of the pulse: Faster than normal. (The prevailing sense.) 1604. **5.** Addicted *to*; accustomed *to do*; given to repetition *in* 1560. **6.** †**a.** That is often *at* or *in* (a place) –1624. **b.** Constant, habitual 1628. †**c.** That is often *with* (a person), familiar; conversant *in* (a subject) –1632. **7.** quasi- *adv.* 1614.

1. In a ful and f. assemblie HOLLAND. **2.** Populous cities..f. Hospitals [etc.] CAMDEN. **4.** You may expect frequente letters MARVELL. F. forgeries 1750, blights 1795. **5.** Lesse f. to his Princely exercises then formerly SHAKS. **6. a.** In prisons more f.: in deaths oft 2 *Cor.* 11:23. **b.** A f. Comunicant 1628.

Frequent (frī·kwe·nt), *v.* 1477. [– (O)Fr. *fréquenter* or L. *frequentare*, f. *frequent-*; see prec.] **1.** *trans.* To visit often; to resort to habitually 1555. †**2.** To use habitually; to practise; to attend (a meeting) –1667; to honour with observances –1581. †**3.** *intr.* To resort *to* or *unto*; to associate *with*; to be often *in* or *about* –1810. †**4.** *trans.* To crowd, fill –1667.

1. A Coffee-house which I myself f. STEELE. To f. good company BERKELEY. **3.** Far from all the ways where men f. POPE. **4.** MILT. *P.L.* x. 1091.

Hence **Freque·ntable** *a.* that may be frequented, easily accessible. **Frequenta·tion,** the action or habit of frequenting or resorting to; habitual visiting. **Freque·nter,** one who frequents or resorts to.

Fre·quentage. 1814. *rare.* [f. prec. + -AGE.] The practice or habit of frequenting.

Frequentative (frīkwe·ntătiv). 1530. [– Fr. *fréquentatif, -ive* or L. *frequentativus*, f. *frequentare*; see FREQUENT *v.*, -ATIVE.]

A. *adj.* †**1.** Versed *in*. *Obs.* *Sc.* ROLLAND. **2.** *Gram.* Of a verb or verbal form: Expressive of the frequent repetition of an action 1533.

B. *sb.* A frequentative verb, verbal form, or conjugation 1530.

Frequently (frī·kwěntli), *adv.* 1531. [f. FREQUENT *a.* + -LY[2].] At frequent or short intervals, often repeatedly; †numerously –1638.

Frere, obs. FRIAR.

Frescade (freskā·d). 1656. [– Fr. †*frescade* (COTGR.) – It. *frescata*, f. *fresco* cool, fresh; see -ADE.] A cool walk; a shady alley.

Fresco (fre·sko), *sb.* Pl. **frescos, -oes.** 1598. [– It. *fresco* cool, fresh; orig. *in fresco*, †*al fresco* (see ALFRESCO), †*a fresco*, repr. It. *affresco*, i.e. *al fresco* 'on the fresh (plaster)'. See FRESH.] †**1.** Cool, fresh air; occas. a fresh breeze –1785. **2.** A kind of painting executed in water-colour on mortar or plaster which is not quite dry; a painting so executed 1598. Also *attrib.*

2. The grand sibyls..painted in f. by Michel Angelo EMERSON. Hence **Fre·sco** *v.* to paint in fresco.

Fresh (freʃ). [ME. *fresch* – OFr. *freis*, fem. *fresche* (mod. *frais, fraîche*) – Rom. **friscus* – Gmc. **friskaz*, repr. by OE. *fersċ* in senses 'not salted, not salt' = OFris., MDu. *fersc* (Du. *vers*), OHG. *frisc* (G. *frisch*), ON. *ferskr*.]

A. *adj.* **I. 1.** New, novel ME.; additional, other, further ME. **2.** Recent; newly made, received, or taken in ME. **3.** Raw, inexperienced; 'green' 1595. Also (*Univ. slang*) characteristic of a freshman. **b.** [Cf. G. *frech* impudent]. Forward, impertinent, free in behaviour (orig. *U.S.*) 1848.

1. MILT. *Lycidas* 193. **3.** SHAKS. *John* III. iv. 145.

II. 1. New; not artificially preserved; not salted, pickled, or smoked. late ME. **2.** Of water: Not salt or bitter; †(of a marsh) containing fresh as opp. to salt water late ME. **b.** Of or pertaining to such water ME. **3.** Untainted, pure; hence, invigorating, refreshing. Said *esp.* of air and water. ME. †**b.** Cool (*rare*) –1697. **4.** Retaining its original qualities; not stale, musty, or vapid. Also *transf.* of immaterial things. ME. **5.** Not faded or worn ME. **6.** Not sullied or tarnished; blooming ME.; †gaily attired –1587. **7.** Not exhausted or fatigued ME. **8.** Of the wind: Strong. Hence, of the way of a ship: Speedy, steady. 1533. **9. a.** Sober. Now only *Sc.* ME. **b.** Partially intoxicated 1812.

1. F. meat 1648, butter 1864. **2.** He always found the ice f. that floated upon the sea-water BOYLE. **3.** F. dews and flowers MILT. The desire of f. air SCOTT. **4.** F. egges 1632. Burton ale—f. or stale DIBDIN. News f. and f. ADDISON. **5.** My glory was f. in mee *Job* 24:20. When the memory of things was f. BERKELEY. **6.** The fresshe daysy CHAUCER. Hast thou beheld a fresher Gentlewoman SHAKS. 7. I never felt fresher in my life 1863. **8.** If it comes on to blow f. I shall make the signal for Boats to repair on board NELSON. *Comb.* †**f.-new** *a.* unpractised.

B. *adv.* In a fresh manner, freshly (see A.) ME. *Comb.* **f.-run** *a.* (a salmon, etc.) that has freshly run up from the sea.

C. *sb.* [The adj. used *absol.*] **1.** The fresh part or period 1715. **2.** A freshet, flood 1538; also, a gust, squall 1719. **3.** A pool, spring or stream of fresh water 1571. **4.** The part of a tidal river next above the salt water; also, the lands adjoining this part. Freq. in *pl.* Now *U.S.* 1634.

1. The f. of the morning NORTH. **2.** Sometimes there are great freshes in the River of Tyne

1682. **3.** I'le not shew him Where the quicke Freshes are *Temp.* III. ii. 75.

Fresh, *v.* ME. [f. FRESH *a.*] To †make or become fresh or lively.

Freshen (fre·ʃən), fre·ʃ'n), *v.* 1697. [f. as prec. + -EN[5].] **1.** *intr.* To become FRESH; to increase in strength; also with *up*. **b.** To become bright 1819. **c.** To lose salt or saltness (Webst.) 1864. **2.** *trans.* To make FRESH; *esp.* to renew, revive, give freshness to; to remove salt or saltness from 1749. **3.** *Naut.* 'To relieve (a rope) of its strain, or danger of chafing, by shifting or removing its place of nip' (Adm. Smyth) 1855.

1. The wind now freshened fast MARRYAT. To f. into smiles W. IRVING. **2.** Air to f. the room 1801. To f. up my Italian LOWELL, their memory 1874. **3.** *To f. hawse, the nip*: to pay out more cable so as to change the part exposed to friction. *To f. ballast*: to divide or separate it, so as to alter its position. *To f. way*: to increase the speed. Hence **Fre·shener,** something that freshens; *spec.* a spell of exercise for freshening a horse.

Fresher (fre·ʃəɹ). 1882. [f. FRESH *a.* + -ER[1].] **a.** *Univ. slang*: = FRESHMAN. **b.** A fresh breeze.

Freshet (freʃėt). Also *erron.* **fresh shot.** 1596. [prob. – fem. of OFr. *freschet* (as in *fontaine frechette*), f. *frais* FRESH; see -ET.] **1.** A small stream of fresh water. *Obs.* exc. *poet.* 1598. **2.** A stream or rush of fresh water flowing into the sea 1596. **3.** A flood or overflowing of a river caused by heavy rains or melted snow 1654.

3. The f. in the river..was so sudden that cattle ..were in danger of being drowned 1784. Hence **Fre·shet** *v.* to flood as with a f.

Freshly (fre·ʃli), *adv.* ME. [f. FRESH *a.* + -LY[2].] In a fresh manner; newly, recently; with renewed or unabated vigour; briskly; with undiminished strength, purity, distinctness, etc.; with fresh appearance, odour, etc.; †gaily –1523.

F. torn BYRON, pursued STOW. Looks he as f., as he did the day he wrastled *A.Y.L.* III. ii. 243.

Freshman (fre·ʃmæ̆n). 1550. [f. FRESH *a.* + MAN.] **1.** A new-comer; a novice. **2.** A student during his first year, *esp.* his first term, at a University (or *U.S.* a school) 1596.

2. He was but yet a f. in Cambridge NASHE. *Comb.* **f.-class** *U.S.*, 'the lowest of the four classes in an American college' (Webst.). Hence **Fre·shmanship,** the condition of being a f.; the period during which it lasts; also *joc.*, the personality of a f.

†Fre·shment. [f. FRESH *v.* + -MENT.] Refreshing influence. J. CARTWRIGHT.

Freshness (fre·ʃnės). ME. [f. FRESH *a.* + -NESS.] The quality of being FRESH. Also *concr.* a fresh stream (KEATS).

Jollitie, pleasaunce, and freshnesse 1500. The f. of the Aire BACON, of Waters BOYLE, of the Evening 1712. The glory and the f. of a dream WORDSW.

Fre·shwater, *a.* 1528. [f. FRESH *a.* + WATER *sb.*] **1.** Of or pertaining to, yielding, produced by, or living in water that is not salt. **2.** Unaccustomed to salt water, new to the sea 1621; hence, unskilled, raw, insignificant.

1. F. fish 1765, lakes GOLDSM., flowers 1828, shells LYELL. **2.** A f. sailor DE FOE. *fig.* Ignorant, unlearned, and f. critics FIELDING. Hence **†Fresh-watered** *a.* unskilled, raw.

Fresison (frĭsəi·sǫn). 1827. *Logic.* A mnemonic word designating the fifth mood of the fourth syllogistic figure, in which a universal negative major premiss and a particular affirmative minor yield a particular negative conclusion.

Fret (fret), *sb.*[1] ME. [prob. – OFr. *frete* trellis, interlaced work (mod. *frette*) of unkn. origin; see FRET *v.*[2]] **1.** Ornamental interlaced work; a net; an ornament consisting of jewels or flowers in a network. **2.** *Her.* Orig. a figure formed by two bendlets, dexter and sinister, intersecting; = Fr. *frette*. Later, 'a figure formed by two narrow bands in saltire, interlaced with a mascle' (Cussans). 1572. **3.** **†a.** *Arch.* Carved ornament, *esp.* in ceilings, consisting of intersecting lines in relief –1664. **b.** An ornamental pattern composed of continuous combinations of straight lines, joined usually at right angles. Also *attrib.* 1664.

1. A frette of goold sche hadde next hyre her CHAUCER. **3. b.** The f. or herring-bone is of common occurrence on vases of the oldest style BIRCH.

Comb.: **f.-cutting** *vbl. sb.*, the cutting of wood with a fret-saw into ornamental designs; also *attrib.*; **-saw,** a saw used for cutting frets, scrolls, etc.

Fret (fret), *sb.*[2] 1545. [f. FRET *v.*[1]] **1.** A gnawing or wearing away, erosion. Now *rare.* Also *concr.* †a fretting sore; a decayed spot. **2.** Pain in the bowels, gripes, colic. Also *pl.* Now *dial.* 1600. **3.** Agitation of mind; irritation, vexation; also, querulous utterance 1556. **†4.** A gust, squall (of wind) –1734. **5.** Secondary fermentation in liquors 1664.

3. My lord was in as great a f. as I DE FOE. Phr. *F. and fever, f. and fume. On* or *upon the f.*: in a state of agitation, irritation, ill humour, or impatience.

Fret (fret), *sb.*[3] 1500. [Of unkn. origin.] In musical instruments like the guitar, formerly a ring of gut (Stainer), now a bar or ridge of wood, metal, etc., placed on the fingerboard, to regulate the fingering.

Fret, *sb.*[4] *rare.* 1587. [– OFr. *fraite* opening, breach, difficult passage. Cf. next.] A breach or passage made by the sea.

†Fret, *sb.*[5] 1576. [– L. *fretum* strait, sound, channel; perh. confused with prec.] A strait –1661.

Fret (fret), *v.*[1] Pa. t. and pple. **fretted.** Pr. pple. **fretting.** [OE. *fretan* = MLG., MDu. *vrēten* (Du. *vreten*), OHG. *frezzan* (G. *fressen*), Goth. *fraītan*; Gmc. f. **fra-* FOR-[1] + **etan* EAT.] **†1.** *trans.* To eat, devour –ME. **2.** To gnaw; to consume, torture or wear by gnawing. Now only of small animals. Also *intr.* ME. **3.** *transf.* of slow and gradual destructive action, as of frost, rust, disease, corrosives, etc. Const. *into, to* (the result). Also *fig.* Also *absol.* ME. **4.** To form or make by wearing away 1593. **†5.** *intr.* To make a way by gnawing or corrosion (*lit.* and *fig.*) –1676. **†6.** *intr.* for *refl.* To become eaten, corroded, or worn; to waste away; to decay –1804. **7.** *trans.* To chafe, irritate ME. **8.** *intr.* To distress oneself with constant regret or discontent; to chafe, worry. Often with additional notion of querulous utterances. 1551. Also quasi-*trans.* with *away, out* 1605. **9.** *intr.* Of liquor: To undergo secondary fermentation. Now *dial.* 1664. **b.** *trans.* (*causatively*) 1742. **10.** *intr.* Of a stream, etc.: To move in agitation or turmoil; to chafe 1727. **11.** *trans.* (*causatively*). To cause to rise in waves; to ruffle 1794.

2. Like as it wer a moth fretting a garment 1551. **3.** The river frets away the rocks along its banks HUXLEY. Phr. *To f. the heart* (fig.). **4.** With cadent Teares f. Channels in her cheekes *Lear* I. iv. 308. **7.** Horses..fretted into a foam W. IRVING. **8.** He only frets to keep himself employed GOLDSM. quasi-*trans.* A poore Player, That struts and frets his houre vpon the Stage *Macb.* V. v. 25. Hence **Fre·tter. Fre·tting** *vbl. sb.* and *ppl. a.*

Fret (fret), *v.*[2] ME. [Chiefly in pa. pple. †*fret, fretted*; prob. – OFr. *freter* (in pa. pple. *freté* = AL. *frectatus, frictatus*), rel. to *frete* trellis; see FRET *sb.*[1] With sense 2 cf. FRETISH *v.*[2]] **†1.** *trans.* To adorn with interlaced work; to adorn richly with gold, silver, or jewels –1668. **b.** *transf.* To variegate 1601. **2.** *Arch.* To adorn (*esp.* a ceiling) with carved or embossed work in patterns 1602. **3.** *Her.* To interlace 1572.

1. Frenyeis of fyne silk, fretit ful fre 1450. **b.** Yon grey Lines That f. the Clouds SHAKS. **2.** This Maiesticall Roofe, fretted with golden fire SHAKS.

†Fret, *v.*[3] ME. [poss. – OFr. **freiter* = mod. dial. *fretter*, Pr. *fretar*, It. *frettare* :– Rom. **frictiare*, frequent. of L. *fricare* rub.] **1.** *trans.* To rub, chafe. Causatively: To make pass by rubbing. **2.** *intr.* To rub, produce friction; to fray *out* 1643. (Merged in FRET *v.*[1])

Fret (fret), *v.*[4] 1600. [f. FRET *sb.*[3]] *trans.* To furnish (a guitar, etc.) with frets.

Fretful (fre·tfŭl), *a.* 1593. [f. FRET *v.*[1] + -FUL.] **†1.** Corrosive, irritating (*lit.* and *fig.*); also, inflamed –1804. **2.** Disposed to fret, irritable, peevish; impatient 1602. **3.** Of water, etc.: Agitated, broken into waves. Of the wind: Blowing in frets; gusty. 1613. **4.** Characterized by or productive of fretting 1737.

1. 2 *Hen. VI*, III. ii. 403. **2.** The fretfull Porpentine SHAKS. **4.** The f. stir Unprofitable and the fever of the world WORDSW. **Fre·tful-ly** *adv.*, **-ness.**

†Fre·tish, fre·tize, *v.*[1] 1523. [– *frediss-*, lengthened stem of OFr. *fredir, freidir* (mod. *froidir*), f. *freid* (mod. *froid*) :– Rom. **frīgidus* for L. *frĭgidus* FRIGID; see -ISH[1].] *trans.* To chill, benumb. Only in *pass.* –1639.

†Fre·tish, Fre·tize, *v.*[2] Also **frettish.** 1579. [Connected with OFr. *fraitis* (Godefroy) said of capitals of columns, and app. rendering 'quasi in modum retis' in 1 Kings 7:17. Cf. FRET *sb.*[1], *v.*[2]] = FRET *v.*[2] –1703.

Frette, var. of FRET *sb.*[1]

Fretted (fre·tėd), *ppl. a.*[1] 1545. [f. FRET *v.*[1] + -ED[1].] **1.** Eaten or worn into holes, chafed. **2.** Worried, vexed, distressed 1756.

Fretted (fre·tėd), *ppl. a.*[2] ME. [f. FRET *v.*[2] + -ED[1].] **1.** Adorned with fretwork; carved or wrought into frets. Also *transf.* and *fig.* 1552. **2.** *Her.* Interlaced 1586.

Fretty (fre·ti), *a.* 1562. [– OFr. *freté*, f. *frete* (mod. *frette*); see FRET *sb.*[1], -Y[5].] *Her.* 'Covered with a number of narrow bars or sticks, usually eight, lying in the directions of the bend and bend-sinister, interlacing each other' (Cussans). †Of a charge: Fretted or interlaced *with*.

†Fre·twise, -ways, *adv.* ME. [f. FRET *sb.*[1] + -WISE, -WAYS.] In the form of a fret; so as to interlace –1717.

Fre·twork. 1601. [f. FRET *sb.*[1] + WORK *sb.*] **1.** *Arch.* Carved work in decorative patterns consisting largely of intersecting lines, *esp.* as used for ceilings. Also *attrib.* **2.** Woodwork cut with a fret-saw into ornamental designs 1881. **3.** The ornamental part of lead-light work 1859.

Freudian (frọi·diăn), *a.* and *sb.* 1910. [See -IAN.] (A disciple) of Dr. Sigmund *Freud* or his teaching; see PSYCHOANALYSIS. Hence **Freu·dianism.**

Friable (frəi·ăb'l), *a.* 1563. [– Fr. *friable* or L. *friabilis*, f. *friare* crumble into small pieces; see -ABLE.] Capable of being easily crumbled or reduced to powder; pulverizable, crumbly.

A f. substance like rust of iron G. WHITE. Hence **Friabi·lity, Fri·ableness,** the quality of being f.

†Fri·and. 1598. [– (O)Fr. *friand* dainty, in OFr. gay, vivacious, ardent for pleasure, for *friant*, pr. pple. of *frire* FRY *v.*] **A.** *adj.* Dainty; delicious to the palate; fond of delicate food –1818. **B.** *sb.* An epicure 1598.

Friar (frəiᵊɹ, frəi·əɹ), *sb.* [ME. *frere* – (O)Fr. *frère* :– L. *frater, fratr-*. For the phonology cf. *briar, entire, quire.*] **†1.** = BROTHER, in fig. uses –1821. **2.** In the *R. C. Ch.* A brother or member of any religious order, but esp. of one of the four mendicant orders: the Franciscans (†*Friars minors, Minorites*, or *Grey Friars*); the Augustines (*Austin Friars*); the Dominicans (*Friars Preachers, Black Friars*); and the Carmelites (*White Friars*) ME. **b.** *pl.* The quarters or convent of a particular order; hence often a name for the part of a town where the convent was ME. **3.** A name of various fishes; e.g. the silversides, a N. American fish 1603. **4.** An Australian bird of the genus *Philemon*; now usu. *f.-bird* 1798. **5.** *Print.* A white or light place on a printed page 1683. **6.** *White friars*: 'a small flake of light-coloured sediment floating in wine' 1745.

Comb.: **friar's balsam,** tincture of benzoin compound used as an application for ulcers and wounds; **f.-bird**: see sense 4; **friar's cap(s,** the Monkshood, *Aconitum napellus*; **friar's cowl,** the Cuckoo-pint or Wake Robin, *Arum maculatum*; **friar's crown,** *Canduus eriophorus*; **friar's lantern** = *Ignis fatuus*; **f.-skate,** the *Raia alba*.

Hence **†Friar** *v. intr.* to play the f. **Fri·arly** *a.* of or pertaining to friars; friar-like; *adv.* in friarly fashion.

†Friar Rush. 1603. The proper name (G. *Rausch*) of the hero of a popular story, which tells of the adventures of a demon disguised as a friar. ¶Confused by Scott with *Ignis fatuus*.

Friary (frəi·əri), *sb.* 1538. [f. FRIAR *sb.* + -Y³.] **1.** A convent of friars. **2.** A fraternity of friars 1631. †**3.** The institution of friars –1661. **4.** *attrib.* (of or pertaining to a friary or friaries) 1598.

†**Fri·ary** *a.* 1589. [f. FRIAR *sb.* + -Y¹.] Of or pertaining to friars –1605.

Fria·tion. 1656. [f. *friat-*, pa. ppl. stem of L. *friare* crumble + -ION. Cf. FRIABLE.] The action of rubbing or crumbling into small pieces –1743.

Fribble (fri·b'l). 1664. [f. next vb.]

A. *sb.* **1.** A trifler. **2.** A trifling thing or idea 1832. **3.** Frivolity 1881.

1. The fop, the f., and the beau 1771.

B. *adj.* Trifling, frivolous, ridiculous 1798.

Fribble (fri·b'l), *v.* 1627. [Expressive formation.] †**1.** *trans.* To falter, stammer; *intr.* to totter in walking –1709. **2.** *intr.* In early use, to act aimlessly or feebly; to fiddle. Now only: To behave frivolously. 1640.

2. Not as you treat these fools that are fribbling round about you THACKERAY. Hence **Fri·bbler,** a trifler. **Fri·bbling** *vbl. sb.* **Fri·bblery,** frivolity.

Friborgh, -burgh: see FRITHBORH.

†**Fricace,** *sb.* 1533. [Earliest forms *fricasie*, *-cie* – L. *fricatio*.] = FRICATION. –1643.

Fricandeau (frikændō^u·). Pl. **-deaux.** 1706. [– Fr. *fricandeau*.] A slice of veal or other meat fried or stewed and served with sauce; a fricassee of veal.

Fricandel, -elle (frikænde·l). 1872. [In Eng. perh. a var. deduced from prec., but mod. Pr. has *fricandel*, whence Fr. †*fricadelle*; cf. also G. *frikadelle, frikandelle*.] Hashed meat made into balls and fried.

Fricassee (frikăsī·), *sb.* 1568. [– Fr. *fricassée*, pa. pple. fem. of *fricasser* cut up (meat) and stew in sauce.] Meat sliced and fried or stewed and served with sauce. Now usually a ragout of small animals or birds cut in pieces. Also *fig.*

Fricassee (frikăsī·), *v.* 1657. [f. prec. sb. Cf. Fr. *fricasser*.] To make a fricassee of; to dress as a fricassee. Also *transf.*

†**Frica·tion.** 1533. [– L. *fricatio*, f. *fricat-*, pa. ppl. stem of *fricare* rub; see -ION.] **1.** The action of chafing or rubbing –1694. **2.** Friction –1725.

Fricative (fri·kătiv). 1860. [– mod.L. *fricativus*, f. L. *fricare* rub + -ATIVE.]

A. *adj.* **1.** Of a consonant-sound: Produced by the friction of the breath through a narrow opening between two of the speech-organs. **2.** 'Sounded by friction, as certain musical instruments' (*Cent. Dict.*).

B. *sb.* A fricative consonant 1863.

Fricatrice (fri·kătris). 1605. [f. L. *fricare* rub + -TRIX. Cf. TRIBADE] A lewd woman.

†**Frickle.** 1681. [Of unkn. origin.] A basket (for fruit) that holds a bushel. (Dicts.)

Friction (fri·kʃən). 1581. [– Fr. *friction* (Paré) – L. *frictio* (Celsus), f. *frict-*, pa. ppl. stem of *fricare* rub; see -ION.] **1.** The action of chafing or rubbing (the body or limbs). **2.** The rubbing of one body against another; attrition 1704. **3.** *Physics* and *Mech.* The resistance which any body meets with, in moving over another body 1722. **4.** *fig.*; *esp.* of opinions, temperaments, etc. 1761.

1. A cold bath, with f. and a little exercise HAMERTON. **3.** Phr. *Angle of f.*, the maximum slope at which one body will rest upon another without sliding down. *F. at rest*, the amount of f. between two touching bodies that are relatively at rest. **4.** The f. between parent and child 1884.

Comb., chiefly *Mech.*: **f.-ball,** one of the balls used to lessen the f. bearings, etc.; **-block,** a block which is pressed against a revolving body to arrest its motion by f.; **-brake,** a form of dynamometer in which a pair of f.-blocks are screwed to a journal rotating at a given speed; also a brake which measures the amount of work performed by any prime mover, by allowing it during the time of trial to waste all its work on f.; a measurer of the lubricity of oils; a brake operating by means of f.; **-breccia** (*Geol.*) = *fault-rock* (see FAULT); **-clutch, -cone, -coupling, -disc,** contrivances for transmitting motion by frictional contact; **-fremitus** (*Path.*) = *f.-sound*; **-fuse** = *f.-tube*; **-gear, -gearing,** gear or gearing for transmitting motion by frictional contact; **-machine,** an electrical machine, generating electricity by contact with amalgamated silk; **-powder,** a composition of chlorate of potash and antimony, which readily ignites by f.; **-primer,** U.S. name for *f.-tube*; **-roller,** a roller placed so as to lessen the f. of anything passing over it; also, = *f.wheel* (*b*); **-sound** (*Path.*), the auscultatory sound heard when the pleuræ or pericardium are roughened by inflammation and effused lymph; **-tube,** a tube used for firing cannon by means of friction; **-wheel,** (*a*) see *friction-roller*; (*b*) one of the small rollers which revolve in bearings, and sustain an axle in the depression formed by the contiguity of the upper portion of their peripheries. Hence **Fri·ction** *v. trans.* to chafe or rub (the body, etc.). **Fri·ctionless** *a.*, **-ly** *adv.*

Frictional (fri·kʃənăl), *a.* 1850. [f. prec. + -AL¹.] Of or pertaining to friction, moved or produced by friction.

Phr. *F. electricity*, electricity developed by friction. *F. gearing* (*-wheels*), wheels which transmit motion by friction instead of by teeth. Hence **Fri·ctionally** *adv.*

Friday (frəi·de¹, -di). [OE. *frīġedæġ*, corresp. to OFris. *frī(g)endei*, MLG., MDu. *vrīdach* (Du. *vrijdag*), OHG. *frīatag* (G. *freitag*); i.e. day of *Friġ* = ON. *Frigg*, name of the wife of Odin, prop. subst. use of fem. of Gmc. **frijaz* noble, FREE; WGmc. tr. of late L. *Veneris dies* day of the planet Venus (whence Fr. *vendredi*) based on Gr. *Ἀφροδίτης ἡμέρα* 'day of Aphrodite'.] **1.** The sixth day of the week. **2.** A reception or entertainment given on that day 1836. **3.** *attrib.*, as *F. morning*. 1592.

1. *Black F.*: applied to various historic dates of disastrous events which took place on Friday, as May 11, 1866, when a panic ensued on the failure of Overend, Gurney, & Co.; etc. *Good F.*: the Friday before Easter Day, observed in commemoration of Christ's crucifixion.

Fridge (fridʒ), *v.* 1550. [app. echoic; cf. FIG *v.*³, FIDGE *v.*] †**1.** *intr.* To fidget –1681. †**2.** To chafe, rub, scrape (*upon*, etc.) –1651. **3.** *trans.* To rub, fray, chafe. Now chiefly *dial.* 1617.

Fried (frəid), *ppl. a.* ME. [f. FRY *v.* + -ED¹.] Cooked by frying.

Friend (frend). [OE. *frēond* = OFris., OS. *friund* (Du. *vriend*), OHG. *friunt* (G. *freund*), ON. *frændi*, Goth. *frijonds*; Gmc. pres. ppl. formation on **frijōjan* love, f. **frijaz* beloved, FREE]

A. *sb.* **1.** 'One joined to another in mutual benevolence and intimacy' (J.). Not ordinarily used of lovers or relatives. **2.** Applied *loosely*, e.g. to a mere acquaintance, or to a stranger; also, used by members of the 'Society of Friends' as the ordinary mode of address. Also often *ironically*. ME. **3.** A kinsman or near relation. Now only in *pl.* OE. †**4.** A lover or paramour of either sex –1765. **5.** One who wishes (another, a cause, etc.) well; a sympathizer, patron, or supporter. Const. *of, to.* ME. **b.** *transf.* Anything helpful ME. **6.** One not an *enemy*; one who is on good terms with another, not hostile or at variance; one who is on the same side in warfare, politics, etc. OE. **7.** A Quaker 1679.

1. And right as welcome as a f. would fall M. ARNOLD. Phr. *F. of God*: one eminent for piety, and enjoying God's special favour. See *Jas.* 2:23. **2.** 'Nay, keep it, f., keep it,' said Dinah Plait MAR. EDGEWORTH. My learned f. (*mod.*). **3.** Friends agree best at a distance *Sc. Prov.* **4.** *Meas. for M.* I. iv. 29. **5.** Friends to marriage 1782, of order 1878. Phr. *F. in* or *at court*: one influential in high quarters who is disposed to help another. **6.** Phr. *To be, keep, make friends with*: to be or get on good terms with; also absol. *to be friends.*

†**B.** *adj.* Well-disposed, friendly, not hostile. (Cf. ENEMY *a.*) –1690.

Friend (frend), *v.* ME. [f. FRIEND *sb.*] †**1.** *trans.* To make (persons) friends or friendly; to join in friendship –1604. **2.** To act as a friend to, befriend; to assist, help. *arch.* or *poet.* 1562. Also *fig.* of things.

2. Well, the Gods are aboue, time must f. or end SHAKS. Hence **Frie·nded** *ppl. a.* having a f. or friends; befriended (*rare*).

Friendless (fre·ndlės), *a.* OE. [f. FRIEND *sb.* + -LESS.] **1.** Destitute of friends. **2.** = Unfriendly. SHELLEY.

1. †*Friendless man*: in OE. law, an outlaw. Hence **Frie·ndlessness.**

Friendlike (fre·ndləik), *a.* 1559. [f. FRIEND *sb.* + -LIKE.] Like a friend or friends, friendly.

Friendly (fre·ndli). [OE. *frēondlić* adj., *-līće* adv.; see -LY¹,².]

A. *adj.* **1.** Having the qualities or disposition of a friend, disposed to act as a friend, kind. **2.** Characteristic of or befitting a friend or friends; manifesting friendship ME. **3.** Not hostile, on amicable terms. Const *to, with.* 1595. **4.** Well-wishing; disposed to help or support 1535. **5.** Kindly, propitious, favourable; convenient. Const. *to*, †*unto*. ME. †**6.** Of things: Not jarring or conflicting –1793.

2. A f. nod 1868. Phr. *F. lead*, an entertainment given, among the poorer classes in London, for the benefit of a friend in distress, etc. **3.** The King's flag is insulted at every F. Port we look at NELSON. *A f. match* (at *Football*, etc.): one not played in competition for a cup, etc. **4.** The Gods to day stand f. *Jul. C.* V. i. 94. **5.** Trees with f. shade DRYDEN. **6.** F. colours POPE.

Phr. **Friendly Society.** Orig., the name of a particular fire-insurance company. Later, one of various associations, the members of which pay fixed contributions to insure help in sickness and old age, and provision for their families in the event of death.

B. *sb.* A friendly native; also, a friendly match 1870.

C. *adv.* In a friendly manner or spirit OE.

Hence **Frie·ndlily** *adv.* in a f. manner. **Frie·ndliness,** the quality or condition of being f.; occas. *pl.* manifestations of friendliness.

Friendship (fre·ndʃip). [OE. *frēondsćipe*; see -SHIP.] **1.** The state of being a friend; association of persons as friends; a friendly intimacy. **2.** Friendly feeling or disposition felt or shown; friendliness ME. †**3.** A friendly act; friendly aid –1613. †**4.** 'Conformity, affinity, correspondence, aptness to unite' (J.) 1695.

1. Without f., society is but meeting BACON. My college friendships TENNYSON. **2.** Christ's f. to his disciples SOUTH. **3.** *Lear* III. ii. 62. **4.** Colours which have a F. with each other DRYDEN.

†**Friese,** *a.* and *sb.* 1481. [The native name.] = FRISIAN, q.v. Hence **Frie·sic** *a.*, †**Frie·sish** *a.* = FRISIAN.

Frieze (frīz), *sb.*¹ ME. [– Fr. *frise* (whence also G. *fries*) – med.L. *(*lana*) *frisia* Frisian wool (so L. *panni frisii* Frisian cloths).] **1.** A kind of coarse woollen cloth, with a nap, usually on one side only; now *esp.* of Irish make. †**2.** The nap or down on a plant –1688. **3.** An abrasion of the grain in leather 1885.

1. An old calash . . lined with green frize STERNE.

Frieze (frīz), *sb.*² 1563. [– Fr. *frise* – med.L. *frisium*, var. of *frigium*, for L. *Phrygium* (sc. *opus*) Phrygian work; cf. L. *phrygiæ vestes*.] *Arch.* **1.** That member in the entablature of an order which comes between the architrave and cornice. **b.** A band of painted or sculptured decoration 1847. **2.** In a column = HYPOTRACHELIUM. 1569. **3.** *attrib.*, as *f.-work*. Also **f.-panel,** one of the uppermost panels of a six-panelled door. 1678.

1. The . . f. adorned in stucco with sea-monsters H. WALPOLE. **2.** The freezes gold, and gold the capitals POPE.

Hence **Friezed** *ppl. a.* furnished with a f.

Frieze (frīz), *v.*¹ 1509. [– Fr. *friser* or Sp. *frisar*; see FRIZZ *v.*¹] **1.** *trans.* To cover with a nap. *Hist.* †**2.** = FRIZZ *v.*¹ Hence **Frie·zing** *vbl. sb.*; also *attrib.*

Frieze (frīz), *v.*² 1577. [– Fr. *friser*, related to *frise* FRIEZE *sb.*² Cf. med.L. *frisare* embroider (with silver or gold).] **1.** *trans.* To embroider with gold. Now *rare.* **2.** *Naut.* (See quot.) 1769. **3.** To cover (a silver plate) with chased patterns 1678.

2. *Friezing*, ornamental carving or painting above the drift-rails, and likewise round the stern or bow [of a ship] 1850.

Friezed (frīzd), *ppl. a.* Now *Hist.* 1509. [f. FRIEZE *v.*¹ and *sb.*¹ + -ED.] **1.** Of cloth: Having a nap. **2.** Of a plant: Downy 1578.

Friezer (frī·zəɹ). 1557. [f. FRIEZE *v.*¹ + -ER¹.] One who friezes cloth.

Frigate (fri·gĕt). 1585. [– Fr. *frégate* (XVI *fragate*) – It. *fregata*, †*fragata* (whence Sp. *fragata*), of unkn. origin.] **1.** A light and swift vessel, orig. built for rowing, afterwards for sailing. *Obs.* exc. *poet.* **2.** †**a.** A merchantman –1800. **b.** A war-vessel. In the Royal Navy, formerly a vessel of the class next in size and equipment to ships of the line, carrying from 28 to 60 guns on the main deck and a raised quarter-deck and forecastle. Not now applied to a distinct class of vessel. 1630. **3.** A large swift-flying raptorial bird (*Fregata aquila*), found near land in the tropical and warmer temperate seas. Also *f.-bird, -petrel.* 1738. **4.** *attrib.* 1641.

Comb.: **f.-built** *a.* having 'a descent of some steps from the quarter-deck and forecastle into the waist' (Adm. Smyth); **-bird, -petrel** (see 3).

Frigatoon (frigătū·n). 1721. [– It. *fregatone*, augm. of *fregata* FRIGATE.] A Venetian vessel, with a square stern, having only a mainmast, mizzen-mast, and bowsprit. 'Also applied to a ship sloop-of-war' (Adm. Smyth).

†**Fri·gefact,** *v. rare.* 1599. [– L. *frigefactare* (Plautus), f. *frigēre* be cold + *fact-*, pa. ppl. stem of *facere* make.] *trans.* To chill –1656. So †**Frigefa·ction,** the action or process of chilling. †**Frigefa·ctive** *a.* chilling.

Fright (frəit), *sb.* [OE. *fryhto*, metathetic (Northumb.) var. of *fyrhto*, *-u* = Goth. *faurhtei* :– Gmc. **furxtīn*, f. **furxtaz* afraid, repr. by OE. *forht*, OS. *foroht*, *-aht*, OHG. *foraht*, Goth. *faurhts*.] **1.** In OE.: Fear in general. *Obs.* In ME. and in mod. use: Sudden fear, violent terror, alarm. An instance of this. **2.** †Anything that causes terror. Hence (*colloq.*) a person or thing of a shocking, grotesque, or ridiculous appearance. 1634.

1. Least by his clamour..The Towne might fall in f. SHAKS. Hence **Fri·ghtless** *a.* without fear.

Fright (frəit), *v.* [OE. (Northumb.) *fryhta*, var. of *fyrhtan* = OFris. **fruchtia*, OS. *forahtian*, OHG. *furihten*, *for(a)htan* (G. *fürchten*), Goth. *faurhtjan* :– Gmc. **furxtjan*, f. **furxtaz* afraid; see prec.] †**1.** *intr.* To be afraid –ME. **2.** *trans.* To affect with fright; to scare, terrify. Repl. by *frighten*, exc. *poet.* OE.

2. Frighting the maids GOLDSM. Hence **Fri·ghted** *ppl. a.* affected with fright; pervaded with fear (MILT. *P. L.* II. 994). **Fri·ghtedly** *adv.* †**Fri·ghter,** one who or that which causes fright or scares away.

Frighten (frəi·t'n), *v.* 1666. [f. FRIGHT *sb.* + -EN[5]; superseding FRIGHT *v.*] = FRIGHT *v.* 2.

Frightened by a shadow FROUDE.

Frightful (frəi·tful), *a.* ME. [f. FRIGHT *sb.* + -FUL.] †**1.** Full of terror; timid; alarmed –1802. **2.** Alarming (const. *to*); shocking, dreadful, revolting 1700.

1. The wild and frightfull Heards DRAYTON. **2.** The f. effects of jealousy HUME. A f. scandal FROUDE. Hence **Fri·ghtfully** *adv.* (often a mere intensive). **Fri·ghtfulness,** the quality or state of being f.; *esp.* terrorizing of non-combatants as a military resource.

Frightment (frəi·tmĕnt). *rare.* 1607. [f. FRIGHT *v.* + -MENT.] The state of being in a fright; something that causes fright.

Frigid (fri·dʒid), *a.* 1622. [– L. *frigidus*, f. *frigēre* be cold, f. *frigus* cold; see -ID[1].] **1.** Intensely cold, devoid of heat or warmth, of a low temperature 1639. **2.** *transf.* Wanting in sexual vigour; impotent –1660. **3.** *fig.* Destitute of ardour or warmth of feeling, lacking enthusiasm or zeal; cold, apathetic; formal, stiff 1658. Of things: Chilling, depressing 1844. **b.** Dull, flat, insipid 1713; †lacking force or point –1699.

1. Nuns in f. cells LONGF. *Frigid zone*: each of the two regions which lie within the north and south polar circles respectively. **3.** Our reception was f. JOHNSON. A f. adieu T. HARDY: **b.** F. splendours 1888. Hence **Fri·gid-ly** *adv.*, **-ness.**

‖**Frigidarium** (fridʒidēᵊ·riŏm). 1706. [L., f. *frigidus*; see prec., -ARIUM.] The cooling-room in a Roman bath. Also *transf.*

Frigidity (fridʒi·dĭti). ME. [– Fr. *frigidité* – late L. *frigiditas*, f. *frigidus*; see FRIGID, -ITY.] **1.** The state or quality of being frigid; intense coldness. **2.** *transf.* Want of generative heat; impotence 1586. **3.** *fig.* Want of warmth of feeling or zeal; apathy, coldness 1631; lack of fire or spirit; flatness, insipidity; also quasi-*concr.* 1642.

1. The benumming frigiditie of Groenland 1630. The f. of decrepit Age GLANVILL. **3.** To write with f. JOHNSON. The f. of the French drama 1763.

Frigoric (frigǫ·rik). 1812. [f. L. *frigus*, *frigor-* cold + -IC. Cf. Fr. *frigorique* sb.] †**A.** *sb.* An imagined imponderable cause of cold.

B. *adj.* 'Pertaining to or consisting in the application of cold' (*Cent. Dict.*). *rare.* 1887.

Frigorific (frigŏri·fik), *a.* 1667. [– L. *frigorificus* cooling, f. as prec.; see -FIC.] Producing cold, freezing; cooling.

Frill (fril), *sb.*[1] 1591. [contemp. with FRILL *v.*[1]; of unkn. origin. Sense 3, not recorded till XIX, may have been the original, in which case the development would be similar to that of *chitterling*, Fr. *fraise*, and G. *gekröse* (i) mesentery, (ii) ruff.] **1.** An ornamental edging of woven material, of which one edge is gathered and the other left loose so as to give it a wavy or fluted appearance. Also *transf.* **b.** Anything resembling this; e.g. a fringe of feathers round the neck of a bird, a tuft on the neck of a dog, etc. 1878. **2.** A kind of scallop-shell 1803. **3.** Used by butchers for: The mesentery of an animal 1879. **4.** *Photogr.* [f. the vb.] The irregular rising of a gelatine film at the edges of a plate.

1. *fig.* (*pl.*) Showy or useless embellishments or accomplishments.

Comb.: **f.-back,** a variety of pigeon, having an extraordinary frill-like appendage encircling the neck; **-lizard,** an Australian lizard of the genus *Chlamydosaurus*, whose neck is encircled by a broad erectile membrane. Hence **Fri·lly** *a.*, full of or resembling frills; also as *sb. pl.* frilled undergarments.

Frill, *sb.*[2] [f. FRILL *v.*[3]; prob. an etymologizing figment to account for FRILL *sb.*[1]] The ruffling of a hawk's feathers when frilling with cold. WORCESTER.

Frill (fril), *v.*[1] 1574. [See FRILL *sb.*[1]] **1.** *trans.* To furnish or decorate with a frill. †**2.** To furl *up* 1603. **3.** *Photogr.* To raise (a film) in flutes like a frill. Also *intr.* 1891.

†**Frill,** *v.*[2] *rare.* 1677. [imit.] Of the eagle: To scream –1688.

†**Frill,** *v.*[3] [– OFr. *friller* shiver with cold.] To shiver with cold. (Dicts.)

Frilled (frild), *ppl. a.* 1825. [f. FRILL *sb.*[1] or *v.*[1] + -ED[1] or [2].] Having, wearing, or adorned with or as with a frill. Of a photographic plate: Raised in flutes at the edges.

F. lizard = *frill-lizard*. Hence **Fri·lledness.**

Frilling (fri·liŋ), *vbl. sb.* 1815. [f. FRILL *v.*[1] + -ING[1].] **1.** The putting a frill to (a garment); *concr.* frilled edging; frills. **2.** *Photogr.* The rising in flutes along the edge 1880.

Frim, *a.* Now *dial.* [OE. *freme* :– pre-hist. **frami-*, cogn. w. *fram* adj., forward, etc.] **a.** Vigorous, flourishing; plump. **b.** Abundant in sap, juicy; abundant. **c.** Soluble, fusible.

b. The f. sap..From the full root DRAYTON.

‖**Frimaire** (frimę̄·r). 1838. [Fr., f. *frimas* hoar-frost.] The third month of the French revolutionary calendar (Nov. 21 to Dec. 20).

Fringe (frindʒ), *sb.* [ME. *frenge* – OFr. *frenge*, *fringe* (mod. *frange*) :– Rom. **frimbia*, metathetic alt. of late L. *fimbria*, earlier only pl., fibres, shreds, fringe. For the change of e to i before ndʒ cf. *cringe, hinge, singe, swinge*.] **1.** An ornamental bordering, consisting of a narrow band to which are attached threads of silk, cotton, etc., either loose or formed into tassels, twists, etc. **2.** Anything resembling this; a border or edging 1649; an outer edge or margin of any kind; an outer limit of a country, area, etc. 1898. **b.** *fig.* An appendage or sequel; also (*colloq.*) irrelevant matter 1642. **c.** A portion of the front hair brushed forward and cut short 1883. **d.** In plants and animals 1601. **e.** *Anat.* = FIMBRIA. 1857. **f.** *Optics.* One of the coloured spectra produced by diffraction 1704.

1. She had..made many yards of f. JANE AUSTEN. **2.** The f. of the foam BYRON. **b.** In.. the confines of Grace and the fringes of Repentance JER. TAYLOR.

Comb.: **f.-net,** a net to confine a fringe of hair; **-pod,** the Californian name of *Thysanocarpus laciniatus*; **-tree,** *Chionanthus virginica.*

Hence **Fri·ngeless** *a.* having no f.

Fringe (frindʒ), *v.* 1480. [f. prec. sb.] **1.** *trans.* To furnish, adorn, or encircle with or as with a fringe. **2.** To serve as a fringe to 1794.

Fringent (fri·ndʒĕnt), *a. rare.* 1847. [app. formed to correspond with *friction*, on the supposed analogy of *fraction, frangent.*] Exercising friction.

A shower of meteors..lit by f. air, Blaze EMERSON.

Fringilla·ceous, *a.* 1853. [f. L. *fringilla* finch + -ACEOUS.] Pertaining to the finches. **Fringi·llide** [anglicized f. mod.L. *fringillidæ*], a bird of the finch family. **Fringi·lline** *a.* of or pertaining to the finches.

Fringy (fri·ndʒi), *a.* 1750. [f. FRINGE *sb.* + -Y[1].] **1.** Of the nature of or resembling a fringe. **2.** Furnished with a fringe or fringes; covered with fringes 1831.

‖**Fripo·n(n)erie.** *rare.* 1708. [Fr., f. *fripon* rogue; see -ERY.] Roguery.

Fri·pper. 1598. [– Fr. *fripier*, alt. f. OFr. *frepier*; f. *frepe* rag, old clothes, of unkn. origin; see -ER[2] 2.] = next. –1697.

Fripperer (fri·pərəɹ). 1584. [Extended form of prec.; see -ER[1] 3.] A dealer in cast-off clothing.

Frippery (fri·pĕri). 1568. [– Fr. *friperie*, OFr. *freperie*, f. *frepe* rag, old clothes; see FRIPPER, -ERY.] †**1.** Cast-off clothes –1824. **2.** Finery in dress, *esp.* tawdry finery. Also *gen.* 1637. **b.** Trifles 1803. **c.** *fig.* Empty display, *esp.* in speech, etc.; showy talk 1727. †**3.** An old-clothes shop –1635. †**4.** Trade or traffic in old clothes –1606. **5.** Tawdry style (*rare*) 1802.

1. I'll reduce him to f. and rags CONGREVE. **2.** She is as fond of gauze and French f. as the best of them GOLDSM. **b.** Boxes, baskets, and other f. 1803. **3.** *Temp.* IV. i. 225.

Frippery (fri·pĕri), *a.* 1625. [From the sb. used attrib.] Frivolous; contemptible; trumpery.

†**Fri·sco.** 1519. [perh. pseudo-It. form of FRISK *sb.*] A brisk movement in dancing; a caper –1675.

Frisette (frize·t). 1818. [– Fr. *frisette*, f. *friser* curl, frizz; see -ETTE.] A cluster of small curls worn on the forehead.

‖**Friseur** (frizö̆r). Now *rare.* 1750. [Fr., f. *friser* to curl, frizz.] A hairdresser.

Frisian (fri·ziăn). 1598. [f. L. *Frisii* (pl.) – the native name, OFris. *Frisa*, *Frēsa*, whence OE. *Frīsa*, *Frēsa*, MDu. *Vriese* (Du. *Vries*), OHG. *Friaso* (G. *Friese*), ON. *Frísir*; see -IAN.] **A.** *adj.* Of or pertaining to the people of Friesland. **B.** *sb.* An inhabitant of Friesland; the language of Friesland. So †**Fri·sic** *a.* of or pertaining to Friesland.

Frisk (frisk), *sb.* 1525. [f. FRISK *v.*] †**1.** A brisk and lively movement in horsemanship or dancing; a caracole or curvet; a caper. **2.** *transf.* and *fig.* A brisk sportive movement; a frolic; a freak 1665.

2. I'll have a f. with you JOHNSON.

†**Frisk,** *a.* 1528. [– OFr. *frisque* vigorous, alert, lively, merry, var. of *frische, friche*, earlier *frique*, of unkn. origin.] Full of life and spirit; brisk, lively –1705.

Frisk (frisk), *v.* 1519. [f. prec. adj.] **1.** *intr.* To move briskly and sportively; to dance, frolic, gambol. **2.** *trans.* To move (*up, out*, etc.) in a sportive or lively manner 16..

1. As twyn'd Lambs, that did f. i' th' Sun SHAKS. Hence **Fri·sker,** one who or that which frisks. **Fri·skingly** *adv.*

Frisket (fri·skĕt). 1683. [– Fr. *frisquette* – mod. Pr. *frisqueto* – Sp. *frasqueta*.] *Printing.* A thin iron frame hinged to the tympan, having tapes or paper strips stretched across it, for keeping the sheet in position while printing.

Friskful (fri·skfŭl), *a. rare.* 1728. [f. FRISK *sb.* or *v.* + -FUL.] Apt to frisk, frolicsome.

Frisky (fri·ski), *a.* 1500. [f. FRISK *sb.* + -Y¹.] Given to frisking; lively; playful.

Like so many f. buffalo calves 1861. Hence **Fri·skily** *adv.* **Fri·skiness.**

†**Fri·slet.** *rare.* 1607. [perh. f. OFr. *fresel*, dim. of *fraise* ruff + -ET.] 'A kind of small ruffle' (Halliwell).

Frist, *sb. Obs.* exc. *arch.* [OE. *first, frist* = OFris. *ferst, first,* OS., OHG. *frist* (G. *frist*), ON. *frest.*] **1.** A space of time, time; a certain time. **2.** Delay, respite; also, a truce ME. Hence †**Frist** *v. intr.* to delay, grant respite; *trans.* to lend or give on credit; to give credit or time for payment; to grant time for payment of (a debt).

†**Fri·sure.** 1755. [– Fr. *frisure*, f. *friser* to curl, frizz; see -URE.] Fashion of curling the hair –1811.

Frit (frit), *sb.* 1662. [– It. *fritta* (perh. through Fr. *fritte*), subst. use of fem. pa. pple. of *friggere* FRY *v.*] **1.** *Glass-making.* A calcined mixture of sand and fluxes ready to be melted in a crucible to form glass. **2.** *Ceramics.* The vitreous composition from which soft porcelain is made 1791. **3.** *attrib.* and *Comb.*, as *f.-brick*, etc. 1853.

Frit (frit), *v.* 1805. [f. prec. sb.] *trans.* To make into frit; to fuse partially; to calcine.

Fri·t-fly. 1881. [Of unkn. origin.] A small fly of the genus *Oscinis*, destructive to wheat.

Frith, *sb.*¹ *Obs.* exc. *Hist.* [OE. *friþu* (also str. neut. *friþ*), = OFris. *frethu*, OS. *frithu* (Du. *vrede*), OHG. *fridu* (G. *friede*), ON. *friðr*, Goth. **friþus* :– Gmc. **friþuz.*] **1.** Peace; freedom from molestation; security. †**2.** A game-preserve, deer-park –ME.

Comb.: **f.-guild,** a guild for the maintenance of peace; also *attrib.*; **frithsoken** (OE. and *Hist.*), an asylum, a sanctuary.

Frith (friþ), *sb.*² [OE. (*ġe*)*fyrhþe, fyrhþ* :– Gmc. **ʒafurχþjam*, **furχþi*, perh. f. **furχjōn* FIR.] **1.** A wood of some kind, or wooded country collectively. **2.** A piece of land grown sparsely with trees or with underwood only. Also, a plain between woods; unused pasture land. Now only *dial.* 1538. **3.** Brushwood, underwood; occas. hedgewood 1605. **4.** A hedge; also, a hurdle 1511. †The same used as a fish-weir. CAREW.

Frith (friþ), *sb.*³ 1600. [var. of FIRTH².; perh. infl. by L. *fretum* arm of the sea, formerly its supposed origin.] = FIRTH².

†**Frith,** *v.*¹ [OE. *friþian* = OFris. *frethia, ferdia,* OS. *frithon*, OHG. *fridōn*, ON. *friða*, Goth. *gafriþōn*, denominative formations; see FRITH *sb.*¹] **1.** *trans.* To keep in peace, make peace with; to defend, help, preserve, protect –ME. **2.** To free –1470.

Frith (friþ), *v.*² *Obs.* exc. *dial.* ME. [f. FRITH *sb.*²] **1.** *trans.* To fence in. Also *fig.* **2.** *intr.* To wattle; also, to cut underwood 1807.

†**Fri·thborh.** Only *OE.* and *Hist.* [OE. *friðborh* lit. 'peace-pledge'. A mistranslation of the corrupt form *friborg* gave the later name FRANKPLEDGE.] = FRANKPLEDGE.

†**Frith-stool.** *Hist.* [OE., f. *friþ* FRITH *sb.*¹ + *stōl* seat; see STOOL.] **a.** A refuge. OE. only. **b.** A seat, usu. of stone, formerly placed near the altar in some churches, which afforded privilege of sanctuary 1610.

‖**Fritillaria** (fritilēᵊ·riă). 1578. [mod.L., f. L. *fritillus* dice-box; cf. -ARY¹ 3.] A genus of liliaceous plants, including the CROWN IMPERIAL (*F. imperialis*), and the Common Fritillary or Snakeshead (*F. meleagris*) found locally in moist meadows.

Fritillary (friti·lări, fri·tilări). 1633. [– mod.L. *fritillaria*; see prec. and -ARY¹ 3.] **1.** Any plant of the genus *Fritillaria*, esp. *F. meleagris.* **2.** A name for species of butterfly, e.g. the Silver-washed Fritillary (*Argynnis paphia*) and the Queen of Spain Fritillary (*A. lathonia*) 1857.

1. I know what white, what purple fritillaries The grassy harvest of the river-fields Above by Ensham, down by Sandford yields M. ARNOLD.

†**Friti·niency.** [f. L. *fritinnire* twitter. In mod. Dicts. spelt *fritinancy.*] Twittering. SIR T. BROWNE.

Fritter (fri·təɹ), *sb.*¹ ME. [– (O)Fr. *friture* :– Rom. **frictura*, f. *frict-*, pa. ppl. stem of L. *frigere* FRY *v.*; see -URE, and -ER² 3.] **1.** Usu. *pl.* A portion of batter, occas. containing slices of meat, apple, etc., fried in oil, lard, etc. Often qualified as *apple-, oyster-, rice-f.* **2.** *pl.* = FENKS. 1631.

Fritter (fri·təɹ), *sb.*² 1686. [See next.] **1.** *pl.* Minute pieces, fragments, shreds. Also, trifles. Now *rare.* Also *attrib.* **2.** [from the vb.] Excessive breaking-up 1803.

Fritter (fri·təɹ), *v.* 1728. [f. *fritters* (FRITTER *sb.*²), synon. with FLITTERS, alt. of FITTERS *sb. pl.*, perh. rel. to MHG. *vetze* (G. *fetzen*) rag, scrap; see -ER⁵.] **1.** *trans.* To break or tear into pieces or fragments; to subdivide minutely. Now *rare.* Also *intr.* for *refl.* 1772. **2.** With *away, down*: To do away with piece-meal; to attenuate, wear down; to waste on trifles 1728.

1. Frittering and crumbling down the attention by a blind unsystematick observance of every trifle BURKE. **2.** To f. away money in paying debts 1868. Hence **Fri·tterer,** one who fritters or wastes (time).

Frivolity (frivǫ·lĭti). 1796. [– Fr. *frivolité*, f. (O)Fr. *frivole* – L. *frivolus*; see next, -ITY.] **1.** The quality of being frivolous; disposition to trifle, levity. **2.** A frivolous act or thing 1838. So †**Fri·volism.** PRIESTLEY.

Frivolous (fri·vŏləs), *a.* 1549. [f. L. *frivolus* silly, trifling + -OUS.] **1.** Of little or no weight or importance; paltry, trumpery; not worth serious attention. **b.** *Law.* In pleading: Manifestly futile 1736. **2.** Characterized by lack of seriousness, sense, or reverence; given to trifling, silly 1560.

1. F. information 'JUNIUS', ornaments 1776, complaints SCOTT. **b.** The appeal [was] adjudged f. 1736. **2.** From reading f. Books, and keeping as f. Company STEELE. Hence **Fri·volous-ly** *adv.*, **-ness.**

Friz, var. of FRIZZ.

Frize, obs. f. FREEZE, FRIEZE.

Frizel, var. of FRIZZLE *sb.*²

Frizette, Frizeur, vars. of FRISETTE, FRISEUR.

Frizz, friz (friz), *sb.* 1646. [f. next vb.] The state of being frizzed or curled; frizzed hair; a row or wig of crisp curls. Also *attrib.* *fig.* A similar full-bottomed well-curled friz of words HARE.

Frizz, friz (friz), *v.*¹ 1620. [Earliest forms *freeze, frize* – Fr. *friser*, perh. f. *fris-* stem of *frire* FRY *v.*; the vowel appears to have been shortened under the infl. of the earlier FRIZZLE *v.*¹] **1.** *trans.* To curl or crisp (the hair); to form into small crisp curls. **2.** *intr.* Of hair: To stand up in short crisp curls. Also *trans.* To set up (hair) on end. 1696. **3.** *trans.* = FRIEZE *v.*¹ 1806. **4.** In *Leather-dressing*: To rub (wash-leather, etc.) with pumice-stone or a blunt knife, so as to soften the surface, and make uniform in thickness 1697.

1. Dressing of herself with her haire frized short up to her eares PEPYS.

Frizz (friz), *v.*² 1835. [f. FRY *v.* with echoic termination.] To make a sputtering noise in frying.

Frizzle (fri·z'l), *sb.*¹ 1565. [Goes with FRIZZLE *v.*¹] **1.** Frizzled hair; a short crisp curl 1613. **2.** [f. the vb.] The state of being frizzled 1850. **3.** *attrib.* 1565.

Frizzle (fri·z'l), *sb.*² *dial.* 1629. [perh. corruption of FUSIL².] 'In flint and steel guns the piece of iron acted on by the flint to produce the explosion.'

Frizzle (fri·z'l), *v.*¹ 1565. [First in pa. pple. *frisled*, and earlier than FRIZZ *v.*¹, of which it might be supposed to be a derivative. Of obscure origin.] **1.** *trans.* To curl in small crisp curls. **2.** *intr.* for *refl.* To form into crisp curls; to curl or twist *up* 1607. †**3.** *trans.* To touch lightly –1652.

1. Lockes with bodkins frisled fine 1573. Hence **Fri·zzler,** one who frizzles.

Frizzle (fri·z'l), *v.*² 1839. [f. FRIZZ *v.*²; see -LE.] **a.** *intr.* = FRIZZ *v.*² **b.** *trans.* To fry or grill (with a sputter) 1858. Hence **Fri·zzle** *sb.* the action of the vb.

Frizzly (fri·zli), *a.* 1707. [f. FRIZZLE *sb.*¹ + -Y¹.] Full of frizzles or crisp curls.

Frizzy (fri·zi), *a.* 1870. [f. FRIZZ *sb.* + -Y¹.] Of, pertaining to, or resembling a frizz.

Fro (frōᵘ), *Sc.* **Frae** (frę̄). ME. [– ON. *frá*, corresp. to OE. *fram* FROM.]

A. *prep.* (Now only *Sc.* and *dial.*) = FROM in all its senses.

B. *adv.* In a direction or position that is remote or apart; away. Now only in TO AND FRO. ME.

†**C.** *conj.* (Chiefly *north.*) **1.** From the time that; as soon as, when –1513. **2.** Since, seeing that –1609.

Frock (frǫk), *sb.* ME. [– (O)Fr. *froc* – Frankish **hrok*, corresp. to OHG. *hroc* (not identical with OHG. *roc*, G. *rock*, coat).] **1.** A long habit with large open sleeves; the outer dress of a monk. *Rarely*, a cassock. Hence, the priestly office. Cf. UNFROCK *v.* **2.** An upper garment worn chiefly by men; a long coat, tunic, or mantle ME. **3.** An overall; a *smock-frock* 1668. **b.** A woollen guernsey or jersey worn by sailors 1811. **4.** The outer garment, for indoor wear, of women and children, consisting of a bodice and skirt; a gown, dress 1538. **5.** A coat with long skirts; a FROCK-COAT 1719; a similar coat used as a military uniform 1753.

2. Phr. *F. of mail*: a defensive garment, armour (MILT. *Sams.* 133). **5.** A light blue f. with silver frogs 1770. *Frock*, in the British service, the undress regimental coat of the guards, artillery, and royal marines 1881.

Frock (frǫk), *v.* 1828. [f. FROCK *sb.*] *trans.* To provide with or dress in a frock (*lit.* and *fig.*); to invest with priestly office or privilege.

Fro·ck-coa·t. 1823. A double-breasted coat with long skirts which are of the same length in front as behind.

Frocked (frǫkt), *pple.* and *ppl. a.* 1550. [f. FROCK *sb.* and *v.* + -ED.] Dressed in a frock.

Froe, frow (frōᵘ). Now chiefly *U.S.* 1573. [The synon. *fromward* (XIX) suggests that the earliest form *frower* (XVI) repr. a subst. use of FROWARD adj. in the lit. sense 'turned away', the reference being to the position of the handle.] A wedge-shaped tool used for cleaving and riving staves, shingles, etc. It has a handle in the plane of the blade, set at right angles to the back; hence the name.

Froe, obs. f. FROW, Dutchwoman.

Frog¹ (frǫg). [OE. *frogga*, a pet-form similar to *docga* DOG, **stacga* STAG, *wicga* (see EARWIG); rel. to OE. *forsć, frosć, frox*, ME. *frosh*, dial. *frosk* = MLG., Du. *vorsch*, OHG. *frosc* (G. *frosch*), ON. *froskr* :– Gmc. **froskaz.*] **1.** A tailless amphibious animal of the genus *Rana*, or of the family *Ranidæ*. **2.** A name of frog-like animals, e.g. the FROG-FISH or ANGLER 2. 1769. **3.** A name given to certain diseases of the throat or mouth 1656. **4.** *attrib.* 1561.

1. The Pike will eat venemous things (as some kind of Frogs are) WALTON.

Comb.: **f.-crab,** a member of the crustacean genus *Ranina*; **-eater,** one who eats frogs, a term vulgarly applied to Frenchmen; **-hopper,** a group of homopterous insects of the family *Cercopidæ*, so called from their shape and leaping powers; **-pecker,** a heron; **-plate,** a plate for viewing the circulation of the blood in the web of a frog's foot; **-shell,** a name of various species of shells of the genus *Ranella*; **-spit, -spittle,** (*a*) = CUCKOO-SPIT¹; (*b*) = FROG-SPAWN; **-tongue,** a tumour under the tongue. **b.** In plant-names: **f.-bit,** (*a*) *Hydrocharis morsus-ranæ*, an aquatic plant; (*b*) *Limnobium spongia*, a similar plant of America; **-cheese,** (*a*) one of the larger puff-balls when young; (*b*) *Malva sylvestris*; **frog('s-foot,** duckweed (*Lemna*); **-grass,** (*a*) = CRAB-GRASS 1; †(*b*) *Juncus bufonius*; **-stool** = TOADSTOOL; **-wort,** a name of species of *Orchis*.

Frog² (frǫg). 1610. [prob. a transf. use of FROG¹ partly induced by the formal similarity of synon. It. *forchetta* and Fr. *fourchette*, dim. of *forca, fourche* FORK, whence perh. (dial.) FRUSH *sb.*²] An elastic horny substance growing in the middle of the sole of a horse's hoof.

Frog³ (frǫg). 1719. [Of unkn. origin.] **1.** An attachment to the waistbelt for carrying a sword or bayonet or hatchet. **2.** A fastening for the front of a military coat or cloak, consisting of a button, covered with silk, etc., which passes through a corresponding loop on the opposite side of the front of a coat or cloak 1746.

Frog⁴ (frǫg). 1860. *Railroads.* A grooved piece of iron placed at the junction of the rails where one track crosses another.

Frog-fish. 1646. A name of fishes; *esp.* of the Angler or Fishing-frog (*Lophius piscatorius*); also of varieties of the genera *Batrachus* and *Chironectes.*

Frogged (frǫgd), *ppl. a.* 1774. [f. FROG³ + -ED².] Of a coat, etc.: Fastened or ornamented with frogs.

Froggy (frǫ·gi), *sb.* 1840. [f. FROG¹ + -Y⁶.] **1.** A playful designation of a frog. **2.** *slang.* A vulgar term for a Frenchman, from their reputed habit of eating frogs 1872.

Froggy (frǫ·gi), *a.* 1611. [f. as prec. + -Y¹.] **1.** Having or abounding in frogs. **2.** Frog-like 1837.

Frogland (frǫ·glænd). 1721. [f. FROG¹ + LAND *sb.*] Marshy land in which frogs abound, as The Fens, Holland, etc. Also *attrib.* So **Fro·glander** (*slang*), a Dutchman.

Frog-march, frog's-march. *slang.* 1871. The method of carrying a drunken or refractory prisoner face downwards between four men, each holding a limb.

Frog-mouth, frog's mouth. 1851. **1.** The great Snapdragon (*Antirrhinum majus*). **2.** A bird of the family *Podargidæ* 1888.

Frog-spawn, frog's-spawn. 1621. **1.** The ova, spawn, or young of frogs. **2.** Certain freshwater algæ, which form green and slimy masses on the surface of ponds and ditches 1864. **3.** *Sugar-manuf.* A fungus destructive to saccharine solutions 1887.

Froise, fraise (froiz, frēⁱz). ME. [perh. – OFr. **freis, *freise* :– pop.L. **frīxum, -a,* for L. *frīxum, -a,* n. and fem. pa. pple. of *frigere* FRY *v.*] A kind of pancake or omelette, often containing slices of bacon.

Frolic (frǫ·lik), *sb.* 1616. [f. FROLIC *v.*] **1.** An outburst of fun, gaiety, or mirth; a prank 1635; fun, merriment 1676. **2.** A merry-making; a party 1645. **†3.** ? Humorous verses sent round at a feast –1631. **†4.** A toy. FULLER.

1. There's mirth and frolick in 't D'URFEY.

Frolic (frǫ·lik), *a.* 1538. [– Du. *vrolijk,* f. (M)Du. *vro* glad, joyous + *-lijk* -LY¹.] **1.** In early use: Joyous, merry, mirthful. In later use: Frolicsome, sportive, full of pranks. **†b.** *transf.* of colours, wine, etc. –1648. **†2.** Free; liberal (*of*) 1593.

1. The f. wind that breathes the spring MILT. *absol.* Lamb, the f. and the gentle WORDSW. **b.** And yet, each Verse of thine Out-did the meat, out-did the frolick wine HERRICK. Hence **†Fro·licly, fro·lickly** *adv.*

Frolic (frǫ·lik), *v.* Inflected **frolicked, frolicking.** 1583. [f. prec. adj.] **1.** *intr.* To make merry; later, to play pranks, gambol, caper about 1593. **†2.** *trans.* To make joyous or merry –1677.

1. 'Tis Whitsontyde, and we must frolick it MARSTON. Hence **Fro·licker,** one who frolics.

Frolicsome (frǫ·liksǒm), *a.* Also **†frolicksom(e.** 1699. [f. FROLIC *v.* or *sb.* + -SOME¹.] Full of frolic; gay, merry, mirthful.

In their frolicksome malice the Fates had ordered [etc.] W. IRVING. **Fro·licsome-ly** *adv.*, **-ness.**

From (frǫm, frəm). [OE. *fram, from* = OS., OHG., Goth. *fram,* ON. *frá* FRO; f. *fra-* = PRO-¹ + *-m* suffix. The primary sense was 'forward'; the sense-development was 'onward', 'on the way', 'away' (from).]

A. *prep.* **1.** Denoting departure or moving away: indicating a starting-point **a.** in space; **b.** in defining an extent in space OE.; **c.** in a series or statement of limits OE.; **d.** in time OE. **2.** Indicating a place or object which is left at a distance, behind, or on one side, by an object which withdraws or turns away OE. **3.** Denoting (statically) distance, absence, remoteness OE.; also used *simply* = away from, apart from, absent from, etc. (now only in *from home*) ME. **4.** Denoting removal, abstraction, separation, expulsion, exclusion, or the like; also, privation, separation, abstention, freedom, deliverance, etc. (*from* a state, condition, action, etc.) OE. **5.** Indicating a state, condition, etc., which is abandoned or changed for another. Often as if with ellipsis of *being.* ME. **6.** Used after words which signify distinction, difference, unlikeness, etc. ME. **†b.** used *simply* = away from, apart or aside from, out of, alien to –1637. **7.** Indicating the place, quarter, etc. whence something comes or is brought or fetched; often = out of; also after words denoting choice, etc. out of a number 1621. **b.** with ellipsis of vb. or pple. = coming from, taken from, etc. 1745. **8.** Indicating a place or position where action or motion is originated which goes thence, while the originator remains there. Similarly after words which express 'hanging', 'depending', etc. 1592. **9.** Indicating a person as a more or less distant source of action. In OE. = by. OE. **10.** Denoting derivation, descent, or the like; *esp.* 'noting progress from premisses to inferences' (J.) ME. **11.** Indicating a model, rule, copy; also, a person or thing after which another is named 1596. **12.** Denoting ground, reason, cause, or motive. Now repl. in some uses by *for.* OE.

1. She leet no morsel f. hir lippes falle CHAUCER. Phr. *F. post to pillar, f. door to door.* **b.** F. the uprising to the setting Sunne SPENSER. **c.** F. 16 or 20 to 24 Oars DAMPIER. **d.** I knew him f. a boy C. BRONTË. Phr. *F. time to time.* **2.** We will not f. the Helme, to sit and weepe SHAKS. Why speaks't thou f. me BEAUM. & FL. **3.** Phr. *Away, absent, apart f.* Far apart F. wicked men like thee KEATS. **4.** Release me f. my bands *Temp.* Epil. 9. To refrain f. laughing BERKELEY. **5.** F. a slave she became to be a Princesse 1641. Temples.. which tremblingly grew blank F. bright BROWNING. **6.** You can't tell one flower f. another L. CARROLL. **b.** Phr. *†F. oneself* = beside oneself, out of one's wits. **7.** She drew a knife f. her bosom ARNOLD. He came f. Cambridge 1879. **b.** Cavaliers f. the country MACAULAY. **8.** God f. the mount of Sinai..will himself..Ordain them laws MILT. *fig.* F. their point of view they are perfectly right L. CARROLL. **9.** He bad me, f. him, call thee Thane of Cawdor SHAKS. You shall hear f. my attorney 1843. **10.** Eve, who..anomalously proceeded f. Adam SIR T. BROWNE. Cuts f. a sabre 1870. To draw a conclusion f. premisses 1887. **11.** Enos, nam'd f. me DRYDEN. To colour f. nature 1811. **12.** To speak and act f. principle 1796. Remarkable f. the neatness..of its architecture DISRAELI. F. your silence I fear [etc.] 1855.

Phrases. **a.** With obj. an adv., as *f. above, afar,* etc. Also, pleonastically, before *hence, thence,* etc.; see those words. **b.** *F. amidst, beneath,* etc., indicating a static condition. **c.** Followed, pleonastically, by *out, out of, forth, off,* where each prep. strengthens or supplements the sense of the other.

†B. quasi-*adv.* = away. Only in *to and f., f. and back.* –1608.

†C. quasi-*conj.* = from the time when –1602.

†Fro·mward. OE. [f. FROM + -WARD.] **A.** *adj.* = Turned from or away –1576.

B. *adv.* In a direction which leads from, or is turned from, a given place or object. Also, of time. –1711.

C. *prep.* Away from –1713.

So **Fro·mwards** *adv.* and *prep.*

Frond (frǫnd), *sb.* 1785. [– L. *frons, frond-* leaf, applied by Linnæus in a specific sense, in contradistinction to *folium* FOIL *sb.*¹] **1.** *Bot.* The leaf-like organ formed by the union of stem and foliage in certain flowerless plants. Formerly (and still loosely) applied also to the large compound leaves, e.g. of the palm, banana, etc. **2.** *Zool.* A leaf-like expansion found in certain animal organisms 1846. Hence **Frond** *v. intr.* to wave with fronds. **Fro·ndage,** fronds collectively; also, erron., foliage.

†Fronda·tion. *rare.* [– L. *frondatio* pruning, f. *frons, frond-* leaf + *-atio* -ATION.] The act of stripping trees of some of the luxuriant branches and sprays. EVELYN.

‖**Fronde** (froṅd). 1798. [Fr., = 'sling'.] *Fr. Hist.* The name given to the party which rose against Mazarin and the Court during the minority of Louis XIV; hence, a malcontent party; also, violent political opposition.

Was there ever a mixed constitution without a *f.* 1808.

†Fro·nded, *ppl. a.*¹ [f. L. *frons, frond-* leaf + -ED².] Having leaves or foliage. HOWELL.

Fronded (frǫ·ndėd), *ppl. a.*² 1882. [f. FROND *sb.* + -ED².] Having fronds.

Frondent (frǫ·ndĕnt), *a.* 1677. [– *frondent-*, pr. ppl. stem of L. *frondēre* put forth leaves, f. *frons, frond-* leaf; see -ENT.] Full of fronds, leafy.

Frondesce (frǫnde·s), *v.* 1816. [– L. *frondescere,* frequent. of *frondēre* put forth leaves; see prec., -ESCE] *intr.* To put forth leaves. So **Fronde·scent** *a.* springing into leaf; expanding into fronds. **Fronde·scently** *adv.*

Frondescence (frǫnde·sĕns). 1841. [– mod.L. *frondescentia,* f. as prec.; see -ENCE.] The process or period of coming into leaf; the conversion of other organs into leaves; fronds or leaves collectively.

‖**Frondeur** (froṅdör). 1798. [Fr., f. *fronde* (see FRONDE).] **1.** *Fr. Hist.* A member of the Fronde. **2.** *transf.* A malcontent, an irreconcilable 1847.

Frondiferous (frǫndi·fĕrəs), *a.* 1599. [f. L. *frondifer* (f. *frons, frond-* leaf) + -OUS; see -FEROUS.] Bearing leaves or fronds.

Frondlet (frǫ·ndlėt). 1862. [f. FROND *sb.* + -LET.] A little frond.

Frondose (frǫndōᵘ·s), *a.* 1721. [– L. *frondosus,* f. *frons, frond-*; see FROND *sb.*, -OSE¹.] Covered with fronds; resembling a frond. In early use: †Leafy, leaf-like.

Frondous (frǫ·ndəs), *a.* 1828. [– L. *frondosus*; see prec., -OUS.] Leafy; having branches bearing both leaves and flowers.

‖**Frons** (frǫnz). 1856. [L., = forehead, front.] *Entom.* The middle part of the face of insects, between the eyes.

Front (frɒnt), *sb.* (and *a.*) ME. [– (O)Fr. *front* :– L. *frons, front-* forehead, front.]

I. 1. = FOREHEAD 1. Now only *poet.* or *rhet.* **2.** Hence: The whole face ME. **3. †a.** The face as expressive of emotion or character; expression of countenance. **b.** Bearing or demeanour in confronting anything. Also *transf.* ME. **4.** Effrontery, impudence. Now *rare.* 1653.

1. The f. of Ioue himselfe SHAKS. The mark of fool set on his f. MILT. *Sams.* 496. *fig.* The verie head, and f. of my offending SHAKS. **2.** F. to F., Bring thou this Fiend of Scotland and my selfe SHAKS. **3. b.** Who, patient in adversity, still bear The firmest f. FALCONER. The..unclouded f. of an accomplished courtier SCOTT.

II. 1. *Mil.* **a.** The foremost line or part of an army or battalion. Also, in words of command; e.g. *files to the f.* ME. **b.** Line of battle ME. **c.** The foremost part of the ground occupied, or of the field of operations; the part next the enemy. Also, the foremost part of a position, as opposed to *rear.* 1665. **d.** The direction towards which the line faces when formed 1832. **2.** *Arch.* 'Any side or face of a building, but more commonly..the entrance side' (Gwilt); occas. *collect.* in *sing.* and *pl.* = 'the four sides' (of a mansion) ME. **3.** *gen.* The part or side of an object which seems to look out or be presented to the eye; the foremost part of anything. Opp. to *back.* ME. **b.** *transf.* With reference to time: The first period; the beginning (*poet.*) 1600. **c.** A frontage 1766. **d.** *Theatr.* The audience 1810. **†4.** The first part or line of anything written or printed –1697. **5.** False hair, or false curls worn by women over the forehead 1687. **b.** That part of a man's shirt which covers the chest; a shirt-front; also, a 'dicky', or the like 1844. **6.** Forward position or situation 1609. **†7.** [f. the vb.] Encounter, onset. LD. BERNERS. **8.** *attrib.* 1600.

1. a. Both our powers, with smiling Fronts encountring SHAKS. **b.** Preserving an even and unbroken f. THIRLWALL. **c.** British Regiments were wanted..at the F. KIPLING. **d.** Phr. *Change of f.*: see CHANGE *v.* *F. of fortification*: two half bastions, and a curtain. **3.** Had he his hurts before? I, on the F. SHAKS. **b.** In summer's f. SHAKS. **4.** Phr. *In the f.* (of a page, etc.): at the head. **6.** *To come to the f.*: to emerge into publicity. **8.** At the Play, in a F. Row 1718.

Comb., etc.: **f. bench,** the foremost bench on either side of the Houses of Lords and Commons, occupied by ministers and ex-ministers respectively; **f. door,** the principal entrance-door of a house; **f.-stall,** an appendage to the bridle covering the horse's forehead; **-ways, -wise** *advs.* in a position or direction facing to the front.

Front (frɒnt), *v.* 1523. [– OFr. *fronter* in same sense, f. *front* FRONT *sb.*; partly f. the Eng. sb.] **1.** *intr.* To have the front in a specified direction; to face, look. **2.** *trans.* To have the front towards; to face, stand opposite to 1606. **3.** To stand face to face with, face, confront, *esp.* in defiance or hostility. *lit.* and *fig.* Said also of things. 1583. **4.** To set face to face *with* 1617. **5.** To adorn in front; to furnish with a front. Also, to face (with some material). 1635. †6. To preface –1732. 7. To be in front of, serve as a front to 1591. 8. Chiefly *Mil.* a. To turn the front or face in a specified direction. Also, as a word of command. 1635. b. To form a front 1802. c. *trans.* (causatively, from *Front!*): To cause to form a front 1796.

1. Philip's dwelling fronted on the street TENNYSON. 2. Like a gate of steele, Fronting the Sunne SHAKS. The church..was to have fronted the Plaza 1847. 3. He dare now to fronte princes SPENSER. Those Warres Which fronted mine owne peace SHAKS. 5. To new front a house H. WALPOLE. 7. Yonder wals that pertly f. your Towne..Must kisse their owne feet SHAKS. 8. Phr. *To f. about*: to turn round so as to face in another direction. **Fro·ntingly** *adv.*

Frontage (frɒ·ntėdʒ). 1622. [f. FRONT *sb.* + -AGE.] 1. Land which abuts on a river or piece of water, or on a road. 2. Extent of front 1844. 3. The front face or part of a building. Also *collect.* 1861. 4. The action of fronting in a certain direction; exposure, outlook 1859.

Hence **Fro·ntager**, an owner of f. (sense 1).

Frontal (frɒ·ntăl), *sb.* [ME. *frountel* – OFr. *frontel* (mod. *frontal*) – L. *frontale* (in pl. *-alia*), f. *frons, front-* FRONT *sb.*; see -AL[1].] †1. Something applied to the forehead: a. A band or ornament –1611; b. *Med.* a medicament to cure headache –1753. 2. A movable covering for the front of an altar, generally of embroidered cloth, silk, etc., but occas. of metal ME. 3. The façade of a building 1784. †4. *Arch.* 'A little..pediment occasionally placed over a little door or window' –1736.

Frontal (frɒ·ntăl), *a.* 1656. [– mod.L. *frontalis*; see FRONT, -AL[1].] 1. Of or pertaining to the forehead, or to the corresponding part in the lower animals. 2. Of or pertaining to the fore-part or foremost edge 1860. b. Of an attack, etc.: Directed against the front 1884. 3. quasi-*sb.* = *f. bone* 1854.

1. Phr. *F. artery, bone, sinus, vein*, etc. 2. *F. hammer* or *F. helve*, a forge-hammer lifted by a cam, acting upon a tongue immediately in front of the hammer-head.

Frontate (frǫ·-, frɒ·nteᶦt), *a.* 1855. [f. FRONT *sb.* + -ATE[2].] *Bot.* Of the leaf of a flower: Growing broader and broader, and at last terminating in a right line. So **†Fronta·ted** *a.*

Fronted (frɒ·ntėd), *ppl. a.* 1615. [f. FRONT *sb.* or *v.* + -ED.] Having, or formed with, a front.

MILT. *P. L.* II. 532.

Frontier (frǫ·n-, frɒ·ntiᵊɹ). [Late ME. *frounter(e)* – AFr. *frounter*, (O)Fr. *frontière*; Rom. deriv. of L. *frons, front-* FRONT *sb.*] A. *sb.* †1. The front side; the fore-part –1551. †2. The front line or foremost part of an army. Hence, 'attack, resistance'. –1523. 3. *sing.* and *pl.* The part of a country which fronts, faces, or borders on another country; the marches. Also *transf.* and *fig.* ME. b. *U.S.* 'That part of a country which forms the border of its settled or inhabited regions' (*Cent. Dict.*) 1870. †4. A fortress on the frontier; a frontier town –1796; a barrier against attack –1690.

4. His Navies do carry a moveable Frontire to all the habitable world MARVELL.

B. *adj.* 1. Of, belonging to, or situated on the frontier; bordering 1523. †2. Fronting; opposite. P. HOLLAND.

Frontier (frǫ·n-, frɒ·ntiᵊɹ), *v.* 1579. [f. prec. sb.] †1. *intr.* To be a frontier, or as a frontier; to border *on* –1662. 2. *trans.* To look upon the boundary or coast of; to face (now *rare*); †to stand in front of; to oppose 1579.

Fro·ntierman, fro·ntiersman. 1813. [f. FRONTIER *sb.* + MAN.] One who lives on the frontier, or on the outlying districts of civilization.

Frontignac (frǫntinyæ·k), *sb.* Often *attrib.* 1629. [erron. form of next, after the many southern Fr. names in *-ignac*.] 1. A muscat wine made at Frontignan, France. 2. The grape from which this is made 1641.

†Frontignan. 1756. = prec. –1777.

Frontispiece (frɒ·ntispīs), *sb.* 1597. [– Fr. *frontispice* or late L. *frontispicium* façade of a building, f. L. *frons, front-* FRONT *sb.* + *-spicium* as in *auspicium* AUSPICE; very early assim. in sp. to *piece*.] 1. The principal face or front of a building; more usually, the decorated entrance. 2. The pediment over a door, gate, etc. Also, a decorated panel. 1601. †3. The first page of a book or pamphlet, or what is printed on it; the title-page including illustrations and table of contents; hence, an introduction or preface. Also *fig.* –1721. 4. An illustration facing the title-page of a book or division of a book. (The current sense.) 1682. 5. The front part of anything 1625.

2. A Kingly Palace Gate, With Frontispice of Diamond and Gold Embellisht MILT. *P. L.* III. 506. Hence **Fro·ntispiece** *v. trans.* to furnish *with* as a f.; to represent on the f.; to put as a f.

Frontless (frɒ·ntlės), *a.* 1605. [f. FRONT *sb.* + -LESS.] Having no front; esp. *fig.* unblushing, shameless, audacious (now *rare*).

The..most frontlesse piece Of solid impudence B. JONS. Hence **Fro·ntless-ly** *adv.*, **-ness.**

Frontlet (frɒ·ntlėt). 1478. [– OFr. *frontelet*, dim. of *frontel*; see FRONTAL *sb.*, -LET.] 1. Something worn on the forehead: a. an ornament or band; also *fig.*; b. = PHYLACTERY 1578; c. = *front-stall* 1805. 2. = FOREHEAD 1. Now only of animals. 1659. b. *Ornith.* The margin of the head, behind the bill, of birds, usu. clothed with rigid bristles 1874. 3. = FRONT *sb.* II. 2; also *transf.* 1808. 4. A superfrontal; also, an ornamental border to an altar-cloth 1536.

1. a. *fig.* What makes that F. on? You are too much of late i'th'frowne *Lear* I. iv. 208. b. It shalbe..as frontlets betwene thine eyes BIBLE (Genev.) *Exod.*13:16.

Fronto- (frǫ·nto), used for *fronti-*, comb. f. L. *frons, front-* FRONT, with sense 'pertaining to the front or forehead and to something else', as *f.-nasal, -occipital, -parietal*, etc.

Fronton (frɒ·ntǫn). 1698. [– Fr. *fronton* – It. *frontone*, augm. of *fronte* forehead; see FRONT *sb.*, -OON.] 1. *Arch.* A pediment. 2. = FRONTAL *sb.* 2. 1749. ||3. A building where pelota is played. [Sp.] 1896.

Frontward, -wards (frɒ·ntwǫɹd, -z), *adv.* (*sb.*) 1553. [f. FRONT *sb.* + -WARD(S).] 1. Towards the front; also with *of* 1865. †b. quasi-*sb.* The direction towards the front 1553. 2. With the face in a specified direction. E.B. BROWNING.

†Fro·ppish, *a.* 1659. [perh. f. *frop, var. of FRAP *v.* + -ISH[1].] Froward, fretful, peevish –1784. Hence **†Fro·ppishness.**

Frore (frōᵊɹ), **†froren, †frorn(e,** *pa. pple.* and *ppl. a.* ME. [orig. pa. pple. of FREEZE *v.*] 1. With ppl. sense: FROZEN. *Obs.* exc. *dial.* 2. Intensely cold, frosty, frost-like. Now only *poet.* in form *frore* (after Milton) 1483.

2. The parching Air Burns frore, and cold performs th'effect of Fire MILT. Hence **Fro·ry** *a.* (in sense 2); also, †foamy.

Frost (frǫ̈st), *sb.* [OE. *frost*, usu. *forst* = OFris. *frost, forst*, OS., (O)HG. *frost* (Du. *vorst*), ON. *frost* :- Gmc. *frustaz, -am, f. weak grade of *freusan FREEZE + abstr. suffix *-t*. The form *frost* was doubtless established by ON. influence.] 1. The act or state of freezing or becoming frozen; the temperature of the air when it is below the freezing-point of water; extreme cold. Also *personified* in *Jack Frost*. 2. Frozen dew or vapour. More fully *hoar(y, rime*, or *white f.* OE. 3. *fig.*; *esp.* of a person: Coldness of behaviour or temperament, frigidity; (*slang*) a 'coolness' 1635. 4. *slang* (orig. *Theatr.*). A failure 1886. †5. A colour like that of hoar-frost; silver-grey; also, gold or silver frost-work –1702.

1. *Black f.*: frost unaccompanied by rime; opp. to *white f.* (see sense 2). When rigorous Winter binds you [river] up with F. COWLEY. F. will penetrate eight inches, sometimes more 1891. 2. Seed-time and Harvest, Heat and hoary F., Shall hold their course MILT. *P. L.* XI. 899. 3. Renaissance frosts came, and all perished RUSKIN.

Comb.: **f.-bearer** = CRYOPHORUS; **-bird,** the American Golden Plover; **-blite,** the plant *Chenopodium album*; **-dew,** hoar-frost, rime; **-fern,** a fern-like figure produced by the freezing of a moist surface; **-fish,** (*a*) the Tomcod, *Microgadus tomcodus*, which appears on the coast of N. America as the frost sets in; (*b*) the scabbard-fish, *Lepidophus caudatus*; **-fog** = *f.-mist*; **-grape,** an American species of *Vitis cordifolia* or *riparia*; **-lamp,** an oil-lamp placed beneath the oil-tube of an Argand lamp to keep the oil in a flowing condition; **-mist,** mist caused by the freezing of vapour in the atmosphere; **-nail** *sb.*, a nail driven into the shoe to prevent slipping in frosty weather; so **-nail** *v.*; **-rime** = *f.-smoke*; **-smoke,** a thick mist in high latitudes, arising from the surface of the sea when exposed to a temperature much below freezing; **-valve,** a valve which opens to allow water to escape from the portion of the pipe or pump where it is liable to be frozen; **-weed, -wort,** the plant *Helianthemum canadense*; so called because, late in autumn, crystals of ice shoot from the cracked bark at the root.

Frost (frǫ̈st), *v.* 1572. [f. prec. sb.] 1. *trans.* To freeze, frost-bite, nip with frost 1807. 2. To cover with or as with rime. Chiefly *fig.* 1635. 3. To give a frosted surface to (glass or metal) 1832. 4. To treat by the insertion of frost-nails, roughing, etc., as a protection against slipping in frosty weather; to shoe (a horse) in this way 1572.

2. The rising moon, While with a hoary light she frosts the ground WORDSW.

Fro·st-bi:t, *pple.* and *ppl. a. rare.* 1749. = FROST-BITTEN.

Fro·st-bi:te, *sb.* 1813. The inflamed or gangrenous condition of the skin and adjacent parts produced by exposure to severe cold.

Fro·st-bi:te, *v.* 1593. *trans.* †To injure with intense cold; also *fig.*; †to invigorate by exposure to the frost; to get (oneself or one's limbs) frost-bitten.

My wife up, and with Mrs. Pen to walk in the fields to f. themselves PEPYS.

Fro·st-bi:tten, *pple.* and *ppl. a.* 1593. Injured by exposure to frost.

Frosted (frǫ̈·stėd), *ppl. a.* 1645. [f. FROST *sb.* and *v.* + -ED.] 1. Frozen, frost-bitten 1807. 2. Covered with rime or hoar-frost 1720. 3. Covered as with rime; hoary, white 1645. 4. Of glass, silver, etc.: Having a surface made to resemble a coating of hoar-frost 1689. 5. Made to resemble rough ice 1790.

3. *F. cake*: cake covered with 'icing'. When I, with f. hairs, Should look at what I was G. DANIEL. 4. F. Buttons 1711, tumblers 1852.

Frosting (frǫ̈·stiŋ), *vbl. sb.* 1617. [f. FROST *v.* + -ING[1].] 1. The action of FROST *v.* 2. *concr.* a. A substance powdered and used for frosting purposes; *esp.* pulverized white sugar used for icing cake 1756. b. A frosted surface 1892.

Fro·stless, *a.* 1711. [f. FROST *sb.* + -LESS.] Without frost.

Fro·st-ni:p, *v.* 1642. To nip or injure with frost. FULLER. Hence **Fro·st-ni:pped** *pple.* and *ppl. a.* = FROST-BITTEN.

Frost-work. 1648. 1. Work produced by frost; *esp.* the tracery formed on the surface of glass, etc., by frost 1729. Also *attrib.* 2. Ornamentation in imitation of this.

Frosty (frǫ̈·sti), *a.* [f. FROST *sb.* + -Y[1]; OE. had *fyrstiġ*.] 1. Affected with or characterized by frost; at or below freezing-point; ice-cold OE.; †belonging to the season of frost ME. 2. *transf.* and *fig.* Cold as frost; without ardour or warmth of feeling, frigid ME. 3. Covered with hoar-frost 1577. 4. Covered as with frost; of the hair: Hoary, white ME.; hence, Characteristic of old age 1588. b. *spec.* in *Entom.* Of a glistening white colour 1698.

1. The noise of f. woodlands TENNYSON. The f. feldefare CHAUCER. 2. He red for shame, but f. in desire SHAKS. 4. Blessings on your f. pow BURNS. Hence **Fro·stily** *adv.* **Fro·stiness.**

Frot (frǫt), *v.* Also **†frote,** etc. ME. [– OFr. *froter* (mod. *frotter*), of unkn. origin.] †1. *trans.* To rub, chafe; in early use, to stroke (an animal) –1688. 2. *Tanning.* To work or render supple by rubbing 1853. Hence **†Fro·terer.**

Froth (frǫ̈þ), *sb.* ME. [– ON. *froða* or *frauð*, f. Gmc. *freuþ- *frauþ- *fruþ-, repr. also by the OE. vb. *āfrēoþan* froth.] 1. = FOAM *sb.* 1. Also *transf.* and *fig.* b. *spec.* Foaming saliva issuing from the mouth ME. c. Scum 1533. 2. Something unsubstantial or of little worth 1593. 3. Applied contemptuously to persons. Cf. SCUM. 1598.

1. *fig.* Society is f. above and dregs below LANDOR. 2. The thing I seeke..a f. of fleeting ioy SHAKS. 3. F., and scum thou liest *Merry W.* I. i. 167.

Comb.: **f.-spit** = CUCKOO-SPIT 1; **-stick,** a stick for whipping cream, etc. Also in names given to the frog-hopper, as **f.-fly, -frog-hopper, -insect, -worm.**
Hence **Fro·thery** (*nonce-wd.*), mere f., triviality (CARLYLE). **Fro·thless** *a.* **Fro·thsome** *a.* frothy.

Froth (frǫþ), *v.* late ME. [f. prec. sb.; cf. ON. mutated form *freyða*.] **1.** *intr.* To emit froth or foam. Of liquids: To gather or throw up froth; to run foaming *away, by, over.* **2.** *trans.* To cause to foam; to make froth rise on the surface of 1621. **3.** To bespatter or cover with or as with froth 1771. Hence **Fro·thing** *vbl. sb.* and *ppl. a.*

Frothy (frǫ·þi), *a.* 1533. [f. FROTH *sb.* + -Y¹.] **1.** Full of, covered with, or accompanied by froth or foam; foamy. **2.** Consisting of or resembling froth, spumous 1605; †soft, not firm or solid, flabby –1658. **3.** *fig.* Vain, empty, unsubstantial 1593.
3. A f. mob orator 1884. F. fine writing 1885. Hence **Fro·thily** *adv.* **Fro·thiness.**

‖**Frou-frou** (frū frū). 1870. [Fr., of imit. origin.] A rustling, *esp.* that of a dress.

Frounce (fraunz), *sb.*¹ ME. [– OFr. *fronce* wrinkle, f. *froncir* wrinkle, f. Frankish **hrunkjan*, rel. to ON. *hrukka* wrinkle. See FLOUNCE *sb.*²] †**1.** A wrinkle –1721. †**2.** A fold, crease; a pleat; *fig.* duplicity. ME. only. †**3.** = FLOUNCE *sb.*² 1. 1619. **4.** A piece of foppish display. (Cf. MILT. *Pens.* 123.) 1881. Hence †**Frou·nceless** *a.* unwrinkled. CHAUCER.

†**Frounce,** *sb.*² 1450. [Of unkn. origin.] **1.** A canker or sore in the mouth of a hawk –1820. **2.** A disease in the mouth of a horse –1725.

Frounce (frauns), *v.* ME. [– (O)Fr. *froncer* wrinkle, also OFr. *froncir* wrinkle, fold, f. *fronce* FROUNCE *sb.*¹] †**1.** *trans.* To gather in folds or wrinkles; to knit, purse; occas. to knit the brows of –1628. †**b.** *intr.* To knit the brows; to look angry. Also of the face or forehead: To become wrinkled. –1600. **2.** *trans.* To frizz, curl; also, to curl the hair of 1526. †**3.** To gather into creases or pleats; to pleat –1805.
1. b. They frounced and tooke on most insolently P. HOLLAND. **2.** Not trick'd and frounc'd as she was wont MILT. **3.** Their shurts frounced LD. BERNERS.

Frouzy; var. of FROWZY.

Frow (frau), *sb.* ME. [– Du. *vrouw*.] **1.** A Dutchwoman. **2.** A woman, a lady, a wife. Chiefly with reference to Dutch or German women. 1587. †**3.** Applied to the Mænads or Bacchantes of paganism; also *transf.* –1616. **4.** *dial.* An idle, dirty woman 1781.

Frow; var. of FROE.

Froward (frōᵘ·wəɹd). ME. [f. FRO + -WARD; superseding FROMWARD.]
A. *adj.* (Not now in colloq. use.) **1.** Disposed to go counter to what is demanded or is reasonable; perverse; refractory; also, †bad, evilly-disposed, 'naughty'. (The opposite of *toward.*) **2.** Of things: †**a.** Adverse, untoward; refractory. †Of shape: Ill-formed. **b.** In later use only as *fig.* of sense 1. ME.
1. A F. Retention of Custome BACON. A f. child 1848. **2. a.** The f. chaos of futurity WORDSW. **b.** To take his f. fortune..with..patience 1576.
†**B.** *adv.* **1.** = FROMWARD. –1596. **2.** *fig.* Untowardly, perversely –1580.
C. *prep.* = FROMWARD. *Obs.* (or *arch.*) ME. Hence **Fro·ward-ly** *adv.*, **-ness.**

Frower: see FROE *sb.*

Frown (fraun), *sb.* 1581. [f. next.] **1.** A wrinkled aspect of the brow, expressive of disapprobation or severity, occas. of deep thought or perplexity. Also, the habit of frowning. 1605. **2.** A manifestation of disapprobation.
1. You are too much of late i'th'frowne SHAKS. *fig.* The f. of angry Heav'n 1783. **2.** To this no answer was given, but frowns 1721. Hence **Frow·nful** *a.* full of frowns. **Frow·ny** *a.* habitually frowning.

Frown (fraun), *v.* ME. [– OFr. *frognier, froignier* (surviving in *re(n)frogner*), f. *froigne* surly look, of Celtic origin (cf. W. *ffroen* nose).] **1.** *intr.* To knit the brows in displeasure or (less frequently) in concentration of thought; to look sternly. Said also of the brow. Of inanimate things: To look gloomy or threatening 1642. **2.** To express disapprobation or unfriendliness by a look. Const. *at, on, upon.* 1576. **3.** quasi-*trans.* To enforce, express, produce, etc. by a frown; also with *away, back, down, off,* etc. 1678.
1. He ended frowning, and his look denounc'd Desperate revenge MILT. They saw the times to frowne and trouble to come 1642. **2.** I frowne vpon him, yet he loues me still SHAKS. The heauens..are angry And frowne vpon's SHAKS. **3.** She smiles preferment, or she frowns disgrace SHERIDAN. Hence **Frow·ner. Frow·ningly** *adv.*

Frowst (fraust), *sb. colloq.* 1880. Also **froust.** [Back-formation from *frowsty*; see next.] Fusty heat in a room; hence as vb., to stay in or enjoy this. So **Frow·sty** *a.* 1865.

Frowzy (frau·zi), *a.* 1681. [prob. rel. to earlier synon. (dial.) *frowy* XVI (Spenser), †*frowish*, and later *frowsty* (XIX); ult. origin unkn.] **1.** Ill-smelling, fusty, musty. **2.** Dingy, rusty, slatternly, unkempt. Of the complexion: Red and coarse, blowsy 1710.
1. My study was so f. I couldn't sit in it HUGHES. **2.** A f. dirty-colour'd red Sits on her cloudy wrinkled face SWIFT. *fig.* A drowsy f. poem BYRON. Hence **Frow·ziness.**

Frozen (frōᵘ·z'n), *ppl. a.* ME. [pa. pple. of FREEZE *v.*] **1.** Congealed by extreme cold; subjected to extreme cold. Also *fig.* and of immaterial things. **b.** Of credits, assets, etc.: Impossible to liquidate or realize at maturity or other given time (opp. to LIQUID *a.* II. 5) 1922. **2.** *F.-out, -up*: cut off, stopped, by frost 1885.
1. The nauigation by the frosen sea EDEN. F. Limbs 1698, meat 1872. *fig.* A f. stare 1867.
Hence **Fro·zenly** *adv.* in a f. manner; with a cold look or action; (*U.S.*) stubbornly. **Fro·zenness,** f. condition.

†**Fru·bbish,** *v.* Also †**frobish.** 1570. [var. of FURBISH.] To furbish. †**Fru·bbisher.**

Fructed (frɒ·ktėd), *a.* 1610. [f. L. *fructus* fruit + -ED².] *Her.* Of a tree or plant: Having fruit (of a specified tincture).

Fructescent (frɒkte·sĕnt), *a.* 1862. [f. L. *fructus* fruit + -ESCENT.] Beginning to bear fruit. Hence **Fructe·scence,** the fruiting season, 'when vegetables scatter their..seeds'.

Fructiculose, a spurious wd.; see FRUTICULOSE.

‖**Fructidor** (früktidǫr). 1797. [Fr.; f. L. *fructus* fruit + Gr. δῶρον gift.] The twelfth month of the French revolutionary calendar (Aug. 18 to Sept. 16); the revolution which took place on 18th Fructidor (Sept. 4), 1797.

Fructiferous (frɒkti·fĕrəs), *a.* 1632. [f. L. *fructifer* (f. *fructus* fruit) + -OUS; see -FEROUS.] Bearing or producing fruit. Hence **Fructi·ferously** *adv.*

Fructification (frɒ:ktifikēⁱ·ʃən). 1604. [– late L. *fructificatio*, f. *fructificat-*, pa. ppl. stem of L. *fructificare*; see next, -ION.] **1.** The action or process of fructifying or producing fruit (now *rare* exc. *Bot.*). Also, fecundation. **2.** *concr.* in *Bot.* **a.** The fruit of a plant. **b.** *collect.* The organs of fruiting or reproduction, *esp.* the reproductive parts of ferns and mosses. 1764.

Fructify (frɒ·ktifəi), *v.* ME. [– (O)Fr. *fructifier* – L. *fructificare*, f. *fructus* fruit; see -FY.] **1.** *intr.* To bear fruit, become fruitful. Also *fig.* **2.** *trans.* To make fruitful; to fecundate 1583.
1. Hys land shall frutyfye 1538. **2.** To fructifie and increase the earth 1583. Hence †**Fru·ctifi:le** *a.* capable of bearing fruit. **Fru·ctifier.**

Fructose (frɒ·ktōᵘs). 1864. [f. L. *fructus* fruit + -OSE².] *Chem.* 'Fruit sugar or lævulose. Also applied to the sugar found in fruit' (*Syd. Soc. Lex.*).

Fructuary (frɒ·ktiuări). 1643. [– L. *fructuarius* adj. usufructuary (also sb. in late L.), f. *fructus* fruit; see -ARY¹. Cf. OFr. *fructuaire* sb. in same sense.]
A. *adj.* in *Rom. Law.* Of or belonging to usufruct. Only in *f. stipulation.* 1875. †**B.** *sb.* **1.** A usufructuary –1687. **2.** Something enjoyed by usufruct 1651.

†**Fru·ctuate,** *v. rare.* 1663. [f. L. *fructus* fruit + -ATE³.] *intr.* To bear fruit; to fructify. Hence **Fructua·tion,** the action of the vb.; †*concr.* a crop of fruit.

Fructuous (frɒ·ktiuəs), *a.* ME. [– OFr. *fructuous* or L. *fructuosus*, f. *fructus* fruit; see -OUS.] **1.** Full of, abounding with, or producing fruit. **2.** *fig.* Productive of results; advantageous, profitable ME.
1. An olyue plenteous, fair, f. WYCLIF *Jer.* 11:16. Hence **Fru·ctuous-ly** *adv.*, **-ness.**

†**Fru·cture.** [app. – Fr. †*fructure*, f. L. *fructus* fruit; see -URE.] The use or enjoyment (of something). COTGR.

Frugal (frū·găl), *a.* 1598. [– L. *frugalis*, f. *frugi* indecl. adj. (orig. dat. of *frux* fruit) frugal, economical, useful; see -AL¹.] **1.** Careful or sparing in the use of food, goods, etc.; economical. Const. *of.* **2.** Of things: Sparingly supplied or used; of small cost; opp. to *luxurious* 1603.
1. 'Tis now the cheap and f. fashion, Rather to Hide than Pay the Obligation COWLEY. **2.** A f. meal, which consisted of roots and tea GOLDSM. Hence **Fru·gally** *adv.*

Frugality (frugæ·liti). 1531. [– (O)Fr. *frugalité* or L. *frugalitas*; see prec., -ITY.] **1.** The quality of being frugal; moderate or sparing expenditure or use of provisions, goods, etc. **2.** The product of frugality, wealth amassed by economy; also in *pl.* frugal ways of living, frugal fare 1725.
1. Riches are gotten with industry, and kept by f. HOBBES. **2.** Wastes the wise f. of Kings POPE.

Frugiferous (frudʒi·fĕrəs), *a.* 1633. [f. L. *frugifer* (f. *frux, frug-* fruit) + -OUS; see -FEROUS.] Fruit-bearing, fruitful.

Frugivorous (frudʒi·vŏrəs), *a.* 1713. [f. L. *frux, frug-* fruit + -VOROUS.] Eating or feeding on fruit.

Fruit (frūt), *sb.* ME. [– (O)Fr. *fruit* :– L. *fructus* (enjoyment of) the produce of the soil, harvest, fruit, revenue, f. **frug-*, base of *frui* enjoy, perh. orig. feed on, *fruges* 'fruits' of the earth.] **1.** Vegetable products in general, that are fit to be used as food by men and animals. Now usu. in *pl.* **2.** The edible product of a plant or tree, consisting of the seed and its envelope, *esp.* the latter when juicy and pulpy, as in the apple, orange, plum, etc. ME. †**3.** A fruit-tree; also a food-plant. *rare.* –1767. †**4.** A course of fruit; the dessert –1602. **5.** The seed of a plant or tree, regarded as the means of reproduction, together with its envelope; *spec.* in *Bot.* 'the ripe pistil containing the ovules, arrived at the state of seeds' (Lindley); also, the spores of cryptogams 1794. **6.** Offspring, progeny. Also, an embryo, fœtus. Orig. a Hebraism. Now *rare.* ME. **7.** Anything accruing, produced, or resulting from an action or fact, the operation of a cause, etc.: **a.** material produce, increase; *pl.* products, revenues ME.; **b.** a result, issue, consequence (*sing.* and *pl.*) ME.; **c.** advantage, enjoyment, profit ME.
1. To give and preserve to our use the kindly fruits of the earth *Bk. Com. Prayer.* *fig.* The only f. which he could reap from a victory 1783. **2.** We take Branches from a Tree, to add to the F. POPE. The glow of ripe fruits 1795. **4.** *Haml.* II. ii. 52. **6.** Blessed shalbe the frute of thy body COVERDALE *Deut.* 28:4. **7. a.** Milke..which is the f. of the breasts 2 *Esd.* 8:10. **b.** Riches and Plenty are the natural Fruits of Liberty ADDISON. **c.** She tooke the Fruites of my Aduice *Haml.* II. ii. 145.
Comb.: **f.-bat** (see FLYING FOX); **-bud,** a bud containing a fruit germ, dist. from *leaf-bud*; **-dot** (*Bot.*), the sorus of ferns; **-fly,** a gardener's name for a sort of small black fly found in numbers among fruit-trees in spring; **-frame,** a trellis or espalier; **-mill,** a mill for grinding grapes for must or apples for cider; **-piece,** 'a pictured or sculptured representation of fruit' (*Cent. Dict.*); **-pigeon,** a general name for pigeons of the genera *Carpophaga* and *Treron*; **-press,** an apparatus for extracting the juice from fruit by pressure; **-spur,** a small branch whose growth is; stopped to ensure the development of fruit-buds **-stalk,** a stalk that bears fruit; *spec.* = PEDUNCLE 1; also occas. = CARPOPHORE; **-sugar** = GLUCOSE or LÆVULOSE; **-tree,** a tree cultivated for its fruit; **-wall,** a wall against which fruit-trees are trained; †**-yard,** an orchard.

Fruit (frūt), *v.* ME. [f. prec. sb.] **1.** *intr.* To bear fruit. **2.** *trans.* (*causatively*) To make bear fruit; to cultivate to the point of bearing fruit. *lit.* and *fig.* 1640. Hence **Frui·ted** *ppl. a.* having fruit upon it; fruit-laden.

Fruitage (frū·tėdʒ). 1578. [– OFr. *fruitage*, f. *fruit*; see FRUIT *sb.*, -AGE.] **1.** The process, season, or state of bearing fruit. **2.** Fruit collectively; also *fig.* 1610. †**3.** A decorative arrangement of fruits; a representation of this –1719.

1. In full f. COLERIDGE. 2. Greedily they pluck'd The Frutage fair to sight MILT.

Fruitarian (frutēᵊ·riăn). 1893. [f. FRUIT *sb.* + -ARIAN, after *vegetarian*.] One who adopts a fruit diet. Also as adj.

Fruiter (frū·təɹ). 1483. [– (O)Fr. *fruitier*, f. *fruit* FRUIT *sb.*; see -ER[2]; later prob. f. FRUIT *sb.* + -ER[1].] A dealer in fruit; also, a vessel engaged in the fruit-trade; a tree that produces fruit; a fruit-grower.

Fruiterer (frū·tĕrəɹ). ME. [Extension with -ER[1] 3 of prec.] **1.** A dealer in fruit. **†2.** A fruit-grower –1813. **Frui·teress,** a female f.

Fruitery (frū·tĕri). 1609. [– (O)Fr. *fruiterie*, f. *fruit* FRUIT *sb.*]; see -ERY.] **†1.** A place for growing or storing fruit –1816. **2.** Fruit collectively *c*1600.

†Fruitester. [f. FRUIT *sb.* + -STER.] A fruiteress. CHAUCER.

Fruitful (frū·tfŭl), *a.* ME. [f. FRUIT *sb.* + -FUL.] **1.** Productive of fruit; bearing fruit abundantly. Of soils, etc.: Fertile. Of rain, etc.: Causing fertility. **2.** Productive of offspring; not barren; prolific 1520. **†3.** Abundant, copious. Chiefly in Shaks. –1697. **4.** *transf.* and *fig.* 1535. **5.** Productive of good results ME.

1. Your Summer Fields, and fruitfull Vines SHAKS. **2.** God blessed them, saying, Be fruitfull, and multiply *Gen.* 1:22. **3.** One f. Meale SHAKS. **4.** Golden days, f. of golden deeds MILT. **5.** Fruytfull occupacyoun ME. Hence **Frui·tful-ly** *adv.*, **-ness.**

Fruition (frūi·ʃən). ME. [– (O)Fr. *fruition* – late L. *fruitio*, f. *frui* enjoy; see FRUIT *sb.*, -TION.] The action of enjoying; enjoyment, pleasurable possession, the pleasure arising from possession. ¶Erron. assoc. w. FRUIT.

1. The f. of our bookes HAKLUYT. All desire is for f. 1655. Repaid by such a..brief f. THACKERAY.

Fruitive (frū·itiv), *a.* 1635. [– med.L. *fruitivus* (Thomas à Kempis), f. L. *frui*; see FRUIT *sb.*, -IVE.] Consisting of, arising from, or producing fruition; having the faculty or function of enjoying.

Fruitless (frū·tlĕs), *a.* ME. [f. FRUIT *sb.* + -LESS.] **1.** Not producing fruit; barren, sterile. †*Rarely*: Not producing offspring. 1513. **2.** Yielding no profit or advantage; producing no result; ineffectual, unprofitable, useless; idle, vain ME. **3.** Of persons: unsuccessful 1843.

1. Rotton and fruyteles trees 1546. **2.** The.. fruitlessest of al passions SIDNEY. A..fruitlesse vision SHAKS. Our search was. f. DAMPIER. F. regrets JORTIN. Hence **Frui·tless-ly** *adv.*, **-ness.**

Fruitlet (frū·tlĕt). 1882. [f. FRUIT *sb.* + -LET.] A little fruit; in *Bot.* a single member of an aggregate fruit (see AGGREGATE *ppl. a.*).

Fruity (frū·ti), *a.* 1657. [f. FRUIT *sb.* + -Y[1].] **1.** Of, pertaining to, or resembling fruit. **2.** Of wine: Tasting of the grape 1851. **3.** *colloq.* Full of rough humour or (usu. scandalous) interest 1900. Hence **Frui·tiness.**

Frumentaceous (frūmĕntēⁱ·ʃəs), *a.* 1668. [– late L. *frumentaceus* (f. L. *frumentum* corn) + -OUS; see -ACEOUS.] Of the nature of or resembling wheat or other cereals.

Frumenta·rious, *a. rare.* 1670. [f. L. *frumentarius* (f. as prec.) + -OUS; see -ARIOUS.] Of or pertaining to corn.

Frumentation (frūmĕntēⁱ·ʃən). 1623. [– L. *frumentatio*, f. *frumentat-*, pa. ppl. stem of *frumentari* furnish with corn, f. as prec.; see -ION.] *Rom. Antiq.* A public largesse of corn.

Frumenty (frū·mĕnti), **Furmety** (fɔ̄·ɹmĕti). [ME. *frumentee, furmente* – OFr. *frumentee, four-*, f. *frument, fourment* (mod. *froment* wheat) :– L. *frumentum*, perh. f. *frui*; see FRUIT *sb.*, -Y[5].] **1.** A dish made of hulled wheat boiled in milk, and seasoned with cinnamon, sugar, etc. **†2.** A kind of wheat or spelt –1601.

Frump (frɒmp), *sb.* 1553. [prob. shortening of (dial.) *frumple* wrinkle (XIV), as vb. – MDu. *verrompelen*, f. *ver-* FOR- *pref.*[1] + *rompelen* RUMPLE *v.*] **†1.** ? A derisive snort –1650. **†2.** A flout, jeer –1700. **†3.** A hoax –1791. **4.** *pl.* Sulks, ill-humour. Now *dial.* 1668. **5.** A cross, old-fashioned, dowdily-dressed woman. Also, *rarely*, of a man. 1817.

5. They voted me a prig, a f., a fogram GODWIN. Hence **†Fru·mpery,** abuse; also, a flout, mock. **Fru·mpish** *a.* disposed to mock or flout; ill-tempered, cross. **Fru·mpy** *a.* cross-tempered; also, dowdy.

Frump (frɒmp), *v.* 1566. [Goes with prec.] **1.** *trans.* To mock, flout, jeer; to taunt, insult, snub. *Obs.* or *arch.* 1577. **†2.** *intr.* To scoff, mock. Const. *at.* –1662. **†3.** To sulk 1693. Hence **Fru·mper,** one who frumps.

Frush (frɒʃ), *sb.*[1] *Obs.* exc. *Sc.* ME. [– OFr. *fruis, frois*, f. *fruissier, froissier*; see FRUSH *v.*] **1.** †A rush, charge, collision –1533. **b.** The noise of this ME. **2.** *collect.* Fragments, splinters 1583.

Frush (frɒʃ), *sb.*[2] Now *dial.* 1607. [perh. short for Fr. synon. *fourchette* (Topsell); see FROG *sb.*[2] But cf. Norw., WFris. *frosk* in same sense.] = FROG *sb.*[2] Also, thrush.

Frush (frɒʃ), *a. Sc.* and *n. dial.* 1802. [perh. f. FRUSH *v.*, but cf. synon. Sc. dial. *frough*.] **1.** Liable to break; brittle, dry, fragile. **2.** Soft, not firm in substance 1848.

Frush (frɒʃ), *v.* ME. [– OFr. *fruissier, froissier* (mod. *froisser*) :– pop. L. **frustiare* to shiver in pieces, f. L. *frustum*; see FRUSTUM.] **†1.** *trans.* To strike violently so as to crush, bruise, or smash; also *fig.* –1609. **†2.** *intr.* To rush violently –1450. **†3.** *trans.* The term of art for: **a.** To carve (a chicken) –1708; **b.** To dress (a chub) –1787. **4.** To straighten (the feathers of an arrow). *Hist.* 1548.

1. High Cedars are frushed with tempests, when lowe shrubs are not touched with the wind GREENE.

†Frust (frɒst). 1765. [– L. *frustum* FRUSTUM.] A fragment –1820.

†Fru·strable, *a. rare.* 1674. [– late L. *frustrabilis*, f. L. *frustrari*; see FRUSTRATE *v.*, -ABLE.] Capable of being frustrated –1677.

†Frustra·neous, *a.* 1643. [f. mod.L. *frustraneus* (f. *frustra* in vain, after L. *extraneus*) + -OUS.] Vain, ineffectual, unprofitable –1780.

Frustrate (frɒ·streⁱt), *pa. pple.* and *ppl. a. arch.* ME. [– L. *frustratus*, pa. pple. of *frustrari*, f. *frustra* in vain; see -ATE[2].]

†A. *pa. pple.* In senses of the vb. –1693.

Bid him yeeld, Being so f. *Ant. & Cl.* V. i. 2.

B. *ppl. a.* **1.** Bereft or deprived of; destitute *of*. *Obs.* exc. *arch.* 1576. **2.** Failing of effect 1529. †Of a legal document: Invalid, null –1664. **3.** Of a hope, etc.: Balked, defeated, futile 1588. **†4.** Idle, purposeless –1535.

2. The f. dart POPE. **3.** And multitude makes f. the design DRYDEN.

Frustrate (frɒ·streⁱt), *v.* Pa. pple. **frustrated, †frustrate.** ME. [– *frustrat-*, pa. ppl. stem of L. *frustrari*; see prec., -ATE[3].] **1.** *trans.* To balk, disappoint. Const. *of* (now *rare*). **2.** To render ineffectual; to neutralize, counteract 1471; to make null and void, to do away with 1528. **3.** To render vain; to baffle, defeat, foil. (The current use.) 1500.

1. They were frustrated in their designes WOOD. Frustrated of His End 1754. **2.** To f. the opperacion [of poisons] EDEN. To f. the Laws and Statutes of this Realm R. COKE. **3.** To f. a villany BLACKSTONE, a motion 1809, a negotiation 1844. So **Fru·strative** *a.* tending to f., balk or defeat; disappointing. **†Fru·stratory** *a.* Frustrative.

Frustration (frɒstrēⁱ·ʃən). 1555. [– L. *frustratio*, f. as prec.; see -ION.] The action of frustrating; disappointment; defeat.

An entire f. of the main object of the deed 1884.

Frustule (frɒ·stiul). 1857. [– L. *frustulum*, dim. of *frustum* FRUSTUM; see -ULE.] The siliceous two-valved shell of a diatom, with its contents.

†‖**Fru·stulum.** *Pl.* **-la.** 1700. [L.; see prec.] **a.** A fragment, an atom. **b.** *Math.* A small frustum. –1785. So **Fru:stulo·se** *a.* consisting of small fragments.

Frustum (frɒ·stɒ̆m). *Pl.* **-a, -ums.** 1658. [– L. *frustum* piece cut off.] **1.** *Math.* The portion of a regular solid left after cutting off the upper part by a plane parallel to the base; or the portion intercepted between two planes, either parallel or inclined to each other. **b.** Applied to the sections of the shaft of a column 1835. **2.** *gen.* A portion or fragment. *rare.* 1721.

Frutage, obs. f. FRUITAGE.

Frutescent (frute·sĕnt), *a.* 1709. [irreg. f. L. *frutex* bush + -ESCENT. Cf. med.L. *frutescere*.] *Bot.* Becoming shrubby; having the appearance or habit of a shrub. Hence **Frute·scence,** shrubbiness.

Frutex (frū·teks). 1664. [– L. *frutex*, *frutic-* bush.] *Bot.* A plant having a woody stem, but smaller than a tree; a shrub.

What is meant by trees, frutexes, etc. EVELYN.

†Fru·ticant, *a.* [– *fruticant-*, pr. ppl. stem of L. *fruticari* sprout; see FRUTEX, -ANT.] Putting forth shoots, sprouting. EVELYN.

†Fruti·ceous, *a.* [f. L. *frutic-* FRUTEX + -EOUS.] Shrubby, bushy. SIR T. BROWNE.

Fruticose (frū·tikōᵘ·s), *a.* 1668. [– L. *fruticosus*, f. *frutic-* FRUTEX; see -OSE[1].] **1.** Of the nature of a shrub; having woody stalks. **2.** Shrublike; said *e.g.* of minerals, etc. 1805.

1. The f. Rubi J. HOOKER. **2.** The F. Lichens VINES. var. **Fru·ticous.**

Fruticulose (fruti:kiŭlōᵘ·s), *a.* 1830. [f. *frutic-* FRUTEX + -ULOUS.] Resembling a small shrub. Also in comb. form **Fruticulo·so-.**

Fru·tify, *v. nonce-wd.* A comic blunder put into the mouth of an illiterate person; *notify*, the word meant, is confused with *fructify*. *Merch. V.* II. ii. 142.

†Fruz, *sb.* [perh. suggested by FRIZZ *sb.*] A collection of small branches, producing a frizzy appearance. EVELYN.

Fry (frəi), *sb.*[1] ME. [– ON. **frio, frjó* seed = Goth. *fraiw*; of unkn. origin. Eng. is implied in AL. *frium* XIII–XIV.] **1.** Offspring, young (of human beings); a man's children or family; *rarely*, a child. Now only as transf. from sense 3. ME. **2.** The roe (of a female fish) ME. **3.** Young fishes just produced from the spawn; *spec.* the young of salmon in the second year, more fully *salmon fry* ME. Also *transf.* and *fig.* **4.** Hence, a collective term for: **a.** the smaller kinds of fish or other animals 1666; **b.** young or insignificant persons 1577; **c.** a heap of inanimate things 1587.

1. What you Egge? Yong f. of Treachery SHAKS. **4. a.** Not onely Pike and Carp, but lesser F. 1674. **b.** That indigested heap, and frie of Authors MILT. **c.** The smaller f. of Christmas Books 1861.

Fry (frəi), *sb.*[2] 1634. [f. FRY *v.*] **†1.** Excessive heat 1634. **2.** Food cooked in a frying-pan 1639. **b.** Applied locally to internal parts of animals, usually eaten fried, as *lamb's f.*, etc. 1847.

Fry (frəi), *v.* Inflected **fried, frying.** ME. [– (O)Fr. *frire* :– L. *frigere* (cf. Gr. φρύγειν, Skr. *bhṛjyáti* grill).] **1.** *trans.* To cook with fat in a shallow pan over the fire. **†2.** *transf.* and *fig.* To torture by fire; to burn or scorch –1697. **3.** *intr.* To undergo the operation of cooking with fat in a pan (*rare* in lit. sense) ME. Also *transf.* and *fig.* **†4.** Of water: To be agitated, boil, seethe, foam –1697. **b.** To ferment; to seethe (in the stomach) –1647.

1. Phr. *To have other fish to f.* (see FISH *sb.*[1]). **2.** Raging Sirius fries the thirsty Land 1695. Phr. *To f. a faggot*: to be burnt alive. **3.** Phr. *To f. in one's own grease*: orig. *transf.* e.g. of persons burning alive, and *fig.*; now only, to suffer the consequences of one's own folly. In his owene grece I made him frye For angre, and for verray Jalousye CHAUCER. *fig.* What kindling motions in their breasts do f. 1632. **4. b.** To keep the Oyle from frying in the Stomach BACON. Hence **Fry·er, fri·er,** one who fries (fish); a vessel for frying; *pl.* fish for frying. **Fry·ing** *vbl. sb.*

Fry·ing-pa:n. ME. [f. prec.] A shallow pan, usually of iron, with a long handle, in which food is fried.

Phr. (*To jump*, etc.) *out of the frying-pan into the fire*: to escape from one evil only to fall into a greater one.

Fuage, var., of FEUAGE, hearth-tax.

Fub, var. of FOB *v.*[1]

†Fub(b, fub(b)s. 1614. [perh. blending of *fat* and *chub*; cf. FUBSY.] A small chubby person (a term of endearment) –1694.

†Fu·bbery, *rare.* [f. *fub*, var. of FOB *v.*[1] + -ERY.] Cheating, deception. MARSTON.

Fubby (fɒ·bi), *a. rare.* 1790. [f. FUB *sb.* + -Y[1].] = next.

Fubsy (fɒ·bzi), *a.* 1780. [f. FUB(B, FUB(B)S + -Y[1]; see -SY.] Fat and squat.

Fat and f. fellows of colleges 1826.

Fucaceous (fiukēⁱ·ʃəs), *a.* 1891. [f. mod. L. *fucaceæ* (f. L. *fucus*; see FUCUS) + -OUS.] Of or belonging to the group *Fucaceæ* of seaweeds.

†**Fu·cate,** *a.* 1531. [– L. *fucatus*, pa. pple. of *fucare* colour, paint, dye, f. FUCUS; see -ATE².] Artificially coloured; hence, falsified, disguised, counterfeit –1621. So †**Fucated** *ppl. a.* †**Fuca·tion,** the action of painting the face; counterfeiting.

Fuchsia (fiū·ʃ'ă). 1753. [mod.L., f. Leonhard *Fuchs* (XVI); see -IA¹.] A genus of ornamental shrubs (N.O. *Onagraceæ*) with drooping flowers; a plant of this genus. Also *attrib.*

Fuchsine (fu·ksin). 1865. [f. prec. + -INE⁵. Named from its resemblance to the colour of the flower.] A salt of rosaniline, crystallizing in iridescent green tablets, soluble in water and forming a deep red liquid; used as a dye.

Fucivorous (fiusi·vŏrəs), *a.* 1860. [f. L. *fucus* FUCUS + -VOROUS.] Eating, or subsisting on, seaweed.

Fuck (fɒk), *v.* 1503. [corresp. to a ME. **fuken*; ult. origin unkn. Connection with synon. G. *ficken* cannot be demonstrated. Until recently regarded as a taboo-word and rarely recorded in print.] *vulg.* **1.** *intr.* To copulate. **b.** *trans.* To copulate with. **2.** Used profanely as the coarsest equivalent of DAMN *v.* 5. 1922.

Phrases, in comb. with advs. **F. about.** To fool about, mess about. **F. off.** To go away, make off. **F. up. a.** To ruin, spoil, make a mess of. **b.** as *sb.* (*f.-up*). A mess, muddle.
Hence **Fuck** *sb.* **Fu·cking** *ppl.a.* (*adv.*) used esp. as a mere intensive.

Fucoid (fiū·koid). 1839. [f. FUCUS + -OID.] **A.** *adj.* **a.** Resembling or belonging to seaweeds, *esp.* those of the group *Fucaceæ*. **b.** Characterized by impressions of such seaweeds or markings similar to them.
B. *sb.* **a.** A seaweed of the group *Fucaceæ* 1857. **b.** A fossil marine plant resembling these 1848.
So **Fucoi·dal** (in sense A. b).

‖**Fucus** (fiū·kŏs). *Pl.* ‖**fuci** (fiū·səi); also †**fucus(s)es,** †**fucus's,** †**fucos,** †**fucu's.** 1599. [L. *fucus* rock-lichen, red dye or cosmetic – Gr. φῦκος, of Semitic origin.] †**1.** Paint or cosmetic for beautifying the skin; a wash or colouring for the face –1757. †Also *fig.* –1742. **2.** A genus of sea-weeds with flat leathery fronds. Formerly applied more widely. 1716.

Fud (fŏd). *Sc.* and *n. dial.* 1785. [Of unkn. origin.] **1.** 'The backside or buttocks' (Jam.). **2.** The tail or scut of a hare or rabbit 1787. **3.** *Woollen-manuf.* Woollen waste 1873.

Fudder (fɒ·dəɹ). 1679. [– G. *fuder* (= FOTHER *sb.*).] A tun (of wine).

Fudder, obs. f. FODDER, FOTHER *sb.*

Fuddle (fɒ·d'l), *sb. slang* or *colloq.* 1680. [f. next vb.] †**1.** Drink, liquor, 'booze' –1706. **2.** A drinking bout 1813. **3.** Intoxication; an intoxicated state 1764. **4.** *transf.* The state of being muddled, or the like 1827.

Fuddle (fɒ·d'l), *v.* 1588. [Of unkn. origin.] **1.** *intr.* To have a drinking bout; to tipple, booze. Also quasi-*trans.* with *away*. **2.** *trans.* To confuse with or as with drink 1600. **3.** *transf.* and *fig.* To stupefy, muddle, confuse. Formerly also of joy, etc.: To intoxicate. 1617.

2. A Cup of Ale..under a Pint, yet it almost fuddled him 1706. **3.** He is fuddled with animal spirits 1803. Hence **Fu·ddler,** a tippler.

Fudge (fɒdʒ). 1766. [f. next.] **A.** *interj.* Stuff and nonsense! Bosh! **B.** *sb.* **1.** Contemptible nonsense, stuff, bosh 1791. **2.** A made-up story, a deceit 1797. **3.** A piece of stop-press news inserted in a newspaper page at the last minute 1899. **4.** A soft-grained sweetmeat made from milk, sugar, chocolate, etc. 1897.

Fudge (fɒdʒ), *v.* 1615. [perh. alt. of earlier FADGE *v.*, of unkn. origin.] **1.** *trans.* To put together clumsily or dishonestly; to patch or fake *up*; to cook accounts 1674; to foist *in* 1776. **2.** *intr.* To fit in with what is anticipated, come off; also, to turn out 1615. **3.** [f. prec. sb.] To talk nonsense, tell 'crams'. Also quasi-*trans.* 1834.

1. To f. accounts 1879. That last suppose is fudged in FOOTE. *To f. a day's work* (Naut.): to work a dead reckoning by 'rule of thumb' methods. **2.** We will see how this will f. SCOTT.

Fuel (fiū·ĕl), *sb.* ME. [– AFr. *fuaille*, *fewaile*, OFr. *fouaille* :– Rom. **focalia* (in med.L., obligation to furnish or right to demand fuel), f. L. *focus* hearth, in late L. fire.] **1.** Material for burning, combustible matter for fires, etc. ME; *fig.* something that serves to feed or inflame passion, excitement, etc. 1580. **2.** (With *a.* and *pl.*) A kind of fuel. †Also *pl.* articles serving as fuel. 1626.

1. *fig.* F. for Dissention STEELE. **2.** Turf, and Peat, and Cow-sheards are cheap Fewels, and last long BACON.

Comb.: **f.-economizer,** a contrivance for saving fuel in an engine or furnace: **-gas,** gas for use as fuel.

Fuel (fiū·ĕl), *v.* 1592. [f. prec. sb.] **1.** *trans.* To feed or furnish with fuel. *lit.* and *fig.* **2.** *intr.* To get fuel 1880.

1. Wealth fuel'd Sin KEN. **2.** The right of fuelling in the park DIXON. Hence **Fu·eller** (now *rare*), one who or that which supplies fuel for fires; also *fig.*

Fuff (fɒf), *sb.* Chiefly *Sc.* 1535. [f. next vb.] **1.** A puff of wind; the 'spit' of a cat; a whiff. **2.** A huff, fume 1834.

Fuff (fɒf), *v. Sc.* and *dial.* 1513. [Echoic. Cf. FAFFLE *v.*] **1.** *intr.* To puff. **2.** Of a cat or tiger: To 'spit' 1693. **3.** *trans.* To puff (a tobacco-pipe) 1787.

Fuffy (fɒ·fi), *a. Sc.* and *n. dial.* 1824. [f. FUFF *sb.* + -Y¹.] **1.** Light and soft. **2.** 'Huffy' 1858.

Fug (fɒg), *sb. colloq.*, orig. *dial.* and *school slang*. 1888. [perh. a blending of elements of two or more synonyms, e.g. †FUNK *sb.*² (XVII–XVIII) and †*fogo* offensive smell (early XIX).] A close stuffy atmosphere. Hence **Fug** *v. intr.* to stay indoors in this. **Fu·ggy** *a.* close and stuffy.

Fugacious (fiugēⁱ·ʃəs), *a.* 1634. [f. L. *fugax*, *fugac-*, f. *fugere* flee; see -ACIOUS.] **1.** Apt to flee away or flit; evanescent, fugitive; volatile. **2.** *Bot.* and *Zool.* Falling or fading early; soon cast off. Cf. CADUCOUS. 1750.

1. The f. nature of life and time HT. MARTINEAU. Hence **Fuga·cious-ly** *adv.*, **-ness.**

Fugacity (fiugæ·sĭti). 1656. [f. as prec. + -ITY.] The quality of being fugacious; instability; transitoriness; volatility.

The f. of pleasure, the fragility of beauty JOHNSON.

†**Fu·gacy.** 1600. [f. as prec. + -Y³, after *fallacy*, etc.; see -ACY 1.] Flight; also, the fact of being a fugitive slave –1661.

Fugal (fiū·găl), *a.* 1854. [f. FUGUE + -AL¹.] *Mus.* Of, pertaining to, or of the nature of fugues.

‖**Fugato** (fugā·to), *adv.* 1866. [It. *fugato* fugued, f. *fuga* FUGUE.] In the fugue style, but not in strict fugue form. Also *sb.* Music composed in this style.

-fuge (fiūdʒ), *suffix*, occurring in words (adj. and sb.) f. mod.L. types in *-fugus*. In the medical words *febrifugus*, etc., the ending takes its sense from L. *fugare* put to flight, not from *fugere* flee.

Fu·gie. *Sc.* Now *Hist.* 1777. [perh. f. *fugæ* in the Law L. phr. *in meditatione fugæ*.] A cock that will not fight; a runaway. Hence, a coward.

Comb. **f.-warrant,** a warrant granted against a debtor on sworn information that he intends to flee.

Fugitive (fiū·dʒitiv). ME. [–(O)Fr. *fugitif*, *-ive* – L. *fugitivus*, f. *fugit-*, pa. ppl. stem of *fugere* flee; see -IVE.]

A. *adj.* **1.** Apt or tending to flee; given to, or in the act of running away; also *fig.* 1606. **b.** That has taken flight. †Also, of a debtor: Meditating flight. 1467. †**2.** Driven out, banished, exiled. Const. *from*, *of*. –1598. **3.** Moving from place to place; vagabond; *fig.* fickle 1481. **4.** Evanescent, fleeting 1510; quickly fading or becoming effaced; perishable 1678; volatile (*rare*) 1666. **5.** Of compositions (occas. of writers): Ephemeral, occasional 1766.

1. The Fugitive Parthians SHAKS. *fig.* A f. and cloister'd vertue..that never sallies out and sees her adversary MILT. **b.** Felons fugitif 1495. A f. daughter RICHARDSON, slave 1880. **3.** F. preachers make f. congregations 1883. F. securities 1893. **4.** F. follies 1635, flowers 1830, dyes 1842. **5.** You're a f. writer, I think, sir, of rhymes BYRON.

B. *sb.* **1.** One who flees from danger, an enemy, justice, or an owner ME.; †a deserter –1659; an exile, refugee 1591. **2.** One who shifts about from place to place; a vagabond, wanderer. Also of the lower animals. 1563. **3.** Something fleeting, or that eludes the grasp 1683.

1. Ranke me..A Master leauer, and a fugitiue *Ant. & Cl.* IV. ix. 22. The fugitives from Rome MILMAN. **3.** That airy f., called wit 1774.

Hence **Fu·gitiveness,** the quality or condition of being f. **Fu·gitivi:sm,** the condition of a f.

Fugle (fiū·g'l), *v.* 1837. [Back-formation from next.] *intr.* To do the duty of a fugleman; to act as guide or director; to make signals. *lit.* and *fig.*

Wooden arms with elbow-joints are jerking and fugling in the air, in the most rapid mysterious manner CARLYLE.

Fugleman (fiū·g'lmæn). 1804. [– G. *flügelmann* flank-man, f. *flügel* wing + *mann* MAN.] A soldier especially expert and well-drilled, formerly placed in front of a regiment or company as an example and model to the others. Also *transf.* and *fig.*

This Hohman was now *Flügelmann* ('fugleman' as we have named it, leader of the file) CARLYLE.

Fugue (fiūg), *sb.* 1597. [– Fr. *fugue* or its source It. *fuga* – L. *fuga* flight, rel. to *fugere* flee.] *Mus.* 'A polyphonic composition constructed on one or more short subjects or themes, which are harmonized according to the laws of counterpoint, and introduced from time to time with various contrapuntal devices' (Stainer and Barrett).

Double f., a common term for a f. on two subjects, in which the two start together GROVE. Hence **Fugue** *v. intr.* to compose, or perform, a f. **Fu·guist,** a composer of fugues.

-ful, *suffix*, orig. identical with FULL *a.*

1. Forming adjs., in composition with a preceding sb., orig. with sense 'having', 'characterized by' (the attribute denoted by the sb.). In the 14th c., in a few forms, the suffix had the force of 'possessing the qualities of'; e.g. in *masterful*, *manful*. In mod. Eng. adjs. in *-ful* are sometimes formed directly on verb-stems, the sense of the suffix being 'apt to', 'able or accustomed to', as in *distractful*, *mournful*. See also *bashful*.

2. Forming sbs., orig. not only with its proper sense, but in the transf. sense of 'quantity that fills or would fill' (a receptacle). In mod.Eng. *-ful.* forms derivatives with the general sense 'quantity that fills or would fill' (something). The pl. forms *spoonsful*, *cupsful*, etc., though historically justifiable, are ambiguous, and contrary to good modern usage.

†**Fu·lciment.** 1648. [– L. *fulcimentum*, f. *fulcire* prop up, stay; see -MENT.] A prop or support; usu. *spec.* a fulcrum –1796.

Fulcra, pl. of FULCRUM.

Fulcraceous (fɒlkrēⁱ·ʃəs), *a.* 1866. [f. FULCRUM + -ACEOUS.] *Bot.* Of or pertaining to the fulcra of plants.

Fulcrate (fɒ·lkreⁱt), *a.* 1760. [f. FULCRUM + -ATE².] *Bot.* Supported by or provided with fulcra.

Fulcrum (fɒ·lkrŏm). *Pl.* **-ra.** 1674. [– L. *fulcrum* post or foot of a couch, f. base **fulc-* of *fulcire* support.] **1.** A prop or support; now only *spec.* in *Mech.* the point on which a lever is placed to get purchase or upon which it turns. Also *fig.* **2.** (Chiefly *pl.*) **a.** *Bot.* Accessory organs or appendages of a plant; e.g. bracts, stipules, etc. 1785. **b.** *Ichth.* (*pl.*) The small osseous scales arranged in a row and situated on the anterior ray of the fins of many ganoid fishes 1880. var. **Fu·lcre.**

Fulfil (fulfi·l), *v.* Pa. t. and pple. **fulfilled** (fulfi·ld). [Late OE. *fullfyllan* (once), f. *full* FULL *a.* + *fyllan* FILL *v.*; a formation peculiar to Eng.] **1.** *trans.* To fill up, make full. Const. *of*, *with*. *arch.* †**2.** To satisfy the appetite or desire of –1601. **3.** To make complete; to supply what is lacking in. Also, to supply the place of (something); to compensate for. *Obs.* exc. *arch.* ME. **4.** To carry out (a prophecy, promise, etc.); to satisfy (a desire, prayer). Orig. a Hebraism. ME. **5.** To perform, execute, do; to obey or follow ME.; to answer (a purpose), comply with (conditions) 1784. **6.** To bring to an end, complete ME.

1. All Beastes I byd yow multeply..the earth to fulfill 1500. He..fulfilleth both heaven and earth with his presence 1563. **4.** To fulfill the Prophecies 1633. Full of bright promise never fulfilled BRYCE. **5.** The Law of God exact he shall f. MILT. Every stone fulfils its place inside and out SMEATON. **6.** Whan thy tyme is fulfylled y[t] thou shalt slepe with thy fathers COVERDALE 2 *Sam.* 7:12. Hence **Fulfi·ller,** one who fulfils.

Fulfilment (fulfi·lmĕnt). 1775. [f. prec. + -MENT.] The action or an act or process of fulfilling; accomplishment, performance, completion.

The f. of a condition 1891.

Fulgent (fʊ·ldʒĕnt), *a.* ME. [– *fulgent-*, pr. ppl. stem of L. *fulgēre* shine; see -ENT.] Shining brightly; brilliant, glittering, resplendent. Now *poet.* or *rhet.*

His f. head And shape Starr-bright MILT. Hence †**Fu·lgence,** †**Fu·lgency,** f. quality; brightness, splendour. **Fu·lgent-ly** *adv.*, **-ness.**

Fulgid (fʊ·ldʒid), *a.* 1656. [– L. *fulgidus*, f. *fulgēre* shine; see -ID[1].] **1.** Flashing, glittering, shining. **2.** *Nat. Hist.* A bright, fiery red. Hence **Fulgi·dity,** f. state or condition.

Fulgor, fulgour (fʊ·lgǫɹ, -əɹ). *arch.* 1602. [– L. *fulgor*, f. as prec.; see -OR 1.] A brilliant or flashing light; dazzling brightness, splendour. Also *fig.* Hence **Fu·lgorous** *a. rare*, flashing, brilliant, lustrous (*lit.* and *fig.*).

Fulgurant (fʊ·lgiŭrănt), *a.* 1647. [– *fulgurant-*, pr. ppl. stem of L. *fulgurare*, f. *fulgur* lightning; see -ANT. Cf. Fr. *fulgurant.*] Flashing like lightning.

Fu·lgurate, *v.* 1677. [– *fulgurat-*, pa. ppl. stem of L. *fulgurare*; see prec., -ATE[3].] To emit flashes like lightning. Hence **Fu·lgurating** *ppl. a.*; also *transf.* (of pains) darting like lightning through the body.

Fulguration (fʊlgiŭrē[i]·ʃən). 1633. [– L. *fulguratio* (esp.) sheet-lightning, f. *fulgurat-*; see prec., -ION. Cf. Fr. *fulguration.*] **1.** The action of lightning or flashing like lightning; chiefly in *pl.* flashes of lightning. Now usu. *fig.* **2.** *Assaying.* = BLICK, q.v. 1676.

Fulgurite (fʊ·lgiŭrəit). 1834. [f. L. *fulgur* lightning + -ITE[1] 2b.] **1.** *Geol.* Any rocky substance that has been fused or vitrified by lightning. Also (less correctly) *fulgorite.* **2.** An explosive, consisting of 'nitro-glycerine mixed with some coarsely ground farinaceous substance' 1882.

Fulgurous (fʊ·lgiŭrəs), *a.* 1616. [f. L. *fulgur* + -OUS.] Resembling, full of, or charged with lightning. Also *fig.*

Fulham (fu·lăm). *slang.* 1550. [perh. f. the place-name *Fulham*, once a haunt of gamesters.] A die loaded at the corner. (A *high f.* was loaded so as to ensure a throw of 4, 5, or 6; a *low f.* one of 1, 2, or 3.) See *Merry W.* I. iii. 94.

Fuliginosity (fiuli:dʒinǫ·sĭti). 1758. [f. next + -ITY. Cf. Fr. *fuliginosité.*] The condition or quality of being fuliginous or sooty; sooty matter, soot. Also *fig.*

Fuliginous (fiuli·dʒinəs), *a.* 1574. [– late L. *fuliginosus*, f. *fuligo, fuligin-* soot; see -OUS. Cf. Fr. *fuligineux* (*humeur fuligineuse*, Paré), perh. the immediate source.] **1.** Pertaining to, consisting of, containing, or resembling soot; sooty 1621; blackened with soot (*joc.*) 1763. †**2.** In old physiology applied to certain thick vapours or exhalations said to be formed by organic combustion, and noxious to the head and vital parts –1725. **3.** (Chiefly *Nat. Hist.*) Soot-coloured, dusky 1822.

2. It is not amiss to bore the scull with an instrument to let out the f. vapours BURTON. Hence **Fuli·ginous-ly** *adv.*, **-ness.**

‖**Fuligo** (fiuləi·go), 1646. [L.] Soot.

Fulimart, obs. f. FOUMART.

Full (ful). [OE. *full* = OFris. *foll, full*, OS. *ful* (Du. *vol*), OHG. *foll* (G. *voll*), ON. *fullr*, Goth. *fulls* :– Gmc. **fullaz* :– **fulnaz* :– IE. **pl̥nós*, cogn. w. Gr. πολύς, L. *plenus.*]

A. *adj.* **1.** Having within its limits all it will hold; having no space empty; replete. Const. *of.* **b.** *fig.*; *esp.* of the heart: Overcharged with emotion ME. **2. a.** Containing abundance *of*; charged, crowded OE. †**b.** Of a surface: Covered (with) –1657. **c.** In non-material sense: Abounding (in). Const. *of*, occas. †*with.* OE. **3.** Engrossed with or absorbed in. Now only with *of.* 1607. **4.** Having eaten or drunk to repletion. Now *arch.* (or *vulgar*). OE. **b.** Having had one's fill of anything. *Obs.* exc. in Hebraisms *f. of days, years, children.* ME. **c.** †Sated, weary *of.* Similarly in *full up* (colonial slang). ME. †**5.** Amply supplied with means –1683. **6.** Abundant, copious, satisfying, satisfactory OE.; complete or abundant in detail 1656. **7.** Complete, entire, perfect; answering in every respect to a description OE. **8.** Complete in number, quantity, magnitude, or extent. Of the moon: Having the disc completely illuminated. Of the face or front: Entirely visible to the spectator. OE. **b.** Of an assembly, etc.: One from which none or few are absent 1557. **9.** Possessed of, delivered with, or exerting the utmost force ME. **10.** Having a rounded outline; large, swelling, plump, protuberant OE. **b.** Of portions of dress: Containing plenty of material which is arranged in gathers or folds 1789. **11.** *Naut.* Of a sail: Filled. Of the ship: Having her sails filled with wind. 1627.

1. A f. stomach 1590. Phr. *F. as an egg, f. to the brim* (see BRIM *sb.*[2]), *f. to overflowing, f. up* (colloq.). **b.** Speake, for my heart is f. *Oth.* V. ii. 175. **2.** As f. of spite and ill nature as a Spider with poyson 1621. **b.** The rind..f. of wrinkles 1657. **c.** O f. of all subtilty and all mischiefe *Acts* 13:10. Phr. *A f. man*: One whose mind is richly stored; Reading maketh a f. man BACON. **3.** The king seemed mighty f. that we should have money to do all that we desired PEPYS. F. of business 1853. **4.** The f. soule loatheth an honie combe *Prov.* 27:7. **c.** I am f. of the burnt offerings of rammes *Isa.* 1:11. **5.** I haue all, and abound. I am f. *Phil.* 4:18. **6.** A f. Repast DRYDEN, Experience 1707. The fullest report of a case 1866. **7.** Phr. *F. point, stop* (see those words). When it was f. Day 1717. At f. liberty to speak his mind BP. BERKELEY. In f. possession of his faculties MACAULAY. Phr. *F. brother, sister*: born of the same father and mother (opp. to HALF-BROTHER). The man commands Like a f. soldier *Oth.* II. i. 36. **8.** The ful ordir of preesthod 1463. A f. yeere SHAKS., regiment PURCHAS, Age 1655. The head of a Roman Emperor drawn with a f. face ADDISON. **b.** *Oth.* IV. i. 275. Phr. *F. flood, sea, tide* (*lit.* and *fig.*), indicating the greatest height of the water, or the time when it is highest. **9.** A f. gale of wind 1634, Huzza 1700, pulse 1783. Phr. *F. butt, cry, gallop, sail, speed*, etc. (see those words). **10.** A f. black Eye 1688. F. round Faces..f. Lips, and short Chins DAMPIER. **b.** Sleeves, full and high on the shoulders 1891. **11.** Phr. *Keep her* (i.e. the ship) *f. F. and by*: see BY *adv.*

Comb. **1.** General: as, *f.-draught, -power*, etc.; *f.-fed, -flowing*, etc.; *f.-banked, -blossomed, -fortuned, -rigged, -sized, -statured, -throated*, etc.

2. Special: **f.-back** (*Football*), position in the field behind the other backs; a player in this position; also *attrib.*; **-bodied** *a.*, having a f. body (*esp.* of wine: see BODY); also *fig.*; **-breasted** *a.*, having a f. breast: also *transf.*; **-brimmed** *a.*, f. to the brim; **-centre arch** [Fr. *arc à plein cintre*], a semicircular arch; one describing the f. amount of 180°; **-circle** *adv.*, with the form of a f. circle or disc; **-eyed** *a.*, †(*a*) perfectly visible; seen in the front; (*b*) having f. eyes; **-flavoured** *a.*, having a f. or strong flavour (*esp.* of cigars); also *fig.*; **-front** *v.*, to present a f. front to; †**-mouth,** a chatterer; also *attrib.* = FULL-MOUTHED; **-orbed** *a. poet.* (of the moon), having its disc completely illuminated; also *fig.*

B. quasi-*sb.* and *sb.* **1.** The *adj.* used *absol.*, passing into *sb.* ME. **2.** = FILL *sb.*[1] 1. Now *rare.* ME. **3.** Complete scope; entire amount; completeness, fullness. Now *rare.* ME. **4.** The period, point, or state of the greatest fullness or strength ME.; of a month or season, the height, the middle 1658.

1. Phr. **At (the) f.:** †fully, completely; at the position or moment of fullness; in the state of fullness. **In (†the) f.:** at f. length, in extenso; to the f. amount. *In f. of*: in f. discharge or satisfaction of. **To the f.:** to the utmost extent, completely, fully. **3.** With my opinions, to the f. of which I dare not confess J. H. NEWMAN. **4.** June was not over Though past the f. BROWNING. Phr. *The f. of the moon* (also ellipt. *the f.* and in phr. *at f.*); the period or state of complete illumination of the moon's disc.

C. *adv.* **1.** Simply intensive: Very, exceedingly: **a.** with adjs. of quality (now only *poet.*) OE.; **b.** with adjs. of quantity or indef. numerals (now *arch.*) ME.; **c.** with advs. (now *arch.*) OE. **2.** Completely, entirely, fully, quite: **a.** with adjs., *esp.* numerals OE.; **b.** with advs. (now *rare*) ME.; **c.** with advb. phrases 1529. **3.** Of position or direction: Exactly, directly, straight 1582; due (? *Obs.*) 1559. †**4.** With vbs. or pples.: Fully, completely, quite, thoroughly –1807.

1. a. Anger is like A f. hot Horse SHAKS. **b.** Fulle many a tere 1450. **c.** F. early lost WORDSW. **2. a.** F. fadom fiue *Temp.* I. ii. 396. **c.** Butter..does f. as well MRS. GLASSE. **3.** Winds..f. in our Teeth 1698. The..Wind is..F. East 1708.

Comb.: with pres. and pa. pples., as *f.-acorned*; **f.-blown**[1], filled with wind, puffed out (*lit.* and *fig.*); see BLOW *v.*[1]; **-blown**[2], in full bloom (*lit.* and *fig.*); see BLOW *v.*[2]

Full (ful), *v.*[1] ME. [f. FULL *a.*] †**1.** *trans.* To make full –1647; *intr.* to be or become full (now only *dial.* and in U.S. of the moon) ME. †**2.** *trans.* To fulfil, complete –1640. **3.** *Dressmaking.* To make full; to gather or pleat 1831.

1. The moon fulls at midnight WEBSTER, 1864.

Full (ful), *v.*[2] ME. [prob. back-formation f. FULLER *sb.*[1] infl. by (O)Fr. *fouler* or med.L. *fullare.* See FOIL *v.*[1]] **1.** *trans.* To tread or beat (cloth) for the purpose of cleansing and thickening it; hence, to cleanse and thicken (cloth, etc.). †**2.** *gen.* To beat or trample down; also, to destroy –1641.

†**Fu·llage.** 1611. [Sense 1 is synon. with (O)Fr. *foulage*; sense 2 may be a derivative of Sc. *fulyie* (XV) refuse of streets, manure; cf. also FOIL *v.*[1] III.] **1.** Money paid for the fulling of cloth. (Dicts.) **2.** Refuse, street-sweepings –1780.

Full age. 1622. Adult or mature age, *esp.* (as opp. to *nonage*) the age of 21 years. Hence †**Full-aged** *ppl. a.*; *spec.* of a horse: Exceeding the age of 6 years (now simply *aged*).

Full-blood, *a.* 1882. **a.** Of a brother or sister: Born of the same parents. **b.** Of pure or unmixed race. So **Full-bloo·ded** *a.* = FULL-BLOOD (*lit.* and *fig.*); also, having plenty of blood. Hence **Full-bloo·dedness.**

Fu·ll-bottom. 1713. [f. FULL *a.* + BOTTOM *sb.*] A full-bottomed wig.

Fu·ll-bottomed, *a.* 1711. [f. as prec. + -ED[2].] **1.** Of a wig: Having a full or large bottom. **2.** *Naut.* Epithet of vessels designed to carry large cargoes 1867.

Full dress. 1790. See DRESS *sb.* Also *fig.* Also *attrib.* as in *full-dress dinner, rehearsal*, etc.; also *fig.*, as in *full-dress debate*, a formal debate in which important speeches are delivered on both sides.

Fuller (fu·ləɹ), *sb.*[1] [OE. *fullere* – L. *fullo* (of unkn. origin), with native suffix -ER[1].] One whose occupation is to full cloth.

Comb.: **fuller's clay** = FULLER'S EARTH; **fuller's grass, herb, weed,** *Saponaria officinalis*; **fuller's teazel, thistle,** *Dipsacus fullonum*; **fuller's thorn** ? = prec.

Fu·ller, *sb.*[2] 1855. [f. FULL *v.*[1] + -ER[1].] **1.** *Blacksmithing*, etc. A grooved tool on which iron is shaped by being driven into the grooves 1864. **2.** A groove made by a fuller 1855. Hence **Fu·ller** *v.* to stamp with a f.; to groove by stamping; *dial.* to goffer (linen).

Fu:ller's ea·rth. 1523. [prob. after Du. *vollersaarde*; cf. G. *walkererde* (see WALKER *sb.*[2]), Fr. *terre à foulon.*] A hydrous silicate of alumina, used in cleansing cloth; also *Geol.* a group of strata containing this. Also *fig.*

Fu:ll-fa·ced, *a.* 1610. [f. FULL *a.* + FACE *sb.* + -ED[2].] **1.** Having a full face; *esp.* of persons 1622. **2.** Having the face turned fully on the spectator or in some specified direction.

Fu·ll-gro·wn, *a.* 1667. [f. FULL *adv.* + GROWN.] Fully grown; having attained full size or maturity.

Fu·ll-hea·rted, *a.* 1611. [f. FULL *a.* + HEART *sb.* + -ED[2].] **a.** Full of courage and confidence; hence of a work: Carried on with zeal. **b.** Full of feeling.

Fulling (fu·liŋ), *vbl. sb.* 1688. [f. FULL *v.*[2] + -ING[1].] The process of cleansing and thickening cloth by beating and washing; also called *milling.*

Comb. **f.-mill,** a mill in which cloth is fulled or milled (now) by being pressed between rollers and cleansed with soap or fuller's earth.

Full length. 1709. The entire length or extension of any object. **1.** In advb. phr. (*at*) *full length.* **2.** *attrib.*, as *full-length figure*, etc. Also ellipt. *a full-length.* 1822.

Full moon. OE. **1.** The moon with its entire disc illuminated. **2.** The period at which this occurs (L. *plenilunium*) ME. **3.** *attrib.* 1780.

Fu:ll-mou:thed, *a.* 1577. [f. FULL *a.* + MOUTH *sb.* + -ED[2].] **1.** Of cattle: Having the full number of teeth. †**2.** Having the mouth filled with food; hence, festive. Also *transf.* and *fig.* –1701. **3. a.** Sounding or talking loud 1648. **b.** Produced or uttered with a loud voice or with violence 1605.

2. Full-mouth'd Easter's neare QUARLES.

Fullness, fulness (fu·lnės). ME. [f. FULL *a.* + -NESS. The spelling *fullness* is more in accordance with analogy.] **1.** The quality or condition of being FULL, in various senses. **2.** The condition of containing in abundance, or of abounding in; *concr.* all that is contained in (the world, etc.) ME.

1. Fulnesse of ioy *Ps.* 16:11. Phr. *The f. of time* (= Gr. πλήρωμα τοῦ χρόνου): in bibl. language, the proper or destined time. F. of diet 1682, of Body 1698, of colour, sound, etc. 1851. **2.** þe world and þe fulnes of it is myn ME.

Full-summed, *a.* 1486. [f. FULL *adv.* + SUMMED *ppl. a.*] **1.** *Falconry.* In full plumage. **2.** *nonce-use.* Fully developed or accomplished. TENNYSON.

Fu:ll-ti·mer. 1870. [f. phr. *full time* + -ER[1].] A child that attends school during the full school hours; opp. to HALF-TIMER.

Fully (fu·li), *adv.* [OE. *fulliće*, f. FULL *a.* + -LY[2].] In a full manner or degree; completely, entirely; thoroughly, exactly, quite.

I satisfied him f. GOLDSM. Day had f. dawned C. BRONTË. †(*To eat, feed*) *f.* = to satiety. *Comb.* **f.- fashioned** *a.* (of women's stockings), fitting the shape of the leg.

Fullymart, obs. f. FOUMART.

Fulmar (fu·lmǝɹ). 1698. [orig. Hebridean dial., perh. f. ON. *fúll* FOUL (with ref. to the bird's offensive smell) + *már* gull (cf. MEW *sb.*[1]).] A sea-bird of the petrel kind (*Fulmarus glacialis*).

Fulminant (fʊ·lminănt). 1602. [– Fr. *fulminant* or *fulminant-*, pr. ppl. stem of L. *fulminare*; see FULMINATE *v.*, -ANT.]

A. *adj.* **1.** = FULMINATING. **2.** *Path.* Developing suddenly 1876.

1. This F. Gold 1693. **2.** The f. forms of anthrax 1876.

B. *sb.* Something that fulminates; a thunderbolt; an explosive. *rare.* 1808.

Hence **Fu·lminancy,** f. character. CARLYLE.

Fulminate (fʊ·lmineᶦt), *sb.* 1826. [f. FULMIN(IC + -ATE[4].] *Chem.* A compound of fulminic acid with a base, detonating by percussion, friction, or heat.

Fulminate (fʊ·lmineᶦt), *v.* Pa. pple. **fulminate.** 1450. [– *fulminat-*, pa. ppl. stem of L. *fulminare* lighten, strike with lightning, f. *fulmen, fulmin-* lightning; see -ATE[3].]

I. 1. *intr.* To thunder and lighten (*rare*) 1610. **2.** To issue as a thunderbolt 1861. †**3.** *Metall.* Of gold: To become suddenly bright and uniform in colour 1727. **4.** To flash forth like lightning 1630. **5.** †To cause to explode, or (*intr.*) to explode with a loud report 1667.

II. *fig.* [orig. a rendering of med.L. *fulminare* to issue eccl. censures, etc.; afterwards used more widely.] **1.** *trans.* To thunder forth; to utter or publish (a condemnation or censure) upon a person 1450. **2.** To strike with the thunderbolts of eccl. censure; hence *gen.* to condemn vehemently 1687. **3.** *intr.* Of the pope, etc.: To issue censures or condemnations (*against*); *gen.* to inveigh violently *against* 1639.

1. The pope fulminated a bull against him..for having hanged an archbishop 1832. **2.** To f. such vain and impious wretches BURKE. **3.** Pulpits fulminated, presses groaned SIR J. STEPHEN.

Fulminating (fʊ·lmineᶦtiŋ), *ppl. a.* 1626. [f. prec. + -ING[2].] That fulminates (*lit.* and *fig.*); *spec.* detonating, violently explosive.

F. gold, mercury, platinum, silver, various fulminates or salts of fulminic acid. *F. powder*, formerly, a mixture of nitre, potash, and sulphur; now occas. applied to other explosive powders, chiefly containing fulminate of mercury.

Fulmination (fʊlminēᶦ·ʃǝn). 1502. [– L. *fulminatio*, f. as FULMINATE *v.*; see -ION. Cf. Fr. *fulmination.*] **1.** The bursting forth of thunder and lightning. Usu. *fig.* 1623. **2.** The action of fulminating or detonating; loud explosion 1667. †**3.** *Metall.* See FULMINATE *v.* I. 3. 1612. **4.** The formal emission of an ecclesiastical condemnation or censure. Subseq.: Violent denunciation or threatening; an instance of this. 1502.

1. The f. of divine Anger 1650. **4.** These Fulminations from the Vatican were turn'd into Ridicule AYLIFFE.

Fulminatory (fʊ·lminătǝ:ri), *a.* 1611. [– Fr. *fulminatoire*; see FULMINATE *v.*, -ORY[2].] Sending forth fulminations, thundering.

Fulmine (fʊ·lmin), *v.* 1590. [– (O)Fr. *fulminer* or L. *fulminare*; see FULMINATE *v.*] **1.** *trans.* To send forth (lightning or thunder); *fig.* to flash *out* 1847. **2.** *intr.* To thunder, speak out fiercely or energetically. (Now chiefly after Milton.) 1623.

2. Whose resistless eloquence..Shook the Arsenal and fulmined over Greece MILT.

Fulmineous (fʊlmi·niǝs), *a.* ? *Obs.* 1727. [f. L. *fulmineus* (f. *fulmen, fulmin-* lightning) + -OUS; see -EOUS.] Pertaining to thunder or lightning.

Fulminic (fʊlmi·nik), *a.* 1825. [f. L. *fulmen, fulmin-* lightning (with sense derived from FULMINATE *v.* I. 5) + -IC.] *Chem.* In *F. acid*: $C_2H_2N_2O_2$, an acid forming explosive salts with some metals.

Fulminous (fʊ·lminǝs), *a.* 1635. [f. as prec. + -OUS.] Of or pertaining to thunder and lightning; fulminating.

Fulminurate (fʊlminiūᵊ·reᶦt). 1864. [f. as next + -ATE[4]; see URATE.] *Chem.* A salt of fulminuric acid.

Fulminuric (fʊlminiūᵊ·rik), *a.* 1864. [f. FULMIN(IC) + URIC.] *Chem.* Only in *F. acid*: '$C_3H_3N_3O_3$ Isocyanuric acid. An acid isomeric with cyanuric acid' (Watts).

Fulness: see FULLNESS.

†**Fulsa·mic,** *a.* [perh. corruptly f. next + -IC.] = FULSOME. Congreve.

Fulsome (fu·lsǝm), *a.* ME. [f. FULL *a.* + -SOME[1].] †**1.** Abundant, plentiful, full –1583. †**2.** Full and plump, fat, well-grown; also, over-grown –1678. †**b.** App.: Lustful, rank. *Merch. V.* I. iii. 87. †**3.** Of food: Satiating, filling; also *fig.*; coarse, gross –1770; †sickly in taste –1743. †**4.** Strong- or foul-smelling –1725. †**5.** Offensive to the senses; disgusting, foul, or loathsome –1720. **6.** Offensive to normal sensibilities, repulsive, odious ME.; †morally foul, obscene –1726. **7.** Of language, style, behaviour, etc.: Offensive to good taste; *esp.* from excess or want of measure. Now chiefly of flattery, over-demonstrative affection, etc. 1663.

1. F. fieldes 1510. Suche f. pasture made him a double chin 1515. **3.** I dined with the lord-mayor..We had two turtles, and a f. great dinner WILKES. **4.** A rank and f. smell BACON. **5.** SHAKS. *John* III. iv. 32. **6. b.** *Oth.* IV. i. 37. **7.** This fawning and f. court-historian J. WARTON. F. publicity HELPS. Hence **Fu·lsome-ly** *adv.*, **-ness.**

Fulvid (fʊ·lvid), *a.* Now *rare.* 1599. [– late L. *fulvidus*, f. L. *fulvus* FULVOUS; see -ID[1].] = FULVOUS.

Fulvous (fʊ·lvǝs), *a.* 1664. [f. L. *fulvus* reddish-yellow + -OUS.] Reddish-yellow, dull yellowish-brown or tawny.

‖**Fulwa** (fu·lwă). 1835. [Corruptly – Bengali *phulwara*, the native name of *Bassia butyracea.*] A solid buttery oil obtained from *Bassia butyracea.*

†**Fum,** *v.* 1607. [Echoic.] *intr.* To play (on a guitar) with the fingers –1672.

Follow me, and f. as you goe DEKKER & WEBSTER.

Fuma·cious, *a.* [f. L. *fumare* smoke + -ACIOUS.] Fond of smoking. (Dicts.)

Fumade (fiumēᶦ·d). Also †**fumado,** †**fumatho,** and, corruptly, FAIR-MAID. 1599. [– Sp. *fumado*, pa. pple. of *fumar* smoke :– L. *fumare*; see FUME *v.*, -ADE.] A smoked pilchard.

Fu·mage. *Hist.* 1755. [– med.L. *fumagium*, f. L. *fumus* smoke; see -AGE. In OFr. *fumage.*] Hearth-money.

As early as the conquest mention is made in domesday book of f. or fuage, vulgarly called smoke farthings BLACKSTONE.

Fumant (fiū·mănt), *a.* 1828. [– Fr. *fumant*, pr. pple. of *fumer*; see FUME *v.*, -ANT.] *Her.* Emitting vapour or smoke.

Fumarin (fiū·mărin). 1864. [f. mod.L. *Fumaria* fumitory + -IN[1].] *Chem.* An organic base contained in fumitory. So **Fuma·ric acid,** $C_4H_4O_4$, an acid produced by the dehydration of malic acid. **Fu·marate,** a salt of this acid.

Fumarole (fiū·mărōᵘl). 1811. [– Fr. *fumerolle* (*fumarolle*); see FEMERELL.] A hole or vent through which vapour issues from a volcano; a smoke-hole.

Fumatory (fiū·mătǝri). Also erron. **fumitory.** 1530. [– med.L. *fumatorium* chimney, louver, f. *fumat-*, pa. ppl. stem of L. *fumare* smoke; see -ORY[1].] †**1.** A censer 1530. **2.** A place set apart for smoking or fumigating purposes 1704.

Fumble (fʊ·mb'l), *v.* 1508. [– LG. *fummeln, fommeln*, Du. *fommelen*, whence Sw. *fumla.* Cf. FAMBLE *v.*] **1.** *intr.* To use one's hands or fingers awkwardly or ineffectually; to grope about 1534. Also *transf.* and *fig.* **2.** *trans.* To handle awkwardly or nervously. Also with *on, out, over.* 1606. **3.** To wrap up clumsily, huddle together. Also with *up.* 1572. **4.** *slang.* (Cf. FUMBLING *ppl.a.*c.) Also *absol.* and *intr.* 1508. **5.** *intr.* To hesitate in speaking; to mumble, mutter. Also *trans.* 1555.

1. I saw him f. with the Sheets, and play with Flowers SHAKS. **2.** Fumbling two large kid gloves THACKERAY. Phr. *To f. the ball* (e.g. in *Cricket*): to fail to take it cleanly. **3.** So many f. this, last and next weeks devotion all in a prayer FULLER. **5.** Never lose time fumbling and prating about it SCOTT. Hence **Fu·mble** *sb.* a piece of fumbling. **Fu·mbler.**

Fu·mbling, *ppl. a.* 1532. [f. FUMBLE *v.* + -ING[2].] **a.** That gropes about; characterized by fumbling 1847. **b.** *fig.* That does something clumsily or awkwardly; also, hesitating in speech 1532. **c.** Sexually impotent 1576. Hence **Fu·mblingly** *adv.*

Fume (fiūm), *sb.* ME. [– (i) OFr. *fum* :– L. *fumus* smoke; (ii) OFr. *fume*, f. *fumer* :– L. *fumare* to smoke.]

I. 1. The volatile matter produced by and usually accompanying combustion; smoke. Also with *a* and *pl. Obs.* or *arch.* †**b.** Something for producing aromatic vapour –1722. **2.** Odour or odorous exhalation (either fragrant or offensive) ME. **3.** Vapour or steam; *esp.* the vapour given off by acids and volatile substances ME. **4.** A vapour or exhalation produced as an excrement of the body; *esp.* a noxious vapour supposed formerly to rise to the brain from the stomach ME.

1. In fiery flames and f. 1549. The fumes of choice tobacco DICKENS. **2.** Aromatyke lycoure, fragraunt of f. HAWES. The Fumes of the Table 1718. **3.** The inhalation of acrid fumes 1834. **4.** The wine..raise[d] disagreeable fumes from the stomach into the head DE FOE.

II. *fig.* **1.** Something unsubstantial, transient, imaginary, etc. 1531. **2.** Something which goes to the head and clouds the faculties 1574. **3.** A fit of anger or irritation 1522.

1. Loue, is a smoake made with the f. of sighes SHAKS. To smother him with fumes and eulogies BURTON. **2.** Sometimes his head gets a little hot with the fumes of patriotism M. ARNOLD. **3.** Phr. *In a f.* Hence **Fu·meless** *a.* free from fumes.

Fume (fiūm), *v.* ME. [– (O)Fr. *fumer* or L. *fumare*; see prec.] **1.** *trans.* To apply smoke or fumes to, to fumigate ME.; to perfume with incense 1641; †to perfume –1740; †to smoke-dry (provisions) –1661. **2.** *intr.* To emit fumes, smoke, or vapour; also *fig.* 1532. **3.** *intr.* Of smoke, etc.: To issue, rise, pass off 1593. Also with *away.* †**4.** *trans.* To send forth or emit as vapour, disperse in vapour. Also with *away, out*, etc. –1707. †**5.** *intr.* Of the brain: To be clouded with fumes (of liquor). *Ant. & Cl.* II. i. 24. **6.** *fig.* To give way to or exhibit anger or irritation 1522.

1. To f. a ship or house in time of infectious aires 1612. She fum'd the temples with an od'rous flame DRYDEN. *fig.* They demi-deify and f. him so COWPER. Lawne sheetes fum'd with Vyolets MARSTON. **2.** A Censer..fuming all the day and night PURCHAS. **3.** Incense Clouds Fuming from Golden Censers, hid the Mount MILT. **6.** To fret and f. about trifles 1878.

‖**Fumé** (füme), *a.* 1883. [Fr., pa. pple. of *fumer*; see prec.] Of glass: Having a smoky tint. Of oak: Treated with fumes of ammonia.

Fumer (fiū·mǝɹ). 1611. [f. FUME *v.* + -ER[1].] †**1.** A perfumer 1611. **2.** One who fumes or gets into a fume 1894.

Fumerel(l, -ill, obs. ff. FEMERELL.

Fu·met[1]. *Obs.* or *arch.* ME. [app. – AFr.

*fumets (*fumez) pl., f. *fumer* (repr. L. *fimare*) to dung.] The excrement (of a deer).

†**Fumet**[2], **fume·tte.** 1723. [– Fr. *fumet*, f. *fumer* FUME *v.*] The scent or smell of game when high; game flavour –1796.

†**Fu·mid,** *a.* 1597. [– L. *fumidus*, f. *fumus* smoke; see -ID[1].] Fuming, vaporous –1797. Hence †**Fumi·dity,** †**Fu·midness,** f. condition or quality.

†**Fumi·ferous,** *a. rare.* 1656 [f. L. *fumifer* (f. *fumus* smoke) + -OUS; see -FEROUS.] Bearing or producing smoke –1742.

Fumify (fiū·mifəi), *v.* [– L. *fumificare*, f. *fumus* smoke; see -FY.] *trans.* (*joc.*) To fumigate. T. BROWN.

Fumigant (fiū·migănt). 1727. [–*fumigant-*, pr. ppl. stem of L. *fumigare*; see next, -ANT.]

†**A.** *adj.* That fumes 1727.

B. *sb.* That which fumigates (*rare*) 1890.

Fumigate (fiū·mige[i]t), *v.* 1530. [–*fumigat-*, pa. ppl. stem of L. *fumigare*, f. *fumus* FUME *sb.*; see -ATE[3].] **1.** *trans.* To apply smoke or fumes to; *esp.* to disinfect or purify by exposure to smoke or fumes 1781. **b.** To perfume 1530. **2.** To darken (oak) by the process of fuming. See FUMING *vbl. sb.* 18.. Hence **Fu·migator.**

Fumigation (fiūmigē[i]·ʃən). ME. [– (O)Fr. *fumigation* or late L. *fumigatio*, f. as prec.; see -ION.] **1.** The action of generating odorous smoke or flames, *esp.* in incantations; the action of perfuming with herbs, etc. Also *concr.* the preparation used to produce this, or the fumes resulting from it. **2.** The action or process of fumigating 1572. **3.** *Med.* Exposure to fumes, *esp.* in order to produce a therapeutic effect. Also *concr.* the fumes generated for this purpose. ME.

Fumigatory (fiū·migătə:ri). *rare.* 1799. [f. FUMIGATE *v.* + -ORY[2]. Cf. Fr. *fumigatoire.*]

A. *adj.* Having the quality of fumigating.

B. *sb.* 'A room or an apparatus used for fumigation' (*Syd. Soc. Lex.*).

Fuming (fiū·miŋ), *vbl. sb.* 1529. [f. FUME *v.* + -ING[1].] **a.** The action of FUME *v.* **b.** The treatment of oak with fumes of ammonia to give it an antique appearance 1893. **c.** *Photogr.* The process of subjecting albuminized paper to the fumes of ammonia 1889.

Fuming (fiū·miŋ), *ppl. a.* 1575. [f. as prec. + -ING[2].] That fumes (see FUME *v.*).

F. liquor of Boyle: hydroguretted sulphuret of ammonia, first described by Boyle. **Fu·mingly** *adv.*

†**Fu·mish,** *a.* 1519. [f. FUME *sb.* + -ISH[1].] **1.** Emitting smoke or vapour; smoky; seething –1599. **2.** Of the nature of fumes; causing or emitting fumes –1693. **3.** *fig.* Inclined to fume; exhibiting anger or irascibility –1608. Hence **Fu·mish-ly** *adv.*, **-ness.**

†**Fu·mishing.** 1527. [app. f. OFr. *femer*, *fumer* to dung (see FUMET[1]) + -ISH[1] (on the anal. of vbs. f. Fr. vbs. in *-iss-*, *-ir*) + -ING[1].] = FUMET[1]. –1726.

Fumitory (fiū·mitəri). ME. [– (O)Fr. *fumeterre* – med.L. *fumus terræ* 'smoke of the earth'.] A plant of the genus *Fumaria* (or the related *Corydalis*), usually *F. officinalis*.

Fumitory, incorrect f. FUMATORY.

Fummel: see FUNNEL[2], sort of mule.

Fumose (fiūmō[u]·s), *a.* ME. [– L. *fumosus*, f. *fumus* smoke; see -OSE[1].] **1.** Full of fumes, vaporous, flatulent. **2.** Smoky, like smoke ME. **3.** *Bot.* Smoke-coloured 1866.

†**Fumo·sity.** ME. [– OFr. *fumosité* or med.L. *fumositas*, f. L. *fumosus*; see prec., -ITY.] **1.** The quality of being full of fumes or vapours –1652. **2.** The flatulent quality of various foods; the heady quality of wine, etc. –1542. **3.** Vaporous humour rising into the head from the stomach –1678. **4.** The state of giving off fumes; *concr.* a fume; the volatile part given off from a mineral or the like –1750.

Fumous (fiū·məs), *a.* ME. [f. L. *fumosus* FUMOSE; see -OUS.] †**1.** Giving off fumes; *esp.* flatulent –1706. †**2.** Consisting of fumes; vaporous, windy –1678. **3.** Pertaining to smoke or smoking. Now *joc.* 1661. †**4.** Full of passion, angry, furious –1684. **5.** *Bot.* = FUMOSE 3. 1866.

1. Abstaine from Garlick, Onions..and such like f. things 1610. Hence **Fu·mously** *adv.*

Fumy (fiū·mi), *a.* 1570. [f. FUME *sb.* + -Y[1].] Composed of, or full of, fumes, vapours, or smoke; of the nature of fume or fumes.

This fumie Citie [London] WOTTON. Hence **Fu·mingly** *adv.*

Fun (fɒn), *sb.* 1700. [f. FUN *v.*] †**1.** A cheat or trick; a hoax –1719. **2.** Diversion, sport; also, boisterous gaiety, drollery 1727.

2. The mirth and f. grew fast and furious BURNS. Phr. *To make f. of, poke f. at*: to ridicule. *For* or *in f.*: as a joke, not seriously.

Fun (fɒn), *v.* 1685. [prob. dial. var. of FON *v.*] **1.** *trans.* To cheat, hoax; also to cajole. Const. *of, out of.* Now *dial.* **2.** [f. the sb.] *intr.* To make fun or sport; to fool, joke 1728.

†**Funa·mble,** *sb.* [– Fr. *funambule* or L. *funambulus*; see FUNAMBULIST.] A rope-walker. EVELYN.

†**Funa·mbulant.** 1606. [f. Fr. *funambule* or L. *funambulus* (see FUNAMBULIST) + -ANT.] A rope-walker, a funambulist –1623. So **Funa·mbulate** *v.* to walk on a stretched rope (in Dicts.). **Funambula:tion,** the action of walking on a rope. **Funa·mbulator,** a rope-walker. **Funa·mbulatory** *a.* pertaining to rope-walking; that walks on a rope.

Funambulist (fiunæ·mbiŭlist). 1793. [f. Fr. *funambule* or its source L. *funambulus* (f. *funis* rope + *ambulare* walk) + -IST.] A rope-walker, a rope-dancer. So **Funa·mbulism,** rope-walking.

‖**Funa·mbulo.** *arch.* 1605. [Sp. or It. *funambulo* – L. *funambulus*; see prec.] A funambulist.

Function (fɒ·ŋkʃən), *sb.* 1533. [– (O)Fr. *fonction* – L. *functio*, f., *funct-*, pa. ppl. stem of *fungi* perform; see -ION.] †**1.** The action of performing; discharge or performance *of* –1701. †**2.** Activity; action in general, physical or mental; also, bearing –1605. **3.** The special kind of activity proper to anything; the mode of action by which it fulfils its purpose: **a.** of a physical organ (often specialized as *animal, organic, vital*, etc.) 1590; **b.** of the intellectual and moral powers, etc. 1604; **c.** of things in general 1541. **4.** The kind of action proper to a person as belonging to a class, *esp.* to the holder of any office; hence, the office itself, an employment, calling, trade 1533. †**b.** *collect.* The persons following a profession or trade; an order, class –1732. **c.** *pl.* Official duties 1550. **5.** A religious ceremony; orig. in the R. C. Ch. 1640. **b.** A public ceremony; a social or festive meeting conducted with ceremony 1864. **6.** *Math.* A variable quantity regarded in its relation to one or more other variables in terms of which it may be expressed, or on the value of which its own value depends 1779.

1. His hand, his eye, his wits all present, wrought The f. of the glorious Part he beares DANIEL. **2.** *Haml.* II. ii. 582. **3. a.** Dark night, that from the eye his f. takes SHAKS. **b.** The first f. of the conscience 1868. **c.** The f. of money ADAM SMITH. **4.** The quill, which is the badge of his f. LAMB. Our f. as ministers 1878. **5.** The Christmas functions here were showy MRS. PIOZZI. **b.** A F. of some kind—a Launch—a Reception—a Royal Visit 1878. **6.** Let us take a f. a little more complicated, $u = ax^2$. 1816. Hence **Fu·nctioned** *ppl. a.* furnished with a f.

Function (fɒ·ŋkʃən), *v.* 1856. [f. prec., after Fr. *fonctionner.*] *intr.* To fulfil a function; to perform one's part; to act.

Functional (fɒ·ŋkʃənăl), *a.* 1631. [f. FUNCTION *sb.* + -AL[1].] **1.** Of or pertaining to a function or office; official; formal. **2.** *Phys.* Of or pertaining to the functions of an organ; affecting the functions only, not structural; serving a function (opp. to *rudimentary*) 1843. **3.** *Math.* Of or pertaining to a FUNCTION (sense 6) 1806.

2. So-called f. diseases, such as epilepsy, chorea, neuralgia MAUDSLEY. Hence **Functiona·lity,** f. character; in *Math.* the condition of being a function. **Fu·nctionalize** *v.* to place or assign to some function or office (Webst.). **Fu·nctionally** *adv.* with respect to the functions; in the discharge of the functions.

Functionary (fɒ·ŋkʃənări), *sb.* 1791. [f. FUNCTION *sb.* + -ARY[1], after Fr. *fonctionnaire*, a word of the Revolution, to replace terms of royalist flavour.] One who has certain functions to perform; an official.

Their republick is to have a first f. (as they call him) under the name of king or not, as they think fit BURKE. Hence **Fu·nctionarism,** officialism.

Fu·nctionary, *a.* 1822. [f. as prec. + -ARY[2].] **1.** = FUNCTIONAL 2. **2.** Official; = FUNCTIONAL 1. 1862.

Functionate (fɒ·ŋkʃəne[i]t), *v. rare.* 1856. [f. FUNCTION *sb.* + -ATE[3], after Fr. *fonctionner.*] *intr.* To perform one's function; to work; to officiate.

Functionless (fɒ·ŋkʃənlės), *a.* 1836. [f. as prec. + -LESS.] Having no function; chiefly in physiological sense.

Fund (fɒnd), *sb.* 1677. [– L. *fundus* the bottom; also, a piece of land. Cf. FOND *sb.*[1] The senses represent those of Fr. *fond, fonds*, rather than those of L. *fundus.*] †**1.** The bottom; in various applications; occas. *Phys.* = FUNDUS. –1761. †**2.** = FOND *sb.*[1] **1.** –1748. **3.** Source of supply; a permanent stock that can be drawn upon 1695. **4. a.** *sing.* A stock or sum of money, *esp.* one set apart for a particular purpose 1694. **b.** *pl.* Pecuniary resources 1728. **5.** †**a.** A portion of revenue set apart as a security for specified payments –1776. **b.** *The (public) funds*: the stock of the national debt, considered as a mode of investment 1713. **6.** *Printing.* = FOUNT[2]. Also *attrib.* 1683.

2. The..British product, being the f. of its inland trade DE FOE. **3.** There is a f. of good sense in this country, which cannot be deceived 'JUNIUS'. **4. a.** Phr. *Sinking fund*: see SINKING FUND. The f. for decayed musicians 1795. **b.** (*To be*) *in funds*: in possession of money; When he was in funds he preferred a hansom MISS BRADDON. **5. a.** The 500,000*l.* lately proposed without F. or Period 1740. **b.** Look what the funds were on the 1st of March THACKERAY.

Comb.: **f.-holder,** one who has money invested in the funds; **-lord** (coined by Cobbett after *landlord*), a magnate whose position is due to money in the funds; **-monger,** one who speculates in the public funds. Hence **Fu·ndless** *a.*, without funds.

Fund (fɒnd), *v.* 1776. [f. prec. sb.] **1.** *trans.* Orig., to provide a fund (see FUND *sb.* 5) for the regular payment of the interest on (a public debt); hence, to convert (a floating debt) into a more or less permanent debt at a fixed rate of interest. **2.** To put into a fund or store (see FUND *sb.* 3); to collect; to store 1806. **3.** To put (money) in the funds (see FUND *sb.* 5 b); to invest 1855.

1. Exchequer bills, which he says he shall..f. 1802. Hence **Fu·ndable** *a.* capable of being funded.

Fundal (fɒ·ndăl), *a.* 1889. [f. FUNDUS + -AL[1].] Relating to the fundus or base of an organ.

Fundament (fɒ·ndămĕnt). Also †**foundment.** [ME. *funde-, fondement* – (O)Fr. *fondement* :– L. *fundamentum*, f. *fundare* FOUND *v.*[1]; see -MENT.] †**1.** = FOUNDATION 4. –1677. **2.** The lower part of the body, on which one sits; the buttocks; also, the anus. In birds, the vent. ME.

Fundamental (fɒndăme·ntăl). ME. [– Fr. *fondamental* or late L. *fundamentalis*; see prec., -AL[1].]

A. *adj.* **1.** Of or pertaining to the foundation, basis, or groundwork. **2.** Serving as the foundation or base. Now only in immaterial applications. Const. *to* (rarely *of*). 1601. **b.** Primary, original; from which others are derived ME. **3.** Of strata; lying at the bottom 1799. **4.** *Mus.* Applied to the lowest or root note of a chord; also to the tone produced by the vibration of the whole of a sonorous body, as dist. from the HARMONICS produced by that of its parts 1752.

1. The f. analogy of sound and light TYNDALL. **2.** A f. truth 1835. **3.** The f. rock..is a black slate LYELL. **4.** *F. bass*, a low note, or series of notes, forming the root or roots of a chord or succession of chords. *F. chord*, an old name for the common chord; now, any chord formed of harmonics of the fundamental tone.

B. *sb.* **1.** A leading or primary principle, rule, law, or article, which serves as the groundwork of a system; an essential part. Chiefly in *pl.* 1637. **2.** *Mus.* Short for *f. tone* or *note*: see A. 4. (Formerly = *key-note.*) 1727.

1. There is an odd tenacity..in the fundamentals of..legends 1864.
Hence **Fu:ndamenta·lity,** the quality or state of being f. **Fundame·ntally** *adv.*

Fundame·ntalism. 1923. [f. prec. + -ISM.] Strict adherence to traditional orthodox tenets (e.g. the literal inerrancy of Scripture) held to be fundamental to the Christian faith: opposed to *liberalism* and *modernism*. Hence **Fundame·ntalist,** an adherent of f.; also as adj.

Fundatorial (fɒndătōᵊ·riăl), *a.* [f. L. *fundator* founder (f. *fundare* FOUND *v.*¹ + *-or* -OR 2) + -IAL.] Pertaining to a founder. FREEMAN.

Funded (fɒ·ndėd), *ppl. a.* 1776. [f. FUND *v.* + -ED¹.] **1.** Made part of the permanent debt of the state (cf. FUND *v.* 1). **b.** Invested in the funds 1848. **2.** Stored up 1841.
1. The publick debts of Great Britain f. and unfunded ADAM SMITH. **b.** F. property MILL.

Funding (fɒ·ndiŋ), *vbl. sb.* 1776. [f. FUND *v.* + -ING¹.] Conversion of a floating debt into a permanent one. Also *attrib.*
The ruinous expedient of perpetual f. ADAM SMITH.

‖**Fundus** (fɒ·ndɒ̆s). 1754. [L.; = 'bottom'.] *Anat.* The base or bottom of an organ; the part remote from the external aperture.
F. of the eye: 'the back part of the globe of the eye behind the crystalline lens' (*Syd. Soc. Lex.*).

Funebrial (fiunī·briăl), *a.* Now *rare.* Also **funebral.** 1604. [f. L. *funebris*, f. *funus* funeral; see -IAL.] = FUNEREAL. So †**Fune·brious.**

Funeral (fiū·nĕrăl). ME. [The adj. is – OFr. *funeral* – late L. *funeralis*, f. *funus, funer-* funeral, death, dead body. The sb. is – OFr. *funeraille*, collect, fem. sing., – med.L. *funeralia*, neut. pl. of the adj. Used in the pl. with the same sense as in the sing. till c1700, after the Fr. usage.]
A. *adj.* **1.** Of or pertaining to the ceremonial burial (or cremation) of the dead; used, etc., at a burial. Now felt as the sb. used *attrib.* **2.** = FUNEREAL. 1651.
1. Funerall griefe DEKKER. *F. pile, pyre*, the pile of wood, etc. on which a dead body is burned. The F. Pyre was out and the last Valediction over SIR T. BROWNE.
B. *sb.* **1.** The ceremonies connected with the burial (or cremation) of the body of a dead person; obsequies; a burial (or its equivalent) with the attendant observances 1512. Also *fig.* †**b.** pl. with sing. sense –1711. †**2.** *pl.* The expenses attending a funeral –1626. **3.** A funeral sermon or service (now *U.S.*) 1641. **4.** A burial procession 1745. **5.** Indefinitely: **a.** death; **b.** grave; **c.** monument 1575.
1. Went to Mr. Cowley's f., whose corpse..was conveyed to Westminster Abbey in a hearse with six horses EVELYN. **3.** Mr. Giles Laurence preached his Funeralls FULLER. **4.** There is no f. so sad to follow as the f. of our own youth LANDOR.
Hence †**Fu·nerally** *adv.* with f. ceremonies.

Funerary (fiū·nĕrări), *a.* 1693. [– late L. *funerarius*, f. *funus, funer-*; see prec., -ARY¹.] Of or pertaining to a funeral or burial.

†**Fu·nerate,** *v.* 1548. [– *funerat-*, pa. ppl. stem of L. *funerare* inter, f. as prec.; see -ATE³.] To bury with funeral rites –1568. So **Funeration,** the performance of funeral rites.

Funereal (fiunīᵊ·rīăl), *a.* 1725. [f. L. *funereus* (f. as prec.) + -AL¹.] Of, pertaining to, or appropriate to, a funeral. Hence, dark, dismal, melancholy, mournful
Near some lone fane, or yew's f. green SHENSTONE. Hence **Fune·really** *adv.*

Funest (fiune·st), *a.* Now *rare.* 1654. [– (O)Fr. *funeste*–L. *funestus*, f. *funus*; see FUNERAL.] Causing or portending death or evil; fatal, disastrous; deeply deplorable.
The execution was..one of the funeste effects of the war 1671.

Fungaceous (fɒŋgē¹·ʃəs), *a.* 1874. [f. L. *fungus* + -ACEOUS.] Of the nature of a fungus or fungi.

Fungal (fɒ·ŋgăl). 1835. [f. FUNGUS + -AL¹.]
A. *adj.* Of or pertaining to a fungus; of the nature of a fungus.
B. *sb.* A fungus 1845.

Fu·ngate, *sb.* 1821. [f. FUNGUS + -ATE⁴. Cf. Fr. *fongate.*] *Chem.* A salt formed by the combination of fungic acid with a base.

Fungate (fɒ·ŋgē¹t), *v.* 1847. [f. FUNGUS + -ATE³.] *Path.* To grow up with a fungous appearance; to grow rapidly like a fungus. See FUNGUS *sb.* 2.

†**Funge.** ME. [– OFr. *fonge* :– L. *fungus* FUNGUS.] **1.** A mushroom or fungus. ME. only. **2.** A soft-headed fellow. [After L. *fungus.*] 1621.

Fungible (fɒ·ndʒib'l). 1765. [– med.L. *fungibilis*, f. *fungi* perform, enjoy, with meaning as in *fungi vice* take the place of; see -IBLE.] *Law.*
A. *adj.* Said of a thing which is the subject of an obligation when another thing of the same or another class may be delivered in lieu of it 1818.
B. *sb.* A fungible thing.

Fu·ngic, *a.* 1819. [f. FUNGUS + -IC. Cf. Fr. *fongique.*] Of or pertaining to fungi or mushrooms.
F. acid, 'a mixture of citric, malic, and phosphoric acids'.

Fungicide (fɒ·ndʒisəid). 1889. [f. FUNGUS + -CIDE 2. Cf. Fr. *fongicide.*] Something used for destroying fungi.

Fungiform (fɒ·ndʒifǭɹm), *a.* 1823. [f. FUNGUS + -FORM. Cf. Fr. *fongiforme.*] Having the form of a fungus or mushroom. Said esp. of papillæ on the tongue.

‖**Fungillus** (fɒndʒi·lɒ̆s). 1830. [mod.L., dim. of L. *fungus* FUNGUS.] A little fungus. Hence **Fungi·lliform** *a.* = FUNGIFORM.

Fungin (fɒ·ndʒin). (Erron. **fungine.**) 1819. [f. FUNGUS + -IN¹.] The substance which forms the cell-walls of a mushroom or fungus.

†**Fu·ngite.** 1691. [f. FUNGUS + -ITE¹ 2 b.] A kind of fossil coral –1756.

Fungivorous (fɒndʒi·vŏrəs), *a.* 1826. [f. FUNGUS + -VOROUS.] Feeding on mushrooms or fungi.

Fungoid (fɒ·ŋgoid). 1836. [f. FUNGUS + -OID. Cf. Fr. *fongoïde.*]
A. *adj.* Resembling, or of the nature of, a fungus; *spec.* in *Path.* (see FUNGUS 2).
B. *sb.* A fungoid plant. Also *attrib.* 1861.

Fungology (fɒŋgǫ·lŏdʒi). 1860. [f. FUNGUS + -LOGY.] The science or study of fungi. Hence **Fungolo·gical** *a.* **Fungo·logist.**

Fungo·se, *a.* 1713. [– L. *fungosus*, f. FUNGUS; see -OSE¹.] = FUNGOUS 1. Hence **Fungo·sity,** the quality or condition of being fungous; *concr.* a fungous growth.

Fungous (fɒ·ŋgəs), *a.* ME. [f. L. *fungosus*, f. FUNGUS; see prec., -OUS. Cf. Fr. *fongeux.*] **1.** Of or pertaining to fungi; having the nature of a fungus; †spongy. *spec.* in *Path.* (see FUNGUS 2). **2.** Growing suddenly like a mushroom, not durable or substantial 1751.

Fungus (fɒ·ŋgɒ̆s), *sb.* Pl. **fungi** (fɒ·ndʒəi), **funguses.** 1527. [– L. *fungus*, commonly held to be – Gr. σφόγγος, σπόγγος SPONGE *sb*¹. Cf. (O)Fr. *fongus.*] **1.** A mushroom, toadstool, or one of the allied plants, including the various forms of mould. In *Bot.*, a cryptogamous plant, characterized by the absence of chlorophyll, and deriving its sustenance from dead or living organic matter. Also *collect.* in *sing.* Also *transf.* and *fig.* **2.** *Path.* A spongy morbid growth or excrescence, such as exuberant granulation in a wound 1674. †**3.** An excrescence of lamp-black or charred fibre on the wick of a candle or lamp. Also *fig.* (So in L.) –1813. **4.** The vegetable growth employed as tinder 1831. **5.** *attrib.* 1826.

Funic (fiū·nik), *a.* 1857. [f. FUNIS + -IC.] Pertaining to the funis or umbilical cord.

Funicle (fiū·nik'l). 1664. [Anglicized f. FUNICULUS.] = FUNICULUS, *esp.* senses 2, 3.

Funicular (fiuni·kiŭlăɹ), *a.* 1664. [f. L. *funiculus*, dim. of *funis* rope + -AR¹.] **1.** Of or pertaining to a FUNICULUS. **2.** Of or pertaining to a rope or its tension 1828. **3.** Resembling a cord; *spec.* in *Anat.* and *Bot.* 1835.
1. †*F. hypothesis*: see FUNICULUS 2. **2.** *F. machine*: an arrangement of a cord, pulleys, and suspended weights, designed to illustrate statical principles. *F. polygon*: the figure assumed by a cord supported at its extremities, and having weights suspended from it at various points. *F. railway* (also simply *funicular*): a cable railway, esp. one for the ascent of a mountain; *spec.* one in which the weight of an ascending car is partly or wholly counterbalanced by the weight of a descending car.

Funiculate (fiuni·kiŭlē¹t), *a.* 1826. [f. FUNICULUS + -ATE².] *Bot.* and *Zool.* Having a funiculus.

‖**Funiculus** (fiuni·kiŭlɒ̆s). 1662. (L., dim. of *funis* rope.] †**1.** A little rope (*rare*) 1706. †**2.** A hypothetical string or filament of extremely rarefied matter, imagined to be the agent in the Torricellian experiment 1662. **3.** The umbilical cord; = FUNIS. Hence *transf.* in *Bot.* A little stalk by which a seed or ovule is attached to the placenta. 1830. **4.** *Entom.* 'A term for the part of the antenna which lies between the scape and the club in certain insects' (*Syd. Soc. Lex.*) 1877. **5.** *Anat.* 'Applied to the primitive cord or bundle of nerve fibres, bound together in a sheath of connective tissue, called the perineurium or neurilemma' (*Syd. Soc. Lex.*).

Funiform (fiū·nifǭɹm), *a.* 1865. [f. L. *funis* rope + -FORM.] Having the form of a cord or rope.

Funiliform (fiuni·lifǭɹm), *a.* 1856. [f. L. *funis* rope + -ILE + -FORM.] *Bot.* 'Tough, cylindrical, and flexible, like a chord'. HENSLOW.

Funipendulous (fiū:nipe·ndiŭləs), *a.* 1706. [f. L. *funis* rope + PENDULOUS.] Hanging from a rope; connected with a hanging rope.

‖**Funis** (fiū·nis). ME. [L.; = 'rope'.] *Anat.* †**a.** Short for *funis brachii*, 'an old name for the median vein' (*Syd. Soc. Lex.*). **b.** The umbilical cord.

†**Funk,** *sb.*¹ ME. [In sense 1 – MDu. *vonke* (Du. *vonk*); with sense 2 cf. PUNK², SPUNK.] **1.** A spark. ME. only **2.** Touchwood –1825.

†**Funk,** *sb.*² 1623. [f. FUNK *v.*¹] A strong smell or stink –1725.

Funk (fɒŋk), *sb.*³ *slang.* 1743. [First recorded by Lye as Oxford slang; perh. identical with sl. *funk* tobacco smoke (see prec.); cf. slang *smoke* fear.] **1.** Cowering fear; a state of panic. *Blue f.*: see BLUE *a.* **2.** One who funks 1860.
1. *Comb.* **F.-hole** (*Mil. slang*), a trench dug-out; employment used as a pretext for evading military service. Hence **Fu·nky** *a.* in a state of f.

Funk (fɒŋk), *v.*¹ *slang.* 1699. [perh. – Fr. dial. *funkier* = OFr. *funkier, fungier* :– pop. L. **fumicare* (It. *fumicare*), late L. *fumigare*, f. L. *fumus* smoke.] **1.** *trans.* To blow smoke upon (a person) 1699; to smoke (a pipe, tobacco) 1704; *intr.* to smoke 1829. **2.** To cause an offensive smell 1708.

Funk (fɒŋk), *v.*² *slang.* 1737. [Belongs to FUNK *sb.*³] **1.** *intr.* To flinch or shrink through fear; to try to back out of anything. **2.** *trans.* To fight shy of, wish or try to shirk or evade 1857. **3.** To be afraid of (a person) 1836. **4.** To scare 1819.
1. To F. right out o' p'lit'cal strife aint thought to be the thing LOWELL. **3.** 'I rather f. the governor' 1849. **4.** The jury, 'funked' by the Anarchists, returned [etc.] 1892. Hence **Fu·nker.**

Funnel (fɒ·nĕl), *sb.*¹ [Late ME. *fonel* (prob. orig. a term of the wine trade with the South of France) – Pr. *fonilh*, also *enfonilh* :– L. *infundibulum*, (late) *fundibulum*, f. (*in*)-*fundere* pour (in).] **1.** A cone-shaped vessel usually fitted at the apex with a short tube, by means of which a liquid, powder, etc. may be conducted through a small opening. **b.** *spec.* in *Casting.* The hole through which the metal is poured into the mould 1874. **c.** *Anat.* and *Zool.* A funnel-shaped organ or limb; an infundibulum 1712. **2.** A tube or shaft for lighting or ventilating purposes; also, the metal chimney of an engine, steamboat, etc. 1555. **b.** The flue of a chimney 1688. **3.** Applied to a funnel-shaped opening, shaft, or channel in rocks, etc. 1774. **4.** A cylindrical band of metal; *esp.* that fitted on to the head of a mast, to which the rigging is attached 1694.
Comb.: **f.-form** = *f.-shaped*; **-shaped** *a.* shaped like a funnel, infundibuliform, *esp.* in *Bot.*; **-stays,** ropes or chains leading from eye-plates near the top of the funnel to the ship's sides.
Hence **Fu·nnelled** *ppl. a.* funnel-shaped; also *fig.*; in *Bot.* unfundibuliform.

Funnel (fɒ·nĕl), *sb.*² *dial.* 1835. [Of unkn. origin.] A mule whose sire is an ass.

Funny (fɒ·ni), *a.* 1756. [f. FUN *sb.* + -Y¹.] **1.** Affording fun, comical, facetious. **2.** Queer, odd, strange. *colloq.* 1806. †**3.** *slang.* Tipsy 1756. *Comb.* **f.-bone,** that part of the elbow over which the ulnar nerve passes, so called from the peculiar sensation experienced when it is struck. Hence **Fu·nnily** *adv.* in a f. manner. **Fu·nniment** *joc.*, drollery, humour; also, a joke. **Fu·nniness,** the quality or state of being f.; a f. saying or joke.

Fur (fɔ̄ɹ), *sb.* ME. [f. FUR *v.*] **1.** A trimming or lining for a garment, made of the dressed coat of certain animals; *hence*, the coat of such animals as material for such use. Also, a garment made of, or trimmed or lined with, this material; now chiefly *pl.* **2.** The short, fine, soft hair of the sable, ermine, beaver, otter, bear, etc., growing thick upon the skin, and dist. from the ordinary hair ME. **3.** *pl.* Skins of such animals with the fur on them 1555. **4.** *Her.* A tincture representing tufts upon a plain ground, or patches of different colours supposed to be sewn together. (The eight principal furs are ermine, ermines, erminois, pean, vair, countervair, potent, and counterpotent.) 1610. **5.** *collect.* Furred animals 1827. **6.** Anything resembling fur, or coating a surface like fur; e.g. a coat or crust of mould, of deposit from wine, etc. 1843. **b.** *esp.* A coating formed on the tongue in certain diseased conditions of the body 1693. **c.** A crust formed by the deposit of carbonate of lime on the interior surface of a kettle, boiler, etc. 1805. **7.** *Carpentry.* A piece nailed upon a rafter to strengthen it when decayed 1703. **8.** *attrib.* 1597.

1. Furred with no menivere, But with a furre rough of here, Of lambe-skinnes CHAUCER. **2.** To want the strength of Bulls, the f. of Bears POPE. Phr. *To stroke the f. the wrong way* (fig.): to cause irritation. *To make the f. fly* (U.S. slang): to claw, scratch, wound severely. **3.** Bargains for hides and furs SCOTT. **5.** Phr *F. and feather*: furred and feathered game.

Comb. **1.** General: as *f.-trader*; *f.-dressing*; *f.-clad*, *f.-collared*, etc.

2. Special: **f.-puller,** one who scrapes the loose down off rabbit and other skins; **-seal,** the seal which affords the fur known as seal-skin.

Fur (fɔ̄ɹ), *v.* ME. [– AFr. **furrer*, OFr. *forrer* (mod. *fourrer*) line, encase, sheathe, f. OFr. *forre, fuerre* – Gmc. **fōðram* sheath; see FOTHER.] **1.** *trans.* To line, or serve to line, trim, or cover with fur. **2.** To clothe or adorn with fur ME. **3.** To coat or cover with or as with fur or morbid matter 1593. **4.** *intr.* To become furred or coated with morbid matter. Also, to collect as fur. 1550. **5.** *trans.* To clean off the fur of (a boiler) 1867. **6.** *Carpentry.* To fix strips of wood to (floor-timbers, rafters, etc.) in order to bring them to a level, or the like 1678. **7.** (? after Fr. *fourrer*). To foist or thrust *in*. BACON.

1. A mantell furryd with ermyns LD. BERNERS. **3.** It [the water]..furs every thing in which it is kept 1839. **4.** Teeth..Which though they furre, will neither ake nor rot HERRICK.

Furacious (fiurēⁱ·ʃəs), *a.* Now *pedantic* or *joc.* 1676. [f. L. *furax, furac-* (f. *furari* steal) + -IOUS; see -ACIOUS.] Given to thieving, thievish. Hence **Fura·city,** the quality of being f.; tendency to steal.

Furbelow (fɔ̄·ɹbĭlo), *sb.* 1705. [alt. f. synon. and contemp. FALBALA.] **1.** A flounce; the pleated border of a petticoat or gown. Now often in *pl.* as a contemptuous term for showy ornaments or trimming. 1706. **2.** Anything resembling a flounce 1742. **3.** A name for *Laminaria bulbosa*, a seaweed with a large wrinkled frond 1846. **4.** *attrib.* = 'having furbelows' 1705.

3. The dimpled flounce of the sea-f. TENNYSON.

Furbelow (fɔ̄·ɹbĭlo), *v.* 1701. [f. prec. sb.] To ornament with or as with a furbelow.

Furbish (fɔ̄·ɹbiʃ), *v.* ME. [– OFr. *forbiss-*, lengthened stem (see -ISH²) of *forbir* (mod. *fourbir*) – Gmc. **furbjan* (OHG. *furben*).] **1.** *trans.* To remove rust from; to brighten by rubbing, burnish. Also *fig.* **2.** To brush or clean up; to do up afresh, renovate, revive. Chiefly with *up*. 1587.

1. The swerd is whettid and furbishid WYCLIF *Ezek.* 21:9. *fig.* F. new the name of John a Gaunt SHAKS. **2.** To f. up old baronies DISRAELI. Hence **Fu·rbisher.**

Furcate (fɔ̄·ɹkeⁱt, -ĕt), *a.* 1819. [– late L. *furcatus*, f. L. *furca* FORK; see -ATE².] Formed like a fork; forked and branched; as, a *furcate* tail. Hence **Fu·rcately** *adv.* Also **Furca·to-** = forkedly-. So **Fu·rcated** *ppl. a.*

Furcation (fɔ̄ɹkēⁱ·ʃən). 1646. [f. L. *furca* FORK + -ATION, prob. extracted from BIFURCATION.] A forking; hence, a fork-like division or branch.

Furciferous (fɒɹsi·fĕrəs), *a.* 1823. [f. L. *furcifer* fork-bearer, hence (with ref. to the 'fork' or yoke placed on the necks of criminals) rascal, jail-bird + -OUS; see -FEROUS.] **1.** *Entom.* Bearing a forked process; said of the larvæ of some butterflies. **2.** Rascally. DE QUINCEY.

‖**Furcula** (fɔ̄·ɹkiŭlă). 1859. [L., dim. of *furca* fork; see -ULE.] *Ornith.* A forked bone below the neck of a bird, consisting of the two clavicles and an interclavicle; the merry-thought or wish-bone. Hence **Fu·rcular** *a.* of or pertaining to the f.; in early use, to the collar-bone

‖**Furculum** (fɔ̄·ɹkiŭlŏm). 1833. [mod. L., incorrectly formed dim. of *furca.*] = FURCULA.

†**Fu·rdel, fu·rdle,** *v.* 1594. [alt. f. FURL *v.* by contamination with FARDEL *sb.*¹; see also FARDEL *v.*] *trans.* To furl or fold. Also with *up*. –1682.

Furfur (fɔ̄·ɹfɔ̄ɹ). *Pl.* **furfures.** 1621. [– L. *furfur* bran.] Dandruff, scurf; *pl.* particles of epidermis or scurf. Hence **Furfura·ceous** *a.* resembling bran; scurfy; in *Bot.* covered with bran-like scales. **Furfura·tion** (*rare*), 'the shedding of the skin in small branny particles' (*Syd. Soc. Lex.*).

Furfurine (fɔ̄·ɹfiŭrin). 1845. [f. L. *furfur* bran + -INE⁵.] *Chem.* An organic base, isomeric with furfuramide, and produced therefrom under the influence of caustic potash, or of heat.

Furfurol (fɔ̄·ɹfiŭrǫl). 1845. [f. as prec. + -OL 3.] A volatile oil obtained by distilling bran with dilute sulphuric acid.

Furfurous (fɔ̄·ɹfiŭrəs), *a.* 1547. [f. as prec. + -OUS.] Resembling or containing bran; made of bran.

†**Fu·rial,** *a.* ME. [– OFr. *furial* – L. *furialis*, f. *furia* FURY.] Furious, raging –1640.

Furibund (fiūᵊ·ribɒnd), *a.* 1490. [– L. *furibundus*, f. *furere* rage; in early use through (O)Fr. *furibond.*] Furious, raging, mad. So †**Fu·ribundal.**

Furiosity (fiuri,ǫ·sĭti). ME. [– OFr. *furiosité* in same senses or late L. *furiositas* fury, in med.L. fury, madness, f. L. *furiosus*; see FURIOUS, -ITY.] **1.** The quality or state of being FURIOUS; fury. Now *rare.* 1509. **2.** Madness, *esp.* in *Sc. Law.*

‖**Furioso** (fūriō·so). 1670. [It.; = L. *furiosus*; see FURIOUS *a.*]

A. *adj.* (*Mus.*) A direction: With vehemence 1823.

B. *sb.* A furious person. (Also **furiosa** fem.)

Furious (fiūᵊ·riəs), *a.* ME. [– OFr. *furieus* (mod. *-eux*) – L. *furiosus*, f. *furia* FURY; see -OUS.] **1.** Full of fury or fierce passion; proceeding from or exhibiting fury; fierce, raging, frantic. Also *transf.* of the elements; also of pains, diseases, etc. **2.** *Hyperbolically* (after Fr. use): Excessive, extravagant. *rare.* 1668. **3.** Mad, insane. *Obs.* exc. in *Sc. Law.* 1475.

1. Parties of religion are more f. HUME. *transf.* The f. Winters rages *Cymb.* IV. ii. 259. F. agues GERARDE. Hence **Fu·rious-ly** *adv.*, **-ness.**

Furl (fɔ̄ɹl), *sb.* 1643. [f. next vb.] **1.** A roll, coil, or curl of any furled body. **2.** The action of furling or state of being furled, the manner in which a sail is furled 1836.

Furl (fɔ̄ɹl), *v.* 1556. [– (O)Fr. *ferler*, earlier *ferlier, fermlier*, f. *fer(m* FIRM + *lier* bind (:– L. *ligare*), the change of *-lier* to *-ler* following the general reduction of inf. *-ier* to *-er.*] **1.** *trans.* 'To roll up and bind (a sail) neatly upon its respective yard or boom' (Adm. Smyth); to roll up (a flag) into small compass. Also *transf.* and *fig.* †**2.** To furrow, wrinkle (a surface) –1763. **3.** *intr.* To become furled; to curl *up* 1676.

1. Till..the battle-flags were furl'd TENNYSON.

Furlong (fɔ̄·ɹlǫŋ). [OE. *furlang*, f. *furh* FURROW + *lang* LONG *a.*¹] **1.** Orig., the length of the furrow in the common field; usually understood to be equal to 40 poles (rods, perches). Early regarded as = the Roman *stadium*, which was ⅛ of a Roman mile; and hence always used as a name for the eighth part of an English mile. The present statute furlong is 220 yards, and is equal both to the eighth part of a statute mile, and to the side of a square of 10 statute acres. **2.** An area of land a 'furlong' each way, containing ten acres 1819. **3.** The headland of a common field. *Obs.* exc. *dial.* OE. **4.** An indefinite division of an unenclosed field ME. **5.** 'The line of direction of plowed lands' (Marshall) 1787.

1. †*F. way*: a short distance, hence a brief space; They sitten stille wel a f. way CHAUCER.

Furlough (fɔ̄·ɹloᵘ), *sb.* 1625. [Early forms are *vorloffe, fore-loofe, furlogh* – Du. *verlof*, modelled on G. *verlaub*, f. *ver-* FOR-¹ + **laub-* LEAVE *sb.* The stress on the first syll. seems to show infl. of synon. Du. *oorloof* = G. *urlaub*, abstr. sb. f. *erlauben* permit.] **1.** Leave of absence, *esp.* a permit given to a soldier to be absent from duty for a stated time. Also *attrib.* †**2.** A passport; a licence, or permit –1826.

1. Like a Low-Countrey vorloffe, or Welsh-briefe B. JONS. Hence **Fu·rlough** *v.* (chiefly *U.S.*), to grant (a person) a f.; to give leave of absence to.

Furmente, -ty, furmety, -ity, vars. of FRUMENTY.

Furnace (fɔ̄·ɹnės), *sb.* ME. [– OFr. *fornais* m. and *fornaise* fem. (mod. *fournaise*) :– L. *fornax, fornac-* and pop. L. **fornatia*, f. L. *fornus, furnus* oven.] **1.** An apparatus consisting essentially of a chamber to contain combustibles for the purpose of subjecting minerals, metals, etc., to the continuous action of intense heat. **b.** *transf.* A volcano 1660. **c.** *fig.*, esp. used to express any severe test or trial. Also, a place of excessive heat; a hot-bed. ME. †**2.** Used of an incubating chamber –1585. **3.** A closed fireplace for heating a building by means of hot-air or hot-water pipes; also, 'the fireplace of a marine boiler' (Smyth) 1691. **4.** A boiler, cauldron, crucible. *Obs.* exc. *dial.* ME. **5.** *attrib.*, as *f. air-pipe*, etc. ME.

1. The Louer, Sighing like F. SHAKS. **c.** I have chosen thee in the fornace of affliction *Isa.* 48:10. Nablous is the very f. of..bigotry KINGLAKE.

Comb.: **f.-bar** = *fire-bar* (see FIRE-.); **-bridge,** 'a barrier of fire-bricks or of iron plates containing water thrown across the furnace at the extreme end of the fire-bars, to prevent the fuel being carried into the flues, and to quicken the draft' (Knight); **f. cadmia** or **cadmium,** the oxide of zinc which accumulates in the chimneys of furnaces smelting zinciferous ores; **-tube,** the tube within which the fuel is enclosed in an internally fired boiler.

Furnace (fɔ̄·ɹnės), *v.* 1598. [f. prec. sb.] **1.** *trans.* To exhale like a furnace; *intr.* to issue as from a furnace. **2.** *trans.* To subject to the heat of a furnace 1612.

1. He furnaces The thicke sighes from him SHAKS.

Fu·rnage. Now *Hist.* 1468. [XV *fornage* – OFr. *fornage* (mod. *fournage*), f. OFr. *forn* (mod. *four*) :– L. *furnus* oven; in med.L. *furn-, fornagium*; see -AGE.] The process of baking; the price paid for baking; in *Feudal Law*, the fee paid to the lord by tenants, bound to bake in the lord's oven, for permission to use their own.

†**Fu·rniment.** 1553. [– OFr. *fornement* decoration(s, fitting(s (mod. *fourniment* (XVII) – It. *fornimento*), f. *fornir* (mod. *fournir*) FURNISH; see -MENT.] The condition of being furnished; *pl.* accoutrements, decorations, fittings –1596.

Furnish (fɔ̄·ɹniʃ), *sb.* 1500. [f. next. vb.] †A furnishing or providing; *concr.* a provision of anything; *colloq.* a setting off or embellishing.

Furnish (fɔ̄·ɹniʃ), *v.* 1477. [– OFr. *furniss-*, lengthened stem (see -ISH²) of *furnir* (mod. *fournir*) :– Rom. **fornire*, alt. of **formire*, **fromire* – Gmc. **frumjan* promote, accomplish, supply, f. **frum-*; see FRAME *v.*, FROM.] †**1.** *trans.* To accomplish; to ensure *that* –1551. †**2.** To fill, occupy –1692. †**3.** To supply, provide for (needs, etc.) –1666. **4.** To provide or supply *with* (something necessary, useful, or desirable). †Also const. *in, of.* 1529. **†5.** *simply.* To supply with what is necessary –1743; to decorate, embellish –1690. **6.** To fit up (an apartment, a house) with all that is requisite, including movable furniture (see FURNITURE), which is now the predominant notion 1650. **7.** To provide, contribute, afford, supply, yield. (Perh. due to mod. Fr. influence.) 1754.

1. To f. a message LD. BERNERS. **3.** To f. his Majestye's present occasions MARVELL. **4.** Let your wiues. .furnishe them selues with al pointes of honest housewifery 1550. He [Plato] has furnished us with the instruments of thought JOWETT. **5.** We haue two houres To f. vs SHAKS. Six led Horses, all. .nobly furnish'd 1703. **6.** He had taken more pains to f. his house, than his mind THIRLWALL. **7.** The idea of inheritance furnishes a sure principle of conservation BURKE.

Comb. with advs. **F. forth.** Used by Shaks. with the sense = 5 above; by Scott in sense 7. **F. out.** (*a*) To supply what is lacking in; to complete. (*b*) To supply adequate provision for.

Hence **Fu·rnishable** *a.* **Fu·rnisher** *spec.* one who supplies furniture. **Fu·rnishing** *vbl. sb. spec. pl.* furniture, fixtures, apparatus, etc. **Fu·rnishment,** the action of furnishing; *spec. pl.* supplies; munitions of war (now *rare*).

Furniture (fǒ·ɹnitiŭɹ). 1529. [– Fr. *fourniture* (OFr. *forneture*, AL. *furnitura*), f. *fournir* FURNISH. Sense 7 is peculiarly English.] **†1.** The action of furnishing (see FURNISH *v.* 1. 5, 7) –1699. **2.** The condition of being equipped; preparedness for action; mental cultivation, culture. *Obs.* exc. *arch.* 1560. **3.** †That with which one is provided; a provision of anything (whether material or immaterial); stores in general; necessaries –1787. **b.** Something to fill or occupy (a receptacle, etc.), contents. Now *rare.* 1612. **4.** Means of equipment; *esp.* the harness, housings, etc. of a horse or other draught animal (rarely in *pl.*) 1553. **5.** Apparatus, appliances, or instruments for work: **a.** material (now chiefly *Naut.*) 1577; **b.** immaterial (now only with *mental* or the like) 1561. **6.** Accessories, appendages (formerly also *pl.*). Now only *techn.*; used, e.g., for the finger-plates, handles, locks, etc. of a door; the plates and handles, etc. of a coffin and the like 1568. **†b.** *pl.* Adjuncts of a salad –1727. **c.** *Printing.* 'The wooden inclosing strips and quoins which surround the matter in the chase' (Knight) 1683. **7.** Movable articles in a dwelling-house, place of business, or public building. (The prevailing sense.) 1573. **8.** *Mus.* 'The name of one of the mixture stops in an organ' (Stainer and Barrett) 1690.

1. Exercises, apt to the f. of a gentilemannes personage ELYOT. They. .stop all f. of food and victuals DRUMM. OF HAWTH. **2.** Great defect of inward F. and Worth HALES. **3.** A noble F. of Divine Learning 1683. **4.** Rachel had taken the images, and put them in the camels f. *Gen.* 31:34. The saddles and rich f. of the cavalry GIBBON. **5. a.** Ladders, bridges, shot, powder, and other furnitures 1601. *Furniture*, the rigging, sails, spars, anchors, cables, boats, tackle, provisions, and every article with which a ship is fitted out SMYTH. **b.** The statesmanlike f. of his mind LOWELL.

Comb.: **f.-pad,** a piece of india-rubber or the like attached to a piece of furniture to prevent rubbing or striking against objects; **-picture,** one painted for the trade; a 'pot-boiler'; **-stop** (*Mus.*), see 8.

‖**Furor** (fiū̆ə·rǫɹ). 1477. [L. *furor*, f. *furere* rage; see -OR 1.] **1.** Fury, rage, mania. **2.** The inspired frenzy of poets and prophets; an excited mood 1589. **3.** A rage or craze 1704.

2. Rises into f. almost Pythic CARLYLE. **3.** The athletic f. 1868.

‖**Furore** (fūrǭre). 1851. [It. form of prec.] Enthusiastic popular admiration; a rage, craze.

Furred (fǒɹd), *ppl. a.* ME. [f. FUR *sb.* and *v.* + -ED.] **1.** In the senses of FUR *v.*; *esp.* covered or coated with morbid matter, encrusted. **2.** Of an animal: Provided with or having fur 1545.

1. Teeth f., and throat sore 1803. A f. tongue 1878. **2.** Thou maist know a foxe by his f. tayle 1545.

†Fu·rrier¹. 1525. [– Fr. *fourrier* (OFr. *forrier*); see FORAYER.] One who went in advance of an army, etc., to secure accommodation, etc.; hence also a courier, harbinger –1704.

Furrier (fɒ·riəɹ). ME. [alt., after *clothier*, etc., of ME. *furour* – OFr. *forreor* (mod. *fourreur*), f. *forrer* trim with fur.] A dealer in or dresser of fur or furs. Hence **Fu·rriery,** †furs collectively; the business of a furrier.

Furring (fǒ·riŋ), *vbl. sb.* ME. [f. FUR *v.* + -ING¹.] **1.** The action of clothing or adorning with fur; *concr.* a lining or trimming of fur. Also *collect.* **2.** The process of becoming furred or encrusted; furred state; also a coating of fur 1601. **3. a.** *Shipbuilding.* The action or process of double planking a ship's side; also, a piece of timber used for this 1622. **b.** *Building.* The nailing on of thin strips of board in order to level or raise a surface for lathing, boarding, etc. Also, the strips laid on. 1678. **c.** *Building.* 'A lining of scantling and plasterwork on a brick wall, to prevent the dampness of the latter reaching the room' (*Cassell*).

Furrow (fɒ·roᵘ), *sb.* [OE. *furh* = OFris. *furch*, MLG., MDu. *vore* (Du. *voor*), OHG. *furuh* (G. *furche*), ON. *for* trench, drain; Gmc. base **furχ-* :– IE. **pṛk-* (L. *porca* ridge between furrows).] **1.** A narrow trench made in the earth with a plough, esp. for the reception of seed. Also *transf.* and *fig.* **b.** *poet.* Used *loosely* for ploughed land, the cornfields ME. **2.** A trench, drain; *spec.* a water-furrow. **3.** Anything resembling a furrow; e.g. a rut or track, a groove, indentation, or depression narrow in proportion to its length ME.; a deep wrinkle 1589; etc.

1. *fig.* When in thee times forrwes I behould SHAKS. **b.** What time the laboured ox In his loose traces from the f. came MILT. **3.** They make. . furrows in the cheeks of the sufferers HELPS.

Comb.: **f.-board** = MOULD-BOARD; **-weed,** a weed that grows on the furrow or ploughed land.

Hence **Fu·rrowy** *a.*, full of furrows or wrinkles.

Furrow (fɒ·roᵘ), *v.* ME. [f. prec. sb.] **1.** *trans.* To make furrows in with a plough; to plough; also *transf.* **2.** To make furrow-like depressions, channels, or wrinkles in 1523. **3.** *intr.* To make furrows or grooves; to make wrinkles 1576. **b.** quasi-*trans.*, as in to *f.* (*out, up*) *one's way* 1613.

1. *transf.* To f. large space of stormy seas SURREY. **2.** Thou canst helpe time to f. me with age SHAKS. Fair cheeks were furrowed with hot tears BYRON.

Furry (fǒ·ri), *a.* 1674. [f. FUR *sb.* + -Y¹.] **1.** Consisting of fur; composed of furs. **2.** Covered with fur; wearing fur 1687. **3.** Made of fur, lined or trimmed with fur. Also *transf.* and *fig.* 1691. **4.** Resembling fur 1876. **5.** Of the nature of, or coated with, fur or morbid matter 1739.

1. F. spoils of beasts POPE. **2.** His [the Czar's] F. Troops 1717. **4.** Cushions of f. moss T. HARDY.

Furry (fɒ·ri), *sb. dial.* 1790. [perh. conn. w. FAIR *sb.*¹, L. *feria.*] A festival observed at Helston, Cornwall, on the eighth of May; also, a dance used on that occasion. (Also called *Flora.*) Also *attrib.*

Further (fǒ·ɹðəɹ), *a.* [OE. *furþra* = OFris. *fordera*, OS. *furð(i)ro, forðro*, OHG. *fordaro* :– Gmc. **furþer-*, f. **furþ-* FORTH + comp. suffix -ER³; see next.] **†1.** That is before another in position, order, or rank; front –1609. **2.** More extended, going beyond; additional, more ME. **3.** More distant, remoter, esp. the remoter of two. Of a horse: The off (side). 1578.

2. Without f. ambiguity 1634, Preface ADDISON. **3.** They would. .goe foorth into a f. countrey 2 *Esd.* 13:41.

Further (fǒ·ɹðəɹ), *adv.* [OE. *furþor, -ur*, corresp. to OFris. *further*, OS. *furðor* (early mod. Du. *voorder*), OHG. *furdar, -ir*, f. Gmc. **furþ-* FORTH + compar. suffix (see -ER³).] **1.** To or at a more advanced point: **a.** of space (*lit.* and *fig.*); **b.** of time ME. **2.** To a greater extent, more OE. **3.** In addition; moreover ME. **4.** At a greater distance in space ME.

1. a. Hither to shalt thou come, but no f. *Job* 38:11. Proverb, *To go f. and fare worse.* **2.** Men who pretend to believe no f. than they can see BP. BERKELEY. **4.** Your best Friends shall wish I had beene f. SHAKS.

Further (fǒ·ɹðəɹ), *v.* [OE. *fyrðr(i)an*, f. *furðor, -ðra* FURTHER *adv.* and *adj.*] **1.** *trans.* To help forward, assist (usu. things); to promote, favour. **†2.** To honour. ME. only. **3.** *intr.* To go on, continue; to make progress. *Obs.* exc. *Sc.* ME. **†4.** *trans.* To put further, defer. WOLSEY.

1. Ire. .furthereth all euyl 1477. To f. a general system of school training 1869. Hence **Furtherer,** a promoter; an aid.

Furtherance (fǒ·ɹðərǎns). ME. [f. FURTHER *v.* + -ANCE.] The fact or state of being helped forward; the action of helping forward; advancement, aid. Also *concr.* a means or source of help.

The pompes of the funeralls are rather solaces to the liuing then furtherances to the dead HEALEY. Some few furtherances have been shown HELPS.

Furthermore (fǒ·ɹðəɹmōᵊɹ), *adv.* See also FARTHERMORE. ME. [f. FURTHER *adv.* + MORE *adv.*] **†1.** Still further; = FURTHER *adv.* 1 a. –1552. **†2.** = FURTHER *adv.* 2. –1450. **3.** = FURTHER *adv.* 3. ME.

Furthermost (fǒ·ɹðəɹmoᵘst), *a.* ME. [f. FURTHER *a.* + -MOST.] **†1.** Foremost, first. ME. only. **2.** Most distant 1765.

Furthersome (fǒ·ɹðəɹsǒm), *a.* 1626. [f. FURTHER *v.* or *adv.* + -SOME¹.] Adapted to further or help forward, advantageous, helpful. Const. *to.*

F. to the interests of the drama 1880.

Furthest (fǒ·ɹðėst). ME. [Formed as superl. to FURTHER.]

A. *adj.* **1.** Most advanced in any direction. Also as superl. of FAR *a.* (now usu. repl. by FARTHEST): Most remote (*lit.* and *fig.*). **2.** Most remote in time; †earliest; latest. *Obs.* exc. *absol.* in *at* (*the*) *f.* 1552.

1. The f. corner of Naboth's vineyard SWIFT.

B. *adv.* To or at the greatest distance, farthest ME.

Furtive (fǒ·ɹtiv), *a.* 1490. [– (O)Fr. *furtif, -ive* or L. *furtivus, -iva*, f. *furt-* in *furtum* theft; see -IVE.] **1.** Done by stealth; clandestine, surreptitious, secret. **2.** Of a person, etc.: Stealthy, sly 1858. **3.** Stolen; also, taken by stealth or secretly 1718. **4.** Thievish 1816.

1. A f. glance W. IRVING. **2.** That f. mien M. ARNOLD. **3.** Columba's f. copy from St. Finnian's psalter 1894. **4.** The f. Indian 1816. Hence **Fu·rtive-ly** *adv.*, **-ness.**

Furuncle (fiū̆ə·rɒŋk'l). 1676. [– L. *furunculus* petty thief, boil, dim. of *fur* thief.] A boil or inflammatory tumour. Hence **Furu·ncular, Furu·nculous** *adjs.* of, pertaining to, or characterized by boils.

Fury (fiū̆ə·ri), *sb.* ME. [– (O)Fr. *furie* – L. *furia*, f. *furiosus*, f. *furere* rage; see -Y³.] **1.** Fierce passion, disorder or tumult of mind approaching madness; *esp.* wild anger, frenzied rage. Also, a fit of this. **2.** Fierce impetuosity or violence. †Rarely, fierce cruelty. 1534. **b.** Hist. *The* (*Spanish*) *Fury*: the massacre perpetrated by the Spaniards at Antwerp in Oct.–Nov. 1576. **3.** *transf.* (e.g. of a tempest, a wind, etc.) 1585. **4.** Inspired frenzy; esp. poetic 'rage'. Now *rare.* 1546. **5.** One of the avenging deities (L. *Furiæ, Diræ*, Gr. Ἐρινύες, Εὐμενίδες), sent from Tartarus to avenge wrong and punish crime: in later accounts, three in number (Tisiphone, Megæra, Alecto). Hence *gen.* An avenging or tormenting infernal spirit. ME. **b.** One of the three 'Fates' or *Parcæ.* MILT. *Lycidas* 75. **6.** *transf.* One like an infernal spirit; *esp.* a ferociously angry or malignant woman ME.

1. Suche folk as falle in furye LYDG. The vnreasonable Furie of a beast SHAKS. **2.** The furies of the Border war SCOTT. **3.** The F. of the Heats 1698, of the Storm 1726. **4.** Whatsoeuer they write, proceeds of a diuine f. SIDNEY. **5.** The furies three with alle hir mortel brond CHAUCER. **6.** Remember, sir, your f. of a wife DRYDEN.

†Fu·ry, *v.* [f. prec.] *refl.* To drive oneself to fury. FELTHAM. So **Fu·rying** *ppl. a.* raging. CLOUGH.

Furze (fǒɹz). [OE. *fyrs*, of unc. origin.] **1.** The pop. name of *Ulex europæus*, a spiny evergreen shrub with yellow flowers, growing abundantly on waste lands throughout Europe. Also named *gorse, whin.* Also *transf.* and *fig.* **2.** In pop. names of other plants, as **Dwarf furze** (*Ulex nanus*); etc.

1578. **3.** *attrib.*, *esp.* in *f.-bush*, also (*obs.* and *dial.*) **furzen bush;** also in pop. names of birds, as **furze-chat,** the whinchat (*Pratincola rubetra*); **-chucker,** the mountain finch or brambling; **-lark,** the tit-lark; **-wren** = FURZELING.

Hence **Fu·rzeling,** the Dartford Warbler (*Melizophilus undatus*).

Furzy (fɒ̄·ɹzi), *a.* 1613. [f. FURZE *sb.* + -Y[1].] **1.** Composed of furze; overgrown with furze; of or pertaining to furze. **2.** Fuzzy 1719.

‖**Fusain** (füsæ̃n). 1870. [Fr.; = 'spindle-tree'.] A charcoal crayon made of the wood of the Spindle Tree; also *attrib.* as *f. drawing.* **b.** A drawing executed with this.

Fusarole (fiū·zărōᵘl). 1664. [– Fr. *fusarolle*, – It. *fusaruola*, f. (ult.) L. *fusus* spindle.] *Arch.* 'A member whose section is that of a semicircle carved into beads. It is generally placed under the echinus. . in the Doric, Ionic, and Corinthian orders' (Gwilt.)

Fuscin (fɒ·sin). Also **-ine.** 1864. [f. L. *fusc-us* (see FUSCOUS) + -IN[1].] *Chem.* A dark-coloured substance obtained from various animal oils when they are decomposed by heat.

Fusco- (fɒ·sko), comb. f. L. *fuscus* 'dusky', as in **fusco-ferruginous** *a.* dull rust-coloured; etc.

Fuscous (fɒ·skəs), *a.* 1662. [f. L. *fuscus* dark, dusky + -OUS.] Of a dark or sombre hue; dusky, swarthy. (Chiefly *Nat. Hist.*)

Fuse *sb.*[1] 1611. [perh. – OFr. *fuies*, pl. of *fuie* flight :– L. *fuga* flight.] The track of an animal. Also *fig.*

Fuse, fuze (fiūz), *sb.*[2] 1644. [– It. *fuso* (:– L. *fusus*) spindle, (hence) spindle-shaped tube orig. used for a bomb, etc.] **1.** A tube, casing, cord, etc., filled or saturated with combustible material, by means of which a military shell, the blast of a mine, etc., is ignited and exploded. **2.** *attrib.* as *f.-hole*, etc. 1692.

†**Fuse, fuze,** *sb.*[3] *rare.* 1674. [alt. of FUSEE[2], assim. to prec.] = FUSEE[2] 2. –1701.

Fuse, *sb.*[4] 1884. [f. FUSE *v.*[1]] *Electr.* A wire or strip of fusible metal inserted in an electric circuit; it melts when the current increases beyond a certain safe strength.

Fuse (fiūz), *v.*[1] 1681. [f. *fus-*, pa. ppl. stem of L. *fundere* pour, melt; see FOUND *v.*[2]] **1.** *trans.* To make fluid by means of intense heat; to liquefy, melt. Also *transf.* **b.** *fig.* Often with the sense: To blend, unite into one whole, as by melting together 1817. **2.** *intr.* To become fluid or liquefied with heat; to melt; also *fig.* 1800. **b.** Of an electric light: To be extinguished owing to the melting of a fuse (*colloq.*) 1930. **3.** *Anat.* Of contiguous vessels, bones, etc.: To coalesce 1870.

Fuse, fuze, *v.*[2] 1802. [f. FUSE *sb.*[2],[4].] To furnish with a fuse.

Fusee, fuzee[1] (fiuzī·). Now *Hist.* 1661. [– Fr. *fusil* (pronounced *füzi*).] = FUSIL[2] 2.

Fusee, fuzee[2] (fiuzī·). 1589. [– Fr. *fusée* – pop. L. **fusata* 'spindleful', f. L. *fusus* spindle.] †**1.** A spindle-shaped figure. PUTTENHAM. **2.** A conical pulley or wheel, *esp.* the wheel of a watch or clock upon which the chain is wound and by which the power of the mainspring is equalized 1622. **3.** = FUSE *sb.*[2] 1. 1704. **4.** *Farriery.* An exostosis upon one of the cannon-bones 1720. **5.** A kind of match with a large head of combustible material; a lucifer, vesuvian 1832.

Fusel (fiū·zĕl). 1850. [– G. *fusel* bad brandy or other spirits, a LG. word applied also to bad coffee and tobacco; cf. FOOZLE *v.*] *attrib.* in *Fusel oil*, an acrid oily liquid accompanying various alcoholic liquids, and consisting of several alcohols, chiefly amyl alcohol, to which the name is esp. applied.

Fuselage (fiū·zélāʒ, -édʒ). 1909. [– Fr. *fuselage*, f. *fuseler* shape like a spindle, f. *fuseau* spindle; see FUSIL[1], -AGE.] The body of an aeroplane, containing the cockpit, engine, etc.; so called from its shape.

Fusible (fiū·zib'l), *a.* ME. [– med.L. *fusibilis*, f. *fus-* (see FUSE *v.*[1]) + *-ibilis* -IBLE. Readopted in XVII, partly through Fr. *fusible*.] Capable of being fused.

The fusible metal consisting of 8 parts of bismuth, 5 of lead, and 3 of tin. . melts at the heat of boiling water or 212° Fahr. URE. *Fusible plug*, one placed in the skin of a steam-boiler, so as to be melted and allow the discharge of the contents when a dangerous heat is reached. Hence **Fusibi·lity. Fu·sibleness.**

Fusiform (fiū·zifǭɹm), *a.* 1746. [f. L. *fusus* spindle + -FORM. Cf. Fr. *fusiforme*.] Spindle-shaped; esp. in *Bot.*, *Entom.*, and *Zool.*

Root caulescent, f. 1805. Shell f., elongated 1854.

Fusil[1] (fiū·zil). 1486. [– OFr. *fusel* (mod. *fuseau*) :– Rom. **fusellus*, dim. of *fusus* spindle; see FUSE *sb.*[2], -EL[2].] *Her.* A bearing in the form of an elongated lozenge; orig. a representation of a spindle covered with tow.

Fusil[2] (fiū·zil). 1580. [– (O)Fr. *fusil* :– pop. L. **focile*, f. *focus* (in pop. L. fire); see FOCUS.] †**1.** A fire steel for a tinder-box 1580. **2.** A light musket or firelock 1680.

Fusile (fiū·zil), *a.* Also **fusil.** ME. [– L. *fusilis* molten, etc.; see FUSE *v.*[1], -ILE.] **1.** Capable of being melted. Now *rare.* 1605. **2.** Running or flowing by the force of heat. Now *rare.* 1631. **3.** Formed by melting or casting. Also *fig.* ME.

2. And o'er the silver pours the fusil gold POPE. **3.** What might else be wrought Fusil or grav'n in mettle MILTON.

Fusilier (fiūzilīᵊ·ɹ). 1680. [– Fr. *fusilier*, f. *fusil* FUSIL[2]; see -IER.] Orig., a soldier armed with a fusil (see FUSIL[2] 2). The designation 'Fusiliers' is still retained by certain regiments in the British army which are distinguished from other regiments of the line only by some small peculiarities of costume. Also *attrib.*

Fusillade (fiūzilēⁱ·d), *sb.* Also **fusilade.** 1801. [– Fr. *fusillade* (1796), f. *fusiller* shoot; see -ADE.] A simultaneous discharge of fire-arms; a wholesale execution by this means. Also *transf.* and *fig.* Hence **Fusilla·de** *v.* to assault (a place), to shoot down (persons) by a simultaneous discharge of fire-arms.

Fusing (fiū·ziŋ), *vbl. sb.* 1832. [f. FUSE *v.*[2] + -ING[1].] The action or process of fusing (see FUSE *v.*[2]).

Phr. *Fusing point* or *temperature*, the point or temperature at which fusion takes place.

Fusion (fiū·ʒən). 1555. [– Fr. *fusion* or L. *fusio*, f. *fus-*, pa. ppl. stem of *fundere* pour; see -ION, FOUND *v.*[2]] **1.** The action or operation of fusing or rendering fluid by heat; the state of flowing or fluidity in consequence of heat. †**2.** *Path.* and *Phys.* Thinning, attenuation of the blood –1725. **3.** The union or blending together of different things as if by melting; the result or state of being so blended. Const. *into*, *with.* 1776. **b.** *Politics.* The coalition of parties 1845. Also *attrib.*

1. †*Watery f.*: the melting of certain crystals by heat in their own water of crystallization. **3.** Everything English is a f. of distinct and antagonistic elements EMERSON. **b.** The f. of parties [became] the babble of the clubs DISRAELI.

Fusionless, var. of FOISONLESS.

Fusk, *a. rare.* Also **fusc.** 1599. [– L. *fuscus* in same sense.] Dark brown, fuscous.

Fusoid (fiū·zoid), *a.* 1889. [f. L. *fusus* spindle + -OID.] = FUSIFORM.

Fuss (fɒs), *sb.* 1701. [perh. Anglo-Ir., but of unkn. origin.] **1.** A bustle or commotion out of proportion to the occasion; ostentatious or officious activity. **2.** A state of (more or less ludicrous) consternation or anxiety 1705. **3.** [f. the vb.] One who fusses 1875.

1. She got under weigh with very little f. R. DANA. **2.** Madame Legoux. . had been in a fine f. about us 1813.

Fuss (fɒs), *v.* 1792. [f. prec. sb.] **1.** *intr.* To make a fuss; to be in a bustle; to busy oneself restlessly about trifles. Also *transf.* **2.** *trans.* To put into a fuss; to worry; to bother about trifles 1816.

Fussy (fɒ·si), *a.* 1831. [f. FUSS *sb.* + -Y[1].] **1.** Fond of fuss; habitually busy about trifles. **2.** Of places: Full of bustle. *dial.* and *U.S.* 1848. **3.** Of dress, etc.: Full of petty details 1858.

1. No f. visiting of the poor 1892. *transf.* The f. little Conservancy tug 1895. Hence **Fu·ssily** *adv.* in a f. manner. **Fu·ssiness,** f. quality or habit.

†**Fust,** *sb.*[1] 1481. [– OFr. *fust* (mod. *fût*); see FOIST *sb.*[2]] **1.** A wine-cask –1601. **2.** A strong, musty smell 1755. **3.** *Arch.* The shaft of a column, or trunk of a pilaster –1819.

Fust, *sb.*[2] Now *dial.* 1703. [var. of (dial.) *first*, OE. *fyrst* = OHG., G. *first.*] The ridge of the roof of a house.

Fust (fɒst), *v.* 1592. [f. FUST *sb.*[1] 1, 2. Cf. FOIST *v.*[2]] *intr.* To become mouldy or stale-smelling; *esp.* Of wine: To taste of the cask; also *fig.*

Fustanella (fɒstăne·lă). 1849. [– It. *fustanella*, f. mod. Gr. φουστάνι (also φουστανέλλα), Alb. *fustan*, prob. – It. *fustagno* FUSTIAN.] A stiff full petticoat of white cotton or linen worn by men in Modern Greece.

Fusteric (fɒstĕ·rik). 1860. [f. FUST(ET; after *turmeric*.] The colouring matter of fustet.

Fustet (fɒ·stét). 1821. [– (O)Fr. *fustet* – Pr. *fustet* = Sp. *fustete*, an etymologizing corruption (as if dim. of Pr. *fust*, Sp. *fuste* stick) of the Arab. source of FUSTIC.] A small European shrub (*Rhus cotinus*), from which a yellow dye is extracted; called also *young fustic.*

Fustian (fɒ·stiăn). ME. [– OFr. *fustaigne* (mod. *futaine*), repr. med.L. *fustaneum*, (*tela*) *fustanea*, (*pannus*) *fustaneus*, i.e. cloth of *Fostat*, suburb of Cairo, from which such cloth was exported.]

A. *sb.* **1.** Formerly, a coarse cloth made of cotton and flax. Now, a thick, twilled, cotton cloth with a short pile or nap, usually dyed of a dark colour. †Also, a blanket of this material. **2.** *fig.* Inflated, turgid, or inappropriately lofty language; bombast, rant; in early use also †jargon, gibberish 1590.

2. With humble service, and such other F. 1651. Between f. in expression, and bathos in sentiment HAZLITT.

B. *adj.* **1.** [The sb. used attrib.] Made of fustian 1537. Also *fig.* **2.** Of language: Ridiculously lofty in expression; bombastic, inflated, pompous 1592. †Hence of a writer or speaker –1782. **3.** Worthless, sorry, pretentious 1523; †imaginary B. JONS.

2. Then comes he out. . with his f. eloquence GREENE. **3.** Such a F. Rascall 2 *Hen. IV*, II. iv. 203.

Hence **Fu·stianist,** one who writes f

Fustic (fɒ·stik). 1545. [– Fr. *fustoc* – Sp. *fustoc* – Arab. *fustuḳ* – Gr. πιστάκη PISTACHIO. The ending has been assim. to -IC.] **1.** The name of two kinds of wood, both used for dyeing yellow. **a.** The wood of the Venetian sumach (*Rhus cotinus*). Now only as *young* or *Zante f.* **b.** The wood of the *Cladrastis* (*Chlorophora*, *Maclura*) *tinctoria* of America and the West Indies. Occas. called *old f.* **2.** A yellow dye extracted from the wood of these trees 1858. **3.** *attrib.*, as *f.-tree*, *-wood* 1630.

Fustigate (fɒ·stigeⁱt), *v.* Now *joc.* 1656. [– *fustigat-*, pa. ppl. stem of late L. *fustigare*, f. *fustis* cudgel; see -ATE[3].] *trans.* To cudgel, beat. Hence **Fustiga·tion,** the action of cudgelling or beating. **Fu·stigator.**

†**Fustila·rian.** (? *nonce-wd.*) [perh. a comic formation on next; see -ARIAN.] ? = next. 2 *Hen. IV*, II. i. 66 (Qo. 1600).

Fustilugs (fɒ·stilɒgz). 1607. [app. f. FUSTY *a.* + LUG in the sense of something heavy or slow.] A person, esp. a woman, of gross or corpulent habit; a fat, frowzy woman.

Fusty (fɒ·sti), *a.* ME. [– OFr. *fusté*, f. *fust* trunk of a tree, barrel :– L. *fustis* club, stake. See FUST *sb.*[1], -Y[5].] **1.** Stale-smelling, musty; smelling of mould or damp. **2.** *fig.* That has lost its freshness and interest; fogyish 1606; †peevish PEPYS.

1. As good cracke a fustie nut with no kernell SHAKS. **2.** F. Latin and Greek 1842. Hence **Fu·stily** *adv.* **Fu·stiness.**

†**Fut,** *interj.* An exclamation of surprise. MARSTON. Also, variant of PHUT.

Futchel(l (fɒ·tʃĕl). 1794. [Of unkn. origin.] One of the pieces of timber carrying or supporting the shafts, or pole, or splinter-bar of a carriage.

Futhorc (fū·þǫɹk). Also **-ark, -ork.** 1851. [Named from the first six letters, *f, u, þ, ǫ* or *a, r, k*.] The Runic alphabet.

Futile (fiū·təil, -il), *a.* 1555. [- L. *futilis* (better *futtilis*), f. **fud-*, base of *fundere* pour; see -ILE.] **1.** Incapable of producing any result; useless, ineffectual, vain. **2.** Addicted to trifling; lacking in purpose. ? *Obs.* 1736. †**3.** Unable to hold one's tongue, loquacious. [From the etymological sense, 'leaky'.] BACON.

1. As f. in its effects, as it is feeble in its principle BURKE. **2.** 'Davy..'tis a f. fellow' BOSWELL. **3.** Talkers and F. Persons BACON. Hence **Fu·tile-ly** *adv.*, **-ness.** var. †**Futi·litious** *a.* [irreg. f. FUTILITY + -OUS]. STERNE.

Futility (fiuti·lĭti). 1623. [- Fr. *futilité* or L. *futilitas*; see prec., -ITY.] **1.** The quality of being futile; want of weight or importance; ineffectiveness, uselessness. **2.** Lack of purpose, frivolousness 1692. †**3.** Loquacity, inability to hold one's tongue –1692. **4.** Something that is futile 1667.

1. The f. of a reply 1777, of contending against the most rooted of prejudices M. ARNOLD. **4.** His mouth full of loud futilities CARLYLE. Hence **Futilita·rian** *a.* devoted to f.; *sb.* one who is devoted to f. (A humorous coinage.) SOUTHEY.

†**Fu·tilous.** 1607. [f. FUTILE + -OUS.] = FUTILE. –1703.

Futtock (fɒ·tək). 1611. [ME. (pl.) *votekes, futtokes, foteken*, f. MLG., f. *fōt* foot + *-ken* -KIN.] **1.** One of the middle timbers of the frame of a ship, between the floor and the top timbers.

Comb.: **f.-hoop,** a hoop encircling the mast at a point below the head, and serving for the attachment of the shackles of the f.-shrouds; **-plate,** one of the iron plates crossing the sides of the top-rim perpendicularly, to which the f.-shrouds are secured; **-shroud,** one of the small shrouds which secure the lower dead-eyes and f.-plates of topmast rigging to a band round a lower mast.

†**Fu·turable,** *a.* [f. FUTURE + -ABLE.] That may happen in the future. FULLER.

Future (fiū·tiŭɹ, fiū·tʃəɹ). ME. [- (O)Fr. *futur, -ure* - L. *futurus, -ura*, fut. pple. of *esse*, f. **fu-* (see BE).]

A. *adj.* **1.** That is to be, or will be, hereafter. Often qualifying a sb., with sense: The person or thing that is to be (what the sb. denotes). Also *absol.* or *ellipt.*; esp. in phr. *in future.* **2.** Of or pertaining to time to come; esp. in *Gram.* of a tense: Relating to time to come; describing an event yet to happen. Also *ellipt.* (= *future tense*) 1530. ¶**3.** Loosely used for: Subsequent 1600.

1. I wish I were the f. Lady Vargrave LYTTON. Phr. *A f. state, life*: existence after death.

B. *sb.* †**1.** *pl.* Future events –1654. **2.** *The future.* **a.** Time to come ME. **b.** What will happen in the future 1607. **3. a.** A condition in time to come different from the present 1852. **b.** The prospective condition (of a person, country, etc.) 1858. **4.** *Gram.* = *future tense*: see A. 2. 1881. **5.** One's betrothed 1827. **6.** *Comm.* in *pl.* Goods and stocks sold for future delivery. Also contracts to sell or buy on these terms. 1880.

2. b. The f. comes apace *Timon* II. i. 157. **6.** American futures are in better demand 1880.

Hence †**Fu·ture** *v.* to make f., put off to a f. day. **Fu·tureless** *a.* without a f. †**Fu·turely** *adv.* in f., at a f. time, hereafter. Also *loosely*, thereafter.

Futurism (fiū·tiŭriz'm, -tʃər-). 1909. [- Fr. *futurisme* – It. *futurismo*; see prec., -ISM.] A movement in art, literature, etc., orig. in Italy, marked by violent departure from traditional forms and by the use of arbitrary symbols in the expression of emotion. So **Fu·turist** [cf. It. *futurista*, Fr. *futuriste*]. **a.** *Theol.* one who believes that the Scripture prophecies are still to be fulfilled in the future; **b.** an adherent of futurism; also *attrib.* Hence **Futuri·stic** *a.*

Futurition (fiūtiuri·ʃən). 1641. [- med.L. *futuritio*, used by St. Bonaventura in discussions of God's foreknowledge; an irreg. formation (see FUTURE, -ITION). Cf. Fr. *futurition* (Fénelon).] *Philos.* **1.** Existence or occurrence in the future. Now *rare.* **b.** A future event or existence 1668. **2.** The quality or fact of being future; the fact that (something specified) will be 1666.

1. The f. of salvation 1659. **b.** Some mere f., as metaphysicians love to speak, some event in futurity 1840. So **Futuri·tial** *a.* relating to what is to come (Dicts.).

Futurity (fiutiū^ə·rĭti). 1604. [f. FUTURE + -ITY.] **1.** = FUTURITION 2. *rare.* 1637. **2.** Future time 1604. **3.** Future condition; also, existence after death 1651.

2. Purpos'd merit in f. *Oth.* III. iv. 117. Futurity's blank page S. ROGERS. **3.** A secret dread of f. BP. BERKELEY. The f. of representative governments MILL.

Fuzil, var. of FUSIL^{2}.

Fuzz (fɒz), *sb.*^{1} 1601. [prob. of LDu. origin; cf. Du. *voos*, LG. *fussig* spongy. Cf. FOZY *a.*] **1.** Loose volatile matter 1674. †**2.** = FUZZ-BALL. –1702. **3.** *Photogr.* = FUZZINESS. 1889. *Comb.* **f.-wig,** a wig of crisp curls.

†**Fuzz,** *sb.*^{2} [Cf. FUZZ *v.*^{1}] A fuddled or muddled state. SWIFT.

†**Fuzz,** *v.*^{1} [perh. conn. w. next through the notion of blurring or confusing.] *trans.* To make drunk, fuddle. WOOD.

Fuzz (fɒz), *v.*^{2} 1702. [f. FUZZ *sb.*^{1}] **1.** *intr.* To fly out in light particles. **2.** *trans.* To cover with fine particles 1851.

Fuzz-ball (fɒ·zbǭl). 1597. [f. FUZZ *sb.*^{1} + BALL *sb.*^{1}] A pop. name of the fungus *Lycoperdon bovista*, puff-ball. Also *transf.* and *fig.*

†**Fuzzle** (fɒ·z'l), *v.* 1621. [Cf. FUZZ *v.*^{1}, FUDDLE.] *trans.* To make drunk, confuse, muddle; = FUZZ *v.*^{1} –1632.

Fuzzy (fɒ·zi), *a.* 1616. [See FUZZ *sb.*^{1} and FOZY *a.*] **1.** Not firm or sound in substance; spongy. **2.** Frayed into loose fibres; covered with fuzz; fluffy 1713. **3.** Blurred 1778. **4.** Of hair; Frizzy, fluffy 1825.

1. A f. sort of Earth, that we call Moss 1725. **3.** It makes the picture more 'f.' 1871. *Comb.* **f.-wuzzy** a nickname for the Sudanese warrior, from his method of dressing his hair. **Fu·zzily** *adv.* **Fu·zziness.**

Fy, obs. f. FIE. **Fy-**: see also FI-.

-fy, *suffix*, forming *verbs.* The older Eng. vbs. in *-fy* are adoptions from Fr. vbs. in *-fier* (:- L. *-ficare*). In med.L. *-ficare* was often substituted for *-facere* in L. vbs. so ending, and hence Fr. and Eng. vbs. in *-fier*, *-fy* sometimes correspond to L. vbs. in *-facere*; e.g. Fr. *liquéfier* liquefy, etc. Exc. in the case of these vbs. the ending has normally the form *-ify* (see -FIC).

Fyke (fəik). *U.S.* 1860. [- Du. *fuik* fish-trap, etc.] A bag-net used for catching fish, esp. shad; called also *f.-net.*

Fylfot (fi·lfǫt). 1500. [perh. simply *fill-foot*, a pattern for filling the foot of a painted window.] A name for the figure called also a cross cramponnee (see CRAMPONNEE), and identified with the SWASTIKA of India, the *gammadion* of Byzantine ornament. Also *f. cross.*

Fyrd (fɔ̄ɹd, fiᵊɹd). 1832. [OE. *ferd, fierd, fyrd* = OFris. *ferd*, OS. *fard*, OHG. *fart* (G. *fahrt*), ON. *ferð* :- Gmc. **far-*; see FARE *v.*^{1}] The military array of the whole country before the Conquest; also the obligation to military service.

Fytte: see FIT *sb.*^{1} *Obs.*

G

G (dʒī), the seventh letter of the Roman alphabet, was orig. a differentiated form of C, q.v. In Latin, G represented the voiced guttural stop; but in the later period of the language it was probably pronounced before front vowels as a palatal.

In OE. the letter stood for four different sounds, viz. the voiced guttural and palatal stop (g, ɡ), and the voiced guttural and palatal spirant (ȝ, ȝ). In early ME. the palatal stop developed into the complex sound (dʒ).

The form ȝ, here employed for ME. words, was commonly used in ME. for the sound of (y) initial and final, for the guttural and palatal unvoiced spirant final or before *t* (as in *inouȝ, auȝt, niȝt*), and so long as the sound was in use, for the guttural voiced spirant. From XIII, however, the ȝ was by some scribes wholly or partly discarded for *y* or *gh*; a few texts have *yh.*

See also KEY TO THE PRONUNCIATION.

II. 1. G, g, *g* is used to denote anything occupying the seventh place in a series. **2.** *Mus.* G. is the name of the 5th note of the diatonic scale of C major; called *sol* in France and Italy. Also the scale or key which has that note for its tonic. *G clef*: the treble clef (see CLEF^{1}) placed on the line in the stave appropriated to the note G.

III. *Abbreviations.* **1.** In *Physics* g is the symbol for acceleration by gravity = about 32 ft. per second per second. **2.** *Math.* G.C.F. or G.C.M. = Greatest Common Factor or Measure. **3.** In *Freemasonry*, G.M. = Grand Master. **4.** G.B.E. = (Knight; or Dame) Grand (Cross of the Order of the) British Empire.

Gab (gæb), *sb.*^{1} ME. [- OFr. *gab, gabe* mockery, idle vaunt – ON. *gabb* mockery. See GAB *v.*^{1}] †**1.** Mockery, deception; a deceit. ME. only. **2.** A piece of brag; a gasconade 1737.

Gab (gæb), *sb.*^{2} *colloq.* or *vulgar.* 1681. [var. of GOB *sb.*^{3} talk, which is prob. a use of GOB *sb.*^{2} mouth, which has a var. GAB *sb.*^{3}] The action of gabbing; conversation, prattle, twaddle 1790.

Phr. *The gift of the g.*: a turn for speaking.

Gab, *sb.*^{3} *Sc.* 1724. [var. of GOB *sb.*^{2} mouth; see GAB *sb.*^{2}] The mouth.

Gab (gæb), *sb.*^{4} 1792. [Of obsc. origin; cf. Flem. *gabbe* notch, gash (in Kilian glossed '*incisura*').] A hook, or open notch, in a rod or lever, which drops over a spindle, and forms a temporary connection between valve or other motions. *Comb.* **g.-lever,** the lever which forms the connection between the slide valve spindle and the eccentric rod in some forms of marine engine valve; also *gen.*

Gab (gæb), *v.*^{1} ME. [- (O)Fr. *gaber* mock, deride, vaunt oneself, f. *gab* GAB *sb.*^{1}] †**1.** *intr.* To speak mockingly –1573. †**2.** To tell lies –1475; †also (*trans.*) to deceive –1460. **3.** *intr.* To brag (quasi-*arch.* and *Hist.*) 1825.

3. [He] gabbed; and his boast was [etc.] WRIGHT.

Gab (gæb), *v.*^{2} 1786. [perh. short for GABBLE *v.*] *intr.* To talk much or glibly.

†**Gab,** *v.*^{3} [Cf. dial. *gobber-tooth*; also GAG-TOOTH; also GAG *v.*^{2} 3.] *intr.* Of teeth: To project. P. HOLLAND.

Gabardine (gæbădī·n). 1904. [var. of GABERDINE, q.v.] A dress material of cotton or silk with a wool lining.

Gabber (gæ·bəɹ), *sb.*^{1} ME. [f. GAB *v.*^{1} + -ER^{1}.] †**1.** A mocker; a deceiver –1450. **2.** A vaunter 1869.

Gabber (gæ·bəɹ), *sb.*^{2} 1793. [f. GAB *v.*^{2} + -ER^{1}.] A chatterer.

†**Ga·bber,** *v.* 1706. [f. GAB *v.*^{2} + -ER^{5}. Cf. JABBER, GIBBER.] *trans.* To talk volubly, to jabber –1808. Hence **Ga·bber** *sb.* jabber.

Gabble (gæ·b'l), *sb.* 1601. [f. the vb.] **1.** Voluble, noisy, incoherent talk 1602. **2.** Inarticulate noises made by animals.

1. MILT. *P.L.* XII. 56. **2.** Choughs language, g. enough, and good enough *All's Well* iv. i. 22.

Gabble (gæ·b'l), *v.* 1577. [- MDu. *gabbelen*, of imit. origin.] **1.** *intr.* To talk volubly, inarticulately and incoherently; to chatter, jabber, prattle. **2.** *trans.* To utter rapidly and unintelligibly 1758. **3.** Of geese, etc.: To GAGGLE 1697.

1. To g. like Tinkers SHAKS. **3.** I..g. like a Goose, amidst the Swan-like Quire DRYDEN. Hence **Ga·bblement. Ga·bbler,** one who gabbles.

Gabbro (gæ·bro). 1837. [- It. (Tuscan) *gabbro* :- L. *glaber, glabr-* smooth.] *Geol.* A name given by Italian artists to a rock essentially composed of felspar and diallage. Hence **Gabbro·ic** *a.*

Gabelle (gabe·l). Also †**gabel(l,** †**gable,** ME. [- Fr. *gabelle* – It. *gabella*, corresp. to Sp. *alcabala*, Pg. *alcavala* – Arab. *al-ḳabāla*, i.e. *al* AL-^{2}, *ḳabāla* tribute.] **1.** A tax; *spec.* the salt-tax imposed in France before the Revolution. **2.** *attrib.* as *g.-man*, etc. 1650.

The thre estates ordenid..that the gabell of salt shulde ron through the realme LD. BERNERS. Hence **Ga·belled** *ppl.a.* liable to a tax. †**Gabe·ller,** a tax-gatherer.

Gaberdine (gæ·bəɹdīn). 1520. [Earliest form *gawbardine* – OFr. *gauvardine, gallevardine* (whence It. *gavardina*), perh. f. MHG. *wallevart* pilgrimage (cf. *pelerine* for the sense); Sp. *gabardina* is closest to the present form, which is used by SHAKS.] **1.** A loose

upper garment or frock of coarse material, worn formerly by Jews, almsmen, and beggars. **2.** *trans.* and *fig.* Dress, covering; also (see *Temp.* II. iii. 40), protection 1594.
1. You..spet vpon my Iewish g. *Merch. V.* I. iii. 113.

Gaberlunzie (gæ:bəɹlɒ·nzi, -yi). *Sc.* 1508. [Of unkn. origin; *-lunzie* = *-lunyie*, which would be pronounced (-lü·nyi).] A strolling beggar. Also, a BEADSMAN.
Barking at a g. SCOTT.

Gabion (gē[i]·biən). 1579. [– Fr. *gabion* – It. *gabbione*, augm. of *gabbia* CAGE.] **1.** A wicker basket, of cylindrical form, usually open at both ends, to be filled with earth, for use in fortification and engineering. **¶2.** Used *fig.* by Scott for a curiosity of small value 1832. **3.** *attrib.* 1633.

Gabionade (gē[i]·bioneɪ·d). Also **†gabionnade.** 1706. [– Fr. *gabionnade*, f. *gabionner*, f. *gabion*; see prec., -ADE.] A work formed of gabions.

Gabionage (gē[i]·biənėdʒ). 1864. [– Fr. *gabionnage*, f. as prec.; see -AGE.] Gabions collectively.

Gabioned (gē[i]·biənd), *ppl. a.* 1589. [f. GABION + -ED[2].] Having gabions; protected with or as with gabions.

Gable (gē[i]·b'l), *sb.*[1] [ME. *gavel, gable*, orig. of twofold origin; – (i) ON. *gafl* and (ii) OFr. *gable*, itself prob. – the ON. word; the corresp. words in the other Gmc. languages mean 'fork'.] **1.** The vertical triangular piece of wall at the end of a ridged roof, from the level of the eaves to the summit. **b.** Any architectural member having the form of a gable 1850. **2.** The triangular-topped end wall of a building; a gable-end ME. **4.** *attrib.* ME.
Comb.: *g.-roof* (hence *-roofed* adj.), *-wall*; **g.-window**, a window in the gable or gable-end of a building.

†Ga·ble, *sb.*[2] ME. Var. of CABLE *sb.*, frequent in XV-XVI. Also *fig.* Also *attrib.* –1615.

Gable (gē[i]·b'l), *v.* 1848. [f. GABLE *sb.*[1]] *trans.* To make (a roof) end in a gable; *intr.* to form gables.

Gabled (gē[i]·b'ld), *ppl. a.* 1849. [f. GABLE *sb.*[1] or *v.* + -ED.] Furnished with a gable or gables.

Ga·ble-e:nd. ME. **1.** An end-wall that is surmounted by a gable. **†2.** = GABLE *sb.*[1] 1, 1 b. –1703.

Gablet (gē[i]·blėt). ME. [– AFr. *gablet*; see GABLE *sb.*[1], -ET.] A little gable, esp. one constructed as an ornament over a tabernacle, niche, buttress, etc.

Gablock (gæ·blǫk). Now *dial.* 1688. [var. of GAVELOCK.] **†1.** An artificial metallic spur for a fighting cock (Dicts.). **2.** *dial.* An iron crowbar 1746.

Gaby (gē[i]·bi; *dial*, gǭ·bi). *colloq.* and *dial.* 1796. [Of dial. and slang origin; cf. synon. dial. *gaups*; see -Y[6].] A simpleton.

Gad (gæd), *sb.*[1] ME. [– ON. *gaddr* goad, spike, sting = OHG. *gart*, Goth. *gazds* :– Gmc. **gazdaz*; see YARD *sb.*[2]] **1.** A sharp spike of metal. Now *Hist.* **†b.** Applied to a stylus –1588. **2.** A bar of metal; also, an ingot. ?*Obs.* ME. **b.** *Mining.* A pointed tool of iron or steel; e.g. a wedge, or a small iron punch with a wooden handle 1671. **3.** A spear. *Hist.* 1548. **4.** A goad ME. **5.** *dial.* A rod or wand, esp. a fishing rod. Also, a stake. 1535. **6.** A measuring rod for land; hence, a measure of length ME. **b.** A division of an open pasture; = SWATH. 1593.
1. b. I will goe get a leafe of brasse, And with a G. of steele will write these words SHAKS. **2.** Flemish-steel is made—some in Bars and some in Gads MOXON. **4.** Phr. †*Upon the g.*: as if pricked with a g.; suddenly. *Lear* I. ii. 26.

Gad (gæd), *sb.*[2] 1815. [f. GAD *v.*[2]] The action of gadding. Only in phr. *On, upon the g.*

Gad (gæd), *sb.*[3] 1728. [– Ir. and Gael. *gad.*] *Mil.*, etc. A band or rope made of twisted fibres of rough twigs.

Gad (gæd), *sb.*[4] Now *arch.* 1611. [Minced pronunc. of GOD. Cf. EGAD, BEGAD.] **1.** Substituted for *God*; esp. in *By Gad!* **2.** quasi-interj. (?'by' omitted) 1608. **3.** In *Gadswoons*, *Gadzooks*, etc. 1695.
1. Phr. *Gads me, Gads my life*: ? God save me, my life. **2.** G., that's exceeding foolish DRYDEN.

Gad (gæd), *v.*[1] 18.. [f. GAD *sb.*[1]] **a.** *trans.* To furnish with a gad or gads. **b.** (*Mining.*) *intr.* To use a gad; *trans.* to break up (rock) by means of a gad. **c.** *trans.* To fasten with a gad-nail.

Gad (gæd), *v.*[2] 1460. [Back-formation from GADLING[2].] **1.** *intr.* To go from one place to another, to wander about; †*rarely*, to rush madly about. **2.** *fig.* To go wandering, in desire or thought. Now *rare.* 1579. **3.** Of a plant, tree, etc.: To straggle in growth (*arch.*) 1637.
1. He was alwayes gadding up and downe the world CAMDEN. **2.** Yet, idle eye, wilt thou be gadding still HEYWOOD. **3.** Wild thyme and the gadding vine MILT. Hence **Ga·ddingly** *adv.*

Gadabout (gæ·dăbaut). 1817. [f. prec. + ABOUT.]
A. *adj.* Given to gadding, wandering.
B. *sb.* One who gads about 1837.

Ga·d-bee:. 1530. [f. GAD *sb.*[1]] = GADFLY 1.

Gadder[1] (gæ·dəɹ). 1887. [f. GAD *v.*[1] + -ER[1].] An instrument for splitting rock.

Gadder[2] (gæ·dəɹ). 1550. [f. GAD *v.*[2] + -ER[1].] One who gads.

Gadding (gæ·diŋ), *vbl. sb.* 1753. [f. GAD *v.*[1] + -ING[1].] The action or process of splitting rock with gads.
Comb. **g.-car** (*Quarrying*), one which carries a drilling machine so arranged as to drill a series of holes in line.

Gade (gē[i]d). 1836. [– mod.L. *gadus* – Gr. γάδος. Cf. Fr. *gade.*] A fish of the genus *Gadus*; a codfish.

Gadean (gē[i]·dĭăn). 1854. [f. mod.L. *gadus* (see prec.) + -(E)AN.] A fish of the family *Gadidæ*, of which the typical genus is *Gadus* (cod).

Gader, obs. f. GATHER.

Ga·d-fly:. 1591. [f. GAD *sb.*[1]] **1.** The pop. name of a fly which bites and goads cattle, *esp.* a fly of the genus *Tabanus* or of the genus *Œstrus*; a bot-fly, breeze 1626. **2.** *fig.* One who torments or worries another. Also (after L. *œstrus*), an irresistible impulse. 1649.

Gadget (gæ·dʒėt). *colloq.* 1886. [Origin obsc.; orig. in nautical use.] A small tool or piece of mechanism. **b.** *gen.* An accessory or adjunct, esp. of a trivial character 1915.

Gadhelic (gădeˑlik), *a.* and *sb.* Cf. GOIDELIC. 1796. [f. Ir. *Gaedheal*, pl. *Gaedhil*, (OIr. *Góidel*; see GOIDEL); see -IC.] Pertaining to the Gaels (in the widest sense).

Gadid (gē[i]·did). 1889. [f. mod.L. *gadus*; see GADE, -ID[1].] = GADOID *sb.* So **Ga·dine.**

Gadinic (gădi·nik), *a.* 1864. [f. as prec. + -INE[1] + -IC.] *Chem.* In *Gadinic acid*: a crystalline fatty acid, obtained from cod-liver oil.

†Gaditan. 1607. [– L. *Gaditanus*, f. *Gades* Cadiz; see -AN.]
A. *adj.* Of or belonging to Cadiz –1626.
B. *sb. pl.* The inhabitants of Cadiz. var. **Gadita·nian** *a.* and *sb.*

Gadite (gē[i]·dəit), *a.* [f. L. *Gades* Cadiz + -ITE[1].] Belonging to Cadiz. SCOTT.

Gadling[1] (gæ·dliŋ). 1502. [f. GAD *sb.*[1] + -LING[1].] One of the metal spikes on the knuckles of a gauntlet.

†Gadling[2]. [OE. *gædeling* = OS. *gaduling*, OHG. *gateling*, Goth. *gadiliggs* cousin; f. Gmc. base **ʒad-*, repr. by OE. *gæd* fellowship, *ġegada* companion, rel. to GATHER.] **1.** Orig., a companion or fellow –ME. **2.** In bad sense: A 'fellow' ME. **3.** A vagabond –1565. **4.** Hence *attrib.* (in sense of 'wandering'); also as *vbl. sb.* 1594.

†Gadman. Chiefly *Sc.* 1450. [f. GAD *sb.*[1]] A goadsman –1827.

Gadoid (gē[i]·doid). 1842. [f. mod.L. *gadus*; see GADE, -OID.] **A.** *sb.* A fish of the family *Gadidæ*, of which the cod is the type. **B.** *adj.* Of, belonging to, or resembling the *Gadidæ*.

Gadolinite (gæ·dŏlinəit). 1802. [Named from *Gadolin*, a mineralogist; see -ITE[1] 2 b.] *Min.* Silicate of yttrium, found in black crystals. So **Gadoli·nic** *a.* derived from g.

Gadroon (gădrūˑn). Also in mod. Dicts. **godroon.** 1723. [– Fr. *godron*, prob. rel. to *goder* pucker, crease; see -OON.] One of a set of convex curves or arcs joined at their extremities to form a decorative pattern used in ornamenting plate, in architecture, costume, etc. Chiefly in *pl.* Also *attrib.* Hence **Gadroo·ned, godrooned** *ppl. a.* ornamented with gadroons.

Gadso (gæ·dso), *interj.* 1687. [var. of CATSO, infl. by GAD *sb.*[4]] An exclam. of asseveration.

Gaduin (gæ·diuin). 1861. [irreg. f. mod.L. *gadus*; see GADE, -IN[1].] A fatty substance found in cod-liver oil.

Gadwall (gæ·dwǫl). 1666. [Of unkn. origin.] A freshwater duck, *Anas strepera* or *Chaulelasmus streperus*, of the north of Europe and America; the grey duck or grey.

†Gaedelian, *a. rare.* [Literary formation on Sc. Gaelic *Gaidheal* GAEL; see -IAN.] Belonging to the Gaelic branch of the Celtic race. MORSE.

Gael (gē[i]l). 1810. [– Sc. Gaelic *Gaidheal* (gai·əl), corresp. to Ir. *Gaoidheal.*] A Scottish Highlander or Celt; also, in more recent use, an Irish Celt.

Gaelic (gē[i]·lik). 1774. [f. GAEL + -IC.]
A. *adj.* Of or pertaining to the Gaels or Celtic Highlanders of Scotland; occas. in wider sense, including the Irish and Manx.
B. *sb.* The Gaelic language 1775.

Gaff (gæf), *sb.*[1] ME. [– Pr. *gaf* hook, whence Fr. *gaffe* boat-hook] **1. a.** An iron hook; a staff armed with this. Now *dial.* **b.** *spec.* A barbed fishing spear; also, a stick with an iron hook for landing salmon, etc. 1656. **2.** *Naut.* 'A spar used in ships to extend the heads of fore-and-aft sails which are not set on stays' (Adm. Smyth) 1769. **3. a.** = GABLOCK 1. 1688. **b.** The spike of a spur 1808.

Gaff (gæf), *sb.*[2] *slang.* 1812. [Of unkn. origin.] **1.** Stuff and nonsense 1877. **2.** In phr. *To blow the g.*: (*fig.*) to reveal a secret or a plot.

Gaff (gæf), *sb.*[3] *slang.* 1753. [orig. thieves' slang; of unkn. origin.] **1.** A fair. **2.** Any public place of amusement. Hence, a low-class theatre or music hall. Also *penny-gaff.*

Gaff (gæf), *v.*[1] 1837. [f. GAFF *sb.*[1]] To strike or to draw *out* with a gaff.

Gaff (gæf), *v.*[2] *slang* and *colonial.* 1812. [orig. thieves' slang; of unkn. origin.] *intr.* To gamble; *esp.* to toss up.

Gaffe (gæf). 1909. Also **gaff.** [Fr.] A blunder, an indiscreet act or remark, a 'faux pas'.

Gaffer (gæ·fəɹ). 1575. [f. contracted form (ga·fəðə), resulting from loss of stress, of GODFATHER; cf. GAMMER and synon. Fr. *compère, commère*, G. *gevatter* gossip.] **1.** A term of respect prefixed to a proper name, the designation of a calling, office, etc. In XVII–XVIII = GOODMAN. **b.** = *My good fellow* 1590. **2.** An elderly rustic. Also, a fellow. 1589. **3.** A master. Now *dial.* 1659. **b.** A foreman; a headman 1841.
1. G. Bishops 1635, Phoebus 1651, Homer 1806, Glover SCOTT. **b.** I pray your blessing, g. 1628. **2.** Go to each g. and each goody 17..

†Ga·ffle. 1497. [Sense 1 prob. – Du. *gaffel* fork; the application of such a word in sense 2 (see RACK *sb.*[3] 3) is unlikely.] **1.** A steel lever for bending the cross-bow –1672. **2.** A steel spur for fighting cocks –1790.

Gaff-topsail. 1794. **1.** 'A light triangular or quadrilateral sail, the head being extended on a small gaff which hoists on the topmast, and the foot on the lower gaff' (Smyth). Also *attrib.* **2.** *U.S.* 'A kind of sea-catfish, *Ælurichthys marinus*' (Cent. Dict.).

Gag (gæg), *sb.*[1] 1553. [f. GAG *v.*[1]] **1.** Something thrust into the mouth to keep it open and prevent speech or outcry. **b.** *fig.* (Now often applied to the 'closure' in parliamentary proceedings.) 1623. **c.** *School slang.* (See quot.) 1820. **2.** *Theatr.* Matter interpolated in a written piece by the actor 1847.
1. c. The repugnance of the school to gags, or the fat of fresh beef boiled LAMB. **2.** The performance consisted of all g. MAYHEW.
Comb.: **g.-bit**, a powerful bit, used for breaking horses, etc.; **-law** (*U.S.*), 'a law or regulation made or enforced for the purposes of preventing or restricting discussion (*Cent. Dict.*); **-rein** (*Saddlery*), a rein passing through a g.-runner, so as to draw the bit upward in the horse's mouth; **-runner**, a loop depending from the throat-latch, through which the g.-rein passes to the bit.

Gag (gæg), *sb.*[2] *slang.* 1805. [f. GAG *v.*[3]] A made-up story; an imposture, a lie. **b.** *U.S.* A laughing-stock 1840.

Gag (gæg), *v.*[1] ME. [perh. imit. of the sound made by a choking person, though a poss. Scand. origin may be seen in ON. *gaghdls* with the neck thrown back.] †**1.** *trans.* To strangle. ME. only. **b.** *intr.* To choke (*lit.* and *fig.*) Also, to retch. Also *trans.* (*causatively*). Now *dial.* 1707. **2.** *trans.* To stop up the mouth of (a person) with a gag in order to prevent speech or outcry; *spec.* in *Surg.* 1509. **b.** *transf.* and *fig.*, esp. to deprive of power or freedom of speech 1601. **3.** To apply a gag-bit to (a horse); to obstruct the working of (a valve); to stop up the valves of (an engine) 1833. **4.** *Theatr. intr.* To introduce 'gag' into a piece 1852; *trans.* to fill *up* with 'gag' 1861.

2. G. him, we may haue his silence B. JONS. **b.** The time was not yet come when eloquence was to be gagged, and reason to be hoodwinked MACAULAY.

Gag, *v.*[2] 1570. [perh. of symbolic formation; cf. JAG *v.*[1], JOG *v.*, RAG *v.*[1]] †**1.** *trans.* To jerk. Also, to toss *up* (the head). –1617. †**2.** *intr.* To make thrusts or pricks (*at*) 1622; *trans.* ?to prick 1570. **3.** *intr.* To stick out. [Cf. GAG-TOOTH.] 1599.

Gag (gæg), *v.*[3] *slang.* 1777. [perh. fig. use of GAG *v.*[1] with the notion of thrusting something 'down the throat' of a credulous person.] *trans.* To impose upon (a person), to 'stuff'; *intr.* to practise imposture.

†**Gagate.** OE. [– L. *Gagates* – Gr. Γαγάτης, f. Γάγαι town in Lycia in Asia Minor. See JET *sb.*[1]] **1.** Jet –1708. **2.** Occas. used for AGATE (*Achates*). FULLER.

Gage (gēⁱdʒ), *sb.*[1] ME. [– (O)Fr. *gage* :– Rom. **gwadjo* – Gmc. **waðjam* WED *sb.* Cf. WAGE.] **1.** Something deposited to ensure the performance of some action, and liable to forfeiture in case of non-performance; a pawn, pledge 1457. **2.** *spec.* A pledge (usu. a glove thrown down) of a person's appearance to do battle in support of his assertions. Hence, a challenge. Also *g. of battle.* ME.

1. He also left Philip. .for the g. of his promises to Pelopidas RALEGH. **2.** Caste downe your g. in that quarrell, and ye shall fynde him that shall take it vp 1523.

Gage, *sb.*[2] *slang.* ME. [var. of GAUGE *sb.*] A quart pot; a quart pot full.

Gage (gēⁱdʒ), *sb.*[3] 1888. = GREENGAGE.

Gage (gēⁱdʒ), *v.* 1489. [– (O)Fr. *gager* or aphetic of ENGAGE.] †**1.** *trans.* = ENGAGE *v.* 1. –1592. **2.** To stake, wager; to risk or bet. *Obs.* or *arch.* 1599. Also *fig.* to pledge 1529. †**3.** To bind as by a formal promise –1606. **4.** *intr.* for *refl.* To assert on one's own responsibility *that* 1811. †**5.** *trans.* To fix *in* or *upon.* MOXON. †**6.** To bind or entangle *in* 1596.

1. Phr. †*To g. battle*: to pledge oneself to judicial combat. **2.** Against the which, a Moity competent Was gaged by our King *Haml.* I. i. 91. *fig.* To all which pointes I g. myne honour and faith ESSEX. **6.** The great debts Wherein my time something too prodigall Hath left me gag'd *Merch. V.* I. i. 130.

Gage, Gager, obs. ff. GAUGE, GAUGER.

Gagger[1] (gæ·gəɹ). 1621. [f. GAG *v.*[1] + -ER[1].] One who gags (see GAG *v.*[1]).

Ga·gger[2]. 1858. [perh. f. GAG *v.*[2] + -ER[1].] 'A lifter used by the founder, consisting of a light T-shaped piece of iron' (Simmonds).

Ga·gger[3]. *slang.* 1781. [f. GAG *v.*[3] + -ER[1].] One who gags, cheats, or hoaxes.

Gaggle (gæ·g'l), *sb.* 1470. [f. the vb.] **1.** A flock (of geese); also, a company (of women). **2.** Chatter, gabble 1668.

Gaggle (gæ·g'l), *v.* ME. [imit.; cf. MHG. *gāgen, gāgern* cry like a goose; Du. *gaggelen* gabble; ON. *gagl* gosling; and OHG. *gackizōn, gackazzen* (G. *gacksen*, also *gackeln, gackern*). Cf. GABBLE, CACKLE.] **1.** *intr.* Of geese: To cackle. †**2.** *transf.* and *fig.* To make a noise like geese; to gabble, chatter –1706. †**3.** *trans.* To express with gaggling or chattering; to babble. Also with *out.* –1650.

†**Gag-tooth.** 1585. [Cf. GAG *v.*[2] 3.] A projecting or prominent tooth –1680. Hence **Gag-toothed** *a.*

Gahnite (gā·nəit). 1808. [f. *Gahn*, a Swedish chemist + -ITE[1] 2 b.] *Min.* An oxide of zinc and alumina, or zinc aluminate occurring in octahedrons; called also *zinc-spinel.*

Gaiety (gēⁱ·ėti). Also, now *U.S.*, **gayety.** 1634. [– (O)Fr. *gaieté* (mod. also *gaîté*), f. *gai* GAY; see -TY[1], -ITY.] **1.** The quality or condition of being gay; cheerfulness, mirth 1647; †levity CLARENDON. **2.** Merrymaking, festivity; a festive occasion; freq. in *pl.* 1634. **3.** Bright appearance; showiness; showy dress; occas. *pl.* 1657.

1. Health and gayety of heart COWPER. **2.** The gaieties of Paris 1791. **3.** To lay aside all g. in dress 1866.

Gail(e, Gailer, -or, obs. ff. GAOL, GAOLER.

Gaillard, Gaillard-: see GALLI-.

‖**Gaillardia** (gēⁱlā·ɹdiă). 1888. [mod.L.; after M. *Gaillard*, an amateur botanist, see -IA[1].] *Bot.* A genus of composite plants, producing showy flowers, for the most part red with a border of yellow.

Gaily, gayly (gēⁱ·li), *adv.* ME. [f. GAY *a.* + -LY[2]. Usually spelt *gaily*; cf. *daily.*] In a gay manner. **1.** Brightly, showily, smartly. **2.** Cheerfully, joyously, festively; airily, jauntily ME.

1. Like some fair flow'r. .That gayly blooms POPE. To dance and sing, be gaily drest TENNYSON. **2.** Dr. Johnson was gaily sociable MME. D'ARBLAY.

†**Gain,** *sb.*[1] ME. only. [– ON. *gagn, gegn*, adj. used subst. (see GAIN *a.*).] Advantage, use, avail; remedy, help.

Gain (gēⁱn), *sb.*[2] 1473. [– OFr. *ga(a)in* (mod. *gain*) m., *ga(a)igne* (mod. †*gagne*) fem., f. *ga(a)igner* (mod. *gagner*); see GAIN *v.*[2]] †**1.** Booty, prey, spoil –1490. **2.** Increase, of possessions, resources, or advantages, consequent on some action or event; profit, emolument; opp. to *loss.* Also 'lucre', 'pelf', as an object of desire. 1496. **b.** In *pl.* Sums acquired by trade, etc.; emoluments, profits, etc. 1546. **c.** An increase in amount, magnitude, or degree. Opp. to *loss.* 1851. **3.** The action of acquiring, winning, etc. (*rare*) 1576.

2. Wythout regard of pryuate gayne and profyt 1538. Greedy as they were of g., they seldom became rich MACAULAY. **b.** Their dubious gains 1893. **c.** I was weighed yesterday and found a g. of five pounds CARLYLE.

Gain (gēⁱn), *sb.*[3] 1679. [Of obscure origin; in sense 1 poss. a use of GAIN *sb.*[2]; sense 2 may be a different word.] **1.** *Carpentry.* = TUSK. **2. a.** *Carpentry*, etc. A notch, groove, niche (?*U.S.*) 1848. **b.** *Coal-mining.* A transverse cutting made in the sides of an underground roadway 1883.

Gain, *a.* Now *dial.* OE. [– ON. *gegn* adj., straight, direct, favourable, helpful :– Gmc. **ʒaʒan-*, **ʒaʒin-*, direct, straight (cf. OE. *ġeġn* straight).] **1.** Of roads or directions: Near, straight; esp. in superl. **2.** Of persons: Ready, well-disposed, kindly ME. **3.** Of things: Available, handy, convenient ME.

1. Fur I wur a Baptis wonst. .Till I fun that it warn't not the gaäinst waäy to the narra Gaäte TENNYSON.

†**Gain,** *v.*[1] ME. [– ON. *gegna*, primarily, meet, encounter, hence, be meet, fit, or suitable, from the adj. and adv. *gegn* against, opposite to (cf. GAIN *a.*).] **1.** *intr.* To be suitable, or useful; to avail, help; to serve, suffice (*for*). Const. *dat.* of person. –1724. **2.** *trans.* **a.** To be an equipoise *to.* **b.** Of sleep: To come upon. **c.** To meet, encounter, oppose. –1500.

1. Us gayneth no raunsoun CHAUCER.

Gain (gēⁱn), *v.*[2] 1530. [– OFr. *ga(a)ignier* (mod. *gagner*) :– Rom. **gwadanjare* – Gmc. **waiþanjan* (OHG. *weidenen* graze, pasture, forage, hunt, fish), f. **waiþō* (OHG. *weida* fodder, pasture, hunting, OE. *wāþ*, ON. *veiðr* hunting).] **1.** *trans.* To obtain (something desired or advantageous) 1570. **2.** To obtain as profit; to earn, 'make' (a livelihood) 1530. Also, To obtain by way of increment or addition 1612. **3.** *absol.* or *intr.* To make a gain or profit; to be advantaged 1572; also with *in* 1841. **4.** *trans.* To acquire or reclaim (land) from the sea 1641. **5.** To obtain or win as the result of a contest; †to capture in fight 1548. **6.** To bring over to one's side, to persuade (often in bad sense, to bribe); also *to gain over* 1582. **7.** To reach, arrive at 1605; to accomplish (now *rare*) 1733.

1. To gaine pardon of the sinne to Rosemond 1595. Sirs, ye should have hearkened unto me, and not have loosed from Crete, and to have gained (? = 'gotten', as in R.V., or = 'spared', as in De Wette, etc.) this harm and loss *Acts* 27:21. Phr. *To g. time* [= Fr. *gagner du temps*]: to obtain a delay by pretexts, etc. *To g. the ear of*: see EAR *sb*[1]. *To g. the wind* (Naut.): to arrive on the weather-side of some other vessel. **2.** Lord, thy pound hath gained ten pounds *Luke* 19:16. To g. a scanty sustenance TENNYSON. **3.** To g. in moral height TENNYSON. **5.** To g. the prize COWPER. He that gain'd a hundred fights TENNYSON. **6.** I have gain'd the guard BYRON. **7.** To gayne the timely inne *Macb.* III. iii. 7.

Phrases. **1.** *To g. ground* [= Fr. *gagner du terrain*]: orig. *Mil.* to conquer ground from the enemy; hence **a.** To make progress; to acquire ascendency. **b.** *To g. ground on*: to make progress at the expense of. **c.** *To g. ground upon*: to get nearer to. **2.** *To g. on* or *upon* [= Fr. *gagner sur*]: **a.** To encroach upon (now only of the sea encroaching on the land). **b.** To come closer to some object pursued. **c.** To win favour with.

Gain (gēⁱn), *v.*[3] ?*U.S.* 1874. [f. GAIN *sb.*[3]] To mortise; to cut gains in (wood).

Gain-, *prefix*, OE. *ġeġn-, ġēan-* (see GAIN *a.*) was formerly employed to form various combinations, chiefly verbal, in the same way as AGAIN-, which was in more frequent use. Its senses are chiefly those of opposition, return, or reversal, answering to L. *re-*. These combs. are now obsolete, with the exception of GAINSAY.

Gainable (gēⁱ·năb'l), *a.* 1611. [f. GAIN *v.*[2] + -ABLE.] Capable of being gained or won over.

†**Gainage.** ME. [– AFr. *gaignage* (AL. *gai(g)nagium, wain-*), f. *gaignier*; see GAIN *v.*[2], -AGE.] **1.** Profit or produce from the tillage of land. ME. only. **2.** Husbandry. MARKHAM. **3.** In Law Dicts. of XVII–XVIII: Implements of husbandry –1706.

Gained (gēⁱnd), *ppl. a.* 1598. [f. GAIN *v.*[2] + -ED[1].] Acquired. Of time: Saved.

Gained day (Naut.): the twenty-four hours gained by circumnavigating the globe to the eastward. SMYTH.

Gainer (gēⁱ·nəɹ). 1538. [f. as prec. + -ER[1].] One who gains, or derives advantage.

Gainful (gēⁱ·nful), *a.* 1555. [f. GAIN *sb.*[2] + -FUL.] **1.** Productive of gain or profit; *esp.* pecuniary gain. **2.** Bent upon making gain; adapted to make gain (*rare*) 1870.

1. A g. undertaking 1791. A g. (= paid) occupation (chiefly *U.S.*). **Gain·ful-ly** *adv.*, **-ness.**

Gain-giving, *vbl. sb.* ME. [f. GAIN- *pref.* + GIVING *vbl. sb.*] †**1.** A giving in return. ME. only. **2.** A misgiving (*arch.*) 1602.

Gaining ((gēⁱ·niŋ), *vbl. sb.* 1874. [f. GAIN *v.*[3] + -ING[1].] The cutting of gains (see GAIN *sb.*[3]) in wood. *Comb.* **g.-machine,** a machine for cutting gains in a beam.

Gai·ning, *ppl. a.* 1642. [f. GAIN *v.*[2] + -ING[2].] That gains. Phr. *Gaining-twist*: in rifled firearms, a twist of the grooves that increases regularly towards the muzzle.

Gainless (gēⁱ·nlės), *a.* 1640. [f. GAIN *sb.*[2] + -LESS.] Producing no gain; unprofitable. Hence **Gai·nlessness.**

Gainly (gēⁱ·nli), *a.* ME. [f. GAIN *a.* + -LY[1].] **1.** Proper, becoming. *Obs.* exc. *Sc. dial.* **2. a.** Tactful. **b.** The reverse of ungainly; graceful, shapely. 1855. Hence **Gai·nliness.**

†**Gai·npain.** ME. [– OFr. *gaignepain* (XIII *wagnepan*) a sort of gauntlet. Commonly identified with the Fr. *gagnepain* 'breadwinner' (XVII, but prob. much older), but the OFr. word = gauntlet is prob. a different word.] **1.** A sort of gauntlet –1500. ¶**2.** Explained after Fr. dicts., as 'The sword of a hired soldier'. Not in Eng. use. (Dicts.)

Gainsay (gēⁱ·nsēⁱ), *sb.* 1559. [f. next.] †**a.** A moot question 1559. **b.** Contradiction 1601.

Gainsay (gēⁱ·nsēⁱ, gēⁱ:nsēⁱ·), *v.* Infl. **-saying, -said** (rarely **-sayed**). ME. [f. GAIN- *pref.* + SAY *v.* Prob. modelled on ON. *gagnmæli* gainsaying; cf. also (O)Fr. *contredire* CONTRADICT. Now only literary. In *gainsaid* the last syllable is usually (-sĕ·d), not (-sed).] **1.** *trans.* To deny. **2.** To contradict ME. **3.** To speak or act against, oppose, hinder ME. **4.** To refuse (*rare*) ME.

1. Facts which cannot be gainsayed FREEMAN. **2.** Evidence that can scarcely be gainsaid 1874. **3.** Too facil then thou didst not much g., Nay, didst permit MILT. *P. L.* IX. 1158.

Gainsayer (gēⁱ·nseⁱ,əɹ). ME. [f. prec. + -ER[1].] One who gainsays.

Such proofe. .may satisfie gaine-sayers HOOKER.

†**Gai·nsome,** *a.*[1] *rare.* 1569. [f. GAIN *sb.*[2] + -SOME[1].] Lucrative, advantageous –1646.

Gai·nsome, *a.*^{2} Now *dial.* [f. GAIN *a.* + -SOME^{1}.] Ready, prompt, ?†willing to assist. MASSINGER.

Gainst, *prep.* Also **'gainst.** 1590. Aphet. f. AGAINST. *poet.*

Gainstand (gē^{i}nstæ·nd), *v.* *Obs.* or *arch.* ME. [f. GAIN- *pref.* + STAND *v.*] *trans.* To withstand, resist.
Vtterly to impugne & g. the scripture FOXE.

†Gainstri·ve, *v.* 1549. [f. GAIN- + STRIVE *v.*] *trans.* To strive against, oppose –1590; *intr.* to make resistance –1596.

Gairfish, obs. f. GARFISH.

Gairfowl, Gairish: see GAREFOWL, GARISH.

Gait (gē^{i}t), *sb.* Also **†gate, †gaite.** 1509. [A spec. use of GATE *sb.*^{2}, q.v. The spelling *gait* was orig. Sc.] Manner of walking or stepping, carriage. **b.** *pl.*, esp. of a horse: Paces 1684. **c.** *U.S.* Rate of movement; pace.
Scarse thy legs uphold thy feeble gate SPENSER. Hence **Gai·ted** *ppl.a.* having a (specified) g., as *slow gated* (SHAKS.).

Gaiter (gē^{i}·təɹ), *sb.*^{1} 1775. [– Fr. *guêtre*, †*guietre*, †*guestre* (XV), perh. (in spite of the lateness of date) repr. **wistr-*, metathetic form of Gmc. **wirst-* (OHG. **wrist*, G. *rist* ankle) WRIST.] **1.** A covering of cloth, leather, etc. for the ankle, or ankle and lower leg. **2.** *U.S.* A kind of shoe of similar form 1864. **3.** *attrib.* 1862. Hence **Gai·ter** *v.* to dress or furnish with gaiters.

Gai·ter, *sb.*^{2} Now *dial.* OE. [Based on OE. *gāte trēow* = goat's tree.] Prop. the Dogwood (*Cornus sanguinea*); also, the Spindle-tree (*Euonymus europæus*), etc. Also *attrib.*

Gala (gē^{i}·lă). 1625. [– Fr. *gala* or its source It. *gala* – Sp. *gala* – Arab. *ḵhil'a* presentation garment.] **1.** Gala dress. Now only in phr. *in gala.* **†2.** Festivity, rejoicing –1809. **3.** A festive occasion 1800.
Comb.: **g. day**, a day of festivity, finery and show; **g. dress**, a dress for a g.; fine or showy dress; **g. meet**, a (hunting) meet attended with festivities.

Galactic (gălæ·ktik), *a.* 1839. [Sense 1 f. Gr. γάλα, γαλακτ- milk + -IC, after LACTIC; sense 2 f. Gr. γαλακτίας, var. of χαλαξίας Milky Way + -IC; see GALAXY.] **1.** Of or pertaining to milk; = LACTIC. 1844. **2.** *Astron.* Of or pertaining to the Galaxy or Milky Way 1839.
2. *Galactic circle*, the mean or centre line of the Galaxy, or Milky Way zone. *G. poles*: the two opposite points of the heavens, situated at 90° from the g. circle.

Galactin (gălæ·ktin). 1838. [f. Gr. γάλα, γαλακτ- milk + -IN^{1}.] **a.** A vegetable substance, obtained from the sap of the Cow-tree (*Galactodendron utile*) of S. America, and used as cream. **b.** 'The coagulating principle of milk' (Mayne) 1854. **c.** A gelatin-yielding substance said to exist in milk (Watts) 1864. **d.** = LACTIN (*Syd. Soc. Lex.*) 1885.

Galacto- (gălækto), bef. a vowel *galact-*, comb. f. Gr. γάλα, γαλακτ-, milk.
gala·ctagogue [+ Gr. -αγωγός] *a.*, inducing a flow of milk; also *sb.* anything that does this; **galacto·meter** [+ Gr. μέτρον] = LACTOMETER; **galacto·phagist** [Gr. γαλακτοφάγος + -IST] *a.*, milk-fed; **galacto·phorous** [Gr. γαλακτοφόρος + -OUS] *a.*, conveying milk, as the excretory ducts of the mammary gland; **gala:ctopoe·tic, -poie·tic** [+ Gr. ποιητικός] *a.*, that tends to produce milk; also *sb.* anything that does this; **galactorrhœ·a** [+ Gr. ῥοία], an excessive flow of milk.

Galactose (gălæ·ktōᵘs). 1869. [f. as prec. + -OSE^{2}. Cf. DEXTROSE.] (See quot.)
Dilute acids convert lactose into a peculiar glucose, called g. ROSCOE.

Galago (gălē^{i}·go). 1848. [– mod.L. *galago.*] A genus of *Lemuridæ*, of nocturnal habits, found in parts of Africa.

Galam butter. 1855. [f. *Galam*, on the Senegal.] A solid oil or fat which is expressed from the seeds of *Bassia butyracea*; much used as food.

Galanga (gălæ·ŋgă). 1485. [– med.L. *galanga*; see GALINGALE.] = GALINGALE.

Galantine (gæ·lăntin). ME. [– (O)Fr. *galantine*, alt. of *galatine* – med.L. *galatina.*] **†1.** A kind of sauce for fish or fowl. –1658. **2.** A dish of white meat, freed from bones, tied up, boiled, and served cold 1725.
1. Pyk walwed in galauntyne CHAUCER.

Galanty show (gălæ·nti,ʃōᵘ·ʃ). 1821. [perh. – It. *galanti*, pl. of *galante* GALLANT.] A shadow pantomime produced by throwing shadows of miniature figures on a wall or screen.

‖Galapee·. 1756. [Of unkn. origin] A W. Indian tree, *Sciadophyllum brownei.*

Galatea (gælătī·ă). 1882. [f. name of H.M.S. *Galatea*, commanded by the Duke of Edinburgh in 1867.] A cotton material striped in blue on a white ground.

Galaxy (gæ·lăksi), *sb.* ME. [– (O)Fr. *galaxie* – med.L. *galaxia*, late L. *galaxias* – Gr. γαλαξίας (sc. κύκλος circle), f. γάλα, γαλακτ- milk; see -Y^{3}.] **1.** A luminous band or track, encircling the heavens irregularly, consisting of innumerable stars, perceptible only by the telescope; the Milky Way. Also extended to other groups of stars of similar extent. **2.** *transf.* and *fig.*; now chiefly a brilliant crowd of beautiful women or distinguished persons 1590.
1. Lo, the Galaxyë Which men clepeth the Milky Wey, For hit is whyt CHAUCER. **2.** Those beauties, who form a g. around the throne of England SCOTT. Hence **Ga·laxy** *v. trans.* to gather like a g. *into* (something). C. MATHER.

Galbanum (gæ·lbănŏm). ME. [– L. *galbanum* – Gr. χαλβάνη, of Semitic origin (cf. Heb. *ḥelbᵉnāh*).] **1.** A gum resin obtained from certain Persian species of *Ferula*. **2.** *fig.* after Fr. usage: Bosh, humbug 1764. var. **†Galbane**; also **†Galban.**

Galbulus (gæ·lbiŭlŏs). 1706. [– L. *galbulus* the fruit of the cypress.] *Bot.* 'A cone when spherical, and of thickened scales with narrow base, as that of Cypresses' (Gray).

Gale (gē^{i}l), *sb.*^{1} [OE. *gagel, gagelle* = MDu. *gaghel*, Du., G. *gagel*; the present form is unexpl.] The bog-myrtle, *Myrica gale*; also *Sweet gale.*

†Gale, *sb.*^{2} ME. only. [perh. repr. two words: (1) ME. *gal* (f. *galen*, OE. *galan* sing); (2) OFr. *gale* gaiety = It. *gala*; see GALA.] **1.** Singing, a song; mirth. **2.** Speech, talk.

Gale (gē^{i}l), *sb.*^{3} 1547. [Of unkn. origin; perh. orig. *gale wind*, in which *gale* is an adj.; perh., in spite of the late date, was of Scand. origin, and to be connected with MSw., Norw. *galen* bad (of weather), ON. *galenn* mad, frantic.] **1. a.** A wind of considerable strength, implying, in naut. use, 'what on shore is called a storm' (Smyth); in pop. lit. use, 'a wind not tempestuous, but stronger than a breeze' (J.). **b.** *poet.* and *rhet.* A gentle breeze 1728. **c.** *transf.* and *fig.* 1623. **2.** *fig.* A state of excitement or hilarity. *U.S.* 1838.
1. A calme, a brese, a fresh gaile, a pleasant gayle, and a stiffe gayle CAPT. SMITH. A common brisk g. is about 15 miles an hour 1772. *Equinoctial g.* (see EQUINOCTIAL). **b.** While every g. is peace, and every grove Is melody THOMSON. **c.** Some unexpected gaile of opportunity MARVELL. The music. . Storm'd in orbs of song, a growing g. TENNYSON.

Gale (gē^{i}l), *sb.*^{4} 1640. [contr. of GAVEL *sb.*^{1}] **1.** A periodical payment of rent, the amount paid periodically 1672. **2.** An instalment (*rare* exc. *local U.S.*) 1789. **3.** In the Forest of Dean: The royalty paid for a plot of land, with the right to dig for coal, iron, or stone; a licence or grant of land for this purpose; the area granted 1775. **4.** *attrib.*, as (sense 1) *g.-day*; (sense 3) *g.-book, -fee* 1832.
Hence **Ga·leage** (sense 3), **galiage**, royalty paid for a g.

†Gale, *v.*^{1} [OE. *galan* = OHG. *galan*, ON. *gala*; cogn. w. GALE *sb.*^{2}, *-gale* in NIGHTINGALE; cf. YELL.] **1.** *intr.* and *trans.* To sing –1480. **2.** *intr.* Of a dog: To bark, yelp. Of a bird: To utter its note. –1560. **3.** *transf.* To make an outcry. ME. only.
1. '*Domine labia*' gan he crye and g. 1480. **3.** Thogh that the Somnour g. CHAUCER.

Gale (gē^{i}l), *v.*^{2} 1692. [f. GALE *sb.*^{3}] *Naut.* To sail *away* before a gale.

Gale (gē^{i}l) *v.*^{3} 1832. [f. GALE *sb.*^{4}] To grant or take the gale of a mine.

Galea (gē^{i}·lĭă). 1706. [– L. *galea* helmet.] **1.** *Bot.*, *Zool.*, etc. Any structure resembling a helmet in shape, function, or position; e.g. the upper part of a labiate flower; the membrane covering the jaws of the Orthoptera and some other insects; etc. 1834. **2.** *Med.* **a.** A headache which 'takes in the whole Head like a helmet' (Phillips) 1706. **b.** A kind of bandage for the head 1854.

Galeas(s(e, obs. ff. GALLIASS.

Galeate (gæ·lĭĕt), *a.* 1706. [– L. *galeatus*, f. *galea* helmet; see -ATE^{2}.] = GALEATED 1, 2.

Galeated (gæ·lĭe^{i}tĕd), *ppl. a.* 1686. [f. as prec. + -ED^{1}.] **1.** Shaped like a helmet. **2.** *Zool.* Covered as with a helmet 1728. **3.** Furnished with a helmet; wearing a helmet 1760. Also *fig.*
3. The g. head of Minerva 1879.

Galeeny (gălī·ni). 1796. [– Sp. *gallina* (*morisca*) '(Moorish) hen' (so in Pg. and It.) – L. *gallina*; the ending assim. to -Y.] A guinea-fowl.

Galeid (gē^{i}·lĭid). [– mod.L. *Galeidæ*, f. *Galeus* = Gr. γαλεός, name of the typical genus; see -ID^{3}.] A shark of the family *Galeidæ* (*Cent. Dict.*). Hence **Gale·idan** = prec.

Galen (gē^{i}·lĕn). Also **†Galien.** 1598. [– L. *Galenus* (in med.L. also *Galienus*) – Gr. Γαληνός.] A celebrated physician of the 2nd century A.D., born at Pergamus in Asia Minor. Hence joc.: A physician.
What saies my Esculapius? my Galien *Merry W.* II. i ii. 29. Hence **Gale·nian** *a.* = GALENIC *a.*^{1} **Ga·lenism**, the medical principles or system of G.

Galena (gălī·nă). Also **†galæna.** 1671. [– L. *galena* lead at a certain stage of smelting (Pliny).] *Min.* Native lead sulphide; the common lead ore. *False* or *pseudo-g.* = BLACK JACK 2. Also called *lead glance.*

Galenic (găle·nik), *a.*^{1} 1668. [f. GALEN + -IC.] Of or pertaining to Galen, to his followers, to his principles and practice; *esp.* pertaining to vegetable preparations, as dist. from chemical remedies. Also *joc.*: Medical. *G. figure* (Logic): see GALENICAL.

Galenic (găle·nik), *a.*^{2} 1828. [f. GALENA + -IC.] Pertaining to or containing galena. (Dicts.)

Galenical (găle·nikăl). 1652. [f. GALENIC *a.*^{1} + -AL^{1}; see -ICAL.]
A. *adj.* = GALENIC *a.*^{1}
G. figure (Logic): the fourth syllogistic figure, added by Galen. Hence **Gale·nically** *adv.* with g. or vegetable remedies.
B. *sb.* A galenical or vegetable remedy, a simple 1768.

Galenist (gē^{i}·lĕnist). 1594. [f. GALEN + -IST.] A follower of Galen. So **†Ga·lenite**^{1}.

Galenite^{2} (gălī·nəit). 1868. [f. GALENA + -ITE^{1} 2 b.] *Min.* = GALENA.

Galenoid (gălī·noid). 1882. [f. GALENA + -OID.]
A. *adj.* Resembling galena 1884.
B. *sb. Crystall.* The Trigonal Trisoctahedron. (The form occurs most freq. in galena, hence the name.)

Galeod (gē^{i}·lĭǫd). 1868. [– Gr. γαλεώδης; see next.] *Ichth.* A shark.

Galeoid (gē^{i}·lĭoid), *a.* 1847. [– Gr. γαλεοειδής, f. γαλεός a kind of shark; see -OID.] **a.** *Ichth.* Resembling a shark or dog-fish. **b.** *Entom.* Belonging to the arachnidans of the family *Galeodidæ.*

Galeopithecus (gē^{i}:lĭopiþī·kŏs). 1835. [mod.L., f. Gr. γαλέη marten-cat + πίθηκος ape.] A flying lemur.

Galericulate (gæ:lĭᵊri·kiŭlĕt), *a.* 1706. [f. L. *galericulum* (dim. of *galerum* cap) + -ATE^{2}.] *Bot.* = GALEATE.

Galerite (gălīᵊ·rəit). 1828. [– mod.L. *galerites*, f. *galerum* cap; see -ITE^{1} 2 a.] A fossil sea-urchin of the genus *Galerites.* (Dicts.)

†Ga·lianes, *sb. pl.* [f. *Galien* GALEN.] 'Drinks named after Galen' (Skeat). CHAUCER.

Galilean (gælilī·ăn), *a.*^{1} and *sb.* 1611. [f. L. *Galilæa* (Gr. Γαλιλαία *Galilee*) + -AN.]
A. *adj.* Of or belonging to Galilee, in Palestine 1637.
The Pilot of the G. lake MILT.
B. *sb.* A native or inhabitant of Galilee; used by pagans as a contemptuous designation of Christ, and hence as = 'Christian'. Also, a member of a fanatical sect which arose in Galilee in the 1st c.
Are not all these which speake, Galileans *Acts* 2:7. And dying, *Thou hast conquered,* he said, *Galilean* SWINBURNE.

Galilean (gælilī·ăn), *a.*^{2} 1727. [f. *Galileo* the astronomer + -AN.] Epithet of the form of telescope invented by Galileo.

Galilee (gæ·lilī). 1593. [– OFr. *galilée* – med.L. *galilea*, a use of the proper name of a province of Palestine. See GALLERY.] A porch or chapel at the entrance of a church. Also *attrib.*

Galimatias (gælimæ·tiăs, gælimē[i]·ʃ[i]ăs). 1653. [– Fr. *galimatias* (Montaigne), of unkn. origin.] Confused language, meaningless talk, gibberish. Also *transf.*

transf. Her dress, like her language, is a g. of several countries H. WALPOLE.

Galingale (gæ·lingē[i]l). OE. [– OFr. *galingal* – (prob. through Arab. *ḵalanjān*, Pers. *ḵūlinjan*, Skr. *kulañjana*) Chinese *ko liang kiang* 'mild ginger of Ko' (a district of Canton). Cf. med.L., med.Gr., It. *galanga* (Fr. *galangue*); see GALANGA.] **1.** The aromatic root of certain East Indian plants of the genera *Alpinia* and *Kæmpferia*, formerly used in medicine and cookery. Hence, †a dish seasoned with galingale. BEAUM. & FL. **2.** An English species of sedge, *Cyperus longus*, sometimes dist. as 'English galingale', the root of which is also aromatic 1578.

2. Many a..meadow, set with slender g. TENNYSON.

Galiot: see GALLIOT.

Galipot (gæ·lipǫt). Also **gallipot.** 1791. [– Fr. *galipot*, also †*garipot* kind of pine XVI (cf. Pr. *garapot* pine-tree resin).] The turpentine or resin which exudes from, and hardens upon, the stem of certain pines.

Galipot, obs. f. GALLIPOT.

Galium (gē[i]·liǒm). 1548. [– mod.L. *galium* – Gr. γάλιον BEDSTRAW 2.] *Bot.* = BEDSTRAW 2.

Gall (gǭl), *sb.*[1] [– ON. *gall* n., corresp., with variety of gender, to OE. *ġealla*, OS. *galla* (Du. *gal*), OHG. *galla* (G. *galle*) :– Gmc. **ȝallam*, **ȝallon*, *-ōn*; cogn. w. Gr. χολή, χόλος, L. *fel* bile.]

I. 1. The secretion of the liver, bile. Now applied only to that of the lower animals, esp. to *ox g.* (see OX). Used as the type of an intensely bitter substance. Also *fig.* **2.** The gall-bladder and its contents ME. **3.** Bitterness of spirit, asperity, rancour (supposed to have its seat in the gall) ME. †**b.** Spirit to resent injury or insult –1680. **4.** *U.S. slang.* Assurance, impudence 1890.

1. *fig.* For I perceive that thou art in the g. of bitterness *Acts* 8:23. **2.** The drie coler with his hete, By wey of kinde his propre sete Hath in the galle, where he dwelleth GOWER. **3.** Full of mirth without g. HOLINSHED. **b.** †*To break one's g.*: to break the spirit, cow.

II. *transf.* †**1.** Poison, venom –1450. **2.** *G. of the earth* [L. *fel terræ*], the Lesser Centaury, from its bitterness 1567. **3.** The scum of melted glass [Fr. *fiel de verre*]; see GLASS-GALL.

Comb.: **g.-bladder**, the vessel in the animal system which contains the g. or bile; **-duct, -pipe,** the tube through which the g. passes †**-sickness,** a form of intermittent fever, common in the Netherlands.

Gall (gǭl), *sb.*[2] [– MLG., MDu. *galle* (Du. *gal*), corresp. to OE. *ġealla* sore on a horse, (M)HG. *galle*, ON. *galli* (MSw. *galle*) fault, flaw, perh. identical with GALL *sb.*[1], the progress of sense being 'bile', 'venom', 'envenomed sore', 'blemish'.] **1.** Orig., A painful swelling, pustule, or blister, esp. in a horse (cf. WINDGALL). Later, a sore produced by rubbing or chafing. **2.** *fig.* Something galling; a state of mental soreness or irritation 1591. †**3.** A person or thing that harasses. SPENSER. †**b.** Galling effect. HALL. **4.** A place rubbed bare; an unsound spot, fault or flaw. Now only *techn.* 1545. **5.** A bare spot in a field or coppice 1573. †**6.** Filth, impurity; *fig.* refuse. ME. only.

2. They did great hurt unto his title, and have left a perpetuall g. in the myndes of that people SPENSER. **3. b.** The smart, and gaules of the arrowes HALL.

Gall (gǭl), *sb.*[3] ME. [– (O)Fr. *galle* :– L. *galla* (Pliny) oak-apple, gall-nut.] **1.** An excrescence produced on trees, esp. the oak, by the action of insects, chiefly of the genus *Cynips*. Oak-galls are largely used in the manufacture of ink and tannin, as well as in dyeing and in medicine. **2.** *attrib.* esp. in the names of insects producing galls, as *g.-beetle, -gnat, -insect*, etc. 1759.

Comb.: **g.-apple** = sense 1; **-leaf,** a leaf on which a g. is formed; **-oak,** †**-tree,** the oak (*Quercus infectoria*) upon which are produced the galls of commerce; **-steep,** 'a bath of nutgalls, for the process of galling in Turkey-red dyeing' (Cassell).

Gall (gǭl), *v.*[1] ME. [Back-formation from GALLED *ppl. a.*[2]] **1.** *trans.* To make sore by rubbing or chafing. **2.** To fret or injure (inanimate objects) by rubbing or contact 1600. †**3.** To break the surface of (ground, soil); to fret or wash *away* –1691. **4.** *fig.* To vex, harass, oppress 1614. **5.** To harass or annoy in warfare 1548. **6.** *intr.* To become sore or chafed 1614.

1. My Horse..gall'd under the Saddle-Bow 1696. **2.** The Gabriell..had her Cable gauld asunder with a piece of driuing yce HAKLUYT. **4.** Neckes..gawled with the yoke of forraine dominion RALEGH. Galled by narrow circumstances BOSWELL. †*To g. at* (intr.): To scoff at *Hen. V*, v. i. 77. **5.** With shot of the English archers were so curried and galled that they were driuen to retire HOLINSHED.

Gall (gǭl), *v.*[2] 1581. [f. GALL *sb.*[3]] *Dyeing.* To impregnate with a decoction of galls.

Gallant (gæ·lănt, gălæ·nt). ME. [– (O)Fr. *galant*, pres. pple. of *galer* make merry, make a show, f. *gale* merry-making, rejoicing; see -ANT. Cf. GALE *sb.*[2], GALA.]

A. *adj.* **1.** Showy in appearance, finely-dressed, smart (*arch.*). †**2.** Of women: Fine-looking –1650. †**3.** Suited to fashionable society; polished, courtier-like –1645. **4.** *loosely*: Excellent, splendid, fine, grand. Now *rare.* 1539. **b.** Of a ship: Noble, stately 1583. **5.** Chivalrously brave, nobly daring 1596. **b.** A conventional epithet of a military or naval officer 1875. **6.** (Usu. *galla·nt.*) Markedly polite and attentive to ladies 1680. **7.** (Usu. *galla·nt.*) Of or pertaining to love, amorous, amatory. Now *rare.* 1673.

1. Garments of Cotten exceeding g. 1578. **3.** Such g. pastyme STUBBES. **4.** A stable of g. horses DE FOE. **b.** Our royall, good, and g. Ship *Temp.* v. i. 237. **5.** Our galant countryman, Sir Philip Sydney STEELE. **b.** The hon. and g. gentleman 1875. **6.** Th' antique Sage, that was g. t' a Goose S. BUTLER. *Comb.* †**g.-springing** *a.*, 'growing up in beauty' (Schmidt).

B. *sb.* **1.** A man of fashion and pleasure; a fine gentleman. (Occas. with added notion of A. 5.) *arch.* ME. †Of a woman: A fashionably dressed beauty –1662. †**2.** As a courteous mode of address, *esp.* in pl.; = 'Gentlemen'. Also used playfully. –1810. **3.** (Occas. *galla·nt.*) A ladies' man (now *rare*). Also, a lover; (in bad sense) a paramour. 1450. †**4.** *Naut.* A name formerly applied to 'all flags borne on the mizen-mast' (Smyth).

1. She would fain be a g. PEPYS. **3.** How few nowadays use the word 'gallant' to describe a lady's man M. ARNOLD.

Hence **Ga·llantness,** the state or quality of being g.

Gallant (gălæ·nt, gæ·lănt), *v.* 1608. [f. the adj.]

I. (?stressed *ga·llant.*) **1.** *intr.* To play the gallant, 'cut a dash'. †**2.** To make gallant or fine 1614.

II. (Usu. *galla·nt.*) **1.** *intr.* To play the gallant, flirt 1744. **2.** *trans.* To play the gallant to, flirt with 1672. **3.** *esp.* To act as cavalier or escort to (a lady) 1690; to conduct, escort, convey 1806. †**4.** *To g. a fan*: To handle or manipulate it 1711.

3. Young Ranter talks to her, gallants to her coach, follows her home 1690. The little black steamer..sometimes gallanting a tall ship in and out HAWTHORNE.

Gallantly (gæ·lăntli, gălæ·ntli), *adv.* 1552. [f. GALLANT *a.* + -LY[2].] In a gallant manner: showily 1552; splendidly, finely 1552; bravely, heroically 1590; with courtesy or politeness (now only as regards women) 1611.

Gallantry (gæ·lăntri). 1606. [– Fr. *galanterie*, f. *galant*; see GALLANT *a.* and *sb.*, -ERY.] †**1.** Gallants collectively –1688. †**2.** Splendour, magnificence –1801. †**b.** An elegant practice or habit –1720. †**c.** *concr.* in *pl.* Knick-knacks –1720. **3.** Bravery, heroic bearing 1647. †**b.** A brave deed –1711. †**4.** Excellence –1657. **5.** Courtliness or polite attention to ladies 1675. **6.** A courtesy 1673. **7.** The occupation or behaviour of a gallant 1632. **8.** Amorous intercourse or intrigue 1678; †an intrigue –1750.

1. Hector..and all the g. of Troy SHAKS. **2.** The old men..who could call to minde the greatness and g. of the former [Temple] FULLER. **3.** The unpremeditated g. of a soldier 'JUNIUS'. **6.** The prince..said a thousand gallantries DRYDEN. **8.** She was not without a charge of g. T. HUTCHINSON.

Gallate (gæ·lēt). 1794. [f. GALLIC *a.*[2] + -ATE[4].] *Chem.* A salt of gallic acid.

†**Ga·llature.** [– It. *gallatura*, f. *gallare* fecundate (an egg), f. *gallo* cock.] The germ in an egg. SIR T. BROWNE.

Galleass: see **Galliass.**

Galled, *ppl. a.*[1] *nonce-wd.* 1604. [f. GALL *sb.*[1] + -ED[2].] Mixed with gall, made bitter.

Galled (gǭld), *ppl. a.*[2] OE. [orig. f. GALL *sb.*[2] + -ED[2], but later as if f. GALL *v.*[1] + -ED[1].] **1. a.** Affected with galls or painful swellings. **b.** Sore from chafing. Often with defining word, as *saddle-g.*, etc. **2.** *fig.* Irritated, unquiet, distressed 1601. **3.** Of land: Having bare patches 1881.

Gallein (gæ·lī,in). 1885. [irreg. f. GALLIC *a.*[2] + -IN[1].] A brown-red powder, or small green crystals, obtained by heating pyrogallol and phthalic anhydride. Used as a dye.

Galleon (gæ·liǒn). 1529. [– MDu. *galjoen* – (O)Fr. *galion*, augm. of *galie* GALLEY or – Sp. *galeon*; see -OON.] A kind of vessel, shorter but higher than the galley; a ship of war, esp. Spanish; also, the large traders used by the Spaniards. **b.** *fig.* A great prize or catch 1706.

We took a Galloon, And the Crew touch'd the Agent for cash to some tune C. DIBDIN.

Gallery (gæ·lĕri), *sb.* 1500. [–(O)Fr. *galerie* – It. *galleria* gallery, †church porch – med.L. *galeria* (IX), perh. alt. of *galilea* GALILEE by dissim. of *l..l* to *l..r.*] **1.** A covered space for walking in, partly open at the side, or having the roof supported by pillars; a piazza, portico, colonnade. **2.** A long, narrow platform or balcony, constructed on the outside of a building, at some elevation from the ground, and open in front except as having a balustrade 1509. **b.** A similar passage on the roof of a house 1535. **c.** *Arch.* A long narrow passage either made in the thickness of a wall, or supported on corbels, open towards the interior of a building 1756. **d.** *Naut.* A balcony built outside the body of a ship, at the stern (*stern-gallery*), or at the quarters (*quarter-gallery*) 1627. **3.** A platform, supported by columns or brackets, projecting from the interior wall of a building; *esp.* **a.** in churches 1630; **b.** in a theatre (now *spec.* of the highest of such platforms, containing the cheapest seats) 1690. **4.** *transf.* **a.** The occupants of the gallery portion of a theatre, the 'gods'; formerly often in *pl.* Hence *fig.* the less instructed portion of the public. 1649. **b.** The body of persons who occupy a public gallery in a senatorial chamber 1817. **5.** A long narrow corridor 1541. **6.** An apartment or building for the exhibition of works of art 1591. **7.** *Mil.* and *Mining.* An underground passage; a level or drift 1631. **b.** *Mil.* 'A covered walk, the sides whereof are musket-proof' 1704. **8.** †A passage made by a deer, etc. through brushwood 1674; also, a passage made by an animal underground, or through a rock 1849. **9.** *Tennis.* *Winning-gallery*, the opening most remote from the dedans 1699. **10.** An ornamental parapet or railing running along the edge of a table, shelf, or the like 1853. **11.** *attrib.* 1480.

2. Our old coaching inns, with their roomy yards and railed galleries 1894. **3.** Phr. *Ladies'-, members'-, press-, strangers'-g.* (in a senatorial chamber). **b.** The people were cracking nuts in the g. DICKENS. **4. a.** Phr. *To play to* (or *for*) *the gallery*: to address oneself to those in the g. (also *fig.*). **6.** For in my G. thy Picture hangs 1 *Hen. VI*, II. iii. 37. **8.** The..galleries made by Crustaceans MURCHISON.

Comb.: **g.-hit,** a piece of showy play (primarily in *Cricket*) intended to gain applause from the uncritical; **-shot, -stroke** (cf. *g.-hit*).

Hence **Ga·llery** *v.* to furnish with a g. or balcony; *Mil.* to make an underground passage.

Galley (gæ·li), *sb.* [– OFr. *galie* (mod. *galée*) – med.L. *galea* (IX), med.Gr. γαλαῖα, of unkn. origin, but rel. to Fr. *galère*, ON. *galeið*, med.L. *galera*, *galeda*, *-ida.*] **1.** A low flat-built sea-going vessel with one deck, propelled by sails and oars, formerly in common use in the Mediterranean. Cf. GALLIASS. The rowers were mostly slaves or condemned criminals. **2.** Applied to the Greek or Roman warships, large vessels with one or more banks of oars 1513. **3.** A large open row-boat, e.g.

one formerly used on the Thames by custom-house officers, and by the press-gang (Smyth); also, a large pleasure-boat 1570. **4.** The cooking-room or kitchen on a ship. Also, a ship's cooking-range. 1750. **5.** *Printing.* [Fr. *galée.*] An oblong tray of brass, wood, or zinc, to which the type is transferred from the composing stick 1652. **6.** [= Fr. *galère.*] An oblong furnace, used to heat stone-ware bottles in the distillation of aqua fortis 1789. **7.** *attrib.* 1599.

1. Phr. *To condemn*, or *send, to the galleys*, also simply *the galleys*, the punishment of a galley-slave.

Comb.: **g.-arch**, a covered structure in Mediterranean ports for the reception of galleys; **-house** = *g.-arch*; **-packet**, a made-up story, lie, yarn; **-press**, 'a small hand-press for pulling proofs in slip form' (Jacobi); **-proof**, a proof in slip form so taken; **-slip** = *g. proof*; **-stick**, one of the long side-sticks used for quoining up galleys.

Ga·lley-man. ME. [f. GALLEY *sb.* + MAN.] **1.** One who rows in a galley. **†2.** A name formerly given to traders, esp. Genoese, from beyond the sea, who 'usually arrived in galleys' –1706.

Galleypot, obs. f. GALLIPOT.

Ga·lley-slave. 1567. [f. GALLEY *sb.* + SLAVE *sb.*] **1.** One condemned to row in a galley. Often *fig.* **†2.** *Printing.* A nickname for a compositor 1683.

†Galley-tile. 1610. [f. GALLEY *sb.* + TILE *sb.*; see GALLIPOT.] A glazed tile used for wall-decoration. Also *collect.* the material of which these are made. –1768.

It is to be known of what stuff galletyle is made BACON.

Galleyworm, gallyworm (gæ·liwɒ̄ɹm). 1658. [f. GALLEY *sb.* + WORM *sb.*, from the resemblance to an oared galley.] An insect of the class *Myriapoda*; an iulus.

Gall-fly (gǭ·lˌfləi). 1822. [f. GALL *sb.*[3]] An insect (esp. of the genus *Cynips*) which produces galls on trees.

Galliambic (gæliæ·mbik). 1846. [f. L. *galliambus* a song of the *Galli* or priests of Cybele (f. *Gallus* + IAMBUS) + -IC.]

A. *adj.* Epithet of a lyric meter (founded on the Ionic a minore tetrameter catalectic, with anaclasis), supposed to have been used by the priests of the Phrygian Cybele in their songs 1876.

B. *sb.* The galliambic metre; a verse written in this metre 1846.

The G. of Catullus may be a relic..of Phrygian poetry LANDOR.

†Gallian (gæ·liăn), *a.* 1591. [f. L. *Gallia* Gaul + -AN.] Gallic, French. Also as *sb. pl.* –1630.

Galliard (gæ̆·liăɹd), *a.* and *sb.*[1] ME. [– (O)Fr. *gaillard*, perh. f. Rom. **gallia* strength, power, of Celtic origin (cf. Ir. *gal*, W. *gallu* be able, valour, prowess); see -ARD. The sb. B. 2, 3 is – Fr. *gaillarde*, subst. use of the fem. adj.]

A. *adj.* **1.** Valiant, 'stout', sturdy (*arch.*). **2.** Lively, brisk, gay (*arch.*) ME. **†3.** Spruce –1605.

2. There lives not..a more frank, galiard, and supine people EVELYN. Hence **†Ga·lliardness.**

B. *sb.* **1.** †A man of courage and spirit –1658; a man of fashion (*arch.*) 1768. **2.** *Hist.* A quick and lively dance in triple time 1533. **†3.** The music for this dance –1674.

2. Why dost thou not goe to Church in a G. SHAKS. Never a hall such a g. did grace SCOTT.

Galliard (gæ·liăɹd), *sb.*[2] 1875. [Of unkn. origin.] *Geol.* A name for very siliceous sandstones with an even close grain.

Galliardise (gæ·liăɹdəi:z). Also **-ize.** *arch.* 1570. [– Fr. *gaillardise*, f. *gaillard*; see GALLIARD *sb.*[1]] Gaiety, mirth, revelry; a merry trick.

No way..disposed for the mirth, and g. of company 1643.

Galliass, galleas (gæ·liǣs). Now *Hist.* 1544. [– OFr. *gal(l)easse* (mod. *galéace*) – It. *galeaza*, augm. of *galea* GALLEY.] A heavy, low-built vessel, larger than a galley, impelled both by sail and oars, chiefly employed in war.

A first-rate galley, otherwise called a galleasse FALCONER.

Gallic (gæ·lik), *a.*[1] and *sb.* 1672. [– L. *Gallicus*, f. *Gallus*, *Gallia* Gaul; see -IC.]

A. *adj.* **a.** Of or pertaining to the Gauls or Gaul; Gaulish 1796. **b.** Often used rhet. or joc. for 'French'.

B. *sb.* A Frenchman 1755.

Gallic (gæ·lik), *a.*[2] 1791. [– Fr. *gallique*, f. *galle* GALL *sb.*[3]; see -IC.] *Chem.* In *g. acid*: a crystalline acid prepared from the oak-gall, etc.

Gallican (gæ·likăn). 1598. [– Fr. *gallican*, †(1) French, (2) pertaining to the Church of France, or L. *Gallicanus*, f. *Gallicus*; see GALLIC *a.*[1], -AN.]

A. *adj.* **a.** *gen.* = GALLIC *a.*[1] **b.** *Eccl.* (= med.L. *Gallicanus*), distinctive epithet of the ancient Church of Gaul or France, and of its characteristic usages, liturgies, etc. Hence applied to that school of French Roman Catholics which maintains the right of the French Church to be in certain respects free from papal control; opp. to *Ultramontane.* 1633.

b. This more correct Psalter..obtain'd first in Gaul about 580..From which circumstance it came to have the name of G., in contradistinction to the Roman WATERLAND.

B. *sb.* A member of the Gallican party in the French Church 1882.

Hence **Ga·llicanist,** one who favours Gallicanism. **Ga·llicanism,** the principles and practice of the G. party.

Gallicism (gæ·lisiz'm). 1656. [– Fr. *gallicisme* (H. Estienne); see GALLIC *a.*[1], -ISM.] **1.** A French idiom or mode of expression, esp. one used by a speaker or writer in some other language; also, free use of French idiom. **2.** A French characteristic, custom, mode of thought, or the like 1715.

1. His [H. Walpole's] style is..deeply tainted with Gallicisms MACAULAY.

Gallicize (gæ·lisəiz), *v.* 1773. [f. L. *Gallicus* + -IZE.] **1.** *intr.* To become Gallic or French in habits, speech, etc. 1775. **2.** *trans.* To render French-like 1773.

Galliform (gæ·lifǭɹm), *a.* [– mod.L. *galliformis*, f. L. *gallus* cock + *forma* form.] *Ornith.* Belonging to the *Galliformes*, an order of birds, including ostriches, gallinaceous birds, rails, cuckoos, and parrots (*rec.*).

Galligaskin (gæ:ligæ·skin). Now chiefly in *pl.* 1577. [Various early forms may point to ult. deriv. from Fr. †*garguesque*, var. of †*greguesque* – It. *grechesca*, subst. use of fem. of *grechesco*, f. *greco* Greek; but the origin of *galli-* remains unknown.] **1.** A kind of wide hose or breeches worn in the 16th or 17th c.; later, a jocose term for loose breeches in general. Also *attrib.* **2.** Leggings, gaiters (*dial.*) 1859. **3.** A variety of the Cowslip (*Primula veris*) 1629.

Gallimatia(s, obs. f. GALIMATIAS.

Gallimaufry (gælimǭ·fri), *sb.* 1551. [– Fr. *galimafrée* (OFr. *calimafrée*), of unkn. origin.] **1.** A hash of odds and ends of food; a hodge-podge, a ragout (*rare* exc. *dial.*) 1591. **2.** *transf.* and *fig.* A ridiculous medley 1551. **3.** *attrib.* 1630.

1. Lattin whole-meats are nowe minc'd, and serude in for English Gallimafries DEKKER. **2.** That G. of Prophesies 1668. A compound of Player, Soldier, Stroller, Sailor, and Tinker! An odd g. ! 1781.

Gallinacean (gæ:linē̆ⁱ·ʃⁱăn). 1842. [f. as next + -AN.]

A. *adj.* = next.

B. *sb.* A bird of the order *Gallinaceæ* or *Gallinæ*.

Gallinaceous (gæ:linē̆ⁱ·ʃəs), *a.* 1783. [f. L. *gallinaceus* (f. *gallina* hen, f. *gallus* cock) + -OUS; see -ACEOUS.] **1.** Of or belonging to the order *Gallinæ*, which comprises the ordinary domestic fowls, pheasants, partridges, etc. **2.** *joc.* 'Cocky' 1879; consisting of fowls 1885. So **Ga·lline** *a.* (*rare*).

Gallinaginous (gæ:linæ·dʒinəs), *a.* 1876. [f. mod.L. *gallinago*, *-gin-* woodcock (f. *gallina* hen) + -OUS.] Of or pertaining to a woodcock.

Gallinaginous crest, transl. of L. *caput gallinaginis*, lit. 'woodcock's head'; the prominent fold of the lining membrane in the prostatic portion of the urethra.

Gallinazo (gæ:linā·zo). 1760. [– Sp. *gallinazo*, augm. of *gallina* hen; see prec.] An American vulture (*Cathartes aura* or *Catharista atrata*).

Galling (gǭ·liŋ), *ppl. a.* 1583. [f. GALL *v.*[1] + -ING[2].] Chafing, irritating, harassing (*lit.* and *fig.*).

Between two g. fires MCCARTHY. *fig.* G. mortifications 1820. Hence **Ga·lling-ly** *adv.*, **-ness.**

Ga·llini:pper. *U.S.* 1818. [Of unkn. origin.] A large mosquito.

Gallinule (gæ·liniul). 1776. [– mod.L. *gallinula*, the name of the genus, dim. of L. *gallina* hen; see -ULE.] Book-name for a genus of birds, typified by the moor-hen (*Gallinula chloropus*). Also used of allied genera.

Galliot (gæ·liŏt). Also **†galiot.** See also GALLIVAT. ME. [– (O)Fr. *galiote* – It. *galeotta*, dim. of med.L. *galea* GALLEY; see -OT[1].] **1.** A small galley or boat, propelled by sails and oars, used for swift navigation; in Eng. applied specially to Mediterranean vessels. **2.** [Du. *galjoot.*] A Dutch cargo-boat or fishing-vessel 1794. **3.** Used of ancient Roman vessels (?*Obs.*) 1718.

Gallipot (gæ·lipǫt). 1465. [Cf. GALLEY-TILE, etc. The first part is perh. identical with GALLEY *sb.* Thus etymologically = pottery brought in *galleys*, i.e. from the Mediterranean. The Du. synonym *gleipot* is a century later, and by some *glei* is taken as a var. of *galei* GALLEY *sb.*] **1.** A small earthen glazed pot, *esp.* one used by apothecaries for ointments, etc. Also *transf.* and *fig.* **2.** Hence *joc.* An apothecary 1785.

Gallium (gæ·liɒ̆m). 1875. [– mod.L. *gallium*, said to be f. L. *gallus* cock, tr. the name of its discoverer, *Lecoq* de Boisbaudran; see -IUM.] *Min.* A soft, tough, bluish-white metal, easily melted, discovered by M. *Lecoq* de Boisbaudran in a zinc-blende from the Pyrenees.

Gallivant (gælivæ·nt), *v.* 1823. [perh. fantastic alt. of GALLANT *v.* as used locally.] *intr.* To gad about, esp. with persons of the other sex. Also = FLIRT.

†Gallivat. 1613. [– Pg. *galeota* through East Indian channels; cf. GALLIOT.] A large boat used in Eastern seas, having oars and a triangular sail –1862.

Galliwasp (gæ·liwǫsp). 1725. [Of unkn. origin.] A small W. Indian lizard (*Celestus occiduus*).

Gallize (gæ·ləiz), *v.* Also **gallisize.** 1888. [From Dr. L. *Gall* of Treves, who invented the process; see -IZE.] *trans.* To treat (unfermented grape-juice) with water and sugar, so as to increase the quantity of wine produced.

Gall-nut (gǭ·lˌnɒt). 1572. [f. GALL *sb.*[3]] = GALL *sb.*[3] 1.

Gallo- (gæ·lo), comb. f. L. *Gallus*, a Gaul.

1. In cl. Latin only in *Gallo-græci*, Gauls who went east and settled in Asia Minor; also *Gallo-græcia*, Galatia. **2.** Used with the sense 'Gallic' (i.e. French); as in **Ga:llo-Ce·ltic** *a.*, belonging to the Celts of France; also in **Ga·lloman** [– Fr. *Gallomane*] = *Gallomaniac*; **Galloma·nia** [Gr. -μανία], unreasoning attachment to France or to what is French; whence **Galloma·niac**; **Ga·llophil** [Gr. -φίλος], a friend of France and of what is French; **Gallo·philism; Gallopho·be** [Gr. -φόβος], one affected with Gallophobia; **Gallopho·bia** [Gr. -φοβία], morbid dread of the French, or of what is French.

Galloglass (gæ·lǒglas). Also **†gallow-.** Now *Hist.* 1515. [– Ir., Gael. *gallóglach*, f. *gall* foreigner + *óglach* youth, servant, warrior, f. *óg* young + *-lach*, abstr. suffix.] **1.** One of a particular class of soldiers or retainers formerly maintained by Irish chiefs. **2.** In the Highlands: = HENCHMAN 2. 1703.

Gallon (gæ·lən). [– ONFr. *galon*, var. of *jalon* :– Rom. **gallone*, f. base of med.L. *galleta* (whence OFr. *jaloie* liquid measure), *galletum* (whence OE. *ġellet* dish, basin, OHG. *gellita*, G. *gelte* pail, bucket), perh. of Celtic origin.] An English cubic measure of capacity. The imperial gallon contains 277¼ cubic inches; the wine-gallon of 231 inches is the standard in U.S. **b.** As a dry measure for corn, bread, etc. 1584.

Me were leuere slepe, Than the beste galon wyn in Chepe CHAUCER.

Galloon (gălū̆·n). 1604. [– Fr. *galon*, f. *galonner* trim with braid; of unkn. origin; see -OON.] A kind of narrow, close-woven ribbon or braid, of gold, silver, or silk thread, used for trimming articles of apparel; a trimming of this.

A Negro Boy..with a broad brimm'd white Hat, edged with Silver G. 1681. Hence **Galloo·ned** *a.*

Gallop (gæ·ləp), *sb.* 1523. [– OFr. *galop*, f. *galoper*; see next, also WALLOP *sb.*] **1.** The most rapid movement of a horse, etc., in which in each stride the animal is entirely off the ground, with the legs flexed under the body. Hence, a ride at this pace. **2.** *transf.* and *fig.* 1651.

2. Horace is always on the amble, Juvenal on the g. DRYDEN. Phr. *False g.*: orig. a canter; now only *fig.* *Full g.*: the extreme pace of a horse; also used *advb.*; also *fig.*

Gallop (gæ·ləp), *v.* 1523. [– OFr. *galoper*; see WALLOP *v.*] **1.** *intr.* Of a horse, etc: To go at a gallop (see GALLOP *sb.* 1) 1533. **2.** *intr.* Of a horseman: To ride at full speed 1523. **3.** *trans.* To make (a horse etc.) go at full speed 1533. †**4.** To traverse (a space) rapidly by means of horses. *Tit. A.* II. i. 7. **5.** *transf.* and *fig.* (from senses 1, 2) 1583. †**6.** To dance a GALOP –1826. **7.** *trans.* To convey rapidly by means of galloping horses 1882.

2. Up the hill Gallopt the gallant three hundred TENNYSON. **3.** Never g. Pegasus to death POPE. **5.** They g. fast that deils and lasses drive A. RAMSAY. Phr. *To g. away*: to talk fast. *To g. over* or *through*: to hurry over, read cursorily. **7.** We galloped the left gun at it 1882.

Gallopade (gælŏpēˑd), *sb.* Also **galopade.** 1753. [– Fr. *galopade*, f. *galoper*, see prec., -ADE. Cf. GALOP *sb.*] **1.** A lively dance, of Hungarian origin 1831. **2.** *Manège.* A side-long or curveting kind of gallop. Hence **Gallopa·de** *v. rare*, to dance a g.

Galloper (gæ·ləpəɹ). 1576. [f. GALLOP *v.* + -ER[1].] **1.** One who, or that which, gallops, esp. a galloping horse. **2.** *Mil.* An aide-de-camp, or orderly officer 1871. **3.** *fig.* One who proceeds at great speed. Also, a gadabout. 1671. **4.** A light field-gun, formerly attached to regiments; also *attrib.* in *g. carriage, -gun* 1746.

Galloping (gæ·ləpiŋ), *ppl. a.* 1641. [f. GALLOP *v.* + -ING[2].] That gallops, in senses of the vb.

Phrases. *Galloping consumption*: a consumptive disease that makes rapid progress. *G. nun*: a temporal religious pensioner, without any vows. *G. carriage* (Mil.) = 'galloper carriage'; see GALLOPER 4.

Gallo-tannate (gæ:loˌtæ·nĕt). 1864. [f. next + -ATE[4].] *Chem.* A compound of gallo-tannic acid with a base.

Gallo-tannic (gæ:loˌtæ·nik), *a.* 1858. [f. *gallo-*, taken as comb. f. L. *galla* GALL *sb.*[3] + TANNIC.] *Chem.* In *gallo-tannic acid*, tannic acid prepared from nut-galls.

Gallow, obs. f. GALLY *v.*, to frighten.

Galloway (gæ·lŏweⁱ). 1597. [A district in the S.W. of Scotland.] **1.** One of a small but strong breed of horses peculiar to Galloway. Also *g.-mare, -nag.* Also *attrib.* **2.** One of a breed of cattle peculiar to Galloway 1805.

Gallows (gæ·loᵘz). [– ON. *gálgi*, also *gálgtré* gallows-tree = OE. *ġ(e)alga*, OFris. *galga*, OS., OHG. *galgo* (Du. *galg*, G. *galgen*), Goth. *galga* :– Gmc. **ʒalʒon*.] **1.** An apparatus for execution by hanging, usually two uprights and a cross-piece, from which the criminal is suspended by the neck. (Orig. both sing. and pl. were used for 'a gallows'; later, the pl. *gallows* became the prevailing form, and is now used as a sing., with pl. *gallowses.*) OE. **2.** The punishment itself 1483. **3.** One deserving of the gallows 1588. **4.** Anything consisting of two or more supports and a cross-piece; e.g. in *Printing*, †'a frame used for supporting the tympans of the old wooden presses when turned up' (Jacobi) 1512. **5.** 'Suspenders' for trousers; braces. Now *dial.* 1730.

1. Let them make a galowe of fiftye cubites hie COVERDALE *Esther* 5:14. Who doth he [Time] gallop withal?..With a theefe to the gallowes SHAKS. Make bonfires of the gallowses 1673. **2.** Phr. *To have the gallows in one's face*: to have the look of one predestined to be hanged. His complexion is perfect Gallowes SHAKS. **3.** 'Now, young g.!' DICKENS.

Comb.: **g.-bitts,** a strong frame of oak about eight inches square, made in the form of a gallows, and fixed at the fore and main hatchway, to support spare top-masts, yards, etc.; also called *gallows*; †**-clapper** = G.-BIRD; **-foot,** the space immediately in front of the gallows; **-ripe** *a.*, ready to be hanged; **-top** = *gallows-bitts.*

Gallows (gæ·loᵘz, gæ·ləs), *a.* ME. [f. the sb. used attrib.] **1.** Fit for the gallows; villainous, wicked. Now only *dial.*; Impish, wild. **2.** *dial.* and *slang.* As an intensive: Very great, 'fine', etc. 1789.

1. *Gallows air* = *hangdog air*: see HANGDOG *a.*

Gallows (gæ·loᵘz, gæ·ləs), *adv. dial.* and *slang.* 1823. [f. the sb.] Extremely, very.

Gallows-bird (gæ·ləzˌbɔ̄ɹd). 1785. [f. GALLOWS *sb.* + BIRD.] One who deserves to be hanged.

Ga·llows-tree. [OE. *ġalg-trēow*, Northumb. *galga-trē* (– ON. *gálgatré*), f. *ġ(e)alga* gallows + *trēow* tree.] **1.** = GALLOWS *sb.* 1. OE. †**2.** An iron support for a pot over a kitchen fire 1590.

Gall-stone (gǭ·lˌstōᵘn). 1758. [f. GALL *sb.*[1] + STONE.] A morbid calculous formation in the gall-bladder.

†**Ga·lly,** *a.*[1] or *sb.* used *attrib.* 1567. [In *gally slopes* (Harman), *breeches, hose*, recorded slightly earlier than, and synon. with, GALLIGASKINS.] In *g. breeches, hose, slops*, app. = GALLIGASKINS. –1622.

Gally (gǭ·li), *a.*[2] ?*Obs.* 1530. [f. GALL *sb.*[1] + -Y[1].] Gall-like, bitter. Chiefly *fig.*

Gally (gǭ·li), *a.*[3] Now *dial.* ME. [f. GALL *sb.*[2] + -Y[1].] **1.** Having galls or sores. ME. only. **2.** Full of bare or wet places 1602.

Gally (gæ·li), *v.* Also †**gallow.** 1605. [repr. OE. *āgælwan* terrify, of unkn. origin.] *trans.* To frighten, daze, scare. Now only *dial.* and in the whale fishery. *Comb.* **g.-** (also **galli-**) **crow,** a scarecrow.

Galoch(e, obs. f. GALOSH.

Galoot (gălū·t). *slang.* 1812. [Of unkn. origin.] **1.** *Naut.* 'A soubriquet for the young or "green" marine' (Smyth). **2.** *U.S.* An awkward or uncouth fellow: often used playfully 1866.

Galop (gæ·lǫ̆p). 1837. [– Fr. *galop* (see GALLOP *sb.*), also *galope.*] A lively dance in $\frac{2}{4}$ time.

†**Galopin.** Also **gall-.** 1567. [– Fr. *galopin*, f. *galoper* gallop.] A turnspit; an errand-boy; a page –1824.

Galore (gălōᵊ·ɹ). 1675. [– Ir. *go leór* or *lór* (= Gaelic *gu leóir*), i.e. *go* to, *leór* sufficiency; prob. popularized by Scott.]

A. *adv.* In plenty.

B. *sb.* Abundance.

Galosh, golosh (gălǫ·ʃ, gŏlǫ·ʃ), *sb.* Also †**galoche.** ME. [–(O)Fr. *galoche*, repr. (with abnormal phonetic development) late L. *gallicula* (Jerome), dim. of L. *gallica* (Cicero), subst. use, sc. *solea* shoe, of *gallicus* GALLIC *a.*[1], prob. 'Gaulish sandal'.] **1. a.** In early use: A patten or clog. **b.** In later use: An over-shoe worn in wet or dirty weather. **2.** A piece of leather running round the lower part of a boot or shoe above the sole 1853.

1. a. Ne were worthy to unbokel his galoche CHAUCER. Hence **Galo·sh, golo·sh** *v.* to furnish with a g.

†**Galp,** *v.* ME. [perh. an expressive alt. of GAPE *v.*; survives as (dial.) *gaup, gawp.*] **1.** *intr.* To gape, yawn –1532. Also *transf.* and *fig.* **2.** *trans.* To vomit *forth* –1558. ¶**3.** Of an animal: To yelp. CAXTON.

Galt (*Geol.*): see GAULT.

Galumph (gălɒ·mf), *v.* 1872. [Invented by C. L. Dodgson (Lewis Carroll) in 'Through the Looking-glass', 1871; a 'portmanteau' word combining *gallop* and *triumphant.* Cf. CHORTLE.] *intr.* To march exultingly with irregular bounding movements. Hence **Galu·mphing** *ppl. a.* (*lit.* and *fig.*).

Galvanic (gælvæ·nik), *a.* 1797. [f. as next, after Fr. *galvanique.*] Of, pertaining to, or produced by galvanism. Also *fig.* with allusion to the effects produced by galvanism.

fig. A sort of g. grin HAWTHORNE. Phr. *G. battery*, an apparatus for the production of galvanic electricity. *G. belt*, a belt containing a galvanic apparatus to be worn round the body. *G. electricity* = GALVANISM. *G. pile*, a pile consisting of thirty pieces of silver, and as many of zinc, with pieces of cloth that were dipped in a saturated solution of common salt. Hence **Galva·nical,** *a.*, **-ly,** *adv.*

Galvanism (gæ·lvăniz'm). 1797. [– Fr. *galvanisme*, f. the name of Luigi *Galvani*, who first described the phenomenon in 1792; see -ISM.] Electricity developed by chemical action. Also, the use of this therapeutically. Hence **Ga·lvanist,** one versed in g. **Ga:lvani·stical** *a.* of, pertaining to, or versed in g.

Galvanization (gælvănəizēⁱ·ʃən). 1860. [f. GALVANIZE *v.* + -ATION.] **1.** The process of applying galvanism to. **2.** The being galvanized. Also *fig.* 1875.

Galvanize (gæ·lvănəiz), *v.* Also **-ise.** 1802. [– Fr. *galvaniser*; see GALVANISM, -IZE.] **1.** *trans.* To apply galvanism to; to stimulate by means of a galvanic current. Also *fig.* **2.** To cover with a coating of metal by means of galvanic electricity. Commonly but incorrectly applied to the coating of iron with zinc. 1839.

1. *fig.* Her approach always galvanized him to new and spasmodic life C. BRONTË.

Phr. *Galvanized iron*, trade name of iron coated with zinc. Hence **Ga·lvanizer.**

Galvano- (gæ·lvăno), comb. f. GALVANIC or GALVANISM.

galvano-caustic *a.*, relating to the use of galvanic heat as caustic; **-cauterization,** cauterization by means of the galvano-cautery; **-cautery,** a cautery heated by galvanism; **-magnetic** *a.*, pertaining to galvano-magnetism; **-magnetism,** magnetism produced by galvanic electricity; **-puncture,** the introduction into the tissues of fine needles, connected with the poles of a galvanic battery; **-therapeutics,** the use of galvanism for the treatment of disease; **-thermometer,** 'an instrument for measuring the heating effect of a galvanic current' (Cassell).

Galvanograph (gæ·lvănogrɑf). [f. GALVANO- + -GRAPH.] 'A plate formed by the galvanographic process; an impression taken from such a plate' (Ogilvie). Hence **Ga:lvanogra·phic** *a.* pertaining to galvanography.

Galvanography (gælvănǫ·grăfi). 1854. [f. as prec. + -GRAPHY.] **a.** 'A method of producing plates for copperplate engraving by the galvanoplastic process without etching' (Ogilvie). **b.** A process by means of which plastic objects may be exactly copied in copper, and bronzed or gilt 1854.

Galvanology (gælvănǫ·lŏdʒi). 1848. [f. as prec. + -LOGY.] A treatise on galvanism, or a description of its phenomena. So **Galvano·logist,** one who describes the phenomena of galvanism.

Galvanometer (gælvănǫ·mĭtəɹ). 1802. [f. as prec. + -METER.] An apparatus for determining the direction and intensity of a galvanic current. Hence **Ga:lvanome·tric, -al** *a.* pertaining to the g., or to galvanometry. **Galvano·metry,** the measurement of galvanic currents.

Galvanoplasty (gæ:lvănoˌplæ·sti). 1870. [f. as prec. + -PLASTY.] The process of coating any substance with metal by galvanism. Hence **Ga:lvanopla·stic** *a.* of or pertaining to g.

Galvanoscope (gæ·lvănoskōᵘ:p). 1832. [f. as prec. + -SCOPE.] An instrument for ascertaining the presence of galvanic electricity. Hence **Ga:lvanosco·pic** *a.* pertaining to, or of the nature of, a g. **Galvano·scopy,** the employment of galvanism in physiological experiment. Also, the use of the g.

Galvano·tropism. 1885. [f. GALVANO- + Gr. τρόπος turning + -ISM.] *Bot.* The phenomenon of curvature produced in growing plant-organs by the passage of electric currents through them.

Galwegian (gælwī·dʒiăn). 1774. [f. *Gal(lo)way*, after *Nor(ro)way, Norwegian.*]

A. *adj.* Belonging to Galloway.

B. *sb.* An inhabitant or native of Galloway.

Gam (gæm), *sb.* 1850. [perh. dial. var. of GAME *sb.*] A herd or school of whales; also, a social meeting of whalers at sea.

Gam (gæm), *v.* 1851. [Cf. prec.] **1.** *intr.* Of whales: To gather together and form a school 1889. **2.** *trans.* Of whalers: To meet and gossip with (another ship). Also *intr.*

Gama grass (gā·măˌgrɑ:s). Also **gamma.** 1858. [perh. alt. f. GRAMA.] A tall and strong fodder grass, the *Tripsacum dactyloides* of Linnæus, native of the south-eastern coasts of N. America.

Gamash (gămæ·ʃ), *arch.* and *dial.*; chiefly in *pl.* 1596. [– Fr. *gamache* – mod.Pr. *gamacho, garamacho* – Sp. *guadamaci* kind of ornamental leather – Arab. *ġadāmasī*, f.

Ghadāmas, a town in Tripoli where an esteemed kind of leather was made.] A kind of leggings or gaiters, worn to protect the legs from mud and wet.

‖**Gamba**[1] (gæ·mbă). [Late L. *gamba* hoof; hock, leg. See JAMB.] *Anat.* 'The elongated metacarpus or metatarsus of the Ruminants and Solipeds.' BRANDE.

Gamba[2] (gæ·mbă). 1598. [Short for VIOL DA GAMBA.] **1.** = VIOL DA GAMBA. Also *gamba viol.* **2.** An organ-stop, resembling a violoncello in tone 1869.

Gambade (gæmbē^i·d). 1821. [– Fr. *gambade* – It. *gambata*, f. *gamba* leg; see -ADE. See GAMBADO[2], GAMBOL.] A leap or bound of a horse; also *fig.* a prank, frolic.

Gambado[1] (gæmbē^i·do). Chiefly in *pl.* **-oes, -os.** 1656. [f. It. *gamba* leg + -ADO.] A kind of large boot or gaiter, attached to the saddle, to protect the rider's legs and feet.

His thin legs tenanted a pair of gambadoes, fastened at the side with rusty clasps SCOTT.

Gambado[2] (gæmbē^i·do). Chiefly in *pl.* **-os, -oes.** Also more correctly **gambadas.** 1820. [– Sp. *gambada*, f. *gamba* leg; see -ADO.] **1.** = GAMBADE. **2.** A fantastic movement; a caper 1859. **3.** *fig.* Any sudden or fantastic action 1857. Hence **Gamba·do** *v. intr.* to prance, caper.

Gambeson (gæ·mbĭsǝn). Now *Hist.* ME. [– OFr. *gambeson*, f. *gambais*, prob. – OFrank. *wamba* belly (see WOMB).] A military tunic of leather or thick cloth, sometimes padded; worn esp. in the 14th c., under the habergeon, but sometimes without other body-armour.

Gambet (gæ·mbėt). 1776. Anglicized f. next.

‖**Gambetta** (gæmbe·tă). 1678. [mod.L. – It., f. *gamba* leg.] *Ornith.* The name of a bird somewhat resembling the Redshank. Now used for the Ruff.

Gambier (gæ·mbiǝɹ). Also **gambeer, gambir.** 1830. [– Malay *gambir* (the decoction is called *getah gambier*; cf. GUTTA-PERCHA).] An astringent extract prepared from an Eastern plant (*Uncaria gambir*), and largely used for tanning and dyeing.

Gambist (gæ·mbist). 1823. [f. GAMBA[2] + -IST.] *Mus.* A performer on the viola da gamba.

Gambit (gæ·mbit). 1656. [In XVI–XVIII *gambett* – It. *gambetto* tripping up, f. *gamba* leg (cf. JAMB); first recorded in 1561 by the Spaniard Ruy Lopez in the form *gambito*, *whence* Fr. *gambit* (XVIII), which was the form finally established in Eng.] *Chess.* A method of opening the game, in which a pawn or piece is sacrificed for position. Also *fig.*

fig. The Widow's g. was played, and she had not won the game 1860.

Gamble (gæ·mb'l), *sb.* Chiefly *colloq.* 1823. [f. GAMBLE *v.*] **1.** An act of gambling 1879. **2.** Any course involving risk and uncertainty.

Gamble (gæ·mb'l), *v.* 1775. [prob. continuing †*gamel* (XVI) play games, sport, alteration (with assim. to -LE) of †*gamene*, early form of GAME *v.*] **1.** *intr.* To play games of chance for money; to stake money on some chance. Also *fig.* **b.** To speculate recklessly 1884. **2.** *trans.* To stake 1885; with *away*: To lose by gambling 1808.

1. *fig.* Gambling against the world for life or for death CARLYLE. **2.** Bankrupts and sots, who have gambled or slept away their estates 1808. Hence **Ga·mbler,** †a fraudulent gamester, a sharper; one who habitually plays for money.

Gamboge (gæmbō^u·dʒ, -bū·dʒ). 1712. [– mod.L. *gambaugium*, var. of *cambugium*, *-bugia*, *-bogia*, f. *Cambodia*, name of a district in Assam whence the substance is derived.] **1.** A gum-resin obtained from trees of the genus *Garcinia*, natives of Cambodia, Siam, etc. It is largely used as a pigment, giving a bright yellow colour, and also as a drastic purgative. **2.** *attrib.*, as *g.-yellow*, etc. 1837. Hence **Gambo·gian** *a.* g.-coloured.

Gambogic (gæmbō^u·dʒik), *a.* Also **gambodic, cambogic.** 1839. [f. GAMBOGE + -IC.] Only in *gambogic acid*, a resin which is the chief constituent of gamboge.

Gambol (gæ·mbǒl), *sb.* 1503. [Earliest form *gambad(e* – Fr. *gambade* (see GAMBADE); the extant forms show the foll. development, *gambade*, *gambaude*, *gambauld*, *gambold*, *gambol* (XVII).] †**1.** The bound or curvet of a horse (*rare*) –1533. **2.** A leap or spring in dancing or sporting; a caper, frisk. Now chiefly *pl.*, of the sportive movements of children or animals. 1513. **b.** *transf.* and *fig.* in *pl.* Frolicsome movements or proceedings. Rarely *sing.*, a frolic. 1596. †**3.** A plaything –1630. †**4.** *attrib.* Playful –1664.

2. b. Those crisped snakie golden locks Which makes such wanton gambols with the winde SHAKS.

Gambol (gæ·mbǒl), *v.* Infl. **gambolled** (-bǒld), **gambolling** (in U.S. often with single *l*). 1507. [f. prec., after Fr. *gambader.*] †**1.** *intr.* Of a horse: To bound or curvet (*rare*) –1533. **2.** To leap or spring, in dancing or sporting; now chiefly of animals or children 1508. Also *transf.* and *fig.* 1602.

2. *fig.* A nation, gamboling in an ocean of superfluity BURKE.

Ga·mbrel. Now *dial.* See also CAMBREL. 1547. [– ONFr. *gamberel*, f. *gambier* forked stick, f. *gambe*, var. of *jambe* leg; see JAMB, -REL.] 1547. **1.** = CAMBREL 1. **2.** = CAMBREL 2. 1601. **3.** *U.S.* Short for *gambrel roof* 1859. *Comb.* **g. roof,** a curved or hipped roof, so called from its resemblance to the shape of a horse's hind leg; hence *g.-roofed* adj.

Gambroon (gæmbrū·n). 1831. [Presumably f. *Gambroon*, a town on the Persian Gulf.] 'A kind of twilled cloth for linings' (Simmonds.)

Game (gē^i m), *sb.* [OE. *gamen*, *gomen* = OFris. *game*, *gome*, OS., OHG., ON. *gaman*; has been regarded as identical with Goth. *gaman* fellowship, (tr. Gr. κοινωνία), f. Gmc. *ʒa- Y- + MAN.] **1.** Amusement, fun, sport. *Obs.* exc. *dial.* †**2.** Jest, as opp. to *earnest.* Also (with *a*), a jest. –1626. **3.** An amusement, diversion. †Also *collect.*, play. ME. †**b.** *spec.* Amorous play. *Tr. & Cr.* IV. v. 63. **c.** *colloq.* A 'lark' 1838. **4.** A diversion of the nature of a contest, played according to rules, and decided by superior skill, strength, or good fortune ME. **b.** *Gr.* and *Rom. Antiq.* Usu. *pl.* (= L. *ludi*): Athletic, dramatic, and musical contests; gladiatorial and other shows ME. **c.** *The game:* the proper method of play 1889. **5.** *fig.* A proceeding, scheme, intrigue, undertaking, followed up like a game ME. **b.** A person's policy; also, the course best suited to one's interests 1698. **c.** *pl.* Tricks, dodges 1660. **6.** A definite portion of play in any GAME (sense 4); 'a match at play' (J.) ME. **b.** Position or advantage in play 1677. **c.** The course or event of a game. Also *fig.* 1827. †**7.** The winning position, the victory, the mastery; also, the prize –1621. **8. a.** A 'set' of players 1741. **b.** *pl.* In trade use: Apparatus for games 1895. **c.** The number of points required for winning. **d.** The state of the game 1898. †**9.** Sport derived from the chase –1719. **10.** The quarry ME. **b.** *transf.* and *fig.* An object of pursuit; an object in view 1573. **11.** *collect.* Wild animals or birds such as are pursued, caught or killed in the chase ME. **b.** The flesh of such animals used for food 1848. **12.** A flock or herd of animals kept for pleasure. *Obs.* exc. in *a g. of swans* 1482. **13.** The characteristics of a game-fowl; spirit for fighting, pluck, endurance. Also predicatively of a person possessing these qualities. 1747. **14.** Short for *game-fowl* 1867.

1. *L. L. L.* V. ii. 360. **2.** *Mids. N.* I. i. 240. Phr. *To make* (†*a*) *g. of*: to make fun of, turn into ridicule. **3.** A wilde pleiere of someres gamenes WYCLIF. **c.** 'Oh, here's a g.', whispered the rest of us HUGHES. **4.** A g. in which there was an agreeable mingling of skill and chance GEO. ELIOT. Phr. *Round g.* (see ROUND *a.*). **c.** He..is not playing the g. 1889. **5.** Alva..resolved to play his g. warily 1650. No man ever knew better how to play a waiting g. WOLSELEY. **b.** In the present state of things, it [a battle] is more Buonaparte's g. than mine MOORE. Phr. *The same old g.* **6.** A Rubber is two games won out of three 1862. Phr. *The game is up* = is lost. *To force the g.* (see FORCE *v.*[1]). *G. and g.*: one g. to each side. (*To play*) *a good*, *a poor*, etc. *g.*: to be a good, a poor, etc., player. **c.** France..held the g. in her hands HALLAM. **9.** 3 *Hen. VI*, IV. v. 11. **10.** Hearke, the G. is rows'd..The G. is vp *Cymb.* III. iii. 98, 107. **b.** Phr. *Fair g.*: a legitimate object of pursuit, attack, etc.; also *forbidden g.* I fly at higher g. MARRYAT. **11.** Sanguinary laws were enacted to preserve the g. GOLDSM. **b.** G. every day THACKERAY. **13.** Phr. *Cock of the g.*: = GAME-COCK. The fifth..died all g. and bottom BYRON.

Comb. **1.** General: as *g.-bird*, *-pie*, etc.; *g.-preserver*, *-stealer*, etc.

2. Special: **g.-act,** an Act of Parliament regulating the killing of g.; **-bag,** a bag for holding the g. killed by a sportsman; **gameball** (Tennis), the position in which one side requires a single point to win; **g. bantam,** a bantam of a fighting breed; **-cast** (*Bowls*), a ball placed so as to make sure of the g.; **-certificate** = *game-licence*; **-hole,** the last hole on a cribbage-board; **-licence,** a licence to kill or deal in g.; **-tenant,** one who rents the shooting or fishing of an estate; **-trespass,** trespassing in pursuit of g.

Game (gē^i m), *a.*[1] 1727. [f. the sb. (sense 13).] Having the spirit of a game-cock; full of pluck, showing fight; spirited. **b.** Having the spirit or will *for* or *to do* (something) 1856.

She [the mare] was evidently g. to the backbone 1851. Phr. *To die g.*: to meet death resolutely; *fig.* to maintain one's pluck to the last. The ruffian lay perfectly still and silent. 'He's gaun to die g., ony how', said Dinmont SCOTT.

Game (gē^i m), *a.*[2] 1787. [Of unkn. origin; cf. dial. synon. *gammy.*] Of a leg or arm: Lame. Also *transf.*

Game (gē^i m), *v.* [A new formation f. the sb. (XIII), distinct from OE. *gam(e)nian*, which continued till XVI in *gamening*. Cf. GAMMON *sb.*[3]] **1.** *intr.* To play, sport, jest; to amuse oneself; *occas.* to indulge in amorous play. Now *dial.* †**2.** *trans.* To amuse, please. ME. only. **3.** *intr.* To play at games of chance for a prize, stake, or wager; to gamble 1510. **b.** With *away*, etc.: To get rid of (money, etc.) by gambling 1634.

3. 'Tis a great pity he..games so deep SHERIDAN.

Ga·me-cock. 1677. [f. GAME *sb.* + COCK *sb.*[1]] A cock of the breed used in cock-fighting.

Ga·me-fowl. 1784. [f. GAME *sb.* + FOWL *sb.*] **a.** A fowl of some species regarded as game. **b.** A domestic fowl of the species used in cock-fighting 1867.

†**Ga·meful,** *a.* ME. [f. GAME *sb.* + -FUL.] **1.** Joyful, playful, sportive, jesting –1725. **2.** Fond of field sports 1704. **3.** Abounding in game –1704. Hence **Ga·mefully** *adv.*

Ga·mekee:per. 1670. [f. GAME *sb.* + KEEPER.] A servant employed to take care of game, prevent poaching, etc.

Ga·me-law. 1714. [f. GAME *sb.* + LAW *sb.*[1]] Usu. *pl.* Laws enacted for the preservation of game.

Gameless (gē^i·mlės), *a.* 1848. [f. GAME *sb.* + -LESS.] Destitute of game.

Gamely (gē^i·mli), *adv.* 1861. [f. GAME *a.*[1] + -LY[2].] With spirit, pluckily.

Gameness (gē^i·mnės). 1810. [f. GAME *a.*[1] + -NESS.] Game quality; endurance, pluck.

Gamesome (gē^i·msǝm), *a.* ME. [f. GAME *sb.* + -SOME[1].] Full of play; frolicsome, sportive.

The Shepherd..piping to his Flocks and g. Kids THOMSON. Hence **Ga·mesome-ly** *adv.*, **-ness.**

Gamester (gē^i·mstǝɹ). 1553. [f. GAME *sb.* + -STER.] †**1.** A player at any game; also, an athlete –1775. **b.** *dial.* (Berks.) A player at backsword or wrestling 1857. **2.** A gambler. Also *fig.* 1553. †**3.** A merry, frolicsome person –1613. †**4.** One addicted to amorous sport; a lewd person –1668. **5.** The keeper of a 'game' of swans. *Hist.* 1880.

2. The G...Oft risks his fortune on one desperate throw GOLDSM. **3.** *Hen. VIII*, I. iv. 45. **4.** *All's Well*, V. iii. 188. Hence **Ga·mestress,** a female g.

Gamete (gæmī·t). 1886. [– mod.L. *gameta* – Gr. γαμετή wife, γαμέτης husband, f. γάμος marriage.] *Biol.* A sexual protoplasmic body which on conjugation with another gives rise to a body called zygote. Also in comb. f. **gameto-,** as **gametophyte,** the sexual form of a thallophyte, as dist. from the sporophyte, or asexual form.

Hence **Ga·metal** *a.* of or pertaining to a g.; conjugating, reproductive. **Ga·metange** [Gr. ἀγγεῖον vessel], the cell or organ in which gametes are produced.

Gamgee (gæ·mdʒi). 1895. The name of S. *Gamgee* (1828–86) used *attrib.* in *Gamgee tissue*, or *absol.*, to designate an absorbent cotton-wool for dressing wounds.

Gamic (gæ·mik), *a.* 1856. [– Gr. γαμικός, f. γάμος marriage; see -IC.] **1.** *Biol.* Having a sexual character; sexual 1864. **2.** *Geom.* *G. edges*, corresponding edges of an autopolar polyhedron. Also as *sb.*

Gamin (gamæ̃n). 1840. [– Fr. *gamin.*] A neglected boy, left to run about the streets; a street Arab.

There are the little gamin smocking him THACKERAY.

Gaming (gē[i]·miŋ), *vbl. sb.* 1501. [f. GAME *v.* + -ING[1].] **1.** Gambling. †**2.** *Gr.* and *Rom. Antiq.* The celebration of games (see GAME *sb.* 4 b) –1606. **3.** *attrib.* 1589.

Gamma (gæ·mă). ME. [Gr. γάμμα.] **1.** The third letter of the Greek alphabet, Γ, γ. †**2.** = GAMUT. –1825. **3.** A common moth, *Plusia gamma*. In full *g. moth.* 1869. **4.** *Comb.* **gamma rays** (or **γ-rays**), specially penetrating rays emitted by radioactive substances.

‖**Gammadion** (gămē[i]·diǫn). Also **gammation.** 1848. [Late Gr. γαμμάδιον, f. γάμμα (prec.).] = FYLFOT.

Gammarid (gæ·mărid). 1852. [– mod.L. *Gammaridæ*, f. L. *gammarus* (*cammarus*) – Gr. κάμμαρος a sea-crab or lobster; see -ID[3].] *Zool.* An individual of the family *Gammaridæ* of amphipodous crustacea, of which the typical genus is *Gammarus*. So **Gamma·rolite,** a fossil crustacean of the genus *Gammarus* or some allied genus.

Gammer (gæ·məɹ), *sb.* 1575. [prob. reduction of GODMOTHER (cf. GAFFER), but a sp. *gandmer* (XVI) shows assoc. with GRANDMOTHER.] A rustic title for an old woman, corresponding to GAFFER for a man.

Gammon (gæ·mən), *sb.*[1] 1486. [– ONFr. *gambon* (mod.Fr. *jambon*) ham, f. *gambe* leg; cf. JAMB.] †**1.** The ham or haunch of a swine. Also *transf.* –1613. **2.** The bottom piece of a flitch of bacon; also, a smoked or cured ham 1529.

Gammon (gæ·mən), *sb.*[2] 1689. [perh. identical with prec., the allusion being to the tying up of a gammon or ham (cf. Fr. *gambes* (*de hune*) futtock shrouds).] *Naut.* The lashing of the bowsprit. Now usu. GAMMONING.

Gammon (gæ·mən), *sb.*[3] 1730. [app. survival of *gamen* GAME *sb.*, esp. as repr. in inflected forms such as (pl.) *gamenes* XIII–XVI, and vbl. sb. *gam(e)ning*, *gamner* gamester, gambler (XVI), f. OE. *gamenian*. See GAME *v.*] **1.** The game of backgammon. Now *rare*. **2.** A term of backgammon, denoting a victory in which the winner removes all his men before the loser has removed any; it scores equal to two 'games' 1735.

Gammon (gæ·mən), *sb.*[4] *slang* or *colloq.* 1720. [perh. f. prec., orig. in thieves' slang.] **1.** *Thieves' slang.* In phrases *To give g.*: 'to side, shoulder, or stand close to a man or a woman, whilst another picks his or her pocket'. *To keep in g.*: to engage (a person's) attention while a confederate is robbing him. **2.** Talk, chatter 1781. **3.** Humbug, rubbish; ridiculous nonsense 1805. **4.** quasi-*interj.* 1825.

Gammon (gæ·mən), *v.*[1] 1694. [f. GAMMON *sb.*[3]] **1.** *trans.* To beat at backgammon by a gammon. †**2.** *intr.* To cheat at play in some particular way 1700.

Gammon (gæ·mən), *v.*[2] 1836. [f. GAMMON *sb.*[1]] To cure (bacon) by salting and smoking.

Gammon (gæ·mən), *v.*[3] 1711. [f. GAMMON *sb.*[2]] To lash (the bowsprit) with ropes to the stem of a ship. Said also of the rope.

Gammon (gæ·mən), *v.*[4] *slang* or *colloq.* 1789. [f. GAMMON *sb.*[4]] **1.** *intr.* To talk (plausibly). **2.** To pretend 1812. **3.** *trans.* To stuff with nonsense, to humbug, hoax. Const. *into*, *out of*. 1812. Hence **Ga·mmoner,** one who gammons; one who gives gammon to an accomplice.

Gammoning (gæ·məniŋ), *vbl. sb.* 1833. [f. GAMMON *v.*[3] + -ING[1].] The lashing of ropes by which the bowsprit is made fast to the stem or cutwater.

Gamo- (gæ:mŏ), comb. f. Gr. γάμος marriage.

gamoma·nia [-MANIA], a form of insanity characterized by strange and extravagant proposals for marriage; **gamomo·rphism** [Gr. μορφή], that stage of development of organized beings in which the spermatic and germinal elements are formed, matured, and generated, in preparation for another act of fecundation. Chiefly in adjs. used in Botany, describing plants or organs in which certain specified parts are united together, as **gamoga·strous** [Gr. γαστήρ], having the ovaries united: said of the pistil; **gamope·talous** [PETAL], having the petals united; **gamophy·llous** [Gr. φύλλον], having the leaves united; **gamose·palous** [SEPAL], having the sepals united.

Gamogenesis (gæmŏdʒe·nėsis). 1861. [f. GAMO- + -GENESIS.] *Biol.* Generation by the conjunction of structures from different individuals; sexual reproduction. Hence **Gamogene·tic** *a.* of or pertaining to g., producing or produced by g. **Gamogene·tically** *adv.* in a gamogenetic manner.

Gamp (gæmp). 1864. [After Mrs. Sarah *Gamp*, a monthly nurse in *Martin Chuzzlewit*, who carried a large cotton umbrella.] **1.** A monthly nurse or sick nurse of a disreputable type. **2.** An umbrella, esp. one tied up in a loose, bulgy fashion 1864. Hence **Ga·mpish** *a.* (in sense 2).

Gamut (gæ·mət). 1529. [contr. of med.L. *gamma ut*; f. GAMMA the name of the symbol Γ (repr. in the Middle Ages a note one tone lower than A) + UT, q.v., first of the six notes forming a hexachord.] **1.** The first or lowest note in the mediæval scale of music, answering to the modern G on the lowest line of the bass stave. Now *Hist.* 1530. **2.** The 'Great Scale' (ascribed to Guido d'Arezzo). Now *Hist.* 1529. **3.** Hence: The whole series of notes that are used by musicians. Occas. also: The major diatonic scale, or any specified scale. 1709. **b.** The full range of notes of a voice or instrument 1639. **4.** *transf.* and *fig.* The whole scale, range, or compass of a thing 1626.

3. b. The gammuth of every municipal fidler MILT. **4.** The painter's g. HOGARTH. The whole g. of Crime DICKENS.

Gamy (gē[i]·mi), *a.* Also †**gamey.** 1844. [f. GAME *sb.* + -Y[1].] **1.** Abounding in game; bent upon game 1848. **2.** Spirited, plucky; showing fight to the last 1844. **3.** Having the flavour of game, esp. when it is 'high' 1863.

1. Any gamey..district 1892. **2.** The g. bass 1883.

Gan, pa. t. of GIN *v.*[1]; obs. inf. of GO.

†**Ganch,** *sb.* Also †**gaunch.** 1625. [– Fr. †*ganche* – mod.Pr. *ganche* hook, boathook – Sp. *gancho* or It. *gancio* hook.] **1.** The apparatus employed in execution by ganching; the punishment itself. **2.** A gash made by a wild boar's tusk 1818.

†**Ganch,** *v.* Also †**gaunch.** 1614. [– Fr. **gancher*, in pa. pple. †*ganché* (Cotgr.), f. †*ganche*; see prec.] **1.** *trans.* To impale upon sharp hooks or stakes as a mode of execution –1783. **2.** Of a boar: To tear or gash with the tusk –1783.

1. G. him, impale him, rid the world of such a monster DRYDEN.

Gander (gæ·ndəɹ). *sb.* [Late OE. *ganra*, *gandra*, corresp. to MLG. *ganre* (LG., Du. *gander*); f. the same base as GANNET.] **1.** The male of the goose. **2.** *fig.* A dull or stupid person 1553. **b.** *slang.* 'A married man; in America one not living with his wife' (Farmer).

Comb. **g.-month, -moon,** the month after a wife's confinement.

†**Gane,** *v.* [OE. *gānian* = OHG. *geinōn* :– WGmc. **ʒainōjan*.] *intr.* To open the mouth wide, to gape or yawn –1570.

See how he ganeth lo this dronken wight CHAUCER.

Gang (gæŋ), *sb.* [– ON. *gangr* m. and *ganga* fem., walking motion, course (Sw. *gång* walk, pace, 'go', time; Da. *gang* (also) set of knitting-needles) = OE., OS., OHG. (Du., G.) *gang*, Goth. *gagg*, Gmc. noun of action to **ʒanʒan* GO.]

I. †**1.** *pl.* Steps, goings, journeyings. OE. only. †**2.** The power of going –ME.; gait or carriage –1626. †**3.** A journey –ME. **4.** A way, road, or passage. Now *dial.* OE. **b.** A walk or pasture for cattle. *Sc.* and *n. dial.* 1808.

II. 1. A set of articles ME.; *esp.* a set of tools so arranged as to work simultaneously 1806. **2.** A company of workmen 1627; a company of slaves or prisoners 1790. **3.** Any company of persons who go about together or act in concert (in mod. use mainly for criminal purposes) 1632.

1. A g. of extremely light harrows A. YOUNG. **2.** A g. of coopers 1863. **3.** Nutt the pirate..with all his g. of varlets 1632. This company, both the ladies and all, are of a g. PEPYS.

attrib. and *Comb.*, as (sense II. 1) *g.-cultivator*, *-drill*, *-plough*, *-press*, *-saw*, etc.; (senses II. 2, 3) *g.-driver*, *-master*, *-robber*, *-system*, *-work*. Also **g.-mill,** a saw-mill in which g.-saws are used; **-rider,** one who rides on mine-cars or trams; **-road** (*local*), a road between a harbour and the buildings.

Gang, *v.*[1] Now *Sc.* and *dial.* [OE. *gangan*, *gongan* = OFris. *ganga*, *gunga*, OS., OHG. *gangan*, ON. *ganga*, Goth. *gaggan* :– Gmc. *ʒanʒan*. Relation to Go is uncertain.] *intr.* To walk, go. Also quasi-*trans.*

False gelden, g. thy gait B. JONS.

Gang (gæŋ), *v.*[2] 1856. [f. GANG *sb.* II. 2.] **1.** *trans.* To arrange in a gang. **2.** *intr.* With *in*: to come in a gang 1891. **3.** *U.S.* To go in company *with* 1928.

Ga·ng-board. 1748. [f. GANG *sb.*] Chiefly *Naut.* **1.** A narrow platform on deep-waisted ships, leading from the quarter-deck to the forecastle. **2.** A plank, usu. with cleats or steps nailed on it, for walking upon, esp. into or out of a boat 1777.

Ga·ng-cask. 1779. [f. GANG *sb.* + CASK.] *Naut.* A water-cask used on board ships for bringing water on board in boats.

Ga·ng-days. *Obs.* exc. *Hist.* OE. [f. GANG *sb.* + DAY; so called from the processions held on these days.] The three days preceding Ascension Day or Holy Thursday; also called Rogation days.

Gange (gændʒ), *v.* 1861. [Of unkn. origin.] **1.** *trans.* To protect (a fish-hook, etc.) with fine wire. Now *dial.* or *arch.* **2.** To fasten (a fish-hook) to the GANGING (*Cent. Dict.*).

Ganger (gæ·ŋəɹ), *sb.*[1] ME. [f. GANG *v.*[1] + -ER[1].] **1.** One who travels on foot. **2.** A fast-going horse 1818.

Ganger (gæ·ŋəɹ), *sb.*[2] 1849. [f. GANG *sb.* or *v.*[2] + -ER[1].] An overseer in charge of a gang of workmen.

Ganger (gæ·ŋəɹ), *sb.*[3] 1860. [perh. short for FOREGANGER 2.] *Naut.* Two or more lengths of chain cable shackled to the sheet anchor.

Gangetic (gænˌdʒe·tik), *a.* 1677. [– L. *Gangeticus*, f. *Ganges* – Gr. Γάγγης.] Belonging to the river Ganges. †Also *sb. pl.* Those who live on the banks of the Ganges.

†**Ga·ng-flower.** 1597. [f. GANG *sb.* + FLOWER.] The milkwort (*Polygala vulgaris*), so called because it blossoms in the Gang or Rogation week.

Ganging (gæ·ndʒiŋ), *vbl. sb.* 1883. [f. GANGE *v.* + -ING[1].] **a.** 'The act of fastening a fish-hook to the line'. **b.** 'A section or part of a fishing-line to the free end of which a hook is ganged' (*Cent. Dict.*).

Gangliac (gæ·ŋgliæk), *a.* 1848. [f. GANGLION + -AC.] Relating to a ganglion. So **Ga·nglial** *a.*, **Ga·ngliar** *a.* pertaining to, or resembling a ganglion.

Gangliated (gæ·ŋgliē[i]tėd), *ppl. a.* 1804. [f. GANGLION + -ATE[3] + -ED[1].] Furnished with ganglia.

Gangliform (gæ·ŋglifǭɹm), *a.* Also **ganglioform.** 1681. [f. as prec. + -FORM.] Having the form of a ganglion.

Ganglion (gæ·ŋgliǫn, -ən). *Pl.* **ganglia;** also **-as, -ons.** 1681. [– Gr. γάγγλιον tumour under the skin, on or near tendons or sinews; used by Galen to denote the complex nerve-centres.] **1.** *Path.* A tumour or swelling of the sheath of a tendon. 'Also..an enlarged bursa mucosa' (*Syd. Soc. Lex.*). **2.** *Phys.* An enlargement or knot on a nerve, forming a centre from which nerve-fibres radiate 1732. **b.** A collection of grey matter (neurine) in the central nervous system, forming a nerve nucleus 1855. **c.** *fig.* A centre of force, activity, or interest 1828. **3.** *Phys.* A lymphatic gland 1831. **4.** 'Applied to the class of organs to which the spleen, the thymus gland, the thyroid body, and the adrenals belong' (*Syd. Soc. Lex.*) 1885. **5.** *Bot.* A swelling on the mycelium of certain fungi 1866.

2. c. A little g., or nervous centre, in the great vital system of immensity CARLYLE.

Comb.: **g.-cell, -corpuscle, -globule,** a nerve-cell in the grey matter of the central nervous system.

Hence **Ga·nglionary** *a.* furnished with ganglia. **Ga·ngliona:ted** *ppl.a.* = GANGLIATED. **Ganglio·nic** *a.* relating to, composed of, or furnished with ganglia.

Ga·ng-plank. *U.S.* 1861. [f. GANG *sb.* + PLANK.] A landing-plank; a gang-board.

Gangrel (gæ·ŋgrĕl). *dial.* and *arch.* 1530. [app. f. GANG *sb.* or *v.*[1]; cf. *haverel, wastrel,* etc.] **1.** A vagabond; a wandering beggar. **b.** *attrib.* or *adj.* Vagabond, vagrant 1538. **2.** A lanky, loose-jointed person 1585. Also *attrib.* as *adj.* 1650.

†**Ga·ngrenate** *v.* 1582. [f. GANGRENE *sb.* + -ATE[3].] To make, or become, gangrenous –1758.

Gangrene (gæ·ŋgrīn), *sb.* 1543. [– Fr. *gangrène* – L. *gangræna* – Gr. γάγγραινα (cf. γόγγρος growth on trees).] **1.** A necrosis of part of the body, extending over some considerable area in a visible mass. Occas., the first stage of mortification. **2.** *fig.* 1602.

2. To the community..corruption is a g. JOHNSON. Hence **Ga·ngrenous** *a.* having the nature of g., or affected with it.

Gangrene (gæ·ŋgrīn), *v.* 1607. [f. prec. sb.] To become or cause to become mortified. Also *fig.* Hence **Gangrene·scent** *a.* becoming gangrenous.

Gangsman (gæ·ŋzmăn). 1793. [f. GANG *sb.* + MAN.] **1.** A dock-porter. **2.** One who has charge of a gang of workmen 1863.

Gangster (gæ·ŋstəɹ). orig. *U.S.* 1896. [f. GANG *sb.* + -STER.] A member of a gang of criminals or toughs.

Gangue (gæŋ). Also **gang.** 1809. [– Fr. *gangue* – G. *gang* vein or lode of metal, techn. use of *gang* course; see GANG *sb.*] The earth or stony matter in a mineral deposit; the matrix in which an ore is found.

Gangway (gæ·ŋwe[i]). [f. GANG *sb.* + WAY; not continuous with OE. *gangweġ.*] **1.** A road, thoroughfare, or passage of any kind. Now *dial.* **2.** A passage in a building; *esp.* one between rows of seats in a public edifice 1702. **b.** In the House of Commons, the cross-passage about half-way down the House, giving access to the rear-benches (rarely *pl.*) 1875. **3.** *Naut.* **a.** = GANG-BOARD 1. 1688. **b.** A narrow passage left in the hold of a laden ship 1780. **c.** The opening in the bulwarks by which persons enter or leave a vessel; now more commonly = GANG-BOARD 2. 1780. **4.** *Mining.* 'A main level, applied chiefly to coal mines' (Raymond) 1776.

Phr. *To bring to the g.*: 'to punish a seaman by seizing him up to a grating, there to undergo flogging' (Smyth).

Comb.: **g.-ladder,** a ladder over the side by which the ship is entered; **g. netting,** in warships, the netting with which the g. between quarter-deck and forecastle is fenced.

†**Ga·ng-week.** [OE. *gangwuce*, f. GANG *sb.* + *wuce* WEEK.] Rogation week, in which the GANG-DAYS fell –1607.

Ganister (gæ·nistəɹ). Also †**gann-.** 1811. [Of unkn. origin.] A close-grained siliceous stone from the lower coal-measures in Yorkshire, used to form furnace-hearths; also in lining Bessemer converters.

‖**Ganja** (gæ·ndʒă). 1800. [Hindi *gānjhā.*] A preparation of Indian hemp (*Cannabis sativa*, variety *indica*), strongly intoxicating and narcotic.

Gannet (gæ·nét). [OE. *ganot*, corresp. to MLG. *gante*, Du. *gent*, MHG. *ganiz, genz,* OHG. *ganazzo*, MHG. *ganze* gander :– Gmc. **ʒanitaz*, **ʒanoton* (whence L. *ganta*; see GOOSE), f. same base as GANDER.] The Solan goose (*Sula bassana*).

Ganocephalan (gæ:nose·fălăn). 1865. [f. mod.L. *ganocephalus* (f. Gr. γάνος brightness + κεφαλή head) + -AN.] A fish of the extinct order *Ganocephala* (so called because their heads were covered with shining bony plates). So **Ganoce·phalous** *a.* belonging to this order.

Ganoid (gæ·noid). 1839. [– Fr. *ganoïde*, f. Gr. γάνος brightness; see -OID.]

A. *adj.* **1.** Of a fish-scale: Having a smooth shining surface, from being covered with a layer of enamel 1854. **2.** Covered with polished bony plates; distinctive epithet of an order of fishes (mod.L. *Ganoidei*) 1847.

B. *sb.* A ganoid fish 1839.

Hence **Ganoi·dal** *a.* = GANOID A. 2. **Ganoi·dean** *a.* and *sb.*, **Ganoi·dian** *a.* and *sb.* = GANOID A. 2 and B.

Ganoin (gæ·no,in). Also **-ine.** 1859. [f. Gr. γάνος brightness + -IN[1].] The hard polished enamel which forms the superficial layer of ganoid scales.

Gansa, gansaw, obs. ff. GANZA.

Gantlet, obs. f. GAUNTLET.

Gantline, erron. f. GIRTLINE.

Gantlope (gæ·ntlo[u]p). Now *rare* exc. as GAUNTLET[2]. 1646. [– Sw. *gatlopp*, f. *gata* lane, GATE *sb.*[2] + *lopp* course (see LEAP); a term introduced through the Thirty Years War (so G. *gassenlaufen*). See GAUNTLET *sb.*[2]] A military punishment in which the culprit had to run stripped to the waist between two rows of men who struck at him with a stick or a knotted cord. *rare* exc. in *to run the g.* Also *transf.* and *fig.*

Gantry, gauntry (gæ·ntri, gǭ·ntri). 1574. [prob. f. GAWN + TREE.] **1.** A four-footed wooden stand for barrels. **2.** A frame or platform for carrying a crane or similar structure 1810.

Ganymede (gæ·nimīd). 1591. [– L. *Ganymedes* – Gr. Γανυμήδης Zeus's cup-bearer.] **1.** A cupbearer; *joc.* a pot-boy 1608. **2.** A catamite 1591. **3.** The largest satellite of the planet Jupiter 1868.

Ganza (gæ·nză). 1633. [Reading of the old edd. of Pliny *N.H.* x. xxii.] One of the birds (called elsewhere 'wild swans') which drew Domingo Gonsales to the moon in Bp. Godwin's romance.

Gaol (dʒē[i]l), **Gaoler** (dʒē[i]·ləɹ), variant spellings of JAIL, JAILER. Both forms are correct, but recent Dictionaries prefer the J forms.

Gap (gæp), *sb.* ME. [– ON. *gap* chasm (Sw. *gap*, Da. *gab* open mouth, opening), rel. to ON. *gapa* GAPE *v.*] **1.** A breach in a wall or hedge; also *fig.* **2.** A notch (now *rare*) 1530. **3.** A mountain pass (common in U.S.) 1555. **4.** An unfilled space or interval; a hiatus 1523.

1. A gappe in the churchyard wall 1584. Phr. *To stand in the g., to open a g.* **3.** Two great Gaps that led thro' this Circuit of Mountains ADDISON. **4.** *spec.* The distance between the upper and lower planes of a biplane, or between the spiral courses of the blades of an aeroplane propeller 1909. **b.** *Electr.* = *spark-gap* (SPARK *sb.*[1]).

Comb.: **g.-bed lathe,** one with an opening in the bed or shears to allow a larger object to be turned; **-window,** a long and narrow window.

Gap (gæp), *v. rare.* 1847. [f. prec.] To become, or make, jagged or notched.

Gape (gē[i]p), *sb.* 1535. [f. GAPE *v.*] **1.** The act of gaping; a yawn. **2.** An open-mouthed stare; also *fig.* 1660. **3.** The expanse of an open mouth or beak 1766; the part of the beak which can be opened 1833. **4.** A rent or opening of any kind 1658.

Phr. *The gapes*: **a.** A disease in poultry, etc., of which frequent gaping is the symptom. **b.** A fit of yawning or staring (*joc.*).

Gape (gē[i]p), *v.* ME. [– ON. *gapa* (Sw. *gapa*, Da. *gabe*) = (M)Du. *gapen*, (M)HG. *gaffen.*] **1.** *intr.* To open the mouth wide, esp. to bite or swallow anything. Said also of the mouth. Also *transf.* of earth, hell, etc. ME. **2.** *intr.* To open as a mouth; to split, crack, part asunder 1577. **3.** *absol.* To stare in wonder or admiration ME. **4.** With *for, after,* †*at*: To be eager to obtain, to long for (something) ME. †**5.** To gasp from pain, heat, etc. –1572. **6.** To yawn, esp. from weariness ME.

1. Opening their Mouths as wide as they could g. 1710. **2.** When the ground gapes with the heate of the Sunne 1577. A wound that gapeth 1688. The seams g., or let in water SMYTH. **3.** And ever he gaped upward into the eire CHAUCER. **4.** A minde that gapeth for nothing but money 1638. **6.** She stretches, gapes, unglues her eyes, And asks if it be time to rise SWIFT.

Comb. **g.-eyed** *a.*, in *Herpetology*, naked-eyed; having apparently no eyelids. Hence **Ga·pingly** *adv.*

Gaper (gē[i]·pəɹ). 1559. [f. prec. + -ER[1].] **1.** One that gapes 1637; †one who gapes for a thing –1628. **2.** *Ornith.* **a.** The open-bill (*Anastomus oscitans*) 1871. **b.** One of the *Eurylæmidæ*; a broad-bill 1884. **3.** A fish, the *Serranus cabrilla*, also called *comber* 1828. **4.** A bivalve mollusc of the family *Myidæ*: also *g.-shell* 1853.

Gape-seed (gē[i]·psī:d). 1600. [f. GAPE *sb.* or *v.* + SEED *sb.*] Something stared at by a gaping crowd; also, the act of staring.

Phr. *To seek, buy,* or *sow gape-seed*: to stare gapingly at a fair or market, instead of doing business.

Gaping (gē[i]·piŋ), *vbl. sb.* ME. [f. GAPE *v.* + -ING[1].] **1.** The action of GAPE *v.* **2.** An opening or chasm in the earth. ?*Obs.* 1539. **3.** *attrib.*, as **g.-stock,** an object of open-mouthed wonder 1817.

Gapped (gæpt), *ppl. a.* 1562. [f. GAP *sb.* or *v.* + -ED.] **1.** Having the edge notched. **2.** Full of holes or breaches 1854.

Gap-toothed (gæ·ptū:þt), *a.* 1567. [f. GAP *sb.* + TOOTHED.] Having the teeth set wide apart.

Gar (gāɹ), *sb.* Also **garr, guard.** 1765. [Short f. GARFISH.] **a.** A fish of the Pike or Esox family of the genus *Belone*, having long bill-like jaws; the gar-fish or gar-pike. **b.** A ganoid fish of the genus *Lepidosteus*, having rhombic scales. *Alligator-gar*, a gar (*L. tristœchus*) with a head like that of an alligator. 1843.

Gar (gāɹ), *v.* Chiefly *Sc.* and *n. dial.* ME. [ME. *gere* – ON. *ger(v)a, gọr(v)a* make, do = OE. *ġierwan* prepare, OS. *garwian, gerwian,* OHG. *garawen* (G. *gerben* tan, curry, polish) :– Gmc. **ʒarwjan*, f. **ʒarwu-* ready; see YARE, GEAR.] †**1.** *trans.* To do, perform; to make, *gare.* –1662. **2.** To make, to cause ME.

Garage (gæ·rāʒ, gæ·rédʒ). 1902. [– Fr. *garage*, f. *garer* shelter, of Gmc. origin; see WARE *v.*[1], -AGE.] A building for the storage or refitting of motor vehicles. Also as vb.

Garancin (gæ·rănsin). Also **-ine.** 1843. [– Fr. *garancine*, f. *garance* madder; see -IN[1], -INE[5].] *Chem.* A dyeing substance obtained from madder.

Garb (gāɹb), *sb.*[1] 1502. [– ONFr. *garbe* (OFr. *jarbe*, mod. *gerbe*) :– Frankish **garba* = OHG. *garba* (G. *gerbe*).] A wheat-sheaf. *Obs.* exc. *Her.*

Garb (gāɹb), *sb.*[2] 1591. [– Fr. †*garbe* (now *galbe*) – It. *garbo* – Gmc. **ʒarwī* (OHG. *garawī* adornment), f. **ʒarw-*; see GAR *v.*] †**1.** Grace, elegance –1670. †**2.** A person's outward bearing –1703. †**3.** Style, manner, fashion –1694. **4.** Fashion of dress, esp. official or other distinctive dress; hence *concr.* dress, costume. Also *transf.* and *fig.* 1622.

3. You thought, because he could not speake English in the natiue g., he could not therefore handle an English Cudgell *Hen. V*, v. i. 80. **4.** Hose and doublet, The horse-boy's g. FLETCHER.

Garb (gāɹb), *v.* 1599. [f. prec. sb.] *trans.* To cover with a garb, to clothe, dress. Also *fig.*

These black dog-Dons G. themselves bravely TENNYSON.

Garbage (gā·ɹbédʒ), *sb.* ME. [– AFr. **garbage*, of unkn. origin.] **1.** The offal of an animal used for food; esp. the entrails. **2.** Refuse in general (in U.S. *esp.* kitchen, etc., refuse); filth. Also *fig.* of literary matter. 1583. †**3.** Wheat straw and the ears, chopped small as food for horses –1617.

†**Garbage** (gā·ɹbédʒ), *v.* 1542. [f. prec. sb.] **1.** *trans.* To remove the offal from; to gut (fish) –1672. **2.** *intr.* To feed on offal 1650.

1. Pilchards..are there taken, garbaged, salted, hanged in the smoke P. HOLLAND.

Garbell, obs. f. GARBOARD.

Garble (gā·ɹb'l), *sb.* 1502. [prob. – It. *garbello*, f. *garbellare*; see next.] †**1.** Refuse (of spices); extraneous matter –1809. †**2.** Goods containing dross or waste –1638. **3.** The process of garbling 1808.

Garble (gā·ɹb'l), *v.* Also †**garbel.** 1483. [In AL. *garbellare*, with *garbelagium* sorting groceries before sale; orig. a term of Mediterranean commerce; – It. *garbellare* sift – Arab. *ġarbala* sift, select, rel. to *ġirbāl* sieve, perh. – late L. *cribellare*, f. *cribellum*, dim. of L. *cribrum* sieve.] †**1.** *trans.* To sift, cleanse (const. *of*); also with *out* –1812. **2.** To select or sort out the best in. Now *rare.* Also with *out.* 1483. **3.** To make selections from with a purpose; to mutilate with a view to misrepresentation 1689.

1. To g. red pepper 1657. **2.** Phr. *To g. the coinage.* **3.** To g. correspondence JAS. MILL, evidence PEEL.

Garbler (gā·ɹbləɹ). 1592. [f. prec. + -ER[1].] **1.** An official who garbled spices, etc. *Obs.* exc. *Hist.* **2.** One who garbles or mutilates (statements, etc.) 1693.

Garbling (gā·ɹbliŋ), *vbl. sb.* 1483. [f. GARBLE *v.* + -ING[1].] **1.** The action of GARBLE *v.* **2.** *concr. pl.* The refuse or remainder of a commodity after selection of the best 1881.

Garboard (gā·ɹbōᵊɹd). Also †**garbell,** †**-ble.** 1626. [– Du. †*gaarboord*, perh. f. *garen*, contr. form of *gaderen* GATHER + *boord* BOARD.] The first range of planks laid upon a ship's bottom, near the keel. Also *transf.* of iron vessels. Also *attrib.*, as **g.-strake** = garboard.

Garboil (gā·ɹboil), *sb. Obs.* exc. *arch.* 1548. [– OFr. *garbouil(le)* – It. *garbuglio.*] Confusion, disturbance, tumult; an instance of this. Hence †**Ga·rboil** *v.* to confuse, agitate, disturb. (Also erron. for GARBLE *v.*)

‖**Garçon** (garsoṅ). 1839. [Fr.] A boy, serving-man, waiter; in Eng. use a waiter in a French hotel or restaurant.

Gard, gard-, vars. of GUARD, GUARD-.

Gardant, obs. f. GUARDANT.

‖**Garde-du-corps** (gardədükor). 1651. [Fr., = body-guard.] A body-guard; a member of a body-guard.

Garden (gā·ɹd'n), *sb.* ME. [– ONFr. *gardin*, var. of (O)Fr. *jardin* :– Rom. **gardino*, f. **gardo* – Gmc. **ʒardon*. See GARTH[1], YARD *sb.*[1]] **1.** An enclosed piece of ground devoted to the cultivation of flowers, fruit, or vegetables; often with defining word, as *flower-*, *fruit-*, *kitchen-*, etc. *g.* **b.** *pl.* Ornamental grounds, used as a place of public resort 1838. **c.** *transf.* of a region of great fertility 1596. **2. a.** Short for *Covent Garden*, *Hatton Garden*, localities in London 1763. **b.** *pl.* In names of squares and streets 1848. **3.** A name for the school of Epicurus (who taught in a garden) 1867.

1. Ile fetch a turne about the G. *Cymb.* I. i. 81. **c.** Fruitful Lombardie, The pleasant g. of great Italy *Tam. Shr.* I. i. 4. *The G. of England*: a name assumed by various counties. **3.** [Neither] the Porch, the G., nor the Academy M. PATTISON.

Comb. **1.** General: **a.** with sense 'of or belonging to a garden, for use in a garden', as *g.-alley*, *-bed*, *-mould*, *-walk*, *-wall*, etc. **b.** with sense 'cultivated or growing in a garden', as *g.-creeper*, *-flower*, etc.; *g.-honesty*, *-mint*, *-pea*, *-poppy*, etc.; †**g.-balsam,** *Trifolium odoratum*. **c.** with sense 'having the garden as its habitat', as *g.-ant*, *-ousel*, etc.; **-warbler,** the bird *Sylvia hortensis*; **-white,** a white cabbage butterfly of the genus *Pieris*. **d.** in the slang phr. *common or g.* = 'common', 'ordinary'.

2. Special: **g. city,** a real estate development combining the advantages of town and country life, as by providing open spaces and garden plots; so **g. suburb;** **-engine,** a portable force-pump used for watering gardens; **-frame** (FRAME *sb.* III. 5c.); **-glass,** (*a*) a bell glass used for covering plants in a g.; (*b*) a round globe of dark-coloured glass, placed on a pedestal, in which the surrounding objects are reflected—much used as an ornament of gardens in Germany; **-party,** one held on a lawn or in a g.; **-plot,** a plot of land used as a g.: **-pot,** †a watering-pot; a flower-pot; **-roller,** a heavy cylinder fitted with a handle or shafts, for smoothing a lawn or path; **g. seat,** a seat for use in a g.; a similar seat fixed on the roof of an omnibus, etc.; hence **-seated** *a.*; **-stuff,** vegetables raised in a g.; **-wall-bond** (*Bricklaying*), a bond consisting of three stretchers and one header in nine-inch walls.

Garden (gā·ɹd'n), *v.* 1577. [f. the sb.] **1.** *intr.* To cultivate a garden; to work as a gardener; †also, to lay out a garden. **2.** *trans.* To cultivate as a garden 1862.

1. When Ages grow to Ciuility..Men come to Build Stately, sooner then to G. Finely BACON.

Gardener (gā·ɹd'nəɹ). ME. [– AFr. **gardiner*, OFr. *gardinier* (mod. *jardinier*), in AL. *gardinarius* (XII); see prec., -ER[2].] One who tends, lays out, or cultivates a garden; *spec.* a servant who does this.

Comb.: **gardener's delight, eye,** *Lychnis coronaria*; **gardener's garters,** the striped garden variety of *Phalaris arundinacea*. Hence **Ga·rdenership.**

Gardenesque (gā·ɹd'nˌesk), *a.* 1838. [f. GARDEN *sb.* + -ESQUE; after *picturesque*.] Partaking of the character of a garden.

Ga·rden-ga·te. ME. [f. as prec. + GATE *sb.*[1]] A gate leading into a garden. Also used *dial.* as a name for Herb Robert, the Pansy, and London Pride.

Ga·rdenhood. [f. as prec. + -HOOD.] Garden-like character. H. WALPOLE.

Ga·rden-house. 1603. [f. GARDEN *sb.* + HOUSE *sb.*[1]] **1.** Any small building in a garden. **2.** A dwelling-house situated in a garden 1607. †**b.** A brothel –1625.

Gardenia (gaɹdī·niă). 1760. [mod.L., f. the name of Dr. Alex. *Garden* (died 1791); see -IA[1].] A genus of trees and shrubs, often spiny (N.O. *Rubiaceæ*), natives of the Cape of Good Hope, etc.

Gardening (gā·ɹd'niŋ), *vbl. sb.* 1577. [f. GARDEN *v.* + -ING[1].] The action or occupation of laying out or cultivating a garden; horticulture. Also *attrib.*

Gardenless (gā·ɹd'nlės), *a.* 1834. [f. GARDEN *sb.* + -LESS.] Destitute of gardens or of a garden.

Gardenly (gā·ɹd'nli), *a. rare.* 1819. [f. as prec. + -LY[1].] Befitting a garden.

Garderobe (gā·ɹdroᵘb). Now *Hist.* ME. [– Fr. *garderobe*, f. *garder* to keep + *robe* ROBE. See WARDROBE.] Prop., a store-room, armoury, wardrobe (occas. also the contents of this); by extension, a private room, a bedchamber.

†**Gardon.** 1611. [– (O)Fr. *gardon.*] A kind of roach (*Leuciscus idus*).

Gardyloo (gāɹdilū·). 1771. [app. f. *gare de l'eau*, pseudo-Fr. for *gare l'eau*, beware of the water. See GARE *v. imp.*] An old Edinburgh cry before throwing slops, etc. from the windows into the street.

†**Gare,** *sb.* 1542. [– AFr. *gare* = OFr. *gard, jart.*] Coarse wool such as grows about the shanks of a sheep –1607.

‖**Gare** (gāɹ), *v. imp.* 1653. [Fr., imper. of *garer*; see GARAGE.] A cry: Look out! Take care!

Gare-fowl (gēᵊ·ɹfaul). Also †**gairfowl.** 1698. [– Icel. *geirfugl.* (Faroese *gorfuglur*, Sw. *garfogl*). The meaning of *geir-* is unknown.] The great auk (*Alca impennis*).

Garfish (gā·ɹfiʃ). ME. [app. f. OE. *gār* spear + FISH, in allusion to its long, sharp nose.] A fish (*Belone vulgaris*) with a long spear-like snout, called also green-bone, horn-fish, sea-pike, etc. In America and Australia a name for other fishes of similar form, e.g. various species of *Lepidosteus* and *Hemirhamphus.*

†**Ga·rgalize,** *v. rare.* 1605. [var. of GARGARIZE, prob. affected by GARGLE.] To gargle –1611.

Garganey (gā·ɹgăni). 1668. [Given by Gesner as the It. name used about Bellinzona.] A species of teal (*Anas querquedula*).

Gargantua (gāɹgæ·ntyuă). 1571. Name of the large-mouthed voracious giant of Rabelais' work (1542); *gen.* a giant. Hence **Garga·ntuan** *a.* gigantic 1596.

You must borrow me Gargantuas mouth first SHAKS.

†**Gargarism** (gā·ɹgăriz'm). ?*Obs.* ME. [– late L. *gargarisma*, *-mum* – Gr. γαργαρισμός, *γαργάρισμα gargle. Cf. (O)Fr. *gargarisme.*] **1.** A gargle. **2.** A disease of the throat which attacks swine –1688. var. (sense 1) †**Gargarise.**

Gargarize (gā·ɹgărəiz), *v.* ?*Obs.* 1533. [– L. *gargarizare* – Gr. γαργαρίζειν. Repl. by GARGLE.] **1.** *trans.* To wash or cleanse (the mouth or throat) with a gargle. **2.** To gargle (a liquid) 1578. **3.** *intr.* To gargle 1569.

†**Garget**[1]. *rare.* ME. only. [– OFr. *gargate*, *garguete*; see next, GARGOYLE.] The throat.

Garget[2] (gā·ɹgėt). 1587. [– OFr. *gargate*, *garguete* – Pr. *gargata*, f. **garg-*; see GARGOYLE.] **1.** An inflamed condition of the head or throat in cattle and pigs. **2.** Inflammation in a cow's or ewe's udder 1725. **3.** *transf.* and *fig.* A distemper, plague 1615. **4.** Short for **g.-plant** (*U.S.*), the Virginian poke-weed 1788.

†**Gargil**[1]. *rare.* 1558. [– OFr. *gargouille* throat; see GARGOYLE.] The gullet –1632.

Gargil[2]. Now *dial.* 1601. [f. prec.]. **1.** A disease in cattle and pigs, also in geese, attacking the head and throat. **2.** = GARGET[2] 2. 1760.

Gargil(l(e, obs. ff. GARGOYLE.

Gargle (gā·ɹg'l), *sb.* 1657. [f. GARGLE *v.*] Any liquid used for gargling.

Gargle (gā·ɹg'l), *v.* 1527. [– Fr. *gargouiller*, f. *gargouille* throat; cf. GARGIL[1].] **1.** *trans.* To hold (a liquid) suspended and rattling in the throat. ?*Obs.* **2.** To wash (the throat or mouth) with a liquid held suspended in the throat 1616. **3.** *fig.* To utter with a sound as of gargling 1635. **4.** *intr.* To perform the act of gargling 1601.

Gargol, obs. f. GARGIL[2], GARGLE.

Gargoyle (gā·ɹgoil). Also †**gurgoyle,** etc. ME. [– OFr. *gargouille* throat, with specialized application from the water passing through the mouth of the figure forming the spout; f. base **garg-*, as repr. in L. *gargarizare* – Gr. γαργαρίζειν, of imit. origin. Cf. GARGARIZE.] A grotesque spout, representing some animal or human figure, projecting from the gutter of a building, in order to carry the rain-water clear of the walls. Also *attrib.*

Garibaldi (gæribæ·ldi). 1862. [Name of an Italian general (1807–82).] **1.** A kind of blouse worn by women, in imitation of the red shirt worn by Garibaldi and his followers. Orig. *attrib.* as *G. jacket.* **b.** *Garibaldi biscuit*, a sandwich biscuit containing a paste of currants 1898. **2.** A red pomacentroid fish (*Hypsypops rubicundus*) of the Californian coast 1885.

Garish (gēᵊ·riʃ), *a.* 1545. [Also †*gaurish*, and perh. f. †*gaure* (Chaucer) to stare, but such a formation with -ISH[1] on a verb is rare.] **1.** Obtrusively or vulgarly bright in colour, showy, gaudy. **2.** Of colour, light, etc.: Excessively bright, glaring 1568. **3.** †Wanting in self-restraint; flighty –1678.

1. The g. service of the Masse 1636. The g. scene W. IRVING. **2.** Som..garment..gaurish in colour ASCHAM. The G. Sun SHAKS. Day's g. eye MILT. The g. day NEWMAN. **3.** Fame and glory makes the mind loose and g. SOUTH. **Ga·rish-ly** *adv.*, **-ness.**

Garland (gā·ɹlănd), *sb.* [ME. *gerland*, *garland* – OFr. *gerlande*, *garlande*, of unkn. origin.] **1.** A wreath made of flowers, leaves, etc., worn on the head like a crown, or hung about an object for decoration. Also *fig.* **2.** A wreath, chaplet, or coronet of gold or silver work, or the like ME. **3.** †**a.** A royal crown or diadem –1615. **b.** The wreath conferred upon the victor in the Greek and Roman games, etc. 1500. †**c.** *fig.* The principal ornament, 'glory' –1637. **4.** *fig.* An anthology, a miscellany 1612. **5.** *Her.* A wreath of laurel or of oak leaves, interspersed with acorns 1828. **6.** Something that resembles a garland: e.g. **a.** *Arch.* an ornamental band surrounding a spire, etc. 1490; †**b.** a ring-like marking or band –1673; **c.** the ring in a target in which the mark was set 1847. **7.** *Mining.* 'A spiral groove, made behind and in the stoning or ginging of a shaft, for collecting the water which oozes out of different strata' (Rees) 1819. **8.** *Naut.* **a.** A band or collar of rope (or iron) used for various purposes; **b.** (also *Mil.*) a receptacle for shot; **c.** a kind of net used by sailors as a locker or cupboard for provisions 1769.

1. The horned Sacrifice mantled with Ghirlonds 1652. **3. a.** *Rich. III*, III. ii. 40. **b.** *To gain, get, win*, etc. *the g.* **c.** You..call..Him vilde, that was your G. *Cor.* I. i. 188.

Comb. **g.-flower,** (*a*) a flower suited for making garlands; (*b*) a common name for *Hedychium*; also applied to *Daphne cneorum*, etc.

Hence **Ga·rlandage** (*rare*), display of garlands. **Ga·rlandless** *a.* **Ga·rlandry,** garlands collectively.

Garland (gā·ɹlănd), *v.* ME. [f. prec. sb.] **1.** *trans.* To form (flowers) into a garland (*rare*). **2.** To deck with or as with a garland 1593.

2. Their hair..gyrlanded with sea grass B. JONS.

Garlic (gā·ɹlik). [OE. *gārlēac*, f. *gār* spear (with ref. to the 'cloves' of the plant) + *lēak* LEEK.] **1.** A plant of the genus *Allium* (usu. *A. sativum*) having a bulbous root, a very strong smell, and an acrid, pungent taste. †**2.** Name of a jig or farce –1630.

1. *Clove of g.* (see CLOVE *sb.*[1] 1). *Oil of g.*, an essential oil obtained from the bulb and stem of g.

Comb.: **g.-pear (tree,** the American plant *Cratæva gynandra*; **-shrub,** *Bignonia alliacea*; also *Petiveria alliacea*; **g. (treacle)-mustard,** †**g. treaclewort,** *Sisymbrium alliaria* (*Alliaria officinalis*); **-wort** = *g. mustard.*

Hence **Ga·rlicky** *a.* savouring or smelling of g.

Garment (gā·ɹmĕnt), *sb.* [ME. *garnement*, *garment* – (O)Fr. *garnement* equipment, f. *garnir* GARNISH; see -MENT.] Any article of dress; in *sing.* esp. an outer vestment; in *pl.* = clothes. Now somewhat *rhet.* Also *fig.*

I do not like the fashion of your garments *Lear* III. vi. 84. Hence **Ga·rmentless** *a.* **Ga·rmenture,** array, attire.

Garment (gā·ɹmĕnt), *v.* 1547. [f. prec.] *trans.* To dress or clothe; chiefly in pa. pple. *garmented.* Also *transf.* and *fig.*

And thus were they garmented CAMDEN.

Garner (gā·ɹnəɹ), *sb.* [ME. *gerner, garner* – AFr. *gerner,* OFr. *gernier* (mod. *grenier*) :– L. *granarium* GRANARY; see -ER².] A storehouse for corn, granary. Also *attrib.* var. †**Ga·rnery.**

Garner (gā·ɹnəɹ), *v.* ME. [f. prec.] **1.** *trans.* To store or deposit in or as in a garner. **2.** *intr.* To accumulate. TENNYSON.

1. But there where I haue garnerd vp my heart *Oth.* IV. ii. 57.

Garnet¹ (gā·ɹnĕt). [ME. *gernet, grenat,* prob. – MDu. *gernate, garnate* – OFr. *grenat* – med.L. *granatus,* perh. transf. use of L. *granatum* POMEGRANATE, the stone being compared in colour to the pulp of the fruit.] A vitreous mineral, commonly found as a distinct crystal, and in the form of a rhomboidal dodecahedron, but also occurring in other shapes. The precious garnet is of a deep transparent red. Also *attrib.* as *g.-red* adj.

Comb.: **g.-berry,** the red currant, *Ribes rubrum*; **-blende,** a sulphide of zinc; **-rock,** a rock consisting mainly of g. Hence **Garneti·ferous** *a.* producing garnets.

Garnet². ME. [– OFr. (*pome*) *garnette, gernate* POMEGRANATE.] The pomegranate; also *g.-apple* –1673.

Garnet³ (gā·ɹnĕt). 1485. [prob. – Du. *garnaat,* of unkn. origin.] *Naut.* A tackle for hoisting light goods into a ship. *Comb.* **clew-garnets,** 'a sort of tackle wove through a g.-block' (Smyth).

Garnierite (gā·ɹniĕrəi:t). 1875. [After Jules *Garnier,* its discoverer; see -ITE¹ 2 b.] *Min.* A hydrous silicate of nickel and magnesium.

Garnish (gā·ɹniʃ), *sb.* ME. [f. GARNISH *v.*] †**1.** A set of vessels for table use, *esp.* of pewter –1674. †**2.** Dress. *Merch. V.* II. vi. 45. **3.** Embellishment, decoration. Also *concr.* an ornament. *lit.* and *fig.* ?*Obs.* 1615. **4.** Things added to a dish for ornament; also *fig.* of literary 'dishes' 1673. **5.** *slang.* Money extorted from a new prisoner as a jailer's fee, or as drink-money for other prisoners (abolished by 4 Geo. IV, c. 43, §12) 1592. **b.** A similar payment among workmen; also *maiden-g.* 1759.

3. To put on some g. and dress of virtue to impose on the world CLARENDON. **5.** [Gaoler, to a prisoner] You know the custom, Sir. G., Captain, G. *Beggar's Opera* II. vii. (1728) 27.

Comb.: **g.-bolt,** a bolt having a chamfered or faceted head; **-money** = sense 5.

Garnish (gā·ɹniʃ), *v.* Pa. t. and pple. **garnished** (-niʃt). ME. [– (O)Fr. *garniss-,* lengthened stem (see -ISH²) of *garnir, guarnir* – Gmc. **warnjan,* prob. rel. to **warnējan, -ōjan* become aware, (hence) guard, defend, provide for (see WARN *v.*¹).] †**1.** *trans.* To furnish with means of defence –1786. †**2.** To equip or arm (oneself) –1750. **3.** To fit out with anything that beautifies; to decorate, embellish (*with,* †*of*). Now somewhat *rhet.* ME. **4.** To decorate (a dish) for the table 1693. †**5.** Of trees: To cover (a wall, etc.). Also *absol.* –1712. **6.** *slang.* To fit with fetters (J.) 1755. **7.** *Law.* **a.** To serve notice on (a person), for the purpose of attaching money belonging to a debtor 1577. **b.** To serve (any one) with notice of payments to be made before he can be returned as an heir (abol. 6 Geo. IV, c. 105) 1585. **c.** To summon as party to a litigation already in process.

3. When he is come he findeth it [the house] empty, swept, and garnished *Matt.* 12:44. **4.** G. the dish with lemon, and send it to table MRS. GLASSE.

Hence **Ga·rnished** *ppl. a.*; *spec.* in *Her.* provided with appendages of different (specified) tincture. **Ga·rnishry,** adornment. BROWNING.

Garnishee (gāɹniʃī·). 1627. [f. GARNISH *v.* 7 + -EE¹.] *Law.* One in whose hands money belonging to a debtor is attached at the suit of the creditor. Also *attrib.,* as *g.-order,* etc. Hence **Garnishee·** *v.* to attach a debtor's money thus.

Garnisher (gā·ɹniʃəɹ). 1515. [f. GARNISH *v.* + -ER¹.] One who garnishes (GARNISH *v.*).

Garnishment (gā·ɹniʃmĕnt). 1550. [f. GARNISH *v.* + -MENT.] **1.** Adornment. **2.** *Law.* A notice, either general, or for (*a*) summoning a third party to appear in a suit, (*b*) attaching money in the hands of a third person 1585.

†**Garnison,** *sb.* ME. [– (O)Fr. *garnison,* f. *garnir* GARNISH. Superseded by GARRISON in XVI.] **1.** Defence; means of defence –1489. **2.** Provisions for an army, a besieged place, etc. –1500. **3.** A body of men stationed in a place for defence –1609. Hence †**Garnison** *v.* (*rare*), to garrison (a place).

Garniture (gā·ɹnitiŭɹ). 1532. [– Fr. *garniture,* f. *garnir* GARNISH.] **1.** Furniture, appurtenances. **2.** Ornament, added to dress 1667; or generally 1685. **3.** Apparel 1827. **4.** Dressing of a dish. Also *fig.* 1725.

2. A man of g. and feather DRYDEN. That train of female g. which passeth by the name of accomplishments LAMB.

‖**Garookuh, garrooka.** 1855. 'A fishing-craft of the Gulf of Persia' (Smyth).

Garotte: see GARROTTE.

†**Garous,** *a.* [f. GARUM + -OUS.] Of or resembling GARUM. SIR T. BROWNE.

Gar-pike (gā·ɹpəi:k). 1776. [f. after GARFISH; see PIKE *sb.*⁴] = GARFISH.

Garran: see GARRON.

Garret (gæ·rĕt), *sb.* [ME. *garite* – OFr. *garite* watch-tower (mod. *guérite*), f. *garir*; see GARRISON.] †**1.** A turret; a watch-tower –1598. **2.** A room within the roof of a house; an attic 1483. **3.** *slang.* The head 1796.

1. She putte her in a garet to see the Kinge Josue passe 1450. **2.** A dissertation upon the advantage of living in garrets L. STEPHEN.

Comb.: **g.-lock,** an inferior lock, made by men who work in a g.; **-master,** a cabinet-maker, locksmith, etc., who works on his own account, supplying both capital and labour.

Garret (gæ·rĕt), *v.* 1845. [perh. var. of synon. and contemp. *gallet* v., f. *gallet* chip or splinter of stone – (O)Fr. *galet* beach pebble.] *Build.* To insert small pieces of stone into the joints of (coarse masonry).

Garreted (gæ·rĕtĕd), *ppl. a.* 1531. [f. GARRET *sb.* + -ED².] **1.** Provided with garrets (see GARRET *sb.* 1). **2.** Lodged in a garret (*rare*) 1837.

2. G., In his ancestral palace WORDSW.

Garreteer (gæ:rĕtīᵊ·ɹ). 1720. [f. GARRET *sb.* + -EER.] One who lives in a garret; *esp.* a literary hack.

Garrison (gæ·risən), *sb.* [– OFr. *garison* defence, safety, provision, store, f. *garir* defend, furnish – Gmc. **warjan* defend. The later meanings are due to the infl. of GARNISON.] †**1.** Store; gift. ME. only. †**2.** Protection; means of defence –1561. **3.** †**a.** A fortress –1494. **b.** (from sense 4) A garrisoned place 1568. **4.** †A troop –1535; hence, a body of soldiers stationed in a place for its defence. Also *fig.* 1542.

4. *fig.* A g. . .of empty. .precepts MILT.

Phrases. *In g.* (*To go* or *be sent*) *into g.*

Comb.: *g.-artillery, -gun,* etc.; **g.-hack,** *slang,* a woman who flirts with the officers of a g.; **-hold,** occupation by means of a g.; **-town.**

Garrison (gæ·risən), *v.* 1569. [f. prec.] **1.** To place troops in for defence. Also *fig.* **2.** To occupy as a garrison. Also *transf.* and *fig.* 1645. **3.** To put 'in garrison' or on garrison-duty. Also *fig.* 1596.

1. *fig.* Garrisoned against. .fears GEO. ELIOT. **3.** *fig.* Garrisoned round about him like a camp Of faithful souldiery MILT.

Garron, -an (gæ·rən). 1540. [– Gael. *gearran,* Ir. *gearrán.*] A small and inferior kind of Irish or Scotch horse.

Garrooka: see GAROOKUH.

Garrot¹ (gæ·rət). 1829. [– Fr. *garrot* (XVIII).] A sea-duck; esp. the Golden-eye (*Clangula glaucion*).

Garrot² (gæ·rət). 1824. [– (O)Fr. *garrot* stick, lever – Pr. *garrot*; see next.] **1.** *Antiq.* A lever for winding a cross-bow. **2.** *Surg.* A tourniquet 1845.

Garrotte, garotte (gărǫ·t), *sb.* 1622. [– Sp. *garrote* orig. cudgel, f. **garr-* (perh. of Celtic origin), whence Pr. *garra* knee-cap, Sp. *garra* claw.] †**1.** A rackpin to tighten cords in packing (*rare*) 1629. **2.** Execution by strangulation, as in Spain; the instrument of this 1622. **3.** Highway-robbery by throttling 1852. Phr. *To tip the g.* (*slang*): to rob thus.

Garrotte, garotte (gărǫ·t), *v.* 1851. [– Fr. *garrotter* or Sp. *garrotear*; see prec.] **1.** *trans.* To execute by means of the garrotte. **2.** To throttle in order to rob 1858. **3.** *transf.* and *fig.* To strangle 1878. Hence **Garro·tter, garo·tter.**

Garrulity (gărū·lĭti). 1581. [– Fr. †*garrulité* – L. *garrulitas,* f. *garrulus*; see next, -ITY.] The quality of being garrulous.

My crime, Shameful g. MILT.

Garrulous (gæ·rŭləs), *a.* 1611. [f. L. *garrulus,* f. *garrire* chatter; see -ULOUS.] **1.** Loquacious; *transf.* of birds, etc.: Chattering, babbling 1854. **2.** Of speech: Wordy 1838.

1. Age. .g., recounts The feats of youth THOMSON. *transf.* Birds grew g. PATMORE. **2.** G. comments DISRAELI, history FREEMAN. Hence **Ga·rrulous-ly** *adv.,* **-ness.**

Garter (gā·ɹtəɹ), *sb.* *Sc.* **gartan, -en.** ME. [– OFr. *gartier,* var. of *jartier* (also *jartière,* mod. *jarretière*), f. *garet, jaret* bend of the knee, calf of the leg, prob. of Celtic origin (cf. GARROTTE *sb.*).] **1.** A band worn round the leg to keep the stocking in place. **b.** *Naut. slang.* Fetters 1769. **2.** *The Garter,* the badge of the highest order of English Knighthood, instituted c1344; membership of this order; the order itself ME. **3.** *Her.* **a.** = BENDLET. 1658. **b.** A strap or ribbon buckled in a circle, with the free end hanging down 1882. **4.** *transf.* Anything resembling a garter in function or in shape; esp. **a.** *techn.* a semi-circular plate, fitting into a groove in the screw of a bench-vice 1874; **b.** the band used in 'prick the g.'; whence, the game itself 1827. **c.** tapes for a circus-performer to leap over 1854. **5.** Short for: **a.** *G. King of Arms* (see KING). **b.** *g.-snake* 1880.

2. Record the Garter's glory; A badge for heroes, and for kings to bear DRYDEN. As well ask. .for the next vacant g. THACKERAY. **4.** Item, for a g. for the sydes [of cucking stool]. .iijᵈ 1556. **5. b.** The g. and the copperhead 1880.

Phrases. *To cast one's g.* (Sc.): to secure a husband. *In the catching up of a g.*: in a moment. *Pricking in the g.* (also *prick-the-g.*): a swindling game (see FAST-AND-LOOSE).

Comb.: **g.-blue,** dark blue, the colour of the G. ribbon; **-fish,** the scabbard-fish (*Lepidopus caudatus*); **-knee,** the left knee; **-robes**; **-snake** *U.S.,* a name of grass- or ribbon-snakes of the genus *Eutænia*; **-webbing,** elastic webbing for garters.

Garter (gā·ɹtəɹ), *v.* ME. [f. prec.] **1.** *trans.* To tie with a garter. Also with *on, up.* Also *absol.* Also *transf.* **2.** *Her.* To surround with a GARTER (sense 3b) 1864. Hence **Ga·rtered** *ppl. a.*; *spec.* wearing the Garter. **Ga·rtering** *vbl. sb.*; *spec.* the material of garters; in *pl.* = garters.

Garth¹ (gāɹþ). ME. [– ON. *garðr* = OE. *ġeard* YARD *sb.*¹] **1.** A piece of enclosed ground, usu. beside a building, a yard, garden, or paddock; freq. with defining word, as *cloister-, willow-g.,* etc. **b.** Short for: Cloister-g. (*rec.*). **2.** = FISHGARTH. 1609.

1. A garden for potatoes. .called a g. A. YOUNG. **b.** The central grassplot of the cloisters—the g. 1890.

Garth² (gāɹþ). *n. dial.* ME. [north. form of *gerth* (see GIRTH).] **1.** A saddle-girth. **2.** A wooden hoop 1483. **3.** Girth 1684.

‖**Garum** (gēᵊ·rŏm). 1587. [L. – Gr. γάρον earlier γάρος.] A Roman sauce made of fermented fish.

Garvie (gā·ɹvi). *Sc.* 1742. [Of unkn. origin.] A sprat.

Gas (gæs), *sb.*¹ Pl. **gases** (gæ·sĕz). 1658. [A word invented by Van Helmont (1577–1644), modelled on Gr. χάος, Du. *g* representing Gr. χ.] †**1.** A supposed occult principle in all bodies, regarded as an ultra-rarefied condition of water –1743. **2.** Any aeriform or completely elastic fluid 1779. *spec.* **a.** Gas for lighting or heating; orig. = COAL-GAS, now including *oil-gas,* etc. 1794. **b.** *Coal-mining.* Fire-damp mixed with air 1853. **c.** Coal-gas used to fill a balloon or airship 1792. **d.** = LAUGHING GAS 1894. **e.** Stomachic vapours 1882. **f.** = POISON-*gas* 1915. **3.** A gas jet 1872. **4.** *slang.* Empty talk; bombast 1847.

2. The three gases which composed the atmosphere HUXLEY. **c.** *fig.* Poltroons Swell'd by the g. of Courage to Balloons WOLCOTT.

Comb. **1.** General: as *g.-globe* (GLOBE *sb.* 6), *-range* (RANGE *sb.*[1] III. 1), *-stove* (STOVE *sb.* 5) *-works* (WORK *sb.* II. 10), etc.

2. Special: **g.-alarm,** (*a*) one to warn of g.; (*b*) one to alarm by explosion of g.; **-bath,** a bath heated by g.; **-battery,** a voltaic battery operating by the generation of gases; **-bill,** (*a*) one granting powers to make and supply g.; (*b*) a bill for g. consumed; **-bleaching,** 'bleaching by means of sulphur dioxide' (*Cent. Dict.*); **-blower,** a stream of g. from a coal-seam; **-bottle,** (*a*) a retort; (*b*) *Med.* a vessel to hold compressed g.; **-buoy,** one with chambers filled with g. to supply the lamp; **-burner** (see BURNER); **-chandelier** = GASELIER; **-check,** a device in guns to prevent an escape of g. at the breach; **-coal,** bituminous coal used in making g.; **-cock,** a tap fitted to the g.-pipe; **-coke,** residuum of coal used in g.-making; **-condenser,** an apparatus for freeing coal-g. from its tar; **-drain** (*Coal-mining*), a heading for carrying off fire-damp; **-dregs,** the refuse of g.-making; **-engine,** one in which the power is obtained by the production or the rhythmical combustion and explosion of g. in a closed cylinder; **-firing,** firing a furnace so that the gaseous products of combustion are utilized as fuel; **-fixture,** a bracket or gaselier for g.; **-furnace,** (*a*) one for making g.; (*b*) one heated by g.; **-helmet** = *g.-mask*; **-holder,** a gasometer; **-indicator,** one for showing the pressure of g.; **-lime,** lime which has been used to purify coal-g.; **-mask,** a mask worn as a protection against poison-gas; **-microscope,** one lit by oxyhydrogen light; **-motor,** a g.-engine; **-pendant,** a g.-pipe hung from the ceiling and fitted with burners; **-pipe,** (*a*) one for conveying g.; (*b*) joc. term for an inferior gun; (*c*) = *gas-drain*; **-plate,** a steel disc, in Krupp guns, to receive the direct force of the powder-gases; **-retort,** a vessel for holding the material of which g. is to be made, **-ring,** (*a*) a thin perforated plate of metal used as a g.-check; (*b*) a hollow iron ring with jets burning g. for heating purposes; **-sand,** sandstone yielding g.; **-shell,** one charged with poison-gas; **-spectrum,** one formed from the rays of an incandescent g.; **-stoker;** **-stoking,** the heating of g.-retorts; **-tar,** COAL-TAR produced in the manufacture of coal-g.; **-tar** *v.*, to coat with g.-tar; **g. thermometer,** one in which g. is the expanding medium; **-washer,** one for removing the ammonia from g.; **-water,** water through which coal-g. has passed; **-well,** a boring in the earth, tapping natural g.

Gas, *sb.*[2] *U.S.* 1905. Colloq. abbrev. of GASOLENE b.

Phr. *To step* or *tread on the g.* (orig. *U.S.*): to accelerate a motor engine by pressing down the accelerator-pedal with the foot; *gen.* to put on speed.

Gas (gæs), *v.* Infl. **gassing, gassed.** 1847. [f. GAS *sb.*[1]] **1.** To supply or light up with gas (*colloq.*) 1886. **2.** To pass through a gas-flame, to remove fibres, as in gassing lace 1859. **3.** To impregnate (slaked lime) with chlorine, in making bleaching-powder 1880. **4.** To affect by or attack with (poison-) gas 1889. **5.** *slang.* To deceive by talking gas (*U.S.*) 1847; *intr.* to vapour, talk idly 1875.

Gasalier, var. of GASELIER.

Ga·s-ba:g. 1827. **1.** A bag in which gas is kept; *spec.* an airship's gas-container. **2.** An inflated bag for plugging a gas-main during repairs 1884. **3.** A 'windbag' 1889.

Gascoign, obs. f. GASKIN.

Gascon (gæ·skŏn), *sb.* ME. [– (O)Fr. *gascon* – L. *Vasco, -ōn-*, whence also BASQUE.] **1.** A native of Gascony. **2.** Hence, a braggart 1771. **3.** *attrib.* or *adj.* Pertaining to Gascony 1488. **4.** *ellipt.* †**a.** Gascon wine 1630. **b.** Gascon dialect 1813.

2. They [the Irish] are the Gascons of Britain SCOTT.

Gasconade (gæskŏnē·d), *sb.* 1709. [– Fr. *gasconnade*, f. *gasconner* brag, prop. talk like a Gascon; see prec., -ADE.] Extravagant boasting. Hence **Gascona·de** *v. intr.* to indulge in gasconades. **Gascona·der,** a braggart.

Gasconism (gæ·skŏniz'm). 1807. [f. after prec. with substitution of suffix -ISM.] A spirit of vaunting.

Gascoyne, obs. f. GASKIN, GASCON.

Gaseity (gæsī·ĭti). 1852. [f. GASE(OUS + -ITY.] The state of being a gas.

Gaselier (gæsĕlīᵊ·ɹ). Also **gasalier.** 1849. [f. GAS *sb.*[1] after CHANDELIER; the older name was *gas-chandelier.*] A frame to hold gas-burners.

Gaseous (gæ·sĭəs, gē·sĭəs), *a.* 1799. [f. GAS *sb.*[1], after AQUEOUS; see -EOUS.] **1.** Having the nature, or in the form, of gas. Also *fig.* **2.** Relating to gases 1805.

1. *fig.* His g., illimitably expansive conceit GEO. ELIOT.

Ga·s-fi:tter. 1858. One who fits up buildings with gas-appliances.

Ga·s-fi:tting. 1865. **1.** *pl.* Pipes, brackets, etc. for the use of gas. **2.** Fixing gas-appliances. Also *attrib.*

Gash (gæʃ), *sb.* 1548. [Later form of †*garsh*, var. of †*garse* (XIII–XVII) – OFr. **garce*, f. *garcer, jarcer* scarify (mod. *gercer* chap, crack). For loss of *r* cf. BASS *sb.*[1], DACE.] **1.** A long and deep cut or slash, made in the flesh, or in any object. Also *fig.* **b.** The act of making such a cut 1829. **2.** *U.S. slang.* The mouth 1852. **3.** *attrib.*, as **g.-vein** (*Austral. Mining*), a V-shaped vein 1869.

1. He..received a mortal g. 1807. To heal..the sloe-tree's g. BROWNING.

Gash (gæʃ), *a.*[1] Now only *Sc.* 1589. [perh. back-formation from GASHFUL or GASHLY (but is recorded earlier than these).] Dismal to look at.

His g. lookes and his abrupt answeres GREENE.

Gash (gæʃ), *a.*[2] *Sc.* 1706. [Cf. Sc. *gash* sb. prattle, and vb. talk, gossip.] **1.** Sagacious. **2.** Wise-looking 1826. **3.** Well-dressed 1785.

Gash (gæʃ), *v.* 1562. [For earlier *garsh, garse* – OFr. *garcer*; see GASH *sb.*] **1.** *trans.* To cut or slash; also *absol.* **b.** With *asunder* TENNYSON. **2.** *intr.* To open in a gash (*rare*) 1750.

1. With barbarous blows they g. the dead BYRON.

Ga·shful, *a.* Now *dial.* 1620. [perh. alt. f. GHASTFUL: cf. GASH *a.*[1], GASHLY.] Ghastly.

Ga·shly, *a.* Now *dial.* 1633. [perh. alt. f. GHASTLY; cf. prec., and GASH *a.*[1]] Ghastly, horrid. Also *advb.* Hence **Ga·shliness.**

By all that is hirsute and g.! I cry STERNE.

Gasifica·tion. 1812. [f. GAS *sb.*[1] + -FICATION.] The process of making into gas.

Gasiform (gæ·sifǭɹm), *a.* 1800. [f. GAS *sb.*[1] + -FORM.] In a gaseous state.

Gasify (gæ·sifəi), *v.* 1828. [f. GAS *sb.*[1] + -FY.] To make or become gaseous. Hence **Ga·sifi:able** *a.*

Gasket (gæ·skėt). 1622. [perh. alt. of †*gassit* (Capt. Smith) – Fr. *garcette* little girl, thin rope, dim. of *garce*, fem. of *gars* boy. For the naut. use of similar words cf. EUPHROE, GRUMMET.] **1.** A small rope for securing a furled sail to the yard. Chiefly in *pl.* **2.** Tow, plaited hemp, etc. for packing a piston or caulking a joint 1829. Hence **Ga·sket** *v.* to tie with gaskets.

Gaskin[1] (gæ·skin). 1573. [perh. due to a false analysis of GALLIGASKINS.] †**1.** A kind of breech or hose. Chiefly *pl.* –1611. **2.** The hinder thigh of a horse 1652.

Ga·skin[2]. *rare.* = GASKET.

Ga·s-light. 1808. **a.** The light of gas. **b.** A jet of lighted gas; chiefly *pl.* Also *attrib.* as *g.-l. paper, plate, print* (in Photography).

Ga·sma:n. 1821. **1.** One who makes or supplies gas. **b.** A collector of gas-accounts. **2.** One who attends to the gas-lights in a theatre 1865. **3.** *Coal-mining.* (*U.S.*) One who examines the workings for fire-damp 1883.

Gasogene, var. of GAZOGENE.

Gasolene, gasoline (gæ·sŏlīn). 1871. [f. GAS *sb.*[1] + -OL + -ENE, -INE[5].] A volatile inflammable liquid, produced in distilling crude petroleum, and used for heating, etc. **b.** *U.S.* The petrol used for motor engines (cf. GAS *sb.*[2]) 1895.

Gasometer (gæsǫ·mĭtəɹ), **gazometer.** 1790. [– Fr. *gazomètre* (Lavoisier, 1789), f. *gaz* GAS *sb.*[1] + *-mètre* -METER.] **1.** An apparatus for holding and measuring gas. **2.** A tank in which gas is stored for distribution 1808.

Gasometry (gæsǫ·mėtri). 1790. [– Fr. *gazométrie*; see prec., -METRY.] The science of measuring gases. Hence **Gasome·tric** *a.* relating to g.

Gasoscope (gæ·sŏskōᵘp). 1858. [f. GAS *sb.*[1] + -SCOPE.] An apparatus for indicating the presence of gas.

Gasp (gɑsp), *sb.* 1577. [f. GASP *v.*] A convulsive catching of the breath from exertion, the lessening of vital action, etc. Also *transf.*

Phr. (*One's*) *last g.*: the last attempt to breathe before death. *At the last g.*: at the point of death.

Gasp (gɑsp), *v.* ME. [Early var. *gayspe* – ON. *geispa*, metath. alt. of **geipsa*, f. base of *geip* idle talk, *geipa* talk idly.] **1.** *intr.* To catch the breath with open mouth, as from exhaustion or astonishment. **2.** *trans.* To exhale (*occas.* to inhale) with convulsive breathings 1534.

1. Names..That would have made Quintilian stare and g. MILT. Phr. *To g. for* (occas. *after*); to pant for (air); also *fig.* The sick, for Air before the Portal g. DRYDEN. **2.** He..lay gasping life away COWPER. Phr. *To g. one's last. To g. out*: to utter with gasps.

Gasper (gɑ·spəɹ). 1914. *colloq.* [f. prec. + -ER[1] 1.] A cheap cigarette.

Ga·s-pla:nt. 1. Bastard Dittany. (U.S. Dicts.) **2.** The apparatus in a gas-works 1889.

Gassendist (gæse·ndist). 1821. [f. *Gassendi* + -IST.] A follower of Gassendi.

Gasserian (gæsīᵊ·riăn), *a.* Also **Casserian.** 1831. [f. Johann Laurentius *Gasser*; see -IAN.] Distinguishing epithet of the ganglion on the sensory trunk of the fifth cranial nerve.

Gassy (gæ·si), *a.* 1757. [f. GAS *sb.*[1] + -Y[1].] **1.** Full of gas; of the nature of gas. **2.** *slang.* characterized by 'gas' (see GAS *sb.*[1] 4); given to 'gassing' 1863. Hence **Ga·ssiness.** *rare.*

†**Gast,** *v.* [OE. *gǣstan* (once) :– Gmc. **ʒaistjan*; see GHOST.] *trans.* To scare, terrify –1616.

Gasted by the noyse I made *Lear* II. i. 57. Hence †**Gast** *ppl. a.* terrified.

†**Ga·ster,** *v.* 1593. [frequent. of GAST *v.*; see -ER[5].] *trans.* To scare, terrify –1787.

Gasteromycetous (gæ:stĕroməisī·təs), *a.* 1861. [f. mod.L. *gasteromycetes* (f. Gr. γαστήρ, γαστερ- stomach + μύκητες pl. of μύκης fungus) + -OUS.] *Bot.* Of, belonging, or relating to the *Gasteromycetes*, one of the orders of Fungi.

Gasteropod, gastropod (gæ·stĕrŏpǫd, gæ·strŏpǫd). Also †**-pode.** 1826. [– Fr. *gastéropode* (XVIII) – mod.L. *gasteropoda* n.pl., f. Gr. γαστήρ, γαστερ- stomach; see -POD.]

A. *sb.* One of the Gasteropoda.

B. *adj.* Gasteropodous 1836.

‖**Gasteropoda, gastropoda** (gæstĕrǫ·pŏdă, gæstrǫ·pŏdă), *sb. pl.* 1828. [See prec.] *Zool.* A class or group of molluscs (including the snails, limpets, etc.) so called from the ventral position of the locomotive organ. Hence **Gastero·podous, gastro·podous** *a.* belonging to the *G.*; pertaining to or marking a gasteropod.

Gastful: see GHASTFUL.

Gastly, obs. f. GHASTLY.

†**Ga·stness.** ME. [f. GAST *ppl. a.* + -NESS.] Terrified condition; terror, dread –1604.

Gastræa (gæstrī·ă). 1877. [mod.L. *gastræa*, f. Gr. γαστήρ, γαστερ- stomach + *-æus*, -αῖος adj. suff.] **1.** = GASTRULA. Huxley. **2.** A primitive sac-like animal, whose existence Haeckel assumes, consisting of two layers of cells, an ectoderm and an endoderm.

Gastræa theory, the theory which makes this the ancestral form of the whole animal kingdom. So **Gastræ·ad,** one of the *Gastreades*, a division of sponges which does not develop beyond the gastrula stage.

‖**Gastralgia** (gæstræ·ldʒiă). 1822. [mod.L., f. as prec. + ἄλγος pain; see -IA[1].] *Path.* Pain in the stomach. Hence **Gastra·lgic** *a.* and *sb.*

Gastric (gæ·strik), *a.* 1656. [– mod.L. *gastricus*, f. Gr. γαστήρ, γαστρ- stomach; see -IC.] Of or pertaining to the stomach; situated in the stomach; of the nature of a stomach.

The g. cavity 1830, artery 1842.

Phr. *Gastric fever*: now usually, enteric or typhoid fever. *G. juice* (formerly also *g. acid, liquor*): thin, clear, almost colourless fluid, of an acid nature, secreted by certain glands in the stomach, where it is the chief agent in digestion. Hence **Ga·stricism,** 'stomach diseases generally' (*Syd. Soc. Lex.*).

Gastriloquist (gæstri·lŏkwist). 1731. [f. as prec., after *ventriloquist.*] = VENTRILOQUIST. So **Gastri·loquous** *a.*, **Gastri·loquy,** etc.

‖**Gastritis** (gæstrəi·tis). 1806. [mod.L., f. as prec. + -ITIS.] *Med.* Inflammation of the coats of the stomach.

Gastro- (gæ·stro), occas. bef. a vowel *gastr-*, comb. f. Gr. γαστήρ, γαστερ-, γαστρ-. **ga·stro-cata·rrhal** *a.*, connected with gastric catarrh; **ga·strocele** [Gr. κήλη tumour], hernia of the stomach; **gastro-co·lic** [Gr. κόλον the colon] *a.*, pertaining to the stomach and the colon; **ga:stro-duode·nal** *a.*, pertaining to the stomach and the duodenum; **-duodeni·tis**, inflammation of the stomach and the duodenum; **-ente·ric** *a.*, pertaining to the stomach and intestines; **-enteri·tis**, inflammation of the stomach and intestines; hence **-enteri·tic** *a.*; **-epiplo·ic** *a.*, pertaining to the stomach and the epiploon; **-hepa·tic** *a.*, pertaining to the stomach and the liver; **-hystero·tomy**, the Cæsarean operation (see CÆSAREAN *a.*); **-intesti·nal** *a.* = *gastro-enteric*; **ga:stro-phre·nic** *a.*, pertaining to the stomach and to the diaphragm; **ga:stro-pneumo·nic** *a.*, pertaining to the stomach and to the lungs; **-pu·lmonary** *a.*, **-pulmo·nic** *a.* = prec.; **-sple·nic** *a.*, pertaining to the stomach and to the spleen; **-va·scular** *a.*, pertaining jointly to the abdominal cavity and to a vessel.

||**Gastrocnemius** (gæ:stro,knī·miŏs). *Pl.* **-cnemii** (knī·miəi). 1676. [mod.L., f. Gr. γαστροκνημία the calf of the leg.] The muscle which gives a 'bellying' form to the calf of the leg. Hence **Ga:strocne·mial, -ian** *adjs.* of or pertaining to the g.

Gastrodisc (gæ·strŏdisk). 1881. [See GASTRO- and DISK.] *Embryol.* The germinal area of a mammal.

Gastrolith (gæ·strŏliþ). 1854. [f. GASTRO- + -LITH.] A calculus in the stomach; *spec.* = CRAB'S-EYE.

Gastrology (gæstrǫ·lŏdʒi). 1810. [– Gr. γαστρολογία; see GASTRO-, -LOGY.] The science of catering for the stomach; hence, cookery, good eating. So **Gastro·loger. Gastrolo·gical** *a.*

||**Gastromalacia** (gæ:stromălē[i]·ʃ[i]ă). 1855. [mod.L., f. GASTRO- + Gr. μαλακία softness.] *Path.* Softening of the coats of the stomach.

Gastromancy (gæ·stromænsi). Now *Hist.* 1610. [f. GASTRO- + -MANCY.] Divination by the belly, i.e. either by figures seen in bellied glass vessels full of water, or by ventriloquism.

Gastronome (gæ·strŏnō[u]m). 1823. [– Fr. *gastronome*, back-formation from *gastronomie* GASTRONOMY.] One versed in good eating. So **Gastro·nomer. Gastro·nomist.**

Gastronomic, -al (gæstronǫ·mik, -ăl), *a.* 1828. [– Fr. *gastronomique*, f. as prec.; see -IC, -ICAL.] Of or pertaining to gastronomy. Hence **Gastrono·mically** *adv.*

Gastronomy (gæstrǫ·nŏmi). 1814. [– Fr. *gastronomie* (Joseph Berchoux, 1800) – Gr. γαστρονομία, alternative of γαστρολογία GASTROLOGY. See -NOMY.] The art and science of good eating.

Gastropod, Gastropodous: see GASTER-.

Gastrorrhaphy (gæstrǫ·răfi). Also **gastroraphy.** 1739. [– Fr. *gastroraphie* – Gr. γαστρορραφία, f. γαστήρ, γαστρ- belly + root of ῥάπτειν sew.] Suture of wounds in the abdomen.

Gastroscopy (gæstrǫ·skŏpi). 1855. [f. GASTRO- + *-scopy* (f. -SCOPE + -Y[3]).] Examination of the abdomen for disease.

Gastrostomy (gæstrǫ·stŏmi). 1854. [f. GASTRO- + Gr. στόμα mouth + -Y[3].] *Surg.* The operation of opening the stomach for the introduction of food.

Gastrotomy (gæstrǫ·tŏmi). 1656. [f. GASTRO- + -TOMY. Cf. Fr. *gastrotomie.*] The opening of the abdomen by incision, or of the stomach through the abdominal walls.

Gastrula (gæ·strŭlă). 1877. [– mod.L. *gastrula*, f. late L. *gaster* belly – Gr. γαστήρ; see -ULE.] *Embryol.* That form of the metazoic germ which consists of a cup with two layers of cells in the wall. Also *attrib.* Hence **Ga·strular** *a.* pertaining to a g., or to gastrulation. **Gastrula·tion,** the formation of a g.

Gastruran (gæstrū[ə]·răn). [f. mod.L. *Gastrura* n.pl. (f. Gr. γαστήρ, γαστρ- stomach + οὐρά tail) + -AN.]

A. *adj.* Of or pertaining to the *Gastrura* or stomatopodous crustaceans.

B. *sb.* [sc. *animal.*] In recent Dicts. So **Gastru·rous** *a.*

Gat (gæt). Also **gate.** 1723. [app. – ON. *gat* (Sw., Da. *gat*) opening, passage; see GATE *sb.*[1]] An opening between sandbanks; a channel, strait; in Kent, an opening in the cliffs.

Gat, pa. t. of GET *v.*

Gate (gē[i]t), *sb.*[1] [OE. *ġæt, ġeat*, pl. *gatu*, corresp. to OFris. *gat* hole, opening, OS. *gat* eye of a needle (LG., Du. gap, hole, breach), ON. *gat* opening, passage (see prec.) :– Gmc. **ȝatam.* Forms with initial *y-*, repr. OE. forms *ġeat*, pl. *ġeatu*, remain in north. dial. *yett, yeat*; but the standard literary form has been *gate* since XVI.] **1.** An opening in a wall for entrance and exit, with a movable barrier for closing it; said with reference to a city or other enclosure, or the enclosure-wall of a large building. **2.** *ellipt.* for *gate(s of the city* as a place of judicial assembly. [A Hebraism.] OE. **3.** *trans.* A mountain-pass. Also *pl.* 1601. **4.** *fig.* A means of entrance or exit ME. **5.** The barrier itself; a framework of wood or iron, either of open-work or solid, turning on pivots or hinges, or sliding in a groove, and used either in a pair or singly OE. **b.** A contrivance for stopping or regulating the passage of water. (Cf. *flood-, lock-, sluice-g.*) 1496. **6.** *techn.* **a.** (*Locksmithing*) One of the apertures in the tumblers for the passage of the stub 1874. **b.** = SASH *sb.*[2] 2. 1874. **c.** An H-shaped arrangement of slots through which a gear-lever is pushed 1906. **7.** The number of persons who pay at the gates to see an athletic contest, etc.; also, the *gate-money* thus received 1888.

1. The Ladies Coach so stopt the G., that the Duke's could not possibly pass COTTON. Phr. *The gate(s of heaven, hell, paradise*, perhaps orig. apprehended in a material sense. Also *the gate(s of death*: a near approach to death. Most like the struggle at the g. of death KEATS. **2.** Then went Boaz up to the g. and sat him down there *Ruth* 4:1. **4.** They [the senses] are the gates and windows of its [the soul's] knowledge DRUMM. OF HAWTH. Phr. *The ivory g., the g. of horn*: in Greek legend, those through which false and true dreams respectively come.

Comb.: **g.-bill** (at Oxford and Cambridge), a record of the times at which a man returns to college (or lodgings) after hours; also, the account of fines charged against a man for staying out late; **-boot,** the right of cutting wood for gates; **-chamber,** a recess in the side wall of a canal-lock, which receives the g.; **-crasher,** an uninvited intruder at a reception, etc. (*colloq.*, orig. *U.S.*); **-leg, -legged** *a.*, designating a table with legs in a gate-like frame swinging back to allow the leaves to be shut down; **-money,** money paid at the gates for admission to an athletic meeting, etc.; **-saw,** a mill-saw which is strained in a g. or sash to prevent buckling; **-vein,** the *Vena portæ* (*Obs.* exc. *fig.*); **-works,** fortifications at the g. of a town, etc. Hence **Ga·ted** *ppl. a.* furnished with a g. or gates.

Gate (gē[i]t), *sb.*[2] Now only *Sc.* and *n. dial.* ME. [– ON. *gata* = OHG. *gazza* (G. *gasse* street, lane), Goth. *gatwō* :– Gmc. **ȝatwōn.* See GAIT.] **1.** A way, road, or path. **2.** A street, as in *Gallowgate*, etc. 1470. †**3.** A going, journey, course (*lit.* and *fig.*) –1677. **4.** Manner of going. *Obs.* exc. *spec.* (see GAIT *sb.*) 1637. **5.** Way, manner, or method of doing or behaving; a peculiar habit ME.

1. Phrases. *To come, go, ride a, the, his, her*, etc. *g. This (that) g.* used advb. = this (that) way, in this (that) direction. *Some, any g.*: somewhere, anywhere.

Gate (gē[i]t), *sb.*[3] 1677. [Cf. synon. Du. *gietgat*, f. *gieten* pour, cast + *gat* opening = GATE *sb.*[1]] *Founding.* **1.** †**a.** The little spout in the brim of casting ladles 1683. **b.** The opening or channel through which the molten metal flows into a mould 1677. **2.** The waste piece of metal cast in the gate 1839.

Gate (gē[i]t), *v.* 1831. [f. GATE *sb.*[1]] *trans.* At Oxford and Cambridge: To confine (an undergraduate) to college.

Gate, obs. f. GOAT.

Gatehouse (gē[i]·t,haus). ME. [f. GATE *sb.*[1] + HOUSE *sb.*] **1.** A house (for a servant) at or over a gate. **2.** The apartment over the gate of a city or palace, often used as a prison; *spec.* that over the gate of the palace at Westminster 1587.

2. [The king's] messenger..was..committed to the G. 1647.

Ga·te-keeper. 1572. [f. GATE *sb.*[1] + KEEPER.] **1.** One who has charge of a gate. **2.** A species of butterfly 1819.

Gateless (gē[i]·tlės), *a.* 1608. [f. GATE *sb.*[1] + -LESS.] Without a gate.

Ga·te-post. 1522. [f. GATE *sb.*[1] + POST *sb.*[1]] A post belonging to a gate, either that on which it hangs, or that against which it shuts.

Ga·teway. 1707. [f. GATE *sb.*[1] + WAY.] **1.** An opening through a fence or wall. ?*Obs.* **2.** A frame or arch in which a gate is hung; a structure built at or over a gate, for ornament or defence. Also *attrib.* 1762. **3.** *transf.* and *fig.* **a.** A means of egress or ingress 1842. **b.** = GATE *sb.*[1] 3. 1884.

3. a. At the gateways of the day TENNYSON.

Gather (gæ·ðəɹ), *sb.* 1555. [f. GATHER *v.*] **1.** The amount gathered, crop. **2.** *The gathers* (pl.), that part, *esp.* of a dress, which is gathered or drawn in 1663. **3.** *techn.* 'The inclination forward of an axle journal, or spindle, usually one-tenth of its diameter' (Knight) 1874.

Gather (gæ·ðəɹ), *v.* [OE. *gaderian* = OFris. *gaderia*, MLG. *gadern*, (M)Du. *gaderen*, MHG. *gatern* :– WGmc. **ȝadurōjan*, f. **ȝadurī* TOGETHER. For the change of OE. d to ð cf. *father.*]

I. *trans.* †**1.** (Only with prefixed *ȝe-.*) To join; to put together. *Obs.* since early ME. **2.** To bring together; to collect OE. **3.** To collect (flowers, etc.) from the place of growth; to cull, pick, pluck; to collect as harvest (also *to g. in*) OE.; to pick up 1715. †**4.** To compile (literary matter) –1677. **5.** To be the means of bringing together or accumulating ME. **6.** To collect (contributions). Also *absol.* to make a collection. Now *rare.* ME. **7.** To collect or acquire by way of increase; to gain 1590. **8.** To collect (knowledge) by observation and reasoning; to infer, deduce, conclude. (= L. *colligere.*) 1535. **9.** To draw into smaller compass, contract 1617; *spec.* to draw together or pucker (part of a dress) by means of a thread 1576. **b.** *Arch.* To contract or make narrower (a drain, chimney, etc.) 1703. **10.** *techn.* **a.** *Glass-making.* To collect (melted glass) on the end of the blowing-tube 1839. **b.** To collect and place in order according to signatures (the printed sheets of a book). Also *absol.* 1683.

2. Up roos our host..And gadrede us togidre, alle in a flok CHAUCER. To g. the materials for nests GOLDSM. Phr. *To be gathered to one's fathers, to one's people*; to be buried with one's ancestors; hence, to die. **3.** But they that have gathered it [the corn] shall eat it *Isa.* 62:9. A Rose just gather'd from the Stalk DRYDEN. **5.** Standing streames geather filth GOSSON. To g. rust 1687. **7.** Phr. *To g. breath*, etc.: to gain or recover breath. *To g. oneself (together).* †*To g. ground*: to gain ground. As Ev'ning Mist.. gathers ground fast at the Labourer's heel MILT. *To g. head*: to acquire strength; also to swell as a festering sore. *To g. way* (Naut.): 'to begin to feel the impulse of the wind on the sails, so as to obey the helm (Smyth). **8.** Pliny supposed amber to be a resin..which he gathered from its smell BP. BERKELEY. **9.** Golden the clasp that gathers her shining robe to her side BOWEN.

II. *intr.* (Chiefly = refl. uses of I). **1.** To congregate, assemble OE. **2.** Of things: To collect; to form or increase by the coming together of material ME. **b.** To accumulate and come to a head. Hence, of a sore, etc.: To develop a purulent swelling. OE. **3.** To contract; to form folds or wrinkles (*rare*) 1577. **4.** *Naut.* To make way (towards an object) 1577.

1. There gathered vnto him..a very great multitude 1 *Esdras* 8:91. **2.** One knows how a story gathers like a snowball MRS. CARLYLE. **b.** *fig.* Now do's my Proiect g. to a head SHAKS. **3.** As fast years flow away, The smooth brow gathers SHELLEY. *To g. into the wind* (Naut.): to sail nearer to the wind.

Hence **Ga·therable** *a.* capable of being inferred.

Gatherer (gæ·ðərəɹ). ME. [f. prec. + -ER[1].] **1.** One who gathers or collects (see GATHER *v.*); often with defining word, as *rent-, tax-g.* (now usu. *-collector*). **2.** One of the front teeth of a horse 1696.

Ga·thering, *vbl. sb.* OE. [f. as prec. + -ING[1].] **1.** The action of GATHER *v.*, in various transitive senses. Also with *in, out, up.* **b.** The action, also the result, of drawing in or contracting 1580. **2.** The action of coming together; the result of this; union, accumulation OE. **3.** *spec.* A suppurated swelling OE. **4.** An assembly or meeting OE.; a signal (by beat of drum, etc.) 1653. **5.** That which is gathered or brought together; *esp.* a collection in money (now *dial.*) ME. **6.** *Bookbinding.* The arrangement of the loose sheets of a book in proper order 1683.

Comb.: **g.-board** (*Bookbinding*), a horseshoe-shaped table on which signatures are laid to be gathered; **-coal,** a large piece of coal, laid on the fire to keep it burning during the night; **-cry,** a summons to assemble for war; **-ground,** area from which the feeding waters of a river etc., are collected; **-hoop,** one used by coopers to draw in the ends of the staves so as to allow the hoop to be slipped on them; **-peat,** a fiery peat which was sent round by the borderers to alarm the country in time of danger; also, a peat put into the kitchen fire at night, to keep it alive till the morning.

Gatling (gæ·tliŋ). 1870. [f. the name of the inventor, Dr. R. J. *Gatling.* First used in the American civil war (1861–5).] *attrib.* in *Gatling gun,* a form of machine gun, with a cluster of barrels into which the cartridges are automatically loaded at the breech. Also *Gatling* simply.

Gatten, var. of GAITER *sb.*[2]

†**Gat-toothed,** *a. rare.* [app. = GAP-TOOTHED, f. GAT *sb.* opening.] Having the teeth wide apart (pop. regarded as a sign of luck and of much travelling). CHAUCER.

‖**Gauche** (gōʃ), *a.* 1751. [Fr., = left-handed, awkward.] **1.** Awkward, clumsy. **2.** *Math.* Skew, not plane 1879.

2. If various points of the line do not lie in one plane, we have in one case..a curve of double curvature, in the other a g. polygon THOMSON & TAIT.

‖**Gaucherie** (gō·ʃəri). 1798. [Fr., f. *gauche*; see prec., -ERY.] Want of tact or manner, awkwardness; a gauche proceeding.

Gaucho (gau·tʃo, gǭ·tʃo). Also erron. **Guacho.** 1824. [Sp., of native origin.] One of a mixed European and Indian race of equestrian herdsmen.

Gaud, *sb.*[1] Also **gaude.** *Obs.* exc. *Hist.* ME. [– AL. *gaudium,* esp. in *quinque gaudia* (XIV) 'the five joyful mysteries' of the B.V.M. Cf. AFr. *gaudes* in the same sense (XIV).] One of the larger beads placed between the decades of 'aves' in a rosary.

Gaud (gǭd), *sb.*[2] [perh. – AFr. deriv. of OFr. *gaudir* – L. *gaudēre* rejoice.] †**1.** A trick, prank; often, a pretence; also a pastime –1796; a scoff, a laughing-stock –1650. **2.** *concr.* A plaything, toy. Also, something gaudy; a gewgaw; a piece of finery. Now *rhet.* Also *fig.* ME. **3.** *pl.* Fine doings, gaieties. Now *rhet.* 1650. **4.** *sing.* Idle display 1800.

2. Solomon..giueth us gaudes to play withall 1591.

†**Gaud,** *v.*[1] ME. [f. GAUD *sb.*[1] and [2].] **1.** *trans.* To furnish with gauds (see GAUD *sb.*[1]) –1552. **2.** To ornament –1607.

2. Their nicely gawded Cheekes *Cor.* II. i. 233.

†**Gaud,** *v.*[2] 1532. [–(O)Fr. *gaudir* (see GAUD *sb.*[2]), or direct f. GAUD *sb.*[2]] *intr.* To make merry; to jest; to scoff (*at*) –1580.

He was sporting and gauding with his Familiars SIR T. NORTH.

‖**Gaudeamus** (gǭdi,ēⁱ·mɒ̆s). 1823. [The first word of the mod.L. students' song: *Gaudeamus igitur, juvenes dum sumus,* 'Then let us be merry while we are young'.] A college-students' merry-making.

Gaudery (gǭ·dĕri). 1597. [f. GAUD *sb.*[2] + -ERY.] Gaudy decoration; finery, fine clothes; a piece of finery.

Vice..trickt up with its alluring gauderies 1663.

†**Gau·dish,** *a.* 1538. [f. GAUD *sb.*[2] + -ISH[1].] Trivial; gaudy, showy –1587. Hence **Gau·dish-ly** *adv.*, **-ness.**

Gaudy (gǭ·di), *sb.* ME. [– L. *gaudium* joy, f. *gaudēre* rejoice, or L. *gaudē,* imper. of this vb.] †**1.** = GAUD *sb.*[1] –1560. †**2.** A taper (one of five, burnt to commemorate the Virgin's five joys) –1852. †**3.** = GAUD *sb.*[2] 2. 1555. †**4.** Rejoicing; a merry-making –1647. **5.** A grand feast or entertainment; *esp.* an annual college dinner 1651. †Hence *pl.* 'Commons' for gaudy-days –1706.

†**Gau·dy,** *a.*[1] [In †*gaudy-green* (XIV–XVI), prop. green dyed with weld, f. (O)Fr. *gaude* WELD *sb.*[1] + -Y[1].] Only in gaudy-green, green dyed with weld, yellowish green –1590.

Gaudy (gǭ·di), *a.*[2] 1529. [Sense 1 perh. f. GAUDY *sb.* 4, sense 2 f. GAUD *sb.*[2]; see -Y[1].] †**1.** Of fare: Luxurious –1601. **2.** Brilliantly (now chiefly glaringly) fine or gay, showy 1583. **b.** *slang.* In neg. sentences: Very good 1884.

1. Where they make reuell and g. chere 1550. **2.** Costly thy habit as thy purse can buy; But not exprest in fancy: rich, not gawdie *Haml.* I. iii. 71. A late notable gawdy Orator BAXTER. G. Dreams SEDLEY. **b.** Not a g. lot 1894. Hence **Gau·dily** *adv.* **Gau·diness.**

Gau·dy, *v.* 1482. [f. GAUDY *sb.* and *a.*[2]] †**1.** *trans.* To furnish (a rosary) with gaudies –1542. **2.** To make gaudy. SOUTHEY.

Gau·dy-day. 1567. [f. GAUDY *sb.* + DAY.] A day of rejoicing; *esp.* the day of a college gaudy. So **Gaudy-night** (*Ant. & Cl.* III, xiii. 183).

Gaudy-green: see GAUDY *a.*[1]

Gauffer, gauffre: see GOFFER.

Gauge, gage (gēⁱdʒ), *sb.* late ME. [– ONFr. *gauge,* var. of (also mod.) *jauge,* of unkn. origin. For the pronunc. cf. *safe* (sēif), formerly †*sauf.* The sp. *gauge* prevails in Eng., exc. in sense I. 5. American Dicts. prefer *gage.*]

I. 1. A standard measure or scale of measurement; *esp.* a measure of the capacity of a barrel, the diameter of a bullet, or the thickness of sheet iron. **b.** *transf.* and *fig.* Capacity, extent; dimensions, proportions 1655. †**2.** A limit of distance or extent. Also *fig.* HOLLAND. **3.** *spec.* The distance between the rails of a railway, tramway, etc.; also, between the opposite wheels of a carriage 1841. **4.** *techn.* **a.** The length of projection or *margin* of a slate or tile beyond that which overlaps it 1703. **b.** A measure of slate, one yard square 1847. **5.** *Naut.* (Usually *gage.*) **a.** The position of one vessel with reference to another and the wind 1591. **b.** The depth to which a vessel sinks in the water with a full cargo 1644. **6.** *Plastering.* The greater or less quantity of plaster of Paris used with common plaster to accelerate its setting 1842.

1. The gadge of Hering 1595. A bullet of 50-gauge 1858. **b.** He [Howard] has visited all Europe ..to take the gage and dimensions of misery, depression, and contempt BURKE. **3.** *Mixed g.*: a broad and narrow g. laid down together. See also BROAD GAUGE, NARROW GAUGE. **5.** Phr. *To have* or *keep the weather gage of*: to be to windward of; also *fig.* to get the better of. Also *lee gage.*

II. †**1.** A gauging-rod –1706. **2.** A graduated instrument or vessel for gauging the force or quantity of a fluctuating object, as wind, etc. Also *rain-, wind-gauge,* etc.: see RAIN, etc. 1688. **3.** A contrivance attached to a boiler, etc., to show the height or condition of its contents; more fully *g.-cock, -glass.* Of an air-pump: An instrument which indicates the degree of exhaustion in the receiver; usu. defined, as *barometer, siphon g.* (see those words) 1794. **4.** An instrument for ascertaining and verifying dimensions 1677. **5.** A carpenter's tool for marking lines parallel to the edge of a board 1678. **6.** A contrivance to regulate the penetration of a cutting tool; as *auger-, boring-g.* **7.** *fig.* A test 1691.

Comb.: **g.-cock,** one of two or three small cocks for ascertaining the height of the water in a steam boiler; **-concussion,** 'the lateral rocking of railway carriages against the rails' (Ogilvie); **-door,** a wooden door fixed in a mine airway for regulating the ventilation; **-glass,** a glass tube attached to a boiler to show the height of the water; **-knife,** a knife with a contrivance for regulating the amount cut off; **-ladder,** a horsing-block for raising the ends of wheeling planks in excavating; **-lathe,** a lathe for turning work to pattern or size; **-pin** (*Printing*), a small steel pin with teeth, for securing the lay on small platen machines; **-point,** a point marked to indicate the diameter of a cylinder one inch high containing a unit of a given liquid measure; **-rod,** a graduated rod for measuring with great accuracy the internal diameters of portions of work; **-saw,** a saw with a frame or clamp to determine the depth of kerf; **-stuff,** mortar containing three-fifths of fine-stuff and one of plaster of Paris; **-weir,** a weir fitted with movable shutters; **-wheel,** one attached to the forward end of a plough-beam, to gauge the depth of furrow.

Gauge, gage (gēⁱdʒ), *v.* ME. [– ONFr. *gauger,* var. of (also mod.) *jauger*; see prec.] †**1.** *trans.* To measure or measure off. ME. only. **2.** To measure the dimensions, proportions, or amount of ME. **3.** To ascertain the capacity or content of (a cask, etc.) by combined measurement and calculation 1483. **4.** *fig.*; esp. to 'take the measure' of (a person, etc.) 1583. **5.** To render conformable to a given standard; also *to g. up.* Hence *fig.* to limit. 1600. **6.** To mark off (a measurement) 1678. **7.** *Plastering.* To mix plaster in the right proportions for any purpose 1686. **8.** *Dressmaking.* To draw up in parallel gatherings 1881.

2. To g. a foord NORTH, the mind CARLYLE, wire 1833, a river PHILLIPS. **3.** To g. beer barrels MACAULAY. **4.** You shall not gage me By what we doe to night *Merch. V.* II. ii. 208. **5.** The stones are gauged and dressed by the hammer GWILT.

Gaugeable (gēⁱ·dʒăb'l), *a.* 1768. [f. prec. + -ABLE.] That may be gauged.

Gauged, gaged (gēⁱdʒd), *ppl. a.* 1678. [f. GAUGE *v.* + -ED[1].] **1.** Marked or measured with a gauge. **2.** *Bricklaying.* Of bricks: Cut or rubbed accurately to size 1823. **3.** *Plastering.* Mixed in the proper proportions for quick drying 1848.

3. *G. stuff* = gauge-stuff (see GAUGE *sb.*).

Gauger (gēⁱ·dʒəɹ). 1483. [– AFr. *gaugeour,* f. *gauger* GAUGE *v.* Cf. (O)Fr. *jaugeur.*] **1.** One who gauges (see the vb.); esp. an exciseman. **2.** A gauging instrument 1580. Hence **Gau·gership.**

Gauging, gaging (gēⁱ·dʒiŋ), *vbl. sb.* ME. [f. GAUGE *v.* + -ING[1].] The action of GAUGE *v.*

Comb.: **g.-line,** a graduated line drawn on a gauging-rod or slide-rule; **-rod** = GAUGE-ROD.

Gauk, var. of GAWK.

Gaul (gǭl). 1601. [*Gaul,* in L. *Gallia* (France and Upper Italy) – Fr. *Gaule* – Gmc. **walxoz* foreigners, pl. of **walxaz* foreign. applied to the Latin and Celtic peoples. Cf. *Wallachian,* WELSH.]

A. *sb.* **a.** An inhabitant of ancient Gaul 1630. **b.** *poet.* and *joc.* A Frenchman (*mod.*). †**B.** *adj.* Gallic –1606.

Gaulish (gǭ·liʃ). 1659. [f. GAUL *sb.* + -ISH[1].]

A. *adj.* Of or pertaining to the ancient Gauls. Also (*poet.* or *joc.*): French.

B. *sb.* The language of the Gauls 1668.

Gault (gǭlt), *sb.* 1575. [Local word of unkn. origin.] *Geol.* Name of a series of beds of clay and marl, which appear between the upper and the lower greensand. Hence **Gault** *v. dial.* to dig g. **Gau·lter.**

Gaultheria (gǭlþīᵊ·riă). 1848. [f. M. *Gaultier,* a Canadian botanist; see -IA[1].] *Bot.* A genus of evergreen aromatic plants (N.O. *Ericaceæ*). The American Wintergreen, *G. procumbens,* yields a volatile oil called *g. oil,* used in the pharmacopœia.

Gaum (gǭm), *v.* 1796. [Cf. GOME[2], COOM *sb.* 3.] *trans.* To smear with a sticky substance; to daub.

Gaunt (gǭnt, gānt), *a.* ME. [Of unkn. origin.] †**1.** Slim, slender, not fat –1736. **2.** Abnormally lean, as from hunger; haggard-looking; tall, thin, and angular ME. **3.** *transf.* Grim or desolate 1814.

2. G. am I for the graue, g. as the graue SHAKS. A tall g. woman 1882. **3.** Like the g. echo of a hollow tomb 1814. Hence **Gau·ntly** *adv.*, **-ness.**

Gauntlet (gǭ·ntlėt, gā·ntlėt), *sb.*[1] [– (O)Fr. *gantelet,* dim. of *gant* glove – Gmc. **want-,* extant only in ON. *vǫttr* (:– **wantuz*) glove (Sw., Da. *vante*); see -LET.] A glove worn as part of mediæval armour, usu. made of leather, covered with plates of steel. **b.** Used for CESTUS[2]. Dryden. **2.** In rec. use: A stout glove, covering part of the arm as well as the hand, used in driving, wicket-keeping, etc. 1858. Also, the part covering the wrist 1882. †**3.** The plant *Campanula trachelium.* LYTE. **4.** *Naut.* 'A rope round the ship to the lower yard-arms, for drying scrubbed hammocks' (Smyth). [? A distinct wd.]

1. Phr. *To throw* (*down*), etc., *the g.* (= Fr. *jeter le gant*): to give a challenge, from the mediæval custom of throwing down a glove or gauntlet on such occasions. *To take up,* etc., *the g.*: to accept a challenge (Fr. *relever le gant*). I cast them my G., take it vp who dares 1590. Hence **Gau·ntleted** *a.* covered or armed with a g. **Gau·ntlet** *v. trans.* to strike with a g. TENNYSON.

Gauntlet (gǭ·ntlĕt, gā·ntlĕt), *sb.*[2] 1661. [Alteration, by assim. to prec., of GANTLOPE.] = GANTLOPE.

Gauntree, gauntrie, -y: see GANTRY.

Gaur (gauᵊɹ). Also **gour, gore.** 1806. [– Hind. *gaur.*] A large species of ox, *Bos gaurus*, found wild in parts of India.

†**Gaure**, *v.* ME. [poss. a frequent. of GAW *v.*] *intr.* To stare, gape –1579.

Gauss (gaus). 1882. [f. Karl F. *Gauss*, the German mathematician (1777–1855).] *Physics.* A unit of intensity of a magnetic field. Hence **Gau·ssage**, the intensity of a magnetic field expressed in gausses. **Gau·ssian** *a.*, discovered or formulated by Gauss. **Gaussi·vity**, the intensity of magnetizing force expressed in gausses.

Gauze (gǭz). 1561. [– Fr. *gaze* (Ronsard), prob. f. *Gaza* name of a town in Palestine. For the pronunc. cf. †*bawman* BATMAN, and (vǭz), var. pronunc. of VASE.] **1.** A very thin, transparent fabric of silk, linen, or cotton; also, any similar fabric, as *wire-g.* **2.** *transf.* A thin transparent haze 1842.

2. A blue g. of smoke T. HARDY. *Comb.* **g.-lamp**, a safety-lamp in which the flame is surrounded by wire-g.

Hence **Gau·zy** *a.* (whence **Gau·ziness**).

Gavel (gæ·vĕl), *sb.*[1] Now *Hist.* [OE. *gafol* tribute, f. *ʒab- rel. to *ʒeb- GIVE.] **1.** †Tribute. Only OE. and early ME. **b.** Rent OE. †**2.** Interest on money lent –1496. **3.** *attrib.*, chiefly in legal terms relating to payments or services exacted from tenants OE.

Gavel (gæ·vĕl), *sb.*[2] Now *dial.* ME. [– ONFr. *gavel* masc., *gavelle* fem. (mod. *javelle*).] A quantity of corn cut and ready to be made into a sheaf.

Phr. *To lie on the g.*: to lie unbound.

Gavel (gæ·vĕl), *sb.*[3] *Pseudo-arch.* 1803. [f. GAVEL(KIND).] A partition of land among the whole tribe or sept at the death of the holder, with reference to Celtic practice. *Comb.*: **g.-act** or **g.-law**, a statute of Ireland (2 Anne) enforcing the principle of (English) gavelkind on Irish Catholics.

Gavel (gæ·vĕl), *sb.*[4] *U.S.* 1860. [Of unkn. origin.] **a.** 'A mason's setting maul' (Knight). **b.** A president's mallet 1866.

Gavel (gæ·vĕl), *v.*[1] Now *dial.* ME. [f. GAVEL *sb.*[2] Cf. (O)Fr. *javeler*, med.L. *gavellare.*] *trans.* To collect mown corn into heaps, for loading.

Gavel (gæ·vĕl), *v.*[2] *Pseudo-arch.* 1828. [f. GAVEL *sb.*[3] Cf. DISGAVEL.] *trans.* To divide (land), according to the practice of gavelkind. Also *fig.*

They 'gavelled' the lands of Papists and made them descendible to all the children equally MAINE.

Gavel, north. var. of GABLE.

†**Gavelet.** ME. [f. GAVEL *sb.*[1] + obscure element. Cf. med.L. *gavelettum.*] *Law.* A legal process against a tenant for non-payment of rent; chiefly relating to lands held in gavelkind –1741.

Gavelkind (gæ·vĕlkəind). [ME. *gavel(i)-kinde, -kende*; repr. OE. **gafolġecynd*, f. *gafol* GAVEL *sb.*[1] + *ġecynd* KIND *sb.*] **1.** The name of a land-tenure existing chiefly in Kent; orig. identical with SOCAGE, but quite early distinguished by the custom under which a tenant's land at his death was divided equally among his sons. **2.** From the 16th c., often used to denote this custom generally 1531. Also *fig.* **3.** *transf.* A similar Welsh custom of dividing property 1542. **b.** *Irish gavelkind*: a custom by which land, on the decease of its occupant, was thrown into the common stock, and the whole area redivided among the members of the sept 1612. **4.** *attrib.* 1570.

Gaveller (gæ·vĕləɹ). ME. [f. GAVEL *sb.*[1] + -ER[1].] †**1.** A usurer. ME only. **2.** *Mining.* In the Forest of Dean: An officer of the Crown who grants 'gales' to the miners 1692. **3.** *Hist.* One who pays gavel for land rented 1862.

Gavelock (gæ·vĕlǫk). *Obs.* exc. *Hist.* and *dial.* [OE. *gafeluc*, in form a dim. of *gafol*, *ġeafel* fork (see GABLE *sb.*).] **1.** A spear or dart. †**2.** = GABLOCK 1. 1698. **3.** An iron crowbar or lever 1497.

Ga·verick. *Cornwall.* 1846. [Local word of unkn. origin.] The Red Gurnard.

Gavial (gēⁱ·viăl). Also **gar(rh)ial**, etc. 1825. [– Fr. *gavial* – Hind. *ghariyāl* (whence the forms *garial, gharrial*, etc.).] A saurian inhabiting the Ganges, dist. by its elongated muzzle from the American alligator and the African crocodile.

Gavotte (găvǫ·t). Also †**gavot(t.** 1696. [– Fr. *gavotte* – mod. Pr. *gavoto*, f. *Gavot* name in Provence for inhabitants of the Alps.] **a.** A dance resembling the minuet, but more lively. **b.** The music for this dance; a piece of music in common time, moderately quick, and consisting of two parts, each of which is repeated.

†**Gaw**, *v.* ME. [– ON. *gá* heed.] *intr.* To gape, stare –1825. Hence †**Gaw·ish** *a.* staring, gaping; gaudy.

Gawk (gǭk), *sb.* 1837. [perh. f. next; but see GAWK *v.*] An awkward person; a fool; a simpleton. (Confounded by Johnson and others with GOWK.) Hence **Gaw·kish** *a.*

Gawk (gǭk), *a.* Also **gauk.** 1703. [Of difficult etymology; app. a contraction of a disyllabic word which appears in many north-Eng. dialects as *gaulick-, galloc-, gaulish- (hand, handed).*] Left, as in *g.-handed.*

Gawk (gǭk), *v. dial. U.S.* Also **gauk.** 1785. [perh. f. GAWK *sb.*, but poss. an iterative f. GAW *v.* (with suffix as in *tal-k, wal-k, lur-k*), in which case it may be the source of the sb.] *intr.* To stare or gape.

Gawky (gǭ·ki). 1724. [f. GAWK *sb.* (? or *v.*) + -Y[1].]

A. *adj.* Of persons: Awkward and stupid; ungainly. Also *transf.* of things. 1759.

A g. Country Boy 1759. A great g. ship L. HUNT.

B. *sb.* An awkward lout; a simpleton 1724.

Gawn (gǭn). Now *dial.* 1565. [contr. from GALLON.] **1.** A gallon. **2.** Any vessel for lading out liquids 1688.

Gay (gēⁱ). ME. [– (O)Fr. *gai*, of unkn. etym.]

A. *adj.* **1.** Full of or disposed to joy and mirth; light-hearted, exuberantly cheerful, sportive, merry. **b.** Airy, off-hand. JOHNSON. †**c.** Applied to women, as a conventional epithet of praise –1802. **2.** Addicted to social pleasures and dissipations; often *euphem.*: Of immoral life 1637. 3. Bright or lively-looking, esp. in colour; brilliant, showy ME. **4.** Showily dressed. Now *rare.* ME. **5.** Brilliant, attractive. †Formerly also of reasonings, etc.: Specious. 1529. †**6.** Excellent, fine –1593. **7.** *dial.* In good health 1855.

1. This Absolon..jolif was and g. CHAUCER. **b.** G. indifference 1779. **c.** The learned man hath got the lady g. SHAKS. Phr. *The gay science* (= Pr. *gai saber*): the art of poetry. **2.** Is this that Haughty, Gallant, G. Lothario ROWE. *euphem.* Two sisters—both g. 1825. **3.** Costumes g. with ribbons 1870. Dressed in his gayest 1842. **4.** Women..sell their soules and bodyes to go g. 1570. **7.** I don't feel very g. (*mod.*).

B. *adv.* †**1.** = GAILY 1, 2. –1754. **2.** Very; also 'pretty'. Freq. in *dial.* Often written GEY. 1686.

C. *sb.* [the adj. used *absol.*] †**1.** A gay lady. Also, rarely, a 'gallant'. –1475. **2.** An ornament (now *dial.*) ME.; †*fig.* a childish amusement –1694. **3.** A picture in a book (now *dial.*) 1646.

‖**Gayal** (gēⁱ·ăl, gayā·l). 1790. [Hindi *gayāl.*] A kind of ox (*Bibos frontalis*), common in Burma, Assam, and Bengal.

Gaydiang (gēⁱ·diæŋ). 1855. An Annamese vessel, somewhat resembling a Chinese junk.

Gayety: see GAIETY.

Gaylussite (gēⁱ·lūsəit). 1826. [f. *Gay-Lussac*, the French physicist + -ITE[1] 2 b.] *Min.* A double carbonate of calcium and sodium, found in white or yellowish crystals.

Gayly, Gayn-: see GAILY, GAIN-.

Gayness (gēⁱ·nĕs). ME. [f. GAY *a.* + -NESS.] The quality, condition, or state of being GAY.

Gaysome (gēⁱ·sŏm), *a.* Now *rare.* 1610. [f. GAY *a.* + -SOME[1].] Full of gaiety; inspiring with gaiety.

Gaze (gēⁱz), *sb.* ME. [f. GAZE *v.*] †**1.** That which is gazed at –1797. **2.** A steady or intent look ME. Also *fig.*

1. Made of my enemies the scorn and g. MILT. *Sams.* 34. **2.** A Lover's ardent G. STEELE. Phr. *At g.*, †*at a* or *the g.*; said of a deer (now chiefly *Her.*), also of persons: in the attitude of gazing, esp. in wonder, expectancy, bewilderment, etc. So in *to stand at g. At g.*: by sight (said of a hunting-dog).

Gaze (gēⁱz), *v.* ME. [Of unkn. origin; prob. rel. to the base of GAW *v.*] †**1.** *intr.* Orig.: To look vacantly; also, to stare. In mod. use: To look fixedly, intently, or deliberately at something. Now chiefly *literary.* **b.** quasi-*trans.* with adv. or phrase 1713. **2.** *trans.* To stare at, look fixedly at. *poet.* 1591.

1. I did make them all g. to see themselves served so nobly PEPYS. The mute rapture with which he would g. upon her in company W. IRVING. quasi-*trans.* So Scotia's Queen..Rose on her couch and gazed her soul away S. ROGERS. **2.** To g. the Skie MILT.

Gazebo (găzī·bo). Also †**gazeebo(o**, etc. 1752. [perh. joc. f. GAZE, in imitation of L. futures in *-ēbō.*] **1.** A turret or lantern on the roof of a house, commanding an extensive prospect; also, a similar erection in a garden, etc. **2.** A projecting window or balcony 1843.

†**Ga·zeful**, *a.* [f. GAZE *sb.* + -FUL.] That gazes intently. SPENSER.

Ga·ze-hound. 1570. [f. GAZE *sb.* + HOUND *sb.*] A species of dog which hunts by sight. Now chiefly *Hist.*

Gazel, var. of GHAZAL.

Gazelle (găze·l). Also †**gazel** (erron. **gazhal**). 1600. [– (O)Fr. *gazelle*, prob. – Sp. *gacela* – Arab. *ġazāl.*] A small delicately-formed antelope, of which the typical species (*Gazella dorcas*) is a native of Northern Africa; other varieties are found in parts of Africa and Asia. The gazelle is noted for the grace of its movements and the softness of its eyes. Also *attrib.*

The turtle-dove, the timid fawn, the soft-eyed g. W. IRVING.

Ga·zement. *rare.* 1596. [f. GAZE + -MENT.] Stare, observation.

Gazer (gēⁱ·zəɹ). 1548. [f. GAZE *v.* + -ER.[1]] **1.** One who gazes. **2.** A fish (*Polyprosopus macer*) 1861.

†**Gaze·t(t.** 1605. [– Fr. *gazette* (now obs. in this sense) – It. *gazzetta.*] A Venetian coin –1682.

Gazette (găze·t), *sb.* 1605. [– Fr. *gazette* or its source It. *gazzetta*, orig. Venetian *gazeta de la novità*, quasi 'a ha'porth of news', so called because sold for a *gazeta*, Venetian coin of small value; see prec., -ETTE.] **1.** A news-sheet; a periodical publication giving an account of current events. Now only *Hist.* 1605. **2.** *spec.* One of the three official journals entitled *The London G.*, *The Edinburgh G.*, and *The Belfast G.*, issued by authority twice a week, and containing legal and government notices. Hence *gen.* the official journal of any government. 1665.

2. Phr. *To be in the g.*: to be published a bankrupt.

The first issues of the *London G.*, published at Oxford while the Court was resident there in 1665, were entitled *The Oxford G.* The official record of the acta and agenda of the university is entitled *The Oxford University G.* In recent times *Westminster G.*, *Pall Mall G.* are examples of the use for general newspapers.

Gazette (găze·t), *v.* 1678. [f. prec.] To publish in a gazette. Chiefly pass. *To be gazetted*: to be announced in the official gazette as appointed *to* a command, or the like.

Phr. *To be gazetted out*: said of an officer whose resignation is announced in the gazette.

Gazetteer (gæzĕtīᵊ·ɹ). 1611. [– Fr. *gazettier* (now *gazetier*) – It. *gazzettiere*; see prec., -EER.] **1.** One who writes in a gazette; a journalist; *spec.* one appointed and paid by Government. †**2.** A newspaper, gazette –1769. **3.** A geographical index or dictionary 1704.

1. *Gazetteer*, it was lately a term of the utmost infamy, being usually applied to wretches who were hired to vindicate the court JOHNSON.

Ga·zing-sto:ck. 1535. [f. GAZING *vbl. sb.* + STOCK.] One on whom others gaze or stare.

Gazogene (gæ·zŏdʒīn). Also **gaso-.** 1853. [– Fr. *gazogène*, f. *gaz* GAS *sb.*[1] + *-gène* -GEN.] A gas-producer; *spec.* an apparatus for the production of aerated waters.

Gazolyte (gæ·zǫləit). 1842. [– Fr. *gazolyte*, f. *gaz* GAS *sb.*[1] + Gr. λυτός soluble, f. λύειν loose.] **a.** A name given by Berzelius to such simple gases as are permanently elastic. These are oxygen, nitrogen, and hydrogen. **b.** Ampère's term for a body which is resolvable into a gas. 1885.

Gazometer, obs. f. GASOMETER.

†**Gazon.** 1704. [– Fr. *gazon* grass; pl. pieces of turf.] A sod or piece of turf, cut wedge-shaped, used to line parapets, etc., in fortification –1768.

Geal (dʒīl), *v.* Now *dial.* ME. [– (O)Fr. *geler* :– L. *gelare* freeze.] To congeal. *trans.* and *intr.*

Gean (gīn). Now chiefly *Sc.* 1533. [Earliest form *guyne* (XVI) – OFr. *guine* (mod. *guigne*).] The wild cherry (*Prunus avium*); also, its fruit.

Geanticlinal (dʒī,æntiklai·năl). 1879. [f. Gr. γῆ earth + ANTICLINAL.] **A.** *adj.* Of the nature of a general upward flexure of the earth's crust. **B.** *sb.* The flexure itself.

Gear (gīᵊɹ). [ME. *gere* – ON. *gervi, gǫrvi*, corresp. to OS. *gerwi, garewi*, OHG. *garawī, gar(e)wī* :– Gmc. **ʒarwīn-*, f. **ʒarwu-* ready; see GAR *v.*, YARE.] **I.** Equipment. **1.** *collect. sing.* Apparel, dress, vestments. Now *rare.* **2.** Armour, arms, accoutrements. Rarely *pl.* *Obs.* exc. *arch.* ME. **3. a.** Riding equipment. (Now always *riding-g.*) ME. **b.** Harness for draught animals. Till 19th c. chiefly *pl.* †Also *fig.* ME.

1. My Lady's geer alone..filld four portmantel trunks 1727.

II. Apparatus. **1.** Appliances, tackle, tools, ME. †**b.** *Weaving.* A leaf of heddles –1839. **2.** *Machinery.* **a.** A combination of wheels, levers, etc. for a given purpose. Often specialized as *expansion-, hand-, steering-, winding-g.* 1523. **b.** Wheels working one upon another, by means of teeth, or otherwise. Often specialized as *bevel-, crown-, spur-g.* 1829. **3.** *Machinery.* = GEARING, *vbl. sb.* 3. 1814. **b.** The relation of the diameter of a wheel of a cycle or motor vehicle to the gearing, indicative of speed capacity; hence *loosely*, speed 1897. **4.** *Naut.* Rigging 1669.

3. Phr. *In, out of g.*: in, out of connection with the motor. So *to get (put, set, throw) in, into, out of g. High, low g.*; so *top, bottom g. fig.* The whole organization of labour was thrown out of g. J. R. GREEN.

III. Stuff. **1.** Goods, movable property, household necessaries ME. †**b.** *Sc.* and *n. dial.* Possessions 1535. †**2.** A material stuff; in depreciatory sense, rubbish –1805; †foul matter, pus –1653. **3.** *fig.* = MATTER, STUFF, in various uses (see quots.) ME.

1. Some harmelesse Villager, Whom Thrift keeps up about his Countrie Geare MILT. 3. Discourse, talk; stuff, nonsense: Priests with prayers and other godly g. DRYDEN. Doings (*arch.* or *dial.*): Our gambols, and our boyish geer K. WHITE. †A matter, business: Whilest this gere was a brewing SIR T. NORTH.

attrib. and *Comb.*, as (sense II. 2 b) *g.-cutter*; **g.-box, -case,** the case enclosing the gearing of a bicycle, etc.; **-wheel,** (*a*) a cog-wheel; (*b*) in a bicycle, etc., the cog-wheel by means of which the motion of the pedals is transmitted to the axle.

Gear (gīᵊɹ), *v.* [ME. *geren*, f. *gere* GEAR *sb.*; see also GAR *v.*] †**1.** *trans.* To array; to dress –1691. **2.** To equip (*arch.*) ME. **3.** To harness 1638. **4.** To put (machinery) into gear; to connect by gearing 1851. **b.** *intr.* Of a toothed wheel, or its teeth: To fit exactly *into*; to be in gear, so as to work smoothly *with* 1734.

4. Phr. *To g. up*: to make the driving wheels go round faster than the pedals. So *to g. down, level.*

Gearing (gīᵊ·riŋ), *vbl. sb.* 1825. [f. GEAR *sb.* and *v.* + -ING[1].] **1.** Harness (*dial.*) 1863. **2.** 'Plant' 1825. **3.** The action of fitting a machine with gear; the manner in which a machine is geared; *concr.* apparatus for the transmission of motion or power, e.g. a train of toothed wheels = GEAR *sb.* II. 3. Often specialized, as *bevel-, spur-*, etc. *g.*; also with advs., as in *g.-down, -up.* 1833.

Comb., as **g.-chain,** an endless chain transmitting motion from one toothed wheel to another.

†**Gea·son.** [OE. *gǣsne, gēsne* barren. Cf. OHG. *keisinī* barrenness.]

A. *adj.* **1.** Producing scantily –ME. **2.** Scantily produced; scarce –1674. **3.** Extraordinary –1583.

B. *sb.* Rarity, scarcity (*rare*) –1557.

Geat(e, obs. f. GATE, GET, JET.

Gebur (gėbūᵊ·ɹ). [OE. *ġebūr* = OS. *gibūr*, OHG. *gibūr, gibūro.* See NEIGHBOUR.] *Hist.* A tenant-farmer (in the early English community).

Gecarcinian (dʒīkarsi·niăn). 1838. [f. mod.L. *Gecarcinius* (Gr. γῆ earth + καρκίνος crab) + -IAN.] A land-crab.

Geck (gek), *sb.*[1] Now *dial.* 1515. [Of LDu. origin; cf. MLG. *geck*, MDu. *gec(k), ghec(k)*, Du. *gek* adj. and sb.; related (either as source or derivative) to *gecken* GECK *v.*] A fool, simpleton; a dupe.

The most notorious gecke and gull *Twel. N.* v. i. 351.

Geck (gek), *sb.*[2] Chiefly *Sc.* 1500. [– Du. (= G.) *geck* vbl. sb. corresp. to *gecken* (see GECK *v.*) as in Du. *in gheck segghen* (Kilian) say in jest, G. (dial.) *in geck sagen*, and *gecken machen* play tricks.] A gesture of derision; an expression of scorn or contempt.

Geck (gek), *v. Sc.* and *n. dial.* 1583. [app. – LG. *gecken* = MDu. *ghecken*, Du. *gekken*, G. *gecken*. See GECK *sb.*[1]] **1.** *trans.* To mock, cheat. **2.** intr. *To g. at*: to scoff at 1603. **3.** To toss the head, as in scorn 1724.

Gecko (ge·ko). *Pl.* **-os, -oes.** 1774. [– Malay *gēkoq* (the *q* is faint), imit. of the animal's cry.] A house-lizard, found in the warmer regions of both hemispheres, remarkable for its cry, and for its power of climbing walls.

Ged (ged). *n.* and *Sc.* ME. [– ON. *gedda*, rel. to *gaddr* GAD *sb.*[1]; cf. the transf. use of *pike.*] The fish *Esox lucius*; the pike.

Gee (dʒī), *sb. colloq.* 1887. [f. GEE *interj.*] A horse (orig. a child's word).

Gee (dʒī), *v. slang.* 1700. [poss. f. GEE *interj.*] *intr.* To go; to fit, suit (only in neg. phrases). Of persons: To agree, get on well (*together*).

Gee (dʒī), *interj.* 1628. A word of command in a horse, variously used to bid it turn to the right, go forward, or move faster.

Geebung (dʒī·bɒŋ). Also **gibong, jibbong.** 1827. [Native Austral.] The fruit of species of *Persoonia*, an Australian tree.

Gee-gee (dʒī·dʒī:). *colloq.* 1869. [redupl. of GEE *interj.*] A horse. Cf. GEE *sb.*

Geer, obs. f. GEAR.

Geese, pl. of GOOSE.

Geest (gīst). 1847. [– Du. *geest* dry or sandy soil. Cf. MDu. *gheest*, MLG. *gēst* (XII).] *Geol.* Old alluvial matter on the surface of land; coarse drift or gravel.

Geet, obs. f. JET.

Gee-up (dʒī·ɒ·p), *interj.* Also **gee-hup.** 1733. [f. GEE *interj.* + HUP *interj.* (confused with UP *adv.*)] = GEE *interj.* Hence **Gee-(h)up** *v.* to say 'gee-up' to; to obey this call.

‖**Gehenna** (gĭhe·nă). 1594. [(Also (XV) anglicized, or – Fr. *gehenne*) – eccl. L. *gehenna* – Hellenistic Gr. γέεννα – Heb. *gē' hinnōm* place of fiery torment for the dead, fig. use of the place-name *gē-ben-hinnōm* valley of the son of Hinnom, where according to Jer. 19:5, children were burnt in sacrifice.] **1.** The place of future torment; hell. **2.** *transf.* A place of torture; a prison 1594.

1. [Moloch] made his Grove The pleasant Vally of Hinnom, Tophet thence And black G. call'd the Type of Hell MILT.

Geic (dʒī·ik), *a.* 1844. [f. Gr. γῆ earth + -IC.] In *g. acid*, a product of the conversion of wood into vegetable mould. Also called *humic* or *ulmic acid.*

Gein (dʒī·in). Also **geine.** 1844. [f. Gr. γῆ earth + -IN[1]; in Fr. *géine* (Berzelius *a* 1848).] *Chem.* A brown precipitate obtained by boiling mould or decayed vegetable matter with alkalies.

†**Geir.** Also **geier.** 1567. [– Du. *gier.*] A vulture –1615.

Comb. **G.-eagle** (= G. *geier-adler*), used in A.V. to render Heb. *raḥam*, a species of vulture. See *Lev.* 11:18.

‖**Geisha** (gē·ʃă). *Pl.* **geisha, -as.** 1891. [Jap. *gēisha* 'person of pleasing accomplishments'.] A Japanese dancing girl.

‖**Geist.** 1871. [G.] Mind; reason; intelligence.

I do exhort..England to get..'Geist'; to search and not rest till it sees things more as they really are M. ARNOLD.

Geitonogamy (gəitǫnǫ·gămi). 1880. [f. Gr. γείτων, γειτον- neighbour + -γαμία.] *Bot.* Fertilization by pollen of other flowers of the same plant.

Gel (dʒel). 1904. [The first syllable of *gelatin.*] A jelly-like material formed by the coagulation of a colloidal liquid. Also as vb.

Gelastic (dʒėlæ·stik), *a. rare.* 1704. [– Gr. γελαστικός, f. γελᾶν laugh; see -IC.] Serving the function of laughter, risible. Also (*nonce-use*) as *sb. pl.*, remedies operating by causing laughter (SOUTHEY).

Gelatification (dʒe:lătifikē·ʃən). 1860. [f. GELATI-N + -FICATION.] The production of, or conversion into, gelatin or jelly.

Gelatigenous (dʒe:lăti·dʒėnəs], *a.* 1854. [f. GELATI-N + -GEN + -OUS.] Producing or developing gelatin; as, *g. tissues.*

Gelatin, gelatine (dʒe·lătin). 1800. [– Fr. *gélatine* – It. *gelatina*, f. *gelata* jelly. In medical L. *gelatina* was orig. 'any sort of clear gummy juice'; its present use is due to scientific chemistry. The pop. spelling is *gelatine*, often pronounced (dʒelătī·n); the scientific form is *gelatin*; see -IN[1], -INE[5].] **1.** The basis of the jellies into which certain animal tissues (skin, tendons, ligaments, etc.) are converted by prolonged boiling. It is amorphous, brittle, without taste or smell, transparent, and of a faint yellow tint; and is composed of carbon, hydrogen, nitrogen, oxygen, and sulphur. **b.** *Vegetable g.*: one of the constituents of gluten, identical with animal gelatin 1852. **2.** An explosive compound (more fully *blasting* or *explosive g.*), made by dissolving collodion-cotton in about nine times its weight of nitroglycerine 1878.

1. Soup..thickened by gelatine 1878.

attrib. and *Comb.*, as (sense 1) *g. capsule, pellicle*; *g.-coated* adj.; (sense 2) *g.-shell.* Also **g. dry-plate,** a plate, usually of glass coated with a film of g., containing sensitive silver bromide; **g. dynamite,** an explosive intermediate between blasting g. and dynamite; it consists of a thin blasting g. mixed with other substances; **g. emulsion,** 'an emulsion of g. containing a sensitive silver compound'; also *attrib.*; **g. paper** (*Photogr.*), paper coated with sensitized g.; **g. picture,** a photograph produced by the action of light on bichromated g.; **g. process,** any photographic process in which g. is employed; **g. sugar** = GLYCOCOLL. Hence **Ge·latined** *a.* coated with g.

Gelatinate (dʒėlæ·tineⁱt), *v.* 1796. [f. GELATIN + -ATE[3].] = GELATINIZE 1, 2. Hence **Gelatina·tion.**

†**Ge·latine.** 1713. [f. med.L. *gelata* (see JELLY) + -INE[1].]

A. *adj.* Of the nature of jelly, gelatinous. DERHAM. **B.** *sb. Zool.* Kirby's name for the Acalephæ of Cuvier, from the gelatinous consistency of their bodies –1855.

Gelatiniferous (dʒėlæ:tini·fėrəs), *a.* 1878. [f. GELATIN + -FEROUS.] Yielding gelatin.

Gelatiniform (dʒelăti·nifǫɹm), *a.* 1830. [f. as prec. + -FORM.] Having the form of gelatin.

Gelatinize (dʒėlæ·tinəiz), *v.* 1809. [f. GELATIN + -IZE.] **1.** *intr.* To become gelatinous. **2.** To render gelatinous or jelly-like 1843. **3.** To coat with gelatin 1890. Hence **Gela:tiniza·tion,** conversion into a gelatinous state.

Gelatino- (dʒe·lătī:no), comb. f. GELATIN, in words denoting its association with other chemical substances, as *g.-albuminous*, etc.; also in *g.-bromide, -chloride*, etc. used *attrib.* to signify the use of gelatin as a vehicle.

Gelatinoid (dʒėlæ·tinoid). 1866. [f. GELATIN + -OID.]

A. *adj.* Resembling gelatin, gelatinous.

B. *sb* [sc. *substance.*] 1882.

Gelatinous (dʒėlæ·tinəs), *a.* 1724. [– Fr. *gélatineux*; see GELATINE, -OUS.] **1.** Having the character or consistency of a jelly; jelly-like. Also *fig.* **2.** Of, pertaining to, or consisting of gelatin 1798.

Gelation (dʒėlēⁱ·ʃən). 1854. [– L. *gelatio*, f. *gelat-*, pa. ppl. stem of *gelare* freeze; see -ION.] Solidification by cold, freezing.

Geld (geld), *sb.* Also *erron.* **gelt.** 1610. [– med.L. *geldum* (in Domesday Book) – OE. *ġeld, ġield*; see GILD *sb.*, GUILD.] *Hist.* The tax paid to the crown by English landholders before the Conquest, and continued under the Norman kings.

Comb.: **g.-acre, -hide** (Domesday *acra, hida ad geldum*), an acre or a hide as reckoned for the purposes of g.

Geld (geld), *a.* Now *dial.* See also YELD. ME. [– ON. *geldr* = OSw. *galder* (Sw. dial. *gall, gåll*, Da. *gold*), OHG. *galt* (G. *gelt*, said of a cow); :– Gmc. **ȝalduz*.] Barren; †also, sexually impotent.

Geld (geld), *v.*[1] Infl. **gelt** and **gelded.** ME. [– ON. *gelda*, f. *geldr* GELD *a.*] **1.** *trans.* To castrate or emasculate; also, to spay. †**2.** *transf.* and *fig.* To deprive *of* some essential part; to mutilate; to expurgate –1729. **3.** †**a.** To cut superfluous shoots, etc. from (a plant or tree) –1664. †**b.** To cut out the old comb from (a bee-hive) –1657.

2. Bereft and gelded of his patrimonie SHAKS. To g. the text [of a book] 1693. **3. a.** G. and prune Strawberries EVELYN. Hence **Ge·lder.**

Geld (geld), *v.*[2] Also *erron.* **gelt.** 1630. [f. GELD *sb.*[1] Cf. med.L. *geldare* tax.] *Hist.* To charge with, or pay, geld. So **Ge·ldable** *a.* liable to pay geld.

Gelder(s rose, obs. f. GUELDER ROSE.

Gelding (ge·ldiŋ), *sb.* ME. [– ON. *geldingr*, f. *geldr* GELD *a.* + *-ingr* -ING[3].] †**1.** A gelded person, a eunuch –1785. **2.** A gelded animal, esp. a horse ME.

1. Putiphar, the geldyng of Pharao WYCLIF *Gen.* 37:36.

Gelding (ge·ldiŋ), *vbl. sb.* ME. [f. GELD *v.*[1] + -ING[1].] The action of GELD *v.*[1]

Gelid (dʒe·lid), *a.* 1606. [– L. *gelidus*, f. *gelu* frost, intense cold; see -ID[1].] Extremely cold, ice-cold, frosty. Also *fig.*

The Brightness of the G. Moon 1695. G. founts THOMSON. Hence **Geli·dity** (?*Obs.*), extreme cold. **Ge·lid-ly** *adv.*, **-ness.**

Gelignite (dʒe·lignəit). 1889. [perh. f. GELATIN + L. *ignis* fire + -ITE[1] 4 a.] A variety of gelatin dynamite.

Gelly, obs. f. JELLY.

†**Gelo·scopy.** Better GELOTOSCOPY. 1730. [f. Gr. γέλως, γελωτ- laughter + -σκοπια looking.] Divination by laughter.

Gelose (dʒilōᵘ·s). 1864. [f. GEL-ATIN + -OSE[2].] *Chem.* An amorphous gelatinous substance obtained from Japan moss and seaweeds.

Gelosie, obs. f. JEALOUSY.

†**Gelotoscopy.** Better form of GELOSCOPY. Evelyn.

‖**Gelsemium** (dʒelsī·miŏm). 1875. [mod.L. f. It. *gelsomino* JASMINE.] **a.** A genus of twining shrubs of the N.O. *Loganiaceæ*. **b.** The roots of a plant of this genus (*G. sempervirens*), or a preparation of them, used as a medicine; also called **gelseminum.** Hence **Ge·lsemine** (also **Gelse·minine**), a colourless, inodorous, bitter alkaloidal substance obtained from the root of *G. sempervirens*. **Gelse·mic acid,** a crystalline substance obtained from the root of *G. sempervirens*.

Gelt (gelt), *sb.*[1] *rare.* [– Ir. *geilt* a frenzied person.] A lunatic. SPENSER.

Gelt (gelt), *sb.*[2] 1529. [– G. *geld* (pron. gelt).] Money; now only *dial.* ¶In Spenser perh. = *gold*.

His whole army cryed out for g. ABP. USSHER.

Gelt (gelt), *ppl. a.* ME. [pa. pple. of GELD *v.*] Gelded. *lit.* and *fig.*

Gelt, obs. f. GELD *sb.*, GILT.

Gelt, var. GILT, young sow.

Gem (dʒem), *sb.* [– (O)Fr. *gemme* :– L. *gemma* bud, jewel; superseded the OE. adoption of the L. word, viz. *ǵim(m)*, ME. *ȝimme*.] **1.** A precious stone of any kind, *esp.* when cut and polished; a jewel. **2.** *transf.* and *fig.*; *esp.* an object of rare beauty or worth; the choicest part of (anything). Now playfully: Something greatly prized, a 'treasure'. 1560. **3.** A precious stone, bearing an engraved design in relief or in intaglio 1791. †**4.** A bud, esp. a leaf-bud –1813. **5.** *Zool.* = GEMMA 2. 1832. **6.** *Printing.* A size of type intermediate between Brilliant and Diamond 1888. **7.** *U.S.* A light muffin.

2. Deliteful dames and gemmes of jolitie GASCOIGNE. A little cabinet picture..which will be quite a g. W. IRVING. **3.** Antique Gems, their Origin, Uses, and Value (*title*) 1860.

Gem (dʒem), *v.* Infl. **gemmed, gemming.** OE. [f. prec.] †**1.** *intr.* To bud; *trans.* to put forth (a blossom, a fruit) –1747. **2.** To adorn with or as with gems 1610. **3.** *trans.* To excavate for gems 1889.

1. MILT. *P. L.* VII. 325. **2.** Gemmed with rubies 1877. A coppice gemm'd with green and red TENNYSON.

‖**Gemara** (gĕmā·ră). 1613. [– Aram. *gᵉmārâ* completion.] The later portion of the Talmud, consisting of a commentary on the older part (the Mishna). Hence **Gema·ric** *a.* pertaining to the G.

‖**Gematria** (gimēⁱ·triă). 1686. [– Aram. *gīmaṭrᵉyâ* – Gr. γεωμετρία GEOMETRY.] A cabalistic method of interpreting the Hebrew Scriptures by interchanging words whose letters have the same numerical value when added.

Gemel (dʒe·mĕl). ME. [– OFr. *gemel* (later *gemeau*, mod. *jumeau* twin) :– L. *gemellus*, dim. of *geminus* twin; see -EL.] †**1.** *pl.* Twins; pairs –1603. †**b.** *attrib.* or *adj.* Twin –1657. **2.** *Her.* in *pl.* Bars, or barrulets, placed together as a couple 1592. **3.** A kind of double ring. Now *Hist.* Also *g.-ring.* Cf. GIMMAL. 1572. **4.** A hinge. Now only in *g.-hinge.* 1536.

Comb.: **g.-hinge** (*Locksmithing*), a hinge consisting of an eye or loop and a hook. var. (in all senses) †**Gemew, gemow.**

[**Geminal:** a spurious word.]

Geminate (dʒe·minĕt). 1598. [– L. *geminatus*, pa. pple. of *geminare*; see next, -ATE[2].]

A. *adj.* Duplicated, combined in pairs, twin, binate; as, *g. leaves.* Hence **Ge·minately** *adv.*

B. *sb.* A doubled consonant (*rec.*).

Geminate (dʒe·mineⁱt), *v.* 1637. [– *geminat-*, pa. ppl. stem of L. *geminare*, f. *geminus* twin; see -ATE[3].] *trans.* To double.

Gemination (dʒeminēⁱ·ʃən). 1597. [– L. *geminatio*, f. as prec.; see -ION.] **1.** A doubling, duplication, repetition. **b.** The union of contiguous teeth 1859. †**2.** *Rhet.* The repetition of a word, phrase, or the like, for effect –1666. **3.** *Gram.* **a.** The doubling of a consonant sound 1877. **b.** The doubling of a letter 1875.

Gemini (dʒe·minəi). ME. [– L. *gemini* (pl. of *geminus*) twins.] **1.** *Astron.* A constellation, otherwise 'Castor and Pollux'; also the third sign of the zodiac, anciently identified with this. †**2.** A couple, a pair; *esp.* in pl. form, a pair of eyes –1700. **3.** A mild oath or exclam. *vulgar.* 1664.

1. When..the starry G. hang like glorious crowns Over Orion's grave TENNYSON. **2.** *Merry W.* II. ii. 8. Hence **Ge·minids** *pl.* the meteoric bodies forming the star-shower that has its radiant point in G. var. **Geminy.**

Geminiflorous (dʒe:mĭniˌflōᵊ·rəs), *a.* 1866. [f. L. *geminus* twin + *flos, flor-* + -OUS.] Having flowers in pairs.

Geminous (dʒe·minəs), *a. rare.* 1646. [f. L. *geminus* twin + -OUS.] Double; occurring in pairs.

‖**Gemma** (dʒe·mă). *Pl.* **gemmæ.** 1770. [L.; see GEM.] **1.** *Bot.* A leaf-bud, as dist. from a flower-bud. In mosses, etc.: A small cellular bulbel. 1830. **2.** *Zool.* A bud-like growth upon animals of low organization, which becomes detached and develops into a new individual 1841. Hence **Gemma·ceous** *a.* pertaining to, or of the nature of leaf-buds.

Gemman (dʒe·mæ̆n). Vulgar pronunc. of GENTLEMAN.

†**Ge·mmary.** ME. [– late L. *gemmarius*, f. *gemma*; see GEM, -ARY[1].]

A. *adj.* Of, pertaining to, or concerned with gems –1682.

B. *sb.* An engraver of gems, a jeweller. ME. only.

Gemmary: see GEMMERY.

Gemmate (dʒe·mĕt), *a.* 1846. [– L. *gemmatus* adorned with jewels, f. *gemma* GEM; see -ATE[2], and cf. next.] *Bot.* and *Zool.* Furnished with buds; reproducing by buds.

Gemmate (dʒe·meⁱt), *v.* 1623. [– *gemmat-*, pa. ppl. stem of L. *gemmare* put forth buds, sparkle with gems (in med.L. deck with gems), f. *gemma* bud, GEM; see -ATE[3].] †**a.** *trans.* To deck with gems –1697. **b.** *intr.* To put forth buds; to propagate itself by buds 1846.

Gemmation (dʒemēⁱ·ʃən). 1760. [– Fr. *gemmation*, f. *gemmer*, f. *gemme* bud; see -ATION.] **1.** *Bot.* **a.** The action of budding. **b.** The time when leaf-buds are put forth. **c.** The arrangement of buds on the stalk; also, of leaves in the bud. **2.** *Zool.* Reproduction by gemmæ; the formation of a new individual by the protrusion and complete or partial separation of a part of the parent; budding 1836.

Gemmeous (dʒe·mĭəs), *a.* 1605. [f. L. *gemmeus* (f. *gemma* GEM) + -OUS.] Of or pertaining to, of the nature of, or resembling a gem. *G. Dragonet*: the fish *Callionymus lyra*.

†**Gemmery** (dʒe·mĕri). Also **gemmary.** 1656. [f. GEM + -ARY[1] B. 2.] A jewel-house –1721.

Gemmiferous (dʒemi·fĕrəs), *a.* 1656. [f. L. *gemmifer* (f. *gemma* GEM) + -OUS; see -FEROUS. Cf. Fr. *gemmifère*.] **1.** Producing gems. **2.** Producing a gemma or bud 1804.

Gemmiparous (dʒemi·părəs), *a.* 1793. [f. mod.L. *gemmiparus* (f. *gemma* GEM) + -OUS. Cf. Fr. *gemmipare* (XVIII).] **a.** Producing offspring by gemmation. **b.** Of or pertaining to gemmation. Hence **Gemmi·parously** *adv.* Also **Gemmipa·rity,** the attribute of being g.

Gemmule (dʒe·miul). 1845. [– Fr. *gemmule* or L. *gemmula* little bud, small gem. dim. of *gemma*; see GEMMA, -ULE.] **1.** *Bot.* **a.** = PLUMULE. 1844. **b.** One of the reproductive cells of cryptogams 1874. **2.** *Zool.* A small GEM (sense 5) or gemma; *spec.* a ciliated embryo of one of the *Cœlenterata*; an encysted mass of sponge-particles, from which new ones are produced 1845. Hence **Gemmuli·ferous** *a.* bearing gemmules.

Gemmy (dʒe·mi), *a.* ME. [f. GEM *sb.* + -Y[1].] **1.** Abounding in gems, covered or set with or as with gems. **2.** Gem-like; glittering 1580.

1. The g. bridle glitter'd free TENNYSON. Hence **Ge·mmily** *adv.* **Ge·mminess.**

†**Ge·monies.** 1598. [– L. (*scalæ*) *Gemoniæ*; of unkn. origin.] *Rom. Antiq.* Steps on the Aventine Hill leading to the Tiber, to which the bodies of criminals were dragged to be thrown into the river. ¶Misapplied *fig.* for 'tortures'. –1683.

Gemot(e (gĕmōᵘ·t). [repr. OE. *ġemōt*, f. *ġe-* Y- + *mōt* MOOT.] *Eng. Hist.* A meeting; an assembly (in England before the Norman Conquest) for judicial or legislative purposes. See also WITENAGEMOT.

‖**Gemsbok** (ge·mzbǫk). 1777. [Du. *gemsbok* prop. chamois – G. *gemsbock*, f. *gemse* CHAMOIS + *bock* BUCK.] S. African name for a large antelope (*Oryx capensis*).

Gemshorn (ge·mzˌhǭɹn). 1825. [– G. *gemshorn* 'chamois horn'; cf. prec.] An organ stop with tapering metal pipes, yielding a tone like that of a horn in quality.

-gen (dʒen), *suffix*, forming *sbs.*; – Fr. *-gène*, repr. (ult.) Gr. -γενής (f. γεν- root of γίγνεσθαι to be born, become, γένος kind, etc.; see KIN) an adjective suffix meaning: (1) 'born in a certain place or condition', as in οἰκογενής born in the house; (2) 'of a (specified) kind', as in ὁμογενής of the same kind. The Fr. *gène* has two applications, both of which have been adopted in Eng.

1. *Chem.* In Lavoisier's *Traité de Chimie* 1789 the etymon of the suffix is said to be 'Gr. γείνομαι, j'engendre'. Hence the sense 'that which produces'. In Eng. *-gène* became *-gene*, and later *-gen*, as in *nitrogen*, etc.

2. *Bot.* The botanical use of *-gène* is due to De Candolle, and is merely a different application of the *-gène* used in chemical terms referred vaguely to a Gr. root meaning 'to produce, to grow'. The adjs. *endogène, exogène* (De Candolle) became in Eng. *endogenous, exogenous*; from these Lindley *c* 1845 formed the sbs. *endogen, exogen*; hence many analogous terms denoting classes of plants.

Genappe (dʒĕnæ·p). 1858. [f. *Genappe* in Belgium, where first made.] A worsted yarn or cord of exceptional smoothness, used in the manufacture of braids, fringes, etc.

‖**Gendarme** (ʒaṅda·rm, dʒendā·ɹm). *Pl.* †**gens d'armes,** †**gensdarmes, gendarmes.** 1550. [Fr. *gendarme*, a sing. formed from the pl. *gens d'armes* men of arms; hence a fresh pl. *gendarmes*. In mod. Fr. the form *gens d'armes* has only the historic sense.] **1.** (Chiefly *pl.*) In the older French army, a horseman in full armour, having others under him; later, a mounted trooper. Now *Hist.* **2.** A soldier, who is employed on police duties, esp. in France. Also *fig.* 1796. **3.** *attrib.*, in *g. blue* 1884.

2. *fig.* Projecting pieces of rock, which are called gendarmes; apparently from their..stopping travellers 1883. Hence **Genda·rmery, -erie,** gendarmes as a body; also *attrib.*

Gender (dʒe·ndəɹ), *sb.* [– OFr. *gendre* (mod. *genre*) – Rom. **genero*, f. L. *genus, gener-*; see GENUS.] †**1.** Kind, sort –1784. **2.** *Gram.* Each of the three (or two) grammatical 'kinds', corresponding more or less to distinctions of sex (or absence of sex), into which sbs. are discriminated according to the nature of the modifications they require in words syntactically associated with them; the property (in a sb.) of belonging to, or (in other parts of speech) of having the form appropriate to concord with, a specified one of these kinds. Also, the distinction of words into 'genders' ME.

Mod. Eng. has 'natural' as opposed to 'grammatical' gender; i.e. nouns are masculine, feminine, or neuter according as the objects they denote are male, female, or of neither sex. For *common, epicene g.*, see those wds.

3. *transf.* Sex. Now only *joc.* ME. †**4.** Offspring –1662.

Gender (dʒe·ndəɹ), *v.* [– OFr. *gendrer* – L. *generare* GENERATE.] **1.** *trans.* To beget, engender (*arch.*) ME. †**2.** *intr.* To copulate –1634. **3.** *trans.* †To generate (heat, etc.) –1653; to engender (a feeling, etc.) (*arch.*) 1450.

Genderless (dʒe·ndəɹlės), *a.* 1887. [f. GENDER *sb.* + -LESS.] Without distinction of gender.

Gene (dʒīn). 1913. Also **gen.** [irreg. f. Gr. γεν- produce.] *Biol.* One of the factors or elements concerned with the development in the offspring of hereditary characters.

Genealogic, -al (dʒe:niˌălǫ·dʒik, -ăl, dʒī-), *a.* 1577. [– Fr. *généalogique* – Gr. γενεαλογικός, f. γενεαλόγος genealogist; see GENEALOGY, -IC, -ICAL.] That belongs to genealogy, or that traces family descent.

Genealogical tree: a table of family descent under the form of a tree with branches. Hence **Ge·nealo·gically** *adv.* Earlier **Ge:nealo·gical** *a.* 1447.

Genealogist (dʒeniˌæ·lŏdʒist, dʒī-). 1605. [f. GENEALOGY + -IST. Cf. Fr. *généalogiste.*] One who traces genealogies, or one interested in the study of them.

Genealogize (dʒeniˌæ·lŏdʒəiz, dʒī-), *v.* 1602. [f. as prec. + -IZE. Cf. med.L. *genealogizare.*] *trans.* To draw up a genealogy of; *intr.* to make out genealogies.

Genealogy (dʒeniˌæ·lŏdʒi, dʒī-). ME. [– (O)Fr. *généalogie* – late L. *genealogia* – Gr. γενεαλογία, f. γενεαλόγος genealogist, f. γενεά race, generation; see -LOGY.] **1.** An account of a person's descent from an ancestor or ancestors, by enumeration of the intermediate ancestors; a pedigree. Also *transf.* †**2.** Lineage, pedigree, family stock –1549. †**3.** Progeny. STERNE. **4.** The investigation of pedigrees as a branch of study or knowledge. TUCKER.

Genera, pl. of GENUS.

Generable (dʒe·nĕrăb'l), *a.* 1450. [– L. *generabilis* that may produce, or be produced, f. *generare*; see GENERATE, -ABLE. Cf. OFr. *generable.*] That may be generated or produced.

General (dʒe·nĕrăl). ME. [–(O)Fr. *général* – L. *generalis*, f. *genus, gener-* class, race, kind; see GENUS, -AL[1].]

A. *adj.* **1.** Pertaining to all, or most, of the parts of a whole; completely or approximately universal within implied limits; opp. to *partial* or *particular*. †**b.** Pertaining in common to various persons or things –1667. **c.** With collect. or pl. sb. All, whole. *Obs.* exc. in *g. body.* 1591. **2.** Concerned with the whole; opp. to *local, sectional*, etc. ME. **3.** Catholic, addressed to all 1611. **4.** Prevalent, widespread, usual ME. **5.** Not specifically limited in application; applicable to a whole class of objects, cases, or occasions ME. **b.** True for a variety of cases; in later use, true in most instances, but not without exceptions (opp. to *universal*) ME. **c.** Of a word, name, etc.: Applicable to each member of a class or genus, COMMON. Of a concept, notion, etc.: Including only what is common to the individuals of a class. 1551. **6.** Not restricted to one department. †Also formerly: Widely accomplished. 1552. †**b.** Open, affable to all –1630. **7.** Not belonging to, or confined to, a class; miscellaneous 1639. **8.** Comprising, dealing with, or directed to the main elements, features, etc. 1563; hence, wanting in details; indefinite, vague (opp. to *precise*) 1601. **9.** *Mil.* Epithet indicating superior rank and extended command 1576. **b.** Applied also to civil and legal functionaries, as *attorney-, postmaster-g.*, etc. (see those wds.) 1591.

1. A g. Battel 1659, Request 1665, peace ADDISON. Phr. *G. average*: see AVERAGE *sb.*[2] *G. paralysis*: see PARALYSIS. **b.** So spake our g. Mother MILT. **c.** The gen'ral sex shall suffer in her shame POPE. **2.** Phr. *G. chapter, council* (see COUNCIL 2), *election* (opp. to *by-election*). *G. ticket* (U.S.): the system by which the whole list of candidates for the representation, e.g. of a state or city, is voted upon by the undivided body of electors (= Fr. *scrutin de liste*). *G. Post*: formerly, the post or mail that was sent from the G.P.O. in London on certain days (opp. to the local 'penny' or 'twopenny' post); hence the first delivery in the morning is still officially called the *G.P.* or *General Post delivery*. Also the name of a game. Also *attrib. G. orders*, the orders issued by the commander-in-chief. **3.** The Generall Epistle of Iames BIBLE 1611. **4.** The g. taste 1752. A g. opinion PALEY. The theme of g. remark 1885. **5.** After we had answered the g. questions, they began to be more particular DE FOE. The *g. costs* of the action 1890. Phr. *G. confession, pardon* (sometimes also in sense 1). *G. issue* (Law): a plea or pleas importing an absolute and general denial of what is alleged in the declaration. **b.** I guess you are right there, as a g. rule LYTTON. **c.** The g. term..Majolica 1875. **6.** Phr. *G. dealer, merchant, agent*, etc. *G. practitioner. G. servant*: a maid-of-all-work. Taking away such a g. and onely man as Mr. Cheeke is ASCHAM. **7.** Not very intelligible to the g. reader 1862. The g. public TYNDALL. Phr. *General ship*, where persons unconnected with each other load goods on board SMYTH. **8.** A g. knowledge was all that could be expected 1860.

Phrases. **In g.:** †(*a*) collectively, universally; †(*b*) in all respects; (*c*) generally; opp. to *in special, in particular*; (*d*) as a general rule, usually. **In the g.:** generally; on a general view; in the main.

B. *sb.* **I.** †**1.** The adj. used *absol.*: The total, the whole, or in weaker sense, the most part –1771. **b.** The public; the multitude (*arch.*) 1601. **2.** Something that is general; chiefly *pl.* Now *rare* (chiefly in antithesis to *particulars*, etc.) 1566. †**b.** That which is common to all. *Tr. & Cr.* I. iii. 180. †**c.** *pl. Oxford Univ.* = RESPONSIONS –1841. †**3.** *Logic.* = GENUS. –1705. †**4.** *Painting.* Name of a neutral colour –1662. **5.** *Mil.* Also as Fr. *générale, generale.* The first beat of the drum for the assembly of all the troops 1706.

1. The g. of people at his time of life MME. D'ARBLAY. **b.** The Play..pleased not the Million, 'twas Cauiarie to the Generall *Haml.* II. ii. 457. **2.** The deceitfull and wrangler walketh in generalles 1566. To whom I refer thee for generals and common news PENN. **5.** The generale was beat at half-past four, the assembly at half-past five WELLINGTON.

II. 1. *Eccl.* The chief of a religious order 1561. **2.** *Mil.* A general officer (see A. 9); orig., the commander of the whole army, subseq. also any divisional commander. In mod. use, designating an officer as holding definite military rank (i.e. the rank next below that of a field-marshal; untechnically extended to those of LIEUTENANT-GENERAL and MAJOR-GENERAL) 1576. Also *transf.* and *fig.* **b.** A tactician, strategist 1615. **c.** The head of the Salvation Army 1882. †**3.** *Naut.* = ADMIRAL –1717. **4.** *colloq.* A maid-of-all-work 1884.

2. Successe vnto our valiant Generall SHAKS. [Waterloo] was perhaps on both sides rather a soldiers' than a general's battle SEELEY. *fig. Rom. & Jul.* V. iii. 219. **b.** Cortez was certainly a great g. PRESCOTT.

Generale: see GENERAL B. I. 5 *sb.*

‖**Generalia** (dʒenĕrēi·liă), *sb. pl.* 1832. [L. neut. pl. of *generālis*, GENERAL *a.*] General principles.

Generalism (dʒe·nĕrăliz'm). 1809. [f. GENERAL *sb.* + -ISM.] A general statement.

‖**Generalissimo** (dʒe:nĕrăli·simo). 1621. [It., superl. of *generale* GENERAL.] The supreme commander of a combined naval and military force, or of several armies in the field. Also *transf.* and *fig.* Hence ‖**Ge:nerali·ssima,** a female g.

Generality (dʒe:nĕræ·lĭti). 1482. [– (O)Fr. *généralité* – late L. *generalitas*, f. *generalis* GENERAL; see -ITY.]

I. 1. The quality or fact of being general (see GENERAL *a.*); now chiefly, applicability to a whole class; also, vagueness. †Formerly also, prevalence. **2.** quasi-*concr.* Something that is general; †a general class; a general proposition or statement; a general point; chiefly in *pl.* 1551. **3.** The main body, the bulk of. (Now only with *sb. pl.* or *collect.*) †Also, people in general. 1563.

1. A method of great g. and power BREWSTER. The g. of a conclusion TYNDALL. **2.** Keep to your sounding generalities, your tinkling phrases HAZLITT. **3.** Some were good scholars, but the g. dunces 1660.

II. Special senses. †**1.** The dignity or office of general 1686. †**2.** The general staff of an army –1676. **3.** *Fr. Hist.* A fiscal and administrative division of the kingdom of France, under an officer called *général des finances* or *intendant* 1630.

Generalization (dʒe:nĕrăləizēi·ʃən). 1761. [– Fr. *généralisation*, f. *généraliser*; see next, -ATION.] **1.** The action or process of generalizing, i.e. of forming general notions or propositions from particulars. **2.** quasi-*concr.* A general inference 1794. **3.** The process of spreading over every part 1897.

1. Hasty g. is the bane of all science 1876. **3.** The g. of an infective disease ALLBUTT.

Generalize (dʒe·nĕrăləiz), *v.* 1751. [– Fr. *généraliser*, f. *général*; see GENERAL, -IZE.] To make general. **1.** *trans.* To reduce to general laws; also, to form a general concept. **2.** *trans.* To infer inductively from particulars 1795. **3.** To draw general inferences from 1828. **b.** *Math.* and *Philos.* To throw (a proposition, etc.) into a general form, including the particular case 1812. **4.** *intr.* To form general notions by abstraction from particular instances; to arrive at general inferences 1785. **5.** *trans.* To render indefinite; to soften down the special features of 1809. **6.** To make general; to popularize. Also, to spread over a system or surface in general. 1818.

1. Generalizing those names, so as to make them represent a class JAS. MILL. Causes which do not admit of being generalized 1849. **2.** A mere conclusion generalized from a great multitude of facts COLERIDGE. **3.** Copernicus generalized the celestial motions..Newton generalized them still more 1828. Knowledge is experience generalized MILL. **5.** Travelling tends to generalise and rub off local habits, prejudices, [etc.] 1835. **6.** To g. the use of the potatoe 1824.

Hence **Ge·nerali:zable** *a.* capable of being generalized. **Ge·neralized** *ppl. a.*; *spec.* of a disease: That has extended itself to the system in general. **Ge·neralizer.**

Generally (dʒe·nĕrăli), *adv.* ME. [f. GENERAL *a.* + -LY[2].] †**1.** So as to include all; as a whole, collectively –1613. †**2.** Universally; with respect to all or nearly all. With neg. = *at all.* –1653. Hence **b.** For the most part, extensively ME. **3.** In a general sense or way; opp. to *specially* ME. **4.** As a general rule; commonly 1654.

1. *Tam. Shr.* I. ii. 274. **2.** Two [sacraments] onely, as g. necessarie to salvation *Bk. Com. Prayer.* **b.** A fact now g. received 1820. **3.** He gave all his lands to Richard, g. CRUISE. Phr. *G. speaking* = 'in general'. **4.** [Winds] from the land are g. dry GEIKIE.

Generalness (dʒe·nĕrălnės). 1561. [f. as prec. + -NESS.] The state, quality, or fact of being GENERAL. Now *rare.*

Generalship (dʒe·nĕrălʃip). 1591. [f. GENERAL *sb.* + -SHIP.] **1.** †The functions of a general; also, conduct in command. **2.** The office, or †tenure of the office, of general 1610. **3.** Skill in the management of an army; strategy 1788; *transf.* skilful management 1768.

1. Cicero..laughs, indeed..at his g. BOLINGBROKE. **3.** Hannibal gave great proofs of g.

LANGHORNE. *transf.* An artful stroke of g. in Trim to raise a dust STERNE.

†**Ge·neralty.** ME. [– OFr. **generalté*, var. of *generauté*, f. *general*; see GENERAL, -TY[1].] = GENERALITY, in all senses –1676.

Generant (dʒe·nĕrănt). 1665. [– *generant-*, pres. ppl. stem of L. *generare*, see next, -ANT.]

A. *sb.* That which generates; in *Math.* = GENERATRIX 1842.

B. *adj.* Productive (*rare*) 1875.

Generate (dʒe·nĕrĕt). *ppl. a.* 1509. [– L. *generatus*, pa. pple. of *generare*; see next, -ATE[2].] Generated.

Generate (dʒe·nĕreᶦt), *v.* 1509. [– *generat-*, pa. ppl. stem of L. *generare* beget, etc., f. *genus, gener-* stock, race; see -ATE[3].] †**1.** *trans.* To beget, procreate, engender –1697. **b.** *absol.* or *intr.* To produce offspring. (Now *rare.*) 1626. **2.** To bring into existence (substances, animals, etc.). Chiefly in *pass.* 1563. **b.** *esp.* To produce, evolve (steam, gas, etc.; also heat, friction, etc.) 1791. **c.** *Math.* To produce or evolve (a line or figure); said chiefly of a point, line, or surface doing this by its own motion 1698. **3.** To bring about, give rise to, produce 1626.

1. b. Some Liuing Creatures g. but at certaine Seasons of the Yeare BACON. **2.** A region where rain was generated TYNDALL. **c.** We know how a circle is generated 1864. **3.** The love of killing game generates a sincere wish to preserve it KINGLAKE. Hence **Ge·nerating** *ppl. a.* that generates; esp. (in mod. use) of electrical apparatus.

Generation (dʒenĕrēᶦ·ʃən). ME. [– (O)Fr. *génération* – L. *generatio*, f. as prec.; see -ION.]

I. 1. The act or process of generating or begetting; procreation; propagation of species. **b.** The fact or manner of being begotten ME. Manner of descent; genealogy (*rare*) ME. **d.** *Theol.* The origin of the Son from the Father 1659. **2.** Production by natural or artificial processes; often opposed to corruption (Aristotle's *φθορά*) ME.

1. Phr. *Equivocal, spontaneous g.*, see the adjs. **c.** The book of the g. of Jesus Christ *Matt.* 1:1. **d.** Strange G. this? Father and Son Co-eval, two distinct and yet but one KEN. **2.** Of the generacyon and cause of stone and metall, and of plantis and herbys 1519. The g. of happiness GODWIN, of heat 1863.

II. That which is generated. †**1.** Offspring –1674; descendants –1704; produce (of the vine) –1565. **2.** Offspring of the same parent regarded as a step in a line of descent from an ancestor; = DEGREE. ME. **3.** The whole body of individuals born about the same period; also, the time covered by the lives of these. (A generation is usually computed at thirty years.) ME. †**4.** Family, breed, race; class, kind, or set of persons –1727.

2. A family party, consisting of three generations 1834. **3.** Why doth this g. seek after a sign *Mark* 8:12. The hopes of the rising g. JOHNSON. **4.** Thy Mothers of my g.: what's she, if I be a Dogge *Timon* I. i. 205. They could not brook the fighting in conjunction with this wicked g. [the Irish] DE FOE.

Generationism (dʒenĕrēᶦ·ʃəniz'm). 1864. [f. prec. + -ISM.] The doctrine that not only the body but the soul comes from the parents; called also *traducianism*.

Generative (dʒe·nĕrĕtiv), *a.* ME. [– (O)Fr. *génératif* or late L. *generativus* (Boethius), f. *generat-*; see GENERATE *v.*, -IVE.] Pertaining to generation; having the power or function of generating (see the *vb.*); productive.

Causes. .generatiue of sedition SPEED.

Generator (dʒe·nĕrēᶦtəɹ). 1646. [– L. *generator*, f. as prec.; see -OR 2. In mod. techn. uses f. GENERATE *v.*] **1.** One who generates or begets. **2.** That which generates or produces; *esp.* an apparatus for producing gases, steam, or electricity 1794. **3.** *Mus.* The fundamental tone of a series of harmonics or of a chord 1825.

Generatrix (dʒenĕrēᶦ·triks). 1657. [– L. *generatrix*, fem. of *generator*; see prec., -TRIX.] †**1.** A female parent –1813. **2.** *Math.* A point, line, or surface conceived as producing by its motion a line, a superficial or a solid figure respectively 1840. **3.** = GENERATOR 2.

Generic (dʒĕne·rik), *a.* 1676. [– Fr. *générique* (Descartes, tr. Gr. *γενικός*, Aristotle), f. L. *genus, gener-* GENUS; see -IC.] Belonging to a genus or class; applied to a large group or class of objects; general (opp. to SPECIAL or SPECIFIC); esp. in *g. character, name, term.* Also *absol.* So **Gene·rical** *a.* generic, general. **Gene·rically** *adv.* with reference to genus. **Gene·ricalness** (*rare*).

Generification (dʒene:rifikēᶦ·ʃən). 1837. [f. L. *genus, gener-* GENUS + -FICATION.] *Logic.* (See quot.)

The abstraction which carries up species into genera, is called. .G., or, more loosely, Generalisation SIR W. HAMILTON.

Generosity (dʒenĕrǫ·sĭti). ME. [– Fr. *générosité* or L. *generositas*, f. *generosus*; see next, -ITY.] **1.** Nobility of birth or lineage. Now only *arch.* **2.** †High spirit, nobility of conduct. Now only: Willingness to forgive injuries; magnanimity. 1623. **3.** Liberality in giving; munificence 1677. **4.** *pl.* Instances of generosity (senses 2, 3). *rare.* 1647.

1. The Virginians especially lay claim to this g. of lineage LOWELL. **2.** G. is never a characteristic of political party warfare SIR T. MARTIN.

Generous (dʒe·nĕrəs), *a.* 1588. [– (O)Fr. *généreux* – L. *generosus* noble, magnanimous, f. *genus, gener-* GENUS; see -OUS.] **1.** Of noble lineage; high-born. Now only *arch.* †**b.** Of animals; Of good breed –1781. **2.** Of actions, character, etc.: Appropriate or natural to one of noble birth or spirit; hence, †gallant; magnanimous 1588. **b.** Of persons: †High-spirited, gallant; magnanimous 1623. †**c.** Of animals: Spirited (*rare*) –1661. **3.** Liberal in giving, munificent 1696; *transf.* of land: Rich 1853. **4.** Furnished liberally; hence, abundant, ample 1615. **b.** Of diet: Ample and rich; strengthening. Also of colour: Rich, full. 1833. **5.** Of wine, etc.: Rich and full of strength; invigorating 1630. †**6.** Of remedies: Vigorous –1677.

1. Most g. sir SHAKS. **b.** A g. race of horses GIBBON. **2.** This is not g., not gentle SHAKS. This g. disposition to defy control SCOTT. **b.** So g. a conqueror GIBBON. **c.** A g. creature a horse is FULLER. **3.** He was himself g. as a giver, parting, indeed, with that which did not altogether belong to himself 1882. **4.** Strong liquors. .in g. portions 1790. **b.** The glow of g. colour KINGLAKE. **5.** It [metheglin] is a most g. liquor FULLER. Hence **Ge·nerous-ly** *adv.*, **-ness.**

Genesial (dʒĕnī·siăl), *a.* 1882. [f. GENESI-S + -AL[1].] Pertaining to generation; as, *genesial cycle.* So **Gene·siology,** the science of generation.

Genesis (dʒe·nesis). OE. [– L. *genesis* – Gr. *γένεσις* generation, creation, nativity, horoscope, name of the O.T. book in LXX, hence in Vulgate, f. **γεν-*, base of *γίγνεσθαι* be born or produced.] **1.** The first of the books of the Old Testament, containing the account of the creation of the world. (So named by the Gr. translators.) †**2.** *Astrol.* Nativity, horoscope –1652. †**3.** = SYNTHESIS (orig. with reference to geometry, opp. to *analysis*; see Aristotle *Eth. Nic.* III. iii) –1674. **4.** Origin, mode of formation or production (freq. in mod. usage) 1604. †**b.** *Math.* = GENERATION –1726.

4. The g. of our Clothes-Philosopher CARLYLE.

-ge·nesis, repr. Gr. *γένεσις* (see GENESIS), in compounds denoting modes of generation, as *abiogenesis, biogenesis, parthenogenesis*, etc.

Genet (dʒe·nĕt). ME. [– OFr. *genete* (mod. *-ette*) – Arab. *jarnayṭ*.] **1.** A kind of civet-cat, a native of Southern Europe, Western Asia, and Africa. The common species (*Genetta vulgaris* or *Viverra genetta*) is found in the south of France. 1481. †**2.** *pl.* Genet skins as fur for garments –1694. **b.** The fur of the genet; also, any imitation of this 1882.

Genet, obs. f. JENNET.

†**Gene·thliac.** 1584. [ult. – Gr. *γενεθλιακός* belonging to one's birth or birthday (= *γενέθλιος*, f. *γενέθλη*, f. **γεν-* bear, bring forth).]

A. *adj.* Relating to the casting of nativities; also, to a birthday –1693.

B. *sb.* **1.** One who calculates nativities (so in L. and Gr.) –1844. **2.** *pl.* = GENETHLIALOGY; also, horoscopes –1755. **3.** A birthday ode 1687.

Genethliacal (dʒeneþləi·ăkăl), *a.* 1613. [f. as prec. + -AL[1].] = GENETHLIAC *a.* Hence **Genethli·acally** *adv.*

‖**Genethliacon** (dʒeneþləi·ăkǫn). 1589. [L. – Gr. *γενεθλιακόν*, n. sing. of *-ιακός*; see GENETHLIAC.] A birthday ode.

Genethlialogy (dʒeneþliæ·lŏdʒi). Also **-ology.** 1656. [– Gr. *γενεθλιαλογία* (L. *genethliologia*), f. *γενεθλιαλογεῖν* cast nativities; see GENETHLIAC, -LOGY.] The science of casting nativities.

†**Genethliatic.** [– Gr. *γενέθλια* n. pl. of *γενέθλιος* of or belonging to one's birthday; see GENETHLIAC, -ATIC.] = GENETHLIAC *sb.* 1. DRUMM. OF HAWTH.

Genetic (dʒĕne·tik), *a.* See also GENETICS. 1831. [f. GENESIS; after *antithesis, antithetic*, etc.] **1.** Pertaining to, or having reference to, origin. ¶ **2.** Occas. misused for: Generative, productive (= Gr. *γεννητικός*) 1838. **3.** quasi-*sb.* (*pl.*) The principles or laws of origination 1872.

1. Phr. *G. affinity, connection, relation(ship)* (Biol.): one that results from a common origin. *G. definition* (Logic): one which defines a thing 'as in the progress to be, as becoming'. var. **Gene·tical** *a.* (in senses 1, 2); †also = SYNTHETIC. Hence **Gene·tically** *adv.* with respect to genesis or origin.

-gene·tic (see prec.), *suffix* forming adjs. corresp. to sbs. in *-genesis* and *-geny*, as *biogenetic*, etc.

Gene·tics. [pl. of GENETIC used as sb., after *politics*, etc.; see -ICS.] That part of biological science which is concerned with the study of heredity and variation. BATESON.

Genetrix, genitrix (dʒe·nitriks). Now *rare.* 1500. [– L. *genetrix, genitrix*, fem. of *genitor*; see GENITOR[2], -TRIX.] A female parent, a mother. Also *fig.*

Geneva[1] (dʒĭnī·vă). 1706. [– Du. *genever*, assim. to next in form and pronunc. – OFr. *genevre* (mod. *genièvre*) :– **jeniperus*, for L. *juniperus* JUNIPER. Cf. GIN *sb.*[2]] A spirit distilled from grain, and flavoured with juniper berries; made in Holland, and also called *Hollands*, formerly *Hollands Geneva.* (Often with capital G by confusion with next.)

Geneva[2] (dʒĭnī·vă). Name of a town in Switzerland, used *attrib.* or quasi-*adj.* with sense 'belonging to, made or originated at Geneva'; often with reference to Calvinism.

Geneva bands, clerical bands resembling those worn by the Swiss Calvinist clergy. **Geneva bible,** the Eng. translation of the Bible first printed at G. in 1560. **Geneva convention** (see CONVENTION). **Geneva Cross,** a red Greek cross on a white ground, used in war time as a badge under the G. convention. **Geneva gown,** a black gown such as was worn by the Calvinist clergy when preaching. †**Geneva hat,** a hat of the style distinctive of the Puritan clergy.

Genevan (dʒĭnī·văn), †**Gene·vian.** 1564. [f. prec. + -AN, -IAN.]

A. *adj.* Of or pertaining to Geneva; esp. Calvinistic 1573.

B. *sb.* A native of Geneva; also, one who adheres to the doctrines of Geneva. Hence †**Gene·vanism,** Calvinism.

Genevese (dʒenĭvī·z). 1650. [f. as prec. + -ESE.]

A. *adj.* Pertaining to Geneva 1860.

B. *sb.* A native of Geneva. (Not now inflected in pl.) var. †**Genevois** *sb.*

Genial (dʒī·niăl), *a.*[1] 1566. [– L. *genialis* nuptial, productive, joyous, pleasant, f. *genius*; see GENIUS, -AL[1].] **1.** Of or pertaining to marriage, nuptial; also, generative. Now *rare.* 1566. †**2.** Of or pertaining to a feast; festive –1762. **3.** Conducive to growth (const. *to*); now chiefly, pleasantly warm, mild 1647. Also *fig.* **4.** Cheering 1746. **5.** Sympathetically cheerful, jovial, kindly 1746. †**6.** Pertaining to 'genius' or natural disposition; natural –1850. **7.** Of, pertaining to, or marked by genius (see GENIUS 5, and cf. G. *genial, genialisch*) 1827.

1. Phr. *G. bed* = L. *lectus genialis.* The bridale bowre and geniall bed SPENSER. The g. Angel (i.e. the angel presiding over marriage or generation) MILT. **2.** G. cups MILT. **3.** The Soil was not G. to the Seed 1705. To seek a more g. climate 1834. **5.** A great broad-shoulder'd g. Englishman TENNYSON. **6.** So much I feel my g. spirits droop MILT.

Genial (dʒĕnəi·ăl), *a.*[2] 1831. [f. Gr. *γένειον* chin (f. *γένυς* jaw = L. *gena*) + -AL[1].] *Anat.* Of or pertaining to the chin; = MENTAL *a.*[2]; as, *g. process, tubercle.*

Geniality (dʒīniæ·lĭti). 1609. [f. GENIAL *a.*[1] + -ITY after late L. *genialitas*.] The quality of being GENIAL; sympathetic cheerfulness, good-nature; mildness (of air, etc.).

Genialize (dʒī·niăləiz), *v.* 1849. [f. GENIAL *a.*[1] + -IZE.] *trans.* To impart geniality to.

Genially (dʒī·niăli), *adv.* 1661. [f. as prec. + -LY[2].] †**1.** By genius or nature; naturally. GLANVILL. **2.** In a genial manner; pleasantly; kindlily 1751.

2. This g. garrulous Fellow of Oriel LOWELL. So **Ge·nialness** = GENIALITY.

Genian (dʒénəi·ăn), *a.* 1885. [f. as GENIAL *a.*[2] + -AN.] *Anat.* = GENIAL *a.*[2]

Geniculate (dʒéni·kiŭlĕt), *a.* 1668. [– L. *geniculatus*, f. *geniculum* knee, knot or joint, dim. of *genu* knee; see -ATE[2].] *Nat. Hist.* Having knots or joints like a knee; bent like a knee; as, a *g. ganglion.*

Geniculate (dʒéni·kiŭleⁱt), *v.* 1623. [– *geniculat-*, pa. ppl. stem of late L. *geniculare* bend the knee, f. L. *geniculum*; see prec., -ATE[3].] To bend like a knee; to form or be formed into joints. *trans.* and *intr.* Hence **Geni:cula·tion,** †genuflexion; the state of being geniculated; *concr.* a kneed part or process.

Genie (dʒī·ni). 1655. [– Fr. *génie* – L. *genius*.] **1.** †**a.** A tutelary spirit –1702. **b.** A JINNEE (see GENIUS 2) 1748. **2. a.** Natural bent. (Common in A. Wood.) 1662. †**b.** A person of genius –1687.

2. a. But his g...led him in the pleasant paths of Poetry WOOD.

Genii, pl. of GENIUS.

†**Genio.** 1609. [– It. *genio* – L. *genius* GENIUS.] = GENIUS 2, 3, 4, and 6. –1710.

Genio- (dʒénəi·o), comb. f. Gr. γένειον (see GENIAL *a.*[2]), with sense 'pertaining to the chin or lower jaw and —'.

geni·o-glossal [see GLOSSAL] *a.* = next; **-hy·o-glossal** *a.*, pertaining to the chin, the hyoid bone, and the tongue; **-hy·oid** [see HYOID] *a.*, pertaining to the chin and to the hyoid bone; also *absol.* quasi-*sb.* = *genio-hyoid muscle*; **-me·ntal** [see MENTAL[2]] *a.*, pertaining to the lower jaw and the chin.

Genip (dʒe·nip). *W. Indian.* 1756. [perh. short for next.] *attrib.* in **genip-tree,** a name of *Genipa americana*, N.O. *Rubiaceæ*; also applied to similar trees of the N.O. *Sapindaceæ*, esp. *Melicocca bijuga* and *paniculata.*

Genipap (dʒe·nipæp). 1613. [app. a native name.] The fruit of *Genipa americana.*

‖**Genista** (dʒéni·stă). 1625. [L., var. of *genesta* (Virgil, Pliny).] *Bot.* A plant of the genus (N.O. *Leguminosæ*) represented by Dyer's Broom or Greenweed (*G. tinctoria*); including, according to some, the Common Broom (*Cytisus scoparia*).

Genital (dʒe·nităl). ME. [– (O)Fr. *génital* or L. *genitalis* (n. sing. and pl. as sb.), f. *genitus*, pa. ppl. of *gignere* beget; see -AL[1].]

A. *adj.* Pertaining to animal generation.

B. *sb.* The †organ or (*pl.*) organs of generation, usually of the male ME.

‖**Genitalia** (dʒenitēⁱ·liă), *sb. pl.* 1876. [L., n. pl. of *genitalis* adj.; see prec.] = GENITALS, see prec. B.

Geniting, obs. f. JENNETING.

Genitival (dʒenitəi·văl), *a.* 1818. [f. next + -AL[1].] Belonging to the genitive case; as, a *g. termination.*

Genitive (dʒe·nitiv). ME. [– (O)Fr. *génitif, -ive* or L. *genitivus, -iva* (*gene-*), f. *genit-*, pa. ppl. stem of *gignere* beget, produce; see -IVE. *Genitivus casus* is a rendering of Gr. γενική πτῶσις 'case of production or origin'.]

A. *adj.* **1.** *G. case*: a grammatical form of sbs., etc., used to denote that the person or thing signified by the word is related to another as source, possessor, or the like. †**2.** Pertaining to generation –1656.

1. There is no g. case in the Persian SIR W. JONES.

B. *sb.* = *genitive case*; also, a part of speech in this case 1620.

The Cumulative or Double G., a peculiarly English combination, where both the *of* and the *'s* are retained, as 'that boy of Norcott's' EARLE.

Genito- (dʒe·nito), mod. comb. f. L. *genitalis* genital, used in terms which refer to the genital organs in conjunction with other parts of the body, as *g.-crural, -urinary*, etc.

†**Genitor**[1], **genitory.** Chiefly *pl.* ME. [– (O)Fr. *génitoires* pl., suffix-variant (-ORY[1]) of synon. †*genitaire(s*, †*genitailles, génitures*; see GENITAL, GENITURE.] A testicle; *pl.* the testicles, but in later use = *genitals* –1708.

Genitor[2] (dʒe·nitŏr). Now *rare.* 1447. [– L. *genitor* begetter, f. **gen-* base of *gignere* beget. The earliest forms are – (O)Fr. *géniteur.*] A male parent, father; in *pl.* = parents.

†**Geniture.** 1548. [– (O)Fr. *géniture* or L. *genitura*, f. as prec.; see -URE.] **1.** Begetting, generation; birth –1759. **2.** *Astrol.* Nativity. horoscope –1819. **3.** Offspring, product –1698. **4.** The generative seed of animals –1683. **5.** *pl.* = Genitals 1548.

Genius (dʒī·niŏs). *Pl.* **-ii** (-iˌəi), **-iuses.** 1513. [– L. *genius* attendant spirit, inclination, appetite, (rarely) intellectual capacity, f. **gen-*, base of *gignere* beget, Gr. γίγνεσθαι be born, come into being.] **1.** The tutelary god or attendant spirit allotted to every person at his birth, to preside over his destiny in life; also, the tutelary spirit of a place, institution, etc. (Now only in *sing.*) †**b.** After L. use: This spirit as propitiated by festivities; hence, one's appetite –1693. **c.** The personification of something immaterial, e.g. of a virtue, a custom, etc. Hence *transf.* a person or thing fit to be this. 1597. **2.** A demon or spirit in general. Now chiefly in pl. *genii*, as tr. Arab. *jinn* (see JINN). (In *sing.* repl. by GENIE.) 1590. **3.** †**a.** Characteristic disposition; inclination; bent –1804. **b.** Prevailing character or spirit (of a nation, age, language, law, etc.) 1639. **c.** The associations or suggestions (of a place) 1823. †**d.** Of material things, diseases, etc.: The natural character, inherent tendency –1747. **4.** Natural ability; quality of mind 1649; natural aptitude (and inclination) †*to, for* 1643. **5.** (Only in *sing.*) Native intellectual power of an exalted type; extraordinary capacity for imaginative creation, original thought, invention, or discovery. Often contrasted with *talent.* 1749. **6.** One who has *great, little*, etc. 'genius' (sense 4); one who has a 'genius' (sense 3); one endowed with 'genius' (sense 5) (now only *geniuses* in pl.) 1647.

1. Vnder him My G. is rebuk'd, as it is said Mark Anthonies was by Cæsar SHAKS. Phr. (*A person's*) *good, evil g.*: the two spirits (also *angels*), good and evil, attendant on every person throughout life. Hence *transf.* of a person who powerfully influences another for good or evil. **c.** He was the very G. of Famine SHAKS. **2.** They mock even the G. of Socrates as a feigned thing STANLEY. **3. a.** My g. is always in extremes JOHNSON. **b.** The G. of the Age BOYLE, of Tragedy BENTLEY, of the British Constitution ADAM SMITH. **4.** The Squire whose active g. [etc.] LYTTON. Walton had a g. for friendships LOWELL. **5.** G. always imports something inventive or creative 1783. G... means transcendent capacity for taking trouble, first of all CARLYLE. **6.** That g. [Inigo Jones] H. WALPOLE. Phrase. ‖**genius loci** [L. = 'genius of the place'], the presiding deity or spirit (see sense 1); but often in sense 3 c.

Genoa (dʒe·noˌă). 1615. [– It. *Genova*, the Fr. form of which, *Gênes*, is repr. by JEAN.] The name of a city of Italy. Used *attrib.* in **G. cake,** a rich currant cake with almonds on the top; **G. treacle** (see TREACLE). Also *absol.* = *G.-velvet.*

Genoblast (dʒe·noblast). 1877. [f. Gr. γένος offspring + -BLAST.] The bisexual nucleus of the impregnated ovum. Hence **Genobla·stic** *a.*

Genocide (dʒe·nosəid). 1944. [f. Gr. γένος race + -CIDE 2.] Annihilation of a race.

Genoese (dʒenoˌī·z). 1553. [f. GENOA + -ESE, after It. *Genovese.*] **A.** *adj.* Of or pertaining to Genoa 1756. †var. **Geno·an. B.** *absol.* and *sb. The G.* (pl.): the Genoese people. var. **Ge·novese** *a.* and *sb.*

Genouillere (ʒənuyę̄r). ME. [– Fr. *genouillère* (OFr. *genoillier, -ère*), f. *genou* knee (OFr. *genoil, genouil*).] **1.** A flexible piece of armour for covering the knees. **2.** *Fortif.* That part of the interior slope of the parapet immediately below the embrasures 1802.

‖**Genre** (ʒaṅr). 1816. [Fr., = kind; see GENDER.] **1.** Kind; sort; style. **2.** A style of painting which depicts scenes and subjects of common life 1873. **3.** *attrib.* as *g.-piece*, etc. 1849.

Gens (dʒenz). *Pl.* **gentes** (dʒe·ntiz). 1847. [– L. *gens*, f. **gen-*, base of L. *gignere* beget, produce.] *Rom. Antiq.* A clan, or sept; a number of families having a supposed common origin, a common name, and common religious rites. Hence as transl. Gr. γένος, and applied to any similar group of families.

Gens d'armerie, Gens d'armes, var. ff. GENDARMERY, GENDARMES.

Gent (dʒent), *sb.* 1564. [Short for GENTLEMAN.] = GENTLEMAN; now *vulgar*, exc. as applied derisively to men of the class who use the word; now frequent in tradesmen's notices.

London audiences of shop-boys and flashy gents 1878.

†**Gent** (dʒent), *a.* ME. [– OFr. *gent* :– pop. L. **gentus* for cl. L. *genitus* born, hence, well-born, noble, etc. Cf. GENTLE.] **1.** Noble, high-born; having the qualities attaching to high birth –1672. **2.** Graceful, elegant, shapely; neat –1824.

1. Jesu so gente ME. **2.** He lov'd..a Lady g. SPENSER.

Genteel (dʒentī·l). 1599. [A re-adoption of Fr. *gentil*, which had become GENTLE. In educated use, slightly sarcastic or playful.]

A. *adj.* **1.** Belonging to the gentry. *Obs.* or *arch.* 1628. **2.** Appropriate to persons of quality 1599; suited to the station of a gentleman or gentlewoman 1602. **3.** Having the habits characteristic of superior station; in early use, †polished, well-bred. (Now chiefly touched with sarcasm.) 1648. †**b.** Of behaviour: Polite, obliging –1814. **4.** Of persons: Gentlemanly or ladylike in appearance; well-dressed. (Now *vulgar*, exc. as depreciatory.) 1629. **5.** Elegant, graceful. *Obs.* of immaterial things. 1678.

1. Thomas Wyatt..of an ancient and gentile family WOOD. **2.** The genteelest dinner..I have seen PEPYS. G. Conversation 1766, accomplishments 1801. A g. maintenance V. KNOX. **3.** Zimri and Cosbi..g. Sinners M. HENRY. The straits of g. poverty 1885. **5.** His countenance beautiful; his limbs g. and slender HUME.

B. *sb.* A genteel person; a gentleman. *Obs.* exc. *occas.* 1675. Hence **Gentee·lish** *a.* somewhat g. **Gentee·l-ly** *adv.*, **-ness.**

Gentian (dʒe·nʃən). OE. [– L. *gentiana* (sc. *herba*), so called, according to Pliny, after *Gentius*, a king of *Illyria*; see -IAN.] **1.** Any plant belonging to the genus *Gentiana* (cf. FELWORT) ; esp. *G. lutea*, the officinal gentian which yields the gentian-root of the pharmacopœia. *Fringed g.* = *G. crinita.* Also *transf.* of other orders and genera. **2.** *attrib.*, as in *g.-blue*, etc.; **g.-bitter,** the tonic principle extracted from g.-root; **g.-worts,** Lindley's name for N.O. *Gentianaceæ.*

Hence **Gentiana·ceous** *a.* of or belonging to the N.O. *Gentianaceæ*; **Gentia·nic** *a.* pertaining to or derived from the g., as *gentianic acid*; **Ge·ntianin** (also †**-ine**) = *gentianic acid.*

Gentianal (dʒe·nʃənăl), *a.* 1846. [f. prec. + -AL[1].] Of or pertaining to the gentians.

Gentianella (dʒe:nʃəne·lă). 1658. [mod.L., dim. of *gentiana* GENTIAN; see -EL[2].] A name for species of gentian, esp. *Gentiana acaulis*, bearing flowers of an intense blue colour.

Gentil, obs. f. GENTEEL, GENTLE.

Gentile (dʒe·ntəil, -til). ME. [– L. *gentilis* of the same family, stock, or nation, (in eccl. use) heathen, pagan, f. *gens, gent-* race, stock, people, f. **gen-*, base of *gignere* beget; see -ILE.]

A. *adj.* **I.** Senses derived from the Vulgate (dʒe·ntəil). Usu. with capital G. **1.** Of or pertaining to any or all of the non-Jewish nations. †**2.** Heathen, pagan –1789.

II. Senses derived from cl. L. (Usu. dʒe·ntil.) **1.** Pertaining to or indicating a nation or tribe. Now *rare.* 1513. **2.** Of or pertaining to a gens or to gentes 1846.

2. There were in every gens or family special g. deities GROTE.

B. *sb.* **I.** From A. I. (dʒe·ntəil). (Usu. with capital G.) **1.** One of any non-Jewish nation ME. (Similarly by Mormons opposed to 'Saint'.) **2.** A heathen, a pagan. Now *rare.* ME. †**b.** *spec.* Of a Hindu, as dist. from a Moslem –1727.

1. No more shalt thou by oracling abuse The Gentiles MILT.

II. From A. II. (dʒe·ntil). **1.** *Gram.* A part of speech indicating the locality or nation to which anything belongs 1612. **2.** *Rom. Law.* A member of the same gens 1875.

1. The words Italian, American..are gentiles 1889.

Gentilesse (dʒe:ntile·s). Now *arch.* ME. [– (O)Fr. *gentillesse*, f. *gentil*; see GENTLE, -ESS².] **1.** Courtesy, politeness, good breeding. **2.** Elegance. CHAUCER.

Gentilic (dʒenti·lik), *a.* 1604. [– late L. *gentilicus* heathen, f. eccl. L. *gentilis*; see GENTILE, -IC.] †**a.** Heathen; var. †**Genti·lical. b.** Tribal, national.

†**Ge·ntilish,** *a.* 1550. [f. GENTILE + -ISH¹.] Of Gentile nature, origin, or character; heathenish –1651.

Gentilism (dʒe·ntiliz'm). 1577. [– OFr. *gentilisme* or med.L. *gentilismus*, f. eccl. L. *gentilis*; see GENTILE, -ISM.] **1.** Heathenism, paganism; a heathen belief or practice. Now only *occas.*, as opp. to *Judaism.* †**b.** *concr.* Heathendom –1654. **2.** The bond uniting the members of a gens (*rare*) 1847.

Gentilitial (dʒentili·ʃăl), *a.* 1611. [f. L. *gentilicius* (national, in eccl. L. pagan) + -AL¹.] **1.** Peculiar to a nation; national 1650. **2.** Of or pertaining to a gens or family 1611. **3.** Of or pertaining to gentle birth. [? f. med.L. *gentilitia* = GENTILESSE.] 1816. var. **Gentili·tian** (in sense 1).

Gentilitious (dʒentili·ʃəs), *a.* 1613. [f. as prec. + -OUS.] †**1.** Pagan (*rare*) 1613. **2.** = GENTILITIAL 1. 1646. **3.** = GENTILITIAL 2; hence, hereditary (? *Obs.*) 1646.

Gentility (dʒenti·lĭti). ME. [In Branch I – (O)Fr. *gentilité*, f. *gentil*; see GENTLE, -ITY. In Branch II eccl. and med. L. *gentilitas* heathenism, paganism, has been at least contributory.]

I. In relation to GENTLE, GENTEEL. **1.** Gentle birth; honourable extraction. Also quasi-*personified.* †**b.** *concr.* Gentlefolks. Also *The g.* –1622. **c.** The heraldic status of a gentleman 1642. **2.** The quality of being gentle (in manners, status, etc.), or genteel 1588. **b.** quasi-*personified.* Also in *pl.* Genteel people; also, marks of gentility. 1840.

1. G. has long since confuted Job's Aphorism, Man is born to labour 1659. 2. There is nothing so vulgar as g. 1872. b. Shabby g. O. W. HOLMES.

II. In relation to GENTILE. †**1.** Heathenism, paganism –1650; †*concr.* heathendom, heathen people –1582. **2.** Relationship between members of the same gens; †the gens itself 1577.

Gentilize (dʒe·ntiləiz), *v.*¹ *arch.* 1581. [f. Fr. *gentil* GENTLE + -IZE.] **1.** *trans.* To make gentle or gentlemanly. †**b.** *intr. To g. it*: to act the gentleman –1613. †**2.** *trans.* To lenify 1679.

Gentilize (dʒe·ntiləiz, dʒe·ntəiləiz), *v.*² 1593. [f. GENTILE + -IZE.] **1.** *intr.* To live like a Gentile or heathen. **2.** *trans.* To make gentile, paganize 1827.

Gentill-: see GENTEEL, GENTIL-, GENTLE, etc.

Gentiopicrin (dʒentiopi·krin). 1875. [f. *gentio-* comb. f. GENTIAN + Gr. πικρός + -IN¹.] *Chem.* 'The bitter principle of gentian, a colourless crystalline glycoside' (*Syd. Soc. Lex.*).

Gentisic (dʒenti·sik), *a.* 1838. [Arbitrarily f. GENTIAN; see -IC.] *Chem.* In *g. acid* = gentianic acid. So **Ge·ntisate** [-ATE], a salt of this acid. **Ge·ntisin** [-IN], a synonym of g. or gentianic acid.

Gentle (dʒe·nt'l). [– (O)Fr. *gentil* high-born, noble (in mod.Fr. pleasant, kind, agreeable) :– L. *gentilis* belonging to the same gens or stock, (Rom.) belonging to a good family; see also GENTEEL, GENTILE.]

A. *adj.* **1.** Well-born; belonging to a family of position; orig. = *noble*, but afterwards designating a lower degree of rank. Also in *Her.*: Having the rank of 'gentleman', and therefore entitled to bear arms. *Obs.* exc. in *gentle and simple*, and in Comb. **b.** Of excellent breed or spirit; now only in *gentle* (also *gentil*) *falcon* ME. †**c.** Of things: Noble, excellent (*rare*) –1556. **2.** Of birth, etc.: Honourable, belonging to the class of 'gentlemen' ME. **b.** Of occupations, etc.: Suitable for one of gentle birth 1592. **3.** Noble, generous, courteous, polite. Now only *arch.* ME. **b.** Used in polite or conciliatory address, or in compliment. *Obs.* exc. *arch.* in 'Gentle Reader'. 1500. **4.** Of a tree, etc.: Cultivated (opp. to *wild*). Now *rare.* ME. Of an animal: Tame, easily managed 1532. †**5.** Not harsh or irritating to the touch; soft, tender; pliant, supple –1769. **6.** Not violent or severe 1563; not rough 1593; not harsh 1605; mild 1576. **7.** Of a slope: Gradual; not steep 1697. **8.** Used advb. = GENTLY (esp. in *compar.*) 1601.

1. Noble men and gentile ne bereð nout packes ME. G. and Simple, Squire and Groom BARHAM. b. A Lion saw I late..Vpon the g. beast to gaze it pleased me SURREY. c. That gentil text CHAUCER. 2. His birth being admitted as g., gave him access to the best society in the county SCOTT. b. *The g. craft* (joc.): †(*a*) shoemaking; (*b*) angling; similarly *the g. art*, now often used transf. 3. [Robin Hood] The gentlest thief that ever was FULLER. b. You g. Romans SHAKS. 4. We marry A gentler sien to the wildest stock SHAKS. 6. As when the Woods by g. Winds are stirr'd DRYDEN. The g. voice of Peace COLLINS. A g. River 1791. A g. heat 1816. G. methods SCOTT. A g. aperient 1835. You have grown g. to me and have left off scolding JOWETT. 8. Hee put it by thrice, everie time gentler then other *Jul. C.* I. ii. 231.

B. *sb.* **1.** One who is of gentle birth or rank (*rare* in *sing.*; *Obs.* in *pl.* exc. *arch.*) ME †**b.** Used in polite address –1641. **2.** = FALCON-GENTLE. 1776. **3.** A maggot, the larva of the flesh-fly or blue-bottle, used as bait by anglers 1578.

1. b. Gentles I would entreat you a courtesie 1641.

Gentle (dʒe·nt'l), *v.* ME. [f. prec.] †**1.** *trans.* To ennoble –1630. **2.** To render mild or pleasant (*rare*) 1651; to break in (a horse, etc.) 1735; to mollify (a person) 1795.

1. Be he ne're so vile, This day shall g. his Condition SHAKS.

Gentlefolk, -folks (dʒe·nt'lfōᵘk, -fōᵘks). 1594. [f. as GENTLE *a.* + FOLK. The sing. is recent.] Persons of good position and family.

The Queene's Kindred are made gentle Folkes SHAKS.

Gentlehood (dʒe·nt'lhud). 1860. [See -HOOD.] Position or character attaching to gentle birth.

Gentleman (dʒe·nt'lmǽn). ME. [f. GENTLE + MAN, after OFr. *gentilz hom* (mod. *gentilhomme*).] **1.** A man of gentle birth; prop., one entitled to bear arms, though not noble, but also applied to any person of distinction. Now chiefly *Hist.* **b.** Used as a complimentary designation of a member of certain societies or professions 1537. **2.** *spec.* A man of gentle birth attached to the household of the sovereign or of a person of rank 1463. **3.** A man of chivalrous instincts and fine feelings ME. **4.** A man of superior position in society; often, a man of money and leisure. In recent use often a courteous synonym for 'man'. 1583. **b.** In *pl.* (†also in *sing.*) a polite term of address without reference to rank 1579. **c.** In legal documents, a person who has no occupation 1862. **5.** In contemptuous or joc. uses; esp. *old g.* = old fellow, *spec.* the devil; *my g.* = 'the fellow' 1622.

1. Early in the 11th century the order of 'gentlemen' as a separate class seems to be forming as something new FREEMAN. b. A gentellman of the Inner Temple 1537. Gentlemen of the faculty 1768. 2. The gentylmen of the kynges housholde and the gentylmen of the Erles housholde 1520. †*G.-pensioner*, now *G.-at-arms*: one of forty gentlemen who act as guards or attendants to the sovereign on state occasions. *G. at large*, †a g. attached to the court but without specific duties; hence *joc.* one who is out of work. 3. Who so is vertuous..he is gentil, bycause he doth As longeth to a gentilman ME. 4. The rich Tradesman..laid the Tradesman down and commenc'd G. DE FOE. b. Your name, honest G. SHAKS. 5. But afterwards..the copy of my Gentlemans countenance was quickly altered MABBE. You *gentlemen's gentlemen* (= valets) are so hasty SHERIDAN.

Phrases. *The g. in black velvet*: a mole (a Jacobite phrase, referring to the belief that the death of William III was caused by his horse's stumbling over a mole-hill). *G. of fortune*: a pirate. *Gentleman's (-men's) agreement*: an agreement binding in honour, but not enforceable at law (orig. *U.S.*).

Hence **Ge·ntlemanhood,** the position or character of a g. **Ge·ntlemanism,** the state of being a g., the affectation of gentlemanliness. **Ge·ntlemani:ze** *v.* to make into a g. **Ge·ntlemanship,** gentlemanhood; the office of a g. (-in-waiting, etc.).

Ge·ntleman-co·mmoner. 1687. [See COMMONER 5.] One of a privileged class of undergraduates formerly recognized in the Universities of Oxford and Cambridge.

Ge·ntleman-farmer. 1749. A country gentleman engaged in farming, usually on his own estate.

Gentlemanlike (dʒe·nt'lmǽnləik). 1542. [f. GENTLEMAN + -LIKE.]

A. *adj.* Appropriate or natural to a gentleman 1557; resembling a gentleman 1581.

†**B.** *adv.* After the fashion of a gentleman –1606.

Ge·ntlemanly. ME. [See -LY¹.] **A.** *adj.* **1.** Having the character, behaviour, or appearance of a gentleman 1454. **2.** Natural or appropriate to a gentleman 1581.

B. *adv.* As befits a gentleman. Now *rare.* ME. Hence **Ge·ntlemanliness,** the attribute of being g.

Ge·ntleman-u·sher. 1485. A gentleman acting as usher to a person of superior rank. *G.-usher of the Black Rod* (see BLACK ROD).

Gentleness (dʒe·nt'lnės). ME. [f. GENTLE + -NESS.] †**1.** The condition of being GENTLE *a.* (sense 1) –1671. **2.** †Good breeding, courtesy, affability; kindliness, mildness ME. **3.** The condition of being gentle (in other senses of the adj.); freedom from harshness or violence, etc. 1614.

Gentleship (dʒe·nt'lʃip). [-SHIP.] The condition or quality of being a gentleman. ASCHAM.

Gentlewoman (dʒe·nt'lwumăn). ME. [f. GENTLE *a.* + WOMAN.] **1.** A woman of good birth or breeding. **2.** A female attendant (orig. a gentlewoman by birth) upon a lady of rank. Now only *Hist.* ME.

Gently (dʒe·ntli), *adv.* ME. [f. GENTLE *a.* + -LY².] In a gentle manner (see GENTLE *a.*); also used as an expression of remonstrance.

G. born and bred TENNYSON. G., Mr. Testy 1806.

Gentoo (dʒentū·), *sb.*¹ and *a.* 1638. [Anglo-Indian – Pg. *gentio* GENTILE.]

A. *sb.* **1.** A Hindu, opp. to a Moslem. **2.** The language of the Gentoos 1698.

B. *attrib.* (*adj.*) Of or pertaining to the Gentoos 1686.

Gentoo (dʒentū·), *sb.*² 1860. [perh. a use of prec.] A kind of penguin frequenting the Falkland Islands. Also *G. Penguin.*

Gentrice. *Obs.* exc. *arch.* (*Sc.*) ME. [– OFr. *genterise*, var. of *gentelise* nobility, kindness, f. *gentil* GENTLE + *ise* -ICE.] **1.** Gentle birth. **2.** Gentle or honourable feeling ME. **3.** Gentility. SCOTT.

Gentry (dʒe·ntri). ME. [prob. alt. of GENTRICE by assoc. with †*gentlery*.] **1.** Rank by birth (usu., high birth). *Obs.* exc. *arch.* **b.** The quality or rank of gentleman (*arch.*) 1447. †**c.** Good breeding; also, courtesy, generosity –1595. **2.** People of gentle birth and breeding; the class to which they belong; now *spec.* the class immediately below the nobility 1585. **3.** Playfully or contemptuously: People, folks 1717.

1. To presume..upon..birth and G. 1647. b. His g. sits as ill upon him, as if he had bought it with his penny OVERBURY. c. True gentrie they have put to flight 1595. 2. Grave G. of estate and name WORDSW. 3. These crusty g. W. IRVING.

Genty (dʒe·nti), *a.* *Obs.* exc. *Sc.* 1721. [var. of †*gentee* – Fr. *gentil*; see JAUNTY.] Neat; graceful; genteel.

‖**Genu** (dʒī·niu). 1854. [L.; = 'knee'.] *Anat.* Name for a knee-like bend in various organs of the body. Hence **Ge·nual** *a.* of or pertaining to the g. **Ge·nuant** *a.* (*Her.*) kneeling. **Ge·nuclast** (*Surg.*), an instrument for breaking down adhesions in the knee-joint.

Genuflect (dʒe·niuflekt), *v.* 1630. [– eccl.L. *genuflectere*, f. L. *genu* knee + *flectere* bend.] *intr.* To bend the knee, esp. in worship. Hence **Genufle·ctory** *a.* of or pertaining to genuflexion or kneeling. var. **Genufle·x.**

Genuflexion, genuflection (dʒeniuflе·kʃən). 1526. [– eccl.L. *genuflexio*, f. L. *genu* knee + *flexio* bending, f. *flectere* bend. See FLEXION.] The act of kneeling or bending the knee, esp. in worship; also *Surg.* as a curative measure in popliteal aneurism.

Genuine (dʒe·niu͡in), *a.* 1596. [– L. *genuinus*, f. *genu* knee; the orig. ref. was to the recognition of a new-born child by a father placing it on his knees; later assoc. with *genus* race; see -INE[1].] †**1.** Natural, not acquired, native –1712. **2.** Pertaining to the original stock, pure-bred 1728. **3.** Not spurious; AUTHENTIC. (The 18th c. distinction between *genuine* and *authentic* is not well founded.) 1661. **4.** Being as represented; real, true, not counterfeit, †unadulterated 1639. **b.** Properly so called 1682.

1. This g. blemish 1644. **2.** [A bull-dog] of a pure and g. breed T. MEDWIN. **3.** Two volumes more.. indubitably g. JOHNSON. **4.** Natural Religion in its g. simplicity BUTLER. **b.** A g. son of the sea SCORESBY. Hence **Ge·nuine-ly** *adv.*, **-ness.**

‖**Genus** (dʒī·nəs). *Pl.* ‖**genera** (dʒe·nĕră). 1551. [– L. *genus* birth, race, stock.] **1.** *Logic.* A class or kind of things which includes subordinate kinds (called SPECIES) as having certain attributes in common; a general concept. (One of the five PREDICABLES, q.v.) **2.** *Zool.* and *Bot.* A classificatory group comprehending (one or) a number of species possessing certain common structural characters distinct from those of any other group. Also *transf.* 1608.

The genus ranks next under the family or subfamily and above the species; it is sometimes divided into sub-genera. The generic and specific names (always in Latin or considered as Latin) together form the scientific proper name of an animal or plant, the generic name standing first and being written with an initial capital.

3. *Mus.* Each of the three scales in ancient Greek music 1763. **4.** *gen.* A kind, class, order, tribe, etc. 1649.

1. *Highest g.* (L. *summum genus*), one which does not become a species of a higher g.; opp. to *subaltern g.* The Highest G. in any special science is the general class, comprehending all the objects whose properties that science investigates MANSEL.

-geny, *suffix* = mod. Fr. *-génie*, added to Gr. stems to form sbs. with sense 'mode of production (of something specified)' as in *anthropogeny*, etc.

Genyplasty (dʒe·niplæsti). 1857. [f. Gr. γένυς jaw, cheek + -PLASTY.] *Med.* An operation for restoring the cheek.

Geo- (dʒī·o-, dʒi͡ǫ·-), repr. Gr. γεω-, comb. f. Gr. γῆ earth. **ge·oblast** [-BLAST], 'a plumule which in germination rises from underground, such as that of the Pea' (GRAY); **ge:obota·nical** *a.*, of or pertaining to geographical botany; **ge:ochro·nic** *a.*, of or pertaining to geological time; **ge:ocy·clic** *a.*, of or pertaining to the revolutions of the earth; also, circling the earth periodically; **geo:dyna·mic, -al** *a.*, of or pertaining to the (latent) forces of the earth; **ge:oi·sotherm,** an underground isotherm; **ge:onaviga·tion,** navigation by dead reckoning —opp. to *Cælo-navigation*; **geo·nomy,** the science of the physical laws relating to the earth; **ge:ophy·sical** *a.*, relating to the physics of the earth; **ge:ophy·sics** *pl.*, the physics of the earth; **ge:osele·nic** *a.*, relating to the earth and the moon; **ge:osta·tic** [Gr. στατικός] *a.*, suited to bear the pressure of earth, as a *geostatic arch*; **ge:osta·tics** *pl.*, 'the statics of rigid bodies' (*Cent. Dict.*); **ge:otecto·nic, -al** *a.*, of or pertaining to the structure of the earth; structural; **ge:othe·rmal** *a.*, of or pertaining to the internal heat of the earth; so **ge:othe·rmic** *a.*; **ge:othermo·meter,** an instrument for measuring terrestrial heat, esp. in mines and artesian wells.

Geocentric (dʒī͡ose·ntrik), *a.* (*sb.*) 1667. [f. GEO-; see CENTRIC. Cf. Fr. *géocentrique.* Opp. to HELIOCENTRIC.] **1.** Referred to the earth as a centre; considered as viewed from the centre of the earth; as, the *g. latitude, longitude, place*, etc. of a planet 1686. **2.** Having, or representing, the earth as centre; also *fig.* 1696. **3.** *sb.* An adherent of the geocentric theory 1667.

2. In the universe of being the difference between a heliocentric and a g. theory is of..small moment M. PATTISON. Hence **Ge:oce·ntrically** *adv.* **Geoce·ntricism,** the g. theory.

Geocronite (dʒī͡ǫ·krŏnəit). 1844. [f. GEO- + Gr. Κρόνος Saturn (in alchemy assoc. with lead) + -ITE[1] 2 b.] *Min.* A sulphide of lead and antimony.

Geodæsia: see GEODESY.

Geode (dʒī·oᵘd). 1676. [– L. *geodes* (Pliny) – Gr. γεώδης earthy, f. γῆ earth. Cf. Fr. *géode.*] A nodular stone, containing a cavity usually lined with crystals or mineral matter. **b.** The cavity itself; also, any similar formation 1849. Hence **Geo·dic** *a.* of, pertaining to, or resembling a g. **Geodi·ferous** *a.*

Geodesy (dʒi͡ǫ·dési). 1570. [– mod.L. *geodæsia* – Gr. γεωδαισία, f. δαίειν divide; see GEO-, -Y[3]. Fr. *géodésie* is later (XVII).] †**a.** Land surveying –1855. **b.** In mod use: That branch of applied mathematics which determines the figures and areas of large portions of the earth's surface, and the figure of the earth as a whole 1853. So †**Geodesian,** a land-surveyor. Hence **Geode·sic** *a.* of or pertaining to g.; *sb.* a geodesic line. **Geode·sical** *a.* = prec. adj. **Geo·desist,** one versed in g.

Geodetic (dʒī͡ode·tik). 1674. [f. mod.L. *geodetes* – Gr. γεωδαίτης land-surveyor; see -IC.]

A. *adj.* Of or pertaining to geodesy 1834.

Phr. *Geodetic line*: the shortest possible line that can be drawn from one point of a surface to another, the plane of curvature of which will be everywhere perpendicular to the surface.

B. *sb.* **1.** A geodetic line (see A. quot.) 1879. **2.** in pl. form **Geodetics** = GEODESY. (Dicts.)

Hence **Geode·tical** a. of or pertaining to geodesy. †**Geode·tically** *adv.*

Geoduck (dʒī·odɒk). 1883. [perh. Amer. Indian.] A large edible clam (*Glycineris generosa*) from the Pacific coast of the U.S.

Geogeny (dʒi͡ǫ·dʒėni). 1855. [f. GEO- + -GENY. Cf. Fr. *géogénie.*] That branch of geology which treats of the formation of the earth's crust. Hence **Geoge·nic** *a.* pertaining to g.; earth-forming.

Geognost (dʒī·ǫ̆gnǫst). 1804. [– Fr. *géognoste* (Werner, 1802), f. Gr. γεω- GEO- + γνώστης one who knows.] One versed in geognosy. Hence **Geogno·stic, -al** *a.* of or pertaining to geognosy. **Geogno·stically** *adv.*

Geognosy (dʒi͡ǫ·gnŏsi). 1791. [– Fr. *géognosie*, f. Gr. γεω- GEO- + γνῶσις knowledge.] **1.** A knowledge of the structure of the earth, its strata, and their relative position. Often = GEOLOGY. **2. a.** A knowledge of the natural position of minerals in particular rocks, and of the grouping, distribution, and relations of those rocks 1811. **b.** Local geology 1839. var. **Geo·gnosis.**

Geogony (dʒi͡ǫ·gŏni). 1828. [f. Gr. γεω- GEO- + γονία production.] The theory of the formation of the earth. Also, an account of this. Hence **Geogo·nic, -al** *a.* of or pertaining to g.

Geographer (dʒi͡ǫ·grăfəɹ). 1542. [f. late L. *geographus* (– Gr. γεωγράφος, see GEO-, -GRAPH) + -ER[1] 4; see -GRAPHER.] One who is versed in, or writes upon, geography. var. †**Ge·ograph.**

Geographic (dʒī͡ogræ·fik). 1610. [– Fr. *géographique* or late L. *geographicus* – Gr. γεωγραφικός, f. γεωγράφος; see prec., -IC.]

A. *adj.* Of or pertaining to geography; of the nature of geography. Now *rare.*

Phr. *Geographic latitude*: the angle made with the plane of the equator by a perpendicular to the surface of the earth at any point.

B. *sb.* pl. **Geographics** (*rare*), geographical science; †a treatise on this 1610.

Geographical (dʒī͡ogræ·fikăl), *a.* 1559. [f. as prec.; see -ICAL.] = GEOGRAPHIC *a.*

Geographical mile: a measure of length = 1′ of longitude on the equator. Hence **Geogra·phically** *adv.*

Geography (dʒi͡ǫ·grăfi). 1542. [– L. *geographia* (partly through Fr.) – Gr. γεωγραφία; see GEO-, -GRAPHY.] **1.** The science that describes the earth's surface, its form and physical features, its natural and political divisions, its climates, productions, etc. Also *transf.* **b.** The subject-matter of geography; the range or extent of what is known geographically 1737. **2.** A treatise on this science 1559.

1. Phr. *Mathematical, physical, political g.* †*Subterranean g.* = GEOLOGY. *transf.* The g. of Mars (*mod.*). **b.** The islands..added to the g. of the globe COOK.

Geoid (dʒī·oid). 1881. [– Gr. γεοειδής earthlike; see GEO-, -OID.] A geometrical solid, nearly identical with the terrestrial spheroid, but having the surface at every point perpendicular to the direction of gravity. Hence **Geoi·dal** *a.*

Geolatry (dʒi͡ǫ·lătri). *rare.* 1860. [f. GEO- + -LATRY.] Earth-worship.

Geologic (dʒī͡olǫ·dʒik), *a.* 1799. [f. GEOLOGY + -IC.] Of, pertaining to, or derived from geology (now used mainly as an epithet of things forming part of the subject-matter of the science, e.g. a *geologic epoch*, as dist. from *geological*). Also *transf.* So **Geolo·gical** *a.* Hence **Geolo·gically** *adv.*

Geologist (dʒi͡ǫ·lŏdʒist). 1795. [f. GEOLOGY + -IST.] One versed in geology. vars. **Geo·loger** (now *rare*), **Geolo·gian** (now *rare*).

Geologize (dʒi͡ǫ·lŏdʒəiz), *v.* 1831. [f. GEOLOGY + -IZE.] **1.** *intr.* To make geological researches. **2.** *trans.* To examine geologically 1834.

1. During Midsummer geologized a little in Shropshire DARWIN.

Geology (dʒi͡ǫ·lŏdʒi). 1735. [– mod.L. *geologia*; see GEO-, -LOGY.] †**1.** The science which treats of the earth in general –1755. **2.** The science which investigates the earth's crust, the strata which compose it, with their mutual relations, and the successive changes to which their present condition and positions are due 1795. **b.** The geological features of a district 1816.

Geomalism (dʒi͡ǫ·măliz'm). 1884. [f. Gr. γεω- GEO- + ὁμαλός level + -ISM.] *Biol.* The tendency of an organism to grow symmetrically in a horizontal plane. So **Geo·maly.**

Geomancy (dʒī·omænsi). ME. [– med.L. *geomantia* (Isidore); see GEO-, -MANCY. Cf. Fr. *géomancie* (XV).] The art of divination by means of lines and figures, formed orig. by throwing earth on some surface, and later by jotting down on paper dots at random. Hence **Ge·oma:ncer,** also **Ge·omant** (*rare*), one who practises g.

Geomantic (dʒī͡omæ·ntik). 1590. [– med.L *geomanticus* geomancer, f. *geomantia*; see prec., -IC.]

A. *adj.* Belonging to geomancy; var. **Geoma·ntical.**

†**B.** *sb.* A geomancer –1652. Hence **Geoma·ntically** *adv.*

Geometer (dʒi͡ǫ·mītəɹ). 1483. [– late L. *geometra*, for cl. L. *geometres* – Gr. γεωμέτρης land-measurer, f. γεω- GEO- + -μέτρης measurer.] **1.** One who studies, or is skilled in, geometry. **2.** The name of a class of caterpillars (so called from their walk) 1816.

Geometric, -al (dʒī͡ome·trik, -ăl), *a.* 1552. [– (O)Fr. *géométrique* – L. *geometricus* – Gr. γεωμετρικός, f. γεωμέτρης; see prec., -IC, -ICAL.] **1.** Belonging to geometry; determined or constructed according to the methods of geometry. **2.** That works by the methods of geometry (*rare*) 1682.

1. †*Geometrical cubit, foot, mile, pace*: measures of length, some of which are app. fixed by geographical computation (1 degree = 60 miles, 1 mile = 1,000 paces, 1 pace = 5 feet). *Geometrical figures*, formerly restricted to those whose construction involved only the straight line and circle, all other curves being called mechanical. *Geometrical ratio* (now usually *ratio* simply): that kind of relation between two quantities which is expressed by dividing the first by the second: the quotient expressing this. *G. proportion*: a proportion which involves an equality of geometrical ratio in its two parts, as 1:3::4:12. *G. progression*; a series in which the ratio between the successive quantities is constant, as 1:3:9:27:81, etc. *Geometric(al spider*, a spider which constructs a web of geometrical form. *Geometrical staircase*, 'one whose opening is down its centre..in which each step is supported by one end being fixed in the wall or partition' (Gwilt). *Geometrical tracery*, tracery in which the openings are of geometrical form (circles, trefoils, etc.). **2.** The g. artist of Laputa KANE. Hence **Geome·trically** *adv.* vars. †**Geometral,** †**Geometrial.**

Geometrician (dʒi͡ǫ:mėtri·ʃăn). 1483. [– OFr. *geometricien*, f. *geometrique*, L. *geometricus* (see prec.) + *-ien* -IAN; see -ICIAN.]

1. One who studies geometry. Now *rare.* †**2.** One who measures the earth or land –1676. var. †**Geometrian** (*rare*).

Geometrid (dʒiˌǫ·mėtrid). 1865. [f. L. *Geometra* mod. name for a genus of moths + -ID[3].]

A. *adj.* Belonging to the family of moths of which *Geometra* is the typical genus; see GEOMETER.

B. *sb.* A moth of this family. So **Geome·triform** *a.* 'resembling in form a moth of the family *Geometridæ*' (*Cent. Dict.*).

Geometrize (dʒiˌǫ·mėtrəiz), *v.* 1658. [f. GEOMETRY + -IZE.] *intr.* To work by geometrical methods; *trans.* to form geometrically. (Cf. Plato's phrase ἀεὶ γεωμετρεῖν τὸν θεόν.)

Knowing that God geometrizes eternally DE QUINCEY.

Geometry (dʒiˌǫ·mėtri). ME. [– (O)Fr. *géométrie* – L. *geometria* – Gr. γεωμετρία; see GEO-, -METRY.] **1.** The science which investigates the properties and relations of magnitudes in space, as lines, surfaces, and solids. (At first regarded as a practical art, and mainly assoc. with Architecture.) †**2.** The art of measuring ground –1621.

Geophagy (dʒiˌǫ·fădʒi). 1850. [f. GEO- + -PHAGY.] The practice of eating earth; also **Geo·phagism.** So **Geo·phagist,** one that eats earth.

Geophilous (dʒiˌǫ·filəs), *a.* 1854. [f. mod.L. *Geophilus* (see GEO-, -PHIL) + -OUS.] *Zool.* and *Bot.* Belonging to one of the genera named *Geophilus* or *Geophila.*

Geoponic (dʒiˌopǫ·nik). 1608. [– Gr. γεωπονικός, f. γεωπόνος husbandman; see -IC.]

A. *adj.* Relating to the cultivation of the ground. Also *joc.* countrified. 1663.

B. *sb.* †**1.** A writer on agriculture. SELDEN. **2.** *pl.* The science of agriculture or husbandry; a treatise on this 1608.

Hence **Geopo·nical** *a.* So **Geo·pony,** agriculture.

Georama (dʒiˌorā·mă). ? *Obs.* 1847. [– Fr. *géorama*, f. Gr. γῆ earth + ὅραμα view. Cf. CYCLORAMA, PANORAMA.] A French invention, in the shape of a hollow sphere, exhibiting a complete view of the seas, lakes, rivers, and mountains on the earth's surface.

Geordie (dʒǭ·ɹdi). *Sc.* and *n. dial.* 1786. [dim. of GEORGE.] †**1.** (*Yellow*) *G.*: a guinea –1893. **2. a.** A coal-pitman 1876. **b.** A collier-boat 1884. **c.** Miner's name for George Stephenson's safety-lamp 1881.

George (dʒǭɹdʒ). [– L. *Georgius* – Gr. Γεώργιος, a saint who suffered martyrdom in the reign of Diocletian. Adopted as patron of the Order of the Garter, and recognized as patron saint of England from the time of Edward III.]

I. Saint George. 1. A cry formerly used by English soldiery 1594. **2.** *St. George's day*: April 23. *St. George's Cross*: an upright and a horizontal bar of red, crossing each other in the centre. 1611.

1. God, and Saint George, Richmond and Victory SHAKS.

II. George. 1. The jewel of the Order of the Garter, with a figure of St. George armed, on horseback, encountering the dragon 1506. †**2.** *slang.* A coin bearing the image of St. George; a half-crown; also, (*yellow*) *G.*, a guinea –1812. **3.** A brown loaf. ? *Obs.* 1755. **4.** *By George* (†*before, for, fore G.*): an exclam. or mild oath 1598.

Comb. †**George-noble,** a gold coin worth 6*s.* 8*d.*

Georgette (dʒǫɹdʒe·t). 1919. [Fr., f. the name of Mme. *Georgette*, a French modiste.) A thin silk dress-material. Also *g. crêpe.*

Georgian (dʒǭ·ɹdʒiăn), *a.*[1] 1787. [f. *George* + -IAN.] **1.** Belonging to the time of the four Georges, Kings of Great Britain 1855. †**2.** *G. planet* = GEORGIUM SIDUS –1812.

Georgian (dʒǭ·ɹdʒiăn), *a.*[2] and *sb.* ME. [f. *Georgia* + -AN.]

A. *adj.* **1.** Belonging to Georgia, in the Caucasus, its inhabitants, or their language 1607. **2.** Belonging to Georgia, one of the United States of America 1762.

B. *sb.* **1.** A native, or the language, of Georgia in Asia ME. **2.** An inhabitant of the State of Georgia 1741.

Georgic (dʒǭ·ɹdʒik). 1513. [– L. *georgicus* – Gr. γεωργικός, f. γεωργός husbandman; see -IC.]

A. *adj.* Relating to agriculture. *Obs.* exc. semi-*joc.* 1711.

B. *sb.* †**1.** A husbandman (*rare*) 1703. **2.** *pl.* **a.** The science of land-culture 1802. **b.** The title of Virgil's poem on husbandry, in four books; hence occas. in *sing.* a poem dealing with rural occupations 1513. So **Geo·rgical** *a.* (now *rare*), agricultural.

‖**Georgium Sidus** (dʒǭ·ɹˌdʒiɒ̆m səi·dɒ̆s). 1783. [mod.L. *Georgium*, n. of *Georgius* GEORGE + *sidus* star.] One of the greater planets (now called Uranus), so named by its discoverer, Sir W. Herschel, in honour of George III.

Geoselenic, -static, etc.: see GEO-.

Geosynclinal (dʒīˌosinkləi·nal). 1873. [f. GEO- + SYNCLINAL.] *Geol.*

A. *adj.* Forming a large depression in the surface of the earth, from the lowest point of which there is a gradual rise to either side. The opposite is *geanticlinal.* 1879.

B. *sb.* A geosynclinal depression.

Geotic: see GOETIC; a *Spurious Word.*

Geotropic (dʒīˌotrǫ·pik), *a.* 1875. [f. next; see -IC.] *Bot.* Pertaining to, marked by, or of the nature of, geotropism. Hence **Geotro·pically** *adv.*

Geotropism (dʒiˌo·trǭpiz'm). 1875. [– G. *geotropismus* (A. B. Frank, 1868), f. Gr. γεω- GEO- + τροπή turning + -ISM. Hence Fr. *géotropisme.*] *Bot.* A term for the phenomena of irritability shown by various parts of plants in relation to the action of gravity.

Positive g.: the tendency (of roots, etc.) to grow towards the centre of the earth. *Negative g.*: the tendency (of stems, etc.) to grow away from the centre of the earth. So also **Geo·tropy.**

Gephyrean (dʒefiri·ăn). 1881. [f. mod.L. *Gephyrea* sb. pl. (f. Gr. γέφυρα bridge) + -AN.]

A. *adj.* Of or pertaining to the *Gephyrea*, a class or group of the *Vermes* or worms.

B. *sb.* A worm of this class.

†**Gepoun,** var. of †GIPON.

Gerah (gīə·ră). 1534. [– Heb. *gērāh.*] *Heb. Antiq.* A Hebrew coin and weight, the twentieth part of a shekel. *Exod.* 30:13.

Geranin (dʒĕrēⁱ·nin). Also **-iin.** 1864. [f. next + -IN[1].] An astringent principle obtained from *Geranium maculatum.*

Geranium (dʒĕrēⁱ·niɒ̆m). 1548. [– L. *geranium* – Gr. γεράνιον, f. γέρανος crane; see -IUM.] **1.** A genus of herbaceous plants (N.O. *Geraniaceæ*), growing wild in temperate regions, and bearing a fruit similar in shape to the bill of a crane; a plant of this genus or its flower. **2.** A plant of the genus Pelargonium (N.O. *Geraniaceæ*), natives of S. Africa, of which many varieties are cultivated in Great Britain 1760. **3.** *U.S. Pharm.* The rhizome of *G. maculatum* used as an astringent 1854.

Geratology (dʒerătǫ·lŏdʒi). 1884. [f. Gr. γῆρας, γηρατ- old age + -LOGY.] The science of the phenomena of decadence, esp. in a species of animals approaching extinction.

Gerbe (dʒɒ̄ɹb). 1698. [– Fr. *gerbe* wheat-sheaf.] †**1.** A wheat-sheaf 1808. **2.** Something resembling a sheaf of wheat; esp. a kind of firework. Also *transf.*

Gerbille (dʒɒ̄·ɹbil). Also **gerbil.** 1849. [– Fr. *gerbille* – mod.L. *gerbillus*, dim. of *gerbo* JERBOA.] Any animal belonging to the genus *Gerbillus.*

Gerbo, obs. f. JERBOA.

†**Gere.** See also GARE *sb.*[1] ME. [Of unkn. origin; superseded by †*gare* (XVII).] A transient fit of passion, feeling, fancy, or the like –1609.

These loveres in hir queynte geres CHAUCER.

Gere, obs. f. GEAR.

Gerent (dʒīə·rĕnt). *rare.* 1576. [– *gerent-*, pr. ppl. stem of L. *gerere* manage; see -ENT.]

A. *sb.* A manager, ruler. Also *attrib.*

B. *adj.* Bearing, carrying. (Dicts.)

Gerfalcon (dʒɒ̄·ɹfǭ:lkǫn, -fǭ:k'n). Also †**jer-,** †**gyr-,** †**gierfalcon,** etc. ME. [– OFr. *gerfaucon* (mod. *gerfaut*) – Frankish **gērfalco* (G. *ger-, gierfalke*) – ON. *geirfálki*, the first element of which is obscure; see FALCON.] Orig., a large falcon, esp. one used to fly at herons; now, any large falcon of the northern regions; esp. the white gerfalcon of Iceland (*Falco islandus*).

†**Ge·rful,** *a.* [f. GERE + -FUL.] Changeful, fitful; wayward. CHAUCER. So †**Ge·rish.**

Gerland, Gerlond, obs. ff. GARLAND.

Germ (dʒɒ̄ɹm), *sb.* 1644. [– (O)Fr. *germe* :– L. *germen* sprout.] **1.** That portion of an organic being which is capable of development into a new individual; a rudiment of a new organism. (In mod. use, *germ-* often signifies the female reproductive element, as opp. to *sperm-*.) **2.** †**a.** The ovary –1829. **b.** The seed (*lit.* and *fig.*) 1823. **3.** In early use, vaguely, the 'seed' of a disease. In mod. use, a micro-organism or microbe, esp. one which causes disease 1803. **4.** *fig.* That from which anything springs or may spring. *In g.*: in a rudimentary form. 1777.

1. Mr. Bonnet supposes..that all the germs of future plants..were really contained in the first g. PRIESTLEY. The germes of existence contained in the earth MALTHUS. **4.** Thereby to eradicate every germe of liberty 1777.

Comb.: **g.-cell,** the first nucleated cell that appears in the impregnated ovum, after the reception of the spermatozoon and the disappearance of the germinal vesicle; also *g.-cellule*; **-cup,** a gastrula; **-gland,** one that produces germs; **-layer** = *germinal layer*; **-membrane** = BLASTODERM; **-plasm,** the protoplasm peculiar to a g. or ovum; **-polyp,** a polyp produced by gemmination; **-pore,** the place of exit for the tubular outgrowths from the spore at the time of germination; **-shield,** the shield-shaped spot which is the first rudiment of the dorsal portion of the embryo; called by Haeckel the *notaspis*; **-stock,** the part of the body from which budding takes place in certain animals; **-theory,** 'the theory of the origin of many diseases in the morbific influence of certain fungi, which are introduced into the organism by means of their germs or spores' (*Syd. Soc. Lex.*); **-tube,** the tube-like growth emitted from a spore in germination; **-vesicle** = *germinal vesicle.*

Germ (dʒɒ̄ɹm), *v.* 1483. [orig. – Fr. *germer*, f. *germe*; now, f. GERM *sb.*] *intr.* To put forth germs or buds. Now only *fig.*

Germain(e, obs. f. GERMAN *a.*

German (dʒɒ̄·ɹmăn), **germane** (dʒəɹmēⁱ·n, dʒɒ̄·ɹmeⁱn), *a.*[1] and *sb.*[1] ME. [–(O)Fr. *germain* (in OFr. also 'brother') :– L. *germanus* genuine, real (as sb. *germanus* brother, *germana* sister).]

A. *adj.* **I.** Closely akin. **1.** 'Own' (brother or sister). *Obs.* exc. in BROTHER-, SISTER-GERMAN. **2.** = 'First' or 'own' (cousin). *Obs.* exc. in COUSIN-GERMAN. ME. †**3.** Closely related; akin –1657. **4.** Closely connected; relevant 1602.

3. *Timon* IV. iii. 344. **4.** The phrase would bee more Germaine to the matter: If we could carry Cannon by our sides *Haml.* v. ii. 165.

II. Genuine, true, thorough. *Obs.* or *arch.* ME.

Sincere, germane and true learning 1542. Hence **Germa·nely** *adv.*

†**B.** *sb.* One sprung from the same stock; a brother, a near relative –1604.

Coursers for Cozens: and Gennets for Germaines SHAKS.

German (dʒɒ̄·ɹmăn), *a.*[2] and *sb.*[2] 1552. [– L. *Germanus*, perh. of Celtic origin (cf. OIr. *gair* neighbour). The earlier names were ALMAIN and DUTCH.]

A. *adj.* **1.** Of or pertaining to Germany or its inhabitants. **2.** *transf.* German-like 1861. **3.** Belonging to, written or spoken in, the German language 1748.

Combs., etc. **a.** In names of things of attributed German origin (sometimes hyphened), as **G. bit,** a wood-boring tool for use in a brace; **G. clock,** in 16–17th c. chiefly one of elaborate construction, often containing automatic figures, etc.; †**G. devil,** ? a sort of screw-jack; **G. flute** (see FLUTE *sb.*[1]); **G. mile,** a distance of between 4 and 5 English miles; **G. paste,** a food for cage birds, made of pea-meal, hemp-seed, lard, etc.; **G. process,** in copper smelting, the process of reduction in a shaft-furnace after roasting, if necessary; **G. sarsaparilla,** a substitute for sarsaparilla; **G.-sausage,** a polony, a cleaned gut stuffed with meat partly cooked; **G. sixth** (*Mus.*), a chord consisting of a note with its major third, fifth, and augmented sixth; **G. steel,** a metal made of charcoal-iron obtained from bog-iron or the sparry carbonate; **G. text,** a black letter resembling Old English or modern G.; also *attrib.*; **G. tinder** = AMADOU; **G. wool** = *Berlin wool* (see BERLIN).

b. In names of plants, as **G. millet,** *Sitaria germanica*, orig. imported from India; **G. wallflower** (see WALLFLOWER); etc.

c. G. measles, an infectious disease of a mild type resembling measles and scarlatina; rubella.

B. *sb.* **1.** A native of Germany 1530. **2.** The German language 1748. **3. a.** Short for *G. cotillon* (see COTILLION); also, a party for dancing this 1879. **b.** = *G. sausage* 1883. **c.** *Coal-mining.* A straw filled with gunpowder to act as a fuse in blasting operations 1883.

2. *High G.*: the variety, orig. confined to 'High' or southern Germany, but now the accepted literary language of Germany. *Low G.*: prop. = 'Plattdeutsch', i.e. all dialects of Germany which are not High G.; applied by philologists to all West Germanic dialects except High G.; and formerly including Gothic and Scandinavian.

Germander (dʒəɹmæ·ndəɹ). ME. [– med.L. *germandra, -drea* (cf. Fr. *germandrée*, OFr. *gemandree*), alt. of *gamandrea* (cf. G. *gamander*), var. of *gamadrea*, for *chamedreos* – late Gr. χαμαίδρυον, earlier χαμαίδρυς 'ground-oak', f. χαμαί on the ground + δρῦς oak.] The name of plants of the genus *Teucrium*, esp. *T. chamædrys*, the Common or Wall Germander. Also *attrib.*

Garlic or Water G. = *T. scordium.* Wood G. = *T. scorodinia.* In the U.S. applied to *T. canadense.* G. Chickweed, *Veronica agrestis.* G. Speedwell or Wild G., *Veronica chamædrys.*

Germane: see GERMAN *a.*[1]

Germanic (dʒəɹmæ·nik). 1633. [– L. *Germanicus*, f. *Germanus* German. Cf. Fr. *germanique.*]

A. *adj.* **1.** Of or pertaining to Germany or to the Germans. Now chiefly *Hist.* in *G. Confederation, Empire.* **2.** Of or pertaining to the Teutonic race, or any of the Teutonic peoples 1841.

2. *East G.*: designation of the group of langs. including Gothic, Burgundian, Vandal, etc. *North G.* = 'Scandinavian'. *West G.*, epithet of the group including High and Low German, English, Frisian, Dutch, etc.

B. *sb.* The language of the Germanic people; Teutonic; see A. 2. 1892.

Germanism (dʒə̄·ɹmăniz'm). 1611. [f. GERMAN *a.*[2] + -ISM.] **1.** A German idiom; esp. one used in a non-German language. **2.** German ideas; German modes of thought or action 1841; attachment to these 1864. **3.** Affectation of what is German 1807.

Germanist (dʒə̄·ɹmănist). 1831. [f. GERMAN *a.*[2] + -IST.] One versed in the German language, or in Teutonic philology; one influenced by German thought.

Germanium (dʒəɹmēⁱ·niŏm). 1886. [f. L. *Germanus* GERMAN *a.*[2] + -IUM.] *Chem.* An element, found in a mineral named Argyrodite, app. intermediate 'between antimony and bismuth.'

Germanize (dʒə̄·ɹmănəiz), *v.* 1598. [f. GERMAN *a.*[2] + -IZE.] **1.** *trans.* To translate into German. **2.** To make German in character, etc. 1609. **3.** *intr.* To become German (in style, tastes, habits, sympathies, etc.) 1665. Hence **Ge:rmaniza·tion,** the action of Germanizing.

Germano-, comb. f. 'German', as in **Ge:rmano-ma·nia,** a mania for things German; **Ge:rmanopho·bia,** a morbid dread of Germany and things German; etc.

Ge·rman si·lver. 1830. A white alloy consisting of nickel, zinc, and copper, orig. obtained from an ore found at Hildburghausen. Also *attrib.*

Germen (dʒə·ɹmen). Also **†germain(e, †germin.** 1605. [– L. *germen, germin-*; see GERM *sb.*] **1.** A germ. Now only *fig.* **†2.** A shoot or sprout –1786. **3.** *Bot.* The rudiment of a seed-vessel, an ovary 1759.

1. Cracke Natures moulds, all germaines spill at once That makes ingratefull Man *Lear* III. ii. 8.

Germicide (dʒə̄·ɹmisəid), *sb.* (*a.*) 1880. [f. GERM *sb.* + -CIDE 1.] **1.** That which kills germs; *spec.* an agent used to destroy disease-germs 1881. **2.** quasi-*adj.* Destructive to germs. So **Ge·rmici:dal** *a.* (in sense 2).

Germiculture (dʒə̄·ɹmikɒltiŭɹ). 18.. [f. GERM *sb.* + CULTURE; after *horticulture*, etc.] The artificial cultivation of the bacteria connected with certain diseases. Hence **Germicu·lturist,** a bacteriologist.

Germigene (dʒə̄·ɹmiˌdʒīn). 1859. [f. GERM *sb.* + *-gene* -GEN.] *Biol.* 'The gland of the female generative apparatus of cestoid and Trematode worms in which the germinal vesicles are formed' (*Syd. Soc. Lex.*).

Germin (dʒə̄·ɹmin), *v.* ME. [– L. *germinare*; see GERMINATE *v.*] *intr.* To put forth shoots; also, to begin to produce vegetation. Also *trans.* To bud or shoot forth into.

Germin, var. of GERMEN.

‖**Germinal** (ʒɛrminal, dʒə̄·ɹminăl), *sb.* 1833. [Fr., f. as next.] The seventh month of the French Revolutionary calendar (Mar. 21–Apr. 19).

Germinal (dʒə̄·ɹminăl), *a.* 1808. [– L. *germen, germin-* sprout + -AL[1].] Of or belonging to a germ or to germs; of the nature of a germ; *transf.* that is in the germ.

G. cell = *germ cell. G. layer*, each of the three layers of cells into which the blastoderm divides. *G. matter*, Beale's term for vitally active matter. *G. membrane* = BLASTODERM. *G. pole*, 'the part or pole of the egg where lies the germinal spot' (*Syd. Soc. Lex.*). *G. spot*, the nucleolus of the permanent ovum, situated in the g. vesicle. *G. vesicle*, the nucleus of the permanent ovum of animals.

Germinant (dʒə̄·ɹminănt), *a.* 1605. [f. *germinant-*, pres. ppl. stem of L. *germinare*; see next, -ANT.] That develops like a germ; germinating, sprouting (*rare* in lit. sense). Also *fig.* of the ground.

Germinate (dʒə̄·ɹmineⁱt), *v.* 1610. [– *germinat-*, pa. ppl. stem of L. *germinare*, f. *germen, germin-* sprout; see -ATE[3].] **1.** *intr.* To sprout, put forth shoots, begin to vegetate. Of a plant: To bud and develop shoots and branches. Also *fig.* 1647. **2.** *trans.* To cause to shoot or sprout. Also *fig.* 1610. **3.** *intr.* Of a salt, etc.: To effloresce. ? *Obs.* 1626.

Germination (dʒə̄ɹminēⁱ·ʃən). 1594. [– L. *germinatio*, f. as prec.; see -ION. Cf. Fr. *germination.*] **1.** The action or process of germinating, sprouting, or putting forth shoots. Used properly of seeds; hence of plants, and of spores in cryptogams. Also *fig.* **2.** *transf.* Efflorescence, ebullition 1665.

1. *fig.* A time of g. in religious history STUBBS.

Germinative (dʒə̄·ɹmineⁱtiv), *a.* 1707. [f. GERMINATE + IVE; see -ATIVE. Cf. Fr. *germinatif.*] Of or belonging to germination; also, having power to bud or sprout, or to develop.

fig. Any vital or g. truth 1865.

Germini·parous, *a.* [f. L. *germen* (see GERMEN) + -PAROUS.] Producing offspring through seeds. H. T. COLEBROOKE.

Germless (dʒə̄·ɹmlės), *a.* 1833. [f. GERM *sb.* + -LESS.] Containing no germs (see GERM *sb.* 3).

†Gernative, *a.* [perh. f. *gern* GIRN *v.* + -ATIVE.] ? Addicted to grumbling. MIDDLETON.

Gerocomy (dʒiᵊrǫ·kŏmi). *rare.* 1818. [–Gr. γηροκομία care of the aged, f. γῆρας, γηρο- old age + -κομία tending; see -Y[3].] The science of the treatment of the aged. Hence **†Geroco·mical** *a.*

Geronomite (dʒĕrǫ·nŏməit). 1754. [– Sp. or It. *geronomita.*] = HIERONYMITE.

Gerontic (dʒĕrǫ·ntik, gĕr-), *a.* 1885. [f. Gr. γέρων, γεροντ- old man + -IC.] Of or pertaining to old age, senile. *sb. pl.* = *GERIATRICS.

Gerontocracy (dʒe:rǫ̆ntǫ·krăsi, ger-). 1830. [f. as prec. + -CRACY.] Government by old men; a governing body of old men.

‖**Geropiga** (dʒeropī·gă). Also **jeru-** and (in Dicts.) **gero-, jerupigia.** 1858. [– Pg. *geropiga* = HIERAPICRA.] A mixture of grape-juice, brandy, sugar, and red colouring-matter, used to adulterate port-wine.

-gerous, in use always **-igerous** (i·dʒerəs), an adjectival suffix f. L. *-ger* bearing (f. root of *gerere*) + -OUS. In mod. scientific language added freely to L. stems, as in *frondigerous*, etc.

Gerrymander (gerimæ·ndəɹ), *sb.* *U.S.* 1868. [f. the surname *Gerry.*] A method of arranging electoral districts so that one party will be enabled to elect more representatives than they could on a fair system. This was done in Massachusetts, in 1812, while Elbridge Gerry was Governor; hence the name.

Gerrymander (gerimæ·ndəɹ), *v.* Also *erron.* (in England) **jerry-.** 1859. [f. the sb.] *trans.* To subject (a state, a constituency) to a gerrymander. Also *transf.* to manipulate in order to gain an unfair advantage.

To g. a bench of magistrates 1893.

Gerund (dʒe·rɒnd). 1513. [– late L. *gerundium*, f. *gerundum*, var. of *gerendum*, gerund of L. *gerere* carry on.] A form of the Latin vb. capable of being construed as a sb., but retaining the regimen of the vb. Hence applied to equivalent forms in other langs., e.g. to the Eng. verbal noun in *-ing*.

Comb.: **g.-grinder,** derisive name for one who instructs in Latin grammar; a pedantic teacher.

Gerundial (dʒėrɒ·ndiăl), *a.* 1846. [f. GERUND + -IAL.] Pertaining to or of the nature of a gerund. Also *ellipt.* = *g. infinitive.*

Gerundival (dʒerɒ̆ndəi·văl), *a.* 1884. [f. GERUNDIVE + -AL[1].] Of, pertaining to, or of the nature of a gerundive.

Gerundive (dʒĕrɒ·ndiv). 1483. [– late L. *gerundivus* (sc. *modus* mood), f. *gerundium* GERUND.]

A. *adj.* **1.** Pertaining to, akin to, or of the nature of, a gerund 1612. **2.** *joc.* Crammed with gerunds 1616.

2. That G. maw of yours, that without *Do* will end in *Di* and *Dum* instantly BEAUM & FL.

B. *sb.* **1.** = GERUND. 1483. **2.** In Latin grammar, a verbal adj., of the nature of a passive pple., expressing the idea of necessity or fitness; its suffix is the same as that of the gerund. Hence *transf.*

Hence **Geru·ndively** *adv.* as, or in place of, a gerund.

Gerusia (gerū·ziă). 1838. [– L. *gerusia* – Gr. γερουσία, f. γέρων old man; see -IA[1].] An assembly of elders, *spec.* the senate in Dorian cities.

†Ge·ry, *a.* ME. [f. GERE + -Y[1].] Changeable, fitful –1529.

Gesling, -lyng, obs. ff. GOSLING.

Gess(e, obs. f. GUESS, and of *guests* pl. of GUEST.

‖**Gesso** (dʒe·so). 1596. [– It. *gesso* :– L. GYPSUM.] **1.** Plaster of Paris; gypsum. **b.** A prepared surface of plaster as a ground for painting 1860. **†2.** A work of art in plaster 1758. **3.** *attrib.*, as *g. work* 1745.

1. No colour is so noble as the colour of a good painting on canvas or g. RUSKIN.

Gest (dʒest), *sb.*[1] ME. [– OFr. *geste, jeste* – L. *gesta* actions, exploits, subst. use of n. pl. of pa. pple. of *gerere* carry, carry on.] **1.** *pl.* Notable deeds, exploits (later also sing.); esp. the deeds *of* a person or people as narrated, history. *Obs.* exc. *arch.* **2.** A romance in verse; also simply, a story, tale. *Obs.* exc. *Hist.* ME. **†3. a.** A lampoon. **b.** An idle tale; now JEST. –1470.

1. The Gestes of the great Charles FABYAN. **2.** Phr. *In g.* = in verse. *The English g., the French g.*: metrical chronicles of England, of France.

Gest (dʒest), *sb.*[2] *Obs.* exc. *arch.* 1509. [– Fr. *geste* – L. *gestus* gesture, bearing, f. *gerere* bear, deport (oneself).] **1.** Bearing, carriage, mien. **2.** A gesture 1521.

1. Look and geste Of buried saint, in risen rest E. B. BROWNING.

†Gest, *sb.*[3] *pl.* **Gesses.** 1550. [Later form of GIST *sb.*[1]] The various stages of a journey, esp. of a royal progress; the route planned and followed. **b.** *sing.* The time allotted for a halt. *Wint. T.* I. ii. 41.

†Gest, *v.*[1] ME. [f. GEST *sb.*[1]] *intr.* To tell a tale –1508.

†Gest, *v.*[2] 1523. [– *gest-*, pa. ppl. stem of L. *gerere* carry on.] To perform; only in phr. *gested and done* –1541.

Gest(e, obs. f. GUEST, JEST.

Gestant (dʒe·stănt), *a. rare.* 1851. [– *gestant-*, pres. ppl. stem of L. *gestare* go with young; see next, -ANT.] Pregnant (*fig.*).

Storm-clouds g. with the heat Of undeveloped lightnings E. B. BROWNING.

Gestation (dʒestēⁱ·ʃən). 1533. [– L. *gestatio*, f. *gestat-*, pa. ppl. stem of *gestare*, frequent. of *gerere* carry; see prec., -ION.] **1.** A carrying or being carried, e.g. on horseback, or in a carriage, by way of exercise. Now *rare.* **†2.** The wearing (of rings). SIR T. BROWNE. **3.** The action or process of carrying young; the condition of being carried in the womb from conception to birth. Also *fig.* 1615.

Gestatorial (dʒe:stătōᵊ·riăl), *a.* 1864. [f. as next + -AL[1].] *G. chair*: a chair in which the Pope is carried on certain occasions.

Gestatory (dʒe·stătəri), *a. rare.* 1682. [– L. *gestatorius*, f. *gestator* one who carries, f. *gestare*; see prec., -ORY[2].] †**a.** Adapted for carrying or wearing. SIR T. BROWNE. **b.** Of or pertaining to carrying as a form of exercise 1804.

†**Ge·ster.** ME. [f. GEST *v.*[1] + -ER[1].] A professional reciter of romances –1496.

Gestic (dʒe·stik), *a.* 1764. [f. GEST *sb.*[2] + -IC.] Of or pertaining to bodily movement, esp. dancing.

The gay grandsire, skill'd in g. lore GOLDSM.

Gesticulant (dʒesti·kiŭlănt), *a. rare.* 1877. [– *gesticulant-*, pres. ppl. stem of L. *gesticulari*; see next, -ANT.] Exhibiting gestures.

The poor g. orator RUSKIN.

Gesticulate (dʒesti·kiŭleᶦt), *v.* 1601. [– *gesticulat-*, pa. ppl. stem of L. *gesticulari*, f. *gesticulus*, dim. of *gestus* action, gesture; see -ATE[3].] **1.** *intr.* To make lively or energetic motions with the limbs or body; *esp.* in speaking or in lieu of speech 1613. **2.** *trans.* To convey by gestures 1601.

1. A Frenchman..gesticulates while he speaks, much more than an Englishman BLAIR. Hence **Gesti·culative** *a.* given to gesticulation. **Gesti·culator. Gesti·culatory** *a.* full of, consisting in, or of the nature of, gesticulation.

Gesticulation (dʒe:stikiŭlēᶦ·ʃən). 1603. [– L. *gesticulatio*, f. as prec.; see -ION.] The action or process of gesticulating. Also, an instance of this (chiefly in *pl.*).

Persons skilled in g. can communicate by it a long series of facts and even complicated trains of thought 1876.

Gestion (dʒe·stiən, dʒe·stʃən). 1599. [– L. *gestio*, f. *gest-*, pa. ppl. stem of *gerere* carry on; see -ION. Cf. Fr. *gestion*.] Conduct, management.

Gestor, -our(e, var. of GESTER.

Gesture (dʒe·stiŭɹ), *sb.* ME. [– med.L. *gestura*, f. as GESTION; see -URE.] †**1.** Bearing, carriage, deportment (rarely in *pl.*) –1810. †**2.** Posture, attitude, *esp.* in prayer or worship –1729. **3.** †**a.** In early use: The employment of bodily movements, attitudes, looks, etc., as a means of giving effect to oratory –1791. **b.** Now only: Movement of the body or limbs as an expression of feeling 1804. **4.** A movement of the body or any part of it; now only as expressive of thought or feeling 1551. **b.** *transf.* A (friendly) move or course of action 1916.

1. *A. Y. L.* v. ii. 69. **2.** As for their g. or position, the men lay downe leaning on their left elbow SIR T. BROWNE. **3.** To put life into words by countenance, voice, and g. HOOKER. G. is the imitation of words JOWETT. **4.** The Shaking of the Head..is a G. of slight refusal BACON. Hence **Ge·stural** *a.* of or pertaining to g.; consisting of gestures. **Ge·stureless** *a.*

Gesture (dʒe·stiŭɹ), *v.* 1542. [f. the sb.] **1.** *intr.* To make gestures, to gesticulate. **2.** *trans.* To express by gestures 1589.

1. The Mayor speaking and gesturing his persuasivest CARLYLE. **2.** It is not orderly read nor gestured as beseemeth HOOKER. Hence †**Ge·sturement** = GESTURE *sb.* 3 b.

Get (get), *sb.* ME. [f. GET *v.*] **1.** What is got or begotten; gain, earnings (now *dial.*); an offspring; *collect.* progeny. **2.** Begetting. Now only in sporting use. ME.

Get (get), *v.* Pa. t. **got** (arch. **gat**). Pa. pple. **got (gotten)**. Pres. pple. **getting.** [– ON. *geta* obtain, beget, guess = OE. **ġietan* (in *beġietan* beget, *forġietan* forget, etc.) :– Gmc. **ʒetan*, **ʒat-*, **ʒētum*, **ʒetanaz*, f. IE. base **ghed-* (**ghod-*) seize, found in L. *præda* (:– **præheda*) booty, PREY, *prædium* estate, *præhendere* lay hold of, Gr. χανδάνειν (aor. ἔχαδον) hold, contain, be able.]

I. *trans.* **1.** To obtain possession of; *absol.* to acquire wealth or property. **2.** To earn ME. **3.** To obtain by way of profit 1490. †Also *absol.* †**4.** To capture (a fortress, etc.) –1676. **5.** To gain (a victory, etc.) ME. **6.** To win, acquire ME. **7.** To learn, commit to memory 1582. **8.** To find out, obtain as a result, by calculation or experiment 1559. **9.** To become possessed of; to receive ME. **10.** To obtain, come to have, attain ME. **11.** To catch, contract (an illness) 1610. **12.** To receive, meet with, suffer ME. **13.** To procure or obtain in any way ME. **14.** To get hold of, capture (a person); also *colloq.* to 'corner' 1596. **15.** The perfect tense is used familiarly as = the present tense of *have* or *possess* 1607.

1. Get Money POPE. **2.** I..get that I weare SHAKS. *absol.* Getting and spending WORDSW. Phr. *To g. a living.* **3.** Alas, he gets nothing by that SHAKS. **5.** Phr. *To g. the upper hand (of)*; *to g. the start, the advantage*, etc. (*of*); *to g. the wind of*; *to g. the better of.* **6.** *Tam. Shr.* II. i. 120. Reason is not..gotten by Experience onely HOBBES. Phr. *To g. wind of*; to hear of. **7.** Phr. *To g. by heart* (see HEART *sb.*); *to g. by rote.* **8.** Dividing nine by three we g. three (*mod.*). **9.** As to salaries, an officer..usually gets sixty pounds 1892. Phr. *To g. the name of*: to have the reputation of (being so-and-so). *To g. mercy, forgiveness, leave*, etc.; *to g. an answer, information*, etc. **10.** When I had gotten my libertye RALEGH. Phr. *To g. one's own way. To g. (a) sight*, etc. *of*, *to g. (a) hold of. To g. religion* (U.S. vulgar): to be converted. **11.** To g. a Cold STEELE. **12.** To g. a Fall SWIFT. Phr. *To g. the worst of it* (cf. 5). To g. six months 1889. *To g. it* (colloq. or slang): to 'catch it'. **15.** The thing has got to be fought out 1889.

†**II.** To gain, reach, arrive at (a place) –1712.

III. To beget, procreate; now only of animals, *esp.* horses ME.

IV. With complement, indicating some change effected in the position or state of the object. **1.** With prep. or adv. of place; as, *to, from, into, out of, through, over*, etc. 1450. Also *refl.* **2.** With pa. pple. as compl. (see quots.) 1500. **3.** With adj.; esp. in *to g. ready* 1590. **4.** With an infinitive 1460.

1. To g. luggage through the custom-house 1859. Phr. *To g. with child. To g.* (a person) *upon* (a subject). **2.** Difficulty..in getting laws obeyed 1877. I got my right wrist dislocated T. JEFFERSON. **4.** To g. them to listen to reason 1771.

V. *intr.* **1.** To succeed in coming or going *to, from, into, out of*, etc.; also, to come in the course or at the end of a journey *to.* Formerly conjugated with *be.* ME. **b.** To come *to* an end aimed at, a condition, a state 1626. **2.** With infinitive: To come (to be or do); to acquire a habit of (doing) 1583. **b.** With pr. pple.: To come to be (doing something) 1727. **3.** With adj., etc. as compl.: To make oneself; to become; to grow (with comparatives) 1596. **4. a.** With pa. pple.: To complete an action. Now only *colloq.* (*rare*). 1716. **b.** With passive pple.: To cause oneself to be treated in a certain way or to undergo a certain action; also, to come to be the object of a certain action. Often = *be* as an auxiliary. 1652.

1. Hercules that year got into Italy NEWTON. **b.** Phr. *To g. to blows. To g. there* (U.S. slang): to succeed. *To g.*, also *git* (U.S. colloq. or slang): to 'clear out'. **2.** To g. to be friends 1891. **b.** Phr. *To g. better, well. To g. drunk. To g. clear, quit of, rid of, shut of.* **4. b.** I..got caught in the storm 1887. Phr. *To g. done with* = to have done with.

VI. *intr.* With preps., in specialized senses. **G. at** —. **a.** To come at, reach. **b.** To find out. **c.** *colloq.* and *slang.* To tamper with (a horse); to bribe. **d.** *slang.* To assail; also, to make game of. **G. off** —. **a.** To dismount from (a horse). **b.** To obtain release from (a contract). **G. on** —. **a.** To mount (a horse). **b.** To enter upon (a subject), esp. by chance. **G. over** —. **a.** To overcome (a difficulty); to evade the force of (evidence); to cease to be surprised or troubled by. **b.** To recover from (a shock, etc.). **c.** To cover (a distance). **d.** To finish (an action). **e.** To circumvent. **G. round** —. To circumvent, cajole. **G. through** —. **a.** To reach the end of. **b.** To be passed by (Parliament, etc.). **c.** To find occupation for (a period of time).

VII. With adverbs.

G. (it) across or **over**: to reach the audience or the public. **G. along** = *get on.* **G. away. a.** *intr.* To escape. Also, in *Hunting*, etc.: To start. **b.** *imper.* = Be off. **c.** *To g. away with it*: to succeed in what one tries; to escape punishment or retribution. **G. back. a.** *intr.* To return. **b.** *trans.* To recover. **G. in. a.** *intr.* To be elected to represent a constituency in Parliament. **b.** *trans.* To gather in (harvest produce). **c.** To collect (contributions of money, esp. sums due). **d.** To sow (seed). **e.** To succeed in planting (a blow). **G. in with. a.** *intr.* To become familiar with. **b.** *Naut.* To come close up to. **G. off. a.** *intr.* To escape; to start. **b.** To escape from punishment or defeat; to be acquitted. **c.** *trans.* To deliver from punishment. **d.** To commit to memory. **G. on. a.** *intr.* To advance; to make haste. **b.** To prosper, succeed. Also, to fare. **c.** To manage (*without, with*). **d.** To agree *with, together.* **G. out. a.** *imper.* = 'Go away' (*colloq.*). **b.** *Stock Exchange.* To get rid of one's shares. **c.** To elicit by inquiry. **G. out of. a.** *intr.* To succeed in issuing from; to escape from; to quit. **b.** To get beyond. **c.** To evade, avoid. **d.** To elicit; also, to succeed in obtaining. **G. round.** *intr.* To recover from illness. **G. through. a.** *intr.* To reach a destination. **b.** Of a bill: To pass in Parliament. **c.** To pass in an examination. **G. under.** *trans.* To subdue, esp. a fire. **G. up. a.** To rise; esp. to rise from bed or to one's feet. **b.** To mount; esp. to mount on horseback; also *fig.* **c.** To come close *to.* **d.** Of fire, wind, the sea; To increase in force or violence. **e.** *Cricket.* Of the ball: To rise off the pitch higher than usual. **f.** To organize, set on foot, make ready. **g.** To dress (linen). **h.** To dress or 'turn out' in a (specified) way. Chiefly in pa. pple. *got up.* Also *intr.* for *refl.* 1782. **i.** To cause to rise; also, to improve (one's health). **j.** To work up.

Get-a·t-able, *a.* 1799. [f. phr. *get at* + -ABLE; cf. COME-AT-ABLE.] Reachable, accessible.

Ge·t-away. 1852. **a.** Breaking cover (of a fox). **b.** Escape (as of a thief with booty) 1890.

Ge·ttable, *a.* 1555. [f. GET *v.* + -ABLE.] That can be got.

Getter (ge·təɹ). ME. [f. GET *v.* + -ER[1].] **1.** One who gets, obtains, acquires, begets, or procreates. **2.** With advs., as with *g.-up* 1820.

Getting (ge·tiŋ), *vbl. sb.* ME. [f. GET *v.* + -ING[1].] **1.** The action of GET *v.*, in various senses. **2.** *concr.* (usually in *pl.*) That which is got; gains, earnings. Now *arch.* ME.

1. He had not the genius for g. THACKERAY.

Get-up. 1847. [See GET *v.*] **1.** Style of equipment or costume. **2.** Style of production or finish, esp. of a book 1865.

‖**Geum** (dʒī·ŏm). 1548. [mod.L. var. of L. *gæum* (Pliny); as L. for 'avens' by Turner (XVI).] A genus of rosaceous plants, including *G. urbanum*, Avens or Herb Bennet, and *G. rivale*, Water Avens.

Gewgaw, gew-gaw (giŭ·gǭ). ME. [Of obscure origin; the phonology of ME. *giuegoue* (Ancr. Riwle) is uncertain, and a rare MDu. *ghiveghave* is of doubtful relevance.] **1.** A gaudy trifle, a toy or bauble. Also *fig.* In *pl.* also, 'vanities'. ME. **2.** *attrib.* Of the nature of a gewgaw; hence *fig.* 'splendidly trifling, showy without value' (J.) 1631.

1. A heavy Gugaw, (call'd a Crown) DRYDEN. **2.** Seeing his g. Castle shine New as his title TENNYSON. Hence **Gew·gawed** *ppl. a.* dressed out with gewgaws.

Gey (gēᶦ), *a.* and *adv. Sc.* 1725. [var. of GAY. Cf. the similar use of JOLLY *adv.* (XVI).] **1.** *adj.* Considerable 1815. **b.** quasi-*advb.* in *g. and* — 1725. **2.** *adv.* Very; 'pretty' 1816.

Geyser (gēᶦ·səɹ, gəi·səɹ, gəi·zəɹ). 1780. [– Icel. *Geysir* proper name of a certain hot spring in Iceland, rel. to *geysa* (ON. *geysa*) gush. Cf. GUST *sb.*[1]] **1.** An intermittent hot spring, throwing up water, etc. in a column. Also *fig.* **2.** An apparatus for rapidly heating water for a bath 1891.

1. The Azores..abound in geysers LADY BRASSEY. Hence **Gey·seric** *a.* pertaining to or of the nature of a g. **Gey·serite** (*Min.*), a concretionary variety of opal, found deposited about the orifices of geysers.

‖**Gharry** (gæ·ri, gɒ·ri). *Anglo-Ind.* 1810. [Hindi *gāṛī*.] A horsed vehicle resembling a bathing-machine.

Ghast (gɑst), *a. arch.* or *poet.* 1622. [Back-formation from GHASTFUL or GHASTLY.] = GHASTLY *a.*

Ghast, var. of GAST *v.*

Ghastful, gastful (gɑ·stful), *a. Obs.* or *arch.* ME. [f. GAST *v.* + -FUL. Cf. next.] **1.** Full of fear. **2.** Dreadful, frightful ME.

2. Here will I dwell apart In gastfull groue SPENSER. Hence †**G(h)a·stful-ly** *adv.*, †**-ness.**

Ghastly, †**gastly** (gɑ·stli), *a.* [ME. *gastlich*, f. GAST *v.* + *lich*, -LY[1]. The sp. with *gh-* (after GHOST) became current through Spenser.] **1.** †Orig.: Causing terror. Now (cf. 2): Affecting like the sight of death or carnage; horrible, frightful, shocking. Also used *hyperbolically.* **2.** (Influenced by GHOST.) Spectre-like, death-like, wan. Of light: Lurid. 1581. †**3.** Full of fear –1634.

1. The g. dreams, That haunt the parting soul 1812. A g. failure (*colloq.*). **2.** G. with wounds PRIOR. A g. grin LYTTON. **3.** *Temp.* II. i. 309. Hence **Gha·stily** (*rare*), **Gha·stlily, Ghastly** *advs.* in a g. manner; fearfully.

‖**Ghaut, ghat** (gǭt). *Anglo-Ind.* 1603. [Hindi *ghāṭ*. Sense 3 is the primary sense.] **1.** *The Ghauts*: the name given by Europeans to the mountain ranges parallel to the east and west coasts of India. **2.** A mountain pass or defile 1698. **3.** A passage or steps leading down to a river; hence, a landing-place, the place of a ford or ferry 1783.

‖**Ghazal** (gæ·zæl). Also **gazel, ghazel,** etc. 1800. [– Pers. – Arab. *ġazal*.] A species of Oriental lyric poetry, usually erotic, having a limited number of verses and a recurrent rhyme.

‖**Ghazi** (gāzi). 1753. [– Arab. *al-ġāzī*, pr. pple. of *ġazā* raid, invade, foray.] A champion, *esp.* against infidels; also as a title of honour. Now used chiefly of Moslem fanatics who devote themselves to the destruction of infidels.

Gheber, -bre, vars. of GUEBRE.

‖**Ghee** (gī). 1665. [– Hindi *ghī* :– Skr. *ghṛitá-*, pa. pple. of *ghṛi* sprinkle.] Butter made from buffalo's milk, clarified by boiling, so as to resemble oil in consistency. Also *attrib.*

Gherkin (gǝ̄·ɹkin). 1661. [– early mod.Du. *(*a*)*gurkkijn* (now *gurkje, augurkje*), dim. of *agurk, augurk, gurk*; ult. – Slav. word repr. by Slov. *ugorek, angurka*, Pol. *ogórek*, Russ. *ogurétś*, deriv. with dim. suffix of late Gr. *ἀγγούριον*. See ANGURIA.] A young green cucumber, or one of a small kind, used for pickling.

Ghess(e, Ghest, obs. ff. GUESS, GHOST.

‖**Ghetto** (ge·to). 1611. [– It. *ghetto* = Pr. *guet* :– L. *Ægyptus* Egypt.] The quarter in a city, chiefly in Italy, to which the Jews were restricted.

The place where the whole fraternity of the Jews dwelleth together, which is called the G. CORYAT.

Ghibelline (gi·bĕlin, -əin). 1573. [– It. *Ghibellino*, supposed to be – G. *Waiblingen* name of an estate belonging to the Hohenstaufen family, said to have been used as a war-cry by partisans of the Hohenstaufen emperor Conrad III at the battle of Weinsberg, A.D. 1140.]

A. *sb.* One of the Emperor's faction in the Italian states; opp. to GUELPH.

B. *adj.* Of or adhering to the Ghibellines 1826. Hence **Ghi·bellinism.**

Ghole, var. of GHOUL. *Obs.*

Ghost (gōᵘst), *sb.* [OE. *gāst* = OFris. *gāst*, OS. *gēst* (Du. *geest*), (O)HG. *geist* :– WGmc. **ʒaista*. The sp. with *gh-* is first recorded in Caxton's works and is there prob. due to Flem. *gheest*; it became established late in XVI.] **1.** The soul or spirit. †**2.** Breath, a blast –1625. †**3.** A person –1590. †**4.** An incorporeal being –1618; a good spirit –1485; an evil spirit –1529. **5.** Formerly used in the sense of SPIRIT (of God). Now only in HOLY GHOST, the Third Person of the Trinity. OE. †**6.** The soul of a deceased person, spoken of as inhabiting the unseen world. Later only = MANES; sometimes *pl.* –1674. **7.** The soul of a deceased person, spoken of as appearing to the living. (The prevailing sense.) ME. Also *transf.* and *fig.* **b.** An apparition; a spectre 1592. †**8.** A corpse. 2 *Hen. VI*, III. ii. 161. **9.** An unsubstantial image; hence, a slight trace or vestige 1590. **10.** *Optics*, etc. **a.** A bright spot or secondary image appearing in the field of a telescope, produced by a defect in a lens 1867. **b.** *Photogr.* = FLARE *sb.*¹ 3. 1864. **11.** One who secretly does artistic or literary work for which his employer takes the credit 1884.

1. He gasped thryse, and gaue away the g. 1574. Whose faire immortal beame Hath darted fyre into my feeble g. SPENSER. **6.** Rainsborough, to whose G. he design'd an ample sacrifice CLARENDON. **7.** There needs no G... come from the Graue, to tell vs this SHAKS. Phr. *To lay a g.*: to cause it to cease appearing. *To raise a g.*: to cause it to appear. **b.** Death—'Grim-grinning g.' SHAKS. **9.** Pitiful ghosts, or rather shadowes of men 1590. Not the g. of a chance (*mod.*).

Comb.: **g.-bird** (*U.S. local*), 'the American yellow-breasted chat (*Icteria virens*)'; **-candle,** one of several kept burning round a corpse to scare away ghosts; **-dance,** a fanatical observance among the N. American Indians; **-moth,** a nocturnal moth (*Hepialus humuli*); **-plant,** the tumble-weed (*Amarantus albus*); **-word,** a word which does not really exist.

Ghost (gōᵘst), *v.* 1586. [f. prec. sb.] †**1.** *intr.* To give up the ghost, expire –1689. **2.** *trans.* To haunt as an apparition 1606. **3.** To prowl as a ghost 1833.

†**Ghostless** (gōᵘ·stlės), *a.* OE. [f. GHOST *sb.* + -LESS.] Without life or spirit; without strength or virtue –1651.

Ghostlike (gōᵘ·stləik). 1611. [f. GHOST *sb.* + -LIKE.] **1.** *adj.* Like a ghost or a place haunted by ghosts. **2.** *adv.* In the manner of a ghost 1859.

Ghostly (gōᵘ·stli), *a.* [OE. *gāstlić*; see GHOST *sb.*, -LY¹.] **1.** Pertaining to the spirit or soul; spiritual. Opp. to *bodily* or *fleshly*; occas. to *natural*. Now *lit.* and *arch.* †**2.** Of persons, etc.: Spiritual, devout –1483. **3.** Concerned with sacred things, or with the church; *spiritual* as opp. to *lay, secular*, or *temporal*. Now *arch.* OE. **4.** Of, pertaining to, or issuing from a ghost; resembling a ghost; *occas.* haunted by ghosts OE.

1. Both worldly and g. comfort SCOTT. Phr. *G. enemy*: the Devil. *G. father*: a father confessor. **3.** His chrism and his rood, his g. weapons FREEMAN. **4.** G. legends LONGF. Hence **Gho·stliness,** the condition or quality of being g.

Ghostly (gōᵘ·stli), *adv.* Now *rare.* [OE. *gāstlīće*; see GHOST *sb.*, –LY².] †In a spiritual manner or sense; opp. to *bodily* or *carnally*; in spirit, as a spirit –1642. Now *rarely*: As a ghost.

Ghostology (gōᵘstǫ·lŏdʒi). 1824. [Badly f. GHOST *sb.* + -LOGY.] Ghost-lore.

Ghoul (gūl). 1786. [– Arab. *ġūl* a desert demon having many shapes.] An evil spirit supposed (in Moslem countries) to rob graves and prey on human corpses.

fig. Ghouls feasting on the fresh corpse of a reputation THACKERAY. Hence **Ghou·lish** *a.* resembling, or characteristic of ghouls.

Ghyll: see GILL *sb.*²

‖**Giallo antico** (dʒa·lˌlo antī·ko). 1741. [It.; = 'ancient yellow'.] A rich yellow marble found among ruins in Italy; identified by some with the *marmor Numidicum*. Also *attrib.* or *adj.*

‖**Giallolino** (dʒalˌlolī·no). ? *Obs.* 1728. [It. *giallolino* (Florio), now *giallorino*, dim. of *giallo* yellow.] A fine yellow pigment, much used as Naples yellow.

Giambeux, Spenser's sp. of JAMBEUX.

Giant (dʒəi·ănt). [ME. *geant* (later infl. by the L. form) – (O)Fr. *géant*, †*jaiant* :– Rom. **gagante*, for L. *gigantem*, nom. *gigas* – Gr. *γίγας, γιγαντ-*.]

A. *sb.* **1.** A supposed being of human form but superhuman stature. In Gr. mythology, used *spec.* (chiefly in *pl.*, with initial capital) as = Gr. *γίγας*, one of *the Giants*, a savage race of men who were destroyed by the Gods. **b.** *fig.* Applied to an agency of enormous power, and prefixed as a title to names of personified qualities 1631. **2.** A human being of abnormally high stature; often *hyperbolical* 1559. Also *transf.* **3.** A person of extraordinary powers, mental or bodily 1535.

1. The Gyaunte Atlas beareth the worlde on hys shoulders 1553. **3.** The schoolmen were mental giants 1868. Giants of Faith 1871.

Comb.: **Giant's causeway,** a collection of basaltic columns in County Antrim, Ireland; **g.-cell,** (*a*) one of the large protoplasmic masses, without cell wall, and containing many roundish nuclei, found in tubercle; (*b*) one of certain large ganglionic cells found in the frontal and the ascending parietal convolutions of the brain; hence **-celled** *a.*; **giant's kettle,** one of the very large pot-holes (moulins) on the coast of Norway; **g.-powder,** also simply *giant*, a form of dynamite, consisting of infusorial earth saturated with nitro-glycerine.

B. *adj.* [the sb. used attrib., or appositively.] Of extraordinary size, extent, or force; gigantic, huge, monstrous 1480. **b.** In the names of plants and animals 1578.

Hence **Gi·antess,** a she-giant. **Gi·antize** *v.* (*rare*), to give the appearance of a g. to. **Gi·antlike** *a.* resembling a g. or what belongs to a g. **Gi·antly** *a.* giantlike (now *rare*); †*adv.* in a giantlike manner. **Gi·antry** (*rare*), giants collectively; g.-mythology. **Gi·antship,** the state of being a g.; the personality of a g.

‖**Giaour** (dʒaur). 1564. [Pers. *gaur, gōr*, pronounced by the Turks (gyaur), var. *gebr*; see GUEBRE.] A term of reproach applied by Turks to non-Moslems, esp. Christians.

Gib (gib), *sb.*¹ ME. [Short for *Gilbert*.] **1.** A familiar name for a cat. **2.** A cat, *esp.* a male cat; later, a castrated cat (*dial.*) 1561. **3.** A term of reproach, esp. for an old woman 1529. **4.** *Gib-cat* = sense 2. 1596.

Gib (gib), *sb.*² 1564. [Of unkn. origin.] **1.** †A hook 1567; a hooked stick 1788. **2.** The hooked gristle which grows at the end of the lower jaw of a male salmon after spawning. Also *g.-fish*, a salmon with a g. 1818. *Comb.* **g.-staff,** a staff to gauge water, or to push a boat.

Gib (dʒib, gib), *sb.*³ 1794. [Of unkn. origin.] A piece of wood or metal used to keep some part of a machine, etc. in place. Also as vb.

†**Gib,** *v.*¹ [f. GIB *sb.*¹] *intr.* To behave like a cat. BEAUM. & FL.

Gib (gib), *v.*² 1883. [var. of GIP.] = GIP. Hence **Gi·bber,** one who disembowels fish.

Gib, var. of JIB *sb.* and *v.*

Gibbed cat. 1633. [orig. var. of *gib-cat* (GIB *sb.*¹ 4); later taken as f. an assumed vb. **gib* geld.] = *Gib-cat*. GIB sb.¹ 2.

Gibber (dʒi·bəɹ, gi·bəɹ), *sb.*¹ 1832. [f. GIBBER *v.*] Rapid inarticulate utterance.

‖**Gibber** (gi·bəɹ), *sb.*² 1857. [L. *gibber*.] *Bot.* A pouch-like swelling at the base of a calyx, corolla, etc.; *gen.* a hump.

Gibber (dʒi·bəɹ, gi·bəɹ), *v.* Occas. **jibber.** 1604. [imit. Cf. JIBBER.] *intr.* To speak rapidly and inarticulately; to chatter. Said also of an ape. *Haml.* I. i. 116.

Gibberish (gi·bəriʃ, dʒi-). 1554. [Earlier than GIBBER *v.*, but presumably to be connected, the ending being based on names of languages in -ISH¹.] **A.** *sb.* Unintelligible speech; inarticulate chatter, jargon.

He repeated some g., which by the sound seemed to be Irish SMOLLETT.

†**B.** *adj.* Of or pertaining to gibberish, expressed in gibberish; unintelligible –1821.

That old entanglement of iniquity, their gibrish Lawes MILTON.

Gibbet (dʒi·bėt), *sb.* [– OFr. *gibet* staff, cudgel, gallows, dim. of *gibe* staff, club, prob. of Gmc. origin.] **1.** Orig. = GALLOWS; later, an upright post with projecting arm from which the bodies of criminals were hung in chains after execution. Also *fig.* ME. **2.** The punishment of death by hanging 1751. **3.** The projecting arm of a crane; also called JIB 1729. †**4.** A cudgel –1691.

Gibbet (dʒi·bėt), *v.* 1646. [f. GIBBET *sb.*] †**1.** *intr.* To hang as on a gibbet. SHAKS. **2.** *trans.* To put to death by hanging 1726; to hang on a gibbet by way of exposure. Also with *up.* 1752. **3.** *transf.* and *fig.* 1646.

3. *fig.* I mean to hang and G. up thy Name OLDHAM.

Gibbier, var. of GIBIER.

Gibble-gabble (gi·b'lˌgæ·b'l). 1600. [Reduplication of GABBLE *sb.* Cf. FIDDLE-FADDLE.] Senseless chatter. †Also as *vb.*

Gibbon (gi·bən). 1774. [– Fr. *gibbon* (Buffon), f. aboriginal name.] *Nat. Hist.* Any long-armed ape of the genus *Hylobates*, esp. one of the species *Hylobates lar* which inhabits the islands of the Indian Archipelago.

Gibbose (gibōᵘ·s), *a.* 1674. [– late L. *gibbosus*; see GIBBOUS, -OSE¹.] **1.** = GIBBOUS *a.* 1. **2.** = GIBBOUS *a.* 2. 1721.

Gibbosity (gibǫ·siti). ME. [– (O)Fr. *gibbosité* hump or med.L. *gibbositas* gibbosity, tumour, f. late L. *gibbosus*; see prec., -ITY.] **1.** The state or quality of being gibbose or gibbous 1547. **2.** A swelling; a protuberance.

Gibboso- (gibōᵘ·so), comb. f. L. *gibbosus* GIBBOUS, with sense 'gibbous and —'.

Gibbous (gi·bəs), *a.* ME. [f. late L. *gibbosus* (f. L. *gibbus* hump) + -OUS.] **1.** Convex, rounded, protuberant. **b.** *Astron.* Said of the moon or a planet when the illuminated portion is more than a semicircle, but less than a circle 1690. **2.** Hunch-backed; having a hump; hump-shaped. 1646.

2. He [William de Longchamp] had a g. chest 1879. Hence **Gi·bbous-ly** *adv.*, **-ness.**

Gibbsite (gi·bzəit). 1822. [f. George *Gibbs*, American mineralogist; see -ITE¹ 2 b.] *Min.* Aluminium hydrate found in stalactitic forms, often as an incrustation.

Gibe, jibe (dʒəib), *sb.* 1573. [f. the verb.] A sneering speech; a taunt, flout, or jeer.

A great master of gibes, and flouts, and jeers DISRAELI.

Gibe, jibe (dʒəib), *v.* 1567. [perh. – OFr. *giber* handle roughly, mod. dial. kick (repr. in mod. Fr. by *regimber* buck, rear; see JIB *v.*²), of unkn. origin.] **1.** *intr.* To speak sneeringly; to utter taunts; to jeer, flout, scoff. Const. *at*, †*with*. **2.** *trans.* To address with scoffs and sneers 1582.

1. Richardson..is always gibing at Fielding STEPHEN. **2.** The deane..would be alwaie gibing him at meales WOOD. Hence **Gi·bingly** *adv.*

Gibel (gi·bĕl). 1841. [– G. *gibel, giebel.*] The Prussian or Crucian Carp, *Carassius* (formerly *Cyprinus*) *gibelio* (see CARP *sb.*¹). Also *g. carp.*

Gibeonite (gi·biənəit). 1798. [f. *Gibeon* + -ITE¹ 1.] A menial, a drudge (see *Josh.* 9 : 27).

Giber, jiber (dʒəi·bəɹ). 1563. [f. GIBE *v.* + -ER¹.] One who utters gibes and taunts.

‖**Gibier** (ʒibie). Also †**gibbier.** Now *rare.* 1514. [Fr.] Game; wild-fowl.

Giblet (dʒi·blėt). [– OFr. *gibelet* game stew, perh. for **giberet*, f. *gibier* game; cf. Walloon *giblè d'awe* goose giblets, Fr. *gibelotte* rabbit stew.] **1.** †**a.** Entrails. ME. only. **b.** *pl.* rarely *sing.* The portions of a goose that are separated before cooking, the liver, gizzard, etc., with the pinions and feet 1539. **c.** *fig.* Odds and ends. Now chiefly *dial.* 1638. **2.** *attrib.*, as *g.-pie* 1693.

Gibraltar (dʒibrǭ·ltăɹ). 1592. **1.** A fortified town on the south coast of Spain, since 1704 a British possession. *fig.* An impregnable stronghold. 1856. †**2.** ? A Gibraltar monkey –1608. **3.** A sweetmeat; a piece of this. Also *G. rock.* 1831. **4.** *attrib.* 1707.

Gibus (dʒəi·bɒ̆s). 1848. [Name of the first maker.] An opera or crush hat. Also *g.-hat.*

Gid¹ (gid). 1601. [Short f. GIDDY *sb.*] Giddiness; *spec.* a brain-disease of a sheep, caused by the hydatid *Cœnurus cerebralis.* Also GIDDY.

Gid², ? *Obs.* 1674. [Of unkn. origin.] Local name for the Jack Snipe.

Gid(d, obs. f. GED.

Giddy (gi·di), *a.* [OE. *gidiġ*, var. of **gydiġ* :– **ʒuđiʒaz*, f. **ʒuđam* god, the primary sense being 'possessed by a god' (cf. OE. *ylfiġ* insane, f. *ælf* ELF, and Gr. ἔνθεος ENTHUSIAST); see -Y¹.] †**1.** Insane, stupid –ME. **2.** Having a sensation of swimming or whirling in the head, with proneness to fall; affected with vertigo, dizzy ME. †**b.** *transf.* Of a ship: Staggering as if giddy –1725. **c.** Rendering dizzy 1585. **d.** Whirling or circling round with bewildering rapidity 1593. **3.** Mentally intoxicated, 'elated to thoughtlessness' (J.); light-headed, frivolous, flighty, inconstant 1547. **4.** *Comb.*, as *g.-head, -headed, -paced* 1652.

2. His brains having been a little g. (like one looking from a great height) DRUMM. OF HAWTH. **c.** The g. footing of the Hatches *Rich. III*, I. iv. 17. **d.** The strong tempestuous treble..Ran into its giddiest whirl of sound TENNYSON. **3.** She said twenty g. things that looked like joy GOLDSM. Hence **Gi·ddily** *adv.* **Gi·ddiness. Gi·ddyish** *a.* somewhat g.

Giddy (gi·di), *v.* 1602. [f. the adj.] To make or become giddy.

Gier-eagle: see GEIR-.

Gierfalcon, obs. f. GERFALCON.

Gieseckite (gi·sĕkəit). 1821. [f. Sir Charles *Giesecke*, who brought it from Greenland; see -ITE¹ 2 b.] *Min.* A variety of pinite, believed to be a pseudomorph after nephelite.

Gif (gif), *conj. Sc.* and *n. dial.* [An alteration of ME. *ʒif* IF prob. due to the infl. of GIVE.] **1.** = IF. Also *gif that.* Now *rare.* ME. †**2.** = WHETHER. Also *gif that.* –1567.

Giff-gaff (gi·f-gæf). *Sc.* and *n. dial.* 1549. [redupl. of GIVE *v.*; cf. MDu. *ghivegave.*] **1.** Give and take. **2.** Interchange of remarks 1787.

Gift (gift), *sb.* [– ON. *gipt*, corresp. to OE. *ġift*, payment for a wife, pl. wedding, OFris. *jeft*, OS. *sundargift* privilege, MDu. *gift, gifte* (Du. *gift* fem. gift, n. poison), OHG. *gift* fem. gift, poison (G. *gift* fem. gift, n. poison), Goth. *fragifts* espousal :– Gmc. **ʒeftiz*, f. **ʒeb-*, base of GIVE.]

I. Giving. **1.** The action of giving; a giving. Also, the power or right of giving. **2.** *Law.* **a.** A transfer of property in a thing, voluntarily and without any valuable consideration 1471. **b.** The conveyance of an estate tail 1818.

1. The rich living was in the g. of the Herberts DISRAELI. *At a g.* (colloq.): for nothing. **2. a.** To complete a g. of goods and chattels delivery is absolutely necessary 1838.

II. The thing given. **1.** Something, the property in which is voluntarily transferred to another without the expectation or receipt of an equivalent ME. Also *transf.* **2.** An offering to God or to a heathen deity ME. **3.** Something given to corrupt; a bribe ME. **4.** A faculty, power, or quality miraculously bestowed; occas. in sense of inspiration OE. **b.** A natural endowment, faculty, ability, or talent ME. **5.** A white speck on the finger-nails, supposed to portend a gift 1708.

1. When we seek, as now, thy g. of sleep MILT. **3.** For giftes the wysest will deceave 1594. **4.** Phr. *The g. of tongues*: see TONGUE. We have not the g. of miracles BERKELEY. The g. of holiness NEWMAN. Faith is..an excellent g. MOZLEY. **b.** Endowed with highest gifts, The vision and the faculty divine WORDSW. The gifts of the wise lawgiver and firm administrator FREEMAN.

Comb.: **g.-book; -horse,** a horse given as a present; see also HORSE *sb.* Hence **Gi·ftling,** a small g.

Gift (gift), *v.* 15... [f. GIFT *sb.*] **1.** *trans.* To endow with gifts (see esp. GIFT *sb.* II. 4); to endow or present *with.* **2.** To make a present of. Chiefly *Sc.* 1619.

1. See how the Lord gifted him above his brethren 1608. Hence **Gi·fted** *ppl. a.* endowed with gifts; †given (MILT.). **Gi·ftedness,** the quality of being gifted; also, a gift.

Giftless (gi·ftlės), *a.* ME. [f. GIFT *sb.* + -LESS.] **1.** That has no gift to offer. **2.** That receives no gift ME. **3.** Untalented 1894.

1. *G. gifts* = gifts that are no gifts (after Gr. ἄδωρα δῶρα).

†**Gi·ft-rope.** 1704. [perh. a spurious word.] *Naut.* = GUEST-ROPE.

Gig (gig), *sb.*¹ ME. [prob. echoic or symbolic.]

I. Something that whirls. †**1.** A whipping-top –1793. **2.** = GIG-MILL. 1842.

1. Thou disputes like an Infant: goe whip thy Gigge *L. L. L.* v. i. 70.

II. †**1.** A flighty, giddy girl –1780. **2.** An oddity; *dial.* a fool. Chiefly *Eton slang.* 1777.

1. The little g. told all the quarrels..she led in her family MME. D'ARBLAY. **2.** What Mr. Daly..called uncommon gigs T. HOOK.

III. †A joke –1821; fun, glee 1777.

Phr. *On the (high) g.*: in a state of hilarity; *dial.* eager.

Gig (gig), *sb*². 1790. [transf. sense of GIG *sb.*¹ I.] **1.** A light two-wheeled one-horse carriage 1791. **2.** *Naut.* A light, narrow, clinker-built ship's boat. Also *cutter-, whale-g.* 1790. **b.** A form of this, used as a rowing boat, for racing purposes 1865. **3.** A wooden box, with two compartments, one above the other, used by miners in ascending and descending a pit-shaft. Also = KIBBLE. 1881.

Comb.: **gigsman** (also simple **gig**), one of the crew of a ship's g.; **g.-pair,** a g. for two rowers; **-work,** practice in rowing in a g.

Gig (gig), *sb.*³ 1722. [Short for FISHGIG or FIZGIG.] A kind of fish-spear.

†**Gig** (gig), *v.*¹ 1651. [f. GIG *sb.*¹ I. 1.] To throw out (a smaller gig); app. referring to a whipping-top of peculiar construction which does this. Hence *fig.* (*trans.* and *intr.*) –1690. Dicts. derive from L. *gignere*, with sense 'to engender'. See DRYDEN *Amphitryon* Prol. 21.

Gig (gig), *v.*² 1693. [perh. symbolic.] †**1.** *intr.* ?To move to and fro. DRYDEN. **2.** *trans.* To move backwards and forwards. Chiefly *U.S.* 1875.

Comb. **g.-saw,** 'a thin saw to which a rapid vertical reciprocation is imparted' (Knight).

Gig (gig), *v.*³ 1789. [perh. back-formation from GIG-MILL.] *trans.* To raise the nap of (cloth) with a gig. Also in *Comb.*, as *g.-machine*, 'a machine for dressing woolen cloth by subjecting it to the action of teasels' (Knight). Hence **Gi·gger,** one who works a g.-machine.

Gig (gig), *v.*⁴ 1816. [f. *Gig sb.*³] To fish, also to spear (fish), with a gig.

Gig, *v.*⁵ 1807. [f. GIG *sb.*²] *intr.* To travel in a gig.

Gig: see JIG.

Gigantean (dʒəigæ̆ntī·ăn), *a.* 1611. [f. L. *giganteus* + -AN.] = GIGANTIC *a.*

Gigantesque (dʒəigæ̆nte·sk), *a.* 1821. [– Fr. *gigantesque* – It. *gigantesco*, f. *gigante*; see GIANT, -ESQUE.] Having the characteristics of a giant; befitting a giant.

How g. the campanile is in its mass and height HAWTHORNE.

Gigantic (dʒəigæ·ntik), *a.* 1612. [f. L. *gigas, gigant-* GIANT + -IC.] †**1.** Of, pertaining to, or characteristic of, a giant or giants –1774. **2.** Having the proportions of a giant 1651. **3.** Hence: Extraordinary; huge, enormous 1797.

1. On each hand slaughter and g. deeds MILT. **3.** This g. telescope 1812. var. †**Gigantal.** Hence †**Gigantical** *a.* = GIGANTIC. **Giga·ntically** *adv.*

Giganticide¹. (dʒəigæ·ntisəid). 1806. [f. as prec. + -CIDE 1.] A giant-killer.

Giga·nticide². 1860. [f. as prec. + -CIDE 2.] The killing of giants.

†**Gigantine,** *a.* 1605. [– Fr. †*gigantin*, f. as prec.; see -INE¹.] = Gigantic. –1696. So †**Gigantive.**

Gigantology (dʒəigæ̆ntǫ·lŏdʒi). 1773. [– Fr. *gigantologie*, f. L. *gigant-*, Gr. γιγαντ-; see GIANT, -LOGY.] Discussions or treatises about giants.

Gigantomachy (dʒəigæ̆ntǫ·măki). Also in Gr. form **-machia.** 1606. [– Gr. γιγαντομαχία, f. γιγαντ- (see GIANT) + -μαχία -MACHY.] The war of the giants against the gods; hence, any similar contest.

†**Gigge,** *v.* [f. *gigge* GUIGE.] *trans.* To fit the GUIGE or arm-strap to (a shield). CHAUCER.

Gigget(t, giggot, obs. ff. GIGOT.

Giggish (gi·giʃ), *a.* 1523. [f. GIG *sb.*¹ III. + -ISH¹.] Lively, flighty, wanton. Hence **Gi·ggishness.**

Giggle (gi·g'l), *sb.* 1611. [f. the vb.] **1.** A minx, a GIGLET. **2.** A giggling laugh 1677.

Giggle (gi·g'l), *v.* 1509. [imit.; cf. Du. *gi(e)chelen*, LG. *giggeln*, MHG. *gickeln*, Russ. *khikhikat'.*] *intr.* To laugh continuously in a manner suggestive of foolish levity or of uncontrollable amusement. Also quasi-*trans.* to utter with a giggle.

A quiet day..giggling and making g. among the kind and frank-hearted young people SCOTT. Hence **Gi·ggler. Gi·ggly** *a.* addicted to giggling.

Gi·g-lamp. 1853. [f. GIG *sb.*² + LAMP.] **1.** One of the lamps at either side of a gig 1888. **2.** *pl.* Spectacles (*slang*) 1853.

Giglet, giglot (gi·glėt, -ət). ME. [perh. f. GIG *sb.*¹ II. 1 + -LET, and later assoc. w. GIGGLE *v.*] †**a.** A wanton woman –1632. **b.** A giddy, romping girl 1725.

attrib. and *Comb.*, as in *g.-fortune, -wench.* Also **g.-fair,** a statute fair for hiring servant-girls.

Gigman¹ (gi·gmæ̆n). 1830. [f. GIG *sb.*² + MAN.] One who keeps a gig: used by Carlyle as one whose respectability is measured by his keeping a gig; a 'Philistine'.

Gi·gman². *U.S.* 1889. [f. GIG *sb.*³] One who fishes with a gig.

Gig-mill. 1551. [f. GIG *sb.*¹ + MILL.] A machine for raising a nap on cloth by the use of teazles; also, a building in which these machines are used.

Gigolo (dʒi·gŏlo). 1927. [– Fr. *gigolo*, masc. correl. of *gigolette* young woman of easy virtue.] A professional male dancing-partner.

Gigot (dʒi·gǫt). 1526. [– Fr. *gigot*, dim. of dial. *gigue* (mod. Pr. *gigo*) leg, f. *giguer* hop, jump, of unkn. origin.] **1.** A leg or haunch of mutton, veal, etc. Now *Sc.* †**2.** A slice –1626.

Comb. **g.-sleeve** = 'leg of mutton sleeve'. Also simply *gigot.*

Gilbertian (gilbɔ̄·ɹtiăn), *a.* 1887. [f. the name of W. S. *Gilbert* (1836–1911), librettist + -IAN.] Of the ludicrously incongruous kind characteristic of Gilbert and Sullivan opera.

Gilbertine (gi·lbəɹtin, -əin). Only *Hist.* 1540. [– med.L. *Gilbertinus*, f. *Gilbertus*; see -INE¹.] **A.** *adj.* Of or belonging to Gilbert of Sempringham in Lincolnshire, or to the religious order founded by him (*c*1140). **B.** *sb.* A canon or nun of this order.

Gild (gild), *sb. Hist.* Also **guild.** 1656. [– med.L. *gildum, geldum*; see GELD *sb.*¹] A payment or tax.

Gild (gild), *v.*¹ Infl. **gilt** and **gilded.** ME. [OE. *gyldan* (in pa. pple. *ġegyld*, see GILT *ppl. a.*) = ON. *gylla* :– Gmc. **ʒulþjan*, f. **ʒulþam*

GOLD.] 1. *trans.* To cover in whole or part with a thin layer of gold. b. *transf.* To smear (with blood) 1595. 2. *Alch.* To impregnate (a liquid) with gold. Also *intr.* (for *refl.*) –1685. 3. *fig.* To supply with gold or money; *esp.* to make attractive by this means 1584. 4. To cover or adorn with a golden colour 1588. 5. *fig.* To adorn with a fair appearance; to give a specious lustre to 1596. †6. To impart a flush to (the face) –1683.

1. To guild a Crown of Silver 1684. b. *K. John* II.i. 316. 3. I will. . guild my selfe With some more ducats SHAKS. 4. Eternal summer gilds them [the Isles of Greece] yet BYRON. 5. To colour and g. blacker Designes 1660. 6. This grand Liquor that hath gilded 'em SHAKS.

†Gild, *v.*[2] Also **guild.** 1645. [var. of GELD *v.*[2]; cf. GILD *sb.* So med.L. *gildare* to pay geld.] *intr.* To pay taxes. *Hist. rare.* –1746.

Gi·lded, *ppl. a.* OE. [f. GILD *v.*[1] + -ED[1]. See also GILT *ppl. a.*] In senses of GILD *v.*[1]

Phr. *G. Chamber*: the House of Lords. *G. spurs*: an emblem of knighthood. *G. youth* (= Fr. *jeunesse dorée*): fashionable young men of wealthy families.

†Gi·lden, *a.* [OE. *gylden* = OFris. *gulden, gelden*, OS. *guldīn* (Du. *gulden*), OHG. *guldīn* (G. arch. *gülden*), ON. *gullenn*, Goth. *gulþeins*:– Gmc *ʒulþīnaz*, f. *ʒulþam GOLD; see -EN[4].] 1. Golden –1591. ¶2. Occas. used instead of GILDED 1530.

Gilder (gi·ldəɹ), *sb.* 1550. [f. GILD *v.*[1] + -ER[1].] One who gilds; one whose occupation is gilding.

Gilder, obs. f. GUILDER, GUELDER (-ROSE).

Gilding (gi·ldiŋ), *vbl. sb.* ME. [f. GILD *v.*[1] + -ING[1].] 1. The action of GILD *v.*[1] 2. The golden surface produced by gilding. Also *transf.* and *fig.* 1634.

2. It was a spacious building Full of barbaric carving, painting, g. BYRON. *Comb.* **g.-metal,** 'an alloy composed of 4 parts of copper, 1 part of Bristol old brass, and 14 ounces of tin, to every pound of copper' (Francis).

Gile, obs. f. GUILE *sb.* and *v.*

Gill (gil), *sb.*[1] Chiefly *pl.* ME. [– ON. *gil (whence Sw. *gäl*, †*gel*, Da. *gjælle*) :– *ʒeliz, rel. to ON. *gjǫlnar* fem. pl. whiskers of the mythical Fenris wolf (cf. ODa. *fiskegæln* fish-gills) :– *ʒelunaz, cogn. with Gr. χελύνη lip, jaw, χεῖλος lip.] 1. The organ of respiration in water-breathing animals, which is so arranged that the venous blood is exposed to the aerating influence of the water. In fishes, the gills are on each side of the neck; in other aquatic animals their position and structure is varied. 2. Applied to organs, etc., resembling the gills of a fish. a. The wattles or dewlap of a fowl 1626. b. The radiating plates arranged vertically in the under side of the cap or pileus of fungi 1715. 3. Attributed to persons: The flesh under the jaws and ears 1626. 4. *slang.* Only in *pl.* The corners of a stand-up collar 1826.

1. The gills or *branchiæ*. These are delicate processes of skin richly supplied with blood, and capable of absorbing oxygen MIVART. 3. Phr. *To be rosy, white, blue, yellow about the gills*: to look well, dejected, ill.

Comb.: **g.-arch, -bar,** one of the cartilaginous arches to which the gills of fishes are attached; **-cavity, chamber,** the cavity or compartment in which the g. is contained; **-cleft** = *gill-opening*; **-comb** = CTENIDIUM; **-cover,** the bony case covering the gills of fish; **-footed** *a.* = BRANCHIOPODOUS; **-lamella, -leaf, -leaflet** = *gill-plate*; **-lid,** the covering of the gills; **-net,** a fishing net so constructed that the fish are caught by the gills; **-opening,** the aperture by which water is admitted to the gills; **-plate,** one of the vascular lamellæ forming part of the gills of fishes, molluscs, etc.; **-plume** = *gill-comb*; **-raker,** one of a line of cartilaginous or bony projections on the inner side of a g.-arch.

Gill (gil), *sb.*[2] Also **†ghyll.** ME. [– ON. *gil* deep glen, cogn. w. *geil* in same sense. The fanciful sp. *ghyll* was introduced by Wordsworth ('Evening Walk' 54).] 1. A deep rocky cleft or ravine, usually wooded and forming the course of a stream. 2. A brook or rivulet 1625

Gill (dʒil), *sb.*[3] ME. [– OFr. *gille, gelle*, in med.L. *gillo, gillus, gellus*, late L. *gello, gillo* water-pot.] 1. A measure for liquids, containing one-fourth (or locally, one-half) of a standard pint. 2. A vessel holding a gill ME. 3. *attrib.*, as *g.-house* 1673.

Gill, jill (dʒil), *sb.*[4] 1460. [Short for *Gillian* – Fr. *Juliane* – L. *Juliana*, orig. fem. adj. (see -AN) f. *Julius*, Roman gentile name.] †1. A lass, wench –1665. 2. *dial.* Short for *Gill-go-by-ground* (see *Comb.*). ? *Obs.* 1727. b. Short for *g.-ale* or *g.-beer* 1755.

1. Phr. *Jack and G.* = lad and lass. Our woing doth not end like an old Play: Iacke hath not G. SHAKS.

Comb.: *G.-creep-* (or *go-*) *by-ground*, dial. name for Ground Ivy (*Nepeta glechoma*); †*attrib.* (sense 2) *g.-ale, -beer, -tea.*

Gill (gil), *sb.*[5] 1839. [poss. transf. use of GILL *sb.*[1]] A flax-comb, used for preparing, drawing, and roving flax and hemp, and for combing and spinning long wool. Also *attrib.*

Gill (gil), *v.*[1] ME. [f. GILL *sb.*[1]] 1. *trans.* To gut or clean (fish). 2. To cut away the gills of a mushroom 1728. 3. To catch (fish) by the gills in a gill-net. Said also of the net. 1884.

Gill (gil), *v.*[2] 1882. [f. GILL *sb.*[5]] *trans.* To dress (flax or wool) by means of a gill.

Gill-flirt (dʒi·lflɔ̄rt). Also **Jil(l)-.** 1632. [f. GILL *sb.*[4] + FLIRT *sb.* Cf. FLIRT-GILL.] A wanton; a giddy young woman or girl. Now only *arch.*

†Gillian. 1573. [See GILL *sb.*[4]] A girl, wench –1685.

Comb. G.-flirt = prec. *G.-spend-all*: an unthrifty woman.

Gillie (gi·li). Also **†gilly.** 1681. [– Gael. *gille* lad, servant = Ir. *giolla* fellow.] 1. *Hist.* An attendant on a Highland chief. †*G.-wetfoot* = Gael. *gille-casfliuch*: Lowlanders' name for a Highland chief's follower; spec. the servant who carried the chief across streams. 2. One who attends a sportsman in the Scottish Highlands 1848.

Gilling (gi·liŋ). *dial.* 1640. [Of unkn. origin; cf. synon. *girling* (1861).] A salmon on his second return from the sea.

Gillyflower (dʒi·liflauᵊɹ). Also **†gilli-, †July-.** ME. [ME. *gilofre, gerofle*, altered (by assim. to *flower*) to *geraflour* (XV), *gelyflour, jillyflower, July-flower* (XVI) – OFr. *gilofre, girofle* :– med.L. *caryophyllum* – Gr. καρυόφυλλον clove-tree, f. κάρυον nut + φύλλον leaf.] †1. A clove –1513. 2. Applied to native plants having clove-scented flowers, esp. to the clove-scented pink (*Dianthus caryophyllus*), and *dial.* to the wallflower (see *Wall-gillyflower*) or to the white stock (see *Stock-gillyflower*) ME. 3. A variety of apple; also *g.-apple* 1657. 4. *attrib.*, as †*g.-grass* –1685.

Comb.: **dame's g.** (see DAME'S-VIOLET); **English g.,** the carnation; **feathered g.,** *Dianthus plumarius*; **mock-g.,** soap-wort (*Saponaria officinalis*); **single g.,** *Dianthus plumarius*; **striped g.,** a variety of *Dianthus caryophyllus*; **yellow g.,** wall-flower. See also *water-, winter-*, etc. *g.*

Gilour(e, var. of GUILER.

Gilra·vage, *v. north.* and *Sc.* 1818. [Of unkn. origin.] *intr.* To feast or make merry in an excessive or riotous manner. Hence **Gilra·vager.**

Gils(e, var. of GRILSE.

Gilt (gilt), *sb.*[1] 1492. [f. GILT *ppl. a.* in *silver and gilt*, etc.] †1. Gilt plate 1492. 2. Gilding. Also *fig.* 1593. 3. Gold, money (cf. GELD, GELT *sbs.*). Now only *slang.* 1598.

2. Phr. *to take the g. off the gingerbread* (see GINGERBREAD). 3. So that some guilt may grease his greedy fist MARSTON.

Gilt (gilt), *sb.*[2] Now *dial.* Late ME. [– ON. *gyltr* :– *gultjō, rel. to *gǫltr* :– *ʒaltuz.] A young sow or female pig.

Gilt (gilt), *ppl. a.* ME. [See GILD *v.*[1]] 1 = GILDED *ppl. a.* 2. *G. youth* (fig.): a transl. of Fr. *jeunesse dorée*, applied first to the dandies who assisted in the downfall of Robespierre in 1794.

1. As a parrot turns Up thro' g. wires a crafty loving eye TENNYSON. *Comb.* **g.-edged,** *lit.* of writing paper or books; applied *fig.* (also **g.-edge**) in commercial slang to 'paper' (i.e. bills) of the best quality; also *absol.* a g.-e. security.

†Gilt, *v.* ME. [f. GILT *ppl. a.* by extension of the participial form to other parts of the verb.] = GILD *v.*[1] –1641. Hence **Gi·lted** *ppl. a.*

Gi·lt-head. ? *Obs.* 1555. [f. GILT *ppl. a.* + HEAD.] A name of fishes which have the head marked with golden spots or lines: The striped tunny or bonito; the dorado or dolphin (*Coryphæna hippuris*); the cunner or golden wrasse (*Crenilabrus melops* or *tinca*).

Gi·lt-tail. 1651. [f. GILT *ppl. a.* + TAIL *sb.*[1]] A little short worm.

Gilty(f, obs. f. GUILTY.

Gim (dʒim), *a.* Now *dial.* 1513. [perh. var. of JIMP *a.*] Smart, spruce.

Gimbal (dʒi·mbăl). 1577. [var. of GIMMAL.] †1. = GIMMAL 1. –1711. †2. *pl.* = GIMMAL 2. –1652. 3. *pl.* A contrivance by means of which articles for use at sea (e.g. the compass, the chronometer) are suspended so as to keep a horizontal position. It usually consists of a pair of rings moving on pivots in such a way as to have a free motion in two directions at right angles, so as to counteract the motion of the vessel. 4. *attrib.*, as *g.-joint.* Also **g.-ring,** a single g. by which the cock-eye of the upper millstone is supported on the spindle to permit vibration. Hence **Gi·mballed** *ppl. a.* fitted with a g.

Gimcrack (dʒi·mkræk). [ME. *gibecrake* (XIV), perh. small ornament; of unkn. origin.]

A. *sb.* †1. App. some kind of inlaid work in wood. ME. only. 2. †a. A fanciful notion; also, a 'dodge' –1639. b. A mechanical contrivance; also *pl.* scientific apparatus 1712. c. Now usually applied to anything showy and useless, a trumpery article, a knick-knack 1676. †3. A fop; in later use applied to women. A term of contempt. –1785. 4. A 'Jack of all trades'. Now only *dial.* 1766.

B. *adj.* Trivial; showy but worthless; trumpery 1750. Hence **Gi·mcrackery,** gimcracks collectively.

Gimlet (gi·mlĕt), *sb.* ME. [– OFr. *guimbelet*, dim. of the Gmc. word which appears in Eng. as WIMBLE *sb.*] A kind of boring-tool; it has a grooved steel body, a cross handle at one end, and a worm or screw at the other.

Comb.: **g.-eye,** (*a*) a squint-eye, (*b*) a piercing eye; hence **-eyed** *a.*; **-hole,** a hole made by a g.

Gimlet (gi·mlĕt), *v.* 1828. [f. prec. sb.] 1. *trans.* To pierce with or as with a gimlet 1840. 2. *Naut.* To turn round (an anchor) by the stock, with a motion like turning a gimlet (Webst.).

Gimmal (dʒi·məl). 1596. [Altered f. GEMEL.] 1. *Antiq.* A finger-ring so made as to divide into two (or three) rings. Also *g.ring.* 1607. †2. *pl.* Joints, links, connecting parts (in machinery) –1867. †3. *pl.* The voussoirs of an arch (*rare*) 1639. †4. = GIMBAL 3. –1793. †5. ? A hinge; = GIMMER[1] 2. 1605. Hence **†Gi·mmaled** *ppl. a.* made with gimmals.

Gimmer[1] (dʒi·məɹ). Now *dial.* 1520. [dial. var. of GIMMAL.] †1. = GIMMAL 1. *rare.* 1570. 2. A hinge. *Obs.* exc. *dial.* 1520. †3. = GIMMAL 2. (Rare in *sing.*) –1668.

Gimmer[2] (gi·məɹ). *Sc.* and *n. dial.* ME. [– ON. *gymbr* ewe lamb one year old (mod. Icel. *gimbur*, Da. *gimmer-lam*); of unkn. origin.] 1. A ewe between the first and second shearing. 2. 'A contemptuous term for a woman' (Jam.) 1774. 3. *attrib.* 1546.

Gimp, gymp (gimp), *sb.*[1] 1664. [– Du. *gimp*, of unkn. origin.] 1. Silk, worsted, or cotton twist with a cord or wire running through it. Now chiefly, a kind of trimming made of this. 2. A fishing-line composed of silk, etc., similarly strengthened 1827. 3. In *Lace-making*: The coarser thread which forms the outline of the design 1839. 4. *attrib.*, as *g.-nail* –1661.

Gimp (gimp), *sb.*[2] 1747. [– Fr. *guimpe* repr. OFr. *guimple, wimple*; see WIMPLE *sb.*] A neckerchief (worn by a nun).

Gimp (dʒimp), *v.*[1] *rare* in lit. use. 1697. [Of unkn. origin.] *trans.* To give a scalloped or indented outline to.

Gimp (gimp), *v.*[2] 1755. [f. GIMP *sb.*[1]] 1. *trans.* To trim with gimp. 2. To 'whip' or twine (wire, etc.) into a plait or twist of something softer. 3. To give a ribbed surface to 1902.

Gimp: see JIMP *a.*

Gin (dʒin), *sb.*[1] ME. [Aphetic – OFr. *engin* ENGINE.] †1. Skill, ingenuity. Also, in bad sense, craft –1470. †2. A scheme, device. Also, an artifice, trick. –1723. 3. A mechanical contrivance; a machine; †a tool; †a spring ME. 4. *spec.* A snare, net, trap, or the like. Also *fig.* ME. †5. An engine of torture;

the rack –1592. †6. A machine used in warfare for casting missiles –1650. †7. A bolt, bar, or the like –1710. **8. a.** An apparatus for hoisting heavy weights; now usually a tripod, with a winch or drum round which the rope is wound ME. **b.** *Mining.* A drum or windlass for hoisting, pumping, etc. 1686. **9.** A machine for driving piles 1682. **10.** A machine for separating cotton from its seeds; also *cotton-g.* 1796. **11.** *Naut.* A small iron frame, having a swivel-hook, furnished with an iron sheave, to serve as a pulley for the use of chain in discharging cargo, etc. 1860. **12.** *attrib.*, as *g.-block, -tackle*, etc. 1497.

Comb.: **g.-horse,** a horse that works a g. (sense 8 b); **-house,** a house where cotton is ginned; **-pit,** a shallow mine- or pit-shaft, worked by a g.; **-race, -ring,** the circle or track in which a g.-horse moves; **-saw,** one used in a cotton-g. for drawing the fibres through the grid, leaving the seed in the hopper; **-wheel,** (*a*) the wheel or drum of a g. for hoisting, etc.; (*b*) a wheel in a cotton g.

Gin (dʒin), *sb.*[2] 1714. [abbrev. of GENEVA[1].] An ardent spirit distilled from grain or malt; see GENEVA[1]. Also *attrib.*

In the form GIN, the name chiefly denotes a spirit of British manufacture, usually flavoured not with juniper but with some substitute; but sometimes GIN and GENEVA are used indiscriminately.

Comb.: **g.-drinker's liver,** 'atrophic cirrhosis of the liver', frequently caused by g.; also **-liver**; **-trap,** (*slang*), the mouth.

Gin (gin), *v.*[1] *Obs.* exc. *arch.* ME. [Aphetic f. BEGIN (or OE. *onginnan*); in ME. chiefly in the pa. t. *gan.* Now sometimes written *'gin*]. **1.** *intr.* To begin. In ME. poetry *gan* is usually a mere auxiliary (= mod. *did*), and periphrastic. **2.** *absol.* To begin, commence ME. **3.** *trans.* To begin (something) ME.

1. Phœbus gins arise *Cymb.* II. iii. 23. **3.** Whence the Sunne gins his reflection *Macb.* I. ii. 25.

Gin (dʒin), *v.*[2] 1625. [f. GIN *sb.*[1]; cf. ENGINE *v.*] **1.** *trans.* To catch in a gin or trap. **2.** To remove the seeds of (cotton) with a gin 1789.

Gin (gin), *prep. Sc.* 17.. [= GAIN *prep.* 3, with vowel-shortening due to want of stress.] Against or by (a certain time).

Gin (gin), *conj. Sc.* and *dial.* 1674. [app. in some way related to GIF.] If; whether.

†**Ging,** *sb.* [OE. *genge* troop, company; f. root of GANG *v.*] **1.** A company or host of armed men. ME. only. **2.** A family, household, train of servants. Also *pl.* One's 'people'; people in general. –1626. **3.** *gen.* A gang, pack, train –1653. **b.** *spec.* The crew of a ship or boat –1670. **c.** A crew, rabble; rout –1659.

3. *transf.* A whole g. of words and phrases MILT.

Gingall, jingall (dʒi·ngǭl). 1818. [– Hindi *janjāl.*] A heavy musket fired from a rest; a light swivel-gun. Used in China and India. Also *attrib.*

Ginger (dʒi·ndʒəɹ), *sb.* and *a.*[1] [ME. *gingivere*, repr. a conflation of OE. *ġinġifer(e)*, *ġinġiber* (directly – med.L.) with OFr. *gingi(m)bre* (mod. *gingembre*) – med.L. *gingiber, zingeber,* L. *zingiber(i* – Gr. ζιγγίβερις – Prakrit *siŋgabēra* – Skr. *çṛŋgavēram*, f. *çṛŋgam* horn + *vēra* body; so named from its antler-shaped root.]

A. *sb.* The rhizome of the tropical plant *Zingiber officinale*, characterized by its hot spicy taste; used in cookery and medicine, and as a sweetmeat. **2.** The plant *Zingiber officinale* ME.; also similar plants 1838. **3.** *slang.* Mettle, spirit (*fig.*) 1843. **4.** *dial.* and *slang.* A light sandy colour 1865; also, a sandy-haired person 1885.

Comb.: **g.-ale,** an effervescing drink flavoured with g.; **-cordial,** a liqueur made from raisins, lemon-rind, g. and water, occas. strengthened with brandy or whisky; **-grass,** (*a*) *Andropogon nardus*, an East Indian grass, yielding an essential oil with a strong smell of g.; (*b*) *Panicum glutinosum*, a coarse grass of Jamaica; **-nut** = GINGERBREAD-NUT; **-snap,** (*a*) a thin brittle cake flavoured with g.; (*b*) a hot-tempered person (*U.S.*); **-spice** = GINGER *sb.* 1; **-wine,** a wine made by the fermentation of sugar, water, and bruised g.; **-wort,** Lindley's name for the order *Zingiberaceæ.*

B. *adj. dial.* Of the colour of ginger. Of a person: Sandy-haired. Of a cock: Having red plumage. 1825.

Gi·nger, *a.*[2] Now *dial.* 1600. [Back-formation from GINGERLY.] = GINGERLY *a.*

Ginger (dʒi·ndʒəɹ), *v.* 1823. [f. the sb.] **1.** *trans.* To put ginger into (a drink) 1825. **2.** To treat (a horse) with ginger; *fig.* to put mettle into, spirit *up.*

Ginger-beer. 1809. [f. GINGER + BEER.] An aerated drink, flavoured with ginger. Also *attrib.*

Gingerbread (dʒi·ndʒəɹbred). [Earliest forms *gingebras*, *gyngebre(e)de* – OFr. *gingembras, -brat* – med.L. *gingibratum, -etum*, f. *gingiber* GINGER + *-atum* -ATE[1]. The final syll. assumed a form resembling or suggesting *bread*, and for sense 1 b the insertion of *r* in the second syll. completed the semblance of a compound; forms of the type *gingebread* remained in Sc.] **1.** †**a.** Orig.: Preserved ginger. **b.** Later: A kind of plain cake, highly flavoured with ginger, and formerly made into fanciful shapes, which were often gilded. **2.** *fig.* Anything showy and unsubstantial 1605. **3.** *slang.* Money 1700. **4.** *attrib.* 1748.

1. Roial spicerye And Gyngebreed CHAUCER. **2.** *To take the gilt off the g.*: to strip something of its attractive qualities. **4.** *G. work*, gaudy and tasteless decorations, orig. of a ship.

Comb.: **g.-nut,** a small round button-like cake of g.; **-tree,** (*a*) = DOUM-PALM; (*b*) *Parinarium macrophyllum*, a West African fruit-tree with a farinaceous fruit; **-plum,** the fruit of *Parinarium macrophyllum.*

Gingerly (dʒi·ndʒəɹli). 1519. [perh. f. OFr. *gensor, genzor*, prop. compar. of *gent* GENT *a.*, but used also as a positive, 'pretty, delicate'. See -LY[1], -LY[2].]

A. *adv.* †**a.** Orig.: Elegantly, daintily; later, mincingly –1607. **b.** Cautiously; also, timidly, fastidiously 1607.

b. But Lord! How g. he answered it PEPYS.

B. *adj.* †**a.** Dainty, delicate. **b.** Extremely cautious or wary. 1533.

Hence **Gi·ngerliness,** the quality of being g.

Gi:nger-po·p. 1827. [f. GINGER + POP *v.*] **1.** *colloq.* = GINGER-BEER. **2.** *slang.* A policeman 1887.

Gingery (dʒi·ndʒəri), *a.* 1852. [f. GINGER + -Y[1].] Ginger-coloured, sandy; also spiced with or as with ginger.

Gingham (gi·ŋăm). 1615. [–(prob. through Du. *gingang*) Malay *ginggang*, orig. adj. striped.] **1.** A kind of cotton or linen cloth, woven of dyed yarn, often in stripes or checks. In *pl.* fabrics of this kind. **2.** *colloq.* An umbrella (prop. of gingham) 1861. **3.** *attrib.* 1793.

Gingival (dʒindʒəi·văl), *a.* 1669. [mod.L. *gingivalis*, f. L. *gingiva* gum; see -AL[1].] **1.** Of or pertaining to the gums. **2.** quasi-*sb.* Sounds in uttering which the tongue is pressed against the gums 1874. So **Gi:ngivi·tis,** inflammation of the gums.

Gingle, obs. f. JINGLE.

Gingles, var. of SHINGLES. Fuller.

Ginglyform (gi·ŋ-, dʒi·ŋglifǭɹm), *a.* 1847. [irreg. f. GINGLYMUS + -FORM.] *Anat.* Hinge-shaped. So **Gi·nglymate** *v. intr.* to form a hinge. **Gi·nglimoid, Ginglymoi·dal** *adjs.* resembling a hinge; hinge-like.

Ginglymus (gi·ŋ-, dʒi·ŋglimŏs). 1657. [mod.L. *ginglymus* – Gr. γίγγλυμος hinge.] *Anat.* 'A diarthrodial joint having some likeness to a hinge, in that its motion is only in two directions, as the elbow-joint' (*Syd. Soc. Lex.*).

Ginkgo (gi·ŋkgo). Also †**gingo,** †**ginko, gingko.** 1808. [Jap. – Chinese *yinhing* 'silver apricot'.] A Chinese tree (*Ginkgo biloba* or *Salisburia adiantifolia*) cultivated for its handsome foliage. Also *attrib.*

Ginn, var. of JINN.

Ginnet, obs. f. JENNET.

Ginney, ginnie, obs. ff. GUINEA.

†**Gi·nning,** *vbl. sb.* ME. [f. GIN *v.*[1] + -ING[1].] = BEGINNING –1463.

Ginny-carriage (dʒi·ni,kærėdʒ). *dial.* 1824. [f. *Ginny*, var. of *Jenny* female name; cf. JENNY II.2.] A stout carriage for conveying materials along a railroad.

Gi·n-pa:lace. 1834. [f. GIN *sb.*[2]] A gaudily decorated public-house.

Ginseng (dʒi·nseŋ). 1654. [– Chinese *jên shên* 'man image' (Giles), with allusion to the form of the root.] **1.** A plant of two species of the genus *Aralia* or *Panax*, found in Northern China, the eastern United States, and elsewhere 1691. **2.** The root of the plant; a preparation of this as a medicine 1654. **3.** *attrib.*, as *g.-farm*, etc. 1758.

Gi·n-shop. 1714. [f. GIN *sb.*[2]] A dram-shop where gin is retailed.

Gin-sling. 1839. [f. GIN *sb.*[2] + SLING *sb.*[5]] A U.S. cold drink, made of gin, etc. flavoured and sweetened.

Giottesque (dʒǫte·sk). 1854. [f. *Giotto* + -ESQUE.] **A.** *adj.* Resembling the style of Giotto (13–14th c.). **B.** *sb.* The style founded by Giotto; also, an artist of the school, or imitating the style, of Giotto.

Gip, *sb.*: see GYP.

Gip (gip), *v.* 1603. [Of unkn. origin. Cf. GIB *v.*[2] (XIX).] To clean (fish) for curing.

†**Gip,** *interj.* 1530. [prob. an involuntary exclam.; cf. GEE-(H)UP and GUP.] **a.** An exclam. of anger or remonstrance addressed to a horse. **b.** Addressed to a person = 'get out' –1660.

Gipon. *Obs.* exc. *arch.* ME. [– OFr. *gip(p)on*, var. of *jup(p)on* tunic (mod. *jupon*, see JUPON, dim. of *gipe, jupe.* See JUPE.] A tunic, frequently worn under the hauberk.

Gippo (dʒi·po). *Army slang.* 1914. [Alteration of dial. *jipper.*] Gravy, soup, stew.

Gipser (dʒi·psəɹ). Also **gipsire (gyp-).** *Obs.* exc. *arch.* ME. [– OFr. *gibecier(e, gibessiere* etc. purse, pouch (mod.Fr. *gibecière* gamebag), of unkn. origin.] A purse, pouch, or wallet, hung from a belt or girdle.

Gipsies, †gips, *sb. pl.* 1644. [Proper name of springs near Bridlington, now called the *Gipsy race.*] Intermitting springs.

Gipsy, gypsy (dʒi·psi), *sb.* Pl. **gipsies, gypsies.** 1537. [Earlier forms †*gicypan*, †*gipsen, -son* (Spenser), aphetic f. EGYPTIAN (in the same use). The form *gipsy* may be directly – L. *Ægyptius*; cf. (*by*) *Mary Gipcy* (Skelton), i.e. Mary of Egypt, Maria Ægyptiaca.] **1.** A member of a wandering race (by themselves called *Romany*), of Hindu origin, formerly believed to have come from Egypt. **b.** Gipsy language, Romany (Recent Dicts.) **2.** *transf.* †**a.** A cunning rogue –1635. **b.** Applied to a woman, as being cunning, deceitful, fickle, or the like. Now merely playful, and applied esp. to a brunette 1632. **3.** Short for *g.-bonnet, -hat, -moth, -winch* 1808. **4.** *attrib.* or *adj.* Resembling what is customary among gipsies 1630.

1. Both in a tune like two gipsies on a horse *A.Y.L.* v. iii. 16. *Ant. & Cl.* IV. xii. 28. More ignorant in his art of divining then any G. MILT. **2. b.** Cursing her [his mother-in-law] for a dissembling hypocritical Gypsie 1673. **4.** A g. tent 1849, breakfast 1850.

Comb.: **g.-bonnet,** one with large side-flaps; so **-hat; -herring,** the pilchard; **-moth,** *Ocneria dispar*; **-ring,** a flat gold ring, with stones (orig. Egyptian pebbles) let into it, at given distances; **-rose,** the wild and garden scabious; **-winch,** a small winch having a drum, ratchet, and pawl, and attachable to a post; **-wort,** *Lycopus europæus.*

Hence **Gi·psydom,** gipsies collectively; also, their way of life (*rare*). **Gi·psyfy, gi·psify** *v.* to make or (*rarely*) become g.-like. **Gi·psyism,** the life and pursuits of gipsies, or what resembles this.

Gipsy (dʒi·psi), *v.* 1627. [f. the sb.] *intr.* To live or act like gipsies; esp. to camp out, picnic, etc.

Giraffe (dʒĭra·f). 1594. [ult. – Arab. *zarāfa*, through Fr. *girafe.*] **1.** A ruminant quadruped found in Africa, remarkable for its long neck and legs, and for its skin, which is spotted like a panther's; also called CAMELOPARD. **2.** *Astron.* The constellation CAMELOPARD 2. 1836. **3.** *Mining.* A form of cage or truck used on inclines 1881. †**4.** A kind of upright spinet. STAINER & BARRETT. Hence **Gira·ffid,** one of the *Giraffidæ*, the animal family of which the g. is the only living representative.

‖**Girandola** (dʒiræ·ndŏlă). 1644. [It.; see next.] **1.** A kind of revolving firework 1670. **2.** A revolving fountain-jet.

Girandole (dʒi·răndoᵘl). 1634. [– Fr. *girandole* – It. *girandola*, f. *girare* – late L. *gyrare* GYRATE.] **1.** = GIRANDOLA 1. **2.** = GIRANDOLA 2. 1813. **3.** A branched support for candles or lights 1769. **4.** An ear-ring or pendant, esp. one with a central stone surrounded by smaller stones 1825. **5.** *attrib.* 1799.

Girasol(e (dʒi·răsǫl, -soᵘl). 1586. [– Fr. *girasol* or its source It. *girasole*, f. *girare* (see prec.) + *sole* sun.] †**1.** A sunflower. SIDNEY. **2.** A variety of opal which reflects a reddish glow in a bright light; a *fire-opal* 1588.

Gird (gǭɹd), *sb.* ME. [f. GIRD *v.*[2]] †**1.** A sharp stroke or blow (*rare*) –1579. **2.** A sudden movement or jerk, a spurt of action. *Obs.* exc. *dial.* 1545. **3.** A spasm of pain. Now *dial* 1614. **4.** A sharp or biting remark; a gibe, 'dig'. Somewhat *arch.* 1566.

3. My Heart relented, and gave me several Girds and Twitches STEELE. **4.** For his girds were oblique, and touched to the quick NORTH.

Gird (gǭɹd), *v.*[1] Infl. **girded** and **girt.** [OE. *gyrdan* = OS. *gurdian* (Du. *gorden*), OHG. *gurten* (G. *gürten*), ON. *gyrða* :– Gmc. **ȝurðjan*; see GIRTH.] **1.** *trans.* To surround, encircle with a belt or girdle. Chiefly *refl.* or *pass.* **b.** *fig.* To prepare (oneself) for action 1450. †**c.** To bind (a horse) with a saddle-girth –1677. **2.** *fig.* To invest or endue *with* attributes OE. **3.** To equip *with* a sword suspended from a belt fastened round the body OE. **4.** To fasten by means of a belt, a girdle, etc. OE.; to put (a cord, etc.) *round* something (*rare*) 1726. **5.** *transf.* and *fig.* †**a.** To tie firmly or confine –1674. **b.** To besiege, blockade 1548. **6.** Said of that which surrounds: To encircle, enclose, confine ME.

1. Let your loins be girded about *Luke* 12:35. Leaves..To g. thir waste MILT. **b.** To g. oneself for one's life's work MOTLEY. **2.** The Son..Girt with Omnipotence MILT. **3.** Upon Easter day..he was gyrde with the sworde of the Duke of Briteyn R. GRAFTON. **4.** He dyd on his helme and gyrte on his sword LD. BERNERS. So they girded sackcloth on their loynes 1 *Kings* 20:32. **5.** Sommers greene all girded up in sheaues SHAKS. **6.** Girt with the iron ring of Fate CARLYLE. Boadicea..Girt by half the tribes of Britain TENNYSON.

Gird (gǭɹd), *v.*[2] ME. [Of unkn. origin. Cf. GRIDE *v.*] †**1.** *trans.* To strike, smite. Also of pain: To touch sharply (*rare*) –1618. †**2.** To impel or move hastily or rudely –1650. **3.** *intr.* To move suddenly or rapidly; to rush, start, spring. *Obs.* exc. *dial* ME. **4.** *fig.* **a.** *absol.* To jest or gibe *at* (rarely *against, upon*). The current sense. 1546. **b.** *trans.* To sneer or scoff at. ? *Obs.* 1573.

4. a. I wonder why many men g. so at the law MIDDLETON. **b.** Hee is still girding the ages vanity EARLE.

Girder[1] (gǭ·ɹdəɹ). 1611. [f. GIRD *v.*[1] + -ER[1].] **1. a.** A main beam in a framed floor, supporting the system of joisting that carries the flooring. **b.** An iron or steel longitudinal beam used for the same purpose; esp., a latticed plate, or other compound structure used to form the span of a bridge 1853. †**2.** In masonry. **a.** A bond-stone. **b.** A bonding-course. 1726. **3.** *attrib.*, as **g.-bridge,** a bridge whose superstructure consists of longitudinal girders carrying the platform or roadway; **-rail,** a form of tramway rail, resembling in its section that of the ordinary iron girder used in construction. 1854. Hence **Gi·rderage,** girders collectively.

†**Gi·rder**[2]. *rare.* 1584. [f. GIRD *v.*[2] + -ER[1].] One who sneers or cavils –1611.

Girding (gǭ·ɹdiŋ), *vbl. sb.* ME. [f. GIRD *v.*[1] and *v.*[2] + -ING[1].] **1.** The action of GIRD *v.*[1] and [2]. **2.** That which girds; esp. †a girdle ME.

2. Instead of a stomacher a g. of sackcloth *Isa.* 3:24.

Girdle (gǭ·ɹd'l), *sb.*[1] [OE. *gyrdel* (earlier *gyrdels*) = MDu. *gurdel* (Du. *gordel*), OHG. *gurtil, -ila* (G. *gürtel*), ON. *gyrðill*, f. **ȝurðjan* GIRD *v.*[1]; see -LE.] **1.** A belt worn round the waist to secure or confine the garments; also used to carry a weapon, a purse, etc. †**2.** The part of the body round which the girdle is worn –1732. Also *transf.* and *fig.* **3.** *transf.* uses of 1. **a.** That which surrounds as a girdle; †a zone OE. **b.** That which confines; a restraint, limit 1616. **4.** *spec.* **a.** *Anat.* In mod. use applied chiefly to the bony supports for the upper and lower limbs, the *shoulder* (or *pectoral*) and *pelvic* (or *hip*) g. 1601. **b.** The line or rim dividing the two faces of a brilliant 1819. **c.** *Arch.* A small circular band round the shaft of a column 1727. **d.** A belt or ring made round the trunk of a tree by the removal of the bark 1896. **e.** *Mining.* A term applied locally to very thin beds of stone 1819.

1. By hire girdel heeng a purs of lether CHAUCER. Phr. (*To have, hold*) *under one's g.*: in subjection, under one's control. **3. a.** †*The g. of the world*: the ecliptic, the equator. The billows roll, From the world's g. to the frozen pole COWPER. †*To put* (*make, cast*) *a g.* (*round*) *about*: to go round, make the circuit of. Ile put a g. about the earth, in forty minutes SHAKS. **b.** The iron g. of a solemn.. oath 1833.

Comb.: **g.-beds,** alternations of thin sandstones and sandy shales; **-bone,** the sphenethmoid bone; **-wheel,** a spinning wheel small enough to be hung at the g.

Girdle (gǭ·ɹd'l), *sb.*[2] *north* and *Sc.* ME. [Metathetic form of GRIDDLE.] A circular plate of iron which is suspended over a fire and upon which cakes are baked.

Girdle (gǭ·ɹd'l), *v.* 1582. [f. GIRDLE *sb.*[1]] **1.** *trans.* To surround with a girdle. Also with *about, in, round.* (Chiefly *transf.* and *fig.*) **2.** To cut through or remove the bark of a tree in a circle extending round the trunk, either to kill it, or to render it more fruitful. Also with *round.* 1662.

1. The Noble Talbot, Who now is girdled with a waste of Iron, And hem'd about with grim destruction 1 *Hen. VI*, IV. iii. 20.

Girdler (gǭ·ɹdləɹ). ME. [f. GIRDLE *sb.*[1] + -ER[1].] **1.** A maker of girdles. **2.** One that encompasses 1879.

Girdlestead (gǭ·ɹd'lste:d). *arch.* ME. [f. as prec. + STEAD *sb.*] That part round which the girdle passes; the waist. **b.** Used for 'lap' 1882.

Smalish in the girdilstede CHAUCER.

Gire, var. of GYRE.

Girkin, obs. f. GHERKIN.

Girl (gǭɹl), *sb.* [The ME. vars. *gurle, girle, gerle* suggest an original *ŭ*, and an OE. **gyrela, *gyrele* has been proposed, based on **ȝur-*, repr. prob. in LG. *gör* n. boy, girl, also *göre* fem.; but, as with *boy, lad,* and *lass,* certainty is not attainable on the evidence.] †**1.** A child or young person of either sex. Chiefly in *pl.* ME. only. **2.** A female child; applied to all young unmarried women 1530. **b.** A maid-servant 1668. **c.** A sweetheart. Also (*U.S. colloq.*) *best g.* 1791. †**3.** A roebuck in its second year –1726. **4.** *attrib.* 1589.

1. *Knave g.*: a boy. **2.** *G. Guide*: see GUIDE *sb.* 2 d. *Old g.*: applied *colloq.* to a woman of any age, either disrespectfully or by way of endearment; also to a mare.

Girland, -ond, obs. f. GARLAND.

Gi·rlery. [f. GIRL *sb.* + -ERY.] Girls collectively. LAMB.

Girlhood (gǭ·ɹlhud). 1785. [f. GIRL *sb.* + -HOOD.] The state or time of being a girl; girls collectively.

Girlie (gǭ·ɹli). 1860. [See -IE, -Y[6].] A little girl.

Girlish (gǭ·ɹliʃ), *a.* 1565. [f. GIRL *sb.* + -ISH[1].] Of or pertaining to a girl or to girlhood; characteristic of or like a girl.

G. laughter DRAYTON. **Gi·rlish·ly** *adv.*, **-ness.**

Girn (gǭɹn), *v.* ME. [Metathetic form of GRIN *v.*] **1.** *intr.* To show the teeth in rage, pain, disappointment, etc.; to be fretful or peevish. Now only *north.* and *Sc.* †**2.** To show the teeth in laughing; to grin –1711. Hence **Girn** *sb.* a snarl; †also (*rare*) = GRIN *sb.*[2]

‖**Giro** (dʒī·ro) 1607. [It., = round, circuit.] A tour, circuit; a 'turn'.

Gironde (ʒirǭ·nd, dʒirǫ·nd). 1876. [See next.] The Girondist party.

Girondist (dʒirǫ·ndist), *sb.* (*a.*) 1801. [– Fr. *Girondiste* (now *Girondin*), f. *Gironde* (see def.) + *-iste* -IST.] A member of the moderate republican party (in the French assembly 1791–1793); its leaders were the deputies from the department of the Gironde. Also *attrib.* or *adj.*

‖**Girouette** (ʒiruẹ·t). 1822. [Fr., = weather cock, -vane.] A weather-cock. Also *fig.*

Girrock. ?*Obs.* [Of unkn. origin.] A sea-fish, *Acus major.* RAY.

Girt (gǭɹt), *sb.* 1563. [var. (XVI) of GIRTH *sb.* surviving in techn. uses, infl. by pa. pple. *girt* of GIRD *v.*[1]] = GIRTH *sb.*[1] 1, 2, 6. Also *attrib.*

Girt (gǭɹt), *v.* Now *rare.* ME. [f. GIRT *sb.* (prec.), infl. by pa. pple. *girt* of GIRD *v.*[1]] **1.** *trans.* = GIRD *v.*[1] **2.** To measure the girth of; also *intr.* 1663. **3.** Of trees, etc.: To measure (so much) in girth or girt 1750.

1. The..Ceremony..consisted.. in Girting the Grand Signior with a Sword 1688. **3.** The tree 'girts' eighteen and a half feet, and spreads over a hundred O. W. HOLMES. Phr. *To g. against*: to press against (said of a ship's cable).

Girt (gǭɹt), *ppl. a.* 1627. [pa. pple. of GIRD *v.*[1]] **1.** In senses of GIRD *v.*[1] 1791. **2.** *Naut.* Said of a ship which is moored so rigidly by her cables, extending from the hawse to two distant anchors, as to be prevented from swinging or turning about.

Girth (gĕɹþ), *sb.* [ME. *gerth* = ON. *gjǫrð* girdle, girth, hoop (:– **ȝerðu*) = Goth. *gairda* girdle :– Gmc. **ȝerdō.* See GARTH, GIRD *v.*[1], GIRDLE.] **1.** A belt or band of leather or cloth, placed round the body of a horse, etc. and drawn tight, so as to secure a saddle, pack, etc. upon its back. **2.** Measurement round the human body, the trunk of a tree, or any object which is more or less circular 1664. **3.** *Mining.* 'A horizontal brace in the direction of the drift' (Raymond) 1881. **4.** *transf.* That part of a horse where the girth is fastened 1846. **5.** *fig.* Something that encircles 1871. **6.** *U.S.* 'A small horizontal beam or girder' (Webst.) 1864.

2. A leafy olive..pillar-like in g. COWPER. **5.** Girdled about with the round sea's g. As a town with its wall SWINBURNE.

Girth (gǭɹþ), *v.* 1450. [f. GIRTH *sb.*] **1.** *trans.* To gird, surround, encompass. **2.** To fit or bind with a girth 1580. **3.** To secure by means of a girth 1819. **4.** To draw (a string) close round a surface which is being measured. Also *absol.* 1825. **5.** *intr.* To measure in girth 1858.

Gi·rth-we:b. ME. [f. GIRTH *sb.* + WEB *sb.*] Woven material of which girths are made; a band made of this.

Gi·rt-li:ne. 1769. [The first element (later also *gant-*) is unexplained.] *Naut.* A rope taken up to the mast-head from which the stay leads, and rove through a block, to hoist up the rigging. Also (erron.) **Ga·ntline.**

Girtonian (gəɹtōᵘ·niăn). 1887. [f. *Girton* + -IAN.] One who is, or has been a student at Girton, a Cambridge college for women.

†**Gis, jis.** 1528. [Minced f. *Jesus.*] An oath or exclam.: *By Gis!* see *Haml.* IV. v. 58.

Gisarme (gizā·ɹm). *Obs.* exc. *Hist.* ME. [– OFr. *g(u)isarme, wisarme* – Frankish *wīs-arm* 'guide-arm', cf. OS. *wīsian* (= OE. *wīsan,* OHG. *wīsen*) show, teach.] A kind of battle-axe, bill, or halberd, having a long blade in line with the shaft, sharpened on both sides and ending in a point.

Gise (dʒəis), *v. dial.* 1695. [var. of, or back-formation from GIST *v.*] To put cattle out to grass at so much per head.

Gise, obs. f. GUISE *sb.*

†**Gi·sel.** ME. only. [– ON. *gisl* = OE. *ǧīs(e)l,* OS., OHG. *gīsal* (G. *geisel*).] A hostage.

Gisement (dʒəi·zmĕnt). 1695. [var. of *gistment,* aphetic of AGISTMENT.] Cattle taken in to graze at a certain price; also, the money received for this.

Gismondine, gismondite (gizmǫ·ndin, -əit). 1823. [f. Prof. *Gismondi,* who first described it; see -INE[5], -ITE[1] 2 b.] *Min.* A hydrous silicate of aluminium and calcium, found near Rome.

†**Gist,** *sb.*[1] ME. [– OFr. *giste* (mod. *gîte*) resting-place, etc.; related to *gésir, gis-* lie. See GEST *sb.*[3], GIST *sb.*[3]] A halting-place or lodging –1601. Also *pl.* a list of stages in a royal progress –1706.

These Quailes have their set gists, to wit, ordinarie resting and baiting places P. HOLLAND.

†**Gist,** *sb.*[2] 1493. [f. GIST *v.*] = AGISTMENT. –1641.

Gist (dʒist), *sb.*[3] Also (sense 1 only) in later Fr. form †**gît,** corruptly **gite,** †**gîte,** †**jet.** 1726. [– OFr. *gist* (mod. *gît*), 3rd sing. pres. ind. of *gésir* lie (:– L. *jacēre*), as in law-Fr. phr. *cest action gist* this action lies; cf. also phr. *gésir en* consist in, depend on.] **1.** *Law.* The real ground or point (of an action, etc.). **2.** The substance or pith of a matter, the essence 1823.

2. This is the g. Here lies the whole of it COBBETT.

Gist (dʒəist), *v.* Now *dial.* 1483. [aphet. f. AGIST; cf. also GISE *v.*] = AGIST *v.* 1, †2.

Git, var. of GATE *sb.*[3]

‖**Gitano** (dʒitāno; in Sp. χitā·no). 1834. [Sp. repr. pop. L. **Ægyptanus* Egyptian.] A male (Spanish) gipsy. So **Gita·na,** a female gipsy.

†**Gite**[1], **gide.** ME. [app. – OFr. *guite*, some article of clothing (according to Godefroy, a hat).] A dress or gown –1614. ¶ Used by Peele for: Splendour.

She cam after in a gyte of reed CHAUCER.

‖**Gite**[2] (ʒīt). Also **gîte.** *rare.* 1798. [Fr. *gîte*; see GIST *sb.*[1]] A halting-place, lodging.

Gite, gîte: see GIST *sb.*[3]

Gith (giþ). ME. [– L. *gīt, gith, gicti.*] Any plant of the genus *Nigella*, esp. *N. sativa.* **b.** The Corn-cockle, *Lychnis githago* 1597.

Gitter (gi·təɹ). 1876. [G.; = lattice, grating.] *Optics.* A diffraction grating.

Gittern (gi·təɹn), *sb. arch.* ME. [– OFr. *guiterne* (perh. through MDu. *giterne*), obsc. rel. to CITHERN and GUITAR.] A cithern.

Of harpis, luttis, and getarnys ME. Hence †**Gi·ttern** *v.* to play on the g.

‖**Giunta** (dʒu·nta). *Hist.* See also JUNTA [It. *giunta* (= Sp., Pg. *junta*: see JUNTA). f. *giungere* join.] In the Venetian republic a number of patricians chosen to act as assessors to the Council of Ten in emergencies; later, the name of the 60 co-opted members of the council of *pregadi*, by whom the affairs of the state were administered.

†**Giust,** Spenser's quasi-It. sp. of JOUST.

Give (giv), *sb.* 1887. [f. GIVE *v.*] A yielding, giving way.

The apparent 'give' in the weather 1893.

Give (giv), *v.* Infl. **gave** (gēⁱv), **given** (gi·v'n), **giving** (gi·viŋ). [OE. *ġiefan, ġefan* = OFris. *jeva*, OS. *geban* (Du. *geven*), OHG. *geban* (G. *geben*), ON. *gefa*, Goth. *giban* :– Gmc. **ʒeban*, with no certain IE. cognates. OE. *ġ(i)efan* was repr. by ME. *yive, yeve*; the present form with initial g appears *c*1200 and is due to Scand. Cf. the phonetic history of GET.]

I. *trans.* To bestow gratuitously. **1.** To hand over as a present; to confer gratuitously the ownership of on another person. **b.** To render (a service) without payment 1719. **2.** To confer, grant, or bestow OE. **3.** To bequeath or devise ME. **4.** To sanction the marriage of (a daughter or female ward) OE.

1. Good sir, this ring was giuen me by my wife SHAKS. *absol.* When Maidens sue Men giue like gods SHAKS. **b.** We gave him his passage, that is to say bore his charges DE FOE. **2.** To g. a Lordship 1584, one's heart (see HEART *sb.*), true love TENNYSON. Hee takes pleasure in those gifts, hee gave QUARLES. Phr. *God, Christ g.*, etc. *Give me*: = 'what I would have is —'. G. me the good old times LYTTON. **4.** Take not a wife of another Law nor g. your daughters to men of another Law PURCHAS.

II. To deliver, hand over. **1.** To deliver or hand (something) to a person; to put (food and drink) before a person ME.; to deliver (a message, etc.) 1611. **2.** To commit, consign, entrust OE. **3.** To hand over as a pledge. Also *fig.* to pledge (one's word, etc.). ME.

1. Giue me some Sack SHAKS. *To g. to eat, drink*, etc. (now only *literary*). G. my love to Clive THACKERAY. **2.** We gaf hem the sovrante LYDG. Phr. *To g. into custody*: in recent use, to direct a policeman to take as a prisoner. **3.** I gave them the word of a sailor DOYLE.

III. 1. To make over to another in exchange for something else; to pay (a sum of money); to sell for a price ME. **2.** To hand over to a superior; to pay (taxes, tithes, etc.). *Obs.* exc. with Biblical reference. OE.

1. For as much money as it is worth he shall g. it me *Gen.* 23:9. Phr. *To g. (one) as good as he brings, to g. (one) his due* (DUE *sb.* 2), *a Roland for an Oliver. To g. the world, etc., one's ears* (see EAR). **2.** Is it lawful to g. tribute unto Cæsar *Matt.* 22:17.

IV. 1. To sacrifice for some object. Also *refl.* ME. **2.** To devote, dedicate. Also to consign *to*, to commend *to* ME. **3.** To addict, devote oneself *to* ME.

1. The Abbots of Peterborough..had given their lives in the cause of England FREEMAN. **2.** Thus I let you go, And giue you to the Gods *Ant. & Cl.* III. ii. 64. **3.** To my great task..I gave me wholly CARY.

V. 1. To put forth from oneself ME. **b.** *absol.* or *intr.* To deal a blow, make an attack or charge (*at, on, upon*). *Obs.* exc. in *Pugilism.* ME. **2.** To make, esp. suddenly; to put forth, emit ME. **3.** To put forth in words; to address (words) *to*; to impose and make known; to pronounce (a blessing, curse) ME. **4.** To deliver authoritatively; to award (costs, etc.) *to, against* ME. **5.** *pa. pple.* (cf. DATE *sb.*[2]): Dated ME. **6.** To provide as host 1523.

1. Phr. *To g. a kiss, a blow, look, push*, etc.; also *a scolding*, etc. *To g. the point* (Sword exercise): to make a direct thrust. *To g. a broadside, a volley, a shot* (see the sbs.). *To g. fire* (see FIRE *sb.*). **2.** They..gave three cheers 1822. Some bitter notes my harp would g. TENNYSON. **3.** G. them good words DE FOE. To g. the word of command 1890. Phr. *To g.* (= to wish) *good day, a merry Christmas*, etc. (now *obsolescent*). Hence (now *dial.*) *To g. the (time of) day (to)*: to salute with 'good morning', 'good evening', etc. (as the case may be). **4.** Judgment had been given against him MACAULAY. Phr. *To g. the case* (idiomatically *to g. it*): to declare *for* or *against*. The umpire gave (= declared) it out 1891. **6.** To g. a ball POPE, a dinner TENNYSON, a treat 1892.

VI. 1. To present; to hold out to be taken OE. †**2.** Of one's heart, mind, conscience, etc.: To suggest (to one) *that*; also, to misgive. Also, to prompt (one) *to* do something. –1820. **3.** To expose or offer to view or observation; to mention, include in a list, etc. ME. **b.** To indicate; to state *at* 1665. †**4.** To display as an armorial bearing; to bear –1640. **5.** To represent. †Also refl.: To present itself as. 1607. **6.** To read, recite, sing, act in the presence of auditors or spectators 1460. **7.** To offer as a sentiment or toast 1728.

1. To g. the breast to a child PURCHAS, sails to the wind S. ROGERS. He holds out his hand; she gives her own HAWTHORNE. **3.** So can I giue no reason SHAKS. The far-off farms..gave no sign of life 1889. **b.** He gives the average..at 0·81 lbs. 1856. **4.** Teare the Lyons out of England's Coat;..giue Sheepe in Lyons stead SHAKS. **6.** Who will g. us a song THACKERAY.

VII. To communicate, impart 1470; to supply 1639.

The broom which gives their title to the Plantagenets M. PATTISON. Phr. *To g.* (a person) *a piece of one's mind* (colloq.): usually, to express emphatically one's disapprobation. *To g. to the world, to the public*: to publish. *To g.* (a person) *to believe, understand*, etc.: to impart to him that which will lead him to believe, etc.

VIII. 1. To allot, apportion OE.; to assign (a name) ME. **2.** To ascribe, assign 1559. **3.** In pa. pple. (cf. GIVEN *ppl. a.*): Posited as a basis of calculation or reasoning 1667.

1. He was given the contract 1891. To give a child a name PURCHAS. **2.** They give it [a pamphlet] to Lord Camden BURKE. †*To g. for*: to set down as. All gave her for a Papist MARVELL.

IX. 1. To yield as a product or result ME. †**2.** To fetch (a price) –1799. †**3.** Of experience, reasoning, etc.: To yield the conclusion *that.* Of a name: To import. –1677.

1. The lamps gave an uncertain light 1891. [His] name in Hebrew characters gives 666—the mystic number of the Antichrist 1890.

X. 1. To cause to have; to produce in a person or thing. Said both of persons and things. ME. ¶**2.** *To give to reflect, think*: to supply material for reflection or thought. (A Gallicism.) 1890.

1. Finding the Army a meere Chaos, he had given it forme MORYSON. *refl.* We ought not to g. ourselves airs JOWETT.

IX. 1. To concede, yield 1548. **2.** *intr.* To yield, give way. **a.** To yield to pressure or strain 1577. **b.** Of a joint, the nerves, etc.: To lose tension, become relaxed, fail 1892. **c.** (Of persons): To accommodate one's attitude *to*; (of a dress) to adjust itself *to*. Also, to allow free play *to*. Also, to give ground. 1823. **d.** To be affected by atmospheric influences; (*a*) of colours, to fade 1546; (*b*) to deliquesce, effloresce, soften, etc. from damp 1677; (*c*) to become damp, exude moisture 1590; (*d*) of timber, to shrink from dryness 1627. **e.** Of frosty weather: To become mild, to thaw 1678.

1. They never gave their enemies one daye to repose HALL. She said she would never g. the *pas* to a tradesman's daughter THACKERAY. **2. a.** My boots had begun to g. 1872. **b.** Rendered..useless by his knee giving 1892. **c.** Dare we to this fancy g. TENNYSON. **d.** *fig.* Flinty mankinde: whose eyes do neuer giue But thorow Lust and Laughter SHAKS.

XII. *intr.* †**1.** Of the sun: To direct its rays 1616. **2.** To look, open, lead. (A Gallicism.) 1840.

2. No window giving on to the Street 1885.

XIII. Phrases.

1. G. birth to. a. To bear; bring forth. **b.** *fig.* To produce; result in. **2. G. ground. a.** To retire before a superior force. **b.** *fig.* To yield; to relax effort. **3. G. it. a.** With *dat.* or *to*: To make an attack. Also colloq., *to g. it hot.* †**b.** = *to g. tongue* (see TONGUE). **4. G. place** (const. *to*). †**a.** To give ground. **b.** To yield precedence. †**c.** To defer (to advice). **d.** To be succeeded or superseded (by another person or thing). **5. G. rise to.** To be the origin of; to produce. **6. G. way. a.** Of fighting men: = *g. ground.* Also *transf.* and *fig.* Const. *to.* †**b.** To make way. **c.** To be superseded by. Const. *to.* †**d.** To allow free scope or liberty of action *to.* **e.** Of things: To yield, break down, fail. **f.** Of persons: To make concessions; to defer to the will of another. Const. *to.* **g.** To abandon oneself *to.* **h.** To allow one's self-control or fortitude to be broken down. **i.** Of stocks and shares: To fall in price. **j.** *Naut.* The order to renew rowing, or to row harder.

XIV. Used *intr.* with preps. in specialized senses.

†**1. G. against—.** To impinge against; to attack, run counter to. †**1. G. into —.** [After Fr. *donner dans.*] To enter into, fall in with; to engage deeply in; to fall into. Now repl. by *g. in to.*

XV. Idiomatically combined with adverbs.

1. G. about. †**a.** *trans.* To encompass (L. *circumdare*). **b.** To distribute; to spread (a rumour). **2. G. again. a.** *trans.* To g. back or in return. **b.** *intr.* To soften; to yield. *lit.* and *fig.* **3. G. away. a.** *trans.* To alienate from oneself by gift; to dispose of gratuitously. **b.** To hand (a bride) to the bridegroom at a marriage. †**c.** To sacrifice (another's interest or rights). **d.** *slang.* To betray, expose to detection or ridicule; to let slip (a secret). **e.** To distribute. **f.** = *g. way* (now *U.S.*). **4. G. back. a.** *trans.* To restore; to surrender again; to reciprocate; to reflect, to echo, etc. †**b.** *intr.* To retreat. †**c.** To yield to pressure. **5. G. forth.** †**a.** *trans.* To hold out. **b.** To emit. **c.** To spread abroad ;to report, rumour. **6. G. in. a.** *intr.* To yield; to acknowledge oneself beaten. **b.** To yield *to* (a habit, opinion, etc.). [prob. due to a false analysis of *give into* (see XIV. 2).] †**c.** To intervene. Also, to rush into conflict. **d.** *trans.* To hand in, deliver to the proper person. *To g. in one's adhesion to*: to notify formally one's acceptance of. **e.** To bestow in addition. **7. G. off.** †**a.** *trans.* To relinquish; to leave off. †**b.** *intr.* To cease; to withdraw. **c.** *trans.* To emit. **d.** To send off as a branch. †**8. G. on.** *intr.* To make an assault. **9. G. out. a.** *trans.* To utter, publish; to report, proclaim. **b.** To announce (a hymn) to be sung; to read out for the congregation to sing. **c.** To emit. †Also, to put forth, utter (prayers). **d.** To issue; to distribute. **e.** *intr.* Of persons: To desist (now, to desist through exhaustion of strength or patience). **f.** Of a limb, a machine, etc.: To break down, fail. Of a supply: To fail. **10. G. over. a.** *trans.* To leave off, finish; to give up. **b.** *absol.* or *intr.* To cease; desist. †**c.** *trans.* To abandon, desert. **d.** To devote, resign, surrender, hand over. **e.** To pronounce incurable so far as concerns the speaker. **f.** To abandon the hope of seeing, finding, overtaking, etc. Also, *To g. over for (dead, lost)*: cf. FOR A. VI. **11. G. up. a.** *trans.* To resign, surrender; to hand over. †Also *ellipt.*, to yield (precedence) to. **b.** To forsake, relinquish, desist from, relinquish the prospect of; to cease to have to do with (a person); to sacrifice (one's life). **c.** *intr.* To leave off; to cease from effort; to stop. Also, to succumb. **d.** *trans.* To devote entirely *to*; to abandon, addict *to.* †**e.** To give in (an account, etc.); to present (a petition, etc.). **f.** To emit; to utter (a cry). *Obs.* exc. in *To g. up the ghost.* **g.** To divulge. **h.** (*a*) To pronounce incurable, insoluble as far as concerns the speaker. (*b*) To renounce the hope of seeing. *To g. up for (lost)*: cf. FOR A.VI.

Give and take, *sb.* 1769. [See GIVE *v.*] **1.** *Sporting.* **a.** In *give and take plate*, a prize for a race in which horses above a standard height carry more, and those under it less, than the standard weight. **b.** Implying the alternation of favourable and unfavourable conditions 1769. **2.** Compromise, exchange of equivalents. Also *attrib.* 1816. **3.** Exchange of talk, esp. of repartee, jest, or raillery 1837.

Give, obs. f. GYVE.

Given (giv'n), *ppl. a.* ME. [pa. pple. of GIVE *v.*] **1.** Bestowed as a gift. **2.** Used predicatively: Inclined, addicted, prone. Const. *to.* ME. **3.** Granted as a basis of calculation, reasoning, etc.; definitely stated, fixed, specified 1570.

1. G. goods never prosper 1892. Phr. *Given name*: the name given at baptism, the Christian name. ?Chiefly *Sc.* and *U.S.* **2.** I'm not g. that way myself 1885.

Giver (gi·vəɹ). ME. [f. GIVE *v.* + -ER[1].] One who gives. Often specialized as *alms-*, *law-*, etc. *g.*

Giving (gi·viŋ), *vbl. sb.* ME. [f. GIVE *v.* and -ING[1].] The action of GIVE *v.* **1.** In trans. senses. Occas. *pl.* **2.** In intr. senses 1710. **3.** With adverbs, as *giving in, over, out*, etc. Also *giving way*. 1530. †**4.** *concr.* That which is given; a gift –1667.

1. His gains were sure; his givings rare POPE. **2.** Upon the first G. of the Weather ADDISON. **4.** MILT. *P. L.* VI. 730.

Gizzard (gi·zăɹd). [ME. *giser* – OFr. *giser*, *gesier*, *juisier*, also *guisier* (mod. *gésier*) :– Rom. **gicerium*, for L. *gigerium*, only in pl. *-ia*. For the final *d* (XVI), cf. †*garnard*, var. of *garner*, and dial. *scholard*, var. of *scholar*.] **1.** The second or muscular stomach of birds, in which the food is ground, after being mixed with gastric juice in the proventriculus or first stomach. **b.** The stomach of the red Irish trout 1776. **c.** *Entom.* The proventriculus of certain insects 1826. **d.** *Zool.* The thickened muscular stomach of certain molluscs 1841. **2.** Attributed joc. to persons 1668. ¶**3.** Used to translate L. *jecur*, liver. CHAUCER. **4.** *attrib.*, as *g.-trout*; etc. 1765.

2. Phr. *To fret one's g.*: to worry oneself. *To stick in one's g.*: to remain as something unpleasant or distasteful. Don't let that stick in your g. SWIFT.

‖**Glabella** (glăbe·lă), **glabellum** (glăbe·lŏm). 1823. [mod.L.; spec. application of L. *glabella, -um*, fem. and n. of *glabellus* adj., dim. of *glaber* smooth. Cf. Fr. *glabelle*.] **1.** *Anat.* The space between the eyebrows and immediately above a line from one to the other. **2.** 'The smooth median portion of the cephalic shield of a Trilobite' (*Syd. Soc. Lex.*) 1849. Hence **Glabe·llar** *a.* pertaining to the g. **Glabello-**, comb. f. GLABELLA, 'pertaining to the g. and —'.

Glabrate (glē^i·brĕt), *ppl. a.* 1857. [f. L. *glabrus* glabrous + -ATE[2].] *Bot.* and *Zool.* Smooth; bald; glabrous; having no hair or other appendages.

Glabreity (gle^ibrī·ĭti). 1885. [– Fr. *glabréité*.] Smoothness; baldness. var. †**Gla·brity.** (Dicts.)

Glabrescent (gle^ibre·sĕnt), *a.* 1857. [f. L. *glaber* glabrous + -ESCENT.] *Bot.* Used of a surface, hairy when young, but smooth when mature.

Glabrous (glē^i·brəs), *a.* 1640. [f. L. *glaber* + -OUS.] Free from hair, down, or the like; smooth. Now only as a scientific term.

‖**Glacé** (glase), *a.* 1850. [Fr., pa. pple. of *glacer* ice, give a gloss to, f. *glace* ice.] **1.** Having a smooth surface with a high polish. Also *absol.* = *g. silk*, and *attrib.* as *g. finish*. **2.** Of fruits: Covered with icing 1882.

†**Gla·ciable.** [f. L. *glaciare* freeze + -BLE.] That may be frozen. SIR T. BROWNE.

Glacial (glē^i·ʃiăl, -ʃăl), *a.* 1656. [– Fr. *glacial* or L. *glacialis* icy, f. *glacies* ice; see -AL[1].] **1.** Full of, or having the nature of, ice; icy. *rare.* **b.** Consisting of ice 1794. **2.** Glass-like; crystallized. (*Obs.* exc. as in quots.) 1681. **3.** *Geol.* Characterized by the presence of ice 1846. **b.** Produced by glacier-ice, or by its action; pertaining to glaciers or ice-sheets 1858.

1. *fig.* His manner..g. and sepulchral MOTLEY. **b.** Enormous g. masses 1794. **2.** *G. acetic acid*, pure acetic acid in crystals; *g. phosphoric acid*, metaphosphoric acid (HPO_3); *g. sulphuric acid*, †*g. oil of vitriol*, pure sulphuric acid in crystals. **3.** *G. epoch, era, period* (called also in U.S. *drift epoch, ice-age*, etc.), a geological period during which the northern hemisphere was largely covered by an ice-sheet. *G. sea*: the sea of the g. epoch. **b.** G. denudation HUXLEY.

Hence **Gla·cialism,** the theory of the action of ice upon the earth's surface. **Gla·cialist,** a student of g. phenomena; one who explains certain geological phenomena as due to g. action. **Gla·cially** *adv.* by means of g. action; icily (*lit.* and *fig.*).

Glaciate (glē^i·ʃi,e^it), *v.* 1623. [– *glaciat-*, pa. ppl. stem of L. *glaciare* freeze, f. *glacies* ice; see -ATE[3].] **1.** To freeze. *trans* and †*intr.* **2.** *Geol.* In pa. pple. *glaciated*. **a.** Rubbed or polished by glacial action 1865. **b.** Furnished with glaciers 1880. **3.** *techn.* 'To give an ice-like or frosted appearance to' 1887. Hence **Glacia·tion,** †freezing; †a result of this; *Geol.* the condition of being covered by an ice-sheet or by glaciers; glacial action or its result.

Glacier (glæ·siəɹ, glē^i·ʃ^iəɹ). 1744. [– Fr. *glacier*, earlier *glacière* (an Alpine word), f. *glace* ice :– Rom. **glacia*, for L. *glacies* ice.] An immense mass or river of ice in a high mountain valley, formed by the descent and consolidation of the snow that falls on the higher ground. Also *attrib.*, as *g.-drift, -moraine, -water*, etc.

Comb.: **g.-mill** = MOULIN; **-mud,** an unstratified mass of coarse gritty mud, containing pebbles, boulder, and stony particles, found resting on the surface of ice-worn rocks; **-silt** = *glacier-mud*; **-snow,** the snow at the upper end of a g., not yet hardened into ice by pressure; **-table,** a flat mass of rock, raised high upon a column of ice.

Hence **Gla·ciered** *ppl. a.* covered with glaciers. **Gla·cierist,** one who studies glaciers WHEWELL.

†**Gla·cious,** *a.* [– Fr. †*glacieux*, f. *glace* ice; see -IOUS.] Resembling ice. SIR T. BROWNE.

Glacis (glē^i·sis, glasi). 1672. [– Fr. *glacis*, f. OFr. *glacier* slide, f. *glace* ice; see GLACIER. Cf. ABATIS.] **1.** A gently sloping bank. **2.** *Fortif.* 'The parapet of the covered way extended in a long slope to meet the natural surface of the ground, so that every part of it shall be swept by the fire of the ramparts' (Voyle) 1688.

†**Glad,** *sb.* OE. [f. the adj.] Gladness, joy –1608.

Glad (glæd), *a.* [OE. *glæd* = OS. *glad* (in comp. *gladmōd*), ON. *glaðr* bright, joyous. The orig. sense survives in OHG. *glat* (G. *glatt*) smooth; Gmc. **ʒladaz* is rel. to L. *glaber* smooth, glabrous.] †**1.** Bright, shining, beautiful –1500. **2.** †Cheerful in disposition; joyful, happy (*arch.*) OE. **3.** = FAIN *a.*; pleased. Now only *predicative*. OE. **4.** Of feelings, looks, etc.: Filled with, marked by, or expressive of joy or delight OE. †**b.** Acceptable –1690. **5.** Full of brightness or beauty; suggesting feelings of delight 1667. **6.** quasi-*adv.* = GLADLY *adv.* (*poet.*) ME.

2. Be mirry and glaid, honest and vertewous DUNBAR. Often, g. no more, We wear a face of joy, because We have been g. of yore WORDSW. **3.** A wise son maketh a g. father *Prov.* 10:1. Phr. *G. of*: †(*a*) made happy, pleased with (a thing possessed); (*b*) = g. to have or get; (*c*) joyful on account of (an event, etc.). Also const. *at, for*, †*in*, †*with*. When his heart is g. Of the full harvest TENNYSON. I am g. I came 1855. I was g. to see the mangrove-belt 1897. **4.** So yong so lusty with hire eyen glade CHAUCER. *Luke* 8:1. *G. eye*: see EYE *sb.*[1] I. 4. *G. rags* (U.S. slang), (one's) best or ceremonial clothes; esp. evening dress 1904. **5.** G. Eevning and g. Morn crownd the fourth day MILT.

Glad (glæd), *v.* Pa. t. and pple. **gladded.** [OE. *gladian* intr. = ON. *glaða* trans.; f. **ʒladaz*; see GLAD *a.*] †**1.** *intr.* To become or to be glad –1622. **2.** *trans.* To make glad OE. Also *transf.* and *refl.* (now *arch.*).

2. They were greatly gladded thereat BUNYAN. *transf.* Now bright Arcturus glads the teeming grain POPE.

Gladden (glæ·d'n), *v.* ME. [f. GLAD *a.* + -EN[5].] **1.** *intr.* To be glad; to rejoice; ? *Obs.* **2.** *trans.* To make glad, joyous, or bright 1558.

1. As we climb Hills and g. as we climb BLOOMFIELD. **2.** [An orchard] gladdened..by flushes of almond and double peach blossom RUSKIN.

†**Gladder.** ME. [f. GLAD *v.* + -ER[1].] **1.** One who rejoices. ME. only. **2.** One who makes glad –1700.

Gladdon (glæ·d'n). Now chiefly *dial.* [OE. *glædene* – **gladina*, f. L. GLADIOLUS.] Pop. name of the iris (*Iris pseudacorus* and *Iris fœtidissima*). *Corn-g.* = CORN-FLAG. Also *attrib.*

†**Glade,** *sb.*[1] ME. [perh. of Scand. origin; cf. Sw. dial. *gladas, gla(d)na* set (of the sun), Norw. dial. *gla* set (of sun and moon).] *To go to g.*: to set, sink to rest (said of the sun) –1788.

Glade (glē^id), *sb.*[2] 1529. [Of unkn. origin; cf. synon. †*glode* (XIV).] **1.** A clear open space or passage in a wood or forest. **2.** *U.S.* **a.** An everglade 1644. **b.** An opening in the ice of rivers or lakes, or a place left unfrozen. (*Local, U.S.*) 1698. †**3.** A clear or bright space in the sky; a flash –1741.

Comb.: **g.-net,** a net hung across an opening in a wood, for the purpose of snaring birds.

Gladen(e, var. of GLADDON.

Gladful (glæ·dful), *a.* ME. [f. GLAD *sb.* + -FUL.] Full of gladness or joy. Now only *arch.* Hence **Gla·dful-ly** *adv.*, **-ness.**

Gladiate (glē^i·diĕt), *a.* 1793. [f. L. *gladius* + -ATE[2].] *Bot.* Sword-shaped, as the leaves of an iris.

Gladiator (glæ̆·diē^itəɹ). 1541. [– L. *gladiator*, f. *gladius* sword; see -ATOR.] **1.** *Roman Hist.* One who fought with a sword or other weapon at public shows. Also *fig.* †**2.** A professional swordsman or fencer –1769.

1. *fig.* The gladiators in the lists of power feel.. the presence of worth EMERSON. Hence **Gla:diato·rial, Gladiato·rian** *adjs.* of or pertaining to gladiators; also *fig.* **Gla·diatorism,** the practice of fighting after the fashion of gladiators; also *fig.* **Gla·diatorship,** the occupation or skill of a g. So †**Gla·diature,** gladiatorship.

†**Gla·diatory.** 1602. [– L. *gladiatorius*, f. *gladiator*; see -ORY.]

A. *adj.* Gladiatorial –1730.

B. *sb.* Gladiatorial art or practice. Also *fig.* 1653.

Gladiole (glæ·diō^ul). ME. [– L. *gladiolus*; see next.] = next.

‖**Gladiolus** (glædəi·ŏləs, glædiō^u·ləs). *Pl.* **-i, -uses.** OE. [– L. *gladiolus* (Pliny), dim. of *gladius* sword.] **1.** †**a.** The corn-flag or GLADDON. **b.** An iridaceous plant having sword-shaped leaves and spikes of brilliant flowers. **2.** *Anat.* 'The second piece or body of the sternum' (*Syd. Soc. Lex.*) 1885.

‖**Gladius** (glē^i·diŏs). 1520. [L.] **1.** A sword (*nonce-use*) 1873. **2.** The sword-fish. **3.** *Anat.* 'The horny endoskeleton or pen of cuttle-fishes' (*Syd. Soc. Lex.*) 1872.

Gladless (glæ·dlės), *a.* *rare.* 1590. [f. GLAD *sb.* + -LESS.] Devoid of gladness or joy.

Gladly (glæ·dli), *a.* *Obs.* exc. *arch.* OE. [f. as prec. + -LY[1]; in later use f. GLAD *a.*] †**a.** Bright, beautiful, precious. OE. only. **b.** Glad, joyous.

Gladly (glæ·dli), *adv.* Compared **gla·dlier, gla·dliest**; also (now usually) with *more, most.* OE. [f. GLAD *a.* + -LY[2].] **1.** With gladness or joy. Also, willingly, with alacrity. †**2.** Aptly, naturally –1483.

1. Will you doe this g. and willingly *Bk. Com. Prayer.* So **Gla·dness,** joy, rejoicing; †also, alacrity (in action). †**Gla·dship,** gladness.

Gladsome (glæ·dsŏm), *a.* ME. [orig. f. GLAD *sb.* + -SOME[1]; later apprehended as being f. GLAD *a.*] **1.** Productive of gladness; cheering, pleasant. **2.** Expressive of, or characterized by, gladness. Also *transf.* of nature, etc. ME. **3.** Having a glad or joyous nature or mood; filled with gladness ME.

1. G. tidings SPEED. **2.** G. countenances 1832. The g. sunshine 1868. **3.** Like g. birds in May WORDSW. Hence **Gla·dsome-ly** *adv.*, **-ness.**

Gladstone (glæ·dstən). 1864. [f. W. E. *Gladstone* (1808–98).] **a.** *Gladstone* (*claret*): a jocular name for the light French wines which Gladstone sought to popularize by a reduction of the Customs duty in 1860. **b.** *G.* (*bag*): a light kind of travelling-bag 1882. **c.** 'A roomy four-wheeled pleasure carriage with two inside seats, calash top, and seats for driver and footman' (Webster) 1864.

Gladstonian (glædstō^u·niăn). 1847. [f. prec. + -IAN.]

A. *adj.* Belonging to or characteristic of W. E. Gladstone; *spec.* (since 1886) the designation of the party which supported Gladstone's proposals for establishing Home Rule in Ireland 1861.

B. *sb.* **1.** A supporter of Gladstone; a member of the Gladstonian party 1847. **2.** = GLADSTONE a. 1864.

Gladwin(e, -wyn, vars. of GLADDON.

Gla·dy, *a.* *rare.* 1837. [f. GLADE *sb.*[2] + -Y[1].] Glade-like; full of glades.

Glair (glē^əɹ), *sb.*[1] ME. [– (O)Fr. *glaire* :– med.L. *glarea*, obscure var. of **clarea*, subst. use of fem. of L. adj. *clarus* clear.] **1.** The white of an egg. Also a technical term for preparations made from the whites of eggs. **2.** *transf.* Anything viscid or slimy 1529. Hence **Glai·reous** *a.* glairy. **Glairi·genous** *a.* producing slime, mucus, or glairin.

†**Glair,** *sb.*[2] [– OFr. *glaire* :– L. *glarea*.] Gravel. CAXTON.

Glair (glēəɹ), *v.* 1563. [f. GLAIR *sb.*[1]] *trans.* To smear with glair; †also *gen.* to daub.

Glairin (glēə·rin). Also **-ine.** 1838. [f. GLAIR *sb.*[1] + -IN[1].] A glairy organic substance found in many mineral waters after exposure to the air.

Glairy (glēə·ri), *a.* 1662. [f. GLAIR *sb.*[1] + -Y[1].] Of the nature of glair; viscid, slimy. Chiefly *Path.* Hence **Glai·riness,** viscidity.

Glaive (glēiv), *sb.* ME. [– (O)Fr. *glaive*, †*glavie* †lance, (now) sword, presumed to be – L. *gladius* sword; but the sense 'lance' (which is also that of MHG., MDu. *glavie*) is not thus accounted for.] †**1.** A lance or spear –1592. †**b.** A lance set up as winning-post in a race, and given as a prize to the winner; hence, a prize –1555. †**2.** A weapon consisting of a blade fastened to a long handle; a soldier armed with a glaive –1678. **3.** A sword; *esp.* a broadsword. *arch.* and *poet.* 1470.

3. The g. and brown-bill, the good old weapons of his country SCOTT.

Glamour (glæ·məɹ), *sb.* Also †**glamer.** 1720. [Alteration of GRAMMAR with the sense of GRAMARYE; introduced by Scott. For the form with *gl-* cf. med.L. *glomeria* grammar, *glomerellus* schoolboy learning grammar.] **1.** Magic, enchantment, spell. **2.** A magical or fictitious beauty attaching to any person or object; a delusive or alluring charm 1840. **3.** *attrib.*, as *g.-gift, -might* 1805.

1. When devils, wizards or jugglers deceive the sight, they are said to cast *g.* o'er the eyes of the spectator A. RAMSAY. **2.** That scene of g. HOOD. Hence **Gla·morous** *a.* full of g. **Gla·morously** *adv.* **Gla·mour** *v.* to affect with g. var. **Gla·moury, -ie.**

Glance (glɑns), *sb.*[1] 1503. [f. GLANCE *v.*[1]] **1.** A swift oblique movement or impact. Also *fig.* ? *Obs.* 1570. †**2.** *fig.* **a.** A satirical hit, a jest *at* (or *upon*) something –1697. **b.** Allusion, reference –1702. **3.** A sudden movement producing a flash or gleam; also, the flash or gleam 1503. **4.** A brief or hurried look 1591.

1. The stroke [in *Cricket*]..best described as the leg g. 1892. **2. a.** This was but the glaunce of Diogenes, who made more accompt of his scoffe then his state FULBECKE. **3.** The ruby g. DUNBAR. Fish..sporting with quick g. MILT. **4.** G. or toy Of amorous intent MILT.

Comb.: **g.-pitch,** a substance of the nature of petroleum in a bituminous form; **-wood,** a hard wood grown in Cuba, and used for carpenters' rules, etc.

Glance (glɑns), *sb.*[2] 1828. [– G. *glanz* lustre, also glance-ore.] A variety of ore having a lustre which indicates its metallic nature. *Obs.* exc. in *antimony-, bismuth-, copper-, iron-, lead-, silver-g.*, q.v.

Comb. **g.-coal,** a variety of anthracite.

Glance (glɑns), *v.*[1] 1450. [The earliest forms *glench, glence, glanch* suggest an alt. of †*glace* (XIV) glance, glide (– OFr. *glacier*; see GLACIS) by crossing with synon. †*glent* (XIII; see GLINT *v.*) and *lanch,* LANCE *v.* Perh. orig. two words.] **1.** *intr.* To strike and glide off an object. †**2.** To move rapidly, esp. in an oblique or transverse direction; to dart, shoot; to spring *aside* –1786. **3.** With reference to discourse: To pass quickly *over*, glide *from, off* 1570. **4.** To cause a flash of light by rapid movement. Of light: To dart, flash, gleam. 1568. **5.** Of the eye: To move quickly, to cast a momentary look, to flash 1583. **6.** *trans.* **a.** To catch a glimpse of 1635. **b.** To convey with a glance (of the eye) 1717. †**7.** To touch obliquely; to graze; also *fig.* –1651. **8. a.** To direct obliquely (*lit.* and *fig.*) 1656. **b.** To emit with a flash or gleam 1746.

1. The blow only glanced on the bone, and scarce drew blood SCOTT. **2.** The warre..glanced into Asia BOLTON. **3.** Verses..wherein he glanced at a certain reverend doctor SWIFT. **4.** In thee [Sion] fresh brooks and soft streams g. MILT. **5.** Phr. *To g. one's eye, look*: †(*a*) to turn aside one's gaze; (*b*) to give a quick look; also, to look quickly *at* or *upon*. **7.** In company I often glanced it *Com. Err.* V. i. 66. **8. a.** To g. an Innuendo SWIFT, a censure at the General CARLYLE. **b.** The..pewter and earthenware..glanced back the flame of the lamp merrily SCOTT. Hence **Gla·ncer** (*nonce-wd.*). **Gla·ncingly** *adv.* in a glancing fashion.

Glance, *v.*[2] *U.S.* 1894. [perh. – Du. *glanzen*, f. *glans* lustre.] To planish (metals).

Gland[1] (glænd). 1631. [– L. *glans, gland-* acorn, perh. through Fr. *gland*.] **1.** An acorn. *Obs.* exc. (occas.) *Bot.* = GLANS 2. **2.** = GLANS 1. 1854.

Gland[2] (glænd). 1692. [– Fr. *glande*, later form of OFr. *glandre*; see GLANDER.] **1.** *Phys.* An organ, composed of nucleated cells, and either simple or complex in structure, which separates from the blood certain constituents for use in the body, or for ejection from it.

Certain organs, such as the spleen, thymus, thyroid, and adrenals, which perform the function of glands but have no excretory duct, are known as DUCTLESS (also *aporic*) glands.

2. *Bot.* A secreting cell or group of cells on the surface of a plant-structure 1785. **3.** *attrib.*, as *g.-cell, -cyst*, etc. 1849. Hence **Gla·ndless** *a.*

Gland[3] (glænd). 1825. [perh. var. of earlier *glam, glan*; cf. Sc. *glaun(d)* 'A clamp of iron or wood'.] *Mech.* **1.** A sleeve employed to press a packing tight on a piston-rod (cf. FOLLOWER) 1839. **2.** A cross-piece or clutch made fast to a shaft, and communicating motion to a machine by engaging with part of the gearing 1825. **3.** *Founding.* **a.** A hooked bar for clamping together the parts of a moulder's flask. **b.** A clip-plate. 1875.

Glander (glæ·ndəɹ). 1483. [– OFr. *glandre* :– L. *glandulæ* pl. throat glands, swollen glands in the neck. See GLANDULE.] †**1.** A glandular swelling about the neck –1523. **2.** *pl.* (const. as *sing.*) (*The*) *glanders*: a contagious disease in horses, marked by swellings beneath the jaw and discharge of mucous matter from the nostrils 1523. **b.** The same disease given to man 1871. Hence **Gla·ndered** *ppl. a.* affected with glanders. **Gla·nderous** *a.* affected with, or of the nature of, glanders.

Glandiferous (glændi·fěrəs), *a.* 1647. [f. L. *glandifer* (f. *glans, gland-* acorn) + -OUS; see -FEROUS.] Bearing acorns or similar fruit.

Glandiform (glæ·ndifǭɹm), *a.* 1822. [f. L. *glans, gland-* acorn + -FORM.] Acorn-shaped; also, resembling a gland.

Glandular (glæ·ndiŭlăɹ), *a.* 1740. [– Fr. *glandulaire*; see GLANDULE, -AR[1].] Of or pertaining to a gland; of the nature of a gland; containing, bearing, or consisting of, a gland or glands.

Glandulation (glændiŭlēi·ʃən). 1760. [f. GLANDULE + -ATION.] 'The mode of occurrence or presence of glands in plants' (*Syd. Soc. Lex.*).

Glandule (glæ·ndiul). Chiefly *pl.* ME. [– L. *glandulæ* pl. glands of the throat, esp. tonsils; in sing. partly through Fr. *glandule*; see GLAND[2], -ULE.] †**1.** A gland –1748. **b.** A small gland 1751. †**2.** *pl.* A swelling of the glands in the throat or neck (so L. *glandulæ*). *rare.* –1616. **3.** A morbid swelling or growth in the body 1656. So **Glanduli·ferous** *a.* bearing glands or glandules. **Gla·nduliform** *a.* having the appearance of a gland or g.

Glandulous (glæ·ndiŭləs), *a.* ?*Obs.* ME. [– (O)Fr. *glanduleux* or med.L. *glandulosus* tumorescent; see prec., -OUS.] Of or pertaining to a gland or glandule; having the nature of a gland; containing, or consisting of, glands. So **Gla·ndulose** *a.* †**Glandulo·sity** (*rare*), a gland-like formation.

‖**Glans** (glænz). 1650. [L. *glans* acorn] **1.** *Anat.* The *glans penis.* **2.** *Bot.* A name for nuts enclosed or surrounded by a cupule, as the acorn, etc. 1704.

Glare (glēəɹ), *sb.*[1] ME. [f. GLARE *v.*] **1.** Dazzling brilliance (of a light, etc.); a strong fierce light. Also *absol.* dazzling or oppressive sunshine, esp. when reflected and unrelieved. **b.** The glistening of some surface 1658. **2.** *fig.* 1706. **3.** A fierce or piercing look 1667.

1. The naked negro, panting at the line..Basks in the g. GOLDSM. **2.** The pomp and g. of rhetoric 1856. **3.** About them round A Lion now he [Satan] stalkes with fierie g. MILT.

Glare (glēəɹ), *sb.*[2] 1567. [Of obscure origin; cf. GLARE *sb.*[1] 1b.] †Frost, icy condition; also *U.S.* a sheet of ice.

Glare (glēəɹ), *a.* *U.S.* Also **glair.** 1856. [perh. prec. used attrib.] Smooth and translucent, glassy. Chiefly of ice.

Glare (glēəɹ), *v.* ME. [– MLG., MDu. *glaren* gleam, glare.] **1.** *intr.* To shine with a brilliant or dazzling light. Also of the light. Also *fig.* **2.** To look fixedly and fiercely (*at, on, upon*) 1609. Also *fig.* **3.** *trans.* To give out or reflect with a glare 1667.

1. Hyt is not al golde that glareth CHAUCER. The morning light glared strangely TYNDALL. *fig.* She glares in Balls, front Boxes, and the Ring POPE. **2.** And each upon his rival glared SCOTT. **3.** Every eye Glar'd lightning MILT.

Glareous (glēə·riəs), *a.*[1] ME. [f. L. *glareosus* (f. *glarea* gravel) + -OUS. Cf. OFr. *glaireus*.] †**a.** Of soil: Gravelly –1675. **b.** *Bot.* Growing in gravel 1880. var. **Gla·reose.**

Glareous, *a.*[2]: cf. GLAIRY.

Gla·ring (glēə·riŋ), *ppl. a.* ME. [f. GLARE *v.* + -ING[2].] **1.** Of the eyes: Staring fiercely and wildly. **2.** That gives out or reflects a dazzling light; excessively bright 1515. **3.** Obtrusively conspicuous. Now chiefly with sbs. like *fault, falsehood*, etc. 1706.

3. This g. absurdity 1812. Hence **Gla·ring-ly** *adv.*, **-ness.**

Glary (glēə·ri), *a.* 1632. [f. GLARE *sb.*[1] + -Y[1].] Full of glare; dazzling, glaring. Hence **Gla·riness.**

Glass (glɑs), *sb.* [OE. *glæs* = OS. *glas, gles*, (O)HG. *glas* :– WGmc. var. of Gmc. *ʒ*lazam*, repr. by ON. *gler* glass, prob. rel. to OE. *glǣr*, MLG. *glār* amber.]

I. As a substance. **1.** A substance, in its ordinary forms transparent, lustrous, hard, and brittle, produced by fusing sand (silica) with soda or potash (or both), usually with the addition of lime, alumina, or lead oxide. **2.** Applied to similar substances 1579. **3.** The substance as made into things. Hence as collect. sing. = things made of glass; e.g. vessels of glass, window-panes, etc. 1625. **b.** *esp.* as used for greenhouses, frames, etc. Hence, greenhouses, etc., collectively. 1838.

1. CROWN-, FLINT-, PLATE-, WATER-G.; also *bottle-, crystal-, cut-g.*, etc. (see the different words). **2.** *G. of Antimony*, a vitreous oxy-sulphide fused. *G. of Borax*, a vitreous transparent substance obtained by exposing to heat the crystals of sodium biborate. *G. of lead*, a g. made with the addition of a large quantity of lead, and used in making counterfeit gems. *G. of phosphorus*, a transparent substance consisting of phosphoric acid, with phosphate, and a little sulphate of lime. **3.** The g. blew in TENNYSON. **b.** Fruit Culture under g. (*title*) 1873.

II. Something made of glass. **1.** A glass vessel or receptacle. (Now usu. *spec.* as in 2.) Also, its contents. ME. **2.** *spec.* A drinking-vessel made of glass; hence, its contents, and *fig.* drink ME. **3.** A SAND-GLASS for measuring time; *esp.* an HOUR-GLASS, and *Naut.* the half-hour glass, the half-minute and quarter-minute glasses 1557. **b.** The time taken by the sand of these to run out. *Naut.* Usually said of the half-hour glass; hence, a glass = half an hour. 1599. **c.** *fig.* 1638. **4.** A pane of glass, esp. the window of a coach; a glazed frame or case (e.g. for protecting plants) ME. **5.** A glass mirror. Also *transf.* and *fig.* ME. **b.** A magic mirror, a crystal, etc. 1566. **6.** A piece of glass shaped for a purpose, a lens, a watch-glass, a burning-glass 1545. **7.** An optical instrument used as an aid to sight; a telescope (more explicitly SPY-, FIELD-, OPERA-GLASS) 1613; a microscope or *magnifying-g.* 1646; an EYE-GLASS; also in *pl.* spectacles 1660. †**8.** *transf.* The eye-ball, the eye (*poet.*) –1621. **9.** A WEATHER-GLASS, a barometer 1688.

2. A deepe g. of Reinish wine SHAKS. **3.** The g. that bids man mark the fleeting hour COWPER. **b.** Our Ship, Which but three glasses since, we gaue out split Is tyte SHAKS. **4.** Bang went the door, up went the g. T. HOOK. **5.** A Fop who admires his Person in a G. ADDISON. *poet.* The cleer Sun on his wide watrie G. Gaz'd hot MILT. **b.** *Macb.* IV. i. 119. **7.** My eyes were so dim, that no glasses would help me WESLEY. **8.** Euen in the glasses of thine eyes I see thy greeued heart SHAKS.

†**III.** [?another word.] = GLOSS *sb.*[2] 1. –1622.

attrib. and *Comb.* **1.** *simple attrib.* **a.** Made of glass; as a *g. vessel, g.-bead factory*, etc. **b.** Glazed, having pieces of glass set in a frame; as G.-COACH, -HOUSE, etc.

2. Special comb.: **g.-artist,** who one designs coloured or stained g. windows; **-bell** = BELL-GLASS; **-blower,** one who blows and fashions g.; **-crab,** the larva of a palinuroid or scyllaroid shrimp; **-culture,** culture of fruit, etc. under g.; **-dust,** powdered g.; **-enamel,** an opaque g., which owes its milkiness to the addition of dioxide of tin; **-faced** *a.*, reflecting, like a mirror, the looks of another; **-furnace; -gall,** a whitish salt scum cast up from g. in a state of fusion; **-gazing** *a.*, given to contemplating oneself in a mirror; **-glazed** *a.*, (of pottery) having a glaze of substantial thickness; **-grenade,** one made with a case of g.; **-height-gauge,** an instrument for measuring the height of watch-glasses; **-metal,** g. in a state of fusion; **-mosaic,** a mosaic formed of small squares of coloured g.; **-mould,** a metallic shaping-box in which g. is pressed or blown to form; **-oven,** a heated chamber for cooling gradually new-made articles of g.; **-paper,** paper covered with finely powdered g. for polishing bone etc.; so **-paper** *v.*; **-pock, -pox,** an eruptive disease, *Varicella coniformis*; **-pot,** a pot or crucible used for fusing the materials of g. in a g.-furnace; **-press,** a device to apply pressure to g. in a mould while plastic; **-rope (sponge),** the genus HYALONEMA; **-sand,** sand used in making g.; **-shell,** a name of certain molluscs, species of *Hyalea*, whose shells look like the thinnest g.; **-shrimp,** a larval form of stomatopodous crustaceans; **-slag,** refuse of g.-manufacture; **-snail,** one of the genus *Vitrina*, having a translucent shell; **-snake,** (*a*) a lizard, *Ophiosaurus ventralis* with a very brittle tail; (*b*) a lizard of the genus *Pseudopus*; **-sponge** = *glass-rope sponge*; **-tinner,** the workman who applies tin-foil to g.; **-ware,** articles made of g.; **-wool,** g. spun out to a very fine fibre; used in the filtration of acids; **-worm,** the glow-worm.

Glass (glas), *v.* 1540. [f. GLASS *sb.*; cf. GLAZE *v.*[1]] **1.** *trans.* = GLAZE *v.*[1] 1. Now *rare.* **2.** To protect by a covering of glass, to enclose in glass 1588. †**3.** = GLAZE *v.*[1] 2. –1661. **4.** To set (an object, oneself) before a mirror; also to see as in a mirror 1586; (of a mirror), to reflect 1628. **5.** *techn.* To dress (leather) with a glassing-machine 1885.

4. Thou glorious mirror, where the Almighty's form Glasses itself in tempests BYRON. Never more Shall the lake g. her, flying over it M. ARNOLD.

Gla·ss-cloth. 1851. **1.** A linen cloth used for drying glass-ware, etc. **2.** A woven fabric made of fine-spun glass thread. (Only as two wds.) 1875. **3.** Cloth covered with powdered glass, used like sand-paper 1873.

†**Glass-coach.** 1667. Original name of a coach with glass windows; esp. applied to a 'private' coach let out for hire, as dist. from those on public stands.

Gla·ss-cu:tter. 1703. **1.** One whose occupation is to cut glass (e.g. to sizes), or to ornament glass-ware by grinding. **2.** A glazier's diamond 1881.

Gla·ssen, gla·zen, *a.* Now *dial*, or *arch.* [OE. *glæsen*, f. *glæs* GLASS *sb.* + -EN[4].] **1.** Made of glass. Also *fig.* **2.** Resembling glass. Of eyes: Glassy, glazed. ME.

2. [The palsied gamester] pursues The Dice with glassen eyes B. JONS.

Glass eye. 1605. †**1.** An eye-glass; usu. *pl.* –1721. **2.** A false eye made of glass 1687. **3.** *Farriery.* A species of blindness in horses 1831. **4. a.** A Jamaican thrush (*Turdus jamaicensis*), so called from its glass-like iris 1847. **b.** *U.S.* The wall-eyed pike (*Stizostedion vitreum*) 1884.

1. Get thee glasse-eyes, and like a scuruy Politician, seeme to see the things thou dost not *Lear* IV. vi. 174.

Glassful (gla·sful), *sb.* Pl. **-fuls.** 1663. [f. GLASS *sb.* + -FUL 2.] As much as fills a glass.

†**Gla·ssful,** *a. rare.* [f. GLASS *sb.* + -FUL 1.] ? Mirror-like. MARSTON.

Glass-house. ME. **1.** The building where glass is made. **2.** A building made chiefly of glass, *esp.* a greenhouse 1838.

Glassing (gla·siŋ), *vbl. sb.* 1544. [f. GLASS *v.* + -ING[1].] The action of GLASS *v.* 1617. **b.** *attrib.* and *Comb.* as *g. effect*; **g.-jack, -machine,** machines used in dressing leather.

Glassite (gla·səit). 1772. [f. the name *Glass* + -ITE[1] 1.] A member of the religious sect founded by the Rev. John Glass, a minister of the Established Church of Scotland (deposed in 1728). The Glassites are also called *Sandemanians.*

Gla·ss-man. 1597. **1.** A dealer in glass-ware. **2.** A man engaged in glass-making 1610.

Gla·ss-work. 1611. **1.** *pl.* (rarely *sing.*) The works where glass is made 1626. **2.** The manufacture of glass and glass-ware. Also, glazing. **3.** Articles made of glass; glass as manufactured 1725. Hence **Gla·ss-wo:rker,** one who works in glass.

Glasswort (gla·swɒɹt). 1597. A name for plants containing much alkali, and on that account formerly used in glass-making. **a.** A plant of the genus *Salicornia*, esp. *S. herbacea*; called also *jointed glasswort.* **b.** *Salsola kali*; called also *prickly glasswort.*

Glassy (gla·si), *a.* ME. [f. GLASS *sb.* + -Y[1].] **1.** Having the nature or properties of glass, vitreous; resembling glass in its properties; appearing as if made of glass. †**b.** *fig.* Brittle and frail as glass –1785. **2.** Of the eye: Lacking fire or life, dull ME. †**3.** Of glass; made of glass –1807.

1. *G.* (now usu. VITREOUS) *humour* (of the eye): so called as resembling melted glass. The clear hyaline, the g. sea MILT. A g. calm 1871. **b.** G. and slippery youth 1637. **2.** His eyes have an odd g. stare MACAULAY. **3.** The g. globe that Merlin made SPENSER. Hence **Gla·ssi-ly** *adv.*, **-ness.**

Glastonbury (gla·stənbəri). 1691. [A town in Somersetshire, famous for its abbey.] Used *attrib.* in **Glastonbury chair,** a kind of armchair, designed after that of 'the Abbot of Glastonbury'; **G. thorn,** a variety of hawthorn.

Glau·ber. 1799. Short for GLAUBER'S SALT(S.

Glauberite (glǭ··, glau·bərəit). 1809. [f. *Glauber* (see next) + -ITE[1] 2 b.] *Min.* Sulphate of calcium and sodium.

Glauber's salt, -s. Also **Glauber salt, -s.** 1736. [f. Johann Rudolf *Glauber*, German chemist (1604–1668).] Sulphate of sodium (first artificially made by Glauber).

Glaucescent (glǭse·sĕnt), *a.* 1829. [f. L. *glaucus* + -ESCENT. Cf. Fr. *glaucescent.*] Somewhat glaucous. Hence **Glauce·scence,** g. condition. var. **Glau·cine.**

Glaucic (glǭ·sik), *a.* 1844. [f. mod.L. *Glaucium* a genus of papaveraceous plants + -IC.] *Chem.* In *Glaucic acid*, 'an acid obtained from *Glaucium luteum*, identical with *Fumaric acid*' (*Syd. Soc. Lex.*).

Glaucodot (glǭ·kŏdǫt). Also **-dote, glaukodot.** 1850. [– G. *glaukodot* (Breithaupt, 1849), said to be f. Gr. γλαυκός (see GLAUCOUS) + δοτήρ giver, the mineral being used in making smalt.] *Min.* A sulph-arsenide of cobalt and iron, occurring in tin-white, orthorhombic crystals.

Glaucoma (glǭkōᵘ·mă). 1643. [– Gr. γλαύκωμα, f. γλαυκός; see GLAUCOUS, -OMA.] A disease of the eye, characterized by increased tension of the globe and gradual impairment or loss of sight. Formerly used for cataract. Hence **Glaucoma·tic** *a.* of or pertaining to g. **Glauco·matous, Glauco·matose** *adjs.* glaucomatic; affected with g.

Glauconite (glǭ·kŏnəit). 1836. [– G. *glaukonit* (Keferstein, 1828), f. Gr. γλαυκόν, n. of γλαυκός; see GLAUCOUS, -ITE[1] 2b.] *Min.* Hydrous silicate of iron, potassium, and other bases, commonly called green earth. Hence **Glauconi·tic** *a.* containing or resembling g.

Glaucophane (glǭ·kŏfeⁱn). 1849. [– G. *glaukophan* (Haussmann, 1845), f. Gr. γλαυκός (see GLAUCOUS) + -φανής shining.] *Min.* A mineral closely resembling Amphibole.

Glaucosis (glǭkōᵘ·sis). 1706. [– Gr. γλαύκωσις, f. γλαυκός; see next, -OSIS.] 'The origination of *Glaucoma.* Also, blindness from *Glaucoma.*' (*Syd. Soc. Lex.*)

Glaucous (glǭ·kəs), *a.* 1671. [f. L. *glaucus* (– Gr. γλαυκός bluish-green or grey) + -OUS.] Of a dull green colour passing into greyish blue; *spec.* in *Bot.* covered with 'bloom'.

‖**Glaucus** (glǭ·kŏs). 1520. [mod.L.; sense 1 echoes Pliny's use of L. *glaucus* – Gr. γλαῦκος, prob. a subst. use of γλαυκός adj. (see prec.); the other senses are direct applications of the L. adj.] †**1.** Some kind of fish –1706. **2.** The burgomaster gull (*Larus glaucus*) 1785. **3.** A genus of nudi-branchiate molluscs, found in the warmer seas, beautifully coloured with blue 1847.

Glaum (glǭm), *v. Sc.* Also **glam.** 1715. [Of unkn. origin.] *intr.* To snatch *at.* Also, to make threatening movements.

†**Glave,** var. of GLAIVE.

†**Gla·ver,** *v.* ME. [Of unkn. origin.] **1.** *trans.* To flatter, deceive with flattery –1594. **2.** *intr.* To talk plausibly and deceitfully; to flatter –1681. Hence †**Gla·verer.**

Glaymore, var. of CLAYMORE.

Glaze (glēⁱz), *sb.* 1700. [f. GLAZE *v.* Not in J.] **1.** The vitreous composition used for glazing pottery, etc. 1807. **2.** *gen.* Any coating used to produce a glazed or lustrous surface; *spec.* in *Cookery.* 1784. **3.** A smooth and glossy surface 1791. **4.** *U.S.* A coating of ice; also, a stretch of ice 1752. **5.** *Painting.* A thin coat of transparent colour laid over another colour 1860. **6.** *slang.* A window 1700.

2. *Glaze* is made from clear stock, boiled down until it forms a sort of meat varnish or strong jelly 1877.

Comb.: **g.-kiln,** a kiln in which glazed ware is placed for firing; **-wheel,** a wooden wheel used by cutlers for polishing knives, etc.; **-worm,** a glow-worm.

Glaze (glēⁱz), *v.*[1] [ME. *glase*, f. obl. form of GLASS.] **1.** *trans.* To furnish or fill in with glass or windows of glass, to cover with glass. **2.** To cover (pottery, etc.) with a vitreous substance which is fixed by fusion. Also, to vitrify the surface of. ME. **b.** *fig.* To gloss *over* 1605. **3.** To overlay or cover with a smooth and lustrous coating. Also, to cover (the eyes) with a film. 1593. **4.** *Painting.* To cover (a painted surface) with a thin coat of a different transparent colour. Also, to lay (a transparent colour) *over* another. 1622. **5.** To make to shine like glass; to polish, render brilliant ME. **6.** *intr.* To become glazed 1747.

1. A portrait framed and glazed 1878. **3.** Sorrowes eye, glazed with blinding teares SHAKS. Where winter..doth g. the Scythian seas 1627.

Glaze, *v.*[2] Now *dial.* [perh. blending of GAZE, GLARE.] *intr.* To stare. *Jul. C.* I. iii. 21.

Glazen, var. of GLASSEN.

Glazer (glēⁱ·zəɹ), *sb.* ME. [f. GLAZE *v.*[1] + -ER[1].] †**1.** = GLAZIER 2. –1466. **2.** A polisher or burnisher; one who applies glaze to pottery, etc. 1586. **3.** An implement for glazing; *esp.* a wheel used in roughly polishing knives, etc. 1812.

Glazier (glēⁱ·ziəɹ, glēⁱ·ʒⁱəɹ). ME. [f. as prec.; see -IER.] †**1.** A glass-maker –1477. **2.** One whose trade is to glaze windows, etc. ME. **3.** = GLAZER 3. 1688. †**4.** *old slang. pl.* The eyes –1785. Hence **Gla·ziery,** glazier's work; also *attrib.*

Glazing (glēⁱ·ziŋ), *vbl. sb.* ME. [f. GLAZE *v.*[1] + -ING[1].] **1.** The action of furnishing a building with windows or filling windows with glass; the trade of a glazier. *concr.* Glazier's work. **2.** The action of polishing or burnishing ME. **3.** The action of coating with a glaze 1677. **b.** *concr.* = GLAZE *sb.* 2, 3. 1694. **4.** *Painting.* The application of a thin coat of transparent colour over another colour in order to modify the tone; the colour thus applied 1706.

Comb.: **g.-wheel,** a wooden wheel charged with emery and used for polishing.

Glazy (glēⁱ·zi), *a.* 1724. [f. GLAZE *sb.* or *v.*[1] + -Y[1].] **1. a.** Glass-like, glassy. **b.** Having the appearance of a glaze or glazed surface 1768. **2.** Of the eye, etc.: = GLASSY *a.* 2. 1838. Hence **Gla·zily** *adv.* **Gla·ziness.**

Glead, obs. f. GLEED *sb.*

Gleam (glīm), *sb.* [OE. *glǣm* (:– *ʒlaimiz), corresp. to LG. *glēm*, OHG. *gleimo* glow-worm, and rel. to OS. *glīmo* brightness, OHG. *glimo* glow-worm, MHG. *glimen* shine, glow, and further to GLIMMER *v.*] **1.** Orig. a brilliant light (e.g. of the sun). Now, a subdued or transient appearance of light. **b.** *fig.* ME. †**2.** *transf.* Brightness, radiance; radiant beauty –1683. **b.** A bright look 1769.

1. The dying lamp feebly emits a yellow g. GOLDSM. **b.** A g. of hope MACAULAY, of good fortune STEPHEN. **2. b.** His black visage lighted up with a curious, mischievous g. 1852.

Gleam (glīm), *v.*[1] ME. [f. prec.] **1.** *intr.* To emit gleams; in mod. use chiefly, to shine with a subdued brightness. Also *fig.* Also quasi-*trans.* †**2.** To glance, look (*rare*) –1508.

1. The palace gleams with shining swords DRYDEN. There g. the columns of Capua LYTTON. quasi-*trans.* Dying eyes gleem'd forth their ashie lights SHAKS. Hence **Glea·mingly** *adv.*

Gleam, *v.*[2] ? *Obs.* 1575. [Later f. obs. *gleim* v.] *Falconry.* Of a hawk: To cast filth from her gorge.

Gleamy (glī·mi), *a.* 1593. [f. GLEAM *sb.* + -Y[1].] **1.** That gleams or sends forth gleams (of light). **2.** That is lighted up by gleams, e.g. of intermittent sunshine. Now *rare.* 1681.

3. Of light or colour: Having the nature of a gleam 1700.

1. Fish, g. with prismatic hues DISRAELI. **2.** Antique castles seen through g. showers WORDSW.

Glean (glīn), *sb.*[1] Now *dial.* ME. [– OFr. *glene, glane*, f. *glener*; see GLEAN *v.* Hence med.L. *glena, glana.*] Something gleaned or gathered; e.g. a handful of corn, a sheaf of hemp, etc.

transf. The Gleans of yellow Thime distend his Thighs DRYDEN.

†**Glean,** *sb.*[2] 1601. [var. of *clean* (perh. f. CLEAN *v.*), which has the same sense in some mod. dialects.] The placenta or after-birth, esp. of a cow –1750.

Glean (glīn), *v.* ME. [– OFr. *glener* (mod. *glaner*) :– late L. (Gallo-Roman) *glennare* (VI), prob. f. Gaulish **glenn-* :– Celtic **glendn-* (in OIr. *dighlaim* :– **dēglendsmn*).] **1.** *intr.* To gather ears of corn left by the reapers. **2.** *trans.* To pick up (ears of corn, etc.) after the reapers, etc. ME. **b.** To strip (a field, vineyard, etc.) of what is left 1533. **3.** *transf.* and *fig.* To gather or pick up in small quantities. Now chiefly with immaterial object. ME. †**b.** To cut off (a remnant or stragglers) in warfare –1726.

1. I pray you, let mee gleane and gather after the reapers amongst the sheaues *Ruth* 2:7. **2.** To gleane the broken eares after the man That the maine haruest reapes SHAKS. **b.** *Lev.* 19:10. **3.** To g. materials for history 1759, a joy BYRON. **b.** *Judges* 20:45. Hence **Glea·nable** *a.* **Glea·ner,** one that gleans.

†**Glean,** var. of GLEEN *sb.*

Gleaning (glī·niŋ), *vbl. sb.* ME. [f. GLEAN *v.* + -ING[1].] The action of GLEAN *v.*; also (chiefly *pl.*) that which is or may be gleaned. Humble gleanings in Divinity B. JONS.

Glebe (glīb), *sb.* ME. [– L. *gleba, glæba* clod, land, soil.] **1.** The soil of the earth, as the source of vegetable products; land. Now only *poet.* or *rhet.* **2.** A piece of cultivated land; a field. Now *poet.* ME. **b.** *spec.* A portion of land assigned to a clergyman as part of his benefice ME. †**3. a.** A clod or piece of earth, ore, etc. –1766. **b.** A small grain or speck –1765. †**4.** An earth, earthy mineral –1723.

1. Howses..he raseth, To make the common gleabe, his priuate land 1598. **2. b.** This parish is a rectory; it has a g., and a good solid house COBBETT.

Comb.: **g.-house,** a parsonage, manse (now only in Ireland); **-land(s** = 2 b. above.

Hence **Glebe** *v.* (*rare*) to furnish with a g. **Gle·beless** *a.*

Glebous (glī·bəs), *a. rare.* 1671. [– L. *glebosus*, f. *gleba* GLEBE; see -OUS.] Earthy; abounding in clods.

Gleby (glī·bi), *a.* ?*Obs.* 1566. [f. GLEBE *sb.* + -Y[1].] Of soil: Full of clods; rich, fertile.

Glede, gled (glīd, gled). [OE. *glida*, corresp. to MLG. *glede*, ON. *gleða* :– Gmc. **ʒliðon* (**ʒleðon*), f. **ʒlið-*, weak grade of **ʒlīðan* GLIDE.] The kite (*Milvus regalis*). Now chiefly *north.* and *Sc.* (in form *gled*). Also applied locally to the buzzard, osprey, and peregrine falcon.

Glede, obs. f. GLEED.

†**Gle·dy,** *a.* [f. *glede* GLEED + -Y[1].] Glowing hot. CHAUCER.

Glee (glī), *sb.* [OE. *glēo, glīo* = ON. *glý* :– **ʒliujam* (not repr. in other Gmc. languages).] †**1.** Entertainment, play; *occas.* scornful jesting –1607. †**2.** Musical entertainment; music, melody. Also *fig.* of other sounds. –1523. **b.** A musical composition, grave or gay, for three or more voices (one voice to each part), (in strict use) without accompaniment 1659. **3.** Mirth, joy, rejoicing; in mod. use, a lively feeling of delight caused by special circumstances ME. †**b.** A state of exaltation –1588. †**4.** Bright colour, beauty –1580. *Comb.* **g.-club.**

Glee *v.*, var. of GLEY.

Gleed (glīd), *sb.* [OE. *glēd* = OFris. *glēd*, OS. *glōd-* (Du. *gloed*), OHG. *gluot* (G. *glut*), ON. *glóð* :– Gmc. **ʒlōðiz*, f. base of GLOW *v.*[1]] **1.** A live coal; an ember. Now only *dial.* exc. *arch.* Also *fig.* †**2.** A fire –1755. †**3.** A beam (of light) –1566. **4.** *local. pl.* Cinders, coke used as fuel 1853.

Gleeful (glī·ful), *a.* 1586. [f. GLEE *sb.* + -FUL.] Full of glee; feeling or showing glee. Hence **Glee·fully** *adv.*

Gleek (glīk), *sb.*[1] 1533. [– OFr. *glic*, also *ghelicque* – MDu. *ghelic* (mod. *gelijk*) LIKE *a.*, perh. the immediate source.] **1.** A game at cards, played by three persons. *Hist.* †**2.** A set of three court cards of the same rank in one hand, in this game –1670; hence, three of anything, a trio –1710.

†**Gleek,** *sb.*[2] 1550. [Possibly dim. of GLEE, *sb.* Cf. synon. (dial.) *glaik.*] **1.** A gibe, jest, gird –1819. **2.** A coquettish glance (*rare*) –1623.

2. A pretty g. coming from Pallas' eye 1623.

†**Gleek,** *v.* 1534. [f. prec.] **1.** *trans.* To trick, circumvent –1653. **2.** *intr.* To make a jest or jibe (*at* a person) –1687.

2. Nay, I can gleeke vpon occasion SHAKS.

Gleeman (glī·mæ̆n). *Obs.* exc. *Hist.* OE. [f. GLEE *sb.* + MAN.] A professional entertainer; esp. a singer, musician, or minstrel.

Gleen (glīn), *sb.* Also **glean.** *Obs.* exc. *arch.* 1656. [prob. a dial. word of Scand. origin; cf. Sw. (dial.) *glena*, Da. (dial.) *glene* clear strip or patch of sky.] A gleam of light; a warm blaze of sunlight.

†**Gleen,** *v. rare.* 1547. [See prec., and cf. Sw. (dial.) *glena* shine.] = GLEAM *v.*[1] –1709.

Gleesome (glī·sǒm), *a.* 1603. [f. GLEE *sb.* + -SOME[1].] = GLEEFUL. Hence **Glee·some-ly** *adv.*, **-ness.**

Gleet (glīt), *sb.* [ME. *glet*, Sc. *glit* – (O)Fr. *glette* slime, filth, (now) litharge, of unkn. origin. The present form is unexpl.] **1.** Slimy matter. Also *fig. Obs.* exc. *Sc.* **2.** Phlegm collected in the stomach, esp. of a hawk. *Obs.* exc. *Sc.* ME. **3.** A morbid discharge of thin liquid from a wound, ulcer, etc. Now *rare.* 1535. **b.** *spec.* A morbid discharge from the urethra 1718. Hence **Glee·tous** *a.* (of a hawk), afflicted with phlegm. **Glee·ty** *a.* slimy (now *Sc.* and *north.*); of the nature of g.

Gleet, *v.* 1527. [f. prec.] †**1.** *intr.* Of a morbid discharge, also of water: To ooze, flow slowly –1725. **2.** To discharge a thin purulent matter. Also quasi-*trans.* 1676.

Gleg (gleg), *a. north.* and *Sc.* ME. [– ON. *gleggr, gløggr* clear, clear-sighted, corresp. to OE. *glēaw* wise, clever, OS., OHG. *glau* clever, Goth. **glaggwus*, whence *glaggwuba* adv. accurately :– Gmc. **glawwu-*.] **1.** Quick in perception by the senses; esp. sharp-sighted. **2.** Quick in action; sharp, smart 1755. **3.** Sprightly 1818.

2. Phr. *G. at the uptake*: quick in understanding a thing. Hence **Gle·gly** *adv.* **Gle·gness.**

Gleir(e, obs. f. GLAIR *sb.*[1]

Glen (glen). 1489. [– Gael., Ir. *gleann*, earlier *glenn* = W. *glyn.*] A mountain-valley, usually narrow, and forming the course of a stream.

Your lowly glens o'erhung with spreading broom COLLINS.

Glendoveer (glendovīə·ɹ). 1810. [Altered f. *grandouver* in Sonnerat *Voy. aux Indes* (1782); app. repr. Skr. *Gandharvas*, a kind of semi-divine spiritual being.] One of a race of beautiful sprites in Southey's quasi-Hindu mythology.

‖**Glene** (glī·ni). 1706. [mod.L. – Gr. γλήνη ball or pupil of the eye; used by Galen for a shallow joint-socket.] *Anat.* **a.** The ball or socket of the eye. **b.** A glenoid cavity. (Dicts.)

Glengarry (glengæ·ri). 1858. [f. *Glengarry* in Inverness-shire.] A kind of man's cap, higher in front than at the back, of Highland origin.

Glenlivet (glenlī·vėt, Sc. -lī·vėt). 1822. [f. *Glenlivet* in Banffshire, where made.] A variety of Scotch whisky.

Gleno-, comb. f. GLENE, as in *g.-humeral*, belonging to the glenoid cavity and the humerus; etc.

Glenoid (glī·noid), *a.* 1709. [– Fr. *glénoïde* – Gr. γληνοειδής, f. γλήνη; see GLENE, -OID.] *G. cavity, fossa, surface*, a shallow cavity on a bone (esp. the scapula) which receives a projection of another bone to form a joint. So **Glenoi·dal** *a.*

Glent, *sb.* and *v.* ME. [prob. of Scand. origin; cf. Sw. (dial.) *glänta, glinta* slip, slide; shine, gleam.] = GLINT.

‖**Gle·tscher.** *rare.* 1762. [G., adopted XVI from Swiss dialect = Fr. *glacier.*] A glacier.

Glew, obs. f. GLUE.

Gley (gləi). *v. Obs.* exc. *north.* and *Sc.* Also **glee.** ME. [Northern vars. of an orig. ME. *glēʒen.* Of obscure origin.] *intr.* To squint; to look obliquely.

Gliadin (gləi·ădin). 1830. [– Fr. *gliadine*, irreg. f. Gr. γλία glue; see -IN[1], -INE[5].] *Chem.* The viscid portion of gluten. Called also *glutin.*

Glib (glib), *sb.* 1537. [– Irish *glib.*] A thick mass of matted hair hanging over the eyes, formerly worn by the Irish. Also, a man who wears this. Now *Hist.*

Glib (glib). 1594. [rel. to GLIBBERY.]

A. *adj.* **1.** Smooth and slippery; easy, unimpeded. Now *rare* exc. *dial.* 1599. **2.** Of an action, method, etc.: easy; off-hand 1598. **3.** Of speech, etc.: Ready and fluent. Chiefly *contemptuous.* 1602.

1. The snow lies g. as glass and hard as steel BROWNING. **3.** That g. and oylie Art, To speak and purpose not SHAKS. Hence **Gli·b-ly** *adv.*, **-ness.**

B. *adv.* **1.** Smoothly, easily. Now *rare.* 1594. **2.** Volubly, fluently 1628.

1. The Bill did not pass g. NORTH.

Glib (glib), *v.*[1] 1598. [f. the adj.] **1.** *trans.* To render glib (see GLIB *a.*). **2.** *intr.* To talk volubly. Now *dial.* 1602.

†**Glib,** *v.*[2] *rare.* 1611. [app. a corruption of LIB *v.*[1]] *trans.* To castrate; to geld –1640. *Wint. T.* II. i. 149.

†**Gli·bbery,** *a.* 1601. [corresp. formally to Du. *glibberig*, MLG. *glibberich* (LG. *glibbrig*), f. base **ʒlib-* (cf. OHG. *gleif* sloping); for expressive *gl-* cf. GLIDE. See GLIB *a.*] Slippery (*lit.* and *fig.*) –1646.

The g. ice Of vulgar favour MARSTON.

Glick(e, obs. f. GLEEK *sb.*[1]; var. of GLEEK *sb.*[2] and *v.*

Glidder (gli·dəɹ), *a. Obs.* exc. *dial.* [OE. *glid(d)er*, f. *glid-*, the weak grade of the base of GLIDE *v.*] Slippery. Hence **Gli·dder** *v. dial.* to glaze over; to cover with ice. **Gli·ddery** *a. dial.* slippery.

Glide (gləid), *sb.* 1590. [f. next.] **1.** The action of gliding (see GLIDE *v.*) 1596. **2.** *concr.* †A stream; also, the part of a stream which glides, a shallow. **3.** *Mus.* and *Phonetics.* (See quots.) 1835.

1. [The snake] with indented glides, did slip away Into a bush SHAKS. **2.** Eurotas silver g. GREENE. **3.** *Glide*, the slur, to join two successive sounds without articulation, also the unaccented notes or anticipations in a *portamento* passage (Wilson *Dict. Mus.*) 1835. A series of semi-consonant, semi-vowel sounds..which we call 'Glides' A. M. BELL. The 'glide', or sound produced in passing from the one position [of the organs of speech] to the other SWEET. *Comb.* **g.-vowel,** a vowel which cannot form a syllable by itself.

Glide (gləid), *v.* Pa. t. and pple. **glided.** [OE. *glīdan* = OFris. *glīda*, OS. *glīdan* (Du. *glijden*), OHG. *glītan* (G. *gleiten*) :– WGmc. str. vb. **ʒlīðan*, of which no cogns. are known.] **1.** *intr.* To pass along by a smooth and continuous movement, without effort or difficulty. **b.** *Aeronautics.* To fly without motor power 1894. **2.** To go unperceived, quietly, or stealthily ME. †**3.** *poet.* To go or come –1596. **4.** To slide. Also †to slip, lose one's footing on ice, etc. ME. **b.** To slip *away*, like something greasy 1510. **5. a.** Of time, one's life, etc.: To pass gently and imperceptibly ME. **b.** *To g. into*: to pass by imperceptible degrees into 1800. **c.** Phonetics. *To g. on to*: (of a consonant or vowel) to be uttered continuously with 1867. **6.** *trans.* = to cause to glide 1650.

1. The river glideth at his own sweet will WORDSW. **3.** Like sparke of fire that from the andvile glode SPENSER. **5. b.** To g. hopelessly into debt 1869. Hence **Gli·der** *spec.* an engineless aeroplane 1897.

Gliff (glif), *sb.* Now *Sc.* or *north.* 1570. [f. next.] **1.** A passing sight; a glance, glimpse. **2.** A moment 1816. **3.** A sudden fright; a scare 1732.

2. Bide a g. SCOTT.

Gliff (glif), *v.* Now *Sc.* or *north.* ME. [Of obscure origin.] †**1.** To slip (*lit.* and *fig.*). ME. only. †**2.** To look quickly; also quasi-*trans. to g. one's eyes* –1570. **3.** *trans.* To frighten 1823.

†**Glike,** var. of GLEEK *sb.*[2] and *v.*

Glim (glim), *sb.* ME. [perh. shortening of GLIMMER *sb.*[1] or GLIMPSE.] †**1.** ?Brightness. ME. only. **2.** *Sc.* †A passing look. Hence, a scrap. 1620. **3.** *slang.* **a.** A light; a candle, a lantern. 1700. **b.** An eye 1820.

3. a. Phr. *Douse the g.* (see DOUSE *v.*[1]). Sure enough, they left their g. here STEVENSON.

Glimmer (gli·məɹ), *sb.*[1] 1567. [f. the vb.] **1.** A feeble or wavering light; a sheen, shimmer 1590. **2.** *fig.* A faint gleam (of knowledge, hope, etc.) 1837. **3.** *slang.* †**a.** A fire –1665. **b.** *pl.* The eyes 1814.

1. In gloss of satin and g. of pearls TENNYSON.

Glimmer (gli·məɹ), *sb.*[2] 1683. [– G. *glimmer*, f. *glimmen* glow.] Mica.

Glimmer (gli·məɹ), *v.* [prob. of Scand. origin (cf. Sw. *glimra*, Da. *glimre*, to which correspond (M)HG., Du.*gli mmern*); f. Gmc. **ʒlim-*, **ʒlaim-*; see GLEAM *v.*[1], -ER[5].] †**1.** *intr.* To glitter; to flash –1530. **2.** To give a faint or intermittent light; to shine faintly. Also *transf.* and *fig.* 1483. **3.** To look or glance with half-closed eyes (*rare*) 1579.

2. The West yet glimmers with some streakes of Day SHAKS. *transf.* The voice came glimmering and bubbling up a flight of stone steps HAWTHORNE.

Comb. **g.-gowk** (*dial.*), an owl.

Glimmering (gli·məriŋ), *vbl. sb.* ME. [See -ING[1].] **1.** The shining of a faint or wavering light. **2.** A partial view; a glimpse, an inkling; a faint notion ME.

1. Shadows and sunny glimmerings WORDSW. **2.** Syre Percyuale hadde a glemerynge of the vessel and of the mayden that bare hit MALORY.

Glimpse (glimps), *sb.* 1540. [f. the vb.] **1.** A momentary shining, a flash (*lit.* and *fig.*) 1602. **2.** A faint and transient appearance. †Also, a tinge or trace. 1540. **3.** A momentary and imperfect view (*of*), a passing sight. (The current sense.) Also *fig.* 1570.

1. *The glimpses of the moon*: the earth by night; often quoted as = sublunary scenes. *Haml.* I. iv. 53. **2.** In his face The glimpses of his Father's glory shine MILT. **3.** A g.. of the whole of Coniston Lake 1872, of the inner history of an English town 1874.

Glimpse (glimps), *v.* ME. [deriv. of the base of GLIMMER *v.*, perh. repr. an OE. **glimsian* = MHG. *glimsen* :– WGmc. **ʒlimisōjan*.] **1.** *intr.* To shine faintly or intermittently (*lit.* and *fig.*) **b.** To appear faintly; to dawn. Now only *poet.* or *arch.* 1603. **2.** *trans.* To give a glimpse of (*rare*) 1663. **3.** To catch a glimpse of; to see by glimpses 1779. **4.** *intr.* To cast a passing glance. Const. *at*, *upon*, etc. 1833.

1. Little glow-worms glimpsing in the dark 1601. Yet sometimes glimpses on my sight, Through present wrong, the eternal right 1851.

Glint (glint), *sb.* ?1541. [f. the vb.] **1.** A gleam. **2.** A passing look; a glance; a glimpse. Chiefly *Sc.* or *north.* 1832.

1. The earliest g. o' morn 1826.

Glint (glint), *v.* ME. [alt. of earlier (dial.) GLENT (XIII).] **1.** *intr.* To move quickly, esp. obliquely; to glance aside. **2.** To shine with a flashing light; to gleam, glitter ME. Also *causative* (trans.) 1844. **3.** *intr.* To peep 1888.

2. The specks of sail that glinted in the sunlight far at sea DICKENS.

Glioma (gləi,ō^u·mă). *Pl.* **-mata.** 1870. [mod.L. *glioma* (Virchow), f. Gr. γλία glue; see -OMA.] *Path.* 'A tumour originating from, and largely consisting of, the neuroglia cells of the central nervous system, esp. of the brain' (*Syd. Soc. Lex.*). Hence **Glio·matous** *a.* of the nature of g.

Glirine (gləi^ə·rin), *a.* 1836. [f. L. *glis, glir-* dormouse + -INE[1].] Pertaining to the order *Glires* of mammals. So **Gli·riform** *a.* resembling the *Glires* in form or character.

Glissade (glisā·d, -ē^i·d), *sb.* 1843. [– Fr. *glissade*, f. *glisser* slip, slide; see -ADE.] **1.** *Mountaineering.* The action of sliding down a snow slope or the like 1862. Also *fig.* **2.** *Dancing.* A step consisting of a glide to right or left 1843. Hence **Glissa·de** *v. intr.* to perform a g. **Glissa·der.**

Glissette (glise·t). 1870. [f. Fr. *glisser* slide + -ETTE as a correlative of ROULETTE (sense 3).] *Math.* (See quot.).

Glissettes are the curves traced out by points, or enveloped by curves, carried by a curve, which is made to slide between given points or given curves 1870.

Glist (glist), *sb.* *rare.* 1715. [app. a shortened form of GLISTEN *v.*] **1.** A gleam, glistening 1864. **2.** = MICA. 1715.

Glisten (gli·s'n), *sb.* 1840. [f. the vb.] Glitter; sparkle.

Glisten (gli·s'n), *v.* [OE. *glisnian*, f. base of *glisian* (= OFris. *glisa*, MLG. *glisen*), f. Gmc. **ʒlis-*, extension of **ʒli-*; see -EN[5], cf. GLISTER *v.*] *intr.* To shine with a twinkling light; to glitter; to sparkle (*lit.* and *fig.*).

The ladies eyes glistened with pleasure RICHARDSON. A mass glistens white as if it were snow GEIKIE. Hence **Gli·steningly** *adv.*

Glister (gli·stəɹ), *sb.* 1535. [f. the vb.] **1.** A glistering; brilliance, lustre. Also *fig.* **2.** *Min.* = GLIST *sb.* 2. 1722.

Glister (gli·stəɹ), *v.* *arch.* and *dial.* ME. [corresp. to and prob. – MLG. *glistern*, (M)Du. *glisteren*, f. Gmc. **ʒlis-*; see GLISTEN, -ER[5].] *intr.* To sparkle; to glitter; to be brilliant. †**b.** quasi-*trans.* SIDNEY.

All that glisters is not gold SHAKS. Hence †**Gli·sterer,** a showy person. **Gli·steringly** *adv.*

Glister, obs. or dial. f. CLYSTER.

Glitter (gli·təɹ), *sb.* 1602. [f. the vb.] **1.** Brilliant or sparkling light; lustre, splendour. Also *fig.* **2.** Erron. for GUTTER *sb.* 5 (Goldsm. *Nat. Hist.* III. v. 114.).

1. Tinsill g. MARSTON. False g. MILT. The g. of gold 1788, (*fig.*) of Junius STEPHEN.

Glitter (gli·təɹ), *v.* ME. [– ON. *glitra* = MHG., G. *glitzern* sparkle, frequent. (see -ER[5]) f. Gmc. **ʒlīt-*, in OS. *glītan*, OHG. *glīʒan* (G. *gleissen*) shine, ON. *glita* glitter, Goth. *glitmunjan* (of clothes) shine bright.] **1.** *intr.* To shine with a brilliant but broken and tremulous light; to emit bright fitful flashes of light; to gleam, sparkle. **2.** *fig.* To be showy or splendid (in dress, etc.) 1548.

1. Many helmes gletred agaynst the sonne LD. BERNERS. All is not gold that glitters *Prov.* **2.** I saw her [the queen of France]. .glittering like the morning star BURKE. Hence **Gli·tterance** (*rare*), glittering appearance. **Gli·tteringly** *adv.*

Gloam (glō^{u}m), *sb.* *rare.* 1821. [Back-formation f. GLOAMING.] Twilight.

Gloam (glō^{u}m), *v.* *Sc.* 1819. [f. as prec.] *intr.* To darken, become dusk.

Gloaming (glō^u·miŋ). [repr. OE. *glōmung*, f. (on the anal. of *ǣfning* evening) *glōm* twilight, prob. f. Gmc. **ʒlō* (see GLOW). In the literary language an early XIX adoption from Sc. writers.] **1.** Evening twilight OE. Also *fig.* 1785. **2.** *attrib.* (occas. *adj.*) as **g.-shot,** (*a*) a shot in the twilight; (*b*) the beginning of twilight; etc. 1788.

1. 'Tween the g. and the mirk HOGG.

Gloat (glō^{u}t), *v.* 1575. [Of unkn. origin; poss. f. Scand. (cf. ON. *glotta* grin, Sw. dial. *glotta* peep, corresp. to (M)HG. *glotzen* stare).] †**1.** *intr.* To look askance –1727. †**2.** To cast amorous or admiring glances. Const. *on*, *upon*. –1727. **3.** To gaze with intense or passionate (usu. lustful, avaricious, or malignant) satisfaction 1748.

3. Phr. *To gloat on, upon,* or *over*: to feast one's eyes upon, to dwell upon with fierce or unholy joy. Never did miser g. on his money with more delight W. IRVING. To g. over the mysteries of iniquity STEPHEN. Hence **Gloat** *sb.* **Gloa·tingly** *adv.*

Global (glō^u·băl), *a.* 1676. [f. GLOBE *a.* + -AL[1].] **1.** Globular. *rare.* **2.** [after Fr.] Pertaining to or embracing the totality of a group of items, categories, or the like 1892.

Globate (glō^u·be^{i}t, -ĕt), *a.* *rare.* 1847. [f. GLOBE + -ATE[2].] Having the form of a globe. So **Glo·bated** *a.* formed into or as into a globe.

Globe (glō^{u}b), *sb.* 1551. [– OFr. *globe* or L. *globus.*] **1.** A body having a spherical form. **b.** *fig.* A complete or perfect body, a 'full-orbed' combination 1607. **2.** *The* (or *this*) *globe*: the earth 1553. **b.** Any planetary or celestial body 1566. **3.** A spherical structure showing the geographical configuration of the earth (*terrestrial globe*), or the arrangement of the stars (*celestial globe*) 1553. **4.** The golden ball borne along with the sceptre as an emblem of sovereignty (cf. BALL *sb.*) 1614. **5.** *Globe of the eye*, the eye-ball 1774. **6.** A glass vessel of approximately spherical shape; esp. a lamp-shade 1665. **7.** A compact body (of persons). After L. use. 1610.

1. b. In the discharge of thie place, sett before thee the best Exemples; For Imitacion is a G. of Preceptes BACON. **2.** We the G. can compasse soone SHAKS. **4.** With crown, with sceptre, and with g., Emblems of empery SCOTT. **7.** Him round A G. of fierie Seraphim inclos'd MILT. Phrase *G. of compression* (= Fr. *globe de compression*): an overcharged mine, the explosion of which produces a crater of greater radius than depth.

Comb.: **g.-amaranth(us** (see AMARANTH); †**-animal, -animalcule,** a minute globular locomotive organism (*Volvox globator*); **-artichoke** = ARTICHOKE 1; **-crowfoot** = *globe-flower*; **-daisy,** *Globularia vulgaris*; **-fish,** a fish of globular form, esp. one of the *Tetrodontidæ* or *Diodontidæ*, which assume this form by inflation; **-flower,** *Trollius europæus*, a ranunculaceous plant with yellow flowers; **-ranunculus** = *globe-flower*; **-sight,** a sight for a rifle, etc., consisting of a ball or disc; **-slater,** a sessile-eyed crustacean of the genus *Sphæroma*; **-thistle,** a name for species of the genus *Echinops*; **-trotter; -trotting,** extensive and hurried travelling over the g.; **-valve,** (*a*) a ball-valve; (*b*) a valve enclosed in a spherical chamber.

Globe (glō^{u}b), *v.* 1641. [f. prec.] To form into, or have the form of, a globe. Hence **Globed** *ppl. a.*; *spec.* furnished with a globe.

Globical (glǫ·bikăl, glō^u·bikăl), *a.* 1612. [f. GLOBE *sb.* + -ICAL.] †**1.** Globular –1698. **2.** *Her.* Having the general outline circular 1688.

Globiferous (glo^{u}bi·fĕrəs), *a.* 1826. [f. GLOBE *sb.* + -FEROUS]. *Entom.* Having a globe or bulb at the end of the antennæ.

‖**Globigerina** (glō^{u}bi,dʒĕrəi·nă). *Pl.* **-næ.** 1847. [mod.L., f. *globus* GLOBE + *-ger* carrying + -INA[2].] A foraminiferous rhizopod, found in numbers in deep parts of the ocean. Also *attrib.*, as *g.-mud*, *-ooze*, deep-sea mud or chalky ooze, consisting of decayed globigerinæ. Hence **Globi·gerine** *a.*

Globin (glō^u·bin). 1877. [Extracted from HÆMOGLOBIN.] The proteid which is precipitated when a solution of hæmoglobin is exposed to the air.

Globoid (glō^u·boid). 1875. [f. GLOBE *sb.* + -OID.]

A. *adj.* Somewhat globular in form 1887.

B. *sb.* Non-crystalline, roundish, or clustered granules, consisting of a double calcium and magnesium phosphate, the latter base greatly in excess.

Globose (glo^{u}bō^u·s), *a.* 1475. [– L. *globosus*, f. *globus* GLOBE; see -OSE[1].] Having the form of a globe; spherical, or nearly so. Now only in scientific use. Hence **Globo·se-ly** *adv.*, **-ness.**

Globosity (glo^{u}bǫ·sĭti). 1657. [– Fr. †*globosité* or late L. *globositas*; see prec., -ITY, -OSITY.] The condition of being globose; roundness. Also a rounded part.

Globous (glō^u·bəs), *a.* 1610. [– Fr. †*globeux* or L. *globosus*, f. *globus* GLOBE; see -OUS.] = GLOBOSE. Now *rare.*

Globular (glǫ·biŭlăɹ), *a.* 1656. [f. L. *globulus* (see next) + -AR[1]; freq. used as the adj. of *globe* rather than of *globule*; see -ULAR.] **1.** Having the form of a globe; spherical, round. **2.** Composed of globules 1733.

1. In this station two g. hills appeared COOK. Phr. *Globular projection*, that method of map-making in which the sphere is represented as it would appear if viewed from a distance = half the chord of 90°. *G. chart*, a chart on this projection. *G. sailing*, sailing over an arc of a great circle, or the shortest distance between two places. Hence **Globula·rity, Glo·bularness,** the property of being g. **Glo·bularly** *adv.*

Globule (glǫ·biul). 1664. [– Fr. *globule* (Pascal) or L. *globulus*, dim. of *globus* GLOBE; see -ULE.] **1.** A small globe; a round drop (of water, oil, etc.). **b.** *Biol.* Applied to various minute spherical structures. **2.** *Bot.* The antheridium of *Characeæ* 1830. **3.** A small pill or pilule, such as homœopathists use 1849.

1. Exceedingly minute globules of water BREWSTER. **3.** Prescribe sometimes for myself the globules 1876. Hence **Glo·bulet** (*rare*), a minute g. **Glo:buli·ferous** *a.* that bears or produces globules. **Globuli·meter** = HÆMATOMETER b. **Glo·bulism,** occas. term for homœopathy.

Globulin (glǫ·biŭlin). Also **-ine.** 1845. [f. prec. + -IN[1], -INE[5].] *Biochem.* Any of a group of proteins, as fibrinogen, etc., insoluble in pure water, but soluble in dilute solutions of neutral salts.

Globulite (glǫ·biŭləit). 1879. [f. GLOBULE + -ITE[1].] *Min.* (*pl.*) Minute rounded bodies developed in the process of devitrification. Hence **Globuli·tic** *a.*

Globulous (glǫ·biŭləs), *a.* Now *rare.* 1668. [– Fr. *globuleux*, f. *globule*; see GLOBULE, -OUS.] Globular in form; consisting of globules. var. **Glo·bulose.** Hence †**Glo·bulousness.**

‖**Globus** (glōᵘ·bɒ̆s). 1794. [L. *globus* GLOBE.] *Path.* Short for *globus hystericus*, a choking sensation, as of a lump in the throat, to which hysterical persons are subject.

Glo·by, *a.* 1600. [f. GLOBE *sb.* + -Y[1].] Globular.

Glochidiate (glōᵘki·diĕt), *a.* Also **-date.** 1829. [f. mod.L. *glochidium* barbed hair of a plant (f. Gr. γλωχίς point of an arrow + dim. suff. -ιδιον) + -ATE[2].] *Bot.* Barbed at the tip.

Glockenspiel (glǫ·kenʃpīl, -spīl). 1876. [G., lit. bell-play.] **1.** = CARILLON 1. **2.** A musical instrument consisting of a series of metal bars which are struck with two hammers. **b.** A similar instrument with tubes or bells instead of bars. **3.** An organ stop 1898.

Glod, glode, obs. str. pa. t. of GLIDE.

Glome (glōᵘm). 1643. [– L. *glomus*, ball or clue of yarn.] †**1.** A ball or clue of yarn, etc. –1656. **2.** *Bot.* = GLOMERULE 1. 1793.

Glome of frog: name for the two rounded, elastic eminences, separated by a cleft, which form the posterior extremity of the frog of the horse's foot.

Glomerate (glǫ·merĕt), *a.* 1793. [– L. *glomeratus*, pa. pple. of *glomerare*; see next, -ATE[2].] Compactly clustered, having the form of a rounded mass or cluster. Chiefly *Bot.*; also *Anat.*

†**Glo·merate,** *v.* 1634. [– *glomerat-*, pa. ppl. stem of L. *glomerare*, f. *glomus*, *glomer-* ball or clue of yarn, etc.; see -ATE[3].] **a.** *trans.* To roll or wind up into a ball; to gather into a rounded mass. **b.** *intr.* To wind or twist about. –1798.

Glomeration (glǫmĕrēⁱ·ʃən). *rare.* 1626. [f. GLOMERATE *v.* + -ATION.] The process of forming into a ball or rounded mass; more widely, a heaping together, agglomeration; also quasi-*concr.*

Glomerule (glǫ·mĕrŭl). 1793. [– Fr. *glomérule* or mod.L. *glomerulus*, dim. of *glomus*; see GLOME, -ULE.] **1.** *Bot.* **a.** A cluster or head of flowers. **b.** A soredium 1855. **2.** A compact cluster of small organisms, animal tissues, etc.; esp. a plexus of capillary blood-vessels, as those in the Malpighian corpuscles of the kidney 1856. Hence **Glome:ruli·tis,** inflammation of the glomerules of Malpighi and their capsule. **Glome·rulose** *a.* gathered in small clusters.

Glonoin(e (glǫ·noᵢin). 1860. [app. f. GL(YCERINE + O (oxygen) + NO_3 (nitric anhydride) + -IN[1], -INE[5].] A name for nitroglycerine, esp. as used in medicine.

Glood(e, obs. pa. t. of GLIDE.

Gloom (glŭm), *sb.*[1] 1596. [In sense 1 f. GLOOM *v.*; in senses 2–3 perh. back-formation from GLOOMY.] **1.** (Only *Sc.*) A sullen look, frown, scowl. ?*Obs.* **2.** An indefinite degree of darkness or obscurity. In recent use: A painful or depressing darkness. Sometimes *pl.* 1629. **b.** A deeply shaded or darkened place 1706. **3.** A state of melancholy or depression; a despondent look. Also in *pl.* fits of melancholy. 1744.

2. This mournful g. For that celestial light MILT. A g. unbroken, except by a lamp burning feebly GEO. ELIOT. **b.** Through glades and glooms the mingled measure stole COLLINS. **3.** A comet.. aggravated the general g. 1786. A fit of the glooms MARY LAMB. Hence **Gloo·mful** *a.*

Gloom, *sb.*[2] 1577. [poss. repr. OE. *glōm*; see GLOAMING.] *Hot gloom*, excessive heat (of the sun). *Comb.* **g.-stove** (also **gloom** simply), a drying-oven used in the manufacture of gun-powder.

Gloom (glŭm), *v.* [Late ME. *gloum(b)e*; of unkn. origin. Earliest evidence is predominantly northern; for the vocalism cf. ROOM (ME. *roum*). See GLUM *v.*] **1.** *intr.* To look sullen or displeased; to frown, scowl, lower. In recent use (infl. by GLOOMY): To look dismal or dejected. **2.** Of the sky, etc.: To lower, look dark or threatening; to be or become dull and cloudy. Also *fig.* ME. **b.** = GLOAM *v.* 1595. **3.** To have a dark or sombre appearance 1770. **4.** *trans.* To make dark or sombre 1576; *fig.* to make dark, dismal, or melancholy 1745.

1. He gloomed from beneath his Eyes, bit his Lips [etc.] 1720. Her father, sitting glooming in his place at the other end of the table THACKERAY. **2.** The sky gloomed through the dusty garret windows HAWTHORNE. **b.** This long weary day.. at last I see it gloome SPENSER. **3.** The black gibbet glooms beside the way GOLDSM. **4.** A black yew gloom'd the stagnant air TENNYSON. *fig.* Such a mood as that, which lately gloom'd Your fancy TENNYSON. Hence **Gloo·mingly** *adv.*

Glooming (glŭ·miŋ), *vbl. sb.* 1572. [f. prec. + -ING[1].] **1.** Frowning, etc.; a frown, scowl; a fit of sullenness. **2.** *poet.* Twilight, gloaming; also, early dawn 1842.

2. Or while the balmy g., crescent-lit, Spread the light haze along the river-shores TENNYSON.

†**Gloo·mth.** [f. GLOOM *v.* or *sb.*[1] + -TH[1].] Gloom. H. WALPOLE.

Gloomy (glŭ·mi), *a.* 1588. [f. GLOOM *sb.*[1] + -Y[1].] **1.** Full of gloom; dark, shaded, obscure. **2.** Affected with gloom or depression of spirits; having dark or sullen looks 1590. **3.** Causing gloom; dismal, disheartening 1710.

2. The ruthlesse, vast, and g. woods *Tit. A.* IV. i. 53. Gloomie clouds MARSTON. **2.** His countenance being dark, bilious, and g. EARL ORRERY. **3.** G. apprehensions GIBBON, reflections THIRLWALL. The gloomiest view of the position 1873. Hence **Gloo·mily** *adv.* **Gloo·miness.**

Gloppen (glǫp'n), *v.* Now *dial.* [ME. *glopne, glope* – ON. *glúpna* be downcast.] †**1.** *intr.* **a.** To be downcast. **b.** To be startled or frightened. ME. only. **2.** *trans.* To startle, frighten, astound ME.

Glore, *v.* Now *dial.* ME. [– LG. *glōren* or Scand. (cf. Icel. *glóra* gleam, stare); rel. to GLOW. See GLOWER.] †**1.** *intr.* = GLARE *v.* 1. –1540. **2.** = GLARE *v.* 2, GLOWER *v.* ME.

‖**Gloria** (glōᵊ·riă). Pl. *occas.* **glorias.** ME. [L. *gloria* GLORY.] **1: a.** A name for: (*a*) *Gloria Patri*, the doxology beginning 'Glory be to the Father', which follows the recitation of the psalms, etc. (*b*) *Gloria tibi*, the response 'Glory be to Thee, O Lord', which follows the announcement of the gospel in the communion mass or service. (*c*) *Gloria in excelsis*, the hymn 'Glory be to God on high' (*Luke* 2:14), forming part of the communion service or mass. **b.** The music to which the last-mentioned is set 1597. **2.** An aureole or nimbus 1784.

Gloriation (glōᵊriēⁱ·ʃən). 1504. [– L. *gloriatio*, f. *gloriat-*, pa. ppl. stem of *gloriari*; see GLORY *v.*, -ION. Cf. OFr. *gloriation.*] The action of glorying; boasting; triumphing.

But al this g. is vain 1669.

Glorification (glōᵊ:rifikēⁱ·ʃən). 1460. [– eccl.L. *glorificatio*, f. *glorificat-*, pa. ppl. stem of *glorificare*; see next, -ION. Cf. Fr. *glorification.*] †**1.** *Alch.* The action of refining; the state of being refined –1470. **2.** The action of glorifying; the condition of being glorified 1549. **b.** *esp.* The exaltation (of Christ) to the glory of heaven 1502. **c.** *joc.* A festive occasion 1843. **3.** The ascription of glory to 1850; a doxology 1660.

3. The g. of Labour 1862, of 'science' 1892.

Glorify (glōᵊ·rifəi), *v.* ME. [–(O)Fr. *glorifier* – eccl.L. *glorificare*, f. late L. *glorificus*, f. *gloria*; see GLORY, -FY.] **1.** *trans.* To render glorious; to invest with glory or radiance. **2. a.** To advance the glory of (God, His name) by faithful action or suffering. **b.** To ascribe glory in adoration to (God). ME. **3.** To extol, honour, magnify with praise 1557. **4.** *refl.* To make one's boast, exult. Now *rare.* ME. **5.** *Alch.* To sublime 1657.

1. Jesus was not yet glorified *John* 7:39. As the bright sunne glorifies the skie SHAKS. To g. common life 1880. **2. b.** I bless and glorifie thy name JER. TAYLOR. Hence **Glo·rified** *ppl. a.* in senses of the vb.; *colloq.* transformed into something glorious (often used sarcastically). **Glo·rifier.**

Gloriole (glōᵊ·rioᵘl). 1813. [– Fr. *gloriole* – L. *gloriola*, dim. of *gloria* GLORY.] †A scrap of glory; an aureole, a halo.

†**Glorio·so.** 1589. [– It. *glorioso* – L. *gloriosus* boastful. See next.] A boaster –1661. Hence †**Glorio·ser.**

Glorious (glōᵊ·riəs), *a.* ME. [– AFr. *glorious*, OFr. *glorios, -eus* – L. *glorioseus*, f. *gloria* GLORY; see -OUS.] †**1.** Boastful; ostentatious; haughty; vainglorious –1734. †**2.** Eager for glory –1704. **3. a.** Possessing glory; illustrious. (Now somewhat *rare*). ME. **b.** Of an action, state of things, etc.: Conferring glory; entitling to brilliant and lofty renown. Const. *to.* 1548. **4.** Splendid in beauty or adornment. Now only with emotional connotation. †Formerly also: Brilliant, shining, lustrous. ME. **5.** Vaguely: Splendid, magnificent, intensely delightful. Often with jocular hyperbole. 1623. **6.** *joc.* Ecstatically drunk 1790.

3. a. Her late g. majesty SWIFT. By nothing is England so g. as by her poetry M. ARNOLD. **b.** The g. Battel (but with small fruit) of Lepanto 1659. **4.** The sunshine is a g. birth WORDSW. **5.** G. John [Dryden] touches them off a little sharply SCOTT. The g. uncertainty of the law 1759, of cricket 1899. **6.** Kings may be blest, but Tam was g. BURNS. Hence **Glo·rious-ly** *adv.*, **-ness.**

Glory (glōᵊ·ri). ME. [– AFr., OFr. *glorie* – L. *gloria.*] **1.** Boastful spirit. *Obs.* exc. in VAINGLORY. **2.** Exalted (and, in mod. use, merited) praise, honour, or admiration accorded by common consent to a person or thing; honourable fame, renown ME. **3.** Something that brings honour or renown; a subject for boasting; a distinguished ornament; a special distinction; a 'boast and pride'. Also *pl.* ME. **4.** Praise, honour, and thanksgiving offered in adoration ME. **5.** *The glory of God*: the majesty and splendour attendant upon a manifestation of God ME. **6.** Resplendent beauty or magnificence (now often with a tinge of sense 5 or 7). Also *pl.* splendours. ME. **7.** The splendour and bliss of heaven ME. **8.** A state of exaltation and splendour 1613. **9.** The circle of light represented as surrounding the head, or the whole figure, of the Saviour, the Virgin, or Saints; an AUREOLE or NIMBUS 1646. **b.** *transf.* Any circle or ring of light 1693. **10.** In names of insects and plants 1819.

1. G., or internal gloriation or triumph of the Minde HOBBES. **2.** What..abatynge of the glorie of a kynge FORTESCUE. The g. of Malebranche HUME. Phr. *The g. of God*: the honour of God, considered as the final cause of creation, and as the highest moral aim of intelligent creatures. **3.** Are all thy Conquests, Glories, Triumphes, Spoiles, Shrunke to this little Measure *Jul. C.* III. i. 149. The glories of Mr. Pitt's administration 1792. **4.** G. to God in the highest *Luke* 2:14. **6.** There hath past away a g. from the earth WORDSW. *pl.* I have seen The glories of the world 1693. **7.** Thou, bright Saint, high sitt'st in g. MILT. *To go to g.* (colloq.): to die. **8.** Phr. *In one's g.*: in one's highest state; also *colloq.* in a state of unbounded gratification.

Comb.: **g.-pea,** a name for the Australasian genus *Clianthus*; **-tree,** a shrub of the genus *Clerodendron*.

Glory (glōᵊ·ri), *v.* ME. [– L. *gloriari*, f. *gloria* GLORY.] **1.** *intr.* To exult with triumph, rejoice proudly. †**2.** To boast –1673. †**3.** *trans.* To give glory to; also, to make glorious, adorn –1661. †**4.** *intr.* Of light: To spread like a 'glory'. N. BACON.

1. Let 'em looke they g. not in mischiefe SHAKS. **2.** *Gal.* 4:14. **3.** The troop That gloried Venus at her wedding-day 1594.

Glo·ry-hole. 1845. [Of unkn. origin.] **1.** *dial.* A receptacle (as a drawer, room, etc.) in which things are heaped together without order or tidiness. **2.** *Glass-making.* An opening in the wall of a blast-furnace, disclosing the white light of the interior 1849.

Glos(e, Glos-, vars. of GLOZE, GLOZ-.

Gloss (glǫs), *sb.*[1] 1548. [Refashioning of GLOZE *sb.* after L. *glossa.*] **1.** A word inserted between the lines or in the margin as an explanatory rendering of a word in the text; hence a similar rendering in a glossary or dictionary. Also, a comment, explanation, interpretation. Often in bad sense: A sophistical or disingenuous interpretation. **b.** A collection of such explanations, a glossary; also, an interlinear translation or explanation of a text 1579. ¶**c.** In sense of Gr. γλῶσσα: A foreign or obscure word, requiring explanation. *Obs.* 1603. **2.** *attrib.* 1624.

1. Malicious Glosses made upon all he had said CLARENDON. A parenthesis or g. slipt into the text COLERIDGE. **b.** Mostly obscure words, only found in glosses 1894.

Gloss (glǫs), *sb.*[2] 1538. [Of unkn. origin.] **1.** Superficial lustre. Also *pl.* **b.** *fig.* A deceptive appearance, fair semblance, plausible pretext 1548. **2.** A layer of glowing matter (*rare*) 1762. †**3.** = GLAZE *sb.* 1. 1825.

1. G. of satin TENNYSON. **b.** Yet all his vertues.. Doe in our eyes, begin to loose their glosse SHAKS. Art, that sets a G. on what's amiss S. BUTLER. The g. of novelty GOLDSM.

Gloss (glǫs), *v.*[1] 1579. [f. GLOSS *sb.*[2], infl. by GLOSS *sb.*[1]] **1.** *trans.* = GLOZE *v.* 1. 1603. **b.** *intr.* 1579. **2.** *trans.* To veil with glosses; to explain away; to read a different sense into 1638.

1. b. The Celts seem to have had a special habit of glossing MAINE. **2.** Who have gloss'd and warp'd all the severe Rules of the Gospel about Chastity BENTLEY.

Gloss (glǫs), *v.*[2] 1656. [f. GLOSS *sb.*[2]] *trans.* To put a gloss upon. **a.** To veil in specious language. **b.** To render bright and glossy; to glaze 1762.

a. His friends..g. over his foible, by calling him an agreeable novelist FOOTE. **b.** Back black, glossed with blue BEWICK.

Glossal (glǫ·săl), *a.* 1860. [f. Gr. γλῶσσα tongue + -AL[1].] Of or pertaining to the tongue.

Glossanthrax (glǫs,æ·nþræks). 1849. [f. Gr. γλῶσσα tongue + ANTHRAX.] A disease of the tongue and mouth in horses and cattle, attended by ulceration.

Glossary (glǫ·sări). 1483. [– L. *glossarium*, f. *glossa*; see GLOZE *sb.*, -ARY[1].] A collection of glosses; a list with explanations of abstruse, antiquated, dialectal, or technical terms; a partial dictionary. Hence **Glossa·rial** *a.* of, pertaining to, or of the nature of, a g. **Glossa·rian, Glo·ssarist,** one who writes a gloss or commentary; one who compiles a g.

Glossator (glǫsē[i]·təɹ). ME. [– med.L. *glossator*, f. *glossare*, f. *glossa* GLOSS *sb.*[1]] A writer of glosses; a commentator, esp. on the texts of Civil and Canon Law.

†**Glo·ssem.** [– Gr. γλώσσημα, f. γλῶσσα; see GLOSS *sb.*[1], GLOZE *sb.*] A gloss, comment. BP. HALL.

Glosser[1] (glǫ·səɹ). 1603. [f. GLOSS *v.*[1] + -ER[1].] = GLOSSATOR.

Glosser[2] (glǫ·səɹ). 1828. [f. GLOSS *v.*[2] + -ER[1].] One who puts on a gloss.

Glossic (glǫ·sik), *a.* and *sb.* 1871. [f. Gr. γλῶσσα + -IC.] Applied by A. J. Ellis to a phonetic system of spelling in which each letter or digraph represents the sound it most commonly expresses in English. Usu. *absol.* as *sb.*

Glossist (glǫ·sist). 1641. [f. GLOSS *sb.*[1] + -IST.] A commentator.

Glossitis (glǫsəi·tis). Also **Glottitis.** 1822. [f. Gr. γλῶσσα + -ITIS.] *Path.* Inflammation of the tongue. Hence **Glossi·tic** *a.* pertaining to, or affected with g.

Glosso- (glǫ·so), rarely **glotto-** (glǫ·to), occas. **gloss-** bef. vowels, comb. f. Gr. γλῶσσα, γλῶττα tongue.

Glo:ss(o)-epiglo·ttic (also **glo:tto-), -epiglo·ttid, -epiglotti·dean** *adjs.*, pertaining to the tongue and to the epiglottis. **Glo:ssohy·al** [HY(OID) + -AL] *a.* pertaining to the tongue and to the hyoid bone; *sb.* a bone or cartilage extending forward from the basi-hyal, and constituting the hard basis of the tongue. **Glo:ssolary·ngeal** *a.*, pertaining to the tongue and to the larynx. **Glo:sso-phary·ngeal** *a.*, pertaining to the tongue and to the pharynx or gullet.

†||**Glo:ssoco·mium.** 1676. [mod.L. – Gr. γλωσσοκομεῖον a case for the reeds or tongues of musical instruments, f. γλῶσσα + κομεῖν take care of.] A case or frame for reducing a fractured or dislocated limb.

Glossograph (glǫ·sŏgraf). 1883. [(1) f. GLOSSO- + -GRAPH; (2) – Gr. γλωσσογράφος.] **1.** A contrivance for reproducing speech automatically by electric action. **2.** = next. 1885.

Glossographer (glǫsǫ·grăfəɹ). Also **glottographer.** 1607. [f. Gr. γλωσσογράφος (f. γλωσσο- + -γράφος); see GLOSSO-, -GRAPHER.] A writer of glosses or commentaries.

Glossography (glǫsǫ·grăfi). 1623. [Sense 1 f. GLOSSOGRAPHER; see -GRAPHY. Senses 2, 3, f. GLOSSO- + -GRAPHY.] **1.** The writing of glosses or commentaries; the compiling of glossaries. **2.** A description of the tongue 1842. **3.** A description or grouping of languages 1889. Hence **Glo:ssogra·phical** *a.*

||**Glossolalia** (glǫ:solæ·liă). Also **-laly.** 1879. [mod.L. *glossolalia*, f. Gr. γλωσσο- GLOSSO- + -λαλία speaking, in allusion to Acts 10:46, 1 Cor. 14 : 6, 23. Cf. Fr. *glossologie.*] The gift of speaking with 'tongues'.

Glossology (glǫsǫ·lŏdʒi). 1716. [f. GLOSSO- + -LOGY.] **1.** †**a.** The study of a language or languages –1857. **b.** The science of language (= GLOTTOLOGY) 1874. **2.** = TERMINOLOGY 1832. **3.** *Med.* The study of the tongue (*rare*) 1844. Hence **Glossolo·gical** *a.* of or pertaining to g. **Glosso·logist,** one who defines and explains terms; one versed in g.

Glossotomy (glǫsǫ·tŏmi). 1842. [f. GLOSSO- + -TOMY.] Dissection, amputation, or excision of the tongue.

Glossotype, earlier f. GLOSSIC, q.v.

Glossy (glǫ·si), *a.* 1556. [f. GLOSS *sb.*[2] + -Y[1].] Having a gloss; smooth and shining; polished; lustrous; *spec.* in *Path.*, designating morbid symptoms, as *g. skin, tongue.* Also *fig.*

fig. He [Ld. Chesterfield], however, with the g. duplicity which was his constant study, affected to be quite unconcerned BOSWELL. Hence **Glo·ssily** *adv.* **Glo·ssiness.**

Glost (glǫst). 1875. [app. a dial. alteration of GLOSS *sb.*[2] 3.] *Ceramics.* The lead glaze used for pottery. In **g.-fireman,** the man who attends to a g.-oven; **-oven,** the oven in which glazed ware is fired.

Glottal (glǫ·tăl), *a.* 1846. [f. GLOTTIS + -AL[1].] Pertaining to, or produced in, the glottis.

The most familiar example of this 'glottal catch' is an ordinary cough SWEET.

Glottic (glǫ·tik), *a.*[1] 1802. [– Gr. γλωττικός of the tongue, f. γλῶττα; see GLOTTIS, -IC.] Linguistic.

Glottic (glǫ·tik), *a.*[2] 1839. [f. GLOTTIS + -IC.] Of or pertaining to the glottis. So **Glotti·dean** *a.*

Glottid (glǫ·tid). 1880. [f. Gr. γλωττίς, γλωττιδ- GLOTTIS; see -ID[2].] A vocal sound produced by the glottis.

Glottis (glǫ·tis). 1578. [– mod.L. *glottis* – Gr. γλωττίς, f. γλῶττα, Attic form of γλῶσσα tongue.] The opening at the upper part of the trachea, or wind-pipe, and between the vocal chords.

Glotti·tis. *Path.* = GLOSSITIS.

Glotto-: see GLOSSO-.

Glottology (glǫtǫ·lŏdʒi). 1841. [f. GLOTTO- (see GLOSSO-) + -LOGY.] The science of language. Hence **Glottolo·gic, -al** *a.* **Glotto·logist.**

Gloucester (glǫ·stəɹ). Name of an English county; hence *single-, double-G.*, the name of a cheese made there, seldom in full *Gloucester cheese* 1802.

Glout (glaut), *v.* Now *rare.* ME. [app. var. of GLOAT *v.*] *intr.* To look sullen, frown. Also *transf.*

transf. Heavy clouds that hung glouting H. WALPOLE. Hence **Glout** *sb.* (*rare*), a frown; a sullen look.

Glove (glɒv), *sb.* [OE. *glōf* corresp. to ON. *glōfi*, by some taken to be :– Gmc. *ʒalōfō, -on,* f. *ʒa- Y- + base of ON. *lófi* (whence ME., Sc. *loof*), Goth. *lofa* hand.] **1.** A covering for the hand, usu. one with a separate sheath for each finger. **2.** = *Boxing-glove* 1725. **3.** In *Hat-making*, a smooth piece of wood, fastened to the hand by a string, employed in rubbing the sheets of felt at the 'battery' 1875.

1. Phr. *To take up, throw (down) the g.* (as a pledge or challenge to battle). Heere's my Gloue: Giue mee another of thine SHAKS. *To fit like a g.*: to fit perfectly. *To handle without gloves*: to treat without mercy. Also HAND AND GLOVE.

Comb.: **g.-finger** (see FINGER *sb.*); **-money,** (*a*) a gratuity given to servants ostensibly to buy gloves with; (*b*) *Law*, extraordinary rewards formerly given to officers of English courts, etc.; *esp.* money given by the sheriff of a county, in which no offenders were left for execution, to the clerk of assize and the judges' officers; **-sponge,** a kind of sponge in the shape of a g.; **-stretcher.**

Glove (glɒv), *v.* 1573. [f. prec.] *trans.* To cover with, or as with, a glove; to provide with gloves.

Glover (glɒ·vəɹ). ME. [f. GLOVE *sb.* + -ER[1].] One who makes or sells gloves.

Comb.: **glover's stitch,** (*a*) the stitch used in sewing the seams of gloves; (*b*) a stitch resembling this, used in sewing up wounds; **glover's suture,** a suture made with the *glover's stitch.*

Glow (glō[u]), *sb.* 1600. [f. next vb.] **1.** The state or condition of glowing with heat 1793. **2.** Brightness and warmth of colour; a flush. Applied esp. to the warm red of the cheeks in youth or health. 1600. **3.** Warmth of feeling or passion; ardour 1748.

2. The red glowe of scorne SHAKS. The transmutation—Jura's black to one gold g. BROWNING. **3.** The g. of self-approbation J. H. NEWMAN.

Comb.: **g.-beetle** = GLOW-WORM; **-fly** = FIREFLY; **-lamp,** a lamp in which the light results from the incandescence of a resisting substance, e.g. carbon, produced by the passage of an electric current; **-lighting,** lighting by g.-lamps.

Glow (glō[u]), *v.*[1] Pa. t. and pple. **glowed.** [OE. *glōwan* str. vb. corresp. to the weak vbs. OS. *glōjan* (Du. *gloeien*), OHG. *gluoen* (G. *glühen*), ON. *glóa*; f. Gmc. *ʒlō-; cf. GLEED.] **1.** *intr.* To be incandescent; to emit bright light and heat without flame. Said also of a fire. **2.** To shine, emit light, appear suffused with radiance, like something intensely heated ME.; to gaze with glowing eyes (E. B. BROWNING). **3.** To be brilliant and warm in colouring ME. **4.** To be excessively hot; to be on fire, to burn (*lit.* and *fig.*) ME. **5.** To burn with bodily heat; usually with the accompaniment of a heightened colour ME. **6.** To burn with the fervour of emotion or passion. Said of persons and their feelings. 1649. †**7.** *trans.* To make hot; to heat –1683.

1. I..found it [Newgate] in ruins, with the fire yet glowing JOHNSON. **2.** Now glow'd the Firmament With living Saphirs MILT. The eye [of Burns]..glowed (I say literally glowed) when he spoke with feeling or interest SCOTT. **3.** A gown that glows with Tyrian rays DRYDEN. **4.** The rapid axles g. 1789. **5.** Girls, all glowing with the flush of life 1884. **6.** The courage of the first ages of the republic glowed in his breast GIBBON. The Tories, glowing with resentment [etc.] MACAULAY. **7.** *Ant. & Cl.* II. ii. 209. Hence **Glow·ingly** *adv.*

Glow, *v.*[2] *Obs.* exc. *dial.* ME. [poss. a use of prec.; but cf. Sw., Da. *glo* stare, look sullen.] *intr.* To stare.

†**Glowbard.** 1475. [f. GLOW *v.*[1] + BIRD, cf. LADY-BIRD.] A glow-worm –1607.

Glower (glau[ə]ɹ, glau·əɹ), *v.* 1500. [perh. Sc. var. of synon. GLORE, or f. GLOW *v.*[2] + -ER[5].] **1.** *intr. Sc.* To stare with wide-open eyes; to gaze intently. **2.** To look crossly; to scowl. Also *dial.* of the weather: To be gloomy. 1775. Hence **Glower** *sb.* (chiefly *Sc.*), the action of glowering.

Glow-worm (glō[u]·wəɹm). ME. [f. GLOW *v.*[1] + WORM.] A coleopterous insect (*Lampyris noctiluca* Linn.), the female of which emits a shining green light from the extremity of the abdomen. The female is wingless; the male is winged, but non-luminous. Also *fig.* Also *attrib.*

The Glowworme..gins to pale his vneffectuall Fire SHAKS. *attrib.* My..Glow-worme Muse 1630.

Gloxinia (glǫksi·niă). 1816. [mod.L., named by L'Héritier after B.P. *Gloxin*, who described the plant in 1785; see -IA[1].] An American tropical plant (N.O. *Gesneraceæ*) with large bell-shaped flowers.

Gloze (glō[u]z), *sb.* ME. [– (O)Fr. *glose* – med.L. *glosa, gloza*, for L. *glossa* word needing explanation, the explanation itself. See GLOSS *sb.*[1]] **1.** = GLOSS *sb.*[1] 1. *arch.* **2.** Flattery, deceit; a flattering speech, etc. Now *rare.* ME. **b.** A pretence, specious show; also, a disguise. Now *rare.* ME.

2. This is a verray sooth with outen glose CHAUCER. **b.** Gloses, and goodly shews of words P. HOLLAND.

Gloze (glō[u]z), *v.* ME. [– (O)Fr. *gloser*, f. *glose* (see prec.); in med.L. *glossare.*] †**1.** *trans.* To make glozes or glosses upon; to comment upon, interpret. Also *absol.* or *intr.* –1872. **2.** *trans.* To veil with specious comments; to palliate; to explain away. Freq. with *over.* ME. **3.** *intr.* To talk smoothly and speciously; to fawn ME. **4.** *trans.* To flatter; to coax, wheedle ME.

1. *Hen. V*, I. ii. 40. **3.** I kan nat glose, I am a rude man CHAUCER. **4.** The parasite glozes his master with sweet speeches CARLYLE. Hence †**Glo·zer,** one who writes glosses; a flatterer, sycophant. **Glo·zing** *vbl. sb.* the action of glossing; flattery, specious talk.

Glucate (glᴵū·kĕt). 1840. [f. GLUC(IC + -ATE⁴.] *Chem.* A salt of glucic acid.

Glucic (glᴵū·sik), *a.* 1840. [– Fr. *glucique*, f. Gr. γλυκύς sweet; see -IC.] *Chem.* In *glucic acid*, an acid obtained by the action of alkalis or acids on glucose.

Glucina (glᴵusəi·nă). Formerly also **glucine, glycine.** 1800. [Latinized form of Fr. *glucine* (Vauquelin, 1798), f. Gr. γλυκύς sweet; see -INE⁵.] *Chem.* The oxide of glucinum or beryllium.

Glucinum (glᴵusəi·nŏm). Also **glucinium.** 1812. [f. *glucina*; see prec., -IUM.] *Chem.* A white metal obtained from beryl. Also called BERYLLIUM. Symbol Be or Gl.

Glucogene, -genic: see GLYCOGEN, -GENIC.

Glucose (glᴵū·kōᵘs). Also **glycose.** 1840. [– Fr. *glucose* (1838), irreg. – Gr. γλεῦκος must, sweet wine, rel. to γλυκύς sweet; see -OSE². Gr. *υ* is abnormally repr. by *u* in these words; contrast GLYCERINE, GLYCO-.] *Chem.* **a.** = DEXTROSE or grape-sugar; now chiefly a trade name for dextrose obtained from starch by the action of sulphuric acid. **b.** Any member of the group of sugars having the common formula $C_6H_{12}O_6$, and including dextrose, lævulose, mannitose, galactose, etc. Hence **Gluco·sic** *a.* of or pertaining to g.

Glucoside (glᴵū·kŏsəid). 1866. [f. GLUCOSE + -IDE.] *Chem.* One of a class of vegetable substances which being treated with dilute acids or alkalis, or subjected to the action of ferments, are resolved into glucose and some other substance.

Glue (glᴵū, glū), *sb.* ME. [– (O)Fr. *glu* :– late L. *glus, glut-* for L. *gluten.*] †**1.** Bird-lime. Also *fig.* –1704. **2.** A hard, brittle, brownish gelatin, obtained by boiling the hides and hoofs of animals to a jelly; when gently heated with water, it is used as a cement for uniting substances ME. **3.** Used loosely for any substance that serves as a cement ME. Also *fig.* **4.** *Soap-making.* A name for the condition of soap at an early stage of its manufacture 1885. **5.** *attrib.* 1755.

2. *Fish-g.* (see FISH *sb.*¹). *Dutch* or *Flanders g.*: a very fine kind of g. **3.** *Marine g.*: a solution of caoutchouc in naphtha, to which a proportion of shellac is added. *Comb.* **g.-plant,** a sea-weed, *Plocaria tenax.*

Glue (glᴵū, glū), *v.* ME. [– (O)Fr. *gluer*, f. *glu* GLUE *sb.*] **1.** *trans.* To join or fasten with glue or other viscous substance. **2.** *transf.* and *fig.* To fix or attach firmly (as if by gluing). Formerly often: To attach in sympathy or friendship. ME. †**3.** *intr.* **a.** To stick together. Also *fig.* **b.** To admit of being fastened by glue. –1701. †**4.** *trans.* To smear with glue or other viscous substance –1808.

1. Two boards glued up edge to edge GWILT. Phr. *To g. up*: to seal up as with glue. **2.** My Loue and Feare, glew'd many Friends to thee SHAKS. He glued the huge flagon to his lips SCOTT. Hence **Glu·er.**

Glue·-pot. 1483. A pot in which glue is melted by the heat of water in an outer vessel.

Gluey (glᴵū·i, glū·i), *a.* ME. [f. GLUE *sb.* + -Y¹.] Resembling, or of the nature of, glue; viscous, glutinous, sticky. In early use: †Bituminous. Hence **Glu·eyness.**

Gluish (glᴵū·iʃ, glū·iʃ), *a.* ME. [f. GLUE *sb.* + -ISH¹.] Somewhat gluey.

Glum (glɒm), *sb. rare.* 1523. [f. GLUM *v.* or *a.* Cf. GLOOM *sb.*¹] †**1.** A sullen look –1530. **2.** Glumness. LOCKHART.

Glum (glɒm), *a.* 1547. [Related to GLUM *v.*] **1.** Sullen, frowning. **2.** Gloomy, dark; dismal. Now only *fig.* from sense 1. 1557.

1. [He] sat g. BESANT. **2.** The g. old bridge THACKERAY. Hence **Glu·mly** *adv.* †**Glu·mmish** *a.* somewhat g. **Glu·mmy** *a.* †gloomy; glum. **Glu·mness,** the condition of being g.

Glum, *v. Obs.* exc. *dial.* 1460. [var. of †*glom(e)*, †*gloumbe* GLOOM *v.*; for the vocalism cf. *thumb* :– OE. *þūma.*] *intr.* To look sullen; to scowl.

Glumaceous (glᴵu-, glumēᴵ·ʃəs), *a.* 1828. [f. GLUME + -ACEOUS.] Of the nature of glumes; bearing glumes. Also, belonging to the N.O. *Glumaceæ* of plants, which includes the grasses and sedges.

Glumal (glᴵū-, glū·măl), *a.* 1846. [f. GLUME + -AL¹.] = prec.: Lindley's name for an alliance of glume-bearing endogens. Also **Glu·mal** *sb.* a member of this alliance.

Glume (glᴵūm, glūm). 1789. [– L. *gluma* hull, husk, rel. to *glubere* shell, peel.] *Bot.* One of the chaff-like bracts which form the calyx or outer envelope in the inflorescence of grasses and sedges; the husk of corn or other grain.

‖**Glumella** (glᴵu-, glume·lă). 1861. [mod.L., dim. of L. *gluma.*] *Bot.* An inner glume or palea. So **Glume·lle** (*rare*). Hence **Glume·llule,** one of the scales frequently found at the base of the ovary in grasses; a lodicule.

Glumose (glᴵu-, glumōᵘ·s), *a.* 1793. [– mod.L. *glumosus*, f. *gluma*; see GLUME, -OSE¹.] Furnished with a glume or husk. var. **Glu·mous.**

Glump (glɒmp), *v. dial.* 1746. [Cf. GLUM, DUMP, etc.] *intr.* To sulk, be glum or sullen. Hence **Glump** *sb.* a sulky person; (*pl.*) the sulks. **Glu·mpish, Glu·mpy** *adjs.* glum, sullen, sulky.

Glunch (glɒnʃ), *v. Sc.* 1719. [Cf. GLUM *a.* and CLUNCH *a.*] *intr.* To look sour or glum. Hence **Glunch** *sb.* a sour look; *a.* sulky.

†**Glunimie.** *Sc.* Also **glune-amie.** 1745. [perh. corruption of Gael.] Lowland name for a Highlander –1828.

Glut, *sb.*¹ *Obs.* exc. *dial.* 1533. [– OFr. *glout* gulp, sb. rel. to *gloutir* GLUT *v.*¹,².] A gulp; the amount swallowed at a gulp.

Glut (glɒt), *sb.*² 1579. [f. GLUT *v.*¹] **1.** The act of glutting or condition of being glutted with food, etc.; indulgence to satiety or disgust; one's fill; a surfeit 1594. **2.** *Comm.* A supply of a commodity which greatly exceeds the demand 1594. **3.** An excessive number or quantity. Now *rare.* 1636. †**4.** An excessive flow of saliva, bile, etc. –1719. †**5.** That which gluts or chokes up –1704.

1. This g. of wealth, and a full satiety of all pleasure 1659. **2.** Phr. *A g. in the market.* **3.** Extream gluts of rain 1661.

†**Glut,** *sb.*³ 1611. [Altered f. *glit* GLEET *sb.*] = GLEET *sb.* 2. –1615.

Glut (glɒt), *sb.*⁴ *techn.* or *dial.* 1790. [perh. altered f. *clut*, dial. var. of CLEAT.] †**1.** A wedge of wood or iron. **2.** 'A small brick or block introduced into a course to complete it' (Knight) 1875. **3.** *Naut.* 'A piece of canvas sewed into a sail, near the head' (Dana) 1841.

Glut, *sb.*⁵ [Cf. dial. *gloat* (XVIII); of unkn. origin.] A kind of eel.

Glut (glɒt), *v.*¹ ME. [Earliest forms *gloute, glotte, glotye*, prob. – OFr. *gloutir* swallow (with causative sense perh. developed in AFr.) :– L. *gluttire* (see GLUTTON).] **1.** *trans.* To feed to repletion; to gorge. Chiefly *refl.* and *pass.* Const. *with.* **2.** *fig.* To gratify to the full (esp. a ferocious or lustful desire) 1549. **b.** *intr.* To take one's fill of thinking, gazing, etc. *on*; to gloat *on.* Also to long greedily *for* (*rare*). 1632. **3.** To surfeit with food; hence, to surfeit, cloy, or sicken with excess of anything ME. **4.** To fill to excess; to choke up; to saturate, impregnate thoroughly *with* some substance. Now *rare.* 1471. **5.** To overstock with mercantile goods 1624.

1. Grim Slaughter strides along Glutting her greedy Jaws SOMERVILLE. Horses that have broken fence, And glutted all night long breast-deep in corn TENNYSON. **2. b.** Love doth with an hungry eye G. on Beauty CAREW. **3.** I found The fickle ear soon glutted with the sound M. PRIOR. **5.** Phr. *To g. the market.*

Glut (glɒt), *v.*² Now *rare.* 1600. [– OFr *gloutir* swallow; see prec. Cf. ENGLUT.] *trans.* To swallow greedily, gulp down.

Hee'l be hanged yet, Though euery drop of water sweare against it, And Gape at widst to g. him SHAKS.

Glut-, abbreviated comb. f. GLUTEN, as in **Glutaco·nic** *a.*, derived from gluten and aconitine; *g. acid*, $C_5H_6O_4$. **Gluta·mic** or **Glutami·nic** *a.*, derived from gluten and amidogen; *g. acid*, $C_5H_9NO_4$. **Gluta·mine** = *glutamic acid.* **Gluta·ric** *a.*, derived from gluten and tartaric acid $(CO_2H)_2\ (CH_2)_3$. **Glu·tazine,** $C_5H_6N_2O_2$, a white crystalline compound derived from pyridine.

Glutæal, gluteal (glᴵū-, glutī·ăl), *a.* 1804. [f. next + -AL¹.] Of or belonging to the glutæi. So **Glute·an** *a.*

‖**Glutæus, gluteus** (glᴵu-, glutī·ɒs). *Pl.* **-tæi, -tei** (-tī·əi). 1681. [mod.L., f. Gr. γλουτός rump, buttock.] One of the three large muscles (dist. as *g. maximus, medius, minimus*) which form the buttock, and serve to move the thigh in man; occas. the analogous muscle in the lower animals. Also *attrib.*, in *g. muscle, glutæi muscles.*

Gluten (glᴵū-, glū·ten). 1597. [– Fr. *gluten* (Paré) – L. *gluten* GLUE.] **1.** Any sticky substance (*rare*) 1639. †**2.** The albuminous element of animal tissues, now called FIBRIN –1834. **3.** The nitrogenous part of the flour of wheat or other grain, which remains behind as a viscid substance when the starch is removed by kneading the flour in a current of water 1803.

Comb.: **g.-bread,** bread containing a large proportion of g., prescribed in cases of diabetes; **-casein, -fibrin,** the vegetable casein and fibrin which form constituents of g.

Glutin (glᴵū, glū·tin). Also **-ine.** 1825. [– Fr. *glutine* (obs.) vegetable albumen, prob. f. L. *gluten* + *-ine* -IN¹, -INE⁵.] †**1.** = GLUTEN 1 and 3. **2.** = GLIADIN 1838. **3.** A distinct form of gelatin obtained from skin, hoof, bone, etc. 1845.

†**Glu·tinate,** *v.* 1564. [– *glutinat-*, pa. ppl. stem of L. *glutinare* glue together, close up (a wound), f. *gluten, glutin-*; see GLUTEN -ATE³. Cf. Fr. †*glutiner.*] **1.** *trans. Med.* To close up, heal (a wound); to constipate (the bowels, veins, etc.). Also *absol.* –1748. **2.** To glue together. (Dicts.) Hence †**Glutina·tion.** †**Glu·tinative** *a.* constrictive; *sb. pl.* medical preparations which serve to close up or bind together.

Glutinosity (glᴵū-, glūtinǫ·sīti). ME. [– med.L. *glutinositas*, f. L. *glutinosus*; see next, -ITY.] The quality of being glutinous.

Glutinous (glᴵū-, glū·tinəs), *a.* 1576. [– (O)Fr. *glutineux* or L. *glutinosus*, f. *gluten, glutin-* + *-osus* -OUS.] Of the nature of glue or gluten; viscid, sticky, gluey. var. **Glu·tinose.** Hence **Glu·tinous-ly** *adv.*, **-ness.**

Glutton (glɒ·t'n). ME. [– OFr. *gluton, gloton* (mod. *glouton*) :– L. *glutto, -ōn-*, rel. to *gluttire* swallow (GLUT *v.*¹,²), *gluttus* greedy, *gula* throat.]

A. *sb.* **1.** One who eats to excess; a gormandizer. Also of animals. **2.** *fig.* One who is inordinately fond of some specified object or pursuit, esp. *a g. of books*, L. *helluo librorum* 1704. **b.** *Sporting slang.* 'One who takes a deal of punishment before he is satisfied' 1809. †**3.** As a general term of reproach or contempt –1523. **4.** A voracious animal, *Gulo luscus* or *arcticus*, belonging to the *Mustelidæ* or weasels and martens, but much larger than other members of that family. The American variety is called WOLVERENE or CARCAJOU. 1674.

1. *fig.* Suche a gredie glotton is avarice HALL. **2.** Foes alike to Good, Gluttons in Murder, wanton to destroy 1706.

B. *adj.* = GLUTTONOUS; also (see A. 3) †villainous ME.

In pleasure some their g. souls would steep DRYDEN.

†**Glu·tton,** *v.* 1600. [f. the sb.; cf. OFr. *gloutoner.*] *intr.* To feed voraciously or to excess –1781.

Glutton'd at last, [you] return at home to pine LOVELACE.

Gluttonish (glɒ·təniʃ), *a. rare.* 1586. [f. GLUTTON *sb.* + -ISH¹.] Glutton-like, voracious.

Gluttonize (glɒ·tənəiz), *v.* 1656. [f. as prec. + -IZE.] *intr.* To feast gluttonously.

Gluttonous (glɒ·tənəs), *a.* ME. [f. GLUTTON *sb.* + -OUS.] Given to excess in eating; characterized by, or of the nature of, gluttony. Also *transf.* Hence **Glu·ttonously** *adv.*

Gluttony (glɒ·təni). [– OFr. *glutonie*, etc. (mod. *gloutonnerie*), f. *gluton* GLUTTON; see -Y³.] The vice of excessive eating. (One of the seven deadly sins.) Also *personified.*

Their sumptuous gluttonies MILT. Swinish g. MILT.

Glyceral (gli·sĕrăl). 1872. [f. GLYCER(INE + -AL(DEHYDE.] *Chem.* A compound obtained by heating glycerine with an aldehyde.

Glycerate (gli·sĕrĕt). 1864. [f. GLYCER(IC + -ATE⁴.] **1.** *Chem.* A salt of glyceric acid.

2. 'A solution of some substance in glycerin' (*Syd. Soc. Lex.*) 1885.

Glyceric (glise·rik, gli·sĕrik), *a.* 1864. [f. GLYCER(INE + -IC.] *Chem.* Of, derived from, or relating to glycerine.

G. acid, an acid obtained by the action of nitric acid on glycerine.

Glyceride (gli·sĕrəid). 1864. [f. GLYCERINE + -IDE.] *Chem.* A compound ester of glycerine.

Glycerine, glycerin (gli·sĕrin). 1838. [– Fr. *glycerin* (Chevreul), f. Gr. γλυκερός sweet; see -IN[1], -INE[5].] **1.** A colourless, sweet, syrupy liquid obtained from animal and vegetable oils and fats by saponification. Chemically it is a triatomic alcohol, the hydrate of glyceryl. The name GLYCEROL is now preferred. **2.** Formerly a general name for the group of alcohols of which glycerine is a member 1866. **3.** *Pharm.* Any preparation consisting of a specified substance dissolved or suspended in glycerine 1879.

Glycerite (gli·sĕrəit). 1875. [f. GLYCER(INE + -ITE[1] 4.] *Pharm.* A preparation dissolved or suspended in glycerine.

Glycero- (gli·sĕro), comb. f. GLYCERINE. **Gly:cerophosphate**, a salt of glycerophosphoric acid. **Gly:cerophospho·ric acid**, an acid produced by the action of phosphoric acid or phosphoric anhydride on glycerine.

Glycerol (gli·sĕrǫl). 1884. [f. GLYCER(INE + -OL.] *Chem.* = GLYCERINE 1.

Glycerole (gli·sĕroᵘl). 1861. [f. GLYCER(INE + *-ole* (used arbitrarily).] *Pharm.* A preparation in which glycerine is the vehicle.

Glyceryl (gli·sĕril). Also **-yle.** 1845. [f. GLYCER(INE + -YL.] *Chem.* The triatomic radical of glycerine and the glycerides.

Glycic (gli·sik), *a. Chem.* Corrected form of GLUCIC (acid).

Glycide (gli·səid). 1864. [f. GLYC(ERINE + -IDE.] *Chem.* $C_3H_6O_2$, the hypothetical radical corresponding to the glycidic ethers. Hence **Glyci·dic** *a.* pertaining to, or derived from g. *Glycidic ethers*, a class of diatomic ethers, produced from the glycerides by the action of alkalis.

Glycin (gli·sin). Also **-ine.** 1881. [f. Gr. γλυκύς + -IN[1].] *Chem.* = GLYCOCOLL.

Glyco- (gləi·ko, gli·ko), irregularly used (instead of *glycy-*) as comb. f. Gr. γλυκύς sweet, and in names of chemical compounds to indicate the presence of *glycerol* or some other substance with a name beginning with *glyc-*, as in **Glyco-gelatin**, a combination of glycerine and gelatin used in the making of lozenges and pastilles.

Glycocholate (gləikokǫ·lĕt, glik-). 1872. [f. as next + -ATE[4].] *Chem.* A salt of glycocholic acid.

Glycocholic (gləikokǫ·lik, gliko-), *a.* 1864. [f. GLYCO- + CHOLIC *a.*] *Chem. Glycocholic acid*, the principal acid in ox-gall.

Glycocin (gləi·kŏsin, gli·-). 1852. [app. after prec.; see -IN[1].] *Chem.* = GLYCOCOLL. Now little used.

Glycocoll (gləi·kŏkǫl, gli·-). 1840. [f. GLYCO- + Gr. κόλλα glue.] *Chem.* A crystalline substance contained in bile and formed when glycocholic acid and hydrochloric acid are boiled together. Also called *gelatin-sugar*.

Glycogen (gləi·kŏ₁dʒən, gli·kŏ-). Also **glu-.** 1860. [f. GLYCO- + -GEN; the substance being the source of the sugar in animal tissues.] *Chem.* A white, amorphous, tasteless, inodorous, starch-like substance found in animal tissues, esp. the liver; it is converted into dextrose by boiling in dilute acid.

Glycogenic (gləikodʒe·nik, gliko-), *a.* Also **glu-.** 1859. [f. as prec. + -IC.] Of or pertaining to the formation of sugar, esp. in the animal body. So **Glycoge·nesis**, the formation of sugar, esp. in the animal body. **Glycogene·tic, Glyco·genous** *adjs.* ? = GLYCOGENIC. **Glyco·geny** = *glycogenesis*.

Glycol (gləi·kǫl, gli-). 1858. [f. GLYC(ERINE + -OL; orig. meant as a name for a substance intermediate between glycerine and alcohol.] *Chem.* **a.** Formerly applied to the compound now called *ethyl glycol* or *ethylene alcohol* $C_2H_4(OH)_2$, a sweetish, colourless, inodorous, viscid liquid obtained from the decomposition of ethylene dibromide. **b.** A general name for the group of fatty dihydroxy alcohols of which this is the type, having the general structure $C_nH_{2n}(OH)_2$. Hence **Glyco·llate**, a salt of glycollic acid.

Glycollic, glycolic (gləikǫ·lik, gli-), *a.* 1852. [f. GLYCO- + Gr. λυτικός resolvent, f. λύειν loose, resolve; see -IC.] Of or containing glycol. *Glycollic acid*, an acid obtained by the oxidation of glycol.

Glycollide. [f. GLYCOL + -IDE.] *Chem.* $C_2H_2O_2$, a compound isomeric with glyoxal, and differing from glycollic acid by 1 at. water. WATTS.

Glycolytic (gləikoli·tik, gliko-), *a.* 1897. [f. GLYCO- + Gr. λυτικός, f. λύειν loose, resolve; see -IC.] Having the property of decomposing sugar.

Glycone·an, glyco·nian, *a. rare.* 1727. [f. late L. *Glyconius* – Gr. Γλυκώνειος, f. Γλύκων name of a Greek lyric poet; see -AN, -EAN, -IAN.] = next.

Glyconic (gləikǫ·nik). 1670. [f. Γλύκων (see prec.) + -IC.]

A. *adj.* Epithet of a lyric metre or verse, essentially a logaœdic tetrapody consisting of three trochees and a dactyl; also, composed or consisting of such verses 1779.

B. *sb.* A glyconic verse.

‖**Glycosuria** (gləi:kosⁱūᵊ·riă, gliko-). 1860. [quasi-L., f. Fr. *glycose* GLUCOSE + Gr. οὖρον urine; see -IA[1].] *Path.* A condition in which sugar appears in the urine. Hence **Glycosu·ric** *a.* relating to or affected with g.

†**Gly·cyrize.** 1599. [– L. *glycyrrhiza* (see next).] Liquorice –1661.

Glycyrrhizin (glisirəi·zin). 1838. [f. late L. *glycyrrhiza* – Gr. γλυκύρριζα LIQUORICE + -IN[1].] *Chem.* The glucoside contained in the root of liquorice (*Glycyrrhiza glabra*).

Glyn(n, obs. f. GLEN.

Glyoxal (gləi₁ǫ·ksăl). 1858. [f. GLY(COL + OX(ALIC + -AL[2].] *Chem.* A white amorphous solid, called also *oxalic aldehyde.* Hence **Glyoxa·lic** *a.*, in *glyoxalic acid*, an acid obtained by treating ethylic alcohol with nitric acid.

Glyoxilin (gləiǫ·ksilin). Also **-yline.** 1875. [perh. f. *glyoxyl(ic*, var. of *glyoxalic* (f. prec. + -IC) + -IN[1].] An explosive, gun-cotton saturated with nitroglycerine.

Glyph (glif). 1775. [– Fr. *glyphe* – Gr. γλυφή carving, rel. to γλύφειν carve.] **1.** A sculptured mark or symbol (*rare*) 1825. **2.** *Arch.* A groove or channel, usually vertical, used esp. in the Doric frieze. Cf. TRIGLYPH. Hence **Gly·phic** *a.* carved, sculptured; *sb.* = GLYPH 1.

Glyphograph (gli·fŏgrɑf), *sb.* 1855. [Back-formation f. next.] A plate made by glyphography, or an impression taken from such a plate. So **Glypho·grapher**, one who practises glyphography. **Glyphogra·phic** *a.* relating to or produced by glyphography.

Glyphography (glifǫ·grăfi). 1843. [f. Gr. γλυφή (see GLYPH) + -GRAPHY.] An electrotype process by which a copy of an engraved plate is obtained with a raised surface, suited for letter-press printing.

Glyptic (gli·ptik). 1818. [– Fr. *glyptique* or Gr. γλυπτικός, f. γλύπτης carver, f. γλύφειν carve; see -IC.]

A. *adj.* **1.** Of or pertaining to carving or engraving, esp. on gems. 1847. **2.** *Min.* Figured (Webster) 1864.

B. *sb.* The art of carving or engraving, esp. on gems. Also *pl.* Hence **Gly·ptical** *a.* = A. 1.

Glyptodon (gli·ptŏdǫn). Also **-dont.** 1838. [mod.L., f. Gr. γλυπτός sculptured + ὀδούς, ὀδοντ- tooth.] An extinct S. American quadruped allied to the armadillos, of the size of an ox, covered with a solid carapace, and having fluted teeth. Hence **Glyptodo·ntoid** *a.* resembling (that of) a g.

Glyptography (gliptǫ·grăfi). 1797. [f. Gr. γλυπτός carved + -GRAPHY. Cf. Fr. *glyptographie.*] The art of engraving upon gems; the descriptive science of engraved gems. So **Gly·ptograph**, an engraving on a gem. **Glypto·grapher. Glyptogra·phic** *a.* pertaining to g.

Glyster(e, var. of CLYSTER.

Gmelinite (gme·linəit). 1825. [f. Professor C. A. *Gmelin*; see -ITE[1] 2 b.] *Min.* Hydrous silicate of aluminium, calcium, and sodium, found in colourless, yellow, and flesh-coloured crystals.

Gnapweed, Gnar, var. ff. KNAPWEED, KNAR.

Gnar (nāɹ), *v.* Also **Gnarr.** 1496. [Echoic; cf. MLG. *gnarren*, etc.] *intr.* To snarl, growl. *fig.* A thousand wants Gnarr at the heels of men TENNYSON.

Gnarl (nāɹl), *sb.*[1] 1824. [Back-formation from GNARLED.] A contorted knotty protuberance, esp. on a tree. Hence **Gna·rly** *a.*

Gnarl, *sb.*[2] [f. GNARL *v.*[1]] A snarl. E. BRONTË.

†**Gnarl** (nāɹl), *v.*[1] 1593. [frequent of GNAR *v.*] *intr.* To snarl –1814.

Wolues are gnarling, who shall gnaw thee first SHAKS.

Gnarl (nāɹl), *v.*[2] Chiefly in pa. pple. 1814. [Back-formation from GNARLED.] *trans.* To contort, twist, make knotted and rugged like an old tree. Also *transf.* and *fig.*

Her lean large hands, So gnarl'd with bone 1814.

Gnarled (nāɹld), *ppl. a.* 1603. [var. of *knarled*, **knurled*, f. KNARL, KNURL, extensions of KNAR, KNUR.] Of a tree: Covered with protuberances; distorted, twisted; rugged, knotted.

The vn-wedgable and g. Oke *Meas. for M.* II. ii. 116.

Gnash (næʃ), *sb. rare.* 1804. [f. GNASH *v.*] A gnashing or snap of the teeth.

Gnash (næʃ), *v.* 1496. [alt. of †*gnacche* (XIV) or GNAST.] **1.** *intr.* To strike together or grind the teeth, esp. from rage or anguish. Also said of the teeth. **2.** *trans.* To strike (the teeth) together, as in rage or anguish 1590. **3.** To bite upon, grind the teeth upon 1812.

1. There they him laid, Gnashing for anguish and despite and shame MILT. **3.** I strove..To rend and g. my bonds in twain BYRON.

†**Gnast.** *v.* ME. [– ON. base of echoic origin, repr. by *gnastan*, *gnastran* gnashing of teeth, *gneista* emit sparks, *gnesta* crash, clatter.] **1.** *intr.* = GNASH *v.* 1. –1530. **2.** *trans.* = GNASH *v.* 2. –1460.

Gnat[1] (næt). [OE. *gnætt*, corresp. to LG. *gnatte*, G. dial. *gnatze*, rel. to MLG. *gnitte*, G. *gnitze.*] **1.** A small two-winged fly of the genus *Culex*, esp. *Culex pipiens*, the female of which has a sharp pointed proboscis, by means of which it punctures the skins of animals and sucks their blood. In U.S., the common mosquito, *Culex mosquito.* **2.** Applied to insects resembling this; in U.S., to a small stinging fly of the genus *Simulium* 1787.

1. Her Waggoner, a small gray-coated G. SHAKS. *Comb.*: **g.-catcher**, an American bird of the genus *Polioptila*, esp. *P. cærulea*; **-flower**, *Ophrys apifera*; **-snap, -snapper**, a name of various small birds; see also GNAT[2]; also *fig.*, as a term of contempt; **-strainer**, one who places too much importance on little things (after Matt. 23:24); **-worm**, the larva of a g.

Gnat[2] (næt). *Obs.* exc. *dial.* 1616. [var. of KNOT *sb.*[2], prob. infl. by the synonyms *gnat-snap*, *-snapper* (see prec.).] A kind of Sandpiper (*Tringa canutus*); also, local name for the Lesser Tern (*Sterna minuta*).

Gnathic (næ·þik, nēⁱ·þik), *a.* 1882. [f. Gr. γνάθος jaw + -IC.] Of or pertaining to the jaws; *spec.* alveolar.

Skulls with a g. index below 98 are orthognathous 1882. So **Gna·thal** *a.*

Gnathite (nēⁱ·þəit). 1870. [f. as prec. + -ITE[1] 3.] *Zool.* One of the mouth-appendages of Arthropoda.

‖**Gnathitis** (neⁱþəi·tis). 1847. [mod.L., f. as prec. + -ITIS.] *Med.* Inflammation of the cheek or upper jaw.

†**Gna·tho.** 1533. [– L. *Gnatho* – Gr. γνάθων, used as the proper name of a parasite, (f. γνάθος jaw).] A person resembling the Gnatho of Terence; a parasite, sycophant –1704. Hence **Gnatho·nic, †-al** *a.* parasitical, toad-eating. **Gna·thonism**, sycophancy (COLERIDGE). †**Gna·thonize** *v. rare*, to behave as a sycophant.

Gnathopod (nēⁱ·pŏpǫd). 1887. [f. Gr. γνάθος jaw + πούς, ποδ- foot.] *Zool.* = next.

Gnathopodite (neⁱþǫ·pŏdəit). 1882. [f. as prec. + -ITE[1] 3.] *Zool.* 'One of those limbs which, in crustaceans, have been modified into accessory organs of mastication' (Ogilvie.)

Gnathostegite (neɪþǫ·stĕdʒəit). 1877. [f. as prec. + *στέγειν* to cover + -ITE[1] 3.] *Zool.* (See quot.)

A broad plate, which, with its fellow, covers over the other organs, and hence receives the name of the g. HUXLEY.

Gnatling (næ·tliŋ). 1614. [f. GNAT[1] + -LING[1].] A small gnat; also *fig.*

‖**Gnatoo** (nătu·; prop. ŋa·tu). 1817. [Polynesian; now spelt *gatu* (g = ŋ).] The substance prepared from the bark of the Chinese paper mulberry tree; used for clothing.

Gnaw (nǭ), *v.* Pa. t. **gnawed.** Pa. pple. **gnawed, gnawn.** [OE. *gnagan* = OS. *gnagan*, OHG. *(g)nagan* (G. *nagen*), ON. *gnaga*; of imit. origin.] **1.** *trans.* To bite persistently so as to injure or remove portions; to wear away by a continued biting or nibbling. Also *absol.* or *intr.* ME. **2.** To corrode, waste away, consume 1530. **3.** *fig.* Said esp. of passion, remorse, etc. ME. Also *absol.* and *intr.* 1598.

1. They gnawed their tongues for pain *Rev.* 16:10. [He] gnaw'd his pen, then dash'd it on the ground POPE. **2.** When eating Time shal g. the proudest towers P. FLETCHER. **3.** As the flower is gnawed by frost, so every human heart is gnawed by faithlessness RUSKIN. Hence **Gnawed** *ppl. a.*; *spec.* in *Bot.* having the margin irregularly toothed as if bitten by some animal. **Gnaw·er,** one that gnaws; a rodent. Chiefly *Zool.* **Gnaw·ing** *vbl. sb.* a persistent fretting pain (in the bowels); *pl.* pangs of hunger. **Gnaw·ingly** *adv.* **Gnawn** *ppl. a.* bitten away, corroded.

Gneiss (nəis, gnəis). 1757. [– G. *gneiss.*] *Geol.* A metamorphic rock, composed, like granite, of quartz, feldspar or orthoclase, and mica, but dist. from it by its foliated or laminated structure. Hence **Gnei·ssic** *a.* of the nature of g. So **Gneissi·tic** *a.* **Gnei·ssoid** *a.* resembling g.; imperfectly gneissic. **Gnei·ssose** *a.* = *gneissic*; also quasi-*sb.* = gneissic rock. **Gnei·ssy** *a.* = *gneissic.*

Gneu, gnew(e, obs. pa. t. of GNAW *v.*

†**Gnide,** *v.* [OE. *gnīdan* = OHG. *gnītan, knītan*, ON. *gníða.*] *trans.* To rub with or between the hands; to bruise, crush. Also *intr.* to crumble away. –ME.

†**Gnoff.** Also **gnof.** ME. [Cf. EFris. *knufe* lump.] A churl, boor, lout –1610.

Gnome[1] (nōᵘm, nōᵘ·mi). 1577. [– Gr. *γνωμή* thought, judgement, opinion; pl. *γνῶμαι* sayings, maxims, f. *γνω-*, base of *γιγνώσκειν* KNOW.] A general maxim; proverb, aphorism, or apophthegm.

Gnome[2] (nōᵘm). 1712. [– Fr. *gnome* – mod.L. *gnomus*, used by Paracelsus as a synonym of *Pygmæus.*] **1.** One of a race of diminutive spirits fabled to inhabit the interior of the earth and to be the guardians of its treasures; a goblin, dwarf. **2.** *U.S.* A name of humming-birds, as the Giant Gnome (*Patagona gigas*) 1889. *Comb.* **g.-owl** *U.S.*, a small owl of the genus *Glaucidium.* Hence **Gnomed** *ppl. a.* inhabited by gnomes.

Gnomic (nōᵘ·mik). 1815. [– Gr. *γνωμικός* (perh. through Fr. *gnomique*), f. *γνώμη* opinion see GNOME[1], -IC.]

A. *adj.* Of the nature of, or consisting of, gnomes or general maxims.

In Euripides [the poetical faculty developed itself] in g. wisdom 1838. *G. poet*, a composer of g. verses. *G. aorist* (Gram.), the aorist used in proverbs, etc. to express what *once happened* FARRAR. So **Gno·mical** *a.*

B. *sb. pl. The gnomics* (= Fr. *les gnomiques*), the older Greek g. poets 1821. So **Gno·mist** (*rare*), a g. poet or writer.

Gnomology (nōᵘmǫ·lŏdʒi). 1645. [– Gr. *γνωμολογία*, f. *γνώμη* GNOME[1]; see -LOGY.] **1.** A collection of general maxims or precepts. **2.** GNOMIC discourse; the sententious element in writing 1806.

1. Gnomologies, or collections of moral sentences from the poets HALLAM. Hence **Gnomolo·gic, -al** *a.* of the nature of general maxims; sententious. **Gnomo·logist** (*rare*), a gnomic writer.

Gnomon (nōᵘ·mǫn). 1546. [– Fr. *gnomon* or L. *gnomon* – Gr. *γνώμων* inspector, indicator, carpenter's square, f. **gnō-*; see KNOW.] **1.** A pillar, rod, etc. which by its shadow indicates the time of day; esp. the pin or triangular plate in an ordinary sun-dial. **b.** A column or style employed in observing the meridian altitude of the sun 1625. †**c.** *joc.* The nose –1803. †**2.** A rule, canon of belief or action –1698. **3.** *Geom.* That part of a parallelogram which remains after a similar parallelogram is taken away from one of its corners. (So Gr. *γνώμων*, from the resemblance to a carpenter's square.) 1570. †**4.** Something shaped like a carpenter's square; an L-shaped bar, etc. –1777.

Gnomonic (nōᵘmǫ·nik). 1601. [– L. *gnomonicus* – Gr. *γνωμονικός*, f. *γνώμων*; see prec., -IC.]

A. *adj.* **1.** Of or pertaining to the gnomon or sun-dial, or to the measuring of time, etc. by means of this. **2.** *transf.* That indicates like a gnomon. COLERIDGE.

1. *G. column*: a cylinder, on which the hour of the day is represented by the shadow of a style. *G. projection*: a projection in which the point of sight is the centre of a sphere. So called from its relation to the art of dialling. So **Gnomo·nical** *a.* Hence **Gnomo·nically** *adv.*

B. *sb. pl. Gnomonics* (rarely sing. *gnomonic*): the art of dialling. *Obs.* exc. *Hist.* 1656.

Hence †**Gno·monist**, one skilled in gnomonics.

‖**Gnosis** (nōᵘ·sis). *Pl.* (rare) **gnoses** (nōᵘ·siz). 1703. [Gr. *γνῶσις* investigation, knowledge, f. **gnō-* KNOW.] A special knowledge of spiritual mysteries. Often: Gnostic philosophy, Gnosticism.

Gnostic (nǫ·stik). 1585. [– eccl. L. *gnosticus* (sb. pl. Tertullian) – Gr. *γνωστικός* (Plato, Aristotle), f. *γνωστός* known; see -IC.]

A. *adj.* **1.** Relating to knowledge; cognitive; intellectual 1656. **b.** Possessing esoteric spiritual knowledge 1800. **c.** *joc.* Clever, knowing 1819. **2.** Pertaining to the Gnostics; occult 1838.

1. c. I said you were a d—d g. fellow SCOTT.

B. *sb.* **1.** *Hist.* Chiefly *pl.* The name of certain heretical sects among the early Christians who claimed to have superior knowledge of spiritual things, and interpreted the sacred writings by a mystic philosophy (cf. GNOSIS) 1585. **2.** †One skilled or learned in any subject 1641; 'a knowing one', an adept in dishonest acts 1819.

1. The ghastly dream of G. and Manichæan TRENCH. Hence **Gno·stical** *a.* = GNOSTIC *a.* **Gno·stically** *adv.* **Gno·sticism,** the system or principles professed by the Gnostics. **Gno·sticize** *v. intr.* to adopt or expand G. views; *trans.* to interpret on G. principles.

Gnow(ȝ)e, obs. pa. t. of GNAW *v.*

Gnu (nū). 1777. [ult. – Kaffir *nqu*, prob. through Du. *gnoe*; so G. *gnu.*] A S. African quadruped (*Catoblepas gnu*) belonging to the antelope family, but resembling an ox or buffalo in shape; also known as *wildebeest.* The brindled gnu (*C. gorgon*) is a distinct species.

Go (gōᵘ), *sb.* Pl. **goes.** 1680. [f. the vb.] **1.** The action of going, in various senses. Also gait (*rare*). 1727. **2.** *colloq.* Orig. of a horse: Power of going, mettle. Hence: Dash, energy; animation, 'swing'. 1825. **3.** *colloq.* or *vulgar.* A proceeding; an (awkward) turn of affairs 1796. **4.** *colloq.* A turn (at doing something); an attempt *at* 1835. **5.** A quantity of anything supplied at one time 1799. **6.** *Cribbage.* A cry uttered by the player if he cannot play a card in his turn; the position thus disclosed (for which the adversary scores one point) 1821. **7.** *colloq.* Something that 'goes'; a success. *U.S.* 1877.

1. Phr. *Come and go*: see COME *sb.* **2.** A queer man..full of 'go', but never getting on 1864. The 'swing' and 'go'..of..ballads 1884. **3.** It might have been a *pretty go* 1833. **3.** I..sat down, and they had a go 1889. **5.** The goes of stout.. passed round merrily THACKERAY.

Phrases. (*It's*) *no go* (colloq.): the attempt is hopeless. *The go* (now only *all* or *quite the go*): the height of fashion; the 'correct thing'; the 'rage' (*colloq.*). *Near go*: a 'close shave'. *On the go*: in constant motion, in a restless state. *Great go, Little-go*, see GREAT GO, LITTLE-GO.

Go (gōᵘ), *v.* Pa. t. **went** (went); pa. pple. **gone** (gǫn). [OE. *gān* = OFris. *gān, gēn*, OS. *gan* (Du. *gaen*), OHG. *gan* (G. *gehen*), f. Gmc. **ȝai-*, **ȝǣ-*; the relation to GANG *v.*[1] is uncertain. The pa. t. OE. *ēode*, ME. *ȝede, yede*, *yode* was superseded XV by *went*, pa. t. of WEND in the south, and by *gaed* in Sc. and n. dial.]

gen. Intransitive verb of motion, expressing a movement (I) irrespective of the point of departure or destination; (II) *away from* the position occupied by the speaker; and (III) *to* or *towards* a point not occupied by the speaker either in fact or in thought. *spec.* In addition, it had formerly the special sense of *walking.* The movement may be either self-originated or impressed.

I. Of movement, irrespective of the point of departure or destination.

†**1.** = To walk (opp. to *creep, ride*, etc.); to walk at an ordinary pace (opp. to *run*, etc.); –1836. **b.** *To go upon the earth* (also simply): to live and move –1579. **c.** To walk or step in a certain manner; *esp.* of a horse: *to go narrow, wide* (see advs.); *to go above his ground* = to step high –1838. **2.** To move along, travel. Of persons and things. OE. **b.** with *adj.* or *adv.*: *lit.* and *fig.* *Go bet* (see BET *adv.*[2]). *To go like blazes* (see BLAZE *sb.*[1] 2), *even* (see EVEN *adv.* I. 2), *full drive, tilt* (see sbs.). ME. **c.** with advb. acc. of the way pursued, distance, speed ME. **d.** with cognate obj. *to go (the) circuit, a cruise*, etc. 1526. †**e.** Hence occas. *trans.*: To go through, over –1683. **3.** *spec.* In *Hunting* = to ride (to hounds) 1841. **4.** To take a specified course (physical or moral), often with adv. acc. Of persons and things. OE. **b.** *Naut. As you go! As she goes* = on the same tack 1692. **c.** Of a line, etc.: To 'run' (in a certain direction) 1889. **d.** with various advs., as *aside, astray, counter*, etc.: see advs. ME. **5. a.** Of persons: To be guided *by.* *To go with the tide* or *the times.* 1485. **b.** Of things: To be regulated *by*; to proceed *upon* (an idea, etc.) 1590. **6.** with adj. or phr.: To be habitually, *esp.* as to attire or circumstances. Cf. *to go without* (see VI), *short* (see SHORT *a.* III.). OE. **7.** Of a female: To pass (a period) in gestation. In full, *to go with calf, child*, etc. ME. **8.** To be moving. **a.** Of persons, *esp.* in *Who goes? Who goes there?* 1593. **b.** Of the sea (with defining word) 1611. **c.** Of a piece of mechanism: to act, work 1680. *transf.* and *fig.* 1565. **d.** *esp.* Of a watch, etc. (with defining word or phr.): To keep (good or bad) time 1588. **9.** with reference to sound. **a.** Of a musical instrument: To sound. Of a gun: To be fired. 1503. **b.** Of a clock: To strike (the hour) 1709. **10.** In senses 8 and 9, with imitative additions, e.g. *to go bang, crash, smash, snap*, etc. 1791. **11.** Of time: To pass ME. **12.** Of coin, etc.: To circulate; to pass current *at* a certain value ME. **13.** Of a report, etc.: To pass from mouth to mouth. Const. *of*, †*on*, †*upon.* 1542. **14.** *To go by* or *under the name* or *title of*: to be known as; to be ascribed to 1599. **15.** To be ordinarily. *As men, things*, etc. *go.* 1545. **16.** Of a document, etc.: To run 1605. **17.** Of verses; To glide along. Of a song: To admit of being sung; to follow the measure of (a tune). 1589. **18.** Of a series of events, etc.: To turn out (well or ill). Const. *with*, (†*for*). 1489. **b.** Of a war, etc., a vote, an election; To result in a specified manner. Also of a constituency or a politician; *colloq.* with adj. 1597. **c.** To take its course; *esp.* in phr. *to let (judgement*, etc.) *go by default* 1820. **d.** *What has gone of —? What is gone with—?* = 'What has become of—?' or 'What ails—?' 1771. **19.** Of a performance, etc.: To proceed *well, badly*, etc. 1665. **b.** To succeed 1742. ¶**20.** *That goes without saying* = 'that is a matter of course'; tr. Fr. *cela va sans dire.* 1878.

1. I have resolved to run when I can, to go when I cannot run, and to creep when I cannot go BUNYAN. **2.** And so she went, and she went, and never rested the evening, where she went in the morning, till [etc.] SIDNEY. **b.** The Government.. are going very strong, as the rowing-man says 1893. **c.** To go three miles in an hour MIEGE. **e.** I went the wastefull woodes and forest wyde SPENSER. **4.** They didna gang the road by the turnpike,..they gaed by the sands SCOTT. **d.** There are more ways of going wrong than of going right H. SPENCER. **5. a.** Had he gone on the chances, he would have won 'CAVENDISH'. **b.** Promotion goes solely by length of service 1892. **6.** Why, he us'd to go very fine, when he was here in Town SWIFT. **7.** The mother of man is said to *go* nine months in producing him 1841. **8. b.** The sea went very high DE FOE. **c.** [The] church clock has not gone for twenty years 1890. *transf.* Those who believe that democracy..will go of itself LOWELL. **9. b.** The clock on the mantel-piece went eight WESTALL. **10.** Clatter, clatter, went the horses' hoofs BARING-GOULD. **12.** Bank-notes, she supposes, will go everywhere 1872. **13.** Now the story goes that he [the young

Pretender] is in the Highlands 1745. **14.** Shakespeare did not write that play, though it generally goes under his name 1879. **16.** You shall be King. And Thane of Cawdor too: went it not so? SHAKS. **17.** This is a passing merry one, and goes to the tune of two maids wooing a man SHAKS. **18.** All went merry as a wedding-bell 1885. **b.** A general election went decidedly against him T. F. TOUT. **d.** What's gone with that boy? DICKENS. **19.** The annual dinner..never goes better than when he is in the chair 1892. **b.** It became evident from an early point in the play that it would 'go' 1893.

II. Uses in which movement *from* a place is the primary notion.

1. To depart. Const. *from*, †*of*. Cf. *go away* (VII below) OE. **b.** with cognate acc. *To go one's way*, etc. ME. **c.** *fig.* e.g. *to go from one's word*, etc. 1530. †**d.** In *imper.* as a rebuke. SHAKS. **e.** *To let go* (see LET *v.*[1]). **2.** To begin to move from a given point or state; *esp.* in *go!* said by the starter in a race, etc. Of an explosive = *to go off* (see VII); also *fig.* HERE *goes*, THERE *goes*, TOUCH *and go*. *From the word Go:* from the start (*U.S. colloq.*). ME. **3.** with adjs. like *quit, unpunished*, etc.: orig. to leave court, now to continue 'quit', etc. ME. *To go free* (see FREE *a.*) ME. **4.** To pass by sale. Const. *at, for*; also *to go cheap*. So *Going!* = on the point of being sold! *Gone!* = sold! ME. **5.** Of money: To be parted with, spent. Const. *in*. ME. **6.** To be given up, sacrificed 1715. **7.** To cease to exist; to be taken away; to come to an end ME. **b.** *Cricket.* Of a wicket: To be 'lost' 1890. **8.** To 'depart this life', die ME. **b.** In phrases, e.g. *to go the way of all the earth* (1 *Kings* 2:2), *to a better world*, etc.; also joc. and slang, *to go aloft, off the hooks, to (the) pot*, etc. **9.** To fail, give way. **a.** Of a material object: To break, to crack; to wear 1798. **b.** To faint 1768. **c.** Of a crop, etc. 1735. **d.** Of living beings, their organs, or faculties 1809.

1. Go, baffled coward, lest I run upon thee MILT. **d.** Go, go, you are a counterfeit cowardly Knaue SHAKS. **2.** On the word 'to go' being given Oxford started well 1892. **3.** Such forays usually went unpunished 1877. **4.** I'll knock 'em down at forty pounds. Going—going—gone SHERIDAN. **6.** The house must go, the carriage must go, the horses must go, and yet [etc.] F. A. KEMBLE. **7.** One of the results of using those..drugs is, that the will entirely goes W. BLACK. **8.** Thy neighbour's wife..dyeth. Every one can say, Why! wee are all mortall;..but when his owne goes, then [etc.] HEALEY. **9. a.** About half-past three the foremast went in three places NELSON. **d.** Omnibus-horses generally go first in the loins 1892.

III. Of movement *not* towards the speaker or the position occupied by him in thought.

******of self-originated movement or action.*

1. To move, or proceed to or towards a place, into the presence of a person, or in a specified direction. Const. *to, towards, into*, or with any prep. or adv. of motion whither. OE. **b.** *To go to Jericho, Bath, Hong Kong, Putney*, etc.: used in imper. etc. to imply that one desires to see no more of a person. So *to go to Halifax* (see GIBBET). 1648. **c.** *transf.* Of a road, passage, etc. To 'lead' *to, into*, etc. ME. **2.** With an additional meaning implied. **a.** The destination implies what is done there, as in *to go to the* BALL, *to* BED, CHURCH, PRESS, SCHOOL, etc. **b.** Of female animals: *To go to (the) bull, horse*, etc. = to copulate with 1577. **c.** As in *to go to college, the university*, etc.: to enter on the mode of life associated with college, etc. So *to go to the bar*, †*on the highway* (or †*the road*), *the stage, the streets*: to become a barrister, a highwayman, an actor, a prostitute. 1727. **d.** *To go to sea*: to go a voyage; usu. to become a sailor. Of rigging: To be carried adrift. 1599. **3.** The motive of going is often indicated: e.g. **a.** by the simple *inf.* (*arch.* and *dial.*) OE. **b.** by the *inf.* with *to* ME. **c.** by *and* with a verb, where the force of *go* tends to disappear. *To go and* (do something) = to be so foolish, unreasonable, or unlucky as to —. OE. **d.** by a sb. (governed by *to*) denoting an action, a ceremony, etc. ME. **e.** by the vbl. sb. governed by *a* (= *on*; now often omitted); also by ordinary sbs. denoting an action, governed by †*in, on, upon*. *Go a begging*. ME. **f.** by a sb., denoting function or capacity. *Obs.* exc. in *to go apprentice*, and *to go bail*, now usu. *fig.* = 'I will be bound', I am certain. 1665. **4.** To have recourse, appeal *to* (an authority, etc.); to carry one's case *to* or *before* (a tribunal, etc.). *To go to the country* (see COUNTRY 6). ME. **5.** To turn *to* (an occupation, etc.); to resort to a specified course of action. *To go to law, war, work*, etc. ME. **b.** *To go (for) to* (do something); *vulg.* = 'To be so foolish, bold, or severe as to —' 1752. **6.** To carry one's action so far as, etc. Const. *to*; also with adv. or advb. phr., or cognate or advb. acc., e.g. *to go the* LENGTH *of*. For phrases see FAR, NEAR, NIGH. 1577. **b.** *esp.* of offers or abatements in negotiations. †*To go less*: to offer or accept less. 1626. **c.** 'To share equally in', as in *to go halves (with), to go shares, snacks*, etc.; or *to go sharer, mates, partners* (see sbs.). **d.** To put oneself *to* (trouble, etc.) 1842. **e.** *trans.* (as with cognate accs.). To go to the extent of. *To go the whole hog* (see HOG). 1855. **7.** *trans.* To risk, stake. Also *absol.* *To go better*, at cards, to stake more. Also *to go one better*: hence *fig.* to outbid or outdo. 1605.

1. That he do appoint a fleet to go to the Northward PEPYS. **b.** 'She may go to Tunbridge, or she may go to Bath, or she may go to Jericho for me' THACKERAY. **2. c.** I..advise you to go upon the road..the only post of honour left you SWIFT. **d.** I should like to go to sea with uncle Maurice NELSON. **3. a.** Your Streatham and my Bookham may go hang JANE AUSTEN. **c.** Would'st thou haue me go & beg my food SHAKS. **d.** When they were all gone one day to dinner SIDNEY. **e.** I was resolved not to go sneaking to the lower professors GOLDSM. **f.** He won't marry her now, I'll go bail RIDER HAGGARD. **4.** You must go to Aristotle for that BLACKIE. **5.** He that..goes to Law to be Relieved Is sillier than a sottish Chews BUTLER (*Hud.*) **6.** The generality..want either force or inclination to go to the bottom, and try the merits COLLIER. **b.** Lewis consented to go as high as twenty-five thousand crowns MACAULAY. **7.** Men that would go forty guineas on a game of cribbage GOLDSM.

*******of passive movement, change of state*, etc.

8. To be carried, moved, etc. *to, towards, into*, etc. (*lit.* and *fig.*) OE. *To go to the bottom* (see BOTTOM *sb.*). **b.** fig. *To go to one's heart*: to cause one great sorrow. 1481. **9. a.** To be capable of passing *into, through*, etc. Of a number, to be contained *in*; also *impers.* ('won't go') in division or subtraction. 1686. **b.** To be usually or properly placed 1729. **10.** To pass *to*; to be allotted to 1607. **b.** To pass by inheritance, or succession 1818. **11.** To be applied or appropriated to. Const. *to, towards, to* with *inf.* ME. **12.** To contribute to a result. Const. *to, towards, to* with *inf.* 1607. **b.** To amount *to* 1841. **13.** To conduce, tend *to*; with *sb.* or *v.* in *inf.* †To have a result amounting *to*. 1781. **14.** To reach, extend; with advb. phr. 1586. **b.** *As* (or *so*) *far as it goes*: a phrase of limitation ME. **c.** *To go a good, great, short way* (*to* or *towards*): to have a great, little effect; to have great influence *with* 1697. **d.** With *far, as* or *so far, further, a long way*, etc. Of provisions, etc.: To hold out. Of clothing: To last. Of money: To have purchasing power. ME. **15.** To pass into a condition. **a.** With adj.: To become, get to be. (Cf. COME *v.* III. 5.) 1583. **b.** To turn *to*; to be reduced *to*. 1591. **c.** Const. *to* with *sb.* in phr. *to go to pieces, to rack, ruin, smash*, etc. (see *sbs.*).

8. I am further of opinion..that there was evidence of negligence to go to the jury 1895. **9. a.** Elzevirs..go readily into the pocket A. LANG. Four from three won't go—borrow one 1890. **10.** American ships..divide the freights which formerly went to the British..shipowner 1849. **11.** All the Revenue goes to the keeping up of the Magnificence of the Court 1688. **12.** Whole gardens of roses go to one drop of the attar 1890. **13.** The bill, therefore, went to the confiscation of the whole of the Company's property JAS. MILL. It goes to show that the Dutch are not the equals of the English 1889. **14.** But the difference goes still further 1874. **b.** The poor law system..is, so far as it goes, Socialism pure and simple 1885. **d.** £4 a year..in those days would go as far as forty would do now 1879. **15. a.** He went bankrupt 1861. **b.** The devil's corn all goes to bran 1889.

IV. Quasi-*trans.* with pronoun as obj.

1. With pleonastic refl. pron. *arch.* [Cf. Fr. *s'en aller.*] ME. **2. Go it.** †**a.** To direct one's course. 1689. †**b.** *imp.* = Be off! 1797. **c.** *colloq.* and *slang*. To go along at great speed; to engage recklessly in dissipation. *To go it blind*: without regarding the consequences. 1821.

V. Special uses of the pples.

Of **going. a.** *Going in*, or *of* —: about to attain (a specified age); also without prep. **b.** *Going to* (with inf.): on the way to, preparing to. Now = *about to*. Cf. Fr. *je vais*. (*To be*) *just going to*. Of **gone. a.** *To be gone*: to take oneself off. Cf. BEGONE. So *to get oneself gone* (see GET *v.*). **b.** In *Archery*, beyond the mark. In *Bowls*, beyond the jack (*transf.* of the player). **c.** Dead. *Dead and gone* (see DEAD). **d.** In a swoon. Dead drunk. **e.** Infatuated. *Gone on* (colloq. or vulg.): infatuated about. **f.** *Far gone*: in disease; deeply entangled; exhausted, etc. **g.** Lost, ruined, undone. Of a battle, game, etc. †**h.** = AGO, SINCE. **i.** = reckoned from a past date. **j.** = over the age mentioned.

VI. With preposition, in specialized uses.

Go about —. †**a.** To encompass. **b.** To busy oneself about; also †to seek after. (Cf. *to be* ABOUT.) **Go after** —. To pursue; to visit as a wooer, or a disciple. **Go against, †again** —. †**a.** To go to meet. **b.** Of an enterprise, etc.: To result unfavourably to. **c.** To run counter to. **d.** *To go against the* GRAIN, HAIR, †*heart* (also *against me* = against my feelings): to be uncongenial (see AGAINST). **Go at** —. To attack; take in hand vigorously. *To go at it:* to enter upon with energy. **Go before** —. **a.** To precede in time or order. †**b.** To take precedence of. **Go behind** —. To reopen a question previously closed. **Go by** —. †**a.** To pass without notice. (Cf. GO-BY *sb.*) †**b.** *To go by the worse, worst*: to be worsted. **Go for** —. †**a.** To start for. **b.** To go to fetch. **c.** To pass as; to be valued as. Now *to go for nothing, little, something*. **d.** To have for one's aim; †also = *to go in for*; to exert oneself to attain. **e.** *colloq.* To assail, attack. **Go into** —. **a.** See simple senses and INTO. †*To go into the field*: i.e. to fight a duel. *To go into (a cabinet, Parliament)*. *To go into society*. **b.** To take part in. †**c.** To accede to. **d.** To enter upon a state, condition, or process; to take up an attitude. **e.** To pass *into* (ecstasies, hysterics, etc.). **f.** To enter as a profession, etc. **g.** To adopt as a style of dress, to dress in (*esp.* mourning). **h.** *To go into* (†*a*, †*the*) *committee* (see COMMITTEE). Said also of a bill. **i.** To examine minutely. *To go into detail(s* (see DETAILS *sb.*). **Go off** —. **a.** See simple senses and OFF. *To go off one's head* or *chump* (see HEAD *sb.*, CHUMP *sb.*). *To go off milk*: (of a cow) to cease to yield. **b.** To fail to fulfil. **Go on** —. **a.** See simple senses and ON. *To go on a wind:* to avail oneself of it for sailing. *To go on board* (see BOARD *sb.*). *To go on one's knees* (see KNEE). †**b.** To approach (a point of time). †**c.** *U.S. colloq.*: To care for. **d.** To become chargeable to (the PARISH, etc.). **Go over** —. **a.** To cross. **b.** To visit and inspect. **c.** To admit of being laid over. **d.** To consider seriatim. **e.** To rehearse. **f.** To repeat. **g.** To examine in detail; to revise and retouch throughout. **Go through** —. **a.** To deal in succession with all the stages of (a business, etc.). **b.** To examine seriatim. **c.** To declaim, recite, etc. at length; to perform in detail. **d.** To experience, undergo. **e.** Of a book: To have all the copies sold of (an edition); now, to be published successively in (so many editions). (Cf. *pass, press through.*) **Go upon** —. (See simple senses and UPON.) **a.** To take in hand. **b.** To proceed upon as a foundation. **Go with** —. **a.** To accompany; to 'keep company with' (vulg.). **b.** To be associated with. **c.** To side with. **d.** To match. **e.** To follow intelligently. **Go without** —. Not to have; put up with the want of. Also *absol.* or *ellipt.*

VII. Combined with adverbs.

Go about. a. To go to and fro, travel; to be current; also †to complete a cycle. **b.** *Mil.* To turn round. †**c.** To use circumlocution. **d.** *Naut.* (See ABOUT A). **e.** *To go about to* (see ABOUT A). **Go abroad.** (See simple senses and ABROAD.) **a.** Of a report, etc.: To circulate (*arch.*). **b.** To go out of doors (*obs.* exc. *dial.*). **c.** To go to a foreign country. **Go ahead.** (See AHEAD.) To make one's way to the front in a race, etc. Also (chiefly U.S.), to make rapid progress. **Go along. a.** See simple senses and ALONG *adv.* In imper. *Go along! Go along with you!* = 'Be off'; also = *Go on*. **b.** *To go along with*: to proceed in company with; †to follow intelligently; to approve of (up to a point); to attend upon; to be the regular concomitant of; †to be classed with. **Go away.** (See simple senses and AWAY.) **a.** To depart *from*. †Of time: To pass. **b.** *To go away with*: to carry off. **c.** To go freely. **Go back.** (See simple senses and BACK *adv.*) **a.** To return; *fig.* to revert to a former state or mode of action; †to lose ground. **b.** To carry one's view backward in time. **c.** *To go back from* (colloq. *of, on, upon*): to withdraw from (an engagement, etc.). **d.** *To go back on*: to betray (*colloq.*); orig. U.S. **e.** To extend backwards (in space or time). **Go backward(s. a.** See simple senses and BACKWARD, BACKWARDS. †To change for the worse. **Go before.** (See simple senses and BEFORE.) **a.** *lit.* To go in advance. **b.** To precede in time or order. **Go by. a.** To go past (see BY *adv.*). †**b.** To go unregarded, etc. **Go down.** (See simple senses and DOWN *adv.*) **a.** To proceed to a lower place or condition; to descend (*from*, †*of*);

transf. (of a road, etc.) to lead downwards. Of a vessel: to sink. *To go down on one's knees* (see KNEE). **b.** To be continued down *to*. **c.** To be overthrown. **d.** To be set down in writing. **e.** Of waves, wind, etc.: To subside. **f.** To be swallowed. **g.** *fig.* To find acceptance *with*. **Go forth.** (Now *arch.* or *rhet.*) **a.** See simple senses and FORTH. (Cf. FORTHGO.) **b.** Of a decree, etc.: To be issued. **Go forward:** see FORWARD *adv.* **Go in.** **a.** See simple senses and IN. **b.** To enter as a competitor. Phr. *go in and win.* In *Poker* = to play for the pool. **c.** *Cricket.* To take the batting. Also *to go in to bat.* **d.** Of the sun, etc.: To be obscured. **e.** *To go into* or *unto* (O.T. after Heb.): To have carnal knowledge of. **f.** *To go in at*: To assail vigorously (*colloq.*). **Go in** *for.* (*Rec.* and *colloq.*) **a.** To make one's object; select as one's 'line', style, or fashion; commit oneself to (a principle, etc.); to venture on acquiring or wearing; to indulge in. **b.** To offer oneself for examination in; as a candidate *for*. (Cf. *to be* IN *for*.) **Go in** *with*. †**a.** To agree with. **b.** To join. **Go off.** (See simple senses and OFF.) **a.** To depart (suddenly); to set out. Of an actor: To leave the stage. At cards: to lead. *To go off at score* (see SCORE). *To go off at a tangent* (see TANGENT). **b.** To be taken off (esp. quickly). **c.** Of firearms, etc.: To be discharged, explode. **d.** To pass away, die. **e.** Of a sensation: To pass away. **f.** To deteriorate. **g.** To start into sudden action; to break *into* a fit of laughter, etc. **h.** To pass into unconsciousness; *to go off to sleep*, *in* or *into a fit*, etc. **i.** To fall through **j.** To be disposed of by sale. Of daughters, to be married (*colloq.*). **k.** Of a performance, etc.: To succeed. **Go on.** (See simple senses and ON.) **a.** To continue a journey. **b.** To continue in a course of action; in speech. Const. *in*, *with*, †*to* with inf.; also *simply*. Also with pr. pple. **c.** To proceed *to*, as the next step. **d.** To get on; to 'manage'. **e.** To continue further; also, to be in progress. Of time: To pass. **f.** To behave (reprehensibly). **g.** *colloq.* To talk volubly; to rail *at*. **h.** Of dress: To admit of being put on. **i.** *Cricket.* To take up the bowling. *Theatr.* To appear in a part. **j.** *imper.* (*int.*) = Go your ways (*colloq.*). **k.** *Going on for*: approaching (an age or period). Also = 'nearly'. †**l.** To make an attack. **Go out.** **a.** *lit.* To go from within; *esp.* from one's house. (See simple senses and OUT.) **b.** To take the field (chiefly *Hist.* with reference to 1715 and 1745); to fight a duel. *To go out to fight.* **c.** Of a fire, etc: To be extinguished. Also *transf.* and *fig.* **d.** In University use. †(*a*) To take the degree of (doctor, etc.). (*b*) At Cambridge: To take the degree of B.A. *in* a subject, or *in* honours. **e.** To die. *To go out of the world.* **f.** Of the tide: To recede. **g.** To retire from office. **h.** *ellipt.* for *to go out of date, fashion*, etc. **i.** Of a year: To terminate. **j.** To go *to* another country as a colonist, ambassador, etc. **k.** Chiefly of girls and women: To find work away from home. Const. *to*. **l.** To mix in general society. **m.** To be published. **n.** To abandon work. In full, *to go out on strike*. **o.** To be drawn *to*, by affection or sympathy. Also of the feeling: To go forth *to*. **Go out of.** See simple senses and OUT. *To go out of the stable*: to be entered for a race. *To go out of hand* (see HAND). **b.** *To go out of cultivation, fashion*, etc.: to cease to be cultivated, fashionable. *To go out of print*: Of a book, etc., when all the printed copies are sold off. *To go out of gear* or *order*: to become disarranged. *To go out of one's mind* or *senses*: to become deranged. **Go over.** See simple senses and OVER; often, to cross a piece of water, a hill, etc. **b.** To pay a visit at some distance. **c.** To pass *to* another owner. **d.** To change one's party. *To go over* (*to Rome*): to become Roman Catholic. *To go over to the majority* (= L. *abire ad plures*): to die (see MAJORITY). **e.** Of a vehicle. To be upset. So of driver, or passengers. **Go round.** **a.** To rotate. Of the head: To 'swim'. **b.** To complete a revolution. **c.** To make a circuit; to visit various places in succession. **d.** To pass from one to another in a company. **e.** To make a detour. Also *colloq.* to visit informally. **f.** To be long enough to encompass. **g.** Of food, etc.: To be sufficient to supply every one. In *cards*, when all the players can follow suit. **Go through.** **a.** See simple senses and THROUGH. †**b.** To complete what is begun. **c.** Of a proposition: To be carried. **Go through** *with.* To carry to completion. **Go to,** †**go till.** †**a.** To set to work. In *imper.* = Come on! L. *age.* **b.** In *imper.*, to express disapprobation or the like = Come, come! **Go together.** **a.** See simple senses and TOGETHER. *To go together by the ears* (see EAR *sb.*[1]). **b.** To be mutually concomitant. **Go under.** Of persons: To fail; to disappear from society; in *U.S. slang*, to die. Of a literary work: To drop out of sight. **Go up.** **a.** To pass to a higher place or position; to rise. †Of a sword: To be put *up* (into the sheath). **b.** Chiefly *U.S.* To go to ruin; become bankrupt. **c.** Of a cry, etc. = ASCEND 1. **d.** To be put up. **e.** To increase in number, price, or value. **f.** *To go up and down* (see UP).

VIII. Phraseological combs. (*colloq.* or *techn.*) serving as sb. or adj.

Go-ashore (*a*) *adj.*, characteristic of a sailor when ashore; (*b*) *sb. pl.*, clothes worn by him when ashore; (*c*) *New Zealand*, an iron cauldron with three feet and attachments for hanging it over a fire; **go-as-you-please** *a.*, unfettered by regulations; **go-getter** (*U.S. colloq.*), an enterprising, pushing person; so **-getting** *ppl. a.*; **go-no-further,** a kind of apple; **go-out,** a sluice for allowing water to escape from tidal lands; **go-slow** *a.* (cf. CA'CANNY); **go-to-bed,** one who is sleepy; **go-to-bed-at-noon** = GOAT'S-BEARD 2; **go-to-meeting** *a.*; **go-within-each-other** *a.*, of boxes.

Goa (gōᵘ·ă). 1846. [– Tibetan *dgoba*.] A Tibetan antelope, *Procapra picticauda*.

Goad (gōᵘd). [OE. *gād* = Lombard *gaida* arrow-head :– Gmc. **ȝaidō*.] **1.** A stick, pointed at one end, for driving cattle, esp. oxen used in ploughing. **2.** *fig.* Anything that pricks or wounds like a goad 1561. **3.** †**a.** A cloth-measure = 4½ feet –1727. **b.** A land-measure = 15, or (locally) 9, feet 1587. **4.** = GAD *sb.*[1] 1. 1855.

Goad (gōᵘd), *v.* 1579. [f. prec.] **1.** *trans.* To prick with a goad; to drive or urge on *to* something by such means 1619. **2.** *fig.* To assail or prick as with a goad; to instigate or impel by mental pain or annoyance 1579.

2. This [mutiny] shall seeme..their owne, Which we haue goaded on-ward *Cor.* II. iii. 271. Hence **Goa·dster,** a driver who uses a goad. CARLYLE.

Goaf (gōᵘf). Also **goave.** 1839. [Cf. synon. GOB *sb.*[4]] *Coal-mining.* The empty space from which the coal has been extracted. Hence **Goa·fing** (in same sense); also, the refuse left behind in working coal.

Go-ahead (gōᵘ·ă,he:d), *a.* *colloq.* (orig. *U.S.*) 1834. [orig. phr. *go ahead.*] Forward and energetic; pushing, enterprising.

What a go-ahead place France is! KINGSLEY.

Goal (gōᵘl), *sb.* [perh. identical with ME. *gōl* boundary, limit (Shoreham, XIV), which may have survived colloq. in some local game, but the origin is unknown.] †**1.** A boundary, limit. SHOREHAM. **2.** The terminal point of a race; any object by which this is marked; a winning-post, or the like 1531. Also *fig.* of the object of effort or ambition, or the destination of a (difficult) journey 1608. **3.** In football, and similar games, the posts between which the ball is driven to win a point in the game. Also, the winning of a goal, the point scored for this. 1548. **4.** **a.** *Rom. Antiq.* As tr. L. *meta*, the conical column marking each of the two turning-points in a chariot-race. Also *fig.* 1634. ¶**b.** The starting-point of a race. Also *fig. rare.* 1697.

2. *fig.* Then Honour be but a Goale to my Will, This day Ile rise SHAKS. **3.** Phr. *To get, take, win a g.* (often *fig.*). *To make, score a g. To drop a g.*: see DROP *v.* **4.** **a.** Part curb thir fierie Steeds, or shun the G. With rapid wheels MILT. **b.** Hast thou beheld, when from the G. they start DRYDEN.

Comb.: **g.-keeper,** a player whose special duty is to protect the g.; **-line,** the line which bounds each end of the field of play, and in the centre of which the g. is placed; **-post.**

Goar, obs. f. GORE.

Goat (gōᵘt). *Pl.* **goats.** [OE. *gāt* she-goat (the male being called *bucca* BUCK *sb.*[1] and *gātbucca*), pl. *gēt* = OS. *gēt* (Du. *geit*), OHG. *geiz* (G. *geiss*), ON. *geit*, Goth. *gaits* :– Gmc. **ȝaitaz*, rel. to L. *hædus* kid :– IE. **ghaidos*. The sexes began to be distinguished by *he-* and *she-* in late XIV.] **1.** A ruminant quadruped of the genus *Capra*. Occas. used with reference to *Matt.* 25:32, 33. **b.** Used *Zool.* in *pl.* = mod.L. *Caprinæ*, the name of the sub-family to which the genus *Capra* belongs. Also applied to certain antelopes. 1731. **2.** *transf.* **a.** The zodiacal sign Capricorn ME. †**b.** The star Capella (Alpha Aurigæ) –1674. †**c.** [tr. Gr. αἴξ.] A fiery meteor. STANLEY. **3.** *fig.* A licentious man 1675. **4.** *To play* or *act the* (*giddy*) *g.*: To play the fool 1879. **5.** *To get* (a person's) *g.*, to annoy him 1912.

1. A jet-black g. white-horned, white-hooved TENNYSON. **b.** †**Blue g.** = BLAUWBOK. **Rocky Mountain g.,** *Haplocerus montanus.* **Yellow g.** = DZEREN.

Combs.: **a.** **g.-antelope,** an antelope of the genus *Nemorhædus*; **-chafer,** a capricorn beetle; **-fig** (= L. *caprificus*), the fig-tree in its wild state; **-fish,** the *Balistes capriscus* and the *Phycis furcatus* of Europe, the *Upenens maculatus* of America, etc.; **-leap** = *goat's-leap*; **-moth,** *Cossus ligniperda*; **-owl** = GOAT-SUCKER; **-root,** the plant *Ononis natrix*; **-rue** = *goat's rue*; **-singing, -song,** renderings of Gr. τραγῳδία TRAGEDY; **-star** = GOAT 2 b; **-weed,** a name for the W. Indian plants *Capraria biflora* and *Stemodia durantifolia*; **-willow,** *Salix capræa*.

b. Comb. with *goat's*: **goat's bane,** *Aconitum tragoctonum*; **goat's foot,** a name for the S. African plant *Oxalis caprina*; **goat's leaf,** the foliage of the Woodbine; †**goat's leap** = CAPRIOLE; **goat's-rue,** *Galega officinalis*; **'goat's thorn,** a name for *Astragalus tragacanthus* and other species; **goat's-wheat,** the genus *Tragopyrum*, allied to the buck-wheat; **goat's-wool,** (*a*) something non-existent; (*b*) the fine wool mingled with the hair of some species of goats.

Goatee (gōᵘtī·). 1844. [f. GOAT + -EE[2].] A beard trimmed in the form of a tuft hanging from the chin, resembling that of a he-goat.

Goat-herd, goatherd (gōᵘ·t,həɹd). OE. [f. GOAT + HERD *sb.*[2]] One who tends goats.

Goatish (gōᵘ·tiʃ), *a.* 1529. [f. GOAT + -ISH[1].] Characteristic of, or resembling, a goat; *spec.* lascivious.

A g., ram-faced rascal SMOLLETT. Hence **Goa·tish-ly** *adv.*, **-ness.**

Goatling (gōᵘ·tliŋ). 1870. [f. GOAT + -LING[1].] A goat above 12 months and under 2 years old.

Goa·t's-bea:rd. 1548. A name of plants. **1.** *Spiræa ulmaria*, meadow-sweet 1578. **2.** *Tragopogon pratensis*; also *T. porrifolius*, salsify. **3.** Some species of mushroom. ?*Obs.* 1688.

Goatskin (gōᵘ·t,skin). ME. The skin of a goat, esp. one used for a garment, a wine-bottle, etc. Also *attrib.*

Goa·tsu:cker. 1611. [tr. L. *caprimulgus* (f. *capra* goat + *mulgēre* to milk), Gr. αἰγοθήλας (f. αἰγο-, αἴξ goat + θηλάζειν suck).] The bird *Caprimulgus europæus*, supposed to suck the udders of goats. Also applied to other birds of the same genus, or of the family *Caprimulgidæ*.

Goaty (gōᵘ·ti), *a.* 1600. [f. GOAT + -Y[1].] Goat-like; goatish.

Gob (gǫb), *sb.*[1] ME. [– OFr. *gobe*, *goube* mouthful, lump (mod. *gobbe* food-ball, pill), f. *gober* swallow, gulp, perh. of Celtic origin; see GOB *sb.*[2] Cf. GOBBET.] A mass or lump (now *dial.*); a lump, clot of some slimy substance (now *dial.* or *vulgar*) 1555.

Gob (gǫb), *sb.*[2] *n. dial.* and *slang.* 1550. [poss. – Gael., Ir. *gob* beak, mouth. Cf. GAB *sb.*[3]] The mouth.

Gob (gǫb), *sb.*[3] *dial.* 1695. [= GAB *sb.*[2], but prob. apprehended by speakers as a fig. sense of prec.] Talk, language.

Gob (gǫb), *sb.*[4] 1839. [perh. alt. f. GOAF, infl. by GOB *sb.*[1]] *Coal-mining.* The empty space from which the coal has been extracted in the 'long-wall' system of mining (cf. GOAF); also, the rubbish used for packing such a space. Also *attrib.*

Gob (gǫb), *v.* 1863. [perh. f. GOB *sb.*[1]] *trans.* To choke up (a furnace). *intr.* Of a furnace: To become choked.

Gobang (gōᵘbæ·ŋ). 1886. [– Jap. *goban*, said to be – Chinese *k'i pan* chessboard.] A game played on a chequer-board, each player endeavouring to be the first to get five pieces into line.

Gobbet (gǫ·bėt), *sb.* Now *rare* or *arch.* ME. [– OFr. *gobet*, dim. of *gobe* GOB *sb.*[1]; see -ET.] **1.** †A piece or fragment of anything that is divided, cut, or broken –1878; *spec.* a piece of raw flesh ME. Also *fig.* †**2.** A lump or mass –1712. **3.** †A large lump or mouthful of food; *spec.* a ball of flour, etc. used in feeding poultry [= Fr. *gobbe*] –1862. **b.** A lump of half-digested food. Also *fig.* 1553.

1. Gobbettes of wodde vnder yᵉ name of percelles of the holy crosse 1538. *spec.* an extract from a text set for translation or comment. **3.** **b.** Belching raw gobbets from his maw, o'ercharged ADDISON. Hence †**Go·bbetmeal** *adv.*, in gobbets; piecemeal.

†**Gobbet,** *v.* 1450. [– OFr. *gobeter*, f. *gobet* GOBBET *sb.* (mod. *gobeter* point a wall), but in some cases directly f. the sb.] **1.** *trans.* To swallow as a gobbet or in gobbets –1692. **2.** To divide into portions or gobbets –1726.

Gobbing (gǫ·biŋ), *vbl. sb.* 1839. [f. GOB *sb.*[4] + -ING[1].] *Coal-mining.* Packing with waste rock; the material used for this. var. (dial.) **Go·bbin.**

Gobble (gǫ·b'l), *sb.* 1878. [prob. f. next.] *Golf.* A rapid straight putt into the hole.

Gobble (gǫ·b'l), *v.*[1] 1601. [prob. of dial. origin, f. GOB *sb.*[1] + -LE 3.] **1.** *trans.* To swallow hurriedly in large mouthfuls, esp. in a noisy fashion. **2.** *U.S. slang.* To snatch up, lay hold of, 'collar' 1825.

1. The Supper gobbled up in haste SWIFT.

Gobble (gǫb'l), *v.*[2] 1680. [imit., but perh. suggested by prec.] *intr.* Of a turkey-cock: To make its characteristic noise in the throat; also (rarely) *transf.*

transf. A tiny geyser gobbled. KIPLING. Hence **Gobble** *sb.* the noise made by a turkey-cock. **Go·bbler,** a turkey-cock.

Gobelin (gobəlæ̃n, gǫ·bəlin). Also **Gobelins.** 1823. [f. *Gobelins*, the state-factory of tapestry in Paris, so named after its founders.] **1.** Used *attrib.*, as in *G. tapestry*, a tapestry made at Gobelins, and imitations of this. **2.** *absol.* 'A variety of damask used for upholstery, made of silk and wool or silk and cotton' (*Cent. Dict.*).

‖**Gobemouche** (gobəmuʃ). 1818. [Fr. *gobemouches*, f. *gober* swallow (see GOB *sb.*[1]) + *mouche* fly.] One who creduously accepts all news. Also *attrib.*

The g. expression of countenance with which he is swallowing an article in the National KINGLAKE.

Gobet, obs. f. GOBBET.

Go·-betwee:n. 1598. [f. GO *v.* + BETWEEN.] **1.** One who passes to and fro between parties, with messages, proposals, etc.; an intermediary. **2.** Anything that goes between or connects two other things. Also *attrib.* 1862.

Gobiid (gōᵘ·bi,id). 1884. [f. L. *gobius* GOBY + -ID[3].]

A. *adj.* Belonging to the *Gobiidæ* or gobies proper.

B. *sb.* One of these; a goby.

Gobioid (gōᵘ·bi,oid). 1854. [f. as prec. + -OID.]

A. *adj.* Belonging to the family *Gobioides* of Cuvier or to the *Gobioidea*, comprising fishes allied to the goby.

B. *sb.* A fish of this kind.

Goblet[1] (gǫ·blėt). ME. [– (O)Fr. *gobelet*, dim. of *gobel* cup, of unkn. origin; see -ET.] **1.** A drinking-cup, properly bowl-shaped and without handles, sometimes mounted on a foot and fitted with a cover. Later, a wine-cup. Now only *arch.* **b.** A glass with a foot and stem, as dist. from a tumbler. †**2.** A conical cup or thimble used by conjurers –1692.

1. I doe thinke him as concaue as a couered g., or a Worme-eaten nut SHAKS.

†**Goblet**[2]. 1530. [alt. f. GOBBET by substitution of suffix -LET.] = GOBBET *sb.*–1742.

Goblin (gǫ·blin). ME. [prob. – AFr. **gobelin* (recorded in Fr. XV and surviving in Norman dial.), med.L. *gobelinus* (XII, in Ordericus Vitalis as the name of a spirit haunting Evreux, France); prob. appellative use of a proper name, dim. of *Gobel* (now *Gobeau*), which appears to be rel. to *Kobold* (see COBALT).] **1.** A mischievous and ugly demon. **2.** *attrib.* (or *adj.*) 1649.

1. To whom the G. [Death] full of wrath replied MILT. **2.** The affrightment of this G. word, *Demagogue* MILT. Hence **Go·blinize** *v.* to convert into a g. **Go·blinry,** the acts or practices of goblins.

Gob-line. 1841. [Of unkn. origin.] *Naut.* A rope leading from the martingale inboard R. H. DANA).

Goby (gōᵘ·bi). 1769. [– L. *gobius*, var. of *cobius* – Gr. κωβιός some small fish; see GUDGEON.] One of a genus (*Gobius*) of small acanthopterygian fishes having the ventral fins joined into a disc or sucker. Also, a member of the family *Gobiidæ*.

Go-by (gōᵘ·bəi). 1611. [f. GO *v.* + BY *adv.*] **1.** The action of going by. *Obs.* exc. in *nonce-uses.* 1673. **2.** *Racing*, etc. The action of getting in front of another dog or horse 1611.

1. Phr. *To give the go-by to*: **a.** To outstrip. †Also, to leave. **b.** To give the slip to, elude. **c.** To pass without notice; to 'cut'; to evade.

Go·-cart. 1676. [f. GO *v.* + CART.] **1.** A light framework, moving on castors, in which a child may learn to walk without falling. Also *fig.* 1689. **b.** A child's carriage drawn by hand 1854. **2.** A litter, palankeen, or the like 1676. **3.** A hand-cart 1759. **4.** A kind of light open carriage 1828.

Goclenian (goklī·niăn), *a.* Epithet of a variety of the sorites due to Rudolf *Goclenius* (1547–1628). See SORITES.

God (gǫd). [OE. *god* (pl. *gudu* n., *godas* m.) = OFris., OS. (Du.) *god* m., OHG. *got* (G. *gott*) m., ON. *god* n., heathen god, *guð* m. and n., God, Goth. *guþ* (pl. *guda* n.). A Gmc. **ȝuð-* points to IE. **ghut-*, pa. ppl. formation of uncertain origin, but prob. f. **ghu-*, repr. by Skr. *hū* invoke the gods.]

I. Pre-Christian senses. **1.** A superhuman person (regarded as masc.: see GODDESS) who is worshipped as having power over nature and the fortunes of mankind; a deity. (Chiefly of heathen divinities, but often with a Christian colouring.) **2.** An image or other object which is worshipped; an idol OE. **3.** *transf.* of persons OE.; of things 1586. **4.** *Theatr. pl.* The occupants of the gallery, so called because seated on high. Also *rarely* in *sing.* 1752.

1. They conteyne the wicked actes and whoredomes of the goddes 1577. Come, let us go—to a land wherein gods of the old time wandered CLOUGH. Phr. *The g. of day*: the Sun. *The g. of war*: Mars (Ares). *The g. of love, the blind g.*: Amor (Eros), or Cupid. *The g. of wine*: Bacchus. *A feast, sight,* etc. *fit for the gods.* **2.** Thou shalt make thee no molten gods *Exod.* 24:17. **3.** Sweare by thy gratious selfe, Which is the G. of my Idolatry SHAKS. The old mans g., his gold, has wonne upon her J. FLETCHER.

II. In the Christian and monotheistic sense. The One object of supreme adoration; the Creator and Ruler of the Universe. (Now always with capital G.) OE. †**b.** In ME. often used for Christ. So, in 16th c., *in the year of G.* = Anno Domini. (Cf. *Mother of God.*) –1565.

Phrases. *With G.*, in heaven. *Act of God* (Law): see ACT *sb. God's truth*: the absolute truth. *On God's earth*: emphatic for 'on earth'. *God eyld* (*ild, dild*) *you* = God yield you (see YIELD). *God wot* (arch.), *God knows.* **b.** By god that for us deyde CHAUCER.

Comb.: **a. g.-bote,** a fine for crimes and offences against God; also an eccl. fine; **-home** *nonce-wd.*, the home of God, heaven; also as transl. of ON. *Goðheimr*, the abode of the gods (W. MORRIS).

b. possessive, as †**God's body,** the sacramental bread; **God's book,** the Bible; †**God's house,** (*a*) ? a pyx, (*b*) an almshouse [cf. Fr. *maison Dieu*]; **God's image,** the human body (*Gen.* 1:27); **God's service** = worship, an act of worship; **God's Sunday,** Easter day.

God (gǫd), *v.* Now *rare.* 1576. [f. the sb.] **a.** *trans.* To deify. **b.** quasi-*trans. To god it*: to play the god. 1595.

God-almighty (gǫdǭlməi·ti). Also (*colloq.* and *dial.*) **God-a-mighty.** OE. **a.** = GOD *sb.* II. **b.** In derisive use (with *a* and in *pl.*): One who poses, or is regarded, as omnipotent 1682.

†**God-a-mercy,** *int. phr.* ME. [= *God have mercy*, i.e. 'God reward you' (see MERCY); hence used as an expression of thanks.] **1.** An exclam. of applause or thanks. Const. *of.* –1828. **2.** quasi-*sb.* = 'thank you' –1692.

2. It would not be worth God-ha-mercy 1626.

Go·d-chi:ld. ME. [f. GOD *sb.* + CHILD (see GODFATHER).] A person considered in relation to his or her god-parent or god-parents; a godson or god-daughter.

God-da·mn(-me). ME. [f. GOD *sb.* and DAMN *v.*] **1.** The utterance of this as a profane oath. Also *attrib.* 1640. †**2.** One who is addicted to swearing. Also *attrib.* –1713. ‖**3.** (After Fr. *goddam.*) An Englishman ME.

Go·d-dau:ghter. OE. [See GODFATHER.] A female considered in relation to her sponsors.

Goddess (gǫ·dės). ME. [f. GOD *sb.* + -ESS[1].] **1.** A female deity. **2.** Applied to a woman 1579.

1. A Goddesse that was clept Deane ME. Phr. *G. of love, night,* etc. **2.** He call'd her his G., she call'd him an Ass 1729.

Gode, obs. f. GOOD.

Godelich, godely, obs. ff. GODLY, GOODLY.

Godet (gode·t, ‖gode). 1580. [– (O)Fr. *godet.*] †**1.** A drinking-cup –1629. **2.** A triangular piece of stuff inserted in a dress, glove, etc. 1923.

Go·dfa:ther, *sb.* OE. [f. GOD *sb.* + FATHER *sb.*] **1.** A male sponsor considered in relation to his god-child.

The sponsors, in making profession of the Christian faith on behalf of the person baptized, and guaranteeing his or her religious education, were held to enter into a spiritual relationship with the person baptized and with each other, and were in OE. denoted by designations formed by prefixing *god-* to the words expressing natural relationship, as *godfæder, godmōdor, godbearn*, etc.

b. A male sponsor at Confirmation 1549. **c.** A sponsor at the consecration of a bell 1498. **2.** *transf.* and *fig.* 1588. †**b.** *pl.* (*joc.*) Jurymen –1634.

1. Right so as he that engendreth a child is his flesshly fader right so is his g. his fadere spiritueel CHAUCER. **2.** These earthly Godfathers of heauens lights, That giue a name to euery fixed Starre SHAKS. **b.** *Merch.V.* IV. i. 398.

Go·dfather, *v.* 1780. [f. prec.] *trans.* To act as godfather; to take under one's care; to give a name to.

Go·d-fea:ring, *ppl. a.* 1835. That fears God, deeply religious.

A grave and staid God-fearing man TENNYSON.

Godhead (gǫ·dhed). ME. [f. GOD *sb.*; see -HEAD.] **1.** The quality of being God or a god; divine nature or essence; deity. **2. a.** *The Godhead* = GOD *sb.* II. ME. **b.** A deity (now *rare*) 1586.

1. Man..sinns Against the high Supremacie of Heav'n, Affecting God-head MILT. **2. a.** 'Tis true I am alone; so was the G., ere he made the world DRYDEN.

Godhood (gǫ·dhud). ME. [f. GOD *sb.*; see -HOOD.] **1.** = GODHEAD 1. †**2.** = GODHEAD 2 b. 1602.

Go·dkin. 1802. [See -KIN.] = GODLING.

Godless (gǫ·dlės), *a.* 1528. [f. GOD *sb.* + -LESS.] Without God or a god; irreligious, ungodly; impious, wicked. **Go·dlessness.**

Godlike (gǫ·dləik), *a.* 1513. [f. GOD *sb.* + -LIKE.] **1.** Resembling God (or a god); divine. **b.** quasi-*adv.* After the fashion of a god 1667. **2.** Appropriate to a god; resembling (that of) God or a god 1555. **b.** *absol.* CARLYLE.

1. The G. Angel MILT. **2.** The God-like faculty of reason COLERIDGE. Hence **Go·dlikeness.**

Godling (gǫ·dliŋ). 1500. [f. as prec. + -LING[1].] A little god. (Chiefly joc.)

Godly (gǫ·dli), *a.* ME. [f. GOD *sb.* + -LY[1].] **1.** Of or pertaining to God; coming from God; divine; spiritual. *Obs.* exc. *arch.* **2.** Observant of the laws of God; religious, pious. Also *absol.* 1526.

2. For g. sorowe causeth repentaunce TINDALE 2 *Cor.* 7:9. *absol.* The g. are not better than other men MACAULAY. Hence **Go·dli-ly** *adv.*, **-ness.**

Godly (gǫ·dli), *adv.* Now *rare.* 1530. [f. GOD *sb.* + -LY[2].] In a godly fashion. *Comb.*: †**g.-learned** *a.*, learned in divinity; †**-wise** *a.* wise in divine things.

Go·d-mamma:. 1828. Childish or fam. for GODMOTHER.

Go·d-ma·n. 1559. [tr. eccl.Gr. θεάνδρος, θεάνθρωπος, whence eccl.L. *deus-homo* (Origen); cf. Fr. *Homme-Dieu* (late L. *homo-deus* (Boethius)), Du. *Godmensch*, G. *Gottmensch.*] One who is both God and man; said of Christ.

Go·dmo:ther. OE. [Cf. GODFATHER.] A female sponsor in relation to her god-child.

Go-dow·n. 1641. [f. phr. *go down*; see GO *v.*] **1.** A draught, gulp. ?*Obs.* **2.** *Sc.* A drinking match. SCOTT. **3.** *U.S.* (Western). 'A cutting in the bank of a stream for enabling cattle to..get to the water' (*Cent. Dict.*).

Godown (gōᵘdau·n). *Anglo-Ind.* 1588. [– Pg. *gudão* – Malay *godong, gadong*, perh. – Telugu *giḍaṅgi* place where goods lie (Tamil *kiḍaṅgu*), f. *kiḍu* lie.] A warehouse or store for goods in the East.

Go·d-papa:. 1826. Childish or fam. for GODFATHER.

Go·d-pa:rent. 1865. A godfather or godmother.

†**Go·d-phere.** [app. f. *phere* FERE *sb.*[1] 'companion'; but perh. a misunderstanding of the rustic *godfer, godfar* GODFATHER.] A god-father. B. JONS.

Godroon, mod. var. of GADROON.

God's acre. 1617. [– G. *Gottesacker.* Properly, 'God's seed-field', in which the bodies of the departed are 'sown' (1 *Cor.* 15:36–44).] A churchyard.

Godsend (gǫ·dsend). 1814. [For *God's send* (XVII), alt. of ME. *goddes sand* God's message, dispensation, or ordinance (OE. *sand* message, messenger, rel. to SEND *v.*[1]).] **1.** Something sent by God, esp. something unexpected of which the recipient is greatly in want. **b.** *spec.* A wreck (*dial.*) 1814. **2.** A welcome event; a happy chance 1831.

1. Mr. Telford..has left me £500..This is truly a G. SOUTHEY.

Godship (gǫ·dʃip). 1553. [f. GOD *sb.* + -SHIP.] The position or personality of a god: esp. as a joc. title.

I..beg his British godship's humble pardon BYRON.

Godsib, -sip, obs. ff. GOSSIP *sb.*

Godson (gǫ·dsɒn). OE. [Cf. GODFATHER.] A male god-child.

Go·d-spee·d. 1526. [f. phr. *God speed* 'May God prosper' (one); see SPEED *v.* I. 4.] **1.** *To bid* (*wish*) *one God-speed*, to utter the words 'God speed (you)'; *esp.* to wish one success in an enterprise, etc. **2.** In subst. use, *a God-speed*, a parting wish for one's success 1856. Also *attrib.* **3.** *fig.* 1606.

1. A brace of Draymen bid God speed him well SHAKS. **2.** *attrib.* A Godspeed dinner 1867. **3.** †*The Godspeed* (of a thing), the finish.

Go·d's-pe:nny. ME. [tr. med.L. *denarius Dei* (whence Fr. *denier à Dieu*, Du. *godspenning*, G. *gottespfennig*), so called from being orig. devoted to some religious or charitable purpose. Cf. *denarius Sancti Petri* c1080) PETER'S PENNY, PENCE, *d. Rome* ROME PENNY, etc.] **1.** A small sum paid as earnest-money on striking a bargain (cf. ARLES-, EARNEST-PENNY). Now only *dial.* †**2.** A penny given in charity 1550.

Godward (gǫ·dwəɹd). ME. [f. GOD *sb.* + -WARD.]

A. *adv.* **1.** Towards God; in the direction of God. **2.** In relation or with reference to God ME. So **Go·dwards** *adv.*

B. *adj.* Tending or directed towards God 1861.

Godwit (gǫ·dwit). 1552. [Of unkn. origin.] A marsh-bird (genus *Limosa*) resembling a curlew, but having the bill slightly curled upwards. The black-tailed godwit (*L. ægocephala* or *melanura*) and the bar-tailed godwit (*L. lapponica* or *rufa*) are British species; others are natives of northern Europe and America. Formerly in great repute for the table.

Godwyts..accounted the daintiest dish in England; and I think, for the bigness, of the biggest price SIR T. BROWNE.

Goen, obs. f. *gone*: see GO *v.*

Goer (gō"·əɹ). ME. [f. GO *v.* + -ER[1].] **1.** One who or that which goes (see GO *v.*). †**2.** A foot. CHAPMAN.

1. A g. to tauernes LANGL. Goers betweene SHAKS. A light grey Nag..a very good G. 1697.

Goethian (gö·tiăn). Also **-ean.** 1840. [f. Johann Wolfgang von *Goethe* (1749–1832) + -IAN.]

A. *adj.* Of, pertaining to, or characteristic of Goethe, his writings, opinions, etc.

The G. paganism 1856.

B. *sb.* An admirer or follower of Goethe 1850.

Goety (gō"·ĭti). *Obs.* exc. *arch.* 1569. [– late L. *goetia* (Augustine) – Gr. γοητεία witchcraft, f. γόης, γοητ- sorcerer. Cf. Fr. *goétie* (XVI).] Witchcraft or magic performed by the invocation and employment of evil spirits; necromancy. Hence **Goe·tic** *a.* of or pertaining to g.; *sb.* a magician, sorcerer.

Goff (gǫf). *Obs.* exc. *dial.* 1570. [app. – Fr. *goffe* awkward, stupid – It. *goffo* – med.L. *gufus* coarse (Isidore).] A dolt, a stupid fellow.

Goff, var. of GOLF.

Goffer (gǫ·fəɹ), *sb.* 1865. [– Fr. *gaufre*; see next. In sense 1 the mod.Fr. term is *gaufroir*.] **1.** A goffering-tool. **2.** 'An ornamental plaiting used for the frills and borders of women's caps, etc.' (Ogilvie).

Goffer (gǫ·fəɹ, gō"·fəɹ), **gauffer** (gǭ·fəɹ), *v.* 1706. [– Fr. *gaufrer* impress with a pattern-tool, f. *gaufre* honeycomb, pastry made on a mould, impressed pattern, AFr. *walfre* – MLG. *wāfel*; see WAFFLE, WAFER.] *trans.* To make wavy by means of heated goffering-irons; to flute or crimp (lace, etc.). Hence **Go·fferer.**

Goffered (gǫ·fəɹd), *ppl. a.* 1706. [f. prec. + -ED[1].] **1.** Of frills, etc.: Fluted, crimped. **2.** *Bookbinding* and *Printing.* Embossed or impressed with ornamental figures, esp. *goffered edges* 1866. **3.** *Entom.* Of the elytra of certain beetles: Having very prominent longitudinal lines or carinæ, which in many cases diverge from the base and converge towards the tip (*Cent. Dict.*).

Goffering (gǫ·fəriŋ), *vbl. sb.* 1848. [f. as prec. + -ING[1].] The action of GOFFER *v.*; also its results; goffered lace, frills, etc.

Comb.: **g.-iron, -tongs,** an iron tool used for goffering lace, frills, etc.; **-press,** a press for crimping the material used in making artificial flowers.

†**Gog**[1]. ME. Euphemistic perversion of *God* in oaths, etc. –1602.

†**Gog**[2]. 1573. [app. f. *on gog*, substituted for earlier AGOG (q.v.).] *To set on g.*, to excite, make eager –1673.

Goggle (gǫ·g'l), *sb.* 1616. [f. the vb.] **1.** One who goggles (*rare*). †**2.** A goggling look; a squint, leer, stare –1688. **3.** *slang.* In *pl.*: The eyes 1710. **4.** *pl.* (rarely *sing.*) A kind of spectacles, having glasses (usually coloured) or fine wire-netting, fixed in short tubes, and worn to protect the eyes from dust, excess of light, etc.; formerly also to correct squinting. Also (*colloq.* and *joc.*) Spectacles with round glasses. 1715. **b.** Blinds for horses 1808.

Phr. *The goggles*, a disease of sheep; the staggers 1793.

Goggle (gǫ·g'l), *a.* 1540. [prop. the vbl. stem GOGGLE in comb., the purely adjectival use being a modern development.] Of the eye: Protuberant, full and rolling; also, †squinting.

His g. eyes were always rolling about wildly THACKERAY.

Goggle (gǫ·g'l), *v.* ME. [prob. frequent. of a base **gog*, expressive of oscillating movement; cf. JOG, JOGGLE *v.*[1], and see -LE 3.] **1.** *intr.* To turn the eyes to one side or other, to look obliquely, to squint. In later use, to roll the eyes about. Now *rare.* **b.** Of the eyes: To squint. In mod. use, to project and move unsteadily, to roll. 1540. **2.** *trans.* To turn (one's eye) to one side, or (now) from side to side with an unsteady motion 1583. **3.** *intr.* To sway or roll about ME.

1. b. The frog's hideous large eyes were goggling out of his head THACKERAY. Hence **Go·ggled** *ppl. a.* (now *rare*) = GOGGLE *a.*

Goggle-eye (gǫ·g'l,əiː). ME. [See GOGGLE *a.* and *v.*] †**a.** One who squints. †**b.** Squinting. **c.** *U.S.* = GOGGLER 2. **d.** 'One of two or more species of American fresh-water fishes of the family *Centrarchidæ*' (Webster).

Goggle-eyed (gǫ·g'l,əid), *a.* ME. [f. *goggle eye* (see GOGGLE *a.*) + -ED[2].] Having prominent, staring or rolling eyes; also, †squint-eyed.

Goggler (gǫ·gləɹ). 1821. [f. GOGGLE *v.* + -ER[1].] **1.** *slang.* An eye. **2.** *U.S.* The big-eyed scad, *Trachurops crumenophthalmus* 1884.

Goglet (gǫ·glėt), **gugglet** (gɒ·glėt). *Anglo-Ind.* Also †**gurglet.** 1698. [– Pg. *gorgoleta.*] A long-necked vessel of porous earthenware for keeping water cool by evaporation.

†**Go·gmago:g.** ME. [f. *Goemagot*, a British giant; altered after the names *Gog* and *Magog* (Ezek. 38–39).] A giant, a man of immense stature and strength –1630.

Goidel (goi·dėl). *Hist.* 1882. [– OIr. *Góidel*; see GAEL.] A GAEL in the widest sense, including the Irish and the Highlanders of Scotland. Hence **Goide·lic** *a.* of or pertaining to the Goidels; *sb.* the language of the Goidels.

Going (gō"·iŋ), *vbl. sb.* ME. [f. GO *v.* + -ING[1].] **1.** The action of GO *v.*; *esp.* departure ME.; †the faculty of walking –1635. †**2.** Manner of going; gait –1805. **3.** *Building.* Width of passage (of a stair) 1712. **4.** Condition of the ground for walking, driving, hunting, etc. 1859.

1. Stand not vpon the order of your g. SHAKS. The day is placid in its g. WORDSW. **4.** The fences are fair, and the g. pretty good 1887.

Phrases. *Going down*: setting (of the sun). *Goings-on*: proceedings, actions, doings (usu. with implied censure). †*Goings-out*: expenses, outgoings. *To set g.* (or *a-going*): To set in motion.

Comb.: **g.-barrel,** the barrel of a watch or clock round which are teeth for driving the train direct without the intervention of a fusee; also *attrib.*; **in g. order** (primarily of a clock), in a condition for going properly; **-train,** a train of wheels in a clock, answering the same purpose as the g.-barrel in a watch; **-wheel,** an arrangement for keeping a clock in motion while it is being wound up.

Going (gō"·iŋ), *ppl. a.* ME. [f. GO *v.* + -ING[2].] That goes; departing; current; working.

Phr. *A g. concern*: one in actual operation.

Goitre (goi·təɹ). Also **goître,** *U.S.* **goiter.** 1625. [– Fr. *goitre*, either (i) – Pr. *goitron* (also in OFr.) :– Rom. **gutturio, -ōn-*, f. L. *guttur* throat, or (ii) back-formation from Fr. *goitreux* :– L. **gutturiosus* adj.] *Path.* A morbid (often enormous) enlargement of the thyroid gland of the neck; bronchocele. **2.** A swelling of the neck in some lizards 1834.

Goi·tral, Goi·tred *adjs.* = next.

Goitrous (goi·trəs), *a.* 1796. [– Fr. *goitreux*; see prec. and -OUS.] Affected with, like, or pertaining to, goitre. Of a locality: Characterized by the prevalence of goitre.

Golconda (gǫlkǫ·ndă). 1780. Old name of Hyderabad, formerly celebrated for its diamonds, used as = 'a mine of wealth'.

Gold (gō"ld). [OE. *gold* = OFris., OS., OHG. *gold* (Du. *goud*, G. *gold*), ON. *goll, gull*, Goth. *gulþ* :– Gmc. **ʒulþam* :– IE. **ghl̥tom*, f. **ghel-* YELLOW + pa. ppl. suffix **-to-*.] **1.** The most precious metal; characterized by its yellow colour, non-liability to rust, high specific gravity, and great malleability and ductility. Chemical symbol Au. **2.** The metal as a valuable possession or as a medium of exchange; hence, gold coin; also, in rhet. use, wealth OE. **3.** *fig.* Something brilliant, beautiful, or precious 1553. **b.** Gilding. *Merch. V.* II. vii. 36. **c.** *pl.* Kinds of gold (*rare*) 1683. †**4.** The metal as used to ornament textile fabrics; gold thread; as in *g. of Venice*, etc. Hence textile materials embroidered with or partly made of this. ME. **5.** Used with defining words in the names of kinds of gold, alloys, imitations of gold, etc. 1839. **6.** The colour of the metal ME. **7.** *Archery.* The gilt centre or bull's-eye of a target 1876. **8.** *attrib.* or *adj.* **a.** Made or consisting of gold ME. **b.** Gold-coloured, golden yellow 1590. **c.** With reference to the use of gold for coinage and as a standard of value, as *g. standard*; also, of sums in depreciated currencies: reckoned at par 1776.

1. The roof was fretted g. MILT. **2.** Where g. makes way Ther is no interruption 1616. **3.** *Heart of g.*: a noble-hearted person (= Fr. *un cœur d'or*). The King's..a Heart of G. SHAKS. Time will run back and fetch the Age of G. MILT. **4.** Vallens of Venice g., in needle worke SHAKS. **5.** ANGEL, DUTCH, FULMINATING, etc. G.: see these words. *Dead g.*, unburnished g. or g. without lustre; *jeweller's g.*, 'an alloy containing three parts of g. to one of copper' (Webster); *red g.*, g. alloyed with copper. *Fairy g.* = fairy money (see FAIRY). **6.** Many a colourd plume sprinkl'd with G. MILT. **7.** *To make a g.*: to hit the bull's-eye. **8. a.** That Booke..That in G. claspes, Lockes in the Golden storie SHAKS. **b.** *Old g.*, of a dulled golden yellow with a brownish tinge. Gowns of old g. sateen 1882.

Combs. **1.** General: as *g.-coast, -ore, -vein*, etc; *-bearing, -broker*, etc.; *-embroidered, -inlaid, -mounted*, etc.; *-red* etc.; *-hilted, -striped*, etc.

2. Special: **g.-amalgam,** g. combined with mercury in a soft or plastic state (found native in 1848); †**-beat,** †**-beaten** *ppl. adjs.*, adorned with beaten g.; **-beating,** the process of beating out g. into a leaf; **g. beetle** *U.S.*, any of various beetles of the family Chrysomelidæ and Cassididæ; **g. beryl** = CHRYSOBERYL; **-bug** *U.S.*, (*a*) = *gold-beetle*; (*b*) a plutocrat; also, an advocate of a single (gold) standard; **-carp** = GOLD-FISH; **-cloth,** cloth of g. (see CLOTH *sb.*); **-digging,** (*a*) digging for g.; (*b*) *pl.* the place where g.-digging is carried on; **-driver** = GOLD-BEATER 1; †**-end-man,** one who buys up broken pieces of g.; **-fever,** the rage for going in search of g.; **goldfinny,** a fish of the wrasse family; †**-flint,** flint containing g.; **-flux** = AVENTURINE 1; **-fringe,** a moth, *Pyralis costalis*; **-mill,** a mill in which g. ore is crushed; also *fig*; **-mouthed** *a.*, whose speech is golden; **-note** *U.S.*, one payable only in g.; **g. plate,** vessels made of g.; **-plating,** g. in thin sheets; **-purple,** the compound oxide which is precipated upon mixing the solutions of g. and tin; **-rush,** a rush to the gold-fields; **-sand,** sand containing particles of g.; also *fig.*; **-shell,** a shell on which powdered g. mixed with gum water is spread for painters' use; **goldsinny** = *goldfinny*; **-size,** a size laid on as a surface on which to apply g.-leaf; **-solder,** †(*a*) = CHRYSOCOLLA 1; (*b*) an alloy for soldering g.; **-spangle,** a moth, *Noctua bractea*; **-spot,** a moth, *Noctua festucæ*; **-stone,** †(*a*) the yellow topaz; (*b*) a piece of g. ore; (*c*) pop. name of breccia; (*d*) = AVENTURINE 1; **g. swift,** a moth, *Hepialus hectus*; **-tail (moth),** *Porthesia chrysorrhœa*; **-thread,** spun g., a flatted g. wrapped or laid over a thread of silk, by twisting it with a wheel, etc.; **-web,** †(*a*) cloth of g.; (*b*) a covering for sweetmeats made of melted sugar, spun with a knife; †**-worm,** a glow-worm.

b. in names of plants, as **g.-balls,** old name for buttercups; **-bloom,** the marigold; **-flower,** †(*a*) *Helichrysum stœchas*; (*b*) the S. African genus *Gorteria*; **g. of pleasure,** *Camelina sativa*; **-shrub,** *Palicourea speciosa*; **-thread,** *Coptis trifolia*, so called from its fibrous yellow roots.

c. in names of birds, as **g.-breasted trumpeter,** *Psophia crepitans*; **-capped weaver bird,** *Ploceus icterocephalus*; **goldcrest** = *golden-crested wren* (see WREN); **-hammer,** the yellow-hammer; **-head,** the pochard; *Fuligula ferina*; **g. robin,** the Baltimore oriole.

Go·ld-bea:ter. ME. **1.** One who beats out gold into gold leaf. **2.** *pl.* A genus of Coleopterous insects remarkable for their golden-green and copper colours.

1. *Goldbeater's skin*, a prepared animal membrane used to separate the leaves of gold-foil during the process of beating; also, occas., to cover wounds.

Gold dust, go·ld-dust. 1703. **1.** Gold in very fine particles, as commonly obtained in a natural state. **2.** *Bot.* A pop. name of *Alyssum saxatile*. Also of *Sedum acre*. 1866.

Golden (gōᵘ·ld'n), *a.* ME. [f. GOLD + -EN[4], superseding GILDEN.] **1.** Made of, consisting of, gold. **2.** Containing gold; auriferous. Of a district: Abounding in gold. ME. **3.** Of the colour of gold. Also *fig.* ME. **4.** Most excellent, important, or precious 1498. **5.** Of rules, precepts, etc.: Of inestimable utility; often *spec.* with reference to Matt. 7:12. 1542. **6.** Of a time or epoch: Flourishing, joyous 1530. †**7.** Pertaining to gold (as the object of desire, pursuit, etc.) –1720.

1. *The g. fleece*, the fabulous fleece of gold in search of which Jason went to Colchis; (*Order of the*) *G. Fleece* (see FLEECE *sb.*). *G. ball*, the apple of discord (see APPLE). *G. gates*, the gates of Heaven. **2.** Some, bound for Guinea, g. Sand to find DRYDEN. **3.** G. corn POPE, (*fig.*) promises SHAKS. **4.** I haue bought G. Opinions from all sorts of people SHAKS. **5.** *The g. mean*, the avoidance of excess and defect [tr. L. *aurea mediocritas*]. *G. number* [tr. med.L., *aureus numerus*; so called from its importance in calculating the date of Easter]: the number of any year in the Metonic lunar cycle of 19 years. The number for a year *n* of the Christian era is the remainder of the operation $(n + 1) \div 19$.

Combs., etc.: **g. book,** a register of the nobility of the state of Venice; **g. ear,** a moth, *Hydrœcia nictitans*; **g. earth,** yellow arsenic or orpiment; **g. maid,** the fish *Crenilabrus melops* or *tinca*; **-mouth,** used to render the name *Chrysostom*; **-mouthed** *a.*, whose speech is g. (used chiefly as prec.); **g. perch,** 'a fresh-water fish of Australia, *Ctenolates ambiguus*' (Morris); **g. rain,** a kind of firework; **-ring,** a worm that gnaws the vine and wraps itself up in its leaves; **g. spur,** a papal order, the order of St. Sylvester; **g. star,** 'a kind of monstrance or ciborium used at Rome in the Papal High Mass on Easter-day' (Lee); **g. sulphide, sulphuret,** persulphide of antimony or antimony pentasulphide, Sb_2S_5 (Watts); **g. syrup** (see SYRUP); **-wasp,** a brightly coloured hymenopterous insect of the family *Chrysididæ*, esp. *Chrysis ignita*; **g. wedding** (see WEDDING); **g. wrasse** = *golden maid*.

b. in names of plants, as †**g. apple,** the tomato; **-club,** the American plant *Orontium aquaticum*; **-crown,** the American genus *Chrysostemma*; **g. cudweed,** *Helichrysum orientale*; also *Pterocaulon virgatum*; **-cup,** pop. name of species of *Ranunculus, Caltha, Trollius*; **g. feather,** the common g.-leaved *Pyrethrum*; **g. flower,** the corn marigold; **g. flower of Peru,** the sunflower; **-hair,** *Chrysocoma comaurea*; **g. herb,** the orach; **-locks,** the fern *Polypodium vulgare*; also *Pterocaulon virgatum*; **g. moss,** †(*a*) the moss *Polytrichum commune*; (*b*) the Stonecrop, *Sedum acre*; **g. nugget,** *Balsamita grandiflora*; **g. oat,** the yellow oat-grass; **g. osier,** (*a*) *Salix vitellina*; (*b*) *Myrica gale*; **g. samphire,** *Inula crithmoides*; **g. saxifrage,** the genus *Chrysosplenium*; **-seal,** *Hydrastis canadensis* of N. America; **g. spur,** a variety of daffodil; **g. thistle,** the composite genus *Scolymus*, esp. *S. hispanicus*; **g. trefoil,** *Hepatica triloba*; **g. tuft,** *Pterocaulon virgatum*; **-withy,** *Myrica gale*.

c. in names of birds, as **g. back,** 'the American golden plover, *Charadrius dominicus*' (*Cent. Dict.*); **-wing,** the g.-winged woodpecker (*Colaptes auratus*); etc.

Golden (gōᵘ·ld'n), *v. rare.* 1850. [f. GOLD + -EN[5].] To make or become golden.

Golden age. 1555. [tr. L. *aurea ætas*; see GOLDEN *a.* 6 and AGE *sb.*] The first and best age of the world, in which, according to the Greek and Roman poets, mankind lived in a state of ideal prosperity and happiness, free from all trouble or crime. Hence, the period in which a nation, literature, etc., is at its acme.

With Ovid ended the g. age of the Roman tongue DRYDEN. The g. age of Roman law 1869.

†**Go·ldeney.** 1552. [perh. f. GOLDEN + -Y[6].] The name of some fish, perh. the golden wrasse, but commonly = L. *aurata* or *scarus* –1661.

Go·lden-eye. 1678. **1. a.** A sea-duck of the genus *Clangula*, esp. *C. glaucion*. **b.** 'The bird *Melithreptus lunulatus*' (Morris) 1827. **c.** The Tufted Duck, *Fuligula cristata* (Newton). **2.** A fish, *Hyodon chrysopsis* (*Cent. Dict.*). **3.** A neuropterous insect of the genus *Chrysopa* 1753.

Goldenly (gōᵘ·ld'nli), *adv.* 1600. [f. GOLDEN *a.* + -LY[2].] **1.** Excellently, splendidly. **2.** Like gold 1827. **3.** As with gold 1825.

Go·lden-ro:d. 1568. [tr. mod.L. *virga aurea*. Cf. Fr. *verge d'or*.] A plant of the genus *Solidago*, esp. *S. Virgaurea*, having a rod-like stem and a spike of bright yellow flowers. **b. Goldenrod-tree,** a shrub (*Bosea yervamora*), a native of the Canary Isles 1829.

Go·ld-field. 1852. A district in which gold is found. Also *attrib.*

Goldfinch (gōᵘ·ldfinʃ). [OE. *goldfinċ*, f. GOLD + FINCH. Cf. Du. *goudfink*, G. *goldfink*.] **1.** A bright-coloured singing-bird (*Carduelis elegans*) of the family *Fringillidæ*, with a patch of yellow on its wings. **b.** *U.S.* Applied to other yellow finches, esp. *Spinus tristis*, the thistle-bird 1858. **2.** A kind of artificial salmon-fly 1867. **3.** *slang.* †**a.** One who has gold –1700. **b.** A guinea or sovereign 1602.

Go·ld-fi:nder. 1611. **1.** One whose occupation is to find gold 1631. †**2.** A scavenger –1755.

Go·ld-fish. 1698. †**a.** A fish with gold markings found in the South Seas. **b.** A small golden-red fish (*Cyprinus auratus*) of the carp family, a native of China, commonly bred and kept for ornament in tanks, glasses, etc. **c.** = GARIBALDI 2.

Go·ld-foil. ME. [FOIL *sb.*[1]] Gold beaten out into a thin sheet. (Techn. *gold leaf* is thinner than *gold-foil*.)

Goldilocks (gōᵘ·ldilǫks). 1550. [f. GOLDY *a.* + LOCK *sb.*] †**1.** Golden hair; woman's hair in general –1596. †**2.** One who has golden hair –1687. **3.** A name of plants, esp. **a.** *Ranunculus auricomus*, a kind of buttercup; **b.** *Chrysocoma linosyris*; **c.** *Helichrysum stœchas*; **d.** *Trollius europæus*.

†**Go·lding.** 1580. [f. GOLD + -ING[3]. Still used locally as a name of the marigold, and in Kent of the ladybird.] **1.** A gold coin. **2.** A kind of apple –1660.

Go·ldish, *a.* ME. [f. GOLD + -ISH[1].] Somewhat golden.

Go·ld-laced, *a.* 1630. Ornamented with gold lace.

Gold leaf. (Often *hyphened.*) 1727. **a.** (with *pl.*) A minute quantity of gold, beaten out into an extremely thin sheet, from 3 to 3½ inches square. **b.** (*sing.* only.) Gold in this form for gilding, etc.

Gold leaf electrometer, electroscope, galvanoscope, appliances in which gold leaf is used as a detector.

Go·ldless, *a. rare.* ME. [f. GOLD + -LESS.] Without gold.

Gold-mine. 1483. A mine from which gold is obtained. Also *fig.* a source of wealth.

Goldney, -nie, -ny, var. ff. GOLDENEY.

Goldsmith (gōᵘ·ldsmiþ). [OE. *goldsmiþ*.] **1.** One who fashions gold into jewels, ornaments, etc. ¶Down to the 18th c. goldsmiths acted as bankers. **2.** Short for *goldsmith-beetle* 1863. *Comb.* **g.-beetle,** a large scarabæid beetle (*Cotalpa lanigera*) having wing-covers of golden lustre; also *Cetonia aurata* or other species. Hence **Go·ldsmi:th(e)ry,** the art or trade of a g.; goldsmith's work; articles made by a g.

Gold stick, go·ld-stick. 1804. **a.** The gilt rod carried on occasions of state by the colonel of the Life-guards or the captain of the Gentlemen-at-arms. **b.** The bearer of this; also *gold-stick in waiting*.

Go·ld-wa:sher. 1515. †**a.** One who sweats gold coins. **b.** One who washes auriferous soil to separate the gold. **c.** An appliance for gold-washing. So **Go·ld-wash,** a place where gold-washing is carried on. **Go·ld-washing,** (*a*) the process of obtaining gold by washing; (*b*) = *gold-wash* (chiefly in *pl.*).

†**Gold-weight.** 1500. **a.** *pl.* Scales for weighing gold –1683. **b.** *sing.* Exact weight, such as is sought in weighing gold –1727.

Go·ld-work, -works. 1683. **a.** *sing.* The art or process of working in gold. **b.** Goldsmith's work. **c.** *pl.* A place where gold is washed, mined, or smelted. So **Go·ld-worker,** one engaged in the obtaining or working of gold. **Go·ld-workings,** a place or places where gold is mined or washed.

Go·ldy, *sb. dial.* 1802. [f. GOLD + -Y[6].] **a.** The goldfinch. **b.** The yellow-hammer.

Goldy (gōᵘ·ldi), *a.* 1605. [f. GOLD + -Y[1].] Gold-like, resembling gold in colour and sheen. *Comb.* **g.-stone** = AVENTURINE.

Goldylocks: see GOLDILOCKS.

†**Golee.** *rare.* Also **gole.** ME. only. [– OFr. *golee* (mod. *gueulée*), f. *gole* (mod. *gueule*) throat :– L. *gula* mouth, throat; see -EE[1].] A mouthful, throatful (of words). CHAUCER.

Golet(te, obs. f. GULLET.

Golf (gǫlf, gǫf), *sb.* 1457. [Of unkn. origin.] A game in which a small hard ball is struck with various clubs into a series of small cylindrical holes made at intervals on the surface of a moor, field, etc.

Comb.: **g.-club** (see CLUB *sb.* I. 2); **-links,** the ground on which g. is played. Hence **Golf** *v.* **Go·lfer.**

Golgotha (gǫ·lgǒþă). 1593. [– Vulgate L. – Gr. γολγοθά – by metathesis Aram. *gogoltâ*, perhaps under influence of Heb. *gulgōleṯ*; see CALVARY.] **1.** A place of interment; a graveyard, a charnel-house. †**2.** *Univ. slang.* (See quot.) –1803.

2. Golgotha, that is, the place of sculls or heads of colleges and halls, where they meet and debate 1726.

Goliard (gōᵘ·liaɹd). Now *Hist.* 1483. [– OFr. *goliard* glutton, f. *gole* (mod. *gueule*) :– L. *gula* gluttony; see -ARD.] One of the class of educated jesters, buffoons, and authors of ribald Latin verse, who flourished chiefly in the 12th and 13th c. Hence **Goliardery,** the practices of a g.

†**Goliardeys.** ME. [– OFr. *goliardeis* adj. and sb., f. *goliard* + *-eis*; see prec., -ESE.] = GOLIARD –1643.

Goliath (gǒlai·ăþ). Often erron. **Goliah.** 1591. [– Vulgate L. *Goliath*, Heb. *golyaṯ* the giant slain by David, 1 Sam. 17.] **1.** A giant; often allusively. **2.** A very large lamellicorn beetle of the genus *Goliathus* 1826. **3.** (Also *g. crane*) A powerful travelling crane 1888.

1. The G. of English literature 1846.

†**Goll.** 1586. [Also †*golly*, freq. in XVII dramatists; of unkn. origin.] A hand –1690.

Golly (gǫ·li), *interj.* 1848. [Substitute for *God* in exclamations; cf. *goles* (Fielding) and U.S. *goldam, -darn, -dasted* for *goddam, -blasted*.]

Gollywog (gǫ·liwǫg). 1895. [– *Golliwogg*, invented name of a doll character in books by B. Upton, d. 1912, U.S.A. Perh. suggested by GOLLY and POLLIWOG.] Also **golliwog(g.** A black (male) grotesque doll, with staring eyes and fuzzy hair.

Golosh, goloshoe, etc.: see GALOSH.

Goluptious (gǒlʋ·pʃəs), *a. joc.* 1856. [perh. perversion of *voluptuous*.] Luscious, delightful.

Gomarist (gōᵘ·mărist). 1674. [f. *Gomar* + -IST.] A follower of Francis Gomar (1563–1641), Professor of Divinity at Leyden, who defended Calvinism as against Arminianism. So **Goma·rian.**

Gombeen (gǫmbī·n). *Anglo-Ir.* 1862. [– Ir. *gaimbín*, according to Whitley Stokes, repr. a deriv. of OCelt. **kmbion*, whence med.L. *cambium* CHANGE.] Usury. Chiefly *attrib.*, as **g.-man,** a usurer. Hence **Gombee·nism,** borrowing or lending at usury.

Gombroon, gomroon (gǫmbrū·n, gǫmrū·n). 1698. [Name of a town on the Persian Gulf. Cf. GAMBROON.] A kind of Persian pottery, imitated in Chelsea ware.

†**Gome**[1]. [OE. *guma* = OS. *gumo, gomo,* OHG. *gomo,* ON. *gumi,* Goth. *guma* :- IE. *ghəmón-,* cogn. w. L. *homo, homin-.* Cf. BRIDEGROOM.] A man -1515.

Gome[2]. 1611. [Cf. COOM *sb.*] The black and oily grease on the axle of a cart wheel.

†**Gomer**[1]. OE. [Vulgate L. *gomor,* Gr. γομόρ, transliteration of Heb.; see OMER.] A Heb. measure; = OMER -1631.

Gomer[2] (gōᵘ·məɹ). 1828. [f. the inventor's name.] *Gomer chamber,* a conical chamber with spherical bottom used in smooth-bore guns and mortars.

Gomerel (gǫ·məɹĕl), *sb. Sc.* and *north.* 1814. [Of obscure formation; see -REL.] A fool, a simpleton.

†**Gomorr(h)ean.** 1522. [f. *Gomorrah, Gomorrha,* after names in *-ean.*]
A. Of or pertaining to Gomorrah (see *Gen.* 18, 19) -1593.
B. *sb.* An inhabitant of Gomorrah; hence, one who follows the practices of its inhabitants -1613.

Gomphiasis (gǫmfəi·ăsis). 1706. [- Gr. γομφίασις toothache, f. γομφίος molar tooth; see -ASIS.] *Path.* Disease of the (molar) teeth, causing them to become loose in their sockets.

Gomphodont (gǫ·mfŏdǫnt), *a.* 1889. [f. Gr. γόμφος bolt + ὀδούς, ὀδοντ- tooth.] *Path.* Having the teeth inserted by gomphosis.

‖**Gomphosis** (gǫmfōᵘ·sis). 1578. [mod.L. - Gr. γόμφωσις, f. γομφοῦν bolt together, f. γόμφος bolt; see -OSIS.] *Anat.* A form of immovable articulation, in which one hard part (e.g. a tooth) is received into the cavity of another.

Gon, obs. inf. (etc.) of GO *v.*

-gon (gǫn), *suffix.* The second element (repr. Gr. -γων-ος, -ον, -angled) of HEPTAGON, etc., sometimes used with algebraic symbols (as *m*-gon, *n*-gon).

Gonad (gǫ·næ̆d). 1880. [- mod.L. *gonas,* pl. *gonades,* f. Gr. γονή, γόνος generation, seed, etc.; see -AD. Cf. Fr. *gonade.*] *Biol.* An undifferentiated germ-gland, serving both as ovary and spermary. Hence **Go·naduct** (for *gonad-duct*).

‖**Gonangium** (gǫnæ·ndʒiŏm). *Pl.* **-ia.** 1871. [mod.L., f. Gr. γόνος generation + ἀγγεῖον vessel; see -IUM.] *Zool.* An external chitinous receptacle within which, in the calyptoblastic genera of Hydrozoa, the sporosacs or planoblasts are developed. Hence **Gona·ngial** *a.*

Gondola (gǫ·ndŏlă). 1549. [- (Venetian) It. *gondola,* f. Rhæto-Romanic (of Friuli) *gondolà* rock, roll.] **1.** A light flat-bottomed boat in use on the Venetian canals, having a cabin amidships and rising to a sharp point at either end; it is usually propelled by one man at the stern with a single oar. Also *transf.* †**2.** A ship's boat 1626. **3.** *U.S.* A large flat-bottomed river boat for freight; used also as a gun-boat 1774. **4.** = *gondola car* 1875. **b.** [cf. G., Du. *gondel*] A car attached to the under side of a dirigible balloon or airship 1914.

1. The far lights of skimming gondolas BYRON. *transf.* In cabs, those gondolas on wheels 1827. *Comb.* **g.-car** *U.S.,* a railway car having a platform body with low sides.

Gondolet (gǫndŏle·t). 1602. [- It. *gondoletta,* dim. of *gondola,* see -ET.] A small gondola.

Gondolier (gǫndŏliᵊ·ɹ). 1603. [- Fr. *gondolier* - It. *gondoliere,* f. *gondola* GONDOLA; see -IER.] One who rows a gondola.
And silent rows the songless g. BYRON.

Gone (gǫ̀n), *ppl. a.* 1598. [pa. pple. of Go *v.*] **1.** Lost, ruined, undone. **2.** That has departed or passed away 1820.

1. *A g. case,* a hopeless case. *A g. sensation (feeling),* a feeling of faintness or exhaustion. *G. coon* (U.S.): see COON. **2.** *Past and g. Dead and g.* Hence **Go·ner** (*slang*), one who is dead or undone.

Goneness (gǫ̀n,nės). 1853. [f. prec. + -NESS.] Faintness; lassitude; exhaustion.

Gonfalon (gǫ·nfălǫn). 1595. [- It. *gonfalone* = Fr. *gonfalon,* later form of *gonfanon,* whence GONFANON.] A banner or ensign, frequently with tails or streamers, suspended from a cross-bar instead of being fastened to the pole, esp. as used by the Italian republics or in eccl. processions.

Gonfalonier (gǫ:nfălŏnīᵊ·ɹ). 1586. [- Fr. *gonfalonier* (OFr. *gonfanonier*); see prec., -IER.] The bearer of a gonfalon, a standard-bearer; *spec.* (*a*) the title of the chief magistrate in several Italian republics; (*b*) the Pope's standard-bearer, an office claimed as hereditary by the Dukes of Parma. Hence **Go:nfalonie·rship.**

Gonfanon (gǫ·nfăn ŏn). Now *Hist.* ME. [- OFr. *gonfanon* (XII) - Frankish **gundfano* (= OE. *gūþfana,* OHG. *gundfano,* ON. *gunnfani*), f. Gmc. **ʒund-, *ʒunþjō* war + *fano* banner, FANON.] **1.** = GONFALON. In the middle ages chiefly applied to the small pennon immediately beneath the steel head of a knight's lance. Also *fig.* †**2.** A lance carrying a gonfanon. CAXTON.

†**Gong**[1]. [Special use of OE. *gang, gong;* see GANG *sb.*] A privy -1576.

Gong[2] (gǫŋ). 1600. [- Malay *gŏng, gŭng,* of imit. origin.] A metallic disc with upturned rim (usu. made of an alloy of four parts copper to one of tin) which produces resonant musical notes when suspended and struck with a soft mallet. **b.** A saucer-shaped bell, struck by a hammer or tongue moved by some mechanical device; used chiefly as an alarm or a call-bell 1864. *Comb.* **g.-bell** = b. Hence **Go·ng-go:ng,** a name given to various analogous instruments in use among barbarous peoples. ?*Obs.*

Gongorism (gǫ·ŋgŏriz'm). 1813. [f. *Gongora* + -ISM.] An affected type of diction and style introduced into Spanish literature by the poet Gongora y Argote (1561–1627). So **Go·ngorist.** Also **Go·ngoresque.**

Goniatite (gōᵘ·niătəit). 1838. [- mod.L. *goniatites* (de Haan, 1825), f. Gr. γωνία angle; see -ITE[1] 2 a.] *Palæont.* A genus of fossil cephalopods with angular markings.

‖**Gonidium** (goni·diŏm). *Pl.* **-ia.** 1845. [mod.L., dim. on Gr. type of γόνος child, produce. See -IUM. Cf. Fr. *gonidie.*] *Bot.* **1.** One of the cells filled with chlorophyll which are formed beneath the cortical layer in the thallus of lichens; now known to be imprisoned algæ. **2. a.** A reproductive cell produced asexually in algæ. **b.** The conidium in fungi. 1882. Hence **Goni·dial, Goni·dic** *adjs.* of or pertaining to gonidia. **Gonidio·genous** *a.* producing or having the power to produce gonidia. **Goni·dioid** *a.* resembling the gonidia of lichens. **Goni·diose** *a.* containing or provided with gonidia. Also **Goni·diophore** = CONIDIOPHORE.

Gonimic (goni·mik), *a.* 1857. [f. mod.L. *gonimon* (f. Gr. γόνιμον n. of γόνιμος producing offspring) + -IC.] In *g. layer, stratum,* orig. = 'gonidial layer'. The adj. is now taken to mean: Relating to gonimia; containing gonimia. var. **Go·nimous** *a.* (in the orig. sense).

‖**Gonimium** (goni·miŏm). *Pl.* **-ia.** 1882. [mod.L., f. *gonimon* (see prec.) + -IUM.] *Bot.* A gonidium which is not of an absolutely green (grass-green) colour.

Goniometer (gōᵘniǫ·mĭtəɹ). 1766. [- Fr. *goniomètre,* f. Gr. γωνία angle + *-mètre* -METER.] An instrument used for measuring angles. (In measuring the angles of crystals two kinds are used, the old *contact-* or *hand-goniometer,* and the more accurate *reflecting goniometer* invented by Wollaston.) So **Gonio·metry,** measurement of angles. Hence **Go:niome·tric, -al** *a.* of or pertaining to goniometry.

Gono- (gǫ·no), *prefix,* bef. a vowel **gon-,** repr. Gr. γονο-, comb. f. γόνος, γονή generation, offspring, semen, etc.

Go·noblast [see -BLAST], *Biol.* a cell which takes part in reproduction; hence, **Go:nobla·stic** *a.* ‖**Go:noblasti·dium** (pl. *-idia*) [f. GONOBLAST + Gr. -ίδιον dim. suffix], *Zool.* = BLASTOSTYLE; hence **Go:noblasti·dial** *a.* ‖**Go·nocalyx** [see CALIX], *Zool.* the bell-shaped disc forming the swimming organ of a medusiform gonophore; hence **Gonoca·lycine** *a.* **Go·nocheme** [Gr. ὄχημα vehicle], *Zool.* a medusiform planoblast which gives origin directly to the generative elements. **Gonoco·ccus** [see COCCUS], *Path.* the micrococcus found in the discharge of gonorrhœa. **Go·nosome** [Gr. σῶμα], *Zool.* name for the collective body of reproductive zooids of a hydrozoan; hence **Go:noso·mal** *a.* **Go·nosphere** [SPHERE], *Bot.* the irregular globule formed by the condensation of the protoplasm of the oogonium in certain fungi; also ‖**Gonosphæ·rium** (pl. *-ia*). ‖**Gonothe·ca** [Gr. θήκη case], *Zool.* = GONANGIUM; hence **Gonothe·cal** *a.* **Gonozo·oid** [ZOOID], *Zool.* one of the sexual zooids enclosed in certain of the gonophores of the *Hydrozoa;* also *attrib.*

Gonoph (gǫ·nǫ̆f). *slang.* 1852. [- Yiddish *ganef* - Heb. *gannāb* thief.] A pickpocket.

Gonophore (gǫ·nŏfoᵊɹ). 1835. [- Fr. *gonophore;* see GONO-, -PHORE.] **1.** *Bot.* The short stalk which bears the stamens and carpels in *Anonaceæ,* etc., due to the elongation of the receptacle above the corolla. **2.** One of the medusoid buds which contain the reproductive elements in *Hydrozoa* 1859.

Gonorrhœa (gǫnŏrī·ă). Also †**-rhea,** etc. 1547. [- late L. - Gr. γονόρροια, f. γόνος semen + ῥοία flux; so called because it was supposed to be a discharge of semen.] An inflammatory discharge of mucus from the membrane of the urethra or vagina. Hence **Gonorrhœ·al, -e·al,** †**Gonorrhœ·an** *adjs.* of, pertaining to, or affected with g.

Gonosome, -sphere, etc.: see GONO-

Gonys (gǫ·nis). 1836. [app. a mistake for *genys* = Gr. γένυς under-jaw.] *Ornith.* The keel of a bird's bill; the inferior margin of the symphysis of the lower jaw. Hence **Gony·deal** *a.* of or pertaining to the g.

Goober (gū·bəɹ). *U.S.* 1885. [- Angolese *nguba.*] The peanut, *Arachis hypogæa.*

Good (gud), *a., adv.* and *sb.* [OE. *gōd* = OFris., OS. *gōd* (Du. *goed*), OHG. *guot* (G. *gut*), ON. *góðr,* Goth. *gōþs* :- Gmc. **ʒōðaz,* f. var. of the base **ʒað-* bring together, unite, as in *gaderian* GATHER, the primary sense being 'fitting, suitable'.]

A. *adj.* **I.** A term of general or indefinite commendation. **1.** Of things: Being what they are called or ought to be. **2.** Of persons: (originally) Of high rank or valour OE. **3.** Of personal qualities: Commendable in the person OE. **4.** Of a state of things, a purpose, etc.: Right, sound OE. Chiefly *predicative.* Also *absol.* as an exclam., expressing satisfaction.

1. Plates of siluer god (= 'pure' *obs.*) ME. A ryght g. dyner CAXTON. To g. wine they do vse g. bushes SHAKS. Phr. *That's a good'un:* used ironically to characterize a statement that is incredibly mendacious or absurdly exaggerated (*slang*). G. townes, G. shyppes ME. (now conventional, as in 'the g. ship A—'; 'the g. town of B—'). **2.** Rare in orig. sense, exc. in phr. *g. men and true, as g. as.* †In forms of address, or courtesy, as, Gode sirs 1420. She's my g. Lady SHAKS. G. your Ladyship 1742. (*Obs.* exc. in jocular use) 'My g. friend', 'the g. woman of the house'; and euphemistically in 'the g. people' = fairies. **3.** An. .emulator of euery mans g. parts SHAKS. G. qualities (*mod.*). Of a g. Family DE FOE. Of g. birth (*mod.*). Take G. herte CHAUCER. *G. cheer* (see CHEER *sb.*). G. name in Man, and woman SHAKS. G.-fame EMERSON. A g. face SHAKS. A g. leg THACKERAY. **4.** Hell is full of g. meanings HERBERT. It was. .g. that they should be respected MACAULAY. *absol.* It is a promise, g. DISRAELI. Very g., my lord 1829.

II. 1. Morally excellent: **a.** of persons. ME. **b.** Of conduct. OE. **2.** Applied to God, and in exclams. *G. God! gracious!* etc. OE. **3.** Kind. OE. Const. *to.* OE. **4.** Pious, holy OE.

1. a. The hand that hath made you faire, hath made you g. SHAKS. **b.** Gode dæda, *opp. to* misdæda *A.-S. Chron.* A. .g. conscience CLARENDON. Be g., sweet maid, and let who can be clever KINGSLEY. Be a g. girl (= well-behayed) 1695. **2.** It was a wicked woman's curse—God's g., and what care I COLERIDGE. 'G. Lord! What Fools!' said the Physician 1890. **3.** Be g. to Rome SHAKS. G. to me (*mod.*). It is the goodest soule B. JONS. *To be g. enough* (or *so g. as*) *to* (do something) 1652. *G. offices, turn* (see TURN). †*G. words* (= *bona verba*) -1592. G. words are worth much and cost little HERBERT. To say a g. word for 1892. Good (= simple) easie Man SHAKS. **4.** Reading g. books and drinking tea TROLLOPE.

III. 1. Agreeable OE. **2.** Amusing 1530. **3.** Salutary, wholesome OE. **4.** Favourable, laudatory 1601.

1. ȝef us alle god endyng ME. G. fortune 1481, newes 1573. G. wynd and whedyr ME. Wine, and g. fare 1755. So in *g. morning,* etc. with ellipse of *to you* ME.; *to have a good time of it* (now an Americanism); had as g. a time as heart could wish PEPYS; *to have a g. night* 1701. A g. smell 1684. **2.** *G. Company* 1530. *As g. as a play.* **3.** Godne mete OE. G. for the short winded 1599, for a cold STEELE; also †*g. against.* **4.** Purchase vs a g. opinion *Jul. C.* II. i. 145. God is in a g. sence. .jelous 1617. The Apostles were Fishers of men in a g. sense 1665. *To take in g. part* (see PART *sb.*).

IV. Useful, reliable for a purpose, or efficient in a function, pursuit, creed, etc. (either specified or understood) OE. Const. *for*, †*to*, *to* with *inf.*

Which of the Goods d'ye mean? g. for something, or g. for nothing? SWIFT. He was not now g. for much CARLYLE. *In g. time* (see TIME *sb.*). G. fightyng men 1548. G. Saracens PURCHAS. G. Shepherds after Sheering drench their Sheep DRYDEN. G. Latin scholars MACAULAY. A g. writer, hater, shot (*mod.*). †*G. under sail* –1561. Good *at*, e.g. the needle 1617, descriptions THACKERAY. G. men of their hands MACAULAY. He is called..a G. Man upon the exchange, who hath a responsible estate FULLER (cf. SHAKS. *Merch. V.* I. iii. 15). A g. life (for purposes of insurance) 1828. G. debts (= debts good as assets); hence **Good-for** *sb.* S. Afr. = IOU. G. for.. twenty years 1893, for a ten-mile walk 1900. We had seven Minutes g. (= available) 1711.

V. 1. Adequate ME., effectual, thorough; valid (esp. in *Law*) OE. **2.** Used as an intensive, before another adj. or with statements of quantity, etc. OE.

1. *G. heed, g. speed* (see sbs.). *In g. earnest, faith, sooth* (see sbs.). [He] made a very g. stand 1617. My Lord..will giue a very g. accompt of them 1617. I..gave him a g. Blow SWIFT. Administering a g. beating to his wife 1878. I have taken g. care That shall not be SHELLEY. Licences g. only for one Year 1562. It is g. in law too MASSINGER. G. claim, prize, reason, cause, excuse (*mod.*). *To have a g. mind to* (see MIND). **2.** A g. smart cut 1787. He writes a g. bold hand 1900. *A g. deal, few, many* (see those wds.). Gode hand fulle OE. Geve to everyone three spoonefulles g. 1577. We have three quarters g. to a voyage of half an hour 1834, a g. two miles off 1842, he played a g. hour on the violoncello GEO. ELIOT.

VI. Phrases.

1. As good. Orig. *adj.* Me had been as g. to goo ME. To be as g. as one's word 1577. Later, *semi-adv.*: I were as g. (= I might as well); or *adv.*: We had as g. make tracks 1843. *As g. as*: advb. phr. = Practically. As g. as gone ME. **2. Make good.** To make up for (a deficiency) ME. To perform (a promise); to effect (a purpose) 1535. To substantiate (a charge), esp. make g. *on any one, on his person* 1523. To make secure (a kingdom, walls, prisoners) 1606. To repair (a building) 1568. To succeed (orig. *U.S.*) 1901.

B. *adv.* **a.** qualifying a vb.: Well. Now *vulgar* or *slang.* Also in †*as good as* = 'as well as'. †**b.** Qualifying an adj. or adv., with intensive force: In a high degree. **c.** In *as good* (see A. VI) the adj. occas. becomes an adv.

C. quasi-*sb.* and *sb.* **1.** The adj. used *absol.* as *pl.* Good persons. Now only with *the* (exc. in *good and bad*) ME. **2.** The neut. adj. used *absol.* That which is good: **a.** *gen.* OE. **b.** The good portion, side, or aspect 1670. **c.** Well-being, profit, benefit, advantage OE. **3.** A particular thing that is good: **a.** That which it is good to attain or possess OE.; †**b.** *occas.* A good quality, virtue, grace –1563. **c.** *pl.* Property; now movable property; also *sing.* (*obs.* exc. *arch.*) OE.; †**d.** *sing.* Money –1548; **e.** *pl.* Live stock (now *dial.*) 1485. **4.** *spec.* (Now only *pl.*) Merchandise, wares (now chiefly manufactured articles) 1460. Also attrib. as *goods agent, engine, train*, etc. 1858.

2. a. To know G. from Evil 1688. **b.** The g. and bad of an affair 1670. **c.** Zeale to promote the common g. BIBLE *Transl. Pref.* To drink..for the g. of the house GOLDSM. As much as he can see the g. of E. IRVING. Phr. *To do g., much g. may it do you, to do any g. To the g.*: as a balance on the right side. *To come to g.*: orig. of a dream, †to come true; later, to yield a g. result. *For g.* (*and all*): as a valid conclusion; hence, finally. *To be any, some, no g.* (colloq.). **3. a.** The goods of the mind SIR T. BROWNE, of fortune BURKE. Life.. is a doubtful g. to many GEO. ELIOT. **b.** The goods and graces wherewith they were indued 1563. **c.** Misers will as easily part with their blood, as with their g. TRAPP. **d.** (*A*) *great g.*: a great sum of money. *Marriage g.*: a marriage portion. **4.** Phr. *To deliver the goods*: to supply the objects contracted for; to carry out one's part of the agreement; to come up to expectations (chiefly *U.S.*). *The goods*: what is supplied or provided; what is expected or required; the real thing; the genuine article (chiefly *U.S.*).

Comb. **1.** †**a.** denoting a grandparent, as *good-dame, -sire*; **b.** denoting a relation by marriage, = -in-law, or step-, as GOOD-FATHER, -MOTHER, *-brother*, -SISTER, -SON, -DAUGHTER.

2. Special: as †**g.-deed** *adv.*, in very deed; **-enough** *a.*, that has a quality in a sufficient degree; **-face**, one that carries a fair or smooth face; **-for-little** *a.*, of little use, insignificant; **-for-something**, one who is of some use; cf. GOOD-FOR-NOTHING; **-woolled** *a.*, (of a sheep) having a g. fleece; (of persons) having plenty of pluck and go (*dial.* or *slang*).

†**Good**, *v.* OE. [f. the adj.] **1.** *intr.* To improve –ME. **2.** *trans.* To endow (a church, etc.). OE. only. **3.** To improve; to manure (land) –18.. **4.** To benefit (a person). Also *absol.* –1620.

Good-bye (gu:dbəi·). 1573. [A contr. of *God be with you* (or *ye*), with later substitution of *good* for *God*, after *good day* (XIII), *good night* (XIV).] **1.** As an exclam.: Farewell. **2.** *sb.* A saying 'good-bye' 1573. Also *attrib.*

2. He hurried through his good-byes 1879.

Good-daughter. *Sc.* and *north.* 1513. [See GOOD C. *Comb.* 1. b.] A daughter-in-law.

Good day. ME. [See GOOD *a.* III. 1.] **1.** A phrase of salutation at meeting or parting. **2.** The salutation expressed by this phrase ME.

1. God so ȝeve ȝou god day CHAUCER. A good day, thou, and thou 1460. **2.** *To bid*, (*give* a person) *good day.*

Good-den: see GOOD EVEN.

Goo·d-do·er. ME. [f. GOOD *sb.* + DOER.] **1.** Now commonly *a doer of good*; a benefactor. **2.** *dial.* An animal or plant that thrives well 1877.

Good even. *Obs.* exc. *dial.* ME. [See GOOD *a.* III. 1.] A form of salutation; = Good evening (but used at any time after noon: see *Rom. & Jul.* II. iv. 116 ff.) 1481.

Oh, 'giue ye-good-ev'n *Two Gent.* II. i. 104. God-den to your Worships *Cor.* II. i. 103.

Good-father. *Sc.* 1533. [See GOOD C. *Comb.* 1 b.] A father-in-law; also, a stepfather.

Good-fellow, *sb.* ME. [See FELLOW *sb.* 2.] **1.** An agreeable companion; *esp.* a boon companion, a convivial person. †**2.** A thief or robber –1633. Hence †**Goodfellow** *v.* (*rare*), to call (a person) a good fellow. **Good-fe·llowship**, the spirit or habits of a good fellow, conviviality; now also, the spirit of true friendship or companionship.

Goo·d-for-no:thing. 1711. [The phr. *good for nothing* used *attrib.* or as *sb.*: see GOOD *a.* IV.]

A. *adj.* Of no service or use; worthless.

We reckon him here a good-for-nothing fellow SWIFT.

B. *sb.* One who is good for nothing; a worthless person (†or thing). So **Goo·d-for-nou:ght** *a.* and *sb.*

Good Friday. ME. [See GOOD *a.* II. 4.] The Friday before Easter-day, observed as the anniversary of the death of Christ.

Goodhap (gu·dˌhæp). *arch.* 1557. [See GOOD *a.* and HAP *sb.*[1] 1; = *good hap.*] Good fortune.

Good humour. 1616. The condition of being in a cheerful and amiable mood; also, the disposition or habit of amiable cheerfulness.

Her good humour made her willing to divert me 1718. Hence **Good-humoured** *a.* possessed of or characterized by good humour; indicative of good humour. **Goodhu·mouredly** *adv.*

Goodish (gu·diʃ), *a.* 1756. [f. GOOD *a.* + -ISH[1].] Somewhat good.

A g. sort of woman MRS. DELANY. A g. sum 1894.

†**Goo·dless**, *a.* OE. [f. GOOD *sb.* + -LESS.] Devoid of good or of goods –1581.

Goo·dlihead. ME. [f. GOODLY *a.* + -HEAD.] **1.** Comeliness (*arch.*). †**2.** Excellence, goodness –1503. †**3.** The personality of one who is goodly. SPENSER.

Goo·dlike, *a.* Now *dial.* 1572. [f. GOOD *a.* + -LIKE.] **a.** Goodly; good-looking. **b.** Resembling what is good.

Good-liking. ?*Obs.* 1583. [See GOOD *a.* I. 4, LIKING *vbl. sb.*] **1.** Kindly feeling towards a person 1586. **2.** Good-will; satisfaction 1583. †**3.** Personal fancy. LOCKE. †**4.** Good condition, embonpoint –1656.

1. A match of prudence and common good-liking SWIFT. **4.** Their yong ones are in good liking *Job* 39:4.

Goodliness (gu·dlinės). ME. [f. GOODLY *a.* + -NESS.] The quality or condition of being goodly; comeliness; †kindness –1555; excellence, value (*rare*) 1832.

Her goodlinesse was full of harmony to his eyes SIDNEY.

Good-looking, *a.* 1780. Having a good appearance; *esp.* with reference to beauty of countenance. So **Goo:d-loo·ker** (chiefly *U.S.*).

Goodly (gu·dli), *a.* [OE. *gōdlić*; see GOOD, -LY[1].] **1.** Of good appearance; well-favoured or proportioned; comely, fair, handsome. **2.** Considerable in size, quantity, or number (freq. with mixture of sense 1) ME. **3.** Of good quality. Also, good for a purpose, proper, convenient (often with mixture of sense 1). Often *ironical.* ME. †**4.** Gracious, kind. ME. only.

1. Þe goodlieste mayde..in al þe toun CHAUCER. **2.** Surely a g. stature is most majestical FULLER. **3.** G. Corne B. GOOGE. Heere's a g. Watch indeed SHAKS.

Goodly (gu·dli), *adv.* [ME. *godliche*; see GOOD, -LY[2].] †**1.** Beautifully, gracefully –1556. †**2.** Graciously, kindly; courteously –1677. **3.** In a goodly fashion; excellently. Also *ironical.* Now *rare.* ME. †**4.** Conveniently –1513. †**5.** In neg. clauses: Easily, readily –1652.

Goodman (gu·dmæ̆n). ME. [GOOD *a.* + MAN.] †**1.** = *Good man.* Perh. really two wds. ME. only. **2.** The male head of a household; †the host (of an inn), †the keeper (of a prison) ME. **b.** Hence, a husband (now only *Sc.* or *arch.*) 1513. †**3.** Prefixed to designations of occupation –1638. **4.** A man of substance, not of gentle birth; a yeoman, etc. *Obs.* exc. *Hist.* or *poet.* 1587. †**b.** *Sc.* The laird or tenant *of* a specified estate or farm –1824.

2. When the g. mends his armour MACAULAY. **3.** Nay, but heare you, g. deluer *Haml.* V. i. 13. **4.** He is called a Good Man in common discourse, who is not dignified with Gentilitie FULLER. **b.** The G. of Primrose Knowe SCOTT.

Good morrow, good-mo·rrow. ME. **1.** A salutation equiv. to the later *good morning* (see GOOD *a.* III. 1). Now *arch.* †**2.** Something as empty as 'good-morrow'; a trivial saying or matter –1704.

1. Giue you good-morrow, sir SHAKS.

Good-mother. *Sc.* 1536. [See GOOD C. *Comb.* 1 b.] A mother-in-law; also, a stepmother.

Good nature, good-na·ture. 1450. **1.** Pleasant or kindly disposition; chiefly denoting undue easiness of disposition. †**2.** Natural goodness of character; virtue (*rare*) –1677.

Good-natured. (The stress varies.) 1577. [f. prec. + -ED[2].] Characterized by good nature (see prec.).

If it is abuse,—why, one is always sure to hear of it from one damn'd goodnatur'd friend or another SHERIDAN. Hence **Good-natured-ly** *adv.*, **-ness.**

Goo:d-nei·ghbourhood. 1817. [f. *good neighbour* + -HOOD.] The disposition and behaviour characteristic of a good neighbour; friendly feeling and intercourse. So **Goo:d-nei·ghbourliness.**

Goodness (gu·dnės). [OE. *gōdnes*; see GOOD, -NESS.] **1.** The quality or condition of being good, in various senses; esp. moral excellence; benevolence; also beneficence OE.; kindly feeling OE. †**2.** Advantage, profit –1583. †**3.** quasi-*concr.* A good act or deed –1568. **4.** In exclams., orig. with reference to the goodness of God 1613.

1. Vertue is bold, and goodnes neuer fearefull SHAKS. The g. of the Lord WESLEY, of a custom STEPHEN, of a cause 1870. Phr. *Have the g. to*..: a form of polite request. **4.** *G. gracious! G.* (*only*) *knows! For goodness' sake! I wish to g.! Surely to g.! Thank g.! Goodness!*

Good night. (Also *hyphened.*) ME. [See GOOD *a.* III. 1.] **1.** A customary phrase used at parting at night or going to sleep; †orig. *have good night*, (*God*) *give you good night*, etc. Also *fig.* Also *attrib.* **2.** *transf.* Any parting salutation at night 1597.

1. *fig.* When our beauty fades, godnight with vs MARSTON. *attrib.* One good-night carol more BYRON.

Good now, goo·d-now:. *Obs.* exc. *dial.* 1579. [See GOOD *a.* I. 4 and NOW.] An exclam. of acquiescence, entreaty, expostulation, or surprise.

Goods. See GOOD C. quasi-*sb.* and *sb.*

Good sense. 1688. [Cf. Fr. *bon sens.*] Native soundness of judgement.

†**Goo·dship.** OE. [f. GOOD *a.* + -SHIP.] Goodness. *pl.* Kindnesses. –ME.

Good-sister. *Sc.* 1666. [See GOOD C. *Comb.* 1 b.] A sister-in-law. So **Good-son** (*Sc.*), a son-in-law.

Good-tempered, *a.* (The stress varies.) 1768. [f. *good temper* (see TEMPER *sb.*) + -ED[2].] Having a good temper; not easily vexed.

Good Templar. 1874. One of an order of total abstainers established in the U.S. in 1851, and introduced into England in 1868.

Good thing. 1694. [See GOOD *a.*] A successful act or speculation; a witty saying; *pl.* dainties.

Goodwife (gu·dwəif). ME. [Cf. GOODMAN; see GOODY *sb.*[1]] **1.** The mistress of a house, etc. Now chiefly *Sc.* †**2.** = Mrs. Also, a civil form of address. –1824.

Goodwill (gudwi·l). OE. [orig. two wds. (still often so written exc. in sense 4): see GOOD *a.* II. 1, 2.] †**1.** Virtuous, pious, upright disposition or intention. (In *Luke* 2:14, *good will* has this sense in the pre-Reformation versions, in 16th c. versions and in A.V. it has sense 2, while R.V. renders 'On earth peace among men in whom he is well pleased'.) –1602. **2.** The state of wishing well to a person, a cause, etc. OE. **3.** Cheerful acquiescence or consent; readiness, zeal ME. **4.** *Comm.* The privilege, granted by the seller of a business to the purchaser, of trading as his recognized successor; the possession of a ready-formed connection of customers, considered as a separate element in the saleable value of a business 1571.

2. Peace vpon earth, and vnto men a good wyll COVERDALE. **3.** And, though my portion is but scant, I give it with good will GOLDSM.

Goody (gu·di), *sb.*[1] 1559. [Hypocoristic f. GOODWIFE, as *hussy*, f. *housewife*.] A term of civility formerly applied to a (married) woman in humble life. Hence such a woman. **b.** *U.S.* A woman who looks after students' rooms 1827.

G. Blake and Harry Gill WORDSW.

Goody (gu·di), *sb.*[2] 1745. [f. GOOD *a.* + -Y[6].] A sweetmeat.

Goo·dy, *sb.*[3] 1859. *U.S.* = LAFAYETTE 1.

Goo·dy, *a.* and *sb.*[4] 1810. [f. GOOD *a.* + -Y[6].] **A.** *adj.* **1.** ?Cosy. MOORE. **2.** Weakly or sentimentally good. Also, *to talk g.* 1830. **B.** *sb. U.S.* A goody person 1878. Hence **Goo·dyness, goo·diness,** the quality of being g.

†**Goodyear.** Also in pseudo-etym. form **goujeres, goujeers.** 1555. [GOOD *a.* + YEAR. Perh. elliptical = 'as I hope for a good year'.] **a.** A meaningless expletive, chiefly in *What a* (or *the*) *good year.* **b.** Some malefic power or agency (app. from its equivalence with *what the plague, what the pox*, etc.) 1591.

b. The good yeares shall deuoure them, flesh and fell *Lear* V. iii. 24.

Goo·dy-goo·dy, *a.* (and *sb.*). 1871. Reduplic. GOODY *a.* and *sb.*[4] **Goo·dy-goo·d** *a.* 1851.

Goof (gūf). *slang.* [Cf. dial. *goof*, GOFF.] A silly stupid person. Hence **Goo·fy** *a.*, silly.

Go:-o·ff. *colloq.* 1851. [f. phr. *go off*; see GO *v.*] **1.** The action or time of going off; commencement. **2.** *Banking.* The amount of loans falling due (and therefore going off the books) in a certain period 1900.

Googly (gū·gli). 1904. [Of unkn. origin.] *Cricket.* An off-break ball bowled with leg-break action. Hence **Goo·gle** *v.* of the ball or the bowler. **Goo·gler.**

Gooroo, var. of GURU.

Goosander (gusæ·ndəɹ). 1622. [prob. f. GOOSE + second element of BERGANDER.] The bird *Mergus merganser*, allied to the ducks but having a sharply serrated bill.

Goose (gūs), *sb.* Pl. **geese** (gīs). [OE. *gōs*, pl. *gēs* = OFris., MLG. *gōs*, (M)Du., OHG., G. *gans*, ON. *gás* :- Gmc. **ʒans-* :- IE. **ghans-*, whence also L. *anser*, Gr. χήν, Skr. *haṅsás* m., *haṅsī́* fem.] **1.** Any large web-footed bird of the sub-family *Anserinæ* (family *Anatidæ*), including *Anser* and allied genera.

The word is applied without addition to the common tame goose (*Anser domesticus*), which is descended from the wild or greylag goose (*A. ferus* or *cinereus*). The other species are dist. by adjuncts, as *black, blue*, etc. *g.*; *fen-, marsh-g.*; *American* (*wild*), etc. *g.*

b. *spec.* The female bird; the male being the GANDER, the young GOSLINGS ME. **c.** *fig.* A simpleton 1547. **d.** Hissing; sibilation; esp. *Theatr. slang.* 1805. **2.** Applied to other birds of the same or a related family, or resembling the true goose, as **Cape Barren g.** (*Coreopsis novæ-hollandiæ*), **Egyptian** or **Nile g.** (*Chænalopex ægyptiaca*), **Spur-winged g.** (the African genus *Plectropterus*), etc.; also the SOLAN *goose* 1772. †**3.** *Winchester goose*: a venereal disorder; also, a prostitute –1778. †**4.** (*Game* of) *goose*: A game played with counters on a board divided into compartments, in some of which a goose was depicted –1801. **5.** A tailor's smoothing-iron. Pl. *gooses.* [The handle resembles in shape a goose's neck.] 1605.

1. Phr. *All* (*his*) *geese are swans*: he always overestimates. *To cook one's g.*: to do for a person or thing; to ruin or kill (*slang*). *To kill the g. that laid* or *lays the golden eggs*: to sacrifice future advantage to present necessities. *To say bo to a g.* (see BO *interj.*). **5.** Come in Taylor, here you may rost your G. SHAKS.

Comb.: **g.-barnacle** = BARNACLE *sb.*[2] 2; **-bone,** a bone of a g., esp. one used as a weather-guide; **-chase** (see WILD GOOSE CHASE); **-club; -dung-ore,** *Min.* an impure iron sinter containing silver; **-file** = *single* or *Indian file*; **-fish** *U.S.*, the fishing-frog, *Lophius piscatorius*; **-pen,** (*a*) a pen or enclosure for geese: †(*b*) a quill-pen; **-silver-ore** = *goose-dung-ore* (above); **-teal,** 'the English name for a very small goose of the genus *Nettopus*' (Morris); †**-trap,** a trap for a g., a quibble, sophism; **Mother Carey's g.,** the largest of the petrels.

Goose (gūs), *v.* 1808. [f. the sb.] **1.** *trans.* To press or iron with a tailor's goose. **2.** *Theatr. slang.* To hiss, to express disapproval of by hissing 1853.

Gooseberry (gū·zbĕri). 1532. [The first element may be alt. (by unexpl. assim. to *goose*) of forms such as (dial.) *groser* (XVI) and *gozell* (XVII), repr. remotely (O)Fr. *groseille*, †*grozelle*, of disputed origin; but immed. deriv. from GOOSE + BERRY *sb.*[1] is possible.] **1.** The edible berry of any of the thorny species of the genus *Ribes*; also the shrub itself. **2.** Applied to shrubs resembling the gooseberry in some way 1847. **3.** Short for *gooseberry-wine* 1766. **4.** A chaperon, esp. in *to play g.* 1837.

1. Not woorth a Goose berry SHAKS. **2. Barbados g.,** *Pereskia aculeata*; **Cape g.,** *Physalis edulis* or *P. peruviana*; **Coromandel g.,** *Averrhoa carambola.* Phr. *Old g.* (slang) = the deuce (see DEUCE[2]); esp. *to play old g.*, to make havoc.

Comb.: **g.-caterpillar,** the caterpillar of the g.-moth; **-louse** = HARVEST-BUG; **-moth,** the magpie-moth (*Abraxas grossulariata*); **-season,** the time when gooseberries are ripe, *esp.* in *big. g. season*, the time of year when the newspapers record marvels.

Goo·seberry foo·l. 1719. [FOOL *sb.*[2]] **1.** A dish made of gooseberries stewed or scalded and pounded with cream. **2.** A plant-name: **a.** Willow-herb (*Epilobium hirsutum*), also called *gooseberry-pie;* **b.** Lungwort (*Pulmonaria officinalis*) 1794.

Goo·se-bill. 1597. [From the resemblance.] **1.** The plant *Galium aparine*; = GOOSE-GRASS 2. †**2.** A kind of forceps for extracting bullets, etc. –1823.

Goo·se-egg. ME. The egg of a goose; hence *U.S.* the score zero or 'O'. (Cf. DUCK'S EGG.)

Goo·se-flesh, goo·seflesh. ME. **1.** The flesh of a goose. **2.** A rough pimply condition of the skin, produced by cold, fear, etc.; horripilation. (Cf. GOOSE-SKIN.) 1810.

Goo·se-foot. 1516. [From the resemblance.] **1.** A plant of any of various species of the genus *Chenopodium*; so called from the shape of the leaves. Pl. *goosefoots.* 1548. **2.** Anything suggesting the shape of a goose's foot; *e.g.* a three-branching hinge, or roads diverging from a common point. Pl. *goose-feet.*

Goo·se-grass. Also *erron.* **goose-grease.** ME. [See GOOSE and GRASS.] A name of plants, mostly used at some time as food for geese. **1.** Silver-weed (*Potentilla anserina.*). **2.** Cleavers (*Galium aparine*) 1530. †**3.** **Purple goose-grass,** field-madder or spurwort (*Sherardia arvensis*) 1548. **4.** The wild grass, *Bromus mollis* 1853. **5.** *U.S.* **a.** *Polygonum aviculare.* **b.** *Poa annua.*

Goo·se-grease. ME. The melted fat of the goose.

Goo·se-neck. 1688. Anything shaped like the neck of a goose; e.g. *Mech.* a pipe or piece of iron; *Naut.* a curved iron, fitted outside the after-chains, to receive a spare spar; etc.

Goo·se-quill. 1552. One of the wing-feathers of a goose; hence, a pen made of this.

Goosery (gū·sĕri). 1642. [f. GOOSE *sb.* + -ERY.] **1.** Silliness as attributed to the goose (*rare*). **2.** A place in which geese are kept; a collection of geese 1828.

1. The finicall g. of your neat Sermon-actor MILTON.

Goo·se-skin. 1700. **1.** The skin of a goose. FLOYER. **2.** = GOOSE-FLESH 2. 1785. **3.** A thin soft kind of leather. Also *attrib.* 1826. **4.** The impression made upon copal by sand 1859.

Goo·se-step. 1806. *Mil.* An elementary drill in which the recruit balances his body on either leg alternately, and swings the other; also, the German stiff-legged parade step. Also as *v. intr.*, to perform this step.

Goo·se-wing. ME. **1.** The wing of a goose. **2.** *Naut.* One of the clues or lower corners of a ship's main-sail or fore-sail, when the middle part is furled or tied up to the yard 1626. Hence **Goo·se-winged** *a.*

Goo·sish *a.* ME. [f. GOOSE *sb.* + -ISH[1].] Goose-like, silly. So **Goo·sy** *a.*; also, like 'goose-flesh' (1857).

Gopher (gōᵘ·fəɹ), *sb.*[1] *U.S.* Also †**gophir.** 1791. [Said to be – Canadian Fr. *gaufre*, a use of the word meaning 'honeycomb', with ref. to burrowing habits; but this is very doubtful (*magofer* occurs earlier in sense 3).] **1.** A burrowing rodent of the genera *Geomys* and *Thomomys*; a pocket gopher or pouched rat 1812. **2.** A burrowing or ground squirrel of the genus *Spermophilinæ*; a spermophile 1874. **3.** A burrowing land-tortoise (*Testudo carolina*), of nocturnal habits 1791. **4.** A large burrowing snake of the southern U.S. Also *g.-snake.* 1884. **5.** *Mining.* A *gopher-drift*, q.v. 1881.

Comb.: **g.-drift,** an irregular prospecting drift, following the ore without regard to maintenance of a regular grade or section; **-hole,** (*a*) the opening of a gopher's burrow; (*b*) a mine-opening begun without any reference to future permanent development; **-plum,** the Ogeechee lime (*Nyssa capitata*).

Gopher (gōᵘ·fəɹ), *sb.*[2] 1611. [– Heb.] The tree of the wood of which the ark was made. Chiefly in comb. **g.-wood:** applied in U.S. to the yellow-wood (*Cladrastis tinctoria*).

Make thee an Arke of Gopher-wood *Gen.* 6:14.

Gopher (gōᵘ·fəɹ), *v. U.S.* 1893. [f. GOPHER *sb.*[1]] **1.** *intr.* To burrow. **2.** *Mining.* To mine without any reference to future permanent development 1889.

‖**Goral** (gō·răl). Also **gooral.** 1834. [Native name.] *Zool.* An Indian antelope (*Cemas goral*).

Gor·belly, *sb.* (and *a.*) *Obs.* exc. *dial.* 1519. [perh. f. *gor*, GORE *sb.*[1] 1 + BELLY; cf. Sw. dial. *går-bälg.*] †**1.** A protuberant belly –1790. **2.** A person with a protuberant belly 1530. †**3.** *attrib.* –1603. Hence †**Go·rbellied** *a.* corpulent.

†**Gorce.** 1480. [– AFr. *gortz*, pl. of *gort* (OFr. *gord, gourt*) :- L. *gurges, gurgit-* whirlpool.] **a.** A whirlpool. **b.** Any stop in a river, such as weirs, mills, stakes –1741.

Gorcock (gǭ·ɹkǫk). *Sc.* and *n. dial.* 1620. [f. *gor* of obscure origin + COCK *sb.*[1]] The male of the Red Grouse.

Gorcrow (gǭ·ɹkrōᵘ). 1605. [f. *gor* GORE *sb.*[1] + CROW *sb.*[1]] The Carrion Crow.

Gordian (gǭ·ɹdiăn). 1561. [f. L. *Gordius* or *Gordium* (see sense 1) + -AN.] **A.** *adj.* **1.** *Gordian knot*: an intricate knot tied by Gordius, king of Gordium in Phrygia. The oracle declared that whoever should loosen it should rule Asia, and Alexander the Great cut it through with his sword 1611. Also *fig.* or allusively 1579. **2.** Resembling the Gordian knot; intricate, involved 1606.

1. *fig.* Turne him to any Cause of Pollicy, The Gordian Knot of it he will vnloose SHAKS. **2.** Tedious and G. difficulties MILTON.

†**B.** *sb.* **1.** = *Gordian knot* –1709. **2.** An inhabitant of Gordium; one who ties intricate knots 1606.

Hence †**Go·rdian** *v. trans.* to tie in a Gordian knot. KEATS.

Gore (gōᵊɹ), *sb.*[1] [OE. *gor* = (M)Du. *goor* mud, filth, OHG. *gor*, ON. *gor* cud, slimy matter, rel. to OIr. *gor*, W. *gôr* matter, pus.]

1. Dung, fæces; filth of any kind. *Obs.* exc. *dial.* 2. Blood in the thickened state that follows effusion. Often *poet.* Blood shed in carnage. 1563.

2. Phr. †(*All*) (*in*) *a g. of blood*: bathed in or besmeared with blood. PEPYS.

Gore (gōᵊɹ), *sb.*² [OE. *gāra* = OFris. *gāra*, MDu. *ghēre* (Du. *geer*), OHG. *gēro* (G. *gehre*), ON. *geiri*, rel. to *gār* spear (a spear-head being triangular).] 1. A triangular piece of land. †2. *poet.* The front section of a skirt, wider at the bottom that at the top; the lap of a gown, an apron. Hence, a skirt, petticoat, or gown. –1570. 3. Any wedge-shaped or triangular piece of cloth forming part of a garment, sail, etc., and serving to produce difference of width at different points ME. 4. *Her.* A charge formed by two curved lines meeting in the fesse-point, the one drawn from the sinister or dexter chief and the other from the lowest angle of the base 1562. 5. Any triangular or lune-shaped piece forming part of the surface of a globe, a balloon, the covering of an umbrella, a dome, etc. 1796.

Gore (gōᵊɹ), *v.*¹ ME. [Of unkn. origin.] 1. *trans.* To pierce or stab deeply, with a sharp weapon, spike, spur, or the like. *Obs.* exc. as in sense 2. 2. *spec.* To pierce, or wound, as with horns, or (*rarely*) the tusk. Also *transf.* and *fig.* Also *absol.* 1523.

2. It is the nature of bulls to g. each other 1865. *fig.* Aquinas..was called bos mutus, a dumbe Oxe; and..with two hornes..gored all unbeleevers 1641.

†**Gore**, *v.*² Only in **Gored, Goring**. 1566. [f. GORE *sb.*¹] 1. *trans.* To cover with or as with gore. Only in pa. pple. –1655. 2. *intr.* To lie soaking *in* blood. STANYHURST.

Gore (gōᵊɹ), *v.*³ 1548. [f. GORE *sb.*²] 1. *trans.* To cut into a gore or gores; to furnish with gores. †2. *Naut. intr.* To swell or jut *out* 1627.

Go·rebill. *local.* 1862. [perh. f. *gore*, var. of †*gare* spear + BILL *sb.*¹; cf. GAR, GARFISH.] The Garfish.

Gore-fish. 1839. [See prec.] ? = GARFISH.

Gorge (gǭɹdʒ), *sb.*¹ ME. [– (O)Fr. *gorge* throat :– Rom. **gurga*, for L. *gurges* whirlpool.]

I. 1. The external throat; the front of the neck. *Obs.* exc. *arch.* 2. The internal throat. Now only *rhet.* ME. 3. *Falconry.* The crop of a hawk. Hence, opprobriously, of the 'maw', devouring capacity, of a monster, a person, etc. *Obs.* exc. *arch.* Also *fig.* 1450. †4. A meal for a hawk –1677. 5. What has been swallowed; in phrases (primarily of *Falconry*) †*to cast up, heave*, etc. *one's g.* Freq. used *fig.* to express disgust or violent resentment. 1532.

3. *fig.* The first are in destruction's g. SCOTT. Phr. *A full g.* (often taken erron. in sense 4). 5. How abhorred my Imagination is, my g. rises at it SHAKS.

II. 1. *Fortif.* The neck of a bastion or other outwork; the entrance from the rear to the platform or body of a work 1669. 2. A narrow opening between hills; a ravine, *esp.* one that gives passage to a stream 1769. 3. *Arch.* The neck of a column; also, a kind of moulding, hollow on the inside 1706. 4. *Mech.* The groove of a pulley 1812. 5. *Angling.* A solid object, intended to be swallowed by the fish 1883. 6. *U.S.* A mass choking up a narrow passage; esp. in *ice-g.* 1884. †7. *Pottery. pl.* Pitchers. [?a distinct wd.; cf. BROWN GEORGE.] 1684.

2. Through the g. of this glen they found access to a black bog SCOTT.

Comb., as (sense II. 5) *g.-hook*; also **g.-circle**, in gearing, 'the outline of the smallest cross-section of a hyperboloid of revolution' (Webster).

Gorge (gǭɹdʒ), *sb.*² 1854. [f. next vb.] An act of gorging oneself; a glut (of food, etc.).

Gorge (gǭɹdʒ), *v.* ME. [– (O)Fr. *gorger*, f. *gorge* GORGE *sb.*¹] 1. *intr.* To fill the gorge; to feed greedily. Const. *on, upon.* 2. *trans.* To fill the gorge of; to glut, satiate. Also *transf.* and *fig.* 1486. 3. To swallow; to devour greedily 1614. 4. To fill full, distend; to choke, choke up. Chiefly in *pa. pple.* 1508.

1. To..g. upon the Church MILT. 2. Messes To g. his appetite *Lear* I. i. 120. *fig.* Gorged with wealth 1639. 3. You must..let him have time to g. your hook WALTON. 4. During excessive laughter..the head and face become gorged with blood DARWIN.

Gorged (gǭɹdʒd), *ppl. a.* 1610. [f. GORGE *sb.*¹ + -ED².] *Her.* Having the gorge or neck encircled (with a coronet, etc.).

Gorgelet (gǭ·ɹdʒlėt). 1872. [f. as prec. + -LET.] A patch of colour on the throat of a bird.

Gorgeous (gǭ·ɹdʒəs), *a.* 1495. [Early forms *gorgayse, gorges, gorgyas* – OFr. *gorgias* fine, stylish, elegant, of unkn. origin; assim. in ending to words in -EOUS.] 1. Adorned with rich or brilliant colours; showy, magnificent. b. *transf.* of literary phraseology, etc.: Dazzling 1561. 2. *colloq.* As an epithet of approbation. (Cf. *splendid.*) 1883.

1. I am not gorgious in attire DEKKER. The land of g. sunsets W. BLACK. *transf.* G. and fine woordes 1561. 2. A g. time 1883. Hence **Go·rgeous-ly** *adv.*, **-ness**.

Go·rgeret. 1758. [– Fr. *gorgeret* (XVIII), f. *gorge* throat, from the tubular shape of the instrument.] *Surg.* = GORGET².

Gorgerin (gǭ·ɹdʒėrin). 1664. [– Fr. *gorgerin* (XV) gorget; mod. also frieze of a Doric capital, f. *gorge* GORGE *sb.*¹] 1. *Arch.* = HYPOTRACHELIUM. 2. = GORGET¹ 1. 1849.

Gorget¹ (gǭ·ɹdʒėt). 1470. [– OFr. *gorgete*, f. *gorge* GORGE *sb.*¹; see -ET.] 1. A piece of armour for the throat. Now *Hist.* b. *transf.* A collar 1629. 2. An article of female dress, covering the neck and breast; a wimple. Now *Hist.* 1575. 3. An ornament for the neck; a necklace 1570. 4. *Mil.* A gilt crescent-shaped badge suspended from the neck, formerly worn by officers on duty 1786. 5. *Zool.* A patch of colour on the throat of a bird, etc. 1801.

1. Cavaliers with ruff, rapier, buff-coat, and g. THACKERAY. 2. Goodly dames in ruff and g. SCOTT.

Gorget² (gǭ·ɹdʒėt). 1740. [Corruption of GORGERET.] *Surg.* A steel instrument having the form of a channel, used in operations for the stone, etc.

‖**Gorgio** (gǭ·ɹdʒio). 1851. [Romany; in G. *gadscho*, in Sp. *gacho*.] Gipsy term for a non-gipsy.

Gorgon (gǭ·ɹgǭn), *sb.* (and *a.*) 1529. [Generalized use of the proper name *Gorgon* – L. *Gorgo, Gorgon-* – Gr. Γοργώ, f. γοργός terrible.] 1. Gr. *Myth.* One of three mythical sisters, with snakes for hair, whose look turned the beholder into stone. Medusa, the only one mortal, was slain by Perseus, and her head fixed on Athene's shield. 1614. b. Short for *Gorgon's head*. BURKE. †2. An African quadruped; ?the gnu. TOPSELL. 3. A very terrible or very ugly person 1529. 4. *attrib.* Petrifying, terrible 1575.

1. Gorgons and Hydra's, and Chimera's dire MILT. 4. Your G. looks Turn me to stone MASSINGER. *Comb.* **Gorgon's head**, (*a*) the head of Medusa; (*b*) 'a kind of basket-fish' (*Cent. Dict.*).

Gorgoneion (gǭɹgonəi·ǭn). 1842. [– Gr. γοργόνειον, n. of -ος, pert. to a GORGON.] A representation of a Gorgon's head.

Gorgonia (gǫɹgōᵘ·niă). Pl. **-iæ, -ias.** 1767. [– mod.L., *gorgonia*, fem. of *-ius*, f. L. *Gorgo* GORGON. The name was intended to express its petrified character.] *Zool.* A genus of polyps (family *Gorgoniaceæ*); one of these; a sea-fan, sea-plume. Hence **Gorgo·nian** *a.*¹ pertaining to the gorgonias or their family; *sb.* a polyp of the family.

Gorgonian (gǫɹgōᵘ·niăn), *a.*² 1616. [f. GORGON + -IAN; cf. L. *gorgoneus*.] Of or pertaining to the Gorgon; Gorgon-like, terrible. Of a shield: Bearing the Gorgon's head.

The rest his look Bound with G. rigor not to move MILT.

Gorgonize (gǭ·ɹgǭnəiz), *v.* 1609. [f. GORGON + -IZE.] *trans.* To petrify as by the glance of a Gorgon; to render hard or stony.

Gorgonzola (gǭɹgǭnzōᵘ·lă). 1885. A ewe-milk cheese made at Gorgonzola, near Milan, Italy. *G.-Hall* (joc.), the Stock Exchange.

Gorilla (gŏri·lă). 1853. [An alleged African word, found (in acc. pl. γορίλλας) in the Greek account of the voyage of the Carthaginian Hanno, adopted as the specific name of the ape *Troglodytes gorilla* by Dr. Savage in 1847.] The largest of anthropoid apes, a native of western equatorial Africa; it closely resembles man in its structure, is very powerful and ferocious, and arboreal in its habits.

Goring (gōᵊ·riŋ), *vbl. sb.* 1626. [f. GORE *v.*³ + -ING¹.] a. The action of GORE *v.*³; the act of cutting out, or fitting with, gores. b. A piece of cloth used as a gore; esp. *Naut.* Also *g.-cloth.*

Gorman, gormand(e: see GOURMAND.

Gormandize (gǭ·ɹmăndəiz), *sb.* 1450. [– Fr. *gourmandise*, f. *gourmand*; see GOURMAND. Early sp. in *-ise*; from XVI assim. to -IZE.] †a. Gluttony. b. Indulgence or connoisseurship in good eating. Now chiefly as Fr. (spelt *gourmandise*).

Gormandize (gǭ·ɹmăndəiz), *v.* 1548. [f. prec. sb.] 1. *intr.* To eat like a glutton. 2. *trans.* To devour greedily, gobble up (*lit.* and *fig.*) 1603. Hence **Go·rmandizer**, a glutton.

Gorse (gǭɹs). [OE. *gors, gorst*, which has no immed. Gmc. cogns., but points to IE. base **ghṛzd-* be prickly or rough, repr. in L. *hordeum* barley (:– **ghṛzdejum*) and so rel. to Gr. κριθή, OHG. *gersta* (G. *gerste*) barley.] 1. Common furze or whin. 2. = JUNIPER. OE.

Comb.: **g.-bird, -linnet**, the common linnet; **-chat, -hatch, -hatcher, -thatcher**, local names for the whinchat, stonechat, wheatear, and linnet; **-duck**, the landrail; **-kid**, a bundle of g. Hence **Go·rsy** *a.* abounding in g.; of or pertaining to g.

Gory (gōᵊ·ri), *a.* 1480. [f. GORE *sb.*¹ + -Y¹.] †1. Of blood: Gore-like, clotted –1590. 2. Covered with gore 1480. 3. = BLOODY 4. 1586. 4. Blood-red (*rare*) 1822.

2. Neuer shake Thy goary lockes at me SHAKS. 3. Goarie blowes 1586. 4. *G. dew*: a minute freshwater alga, *Palmella cruenta*.

Gos, short for GOSHAWK. Burns.

Gosh (gǫʃ). 1757. [Minced f. GOD.] An exclam., (*By*) *g.!*

Goshawk (gǫ·shǭk). [OE. *gōshafoc*, f. *gōs* GOOSE + *hafoc* HAWK; cf. ON. *gáshaukr*.] A large short-winged hawk (*Astur palumbarius*, and other species).

Shrill As goss-hawk's whistle on the hill SCOTT.

Goshen (gōᵘ·ʃĕn). 1611. [Heb., the fertile land allotted to the Israelites in Egypt, in which there was light during the plague of darkness.] Allusively: A place of plenty or of light.

Go·slet. *U.S.* 1884. [f. GOOSE + -LET.] One of a few diminutive species of geese, of the genus *Nettepus*.

Gos-lettuce, var. of *Cos lettuce*; see COS.

Gosling (gǫ·zliŋ). ME. [orig. *gesling* – ON. *gæslingr* (Sw., Da. *gäsling*), f. *gás* GOOSE; assim. (XV) to Eng. *goose*; see -LING¹.] 1. A young goose. 2. *fig.* One who is young and 'green' 1607. 3. A catkin 1706.

Comb.: **g.-colour, -green**, a pale yellowish green; **-grass, -weed**, local names for GOOSE-GRASS 2.

Gospel (gǫ·spĕl), *sb.* [OE. *gōdspel*, i.e. *gōd* GOOD, *spel* news, tidings (see SPELL *sb.*¹), rendering of eccl.L. *bona annuntiatio, bonus nuntius*, used as literal renderings of eccl.L. *evangelium*, Gr. εὐαγγέλιον EVANGEL. Later assoc. with *God*, as in all the forms adopted in the Gmc. langs. of peoples evangelized from England, viz. OS. *godspell*, OHG. *gotspell*, ON. *guð-, goðspjall*.] 1. 'The glad tidings (of the kingdom of God)'; see Matt. 4:23. Hence, the Christian revelation, religion, or dispensation. Often contrasted with the *Law*, i.e. the O.T. dispensation. b. *gen.* Any revelation from heaven 1481. 2. The record of Christ's life and teaching, contained in the books written by the four evangelists OE. b. One of these books. Also applied to certain *apocryphal* lives of Christ, as the *G. of Nicodemus*, etc. ME. 3. Eccl. *The g.* (*for* or *of the day*): the portion from one of the four Gospels read at the Communion Service OE. 4. Something as 'true as the gospel' ME. 5. a. Something that serves as a guide to human action 1652. b. A doctrine preached with fervour as a means of social or political salvation 1790. 6. *attrib.* 1538.

1. The Jews saw Christ in the law; the Christians see Christ in the g. JEWEL. 2. b. The four gospels are particularly mentioned by Julian PRIESTLEY. 5. Phr. *To take for g.* And all was g. that a monk could dream CRABBE. 5. a. Hireling wolves, whose G. is their maw MILT. b. The g. of the intellect in the kitchen HAMERTON.

Comb.: **g.-oath**, an oath sworn upon the Gospels, or one equally binding; **-shop**, derisive name for a Methodist chapel; **-side**, the side of the altar at which the g. is read, the north side; **-true** *a.*; **-truth**. Hence **Go·spelless** *a.*

Go·spel, *v.* [f. prec. sb.; in OE. *gōdspellian*, repr. eccl.L. *benenuntiare*, Gr. εὐαγγελίζεσθαι.]

†**a.** *trans.* = EVANGELIZE *v.* 3. –1659. **b.** *intr.* To preach the gospel (*rare*) 1565.

Gospelize (gǫ·spĕləiz), *v.* 1643. [f. GOSPEL *sb.* + -IZE.] †**1.** *trans.* To modify according to the spirit of the gospel –1658. **2.** = EVANGELIZE 3. Now *rare*. 1646.

1. This command thus Gospelliz'd to us MILT. **2.** To fetch the Jew to Gospellize his Child 1704.

Gospeller (gǫ·spĕləɹ). Also †**gospeler.** OE. [f. GOSPEL *sb.* and *v.* + -ER[1]; in OE. *gōdspellere.*] †**1.** One of the four evangelists –1674. **2.** A missionary (*rare*) 1673. **3.** One who reads the Gospel in the Communion Service 1506. †**4.** A book containing the Gospels (see GOSPEL *sb.* 3). **5.** One who identifies the gospel with himself and his party 1533.

1. Marke the G., who followed Peter for instruction 1623. **3.** I was g. at my Ordination W. C. RUSSELL. Phr. *Hot g.*: a zealous Protestant or Puritan.

Goss (gǫs). 1906. A kind of crest china invented by W. H. *Goss* of Stoke-on-Trent.

Goss, var. of GORCE, GORSE.

Gossamer (gǫ·sǎməɹ). [ME. *gos(e)somer(e,* app. f. GOOSE *sb.* + SUMMER *sb.*[1] Perh. primarily 'St. Martin's summer', when geese are in season; hence, gossamer, which is then chiefly observed. Cf. G. *mädchensommer, altweibersommer,* which also have these meanings.]

A. *sb.* A fine filmy substance, consisting of cobwebs, spun by small spiders, which is seen floating in the air, esp. in autumn, or spread over a grassy surface. Occas. with *a* and *pl.*, a thread or web of gossamer. Also *transf.* and *fig.* **2.** A very delicate kind of gauze 1872. **3. a.** In England: A very light silk hat (so named by a hatter) 1837. **b.** *U.S.* A very light kind of waterproof 1888. **4.** *attrib.* 1802.

1. All the silvery gossamers That twinkle into green and gold TENNYSON. *fig.* A decent g. of conventional phraseology MOTLEY.

B. *adj.* Light, flimsy; (of persons) frivolous, volatile 1806. Hence **Go·ssamered** *ppl. a.* coated with g., g.-like. **Go·ssamery** *a.* = GOSSAMER *a.*

Gossan (gǫ·zǎn). 1776. [Cornish dial.] *Min.* Decomposed rock, of a reddish or ferruginous colour (due to oxidized iron pyrites), forming a part of the outcrop of a metallic vein. Also *transf.* of a rusty wig. Hence **Gossani·ferous** *a.* producing g.

Gossep(pe, obs. forms of GOSSIP.

Gossip (gǫ·sip), *sb.* [Late OE. *godsibb,* corresp. to ON. *guðsefi* godfather, *guðsifja* godmother, comp. of GOD and SIB *a.* denoting the spiritual affinity of the baptized and their sponsors.] **1.** A godfather or godmother; a sponsor. Now only *arch.* and *dial.* **2.** A familiar acquaintance, friend, chum. Now only (somewhat *arch.*) of women. ME. **3.** A person, mostly a woman, who delights in idle talk; a tattler 1566. **4.** The tattle of such a person; idle talk; trifling or groundless rumour 1811. **5.** Some kind of game. THACKERAY.

1. Fully designed to come and stand g. in person to Dr. Hudson's child HEARNE. **2.** She is to her Gossypes gone to make mery 1560. All the gossips present at their mothers labours FULLER. **3.** A negligent, busy, prating G. HEARNE. **4.** All this g. about their neighbours HT. MARTINEAU.

Gossip (gǫ·sip), *v.* 1590. [f. prec.] †**1.** *trans.* To give a name to –1716. †**2.** *intr.* To act as a gossip; to take part; to make oneself at home –1645. **3.** To talk idly, mostly about other people's affairs; to go about tattling 1627. Also *transf.* and *fig.* 1627. **4.** *trans.* To tell like a gossip 1611.

1. *All's Well* I. i. 189. **2.** Ile G. at this feast SHAKS. **3.** You g. everywhere, of every thing 1846. **4.** It is so Gossipt in the Queenes chamber HEYWOOD. Hence **Go·ssiper.**

Gossipred (gǫ·sipred). ME. [f. GOSSIP *sb.* + -RED.] **1.** The relation of gossips (see GOSSIP *sb.* 1, 2); spiritual affinity. Now only *Hist.* ¶**2.** In some mod. writers = GOSSIP *sb.* 4. 1828.

Gossipry (gǫ·sipri). 1550. [f. GOSSIP *sb.* + -RY.] **1.** = GOSSIPRED 1. **b.** *concr.* A relative in general. BROWNING. **2.** Small talk, gossip; also, a gossiping conversation 1818. **b.** *concr.* A body of gossips 1853.

Gossipy (gǫ·sipi), *a.* 1818. [f. as prec. + -Y[1].] Full of, or devoted to, gossip.

Gossoon (gǫsū·n). Chiefly *Anglo-Ir.* 1684. [alt. of †*garsoon* (XVII), earlier †*garsoun* – (O)Fr. *garçon.*] A boy; a servant-boy, lackey.

Gossypine (gǫ·sipəin), *a.* [f. mod.L. *Gossypium* the generic cotton-plant + -INE[1].] Cottony, flocculent.

Got (gǫt), *ppl. a.* 1593. [Shortened pa. pple. of GET *v.*; see GOTTEN.] Gained, acquired; gathered as a crop. Now only with adv., as *ill got,* etc.

Gote (gōᵘt). Chiefly *n. dial.* ME. [f. *got-,* wk. root of OE. *gēotan* pour; cf. MLG., MDu. *gote* (Du. *goot*) of similar meaning. See GOUT *sb.*[2]] **1.** A channel for water; a stream. **2.** A sluice 1531.

Goter(e, obs. f. GUTTER.

Goth (gǫþ). [OE. *Gota,* usu. in pl. *Gotan,* was superseded in ME. by the adoption of late and med.L. *Gothi* pl. = Gr. Γόθοι, Γότθοι pl. – Goth. **Gutos* or **Gutans* pl. (cf. *Gutþiuda* the Gothic people).] **1.** One of a Germanic tribe, who in the third, fourth, and fifth centuries, invaded both the Eastern and Western empires, and founded kingdoms in Italy, France, and Spain. **2.** *transf.* One who behaves like a barbarian; a rude, uncivilized, or ignorant person. Often with *Vandal.* 1663.

1. Till Goths and Vandals, a rude northern race, Did all the matchless monuments deface DRYDEN.

Gotha (gōᵘ·tǎ). 1919. [A town in Germany.] A large German aeroplane.

Gotham (gǫ·tǎm; often erron. gōᵘ·þǎm). 1460. **1.** The name of a village, proverbial for the folly of its inhabitants ('wise men of Gotham'). (There is a village so named in Notts.) †**2.** A 'man of Gotham', a simpleton. CROWNE. †**3.** *attrib.* (or *adj.*): Of or pertaining to Gotham; foolish, stupid –1694. Hence †**Go·thamist,** a blunderer, a simpleton. **Go·thamite,** (*a*) = *Gothamist;* (*b*) a New-Yorker.

Gothic (gǫ·þik). 1611. [– Fr. *gothique* or late L. *Gothicus,* f. *Goti*; see GOTH, -IC.]

A. *adj.* **1.** Of, pertaining to, or concerned with the Goths or their language. †**2.** = TEUTONIC or GERMANIC –1685. **3.** †**a.** Mediæval, romantic, as opp. to classical. In early use: Belonging to the dark ages. –1782. **b.** Applied to the style of architecture prevalent in Western Europe from the 12th to the 15th c., of which the chief characteristic is the pointed arch. Applied also to buildings, architectural details, and ornamentation. 1641. **4.** Barbarous, rude, uncouth, in bad taste. Of temper: Savage. 1695. **5.** *Writing* and *Printing.* **a.** In England, the name of the type used for printing German, as dist. from roman and italic characters. (Formerly = *black letter*). 1781. **b.** In U.S., applied to the type called in English GROTESQUE (formerly *stone letter*).

1. Vlpilas is reported..to haue translated the Scriptures into the Gothicke tongue BIBLE *Transl. Pref.* **2.** He raised up the G. or Teutonic race MAURICE. **3. a.** The Castle of Otranto, a G. story H. WALPOLE (*title*). **b.** The Gothick Manner of Architecture (so the Italians called what was not after the Roman style) WREN. **4.** The G. crime of duelling BP. BERKELEY. Hence **Go·thically** *adv.* in a g. manner.

B. quasi-*sb.* or *sb.* **a.** The Gothic language. **b.** Gothic architecture or ornamentation. 1644.

Gothicism (gǫ·þisiz'm). 1710. [f. GOTHIC *a.* + -ISM.] **1.** Rudeness, barbarism; absence of polish. **2.** Conformity to the Gothic style of architecture 1754. **3. a.** Conformity to Teutonic notions 1847. **b.** A Gothic idiom 1818. So **Go·thicist,** one who affects what is Gothic, esp. in architecture.

Gothicize (gǫ·þisəiz), *v.* 1750. [f. GOTHIC *a.* + -IZE.] †**1.** *intr.* To indulge one's taste for what is Gothic or mediæval. H. WALPOLE. **2.** *trans.* **a.** To render mediæval 1808. **b.** To give an architecturally Gothic character to 1798.

2. b. Arabic forms of parapet, more or less Gothicised RUSKIN.

Gothish (gǫ·þiʃ), *a.* 1602. [f. GOTH + -ISH[1].] **1.** †**a.** = GOTHIC *a.* 1. **b.** Looking Gothic, or like a Goth. 1605. **2.** Goth-like, barbarous, tasteless 1602. †**3.** = GOTHIC *a.* 3. –1663.

Gotten (gǫ·t'n), *ppl. a.* ME. [pa. pple. of GET *v.*] **1.** Obtained, acquired, won (usu. with adv.). Now *rare,* exc. in ILL-GOTTEN. †**2.** = BEGOTTEN –1637.

Gou-: see GOV-.

‖**Gouache** (guaʃ). 1882. [Fr. – It. *guazzo.*] A method of painting with opaque colours ground in water, and mixed with gum and honey. Also, a painting thus executed, and the pigment itself.

Gouge (gaudʒ, gūdʒ), *sb.*[1] 1495. [– (O)Fr. *gouge* :– late L. *gubia, gulbia* (Vegetius, Isidore), perh. of Celtic origin (cf. OIr. *gulba* sting, W. *gylf* beak, Corn. *gilb* borer).] **1.** A chisel with a concave blade for cutting rounded grooves or holes in wood. In *Surgery,* a similarly-shaped tool for removing portions of bone, etc. **b.** A stamping tool for cutting out forms in leather, paper, etc. 1875. **c.** *Book-binding.* An instrument for impressing curved lines or segments of a circle upon leather 1885. **2.** *Mining.* A layer of soft material along the wall of a vein, which the miner can gouge out with a pick 1877. **3.** *U.S. colloq.* **a.** A scooping out. **b.** A swindle. Also, an imposter. 1845.

Comb. **g.-bit,** a bit shaped at the end like a g.

†**Gouge,** *sb.*[2] [– mod.Fr. *gouge* wench.] A wench. SCOTT.

Gouge (gaudʒ, gūdʒ), *v.* 1570. [f. GOUGE *sb.*[1]] **1.** *trans.* To make or cut holes in, with or as with a gouge. Also *intr.* **2.** *trans.* To cut *out,* hollow or scoop *out,* with or as with a gouge. Also, to hollow *into* (a certain form). 1616. **3.** To cut or force out with or as with a gouge; to push out (a person's eye) with the thumb. 1800. **b.** To force out the eye of (a person). Also *absol.* 1785. **4.** *U.S.* to cheat, impose upon. Also *absol.* 1875.

3. b. When they had gotten him on his back, one gouged him like a Yankee 1827. **4.** He's regularly gouged me in that ere horsehair spekilation B. HARTE. Hence **Gou·ger,** one who gouges (senses 3, 4).

‖**Goujat** (guʒa). 1776. [Fr.] A soldier's boy.

Goujeers, goujeres: see GOODYEAR.

Goulan(d, var. *gollan(d*: see GOWAN.

Goulard (gulā·ɹd). 1806. [f. Thomas *Goulard,* a French surgeon.] In full, *Goulard's extract* or *G. water*: a solution of subacetate of lead, used as a lotion in cases of inflammation.

Goulash (gū·laʃ). 1900. [– Magyar *gulyáshús,* f. *gulyás* herdsman + *hús* meat.] **1.** A highly-seasoned stew of beef or veal and vegetables. **2.** *Contract Bridge.* A re-deal before which each player arranges his cards in suits and order of value 1927.

Gour, var. of GAUR; obs. f. GIAOUR.

‖**Goura** (gūᵊ·rǎ). 1855. [Native name.] A genus of large crested pigeons inhabiting New Guinea and adjacent islands; one of these.

Gourd (gōᵊɹd, gūᵊɹd). ME. [– AFr. *gurde* (William of Wadington), (O)Fr. *gourde,* repr. ult. L. *cucurbita* (Columella, Pliny).] **1.** The large fleshy fruit of the trailing or climbing plants of the N.O. *Cucurbitaceæ*; *spec.* the fruit of *Lagenaria vulgaris,* used as a vessel when dried and hollowed out. †**b.** *Wild g.* = COLOCYNTH –1560. **2.** A plant of this order; esp. *Lagenaria vulgaris,* the bottle-gourd. *Bitter g.* = COLOCYNTH. ME. Also *transf.* **3.** The shell of the fruit dried and excavated, used as a water-bottle, float, rattle, etc. 1624. **4.** *transf.* †**a.** A bottle or cup –1583. **b.** = CUCURBIT[1] 1. –1683.

2. And the Lord God prepared a gourde, and made it to come vp ouer Ionah BIBLE (Genev.) *Jonah* 4:6. **4. b.** Distill this liquor in a glasse g. FRENCH.

Comb.: **g.-pear,** a pear shaped like a g. (L. *pirum cucurbitinum*); **-shell** = sense 3; **-tree,** the calabash-tree (see CALABASH); **-worm,** a name for the fluke, and for the segments of the tapeworm, from the likeness to the seeds of the g.

†**Gourd**[2]. 1545. [– OFr. *gourd* swindle, 'fourberie'.] A kind of false dice –1610.

Gou·rdy, *a.* 1540. [– OFr. *gourdi,* swollen, pa. pple. of *gourdir* (mod. *s'engourdir*) swell.] †**1.** Stuffed out. PALSGR. **2.** *Farriery.* Swollen in the legs. ?*Obs.* 1704. Hence **Gou·rdiness.**

Gourmand (gūᵊ·ɹmǎnd, ‖gurmaṅ). 1491. [– (O)Fr. *gourmand,* of unkn. origin.]

A. *adj.* Gluttonous; fond of eating 1530. The insatiable and gurmand throate SIR T. NORTH.

B. *sb.* †**1.** A glutton; also *fig.* –1692. **2.** A judge or devotee of good eating. In this sense often as Fr. 1758.

1. That great gourmond, fat Apicivs B. JONS. **2.** Their table is always good, for the Landgrave is a

G. CHESTERF. So †**Gourmand** *v.* to eat greedily. **Gou·rmandism,** love of good fare.

‖**Gourmet** (gurme). 1820. [Fr. *gourmet* (earlier pl. *grommes*) †wine-merchant's assistant, wine-taster, infl. in sense by GOURMAND.] A connoisseur in eating and drinking.

Gournard, gournit, obs. ff. GURNARD.

Gout (gaut), *sb.*[1] ME. [– OFr. *goute* (mod. *goutte*) drop, gout :– L. *gutta* drop, in med.L. applied to diseases attributed to a defluxion of humours.]

I. 1. A constitutional disease occurring in paroxysms, usually hereditary and in male subjects; characterized by painful inflammation of the smaller joints, esp. that of the great toe, and the deposition of sodium urate in the form of chalk-stones; it often spreads to the larger joints and the internal organs. **a.** With *a* and *pl.*: orig. perh. an affection of a particular joint; later = a fit of the disease, or simply, the disease itself. **b.** *sing.* only (often *the g.*) ME. **†2.** A disease in hawks, etc.; esp. a hard swelling on the feet –1600. **3.** A disease in wheat, caused by the larva of the gout-fly (see *g.-fly*) 1828.

1. a. In foote and hand A grievous g. tormented him full sore SPENSER.

II. 1. A drop, esp. of blood. Later, usually: A large splash or clot. 1503. **2.** A spot of colour resembling a drop. (Cf. GOUTTE *Her.*) 1833.

1. On thy Blade, and Dudgeon, Gouts of Blood SHAKS. *Comb.*: **g.-fly,** the fly (*Chlorops tæniopus* or *lineata*) whose larva causes the g. in wheat; **-stone** = CHALK-STONE; **-weed, -wort,** the plant *Ægopodium podagraria.*

Gout (gaut), *sb.*[2] ME. [Sense 1 var. of GOTE; sense 2 prob. aphetic f. Fr. *égout* sewer, etc.] **†1.** ?A flow of water. Only ME. **2.** A channel for water; a sluice; a culvert 1598.

‖**Goût** (gū). 1586. [Fr., earlier *goust* :– L. *gustus* taste. Cf. GUST *sb.*[2], GUSTO.] = TASTE, in various senses.

Goutify (gau·tifəi), *v.* 1749. [GOUT *sb.*[1] + -FY.] To make gouty, afflict with gout.

Goutish (gau·tiʃ), *a.* ME. [f. GOUT *sb.*[1] + -ISH[1].] **a.** Somewhat gouty; predisposed to gout. **b.** Pertaining to, or of the nature of, gout 1700.

‖**Goutte** (gūt). ME. [Fr.] *Her.* A small drop-shaped figure (of specified tincture), used as a charge.

Goutté, goutty, *Her.*, vars. of GUTTÉ.

Gouty (gau·ti), *a.* ME. [f. GOUT *sb.*[1] + -Y[1].] **1.** Affected with, or subject to, gout. Also *fig.* **†b.** Of a horse's legs: Swollen –1577. **2.** Of, pertaining to, or of the nature of, gout 1615. **b.** Used during a fit of gout 1733. **c.** Having a tendency to produce gout 1802. **3.** *transf.* and *fig.* Swollen or bulging; †knotty 1595. **†4.** Of land: Boggy –1790.

1. A man aged and gowtie 1581. **2.** G. Matter 1724, concretions 1846. A g. diathesis M. PATTISON. **b.** My g. shoes BP. BERKELEY. **c.** G. wines 1897. *Comb.* **g.-stem** (tree), the Australian baobab (*Adansonia gregorii*). Hence **Gou·tily** *adv.* **Gou·tiness,** tendency to gout (*lit.* and *fig.*). **Gou·tyish** *a.* somewhat g.

Gouv-: see GOV-.

‖**Gouvernante** (guvęrnānt). 1716. [Fr., fem. pr. pple. of *gouverner* GOVERN]. **†1.** A female ruler –1772. **2.** A housekeeper (*rare*) 1772. **b.** A chaperon or duenna 1716. **c.** A governess 1781.

2. a. Rousseau..crossed the country with his g. H. WALPOLE

Govern (gɒ·vəɹn), *v.* ME. [– OFr. *governer* (mod. *gouverner*) :– L. *gubernare* steer, direct, rule – Gr. κυβερνᾶν steer.] **1.** *trans.* To rule with authority, esp. with that of a sovereign; to direct and control the actions and affairs of (a people, etc.), whether despotically or constitutionally; to regulate the affairs of (a body of men). Also *absol.* **2.** To sway, influence; to direct, guide, or regulate ME. **†b.** To prevail over. SHAKS. **3.** *intr.* To hold sway, prevail, have decisive influence 1596. **†4.** *trans.* To administer, manage, order –1741. **†5.** To attend to; *esp.* to tend in respect to health –1680. **†6.** To work or manage (a ship, etc.) –1697. **†7.** To control the working of; to regulate –1807. **8.** To hold in check, curb, bridle 1513. **9.** To constitute a law or rule for; *esp.* in *Law*, to serve in determining or deciding (a case) 1818. **10.** *Grammar.* To require (a noun or pronoun) to be *in* a particular case, or a verb to be *in* a certain mood; to be necessarily followed by (a particular case or mood) 1530.

1. She must..gouerne the maides, and keepe them at their woorke B. GOOGE. Those that think must g. those that toil GOLDSM. *absol.* The king reigned, but his ministers governed MAY. **2.** Ordinary Minds are wholly governed by their Eyes and Ears STEELE. He really helped to g. the events KINGLAKE. **3.** Let it be as humors and conceits shall gouerne SHAKS. Fooles that want wit to gouerne themselves well 1608. **8.** To g. the tongue SHAKS., the temper DICKENS. **9.** The law there stated clearly governs this case 1890. **10.** Prepositions governing the dative 1881.

Hence **Go·vernable** *a.* capable of being governed (in various senses). **Go:vernabi·lity, Go·vernableness,** the state or quality of being governable. **Go·vernably** *adv.* in a governable manner.

†**Gouvernail.** ME. [– OFr. *governail* (mod. *gouvernail*) :– L. *gubernaculum*, pl. *gubernacula* rudder, f. *gubernare*; see prec.] **1.** A rudder; also, steering –1561. **2.** Government; authority. (In early use often *pl.*) –1597. **b.** Management; also, tending (of plants, wounds) –1590. **c.** Behaviour; rule of conduct –1598.

Governance (gɒ·vəɹnăns). ME. [– OFr. *governance* (mod. *gouvernance*); see GOVERN, -ANCE.] **1.** The action or manner of governing (see the vb.); the fact that (a person, etc.) governs. **b.** Control ME. **†c.** The state of being governed –1590. **2.** The office, function, or power of governing ME.; †governing person or body –1643. **†3.** Method of management, system of regulations –1660. **†4.** Mode of living, behaviour, demeanour. **†b.** Wise self-command –1600.

1. Goddes gouvernaunce UDALL. **b.** An irascible spirit under no great g. 1789. **2.** To han the gouernance of hous and lond CHAUCER. **3.** Of the Foundation, Erection, and G. of Hospitals R. COKE. **4. b.** In him is bountee, wisdom, governaunce CHAUCER. So †**Go·vernancy** (in sense 2).

†**Go·vernante.** 1639. Anglicized f. GOUVERNANTE, q.v. –1823.

†**Governeress.** ME. [– OFr. *governeresse*, fem. of *governeor*; see GOVERNOR, -ESS[1].] A female governor; = GOVERNESS, in various senses –1652.

Governess (gɒ·vəɹnės), *sb.* 1483. [Shortened f. prec.] **1.** A woman who governs; a female ruler. *Obs.* exc. as *nonce-use.* †Also *fig.* –1706. **2.** †A woman who has charge of a person, esp. of a child –1771; a female teacher; now chiefly, one so employed in a private household. (The current use.) 1712. **3.** The wife of a Governor. *Obs.* exc. *joc.* 1697. *Comb.* **g.-car, -cart,** a light two-wheeled vehicle with seats at the sides only. Hence **Go·verness** *v.* to learn one's living as a g.

Governing (gɒ·vəɹniŋ), *ppl. a.* 1635. [f. GOVERN *v.* + -ING[2].] That governs, in senses of the vb.

G. body: the body of managers of a hospital, public school, etc. Hence **Go·verningly** *adv.*

†**Go·vernless,** *a.* 1621. [f. GOVERN *v.* + -LESS.] Without government –1679.

The sad ends of many dissolute and g. persons SIR T. BROWNE.

Government (gɒ·vəɹnmĕnt). 1483. [– OFr. *governement* (mod. *gouvernement*), f. *governer*; see GOVERN *v.*, -MENT.] **1.** The action of governing (see the vb.); *spec.* the action of ruling and directing the affairs of a state 1566. **†2.** The manner in which one's action is governed; movements, demeanour; regimen –1612; conduct; discretion –1639. **3.** The office or function of governing; authority to govern 1584; †an appointment as governor –1769. **†4.** Period of rule, tenure of office –1664. **5.** The portion of country ruled over by a governor. Also, *occas.*, the territory united under a common rule, as a kingdom, etc. 1603. **6.** Form or kind of polity 1553. **7.** The governing power in a state; the body of persons charged with the duty of governing; in England esp. the *ministry* or *administration* 1702. **8.** *Grammar.* The influence of one word over another in determining the case of a noun or pronoun or the mood of a verb 1755.

1. The g. of the tongue BUTLER. The business of g. is to promote the happiness of the society by punishing and rewarding BENTHAM. **3.** The G. I cast vpon my brother SHAKS. **6.** Phr. *Civil* or *political, church* or *ecclesiastical g.*; *monarchical, oligarchical, republican g.*; *episcopal, presbyterian g.* **7.** The Liberal G. DUFF. The United States g. JEVONS. In America people usually speak of the President and his ministers as the 'administration', not as the 'government' BRYCE. **8.** Adverbs have no g. 1762.

Comb.: †**g.-general,** the territory under a governor-general; **-house,** a governor's official residence; **-man,** (*a*) a man connected with the g.; (*b*) *Austral.* a convict; **-paper,** bonds, exchequer bills, etc. issued by a g.; **-securities,** (*a*) = prec.; (*b*) *slang*, fetters; **-valve** = SAFETY-VALVE.

Hence **Governme·ntal** *a.* of or pertaining to g., or to the g. of a country, etc. **Governme·ntally** *adv.*

Governor (gɒ·vəɹnəɹ). ME. [– AFr. *governour*, OFr. *governëo(u)r* (mod. *gouverneur*) :– L. *gubernator*; see GOVERN *v.*, -OR 2.] **†1.** A steersman, pilot, captain –1611. **2.** One who governs ME. **3.** An official appointed to govern a province, country, town, etc. Now the official title of the representative of the Crown in a colony or dependency; also of the executive head of each of the United States. ME. **b.** The commander of a fortress or garrison 1647. **4.** One who bears rule in an establishment, institution, society, etc. Now chiefly as an official title. ME. **†5.** The commander of a company, esp. an armed force –1625. **†6.** A tutor, esp. of a prince or young noble –1788. **7.** *colloq.* or *slang.* **a.** An employer 1802. **b.** Applied by sons to their fathers 1827. **c.** A vulgar form of address to a man 1866. **8.** *Machinery.* A self-acting contrivance for regulating the passage of gas, steam, water, etc., esp. in order to ensure an even and regular motion in a machine 1819. **9.** *Angling.* A particular fly 1867.

1. *Jas.* 3:4. **2.** History is full, down to this day, of the imbecility of kings and governors EMERSON. The..moral G. of the world 1817. **3.** Wm. Penn..Governer of Pensilvania 1683. **b.** The g. of Portsmouth CLARENDON. **5.** My hopes do shape him for the Guernor *Oth.* II. i. 55.

Go·vernor-ge·neral. 1586. A governor who has under him deputy- or lieutenant-governors, as, the *Governor-General of India*, Hence **Go·vernor-ge·neralship.**

Governorship (gɒ·vəɹnəɹʃip). 1644. [f. GOVERNOR + -SHIP.] **1.** The office of a governor 1658. **2.** The exercise or tenure of this office.

Gowan (gau·ăn). *Sc.* and *n. dial.* 1570. [prob. alt. of (dial.) *gollan* (XIV) ranunculus, caltha, chrysanthemum, which is prob. rel. to *gold* in MARIGOLD.] A name for various yellow or white field flowers, esp. the Common Daisy (*Bellis perennis*).

Whare gowans grew, Sae white and bonie BURNS. Hence **Go·waned** *ppl. a.*, **Go·wany** *a.* covered with gowans.

Gow·die. *Sc. dial.* 1810. [Local pronunc. of GOLDY.] The fish *Callionymus lyra.*

Gowk (gauk), *sb.* Orig. *Sc.* and *n. dial.* ME. [– ON. *gaukr* = OE. *ġēac*, OFris., OS. *gāk*, OHG. *gouh* (G. *gauch* cuckoo, fool) :– Gmc. *ʒaukaz, of imit. origin.] **1.** The cuckoo. **2.** A half-witted person; a fool 1605.

Gowk, *v. rare.* 1513. [Of unkn. origin. Cf. GAWK *v.*] *intr.* To stare foolishly.

Gowl (gaul), *v.* Chiefly *Sc.* and *n. dial.* ME. [– ON. *gaula*, perh. f. root *gau- to bark. But cf. YOWL.] *intr.* To howl, yell; also, to whine. Also *transf.* of the wind. Hence **Gowl** *sb.* a howl, a yell, a loud cry.

Gown (gaun), *sb.* ME. [– OFr. *goune, gon(n)e* :– late L. *gunna* fur garment (cf. Byz. Gr. γοῦνα fur, fur-lined garment).] **1.** A loose flowing upper garment; esp. in mod. use, a woman's garment fitting close to the upper part of the body with flowing skirts; a FROCK ME. **†2.** = DRESSING-*gown*, NIGHT-GOWN –1778. **3.** Used as the name of the Roman toga. Hence: 'The dress of peace' (J.). ME. **4.** A more or less flowing robe as worn: **a.** by an alderman, a judge or magistrate; also *collect.* the magistracy ME.; **b.** by members of the legal or clerical profession; hence the profession itself, and *collect.* the members of it 1564; **c.** by members of a University 1665. **5.** *collect. sing.* The resident members of a university; opp. to *town* (now only without article) 1659.

1. The Queene..hath bespoke herself a new gowne PEPYS. 2. I came down..in my g. and slippers DE FOE. 3. He Mars deposed, and arms to gowns made yield DRYDEN. 4. a. The Maire and Aldermen, cled in long gownys of skarlet 1486. b. The Cut-throat Sword and clamorous G. shall jar DRYDEN. I have now taken the g. [i.e. holy orders] 1784. *Comb.* **g.-boy**, a boy belonging to a scholastic foundation, e.g. that of the Charterhouse. Hence **Gown** *v. trans.* to dress in a g.; *intr.* (for *refl.*) to put on a g. **Gowned** *ppl. a.* dressed in a g.; in *g. war*, warfare waged in the law-courts (COWLEY).

Gownsman (gau·nzmăn). Also **gown-man.** 1579. [f. GOWN *sb.* + MAN; cf. *craft(s)-man*, etc.] †**1.** An adult Roman. SIR T. NORTH. **2.** One wearing the gown, or 'dress of peace'; a civilian 1607. **3.** One who wears a gown: **a.** as a lawyer, barrister, or judge 1627; **b.** as a clergyman (now *rare*) 1641; **c.** as a member of a University (often opp. to *townsman*) 1665.

2. It was rather a military spirit than that of the gownman BURKE. 3. a. A gownman's lie 1735.

Gozzard (gǫ·zăɹd). ME. [repr. OE. **gōshierde*; see GOOSE, HERD *sb.*[2]] One who takes care of geese.

Graafian (grā·fiăn), *a.* 1841. [f. R. de *Graaf*, a Dutch anatomist (1641–73) + -IAN.] *Anat.* In *G. follicle, vesicle*, one of the small sacs in the ovary of mammals in which the ova are matured.

Grab (græb), *sb.*[1] *Anglo-Ind.* 1680. [– Arab. *ġurāb* galley.] A large coasting-vessel, built with a prow and usually two-masted; used in the East.

Grab (græb), *sb.*[2] 1777. [f. GRAB *v.*] **1.** A quick sudden clutch, grasp, or attempt to seize 1824. **b.** The action or practice of grabbing 1883. **2.** The thing grabbed. *Sc.* 1777. **3.** One who grabs; a resurrectionist, a catch-poll, etc. ?*Obs.* 1823. **4.** A mechanical device for clutching or gripping objects; *esp.* one for withdrawing drills, etc. from artesian and other wells 1875. **5.** A children's game at cards.

Comb.: **g.-bag** (*U.S.* at fancy fairs), a bag containing various articles, into which one may dip on payment of a certain sum; also *fig.*; **-game,** a mode of stealing, in which one of several confederates grabs the money at stake in a dispute and runs off.

Grab (græb), *v.* 1589. [– MLG., MDu. *grabben*, f. **grab-*, perh. modification of the base of GRIP *v.*[1], GRIPE *v.*[1], GROPE *v.*] **1.** *trans.* To grasp or seize suddenly and eagerly; hence, to appropriate unscrupulously. **2.** To capture or arrest 1800. **3.** *intr.* To make a grab *at* (U.S. *for*) 1852. Hence **Gra·bber,** one who or that which grabs; *esp.* in (or short for) **land-grabber**, used chiefly in Ireland for one who takes a holding from which another has been evicted.

Grabble (græ·b'l), *v.* 1579. [prob. – Du., LG. *grabbeln* scramble for a thing, frequent. of *grabben*; see prec., -LE 3.] **1.** *intr.* To feel or search with the hands, to grope about. Also *trans.* **2.** *intr.* To sprawl or tumble about on all-fours 1736. †**3.** *trans.* To handle rudely or roughly –1790. **4.** To seize 1796.

1. Thou must stoop..And g. for't [gold] in ground SHIRLEY.

Gra·bby. *slang.* 1868. [Of unkn. origin.] An infantryman.

Grace (grēis), *sb.* ME. [– OFr. *grace* (mod. *grâce*) – L. *gratia*, f. *gratus* pleasing; cf. GRATEFUL.]

I. 1. Attractiveness, charm; now usually, the charm belonging to elegance of proportions, or (esp.) ease and refinement of movement, action, or expression. **b.** Becomingness, creditable aspect. Hence, *a bad, an ill g.*, an unbecoming appearance. 1586. **c.** Hence, *with a good g.*, with a show of willingness; *with a bad* or *ill g.*, ungraciously 1754. **2.** An attractive or pleasing quality or feature ME. †**b.** An ornament –1700. **c.** An attitude, etc. adopted with a view to grace 1607. **3.** *Mus.* An embellishment consisting of additional notes introduced into vocal or instrumental music, not essential to the harmony or melody 1657. **4.** *Myth.* One of the sister goddesses (= L. *Gratiæ*, Gr. Χάριτες) regarded as the bestowers of beauty and charm, and portrayed as women of exquisite beauty. Usually spoken of (after Hesiod) as three in number, Aglaia, Thalia, and Euphrosyne. 1579. **5.** *The graces*: a game played with hoops and pairs of slender rods 1842.

1. G., indeed, is beauty in action DISRAELI. b. Henry..retired with a good g. from an impossible position FROUDE. 2. Graces of Mind and Person RICHARDSON. c. Old Sir Pitt..chuckled at her *airs and graces* THACKERAY. 4. Euphrosyne.. Whom lovely Venus, at a birth, With two sister Graces more, To ivy-crownèd Bacchus bore MILT.

II. Favour. **1.** Favour or its manifestation (now only on the part of a superior); favour or goodwill, as dist. from right or obligation, as the ground of a concession. Rather *arch.* ME. **2.** The condition or fact of being favoured 1463. **3.** An instance of favour; an exceptional favour, a privilege, a dispensation (now only *Hist.*) ME. **4.** In University use. **a.** †Orig., a dispensation from some of the statutable conditions required for a degree. Hence **b.** Leave of Congregation to take a degree. **c.** Other decrees of the Governing Body, being very often dispensations from the permanent statutes. **d.** In mod. use, the permission which a candidate for a degree is required to obtain from his College or Hall. ME. †**5.** Hap, luck, or fortune (good or bad) –1591. **6.** *Theol.*, etc. **a.** The free and unmerited favour of God ME. Hence, The source of grace, God. *All's Well* I. iii. 226. **b.** The divine influence which operates in men to regenerate and sanctify, and to impart strength to endure trial and resist temptation ME. **c.** The condition of one who is under such influence ME. **d.** An individual virtue or excellence, divine in its origin ME. Also *transf.* **7.** Favour shown by granting a delay, or immunity from penalty during a specified period 1711. **b.** Comm. *Days of grace*, the period (in England 3 days) allowed by law for the payment of a bill of exchange, after the expiration of the term for which it is drawn. Similarly, the period allowed for payment of a premium of insurance or the like, after the date at which it is said to be due. 1731. **8.** Mercy, clemency; hence, pardon. Now *rare* or *arch.* ME. **9.** A courtesy-title now given only to a duke, a duchess, or an archbishop. Formerly used in addressing a king or queen. (Usu. written with capital.) 1500.

1. The marks of g. which Elizabeth..shewed to young Raleigh SCOTT. Phr. *By the g. of God* (tr. L. *Dei gratiâ*), appended to the formal statement of the titles of sovereigns, etc. †*Save your g.*: = 'by your leave'. †*Hard g.*: displeasure, ill will (CHAUCER) 2. Till all graces be in one woman, one woman shall not come in my g. SHAKS. Phr. *A person's good graces*: his favour and good opinion. 3. But, to return and view the chearful Skies,.. To few great Jupiter imparts this G. DRYDEN. *Expectative g.* (see EXPECTATIVE). 5. *Two Gent.* III. i. 146. 6. a. *Doctrines of g.*: by Calvinists applied esp. to the doctrines of election, predestination, etc. b. *Prevenient g.*: that which produces the repentance and faith without which the *g. of justification* cannot be received. *Sufficient g.*: that which (merely) renders the soul capable of performing a supernatural act, as dist. from *efficacious g.*, that which really effects the end for which it is given. c. Phr. *To fall from g. transf.* I think the Boy hath g. in him, he blushes SHAKS. The powerful g. that lies In Plants SHAKS. Phr. *transf. To have the g.* (to do something). 7. Phr. *Year of G.*: orig., a year as reckoned from the birth of Christ (*arch.*); (at the Universities), a year allowed to the person chosen to succeed to a college living, at the end of which he must resign either his living or his fellowship. *Time of g.*, a close time (for beasts of the chase). *Day of g.* (Theol.): the time allowed for repentance. 8. [Thou] Stand'st at our g., a captiue HEYWOOD. Phr. *Act of g.*: a formal pardon, *spec.* a free and general pardon, granted by Act of Parliament.

III. †**1.** *pl.* Thanks, thanksgiving –1533. **2.** (Till 16th c. usu. *pl.* in sing. sense; now only *sing.*) A short prayer either asking a blessing before, or rendering thanks after, a meal ME.

2. A youth came forward..and pronounced the ancient form of g. before meals EMERSON.

Comb.: **g.-hoop,** 'a hoop used in playing the game called *graces*'; **-note** = sense I. 3; †**-term,** a term of the period required for a degree, in which residence was customarily dispensed with.

Grace (grēis), *v.* ME. [In sense 1 – OFr. *gracier* thank; in other senses f. prec.] †**1.** *trans.* To thank. ME. only. †**2.** To show favour to; to countenance –1626. †**3.** To endow with (heavenly) grace –1701. **4.** To adorn, embellish, set off 1586; *Mus.* to add grace-notes, cadenzas, etc., to 1659. **5.** To confer honour or dignity upon; also, to do honour or credit to 1585. †**b.** To name honourably. MILT. †**6.** To gratify, delight –1703. **7.** To address by the title, 'your Grace' 1610.

4. He left nothing unassayed..to g. his friend SIDNEY. 5. Pleas't your Highnesse, To g. vs with your Royall Company SHAKS.

Gra·ce-cup. 1593. The cup of liquor passed round after grace is said; the last cup drunk before retiring, a parting draught. Also *fig.*

Graced (grēist), *ppl. a.* 1593. [f. GRACE *sb.* or *v.* + -ED.] Endowed with grace; favoured; having a grace or graces; embellished, etc.

A well grac'd Actor SHAKS. Their well g. fourmes of speech BACON.

Graceful (grēi·sfŭl), *a.* ME. [f. GRACE *sb.* + -FUL.] †**1.** Full of divine grace –1611. †**2.** Favourable. *Ant. & Cl.* II. ii. 60. **3.** Possessed of pleasing or attractive qualities; now usually, elegant in form, proportions, action, etc. (see GRACE *sb.* I. 1) 1586.

1. *Wint. T.* V. i. 171. 3. A fine queint gracefull and excellent fashion SHAKS. A g. speaker upon any subject CLARENDON. A g. dome STANLEY. Hence **Graceful-ly** *adv.*, **-ness.**

Graceless (grēi·slės), *a.* ME. [f. GRACE *sb.* + -LESS.] **1.** Not in a state of grace, unregenerate; hence depraved, wicked ME.; wanting sense of propriety 1508. Also *absol.* †**2.** Lacking favour –1579. †**3.** Merciless, unfeeling –1658. **4.** Wanting grace, charm, or elegance, unlovely 1638.

1. G. zealots POPE. The g. Youth ADDISON. 3. Asking grace of a graceles face 1658. 4. The composition is g. 1884. **Graceless-ly** *adv.*, **-ness.**

Gracile (græ·sil), *a.* 1623. [– L. *gracilis* slender.] Slender, thin, lean. ¶Recently misused (through association w. *grace*) for: Gracefully slender. Hence **Graci·lity, g.** state; slenderness, leanness.

Graciosity (greiʃiǫ·sĭti). 1477. [– Fr. *gracieuseté* or late L. *gratiositas*; see GRACIOUS, -ITY.] Graciousness.

‖**Gracioso** (greiʃiōu·so; in Sp. graþiō·so). 1650. [Sp.; = GRACIOUS *a.*] †**1.** A court favourite –1670. **2.** The buffoon of Sp. comedy 1749.

Gracious (grēi·ʃəs), *a.* ME. [– OFr. *gracious* (mod. *gracieux*) – L. *gratiosus*, f. *gratia*; see GRACE, -OUS.] †**1.** Enjoying favour; acceptable, popular. Const. *to, with.* –1821. **2.** Having pleasing qualities. Somewhat *arch.* or *poet.* ME. †**b.** Attractive; also, graceful, elegant –1649. **3.** Characterized by or exhibiting kindness or courtesy. Now *rare* (chiefly *poet.*). ME. **4.** Condescendingly kind, indulgent and beneficent to inferiors. Now only of exalted personages, or playful or sarcastic. ME. **5.** Of the Deity, Christ, the Virgin Mary: Disposed to show grace, merciful, benignant ME. **b.** *ellipt.* for God (in exclams.) 1713. †**6.** Godly, pious, regenerate –1757. †**7.** Happy, fortunate –1611. †**8.** Given by way of indulgence or mercy –1726.

2. A Citie, to the sight most gratious 1601. G. herbs HAWTHORNE. 3. Sir Lancelot..Was g. to all ladies TENNYSON. 4. The g. intentions of his sovereign BURKE. A g. master MACAULAY. 5. Under the shadow of Thy gratious Wing 1635. b. *Gracious! Good gracious! Gracious me!* 7. Goe: fresh Horses, And g. be the issue SHAKS. Hence **Gra·cious-ly** *adv.*, **-ness.**

Grackle (græ·k'l). 1772. [Anglicized f. *Gracula* generic name, a mod.L. fem. corresp. to L. *graculus* jackdaw.] **1.** A name for various birds included in the genus *Gracula.* **2.** *Angling.* Name of an artificial fly 1894.

1. *Grackle*..a word..restricted to members of the families *Sturnidæ* (starling) belonging to the Old World, and *Icteridæ* belonging to the New.. In the New World the name G. has been applied to several species of the genera *Scolecophagus* and *Quiscalus*...The best known are the Rusty G., *S. ferrugineus*..and *Q. purpureus*, the Purple G. or Crow-Blackbird 1893.

Gradate (grădēi·t), *v.* 1753. [Back-formation f. GRADATION.] **1.** To pass or cause to pass by imperceptible grades from one tone or shade to another; to shade off. Also *absol.* **2.** *trans.* To arrange in steps or grades.

?Only in *pass.* 1869. **3.** *Chem.* (?*U.S.* only.) 'To bring to a certain strength or grade of concentration' (Webster); 'to concentrate as by evaporation' (Funk).

1. Retiring shades, which g. or go off by degrees 1753.

‖**Gradatim** (grădē¹tim), *adv.* 1583. [L. *gradatim* by degrees, f. *gradus* step.] Step by step, gradually.

Gradation (grădē¹ʃən). 1538. [– L. *gradatio*, f. *gradus* step; see GRADE, -ATION. Cf. Fr. *gradation.*] †**1.** The process of advancing step by step –1750. **2.** A series of successive stages in a process or course. ?*Obs.* 1549. **3.** *pl.* Steps, progressive movements; stages of transition 1599. †**4.** *pl.* Arrangements resembling a flight of steps –1802. **5.** A scale or series of degrees; the fact or condition of including or being arranged in a series of degrees 1677. **6.** *pl.* Degrees of rank, merit, intensity, etc. 1605. **7.** The action of arranging in steps or grades. WHEWELL. **8. a.** *Rhet.* = CLIMAX 1. ?*Obs.* 1538. †**b.** *Logic.* = SORITES (*rare*) 1727. †**9.** *Alch.* Exaltation –1641. **10.** *Fine Arts.* **a.** *Painting.* An insensible passing from one colour or shade to another 1727. **b.** *Mus.* 'A diatonic ascending or descending succession of chords' (Brande) 1842. **11.** *Philol.* = ABLAUT; also, a modification resulting from ablaut 1870.

2. The regular g. of civil honours GIBBON. **5.** A g. of ranks in society HT. MARTINEAU. **6.** Who shall enumerate the gradations between insect and man 1793. **10. a.** What curvature is to lines, g. is to shades and colours RUSKIN. Hence **Grada·tional** *a.* pertaining to, or characterized by, g.

Gradatory (grē¹·dătəri), *sb.* 1670. [– med.L. **gradatorium*, var. of *gradatarium* (Du Cange) flight of steps, f. *gradatio*; see GRADATION, -ORY¹.] A flight of steps, esp. from the cloisters to the choir of a church.

Gradatory (grē¹·dătəri), *a.* 1793. [f. GRADATION + -ORY².] **1.** Proceeding by steps or grades (*rare*). **2.** Adapted for stepping; said of the extremities of a quadruped which are adapted for ordinary progression on dry land 1842.

Grade (grē¹d), *sb.* 1511. [– L. *gradus* step, or Fr. *grade.*] †**1.** *Math.* A degree; the 90th part of a right angle or quadrant –1593. **2.** A step or stage in a process; rarely *spec.* a step in preferment 1796. **3.** A degree in the scale of rank, dignity, proficiency, etc. 1808; a number of persons holding the same position in the scale; a class 1827. **4.** A degree of comparative quality or vâlue; a class of things of the same quality or value 1833. **5.** *Path.* Degree of intensity (of a disease) 1803. **6.** A result of cross-breeding, a hybrid. Also *attrib.* 1796. **7.** *Zool.* A group of animals presumed to have branched from the common stem at about the same point of its development 1877. **8.** *Philol.* The position occupied in an ablaut-series by a particular vowel or form of a root 1891. **9.** *U.S.* = GRADIENT *sb.* 1835. **b.** An inclined portion of a railway or road. Also DOWN G., UP G. 1883. **c.** *U.S. local.* In mining districts: A portion of road 1877. **10.** Of a surface: Degree of altitude; level (*rare*) 1851.

2. Grades of depreciation 1796. **3.** Teachers of every grade BUCKLE. All grades of railway employés 1897. **4.** Low grades of cotton 1880. Ore of low g. 1893. **b.** (*U.S.*) A class at school in relation to advancement 1852.

Comb.: **g.-crossing** (U.S.), a place where a road and a railway, or two railways cross each other at the same level; **g. school** = *graded school* (see GRADED *ppl. a.*).

Grade (grē¹d), *v.* 1563. [f. GRADE *sb.*] †**1.** *trans.* To admit to a (specified) degree. FOXE. **2.** To arrange in grades or classes; to class; to sort; to determine the grades or degrees of 1659. **b.** To blend so as to affect the grade of 1889. **3.** *trans.* To reduce (the line of a road, railway, or canal) to levels or practicable gradients 1835. **4.** *Stock-breeding.* To cross with some better breed 1887. **5.** *Philol.* In *pass.*: To be altered by gradation or ablaut 1887. **6.** To cut (steps) at regular intervals 1896. **7.** *intr.* To pass imperceptibly from one grade *into* another. Also *down, up, off.* 1903.

Graded (grē¹·dĕd), *ppl. a.* 1840. [f. GRADE *sb.* and *v.* + -ED.] **1.** Formed like a flight of steps 1850. **2.** Divided according to grades of rank, quality, etc. 1859. **3.** Of a road, etc.: See GRADE *v.* 3. **4.** Of cattle: Improved by crossing 1887.

2. *Graded school* (chiefly U.S.): 'a school divided into departments..in which the children pass from the lower departments to the higher as they advance in education' (*Cent. Dict.*).

Gradely (grē¹·dli), *a.* Now only *dial.* [ME. *grayþly, graydely* – ON. *greiðligr*, f. *greiðr* GRAITH *a.*; see -LY¹.] **1.** Of persons, their actions, etc.: Decent, respectable, worthy; *occas.* of a girl, comely. Also 'regular', thorough (*dial.*) 1746. **b.** *predicatively.* Well in health 1851. **2.** Of things: Excellent, suitable, handsome ME.; real, proper (*dial.*) 18... So **Gra·dely** *adv.* †promptly; carefully, exactly; properly; really; well.

Grader (grē¹·dəɹ). 1868. [f. GRADE *v.* + -ER¹.] **1.** One who grades 1870. **2.** A machine for grading 1868.

Gradient (grē¹·diĕnt). 1641. [– *gradient-*, pres. ppl. stem of L. *gradi* walk, f. *gradus* step; see -ENT. As *sb.* prob. f. *grade* with ending suggested by *salient*; not connected with adj.]

A. *adj.* **1.** Of animals: Walking, ambulant. **2.** Of a railway line: Rising or descending by regular degrees of inclination. (Only in Dicts.)

B. *sb.* Of a road or railway: Amount of inclination to the horizontal 1835. **b.** A portion of a way not level (Webster). **2.** *transf.* The proportional amount of rise or fall of the barometer or thermometer in passing from one region to another 1870. **3.** *Math.* A rational integral function of a number of quantics of assigned weights, which is of one degree and one weight throughout (Prof. Elliott) 1887.

2. A g. of 4 means that over a distance of 60 nautical miles, the barometer rises $\frac{4}{100}$ or $\frac{1}{25}$ of an inch HUXLEY.

Gradin, gradine¹ (grē¹·din, grădī·n). 1834. [– It. *gradino*, dim. of *grado* step; cf. Fr. *gradin* (XVII).] **1.** One of a series of low steps or seats raised one above the other. **2.** A shelf or ledge at the back of an altar 1877.

Gradine² (gradī·n). 1860. [– Fr. *gradine.*] A toothed chisel used by sculptors.

Grading (grē¹·diŋ), *vbl. sb.* 1835. [f. GRADE *v.* + -ING¹.] The action of GRADE *v.*; *spec.* the action or process of reducing a road to practicable gradients.

‖**Gradino** (gradī·no). 1883. [It.: see GRADIN.] **a.** = GRADIN 2. **b.** A work of painting or sculpture to ornament the gradin of an altar.

Gradual (græ·diuăl), *sb.* 1563. [– med.L. *graduale*, n. of *gradualis* used subst.; see next, and cf. GRAIL¹.] **1.** An antiphon sung between the Epistle and the Gospel at the Eucharist; it was sung at the steps of the altar or while the deacon was ascending the steps of the ambo. **2.** A book of such antiphons 1619. †**3.** The steps of an altar. DRYDEN.

Gradual (græ·diuăl), *a.* 1541. [– med.L. *gradualis*, f. L. *gradus* step; see -AL¹.] †**1.** Of or pertaining to degree; only in *g. difference* = difference in degree –1658. †**2.** Arranged in, or admitting of, degrees or gradation –1712. **3.** Of a process: Taking place by degrees; advancing step by step. Of a slope: Gentle. 1692. **b.** *poet.* Tapering; sloping gradually; moving or changing gradually 1739. **c.** quasi-*adv.* (*poet.*) 1736.

3. Isabel By g. decay from beauty fell KEATS. **b.** Thy dewy fingers draw The g. dusky veil COLLINS. **c.** The distant view, That g. fades G. WHITE. Phr. *G. psalms*: fifteen psalms (120–134) each of which is entitled in the A.V. 'Song of Degrees', in R.V. 'Song of Ascents', in the Vulgate *Canticum graduum*, in LXX ᾠδὴ ἀναβαθμῶν. Hence **Gra·dualness.**

Gradualism (græ·diuăliz'm). 1835. [f. GRADUAL *a.* + -ISM.] The principle or method of gradual as opp. to immediate change, e.g. in the abolition of slavery.

Graduality (grædiu,æ·lĭti). 1646. [In XVII – med.L. *gradualitas*, f. *gradualis*; see GRADUAL, -ITY. In later use directly from the Eng. adj.] The quality or condition of being gradual.

Gradually (græ·diuăli, græ·dʒ¹uăli), *adv.* 1646. [f. GRADUAL *a.* + -LY².] †**1.** In respect of degree –1701. †**2.** In a graduated scale; by degrees of rank, etc. –1755. **3.** Little by little 1646.

3. You must understand it g...a little at a time DE FOE.

Graduate (græ·diu,ĕt). 1479. [– med.L. *graduatus*, pa. pple. (used subst.) of *graduari* GRADUATE *v.*; see -ATE¹, -ATE².]

A. pa. pple. and *ppl. a.* **1.** Admitted to or holding a University degree. *Obs.* exc. as attrib. use of the sb. 1494. **2.** Arranged by steps or degrees (now *rare*) 1628.

2. The starry ranks..In g. scale of might 1855.

B. *sb.* **1.** One who has obtained a degree from a University, college, etc. In U.S. occas.: A pupil who has completed a school course. 1479. **2.** *transf.* A proficient in an art, etc. (now *rare*) 1582. **3.** A graduated cup, tube, or flask; a measuring glass used by apothecaries and chemists; the quantity this holds 1883. **4.** *attrib.* 1895.

2. Your gradiate in the schoole of warre 1642. **4.** G. members of the University (*mod.*).

Graduate (græ·diu,e¹t), *v.* 1588. [– *graduat-*, pa. ppl. stem of med.L. *graduari* take a degree, f. *gradus* degree; see -ATE³.]

I. 1. *trans.* To admit to a University degree. Now *rare* exc. *U.S.* Also *fig.* †**2.** Of an acquirement, etc.: To qualify (a person) for a degree or as a proficient in an art, etc. –1829. **3.** *intr.* To take a University degree 1807; also *transf.* to qualify (*as*); also, to train in order to qualify 1829.

1. Thence to Oxford, to be graduated HOWELL. **3.** He (Mandeville) graduated at Leyden 1808. *transf.* To g. as a Saint SOUTHEY.

II. *gen.* **1.** *trans.* To divide into degrees 1594. **b.** To arrange in gradations; to adapt *to* by graduating. Also *intr.* for *refl.* 1610. †**2.** To improve the scale or quality of; *spec.* in *Alch.* to transmute (a metal, an essence) into one of a higher grade –1669. **b.** To concentrate (a solution) by evaporation. So Fr. *graduer* (Littré). 1828. **3.** *intr.* To pass by degrees or gradations; to change gradually; *spec.* in *Geol., Bot.,* and *Zool.* 1786.

1. The thermometer..graduated according to the method of Farenheit 1748. **b.** The proposal to g. the Income-tax FAWCETT. **2.** Dyars..advance and g. their colours with Salts SIR T. BROWNE. **3.** This sandstone graduates into the inferior conglomerates 1832. Carriers..g...into the rock-pigeon DARWIN.

Graduated (græ·diu,e¹tĕd), *ppl. a.* 1655. [f. prec. + -ED¹.] In senses of the vb.; esp.: **a.** Qualified 1665. **b.** Marked with lines to indicate degrees, grades, or quantities 1762. **c.** Arranged in grades or gradations; advancing or proceeding by degrees 1678.

b. A g. measure 1806. **c.** G. taxation MILL, privilege 1896. *Graduated*, in Ornithology, when the quill-feathers of the tail increase in length by regular gradations BRANDE.

Graduateship (græ·diu,ĕt,ʃip). 1644. [f. GRADUATE *sb.* + -SHIP.] The period during which one is a graduate; the condition of being a graduate.

A topic folio, the gatherings and savings of a sober graduatship MILTON.

Graduation (grædiu,ē¹·ʃən). 1477. [f. GRADUATE *v.* + -ION; see -ATION.] The action of graduating. **1. a.** The action of dividing into degrees, etc. on a graduated scale 1833. **b.** *pl.* Lines to indicate degrees of latitude and longitude, quantity, etc. 1594. **c.** The manner in which something is graduated 1653. **2.** Arrangement in degrees or gradations; 'regular progression by succession of degrees' (J.) 1658. **b.** An elevation by degrees into a higher condition; also quasi-*concr.* a degree 1643. †**3.** *Alch., Chem.,* etc. The process of tempering the composition of a substance, or of refining an element, a metal –1683. **b.** Concentration by evaporation. Also *attrib.* 1839. †**4.** *U.S. Railways.* Formerly used for GRADIENT. **5.** The action of receiving or conferring a University degree, or the like. Also, the ceremony of conferring degrees. Chiefly *Sc.* and *U.S.* 1639.

2. b. [Justice] Silence [in 2 *Hen. IV*] is an embryo of a man..a g. from nonentity towards intellectual being 1863.

Graduator (græ·diu,e¹təɹ). 1828. [f. GRADUATE *v.* + -OR 2.]. One who or that which graduates. **a.** One who graduates glasses, instruments, etc. **b.** An instrument for dividing any line, straight or curved, into small regular portions. **c.** A contrivance for concentrating a solution by rapid evaporation.

‖**Gradus** (grēⁱ·dŏs). 1764. Short for *Gradus ad Parnassum* 'a step to Parnassus', the L. title of a dictionary of prosody until recently used in public schools as an aid in writing Latin verses. Hence applied to other similar works.

attrib. A commonplace or g. epithet 1887.

Græcian, obs. f. GRECIAN.

Græcism, Grecism (grī·siz'm). 1450. [– Fr. *grécisme* or med.L. *Græcismus*, f. *Græcus* Greek; see -ISM.] †**1.** The *Græcismus*, a 12th c. grammatical treatise (*rare*). **2.** An idiom, or other feature, belonging to the Greek language; esp. as used by a speaker or writer in another language 1570. **3.** The Greek spirit or style in art, mode of thought, etc.; adoption or imitation of these 1609.

2. Milton..has infused a great many..Græcisms ..into the language of his poem ADDISON. **3.** The singular Grecism in Shakespeare's mind RUSKIN.

Græcize, Grecize (grī·səiz), *v.* 1692. [– L. *Græcizare* imitate the Greeks, f. *Græcus* Greek; see -IZE.] **1.** *trans.* To give a Greek cast, character, or form to. **2.** *intr.* To become Greek-like; to adopt Greek expressions, idioms, modes of life, etc. 1840.

Græco-, Greco- (grī·ko), comb. f. L. *Græcus* GREEK, with sense 'relating to the Greek settlements or states established in certain regions abroad', as in *Græco-Asiatic*, etc., or 'partly Greek and partly —', as in *Græco-Latin*, etc.

Græcomania (grīːkomēⁱ·niă). 1800. [f. GRÆCO- + -MANIA.] A mania for things Greek. Hence **Græcoma·niac.**

Græcophil (grī·kŏfil). 1889. [f. as prec. + Gr. φίλος; see -PHIL. A newspaper wd.] A lover of Greece or of what is Greek.

‖**Graf** (grāf). 1630. [G.; see GRAVE *sb.*³] German equivalent of COUNT and EARL.

Graff (grɑf), *sb.*¹ *arch.* ME. [– OFr. *grafe, grefe*, (also mod.) *greffe* – L. *graphium* – Gr. γραφίον, γραφεῖον stylus, f. γράφειν write.] = (and repl. by) GRAFT *sb.*¹ 1, 2.

Graff (grɑf), *sb.*² Now *Hist.* 1637. [prob. – MDu. *grave* = GRAVE *sb.*¹] A trench serving as a fortification; a foss or moat; *rarely*, a canal (in Holland).

Graff (grɑf), *sb.*³ 1523. [perh. var. of GRAFT *sb.*²] **1.** = GRAFT *sb.*² 1. **2.** *dial.* = GRAFT *sb.*² 2. 1875.

Graff (grɑf), *v. arch.* ME. [f. GRAFF *sb.*¹] Superseded by GRAFT *v.*¹, q.v.

Graffage (grɑ·fėdʒ). *dial.* 1798. [perh. f. GRAFF *sb.*² + HEDGE.] A railed fence at the junction of two ditches, or where a ditch abuts on a road at right angles.

†**Graffer.** 1513. [– Fr. *greffier*; see GREFFIER.] A notary –1615.

‖**Graffito** (grɑfˌfī·to). *Pl.* **-ti.** 1851. [– It. *graffito*, f. *graffio* scratching.] A drawing or writing scratched on a wall or other surface, as at Pompeii and Rome. Also, a method of decoration by scratches through a superficial layer of plaster, glazing, etc., on a ground of different colour; chiefly *attrib.*, as in *g.-pottery*, etc.

Graft (grɑft), *sb.*¹ 1483. [alt., with parasitic *t*, of GRAFF *sb.*¹; the transf. of meaning was suggested by the similarity of shape.] **1.** A shoot or scion inserted in a groove or slit made in another stock, so as to allow the sap of the latter to circulate through the former. †**2.** A twig fit for use in grafting; a scion, a sucker; hence *gen.* a branch, plant. Also *fig.* –1624. **3.** *Surg.* 'A portion of living tissue transplanted from one place to another on the same or another organism, with a view to its adhesion or growth' (Billings); also, the operation or its result 1886. **4.** [f. the vb.] **a.** The process or product of grafting. **b.** The place where the scion is inserted in the stock. 1802.

Comb.: **g.-hybrid,** a plant produced by the union of the cellular tissue of two distinct species, bearing leaves and sterile flowers intermediate in character between the scion and the stock; **-hybridism, -hybridization,** hybridizing by means of a g.

Graft (grɑft), *sb.*² 1620. [– (or perh. cogn. w.) ON. *groftr* action of digging :– Gmc. **ȝraftuz*, f. **ȝrab-* dig; see GRAVE *v.*¹] **1.** A 'spit' of earth. Often *spade('s) g.* **2.** A kind of spade for digging drains 1894.

Graft (grɑft), *sb.*³ orig. *U.S. slang.* 1889. [Of unkn. origin; perh. extension of dial. sense 'work' of *graft* (cf. *job*).] A means of making illicit profit; dishonest gains or illicit profits, esp. in connection with political or municipal business.

Graft (grɑft), *v.*¹ 1483. [alt. of GRAFF *v.*; see GRAFT *sb.*¹] **1.** *trans.* To insert (a shoot from one tree) as a graft into another tree. Const. *in, into, on, upon.* Also *transf.* and *fig.* **2.** *absol.* and *intr.* To insert a graft or grafts 1626. **3.** *trans.* To fix a graft or grafts upon (a stock). Also *vaguely*, to perform the operation of grafting on (a tree), to produce (fruits) by grafting 1624. **4.** *transf.* To plant, implant 1562. **5.** *Naut.* To cover (a ring-bolt, block-strop, etc.) with a weaving of small cord or rope-yarns 1860. **6.** *Surg.* To transplant (skin, tissue, etc.): cf. GRAFT *sb.*¹ 3. 1868.

1. *fig.* No Art can be grafted with success on another art SIR J. REYNOLDS. **3.** G. thy pears, O Daphnis, the fruit thy sons shall enjoy BOWEN.

Graft (grɑft), *v.*² orig. *U.S. slang.* 1903. [f. GRAFT *sb.*³] *intr.* To practise or make 'graft'. Hence **Gra·fter. Gra·fting** *vbl. sb.* and *ppl. a.*

Grafter (grɑ·ftəɹ). 1599. [f. GRAFT *v.*¹ + -ER¹.] **1.** One who grafts trees 1616. †**2.** The original tree from which a scion has been taken for grafting on another –1770. **3.** A kind of hand-saw used in grafting 1884.

2. *Hen. V*, III. v. 9.

Grafting (grɑ·ftiŋ), *vbl. sb.* 1483. [f. GRAFT *v.*¹ + -ING¹.] **1.** The action of GRAFT *v.*¹ **2.** In techn. senses: **a.** *Naut.* 'An ornamental weaving of fine yarns, etc., over the strop of a block; or applied to the tapered ends of the ropes, and termed pointing' (Smyth). **b.** *Surg.* The transference of a portion of skin, etc., to another part of the body or to another body 1896. **c.** *Carpentry.* 'A scarfing or endwise attachment of one timber to another' (Knight). **d.** Knitting new feet to stockings 1858.

1. *Cleft-, crown-, saddle-, tongue-, whip-*, etc. *g.*, see the sbs. CLEFT, etc. *Comb.*: **g. clay, wax,** a mixture of clay or wax and other ingredients, forming a composition with which to cover the united parts of a scion and stock in grafting.

Grahamism (grēⁱ·ămiz'm). *U.S.* 1845. [f. *Graham* + -ISM.] The vegetarian principles advocated by Sylvester Graham (1794–1851). So **Gra·hamite,** a follower of Graham.

Grail¹ (grēⁱl). [ME. *grael* – OFr. *grael* :– med.L. *gradale*, for *graduale* GRADUAL *sb.*] = GRADUAL *sb.* 1, 2.

Grail² (grēⁱl). Also †**greal,** †**graal.** ME. [ME. *greal, graal* – OFr. *graal, grael, greel, greil* :– med.L. *gradalis* dish, of unkn. origin.] *The (Holy) Grail, the Saint Grail* or SANGRAIL: in mediæval legend, the platter used by our Saviour at the Last Supper, in which Joseph of Arimathea received the Saviour's blood at the cross. According to one story it was brought by Joseph of Arimathea to Glastonbury. ¶Sometimes supposed erron. to be the cup or chalice used at the Last Supper.

Three angels bear the holy Grail TENNYSON.

Grail³ (grēⁱl). *poet.* 1590. [perh. contraction of GRAVEL.] Gravel.

Grail⁴ (grēⁱl). Also †**graille.** 1688. [– Fr. *grêle*, f. *grêler* make slender, *spec.* to taper and smooth (the teeth of a comb).] A comb-maker's file.

Grain (grēⁱn), *sb.*¹ ME. [Branches I and II: – OFr. *grain, grein* (mod. *grain*) :– L. *granum* grain, seed; Branch III: – (O)Fr. *graine* :– Rom. **grana* fem., orig. pl. of *granum* n.]

I. Seed; corn. †**1.** A single seed, esp. one which is small, hard, and roundish. (After 15th c. usually: The stone or pip of a fruit.) –1823. Also *fig.* **2.** *spec.* A seed or corn of a cereal plant ME. **3.** *collect. sing.* The fruit or seed of wheat and the allied fruit-plants or grasses (†*rarely* of beans, etc.); the plants themselves ME. **b.** A particular species of corn. †Also *pl.* Crops of grain. ME. **4.** Spec. uses of the pl. **a.** (in full *grains of Paradise*): The capsules of *Amomum melegueta*; called also *Guinea grains* (see GUINEA) ME. **b.** Refuse malt after brewing or distilling 1583. †**c.** = DUCKWEED –1597. **5.** †**a.** A berry, grape –1693. **b.** One part of a collective fruit 1674. **c.** *Bot.* A tubercle (see GRAINED *ppl. a.*²) 1829.

1. The G. of a Grape 1684. *fig.* No greine of pite GOWER. Phr. †*In the g.*: in the stage of forming seed. **2.** A Caryopsis or G. GRAY. **3.** The lab'ring Swain Scratch'd with a Rake, a Furrow for his G. DRYDEN. **b.** Barley is a summer g. 1704.

II. Senses orig. transf. from I. 1 and 2. †**1.** A bead, esp. a bead of a rosary; also, a pearl –1662. **2.** A small, round, usually hardish particle (e.g. of sand, salt, etc.) ME. **b.** *spec.* Of gunpowder: A particle of definite size. Also *attrib.* in *large, small*, etc. *g. powder.* 1667. **3.** The smallest English and U.S. unit of weight (orig. the weight of a grain of wheat taken out of the middle of the ear); now = $\frac{1}{5760}$ of a lb. Troy, $\frac{1}{7000}$ of a lb. avoirdupois 1542. **4.** *fig.* (from 2 prec. senses): The smallest possible quantity; esp. in neg. contexts ME.

2. A g. of Mustard-seed HOBBES. *With a g. of salt* (see SALT). **3.** From eight to twelve Grains of Calomel WESLEY. A diamond g. is but ·7925 of a true g. 1883. *Fine g.* (see FINE *a.*). **4.** A..stupid Blockhead, without one G. of Learning HEARNE.

III. With reference to dyeing. [OFr. *graine.*] **1.** *Hist.* The Kermes or Scarlet Grain (see ALKERMES); later also Cochineal. Also the dye from either of these. ME. **2.** Dye in general, esp. a fast dye; colour, hue. Now only *poet.* ME.

1. The chief reds were scarlet..and g. 1883. Phr. *To dye in g.*: orig. to dye in scarlet g.; subseq., to dye in any fast colour, to dye in the fibre, or thoroughly. *In g.* [short for *dyed in g.*], adjectival phr. = dyed scarlet or crimson, fast dyed; hence in fig. use, esp. with *ass, fool*, etc.: Downright, by nature, thorough. Also as *predicate*, ineradicable, INGRAINED. ME. **2.** All in a robe of darkest g. MILT. *fig.* Sins of so deep a graine 1660.

IV. 1. Granular texture; hence in an engraving, etc. a granular appearance produced by dots or lines ME. **2.** *spec.* Of leather: **a.** The rough surface resulting from the growth of papillæ 1607. Also *transf.* **b.** = *grain-side* 1851. **3.** The arrangement and size of the constituent particles of any substance, determining its texture 1600. **b.** *concr.* Internal substance 1579. **4.** The longitudinal arrangement of fibres or particles in wood 1565; the plane of cleavage in coal, stone, etc. 1664. **5.** *fig.* (from 2 prec. senses): Quality, nature, temper; inclination, tendency 1641. **6.** *pl.* A preparation used in graining leather. (Recent Dicts.)

3. Coarse complexions, And cheeks of sorry g. MILT. The clouded olive's easy g. POPE. A.. stone, of a close g. SMEATON. **b.** The graine of the bone is somewhat more yellow than the Ivorie HAKLUYT. **4.** *Tr. & Cr.* I. iii. 8. As the gun-flint makers observe, 'flint has no g.'. It has not in fact the slightest cleavage. 1860. **5.** Crossing the G. of our Nature and Desires BARROW. Phr. *Against* (also, *contrary to*) *the g.* Cut Prejudice against the g. TENNYSON.

V. *attrib.* and *Comb.* **1.** General: as *g.-farm, -merchant*, etc.; *g.-weight*; *g.-dyer*; *g.-eating*, etc.; *g.-fed* adj.

2. Special: **g.-colour,** (*a*) scarlet dye; (*b*) a fast colour; also a cloth dyed with this; **-cut,** *a.* (*Shipbuilding*), of timber, cut athwart the g.; **-founder** = *grain-sick*; **-gold,** gold formed into grains by heat after parting; **-intoxication,** that arising from the use of musty g.; **-leather,** leather dressed with the g.-side outwards; **-moth,** a moth (esp. *Tinea granella*) whose larvæ devour g. in storehouses; **-poisoning,** see *grain-intoxication*; **-process** (*Photogr.*), a process in which a granular texture is given to the plate; **-sick,** a disease in cattle, consisting of an excessive distension of the rumen with food; **-side,** the side of a skin on which the hair grew, opp. to *flesh-side*; **-soap,** in soap-making, soap that has become solid; **g. tin** (see TIN); **-tree** (*Her.*), an imaginary plant bearing kermes grains; **-weevil,** a small weevil which injures stored g.; **-whisky,** whisky made of barley in the g. stage.

Grain (grēⁱn), *sb.*² [– ON. *grein* division, distinction, branch (Sw. *gren*, Da. *green*), of unkn. origin.] †**1.** *pl.* The fork of the body –1612. **2.** A bough or branch. *Obs.* exc. *dial.* 1501. **3.** †**a.** An arm (of the sea); a branch (of a stream) –1533. **b.** A valley branching out of another (*dial.*) 1542. **4.** A prong of a fork. *Obs.* exc. *dial.* 1486. *pl.* (formerly also *grainse* constr. as *sing.*): A fish-spear or harpoon with two or more prongs 1815.

Grain (grēⁱn), *v.*¹ ME. [f. GRAIN *sb.*¹] †**1.** *intr.* To yield grain. Of corn: To form its grains. –1604. **2. a.** *trans.* To cause to deposit grains; to form into grains. **b.** *intr.* for *refl.* Of salt, etc.: To form into grains. 1706. **3.** *Brewing.* To free from grain 1882. **4.** To dye in grain (see GRAIN *sb.*[1]) 1530. **5.** To give a granular surface to 1888. **6.** *Leather-dressing.* **a.** To remove the hair from (skins). **b.** To soften or raise the grain of (leather, etc.). 1530. **7.** To paint in imitation of the grain of woods or of marble. Also *absol.* 1798.

†**Grain,** *v.*[2] *rare.* [f. GRAIN *sb.*[2]] To divide 1664.

Grainage (grēi·nėdʒ). 1610. [f. GRAIN *sb.*[1] + -AGE.] †**1.** Crop of grain. W. FOLKINGHAM. **2.** *Farriery.* Mangy tumours on the legs of horses 1847.

Grained (grēind), *ppl. a.*[1] ME. [f. GRAIN *v.*[1] + -ED[1].] **1.** Dyed in grain. Also *fig.* **2.** Formed into grains 1800. **3.** Of leather (see GRAIN *v.*[1] 6) 1714. **4.** Painted to imitate the grain of woods or of marble 1798.

1. *fig.* Thou turn'st mine eyes into my very soule, And there I see such blacke and g. spots, As will not leaue their Tinct SHAKS.

Grained (grēind), *ppl. a.*[2] 1529. [f. GRAIN *sb.*[1] + -ED[2].] **1.** Having grains, seeds, or particles. *Obs.* exc. in *large-, small-g.*, etc. 1611. **2.** Of wood, stone, leather, flesh, etc.: Having a grain, or granular structure or surface (see GRAIN *sb.*[1] IV. 1–4) 1529. **3.** *Bot.* Having tubercles, as the segments of the flowers of the *Rumex* 1818.

Grained (grēind). *ppl. a.*[3] 1513. [f. GRAIN *sb.*[2] + -ED[2].] Having tines or prongs; forked.

Grainer (grēi·nəɹ). 1813. [f. GRAIN *v.*[1] + -ER[1].] One who or that which grains. **1.** *Leather-dressing.* **a.** An alkaline lye consisting of water impregnated with pigeon's or hen's dung; also, the pit or vessel containing it. Cf. BATE *sb.*[4] **b.** A tool for graining skins 1839. **2.** A house-painter's graining-tool 1858. **3.** One who paints in imitation of the grain of woods or of marble 1837.

Graining (grēi·niŋ), *vbl. sb.* 1664. [f. GRAIN *v.*[1] + -ING[1].] **1.** The action of GRAIN *v.*[1] 1823; quasi-*concr.* the result of this action, *esp.* in house-painting 1834. **2.** *Coinage.* †**a.** A ring of grain-like protuberances on the face of a coin, close to its edge (= Fr. *grènetis*) EVELYN. **b.** = MILLING 1691. *Comb.* **g.-comb,** a tool resembling a comb, used by house-painters in graining.

Graining (grēi·niŋ), *sb.* 1772. [Of unkn. origin.] A small freshwater fish, *Leuciscus lancastrensis.*

Grainy (grēi·ni). *a.* 1611. [f. GRAIN *sb.*[1] + -Y[1].] **1.** Granular; grain-like. **2.** Full of grain or corn 1755.

Graip (grēip). *Sc.* and *n. dial.* 1459. [– ON. *greip* corresp. to OE. *grāp* grasp; see GRIP *sb.*[1], GROPE.] A three- or four-pronged fork used as a dung-fork, etc.

Graith (grēiþ), *sb.* In later use only *Sc.* ME. [– ON. *greiðe* wk. masc., cogn. w. OE. *ġerǣde* str. n. trappings, equipage :– Gmc. *ʒaraiðon or -*jon*, *ʒaraiðjam, f. *ʒa- Y- + *raið-; see READY. For the sense-development cf. GEAR.] †**1.** A state of preparation –1460. **2.** Equipment; dress, articles of dress; armour ME.; harness 1663. **3.** Apparatus, gear, tackle; a contrivance ME. †**4.** Wealth, money –1786. **5.** Material, stuff (for a purpose) 1513.

1. *In g.*: in proper order; also, without delay. *Out of g.*: out of order. **2.** I will sleep like a sentinel, with my g. about me SCOTT.

†**Graith,** *a.* and *adv.* ME. [– ON. *greiðr* = OE. *ġerǣde* ready, f. Gmc. *ʒa- Y- + *raið-; see prec.]

A. *adj.* **1.** Ready –1475. **2.** Of a road: Direct. Of a measure: Exact. Of a sign, truth, etc.: Plain. ME. only.

B. *adv.* Readily; clearly, plainly –1450.

Graith (grēiþ), *v. Obs.* exc. *dial.* ME. [– ON. *greiða*, f. *greiðr* ready; see prec.] **1.** *trans.* To make ready; also, to procure. **2.** To equip, furnish; to array; to bedeck ME. †**3.** = MAKE in various senses. ME. only. Hence **Grai·thing** *vbl. sb.* (now *dial.*), preparation; furnishing; furniture, attire.

Grakle, var. of GRACKLE.

Grallatorial (grælătō°·riăl), *a.* 1835. [f. mod.L. *grallatorius*, f. L. *grallator* walker on stilts, f. *grallæ* stilts; see -ATOR, -IAL.] *Ornith.* Pertaining to the order *Grallatores*, which consists of long-legged wading birds, such as the crane, heron, etc. So **Gra·llatory** *a.*

Grallic (græ·lik), *a. rare.* 1828. [f. L. *grallæ* stilts + -IC.] *Ornith.* Of or pertaining to the *Grallæ* or wading birds. So **Gra·lline** *a.*

Gralloch (græ·lǫχ), *sb.* 1882. [– Gael. *grealach* entrails.] The viscera of a dead deer. Hence **Gra·lloch** *v.* to disembowel (prop. a deer) 1848.

Gram[1] (græm). 1702. [– Pg. †*gram*, *grão* :– L. *granum* GRAIN *sb.*[1]] The chick-pea, *Cicer arietinum*. Hence, any kind of pulse used as food for horses. Also *attrib.*

Gram[2]: see GRAMME.

-gram (græm), repr. (chiefly) Gr. γράμμα something written, letter (of the alphabet). The older Eng. sbs. with this ending are: (1) adaptations of Gr. sbs. in -γραμμα, derived from vbs. f. prep. + γράφειν, as *anagram, diagram*, etc.; (2) compounds of a Gr. sb. with γράμμα, as *chronogram*, etc.; (3) compounds of a numeral with γράμμα, or γραμμή line, of which the Gr. type is a neut. adj. in -γραμμον, as *monogram, hexagram*, etc. In 1857 *telegram*, which violates Gr. analogy, was introduced as a shorter term for 'telegraphic message'. Similar formations are *cablegram* for 'cable telegram', *pistolgram* for an instantaneous photograph.

Grama, gramma (grā·mă, græ·mă). See GAMA GRASS. 1851. [– Sp. *grama* a sort of grass.] A name for several low pasture grasses found in the western U.S., esp. *Bouteloua oligostachya*.

Gramarye (græ·mări). *Obs.* exc. *arch.* ME. [– AFr. *gramarie* = OFr. *gramaire* GRAMMAR; cf. Fr. *grimoire* book of magic, earlier †*gramoire* (dial. var. of *gramaire*) †Latin grammar.] †**1.** Grammar; learning –1483. **2.** Occult learning, magic, necromancy. (Revived by Scott.) 1470.

Gramash (grămæ·ʃ). 1681. [Sc. var. of GAMASH.] = GAMASH.

Grame (grēim), *sb. Obs.* exc. *arch.* [OE. *grama*, rel. to *gram* GRAME *a.*, whence GRAME *v.*] †**1.** Anger, wrath, ire –1621. **2.** Grief, sorrow; harm. In *pl.* Troubles. OE. So †**Grame** *a.* angry; vexed; furious; of heat, fierce. †**Grame** *v.* to be vexed or displeased; also *trans.* to vex.

Gramercy (grămɔ̄·ɹsi), *interj. phr. Obs.* exc. *arch.* ME. [– OFr. *grant merci*, i.e. *grant* great, *merci* reward, favour (the etymol. sense being 'May God reward you greatly'); see GRAND, MERCY.] **1.** = Thanks; thank you. †**b.** with *dat.* or *to*: = Thanks *to*; by the instrumentality of –1734. **2.** ?As an exclam. of surprise, etc. = 'mercy on us!' 1607. †**3.** quasi-*sb.* The salutation 'thanks' or 'thank you' –1670.

1. G. for thy caution SCOTT. **b.** Gromesty God, and that good Man 1450. **2.** G.! they for joy did grin COLERIDGE. **3.** *Worth g.*, worth a 'thank you', of some value. What g. [= what special merit] to be sober, just, or continent MILTON.

Gramineous (grēimi·nĭəs), *a.* 1658. [f. L. *gramineus*, f. *gramen, gramin-* grass; see -EOUS.] Of, pertaining to, or resembling grass; grassy; *spec.* belonging to the N.O. *Gramineæ*. So **Gramina·ceous, Grami·neal** *adjs.* (in same sense). var. **Gra·minous.** ?*Obs.*

Graminiferous (græmini·fĕrəs), *a.* 1834. [f. as prec. + -FEROUS.] Producing grass.

Graminivorous (grămini·vŏrəs), *a.* 1739. [f. as prec. + -VOROUS.] Eating or feeding on grass.

Grammalogue (græ·mălǫg). 1845. [irreg. f. Gr. γράμμα letter + λόγος word; cf. *analogue, catalogue*.] *Shorthand.* A letter-word; a word represented by a single sign; also, a letter or character representing a word (more correctly LOGOGRAM).

Grammar (græ·məɹ), *sb.* [ME. *gramer(e* – AFr. *gramere*, OFr. *gramaire* (mod. *grammaire*) :– **gramadie* – L. *grammatica* – Gr. γραμματική, subst. use (sc. τέχνη art) of fem. of γραμματικός pertaining to letters, f. γράμμα, γραμματ- letter.] **1.** That department of the study of a language which deals with its inflexional forms or their equivalents, and with the rules for employing these correctly; usually treating also of the phonetic system of the language and its representation in writing. (Till the 16th c. *grammar* in Eng. use meant mainly Latin grammar.) **2.** A treatise or book on grammar 1530. **3.** An individual's manner of using grammatical forms; speech or writing as it conforms to or violates grammatical rules; also speech or writing that is correct according to these rules 1586. **4.** The system of inflexions and syntactical usages characteristic of a language 1846. †**5.** Used for LATIN, or the Latin language. *By g.*: in Latin (Cf. GRAMMAR-SCHOOL.) –1576. **6.** *transf.* **a.** The fundamental principles or rules of an art or science. **b.** A book presenting these methodically (now *rare*). 1642.

1. Concerning speech and words, the consideration of them hath produced the science of G. BACON. *Historical G.*: the study of the historical development of the inflexional forms and syntactical usages of a language. *Comparative G.*: the comparative treatment of the phenomena of two or more related languages, with reference to the nature and degree of their relationship. *General, Philosophical* or *Universal G.*: the science concerned with the general principles which underlie the grammatical phenomena of all languages. **2.** I read it in the Grammer long agoe SHAKS. **3.** He had German enough to scold his servants..but his g. and pronunciation were very bad MACAULAY. **6. a.** Manly sports are the Grammer of Military performance FULLER.

Grammar (græ·məɹ), *v. rare.* 1593. [f. the sb.] †**a.** *intr.* To discuss grammar. BEAUM. & FL. †**b.** To ground *in* something, as in the rudiments of grammar. BUNYAN. **c.** To classify, as the parts of speech in grammar 1883.

Grammarian (grămē°·riăn). ME. [– OFr. *gramarien* (mod. *grammairien*), f. *gramaire* GRAMMAR; see -IAN.] **1.** One versed in the knowledge of grammar, or of language; a philologist; a writer upon, or teacher of grammar. †**2.** A grammar-school boy –1607.

1. I have seene a G. toure, and plume himselfe over a single line in Horace SIR T. BROWNE. Hence **Gramma·rianism,** the principles or practice of a g.

Grammarless (græ·məɹlės), *a.* 1823. [f. GRAMMAR *sb.* + -LESS.] Having no grammar; said of a language, also of persons, speech, etc.

Gra·mmar-school. ME. A school for teaching grammar. **1.** In England a class of schools founded in the 16th c. or earlier for the teaching of Latin grammar. They are now secondary schools of various degrees of importance. Also *attrib.* **2.** *U.S.* In the system of graded common schools in the United States, the grade or department in which English grammar is taught 1860.

1. Thou hast most traiterously corrupted the youth of the Realme, in erecting a Grammar Schoole SHAKS.

†**Grammates,** *sb. pl.* [perh. – Gr. γράμματα.] Rudiments. FORD.

Grammatic (grămæ·tik), *a.* 1599. [– OFr. *gramatique* or L. *grammaticus* – Gr. γραμματικός; see GRAMMAR, -IC.] = GRAMMATICAL *a.* 1.

Grammatical (grămæ·tikăl), *a.* 1526. [– Fr. *grammatical* or late L. *grammaticalis*, f. as prec.; see -AL[1], -ICAL.] **1.** Of or pertaining to grammar 1526. **2.** Conforming to the rules of grammar 1752. **3.** *transf.* Of the grammar of an art 1833. †**4.** *absol.* as *sb. pl.* The subjects taught in a grammar-school –1716.

1. *Grammatical gender*: gender which is not determined by the real or attributed sex; opp. to *natural gender*. *G. sense*: the sense obtained by the simple application of the rules of grammar to a text. So *g. meaning, interpretation, †translation.* **3.** The..g. accuracy of the tones of Turner RUSKIN. *G. accent* (Mus.): the accent regularly occurring at the beats of a bar; opp. to *oratorical accent.* Hence **Gramma·tically** *adv.*

Grammaticaster (grĕmæ·tikæstəɹ). 1601. [– med.L. *grammaticaster* 'scribe, notarius' (Du Cange); see GRAMMATIC, -ASTER.] A petty grammarian. (Contemptuous.)

†**Grammatication.** 1582. [f. med.L. *grammaticare*; see GRAMMATIC, -ATION.] A discussion of points in grammar –1680.

Gramma·ticism. Now *rare.* 1610. [f.

GRAMMATIC + -ISM.] A point or principle of grammar; a grammatical definition.

Grammaticize (grămæ·tisəiz), *v.* 1673. [f. as prec. + -IZE. Cf. med.L. *grammatizare.*] **1.** *trans.* To render grammatical 1780. **2.** *intr.* To discuss grammatical points 1673.

Grammatist (græ·mătist). 1589. [– Fr. *grammatiste* or its source L. *grammatista* (Suetonius) – Gr. *γραμματιστής*, f. *γράμμα, γραμματ-* letter; see -IST.] **a.** A grammarian. (Usu. disparaging.) **b.** A teacher of letters 1849. Hence **Grammati·stical** *a.* befitting a g.

Grammatolatry (græmătǫ·lătri). 1847. [f. Gr. *γράμμα, γραμματ-* letter + -LATRY.] The worship of letters; adherence to the letter (of Scripture).

Gramme, gram² (græm). 1797. [– Fr. *gramme* – Gr. *γράμμα* (whence late L. *gramma*) small weight.] In the Metric system, the unit of weight; the weight of a cubic centimetre of distilled water at the maximum density, weighed *in vacuo*; = 15.432 Troy grains. Also *attrib.*

Comb.: **g.-centimetre,** a unit equivalent to the work done in raising one gramme vertically one centimetre; **-degree,** the quantity of heat required to raise a gramme of water 1° (Centigrade); **-equivalent** (*Electrolysis*), that quantity of the metal which will replace one gramme of hydrogen.

Gramophone (græ·mŏfōᵘn). Also **grammophone.** 1888. [Formed by inverting the first and last sylls. of PHONOGRAM. Preceded by *graphophone*, 1885, from PHONOGRAPH. The sp. *grammo-* is an attempt to correct the formation.] An instrument for recording and reproducing vocal, instrumental, and other sounds; *esp.* a reproducing instrument consisting essentially of a revolving turntable capable of carrying discs on which are impressed, in a spiral track, wave-forms corresp. to sound vibrations, to reproduce which a stylus, attached to an acoustic device or electric system, travels along the track.

Grampus (græ·mpŏs). 1529. [Earliest forms *graundepose*, *grampoys*, alt. (by assim. to GRAND) of †*gra(s)peys* GRAPEYS.] One of various kinds of blowing, spouting, blunt-headed delphinoid cetaceans. **b.** *transf.* A person who breathes loudly 1836.

1. Coughing like a g. DICKENS. **b.** The blustering old g. of a governor 1851.

Granada, -ade, obs. ff. GRENADO, -ADE.

Granadilla, grenadilla (grænă-, grenădi·lă). 1613. [– Sp. *granadilla*, dim. of *granada* POMEGRANATE.] A name of tropical species of the Passion-flower; esp. of *Passiflora quadrangularis* or its fruit, which is esteemed as a dessert fruit. Also *attrib.*

†**Grana·do.** 1582. [pop. Eng. form of the Spanish city *Granada*; see -ADO.] Only in *G. silk*, *silk of G.* –1618.

†**Gra·nage.** In mod. Dicts. **grainage.** 1582. [– AFr. *granage*, formally corresp. to OFr. *grenage* duty on grain, f. *grain* GRAIN *sb.*¹ + *-age* -AGE. The AFr. sense is unaccounted for.] A duty in London on salt imported by an alien –1820.

Granary (græ·nări). 1570. [– L. *granarium* (usu. pl. *-ia*), f. *granum* GRAIN *sb.*¹; see -ARY¹.] A storehouse for grain after it is threshed. **b.** *transf.* and *fig.* 1570. Also *attrib.*

b. Sicily..when 'twas styled the G. of Great Rome 1632.

†**Gra·nat.** [– Du. *granaat.*] = GRENADE¹. B. Jons.

†**Gra·nate,** *sb.*¹ ME. [– med.L. *granatus*; see GARNET¹.] = GARNET¹ –1796.

†**Gra·nate,** *sb.*² 1568. [– med.L. *pomum* (cl.L. *malum*) *granatum*, OFr. (*pome*) *grenate*. See POMEGRANATE.] **1.** The pomegranate –1698. **2.** Short for 'granate-colour' –1805.

Granatite (*Min.*), var. of GRENATITE.

Grand (grænd). [ME. *graunt(e* – AFr. *graunt*, OFr. *grant* m. and fem. (mod. *grand*, *grande*); later *grand* (XVI) – Fr. *grand* or its source L. *grandis*, which in Rom. superseded L. *magnus* in all its uses.]

A. *adj.* †**1.** *The Grand*: = 'the Great' –1529. **2.** In titles: Chief, highest in rank or office. Now chiefly *Hist.* or with reference to foreign countries. 1609. **3.** [Orig. transf. of 2; cf. ARCH- *pref.* 2.] Pre-eminent, chief; most properly so called. ?*Obs.* 1584. **4.** *Law.* Great; principal, chief; opp. to *petty* or *common* 1562. **5.** Of things, events, etc.: Specially great or important; chief, main 1597. **b.** With *a*, or with sb. in pl.: Of first-rate magnitude, scale, or importance 1611. **6.** Used to designate a comprehensive unity in relation to its constituent portions. Now only in *grand total.* 1576. **7.** Main, principal 1601. **8.** = GREAT in various senses 1660. **9.** Characterized by great solemnity, splendour, or display; conducted with great form and on a great scale 1735. **b.** Of persons, their belongings, etc.: Fine, splendid, gorgeously arrayed. Also more widely: Giving evidence of wealth or high social position. 1766. **10. a.** Of natural objects, architecture, etc.: Imposing by reason of beauty coupled with magnitude 1712. **b.** Of ideas, style, design, etc.: Lofty and dignified in conception, treatment, or expression 1755. **c.** Of persons; Imposing morally or intellectually; also, stately, noble, dignified 1832. **d.** In recent use, coupled with sbs. qualified by *old* 1833. **11.** As a general term of admiration (*colloq.*) 1816.

2. *G. Almoner, Falconer* (see the sbs.). *G. Pensionary, Pensioner*, the prime minister or president of the Council of Holland, when a republic. *G. Vizier*, the chief minister of the Turkish empire. *G. Turk*, the Sultan of Turkey. **3.** Sin and Death, the two g. foes MILT. **4.** *G. assize, compounder, distress, larceny*, etc. (see the sbs.). *Grand* (or *Gaudy*) *days*: Ascension day, St. John Baptist's day, All Saints' Day, and Candlemas, four days, one in every term, which are observed as holidays in the Inns of Court and Chancery. 'And these are no days in Court.' **5.** The g. rebellion SWIFT. The g. article of my expense is food WESLEY. **b.** A g. imposture 1842. **7.** The g. entrance 1855, staircase 1860. **8.** A g. sonata or a g. concerto meant one in complete classical form 1879. *G. Opera*, a French term, denoting a lyric drama in which spoken dialogue is excluded 1879. **9.** G. wedding festivities 1893. G. company 1860. A very g. lady on state occasions THACKERAY. **10. b.** *G. style*: a style fitted to the expression of lofty ideas and great subjects in literature and art. In what used to be called the g. style, at once noble and natural LOWELL. **d.** Since, 'gainst the classes, He heard, of late, the Grand Old Man [= W. E. Gladstone] Incite the masses M. ARNOLD.

Comb.: **g. action,** the action of a g. pianoforte; **g. committee** (*Parliament*), (*a*) *Hist.* each of the four committees (for religion, for grievances, for courts of justice, and for trade) annually appointed by the House of Commons until 1832; †also, in 17th c., 'committee of the whole house'; (*b*) now, applied to the two 'standing committees' (each of 60 to 80 members) since 1882 appointed every session to consider bills relating to matters of Law and Trade; **G. Fleet,** the main part of the British fleet in the war of 1914–18; **g. lodge** (see LODGE); **g. pianoforte, piano,** a large pianoforte, usually harp-shaped and horizontal, whose size admits of the most effective arrangement of the mechanism (see also UPRIGHT *a.*); **g. stand,** the principal stand for spectators at a racecourse, etc.; also *fig.* and *attrib.* (U.S.).

b. used (after Fr.) to denote the second degree removed in ascent or descent of relationship, as GRANDFATHER, GRANDSON, etc.

B. quasi-*sb.* and *sb.* **1.** quasi-*sb. The grand*: that which is grand 1742. †**2.** *sb.* = GRANDEE –1669. **3. a.** Among Freemasons, any officer whose title contains the adj. **b.** In some clubs, the title of the chairman. Also *Noble Grand, Vice Grand*, the chairman and vice-chairman of a lodge of Odd Fellows. 1747. **4.** A grand pianoforte 1840. **5.** *Sugar Manuf.* The largest evaporating pan of a battery 1839. **6.** *U.S.* A thousand dollars 1930.

Grand air. 1775. [prop. Fr., but pronounced as Eng.] An air of distinction; also (in bad sense) an affected loftiness of manner.

Grandam, grandame (græ·ndăm, -dēⁱm). ME. [– AFr. *graund dame*; see GRAND, DAME (the use of *dame* for 'mother' seems to be AFr. only). See also GRANNY, and cf. GRANDSIRE.] **1.** = GRANDMOTHER 1, 2. **2.** An old woman; a gossip 1550. **3.** *fig.* 1602. **4.** *attrib.* (quasi-*adj.*) 1598.

Gra·nd-aunt. 18.. [See GRAND *a. Comb.* b.] One's father's or mother's aunt; a great-aunt.

Grandchild (græ·nd-, græ·nˌtʃəild). 1587. [See GRAND *a. Comb.* b.] The child of one's son or daughter. Also *fig.*

Grand-dad, grandad (græ·ndˌdæd, græ·ndæd). 1819. [See GRAND *a. Comb.* b., DAD.] Childish or affectionate for GRANDFATHER.

Gra·nd-daughter. 1611. [See GRAND *a. Comb.* b.] The daughter of one's son or daughter.

Grand duchess. 1757. [See GRAND *a.* A. 2.] **a.** The wife or widow of a Grand Duke. **b.** A lady holding in her own right the sovereignty of a duchy. **c.** A daughter of the Czar of Russia. So **Grand Duchy,** the territory ruled by a Grand Duke or Duchess.

Grand duke. 1693. [See GRAND *a.* A. 2.] **1. a.** The title of the sovereigns of Grand Duchies, who rank one degree below kings. **b.** In Russia, any son of an emperor. **2.** The Great Eagle Owl (*Bubo ignavus*) 1855. Hence **Grand-du·cal** *a.* of or belonging to a Grand Duke. **Grand-du·kedom.**

Grandee (grændī·). 1598. [– Sp., Pg. *grande*, subst. use of *grande* adj. GRAND, the ending assim. to -EE¹.] A Sp. or Pg. nobleman of the highest rank. Also *transf.* and *gen.* Hence **Grandee·ship,** the position or dignity of a g.

Grandeur (græ·ndiŭɹ). 1500. [– (O)Fr. *grandeur*, f. *grand* great, GRAND.] †**1. a.** Height; tall stature. **b.** Greatness (in amount or degree). –1658. **2.** Greatness of power or rank. Now somewhat *rare.* 1616. **3.** Transcendent greatness or nobility of intrinsic character 1669. **4.** The quality of being GRAND; sublimity, majesty. Also an instance of this. 1662. **5.** Conscious greatness, lofty dignity. †Also, arrogance. 1644. **6.** Magnificence of appearance, style of living, trappings, etc. Also *pl.* 1652.

4. The Majesty and Grandure of Tragedy BENTLEY. **6.** The English go to their estates for g. The French live at court, and exile themselves to their estates for economy EMERSON.

Grandeval (grændī·văl), *a. rare.* 1650. [f. L. *grandævus* aged (f. *grandis* great + *ævum* age) + -AL¹.] Of a great age, old, ancient.

†**Grande·vity.** 1623. [– L. *grandævitas*, f. *grandævus*; see prec., -ITY.] Great or old age –1688.

†**Grande·vous,** *a.* [f. L. *grandævus* (see prec.) + -OUS.] Aged, old. HY. MORE.

†‖**Grande·zza, grande·za.** 1642. [It. *grandezza*, Sp. *grandeza*, f. *grande* GRAND; see -ESS².] Grandeur, greatness, magnificence; also, an instance of this –1675.

Grandfather (græ·nd-, græ·nfāðəɹ), *sb.* ME. [f. GRAND (*Comb.* b.) + FATHER, after Fr. *grandpère.*] **1.** The father of one's father or mother. Also *fig.* **2.** A male ancestor 1613.

1. Who begot thee? Marry, the son of my G. SHAKS. **2.** Our g. Adam HIERON. *Comb.* **g.-long-legs** = DADDY-LONG-LEGS; **grandfather clock** [suggested by a popular song about 1880], the weight-and-pendulum eight-day clock in a tall case formerly in common use. Hence **Grandfatherly** *a.* of, befitting, or resembling a g.

Gra·ndfather, *v. rare.* 1748. [f. the sb.] *To g.* (a thing) *on*: *fig.* [after FATHER *v.*] to impute to (a person) as its mediate originator.

Grand Guignol (grañ ginʸol). 1920. [Fr.] A dramatic entertainment consisting of a succession of short sensational pieces.

Grandiloquent (grændi·lŏkwĕnt), *a.* 1593. [f. L. *grandiloquus*, f. *grandis* + *-loquus*, f. *loqui* to speak; after *eloquent*, etc.] Characterized by swelling or pompous expression. Hence **Grandi·loquence,** the quality of being g. **Grandi·loquently** *adv.* So **Grandi·loquous** *a.*

Grandiose (græ·ndiōᵘs), *a.* 1840. [– Fr. *grandiose* – It. *grandioso*, f. *grande* GRAND, after *glorioso*, etc.; see -OSE¹.] **1.** Producing an effect of grandeur; characterized by largeness of plan or nobility of design 1843. **2.** Of speech, style, etc.: Characterized by formal stateliness; in bad sense, pompous.

1. Things painted by a Rubens..all more g. than the life BROWNING. **2.** With a strut more than usually g. 1847. Hence **Gra·ndiosely** *adv.* **Grandio·sity,** g. quality.

Grandisonant (grændi·sŏnănt), *a. rare.* 1684. [f. late L. *grandisonus* (f. *grandis* GRAND + *sonus* sounding) + -ANT.] Stately-sounding. So **Grandi·sonous** *a.*

Grandisonian (grændisōᵘ·niăn), *a.* 1829. [f. *Grandison* (see below) + -IAN.] Of deportment, manner, etc.: Of or resembling that of Sir Charles Grandison in Richardson's novel of that name.

†**Gra·ndity.** 1589. [– L. *granditas*, f. *grandis*; see GRAND, -ITY. Cf. OFr. *grandité*.] Grandeur, stateliness. Also, a mark of greatness. –1839.

Grandly (græ·ndli), *adv.* 1654. [f. GRAND *a.* + -LY².] In a grand manner; magnificently, grandiosely, etc.

A mind that is g. simple. EMERSON

Grandmamma (græ·nd-, græ·nmămā). 1763. [See GRAND *Comb.* b.] = GRANDMOTHER. *colloq.*

Grand master. 1549. [See GRAND A. 2.] †**1.** The chief officer of a royal household –1748. **2.** The head of one of the military orders of knighthood, *e.g.* the Hospitallers, Templars, etc. 1553. **b.** The head of the order of Freemasons, or of the Odd Fellows, etc. 1724. Hence **Grandma·stership.**

Grandmaternal (græ:ndmătə̄·ɹnăl), *a.* 1790. [f. GRAND *a. Comb.* b. + MATERNAL *a.*] = GRANDMOTHERLY. Somewhat *joc.*

Grandmother (græ·nd-, græ·nmɒðəɹ). ME. [f. GRAND (*Comb.* b.) + MOTHER, after Fr. †*grant mère*, mod. *grand'mère*.] **1.** The mother of one's father or mother. Also *fig.* **2.** A female ancestor 1526. **3.** *attrib.* 1649. Also as vb.

Grandmotherly (græ·nd-, græ·nmɒðəɹli), *a.* 1842. [f. prec. + -LY¹.] Pertaining to or befitting a grandmother. Now often *fig.* of government, legislation, etc.

Grand-nephew. 1639. [See GRAND *Comb.* b.] The son of a nephew or niece.

Grandness (græ·ndnės). 1722. [f. GRAND + -NESS.] The state or quality of being grand. Also, a grand action (BROWNING).

Grand-niece. 1830. [See GRAND *Comb.* b.] The daughter of a nephew or niece.

Grandpapa (græ·nd-, græ·npăpā). 1753. [See GRAND *Comb.* b.] = GRANDFATHER. *colloq.* Also **Grandpa.**

Grandparent (grændpēᵊrĕnt). 1830. [See GRAND *Comb.* b.]. The parent of a parent. So **Grandparentage.**

Grandpaternal (græ:ndpătə̄·ɹnăl), *a.* 1844. [f. GRAND *Comb.* b. + PATERNAL *a.*] = GRANDFATHERLY. Somewhat *joc.*

Grand signior. 1592. [– It. *gran signore* (whence Fr. *grand seigneur*); see GRAND, SIGNOR.] **1.** *The Grand Signior*: the Sultan of Turkey. †**2.** A great noble. P. HOLLAND.

Grandsire (græ·nd-, græ·nsəiᵊɹ). ME. [– AFr. *graunt sire*; see GRAND, SIRE, and cf. GRANDAME.] **1.** = GRANDFATHER 1 (*arch.* and *dial.*). Also *transf.* of a horse, etc. 1881. **2.** A forefather (*arch.*) ME. **3.** An old man (*arch.*) 1596. **4.** *attrib.* 1592. **5.** *Bell-ringing.* A particular method of ringing the changes on a peal of bells 1671.

1. By Woden wild, (my grandsire's oath) SCOTT. **2.** Our Grand-sire Adam 1599. **3.** *Tam. Shr.* IV. v. 50. **4.** I am prouerb'd with a Grandsier Phrase SHAKS.

Grandson (græ·nd-, græ·nsɒn). 1586. [See GRAND *Comb.* b.] A son's or daughter's son. Also *transf.* of a horse.

Grand tour. 1748. [– Fr. *grand tour* 'great circuit', but now apprehended as an Eng. phrase.] A tour of the principal cities and places of Europe, formerly supposed to be necessary to complete the education of young men of position.

Gra·nd-uncle. 1475. [See GRAND *Comb.* b.] One's father's or mother's uncle.

Grane, north. f. GROAN.

Grange (grēⁱndʒ), *sb.* ME. [– AFr. *graunge*, (O)Fr. *grange* :– med.L. *granica*, subst. use (sc. *villa*) of fem. of **granicus* pertaining to grain, f. L. *granum* GRAIN.] **1.** A repository for grain; a granary. **2.** An establishment where farming is carried on. Now, A country house with farm buildings attached, usually the residence of a gentleman-farmer. ME. **b.** *esp.* An outlying farm-house with barns, etc. belonging to a monastery or a feudal lord, for storing tithes in kind etc. ME. †**3.** A country house –1633. **4.** *U.S.* A lodge of the order of 'Patrons of Husbandry'; an association for promoting the interests of agriculture 1875.

2. The thousand waves of wheat, That ripple round the lonely g. TENNYSON. **b.** A g. of the monks of Abingdon J. R. GREEN.

Granger (grēⁱ·ndʒəɹ). ME. [– AFr. *graunger* = OFr. *grangier*, f. *grange* GRANGE; see -ER² 2.] **1.** A farm-bailiff. **2.** *U.S.* **a.** A member of a grange (see GRANGE 4) 1875. **b.** A farmer 1887. **c.** *pl.* Short for *granger shares* 1885. **3.** *attrib.* (sense 2), as **g. road** (*U.S.*), one of the railways which convey grain from the Western States; **g. shares,** shares in the g. roads 1892.

Grangerize (grēⁱ·ndʒərəiz), *v.* 1882. [f. James *Granger* who in 1769 published a 'Biographical History of England', with blank leaves for engraved portraits, etc. See -IZE.] To illustrate (a book) by the addition of prints, engravings, etc., usually cut out of other books. Hence **Gra·ngerism,** the practice of grangerizing. **Gra·ngerite,** one who grangerizes.

Graniferous (grăni·fĕrəs), *a.* 1656. [f. L. *granum* GRAIN *sb.*¹ + -FEROUS.] Bearing grain or seed like grain.

Graniform (græ·nifǭɹm), *a.* 1778. [f. as prec. + -FORM.] Formed like grains of corn; *spec.* in *Anat.* and *Bot.*

‖**Granilla** (grăni·lă). 1812. [Sp., dim. of *grana*; see GRAIN *sb.*¹] The refuse of cochineal, consisting of the dried bodies of small or half-grown cochineal-insects.

Granite (græ·nit). 1646. [It. *granito* lit. grained, granular, pa. ppl. formation on *grano* GRAIN *sb.*¹] **1.** A granular crystalline rock, consisting essentially of quartz, orthoclase-feldspar, and mica, and usually light grey, white, or light red in colour. **2.** *attrib.* Consisting or made of granite 1703.

1. The tremendous granites of the Grimsel RUSKIN. **2.** *The g. City*, Aberdeen. *The g. State*, New Hampshire, U.S. *Comb.*: **g.-quartzy** *a.*, intermediate between g. and quartz; **g. ware,** (*a*) pottery with a colouring imitating that of g.; (*b*) a kind of enamelled ironware. Hence **Grani·tic, -al** *a.* pertaining to, or of the nature of g.; composed of, or containing g.; (of water) obtained from g. soils; also *fig.* **Graniti·coline** *a.* growing upon g., as a lichen. **Graniti·ferous** *a.* g.-bearing. **Grani·tiform** *a.* resembling g. **Gra·nitoid** *a.* resembling, or having the structure of g.; *sb.* [sc. *rock*].

Granivorous (grani·vŏrəs), *a.* 1646. [f. L. *granum* GRAIN *sb.*¹ + -VOROUS.] That feeds on grain.

Grannam (græ·nəm). 1597. Colloq. pronunc. of GRANDAM.

Granny, grannie (græ·ni). 1663. [f. GRANNAM (prec.) + -Y⁶, -IE.] A grandmother; also, an old woman, a gossip.

Comb.: **granny's bend** (*Naut.*), a slippery hitch made by a lubber; **granny's knot** (*Naut.*), a reef-knot crossed the wrong way, which cannot be untied when it is jammed.

Granolithic (grænoli·þik), *a.* 1883. [f. L. *grano-* irreg. comb. form of L. *granum* + Gr. λίθος stone + -IC.] A kind of concrete. Hence, of buildings, etc.: Made of granolithic concrete.

Granose (grēⁱnōᵘ·s), *a. rare.* 1889. [– L. *granosus*, f. *granum* GRAIN *sb.*¹; see -OSE¹.] *Entom.* Having the form of a string of grains, as the antennæ of many insects.

Grant (grɑnt), *sb.* ME. [f. the vb.] The action of granting; the thing granted. †**1. a.** Consent –1648. **b.** Promise –1575. **c.** Admission –1700. Also, what is agreed to, promised, etc. **2.** The action of according (a request, etc.) ME. **3.** An authoritative bestowal or conferring of a right, etc.; a gift or assignment of money, etc., out of a fund ME. **b.** The thing which is the subject of the grant 1815. **4.** *Law.* **a.** A conveyance by deed. †**b.** Formerly: A conveyance of such property (viz. incorporeal hereditaments) as can pass only by deed. 1596. **5.** Chiefly *U.S.* The name given to a portion of land in the occupation of specified persons. *The Hampshire Grants*: now the State of Vermont. 1719.

3. The g. of a patent 1824, of certain Customs duties 1874. **b.** I am an enemy of the present system of what are called *grants in aid* GLADSTONE. *Capitation-grant* (see CAPITATION). **4. b.** A thing is said *to lie in graunte* which cannot be assigned with out deed 1607.

Grant (grɑnt), *v.* Pa. t. and pple. **granted.** ME. [– OFr. *granter*, *graanter*, *greanter*, alt. of *creanter* guarantee, assure :– Rom. **credentare*, f. *credent-*, pres. ppl. stem of L. *credere* believe, trust.] †**1.** *intr.* To agree, consent –1593. **2.** *trans.* To agree to, promise, undertake. *Obs.* exc. in legal documents. ME. **3.** To accede to, consent to fulfil ME. **4.** To allow as an indulgence; to bestow as a favour, or in answer to a request ME. †**b.** To permit (an action). CHAUCER. **5.** To bestow by a formal act. Also in *Law*, to transfer (property), esp. by deed. ME. †**6.** To give up –1613. **7.** To admit, confess, acknowledge. Now only of conceding a proposition to be used as a basis of argument. ME.

2. A. covenanted, granted, and agreed that [etc.] CRUISE. **3.** Iesus g. him his praier ME. **4.** To g. better conditions to a garrison 1711. **5.** They granted charters to the towns and privileges to the inhabitants BUCKLE. **7.** If thus much be granted ..how is not our principle conceded KEBLE. I g. him brave, But wild SCOTT. Phr. *To take for granted*: to regard as not requiring proof, or as likely to be generally admitted. Hence **Gra·ntable** *a.* capable of being granted.

Grantee (grɑntī·). 1491. [f. prec. + -EE¹.] *Law.* The person to whom a grant or conveyance is made.

Grantor (grɑntǭ·ɹ). 1626. [– AFr. *grantor*; see GRANT *v.*, -OR 2.] *Law.* One who makes a conveyance in legal form.

‖**Granula** (græ·niŭlă). *Pl.* **-læ**; also †**laes.** 1658. [mod. L., irreg. dim. of *granum* = late L. *granulum*.] = GRANULE.

Granular (græ·niŭlăɹ), *a.* 1794. [f. late L. *granulum* (see prec.) + -AR¹.] **1.** Consisting of grains or granules. **2.** Having a granulated surface or structure 1833. **3.** Of the nature of a granule or granules 1834.

1. Dynamite..is a solid g. explosive 1868. Hence **Gra·nularly** *adv.* So **Gra·nulary** *a.*

Granulate (græ·niŭlĕt), *a.* 1793. [f. late L. *granulum* GRANULE + -ATE².] = GRANULATED *ppl. a.* 2. ¶Also in pseudo-L. comb. form *granulato-*.

Granulate (græ·niŭleⁱt), *v.* 1666. [f. as prec. + -ATE³.] **1.** *trans.* To form into granules or grains; *intr.* for *refl.* to become granular. **2.** *trans.* To raise in granules or small asperities; to roughen the surface of 1691. **3.** *intr.* in *Path.* Of a wound, etc.: To develop small prominences, producing a roughened surface, as if sprinkled with granules 1737.

Granulated (græ·niŭleⁱtėd), *ppl. a.* 1677. [f. GRANULATE *v.* + -ED¹.] **1.** Formed into, or consisting of, granules, or grain-like bodies 1694. **2.** Having the surface raised in granules or small prominences. **3.** *Path.* = GRANULAR *a.* 2. 1835.

2. *G. glass*, a kind of roughened glass used in stained windows.

Granulation (græniŭlēⁱ·ʃən). 1612. [f. as prec.; see -ATION. With sense 1 cf. mod.L. (*Alch.*) *granulatio*.] **1.** *gen.* The act or process of forming into granules or grains; the being so formed; *concr.* a granular formation. **2.** *Path.* The formation of grain-like prominences on sores when healing 1786; *concr.* in *pl.* the grain-like bodies, so formed 1739. **3.** *Bot.* and *Zool.* **a.** The formation of granular bodies on the surface of a plant, a crustacean, etc. **b.** *concr.* The granular structure, or (*pl.*) the granules, so formed. 1796. **4.** *attrib.*, as *g.-tissue*, etc. 1873.

2. b. Granulations formed, and a cicatrix took place ABERNETHY.

Granulator (græ·niŭleⁱtəɹ). 1839. [f. as prec. + -OR 2.] One who or that which granulates; *spec.* a granulating-machine.

Granule (græ·niul). 1652. [– late L. *granulum*, dim. of L. *granum* GRAIN *sb.*¹; see -ULE.] A small grain; a small compact particle; a pellet. Also *attrib.*

G. is the best word to describe the luminous particles on the Sun's surface 1867.

Granuliferous (græniŭli·fĕrəs), *a.* 1840. [f. late L. *granulum* (see prec.) + -FEROUS.] Bearing granules or granulations.

Granuliform (grĕniŭ·lifǭɹm), *a.* 1847. [f. as prec. + -FORM.] Having a granular structure.

Granulite (græ·niŭləit). 1849. [f. GRANULE + -ITE[1] 2 b.] *Geol.* A rock consisting of feldspar and quartz intimately mixed. Hence **Granuli·tic** *a.*

Granulo- (græ·niŭlo), comb. f. L. *granulum* GRANULE, with sense 'granular and —', as in *g.-adipose*, etc.

Granulose (græniŭlōᵘ·s). 1852. [A. *sb.*, f. GRANULE + -OSE[2]; B. *adj.* + -OSE[1].]
A. *sb.* The main constituent (the other being cellulose) of the starch granule, which gives a blue colour with iodine, and is converted into sugar by the saliva 1875.
B. *adj.* = GRANULAR.

Granulous (græ·niŭləs), *a.* 1547. [– Fr. *granuleux* or med.L. *granulosus*; in later use directly f. GRANULE + -OUS.] = GRANULAR, in various senses.

Grape (grēⁱp), *sb.* ME. [Earlier in *win grape* 'wine-cluster', cluster of grapes (XIII), f. OE. *win* WINE + *grape* – OFr. *grape* (mod. *grappe* bunch of grapes), prob. a verbal sb. f. *graper* gather (grapes), f. *grape, grappe* hook :– Rom. **grap(p)o* – Gmc. **krăppon* (OHG. *krāpfo*) hook, rel. to CRAMP. See WINEBERRY.] **1.** One of the berries, growing in clusters on a vine, from the juice of which wine is made. Chiefly *pl.* **b.** Put for wine 1636. †**2.** *transf.* The berry of other plants –1601. **3.** The plant that produces grapes; the vine; chiefly with some word prefixed, as *Frontignac, Muscatel*, etc. *g.* ME. **4.** *Mil.* = GRAPE-SHOT. Now only *collect. sing.* 1687. **5.** *Farriery. pl.* A diseased growth resembling a bunch of grapes on the pastern of a horse, mule, etc.; also on the pleura 1600. **6.** The knob or pommel at the rear end of a cannon; formerly called the CASCABEL 1864.
1. Do men gather grapes of thorns *Matt.* 7:16. **b.** He bad me taste of it; and 'twas—the Grape FITZGERALD. **3.** *Seaside g.* = *g.-tree* (q.v.).
Comb.: **g.-berry-moth** (*U.S.*) = *grape-moth*; **-cure,** treatment by a diet of grapes; **-eater,** the Australian bird *Zosterops chloronotus*; **-fern,** a plant of the genus *Botrychium*, from the appearance of its fructification; †**-flower** = *grape-hyacinth*; **-fruit** (*U.S.*), the pomelo; **-fungus,** a mould (*Oidium tuckeri*) on vines, vine-mildew; **g. hop,** a variety of hop, so called because the cones hang in clusters like bunches of grapes; **-hopper** (*U.S.*), an insect destructive to vine-leaves; **-hyacinth** (see HYACINTH); **-louse** (*U.S.*) the phylloxera; **-moth** (*U.S.*), *Eudemis botrana*, the larva of which devours grapes; **-pear,** *Amelanchier botryapium*; **-sugar** = DEXTROSE or GLUCOSE; **-tree,** (*a*) in W. Indies, a tree of the genus *Coccoloba*; (*b*) a grape-vine; **-weevil** (*U.S.*), a weevil (*Cœliodes* or *Craponius inæqualis*) which destroys green grapes; **-worm** (*U.S.*), the larva of the g.-moth.
Hence **Gra·peless** *a.* having no grapes; wanting the flavour of grapes. **Gra·pelet,** †**Gra·peling,** a small g.; also *transf.*

Grapery (grēⁱ·pěri). 1812. [f. GRAPE *sb.* + -ERY.] A building in which grapes are grown; a plantation of vines; a vinery.

Gra·pe-shot. 1747. [f. GRAPE *sb.* + SHOT *sb.*[1]] Small cast-iron balls, strongly connected together, so as to form a charge for cannon.

Gra·pe-stone. 1589. [f. GRAPE *sb.* + STONE.] **1.** The seed of a grape. **2.** *Min.* Occas. used for BOTRYOLITE 1860.

Gra·pe-vine. Now chiefly *U.S.* and *Austral.* 1736. **1.** The vine which bears grapes; any species of the genus *Vitis*, esp. *V. vinifera*. **2. a.** A canard: current during the American Civil War, and short for 'a despatch by grape-vine telegraph' 1867. **b.** A figure in skating 1868.

Grapeys. ME. [– OFr. *grapois, graspeis*, also *craspois* :– med.L. *craspiscis*, f. L. *crassus* fat, CRASS + *piscis* fish. See GRAMPUS.] The flesh of the grampus.

Graph (grɑf), *sb.* 1878. [orig. short for 'graphic formula'; see GRAPHIC.] **1.** A symbolic diagram expressing a system of chemical or mathematical connections. **2.** *Alg.* A graphical representation of the locus of a function; the traced curve of an equation 1886. **3.** A line or system of lines symbolizing variations of occurrence or intensity.

Graph (grɑf), *v.* 1898. [– Gr. γράφειν.] *Math.* To trace (a curve) from its equation; to trace the curve corresponding to (a given equation).

-graph (grɑf), repr. Fr. *-graphe*, L. *-graphus*, Gr. -γραφος. The Greek termination was chiefly used in the sense 'written', whence *autograph, holograph, photograph*, etc.; sometimes in the active sense 'that writes'. In many of the words in *-graph* this element expresses the meaning 'instrument that marks, portrays, or records', as *heliograph, seismograph*; the earliest of these is *telegraph* (1794), from French.

-grapher (grăfəɹ), an ending first found early in XVI. The normal mode of anglicizing a real or assumed Gr. word in -γραφος denoting a personal agent, and of providing a personal designation correlative to sb. in -GRAPHY denoting an art or science.

Graphic (græ·fik), *a.* 1637. [– L. *graphicus* – Gr. γραφικός, f. γραφή drawing, writing.] †**1.** Drawn with a pencil or pen. B. JONS. **2.** Of or pertaining to drawing or painting 1756. **3.** Vividly descriptive, life-like 1669. **4.** Of or pertaining to writing 1774. **b.** Of a mineral: Presenting an appearance of written or printed characters 1814. **5.** Pertaining to the use of diagrams, linear figures, or symbolic curves 1866. **b.** Concerned with position and form; opp. to *metric*. CLIFFORD. **6.** quasi-*sb.* in **Graphics:** the use of diagrams as a means of calculation 1889.
2. *G. arts*: drawing, painting, engraving, etching, etc. G. representations LAMB. **4. b.** *G. granite*..a binary compound of felspar and quartz—the quartz being disposed through the felspar matrix like lines of Arabic writing PAGE. *G. gold, ore*, or *tellurium*: = SYLVANITE. **5.** *G. formula*: in *Chem.*, a formula in which lines are employed to indicate the connections of the elements represented by the symbols. *G. method, solution*: a method of solving problems (e.g. in *Statics*) by the construction of a diagram from which the result is obtained by direct measurement instead of calculation. *G. method*: the method of recording movements of a part of the body by some automatic instrument, e.g., those of the pulse by the sphygmograph. Hence **Gra·phicness,** vividness of description.

-graphic (græ·fik), repr. Gr. -γραφικός, as in *historiographic*. In Eng. adjs. prob. formed on sbs. in *-graphy* (or *-graph*) + -IC. The prevailing sense is 'of or pertaining to ——graphy.'

Graphical (græ·fikăl), *a.* 1610. [f. as GRAPHIC; see -ICAL.] = GRAPHIC *a.* 1–5. Hence **Gra·phical-ly** *adv.*, **-ness.**

Graphiology (græfiǫ·lŏdʒi). 1854. [irreg. f. Gr. γράφειν + -LOGY.] = GRAPHOLOGY 2.

-graphist, sometimes used instead of -GRAPHER in anglicizing Gr. words in -γράφος or forming derivs. from sbs. in *-graphy*; as in *telegraphist*, etc.

Graphite (græ·fəit). 1796. [– G. *graphit* (Werner, 1789), f. Gr. γράφειν write (the stuff being used for pencils); see -ITE[1] 2b.] A crystalline allotropic form of carbon (see CARBON), called also BLACK LEAD and PLUMBAGO. Hence **Gra·phitoid, Graphitoi·dal** *adjs.* having the appearance of g.

Graphitic (grafi·tik), *a.* 1864. [f. prec. + -IC.] Of, pertaining to, or of the nature of graphite.
Graphitic acid, an acid produced from graphite by the repeated action of chlorate of potassium and nitric acid. *G. carbon*, that portion of the carbon in iron and steel which is present as graphite.

Grapholite (græ·fŏləit). 1796. [f. Gr. γραφο-, comb. f. γραφή writing + -LITE.] Any species of slate suitable for writing on.

Graphology (grăfǫ·lŏdʒi). 1878. [f. as prec. + -LOGY.] **1.** The study of handwriting 1882. **2.** *esp.* The art or science of inferring character, disposition, and aptitudes from handwriting 1886. **3.** The system of graphic formulæ 1878. Hence **Grapholo·gic, -al** *a.* of or pertaining to g.

Graphometer (grăfǫ·mĭtəɹ). 1696. [– Fr. *graphomètre* (1597), f. as prec. + *-mètre* -METER.] A semicircle, used for measuring angles in surveying. †Also, a goniometer used in crystallography.

Graphoscope (græ·fŏskōᵘp). 1879. [f. Gr. γραφο-, comb. form of γραφή writing + -SCOPE.] An apparatus containing a magnifying lens arranged for viewing engravings, photographs, etc.

Graphotype (græ·fŏtəip), *sb.* 1866. [f. as prec. + -TYPE.] A process for producing a design in relief for surface-printing; also, the block or plate so produced. Hence **Gra·photype** *v. trans.* to print by means of the g.

-graphy (grăfi) = Fr., G. *-graphie*, L. *-graphia*, repr. Gr. -γραφία in Gr. or quasi-Gr. sbs. Some of the sbs. with this ending denote processes or styles of writing, drawing, or graphic representation, as *stenography, lithography, photography*, etc. More commonly they are names of descriptive sciences, as *geography, bibliography*, etc.

Grapnel (græ·pnĕl), *sb.* ME. [– AFr. **grapenel*, f. synon. OFr. *grapon* (mod. *grappin*) – Gmc. **krăppon*; see GRAPE, -EL[2].] **1.** An instrument with iron claws for throwing in order to seize and hold an object, esp. an enemy's ship. **2.** A small anchor with three or more flukes, used esp. for boats, and for securing a balloon on its descent ME. **3.** Any of various instruments for grasping or clutching 1875. Hence **Gra·pnel** *v.* to catch or seize with a g.

Grapple (græ·p'l), *sb.* 1530. [– OFr. *grapil* – Pr. *grapil*, f. *grapa* hook; see prec., GRAPE.]
I. 1. = GRAPNEL 1. Also *transf.* and *fig.* †**2.** = GRAPNEL 2. –1807. **3.** = GRAPNEL 3. 1593.
1. The end of the lever, with an iron g. affixed to it, was lowered upon the Roman ships ARNOLD.
II. [f. the vb.] The action of grappling, or grappling *with*; the state of being grappled; the grip of a wrestler; a contest in which the combatants grip one another. Said also of immaterial contests. 1601.
In the G., I boorded them *Haml.* IV. vi. 18.
Comb: **g.-plant,** a S. Afr. herb, *Uncaria procumbens*, the fruit of which has many projecting claw-like hooks; **-shot,** a projectile attached to a cable, with hinged flukes which catch in the rigging of a ship in distress.

Grapple (græ·p'l), *v.* 1530. [f. GRAPPLE *sb.*] **1.** *trans.* To seize or hold (a ship, etc.) with a grapnel; to fasten *to* something with grappling-irons. Also *fig.* **2.** *intr.* for *refl.* To fasten oneself firmly (*to* an object) by means of a grapple. Also *fig.* 1563. **3.** *trans.* To take hold of with the hands; to seize; to grip firmly; *hence*, to come to close quarters with 1583. **4.** *intr.* To take a firm hold, as with a grapple, esp. in wrestling; to get a tight grip; to contend in close fight. Also with *together*. 1583. **5.** To grope (*rare*). ?*Obs.* 1596.
1. *fig.* The friends thou hast, and their adoption tride, G. them to thy Soule, with hoopes of Steele *Haml.* I. iii. 62. **3.** Man grapples man COWPER. **4.** To tug or g., and to close MILT.
Phr. **To g. with** —. **a.** To make fast one's ship to (an enemy) with grappling-irons; to come to close quarters with. **b.** To grip as in wrestling; to close with bodily. **c.** To encounter hand to hand; also *fig.* **d.** *esp.* To try to overcome (a difficulty); to take in hand (a task, etc.).

†**Gra·pplement.** *rare.* [f. GRAPPLE *v.* + -MENT.] A grappling. SPENSER.

Grappler (græ·pləɹ). 1628. [f. GRAPPLE *v.* + -ER[1].] One who or that which grapples; a grappling-iron, a grapnel; *slang*, a hand.

Grappling (græ·pliŋ), *vbl. sb.* 1598. [f. as prec. + -ING[1].] **1.** The action of GRAPPLE *v.* 1601. †**2.** A place where one may grapple a vessel –1784. **3.** *concr.* = GRAPPLE *sb.* I. 1, 2. 1598.
2. *To come, bring to a g.*: to come to anchor. **3.** The crooked Grappling's steely Hold they cast ROWE. *Comb.* **g.-hook, -iron** = GRAPNEL.

Grapsoid (græ·psoid), *a.* 1852. [f. mod.L. *grapsus* (cf. Gr. γραψαῖος crab) + -OID.] Of or pertaining to the genus *Grapsus* of crabs, or the family *Grapsidæ*.

Graptolite (græ·ptŏləit). 1838. [f. Gr. γραπτός painted or marked with letters + -LITE; in 1 – mod.L. *graptolithus* (Linn.).] †**1.** Any stone showing a resemblance to a drawing –1847. **2.** A fossil zoophyte of the genus *Graptolites* (or *Graptolithus*), or of the family of which this genus is the type 1841. Hence **Graptoli·tic** *a.* of, pertaining to, or containing graptolites.

Grapy (grēⁱ·pi). *a.* ME. [f. GRAPE *sb.* + -Y[1].] **1.** Of or pertaining to grapes or to the vine; composed or savouring of grapes 1594. †**2.** Epithet of the CHOROID coat of the eye. (Cf. UVEA.) –1696.
1. His soul quite sousèd lay in g. blood P. FLETCHER.

Grasp (grasp), *sb.* 1561. [f. the vb.] **1.** That which grasps or is grasped; the fluke of an anchor, a handle. Now only *Naut.* the handle of an oar. **2.** The action of grasping; the grip of the hand; †an embrace 1606. **3.** *fig.* **a.** Firm hold or control; mastery 1605. **b.** Intellectual hold; *esp.* mastery of the whole of a subject; hence, mental comprehensiveness 1683.

2. Beshrew the witch!..she..flies the graspes of loue SHAKS. Phr. *Within, beyond* (*one's*) *g.* **3. a.** To rescue liberty from the g. of executive power 1852. **b.** Men of immense mental g. RUSKIN.

Grasp (grasp), *v.* [Late ME. *graspe*, also *grapse*, perh. :– OE. **græpsan* :– Gmc. **ȝraipisōn*, parallel to **ȝraipōjan* GROPE; but perh. of LG. origin (cf. LG., EFris. *grapsen*).] **1.** *intr.* To make clutches with the hand; often = GROPE. *Obs.* exc. in *to grasp at.* †**b.** To grapple *with* –1766. **2.** To clutch at; to seize greedily 1642. **3.** To seize and hold firmly (*lit.* and *fig.*) 1586. †**4.** To clasp in the arms, embrace –1766. **5.** To grip 1774. **6.** To lay hold of with the mind; to become completely cognizant of or acquainted with; to comprehend 1680.

1. 2 *Hen. VI*, III. ii. 172. Like quicksilver [which] ..grasped at, slips away COWPER. To g. at a proposal W. IRVING. **2.** *Provb.* G. all, lose all. **3.** Thy Hand is made to graspe a Palmers staffe SHAKS. *To g. the nettle*: *fig.* to attack a difficulty boldly. To g. an argument JOWETT. **6.** To g. the eternal and unchangeable JOWETT. Hence **Gra·spable** *a.* that may be grasped. **Gra·sper,** one who or that which grasps; esp. a grasping person.

Grasping (gra·spiŋ), *ppl. a.* 1577. [f. GRASP *v.* + -ING².] **1.** That grasps; tenacious. **2.** *fig.* Eager for gain, greedy, avaricious 1748.

2. The corrupt, g. and ambitious part of human nature BURKE. Hence **Gra·sping-ly** *adv.*, **-ness.**

Graspless (gra·splės), *a.* 1794. [f. GRASP *sb.* + -LESS.] Without grip; relaxed.

In its g. hold her hand Felt that the sceptre shivered 1886.

Grass (gras), *sb.* [OE. *græs*, *gærs* = OFris. *gres, gers*, OS. (Du.), OHG. (G.), ON., Goth. *gras* :– Gmc. **ȝrasam*, f. **ȝra-* **ȝro-* (see GREEN, GROW).] **1.** Herbage in general, the blades or leaves and stalks of which are eaten by horses, cattle, etc. Also, in a narrower sense = 2 b. Now only *collect. sing.* **2.** A kind of grass. †**a.** A (medicinal) herb –1587. **b.** One of the non-cereal *Gramineæ*, or other similar plants. Often defined as *blue-, bunch-, dog-*, etc. *g.* (see those wds.). *Grass of the Andes*: an oat-grass, *Arrhenatherum avenaceum. G. of Parnassus*: a name for *Parnassia palustris.* 1548. **c.** Any species of plants grown for pasture 1677. **d.** *Bot.* Any plant belonging to the order *Gramineæ* (*Graminaceæ*), which includes grass (sense 1) together with the cereals (barley, oats, rye, wheat, etc.), the reeds, bamboos, etc. 1611. **3.** An individual plant of grass or †corn; a blade or spire of grass. Now only in *pl.* and *rare.* ME. †**4.** The blade stage of growth; corn in the blade –1733. **5.** Pasture; the condition of an animal at pasture 1471. **b.** *fig.* of persons rusticated, or going away for a holiday, etc. 1589. **6.** Grazing OE. **7.** Pasture-land 1609. **8.** The yearly growth of grass; hence, spring and early summer, when the grass grows 1485. **9.** Grass-covered ground ME.; the earth's surface above a mine 1776; *slang*, the ground 1625. **10.** Short for *sparrow-grass*, corrupt f. ASPARAGUS. Now *vulgar.* 1747.

1. Her treading would not bend a blade of grasse B. JONS. *fig.* All flesh is grasse *Isa.* 40:6. Phr. *To cut the g. from under a person's feet*: to thwart, trip him up. *To let no g. grow under one's feet*: to make the most of one's time. **3.** Strange grasses were sometimes perceived in her hair DICKENS. **4.** *fig.* Our faith is yet in the grasse 1579. **5.** In Cheapside shall my Palfrey go to grasse SHAKS. *fig.* If to g. sent from Oxon or Granta 1801. **6.** Not as much as the g. of a goat 1880. **7.** Half the lands of a farm..ought to be g. A. YOUNG. **8.** Six years old last G. 1685. **9.** About 70 tons [of quartz] are now at g. awaiting crushing 1890.

Comb.: **g.-bass,** a freshwater edible fish (*Pomoxys sparoides*) of the U.S.; **-beef,** the flesh of g.-fed oxen; **-bird,** (*a*) a name for *Tringa maculata*, and other American sandpipers; (*b*) in Australasia, one or more species of *Sphenœacus*; **-bleached** *ppl. a.* bleached by exposure on g.; so *g.-bleaching* vbl. sb.; **-butter,** that made from the milk of cows at g.; **-chat** = WHINCHAT; **-comber,** a sailor's term for one who has been a farm-labourer; **-drake** = CORN-CRAKE; **-finch,** (*a*) a common American sparrow (*Poœcetes gramineus*); (*b*) any Australian finch of the genus *Poëphila*; **-flesh,** the flesh gained by an animal at g.; **-hand,** (*a*) a compositor temporarily engaged; (*b*) an irregular cursive hand used by the Chinese and Japanese in business and private writing; **-ill,** a disease of lambs; **-lamb,** (*a*) a lamb suckled by a dam which is running on pasture land; (*b*) the flesh of the same; **-lawn,** a fine gauze-like material, the colour of unbleached linen; **-moth,** one of many small moths of the genus *Crambus* or family *Crambidæ*, found in dry meadows; **-oil,** one of several fragrant essential oils obtained in India by distillation from grasses (*Andropogon* and other genera); **-parakeet,** an Australian parakeet of the genus *Euphema* or *Melopsittacus*; †**-poly,** *Lythrum hyssopifolia*; **-quit,** one of several finches of tropical America, esp. species of *Phonipara*; **-rope** (*Naut.*), a rope made of coir; **-snake** (*a*) the common ringed snake (*Tropidonotus natrix*); (*b*) the common green snake of U.S.; **-snipe** *U.S.* = *grass-bird* (*a*); **-sparrow** = *grass-bird* (*a*); **-sponge,** an inferior kind of sponge from Florida and the Bahamas; **-table** (*Arch.*) = EARTH-*table*; **-warbler** *Austral.*, a bird of the genus *Cisticola*; **-wrack,** a seaweed (*Zostera marina*), with g.-like leaves.

Grass (gras), *v.* 1460. [f. prec. sb. Cf. GRAZE *v.*¹] †**1.** *trans.* To plunge or sink in grass –1670. **2.** *trans.* †**a.** To GRAZE (cattle). **b.** To supply (cattle) with grass. 1500. **3.** To cover, or (*intr.*) become covered, with grass or turf 1573. **4.** To lay or stretch on the grass or on the ground (see quots.) 1765. **5.** *intr. Printing.* To do casual or jobbing work 1894. **6.** *Mining.* To bring to the surface 1890.

3. The graves being levelled and grassed over 1895. **4.** To g. flax for bleaching 1765. A blow ..which floored or grassed him 1814. To g. a fish 1856. **6.** Stone grassed from the 50 foot shaft 1890.

†**Grassant,** *a.* 1659. [– *grassant-*, pres. ppl. stem of L. *grassari* lie in wait; see -ANT.] Roaming about, or lying in wait, with evil intent –1734.

†**Grassation.** 1610. [L. *grassatio* rioting (Pliny), f. *grassat-*, pa. ppl. stem of *grassari*; see prec., -ION.] The action of making violent assaults; also, lying in wait to attack –1680. So †**Grassator,** a footpad, violent assailant.

Gra·ss-cloth. 1857. **a.** A fine light cloth, resembling linen, woven from the fibres of the inner bark of the **grass-cloth plant** (*Bœhmeria nivea*). **b.** A thick fabric made in the Canary Islands from vegetable fibre.

Grassed (grast), *ppl. a.* 1731. [f. GRASS *sb.* and *v.* + -ED.] **1.** Grown or covered with grass. **2.** *Golf.* Of a driver, etc.: Having a slightly filed-back face 1878.

Grass-green, *a.* (Stress variable.) [OE. *græsgrēne.*] **1.** Of the colour of grass. Also *absol.* **2.** Green with grass 1602.

2. At his head a grasse-greene Turfe *Ham.* IV. v. 31.

†**Grasshop.** [OE. *gærshoppa, -e*, Orm *gresshoppe* (f. *gærs* GRASS + *hoppa*, agent-noun of *hoppian* HOP *v.*¹), perh. after OSw. *gräshoppare* or LG. *grashüpper* (G. *grashüpfer*); cf. synon. OS. *feldhoppo* 'field-hopper'.] A grasshopper, locust –1607.

Grasshopper (gra·shǫpəɹ). ME. [Extended form of GRASSHOP.] **1.** Any orthopterous insect of the families *Acridiidæ* and *Locustidæ*, remarkable for their powers of leaping, and the chirping sound produced by the males. **2.** In a pianoforte: = HOPPER¹. 1807. **3.** An artificial bait for fish 1867.

1. The grashopper shall be a burden *Eccles.* 12:5. *Comb.*: **g.-beam,** a form of working-beam in steam-engines, pivoted at one end instead of in the centre (hence *g.-engine, -principle*); **-lark** = *grass-warbler*; **-sparrow,** a small U.S. sparrow of the genus *Coterniculus*, named from its note; **-warbler,** a small warbler, *Locustella nævia*, named from its note.

Grass land. 1689. Pasture or grazing land.

Gra·ssless, *a.* 1591. [f. GRASS *sb.* + -LESS.] Without grass.

Gra·ss-plat, -plot. 1610. [f. GRASS *sb.* + PLAT *sb.*², PLOT *sb.*] A piece of ground covered with turf, sometimes ornamented with flower-beds.

Here on this grasse-plot..To come, and sport SHAKS.

Gra·ss-tree. 1802. A name of several Australasian trees. The liliaceous genus *Xanthorrhœa*; *Richea dracophylla* and *R. pandanifolia* of Tasmania; the *Pseudopanax crassifolium* of N. Zealand; the cabbage-tree of N. Zealand, *Cordyline australis*; the juncaceous plant *Kingia australis.*

Grass widow. 1528. [Cf. MLG. *graswedewe*, Du. *grasweduwe*, Sw. *gräsenka*, Da. *græsenke*; also G. *strohwitwe* 'straw widow'.] **1.** An unmarried woman who has cohabited with one or more men. ?*Obs.* **2.** A married woman whose husband is absent from her 1859.

1. I have made more matches in my time than a grass widow GOLDSM. Hence **Grass-wi·dowhood.** So **Grass-widower,** a man living apart from his wife.

Grassy (gra·si), *a.* 1513. [f. GRASS *sb.* + -Y¹.] **1.** Covered with or abounding in grass. **2.** Pertaining to, consisting of, or containing grass 1697. **3.** Resembling grass 1567.

1. The grassye ground with daintye Daysies dight SPENSER. **2.** G. Fare DRYDEN. **3.** Grassie colour 1567. Hence **Gra·ssiness** (*rare*).

Grate (grēⁱt), *sb.* ME. [– OFr. *grate* (Aimé), Sp. *grada* hurdle, corresp. to It. *grata* grate, gridiron, hurdle (cf. med.L. *grata* hurdle), pointing to Rom. **crata*, **grata*, for L. *cratis* hurdle. See CRATE.] **1.** A framework of bars or laths, parallel to or crossing each other, fixed in a door, etc., to permit communication while preventing ingress. Now somewhat *rare.* **2.** A similar framework for other purposes; *rarely*, †a gridiron ME. †**3.** The railing round a monument, building, etc. –1645. **4.** A frame of metal bars for holding the fuel in a fireplace or furnace. Hence, the fireplace itself. 1605. **5.** *Mining.* A screen used when stamping ores 1776. †**6.** A barred place of confinement, a prison or cage –1777. †**7.** One of the spaces between the bars of a grate (*rare*) –1649.

1. But in the same [doore] a little g. was pight, Through which he sent his voyce SPENSER. **4.** An old-fashioned G. consumes Coals, but gives no Heat STEELE. **6.** Else you had look'd through the g., like a Geminy of Baboones SHAKS. *Comb.* **g.-area, -surface,** the area in square feet covered by the fire-bars of a furnace or boiler.

†**Grate,** *a.* 1523. [– L. *gratus* pleasing, thankful. Cf. Fr. †*grate* (Cotgr.).] **1.** Pleasing, acceptable –1665. **2.** Grateful –1596. Hence †**Gra·tely** *adv.*

Grate (grēⁱt), *v.*¹ ME. [– OFr. *grater* (mod. *gratter*) :– Rom. **grattare* – Gmc. **krattōn* (OHG. *krazzōn*, G. *kratzen* scratch).] †**1.** *trans.* To scrape, file, abrade; to rub harshly –1660. **2.** To reduce to small particles by rasping or rubbing against a rough or indented surface. Often with *in, into, over.* ME. **3.** *fig.* To fret, harass, irritate. Now *rare.* 1555. **4.** *intr. To grate on* or *upon*: †**a.** To oppress with exactions or importunities –1705. **b.** To have an irritating effect *on* or *upon* 1635. †**5.** *trans.* To obtain by oppression or importunity –1542. †**6.** *trans.* To make (a weapon) strike or bite. *intr.* Of a weapon: To strike or bite. –1700. **7.** *trans.* To rub harshly against (something) 1555. **8.** *intr.* To rub *against* with a harsh, grinding noise; to sound harshly; to move creakingly 1596. **b.** *trans.* To produce by jarring movement. MILT. †**9.** *intr.* To dwell querulously *upon* a subject –1698.

1. *Tr. & Cr.* III. ii. 195. **2.** To g. a Nutmeg 1732. **3.** This outrageous merriment grates my spirits 1826. **4. a.** *Merry W.* II. ii. 6. **b.** To choose What grates upon the sense GEO. ELIOT. **7.** His galley now Grated the quay-stones KEATS. **8.** Their lean and flashy songs G. on their scrannel pipes of wretched straw MILT. A key grated in the lock 1797. **b.** Th' infernal dores..on thir hinges g. Harsh Thunder MILT.

Grate (grēⁱt), *v.*² 1528. [f. GRATE *sb.*] †**1.** *trans.* To confine within grates or bars. MORE. **2.** To fit or furnish with a grate or grating 1547.

2. The windows grated with iron MASSINGER.

Grateful (grēⁱ·tfŭl), *a.* 1552. [f. GRATE *a.* + -FUL; the unusual formation with an adj. may have been suggested by It. *gradevole* pleasing.] **1.** Pleasing to the mind or the senses, agreeable, acceptable. Now only of things. 1553. **2.** Of persons, their actions, etc.: Feeling gratitude; actuated by or manifesting gratitude; thankful 1552. **b.** Of land: Responsive to labour, fertile 1832.

1. The g. and cooling shade SCOTT. **2.** I cannot giue thee lesse to be cal'd gratefull SHAKS. A g. Sacrifice WESLEY. **Gra·teful-ly** *adv.*, **-ness.**

Grater (grēⁱ·təɹ). ME. [Partly – OFr. *grateor, -our*, partly f. GRATE *v.*¹; see -ER¹, -ER².] **1.** An instrument with a rough indented surface used for grating or rasping; *esp.* a kitchen utensil for grating ginger, nutmegs, etc. †**2.** One who or that which grates; chiefly *fig.* –1628.

2. He is no base G. of his Tythes, and will not wrangle for the odde Egge 1628.

‖**Gratia Dei** (grēⁱ·ʃiă dī·əi). ME. [med.L. = 'grace of God'; cf. HERB-GRACE, Fr. *grace Dieu*.] The Hedge Hyssop (*Gratiola officinalis*); formerly also the Lesser Centaury (*Erythræa centaureum*) and *Geranium pratense*.

Graticulation (grătikiŭlēⁱ·ʃən). 1727. [– Fr. *graticulation*, f. *graticuler*, f. *graticule*; see next, -ATION.] The division of a design or plan into squares with the object of reproducing it accurately on a different scale; *concr.* a surface so divided.

Graticule (græ·tikiul). 1887. [– Fr. *graticule* – med.L. *graticula* for (also cl.L.) *craticula* small gridiron, dim. of L. *cratis* hurdle. See GRATE *sb.*] A design or plan divided into squares to facilitate its reproduction on other scales; the style or pattern of such division.

Gratification (grætifikēⁱ·ʃən). 1576. [–(O)Fr. *gratification* or L. *gratificatio*, f. *gratificat-* pa. ppl. stem of L. *gratificari*; see next, -ION.] **1.** The act of gratifying 1598. **2.** The state or fact of being gratified or pleased; enjoyment, satisfaction 1712. **b.** with *a.* and *pl.* An instance of this; a thing that gratifies or pleases 1711. **3.** A reward, recompense, gratuity; a bribe 1576.

1. The g. of his love of domineering MILL. **2.** G. is of the mind when receiving wisdom and knowledge JOWETT. **3.** Giveing the g. of twoe thowsand poundes 1624.

Gratify (græ·tifəi), *v.* 1540. [– Fr. *gratifier*, or its source L. *gratificari* do a favour to, make a present of, f. *gratus* pleasing, thankful; see GRATE *a.*, -FY.] †**1.** *trans.* To show gratitude to; to reward, requite –1655. **2.** To make a present (usually of money) or give a gratuity to, esp. as a recompense, or as a bribe. Now *arch.* 1590. †**3.** To express pleasure at –1612. **4.** To give pleasure to; to please, oblige; to do a favour to 1568. **5.** To please by compliance; to humour, indulge 1665; †to comply with; to concede (an objection) –1703. †**6.** To render acceptable –1698.

1. It remaines..To gratifie his Noble seruice SHAKS. **2.** The Messenger he richly gratifies 1613. **4.** Pilate himself (to gratifie the Jews) delivered him to be crucified HOBBES. **5.** Mankind have ungoverned passions which they will g. at any rate BUTLER. **6.** *L. L. L.* IV. ii. 161. Hence **Gra·tifiedly** *adv.* with pleasure or satisfaction. **Gra·tifier. Gra·tifying** *ppl. a.* affording pleasure. **Gra·tifyingly** *adv.*

Gratility (grăti·lĭti). Joc. perversion of *gratuity* in *Twel. N.* II. iii. 27.

‖**Gratin** (gratæṅ). 1846. [Fr., f. *gratter*, earlier *grater* GRATE *v.*¹] *Cookery.* A manner of preparing viands by treating them with raspings of bread and cooking them between two fires so as to produce a light crust; hence, the dish so cooked.

Grating (grēⁱ·tiŋ), *vbl. sb.*¹ ME. [f. GRATE *v.*¹ + -ING¹.] **1.** The action of GRATE *v.*¹ **2.** The discordant sound made by rubbing harshly against something 1611. **3.** *fig.* Irritation, fretting. SOUTH.

Grating (grēⁱ·tiŋ), *vbl. sb.*² 1597. [f. GRATE *sb.* and *v.*² + -ING¹.] **1.** The action of GRATE *v.*² (*rare*). **2.** = GRATE *sb.* 1, 2. 1739; *esp. Naut.* the open wood-work cover for the hatchway 1626. **3.** *Optics.* An arrangement of parallel wires in a plane, or a surface of glass or polished metal ruled with a series of very close fine parallel lines, designed to produce spectra by diffraction 1877. *Comb.* **g. spectrum,** a diffraction spectrum produced by a g.

Grating (grēⁱ·tiŋ), *ppl. a.* 1563. [f. GRATE *v.*¹ + -ING².] **1.** That grates, in senses of the vb. **2.** That makes a grinding or creaking sound; hence, sounding harsh or discordant 1718. Hence **Gra·tingly** *adv.*

‖**Gratiola** (grǣtəi·ŏlă). 1579. [mod.L., f. *gratia* grace; so called from its supposed medicinal virtues. Cf. Fr. *gratiole* (XVI), and see GRATIA DEI.] *Bot.* A genus of scrophulariaceous plants, of which the best known species is *G. officinalis*, the Hedge Hyssop.

Gratiolin (grǣtəi·ŏlin). 1886. [f. prec. + -IN¹.] *Chem.* A bitter resinous principle obtained from *Gratiola officinalis*.

Gratis (grēⁱ·tis). 1477. [L. *gratis*, contr. f. *gratiis* lit. out of favour or kindness, abl. pl. of *gratia*, grace, favour.]

A. *adv.* **1.** For nothing; without charge, cost, or pay; gratuitously. †**2.** Without a reason or due cause –1818.

B. *adj.* Given or done for nothing; free, gratuitous 1659.

No Chinke no Drink; Nothing is G. now 1659.

Gratitude (græ·titiūd). 1500. [– Fr. *gratitude* or med.L. *gratitudo*, f. *gratus*; see GRATE *a.*, -TUDE.] **1.** The quality or condition of being grateful; a warm feeling of goodwill towards a benefactor; gratefulness. Also with *a.* and *pl.* 1565. †**2.** Grace, favour; a favour. Chiefly *Sc.* –1557. †**3.** A free gift; a gratuity, reward –1699.

1. Which g. Through flintie Tartars bosome would peepe forth, And answer thankes SHAKS.

Gratuitous (grătiū·itəs), *a.* 1656. [f. L. *gratuitus* freely given, spontaneous; for the formation cf. FORTUITOUS, and OFr. *gratuiteus* (Fr. †*-eux*), which may be the source.] **1.** Freely bestowed or obtained; granted without claim or merit; costing nothing to the recipient; free. **2.** Done, made, adopted, or assumed without any good ground or reason; uncalled-for; unjustifiable 1691. **b.** Of the agent: Acting without reason or justification 1864. †**3.** Requiring no proof. JOHNSON.

1. We..Mistake the G. Blessings of Heaven, for the Fruits of our Own Industry L'ESTRANGE. **2.** A g. interference with private rights 1844, supposition LINGARD. **b.** A g. liar SALA. Hence **Gratu·itous-ly** *adv.*, **-ness.**

Gratuity (grătiū·ĭti). 1523. [– OFr. *gratuité* or med.L. *gratuitas* gift, f. L. *gratus*; see GRATE *a.*, -ITY.] †**1.** Graciousness, favour; a favour, a kindness –1646. **2.** A gift or present (usu. of money), often in return for favours or services, the amount depending on the inclination of the giver; in bad sense, a bribe. Now, a 'tip'. 1540. †**b.** Payment, wages –1832. **3.** *spec.* A bounty, esp. that given to soldiers on re-enlistment, retirement, or discharge 1804. †**4.** = GRATITUDE 1. –1660. **5.** Gratuitousness (*rare*) 1858.

2. I..had a small g. above my wages JOHNSON. **b.** A large hundred marks annuitie, To be given me in gratuitie for done service and to come B. JONS.

Gratulant (græ·tiŭlănt), *a.* 1471. [f. *gratulant-*, pres. ppl. stem of L. *gratulari*; see next, -ANT.] Expressing joy or satisfaction; congratulatory.

†**Gra·tulate,** *a.* [– L. *gratulatus*, pa. pple. of *gratulari*; see next, -ATE².] To be rejoiced at. SHAKS.

There's more behinde that is more g. *Meas. for M.* V. i. 535.

Gratulate (græ·tiŭleⁱt), *v.* Now *arch.* and *poet.* 1556. [– *gratulat-*, pa. ppl. stem of L. *gratulari*, f. *gratus*; see GRATE *a.*, -ATE³.] **1.** *trans.* To express joy at the appearance of; to welcome; to greet. **2.** = CONGRATULATE 2. 1584. **3.** = CONGRATULATE 4. Const. *on, upon*, †*in*. 1598. Also *absol.* †**4.** To be grateful or show gratitude for; to thank –1673. †**5.** To recompense (a service, etc.) –1633. †**6.** To gratify, please –1809.

1. To g. the sweet return of morn MILT. **2.** I g. the newes B. JONS.

Gratulation (grætiŭlēⁱ·ʃən). 1482. [– OFr. *gratulation* or L. *gratulatio*, f. as prec.; see -ION.] **1.** A feeling of gratification, joy, or exultation. (Now only with mixture of sense 3.) **2.** Manifestation, or a manifestation, of joy 1549. **3.** The expression of pleasure at a person's success, good fortune, or the like; compliment, congratulation 1542; a complimentary or congratulatory speech 1614. †**4.** A welcome –1638. †**5.** Thanksgiving; also, an instance of this –1677. †**6.** = GRATIFICATION 3. –1628.

1. With great ioie of hart and godlie g. 1577. **3.** After this Complement, and some g. for the Kings victorie BACON.

Gratulatory (græ·tiŭlĕtəri), *a.* (*sb.*) 1555. [– late L. *gratulatorius*, f. as prec.; see -ORY². Cf. OFr. *gratulatoire*.] **1.** Expressing joy for the good fortune, etc. of another; congratulatory, complimentary 1577. †**2.** Expressing gratitude or thanks –1739. †**3.** *sb.* A congratulatory speech. NORTH.

1. G. poems 1763, cries 1867. **2.** No propiciatorie sacrifice but a gratulatorie sacrifice 1555. Hence **Gra·tulatorily** *adv.*

Graunt, obs. f. GRANT.

‖**Grauwacke** (grau·vakə). 1794. [G., f. *grau* GREY + *wacke* WACKE.] *Geol.* = GREYWACKE.

Gravamen (grăvēⁱ·men). *Pl.* **gravamina** (grăvēⁱ·mină). 1602. [– late L. *gravamen* physical inconvenience, in med.L. grievance, f. L. *gravare* weigh upon, oppress, f. *gravis* GRAVE *a.*¹] **1.** A grievance 1647. **2.** †**a.** A formal complaint or accusation –1880. **b.** *Eccl.* A memorial presented by the Lower House of Convocation to the Upper representing the existence of disorders or grievances in the church 1602. **3.** The part of an accusation that bears most heavily on the person or thing accused 1832.

3. The g. of the charge against the principle of utility MILL. So †**Gravament** (in sense 1).

Grave (grēⁱv), *sb.*¹ [OE. *græf* = OFris. *gref*, OS. *graf*, OHG. *grap* :– WGmc. **ȝraba*, parallel to N. and EGmc. **ȝrabō*, repr. by ON. *grǫf*, Goth. *graba*; f. **ȝrab-* GRAVE *v.*¹ The present form descends from OE. obl. forms.] **1.** A place of burial; an excavation in the earth for the reception of a corpse; formerly, †a mausoleum or the like. **b.** A grave-mound 1868. **2.** *occas.*, The condition or state of being buried, death ME. **3.** *rhet.* Anything that is, or may become, the receptacle of what is dead 1559. **4.** A pit or trench. *Obs.* exc. in sense of a trench for earthing up potatoes, etc. 1526.

1. Phr. *Secret as the g. Enough to make a person turn in his g.*: said hyperbolically of something which was abhorrent to the person in his lifetime. **2.** Both Rich and Poore are equal'd in the g. QUARLES. The path of glory leads but to the g. GRAY. **3.** His vast and wandering g. TENNYSON. *Comb.*: **g.-mound,** a hillock, or a barrow or tumulus, indicating the site of an interment; **-plant,** *Datura sanguinea*; †**-wax** = ADIPOCERE.

Grave (grēⁱv), *sb.*² *local.* ME. [– ON. *greifi* – OLG. *grēve*; cf. GRAVE *sb.*³] †**a.** A steward, a person placed in charge of property. **b.** In parts of Yorkshire and Lincolnshire, each of a number of administrative officials formerly elected by the inhabitants of a township.

†**Grave,** *sb.*³ 1605. [Now only as the second element in LANDGRAVE, MARGRAVE, PALSGRAVE, RHINEGRAVE; – OLG. *grēve*, whence ON. *greifi*; see prec.] A foreign title = COUNT *sb.*²; chiefly used of the counts of Nassau –1718.

Grave (grēⁱv), *a.*¹ (*sb.*) 1541. [–(O)Fr. *grave* or L. *gravis* heavy, important.]

A. *adj.* †**1.** Of persons: Having weight or importance; influential; authoritative –1749. **2.** Of works, employments, etc.: Weighty, important; requiring serious thought 1592. **b.** Now *esp.* of faults, evils, difficulties, etc.: Highly serious. Of diseases or symptoms: Threatening a fatal result, serious. 1824. **3.** Marked by dignity and weight; in later use, serious, not mirthful or jocular; opp. to *gay* 1549. **4.** Of colour, dress, etc.: Dull, sombre, not gay or showy 1611. **5.** Physically ponderous, heavy. *Obs.* or *arch.* 1570. **6.** Of sounds: Low in pitch, deep in tone; opp. to *acute* 1609.

1. Most reuerend and graue Elders SHAKS. **2.** When our council is assembled, we will treat of graver matters SCOTT. **b.** G. errors 1858, doubts 1866, news from the front 1900. **3.** With g. Aspect he rose, and in his rising seem'd A Pillar of State MILT. **6.** *G. accent* (cf. ACCENT *sb.* 1, 2). *G. harmonic* = differential tone.

B. *sb.* A grave accent; †a grave note. 1609.

‖**Grave** (grăv, grā·ve), *a.*² 1683. [Fr. or It. *grave* = GRAVE *a.*¹] *Mus.* A term indicating a slow and solemn movement.

Grave (grēⁱv), *v.*¹ [OE. *grafan* str. vb. dig, engrave, also in *begrafan* bury = OLFrankish *gravan* (Du. *graven*) dig, OHG. *graban* dig, carve (G. *graben* dig, *begraben* bury), ON. *grafa* dig, bury, Goth. *graban* dig :– Gmc. **ȝraban*, f. **ȝrab-* (see GRAVE *sb.*¹), **ȝrōb-*

(see GROOVE). The strong pa. t. *grove* died out in XV; pa. pple. *graven* survives as a literary arch.]

I. 1. *intr.* To dig. *Obs.* exc. *dial.* **2.** *trans.* To dig, form by digging; to excavate. Also with *out, up.* Now *rare* exc. *dial.* OE.

2. And next the shryne a pit thann doth she g. CHAUCER.

II. To deposit (a corpse) in the ground, in a tomb; to bury ME.; †to hide under ground (ME. only); †to swallow up in or as in a grave –1611.

Ditches graue you all *Timon* IV. iii. 116.

III. 1. To form by carving, to carve, sculpture (*lit.* and *fig.*); also *absol. Obs.* exc. *poet.* OE. †**2. a.** To cut into (a hard material). **b.** = ENGRAVE *v.* 2. –1677. **3.** To engrave (letters, etc.) upon a surface, (a surface) *with* letters. Hence, to record by engraved or incised letters. *arch.* ME. **b.** *fig.* = ENGRAVE *v.* 3b. ME. †**4.** = ENGRAVE *v.* 4. –1818.

1. Ymages..craftely grauen ME. **2.** Hard was it youre herte for to graue CHAUCER. **3.** There.. graving our names in the trees CAPT. SMITH. **b.** His wrinkles and furrows were inscriptions that Time had graved HAWTHORNE.

Grave (grēⁱv), *v.*² 1461. [prob. f. dial. Fr. *grave* (OFr. = gravel), var. of (O)Fr. *grève* shore – Celtic **gravo-* gravel, pebbles, repr. by Breton *grouan* GROWAN.] *trans.* To clean (a ship's bottom) by burning off the accretions, and paying it over with tar, while aground on a beach, or placed in a dock.

Grave-clothes, *sb. pl.* 1535. The clothes or wrappings in which a corpse is laid out for burial.

Grave-digger (grēⁱ·vˌdigəɹ). 1593. [f. GRAVE *sb.*¹] **1.** One who digs graves. **2.** A name given to insects that bury the bodies of small animals and insects, for the use of their larvæ on quitting the egg; *esp.* a beetle of the genus *Necrophorus*; also, a digger-wasp, e.g. one of the genus *Sphex* 1851.

‖**Gravedo** (grăvī·do). 1706. [L.; = heaviness (in the limbs or head), f. *gravis* heavy.] A cold in the head; coryza.

Gravel (græ·vĕl), *sb.* ME. [– OFr. *gravel* masc., *gravel(l)e* fem., dim. of OFr. *grave* gravel, coarse sand; see GRAVE *v.*², -EL². Sense 4 is – mod.Fr. *gravelle.*] †**1.** Sand –1712. **2.** Coarse sand and waterworn stones, often slightly intermixed with clay, much used for laying roads and paths ME. Also *fig.* **b.** *Geol.* and *Mining.* A stratum of this material, *esp.* one that contains gold 1849. **3.** *U.S.* Ballast 1868. **4.** *Path.* An aggregation of urinary crystals which can be recognized as masses (as dist. from *sand*); also, the disease of which these are characteristic. Also, pop., pain or difficulty in passing urine with or without any deposit. ME. **5.** *Financial slang.* A term used when the supply of money in the market is growing bare 1884. **6.** *attrib.* 1450.

1. *Quick g.*: quicksand. *Golden g.* (see GOLDEN 2). **2.** Proofes as cleere as Founts in July, when Wee see each graine of grauell SHAKS. **b.** *Pay g.*: g. containing gold enough to yield a profit. *Comb.*: **g.-grass,** *Galium verum*: **-plant,** *Epigæa repens*, **-powder,** coarse gunpowder, pebble-powder; **-root,** *Eupatorium purpureum.*

Gravel (græ·vĕl), *v.* 1543. [f. prec. sb.] **1.** *trans.* To cover (a path, etc.) with gravel or sand. †Also with *up.* †**2.** To bury in gravel or sand; to overwhelm with gravel; hence *fig.* to suppress, stifle –1686. †**3.** To run (a ship) aground on the gravel or beach, mud, etc. Also in *pass.*, of a person. Also *fig.* –1682. **4.** *fig.* **a.** To set fast, nonplus, perplex 1548. **b.** Of a question, etc.: To confound, perplex, puzzle. Also *U.S.* To go against the grain with. 1601. **5.** *Farriery.* in *pass.* and *intr.* Of a horse or its feet: To be injured by gravel lodged between the shoe and the hoof 1593.

3. When we were fallen into a place betwene two seas, they graveled the ship N.T. (Rhem.) *Acts* 27:41. *fig.* I was gravell'd, like a ship that's grounded WITHER. **4. a.** When you were grauel'd for lacke of matter SHAKS. **b.** It will perhaps g. even a philosopher to comprehend it BERKELEY.

Gravel-blind, *a.* 1596. Orig. *high-gravel-blind*, in *Merch. V.* II. ii. 38, a jocular intensive synonym for SAND-BLIND. Hence, in later writers, 'nearly stone-blind'. Also *fig.*

Graveless (grēⁱ·vlės), *a.* 1606. [f. GRAVE *sb.*¹ + -LESS.] Having no grave or graves.

Graveling (græ·vĕliŋ). Also **gravelling.** 1587. [Of unkn. origin.] The parr or young salmon.

Gravelling (græ·vĕliŋ), *vbl. sb.* 1523. [f. GRAVEL *v.* + -ING¹.] **1.** The action of laying down gravel. Also, a gravelled surface. 1577. †**2.** *Farriery.* A disease in a horse's foot (see GRAVEL *v.* 5) –1639.

Gravelly (græ·vĕli), *a.* ME. [f. GRAVEL *sb.* + -Y¹.] **1.** †Sandy; full of or abounding in gravel; consisting of gravel; strewn with gravel. Also, resembling gravel. **2.** *Path.* Of the nature of gravel (see GRAVEL *sb.* 4); characterized by or arising from, the presence of gravel 1607. †**3.** Containing gritty particles –1727.

†**Gra·velous,** *a.* ME. [– (O)Fr. *graveleux*, f. *gravel* GRAVEL *sb.*; see -OUS.] **a.** Gravelly. **b.** Granular. –1758.

Gra·vel-pit. ME. An excavation from which gravel (or †sand) is or has been obtained.

Gra·vel-stone. ME. [f. GRAVEL *sb.* + STONE *sb.*] **1.** A pebble. Also *fig.* †**2.** = CALCULUS 1. P. Holland.

Gravel-walk. 1663. An alley or path laid with gravel.

Gravely (grēⁱ·vli), *adv.* 1553. [f. GRAVE *a.*¹ + -LY².] In a grave manner (see GRAVE *a.*¹).

Graven (grēⁱ·v'n), *ppl. a.* ME. [pa. pple. of GRAVE *v.*¹] **1.** Sculptured, hewn. **b.** quasi-*sb.* A graven image BIBLE (Douay) *Ps.* 77:58. **2.** Carved on a surface, engraved 1821.

1. Thou shalt not make unto thee any g. image *Exod.* 20:4.

Graveness (grēⁱ·vnės). 1577. [f. GRAVE *a.*¹ + -NESS.] The quality or state of being grave (see GRAVE *a.*¹).

Had put off levity and put g. on TENNYSON.

Graveolent (grăvī·ŏlĕnt), *a.* 1657. [– L. *graveolens, -ent-*, f. *grave* adv. n. of *gravis* heavy (GRAVE *a.*¹) + *olens*, pres. pple. of *olēre* have a smell; see -ENT.] Having a rank smell; fetid. So **Graveolence, -ency,** a rank offensive smell. (Dicts.)

Graver (grēⁱ·vəɹ). ME. [f. GRAVE *v.*¹ + -ER¹. Cf. (O)Fr. *graveur* engraver.] **1.** One who carves or engraves: †a sculptor –1628; an ENGRAVER (sense 1) (now *rare*) ME. **2.** A cutting or shaving tool; an engraver's tool, a burin (now the principal use) 1548.

†**Gra·very.** 1601. [f. GRAVE *v.*¹ + -ERY.] The employment of an engraver; engraving –1695.

Graves, obs. f. GREAVES.

Graves's disease. 1868. [f. Dr. R. J. *Graves* of Dublin.] *Med.* Exophthalmic goitre; also called Basedow's disease.

Gravestone, grave-stone (grēⁱ·vˌstōᵘn). ME. [f. GRAVE *sb.*¹ + STONE *sb.*] A stone placed over or at the head or foot of a grave, or at the entrance of a tomb.

Graveyard (grēⁱ·vˌyaɹd). 1825. [f. GRAVE *sb.*¹ + YARD *sb.*¹] A burial-ground.

The..desolate g. of Donore MACAULAY.

Gra·vic, *a.* 1864. [irreg. f. L. *gravis* GRAVE *a.*¹ + -IC.] Pertaining to or causing gravitation. (Dicts.)

Gravid (græ·vid), *a.* 1597. [– L. *gravidus* laden, pregnant, f. *gravis* heavy; see GRAVE *a.*¹, -ID¹.] Pregnant, heavy with young. Also *fig.*

A carefull husband [*sc.* a dolphin] over his g. associate 1638.

†**Gra·vidate,** *v. rare.* 1623. [– *gravidat-*, pa. ppl. stem of L. *gravidare* burden, impregnate, f. *gravidus*; see prec., -ATE³.] *intr.* To be gravid or pregnant; *trans.* to make heavy or gravid. Hence **Gra·vidated** *ppl. a.* pregnant. †**Gravida·tion,** pregnancy.

Gravidity (grăvi·dĭti). 1651. [– L. *graviditas* pregnancy, f. *gravidus*; see GRAVID, -ITY.] The state of being gravid; pregnancy.

Gravific (grăvi·fik), *a.* 1807. [– Fr. *gravifique*, f. L. *gravis* heavy + *-fique* -FIC.] That makes heavy or produces weight.

Gravigrade (græ·vigrēⁱd). 1847. [– Fr. *gravigrade* (whence mod.L. *Gravigrada*), f. L. *gravis* heavy + *-grade*, L. *-gradus* going. Cf. PLANTIGRADE, TARDIGRADE.] *Zool.*

A. *adj.* 'Walking heavily'; of or belonging to the extinct edentate group *Gravigrada*, which includes the Megatherium and the Mylodon 1884.

B. *sb.* Formerly, a heavy-paced animal, e.g. an elephant; now, one of the *Gravigrada* (see A).

Gravimeter (grăvi·mĭtəɹ). 1797. [– Fr. *gravimètre* (Guyton de Morveau, 1797), f. L. *gravis* heavy; see -METER.] *Physics.* A kind of hydrometer for determining the specific gravity of bodies, whether liquid or solid. Hence **Gravime·tric, -al** *a.* pertaining to the g., or to gravimetry. **Gravime·trically** *adv.* in respect of measurement by weight. **Gravi·metry,** measurement of weight.

Graving (grēⁱ·viŋ), *vbl. sb.*¹ ME. [f. GRAVE *v.*¹ + -ING¹.] †**1.** Digging –1486. †**2.** Carving, sculpturing; incision of lines, etc. in stone, metal, and the like –1727; *concr.* a carving, sculpture; an inscription –1801. **3.** The engraving (of a design, etc.) on metal or wood; an engraved plate, or an impression from it. *Obs.* or *arch.* 1646. **4.** *attrib.*, as *g. tool*, etc. ME.

2. *concr.* The g. of palme-trees in the front therof 1609.

Graving (grēⁱ·viŋ), *vbl. sb.*² 1627. [f. GRAVE *v.*² + -ING¹.] The cleaning of a ship's bottom by scraping or burning, and coating with tar. *Comb.* **g.-dock,** a dock into which vessels are floated to be graved; = DRY DOCK.

Gra·vitate, *a.* [f. L. *gravitas* + -ATE².] Endowed with gravity. COLERIDGE.

Gravitate (græ·viteⁱt), *v.* 1644. [– *gravitat-*, pa. ppl. stem of mod.L. *gravitare* (Newton), f. L. *gravitas* gravity; see -ATE³.] †**1.** *intr.* To exert weight or pressure; to move or tend to move downward –1808. **2.** *intr.* To be affected by gravitation; to move or tend to move by the force of gravity *towards* a body 1692. **b.** To sink or fall by, or as by, gravitation (*lit.* and *fig.*) 1823. **c.** *trans.* To cause to descend or sink by gravitation 1894. **3.** *transf.* and *fig.* (*intr.*) To move or tend to move towards (some centre of influence) 1673.

2. Systems of bodies which g. round a central body LOCKYER. **3.** The market price..is continually gravitating towards the natural price ADAM SMITH.

Gravitation (grævitēⁱ·ʃən). 1644. [– mod.L. *gravitatio*, f. as prec.; see -ION.] **1.** *Physics.* The action or process of gravitating; now in wide sense, the moving or tending to a centre of attraction 1645. **b.** The degree of such attraction 1812. **2.** The attraction of one body for another; the tendency of every particle of matter towards every other particle 1646. **3.** *transf.* and *fig.* Natural tendency (*to* or *towards*); in bad sense, tendency to sink to a low level 1644. **4.** *attrib.* 1850.

1. The mutual g. of bodies BERKELEY **2.** Phr. *The law of gravitation*, the law according to which the attractive force of bodies varies directly as their masses and inversely as the square of the distance between them. **3.** That strong g. towards evil 1876.

Gravitational (grævitēⁱ·ʃənăl), *a.* 1855. [f. GRAVITATION + -AL¹.] Of, pertaining to, or caused by gravitation.

Gravitational astronomy: a system based, as by Sir Isaac Newton, on the theory of gravitation.

Gravitative (græ·viteⁱtiv), *a.* 1799. [f. GRAVITATE *v.* + -IVE.] Of, pertaining to, or produced by gravitation.

Gravity (græ·vĭti). 1509. [– (O)Fr. *gravité* or L. *gravitas*, f. *gravis* GRAVE *a.*¹; see -ITY.]

I. 1. †Weight, influence –1741; solemnity 1647; a grave subject, speech, or remark (now *arch.*) 1609. **2.** Grave character or nature; importance, seriousness 1519. **3.** Weighty dignity of conduct or demeanour; staidness. In later use opp. to *levity* and *gaiety.* 1509.

1. The g. of that supreme court CLARENDON. **2.** The g. of the offence SIR T. MORE, of the occasion 1878. **3.** A man of his place, grauity, and learning SHAKS. The settled g. of his face 1894.

II. In physical senses. **1.** †**a.** The quality of having weight, ponderability; tendency to downward motion (opp. to *levity*, or upward tendency, as e.g. of fire) –1678. **b.** Weight, heaviness; chiefly = *specific gravity.* Now mainly in *centre of g.* (see CENTRE *sb.*). 1641. **c. Specific gravity.** The degree of relative heaviness characteristic of any kind or portion of matter; expressed by the ratio of the weight of a given volume to that of an equal volume of some substance taken as a standard (viz. usually water for liquids and solids, air for gases). Now sometimes called *density*. Abbrev. *sp. gr.* 1666. **2.** The attractive force by which all bodies tend to move towards the centre of the earth. Also often more widely, the degree of intensity with which one body is affected by the attraction of gravitation exercised by another body. 1692. **3.** Of sounds: Lowness of pitch 1669.

Comb.: **g. battery, cell,** a galvanic battery or cell in which the liquids are kept apart by the force of g. alone; **-railroad,** a railroad in which the cars descend under the action of g. alone.

Gravo-, bad comb. form of GRAVE *a.*[1]

Gravure (gravūr, græ·viu^{ə}ɹ). 1893. [Short for PHOTOGRAVURE.] Engraving by means of photography; a print thus produced. Also *attrib.*

Gravy (grē^{i}·vi). [Late ME. *grauey, graue,* perh. originating in a misreading of *grane* – OFr. *grané* (in printed texts often *gravé*), prob. f. *grain* spice (cf. OFr. *grenon* stew); see GRAIN *sb.*[1], -Y[5].] †**1.** A dressing of some sort used for white meats, fish, and vegetables –1513. **2.** The fat and juices which exude from flesh in cooking; a dressing for meat and vegetables made from these 1591. **3.** *attrib.* 1694.

Gray, etc.: see GREY.

Graybeard; see GREYBEARD.

Graylag, var. of GREY LAG.

Grayling (grē^{i}·liŋ). 1450. [f. *gray* GREY + -LING[1].] **1.** A freshwater fish of the genus *Thymallus* (family *Salmonidæ*), of a silvery-grey colour and characterized by a long and high dorsal fin. The European grayling is *Thymallus vulgaris*; other species are *T. signifer*, the American or Alaskan grayling, and *T. ontariensis*, the Michigan grayling. **2.** A common butterfly (*Hipparchia semele*), so called from the grey underside of the wings 1819.

1. In this riuer [Wie] be vmbers, otherwise called grailings 1577.

Graymalkin, var. of GRIMALKIN.

Graze (grē^{i}z), *sb.* 1692. [f. GRAZE *v.*[2]] **1.** An act or instance of grazing; said esp. of shot. **2.** A superficial wound or abrasion, caused by an object rubbing against the skin 1847.

Graze (grē^{i}z), *v.*[1] [OE. *grasian*, f. *græs* GRASS; cf. MDu., MHG. *grasen*.] **1.** *intr.* To feed on grass or growing herbage. **2.** *transf.* and *fig.* **a.** 'To move on devouring' (J.). ?*Obs.* **b.** *joc.* of persons: To feed. 1579. **3.** *trans.* To feed on, eat (growing herbage). Chiefly *poet.* 1667. †Also said of fish (DRYDEN). **4.** *causal.* To put (cattle) to feed on pasture 1564. **5.** *intr.* (or *absol.*) To pasture cattle 1645. **6.** *trans.* To put cattle to feed on (grass, land, etc.); also, to tend while feeding 1601. **7.** *intr.* Of land: To produce grass. *Obs.* exc. *dial.* 1625.

1. The..horses were turned out to g. W. IRVING. **2. b.** *To send to g.*: to send packing. Will you.. Send the clergy all to g. SWIFT. **4.** When Iacob graz'd his Vncle Labans sheepe SHAKS. **7.** The Quarters to G., being kept Shorne BACON. Hence **Gra·zer,** an animal that grazes.

Graze (grē^{i}z), *v.*[2] 1604. [perh. a spec. use of prec., as if 'to take off the grass close to the ground'; cf. G. *grasen* browse, pasture, scythe, glance off, Sw. *gräsa* (of a shot) graze, Da. *græsse* pasture, (of a bullet) ricochet.] **1.** *trans.* To touch lightly (a surface) in passing; *esp.* to roughen or abrade (the skin, etc.) in brushing past. Also *fig.* **b.** Said of a ray of light 1839. **2.** *intr.* To move so as to touch lightly in passing, or so as to produce slight abrasion. †Also, of a bullet: To ricochet. 1632.

1. Our little canoe grazed the steps 1863. **b.** The sun's..rays..grazing the summit of the mountain TYNDALL. **2.** Points Of slander, glancing here and grazing there TENNYSON.

Grazier (grē^{i}·ziəɹ). 1502. [f. GRASS *sb.*; see -IER. Formerly assoc. with Fr. *graissier* fattener.] †**1.** = VERDERER. **2.** One who feeds cattle for the market 1523.

2. The savage..chooses to be a g. rather than to till the ground 1853.

Graziery (grē^{i}·ʒ^{i}əri). 1731. [f. prec.; see -ERY.] **a.** The business of a grazier. **b.** Grazing-ground, pasture (*rare*).

Grazing (grē^{i}·ziŋ), *vbl. sb.* ME. [f. GRAZE *v.*[1] + -ING[1].] **1.** The action of GRAZE *v.*[1]; pasturing. Also *fig.* **2.** Grazing-ground, pasture-land, pasture 1517. **3.** *attrib.*, as g. guard, a guard placed over the cattle of an army whilst grazing 1626.

Gre, var. of GREE.

Grease (grīs), *sb.* ME. [– AFr. *grece, gresse,* (O)Fr. *graisse* :– Rom. **crassia*, f. L. *crassus*; see CRASS.] †**1.** The fat part of the body of an animal; also, fatness, corpulence –1672. **2.** Melted or rendered fat of animals, esp. when in a soft state. Hence, oily or fatty matter in general, esp. such as is used as a lubricant. ME. **3.** A disease which attacks the heels of a horse (see quot.) 1674. **4.** The oily matter in wool; also, wool before it has been cleansed of this 1835.

3. Grease is a specific inflammation of the sebaceous follicles of the skin of the heels, followed by an increased morbid secretion YOUATT.

Comb.: **g.-band,** a band coated with cart-grease mixed with tar fastened round a tree-trunk to prevent the ascent of flightless moths; hence as vb.; **g. bird,** the Canada Jay; **g.-bush** = *grease-wood*; **-season, -time,** the period when the deer are fat and fit for killing; **-trap,** an appliance for catching g. in a drain; **-wood,** a name for various stunted and prickly chenopodiaceous shrubs of the genera *Sarcobatus*, *Atriplex*, etc., which contain oil and are found in dry alkaline valleys of the western U.S.

Grease (grīz, grīs), *v.* ME. [f. prec. Cf. Fr. *graisser*.] **1.** *trans.* To smear, anoint, or lubricate with grease; to make greasy 1613. **2.** To apply a salve of tallow and tar to (sheep). Also *absol.* ME. **3.** *fig.* **a.** Phr. *To g. the wheels*: to make things run smoothly; to pay the expenses ME. **b.** To ply with money, to bribe 1526. †**c.** To gull, cheat –1634. **4.** To cause (a horse) to become affected with grease. Also *intr.* of a horse. 1737.

3. b. While pluralities greas'd them thick and deepe MILT. Phr. *To g. a person's hand, palm.*

Greaser (grī·zəɹ, -səɹ). 1641. [f. prec. + -ER[1].] **1.** †One who greases (sheep); one who cleans and lubricates machinery, etc. with grease; *U.S.* the head fireman on a steamer. **2.** *U.S. slang.* A nickname for a native Mexican or a native Spanish American 1849.

Greasy (grī·zi, -si), *a.* 1514. [f. GREASE *sb.* + -Y[1].] **1.** Smeared, covered, or soiled with grease. †**2.** Anointed or smeared with grease or chrism. (Applied contemptuously to R.C. priests in reference to unction.) –1583. **3.** Composed of or containing grease; of the nature of grease. Of food: Containing too much grease. 1592. **4.** Of wool: Containing a natural grease; used *spec.* of wool not cleansed of this. Also of flannel. 1600. **5.** Of a horse: Affected with the grease 1701. **6.** Having the feel of grease 1703; (of a road) slimy with mud or moisture 1801. **7.** Filthy, obscene, low 1588. **8.** Of manners, voice, etc.: 'Unctuous', oily 1848.

1. Greasie Napkins SHAKS. Sweepe on you fat and greazie Citizens SHAKS. G. sophisters MILT. **3.** When a German dish is not sour it is sure to be g. HOOD. **4.** *A. Y. L.* III. ii. 55. **7.** His g. Jest 1687. **8.** A g. simper THACKERAY.

Comb.: **g. fritillary,** a species of butterfly, *Melitæa artemis*; **g. pole,** a pole rubbed with g. to make it harder to climb or walk upon (used at fairs or village sports); **g. steam,** steam which becomes its own lubricant by a mechanical admixture of g. with it.

Great (grē^{i}t). [OE. *grēat* = OFris. *grāt*, OS. *grōt* (Du. *groot*), OHG. *grōz* (G. *gross*) :– WGmc. **ʒrauta*, of unkn. origin.] **A.** *adj.*

I. 1. Coarse of grain or texture. Of diet: Coarse, not delicate. *Obs.* exc. *Sc.* **2.** Thick, stout, massive, bulky, big. (Opp. to *small* in sense of 'slender'.) OE. **3.** Pregnant, far advanced in pregnancy. Chiefly with *with* (*child*, etc.). *arch.* and *dial.* ME. †Also *fig.* –1654. †**4.** Full or big with courage, emotion, etc.; angry, grieved; proud, arrogant –1832. **5.** Of the sea, a river: In high flood 1670.

3. Hyr body is grete, and she with childe 1460. *fig.* I am g. with woe, and shall deliver weeping SHAKS. **4.** My harte is g.: but it must break with silence SHAKS.

II. Having a high position in a scale of measurement. (Opp. to *small, little.*) **1.** Of material objects, with reference to size (see quots.) ME. †**2.** Grown up; full-grown. Chiefly in *Hunting* language. –1774. **3.** Of collective unities, numbers, quantities, dimensions, etc. OE. **4.** Of qualities, emotions, conditions, actions, or occurrences; with reference to degree or extent ME.

1. The g. Globe it selfe SHAKS. A g. big Man 1766. A g. oak stump SHELLEY. Of letters: = CAPITAL, as *g. A*, capital A. Thus makes she her g. P's SHAKS. Of animal and vegetable species of larger size than others so named: The g. Horn-Owl RAY. The black or g. ostrich 1802. In names of constellations, as *G.* (formerly *Greater*) *Bear*, *G. Dog*; of anatomical structures, as *G. artery*, *pelvis*, etc. G. Malvern (opp. to *Little* Malvern), G. Ouse, G. Portland Street, etc. = Main, principal; William Rufus builded the g. hall there [Westminster] about..1097 STOW. **2.** ij hennes, or a grete ghoos CAXTON. **3.** *G. deal*, *many* (see those words). Grete possescions 1460. G. Dust they raised HOBBES. *G. gross*, twelve gross, 1728. *G. hundred*, a long hundred,120. **4.** The g. heates are abated 1573. I will take g. care of them HEARNE. G. agitation 1849, ignorance, poverty BUCKLE.

III. In fig. extensions of II. **1.** Important, elevated, distinguished ME. **2.** Of persons: Eminent by reason of birth, rank, wealth, power, or position. **b.** Applied (more or less conventionally) to the Deity, or deities; also to saints. ME. **c.** = GRAND *a.* 2. 1532. **3.** Of things: Pertaining to or occupied by persons of high place or rank ME. †**4.** 'Of elevated mien' (J.) –1697. **5.** (usually qualifying *man*) Eminent in point of attainments or achievement; exhibiting signal excellence in some important work. In recent use, often with an implication of more or less loftiness and integrity of character. 1709. **b.** Lofty, magnanimous, noble 1726. **6.** Hence: **a.** *predicatively*. Having considerable knowledge (of a subject) or skill (in doing something); const. *at*, †*in* 1784. **b.** Of surpassing excellence; hence, Magnificent, splendid, grand, immense. *U.S.* and *colloq.* 1809. **7.** Qualifying a descriptive sb. (see quots.) ME. **8.** Favourite; high in favour *with* ME. **9.** Intimate, familiar, friendly; 'thick' *with* 1483.

1. G. matters..could not but be full of g. difficulties 1655. A name g. in story BYRON. The g. day of the Exclusion Bill MACAULAY. The g. attraction was [etc.] DICKENS. The g. sin of g. cities HELPS. **2.** The g. man, at whose frown, a few days before, the whole kingdom had trembled MACAULAY. *The g. world* [= Fr. *le grand monde*]: aristocratic society. *The Great* (following a proper name): (*a*) as merely honorific (*obs.* or *arch.*); (*b*) implying both that the person so designated is the most famous person of the name, and that he ranks among the great men of history. *The G. King*; in *Gr. Hist.*, the King of Persia. *The G. Cham, Mogul, Turk*, see CHAM, etc. **c.** *The Lord Great Chamberlain* 1727. **3.** Of G. Place BACON (*title*). **4.** Dido..Amidst the Crowd, she walks serenely g. DRYDEN. **5.** He is a g. man, eloquent in conception and in language BURKE. **b.** Nothing can be g. which is not right JOHNSON. **6. a.** He is very 'great' on dogs JEFFERIES. **b.** Phr. *To run a g. filly. dog*, etc.: said of one that runs a fine race. **7.** With sense: Eminently entitled to the designation; A g. scoundrel 1828. With sense: That is much in the habit of performing the action; also, that is on a large scale. I am a g. eater of beefe SHAKS. The g. Dealers in Wit POPE. **9.** The Duchess of York and the Duke of York are mighty g. with her PEPYS.

Combs. **1.** With sbs., and normally preceded by the definite article. **Great Bible,** usually applied to the version by Coverdale in 1539; occas. also to revised versions of this, esp. to Cranmer's Bible of 1540. **G. day,** (*a*) the Day of Judgement; (*b*) Easter Day; (*c*) a feast- or fast-day of high importance. **G. fast,** the season of Lent. **G. organ,** one of the divisions of a large organ, having the pipes of largest scale and loudest tone; **G. week** = HOLY WEEK. See also *Great* ASSIZE, etc.

2. Prefixed to terms denoting kinship, to form designations for persons one degree further removed in ascending or descending relationship. [After Fr. *grand*, which follows L. *avunculus magnus*, etc.] **a. Great-uncle, -aunt,** a father's or mother's uncle, aunt; **great-nephew, -niece,** a nephew's or niece's son, daughter. **b. Great-grandfather, -grandmother,** a grandfather's or grandmother's father, mother (also *transf.* a remote male or female ancestor); **-grandchild,** grandchild's child; **-grandson, granddaughter,** a grandson's or granddaughter's son, daughter; etc. Similarly with repetition of *great*.

3. In parasynthetic adjs., as **g.-bellied,** having a big belly, pregnant; *fig.* big with events, etc.; **-eyed,** *lit.* having large or prominent eyes;

fig. far-seeing, taking a large view; **-mouthed,** *fig.* loud-voiced, boastful, bragging; †**-stomached,** high-spirited.

B. *adv.* In a great degree; to a great extent; greatly, exceedingly, highly; much; very. *Obs.* exc. *dial.* ME.

Say that he thriue, as 'tis g. like he will SHAKS.

C. as quasi-*sb.* and *sb.*

I. The adj. used *absol.* **1. a.** As *pl.*: Great persons; freq. in *g. and small.* Now usually *the g.* ME. **b.** (With *the.*) That which is great; great things, aspects, qualities, etc. collectively 1557. **2. By the g.,** †**by g. a.** Of work done: At a fixed price for the whole amount; by task; by the piece. Now *dial.* 1523. †**b.** In gross, wholesale –1640. †**c.** *transf.* and *fig.* In the mass; by wholesale –1755. †**3. In g.** [Cf. Fr. *en grand, en gros.*] **a.** In the mass, in the bulk; in the gross, wholesale; by the piece –1792. **b.** On a large scale –1795.

II. As *sb.* †**1.** A great person –1649. †**2.** The chief part; the main point; the sum and substance; the general drift or gist. ME. only. †**3. a.** Thickness. **b.** Greatness, magnitude (*rare*). –1629. **4. Greats** (*Oxford Univ. colloq.*). The final examination for the degree of B.A.; *esp.* the examination for Honours in Literæ Humaniores. Formerly GREAT GO. 1853.

Great-coat, greatcoat (grēⁱ·tkōᵘ·t). 1661. A large heavy overcoat, a top-coat. Hence **Great-coated** *a.* dressed in or wearing a g.

Greaten (grēⁱ·t'n), *v.* Now *arch.* ME. [f. GREAT + -EN⁵.] †**1.** *intr.* To become pregnant. ME. only. **2.** *trans.* To render great or greater in size or amount 1626. **3.** To render eminent, prominent, distinguished, or important; to exalt, aggrandize. Also *absol.* 1614. **b.** To exalt mentally or spiritually; chiefly in good sense 1647. **4.** *intr.* To become great or greater 1716.

2. Every thing concurred to g. the fire PEPYS. **3.** So much doth the means of facilitating carriage g. a city PETTY. **4.** My blue eyes greatening in the looking-glass E. B. BROWNING.

Greater (grēⁱ·təɹ). [OE. *grȳttra* (**grīetra*, Angl. **grētra*); but most later forms are refashioned on the positive. See -ER³.]

A. *adj.* **1.** The comparative of GREAT. †**2.** Older, elder. [A Latinism.] –1535. **3.** In special or technical use, opp. to *lesser* 1551.

1. Lesser then Macbeth, and g. SHAKS. **3.** In names of constellations, as *the G. Dog*, etc. Also †*g. circle* = 'great circle': see CIRCLE. *Mus.* Applied to intervals now usu. called MAJOR. In names of plants, as *G. Knapweed*, of birds, etc., and in *Anat.*

†**B.** *adv.* In a greater degree 1496.

C. quasi-*sb.* and *sb.* The adj. used *absol.* and *ellipt.*

The g. scornes the lesser SHAKS. Thou Sun, of this great World both Eye and Soule, Acknowledge him thy G. MILT.

Greatest (grēⁱ·tėst). ME. [f. GREAT *a.* + -EST; app. not recorded in OE.]

A. *adj.* The superlative of GREAT. †**2.** Eldest 1535. **3.** *absol* and *ellipt.* (quasi-*sb.*) ME.

1. The world knows nothing of its g. men SIR H. TAYLOR. *G. happiness of the g. number* (see HAPPINESS). *G. common measure* (see MEASURE). **3.** Our g. yet with least pretence TENNYSON.

†**B.** *adv.* Most greatly or highly; most 1553.

Great go. 1820. [See GREAT *a.* and GO *sb.*] *Univ. slang.* The final examination for the degree of B.A. (At Oxford now called *Greats.*)

Great-grandfather, etc. [See GREAT *a.* *Combs.* 2.]

Great-great-: see GREAT *a.*

Great-head (grēⁱ·thed). *U.S.* 1844. [f. GREAT *a.* + HEAD *sb.*] U.S. name for the golden-eye, *Clangula glaucion.*

Great-hearted, *a.* (Stress variable.) ME. [f. GREAT *a.*; see HEARTED.] †**a.** High-spirited; proud –1647. **b.** Having a noble or generous heart or spirit; magnanimous. Hence **Greathea·rtedness.**

Greatly (grēⁱ·tli), *adv.* ME. [f. GREAT *a.* + -LY².] **1.** To a great extent, in a great degree; much, very. **2.** Largely 1670; mainly, chiefly (*rare*) 1742. **3.** In a great manner; magnanimously, nobly; †illustriously; with brilliant success ME. **4.** In or to a high rank or position (*rare*) 1800.

1. To heare Musicke, the Generall do's not g. care *Oth.* III. i. 18. It is g. probable H. WALPOLE. **3.** Small time: but in that small, most g. liued This Starre of England SHAKS. **4.** G. born 1800. To expect to marry g. JANE AUSTEN.

Greatness (grēⁱ·tnės). [f. GREAT *a.* + -NESS; in OE. *grētnys.*] †**1.** Thickness, coarseness; stoutness –1536; pregnancy –1634. **2.** The attribute of being great in size, extent, or degree ME. †**3.** Magnitude –1765. **4.** Eminence, distinction, importance. *Occas.* in *pl.* ME. **5.** Inherent nobility or dignity; grandeur 1597. **6.** Intimacy *with.* *Obs.* or *arch.* 1625.

3. An elephant excedeth in greatnes thre wilde oxen EDEN. **4.** Some atcheeues greatnesse SHAKS. **5.** This Language..has a Natural G. in it DRYDEN.

†**Greave¹.** [OE. *grǣfa, grǣfe* brushwood, thicket :– **ȝraibjon, -jōn,* f. **ȝraib-*; see GROVE.] **1. a.** Brushwood. (OE. only.) **b.** *pl.* Branches, twigs –1612. **2.** A thicket –1609.

Greave² (grīv). Chiefly *pl.* ME. [– OFr. *greve* calf of the leg, shin, armour (mod.Fr. dial. *grève, graive* upper part of the leg) = Sp. *greba*, of unkn. origin.] **1.** Armour for the leg below the knee. †**2.** The shin 1600. Hence **Greaved** *ppl. a.* furnished with greaves.

Greaves, graves (grīvz, grēⁱvz), *sb. pl.* 1614. [orig. a whaler's term – LG. *greven* pl. (whence also Da. *grever*), corresp. to OHG. *griubo, griobo* (G. *griebe* refuse of lard or tallow), of unkn. origin.] The fibrous matter or skin found in animal fat, which forms a sediment on melting and is pressed into cakes for dogs'-food, fish-bait, etc.; the refuse of tallow; cracklings.

Grebe (grīb). 1766. [– Fr. *grèbe*, of unkn. origin.] **1.** The name for the diving birds of the genus *Podiceps* or family *Podicipedidæ*, characterized by a short body, flattened and lobed feet set far behind, and the virtual absence of tail. **2.** The plumage of the grebe 1859. *Comb.* **g.-cloth,** a cotton cloth with a downy surface on one side.

Grece (grīs). *Obs.* exc. *dial.* [ME. *grese* – OFr. *gres, grez, greis*, pl. of *gré* GREE *sb.*¹] **1.** A flight of stairs or steps; a stairway ME. **2. a.** *pl.* Steps or stairs collectively; = sense 1. ME. **b.** *pl.* Steps or stairs (in a flight); *spec.* in *Her.* with spelling **grieces** (whence GRIECED *a.*) ME. **c.** *sing.* A single step or stair 1448.

Grecian (grī·ʃ'ăn). 1547. [– OFr. *grecien* or med.L. **græcianus*, f. L. *Græcia* Greece; see -IAN.]

A. *adj.* Of or pertaining to Greece or the Greeks; Greek. Now *rare* exc. with reference to architecture and facial outline. 1577.

Comb.: **G. bend,** an affected carriage of the body, in which it is bent forward from the hips; †**G. calends** (see CALENDS); **G. fire,** (*a*) = Greek fire (see FIRE *sb.*); (*b*) a kind of firework; **G. horse,** the wooden horse by means of which Troy was captured.

B. *sb.* **1.** A Greek. *Obs.* or *arch.* 1547. **b.** [tr. Gr. Ἑλλανιστής.] = HELLENIST 1. 1611. **2.** One learned in the Greek language; a Greek scholar 1557. **b.** A boy in the highest class at Christ's Hospital 1820. †**3.** A member of the Greek Church –1766. **4.** *slang.* An Irishman 1853.

1. Was this faire face the cause, quoth she, Why the Grecians sacked Troy SHAKS. **b.** There arose a murmuring of the Grecians [*R.V.* Grecian Jews] against the Hebrewes *Acts* 6:1.

Grecing (grī·siŋ). *Obs.* exc. *dial.* ME. [f. GRECE *sb.* + -ING¹.] Chiefly *pl.* Steps in a flight; flights of steps; stairs. Rarely *sing.* A step.

Grecism, Grecize, Greco-: see GRÆC-.

‖**Grecque** (grek, as Fr. grẹk). 1836. [Fr., fem. of *grec* GREEK.] *Arch.* A Greek fret.

Gree (grī), *sb.*¹ *Obs.* exc. *Sc.* ME. [– OFr. *gré* :– L. *gradus* step. See GRECE.] †**1.** = DEGREE I. 1. –1693. †**2.** *fig.* = DEGREE I. 2. –1589. †**3.** = DEGREE I. 3. –1617. †**4.** = DEGREE I. 4. –1590. **5.** Pre-eminence; superiority; mastery; victory in battle; hence, the prize for a victory. Now *Sc.* ME. †**6.** = DEGREE I. 6, II. 1, 3. –1563.

Gree (grī), *sb.*² Now *arch.* ME. [– (O)Fr. *gré* pleasure, goodwill, will :– L. *gratum*, subst. use of n. of *gratus* pleasing. Cf. MAUGRE.] †**1.** Favour, goodwill –1590. **2.** *To do* or *make gree*: to give satisfaction for an injury ME. †**3.** (One's) good pleasure; will, desire, consent –1734.

1. In gree: with goodwill or favour, in good part. Accept in g... the words I spoke 1600.

Gree, *v.* *Obs.* exc. *dial.* ME. [aphet. f. AGREE *v.*, or f. GREE *sb.*² Cf., however, OFr. *gréer* which may be the direct source.] = AGREE *v.*

Greed (grīd), *sb.* Orig. *Sc.* 1609. [Back-formation from GREEDY.] Inordinate or insatiate longing, esp. for wealth; covetous desire. Const. *of.*

Greedily (grī·dili), *adv.* [Coalescence of: (1) OE. *grǣdelīċe*, f. **grǣd* (*u-stem*, = ON. *gráðr*) + *-līċe* -LY²; (2) OE. *grǣdi(ġ)līċe*, f. *grǣdiġ* GREEDY + *-līċe* -LY².] In a greedy manner; hungrily, rapaciously OE.; eagerly, zealously ME.

Greediness (grī·dinės). OE. [f. GREEDY + -NESS.] The attribute of being greedy; gluttony ME.; avarice, rapacity OE.; excessive longing or desire in general 1553.

The greedinesse of the Wolfe 1641. The g. and extortion of the Court of Rome 1661. A G. of Knowledge, that is impatient of being confin'd BOYLE.

Greedy (grī·di), *a.* [OE. *grēdiġ, grǣdiġ* = OS. *grādag*, OHG. *grātac*, ON. *gráðugr*, Goth. *grēdags* :– Gmc. **ȝrǣðaȝaz, -uȝaz*, f. **ȝrǣðuz* hunger, greed, of unkn. origin.] **1.** Having an intense desire or inordinate appetite for food or drink; ravenous, voracious, gluttonous. †In early use: Hungry. Const. *of* (OE. *genitive*). Also *transf.* and *fig.* **2.** Eager for gain, wealth, and the like; avaricious, covetous, rapacious OE. **3.** Eager, keen; †zealous ME. †**4.** *transf.* Of spoil, prey: Greedily pursued –1648.

1. Two gredy sowes LANGL. *fig.* The..noise of g. Acheron CARLYLE. *transf.* Air..g. of moisture 1800. **2.** A wolvish, g., and covetous heart GAGE. **3.** With g. hope to find His wish MILT. G. of novelty 1734. **4.** Running headlong after g. spoils MARLOWE.

Gree·dy-gut(s. Now *dial.* and *vulgar.* 1550. [See GUT.] A voracious eater; a glutton.

Greegree (grī·grī). Also †**griggory,** †**gri-gri.** 1698. [Of native origin. Cf. Fr. *grisgris.*] **1.** An African charm, amulet, or fetish. **2.** The ordeal-tree of Guinea, *Erythrophleum guineense* 1847. **3.** *attrib.*, as **greegree man,** a 'medicine-man' 1788.

Greek (grīk), *sb.* [OE. *Grēcas* (pl.; and so for the most part till XVI), corresp. to MLG. *Grēke*, MDu. *Grieke*, G. *Grieche*, ON. *Grikkir* (pl.) of which the earlier forms are OE. *Crēcas*, OHG. *Chrēch*, Goth. *Krēks* :– Gmc. **Krēkaz* – L. *Græcus* (applied by the Romans to the people who called themselves Ἕλληνες; see HELLENE) – Gr. Γραικός (acc. to Aristotle a prehistoric name of the Hellenes), adj. deriv. of **Graios*, which was used by the Romans in pl. *Graii* as a poet. syn. of *Græci.*]

I. 1. A native of Greece; a member of the Greek race OE. **2.** A member or adherent of the Greek Church ME. †**3.** A Hellenized Jew –1685. **4.** A cheat, sharper, esp. one who cheats at cards. (Cf. Fr. *grec.*) 1528. **5.** Qualified by *merry, mad, gay*: A merry fellow; a roysterer; a person of loose habits 1536. **6.** *slang.* An Irishman 1823.

1. Come worthy Greeke, Ulisses, come DANIEL. When Greeks joyn'd Greeks, then was the tug of War LEE. **4.** In carde playinge he is a goode greke 1528.

II. [the adj. used *absol.*] **1.** The Greek language ME. **2.** Unintelligible speech, gibberish 1600.

1. Though thou hadst small Latine, and lesse Greeke B. JONS. in *Shaks. Wks.* Pref. verses. **2.** I knew this was heathen G. to them WESLEY. *St. Giles's G.*: slang.

Greek (grīk), *a.* ME. [f. GREEK *sb.*, infl. by L. *Græcus* and Fr. *grec* adjs.] **1.** Of or pertaining to Greece or its people; Hellenic; Grecian. **2.** As the designation of a language (see GREEK *sb.* II. 1). Hence: Belonging to, or written in, the Greek language. 1548. **3.** Distinctive epithet of the *Eastern* or (*Holy*) *Orthodox Church*, now representing the Christianity of Greece, Russia, and the Turkish Empire, which acknowledges the primacy of the Patriarch of Constantinople and which formally renounced communion with the Roman see in the ninth century A.D. Also applied to its clergy, rites, buildings, etc. 1560.

1. Thise noble clerkes grekes CHAUCER. The straight G. nose 1888. 2. This small packet of Greeke and Latine bookes SHAKS. *G. fathers*: those early Christian fathers (see FATHER *sb.*) who wrote in G. 3. The Romanists called the G. church the G. schism E. CHAMBERS.

Comb., etc.: **G. braid** (*ornament*), ornament arranged in the pattern of a fret (see FRET *sb.*[1]); **G. Calends** (see CALENDS); **G. cross** (see CROSS *sb.*); **G. gift,** a gift covering some act of treachery (see Virgil *Æn.* II. 49); **G. masonry,** that in which every alternate stone is made of the whole thickness of the wall; †**G. pitch** (L. *pix Græca*) = COLOPHONY; **G. point,** a kind of needle-made lace; **G. rose** [tr. L. *rosa græca*], a book-name for the Campion.

†**Greek,** *v.* 1615. [f. GREEK *sb.* Cf. L. *Græcari*.] **1.** *To Greek it*: to follow the practice of the Greeks; to play the Greek scholar –1799. **2.** Only in *Greeking*: To cheat at cards –1825. So **Gree·kery,** card-sharping.

Greekish (grī·kiʃ), *a.* [In I, repr. OE. *Crēcisc, Grēcisc*, f. *Crēcas, Grēcas* (see GREEK *sb.*) + *-isc* -ISH[1]. In II, f. GREEK *sb.* or *a.* + -ISH[1].]

I. 1. Of or pertaining to Greece or the Greeks; Greek, Grecian (*arch.*) ME. †**2.** = GREEK *a.* 2. –1647. †**3.** = GREEK *a.* 3. –1639.

1. The..famous light of all the G. hosts SPENSER.

II. Somewhat Greek; resembling Greek persons or things; characteristic of a Greek or Greeks 1568. **b.** Pagan. CARLYLE. Hence **Gree·kishly** *adv.* after the Greek fashion.

Greekize (grī·kəiz), *v. rare.* 1796. [f. GREEK *sb.* + -IZE.] = GRÆCIZE 1. So **Gree·kism** = GRÆCISM 2. **Gree·kist,** a student of Greek.

Greekling (grī·kliŋ). 1636. [f. GREEK *sb.* + -LING[1], after L. *Græculus* (Juvenal), dim. of *Græcus* Greek.] A little Greek; a degenerate, contemptible Greek.

Green (grīn). [OE. *grēne* = OFris. *grēne*, OS. *grōni* (Du. *groen*), OHG. *gruoni* (G. *grün*), ON. *grœnn* :– Gmc. **ȝrōnjaz*, f. **ȝrō-*, base of GROW; cf. GRASS.] **A.** *adj.*

I. 1. Of the colour which in the spectrum is intermediate between blue and yellow; in nature chiefly conspicuous as the colour of growing herbage and leaves. **2.** Covered with a growth of herbage or foliage; verdant; (of trees) in leaf OE. **b.** Of a season of the year: Characterized by verdure; hence, of a winter or Christmas: Mild, temperate ME. **3.** Of the complexion: Having a pale, sickly, or bilious hue, indicative of fear, jealousy, ill-humour, or sickness. (Cf. Gr. χλωρός green, pale.) ME. **4.** Consisting of green herbs, plants, or vegetables 1460. **5.** When applied to fruits or plants, often implying some additional sense: (*a*) Unripe; (*b*) young and tender; (*c*) vigorous, flourishing; (*d*) retaining the natural moisture, not dried OE.

1. How lush and lusty the grasse lookes? How greene SHAKS. The g. Wave MILT. Wing-coverts g. STARK. Meat g. [i.e. putrid from long keeping] before cooking 1863. Phr. †*To give a woman a g. gown*: to roll her, in sport, on the grass so that her dress is stained with g.; hence *euphem.* to deflower her. 2. Yonder Allies g. MILT. The broad way and the g. [cf. *primrose path*] MILT. b. A g. Christmas is neither handsome nor healthfull FULLER. 3. The duke..waxed pale and grene as a lefe LD. BERNERS. 4. G. food for cattle 1804. 5. Hurte the grene blade, & you shall haue no whete there 1526. *Green corn* (U.S.), the unripe and tender ears of maize, commonly cooked as a table vegetable.

II. *transf.* and *fig.* **1.** Full of vitality; not withered or worn out OE. †**2.** Of tender age, youthful –1818. **3.** Unripe, immature, undeveloped. Often with mixture of sense 4 below. ME. **b.** Raw, untrained, inexperienced 1548. **c.** Simple, gullible 1605. **4.** That has not been prepared by drying; hence, not ready for use or consumption 1460. **5.** Unaltered by time or natural processes; fresh, new ME.

1. The example is fresh and greene 1579. He is yet in g. and vigorous senility LAMB. *In the g. tree* (after Luke 23:31): under conditions not involving pressure or hardship. 2. In that new world and greene age of the Church A.V. *Transl. Pref.* 4. 3. The Regency..was still g. and raw BURKE. G. probationers in mischief LAMB. Another young fellow almost as g. as myself 1871. *G. hand* (cf. HAND). 4. Like greene timber SHAKS. Fish-Cod dry..*Ditto* G. 1714. A g. ham wants no soaking MRS. GLASSE. The g. hide of an eland bull 1893. *G. sand*: 'sand used for moulds without previous drying or mixture' (Raymond). 5. A Man that studieth Revenge, keepes his owne Wounds greene BACON. G. Mortar 1776. It [Port] strengthens Digestion..which g. Wines of any kind can't do STEELE. Phr. *G. in earth*: just buried (*Rom. & Jul.* IV. iii. 42).

Comb. **1.** General: as *g.-backed, -curtained*, etc.; *g.-dropping, -glimmering*, etc.; *g.-black, -blue, -yellow* adjs. (occas. sbs.).

2. Special: **g.-book,** a book with a g. cover, *spec.* an official publication of the Indian Government; **-charge,** gunpowder of which the ingredients have been mixed but have not yet undergone the incorporating process; **g. crop,** a crop used for food while in an unripe state, as opp. to a grain crop, hay crop, etc.; **g. ebony,** the wood of the W. Indian tree *Jacaranda ovalifolia*; also of *Excæcaria glandulosa*; **g. fat,** the g. gelatinous portion of the turtle, highly esteemed by epicures; **g. fire,** a pyrotechnical composition, consisting of sulphur, potassium chlorate, and a salt of barium, which burns with a g. flame; **g. gill** (*U.S.*), the condition of oysters when tinged g. by feeding on confervæ; so **g.-gill, -gilled** *adjs.*, affected with g. gill; **g. gland,** 'one of a pair of large glands in Crustacea, supposed to serve as kidneys' (Webster); **g. glass,** bottle-glass; **g. goods** *pl.*, counterfeit greenbacks (see GREENBACK *sb.* 1); also *attrib.* **-jerkin,** one who wears a g. jerkin, a forester; **g. manure,** a mass of growing plants ploughed while g. into the soil, to enrich it; **g. oak,** the wood of oak branches stained g. by a parasitic fungus (used in making Tunbridge ware); **g. oyster,** an oyster coloured g. (see GREEN *v.*) formerly regarded as a delicacy; **g. ribbon,** a ribbon of g. colour worn (*a*) as the badge of the King's Head Club, consisting of supporters of the Duke of Monmouth (1679–85); (*b*) as part of the insignia of the Order of the Thistle; †**g. rushes,** fresh rushes spread on the floor of a house in honour of a guest who is a great stranger; hence used as an exclam. of surprise or welcome; **-salted** *a.*, salted down without tanning; **-soil,** soil in which g. crops are raised; hence **-soil** *v.*, to provide with such a soil; **-stick** *Path.*, a form of fracture of a long bone in which whilst one side of the bone is broken the other is only bent; **-stuff,** vegetation, herbage; *pl.* a commercial term for g. vegetables; **g. syrup** (*Sugar-making*), the syrup which flows off from the loaves; **g. table,** a table covered with g. cloth; hence (*a*) *Hist.* the board of Covenanting notables which ruled Scotland in 1638–41; (*b*) a gaming-table; **-ware,** †(*a*) = *greenstuffs*; (*b*) *Ceramics*, articles just moulded or otherwise shaped, before drying and baking; **g. water,** †(*a*) some remedy for venereal disease; (*b*) *Med.* a name for lochia in the later stage; (*c*) the condition of the Nile when the water is low and unwholesome. For *g. apron, hasting*, etc., see the sbs.

b. In names of animals: **g. bass,** the black bass (see BASS *sb.*[1]); **g. blights,** plant-lice, aphides; **g. bone,** (*a*) the garfish; (*b*) the viviparous blenny; **-bottle,** a fly, *Musca cæsar*; **-cod,** (*a*) = GREENFISH 1; (*b*) the Coal-fish, *Gadus virens*; (*c*) the Cultus Cod, *Ophiodon elongatus*; **g. cormorant,** the shag, *Phalacrocorax graculus*; **g. crab,** the common shore crab, *Carcinus mænas*; **g. drake,** the common May-fly, *Ephemera vulgata*; **g. grosbeak** = GREENFINCH 1; **-leek,** an Australian parrakeet, *Polytelis barrabandi*; **g. linnet** = GREENFINCH 1; **-louse,** a plant-louse or aphis; **g. plover,** the lapwing; **-pollack,** the coal-fish; **-tail** (*fly*), the grannom fly; **-wing,** the green-winged teal, *Querquedula crecca* of Europe, *Q. carolinensis* of America. For *g. turtle, woodpecker*, etc., see the sbs.

c. In names of plants and fruits: **g. ash,** a variety of the ash tree, so called from the colour of the young shoots; **g. brier,** American name for *Smilax*; **g. broom,** the common broom, *Sarothamnus* or *Cytisus scoparius*; **g. dragon,** (*a*) the plant *Dracunculus vulgaris* (formerly *Arum D.*); (*b*) the U.S. plant *Arisæma Dracontium*-dragon-root (Webster); **g. laver,** an edible sea, weed, *Ulva lactuca* and *U. latissima*, also called locally *g. oyster*; **-wort,** sneezewort, *Achillea ptarmica*. For *g. hellebore, rose*, etc., see the sbs.

d. In names of mineral and chemical substances: †**g. brass** = VERDIGRIS; **g. diallage,** (*a*) DIALLAGE[2], a variety of pyroxene; (*b*) = SMARAGDITE, a variety of amphibole; **g. earth** = GLAUCONITE; **g. gold** ?*Obs.*, an alloy of gold and silver; **g. iron ore** = DUFRENITE; **g. lead ore** = PYROMORPHITE; **g. marble** = SERPENTINE; **g. mineral** = MALACHITE. For *g. bice, copperas*, etc., see the sbs.

B. *sb.* **1.** The adj. used *absol.* That which is green; the green part of anything OE. **2.** Green colour. In *pl.* = different tints of green ME. **3.** A green dye or pigment; usu. defined as *Brunswick, emerald*, etc. 1611. **4.** Green clothing or dress (*lit.* and *fig.*) ME. **5.** *Antiq.* As the distinctive colour of one of the factions in the circus. Also *pl.* the adherents of this faction. 1693. **6.** The emblematic colour of Ireland; hence adopted as the colour of the 'nationalist' party 1797. **7.** Greenness, as indicative of vigour, youthfulness, virility 1586. **8.** Verdure, vegetation, greenery ME. †**9.** A tree, herb, or plant. (Mostly in pl.) –1719. **10.** *pl.* **a.** Freshly cut greenery used for decoration. Now *U.S.* 1697. **b.** Green vegetables such as are boiled for the table (*colloq.*) 1725. **11.** Grassy ground; a grassy spot. Now *rare.* ME. **b.** A piece of grassy land situated in or near a town or village 1477. **c.** A piece of grassy land used for some particular purpose, as BOWLING-GREEN. In *Golf*, the putting-ground; sometimes = the whole links. 1646. **12.** *attrib.* Of or pertaining to a bowling-green or golf-links, as *g.-keeper* 1705.

4. A hunter all in grene ME. 6. They are hanging men and women for the wearing of the green 1798. 7. Phr. *In the g.*: in the period of youthful vigour. Thy leaf has perish'd in the g. TENNYSON. 10. b. Bacon and Greens WESLEY. 11. Goodly gardens and pleasant greenes KNOLLES. b. Every Holiday, she danced upon the G. 1718.

Green (grīn), *v.* [OE. *grēnian*, f. *grēne*; see prec.] **1.** *intr.* To become green, as growing herbage; *occas.* to appear or look green. **2.** *trans.* To impart a green colour to; to clothe with green 1570. **b.** *Oyster-culture.* To turn oysters green in the gills by putting them in pits. Also *absol.* 16.. **3.** *slang.* To make to appear green; to hoax, take in 1884.

2. Have not rains Green'd over April's lap KEATS. 3. To g. a visitor 1884.

Greenback (grī·nbæk), *sb.* 1778. [f. GREEN *a.* + BACK *sb.*[1]] **1.** One of the legal-tender notes of the U.S., first issued in 1862 and so called from the devices printed in green ink on the back. Hence 'any note issued by a national bank in the U.S.' (Funk). Also *attrib.*, as in **Greenback party,** a party in U.S. politics, which advocated that greenbacks should be made the sole currency of the country. **2. a.** The garfish, *Belone vulgaris*. **b.** The American golden plover, *Charadrius dominicus*. **c.** *slang.* A frog. 1778. Hence **Gree·nbacker,** a member of the g. party.

Green bag, green-bag. 1677. A bag made of green material used formerly by barristers and lawyers for documents and papers. Also *attrib.*

Gree·n-blind, *a.* 1881. Suffering from colour-blindness in respect of green light-rays. Hence **Green-blindness.**

Green cheese. ME. **a.** New or fresh cheese. **b.** An inferior kind of cheese made from skim milk or whey. **c.** Cheese coloured green with sage; also called *sage cheese*.

Green cloth, greencloth. 1536. **1.** In full, *Board of Green Cloth*: A department of the Royal Household, consisting of the Lord Steward and his subordinates, which has control of various matters of expenditure, and legal and judicial authority within the sovereign's court-royal, with power to correct offenders, and to maintain the peace of the verge of the court-royal, which extends every way two hundred yards from the gate of the palace. (So called from the green-coloured table at which its business was originally transacted.) Also *attrib.* **2.** *colloq.* The green baize covering of a billiard, etc. table; hence, the table itself 1871.

Greenery (grī·nəri). 1797. [f. GREEN *a.* or *sb.* + -ERY.] **1.** Green foliage or vegetation; verdure. **2.** Green branches or leaves for decoration. (Rarely *pl.*) 1867. **3.** A place where plants are reared or kept 1847.

Green-eyed (grīn,əid), *a.* (Stress variable.) 1596. [f. GREEN *a.* + EYE *sb.*[1] + -ED[2]. Cf. EYED 1.] Having green eyes. *The green-eyed monster* (Shaks.): jealousy. Hence *fig.* Viewing everything with jealousy.

Oh, beware my Lord, of ielousie, It is the greene-ey'd Monster *Oth.* III. iii. 166.

Greenfinch (grī·nfinʃ). 1532. [See GREEN *a.* and FINCH.] **1.** A common European bird of the family *Fringillidæ*, *Coccothraustes* or *Ligurinus chloris*, so called from its green and gold plumage. Called also *green linnet*. **2.** The Texas sparrow (*Embernagra rufivirgata*) 1883. **3.** *slang.* One of the Pope's Irish guard 1865.

Green-fish (grī·nfiʃ). 1460. [See GREEN *a.* II. 4.] †**1.** Fresh, unsalted fish; *spec.* applied to cod –1867. **2. a.** *local.* The coal-fish 1880. **b.** *U.S.* The blue-fish (*Pomatomus saltatrix*) 1884.

Gree·n-fly. 1686. **1.** *Angling.* A particular kind of artificial fly. **2.** An aphis or plant-louse, from its colour. Usually *collect. sing.* 1744.

Greengage (grīngē[i]dʒ). 1759. [f. GREEN *a.* and the surname of Sir William *Gage.*] A variety of plum of roundish shape, green colour, and fine flavour. Also *attrib.*

Green goose. 1564. [See GREEN *a.*; the use of the word in opposition to *stubble-goose* suggests GREEN *sb.*] **1.** A young goose, a gosling. ?Now *dial.* (See also quot.) **2.** A simpleton (*rare*) 1768.

1. The greene goose is better than the stubble goose 1589.

Greengrocer (grī·ngrō[u]:səɹ). 1723. [See GREEN and GROCER.] A retail dealer in vegetables and fruit. Hence **Gree·ngro:cery,** the business of a g.; the articles retailed by a g.; also *attrib.*

Green head, gree·nhead. 1569. [f. GREEN *a.* + HEAD *sb.*] †**1.** A young, immature, or untrained intellect –1694. **2.** A simpleton, an ignoramus. ?*Obs.* 1589. †**3.** One entitled to wear the green turban, a descendant of Mohammed –1625. Hence †**Green-headed** *a.* raw.

Greenheart (grī·nhāɹt). 1756. [See GREEN *a.* and HEART *sb.* IV. 3.] **1.** The name of several W. Indian trees. **a.** A large lauraceous tree of Guiana, *Nectandra rodiæi*, which furnishes very hard timber. **b.** The cog-wood tree, *Ceanothus chloroxylon*. **c.** A small rhamnaceous tree, the *Colubrina ferruginosa* of Jamaica. **d.** *Bastard* or *False Greenheart*, a small myrtaceous tree, *Calyptranthes chytraculia*. **2.** The timber of 1a, used in shipbuilding, for fishing-rods, etc. Also *attrib.* 1794. **b.** A fishing-rod of this wood 1884.

Gree·nhew. *Obs.* exc. *Hist.* 1598. [app. f. GREEN *a.* + HEW *v.*] **1.** = VERT *sb.*[1] 1. Also *attrib.* **2.** The right to cut greenery for fodder; payment for this right 1869.

Greenhorn (grī·nhǭɹn). 1650. [GREEN *a.*] **1.** A raw recruit –1682. **2.** A raw, inexperienced person; an ignoramus; hence, a simpleton 1682. Hence **Gree·nhornism,** inexperience.

Green-house, greenhouse (grī·nhaus). 1664. **1.** [f. GREEN *sb.* 9.] A glass-house in which delicate and tender plants are reared and preserved. Also *attrib.* **2.** *Pottery.* A house in which 'green ware' (see GREEN *a.*) is left to dry before being placed in the kiln 1875.

Greening (grī·niŋ), *sb.* 1600. [prob. – MDu. *groeninc* (Du. *groening*) kind of apple; see GREEN *a.*, -ING[3].] **1.** †**a.** A variety of pear –1632. **b.** An apple, which is green when ripe 1664.

Greenish (grī·niʃ), *a.* ME. [f. GREEN *a.* + -ISH[1].] Somewhat green. **b.** Qualifying adjs. or sbs. of colour, as *g.-blue* 1644.

Greenland (grī·nlănd). 1678. [f. GREEN *a.* + LAND *sb.*, ult. after ON. *Grœnland*. So named by its discoverer, 'because it would induce settlers to go there, if the land had a good name'.] **1.** A large island or small continent to the north-east of N. America. Also *attrib.* **2.** *slang.* The country of greenhorns. DICKENS. Hence **Gree·nlander,** a native or inhabitant of G. **Greenla·ndic** *a.* of or pertaining to G., its language and its inhabitants; *sb.* the language of G.

Greenless (grī·nlės), *a.* 1618. [f. GREEN *sb.* + -LESS.] Without greenness or verdure.

Greenlet (grī·nlėt). 1831. [f. GREEN *a.* + *-let*; app. formed to render the etym. sense of L. *vireo.*] A name for the numerous species of small greenish American singing-birds of the genus *Vireo* or family *Vireonidæ*.

Greenling (grī·nliŋ). *rare.* 1440. [f. GREEN *a.* + -LING[1].] = GREEN-FISH 1 and 2a.

Greenly (grī·nli), *adv.* 1583. [f. GREEN *a.* + -LY[2].] **1.** With a green colour; with green vegetation. **2.** *fig.* Freshly, vigorously, youthfully 1633. **3.** In an inexperienced or unskilful manner (*arch.*) 1599.

3. We haue done but g. SHAKS.

Green man, greenman. 1638. †**1.** A man dressed up with greenery to represent a wild man of the woods; a Jack-in-the-green –1810. **2.** A fresh, raw, or inexperienced man; *spec.* in whale-fishing, one who has not been to sea before. *Obs.* exc. *Hist.* 1682. **3.** A name for *Aceras anthropophora* 1829.

Greenness (grī·nˌnės). [OE. *grēnnes*, f. *grēne* GREEN; see -NESS.] **1.** The quality or condition of being green; *concr.* or semi-*concr.* verdure. **2.** Unripeness; immaturity; crudity; inexperience; gullibility ME. **3.** The vigour or freshness of growth; vitality 1649. **4.** Freshness, newness. ?*Obs.* 1553.

1. The g. of fields LAMB, of the sea TYNDALL **2.** The g. of his yeares 1579, of his troops 1875.

Greenockite (grī·nəkəit). 1844. [Named after Lord *Greenock* by Jameson in 1840; see -ITE[1] 2 b.] *Min.* Native sulphide of cadmium, found usually in yellow coatings, rarely in crystals.

Green-peak (grī·nˌpīk). Also **-peek.** 1598. [tr. It. *picchio verde* or Fr. **pic-vert* (now *pivert*).] The Green Woodpecker, *Gecinus viridis*.

Gree·n-room. 1701. **1.** A room in a theatre for actors and actresses when not required on the stage, perh. orig. painted green. *transf.* The players who frequent the green-room. **2.** A room in a warehouse or factory for the reception of goods in a 'green' state, such as fresh cloth, undried pottery, etc. (Recent Dicts.)

Gree·n-sand, gree·nsand. 1796. **1.** *Min.* and *Geol.* **a.** = GLAUCONITE. **b.** A variety of sandstone, usually imperfectly consolidated, consisting largely of glauconite. **c.** A formation consisting largely of this sandstone; denominated *Upper* or *Lower Greensand* from the position of the stratum relatively to the gault. **2.** See GREEN *a.* II. 4.

Greenshank (grī·nʃæŋk). 1766. A large sandpiper, *Totanus glottis*; prob. so called from its olive-coloured legs.

Green sickness, green-sickness (grī:nsi·knės). 1583. [See GREEN *a.* I. 3.] An anaemic disease which mostly affects young women about the age of puberty and gives a pale or greenish tinge to the complexion; chlorosis. Also *transf.* and *fig.* (often with reference to the morbid appetite which characterizes chlorosis). Also *attrib.*

attrib. Out you greene sicknesse carrion, out you baggage, You tallow face SHAKS.

Green-sleeves. 1580. A woman wearing green sleeves; the name given to an inconstant lady-love in a ballad published in 1580; hence, the ballad and the tune themselves.

Let it thunder to the tune of Greene-sleeues SHAKS.

Green snake. *U.S.* 1791. **1.** One of two green harmless snakes of the U.S. **2.** An air-plant resembling the snake 1883.

Green-stone, gree·nstone. 1772. [f. GREEN *a.* + STONE *sb.*; in sense 1 from G. *grünstein.*] **1.** *Geol.* A wide term, usually comprising the greenish-coloured eruptive rocks containing feldspar and hornblende (or augite), such as diorite, melaphyre, etc. 1805. Also *attrib.* **2.** *Min.* = NEPHRITE, a variety of jade 1772. **3.** A hard and close-textured stone used for putting the last edge on delicate surgical instruments (*Cent. Dict.*).

Greensward (grī·nswǭɹd). 1600. [SWARD *sb.*] Turf on which grass is growing.

Greenth (grīnþ). 1753. [f. GREEN *a.* + -TH[1] (H. Walpole).] Verdure.

Green wax, gree·nwax. *Obs.* exc. *Hist.* ME. Sealing-wax of a green colour; hence **b.** A seal of green wax, as affixed to documents delivered by the Exchequer to sheriffs. **c.** An estreat, etc. bearing this seal; also *process of green wax.* **d.** The fines or amercements exacted in accordance with such a document.

Greenweed (grī·nwīd). 1599. [f. GREEN *a.* + WEED *sb.*[1]] **1.** The plant *Genista tinctoria*; used for dyeing. **2.** A green sea-weed 1856.

Greenwich (gri·nidʒ). A town on the south bank of the Thames, adjoining London on the east, famous for its astronomical observatory and its hospital; used *attrib.* in **G. stars,** 'those used for lunar computations in the nautical ephemeris' (Smyth); **Greenwich time,** mean time for the meridian of Greenwich, the standard time for English astronomers.

Greenwood (grī·nwud). ME. [See GREEN *a.* I. 2.] A wood or forest when in leaf. Also *attrib.*

Phr. *To go to the g.*: to become an outlaw. I muste too The grene wode goo Alone a bannysshed man 1500

Greeny (grī·ni), *a.* 1593. [f. GREEN *a.* + -Y[1].] †**1.** Green, verdant. Also *fig.* Vigorous. –1674. **2.** = GREENISH *a.* 1826.

Green-yard, greenyard (grī·nyāɹd). 1578. An enclosure covered with grass or turf (not paved); *spec.* a pound for stray animals, etc.; also, a grass yard for hounds to take exercise in.

†**Greet,** *sb.*[1] 1590. [f. GREET *v.*[1]] A greeting –1634.

Greet (grīt), *sb.*[2] *Obs.* exc. *Sc.* ME. [f. GREET *v.*[2]] Weeping, lamentation; a cry of sorrow.

Greet (grīt), *v.*[1] [OE. *grētan*, **grǣtan* handle, touch, visit, attack, treat, salute = OFris. *grēta* salute, complain, OS. *grōtian* call upon (Du. *groeten* salute), OHG. *gruozzen* address, attack (G. *grüssen* salute, greet) :– WGmc. **ȝrōtjan* cry out, call upon, (hence) provoke to action, assail, address.] †**1.** *trans.* To approach, come up to; to begin upon. OE. only. †**2.** To assail, attack –ME. **3.** To address with expressions of goodwill or courtesy; to offer in speech or writing to (a person) the expression of one's own or another's friendly or polite regard. Now only *literary.* Also *absol.* OE. **b.** To salute *with* words or gestures; also *transf.* OE. †**c.** In Spenser: to offer congratulations on (an achievement, etc.); const. *unto* or *dative.* †**d.** To gratify. *Per.* IV. iii. 38. **4.** To receive or meet with demonstrations of welcome 1605. **5.** Of a thing (now only of sights or sounds.): To meet 1698.

3. There's other of our friends Will g. vs heere anon SHAKS. *absol.* There greete in silence as the dead are wont SHAKS. **b.** To g. the strangers with a nod DICKENS. **4.** We will g. the time SHAKS. **5.** A wide extent of sea greets the eye 1872.

Greet (grīt), *v.*[2] Now *Sc.* and *n. dial.* [(i) OE. (Anglian) *grētan*, **grǣtan* = OS. *grātan*, MHG. *grāzen* cry out, rage, storm, ON. *grāta*, Goth. *grētan* :– Gmc. **ȝrǣtan*, orig. redupl. str. vb. rel. to prec. (ii) OE. *grēotan* (= OS. *griotan*), perh. f. Gmc. **ȝa-* Y- + vb. repr. by synon. OE. *rēotan.*] **1.** *intr.* To weep, cry, lament, grieve. †**2.** To cry or call out in supplication or in anger –1513.

Greet(e, obs. f. GREAT *a.*

Greeter[1] (grī·təɹ). 1552. [f. GREET *v.*[1] + -ER[1].] One who greets or salutes.

Greeter[2] (grī·təɹ). *Sc.* 17.. [f. GREET *v.*[2] + -ER[1].] One who greets or cries.

Greeting (grī·tiŋ), *vbl. sb.* OE. [f. GREET *v.*[1] + -ING[1].] The action of GREET *v.*[1]; a salutation.

Health, and faire g. from our Generall SHAKS. Phr. *Sendeth g.*: a transl. (now *arch.*) of L. *salutem (dicit)*, Gr. χαίρειν; also with ellipsis of the vb.

Greeve, obs. f. GRIEVE.

Greffier (gre·fiəɹ, Fr. gręfye). 1590. [– Fr. *greffier* – med.L. *graphiarius* registrar, f. *graphium* register; see GRAFF *sb.*[1]] **1.** A registrar, clerk, or notary. **2.** A white hunting dog. TURBERV.

Gregal (grī·găl), *a.* 1540. [– L. *gregalis*, f. *grex, greg-*; see -AL[1].] **1.** Pertaining to a flock, or to the multitude (*rare*). †**2.** = GREGARIOUS –1658.

‖**Gregale** (gregā·le). Also **grigale, grecale.** 1804. [It.; app. repr. a late L. **græcalis*, f. L. *Græcus.*] The north-east wind in the Mediterranean.

Gregarian (grėgē[ə]·riăn), *a. rare.* 1632. [f. L. *gregarius* (see GREGARIOUS) + -AN.] Belonging to the herd or common sort. Of a soldier: Common, private.

Gregarine (gre·gărin). 1867. [f. mod.L. *Gregarina* (f. L. *gregarius*: see next), the typical genus of the *Gregarinidæ*. See -INE[1].]

A. *adj.* Of or pertaining to the genus *Gregarina* or class *Gregarinida* of protozoans, parasitic chiefly in insects, molluscs, and crustacea. (Rec. Dicts.).

B. *sb.* One of the *Gregarinida.*

Gregarious (grĕgēᵊ·riəs), *a.* 1668. [f. L. *gregarius*, f. *grex, greg-* flock, herd + -OUS; see -ARIOUS.] **1.** *Nat. Hist.* Of animals: Living in flocks or communities, given to association with others of the same species. **b.** *transf.* of persons 1789. **2.** *Bot.* Growing in open clusters 1829. **3.** *Path.* Clustered 1822. **4.** Of or pertaining to a flock or community; characteristic of persons gathered together in crowds 1833.

1. Stares are g. birds, living and flying together in great flocks RAY. **4.** Mere religious zeal is a g. thing MOZLEY. Hence **Grega·rious-ly** *adv.*, **-ness.**

‖**Grège** (greⁱʒ). Also **greige.** 1927. [Fr., in *soie grège* raw silk – It. *greggio* raw, crude, unprocessed.] (Of) a colour between beige and grey.

†**Greg(g)e,** *v.* ME. [Aphetic f. *agrege* AGGREGE.] = *agregge*, AGGREGE.

‖**Grego** (grē·go). Also †**greiko.** 1747. [– some Rom. form of L. *Græcus* GREEK *a.*] A coarse jacket with a hood, worn in the Levant. Also *slang*, a rough great-coat.

Gregorian (grĭgōᵊ·rĭan). 1598. [– med.L. *Gregorianus* (in *cantus Gregorianus* XII), f. late L. *Gregorius* – Gr. Γρηγόριος; see -IAN.] A man's name; in some senses used with reference to the Eng. surname Gregory.]

A. *adj.* **1.** Of or pertaining to Pope Gregory I (who reigned 590–600); chiefly applied to the ancient system of ritual music, also known as *plain-chant* or *plain-song* (characterized by free rhythm, a limited scale, etc.), which is founded on the *Antiphonarium* ascribed to Pope Gregory. So *G. chant, music, tones*, etc. 1653. **2.** Of, pertaining to, or established by Pope Gregory XIII. 1642. **3.** Distinctive epithet of the reflecting telescope invented by J. Gregory (died 1675) 1761. †**4.** *G. tree*, the gallows, so named from Gregory Brandon, a hangman –1785.

2. *G. calendar:* see CALENDAR 1; so *G. style* = 'new style'. *G. epoch*, the time from which the G. calendar dates (1582).

B. *sb.* **1.** A variety of wig, named after one Gregory, a Strand barber 1598. **2.** A member of an 18th c. society (often classed with the Freemasons) 1742. **3.** A Gregorian chant; †also, one versed in Gregorian music 1609.

1. A quaint G. to thy head to binde HARINGTON. Hence **Grego·rianist,** one who advocates the use of G. chants.

Gregory-powder. Also **gregory.** 1886. [f. James *Gregory*, a Scottish physician (1758–1822).] The 'compound powder of rhubarb' (*Pulvis rhei composita*) of the British Pharmacopœia. Usually called *Gregory's powder.*

Greisen (grəi·z'n). 1878. [G.; a dial. var. of *greiss*, f. *greissen* to split.] *Min.* A granitic rock with crystalline granular texture, consisting chiefly of quartz and mica.

Greit, obs. f. GREET *sb.*², *v.*²

Greith(e, obs. form of GRAITH.

Gremial (grī·miăl). 1563. [– med.L. *gremialis* alumnus, *gremiale* bishop's apron, f. L. *gremium* lap, bosom; see -IAL.]

A. *adj.* **1.** Of or pertaining to the bosom or lap. Of a friend: Intimate (cf. *bosom-friend*). *Obs.* exc. in *g. veil* = B. 2. 1631. **2.** Dwelling within the bosom of a University or society, resident. Also opp. to *honorary. Obs.* exc. *Hist.* 1730.

B. *sb.* **1.** A resident member (of a University, etc.). *Obs.* exc. *Hist.* 1563. **2.** *Eccl.* A silken apron placed on the bishop's lap when celebrating Mass or conferring orders 1811.

Grenade¹ (grĕnēⁱ·d). 1532. [– Fr. *grenade* (XVI), alt. of OFr. (*pome*) *grenate* POMEGRANATE after Sp. *granada.*] †**1.** A pomegranate –1664. **2.** A small explosive shell, usually of metal, thrown or shot into the trenches or among clusters of the enemy 1591. See HAND-GRENADE, RIFLE-*grenade.* **b.** A glass receptacle to be thrown in order to burst and disperse its contents 1891.

2. b. *Drain g.*, one filled with a strong-smelling fluid, to be used in detecting a leakage in a drain. *Fire-g.* = HAND-GRENADE 2.

Grenade² (grĕnēⁱ·d). 1706. [Alleged to be Fr.; perh. f. *grain* GRAIN *sb.*¹, with sense 'something spiced' (cf. OFr. *grané* mentioned s.v. GRAVY). Cf. GRENADINE¹.] *Cookery.* 'A dish of larded veal-collops, with six pigeons and a ragoo in the middle, and covered on the top and underneath with thin slices of bacon.'

Grenadier (grenădīᵊ·ɹ). 1676. [– Fr. *grenadier*, f. *grenade* GRENADE¹ 2; see -IER.] **1.** Orig., a soldier who threw grenades. At first four or five were attached to each company, but, later, each battalion or regiment had a company of them. When grenades went out of general use, the name of 'grenadiers' was retained for a company of the finest and tallest men in the regiment. Now, in the British army, the word is retained only in the name of the Grenadier Guards (*colloq.* Grenadiers), the first regiment of household infantry. Also *attrib.* **2. a.** A S. African weaver-bird, *Pyromelana* (or *Ploceus*) *oryx*, with vivid red and black plumage. Also *g. grosbeak, g. waxbill.* 1751. **b.** The fish *Macrurus fabricii* or *M. rupestris* 1889.

1. Now were brought into service a new sort of soldiers call'd *Granadiers*, who were dextrous in flinging hand granados EVELYN.

Grenadilla: see GRANADILLA.

Grenadine¹ (gre·nădin). 1706. [– Fr. *grenadin*; cf. GRENADE².] *Cookery.* A dish of veal or of fillets of poultry, etc., smoothly trimmed, larded, and brightly glazed.

Grenadine² (gre·nădin). 1865. [– Fr. *grenadine*, formerly *grenade* silk of a grained texture, f. *grenu* grained, f. *grain* GRAIN; see -INE⁴.] An open silk or silk and wool textile used for dresses.

Grenado (grĕnēⁱ·do). *arch.* 1611. [– Sp. *granada*; see GRENADE¹ and -ADO.] = GRENADE¹ 2. Also *attrib.*

Grenatite (gre·nătəit). Also **granatite.** 1804. [– Fr. *grenat* garnet + -ITE¹ 2 b.] *Min.* = STAUROLITE.

Grene, obs. f. GRAIN, GREEN.

Gres, obs. f. GRASS, GREASE.

†**Gre·ssible,** *a.* 1600. [– late L. *gressibilis*, f. *gress-*, pa. ppl. stem of L. *gradi* walk; see -BLE.] Able to walk –1610.

A two legd liuing creature, g., vnfeathered *Timon* v. iv. 86. So †**Gre·ssile** *a.* (*rare*).

Gressorial (gresōᵊ·riăl), *a.* 1842. [– mod.L. *gressorius* f. *gress-* (see prec.) + -ORIAL.] Adapted for stepping or walking, ambulatory.

Gressorial, in Ornithology, is applied to the feet of birds which have three toes forward, two of which are connected, and one behind 1842. So **Gresso·rious** *a.*

Gret, obs. f. GREAT, GREET *sb.*²; obs. pa. t. of GREET *v.*¹ and ².

Grete, obs. f. GREAT, GREET.

Grew, pa. t. of GROW *v.*

Grewsome, obs. f. GRUESOME.

Grey, gray (grēⁱ). [OE. *grǣġ* = OFris. *grē*, MDu. *grau, gra* (Du. *grauw*), OHG. *grāo* (G. *grau*), ON. *grár* :– Gmc. **ʒrǣwaz.* Both spellings have analogies in two words in gen. use derived from OE. forms in *-ǣġ* and pronounced with *ē*ⁱ, viz., *clay* and *whey*; the practice of printing houses is various and individuals tend to use the vars. with a difference of implication; the *-ey* form is established in *Scots Greys* and *a pair of greys.*]

A. *adj.* **1.** Of the colour intermediate between black and white, or composed of a mixture of black and white with little or no positive hue; ash-coloured, lead-coloured. Also *fig.* ¶**b.** (See quot.) 1885. **2.** Epithet of (*a*) the Cistercian monks, (*b*) the Franciscan friars, (*c*) the sisters of the third order of St. Francis, on account of the colour of their habits. See also GREY FRIAR. ME. **3.** Of the eyes: Having a grey iris ME. **4.** Of a horse: Having a grey coat ME. **5.** Of the hair or beard: That is turning white (with age or grief) ME. **b.** Of a person: Grey-haired 1483. **c.** *fig.* Ancient, old 1662. **d.** Belonging to old age; hence (of experience, etc.), mature 1602.

1. The night is chill, the cloud is gray COLERIDGE. The grass path grey with dew BROWNING. **b.** Grey is composed only of black and white; the term gray is applied to any broken colour of a cool hue, and therefore belongs to the class of chromatic colours 1885. **2.** It was the Friar of Orders gray SHAKS. **3.** With kamuse nose and eyen greye as glas CHAUCER. **4.** My horse, gray Capilet SHAKS. Proverb. *The grey mare is the better horse*: the wife rules the husband. **5.** I..with grey haires and bruise of many daies, Do challenge thee SHAKS. **c.** Mac-Kinnon's chief, in warfare grey SCOTT. **d.** Type of grey honour, and sweet rest RUSKIN.

Comb.: **1.** General: as *grey-black, -blue*, etc.; *grey-eyed, -haired*, etc.

2. Special: as **grey band**, a grey laminated quartzose sandstone; **grey groat**, emphatic for *groat*; also a type of something of little value; **grey matter**, the grey-coloured matter of which the active part of the brain is composed; also *fig.*; **grey millet** = GROMWELL, q.v.; **grey powder**, a powder consisting of mercury and chalk; **grey russet**, coarse cloth of a dull grey colour; **grey wethers**, detached oolitic sandstones of various sizes; applied also in Devonshire to two circles of stones which nearly touch each other, and look like sheep, when seen from a distance.

b. In names of animals, as **grey bass**, a sea-fish of the perch family, but resembling the mullet in taste; **grey crow**, the Hooded Crow, *Corvus cornix;* **grey duck**, the gadwall; **grey falcon**, (*a*) the hen-harrier; (*b*) the common or Peregrine Falcon; **grey fly**, perh. a dor-beetle; **grey fowl**, grouse in winter plumage; **grey mullet** (see MULLET¹); **grey owl, parrot** (see the sbs.); **grey pike** = HORN-FISH 2; **grey plover, sandpiper**, etc. (see the sbs.); **grey snipe**, 'the dowitcher in winter plumage' (Webster); **grey trout** (see TROUT); **grey whale**, *Rhachianectes glaucus.*

c. In names of minerals, as **grey antimony, cobalt** (see the sbs.); **grey copper (ore)**, tetrahedrite; **grey ore**, chalcocite.

B. *sb.* **1.** Grey material or clothing ME.; *techn.* unbleached material 1884. †**2.** *spec.* Grey fur; usu. of badger skin –1702. **3.** A grey or subdued light; esp. in phr. *the g. of the morning* 1592. **4.** Grey colour. In *pl.* = shades of this 1825. **b.** *Gunmaking.* A grey spot indicating a flaw 1881. **c.** A grey-coloured pigment 1888. †**5.** A grey-haired person –1513. †**6.** A badger –1686. **7.** A grey horse. Chiefly *pl.* 1760. **8.** *pl.* (in full *Scots Greys*). A regiment of dragoons, now the 2nd Dragoons 1751. **9.** A kind of fish; ?a GRILSE 1686.

1. A Gown of gray 1640. **3.** Yon gray is not the mornings eye SHAKS. **7.** Mrs. Mantrap..drives her greys in the Park THACKERAY.

Grey (grēⁱ), *v.* Also **gray.** ME. [f. GREY *a.*] **1.** *intr.* To become or grow grey. **2.** *trans.* To make grey 1879.

Grey-back, greyback (grēⁱ·bæk). 1864. **1.** *U.S. colloq.* A Confederate soldier in the American civil war. **2.** *dial.* and *U.S. colloq.* A louse 1864. **3.** A name of birds. **a.** The Hooded Crow, *Corvus cornix.* Also *g. crow.* **b.** *U.S.* The N. American Knot, *Trigla canutus.* **c.** *dial.* and *U.S.* The scaup duck, *Fuligula marila.* 1888. **4.** *U.S.* The grey whale 1884.

Greybeard (grēⁱ·bīᵊɹd). Also **graybeard.** 1579. **1.** A man with a grey beard; hence, an old man. **2.** A large earthenware or stoneware jug or jar, used for holding spirits 1788. **3.** A hydroid polyp which infests oyster-beds, *Sertularia argentea.* (Rec. Dicts.). **4.** *attrib.* **Greybeard lichen,** *Usnea barbata.* Hence **Greybearded** *a.*

Grey·-coat. 1644. One who wears grey clothing; *spec.* a Cumberland yeoman. **b.** *attrib.*: **Grey-coat Hospital**, a charity school, where the scholars were clothed in grey; **grey-coat parson**, an impropriator; a holder of lay tithes. Hence **Grey-coated** *a.*

Grey friar. ME. [See GREY *a.* 2.] A member of the order of Franciscan or Minor frairs, founded by St. Francis of Assisi in 1210. *Grey Friars*, a convent of this order.

Grey goose. OE. The greylag goose.

Grey-hen (grēⁱ·hen). late ME. Female of the black grouse (*Tetrao tetrix*), the heath-hen. (The male is called the BLACKCOCK.)

Greyhound (grēⁱ·hαund). [OE. *grīġhund*, **grīeġhund* (= ON. *greyhundr*), f. **grīeġ* (= ON. *groy* n. bitch :– Gmc. **ʒraujam*) + *hund* dog, HOUND. The etym. of the first element is unknown.] **1.** A variety of dog used in the chase, characterized by its long slender body and long legs, its keenness of sight, and its great speed in running. **2.** *transf.* An ocean steamship specially built for speed. Also *ocean g.* 1887. *Comb.* **g. fox**, a name given to the largest and boldest variety of the fox kind; **g. racing** (contr. **greycing**), a sport in which a mechanical hare is coursed by greyhounds.

Greyish (grēⁱ·iʃ), *a.* Also **grayish.** 1508. [f. GREY *a.* + -ISH¹.] Somewhat grey.

Grey lag goose, grey·lag (goose). 1713. [orig. three words. The bird remains longer in England than the other migratory species;

hence the use of LAG *a.*] The common wild goose of Europe, *Anser cinereus* or *ferus*.

Greyling, obs. f. GRAYLING.

Greyness, grayness (grēⁱ·nės). 1483. [f. GREY *a.* + -NESS.] The state or quality of being grey; grey colour. Also *fig.*

Greystone, graystone (grēⁱ·stōᵘn). 1815. [f. GREY *a.* + STONE *sb.*] *Min.* A grey volcanic rock, composed of feldspar (sometimes replaced by leucite or melilite), augite, or hornblende, and iron.

Greywacke (grēⁱ·wækə). Also **graywacke, greywack.** 1811. [Anglicized f. GRAUWACKE.] *Geol.* A conglomerate or grit rock consisting of rounded pebbles and sand firmly united together; orig. applied to various strata of the Silurian series; now little used. Rarely *pl.*

Gribble (gri·b'l). 1838. [perh. cogn. w. GRUB *v.*] A small marine boring crustacean, *Limnoria terebrans*, resembling a wood-louse.

Grice (grəis). *Obs.* exc. *Sc.* and *arch.* ME. [– ON. *griss* (Sw., Da. *gris*) young pig, pig.] A pig, *esp.* a young pig, a sucking pig; †*occas.* and *spec.* in *Her.*, a wild boar.

Provb. Bring the head of the sow to the tail of the g.: balance your loss with your gain.

Grice, obs. f. GRECE, steps.

Grid (grid). 1839. [Back-formation from GRIDIRON.] **1.** A grating. **2.** = GRIDIRON 1. 1875. **3.** = GRIDIRON 3. *Naut.* 1867. **4.** The wire spiral between the filament and the plate of a wireless valve 1922. **5.** A network of lines on a map 1918. **6.** A network of electric lines, etc. 1926.

Griddle (gri·d'l), *sb.* [– OFr. *gredil, gridil* gridiron (mod. *gril*) :– Rom. **graticulum*, **craticulum* (see GRILLE *sb.*, GRILL *sb.*³), dim. of L. *cratis* (see CRATE, GRATE *sb.*).] †**1.** = GRIDIRON 1. –1746. **2.** = GIRDLE *sb.*² ME. **3.** *Mining.* A wire-bottomed sieve 1776.

Comb.: **g.-bread, -cake,** bread or cake baked on a g.; †**-iron** = sense 2.

Griddle (gri·d'l), *v.* ME. [f. the sb.] **1.** *trans.* To cook on a griddle. **2.** *Mining.* *To g. out*: To screen ore with a griddle 1776.

Gride (grəid), *sb.* 1830. [f. GRIDE *v.*] A strident or grating sound.

Gride (grəid), *v.* Chiefly *poet.* ME. [Metathetic f. GIRD *v.*², adopted by Spenser from Lydgate.] **1.** *trans.* To pierce with a weapon; to wound; †also, to inflict (a wound) by piercing. Also *fig.* **2.** *intr.* To pierce *through*. Now usually, To cut, scrape, or graze *along*, etc., with a strident, grating, or whizzing sound, or so as to cause rasping pain 1590. **3.** *trans.* To clash or graze against with a strident sound; to cause to grate 1821.

2. Through his thigh the mortall steele did gryde SPENSER. **3.** The wood which grides and clangs Its leafless ribs and iron horns Together TENNYSON.

Gridelin (gri·dělin). Also †**gridaline,** †**grizelin.** 1640. [– Fr. *gridelin, gris-de-lin* 'grey of flax', flax-grey.]

A. *sb.* The name of a colour, a pale purple or grey violet; occas., a pale red.

B. *adj.* Having this colour.

Gridiron (gri·dəiᵊɹn), *sb.* [ME. *gredire*, appearing in the same text with *gredile* GRIDDLE. The *-ire* was early identified with ME. *ire* = *iren* IRON *sb.*¹ See also ANDIRON.] **1.** A framework of parallel metal bars, used for broiling flesh or fish over a fire. †Also formerly, a griddle. **b.** A similar structure used in torture by fire. (The first sense in Eng.) ME. **2.** *fig.* 1590. **3.** Any object resembling or likened to a gridiron; esp. *Naut.* a heavy framework of beams in parallel open order used to support a ship in dock. (So Fr. *gril.*) 1846.

3. b. A football field (*U.S.*) 1896. *Comb.*: **g. pendulum,** a compensation pendulum composed of parallel rods of different metals; **g. valve,** a sliding valve in which the cover and seat are both composed of parallel bars with spaces between them.

Gri·diron, *v.* 1857. [f. the sb.] *trans.* To mark with parallel lines suggesting the form of a gridiron; said *esp.* of railways as they appear on a map.

Grieced (grīst), *a.* [f. *griece*, var. of GRECE + -ED².] *Her.* = DEGRADED *a.*

Grief (grīf), *sb.* Pl. **griefs.** [ME. *gref* – AFr. *gref*, OFr. *grief* (mod. *grief* grievance, injury, complaint), f. *grever*; see GRIEVE *v.*] †**1.** Hardship, suffering; a kind, or cause, of these –1722. †**2.** Hurt, harm, mischief inflicted or suffered; molestation, trouble, offence –1584. †**b.** A wrong or injury which is the subject of formal complaint or demand for redress. Also, a document stating the grievance. –1651. †**3.** Feeling of offence; displeasure, anger –1573. †**4.** A sore, wound; a blemish of the skin; a disease, sickness –1727. **b.** The seat of this –1624. †**5.** Physical pain or discomfort –1621. **6.** Mental pain, distress, or sorrow. In mod. use: Deep or violent sorrow caused by loss or trouble; keen or bitter regret or remorse ME. **b.** A cause or subject of grief 1535.

6. Griefe of my Sonnes exile hath stopt her breath SHAKS. Their father died of g. for his eldest son 1883. **b.** The one g. of having no children RUSKIN.

Phr. *To come to g.*: to meet with disaster; (*Sporting*) to have a fall; to fail. So *to bring to g.* Chiefly *colloq.*

Comb. **g.-muscles,** Darwin's name for certain muscles concerned in the facial expression of g. Hence **Grie·fful** *a.* painful, sorrowful; †grievous. **Grie·fless,** *a.* free from g. **Grie·flessness,** griefless condition.

Grieko, var. of GREGO.

†**Grie·vable,** *a.* ME. [– OFr. *grevable*, f. *grever* to GRIEVE.] Causing grief or pain –1500.

Grievance (grī·văns). [ME. *grevance* – OFr. *grevance, grievance*, f. *grever* to harm, GRIEVE; see -ANCE.] †**1.** The infliction of wrong or hardship on a person; injury, oppression; a cause or source of injury –1768. **b.** = GRIEF 2 b. †**2.** The state or fact of being oppressed, injured, or distressed; distress; suffering, pain –1592. **3.** A circumstance or state of things felt to be oppressive. In mod. use, something (real or supposed) which is considered a legitimate ground of complaint. 1481. †**4.** A disease, ailment, hurt –1761. †**5.** Displeasure, indignation, offence –1523.

3. Irregular and grinding courts, the maine grievances MILT. The length of Chancery suits was a real public g. 1882. Hence †**Grie·vancer,** one who gives ground for complaint FULLER.

Grieve (grīv), *sb.* [OE. (Northumb.) *grǣfa* = WS. *ġerēfa*; see REEVE *sb.*¹] **1.** A governor of a province, town, etc. Now only Hist. = SHERIFF. **2.** *Sc.* and *north.* The overseer, manager, or head-workman on a farm; a farm-bailiff 1480.

2. He has got a ploughman from Scotland who acts as g. SCOTT *Diary*. Hence **Grie·veship,** a district under charge of a g.

Grieve (grīv), *v.* [ME. *greve* – OFr. *grever* :– Rom. **grevare*, alt. of L. *gravare*, f. *gravis* GRAVE *a.*¹] †**1.** *trans.* To press heavily upon. Only in *pass.* ME. only. †**2.** To harass, trouble; to oppress –1651; to cause damage to –1574. †**3.** To hurt, injure –1810. †Also *absol.* †**4.** To affect with pain or disease –1592. **5.** To affect with grief or deep sorrow. †Formerly, To cause pain, anxiety, or vexation to; to annoy. ME. †**6.** To make angry; to incense, offend –1535. **7.** *intr.* To feel grief; to sorrow deeply. Const. *at, for, over*, or *to* with *inf.* ME. **b.** *trans.* To feel or show grief at or for; to regret deeply (*poet.*) 1598.

2. The whiche garyson hadde greuyd sore the towne of Cambray LD. BERNERS. **5.** It greveth me to se hym in this case PALSGR. Griev'd at his heart, when looking down he saw The whole Earth fill'd with violence MILT. **6.** How oft did they . . grieue him in the desert *Ps.* 78:40. **7.** Grieving, if aught inanimate e'er grieves, Over the unreturning brave BYRON. **b.** Sorrow doth utter what it still doth g. DRAYTON. Hence **Grie·vedly** *adv.* †**Grie·vement,** a hurt, injury.

Griever (grī·vəɹ). 1598. [f. GRIEVE *v.* + -ER¹.] †**1.** One who molests or troubles another –1660. **2.** A person or thing that grieves or distresses 1641. **3.** One who feels or shows grief 1819.

Grieving (grī·viŋ), *ppl. a.* 1450. [f. GRIEVE *v.* + -ING².] **a.** That causes grief, pain, or annoyance. **b.** That feels or expresses grief. Hence **Grie·vingly** *adv.*

Grievous (grī·vəs), *a.* [ME. *grevous* – Fr. *grevos, -eus*, f. *grever*; see GRIEVE *v.*, -OUS.] †**1.** Burdensome, oppressive; in later use only of public grievances –1765. †**b.** Of penalties, etc.: Heavy, severe –1659. **2.** Bringing serious trouble or discomfort; having injurious effects; †causing hurt or pain. (Now only with mixture of sense 5— 'grievous to think of'.) ME. **3.** Of a disease, wound, or pain: Acute, severe, Now *rare.* ME. **4.** Of a fault, crime, etc.: Deserving heavy penalties. Later: Atrocious, flagrant, heinous. Now only *arch.* ME. **5.** Causing mental pain or distress. Now less widely: Exciting grief or intense sorrow. ME. **6.** Full of grief (*rare*) ME.

1. Thy father made our yoke grieuous 1 *Kings* 12:4. **2.** A g. delusion 1864. **4.** A Heynous and Grevious Crime 1683. **5.** The Loss [of Sight] must be very g. STEELE. **6.** A deep g. expression of countenance HAWTHORNE. Hence **Grie·vous-ly** *adv.*, **-ness.**

Griff (grif), *sb.*¹ *Anglo-Ind.* 1829. [abbrev. of GRIFFIN².] = GRIFFIN². Hence **Griff** *v.* to take in (anyone).

Griff (grif), *sb.*² *rare.* 1820. [– Fr. *griffe* (anglicized as *griff* by Shelley), f. *griffer* seize as with a claw, f. OFr. *grif* claw.] A claw.

Griff (grif), *sb.*³ Also **Griffe, griffo(n,** etc. 1850. [Of unkn. origin. See GRIFFIN³.] The offspring of a mulatto and a negro, three parts black.

Griff (grif), *sb.*⁴ 1860. [Of unkn. origin.] *Weaving.* A frame composed of horizontal bars employed in pattern-weaving. Also *g.-frame.*

Griffe, obs. f. GRAFF *sb.*¹, *sb.*³, *v.*

Griffin¹ (gri·fin), **griffon, gryphon** (gri·fən). ME. [– OFr. *grifoun* (mod. *griffon*) :– Rom. **grypho, -ōn-*, augm. of late L. *gryphus*, f. *gryps, gryph-* – Gr. γρύψ, γρυπ-. Now usually spelt *griffin* exc. in sense 2; *gryphon* is supposed to be dignified.] **1.** A fabulous animal having the head and wings of an eagle and the body and hind quarters of a lion. (Believed by the Greeks to inhabit Scythia and to guard its gold.) **b.** A representation or figure of a griffin ME. **2.** A vulture; now = griffon-vulture (see 3) ME. **3.** *attrib.*, as **griffin's foot,** a surgical instrument, so called from its shape; **griffon-vulture,** a vulture of the genus *Gyps*, esp. *G. fulvus* 1641.

1. As when a Gryfon through the Wilderness . . Pursues the Arimaspian, who by stealth Had from his wakeful custody purloind The guarded Gold MILT. **b.** Grim stone griffins surmount the terrace-steps 1863.

Griffin² (gri·fin). *Anglo-Ind.* 1793. [perh. fig. use of prec., but there is no evidence. See GRIFF *sb.*¹] A European newly arrived in India, and unaccustomed to Indian ways; a novice, newcomer, greenhorn. Hence **Gri·ffinage,** the state of being a g.; one's first year in India.

Griffin³. [Of unkn. origin. See GRIFF *sb.*³] *U.S.* A mulatto.

Griffon (gri·fən). 1882 [– Fr. *griffon* (applied to an Eng. dog 1829) GRIFFIN¹.] A species of coarse-haired dog, resembling a terrier.

Griffon-vulture: see GRIFFIN¹ 3.

Grig (grig), *sb.*¹ ME. [Of unkn. origin.] †**1.** A dwarf –1629. **2.** A short-legged hen. *Obs.* exc. *dial.* 1589. **3.** A species of eel; a small or young eel. Also *g.-eel* 1611. **4.** A *merry* (or †*mad*) *g.*: an extravagantly lively person. Also in phr. *as merry as a g.* [?from sense 3 or 2.] 1566. **5.** *slang.* A farthing; *pl.* cash, 'dibs' 1656.

Grig (grig), *sb.*² *dial.* 1674. [– W. *grug*, Cornish *grig.*] The common heath or heather, *Calluna vulgaris*; also, cross-leaved heath, *Erica tetralix.*

†**Grill,** *sb.*¹ *rare.* 1597. [After Spenser's *Gryll*, which is – Gr. γρύλλος a pig.] Quasi-proper name for a low or lazy person –1644. Grains are fitter for G., then Pearles QUARLES.

Grill (gril), *sb.*² 1766. [f. GRILL *v.*] **1.** Meat, fish, etc. broiled on a gridiron. Also *fig.* **2.** Short for *g.-room* 1896. **3.** A spell of grilling 1842. **4.** *attrib.*, as **grill-room,** a room in a restaurant, etc., in which grills are served 1883.

Grill (gril), *sb.*³ 1685. [– (O)Fr. *gril*, earlier *graïl, greïl*, masc. form (see GRIDDLE) based on fem. *grille*, see GRILLE *sb.*] A gridiron.

Grill, *sb.*⁴: see GRILLE *sb.*

†**Grill,** *a.* ME. [Cf. Du. *gril* (*grel*) fierce, angry, rough (of persons, etc.), shrill (of sound), glaring (of colour), LG. *grel, grell* (in the same senses).] **1.** Of persons: Fierce, harsh, cruel –1529. **2.** Of things, etc.: Cruel, painful, bitter, severe, terrible –1570.

Grill (gril), *v.* 1668. [– Fr. *griller*, f. *gril*

(*grille*) GRILL *sb.*[3]] **1.** *trans.* To broil on a gridiron or the like over or before a fire. **b.** To scallop (oysters or shrimps) 1727. **c.** *transf.* To torment with heat 1825. **d.** To subject to severe questioning (*U.S.*) 1928. **2.** *intr.* To undergo broiling. Chiefly *fig.* 1842.

1. c. Oh, Barton man! but I am grilled here FITZ-GERALD. **2.** The spleen which was..grilling within him 1883.

†Grilla·de, *sb.* 1656. [– Fr. *grillade*, f. *griller* GRILL *v.*; see -ADE.] **1.** Something grilled, a broiled dish –1727. **2.** *Cookery.* The browning of any dish with a hot iron. CHAMBERS. Hence **†Grilla·de** *v. trans.* to grill.

Grillage (gri·lėdʒ). 1776. [– Fr. *grillage*, f. *grille* GRILLE *sb.*; see -AGE.] *Engineering.* A heavy framework of cross-timbering, sometimes resting on piles, serving as a foundation on treacherous soil.

Grille, grill (gril), *sb.* 1661. [–(O)Fr. *grille*, earlier *graïlle* :– med.L. *graticula*, *craticula* = L. *craticula*, dim. of *cratis* (see CRATE, GRATE *sb.*).] **1.** A grating; an arrangement of parallel or cross bars, or structure of open metal-work, used to close an opening or separate one part of a room, etc. from another 1686. **†2.** One of the bars in the visor of a helmet 1661. **3.** *Tennis.* The square opening in the end wall on the hazard side of the court, adjacent to the main wall 1727. **4.** *Pisciculture.* A wooden frame fitted with glass tubes, between which the fish-eggs lie during incubation 1883. **5.** A rectangular pattern of small dots impressed on postage stamps 1898. Hence **Grille** *v.* to fit or impress with a g.

†Gri·lly, *v. rare.* [– Fr. *griller*; the *lly* is meant to give the sound of Fr. *ll*.] = GRILL *v.* BUTLER *Hud.*

Grilse (grils). ME. [Of unkn. origin.] The name given to a young salmon on its first return to the river from the sea and retained for the year.

Grim (grim). [OE. *grim* = OFris., OS. (Du.), OHG. *grim* (G. *grimm*), ON. *grimmr* :– Gmc. **ʒrimmaz*, f. **ʒrem-* **ʒram-*. See GRAME *a.*]

A. *adj.* **1.** Of persons and animals: Fierce, cruel, savage, or harsh. Also, daring, determined, bold. (Now merged in sense 4). **2.** Of actions, character, feelings, etc. **a.** Fierce, furious, cruel. (*Obs.* or *arch.*) **b.** In mod. use: Stern, merciless; resolute, uncompromising. OE. **3.** Of pain, wounds, conditions, etc.: Cruel, terribly severe OE. **†b.** Of weapons, etc.: Cruel, formidable –1485. **4.** Of stern, forbidding, or harsh aspect. †Also, hard-featured, ugly. ME. **5.** *transf.* Of things, scenes, etc.: Harsh or repellent of aspect; uninviting 1820. **6.** Of laughter, jests, etc.: Stern, implying no softening. In recent use often: Dealing with ghastly or painful subjects. 1641.

1. The g. Woolf with privy paw MILT. **2.** The ridges of g. Warr MILT. G. earnestness 1853. **3.** Wind and weather wax'd so g. SCOTT. **4.** The g. face of law DENHAM. Phr. *To hold on, cling*, etc. *like g. death.* A g. and crabbed look EVELYN. **6.** One of those g. pleasantries in which Oliver took delight MILMAN.

B. *adv.* (OE. *grimme*) or quasi-*adv.* In a grim manner or mood; fiercely, savagely, horribly.

Thus chides she Death, Grim-grinning ghost SHAKS.

Grim (grim), *v.* ME. [In 1 – Du. *grimmen*, *grim(m* adj. GRIM. In 2, f. GRIM *a.*] **†1.** *intr.* To be angry, look fierce –1848. **2.** *trans.* To make grim or fierce; to give a grim look to 1710.

2. The sculptured effigies That g. the silence of chivalric aisles GALT.

Grimace (grimēi·s), *sb.* 1651. [– Fr. *grimace*, earlier †*grimache* – Sp. *grimazo* caricature, f. *grima* fright.] **1.** A distortion of the countenance whether spontaneous or involuntary, expressive of some feeling or tending to excite laughter; a wry face. **2.** An affected look or †gesture 1678. **3.** *fig.* Affectation, pretence, sham. ?Now *rare.* 1655.

1. I tried to laugh, but could only make a g. W. IRVING. **2.** Our Conferences go no further than a Bow and a G. ADDISON. **3.** All this my parade and g. of philosophy CIBBER. Hence **Grima·ce** *v. intr.* to distort the countenance; to make a wry face; †to put on an affected air. **Grima·ced** *ppl. a.* affected (*rare*). **Grima·cer.**

Grimalkin (grimæ·lkin, -mǭ·lkin). 1630. [f. GREY + MALKIN.] A name given to a cat; hence, a cat, *esp.* an old she-cat; *contemptuously* applied to a jealous or imperious old woman.

Grime (grəim), *sb.* 1590. [f. GRIME *v.*] Soot, smut, coal-dust, or other black particles, deposited upon or ingrained in some surface. *fig.* The dirt and g. of human affairs DE FOE.

Grime (grəim), *v.* 1470. [– MLG., MDu. **grīmen* (cf. Flem. *grijmen*, beside LG. *gremen*); cf. BEGRIME.] *trans.* To cover with grime, to blacken, befoul. Also *fig.*

Grimgribber (gri·mgri:bəɹ). 1786. In Steele the name of an imaginary estate, extemporized in a discussion between two sham counsel respecting a marriage settlement. Hence: Legal or other technical jargon, learned gibberish. Also *attrib.*

Griminess (grəi·minės). 1650. [f. GRIMY *a.* + -NESS.] The quality or state of being grimy.

Grimly (gri·mli), *a. Obs.* or *arch.* [OE. *grimlić*; see GRIM *a.* and -LY[1].] Grim-looking; grim in nature. Hence **Gri·mliness,** the state of being g.

Grimly (gri·mly), *adv.* [OE. *grimlīće*; see GRIM *a.* and -LY[2].] **1.** In a grim fashion; fiercely, cruelly; also, in mod. use, austerely, rigidly. **†2.** Dreadfully –1470. **3.** With a grim look or air ME.

3. The Auguries..looke g. SHAKS.

Grimm(e (grim). 1834. [– Fr. *grimme* (Buffon 1764) – mod.L. (*Capra*) *grimmia*, the name given by Linnæus to a S. African antelope described by Herm. Nic. Grimm (1641–1711).] A West African antelope, the coquetoon.

Grimness (gri·mnės). OE. [f. GRIM *a.* + -NESS.] The quality or condition of being grim; fierceness; sternness; formidable aspect.

†Gri·msir(e. 1450. [f. GRIM *a.* + SIR, SIRE.] An austere, stern, morose, or overbearing person –1621.

Grimy (grəi·mi), *a.* 1612. [f. GRIME *sb.* + -Y[1].] Covered with grime; begrimed, dirty. Also, swarthy.

Grin, *sb.*[1] [OE. *grin*, *gryn*.] **1.** A snare for catching birds or animals, made of cord, etc., with a running noose. *Obs.* exc. *dial.* or *arch.* Also *fig.* **†2.** A noose; also, a halter –1591.

Grin (grin), *sb.*[2] 1635. [f. GRIN *v.*[2]; cf. GIRN *sb.*] An act of grinning.

On the (*broad* or †*high*) *g.*: grinning (openly).

Grin, *v.*[1] *Obs.* exc. *dial.* OE. [f. GRIN *sb.*[1]] *trans.* To catch in a noose; to snare, ensnare; to choke, strangle.

Grin (grin), *v.*[2] [OE. *grennian*, rel. to OHG. *grennan* mutter (MHG. *grennen* wail, grin) and OHG. *granōn* grunt, ON. *grenja* howl, OSw. *gränia* roar, gnash the teeth; f. Gmc. **ʒran-*. Cf. GROAN, GIRN *v.*] **1.** *intr.* Of persons and animals: To draw back the lips and show the teeth: **a.** generally, or as an indication of pain or †anger; **b.** by way of a forced or unnatural smile, or of a broad smile 1480. **2. a.** *trans.* To express by grinning 1681. **b.** *intr.* Of a feeling: To find expression by grinning. FIELDING.

1. a. As the wolfe doth g. before he barketh SHAKS. **b.** They often grinned and capered with heavy hearts W. IRVING. **2. a.** The surgeon grinned approbation SMOLLETT.

Phr. *To g. and bear it*: to submit with no other sign of impatience than a grin. *To g. like a Cheshire cat* (see CAT *sb.*[1]).

Grind (grəind), *sb.* ME. [f. GRIND *v.*] **1.** The action of grinding (*lit.* and *fig.*). **2.** *colloq.* Steady hard work; *esp.* close and hard study; a dull and laborious task 1851. **3.** *Univ. slang.* **a.** A steeplechase; also, a 'constitutional' 1857. **b.** *U.S.* A hard student 1896.

Grind (grəind), *v.* Pa. t. and pple. **ground.** [OE. *grindan*, of which there are no Gmc. cognates. An IE. base **ghrendh-* is repr. by L. *frendere* rub away, gnash.] **1.** *trans.* To reduce to small particles or powder by crushing between two hard surfaces; *esp.* to make (grain) into meal or flour in a mill. **b.** Denoting the action of teeth; = to masticate ME. **c.** *transf.* and *fig.* 1535. **d.** *intr.* To admit of being ground (fine, etc.). **2.** *fig.* To crush, to oppress; to harass with exactions 1626. **3.** *fig.* To torment. Also *absol.* Now only *U.S.* to annoy, vex. ME. **4.** To produce by grinding ME. **5.** To wear down by friction so as to make sharp or smooth (a tool, a weapon, glass, etc.) ME. **6.** *intr.* or *absol.* To perform the operation of grinding OE. **7. a.** *intr.* To work as if grinding with a hand-mill 1840. **b.** quasi-*trans.* To produce (music) on a barrel-organ, etc. 1784. **8.** *intr.* To work laboriously and steadily; *esp.* to study hard. Const. *at.* Also with *away*, *on.* 1855. **b.** *trans.* To teach (a subject) in a steady laborious manner; also, to prepare (a pupil) in a subject 1815. **9.** *intr.* To scrape or rub *on* or *against* something; to make a grating noise OE. **b.** *trans.* To rub gratingly *against* or *upon*; to force *into* by grinding; also quasi-*trans.* to make (one's way) by grinding 1644. **10. †a.** *intr.* To gnash *with the teeth.* Const. *at.* –1581. **b.** *trans.* To rub the teeth together with a grating sound. Const. *at.* ME.

1. Any corne or meale, ground or to be grynded 1568. **b.** *Ant. & Cl.* III. v. 16. **c.** He grinds divinity of other days Down into modern use COWPER. **2.** Laws g. the poor, and rich men rule the law GOLDSM. Phr. *To g. the faces* (or *face*) *of* (a Hebraism). **5.** The bristled Boar..New grinds his arming Tusks DRYDEN. **6.** Though the mills of God g. slowly, yet they g. exceeding small LONGF. **8.** So..Ground he at grammar BROWNING. **9.** The villainous centre-bits G. on the wakeful ear TENNYSON.

Grinded (grəi·ndėd), *ppl. a.* 1613. [f. GRIND *v.* + -ED[1].] = GROUND *ppl. a.*

Grinder (grəi·ndəɹ). ME. [f. GRIND *v.* + -ER[1]; in sense 1 tr. L. *molaris* MOLAR[1].]

I. 1. That which grinds; e.g. a molar tooth; hence *joc.* in *pl.*, the teeth generally. **2.** The upper millstone or runner; †a muller or pestle 1688.

II. 1. A person who grinds 1483. **2.** A crammer 1813. **3.** One who sweats workmen 1851. **4.** A bird that makes a grinding noise: **a.** The flycatcher (*Sisura inquieta*) of Australia 1848. **b.** The night-jar or goat-sucker.

Comb. **grinder's asthma, phthisis, rot** (*Path.*), 'a lung disease produced by the mechanical irritation of the particles of steel and stone given off in the operation of grinding' (Webster).

Grindery (grəi·ndəri). 1805. [f. GRIND *v.* + -ERY.] **1.** Materials, tools, etc. used by shoemakers and other workers in leather. (Orig. applied only to the whetstone.) Also *attrib.* **2.** A place for grinding tools, weapons, etc. 1884.

Grinding (grəi·ndiŋ), *vbl. sb.* ME. [f. GRIND *v.* + -ING[1].] **1.** The action of GRIND *v.* **2.** *attrib.* **a.** Adapted for, or connected with, grinding, as *g.-clamp*, *-machine*, etc. **b.** Suitable for being ground, as *g.-barley*, etc. *Comb.* **g.-wheel,** (*a*) a wheel for grinding or polishing; (*b*) a building fitted up with water or steam power for grinding cutlery or tools.

Gri·nding, *ppl. a.* OE. [f. GRIND *v.* + -ING[2].] That grinds. Hence **Gri·ndingly** *adv.* in a g. manner.

Grindle (gri·nd'l). *U.S.* 1884. [– G. *gründel*, f. *grund* GROUND, bottom.] The mud-fish, called also 'John A. Grindle', or lawyer.

Grindle stone. *Obs.* exc. *dial.* ME. [prob. repr. OE. **grindelstān*, f. **grindel* (instrumental n., f. *grindan* grind) + *stān* STONE.] A grindstone; = †also, a piece, or kind, of stone suitable for making grindstones.

Grindstone (grəindstōᵘn). [ME. *grinstone* (still dial. *grinston*), f. GRIND *v.* + STONE.] **1.** A millstone. *Obs.* exc. in *nonce-use.* **2.** A disc of stone revolving on an axle, and used for grinding, sharpening, and polishing ME. **3.** A kind of stone suitable for making grindstones. Also *g. grit.* 1703.

2. Phr. *To hold* (*keep, bring, put*) *one's nose to the g.*: to grind down or oppress; also, in mod. use, to keep continually engaged in hard and monotonous labour.

‖**Gringo** (gri·ŋgo). 1884. [transf. use of Sp. *gringo* gibberish.] Among Spanish Americans, a contemptuous name for an Englishman or an Anglo-American.

Grinner (gri·nəɹ). 1440. [f. GRIN *v.*[2] + -ER[1].] One who grins.

Grinning (gri·niŋ), *ppl. a.* ME. [f. as prec. + -ING[2].] That grins. Hence **Gri·nningly** *adv.* in a g. manner.

†**Grint**, *v.* ME. [app. imit., after GRIND, GRUNT, etc.] *intr.* To grind or gnash the teeth. Said also of the teeth –1491.
He grynte with his teeth, so was he wrooth CHAUCER.

Grip (grip), *sb.*[1] [Two formations: (i) OE. *gripe* grasp, clutch, corresp. to OHG. *grif-* in comb., MHG. *grif* (mod. *griff*) grasp, handle, claw, ON. *grip* grasp, clutch; (ii) OE. *gripa* handful, sheaf; both f. weak base of *grīpan* GRIPE *v.*[1]] **1.** Firm hold or grasp; the action of gripping, grasping, or clutching; also, grasping power. **b.** Sometimes used with reference to the mode of grasping the hand by which members of a secret society, e.g. Freemasons, recognize one another 1785. **2.** *fig.* Firm or tenacious hold, grasp, or control; power, mastery (esp. now assoc. with the idea of irresistible force) 1450. **b.** Power to apprehend or master a subject 1861. **3.** A seizure or twinge of pain; a spasm ME. **4.** A handful OE. **5.** Something which grips or clips 1800. **6.** That which is gripped or clasped; e.g. the handle of a sword, a golf-club, etc. 1867. **7.** *U.S.* = GRIPSACK 1883.
1. The horrors of the bear's g. 1885. **b.** Masons' mystic word and g. BURNS. Phr. *At grips*: in close combat. **2.** The g. of poverty 1894, of malarial fever 1897. **b.** A g. of the essential facts 1894. **4.** Phr. *To lie in g.*: (of corn) to lie as left by the reapers (*dial.*).
Comb.: **g.-brake,** a brake worked by gripping with the hand; **-car** (*U.S.*), a tramcar worked on an endless cable to which the car is attached by a g. (sense 5), a cable-car; **-man,** the man who manipulates the g. of a cable-car.

Grip (grip), *sb.*[2] Now only *Hunting* or *dial.* [OE. *grypa* (or *-e*) sewer, rel. to *grēop* burrow and MLG. *grüppe*, MDu. *grippe*, *greppe*; f. Gmc. **ʒrup-* **ʒreup-* hollow out.] **1.** A small open furrow or ditch; a trench, drain. **2.** The gutter in a cowhouse 1825.

Grip (grip), *v.*[1] [OE. (late Northumb.) *grippa*, corresp. to MHG. *gripfen.*] **1.** *trans.* To grasp or seize firmly or tightly with the hand; to seize with the mouth, claw, beak, etc. Also *transf.* of a disease. **2.** *absol.* and *intr.* To take firm hold; to get a grip (*lit.* and *fig.*) ME. **3.** *trans.* To join firmly *to* something, as with a grip, etc. 1886. **4.** *fig.* To take hold upon (the mind, the emotions) 1891.
1. The gout..grips him by both legs DICKENS. **2.** *Grip*..to hold, as 'the anchor grips' SMYTH.

Grip (grip), *v.*[2] Now *dial.* 1597. [f. GRIP *sb.*[2]] *trans.* To make grips in; to ditch, trench.

Gripe (grəip), *sb.*[1] ME. [f. GRIPE *v.*[1]] **1.** The action of griping, clutching, or seizing tenaciously, *esp.* with the hands, arms, claws, and the like. **b.** *fig.* Grasp, hold, control, grip ME. **c.** *Surg.* An act of compressing (e.g. an artery) with the fingers 1676. **2.** *transf.* and *fig.* **a.** The clutch or pinch of something painful. Formerly often in *pl.*: Spasms, pangs. ?*Obs.* 1547. **b.** An intermittent spasmodic pain in the bowels. Usu. *pl.* colic pains. 1601. †**3.** The hand held in the position for grasping or clutching –1791. **4.** A handful 1570. **5.** = GRIP *sb.*[1]6. 1610. †**6.** *slang.* A covetous person, a usurer. Also *Gripes* (as quasi-proper name). –1700. **7.** Something which gripes or clutches; *esp.* a BRAKE 1578. **8.** *Naut. pl.* Lashings formed by an assemblage of ropes, etc., to secure a boat in its place on the deck; also, two broad bands passed respectively round the stem and stern of a boat hung in davits, to prevent swinging 1762. **9.** *attrib.* as *g. mixture* 1891.
1. All the Locks and Gripes of Wrestling MILT. **b.** I take my cause Out of the gripes of cruell men SHAKS. **2. a.** Heart-strook with chilling g. of sorrow MILT.

Gripe (grəip), *sb.*[2] 1674. Dial. var. of GRIP *sb.*[2]

†**Gripe,** *sb.*[3] [ME. *grip(e, gryp(e* – OFr. *grip* griffin, corresp. to med.L. *grypus, -is, gripes, grippis, gripa* griffin, vulture, vars. of *gryphus* – L. *gryps, gryph-* (*gryphus*) – Gr. γρύψ, γρυπ-; see GRIFFIN[1].] **1.** A griffin –1592. **2.** A vulture –1767.
2. Like a white hind under the gripe's sharp claws SHAKS. *Comb.* **g.-shell** = GRIPE'S-EGG.

†**Gripe,** *sb.*[4] Also †**grype.** 1506. [– Fr. †*grip* (XV) small war-ship, in med.L. *grippa* (XV) 'genus navis'.] A vessel used in the Levant –1599.

Gripe (grəip), *sb.*[5] 1580. [orig. *greepe* – Du. *greep*, but later assim. to GRIPE *sb.*[1]] *Naut.* The piece of timber terminating the keel at the forward extremity; occas. taken as = FOREFOOT 2.

Gripe (grəip), *v.*[1] [OE. *grīpan* = OFris. *grīpa*, OS. *grīpan* (Du. *grijpen*), OHG. *grīfan* (G. *greifen*), ON. *gripa*, Goth. *greipan*; f. Gmc. **ʒrīp-*; see GRIP *sb.*[1], GROPE.] †**1.** *intr.* To make a grasp or clutch, to seek to get a hold (*lit.* and *fig.*) –1820. **2.** *trans.* To lay hold of, seize; to get into one's power or possession. *Obs.* exc. *arch.* OE. **3.** To grip ME. †**b.** To encircle tightly –1758. **c.** *absol.* 1597. †**4.** To clench (the fist, etc.) (*rare*) –1728. †**5.** *fig.* To apprehend; to comprehend (*rare*) –1742. **6.** To pinch, squeeze. (Said also of poverty.) 1645. **7.** To grieve, afflict, distress. Now *rare.* 1559. **8.** To affect with gripes. Now chiefly in pa. pple. 1611. **b.** *absol.* To produce pain in the bowels as if by constriction or contraction; to cause gripes 1702. **9.** *Naut.* **a.** *trans.* To secure (a boat) with gripes. (In *pa. pple.* only.) 1840. **b.** *intr.* Said of a ship which has a tendency to come up into the wind in spite of the helm 1627.
1. Upon whose heart may all the Furies g. MARLOWE. **2.** Woldest thou g. both gaine and pleasure 1551. **3.** Let each..g. fast his orbed Shield MILT. **6.** For this, he grip'd the Poor, and Alms denied SAVAGE. **7.** How inly Sorrow gripes his Soule SHAKS. *Comb.*: **g.-all,** a grasping, avaricious person; †**-money, -penny,** a miser, niggard. Hence **Gri·ping-ly** *adv.*, **-ness.**

Gripe, *v.*[2] 1597. Dial. var. of GRIP *v.*[2]

Gripeful (grəi·pful), *sb. rare.* 1727. [f. GRIPE *sb.*[1] + -FUL.] As much as can be grasped in the hand.

Gripeful (grəi·pfŭl), *a. rare.* 1864. [f. GRIPE *v.*[1] + -FUL.] Apt to gripe; gripy.

Griper (grəi·pəɹ). 1573. [f. GRIPE *v.*[1] + -ER[1].] One who, or that which, gripes; an extortioner (now *rare*); †an instrument of torture.

Gripe's egg. ME. [GRIPE *sb.*[3]]. A large egg supposed to be that of a gripe; a vessel shaped like this; an oval-shaped cup.

†**Griph.** 1652. [– L. *griphus* (also used) – Gr. γρῖφος creel, (fig.) riddle.] A puzzling question; a riddle, enigma –1796.

‖**Grippe** (grip). Also (anglicized) **grip.** 1776. [Fr., vbl. sb. f. *gripper* seize.] = INFLUENZA.

Grippe, obs. f. GRIP.

Gripper (gri·pəɹ). 1570. [f. GRIP *v.*[1] + -ER[1].] †**1.** One who grips. **2.** *spec.* **a.** 'In Ireland, a sheriff's officer; a bailiff' (Cassell) 1884. **b.** *Austral. slang.* One who catches sheep for the shearers 1886. **3.** Any contrivance for gripping, clutching, or grasping tightly 1857. **4.** *attrib.*, as *g. mechanism* 1871.

†**Gri·pple,** *sb. rare.* 1530. [f. root of GRIP *sb.*[1], GRIPE *v.*[1]; cf. GRAPPLE *sb.*] **1.** A hook to seize things with. **2.** Grasp. SPENSER.

Gri·pple, *a.* Now only *dial.* or *arch.* [OE. *gripul*, f. *grip-*, wk. base of *grīpan* GRIPE *v.*[1]] **1.** Griping, niggardly, usurious. **2.** Gripping; tenacious 1513.
1. While g. owners still refuse To others what they cannot use SCOTT.

†**Gri·pple,** *v.* 1591. Altered f. GRAPPLE *v.*, perh. infl. by GRIP *v.*[1] –1630.

Gripsack (gri·pˌsæk). *U.S. colloq.* 1883. [f. GRIP *v.*[1] + SACK.] A traveller's handbag.

†**Gris,** *sb.* ME. [– OFr. *gris*, subst. use of adj. *gris*; see next.] A kind of grey fur –1575.

†**Gris,** *a. rare.* ME. [– (O)Fr. *gris* adj. – Frankish **gris* (OS., MLG. *grīs*) of unkn. origin.] Grey –1513.

Grisaille (grizēⁱ·l, as Fr. grizay). 1848. [– Fr. *grisaille*, f. *gris* (see prec.) + *-aille* -AL[2].] *Painting.* Decorative painting in grey monotone to represent objects in relief. **b.** *attrib.* or *adj.* Executed in grisaille 1860.

Gris-amber: see AMBERGRIS.

Grisard (gri·săɹd). *rare.* 1607. [– (O)Fr. *grisard*, f. *gris*; see GRIS *a.*, -ARD.]
†**A.** *adj.* Greyish. TOPSELL.
B. *sb.* A grey-haired man. BROWNING.

Grise, var. of GRIS *sb.*; obs. f. GRECE.

Griseous (gri·ziəs), *a.* 1819. [f. med.L. *griseus* + -OUS.] Grey; *spec.* in *Zool.* and *Bot.*, bluish grey, pearl-grey.

‖**Grisette** (grize·t). 1700. [– Fr., f. *gris* grey; see -ETTE.] **1.** A cheap grey dress fabric, formerly worn by working girls in France. **2.** A French girl or young woman of the working class, e.g. a shop assistant or a seamstress 1723. **3.** A noctuid moth, *Acronycta strigosa* 1869.

Griskin (gri·skin). 1700. [Obscurely f. *gris* GRICE + -KIN.] The lean part of the loin of a bacon pig.

Grisled, var. of GRIZZLED *a.*

Grisly (gri·zli), *a.* Now *arch.* or *literary.* [Late OE. *grislić*, f. wk. base of **grīsan* (in *āgrīsan* terrify) = MLG., MDu. *grīsen.* See -LY[1].] **1.** Causing horror, terror, or extreme fear; horrible to behold or hear. Now: Causing uncanny or unpleasant feelings; grim, ghastly. **2.** Ugly (*dial.*) 1674. †**3.** Inspired by fear –1698.
1. A man of grislie and sterne grauitie 1551. Grieslie ghostes, night SPENSER. G. Grones SIDNEY, oaths SCOTT. **3.** G. drede CHAUCER. Hence **Gri·sliness,** g. quality or condition. **Gri·sly** *adv.* (*Obs.* exc. *arch.*)

Grisly, obs. f. GRIZZLY *a.* and *sb.*[1]

Grison (gri·zən), *sb.* 1796. [– Fr. *grison*; app. the same word as next. (Both animals are grey.)] **1.** A carnivorous quadruped of S. America, of the family *Mustelidæ*, allied to the glutton and marten. **2.** A S. American monkey (*Lagothrix canus*), said to be a remarkable glutton 1840.

†**Grison,** *a.* 1438. [– Fr. *grison* adj. (XV), f. *gris* grey; see -OON.] Grey.

Grist (grist), *sb.*[1] [OE. *grist* :– Gmc. **ʒrinst-*, f. **ʒrindan* GRIND *v.*] †**1.** The action or an act of grinding –1676. **2.** Corn to be ground; also (with *pl.*) a batch of this ME. Also *fig.* **b.** *U.S.* A lot, number, quantity (*of*) 1840. **3.** Corn that has been ground 1566. **4.** Malt crushed or ground for brewing 1822. **5.** *attrib.*, as *g.-cart* 1602.
1. Phr. *To bring g. to the (one's) mill*: to bring one business or advantage. *All is g. that comes to his mill*: he turns everything to account. **b.** There's an onaccountable g. on 'em [bees] J. F. COOPER. *Comb.* **g.-mill,** a mill for grinding corn.

Grist (grist), *sb.*[2] 1733. [poss. conn. w. GIRD *v.*[1]] The size or thickness of yarn or rope.
Common g. is a rope 3 inches in circumference, with twenty yarns in each of the three strands KNIGHT.

Grist, *v.* 1825. [f. GRIST *sb.*[1]] *trans.* To grind (corn). Hence **Gri·sting** *vbl. sb.* the action of grinding corn, or its result.

Gristle (gri·s'l). [OE. *gristle* = OFris., MLG. *gristel*, *gerstel*, OHG. *chrustila*, MHG. *krustel*, rel. to OE. *grost* gristle; ult. origin. unkn.] **1.** = CARTILAGE. Also *fig.* and †*transf.* †**2.** *fig.* A tender or delicate person –1652. **3.** *attrib.* ME.
1. *fig. In the g.*: in an initiatory, or unformed stage of existence. BURKE.

Gristly (gri·sli), *a.* ME. [f. GRISTLE *sb.* + -Y[1].] **1.** Pertaining to, or of the nature of gristle; consisting or full of gristle; cartilaginous. **2.** Having a texture resembling that of gristle, in toughness, etc. 1601.

Grit (grit), *sb.*[1] [OE. *grēot* = OS. *griot*, OHG. *grioz* (G. *griess*), ON. *grjót* :– Gmc. **ʒreutam*; see next.] **1.** *collect. sing.* Formerly: Sand, gravel. Now: Minute particles of stone or sand, as produced by attrition or disintegration. **b.** A particle of sand (*rare*) 1601. **2.** Coarse sandstone, esp. of the kinds used for millstones and grindstones; grit-stone ME. **3.** Earth, soil, mould; †the ground. *Obs.* exc. *dial.* ME. **4.** The grain or texture of a stone 1529. **5.** *colloq.*; orig. *U.S. slang.* Firmness or solidity of character; indomitable pluck or spirit; stamina 1825. **b.** In Canadian politics, a Radical or Liberal. Formerly *clear g.* 1884.
4. These stonis at Stonehenge be all of one gryt, without chaunge of colour, or vayne 1529. **5.** If you were a chip of the old block you would be just what he called 'the grit' (= the right sort) THACKERAY.
Comb.: **g.-berry,** the genus *Comarostaphylis*; **-board,** the earth-board of a plough; **-emery,** coarse emery; **-rock** = sense 2.

Grit (grit), *sb.*[2] Now only *pl.* and *dial.* [OE. *grytt(e* = MLG., Du. *grutte*, OHG. *gruzzi* (G. *grütze*) :– WGmc. **ʒrutjō, -jon*, f. Gmc. **ʒreut-* **ʒraut-* **ʒrŭt-*, whence also GRIT *sb.*[1], GROATS, GROUT *sb.*[1]] †**1.** Bran, chaff, mill-dust –ME. **2.** Oats husked but not ground (or only coarsely); coarse oatmeal 1579.

Grit (grit), *v.* 1762. [f. GRIT *sb.*[1]] **1.** *intr.* To produce a grating sound, as of the crushing of grit; to move with such a sound. **2.** *trans.* To cover with grit or sand 1842. **3.** To grind or grate (the teeth) 1848.

1. The sanded floor that grits beneath the tread GOLDSM.

Grith (griþ). Now *Hist.* [Late OE. *griþ* – ON. *grið* domicile, home, pl. truce, peace, pardon, quarter.] †**1.** Protection, defence; safe conduct –1650. **2.** *spec.* in *OE. Law.* Security, peace, or protection guaranteed under limitations OE. **3.** *concr.* A sanctuary, asylum ME. †**4.** Peace –1460. †**5.** Quarter (in battle) –1475. **6.** *attrib.* ME.

2. *Church-g.* (OE. *ciric-grið*), security within the precincts of a church. To ask the privilege of girth and sanctuary SCOTT. Hence **Grithbreach,** breach of the peace, or its penalty.

Gritstone (gri·tstōᵘn). 1555. [f. GRIT *sb.*[1] + STONE *sb.*] = GRIT *sb.*[1] 2.

Gritty (gri·ti), *a.* 1598. [f. GRIT *sb.*[1] + -Y[1].] **1.** Of the nature of or resembling grit; containing, consisting of, or full of grit; sandy. **2.** Full of or containing minute hard particles; also *fig.* of literary style, with allusion to the quality of gritty bread 1882. **3.** *U.S. colloq.* Having grit (see GRIT *sb.*[1] 5) 1847.

Grivet (gri·vėt). 1859. [Of unkn. origin.] A small greenish-grey monkey of north-east Africa (*Circopithecus griseiviridis*); the tota.

Grize, rare obs. form of GRECE, stairs.

Grizel (gri·zĕl). 1565. Later form of *Grisilde* (= *Griseldis, Griselda*) in Chaucer's *Clerk's Tale*, the proverbial type of a meek, patient wife.

For patience shee will proue a second Grissell *Tam. Shr.* II. i. 297.

Grizelin, obs. f. GRIDELIN.

Grizzle (gri·z'l). [ME. *grisel* (earlier as sb.) – OFr. *grisel*, f. *gris* grey; see GRIS *a.*, -EL[1].]

A. *adj.* Of grey colour, grey, grizzled. †Of a horse: Roan.

B. *sb.* †**1.** A grey-haired old man. ME. only. **2.** A grey horse or other animal 1620. **3.** Grey hair; a sprinkling of grey hair 1601; a grey wig 1755. **4.** Grey colour; the colour grey; †light roan 1611. **5.** A second-class stock brick, so called from its colour 1843.

3. O thou dissembling Cub: what wilt thou be When time hath sow'd a g. on thy case SHAKS.

Grizzle (gri·z'l), *v.* 1740. [f. GRIZZLE *a.* or back-formation from GRIZZLED.] **1.** *trans.* To render grey or grey-haired. **2.** *intr.* To become grey, etc. 1875.

Grizzled (gri·z'ld), *a.* 1458. [f. GRIZZLE *a.* + -ED[2].] **1.** Grey, grizzly; roan-coloured (*dial.*). **2.** Having grey hair 1606.

2. To the Boy Cæsar send this grizled head SHAKS.

Grizzly (gri·zli), *a.* and *sb.*[1] 1594. [f. GRIZZLE *a.* + -Y[1].]

A. *adj.* Grey; greyish; grey-haired; grizzled. Old Squirrels, that turne Grisly BACON. **Grizzly bear:** a large and ferocious bear, *Ursus horribilis*, peculiar to the mountainous districts of western North America 1791.

B. *sb.* The grizzly bear 1808.

Grizzly (gri·zli), *sb.*[2] 1877. [Of unkn. origin.] *Mining. U.S.* A grating of parallel iron bars with interstices between to allow the finer material to fall into the sluices below while the larger stones are screened off.

Grizzly, var. of GRISLY *a.*

Groan (grōᵘn), *sb.* ME. [f. GROAN *v.*] An act of groaning; a low vocal murmur emitted involuntarily in pain or great distress; *occas.*, an expression of strong disapprobation. **b.** attributed to inanimate things 1605.

b. Such groanes of roaring Winde *Lear* III. ii. 47.

Groan (grōᵘn), *v.* [OE. *grānian* :- **ʒrainōjan*, f. Gmc. **ʒrain-* **ʒrīn-*, whence also OHG. *grīnan* grin with laughing or weeping (G. *greinen*), MHG. *grinnen* gnash the teeth (G. *grinsen* laugh, weep); cf. MDu. *grinsen* (Du. *grijnsen*) grin. Cf. GRIN *v.*[2]] **1.** *intr.* To breathe with a deep-toned murmur; to utter a low deep sound expressive of grief or pain. Also quasi-*trans.* Also *fig.* 1642. **b.** attributed to inanimate things 1602. †**2.** *spec.* Of the buck: To utter its cry at rutting time –1686. **3.** *trans.* To utter with groans 1606; †to bewail (*rare*) –1766. **4.** *intr.* To be oppressed to the point of groaning. Const. *beneath, under, with.* 1613. Also *fig.* and *transf.* 1513. **5.** To express earnest longing by groans; to yearn, as if with groans; hence *fig.* of things. Const. *for, to* with inf. 1560. **6.** *trans.* To express disapproval by means of groans 1799.

1. *fig.* Beshrew that heart that makes my heart to groane SHAKS. quasi-*trans.* He fell, and deadly pale, Groand out his Soul MILT. **3.** 'No trifle', groan'd the husband TENNYSON. **4.** Modest merit..Is left in poverty to g. CHURCHILL. The press groans with productions JEFFERSON. The door upon its hinges groans KEATS. **5.** *Jul. C.* III. i. 275. Hence **Groa·ner,** one who groans; also *slang*, a thief who attends funerals, etc. **Groa·ningly,** in a groaning manner.

Groanful (grōᵘ·nfŭl), *a. rare.* 1590. [f. GROAN *sb.* + -FUL.] Full of groans or groaning; lugubrious.

Groat (grōᵘt, grǫt). ME. [– MDu. *groot*, MLG. *grōte*, subst. use of the adj. (= GREAT) in the sense 'thick' (cf. MHG. *grōȝe pfennige* 'thick pennies', and GROSCHEN).] **1.** *Hist.* A denomination of coin (med.L. *grossus*, Fr. *gros*, It. *grosso*, MDu. *groot*), recognized from the 13th c. in various countries of Europe. Its standard was theoretically one-eighth of an ounce of silver. **2.** The English groat coined in 1351–2 was made equal to four pence. The groat ceased to be issued for circulation in 1662. **3.** *attrib.*, as **g.-silver,** a customary gratuity of a g. ME.

1. A Pin a Day, says our frugal Proverb, is a G. a Year ADDISON. I do not care a g. what it is CHESTERF. *A cracked* or *slit g.*: a type of something worthless.

Groats (grōᵘts, grǫts), *sb. pl.* [Late OE. *grotan* pl., rel. to *grot* fragment, particle (**ʒrut-*), *grēot* GRIT *sb.*[1] (**ʒreut-*), *grytt* bran, chaff, coarse oatmeal, dial. *grit* GRIT *sb.*[2], and *grūt* GROUT *sb.*[1]] **1.** Hulled, or hulled and crushed grain, chiefly oats, but also wheat, barley, and †maize. *Embden groats*: crushed barley or oats. †**2.** Naked oats –1725. *Comb.* †**g.-sugar,** coarse sugar.

†**Groa·tsworth.** 1562. [f. *groat's*, genitive of GROAT *sb.* + WORTH *sb.*[1]] As much as a groat will buy; *fig.* a small amount –1678.

Grobian (grōᵘ·biăn). 1609. [– G. *grobian* or its source med.L. *Grobianus* type of boorishness in Germany (XV–XVI), f. G. *grob* coarse, rude, GRUFF.] A clownish slovenly person. Also as *adj.*

Grobians and sluts, if once they be in loue, they will be most neat and spruce BURTON.

Grocer (grōᵘ·səɹ). [ME. *grosser* – AFr. *grosser*, OFr. *grossier* :- med.L. *grossarius*, f. *grossus* GROSS *a.* The sp. with *c* (XV) followed that of †SPICER[1].] †**1.** One who buys and sells in the gross, a wholesale dealer or merchant. (The company of Grocers consisted of wholesale dealers in spices and foreign produce; hence prob. sense 2.) 1689. **2.** A trader who deals in spices, dried fruits, sugar, etc. 1465.

2. What should an Irenmonger meddle with Grocer's ware 1510. *Grocer's itch*, eczema caused by handling sugar.

Grocery (grōᵘ·səri). ME. [f. prec. + -Y[3]; see -ERY.] **1.** *collect. sing.* The goods sold by a grocer; *pl.* various sorts of such goods. **2.** The trade of a grocer 1689. **3.** *U.S.* A grocer's shop 1828; a dram-shop 1846. **4.** *attrib.*, as *g.-warehouse* 1554.

1. A deal box..to bring home groceries in GOLDSM. A parcel of g. 1865. *Comb.* **g.-captain,** the captain of an East Indiaman.

Grog (grǫg), *sb.* 1770. [Said to be short for GROGRAM; applied first as a nickname to Admiral Vernon, who wore a grogram cloak, and afterwards to the mixture which he ordered in 1740 to be served out instead of neat spirit.] A drink consisting of spirits (orig. rum) and water. *Seven-water g.*, a sailor's term for very weak grog.

Comb.: **g.-blossom,** a redness or pimple on the nose caused by excessive drinking; **-shop,** a dram-shop; also (*pugilistic slang*) the mouth.

Grog (grǫg), *v.* 1833. [f. the sb.] **1.** *intr.* To drink grog. **2.** *trans.* To extract spirit from (an empty cask) by pouring hot water into it, and letting it stand 1878.

Groggery (grǫ·gəri). *U.S.* 1855. [f. GROG *sb.* + -ERY.] A grog-shop.

Groggy (grǫ·gi), *a.* 1770. [f. GROG *sb.* + -Y[1].] **1.** Intoxicated; also, bibulous. **2.** *Farriery.* Of a horse: Having a weakness in the forelegs, which causes a hobbling or tottering movement 1828. **3.** *slang.* Weakened in a fight, so as to stagger; hence *gen.* shaky 1832. Hence **Gro·gginess,** g. condition or state.

Grogram (grǫ·grăm). 1562. [Early forms also *grow graine, grograyn, grogerane* – Fr. *gros grain* 'coarse grain'; see GROSS *a.*, GRAIN *sb.*[1] For the change of final *n* to *m* cf. BUCKRAM, LOCKRAM.] **1.** A coarse fabric of silk, of mohair and wool, or of these mixed with silk; often stiffened with gum. **2.** A garment made of grogram 1633. **3.** *attrib.*, as *g.-cloak*, etc. 1582.

Groin (groin), *sb.*[1] *Obs.* exc. *dial.* ME. [– OFr. *groign* (= med.L. *grugnum* XIII), mod. *groin* :- late L. *grunium, -ia*, med.L. *grunnium* snout – L. *grunnire* grunt like a swine.] †**1.** A grunting, grumble. CHAUCER. **2.** The snout, *esp.* of a swine ME. †**3.** *Naut. The groin (of Spain)* [an etymological perversion of Sp. *Coruña*]: a sailor's name for Corunna –1719.

Groin (groin), *sb.*[2] [ME. *grynde*, early mod.Eng. *gryne*, in late XVI *groin*; perh. transf. use of OE. *grynde* (orig. perh. 'depression'); cf. dial. *grindle* (XV) narrow ditch or drain (cf. GRIP *sb.*[2]). The change of (ī) to (oi) in the pronunc. is paralleled in BOIL *sb.*[1], HOIST, JOIST.] **1.** The fold or depression on either side of the body between the abdomen and the upper thigh. †*fig.* The seat of lust. B. JONS. †**2.** A deep trench –1587. **3.** *Arch.* The edge formed by the intersection of two vaults. Also, the rib or fillet of stone or wood with which this is usually covered. 1725.

1. *fig.* To see The fury of mens gullets, and their groines B. JONS.

‖**Groin,** *v.*[1] ME. [– OFr. *grognir*, (also mod.) *grogner* :- L. *grunnire* grunt like a swine; cf. GROIN *sb.*[1]] **1.** *intr.* Of animals: To grunt; to growl –1596; *esp.* of the buck: To utter its cry at rutting-time (cf. GROAN *v.*) –1711. **2.** *transf.* Of persons: To grumble, murmur –1583.

Groin (groin), *v.*[2] 1805. [f. GROIN *sb.*[2]] *Arch.* **1.** To form into or furnish with groins; to build with groins 1812. **2.** *intr.* Of an arch, etc.: To spring as a groin.

Groin: see GROYNE *sb.* and *v.*

Groined (groind), *ppl. a.* 1789. [f. GROIN *sb.*[2] and *v.*[2] + -ED.] Built or furnished with groins.

Grom(m)et, -it: see GRUMMET.

Gromil, -ill, -ille, obs. ff. GROMWELL.

Gromwell (grǫ·mwĕl). [ME. *gromil* – OFr. *gromil, grumil* (mod. *grémil*) prob. :- med.L. **gruinum milium* 'crane's millet', i.e. n. of late L. *gruinus*, f. *grus* crane, and *milium* MILLET.] Any of the plants of the genus *Lithospermum* (N.O. *Boraginaceæ*), characterized by hard stony seeds; formerly used in the cure of gravel. Also *attrib.*

Grond, obs. pa. t. of GRIND *v.*

Gront(e, vars. of GRUNT.

Groof, grufe (grūf), *adv.* ME. [– ON. *grúfa*, in phr. *á grúfu* face downwards. The occurrence of *f* instead of the normal *v* is unexpl. See GROVEL.] On the face, on the belly; prone –1567.

She on here armes two Fil gruf, and gan to wepe CHAUCER.

Groo-groo, gru-gru (grū·grū). 1796. [prob. Native name.] **1.** In the W. Indies and S. America, a name for two species of palm, *Astrocaryum aculeatum* and *Acrocomia sclerocarpa*. **2.** Usu. *groo-groo worm*: The grub of the coleopterous insect *Calandra palmarum* 1796.

Groom (grūm), *sb.* [ME. *grōm* (with tense *ō*), of unkn. origin. AFr. *gromet*, AL. *gromus* (c1410), *grometus* (XVI) are used in sense 3.] †**1.** A man-child, boy –1675. **2.** A man, male person. Sometimes *contemptuous* = 'fellow'. *Obs.* exc. *arch.* ME. **3.** A manservant; a male attendant. *Obs.* exc. *arch.* ME. **4.** The specific designation of several officers of the English Royal Household, chiefly in the Lord Chamberlain's department; as *Groom of the Chamber, of the Stole, in waiting*, etc. 1464. **5.** A servant who attends to horses.

(Orig. a contextual use of 3; now the current sense.) 1667. **6.** Short for BRIDEGROOM. (Usu. in context with *bride*.) 1604. **7.** *attrib.* 1483.

2. *Tit. A.* IV. ii. 164. **3.** You logger-headed and vnpollisht groomes, What? no attendance SHAKS. **5.** Horses led, and Grooms besmeared with Gold MILT. **6.** Drinking health to bride and g. TENNYSON.

Groom (grūm), *v.* 1809. [f. GROOM *sb.*] **1.** *trans.* To curry, feed, and generally attend to (a horse); to 'fettle'. **2.** *transf.* To tend or attend to carefully; to give a smart appearance to 1843. **3.** *pass.* To be made a bridegroom. BYRON. **4.** *U.S.* To prepare as a political candidate 1889.

Groo·mer. 1884. [f. prec. + -ER[1].] A brush rotated by a flexible or jointed revolving shaft, for the mechanical grooming of horses.

Groom-porter. *Obs.* exc. *Hist.* 1502. An officer of the English Royal Household, abolished under George III, whose principal functions were to regulate gaming within the precincts of the court, to furnish cards and dice, and to decide disputes arising at play.

Groomsman (grū·mzmæn). 1698. [f. *groom's* + MAN, after BRIDESMAID, q.v.] A young man acting as friend or attendant on the bridegroom at a marriage, either alone (as 'best man') or as one of a company.

Grooper, obs. f. GROUPER.

Groove (grūv), *sb.* ME. [– Du. †*groeve* furrow, ditch (mod. *groef*) = OHG. *gruoba* (G. *grube* pit, ditch), ON. *gróf*, Goth. *grōba*; f. Gmc. *ʒrōb-, rel. to *ʒrab- GRAVE *sb.*[1], *v.*[1]] **1.** A mining shaft; a mine, pit. Now *dial.* **2.** A channel or hollow, cut by artificial means, in metal, wood, etc. 1659. **3.** A channel or furrow of natural formation; *spec.* in *Anat.* and *Zool.* 1787. **4.** *transf.* and *fig.* A channel or routine of action or life. Often, in bad sense: A rut. 1842. †**5.** A gardener's transplanting tool –1726.

4. His ideas were wont to travel rather in a g. HELPS. *Comb.* **g.-board** (in an organ), a second upper board in which grooves are cut to supply room for the larger pipes, etc.

Groove (grūv), *v.* 1483. [f. GROOVE *sb.*] **1.** *intr.* To sink a mining shaft; to mine (*dial.*). **2.** *trans.* To cut a groove or grooves in; to provide with grooves 1686. **3.** To cut in the form of a groove or channel; to excavate (a channel) 1866. **4.** *pass.* and *intr.* To fit or be fitted as *into* a groove (*rare*) 1854.

Groover (grū·vəɹ). 1610. [f. GROOVE *v.* + -ER[1].] One who or that which grooves; a miner (now *dial.*); a gouge (*rare*) 1865.

Grooving (grū·viŋ), *vbl. sb.* 1678. [f. GROOVE *v.* + -ING[1].] **1.** The action of GROOVE *v.*; mining (*dial.*) 1892. **2.** The making or forming of grooves or channels; a groove or set of grooves. Also *fig.* 1728. **3.** *attrib.*, as *g.-plane*, etc. 1678.

Grope (grōᵘp), *sb.* 1500. [f. GROPE *v.*] The action or an act of groping (*lit.* and *fig.*).

Grope (grōᵘp), *v.* [OE. *grāpian* = OHG. *greifōn* :– WGmc. *ʒraipōjan, f. Gmc. *ʒraip- *ʒrīp- (see GRIPE *v.*[1]).] †**1.** *intr.* To use the hands in feeling, touching, or grasping; to handle or feel something –1568. **2.** To attempt to find something by feeling about as in the dark or as a blind person; to feel about in order to find one's way OE. Also *fig.* †**3.** *trans.* To touch with the hands; to handle, feel; to probe (a wound). Also, to take hold of, grasp, seize. –1738. **b.** To search, rummage. *Obs.* exc. *Sc.* 1526. †**4.** *fig.* **a.** To apprehend as something palpable –1642. †**b.** To examine, sound, probe; to investigate –1651.

2. She gropeth alwey forther with hir hond And foond the bed CHAUCER. Fish must be grop't for, and be tickled too BUNYAN. *fig.* As blindly groped they for a future state DRYDEN. Phr. *To g. one's way*: to find one's way by groping (*lit.* and *fig.*). **4. b.** Felix gropeth him, thinking to haue a bribe N.T. (Genev.) *Acts* 24. *Contents.* Hence **Gro·pingly** *adv.* in a groping manner.

Groroilite (groroi·ləit). 1844. [f. *Groroi* in France + -LITE.] *Min.* Earthy manganese, occurring in roundish masses, of a brownish-black colour with reddish-brown streaks.

Grosbeak (grōᵘ·sbīk). Also †**gross-beak.** 1678. [– Fr. *grosbec*, f. *gros* GROSS *a.* + *bec* BEAK *sb.*[1]] Any of various small birds having a large stout bill, chiefly of the families *Fringillidæ* and *Ploceidæ*. The common grosbeak is the hawfinch (*Coccothraustes vulgaris*.) Other species are: **green g.** = GREENFINCH 1; **pine g.,** *Pinicola enucleator;* **cardinal g.** (see CARDINAL *sb.*); **grenadier g.** (see GRENADIER 2a); also (in U.S.) **blue g.** (*Guiraca cærulea*), **evening g.** (*Hesperophona vespertina*), **rose-breasted g.** (*Hedymeles ludovicianus*).

‖**Groschen** (grōᵘ·ʃĕn). 1617. [G., (Bohemian) alteration of late MHG. *grosse, gros,* in med.L. *denarius grossus* 'thick penny'; see GROSS *a.*, GROAT.] A small silver coin and money of account variously = $\frac{1}{24}$, $\frac{1}{30}$, or $\frac{1}{36}$ of a thaler. Not a part of the present German monetary system.

‖**Gros de Naples** (gro də nap'l). 1799. [Fr. *gros* GROSS *a.*, used subst.] A heavy silk fabric, made originally at Naples. Also *attrib.* So ‖**Gros de Tours.**

‖**Gros grain.** [See GROGRAM.] Commercial name of a strong corded silk fabric. (Recent.)

†**Gross,** *sb.*[1] 1638. [repr. Fr. *gros*, It. *grosso*.] A name for various foreign coins; e.g. the German GROSCHEN, and the Italian *grosso*, worth about 3*d*. Cf. GROAT. –1705.

Gross (grōᵘs), *sb.*[2] ME. [– Fr. *grosse*, subst. use (sc. *douzaine* dozen) of fem. of *gros* great; see next and cf. Sp. *gruesa*, Pg., It. *grossa*.] Twelve dozen. Not found in *pl.* Also *small g.*, in opposition to *great g.* = 12 gross.

Bowe stringes, xl gros 1549.

Gross (grōᵘs), *a.* and *sb.*[3] ME. [–(O)Fr. *gros*, fem. *grosse* :– late L. *grossus* (freq. in Vulgate), of similar formation to *bassus* BASE *a.*, *crassus* CRASS.]

A. *adj.*

I. †**1.** Thick, stout, massive, big –1794. **2.** Big-bodied, corpulent, burly. (Now only *dial.*) Hence, Overfed, unwholesomely fat and corpulent. Hence said also of the habit of body. 1577. †**3.** Of conspicuous magnitude; palpable, striking; plain, evident –1793. **4.** Glaring, flagrant, monstrous 1581.

1. The Foe Approaching g. and huge MILT. In a strong g. hand BLACKSTONE. Phr. †*To fly g.* (Hawking), i.e. at great birds. **2.** One of them is well knowne..a grosse fat man SHAKS. A full g. Habit of Body ARBUTHNOT. **3.** Lyes.. grosse as a Mountain, open, palpable SHAKS. **4.** G. Folly and Stupidity BENTLEY, sophistry 1781, imposters 1817, perfidy GROTE, credulity 1884.

II. †**1.** Of a denomination of value or weight: Relatively large; containing lower denominations –1801. **2.** Entire, total, whole. Now only as opp. to *net*. 1523. †**b.** Main, the great majority of –1793. **3.** Concerned with large masses or outlines; general, opp. to *particular* ME.

1. Phr. *A hundred g.* = 112 lb. or 1 cwt. **2.** The g. personal estate is sworn at £37,405..the net at £29,389. **3.** †*G. average* = general average (see AVERAGE *sb.*[2]).

III. 1. Dense, thick 1460. †**2.** Solid; having three dimensions. DIGGES. †**3.** Of a body of armed men: Compact, solid –1670.

1. Darkness..so g. that it might be felt 1592. Spirits of purest light, Purest at first, now g. by sinning grown MILT.

IV. †**1.** Consisting of comparatively large parts or particles. Hence, Wanting in fineness or delicacy. –1793. **2.** †Of commodities, etc.: Coarse, inferior, common –1763. **b.** Of diet: †(*a*) In early use, plain, not delicate; (*b*) in recent use, repulsive in quality. *G. feeder*, one who feeds grossly; said *transf.* of plants. 1599. **3.** Lacking in delicacy of perception; dull, stupid. *Obs.* of persons, their opinions, etc.; *arch.* of faculties, after Matt. 13:15. 1526. †**b.** Rough, rough and ready, clumsy –1675; approximate, general, indefinite –1818. **4.** Rude, uninstructed (now *rare*) 1561; †uncultivated; †unlearned, untechnical –1781. **5.** Extremely coarse in behaviour or morals 1532.

2. Fish and oil, and such g. commodities DE FOE. **3.** Men..g. of ear, of vision dim WHITTIER. G. and confus'd Conceptions LOCKE. **4.** Peter and John..grosse vnlerned men 1561. The vulgar dialect of the city was g. and barbarous GIBBON. **5.** Agamemnon's Wife Was a g. Butcher DRYDEN. Terms of the grossest abuse 1850.

B. quasi-*sb.* (the adj. used *absol.*) and *sb.* †**1. By gross:** in large quantities, wholesale –1660. **2. In gross, in the gross.** [Fr. *en gros.*] **a.** In a general way, generally; in the main (now *rare*) ME. †**b.** 'En masse' –1647. †**c.** In bulk, wholesale; opp. to *by retail* –1818. †**d.** Nothing being omitted or withheld –1774. **e.** *Law.* [med.L. *in grosso.*] Said of that which is absolute and independent, belonging to the person, and not to a manor; esp. in *advowson, villain in g.* 1626. **3.** †The greater part; the majority, the bulk –1766; *esp.* of an army, etc.: The main body (now *arch.*) 1600; †the sum; the whole –1728. †**4.** Chiefly *Mil.* A large body; a mass –1700.

2. a. You cannot refuse in the g., what you have so often acknowledged in detail BURKE. **3.** The g. of an audience STEELE, of Mankind BUTLER.

Gross-beak, obs. f. GROSBEAK.

†**Gro·sshead.** 1580. [f. GROSS *a.* + HEAD.] A thick-headed person, a dullard –1606.

Grossification (grōᵘ:sifikēⁱ·ʃən). 1835. [f. GROSS *a.* + -FICATION.] *Bot.* The swelling of the ovary after fertilization.

Grossly (grōᵘ·sli), *adv.* 1526. [f. GROSS *a.* + -LY[2].] In a gross manner; †plainly –1771; excessively, flagrantly 1594; †coarsely –1823; †materially –1601; †stupidly, †awkwardly, roughly 1526; indelicately, indecently 1547.

Grossness (grōᵘ·snės). 1494. [f. GROSS *a.* + -NESS.] The quality or condition of being gross (see GROSS *a.*).

The G. of a City Feast DRYDEN. That chastity of honour..under which vice itself lost half its evil, by losing all its g. BURKE. The very g. of this flattery DICKENS.

Grossular (grǫ·siŭlăɹ). Also **-are.** 1819. [– mod.L. *grossularia*, an application of the specific name of the gooseberry (Werner in 1811).] *Min.* A pale-green variety of garnet from Siberia, often called the gooseberry garnet. So **Grossula·rious, Gro·ssularite** *adjs.* of the nature of, or resembling, the gooseberry.

†**Grot**[1]. [OE. *grot*, related to GRIT *sb.*[1], GRIT *sb.*[2], GROUT; see also GROATS.] A fragment, particle, atom –ME.

Grot[2] (grǫt). Now only *poet.* 1506. [– Fr. *grotte* – It. *grotta* :– Rom. **crupta*, **grupta* (L. *crypta*) – Gr. κρύπτη vault, CRYPT.] = GROTTO.

Grote, obs. f. GROAT, GROATS.

Grotesque (grote·sk). 1561. [Earliest *crotesque*, etc. – Fr. *crotesque* – (with assim. to OFr. *crote* GROT[2]) It. *grottesca*; ellipt. use (for *opera* or *pittura grottesca* grotto-like work or painting) of fem. of *grottesco*, f. *grotta*; finally assim. to Fr. *grotesque*; see GROT[2], -ESQUE.]

A. *sb.* **1.** A kind of decorative painting or sculpture, in which portions of human and animal forms are fantastically interwoven with foliage and flowers. **b.** A work of art in this style. Chiefly *pl.*; in pop. use, figures or designs comically distorted or exaggerated. 1643. **2.** A clown, buffoon, or merry-andrew 1864. **3.** *Printing.* A square-cut letter without ceriph. THUS; formerly called *stone-letter* 1875.

B. *adj.* **1.** *Arch.* Having the character of the work described in A. 1. 1603. **2.** More widely: Characterized by distortion or unnatural combinations; fantastically extravagant; bizarre, †quaint. Also *transf.* of literary style, etc. 1653. †**b.** Of landscape: Romantic, picturesquely irregular –1764. **3.** Ludicrous from incongruity 1747.

2. Those G. monsters..with which the spouts..of ancient buildings are decorated H. WALPOLE. **b.** MILT. *P.L.* IV. 136. **3.** But what added most to the g. expression of his face, was a ghastly smile DICKENS. Hence **Grote·sque** *v.* to caricature, travesty. **Grote·sque-ly** *adv.*, **-ness. Grote·squerie,** g. objects collectively; g. quality; a piece of grotesqueness.

Grotto (grǫ·to). *Pl.* **-os, -oes.** 1617. [Earliest *grotta* – It. *grotta*; see GROT[2].] **1.** A cave or cavern, esp. one which is picturesque or an agreeable retreat. **2.** An excavation or structure made to imitate a rocky cave, often adorned with shell-work, etc. 1625. *Comb.* **g.-work** = sense 2.

Grouch (grautʃ), *sb.* *U.S.* 1903. [var. of GRUTCH.] Grumbling; a fit of the sulks; a grumbler. Hence **Grouch** *v.* **Grou·chy** *a.*

Ground (graund), *sb.* [OE. *grund* = OFris., OS. *grund* (Du. *grond*), OHG. *grunt* (G. *grund*), Goth. **grundus* :– Gmc. **ʒrunduz*. No cognates outside Gmc. are known.]

I. †**1.** The bottom; the lowest part or downward limit of anything –1824. **2.** The solid bottom or earth underlying the sea (†or other water). Now only *Naut.* OE. **3.** *pl.* The particles deposited by a liquid in the bottom of a vessel; dregs, lees. †Also *sing.* a sediment. ME. Also *fig.* **b.** Refuse (of meal, wool, etc.) (*rare*) 1629.

1. A customer..that's near the grund of the purse SCOTT. *fig.* Let vs rather blesse God from the g. of our heart BIBLE *Transl. Pref.* **2.** The bottome of the deepe, Where Fadome-line could neuer touch the g. SHAKS. *To break g.* (Naut.): to heave the anchor clear of the bottom. *To strike g.*: to obtain soundings. *To take the g.*: to run ashore, strand. **3.** Smoking black coffee (half grounds) 1860.

II. †**1.** The solid base or foundation on which a structure is raised. In early use also *pl.* (cf. *foundations*). –1715. **2.** In immaterial applications: **a.** The basis, foundation ME. †**b.** A fundamental principle; also *pl.* rudiments –1762. **c.** A reason, motive; often, a valid reason, etc. ME. **3.** The foundation on which other parts are overlaid, or on which they rest for support or display: **a.** in a composite textile fabric ME. **b.** Any material surface which is taken as a basis to work upon; *esp.* in painting and decorative art, a main surface or first coating of colour serving as a support for other colours or as a background for designs; the prevailing colour of any object, picture, etc.; the portion of a surface which is not operated upon. Also *pl.* ME. †**c.** *Mus.* The plain-song or melody on which a descant is raised. Also = *ground-bass.* –1811. **d.** *Etching.* (See quot.) Also *etching-ground.* 1727. **e.** *Carpentry.* (See quot.) Usu. *pl.* 1823. †**4.** The main constituent or the essential part of anything –1737.

1. Salomon..buylded the walles..from the grounde of y[e] house vnto the rofe COVERDALE 1 *Kings* 6:15. **2. a.** Which of all goodly manners is the g. SPENSER. **b.** There is a g. in the law, that inheritance may..not lyneally ascend *Littleton's Tenures.* **c.** Hee refus'd; his grounds I know not 1657. What grounds for apprehension SHERIDAN. **3. a.** To weave coarse work upon a precious g. DRYDEN. **b.** Mosaick work of Green, upon a G. of fine Gold 1687. **c.** SHAKS. *Rich. III*, III. vii. 49. **d.** Ground in etching denotes a gummous composition, smeared over the surface of the metal to be etched; to prevent the aqua fortis from eating, or having effect, except in places where this *ground* is cut through, or pared off E. CHAMBERS. **e.** *Grounds*—Pieces of wood concealed in a wall, to which the facings or finishings are attached P. NICHOLSON.

III. The surface of the earth or a part of it. **1.** The earth as the surface upon which man and his surroundings rest or move. Also *fig.* OE. **b.** The portion of the earth's surface on which a person or thing stands or moves; often *fig.* 1530. **c.** The bare floor (= pit) of a theatre. B. JONS. **d.** *Fox-hunting.* (*To run*) *to g.*: into a burrow or hole, 'to earth' 1797. †**2.** The earth as contrasted with (*a*) heaven –1742. (*b*) the sea –1697. **3.** With *a* and *pl.* †**a.** A region, land, country (*rare*) –1609. †**b.** A piece or parcel of land –1733. **c.** *pl.* Enclosed land surrounding or attached to a dwelling-house or other building, serving chiefly for ornament or recreation. †Formerly = lands, fields 1460. **4.** Area or distance on the face of the earth. (Usu. without article.) ME. **b.** *fig.* Subject-matter; things that may be the object of study or discourse 1796. **5.** Area or space having a specified extent or character, or adapted for a specific purpose ME. **6.** With reference to possessor or occupier, denoted by a genitive, etc. ME. **7.** The space or area under consideration, or one used for some special purpose, *esp.* the scene of any contest or meeting ME. **8.** *Telegraphy.* The contact of the conductor of an electric circuit with the earth; the escape of current resulting from this 1870.

1. The grassye g. with daintye Daysies dight SPENSER. *fig.* Phr. †*To bring to the g.*: To cast down, overthrow, overcome. *To fall to the g.*: (of schemes) to come to nothing; so *to be dashed to the g.* (of hopes). *Down to the g.*: completely (*colloq.*). *Above g.*: unburied, alive. **b.** *To cut the g. from under one* or *one's feet.* **2.** 'Twixt sky and g. SHAKS. **3. c.** Like a Theefe to come to rob my grounds; Climbing my walles inspight of me the Owner SHAKS. **4.** Phr. *To gain, gather, get g.*: to advance, make progress (*lit.* and *fig.*). *To give g.*: to recede, retire. *To lose g.*: to fall back, decline. *To take g.*: to take up, or move into, a certain position. **b.** *fig.* The learned Dr. Robertson has travelled partly over the same g. 1804. **5.** From a g. of advantage 1618. On some spot of English g. SHELLEY. **6.** A fair house, built on another mans g. SHAKS. Phr. *To hold, keep, maintain, stand, shift one's g.* (now usu. *fig.*). **7.** *On the g.*: engaged, in a duel. He has been 'on the ground' I don't know how many times THACKERAY. *The g.* (Cricket): (*a*) The space on which the game is played; (*b*) the space within which a player may lawfully stand, e.g. while batting; (*c*) the paid staff of players attached to a club (also *g.-staff*).

IV. The soil of the earth. Also without article: Soil, earth, mould; now only in *Mining.* With *a* and *pl.* A kind or variety of soil. ?*Obs.* ME.

There be many maner of groundes and soyles FITZHERB.

Comb. **1.** General: **a.** *g.-level, -pipe, -sward,* etc.; **b.** with sense 'fundamental', †'deep-seated', etc.: *g.-idea, -principle, -root, -thought, -tint, -tone,* etc. (mostly recent imitations of German compounds); †**c.** with sense 'to the bottom', hence 'completely, thoroughly, extremely': *g.-hot, -stalwart,* etc.

2. Special: **g.-air,** the air contained in the soil, which contains a large portion of carbonic acid gas, due to the disintegration of organic substances; **-angling,** fishing with a weighted line, without a float; **-bailiff,** a superintendent of mines; **-bass** (*Mus.*), a bass-passage of four or eight bars in length, constantly repeated with a varied melody and harmony (Stainer & Barrett); **-bundle** (*Anat.*), one of the bundles of nerve-fibres lying on either side of the grey matter of the spinal cord; **-cable,** that part of a mooring-cable which lies on the sea-bottom; **-chamber,** one on the ground-floor; **-colour,** (*a*) a first coating of paint; (*b*) the prevailing colour of an object having markings of other colours; **-crab,** a kind of hoisting apparatus used in mining; †**-ebb,** low water; also as *adj.*, at low water; **-fast** *a.*, firmly fixed in the g.; **-fish,** a fish which lives at the bottom of the water; **-fishery, -fishing,** fishing with the bait at or near the bottom of the water; **-game,** game which lives on the g., as hares and rabbits; †**-hold,** the anchors of a vessel; **-joint,** the joining of one stone or course in masonry with the g. or course immediately below; **-joist,** a joist supporting the ground floor of a building; **-landlord,** the owner of land which is leased for building on; **-mail,** *Sc.*, payment for burying-ground; **-mass,** the compact basal part of an igneous rock, in which the distinctive crystals are embedded; **-moraine,** subglacial till, boulder-clay; also *attrib.*; **-net,** a trawl or drag-net; **-note** (*Mus.*), the note on which a common chord is built, called also the *fundamental bass*; also *fig.*; **-officer,** one who has charge of the grounds and lands of an estate; **-plane,** the horizontal plane of projection in perspective drawing; **-rope,** a rope by which the lower edge of a trawl is kept on the g.; **-row,** a row of gas-jets on the floor of a theatre-stage; **-seine,** a form of seine or drag-net; **-sluice** *sb.* (*Mining*), a channel cut in the bottom or bed-rock, into which the earth is conveyed by a stream of water; **-story** = GROUND-FLOOR; **-substance** (*Phys.*), the homogeneous matrix in which the structural elements of a tissue are embedded; **-sype,** water filtering through from the surface, opp. to *spring water*; **-table** (*Arch.*), the plinth or projecting course resting on the foundation of a wall; an earth-table; **-tier,** (*a*) the lowest tier of goods in a vessel's hold; (*b*) the lowest range of boxes in a theatre; **-timbers,** the main timbers laid on the keel of a ship, floor-timbers; **-tissue** (*Bot.*), the mass of cells separating the vascular bundles from each other and from the epidermis; **-torpedo,** a torpedo fixed to the g. or bottom of the sea; **-tow,** the loose hemp that comes from the sides of the hatchellers and spinners; **-water,** all water found in the surface soil of the crust of the earth, except such as may be in combination with the materials of the crust of the earth; **-ways,** the large blocks and thick planks which support the cradle on which a ship is launched; **-wire** (*Telegraphy*), a metaphorical term applied to the earth when used as a return circuit; **-worm,** an earth-worm. See also Main Words.

b. In names of animals (esp. birds of terrestrial habits, and animals that burrow, or lie in holes or on the ground); as **g.-bear,** the common brown bear, *Ursus arctos*; **-beetle,** a general name for all beetles of the family *Carabidæ*; **-cuckoo,** a member of one of the four genera of *Neomorphinæ*, a sub-family of the *Cuculidæ*; **-dove,** a dove or pigeon of terrestrial habits, esp. of the genera *Chamæpelia* and *Geopelia*; **-finch,** (*a*) a bird of Swainson's sub-family *Fringillinæ* or true finches; (*b*) an American finch of the genus *Pipilo*; **-gudgeon,** the loach; **-hornbill,** the African genus *Bucorvus* (or *Bucorax*) of hornbills; **-hornet,** a hornet that has its nest on the g.; **-lackey,** *Bombyx castrensis*; **-lark,** the tree pipit; also the bunting; **-lizard,** *Ameiva dorsalis*; **-parrakeet,** any bird of the genera *Geopsittacus* and *Pezoporus*; **-parrot,** (*a*) = prec.; (*b*) the Kakapo of New Zealand; **-pearl,** an insect which lives beneath the soil in crevices frequented by ants, and acquires a shell-like calcareous scaly covering; **-pig,** the ground-rat (*Aulacodus swinderianus*); **-pigeon,** a pigeon which passes most of its time on the ground; esp. one of the family *Gouridæ*; also = *ground-dove*; **-puppy** = HELL-BENDER 1; **-rat** (see *ground-pig*); **-scratcher,** a name for the *Rasores* or gallinaceous birds; **-shark,** any species of shark that rarely comes to the surface, *esp.* the spinous shark (*Echinorrhinus spinosus*); **-sloth,** one of an extinct group intermediate between the existing sloths and ant-eaters; **-snake,** *Coronella australis*; **-sparrow** *U.S.*, one of several sparrows of terrestrial habits, e.g. the grass-finch and savannah-sparrow; **-spearing,** a fish, *Trachinocephalus myops*; **-spider,** any kind of spider that burrows or lives under stones; **-thrush,** (*a*) a thrush of the genus *Geocichla*; (*b*) a bird of the Australian genus *Cinclosoma*; (*c*) the pitta or ant-thrush; **-tit,** a small Californian bird (*Chamæa fasciata*), allied to the wrens and titmice; **-wasp,** a wasp that has its nest on the g.; **-wren,** (*a*) the willow wren, *Sylvia trochilis*; (*b*) = *ground-tit.* See also Main Words.

c. In names of plants, generally denoting dwarfish plants and sometimes those of a trailing habit; as **g.-archil,** *Lecanora parella*, a lichen used in dyeing; **-berry,** (*a*) *U.S.* = CHECKER-BERRY; (*b*) *Austral.* a name for *Astroloma humifusium* and *A. pinifolium*; **-box,** *Buxus sempervirens*, the small variety used for edgings; **-cedar,** a cedar-like trailing plant; **-cherry,** (*a*) the Dwarf Cherry, *Cerasus chamæcerasus*; (*b*) an American plant of the genus *Physalis*; **-cistus,** *Rhododendron chamæcistus;* **-cypress,** *Santolina chamæcyparissus;* **-elder,** a name for *Sambucus ebulus, Angelica sylvestris, Ægopodium podagraria*, and *Mercurialis perennis*; **-fir** = GROUND-PINE; **-flax,** the genus *Camelina*; **-hemlock,** an American variety of the common yew, *Taxus baccata*; **-holly** = CHECKER-BERRY; **-jasmine,** *Passerina stelleri*; **-laurel,** the Trailing Arbutus (*Epigæa repens*) of N. America; †**myrtle,** Butcher's Broom (*Ruscus aculeatus*); **-oak,** (*a*) an oak-sapling; (*b*) a species of dwarf oak; **-pea** = GROUND-NUT 2; **-plum,** *Astragalus caryocarpus*, the fruit of which, a pod, closely resembles a plum; **-thistle,** the cardoon (*Cynara cardunculus*); **-willow,** a dwarf willow; **-yew** = CROWBERRY. See also Main Words.

Ground (graund), *v.* ME. [f. GROUND *sb.*] †**1.** *trans.* To lay the foundations of (a house); to found; to fix or establish firmly. Also *fig.* –1684. **2.** To set on a firm basis, to establish. Const. *on*, also *in* (now only in *pass.*). ME. †**3.** To establish, settle (a person in respect of his position, beliefs, etc.). Const. *in*, *of*. –1657. †**4.** *refl.* To rest or rely *upon* –1812. †Also *intr.* for *refl.* –1682. **5.** *trans.* To instruct *in* main or elementary principles ME. **6.** To form or supply a basis, ground, or reason for (*rare*) 1667. **7.** To furnish with a ground (see GROUND *sb.* II. 3) ME. **8.** To knock down ME.; †*fig.* to 'floor', 'gravel' (*rare*) –1598. **9.** To set on the ground; to cause to touch the ground; to lay down 1650. **b.** *Electr.* To connect with the earth as a conductor 1883. **c.** *intr.* To come to or strike the ground 1751. **10.** *intr.* Of a vessel: To run ashore or aground; to strand. Const. *on.* c1430. **b.** *trans.* To cause to run ashore. Also *fig.* 1658.

1. That house..was grounded vpon ye rocke COVERDALE *Luke* 6:48. **2.** Moral vertue grounded vpon trouþe CHAUCER. Their suspicions and fears were not ill grounded THIRLWALL. **5.** He came young and not well grounded from Oxford University 1617. **7.** Whether he grounds a head.. or whether he grounds the whole picture RUSKIN. **9.** To g. one's bat STRUTT. Phr. *To g. arms* (Mil.): to lay one's arms upon the ground, *esp.* as an act of surrender. **10.** Three of our ships seemed to be grounded 1806. Hence **Grou·nded-ly** *adv.*, †**-ness** (*rare*).

Ground (graund), *ppl. a.* 1765. [pa. pple. of GRIND *v.*] **1.** Reduced to fine particles by grinding or crushing. **2.** Having the surface abraded or fashioned by grinding, esp. of joints, stoppers, etc. intended to fit closely 1807. **3.** *Ground glass.* †**a.** Plate glass –1823. **b.** Glass made opaque by grinding, etc.; also *attrib.* 1848.

Groundage (grau·ndédʒ). 1440. [f. GROUND *sb.* + -AGE.] **1.** †**a.** Some kind of toll or tax. ME. only. **b.** A duty levied on vessels lying upon a shore or beach, or entering a port 1567. **c.** *Mining.* = ROYALTY 6b. 1852.

Ground-ash. 1664. **1.** A young ash-plant; an ash sapling. Also *attrib.* **2.** *dial.* The gout-weed, *Ægopodium podagraria* 1796; also, *Angelica sylvestris* 1853.

Grou·nd-bait. 1651. **1.** †**a.** A bait used in bottom-fishing (*rare*). T. BARKER. **b.** A bait thrown to the bottom of the water, in order to lure the fish. Also *fig.* 1655. **2.** *Northumb.* The loach or groundling 1867.

Ground-bird. 1560. †**1.** One, or perh. more than one, swan out of a 'game', ?as the due of the owner of the land –1887. **2.** Any columbine, gallinaceous, grallatorial, or struthious bird 1840. **3.** *U.S.* The grass-finch or ground-sparrow 1856.

Grou·nden, obs. pa. pple. of GRIND *v.*

Grounder (grau·ndəɹ). ME. [f. GROUND *v.* + -ER[1].] **1.** One who, or that which, grounds (see GROUND *v.*). **2.** *colloq.* **a.** A catching the ground (in angling) 1847. **b.** A knock-down blow 1889. **c.** In *Cricket*, etc.: A ball sent along the ground.

Grou·nd-floor. 1601. The floor in a building which is more or less on a level with the ground outside. Also *attrib.*

Phr. *To get* (or *be let*) *in on the ground-floor* (U.S.): to be allowed to share in a speculation on the same terms as the original promoters.

Ground-hog. 1840. **1.** = AARD-VARK. **2.** The American marmot (*Arctomys*) 1843.

Ground-ice. 1694. [Cf. Du. *grondijs*, G. *grundeis.*] Ice formed at the bottom of the water; *anchor-ice.*

Grounding (grau·ndiŋ), *vbl. sb.* ME. [f. GROUND *v.* and *sb.* + -ING[1].] **1.** The action of founding or establishing; chiefly in immaterial sense. Also quasi-*concr.* That on which something is grounded (now *rare*). **2.** Elementary instruction 1644. **3.** The preparation or laying of a ground in arts and manufactures. Also *grounding-in*, the application of the secondary colours in calico-printing. 1466. **4.** The action of laying, or of running, a ship aground 1691. **5.** *attrib.* 1790.

Comb.: **g.-machine,** a machine for grounding in the manufacture of wall-paper; **-tool,** in mezzotint engraving the tool with which the plate is roughened.

Ground-ivy. ME. **1. a.** The herb ale-hoof, *Nepeta glechoma* or *Glechoma hederacea*, a common labiate plant having bluish-purple flowers and kidney-shaped leaves. †**b.** The periwinkle, *Vinca minor* (*rare*). (These plants were classed as *hedera* solely on account of their creeping stems.) †**2.** The barren trailing ivy (*Hedera helix*). GERARD. †**3.** The ground-pine (*Ajuga chamæpitys*). Parkinson.

Groundless (grau·ndlės), *a.* [OE. *grundlēas*, f. *grund* GROUND *sb.* + *-lēas* -LESS.] †**1.** Bottomless, unfathomable (*lit.* and *fig.*)–1605. **2.** Destitute of foundation, authority, or support; having no real cause or reason; unfounded 1620.

1. Ground-less gulfs SYLVESTER. **2.** A g. fiction that cannot be proved BAXTER. Hence **Grou·ndless-ly** *adv.*, **-ness.**

Ground-line. 1450. [Cf. Du. *grondlijn*, G. and Sw. *grundlinie* (in senses 2 and 3).] **1.** A line used for bottom-fishing. **2.** *Geom.* †**a.** The base upon which a diagram is constructed –1659. **b.** The intersecting line of the vertical and horizontal planes of projection 1857. **3.** *pl.* Outlines (*lit.* and *fig.*) 1624.

Groundling (grau·ndliŋ). 1601. [f. GROUND *sb.* + -LING[1]. Cf. MDu. *grundelinck* (Du. *grondeling*), MHG. *grundelinc* (G. *gründling*) gudgeon.] **1.** A name for various small fishes which live at the bottom of the water, *esp.* a gudgeon or loach. **2.** A creeping plant, or one of low growth 1822. **3.** A frequenter of the ground or pit of a theatre; hence, an uncritical or unrefined person. (Only in literary use, after *Haml.* III. ii. 12.) 1602. †**4.** One of humble rank (*rare*) –1630. **5.** *attrib.* or *adj.* 1825.

3. But how do you like sharing the mirth of the groundlings LYTTON.

†**Grou·ndly,** *adv.* ME. [f. GROUND *sb.* + -LY[2].] Firmly established; in relation to the ground or root; profoundly –1602. †Also as *adj.*

Ground-man. Also **groundsman.** 1785. **a.** A labourer employed to dig or work on the ground. **b.** (Now always *groundsman*) One who is employed to keep a cricket, etc. ground in order 1886.

Ground-nut. 1636. [With 1, cf. Du. *grondnoot.*] **1.** One of the small farinaceous edible tubers of the wild bean (*Apios tuberosa*), a climbing plant of N. America; also, the plant. **2.** The pea-nut or ground-pea (*Arachis hypogæa*), the fruit of which is a pod ripening under ground 1769. Also *attrib.* **3.** The earth-nut (*Bunium flexuosum*) 1653.

Ground-pine. 1551. **1.** The plant *Ajuga Chamæpitys*, said to be named from its resinous smell. **2.** The club moss (*Lycopodium clavatum*), or other species of *Lycopodium* 1847.

Ground-plan. 1731. [Cf. Du. *grondplan.*] **1.** The representation on a plane of the arrangements, divisions, etc. of a building or other structure, at the ground-level. **2.** *fig.* The outline, general plan or basis upon which any work is constructed or composed 1831.

Ground-plate. 1663. [Cf. Du. *grondplaat*, G. *grundplatte.*] **1.** The lowest horizontal timber in a framing; a ground-sill. **2. a.** A bed-plate carrying railway sleepers or ties (Knight) 1875. **b.** A piece of flattened metal on which anything is fixed 1871. **c.** *Electr.* A metal plate sunk in the ground and connecting an electric current with the earth 1875.

Ground-plot. 1563. **1.** The portion of ground covered by a building, etc.; foundation. ?*Obs.* †**2.** = GROUND-PLAN 1, 2. –1794.

Ground-rent. 1667. [Cf. Du. *grondrente*, G. *grundrente.*] The rent paid to the owner of land which is let for building upon.

Ground-sea. 1642. A heavy sea in which large waves rise and dash upon the coast without apparent cause.

Groundsel (grau·ndsěl), *sb.*[1] [OE. *grundeswyliġe*, earlier *gundæswelġ(i)æ*, presumably f. *gund* pus (cf. REDGUM[1]) + **swulʒ- *swelʒ-* SWALLOW *v.*, the etymol. meaning being 'pus-absorber', with ref. to its use in poultices to reduce abscesses.] Any plant belonging to the genus *Senecio* (N.O. *Compositæ*), esp. *S. vulgaris* ('common groundsel'), given as food to cage-birds and formerly largely used for medical purposes.

Comb. **g.-tree,** a N. American shrub, *Baccharis halimifolia.*

Groundsel (grau·ndsěl), *sb.*[2], **ground-sill** (-sil). ME. [app. f. GROUND *sb.* + SILL[1], but the second element early became a mere termination.] **1.** A timber serving as a foundation to carry a superstructure, esp. a wooden building; the lowest member of a wooden framework; a ground-plate; hence, the foundation of any structure. Now chiefly *techn.* **b.** *fig.* An underlying principle 1604. **2.** The lower framing-timber of a door; a door-sill, threshold. †Also, a window-sill. 1523. **3.** *attrib.* 1625. Hence †**Grou·ndsel, grou·ndsill** *v. trans.* to lay the foundation or threshold of.

Groundsman: see GROUND-MAN.

Ground-squirrel. 1772. **1.** A terrestrial squirrel-like rodent: **a.** of the genus *Tamias*; esp. the chipmunk (*T. striatus*) of the *U.S.*; **b.** = GOPHER *sb.*[1] 2. **2.** An African squirrel of the genus *Xerus* 1867.

Ground-swell. 1818. A deep swell or heavy rolling of the sea, the result of a distant storm or seismic disturbance. Also *fig.*

fig. The deep-raking, g. of passion, as we see it in the sarcasm of Lear LOWELL.

Ground-tackle. 1556. [Cf. Du. *grondtakel*, G. *grund-takelage.*] A general name for all tackle made use of in anchoring, mooring, or kedging a vessel.

Grou·ndward. 1562. [See -WARD.]

A. *adv.* Towards the ground. Now *rare.*

B. *adj.* Turned or inclined towards the ground 1878.

Groundwork (grau·ndwəɹk). 1550. [Cf. MDu. *gront-werck* (mod. *grondwerk*), G. *grundwerk.*] **1.** The solid base on which a structure is built; foundation. Now *rare.* Also *fig.* **2.** The body or foundation on which other parts are overlaid, or on which they rest for display, as in painting, etc. 1655. **b.** The principal ingredient (*rare*) 1822.

1. *fig.* No Thought can be valuable, of which good Sense is not the G. ADDISON. **2.** Cushions of flower'd Satin, the g. thereof Gold and Silver 1662.

Group (grūp), *sb.* Also †**groupe.** 1686. [– Fr. *groupe* – It. *gruppo* – Gmc. **kruppaz* round mass (see CROP *sb.*). The etymol. sense is app. 'lump' or 'mass'.] **1.** *spec.* **a.** *Fine Art.* An assemblage of figures or objects forming together either a complete design, or a distinct portion of one. **b.** *Mus.* (*a*) A series of notes, of small time-value, grouped together; a division or run. (*b*) The method of setting out band parts in score. 1727. **2.** *gen.* An assemblage of objects standing near together, and forming a collective unity; a knot (of people), a cluster (of things). In early use there is often a notion of confused aggregation. 1736. **3.** A number of persons or things in a certain relation, or having a certain degree of similarity 1729. **4.** *esp.* in scientific classification. Chiefly used as an indefinite term for any classificatory division, whatever its relative rank (so, e.g., in *Zoology*) 1826. **5.** *Math.* A set or system of operations so constituted that the product of any number of these operations is always itself a member of the group 1854.

1. The beautiful Grouppe of Figures in the Corner of the Temple STEELE. **2.** They stood, clustered in a dark and savage g. J. F. COOPER. A fine groupe of crystals HERSCHEL. **3.** Man can only make progress in co-operative groups BAGEHOT. Natural groups of languages 1892. (*Oxford*) *g. movement*: a movement characterized by the 'sharing' of religious experiences by groups of persons. **4.** The forms of life..become divided into groups subordinate to groups DARWIN. *attrib.* **g. captain,** a rank in the Royal Air Force equivalent to colonel in the army.

Group (grūp), *v.* 1718. [f. the sb., or – Fr. *grouper.*] **1.** *trans.* To make a group of, to form into a group; to place in a group *with* 1754. **b.** *intr.* for *refl.* To form a group or part of a group; to gather in a group or groups 1801. **2.** *trans.* To dispose (colours, figures, etc.) so as to form a harmonious whole. Also with *about*, *together.* 1718. Also *intr.* for *refl.* **3.** *trans.* To arrange in groups with reference to some common feature or property 1862.

1. Scattered huts or cells grouped around a church or oratory 1894. **2.** Six figures will form too many for a sculptor to g. to advantage LOCKHART. Hence **Group·age,** arrangement in a g. or groups.

Grouped (grūpt), *ppl. a.* 1702. [f. prec. + -ED[1].] Arranged or forming a group or groups.

Grouped columns: three, four, or more columns placed upon the same pedestal.

Grouper (grū·pəɹ). 1687. [– Pg. *garupa*, prob. native S. Amer. name. For the perversion of form cf. BREAKER[2].] **1.** One of several species of the genus *Epinephelus* of serranoid fishes, inhabiting W. Indian waters and the Mexican gulf. The chief species are the Red G. (*E. morio*) and Black G. (*E. nigritus*). In California, a name of the rock-fish (*Sebastichthys*). **2.** *Austral.* A percoid fish of the genus *Oligorus* 1865. *Blue groper*: a labroid fish, *Cossyphus gouldii* 1880.

Grouping (grū·piŋ), *vbl. sb.* 1748. [f. GROUP *v.* + -ING[1].] The action of placing in groups, a manner in which things are grouped.

Grouse (graus), *sb.* 1531. [poss. pl. of orig. **grue*, to be referred to med.L. *gruta* (Giraldus Cambrensis), or W. *grugiar*, f. *grug* heath + *iar* hen.] **1. a.** Any of the gallinaceous birds having feathered feet (the family *Tetraonidæ* of many naturalists, of which the largest genera are *Tetrao* and *Lagopus*). **b.** In pop. use, restricted to *Lagopus* (formerly *Tetrao*) *scoticus*, more particularly called **Red Grouse,** and also Moor Fowl or Moor Game. **c.** Applied to birds of the genera *Syrrhaptes* and *Pterocles*, the SAND-*grouse*, q.v. 1772. **d.** The flesh of the bird 1786. †**2.** As a term of contempt. B. JONS. **3.** *attrib.*, as *g.-drive*, etc. 1814.

1. a. Besides the Red Grouse, the most important British varieties are: **Black G.,** *Tetrao tetrix*, Black Game or Heath Fowl, the male being called BLACK-COCK and the female GREY-HEN. **Wood** or **Great G.,** the capercailye, *Tetrao urogallus.* **White G.,** *Lagopus mutus*, the ptarmigan, locally called also Rock Grouse. Other varieties are: **Canada G.,** *Canace* or *Dendragapus canadensis*, called also Spotted Grouse. **Dusky G.,** *Canace* or *Dendragapus obscurus.* **Pinnated G.,** *Cupidonia cupido.* **Ruffed G.,** *Bonasa umbellus*; another species is the HAZEL-GROUSE, *B. silvestris.* **Sage G.,** *Centrocircus urophasianus.* **Sharp-tailed G.,** a g. of the genus *Pediœcetes. Comb.* **g.-pigeon,** the sand-grouse.

Grouse (graus), *v.*[1] 1798. [f. prec.] *intr.* To shoot grouse. Also *transf.* (cf. *snipe* v.).

Grouse (graus, grūs), *v.*[2] orig. *Army slang.* 1892. [Of unkn. origin.] *intr.* to grumble. Also as sb.

Grouser (grau·səɹ). 1876. [Of unkn. origin.] *Hydraulics.* An iron-pointed pile or timber attached to a boat, etc. as a means of anchorage or of keeping it in position.

Grout (graut), *sb.*[1] [OE. *grūt*, corresp. to MDu. *grūte, gruut* coarse meal, peeled grain, malt, yeast (Du. *gruit* dregs), MHG. *grūz* (G. *grauss*) grain, small beer; f. **ʒrūt-*, var. of **ʒraut-* **ʒreut-* **ʒrut-* (see GRIT *sb.*[2], GROATS).] **1.** Coarse meal, peeled grain. In *pl.* = GROATS. Now *rare.* **2.** The infusion of malt before and during fermentation. Also, small beer. *Obs.* exc. *dial.* OE. †**b.** (= Du. *grute*) app. some plant formerly used for flavouring beer –1671. **3.** Whole meal porridge. ?*Obs.* 1587. **4.** Sediment; dregs; lees; grounds 1697.

4. Wherefore should we turn the g. In a drained cup ROSSETTI.

Grout (graut), *sb.*[2] 1638. [perh. a use of prec., but cf. Fr. dial. *grouter* grout a wall.] Thin fluid mortar, which is poured into the interstices of masonry and wood-work. Also *attrib.*

Grout (graut), *v.* 1838. [f. prec.] *trans.* To fill up or finish with grout or liquid mortar; to cement. Also with *in.* Hence **Grou·ting** *vbl. sb.* filling of chinks, etc. with grout; chiefly *concr.* the material used in this operation.

†**Grout-head.** Also **growthed.** 1550. [f. GROUT *sb.*[1]; in 2 confused with *great.* Cf. *pudding-head.*] **1.** A blockhead, thickhead, dunce –1649. **2.** A big head; a person with a big head –1706. So **Grout-headed** *a.* thick-headed, stupid (now *dial.*).

†**Groutnoll.** 1578. [f. GROUT *sb.*[1] + NOLL.] = prec. –1658.

Grouty (grau·ti), *a. U.S.* 1836. [f. *grout* vb. to grumble + -Y[1]. Cf. GROUCHY.] Sulky, cross, ill-tempered. Hence **Grou·tiness.**

Grove (grōᵘv). [OE. *grāf* (:– **ʒraibaz, -am*), rel. to *grǣfa* brushwood, thicket (:– **ʒraibon*).] **1.** A small wood; a group of trees affording shade or forming avenues or walks. Also *transf.* and *fig.* ¶**2.** In Eng. versions of the Bible, an erron. rendering: **a.** of Heb. *'ᵃšērāh*, now understood as the name of a goddess or of a pillar serving as an idol 1535; **b.** of Heb. *'ēšel* (R.V. 'tamarisk tree') 1535. **3.** *attrib.* 1535.

1. I, ..like a Forrester, the groues may tread SHAKS. *transf.* Through Groves Of Coral MILT. *Comb.* **g.-dock**, *Rumex nemolapathum*; **-snail**, *Helix sylvatica.* Hence †**Grovet**, a little g.

Grovel (grǫ·v'l), *v.* 1593. [Back-formation (cf. *suckle*) from GROVELLING adj., attrib. use of the †adv., earlier †*grovellings* (XIII), f. *gruf* on the face, on the belly (for phr. *on grufe, ogrufe*) – ON. *á grúfu* face downwards (cf. *grúfla* go on all fours); see GROOF, GRUFE *adv.*, -LING[2], -LIN(G)S.] *intr.* To lie prone or with the face downwards; to move with the body prostrate upon the ground 1593. Also *fig.*

Gaze on, and grouell on thy face SHAKS. *fig.* The vindictive Laud grovelled in a meaner..victory D'ISRAELI. Hence **Grovel** *sb.* the action of grovelling. **Gro·veller, gro·veler**, one who grovels, chiefly *fig.*

Grovelling, groveling (grǫ·v'liŋ), *a.* (*ppl. a.*) 1538. [See prec.] **1.** Having the face or belly towards or on the ground; prone. Applied also to a low-growing plant. **2.** *transf.* and *fig.* Of persons, qualities, etc.: Abject, base, low, mean, sordid 1608.

1. Circe..Whose charmed Cup Whoever tasted, lost his upright shape, And downward fell into a groveling Swine MILT. **2.** Our groueling earth-desires SYLVESTER. Hence **Gro·vellingly** *adv.*

Grovelling, groveling (grǫ·v'liŋ), *adv.* [ME. See GROVEL *v.*] Face downward; in or to a prone or prostrate position.

Sir launcelot..pulled hym grouelyng doune MALORY. So **Gro·vellings** *adv.* (*Obs.* exc. *dial.*)

Grovy (grōᵘ·vi), *a.* Also †**grovey.** 1594. [f. GROVE + -Y[1].] Of, pertaining to, or resembling a grove; abounding in groves; situated in a grove.

Grow (grōᵘ), *v.* Pa. t. **grew** (grū, grⁱū). Pa. pple. **grown** (grōᵘn). [OE. *grōwan* = OFris. *grōwa, grōia*, MDu. *groeyen* (Du. *groeien*), OHG. *gruoan*, ON. *gróa*; Gmc. str. vb. f. **ʒrō-* (see GRASS, GREEN).]

I. Intr. senses. (In early use always with *be*, and still when a state or result is implied.) †**1.** Of a plant: To manifest vigorous life; to put forth foliage, flourish, be green –ME. **2.** In weaker sense: To have vegetative life. Hence also, to exist as a living plant in a specified habitat, or with specified characteristics. OE. **b.** *transf.* †(*a*) Of minerals: To be native in a certain situation; (*b*) *joc.*, of other things ME. **c.** *Naut.* Of a cable: To stretch out forward towards the starboard side 1780. **3.** With advs. or preps. forming phrases chiefly used *transf.* or *fig.* 1593. **4.** With especial reference to the beginning of vegetable, or (*transf.*) animal life OE. **5.** *fig.* Of immaterial things: To spring up; to arise, originate, be developed as from a germ; to spring naturally as from a stock OE. **6.** To increase gradually in size by natural development. (Cf. WAX *v.*[1]) OE. **7.** To increase gradually in magnitude, quantity, or degree ME. **8.** To increase in some specified quality or property. Const. *in*, †*of.* ME. **9.** To advance in age (now *arch.*) 1477. **10.** To come or pass by degrees *into* some state or condition. Also const. *to* with *inf.* Now *rare.* 1450. **11.** To become or come to be by degrees, sometimes with inclusion of the literal sense ME.

2. [They] show you slips of all that grows From England to Van Diemen TENNYSON. **b.** There groweth Yron, Steele and Copper, and what not LYLY. **3.** For euer may my knees g. to the earth, ..Vnless [etc.]. SHAKS. †*To g. to*: to be an organic or integral part of. 2 *Hen. IV*, I. ii. 100. **4.** Sugar-canes g. without planting 1660. Here grows..this Fruit Divine MILT. *transf.* Horns only g. upon the Male 1677. **5.** Rumour of battle grew TENNYSON. [The States] g. out of human characters JOWETT. Phr. †*To g. to*: to arise or come into existence to the benefit or injury of (a person, etc.). Also *absol.* without *to. The law of growing-to*: reversion, escheat. **6.** Great Weeds do g. apace SHAKS. She plumes her feathers, and lets g. her wings MILT. **7.** New moons may g. or wane, may set or rise M. PRIOR. **8.** Growe in grace TINDALE. He grew to no place of more honour FULLER. Phr. *To g. on* or *upon* (a person, etc.): (*a*) To increase so as to be more troublesome to. (*b*) To acquire more and more influence over. Hence: To gain more and more of (a person's) liking or admiration. **9.** *To g. on*: to advance, make progress. My houre grows on a pace BEAUM. & FL. **10.** To g. into a Consumption 1616, into gentility LAMB. **11.** To g. old with a good Grace STEELE. The soldiers grew..out of all discipline DE FOE.

Comb. **Grow up. a.** To advance to or towards maturity. **b.** Of plants: To emerge from the soil, spring up; also, to g. to full size. **c.** Of a custom, state of things, etc.: To arise gradually.

II. Trans. senses. **1.** *causative.* To cause to grow 1774; to produce, *esp.* by cultivation 1847; to let grow on the body 1819. **2.** *pass.* Of land, etc.: To be covered with a growth of something. Also with *over.* 1470.

1. Wool, grown in Norfolk 1842. To g. potatoes 1847. To g. quills SOUTHEY, a beard 1860. **2.** It was all growen ouer with thornes *Prov.* 24:31.

Hence **Grow·able** *a.* capable of being grown or cultivated. **Grow·ingly** *adv.*

Growan (grōᵘ·ăn). *Cornish dial.* Also **grouan.** 1753. [f. Cornish *grow*, W. *gro*; see GRAVEL.] A soft decomposed granite, overlying the veins of tin in Cornwall. *Hard g.*: granite or moorstone.

Grower (grōᵘ·əɹ). 1562. [f. GROW *v.* + -ER[1].] **1.** Of a plant: One that grows (in a specified way). **b.** 'A thick limb of a thorn hedge' (*E. Dial. Dict.*) 1829. **2.** One who grows (produce) 1687.

Growing (groᵘ·iŋ), *vbl. sb.* ME. [f. GROW *v.* + -ING[1].] **1.** The action of GROW *v.*: **a.** in intr. senses; **b.** in trans. senses 1889. †**2.** Growth; the faculty, period, or process of growth. Rarely *pl.* –1561. †*concr.* A growth, a crop –1722. †**3.** Advance, progress. *Wint. T.* IV. i. 16. **4.** *attrib.* ME.

Comb.: **g.-cell**, a microscopic-slide on which minute objects are kept growing in water; **-pains**, the neuralgic pains common in young persons during the period of growth; **-point** (*Bot.*), the terminal portion of an organ with permanent apical growth, consisting entirely of primary meristem; **-slide** = *growing-cell*; **g. weather**, weather conducive to the growth of plants.

Growl (graul), *sb.* 1727. [f. GROWL *v.*] **1.** An act of growling; a low angry guttural sound uttered by an animal. Also *transf.* of cannon, earthquake, thunder, etc. 1833. **2.** An expression of anger or dissatisfaction uttered by human beings 1821.

Growl (graul), *v.* ME. [The mod. word (XVII) is prob. an imit. formation, not continuous with late ME. *grolle, groule, gurle* rumble (said of the belly and thunder).] **1.** *intr.* †**a.** Of the bowels: To rumble. ME. only. **b.** Of an animal: To utter a low guttural sound, expressive of rising anger 1719. **c.** *transf.* Of thunder: To rumble 1727. **2.** Of persons: **a.** *intr.* To murmur angrily 1707. **b.** To utter or express with a growl. Also with *out.* 1758.

2. a. He Growls, he Rages, he Swears 1707. **b.** To g. out criticisms STEPHEN. **Grow·lingly** *adv.*

Growler (grau·ləɹ). 1753. [f. GROWL *v.* + -ER[1].] **1.** One who or something which growls. **2.** *colloq.* A four-wheeled cab 1865. **3.** *U.S.* A species of black-bass (*Grystes salmonoides*) 1880. Also, the grunt or pig-fish (*Cent. Dict.*).

Growlery (grau·ləri). 1852. [f. GROWL *v.* + -ERY.] A place to growl in; applied joc. to a person's private sitting-room.

'This, you must know, is the G. When I am out of humour I come and growl here' DICKENS.

Grown (grōᵘn), pa. pple. of GROW *v.*

Grown up. 1633. [See GROW *v.*] *ppl. a.* Having reached the age of maturity; adult. *sb.* An adult 1813.

sb. No children for me. Give me grown-ups DICKENS.

Growth (grōᵘþ). 1557. [f. GROW *v.* + -TH[1].] **1.** The action, process, or manner of growing; vegetative development; increase 1587. **2.** Stage in the process of growing; size or stature attained by growing. *Obs.* exc. in *full growth.* 1557. **3.** Production by cultivation 1663. **4.** *concr.* Produce, product 1580. In *Path.* often *spec.* a morbid formation 1847.

1. When I haue pluck'd thy Rose, I cannot giue it vitall g. againe *Oth.* V. ii. 14. The g. of Anabaptism *Bk. Com. Prayer* Pref. Of foreign g. 1879. **2.** Men are but Children of a larger g. DRYDEN. **4.** Hogsheads of Claret, the best Growths in France 1715. *Comb.* **g.-line** (*Phys.*), a line indicating a stage of g. Hence **Grow·thful** *a.* full of g.; capable of growing.

Groyne (groin), *sb.* Also †**groin,** †**groyn.** 1582. [transf. use of (dial.) *groin* (XIV) snout; see GROIN *sb.*[1]] A framework of timber, or now sometimes a low broad wall of concrete or masonry run out into the sea, to arrest and retain the washed-up sand and shingle.

Groyne (groin), *v.* 1872. [f. prec.] *trans.* **a.** To build groynes or breakwaters against the sea. **b.** To furnish with groynes or breakwaters. Hence **Groy·ning** *vbl. sb.* the building of groynes; a system of groynes.

Grozing-iron (grōᵘ·ziŋ əi·əɹn). Also **grosing-.** 1688. [After Du. *gruisijzer*, f. *gruisstem* of *gruizen* trim glass, crush, f. *gruis* fragments.] †**1.** A tool in the form of nippers formerly used by glaziers in cutting glass –1847. **2.** An iron tool terminating in a bulb, used, when heated, for smoothing the solder joints of lead pipes 1825.

Grub (grʋb), *sb.* ME. [Presumably f. GRUB *v.*] **1.** The larva of an insect, esp. of a beetle; a caterpillar, maggot; also (now *dial.*) a worm. **2.** *contemptuous.* †**a.** A short, dwarfish fellow –1706. **b.** A dull industrious drudge, a literary hack; in recent use, an ill-dressed, unpleasant fellow 1653. **c.** *U.S.* A hard-reading student 1847. **3.** *Cricket.* A ball bowled along the ground 1894. **4.** *slang.* Food or provender 1659. **5.** *U.S.* A root left in the ground after clearing 1875.

2. b. Mr. Nahum Tate:—this poor g. of literature DE QUINCEY. **4.** How you'll relish your g. MARRYAT. *Comb.* **g.-stake** *U.S.*, 'the outfit, provisions, etc. furnished to a prospector on condition of participating in the profits of any find he may make, a lay-out (*Cent. Dict.*); **-worm** = sense 1, also *contemptuous.*

Grub (grʋb), *v.* [perh. to be referred to an OE. **grybban*:–**grubbjan*; cf. OHG. *grubilōn* dig, search closely, MDu. *grobben* scrape together, Du. *grobbelen* root out; f. Gmc. **ʒrub-*, rel. to **ʒrab-* GRAVE *sb.*[1], *v.*[1]] **1.** *trans.* To dig superficially; to clear (ground) of roots and stumps. Said *occas.* of animals. **2.** To dig up by the roots; to root up, uproot; *esp.* with *up.* Also *transf.* and *fig.* 1555. **3.** With *up, out*: To extract by digging. Also *transf.* and *fig.* ME. **4.** *intr.* To dig. In recent use, connoting the idea of mean and laborious occupation. ME. Also *transf.* of animals 1647. **5.** *transf.* and *fig.* To rummage 1800. **6.** To lead a grovelling existence; to toil, 'fag' 1735. **7.** [?f. the sb.] *slang.* **a.** To take grub; to feed 1725. **b.** *trans.* To provide with food 1812.

1. To manure grounds that are newly grubb'd 1653. Like the swine That grubb'd the turf 1827. **2.** *fig.* To g. up morality 1807. **4.** I met plenty of people, grubbing in little miserable fields STEVENSON. **5.** Grubbing among Roman remains and relics A. LANG.

Comb.: **g.-axe** (corruptly †*grubbage*), **-hoe, -hook,** implements used in grubbing up roots, stumps, etc.; **-fell** *v. trans.*, to bring down (a tree) by cutting at the root; **-saw,** a hand-saw used for sawing marble.

Grub- (in *Grub-Pegasus*), = GRUB-STREET (sense 2). SWIFT.

Grubber (grɒ·bəɹ). ME. [f. GRUB *v.* + -ER[1].] **1.** One who grubs (*lit.* and *fig.*). **2.** An implement for grubbing up roots, stumps, etc. (*local*) 1598. **3.** An eater, a feeder 1861.

Grubble (grɒ·b'l), *v.* 1690. [var. of GRABBLE *v.*, infl. by GRUB *v.*] †**1.** *intr.* and *trans.* To grope –1719. **2.** *intr.* To root (*rare*) 1867.

Grubby (grɒ·bi), *a.* 1611. [f. GRUB *sb.* + -Y[1].] **1.** Infested with grubs; also, grub-like 1725. **2.** Stunted, dwarfish. Now *dial.* 1611. **3.** Dirty, grimy; also, underbred 1845.

3. A g. lot Of sooty sweeps HOOD. Hence **Gru·bbiness.**

Grub-street (grɒ·bstrīt). 1630. **1.** *orig.* The name of a street near Moorfields in London (now Milton Street), 'much inhabited by writers of small histories, dictionaries, and temporary poems' (J.); hence, the tribe of literary hacks. **2.** *attrib.* or as *adj.* Pertaining to, emanating from, or characteristic of Grub-street; of the nature of literary hack-work 1648.

1. The very Spirit of Grubstreet Reigns in you SHADWELL. **2.** Grubstreet and Polemical Divinity MARVELL. Hence †**Grubean** *a.* (*joc.*) of or belonging to Grub-street. SWIFT.

Grucche, obs. f. GRUTCH.

Grudge (grɒdʒ), *sb.* 1477. [f. GRUDGE *v.*, or var. of GRUTCH *sb.*] †**1.** Murmur, grumbling; discontent; reluctance –1611. †**2.** Murmuring of the conscience; scruple, doubt, misgiving –1598. **3.** Ill will or resentment due to some special cause. (*Obs.* exc. as in b.) 1477. **b.** An instance of this: const. *against* (a person) 1531. †**4.** = GRUDGING *vbl. sb.* 2. –1678. †**5.** Injury (*rare*) –1641.

3. Queen Elizabeth bare..secret g. against her 1635. **b.** Public affairs were mingled with private grudges SIDNEY. Phr. *To have a g. against, to bear, owe* (a person) *a g.*, etc. **5.** Struggling against the grudges of more dreadfull Calamities MILTON. Hence **Gru·dgeful** *a.* resentful; **-ly** *adv.*

Grudge (grɒdʒ), *v.* 1450. [alt. of GRUTCH *v.*] †**1.** *intr.* To murmur; to grumble, complain; to be discontented –1632. **2.** *trans.* To be unwilling to give, grant, or allow; to begrudge 1500. †**3.** *trans.* To envy (a person); *intr.* to be envious (*rare*) –1661. †**4.** *trans.* To trouble or vex mentally. Also *impers.* –1558. †**5.** *pass.* and *intr.* To be seized *with* a disease; to have the first touch or access of a fever –1549. †**6.** To cram [? for *gregge*]. 1642.

1. To g. or complain of injustice HOOKER. Phr. †*To g. a thought*: to think an envious thought. 1 *Hen. VI*, III. i. 176. **2.** The English are very good Sea-men..never grudging their labour 1687. Long the Gods..Have grudg'd thee, Cæsar, to the World below DRYDEN. Hence **Gru·dger,** one who grudges. **Gru·dging-ly** *adv.*, **-ness.**

Grudgeons, obs. f. GURGEONS.

Grudging (grɒ·dʒiŋ), *vbl. sb.* ME. [f. GRUDGE *v.* + -ING[1].] **1.** The action of GRUDGE *v.* †**2.** A slight symptom or trace of an illness; a touch –1796. †**3.** A secret longing or inclination –1694.

2. The g. of my ague yet remains DRYDEN.

Gruel (grū·ĕl), *sb.* ME. [– OFr. *gruel* (mod. *gruau*) :– Gallo-Romanic **grutellum* (med.L. *grutellum*), dim. f. Frankish **grūt*; see GROUT *sb.*[1], -EL[2].] **1.** Fine flour, meal, or the like. *Obs.* or *dial.* **2.** A light, liquid food made by boiling oatmeal or other farinaceous substance in water or milk ME. †**3.** Broth or pottage of oatmeal in which chopped meat has been boiled –1601.

Phr. *To have* or *get one's g.*: to receive one's punishment. Hence **Gru·el** *v. trans.* to exhaust or disable; to punish; also (*nonce-use*) to feed with g. **Gru·elly** *a.* of the nature of or resembling g.

Grueller (grū·ĕləɹ). 1691. [f. GRUEL *sb.* and *v.* + -ER[1].] †**1.** One who feeds on gruel; a name given to a set of Oxford students in the 17th c. –1708. **2.** *colloq.* A poser, settler. KINGSLEY.

Gruesome (grū·sɒ̆m), *a.* *dial.* Also †**grewsome.** 1570. [f. *grue* (XIII), now Sc. and north., feel horror – Scand. word repr. by OSw. *grua*, ODa. *grue* (= OHG. *ingrūēn* shudder, G. *grauen* be awed, Du. *gruwen* abhor), see -SOME[1].] **1.** Inspiring fear, awe, or horror; fearful, horrible; grisly. **2.** Full of or inspired by fear (*rare*) 1869.

1. As grave and grewsome an auld Dutchman as e'er I saw SCOTT. **Grue·some-ly,** *adv.*, **-ness.**

Gruf, obs. f. GROOF.

Gruff (grɒf). 1533. [First in Sc. and prob. orig. in commercial use – Flem. (Du.) *grof* 'crassus, spissus, densus, impolitus, rudis' (Kilian) = MLG. *grof* coarse, (OH)G. *grob* :– WGmc. **ʒaxruba*, f. **ʒa-* Y- + **xrub-* **xreub-* (OE. *hrēof* ROUGH).]

A. *adj.* **1.** Coarse, coarse-grained (now only *techn.*); of immaterial things, rude, gross, unpolished 1681. **2.** Rough of aspect, voice, or manner, surly, sour 1690.

1. The..purchase of sugar and other g. goods 1800. **2.** A g. religionist 1862. Hence **Gru·ffish** *a.* somewhat g. **Gru·ffly** *adv.* in a g. manner, with a g. voice. **Gru·ffness,** g. condition or quality.

B. *sb.* **1.** *Pharmacy.* The coarse residue, which will not pass through the sieve in pulverization 1853. **2.** A quarrel, tiff. ?*local U.S.* 1857.

Gruft (grɒft). *local.* 1803. [Of unkn. origin.] Particles of soil which are washed up by rain among the grass. Hence **Gru·fted** *ppl. a.* begrimed, dirty. TENNYSON.

Gru-gru; see GROO-GROO.

Grum (grɒm), *a.* 1640. [prob. due to blended reminiscence of words like *grim, glum, gruff, grumble.* Cf. Da. *grum* cruel.] = GLUM *a.* 1. †**b.** *dial.* Of the voice: Gruff, harsh, and deep in tone 1744.

The King replyed nothing but Look'd very g. 1640. Hence **Gru·mness,** g. quality.

Grumble (grɒ·mb'l), *sb.* 1623. [f. GRUMBLE *v.*] **1.** An act of grumbling; a subdued utterance of complaint. **2.** *The grumbles* (*joc.* as if a malady): ill humour, vented in grumbling 1861.

Grumble (grɒ·mb'l), *v.* 1586. [frequent. of †*grumme* (XV–XVI) + -LE 3. Cf. (M)Du. *grommen*, MLG. *grommelen*; f. imit. Gmc. **ʒrum-* (cf. GRIM, GRUM).] **1.** *intr.* To utter dull inarticulate sounds; to mutter, mumble; to growl faintly 1596. Of thunder, a drum, etc.: To rumble, esp. faintly 1621. **2.** To utter murmurs of discontent; hence *gen.* to complain 1586. **3.** *trans.* To express or utter with mumbling, muttering, or complaining 1824.

1. What art thou that dost g. there i' th' straw SHAKS. The Lion..with sullen pleasure, grumbles o'er his prey DRYDEN. **2.** He was always grumbling about his food TROLLOPE. **Gru·mbler,** one who grumbles; a name for the GURNARD. **Gru·mblingly** *adv.*

Grumbletonian (grɒmb'ltōᵘ·niăn). 1690. [f. GRUMBLE *v.* after *Muggletonian*, etc.] †**1.** A nickname for the members of the 'Country Party' in English politics after the Revolution, who were accused by the 'Court Party' of being actuated by dissatisfied personal ambition. Also *attrib.* –1855. **2.** A grumbler. GOLDSM.

1. No more of your g. morals, brother; there's preferment coming DRYDEN.

Grume (grūm). 1555. [– L. *grumus* little heap. Cf. Fr. †*grume* (mod. *grumeau*) clot.] †**1.** A lump. EDEN. **2.** *Med.* A clot of blood; blood in a viscous condition. Also, any viscous fluid. 1619.

Grummet, grommet (grɒ·met). 1626. [– Fr. †*grom(m)ette, gourmette* curb chain, f. *gourmer* to curb, bridle, of unkn. origin.] A ring or wreath of rope, *spec.* one consisting of a single strand laid three times round. **a.** One of those used to secure the upper edge of a sail to its stay. **b.** A ring of rope or an eyelet of metal used for a rowlock. 1802. **c.** A wad for keeping the shot steady in the bore when firing at a depression 1828.

Grumose (grumōᵘ·s), *a.* *rare.* 1753. [See next, and -OSE[1].] = GRUMOUS 3.

Grumous (grū·məs), *a.* 1665. [f. GRUME + -OUS, perh. through mod.L. **grumosus.*] **1.** Containing, consisting of, or resembling grume; clotted; thick, viscid. **2.** *transf.* Of diseases, etc.: Characterized or caused by grume 1779. **3.** *Bot.* Of roots, etc.: Consisting or formed of clustered grains 1688.

2. A small g. tumour PALEY. **Gru·mousness.**

Grump (grɒmp), *sb.* 1727. [In †*humps* and *grumps*, surly or ill-tempered remarks, based on inarticulate noises betokening displeasure.] †**1.** *Humps and grumps*: slights and snubs –1760. **2.** *pl.* The sulks. W. CORY. Hence **Gru·mpish, Gru·mpy** *adjs.* surly, ill-tempered.

Grundel (grɒndĕl). ME. [f. *grund* GROUND *sb.* + -EL[1]. Cf. MDu., Du. *grondel*, G. *grundel*; also GRINDLE.] A fish; = GROUNDLING 1.

Grundsil(l, obs. f. GROUNDSEL *sb.*[2]

Grundy (grɒ·ndi). 1798. The surname of an imaginary personage (*Mrs. Grundy*), in the play *Speed the plough*, proverbially referred to as a personification of the tyranny of social opinion in matters of conventional propriety.

'If shame should come to the poor child—I say, Tummas, what would Mrs. Grundy say then' T. MORTON.

Grunswel(l, obs. f. GROUNDSEL *sb.*[1]

Grunt (grɒnt), *sb.* 1553. [f. GRUNT *v.*] **1.** The characteristic low gruff sound made by a hog; a similar sound made by other animals 1615. **2.** A similar sound made by a man. In early use, a groan. 1553. **3.** A name for American fishes of the genus *Hæmulon* and allied species (as *Orthopristis chrysopterus*). So called from the noise they make when taken. 1713. **b.** An Eng. fish, ?the perch 1851.

Grunt (grɒnt), *v.* [OE. *grunnettan* = OHG. *grunnizōn* (G. *grunzen*), intensive formation on the imit. base **ʒrun-* (OE. *grunian* grunt), which has an analogue in L. *grunnire.*] **1.** *intr.* Of a hog: To utter its characteristic low gruff sound. Also of other animals and of persons: To utter a sound like this. †**b.** To groan –1602. **2.** To grumble, murmur ME.; *trans.* to utter or express with a grunt 1613. †**3.** *trans.* To grind (the teeth) –1483.

1. Sneak with the scoundrel fox, or g. with glutton swine BEATTIE. **b.** *Haml.* III. i. 77. Hence **Gru·ntingly** *adv.*

Grunter[1] (grɒ·ntəɹ). ME. [f. GRUNT *v.* + -ER[1].] **1.** An animal or person that grunts; *esp.* a pig. **2.** A name for fishes making a grunting noise (cf. GRUNT *sb.* 3) 1726.

1. Jerome has no name for him but the 'grunter', FARRAR.

Grunter[2] (grɒ·ntəɹ). 1858. [Of unkn. origin.] An iron rod bent like a hook, used by mechanics.

Gru·nting, *ppl. a.* 1567. [f. GRUNT *v.* + -ING[2].] That grunts.

Comb.: **g.-ox,** the yak, *Poëphagus grunniens* (*Cent. Dict.*); **-peck** *slang.* pork.

Gruntle (grɒ·nt'l), *v.* ME. [f. GRUNT *v.* + -LE 3. Cf. DISGRUNTLE.] **1.** *intr.* To utter a little or low grunt. *Rarely* of persons. *Obs.* exc. *dial.* **2.** To grumble, murmur, complain 1589.

Gruntling (grɒ·ntliŋ), *sb.* 1686. [f. GRUNT *v.* + -LING[1].] A young pig.

†**Grutch,** *sb.* ME. [f. GRUTCH *v.*] = GRUDGE *sb.* 1–3. –1687.

Grutch (grɒtʃ), *v.* Now *dial.* or *arch.* [ME. *gruce, gruche* – OFr. *groucier, grouchier* murmur, grumble, of unkn. origin. Cf. GROUCH, GRUDGE.] **1.** = GRUDGE *v.* 1, 2. †**2.** To make a jarring or grating sound –1509.

‖**Gruyère** (gruyēᵊ·ɹ; Fr. grüyẹr). 1826. [Name of a town in Switzerland, used *attrib.* in 'Gruyère cheese', also with 'cheese' omitted.] A cheese made of cow's milk, of firm consistence, containing numerous cavities.

†**Gry.** 1679. [– L. *gry* (in Plautus *Most.* I. iii. 67) – Gr. γρῦ in the phr. οὐδὲ γρῦ, and explained as meaning (1) the grunt of a pig, (2) the dirt under the nail; hence the veriest trifle.] The smallest unit in Locke's proposed decimal system of linear measurement, being the tenth of a line –1813.

Gry-: see GRI-.

†**Grylle.** *rare.* [– L. *gryllus* – Gr. γρύλλος.] A cricket. EDEN.

Gryllotalpa (gri:lotæ·lpă). 1791. [f. L. *gryllo-*, comb. f. *gryllus* cricket + *talpa* mole.] The mole-cricket.

Grype: see GRIPE.

†**Gryph(e.** ME. [A perversion of GRIPE *sb.*[3], after L. *gryphus*; see GRIFFIN[1].] **1.** A griffin –1579. **2.** A vulture. Also *fig.* –1586.

Gryphite (gri·fəit). 1796. [– mod.L. *gryphites*, f. L. *gryphus*; see GRIFFIN[1], -ITE[1] 2 b.] *Min.* A fossil oystershell of the genus *Gryphæa.* (Cf. CROW-STONE.)

Gryphon: see GRIFFIN.

Grysbok (grəi·sbǫk). Also †**greisbok.** 1786. [S. Afr. Du., f. Du. *grijs* grey + *bok* BUCK *sb.*[1]] A small grey S. African antelope (*Antilope melanotis*).

‖**Guacharo** (gwa·tʃăro). 1830. [Sp., of S. Amer. origin.] A nocturnal bird, *Steatornis caripensis*, of S. America and Trinidad, valued for its oil; the oil-bird. Also *attrib.*

Guacho, erron. sp. of GAUCHO.

‖**Guaco** (gwā·ko). 1822. [Sp.-Amer.] The name given to *Mikania guaco*, *Aristolochia anguicida*, and other plants used as an antidote to snake-bites. Also, the substance obtained from these. Hence **Gua·conize** *v. trans.* to treat with g.

Guaiac (gwai·ăk). 1558. [Anglicized f. next. Cf. Fr. *gaïac* (XVI).] = GUAIACUM 2, 3. Also *attrib.*, as *g.-resin*, etc.

‖**Guaiacum** (gwai·ăkŏm). 1533. [mod.L. – Sp. *guayaco, guayacan*, of native Haitian origin.] **1.** A genus of trees and shrubs (N.O. *Zygophallaceæ*), native to the W. Indies and tropical America; a tree of this genus, esp. *Guaiacum officinale* and *G. sanctum* 1553. **2.** The hard and heavy brownish-green wood of *G. officinale* and *G. sanctum*, used in medicine; lignum vitæ 1533. **3.** A resin obtained from the tree; also, the drug made from it. Also *gum g.* 1553. **4.** *attrib.* 1596.

Hence **Guai·acene,** *Chem.* a light colourless oil, obtained by the dry distillation of g. resin. **Guaia·cic** *a.*, in *Guaiacic acid* $C_6H_8O_3$, a substance obtained from g. resin and wood. **Guai·acin, -ine,** *Chem.* a non-nitrogenous vegetable principle discovered in the wood and bark of *G. officinale*, having a sharp acrid taste.

Guan (gwān). 1743. [prob. a native name.] One of a family or subfamily (*Pelopinæ*, Newton) of gallinaceous birds of S. America, allied to the curassows.

Guana (gwā·nă). Also *Austral.* †**go(h)anna.** 1607. [var. of IGUANA.] **1.** The IGUANA, a large arboreal lizard of the W. Indies and S. America. **2.** *Colonial.* Any large lizard, e.g. *Sphenodon punctatum* of New Zealand 1802.

Guana, var. of GUANO.

‖**Guanaco** (gwănā·ko). 1604. [Quechua *huanaco, huanacu.*] A S. Amer. mammal, *Auchenia huanaco*, a kind of wild llama producing a reddish-brown wool.

Guanamine (gwæ·năməin). Also **-in.** 1881. [f. GUAN(O + AMINE.] *Chem.* One of a series of bases formed by the action of heat on the guanidine salts of the fatty acids.

Guanidine (gwæ·nidin.) Also **-in.** 1864. [Modified from GUANIN, see -INE[5].] *Chem.* A strongly alkaline base CN_3H_5, formed by the oxidation of guanin. Hence **Gua·nidinic** *a.*

Guaniferous (gwăni·fĕrəs), *a.* 1844. [f. GUANO + -FEROUS.] Producing guano.

Guanin (gwā·nin). Also **-ine.** 1850. [f. GUANO + -IN[1], -INE[5].] *Chem.* A white amorphous substance obtained from guano, forming a constituent of the excrement of birds, and found in the liver, pancreas, etc. of animals.

Guano (gwā·no, giu,æ·no), *sb.* Also †**guana.** 1604. [–Sp. *guano*, S. Amer. Sp. *huano*, – Quechua *huanu* dung.] **1.** A natural manure found in great abundance on some seacoasts, esp. on the islands about Peru, consisting of the excrement of sea-fowl. Also *fig.* **2.** *transf.* Artificial manure, esp. that called *fish-manure* or *fish-g.* 1844. **3.** A general name for sea-birds which produce guano. ? *Obs.* 1697. **4.** *attrib.* 1844. Hence **Gua·nize, Gua·no** *vbs.*, to treat with g.

‖**Guara**[1] (gwā·ră). 1678. [mod.L. – Tupi *guará* 'bird'.] The Scarlet Ibis, *Eudocimus ruber.*

‖**Guara**[2] (gwā·ră). Also **aguara.** 1884. [Tupi *jagoára* 'dog, ounce' (Dias); cf. JAGUAR.] A large-maned wild dog of S. America, *Canis jubatus.*

‖**Guaracha** (gwara·tʃa). Also *erron.* **guaracia.** 1828. [Sp.] 'A lively Spanish dance in $\frac{3}{8}$ or $\frac{3}{4}$ time, usually accompanied on the guitar by the dancer himself' (Stainer and Barrett).

‖**Guarana** (gwărā·nă). 1838. [Tupi *guaraná.*] A Brazilian shrub, *Paullinia sorbilis*; a paste prepared from its seeds (*g. bread, paste*).

Guarani (gwarā·ni). [(Language of) a S. American Indian race inhabiting Paraguay and Uruguay, forming a group with TUPI.] The unit of currency in Paraguay since November 1943, superseding the peso.

Guaranin (gwărā·nin). Also †**-ina, -ine.** 1838. [f. GUARANA + -IN[1].] *Chem.* A crystalline principle (? = caffeine) contained in guarana.

Guarantee (gærăntī·), *sb.* 1679. [The earliest forms, *garanté, garante*, are perh. – Sp. *garante* = Fr. *garant* WARRANT; in its later use the word was identified with Fr. *garantie* GUARANTY.] **1.** A person or party that makes a guaranty or gives a security. **2.** = GUARANTY *sb.* 1. 1786. **3.** = GUARANTY *sb.* 3. 1832. **4.** A person to whom a guaranty is given: the correl. of *guarantor* 1853. **5.** *attrib.*: **guarantee fund,** a sum of money pledged as a contingent indemnity for possible loss; **g. society,** a joint-stock company, which, for a premium, guarantees to an employer the honesty of a person employed, and undertakes to make good any defalcations in his accounts.

1. That promise, of which our King was the Garante 1683. **2.** This I relate as I heard it, without g. STEVENSON. **3.** This announcement was received as a g. of their personal safety KANE. Hence **Guarantee·ship.**

Guarantee (gærăntī·), *v.* 1791. [f. prec. sb.] **1.** *trans.* To be a guarantee, warrant, or surety for; *spec.* to undertake with respect to (a contract, the performance of a legal act, etc.) that it shall be duly carried out; to make oneself responsible for the genuineness of (an article); *hence*, to assure the existence or persistence of. **b.** with *inf.* or *obj. cl.*: To engage to do something; to warrant that something will happen or has happened 1820. **2.** To secure the possession of (something) *to* a person, etc. 1838. **3.** To secure (a person) *against* or *from* (risk, etc.); to secure *in* (the possession of anything) 1804.

1. By the treaty of alliance she guaranteed the Polish constitution in a secret article LD. BROUGHAM. **b.** I'll g. that he'll never return 1884. **2.** Liberty to follow the Confession of Augsburg.. was guaranteed to the city S. AUSTIN. **3.** To g. them against all exactions WELLESLEY.

Guarantor (gærăntǫ·ɹ). 1853. [f. GUARANT(EE *v.* + -OR 2, after WARRANTOR.] One who makes or gives a guaranty or security. Hence **Guaranto·rship.**

Guaranty (gæ·rănti), *sb.* 1592. [– AFr. *guarantie*, (O)Fr. *garantie*, var. of *warantie* WARRANTY.] **1.** The action or an act of securing, warranting or guaranteeing; security, warranty; *spec.* a written undertaking made by a *guarantor* to be answerable for the payment of a debt or the performance of an obligation by another person who is in the first instance liable to such payment or obligation. †**2.** A person who gives a guaranty (sense 1) –1692. **3.** Something which guarantees the existence or persistence of a thing 1697.

1. Our g. of the pragmatic sanction 1792. **3.** The best G. of a Peace, is a good Force to maintain it 1697.

Guaranty (gæ·rănti), *v.* 1732. [f. the sb. Now repl. by GUARANTEE *v.*] = GUARANTEE *v.*

Guard (gāɹd), *sb.* [– (O)Fr. *garde*, f. *garder* :– Rom. **wardare* – WGmc. **warðo* WARD *sb.*] †**1.** Keeping, guardianship, custody, ward; used *spec.* in *Law.* –1711. **2.** Protection, defence. (*Obs.* or *arch.*) 1576. **3.** *Sword-exercise, Boxing*, etc. A posture of defence; hence, the weapons or arms in such a posture 1596. **4.** The condition or fact of guarding, protecting, or standing on the defensive; watch; *esp.* in *to keep g.* 1596. **5.** †**a.** Caution, precaution. **b.** (with *pl.*) A precaution (now *rare*) 1597. **6.** One who keeps, protects, or defends; *spec.* one of a guard (sense 8), a sentry, sentinel ME. **b.** The man who has general charge of a stage-coach or a railway train. (Orig. an armed man to protect a mail-coach against robbery; hence the name.) 1788. **7.** *pl.* The household troops of the English army, consisting of the FOOT-GUARDS, the HORSE-GUARDS, and the LIFE-GUARDS. Also applied to the Dragoon Guards. 1661. **8.** A body of persons, esp. soldiers (†also *occas.* ships), engaged to protect or control a person or position. Also *transf.* and *fig.* 1494. **9.** A protection, defence (*lit.* and *fig.*) 1606. **10.** An ornamental border or trimming on a garment. *Obs.* exc. *Hist.* or *arch.* Also *fig.* 1529. †**b.** *transf.* A stripe, band of colour –1613. †**11.** *Astr. pl.* The stars Beta and Gamma of the Lesser Bear; also *guards of the pole.* Also, the two 'pointers' of the Great Bear. –1819. **12.** A contrivance of metal, wood, etc. made to protect an object from injury, prevent accidents by falling, etc.; often in comb., as *fire-g.* etc.

a. *gen.* 1774. **b.** That part of the hilt of a sword that protects the hand 1596. **c.** Protections to a book 1892. **d.** A piece of metal to protect the trigger of a gun 1687. **e.** *pl.* The wards of a lock 1677. **f.** = *fire-guard* (see FIRE *sb.*) 1845. **g.** *Archery* = BRACER[2]. 1853. **h.** *Railway.* An iron placed in front of a locomotive engine to catch and remove obstacles; *U.S.* a cow-catcher 1838. **i.** A lateral extension of the deck of a steamboat beyond the lines of the hull so as to overhang the water 1850. **j.** *Conch.* In cephalopods, a calcareous structure enveloping the apex of the phragmacone; the rostrum. **k.** A light frame in which the nuts of bolts fit to prevent their unscrewing by the vibration of the engine (Knight) 1875. **l.** A welt inserted between the leaves of a scrap-book, etc. for the attachment of additional leaves 1708. **m.** *Electr.* A device for protecting electrical apparatus from leakage currents, or for rearranging the magnetic or electric field (cf. *g.-ring*).

†**13.** Short for *g.-room* or *g.-house.* PURCHAS.

1. He broke from those that had the g. of him SHAKS. **3.** Phr. *At open g.*: a position which leaves the swordsman open to attack. **4.** Haue you had quiet G. SHAKS. **6.** Thy cries will wake the guards, and they will seize thee B. TAYLOR. **b.** In the winter [c1820] the g. carried a blunderbuss for protection in a box near him 1893. **8.** Phr. *To mount, relieve* (†*the*) *g. G. of honour*: a body of soldiers, sailors, policemen, etc. appointed to receive a person of distinction and to attend at state ceremonials. *Yeoman of the G.*: see YEOMAN. **9.** His greatnesse was no gard To barre heauens shaft SHAKS.

Phrases. **On** or **upon one's g., on g.:** in a position of defence, on the defensive (*orig.* with reference to fencing and sentry duty). **Off one's g.:** in or into a defenceless condition; unsuspicious of danger. †**Out of (one's) g.:** = *off (one's) g. Twel. N.* I. v. 93.

Comb.: **g.-bolt,** a flat-headed screw-bolt, fully counter-sunk, for fastening the guards of mowing machines to the bars; **-brush,** on an electric railway, a metallic brush by means of which the current is conveyed to the motor; **-cell** (*Bot.*), one of the two cells that embrace the stomata of plants; **-chamber** = GUARD-ROOM; **-detail,** 'men from a company, regiment, etc. detailed from g. duty' (Webst.); **-duty,** the duty of watching, patrolling, etc.; **-finger,** 'one of the teeth projecting forward from the cutter-bar of a harvester and through which the knife plays' (Knight); **-book,** a blank book, furnished with guards (sense 12 l); **-iron,** (*a*) *Naut.* one of certain curved or arched bars of iron placed over the ornamental figures on a ship's head or quarter, to protect them from injury; (*b*) = 12 h; **-lock,** a *tide-lock*, forming a communication between a basin and tide-water; **-pin,** (*a*) *Horol.* a pin in the lever escapement that prevents the pallets leaving the escape wheel when the hands of the watch are turned back; (*b*) in a rifle, the pin by which the guard (sense 12 l) is attached; **-plate,** (*a*) in an electrometer = *guard-ring*; (*b*) 'the plate which closes the opening in front of a cupola furnace to whose iron casing it is attached by staples' (Knight); **-polyp** (*Zool.*), a zooid modified to serve a defensive function, as in the nematophore of a cœlenterate, a macho-polyp; **-ring,** (*a*) a keeper; (*b*) *Electr.* an annular horizontal surface surrounding the balanced disc in the absolute electrometer; **-stops,** the two points placed one on each side of a numeral, letter, figure, etc.; **-tube** (*Electr.*), a metal tube surrounding a dry pile used with a quadrant electrometer, or its like.

Guard (gāɹd), *v.* 1500. [f. GUARD *sb.* or – (O)Fr. *garder*, †*guarder*, f. *garde*; see prec.] **1.** *trans.* To keep in safety from injury or attack; to stand guard over; to take care of, protect, defend 1583. **b.** To accompany as a guard (*arch.*) 1597. **2.** To provide with safeguards, or (*Med.*) correctives 1726. **3.** To keep watch over; to keep in check, control (thoughts, etc.) 1742. †**4.** To parry (a blow) –1695. **5.** To ornament with guards; to trim; also *transf.* to stripe 1500. Also *fig.* **6.** *intr.* To be on one's guard; to stand as a sentinel; to take up or maintain a position of defence 1590. **7.** *Curling.* **a.** *trans.* To cover a stone by planting one in a line between it and oneself. Also *absol.* **b.** *intr.* Said of a stone so planted. Similarly in *Bowls.* 1685. **8.** *Chess. trans.* To support a piece or pawn with another 1761. **9.** *Bookbinding.* To supply (a guard book) with guards.

1. Draw not thy sword to gard iniquitie SHAKS. Guarding realms and kings from shame TENNYSON. **b.** My blessing. .like a beacon, guards thee home TENNYSON. **2.** To g. oneself from being supposed [etc.] 1891. **3.** He that guardeth his mouth keepeth his life R.V. *Prov.* 13:3. **5.** *fig.* To g. a Title, that was rich before; To gilde refined Golde *John* IV. ii.10. Also *Much Ado* I. i. 288. Hence **Gua·rdable** *a.*

‖**Guarda-costa** (gā·ɹdǎkǫ·stǎ, Sp. gwa·rda-). 1731. [Sp., f. *guarda-* stem of *guardar* GUARD *v.* + *costa* coast.] A Spanish vessel used for the protection of the coast; a custom-house cutter.

†**Gua·rdage.** *rare.* 1604. [f. GUARD *v.* + -AGE.] Keeping, guardianship –1621.

Guardant (gā·ɹdǎnt). 1572. [– Fr. *gardant*, pr. pple. of *garder*; see GUARD *v.*, -ANT.]

A. *adj.* **1.** Guarding, watching; on guard 1574. **2.** *Her.* Of a beast: Having the full face towards the spectator. (Cf. AFFRONTEE and GAZE *sb.*) Also *fig.* 1572.

B. *sb.* A keeper, guardian, protector 1591.

Guard-boat (gā·ɹdbōᵘt). 1696. **a.** A boat appointed to row the rounds among the ships of war in a harbour, to observe that a good look-out is kept. **b.** A boat employed to enforce custom-house or quarantine regulations.

Guarded (gā·ɹdėd), *ppl. a.* 1509. [f. GUARD *v.* or *sb.* + -ED.] **1.** Protected, watched; having a guard or sentinel 1570. **2.** Reserved, restrained; on one's guard; hence: Careful; prudent; cautious 1709. **3.** Ornamented, as with lace, etc.; tricked out; having guards. *Obs.* exc. *Hist.* and *spec.* in *Her.* of a garment: Trimmed or turned up with some material 1509. **4.** Of a book: Having guards (see GUARD *sb.* 12 l) 1888.

1. The g. mount, gold MILT., pass SCOTT. **2.** Learn to be more g. GAY. **Gua·rded-ly** *adv.*, **-ness. Gua·rder,** one who or that which guards (*lit.* and *fig.*)

Guard-fish, var. of GARFISH.

Guardful (gā·ɹdfŭl), *a.* Now *rare.* 1611. [f. GUARD *sb.* + -FUL.] Watchful, careful. Hence **Gua·rdfully** *adv.*

Guard-house (gā·ɹdhaus). 1592. **a.** A building to accommodate a (military) guard. **b.** A building in which prisoners are kept under guard.

Guardian (gā·ɹdiǎn). [Late ME. *gardein* – AFr. *gardein*, OFr. *garden*, earlier *gardenc* (mod. *gardien* (XIII), with assim. of suffix to *-ien*, -IAN, which was followed in Eng.) :– Frankish **warding*, f. **wardo* WARD *sb.* + *-ing* -ING³. Cf. WARDEN¹.] **1.** One who guards, protects, or preserves; 'one to whom the care or preservation of any thing is committed' (J.); occas. = *guardian angel* 1477. Also *occas.* used of things. **2.** *spec.* in *Law.* One who has or is entitled to the custody of the person or property (or both) of an infant, an idiot, or other person legally incapable of managing his own affairs; a tutor. (Correl. of *ward.*) 1513. †**3.** In official titles; now more commonly WARDEN. –1632. **4.** The superior of a Franciscan convent. (L. *custos.*) 1466. **5.** *attrib.*, as **g.-cell** = *guard-cell* 1880; also as *adj.* with sense 'protecting, tutelary', in **g.-angel.**

1. The attorney-general is *ex officio* the G. of liberty 'JUNIUS'. The Sacred Store-house of his Predecessors, And G. of their Bones SHAKS. *G. of the Poor* (often simply *G.*): one of a board elected to administer the poor laws in a parish or district. **2.** A wastefull Prince, that had neede of a G., or ouerseer A. V. *Transl. Pref.* Phr. *G. in chivalry*: the g. of a minor holding by knight service. *G. in socage*: the g. of a tenant in socage. *G. by nature*: the father. *G. by nurture*: the father, and, after his death, the mother, until the minor is 14. (These four are guardians *by the common law.*) *G. ad litem*: one appointed by the courts, to defend a prosecution or suit instituted by or against an infant.

Hence †**Gua·rdianage** (*rare*), †**Gua·rdiance, Gua·rdiancy** (*rare*), = GUARDIANSHIP. **Gua·rdianess,** a female g. **Gua·rdianless** *a.* having no g.

Guardianship (gā·ɹdiǎnʃip). 1553. [f. GUARDIAN + -SHIP.] The condition or fact of being a guardian; the office or position of a guardian; used *spec.* in *Law.*

Guardless (gā·ɹdlės), *a.* 1611. [f. GUARD *sb.* + -LESS.] **1.** Without a guard; without safeguards; unprotected. **2.** Off one's guard 1654. **3.** Of a sword: Having no guard 1882.

Guard-rail (gā·ɹd,rēˈl). 1860. **1.** A hand- or other rail to guard against accidents. **2.** *Railway.* A short rail placed on the inside of a main rail, so as to keep a wheel on the track; used in switches, crossings, etc. 1875.

Guard-room (gā·ɹd,rūm). 1762. = GUARD-HOUSE.

Guardship¹ (gā·ɹdʃip). *rare.* 1624. [f. GUARD *sb.* + -SHIP.] The condition or position of a guard or guardian.

Guard-ship, guardship² (gā·ɹdʃip). 1689. **a.** A vessel of war appointed to protect and regulate a harbour, and to receive seamen until they can join their ships. **b.** 'The ship (of the squadron) having guard-duty for the day' (Funk).

Guardsman (gā·ɹdzmǎn). 1817. [In 1 f. *guard's*; in 2 f. *Guards* pl.] **1.** A man who acts as a guard; a member of a guard 1854. **2.** A soldier, usu. an officer, of the household guards.

‖**Guariba** (gwarī·bǎ). 1753. [Native Brazilian.] The Howling Monkey.

†**Gua·rish,** *v.* 1474. [– OFr. *g(u)ariss-*, extended stem of *g(u)arir* (mod. *guérir*) :– Frankish **warjan* defend; see -ISH². Cf. GARRISON.] **1.** *trans.* To cure, heal –1596. **2.** *intr.* for *pass.* To recover. Const. *of.* CAXTON.

‖**Guava** (gwā·vǎ). 1555. [– Sp. *guayaba*, *-abo*, of S. Amer. origin.] **1.** A tree of the myrtaceous genus *Psidium* of tropical America, esp. *P. guayava*, which yields a fruit of an acid flavour, used to make jelly, etc. **2.** This fruit 1555. **3.** *attrib.* 1630.

1. White G., *Psidium pyriferum.* **Red G.,** *P. pomiferum.*

‖**Guazzo.** 1722. [It.] = GOUACHE.

Gubernaculum (giūbəɹnæ·kiŭlǒm). Pl. **-la.** 1661. [– L. *gubernaculum*, f. *gubernare* steer, rule, govern.] Applied to several animal and vegetable structures which are used for steering (e.g. in flight), or for regulating the (embryonic) development or course of an organ. Hence **Guberna·cular** *a.*

†**Gubernance.** 1455. [– OFr. **gubernance* (cf. next) or late L. *gubernantia*, f. as GOVERN, -ANCE. Cf. GOVERNANCE.] Governance, government –1550.

Gubernation (giūbəɹnēˈ·ʃən). Now *rare.* ME. [– OFr. *gubernation* or L. *gubernatio*, f. *gubernat-*, pa. ppl. stem of *gubernare* steer, govern; see -ION.] The act or fact of governing; government.

Gubernative (giū·bəɹnėtiv), *a.* Now *rare.* ME. [– OFr. *gubernatif*, *-ive* or late L. *gubernativus*, f. as prec.; see -IVE.] Of or pertaining to government; governing.

Gubernator (giū·bəɹneˈtǫɹ). *rare.* 1522. [– L. *gubernator*, f. as prec.; see -OR 2.] A ruler, governor. Hence **Gu:bernato·rial** *a.* (chiefly *U.S.*), of or pertaining to a governor or government, or to 'the governor', i.e. one's father. So ‖**Guberna·trix,** she that rules or governs.

Gudgeon (gɒ·dʒən), *sb.¹* [Late ME. *gogen*, *gojo(u)n* – OFr. *goujon* :– L. *gobio*, *-ōn-*, f. *gobius* GOBY.] **1.** A small European freshwater fish (*Gobio fluviatilis*), much used for bait. †**b.** Applied to fishes of the genus *Gobius* or family *Gobiidæ*; see GOBY –1774. **2.** *fig.* **a.** One that will swallow anything; a gullible person 1584. **b.** A bait 1579. **3.** *attrib.* 1599.

1. The Gudgion is an excellent fish to eat WALTON. **2. a.** In vain at glory g. Boswell snaps WOLCOT. **b.** The Gullings and Gudgeons that he had given him 1620. Hence **Gu·dgeon** *v.* to play the g.; also *trans.* to cheat.

Gudgeon (gɒ·dʒən), *sb.²* ME. [–OFr. *goujon* pin, dowel, tenon, dim. of *gouge* GOUGE *sb¹.*] **1.** A pivot, usually of metal, fixed on or let into the end of a beam, spindle, axle, etc., and on which a wheel turns, a bell swings, or the like; now used more widely of various kinds of journals, etc. **2.** The ring or eye in the heel of a gate which turns on the hook or pintle in the gate-post 1496. **3.** *Naut.* A metal socket in which the pintle of a rudder turns 1558. **4.** A metallic pin used for securing together two blocks of stone, etc. (Spon). **5.** *attrib.*, as *g.-pin*, etc. 1839.

†**Gue.** [– Fr. *gueux* beggar.] A rogue. J. WEBSTER.

Guebre (gī·bəɹ, gēˈ·bəɹ). 1687. [– Fr. *guèbre* – Pers. *gabr.* Cf. *giaour.*] A Zoroastrian, fire-worshipper, Parsee.

Guelder rose (ge·ldəɹ,rōᵘz). 1597. [– Du. *geldersche roos*, f. *Gelderland* or *Gelders*, province of Holland.] The plant *Viburnum opulus*, esp. the cultivated form; the snowball-tree. Also, the flower of this plant.

Guelph (gwelf). Also †**Guelf.** 1579. [– It. *Guelfo*, med.L. *Guelphus* – MHG. *Welf*, name of the founder and of many chiefs of the family now represented by the ducal house of Brunswick and the present dynasty of Great Britain and Ireland.] A member of one of the two great parties in mediæval Italian politics, characterized chiefly by supporting the popes against the emperors. (Cf. GHIBELLINE.)

Guelphic (gwe·lfik), *a.* Also †**Guelfic.** 1823. [f. GUELPH + -IC.] **1.** Of or pertaining to the family or the faction of the Guelphs.

‖**Guenon** (gənoṅ). 1838. [Fr.; of unkn. origin.] Name for a group of African monkeys, of which the Green Monkey, *Cercocebus sabæus*, is typical.

Guepard (ge·pāɹd). Also **gepard.** 1882. [– Fr. *guépard* (Buffon).] **a.** = CHEETAH. **b.** A kind of leopard, *Cynailurus guttata.*

Guerdon (gə̄·ɹdən), *sb.* Now *poet.* and *rhet.* ME. [– OFr. *guer(e)don* :– Rom. (med.L.) *widerdonum* – WGmc. **widarlōn* (= OHG. *widarlōn*, OE. *wiþerlēan*, f. *wiþer* again + *lēan* payment) with assim. of the second element to L. *donum* gift.] A reward, requital, or recompense.

Death in g. of her wrong Giues her fame *Much Ado* V. iii. 5. The g. of our wicked works H. COGAN. Hence **Gue·rdonless** *a.* without g.

Guerdon (gə̄·ɹdən), *v.* Now *poet.* and *rhet.* ME. [– OFr. *guer(e)doner*, f. the sb.; see prec.] *trans.* To reward, recompense. Also *absol.*

She may right wel g. hym for hys seruice LD. BERNERS. Confusion g. his base villainie HEYWOOD. Hence **Gue·rdonable** *a.* that may be guerdoned.

‖**Guereza** (ge·rīzǎ). 1859. [prob. African.] An Abyssinian monkey (*Colobus guereza*) with long hair and a bushy tail.

Guerilla: see GUERRILLA.

Guérite (gerit). 1706. [– Fr. *guérite*; see GARRET *sb.*] A turret or box of wood or stone for a sentry.

Guernsey (gə̄·ɹnzi). The name of one of the Channel Islands. Cf. JERSEY¹. **1.** Used *attrib.* in †**G. flower, lily,** a ? Japanese or S. African plant (*Nerine sarniensis*), with handsome lily-like flowers, naturalized in Guernsey 1578. **2.** (orig. *ellipt.*) A thick, knitted, closely-fitting vest or shirt, usu. made of blue wool, worn by seamen 1851. **b.** One of a breed of cattle of the Channel Islands 1834.

Guerrilla, guerilla (geri·lǎ, gĕri·lǎ). 1809. [– Sp. *guerrilla*, dim of *guerra* war, introduced into Fr. and Eng. during the Peninsular War (1808–14).] **1.** An irregular war carried on by small bodies of men acting independently 1819. **2.** One engaged in such warfare 1809. **3.** *attrib.* (or *adj.*), esp. in *g. war* (= sense 1) 1811. Also *fig.*

1. Arkansas is now the theatre of a large g. 1862. So ‖**Guerrillero, guerillero** (= sense 2).

Guess (ges), *sb.* ME. [f. GUESS *v.*; cf. MDu. *gisse* (Du *gis*).] **1.** The action or an act of guessing; a conjecture, rough estimate; a supposition based on uncertain grounds. **2.** *attrib.* 1863.

1. *By g.*: at haphazard, by rough estimation; by conjecture. By my g. we should come upon Crackskull common GOLDSM.

Guess (ges), *v.* [ME. *gesse*, perh. orig. naut. and – vars. with *-e-* of MLG., MDu. (Du., Fris.) *gissen*, or OSw. *gissa*, ODa. *gitse*; ult. f. base of GET (cf. ON. *geta* guess). The sp. with *gu-* and *gh-* dates from XVI; cf. GUEST.] **1.** *trans.* To form an approximate judgement of without actual measurement or calculation; to estimate. Also *absol.* †**2.** *intr.* To take aim (const. *to*) –1530. †**3.** *trans.* To esteem, account, reckon. ME. only. †**4.** To think, judge, suppose. ME. only. **5.** To form an opinion or hypothesis respecting (some unknown state of facts), either at random or from uncertain indications; to conjecture. Const. *by, from.* Also *absol.* and *ellipt.* ME. **6.** *I guess*: sometimes used playfully in reference to a fact or secure inference. Hence *colloq.* in U.S. = 'I am pretty sure'. 1692. **7.** *intr.* To form conjectures ME. **b.** *To keep* (a person) *guessing*: to keep in a state of uncertainty (*colloq.*, orig. *U.S.*) 1905. **8.** *trans.* 'To conjecture rightly' (J.); to divine 1548.

1. Mo than a thousand stories as I gesse Koude I now telle CHAUCER. To g. Time 1726. **5.** I g. it to have been a Piece of the Chapell HEARNE. I.. little guessed the end E. B. BROWNING. He went Alone, as you may g., to banishment SHELLEY. **6.** I g...you winna be the waur o' a glass of the right Rosa Solis SCOTT. Hence **Gue·ssable** *a.* **Gue·sser. Gue·ssingly** *adv.* by guess-work.

†**Gue·ssive,** *a.* [f. GUESS *sb.* + -IVE.] Conjectural. FELTHAM.

Guess-rope: see GUEST-ROPE.

Guess-warp (ge·s,wǭɹp). 1495. [The first element is of unknown origin (earliest form *gyes warpe* XV); the second is WARP *sb.* See GUEST-ROPE.] *Naut.* **1.** 'A rope carried to a distant object, in order to warp a vessel round it, or to make fast a boat' (Adm. Smyth). By some used of any rope attaching a boat astern of a vessel. **2.** = GUEST-ROPE 2. Also *attrib.* 1833.

Gue·ss-work. 1725. [f. GUESS *sb.*] Procedure consisting in or based on guessing.

Guest (gest), *sb.* [– ON. *gestr*; superseding OE. *ġiest, ġest* = OS., OHG. (Du., G.) *gast*, Goth. *gasts* :– Gmc. **ȝastiz* :– IE. **ghostis*, repr. also by L. *hostis* enemy, orig. stranger. The sp. *gu-* (XVI) marks the stopped g, like the earlier var. with *gh-*; cf. GUESS *v.*] **1.** One who is entertained at the house or table of another. Also *transf.* and *fig.* †**2.** A stranger –1578. **3.** A temporary inmate of an hotel, inn, or boarding-house ME. **4.** A man, 'fellow'. *Obs.* exc. *dial.* ME. **5.** A parasite animal or vegetable. Also *g.-fly.* 1864.

1. The sacred name of g. SCOTT. *fig.* I thought of times when Pain might be thy g., Lord of thy house and hospitality, And Grief WORDSW. **3.** If our landlord supplies us with beef and with fish Let each g. bring himself GOLDSM.

Comb.: **g.- (gall-) fly** (see INQUILINE 2); **-moth,** an inquiline moth; **-night,** the night on which guests are entertained at a club, college, etc.; **-room** = GUEST-CHAMBER.

Guest (gest), *v.* ME. [f. GUEST *sb.*] **1.** *trans.* To make a guest of; to entertain, lodge, put up. **2.** *intr.* To be or become a guest; to lodge (*rare*) 1615.

2. Tell me..who he was That guested here so late CHAPMAN.

Gue·st-cha:mber. 1526. A room used for the lodging or entertainment of a guest.

Guest house. [OE. *ġiest-hūs* = Du. *gasthuis*, G. *gasthaus*; see GUEST *sb.* and HOUSE.] †**1.** An inn –ME. **2.** A house or apartment for the reception of strangers or guests. Also *attrib.* OE. †**b.** A hospital –1641.

Guestless (ge·stlės), *a.* 1598. [f. GUEST *sb.* + -LESS.] Having no guests; also *occas.*, as tr. Gr. ἄξενος, inhospitable.

Gue·st-rope, gue·ss-rope. 1623. [The first element (*guest*) may be a var. of *guess-* in GUESS-WARP, of which *guest-rope* may be a later parallel formation.] **1.** A second rope, fastened to a boat in tow, to keep it steady. **2.** A stout rope slung outside a vessel fore and aft, formerly also fastened to the end of a boom, to give a hold for boats coming alongside.

Gu·estwise. 1548. [f. GUEST *sb.* + -WISE.] †**A.** *sb. In, on, a g.*: as a guest –1641. **B.** *adv.* After the manner of a guest or stranger *Mids. N.* III. ii. 171.

Guffaw (gɒfǭ·), *sb.* Orig. *Sc.* 1720. [Echoic.] A burst of coarse laughter. So **Guffaw·** *v. intr.* to laugh coarsely or harshly; *trans.* to say with a g.

Guffer (gɒ·fəɹ). *Sc.* 1684. [Of unkn. origin.] The Viviparous Blenny (*Zoarces viviparus*). Also *g.-eel.*

Guggle (gɒ·g'l), *sb.* 1680. [f. GUGGLE *v.*] **1. a.** *slang.* The windpipe. **2.** A guggling sound 1821.

Guggle (gɒ·g'l), *v.* 1611. [Echoic.] **1.** *intr.* = GURGLE *v.* 2, 2 b. **2.** *trans.* To bring *up* or pour *forth* with a guggling sound 1731.

‖**Guglio** (gū·lyo). *Pl.* **guglio(e)s.** 1644. [It. *guglia*, aphet. var. of *aguglia* needle.] An obelisk, needle.

‖**Guhr** (gūr). 1686. [G. dial., lit. 'ferment'.] *Min.* A loose earthy deposit from water found in the cavities of rocks.

Guiac, -an, -ol, -um, obs. ff. GUAIAC, etc.

Guib (gwib). Also †**guiba.** 1774. The harnessed Antelope of W. Africa, *Tragelaphus scriptus.*

Guidage (gəi·dėdʒ). 1440. [Sense 1 – AFr. *guidage* (AL. *guidagium* escort XIII, toll or custom XV); sense 2 f. GUIDE *v.* + -AGE.] †**1.** *Old Law.* A fee or tax paid for guidance or safe conduct –1800. **2.** Guidance. SOUTHEY.

Guidance (gəi·dăns). 1538. [f. GUIDE *v.* + -ANCE.] **1.** The action of guiding; directing agency; leadership, direction. **2.** Something which guides or leads 1712.

1. They steered by the g. of the stars GIBBON. Instructions..for the g. of his son MACAULAY.

Guide (gəid), *sb.* ME. [– (O)Fr. *guide*, alt. of †*guie* (whence GUY *sb.*[1]), f. *guider* GUIDE *v.*]

I. 1. One who leads or shows the way, esp. to a traveller in a strange country; *spec.* one who is hired to conduct a traveller or tourist, and to point out objects of interest. Also *transf.* and *fig.* **2.** *Mil.* One employed or forced to accompany an invading army, in order to show the way, etc. 1540. **b.** *pl.* Men formed into corps for this service 1802. **c.** One of the two officers of a company, called respectively the *right* and *left guide*, superintending and acting as pivots, etc. in evolutions. Also a vessel which guides the others in the manœuvres of a fleet. 1870. **d.** (In full *Girl Guide*) A member of an organization of girls corresp. to the Boy Scouts 1908. **3.** One who directs another in his ways or conduct; †a ruler. Also *transf.* of things ME. **4.** In the titles of books: **a.** A book of elementary instruction or information 1617. **b.** A guide-book 1759.

1. He which is the g. goeth before mounted on a cammel 1585. *transf.* The World was all before them..and Providence thir g. MILT. **3.** Now God be his gide for his grete pite 1450. *transf.* They were dangerous guides, the feelings TENNYSON.

II. 1. *gen.* Something that guides 1700. **2.** *Mech.* Something which serves to steady or direct the motion of a thing, and upon, through, or against which it moves, slides, or is conducted in the required direction; *esp.* a bar, rod, etc. which guides or 'bears' machinery having reciprocating motion; often in *pl.* 1763. **b.** Something which guides a tool or the work operated upon; *spec.* in *Surgery*, a director 1680. **3.** Something which marks a position or serves to guide the eye 1875. **4.** *Mus.* = DUX 2. 1753. **5.** *Mining.* A cross-course or -vein 1874.

III. The action of GUIDE *v.*; direction; conduct; guidance. Now *rare.* 1500.

Goats, which now he had in g. CHAPMAN.

Combs. **1.** General: as *g.-bar, -chain, -curve*, etc. **2.** Special: **g.-block,** a block or piece of metal which slides between or upon guides or guide-bars; **-board,** a board erected at a fork in a road, for the direction of travellers; **-pulley,** (*a*) *Oval-turning*, a pulley by means of which motion is communicated to the guide (sense II. 2 b); (*b*) a pulley over which a band or cord is passed, where its course is altered or where it needs support; **-screw,** a screw-thread in a screw-cutting lathe which regulates the thread of the screw being cut; **-tackle,** a rope secured to the top of a pole, etc., to steady it; **guideway,** a groove, track, or way along which a thing is moved or run in the required direction.

Guide (gəid), *v.* ME. [– (O)Fr. *guider*, alt. of †*guier* (whence GUY *v.*[1]) :– Rom. **widare* – Gmc. **wītan*, f. **wīt-*, gradation-var. of **wit-* (see WIT *v.*[1]), repr. by OE. *wīse* direction (see WISE *sb.*[1]), *wissian* direct, guide.] **1.** *trans.* To act as guide to; to go with or before for the purpose of leading the way. **b.** To direct the course of (a vehicle, tool, etc.) 1460. **2.** *fig.* and in immaterial senses: To lead or direct in a course of action, etc.; to determine the course of (events, etc.) ME. †**3.** To lead or command (an army, etc.) –1548; to lead and tend (a flock) –1615. **4.** To conduct the affairs of (a household, state, etc.) ME.; to manage (money, etc.); also *absol.*; now *Sc.* 1465. **5.** *trans.* To use (a person) in a specified manner. *Sc.* and *n. dial.* 1768.

1. Some heauenly power g. vs Out of this fearefull Country *Temp.* V. i. 105. The stars will g. us back 1868. **b.** Men Who g. the plough CRABBE. **2.** The spirit of trueth..wil g. you into all trueth *John* 16:13. Guided by the reports of the Board 1863. **3.** [He] guided them in the wildernesse like a flocke *Ps.* 78:52. Hence **Gui·der,** one who, or something which, guides.

Gui·de-book. 1823. A book for the guidance of visitors or strangers in a district, town, building, etc.

Guideless (gəi·dlės), *a.* 1557. [f. GUIDE *sb.* + -LESS.] **1.** Without a guide or †steersman. **2.** Without a director or ruler 1561.

Gui·de-post. 1774. A post with a direction-board affixed, set up for the guidance of travellers, *e.g.* at a fork of a road. Also *transf.* and *fig.*

Great men are the guide-posts and land-marks in the state BURKE.

†**Gui·deress.** ME. [f. GUIDER + -ESS[1].] A female who guides –1650.

Guidon (gəi·dən, -dǭn). 1548. [– Fr. *guidon* – It. *guidone*, f. *guida* GUIDE; see -OON.] **1.** A flag or pennant, broad at the end next the staff and forked or pointed at the other. It is the standard now used by dragoon regiments. **2.** An officer who carries such a standard 1591. †**3.** A troop –1610. **4.** *Mus.* A direct. 1811.

2. The Cornet or Guydon is the same that the Ensigne on foot is 1622.

Guidonian (gwidōᵘ·niăn), *a.* 1721. [f. *Guidon-*, stem of *Guido* + -IAN.] *Mus.* Of or pertaining to the Italian musician *Guido* d'Arezzo (11th c.), the reputed inventor of the system of hexachords.

‖**Guige** (gīʒ). [ME. *gyge* – OFr. *guige*, recently re-adopted.] *Hist.* An extra strap, forming an additional support for the shield.

Guild, gild (gild). [The present form is prob. – MLG., MDu. *gilde* (Du. *gild*; G. *gilde* is from LG.) :– **ȝelðjōn*, rel. to OE. *ġield, ġild* payment, offering, sacrifice, idol, (also) guild (continued as *ȝild, yeld*), OFris. *geld, ield* money, OS. *geld* payment, sacrifice, reward, OHG. *gelt* payment, tribute (Du., G. *geld* money), ON. *gjald* payment, Goth. *gild* tribute :– Gmc. **ȝelðam* and ON. *gildi* guild, payment :– Gmc. **ȝelðjam.*] **1.** A confraternity or association formed for the mutual aid and protection of its members, or for the furtherance of some common purpose. The term is *primarily* applied to associations of mediæval origin, but is also used in the names of various modern associations, more or less imitating these. **b.** *transf.* Any company or fellowship 1630. †**2.** The place of meeting of a guild; the home of a religious guild –1644.

1. The *g. of merchants, merchant g.* (or *g. merchant*, late OE. *céapmanna ȝild*) was an incorporated society of the merchants of a town or city, having exclusive rights of trading within the town. It often became the governing body of the town. (Cf. *Dean of Guild* s.v. DEAN[1].) The *trade guilds* were associations of persons exercising the same craft, formed to protect and promote their common interests. They are historically represented in London by the Livery Companies. St. George's G. RUSKIN. The Church and Stage G. 1900. **b.** Names..enrolled in the guilds of the learned COLERIDGE.

Comb.: **g.-rent,** rent payable to the Crown by a g.; **g. socialism,** a system by which an industry is to be controlled by a council of its members; **-wite,** a fine levied by a g.

Guild-brother. ME. A member of a guild.

Guilder (gi·ldəɹ). 1481. [alt. (perh. after

kroner) of Du. GULDEN, prop. adj. of gold, golden; see GILDEN *a.*, GOLDEN *a.*] **a.** A gold coin formerly current in the Netherlands and parts of Germany. **b.** A Du. silver coin, worth about 1*s.* 8*d.* English.

Guild-hall. (Stress level or variable.) OE. [See GUILD and HALL.] The hall in which a guild met. Often synon. with 'town-hall'. *spec.* (*the Guildhall*) the hall of the Corporation of the City of London, used for meetings, etc.

Guildship (gi·ldʃip). [OE. *ġieldsċipe*; see GUILD, -SHIP.] **1.** = GUILD 1. **2.** Membership of a guild 1844. So **Gui·ldsman,** a member of a guild.

Guile (gəil), *sb.* ME. [– OFr. *guile* – Scand. **wihl*- WILE *sb.*] **1.** Insidious cunning, deceit, treachery. **†2.** A deceit, stratagem, wile, trick –1767.

1. Behold an Israelite indeed, in whom is no g. *John* 1:47. Jael, who with inhospitable g. Smote Sisera sleeping MILT. **2.** I..count thy specious gifts no gifts but guiles MILT. Hence †**Guiled** *ppl. a.* full of g.; treacherous SHAKS.

Guile (gəil), *v. Obs.* or *arch.* ME. [– Fr. *guiler*, f. *guile*; see prec. Cf. WILE *v.*] *trans.* To beguile; to deceive.

Guileful (gəi·lfŭl), *a.* Now only *literary.* ME. [f. GUILE *sb.* + -FUL.] Full of guile; deceitful, treacherous.

Gylefull wyles of women CAXTON. Hence **Gui·leful-ly** *adv.*, **-ness.**

Guileless (gəi·l,lės), *a.* 1728. [f. GUILE *sb.* + -LESS.] Devoid of guile.

G. youth 1844. Hence **Gui·leless-ly** *adv.*, **-ness.**

†**Gui·ler.** [ME. *guilour* – OFr. *guileor*, etc., f. *guiler*; see GUILE *v.*, -OUR, -ER[2].] A beguiler; a deceiver –1590.

To beguile the Guyler of his pray SPENSER. So **Gui·lery** (now *dial.*), deception, deceit, trickery; also with *a* and *pl.* a trick, etc.

Guilfat, var. of GYLE-FAT.

Guillem (gi·lĕm). 1603. [– W. *Gwilym* William. Cf. next.] = GUILLEMOT.

Guillemot (gi·lĭmǫt). 1678. [– Fr. *guillemot*, deriv. of *Guillaume* William.] A name of species of sea-birds of the genus *Alca* or *Uria*; esp. *Uria* or *Alca troile*, the Common or Foolish Guillemot, and *Uria grylle*, the Black Guillemot.

Guillevat, var. (in Dicts.) of GYLE-FAT.

Guilloche (gilōᵘ·ʃ, Fr. giyoʃ), *sb.* 1842. [Formally repr. Fr. *guilloche* burin, graver used in making the ornament called *guillochis.*] *Arch.* 'An ornament in the form of two or more bands or strings twisting over each other, so as to repeat the same figure, in a continued series, by the spiral returning of the bands' (Gwilt). So **Guillo·che, Guillochee·** *vbs., trans.* to decorate with guilloches.

Guillotinade (gi:lŏtinē¹·d). 1835. [– Fr. *guillotinade* (Dupré, 1801); see next, -ADE.] An execution by means of the guillotine.

Guillotine (gilŏtī·n), *sb.* 1793. [–Fr. *guillotine* (1790), f. name of Joseph-Ignace *Guillotin*, French doctor who recommended its use.] **1.** An instrument for beheading, consisting of a heavy knife-blade sliding between grooved posts. Also, execution by means of this. **2.** The name of instruments of similar action; *esp.* **a.** *Surg.*, an instrument for excising the tonsil or uvula, etc. 1866. **b.** A machine for cutting the edges of books, paper, straw, etc. 1883. **3. a.** *U.S.* The dismissal of Government officials on the coming in of a new President 1883. **b.** The method of closure by compartments, applied to shorten or prevent discussion of a bill in Parliament 1893.

1. One makes new noses, one a g. BYRON.
Comb.: **g.-cravat,** a fashion of cravat current during the French Revolution; **-window** [Fr. *fenêtre à guillotine*], an ordinary sash window, the sashes of which slide in grooves.

Guillotine (gilŏtī·n), *v.* 1794. [– Fr. *guillotiner*; see prec.] **1.** *trans.* To behead by the guillotine. Also *transf.* and *fig.* **2.** To cut (the edges of a book) with a guillotine; to cut short discussion upon (a bill, a clause); etc. 1893.

Guilt (gilt), *sb.* [OE. *gylt*, of unkn. origin.] **†1.** A failure of duty, delinquency; offence, crime, sin –ME. **†2.** The fault of (some person) –1671. **†3.** Desert (*of* a penalty) –1625. **4.** The fact of having committed, or of being guilty of, some specified or implied offence; guiltiness ME. **5.** The state of having wilfully committed crime or heinous moral offence; criminality, great culpability 1510. **b.** An instance, kind, or degree of guilt (*rare*) 1500. **c.** Conduct involving guilt; heinous sin or crime 1729. **¶d.** Misused for 'sense of guilt'. TILLOTSON. **6.** In legal use: The state of being justly liable to penalty 1765.

3. Phr. *Without g.*: innocently. **4.** The g. of blood is at your door TENNYSON. **5.** G. resides in the intention BURKE. **b.** Close pent-vp guilts *Lear* III. ii. 57. **c.** One chain of g. from the cradle to the gallows 1780. **6.** A ship contracts g. by a breach of blockade KENT. *Comb.*: *g.-sick* adj.; †**guiltwite,** penalty for commission of crime.

†**Guilt,** *v.* [OE. *gyltan*, rel. to prec.] **1.** *intr.* To commit an offence or trespass, to sin –1530. **2.** [f. the sb.] *trans.* To render guilty 1553.

Guiltless (gi·ltlės), *a.* [Late OE. *gyltlēas*, f. *gylt* GUILT + *lēas* -LESS.] **1.** Free from guilt; innocent. **†b.** *transf.* Of things, places, etc.: Free from the stain of crime –1784. **2.** Having no acquaintance, dealings, or familiarity with, no experience or use of (something) 1667.

1. Some Cromwell, g. of his country's blood GRAY. **2.** The teeming earth, yet g. of the plough DRYDEN. Hence **Gui·ltless-ly** *adv.*, **-ness.**

Guilty (gi·lti), *a.* [OE. *gyltiġ*; see GUILT *sb.*, -Y[1].] **1.** That has been in fault; delinquent, criminal. Now: That has incurred guilt; deserving punishment and moral reprobation; culpable. Often *absol.* **b.** *transf.* of the instrument, the scene of crime, etc. 1588. **2.** That has committed, or is justly chargeable with, a particular offence or fault. Const. *of.* ME. **†3.** *Guilty of*: culpably responsible for; to blame for the loss or destruction of –1715. **†4.** Deserving *of*, liable *to* (a penalty). Also bound to the performance *of* (a vow) = L. *reus voti.* –1700. **5.** Of actions, etc.: Involving guilt 1591. **6.** Of the conscience, etc.: Laden with guilt. Of feelings, etc.: Prompted by sense of guilt. 1593. **†7.** Conscious, cognizant, privy –1691.

1. The guiltiest still are ever least ashamed COWPER. **b.** Vpon me the guiltie doores were shut SHAKS. **2.** You must plead to the Court, G. or not G. 1681. He finds his fellow g. of a skin Not coloured like his own COWPER. **3.** Severn swift, g. of Maiden's death MILT. **5.** His Trespas yet liues guiltie in thy blood SHAKS. **6.** Naked left To g. Shame MILT. *Comb. g.-like* adv. SHAKS. Hence **Gui·ltily** *adv.* **Gui·ltiness.**

Guinea (gi·ni). 1598. [Occurs first in Pg. as *Guiné*; of unkn. origin.]

I. 1. The European name of a portion of the West Coast of Africa, extending from Sierra Leone to Benin, used *attrib.* and *Comb.* in the following:

G. bird, a G.-hen or G.-fowl (also *fig.*); **G. corn** (also with small *g*), DURRA or Indian millet, *Sorghum vulgare*; **G. cubebs,** *Piper afzelii*; **G. deer,** the CHEVROTAIN; **G. goose,** the Chinese goose or swan-goose, *Anser* or *Cygnopsis cygnoides*; **G. grains,** grains of Paradise; **G. grass** (also with small *g*), *Panicum maximum*; **G. hog,** the river-pig of G., *Potamochœrus pictus*; **G. merchant,** one who trades with G.; hence, a slave-dealer; **G. (oil) palm,** *Elais guineensis*; **G. peach,** a strong climbing shrub of western tropical Africa, *Sarcocephalus esculentus* (N.O. *Rubiaceæ*), yielding a peach-like fruit; **G. plum,** the plum-like fruit of a large W. African tree, *Parinarium excelsum*; **G. pods,** the fruit of *Capsicum frutescens*; **G. ship,** a ship trading to G., a slave-ship; **G. sorrel,** *Hibiscus sabdariffa*; **G. trader** = *Guinea merchant*; **G. weed,** *Petiveria alliacea*; †**G. wheat,** Indian corn; †**G. wood** = RED-WOOD.

†2. Short for GUINEA-FOWL, GUINEA-HEN –1661.

II. The coin so called. **1.** An English gold coin, not coined since 1813, first struck in 1663 with the nominal value of 20*s.*, but from 1717 current as legal tender at the rate of 21*s.* **2.** A name for the sum of 21*s.* 1688.

When first coined, 'in the name and for the use of the Company of Royal Adventurers of England trading with Africa', these pieces were to bear for distinction the figure of a little elephant, and were made of gold from Guinea. They received the popular name of *guineas* almost at once.
1. *Double g.*: a coin of the value of two guineas. *Spade g.*: a g. of the pattern of 1787–1800, so called from the form of the escutcheon on the reverse. **2.** Such substitutes..shall be paid at the rate of seven guineas per day 1885. *Comb.* **g.-gold,** †(*a*) *collect.* guineas; (*b*) gold of which guineas were coined, gold of 22 carats.

†**Guinea-cock.** 1577. **1.** An early name for the Turkey-cock –1601. **2.** = GUINEA-FOWL. 1599.

Gui·nea-fowl. 1788. [Imported from Guinea in XVI.] A gallinaceous bird of the genus *Numida*, esp. *N. meleagris*, a common domestic fowl in Europe. It has slate-coloured plumage with white spots.

Gui·nea-hen. 1578. **†1.** The Turkey-hen or Turkey –1698. **2.** The Guinea-fowl, or the female of this 1599. **†b.** *slang.* A prostitute –1708.

2. b. *Oth.* I. iii. 317. *Comb.*: **guinea-hen flower,** the fritillary, *Fritillaria meleagris*; **guinea-hen weed,** a W. Indian herb, *Petiveria alliacea.*

Guinea-man (gi·nimæ̆n). 1695. **1.** = *Guinea ship. Obs.* exc. *Hist.* **†2.** A Guinea merchant (*rare*) 1756. **3.** A native of Guinea 1830.

Guinea pepper. 1597. **†a.** Cayenne pepper. **b.** The seeds of two species of *Amomum*, found on the west coast of Africa, within the tropics; they are aromatic, stimulant, and cordial.

Guinea-pig (gi·nipig). 1664. [Confusion with *Guiana* seems unlikely.] **1.** A rodent mammal (*Cavia cobaya*) of the genus *Cavia*, originating in S. America, but now widely distributed. **2.** *Naut.* A midshipman in the E. Indian service 1747. **3.** *joc.* or *contempt.* One who receives a fee of a guinea; e.g. a clergyman performing temporary duty, a director of a company 1821.

Guinea trade. 1673. **†1.** Trade with Guinea. **2.** *joc.* Taking of guinea fees 1808.

Guinea worm. 1699. A parasitic nematoid worm (*Filaria medinensis*) frequent in Guinea, whence its name; it is long and thread-like, of a white colour, inhabiting the human skin, where its presence causes painful suppuration. Also, the disease occasioned by this.

Guinness (gi·nės). 1842. (A bottle or glass of) stout made by the firm of Guinness of Dublin.

‖**Guipure** (gĭpür). 1843. [– Fr. *guipure*, f. *guiper* cover with silk, wool, etc. – Gmc. **wīpan* wind round.] **1.** A kind of lace 'where the flowers are either joined by.. large coarse stitches, or lace that has no ground at all' (Mrs. Palliser). **2.** A kind of gimp 1864.

Guirlande, obs. f. GARLAND.

†**Gui·sard,** *sb.*[1] 1607. [– Fr. *guisard*, f. (*duc de*) *Guise*; see -ARD.] A partisan of the Guise faction in France in the 16th c. –1683.

Guisard (gəi·säɹd), *sb.*[2] Chiefly *Sc.* 1626. [f. GUISE *v.* + -ARD.] A masquerader, a mummer.

Guise (gəiz), *sb.* ME. [– (O)Fr. *guise* :– Rom. **wīsa* – Frankish **wīsa* (= OS. *wīsa*) :– Gmc. *wīsō*; see WISE *sb.*[1]] **†1.** Manner, method, way; fashion, style. Rarely *pl.* –1782. **†2.** Usual manner; custom, habit, practice; the 'ways' (of a country) –1725. **†3.** Manner of carrying oneself; behaviour, conduct, course of life –1813. **4.** Attire, costume, garb. Now only *arch.*, as in *in the g. of...*, *in lowly*, etc. *g.* ME. **5.** External appearance, aspect, semblance. Also *fig.* and in immaterial sense. ME. **b.** In bad sense: Assumed appearance, pretence 1662. **†6.** *Sc.* A disguise, a mask. Also, a masquerade, show –1801.

1. He began in artful g. to sound the Marquis H. WALPOLE. **2.** It never was our g. To slight the poor POPE. **3.** By thir g. Just men they seemd MILT. **5.** A fox in the g. of a priest M. CONWAY. *fig.* He will put on the g. of benevolence 1773.

Guise (gəiz), *v.* ME. [f. GUISE *sb.*] **1.** *trans.* To attire, attire fantastically; dress, 'get up' (*arch.*). **2.** *intr.* To go about in disguise, or in masquerade dress. Chiefly *Sc.* and *north.* 1876. Hence **Gui·ser,** a masquerader, a mummer.

Guisian (gī·ziăn). 1562. [f. Fr. (*duc de*) *Guise* + -IAN.]

A. *adj.* Of or pertaining to the duke of Guise, or his family or faction 1579.

B. *sb.* = GUISARD[1].

B. To give the watch-word like a G. of Paris to a mutiny or massacre MILTON.

Guitar (gitā·ɹ), *sb.* 1621. [orig. – Sp. *guitarra*, later – Fr. *guitare* (superseding

OFr. *guiterne* GITTERN) – Sp. itself – Gr. κιθάρα, which was adopted in L. as *cithara*, whence Pr. *cedra*, It. *cetera*, and OHG. *cithara* (G. *zither*); see also CITHERN, CITOLE, ZITHER.] A musical instrument of the lute class, with six strings, and a handle or finger-board provided with frets for stopping the notes—played upon with the fingers. Hence **Guita·r** *v.* to serenade with a g. **Guita·rist,** one who plays the g.

Guit-guit (gwit gwit). 1893. [imit.] A name used for any species of the Neotropical genera *Cæreba*, *Dacnis*, and their allies.

‖**Gul** (gul). 1813. [Pers.] The Pers. word for flower, in poet. use 'rose'.

Where the light wings of Zephyr..Wax faint o'er the gardens of Gúl in her bloom BYRON.

‖**Gula** (giū·lă). ME. [L. *gula* throat (hence, appetite).] †**1. a.** The external throat. ME. only. **b.** The gullet, or its analogues 1661. **2.** *Entom.* 'The chitinous plate which supports the submentum in many Insecta' (*Syd. Soc. Lex.*) 1826. **3.** = CYMA 1. 1664.

Gular (giū·lăɹ), *a.* (*sb.*). 1828. [f. GULA (in sense 2 f. L. *gula*) + -AR¹.] **1.** Of, pertaining to, or situated upon the gula. **2.** Devoted to good eating (*nonce-use*) 1854. **3.** *sb.* A gular plate beneath the throat of a serpent or a fish 1884.

Gulaund. 1784. [Icel. *gulönd*, f. *gulr* yellow + *önd* (formerly *aund*) duck.] The Icelandic name of the Goosander. (Dicts.)

†**Gulch,** *sb.*¹ 1601. [f. GULCH *v.*] A glutton or drunkard –1611.

Gulch (gɒlʃ), *sb.*² *U.S.* 1850. [perh. f. GULCH *v.*] A narrow and deep ravine, with steep sides, marking the course of a torrent; esp. one containing gold.

Gulch, *v. Obs.* exc. *dial.* ME. [imit.; cf. Norw. *gulka*, Sw. dial. *gölka*.] **1.** *trans.* To swallow or devour greedily. †**2.** *To g. out*: to vomit. ME. only.

Guld = *Gold-bloom*, marigold.

‖**Gulden** (gu·ldĕn). 15.. [– Flem., G. *gulden*, subst. use of adj. of GOLD, golden, = OE. *gylden*, etc. Cf. GUILDER.] †**a.** A gold coin, *spec.* one of various obs. gold coins of Germany and the Netherlands. **b.** A silver coin, which survives with the value of about 1*s.* 8*d.* in Holland (see GUILDER) and Austria-Hungary.

†**Gule,** *sb.*¹ ME. [– L. *gula*; see GULA.] **1.** The gullet –1750; in *Arch.*, the neck of a column 1706. **2.** Gluttony –1535.

Gule (giūl), *sb.*² 1543. [– OFr. *gule, goule*, med.L. *gula Augusti*, of unkn. etym.] *The Gule of August*: Lammas Day, Aug. 1.

†**Gule,** *v. rare.* 1609. [f. *gule* GULES.] *trans.* To stain or dye gules –1632.

Gules (giūlz). ME. [Late ME. *goules, gols, gulles* – OFr. *goules, goles* (mod. *gueules*), pl. of *gole, gueule* throat, used like med.L. pl. *gulæ*, for pieces of fur used as a neck-ornament and dyed red.] Chiefly *Her.*

A. *sb.* Red, as one of the heraldic colours; in engraving represented by vertical lines. Hence *poet.* and *rhet.*, red generally.

The wintry moon..threw warm g. on Madeline's fair breast KEATS.

B. quasi-*adj.* and *adj.* Red in colour 1503.

Follow thy Drumme, With mans blood paint the ground Gules, Gules *Timon* IV. iii. 59.

Gulf (gɒlf), *sb.* [–(O)Fr. *golfe* (in sense 1) – It. *golfo* :– Rom. **colpus*, **colphus* – Gr. κόλπος, (late) κόλφος bosom, fold, gulf. For the sense cf. L. *sinus*, G. *busen* bosom, bay.] **1.** *Geog.* A portion of the sea partially enclosed by a sweep of the coast. (Not always clearly dist. from a *bay*.) **2.** A profound depth (in a river, the ocean); the deep (*poet.*) ME. Also *transf.* **3.** An absorbing eddy; a whirlpool. In later use chiefly *fig.* 1538. **b.** A voracious appetite 1566. **4.** A yawning chasm or abyss; a vast ravine or gorge 1533. Also *fig.* **b.** (After Luke 16:26.) An impassable gap 1557. **5.** *Univ. slang.* The position of candidates for honours who fail, but are allowed (at Oxford) to take a pass, or are allowed (at Cambridge) the ordinary degree 1827. †**6.** [f. GULF *v.*] = GULP *sb.* –1771. **7.** *Mining.* A large deposit of ore in a lode 1778.

1. The Goulf of Venyse MAUNDEV. **2.** Slippery cliffs arise Close to deep gulfs BRYANT. *transf.* Gulphs of air BLACKMORE. **3.** England his approaches make as fierce, As Waters to the sucking of a Gulfe SHAKS. **b.** Maw and Gulfe Of the rauin'd salt Sea sharke SHAKS. **4.** Phr. *A fiery g., g. of fire*: an abyss full of flame. *fig.* The g. of his debts 1894. **b.** Betwene you and vs there is a great gulfe [χάσμα] set N.T. (Geneva) *Luke* 16:26.

Comb.: **g.-dream,** a dream of drowning in, or falling into, a g.; **G. State,** any State on the G. of Mexico.

Gulf (gɒlf), *v.* 1538. [f. GULF *sb.*] †**1.** *intr.* To rush along like a gulf; to eddy, swirl –1658. **2.** *trans.* To swallow like, or as in, a gulf; to engulf (*lit.* and *fig.*) 1807. **3.** *Univ. slang.* To place the name of (an undergraduate) in the gulf (see GULF *sb.* 5) 1831. ¶**4.** Used for GULP *v.* 1650.

2. *fig.* A yawning valley, gulfed in blackness STEVENSON.

Gulf Stream, Gulf-stream. 1775. *Geog.* A great oceanic current of warm water that issues from the Gulf of Mexico and runs parallel to the American coast as far as Newfoundland, and thence in the direction of Europe. Occas. also applied to a similar current along the shore of Japan.

Gulf-weed. 1674. A species of sea-weed (*Sargassum bacciferum* of the sub-order *Fucaceæ*) found in the Gulf Stream, the Sargasso Sea, and elsewhere; it has a number of berry-like air-vessels.

Gulfy (gɒ·lfi), *a. poet.* 1594. [f. GULF *sb.* + -Y¹.] Full of eddies or whirlpools; *fig.* full of hollows or depths.

†**Gulist.** 1632. [f. L. *gula* GULA + -IST.] A glutton.

Gull (gɒl), *sb.*¹ ME. [prob. – W. *gwylan*, Cornish *guilan* = Breton *gwelan, goelann* (whence Fr. *goéland*), OIr. *foilenn* :– OCeltic **voilenno-*.] Any long-winged, web-footed bird of the family *Laridæ* and sub-family *Larinæ*, which contains several genera, *Larus* being the largest. In pop. use the name includes the Terns and Skuas.

The **Common Gull** is *Larus canus*. Other species are the **Greater Black-backed G.,** *Larus marinus*; the **Lesser Black-backed G.,** *Larus fuscus*; **Glaucous G.,** *Larus glaucus*, the BURGOMASTER; **Herring G.,** *Larus argentatus*; etc.

Comb.: **g.-billed tern,** *Sterna anglica*; **-teaser,** a bird that torments gulls, as a tern or jäger.

Gull (gɒl), *sb.*² Now *dial.* ME. [prob. GULL *a.* yellow used subst.] An unfledged bird, *esp.* a gosling.

Gull (gɒl), *sb.*³ 1594. [perh. f. GULL *a.*, but cf. the earlier GULL *v.*³] **1.** A credulous person; a dupe, simpleton, fool. †**2.** [f. the vb.] A trick, deception, fraud; a false report –1668. **3.** *slang.* A trickster, cheat 1700.

2. I should thinke this a g., but that the white-bearded fellow speakes it SHAKS.

Gull (gɒl), *sb.*⁴ ME. [perh. var. of GOLE(E.] †**1.** The gullet –1663; *transf.* an orifice (RAYNOLD). **2.** A breach or fissure made by a torrent; a chasm, gully; a channel made by a stream. *Obs.* exc. *dial.* 1553.

†**Gull,** *a.* ME. [– ON. *gulr* yellow.] Yellow, pale –1600.

†**Gull,** *v.*¹ 1530. [rel. to GULL *sb.*⁴] **1.** *trans.* To swallow, guzzle; also *transf.* and *fig.* Also *absol.* –1674. **2.** *trans.* To gorge –1604.

Gull (gɒl), *v.*² Now *dial.* and *techn.* 1577. [f. GULL *sb.*⁴] **1.** *transf.* Of water: To make channels or ruts in; to hollow out; to sweep *away*, wear *down*. Also *absol.* **2.** *intr.* To become worn away or hollowed out 1763.

Gull (gɒl), *v.*³ 1550. [Related to GULL *sb.*³] **1.** *trans.* To make a gull of; to dupe, take in, deceive. Also *absol.* †**2.** To cheat *out of*, deprive *of* by trickery –1783.

1. Nothing is so easy as to g. the public W. IRVING. **2.** To g. people of their money DE FOE. Hence **Gu·llable** *a.* gullible. †**Gu·llage,** deception, cajolery. †**Gu·ller,** one who dupes; a cheat. **Gu·llery** (now *arch.*), deception, trickery; a deception, trick.

Gullet (gɒ·lĕt), *sb.* [– OFr. **golet, goulet*, dim. of *gole, goule* (mod. *gueule*) :– L. *gula* throat; see -ET.] **1.** The passage by which food and drink pass from the mouth to the stomach; the œsophagus; also, *loosely*, the throat, neck. **2.** †A piece of armour for the neck. ME only. **b.** The lower end of a horse-collar 1875. **3.** A water channel; a strait, estuary, river mouth, etc. Now *local.* 1515. **4.** A defile; a gully or ravine; a narrow passage. ?*Obs.* or *dial.* 1600. †**5.** The flue of a chimney –1672. **6.** A concave cut made in the teeth of some saw-blades (Webst.) 1864.

Gulleting (gɒ·lĕtiŋ), *vbl. sb.* 1869. [f. GULLET *sb.* or *v.* + -ING¹.] **1.** Making gullets in saws 1875. **2.** *Shipbuilding.* The groove to receive the rudder.

Gullible (gɒ·lĭb'l), *a.* 1825. [f. GULL *v.*³ + -IBLE.] Capable of being gulled; easily duped. Also *absol.* So **Gullibi·lity** 1763. (Cf. CULLIBILITY, CULLIBLE.)

Gullish (gɒ·liʃ), *a.* 1598. [f. GULL *sb.*³ + -ISH¹.] Of the nature of a gull; foolish, simple.

Gully (gɒ·li), *sb.*¹ 1538. [– Fr. *goulet* neck of a bottle, outlet, narrow passage of water; see GULLET.] †**1.** The gullet –1552. **2.** A channel or ravine worn in the earth by the action of water, esp. in a mountain or hill side 1657. **b.** *Cricket.* The part of the field lying behind the slips 1920. **3.** A deep gutter, sink, or drain 1789.

Comb.: **g.-drain,** a drain, generally of earthenware piping, which is the means of communication between the sewer and the g.-hole; **-hole,** the opening from the street into a drain or sewer; **-squall** (*Naut.*), a violent gust of wind from a mountain ravine.

Gully (gɒ·li), *sb.*² *Sc.* and *north.* 1582. [Of unkn. origin.] A large knife. Also *attrib.*, as in *g.-knife*.

Gully (gɒ·li), *sb.*³ Also **gulley.** 1800. [Of unkn. origin.] An iron tram-plate or -rail.

Gully (gɒ·li), *v.* 1775. [f. GULLY *sb.*¹] *trans.* To make gullies or deep channels in; to form (channels) by the action of water. Also with *out*.

‖**Gulo** (giū·lo). 1607. [L.; = 'glutton', f. *gula*.] Formerly, the glutton, *Gulo luscus*; now, the name of its genus.

Gulosity (giulǫ·sĭti). Now *rare.* 1500. [– late L. *gulositas*, f. *gulosus* gluttonous, f. *gula* gullet, gluttony; see -ITY. Cf. OFr. *gulosité, -eté*.] Gluttony, greediness, voracity.

Gulp (gɒlp), *sb.* 1568. [f. GULP *v.*] **1.** The action or an act of gulping. Also *transf.* and *fig.* **b.** Capacity for gulping, swallow. CARLYLE. **c.** An effort to swallow 1873. **2.** A mouthful 1611.

Gulp (gɒlp), *v.* ME. [prob. – MDu. *gulpen* swallow, guzzle, of imit. origin.] **1.** *trans.* To swallow in large draughts or morsels hastily or with greediness. Chiefly with *down*. Also *absol.* Also *transf.* and *fig.* **2.** *intr.* To gasp or choke when or as when drinking large draughts 1530.

1. *fig.* The worthy knight fairly gulped down the oaths SCOTT. [She] had gulped down her sobs TROLLOPE. Hence **Gu·lpin,** one who will swallow anything; *Naut.* a marine.

Gulph, obs. f. GULF, GULP.

Gult, obs. f. GILT *ppl. a.*

Gult(e, Gulti(f, -y, obs. ff. GUILT, GUILTY.

†**Gu·ly,** *a.* 1592. [f. GULE-S + -Y¹.] *Her.* Of the colour gules –1641.

Those fatall g. Dragons MILT.

Gum (gɒm), *sb.*¹ [OE. *gōma*, corresp. to OHG. *guomo* gum, ON. *gómr* roof or floor of the mouth, finger-tip, rel. to OHG. *guomo* (G. *gaumen*).] †**1.** *sing.* or *pl.* The inside of the mouth or throat –ME. **2.** *pl. collect.* The firm fleshy integument of the jaws and bases of the teeth. Also *sing.* the portion of this attached to a single tooth. ME. **3.** *slang.* 'Jaw'. SMOLLETT.

Comb.: **g.-rubber,** something for a child to rub its gums on; **-stick** = prec.; **-tickler** *U.S.*, the first stage in dram-drinking; **-tooth,** a molar tooth.

Gum (gɒm), *sb.*² ME. [– OFr. *gomme* :– Rom. **gumma*, for L. *gummi*, var. of *cummi* – Gr. κόμμι – Egyptian *kemai*.] **1.** A viscid secretion of many trees and shrubs, which hardens in drying, but is usually soluble in water, unlike resin. Occas. including resins (cf. 2). Also with *a* and *pl.* **b.** *British gum* (see BRITISH). †**2.** Chiefly *pl.* Products of this kind employed as drugs or perfumes, or for burning as incense –1780. Often qualified (see quots.). **3.** The sticky secretion that collects in the corner of the eye 1599. **4.** Short for GUM-TREE. Also specialized as *black, blue, white, mountain, spotted*, etc. *g.* 1802. **b.** *U.S.* A log cut from a gum-tree, hollowed out for a bee-hive, a water-trough, or a well-curb 1817. **5.** *U.S. colloq.* Short for *elastic gum*, i.e. india-rubber; *occas.* an india-rubber garment.

Also *pl.* Galoshes. 1859. **6.** A disease in fruit-trees consisting in a morbid secretion of gum 1721. **7.** A hard transparent sweetmeat made of gelatine, etc. 1921.

1. As for to speke of gomme or erbe or tre CHAUCER. **2.** Altars I would reare..and thereon Offer sweet smelling Gumms MILT. *G. acacia, ammoniac, copal, elemi, guaiacum, lac, ladanum, olibanum, sandarac, tragacanth* (see the second member); **g.-arabic** (see ARABIC); **-dragon** = TRAGACANTH; **-juniper** = SANDARAC; **-senegal** or †**-senega,** a variety of gum-arabic, obtained from Senegal. **G. elastic** [after Fr. *gomme élastique*], india-rubber, caoutchouc (also *elastic-gum*; see ELASTIC); rarely applied to gutta-percha. **G. ivy,** †**g. of ivy:** the inspissated juice of the stem of the ivy. **3.** *Hen. V*, IV. ii. 48.

Comb.: **g.-animal,** the Senegal galago, which feeds much on gums; **-boots** *U.S.*, boots made of g. or india-rubber; **-flowers** *Sc.*, artificial flowers; **-shoe** *U.S.*, a galosh; also *attrib.* and *fig.* and as vb.; **-sucker** *Austral.*, a native Australian (esp. a Victorian) or Tasmanian; †**-taffeta,** taffeta stiffened with gum; **-water,** a solution of gum-arabic in water; **-wood,** the wood of the gum-tree; the tree itself; also *attrib.*

b. In names of plants yielding g.; **g.-cistus,** one of the shrubs of the genus *Cistus* which yield ladanum; **-plant,** a plant of the genus *Grindelia*, which is covered with a viscid secretion; **-succory,** (*a*) *Chondrilla juncea*; also, the g. from this; *Lactuca perennis*; **-thistle,** *Onopordium acanthium.*

Gum, *sb.*[3] See RED-GUM[1].

Gum (gɒm), *sb.*[4] *dial.* and *vulgar.* 1832. Deformation of *God*: in phr. *by* (or *my*) *g.*

Gum (gɒm), *v.*[1] ME. [f. GUM *sb.*[2]] †**1.** *trans.* To treat with aromatic gums –1485. **2.** To stiffen with gum; to coat or smear with or as with gum 1610. **3.** To fasten, or fix in position with gum or the like 1592. **4.** *intr.* To exude gum as a morbid secretion 1794. **5.** To become gummous 1874. **6.** *trans.* To cheat, delude, humbug. *U.S. slang.* 1848.

6. You can't g. me, I tell ye now LOWELL.

Gum (gɒm), *v.*[2] 1859. [f. GUM *sb.*[1]] *trans.* To deepen and enlarge the spaces between the teeth of (a worn saw). See GUMMER.

Gumbo (gɒ·mbo). *U.S.* Also **gombo.** 1859. [Of Negro origin; cf. Angola *kingombo* (in Marcgraf, 1648, *quingombo*), f. Bantu prefix *ki-* + *ngombo*.] **1. a.** The okra plant or its pods (*Hibiscus esculentus*). Also *attrib.* **b.** A soup thickened with the mucilaginous pods of this plant. Also *g. soup.* **2. a.** *Geol.* 'The stratified portion of the lower till of the Mississippi valley' (Funk). **b.** *Colloq. Western U.S.* The mud of the prairies. Also *g. mud.* 1881. **3.** A Creole patois in New Orleans, etc. Also *attrib.* 1882.

Gumboil (gɒ·mboil). 1753. [f. GUM *sb.*[1] + BOIL *sb.*[1]] An inflammatory swelling or small abscess on the gum.

Gum-gum (gɒ·m,gɒm). 1700. [Presumably Malay. Cf. *gong-gong* s.v. GONG[2].] A hollow iron bowl, which is struck with an iron or wooden stick; a series of these.

'What is a gum-gum?' eagerly enquired several young ladies DICKENS.

‖**Gumma** (gɒ·mă). *Pl.* **-as, -ata.** 1722. [mod.L. (neut.), f. L. *gummi* GUM *sb.*[2]] *Path.* A tumour usually of syphilitic origin, so called from the gummy nature of its contents. Hence **Gu·mmatous** *a.* of the nature of or resembling a g., as *gummatous tumour.*

Gummer (gɒ·məɹ). *U.S.* 1859. [f. GUM *v.*[2] + -ER[1].] A workman who enlarges the spaces between the teeth of a saw; a machine for this purpose.

Gummic (gɒ·mik), *a.* 1838. [f. L. *gummi* GUM *sb.*[2] + -IC.] In *G. acid*: an acid obtained from gum = *Arabic acid* (see ARABIC *a.*). So **Gummi·ferous** *a.* producing gum.

Gumminess (gɒ·minės). 1600. [f. GUMMY *a.*[1] and [2] + -Y[1].] The quality or condition of being gummy. Also quasi-*concr.*, a gummy concretion, etc.

Gummite (gɒ·məit). 1868. [f. L. *gummi* GUM *sb.*[2] + -ITE[1] 2 b.] *Min.* A hydrate of uranium of reddish-yellow colour, which looks like gum.

Gummosity (gɒmǫ·sĭti). ME. [– med.L. *gummositas*, f. *gummosus*; see GUMMOUS *a.*[1], -ITY. Cf. OFr. *gommosité* gum, gumminess.] The quality of being gummous 1651; †*concr.* a gummy substance, deposit, concretion, etc. –1683.

Gummous (gɒ·məs), *a.*[1] 1669. [– L. *gummosus*, f. *gummi* GUM *sb.*[2]; see -OUS. Cf. Fr. *gommeux*.] **1.** Of the nature of gum, gum-like. †**2.** = GUMMY[1] 2. 1693. var. **Gummo·se.**

Gummous (gɒ·məs), *a.*[2] 1588. [f. GUMMA + -OUS.] = GUMMATOUS.

Gummy (gɒ·mi), *a.*[1] ME. [f. GUM *sb.*[2] + -Y[1].] **1.** Of the nature of gum; viscid, sticky. **2.** Abounding in gum ME. **3.** Suffused with or exuding gum, or its like 1580; †*transf.* sticky, dirty –1720. **4.** Of the ankles, legs, etc.: Puffy, swollen 1737.

1. The gummie fatte of a fygge 1575. **3.** Foul teeth, and g. eyes SWIFT. G. chestnutbuds TENNYSON.

Gummy (gɒ·mi), *a.*[2] 1861. [f. GUMMA + -Y[1].] = GUMMATOUS.

Gump (gɒmp), *sb. dial.* and *U.S.* 1825. [Of unkn. origin.] A foolish person, a dolt.

Gumption (gɒ·mᵖʃən). *colloq.* 1719. [orig. Sc., of unkn. origin. Cf. *rum-*, *rumble-gumption.*] **1.** Common sense, mother wit, shrewdness. **2.** *Painting.* **a.** The art of preparing colours. SIR W. SCOTT. **b.** A vehicle for colour 1854.

Gum resin, gum-re·sin. 1712. [f. GUM *sb.*[2] + RESIN.] A vegetable secretion consisting of resin mixed with gum or mucilage; e.g. ammoniac, euphorbium, gamboge.

Gu·m-tree. 1676. [f. GUM *sb.*[2] + TREE.] Any tree that exudes gum: *spec.* **a.** Any tree of the genus *Eucalyptus*; **b.** Various species of the N. American genus *Nyssa*; **c.** *Sweet gum tree* of the U.S., *Liquidambar styraciflua.*

Phr. (*U.S.*) *To be up a gum-tree*: to be on one's last legs. (*Austral.*) *He has seen his last gum-tree* = it is all up with him.

Gun (gɒn), *sb.* [ME. *gunne, gonne* (1339 instrumenta de latone, vocitata Gonnes; whence AL. *gunna, gonna*), prob. repr. pet-form (**Gunna*; in Sw. dial. *Gunne*) of the Scand. female name *Gunnhildr* (f. *gunnr* + *hildr*, both meaning 'war'), which may have been orig. applied to ballistæ or the like; cf. 'una magna balista de cornu quæ vocatur Domina *Gunilda*' (1330–1 in Exchequer Accounts) and '*gonnylde* gnoste', i.e. Gunnild's spark (Political Song temp. Edward II).]

I. 1. A weapon consisting essentially of a metal tube from which heavy missiles are thrown by the force of gunpowder, or (in later use) by explosive force of any kind; a piece of ordnance, cannon, great gun. Also *fig.* †**2.** In 15th c. used vaguely for a large engine of war –1534. **3.** (Orig. *Handgun.*) Any portable firearm (in U.S., a pistol or revolver); a musket, fowling-piece, rifle, etc. ME. †**4.** A missile hurled from an engine of war. CHAUCER. **5.** *transf.* One of a shooting party 1870; an artilleryman 1896.

1. Bowes of brake and brasene gonnes LANGL. The guns of the British nation may be divided into four classes—Park, or Field artillery, Siege guns,..garrison guns, and marine artillery 1858. *Morning* and *evening g.* (in the navy), 'warning-pieces' fired at morning and evening respectively; hence, the times at which these guns are fired. [I slept] till the morning g. 1899. **2.** The gones [L. *aries*] beare downe the walls 1534. **5.** Five guns went before breakfast 1870.

Phrases. *As a g.* = perfectly, absolutely, *esp.* in (*as*) *sure as a g.*: to a dead certainty. *To stand* or *stick to one's gun(s*: to maintain one's position. *Son of a g.*, depreciatory for 'man, fellow'. **Great gun,** a fire-arm of the larger kind which requires to be mounted for firing; hence, a person of distinction or importance. *To blow great guns*: to blow a violent gale.

II. Transf. uses. **1.** *Mining.* A hollow cylinder or plug used in cleaving rocks with gunpowder 1747. **2.** *slang* and *dial.* A flagon (of ale) 1645. **3.** *joc.* A tobacco pipe 1708. **4.** *slang.* A thief; also 'rascal', 'beggar' 1858. **5.** *attrib.*, esp. with a prefixed numeral, qualifying *ship, frigate*, etc. 1485.

Comb.: **g. apron,** a cover for the protection of the vent and tangent blocks of guns against rain and dirt; **g. barrel** (see BARREL *sb.*); **-brig,** a two-masted ship of war, now obsolete; **-brush,** a brush for cleaning the bore of a g.; **-carriage** (see CARRIAGE); **-fire,** the firing of a g. or guns; *Naut.* and *Mil.* the time at which the morning or evening g. is fired; **g. flint** (see FLINT *sb.* 2); **-harpoon,** a harpoon which is fired from a g.; **g. hoop,** one of the coiled or forged steel envelopes shrunk on the central tube of a modern cannon; **-iron,** (*a*) the iron used in making guns; (*b*) a gun-harpoon; **-money,** (*a*) = GUNNAGE; (*b*) money coined (by James II in Ireland) from the metal of old guns; **-pendulum,** 'a device employed to determine the initial velocity of projectiles by means of the recoil of the gun' (Hamersly); **-pit,** (*a*) *Fortif.* an excavation made to receive guns for protection from the enemy's fire; (*b*) 'a pit for receiving the mold used in casting a gun, or for receiving the tube or jacket in assembling a built-up gun' (*Cent. Dict.*); **-port,** a port-hole for a g.; **-runner** *colloq.*, one engaged in **g.-running,** i.e. illegally conveying firearms and ammunition into a country; **-searcher,** an iron instrument used to find whether the bore of a g. is honey-combed; **-slide,** in naval guns, 'the chassis on which the top-carriage carrying the gun slides in recoiling' (*Cent. Dict.*); **-sling,** long rope grommets used for hoisting in and mounting guns; **-stick,** a ramrod, rammer; **-tackle,** (*a*) *Naut.* in full *gun-tackle-purchase*, 'a tackle composed of a rope rove through two single blocks' (Smyth); also *attrib.*; (*b*) an arrangement of blocks and ropes for moving guns; **-work,** (*a*) any labour performed in connection with ordnance; (*b*) shooting with a g. or rifle.

Gun (gɒn), *v.* Infl. **gunned, gunning.** 1622. [f. prec.] †**1.** To provide with guns; to assail with guns –1698. **2.** *intr.* To shoot with a gun; hence, to make war. Chiefly *to go gunning* (= *a-gunning*). 1622.

‖**Guna** (gu·nă), *sb.* 1804. [Skr. *guṇa.*] In *Skr. Grammar*, the middle grade of an ablaut-series of vowels; the process of raising a vowel to the middle grade by prefixing *ă*. Hence sometimes used in Indo-germanic comparative grammar for the *ĕ* grade of the o:ĕ:ŏ series. Also *attrib.* Hence **Gu·na** *v. trans.* to GUNATE.

Gunarchy, obs. f. GYNARCHY.

Gunate (gu·neᶦt), *v.* 1864. [f. GUNA + -ATE[3].] *trans.* In *Skr. Grammar*, to subject to the change known as guna. Hence **Guna·tion.**

Gun-boat, gunboat (gɒ·nbōᵘt). 1793. A boat or small vessel of light draught carrying one or more large guns. Also *attrib.*

Gun-cotton (gɒ·nkǫ:t'n). 1846. A highly explosive compound prepared by steeping cotton in nitric and sulphuric acids, now almost superseded by dynamite. Chemically, it is one of a series of nitrates of cellulose, from other members of which are obtained celluloid and collodion. See also PYROXYLIN.

Gun-deck. 1677. *Naut.* A deck which carries guns; *esp.* in an old-fashioned ship of the line, the lowest of the decks on which guns are placed. Also *attrib.*

Gundelet, -olet, obs. ff. GONDOLA.

‖**Gunge, gunj** (gɒndʒ). Also †**gunja.** 1776. [– Hind. *ganj* store, store-house, market.] A market.

Gunja, var. of GANJA; obs. f. GUNGE.

Gun-lock (gɒ·nlǫk). 1731. That part of the mechanism of a gun which by the charge is exploded. (See LOCK *sb.*[2]) Also *attrib.*

Gunmaker (gɒ·nmēᶦkəɹ). ME. One who manufactures guns.

Gun-man, gunman (gɒ·nmăn). 1624. **1.** One who is armed, or who shoots, with a gun. Now (esp. from *U.S.* use 1903) a lawless man who uses fire-arms, an armed robber. **2.** One who has to do with guns or their making 1881.

Gu·n-metal. 1541. A bronze formerly much used for cannon; now, a name for alloys of copper and tin, or zinc.

Gunnage (gɒ·nėdʒ). 1703. [f. GUN *sb.* + -AGE.] The money distributed among the captors of a ship, assigned in proportion to the number of guns on the captured ship. ? *Obs.*

Gunnel (gɒ·nĕl). 1686. [Of unkn. origin.] A small, eel-shaped marine fish, *Centronotus* or *Murænoides gunnellus*; the butter-fish. Also *spotted g.*

Gunnel; see GUNWALE.

Gunner (gɒ·nəɹ). [ME. *gonner, gunner*, f. *gunne* GUN, after AFr. analogies; see -ER[2]. Cf. AL. *gunnarius* (1347).] **1.** One whose office it is to work a cannon. In the British army, now applied to all privates of artillery except the drivers. **b.** In the navy, a warrant officer who has special charge of the battery, small arms, ordnance stores, etc. 1495. **c.** *fig.* 1657. **2.** A gun-maker, gunsmith. *Obs.* exc. *dial.* 1463. **3.** One who goes shooting game 1753. **4.** With number prefixed: A vessel carrying (so many) guns 1829. **5.** *dial.* **a.** The Sea Bream 1859. **b.** The Great Northern Diver, *Colymbus glacialis* 1837. **6.** *attrib.* 1628.

1. The nimble g. with lynstock now the devilish cannon touches SHAKS. †*Master g.*: the chief g. in charge of ordnance. Phr. *Gunner's daughter*: joc. name for the gun to which sailors were 'married', i.e. lashed, to receive punishment. *Gunner's quadrant* (see QUADRANT 3.).

Gunnery (gʊ·nəri). 1497. [f. GUN + -ERY.] **1.** The science and art of constructing and managing guns 1605. **2.** The firing of guns; the use of guns for sporting purposes 1816. **3.** *concr.* Guns collectively 1497. **4.** *attrib.*, as **g.-lieutenant,** 'one who, having obtained a warrant from a g.-ship, is eligible to large ships to assist specially in supervising the g. duties' (Smyth); **-ship,** a ship for training men in g.

Gunnies (gʊ·nis). *Cornwall.* [Local, of unkn. origin.] Also (in Dicts.) **gunnis(s.** 1778. A crevice in a mine or lode; 'the vacant space left where the lode has been removed' (Raymond); hence (app.) taken as a measure of breadth or width. (By some writers used as *pl.*)

Gunning (gʊ·niŋ), *vbl. sb.* 1562. [f. GUN *sb.* and *v.* + -ING¹.] **1.** Gunnery 1570. **2.** Shooting with a gun; esp. the act or practice of hunting game with guns 1624. †**3.** Provision of guns. MARVELL. **4.** *attrib.* 1562.

Gunny (gʊ·ni). 1711. [– Hindi, Marathi *gōnī* :– Skr. *gōṇī* sack.] A coarse material used chiefly for sacking and made from the fibres of jute or from sunn-hemp; a sack made of this. Also *attrib.*

Gunpowder (gʊ·npaudəɹ). ME. [f. GUN *sb.* + POWDER *sb.*¹] **1.** An explosive mixture of saltpetre, sulphur, and charcoal, used chiefly in gunnery and blasting. Also *fig.* **2.** (In full, *g. tea.*) A fine kind of green tea, each leaf of which is rolled up into a pellet 1771. **3.** *attrib.* Explosive; also *fig.* 1550.

1. The best g...is composed of 70 parts (in weight) of nitre, 18 parts of sulphur, and 16 parts of charcoal 1797. *White g.*: **a.** a tri-nitro-cellulose, prepared from sawdust; **b.** a blasting mixture made of chlorate of potash, potassium ferro-cyanide, and sugar. **3.** Such Gunne-powder Oathes 1604.

Comb.: **g.-cake,** g. in a cake, i.e. before it is corned; **-engine,** a gas-engine in which the movement of the piston is produced by the evolution of gas resulting from the combustion of g. (Knight); **-hammer,** a pile-driving machine worked by the explosion of g.; **-press,** a press for compacting mill-cake into hard cake for granulation; **g. tea** (see 2). **b. Gunpowder plot:** the plot to blow up the Houses of Parliament on Nov. 5, 1605, while the King, Lords, and Commons were assembled. (So *g. treason, traitor*, etc.)

Hence **Gu·npowderous** *a.* pertaining to or characteristic of g.; of the bluish colour of g.; also *fig.*

Gun-room (gʊ·nrum). 1626. **1.** In large ships of war, a compartment orig. occupied by the gunner and his mates, but now by the junior officers; in smaller vessels, the lieutenants' mess-room. Also *attrib.* **2.** A room in which guns are kept. 1773.

2. The story of Ould Grouse in the gun-room GOLDSM.

Gun-shot (gʊ·nʃǫt). 1471. [f. GUN *sb.* + SHOT *sb.*¹] **1.** Shot fired from a gun or cannon; †also the shooting of guns. Now *rare.* Also *fig.* **2.** The range of a gun; the distance to which a shot can be effectively thrown from a gun 1532. †Also *transf.* and *fig.* –1687. ¶**3.** A pistol. BUTLER *Hud.* **4.** *attrib.*, as in *g. fracture* 1672.

2. They [mallards] were always out of g. JEFFERIES. *fig.* Not yet out of the gun-shot of the Devil BUNYAN.

Gun-shy (gʊ·nʃəi), *a.* 1884. Frightened at the report of a gun; said *esp.* of a sporting dog.

Gunsmith (gʊ·nsmiþ). 1588. **1.** One who makes and repairs small fire-arms. **2.** *slang.* A thief 1869. Hence **Gu·nsmithery,** the trade of a g.; also, the place where the work is carried on.

†**Gu·nster.** *slang.* 1709. [f. GUN *sb.* + -STER.] 'A Cracker, or bouncing Fellow' (*un Bavard*). Boyer. See STEELE *Tatler* No. 88 ¶2. –1727.

Gun-stock (gʊ·nstǫk). 1495. [f. GUN *sb.* + STOCK *sb.*¹ II. 1.] The wooden stock or support to which the barrel of a gun is attached; †a support on which to place a cannon on board ship.

†**Gu·nstone.** ME. [f. GUN *sb.* + STONE *sb.*] **1.** A stone used for the shot of a cannon or gun; a cannon-ball –1808. **2.** *Her.* = PELLET, OGRESS². –1847.

Gunter (gʊ·ntəɹ). 1679. [The name of a distinguished English mathematician, Edmund *Gunter* (1581–1626).] **1.** In *Gunter's chain*: the chain of 4 poles' length now in general use for land-surveying (see CHAIN *sb.*). *Gunter's line*: a logarithmic line on Gunter's scale used for multiplying and dividing mechanically; also called *Gunter's proportion. Gunter's quadrant*: an apparatus for finding the hour of the day, the azimuth, etc. **b.** Short for *Gunter's scale*: A flat rule, two feet long, marked on one side with scales of equal parts, of chords, sines, tangents, etc., and on the other with scales of the logarithms of those parts; much used in surveying and navigation 1706. **2.** *Naut.* Applied to a method of rigging in which the topmast slides up and down the lower mast on rings or hoops; a mast so rigged or a sail attached to such a mast (more fully *sliding-g.*) 1794.

Gunwale, gunnel (gʊ·nĕl). 1466. [f. GUN *sb.* + WALE *sb.*¹, the gunwale having formerly served to support the guns. The usual spelling is *gunwale*, but the pronunc. (gʊ·nwē¹l) is not favoured.] The upper edge of a ship's side; in large vessels, the uppermost planking, which covers the timber-heads and reaches from the quarter-deck to the forecastle on either side; in small craft, a piece of timber extending round the top side of the hull.

†**Gup,** *interj.* 1529. [Contr. f. *go up.*] **a.** A cry of anger or chiding addressed to a horse. **b.** An exclam. of derision, remonstrance, or surprise; often with *marry.* –1682.

Gurge (gɔ̄ɹdʒ), *sb. rare.* 1667. [– L. *gurges* abyss, whirlpool.] A whirlpool (*lit.* and *fig.*). MILT. *P.L.* XII. 41.

Gurge (gɔ̄ɹdʒ), *v.* 1523. [– L. *gurges* (prec.).] †**1.** *trans.* To turn into a whirlpool. LD. BERNERS. **2.** *intr.* To swirl, surge 1578.

Gurgeons (gɔ̄·ɹdʒənz), *sb. pl.* Now *dial.* 1483. [Cf. Fr. †*grugeons* (Cotgr.) lumps of crystalline sugar in brown sugar, conn. with *gruger* crunch.] Coarse meal; the coarse refuse from flour; pollards.

Gurgitation (gɔ̄ɹdʒitē¹·ʃən). 1542. [– mod.L. **gurgitatio*, f. *gurgitat-*, pa. ppl. stem of late L. *gurgitare* engulf, f. *gurges, gurgit-* gulf, abyss; see -ION.] †**1.** = INGURGITATION –1658. **2.** Surging or whirling up and down 1864.

Gurgle (gɔ̄·ɹg'l), *sb.* 1562. [f. the vb.] †**1.** = GARGLE *sb.* **2.** The action or an act of gurgling; the noise of a stream flowing over a stony bed, or the like 1757. **b.** A guttural sound produced by gargling, etc. 1862.

2. A g. of innumerable emptying bumpers CARLYLE.

Gurgle (gɔ̄·ɹg'l), *v.* 1562. [prob. imit., if not directly – similarly formed vbs., e.g. MLG., Du. *gorgelen*, G. *gurgeln*, med.L. *gurgulare*, f. L. *gurgulio* gullet.] †**1.** *intr.* = GARGLE *v.* –1611. **2.** Of water, etc.: To flow in a broken irregular current, with intermittent low noises 1713. **b.** *tranf.* To utter intermittent guttural sounds 1779. **3.** *trans.* To utter with gurgling sounds 1814.

2. Ayr gurgling kiss'd his pebbled shore BURNS. **3.** He gurgled-out his pursy chuckle of a cough-laugh CARLYLE. Hence **Gu·rglingly** *adv.* with a gurgle.

Gurglet, obs. f. GOGLET.

Gurgoyl(e, var. of GARGOYLE.

Gurjun (gɔ̄·ɹdʒən). Also **gurjon.** 1858. Native name for a large E. Indian tree, *Dipterocarpus alatus*, from which and other species a viscid balsamic liquid is obtained, called *g. balsam* or *g. oil*, used as a varnish and medicinally. Hence **Gurju·nic** *a.* in *gurjunic acid*, $C_{34}H_{14}O_{51} + 3H_2O$.

Gurle, obs. f. GIRL.

‖**Gurlet** (gɔ̄·ɹlĕt). 1875. [Fr. *gurlet, grelet* (mason's) gurlet.] 'A pickaxe with one sharp point and one cutting-edge' (Knight).

[**Gurmie,** spurious wd. in Dicts.: see GUNNIES.]

Gurnard (gɔ̄·ɹnăɹd), **gurnet** (gɔ̄·ɹnĕt). ME. [– OFr. *gornart*, for **gronart*, f. *gronir*, by-form of *grondir* :– L. *grundire, grunnire* GRUNT *v.*; see -ARD. Cf. AL. *gurnardus* XIII.] One of the marine fishes of the genus *Trigla* or family *Triglidæ*, characterized by a large spiny head with mailed cheeks and three free pectoral rays. Applied also to allied genera 1704.

†*Soused g.*: a term of opprobrium. 1 *Hen. IV*, IV. ii. 12. *Flying g.*, a flying fish of the family *Cephalacanthidæ* or *Dactylopteridæ*.

Gurry¹ (gʊ·ri). Now *dial.* 1523. [Of unkn. origin.] Diarrhœa.

‖**Gurry**² (gʊ·ri). *Anglo-Ind.* 1786. [Hind. *gaṛhī, gaṛh* a hill fort.] A small native Indian fort.

Gurry³ (gʊ·ri). Chiefly *U.S.* 1850. [Of unkn. origin.] *Whale-fishing.* The refuse from cutting-in and boiling out a whale. Also, fish-offal.

Gurt (gɔ̄ɹt). *dial.* 1633. [perh. – AFr. *gort*; see GORCE. Cf. Fr. dial. (Beauce) *gort* trench, conduit.] A trench or gutter, *esp.* in *Mining.*

Gurts, obs. dial. pl. of GRIT *sb.*²

Guru, gooroo (gu·ru, gurū·). 1613. [– Hind. *gurū* teacher, Hindi *guru* priest, subst. use of Skr. *gurús* weighty, grave, dignified.] A Hindu spiritual teacher or head of a sect. Hence **Guruship.**

Gush (gʊʃ), *sb.* 1682. [f. the vb.] **1.** The action or an act of gushing; a copious or sudden emission of fluid; a rush; also *concr.* a quantity of fluid so emitted. **2.** *transf.* and *fig.* A sudden and violent outbreak; a burst 1704. **3.** *colloq.* Objectionably effusive or sentimental display of feeling 1866.

1. One G. of Tears STEELE. A red g. spurted over the garments of the Indian 1851. **2.** A g. of wind 1704, of light DICKENS, of violets RUSKIN, of rhetoric STEPHEN. **3.** G. and twaddle 1869.

Gush (gʊʃ), *v.* [ME. *gosshe, gusche*; prob. of northern, imitative origin.] **1.** *intr.* 'To flow or rush out with violence' (J.); to issue suddenly or copiously, as water when released from confinement. Freq. with *down, in, forth, out, up.* Also *transf.* and *fig.* **2.** Of a person, parts of the body, etc.; To have a copious flow of blood, tears, etc. 1530. **3.** *trans.* 'To emit in a copious effusion' (J.) 1553. **4.** *intr.* (*colloq.*) To act or speak in an over-effusive, exaggerated, or sentimental fashion. Also *trans.* 1864.

1. He brought waters out of the stony rocke, so that they gusshed out like the ryuers COVERDALE *Ps.* 77[78]. Then gush'd the tears POPE. **2.** Myne eyes gusshe out with water COVERDALE *Ps.* 118 [119]. **3.** Davids eyes gusht out rivers of waters BP. HALL.

Gusher (gʊ·ʃəɹ). 1864. [f. GUSH *v.* + -ER¹.] One who or that which gushes; *spec.* in *U.S.*, a gas-well or oil-well from which the material flows profusely without pumping.

Gushing (gʊ·ʃiŋ), *ppl. a.* 1583. [f. GUSH *v.* + -ING².] That gushes. **1.** Flowing or issuing with violence or in copious streams. **2.** Emitting fluid copiously; also *transf.* 1717. **3.** *fig.* Effusive, overflowing, displaying itself impulsively 1807. **b.** Given to or characterized by gush (*colloq.*) 1864.

1. G. fountains W. IRVING. **2.** My g. eyes o'erflow POPE. **3.** A g. affluence of imagery MRS. CARLYLE. **b.** A g. speech 1878. Hence **Gu·shing-ly** *adv.*, **-ness.**

Gusset (gʊ·sĕt). ME. [– (O)Fr. *gousset* in similar senses, formally dim. of *gousse* pod, shell, clove (of garlic), (though this is much later), of unkn. origin.] **1.** In a suit of mail, a piece of chain-mail protecting a joint. **2.** A triangular piece of material let into a garment to strengthen or to enlarge some part 1570. **b.** *pl.* The flexible sides of a pair of bellows 1861. **c.** An elastic insertion in the side of a boot 1881. **3.** *transf.* A triangular piece of land 1650. **4.** *Her.* An abatement formed by a line drawn from the dexter or sinister chief to a central point and continued perpendicularly to the base of the escutcheon. (Cf. GORE *sb.*²) 1562. **5.** *techn.* A bracket or angular piece of iron fixed at the angles of a structure to give strength or firmness 18..

2. The gussets of his waistcoat 1878. **3.** Which gore, or gusset of ground, was called Apherema FULLER. *Comb.* **g. needle** (*Knitting*), one of the two side needles used in knitting the foot of a stocking. Hence **Gu·sseted** *a.* having a g. or gussets. **Gu·sseting** *vbl. sb.* insertion or making of gussets; *concr.* a g.

Gust (gʊst), *sb.*¹ 1588. [– ON. *gustr*, f. **ȝus-*, weak grade of the base of ON. *gjósa* gush.

Cf. GEYSER.] **1.** A sudden violent rush or blast of wind; †formerly often, a whirlwind. Also *transf.* **2.** *fig.*; also *gen.*, a burst, outbreak, outburst 1611.

1. The stormy gusts of winters day SHAKS. **2.** The first little sudden g. of passion against these gentlemen BURKE.

Gust (gɒst), *sb.*² Now *arch.* ME. [– L. *gustus* taste; cf. GOÛT, GUSTO.] = TASTE *sb.*¹, in various senses. **1.** The sense or faculty of taste. †**2.** Individual taste or liking –1732. †**3.** Æsthetic or artistic taste (*rare*) –1716. **4.** Keen relish, appreciation, or enjoyment 1627. **5.** Savour or flavour (of food, etc.) 1536. **b.** Pleasing taste or flavour; relish 1649. †**6.** A taste of something; also, a foretaste –1698.

1. I am for a Set-meal, where I may enjoy my full G. DRYDEN. **4.** He drinks his simple beverage with a g. COWPER. I had no g. to antiquities DE FOE. **5.** The whole vegetable tribe have lost their g. with me LAMB. **b.** The g. of novelty D'ISRAELI.

Gust (gɒst), *v.* Now only *Sc.* ME. [f. GUST *sb.*² or L. *gustare*, f. *gustus* GUST *sb.*²] *trans.* To taste, to relish. Also *absol.*

Gustable (gɒ·stăb'l). Now *rare.* 1480. [– late L. *gustabilis*, f. L. *gustare* taste; see prec., -ABLE.]

A. *adj.* **1.** That can be tasted; also, having a pleasant taste, appetizing. **2.** Of qualities: Perceptible by the sense of taste. Of perceptions: Gustatory. 1657.

1. Mylk, hony & herbes g. CAXTON. **2.** G. and olefactible perceptions BP. BERKELEY.

B. A thing that can be tasted; an article of food 1642.

†**Gustard.** *Sc.* 1536. [f. GOOSE + (BUS)-TARD.] A bustard –1655.

Gustation (gɒstēⁱ·ʃən). 1599. [– Fr. *gustation* or L. *gustatio*, f. *gustat-*, pa. ppl. stem of *gustare*, f. *gustus* taste; see -ION.] The action or faculty of tasting, taste.

Gustative (gɒ·stătiv), *a.* 1620. [– med.L. *gustativus*, f. as prec.; see -IVE.] Having the function of tasting; also, concerned with tasting.

Gustatory (gɒ·stătəri), *a.* 1684. [f. as prec. + -ORY².] Pertaining to or concerned with tasting or the sense of taste. *G. nerve* (Anat.): the lingual nerve upon which the sense of taste depends.

Gustful (gɒ·stfŭl), *a.*¹ *Obs.* exc. *arch.* 1645. [f. GUST *sb.*² + -FUL.] **1.** Full of gust or flavour; tasty. **2.** *fig.* Pleasant to the mind or feelings 1645. Hence **Gu·stful-ly** *adv.*, **-ness.**

Gustful (gɒ·stfŭl), *a.*² *rare.* 1825. [f. GUST *sb.*¹ + -FUL.] Gusty.

†**Gu·stless,** *a.* 1597. [f. GUST *sb.*² + -LESS.] Tasteless. insipid –1695.

‖**Gusto** (gɒ·sto). 1629. [It. *gusto* :– L. *gustus* GUST *sb.*²] **1.** Particular liking, relish, or fondness 1647. **2.** Zest 1629. **3.** Artistic style; *occas.* fashionable style in matters of taste. Often qualified as *great* (= It. *gran gusto*), *high, noble.* 1662. †**4.** Æsthetic perception –1711. †**5.** Flavour or savour (of food). DERHAM.

2. He read me, though with too much g., some little poems of his own PEPYS.

Gusty (gɒ·sti), *a.*¹ 1600. [f. GUST *sb.*¹ + -Y¹.] **1.** Characterized by gusts 1600; blown upon, tossed, or disturbed by gusts of wind 1725. **2.** *fig.* Given to or marked by fits or bursts 1690.

1. Great store of snowe, with some gustie weather HAKLUYT. The long carpets rose along the g. floor KEATS. Hence **Gu·stily** *adv.*

Gusty (gɒ·sti), *a.*² Chiefly *Sc.* 1721. [f. GUST *sb.*² + -Y¹.] Tasty, savoury, appetizing.

Gut (gɒt), *sb.* [OE. pl. *guttas*, prob. f. base *ʒut- of OE. *ġēotan*, Goth. *giutan* pour.] **1.** *collect. pl.* The contents of the abdominal cavity; the bowels, entrails. Formerly in dignified use with regard to man. In the Bible occas. *fig.* = 'inward parts'. **b.** *transf.* The inside, contents of anything 1663. **c.** Spirit; force of character (*slang*) 1893. **2.** = INTESTINE *sb.* ME. **b.** Hence, the whole of the alimentary canal or its lower portion 1460. **3.** *sing.* The belly or stomach, *esp.* as the seat of appetite or gluttony. Now *dial.* and *vulgar.* ME. **b.** *pl.* A corpulent or gluttonous person. Now *rare* or *dial.* 1550. **4.** The intestines of animals employed for various purposes (see quots.) 1602. **5. a.** A narrow passage of water 1538. **b.** On land: A narrow passage between two declivities; hence, any narrow passage 1615.

1. Falstaffe, you caried your Guts away..nimbly SHAKS. **b.** Phr. †*To have guts* (= 'something') *in one's brains.* **2.** BLIND GUT, the cæcum; *transf.* a cul-de-sac. **3. b.** Thou Clay-brayn'd Guts SHAKS. **4. a.** *pl.* = OFFAL 2a. 1602. **b.** For making violin strings; now *sing.* as the name of a material; Seven strings of very fine g. GOLDSM. **c.** *sing.* The silken fibre obtained from the intestine of the silkworm; Silkworm g. for angling URE. **5. a.** The G. of Gibraltar 1829. *The Gut* (Oxford and Cambridge): a bend of the river in the racing-course. **b.** The signal-box in this narrow g. of traffic 1896.

Comb.: **g.-bread,** sweetbread, pancreas; **-scraper** (*joc.*), a violin-player; **-weed,** *Sonchus arvensis.*

Gut (gɒt), *v.* ME. [f. GUT *sb.*] **1.** *trans.* To take out the guts of; to eviscerate. **2.** *transf.* To clear out the contents or inside of; *esp.* to remove or destroy the internal fittings of (a building). Const. *of.* 1688. Also *fig.* **3.** *intr.* To cram the guts (*vulgar*) 1616.

2. We took an Arabian junk..We gutted him of the pearl DE FOE. *fig.* T–m Br–wn, of facetious Memory..having gutted a proper Name of all its intermediate Vowels, used to..make as free with it as he pleased ADDISON. To g. a book 1888.

‖**Gutta**¹ (gɒ·tă). *Pl.* **guttæ** (gɒ·ti). ME. [L.; = 'a drop'. Cf. GOUT *sb.*¹] **1. a.** *Pharmacy* and *Path.* A drop. In prescriptions *gt.*, pl. *gtt.* 1562. **b.** *Arch.* = DROP *sb.* 8b. 1563. **c.** *Her.* = GOUTTE. 1868. †**2.** A kind of gum. In 18th c. = GAMBOGE. –1712.

1. b. **Guttæ band** (*Arch.*), the listel from which the guttæ seem to hang. *Comb.*: **gutta opaca,** cataract; **g. serena** = AMAUROSIS; also *fig.*

Gutta² (gɒ·tă). 1852. [– Malay *getah* gum; see next.] **1.** Short for GUTTA-PERCHA. **2.** *Chem.* A white amorphous substance $C_{10}H_{16}$, the principal constituent of gutta-percha. WATTS.

Gutta-percha (gɒ'tă,pə·ɹtʃă). 1845. [– Malay *getah percha*, i.e. *getah* gum, *percha* tree yielding the juice; assim. to L. *gutta* drop, used in med. and mod.L. for gum.] **1.** The inspissated juice of various trees found chiefly in the Malayan archipelago (see sense 2), now much used in the arts. **2.** (Short for *gutta-percha tree.*) One of the trees that yield this juice, esp. *Isonandra* (or *Dichopsia*) *gutta* (N.O. *Euphorbiaceæ*) 1860.

Comb.: **gutta-percha-tissue,** 'gutta-percha in a very thin leaf, used as a waterproof covering to dressings to prevent evaporation' (*Syd. Soc. Lex.*); **gutta-percha-wire** (*Telegraphy*), wire covered with gutta-percha.

Guttate (gɒ·teⁱt), *a.* 1826. [– L. *guttatus* speckled, spotted, f. *gutta* drop + *-atus* -ATE².] In the form of drops; furnished with drops, spotted as if by drops. So **Gutta·ted** *a.* spread about as if in drops or spots 1727.

‖**Guttatim** (gɒtēⁱ·tim). 1694. [L.; = 'by drops', f. *gutta.*] Drop by drop.

‖**Gutté** (gute), *a.* 1572. [AFr. *gutté* = OFr. *gouté* spotted, f. *goute* (mod. *goutte* drop) + *-é* -ATE².] *Her.* Besprinkled with drops; as in *gutté de sang*, etc. *Gutté reversed*: charged with drops having the bulb or globe upwards. vars. †**Gu·tted** *a.*, **Guttee.**

Gutter (gɒ·təɹ), *sb.* ME. [– AFr. *gotere*, OFr. *gotiere* (mod. *gouttière*) :– Rom. **guttaria*, f. L. *gutta* drop; see -ER² 2, -ARY¹.] †**1.** A watercourse; later, a small brook or channel –1797. **b.** A furrow or track made by running water 1586. **c.** *Austral. gold-mining.* The lower part of the channel of an old river of the Tertiary period containing auriferous deposits 1864. **2.** A shallow trough fixed under the eaves of a roof, etc., to carry off the rain-water ME. **3.** A hollowed channel at the side of a road or elsewhere, to carry away the surface water ME. Also *fig.* as the haunt of children, etc., of low birth or breeding 1846. **b.** A sink (*lit.* and *fig.*). Now *dial.* 1440. **c.** Mud, filth. Chiefly *Sc.* (only *pl.*). 1785. **4.** A shallow trough or open conduit or pipe for the outflow of fluid 1657. †**5.** A groove in an animal or vegetable body. *Obs.* in gen. sense. –1712. **6.** An artificial groove or channel. Now only *techn.* 1555. **7.** In *Printing* = *gutter-stick* (see Comb.). Also in *Bookbinding*, 'the white space between the pages of a book'. 1841.

3. The gutters run blood ZANGWILL. *fig.* To die in the g. HALL CAINE.

Comb.: **g.-bird,** the sparrow, hence *fig.* a disreputable person; **-board,** a board forming the foundation on which is laid the lining-material forming the g. itself; **-child,** a child such as haunts the gutters; **-drift** = sense 1 c; **-flag** *Austral.*, a flag fixed on the surface to denote where the course of a g. has been discovered; **-member** (*Arch.*), a member made by decorating the outside face of a g. with regularly spaced ornaments; **g. plane,** a moulding plane with a semi-cylindrical sole for planing gutters; **-snippet,** app. a dim. of GUTTER-SNIPE (Kipling); **-stick** (*Printing*), one of the pieces of furniture which separate pages in a forme; **-tree,** the Wild Cornel or Dogwood, *Cornus sanguinea* (*Syd. Soc. Lex.*).

b. *attrib.* (or *adj.*) Brought up in or appropriate to the g.; low, disreputable; as the *gutter Press, g. journalism* 1851.

Gutter (gɒ·təɹ), *v.* ME. [f. prec.] **1.** *trans.* To make gutters in; to furnish with gutters; to furrow with streams, tears, etc. **2.** *intr.* Of water: To form gutters or gullies 1632. **3.** To flow in streams, to stream *down* 1583. **4.** Of a candle: To melt away rapidly by becoming channelled on one side; to sweal. (The chief current sense.) 1706.

Gutter-blood (gɒ·təɹblɒd). *Sc.* One of the rabble. SCOTT.

Gutter-snipe (gɒ·təɹsnəip). 1869. **1. a.** *dial.* The common snipe, *Gallinago cælestis* 1893. **b.** The common American snipe, *Gallinago wilsoni* or *delicata* 1874. **2. a.** A gatherer of refuse from the gutter 1869. **b.** A street arab 1882. **3.** *Printing.* (*U.S.*) A small and narrow poster for pasting on curbstones 1871.

Guttifer (gɒ·tifəɹ). 1846. [– mod.L. *guttifera* (sc. *planta*), f. L. *gutta* drop (in med. and mod.L. used for 'gum') + *-fer* bearing; see -FEROUS.] *Bot.* A plant that exudes gum or resin; a plant of the order *Guttiferæ.*

Guttiferous (gɒti·fĕrəs), *a.* 1847. [f. as prec.; see -FEROUS.] Yielding gum or resinous substances; pertaining to N.O. *Guttiferæ*, of trees and shrubs remarkable for their abounding in a resinous sap. So **Gutti·feral** *a.* epithet of an alliance including the order *Guttiferæ*; *sb.* a plant belonging to this alliance. LINDLEY.

Guttiform (gɒ·tifǭɹm), *a.* 1874. [f. L. *gutta* drop + -FORM.] Drop-shaped.

Guttle (gɒ·t'l), *v.* 1654. [f. GUT *sb.*, after GUZZLE *v.*] **1.** *intr.* To eat voraciously; to gormandize. **2.** *trans.* To devour or swallow greedily 1685. Hence **Gu·ttler,** a glutton; a gormandizer.

‖**Guttula** (gɒ·tiŭlă). 1887. [L., dim. of *gutta* drop; see -ULE.] A small drop or drop-like spot. Hence **Gu·ttular** *a.* spotted. **Gu·ttulate** *a.* (*Nat. Hist.*), having drops or spots, as 3-*guttulate.* †**Gu·ttulous** *a.* in drop-like form –1651.

‖**Guttur** (gɒ·tŏɹ). 1562. [L.; = 'throat'.] The throat; used rarely in techn. applications.

Guttural (gɒ·tŏral). 1594. [– Fr. *guttural* or med.L. *gutturalis*, f. *guttur* throat; see -AL¹.]

A. *adj.* Of or pertaining to the throat 1625; (of sounds) produced in the throat.

The g. orifice of the Eustachian tube 1836. The g. nasal seems to have been the regular pronunciation of *ng* in English 1867.

B. *sb.* [*sc.* sound; *occas.* utterance.] 1696. His speech was..all gutturals DE FOE.

Hence **Gu·tturalism,** g. quality or characteristics. **Guttura·lity,** g. nature, character, or condition. **Gu·tturalize** *v. trans.* to pronounce or utter gutturally; to render g. in character. **Gutturaliza·tion.** **Gu·ttural-ly** *adv.* in a g. manner; **-ness,** gutturality.

†**Gutturine,** *a.* [f. GUTTUR + -INE¹.] Pertaining to the throat. RAY.

Gutturize (gɒ·tŏrəiz), *v.* [f. as prec. + -IZE.] *trans.* To enunciate gutturally. COLERIDGE.

Gutturo- (gɒ·tŏro), taken as comb. f. L. *guttur* throat; as in *g.-maxillary*, relating to the throat and the jaw; *g.-nasal*, guttural and nasal; etc.

Gutty (gɒ·ti), *sb. Golfers' slang.* 1890. [f. GUTTA² + -Y⁶.] A gutta-percha ball.

Gutty (gɒ·ti), *a.* Chiefly *Sc.* 1785. [f. GUT *sb.* + -Y¹.] Pot-bellied.

Gutwort (gɒ·twɒɹt). ?*Obs.* 1597. [f. GUT *sb.* + WORT¹.] The plant *Globularia alypum*, a violent purgative, of S. Europe and Africa.

Guy (gəi), *sb.*[1] ME. [Sense 1: – OFr. *guie* guide, f. *guier* GUY *v.*[1] Sense 2: first in *guy-rope* (*girap* XIV, *gyerope* XV), prob. of LG. origin, as are Du. *gei* brail, *geitouw* clew-garnet, *geiblok* pulley, G. *geitau* clew-line, (pl.) brails (cf. *aufgeien* brail up).] †**1.** A guide; a conductor or leader (*rare*) –1520. **2.** Chiefly *Naut.* A rope used to guide and steady a thing which is being hoisted or lowered; a rope, chain, rod, etc., to secure and steady anything likely to shift its position or to be carried away, as the mast, funnel, etc., of a vessel, a derrick, a suspension-bridge, etc. 1623. **3.** *attrib.*, as in **guy rein,** a guiding or leading rein 1793.

Guy (gəi), *sb.*[2] *Pl.* **guys.** 1806. **1.** An effigy of Guy Fawkes carried about in the streets on the anniversary of Gunpowder Plot (Nov. 5), and burnt in the evening. **2.** A person of grotesque looks or dress; a fright 1836. **3.** A man, fellow (*U.S. slang*) 1896.

1. Dressed up..like a g. TROLLOPE. **2.** Grisly Guys some of them turn out 1836.

†**Guy,** *v.*[1] ME. [– OFr. *guier*; see GUIDE *v.*] = GUIDE *v.* 1–4. –1600.

Guy (gəi), *v.*[2] 1712. [f. GUY *sb.*[1] 2.] *trans.* To fasten or secure with a guy or with guys. Chiefly *Naut.* Also *transf.*

Guy (gəi), *v.*[3] 1851. [f. GUY *sb.*[2]] **1.** *intr.* To carry an effigy of Guy Fawkes about the streets on Nov. 5. **b.** *trans.* To exhibit a person in effigy 1894. **2.** *trans.* (Orig. *Theatr. slang.*) To make an object of ridicule 1872.

Guze (giūz). 1562. [Of unkn. origin.] *Her.* A roundle of a sanguine tint.

Guzzle (gɒ·z'l), *sb.* 1598. [app. f. the vb.] **1.** A gutter, drain. Also *fig.* Now *dial.* **2.** Drink, liquor 1704. **3.** A debauch 1836.

1. That sinke of filth, that g. most impure MARSTON.

Guzzle (gɒ·z'l), *v.* 1579. [poss. – OFr. *gosillier*, a deriv. of *gosier* throat, but found only in the senses 'chatter' and 'vomit'.] **1.** *trans.* To swallow (liquor, *rarely* food) greedily or to excess 1583. **2.** To consume (time, money, etc.) in guzzling 1653. **3.** *intr.* To drink largely or greedily, to swill 1579.

1. How it annoyed me to behold Belvidera [Mrs. Siddons] g. boiled beef and mustard 1808. **2.** To g. away money 1797. **3.** To shoot and g. at his country seat MACAULAY. Hence **Gu·zzler,** one who guzzles.

Gwyniad (gwi·niæd). Also †**guiniad,** †**gwiniad,** †**gwinead.** 1611. [– Welsh *gwyniad*, f. *gwyn* white.] A fish of the salmon or trout kind (*Coregonus pennantii*) with white flesh, found in lakes, esp. Bala.

Gy-, in wds. of Gr. etym., is herein marked to be pronounced with (dʒ), but with regard to the less common words there are many, esp. among scholars, who prefer the 'hard *g*'.

Gyal, obs. f. GAYAL.

Gybe, *sb.*[1] *Thieves' slang.* ?*Obs.* 1561. [Of unkn. origin.] A counterfeit pass or licence.

Gybe (dʒəib), *sb.*[2] 1880. [f. next.] *Naut.* An act of gybing.

Gybe (dʒəib), *v.* 1693. [– Du. †*gijben* (mod. *gijpen*, whence G. *geipen*); but initial (dʒ) is unexplained. Cf. JIB *v.*[1]] **1.** *intr.* Of a fore-and-aft sail and its boom: To swing from one side of the vessel to the other. Also *trans.* **2.** *intr.* To put about or alter the course of a boat so that her boom-sails gybe. Said also of the boat. Also *trans.* with the boat as object; also, to sail round by gybing. 1693.

Gye, obs. f. GUY *sb.*[1]; obs. var. of GUY *v.*[1]

Gyle (gəil). 1440. [– MDu. *ghijl* (Du. *gijl*), rel. to *gijlen* ferment, of unkn. origin.] *Brewing.* **1.** A brewing; the quantity brewed at one time 1594. **2.** Wort in process of fermentation 1440. **3.** A gyle-tun 1836. **4.** *attrib.*, as **gyle-tun** = GYLE-FAT; etc. 1498.

Gyle-fat. *Obs.* exc. *dial.* ME. [See prec. and FAT *sb.*[1]] The vat in which the wort is left to ferment.

Gym (dʒim). 1889. Colloq. abbrev. of GYMNASIUM.

Gymkhana (dʒimkā·nă). Orig. *Anglo-Ind.* 1861. [Alteration, by assim. to *gymnastic*, of Hind. *gendkhāna* 'ball-house', racket court.] 'A place of public resort at a station where the needful facilities for athletics and games..are provided' (Yule). Hence, an athletic sports display. Also *attrib.*

Gymmal(l, obs. ff. GIMMAL.

Gymnasial (dʒimnē·ziăl), *a.* 1852. [f. GYMNASIUM + -AL[1].] Of or pertaining to the Continental gymnasia or similar educational establishments.

Gymnasiarch (dʒimnē·ziaɹk). 1658. [– L. *gymnasiarchus*, *-archa* – Gr. γυμνασίαρχος, -άρχης, f. γυμνάσιον GYMNASIUM; see -ARCH.] **1.** *Gr. Antiq.* An Athenian official who superintended athletic schools and games. **b.** *transf.* A leader among athletes 1825. **2.** A governor of a school or college; a head instructor 1682. So **Gymna·siarchy,** the office or function of g.

Gymnasiast (dʒimnē·ziæst). 1828. [f. Gr. γυμνάσιον GYMNASIUM; in sense 1 after G. *gymnasiast.*] **1.** A student in a (Continental) gymnasium. **2.** A gymnast 1857.

Gymnasium (dʒimnē·ziŏm). *Pl.* **-ia, -iums.** 1598. [– L. *gymnasium* – Gr. γυμνάσιον, f. γυμνάζειν train naked, f. γυμνός naked. See -IUM.] **1.** A place or building for practice of or instruction in athletic exercises; a gymnastic school. Also *transf.* Also *attrib.* **2.** †A high school, college, or academy; *spec.* in Germany and elsewhere, a school of the highest grade preparatory for the universities. Now often as Ger. (gimnā·zium). 1691.

1. Galen..inveighs against the..violent Practices of the G. 1704. **2.** Cambridge and Oxford..surpass..the gymnasia of foreign countries JOHNSON. Hence **Gymna·sic** *a.* pertaining to the g. (sense 2). CARLYLE.

Gymnast (dʒi·mnæst). 1594. [– Fr. *gymnaste* or Gr. γυμναστής trainer of athletes; see prec.] One skilled in gymnastic exercises; a gymnastic expert.

Gymnastic (dʒimnæ·stik). 1574. [– L. *gymnasticus* – Gr. γυμναστικός; see GYMNASIUM, -IC.]

A. *adj.* **1.** Pertaining to or connected with athletic exercises of the body; concerned with gymnastics (see B. 2). **b.** Physically active (*rare*) 1784. **2.** *fig.* 'Pertaining to disciplinary exercises for the intellect' (Webster) 1710.

1. b. A form not now g. as of yore COWPER. **2.** The difference of the g. and dogmatic styles GIBBON.

B. *sb.* **1.** *sing.* [= Gr. ἡ (τέχνη) γυμναστική.] = 2. 1598. Also *fig.* **2.** *pl.* **Gymnastics** [see -ICS, -IC 2]. **a.** The practice of athletic exercises for the development of the body, now esp. of such as are performed in a gymnasium (sense 1) 1652. Also *fig.* †**b.** A treatise on athletic exercises. SIR T. BROWNE.

1. Good gymnastic..will give health to the body JOWETT. **2. a.** Gymnastics..have not until lately been practised HONE. *fig.* I think Hindoo books the best gymnastics for the mind EMERSON. Hence **Gymna·stical** *a.* = A. **Gymna·stically** *adv.* (*rare*), in a g. manner; in respect of gymnastics.

Gymnic (dʒi·mnik). Now *rare.* 1601. [– L. *gymnicus* – Gr. γυμνικός pertaining to bodily exercises, f. γυμνός naked; see -IC. Cf. Fr. *gymnique.*]

A. *adj.* = GYMNASTIC *a.* 1.

Have they not Sword-players, and ev'ry sort of G. Artists, Wrestlers, Riders, Runners, Juglers and Dancers MILT.

B. *sb. pl.* **Gymnics:** = *gymnastics* (see GYMNASTIC *sb.* 2) 1621. Hence †**Gy·mnical** *a.* = A.

Gymnite (dʒi·mnəit). 1843. [f. Gr. γυμνός naked, in allusion to Bare Hills, Maryland, where found; see -ITE[1] 2 b.] *Min.* A hydrated silicate of magnesium.

Gymno- (dʒimnŏ), bef. a vowel **gymn-,** comb. f. Gr. γυμνός naked, bare.

Gymnobla·stic [Gr. βλαστός (see -BLAST)] *a., Zool.* having the nutritive or generative buds unprotected by an external receptacle (hydrotheca or gonangium); so **Gymnobla·stous** *a.* **Gymnobra·nchiate** [Gr. βράγχια *pl.*, gills] *a.*, belonging to the *Gymnobranchiata*, a group of gastropods having naked gills; *sb.* an animal of this group. **Gymnoce·ratous** [Gr. κερατ-, κέρας horn] *a., Entom.* belonging to the *Gymnocerata*, a group of heteropterous insects having exposed antennæ. ‖**Gymnocyta, -cyte** [Gr. κύτος cell], *Biol.* 'Haeckel's term for a naked or wall-less cytode having a nucleus' (*Syd. Soc. Lex.*). **Gy·mnodont** [Gr. ὀδοντ-, ὀδούς], *Ichthyol., a.* belonging to the *Gymnodontes*, a group of plectognath fishes having the jaw prolonged into a beak covered with a dental plate; *sb.* a fish of this group. **Gy·mnogen** [see -GEN], *Bot.* = GYMNOSPERM. **Gymno·genous** [see -GEN 2] *a., Bot.* = GYMNOSPERMOUS. **Gy·mnogram** [Gr. γραμμή line, mark], *Bot.* a fern of the genus *Gymnogramme* or *-gramma*, having the lines of spore-cases on the lower side of the frond uncovered. **Gymno·gynous** [see -GYNOUS] *a., Bot.* having a naked ovary. **Gymnolæ·matous** [Gr. λαιμός throat, gullet] *a., Zool.* belonging to the *Gymnolæmata*, a division of Polyzoa having no epistome or valve to close down upon the mouth. **Gymno·merous** [Gr. μηρός thigh] *a., Zool.* pertaining to the *Gymnomera*, a division of cladocerous crustaceans. **Gymnomy·xine** [Gr. μύξα slime] *a., Zool.* pertaining to the *Gymnomyxa*, a low grade of Polyzoa which are naked or not corticate. **Gymnophtha·lmate, -ophtha·lmatous, -ophtha·lmic, -ophtha·lmous** [Gr. ὀφθαλμός] *adjs., Zool.* belonging to the *Gymnophthalmata* or naked-eyed medusæ. **Gymno·pterous** [Gr. πτέρον] *a., Entom.* having naked wings, without hairs or scales; having sheathless wings. **Gymnorhi·nal** [Gr. ῥίς, ῥιν- nostril] *a., Ornith.* having naked or unfeathered nostrils. **Gymnoso·mate, -so·matous, -so·mous** [Gr. σωματ-, σῶμα] *adjs., Zool.* pertaining to the *Gymnosomata*, an order of pteropods having a naked body. **Gy·mnospore** [SPORE], *Bot.* a naked spore; so **Gymno·sporous** *a.*, having uncovered spores. **Gymnotetraspe·rmous** [Gr. τετρα- four, σπέρμα seed] *a., Bot.* having such a four-lobed ovary as is found in labiates, which was formerly thought to consist of four naked seeds. **Gymno·tocous** [Gr. τόκος] *a., Zool.* having the genital products uncovered, as certain hydroids. **Gymnozo·idal** [Gr. ζῷον; see -ID[3]] *a., Zool.* pertaining to the *Gymnozoida*, a section of Infusoria in Saville Kent's classification.

Gymnocarpous (dʒimnŏkā·ɹpəs), *a.* 1856. [f. Gr. γυμνόκαρπος huskless (f. γυμνός naked, bare + καρπός fruit) + -OUS.] *Bot.* Having a naked fruit; applied to lichens with open or expanded apothecia, or to a fructification of this character.

Gymnogene (dʒi·mnŏdʒīn). 1875. [– mod. L. *Gymnogenys* naked-chinned, f. GYMNO- + γένυς chin.] A book-name for an African hawk, *Polyboroides typicus* or *P. capensis*.

Gymnopædic (dʒimnŏpī·dik), *a.* 1850. [– Gr. γυμνοπαιδικός, f. γυμνός naked + παῖς, παιδ- boy; see -IC.] *Gr. Antiq.* Distinctive epithet of the dances, etc., performed by naked boys at public festivals.

Gymnosophist (dʒimnǫ·sŏfist). ME. [– Fr. *gymnosophiste* – L. (pl.) *gymnosophistæ* – Gr. (pl.) γυμνοσοφισταί, f. γυμνός GYMNO- + σοφιστής SOPHIST.] One of a sect of ancient Hindu philosophers of ascetic habits, who wore little or no clothing, denied themselves flesh meat, and gave themselves up to mystical contemplation. They were known to the Greeks through the reports of the companions of Alexander. Also *occas.*, an ascetic or mystic. So **Gymno·sophy,** the doctrine or system of gymnosophists. var. **Gy·mnosoph** (*rare*). COLERIDGE.

Gymnosperm (dʒi·mnŏspəɹm). 1838. [– mod.L. *gymnospermus* – Gr. γυμνόσπερμος, f. γυμνός naked + σπέρμα seed.] *Bot.* A plant which has naked seeds, as the pine, hemlock fir, etc.; one of the *Gymnospermæ*, a class of exogenous plants so characterized.

Gymnospermous (dʒimnŏspə·ɹməs), *a.* 1727. [f. as prec. + -OUS.] *Bot.* Naked-seeded, i.e. not provided with a seed-vessel; belonging to the class *Gymnospermæ*. So **Gymnospe·rmal, -spe·rmic** *adjs.* in same sense.

Gymnostomous (dʒimnǫ·stŏməs), *a.* 1861. [f. Gr. γυμνός naked + στόμα mouth + -OUS.] *Bot.* Naked-mouthed; applied to mosses in which the mouth of the sporangium has no peristome. So **Gymnosto·matous** *a.* in same sense.

Gymnotus (dʒimnō[u]·tŏs). *Pl.* **-ti** (-təi). 1775. [mod.L. (Linnæus), for *gymnonotus, f. Gr. γυμνός naked + νῶτον back, with ref. to the absence of dorsal fins.] A freshwater eel-like fish of S. America, *Electrophorus* (formerly *Gymnotus*) *electricus*, capable of giving an electric shock; an electric eel.

Gyn, obs. f. GIN *sb.*[1]

‖**Gynæceum** (dʒəi-, dʒinīsī·ŏm). 1610. [L. – Gr. γυναικεῖον, f. γυνή, γυναικ- woman.] **1.** *Gr. and Rom. Antiq.* **1.** The women's apartments in a house; any building set apart for women 1723. †**b.** Under the Roman empire: A textile manufactory –1781. **2.** *Bot.* The female organs of a flower 1832. Now usually spelt **gynœcium,** as if from Gr. οἰκίον house, with correl. ANDRŒCIUM.

Gynæcian, *a. rare.* Also **gynecian** (in Dicts.) 1640. [f. Gr. γυνή, γυναικ- woman + -IAN.] Pertaining or relating to women.

Gynæcic (dʒəinī·sik), *a.* Also **gynecic.** 1878. [– Gr. γυναικικός, f. as prec.; see -IC.] Relating to diseases peculiar to women.

Gynæco- (dʒəi-, dʒinī·kŏ), also (esp. *U.S.*) **gyneco-,** repr. Gr. γυναικο-, comb. f. γυνή woman, female.

gynæco-cœ·nic [Gr. κοινός] *a.*, having women in common; **-phore** [Gr. -φορος bearing], *Zool.* in certain invertebrate animals, as some trematodes, a receptacle in the male in which the female is borne; hence **-phoric** *a.*; **-physiology,** the PHYSIOLOGY of the female generative organs.

Gynæcocracy (dʒəi-, dʒinīkǫ·krăsi). 1612. [– Fr. *gynécocratie* or mod.L. – Gr. γυναικοκρατία see GYNÆCO-, -CRACY.] Government by a woman or women; female rule; petticoat government. Hence **Gynæcocra·tic, -al** *a.* pertaining to g.

Gynæcology (dʒəi-, dʒinīkǫ·lŏdʒi) Also **gynecology.** 1847. [f. GYNÆCO- + -LOGY.] That branch of medical science which treats of the functions and diseases peculiar to women. Also *loosely*, the science of womankind. Hence **Gynæcolo·gical** *a.* pertaining to or relating to g. **Gynæco·logist,** an expert in g.

Gynander (dʒəinæ·ndəɹ). 1828. [– Gr. γύνανδρος (see GYNANDROUS).] A plant of the class *Gynandria*.

Gynandrian (dʒəi-, dʒinæ·ndriăn), *a.* 1828. [f. mod.L. *Gynandria* (Linn.), f. Gr. γυνή + ἀνήρ, ἀνδρ- (see GYNANDROUS) + -IAN.] Pertaining to the class *Gynandria* of plants having gynandrous flowers.

Gynandro- (dʒəi-, dʒinæ·ndro), comb. f. Gr. γύνανδρος (see GYNANDROUS).

Gynandromo·rphism, *Entom.* the condition of being gynandromorphous. **Gynandromo·rphous** [Gr. μορφή] *a.*, having both male and female characters; applied to some insects. **Gyna·ndrophore,** *Bot.* a gonophore which bears both the stamens and the pistil.

Gynandrous (dʒəi-, dʒinæ·ndrəs), *a.* 1807. [f. Gr. γύνανδρος 'of doubtful sex' + -OUS; cf. GYNO- and -ANDROUS.] *Bot.* Applied to those flowers and plants in which the stamens and pistil are united in one column, as in orchids; said also of the stamens.

Gynantherous: see GYNO-.

Gynarchy (dʒəi·naɹki). 1577. [f. Gr. γυνή woman + αρχία, ἀρχή rule.] Government by a woman or women.

Gyneocracy (dʒəi-, dʒinĭ,ǫ·krăsi). *rare.* 1611. [f. as prec. + -CRACY.] Incorrect f. GYNÆCOCRACY.

Gyniolatry (dʒəi-, dʒini,ǫ·lătri). 1876. [irreg. f. as prec. + -LATRY.] Adoration or worship of women. LOWELL.

Gyno- (dʒəino, dʒinŏ), bef. a vowel **gyn-** (dʒəin, dʒin), reduced form of GYNÆCO-, used chiefly in *Bot.* with the meaning 'pistil', 'ovary'.

Gyna·ntherous [ANTHER] *a.*, *Bot.* pertaining to an abnormal condition of the flower in which the stamens are converted into pistils. **Gynodiœ·cious** [DIŒCIOUS] *a.*, *Bot.* having perfect and female flowers on different plants; so **Gynodiœ·cism,** the condition of being gynodiœcious. **Gynomonœ·cious** [MONŒCIOUS] *a.*, *Bot.* having both perfect and female flowers on the same plant. ‖**Gynoste·gium** [Gr. στέγη roof], *Bot.* the sheath of a gynæceum. ‖**Gynoste·mium** [Gr. στήμων thread, stamen], *Bot.* the column consisting of the united stamens and pistil, as in the orchis.

Gynobase (dʒəi·n-, dʒi·nŏbēˈs). Also in mod.L. form **gynobasis.** 1830. [f. GYNO- + BASE *sb.*[1]] *Bot.* The flat or conical enlargement of the receptacle of a flower supporting the gynæceum. Hence **Gynoba·sic** *a.* pertaining to or having a g.; *gynobasic style*, one rising from the base of the ovary.

Gynocracy (dʒəi-, dʒinǫ·krăsi). 1728. [f. GYNO- + -CRACY.] = GYNÆCOCRACY; also quasi-*concr.*

‖**Gynœcium:** see GYNÆCEUM.

Gynophore (dʒəi·n-, dʒi·nŏfōᵊɹ). 1821. [f. GYNO- + -PHORE. Cf. Fr. *gynophore.*] **1.** *Bot.* The pedicel or stalk which in some flowers supports the ovary. **2.** *Zool.* One of the branches bearing the female gonophores in certain Hydrozoa 1861.

-gynous (dʒinəs), *Bot. suffix* forming adjs., f. mod.L. *-gynus* (– Gr. -γυνος, f. γυνή) + -OUS; used as = 'having... female organs or pistils', as in *monogynous* having one pistil, etc.

Gyp[1] (dʒip). Also †**gip.** 1750. [perh. short for †*gippo* scullion (XVII), transf. use of †*gippo* tunic – (O)Fr. *jupeau*, dim. of *jup(p)e*.] **1.** At Cambridge and Durham, a college servant or bed-maker. **2.** *U.S. slang.* A thief 1889.

Gyp[2]. *dial.* or *colloq.* 1898. [app. contr. of GEE-UP.] *To give* (a person or thing) *gyp*: to punish, thrash, treat roughly.

Gyps (dʒips). ME. Anglicized f. GYPSUM.

Gypseous (dʒi·psĭəs), *a.* 1661. [f. late L. *gypseus* (f. *gypsum*) + -OUS.] **1.** Like or having the nature of gypsum. **2.** Containing or consisting mainly of gypsum 1771. var. **Gy·psous.**

Gypsi·ferous, *a.* 1847. [f. GYPSUM + -FEROUS.] Yielding or containing gypsum.

†**Gy·psine,** *a. rare.* 1695. [f. as prec. + -INE[1].] = GYPSEOUS. –1753.

Gypsography (dʒipsǫ·grăfi). *rare.* 1840. [f. as prec. + -GRAPHY.] The art or practice of engraving on gypsum, or on plaster of Paris.

Gypsum (dʒi·psŏm), *sb. Pl.* **-sa, -sums.** 1646. [– L. *gypsum* – Gr. γύψος chalk, gypsum.] *Min.* Hydrous calcium sulphate, the mineral from which plaster of Paris is made. Hence **Gy·psum** *v.* to dress (land or a crop) with g.

Gypsy, alternative form of GIPSY.

Gyral (dʒəiᵊ·răl), *a.* 1750. [f. GYRE or GYRUS + -AL[1].] **a.** Moving in a circle or spiral; whirling, gyratory. **b.** Pertaining to a gyrus or gyri (see GYRUS). Hence **Gy·rally** *adv.*

Gy·rant, *a.* Also †**girant.** [– *gyrant-*, pres. ppl. stem of late L. *gyrare*; see GYRE *v.*, GYRATE *v.*, -ANT.] Moving in a circle or spiral. E. B. BROWNING.

Gyrate (dʒəiᵊ·rĕt), *a.* 1830. [– L. *gyratus* (Pliny) f. *gyrus*; see GYRE *sb.*, -ATE[2].] Arranged in rings or convolutions. *Bot.* = CIRCINATE; also, surrounded by an elastic ring, as the theca of ferns.

Gyrate (dʒəiᵊ·reⁱt), *v.* 1822. [– *gyrat-*, pa. ppl. stem of late L. *gyrare*; see GYRE *v.*, -ATE[3].] *intr.* To move in a circle or spiral; to revolve round a fixed point or axis; to rotate, whirl. Also *fig.* Hence **Gyra·tor.**

Gyration (dʒəiᵊrēⁱ·ʃən). 1615. [– late L. *gyratio*, f. *gyrat-*; see prec., -ION.] **1.** The action or process of gyrating; motion in a circle or spiral; revolution round a fixed centre or axis, wheeling, whirling; an instance of any of these. Also *fig.* **2.** *concr.* in *Conch.* One of the whorls of a spiral univalve shell.

1\. If a burning Coal be nimbly moved round in a Circle with Gyrations continually repeated NEWTON. In the gyrations of the storm MAURY. *fig.* His life was a g. of energetic curiosity DISRAELI.

Gyratory (dʒəiᵊ·rătəri), *a.* 1816. [f. GYRATE *v.* + -ORY[2].] Moving in a circle or spiral; revolving, whirling.

Gyre (dʒəiᵊɹ), *sb.* 1566. *poet.* and *literary.* Also †**gire.** [– L. *gyrus* – Gr. γῦρος ring, circle. Cf. GIRO.] **1.** A turning round, revolution, whirl; a circular or spiral turn. **2.** *concr.* A ring, circle, spiral; also, a vortex 1590.

1\. Be thy wheeling gyres Of ample circuit, easy thy descent CARY. Others run still in the same g., to weariness BP. HALL. Hence †**Gy·reful** *a.* circling, whirling.

Gyre (dʒəiᵊɹ), *v. poet.* Also †**gire.** ME. [– late L. *gyrare*, f. L. *gyrus*; see prec.] To turn or whirl round (*rare*). *trans.* and *intr.* Hence **Gy·ringly** *adv.* with revolving motion.

Gyrencephalate (dʒəiᵊrĕnse·fălĕt), *a.* 1859. [f. mod.L. *Gyrencephala* (see below), f. GYRUS + ENCEPHALON + -ATE[2].] *Zool.* Of or pertaining to the *Gyrencephala*, in which the cerebrum is convoluted. Also **-ous** *a.*

Gyrfalcon, obs. f. GERFALCON.

Gyro- (dʒəiᵊ·rŏ), comb. f. Gr. γῦρος ring, circle, spiral: **Gy·ro-co:mpass,** a form of gyroscope used as a compass, being continuously driven and thus retaining a fixed direction 1913.

Gyrogonite (dʒəiᵊrǫ·gŏnəit). 1832. [f. GYRO- + Gr. γόνος seed + -ITE[1] 2b.] *Geol.* A petrified seed-vessel of plants of the genus *Chara*, spiral in form, and formerly supposed to be a shell.

Gyroidal (dʒəiᵊroi·dăl), *a.* 1864. [f. GYRE or GYRUS + -OID + -AL[1].] **1.** *Crystall.* Having a spiral arrangement, as certain planes, etc. in some crystalline forms. **2.** *Optics.* Turning the plane of polarization to the right or left; rotatory in respect to polarized light 1864. Hence **Gyroi·dally** *adv.*

Gyromancy (dʒəiᵊ·rŏmænsi). 1557. [– med.L. **gyromantia* (whence also Fr. *gyromantie* (XVI); see GYRO-, -MANCY.] A mode of divination by walking in a circle till the person fell down from dizziness, the inferences being drawn from the place in the circle at which he fell.

Gyron (dʒəiᵊ·rǫn). 1572. [– (O)Fr. *giron*, †*geron* gusset – OFrank. **gēro* = OHG. *gēro*; see GORE *sb.*[2]] *Her.* An ordinary of triangular form made by two lines drawn from the edge of the escutcheon to meet in the fesse-point and occupying half of the quarter. Also *attrib.*

Gyronny (dʒəiᵊrǫ·ni), *a.* ME. [– Fr. *gironné*; see prec., -Y[5].] *Her.* Of an escutcheon: Divided into or having gyrons; *g. of eight*, having eight gyrons.

Gyroscope (dʒəiᵊ·rŏskōᵘp). 1856. [– Fr. *gyroscope* (Foucault, 1852); see GYRO-, -SCOPE.] *Dynamics.* A solid rotating wheel mounted in a ring, and having its axis free to turn in any direction; designed to illustrate the dynamics of rotating bodies. Foucault's gyroscope is contrived so as to render evident the rotation of the earth, through the tendency of the wheel to maintain its rotation in a fixed plane independently of the earth's motion. Hence **Gyrosco·pic** *a.* pertaining to or of the nature of the g.; rotatory.

Gyrose (dʒəiᵊ·rōᵘs), *a.* 1836. [f. GYRUS + -OSE[1].] *Bot.* Folded and waved, marked with wavy lines.

Gyrostat (dʒəiᵊ·rŏstæt). 1879. [f. GYRO- + -STAT.] *Dynamics.* An instrument used to illustrate the dynamics of rotating bodies: a rapidly rotating fly-wheel pivoted as finely as possible within a rigid case, having a convex curvilinear polygonal border, in the plane perpendicular to the axis through the centre of gravity of the whole. Hence **Gyrosta·tic** *a.* pertaining to the g. or to gyrostatics; connected with the theory that a rotating body tends to maintain its plane of rotation. **Gyrosta·tically** *adv.* **Gyrosta·tics** *sb. pl.* that part of physical science which deals with the rotation of solid bodies.

‖**Gyrus** (dʒəiᵊ·rŏs). *Pl.* **gyri** (-rəi). 1846. [L. – Gr. γῦρος ring, circle.] *Anat.* A convoluted ridge between grooves or sulci; *esp.* a convolution of the brain.

Gyse, obs. f. GUISE.

Gyte (gəit), *a. Sc.* 1725. [Of unkn. origin.] Out of one's senses.

Gyve (dʒəiv), *sb.* Usu. *pl.* Now *arch.* or *poet.* [ME. *give*, of unkn. origin. Orig. pronounced (gəiv).] A shackle, esp. for the leg; a fetter. Also *transf.* and *fig.*

Eugene Aram walked between With gyves upon his wrist HOOD.

Gyve (dʒəiv), *v.* ME. [f. GYVE *sb.*] *trans.* To fasten with, or as with gyves; to fetter, shackle. Also *fig.*

fig. Oth. II. i. 171.

H

H (ēⁱtʃ), the eighth letter of the Roman alphabet, repr. historically Semitic ⊟, *Hheth* or *Kheth*, through Gr. H, *Heta, Eta*. The Semitic letter represented a laryngal or guttural spirant, or a rough aspirate, and it was with the aspirate value that the letter was orig. used in Gr. and passed thence into Roman use. In OE., *h* occurred not only bef. the vowels, but also bef. the consonants *l, n, r, w*, as in *hláf* loaf, *hræfn* raven, etc.; it now stands initially only bef. vowels. Its power is that of a simple aspiration or breathing, with just sufficient narrowing of the glottis to be heard bef. a vowel. It is also used to form consonantal digraphs (*sh, th*, etc.) with simple sounds; and it is often silent, or merely lengthens a preceding vowel.

The name *aitch* goes back through ME. *ache* to OFr. *ache*, pointing to a late L. **accha*, **ahha*, or **aha*, exemplifying the sound. (The earlier L. name was *ha*.) Pl. *aitches, aches, hs, h's*.

Comb. H-piece, in a force-pump, a piece standing on the wind-bore, under the door-piece, by which the water is forced through the door-piece into the stand-pipe.

II. Besides serial order, *H* or *h* signifies *spec.* **1.** *Mus.* The note B natural in the German system of nomenclature (the letter B being used only for B flat). **2.** *Math.* In the differential calculus, *h* denotes a small increment. **3.** In *Cryst., h, k, l* are used for the quantities which determine the position of a plane.

III. Abbreviations. H. = *Henry, Helen*, etc. H. (*Chem.*) = Hydrogen. H. in the Shipping Register = *Hoy*. h. (in a ship's log) = hail. H or h. = hour. H or h (*Physics*) = horizontal force. H (on lead pencils) = hard; the various degrees of hardness being denoted by HH, HHH, etc. H (*Mus.*), as a direction = horns. HB (on lead pencils) = hard black (i.e. of a medium hardness). H.B.C. = Hudson's Bay Company. H.B.M. = His (or Her) Britannic Majesty. H.C. = Heralds' College, House of Commons. H.C.F. (*Math.*) = Highest Common Factor. H.E.I.C. = Honourable East India Company. H.G. = Horse Guards. H.H. = His (or Her) Highness, or His Holiness. H.I.M. = His (or Her) Imperial Majesty. H.M. = His (or Her) Majesty. H.M.C. = His (or Her) Majesty's Customs. H.M.S. = His (or Her) Majesty's Ship or Service. H.P. = horse-power, half-pay. H.R.H. = His (or Her) Royal Highness. †H.q. = L. *hoc quære*, seek this, q.v. H.T., h.t., high tension.

H', formerly used for *he* bef. a vowel or *h*: see HE.

Ha (hā), *int.* (*sb.*) ME. [Not in OE., exc. in the HA HA of laughter. Cf. HE *int.*, HO *int.*] **1.** An exclam. of surprise, wonder, joy, suspicion, indignation, etc., according to the intonation. **b.** Repeated, *ha ha!* it represents laughter: see HA-HA. **2.** esp. after a question; = EH 2. (Chiefly in SHAKS.) 1594. **3.** Expressing hesitation or interruption in speech (hə or ə). Often with *hum.* 1606. **4.** *sb.* The interjection as a name for itself; see HUM, also HAW 1610.

1. Ha? Let me see: I, giue it me, it's mine SHAKS. **2.** What saies that foole of Hagars offspring? ha SHAKS. Hence **Ha** *v.*, also **hah,** to utter 'ha!' in hesitation.

Ha, pron., ME. form of HE, HEO she, HI they.

Ha, ha', worn-down form of HAVE *v.*

Ha' (hā), Sc. form of HALL. *Comb.*: **ha'-Bible,** the great Bible that lay in the *ha'* or principal apartment; **ha' house,** the manor-house.

Haaf (hāf, haf). 1809. [– ON. *haf* (Sw. *haf*, Da. *hav*) sea, high sea, ocean.] In Shetland and Orkney: The deep or main sea: now used only in connection with deep-sea fishing; hence, deep-sea fishing ground or station. Also *attrib.*

Haak, dial. f. HAKE.

Haar (hāɹ). *local.* 1671. [perh. – ON. *hárr* hoar, hoary; cf. *hoar-frost*.] A wet mist or fog; esp. a cold sea-fog.

Hab (hæb), *adv.* (*sb.*) *Obs.* exc. *dial.* 1530. [repr. OE. *hæbbe*, early south. ME. *habbe*, pres. subj. of HAVE *v.*, in conjunction with the corresp. neg. form OE. *næbbe*, ME. *nabbe*. See HOB-NOB.] **1.** In the phrases *hab or nab, hab nab* (*habs-nabs*), get or lose, hit or miss; anyhow; at a venture 1542. **2.** quasi-*sb.* In phr. *at* (*by*) *hab or nab* = prec. So †**Hab** *v.* in *hab or nab*, have or not have.

‖**Habeas corpus** (hēⁱ·bi,ǣs kǭ·ɹpǒs). 1465. [L.; = thou (shalt) have the body (*sc.* in court).] A writ requiring the body of a person to be brought before a judge or into court for the purpose specified in the writ; *spec.* the prerogative writ *habeas corpus ad subiiciendum*, requiring the body of a person restrained of liberty to be brought before the judge or into court, that the lawfulness of the restraint may be investigated and determined. Also *fig.*

Habeas Corpus Act: the Act 31 Chas. II. c. 2 (1679), facilitating the granting and enforcing of the prerogative writ.

‖**Habendum** (hăbe·ndǒm). 1607. [L. = 'to be had' or 'to be possessed', gerundive of *habēre* have.] *Law.* That part of a deed (beginning in Law Latin with the words *habendum et tenendum*, and in Eng. deeds 'to have and to hold') which defines what estate or interest is thereby granted.

†**Ha·berdash,** *v.* [Back-formation from next.] *intr.* To deal in haberdashery. QUARLES.

Haberdasher (hæ·bəɹdæʃəɹ). ME. [prob. – AFr. **haberdasser* (cf. AL. *habardasshator* XV), **hapertasser* (cf. *haberdasshrie* XV), presumably f. recorded *hapertas* of unkn. origin and unc. meaning (Eng. †*haberdash* was used for 'small wares' XV–XVII); see -ER².] Formerly, a dealer in a variety of articles, including caps, and probably hats. In the 16th c.: **a.** A dealer in, or maker of, hats and caps, a hatter –1711; in *U.S.*, a dealer in men's hats, collars, cuffs, and underwear. **b.** A dealer in thread, tape, ribbons, and the like 1611. Also *fig.*

a. The H. heapeth wealth by hattes GASCOIGNE.

Haberdashery (hæ·bəɹdæ:ʃəri). ME. [See prec. and -ERY.] **1.** The goods and wares sold by a haberdasher. **2.** The shop of a haberdasher 1813. **3.** *attrib.*, as *h.-ware*, etc. 1547.

†**Haberdine** (hæ·bəɹdīn, -din). ME. [repr. MDu. *abberdaen* (Du. *abberdaan*), var. of *labberdaen*, connected by De Vries with the name of a Basque district, *le Labourd*, or from *Lapurdum* ancient name of Bayonne.] The name of a large sort of cod, used esp. for salting; salt or sun-dried cod –1708. Also *attrib.*

Habergeon (hæ·bəɹdʒən, hăbə̄·ɹdʒən), **hau-bergeon** (hǭ·bəɹdʒən). ME. [– (O)Fr. *haubergeon*, f. OFr. *hauberc* (mod. *haubert*); see HAUBERK, -OON. Since XVI only *Hist.*] A sleeveless coat or jacket of mail or scale armour, orig. smaller than a HAUBERK, but sometimes app. the same as that.

Habilatory (hăbi·lătəri), *a. rare.* 1827. [Arbitrary f. Fr. *habiller*, after adjs. in *-atory*.] Having reference to dressing.

Habile (hæ·bil), *a.* ME. [var. of ABLE (formerly *hable, abil*, etc.), conformed to mod. Fr. *habile* or L. *habilis*.] †**1.** Suited; suitable; competent. Chiefly *Sc.* –1795. †**2.** Manageable 1741. †**3.** Having the capacity or power (*to do* a thing) –1678. **4.** Handy; skilful, adroit, dexterous 1485.

Habiliment (hăbi·limĕnt). [Late ME. *abylement*, etc. – OFr. *abillement* (later and mod. *hab-*), f. *habiller* render fit, fit out, (hence, by assoc. with *habit*) clothe, dress, f. *habile* ABLE; see -MENT.] **1.** (without *pl.*) Outfit, array, attire. (Now only of personal attire.) 1470. †**2.** *pl.* Munitions, or apparatus of war. (In this sense usually spelt without *h*, quasi 'things making *able* for war'.) –1686. †**b.** *esp.* Armour, warlike apparel; trappings (of a horse) –1816. **3.** *pl.* The vestments appropriate to any office or occasion. Also *joc.* Ordinary clothes. (The chief extant sense.) Also *fig.* 1491. †**4.** = BILIMENT –1621. †**5.** *fig.* Mental equipment; *pl.* abilities, faculties, powers –1640.

3. My riches, are these poore habiliments SHAKS. Hence **Habi·limented** *ppl. a.* equipped, apparelled, dressed.

†**Habi·litate,** *ppl. a.* [– med.L. *habilitatus*, pa. pple. of *habilitare*; see next, -ATE².] Endowed with ability; capacitated, qualified. BACON.

Habilitate (habi·litēⁱt), *v.* Also **abilitate.** 1604. [– *habilitat-*, pa. ppl. stem of med.L. *habilitare*, f. *habilitas* ABILITY; see -ATE³.] †**1.** *trans.* To capacitate, qualify –1819. **2.** *intr.* for *refl.* To qualify oneself for office. [After Ger. *habilitiren*.] 1881. **3.** *trans.* To clothe, dress (*rare*) 1885. Hence **Habi:lita·tion,** also *abilitation*, the action of enabling; capacitation, qualification; *spec.* in *U.S.*, the furnishing of means to the owner of a mine, to enable him to work it. **Habi·litator** [Sp. *habilitador*], one who furnishes means for the working of a mine under contract with the owner.

Hability (hăbi·liti). ME. Early form of ABILITY (not recorded after 1723), after OFr. *habileté*; in XIX sometimes restored with the mod.Fr. sense of *habilité*, the quality of being habile.

Habit (hæ·bit), *sb.* [ME. (*h*)*abit* – OFr. *abit* (later and mod. *habit*) :– L. *habitus*, f. *habit-*, pa. pple. stem of *habēre* have, hold, refl. be constituted, be. In mod.Fr. the word is narrowed down to branch I below, other senses being supplied by *habitude*.]

I. Dress. **1.** Bodily apparel or attire; dress (*arch.*). **b.** with *a* and *pl.* A set or suit of clothes, a dress (of a specified kind) (*arch.*) ME. **c.** *pl.* Clothes, garments 1477; hence in *sing.* A garment (*arch.*) 1714. **d.** *transf.* and *fig.* 1549. **2.** *spec.* The dress of a particular rank, degree, profession, or function; *esp.* the dress of a religious order ME. **3.** = RIDING-HABIT. 1798.

1. It is her habite onely, that is honest SHAKS. **c.** MILT. *Comus* 157. **d.** Tory to-day, and Whig to-morrow, All habits and all shapes he wore 1839. **2.** *The habit*, the monastic order or profession (cf. 'the cowl').

II. †**1.** Bearing, deportment, behaviour; posture –1687. **2.** Bodily condition or constitution 1576; †the bodily system –1733; †the outer part, surface, or external appearance of the body –1725. **3.** *Zool.* and *Bot.* The characteristic mode of growth and appearance of an animal or plant. Hence *transf.*, e.g. in *Crystall.* 1691. †**4.** Habitation (*rare*). FLORIO.

2. Originally..of a spare h., but now..inclined to corpulency DISRAELI. **3.** Plants..of a tufted h. HOOKER.

III. 1. Mental constitution, disposition, character ME. **2.** A settled disposition or tendency to act in a certain way, esp. one acquired by frequent repetition of the same act; a settled practice, custom, usage; a customary manner of acting. (The chief sense.) Said occas. of inanimate things. 1581. **b.** without *a* or *pl.*: Custom, use, wont 1605. **c.** (Usu. in *pl.*) Applied *transf.* to animals and plants 1774. †**3.** The condition of being accustomed to something; familiarity –1859.

1. If we respect more the outward shape, then the inward habit LYLY. **2.** How vse doth breed a h. in a man SHAKS. *Disposition* properly denotes a natural tendency [to action], *habit* an acquired tendency SIR W. HAMILTON. **c.** The h. of cotyledons rising vertically at night DARWIN. **3.** The h. of affairs BURKE.

†**IV.** *Logic.* The eighth of the categories or predicaments of Aristotle: Having or possession: in Gr. ἔχειν, L. *habitus*. (See CATEGORY 1.) –1837.

Habit (hæ·bit), *v.* ME. [– (O)Fr. *habiter* – L. *habitare* have possession of, inhabit, f. *habit-*; see prec.] †**1.** *intr.* To dwell, abide –1649. **2.** *trans.* To dwell in 1598. **3.** To attire. (Usu. in *pa. pple.*) 1588. †**4.** To habituate –1814; to render habitual –1660.

1. Although he h. on the earth GREENE. **3.** Or is it Dian habited like her SHAKS. **4.** Men..habited in falsehood FELTHAM.

Habitable (hæ·bităb'l), *a.* Also †**abitable.** ME. [– OFr. *abitable* (later and mod. *habitable*) – L. *habitabilis*, f. *habitare*; see prec., -ABLE.] Suitable for habitation; fit to live in, inhabitable; also *absol.* the habitable globe (MILT. *P. L.* VIII. 157). Hence **Ha:bitabi·lity, Ha·bitableness. Ha·bitably** *adv.*

Ha·bitacle. *Obs.* exc. *Hist.* ME. [– (O)Fr. *habitacle* – L. *habitaculum* dwelling-place, f. *habitare* inhabit.] **1.** A dwelling-place. Also *transf.* and *fig.* **2.** A canopied niche in the wall of a building ME. var. †**Habita·cule** (in sense 1).

Ha·bitance. [– OFr. *habitance*, f. *habiter*; see HABIT *v.*, -ANCE.] A habitation. SPENSER.

Habitancy (hæ·bitănsi). 1792. [f. next; see -ANCY.] **1.** Residence as an inhabitant. **2.** Inhabitants collectively 1832.

Habitant (hæ·bitănt). 1490. [– (O)Fr. *habitant*, pres. pple. of *habiter*; see HABIT *v.*, -ANT.]

A. *adj.* Indwelling. 1856.

B. *sb.* **1.** One who dwells in a place; an inhabitant 1490. ‖**2.** (pronounced abitañ; pl. often *habitans*). A native of Canada (also of Louisiana) of French descent; one of the race of original French colonists, chiefly small farmers.

1. *fig.* O Love! no h. of earth thou art BYRON. **2.** To ascertain the feelings of the *habitans*, or French yeomanry W. IRVING.

Habitat (hæ·bitæt). 1796. [– L. *habitat*, *lit.* 'it inhabits', in Floras and Faunas, written in Latin.] *Nat. Hist.* The locality in which a plant or animal naturally grows or lives; habitation. Applied (*a*) to the *geographical area* over which it extends; (*b*) to the particular *station* in which a specimen is found; (*c*) but chiefly used to indicate the kind of locality, as the sea-shore, chalk hills, or the like. Hence *gen.* Habitation 1854.

The Black Spleenwort..occurs on rocks as a native h. E. NEWMAN. *gen.* Brook Street, the favourite h. of physicians 1869.

Habitation (hæbitē^i^·ʃən). ME. [– (O)Fr. *habitation* – L. *habitatio*, f. *habitat-*, pa. ppl. stem of *habitare*; see HABIT *v.*, -ION.] **1.** The action of dwelling in or inhabiting; occupancy by inhabitants. **2.** *concr.* A place of abode or residence ME. Also *fig.* **3.** The name adopted for local branches of the 'Primrose League' in 1883. **4.** A settlement. [After Fr.] 1555.

1. Every Starr perhaps a World Of destind h. MILT. **2.** They had no Cities, nor setled Habitations 1662. *fig.* The Sonne and Mone remayned still in their habitacion COVERDALE *Hab.* 3:11.

†**Ha·bitator.** [– L. *habitator*, f. as prec.; see -OR 2.] A dweller, inhabiter. SIR T. BROWNE.

Habited (hæ·bitėd), *ppl. a.* 1605. [f. HABIT *v.* + -ED^1^.] **1.** Inhabited 1866. **2.** Clothed, dressed 1807. †**3.** That has become habitual; accustomed –1651.

2. Statues of the Habited Graces 1807.

Habitual (hăbi·tiuăl). 1526. [– med.L. *habitualis*, f. *habitus*; see HABIT *sb.*, -AL^1^.]

A. *adj.* †**1.** Belonging to the habit or inward disposition (see HABIT *sb.* III. 1); inherent or latent in the mental constitution. **2.** Of the nature of a habit; fixed by habit; constantly repeated; customary 1611. Hence *transf.* of an agent 1825. **3.** Constantly used; usual 1654.

1. I distinguish between habituall and actuall Jurisdiction BRAMHALL. **2.** H. dissoluteness of manners BURKE, diffidence and awkwardness of address W. IRVING, actions DARWIN. *transf.* A h. drunkard MACAULAY, volcano LYELL, tea-drinker 1875. **3.** Romola's h. seat GEO. ELIOT.

B. *ellipt.* as *sb.* A habitual criminal, drunkard, etc. (*colloq.*) 1884.

Hence **Habi·tualize** *v. trans.* to render h. **Habi·tual-ly** *adv.*, **-ness.**

†**Habituate** (hăbi·tiu,ĕt), *ppl. a.* 1526. [– late L. *habituatus*, pa. pple. of *habituare*; see next, -ATE^2^.] **1.** Made or become habitual –1720. **2.** Of a person: Grown accustomed (*to* a thing); established in a habit –1679.

Habituate (hăbi·tiu,e^i^t), *v.* 1530. [– *habituat-*, pa. ppl. stem of late L. *habituare*, f. L. *habitus*; see HABIT *sb.*, -ATE^3^.] †**1.** *trans.* To form (anything) into a habit –1649. **2.** To fix (any one) in a habit; to accustom *to*. *Pa. pple.* Used, accustomed. 1530. †**3.** To settle as an inhabitant (*in* a place). [After Fr.] –1695. **4.** To frequent. *U.S.* 1872.

2. Minds not habituated to accurate thinking 1864.

Habituation (hăbitiu,ē^i^·ʃən). 1449. [– Fr. *habituation* or med.L. *habituatio*; in mod. use f. HABITUATE *v.* + -ION.] †**1.** The action of rendering or becoming habitual –1673. **2.** The action of habituating or accustoming, or the being habituated (*to* something) 1816.

Habitude (hæ·bitiud). ME. [– (O)Fr. *habitude* – L. *habitudo*, f. *habit-*, pa. ppl. stem of *habēre*; see HABIT *v.*, -TUDE. For the formation, cf. DECREPITUDE.] **1.** = HABIT *sb.* II. 2, III. 1. †**2.** Relation, respect (to something else) –1732. †**3.** Familiar relation or acquaintance; familiarity, intimacy; intercourse –1796. **4.** = HABIT *sb.* III. 2. 1603. †**5.** *Chem.* (*pl.*) Behaviour of one substance *with* another; reaction –1832.

1. Helth is a temperat habytude of the bodye 1540. **2.** The h. (which we call proportion) of one sound to another MORLEY. †*In full h.*: entirely. **4.** Many habitudes of life, not given by nature BUTLER. The fetters of h. 1889.

Habitué (abitüe). 1818. [Fr., pa. pple. of *habituer* – L. *habituare*; see HABITUATE *v.*] One who has the habit of frequenting a place. Old *habitués* of the boxes THACKERAY.

†**Ha·biture.** [f. HABITUDE by substitution of suffix -URE.] = HABITUDE. Marston.

‖**Habitus** (hæ·bitŏs). 1886. [L.] = HABIT *sb.* II. 2, 3.

Hable, early f. ABLE; see also HABILE.

Hab-nab, Hab or nab: see HAB.

‖**Hachure** (haʃū·r), *sb.* 1858. [Fr., f. *hacher* HATCH *v.*^2^; see -URE.] *pl.* The lines used in hill-shading to indicate the more or less steep slope of the surface. Also *attrib.*, as *hachure lines*. Hence **Ha·chure** *v.* to shade (a map) with hachures.

‖**Hacienda** (asi,e·ndă). 1760. [Sp. (aþye·nda) :– L. *facienda* things to be done, f. *facere*.] In Spain, and Sp. colonies, etc.: An estate or plantation with a dwelling-house upon it; a farming, mining, or manufacturing establishment in the country; *occas.*, a country-house. ‖**Haciendado** (a:siendā·do), the owner of an h.

Hack (hæk), *sb.*^1^ ME. [Partly – MLG. *hakke*, f. *hacken* HACK *v.*^1^; partly f. the vb.] **1.** A tool or implement for breaking or chopping up: **a.** Any tool of the mattock, hoe, and pick-axe type. **b.** A two-pronged tool like a mattock, for dragging dung, etc. 1797. **c.** A miner's pick for breaking stone 1681. **d.** A bill for cutting wood 1875. **2.** A gash or wound made by a cutting blow; *spec.* a notch made in a tree to serve as a guide; a 'blaze' (*U.S.*); a chap in the skin 1575. **b.** *Football.* A cut or gash in the skin caused by a kick 1857. **3.** A ridge of earth thrown up by ploughing or hoeing. *Obs.* exc. *dial.* 1744. **4.** Hesitation in speech 1660. **5.** A short dry hard cough 1885.

Hack, *sb.*^2^ 1575. [In sense 1 by-form of HATCH *sb.*^1^; prob. due to assoc. with its north. dial. var. HECK; in sense 2 a fusion of HATCH *sb.*^1^ and HECK.] **1.** *Falconry.* The board on which a hawk's meat is laid. Hence applied to the state of partial liberty in which eyas hawks are kept before being trained. **2.** A rack to hold fodder for cattle. ? *Obs.* exc. *dial.* 1674. **3.** A frame on which bricks are laid to dry before burning; a row of bricks laid out to dry 1703. **4.** = HAKE *sb.*^3^ 1. 1808.

2. Phr. *To live at h. and manger*, i.e. in plenty. *Comb.* **h.-board** = sense 1.

Hack, *sb.*^3^ (*a.*) 1687. [An abbrev. of HACKNEY, mostly familiar or contemptuous.] **1.** A hackney horse. **a.** A horse let out for hire; hence, a sorry jade 1721. **b.** *spec.* A horse for ordinary riding; a saddle-horse for the road. (Technically a half-bred horse with more bone and substance than a thorough-bred.) 1798. **2.** = HACKNEY 5. Now only *U.S.* 1704. †**3.** The driver of a hackney carriage –1713. **4.** A common drudge; *esp.* a literary drudge; hence, a poor writer, a mere scribbler 1700. **b.** *slang.* A prostitute; a bawd 1730. †**5.** Anything that is hackneyed; a hackneyed sermon, book, quotation, etc. –1805. **b.** Applied to persons; as, a *garrison hack* 1876. **6.** *Naut.* A watch used, in taking observations, to obviate the necessity of moving the standard chronometer. Also *hack-*, *job-watch*. 1851.

1. a. Butcher's hacks That 'shambled' to and fro HOOD. **b.** *Covert-hack*, a horse for riding to the meet, or to the cover, as dist. from the hunter. **4.** Here lies poor Ned Purdon..Who long was a bookseller's h. GOLDSM.

attrib. and *Comb.* **1.** In apposition or *attrib.*, as *h.-horse* (= sense 1); *-cab*, etc.; also *h.-attorney*, *-author*, *-moralist*; *h.-rider*, *-stand*, etc. **2.** *attrib.* or *adj.* **a.** Hackneyed; trite, commonplace, as a *hack speech*. **b.** Of a hired sort, as HACK-WORK.

Hack (hæk), *v.*^1^ [OE. (*tō*)*haccian* cut in pieces = OFris. (*tō*)*hakia*, MLG., MDu., (M)HG. *hacken* (Du. *hakken*); WGmc. deriv. of imit. base **xak-*; cf. synon. OE. *hæććan*, OHG. *hecken*.]

I. Trans. senses. **1.** To cut with heavy blows irregularly or at random; to notch; to mangle by jagged cuts. In earlier use chiefly, To chop *up* or into pieces, to chop *off*. **2. a.** Of frost: To chap or crack the skin (*dial.*) 1673. **b.** *Football.* To kick the shin of (an opponent) 1866. **3.** *Agric.* Applied to various operations involving cutting and chopping 1620. **4.** To hoe or plough up (the soil) into ridges; to rake (hay) into rows (*dial.*) 1744. †**5.** *Mus.* To break (a note) –1496. †**6.** *fig.* To mangle (words) in utterance. Also *absol.* –1676.

1. My Sword hackt like a Hand-saw SHAKS. **6.** Let them keepe their limbs whole, and h. our English SHAKS.

II. Intr. senses. **1.** To make rough cuts, to deal cutting blows 1450. **2.** Of the teeth: To chatter. *Obs.* exc. *dial.* ME. **3.** To hesitate in speech; to stammer. *Obs.* exc. *dial.* 1553. †**4.** To haggle –1613. **5.** To cough with short, dry, oft-repeated cough 1802.

5. *Hacking cough*, a short, dry, frequently repeated cough.

Hack, *v.*^2^ 1875. [f. HACK *sb.*^2^] **1.** *trans.* To place (bricks) in rows upon hacks. **2.** *Falconry.* To keep (young hawks) 'at hack' or in a state of partial liberty 1883.

Hack, *v.*^3^ 1745. [f. HACK *sb.*^3^] **1.** *trans.* To put to indiscriminate or promiscuous use; to make common by such treatment; to hackney. **2.** To employ as a literary hack 1813. **3. a.** *trans.* To employ (a horse) as a hack. **b.** *intr.* To ride on the road; dist. from *cross-country* or *military* riding. 1857. **4.** *intr.* To ride in a cab. *U.S.* 1879.

1. If ever tale was hackt about, Grown obsolete, [etc.] 1762. ¶The sense of *hack* in *Merry W.* II. i. 52, 'These knights will hack', is doubtful. The history and chronology of the vb. are against the senses suggested in Johnson and Nares.

Hack-, stem of HACK *v.*^1^ in Comb., in sense 'hacking, chopping'. Hence **h.-saw,** a saw used in metal-cutting; etc.

Hackamore (hæ·kămo^ə^ɹ). *U.S.* 1889. [perh. corruption of Sp. *jaquima*, formerly *xaquima*, halter.] A halter of horse-hair or raw hide having a nose-piece fitted to serve as the head-piece of a bridle.

Hackberry (hæ·kberi). 1796. [Phonetic var. of HAGBERRY, q.v.] **1.** = HAGBERRY. **2.** In N. America, the fruit of the tree *Celtis occidentalis*, which resembles the bird-cherry in size; also the tree itself 1796.

Hackbolt (hæ·kbo^u^lt). Also **hagbolt.** 1843. [Of unkn. origin.] The greater Shearwater, *Puffinus major*.

†**Ha·ckbush, ha·gbush.** Also †**hackbus.** 1484. [– Fr. *haquebusche*; see next.] = HACKBUT.

Hackbut, hagbut (hæ·k-, hæ·gbŏt). *arch.* and *Hist.* 1541. [– Fr. *haquebut*(*e*, alt. of *haquebusche* (see prec.) – MDu. *hakebus*, *hagebus* (Du. *haakbus*), MLG. *hakebusse*, f. *hake*(*n* HOOK + *bus*(*se* gun, firearm (cf. BLUNDERBUSS), so called from the hook orig. cast on the gun as an attachment. Cf. HARQUEBUS.] An early form of portable fire-arm; = prec.

†**Hackbut à croc:** see HARQUEBUS 2.

Hackbutter, hagbutter (hæ·kbɒtəɹ, hæ·g-). *arch.* and *Hist.* 1544. [f. prec. + -ER^1^.] A soldier armed with a hackbut; a harquebusier. vars. **Hackbutee·r, -ier.**

Hacked (hækt), *ppl. a.* ME. [f. HACK *v.*^1^ + -ED^1^.] In the senses of the vb.; *spec.* in *Her.*, indented, with the notches curved on both sides, as a bend, etc.

Hackee (hæ·ki). 1860. [After the animal's cry.] A species of ground squirrel, the Striped Squirrel, or Chipmuck, of N. America.

Hacker (hæ·kəɹ), *sb.* 1481. [f. HACK *v.*^1^ + -ER^1^.] **1.** One who hacks, in various senses 1581. **2.** That which hacks; *spec.* in *U.S.*, a tool for making an oblique incision in a tree, as a channel for the passage of sap, gum, or resin 1875.

Hackery (hæ·kəri). *Anglo-Ind.* 1698. [– Hindi *chhakṛā* two-wheeled cart.] A bullock-cart for the transport of goods; also, locally, a lighter carriage (drawn sometimes by horses) for the conveyance of persons.

Hackle (hæ·k'l), *sb.*¹ [OE. *hacele, hæcile* cloak, mantle, corresp. (exc. in formative suffix) to OHG. *hachul*, MHG. *hachel*, ON. *hǫkull*, Goth. *hakuls*.] †**1.** A cloak, outer garment; a chasuble –ME. **2.** A covering of any kind, as a bird's plumage, a serpent's skin, etc. *Obs.* exc. *dial.* ME. **3.** The straw roofing of a beehive; the straw covering of the apex of a rick; the case of a Florence flask 1609.

Hackle (hæ·k'l), *sb.*² ME. [By-form of HATCHEL *sb.*; cf. HECKLE *sb.*] **1.** A comb for splitting and combing out the fibres of flax or hemp; = HECKLE, HATCHEL. 1485. **2.** Local name of the stickleback 1655. **3.** The long shining feathers on the neck of the domestic cock, peacock, pigeon, etc. ME. **4.** *Angling.* An artificial fly, dressed with a hackle-feather, or something like this; a 'palmer'. Also *h.-fly.* 1676. **5.** *attrib.* 1681.

3. Phr. *To show h.*, to be willing to fight (*slang*). *With the hackles up*, as in a cock when he is angry; said also of a dog on the point of fighting, also *transf.* of a man. The 42nd [1st Batt. Royal Highlanders]..received the red h. as an honourable distinction 1884. Hence *hackles* is sometimes put for hair, whiskers, etc.

Hackle, *v.*¹ 1579. [dim. and frequent. of HACK *v.*¹ Cf. HAGGLE *v.*] **1.** *trans.* To cut roughly, hack, mangle by cutting. †**2.** *intr.* To make a hacking. NASHE.

Hackle, *v.*² 1616. [f. HACKLE *sb.*² 1; cf. HECKLE *v.*] *trans.* To dress (flax or hemp) with a hackle; also *fig.* = HECKLE. Hence **Ha·ckler,** a flax-dresser, heckler.

Hackle, *v.*³ 1867. [f. HACKLE *sb.*² 3.] *trans.* To dress (a fly) with a hackle-feather.

Hackly (hæ·kli), *a.* 1796. [f. HACKLE *v.*¹ + -Y¹.] Rough or jagged, as though hacked; *esp.* of metals, etc.: Having the surface rough with short sharp points.

Hackman (hæ·kmæ̆n). 1850. *U.S.* [f. HACK *sb.*³ 2.] The driver of a hack or hackney-carriage; a cab-driver.

Hackmatack (hæ·kmătæk). 1792. [Amer. Indian (cf. Abnaki *akemantak*).] The American Larch or Tamarack (*Larix americana*). Also *attrib.*

Hackney (hæ·kni), *sb.* (*a.*) ME. [In AFr. *hakenei* (XIV), AL. *hakeneius* (XIII), prob. f. ME. *Hakenei* Hackney in Middlesex, Skeat's view being that horses were raised on the pasture land there and taken to Smithfield market through Mare Street. Hence (O)Fr. *haquenée*.]

A. *sb.* **1.** A horse of middle size and quality, used for ordinary riding; now techn. = HACK *sb.*³ 1 b. †**2.** Often taken as, A horse kept for hire 1614. Also *fig.* †**3.** One who does mean work for hire; a common drudge. Also *fig.* –1784. †**4.** A prostitute –1679. **5.** A HACKNEY-COACH. 1664.

1. He rode..a strong h. for the road, to save his gallant warhorse SCOTT. **2.** *fig.* Hector of Troy was an h. to him DEKKER. **3.** Public hacknies in the schooling trade COWPER.

attrib. and *Comb.* **1. a.** in apposition, as **hackney horse** = senses 1, 2. **b.** *attrib.* Of or pertaining to a hackney (horse), as *h. hire, stable, stud*, etc. **c.** Plying for hire, as HACKNEY-CARRIAGE, -CHAIR, -COACH, etc. †**2. a.** in apposition, or as *adj.* Hireling (also *fig.*), as *h. author, pen, tongue, writer*, etc. **b.** *attrib.* or *adj.* Done by a hackney or for hire, as *h. job, writing.* †**c.** Prostitute, as *h.-wench.*

†**B.** as *adj.* Worn out, like a hired horse, by indiscriminate use; trite, commonplace; hackneyed –1792.

Ha·ckney, *v.* Now *rare* exc. in *ppl. a.* HACKNEYED. 1577. [f. HACKNEY *sb.*] **1.** *trans.* = HACK *v.*³ 3 a. Also *fig.* †**2.** To convey in a hackney-carriage. COWPER. †**3.** *fig.* To drive hard; to post; to hurry. Also *intr.* (for *refl.*) –1798. †**4.** To let *out* for hire. Also *intr.* for *pass.* –1736. **5.** To make common by indiscriminate everyday usage; to render vulgar, trite, or commonplace 1596; †to undo the freshness or delicacy of –1808. **6.** To render habituated, practised, or experienced *in.* Often dyslogistic. 1751.

3. How are thy Angels hackney'd up and down To visit man QUARLES. **5.** So common hackney'd in the eyes of men SHAKS. **6.** Persons a little hackneyed in the world LYTTON.

Ha·ckney-ca·rriage. 1831. [f. HACKNEY *sb.* + CARRIAGE.] Any vehicle standing or publicly plying for hire.

Ha·ckney-chai·r. 1710. Formerly, a sedan chair, now a bath chair or the like, plying publicly for hire. Hence **Hackney-chairman.**

Ha·ckney-coa·ch. 1610. [f. HACKNEY *sb.* + COACH.] A four-wheeled coach, drawn by two horses, and seated for six persons, kept for hire. Hence **Ha·ckney-coa·chman.**

Hackneyed (hæ·knid), *ppl. a.* 1749. [f. HACKNEY *v.* + -ED¹.] †**1.** Hired; kept for hire –1818. **2.** Made trite and commonplace; stale 1749. **3.** Experienced, *occas.*, to disgust or weariness 1760.

2. A h. expression HURD, objection BOSWELL, subject 1887. **3.** Hacknied statesmen D'ISRAELI.

Hackney-man (hæ·knimæn). ME. [f. HACKNEY *sb.* + MAN.] A man who keeps hacks or hackney-carriages for hire.

Hackster. *Obs.* exc. *dial.* 1581. [f. HACK *v.*¹ + -STER.] **1.** *lit.* One who hacks; a cut-throat; a swashbuckler. **2.** A prostitute 1594.

Hackthorn (hæ·kþǭɹn). 1863. [– Du. *haakedorn*, hook-thorn.] A S. African thorny shrub (*Acacia detinens*), also termed 'Wait-a-bit thorn'.

Hack-work (hæ·k₁wɒ̄ɹk). 1851. [HACK *sb.*³] Work (esp. literary work) done by a hack or hired drudge.

Hacqueton, hacton, vars. of HAQUETON, ACTON.

Had, pa. t. and pple. of HAVE *v.*

Hadder, obs. Sc. f. HEATHER.

Haddie (hæ·di). 1816. A Sc. dial. var. of *haddo'* = HADDOCK.

Haddock (hæ·dǫ̆k). ME. [In AL. *haddocus* (XIII); prob. – AFr. *hadoc*, var. of OFr. (*h*)*adot*, pl. *hadoz, haddos*, of unkn. origin. For the final cons. cf. HAVOC.] A fish (*Gadus æglefinus*) allied to the cod, but smaller, abundant in the North Atlantic and the British seas, and much used for food. Also applied to allied fishes, as the *Norway* or *Norwegian h.*, the Bergylt or Sea Perch; etc. Hence **Ha·ddocker,** a person or vessel employed in fishing for h.

Hade (hēⁱd), *sb.* 1789. [Goes with next, from which it is app. derived.] *Mining* and *Geol.* The inclination of a mineral vein or fault from the vertical; the complement of the *dip.* Also called *underlay* or *underlie.*

Hade (hēⁱd), *v.* 1681. [perh. a dial. form of *head*, retaining the older pronunc. of that word; cf. *tread, trade.*] *Mining*, etc. *intr.* To incline or slope from the vertical, as a shaft, a vein, a fault.

‖**Hades** (hēⁱ·dīz). Also formerly **Ades.** 1597. [– Gr. ᾅδης (orig. αἴδης, or ἀΐδης) of unkn. origin; in LXX and N.T. Greek used as tr. Heb. *šᵉʼôl*, the abode of departed spirits.] **1.** *Gr. Myth.* Oldest name of the god of the dead, also called Pluto; hence, the kingdom of Hades, the lower world, the abode of shades 1599. **2.** In N.T. (R.V.): The state or abode of the dead, or of departed spirits after this life; = Heb. *Sheol* 1597.

1. Orcus and Ades, and the dreaded name Of Demogorgon MILT. The enthroned Persephone in Hades TENNYSON. **2.** Neither was he left in Hades, nor did his flesh see corruption R.V. *Acts* 2:31.

‖**Hadj** (hæ·dʒ). 1704. [Arab. *ḥājj* pilgrimage.] The greater pilgrimage to Mecca.

‖**Hadji, hajji** (hæ·dʒī). 1612. [– Pers., Turk. *ḥājjī, ḥājī* pilgrim, f. *ḥājj* (prec.).] A title given to one who has made the greater pilgrimage (on 8th to 10th day of the 12th month) to MECCA (q.v.). **b.** An Oriental Christian who has visited the Holy Sepulchre at Jerusalem 1835.

Hadrosaur (hæ·drosǭɹ). 1877. [– mod.L. *Hadrosaurus* (name of the genus), f. Gr. ἁδρός thick, stout + σαῦρος (= σαύρα) lizard.] A genus of gigantic fossil saurian reptiles found in N. America.

Hæcceity (heksī·ĭti, hīk-). 1647. [– med.L. *hæcceitas* 'thisness' (Dun Scotus), f. L. *hæc*, fem. of *hic* this + *-itas* -ITY; cf. *quidditas* QUIDDITY, *seitas* SEITY.] *Scholastic Philos.* The quality implied in the use of *this*, as *this man*; 'thisness', 'hereness and nowness'; individuality.

Hæma-, hema-, repr. Gr. αἷμα blood, sometimes improp. used for HÆMATO- or HÆMO-. For words in *hæma-* see HÆMO-. The sp. *he-* in words from Gr. αἷμα is favoured in U.S., but is rare in Gt. Britain.

Hæmad (hī·mæ̆d), *sb.* 1891. [f. Gr. αἷμα blood + -AD, after *monad*, etc.] A blood-corpuscle.

Hæmal, hemal (hī·măl), *a.* 1839. [f. Gr. αἷμα blood + -AL¹.] *Anat.* Of or belonging to the blood or blood-vascular system; belonging to or situated on or towards that side or region of the body which contains the heart and great blood-vessels: opp. to *neural*; in the case of the Vertebrata and Tunicata, synonymous with *ventral.*

Hæmal arch, Owen's term for the inferior arch of a typical vertebra. *H. cavity*, the cavity formed by a series of h. arches (constituted by the ribs, costal cartilages, and breast-bone). *H. spine*, the ventral element of a h. arch.

Hæmapophysis (hīmăpǫ·fisis). 1849. [mod.L.; see HÆMO- and APOPHYSIS. (So called as situated towards the hæmal aspect of the body.)] *Anat.* Owen's term for that portion of the hæmal arch of a typical vertebra situated between the pleurapophysis and the hæmal spine. Hence **Hæ:mapophy·sial** *a.*

‖**Hæmatemesis** (hīmăte·mĭsis). 1800. [mod.L., f. HÆMATO- + Gr. ἔμεσις vomiting.] *Path.* Vomiting of blood.

Hæmatic, hem- (hĭmæ·tik). 1854. [– Gr. αἱματικός, f. αἷμα, αἱματ- blood; see -IC.]

A. *adj.* Pertaining to blood; containing blood, sanguineous; acting upon the blood; of the colour of blood.

B. *sb.* **1.** A medicine that acts upon the blood 1854. **2. Hæmatics:** that branch of physiology or medicine which treats of the blood 1854.

Hæmatin, hem- (hī·mătin, he·m-). 1819. [f. Gr. αἷμα, αἱματ- blood + -IN¹.] *Chem.* **1.** Earlier name of HÆMATOXYLIN. **2.** A bluish-black amorphous substance with metallic lustre, obtained from red blood-corpuscles, in which it exists as a constituent of hæmoglobin 1845. Hence **Hæmati·nic** *a.* of or relating to h. (sense 2); *sb.* a medicine which increases the h. in the blood. **Hæ:matino·meter,** an instrument for measuring the h. in the blood; **Hæ:matinome·tric** *a.* relating to such measurement. ‖**Hæ:matinu·ria,** the passing of urine containing the colouring matter of the blood without the corpuscles (now called *hæmoglobinuria*).

Hæmatite, hem- (he·mătəit, hī·m-). 1543. [– L. *hæmatites* – Gr. αἱματίτης (sc. λίθος stone); see -ITE¹ 2 b. The commercial and economic sp. is *hem-*.] *Min.* Native sesquioxide of iron (Fe_2O_3), a widely distributed iron ore, occurring in crystalline, massive, or granular forms; in colour, red, reddish-brown, or blackish with a red streak. Also *attrib.*

Brown hæmatite: a brown or brownish yellow mineral, consisting of hydrated sesquioxide of iron; also called *limonite*. Hence **Hæmati·tic** *a.*, also **hem-,** pertaining to, consisting of, or resembling h.

Hæmato-, hemato- (hīmăto, hemăto), bef. a vowel **Hæmat-, hemat-,** = Gr. αἱματ-, comb. f. αἷμα blood. See also HÆMO- for some shorter forms. The spelling *hemato-* is chiefly U.S.

hæ·matochro:me [Gr. χρῶμα], a red colouring matter developed in some Protozoa at a certain stage of existence; **hæ:matocry·al** [Gr. κρύος cold, frost] *a.*, belonging to the *Hæmatocrya* or cold-blooded Vertebrata; **hæ·matocy:st, -cy·stis,** a cyst containing blood; **hæ:matodyna·mics, -dynamo·meter** (see HÆMO-); **hæ:matoge·nesis** [see GENESIS], the formation of blood; **hæ:matoge·nic** *a.*, relating to hæmatogenesis; also = next; **hæmato·genous** *a.*, originating in the blood; **hæmato·phagous** [Gr. -φαγος] *a.*, feeding upon, or living in, the blood; **hæ·matophy:te** [Gr. φυτόν], a vegetable parasite inhabiting the blood; ‖**hæ:matopoie·sis** [Gr. ποίησις], the formation of blood; whence **hæ:matopoie·tic** *a.*; **hæ·matosco:pe, hæ:matospe·ctroscope,** an instrument for the determination of the quantity of oxyhæmoglobin in the blood; **hæmato·scopy,** a (spectroscopic) method of examining the blood; **hæ:matothe·rmal** *a.*, warm-blooded; **hæmatotho·rax,** hæmorrhage into the pleural cavities; **hæ:matozo·on** (pl. *-zo·a*) [Gr. ζῷον], an animal parasite inhabiting the blood; hence **hæ:matozo·an** = prec.; **hæ:matozo·ic** *a.*, of or pertaining to a hæmatozoon.

Hæmatoblast (hī·matoblɑːst). 1876. [f. HÆMATO- + -BLAST.] **a.** *Phys.* Name given to certain yellowish or greenish discs, smaller than the ordinary blood-corpuscles, found in the blood of viviparous Vertebrata; also called *blood-plates*. **b.** *Embryol.* Name given to cells of the mesoderm from which the first blood-corpuscles and blood-vessels originate. Hence **Hæmatobla·stic** *a.*

Hæ·mato-cry·stallin. 1863. [f. as prec. + CRYSTALLIN.] **a.** The special form of CRYSTALLIN or GLOBULIN found in the blood-corpuscles. **b.** Hæmoglobin when obtained in a crystalline condition.

Hæ:mato-glo·bulin. 1845. [for *hæmatino-globulin*, f. HÆMATIN + GLOBULIN, as being composed of the two.] *Chem.* The colouring matter of the red corpuscles of the blood; also called **Hæmatoglo·bin;** now usu. shortened to HÆMOGLOBIN.

Hæmatoid, hem- (hī·mătoid, he·m-), *a.* 1840. [– Gr. αἱματοειδής; see HÆMATO-, -OID.] **a.** Resembling or containing blood. **b.** Consisting of hæmatoidin.

Hæmatoi·din, hem-. 1855. [f. prec. + -IN[1].] *Chem.* A yellow or yellowish-red crystalline substance found in extravasated blood; by some identified with bilirubin.

Hæmatoin (hīmătōᵘ·in). 1876. [Differentiated from *hæmatin*; see HÆMATO-, -IN[1].] *Chem.* A derivative of hæmoglobin containing no iron.

Hæmatology (hīmătǫ·lŏdʒi). 1811. [f. HÆMATO- + -LOGY.] That branch of animal physiology which relates to the blood.

Hæmatometer, hem- (hīmătǫ·mĭtəɹ). 1854. [See HÆMATO- and -METER.] **a.** = *hæmodynamometer* (see HÆMO-). **b.** An instrument for numbering the blood-corpuscles.

Hæmatosin, hem- (he·m-, hī·mătosin). 1834. [– Fr. *hématosine* (Chevreul, 1814), irreg. f. Gr. αἵματος, gen. of αἷμα blood + -IN[1].] = HÆMATIN 2.

||**Hæmatosis** (hīmătōᵘ·sis). 1696. [med. or mod.L. – Gr. αἱμάτωσις (Galen), f. αἱματοῦν make into blood.] **a.** The formation of blood, esp. of blood-corpuscles; sanguification. **b.** Old name for hæmorrhage. **c.** The oxygenation of the blood in the lungs.

Hæmatoxylin, hem- (hīmătǫ·ksilin). 1874. [f. mod.Bot.L. *hæmatoxylon, -um* logwood (f. HÆMATO- + Gr. ξύλον wood) + -IN[1].] *Chem.* A crystalline substance ($C_{16}H_{14}O_6$) obtained from logwood; colourless when pure, but affording fine red, blue, and purple dyes by the action of alkalis and oxygen. Hence **Hæmatoxy·lic** *a.* derived from h.

||**Hæmaturia** (hīmătiūᵊ·riă). 1811. [f. HÆMATO- + URIA.] *Path.* The presence of blood in the urine. Hence **Hæmatu·ric** *a.*

Hæmic (hī·mik), *a.* 1857. [Arbitrary f. Gr. αἷμα + -IC; prop. HÆMATIC.] Pertaining or relating to the blood, as *hæmic asthma*.

Hæmin (hī·min). 1857. [f. Gr. αἷμα + -IN[1]; cf. *hæmatin*.] *Chem.* A deep red crystalline substance obtained from blood, containing hæmatin and hydrochloric acid.

Hæmo-, hemo- (hīmo, hemo), bef. a vowel **hæm-, hem-** (hīm, hem), repr. Gr. αἱμο-, shortened f. αἱματο- HÆMATO-, comb. f. αἷμα blood.

hæ·mochrome (erron. *hæma-*) [Gr. χρῶμα] = HÆMOGLOBIN; hence **hæ:mochromo·meter**, 'an apparatus for calculating the amount of hæmoglobin in a liquid by comparison with a standard solution of normal colour' (*Syd. Soc. Lex.*); **hæ·mocœle** [Gr. κοῖλος, κοιλία], the body-cavity of an arthropod or mollusc, analogous to the cœlome of a vertebrate; **hæ:mocyto·meter** (erron. *hæma-*), an instrument for ascertaining the number of blood-corpuscles; **hæ:modromo·meter** (also **-dro·meter**), **-dro·mograph** [Gr. -δρομος: see -METER, -GRAPH], instruments for measuring and registering the velocity of the blood-current; **hæ:modyna·mics** [see DYNAMICS], 'the science of the forces connected with the circulation of the blood' (*Syd. Soc. Lex.*); **hæ:modynamo·meter** (erron. *hæma-*), an instrument for measuring the pressure of the blood; **hæmoglo·bulin** = HÆMOGLOBIN; **hæmoly·tic** [Gr. λυτικός] *a.*, destructive of the blood or of the blood-corpuscles; **hæ:mopatho·logy**, the pathology of the blood; **hæmopoie·tic** (see HÆMATO-); **hæ·moscope**, an apparatus for examining the blood; so **hæmo·scopy** (erron. *hæma-*), examination of the blood: see HÆMATO-; **hæ:motacho·meter** (erron. *hæma-*) [Gr. τάχος; see -METER], an instrument for measuring the velocity of the blood-current; so **hæ:motacho·metry; hæmotho·rax** (see HÆMATO-).

Hæmocyanin, hemo- (hīmoˌsəi·ănin). Also erron. *hæma-*. 1845. [f. HÆMO- + CYANIN.] **a.** A blue colouring matter which has been found in human blood. **b.** A substance containing copper, blue when oxidized and colourless when deoxidized, found normally in the blood of some invertebrates.

Hæmoglobin, hemo- (hīmoglōᵘ·bin). 1869. [Shortened f. HÆMATO-GLOBULIN.] *Chem.* The colouring matter of the red corpuscles of the blood, which serves to convey oxygen to the tissues in the circulation; it occurs in reduced form (*reduced h.*) in the blood of the veins, and, combined with oxygen (*oxyhæmoglobin*), in that of the arteries. Formerly called *cruorin, hæmatoglobulin, hæmoglobulin, hæmatoglobin*. Hence ||**Hæ:moglobinæ·mia**, *Path.* the presence of free h. in the fluid part of the blood. **Hæ:moglobini·ferous** *a.* containing h. **Hæ:moglobino·meter**, an instrument for measuring the h. in blood; whence **Hæ:moglobino·metry.** ||**Hæ:moglobinu·ria**, *Path.* the presence of free h. in the urine; whence **Hæ:moglobinu·ric** *a.* characterized by hæmoglobinuria.

Hæmometer (hīmǫ·mĭtəɹ). 1872. [f. HÆMO- + -METER.] An instrument for measuring (*a*) the quantity of blood passing through a vessel in a given time; (*b*) the pressure of the blood (= *hæmodynamometer*); or (*c*) the amount of hæmoglobin in the blood (= *hæmoglobinometer*).

†**Hæmony** (hī·mŏni). [f. Gr. αἷμα blood, after *agrimony*.] An imaginary plant having supernatural virtues. MILT. *Comus* 638.

||**Hæmophilia** (hīmofi·liă, hemo-). Also **hæmo·phily** (*rare*). 1854. [mod.L., f. HÆMO- + Gr. φιλία affection. Cf. G. *hämophilie* (1828).] *Path.* A tendency to bleeding, either spontaneously, or from very slight injuries; hæmorrhagic diathesis. Hence **Hæmophi·liac** *a.* and *sb.*

||**Hæmoptysis** (hīmǫ·ptisis). 1646. [mod. L. *hemoptysis*, f. HÆMO- + Gr. πτύσις spitting.] *Path.* Spitting of blood; expectoration of blood, or of bloody mucus, etc., from the lungs or bronchi. Hence **Hæmopty·sic, -al** *a.* relating to or affected with h.

Hæmorrhage, hemo- (he·mŏrėdʒ). 1671. [Later form of HÆMORRHAGY.] An escape of blood due to rupture of a blood-vessel; bleeding, esp. when profuse or dangerous. Also *fig.*

Hæmorrhagic, hemo- (hemŏræ·dʒik), *a.* 1804. [– Gr. αἱμορραγικός; see HÆMORRHAGY, -IC.] Belonging to, of the nature of, accompanied with, or produced by hæmorrhage.

†**Hæ·morrhagy, hemo-.** 1541. [In XVI *emorogie, hemoragie* – Fr. *hémorr(h)agie*, †*emorogie* – L. *hæmorrhagia* (Pliny) – Gr. αἱμορραγία, f. αἱμο- HÆMO- + *rhag-, base of ῥηγνύναι break, burst. Superseded by HÆMORRHAGE.] = HÆMORRHAGE. –1838.

Hæmorrhoid[1], **hemo-** (he·mŏroid); usu. in pl. [Late ME. *emeroudis* (see EMERODS) – OFr. *emeroyde*, later *hémorrhoïdes* (XVI) – L. *hæmorrhoida* – Gr. αἱμορροΐς, -ίδ- discharging blood, pl. -οἶδες (sc. φλέβες veins) bleeding piles, f. αἱμόρροος, f. αἱμο- HÆMO- + -ροος flowing; assim. to L. form in XVI.] **1.** *pl.* A disease characterized by tumours of the veins about the anus; = PILE *sb.*[5], q.v. Rarely *sing.* †**2.** *pl.* Hæmorrhoidal veins –1541.

†**Hæmorrhoid**[2]. Also **hæmorrhe,** and in L. form **hæmorrhoïs, -rhus.** ME. [– L. *hæmorrhois, -id-* (Pliny) kind of poisonous serpent – Gr. αἱμορροΐς; etym. as in prec.] A serpent whose bite was fabled to cause unstanchable bleeding –1774.

Hæmorrhoidal, hemo- (hemŏroi·dăl), *a.* (*sb.*) 1541. [f. HÆMORRHOID[1] + -AL[1].] **1.** *Path.* Of or pertaining to hæmorrhoids 1651. **2.** *Anat.* Applied to those arteries, veins, and nerves which are distributed to the rectum and adjacent parts 1671. **3.** *sb.* (in sense 2) 1541.

Hæmostatic, hemo- (hīmostæ·tik, hem-). Also erron. **hæma-, hema-.** 1706. [f. HÆMO- + Gr. στατικός causing to stand still; see -IC.] **A.** *adj.* Having the property of stopping hæmorrhage; styptic 1854. **B.** *sb.* A styptic.

Haf, obs. pa. t. of HEAVE.

Hafnium (hæ·fniŏm). 1923. [mod.L., f. *Hafnia*, L. name of Copenhagen (Da. *Kjøbenhavn*, orig. *Havn*) Denmark; see -IUM.] *Chem.* A metallic element: symbol Hf, atomic number 72.

Haft (hɑft), *sb.*[1] Also **heft.** [OE. *hæft, hæfte*, corresp. to MLG. *hechte* (Du. *hecht, heft*), OHG. *hefti* (G. *heft*), ON. *hepti* :– Gmc. **χaftjam*, f. **χaf-* HEAVE; see -T[1].] A handle; esp. that of a cutting or piercing instrument, as a dagger, knife, sickle, etc.

The h. of a razor GOLDSM. Hilt and heft BROWNING.

Haft, *sb.*[2] *Sc.* and *n. dial.* Also **heft.** 1785. [Goes with HAFT *v.*[3]] **1.** Fixed place of abode. **2.** Accustomed pasture-ground 1800.

Haft, *v.*[1] Also **heft.** ME. [f. HAFT *sb.*[1]] **1.** *trans.* To fit with, or fix in, a haft or handle. †**2.** To drive *in* up to the haft 1583.

†**Haft,** *v.*[2] 1519. [perh. repr. OE. **hæftian*, corresp. to OS. *hafton*, OHG. *haftēn* (cf. MHG., G. *haften* intr.) remain fixed or fast.] *intr.* To use subtlety or deceit, to use shifts or dodges; to haggle, cavil; to hold off, hang back –1644. Hence †**Ha·fter** *sb.* a caviller, wrangler, haggler, dodger.

Haft, *v.*[3] *Sc.* and *n. dial.* Also **heft.** 1725. [Goes with HAFT *sb.*[2]; for the sense, cf. OE. *hæftan* = OS. *heftjan*, OHG., G. *heften*, Goth. *haftjan* make fast.] **1.** *trans.* To establish in a situation or place of residence; *spec.* to accustom (sheep, cattle) to a pasturage. Also *intr.* for *refl.* 1725. **2.** *transf.* and *fig.* To set or plant firmly, fix, root, settle 1755.

Hag (hæg), *sb.*[1] [ME. *hegge, hagge*, perh. shortening of OE. *hægtesse, hegtes* fury, witch = MDu. *haghetisse* (Du. *hecse*), OHG. *hagazissa* (G. *hexe*), of unkn. origin.] **1.** An evil spirit, dæmon, or infernal being, in female form; applied to the Græco-Latin Furies, Harpies, etc.; also to the Teut. 'fairies' 1552. †**b.** Applied to ghosts, hobgoblins, and other terrors of the night –1634. **2.** A witch; sometimes an infernally wicked woman. Now assoc. w. 3. 1587. **3.** An ugly, repulsive old woman; often with implication of viciousness or maliciousness ME. Also *fig.* and †*transf.* of a man. **4.** †**a.** A kind of light said to appear at night on horses' manes and men's hair –1656. **b.** *dial.* A white mist usu. accompanying frost 1825. **5.** A cyclostomous fish (*Myxine glutinosa*) allied to the lamprey, eel-like in form, and living parasitically upon other fishes. Also *h.-fish*. 1611.

1. Noontide h. or goblin grim SCOTT. **b.** Blue meagre h., or stubborn unlaid ghost MILT. **2.** How now you secret, black, and midnight Hags SHAKS. **3.** *fig.* The h. Evil TENNYSON. *transf.* That old h. [Silenus] GOLDING.

Comb., as *h.-seed* (from 2); also **h.-fish** (see 5); **hag's teeth,** irregularities in a matting or pointing such as to spoil the uniformity; **-track** = FAIRY-RING.

Hag, *sb.*[2] *n. dial.* 1470. [– ON. *hagi* enclosed field, pasture, rel. to OE. *haga*; see HAW *sb.*[1]] †**1.** ? A hedge. **2.** A wooded enclosure; a coppice or copse 1589.

2. He led me ouer holts and hags FAIRFAX.

Hag, *sb.*[3] *Sc.* and *n. dial.* 1615. [repr. ON. *hǫgg* cutting blow or stroke; see next.] **1.** A cutting, hewing, or felling 1808. **2.** The stump of a tree left after felling. Also *hagsnare*. 1615. **3.** A portion of a wood marked for cutting; hence, a lot of felled wood 1796.

3. Edward learned from her that the *dark hag*.. was simply a portion of oak copse..to be felled that day SCOTT.

Hag, *sb.*[4] *Sc.* and *n. dial.* ME. [– ON. **haggw-*, *hǫgg* gap, breach, orig. cutting blow whence HAG *sb.*[3]), f. **haggwa, hǫggva* HEW *v.* See HAG *v.*[1]] †**1.** A break, gap, or chasm (in a crag or cliff). ME. only. **2.** 'Moss-ground that has formerly been broken up; a pit or break in a moss', i.e. marsh or bog (Jam.) 1662. **3.** The vertical margin of a peat-cutting; the shelving margin of a stream 1893.

Hag, *v.*[1] *n. dial.* ME. [– ON. *hǫggva*; see prec., HEW *v.*] *trans.* = HACK *v.*[1] 1. Also *absol.* or *intr.*

Hag, *v.*[2] *Obs.* exc. *dial.* 1587. [In sense 1 f. HAG *sb.*[1]; senses 2–3 may be of different origin.] †**1.** *trans.* To torment or terrify as a hag; to trouble as the nightmare –1700. **2.** To urge; to egg *on.* Now *dial.* 1587. **3.** To tire out, fag. Now *dial.* 1674.

Hagarene (hæ̆găr͞ī·n). 1535. [– med.L. *Agarenus, Hagarenus*, f. (Vulg.) *Agar*, Hagar.] A reputed descendant of Hagar the concubine of Abraham and mother of Ishmael; an Arab, a Saracen. Also *transf.*

transf. Hagarenes, sons of fornication and wrath MILMAN.

Hagberry (hæ·gberi). Also **hack-, heck-, heg-berry.** 1597. [Of Norse origin: Da. *hæggebær*, Norw. *hagge-bār*, etc.] A northern name of the bird-cherry, *Prunus Padus.*

Hag-boat. Rarely **hag.** 1700. [Of unkn. origin.] A kind of vessel formerly used both as a man-of-war, and in the timber and coal trade; latterly, 'a clincher-built boat with covered foresheets and one mast with a trysail' (Smyth).

Hagbolt: see HACKBOLT.

Hagbush, -but(t, obs. ff. HACKBUSH, HACKBUT.

‖**Haggadah** (hăgā·dă). Also **Hagada(h, Agadah.** 1856. [Rabbinical Heb.; = 'tale', esp. 'edifying tale', f. bibl. Heb. *higgîḏ* declare, tell, expound something mysterious.] A legend, anecdote, parable, or the like, introduced in the Talmud to illustrate a point of the Law; hence, the legendary element of the Talmud, as dist. from the *Halachah.* Hence **Hagga·dic** *a.* of, pertaining to, or of the nature of H. **Hagga·dist**, a writer of H. **Haggadi·stic** *a.*

Haggard (hæ·găɹd), *sb.*[1] 1586. [repr. ON. *heygarðr*, f. *hey* hay and *garðr* GARTH.] In Ireland and Isle of Man: A stackyard.

Haggard (hæ·găɹd), *sb.*[2] 1567. [HAGGARD *a.* 1, used absol.] **1.** A wild (female) hawk caught when in her adult plumage. (With some, in 17–18th c. = peregrine falcon.) †**2.** *fig.* A wild and intractable person (at first, a female); one not to be captured –1680.

2. *Tam. Shr.* IV. ii. 39.

†**Haggard,** *sb.*[3] 1658. [f. HAG *sb.*[1] + -ARD.] A hag –1715.

Haggard (hæ·găɹd), *a.* 1567. [– (O)Fr. *hagard*, perh. f. Gmc. **haȝ-* hedge, bush (see HAG *sb.*[2], HAW *sb.*[1]); see -ARD. Later infl. in sense by HAG *sb.*[1] (cf. HAGGARD *sb.*[3]); cf. also HAGGED 2.] **1.** Of a hawk: Caught after having assumed the adult plumage; hence, wild, untamed. †**2.** *transf.* and *fig.* **a.** Wild, unreclaimed, untrained. **b.** 'Froward, contrarie, crosse, vnsociable' (Cotgr.) –1695. †**3.** In ragged plumage –1798. †**4.** Half-starved; gaunt, lean –1796. **5.** Of a person: Wild-looking; in early use applied esp. to the wild expression of the eyes, afterwards to the expression induced by privation, want of rest, anxiety, terror, or worry. Also *transf.* and *fig.* 1697. **b.** Gaunt or scraggy-looking, from the loss of flesh with age 1807.

1. In time all haggred Haukes will stoope the Lures T. WATSON. **4.** The gaunt hagard forms of famine and nakedness BURKE. **5.** Staring his eyes, and h. was his look DRYDEN. **b.** H. beyond the power of rouge CARLYLE. Hence **Ha·ggardly** *a.* and *adv.* **Ha·ggardness.**

Hagged (hægd, hæ·gĕd), *a.* Now *dial.* 1694. [f. HAG *v.*[2] 1; with sense 2 cf. HAGGARD *sb.*[3], and prec.] **1.** Bewitched; also, hag-like. ? *Obs.* 1700. **2.** Lean, gaunt; haggard; worn-out.

Haggis (hæ·gis). ME. [Of unkn. origin.] A dish consisting of the heart, lungs, and liver of a sheep, calf, etc. (or sometimes of the tripe and chitterlings), minced with suet and oatmeal, seasoned with salt, pepper, onions, etc., and boiled like a large sausage in the maw of the animal. (A popular English dish till 18th c., but now considered specially Scottish.)

Antinous a haggas brought, fill'd up With fat and blood CHAPMAN.

Haggish (hæ·giʃ), *a.* 1583. [f. HAG *sb.*[1] + -ISH[1].] Like, resembling, or of the nature of a hag. Hence **Ha·ggish-ly** *adv.*, **-ness.**

Haggle (hæ·g'l), *v.* 1583. [f. ON. **haggw-*, *hǫggva* (see HAG *v.*[1]) + -LE.] **1.** *trans.* To mangle with repeated irregular cuts; to cut clumsily; to hack, mangle, mutilate 1599; *intr.* to hack 1768. **2.** *intr.* To cavil, wrangle, dispute as to terms; *esp.* to make difficulties in settling a bargain 1602; *trans.* to harass with haggling 1648. **3.** *intr.* To advance with difficulty 1583.

1. Suffolke first dyed, and Yorke all hagled ouer Comes to him, where in gore he lay *Hen. V*, IV. vi. 11. **2.** There were two points on which he haggled SCOTT. Hence **Ha·ggle** *sb.* wrangling about terms. **Ha·ggler**, a bungler (now *dial.*); one who haggles in making a bargain; also, a huckster, a CADGER.

Hagio-, hagi, comb. ff. Gr. ἅγιος holy, saintly; as in **Ha·giarchy** [Gr. ἀρχή], the rule or order of saints; etc.

Hagiocracy (hægiǫ·krăsi). 1846. [f. HAGIO- + -CRACY.] A government or sovereignty of persons esteemed holy.

‖**Hagiographa** (hægi,ǫ·grăfă), *sb. pl.* 1583. [Late L. – Gr. ἁγιόγραφα; see HAGIO-, -GRAPH.] The Greek name (lit. 'sacred writings') of the last of the three divisions of the Hebrew scriptures (called in Heb. *kᵉṯûḇîm* writings) comprising all the books not included under 'the Law' and 'the Prophets'. (These are Psalms, Proverbs, Job; Canticles, Ruth, Lamentations, Ecclesiastes, Esther; Daniel, Ezra, Nehemiah, Chronicles.) Hence **Hagio·graphal** *a.* of or pertaining to the H.

Hagiographer (hægi,ǫ·grăfəɹ). 1656. [f. late L. *hagiographus* (Jerome) + -ER[1] 4; see -GRAPHER.] **1.** A sacred writer; *esp.* one of the writers of the Hagiographa. **2.** A writer of saints' lives; a hagiologist 1849. So **Hagiogra·phic, -al** *a.* of or pertaining to sacred writings or the sacred Scriptures; of or relating to the Hagiographa; pertaining to the writing of saints' lives. **Hagio·graphy,** the writing of the lives of saints; also = HAGIOGRAPHA.

Hagiolatry (hægi,ǫ·lătri). 1808. [f. HAGIO- + -LATRY.] The worship of saints.

Hagiology (hægi,ǫ·lŏdʒi). 1807. [f. HAGIO- + -LOGY.] The literature that treats of the lives and legends of saints; also, of great men or heroes; a work on the lives and legends of the saints. Hence **Hagiolo·gic, -al** *a.* **Hagio·logist,** a writer of h.; one versed in h.

Hagioscope (hæ·gioskōᵘp). Also **agioscope.** 1839. [f. HAGIO- + -SCOPE.] A small opening, cut through a chancel arch or wall, to enable worshippers in an aisle or side chapel to see the elevation of the host; a squint; also, a kind of chancel window. Hence **Hagiosco·pic** *a.*

Hag-ridden (hæ·g,rid'n), *ppl. a.* 1684. [f. HAG *sb.*[1] + RIDDEN *ppl. a.*] **1.** Ridden by a hag; *esp.* afflicted by nightmare. **2.** Oppressed in mind 1702. So **Ha·g-ride** *v.* to ride as a hag.

Hagseed: see HAG *sb.*[1]

Hagship (hæ·gʃip). 1604. [f. HAG *sb.*[1] + -SHIP.] The personality of a hag; used as a mock title.

Hag-taper (hæ·g,tēⁱpəɹ). 1548. [The first element is unexpl.; the second is TAPER *sb.*[1] Cf. G. *kerzenkraut* 'taperwort', Du. *tortsecruyt* 'torchwort'.] A plant, the Great Mullein (*Verbascum thapsus*).

Hah, var. of HA *interj.* and *vb.*

Ha ha (hā hā·), *interj.* and *sb.*[1] OE. [See HA, AHA.]

A. *interj.* The ordinary representation of laughter.

B. *sb.* A loud or open laugh 1806. Hence **Ha ha** *v.* to utter *ha ha* in laughter, to laugh aloud.

Ha-ha (hahā), *sb.*[2] Also **haw-haw.** 1712. [– Fr. *haha* (XVII), usu. taken to be so named from the expression of surprise at meeting the obstacle; redupl. of HA.] A boundary to a garden, pleasure-ground, or park, of such a kind as not to interrupt the view from within, and not to be seen till closely approached; a sunk fence. Also *attrib.*

Haidingerite (hai·diŋərəit). 1827. [f. von *Haidinger*, Austrian mineralogist + -ITE[1] 2 b.] *Min.* **1.** A hydrated arsenate of calcium, occurring in minute white crystals. †**2.** = BERTHIERITE –1868.

Haiduck, obs. f. HEYDUCK.

‖**Haik, haick** (haik, həik). Also †**hyke,** etc. 1713. [Moroccan Arab. *ḥā'ik.*] An oblong piece of cloth which Arabs wrap round the head and body, as an outer garment.

Hail (hēⁱl), *sb.*[1] [OE. *hagol, hæǧl*, corresp. to OFris. *heil*, OS., OHG. *hagal* (Du., G. *hagel*), ON. *hagl* :– Gmc. **haȝ(a)laz, -am*, rel. to Gr. κάχληξ pebble.] **1.** Ice (frozen raindrops) falling in pellets or masses in a shower from the atmosphere. (In spring and summer usu. accompanying a thunderstorm.) **2.** With *a* and *pl.* A shower or storm of hail. Now usu. only *transf.* or *fig.* **3.** *attrib.*, as *hail-shower* (OE. *hæǧlscūr*), *-storm.*

1. Down comes a deluge of sonorous h. THOMSON. **2.** *All's Well* V. iii. 33. *transf.* A perfect h. of round-shot assailed us 1893.

†**Hail,** *sb.*[2] Chiefly *north.* ME. [– ON. *heill* health, prosperity, good luck, rel. to OE. *hǣl*; see HEAL *sb.*] Health, safety, welfare –1549.

Phr. *To drink h.*, to drink wishing health, etc. to another.

Hail, *sb.*[3] 1500. [A later subst. use of HAIL *int.*, and noun of action f. HAIL *v.*[2]] **1.** An exclam. of 'hail'; a (respectful) salutation. **2.** The act of hailing some one; a shout of welcome; a call to attract attention 1811.

1. The Angel Haile Bestow'd, the holy salutation MILT. **2.** Phr. *Within h.*: within call; so *out of h.*, beyond call. Orig. *Naut.*

†**Hail,** *a.* [ME. *heil* – ON. *heill* hale, sound, whole = OE. *hāl*; see HALE, WHOLE, WASSAIL.] = HALE, WHOLE. Also *fig.* –1725.

Phr. *Hail be thou*, etc., an exclam. of well-wishing or reverence.

Hail (hēⁱl), *v.*[1] [f. HAIL *sb.*[1] Earlier ME. †*haweli* :– OE. *hagalian* = ON. *hagla.*] **1.** *intr.* **a.** In *it hails* = hail falls. **b.** with subject: To pour or send down hail ME. **2.** *trans.* To pour, throw, or send down with force like hail in a storm 1570.

2. He hail'd downe oathes that he was onely mine SHAKS.

Hail (hēⁱl), *v.*[2] ME. [An early deriv. of HAIL *sb.*[2] and *int.*, which has superseded HAILSE *v.*] **1.** *trans.* To salute with 'hail'; to salute, greet; to welcome. **2.** To call to (a ship, a person, etc.) from a distance, in order to attract attention. (Orig. and chiefly *Naut.*) 1563. **3.** *intr.* or *absol.* To call out in order to attract attention. (Formerly with *to*; now only *absol.*) 1582.

1. Such a Son as all Men hail'd me happy MILT. The restoration of the Stuarts had been hailed with delight MACAULAY. **2.** To h. a cab (*mod.*). **3.** Phr. *To h. from*: said of a vessel in reference to the port from which she has sailed; hence *transf.* of a person, to come from.

Hail (hēⁱl), *interj.* ME. [ellipt. use of HAIL *a.*, from phrases like *hail be thou* (XIII-XV), *wæs hail* (cf. WASSAIL), etc.] An exclam. of greeting or salutation; now *poet.* and *rhet.*, and usually implying respectful or reverential salutation; = L. *ave, salve.*

H. holy Light, ofspring of Heav'n first-born MILT. H. to thee, blithe spirit SHELLEY.

Hail-fellow. 1580. [The greeting 'Hail, fellow!' (now *obs.* or *arch.*), used variously.]

A. *adj.* On a most intimate footing; over familiar. So *Hail fellow well met.*

All's hail-fellow, here SCOTT.

B. *adv.* On most intimate terms 1670.

†**C.** *sb.* The state or footing of intimate friends –1687.

This Youth hail Fellow with me made COTTON.

Hail Mary, *phr.* and *sb.* ME. **1.** The angelic salutation (cf. Luke 1:28) = L. *Ave Maria.* **2.** As a devotional recitation = AVE MARY. ME.

†**Hailse,** *v.* ME. [– ON. *heilsa* to say hail (*to* a person); cf. HALSE *v.*[1]] *trans.* To greet, salute –1596.

†**Ha·il-shot.** 1485. [f. HAIL *sb.*[1] + SHOT *sb.*[1]] **1.** Small shot which scatters like hail. Also *fig.* –1830. **2.** The discharge of such shot. Also *fig.* –1696.

Hailstone (hēⁱ·lstōᵘn). [f. HAIL *sb.*[1] + STONE *sb.* OE. *hagolstān.*] A pellet of hail.

Hai·lstorm, hail-storm. 1697. [f. HAIL *sb.*[1] + STORM *sb.*] A violent fall or storm of hail. Also *fig.*

Haily (hēⁱ·li), *a.* 1552. [f. HAIL *sb.*[1] + -Y[1].] Consisting of or characterized by hail or hailstorms.

Hain (hēⁱn), *v.* Now *Sc.* and *dial.* ME. [– ON. *hegna* to hedge, fence, protect :– Gmc. **haȝ-* fence, hedge.] **1.** *trans.* To enclose or protect with a fence or hedge; *esp.* to preserve (grass) from cattle. **2.** To spare, save. *Sc.* 1508. Also *absol.* or *intr.*

1. The uplands are usually 'hayned' or laid up at Candlemas 1834.

Hain't, haint, vulgar contr. of *have not.*

Hair (hēᵊɹ), *sb.* [OE. *hǽr, hēr* = OFris. *hēr*, OS., OHG. *hār* (Du., G. *haar*), ON. *hár* :- Gmc. **χǣram*, of unkn. origin.] **1.** One of the filaments that grow from the skin or integument of animals, esp. of most mammals, of which they form the characteristic coat; applied also to similar-looking filamentous outgrowths from the body of insects and other invertebrates, although these are generally of different structure. **b.** *pl. Hairs* = collective sense 2. [Cf. L. *crines*, Fr. *les cheveux*, etc.] Now *obs.* or *arch.* as in *grey hairs.* OE. **2.** *collect.* The aggregate of hairs growing on the skin of an animal; also, hairs collectively, as used in manufactures, etc. OE. **b.** *fig.* 1594. **3.** In plants: An outgrowth of the epidermis, consisting of an elongated cell, or a row of cells, usually soft and flexible like the hair of animals. In *Bot.* sometimes extended to prickles, spore-capsules, etc.: = TRICHOME. **4.** *transf.* as in MAIDENHAIR, *Venus' hair*, etc. 1551. **b.** A spring mechanism which is freed by the HAIR-TRIGGER, q.v. 1864. **5.** A jot or tittle; an iota; the slightest thing; the least degree ME. †**6.** *Of one hair*: of one colour and external quality; hence = sort; stamp, character –1625. **7.** A haircloth 1485. **8.** *attrib.*, as *h.-cell*, etc. 1565.

1. A sword..hanging by a haire over his head 1581. **b.** He rends his hairs in sacrifice to Jove POPE. **2.** My h. is grey, but not with years BYRON. *fig.* Like a Comet..That..from his horrid h. Shakes Pestilence and Warr MILT. **6.** Two notable knaues, both of a haire GREENE.

Phr. *Against the h.*: contrary to the direction in which an animal's h. naturally lies; against the grain, inclination, or sentiment. *To a h.*: to a nicety, with complete exactness. *A h. of the dog that bit you, of the same dog* (or *wolf*): see DOG *sb.* *To split hairs*: to make cavilling distinctions. *To keep one's h. on* (slang): to keep cool. *To put up her hair*: said of a girl when she passes into womanhood. *Not to turn a h.*: *lit.* of a horse, not to show sweat by the roughening of his hair; *fig.* not to show any sign of being ruffled, or affected by exertion.

Comb.: **h.-ball,** one of the masses of hair of different shapes and sizes found in the stomachs of cows, deer, etc.; **-bracket,** the moulding at the back of a ship's figure-head; **-compasses,** compasses which can be regulated to the breadth of a h.; **-drawn** *a.*, drawn out as fine as a hair; **-eel,** a kind of filiform worm inhabiting stagnant water; **-follicle,** the cylindrical depression in the skin from which a h. grows, extending through the corium to the subcutaneous connective tissue; **-hygrometer,** a hygrometer depending upon the expansion of hair when exposed to damp; **-kiln,** a hop-kiln covered with a haircloth on which the hops are spread out to dry; **-lead,** a very thin lead used for spacing in printing; **-lichen,** an eruption attacking the roots of the hair; **-mole** (†**-mold**), a mole on the skin having a h. or hairs on it; **-moss,** a moss of the genus *Polytrichum*; **-pencil,** a painter's brush made of camel's hair or the like; **-plate,** the plate at the back of a bloomery; **-pyrites** = MILLERITE; **-sac** = *hair-follicle*; **-salt** [Ger. *haarsalz*], alunogen; **-seal,** an eared seal of the family *Otariidæ*, sub-family *Tricophocinæ*; **-space,** a very thin space used in printing; **-spring,** the fine hair-like spring in a watch which regulates the movement of the balance-wheel; **-stone** [Ger. *haarstein*] = SAGENITE; †**-tail,** a name of fishes of the family *Trichiuridæ*; **-tail worm** = *hair-eel*; **-trunk,** a trunk covered with skin retaining the h.; †**-weed,** a conferva.

Hair, *v.* 1802. [f. prec.] **1.** *trans.* To free from hair; to depilate. **2.** *intr.* 'To produce or grow hair' (*Cent. Dict.*).

Hairbell, -brain, etc.: see HARE-.

Hairbreadth (hēᵊ·ɹbredþ). 1561. **1.** The breadth or diameter of a hair; an infinitesimally small space or distance. **2.** *attrib.* or as *adj.*: Very narrow or close, as *h. difference, escape*; hence, *h. adventure* 1604.

2. Haire-breadth scapes i' th' imminent deadly breach SHAKS.

Hairbrush (hēᵊ·ɹbrɒʃ). 1599. A toilet-brush for the hair.

Haircloth (hēᵊ·ɹklǫþ). 1500. [See HAIRE.] **1.** Cloth or fabric made of hair, used for tents, towels, shirts of penitents or ascetics; also in drying malt, hops, etc. Also *attrib.* **2.** An article made of this fabric 1548.

Hai·rdresser. 1771. One whose business is to dress and cut the hair. So **Hairdressing,** the business of a h.

†**Haire.** [Two types: 1. ME. *hēre, heare, heere, heer*; 2. ME. *haire*, through OFr. *haire*; both :- Frankish **hārja* = OHG. *hār(r)a*. The form from French, which survived longest, is now merged in HAIR *sb.* (sense 7).] Cloth made of hair, haircloth; *esp.* a hair shirt worn by penitents and ascetics; extended later to sackcloth or the like –1601.

Haired (hēᵊɹd), *a.* ME. [f. HAIR *sb.* + -ED².] Having hair. Often with adj. prefixed, as *black-haired*, etc.

He that hath not his Browes heyred is not seemely 1548.

Hai·ren, *a. Obs.* exc. *dial.* [OE. *hǽren*, **hēren* = OHG. *hārin*; see HAIR, -EN⁴.] Made or consisting of hair; hair-.

More..afflictive than his h. shirt JER. TAYLOR.

Hai·r-grass. 1759. [After L. generic name *Aira*, with reference to the slender hair-like branches.] A name for grasses of the Linnæan genus *Aira*.

Hairiness (hēᵊ·rinės). ME. [f. HAIRY + -NESS.] The quality or state of being hairy; hirsuteness.

†**Hair-lace.** ME. [f. HAIR *sb.* + LACE.] A string or tie for binding the hair; a fillet; also, a fillet in *Archit.* –1738.

Hai·rless, *a.* 1552. [f. HAIR *sb.* + -LESS.] Destitute of hair.

Hai·r-line. 1731. **1.** A rope or line made of hair. **2.** A very thin line, as the up-stroke of a written letter 1846. **3.** *Printing. Hair-line letter*: A very thin-faced type, generally used for lettering of mounts 1888.

Hair-lip, erron. f. HARE-LIP.

Hai·rpin, hai·r-pin. 1818. A kind of pin used in dressing and fastening up the hair, etc. **b.** In full *hairpin bend*: A sharp bend in a road likened to a hairpin in form 1923.

Hair-powder. 1663. A scented powder for the hair; now chiefly used by men-servants.

Hair's-breadth, hair's breadth (hēᵊ·ɹzbredþ). 1584. = HAIRBREADTH. Also *attrib.* or as *adj.* **b.** *Bot.* The twelfth part of a line. LINDLEY.

Hair-shirt. 1737. A shirt made of haircloth, worn by ascetics and penitents. (Cf. HAIRE.)

Hair-sieve (hēᵊ·ɹ,si·v). ME. A sieve with the bottom made of hair finely woven; usu. for straining liquid.

Hai·r-splitter. 1849. One who 'splits hairs', or makes minute or cavilling distinctions. So **Hai·r-splitting** *vbl. sb.* the splitting of hairs; *ppl. a.* that splits hairs.

Hai·r-streak. 1816. In full, *hair-streak butterfly*: A butterfly of the genus *Thecla*; so called from the markings on the wings of some species.

Hai·r-stroke. 1634. **1.** A very fine line made in writing or drawing; *esp.* a fine up-stroke in penmanship. **2.** *Printing.* A CERIPH. 1875.

Hai·r-trigger. 1830. A secondary trigger in a firearm, which acts by setting free a spring mechanism called the *hair*, and, being delicately adjusted, releases the main trigger by very slight pressure. Also *attrib.* Hence **Hai·r-triggered** *a.* having a hair-trigger.

Hair-worm (hēᵊ·ɹwɒɹm). 1658. A nematode worm of the genus *Gordius*; spec. *G. aquaticus*. (Sometimes applied to the Guinea-worm, *Dracunculus medinensis*.)

Hairy (hēᵊ·ri), *a.* ME. [f. HAIR *sb.* + -Y¹.] **1.** Having much hair; hirsute. Also *transf.* **2.** Consisting of hair; hair-like (now *rare*); made of hair 1535. **3.** *Bot.* Covered with short weak thin pubescence 1597.

1. Esau my brother is an heeri man WYCLIF *Gen.* 27:11. *transf.* Comets or hairie starres HOLLAND. **2.** The h. gown and mossy cell MILT. *Comb.*: **h.-back,** a fish of the family *Trichonotidæ*; **h.-crown, -head,** species of Merganser.

Hait, heit (hēⁱt), *interj.* ME. [Cf. G. *hott* go right!] A word of encouragement or command given to horses to urge them forward.

Hake (hēⁱk), *sb.*¹ ME. [perh. for **hakefish*, f. (dial.) *hake* hook (– ON. *haki*; see HOOK); cf. Norw. *hakefisk* applied to fishes having a hooked under-jaw, and OE. *hacod* pike.] A gadoid fish, *Merlucius vulgaris*, resembling the cod. Applied also to the genus *Merlucius*, and to other gadoid fish, esp. to species of the genus *Phycis* found on the coast of N. America, and to the New Zealand *Lotella rhacinus*. Also *attrib.*

Hake, haik, *sb.*² 1768. [poss. f. the base *hak-* of HATCH *sb.*¹ and HECK, if not merely a dial. var. of the latter; cf. HACK *sb.*²] **1.** A wooden frame suspended from the roof for drying cheeses, etc.; a wooden frame for holding plates. *Sc.* **2.** = HACK *sb.*² 3. 1840. **3.** = HECK. 1863.

†**Hake,** *sb.*³ Also **hack(e, hag(g, haque.** 1538. [app. an abbrev. of *haquebut, hagbut.*] A short 16th c. fire-arm –1656.

Hake, haik (hēⁱk), *v. Sc.* and *n. dial.* 1450. [Cf. Du. *haken* to long, to hanker.] **1.** *intr.* 'To go about idly from place to place'. **2.** To go, advance; 'to tramp, trudge, or wend one's way' (Jam.) 1450. **3.** *trans.* To urge, to pester 1855.

‖**Hakeem, hakim** (hăkī·m). *Oriental.* 1638. [Arab. *ḥakīm* wise, learned, philosopher, physician.] A physician or doctor, in Moslem countries and in India.

‖**Hakim** (hā·kim). *Oriental.* 1615. [Arab. *ḥākim* governor.] A judge, ruler, or governor in Moslem countries and in India.

‖**Halachah, halakah** (hălā·kă). 1856. [Aramaic *hᵉlāḵāh* law.] A legal decision regarding a matter or case for which there is no direct enactment in the Mosaic law, deduced by analogy, and included as a binding precept in the Mishna. Hence **Hala·chist,** one who deduces laws from the Bible.

‖**Hala·lcor.** *E. Indies.* Also †**halichore.** 1662. [Hind. *ḥalāl-ḵōr*, f. Arab. and Pers.] One of the lowest and vilest class in India, etc., to whom everything is lawful food.

He is wholly driven from all honest society..He becomes an Halichore BURKE.

Halation (hălēⁱ·ʃən). 1859. [irreg. f. HALO + -ATION.] *Photogr.* The term for the spreading of light beyond its proper boundary in the negative image upon the plate, producing local fog around the high lights, etc.

Halberd, halbert (hæ·lbəɹd, -əɹt), *sb.* 1495. [– Fr. *hallebarde*, †*alabarde* – It. *alabarda* – MHG. *helmbarde* (G. *hellebarde*), f. *helm* handle, HELM *sb.*² + *barde, barte* hatchet, rel. to *bart* beard (cf. ON. *skeggja* halberd, lit. 'the bearded', f. *skegg* beard).] **1.** A military weapon; a kind of combination of spear and battle-axe, consisting of a sharp-edged blade ending in a point, and a spear-head, mounted on a handle five to seven feet long. †**2.** *transf.* A soldier armed with a halbert –1603.

Comb.: **halberd-headed, -shaped,** *adjs. Bot.* (of leaves) shaped like the axe of a halberd; **-weed,** the W. Indian shrub *Neurolæna lobata.*

Halberdier (hælbəɹdīᵊ·ɹ). 1548. [– Fr. *hallebardier*; see prec., -IER.] A soldier armed with a halberd; *spec.* a member of certain civic guards carrying a halberd as a badge of office. So **Ha·lberdman.**

Halcyon (hæ·lsiən, hæ·lʃiən). ME. [– L. *halcyon, alcyon* – Gr. ἀλκυών kingfisher (ἁλκυών by assoc. with ἅλς sea and κύων conceiving), rel. to L. *alcedo.*]

A. *sb.* **1.** A bird anciently fabled to breed about the time of the winter solstice in a nest floating on the sea, and to charm the wind and waves so that the sea was then specially calm; usu. identified with a species of kingfisher, hence a poetic name of this bird. Also *fig.* **b.** In *Zool.* a kingfisher of the Australasian genus *Halcyon*, or of the sub-family *Halcyoninæ* 1772. †**2.** Calm, quietude, halcyon days –1797.

1. There came the h., whom the sea obeys, When she her nest upon the water lays SHENSTONE. var. †**Ha·lcydon.**

B. *attrib.* or *adj.* **1.** Of, or pertaining to, the halcyon or kingfisher 1601. **2.** Calm, quiet, peaceful, undisturbed. (Usu. qualifying *days.*) 1578.

1. Phr. *Halcyon days* [Gr. ἀλκυονίδες ἡμέραι L. *alcyonei dies, alcyonides, alcedonia*]: fourteen days of calm weather, anciently believed to occur about the winter solstice when the h. was brooding.

Hence †**Halcyo·nian** *a.* = B.

Halcyonic, -ite, -oid, vars. of ALCYONIC, etc.

Ha·lcyonine, *a.* [See HALCYON, -INE[1].] *Ornith.* Of or pertaining to the sub-family of kingfishers (*Halcyoninæ*) of which the genus *Halcyon* is the type.

†**Hale,** *sb.*[1] ME. [A parallel form to HEAL *sb.*, ME. *hele*, and HAIL *sb.*[2], conformed in vowel to the adj., OE. *hāl.*] = HAIL *sb.*[2], HEAL *sb.* –1795.

†**Hale,** *sb.*[2] ME. [– (O)Fr. *halle* covered market-place – Frankish *halla = OS. *halla*, OE. *heall*; see HALL.] A place roofed over, but usually open at the sides; a pavilion; a tent; a booth, etc. –1606.

Hale (hēⁱl), *sb.*[3] Now *rare* or *Obs.* 1470. [f. HALE *v.*[1] See also HAUL *sb.*] In *hoise and h., h. and how*, exclams. of sailors in hauling; also, the act of haling or hauling.

Hale (hēⁱl), *a.* (*adv.*) [The n. dial. repr. of OE. *hāl*, which became in s. and midl. dial. *hōl, hool, hole*, WHOLE.]
I. 1. Free from injury; safe, sound. Now only *Sc.* and *n. dial.* **2.** Free from disease, well; 'whole'. Now *Sc.* and *n. dial.* OE. **3.** Free from infirmity; sound, vigorous. (The current literary sense; usu. of old persons.) 1734.
3. Finding my old friend..so h. at 83–4 JARVIS.
II. = WHOLE, in its current senses ME.

Hale (hēⁱl), *v.*[1] ME. [– (O)Fr. *haler* – ON. *hala* = OS. *halon*, OHG. *halōn, holōn* (Du. *halen*, G. *holen* fetch); cf. OE. *ġeholian* acquire.] **1.** *trans.* To draw or pull. †**a.** = DRAW *v.* in various senses –1842. **b.** Now repl. by HAUL. ME. **2.** *fig.* ME. †**b.** To harry, molest –1641. **3.** *absol.* or *intr.* To pull, tug ME. †**4.** *intr.* To move along as if drawn or pulled; to move with force; *spec.* of a ship, to proceed before the wind with sails set, to sail. Also *fig.* –1727. **b.** To flow, run down in a stream. *Obs.* exc. *Sc.* and *n. dial.* (Later, written *hail.*) ME.
1. a. The rope that haled the buckets from the well TENNYSON. **b.** As one hal'd to execution JER. TAYLOR. **2.** Texts..haled to their purposes by force of wit HOBBES. **b.** To let them still h. and worrey us with their band-dogs MILT.

†**Hale,** *v.*[2] ME. [Either f. HALE *a.*, or a var. of HEAL *v.*[1] assim. to HALE *a.*] *trans.* To make hale or whole; to heal –1530.

‖**Halesia** (hēⁱlĭ·siă). 1760. [f. Stephen *Hales*, an English botanist (1677–1761) + -IA[1].] *Bot.* A genus of plants (N.O. *Styraceæ*), containing the Snowdrop or Silver-bell tree of southern U.S., *Halesia tetraptera*, and other species.

Half (hăf), *sb.* Pl. **halves** (hăvz); †**halfs.** [OE. *healf* fem. = OFris. *halve*, OS. *halba*, OHG. *halba*, ON. *hálfa*, Goth. *halba* side, half. The oldest sense in all the languages is 'side'.]
I. †**1.** Side; one of the (two) sides; the right or left side (of any one); the direction indicated by the side or hand –1532. †**2.** *fig.* One of the opposite sides in a conflict, sexes in descent, etc. –1563. †**b.** Side, part (as of one of the parties to a transaction) –1526.
1. On this halfe the fest of Ester 1495. **2.** He was, in hys moder alf, Seynt Edwardes broþer R. GLOUC. **b.** It shal not lakke, certeyn, on myn halve CHAUCER. Phr. †*On God's h.*: in God's name, for God's sake.
II. 1. One of two opposite, corresponding, or equal parts into which a thing is or may be divided OE. **2.** More vaguely: One of two (†or more) divisions more or less approaching equality; esp. with comparatives ME. †**3.** One of two partners or co-sharers –1596. **4.** In various ellipt. uses of HALF *a.*, some sb. being omitted (*colloq.*). See quots. 1659.
1. The two Sides, or Halves of the Float 1717. One-half or three-fourths of an inch thick SCORESBY. Phr. *One and a h.* (see HALF *a.*). **2.** Swear..it broke into three halves SWIFT. Phr. *Better half*, a wife (or †husband). **3.** *Tam. Shr.* v. ii. 78. Phr. *To go halves.* **4. a.** = Half-year, or -term. It..has..stopped the boats for this h. 1820. **b.** = Half-boot; There's two pair of halves in the commercial DICKENS. **c.** = Half-pint, half-gill of spirits; Two halves of ale and a cigar 1891. **d.** = Half-back (at Football). **e.** = Half-mile (race); etc.
Phrases. *To (the) halves* (now *U.S.*) = so as to have a half-share in the profits (in letting or hiring a house, a piece of land, etc.). *By halves*: to the extent of a h. only; half-heartedly; imperfectly. *By h.*: by a great deal. *To go halves* (cf. II. 3): to share equally (with a person). *To cry halves*: to claim a half-share in what is found by another.
Comb. **a.** *attrib.*, as *h.-share.* **b.** quasi-*adv.*, as *h.-partner*, etc.

Half (hăf), *a.* [OE. *half* (*healf*) = OFris., OS. (Du.) *half*, (O)HG. *halb*, ON. *hálfr*, Goth. *halbs* :– Gmc. *xalbaz.] **1.** Forming a half or moiety (see quots.). **2.** Half the length (or breadth) of. Now *rare* or *Obs.* 1481. **3.** As a measure of degree: Attaining only half-way to completeness; partial, imperfect. (In this use now usu. hyphened: see HALF-.) ME.
1. A h. length, share (*mod.*). *H. the length* (in mod. use occas. viewed as a *sb.* with *of* suppressed). The..wind blew h. a gale BYRON. *H. a crown* (= the equivalent of *a half-crown*, e.g. five sixpences; see HALF-). **2.** Within h. Pistol shot 1681. **3.** A h. toleration, known by the name of the Indulgence MACAULAY.
Phr. †OE. *þridda healf*, †ME. *thridde half* or *half thrid* = two and a half, i.e. a half-unit less than the corresponding cardinal number. Cf. G. *dritte halb*, etc.

Half, *v.* Obs. and dial. f. HALVE *v.* (q.v.); also *mod. colloq.* in sense To 'be half', go halves.

Half (hăf), *adv.* [OE. *half, healf*, in composition; written separate or hyphened, with no difference of sense; see HALF- I.] **1.** To the extent of half. Hence loosely: In part, partially; in some degree. **2.** Used correlatively: *Half..half..* OE. **3.** Idiomatic uses, in which *half* may have been orig. the adj. or sb. (see quots.) 1726.
1. She ran..Like one h. mad 1600. In her halfe ruin'd cell 1615. The lily was not h. so fair ADDISON. **2.** He was h. man and h. beste GOWER. **3.** *Half past* (or *after*) *one* or *one o'clock*, etc. = half an hour past the time named. *Half* (Naut.) = half a point (i.e. $5\frac{5}{8}$°) from the first towards the second of two points (of the compass) mentioned. *Half four* (in soundings) = $4\frac{1}{2}$ fathoms.
Phr. *Not half*: a long way from the due amount; in mod. *slang* and *colloq.* use = not at all, as 'not half bad'.

Half- in *comb.* [OE. *half-, healf-* was regularly combined with an adj. or pple., or with a sb. In OTeut. *halb-* was app. a later substitute for the original *sāmi-*, OE. *sam-*, = L. *semi-*, Gr. ἡμι-, Skr. *sāmi-*, etc.]
I. In advb. relation. **1.** With adjs. and pa. pples. The two elements are often written separately when the adj. is in the predicate; when it is attributive the hyphen is regularly used as implying a feeling of closer unity of notion in the compound attribute, as in *h.-thought-out recollections* OE. **2.** With advs., as *h-angrily, -questioningly*, etc. 1700. **3.** With vbs., as *h.-murder*, etc. 1674.
Comb.: **h.-equitant** *a. Bot.* = OBVOLUTE; **-imperial** *a.*, half imperial-folio size; **-large** *a.*, (a card) 3 × $2\frac{1}{4}$ inches (Jacobi *Printer's Vocab.*); **-saved** *a.*, half-witted (*dial.*).
II. In attrib. relation to a sb. The number of these has latterly become enormous, esp. through the practice of hyphening an adj. and sb. when these have a special or individualized application.
a. In names of *Coins, Weights, Measures, h.-barrel, -farthing, -florin, -inch*, etc. Also HALF-CROWN, -DOLLAR, -HOUR, -MINUTE, etc. **b.** In *Her.* = DEMI- B 1, as *h.-belt*, etc. **c.** In *Artillery*, etc., *h.-cannon, -lance*, etc. (cf. DEMI-). Also HALF-PIKE, -SWORD, etc. **d.** In Mil., *h. -squadron, -turn, -wheel*, etc.; **h.-battery** = three subdivisions; **-company,** same as subdivision; **-distance,** the regular interval or space between troops drawn up in ranks, or standing in column; **-file,** half the given number of any body of men drawn up two deep. Also HALF-FACE, etc. **e.** In *Fortif.*, **h.-bastion, -caponier, -sap** (see DEMI-BASTION, etc.); **h.-merlon,** that solid portion of a parapet which is at the right or left extremity of a battery. Also HALF-MOON. **f.** *Naut.* and *Shipbuilding*: **h.-beam,** a short beam introduced to support the deck where there is no framing; **-breadth staff,** a rod having marked upon it half the length of each beam in the ship; †**-wind,** a side-wind. **g.** In *Mus.*, **h.-cadence, -close,** an imperfect cadence; **-demisemiquaver; -rest** (*U.S.*), a minim rest; **-shift,** a position of the hand in violin playing; it lies between the open position and the first shift. Cf. DEMI-. Also HALF-NOTE, -TONE. **h.** Applied to a stuff which is half of inferior material, as *h.-silk, -yarn*, etc. **i.** In *Games*, **h.-back** (*Football*), a position immediately behind the 'forwards'; a player in this position; **-ball** (*Billiards*), a contact in which the half of one ball is covered by half of the other; **-hit** (*Cricket*), a mistimed hit that sends the ball into the air; **-volley** (*Cricket, Football*, etc.), a ball which pitches so that it can be hit or kicked as soon as it rises from the ground. Also *half-bowl*, etc. **j.** In *Bookbinding*, 'half' signifies that only the back and corners of the binding are of the materials specified; e.g. *h.-calf*, etc. **k.** In various connections; as *h.-door, -honesty, -knowledge, -quotation, -reasoning, -whisper*, etc.
Special combs.: **h.-arm,** half arm's length; **-barrel** *a.*, semicylindrical (vaulting); **-bend,** a half fillet for the head; **-bent,** (*a*) the condition of being half-bent; (*b*) the catch by which the hammer of a gun is placed at half-cock; **-boarder,** one who has half his board, a day-boarder; **-box,** a box open at one side; **-chronometer,** *orig.*, a watch having an escapement compounded of the lever and chronometer; *now*, a fine lever watch which has been adjusted for temperature; **-column,** a column or pilaster half projecting from a flat surface; **-communion,** communion in one kind, as practised in the R.C. Ch.; †**-compass,** hemisphere; **-course** (*Mining*), half on the level and half on the dip; **-dike,** a sunk fence; **-hatchet,** 'a hatchet with one straight line, all the projection of the bit being on the side towards the hand' (Knight); **-header,** a half-brick used to close the work at the end of a course; **-house,** a shed open at the side; **-margin,** applied to paper folded in the centre, lengthways; **-plate,** a watch in which the top pivot of the fourth wheel pinion is carried in a cock so as to allow the use of a larger balance; **-plate paper,** machine-made paper of fine and soft quality used for woodcuts; **-press,** the work done by one man at a printing-press; **-principal** (*Carpentry*), 'a rafter which does not extend to the crown of the roof' (Knight); **-relief** = *demi-relief* (see DEMI-); **-royal,** a kind of millboard or pasteboard; **-shade** (*Painting*), a shade of half the extreme depth; **-sheet** (*Printing*), the off-cut portion of a duodecimo (Knight); **-space** = HALF-PACE 2; **-stitch,** a loose open stitch in braid work or pillow-lace making (Caulfield); **-storey,** an upper storey half the height of which is in the walls and half in the roof; **-stuff** (*Paper-making*), partly prepared pulp; **-swing plough,** a plough in which the mould-board is a fixture; **-text,** a size of hand-writing half the size of 'text' or large hand; **-throw, -travel,** half the full movement of a piston, valve, etc.; **-tint,** in a monochrome, all gradations between white and black; **-title,** the short title of a book; **-tongue** (*Law*), a jury of which one half were foreigners, formerly allowed to a foreigner tried on a criminal charge; **-trap,** a semicircular depression in a sewer pipe; **-uncial** = SEMI-UNCIAL; **-water** = HALF-TIDE; **h. wave,** one-half of a complete wave of electricity, light, or sound; chiefly *attrib.*; **h.-world,** hemisphere; the demi-monde.

Halfa (hæ·lfă). Also **alfa, alpha, halfeh,** etc. 1857. [– Arab. *ḥalfā', ḥalfa.*] The N. African name of Esparto (*Stipa tenacissima*) used in paper-making, etc.

Half-and-half, *phrase.* 1715. **1.** A mixture of ale and porter, or the like 1756. **2.** Something that is half one thing and half another, or half this and half that 1814. Also *attrib.* or *adj.* **3.** as *adv.* In two equal parts; half..and half not 1818. **4.** Half-intoxicated 1715.

Ha·lf-ape. 1883. A lemur.

Half-baked (hā·f,bēⁱkt), *a.* 1621. **1.** *lit.* See HALF *adv.* and BAKE *v.*; hence, underdone, not earnest; raw; incomplete, rude. **2.** Silly, half-witted (*dial.*) 1855.

Ha·lf-bapti·ze, *v.* 1836. To baptize privately or without full rites, as a child in danger of death.

Ha·lf-beak. 1880. A fish of the genus *Hemirhamphus*, having the lower jaw long and ensiform, and the upper short.

Ha·lf-bi:nding. 1864. [Cf. HALF-BOUND.] A style of binding of books in which the back and corners are of leather, the sides being of cloth or paper.

Ha·lf-blood. 1553. **1.** The relation between persons having only one parent in common. **2.** A person or group of persons related in this way 1848. **3.** A half-breed 1826.
1. What, is a brother by the half bloud no kinne FULLER. Hence **Half-blooded** *a.* born of different races.

Ha·lf-boot. 1787. [HALF- II.] A boot reaching half-way to the knee, or well above the ankle.

Ha·lf-bound, *ppl. a.* 1775. Of a book: Having a leather back and corners, with cloth or paper sides; cf. HALF-BINDING.

Ha·lf-bred, *a.* (*sb.*) 1701. [See BREED *v.*, BRED *ppl. a.*] **1.** Of mixed breed; mongrel. Also *fig.* †**2.** Imperfectly acquainted with the rules of good-breeding; under-bred. ATTERBURY. **3.** *sb.* A half-bred horse, pigeon, etc. 1856.

Half-breed (hā·fˌbrīd). 1791. [See BREED *sb.*, and cf. HALF-CASTE.] **1.** One who is sprung from parents of two races; esp. in U.S., the offspring of whites or Negroes and American Indians. **2.** *attrib.*, as *half-breed boys* 1837.

Half-brother. ME. [prob. – ON. *hálfbróðir.*] A brother by one parent only.

Ha·lf-cap. 1607. [See CAP *v.*¹ sense 5.] A half-courteous salute, shown by a slight movement only of the cap.

With certaine halfe-caps, and cold mouing nods, They froze me into Silence SHAKS.

Half-caste. Also **half-cast.** 1789. †**1.** A mixed caste; a race sprung from the union of two castes or races. WELLESLEY. **2.** A half-breed; *esp.*, in India, one born or descended from a European father and native mother 1789. **3.** *attrib.* (from 1), as, a *half-caste merchant* 1793.

Half-cheek. 1588. †**1.** A face in profile. **2.** *Naut.*: see CHEEK *sb.* II. 5. 1860.

1. S. Georges halfe-cheeke in a brooch SHAKS.

Half-cock, *sb.* 1701. [See COCK *sb.*¹ III. 2.] †**1.** Part of a watch; cf. COCK *sb.*¹ **2.** Of a fire-arm: The position of the cock or hammer when raised only half-way and held by the catch, from which it cannot be moved by pulling the trigger 1745. Hence *To go off* (*at*) *half-cock*, to go off prematurely, to speak or act without due forethought or preparation, and thereby to fail. So **Half-cock** *v. trans.* to put (a gun) at half-cock.

Half-cousin. 1871. The child of one's father's or mother's cousin; a second cousin. Occas. applied to the child of one's own cousin, or to the cousin of one's father or mother.

Half-crown. 1542. A coin of Great Britain, of the value of two shillings and sixpence; sometimes used for **Half a crown,** the equivalent sum.

Half-dead, *a.* OE. [See HALF *adv.*] In a state in which death seems as likely as recovery.

Ha·lf-deck. 1626. [See DECK *sb.*] **1.** *lit.* A deck covering half the length of a ship or boat, fore and aft. *spec.* **a.** In old ships of war: A deck extending from the mainmast aftward, situated between the then smaller 'quarter-deck' and the upper or main deck. These two were later reduced to one, and called 'quarter-deck'. †**b.** In colliers: A deck under the main deck, containing berths, etc. for the crew. **c.** In merchantmen: Accommodation for cadets and apprentices. 1626. **2.** *U.S. local.* The Slipper-limpet, *Crepidula fornicata*, which has an under half-shell (*Cent. Dict.*). Hence **Ha·lf-decked** *a.* that is about half covered in or decked. **Half-de·cker,** a half-decked boat.

Half-dime. 1796. A U.S. coin, value 5 cents, orig. of silver, but now of copper and nickel; pop. called a *nickel*.

Ha:lf-do·llar. 1786. A silver coin of the U.S. and other countries, equal to 50 cents.

Half-dozen, half a dozen. ME. The half of a dozen; six (or about six). See DOZEN.

Half-eagle. 1824. A gold coin of the U.S., value 5 dollars.

Half-ebb. ME. The state or time of the tide when its reflux is half completed.

†**Halfen,** *a.* [pseudo-arch., perh. taken from next.] Half. SPENSER.

Ha·lfendeal, ha·lven-. *Obs.* exc. *dial.* [OE. *þone healfan dǣl*, accus. case of *se healfa dǣl*, the half part, mechanically retained after the sense of inflexion was lost.]

A. *sb.* 'Half part'; a half, a moiety.

†**B.** *adj.* Half –ME.

†**C.** *adv*, Half, by half –1590.

Halfer: see HALVER.

Half-face, *sb.* 1542. **1.** Half of a face; a profile. Also *attrib.* **2.** *Mil.* The action or position of facing half-way to the right or left, i.e. at an angle of 45 degrees 1833. So **Half-face** *v.* (*Mil.*), *intr.* to make a half-face.

Ha·lf-faced, *a.* 1592. [f. prec. sb. + -ED².] **1.** Presenting a half-face or profile. Of a coin: Having a profile stamped upon it; hence, of persons, having a thin, pinched face 1595. So *half-faced groat*, applied contemptuously to a thin-faced man (*John* I. i. 94). **2.** With only half of the face visible 1593. **3.** Half-and-half, incomplete 1592.

Ha·lf-fish. 1677. A half-grown salmon, usually about twenty or twenty-two inches.

Half-flood. ME. The state or time of the flowing tide half-way between low and high water.

Ha:lf-gui·nea. 1696. An English gold coin worth (in 19th c.) 10*s.* 6*d.*, coined from Charles II to 1813.

Ha·lf-headed, *a.* 1621. Half-intelligent; stupid.

Ha·lf-hearted, *a.* 1611. Not having one's whole heart in a matter; wanting in courage, earnestness, or zeal. †**b.** Illiberal, ungenerous, unkind (Webster, citing Ben Jonson) 1864. Hence **Half-hea·rted-ly** *adv.*, **-ness.**

Half-hitch. 1769. [See HITCH *sb.*] *Naut.* A hitch formed by passing the end of a rope round its standing part, and then through the bight; the simplest form of hitch.

Half-ho·liday. Also †**-holyday.** 1552. †**1.** A day which is considered only half a holy day; a saint's day or holy day other than Sunday –1631. **2.** †**a.** The half of a holy day (used for recreation). **b.** The (latter) half of a working day, given up to recreation. **c.** A day of which the latter half is taken as a holiday. 1631.

†**Ha·lf-horse.** 1588. A centaur –1621.

Half-hour. ME. The half of an hour; thirty minutes. Also **b. Half an hour** (not used with a defining word) ME. Hence **Half-hou·rly** *adj.* occurring every half-hour; lasting half an hour; *adv.* every half-hour.

Half-impe·rial, *sb.* 1839. **1.** A gold coin of Russia valued orig. at 5 and later at 7½ silver roubles. **2.** A size of mill-board 1858.

Half-island, half-isle. *Obs.* or *arch.* 1600. A peninsula.

Ha·lf-length. 1699. A portrait of half the full length. Also *attrib.* or *adj.*

Half-light. 1625. A light of half the full intensity; a dim, imperfect light. Also *fig.* *At half lights*: vaguely, dimly.

Half-mast. 1627. The half of a mast, half the height of a mast; in *at half-mast, half-mast* (*high*); said esp. of the position of a flag lowered to half the height of the staff as a mark of respect for the dead. Hence **Half-mast** *v. trans.* to hang half-mast high.

Half-measure. 1798. [See HALF *a.*] A measure, plan, effort, etc., wanting in thoroughness or energy; procedure marked by compromise.

Half-minute. 1684. [See HALF *a.*] The half of a minute; thirty seconds; also **Half a minute. b.** *attrib.* and *Comb.*, as *half-minute gun*; **half-minute glass** (*Naut.*), a sand-glass which marks the time for the running out of the log-line.

Half-moon, *sb.* 1530. **1.** The moon, when only half its disc appears illuminated; *loosely*, a crescent. Also *transf.* of things in the shape of a half-moon or crescent. **2.** *Fortif.* = DEMILUNE 2. 1642. †**3.** A cuckold (in allusion to his horns). SHIRLEY. **4.** *Mining.* Scaffolding filling up one half the sectional area of a *pit-shaft*, on which repairs are done (Gresley). **5.** *attrib.* Shaped like a half-moon, as *half-moon battery*, etc.; **half-moon knife,** a double-handed knife used by the dresser of skins for parchment (Knight).

1. *transf.* And cuts me from the best of all my Land, A huge halfe-Moone, a monstrous Cantle out SHAKS. Hence **Half-moon** *v. trans.* to surround like a half-moon; *intr.* to move in a half-moon formation.

Half-mou·rning. 1820. **1.** The second stage or period of mourning, after full mourning. **b.** Attire in which black is relieved or replaced by white, or by such colours as grey, lavender, or purple. **2.** The Marbled White Butterfly; also called *half-mourner* 1832.

Half-nephew. 1824. The son of one's half-brother or -sister.

Halfness (hā·fnės). 1530. [f. HALF *a.* + -NESS.] The condition or quality of being half or incomplete, or of being half one thing and half another.

Such H., such halting between two opinions 1831.

Half-niece. 1824. The daughter of one's half-brother or -sister.

Half-noble. 1480. A gold coin issued from Edw. III to Edw. IV.

Ha·lf-note. 1597. **1.** *Mus.* †**a.** A half-tone; a semitone –1763. **b.** A minim 1847. **2.** The half of a bank-note, cut in two for safe transmission by post 1882.

Half-pace. 1569. [alt. of HALPACE.] **1.** A step, raised floor, or platform on which a throne, a dais, etc., is to be placed or erected. **b.** The platform at the top of steps on which an altar stands. **2.** A broad step or landing between two half flights in a staircase 1611. Hence **Ha·lf-paced** *a.* having a half-pace.

Half-pay. 1664. **1.** Half the usual or full wages or salary; a reduced allowance to an officer when not in actual service, or after retirement at a stated time. **2.** An officer in receipt of half-pay 1826. **3.** *attrib.*, as *half-pay officer*, etc. 1715.

Halfpenny (hēⁱ·pěni, *dial.* hā·fpěni, hā··pěni, ha·pěni, ha·pni.) *Pl.* **Halfpennies** (hēⁱ·pěniz), **halfpence** (hēⁱ·pěns). ME. [f. HALF *a.* + PENNY. The pl. *halfpennies* means the individual coins only; *halfpence*, usually, the sum.] **1.** A coin (formerly of copper, now of bronze) of half the value of a penny; a sum = two farthings. †**2.** A small fragment. *Much Ado* II. iii. 147. **3.** *attrib.* That costs a halfpenny, as *h. ballad*, etc.; of contemptible value (also *twopenny-halfpenny*) ME.

1. *H. under the hat*, a low game of chance. THACKERAY. *More kicks than halfpence*: see KICK *sb*¹.

Halfpennyworth (hēⁱ·pěniwɒɹþ), *sb.*, contracted **ha'porth, ha'p'orth** (hēⁱ·pəɹþ). [OE. *healfpeniȝwurþ*; see WORTH *sb.*¹] As much as a halfpenny will purchase; a very small quantity.

Phr. *To lose the ship* (orig. and prop. *sheep, ewe, hog*) *for a h. of tar*: to lose an object by trying to save in a small detail. (*Sheep* is dialectally pronounced *ship* in many parts of England, and the tar was used to protect sore places on sheep from the attacks of flies.) Rather..to lose ten sheepe, than be at the charge of a halfe penny worth of Tarre 1631. Hence †**Ha·lfpennyworth** *v. intr.* to haggle about minute expenses (RALEGH); *trans.* to deal *out* by halfpenny-worths (MARVELL).

Half-pike. Now *Hist.* 1599. [Cf. DEMIPIQUE, Fr. *demi-pique.*] A short pike. There were two kinds; one, also called a *spontoon*, formerly carried by infantry officers; the other, used in ships for repelling boarders, a *boarding pike*.

Half-price. 1720. **1.** Half the usual or full price. Also, the time at which people are admitted to an entertainment or the like at half-price. Also *attrib.* or quasi-*adj.*

Half-round. 1662.

A. *adj.* Semicircular, in shape or section; semicylindrical, as *half-round bit*, etc.

B. *sb.* A semicircle; a hemispherical figure 1718. **b.** *Arch.* 'A semicircular moulding which may be a bead or torus' (Gwilt) 1842. Hence †**Half-rounding** *a.* forming a semicircle (MILT.).

†**Half-seal.** 1509. The impression of the reverse side or foot of the Great Seal, with which certain documents used to be sealed. Abolished in 1833.

Half-seas-over. 1551. [*Seas* was prob. a genitive case; *half sea's* = half of the sea.] **1.** Halfway across the sea. **b.** *transf.* and *fig.* Half through with a matter; halfway between one state and another 1697. **2.** Half-drunk (*joc.*) 1700.

1. About half Seas over, we discovered the Dutch Fleet 1688. **b.** I am half-seas over to death DRYDEN.

Half-sister. ME. [prob. – ON. *hálfsystur* (pl.).] **1.** A sister by one parent only. Also *fig.* †**2.** A lay sister in a convent 1482.

1. *fig.* Raw Haste, half-sister to Delay TENNYSON.

Ha·lf-snipe. 1766. The jack snipe or lesser snipe.

Ha:lf-so·vereign. 1503. **1.** An English gold coin worth 10*s.* The sum, as dist. from the coin, is also expressed by *half a sovereign*. **2.** A pavior's name for a 6-in. Purbeck stone pitcher; also for a granite pitching 1851.

†**Half-strain.** 1673. The quality of being half of a good strain or stock and half of an inferior one; half-breed. Also *attrib.* DRYDEN. Hence †**Ha·lf-strained** *a.*

†**Ha·lf-sword.** 1552. **1.** A small-sized sword –1611. **2.** Half a sword's length –1616.
2. Phr. *To be at half-sword*, to be at close quarters with swords.

Ha·lf-tide. 1669. **1.** The state of the tide half-way between flood and ebb. **2.** *attrib.* and *Comb.* Left dry or accessible at half-tide, as *half-tide cavern*; **half-tide basin** or **dock,** one fitted with gates which are closed at half-ebb.

Ha·lf-ti:mber. 1842.
A. *sb. Shipbuilding.* (See quot.)
Half-timbers..those timbers in the cant bodies which are answerable to the lower futtocks in the square body WEALE.
B. *adj.* **1.** Built half of timber 1842. **2.** Made of timber split in half 1874.
1. *Half-timber building*, a structure formed of studding, with sills, lintels, struts, and braces, sometimes filled in with brickwork and plastered over on both sides GWILT. Hence **Half-timbered** *a.* = B.1.

Half-time. 1645. **1.** Half of a (particular) period of time; *esp.* half the usual or full time during which work is carried on. (Occas. as *adv.*) 1861. **2.** *Football*, etc. The time at which the first half of the game is completed 1871. **3.** *attrib.* 1861.
3. *Half-time system*, the system by which children were allowed to attend school for half the usual time and spend the other half in earning money; so *half-time register*, a register of half-time scholars.

Half-timer. 1865. One who spends half the usual or full time at anything; *esp.* a half-time scholar (see prec.).

Half-tone, *sb.* 1875. **1.** *Mus.* = SEMITONE 1. 1880. **2.** *Art.* A tone intermediate between the extreme lights and extreme shades. Also *attrib.*

Half-truth. 1658. A proposition which is or conveys only one half or a part of the truth.
A half-truth is often a falsehood J. H. NEWMAN.

Half-way, halfway (hāfwēⁱ: see below). ME. [f. HALF *a.* + WAY *sb.*]
A. *adj.* (Stressed *ha·lfway* before, *ha:lf-way·* when following, the word it qualifies.) At or to half the distance. *To meet half-way*: see MEET *v.*
B. *adj.* (Usu. *ha·lfway.*) **1.** Midway or equidistant between two points 1711. **2.** *fig.* Half one thing and half another 169..
1. *Half-way house*, a house (often an inn) situated midway between two towns or stages of a journey, and therefore a convenient halting-place. Also *fig.* **2.** Half-way measures PRESCOTT.
C. *sb.* A half-way place or house 1634.

Ha·lf-wit. 1678. [See WIT *sb.*] †**1.** One who is only half a wit –1720. **2.** One who has not all his wits 1755. So **Ha·lf-wi:tted** *a.* †simple, senseless; imbecile.

Ha·lf-word. ME. A word or speech which insinuates something, instead of fully asserting it; a hint, suggestion.

Half-year. OE. The half of a year; six months. As a space of time, expressed by *half a year*. In Schools, etc. = HALF *sb.* II. 4 a. Hence **Half-yearly** *a.* and *adv.*

Halibut (hæ·libɒt), **holibut** (hǫ·libɒt). [f. *hāly*, HOLY + BUTT *sb.*[1] For the first element cf. LG. *heilbut, heilige but*, Du. *heilbot*, G. *heilbutt*, ON. *heilagr fiskr* (Icel. *heilagfiski*, Sw. *helgeflundra*, Da. *hellefisk, -flyndre*).] A large flat fish (*Hippoglossus vulgaris*), abundant in the northern seas, and much used for food. (Pl. *halibuts*, also collect. *halibut.*) Also applied to other flat fish of the family *Pleuronectidæ*.

Halichondroid (hælikǫ·ndroid), *a.* 1887. [f. mod.L. *Halichondria*, name of a genus of sponges (f. Gr. ἅλς, ἁλι- sea + χόνδρος cartilage) + -OID.] *Zool.* Related to a group of sponges including *Halichondria palmata*, the largest British sponge.

‖**Halicore** (hăli·kŏri). 1828. [f. Gr. ἅλς, ἁλι- sea + κόρη maiden, lit. 'mermaid'.] *Zool.* Name of the group of Sirenians, found in the Red Sea and Indian Ocean, to which the Dugong belongs.

Halidom (hæ·lidəm), **-dome** (dōᵘm). *Obs.* or *arch.* [OE. *hāligdōm* sanctity, holy place or thing = MDu. *heilichdoem*, OHG. *heilagtuom* (cf. ON. *helgidómr*); see HOLY, -DOM. *By my halidom* (XVI) is due to misunderstanding.] †**1.** Holiness, sanctity –1626. **2.** A holy place, chapel, sanctuary (*arch.*) OE. **3.** A holy relic; anything regarded as sacred. Formerly much used in oaths and adjurations. OE.
2. The men of the Halidome, as it was called, of St. Mary's SCOTT. **3.** As help me God and halidome MORE. By my hallidome, I was fast asleepe SHAKS.

Halieutic (hæliyū·tik). 1646. [- L. *halieuticus* - Gr. ἁλιευτικός, f. ἁλιευτής fisher; see -IC.]
A. *adj.* Of or belonging to fishing 1854.
B. *sb. pl.* **Halieutics:** The art or practice of fishing; a treatise on fishing.

†**Halio·graphy.** 1656. [f. Gr. ἅλς, ἁλι- sea + -GRAPHY.] A description of the sea. So †**Halio·grapher.**

‖**Haliotis** (hæli͵ōᵘ·tis). 1752. [f. as prec. + οὖς, ὠτ- ear; so named from their resemblance to the ear.] *Zool.* A genus of univalve shells, the Ear-shells. Hence **Halio·toid** *a.* akin to the Ear-shell.

Halitosis (hælitōᵘ·sis). 1885. [f. L. *halitus* breath, exhalation + -OSIS, used irreg.] *Med.* Abnormally foul breath.

Halituous (hăli·tiuəs), *a.* 1616. [f. L. *halitus* (prec.) + -OUS.] Of the nature of breath; vaporous.

‖**Halitus** (hæ·litŏs). 1661. [L.; = 'breath'.] A vapour, exhalation.

†**Halke.** ME. only. [perh. dim. of OE. *halh, healh* a corner; see HALE *sb.*[2]] A corner, recess, hiding-place.

Hall (hǫl), *sb.* [OE. *hall, heall* = OS., OHG. *halla* (Du. *hall*, G. *halle*), ON. *hǫll* :- Gmc. **χallō*, f. **χal-* **χel-* cover, conceal. Cf. HELE *v.*, HELL *sb.*] †**1.** A large place covered by a roof; a temple, palace, court, royal residence. *Obs.* in gen. sense. **2.** The large public room in a mansion, palace, etc., used for receptions, banquets, etc., which till 1600 greatly surpassed in size the private rooms or 'bowers' (see BOWER *sb.*[1]); a large or stately room in a house ME. **3.** The residence of a territorial proprietor, a baronial or squire's hall OE. **4.** A term applied, esp. in the English universities, to buildings set apart for the residence or instruction of students, and, hence, to the body of students occupying them. **a.** Orig. applied at Oxford and Cambridge to all residences of students, including the Colleges. Now only *Hist., arch.*, or *poet.* for 'academic buildings'. ME. **b.** Later, halls were distinguished from colleges, as being governed by a head only, and having their property held in trust for them, they not being bodies corporate 1535. **c.** In recent times applied variously: e.g. at Oxford, to private halls for the residence of undergraduates, under the charge of a member of Convocation; to theological halls (e.g. Wycliffe Hall), halls for women students (e.g. Lady Margaret Hall), etc. 1879. **5.** In English colleges, etc.: The large room in which the members and students dine in common 1577; *transf.* dinner in hall 1859. **6.** A house or building belonging to a guild or fraternity of merchants of tradesmen ME. **7.** A large room or building for the transaction of public business, the holding of public meetings, or the like ME. †**b.** *The Hall*, Westminster Hall, formerly the seat of the High Court of Justice in England; hence, the administration of justice –1738. †**c.** A formal assembly held by the sovereign, or by the mayor, etc. of a town; usu. in phr. *to keep h., call a h.* –1684. **8.** The entrance-room or vestibule of a house; hence, the lobby or entrance passage 1663. †**9.** *A hall! a hall!* a cry or exclam. to clear the way or make room, esp. for a dance; also to call people together –1808. **10.** *attrib.*, as *h.-bible*, etc. 1460.
2. In halle & i bure ME. *Servants' hall*: see SERVANT *sb.* **6.** At Stationers H. 1654. **7. b.** *Hen. VIII*, II. i. 2. **9.** *Rom. & Jul.* I. v. 28. **10. h. bedroom** *U.S.*, a small bedroom over the entrance hall; **hallway** *U.S.*, = sense 8; also, a corridor or passage on other floors.

†**Hallage** (hǫ·lėdʒ). 1607. [-(O)Fr. *hallage*, f. *halle* market-hall + -AGE.] A fee or toll paid for goods sold in a hall or market –1720.

Hall-door. ME. **a.** The door of a hall or mansion. **b.** The door leading into the hall; the front door.

‖**Hallel** (hæ̆lē·l, hæ·lel). 1702. [Heb., *hallēl* praise.] A hymn of praise, consisting of Psalms 113 to 118 inclusive, sung at the four great Jewish feasts. Also *attrib.*

Hallelujah, -iah (hælĭlū·yă), *interj.* and *sb.*[1] 1535. [- Heb. *hallᵉlûyāh* praise Jah (i.e. Jehovah), f. imper. pl. of *hallēl* praise (prec.).] The exclam. 'Praise (ye) the Lord (Jah, or Jehovah)', which occurs in many psalms and anthems; hence, a song of praise to God; = ALLELUIA *interj.* and *sb.*[1]
And the Empyrean rung With Halleluiahs MILT.
Comb.: **H. Chorus,** a musical composition based on the word 'hallelujah'; **h.-lass,** a female member of the Salvation Army.
Hence **Ha:lleluja·tic, -ia·tic** *a.* of or pertaining to the h. So †**Hallelu·jous, -u·ious** *a.* QUARLES.

Hallelu·jah, *sb.*[2] = ALLELUIA *sb.*[2]

Hallidome: see HALI-.

†**Hallier.** 1479. [f. HALE *v.*[1]; see -IER 1.] **1.** A hauler –1644. **2.** A kind of net for catching birds. BRADLEY. **3.** Earlier form of HALYARD.

Ha·ll-mark, *sb.* 1721. [f. HALL *sb.* 6.] The official mark or stamp of the Goldsmiths' Company, used in marking the standard of gold and silver articles assayed by them; hence, generally, a mark used by Government assay offices for the same purpose. Also *fig.*
fig. The hall-mark of real military genius WOLSELEY. Hence **Hall-mark** *v.* to stamp with a hall-mark (*lit.* and *fig.*).

Hallo, halloa (hălōᵘ·), *interj.* and *sb.* 1840. [A later form of HOLLO, HOLLOA.] A shout or exclam. to call attention or to express surprise (e.g. on meeting some one unexpectedly). Cf. HALLOO.

Halloo (hălū·), *interj.* and *sb.* 1700. [Goes with next; survives in VIEW-HALLOO.] An exclam. to incite dogs to the chase, to call attention at a distance, to express surprise, etc.
To horse! halloo! halloo! SCOTT. The far h. 1810.

Halloo (hălū·), *v.* 1568. [perh. var. of HALLOW *v.*[2]] **1.** *intr.* To shout 'halloo' to dogs in order to urge them on; *trans.* to urge on with shouts 1606. **2.** *intr.* To shout in order to attract attention 1722. **3.** *trans.* To shout (something) aloud 1602.
1. Old John halloos his hounds again M. PRIOR. **2.** Phr. *Not to h. until one is out of the wood*, not to shout till one is safe from robbers in the forest; esp. *fig.* not to exult till danger or difficulty is past.

Hallow (hæ·lo͝ᵘ), *sb.*[1]; usu. in pl. **hallows.** [OE. *hālga*, subst. use of definite form of *hālig* HOLY.] **1.** A holy personage, a SAINT. (Now preserved only in ALL-HALLOWS and its combs., q.v.) **2.** In *pl.*, the shrines or relics of saints; the gods of the heathen or their shrines ME. **3.** HALLOW- in *Comb.* (chiefly in *Sc.*) is used for ALL-HALLOW- = All Saints'-, in HALLOW-E'EN, etc. 1795.

Hallow (hæ·loᵘ), *sb.*[2] 1440. [f. HALLOW *v.*[2] Often identified in spelling with HALLOO, although differently stressed.] A loud shout or cry, to incite dogs in the chase, to assist combined effort, or to attract attention.

Hallow (hæ·loᵘ), *v.*[1] [OE. *hālgian* = OS. *hēlagon*, OHG. *heilagōn* (G. *heiligen*), ON. *helga*; Gmc. vb. f. **χailaʒ-* HOLY.] **1.** *trans.* To make holy; to sanctify. **2.** To consecrate, set apart (a person or thing) as sacred to God; to dedicate to some sacred or religious use or office; to bless a thing OE. †**b.** To consecrate (a person) to an office, as bishop, king, etc. –ME. **3.** To honour as holy (esp. God or his name) OE. **4.** *trans.* To keep (a day, festival, etc.) holy; to observe solemnly OE.
1. Those women whose teares Antiquitie hath hallowed 1638. **2.** Leo..entered France..to h. the newly built church of his monastery FREEMAN. **3.** Our father..hallowed be thy Name *Matt.* 6: 9. **4.** To h. the Sabboth day ABP. HAMILTON.

Hallow (hæ·loᵘ), *v.*[2] ME. [prob. - OFr. *halloer*, imit. of shouting (cf. HALLOO *v.*).] **1.** *trans.* To pursue with shouts; to urge on with shouts; to call or summon *in, back*, etc., with shouting. **2.** *intr.* To shout, in order to urge on dogs to the chase, attract attention, etc. ME. **3.** *trans.* To shout (something) aloud ME.
1. They [fox hounds] were then halloed back 1812. **2.** The shepherd him pursues, and to his dog doth halow DRAYTON. **3.** H. your name to the reuerberate hilles SHAKS.

Hallow-e'en. *Sc.* 1556. [Shortened from *All-hallow-even*; see ALL-HALLOW.] The eve of All Hallows' or All Saints'; the last night of October. Also *attrib.*

In the Old Celtic calendar the last night of October was 'old year's night', the night of all the witches, which the Church transformed into the Eve of All Saints.

Hallowmas (hæ·lomæ̆s). ME. [Shortened from *All-hallow-mass*: see ALL-HALLOW.] The feast of All Hallows or All Saints. Also *attrib.*

She came adorned hither like sweet May; Sent back like H., or short'st of day SHAKS.

†**Ha·llow-tide.** 1450. [Shortened from *All-hallow-tide*; see ALL-HALLOW.] The season of All Saints; the first week of November –1609.

Halloysite (hăloi·zəit). 1827. [f. *d'Halloy*, a Belgian geologist; see -ITE[1] 2 b.] *Min.* A clay-like earthy mineral, a hydrated aluminium silicate, resulting from the decomposition of felspar.

Hallucal (hæ·lⁱukăl), *a.* 1889. [f. HALLUX (*halluc-*) + -AL[1].] *Anat.* Of or belonging to the hallux or great toe. So **Ha·llucar** *a.* in same sense.

Hallucinate (hæ̆lⁱū·sineⁱt), *v.* 1604. [– *hallucinat-*, pa. ppl. stem of L. *hallucinari*, late form of *alucinari* wander in thought or speech – Gr. ἀλύσσειν be distraught or ill at ease.] †**1.** *trans.* To deceive (*rare*) –1623. **2.** *intr.* To be deceived, entertain false notions, blunder, mistake. *Obs.* or *arch.* 1652. **3.** *trans.* To affect with hallucination 1822.

Hallucination (hæ̆lⁱūsinēⁱ·ʃən). 1646. [– L. *hallucinatio*, f. *hallucinat-*; see prec., -ION.] **1.** The condition of being deceived or mistaken, or of entertaining unfounded notions; with *a* and *pl.*, an illusion 1652. **2.** *Path.* and *Psych.* The apparent perception of an external object when no such object is present. (Dist. from *illusion*, as not necessarily involving a false belief.)

1. Reason. .swept away by the hallucinations of sentiment 1856.. **2** The most celebrated men have been liable to hallucinations, without their conduct offering any sign of mental alienation 1859. So **Hallu·cinative** *a.* productive of h. **Hallu·cinator**, one who hallucinates. **Hallu·cinatory** *a.* characterized by, pertaining to, or of the nature of h.

||**Hallux** (hæ·lŏks). *Pl.* **halluces** (hæ̆·lⁱŭsīz). 1831. [mod.L., corrupted from *allex* (*allic-*) the great toe.] *Anat.* The innermost of the digits (normally five) of the hind foot of an air-breathing vertebrate; the great toe; in birds (when present) usually either the inner or the hind toe.

Halm: see HAULM.

||**Halma** (hæ·lmă). 1890. [– Gr. ἅλμα leap.] A game played on a chequer-board of 256 squares, by two persons with 19 men each, or four persons with 13 each, the characteristic move consisting of a leap over any man in an adjacent square into a vacant square beyond, or of a series of such leaps. Named also *hoppity.*

Halo (hēⁱ·lo), *sb. Pl.* **haloes, halos** (also **halones**). 1563. [– med.L. *halo*, for L. *halos* – Gr. ἅλως threshing-floor, disc of the sun, moon, or a shield. Cf. Fr. *halo* (XVI).] **1.** A circle of light, either white or prismatically coloured, seen round a luminous body and caused by the refraction of light through vapour; *spec.* that seen round the sun or moon. **b.** Applied to other circular luminous appearances; hence, to other things in the form of a circle or a ring 1813. **c.** = AREOLA 3. 1706. **2.** The circle or disc of light with which the head is surrounded in representations of Christ and the Saints; a nimbus 1646. **3.** *fig.* The ideal glory with which a person or thing is invested by feeling or sentiment 1813.

3. A gilded h. hovering round decay BYRON. Hence **Ha·lo** *v.* to surround, encompass, or invest with a h. **Ha·loed** *ppl. a.* surrounded or invested with a h.

Halogen (hæ·lo͟ᵢdʒen). 1842. [f. Gr. ἅλς, ἁλο- salt + -GEN. Cf. Fr. *halogène*.] *Chem.* An element or substance which forms a salt by direct union with a metal. The halogens are chlorine, fluorine, bromine, iodine, and the compound cyanogen. Hence **Halo·genated** *a.* combined with a h. **Halo·genous** *a.* of the nature of a h.

Haloid (hæ·loid, hæ·lo͟ᵢid). 1841. [f. as prec. + -OID.] *Chem.*

A. *adj.* Having a composition like that of common salt (sodium chloride, NaCl); applied to all salts formed by the simple union of a halogen with a metal, as potassium iodide, K1.

B. *sb.* A salt of this nature 1846.

Ha·lomancy. 1864. [f. as prec. + -MANCY.] Divination by means of salt.

Halometer (hæ̆lǫ·mĭtəɹ). 1854. [f. as prec. + -METER.] An instrument for measuring the external form, angles, and planes of the crystals of salts.

Halotrichite (hæ̆lǫ·trikəit). 1849. [f. Gr. ἅλς, ἁλο- salt + θρίξ, τριχ- hair + -ITE[1] 2 b.] *Min.* Iron alum, occurring in yellowish-white, fibrous masses.

Haloxylin, -ine (hæ̆lǫ·ksilin). 1883. [f. Gr. ἅλς, ἁλο- salt + ξύλον wood + -IN[1].] An explosive, in which a powdered cellulose substance and a rapid explosive are added to charcoal and saltpetre.

Halp, obs. pa. t. of HELP.

†**Halpace, haltpace.** 1507. [var. of *hau(l)tepase* HAUT-PAS – Fr. *haut pas* 'high step'; see also HALF-PACE.] = HAUT-PAS; HALF-PACE 1. –1587.

Halse, hals, *sb.* Now *Sc.* and *n. dial.* [OE. *hals, heals* = OFris., OS., OHG. *hals*, ON. *háls*:– Gmc. **xalsaz*, rel. to L. *collum*.] **1.** The neck. **2.** The throat, gullet 1440. †**3.** *transf.* A narrow neck of land or channel of water –1536.

†**Halse,** *v.*[1] [OE. *halsian, healsian*, perh. earlier **hālsian* = OHG. *heilisōn* augur, expiate, ON. *heilsa* hail, greet (with good wishes) :– Gmc. **xailosōjan*, f. **xailaz*. See HEAL *v.*[1], WHOLE.] **1.** *intr.* To augur, divine, soothsay. OE. only. **2.** *trans.* To call upon in the name of something divine or holy; to exorcize, adjure, conjure; to beseech –1553. **3.** To hail, salute, greet –1596.

Halse, *v.*[2] *Obs.* exc. *Sc.* (hās, hǫs). ME. [Either an independent deriv. of HALSE *sb.*, or a sense developed upon HALSE *v.*[1], through assoc. with HALSE *sb.*] *trans.* To embrace. Also *transf.* and *fig.*

Halser, obs. f. HAWSER.

Halt (hǫlt), *sb.*[1] Also †**alt.** 1591. [orig. in phr. *make halt* – G. *halt machen* (whence also Fr. *faire halte*); in the G. phrase *halt* is prob. orig. based on the imper. ('stop', 'stand still') of *halten* HOLD *v.*] A temporary stoppage on a march or journey. **b.** A railway stopping-place for local services only and without regular station buildings, etc. 1910. Hence **Ha·ltless** *a.*

The distant foe. .In motion or in alt MILT.

Halt, *sb.*[2] 1599. [f. HALT *v.*[1] and *a.*] **1.** A halting or limping, a limp (*arch.*). **2.** The disease foot-rot in sheep 1750.

Halt (hǫlt), *a. arch.* and *literary.* [OE. *halt, healt* = OFris., OS. *halt*, OHG. *halz*, ON. *haltr*, Goth. *halts* :– Gmc. **xaltaz*, of unkn. origin.] Lame; crippled; limping.

Halt (hǫlt), *v.*[1] [OE. *healtian*, corresp. to OS. *halton*, OHG. *halzēn*, f. the adj.] **1.** *intr.* To be lame, walk lame, limp (*arch.*). †**2.** To cease haltingly *from* (a way or course); to fall away –1613. **3.** To walk unsteadily or hesitatingly; to waver; to remain in doubt ME. **4.** *fig.* To proceed 'lamely'; to be at fault; to be defective, as a syllogism, metaphor, verse; not to go 'on all fours' ME. †**5.** To play false –1600.

1. I am ready to h. *Ps.* 38:17. **3.** How long h. ye between two opinions 1 *Kings* 18:21. **4.** The Lady shall say her minde freely; or the blanke Verse shall h. for't SHAKS.

Halt (hǫlt), *v.*[2] Also †**alt.** 1656. [f. HALT *sb.*[1]] **1.** *intr.* To make a halt. (At first a military term only, but occas. in later use = 'stop'.) **b.** *Mil.* In the imperative 1796. **2.** *trans.* To cause to halt 1805.

Halter (hǫ·ltəɹ), *sb.*[1] [OE. *hælfter, hælftre*, corresp. to OLG. *heliftra* (MLG. *helchter*, MDu. *halfter, halter*) :– WGmc. **xalftra-*, **xaliftra*, f. (with instr. suffix) **xalƀ* -; see HELVE.] **1.** A rope, cord, or strap with a noose or headstall, by which horses or cattle are led or fastened up. **2.** A rope with a noose for hanging malefactors 1460. Also *fig.* **b.** Used typically for death by hanging 1533.

2. A h. gratis, nothing else for Gods sake SHAKS. **b.** Threats of jail and h. TENNYSON.

Ha·lter, *sb.*[2] 1440. [f. HALT *v.*[1] + -ER[1].] One who halts or limps. **b.** A waverer 1611.

Ha·lter, *v.* 1440. [f. HALTER *sb.*[1]] **1.** *trans.* To put a halter upon; to fasten *up* with a halter. Also *fig.* **2.** To catch or entrap with a noose or lasso 1573. **3.** To put a halter about the neck of (a person); to hang with a halter. Also *fig.* 1616.

3. *fig.* Suffered to have rope enough, till they had haltered themselves in a Præmunire FULLER.

||**Halteres** (hæltīᵊ·rīz), *sb. pl.* Also **alteres.** 1533. [Gr. ἁλτῆρες (in sense 1), f. ἅλλεσθαι to leap.] **1.** Weights held in the hand to give an impetus in leaping. **2.** *Entom.* The pair of knobbed filaments, also called *balancers* and *poisers*, which in dipterous insects take the place of a pair of posterior wings 1823.

†**Halter-sack.** 1598. [f. HALTER *sb.*[1] + SACK *sb.*[1]] A 'gallows-bird'; a term of obloquy –1616.

Ha·lting, *ppl. a.* ME. [f. HALT *v.*[1] + -ING[2].] **1.** That halts or limps; *fig.* maimed; defective. **2.** Wavering 1585.

1. That h. slave, who in Nicopolis Taught Arrian M. ARNOLD. Hence **Ha·lting-ly** *adv.*, **-ness.**

Ha·lvans, *sb. pl.* 1849. [deriv. of *half, halve.*] Refuse ore.

Halve (hāv), *v.* [ME. *halfen, halven*, f. HALF *sb.*; repl. ME. *helfen*, OE. *hielfan* :– **xalbjan*.] **1.** *trans.* To divide into two equal parts; to share equally; to deal *out*, take, or complete the half of; to reduce to half. Also *fig.* **2.** *Carpentry.* To fit (timbers) together by HALVING, q.v. Also *intr.* for *pass.* 1804. †**3.** *intr.* To render half service –1680.

1. The fervid Sun had more than halved the day COLERIDGE. *To h. a hole, a round, a match* (Golf). Hence **Halved** (hāvd), **Ha·lving** *ppl. adjs.*

Halver (hā·vəɹ). 1517. [f. prec. + -ER[1].] **1.** One who halves or has a half-share 1625. **2.** (usu. *pl.*) A half-share (*Sc.* and *dial.*).

Halving (hā·viŋ), *vbl. sb.* ME. [f. HALVE *v.* + -ING[1].] **1.** The action of HALVE *v.* **2.** *Carpentry.* A method of fitting two pieces of timber together by cutting out half the thickness of each, so as to let them into each other 1842.

Halwe, obs. f. HALLOW.

Halyard, halliard, haulyard (hæ·lyăɹd, hǫ·l-). ME. [orig. *halier, hallyer*, f. HALE *v.*[1] + -IER 1; alt. XVII by assoc. with YARD *sb.*[2] (cf. LANYARD).] *Naut.* A rope or tackle used for raising or lowering a sail, yard, etc.

Ham (hæm), *sb.*[1] [OE. *ham, hom* = MLG. *hamme*, OHG. *hamma* (G. dial. *hamm*), rel. to synon. MLG. *hame*, OHG. *hama*, ON. *hǫm*, f. Gmc. **xam-* be crooked.] **1.** That part of the leg at the back of the knee; hence **b.** the back of the thigh; the thigh and buttock collectively (usu. in *pl.*) 1552; **c.** in quadrupeds, the back of the hough; the hough 1607. **2.** The thigh of a slaughtered animal, used for food; *spec.* that of a hog salted and dried; also, the meat so prepared 1637.

1. With supple h., and pliant knee 1679. **b.** Squatting on their hams 1875. **2.** *attrib.*, as *h.-pie*, etc.

Ham, *sb.*[2] The OE. *hām* HOME *sb.*[1], as in *Hampstead, Hampton* (:– *Hāmtūn*), *Oakham*, etc., and, in the shortened form *ham*, sometimes used by historical writers in the sense 'town, village, or manor' of the OE. period.

Hamadryad (hæmădrəi·æ̆d). *Pl.* **-ads;** also in L. form **-ades** (-ădīz). ME. [– L. *Hamadryas, -ad-*, Gr. Ἁμαδρυάς, -αδ-, f. ἅμα together + δρῦς tree.] **1.** *Gr.* and *L. Mythol.* A wood-nymph fabled to live and die with the tree which she inhabited. **2.** *Zool.* **a.** A large, very venomous, hooded serpent of India (*Naja hamadryas*, or *Hamadryas* (*Ophiophagus*) *elaps*), allied to the cobra 1863. **b.** A large baboon of Abyssinia (*Cynocephalus hamadryas*) 1894.

Hamate (hēⁱ·mĕt), *a.* 1744. [– L. *hamatus* hooked, f. *hamus* hook; see -ATE[2].] Furnished with hooks, or hook-shaped; hooked. (Chiefly in *Nat. Hist.*) So **Ha·mated** *a.*

Hamber-line (hæ·mbəɹ ləin). 1853. [Corruption of *Hamburg*.] *Naut.* Small line for seizings, lashings, etc.

Hamble, *v. Obs.* exc. *dial.* [OE. *hamelian* mutilate = OHG. *hamalōn*, ON. *hamla*; from an adj. appearing as OHG. *hamal* maimed, whence G. *hammel* castrated sheep.] **1.** *trans.* To mutilate, maim; to dock; *spec.* to cut off the balls of the feet of (dogs) so as to render them unfit for hunting. (Erron. taken in 17–18th c. as = *Hamstring.*) **2.** *intr.* To walk lame (*dial.*) 1828.

Hamburg, -burgh (hæ·mbɒɹg, -bŏrŏ). 1838. [*Hamburg*, a city of North Germany.] **1.** (Also *Hamburg grape*) A black variety of grape which is specially adapted to hot-house cultivation. **2.** Name of a small variety of the domestic fowl 1857.

Hame (hēⁱm). ME. [– MDu. *hame* (Du. *haam*), corresp. to MHG. *ham(e)* fishing-rod, of unkn. origin.] Each of two curved pieces of wood or metal placed over, fastened to, or forming, the collar of a draught horse.

Hame, obs. and Sc. f. HOME.

Hamel. *Obs.* exc. *dial.* 1514. [–OFr. *hamel* (mod. *hameau*), dim. of *ham* – MLG. *hamm*; see -EL.] = HAMLET.

Hamel, var. of HAMBLE.

Hamesucken, †-soken (hēⁱ·msɒk'n). [OE., f. *hām* home, dwelling + *sōcn* seeking, visiting, attack, assault, ON. *sókn* attack.] *OE.* and *Sc. Law.* **1.** The crime of assaulting a person in his own house or dwelling-place. Now only in Sc. Law. **2.** A franchise of holding pleas of this offence and receiving the penalties imposed on the offender; also the penalty itself. (Variously misunderstood.) OE. So **†Ha·mfare** [f. OE. *hām* + *faru* going] = sense 1.

Hamiform (hēⁱ·mifǫ̈ɹm), *a.* 1849. [f. L. *hamus* hook + -FORM.] Hook-shaped.

Hamiltonian (hæmiltōᵘ·niăn), *a.* (*sb.*) 1826. [f. the surname *Hamilton* + -IAN.] **1. a.** Pertaining to James Hamilton (1769–1831), or to his system of teaching languages. **b.** Pertaining to the Scottish philosopher and logician, Sir William Hamilton (1788–1856). **c.** Pertaining to or invented by the Irish mathematician, Sir William Rowan Hamilton (1805–65), as *Hamiltonian equation*, *function*, etc. **d.** Pertaining to or holding the doctrines of the American statesman, Alexander Hamilton, a leader of the Federalist party (1757–1804). **2.** *sb.* A follower of any of these.

Hamite (hæ·məit), *sb.*¹ and *a.* Also **†Chamite, †Khamite.** 1645. [f. *Ham* (formerly spelt *Cham*, Gr. Χάμ, L. *Cham*), name of the second son of Noah (Gen. 6:10) + -ITE¹ 1.]

A. *sb.* **†1.** A follower of Ham; a term of obloquy. (Cf. Gen. 9:22–5.) PAGITT. **2.** A descendant of Ham (cf. Gen. 9:18, 19); an Egyptian, or an African Negro 1854.

B. *adj.* = Hamitic (see below) 1842.

Hence **Hamitic** (hæmi·tik) *a.* belonging to the Hamites; esp. applied to a group comprising the ancient Egyptian, and the Berber, Galla, and allied extant languages.

Hamite (hēⁱ·məit), *sb.*² 1832. [– mod.L. generic name *Hamites*, f. L. *hamus* hook; see -ITE¹ 2 a.] A fossil cephalopod having a shell of a hooked shape.

Hamlet (hæ·mlėt). ME. [– AFr. *hamelet(t)e*, OFr. *hamelet*, dim. of *hamel*; see HAMEL, -ET.] A group of houses or small village in the country; *esp.* a village without a church. **b.** *transf.* The people of a hamlet (*poet.*) 1726.

A small village or h., where..some thirty or forty families dwelt together SCOTT. Hence **Ha·mleted** *a.* located in a h.

‖**Hammam, hummaum** (hɒmā·m). 1625. [See HUMMUM.] An Oriental bathing establishment, a Turkish bath.

Hammer (hæ·məɹ), *sb.* [OE. *hamor*, *hamer*, *homer* = OFris. *homer*, OS. *hamur* (Du. *hamer*), OHG. *hamar* (G. *hammer*), ON. *hamarr* hammer, back of an axe, crag.] **1.** An instrument having a hard solid head, usu. of metal, set transversely to the handle, used for beating, breaking, driving nails, etc. Hence, a machine in which a heavy block of metal is used for the same purpose (see TILT-HAMMER, etc.). **b.** *fig.* A person or agency that smites, beats down, or crushes, as with blows of a hammer. Cf. L. *malleus.* ME. **2.** *spec.* Anything in form or action resembling a hammer. **a.** A lever with a hard head arranged so as to strike a bell, as in a clock 1546. **†b.** The knocker of a door –1627. **c.** *Fire-arms.* (*a*) In a flint-lock, a piece of steel covering the flash-pan and struck by the flint; (*b*) in a percussion-lock, a spring lever which strikes the percussion-cap on the nipple; (*c*) applied to analogous contrivances in modern guns. 1590. **d.** A small bone of the ear; the malleus 1615. **e.** A small hammer or mallet used by auctioneers to indicate by a rap the sale of an article 1717. **†3.** A disease in cattle –1688. **4.** A match at throwing the hammer 1897.

1. Mechanicke Slaues With greazie Aprons, Rules, and Hammers SHAKS. Phr. *Throwing the h.*, an athletic contest, consisting in throwing a heavy h. as far as possible. **b.** Saladinus..þe strong hamer of Cristen men TREVISA. The h. of affliction 1679. **2. e.** Phr. *To bring* (*send, put up*) *to the h.*; to *go* or *come to* or *under the h.*, to be sold by auction.

Phrases. *H. and tongs* (colloq.): with might and main (like a blacksmith smiting the iron taken with the tongs from the forge-fire). *Thor's h.*, *h. of Thor*: (*a*) the h. carried by the god Thor in Norse mythology; (*b*) = FYLFOT; (*c*) a prehistoric ornament resembling a h.

Comb.: **h.-fish,** the h.-headed shark; **-harden** *v.*, to harden (metals) by hammering; **-mill,** a mill driving a h. in a small forge; **-oyster** = *hammer-shell*; **-scale,** the coating of oxide which forms on red-hot iron and can be separated by hammering (also called *forge-scale*); **-sedge,** *Carex hirta*; **-shark,** the h. headed shark; **-shell,** the h.-shaped shell of a bivalve mollusc of the genus *Malleus* (also called *hammer-oyster*); **-slag, -slough** = *hammer-scale*; **-stone,** a prehistoric stone implement resembling, or used as, a h.; **-toe,** persistent angular flexion of a toe; **-work,** (*a*) work performed with a h.; (*b*) something constructed or shaped with the h.; **-wrought** *a.*

Hammer, *v.* ME. [f. prec. sb.]

I. *trans.* **1.** To strike, beat, or drive with or as with a hammer ME.; to fasten with or as with a hammer 1450; to beat out or shape with a hammer 1522. **2.** *fig.* **a.** To put into shape with much intellectual effort. Often with *out.* ('Used commonly in contempt' J.) 1583. **†b.** To debate. CAREW. **c.** To drive by dint of repetition (as an idea, etc., into a person's head) 1646. **d.** *Stock Exchange slang.* (*a*) To declare (a person) a defaulter 1887. (*b*) To depress (prices, a market) 1865.

1. Armillæ of pure gold, hammered into rounded bars 1851. **2. a.** To h. out an excuse 1751. **c.** Hammering common sense into his head 1866. **d.** The head Stock Exchange waiter strikes three strokes with a mallet..before making formal declaration of default of a member. Thus, to be 'hammered', is to be pronounced a defaulter. 1887.

II. *intr.* **1.** To deal blows with or as with a hammer; to thump ME. **2.** *fig.* **†a.** To devise plans laboriously, 'cudgel one's brains' (*upon, on, at, of*); with *upon*, sometimes, To reiterate, insist upon –1777. **†b.** Of an idea: To be in agitation –1667. **c.** To work hard, toil. Const. *at.* 1755. **3.** To stammer. Now only *dial.* 1619.

1. Hammering away with a geologist's hammer 1886. **2. a.** That Whereon, this month I haue bin hamering SHAKS. **b.** Blood, and reuenge, are Hammering in my head SHAKS.

Hence **Ha·mmerable** *a.* (*rare*), malleable.

Ha·mmer-beam. 1823. *Arch.* A short beam projecting from the wall at the foot of a principal rafter in a roof, in place of a tie-beam.

Hammer-cloth. 1465. [Of unkn. origin.] A cloth covering the driver's seat or box in a state or family coach.

Hammerer (hæ·mərəɹ). 1611. [f. HAMMER *v.* + -ER¹.] **1.** One who hammers or wields a hammer; often, a geologist. **2.** 'The three-wattled bell-bird of Costa Rica, *Chasmorhynchus tricarunculatus*' (Cent. Dict.).

Ha·mmer-head. 1532. **1.** The striking part of a hammer 1562. **†2.** A blockhead. (Cf. *beetle-head.*) –1628. **3. a.** A hammer-headed shark; so called from the great lateral expansions of the head 1880. **b.** An American fish, *Hypentelium nigricans*, having a hammer-shaped head 1861. **4.** An African bird, the shadow-bird or umber-bird (*Scopus umbretta*); from the shape of the head 1890. Hence **Ha·mmer-hea:ded** *a.* having a hammer-shaped head; *fig.* stupid.

Ha·mmerless, *a.* 1875. [f. HAMMER *sb.* + -LESS.] Without a hammer; *esp.* of a gun.

Hammerman (hæ·məɹmæ̆n). 1483. A man who works with a hammer; *esp.* a smith or worker in metal; also, a blacksmith's striker. So **Ha·mmersmith.**

‖**Hammochrysos** (hæmokrəi·sǫ̈s). 1706. [L. (Pliny) – Gr., f. ἄμμος sand + χρυσός gold.] *Min.* A sparkling stone mentioned by the ancients; perhaps yellow micaceous schist, or the sand from it.

Hammock (hæ·mək). 1555. [Earlier *hamaca* – Sp. *hamaca* (whence also Fr. *hamac*), of Carib origin; the ending has been assim. to -OCK.] **1.** A hanging bed, consisting of a large piece of canvas, netting, etc., suspended by cords at both ends; used esp. on board ship, also in hot seasons on land. **2.** *transf.* Applied to the suspended case made by the caterpillars of certain moths, etc. 1859. **†3.** A cloth for the back of a horse 1690.

1. Theyr hangynge beddes whiche they caule *Hamacas* EDEN.

Comb.: **h.-chair,** a folding reclining-chair with canvas support for the body; **-nettings,** *orig.* rope nettings in which the hammocks were stowed away on board ship, these being lashed or hung to the **h.-rails** above the bulwarks; hence, the long troughs afterwards constructed for this purpose on the top of the bulwarks of the spar-deck in a man-of-war; **-shroud,** a h. used as a shroud in which to bury a corpse at sea.

Hamose (hēⁱmōᵘ·s), *a.* 1709. [Pedantic var. of earlier *hamous*, f. L. *hamus* hook + -OUS; see -OSE¹.] Having hooks, hooked. So **Ha·mous** *a.* ?*Obs.*

Hamper (hæ·mpəɹ), *sb.*¹ ME. [Reduced form of AFr. *hanaper* HANAPER; cf. *ampersand.*] **1.** A large basket, with a cover, generally used as a packing-case. In earlier use a case or casket generally; but from 1500 usu. of wickerwork. **b.** *U.S.* In New York, an oyster-basket holding two bushels; in Virginia, a measure of small fish holding about a bushel (*Cent. Dict.*). **†2.** = HANAPER 3. –1714.

2. An annuity of 180 Marks out of the H. 1714.

Ha·mper, *sb.*² 1613. [f. HAMPER *v.*¹] **†1.** Something that hampers; a shackle –1624. **2.** *Naut.* Things which form a necessary part of the equipment of a vessel, but are in the way at times. (See TOP-HAMPER.) 1835.

Hamper (hæ·mpəɹ), *v.*¹ ME. [Of obscure formation; the termination appears to be identical with -ER⁵.] **1.** *trans.* To obstruct the free movement of by fastening something on, or by obstacles or entanglements; to fasten, bind, fetter, shackle, clog; to entangle, catch (*in* something). **b.** To derange (a lock, etc.) so as to impede its working 1804. **2.** *fig.* and *gen.* To obstruct or impede in action; †to fetter; to entangle, encumber, or embarrass. (Now the common use.) ME. **3.** To pack up ME.

1. Such a novice, as to be still hamper'd in his owne hempe MILT. **2.** I believe no officer at the head of an army was ever so hampered WELLINGTON. The builder was hampered by the existence of aisles FREEMAN. Hence **Ha·mperer.**

Ha·mper, *v.*² 1603. [f. HAMPER *sb.*¹] **1.** *trans.* To load or present with a hamper or hampers (*joc.*). **2.** To pack in a hamper 1775.

Hamshackle (hæ·mʃæk'l), *v.* 1802. [perh. f. *ham-* in HAMPER *v.*¹ + SHACKLE *v.*; but the first element occurs also as *hab-*, *hap-*, *hob-*, *hop-*.] *trans.* To shackle (a horse or cow) by a rope or strap connecting the head with one of the forelegs; hence *fig.* to fetter, curb, restrain.

Hamster (hæ·mstəɹ). 1607. [– G. *hamster* :– OHG. *hamustro* = OS. *hamustra* 'curculio', corn-weevil.] A species of rodent (*Cricetus frumentarius*) allied to the mouse and rat, found in parts of Europe and Asia; it is of a stout form, about 10 inches long, and has cheek-pouches for carrying grain to its burrows; it hibernates during the winter. **b.** The fur of the hamster 1895.

Hamstring (hæ·mstriŋ), *sb.* 1565. [f. HAM *sb.*¹ + STRING *sb.*] **a.** In human anatomy, one of the tendons which form the sides of the ham or space at the back of the knee; they are the tendons of the muscles of the thigh. **b.** In quadrupeds, the great tendon at the back of the hough in the hind leg; it is the *tendo Achillis*, corresponding to that of the heel in man.

Hamstring (hæ·mstriŋ), *v.* Pa. t. and pple. **-stringed** (-striŋd), **-strung** (-strɒŋ). 1641. [f. prec. sb.] **1.** *trans.* To cut the hamstrings of, so as to lame or disable 1675. **2.** *transf.* and *fig.* To cripple, destroy the activity or efficiency of 1641.

2. So they have hamstrung the valour of the Subject by seeking to effeminate us all at home MILTON.

Hamular (hæ·miulăɹ), *a.* 1839. [f. L. *hamulus* small hook + -AR[1].] Of the form of a small hook, hooked; applied *spec.* in *Anat.* to processes of certain bones.

Hamulate (hæ·miulĕt), *a.* 1886. [f. as prec. + -ATE[2]. Cf. HAMATE.] **a.** *Bot.* Having a small hook at the tip (*Syd. Soc. Lex.*); also = HAMULOSE a. **b.** *Anat.* = HAMULAR.

Hamulose (hæmiulōᵘ·s), *a.* 1860. [f. as prec. + -OSE[1]. Cf. HAMOSE.] **a.** Covered with little hooked hairs or bristles. **b.** Having a small hook, hamulate. var. **Ha·mulous** 1684.

‖**Hamulus** (hæ·miulŏs). *Pl.* **-li** (-ləi). 1727. [L., dim. of *hamus* hook; see -ULE.] **a.** *Anat.*, *Zool.*, and *Bot.* A small hook or hook-like process, as in certain bones, in feathers, etc.; in *Bot.* a hooked bristle. **b.** *Obstetrics.* A hook-shaped instrument for extracting the fœtus. var. **Ha·mule** (in sense a).

Han = *haven*, obs. inf. and pres. t. pl. of HAVE *v.*

Hanap (hæ·næp). *Obs.* exc. *Hist.* 1494. [– (O)Fr. *hanap* drinking-vessel, cup – Frankish **hnap* = OE. *hnæp*, OHG. *hnapf* (G. *napf*).] A drinking vessel, a wine-cup or goblet; now, a mediæval goblet of an ornate character.

Hanaper (hæ·năpəɹ). *Obs.* exc. *Hist.* 1440. [– AFr. *hanaper*, OFr. *hanapier* (AL. *hanaperium* XIII), f. (O)Fr. *hanap*; see prec., -ER[2].] †**1.** A case for a hanap or hanaps; a plate-basket; a repository for treasure or money –1576. **2.** A round wicker case or small basket in which documents were kept 1768. **3.** The department of the Chancery, into which fees were paid for the sealing and enrolment of charters and other documents. (? So called because documents that had passed the Great Seal were here kept in a hanaper (sense 2); or with reference to the hanaper (sense 1) in which the fees were kept.) 1455.

†**Ha·naster, ha·nster.** [ME. *hauncer*, *hanster* (XIV), in AL. *hansterus*, *hanasterius* XV guild member (Oxford), held to be a deriv. of *hansa* or *hanse* HANSE.] The name given (in the city of Oxford) to persons paying the entrance-fee of the guild-merchant (see HANSE 2), and admitted as Freeman of the City –1608.

Hance (hɑns), *sb.* 1534. [– AFr. **haunce*, alt. f. OFr. *hau(l)ce* (mod. *hausse*), f. *hau(l)cer*; see HANCE *v.*] †**1.** The lintel of a door or window –1618. **2.** *Naut.* **a.** A curved rise, as of the fife-rails or bulwarks from the waist to the quarter-deck. Also erron. *hanch* or *haunch.* 1664. **b.** = HAUNCH *sb.* 4a. 1637. **3.** *Arch.* The arc of smaller radius at the springing of an elliptical or many-centred arch. Now usu. viewed as the HAUNCH of the arch, and so spelt. 1703.

†**Hance,** *v.* ME. [– AFr. **hauncer*, alt. f. OFr. *haucer* (mod. *hausser*) :– Rom. **altiare*; see ENHANCE.] *trans.* = ENHANCE 1, 2. –1583.

Hand (hænd), *sb.* [OE. *hand*, *hond* = OFris. *hānd*, *hōnd*, OS. *hand*, OHG. *hant* (Du., G. *hand*), ON. *hǫnd*, Goth. *handus*; Gmc., of uncertain origin.]

I. 1. The terminal part of the arm below the wrist, consisting of the palm and five digits, forming the organ of prehension characteristic of man. Also applied to the terminal members of all four limbs in the quadrumanous animals or monkeys. **b.** The terminal part of the fore-limb in quadrupeds, esp. when prehensile, or of any limb of an animal when prehensile. In *Anat.* and *Zool.*, the terminal part of the 'arm' or fore-limb in all vertebrates above fishes; also, the prehensile claw or chela in crustaceans. ME. †**c.** *transf.* The whole arm –1751. †**d.** The trunk of an elephant –1859. **e.** *fig.* 1592. **2.** Used to denote possession, custody, charge, authority, power, disposal OE. **b.** *Roman Law.* The power of the husband over his wife (tr. L. *manus*) 1875. **3.** = Agency, instrumentality OE. **b.** Part or share in the doing of something 1597. **4.** Side (right or left); hence *gen.*, side, direction, quarter. Also *fig.* (*arch.* or *dial.*) OE. **5.** As used in making a promise or oath; *spec.* as the symbol of troth-plight in marriage; pledge of marriage; bestowal in marriage ME. †**6.** Hence in oaths and asseverations –1636.

1. Moyses helde up his hond ME. The Gorilla's h. is clumsier. .than that of a man; but no one has ever doubted its being a true h. HUXLEY. **d.** The brutes of mountain back. .with their serpent hands TENNYSON. **e.** The griping Hands of the Law 1724. **2.** Phr. *In* (*into, to,* etc.) *the hands of, in other hands.* **3.** To suffer *by the hands of* the hangman 1639. **b.** Phr. *To have a h. in.* **4.** The mountains on either h. 1884. Phr. *On* (*upon, in, of*) *the mending h.* (fig.), i.e. in the way to mend or recover, getting better. **5.** Have here min honde, I shall the wedde GOWER. **6.** Tarry good Beatrice, by this h. I loue thee SHAKS.

II. As repr. the person. **1.** Often denoting the person in relation to his action 1590; hence *spec.* the person himself, *esp.* an artist, musician, writer, etc. 1644. **2.** One employed to do any manual work 1655; *spec.* each of the sailors belonging to a ship's crew 1669. **3.** *colloq.* Used (with defining adj.) of a person with reference to his ability or skill in doing something. (See also OLD *hand.*) Usu. with *at.* 1792. **b.** Used similarly in reference to a person's action or character. (*colloq.* or *slang.*) 1798. †**4.** Used of or in reference to a person as the source from which something is obtained (see quots.) –1811. **b.** With ordinal numerals, indicating a series of so many persons through whom something passes ME.

1. Except some charitable h. reclaimes him 1615. Paintings, by the most celebrated Hands 1696. **2.** All hands on board perished SCORESBY. **3.** I am a bad h. at criticising men J. H. NEWMAN. **b.** A cool h. 1860. **4.** I have heard it. .from good hands 1614. †*At the best h.*, most profitably or cheaply. **b.** I had it [the tale] at the second h. 1589.

III. As put for its capacity or performance. **1.** Skill in doing with the hand, and hence in doing generally; ability, knack ME. **2.** *Horsemanship.* Skill in handling the reins, etc. ME. **b.** Used for a division of the horse into two parts (see quot.) 1727. **3.** The performance of an artist, etc.; handiwork; style of execution, 'touch'. †Also *concr.* Handiwork. 1667. **b.** Touch, stroke (in phr. *last h.*, etc.) 1648. **4.** *Games.* A turn, innings, etc. 17.. **5.** Handwriting; style of writing ME. **6.** Signature. *Obs.* or *arch.*, exc. in phrases in which *hand* is now understood more literally. 1534.

1. The 'hand for crust' which is denied to many cooks 1881. **2.** A jockey must therefore. .have a h. for all sorts of horses 1881. **b.** The *fore-hand* includes the head, neck, and fore-quarters. The *hind-hand* is all the rest of the horse E. CHAMBERS. **3.** Carved work, the h. of famed artificers MILT. **b.** The compiler did not put his last h. to the work M. ARNOLD. **5.** A running h. 1576. He will recognize my h. LYTTON. **6.** In witness whereof, we have hereunto set our hands and seals 1726.

IV. Something like or of the size of a hand. **1.** An image or figure of a hand; *esp.* a conventional hand (☞) for drawing attention to something OE. **2.** The pointer or index on a dial, esp. that of a clock or watch 1575. **3.** A lineal measure, formerly three inches, now four; a palm, a HANDBREADTH. Now used only in giving the height of horses, etc. 1561. **4.** As a measure of various commodities; e.g. a bundle of tobacco leaves tied together; a cluster of bananas; etc. 1726. **5.** *Cookery.* A shoulder of pork 1825.

2. *Rom. & Jul.* II. iv. 119.

V. That which is held in the hand. **1.** *Cards.* The cards dealt to each player 1630. **b.** The person holding the cards 1589. **c.** A single round in a game 1622. **d.** *fig.* 1600. **2.**† A handle –1764; the part of a gun grasped by the hand 1881.

1. d. To PLAY *into the hands of another, to* FORCE *the h. of, to* SHOW *one's h.*, etc. (see the vbs.).

Phrases. **With governing prep.* **At hand. a.** Near, close by. **b.** Near in time. †**c.** At the start (*Jul. C.* IV. ii. 23). †**d.** = By hand (*John* V. ii. 75). †**e.** *At* (*on, upon*) *any h.*: on any account, in any case. So *at no h.*: on no account. †**f.** *At every h.*: on all hands. **g.** *At the hand(s of*: from the hands of; from. **By hand. a.** With the hand or hands; by manual action. **b.** *By the h.*: expeditiously. **For one's own hand.** For one's own benefit. **In hand. a.** *lit.* (Held or carried) in the hand. †**b.** *In h.*, *in one's h.*: (led) by the hand, or by a string, etc. **c.** In actual possession, at one's disposal; †in early use, Subject to one; in one's charge; in custody. (Also *in hands.*) †**d.** In suspense (with *hold, keep*). **e.** In process: being actually dealt with. **f.** *In h.*: under control, subject to discipline. **g.** Preceded by a numeral: see FOUR-IN-HAND. †**h.** *In any h.*: in any case. **Of. . hands. a.** *Of one's hands* (rarely *hand*): in respect of one's actions, of action, of valour in fight. †**b.** *Of all hands*: on all hands, on all sides; also, in any case (*L.L.L.* IV. iii. 219). **Off hand. a.** See OFF-HAND. **b.** *Off one's hand(s*: out of one's charge or control. **On hand, upon hand. a.** In one's possession, charge, or keeping. *To have on h.*: to have with one; to be charged with; to have in order to deal with or dispose of; to be engaged on. **b.** At hand; in attendance (*U.S.*). **c.** *On, upon one's hands* (rarely *hand*): resting upon one as a charge, burden, or responsibility, or as a thing to be dealt with or attended to. **d.** *On all hands, on every h.*: on all sides, from all quarters. **e.** *On* (*the*) *one h.*, *on the other h.*: used to indicate two contrasted sides of a subject, circumstances, points of view, etc. **f.** *On any h.*: on any account, in any case. **Out of hand. a.** Straight off; extempore. **b.** The opposite of *in h.* (in various senses). **To hand. a.** Within reach, accessible; †near; into one's possession or presence. **b.** *To h.*, *to one's h.*: into subjection, under control. **c.** *To* (*unto*) *one's hand(s*: ready for one. **Under hand. a.** Secretly; see UNDERHAND. **b.** *Under one's hand(s*: under one's action, charge, care, or treatment. **c.** *Under the h. of*: with the signature of.

***With verb and preposition.* (See also *bear in h.* (BEAR *v.*[1]), etc.) **Come to hand. a.** To come to one; to be received or obtained. **b.** *Come to* (*one's*) *hands*: to come to close quarters. **Take in hand,** †**on hand.** To undertake; occas. *spec.* to undertake the discipline, care, or cure of (a person).

****With verb governing* hand. (For BEAR *a h.*, FORCE (*a person's*) *h.*, HOLD (*one's*) *h.*, JOIN *hands*, KISS *the h.*, LAY *hands on*, LEND *a h.*, SET *h.* (*to, on*), SHAKE *hands*, STRIKE *hands*, TRY *one's h.*, WASH *one's hands of*, etc., see the vbs.) **Change hands.** To substitute one hand for the other; to pass from one person's h. or possession to another's. **Give** (one's) **hand.** To hold out the h. to be grasped, in token of salutation, bargaining, etc.; †also *fig.* **Make a hand. a.** To make one's profit; to make a success *of.* Freq. with *fair, fine* (often ironical), *good*, etc. **b.** *To make a hand of* (*with*): to 'do for'. *Obs.* or *dial.* **Put** (one's) **hand.** To exert oneself; now always with *to*: to undertake (a piece of work).

*****With adj. qualifying* hand. (For BLOODY *h.*, FREE *h.*, HIGH *h.*, UPPER *h.*, etc., see the adjs.) **Better hand.** †The 'upper hand'; precedence. **Clean hands.** *fig.* Freedom from wrongdoing.

******With an adverb.* **Hand in, out.** *To have one's h. in*: to be actively engaged; to be in practice. **Hands off!** *colloq.* Keep off! A peremptory order. **Hands up!** A direction to people to hold up their hands to signify assent, etc.; also, a robber's, policeman's, etc., order to preclude resistance. Also as vb.

*******With another noun.* (See also HAND AND GLOVE, etc.) **Hand. . fist. a.** *H. over fist* (colloq.) = HAND OVER HAND. **b.** *H. to fist* (colloq.) = HAND TO HAND. **Hand and foot.** Usually (now always) in adverbial construction; esp. in phr. *to bind h. and foot* (also *fig.*). *To wait upon h. and foot*: to wait upon or serve assiduously. **Hand. . hand. a.** *From h. to h.*: from one person to another. **b.** *H. under h.*: the opposite of HAND OVER HAND. **Hand's turn.** A stroke of work.

*******Phr. **a.** *As bare, flat, as one's h.* **b.** *To have one's hands full*: to be fully occupied. **c.** *In the turn(ing of a h.*: in a moment. **d.** (*To win*) *hands down* (orig. in Racing): with little or no effort.

Combs.: **1.** *attrib.* **a.** Of or belonging to the hand, as *h.-clasp*, etc. **b.** Worn on the hand, as *h.-ruffle*, etc. **c.** Portable, as *h.-anvil, -camera, -lamp*, etc. **d.** Managed or worked by the hand (occas. *spec.* with one hand); driven or operated by manual power; as *h.-bellows, -brake, -pump*, etc. **e.** Made or done by hand, as *h.-embroidery.*

2. Special Combs.: **h.-alphabet,** an alphabet of signs made by the hands; **handbell,** a small bell rung by being swung by hand; **-car** (*U.S.*), a light car propelled by cranks or levers worked by hand, used in the inspection, etc., of a railway line; **-drop,** a name for the paralysis of the h., induced by the action of lead; **-fish,** a pediculate fish, having the pectoral fin articulated; **-flower,** the flower of the *hand-plant* (q.v.); **-gear,** the starting-gear of an engine; **-language,** the art of conversing by signs made with the hands; **-lead** (*Naut.*), a small lead used in taking soundings less than 20 fathoms; **-light** (*Gardening*), a bell-glass; **-mast,** a round spar, of at least 24, and not more than 72 inches in circumference; also *attrib.*; **-mule** (MULE[1] 4 a); **h. orchis,** a name for *Orchis maculata*, from the finger-like lobes of the tubers; **-pick** *v. trans.*, to pick by hand; also *fig.*; **-plant,**

a Mexican tree (*Cheirostemon platanoides*, N.O. *Sterculiaceæ*), having large flowers with bright red stamens, which are united at the base and then spread in five finger-like bundles; **-post,** a guide-post at the parting of roads; a FINGER-POST; **-promise,** a solemn form of betrothal among the Irish peasantry; **-reading** = PALMISTRY; **-screw,** a jack; also *attrib.*; **-spring,** a somersault; **-swipe,** a shadoof worked by h. for raising water; **-tree** = *hand-plant*; **-wave** *v.*, to smooth the surface of (a measure of corn) with the h., instead of using a strike.

Hand (hænd), *v.* 1610. [f. prec. sb.] **1.** *trans.* To touch or grasp with the hand; to manipulate, handle; also *fig.* to treat of. *Obs.* exc. *techn.* **2.** *Naut.* To take in, furl (a sail) 1634. **3.** To lead or conduct by the hand; to assist with the hand 1631. **4.** To deliver or pass with the hand or hands 1650. **b.** *transf.* and *fig.* To deliver, pass, transfer, transmit. Now only with adverbs, as *down, on, over.* 1642. **5.** To join the hands of (*rare*) 1643. †**6.** *intr.* To go hand in hand. MASSINGER.

1. *Temp.* I. i. 25. **3.** He hands her o'er the stile CLARE. **4.** To h. over money 1816. **b.** A story handed by Tradition 1698. The father handed on the work KINGSLEY.

Hand and glove, (also with - -), *pred.* or *adj. phr.* Also (later) **hand in glove.** 1680. In constant close relations; on very intimate terms.

Ha·nd-axe, -ax. ME. An axe to be wielded with one hand; anciently a battle-axe.

Hand-ball. ME. **1.** A ball for throwing with the hand. **2.** A game played with such a ball in a space between two distant goals 1581. **3.** A hollow ball of india-rubber punctured so as to emit a spray when pressed in the hand 1888.

Hand-barrow. ME. [BARROW *sb.*[3]] A flat rectangular frame of transverse bars, having shafts before and behind, by which it is carried.

Handbi·ll[1]. 1523. [BILL *sb.*[1]] A light bill or pruning knife.

Ha·ndbill[2]. 1753. [BILL *sb.*[2]] A printed notice on a single page, to be delivered or circulated by hand.

Handbook (hæ·ndbuk). [OE. *handbōc*, tr. med.L. *manualis liber*, late L. *manuale* (tr. Gr. ἐγχειρίδιον) MANUAL *sb.* But the current word was introduced, after G. *handbuch*, in XIX.] A small book or treatise, such as may be held in the hand: †**a.** in OE. The MANUAL of eccl. offices and ritual; **b.** *spec.* A book containing concise information for the tourist 1836. **c.** *U.S.* A betting book 1903.

Ha·ndbreadth. 1535. A unit of lineal measure, a PALM; formerly taken as three inches, but now as four. So **Ha·ndbrede.** (*Obs.* exc. *n. dial.*)

Ha·nd-ca:nter. 1836. [CANTER *sb.*[2]] A gentle, easy canter.

Ha·nd-cart. 1810. A small cart drawn or pushed by hand.

†**Ha·ndcraft.** OE. = HANDICRAFT 1. –1599. †**Ha·ndcraftman,** †**Ha·ndcraftsman.**

Handcuff (hæ·nd,kɒf), *sb.* Also *dial.* **handy-.** 1775. [HAND *sb.* + CUFF *sb.*[1]] A manacle, consisting of a divided metal ring which is locked round the wrist. Handcuffs are used in pairs, connected by a short chain or jointed bar. So **Ha·ndcuff** *v. trans.* to put handcuffs on; to manacle.

Handed (hæ·ndėd), *a.* 1526. [f. HAND *sb.* + -ED[2].] **1.** Having hands; esp. as specified. **2.** = PALMATE 1854. **3.** Joined hand in hand 1643.

1. H. moles 1791. [An] open-handed master 1894. **3.** Into thir inmost bower H. they went MILT.

Hander[1] (hæ·ndəɹ). 1678. [f. HAND *v.* + -ER[1].] One who hands, delivers, or passes. Also with *down, in, out,* etc.

Ha·nder[2]. 1868. [f. HAND *sb.* + -ER[1] 1.] **1.** A blow on the hand. **2.** *-hander* in comb., **a.** as BACK-HANDER, a back-handed blow; **b.** as LEFT-HANDER, a left-handed man 1882.

†**Ha·ndfast,** *sb.* 1545. [app. f. HAND *sb.* + FAST *a.*, an unusual formation for a *sb.* Senses 3, 4 go with HANDFAST *v.*] **1.** Firm hold or grip with the hands; also *fig.* –1656. *In h.*, in hold, held fast. **2.** A handle, e.g. of a flail (*local*). BARING-GOULD. **3.** The joining of hands in making a bargain. MIDDLETON. **4.** A covenant; *spec.* a betrothal or marriage-contract –1884.

Ha·ndfast, *a.* ME. [In senses 1, 2, orig. pa. pple. of HANDFAST *v.*] †**1.** Contracted by the joining of hands; espoused. Also 'betrothed by joining of hands in order to cohabitation before marriage'. –1610. †**2.** Bound; manacled –1632. **3.** Tight-fisted, close-fisted (*lit.* and *fig.*) 1603.

3. Ludlow, a common, h., honest. . wooden man CARLYLE.

Handfast (hæ·ndfɑst), *v.* Pa. pple. **-ed;** in earlier use **handfast.** *Obs.* exc. *Hist.* [In sense 1, early ME. – ON. *handfesta* strike a bargain by joining hands, etc.; the other senses are f. HAND *sb.* and FAST *a.*] **1.** *trans* To make a contract of marriage between (parties) by joining of hands; to betroth. Also *fig.* †**2.** To grasp, seize with the hand; to take fast hold of. Also *fig.* –1662. †**3.** To manacle –1611.

Ha·ndfasting, *vbl. sb.* *Obs.* exc. *Hist.* 1530. [f. prec. + -ING[1].] Betrothal. **b.** Formerly treated as an uncanonical, private, or even probationary form of marriage. See Jamieson s.v. 1541.

†**Ha·ndfastly,** *adv.* [-LY[2].] By solemn engagement made by joining hands; firmly. HOLINSHED.

Handful (hæ·ndful), *sb.* [OE. *handfull* str. fem.; in OE. and ME. a true sb.; hence in pl. *handfuls*, not *handsful.*] **1.** A quantity that fills the hand; as many as the hand can grasp or contain. **2.** A small company or number; a small amount. (Usu. *depreciative.*) 1525. †**3.** = HAND *sb.* IV. 3. –1737. **4.** *fig.* As much as one can manage 1755.

1. A handfull or two of dried pease SHAKS. **2.** His Page atother side, that handfull of wit SHAKS. **3.** A bay Gelding 14 h. high 1676. **4.** The boy was a h. 1887.

Ha·nd-ga·llop. 1675. An easy gallop, in which the horse is kept well in hand. Also *fig.*

Han·d-glass. 1822. **1.** A magnifying glass held in the hand. **2.** *Hort.* A portable glass shade used for protecting or forcing a plant 1828. **3.** A small mirror with a handle 1882. **4.** A half-minute or quarter-minute sand-glass used for measuring the time in running out the log-line 1875.

Hand-grenade (hæ·nd,grĕnē[i]·d). 1661. **1.** An explosive missile, smaller than a bomb-shell, thrown by hand. Now usually spherical, and made of cast-iron. **2.** A glass bottle containing a chemical, to be broken in order to extinguish a fire 1895.

Handgrip. Also **-gripe, handy-, handi-grip(e.** [OE. *handgripe*, f. *gripan* to gripe, grip.] **1.** Grasp, seizure with the hand. **2.** Grip or firm pressure of the hand in greeting 1884.

†**Hand-habend,** *a.* (*sb.*) [Early ME. form of OE. **hand-hæbbend* 'hand-having'.] *OE. Law.* Of a thief: Having (the thing stolen) in hand. Applied as *sb.* to the offence, and to the franchise of holding plea thereof. –1828.

Handhold (hæ·nd,hō[u]ld). 1643. [See HOLD *sb.*[1]] **1.** Hold for the hand; that by which one can hold on in climbing. Also *fig.* **2.** That part of an implement, e.g. a fishing-rod, that is grasped by the hand 1833.

Handicap (hæ·ndikæp), *sb.* 1653. [app. from the phrase 'hand i' cap', or 'hand in the cap'. Formerly the name of a sport, described under the name of *Newe Faire* in *Piers Plowman*, B. v. 328, where it appears that it was a custom to barter articles, and to give 'boot' or odds, as settled by an umpire, with the inferior article. All the parties, including the umpire, deposited forfeit-money in a cap. The name refers to the drawing out of full or empty hands, to settle whether the match was accepted or not.] **1.** The name of a kind of sport having an element of chance in it, in which one person challenged some article belonging to another, for which he offered something of his own in exchange. Also *fig.* **2.** *Horse-racing.* (orig. *attrib.*) †**a.** *Handicap match*: a match between two horses, the umpire decreeing the weight to be carried by the superior horse, and the parties drawing to declare whether the match should be 'on' or 'off'. If the two agree, the forfeit-money is taken by the umpire; but if not, by the party who is willing that the match should stand. 1754. **b.** *Handicap race* (shortened *handicap*): a horse-race in which an umpire (the handicapper) decrees what weights have to be carried by the various horses entered, according to his judgement of their merits, in order to equalize their chances. So *h. plate, sweepstakes,* etc. 1786. **3.** Any analogous race or competition 1875. **4.** The extra weight or other condition imposed in equalizing the chances; hence, any encumbrance or disability that weighs upon effort 1883. **5.** *attrib.*, as *h. match*, etc. 1754.

Ha·ndicap, *v.* 1649. [f. prec.] †**1.** *trans.* To draw or gain as in a game of chance. **2.** *intr.* To engage or take part in a handicap match 1839. **3.** *trans.* To equalize the parties to a handicap, by decreeing the odds to be given; also *fig.* 1852. **4.** *trans.* To weight race-horses in proportion to their known or assumed powers, in order to equalize their chances 1856. **5.** *trans.* To penalize a superior competitor in any match or contest, so as to equalize his chances with those of inferior competitors. More generally, To weight any one unduly. 1864. Hence **Ha·ndicapper,** one who handicaps; *spec.* the public official who decrees what weights the different horses are to carry in a handicap.

Handicraft (hæ·ndikrɑft). Also formerly **handycraft.** ME. [alt. of earlier HAND-CRAFT (OE. *handcræft*) after HANDIWORK.] **1.** Manual skill; skilled work with the hands. **2.** A manual art, trade, or occupation 1548. †**3.** A handicraftsman –1821. **4.** *attrib.*, passing into *adj.* = 'manual, practical' 1662.

Ha·ndicra:ftsman. Formerly also as two words or hyphened. 1551. [lit. *handicraft's man*, man of handicraft; cf. CRAFTSMAN.] A man who exercises a handicraft; one employed in manual occupation.

The best wit of any handycraft man in Athens SHAKS.

Handicuff. Also **handy-.** 1701. [f. HAND *sb.* or HANDY *a.* + CUFF *sb.*[2]; app. after *fisticuff.*] *pl.* Blows with the hands; fighting hand to hand. Also *fig.*

Ha·ndily, *adv.* 1611. [f. HANDY *a.* + -LY[2].] In a handy manner; expertly; †manually.

Ha·ndiness. 1647. [f. as prec. + -NESS.] **1.** The quality of being handy or expert. **2.** Manageableness, convenience 1877.

Hand in glove: see HAND AND GLOVE.

Hand in hand (also with - -), *adv. phr.* (*a., sb.*). 1500. [HAND *sb.*] **1.** *adv. phr.* With hands mutually clasped; also *fig.* **2.** *attrib.* or *adj.* Going hand in hand or side by side; well-matched 1611. **b.** Name given to a Fire Insurance Office; implying the mutual sharing of risks 1781. **3.** *sb.* **a.** A representation of two hands mutually clasped. STEELE. **b.** Mutual clasping of hands. TENNYSON. **c.** A company of persons hand in hand. G. MEREDITH.

1. They hand in hand, with wandring steps and slow, Through Eden took thir solitarie way MILTON. **2.** A kind of hand in hand comparison *Cymb.* I. iv. 75.

Handiron, obs. form of ANDIRON.

Handiwork (hæ·ndi,wɒɹk). Also **handy-** and as 2 words. [OE. *handġeweorc*, f. *hand* HAND *sb.* + *ġeweorc*, collective formation (see Y-) on *weorc* WORK *sb.*; analysed in XVI as *handy work* (see HANDY).] **1.** A thing or collection of things made by the hands of any one. **2.** Work done by direct personal agency. Sometimes, the work of man's hands as opp. to nature. OE. **b.** Doing, performance 1838. **4.** Manual employment; practical work. [Cf. HANDY.] 1565.

1. The firmament sheweth his handywork *Ps.* 19:1.

Handkerchief (hæ·ŋkəɹtʃif), *sb.* 1530. [f. HAND *sb.* + KERCHIEF, q.v. also for *handkercher* (now dial. and vulgar).] A small square of linen, silk, or other fabric, carried in the hand or pocket (*pocket-h.*), for wiping the face, hands, or nose, or used as a kerchief to cover the head, or worn about the neck (*neck h.* or *neckerchief*).

Ha·nd-labour. 1549. Manual labour; †'art' as opp. to nature; now, usually, manual as opp. to machine work.

Handle (hæ·nd'l), *sb.* [OE. *handle, -la*, f. *hand* HAND *sb.*; see -LE.] **1.** That part of a thing which is grasped by the hand in using or moving it. **2.** *transf.* Something resembling a handle; in *Bot.* = MANUBRIUM. 1639. **3.** *fig.* That by which something is or may be taken hold of, or taken advantage of for some purpose; an occasion, excuse, pretext 1535. **4.** *attrib.* 1532. **Handle-bar,** the steering-bar of a bicycle, etc., with a handle at each end.

3. I would not give this h. to calumny 1732. Phr. *A h. to one's name* (colloq.): a title of rank, honour, or courtesy attached to the name.

Handle (hæ·nd'l), *v.*[1] [Late OE. *handlian* feel with the hands, treat of, corresp. to OFris. *handelia*, OS. *handlon*, OHG. *hantalōn* (G. *handeln*), ON. *hǫndla* seize, treat; see -LE.]

I. 1. *trans.* To subject to the action of the hand or hands: earlier, to touch or feel with the hands; later, to take hold of, turn over, etc., in the hand, to employ the hands on or about. Also *absol.* **b.** *intr.* (for *refl.*) To have a (specified) feel, behaviour, action, etc. when handled 1727. **2.** *trans.* To ply or wield with the hand ME.; *spec.* in *Mil.* 1684. **3.** To manage, direct, conduct, control (sometimes = carry out, perform). †Also *refl.* 1523. **4.** To use; to make due use of 1647.

1. I have handled and felt it 1717. To h. a book BURGON. *absol.* They haue handes and h. not COVERDALE *Ps.* 113:15 [115:7]. Phr. *To h. a horse*, to get him accustomed to the hand. **2.** Iubal..was the father of all such as h. the harpe and organ *Gen.* 4:21. **3.** A smarter officer never handled a regiment 1874. **4.** To h. one's fists GROSE.

II. 1. To deal with, treat 1542. †Also *intr.* –1581. **2.** To treat of, discuss OE. †Also *intr.* or *absol.* –1673. **3.** To treat artistically 1553. **4.** To have in hand or pass through one's hands in the way of business; to deal in; to buy and sell. *U.S.* 1888.

1. I wil h. him, euen as he hath dealte with me COVERDALE *Prov.* 24:29. **2.** The Preacher handeled his matter learnedly 1551. **4.** Export houses which h. steel rails 1897. Hence **Handlable, -eable** *a.* **Ha·ndler**[1].

Handle, *v.*[2] 1600. [f. HANDLE *sb.*] *trans.* To furnish with a handle. Hence **Ha·ndler**[2].

Handled (hæ·nd'ld), *a.* 1785. [f. HANDLE *sb.* and *v.*[2] + -ED.] Furnished with or having a handle. Used in *Her.* when the handle of a tool or weapon is figured of a different tincture from the blade, as 'a sickle or, handled gules'.

Handless (hæ·ndlės), *a.* ME. [f. HAND *sb.* + -LESS.] Without hands; *fig.* incapable in action (now only *dial.*).

Ha·nd-line. 1674. A line to be worked by hand; *esp.* a fishing-line worked without a rod.

Handling (hæ·ndliŋ), *vbl. sb.* OE. [f. HANDLE *v.*[1] + -ING[1].] **1.** The action of HANDLE *v.*[1] **2.** Treatment; management 1530. **3.** Artistic manipulation 1771. **4.** *attrib.* 1866.

1. Satire is one of those edged tools which require careful h. 1795. **3.** H.; that is, a lightness of pencil that implies great practice SIR J. REYNOLDS.

Ha·nd-list, *sb.* 1859. [Cf. *hand-book.*] A list of books, etc. in a form handy for reference. **Handlist** *v.* to enter (books, etc.) in such a list.

†**Ha·ndlock.** 1532. [See LOCK *sb.*] A handcuff –1633. Hence **Ha·ndlock** *v.* to handcuff. Also *transf.*

Ha·nd-loom. 1833. A weaver's loom worked by hand as dist. from a power-loom.

Ha·nd-made, *a.* 1613. Made by hand. Now usually dist. from the work of machinery.

Handmaid (hæ·ndmē[i]d), *sb.* ME. [f. HAND *sb.* + MAID (Wyclif; cf. OE. *handþeġen* manservant, *handprēost* chaplain, and L. *a manu servus* secretary, AMANUENSIS).] **1.** A female attendant or servant. **b.** *fig.* (in common use) 1592. †**c.** A tender. HAKLUYT. **2.** A moth, *Datana ministra*, of the family *Bombycidæ* 1869. **3.** *attrib.* 1629.

1. I am the handmayde of the lorde TREVISA. **3.** Her sleeping Lord with h. lamp attending MILTON. So **Ha·ndmai:den** = 1, 1 b. ME.

Ha·nd-me-down. *dial.* and *U.S.* 1888. = REACH-ME-DOWN.

Ha·nd-mill. 1563. A grinding mill consisting of one millstone turned upon another by hand, a quern. Now also applied to a form of coffee-mill, etc.

Hand of glory. 1707. [tr. Fr. *main de gloire*, a deformation of *mandegloire*, etc., orig. *mandragore* mandrake.] Orig., in French, a charm formed of the root of a mandrake; later, one made of the hand of an executed criminal.

Hand over hand, *adv. phr.* 1736. Chiefly *Naut.* **a.** With each hand brought successively over the other, as in climbing up or down a rope, or rapidly hauling it in. **b.** *fig.* With continuous advances; said of a vessel, etc. approaching another 1830. **c.** *attrib.* 1859.

Hand over head, *adv. phr.* Now *rare* or *Obs.* 1440. **1.** Precipitately, recklessly, without deliberation; †indiscriminately. **2.** *attrib.* or *adj.* (with - -). Precipitate, rash, reckless; †indiscriminate 1693.

Ha·nd-play. *arch.* OE. Interchange of blows in a hand-to-hand encounter. (Recently revived.)

Ha·nd-rail. 1793. A rail or railing supported on balusters, as a guard or support to the hand at the edge of a platform, stairs, etc.

Ha·nd-saw. ME. A saw managed by one hand. **b.** In *Haml.* II. ii. 367, generally explained as a corruption of *heronshaw* or *hernsew*, heron.

Handsel, hansel (hæ·ndsĕl, hæ·nsĕl), *sb.* ME. [corresp. formally to late OE. *handselen* 'mancipatio', delivery into the hand, and ON. *handsal* giving of the hand, esp. in a promise or bargain (OSw. *handsal*, Sw. *handsöl* money handed over, gratuity, Da. *handsel* earnest money); f. HAND *sb.* + base of OE. *sellan* give, SELL.] †**1.** Lucky prognostic, omen, presage; token or omen of good luck –1681. **2.** A gift or present (expressive of good wishes) at the beginning of a new year, or on other occasions; orig., deemed to ensure good luck. [= L. *strena*, Fr. *étrenne.*] ME. **3.** A first instalment of payment; earnest money; the first money taken by a trader in the morning, a luckpenny; anything given or taken as an omen, earnest, or pledge of what is to follow 1569. **4.** The first use, trial, proof, or specimen of anything; often with the notion of its being auspicious of what is to follow 1573. **5.** *attrib.* 1585.

3. Take this..but for hansell, the gaine is to come CAMPION. They say, a fooles handsell is lucky B. JONS. **4.** Such was the handsel, for Scott protested against its being considered as the house heating of the new Abbotsford LOCKHART. *Comb.* **H. Monday,** the first Monday of the year (usu. O.S.), on which New Year's h. is given. (*Sc.*)

Handsel, *v.* ME. [f. prec.] **1.** *trans.* To give handsel to (a person). **2.** To inaugurate with some ceremony or observance of an auspicious nature; to auspicate. Also *fig.* (*ironical*). 1583. **3.** To use for the first time; to be the first to test, try, prove, taste 1605.

3. Haman shall hansell his owne gallowes 1612.

Handsome (hæ·n[d]sŏm), *a.* (*adv.*) ME. [f. HAND *sb.* + -SOME[1].] †**1.** Easy to handle, or to use in any way –1598. **b.** Handy, ready at hand, suitable. (*Obs.* or *dial.*) 1530. **2.** Of action, speech, etc.: Apt, dexterous, clever, happy. ? *Obs.* exc. *U.S.* 1563. **b.** Of an agent: Apt, skilled, clever. ? *Obs.* exc. *U.S.* 1547. †**3.** Proper, seemly, decent –1654. **4.** Of fair size or amount; 'decent', moderately large. Now *unusual.* 1577. **b.** Of a fortune, a gift, etc.: Considerable. Now (by association with 5): Generous, liberal, munificent. 1577. **5.** Of conduct, etc.: Fitting, seemly; courteous, polite. Now: Generous, magnanimous. 1621. **6.** Having a fine form or figure (usually in conjunction with full size or stateliness); 'beautiful with dignity' (J.), 'fine'. (The prevailing current sense.) 1590.

2. Mr. Recorder in a h. speech [etc.] LUTTRELL. **4.** Pretty h. quantities of pickled salmon 1730. **b.** To get h. fortunes by small profits, and large dealings PRIESTLEY. **5.** Through this h. conduct of the dean the dispute was amicably settled 1830. **6.** This Ludouico is a proper man..A very h. man *Oth.* IV. iii. 37. A large and h. room 1849.

B. *adv.* = HANDSOMELY. Now only in vulgar use, exc. in *H. is that h. does.* ME.

†**Ha·ndsome,** *v.* 1555. [f. prec. adj.] *trans.* To make handsome (in various senses) –1657.

Handsomely (hæ·nsŏmli), *adv.* 1547. [f. as prec. + -LY[2].] **1.** In a handsome manner. **2.** Carefully; without haste, gently, gradually. Now only *Naut.* 1550.

2. Ease off the main sheet, h. my lad—not too much 1832.

Handsomeness (hæ·nsŏmnės). 1530. [f. as prec. + -NESS.] The quality of being handsome.

H. is the more animal excellence, beauty the more imaginative HARE.

Handspike (hæ·nd,spəik), *sb.* 1615. [– Du. †*handspaeke* (now *-spaak*), f. *hand* HAND *sb.* + MDu. *spāke* pole, rod; assim. to SPIKE *sb.*[2]] **1.** A wooden bar, used as a lever or crow, chiefly on shipboard and in artillery-service. **2.** Incorrectly for Sc. *handspake*, HANDSPOKE.

Comb. **h.-ring** (*Artill.*), the thimble on the trail transom of a gun, for the h. by which it is manœuvred.

Ha·ndspoke. In Sc. also **-spake, -spaik, -spike.** 1727. [See SPOKE.] A spoke or bar of wood carried in the hand, e.g. in carrying the coffin at a funeral in Scotland.

Ha·nd-staff. ME. **1.** A staff-like handle; *spec.* that part of a flail by which it is held. †**2.** A staff carried as a weapon [tr. Heb.]. *Ezek.* 39:9.

Ha·ndstroke. Also **handi-, handy-stroke.** 1523. [f. HAND *sb.* + STROKE *sb.*[1]] †**1.** A stroke or blow with the hand –1840. **2.** *attrib.*, as *h. pull* (in *Bell-ringing*) 1880.

Hand to hand, *adv. phr.* (*a.*). ME. With close approach of hand; at close quarters; man to man. **b.** *attrib.* or *adj.*, as in *hand-to-hand valour* 1836.

Hand to mouth, *phr.* (*a., sb.*). 1509. **1.** *From hand to mouth*: by consuming food as soon as it is obtained; improvidently, thriftlessly. **2.** *attrib.* or *adj.* (with - -). Involving consumption (or *transf.* disposal of goods) as soon as obtained; improvident 1748. **3.** *sb.* Lack of provision for the future. TENNYSON.

Hand-vice. 1611. A vice that can be held in one hand; a small movable vice.

Handwork (hæ·nd,wɒɹk). [OE. *handweorc.*] †**1.** = HANDIWORK 1. –1594. **2.** Work done with the hands; manual operation or labour; now esp. as dist. from work done by or with machinery OE. So **Ha·nd-worked** *ppl. a.*, **-wo:rker, -working.**

Ha·nd-wrist. *Obs.* exc. *dial.* [OE. *handwrist, -wyrst*, f. HAND + WRIST.] The wrist or joint of the hand. Now *dial.*

Colonel Whalley only cut in the handwrist CROMWELL.

Handwriting (hæ·nd,rəitiŋ). 1500. [Cf. L. *manuscriptum*, Gr. χειρόγραφον.] **1.** Writing with the hand; manuscript; the writing peculiar to a hand or person, time or nation. **2.** That which is written by hand; manuscript; a written document or note. *Obs.* or *arch.* 1534. Also *fig.*

1. A paper in his own h. BURKE. The study of handwritings 1891.

Handy (hæ·ndi), *a.* 1535. [In sense 1 evolved from HANDIWORK; in the later senses f. HAND *sb.* + -Y[1].] †**1.** Of, or done by, the hand; manual –1713. **2.** Ready to hand; near at hand; conveniently ready for use 1650. **3.** Convenient to handle; easy to be manipulated or managed 1694. **4.** Able to turn the hand to anything 1662. **5.** **Handy-** in *comb.*, as **Handy-craft** (see HANDICRAFT); †**-fight,** a hand to hand fight; **-grip(e** (see HANDGRIP); **-stroke** (see HANDSTROKE); **-work** (see HANDIWORK); **-man,** a man useful for all sorts of odd jobs; etc. 1592.

1. H. Artificers 1576, labour 1631. **2.** I happen to have it h. 1894. **3.** The volume is delightfully h. 1897. **4.** Two smart h. boys or girls 1790.

Ha·ndy-da·ndy, *sb.* or *adv. phr.* ME. [A rhyming jingle on *hand*, or its childish dim. *handy.*] **1.** A children's game in which a small object is shaken between the hands of one player, and, the hands being suddenly closed, the other player has to guess in which hand the object is 1585. **b.** The words as used in the game; = 'Choose which you please' 1598. †**2.** Something held in the closed hand; a covert bribe. ME. only.

Hang (hæŋ), *v.* Pa. t. and pple. **hung** (hɒŋ), **hanged** (hæŋd). [The present stem derives from (i) intr. OE. *hangian* = OFris. *hangia*, OS. *hangon*, OHG. *hangēn* (Du., G. *hangen*) :– WGmc. wk. vb. **χaŋʒōjan*, *-*ǣjan*; (ii) trans. ON. *hanga* = OE. *hōn*, OFris. *hua*, OS., OHG. *hāhan*, Goth. *hāhan* :– Gmc. redupl. vb. **χaŋχan*.]

I. *trans.* **1.** To place (a thing) so that it is supported from above; to fasten or attach to an object above; to suspend. Also *fig.* †**b.** To hook (a fish) –1787. **c.** To suspend floating without attachment in the air, or in space ME. **2.** *spec.* To attach or suspend in such a way as to allow of free movement about or on the point of attachment; e.g. to hang a door (on its hinges), a coach (on springs), etc. Also, to attach in a well-balanced position, as to hang a scythe (on its 'snead'). 1535. **3.** To fasten up or suspend on a cross or gibbet; †**a.** formerly, *spec.* to crucify; **b.** now, *spec.* to put to death by suspension by the neck. (In this sense, *hanged* is now the spec. form of the pa. t. and pa. pple.) OE. **b.** *refl.* To commit suicide by hanging ME. **c.** Used as an imprecation, etc. ME. **4.** To let droop or bend downward; to cause to lean or slope over 1593. **5.** To furnish or decorate *with* things suspended about or around; *esp.* to deck or ornament (a place) with tapestry or hangings 1451. **6.** *To hang fire*: (of a fire-arm) to be slow in communicating the fire through the vent to the charge; hence *fig.* to hesitate, be slow in acting (cf. II. 10.) 1781.

1. It were better for him that a millstone were hanged about his neck *Matt.* 18:6. H. it [venison] where the air comes MRS. GLASSE. **c.** He.. hangeth the earth upon nothing *Job* 26:7. **2.** This Rogue's Tongue is well hung SWIFT. **3.** To be hanged by the neck, till he was dead—that was the end DICKENS. 'Beef, sir, is hung, men are hanged' 18.. **c.** *Tam. Shr.* II. i. 301. **4.** Phr. *To h. the head (down)*: i.e. as a sign of shame, contrition, despondency, or sheepishness. *To h. the groin, a leg*: to hold back; to be reluctant or tardy. **6. b.** *To hang a jury* (*U.S.*): to prevent a jury from reaching a verdict; also *intr.* of a jury: to fail to agree; so HUNG *ppl. a.* 1850.

II. *intr.* **1.** To remain fastened or suspended from above; to depend, dangle, swing loose OE. **b.** To be furnished or adorned with things suspended or attached ME. **2.** To be supported or suspended at the side, as on a hinge or pivot ME. **3.** *spec.* Of a person: To be suspended *on* or *upon* a cross, gibbet, gallows, etc.; to suffer death in this way; esp. as a form of punishment. Also as an imprecation (*arch.*). OE. **4.** To bend forward or downward; to lean over; also, to incline steeply OE. **5.** To rest, float (in the air, etc.) ME. Also *fig.* of an evil or doubt 1548. **6.** To rest *on*, *upon* for support or authority; to depend *upon*; to be dependent *on* OE. **b.** To remain in consideration or attention ME. **7.** To attach oneself for support; to cling, hold fast, adhere ME. **b.** To stick close, so as not to leave or let go 1508. **c.** Of the wind: To remain persistently in a certain point of the compass 1671. **d.** To be a hanger-on 1535. **8.** To cling or adhere as an encumbrance or drag; to be a depressing weight 1450. **9.** *fig.* To be attached as an adjunct 1596. **10.** To be or remain in dubious suspense. Also *to h. in the wind.* ME. **11.** Of a note in music: To be prolonged 1597. **12.** To remain with motion suspended 1667. **13.** To remain as unwilling to depart or move on; to loiter, linger, as with expectation or interest 1842. †**14.** To hanker *after* or *for* –1684.

3. If I h., Ile make a fat payre of Gallowes SHAKS. Wretches h. that jurymen may dine POPE. **4.** The high hils which hanged ouer them 1598. **5.** Yon hard crescent, as she hangs Above the wood TENNYSON. *fig.* Uncertainty hung over their movements 1865. **6.** One upon whose hand and heart and brain Once the..fate of Europe hung TENNYSON. **b.** Enoch hung a moment on her words TENNYSON. **7.** Shee hung about my necke SHAKS. **b.** The patient Pack H. on the Scent unweary'd SOMERVILLE. **8.** Contempt and beggery hangs vpon thy backe SHAKS. Time hanging heavy upon our hands 1768. **9.** Wel, thereby hangs a tale SHAKS. **10.** To h. betwixt life and death MRS. CARLYLE. **12.** A noble stroke he lifted high, Which hung not MILT. **13.** The witnesses had to be kept hanging about 1892.

III. In comb. with advs. **Hang back.** *intr.* To resist advance by one's weight or inertia; *fig.* to be backward. **Hang off. a.** *intr.* To leave hold. *Mids. N.* III. ii. 260. **b.** To hang back, demur. **Hang on.** To continue to adhere; usually implying expectation, or the like. **Hang out. a.** *intr.* To protrude with downward direction. **b.** *trans.* To display as a sign or signal. **c.** *intr.* To lodge, live (*colloq.* or *slang*). **Hang together. a.** *intr.* To adhere together loosely. **b.** To be coherent or consistent. **c.** To hold together; *spec.* (of a person) to keep body and soul together. **Hang up. a.** *trans.* To fasten so as to be supported only from above; to suspend on a hook, peg, or the like. **b.** Phr. *To h. up (one's sword, gun,* etc.): to give up using. *To h. up one's hat*: said of a man who marries and goes home to the wife's house to live. †**c.** To hang on a gibbet; hence as an imprecation *L.L.L.* IV. iii. 54. *Rom. & Jul.* III. iii. 57. **d.** To put 'on the shelf' or into abeyance; to keep back indefinitely.

Hang (hæŋ), *sb.* 1797. [f. prec. vb.] **1.** The action of hanging; also, a downward slope or bend; a declivity 1807. **b.** A suspension of motion 1866. **2.** The mode in which a thing hangs or is poised 1797. **3.** *concr.* (*dial.*) Something that hangs; a hanging mass or clump; a crop of fruit; a hang-net 1825.

1. The south-east h. of a hill 1807. **b.** The h. and eddy of a stream 1867. **2.** The h. of a discourse 1864, of a skirt 1885. Phr. *To get the h. of*: to become familiar with the proper wielding of a tool; *fig.* to get to understand, master; to acquire the knack of (*U.S. colloq.*) *Not..a h.* (usu. with *care*): = 'not a bit'.

Hang-, the vb.-stem used in comb.: **hang-bench** (dial. **hing-**), in *Lead-mining*, a piece of timber forming part of a stow, which is pinned to the sole-tree by wooden pins; **-choice,** a choice between two evils; **-nest,** a bird that constructs a pensile nest, a HANGBIRD; **-net,** a kind of net which is set vertically.

Hangar (aṅgār). 1852. [– Fr. *hangar.*] A covered space, shed, or shelter. **b.** (hæ·ŋəɹ). A shed for accommodating aircraft 1902.

Hangbird (hæ·ŋbɜ̄ɹd). 1856. [f. HANG *v.* + BIRD.] A bird that builds a hanging nest; *esp.* an American oriole of the genus *Icteridæ*.

Ha·ng-by. *Obs.* exc. *dial.* 1579. [f. HANG- + BY *adv.* and *prep.*] **1.** A contemptuous term for a dependant or hanger-on. **2.** An appendage, an adjunct 1585. Also *attrib.*

Ha·ng-dog. 1677. [f. HANG *v.* + DOG; cf. *cut-throat.*]

A. *sb.* A despicable fellow fit only to hang a dog, or to be hanged like a dog. Also *attrib.* in *apposition.* 1687.

Paws off..You young hang-dog THACKERAY.

B. *adj.* Of, befitting, or characteristic of a hang-dog; low, degraded; sneaking 1677.

A squinting, meager, hang-dog countenance OTWAY.

Hanged (hæŋd), *ppl. a.* 1451. [f. HANG *v.* + -ED[1].] **1.** Now *Obs.* in the general sense; the form in use being HUNG. **2.** Put to death by hanging by the neck 1470. **b.** As an expletive (also *advb.*): 'Confounded' 1887.

Hanger[1] (hæ·ŋəɹ). [OE. *hangra*, deriv. of HANG *v.* Now identified with the next.] A wood on the side of a steep hill or bank.

Hanger[2] (hæ·ŋəɹ). ME. [f. HANG *v.* + -ER[1].] **1.** One who suspends a thing from above; often in *comb.*, as *paper-h.*, etc. *spec.* One of those who select and hang the pictures for an exhibition. 1791. **b.** One who puts a person to death by hanging, or causes him to be hanged ME. **2.** Something that hangs down or is suspended; e.g. †a bell-rope; a pendent catkin, etc. 1483. **3.** Something that overhangs; in *Mining*, The rock over the vein or lode; the 'roof' 1631. **4.** That by which anything is hung; a rope, chain, or hook used to suspend something; a support for a journal-box, etc. of a shafting. Also *attrib.* 1864. †**b.** A loop or strap on a sword-belt from which the sword was hung –1676. **c.** A chain or iron rod to which a pot or kettle is hung by means of a pot-hook. Hence *transf.* A nursery name for the stroke with a double curve (ɩ); usually in the phr. *pot-hooks and hangers* 1599. **5. Hanger-on. a.** A follower or dependant (often *disparagingly*) 1549. †**b.** An appendage, an adjunct –1674.

Hanger[3] (hæ·ŋəɹ). 1481. [prob. identical with HANGER[2]; cf. early mod. Du. *hangher* rapier, which may be the immed. source.] A kind of short sword, orig. hung from the belt.

Hanging (hæ·piŋ), *vbl. sb.* ME. [f. HANG *v.* + -ING[1].] **1.** The action of HANG *v.*; suspension. **2.** The action of putting to death on the gallows, etc.; the being so put to death ME. **3.** A downward slope or curve; esp. in *Ship-building* 1684. **4.** *concr.* Something that hangs or is suspended; something attached; also *fig.* (Usu. in *pl.*) 1549. **5.** *spec.* A piece of drapery with which a bedstead, the walls of a room, etc., are hung; also the material for this ME. **b.** *pl.* The pieces, folds, or masses of tapestry, etc., with which a room or bed is hung; also extended to wall-paper (*paper-hangings*) 1485. **6.** A steep slope or declivity of a hill. Now *local.* ME.

2. Many a good h. preuents a bad marriage SHAKS. **4.** *Cymb.* III. iii. 63. **5. b.** No more than a picture in the hangings DRYDEN.

Comb.: **h.-committee,** the committee who decide the hanging of pictures in an Exhibition (e.g. that of the Royal Academy); **-head, -post, -stile,** the post or upright which bears the hinges of a door or gate.

Hanging (hæ·ŋiŋ), *ppl. a.* (*prep.*) ME. [f. as prec. + -ING[2].] That hangs. **1.** Supported above, and not below; suspended, pendulous; hanging downwards 1483. **2.** Overhanging; steep ME.; situated on a steep slope, top of a wall, etc., so as to appear to hang over ME. †**3.** Remaining in suspense –1590. †**b.** Pending, during; orig. with a sb. in absolute construction; hence, occas. treated as a prep. –1628. **4.** Having a downward cast of countenance. (Often with play on HANG *v.* I. 3.) 1603. **5.** In trans. sense: Addicted to hanging; as, a *h. judge* 1848.

1. Phr. *H. sleeve*, a loose open sleeve hanging down from the arm. **2.** A man with a heavy h. brow 1847. Phr. *H. Gardens* (of Babylon), a transl. of L. *pensiles horti* (Q. Curtius). **3. b.** This matter thus hangyng, the king [etc.] GRAFTON. **4.** A good fauor you haue, but that you haue a h. look SHAKS.

Comb.: **h. ball** (Golf), a ball lying on a downward slope; **h. buttress,** 'a buttress supported on a corbel, and not standing solid on the foundation' (Webster); **h.-coal, -side, -wall** (*Mining*), that which hangs or leans over the working; **h. gale,** the rent due at the previous gale-day (GALE *sb.*[4]); **-moss,** a lichen or moss that hangs in long fringes from the limbs of a tree; **h. valve,** a hinged valve which falls open by the action of gravity.

Hangman (hæ·ŋmæ̆n). ME. [f. HANG *v.* + MAN.] A man whose office it is to hang condemned criminals; also, an executioner, a torturer, racker. **b.** *transf.* A term of reprobation; also used playfully 1553. Also *attrib.* **Ha·ngmanship,** the office or function of h.

Ha·ng-nail. 1678. [alt. f. AGNAIL.] A small piece of epidermis hanging by one end, near to a nail.

Ha·ng-o:ver. *U.S.* 1894. Something remaining or left over; a remainder or survival.

Hank (hæŋk), *sb.* ME. [– ON. **hanku*, prehistoric form of *hǫnk*, gen. *hankar* (cf. *hanki* hasp, clasp; Sw. *hank* string, tie-band, rowel, Da. *hank* handle, ear of a pot).] **1.** A circular coil or loop of anything flexible 1483. **2.** A skein or coil of thread, yarn, etc.; a definite length of yarn or thread in a coil 1560. **3.** *Naut.* A hoop or ring of rope, wood, or iron, fixed upon the stays, to seize the luff of the fore-and-aft sails, and to confine the staysails thereto, at different distances (Smyth) 1711. **4.** *fig.* A hold; a power of restraint (now *rare* or *dial.*) 1613.

4. 'Twill give me such a h. upon her pride FARQUHAR.

Hank (hæŋk), *v.* ME. [– ON. *hanka* coil, f. *hǫnk*; see prec.] **1.** *trans.* To fasten by a loop or noose; to entangle (now *dial.*). **2.** *intr.* To hang or remain fastened; to 'catch' 1547. **3.** *trans.* To make up (thread) in hanks 1818. †**4.** *intr.* = HANKER *v.* 1. –1716.

Ha·nker, *sb.* 1827. [f. HANKER *v.*] A longing after something.

Hanker (hæ·ŋkəɹ), *v.* 1601. [f. HANK *v.* 4 + -ER[5]; prob. f. **haŋk-*, parallel to **haŋg-* HANG; cf. synon. Du. *hunkeren*, dial. *hankeren.*] **1.** *intr.* To 'hang about', to linger *about* with longing or expectation. Now *dial.* **2.** To have a longing or craving. Const. *after*; occas. with *for* or *infin.* 1642.

2. The mind..always hankering after what she has not TUCKER. Hence **Ha·nkerer. Ha·nkering** *vbl. sb.* a mental craving or longing; **-ly** *adv.*

Hanky-panky (hæ·ŋkiˌpæ·ŋki). *slang.* 1841. [Rhyming jingle based on *hokey pokey*, *hocus pocus*, with possible suggestion of 'sleight of hand'.] Jugglery, legerdemain; trickery, double dealing, underhand dealing. Also *attrib.*

Hanover (hæ·nŏvəɹ, orig. as in G. hanō·vəɹ). [G. *Hannover.*] A North German town, capital of Hanover, formerly an Electorate of the Empire, now a province of Prussia; in 1714 the Elector of Hanover became king of England. Hence **Hanove·rian** *a.* of or pertaining to H. or the House of H.; *sb.* an inhabitant of H.; also an adherent of the House of H. †**Hanoverianize** *v.* to make, or become, Hanoverian.

Hans (hans). 1569. Abbrev. in G. and Du. of *Johannes*, John; hence, a German or Dutchman.

Hans, obs. f. HANSE.

Hansard[1] (hæ·nsăɹd). *Hist.* 1832. [f. HANSE + -ARD.] A member of one of the establishments of the German Hanse.

Hansard[2] (hæ·nsăɹd). 1876. The official report of the proceedings and debates of the Houses of Parliament; long compiled by Messrs. Hansard (*colloq.*). Also *transf.* Hence **Ha·nsardize** *v.* to confront (a member of Parliament) with his former utterances as recorded in 'Hansard'. Also *absol.*

Hanse (hæns, ‖ha·nzə). *Hist.* ME. [First in *hanshus* (*a* 1135) 'hanse-house', guildhall – MLG. *hanshūs*, and in med.L. form *hansa*, – OHG. *hansa*, (M)HG. *hanse* (whence MLG. *hanse*, etc.) = OE. *hōs* (instr. only) troop, company, Goth. *hansa* company, crowd :– Gmc. **χansō* (whence Finn. *kansa* people, company); of unkn. origin.] **1.** A company or guild of merchants in former times; also, the privileges and monopolies possessed by it; *occas.*, the guild-hall or hanse-house. **b.** *spec.* A famous political and commercial league of Germanic towns, which had also a house in London. *pl.* The Hanse towns or their citizens. ME. **2.** The entrance-fee of a mediæval trading guild; also, a toll levied on traders not of the guild ME.

Comb.: **H. city, H. town,** one of the towns of the German H. or Hanseatic League; so *H. association, league, merchant*, etc.; **h.-house,** a guild-hall.

Hanseatic (hænsi,æ·tik), *a.* 1614. [– med.L. *Hanseaticus*; see prec.] Of or pertaining to the German Hanse.

Hansel: see HANDSEL.

†**Hanselin.** [– OFr. *hainselin, hamselin.*] A kind of jacket or slop. CHAUCER.

Hansom cab; also **hansom** (hæ·nsŏm). 1847. [f. name of Joseph Aloysius *Hansom* (1803–82), architect, who registered a Patent Safety Cab in 1834.] A low-hung two-wheeled cabriolet holding two persons inside, the driver being mounted on a dickey behind, and the reins going over the roof. Also *attrib.*

He hailed a cruising hansom..''Tis the gondola of London', said Lothair DISRAELI.

Han't, ha'n't, vulgar contr. of *have not.*

Hantle (ha·nt'l). *Sc.* and *n. dial.* 1692. [Of unkn. origin.] A (considerable) number or quantity.

Hap (hæp), *sb.*[1] *arch.* ME. [– ON. *happ* chance, good luck, rel. to OE. *ġehæp(lić)* fitting, convenient, orderly.] **1.** Chance or fortune (good or bad); luck, lot. **2.** (with *pl.*) A chance, accident, occurrence; often, an unfortunate event, mishap ME. †**3.** Good luck, success, prosperity –1813. **4.** Fortuity. (*Occas.* personified.) ME.

1. He sought them both, but wish'd his h. might find Eve separate MILT. Good h. and evil h. 1884. **3.** Be it h., or be it harm SCOTT. **4.** H. helpeth hardy man alday CHAUCER.

Hap, *sb.*[2] *n. dial.* 1724. [f. HAP *v.*[2]] A covering.

Hap (hæp), *v.*[1] *arch.* ME. [f. HAP *sb.*[1]; superseded by HAPPEN.] **1.** *intr.* To come about by hap or chance; to happen, chance. **2.** To have the hap, fortune, or luck (*to do*, or with cl.) ME. **3.** To come or go by chance; to chance *on* or *upon* ME.

1. Happe how happe may, Al sholde I deye CHAUCER. **2.** If the Skie fal, we may happe to catche Larkes 1566.

Hap, *v.*[2] Now only *Sc.* and *dial.* ME. [Of unkn., prob. Scand., origin.] **1.** *trans.* To cover up or over. †Also *transf.* and *fig.* –1576. **2.** To cover for warmth; to wrap; to 'tuck *up*' (in bed) ME.

2. His chaplain hapt him up in bed KINGSLEY.

Haphazard (hæ·phæ:zăɹd). 1575. [f. HAP *sb.*[1] + HAZARD; lit. 'hazard of chance'.]

A. *sb.* Mere chance or accident; fortuity. Chiefly with *at, by,* †*in.*

It is hap hazard, if you escape undamnified 1576.

B. *adj.* Characterized by haphazard; random 1671.

C. *adv.* In a haphazard manner; casually 1857.

Hapless (hæ·plĕs), *a.* 1568. [f. HAP *sb.*[1] + -LESS.] Destitute of hap or good fortune; luckless.

An..haplesse love 1635. Hence **Ha·pless-ly** *adv.*, **-ness** (*rare*).

Haplo-, comb. f. Gr. ἁπλόος, ἁπλοῦς single, simple:

haplo-ca·rdiac [Gr. καρδία], *a.*, having a heart of simple structure; belonging to the *Haplocardia* or *Brachiopoda*; ‖**-cerus** [Gr. κέρας], generic name of Rocky Mountain sheep; hence **-cerine** *a.*; **-ste·monous** [Gr. στήμων] *a.*, *Bot.* having a single circle or row of stamens; **-tomy** [Gr. ἁπλοτομία], a simple cutting or incision.

Haply (hæ·pli), *adv.* Now *arch.* or *poet.* ME. [f. HAP *sb.*[1] + -LY[2].] By hap; by chance or accident; perhaps.

Lest h. ye be found even to fight against God *Acts* 5:39.

Ha'p'orth: see HALFPENNYWORTH.

Happen (hæ·p'n), *v.* ME. [f. HAP *sb.*[1] + -EN[5]; superseding HAP *v.*[1]] **1.** *intr.* To come to pass (*orig.* by hap or chance); to take place; to occur. The most general verb to express the simple occurrence of an event. †**2.** With *to, unto*: To fall to the lot of; to come in the way of –1764. **3.** To have the hap or fortune (*to do* something) ME. **4.** To chance to be or to come; to 'turn up', occur ME.; also with *on, upon,* occas. *of* 1533.

1. The greatest evill that can h. in this life HOBBES. As it happens JANE AUSTEN. No harm shall h. to you 1815. **3.** I h. to know [etc.] DICKENS. **4.** Phr. *Happen in*: to go or come in casually: *esp.* to drop in (at a house). *U.S.* **Ha·ppening** *vbl. sb.*, the action of the vb.; also (with *pl.*), an event, occurrence 1581.

Happily (hæ·pili), *adv.* Also †**happely.** ME. [f. HAPPY *a.* + -LY[2].] In a happy manner. **1.** = HAPLY (*arch.*). **2.** With or by good fortune; luckily, successfully. (Now often expressing only that it is well that things are so.) ME. **3.** Aptly, fitly, appropriately; felicitously 1577. **4.** With mental pleasure or content 1513.

2. The case h. stands alone in his biography MORLEY. **3.** Minds..h. constituted for the cultivation of science MACAULAY. **4.** He writes How h. he liues SHAKS.

Happiness (hæ·pinĕs). 1530. [f. as prec. + -NESS.] The quality or condition of being happy. **1.** Good fortune or luck; success, prosperity. **2.** The state of pleasurable content of mind, which results from success or the attainment of what is considered good 1591. **3.** Successful or felicitous aptitude, fitness, or appropriateness; felicity 1599.

1. Wish me partaker in thy happinesse, When thou do'st meet good hap SHAKS. **2.** Oh H.! our being's end and aim! Good, Pleasure, Ease, Content! whate'er thy name POPE. Phr. *Greatest h. of the greatest number*: a principle of moral and political action, first enunciated by Hutcheson, 1725; shortened, later, to 'greatest h. principle', 'rule of greatest h.' **3.** How pregnant (sometimes) his Replies are? A happinesse That often Madnesse hits on SHAKS.

Happy (hæ·pi), *a.* ME. [f. HAP *sb.*[1] + -Y[1].] †**1.** Fortuitous; chance (*rare*) –1677. **2.** Having good hap or fortune; lucky, fortunate; favoured by circumstance ME. †**b.** Blessed, beatified –1700. **3.** Characterized by or involving good fortune. (Now used only in association with senses 4 and 5.) ME. **4.** Having the feeling arising from satisfaction with one's circumstances or condition; also: Glad, pleased 1525. **5.** Apt, dexterous; felicitous ME. **6.** *colloq.* (*joc.*) Slightly drunk 1770.

1. Any h. concourse of Atoms HALE. **2.** The h. seat of liberty 1741. **b.** If yee know these things, h. are ye if ye doe them *John* 13:17. Phr. *Of h. memory.* **3.** Many h. returns DICKENS. **4.** Better be h. then wise 1562. H. as a king GAY. **5.** He was apt and happie in armes LD. BERNERS. A most h. thought SHERIDAN, reply (*mod.*). Phr. *Happy dispatch*: see HARA-KIRI.

†**Happy,** *v.* 1600. [f. prec.] To render happy –1632.

Ha·ppy-go-lu·cky. 1672.

A. *adv.* Just as it may happen; haphazard.

B. *adj.* Of persons, etc.: Easy-going 1856.

C. *sb.* A happy-go-lucky person, quality, or character 1851.

Haquebut, var. of HACKBUT.

Haqueton (hæ·ktǫn). *Obs.* exc. *Hist.* ME. [Later modification of ME. *aketoun* ACTON after OFr. *hocqueton* (mod. *hoqueton*).] = ACTON.

‖**Hara-kiri** (hā:răki·ri). Also corruptly **hari-kari.** 1856. [Japanese (colloq. and vulgar), f. *hara* belly + *kiri* cutting.] Suicide by disembowelment, as formerly practised by the samurai class in Japan, when in disgrace, or under sentence of death. Also called (by Englishmen) *happy dispatch.* Also fig.

Harangue (hăræ·ŋ), *sb.* 1450. [– Fr. *harangue*, earlier †*arenge* – med.L. *harenga*, perh. – Gmc. **χariχriŋg-* assembly, f. **χarjaz* host, crowd + **χriŋgaz* RING *sb.*[1]] A speech addressed to an assembly; a loud or vehement address, a tirade; occas., †a formal or pompous speech.

His grave H. 1610. Telemachus, intemp'rate in h. COWPER.

Harangue, *v.* 1660. [– Fr. *haranguer*, f. *harengue*; see prec.] **1.** *intr.* To deliver a harangue; to declaim. **2.** *trans.* To address in a harangue; to make a formal speech to 1682.

1. My wife..undertook to h. for the family GOLDSM. **2.** He often harangued the troops GIBBON. Hence **Hara·nguer.**

Haras (hæ·răs, ‖arā). Now treated as Fr. ME. [– (O)Fr. *haras*, of unkn. origin.] An enclosure or establishment in which horses are kept for breeding; hence, †a stud.

Harass (hæ·răs), *v.* 1618. [– Fr. *harasser*, pejorative deriv. of *harer* set a dog on, f. *hare* cry used for this purpose.] **1.** *trans.* To wear *out*, or exhaust with fatigue, care, trouble, etc. *Obs.* or *dial.* †**2.** To harry, lay waste –1710. **3.** To trouble or vex by repeated attacks 1622. **4.** To worry, distress with annoying labour, care, importunity, misfortune, etc. 1656.

1. Troops..harassed with a long and wearisome march BACON (J.). **3.** The Indians unceasingly harassed their march 1865. **4.** Vext with lawyers and harass'd with debt TENNYSON. Hence **Ha·rass** *sb.* harassment. **Ha·rassedly, Ha·rassingly** *advs.* **Ha·rasser.**

Harassment (hæ·răsmĕnt). 1753. [f. HARASS *v.* + -MENT.] The action of harassing; the being harassed; vexation, worry.

The h. of these applications 1806.

†**Harbergage.** [ME. *herbergage* (also *har-*) – OFr. *herbergage* (rarely *har-*), f. *herbergier*; see HARBINGER.] Lodging.

Harbinge (hā·ɹbindʒ), *v.* 1475. [ME. *herberge* – OFr. *herbergier*; see next, and cf. HARBOUR *v.*] †**1.** *trans.* To lodge. Also *intr.* (for *refl.*, as in OFr.). –1603. **2.** [*nonce-use* from next.] *trans.* To be a harbinger of. WHITMAN.

Harbinger (hā·ɹbindʒəɹ), *sb.* [ME. *herbergere, -geour* – AFr., OFr. *herbergere*, obl. case *-geour*, f. *herbergier* provide lodging for, f. *herberge* lodging – OS. (= OHG.) *heriberga* 'shelter for an army', lodging, f. *heri, hari* host, army (see HARRY *v.*) + **berʒ-* protect (see BOROUGH). The intrusive *n* occurs XV; cf. *messenger, passenger, scavenger, wharfinger.*] †**1.** One who provides lodgings; a host; a HARBOURER –1502. **2.** One sent on before to purvey lodgings for an army, a royal train, etc.; a purveyor of lodgings; in *pl.* an advance company of an army sent to prepare a camping-ground; a pioneer ME. **3.** A forerunner. Mostly in *transf.* and *fig.* senses, and in literary language. 1550.

3. The bright morning star, day's h. MILTON. The prophet and h. of better days STUBBS. **Harbinger of spring:** a small umbelliferous herb of N. America, *Erigenia bulbosa*, closely resembling the Earth-nut.

Ha·rbinger, *v.* 1646. [f. prec. (sense 3).] *trans.* To act as a harbinger to; to announce, presage.

To H. his learned name G. DANIEL.

Harbor, var. sp. of HARBOUR.

†**Harborough, -borow,** etc. ME. ff. HARBOUR *sb.* and *v.*

†**Ha·rborous,** *a.* 1526. [f. HARBOUR *sb.*[1], after words in -OUS from French, e.g. *humorous.*] **1.** Affording harbour; given to hospitality –1632. **2.** Furnished with harbours or havens for ships –1702.

2. A well known sea, called Euxine, or h. C. MATHER.

Harbour, also (now *U.S.*) **harbor** (hā·ɹbəɹ), *sb.*[1] [Late OE. *herebeorg* (perh. – ON.), corresp. to OS., OHG. *heriberga* (Du. *herberg*, G. *herberge*), ON. *herbergi*; see HARBINGER.] **1.** Shelter, lodging, entertainment; sojourn, abode. **2.** A place of shelter or sojourn; lodgings; inn; asylum. *Obs.* exc. *dial.* ME. †**b.** The 'house' of the sun or a planet in the zodiac. CHAUCER. **c.** The covert of wild animals 1576. **d.** *fig.* 1548. **3.** A place of shelter for ships; *spec.* where they may lie sheltered by the shore or by works extended from it; a haven, a port ME. **4.** *Glass-making.* A trough-like box for holding the mixed ingredients and conveying them to the pot for fusion 1891.

1. Our great Want..was Harbor and good Company BUNYAN. **2.** Fair h. that them seems: so in they entred are SPENSER. **3.** A Station safe for Ships, when Tempests roar, A silent H. and a cover'd Shoar DRYDEN.

Comb.: **h.-due,** a charge for the use of a h. (usually in *pl.*); **-master,** an officer who has charge of a h., and of the mooring of ships, etc. therein; **-watch,** a division or subdivision of the watch kept on night-duty, when the ship rides at single anchor.

†**Harbour,** *sb.*[2] 1505. [A form of ARBOUR, intermediate between it and the earlier *herber, erber.*] **a.** = ARBOUR 1. –1820. **b.** A bower covered with climbing plants –1790.

Harbour, also (now *U.S.*) **harbor** (hā·ɹbəɹ), *v.* [Late OE. *herebeorgian*, corresp. to (M)Du. *herbergen*, OHG. *heribergōn*, ON. *herbergja.*]

I. *trans.* †**1.** To provide a lodging for; to shelter; to lodge, entertain. Also *fig.* –1671. †**2.** To quarter (soldiers or retainers); to billet; *refl.* to encamp. Also *absol.* –1648. **3.** To give shelter to, to shelter. Now mostly dyslogistic. Also *fig.* ME. †**b.** Of a place, etc.: To afford room for; to contain, hold –1680. **4.** *fig.* To entertain; to cherish privately; to indulge (esp. evil thoughts or designs) ME. **5.** To shelter in a haven or harbour 1555. **6.** To trace (a stag) to his lair. Also *transf.* 1531.

1. She harbors you as her kinsman SHAKS. *fig.* The anguish of my soul, that suffers not Mine eye to h. sleep MILT. **3.** To h. rebels 1849, vermin 1851, smuggled tobacco 1898. **4.** To h. suspicions 1766, the worst designs MACAULAY, resentment 1850.

II. *intr.* **1.** To lodge, take shelter; to encamp; later, often with some notion of lurking or concealment. (*arch.* or *Obs.*) Also *fig.* ME. **2.** Of a stag, etc.: To have its retreat or resort 1599. **3.** To take shelter or cast anchor in a haven or harbour. Also *fig.* 1583.

1. For this Night, lets harbor herte in Yorke SHAKS. **2.** The place where the turtle were known to h. COOK. Hence **Ha·rbourer, -orer,** one who harbours (now usu. dyslogistic); one whose office it is to trace a deer to its covert.

Harbourage, -orage (hā·ɹbəredʒ). 1570. [f. HARBOUR *sb.*[1] + -AGE.] **1.** = HARBOUR 1. Also *transf.* and *fig.* **2.** = HARBOUR 2. 1651. **3.** Shelter for ships, shelter in a haven 1850.

1. Where can I get me h. for the night TENNYSON.

Harbourless (hā·ɹbəɹlės), *a.* ME. [f. as prec. + -LESS.] **1.** Destitute of shelter, houseless. †**2.** Of a place: That affords no shelter –1589. **3.** Without harbours for ships 1600.

Harbrough(e, Harburrow, obs. ff. HARBOUR *sb.*[1] and *v.*

Hard (hāɹd), *a.* (*sb.*) [OE. *hard, heard* = OFris. *herd*, OS. (Du.) *hard*, (O)HG. *hart*, ON. *harðr*, Goth. *hardus* :- Gmc. **χarðuz* :- IE. **kratús*, whence Gr. κρατύς strong, powerful.]

I. Passively hard. **1.** That does not yield to blows or pressure; not easily penetrated or separated into particles; firm and resisting to the touch; solid, compact in substance and texture. Opp. to *soft.* **2.** Of money: In specie as opp. to paper currency 1706. **3.** Said of the pulse when the blood-tension is high 1727. **4.** Not easy to wear out or cause to give way; formerly, *esp.*, hardy and bold in fight OE. †**b.** Inured, hardened. SHAKS. **5.** Difficult to do or accomplish ME. **b.** Of the subject of an action: Having difficulty in doing something. *Obs.* exc. in *hard of hearing.* ME. **6.** Difficult to understand or explain 1450. **7.** Difficult to deal with, manage, control, or resist 1588. **8.** Obdurate; callous; hard-hearted OE. **9.** Not easily moved to part with money; niggardly, 'close' ME. **10.** Not easily moved by sentiment; practical, shrewdly intelligent 1747.

1. H. stone 1568, egs SIR T. HERBERT. Harder than adamant PUSEY. *H. iron,* iron which retains its magnetic properties when removed from the magnetic field. *H. lead,* lead containing certain impurities, principally antimony. **2.** H. cash to meet a run GALT. **4.** The men..look as h. as nails 1885. **b.** *Ant. & Cl.* III. xiii. 111. **5.** So h. a thing it is to please all BIBLE *Transl. Pref.* A h. thing to manage 1833. **6.** To ask h. questions BURGON. **7.** Phr. *H. case,* a difficult case to treat or deal with; a person that cannot be reclaimed; a 'bad lot'. *U.S.* **8.** With his h. eye, casting envious looks at them LAMB. †*To die h.*: to die obdurate or impenitent. (See also HARD *adv.*) **10.** We Americans have got h. heads 1824.

II. Actively hard. **1.** Difficult to bear or endure; severe, rigorous, oppressive, cruel OE. **2.** Of persons: Harsh or severe in dealing with any one OE.; of things, actions etc.: Unfeeling, cruel, harsh, rough OE.; strict, without concession 1612.

1. Phr. *H. lines*: see LINE *sb.*[2] 6. It was his h. lucke 1576. Money..a very necessary Commodity in H. times 1705. A 'hard' winter 1884. **2.** Colonel, why so h. upon poor Miss? SWIFT. H. words BUTLER, fare COWPER. A h. view of persons and things 1887. To drive a h. bargain 1870.

III. In transf. senses. **1.** Harsh or unpleasant to the eye or ear, or to the æsthetic faculty 1513. **2. a.** Applied to water holding in solution mineral, esp. calcareous salts, which decompose soap and render the water unfit for washing purposes 1660. **b.** Of liquor: Harsh to the taste; acid; sour from being stale. (Now *dial.* or *slang.*) 1581. **c.** Intoxicating, strong (*colloq. U.S.*) 1879. **3.** *Comm.* Of prices: High and unyielding; stiff. Said also of the market, etc. 1882. **4.** *Phonetics.* Applied: **a.** to the letters *c, g,* when they have their original guttural sounds (k, g), as dist. from the palatal and sibilant sounds (tʃ, ts, s, dʒ, etc.); **b.** to the breath consonants (k, t, p, and sometimes χ, ʃ, s, þ, f) as opp. to the corresponding voiced consonants (g, d, b; γ, ʒ, z, ð, v) 1775. **5.** *Electr.* Of or pertaining to an electron tube having a relatively high vacuum.

1. A h. rime SHAKS., face 1622, outline 1854, negative 1894. A Virgin h. of Feature POPE.

IV. †**1.** Intense in force or degree –1807. **2.** Carried on unremittingly; (of study) close; involving great labour or effort; vehement, vigorous, violent OE. **3.** Unremitting, persistent. Qualifying an agent-noun. 1663.

2. H. drinking 1714, study SWIFT. **Hard labour:** hard bodily labour of certain kinds imposed upon certain classes of criminals during their term of imprisonment. *H. swearing,* swearing (as a witness) to one effect regardless of perjury; hence, perjury. **3.** A h. rider KINGSLEY.

Phrases and Combs. **a.** In names of trees and plants: **h.-corn,** a general name for wheat and rye; **-grass,** a name given locally to various coarse dry grasses, e.g. *Dactylis glomerata,* species of *Rottbœllia,* etc.; **-rush,** *Juncus effusus*; **-tinder fungus,** *Boletus igniarius.* **b.** Chiefly techn.: **h. bargain,** a thing or person not worth its cost; **-bread,** a kind of hard-baked cake or biscuit; **h. finish, -ing,** in *Plastering,* the third and last coat, consisting of fine stuff laid on to the depth of about an eighth of an inch; **h. fish,** cod, ling, etc., salted and dried.

B. *sb.* (the adj. used ellipt.) †**1.** That which is hard, something hard; hardship. ME. only. **b.** *In hard,* in hard cash, down. †**2.** Hard or firm ground –1629. **3.** A firm beach or foreshore; also, a sloping stone roadway or jetty at the water's edge for landing, etc. (Hence, at Portsmouth, a street which adjoins the landing.) 1838. **4.** *slang.* = *hard labour* 1890.

Phr. *When h. comes to h.*: when the worst comes to the worst.

Hard, *adv.* [OE. *hearde,* f. HARD *a.*] In a hard manner. **1.** With effort or violence; strenuously, earnestly, vigorously; fiercely. In early use, occas. = exceedingly. **2.** So as to bring or involve pain or hardship; severely; cruelly, harshly ME. †**b.** With an uneasy pace –1824. **3.** With difficulty, hardly; scarcely ME. **4.** Firmly, securely; tightly; fast. Now *rare.* ME. **5.** So as to be hard ME.; on a hard ground, floor, etc. 1577. **6.** Close, of time or place ME. **b.** *Naut.* Expressing the carrying of an action to its extreme limits, as in *hard-a-lee, -a-port,* etc.: see the second elements 1549. †**7.** Parsimoniously. STEELE.

1. Strangers..Who hunt me h. 1586. His majesty looked at me very h. FOOTE. Last night it froze h. (*mod.*). **2.** H. put to it to veil their feelings 1885. **b.** He [Time] trots h. with a yong maid, between the contract of her marriage [etc.] *A. Y. L.* III. ii. 331. Phr. *To go h. with* (a person): to fare ill with him; with *but,* introducing a statement of what will happen unless prevented by overpowering difficulties. **3.** Phr. *To die h.*: to die with difficulty, not without a struggle. **4.** Bound h. and fast 1833. **5.** Lakes..h. frozen 1632. The harder they lie, the sooner they fatte B. GOOGE. **6.** *H. upon* sixty FOOTE. Phr. *To run* (a person) *h.* In *Comb.,* qualifying ppl. adjs., to which *hard* is always united by a hyphen, when they are used attrib., and generally when they are used predicatively: **a.** With effort, strenuously, violently, etc., as *h.-drinking, -fought, -hitting,* etc. **b.** With hardship, severely, etc., as *h.-faring, -living,* etc. **c.** With difficulty, as *h.-bought, -earned,* etc. **d.** So as to be hard, tight, etc., as *h.-baked, -pressed,* etc. **e. h.-boiled** of an egg: boiled till the white and yolk are solid; *fig.* (orig. *U.S.*) callous, hard-headed, shrewd; **-bound,** slow in action; costive; **-drawn,** drawn when cold, as wire; **-spun,** tightly twisted in spinning; etc.

†**Hard,** *v.* [OE. *heardian* = OS. *hardon,* OHG. *hartēn, hartōn*; orig. intr., f. the adj.] To make, be, or become hard (*lit.* and *fig.*) –1620.

Hard and fast, *a.* 1867. **1.** *Naut.* Said of a ship on shore. **2.** Rigidly laid down and adhered to 1867.

Hard-bake (hā·ɹdbēɪk). 1825. [f. HARD *a.* + BAKE *v.* and *sb.*] A sweetmeat made of boiled sugar or treacle with blanched almonds; almond toffee.

Hardbeam (hā·ɹdbīm). ? *Obs.* OE. [f. HARD *a.* + BEAM tree.] The HORNBEAM, *Carpinus betulus.*

Hard-bitten, *a.* 1784. [f. HARD *a.* + BITTEN *pa. pple.* (here used actively; cf. *ill-spoken*).] Given to hard biting; tough in fight.

They will be hard-bitten terriers will worry Dandie SCOTT.

Hard by. *arch.* 1526. [f. HARD *adv.* 6 + BY *prep.* and *adv.*] **A.** *prep.* Close by; close to, very near to. (Now only of place.) **B.** *adv.* Close by; very near; †also *transf.* close at hand in time 1535.

Harden, hurden (hā·ɹd'n, hɔ̄·ɹd'n), *sb.* late ME. [f. HARDS + -EN[4].] Coarse fabric made from hards.

Harden (hā·ɹd'n), *v.* ME. [f. HARD *a.* + -EN[5], after ON. *harðna*; repl. OE. *heardian,* to HARD.]

I. *trans.* **1.** To render or make hard; to indurate. Also *transf.* and *fig.* †**2.** To embolden, confirm; to incite to action –1658. **3.** To make callous or unfeeling ME. **4.** To make persistent or obdurate in a course of action or state of mind ME. **5.** To make firm and tight 1523. **6.** To render hardy, robust, or capable of endurance 1577. **7.** *Phonetics.* To make a sound hard. See HARD *a.* 1871.

1. Snow hardened by frost TYNDALL. *fig.* Hardening customary into written rights 1874. **3.** He hath blinded their eyes, and hardened their heart *John* 12:40. **4.** Harden'd in Impenitence DRYDEN. **6.** It is not true..that cold hardens children 1793.

II. *intr.* **1.** To become hard. Also *fig.* ME. **2.** To become hard in feeling, constitution, etc. 1667. **3.** *Comm.* Of prices: To rise; to stiffen. Cf. HARD *a.* 1674.

1. *fig.* This natural sequence hardened first into custom and then into law 1891. **2.** Now his heart..hardning in his strength Glories MILT.

Hence **Ha·rdened** *ppl. a.* made hard, indurated; rendered callous; hard-hearted; obdurately determined in a course. **Ha·rdener,** one who hardens; *spec.* one who hardens metals; one who case-hardens guns.

Harderian (haɹdīə·riăn), *a.* 1835. [f. J. J. *Harder,* Swiss anatomist (1656–1711) + -IAN.] *Anat.* In *Harderian gland*: the lubricating gland of the nictitating membrane or 'third eyelid' in the inner angle of the eye of birds and some mammals.

Ha·rd-favoured, *a. arch.* 1513. [See HARD *a.* III. 1, FAVOUR *sb.,* -ED[2].] Having a hard or unpleasing 'favour', appearance, or look; ugly.

The Corsicans are in general..rather hard-favoured BOSWELL. Hence **Hardfa·vouredness.**

Ha·rd-featured, *a.* 1748. [See HARD *a.* III. 1, -ED².] Having hard, harsh, or unpleasing features.

Hard fern. 1828. Any fern of the genus *Lomaria*, as the Northern Hard Fern, *Lomaria* (*Blechnum*) *spicant*, of Europe.

Ha·rd-fisted, *a.* 1656. [See HARD *a.* I. 9, -ED².] Stingy, niggardly.

Ha·rdhack. *U.S.* 1851. [f. HARD *a.* + (perh.) HACK *v.*] A low shrub, *Spiræa tomentosa*, common in New England.

Ha·rd-handed, *a.* 1590. [See -ED².] **1.** Having hard hands, from manual labour. †**2.** Niggardly, close-fisted. NORDEN. **3.** Ruling with a cruel hand; severe 1641.

1. Hard handed men..Which neuer labour'd in their mindes till now SHAKS.

Ha·rdhead, hard-head. 1519. **1.** A hard-headed person; one not easily moved; a blockhead. †**2.** A contest of butting with the head. Also *hard-heads*. DRYDEN. **3.** A name of fishes: **a.** The sea scorpion, *Cottus scorpius* 1803. **b.** The grey gurnard, *Trigla gurnardus* 1810. **c.** The menhaden (*New England*) 1837. **4.** The Californian grey whale, *Rhachianectes glaucus*: so named from its habit of butting boats 1860. **6.** The plant Knapweed. Also *hard-heads*. 1794. **6.** A variety of sponge 1883. **7.** A residual alloy of tin, iron, and arsenic, produced in the refining of tin (Raymond).

Ha·rd-headed, *a.* 1583. [See -ED².] **1.** *lit.* Having a hard head. †**2.** Not easily turned, as a horse; *fig.* stubborn –1642. **3.** Not moved by sophistry or sentiment; matter-of-fact, logical, practical 1779. Hence **Hard-hea·ded-ly** *adv.*, **-ness.**

Ha·rd-hearted, *a.* ME. [f. *hard heart* + -ED².] Having a hard heart; unfeeling; unmerciful. Hence **Hardhea·rted-ly** *adv.*, **-ness.**

‖**Hardiesse** (hardie·s). ME. [– (O)Fr., f. *hardi* HARDY. Adopted anew as Fr. in XVIII.] Hardihood, boldness.

Hardihood (hā·ɹdihud). 1634. [f. HARDY *a.* + -HOOD.] **1.** Boldness, hardiness; audacity. **2.** Robustness (of body or constitution) (*rare*) 1794.

1. With dauntless h., And brandish'd blade, rush on him MILT. Phr. *To have the h. to deny*, etc. So **Ha·rdihead** (*arch.*).

Hardily (hā·ɹdili), *adv.* ME. [f. HARDY *a.* + -LY².] **1.** Boldly. †**2.** Robustly; not tenderly (*rare*) –1793. †**3.** *Parenthetically.* = It may be boldly said; freely, assuredly, by all means. Changed later through *hardely* to *hardly*. –1600.

1. H. I make the assertion [etc.] 1799. **2.** Among those h. brought up BEDDOES.

Hardiment (hā·ɹdimĕnt). *arch.* ME. [– OFr. *hardiment* act of daring, f. *hardier* attack, charge, harass + *-ment*, -MENT.] Boldness, hardihood; †a bold exploit.

Now is the time to prove your h. WORDSW.

Hardiness (hā·ɹdinės). ME. [f. HARDY *a.* + -NESS.] **1.** Boldness; audacity; hardihood. Now *rare*. **2.** Capability of endurance. Now chiefly, Physical robustness. 1642. **3.** Catachr. for *hardness* 1539.

1. There being none that had the h. yet to declare..for the King CLARENDON. **2.** The extreme h. of the race 1879.

Ha·rdish, *a.* 1580. [f. HARD *a.* + -ISH¹.] Somewhat hard.

Hardly (hā·ɹdli), *adv.* ME. [f. HARD *a.* + -LY².] In a hard manner. †**1.** With energy; vigorously, forcibly, violently –1818. †**2.** Hardily –1622. **3.** With hard pressure; with severity or rigour; harshly 1523. **4.** With hardship; uneasily, painfully 1535. **5.** Not easily. *Obs.* exc. as in 6. 1535. **6.** Barely, only just; not quite; scarcely. (Formerly with superfluous negative.) 1553. **7.** Closely 1584. †**8.** *Parenthetically.* Certainly, assuredly, by all means.

3. The Sea used us h. BP. HALL. The rule worked h. 1886. **4.** The Husbandmen live h. 1630. **5.** Easily provoked and h. pacified FORDYCE. **6.** When Day broke I could h. believe my Eyes 1698. **7.** They were so h. pursued KNOLLES.

Hard-mouthed (hā·ɹdmauðd, -mauþt), *a.* 1617. **1.** Having a hard mouth: said of a horse not easily controlled by the bit. **2.** *fig.* Self-willed 1686.

Hardness (hā·ɹdnės). OE. [f. HARD *a.* + -NESS.] The quality or condition of being hard; difficulty of penetration, solution, apprehension, performance, endurance; inflexibility, stiffness, harshness; rigour, severity, cruelty; obduracy, obstinacy; hardiness, etc.; see HARD *a.* Also with *a* and *pl.*

†**Ha·rdock.** [app. f. OE. *hār*, ME. *hōr*, HOAR + DOCK *sb.*¹] Some coarse weed; prob. burdock. *Lear.* IV. iv. 4 (Fo. 2).

Ha·rd-pan. *U.S.* 1828. [See PAN *sb.*¹] **1.** A firm subsoil of clayey, gravelly, or sandy detritus; also, hard unbroken ground. **2.** *fig.* Bottom; 'bed-rock' 1852.

Hards, hurds (hāɹdz, hǭɹdz), *sb. pl.* Now *local*. [OE. *heordan* wk. fem. pl., corresp. to OFris., OLG. *hēde* (Du. *heede*); of unkn. origin. (For the phonology cf. OE. *meord*, *mēd*; OS. *mēda* MEED.] The coarser parts of flax or hemp; tow.

Hard-set, *a.* ME. [f. HARD *adv.* + SET *pa. pple.*] **1.** In a difficult position; beset by trouble. **2.** Set so as to be hard or firm 1813. **3.** Obstinate. SCOTT.

Ha·rdshell, ha·rd-shell. 1848. **A.** *adj.* **1.** Having a hard shell; as crabs, clams, etc. **2.** *fig.* Rigid in religious orthodoxy 1857. **B.** *sb.* A hard-shelled crab or clam (*U.S.*) So **Hard-shelled** *a.* = above; also, hardened, callous.

Hardship (hā·ɹdʃip). ME. [f. HARD *a.* + -SHIP.] †**1.** The quality of being hard to bear; hardness; severity –1676. **2.** Hardness of fate or circumstance; severe toil or suffering; extreme privation. Also with *a* and *pl.* ME. †**b.** A piece of harsh treatment –1780.

2. Men to much misery and h. born MILT. **b.** To offer a h. or affront to religious prejudices BURKE.

Hard-tack. 1841. [f. HARD *a.*; see TACK *sb.*⁴] Ship-biscuit; hence, ordinary sea fare in general.

Hard u·p, *advb.* and *adj. phr.* 1612. **1.** *adv. Naut.* Said of the tiller when it is put as far as possible to windward, so as to turn the ship's head away from the wind. (Usu. as a command.) **2.** *adj.* Hard put to it; in want, *esp.* of money. *Hard up for*, sorely at a loss for. *colloq.* (of slang origin). 1821.

Hardware (hā·ɹd,wēᵊɹ). 1515. [See WARE *sb.*²] Small ware or goods of metal; ironmongery. Also *attrib.* Hence **Ha·rdware-man.**

Ha·rdwood, *sb.* 1568. **1.** The wood or timber of broad-leaved deciduous trees as dist. from that of conifers; *locally*, that of oak and ash. Mostly *attrib.* Chiefly *Sc.* and *U.S.* **2. a.** In Australia, any timber resembling teak, esp. *Backhousia bancroftii*. **b.** A W. Indian shrub, *Ixora ferrea*. 1888.

Hardy (hā·ɹdi), *a.* ME. [– (O)Fr. *hardi*, pa. pple. of *hardir* become bold – Gmc. **χarðjan*, f. **χarðuz* HARD *a.*] **1.** Bold, courageous, daring. **2.** *opprobriously.* Presumptuously bold; showing temerity. Cf. FOOLHARDY. ME. **3.** Capable of enduring fatigue, hardship, rigour of the weather, etc.; robust, vigorous 1548. **b.** *Hort.* Able to grow in the open air throughout the year 1852.

1. A good Knight and hardie of his handes GRAFTON. A h. denial of facts JOHNSON. **3.** [Art] Thou then they Less hardie to endure MILT. The h. pine 1783. **b.** Phr. *Half h.*, able to grow in the open air except in winter. *H. annual*, an annual plant that ripens its seed and sows itself year after year. Also *fig.*, a subject that comes up year after year in Parliament, or in the newspapers.

Ha·rdy, *sb.* 1870. [prob. f. HARD, or HARDY *a.*] A movable piece, called also 'fuller', fitting into a socket in an anvil, used by blacksmiths.

Hare (hēᵊɹ), *sb.* [OE. *hara* = OFris. *hasa*, MDu. *haese* (Du. *haas*), OHG. *haso* (G. *hase*), ON. *heri* :– Gmc. **χason*, **χazon*.] **1.** A rodent quadruped of the genus *Lepus*, having long ears and hind legs, a short tail, and a divided upper lip. The common hare of Great Britain and Europe is *L. timidus*. **b.** The buck is sometimes called *Jack hare*. During March (the breeding season) hares are unusually wild; hence the saying *As mad as a March h.* 1529. **2. a.** *fig.* Applied to persons, allusively ME. **b.** He who lays the 'scent' in the sport *hare and hounds*, also called 'paper-chase' 1845. **3.** A southern constellation, *Lepus* 1551. **4.** = SEA-HARE, a molluscous animal, *Aplysia depilans* 1591.

Phrases. *To hold* (or *run*) *with the h. and run* (or *hunt*) *with the hounds; to run with h. and hounds*: to try to keep in with both sides. *First catch your h.* (i.e. as the first step to cooking him): a direction jestingly ascribed to Mrs. Glasse, but much more recent.

Comb.: **h.-eyed** *a.*, having eyes that look all round, or that are never closed; **-hearted** *a.*, timid; **-kangaroo,** a small kangaroo of the genus *lagorchestes*; so called from its resemblance to a h. in size and colour; **hare's eye** = lagophthalmia, a disease arising from the contraction of the upper eyelid, so that the patient is obliged to sleep with the eye half-open; **-sighted** *a.*, short-sighted; †**-sleep,** a very light sleep.

b. In names of plants: **hare's-bane,** *Aconitum lagoctonum*; **hare's-beard,** the Great Mullein; **hare's colewort, house, lettuce, palace, thistle** (also *h.-thistle*), names for the Sow-thistle, *Sonchus oleraceus*; **hare's eye,** the Red Campion; **hare's-meat,** Wood-sorrel; **-parsley,** Wild Chervil; **hare's-tail (grass),** *Lagurus ovatus*; **hare's-tail rush,** Single-headed Cotton-grass.

†**Hare,** *v.* 1523. [With sense 1 cf. HARRY *v.*; sense 2 may be assoc. with prec.] **1.** *trans.* To harry; to worry; to harass –1674. **2.** To scare –1750.

2. To h. and rate them thus at every turn, is not to teach them LOCKE.

Harebell, hare-bell (hēᵊ·ɹbel). Also **hair-bell.** ME. [f. HARE *sb.* + BELL; perh. as growing where hares frequent.] **1.** = BLUE-BELL 2. **2.** = BLUEBELL 1. 1765.

2. E'en the slight hare-bell raised its head Elastic from her airy tread SCOTT.

Ha·re-brain. Also **hair-.** 1550. [f. HARE *sb.* + BRAIN. The sp. *hair-brain* is later.] †**1.** A person who has a brain like a hare's; a giddy or reckless person –1670. **2.** *attrib.* or *adj.* = HARE-BRAINED. 1566.

Ha·re-brained, *a.* Also **hair-.** 1548. [f. *hare-brain* + -ED². For *hair-* see prec.] Having no more brains or sense than a hare; heedless; rash, wild, mad.

They, out of a hare-brained lunacie desire battaile 1615.

Ha·re-finder. A man whose business is to find or espy a hare in form. *Much Ado* I. i. 186.

Harefoot, hare-foot. ? *Obs.* ME. **1.** A foot resembling a hare's; *spec.* a long narrow foot found in some dogs 1748. **2.** A nickname for a fleet-footed person ME. **3.** A plant; = HARE'S-FOOT 1. ME.

Hareld (hæ·rĕld). 1841. [– mod.L. *Harelda* (Stephens, 1824), arbitrary alt. of earlier *Havelda*, f. Icel. name *havelle*.] A species of sea-duck, *Harelda glacialis*.

Hare-lip (hēᵊ·ɹ,li·p). Also †**hair-.** 1567. [perh. immed. – (with accommodation) Du. *hazenlip*, tr. L. *labium leporinum*; cf. OE. *hærscéard* 'hare-cleft', OFris. *has-skerde* adj., G. *hasenscharte*, Da. *hareskaar*; Fr. *bec-de-lièvre*.] Fissure of the upper lip, caused by arrest of development; so called from resemblance to the cleft lip of a hare. Hence **Hare-lipped** *a.*

Harem, haram (hēᵊ·rĕm). Also **hareem, harim** (harī·m). 1634. [– Arab. *ḥarām*, *ḥarīm* (that which is) prohibited, (hence) sacred place, sanctuary, women's apartments, wives, women, f. *ḥarama* prohibit, make unlawful.] **1.** The part of a Moslem dwelling-house appropriated to the women; called also *seraglio*, and in Persia and India *zenana*. Also *transf.* and *fig.* **2.** The occupants of a harem collectively; *esp.* the wives and concubines collectively of a Turk, Persian, or Indian Moslem 1781. Also *transf.* and *fig.* **3.** A Moslem sacred place or area. More usually *haram*, forbidden, sacred place 1855.

Hare·ngiform, *a.* 1828. [f. mod. zool. L. *harengus* HERRING + -FORM.] Having the form of a herring. (Dicts.)

Hare's-ear (hēᵊ·ɹz,iᵊɹ). 1597. [From the shape of the leaves.] The name given to species of *Bupleurum* (N.O. *Umbelliferæ*), and *Erysimum* (N.O. *Cruciferæ*), having auricled leaves.

Hare's-foot. 1562. **1.** A species of clover (*Trifolium arvense*), with soft hair about the flowers. Also called *hare's-foot trefoil*. **2.** The Corkwood tree (*Ochroma lagopus*) of the W.

Indies and Central America; so called from the dehiscent ripe fruit with the cotton of the seeds protruding from it 1866.

Comb.: **Hare's-foot Fern,** a name of *Davallia canariensis*; also of other species, as *D. pyxidata.* **Hare's-foot Sedge,** *Carex lagopina.*

‖**Harfang** (hā·ɹfæŋ). 1774. [– Fr. *harfang* – Sw. *harfång* snowy owl, f. *har(e* hare + *fånga* catch.] The Great Snowy Owl.

Haricot (hæ·riko, -kǫt), *sb.* 1653. [In sense 1 – Fr. *haricot*, OFr. *hericoq, hericot (de mouton)*, prob. rel. to *harigoter* cut up; in sense 2 – Fr. *haricot* in *febves de haricot* (XVII), perh. – Aztec *ayacotli.*] **1.** A ragout (orig. of mutton, now occas. of other meat). Also *attrib.* 1706. **2.** A leguminous plant of the genus *Phaseolus*, esp. *P. vulgaris*, the common Kidney-bean or French-bean; also *Haricot bean.* Applied both to the plant and to the beans. Hence **Haricot, Harico** *v. trans.* to make into a h. (sense 1).

Harier, obs. f. HARRIER.

Hari-kari, erron. f. HARA-KIRI.

†**Ha·riolate,** *v.* 1656. [– *hariolat-*, pa. ppl. stem of L. *hariolari*, f. *hariolus* soothsayer; see -ATE[3].] *intr.* To soothsay; also, in 17th c., to practise ventriloquism –1677. Hence †**Hariola·tion.**

†**Harish** (hēᵊ·riʃ), *a.* 1552. [f. HARE *sb.* + -ISH[1].] Of the nature of a hare; mad, foolish –1581.

Hark (hāɹk), *v.* [ME. *herkien* :– OE. **he(o)rcian* = OFris. *herkia, harkia*, rel. to MLG., MDu., Flem. dial. *horken*, OHG. *hōrechen* (G. *horchen*); cf. HEARKEN.] **1.** *trans.* To give ear or listen to. **2.** *intr.* To give ear, hearken, listen. Also *absol.* (chiefly in *imperative.*) ME. **3.** *intr.* Used in hunting, etc., as a call of attention and incitement 1610.

1. H. what he himself here saith 1680. **2.** Just Lord, to my suit h. SIDNEY. *absol.* Harke, they rore *Temp.* IV. i. 262. *Hark'ee, harkee*: = hark ye (in the imperative); so, less commonly, *hark you*, and by confusion *hark thee.* **3.** *Hark away, forward, in, off*: to proceed or go away, forward, in, draw off. *H. back*: (of hounds) to return along the course taken, till the lost scent is found again; hence *fig.* to retrace one's course or steps. *H. on, forwards* (trans.): to urge on with encouraging cries. *H. back*: to recall.

Hark, *sb.* 1737. [f. HARK *v.*] **a.** An act of harking. **b.** A shout starting or urging on the hounds in the chase; also *hark away.* **c.** *Hark back*: a backward move.

Harken, *v.* etc.: see HEARKEN, etc.

Harl, harle, *sb.* See also HERL. 1450. [app. = MLG. *herle, harle*, etc., LG. *harl*, EFris. *harrel* fibre of flax or hemp.] **1.** A filament or fibre (of flax or hemp) 1649. **2.** A barb or fibre of a feather 1450.

Harleian (haɹlī·ăn, hā·ɹliăn), *a.* 1744. [– mod.L. *Harleianus*, f. surname *Harley.*] Of or belonging to Robert Harley Earl of Oxford (1661–1724), and his son Edward Harley; esp. in reference to the library of books and MSS. collected by them, of which the MSS. were purchased in 1753 and deposited in the British Museum.

Harlequin (hā·ɹlĭkwin, -kin), *sb.* 1590. [– Fr. †*harlequin* (mod. *arlequin*, after It. *arlecchino*), later var. of *Herlequin* (also *Hellequin*, as in OFr. *maisnie Hellequin*, in med.L. *familia Hellequini* or *Herlechini*) leader of the Wild Host or troop of demon horsemen riding by night, also called in med.L. *familia Herlethingi* (Walter Map) which has been plausibly referred (as if for **Herlechingi*) to OE. *Herla cyning* king Herla. For the It. associations cf. COLUMBINE *sb.*[3], PUNCH *sb.*[5], ZANY.] **1.** A character in Italian and French light comedy; in English pantomime a mute character supposed to be invisible to the clown and pantaloon; he has many attributes of the clown (his rival in the affections of Columbine) with the addition of mischievous intrigue; he usually wears particoloured bespangled tights and a visor, and carries a light bat of lath as a magic wand. Also *transf.* **2.** A small breed of spotted dogs 1774. **3.** A northern species of duck, *Histrionicus minutus*, with variegated plumage; also *Harlequin duck* 1772.

1. A piece of patch-work, a mere harlequin's coat FOOTE. In the same manner as dumb h. is exhibited on our theatres JOHNSON.

II. *attrib.* or as *adj.* Resembling a harlequin or his dress; burlesque, ludicrous; particoloured 1779.

Comb.: **h.-bat,** an Indian species, *Scotophilus ornatus*, of pale tawny-brown, with white spots; **h. beetle,** a S. American longicorn beetle, *Acrocinus longimanus*, with particoloured elytra; **h. brant,** the American white-fronted goose, *Anser albifrons gambeli*, also called *pied* or *speckled brant*; **h. cabbage-bug,** an American hemipterous insect, *Murgantia histrionica*, having brilliant markings; **h. duck**: see 3; **h.-flower,** a name of the S. African genus *Sparaxis*, N.O. *Iridaceæ*, with great variety of colouring; **h. garrot,** the golden-eye duck or pied widgeon, a species of *Clangula*; **h. moth,** the magpie moth, *Abraxas grossulariata*; **h. pigeon,** an Australian Bronze-wing pigeon; **h. ring,** a ring so called because set round with variously-coloured stones; **h. rose,** a variety of rose with striped petals; **h. snake,** the coral-snake and other species of *Elaps*, so called from their variegated colouring of orange and black.

Harlequin, *v. rare.* 1737. [f. prec. sb.] **a.** *trans.* To conjure *away*, like harlequin. **b.** *intr.* To play the harlequin 1828.

Harlequinade (hāɹlĭk(w)inēⁱ·d), *sb.* 1780. [– Fr. *arlequinade*, f. *arlequin* HARLEQUIN; see -ADE.] A kind of pantomime; that part of a pantomine in which the harlequin and clown play the principal parts. Also *transf.* Hence **Harlequina·de** *v.* to play the harlequin; to act fantastically.

†**Ha·rlock.** 1631. Some flower not identified. It cannot well be either *hardock* or *charlock.* DRAYTON.

Harlot (hā·ɹlət, -ǫ̆t), *sb.* [ME. *har-, herlot* – OFr. *(h)arlot, herlot* young fellow, knave, vagabond = Pr. *arlot*, med.L. *harlotus, herlotus* vagabond, beggar; cf. also It. *arlotto*, med.L. *arlotus, erlotus* glutton, OSp. *arlote, alrote* lazy, OPg. *alrotar* go about begging.] †**1.** A vagabond, beggar, rogue, villain, low fellow, knave. In 16–17th c., sometimes a man of loose life; also, often, a term of insult. –1699. †**2.** An itinerant jester or juggler –1483. †**3.** A male servant; a menial; cf. KNAVE –1536. †**4.** = 'Fellow' –1634. **5.** Applied to a woman. **a.** As a general term of execration (*rare*) 1485. **b.** *spec.* An unchaste woman; a strumpet ME. Also *fig.* **6.** *attrib.* That is a harlot; of or pertaining to a harlot ME.

4. He [Somonour] was a gentil h. and a kynde A bettre felawe sholde men noght fynde CHAUCER. **6.** And teare the stain'd skin of my H. brow SHAKS.

Phr. *To play the h.* (Of both sexes, but chiefly of women.) Hence **Ha·rlot** *v.* to play the h.

Harlotry (hā·ɹlǫ̆tri), *sb.* (*a.*) ME. [f. HARLOT *sb.* + -RY.] †**1.** Buffoonery; ribaldry; obscene talk or behaviour –1809. **2.** Unchastity; the conduct of a harlot; dealing with harlots; the practice or trade of prostitution ME. **3.** *concr.* A harlot; a term of opprobrium for a woman 1584. **4.** *fig.* Meretriciousness 1768. †**5.** *attrib.* or as *adj.* Base, filthy, trashy –1663.

3. A peeuish selfe-will'd H. SHAKS. **4.** Ev'n as the virgin blush of innocence [eclips'd] The h. of art G. MASON.

Harm (hāɹm), *sb.* [OE. *hearm* = OFris. *herm*, OS., OHG., (G.) *harm*, ON. *harmr* (chiefly) grief, sorrow :– Gmc. **χarmaz.*] **1.** Evil (physical or otherwise) as done or suffered; hurt, injury, damage, mischief. Also with *a* and *pl.* †**2.** Grief, pain, trouble, affliction. Also with *a* and *pl.* –1627.

1. Thou shalt have no harme truely CHAUCER. Of ij harmys the leste is to be taken 1461. Phr. *Out of harm's way*: out of the way of doing or of suffering injury.

Harm, *v.* [OE. *hearmian* = OHG. *harmen, hermen* (G. *(sich) härmen* grieve); f. prec.] To do harm (to); to injure; to hurt, damage. Orig. *intr.* To be hurtful, with dative, which ult. became a simple object, making the vb. *trans.* Also *absol.*

An High Elme..in the midst of a Garden.. harms all round about it 1659. When a man has no sense he is harmed by courage JOWETT.

‖**Harmala** (hā·ɹmălă), **harmel** (hā·ɹmel). OE. [Late L., = Gr. ἅρμαλα, from Semitic.] Wild rue, *Peganum harmala*, a plant native to Southern Europe and Asia Minor. Hence **Harmaline** (hā·ɹmăləin), *Chem.*, a white crystalline alkaloid ($C_{13}H_{14}N_2O$) obtained from the seeds of wild rue.

†**Ha·rman.** *Thieves' Cant.* 1567. [First syll. unexpl.; *-man(s)* as in *crackmans*, DARKMANS, etc.] **1.** pl. *Harmans*, the stocks –1609. **2.** Short for *Harman-beck*: A constable –1829. Hence †**Ha·rman-beck** [*beck*, BEAK *sb.*[3]], a constable.

‖**Harmattan** (haɹmæ·tăn, in 18th c. hā·ɹmătæn). 1671. [f. Fanti or Tshi (W. Africa) *haramata.*] A dry parching land-wind, which blows during December, January, and February, on the coast of Upper Guinea; it obscures the air with a red dust-fog. Also *attrib.*

Harmel: see HARMALA.

Harmful (hā·ɹmfŭl), *a.* ME. [f. HARM *sb.* + -FUL.] Fraught with harm; injurious. **Ha·rmful-ly** *adv.*, **-ness.**

Harmine (hā·ɹməin). 1864. [f. HARMA(LA + -INE[5].] *Chem.* An alkaloid ($C_{13}H_{12}N_2O$) contained in the seeds of HARMALA, or obtained by oxidation of harmaline. **Harmi·nic** *acid*, an acid ($C_{10}H_8N_2O_4$) obtained by oxidation of h.

Harmless (hā·ɹmlės), *a.* ME. [f. HARM *sb.* + -LESS.] **1.** Free from harm; unhurt, uninjured. Now *rare.* **2.** Free from loss, free from liability to punishment, or to pay for loss ME. **3.** Innocent (*arch.*) ME. **4.** Inoffensive, innocuous 1533.

2. *To save* the lessee *h.* from any claiming by, from, or under the covenantor 1818. **3.** To follow h. Nature FELTHAM. **Ha·rmless-ly** *adv.*, **-ness.**

Harmonic (haɹmǫ·nik). 1570. [– L. *harmonicus* – Gr. ἁρμονικός, in neut. pl. ἁρμονικά as sb., theory of music, f. ἁρμονία HARMONY; see -IC.]

A. *adj.* **1.** Relating to music, musical; in reference to ancient music, Relating to melody as dist. from rhythm. *Obs.* exc. in spec. uses. **2.** Harmonious, in harmony, concordant 1667. **3.** *Mus.* Relating to harmony (as dist. from melody and rhythm); belonging to the combination of musical notes in chords 1661. **4.** *Acoustics* and *Mus.* Applied to the tones produced by the vibration of a sonorous body in aliquot parts of its length (see B. 2); relating to such tones 1831. **5.** *Math.* **a.** Applied to the relation of quantities whose reciprocals are in arithmetical progression (e.g. $1, \frac{1}{2}, \frac{1}{3}, \frac{1}{4}, \ldots$); or to points, lines, functions, etc., involving such a relation 1706. **b. Harmonic motion,** a periodic motion, which in its simplest form (*simple h. motion*) is like that of a point in a vibrating string, and is identical with the resolved part, parallel to a diameter, of uniform motion in a circle 1867. **6.** Relating to or marked by harmony, agreement, or concord; harmonizing in aspect or artistic effect; harmonious in feeling, etc. 1756. **7.** *Anat.* Belonging to or of the nature of a false suture 1826.

2. With Heav'nly touch of instrumental sounds In full h. number joind MILT. **4.** *Harmonic scale*: the scale formed by the series of harmonics of a fundamental note. **5. a.** *H. progression*, the relation of a series of quantities whose reciprocals are in arithmetical progression, or such a series itself. *H. proportion*, the relation of three quantities in h. progression; the second is said to be a *h. mean* between the first and third. **b.** *H. function*, a function consisting of a series of terms, each of which expresses a harmonic motion; in a wider sense, any function that satisfies a differential equation of a class of which that expressing a simple harmonic motion is the first example. *H. analysis*, the calculus of h. functions, an important part of modern mathematical analysis. *H. current* (*Electr.*), an alternating current the variations of which follow the law of a harmonic curve.

B. *sb.* **1.** *pl.* A theory or system of musical sounds or intervals; that part of acoustics which relates to music. (Rarely in *sing.*) *Obs.* exc. in reference to ancient systems 1709. **2.** (Short for *h. tone.*) One of the secondary tones produced by vibration of the aliquot parts of a sonorous body (as a string, reed, column of air in a pipe, etc.); usually accompanying the primary tone produced by the vibration of the body as a whole. Also called *overtones* or *upper partials.* 1777. **3.** *Math.* = *H. function* (A. 5 b), in the wider sense. *Spherical h.*, a h. function having a relation to Spherical Geometry akin to that which functions expressing harmonic motion have to Plane Geometry 1867. **4.** *Electr.* In an alternating circuit, a component current whose frequency is a multiple of the fundamental 1894.

Harmonica (haɹmǫ·nikă). 1762. [fem. sing. or n. pl. (used subst.) of L. *harmonicus*; see prec.] **1. a.** An instrument consisting of a row of hemispherical glasses fitted on an axis turned by a treadle and dipping into a trough of water, played by the application of the finger. **b.** An instrument consisting of a row of glass plates mounted on a resonance box and struck with hammers. **c.** A kind of mouth organ. **2.** Name given to different organ-stops 1840.

Harmonical (haɹmǫ·nikăl), *a.* 1531. [f. as HARMONIC + -AL[1].] **1.** = HARMONIC *a.* 6. Now *rare.* **2.** Relating to collation of parallel passages in different books 1612. †**3.** = HARMONIC *a.* 1. –1837. †**4.** = HARMONIC *a.* 2. –1774. **5.** = HARMONIC *a.* 3. ?*Obs.* 1727. †**6.** = HARMONIC *a.* 4. 1727. **7.** *Math.* = HARMONIC *a.* 5. 1569. †**b.** as *sb.* (*pl.*) Quantities in harmonical progression –1796. †**8.** *Anat.* = HARMONIC *a.* 7. 1578.

Harmonically (haɹmǫ·nikăli), *adv.* 1589. [f. prec. + -LY[2].] †**1.** Harmoniously, agreeingly. (Sometimes *fig.* from 2.) –1681. †**2.** With harmony or concord of sounds –1751. **3.** *Mus.* In relation to harmony 1775. **4.** *Math.* In a harmonic relation or proportion 1597.

Harmonicon (haɹmǫ·nikǫ̆n). 1825. [– Gr. ἁρμονικόν, n. sing. of ἁρμονικός HARMONIC.] **a.** = HARMONICA 1 a, b. **b.** A mouth-organ consisting of a row of free reeds arranged in a case so as to give different notes by expiration and inspiration.

Harmonious (haɹmōᵘ·niəs), *a.* 1530. [f. HARMONY + -OUS; cf. (O)Fr. *harmonieux.*] **1.** Marked by harmony, agreement, or concord 1638. **b.** Marked by agreement of feeling or sentiment; consentient, unanimous 1724. **2.** Characterized by harmony of sounds; concordant; tuneful; full of harmony 1549. **b.** *transf.* Of persons: Singing, playing, or speaking tunefully or agreeably 1530.

1. A..h. order of architecture in all its parts HOGARTH. **2.** H. bells G. HERBERT. **b.** The popular air known as 'The Harmonious Blacksmith' GROVE. Hence **Harmo·nious-ly** *adv.*, **-ness.**

Harmoniphon, -phone (haɹmǫ·nifǫ̆n, -fōᵘn). 1839. [– Fr. *harmoniphon*, f. Gr. ἁρμονία HARMONY + -φωνος -sounding; cf. -PHONE.] A musical instrument consisting of a tube like that of a clarinet, enclosing a set of free reeds governed by a keyboard. Also applied to a musical box with a combination of reeds and pipes.

Harmonist (hā·ɹmŏnist). 1570. [Mainly f. HARMONY + -IST.] **1.** One skilled in musical harmony. **a.** A musician. Also *fig.* A poet (cf. *singer*). 1742. **b.** A composer skilled in harmony (as dist. from melody, etc.); one versed in the theory of harmony 1790. **c.** One of a school of ancient Greek musical theorists who founded the rules of music on the subjective effects of tones, not on their mathematical relations, as the *canonists* did 1570. **2.** One who collates and harmonizes parallel narratives, or the like; *esp.* one who makes a harmony of the Gospels 1713. **3.** A harmonizer 1809. **4.** (with capital *H*). One of a communistic religious body in the United States, founded by Geo. Rapp of Würtemberg in 1803; they settled in Pennsylvania, and founded a town called Harmony (whence their name) 1824. Hence **Harmoni·stic** *a.* belonging to the work of a h. (sense 2); *sb.* (also in *pl.*) harmonistic studies. **Harmoni·stically,** *adv.* in the manner of a h.; in relation to a harmony of writings.

Harmonium (haɹmōᵘ·niŏm). 1847. [– Fr. *harmonium* (Debain, *c*1840), f. L. *harmonia* or Gr. ἁρμόνιος harmonious.] A keyboard instrument, the tones of which are produced by free metal reeds, tongues, or vibrators, actuated by a current of air from bellows, usually worked by treadles; a kind of reed-organ.

Harmonization (hā:ɹmŏnəizē[i]·ʃən). 1837. [f. next + -ATION.] The action or process of harmonizing.

Harmonize (hā·ɹmŏnəiz), *v.* 1483. [– Fr. *harmoniser*, f. *harmonie* HARMONY; see -IZE.] †**1.** *intr.* To sing or play in harmony. CAXTON. **2.** To be in harmony (*with*); to accord, agree 1629; to form a concord 1855. **3.** *trans.* To bring into harmony, agreement, or accord 1700. Also *absol.* **b.** To reconcile 1767. **4.** *Mus.* To add notes, usually of lower pitch, to the notes of (a melody) so as to form chords; to add harmony to. Also *absol.* 1790.

2. The colours do not h. 1898. **3.** A music harmonizing our wild cries TENNYSON. When social laws first harmonized the world JOHNSON. Hence **Ha·rmonizer,** one who harmonizes.

Harmonometer (hāɹmŏnǫ·mĭtəɹ). 1823. [– Fr. *harmonomètre*, irreg. f. *harmonie* + *-mètre* (see -METER).] An instrument for measuring the harmonic relations of musical notes.

Harmony (hā·ɹmŏni). ME. [– (O)Fr. *harmonie* – L. *harmonia* – Gr. ἁρμονία joint, agreement, concord, f. *ἁρμο- of ἁρμός joint, ἁρμόζειν fit together.] **1.** Combination or adaptation of parts, elements, or related things, so as to form a consistent and orderly whole; agreement, congruity 1532. **2.** Agreement of feeling or sentiment; peaceableness, concord. (Sometimes as *fig.* from 4.) 1588. **3.** Combination of parts or details with each other, so as to produce an æsthetically pleasing effect; agreeable aspect thus arising 1650. **4.** The combination of musical notes, so as to produce a pleasing effect; melody; music. (The earliest sense in English.) ME. **b.** *gen.* Pleasing combination of sounds 1529. **5.** *Mus.* The combination of (simultaneous) notes so as to form chords (dist. from *melody*, which is the succession of notes forming an air or tune); that part of musical art or science which deals with chords; the structure of a piece in relation to its chords 1526. **6.** A collation of passages on the same subject from different writings, arranged so as to exhibit their consistency; as, a *harmony* of the Gospels 1588. **6.** *Anat.* False suture or union by mere apposition 1615.

1. *Pre-established harmony* (Leibnitz): a harmony between mind and matter established before their creation, whereby their actions correspond though no communication exists between them. **2.** Harmonie to behold in wedded pair MILT. **3.** The h. of a face 1650. **4.** Songes ful o Armonye CHAUCER. Ten thousand Harpes that tun'd Angelic harmonies MILT. *H. of the spheres*: see SPHERE *sb.* 2b. **b.** O mighty-mouthed inventor of harmonies TENNYSON.

Harmost (hā·ɹmǫst). 1775. [– Gr. ἁρμοστής, f. ἁρμόζειν to fit, regulate.] One of the governors sent out by the Spartans during their supremacy to control the subject cities and islands.

Harmotome (hā·ɹmŏtoᵘm). 1804. [– Fr. *harmotome* (Haüy), f. Gr. ἁρμός joint + -τομος cutting, app. in ref. to the way the octahedral crystal divides.] *Min.* A hydrous silicate of aluminium and barium, commonly occurring in cruciform twin crystals of various colours. Also called *cross-stone.*

Harness (hā·ɹnės), *sb.* [ME. *harnais*, *harneis* – OFr. *harneis* military equipment (mod. *harnais*) – ON. **hernest* 'provisions for an army', with assim. of the termination to *-*isk*- (cf. OFr. *harneschier* equip), f. *herr* army (see HARRY *v.*) + *nest* = OE., OHG. *nest* provisions.] †**1.** Tackle, gear, furniture, armament; e.g. of a ship, a fishing-rod, etc. –1632. **2.** Body-armour; all the defensive equipment of an armed horseman, for both man and horse; military equipment or accountrement. *Hist.* or *arch.* ME. Also *fig.* **b.** with *a*; A suit of mail 1489. **3.** The trappings of a horse; now confined to the gear or tackle of a draught horse or other animal ME. **b.** *fig.* Working equipments; the routine of daily work 1841. †**4.** Furniture; apparel –1602. **5.** The apparatus in a loom by which the sets of warp-threads are shifted alternately to form the shed; the mounting 1572. †**6.** Ware, gear; *fig.* affairs, matters. CHAUCER.

2. At least wee'l dye with Harnesse on our backe SHAKS. *fig.* Men who win power, easily put on its h., dignity LYTTON. **3.** Wild horses.. which had never before been in h. 1834. **b.** *In h.*, in the routine of daily work; *to die in h.*, i.e. in the midst of work.

Ha·rness, *v.* ME. [In form *harnesche* – OFr. *harneschier*, f. *harnesc-*, OFr. *harneis*; see prec.] †**1.** To furnish, equip, accoutre; esp. to ornament with fittings of price –1534. **2.** To equip in harness or armour; to arm (*arch.*) ME.; †to fortify (1 *Macc.* 4:7). Also *fig.* **3.** To put harness on (a horse, etc.); now only on draught animals, *esp.* carriage-horses ME. Also *fig.* **4.** To dress, apparel, array. *Obs.* or *arch.* ME.

1. A gay daggere, Harneised wel and sharpe as point of spere CHAUCER. **2.** H. yourselves for the war BUNYAN. **3.** *fig.* Harnessed together in matrimony SHERIDAN. Hence **Ha·rnesser.**

†**Ha·rness-bearer.** 1563. An armour-bearer –1611.

Ha·rness-cask. 1818. *Naut.* A cask or tub with a rimmed cover used on board ship for keeping the salt meats for present consumption. Also *harness-tub.*

Harns, *sb. pl.*, brains.

Harp (hāɹp), *sb.* [OE. *hearpe* = OS. *harpa* (Du. *harp*), OHG. *harfa* (G. *harfe*), ON. *harpa* :– Gmc.* χ*arpōn*, whence late L. *harpa.*] **1.** A musical instrument consisting of a framework, now usually triangular in form, furnished with strings (and now with pedals), and played with the fingers. Also *fig.* **2.** The northern constellation Lyra 1551. †**3. a.** = *harp-groat* (see *Comb.*). **b.** Short for *harp-shilling* (see *Comb.*). –1606. **4.** A screen or sieve. *Sc.* 1768. **5.** Also *harp-shell*: A mollusc of the genus *Harpa* of family *Buccinidæ*, and its shell 1751. **6.** Also *harp-seal*: The Greenland seal: so named from the harp-shaped dark marking on the back 1784.

1. Our pleasures are the feast, the h., the dance COWPER. *Double harp*: one with two sets of strings differently tuned. *Æolian h.*: see ÆOLIAN. *Comb.*: **h.-file,** a wire hook for filing papers, attached to a harp-shaped piece of iron; **-fish,** a fish of the genus *Lyra*, the Piper; †**-groat,** an Irish coin bearing the figure of a h. on the reverse; **-lute,** an instrument having twelve strings and resembling the guitar; **-seal,** see 6; †**-shilling:** see HARPER[1] 2; †**-star,** Vega, the chief star in Lyra.

Harp, *v.* [OE. *hearpian*, ON. *harpa*, f. prec.] **1.** *intr.* To play on a harp. †**2.** *trans.* To play (notes, etc.) upon a harp –1777. †**3.** *trans.* To play upon, twang 1628. **4.** *intr.* To make a sound like that of the harp 1657. **5.** *trans.* To give voice to, to guess 1605. †**b.** *intr. To h. at*: To guess at. MILT.

1. Sworded seraphim..Harping in loud and solemn quire MILTON. *fig. To h. upon, on, a, one, the same* (etc.) *string*: to dwell on a subject to a wearisome or tedious length. *To h. on, upon*: to dwell wearisomely upon in speech or writing; Still harping on my daughter SHAKS. **5.** Thou hast harp'd my feare aright SHAKS.

†**Harpagon.** 1553. [– L. *harpago*, *-ōn-*, f. Gr. ἁρπάγη grappling-hook.] A grappling-hook –1600.

Harper[1] (hā·ɹpəɹ). [OE. *hearpere* = ON. *harpari*; see HARP *sb.*, -ER[1].] **1.** One who harps or plays upon a harp. **2.** Applied to Irish coins, bearing the figure of a harp; *esp.* the *harp-shilling*, worth 9*d.* English. *Obs.* exc. *Hist.* 1598. **3.** The harp-seal (*Cent. Dict.*).

Harper[2] (also *harpier*), app. error for HARPY. *Macb.* IV. i. 3.

Ha·rping, *ppl. a.* 1641. [f. HARP *v.* + -ING[2].] That harps or plays on a harp. Also *transf.*

†**Harping-iron** (hā·ɹpiŋ,əi·əɹn). 1596. [perh. – Fr. *harpin* boat-hook, f. *harper* grasp, grapple. Superseded by HARPOON.] A barbed spear used for spearing whales and large fish; a harpoon –1814.

Harpings (hā·ɹpiŋz), *sb. pl.* Also †**harpins,** †**harpens.** 1626. [Earliest in *cat-harpings*; perh. connected with Fr. *harpe* (see HARPOON).] **1. a.** The fore-parts of the wales which encompass the bow of a ship and are fastened to the stem. **b.** Pieces of oak, forming an extension of the rib-bands, for holding the cant-frames of a vessel in place until the outside planking is worked. 1658. **2.** *Cat-harpings*: the ropes or (now oftener) iron cramps that serve to brace in the shrouds of the lower-masts behind their respective yards. Also *cat-harping legs.*

Harpist (hā·ɹpist). 1613. [f. HARP *sb.* + -IST.] A (professional) harper.

Harpoon (haɹpū·n), *sb.* 1625. [– Fr. *harpon*, f. *harpe* dog's claw, cramp-iron, clamp – L. *harpe, harpa* – Gr. ἅρπη sickle; superseded earlier HARPING-IRON.] †**1.** A barbed dart or spear –1697. **2.** A barbed spear-like missile, to the shank of which a long line of rope is attached; it is used for capturing whales or large fish, being either hurled by the hand or fired from a gun 1694.

Comb.: **h.-fork**, a kind of hay-fork worked by tackle in loading or unloading hay; **-gun**, a gun for firing harpoons; **-rocket**, a bomb-lance for killing whales.

Harpoo·n, *v.* 1774. [f. prec.] *trans.* To strike or spear with a harpoon. Also *transf.* and *fig.*

Harpooneer (hāɹpunīᵊ·ɹ). Now *rare.* Also †**-ier.** 1613. [f. HARPOON *sb.* + -EER, -IER.] = next.

Harpooner (hāɹpū·nəɹ). 1726. [f. HARPOON *v.* + -ER¹.] One who hurls or fires a harpoon.

Ha·rpress. [f. HARPER + -ESS¹.] A female harper. SCOTT.

†**Ha·rpsical** (also **-secol, -sicol,** vulg. **haspicols**). 1616. Corrupt ff. HARPSICHORD, prob. after *virginal* –1773.

Harpsichord (hā·ɹpsikǭɹd). 1611. [– Fr. †*harpechorde* = It. *arpicordo*, mod.L. *harpichordium*, f. late L. *harpa* HARP *sb.* + *chorda* CHORD *sb.*¹; the intrusive *s*, found in the earliest instances, is of obscure origin.] A keyboard instrument of music (resembling in appearance the grand piano), in which the strings were plucked or set in vibration by quill or leather points set in jacks connected by levers with the keys. (In use from 16–18th c.) Also *attrib.*

Harpy (hā·ɹpi). 1540. [– (O)Fr. *harpie* or its source L. *harpyia*, pl. *-iæ* – Gr. ἅρπυιαι 'snatchers', rel. to ἁρπάζειν seize.] **1.** *Gr.* and *L. Myth.* A fabulous monster, rapacious and filthy, having a woman's face and body and a bird's wings and claws, and supposed to act as a minister of divine vengeance. **2.** *transf.* and *fig.* A rapacious, plundering, or grasping person 1589. **3.** The HARPY-EAGLE 1838. **4.** The moor-buzzard, *Circus æruginosus* 1838. **5.** The HARPY-BAT, q.v.

1. Both table and provisions vanished quite With sound of harpies' wings, and talons heard MILT. **2.** The insolent carriage of Prince Rupert, and his Harpyes 1643. The harpies of taxation JOHNSON. Hence **Harpyian** (erron. **-peian, -pyan**) *a.*

Ha·rpy-ba·t. 1883. A name of two or more species of bat found in the East Indies.

Ha·rpy-ea·gle. 1830. A large and powerful bird of prey (*Thrasyaëtus harpyia*, or *Harpyia destructor*) with crested head and fan-shaped tail, a native of S. America.

Harquebus, arquebus (hā·ɹkwibŏs, ā·ɹk-), *sb.* 1532. [– Fr. (*h*)*arquebuse*, ult. – MLG. *hakebusse* (mod. *haakbus*) or MHG. *hake(n)-bühse* (mod. *hakenbüchse*), which in the Fr. form †*haquebusche* was adopted in Eng. as HACKBUSH; f. *hake(n)* hook + *bus(se)* fire-arm (a hook being orig. cast on the gun).] **1.** The early type of portable gun, varying in size, and, when used in the field, supported upon a tripod, trestle, or other 'carriage', or upon a forked rest. The name in German meant literally 'hook-gun', from the hook, cast along with it, by which it was attached to the carriage; but the meaning was forgotten, and the name became generic for portable fire-arms in the 16th c.; see 2. †**2. Harquebus à croc** (corruptly *of crock*): 'An arquebus supported on a rest by a hook of iron fastened to the barrel. From the size of its calibre, it was used to fire through loopholes' (Meyrick) –1693. **3.** *collect.* Soldiers armed with harquebuses 1594.

So **Ha·rquebusa·de, a·rq-,** †a shot from a h.; a continuous discharge of such shots. **Ha·rquebusie·r, a·rq-,** a soldier armed with a h.; vars. †**Ha·rquebusher, -butter.**

†**Harrage,** *v.* A form used by Fuller, app. as = HARRY or HARASS (cf. *ravage*).

Harre, har. *Obs.* exc. *dial.* [OE. *heorr* corresp. to MDu. *herre, harre* (Du. *har, harre*) :– Gmc. *χerrō*, beside *heorra*, corresp. to ON. *hjarri* :– Gmc. **χerron*.] **1.** The hinge of a door or gate. **2.** *fig.* A cardinal point OE.

Harridan (hæ·ridăn). 1700. [Recorded first as a cant word; presumed to be alteration of Fr. *haridelle* old jade of a horse, of unkn. origin.] A haggard old woman; a vixen; 'a decayed strumpet' (J.); usu. a term of abuse.

attrib. The old h. landlady MOORE.

Harrier¹ (hæ·riəɹ). 1556. [f. HARRY *v.* + -ER¹; in sense 3 (early forms *har(r)oer, harrower*), f. HARROW *v.*²] **1.** One who harries, ravages, or lays waste 1596. †**2.** A drover –1598. **3.** (Also †*harrower.*) A name for falcons of the genus *Circus*, and their allies; cf. MARSH-HARRIER, etc. 1556.

Comb.: **H. eagle,** *Circaetus gallicus*; **H.-hawk,** a hawk of the American genus *Micrastur.*

Harrier² (hæ·riəɹ). 1542. [Early forms *hayrere, heirere*, f. *hayre* HARE + -ER¹, after (O)Fr. *lévrier*, repr. med.L. *leporarius* greyhound; assim. to prec.] **1.** A kind of hound, smaller than the fox-hound, used for hunting the hare. **b.** In *pl.* A pack of harriers; including the persons following the chase 1877. **2.** One of a 'hare-and-hounds' team 1891.

Harrovian (hærōᵘ·viăn). 1864. [f. mod. L. *Harrovia* + -AN.] *adj.* Of or pertaining to Harrow school. *sb.* One educated at Harrow.

Harrow (hæ·roᵘ), *sb.* ME. [– ON. **harwjan*, prehistoric form of *herfi, hervi* (Sw. *harf, härf*, Da. *harv*), obscurely rel. to MLG., MDu. *harke* (Du. *hark*) rake.] **1.** A heavy frame of timber (or iron) set with iron teeth or tines, which is dragged over ploughed land to break clods, pulverize and stir the soil, root up weeds, or cover in the seed. **2.** *transf.* A similar contrivance used for other purposes 1548. **b.** *Fortif.* A gate made of timber, well fastened to three or four cross bars, and secured with iron 1788. **3.** A diagonal arrangement of soldiers; also of wild geese in the air 1876.

1. *fig.* Under the h. of affliction LANDOR. *Comb.*: **revolving h.,** a h. of which the teeth are fixed on radiating arms, so as to revolve horizontally; *brake* (or *break*) *h.* (see BRAKE *sb.*³); BUSH-HARROW; *chain-h.* (cf. CHAIN *sb.* I.1.) etc.

Harrow (hæ·roᵘ), *v.*¹ ME. [f. prec.] **1.** *trans.* To draw a harrow over; to break up, crush, or pulverize with a harrow. Also *absol.* †**2.** *transf.* To cut through as a harrow; to plough (the sea, etc.) 1583. **3.** To tear, lacerate, wound (*lit.* and *fig.*) 1602.

1. Canst thou binde the Vnicorne with his band in the furrow? or will he h. the valleyes after thee *Job* 39:10. **3.** The thorns harrowing his sacred head T. ADAMS. *fig.* I could a Tale vnfold, whose lightest word Would h. vp thy soule SHAKS. Hence **Ha·rrower. Ha·rrowing-ly** *adv.*, **-ness.**

Harrow (hæ·roᵘ), *v.*² ME. [A by-form of HARRY *v.*, OE. *herġian*, of which the pa. t. and pa. pple. *hergode, hergod*, and vbl. sb. *hergung* regularly became in ME. *herwede, herwed, herwyng*, whence, by change of *-er* bef. a cons. to *-ar*, and levelling, came ME *harwe, harowe, harrow.*] *trans.* To harry, rob, spoil.

By him [Christ] that harwed helle CHAUCER. These Picts. . did oft-times h. the borders 1606.

†**Harrow, haro** (hæ·roᵘ), *interj.* ME. [– (O)Fr. *harou*, (also mod.) *haro*, of echoic origin; cf. also OFr. *hare* cry to set a dog on (see HARASS).] **1.** A cry of distress or alarm; a call for succour. ‖**2.** In Law of Normandy and Channel Isles, in form *haro!*: A cry repeated thrice, and followed by action in the court, in cases of trespass or encroachment 1682.

To cry h. (on any one): to denounce (a person's) doings. Iohn. . gan to crie h. and weylaway Oure hors is lorn CHAUCER.

Harry (hæ·ri), *sb.* [ME. *Herry*, from *Henry, -er* subseq. becoming *-ar*, as in HARRY *v.*] Familiar for Henry. **1.** The proper name. **2.** A generic name for a young Englishman of a low-class type 1874. **3.** *Harrys* or *King Harrys*: playing-cards of the second quality 1842.

Phrases, etc.: **Old Harry:** A familiar name for the Devil. *To play Old H. with*: to play the devil with; to work mischief upon; to ruin. *By the Lord H.*: a form of swearing; of doubtful origin. *Comb.*: **H.-bird,** the Greater Shearwater (*Puffinus major*). **H. Denchman, H. Dutchman,** local names of the hooded or Danish Crow. **H. groat,** a groat coined by Henry VIII. **H. noble,** a gold coin of Henry VI. **H. sovereign,** a sovereign of Henry VII or Henry VIII.

Harry (hæ·ri), *v.* [OE. *herġian, herian*, corresp. to OFris. *-heria*, OS. *herion*, OHG. *heriōn*, ON. *herja* :– Gmc. **χarjōjan*, **χarjōn*, f. **χarjaz* host, army. Conflation with synon. OFr. *harier, her(r)ier* is probable. See HARROW *v.*²] **1.** *intr.* To make predatory raids; to commit ravages. **2.** *trans.* To overrun with an army; to lay waste, sack, pillage, spoil ME. †**b.** *spec.* To despoil *hell*; as said of Christ after his death –1450. **3.** To worry, goad, harass; to maltreat ME. **4.** To carry off in a marauding raid. Now *Sc.* 1579. **5.** To drag. *Obs.* or *dial.* ME.

1. Harrie and make havock of all P. HOLLAND. **2.** Italie he harried as a conquered countrey 1581. **3.** That your mind should be harried it is no wonder JOHNSON. **5.** Þe holy mayde was haryed forth to turment CHAUCER.

Harsh (hāɹʃ), *a.* 1530. [– MLG. *harsch* (whence G. *harsch*) rough, lit. 'hairy', f. *haer* HAIR; see -ISH¹.] **1.** Disagreeably hard and rough: **a.** to the touch; **b.** to the taste; **c.** to the ear. **2.** Of rough aspect; forbidding 1774; forbidding in general physical effect; rough, rude 1613. **3.** Repugnant to the feelings; severe, rigorous, cruel, rude, unfeeling 1579. **4.** Repugnant to the understanding or taste; strained, lacking smoothness, unpleasing 1594.

1. a. H. haire like goates 1600. **b.** Berries h. and crude MILT. **c.** And with h. din Broke the fair musick MILT. **2.** Wild groups and h. faces W. IRVING. A picture without half tones is h. 1894. H. remedies DRYDEN. **3.** A h. sentence 1659, censure 1709, master JOWETT. The h. administration of Laud MACAULAY. **4.** H. transitions 1841. Hence **Ha·rshen** *v.* to render h. **Ha·rshly** *adv.* in a h. manner. **Ha·rshness,** the quality of being h.

Harslet: see HASLET.

Hart (hāɹt). [ME. *hert*, OE. *heort*, earlier *heorot* = OS. *hirot* (Du. *hert*), OHG. *hir(u)z* (G. *hirsch*), ON. *hjǫrtr* (:– **herutr*) :– Gmc. **χerutaz*.] The male of the deer, esp. of the red deer; a stag; *spec.* a male deer after its fifth year.

As the H. panteth after the water brookes *Ps.* 42:1. †*Hart of grease*, a fat h. *H. of ten*, a h. with ten branches on his horns. *H. royal*, a h. that has been chased by royalty.

Comb.: **h.-berry,** the Bilberry; **-clover, hart's clover,** Melilot; **hart's-balls** = *hart's truffles*; †**hart's eye,** wild dittany; **hart's-trefoil** = *hart-clover*; **hart's-truffle,** a kind of underground fungus (*Elaphomyces*); †**h.-wolf,** a fabulous animal, a hybrid between a deer and a wolf.

‖**Hartal** (hā·ɹtæl). 1920. *India.* [Hindi *hartāl*, for *haṭtāl* 'locking of shops' (Skr. *haṭṭa* shop, *tālaka* lock, bolt).] A day of national mourning when business is suspended, used as a form of boycott.

Hart(e)beest (hā·ɹtĕbīst, hā·ɹtbīst). 1786. [S. Afr. Du. (Afrikaans *hartbees*), f. Du. *hert* HART + *beest* BEAST.] A S.Afr. Antelope (*Alcephalus caama*).

Hartleian (hāɹtlī·an, hā·ɹtliˌăn). 1803. **A.** *adj.* Of or pertaining to the doctrines of David Hartley (1705–57), regarded as the founder of the English associationist school of psychologists. **B.** *sb.* One of the H. school.

Hartshorn (hā·ɹtsˌhǭɹn). OE. [f. *hart's* + HORN.] **1.** The horn or antler of a hart; the substance obtained by rasping, slicing, or calcining the horns of harts, formerly the chief source of ammonia. †**2. a.** Buck's-horn Plantain, *Plantago coronopus* (also **H. Plantain**); **b.** Swine's Cress, *Senebiera coronopus.* –1674.

1. *Spirit of h.*, also simply *h.*: the aqueous solution of ammonia (from any source). *Salt of h.*: carbonate of ammonia; smelling salts.

Comb.: †**h. beetle,** the stag-beetle; **h. jelly,** a jelly made formerly from the shavings of harts' horns, now from those of calves' bones; **h. plantain** (see 2).

Hart's-tongue. ME. [tr. med.L. *lingua cervi*; so named from the shape of the fronds. So G. *hirschzunge*, Da. *hertstong*, Fr. *langue de cerf*, etc.] The common name of *Scolopendrium vulgare*; also given to other species of the genus; occas. also to some other polypodiaceous ferns, as *Olfersia cervina*, etc. So **Hart's-tongue fern.**

Hartwort (hā·ɹtwɒɹt). 1562. [var. sp. of HEARTWORT.] *Herb.* **1.** Formerly applied to the genus *Seseli*. **2.** A book-name for *Tordylium maximum*, one of the plants formerly included in the genus *Seseli* 1787.

Harum-scarum (hēᵊ·rəm,skēᵊ·rəm). *colloq.* 1674. [A rhyming comb., app. f. HARE *v.* + SCARE *v.*] **A.** *adv.* Recklessly, wildly. ? *Obs.* **B.** *adj.* Reckless, heedless; wild, rash 1751. **C.** *sb.* A reckless person; reckless action or behaviour 1784.

B. A dissolute, harum-scarum fellow..always in debt LYTTON.

‖**Haruspex** (hărɒ·speks). *Pl.* **-spices** (-isīz). Also †**aruspex.** 1584. [L., f. a root appearing in Skr. *hirâ* entrails + L. *-spic-* beholding.] One of the ancient Roman soothsayers, of Etruscan origin, who performed divination by inspection of entrails, etc. Hence **Haru·spical (ar-)** *a.* belonging to, or having the function of, a h. So †**Haru·spicate (ar-)** *a.* in same sense. **Haruspica·tion,** divination by inspection of entrails.

Haruspicy (hărɒ·spisi). Also †**ar-**. 1569. [- L. *haruspicium*, f. *haruspex*, *-spic-* HARUSPEX.] The practice or function of a haruspex.

Harvest (hā·ɹvėst), *sb.* [OE. *hærfest* = OFris., (M)Du. *herfst*, OHG. *herbist* (G. *herbst* autumn, in Upper Germany, fruit harvest), ON. *haust* :- Gmc. **χarbistaz*, **-ustaz*, f. **χarb-* :- IE. **karp-*, as in L. *carpere* pluck, Gr. καρπός fruit.] **1.** The third season of the year, autumn. *Obs.* exc. *dial.* **2.** The season for reaping and gathering in the ripened grain. Also *transf.* and *fig.* ME. **3.** The reaping and gathering in of ripened grain; also *transf.* 1526. **4.** The ripened grain or fruit 1526; the sean'yie ossld of any natural product 1607. **5.** *fig.* The product of any action or effort; a 'crop' 1576. **6.** *attrib.* Of or pertaining to the autumn or harvest ME., or to the harvest-home 1602.

2. Seed time and H., Heat and hoary Frost Shall hold thir course MILT. *fig.* It is needful that you frame the season for your owne haruest SHAKS. **3.** A field Of Ceres ripe for h. MILT. Phr. *Lord of the h.*, (*a*) the farmer to whom the crops belong, hence applied to God (*Matt.* 9:8); (*b*) the head reaper. **4.** Along the furrow here, the h. fell COWPER. The grouse h. 1881. **5.** To reape the Haruest of perpetuall peace SHAKS.

Comb.: **h.-bell,** a flower, the Autumn bell, *Gentiana pneumonanthe*; **h. festival, thanksgiving,** a service for the ingathering of the h., at which the church is usually decorated with fruit, grain, etc.; **-fish,** the butter- or dollar-fish of N. America, a species of *Stromateus*; **-fly,** a name in U.S. for species of *Cicada*, which appear during h. time; **-louse, -mite** = HARVEST-BUG; **-spider,** a long-legged spider, *Phalangium*, common in harvest-fields; **-tick,** (*a*) = HARVEST-BUG; (*b*) any small spider of the genus *Leptidæ*; **-work,** the work of reaping and gathering in the h.

Harvest (hā·ɹvėst), *v.* ME. [f. prec. sb.] **1.** *trans.* To reap and gather in (the corn, hence, any ripe crop). Also *intr.* **2.** *transf.* To gather and lay up in store; to husband 1888.

Harvest-bug. 1768. A minute mite or acarid troublesome during harvest; also called *harvester, harvest-louse, -mite, -tick.*

Harvester (hā·ɹvestəɹ). 1589. [f. HARVEST *v.* + -ER¹.] **1.** A reaper. **2.** Applied to various insects: **a.** = *harvesting ant* 1882. **b.** A harvest-bug. **3.** A reaping machine, *esp.* one which also binds up the sheaves 1875.

Harvest-field. 1730. A field in which the corn is being reaped; a corn-field in harvest. Also *transf.* and *fig.*

Harvest home, harvest-home. 1573. **1.** The fact, occasion, or time of bringing home the last of the harvest; the close of the harvesting. Also *fig.* 1596. **2.** The festival to celebrate the successful homing of the corn. (Now rarely held.) 1573.

1. Like a stubble Land at Haruest-home SHAKS. *Comb.* **harvest-home goose,** one killed and eaten at the harvest-home feast; also called *harvest-goose.*

Ha·rvesting, *ppl. a.* 1873. [f. HARVEST *v.* + -ING².] That reaps or gathers in and stores up grain, etc.

Harvesting ant, a kind of ant which gathers and stores up the seeds of grasses; *h. mouse* = HARVEST MOUSE.

Ha·rvestless, *a.* 1868. [f. HARVEST *sb.* + -LESS.] Devoid of harvests; sterile.

H. autumn, horrible agues, plague TENNYSON.

Ha·rvestman. 1552. **1.** A reaper; *esp.* one who leaves home to obtain harvest work. **2.** A name given to insects common in harvest-time; *esp.* a long-legged spider, *Phalangium.*

Harvest month. OE. The month (orig. September, but in Robert of Gloucester, August) during which the harvest is gathered in.

Harvest moon. 1706. The moon which is full within a fortnight of the autumnal equinox (22 or 23 Sept.), and which rises for several nights nearly at the same hour, at points successively farther north on the eastern horizon.

Harvest mouse. 1812. A very small species of mouse (*Mus messorius*, or *Micromys minutus*), which builds its nest in the stalks of growing grain.

Harvest queen. 1579. A name given **a.** to Ceres, the goddess of agriculture and crops; **b.** to a young woman chosen from the reapers, to whom was given a post of honour at the harvest home.

Ha·rvey, *v.* 1894. [f. the inventor's name.] **a.** To harden (steel) by a process invented by H. A. Harvey of New Jersey. **b.** To fit or supply (a ship) with armour plates so treated. Also **Ha·rveyize** *v.*

Has, 3rd sing. pres. ind. of HAVE *v.*

Hasard, Hase, obs. ff. HAZARD, HAZE.

Has-been (hæ·z,bīn), *sb.* (*a.*) 1606. [perf. tense of BE.] One that *has been* but is no longer; a person or thing whose career or efficiency belongs to the past; a back number.

Hash (hæʃ), *v.* 1653. [Also †*hache* (XVII) - (O)Fr. *hacher*, f. *hache* HATCHET.] **1.** *trans.* To cut (meat) into small pieces for cooking; to make into a hash. Also *fig.* **2.** To cut up or hack about; to mangle. Now *Sc.* and *dial.* Also *intr.* 1663. Hence **Ha·sher.**

Hash (hæʃ), *sb.* 1662. [f. HASH *v.*, replacing earlier †*hachee*, *hach(e)y* - Fr. *hachis.*] **1.** Something cut up into small pieces; *spec.* a dish of meat which has been previously cooked, cut small, and warmed up with gravy and sauce. **2.** *transf.* and *fig.* Old matter served up in a fresh form 1672. **3.** A medley; a spoiled mixture; a mess, jumble 1735.

1. I had..at first course, a h. of rabbits, a lamb PEPYS. **2.** Chiefly a well-done h. of my own words DARWIN. Phr. *To make a h. of*: to mangle and spoil in dealing with. *To settle* (a person's) *h.*: to silence, subdue; to 'do for' (*slang* or *colloq.*).

‖**Hashish, hasheesh** (hæ·ʃiʃ, haʃī·ʃ). 1598. [- Arab. *ḥašīš* dry herb, hay, powdered hemp-leaves, intoxicant made therefrom.] The top leaves and tender parts of the Indian hemp (which in warm countries develop intoxicating properties) dried for smoking or chewing, in Arabia, Egypt, Turkey, etc. Cf. BHANG. Also *fig.*

†**Hask, haske,** *sb.* 1579. [Cf. †*hassock* rush basket (XVI).] 'A wicker pad, wherein they vse to cary fish' (SPENSER) -1611.

Haslet (hēⁱ·slėt), **harslet** (hā·ɹslėt). [ME. *hastelet* - OFr. *hastelet* (mod. *hâtelet, -lette*), dim. of *haste* (*hâte*) spit, roast meat - OLG. *harst* piece of roast meat (cf. Du. *harst* sirloin) = OHG. *harst*; see -LET.] A piece of meat to be roasted, *esp.* part of the entrails of a hog; pig's fry.

Hasp (hɑsp), *sb.* [OE. *hæpse, hæsp*, corresp. to MLG. *haspe, hespe*, OHG. *haspa* (G. *haspe*), ON. *hespa*, rel. further to MLG., Du. *haspel*, OHG. *haspil.*] **1.** A contrivance for fastening a door or lid; now chiefly, a hinged clasp of metal which passes over a staple and is secured by a pin or padlock. **b.** A latch for a sash window 1772. **2.** A clasp or catch for fastening two parts of a garment, the covers of a book, etc. ME. **3.** A hank or skein of yarn, thread, or silk; a definite quantity of yarn, the fourth part of a spindle ME. **4.** 'An instrument for cutting the surface of grass-land; a scarifier' (Webster) 1864.

Hasp, *v.* [OE. *hæpsian*, f. *hæpse* HASP *sb.*] **1.** *trans.* To fasten with, or as with, a hasp. †**2.** To confine or fasten in a tight place; to lock *up* -1711.

2. Being hasped up with thee in this publick Vehicle STEELE.

Hassock (hæ·sək), *sb.* [OE. *hassuc*, of unkn. origin; see -OCK.] **1.** A firm tuft or clump of matted vegetation; *esp.* of coarse boggy grass or sedge; a tussock. **b.** *transf.* A shock of hair 1785. **2.** A thick firm cushion or bass, used to rest the feet on, and *esp.* in church to kneel on 1516. **3.** The soft calcareous sandstone which separates the beds of ragstone in Kent. (? A different wd.) 1706.

2. Knees and hassocks are well-nigh divorc'd COWPER. Hence **Ha·ssocky** *a.* abounding in hassocks or clumps; consisting of calcareous h.

Hast, 2nd pers. sing. pres. ind. of HAVE *v.*

Hastate (hæ·steⁱt), *a.* 1788. [- L. *hastatus*, f. *hasta* spear; see -ATE².] Formed like a spear or spear-head 1854. **b.** *Bot.* Of leaves: Narrowly triangular nearly to the base, where two lateral lobes project at right angles to the midrib 1788. So †**Hasta·ted** *a.*

Ha·stately, *adv.* 1831. [f. prec. + -LY².] In a hastate fashion; chiefly in comb. with adjs., as *h.-lanceolate*, etc.

Hasta·to-, comb. f. L. *hastatus*, used like prec.

Haste (hēⁱst), *sb.* ME. [- OFr. *haste* (mod. *hâte*) - WGmc. **χaisti* (OE. *hǣst* violence, fury, ON. *heifst, heipt* hate, revenge, Goth. *haifsts* strife; OE. *hǣste* violent, OFris. *hāste*, OHG. *heisti* powerful); of unkn. origin.] **1.** Urgency or impetuosity of movement tending to swiftness or rapidity; quickness, speed, expedition (properly of voluntary action). **2.** Such quickness of action as excludes due consideration; hurry, precipitancy, rashness ME. **3.** The condition of being obliged to act quickly on account of having little time; hurry ME.

1. This asketh h. CHAUCER. **2.** I said in my h., All men are liars *Ps.* 116:11. Raw H., half-sister to Delay TENNYSON. **3.** The h. to get rich 1872. Phr. *To make h.*: to put forth energy producing speed; to use expedition, to hasten. (Often with *inf.*)

Haste (hēⁱst), *v.* ME. [- OFr. *haster* (mod. *hâter*), f. *haste*; see prec. Superseded by HASTEN.] **1.** *trans.* To cause to move quickly; to urge, drive, or press on; to hurry. **2.** *refl.* = 3. *arch.* ME. **3.** *intr.* To make haste; to come or go quickly; to act with expedition (of time or events) to come on rapidly. (Often with *to* and *inf.*) ME.

1. They were so hastyd and pursewyd LD. BERNERS. **2.** Lorde, I call vpon the; haist the vnto me COVERDALE *Ps.* 140 [41]: 1. **3.** If the reward were good, he would hast to gaine more 1581.

Hasteful (hēⁱ·stfŭl), *a. rare.* 1610. [f. HASTE *sb.* + -FUL.] Full of haste; hurrying, hurried. Hence **Ha·stefully** *adv.*

Hasteless (hēⁱ·stlės), *a.* 1873. [f. HASTE *sb.* + -LESS.] Without haste. Hence **Ha·stelessness.**

Hasten (hēⁱ·s'n), *v.* 1565. [f. HASTE *v.* + -EN⁵.] **1.** *trans.* = HASTE *v.* 1. †**b.** To dispatch in haste -1748. **2.** *intr.* = HASTE *v.* 3. 1568.

1. Sorrowe ne neede be hastened on SPENSER. **2.** So do our minutes h. to their end SHAKS. Hence **Ha·stener,** one who or that which hastens; *esp.* a stand or screen for concentrating the heat of the fire on a roasting joint of meat (*dial.*); also **Haster.**

Hastif, -ly, -ness: see HASTIVE, -LY, -NESS.

Hastifoliate (hæstifōᵘ·liėt), *a.* 1886. [f. L. *hasta* spear + *folium* leaf + -ATE².] *Bot.* Having spear-shaped leaves. So **Hastifo·lious** *a.*

Hastiform (hæ·stifǫɹm), *a.* 1886. [f. L. *hasta* spear + -FORM.] Spear-shaped.

Hastile (hæ·stəil), *a.* 1864. [f. as prec. + -ILE.] *Bot.* = HASTATE.

Hastily (hēⁱ·stili), *adv.* ME. [f. HASTY *a.* + -LY².] In haste. **1.** Quickly, expeditiously; †soon, without delay, suddenly; rapidly. Now usu.: Hurriedly. **2.** With undue haste excluding consideration; precipitately, rashly 1586. **3.** In sudden anger 1573.

1. Over-hastily blooming Trees EVELYN. The Northern nobles marched h. to join their comrades J. R. GREEN. **2.** She had married h., and as h. grown weary of her choice FROUDE.

Hastiness (hēⁱ·stinės). ME. [f. as prec. + -NESS.] The quality or condition of being hasty; †swiftness –1591; precipitancy ME.; quickness of temper; passion ME.

Hasting, *ppl. a.* and *sb.* 1546. [f. HASTE *v.* + -ING.]

A. *ppl. a.* **1.** That hastes 1632. †**2.** That ripens early –1753.

B. *sb.* [the adj. used ellipt.] **1.** An early-ripening fruit or vegetable; *spec.* a kind of early pea. *Obs.* or *local.* 1573. †**2.** Hence applied to persons who hasten or make haste. Only in *pl.* –1700.

1. A day or two ago I heard the cry 'Green Hastings!'..fifty years ago, it was the usual cry for green peas 1878.

†**Ha·stive, ha·stif,** *a.* ME. [– OFr. *hastif, -ive*; see next.] **1.** Speedy, swift (ME. only); (of fruit, etc.) maturing early –1751. **2.** Precipitate, rash. ME. only. **3.** Quick-tempered; angry –1489. Hence †**Ha·stive-, hastif, -ly** *adv.*, †**-ness.**

Hasty (hē[i]·sti), *a.* ME. [– OFr. *hasti, hastif* (mod. *hâtif*), f. *haste* HASTE *sb.* + *-if* -IVE; superseded HASTIVE (cf. *jolly, tardy*).] Marked by haste. **1.** Speedy, expeditious; swift, rapid; sudden. *arch.* exc. as in b. **b.** Hurried 1590. **c.** Requiring speed; made in haste. *spec.* in *Cookery.* ME. †**d.** Early, forward [L. *præcox*] –1693. †**2.** In a hurry. Usu. with *inf.* –1754. **3.** Unduly quick of action; precipitate, rash, inconsiderate ME. **4.** Of persons, etc.: Quick-tempered, irritable. Of words or actions: Uttered or done in sudden anger or irritation. 1526.

1. We wish h. ruin to all Tyrants MILTON. **b.** A h. sketch 1834, glance 1844, reader 1874. **d.** As the hastie fruite before the summer *Isa.* 28:4. **2.** 2 *Hen. IV*, IV. v. 61. **3.** Hastie and furious of heart, and unware of perilles GRAFTON. **4.** Hee that is h. of spirit, exalteth folly *Prov.* 14:29.

Hasty pudding. 1599. A pudding made of flour stirred in milk or water to the consistency of a thick batter; in some parts applied to oatmeal porridge; in U.S. made with Indian meal and water.

Hat (hæt), *sb.* [OE. *hætt*, corresp. to ON. *hǫttr* hood, cowl :– Gmc. **χattuz* (cf. ON. *hetta* hood :– **χatjōn*) :– **χadnús*; see HOOD.] **1.** A covering for the head; in recent use, one having a more or less horizontal brim all round the hemispherical, conical, or cylindrical part which covers the head. Worn by men and women. **2.** A head-dress showing the rank or dignity of the wearer; *esp.* a cardinal's hat (see CARDINAL *sb.*); whence *transf.* the office or dignity of a cardinal; called also *red hat* ME. **3.** *attrib.* 'Forming part of a hat', as *h.-brim*, etc.; 'for supporting or holding hats', as *h.-peg*, etc. 1670.

1. Beaver, felt, silk, straw *h.*; high, tall (chimney-pot, stove-pipe, top) *h.*, the ordinary cylindrical silk h. of the 19th c.; opera, tennis *h.*; Rubens, Gainsborough *h.*; see these words. **2.** †*H. of Maintenance*: see MAINTENANCE.

Phrases. *H. in hand*, with the head uncovered in respect; obsequiously, servilely. (*His*) *h. covers* (*his*) *family*, he is alone in the world. *To send round the h., go round with the h.*, etc.: applied to the collection of money by personal solicitation for charitable or benevolent purposes. *To hang up one's h.*: see HANG *v.* *To talk through one's h.*: see TALK *v.*

Comb.: **h.-block,** a form or mould upon which a man's h. is shaped; **-body,** the unshaped piece of felt from which a h. is formed; **-box,** a box for holding a hat; **-brush; -case** = *hat-box*; **-die** = *hat-mould*; **-homage,** †**-honour,** reverence shown by removing the h., an early Quaker phrase; **-mould,** the die on which a h. or bonnet is formed or shaped by pressing; **-piece,** a metal skull-cap worn under the h. as defensive armour; **-stand; -tree,** a hat-stand with projecting arms for hats and coats; †**-worship** = *hat-homage.*

Hat, *v.* ME. [f. prec.] *trans.* To cover, furnish, or provide with a hat. Also, to bestow the cardinal's hat upon.

Hatable, obs. var. of HATEABLE.

Ha·tband, hat-band. ME. **1.** A band or narrow ribbon, put round a hat above the brim. **2.** A band of crape, etc. worn round the hat as a sign of mourning 1598.

1. †*Gold h.*: a nobleman at the University; a 'tuft'.

Hatch (hætʃ), *sb.*[1] [OE. *hæċċ, heċċ*, corresp. to MLG. *heck*, MDu. *hecke* (Du. *hek*); f. Gmc. **χak-*, of unkn. origin.] **1.** A half-door, gate, or wicket with an open space above; the lower half of a divided door. Also formerly, and still dial., any small gate or wicket. **2.** *Naut.* †**a.** Formerly (usu. in *pl.*), A movable planking forming a kind of deck in ships; hence, also, the permanent deck. **b.** Now: A trap-door or grated framework covering the openings in the deck called hatchways. ME. **c.** A square or oblong opening in the deck, by which cargo is lowered; a hatchway 1793. **3.** *transf.* **a.** An opening in the floor of a timber-shed or other building, which is covered by a trap-door; also, the trap-door itself 1888. †**b.** *Mining.* An opening made in the ground –1753. **4.** A flood-gate or sluice 1531. **5.** 'A contrivance for trapping salmon' (Smyth) 1826. **6.** A wooden bed-frame. ? *Obs.* 1832.

1. In at the window, or else ore the h. SHAKS. Phr. †*To keep a h. before the door* (fig.): to keep silence. **2.** *Under hatches*: *orig.* = below deck, but now assoc. with sense 2 b. *Under* (*the*) *hatches* (fig.): down in position or circumstances; down out of sight. *Comb.* **h.-gate,** (*a*) a wicket; (*b*) = sense 4.

Hatch, *sb.*[2] 1597. [f. HATCH *v.*[1]] The action of hatching; that which is hatched; a brood (of young).

Hatch, *sb.*[3] Also †**hache.** 1658. [f. HATCH *v.*[2]] An engraved line or stroke; esp. for shading in an engraving.

†**Hatch,** *sb.*[4] 1704. [– Fr. *hache* hatchet.] A hatchet –1810.

Hatch, *v.*[1] [ME. *hacche* points to an OE. **hæċċan*, rel. to MHG. *hecken*, Sw. *häcka*, Da. *hække*, of unkn. origin.] **1.** *intr.* To bring forth young birds from the egg by incubation. **2.** *trans.* To bring forth from the egg by either natural or artificial heat ME. **3.** *intr.* for *pass.* **a.** Of the young: To come forth from the egg. **b.** Said of the egg. 1593. **4.** *transf.* (*trans.*) To bring forth, bring into existence, breed ME. **5.** *fig.* To bring to full development, esp. by a covert process; to contrive, devise 1549. Also *intr.* for *pass.*

2. In this fortress the male and female h. and bring up their brood with security GOLDSM. No Reptile hatches its eggs 1834. **3.** Why should.. hateful cuckoos h. in sparrows' nests SHAKS. **5.** The Gunpowder Treason was hatched here in England 1678. *intr.* Treason hatching in his heart TRAPP.

Hatch, *v.*[2] 1480. [– (O)Fr. *hacher*, f. *hache* HATCHET.] **1.** *trans.* To cut, engrave, or draw a series of lines, generally parallel, on; chiefly for shading in engraving or drawing 1598. **2.** To inlay with narrow strips or lines of a different substance. Also *transf.* and *fig.* 1480.

1. Having heated the steel..they h. it over and across with the knife 1833. **2.** The handle or pummell hatcht or inameld HAKEWILL. *fig.* His Sword..Hatch't in Blood Royall G. DANIEL.

Phr. *Hatched moulding*: a kind of moulding used in Norman architecture, formed with two series of oblique parallel incisions crossing each other.

†**Hatch,** *v.*[3] 1581. [f. HATCH *sb.*[1]] To close (a door) with a hatch; to close –1608.

While sleepe begins with heauy wings To h. mine eyes SYDNEY.

Ha·tch-boat. 1858. [f. HATCH *sb.*[1] + BOAT.] **a.** 'A sort of small vessel known as a pilot boat, having a deck composed almost entirely of hatches' (Adm. Smyth). **b.** 'A kind of half-decked fishing-boat; one which has a hatch or well for keeping fish' (Simmonds).

Hatchel (hæ·tʃ'l), *sb.* [Later var. of *hetchel*, ME. *hechele, hechil* (XIII) :– OE. **hæċel* :– WGmc. **χakila*, f. **χak* HOOK *sb.* Cf. HACKLE *sb.*[2], HECKLE *sb.*] An instrument for combing flax or hemp; = HECKLE.

Hatchel, *v.* ME. [f. prec.; cf. HACKLE *v.*[2], HECKLE *v.*] **1.** *trans.* To dress (flax or hemp) with a hatchel; to heckle. **2.** *fig.* To harass, worry (*rare*) 1833.

2. Fleeced, hatchelled, bewildered and bedevilled CARLYLE. Hence **Ha·tcheller,** a flax-dresser, heckler.

Hatcher (hæ·tʃəɹ). 1581. [f. HATCH *v.*[1] + -ER[1].] **1.** One who or that which hatches (eggs) 1632; *spec.* an incubator 1884. **2.** *fig.* A contriver, designer, plotter 1581.

2. A great h. and breeder of business SWIFT.

Hatchery (hæ·tʃəri). 1880. [f. HATCH *v.*[1] + -ERY.] A hatching establishment; *spec.* one for hatching the ova of fish by artificial means.

Hatchet (hæ·tʃėt), *sb.* ME. [– (O)Fr. *hachette*, dim. of *hache* axe :– med.L. *hapia* – Gmc. **χapja* (OHG. *happa, heppa* sickle-shaped knife); see -ET.] A smaller or lighter axe with a short handle, for use with one hand.

Phrases. *To take* or *dig up the h.*: to commence hostilities. *To bury the h.*: to cease from hostilities (Derived from the customs of the N. Amer. Indians.) *Comb.*: **h.-face,** a narrow and very sharp face; so **-fist, -jaw; -faced** *a.*, having a h.-face. Hence **Ha·tchety** *a.* (said of the face).

Hatchettin (hæ·tʃėtin). Also **-ettine, -etin(e.** 1821. [f. C. *Hatchett*, the discoverer of columbium and tantalium; see -IN[1], -INE[5].] *Min.* = next.

Hatchettite (hæ·tʃėtəit). 1868. [f. as prec. + -ITE[1] 2 b.] *Min.* A yellowish-white subtransparent fossil resin or wax-like hydrocarbon found in the coal-measures of South Wales.

Hatching, *vbl. sb.* 1662. [f. HATCH *v.*[2] + -ING[1].] The action of HATCH *v.*[2]; the drawing of parallel lines so as to produce the effect of shading; chiefly *concr.*, the series of lines so drawn; hatches.

Hatchment[1] (hæ·tʃmĕnt). 1548. [Altered f. ACHIEVEMENT (q.v.), through *atcheament, atchement, atch'ment.*] An escutcheon or ensign armorial; = ACHIEVEMENT 3; *esp.* a square or lozenge-shaped tablet exhibiting the armorial bearings of a deceased person, which is affixed to the front of his dwelling-place. Also *transf.*

No Trophee, Sword, nor H. o're his bones SHAKS.

†**Hatchment**[2]. 1616. [f. HATCH *v.*[2] + -MENT.] The hatching with which the hilt of the sword is ornamented –1649.

Five Marks in hatchments to adorn this thigh BEAUM. & FL.

Hatchway (hæ·tʃwe[i]). 1626. [f. HATCH *sb.*[1] + WAY.] **1.** *Naut.* A square or oblong opening in the deck of a ship down which cargo is lowered into the hold; also forming a passage from one deck to another. Qualified, as *after-, fore-, main-h.* **2.** An opening in a floor, etc. which may be closed by a hatch or trap-door. (Applied by Scott to the sliding-door of a box-bed.) 1814.

Hate (hē[i]t), *sb.*[1] OE. [Partly – ON. *hatr* (see HATE *v.*), partly f. HATE *v.* under the infl. of HATRED.] An emotion of extreme dislike or aversion; detestation, abhorrence, hatred. Now chiefly *poet.* **b.** The object of hatred (*poet.*) 1592.

Unimaginable as h. in Heav'n MILT. **b.** My onely Loue sprung from my onely h. SHAKS.

Hate, haet (hēt), *sb.*[2] *Sc.* 1590. *orig.* The words *hae't* in *Deil hae't*, 'Devil have it!' This deprecatory expression became a strong negative, and thus = 'Devil a bit', i.e. not a whit. Hence *haet*, in *not a haet*, or the like, was taken as = 'whit, atom'.

Deil haet do I expect SCOTT.

Hate (hē[i]t), *v.* [OE. *hatian* = OFris. *hatia*, OS. *haton* (Du. *haten*), OHG. *hazzōn, -ēn* (G. *hassen*), ON. *hata*, Goth. *hatan* :– Gmc. **χatōjan*, *-*ǣjan*, f. base of **χatis-*, repr. by OE. *hete* (to XIII), OS. *heti*, OHG. *haz* (G. *hass*), ON. *hatr*, Goth. *hatis.*] **1.** *trans.* To hold in very strong dislike; to detest; to bear malice to. The opposite of *to love.* Also *absol.* **2.** To dislike greatly, be extremely averse (*to do* something). Also constr. with *vbl. sb.* ME.

1. Her presence, hated both of Gods and men TENNYSON. *absol.* She hated easily; she hated heartily; and she hated implacably MACAULAY. **2.** I h. to promise much, and fail WALTON. To h. being bothered 1891.

Hateable (hē[i]·tăb'l), *a.* Also †**hatable.** 1611. [f. HATE *v.* + -ABLE.] Deserving of being hated; odious.

Hateful (hē[i]·tfŭl), *a.* ME. [f. HATE *sb.*[1] + -FUL.] **1.** Full of hate, cherishing hatred, malignant. **2.** Exciting hate; odious, repulsive ME.

1. Hide thee from their hatefull lookes SHAKS. **2.** These Acts of h. strife, h. to all MILT. Hence **Ha·teful-ly** *adv.*, **-ness.**

†**Hatel,** *a.* [OE. *hatol, hetol* = OS. *hatul* (MDu. *hatel*), OHG. *hazzal*, cogn. with HATE *sb.*[1] and *v.*; see -LE.] Full of hatred; malignant, hostile; severe, cruel; bitter –ME.

Hater (hē[i]·təɹ). ME. [f. HATE *v.* + -ER[1].] One who hates.

Haters have I, more than haires C'TESS PEMBROKE.

Hath, arch. 3rd pers. sing. pres. ind. of HAVE *v.*

Ha·tless, *a.* 1450. [-LESS.] Having no hat.

Ha·t-money. 1676. [In Fr. *chapeau*, Sp. *sombrero*, app. because dropped in a hat.] (See quot.).

The word *primage* denotes a small payment to the master for his care and trouble..It is sometimes called the master's hat-money 1808 (*Law Merch. Ships*).

Hatred (hēⁱ·trėd). ME. [f. HATE *v.* + -RED.] The condition or state of relations in which one person hates another; the emotion of hate; active dislike, detestation; enmity, ill-will, malevolence.

Dislike easily rises into h. DARWIN.

Hatte, obs. f. HATE *v.*, HOT *a.*

Hatte, obs. pa. t. of HEAT *v.*, HIGHT *v*[1].

Hatted, *ppl. a.* 1552. [f. HAT *v.* or *sb.* + -ED.] Wearing a hat, having a hat on.

Hatter (hæ·təɹ), *sb.* ME. [f. HAT *sb.* + -ER[1].] **1.** A maker of or dealer in hats. **2.** *Austral. Mining.* One who works alone. [Cf. *Hat covers his family* in HAT *sb.*] 1864.

1. *As mad as a h.*: see MAD *a.*

Hatter, *v.* Now *Sc.* and *n. dial.* 1450. [perh. of imit. origin with frequent. ending; cf. *batter, shatter*, etc.] **1.** *trans.* To bruise with blows; to erode. ? *Obs.* **2.** To harass; to wear *out* 1687.

2. He's hattered out with penance DRYDEN.

‖**Hatti.** In full *α.* **hatti-sherif** (ha:tiˌʃĕrī·f). *β.* **hatti-humayun** (ha:tiˌhumā·yūn). 1688. [Pers.] A decree or edict issued by the government of Turkey bearing the Sultan's special mark, and therefore irrevocable.

Ha·tting, *vbl. sb.* 1796. [f. HAT *v.* and *sb.* + -ING[1].] The trade of making hats; material for hats; also, the covering of a tan-pit with its hat of bark.

Hat trick. 1882. **1.** Any trick with a hat 1886. **2.** *Cricket.* The feat of a bowler who takes three wickets by three successive balls; entitling him to a new hat from his club.

Haubergeon, obs. f. HABERGEON.

Hauberk (hǭ·bəɹk). ME. [– OFr. *hauberc*, also *holberc*, earlier *hausberc* :– Frankish **halsberg* (= OHG. *halsberc*, OE. *healsbeorg*, ON. *hálsbjǫrg*), f. *hals* neck + **berʒ-* protect (cf. HARBOUR *sb.*[1]).] A piece of defensive armour, orig. for the neck and shoulders; but early developed into a long military tunic, usually of ring or chain mail.

H. woven of polished chain BOWEN.

Hauerite (hau·ĕrəit). 1847. [f. von *Hauer*, Austrian geologist + -ITE[1] 2 b.] *Min.* Native disulphide of manganese, occurring in reddish-brown crystals, usually octahedral.

Haugh (hăχ, hăχʷ, hăf). *Sc.* and *n. dial.* Also in north. Eng. **halgh** as in *Greenhalgh*. [ME. *hawch, hawgh*, prob. :– OE. *healh* corner, nook, rel. to *holh* HOLLOW *sb.*] A piece of flat alluvial land by the side of a river, forming part of the floor of the river valley. Also *attrib.*

Haught (hǭt), *a. arch.* late ME. [orig. *haut* (XV) – (O)Fr. *haut* high :– L. *altus* high, infl. by Gmc. **χauh-* HIGH. The sp. with *gh* was induced by assim. to words in which the sound denoted by it had become mute, or to *high, height*.] **1.** High in one's own estimation; haughty (*arch.*). †**2.** High-minded; lofty –1590. †**3.** High-born –1627. †**4.** High, in other senses –1587. Hence †**Hau·ght-ly** *adv.*, †**-ness.**

Haughty (hǭ·ti), *a.* 1530. [An extension of *haut* HAUGHT *a.* with -Y[1].] **1.** High in one's own estimation; proud, arrogant, supercilious. **b.** *fig.* Imposing in aspect; often with a mixture of sense 3. 1585. **2.** Of exalted character, style, or rank; eminent; high-minded, aspiring; of exalted courage (*arch.*) 1563. †**3.** High (in literal sense) –1621.

1. The Fiend..like a proud Steed reind, went hautie on MILT. **b.** His h. Crest DRYDEN. **2.** The hawtye verse, that Maro wrote B. GOOGE. No h. feat of arms I tell SCOTT. **3.** From the toppes of hawtie towres B. GOOGE. Hence **Hau·ghti-ly** *adv.*, **-ness.**

Haul (hǭl), *v.* 1557. (Earliest form *hall*; var. of HALE *v.*[1] For the sp. with *au* cf. CRAWL.] **1.** *trans.* To pull or draw with force; to drag, tug 1581. **b.** To transport by cart or other conveyance 1787. **2.** *intr.* To pull, tug (*at* or *upon* something) 1743. Also *intr.* for *refl.* in passive sense 1797. **3.** *Naut.* (*intr.*) To trim the sails, etc. of a ship so as to sail nearer to the wind (also *to h. up*); hence, to change the ship's course; to sail in a certain course. (Also, *trans.* with the ship as object; also, to sail along *a coast.*) 1557. **b.** *transf.* and *fig.* To change one's course of action; to withdraw; to make one's way, to come or go 1802. **4.** Of the wind: To shift, veer 1769.

1. We hauled anchor, and passed gently up the river COLERIDGE. Phr. *To h. up*: to bring up for a reprimand. Also, *to h. over the coals* (see COAL *sb.*). **2.** I..pull'd and haul'd, to try to turn him [a horse] 1791. **3.** The enemy..hauled up on the Terpsichore's weather-beam A. DUNCAN. Phr. *To h. upon* or *to the wind*, also trans. *to h.* (a ship) *on a wind*, and *to h. the* (*her, our*, etc.) *wind*; to bring the ship round so as to sail closer to the wind. **4.** The wind hauled to the southward R. H. DANA. *H. round*, said when the wind is gradually shifting towards any point of the compass.

Haul (hǭl), *sb.* 1670. [f. prec. vb.] **1.** The act of hauling; a pull, a tug; *spec.* the draught of a fishing-net. **2.** *concr.* **a.** A draught of fish 1854. **b.** *Haul of yarn* in *Rope-making*: about four hundred threads, when ready to be tarred 1794. **3.** *fig.* The act of drawing or making a large profit or gain of any kind; *concr.* the amount thus gained 1776.

1. We caught..at one H...seven Hundred 1670. **3.** A fine h. of prizes 1776. *Comb.*: **h.-rope,** a rope for hauling something; **-seine,** a drag-seine.

Haulage (hǭ·lėdʒ). 1826. [f. as prec. + -AGE.] **1.** The action or process of hauling; the traction of a load in a wagon or the like; the amount of force expended in hauling. **2.** The expense of hauling 1864. **3.** 'A traction-way' (Smyth).

Hauler (hǭ·ləɹ). 1674. [f. HAUL *v.* + -ER[1].] One who or that which hauls; a HAULIER.

Haulier (hǭ·liəɹ). 1577. [f. HAUL *v.* + -IER; cf. *collier*, HALLIER.] A man employed in hauling something, e.g. coal in a mine.

Haulm, halm (hǭm, hām), *sb.* [OE. *halm* (*healm*) = OS., OHG. (Du., G.) *halm*, ON. *hálmr* :– Gmc. **χalmaz* :– IE. **kolmos*; cf. L. *culmus* haulm, Gr. κάλαμος reed.] **a.** *collect. sing.* The stems or stalks of such plants as peas, beans, vetches, hops, potatoes, etc., now less commonly of corn or grass; *esp.* as used for litter and thatching; straw. **b.** with *a* and *pl.* A stalk or stem (of a bean, potato, grass, etc.) OE. Hence **Haulm** *v.* to lay (straw or haulm) straight for thatching. **Hau·lmy** *a.* having (long or large) haulms.

Haulse, obs. f. HALSE *v.*[2]

Haulte, haultie, obs. ff. HALT, HAUGHT, HAUT, HAUGHTY.

Haum(e, obs. f. HAULM.

Haunce, var. of HANCE *sb.* and *v.*

Haunch (hǭnʃ, hānʃ), *sb.* ME. [– (O)Fr. *hanche* = Pr., Sp., It. *anca* of Gmc. origin (cf. LG. *hanke* hind leg of a horse). Till XVIII usu. spelt *hanch*.] **1.** The part of the body lying between the last ribs and the thigh; the lateral expansions of the pelvis. **b.** The leg and loin of a deer, sheep, etc., prepared for table 1481. **c.** *fig.* The latter end. SHAKS. **2.** The coxa or basal joint of the leg in insects, spiders, and crustaceans 1828. **3.** *Arch.* = HANCE *sb.* 3, q.v. Hence, the corresponding part of any arched figure. 1793. **4.** *Naut.* **a.** A sudden decrease in the size of a piece of timber 1823. **b.** = HANCE *sb.* 2 a. 1867.

1. c. A Summer Bird, which euer in the haunch of Winter sings The lifting vp of day 2 *Hen. IV*, IV. iv. 92.

†**Haunch,** *v.*[1] [f. HAUNCH *sb.*] *trans.* To bring down a deer upon its haunches. CAMDEN.

Haunch, *v.*[2] 1794. [f. HAUNCH *sb.* 4.] *trans.* To reduce in thickness. *intr.* Of a piece of timber: To decrease suddenly in thickness.

Hau·nch-bone. ME. The bone of the haunch; occas. the *os innominatum* as a whole, but usu. the *os ilium*.

Haunched, *a.* 1611. [f. HAUNCH *sb.* + -ED[2].] Having haunches; usu. in comb.

Haunt (hǭnt, hānt), *v.* ME. [– (O)Fr. *hanter* – Gmc. **χaimatjan* (repr. by OE. *hāmettan* provide with a home, house, ON. *heimta* get home, recover), f. **χaimaz* HOME *sb.*[1]]

I. *trans.* †**1.** To practise habitually –1573. †**2.** To use or employ habitually or frequently; *refl.* to accustom *oneself* –1588. **3.** To resort to frequently or habitually; to frequent (a place) ME. **4.** To frequent the company of (a person); to 'run after' 1477. **5.** *transf.* and *fig.* Of unseen or immaterial visitants: To visit frequently or habitually; *esp.* as ghosts, etc., with manifestations of a molesting kind. *To be haunted*: to be subject to the visits and molestation of disembodied spirits. 1576.

2. *refl.* Haunte [*exerce*] thi silf to pite WYCLIF 1 *Tim.* 4:7. **3.** To h. the bathes 1585, the Mountains and the Plains DRYDEN. **4.** To h. a minister of state SWIFT, rich men 1890. **5.** Your beauty.. did h. me in my sleepe SHAKS. Spirits haunted this dungeon, and walked there 1722.

II. *intr.* **1.** To resort habitually; to stay or remain usually (in a place); to associate (with a person). Now usu. said of the lower animals. ME. †**2.** To have resort, go *to* –1632.

1. I haue charg'd thee not to h. about my doores SHAKS. Hence **Hau·nted** *ppl. a.* practised; frequented; *esp.* much visited by apparitions, etc. **Hau·nter,** one who or that which haunts.

Haunt (hǭnt, hānt), *sb.* ME. [f. HAUNT *v.*] **1.** Habit, wont (now *dial.*); †habitual practice or use (of anything) –1585. †**2.** The act or practice of frequenting a place, etc.; resort –1712. **3.** *concr.* A place of frequent resort or usual abode; the usual feeding-place of deer, game, fowls, etc.; often, a place frequented by the lower animals or by criminals. Also *fig.* ME. †**4.** ?A topic –1658. **5.** A ghost that haunts a place. *local U.S.* and *Eng.* 1878.

3. We talke here in the publike h. of men SHAKS. Haunts of the buccaneers 1748, of coot and hern TENNYSON.

Haurient (hǭ·riĕnt), *a.* 1572. [– *haurient-* pres. ppl. stem of L. *haurire* draw (water, etc.); see -ENT.] *Her.* Of a fish borne as a charge: Placed palewise or upright with the head in chief, as if raising it above the water to draw in the air.

Hause, hawse (hǭs). *Sc.* and *n. dial.* 1781. [mod. north. f. HALSE neck, used in a special sense.] A narrower and lower neck between two heights; a *col.*; the name in the English Lake district and on the Scottish Border.

‖**Hausen** (hauz'n, hǭ·z'n). 1745. [G. *hausen*, OHG. *hūso*.] The largest species of sturgeon, *Acipenser huso*.

‖**Hausse** (hos). 1787. [Fr., f. *hausser* raise.] A kind of breech-sight for a cannon.

Haussmannize (hau·smănəiz). 1865. [f. Baron Eugène-Georges *Haussmann*, who, when prefect of the Seine (1853–70), remodelled a great part of Paris; see -IZE.] *trans.* To open out, widen, and straighten streets, and generally rebuild.

Haustellate (hǭ·stĕlět). 1835. [– mod.L. *haustellatus*, f. *haustellum*; see next, -ATE[2] 2.]

A. *adj.* **1.** Provided with a haustellum; of or pertaining to the *Haustellata* or suctorial insects. **2.** Adapted for sucking, suctorial 1835.

B. *sb.* A member of the *Haustellata* 1842.

‖**Haustellum** (hǭste·lŏm). *Pl.* **-a.** 1816. [mod.L. dim. of L. *haustrum* machine for drawing water, f. *haust-*, pa. ppl. stem of *haurire* draw (water, etc.).] *Zool.* The sucking organ or proboscis of an insect or a crustacean.

‖**Haustorium** (hǭstǭə·riŏm). *Pl.* **-ia.** 1875. [mod.L., f. late L., *haustor* drainer; see -ORIUM.] *Bot.* A small sucker of a parasitic plant, which penetrates the tissues of the host.

†**Haut.** See also HAUGHT. ME. [– Fr. *haut, haute* high, height (OFr. *halt, hault*).]

A. *adj.* High, lofty, haughty; see HAUGHT. –1648.

B. *sb.* Height, a height –1686.

†**Hau·tain, -tein,** *a.* ME. [– (O)Fr. *hautain*, etc., f. *haut* high; see prec., -AN.] **1.** = HAUGHTY 1. –1549. **2.** Of the voice: Raised –1475. **3.** High-flying. CHAUCER. **4.** = HAUGHTY 2. –1485.

Hautboy, hoboy (hōᵘ·boi). 1575. [– Fr. *hautbois*, f. *haut* high + *bois* wood. Superseded by OBOE.] **1.** A wooden double-reed wind instrument of high pitch, having a compass of about 2½ octaves, forming a treble to the bassoon. (Now usu. OBOE.) **b.** *transf.* One who plays a hautboy 1633. Also *attrib.* †**2.** *Forestry.* Lofty trees, as dist. from shrubs, etc. –1700. **3.** A species of strawberry (*Fragaria elatior*). Also *hautboy strawberry.* 1731. Hence **Hau·tboyist** = OBOIST.

Hautein, -en, -eyn, vars. of HAUTAIN *Obs.*

‖**Hauteur** (hotǭ·r). 1628. [Fr., f. *haut* high + *-eur* -OR 1. For the sense, cf. HAUTAIN.] **1.** Loftiness of manner or bearing; haughtiness. †**2.** A height (*rare*) 1711.

‖**Haut-goût** (hoˌgu). 1645. [Fr.; lit. 'high flavour', f. *haut* + *goût* (formerly *goust*) taste, etc. See HOGO.] †**1.** A high or piquant flavour; a strong relish; seasoning –1752. **b.** *fig.* 'Flavour', 'spice'. [So in Fr.] 1650. **2.** In later use: A high flavour; a taint 1693. †**3.** A highly-seasoned dish –1817.

1. [Garlick] giving a delicious Hault-gust to most meats they eat FULLER.

‖**Haut-pas.** Now only as Fr. (hoˌpa). 1460. [Fr.; lit. 'high step'; anglicized as HALPACE, whence HALF-PACE, etc.] = HALF-PACE 1.

‖**Haut-relief** (ho·rīlī·f). 1850. [Fr. (ho rəlyęf).] High relief, ALTO-RELIEVO; opp. to *bas-relief.*

‖**Haut ton** (hoˌtoṅ). 1801. [Fr.; = high tone. (Now little used.)] High fashion; *ellipt.* people of high fashion.

Haüyne (hā·win). 1814. [– Fr.; named after *Haüy*, the French mineralogist.] *Min.* A silicate of aluminium and sodium with calcium sulphate, occurring in certain igneous rocks in crystals or grains of various shades of blue or green. Hence **Haüynite** (in same sense).

Havana (hăvæ·nă). Also **Havanna(h.** 1826. [Name of the Cuban capital, now in Sp. *Habana.*] (In full, *Havana cigar*): A cigar of the kind made at Havana or in Cuba. (Also applied to the tobacco of which these are made.)

A grilled bone, Havannahs, and Regents punch DISRAELI.

Have (hæv), *v.* [OE. *habban* = OFris. *hebba*, OS. *hebbian* (Du. *hebben*), OHG. *habēn* (G. *haben*), ON. *hafa*, Goth. *haban* :– Gmc. **χabēn*, prob. rel. to **χabjan* HEAVE. In ME. the *habb-* forms were reduced by levelling to *hav-* (*have, having*, etc.); while the original *haf-* (= *hav-*) forms at length lost their *f* (*v*) before the following consonant (*ha-st, ha-th, ha-s, ha-d*).]

A. As a main verb (*trans.* or *intr.*).

I. 1. *trans.* To hold in hand, or in possession; to hold or possess as property, or as something at one's disposal. Also *absol.* **2.** To hold or possess, in a relation other than that of property or tenancy OE. **3.** To possess, bear, contain, as an appendage, organ, subordinate part, or adjunct; to contain as parts of itself OE. **4.** To possess as an attribute, function, right, etc.; to be characterized by; to hold; to be charged with OE. **5.** To be possessed or affected with (something physical or mental); to experience OE. **6.** To possess as an intellectual acquirement, to know; to understand 1591. **7.** To possess as a duty or thing to be done OE.

1. Having an axe in his hand 1483. To h. shares in a company (*mod.*). Phr. *To have and to hold* (cf. law L. *habendum et tenendum*): to have (or receive) and keep or retain, indicating continuance of possession. **2.** Let me haue men about me, that are fat SHAKS. We had fifty-two fathom of water 1748. He having no son at the time CRUISE. They had him to dine with them at the inn THACKERAY. **3.** The sea hath bounds SHAKS. Riches have wings to fly away from their owner LOWELL. The year has twelve calendar months (*mod.*). **4.** They h. a Fashion to cut holes in the Lips DAMPIER. [They] had reason to regret his departure 1795. Their policy had the desired effect 1882. **5.** Such as have the collicque 1599. I have had a real good time 1890. He has bad health (*mod.*). **6.** He hath neither Latine, French, nor Italian SHAKS. You haue me, haue you not SHAKS. 'Ah! I have it!' he added 1839. **7.** He had much to see MILT. *To h. to do* (see DO *v.* IV). The firm had to suspend payment 1883.

II. 1. To hold, keep, retain (*in* some relation to oneself) OE. **2.** To hold or entertain in the mind (a feeling, etc.); to cherish OE.; hence, to show (such sentiment, etc.) in action ME. **3.** To hold in (some specified) estimation; to account or regard as (*arch.*) OE. **4.** To hold, keep up, carry on (some proceeding or performance); to engage in, maintain, or perform, as a chief actor; to engage in and perform some action OE. †**5.** *refl.* To comport oneself –1556. **6.** To assert, maintain; to put it OE.

1. The Government hath had some things in desire CROMWELL. **2.** Let me see..what you h. against it 1656. Sir, haue pacience with me, and I will paye the all BIBLE (Great) *Matt.* 18:26. **3.** They were then had in great reverance M. HANMER. **4.** She and I had some Words last Sunday at Church SWIFT. You will then h. a good shot at him MARRYAT. **6.** All the Town has it, that [etc.] SWIFT. Some will h. it, that I often write to my self ADDISON.

III. 1. To possess by obtaining or receiving; hence, to come into possession of; to obtain, get, gain, accept, to have learned (*from* some source); to take (food, drink) OE. **2.** To get or have got into one's power, or at a disadvantage; to have caught (*fig.*), to have hold upon 1596. **b.** To get the better of, take in, 'do' (*slang*) 1805. **3.** To get into a place or state; to bring, lead, convey, take, put (*arch.*) ME. †**4.** *intr.* (for *refl.*) or *absol.* To betake oneself, go –1849. **5.** *intr.* or *absol.* *Have at*: To go at or get at, esp. in a hostile way; to have a stroke at, make an attempt at. Chiefly in imperative; app. 1st pers. pl., but often singular in sense, announcing the speaker's intention to get at or attack. So with other preps., as *after, with*, etc. ME.

1. [She] had two children at a birthe 1583. They h. it..from his own mouth 1680. There is nothing to be had here (*mod.*). Phr. *To have it*: (*a*) to gain the victory or advantage; to win the match; (*b*) to receive (or have received) a drubbing, punishment, reprimand; *to let one h. it*, to 'give it' one (*colloq.*). **2.** Now infidell I haue thee on the hip SHAKS. I admit that you h. me there 1890. **b.** If you've advanced money on 'em [diamonds], you've been had 1879. **3.** He was had before the Juge CAXTON. Phr. *Have up*: to take up or cause to go before a court of justice in answer to a charge; to call to account. *H. out*: to cause to come out to a duel. To h. their Fortunes told them DE FOE. They are having the pavement up for the electric light (*mod.*). Phr. *To h. something done to one*: receive, experience, or suffer it as the action of others or of fate. So *To h. someone do something, to have something happen to one.* **5.** Well, sith here is no company, h. with ye to Jericho 1575.

Phrases. *To h.* ADO, *h. at* AVAIL, *h.* BUSINESS, *h. in* CHARGE, *h.* DONE, *h. a* HAND *in*, *h. in* HAND, *h. on* HAND, etc.: see the distinctive words.

Idiomatic uses. The past Subjunctive *had* = would have, is used with adjs. (or advs.) in the comparative, as *better, liefer, rather*, etc.: in the superlative, as *best*; or in the positive with 'as', *as soon, as well*, etc., to express preference or comparative desirability. In OE. the adjs. *lēofre, betre* were construed with *be* and the dative, e.g. *him wǣre betere* = it would be better for him. In ME., side by side with this, appears *have* and the nominative, in the sense 'he (I, etc.) would hold or find it better or preferable'. The use of *as soon, sooner, well*, is recent, since *liefer* and *better* began to be felt as advs.

b. The two forms of expression are confused in *he* (*I*, etc.) *were better* (see BE *v.*) and *him* (*me*, etc.) *had liefer, rather.* **c.** *Had like* (*liked, likely*) *to*: see LIKE *a.* *Had need to*: see NEED *sb.*

B. As an auxiliary verb. **1.** The present tense of *have* forms a present of completed action, or 'present perfect'. **a.** To a trans. vb. with object OE. **b.** Extended to vbs. of action without object ME. **c.** Extended to intr. vbs. generally. Used early with *been*, and hence with the passive voice. With vbs. of motion later, partly displacing *be* as an auxiliary. ME. **2.** The past of *have* forms a past tense of completed action or 'pluperfect'. **a.** With trans. vb. and object OE. **b.** With active vbs. without object, and with intr. and passive vbs. ME. **3.** The compound tenses (*shall have*, etc.) are similarly employed ME. ¶**4.** In 15th and 16th c. occur many instances of redundant *have* in the compound tenses 1442.

1. a. Hauing burnt Holyhed POWEL. Phr. *I have got*, colloquially used for *I have*: see GET *v.* I've got a great deal on my hands MARRYAT. **b.** Every age hath abounded in instances WORDSW. **c.** Why haven't you been to see me 1882. **2. a.** Thou hadest chosen me for thy wife 1582. **b.** They had soiourned there in great ease LD. BERNERS. He had been taught to dislike politeness MAR. EDGEWORTH. **3.** I should haue lost the worth of it in Gold SHAKS.

Have (hæv), *sb.* ME. [f. prec. vb.] **1.** Having, possession. *Obs.* exc. as *nonce-wd.* **2.** *colloq.* One who *has* or possesses. (Usu. in *pl.*; and in conjunction with *have-not.*) 1836. **3.** *slang.* 'A swindle; a *take-in*; a *do*' (Farmer).

Haveless, †**havenless,** *a.* *Obs.* exc. *dial.* [OE. *hafenlēas, hæfenlēas*, f. *hæfen* property, possession, f. *haf-, hæf-* stem of *habban* HAVE; see -LESS.] †**1.** Without possessions, indigent –1450. **2.** Without resource, shiftless; slovenly. *Sc.* and *dial.* 1868.

Havelock (hæ·vlǫk). *U.S.* 1861. [f. Gen. Henry *Havelock*, distinguished in the Indian Mutiny 1857.] A white cloth covering for the cap, with a flap hanging over the neck, worn by soldiers as a protection from the sun's heat.

Haven (hēⁱ·v'n), *sb.* [Late OE. *hæfen, hæfne* (XI) – ON. *hǫfn* (*hafn*), gen. *hafnar* = MLG., MDu. *havene*, Du. *haven* (whence G. *hafen*).] **1.** A recess or inlet of the sea, or the mouth of a river, affording good anchorage and a safe station for ships; a harbour, port. **2.** *fig.* A refuge; an asylum ME.

1. Weymouth, a very convenient Harbour and H. CLARENDON. **2.** My sole refuge and only h.. is in the arms of death CARLYLE. Hence **Ha·venless** *a.*

Ha·ven, *v.* ME. [f. prec. sb.] †**1.** *intr.* To put into a haven –1621. **2.** *trans.* To put (a ship, etc.) into a haven 1601.

2. *fig.* Blissfully haven'd both from joy and pain KEATS.

Ha·venage. 1864. [f. HAVEN *sb.* + -AGE.] Harbour-dues.

Ha·vener, -or. 1495. [f. HAVEN *sb.* + -ER[1], -OR 2.] Harbour-master. Hence **Ha·venership,** the office of h.

Haver (hæ·vəɹ), *sb.*[1] ME. [f. HAVE *v.* + -ER[1].] A possessor, owner.

Haver (hæ·vəɹ), *sb.*[2] *dial.* [ME. *haver* (*hayfr*) – ON. *hafre* = OS. *habero*, MLG., MDu. *haver(e)* (Du. *haver*), OHG. *habaro* (G. dial. *haber*; *hafer* – LG.).] Oats. Also *attrib.*, as *h.-meal.* *Comb.*: **h.-cake,** oatcake; **-grass,** 'oatgrass'; species of *Avena* and *Bromus.*

Haver, *sb.*[3], usu. in pl. **havers** (hēⁱ·vəɹz). *Sc.* and *n. dial.* 1787. [Of unkn. origin.] Foolish talk; nonsense. So **Ha·ver** *v.* to talk foolishly; to talk nonsense. **Ha·verel,** one who havers; also *attrib.* or *adj.*

Haversack (hæ·vəɹsæk). 1749. [– Fr. *havresac* – G. *habersack*, orig. bag in which cavalry carried oats for their horses, f. *haber* oats (see HAVER *sb.*[2]) + *sack* SACK *sb.*[1]] A bag of stout canvas, worn with a strap over the shoulder, in which a soldier carries his day's rations. Also, any similar bag used by travellers, etc. †**b.** 'A gunner's case for ordnance, being a leather bag used to carry cartridges from the ammunition-chest to the piece in loading' (Simmonds) 1858.

Haversian (hăvə̄·ɹsiăn), *a.* 1836. [f. Clopton *Havers*, an English anatomist (*c* 1690); see -IAN.] *Anat.* Applied to certain structures in bone discovered by Havers, as in *H. canal*, one of the minute cylindrical passages in bone which form the channels for blood-vessels and medullary matter; *H. system*, 'the H. canal, its concentric lamellæ of bone and the lacunæ with their canaliculi' (*Syd. Soc. Lex.*).

Haversine (hæ·vəɹsəin). 1875. [contr. of *half versin* (= *versed sine*).] *Trigonometry.* A nautical term: Half the versed sine.

‖**Havildar** (hæ·vildāɹ). *E. Ind.* 1698. [Hind. *ḥavildār*, – Pers. *ḥawāl(a)dār* charge or trust holder.] 'A sepoy non-commissioned officer, corresponding to a sergeant' (Yule).

Having (hæ·viŋ), *vbl. sb.* ME. [f. HAVE *v.* + -ING[1].] **1.** Possession. **2.** *concr.* (often in *pl.*) That which one has; possession, property, wealth, belongings ME. **3.** (Often in *pl.*) Behaviour, manners. (Chiefly *Sc.*) ME.

2. Look to my house and havings; keepe all safe BROME. **3.** By and attour her gentle havings SCOTT.

Having, *ppl. a.* ME. [f. HAVE *v.* + -ING[2].] **1.** That has; possessing property. (Now *rare* exc. as pple.) **2.** Desirous of having; grasping. Now only *dial.* 1591.

2. She's as jealous and h. as can be GEO. ELIOT.

Haviour (hēi·viəɹ), †**havour.** ME. [orig. – AFr. *aver* (see AVER *sb.*[2]) = OFr. *aveir*, (also mod.) *avoir* possession, property, etc., subst. use of infin. *aveir*, *avoir* have :– L. *habēre*. The forms *haver*, *havoir*, *havour* (subseq. *-eour*, *-iour*) were infl. by Eng. *have*. Cf. BEHAVIOUR.] †**1.** The fact of having; possession; a possession; estate, substance –1616. **2.** The action of bearing oneself; deportment, behaviour. Also *pl.* manners. *arch.* or *dial.* 1503.

2. A courteous haviour, gent and debonair 1756.

Havoc (hæ·vǫk), *sb.* ME. [– AFr. *havok* (phr. *crier havok* XIV), alt. of OFr. *havo(t)*, of unkn. origin. For the final cons. cf. HADDOCK.] **1.** In the phr. *cry havoc*, orig. to give to an army the order *havoc!*, as the signal for the seizure of spoil, and pillage. In later use (usually after Shaks.) *fig.* **2.** Devastation, destruction; esp. in phr. *to make h.*, *play h.* 1480.

1. Cæsars Spirit..Shall..Cry hauocke, and let slip the Dogges of Warre *Jul. C.* III. i. 273. **2.** What havock the floud had made 1635. Hence **Ha·voc** *v.* (infl. **-ocked, -ocking**), to make h. of; to lay waste; also *absol.* and *intr.* **Ha·vocker.**

Haw (hǫ), *sb.*[1] *Obs.* exc. *Hist.* [OE. *haga* hedge, fence, corresp. to OS. *hago*, MDu. *hage*, *haghe* (Du. *haag*), ON. *hagi* :– Gmc. **χaʒon*, f. **χaʒ-* as in HAG *sb.*[2], HAY *sb.*[2], HEDGE *sb.*] A hedge or encompassing fence (OE); hence, an enclosed piece of ground; a messuage (OE.); generally, a yard, close, or enclosure.

Haw (hǫ), *sb.*[2] [OE. *haga*, identical in form with *haga* hedge (see prec.), connection with which appears to be shown by OE. *haga-*, *haguþorn* HAWTHORN; cf. OE. *hæġþorn* 'hedge-thorn'.] **1.** The fruit of the hawthorn. **2.** The hawthorn, *Cratægus oxyacantha* 1821. †**3.** A head or ear of grass. [Perh. a different wd.] –1825.

1. Stores of Haws and Heps do commonly portend cold Winters BACON.

Haw, *sb.*[3] 1523. [Of unkn. origin.] The nictitating membrane of a horse, dog, etc. †**b.** *transf.* An excrescence in the human eye –1684.

Haw, *interj.* and *sb.*[4] 1679. [imit.] An utterance marking hesitation. Usually with *hum*. See also HAW-HAW.

Haw, *v.* 1632. [f. HAW *interj.*] *intr.* To utter 'haw!' as an expression of hesitation. Usually in *to hum* (*hem*) *and h.*; see HUM *v.*[1]

Hawbuck (hǫ·bǫ̈k). 1805. [perh. f. HAW *sb.*[1] or [2] + BUCK *sb.*[1] 2.] A country bumpkin.

Hawcubite (hǫ·kəbəit). 1712. One of a band of dissolute young men who infested the streets of London *c*1700; a street bully, a ruffian.

†**Hawe-bake.** Usu. taken as = 'haw(s) baken', baked haws, i.e. 'plain fare'; but this is doubtful. CHAUCER *Man of Law's Prol.* 95.

Hawfinch (hǫ·finʃ). 1674. [f. HAW *sb.*[2] + FINCH.] The common grosbeak. *Coccothraustes vulgaris*.

Haw-haw (hǫ·hǫ·). 1834. [imit.; cf. HA HA *int.* + *sb.*[1]]

A. *interj.* An expression of hesitation uttered repeatedly in an affected tone. Also, the representation of loud laughter.

B. *sb.* The utterance of *haw haw*; a guffaw 1834.

C. *attrib.* or *adj.* Characterized by the utterance of *haw haw* 1841. Hence **Haw-haw** *v.* to utter *haw haw*; to laugh boisterously.

Haw-haw, var. of HA-HA *sb.*[2].

Ha·wk (hǫk), *sb.*[1] [OE. *hafoc*, *heafoc*, earlier *hæbuc*, *habuc* = OFris. *havek*, OS. *habuk* (Du. *havik*), OHG. *habuh* (G. *habicht*), ON. *haukr* :– Gmc. **χabukaz*.] **1.** Any diurnal bird of prey used in Falconry; any bird of the family *Falconidæ*. In *Nat. Hist.*, restricted to a bird of the subfamily *Accipitrinæ*, with rounded and shortish wings, which chases its prey near the ground. **2.** *fig.* Applied to a person, in various senses: e.g. one who preys on others, a sharper or cheat; one who is keen and grasping; an officer of the law who pounces on criminals 1548.

1. *H. of the fist*, 'one that flies direct off the fist without mounting or waiting-on'. **Black Hawk,** the American rough-legged buzzard; **Musket-, Small-bird-,** or **Spar-h.,** the Sparrow-h.; **Ringtail H.** (*Falco hudsonius*). *Night-h., dor-h., screech-h.*, applied to the goatsucker. (See these words.) **2.** Phr. *Ware h.*: see WARE *v.*[1] 2 b.

Comb.: **H. eagle,** an eagle of the genus *Nisaetus*; **h.-eye** (*U.S.*), colloq. appellation of a native or inhabitant of Iowa, pop. called the 'Hawk-eye State'; **-eyed** *a.*, very keen-sighted; **-fly,** a fly of the family *Asitidæ*, also called hornet-flies, which prey on other insects.

Hawk (hǫk), *sb.*[2] 1700. [Of unkn. origin. Cf. Fr. *oiseau* (*de maçon*).] 'A small quadrangular tool with a handle, used by a plasterer, on which the stuff required by him is served' (Gwilt.) Hence **Hawk-boy,** the boy who brings him the material.

Hawk, *sb.*[3] 1604. [f. HAWK *v.*[3]] An effort made to clear the throat; the noise thus made.

Hawk (hǫk), *v.*[1] ME. [f. HAWK *sb.*[1]] **1.** *intr.* To chase or hunt game with a trained hawk; to practise falconry. **2.** *intr.* Of birds and insects: To hunt on the wing ME. *trans.* to pursue or attack on the wing 1825.

1. Thei hauke, thei hunt, thei card, thei dyce LATIMER. **2.** The bird [a martin] was hawking briskly after the flies G. WHITE. Phr. *To h. at*: to fly at or attack on the wing, as a hawk does; (of a person) to fly a hawk at. Who does h. at eagles with a dove G. HERBERT. †*To h. after* (*for*): to hunt after.

Hawk (hǫk), *v.*[2] 1542. [Back-formation from HAWKER *sb.*[2]] **1.** *intr.* To practise the trade of a hawker. **2.** *trans.* To carry *about* from place to place and offer for sale; to cry in the street. Also *transf.* and *fig.* 1713. **3.** To traverse with something in hand to dispose of 1865.

2. His works were hawk'd in ev'ry street SWIFT. **3.** Hawking the world, Pragmatic Sanction in hand CARLYLE.

Hawk (hǫk), *v.*[3] 1581. [prob. imit.] **1.** *intr.* To make an effort to clear the throat of phlegm; to clear the throat noisily 1583. **2.** *trans.* To bring *up* by such an effort.

Haw·kbill. 1782. **1.** = HAWK'S-BILL 1. **2.** An instrument, such as 'a pliers with curved nose', etc. 1875. So **Hawk-billed** *a.* having a mouth like a hawk's beak, as the *hawk-billed turtle*.

Hawkbit (hǫ·kbit). 1713. [f. HAWK(WEED + DEVIL'S-)BIT.] A book-name for the genus *Apargia* of composite plants, resembling hawk-weeds.

Hawked (hǫkt), *a.* 1577. [f. HAWK *sb.*[1] + -ED[2]; cf. *hooked*.] Curved like a hawk's beak; aquiline.

Hawker (hǫ·kəɹ), *sb.*[1] [OE. *hafocere*; see HAWK *sb.*[1] and -ER[1].] A falconer.

Hawker (hǫ·kəɹ), *sb.*[2] 1510. [prob. of LDu. origin (cf. MLG. *hoker*, LG. *höker*, Du. *heuker*); see HUCKSTER.] A man who goes from place to place selling his wares, or who cries them in the street. Now technically dist. from *pedlar*, as having a horse and cart, or van.

fig. This broad-brim'd h. of holy things TENNYSON.

Ha·wk-moth. 1785. A moth of the family *Sphingidæ* or *Sphingina*; a sphinx-moth; so called from their manner of flight, which resembles the hovering and darting of a hawk. There are many genera and species, as DEATH'S-HEAD *h.*, ELEPHANT *h.*, etc.

Hawk-nose. 1533. A nose curved like a hawk's beak. Hence **Haw·k-nosed** *a.*

Hawk-owl. 1743. **a.** The Short-eared Owl, *Asio brachyotus*. **b.** The Day-owl, *Surnia ulula* or *funerea*. Both so called from their smaller heads, and habit of hunting in the day.

Hawk's-bell, hawk-bell. 1483. A small spherical bell, for fastening on the leg of a hawk.

Hawk's-bill. 1657. **1.** (Also *hawk's-bill turtle*.) A species of turtle, *Chelone imbricata*, having a mouth resembling the beak of a hawk, and furnishing the tortoise-shell of commerce. **2.** Part of the striking action of a clock 1875.

Hawkweed (hǫ·kˌwīd). 1562. [tr. L. *hieraceum* = Gr. ἱεράκιον, f. ἱέραξ hawk, falcon; but the ancient application of the name was different.] The common name for plants of the large genus *Hieracium* (N.O. *Compositæ*). Also applied to other yellow-flowered composites, as *Senecio hieracioides*, etc.

Hawm (hǫm), *v. dial.* 1847. [Of unkn. origin.] To move about awkwardly; to lounge.

Hawse (hǫz), *sb.*[1] 1497. [Early form *halse* (in AL. *halse* XIV), prob. – ON. *háls* neck, ship's bow, tack of a sail, rope's end (= OE. *heals* neck, prow).] *Naut.* **1.** That part of a ship's bows in which the hawse-holes are cut for the cables to pass through; hence, occas., in *pl.*, the hawse-holes themselves. †**2.** A cable, a hawser –1642. **3.** The space between the head of a vessel at anchor and the anchors, or a little beyond the anchors. Also *fig.* 1630. **4.** 'The situation of the cables before the ship's stem, when she is moored with two anchors out from forward, one on the starboard, and the other on the port bow' (Smyth) 1597.

1. We cut our cable at the h. 1567. **3.** Phr. *Athwart* (†*thwart*) *the h.*, (cf. *athwart-hawses* v. ATHWART), *to cross the h.* **4.** *Clear h.*, *open h.*, when both cables lead directly (without crossing) to their respective anchors. *Foul h.*, when the cables lie across the stern, or bear upon each other. *To clear the h.*, to untwist two cables, which being let out at two several hawses, are wound about one another. *To fresh* (*freshen*) *the h.*, to veer out a little more cable so as to let another part endure the stress.

Comb.: **h.-block,** a block of wood made to fit over the h.-holes when at sea; **-hole,** a cylindrical hole, of which there are two in the bows of a vessel, for the cable to run through; **-piece,** one of the timbers in the bow of a ship through which a h.-hole is cut; **-pipe,** a cast-iron pipe fitted into a h.-hole to protect the wood; **-plug,** a plug made to fit into the h.-pipe to prevent water from entering.

Hawse, *sb.*[2], var. of HAUSE.

†**Hawse,** *v.* 1500. [– Fr. *hausser*, OFr. *haucier* hoist :– Rom. **altiare*, f. *altus* high.] *trans.* To raise, exalt, hoist –1600.

Hawser (hǫ·zəɹ). ME. [– AFr. *haucer*, *hauceour* (in AL. *haucerus, ausorus, auncerus*), f. OFr. *haucier* (mod. *hausser*) hoist :– Rom. **altiare*, f. L. *altus* high; see -ER[2].] **1.** A large rope or small cable, between 5 and 10 inches in circumference; used in warping and mooring; in large ships now made of steel. **2.** Used by confusion for HAWSE *sb.*[1] 3. 1684.

Comb.: **h.-bend,** a kind of hitch or knot; **-laid** *a.*, made of three or four strands laid into one.

Hawthorn (hǫ·þǫɹn). [OE. *haga-*, *haguþorn* = MDu. *hagedorn* (Du. *haagdoorn*), MHG. *hage(n)dorn* (G. *hagedorn*), ON. *hagþorn*; f. *haga* HAW *sb.*[1] + THORN.] **1.** A thorny shrub or small tree, *Cratægus oxyacantha*, N.O. *Rosaceæ*, much used for forming hedges; the White-thorn. It bears white, and, in some varieties, red or pink blossom (called 'may'); its fruit, the haw, is a small round dark red berry. (Also extended to other species of *Cratægus*.) **2.** *Angling.* Short for *h.-fly* 1884.

1. A..bussh of white h. full of floures 1450.

Comb.: **h. china,** a kind of Oriental porcelain, in which the decoration represents branches of the Japanese plum-tree in white on a dark blue ground; **-fly,** a small black fly appearing on h.-bushes when the leaves first come out; an imitation of this for angling; **-grosbeak,** the hawfinch. Also **Hawthorn-tree,** †**Haw-tree,** in sense 1.

Hay (hēi), *sb.*[1] [OE. *hēġ*, *hieġ*, *hīġ* = OFris. *hā*, *hē*, OS. *hōi*, OHG. *hewi*, *houwi* (Du. *hooi*, G. *heu*), ON. *hey* (whence the native word was reinforced), Goth. *hawi* :– Gmc. **χaujam*, f. **χauwan* cut down, HEW *v.*] **1.** Grass cut or mown, and dried for use as fodder; occas. including grass fit for mowing. **2.** *Burgundian* or *Burgundy h.*, Lucerne or Sainfoin.

Phrases. *To carry h. in one's horns*: to be ill-tempered or dangerous (L. *fænum habet in cornu*, Horace). *To look for a needle in a bundle of h.*: see NEEDLE. *To make h.*: (*a*) *lit.*, to mow grass and dry it by spreading it about; (*b*) *fig.* to make confusion. *To make h. of*: to turn topsy-turvy. *To make h. while the sun shines*: to lose no time, to profit by opportunities.

Comb.: **h.-box,** a box stuffed with hay in which heated food is left to continue cooking; **-plant,** an umbelliferous plant of Tibet, *Prangos pabularia*.

Hay, *sb.*[2] Now *arch.* or *dial.* [OE. *heġe* :– **χaʒiz*, f. **χaʒ-*, as in HAG *sb.*[2], HAW *sb.*[1],

HEDGE *sb.*] **1.** A hedge, fence. **2.** An enclosure; a park 1630. †**3.** *Mil.* An extended line of men –1753.

†**Hay,** *sb.*[3] ME. [– AFr. *haie*, conjectured to have been an extension of HAY *sb.*[2], or of the equivalent (O)Fr. *haie*; cf. OFr. *haier* 'chasser à la haie' (Godefroy).] A net used for catching wild animals, *esp.* rabbits, being stretched in front of their holes, or round their haunts –1821.

Hay, hey, *sb.*[4] 1529. [– Fr. †*haie* kind of dance (Godefroy); cf. *haye d'allemaigne* XV.] **1.** A country dance having a serpentine movement. †**2. Hay-de-guy, -guise.** A kind of hay or dance –1694.

To dance the hay or *hays*: to go through varied evolutions like those of a dance.

Hay, *v.*[1] 1556. [f. HAY *sb.*[1]] **1.** *trans.* To furnish with hay; to put (land) under hay 1708. **2.** *intr.* To make hay 1556. **3.** *trans.* To make into hay 1884.

†**Hay,** *v.*[2] [OE. *heġian*, f. *haga* HAW *sb.*[1], *heġe* HAY *sb.*[2]] *trans.* To enclose by a hedge; to hedge –1610.

†**Hay,** *v.*[3] 1440. [f. HAY *sb.*[3]] *intr.* To set hays or nets for rabbits, etc. –1613.

†**Hay,** *v.*[4] 1768. [f. HAY *sb.*[4]] *intr.* To dance the hay –1777.

†**Hay,** *interj.* and *sb.*[5] 1592. [– It. *hai* (pron. ai) thou hast (it). Cf. L. *habet*, exclam. when a gladiator was wounded.]

A. *int.* An exclam. on hitting an opponent. B. JONS.

B. *sb.* A home-thrust. *Rom. & Jul.* II. iv. 27.

Hay-a·sthma. 1827. [Cf. Fr. *asthme de foin*, G. *heuasthma*.] = HAY-FEVER.

Hay·-bird. 1802. **1.** Any bird that builds its nest with hay, *esp.* the Blackcap, Garden Warbler, and Willow-wren. **2.** The Pectoral Sandpiper or Grass-snipe, *Tringa maculata* (U.S.).

Hay·bote. ME. [See HAY *sb.*[2], BOOT *sb.*[1] 2. Cf. HEDGEBOTE.] Wood or thorns for the repair of fences; the right to take this from the landlord's estate or from the common; = HEDGEBOTE.

Haycock (hē[i]·kǫk). 1470. [f. HAY *sb.*[1] + COCK *sb.*[2]] A conical heap of hay in the field.

To the tanned h. in the mead MILT. *L'Allegro* 90.

Hay-de-Guy, -guise. See HAY *sb.*[4]

Hay-fever. 1829. [f. HAY *sb.*[1]] A catarrhal condition of the ocular, nasal, and respiratory mucous membranes, accompanied generally by asthmatic symptoms; a disorder of the early summer, usually caused by the pollen of grasses and some flowers, sometimes also by dust, etc.

Hay·field. 1784. [f. HAY *sb.*[1]] A field in which grass has been cut or is standing to be cut for hay.

Hay-fork. 1552. [f. HAY *sb.*[1]] A long-handled fork used for turning over hay to dry, or in pitching and loading it. **b.** A large fork elevated by a horse and pulley in unloading hay from a wagon to a mow; or *vice versa* (Knight) 1875.

Hayloft (hē[i]·lǫft). 1573. [f. HAY *sb.*[1]] A loft for hay over a stable or barn.

Hay·maker. ME. [f. HAY *sb.*[1]] **1.** A man or woman employed in making hay, *esp.* after it is mown. **2.** An apparatus for shaking up and drying hay 1853. **3.** *pl.* The name of a country dance. Also *haymakers' jig*.

Hay·making, *vbl. sb.* 1588. [f. as prec.] The process of cutting and drying grass for hay. Also *attrib.*, as **h. machine,** an apparatus for drying grass for hay.

Hay-mow (hē[i]·mau). 1483. [f. HAY *sb.*[1] + MOW *sb.*[1]] A rick or stack of hay; in some places applied to the pile of hay stored in a barn, or to the compartment of a barn in which hay is stored.

†**Hayne.** ME. [Of unkn. origin.] A mean wretch, a niggard –1570.

Hay·-rack. 1825. [f. HAY *sb.*[1]] **1.** A rack for holding hay for cattle. **2.** A light framework projecting from the sides of a wagon to increase its carrying capacity for hay, etc. *U.S.*

Hay·-rake. 1725. **1.** A hand-rake used in hay-making. **2.** An implement drawn by a horse for raking hay into windrows 1875.

Hayrick (hē[i]·rik). ME. [f. HAY *sb.*[1] + RICK *sb.*[1]] A haystack.

Hay·-seed, hay·seed. 1577. [f. HAY *sb.*[1]] **1.** The grass seed shaken out of hay. **2.** The redseed, brit, etc., on which mackerel largely feed (*U.S.*) 1889. **3.** Joc. name for a rustic (*U.S.*) 1889.

Haystack (hē[i]·stæk). ME. [f. HAY *sb.*[1]] A stack of hay built in the open air, of regular form.

Haythorn, obs. f. HAWTHORN.

Hayward (hē[i]·wǫɹd). ME. [f. HAY *sb.*[2] + WARD, OE. *weard* guardian.] An officer having charge of the fences and enclosures, *esp.* to keep cattle from breaking through from the common into enclosed fields; sometimes, the herdsmen of the cattle feeding on the common.

Hazard (hæ·zăɹd), *sb.* ME. [– (O)Fr. *hasard* – Sp. *azar* – NAfr. Arab. *al-zahr* chance, luck, gaming die.] **1.** A game at dice in which the chances are complicated by a number of arbitrary rules. **2.** Chance, venture; a chance 1583. **3.** Risk of loss or harm; peril, jeopardy 1548. †**4.** That which is staked. *Merch V.* I. i. 151. **5.** *Tennis.* Each of the winning openings in a tennis-court 1599. †**6.** *Billiards.* One of the pockets in the sides of a billiard table –1751. **b.** Hence, A stroke by which one of the balls is driven into a pocket 1778. **7.** *Golf.* A general term for bunkers, furze, water, sand, loose earth, or any kind of bad ground 1857. **8.** A cab-stand (in Ireland) 1882. **9.** *attrib.* 1570.

1. Who will goe to H. with me for twentie Prisoners SHAKS. **2.** I will stand the h. of the Dye SHAKS. **3.** Profits proportionable to their..h. HUME. **5.** We will..play a set, Shall strike his fathers Crowne into the h. SHAKS. *H. side*, the side of the tennis-court into which the ball is served. **6. b.** *Winning h.*, a stroke in which the object ball is struck with the player's ball and pocketed. *Losing h.*, one in which the striker's ball is pocketed after contact with another.

Ha·zard, *v.* 1530. [– Fr. *hasarder*, f. *hasard*; see prec.] **1.** *trans.* To put to the risk of being lost in a game of chance; to stake; to expose to hazard or risk. **b.** *refl.* To run or incur risks. †Also *intr.* 1549. **2.** *trans.* To run or take the risk of (a penalty, etc.) 1559. †**3.** To endanger (any person or thing) –1786. †**4.** To get by chance –1664. **5.** To take the chance or risk of; to venture upon; to venture (*to do*) 1581. †**6.** *Billiards.* To pocket (a ball). EVELYN.

1. To h. a prize by clutching it too soon FREEMAN. **2.** Ready to h. all consequences 1827. **5.** To h. a battle STEELE, a conjecture 1758, an assertion COLERIDGE. Hence **Ha·zardable** *a.* hazardous, risky; that may be risked. **Ha·zarder,** a player at hazard; a gamester; 'he who hazards' (J.). (Now *rare*.)

†**Ha·zardize,** *v. rare.* 1628. [f. HAZARD *sb.* + -IZE.] To put in hazard, jeopardize, risk –1631.

†**Ha·zardize,** *sb.* [For *hazardise*, f. HAZARD *sb.* + *-ise* as in *merchandise*.] A condition of peril or risk. SPENSER.

Hazardous (hæ·zăɹdəs), *a.* 1580. [– Fr. *hasardeux*; see HAZARD *sb.*, -OUS.] **1.** Of the nature of the game of hazard; casual, fortuitous 1585. †**2.** Venturesome –1651. **3.** Fraught with hazard or risk; perilous 1618.

1. H. contracts, in which the performance depends upon some uncertain future event 1880. **3.** The enterprize so h. and high MILT. Hence **Ha·zardous-ly** *adv.*, **-ness.**

†**Ha·zardry.** ME. [– OFr. *hasarderie; see HAZARD, -ERY. Cf. AL. *hasarderia*.] **1.** The playing at hazard; gambling –1590. **2.** The incurring of risk. SPENSER.

Haze (hē[i]z), *sb.* 1706. [prob., along with HAZE *v.*[2], back-formation from earlier HAZY.] An obscuration of the atmosphere near the earth's surface, caused by an infinite number of minute particles of vapour, etc. in the air. In 18th c. applied to a thick fog or hoar-frost; but now usually to a thin misty appearance, which makes distant objects indistinct, and often arises from heat. Also *transf.* and *fig.*

Till he disappeared in the silvery night h. 1833. A h. of sunshine 1891. *fig.* In the fog and h. of confusion all is enlarged BURKE. Hence **Ha·zeless** *a.*

Haze (hē[i]z), *v.*[1] 1678. [Cf. Fr. †*haser* (XV) tease, anger, insult.] **1.** *trans.* To affright, scare; to scold; also, to punish by blows (*dial.*). **2.** *Naut.* To punish by keeping at disagreeable and unnecessary hard work; to harass by overwork 1840. **3.** To subject to cruel horseplay (as practised by American students); to bully (*U.S.*) 1850. **4.** *intr.* To frolic, lark (*U.S.*) 1848. **5.** *H. about*, to roam about aimlessly; cf. HAZY *a.* 2 b. 1841.

3. 'Tis the Sophomores rushing the Freshmen to h. 1850.

Haze, *v.*[2] 1674. [See HAZE *sb.*] **1.** *intr.* To drizzle (*dial.*) **2.** *trans.* To make hazy 1801.

Haze, *v.*[3] *dial.* 1825. [Of unkn. origin.] *trans.* To dry.

Hazel[1] (hē[i]·z'l). [OE. *hæsel*, corresp. to MDu. *hasel* (Du. *hazelaar* hazel tree, *hazelnoot* hazel-nut), OHG. *hasal*, *-ala* (G. *hasel*), ON. *hasl* :– Gmc. *χasalaz :– IE. *kosolos, *koselos, whence also L. *corylus*, *-ulus*.] **1.** A bush or small tree of the genus *Corylus*, having as its fruit a nut. The European species, *C. avellana*, grows to a small tree; the N. American species are *C. Americana*, a shrub forming dense thickets, and *C. rostrata*. **b.** The wood of this tree 1480. **c.** A stick of this wood 1603. **2.** Applied to other plants; *esp.* WITCH (WYCH) HAZEL, q.v. **3.** The reddish brown colour of the nut when ripe 1774. **b.** *adj.* Of this colour; used esp. of the eyes 1592. **4.** *attrib.* ME.

1. *Oil of h.*, a joc. name for an oil alleged to be contained in a green hazel rod, and to be the efficacious element in a sound drubbing; *to anoint with oil of h.*, to drub with a h. rod. **3. b.** Her full dark eye of h. hue SCOTT.

Hence **Ha·zelly** *a.*[1]

Ha·zel[2], **hazle.** 1613. [First in *hazel ground*, perh. named from its colour and so a transf. use of prec. But HAZELLY *a.*[2] is earlier (XVI).] **1.** A kind of freestone (*local*) 1855. **2.** *attrib.* Consisting of a mixture of sand or gravel, clay, and earth, as *h. earth*, *ground*, *loam*, etc. So **Ha·zelly** *a.*[2]

Hazel grouse. 1783. = next.

Hazel-hen. 1661. [– Du. *haselhoen*, G. *haselhuhn*; see HAZEL[1], HEN.] The European ruffled grouse, *Bonasia sylvestris*.

Hazeline (hē[i]·zĕlīn). 1881. [f. HAZEL[1] + -INE[5].] An alcoholic distillate from the Witch Hazel, *Hamamelis virginica*.

Hazel-nut (hē[i]·z'l,nɒt). [OE. *hæselhnutu*.] The nut of the hazel. Also *attrib.*

Hazel-wood. ME. **1.** A wood or thicket of hazel bushes. **2.** The wood of the hazel 1573.

Phr. †*Hazelwoods shake*, or merely *hazelwood!* (in Chaucer) app. = Of course.

Ha·zelwort. 1578. [– G. *haselwurz*, f. *hasel* HAZEL[1] + *wurz* herb, WORT[1].] *Herb.* A book-name for Asarabacca.

Hazily (hē[i]·zĭli), *adv.* 1833. [f. HAZY + -LY[2].] In a hazy manner; dimly, indistinctly. Also *fig.*

Haziness (hē[i]·zinės). 1709. [f. as prec. + -NESS.] **1.** The quality of being hazy; mistiness, fogginess. **2.** The quality of being intellectually indistinct; vagueness 1872.

Hazle, hazzle (hæ·z'l), *v. dial.* 1642. [frequent. of HAZE *v.*[3]; see -LE.] To dry on the surface. *trans.* and *intr.*

Hazy (hē[i]·zi), *a.* 1625. [The earliest forms *hawsey*, *heysey*, *haizy*, beside *hasie*, *hazy*, together with chronological uncertainty, make the problem of origin difficult.] **1.** Of the atmosphere, etc.: Characterized by the presence of haze; misty. (orig. *Naut.*) In 17–18th c. = foggy. **2.** *fig.* Lacking intellectual distinctness; vague, uncertain 1831. **b.** Somewhat confused with drink 1824.

1. A diffused light, which made the air seem h. 1799. **2.** Some h. idea DICKENS.

He (hī, hĭ), *pers. pron.*, *3rd sing. masc. nom.* [OE. *he*, *hē* = OFris. *hi*, *he*, OS. *hi*, *he*, *hie*; f. Gmc. demons. stem *χi- repr. also in OHG. (Franconian) *er*, *her*, *hē* he, dat. *himo*, ON. *(h)inn* him, Goth. *himma* to him, *hina* (acc.) him. See also HIM, HIS, HITHER, HENCE. In OE. the base *he* supplied all parts of the third personal pronoun, singular and plural. Subseq. some parts were lost; thus the fem. *hio*, *heo* became supplanted by SHE, q.v.; the pl. by a pl. of the demonstrative *that*; and in the neuter the acc. *hit* lost its initial *h* in all constructions. The present inflexion is therefore:

SING.	MASC.	FEM.	NEUT.	PLURAL.
Nom.	he	[she]	it	[they]
Acc. / *Dat.*	him	her	it	[them]
Possess. *adj.*	his	her	its	[their]
absol.	his	hers	its	[theirs]

See the other inflexional parts in their alphabetical places.]

I. As proper masculine pronoun of the third person, nominative case. **1.** The male being in question, or the last mentioned. Used of persons and animals of the male sex. **2.** Of things not sexually distinguished ME. **3.** Used pleonastically along with its noun. Common in ballad style, and now in illiterate speech. OE.

1. He first, and close behind him follow'd she DRYDEN. **2.** The Philosophres stoon Elixer clept..With al oure sleighte he wol nat come vs to CHAUCER. **3.** 'Fair and softly', John he cried COWPER. The skipper he stood beside the helm LONGF.

II. As Antecedent pronoun, followed by relative, etc. (The neut. is *that*, the pl. *they* or *those*.) **1.** The or that man, or person of the male sex (*that* or *who*..). Hence *Indefinitely*, Any man, any one, a person (*that* or *who*). ME. **2.** Followed by a prepositional phrase (*arch.*) 1598.

1. He that hath ears to hear, let him hear *Matt.* 11:15. **2.** If he of the bottomlesse pit had not.. broke prison MILT.

III. As demonstrative pronoun. *He and he*: this and that, the one and the other, both ME.

He snapped me on this hand and he on that 1620.

IV. As *sb.* (not changing in the objective). **1.** Man, person, personage (*arch.* and *poet.*) ME. **2.** Opp. to *she*: Male OE. **b.** A male. (With pl. *hes, he's*, †*hees*.) 1575.

1. The best he in the kingdom FIELDING. **2.** Any one not a poet, whether he or she, might toil [etc.] 1888. **b.** Do we divide dogs into hes and shes JOWETT.

V. *attrib.* (Now usu. hyphened to following noun.) Male. (Now confined to the lower animals, as *he-goat*; in 16–18th c. with nouns denoting persons; this is now contemptuous.) ME. **b.** Occas. with names of plants 1626.

Pope Joan..this He-she FULLER. My he-cosen Harman PEPYS. *spec.* **he-man** (*U.S.*), a masterful or virile man. **b. He-oak**, an Australian tree, *Casuarina stricta*; also *C. suberosa*.

He *v. trans.* to speak to or of (a person) as 'he'.

He (hī), *interj.* OE. [A natural exclam.] Repeated, as *he, he*, or in comb. with *ha, ha*, etc.: A representation of laughter, usu. affected or derisive.

Head (hed), *sb.* [OE. *hēafod* = OFris. *hāved, hād*, OS. *hōbid* (Du. *hoofd*), OHG. *houbit* (G. *haupt*), ON. *haufuð, hǫfuð*, Goth. *haubiþ* :– Gmc. **χaubuðam, -iðam* the relation of which with L. *caput*, Gr. κεφαλή head, Skr. *kapālam* skull, is not clear.]

I. 1. a. The anterior part of the body of an animal, when distinguished from the rest of the body; it contains the mouth and special sense-organs and the brain. **b.** A headache or disordered head 1889. **2. a.** As the seat of mind, thought, intellect, memory, or imagination; cf. BRAIN *sb.* Often contrasted with *heart*, as the seat of the emotions. ME. **b.** As a part essential to life; hence = life OE. **3.** A representation, figure, or image of a head ME. **b.** The obverse side of a coin, when bearing the figure of a head; the reverse being called the *tail* 1684. **4.** The hair on the head ME. †**5.** The hair as dressed in some particular manner; hence, a head-dress –18.. **6.** *Venery.* The 'attire' or antlers of a deer, etc. ME. **7.** Put for the person himself 1535. **b.** As a unit in numbering cattle, game, etc. (Pl., after a numeral, *head.*) 1513. **c.** An indefinite number of animals, esp. of game 1601.

1. The h. of John the Baptist *Mark* 6:24, of a stag 1735. Phr. *Taller by a h.*; *to make shorter by the h.*, i.e. to behead. **2.** They remembered, or it came into their heads 1573. Accounts..which he kept in his h. 1802. **b.** Proofs enough..to cost him his h. 1887. **3. b.** Phr. *Head(s) or tail(s)*, used in tossing a coin to decide a chance. **5.** At my toilette, try'd a new h. ADDISON. **6.** Phr. *Of the first h.*: said of a deer, etc. at the age when the antlers are first developed; hence *fig.* of a man newly ennobled. **7.** Different crowned heads DE QUINCEY. An anna a h. for each boy 1847. See also HOTHEAD. **b.** Thirteen Head of Neat Cattel 1677. **c.** The possible h. of pheasants to be bagged next Christmas 1862.

II. A thing or part resembling a head in form or position. **1.** The upper or principal extremity of various things, esp. when rounded, projecting, or of some special shape ME. **2. a.** Any rounded or compact part of a plant, usually at the top of the stem OE. **b.** The rounded leafy top of a tree or shrub 1523. **3.** A collection of foam or froth on the top of liquor, esp. ale or beer 1545; a collection of cream on the surface of milk 1848. **4.** Techn. uses (see quots.) 1703. **5.** The top, summit, upper end ME. **6.** The top of a page or writing; hence, Something, as a title, written at the top; a heading 1586. **7.** The maturated part of a boil, abscess, etc. 1611. **8.** The upper end of something on a slope or so regarded OE. **9.** *spec.* The source of a river or stream. Also *fig.* ME. **10.** A body of water kept at a height for supplying a mill, etc.; the height of such a body of water, or the force of its fall (estimated in terms of the pressure on a unit of area). Sometimes, the bank or dam by which such water is kept up. 1480. **b.** *transf.* The difference of pressure (per unit of area) of two columns of fluid (liquid or gaseous) of different densities communicating at the base; the pressure (per unit of area) of a confined body of gas or vapour 1862. **c.** = BORE *sb.*[3] 2, EAGRE. 1570. **11.** The foremost part or end; the front ME. †**12.** The beginning (of a word, writing, etc.). **b.** *Astrol.* The commencement of a zodiacal sign, i.e. the point where the sun enters it. –1816. **13.** The thick end of a chisel or wedge 1793. **14.** The forepart of a ship, boat, etc.; the bows 1485. **15.** A cape, headland, promontory ME.; a projecting point of a rock or sandbank 1775. **16.** *Coal-mining.* = HEADING 5. 1664. **17.** An end, extremity (of anything of greater length than breadth). *Obs.* exc. in special uses (cf. HEADER 4). ME.

1. The h. of a spere, an arowe ME., of a golf-club PARK, of a pin, a nail, a screw (*mod.*), of a rib. J. BELL, of a muscle 1877, of a comet 1878, of a gate 1854, of a cask MARRYAT, of an alembic 1800, of a carriage 1868, of an anchor 1706, (*Mus.*) of a note 1727, of a lute, violin, etc. 1611, of a violin-bow 1836. **2. a.** A h. of asparagus (*mod.*). **b.** Oaks..that had once a h. COWPER. **4.** A h. (= a bundle) of flax 1704, of silk 1876. *Head* in *Bricklaying*, a tile of half the usual length, used at the eaves of a roof. *Head* in *Goldmining*, a rammer for crushing quartz. *Heads* (pl.) in *Tin Washing*, the purest ore, which collects at the h. of the table. **5.** The skyish h. of blew Olympus SHAKS. The h. of the stairs 1797. **6.** The heads of chapters 1854. **7.** Phr. *To come to a h.*, to suppurate. **8.** The h. of a bedde 1548, of the table 1786, of the Gulf 1862. **9.** 'Thames H.', or 'the very h. of Isis' PHILLIPS. *fig.* Acquiring facts at the fountain h. COLERIDGE. **10.** The h. of water is 132 feet 1861. **b.** Under a full h. of steam 1862. **11.** The h. of the vast column of troops KINGLAKE, of the pier BORLASE, of a plough 1842. **14.** They were moored by anchors h. and stern GROTE. Phr. *By (down by) the h.*, with the head lower in the water than the stern. *H. on*, with the head directly pointing at something. **15.** It shone on Beachy H. MACAULAY. **17.** The bridge's h. 1843.

III. Fig. uses. **1.** A person to whom others are subordinate; a chief, captain, ruler, principal person, head man OE. **b.** *spec.* The master or principal of a college in a university; also short for HEAD MASTER 1565. **c.** The chief city, capital; the chief part OE. **2.** Position of leadership, chief command, or greatest importance ME. **3.** One of the chief points of a discourse; the section of it pertaining to any such point; hence, a point, topic; a main division, section, chapter of a writing; a division of a subject, class, category 1500. **4.** Advance against opposing force; resistance; insurrection 1597. †**5.** A force raised, esp. in insurrection –1661. **6.** Issue, result; summing up; culmination, crisis; maturity; height; strength, force, power (gradually attained) ME.

1. The heed of the vnyuersall chirche is the pope FISHER. **c.** The h. of Syria is Damascus *Isa.* 7:8. **2.** Men..who thought it better to be at the H. of a Sect, than at the Tail of an Establishment BOLINGBROKE. Phr. *H. of the river* (in Bumping races): the position of being first boat; also the boat, crew, or college which holds this position. **3.** Quarrelling Vpon the h. of Valour SHAKS. **4.** Phr. *To make* or *gain h.*; *to bear* or *keep h. against*, to hold one's own against. **5.** The Gothes have gather'd h. SHAKS. **6.** Phr. *To come, grow, gather to a h.*; *to bring, draw to a h.*; *to gather h.* It might bring things to a h., one way or the other T. HARDY.

Phrases.

With a preposition.* **Off one's **h.** Crazy (*colloq.*). **On** or **upon..h. a.** *On one's h.*: said of evil, vengeance, etc., or of blessing, etc. figured as descending upon a person; also of guilt, 'blood', etc., as resting upon him. †**b.** *On (upon) h.* (*a, the h.*): Headlong, rashly, inconsiderately. **Out of** one's **own h.** From one's own mind or invention. (Somewhat *colloq.*) **Over..h. a.** Overhead, up aloft. **b.** *Over* (one's) *h.*: *lit.* above one, e.g. in the sky or air, or affording shelter; also of something rising and overwhelming one; hence *fig.* of danger or evil impending, etc. **c.** *Over* (some one's) *head*: passing over (a person) who has a prior right, claim, etc. **d.** *Over* (one's) *head*: (of time) past, over. **e.** *Over* (one's) *head*: beyond one's comprehension or mental capacity; without considering or consulting one. **To** (one's) **head.** To one's face. *Obs.* or *dial.*

***With another sb.* **H. and ears. a.** *By the h. and ears*: violently, as one drags a beast. **b.** *Over h. and ears*: completely immersed; also *fig.* **H...foot.** *From h. to foot*: all over the person; *fig.* completely. **H. and front.** Orig. app. = 'summit, height, highest extent or pitch' (*Oth.* I. iii. 80); occas. used by mod. writers in other senses. **H. of hair.** The covering of hair on the head, esp. when copious. **H...heel(s. a.** *From h. to heel*: = from h. to foot (see above). **b.** *H. over heels*: a common corruption of *heels over head* (see HEEL *sb.*[1]). **H. and shoulders. a.** *By h. and shoulders* (*by* occas. omitted): by force, violently; *fig.* of something violently introduced into a speech or writing. **b.** (with *taller*, etc.) By the measure of the h. and shoulders; hence *fig.* considerably, by far. **H. or tail. a.** Either one thing or another; anything intelligible. (With neg.) Now always *to make h. or tail of*. **b.** *Head(s or tail(s*: see sense I. 3 b.

****With a verb.* (*To* BREAK *Priscian's h.*, HIDE, *one's h.* KNOCK *on the h.*, TURN *h.*, etc.: see the verbs.) **Keep one's h.** To keep one's wits about one, keep calm: the opposite of *lose one's h.* **b.** *To keep one's h. above water*: to keep oneself in life; also *fig.* = out of debt. **Lose** one's **h. a.** *lit.* To be beheaded. **b.** *fig.* To lose self-possession or presence of mind. **Make h. a.** To advance, press forward, esp. in opposition to some person or thing; †also *to make a h.* Usually, *To make h. against*: to advance against; to rise in insurrection against; to resist successfully, advance in spite of. †**b.** *To make a h.*: to raise a body of troops. **Put** (a thing) **in** or **into** (a person's) **h.**: to suggest it to his mind; formerly also, to remind him of it. So *to put out of one's h.*, to cause one to forget. †**b.** Hence, by corruption, *to put* (a person) *in the h. of* (a thing): to put him in mind of it. **Take..h.** †**a.** *To take* (one) *in the h.*: to occur to one. **b.** *To take into (in) one's h.*: to conceive the idea or notion of.

*****With adverb.* **H. first, h. foremost**: with the head first or foremost; hence *fig.* precipitately. (Also with hyphen or as one word.)

******Fig. and proverbial phrases.* **To give** (a horse) **the h.,** also *to let him have the h.*: not to check him with the bridle; to let him go freely. Hence *fig.* of persons. **To lay their heads together:** to consult together. **In spite of** or **maugre his h.:** notwithstanding all he can do. **To talk** (etc.) a person's **h. off** (joc.): i.e. until he is too weary to reply, or *ad nauseam*. So *to beat his h. off*, i.e. to beat him out and out. Prov. *Two heads are better than one* (cf. sense I. 2 a. and *Eccles.* 4:9).

attrib. uses. **1.** At the head (sense III.2); in the position of command; chief, principal, capital OE. **2.** Situated at the head, top, or front; coming from the front, as *a head wind* ME.

Combs. **1.** General: as *h.-affection, -brush, -rest*, etc.; *h.-breaking, -breaker*, etc.; *h.-felt* adj.; *h.-lugged* adj.; *h.-high, -like* adjs.

2. Special: **h.** †**-bone,** the skull; **-boom** (*Naut.*), a boom at the ship's head; a jib-boom; **-cap** (*Book-binding*), the leather cap over the head-band; **-cheese** (*U.S.*), pork-cheese, brawn; **-chute** (*Naut.*), a tube leading from the ship's head down to the water, for conveying refuse overboard; **-coal,** the upper portion of a thick seam of coal which is worked in two or more lifts (Gresley); **-cringle** (*Naut.*), a cringle at the upper corner of a sail (Smyth); **-earing** (*Naut.*), an earing attached to a head-cringle (*ibid.*);

-fish (*U.S.*), the sun-fish (Webst.); †**-fountain** = FOUNTAIN-HEAD; **-gate,** (*a*) one of the upper pair of gates of a canal-lock; (*b*) a crown-gate, flood-gate, water-gate; **-hunter,** one who practises head-hunting; **-hunting,** the practice, among some savages, of making incursions for the purpose of procuring human heads as trophies, etc.; **-kidney,** foremost of the three parts of the elementary kidney in a vertebrate embryo, the pronephros; **-lease** (*Law*), a lease granted directly by the freeholder; **-lessee** (*Law*), a person to whom a head-lease is granted; **-light,** a light carried on the front of a locomotive, or on the mast-head of a steamer; *spec.* each of two powerful lamps carried on the front of a motor-vehicle; **-louse,** *Pediculus capitis*; **-netting** (*Naut.*), 'an ornamental netting used in merchant ships instead of the fayed planking to the head-rails' (Smyth); **-page,** a page on which the beginning of a book, chapter, etc. is printed; **-phone,** a telephone or wireless receiver attachable to a listener's ears; **-pump** (*Naut.*), a small pump at the h. of a ship, communicating with the sea, and used for washing the decks; **-rent** (*Law*), rent payable to the freeholder; **-sill,** the upper frame of a door or window; **-timber** (*Shipbuilding*), one of the upright pieces of timber which support the frame of the head-rails; **-tone** = HEAD-NOTE 2; **-valve,** in a steam-engine, 'the delivering valve, the upper air-pump valve' (Knight); †**-well** = HEADSPRING, FOUNTAIN-HEAD; **-word,** a word forming a heading; **-yard** (*Naut.*), one of the yards on the foremast.

Head (hed), *v.* ME. [f. HEAD *sb.* In sense 1 OE. had *behēafdian.*]

I. 1. *trans.* To cut off the head of; to behead. **2.** To top, poll (a tree or plant). Also *to h. down.* 1523.

2. The Willow.. is headed every three or four Years 1712.

II. 1. *trans.* To furnish or fit with a head 1530; to form the head or top of 1637. **2.** To furnish with a heading or head-line 1877; to stand at the head of (a page, list, etc.) 1832. **3.** *intr.* To form a head; to come or grow to a head ME. **4.** Of a stream: To have its head or source; to rise. Chiefly *U.S.* 1762. **5.** *trans.* (with *up*): To collect (water) so as to form a head. Also *fig.* 1829.

1. To h. a pin 1854. *To h. up* (a cask), to close it up by fitting a head on. **2.** Heaven heads the count of crimes With that wild oath TENNYSON. To h. the poll 1885. Phr. *To h. a trick* (at cards): to play a card of higher value. **3.** Cabbages would not h. O. W. HOLMES.

III. 1. *trans.* To be or put oneself at the head of ME. **2.** To go in front of; to lead; to precede; *fig.* to surpass, excel 1711.

1. I in person will my people h. POPE. **2.** The old Dogs.. now headed the Pack 1711.

IV. 1. *intr.* To face 1610; to have an upward slope; opp. to *dip* 1802; *trans.* to cause to face 1610. **2.** *intr.* To shape one's course towards; to make *for.* (Esp. of a ship.) 1835. **b.** *trans.* To direct the course of 1885. **3.** *trans.* To move forward so as to meet; to face, front, oppose; to attack in front 1681. **b.** To get ahead of so as to turn back or aside; now often with *back, off*; also *fig.* 1716. **4.** To go round the head of (a stream or lake) 1657.

1. Two strong veins, heading in the direction of the main lode 1880. **2.** We h. for Venice 1835. **3.** Heading danger in the wars of Tyre 1681. **b.** The Bavarian General.. tried to h. back Bony in his retreat from Leipsic SCOTT.

V. *trans.* To strike or drive with the head e.g. in football 1784.

-head (hed), *suffix,* ME. **hēde, hēd,** not known in OE. Now repl. by *-hood,* exc. in one or two special forms, e.g. *godhead, maidenhead.* See -HOOD.

Headache (he·dₑēᶦk). OE. [See HEAD *sb.* and ACHE *sb.*[1]] **1.** A continuous pain in the cranial region of the head. **2.** The wild poppy (*Papaver rhœas*), so named from the effect of its odour (*local*) 1825.

Comb.: **H.-tree,** a verbenaceous shrub, *Premna integrifolia,* the leaves of which are used to cure h.; **-weed,** a shrub, *Hedyosmum nutans* (N.O. *Chloranthaceæ*), found in the W. Indies.

Hence **Hea·dachy** *a.* suffering from or subject to h.; accompanied with or producing h. **Headachiness.**

Headband (he·dbænd). 1535. **1.** A band worn round the head, a fillet. **2.** A band round the top of trousers, etc. 1818. **3.** *Book-binding.* A band (usually of silk or cotton) fastened to the inner back of a bound book at the head and tail 1611. **4.** *Arch.* = ARCHIVOLT 1723. **5.** *Printing.* A thin slip of iron forming the top of the tympan of a printing-press 1841. Hence **Hea·dbander. Hea·dbanding.**

Head-block (he·dˌblǫk). 1642. †**1.** A block put at the back of the chimney to keep the fire in by night. FULLER. **2.** In a saw-mill: The device for holding the log upon the carriage, while it is sawn 1864. **3.** The piece which connects the wheel-plate or fifth wheel of a carriage with the fore-body 1875.

Head-board (he·dbōᵊɹd). 1730. **1.** A board at the upper end of anything, as a bedstead, etc. **2.** *Naut.* (*pl.*) 'The berthing or close-boarding between the head-rails' (Smyth).

Headborough (he·dbɒːrŏ). 1440. Orig., the head of a *friðborh,* tithing, or frank-pledge (see BORROW *sb.*); afterwards a petty constable; = BORSHOLDER, TITHINGMAN[1]. Also *transf.*

Head-cloth (he·dˌklǫþ). OE. [See CLOTH *sb.* 1.] **1.** A covering for the head; in *pl.* the pieces composing a head-dress. **2.** A piece of cloth at the head of a bed 1730.

Head-court. *Hist.* 1545. A chief court (of justice); for some time used as a court for the registration of county voters.

Head-dress (he·dˌdres). 1703. Any dress or covering for the head; *esp.* an ornamental one worn by women.

Headed (he·dėd), *a.* and *ppl. a.* ME. [f. HEAD *sb.* and *v.* + -ED.] **1.** Having a head (of a specified kind). Freq. in comb., as *clear-h.,* etc. **2.** Of things: Furnished with a head; tipped, as an arrow, etc. 1450. **3.** Of a plant: Grown to a head 1577. **4.** That has come to a head, as a boil. *A.Y.L.* II. vii. 67. †**5.** Of flints: Faced (see FACE *v.* III.3.) –1717. **6.** Furnished with a heading 1838.

6. A five-lined whip, h. 'Most important' 1884.

Header (he·dəɹ). ME. [f. HEAD *v.* and *sb.* + -ER[1].] **1.** One who or that which removes the head; *spec.* a reaping-machine which cuts off only the heads of the grain 1883. **2.** One who puts a head on something, e.g. casks, nails, pins, etc. 1755. **3.** One who heads or leads a party, etc.; a leader (*rare*) 1818. **4.** *Building.* A brick, or stone, laid with its head or end in the face of the wall; opp. to *stretcher.* Also applied to sods, etc. in fortification. 1688. **5.** *Pugilism.* A blow on the head 1818. **6.** A plunge or dive head foremost (*colloq.*) 1849. **7.** One who dives head foremost. CLOUGH. **8.** A collier or coal-cutter who drives a head 1883.

6. Four blacks.. took a h. into the boiling current 1859.

Headfast (he·dfɑst), *sb.* 1569. [f. HEAD *sb.* + FAST *sb.*[2]] *Naut.* A rope or chain at the head of a vessel, to make her fast to a wharf, buoy, etc. Hence **Hea·dfast** *v. trans.* to make fast with a h.

Head-foremost, headforemost, *adv. phr.* and *a.* 1871. **a.** *adv. phr.* See *head foremost,* s.v. HEAD *sb.* **b.** *adj.* Headlong, precipitate (*rare*).

Head-gear (he·dˌgīᵊɹ). 1539. **1.** That which is worn on the head; a head-dress of any kind. **2.** The parts of the harness about a horse's head 1875. **3.** *Mining.* Apparatus at the head of a shaft 1841. **4.** The rigging on the forepart of a vessel.

Headily (he·dili), *adv.* 1450. [f. HEADY + -LY[2].] In a heady manner; hastily, rashly; violently, impetuously; †eagerly. So **Hea·diness,** the quality or condition of being heady.

Heading (he·diŋ), *vbl. sb.* ME. [f. HEAD *v.* + -ING[1].] **1.** The action of HEAD *v.,* in various senses. **2.** *concr.* A distinct part forming the head, top, or front of a thing; that which is at the top 1676. **3.** Material for the heads of casks 1772. **4.** The title or inscription at the head of a page, chapter, etc. 1849; *fig.* a division, section of a subject of discourse, etc. 1859. **5.** A gallery or adit in a mine; a drift; also, the end of a drift or gallery 1819. **6.** A top layer or covering, e.g. foam on beer 1777. **7.** *attrib.* ME

Comb.: **h.-course,** a course of bricks consisting of headers; **-joint** (*Carp.*), the joint of two or more boards at right angles to the fibres; †**-stone,** a faced or pitched stone.

Heading-machine. 1875. **a.** A kind of harvester (see HEADER 1). **b.** A machine for forming heads, as for casks, pins, bolts, etc. 1884.

Headland (he·dlănd). [OE. *hēafodland,* f. HEAD *sb.* + LAND *sb.*] **1.** A strip of land left for convenience in turning the plough at the end of the furrows, or near a fence; in old times used as a boundary. **2.** A point of land projecting into the sea or other expanse of water; a cape or promontory: now usu., a bold or lofty promontory 1527.

2. The Cape or Head-land of St. Bees 1769.

Headless (he·dlės), *a.* OE. [-LESS.] **1.** Without a head; beheaded. **b.** = ACEPHALOUS 3. 1880. **2.** Having no chief or leader ME. **3.** Wanting in brains or intellect 1526; (of actions) senseless, stupid 1586.

1. H. figures 1862, casks 1884. **3.** Headlesse Captaines CHEKE. Headlesse Old-wiues Tales 1619.

Hea·d-line. 1626. **1.** *Naut.* **a.** One of the ropes that make a sail fast to the yard. **b.** The line sewed along the upper edge of flags to strengthen them 1794. **2.** *Printing.* †**a.** The upper line that bounds the short letter. MOXON. †**b.** The line which is drawn across the head of a page. CRABB. **c.** The line at the top of a page in which the running title, pagination, etc., are given; a title or sub-title in a book, etc. 1824. **3.** A rope attached to the head of a bullock, etc. 1889. Hence **Hea·d-line** *v.* to furnish with a head-line. **Hea·d-liner,** one who writes head-lines; also (*U.S.*), one whose name appears in a h.-l.; a chief person or performer.

Headlong (he·dlǫŋ). 1482. [alt. of earlier *headling,* by erron. assim. to -LONG; cf. *sidelong.*]

A. *adv.* **1.** Head foremost; head downmost. Also *fig.* **2.** With ungoverned speed; with blind impetuosity 1576; *fig.* without regard to where one is going; precipitately 1530.

1. *fig.* He casts him selfe head-long to hel 1602.

B. *adj.* **1.** Of heights, etc.: Precipitous. Now *rare.* 1550. **2.** Plunging downwards head foremost, as when one falls or dives: **a.** of actions 1586; **b.** *poet.* of a person 1663. **c.** Hanging head downmost. POPE. **3.** Wildly impetuous. Of actions and agents. 1590. **4.** *fig.* Precipitate; rash, reckless 1566.

1. You tumble down a h. Precipice 1692. **2. a.** H. leaps of waters E.B. BROWNING. **3.** H. torrents MACAULAY. **4.** H. orator COWPER, ire SCOTT. Hence †**Hea·dlong** *v. trans.* to cast h.; *intr.* to proceed in a h. fashion. Also **Hea·dlongs** *adv.* (now *dial.*) = A.

Head-man, headman, head man. [OE. *hēafodman.*] **1.** Chief man, chief, leader. **2.** = HEADSMAN. –1816.

Head Master, hea:d-ma·ster. 1576. The principal master of a school, having assistant masters under him. Hence **Head-ma·stership.**

Head Mistress, hea:d-mi·stress. 1872. The principal mistress of a school, having assistant mistresses under her. Hence **Head-mistress-ship.**

Hea·d-money. 1530. **1.** A fee, tax, etc., paid per head. **2.** A sum paid for each prisoner taken at sea, for each slave recovered, or for each person brought in certain circumstances 1713.

Hea·dmost, *a.* 1628. [f. HEAD *sb.* + -MOST.] **1.** Most forward in order or progression; said *esp.* of the foremost ship of a line. **2.** Topmost (*dial.*) 1798.

Hea·d-note. 1855. **1.** *Law.* A summary prefixed to the report of a decided case, stating the principle of the decision, with, latterly, an outline of the facts. **2.** *Mus.* A note produced in the second or third register of the voice; cf. HEAD-VOICE. 1869.

†**Hea·d-pan.** [OE. *hēafodpanne*; see HEAD *sb.,* PAN *sb.*[1]] Skull, brain-pan –ME.

Hea·d-penny. *Obs.* exc. *Hist.* ME. **1.** A capitation fee. **2.** A personal or individual eccl. payment or offering 1550.

Hea·d-piece. 1530. The piece that covers or forms the head. **1.** A helmet 1535. **2.** A cap 1552. **3.** The head, skull (*arch.*)

1579. **4.** The head, as the seat of intellect; brain 1588. **5.** †**a.** The protective covering of the forehead of a barded horse 1611. **b.** A halter, a head-stall 1530. **6.** The top piece or part 1611. **7.** *Printing.* A decorative engraving placed at the head of a volume, of chapters, etc. 1718.

3. In his headpeace he felt a sore payne SPENSER. **4.** The hurt..had somewhat crazed his h. 1613. Is not this Steward of mine..a rare h. GAY.

Hea·d-plate. 1794. †**1.** An ornament made to fix on the upper quarters of a coach or chariot –1809. **2.** *Artillery.* 'The plate which covers the breast of the cheeks of a gun-carriage' (Knight) 1875. **3.** *Saddlery.* 'The plate strengthening the..cantle of a saddle-tree' (Knight) 1874.

Hea·d-qua·rters, *sb. pl.* (Rarely *sing.*) 1647. **1.** *Mil.* The residence of the commander-in-chief of an army; the place whence a commander's orders are issued. Also, the officers belonging to head-quarters. 1812. **b.** The transport which carries the staff of an expedition (Smyth). **2.** A chief place of residence, meeting, or business; a centre of operations 1851. **3.** *attrib.*, usually in form *head-quarter* 1879.

1. On the way to report himself at head-quarters W. IRVING. **2.** A strong continuous impulse from head-quarters BURGON.

Hea·d-race. 1846. The race or flume which brings water to a mill-wheel. Cf. *tail-race.*

Hea·d-rail[1]. 1823. **1.** One of the rails at the head of a ship. **2.** The upper horizontal piece of a door-frame 1874.

Hea·d-r-ail[2]. *Obs.* exc. *Hist.* [OE. *hēafodhrægl*; see HEAD *sb.*, RAIL *sb.*[1]] The kerchief or head-dress of women in OE. times.

Hea·d-rope. ME. †**1.** One of the stays of a mast –1475. **2.** That part of a bolt-rope which is sewed on the upper edge of any sail. Also, the small rope to which a flag is fastened, to hoist it to the mast-head, etc. 1627. **3.** A rope along the top of a fishing-net 1883. **4.** A rope for leading or tying up a horse 1854.

Head-sail. 1627. *Naut.* Any foremast or bowsprit sail.

Headship (he·dʃip). 1582. [f. HEAD *sb.* + -SHIP.] The position or office of head; leadership; supremacy, primacy.

Hea·dsman. ME. [f. *head's* gen. + MAN; cf. *draughtsman.*] **1.** A chief, head man. Now *rare.* **2.** One who beheads; an executioner 1601. **3.** *Mining.* A labourer in a colliery who pushes coal from the workings to the tramway; a 'putter' 1841.

Hea·dspring. ME. Fountain-head, source.

Head-stall, headstall (he·dˌstǭl), *sb.* 1480. [f. HEAD *sb.* + STALL *sb.*[1]] The part of a bridle or halter that fits round the head. Hence **Head-stall** *v.* (*rare*), to put a h. on (a horse).

Headstock. 1731. [f. HEAD *sb.* + STOCK *sb.*[1]] Name applied to the bearings or supports of revolving parts in various machines; as: **a.** That part of a lathe which carries the mandrel or live stock; **b.** The head which supports the cutters in a planing machine; etc.

Hea·dstone, head stone. 1535. **1.** (*head stone*) The chief stone in a foundation; the cornerstone. Also *fig.* **2.** (*hea·dstone*) An upright stone at the head of a grave 1775.

Headstrong (he·dstrǫŋ), *a.* ME. [f. HEAD *sb.* + STRONG *a.*; *lit.* strong of or in head.] **1.** Determined to pursue one's own course; wilful, obstinate. **2.** Of things, etc.: Characterized by or proceeding from wilfulness or obstinacy 1586.

1. To tie a h. girle from loue GREENE. **2.** Dangerous and h. passions 1796. Hence **Hea·dstrongness.**

Head-tire (he·dˌtəiᵊɹ). Now *arch.* or *dial.* 1560. [f. HEAD *sb.* + TIRE *sb.*[1]] Attire for the head; a head-dress.

An head tyre of fine linnen BIBLE (Geneva) 1 *Esd.* 3:6.

Hea·d-voice. 1849. One of the highest registers of the voice in singing or speaking; applied both to the second register, and to the third register or falsetto.

Headward (he·dwǭɹd). ME. [f. HEAD *sb.* + -WARD.] †**A.** *orig.* in *To the h.*, in the direction of the head. **b.** Of a ship: Ahead. –1674. **B.** *adv.* Towards or in the direction of the head 1798. **C.** *adj.* Being in the region or direction of the head 1667.

Head water, head-water. 1535. **1.** *pl. Head waters*: The streams from the sources of a river. **2.** *H.-w.-mark*, a mark showing the 'head' to be allowed above a weir, etc. 1894.

Headway (he·dweⁱ). 1708. [In I short for **aheadway*; in II f. HEAD *sb.* + WAY *sb.*]

I. 1. Of a ship: Motion ahead or forward; rate of progress 1748. **2.** *transf.* and *fig.* Advance, progress (in general) 1775.

1. The head-way..is..feeble 1769.

II. 1. *Arch.* Room overhead; the clear height of a doorway, arch, tunnel, etc. 1775. **2.** *Mining.* (Also *headways.*) A narrow passage or 'gallery', connecting the broad parallel passages or 'boards' in a coal mine 1708. **3.** The interval of time or the distance between two trains, trams, etc., running on the same route and in the same direction (orig. *U.S.*) 1895.

Hea·d-work. 1843. [f. HEAD *sb.* + WORK *sb.*] **1.** Mental work. **2.** An ornament for the keystone of an arch 1864. **Hea·d-wo:rker.**

Heady (he·di), *a.* ME. [f. HEAD *sb.* + -Y[1].] **1.** Headlong, precipitate, impetuous, violent; headstrong; 'hurried on with passion' (J.). **2.** Apt to affect or 'go to' the head; intoxicating, stupefying 1577. †**3.** Of a tenure: In chief (*in capite*) MARSTON.

1. H. judgements 1545. A Flood, With such a h. currance SHAKS. When a h. Prince comes to the Throne LOCKE. **2.** There is such headie ale 1577.

†**Heal, hele,** *sb. Obs.* exc. *Sc.* [OE. *hǣlu, hǣlo, hǣl*, corresp. to OS. *hēli*, OHG. *heilī*; f. *hāl* adj.; see HALE *a.* Cf. HALE *sb.*[1]] **1.** Health; cure –1795. **2.** Well-being, safety; prosperity –1605.

Heal (hīl), *v.*[1] [OE. *hǣlan* = OFris. *hēla*, OS. *hēlian* (Du. *heelen*), (O)HG. *heilen*, ON. *heila*, Goth. *hailjan* :– Gmc. **χailjan*, f. **χailaz* WHOLE.] **1.** *trans.* To make whole or sound; to cure (*of* a disease or wound). Also *absol.* **2.** To cure (a disease); to restore to soundness (a wound); also to *h. up*, *over.* Also *absol.* OE. **3.** *fig.* To save, purify, cleanse, repair, amend OE. **4.** *intr.* (for *refl.*) To become whole or sound; to recover from sickness or a wound; to get well ME.

1. Physician, h. thyself *Luke* 4:23. *absol.* I wound, and I heale *Deut.* 32:39. **2.** O foolish physick..That heales up one, and makes another wound SPENSER. **3.** So the waters were healed 2 *Kings* 2:22. The breach in our ranks might be healed tomorrow 1887. **4.** Those wounds heale ill, that men doe giue themselues SHAKS. Hence **Hea·lable** *a.* (*rare*), that may be healed.

Heal, *v.*[2], to cover; see HELE *v.*

Heal-all (hī·lˌǭl). 1577. [f. HEAL *v.*[1] + ALL.] **1.** A universal remedy; a panacea. Also *fig.* **2.** *Herb.* A pop. name of plants, e.g. *Rhodiola rosea, Prunella vulgaris*, etc. 1853.

Heald (hīld). [app. same word as OE. *hefel, hefeld*, OS. *hevild*, ON. *hafald*, a deriv. of **hafjan* raise. See HEDDLE.] *Weaving.* = HEDDLE.

Healer (hī·ləɹ). ME. [f. HEAL *v.*[1] + -ER[1].] **1.** One who heals or saves; in early use, Saviour. **2.** That which heals; a remedy 1523.

†**Healful,** *a.* ME. [f. HEAL *sb.* + -FUL.] Fraught with health; wholesome, salutary –1563.

Hea·ling, *vbl. sb.* OE. [f. HEAL *v.*[1] + -ING[1].] The action of HEAL *v.*[1]; *spec.* the touching by English sovereigns for the king's evil 1676. Also *transf.* and *fig.* ME.

Hea·ling, *ppl. a.* ME. [f. as prec. + -ING[2].] **1.** That heals or cures. Also *transf.* and *fig.* **2.** Of a wound: That cicatrizes or closes 1857.

1. The h. waters SCOTT. *fig.* To whom with h. words Adam reply'd MILT. Hence **Hea·lingly** *adv.*

†**Healless,** *a.* [f. HEAL *sb.* + -LESS.] Deprived of health or well-being. CHAUCER.

Health (helþ), *sb.* [OE. *hǣlþ* = OHG. *heilida* :– WGmc. **χailiþa*, f. Gmc. **χailaz* WHOLE; see -TH[1].] **1.** Soundness of body; that condition in which its functions are duly discharged. **2.** Hence, The general condition of the body; usually qualified as *good, bad, delicate*, etc. 1509. †**3.** Healing, cure –1555. **4.** Spiritual, moral, or mental soundness; salvation (*arch.*) OE. †**5.** Well-being, safety; deliverance –1611. **6.** A wish expressed for a person's welfare; a toast drunk in a person's honour 1596.

1. With a..Flush of H. in his Aspect ADDISON. **2.** She enjoyed very tolerable h. 1802. Phr. *Bill of Health*: see BILL *sb.*[3] *Board of H.*, a Government Board which existed 1848–1858 for the control of matters affecting the public health. **4.** There is no health in vs *Bk. Com. Prayer.* **5.** Be thou a Spirit of h., or Goblin damn'd SHAKS.

Comb.: **h.-guard,** an officer appointed to enforce quarantine regulations (Smyth); **-officer,** an officer charged with the administration of the health laws and sanitary inspection; so **h. visitor; -resort; -roll,** a list showing the state of health of a company of people, as of a ship's crew.

Healthful (he·lþfŭl), *a.* ME. [f. HEALTH *sb.* + -FUL.] **1.** Promoting bodily or spiritual health; health-giving, salubrious; salutary. **2.** Of persons, etc.: Full of or characterized by health; healthy (now *rare*) 1550; marked by intellectual or moral soundness 1601.

1. Much subject to Earthquakes, else very h. 1694. H. elements of European civilization 1862. **2.** He was generally h., and capable of much labour JOHNSON. The h. progress of the world 1884. Hence **Hea·lthful-ly** *adv.*, **-ness.**

Healthless (he·lþlės), *a.* Now *rare.* 1568. [f. as prec. + -LESS.] **1.** Destitute of bodily, mental, or spiritual health; unhealthy. **2.** Not conducive to health; unwholesome 1650. Hence **Hea·lthlessness.**

Healthsome (he·lþsŏm), *a.* Now *rare.* 1538. [f. as prec. + -SOME[1].] †**1.** Full of health; healthy –1635. **2.** Bestowing health; wholesome; salutary 1538. Hence **Hea·lthsome-ly** *adv.*, **-ness.**

Hea·lthward, *a.* 1884. [f. as prec. + -WARD.] Tending towards health.

Healthy (he·lþi), *a.* 1552. [f. HEALTH *sb.* + -Y[1].] **1.** Possessing good health; hale or sound (in body). **2.** Conducive to health; wholesome, salubrious; salutary. Also *fig.* 1552. **3.** Denoting health or sound condition (*lit.* and *fig.*); opp. to *morbid* 1597.

1. My abstinence keeps me quite h. 1815. **2.** H. dwelling-houses 1871. *fig.* A h. influence upon society 1884. **3.** The h. habit of the British constitution BURKE. Hence **Hea·lthily** *adv.* **Hea·lthiness.**

Heap (hīp), *sb.* [OE. *hēap* = OFris. *hāp*, OS. *hōp* (Du. *hoop*; cf. FORLORN HOPE), OHG. *houf* (rel. to MLG. *hupe*, OHG. *hūfo*, G. *haufen*) :– WGmc. **χaup-*, **χūp-*.] **1.** A collection of things lying one upon another so as to form an elevated mass roughly conical in form. †**b.** Mass, main body –1709. **2. a.** A heaped measure of capacity. **b.** A pile or mass of definite size, varying with the commodity. 1674. **3.** A great company (esp. of persons); a multitude, a host. Now only as in 4. OE. **4.** Hence, colloq.: A large number or quantity; a (great) deal; a lot. Also *pl.* in same sense. 1547. Also *absol.* and as *adv.* (colloq.) 1834.

1. They haue..made Ierusalem an heape of stones COVERDALE *Ps.* 78(79):1. *Fallacy of the heap*: the fallacy which plays upon the difficulty of saying precisely when a number of things make a h. **4.** She..has a h. of servants TROLLOPE. *pl.* In heaps of time 1856. *absol.* It's nature I should think a h. of him MRS. STOWE. Phrases. *All of a h.*: all in a mass falling or fallen. *To strike all of a h.* (colloq.): to paralyse, cause to collapse. *Comb.*: **h.-cloud** = CUMULUS 2; **-flood,** a heavy sea.

Heap (hīp), *v.* [OE. *hēapian* (corresp. to OHG. *houfōn*), f. prec.] **1.** *trans.* To make, form, gather, or cast into a heap. Often with *up, together, on.* **2.** *transf.* and *fig.* To amass, accumulate; to add many things together. Also *absol.* OE. **3.** *trans.* To fill, load, cumber with a heap or heaps. Also with *up.* 1526. **4.** To bestow in heaps. *Const.* upon. 1573. **5.** To load (a person) *with* (something in large quantities) 1583.

1. Though he heape vp siluer as the dust *Job* 27:16. **2.** Generations of antiquaries have heaped together vast piles of facts M. PATTISON. **3.** The field is heaped with bleeding steeds, and flags, and cloven mail MACAULAY. **4.** To h. insults on his memory BRIGHT. Phr. *Heaped measure*, a dry measure used for certain com-

modities which are heaped up in a cone above the brim of the measure.
Hence **Hea·per**, one who heaps up or accumulates.

Heapy (hī·pi), *a.* 1552. [f. HEAP *sb.* + -Y[1].] Full or consisting of heaps.

Hear (hīᵊɹ), *v.* Pa. t. and pple. **heard** (hɔ̄ɹd). [OE. *hēran* (WS. *hīeran*) = OFris. *hēra, hōra*, OS. *hōrian* (Du. *hooren*), OHG. *hōren* (G. *hören*), ON. *heyra*, Goth. *hausjan* :- Gmc. *χauzjan.] **1.** *intr.* To perceive, or have the sensation of, sound; to possess or exercise the faculty of audition, of which the organ is the ear. The proper verb to express this faculty or function. **2.** *trans.* To perceive (sound or something that causes sound); to have cognizance of by means of the ear OE. **3.** To exercise the auditory function intentionally; to give ear, hearken, listen. **a.** *intr.* ME. **b.** *trans.* To listen to; to give ear to, hearken to; to give audience to. Orig. with dative of the person or thing. OE. **4.** *trans.* To attend and listen to (a lecture, sermon, etc.); to form one of the audience at ME. **5.** *trans.* To listen to judicially in a court of law; to give (one) a hearing; to try (a person or case) ME. **6.** To listen to with compliance; to accede to, grant OE. **7.** To obey. (Only OE., ME., and *arch.*) **8.** To learn by hearing; to be informed of OE. **9.** *absol.* or *intr.* To be informed, learn; to receive tidings *of*, a message or letter *from* ME. *To h. from*: also, to receive a reprimand from 1907. †**10.** To be spoken (well or ill) of. [After Gr. *εὖ, κακῶς ἀκούειν*, L. *bene, male audire.*] –1706. **b.** *To h. rather*: to prefer to be called. (A Latinism.) 1667.

1. He that hath eares to heare, let him here TINDALE *Matt.* 11:15. To heare with eies belongs to loves fine wit SHAKS. **2.** Lay thine eare close to the ground, and list if thou can heare the tread of Trauellers SHAKS. Eye hath not seen, nor ear heard..the things which God hath prepared for them that love him 1 *Cor.* 2:9. Phr. *To h. say, h. tell*, etc., with ellipsis of *people, persons, some one*, before *say, tell*, etc. **3. a.** Speak, Lord, for thy servant heareth 1 *Sam.* 3:9. **b.** Wherfore hearest thou mens words 1 *Sam.* 24:9. **4.** To h. a play SHAKS. **5.** To heare The cause SHAKS. **6.** The prayer is heard KEBLE. Phr. *To h. of* (in U.S. also *to*) (with *will*, etc. and neg.): to refuse to listen to, entertain the notion of, permit. **8.** Adam, soon as he heard The fatal Trespass don by Eve MILT. I h. there are no lodgings to be had 1808. **9.** I too had been looking to h. from you SOUTHEY. Phr. *To h. of it*: to be called to account for it (*colloq.*). **10.** Or hear'st thou rather pure Ethereal stream Whose Fountain who shall tell MILT.

Phr. **Hear!** (imper.), now usu. **Hear! Hear!** (formerly *Hear him! Hear him!*): an exclam. to call attention to a speaker's words, and hence a regular form of cheering (CHEER *sb.* 7). Hence also as *sb.* and *v.*

Hence **Hea·rable** *a.* that can be heard.

Hearer (hīᵊ·rəɹ). ME. [f. HEAR *v.* + -ER[1].] **1.** One who hears: an auditor. **2.** One who attends lectures or sermons; a disciple 1686. **3.** *Eccl. Hist.* One admitted to hear the Scriptures read, but not to the common worship of the church 1697.

Hea·ring, *vbl. sb.* ME. [f. as prec. + -ING[1].] **1.** The action of HEAR *v.*; the faculty or sense by which sound is perceived; audition. **2.** The action of listening (e.g. to a lecture, sermon, play, etc.); *spec.* attendance at preaching (*dial.*); audience. Also *fig.* ME. **3.** The listening to evidence and pleadings in a court of law; the trial of a cause; *spec.* a trial before a judge without a jury 1576. **4.** Knowledge by hearing or being told 1450. **5.** Something heard; report, rumour, news (*dial.*) ME.

1. Captivating..at the first h. PRIESTLEY. The organ of h. is not manifest in insects STARK. Phr. *In one's h. Within h., out of h.*: within, or out of, hearing distance. **2.** We begge your h. Patientlie SHAKS. **3.** I'll..leaue to you the h. of the cause SHAKS. **4.** Phr. *To come to one's h.* **5.** Tis..a harsh h., when women are froward SHAKS.

Hearken, harken (hā·ɹk'n), *v.* [OE. *hercnian, heorcnian*, f. *he(o)rcian*; see HARK, -EN[5]. The sp. with *-ea-* is due to assoc. with *hear.*] **1.** *intr.* To apply the ears to hear; to listen, give ear. Const. *to*, in OE. and ME. with dative. †**2.** *intr.* To listen privily –1588. **3.** *intr.* To apply the mind to what is said; to have regard. Const. *to.* ME. **4.** *trans.* To hear with attention, give ear to; to have regard to; to learn by hearing; to perceive by the ear. Now only *poet.* OE. †**5.** *intr. Hearken to*: Listen, give ear. [As if from *to-hearken*; cf. *Go to*, from vb. *to-go.*] –1535. †**6.** *intr.* To seek to hear tidings; to inquire *after*, ask *for* –1830. †**7.** *intr.* To lie in wait; to wait –1633. †**8.** *trans.* To get to hear of; to search *out* –1637. †**9.** To have regard or relation (*rare*). POPE.

1. She hearkens for his hounds and for his horn SHAKS. **3.** No man wyll herken to it LATIMER. **4.** This King of Naples..hearkens my Brothers suit SHAKS. **6.** *Much Ado* V. i. 216. **7.** *Tam. Shr.* I. ii. 260. **8.** He has imploied a fellow..to harken him out a dumbe woman B. JONS. Hence **Hea·rkener, Hark-.**

Hearsay (hīᵊ·ɹsē[i]). 1532. [orig. in phr. *by hear say*, tr. OFr. *par oüir dire* (now *ouï-dire*), i.e. *par* by, *oüir* hear, *dire* say.] **1.** That which one hears or has heard some one say; report, tradition, rumour, common talk, gossip. With *a* and *pl.* A rumour, a piece of gossip 1642. **2.** *attrib.* becoming an *adj.*, etc.: (*a*) Of the nature of hearsay; (*b*) founded upon what one has heard said, but not within one's direct knowledge; (*c*) of hearsay, speaking from hearsay. 1580.

1. Thou speakest by hearesaye, rather then by anye experience 1577. **2.** An h. account by Bellonius SIR T. BROWNE. The report of h. witnesses CHALMERS. *Hearsay evidence*: evidence consisting in what the witness has heard others say or what is commonly said. H.-evidence is.. rejected in law 1753. Yet..(as in proof of any general customs, or matters of common tradition or repute), the courts admit of h. evidence BLACKSTONE.

Hearse (hɔ̄ɹs), *sb.* ME. [– (O)Fr. *herse* harrow, portcullis (see HERSE), triangular frame for candles (in AL. *hercia* XIII) :- med.L. *erpica*, Rom. **herpica*, for L. *(h)irpex, (h)irpic-* large rake used as a harrow, f. Samnite *(h)irpus* wolf, with ref. to the teeth.] †**1.** A harrow-shaped triangular frame, designed to carry candles, and used at the service of *Tenebræ* in Holy Week. **2. a.** A framework orig. for carrying lighted tapers, etc. over the bier or coffin while placed in the church at the funerals of distinguished persons; also called *castrum doloris, chapelle ardente*, or *catafalco* ME. **b.** A permanent framework of iron or metal. fixed over a tomb to support rich coverings or palls, etc. 1552. **c.** A temple-shaped structure of wood used in royal and noble funerals. It was decorated with banners, lighted tapers, etc., and often had short poems or epitaphs pinned upon it 1575. **3.** A light framework of wood used to support the pall over the body at funerals 1566. †**4.** A funeral pall –1603. **5.** A bier; a coffin; vaguely, a tomb, grave. *Obs.* or *arch.* 1601. †**6.** A dead body –1633. **7.** A carriage or car constructed for carrying the coffin at a funeral. (The current use.) 1650.

2. c. Underneath this sable herse Lyes the subject of all verse B. JONS. Be this my latest Verse With which I now adorn his Herse COWLEY. **5.** As thou my cradle wert, so wilt thou be my herse LISLE. **7.** A h. too, with plenty of plumes MRS. CARLYLE.

Comb.: **h.-cloth,** a black cloth to cover a bier or coffin; a funeral pall; **-like** *a.*, like a h.; mournful.

Hearse, *v.* 1592. [f. the sb.] *trans.* To lay on a bier or in a coffin; to bury with funeral rites. **b.** (in recent use) To carry to the grave in a hearse 1854. **c.** To enclose as in a bier 1608.

1. Would she were hearsed at my foote SHAKS. **c.** Worth may be hears'd but Envy cannot die CHURCHILL.

Hence **Hearsed** *ppl. a.* placed on, in, or under a hearse (*Haml.* I. iv. 47).

Hearst. Also †**hearse.** 1674. [Of unkn. origin.] *Hunting.* A hind of the second or third year.

Heart (hāɹt), *sb.* [OE. *heorte* = OFris. *herte*, OS. *herta* (Du. *hart*), OHG. *herza* (G. *herz*), ON. *hjarta*, Goth. *hairtō* :- Gmc. **χerton*. The IE. base **kĕrd-* **krd-* is repr. also by Gr. *κῆρ, καρδία*, L. *cor, cord-*.]

I. *The bodily organ*, etc. **1.** The hollow muscular or otherwise contractile organ which, by its dilatation and contraction, keeps up the circulation of the blood. **b.** A diseased or disordered heart, as FATTY *h.*, *smoker's h.* 1871. **2.** The seat of life; the vital part or principle; hence occas. = life. *Obs.* or *arch.* OE. **3.** *transf.* The region of the heart; breast, bosom 1450. **4.** The stomach. *Obs.* or *dial.* 1542.

1. Why doe's my bloud thus muster to my h. SHAKS. *fig.* Nature's mighty h. SHELLEY. **2.** Bread which strengtheneth man's h. *Ps.* 104:15. **3.** Lay hand on h., aduise SHAKS. *fig.* He hugged his old conviction to his h. 1887. **4.** Phr. *Next the h.*: on an empty stomach. (*Obs.* or *dial.*).

II. *As the seat of feeling, understanding, and thought.* **1.** = MIND, in the widest sense OE. **2.** The seat of one's inmost thoughts and secret feelings; one's inmost being; the soul, the spirit OE. **3.** Intent, will, purpose, inclination, desire. Now only in phr. *after one's own h.* OE. †**4.** Disposition, temperament, character –1611. **5.** The seat of the emotions generally; the emotional nature; opp. to *head* OE. †**b.** The sentiment one has in regard to a thing –1603. **6.** *esp.* The seat of love or affection; hence, Affection, love, devotion ME. **b.** Kindly feeling (*rare*) 1656. **c.** Sensibility; feeling 1735. **7.** The seat of courage; hence, Courage, spirit OE. **8.** The seat of the intellectual faculties. Often = understanding, intellect, mind, and (less often) memory. *arch.* exc. in phr. *by h.* OE. **9.** The moral sense, conscience. Now only in *my*, etc. *h. smote me*, etc. ME.

1. His Heart's his mouth; What his Brest forges that his Tongue must vent SHAKS. Behould the eares of my hart, are set before thee; open thou them 1620. **2.** Great searchings of h. *Judg.* 5:16. **4.** Not changing h. with habit SHAKS. **5.** Her h. was too full to speak TROLLOPE. **6.** Phr. *To give, lose one's h.* (*to*), *to have, obtain, gain a person's h. Near, nearest, one's h.*, close or closest to one's affection. She..won all hearts 1887. **7.** Thy dauntless h...will urge thee to thy fate DRYDEN. Phr. *To pluck up, gather, keep* (*up*), *lose h. To have the h., take h. To have one's h. in, put one's h. into.* **8.** Ephraim is like a silly dove without h. *Hos.* 7:11.

III. *Put for the person.* **1.** Used as a term of endearment ME. **2.** = Man of spirit. Often in nautical use. 1500. †**3.** As a term of compassion: *Poor h.!* 1682.

1. Alas whan shall I mete yow, herte dere CHAUCER. **2.** Heigh my hearts, cheerely, cheerely my harts SHAKS.

IV. *Something having a central position.* **1.** The central part of anything; the middle ME. **2.** *esp.* A central part of distinct conformation or character (see quots.) 1578. **3.** *spec.* The solid central part of a tree without sap or alburnum ME. Hence fig. *Heart of oak*: a stout courageous spirit; a man of courage or endurance. Also *attrib.* 1609.

1. The H. of England 1658, of the City DE FOE, of the London season DISRAELI. **2.** A goodly apple rotten at the h. SHAKS. The h. of a tree 1681, of a Flower 1707, of a rope 1841, of a cabbage 1866. **2.** He was..a h. of oke, and a pillar of the Land WOOD.

V. *The vital part or principle.* **1.** The vital part; essence 1533. **2.** Of land, etc.: Strength, fertility; capacity to produce; 'proof' (of grass, etc.) 1573. **3.** The best or most important part 1589.

1. Now (Sir John) here is the h. of my purpose SHAKS. **2.** Phr. *In* (*good, strong*, etc.) *h.*: in prime condition. *Out of h.*: in poor condition, unproductive. *In h.*: in good condition.

VI. *Something of the shape of a heart.* **1.** A figure of the human heart; esp. a symmetrical figure formed of two similar curves meeting in a point at one end and a cusp at the other. Also, an ornament in the shape of a heart. 1463. **2.** A playing card marked with one or more figures of a heart; one of the suit so marked; *pl.* the suit of such cards 1529. **3.** *Naut.* A kind of dead-eye, in shape resembling a heart, with one large hole in the middle 1769. **4.** A heart-shaped wheel or cam (Knight) 1875.

1. A costly Iewell..A Hart it was bound in with Diamonds SHAKS.

Phrases.

With prep.* **At heart. Inwardly, secretly; at bottom; in reality. **By heart.** In the memory; from memory; by rote. **From one's heart.** With the deepest feeling. **In..heart. a.** *In* (one's) *h.*: inwardly; secretly; at h. **b.** *In h.*: in good spirits. So *to put in* (or *into*) *h.* **c.** In good condition. **Out of heart. a.** In low spirits. **b.** In poor condition. **With..heart. a.** *With* (OE. *mid*) *all one's h., With one's whole h.*: with great sincerity, or devotion; now, with the utmost goodwill. **b.** *With a h. and a half*: willingly. *With half a h.*: half-heartedly.

***With verb and prep.* **Find** in one's **heart.** To feel willing; to prevail upon oneself (to do something): now chiefly in neg. and interrog. sentences. **Have at heart.** To have as an object in which one is deeply interested. **Lay to heart.** To think seriously about; to be deeply concerned about (a thing). **Take to heart.** To take seriously; to grieve over; †to be solicitous about.

****With governing verb.* **Break the heart of. a.** To crush with sorrow. **b.** To 'break the back of'. **Cry** (*plague, tease, weary*, etc.) one's **heart out:** to cry (etc.) violently or exhaustingly: see the vbs. **Eat** one's **heart.** To suffer or pine away from vexation or longing. See EAT *v.* **Have . . heart.** *To have the h.*: to be courageous, spirited, or (in mod. use, with negs.) hard-hearted enough (to do something). **Take heart.** To pluck up courage. *To take h. of grace*, etc.: see HEART OF GRACE.

*****With another noun.* **Heart and hand.** With will and execution; readily. **Heart . . heart. a.** *H. of hearts* (orig. *h. of h., heart's h.*): the heart's core; one's inmost h. or feelings. Usu. *in one's h. of hearts.* **b.** *A h. and a h.*, a Hebraism = duplicity. **c.** *H.-to-h.*: used to denote conversation, etc., of great intimacy and/or frankness and sincerity. **Heart and soul. a.** The whole of one's affections and energies. **b.** *advb.* With all one's energy and devotion.

******In ejaculations and invocations.* The commonest expressions now are: *Lord* (*God*) *bless my* (*your*, etc.) *h.!* elliptically *Bless my* (etc.) *h.!*

*******Proverbial phrases*, etc. *One's h. sinks in one's shoes*, etc.: hyperbolical for 'one's h. sinks', connoting extreme fear or dejection. *To have one's h. in one's mouth*, etc., referring to the apparent leaping of the h. under the influence of a sudden start. *One's h. is in its right place*: one's sympathies are rightly placed. *To wear one's h. upon one's sleeve*: to expose one's feelings, etc. to every one. *To do one's h. good*: to make one feel gladdened, strengthened, etc.

Comb.: **h.-cam,** a form of cam used for converting a rotary into a reciprocating motion; **-clot,** a clot of blood or fibrin formed in the h., usually after death; **-cockle,** a bivalve mollusc, *Isocordia cor*, so called from its shape; **-moth,** *Dicycla oo*; **-motion,** the motion generated by a heart-cam; **-sac,** the pericardium; **-shake,** a split or cleft in the centre of a tree; **-shell** = *heart-cockle*; **-strand,** the central strand of a rope; **-stroke,** (*a*) the impulse of the contraction of the h., apex-beat; (*b*) = Angina pectoris; **-trace,** 'the record on smoked paper made by the needle of a cardiograph' (*Syd. Soc. Lex.*); **-urchin,** a sea-urchin of the genus *Spatangus*, being heart-shaped; a spatangoid; **-wheel** = *heart-cam.*

b. In names of trees and plants: **h.-cherry,** a heart-shaped variety of the cultivated cherry; **-clover,** *Medicago maculata*; **-liver** = prec.; **-pea, -seed,** a name for plants of the genus *Cardiospermum*, from the heart-shaped scar which marks the attachment of the seed.

Heart (hāɹt), *v.* [OE. *hiertan*, f. *hert, heort*, HEART *sb.* Superseded by HEARTEN.] **1.** *trans.* = HEARTEN 1. *arch.* **†2.** To supply with physical strength or stimulus; to put (land) into good heart. TUSSER. **3.** To take to heart, fix in the heart 1604. **4.** *Building.* To fill up the central space within (a piece of masonry) with rubble, etc. Also with *in.* 1776. **5.** *intr.* Of a cabbage, lettuce, etc.: To form a heart or close compact head 1866.

1. A grief. .Hearted with hope TENNYSON. **3.** I hate the Moore. My cause is hearted; thine hath no lesse reason SHAKS.

Heart-ache (hāɹtˌēⁱk). OE. [f. HEART *sb.* + ACHE *sb.*¹] **1.** Pain in the heart; formerly = HEARTBURN 2. **2.** Pain or anguish of mind 1602.

Hea·rt-blood, heart's-blood. ME. Blood from the heart; life-blood; hence, vital energy, life. Also *fig.*

Hea·rt-bond. 1823. [See BOND *sb.*¹] **a.** A union of hearts, betrothal. **b.** *Arch.* 'The construction of walling in which two stones side by side form the width of the wall, and a third stone of an equal breadth is put over the joint in the course above' 1851.

Hea·rt-break, *sb.* 1583. [See BREAK *sb.*¹] A breaking of the heart; great and overwhelming sorrow or distress of mind. So **Hea·rt-breaking** *ppl. a.* causing intense sorrow or crushing grief. **Hea·rt-breakingly** *adv.*

Hea·rt-broken, *a.* 1586. [f. HEART *sb.* + BROKEN.] Having a broken heart; overwhelmed with grief or anguish. Also *transf.* of feelings, acts, etc. var. **Hea·rt-broke** (*arch.*). **Hea·rt-bro:ken-ly** *adv.*, **-ness.**

Heartburn (hāɹtbɒ̄ɹn), *sb.* ME. [f. HEART *sb.* + BURN *sb.*²] **†1.** Burning of heart; fire of passion. ME. only. **2.** = CARDIALGY. 1597. **3.** = HEART-BURNING *sb.* 1. 1621.

†Hea·rt-burn, *v.* 1540. [f. HEART *sb.* + BURN *v.*¹; cf. next.] **1.** *trans.* To affect with heart-burning. **2.** To regard or treat with jealous enmity 1612.

Heart-burning (hāɹtbɒ̄ɹniŋ), *sb.* 1513. [f. HEART *sb.* + BURNING *vbl. sb.*] **1.** A heated and embittered state of mind, which is not openly expressed; jealousy or discontent; grudge. **b.** *pl.* Grudges 1605. **†2.** = HEARTBURN *sb.* 2. Also *attrib.* –1747.

1. A long continued grudge and hearte brennyng betwene the Quenes kinred and the kinges blood MORE.

Hea·rt-burning, *ppl. a.* 1588. [f. HEART *sb.* + BURNING *ppl. a.*] That kindles or consumes the heart; distressing the heart.

Hearted (hāɹtėd), *ppl. a.* ME. [f. HEART *sb.* and *v.*; see -ED¹, ².] **1.** Having a heart; *esp.* in comb., as FAINT-HEARTED, etc. **†2.** Full of heart; spirited –1595. **3.** Having the shape of a heart; cordate 1834. **4.** Fixed in the heart 1604.

4. *Oth.* III. iii. 448. Hence **-hearted-ly** *adv.*, **-ness** in comb.

Hearten (hāɹt'n), *v.* 1526. [f. HEART *v.* + -EN⁵; repl. HEART *v.*] **1.** *trans.* To put heart into; to embolden; to inspirit, animate, cheer. **†2.** To give physical strength or stimulus to –1792. **3.** *transf.* in weaker sense: To strengthen, help on, further, promote 1615.

1. Where God. .heartened his own people. .by drying up the waters of Jordan FULLER. **2.** Good Ale, which inwardly must h. him 1586. To h. the ground with dung MAY, Punch with Brandy DAMPIER. Hence **Hea·rtener,** one who heartens, encourages, or cheers.

Hea·rt-felt, *a.* 1734. [f. HEART *sb.* + *felt*, pa. pple. of FEEL *v.*] Felt in the heart; hence, sincere, genuine, real.

Hea·rtful (hāɹtfŭl), *a.* ME. [f. HEART *sb.* + -FUL.] Full of heart, feeling, or affection; hearty. Hence **Hea·rtfully** *adv.* cordially, heartily; earnestly. **Hea·rtfulness,** h. quality.

Hearth (hāɹþ). [OE. *heorþ* = OFris. *herth, herd*, OS. *herth* (Du. *haard*), OHG. *hert* (G. *herd*) :– WGmc. **χerþa*.] **1.** That part of the floor of a room on which the fire is made; the floor of a fireplace. **b.** 'Applied to the ship's fire-place, coppers, and galley generally' (Smyth) 1867. **2.** Hence, the home, fireside OE. **3.** Techn. **a.** The fireplace of a smith's forge. **b.** The floor in a furnace on which the ore or metal is exposed to the flame. **c.** The hollow at the bottom of a blast-furnace through which the molten metal descends to the crucible. **d.** A portable brazier used in soldering. ME.

1. A pile of blazing logs on the h. 1849. **2.** Now this extremity, Hath brought me to thy Harth SHAKS. Puissant defenders of the *h. and home* 1857.

Comb.: **h.-book,** a book containing a list of hearths for the purpose of the HEARTH-TAX; **-cinder,** the slag formed on the refinery-hearth; **-cricket,** the common house-cricket; **-fly,** an artificial fly used in angling; **†-yeld** = HEARTH-PENNY.

Hea·rth-money. *Hist.* 1660. **†1.** = CHURCH-SCOT. (Coke.) **2.** A tax upon hearths or fireplaces; *esp.* a tax of two shillings per annum formerly levied on every fire-hearth in England and Wales; = CHIMNEY-MONEY. 1663.

Hearth-penny. *Hist.* OE. [So called because chargeable on every dwelling-house.] The payment also called Peter's pence and Rome-scot, formerly made to the Pope.

Hea·rth-rug. 1824. A rug laid before the fireplace.

Hea·rth-stead. 1475. [f. STEAD place.] The place of a hearth; fireside; hence = homestead.

Hearthstone (hāɹþstōᵘn), *sb.* ME. **1.** The flat stone forming the hearth. Hence, the fireside or home. **2.** A soft kind of stone used to whiten hearths, door-steps, etc.; a composition used for this purpose 1851.

1. Whate'er of peace about our h. clings BYRON. Hence **Hea·rthstòne** *v.* to whiten with h.; also *absol.*

Hea·rth-tax. 1689. = HEARTH-MONEY.

Heartily (hāɹtĭli), *adv.* ME. [f. HEARTY *a.* + -LY².] **1.** In a hearty manner; earnestly, sincerely; with goodwill. **2.** Spiritedly, zealously ME. **3.** With good appetite; abundantly, amply 1613. **4.** Plenteously; to the full, thoroughly; exceedingly, very 1686.

1. Myn lady quod he thanke I hertyly CHAUCER. **2.** To fight h. JOWETT. **3.** To feed h. DE FOE. **4.** They. .were. .h. beaten DE FOE.

Heartiness (hāɹtinės). 1530. [f. as prec. + -NESS.] The quality of being hearty.

The duke with a seeming h. gave his consent BP. BURNET.

Heartless (hāɹtlės), *a.* ME. [f. HEART *sb.* + -LESS.] **1.** *lit.* Without a heart 1586. **2.** Spiritless; out of heart, disheartened, dejected ME.; without warmth or zeal 1658. **3.** Destitute of feeling or affection; callous, unkind, cruel. (The current sense.) 1816. **4.** Of land: Without fertility 1594. **5.** Of food or drink: Without sustaining or stimulating power 1657. **6.** Of plants or trees: **a.** Without core. **b.** Not forming a heart. 1731.

2. In a h. mood Of solitude WORDSW. **3.** H. things Are done and said i' the world SHELLEY. **5.** H. Slops 1674. Bread, black and h. BP. BURNET. Hence **Hea·rtless-ly** *adv.*, **-ness.**

Heartlet (hāɹtlėt). 1826. [f. HEART *sb.* + -LET.] A little heart or core; a nucleus.

Hea·rtlike. 1616. *adj.* Like or having the appearance of a heart. *adv.* Like or after the manner of a heart 1844.

†Hea·rtling. [f. HEART *sb.* + -LING¹.] Little or dear heart. SHAKS.

Ods heartlings!: a minced oath (= God's heart!).

†Hea·rtly, *a.* Also **hertely.** ME. [f. HEART *sb.* + -LY¹.] = HEARTY 3, 4. –1600. So **†Hea·rtly** *adv.* = HEARTILY 1–3.

Heart of grace, *phr.* 1530. [Origin and early form uncertain.] **a.** in phr. *to take h. of gr., h. a gr.*, to pluck up courage. **b.** Hence, *to get, give, keep, gather h. of gr.* 1587. **†c.** Also 16–17th c. *to take heart* (*hart*) *at grass, to grass.*

Hea·rt-piercing, *a.* 1590. [See PIERCE *v.*] That pierces, or is fitted to pierce, the heart; *fig.* that appeals keenly to the emotions. Hence **Hea·rt-piercingly** *adv.*

Hea·rt-quake. 1561. [See QUAKE, and cf. *earthquake.*] Palpitation of the heart; *fig.* sudden and violent terror, delight, etc.

Heartquakes shook the joints Of all the Trojans CHAPMAN. So **Hea·rt-qualm,** in same senses.

Hea·rt-rending, *a.* 1687. [See REND *v.*] That rends the heart; terribly distressing. So **Hea·rt-rendingly** *adv.*

Hea·rt-searching, *a.* 1647. [See SEARCH *v.*] That rigorously examines the heart or feelings. So **Hea·rt-searching** *sb.*

Heartsease, heart's-ease (hāɹtsˌīz). ME. [See HEART *sb.* and EASE *sb.*] **1.** (prop. as two words.) Ease of heart; tranquillity or peace of mind; freedom from care. **2.** The Pansy (*Viola tricolor*). Also formerly the Wallflower. 1530.

Hea·rt-shaped, *a.* 1776. Having the shape of a (conventional) heart; cordate.

Hea·rt-sick, *a.* 1526. [f. HEART *sb.* + SICK *a.*] **1.** Sick at heart; *fig.* depressed or despondent. **2.** Pertaining to or characterized by heart-sickness 1591.

1. Chatham, heart-sick of his country's shame COWPER. Hence **Hea·rt-sickness.**

Heartsome (hāɹtsŏ̆m), *a.* Chiefly *Sc.* 1567. [f. HEART *sb.* + -SOME¹.] **†1.** Spirited. **2.** That gives heart; animating 1596. **3.** Cheerful, blithe 1724. Hence **Hea·rtsomely** *adv.*

Hea·rt-sore, *sb.* ME. [f. HEART *sb.* + SORE *sb.*¹] **1.** Pain or grief of heart; a cause of this. **†2.** A disease of horses, etc. (obs. Fr. *encœur*) 1616.

Heart-sore, *a.* 1591. [f. as prec. + SORE *a.*¹] Sore at heart; characterized by grief. *Two Gent.* I. i. 30.

Hea·rt-spoon. *Obs.* or *dial.* ME. [See SPOON *sb.*] **a.** The depression at the end of the breast-bone. **b.** The pit of the stomach; the navel or midriff.

Hea·rt-strike, *v. rare.* 1637. [See STRIKE *v.*] *trans.* To strike to the heart, deeply affect the feelings of. So **Hea·rt-stricken** *ppl. a.*, **-ly** *adv.*

Heart-strings (hā·ɹtˌstriŋz), *sb. pl.* 1483. [f. HEART *sb.* + STRING *sb.* 2a.] **1.** In old Anatomy, the tendons or nerves supposed to brace and sustain the heart. Also *transf.* and *fig.* **2.** *esp.* The most intense feelings; the deepest affections; the heart 1596.

2. The falsest woman, That ever broke man's heart-strings FLETCHER. To play upon the heart-strings 1887.

Hea·rt-struck, *ppl. a.* 1605. Struck to the heart: †**a.** Keenly distressing the heart; **b.** Smitten with mental anguish or dismay.

a. His heart-strooke injuries SHAKS.

Hea·rt-whole, *a.* 1470. [See WHOLE.] **1.** Having the spirits or courage unimpaired; undismayed. **2.** Having the affections unengaged 1600. **3.** Whole-hearted; free from hypocrisy or affectation; sincere, genuine 1684; unmitigated 1811.

2. Cupid hath clapt him oth' shoulder, but Ile warrant him heart hole SHAKS. **3.** A heart-whole laugh 1886, traitor LAMB. Hence **Hea·rt-wholeness.**

Hea·rt-wise, *adv.* 1727. [See -WISE.] After the manner or shape of a heart.

Hea·rt-wood. 1801. [See HEART *sb.* IV. 3.] A name for the central part of the timber of exogenous trees, hardened and matured by age; duramen.

Ebony..is the heart-wood of the date-tree 1876.

Heartwort (hā·ɹtwɒɹt). ME. [From form of leaves (or ? seeds).] **1.** The plant *Aristolochia clematitis*, also called Birthwort. †**2.** = HARTWORT, q.v. †**3.** A species of Mint. GERARDE.

Hearty (hā·ɹti), *a.* (*adv.*) and *sb.* ME. [f. HEART *sb.* + -Y[1].] Full of heart. **1.** †Full of courage. In later use: Zealous; energetic or thorough in one's support or action. †**2.** Possessed of understanding. WYCLIF. **3.** Full of kindly sentiment or goodwill; cordial, kindhearted, genial, cheery 1440. **4.** Heartfelt, genuine, sincere 1479. **5.** Giving unrestrained expression to the feelings; vehement, vigorous 1661. **6.** In sound health, having good appetite and spirits; vigorous, hale 1552. **7.** Of food or drink: Strengthening, invigorating 1617. **8.** Of a meal, etc.: Satisfying; abundant, ample, full 1593. **9.** Of soil, etc.: In good heart, well fitted to bear crops 1573. **10.** Of timber: Consisting of heart-wood; strong, durable 1624.

1. H. for the government SWIFT, in the common cause MACAULAY. **3.** H. Salutations ADDISON. **4.** With herty thankes 1526. **5.** A h. curse SCOTT, slap on the back DICKENS. **8.** A h. and prolonged repast W. IRVING.

B. *adv.* or quasi-*adv.* = HEARTILY. 1753.

C. *sb.* A hearty fellow; a brave, vigorous man; *esp.* in nautical use. Hence, a sailor, a jack-tar 1839.

Heat (hīt), *sb.* [OE. *hǣtu* = OFris. *hēte*, MDu. *hēte*, OHG. *heizī* :- WGmc. **χaitī(n)*, f. Gmc. **χaitaz* hot; also OE. *hǣte* (:- **haitja*).] **1.** The quality of being hot; often regarded as a substance or thing contained in or issuing from bodies; *esp.* In ordinary use, A high or sensible degree of this quality; high temperature; warmth. **b.** The sensation or perception of this quality or condition; one of the primary sensations, produced by contact with or nearness to fire or any body at a high temperature, by any agency that quickens the circulation of the blood, etc. 1704. **c.** With adjs. of colour, used in reference to the appearance of metals, etc. when at certain high temperatures, as BLUE *h.*, etc.; also with other defining words, as BLOOD-HEAT, etc.: see the defining words 1703. **2.** In *Physics*, formerly supposed to be an elastic material fluid (CALORIC), of extreme subtility, attracted and absorbed by all bodies; now held to be a form of ENERGY, viz. the kinetic and potential energy of the invisible molecules of bodies 1626. **3.** *spec.* A hot condition of the atmosphere or physical environment; hot weather or climate: often spoken of as an agent perceptible by its effects OE. **b.** (with *pl.*) A hot period or season ME. **c.** A fire. *Acts* 28:3. **d.** High temperature produced by fermentation or putrefaction, as in a hotbed; hence *concr.* a hotbed, esp. in phr. *in h.* ME. **4.** As a quality or condition of animal bodies (see quots.) OE. †**5.** In mediæval physiology, as a quality of 'elements', 'humours', and bodies in general: see HOT *a.* -1626. **6.** The quality of being hot in taste 1586. **7.** A redness or eruption on the skin, accompanied by a sensation of heat, or indicating inflammation 1597. **8.** A heating; *esp.* a single operation of heating, as of iron in a furnace; hence *concr.* the quantity of metal heated at one operation 1594. †**b.** A run given to a race-horse in preparation for a race -1751. **9.** *fig.* A single bout of action; a stroke, a 'go'. Chiefly in phr. *at a h.* ME. **10.** A single course in a race, etc. (See also DEAD HEAT.) Also *transf.* and *fig.* 1663. **11.** Intensity or warmth of feeling OE. **b.** (with *pl.*) An access of feeling or intensity ME. **c.** (with *pl.*) A fit of passion or anger; †a quarrel 1549. †**d.** Passionateness, excitability -1718. **12.** The intense or violent stage of any action; height, stress (e.g. of conflict, etc.) 1588. **13.** Sexual excitement in animals during the breeding season 1768.

1. c. Several degrees of Heats Smiths take of their Iron..As first, a Blood-red H. Secondly, a White Flame H. Thirdly, a Sparkling, or Welding H. MOXON. **2.** *Radiant heat*: not properly h. at all, but the energy of vibration of the intervening ether when heat is transmitted from one body to another body not in contact; it is identical, within a certain range of wave-length, with light. *Latent h.* (Physics): the h. required to convert a solid into a liquid or vapour, or a liquid into vapour: formerly regarded as being absorbed and remaining latent in the resulting liquid or vapour; now viewed as the energy absorbed during the change of state. *Specific h.* (Physics): the h. required to raise the temperature of a given substance to a given extent (usually one degree). *Atomic molecular h.* (Chem.): the product of the specific h. of a substance into its atomic or molecular weight. **3.** That knows not parching h. nor freezing cold SHAKS. **b.** The great heates are abated BARET. **4.** *Natural h.*, *vital h.*: the warmth characteristic of a living body. The vital h. Forsakes her limbs DRYDEN. The burning h. of his skin 1782. **6.** The h. of the Ginger SHAKS. **7.** *Prickly h.*: a skin disease (*Lichen tropicus*), characterized by minute papulæ formed by the hyperæmia of the sweat follicles. **9.** Neither can a true just play, which is to bear the test of ages, be produced at a h. DRYDEN. **11.** In suddain h. and passion 1694. **c.** To keep alive heats and animosities WELLINGTON. **12.** To com vpon them, in the heate of their diuision SHAKS.

Comb.: **h.-apoplexy, -asphyxia** = *heat-stroke*; **-engine,** one in which the motive power is produced by h.; **-factor** = ENTROPY; **-spectrum,** the spectrum of heat-rays, visible and invisible; **-stroke,** an affection of the nervous system, often fatal, caused by exposure to excessive h.; **-unit,** a unit quantity of h.; usually reckoned as the amount of h. required to raise the temperature of a unit weight (pound, gramme, etc.) of water one degree.

Heat (hīt), *v.* Pa. t. and pple. **heated,** †**heate** (SHAKS.). [OE. *hǣtan* = (M)Du. *hēten*, OHG. *heizzen*, *heizen* (G. *heizen*), ON. *heita* :- Gmc. **χaitjan*, f. **χaitaz* HOT *a.*]

I. *trans.* **1.** To communicate heat to; to make hot, to warm; to raise the temperature of. **2.** To cause to feel hot or warm; to bring into a condition of bodily heat, to inflame. Also *absol.* 1601. **3.** *fig.* To rouse to intense emotion; to excite in mind or feeling; to inspire with ardour; to inflame ME.

1. When I am cold, he heates me with beating SHAKS. **2.** Men heated with wine WARBURTON. **3.** He hath..cooled my friends, heated mine enemies SHAKS.

II. *intr.* **1.** To contract heat, become hot or warm, rise in temperature OE. **b.** To grow hot; to become inflamed physically ME. **2.** *fig.* To become inflamed or excited in mind or feeling; to wax warm ME.

1. Green hay heats in a mow, and green corn in a bin WEBSTER s.v. **b.** Let my Liuer rather heate with wine SHAKS. **2.** As I heated, so did she 1880.

Hence **Hea·tedly** *adv.* with warmth of temper.

Hea·t-drop. 1615. Usu. in *pl.*: **a.** A few drops of rain ushering in a hot day. Also *fig.*, e.g. of tears. **b.** Drops of sweat.

Heater (hī·təɹ). 1500. [f. HEAT *v.* + -ER[1].] **1.** A person or thing that heats. **2.** *spec.* Any of various contrivances for imparting heat; e.g. an iron made hot, and put into a box-iron, smoothing-iron, tea-urn, etc.; a stove for heating a room, etc.; a vessel in which something is placed to be heated 1755. **3.** *attrib.*, as **h. shield,** a shield shaped like a flat-iron heater 1821.

Heath (hīþ), *sb.* [OE. *hǣþ*, corresp. to OS. *hētha*, MLG., MDu. *hēde*, MHG. *heide* (Du. *heide*, *hei*, G. *heide*), ON. *heiðr*, Goth. *haiþi* :- Gmc. **χaiþiz*.] **1.** Open uncultivated ground; a bare, more or less flat, tract of land, naturally covered with low herbage and dwarf shrubs, esp. with heath, heather, or ling. †**b.** *transf.* Part of a garden left more or less wild. BACON. **2.** A name of plants and shrubs found upon heaths or in waste places. **a.** The ordinary name for species of *Erica*, esp. *E.* (now *Calluna*) *vulgaris*, common heath, heather, or ling, *E. cinerea*, and *E. tetralix* OE. **b.** With distinctive additions, applied to other species of *Erica*, and allied genera; and pop. to some other plants 1617. **c.** In Coverdale's and later versions of *Jer.* 17:6, 48:6, applied to some desert plant, identified variously with Tamarisk, or with Savin, *Juniperus sabina*. **3.** Short for *heath butterfly, moth* 1827. **4.** *attrib.* OE.

1. On holte and hethe the merye somers daye LYDG. An uninteresting flat, with many heaths of ling A. YOUNG. **2. a.** Now would I giue a thousand furlongs of Sea, for an Acre of barren ground: Long heath [= *Erica vulgaris*], Brown firrs, anything SHAKS.

Comb.: **h.-ale, -beer,** a traditional beverage anciently brewed from the flowers of heather; **-cropper,** *lit.* one that crops or feeds on h.; a sheep or pony living on open h.; hence, a person who inhabits a h.; **-fowl** = HEATH-BIRD; **-game,** grouse or moor-fowl; **-tax,** a tax to defray the expenses of repairing the course at Newmarket; **-throstle, -thrush,** the Ring-blackbird or Ring-ouzel, *Turdus torquatus*.

b. In names of trees and plants: applied to any species which grow on heaths, as *h. bedstraw*, etc.; **h.-fern,** the Sweet Mountain Fern, *Lastrea oreopteris*; **-grass,** *Triodia decumbens*; †**-rose,** the rose of Jericho, *Anastatica hierochuntina*.

Hea·th-bell. 1804. **1.** The bell-shaped flower of the Heath; cf. HEATHER-BELL. 1808. **2.** Any bell-shaped flower growing on heaths, esp. the Blue-bell.

Hea·th-berry. OE. A name of various berries growing on heaths, esp. the Bilberry and Crowberry.

Hea·th-bird. 1683. A bird which lives on heaths; *spec.* the Black Grouse, of which the male is the HEATH-COCK and the female the HEATH-HEN.

Hea·th-cock. 1590. The male of the HEATH-BIRD or Black Grouse (*Tetrao tetrix*), the Blackcock; in N. America, the Canada grouse.

Heathen (hī·ðěn, -ð'n). [OE. *hǣþen* = OFris. *hēthin*, OS. *hēthin* (Du. *heiden*), OHG. *heidan* (G. *heide*), ON. *heiðinn*, in Goth. repr. by *haiþnō* Gentile woman (Mk. 7:26, Gr. Ἑλληνίς); gen. regarded as a specific Christian use (perh. as loose rendering of L. *paganus*, and orig. in Gothic) of Gmc. adj. **χaiþanaz*, *-*inaz* inhabiting open country, savage, repr. by the ethnic and personal names Χαιδεινοί people of W. Scandinavia (Ptolemy), OE. (*mid*) *Hǣþnum* ('Widsith' 81), ON. *Heinir* (:- *Heiðnir*), OHG. *theidanrīh*; f. **χaiþiz* HEATH; see -EN[4].]

A. *adj.* **1.** Applied to persons or races whose religion is neither Christian, Jewish, nor Moslem; pagan; Gentile. In earlier times applied also to Moslems; now mostly restricted to those holding polytheistic beliefs. **2.** Pertaining to such persons or races, or to their religion and customs OE. Also *transf.*

1. The h. priests SWIFT, Soldan SCOTT. **2.** In al places crysten and hethen CAXTON. *transf.* Bishops of Durham and naked h. colliers EMERSON.

B. *sb.* (or *adj.* used *subst.*) **1.** One who holds a religious belief which is neither

Christian, Jewish, nor Moslem; a pagan OE. (The adj. pl., *the heathen*, is now collective; in O.T. = the Gentiles; the sb. pl. *heathens* is mostly individual.) **2.** *transf.* One who is no better than a heathen 1818.

1. I was sorry to find more mercy in an h. than in a brother Christian SWIFT. **2.** Puir frightened heathens that they are SCOTT.

Heathendom (hī·ðĕndəm). [OE. *hǣþendōm*, OHG. *heidentuom*, ON. *heiðindómr*; see prec., -DOM.] **1.** = HEATHENISM. **2.** The domain or realm of the heathen; the heathen world 1860.

Heathenesse (hī·ðĕne:s). *arch.* [OE. *hǣðennes, -nys*; see HEATHEN and -NESS.] **1.** Heathenism. **2.** = HEATHENDOM 2. ME.

Heathenish (hī·ðĕniʃ), *a.* [OE. *hǣþenisć*, OHG. *heidanisc*, ON. *heiðneskr*. In mod. use prob. a new formation; see HEATHEN, -ISH[1].] **1.** Of or pertaining to the heathen (now *rare*). †**2.** = HEATHEN *a.* 1. –1718. **3.** *transf.* and *fig.* **a.** Heathen-like; unworthy of a Christian. **b.** *colloq.* Abominable, 'beastly' 1593.

1. The h. temples 1774. **2.** The h. philosopher Plutarch 1652. **3.** Most H., and most grosse SHAKS. Hence **Hea·thenish-ly** *adv.*, **-ness.**

Heathenism (hī·ðĕniz'm). 1605. [f. HEATHEN + -ISM.] **1.** Heathen practice or belief; paganism. Also with *a* and *pl.* **2.** *transf.* Unchristian state of things; unchristian degradation or barbarism 1742.

2. The practical h. of our great cities 1898.

Hea·thenize, *v.* 1681. [f. as prec. + -IZE.] **1.** *trans.* To render heathen or heathenish. **2.** *intr.* To become heathen or heathenish 1769.

Hea·thenly, *adv.* ME. [f. as prec. + -LY[2].] After the manner of the heathen; barbarously.

Heathenness, var. HEATHENESSE.

Heathenry (hī·ðĕnri). 1577. [f. as prec. + -RY.] **1.** Heathen belief, practice, custom, character, or quality; heathenism. **2.** Heathen people. R. F. BURTON.

1. In conuerting the Iland from heathenrie to christianitie 1577.

Heather (he·ðəɹ). ME. [Sc. and north. *hathir, haddyr, hadder, hedder*; the form *hadder* or *hather* (now north. dial.) prevailed in Eng. use from XVI to XVII, where *heather* is first recorded; of unkn. origin, perh. repr. earlier **hǣddre*; the present literary form appears to be due to assim. to *heath.*] **1.** The Scotch name, now in general use, for the native species of *Erica*, called in the north of England LING; esp. *E.* (now *Calluna*) *vulgaris*, Common H., and *E. cinerea*, Fine-leaved Heath or Lesser Bell-h. Also *transf.* **2.** *attrib.* Of, pertaining to, consisting of, or made from heather, as *h.-ale*, etc.; of the colour or appearance of heather, as *h.-mixture*, etc. 1819.

1. In the Northerne..places of this Island.. They dry their malt with ling, or heath, called there hadder 1633. Phr. *To set the h. on fire*: to make a disturbance. *To take to the h.*: to become an outlaw.

Comb.: **h.-cat,** a cat living wild among the h.; hence *fig.* of a person; **-grass** = *heath-grass, Triodia decumbens*; **-owl,** the Short-eared Owl, *Asio accipitrinus*.

Heather-bell. 1725. A name of: **a.** *Erica tetralix* (or its blossom); **b.** *E. cinerea.*

Hea·ther-blea:t(er. *Sc.* [Perversion, after *heather*, of the OE. name *hæfer-blǣte* goat-bleater.] A snipe.

Heathery (he·ðəri), *a.* 1535. [f. HEATHER + -Y[1].] Covered with or abounding in heather; of the nature of heather.

Hea·th-hen. 1591. The female of the HEATH-COCK; applied in N. America to species of grouse.

Heath-pea (hī·þpī). Also †**-pease.** 1633. A tuberous-rooted leguminous plant, *Lathyrus macrorrhizus* (*Orobus tuberosus*), also called *Carmele*.

Heathy (hī·þi), *a.* 1450. [f. HEATH + -Y[1].] Abounding in or covered with heath; of the nature of heath; heathery.

Heating (hī·tiŋ), *vbl. sb.* ME. [f. HEAT *v.* + -ING[1].] The action of HEAT *v.*; imparting of heat or warmth; becoming hot; *techn.* 'getting the steel hot for rolling'.

Hea·ting, *ppl. a.* 1591. [f. as prec. + -ING[2].] That heats or makes hot; making the blood too 'hot', as *h. diet.*

Heating surface, the total surface of a steam boiler, exposed on one side to the fire, on the other to water; the fire-surface. Hence **Hea·ting-ly** *adv.*

Hea·tless, *a. rare.* 1596. [f. HEAT *sb.* + -LESS.] Destitute of heat.

Heat-spot. 1822. **a.** A freckle. **b.** *Physiol.* A spot or point of the skin at which heat can be produced.

Heat-wave. 1878. **a.** A wave of radiant heat; one of those vibrations of ether that produce heating effects. **b.** A wave or access of excessive heat in the atmosphere, esp. when regarded as passing from one place to another.

Heau·me (hōᵘm). *Obs.* or *arch.* 1572. [– Fr. *heaume*; see HELM *sb.*[1]] A massive helmet, reaching down to the shoulders.

Heauto- (hi̯ǫto), bef. vowel **heaut-,** comb. f. Gr. ἑαυτοῦ of oneself, used occas. for AUTO-: as **Heau:tomo·rphism** [Gr. μορφή], ascription of one's own characteristics to another.

Heave (hīv), *v.* Pa. t. and pple. **heaved** (hīvd), **hove** (hōᵘv). [OE. *hebban* = OFris. *heva*, OS. *hebbian* (Du. *heffen*), OHG. *heffen* (G. *heben*), ON. *hefja*, Goth. *hafjan* :– Gmc. **χabjan*, rel to L. *capere* take.]

I. *trans.* **1.** To lift, raise, bear up. (Often with *up.*) In mod. use: To raise with effort or force; to hoist 1715. Also *absol.* **2.** *transf.* and *fig.* To raise OE.; †to exalt; to extol –1641. †**3.** *spec.* To lift (a child) from the font; to stand sponsor to; hence *transf.* to baptize, christen –1571. †**4.** To lift and take away, carry off, remove –1649. †**b.** *Thieves' Cant.* To 'lift', to rob –1700. **c.** *Mining* and *Geol.* To move away or displace (a vein or stratum): said of another intersecting it 1728. **5.** To cause to swell up or bulge out 1573. **6.** To cause to rise in repeated efforts 1612. **7.** To utter (a groan, sigh, sob; *rarely*, words) with effort; to fetch 1600. **8.** To throw, cast, fling, toss, hurl (esp. with effort). Now only *Naut.* and *colloq.* 1592. **9.** *Naut.* To haul up or raise by means of a rope; to haul, pull, draw with a rope or cable; to haul a cable; to weigh (anchor); to unfurl (a flag or sail; also, *to h. out*); to cause (a ship) to move in some direction, as by hauling at a rope. Also *absol.* 1626.

1. How could I once look up, or h. the head MILT. To h. a boat into a sloop SMEATON. **2.** For the prevention of growing schisme the Bishop was heav'd above the Presbyter MILT. **6.** The water was observed..to be heaved up and agitated 1832. **7.** The wretched annimall heau'd forth such grones SHAKS. **8.** The Pirats had heaued me ouer boord GREENE. **9.** We heau'd home our Anker 1633. *Heaving astern*, causing a ship to go backwards, by heaving on a cable fastened to some fixed point behind her.

II. *intr.* **1.** To rise, mount, come up, spring up. *Obs.* exc. in spec. uses. ME. **2.** To swell up, bulge out 1629. **3.** To rise with alternate falling, as waves, etc. Also *fig.* 1618. **4.** To draw in the breath with effort; to pant, gasp 1678. **5.** To make an effort to vomit; to retch; also *fig.* 1601. †**6.** To make an effort to lift or move something; to push or press with force; to endeavour, labour, strive –1742. **7.** To pull or haul (*at* a rope, etc.); to push (*at* the capstan so as to haul in the cable); to move the ship in some direction by such means; of the ship, to move or turn in some direction 1626.

1. Phr. *H. and set*: to rise and fall, as a floating object upon the waves. **2.** Their Petticoats, which began to h. and swell before you left us ADDISON. **3.** When heaved the long and sullen sea 1827. **4.** He heaves for Breath DRYDEN. **5.** (*trans.*) To heaue the gorge SHAKS. **6.** Phr. †*H. at*: to aim at, strive after. †*H. at* (*fig.*): to meditate or threaten an attack upon; to oppose; to aim at with hostile intent. His adversaries heaved at him, to cast him out of his Bishoprick FULLER. **7.** Phr. *Heaving ahead*, is the act of advancing or drawing a ship forward by heaving on a cable or rope made fast to some fixed point before her SMYTH.

Phrases. *To h. a-peak*: to bring (a ship) into the position in which the cable hangs perpendicularly between the hawse and the anchor; see A-PEAK. *To h.* (the ship) *in stays*: to bring her head to the wind in tacking; also *intr.* of the ship. *To h. short*: to h. in on the cable until the vessel is nearly over her anchor. *To h. taut*: to h. at the capstan until the cable is taut. *H. down*: to turn (a ship) over on one side by means of purchases attached to the masts; to careen. (Also *intr.* of the ship.) *H. to*: to bring the ship to a standstill by setting the sails so as to counteract each other; to make her lie to. *H. in sight*: to rise into view, become visible; hence (*colloq.*) *transf.* in general sense.

Heave (hīv), *sb.* 1571. [f. prec. vb.] **1.** An act of heaving, in various senses (see quots.). **2.** *Mining* and *Geol.* A horizontal displacement or dislocation of a vein or stratum, at a fault 1801. **3.** *pl.* A disease of horses, broken wind 1828.

1. When his heaves renew..his heart panteth JEWEL. Divers heaves were made at the Duke of Lauderdale NORTH. *Heave*..3. Effort to vomit JOHNSON. The h. of the sea 1834. A h. of surprise STEVENSON.

Heave ho, *interj.* and *sb.* ME. [app. HEAVE (imper.), with HO *int.*] A cry of sailors in heaving the anchor up, etc.; also, the burden of a song. Also as *vb.* (with *vbl. sb.*)

Heaven (he·v'n), *sb.* [OE. *heofon*, earlier *hefen, heben*, corresp. to OS. *heban*, ON. *himinn* (inflected stem *hifn-* :– **hibn-*), Goth. *himins*; parallel formations with *l*-suffix are OFris. *himul*, OS., OHG. *himil* (Du. *hemel*, G. *himmel*); ult. origin unkn.] **1.** The expanse in which the sun, moon, and stars are seen, which resembles a vast vault or canopy overarching the earth, on the 'face' or surface of which the clouds seem to float. Since 17th c. chiefly *poet.* in the sing. **b.** The pl. *heavens* was formerly used, esp. in O.T., in the same sense as the sing.; it is now the prose form for the visible sky. Hence *maps of the heavens*, etc. OE. **2.** = Climate 1581. **3.** The 'realm' or region of space beyond the clouds, of which the visible sky is poetically viewed as the 'floor' OE. †Also *transf.* **b.** In *pl.*: occas. = the regions of space in which the heavenly bodies move 1678. **4.** Each of the 'spheres' or spherical shells, lying above or outside of each other, into which the realms of space outside the earth were formerly divided. Their number varied from seven to eleven. ME. **5.** The celestial abode of immortal beings; the habitation of God and his angels, and of beatified spirits; the state of the blessed hereafter. Opp. to *hell*. OE. Also in *pl.* **b.** By the Jews seven heavens were recognized; the highest, the 'heaven of heavens', being the abode of God and the most exalted angels. Thence also the seven heavens of Mohammed. OE. **c.** The seat of the celestial deities of heathen mythology ME. **6.** The power or majesty of heaven; Providence, God. (With capital H.) OE. Also in *pl.* The gods; God 1579. **b.** In asseverations and exclams. ME. **7.** *fig.* **a.** A place of supreme bliss ME. **b.** A state of bliss ME. **8.** *transf.* [from 1]. The covering over an Elizabethan stage. [Fr. *ciel*, G. *himmel.*] 1611. **9. a.** simple attrib.: 'of heaven', etc. OE.; *h.-bliss* ME. –1583. **b.** objective, as *h.-kissing* SHAKS. **c.** advb. 'to or towards heaven', etc. 1591.

1. All that is vnder the heauen COVERDALE *Eccles.* 3:1 Heaven's high canopy, that covers all DRYDEN. Trees, As high As h. TENNYSON. **b.** The heauens shal geue their dew COVERDALE *Zech.* 8:12. **2.** Flowers of all heavens..Grew side by side TENNYSON. **3.** Looke how the floore of heauen Is thicke inlayed with pattens of bright gold SHAKS. **b.** Far above the starry heavens CUDWORTH. **4.** Deepening thro' the silent spheres H. over H. rose the night TENNYSON. *fig. Hen. V*, Prol. 2. **5.** H. lies about us in our infancy WORDSW. *pl.* Wee haue a great high Priest, that is passed into the heauens *Heb.*4:14. **b.** The heauen and heauen of heauens cannot conteine Thee 1 *Kings* 8:27. **6.** The will And high permission of all-ruling H. MILT. **b.** By heav'n the story's true ADDISON. Gracious H.! who are you? 1801. Heavens..what an idea 1819. **7.** I follow thee, and make a heauen of hell SHAKS. **b.** O what a h. is loue! O what a hell MIDDLETON & DEKKER. In the *seventh h.* [cf. 4] of delight RITA. **9. a.** Ere the Tower Obstruct Heav'n Towrs MILT. **b.** This h.-aspiring tower HAWTHORNE.

Hea·ven, *v.* 1627. [f. prec. sb.] *trans.* To make heavenly in character; also, to bless with heaven, beatify.

Hea·ven-born, *a.* 1595. **1.** Of celestial birth. **2.** Specially prepared or designed by Heaven for the work. Now often *sarcastic*. 1789.

1. The Heaven-born child MILT. **2.** A heaven-born teacher SCOTT; heaven-born amateur 1858.

Heaven-gate. ME. The gate or portal of heaven.

Heaven-high, *a.* and *adv.* OE. As high as heaven.

†**Hea·venish,** *a,* ME. [f. HEAVEN *sb.* + -ISH¹.] Of or pertaining to heaven –1577. Hence †**Hea·venishly** *adv.* CHAUCER.

Heav·enize, *v.* [f. as prec. + -IZE.] To render heavenly. BP. HALL.

Hea·venlike. 1548. [f. as prec. + -LIKE.] **1.** *adj.* Heavenly. **2.** *adv.* After the manner of heaven. SWINBURNE.

Heavenly (he·v'nli), *a.* (*sb.*) [OE. *heofonlić*, f. as prec. + -LY¹.] **1.** Of, in, or belonging to heaven; celestial. **2.** Of or belonging to the natural heaven or sky; as *h. bodies*, i.e. the stars, planets, comets, etc. Formerly also, Coming from the clouds or atmosphere; as *h. dew*. ME. **3.** Having relation to heaven and divine things; divine ME. **4.** Of more than earthly excellence; 'divine' 1425. **5.** *absol.* in pl. *The heavenlies*: tr. Gr. (ἐν) τοῖς ἐπουρανίοις (Eph. 1:3, 3:10), variously translated '(in) heavenly places' or 'things' 1844.

1. A showr of heauenly bread BIBLE *Transl. Pref.* **3.** A breaking..Of heauenly oaths SHAKS. **4.** The h. Rosaline SHAKS. A H. Voice STEELE, day 1779. Hence **Hea·venliness,** h. state or quality.

Hea·venly, *adv.* [OE. *heofonliće*, f. as prec. + -LY².] **1.** From or by heaven; in a heavenly manner or degree. **2.** To the extent of heaven, as in *h. wide* 1674.

1. Oh she was heauenly true *Oth.* v. ii. 135. Our h.-guided soul MILT.

Hea·venly-mi:nded, *a.* 1656. Having the thoughts and affections set on things above; holy, devout. Hence **Hea:venly-mi·ndedness.**

Hea·ven-sent, *a.* 1649. Sent from heaven.

Heavenward (he·v'nwǫɹd). ME. [f. HEAVEN *sb.* + -WARD.]

A. *adv.* Towards, or in the direction of, heaven. Orig. *to heaven-ward.*

B. *adj.* Directed towards heaven 1795.

So **Hea·venwards** *adv.*

Hea·ve-o:ffering. 1530. [tr. Heb. *tᵉrūmāh* (Tindale, Exod. 25:3).] In the Levitical law: An offering which was heaved or elevated by the priest when offered; also used of other offerings.

Heaver (hī·vəɹ). 1586. [f. HEAVE *v.* + -ER¹.] **1.** A person who heaves; *spec.* a dock-labourer employed in landing goods. **2.** Something that heaves; *spec.* (*Naut.*) a bar used as a lever or purchase 1598.

Heaves, a disease of horses; see HEAVE *sb.* 3.

Heave shoulder. 1530. In the Levitical law: The shoulder of an animal heaved or elevated in sacrifice. Also *transf.* and *fig.*

Hea:vier-than-ai·r, designating a flying machine whose weight is greater than the weight of the air which it displaces 1888.

Heavily (he·vili), *adv.* [OE. *hefiglīce*, f. *hefiġ* HEAVY *a.*¹ + -LY².] **1.** In a heavy manner; with or as with weight (*lit.* and *fig.*); ponderously; burdensomely ME. **2.** With heavy movement; laboriously, sluggishly OE. **3.** With sorrow, grief, or displeasure. *Obs.* or *arch.* OE. **4.** Forcibly, violently; intensely; severely OE. **5.** To a large or heavy amount 1819.

1. A Gentleman leaning upon me, and very h. STEELE. Time hangs h. on her hands 1886. **2.** And broke off their charet wheeles, that they draue them heauily *Exod.* 14:25. **3.** Berkley.. took this refusal very h. CLARENDON. **4.** Thou shalt be heauily punished SHAKS. **5.** H. wooded 1864.

Heaviness (he·vinės). [OE. *hefiġnes*; see prec., -NESS.] The state or quality of being heavy; ponderousness; gravity; weight of impact ME.; burdensomeness OE.; †anger –1590; torpor; dullness; want of animation OE.; dejectedness of mind; †grief ME.

Heaving (hī·viŋ), *vbl. sb.* ME. [f. HEAVE *v.* + -ING¹.] The action of HEAVE *v.*, in various senses.

Comb.: **h.-line** (*Naut.*), a line, usually from 5 to 10 fathoms long, used for casting from a vessel to enable a hawser to be hauled ashore or to another vessel; **-net,** a net that is heaved or hauled up.

Hea·visome, *a.* *Obs.* or *dial.* ME. [f. HEAVY *a.* + -SOME¹.] Of heavy mood, doleful; dull.

Heavy (he·vi), *a.*¹ (*sb.*) [OE. *hefiġ* = OS. *hebig* (Du. *hevig*), OHG. *hebīg*, ON. *hǫfugr*, *hǫfigr* :– Gmc. **χabuʒa-*, **χabiʒa*, f. **χabiz* (OE. *hefe*) weight, f. **χabjan* HEAVE.]

I. 1. Of great weight; ponderous. **b.** Hence, in large quantity or amount, abundant 1728. **c.** *techn.* Possessing (non-negligible) weight 1871. **2.** Of great weight in proportion to bulk OE. **3.** Great with young. Also *fig.* 1622. **4.** Laden *with* (something) 1622. **5.** Applied to classes of goods, animals, etc. of more than a defined or usual weight 1617. Hence **b.** *transf.* Connected or concerned with the manufacture, carriage, etc. of such articles 1888. **6.** *Mil.* Carrying heavy arms or equipments: said chiefly of soldiers 1836.

1. [A coate] too heavie and hote for sommer 1592. Phr. *To lie, sit h. upon*, or *at* (chiefly *fig.*). **b.** H. harvests POPE. **2.** Platinum, the heaviest metal LOCKYER. The pasty is h. 1887. **4.** His men h. and laden with booty BACON. **5.** H. artillery 1727. Phr. *H. metal*: guns or shot of large size; hence *fig.* ability; power; also, a person or persons of great ability or power. **b.** A curate in the H. Woollen District of Yorkshire 1888. **6.** Phr. *H. order* or *h. marching order*, that of a soldier equipped and carrying, besides his arms and ammunition, complete kit and great-coat.

II. 1. Having great momentum; that falls or strikes with force ME. **2.** Of ground, a road, etc.: That clings or hangs heavily to the spade, feet, wheels, etc. Also *transf.* 1577. **3.** That weighs upon the stomach; difficult of digestion 1574.

1. A h. sea GOSSE. **2.** The h. state of the roads 1837. *transf.* H. walking THOREAU. **3.** Bacon is a coarse and h. food 1842.

III. 1. Of great import; weighty; grave. Now *rare* or *Obs.* OE. **2.** Grave, severe, profound, intense OE.

1. Trust him not in matter of heauie consequence SHAKS. **2.** H. complaints 1801, frost DICKENS.

IV. 1. Of the sky, clouds, etc.: Dark with clouds; lowering, gloomy 1583. **2.** Thick, coarse; also, massive; wanting in lightness or delicacy 1818. **3.** Having a sound like that made by a heavy object; loud and deep 1810.

2. H. features SCOTT, renaissance porch 1886, hand-writing 1898. **3.** A deep and h. bell SHELLEY.

V. 1. Ponderous and slow mentally ME. **2.** Acting or moving slowly, clumsily, or with difficulty; sluggish; unwieldy ME. **3.** Of things: Wanting in vivacity; tedious, uninteresting 1601. **4.** *Theatr.* Serious; relating to the representation of sombre or tragic parts 1826.

1. The heaviest man in the country PEPYS. **2.** His heels too h., and his head too light DRYDEN. Sleepless nights and h. days BYRON. If Time be h. on your hands TENNYSON. **3.** So h. a book SWIFT. **4.** As the h. villain at the Surrey Theatre would say HELPS.

VI. †**1.** Of persons: Oppressive; annoying; angry; violent –1703. **2.** Hard to bear; grievous, sore; distressful OE. **3.** Hard to perform; laborious, toilsome ME. **4.** Causing or occasioning sorrow ME. **5.** Oppressive to the bodily sense ME.

1. †*H. friend*: a troublesome or evil friend; an enemy. So *h. father*. **2.** Ile..endure Your heauiest Censure SHAKS. A h. calamity 1844. **4.** A heavie Christmasse GRAFTON. H. news CARLYLE. †*H. hill*: the ascent to Tyburn; the way to the gallows.

VII. 1. Weighed down with sorrow or grief; sorrowful ME. **2.** Weighed down by sleep, weariness, etc.; hence *esp.* weary from sleep, drowsy ME.

2. With eyelids h. and red HOOD.

VIII. That does what is expressed heavily, as in *a h. drinker* 1816.

Comb.: **h. drift-ice, h. ice,** that which has a great depth in proportion, and not in a state of decay; **-earth** = BARYTA; **h. pine,** the *Pinus ponderosa*; **h. swell** (*colloq.*), a man of showy and impressive appearance (with pun on sense II. 1).

B. *sb.* [the adj. used absol.] **1.** *pl. Heavies*: heavy cavalry; the Dragoon Guards. Rarely in *sing.* 1841. Also, heavy artillery. **2.** A stage wagon for the conveyance of goods. DE QUINCEY. **3.** = HEAVY WET.

Heavy (hī·vi), *a.*² 1864. [f. HEAVE *sb.* 3 + -Y¹.] Suffering from the heaves.

Heavy (he·vi), *adv.* [OE. *hefiġe* = OHG. *hefīgo, hevīgo*; f. *hefiġ* HEAVY *a.*¹] = HEAVILY. Now chiefly hyphened to pples. which it qualifies.

†**Heavy,** *v.* [OE. *hefigian* = OHG. *hevīgōn*; f. *hefiġ* HEAVY *a.*¹] To make or become heavy, in various senses –1581.

Heavy-armed (he·vi,ā̆ɹmd), *a.* 1836. Bearing heavy armour or arms.

Hea·vy-ha·nded, *a.* 1633. **1. a.** Having the hands heavy from weariness. **b.** Clumsy 1647. **2.** Full-handed 1864. **3.** Overbearing 1883.

Hea·vy-hea·ded, *a.* 1552. **1.** Having a heavy or large head 1684. **2.** Dull, stupid 1590. **3.** Drowsy 1552.

3. This heavy-headed revel..Makes us traduced SHAKS.

Hea·vy-hea·rted, *a.* ME. **1.** Having a heavy heart; sad. **2.** Caused by a heavy heart; doleful 1562.

Hea·vy-la·den, *a.* 1440. **1.** Loaded heavily. Also *fig.* **2.** Oppressed; weighed down with trouble, etc. 1611.

2. Come vnto mee all ye that labour, and are heauie laden *Matt.* 11:28. Also **h.-loaden** *Isa.* 46:1.

Heavy spar. 1789. [tr. G. *schwerspat* (Werner, 1774); see SPAR *sb.*²] The native sulphate of barium, barytes; also improp. applied to barium carbonate, etc.

Heavy-weight. 1857. A person or animal of more than the average weight; *spec.* a jockey, etc., of more than the average weight; a boxer over 12 st. 7; *transf.* a horse that carries more than the average weight. Also *fig.*

Heavy wet. *slang.* 1821. [WET *sb.*] Malt liquor.

Hebdomad, -ade (he·bdŏmæd, -eᶦd). 1545. [– late L. *hebdomas, -ad-* – Gr. ἑβδομάς, -αδ-, the number seven, period of seven days, f. ἑπτά seven; see -AD.] †**1.** The number seven; a group of seven –1837. **2.** The space of seven days, a week 1600. **3.** In some Gnostic systems, a group of seven superhuman beings; also a title of the Demiurge 1837.

Hebdomadal (hebdǫ·mădăl), *a.* (*sb.*) 1613. [– late L. *hebdomadalis*, f. *hebdomas, -ad-*; see prec., -AL¹.] †**1.** Consisting of or lasting seven days –1651; changing every week 1796. **2.** Meeting, taking place, or appearing once a week; weekly 1711.

1. H. politicians, who run away from their opinions without giving us a month's warning BURKE. **2.** *H. Council*: the representative board of the University of Oxford, which meets weekly. Hence **Hebdo·madally** *adv.*

B. *sb.* (*ellipt.*) A 'weekly' (*joc.*) 1835.

Hebdomadary (hebdǫ·mădări). ME. (*Sc.* **-dar** 1549.) [– late (eccl.) L. *hebdomadarius*, f. as prec.; see -ARY¹.]

A. *sb.* *R.C.Ch.* A member of a chapter or convent, who takes his (or her) weekly turn in the performance of the sacred offices of the Church. var. **He·bdomary, -arian.**

B. *adj.* Weekly; doing duty for a week 1625. var. †**Hebdoma·tical** *a. rare.*

‖**Hebe** (hī·bi). 1606. [– Gr. ἥβη youthful prime; the daughter of Zeus and Hera.] **1.** The goddess of youth and spring, the cup-bearer of Olympus; hence *fig.* **a.** A waitress; **b.** A woman in her early youth. **2.** *Astron.* The sixth of the asteroids 1858. **3.** *attrib.*, as *Hebe bloom*, etc. 1838.

Hebe- (hī·bi-), comb. f. Gr. ἥβη youth, also puberty, down of puberty, taken in senses **a.** Pubescence (in botanical terms), as in **Hebea·nthous** [Gr. ἄνθος] *a.*, having the corolla of the flower pubescent; etc. **b.** Puberty, as in **Hebephre·nia** [Gr. φρήν], a form of insanity incident to puberty.

Heben, Hebeny, -yf, obs. ff. EBON, EBONY.

†**He·benon, Hebon, Hebona.** 1592. In Shakespeare and Marlowe: Some substance having a poisonous juice. Variously identified with *ebon, henbane*, and Ger. *eibe, eibenbaum* the yew.

Hebetate (he·bĭteⁱt), *v.* 1574. [– *hebetat-*, pa. ppl. stem of L. *hebetare*, f. *hebes, hebet-* blunt; see -ATE³.] To make, or become, dull or inert. So **He·betant** *a.* making dull. LAMB. Hence **Hebeta·tion.**

He·betate, *a.* 1858. [– L. *hebetatus*, pa. pple. of *hebetare*; see prec., -ATE².] *Bot.* Having a dull or blunt and soft point.

Hebete (he·bīt), *a. rare.* 1743. [– L. *hebes, hebet-* blunt, dull.] Dull, stupid, obtuse.

Hebetude (he·bĭtiud). 1621. [– late L. *hebetudo*, f. as prec.; see -TUDE.] The condition or state of being blunt or dull.

Hebræan (hĭbrī·ăn). 1509. [f. L. *Hebræus*; see HEBREW and -AN.] †**1.** A Jew. BARCLAY. †**2.** A Hebrew scholar –1801. **3.** One of a school in Holland, whose system rested upon the interpretation of certain hidden truths in the Hebrew language. SCHAFF.

Hebraic (hĭbrēⁱ·ik), *a.* ME. [– Chr.L. *Hebraicus* – late Gr. Ἑβραϊκός, f. Ἑβρα- based on the Aram. form; see -IC.] Pertaining or relating to the Hebrews or to their language; Hebrew. So **Hebra·ical** *a. rare.* Hence **Hebra·ically** *adv.* in Hebrew fashion; after the manner of the Hebrews or the Hebrew language (e.g. as written from right to left or 'backwards').

Hebraism (hī·breˌiz'm). 1570. [– Fr. *hébraïsme* or mod. L. *Hebraismus* = late Gr. Ἑβραϊσμός, see HEBREW, -ISM.] **1.** A Hebrew idiom or expression. **2.** A quality or attribute of the Hebrew people; Hebrew character or nature; Judaism 1847. **b.** Applied by M. Arnold to the moral, as opp. to the intellectual, theory of life; cf. *Hellenism* 1869.

2. b. Self-conquest, self-devotion. .*obedience*, is the fundamental idea of. .the discipline to which we have attached the general name of H. M. ARNOLD.

Hebraist (hī·breˌist). 1753. [f. stem *Hebra-* in HEBRAIC; see -IST.] **1.** A Hebrew scholar. **2.** One who has the qualities of the Hebrew people 1879. **3.** A Jew of Palestine, who used the Hebrew Scriptures, as opp. to a Hellenistic Jew 1892. Hence **Hebrai·stic, -al** *a.* of or pertaining to Hebraists; marked by Hebraism; Hebraic. **Hebrai·stically** *adv.* var. †**Hebrai·cian** (in sense 1).

Hebraize (hī·breˌəiz), *v.* 1645. [– late Gr. Ἑβραΐζειν speak Hebrew, imitate Jews, f. Ἑβρα-; see HEBREW, -IZE.] **1.** *intr.* To use a Hebrew idiom or manner of speech. **b.** To follow Hebraism as an ideal. M. ARNOLD. **2.** *trans.* To make Hebrew 1816.

Hebrew (hī·bru). [ME. *ebreu* – OFr. *ebreu, ebrieu* (mod. *hébreu*) – med.L. *Ebreus*, for L. *Hebræus* – late Gr. Ἑβραῖος – Aram. *'ibray*, for Heb. *'ibrî* lit. 'one from the other side' (sc. of the river), f. *'ēber* the region on the other or opposite side, f. *'ābar* cross or pass over.]

A. *sb.* **1.** A person belonging to the Semitic tribe or nation descended from Abraham, Isaac, and Jacob; an Israelite, a Jew. (In mod. use the term avoids the associations often attaching to *Jew.*) **2.** The Semitic language spoken by the Hebrews, and in which most of the books of the O.T. were written ME. **b.** *colloq.* Unintelligible speech; cf. *Greek* 1705.

1. Thou knows't I am an Ebrew MILT.

B. *adj.* Belonging to the Hebrews; Israelitish, Jewish.

Of H. extraction 1851. A *Hebrew scholar*, one learned in H. (In the N.T. = Aramaic or Syriac.) Hence **He·brew-wise** *adv.* in H. fashion; in the manner of H. writing, from right to left, backwards. **He·brewess,** a Jewess. **He·brewism** = HEBRAISM.

Hebrician (hĭbri·ʃⁱăn). Now *rare* or *Obs.* 1542. [var. of earlier †*Hebraician* (f. HEBRAIC + -IAN); cf. †*algebrician.*] †**1.** A Hebrew –1570. **2.** A Hebrew scholar 1565.

Hebridean (hebridī·ăn, -i·diăn), *a.* and *sb.* Also **–ian.** 1600. [f. *Hebrides* + -AN, -EAN, -IAN.] Belonging to, a native of, the Hebrides, islands off the west coast of Scotland.

An oar-song used by the Hebrideans JOHNSON.

‖**Hecate** (he·kăti). ME. [– Gr. Ἑκάτη, fem. of ἕκατος far-darting, an epithet of Apollo. (Always disyllabic, like Fr. Hécate, in Shaks., exc. once.)] **1.** *Gr. myth.* A goddess, said to be of Thracian origin, daughter of Perses and Asteria; in later times identified esp. with Artemis, and thus (**b.**) with the moon; also with Persephone, and hence (**c.**) regarded as presiding over witchcraft, etc. **d.** *transf.* Hag, witch 1591. **2.** *Astr.* Name of the 100th asteroid, discovered in 1868.

1. c. Stay thy cloudy ebon chair, Wherein thou ridest with Hecat', and befriend Us thy vowed priests MILT. **d.** 1 *Hen. VI*, III. ii. 64. Hence **Hecatæ·an** *a.*

Hecatomb (he·kătǫm, -tūm), *sb.* 1592. [– L. *hecatombe* – Gr. ἑκατόμβη, f. ἑκατόν hundred + βοῦς ox.] **1.** A great public sacrifice (prop. of a hundred oxen); a large number of animals offered or set apart for sacrifice. **2.** *transf.* and *fig.* A sacrifice of many victims; *loosely*, a large number or quantity 1598.

2. Whole Hecatombes of Tribute Rhimes G. DANIEL. A h. of reputations 1713. Hence **He·catomb** *v.* to furnish with a h.

Hecatomped (hekătǫ·mpĕd), *a.* 1703. [– Gr. ἑκατόμπεδος, f. ἑκατόν + πεδ- ablaut-grade of πούς, ποδ- foot.] Measuring a hundred feet in length and breadth; a hundred feet square. So **Hecato·mpedon,** a temple of these dimensions, as the Parthenon at Athens.

Hecatontarchy (hekătǫ·ntaɹki). 1660. [– late Gr. ἑκατονταρχία post or command of a centurion, f. ἑκατοντ(α)-, comb. f. ἑκατόν hundred; see -ARCHY.] Government by a hundred rulers.

†**He·catontome.** [irreg. f. Gr. ἑκατόν hundred + τόμος tome.] A collection of 100 volumes. MILT.

†**He·cco** = HICKWALL. Drayton.

Heck (hek). Chiefly *Sc.* and *n. dial.* [north. form of *hatch* (implied in AL. *heckum* (Yorks.) 1270); see HATCH *sb.*¹ and cf. HACK *sb.*²] **1.** = HATCH *sb.*¹ 1. *n. dial.* **2.** A grating or frame of parallel bars in a river to obstruct the passage of fish, or solid bodies, without obstructing the flow of the water ME. **3.** A rack made with parallel spars to hold fodder. *Sc.* and *n. dial.* ME. **4.** A loose board placed at the back part of a cart (*local*) 1825. **5.** A 'shuttle' or sluice in a drain (*local*) 1877. **6.** A contrivance in a spinning-wheel or warping-mill, by which the yarn or thread is guided to the reel or reels 1824.

Comb.: **h.-door** (see sense 1); **-board** (see sense 4); **-box,** a box used to divide the warp threads into two alternate sets, one for each heddle or heald.

Heckle (he·k'l), *sb.* c1425. [north. and E. Anglian form of HACKLE *sb.*²] = HACKLE *sb.*² 1, 3, 4.

Heckle (he·k'l), *v.* 1325. [f. HECKLE *sb.*; cf. HACKLE *v.*², HATCHEL *v.*] **1.** *trans.* = HACKLE *v.*² **2.** To catechize severely, with a view to the discovery of weak points; *spec.* of the public questioning of parliamentary candidates 1808. Hence **He·ckler.**

‖**Hectare** (he·ktēᵊɹ, or as Fr. (h)ektā·ɹ). 1810. [Fr., irreg. f. Gr. ἑκατόν (see HECTO-) + ARE *sb.*²] In the Metric system, a superficial measure containing 100 ares, or 2·471 acres.

Hectic (he·ktik). [ME. *etik* – OFr. *etique* – late L. *hecticus* – Gr. ἑκτικός habitual, hectic, consumptive, f. ἕξις habit, state of body or mind; superseded XVI by the mod. form, – Fr. *hectique* or late L.]

A. *adj.* **1.** Belonging to or symptomatic of the bodily condition or habit: applied to that kind of fever which accompanies consumption or other wasting diseases, and is attended with flushed cheeks and a hot dry skin. **b.** Belonging to or symptomatic of this fever 1642. **c.** Affected with hectic fever 1664. **2.** *fig.* 1603. †**3.** Habitual, constitutional –1654. **4.** Stirring, exciting, disturbing (*colloq.*) 1904.

1. H. fever is more or less remittent 1807. **b.** A h. cough 1831. **c.** Young people with h. cheeks 1860. **2.** Leaves. .pale, and h. red SHELLEY. Thrill with. .h. feeling 1886.

B. *sb.* [the adj. used ellipt.] **1.** A hectic fever. Also *fig.* ME. **2.** A consumptive person 1653. **3.** A hectic flush. Also *transf.* and *fig.* 1768.

1. *fig.* Wishing, that constant h. of a fool YOUNG. **3.** One man's cheek kindled with the h. of sudden joy DE QUINCEY.

So **He·ctical** *a.* = A. Hence **He·ctically** *adv.*

Hecto-, hect-, Fr., contr. of Gr. ἑκατόν hundred, used esp. in terms of the metric system, as *hectare, hectolitre, hectometre.*

Hectocotyl, -e (hektokǫ·til). 1854. [– mod.L. *Hectocotylus* (also used), f. HECTO- + Gr. κοτύλη cup, hollow thing (cf. COTYLE).] *Zool.* A modified arm in male dibranchiate Cephalopods, which serves as a generative organ, and in some species is detached and remains in the pallial cavity of the female; in this position mistaken by Cuvier for a parasite, which he named *Hectocotylus octopodis.* Hence **Hectoco·tylize** *v. trans.*, (*a*) to convert into a h.; (*b*) to impregnate with a h. **Hectoco·tylism,** the formation of a h.

Hectogramme, -gram (he·ktogræm). 1810. [– Fr. *hectogramme*; see HECTO-, GRAMME, GRAM².] In the metric system, a weight containing 100 grammes, or 3·52 oz. avoirdupois.

Hectograph (he·ktograf), *sb.* 1880. [f. HECTO- + -GRAPH.] An apparatus for multiplying copies of writing; = CHROMOGRAPH. Also, the process of taking copies by means of this. Also as *vb.*

Hectolitre, -liter (he·ktolītəɹ). 1810. [– Fr. *hectolitre*; see HECTO-, LITRE.] In the metric system, a measure of capacity containing 100 litres, or 3·531 cubic feet, or about 2¾ bushels.

Hectometre, -meter (he·ktomītəɹ). 1810. [– Fr. *hectomètre*; see HECTO-, METRE.] In the metric system, a measure of length containing 100 metres, or 328·089 feet.

Hector (he·ktǫɹ), *sb.* ME. [L. *Hector*, Gr. Ἕκτωρ son of Priam and Hecuba, husband of Andromache, 'the prop or stay of Troy'; in origin, as adj. ἕκτωρ = holding fast, f. ἔχειν hold.] **1.** Name of a Trojan hero celebrated in the Iliad; hence *transf.* A warrior like Hector. **2.** A swaggering fellow; a swash-buckler; a blusterer, bully 1655. **3.** A species of butterfly, *Papilio hector* 1863.

2. Muns and Tityre Tus had given place to the Hectors MACAULAY. Hence **He·ctorism,** the quality or practice of a h. or bully. **He·ctorly** *a.* blustering, insolent.

Hector (he·ktǫɹ), *v.* 1660. [f. prec. sb. (sense 2).] **1.** *intr.* To play the hector or bully; to brag, bluster, domineer. **2.** *trans.* To intimidate by bluster or threats; to domineer over; to bully 1664.

1. She does now and then h. a little FOOTE. Hence **He·ctorer.**

Hectostere (he·ktostīᵊɹ, Fr. ęktostę̄r). 1864. [– Fr. *hectostère*; see HECTO-, STERE.] In the metric system, a measure of capacity containing 100 steres.

Heddle (he·d'l), *sb.* 1513. [app.:– OE. *hefedl, earlier f. *hefeld*; see HEALD.] In *pl.*, The small cords (or wires) through which the warp is passed in a loom after going through the reed, and by means of which the warp threads are separated into two sets so as to allow the passage of the shuttle bearing the weft.

Comb.: **h.-eye,** the eye or loop formed in each h. to receive a warp thread. Hence **He·ddle** *v.* to draw (warp-threads) through the eyes of a h.

†**Hede.** Also **hed.** [ME. *hede*, repr. OE. **hǣdu* (accus. *hǣde*) fem., beside *hād* masc.; see -HEAD, -HOOD.] **1.** Rank, order, condition, quality. ME. only. **2.** = mod. Eng. *-head*; see -HEAD –1585.

Heder (hī·dəɹ). *dial.* 1532. [f. HE + (perh.) DEER; cf. dial. *sheder* female sheep.] A male sheep; *spec.* one from eight or nine months old till its first shearing.

Hederaceous (hedĕrēⁱ·ʃəs), *a.* 1727. [f. L. *hederaceus* (f. *hedera* ivy) + -OUS; see -ACEOUS.] Pertaining or allied to ivy.

Hederal (he·dĕrăl), *a.* 1656. [f. L. *hedera* ivy + -AL¹.] Of or pertaining to ivy.

Hederated (he·dĕreⁱtĕd), *a.* [f. late L. *hederatus* (f. L. *hedera* ivy) + -ED¹; see

-ATE².] Adorned or crowned with ivy. FULLER.

Hederic (hĭde·rik), *a.* 1865. [f. L. *hedera* ivy + -IC.] *Chem.* Of or pertaining to ivy; as in *hederic acid.*

Hedge (hedʒ), *sb.* [OE. *heġġ*, **heċġ* = EFris. *hegge*, MDu. *hegghe* (Du. *heg*), OHG. *hegga*, *hecka* (G. *hecke*) :– Gmc. **χaʒja*, rel. to HAG *sb.*², HAW *sb.*¹, HAY *sb.*²] **1.** A row of bushes or low trees (e.g. hawthorn, or privet) planted closely to form a boundary between pieces of land or at the sides of a road. **b.** Locally or spec. applied to other fences 1850. **2.** A fishing weir of faggots or of wattle-work 1653. **3.** *transf.* Any line of objects forming a barrier, boundary, or partition 1523. **4.** *transf.* and *fig.* A barrier, limit, defence; a means of protection ME. **5.** *spec.* (*Betting.*) The act of hedging; a means of hedging; see HEDGE *v.* 6. 1736. **6.** *attrib.* **a.** 'Of or for a hedge', as *h.-shears*, etc. ME. **b.** Born, brought up, sheltering, plying their trade, etc. under hedges, or by the roadside (hence as an attribute expressing contempt), as *h.-bantling, -lawyer, -parson, -wench*, etc. 1530. **c.** Done, performed, etc. under a hedge, or clandestinely, as *h.-marriage, -press*, etc. 1667. **d.** Of mean, common, third-rate quality, as *h.-alehouse, -inn, -wine*, etc. 1594. Hence **e.** Mean, third-rate, paltry, despicable, rascally 1596.

1. *Quickset h., dead h.*: see the adjs. H. and ditch is the most common mode of fencing property FORSYTH. **3.** Hedges of police from our little street to [etc.] HT. MARTINEAU.

Phrases, etc. *To be on the right* (*better, safer*) or *wrong side of the h.*: to be in a right or wrong position. *To take a sheet off a h.*: to steal openly. *To be on the h.* = to sit on the fence.

Combs.: **h.-born** *ppl. a.*, born under a h., of low or mean birth; **-chafer,** the cockchafer; **-chanter, -chat,** the hedge-sparrow; **-green,** the green headland in a ploughed field; **-hook,** a bill-hook for trimming hedges; **-rustic,** the moth *Luperina cespitis*; **-warbler,** the hedge-sparrow.

b. In names of plants and fruits growing on hedges, as **h.-bedstraw,** the white-flowered species, *Galium mollugo*; **-bell(s, -bindweed,** the Greater Bindweed, *Convolvulus* (or *Calystegia*) *sepium*; also erron. *C. arvensis*; **-garlic,** *Sisymbrium alliaria* (*Alliaria officinalis*), also called garlic mustard, a cruciferous weed with an odour like garlic; **-mushroom,** *Agaricus arvensis*; **-mustard,** the cruciferous plant *Sisymbrium officinale*; also applied to plants of the genus *Erysimum*; **-nettle,** any labiate plant of the genus *Stachys*, esp *S. sylvatica*, also called *hedge woundwort*; **-parsley,** common name of the genus *Torilis*, esp. *T. anthriscus*; also applied to species of *Caucalis*; **-taper** = HAG-TAPER; **h. violet,** *Viola sylvatica*; **h. woundwort,** *Stachys sylvatica*.

Hedge, *v.* ME. [f. HEDGE *sb.*] **1.** *trans.* To surround with a hedge or fence as a boundary, or for purposes of defence. **2.** *intr.* or *absol.* To construct hedges or fences ME. **3.** *trans.* To arrange so as to form a barrier 1812. **4.** To surround as with a hedge or fence. Also with *in, about, around.* 1500. **b.** To hem *in*; to restrict 1549. **5.** To obstruct as with a hedge 1535. **6.** *trans.* To secure oneself against loss on (a bet, etc.) by betting, etc. on the other side. Also *fig.* 1672. Also *absol.* or *intr.* 1676. **b.** To insure against risk of loss by entering into contracts which balance one another 1909. **7.** *intr.* To go aside from the straight way; to shift, shuffle, dodge; to leave open a way of retreat or escape 1598.

1. Plauntide a vynʒerd, and heggide it aboute WYCLIF. **4.** England hedg'd in with the maine SHAKS. There's such Diuinity doth h. a King SHAKS. **5.** †*H. in*, to secure (a debt), app. by including it in a larger one which is better secured; to include within the limits of something else. **6.** I kept hedging my bets as I laid them 1813. *intr.* No man should venture to bet, who could not h. well 1819. **7.** Prophesy as much as you like, but always h. O. W. HOLMES.

He·dge-bird. 1. Any bird that lives in or frequents hedges 1884. **2.** *transf.* A vagrant; a footpad 1614.

2. Out, you rogue, you hedge-bird, you pimp B. JONS.

Hedgebote (he·dʒ,bōᵘt). 1565. [See BOOT *sb.*¹ 2.] *Law.* = HAYBOTE.

†He·dge-creeper. 1548. 'One that skulks or creeps under hedges for bad purposes' (J.); a hedge-bird; a sneaking rogue –1708. So **†He·dge-creeping** *a.* clandestine, base.

Hedgehog (he·dʒ,hǫg). 1450. [f. HEDGE *sb.* + HOG; named from its frequenting hedges and from its pig-like snout.] **1.** An insectivorous quadruped of the genus *Erinaceus*, armed with innumerable spines, and able to roll itself up into a ball with these bristling in every direction; an urchin. Also *fig.* **2.** Applied to other animals armed with spines; as, the Porcupine Ant-eater of Australia; the Tenrec of Madagascar; etc. 1598. **3.** A name for prickly seed-vessels or burs borne by plants, and for the plants which bear them, e.g. *Ranunculus arvensis, Medicago echinus*, etc. 1711. **†4.** Applied to a person who is regardless of others' feelings; often as a term of obloquy –1660. **5.** *attrib.* (or *adj.*): Of, belonging to, or resembling a hedgehog 1610.

1. The h. underneath the plantain bores TENNYSON. **4.** *Rich. III*, I. ii. 102.

Comb.: **h. cactus,** a plant of the genus *Echinocactus*, globular and spiny; **h. caterpillar** (*U.S.*), the larva of an insect, *Arctia isabella*, which is thickly covered with stiff black hairs on each end and with reddish hairs on the middle of the body; **h. fruit,** the prickly fruit of an Australian tree, *Echinocarpus australis*; **h. grass** †(*a*) a kind of sedge (*Carex flava*) having prickly fruit; (*b*) name of various grasses of which the spikelets form burs, esp. *Cenchrus tribuloides* of N. America; **h. mushroom,** an edible fungus of the genus *Hydnum*, having prickly hymenium; **h. parsley,** a name for bur-parsley, *Caucalis daucoides*; **h. rat,** rodent of the sub-family *Echinomyinæ*, the coat of which is usually harsh, or bristly, or even mixed with spines; **h. thistle** = *h. cactus.*

Hence **He·dgehoggy** *a.* difficult to get on with.

Hedge-hyssop. 1578. *Gratiola officinalis*, a scrophulariaceous plant of Central Europe, formerly noted for its medicinal properties. Applied also to similar British plants, e.g. *Scutellaria, Lythrum hyssopifolium.*

He·dgeless, *a.* 1802. [f. HEDGE *sb.* + -LESS.] Destitute of hedges.

Hedge-pig. = HEDGEHOG. *Macb.* IV. i. 2.

He·dge-priest. 1550. [See HEDGE *sb.* 6 b.] An illiterate priest of inferior status.

Hedger (he·dʒəɹ). 1515. [f. HEDGE *sb.* or *v.* + -ER¹.] **1.** One who makes, repairs, or trims hedges. **2.** One who hedges in betting, etc. 1803.

Hedgerow (he·dʒ,rōᵘ). [OE. *heġġerǣwe.*] A row of bushes forming a hedge, with the trees, etc. growing in it; a line of hedge. Also *attrib.*

attrib. By hedge-row elms, on hillocks green MILT.

He·dge-school. 1807. A school held by a hedge-side or in the open air, as formerly in Ireland; hence, a poor, low-class school. Hence **Hedge-schoo·lmaster.**

He·dge-sparrow. 1530. A common European bird, *Accentor modularis*, belonging to the *Sylviidæ* or Warblers.

Hedging (he·dʒiŋ), *vbl. sb.* ME. [-ING¹.] **1.** The action of HEDGE *v.* Also *concr.* Matter forming or made into a hedge. **2.** *attrib.*, as *h.-bill*, a bill with a long handle for cutting and trimming hedges 1497.

Hedonic (hidǫ·nik). 1656. [– Gr. ἡδονικός, f. ἡδονή pleasure; see -IC.]

A. *adj.* Of or relating to pleasure.

Mill's H. philosophy 1880.

B. *sb.* **†1.** One who maintains that pleasure is the proper end of action; applied to the Cyrenaics 1678. **2.** *pl.* **Hedonics:** The doctrine of pleasure; the part of ethics which treats of pleasure 1865.

2. Hedonics, or the science of human pleasure 1866.

Hedonism (hī·dŏniz'm). 1856. [f. Gr. ἡδονή pleasure + -ISM.] The doctrine or theory of ethics in which pleasure is regarded as the chief good, or the proper end of action.

Hedonist (hī·dŏnist). 1856. [f. as prec. + -IST.] One who maintains the doctrine of hedonism.

(*Note*) Professor Wilson coined the English word *Hedonist* DE QUINCEY. Hence **Hedoni·stic** *a.* pertaining to hedonists, or of the nature of hedonism. **Hedoni·stically** *adv.*

Heed (hīd), *v.* [OE. *hēdan* = OS. *hōdian* (Du. *hoeden*), OHG. *huoten* (G. *hüten*) :– WGmc. **χōdjan*, f. **χōda* care, keeping (OFris., MLG. *hōde*, OHG. *huota*, G. *hut*).] **†1.** *intr.* To take charge, take. OE. only. **2.** *intr.* To have a care, take notice (*arch.* and *dial.*) OE. **3.** *trans.* To care for, concern oneself about; to give attention to; to regard. (In Eng. now chiefly literary.) ME. **†4.** To observe, see, take note of. Also *intr.* To look. ME. only.

3. Not perceived, or not heeded, by other men HURD.

Heed, *sb.* ME. [f. HEED *v.*] **1.** Careful attention, observation, regard. (Now chiefly literary.) **†2.** That which one heeds. SHAKS.

1. I will..teach your eares to list me with more heede SHAKS. Phr. *To give, pay h.* (*to*). *To take* (†*nim*) *h.* **2.** *L. L. L.* I. i. 82.

Heedful (hī·dfŭl), *a.* 1548. [f. HEED *sb.* + -FUL.] Full of heed; careful, attentive, watchful, mindful. Hence **Hee·dful-ly** *adv.*, **-ness.**

Heedless (hī·dlės), *a.* 1579. [f. HEED *sb.* + -LESS.] Without heed; paying no attention; careless, regardless.

There in the ruin, h. of the dead, The shelter-seeking peasant builds his shed GOLDSM. Hence **Hee·dless-ly** *adv.*, **-ness.**

†Heedy, *a.* 1548. [f. HEED *sb.* + -Y¹.] Heedful, careful, cautious –1645. Hence **†Hee·dily** *adv.* **†Hee·diness.**

Hee-haw (hī·hǭ:), *sb.* 1815. [imit.] **1.** An imitation of the bray of a jackass; a name for this. **2.** A loud coarse laugh 1843. Hence **Hee-haw** *v. intr.* to bray, as an ass.

Heel (hīl), *sb.*¹ [OE. *hēla, hǣla*, corresp. to OFris. *hēla*, MDu. *hiele* (Du. *hiel*), ON. *hæll* :– Gmc. **χāχil-* :– **χaŋχil-*, f. **χaŋχ-* (whence OE. *hōh* heel; see HOUGH).] **1.** In man, the hinder part of the foot; the spurred heel, the spur ME.; the whole foot ME. **2.** The analogous part. **a.** In quadrupeds: the hinder part of the hoof 1674; the hind feet OE.; the hoof OE. **b.** In birds: the spur 1611. **c.** In insects (*rec.*). **3.** Pregnant uses: **a.** *To raise* or *lift the h. against, to make a h.*: to kick OE. **b.** *To set the h. on*: to trample down 1601. **c.** *To have* or *get the heels of*: to outrun 1523. **4.** A stocking or shoe heel 1577. **5.** A part of a thing resembling the human heel in position or shape, esp. *the heel of Italy* 1717; the h. of a golf-club, a ship, a rudder, a mast, a gate, a gun-stock, etc.; a cyma reversa. Also, the bottom (or top) crust of a loaf; the rind of a cheese ME. **6.** The end-part of a period; of a book, etc.; *Astrol.*, of a zodiacal sign 1584.

1. His stockings are about his Heels BUDGELL. Then ply'd, With iron h., his courser's side BUTLER. Fauns with cloven h. MILTON. *Two for his heels*, in *Cribbage* (opp. to *One for his nob*) = two points for turning up a knave. **2. a.** [Horses] fighting with heels and mouth 1658. **b.** A cock which hath a dull h. MARKHAM. **3.** He that etith my breed, schal reyse his heele aʒens me WYCLIF. Friday..had..the heels of the bear DE FOE. **4.** *Mod.* She wears high heels. Slippers have no heels. **5.** The h. of a Dutch cheese DICKENS. **6.** The corps..in a close pursuit at the h. of the day, lost many men WELLINGTON.

Phrases.

At, on, upon, †in (one's) **heel(s.** Close behind ME. Also *fig.* **Down at heel** (*adv.* and *adj.*). **a.** In destitution: cf. next. **b.** Of shoes, etc.; and *fig.* slovenly 1732. **Out at heels** (*adv.* and *adj.*). With shoe or stocking heels worn through 1553; *fig.* in decayed circumstances. **To heel.** Of a dog: close behind; under rule. Also *fig.* **Heel and toe. a.** *adv.* Walking fairly, not running; also as *adj.* and *sb.* (*mod.*). **b.** Of dancing (also *heel over toe*). **Heels over head.** Upside down ME.; *to turn heels over head*, to turn a somersault. Also *attrib.* So (*Sc.*) *heels over gowdy.* **Kick** one's **heels.** To wait idly or impatiently 1760. Cf. *to cool one's heels*, COOL *v.* **Lay, set, clap by the heels.** To put in the stocks; to arrest; *fig.* to overthrow 1510. So *to have by the h.*; *to lie* or *be tied by the h.* **Take** to one's **heels.** To run away 1542. **Trip** (*kick, strike, throw*) **up** a person's **heels.** To trip (him) up 1600; also *fig.* **Turn on** (*upon*) one's **heel.** To turn sharply round 1757. **Turn** (*kick, tumble*) **up** a person's **heels.** To knock (him) down; to kill 1500. So *to turn* (*kick, lay, tip, topple*) *up one's heels*, to die. Also **†a.** *To run* or *hunt heel, take it heel*, to run back on the scent, hunt counter 1674. **b.** *With the heels foremost* or *forward*, as a corpse is carried 1670.

Combs.

1. General: as *h.-leather, -sliding, -hurt* and the like. **2.** Special: **a.** in *Shoemaking*, as **h.-blank,** a set of 'lifts' built up into a heel; **-block,** a block used in heeling a shoe; **-cutter; -fastener;**

-iron = HEEL-PLATE; **-lift,** one thickness of material in a shoe heel; **-maker; -quarters,** the counter; **-seat,** the part to which the heel is attached; **-shave,** a tool for shaping the heel; **-tip** = HEEL-PLATE; **-trimmer. b.** *Naut.* (see sense 5), as **h.-brace,** a piece of iron-work to brace the lower part of a rudder; **-chain,** a chain for holding out the jib-boom; **-jigger,** a light tackle fastened to the heel of a spar; **-knee,** the knee that joins the keel and the stern-post. **c.** Other uses: **h.-cap,** a cap for the heel of a shoe or stocking; whence **-cap** *v. trans.*; **-dog,** esp. a retriever; **-fly,** a fly, *Hypoderma lineata,* that attacks the heels of cattle; **-pad,** a pad in a boot heel; **-ring,** the ring securing the blade of a plough, or scythe; **-string,** the *Tendo Achillis*; **-tool,** a tool used by turners for roughing out iron; **-tree,** the swingle-tree of a harrow; **-way** *adv.*, backward on the scent; **-wedge,** (*a*) a wedge to fasten the coulter, (*b*) a wedge to tighten the heel-ring of a scythe.

Heel (hīl), *sb.*[2] 1698. [A later form of HIELD, after HEEL *v.*[2]] *Naut.* Inclination of a ship to one side.

Heel (hīl), *v.*[1] 1605. [f. HEEL *sb.*[1]] **1.** *intr.* To move the heel rhythmically in dancing; also *trans.* Also *to h. it.* 1606. **2.** *trans.* To add a heel to 1605; esp. to arm (a game-cock) with a spur 1755; hence (*U.S. slang*), to furnish (a person) with something, esp. with a revolver 1755. **3.** To catch by the heel (*nonce-use*); to fasten by the heels 1638. **4.** To follow at the heels of; also *absol.* 18.. **5. a.** *Football.* (*intr.* or *absol.*) To pass the ball *out* with the heels (*mod.*). **b.** *Golf.* To strike (the ball) with the heel of the club 1857. **6.** *Ship-building.* To rest with the heel *on* something 1850.

1. I cannot sing, Nor heele the high Lauolt SHAKS. **4.** *absol.* See that he [the collie] heels properly 18.. **5. a.** Oxford..heeled out quickly 1893.

Heel (hīl), *v.*[2] 1575. [prob. evolved from †*heeld* HIELD, through apprehending final *d* as a pa. ppl. suffix.] Chiefly *Naut.* **1.** *intr.* Of a ship, etc.: To lean to one side. Also *fig.* 1575. **2.** *trans.* To lay (a ship) on her side. Also *absol.* 1667.

1. Eight hundred of the brave..Had made the vessel h. COWPER. Phr. *Heeling error*: the error of the compass caused by the heeling of the vessel. **2.** The Dutch did heele 'the Charles' to get her down PEPYS.

Hee·l-ball, *sb.* 1822. A ball of wax and lamp-black, used **a.** for polishing the sole-edges of new shoes; **b.** for taking rubbings of brasses, etc. Hence **Heel-ball** *v. trans.*

Hee·l-bone. 1598. The bone of the heel; the *calcaneum*.

Heeled (hīld), *ppl. a.* 1562. [f. HEEL *sb.*[1], *v.*[1] + -ED.] **1.** Having a heel; esp. in comb., as *high-heeled.* **2.** Provided; esp. with a revolver (*U.S. slang*) 1883. **3.** *Golf.* Struck or made with the heel of a club 1890.

Heeler (hī·ləɹ). 1638. [f. as prec. + -ER[1].] **1.** One who puts heels on 1665. **2.** A cock that uses his heels 1688. **3.** A supplanter (see HEEL *v.*[1] 3) 1638. **4.** A disreputable follower of a political 'boss'. *U.S.* 1877.

Hee·ling, *vbl. sb.* 1591. [f. HEEL *v.*[1] + -ING[1].] **1.** The action of HEEL *v.*[1] 1859. **2.** *concr.* The heel of a stocking 1591, of a mast or spar 1794.

Hee·lless, *a.* 1841. [f. HEEL *sb.*[1] + -LESS.] Having no heel.

Hee·l-piece, *sb.* 1709. **1. a.** The piece forming, or added to, the heel of a shoe. **b.** Armour for the heel 1828. **c.** The heel of a mast, etc. 1794. **2.** *fig.* The end-piece of a book or play 1761. Hence **Heel-piece** *v. trans.* to put a heel-piece on.

Heel-plate. 1847. A plate on the butt-end of a gun-stock, or the heel of a shoe.

Heel-post. 1846. **a.** The post to which a door or gate is hung 1875. **b.** *Ship-building.* The post supporting the outer end of a propeller shaft 1864. **c.** The outer post which supports a stall-partition in a stable 1846.

Heel-rope, *sb.* 1794. A rope attached to the heel of anything, e.g. of a spar or rudder, or to the heels of a horse. Hence **Heel-rope** *v.*

Hee·l-tap, *sb.* 1688. **1.** A thickness or 'lift' of leather, etc. in a shoe-heel. **2.** The liquor left at the bottom of a glass after drinking 1780. Also *fig.*

1. Ivory heel-taps 1850. **2.** 'Toss it off, don't leave any heeltap' DICKENS. *Heel-tap glass* (attrib.): one without shank or foot.

Heel-way. Longfellow's erron. rendering of *hele-wages*; see HELEWOU.

Heep, obs. f. HIP.

Heer (hīᵊɹ). *Sc.* 1777. [Of unkn. origin.] A measure of yarn; = 2 cuts.

Heer, obs. f. HAIR.

Heeze, heize (hīz), *v. Sc.* and *north.* 1513. [orig. identical with *hysse, hyse, hyce,* early forms of HOISE *v.*] *trans.* To hoist. Also *fig.* Hence **Heeze, heize** *sb.*, also **Hee·zy,** a lift.

Heft (heft), *sb.* 1555. [prob. analogically f. HEAVE *v.*, after *cleave, cleft, weave, weft,* etc.] **1.** Weight (*dial.* and *U.S.*). **2.** The bulk (*U.S. colloq.*) 1816. **3.** †A strain; a heaving effort (SHAKS.); a lift (*dial.*) 1881.

1. *A dead h.*: a weight that cannot be moved (*local*). **2.** The h. of it [the crop] was bad 1816. **3.** He cracks his gorge, his sides, With violent Hefts SHAKS.

Heft, *v. dial.* and *U.S.* 1661. [f. HEFT *sb.*] **1.** To lift, lift up. **2.** To lift to judge the weight 1816. **3.** *intr.* To weigh 1851.

Hefty, *a.* 1867. [f. HEFT *sb.* + -Y[1].] Weighty, heavy (*dial.*); big and strong (*colloq.*).

Hegelian (higī·liăn, hegē·liăn). 1838. [f. G. W. F. *Hegel* (1770–1831) + -IAN.] **A.** *adj.* Pertaining to Hegel or his philosophy.

B. *sb.* A follower of Hegel 1860.

Hence **Hege·lianism,** also **He·gelism,** the H. system. **Hege·lianize** *v. trans.* to render H. So **He·gelize** *v. intr.* to do like Hegel.

Hegemonic (hedʒĭmǫ·nik, hīg-). 1656. [– Gr. ἡγεμονικός capable of command, f. ἡγεμών leader, chief; see -IC.] **1.** *adj.* Ruling. **2.** *sb.* The ruling part, the master-principle 1678. So **Hegemo·nical** *a.*

Hegemony (hĭdʒe·mŏni, he·dʒĭməni, hī·-; or *with* g *hard.*) 1567. [– Gr. ἡγεμονία, f. ἡγεμών leader, f. ἡγεῖσθαι lead; see -MONY.] Leadership, predominance of one state of a confederacy, *orig.* in ancient Greece, whence *transf.*

The headship, or h., was in the hands of Athens GROTE.

‖**Hegira, hejira** (he·dʒĭră, *erron.* hĭdʒəi·ră). 1590. [– med.L. *hegira* – Arab. *hijra* departure from one's country and one's friends, f. *hajara* separate, go away.] **1.** The flight of Mohammed from Mecca to Medina in A.D. 622; hence, the Mohammedan era, which is reckoned from that date. **2.** *transf.* Any exodus 1753.

1. The 38th year of the Hejira 1800. **2.** The London hegira H. WALPOLE. Hence **Hegiric, hejiric** *a.*

Hegumen (hĭgiū·mĕn). 1591. [– late L. *hegumenus* – Gr. ἡγούμενος, subst. use of pres. pple. of ἡγεῖσθαι lead, command.] In the Gr. Ch.: The head of a religious community; *spec.* = abbot; also, prior.

Heh (hē), *interj.* Also **hegh** (DE FOE). 1475. [Cf. Fr. *hé,* and see HEIGH, HEY.] An exclam. used to express sorrow or surprise, or to attract attention.

Heifer (he·fəɹ). [OE. *heahfore, heahfru, -fre,* of unkn. origin.] A young cow that has not had a calf; *fig.* wife.

To plough with one's h. (see *Judges* 14:18). Hence **Hei·ferhood,** the state or age of a h.

Heigh (hēⁱ, hē), *interj.* (*sb.*) 1573. [Later sp. of ME. HE (XIII), HEH (XV); cf. (O)Fr. *hé.*] **1.** A call of encouragement 1599; an expression of inquiry 1848. **2.** *sb.* A name for the exclam. 1573.

1. H. my hearts, cheerely, cheerely my harts SHAKS. **2.** With friskes, and heighs 1595.

Heigh-ho (hēⁱ·ho), *interj.* (*sb., v.*) 1553. [f. prec. + HO.] **1.** An exclam. to express yawning, sighing, languor, weariness, disappointment. **2.** *sb.* An utterance of *heigh-ho!*; an audible sigh 1600. **3.** *vb.* To utter *heigh-ho!* 1824.

1. Heigh ho for a husband SHAKS.

Height (həit), *sb.* [OE. *hēhþu,* (WS. *hīehþu*) = MDu. *hogede, hoochte* (Du. *hoogte*), OHG. *hōhida,* Goth. *hauhiþa* :– Gmc. **xauxiþō*; see HIGH *a.*, -TH[1]. For dissimilation of *-hþ* (*-ʒþ*) to *-ht* see -T[2]. For the development of *ē* to *ī* see HIGH *a.*]

I. 1. Measurement from the base upwards; stature; elevation above a recognized level (e.g. the sea). Also *fig.* (see Eph. 3:18.) ME. **2.** Great comparative altitude ME. **3.** = ALTITUDE 4. 1551. †**4.** *Geog.* = LATITUDE (cf. *high latitude*) –1694; position (at sea) = alongside of, and, hence, *off* some place –1753. †**5.** High pitch (of a note, etc.) –1697. †**6.** High rank, estate, etc. –1718. **7.** High degree of a quality (*arch.*) 1601. **8.** †Haughtiness; *hauteur.* Orig. *Sc.* Also, magnanimity (*arch.*). 1450.

1. Fiftene [elne] on..heit ME. About my height SHAKS. *fig.* The highth..of thy Eternal wayes MILT. **2.** Bodies..named of their height *Meteors* 1563. **3.** A Table of the sonnes height 1559. **4.** Spain lyeth..in the same h. and parallel with the Azores Islands 1622. **6.** Exceeded by the hight of happier men SHAKS. **7.** To such a heighth is licentiousness risen 1762. **8.** A very resolute answer, and full of height CROMWELL. Something of the old Roman height LAMB.

II. Semi-concrete senses. **1.** A high point 1563. **2.** The top *of* anything OE. **3.** The utmost degree (of something immaterial) OE.

1. From what highth fal'n MILT. **2.** From heav'ns highth MILT. *fig.* Scipio the highth of Rome MILT. **3.** Ceasing to be the H. of Folly, it became the H. of Wickedness 1718.

III. Concrete senses. †**1.** The heavens –1615. **2.** An eminence ME. **3.** *Her.* (See quot.)

1. So is God in the height, and in the earth 1615. **2.** The Heights of Abraham close to Quebec 1887. **3.** *A plume of feathers* strictly consists of three..If there be more rows than one they are termed *heights* 1847.

Phrases.

At..height. *At the h.* (arch.), †*At h.*: at the highest point. Now usu. *at its h.* †**In..height.** *In h.*: on high. *In the h.*: in the highest degree. *In h., in the* (*its,* etc.) *h.* = *At height, at the height.* †**On** or **upon height: a.** Aloft. **b.** Aloud. **To the height.** *arch.* To the utmost.

Height, *v. Obs.* or *arch.* 1495. [f. HEIGHT *sb.*] **1.** To heighten, raise on high (*arch.*) 1515. **2.** To raise in amount, quality, etc. (*arch.*) 1528. Hence **Heighting** *vbl. sb.*, increase.

Heighted (həi·tĕd), *a.* 1892. [f. HEIGHT *sb.* + -ED[2].] Having a (certain) height.

Heighten (həi·t'n), *v.* 1523. [f. HEIGHT *sb.* or *v.* + -EN[5].] **1.** *trans.* To make high or higher 1530. **2.** To make high or higher in amount or degree 1523; to augment in description 1731. **3.** *spec.* To render (a colour) more luminous, or, *occas.*, more intense 1622. †**4.** To elate, excite –1692. **5.** *intr.* To become high or higher 1567; to rise in amount or degree 1803.

2. To h. the price ADAM SMITH, the flavour 1853. **4.** Satiate at length, And hight'nd as with Wine MILT. **5.** The Rock seemed to h. marvellously J. H. NEWMAN. Hence **Hei·ghtened** *ppl. a.*; *spec.* in *Her.* having another charge placed higher in the field. **Hei·ghtener.**

†**Heild,** *v. Sc.* 1508. Var. of HELE cover.

†**Heily,** *a. Sc.* 1470. [prob. identical with OE. *hēalič*; see HIGHLY.] Haughty.

Heinous (hēⁱ·nəs), *a.* ME. [– OFr. *haïneus* (mod. *haineux*), f. *haïne* (mod. *haine*), f. (O)Fr. *haïr* – Frankish **hatjan*; see HATE *v.*, -OUS.] **1.** Odious; highly criminal; infamous; chiefly of offences, and offenders. **b.** Hence, of the accusation or charge 1548. †**2.** Grievous, severe –1675. †**3.** Full of hate –1580.

1. The hainous..act Of Satan done in Paradise MILT. H. offenders 1845. **b.** H. charges STUBBS. **3.** To wreke Their hainous wrath SURREY. Hence **Hei·nous-ly** *adv.*, **-ness.**

Heir (ēᵊɹ), *sb.* [ME. *eir, eyr* – OFr. *eir, heir* (later, *hoir*) :– archaic and late L. *hērem,* for regular *hērēdem,* nom. *hērēs.*] **1.** One who on the death of another becomes entitled by law to succeed him in the enjoyment of property or rank; one who so succeeds; pop., one who receives or is entitled to receive property of any kind as the legal representative of a former owner. **2.** *transf.* One who succeeds, or should succeed, to any gift, endowment, or quality of another. Often one to whom something (*e.g.* joy, punishment) is morally due. ME. †**3.** *fig.* Offspring –1593.

1. The onely haire Of a most mighty king SPENSER. *Heir-at-law*: one who succeeds another by right of blood in the enjoyment of his property; in English law confined to one who has such a right in real property. *H. general* = *Heir-at-law*:

used to include heirs female. *H. male*: an h. who is a male, and who derives from the ancestor through males only. *H. presumptive*: he who, if the ancestor should die immediately, would be his h., but whose right may be defeated by the birth of a nearer h., or the like. *Right h.* = *heir-at-law*. **2.** The thousand Naturall shockes That Flesh is heyre too SHAKS. **3.** The first heire of my inuention SHAKS.

Heir, *v.* ME. [f. prec. sb.] *trans.* To inherit; to be heir to. Also *fig.*

Not one son more To h. his goods CHAPMAN.

Heir apparent. [See APPARENT *a.* 3.] Formerly also **apparent heir.** ME. The heir whose right is indefeasible, provided he outlives his ancestor.

Heirdom (ēᵊ·ɹdəm). 1597. [f. HEIR *sb.* + -DOM.] Succession by right of blood; the state of an heir; an inheritance.

Heiress (ēᵊ·rès). 1659. [f. as prec. + -ESS¹.] A female heir. Also *fig.*

Heirless (ēᵊ·ɹlès), *a.* ME. [f. as prec. + -LESS.] Without an heir.

The h. Duke 1892, sceptre PALGRAVE.

Heirloom (ēᵊ·ɹlūm). 1472. [f. HEIR *sb.* + LOOM *sb.*¹] A chattel that, under a will, settlement, or custom, follows the devolution of real estate. Hence, Any piece of personal property that has been in a family for several generations. Also *fig.*

A glass cup, called.. 'The Luck of Muncaster'.. is carefully preserved as a precious h. 1872. *fig.* Political wisdom is the h. of no one class of society STUBBS.

Heirship (ēᵊ·ɹʃip). 1478. [f. as prec. + -SHIP.] The state, condition, or rights of an heir; right of inheritance. Also *fig.*

†*H. movables, goods* (*Sc. Law*), the best of certain kinds of movable goods, which the heir was entitled to take besides the heritable estate. (The right was abolished in 1868.)

Hejira, var. of HEGIRA.

†**Helas,** *interj.* 1484. [– Fr. *hélas*, later form of *ha las*, *a las* ALAS.] An exclam. of grief, sorrow, etc.; alas! –1753.

Helco-, comb. f. Gr. ἕλκος 'festering wound, ulcer', used with sense 'ulcer'; as in **Helco·logy,** the branch of pathology that treats of ulcers; **He·lcoplasty** [Gr. πλαστός], the operation of grafting on an ulcer a piece of healthy skin from another part or person; etc.

Held (held), *ppl. a.* 1820. [pa. pple. of HOLD *v.*] Kept in, restrained.

Hele, heal (hīl), *v.* [OE. *helian* = OS. *bihellian*, OHG. *bihellen* :- WGmc. **χaljan*, causative f. Gmc. **χelan* (whence OE. *helan*), f. **χel-* **χal-* **χul-* conceal, rel. to L. *celare* hide, Gr. καλύπτειν.] †**1.** *trans.* To hide –16.. **2.** To cover; to roof ME. **b.** To set (a plant) in the ground and cover it *in*.

1. But the preest alwey heled his synne CAXTON.

Hele, obs. f. HALE *a.*, HEAL *sb.* and *v.*²

†**Helena** (he·lĭnă). 1563. [– L. *Helena* – Gr. Ἑλένη, the sister of Castor and Pollux, the name given to double meteors at sea; but there was perh. also assoc. with ἑλένη torch.] A meteoric light seen about the masts of ships; cf. CORPOSANT. –1601.

Helenin (he·lĭnin). 1838. [f. botanical name *Helenium* + -IN¹.] *Chem.* A colourless crystalline substance, C_6H_8O, obtained from the root of elecampane (*Inula helenium*). Hence **He·lenene,** a yellow oily hydrocarbon obtained by distilling h. with phosphoric anhydride.

†**Helewou.** ME. [f. dial. *hele* covering, f. HELE *v.* + WOUGH¹.] End-wall.

Heliac (hī·liˌæk), *a.* 1565. [– late L. *heliacus* – Gr. ἡλιακός, f. ἥλιος sun; see -AC. Cf. Fr. *héliaque* (XVIII).] = next.

Heliacal (hĭləi·ăkăl), *a.* 1607. [In sense 1 f. med.L. *heliacus* (in AL. *heliacus ortus* heliacal rising) + -AL¹; in sense 2 f. as prec. + -AL¹.] **1.** *Astron.* Said of the rising of a star when it first emerges from the sun's rays and becomes visible before sunrise, or of its setting when it is last visible after sunset before being lost in the sun's rays. **2.** Solar 1801.

1. *Heliacal year*, the year reckoned from the h. rising of Sirius, the canicular year: see CANICULAR. Hence **Heli·acally** *adv.*

‖**Helianthus** (hīliˌæ·nþŏs). 1776. [mod.L., f. Gr. ἥλιος sun + ἄνθος flower.] *Bot.* The genus including the common sunflower (N.O. *Compositæ*).

Hence **Heliantha·ceous** *a.* allied to the genus *H.* of composite plants. **Helia·nthic** *a.* of or belonging to H. **Helia·nthin,** an aniline dye of orange-yellow colour. **Helia·nthoid** *a.* belonging to the *Helianthoidea*, an order of *Actinozoa*, comprising the sea anemones; *sb.* one of these. Also **Helianthoi·dean** *a.* and *sb.*

Helical (he·likăl), *a.* 1613. [f. L. *helix*, *helic-* (see HELIX) + -AL¹.] Belonging to or having the form of a helix; spiral; as, a *helical spring*. Hence **He·lically** *adv.* spirally.

Helices (he·lisīz), pl. of HELIX.

‖**Helichrysum** (helikrəi·sŏm). Also **-os, -on.** 1551. [L. *helichrysum*, *-os* – Gr. ἑλίχρυσος, f. ἕλιξ spiral + χρυσός gold.] **1.** A creeping plant with yellow flowers, so called by the ancients. **2.** *Bot.* A large genus of composite plants, having mostly yellow flowers, called also *Everlastings* or *Immortelles* 1664.

Heliciform (he·lisifǭɹm), *a.* 1854. [f. L. *helix*, *helic-* HELIX + -FORM.] Having the form of a helix; spirally wound.

Helicin (he·lisin). 1854. [f. L. *helix*, *helic-* spiral, also a kind of snail + -IN¹.] *Chem.* **1.** The glycoside of salicylic acid 1859. **2.** An oily substance extracted from snails.

Helicine (he·lisəin, -in), *a.* 1833. [f. L. *helix*, *helic-* spiral + -INE¹.] *Anat.* **a.** Spiral, coiled; applied to certain arteries of the penis and clitoris. **b.** Pertaining to the helix of the ear.

Helicograph (he·likograf). 1851. [f. *helico-*, comb. f. Gr. ἕλιξ HELIX + -GRAPH.] An instrument for describing the volutes and scroll-work found in Gr. architecture.

Helicoid (he·likoid). 1699. [– Gr. ἑλικοειδής, f. as prec.; see -OID. Cf. Fr. *hélicoïde* (1704).]

A. *adj.* **1.** Having the form of a helix; screw-shaped; spiral 1704. **2.** *Zool.* Belonging to or resembling the *Helicidæ*, gastropodous molluscs including the snail 1876.

1. *Helicoid parabola* (Geom.): the parabolic spiral.

B. *sb.* †**1.** Something of a spiral form (*rare*) 1699. **2.** *Geom.* †**a.** = Helicoid parabola; see A. 1. **b.** A warped surface generated by a moving straight line which always passes through or touches a fixed helix 1855. So **Helicoi·dal** *a.* = HELICOID A. 1. Hence **He·licoidly** *adv.* spirally.

Helicon (he·likǫn). 1529. [– L. *Helicon* – Gr. Ἑλικών. In sense 2 app. assoc. with HELIX.] **1.** (With capital H.) A mountain in Bœotia, sacred to the Muses, in which rose the fountains of Aganippe and Hippocrene; in 16–17th c. often confused with these. **2.** A large brass wind-instrument of a spiral form 1875.

Heliconian (helikōᵘ·niăn), *a.* 1557. [In 1 f. L. *Heliconius* (see prec.). In 2 f. mod.L. *Heliconia*, a genus of butterflies. See -IAN.] **1.** Pertaining to Helicon, or to the Muses. **2.** *Entom.* Belonging to the genus *Heliconia*, or family *Heliconidæ* of butterflies. Also **Heliconi·deous, He·liconine, He·liconoid,** *adjs.*

Helicopter (he·likǫptəɹ). 1872. Also in Fr. form. [– Fr. *hélicoptère*, f. Gr. ἑλικο-, comb. form of ἕλιξ HELIX + πτερόν wing.] A flying machine designed to rise vertically by one or more lifting screws revolving horizontally.

He·lio, colloq. abbrev. of HELIOGRAPH.

Helio-, comb. f. Gr. ἥλιος sun:

helio-engra·ving = HELIOGRAVURE; **-·later** [Gr. -λατρης worshipping], a worshipper of the sun; so **-·latrous** *a.*; **-·latry** [Gr. λατρεία], sun-worship; **-·logist**, one versed in heliology; **-·logy**, the science of the sun's energy and action; **-pho·bia** [Gr. -φοβία], dread of or shrinking from sunlight; so **-phobe** [Gr. -φοβος], one affected with heliophobia; **-pho·bic** *a.*

Heliocentric, -al (hī:liose·ntrik, -ăl) *a.* (*sb.*) 1667. [f. HELIO-; see CENTRIC. Opp. to GEOCENTRIC. See -ICAL.] **1.** Referred to the sun as centre 1685. **2.** Having, or taking, the sun as centre 1834. Also *fig.* †**3.** *sb.* One who takes the sun as a centre 1667.

1. *H. latitude, longitude, place*, etc. of a planet: that in which it would appear to an observer placed at the centre of the sun. Hence **Helioce·ntrically** *adv.* as viewed from the centre of the sun.

Heliochrome (hī·liokrōᵘm). 1853. [f. HELIO- + Gr. χρῶμα colour.] A photograph representing an object in its natural colours. So **Heliochro·mic** *a.* pertaining to *heliochromy*. **Heliochro·motype** = HELIOCHROME. **He·liochromy,** the production of heliochromes.

Heliograph (hī·liograf), *sb.* 1848. [f. HELIO- + -GRAPH.] **1.** An engraving obtained by HELIOGRAPHY (sense 3). Also *attrib.* 1853. **2.** An apparatus for taking photographs of the sun 1848. **3.** An instrument for measuring the intensity of sunlight 1851. **4.** An instrument for signalling by means of flashes of sunlight. Cf. HELIOTROPE 4. Also *attrib.* 1877. Hence **He·liograph** *v.* to communicate by h.; to photograph by h. **Helio·grapher.**

Heliographic, -al (hīliogræ·fik, -ăl), *a.* 1706. [f. HELIO- + -GRAPHIC. See -ICAL.] **1.** Pertaining to the description of the sun. **2.** †Photographic –1855; belonging to photographic engraving 1851. **3.** Pertaining to or obtained by a heliograph (see HELIOGRAPH 4) 1880.

1. *H. charts*: descriptions of the sun's body, and of its *maculæ* or spots. Hence **Heliogra·phically** *adv.* by means of a heliograph.

Heliography (hīliǫ·grăfi). 1730. [f. HELIO- + -GRAPHY.] **1.** The description of the sun. (Cf. *geography*.) †**2.** Photography –1840. **3.** A process of engraving in which a specially prepared plate is acted upon chemically by exposure to light 1845. **4.** The system of signalling by the HELIOGRAPH (sense 4) 1887.

Heliogravure (hīliogrăviūᵊ·ɹ). 1879. [– Fr. *héliogravure*, f. HELIO- + *gravure* engraving.] A process of engraving by means of the action of light on a sensitized surface; an engraved plate, or an engraving, thus obtained; photogravure. Also *attrib.*

Heliometer (hīliǫ·mĭtəɹ). 1753. [– Fr. *héliomètre* (Bouguer, 1747), f. HELIO- + *-mètre* -METER.] **1.** An astronomical instrument originally devised for measuring the diameter of the sun; now much used in determining the angular distance between two stars. †**2.** A complex form of portable sun-dial, used for ascertaining solar time, latitude, and the like (Knight) 1875. Hence **Heliome·tric, -al** *a.* pertaining to, or obtained by, the h.; relating to measurement of the sun.

Heliopore (hī·liopōᵊɹ). [– mod.L. *Heliopora*, f. Gr. ἥλιος sun + πόρος pore; cf. MADREPORE.] A coral of the genus *Heliopora*; a sun coral.

Helioscope (hī·lioskoᵘp). 1675. [– Fr. *hélioscope* (1671), f. HELIO- + -SCOPE.] An apparatus for observing the sun without injury to the eye, as through smoked or coloured glass, by reflectors, etc.; a telescope fitted with such an apparatus. So **Heliosco·pic** *a.* **Helio·scopy.**

Heliostat (hī·liostæt). Also **-stata, -state.** 1747. [– Fr. *héliostat*, f. HELIO-; see -STAT.] An apparatus consisting of a mirror turned by clockwork so as to reflect the light of the sun in a fixed direction. (Also applied to an apparatus worked by hand, a *porte-lumière*.) Hence **Heliosta·tic** *a.*

Heliotrope (hī·liotroᵘp). OE. [– L. *heliotropium*, med.L. also *eliotropus*, *-ius*, etc. (formerly used in Eng.) – Gr. ἡλιοτρόπιον, f. ἥλιος sun + -τροπος turning, τρέπειν turn.] **1.** A name given orig. to plants of which the flowers turn so as to follow the sun; as the sunflower, marigold, etc.; now, a plant of the genus *Heliotropium*; esp. *H. peruvianum*, commonly cultivated for its fragrance. Also *fig.* **b.** The shade of purple of the flowers of the heliotrope. Also *attrib.* 1882. **2.** *Min.* = BLOOD-STONE, q.v. ME. **3.** An ancient kind of sun-dial 1669. **4.** An instrument with a movable mirror for reflecting the sun's rays, used for signalling, etc., esp. in geodesy; cf. HELIOGRAPH (sense 4) 1822.

2. The pretious stone Heliotropium..is a deepe green in maner of a leeke..garnished with veins of bloud P. HOLLAND. Hence **He·liotroper,** one who manages a HELIOTROPE (sense 4). **Heliotro·pian** *a.* (*rare*), pertaining to or of the nature of the h. (1 and 2); †*sb.* = HELIOTROPE 2. **Helio-tro·pic** *a. Bot.* bending or turning under the influence of light; pertaining to or marked by heliotropism.

Heliotropism (hīliǫ·tropiz'm). 1854. [See prec. and -ISM. Cf. Fr. *héliotropisme* (De Candolle, 1832).] *Bot.* The property of bending or turning in a particular manner under the influence of light. Some restrict the term to the case of bending towards the light (*positive h.*).

Heliotype (hī·liotəip). 1870. [f. HELIO- + -TYPE.] A picture obtained by printing from a film of gelatine which has been sensitized with bichromate of potash and exposed to light under a negative; also, this process. Also *attrib.* So **He·liotyped** *ppl. a.* produced by *heliotypy*. **Helioty·pic** *a.* of or belonging to *heliotypy*. **He·liotypy,** the heliotype process.

Heliozoan (hīlio,zōᵘ·ăn). [f. mod.L. *Heliozoa* sb. pl. (f. Gr. ἥλιος sun + ζῷον animal) + -AN.] **1.** *adj.* Belonging to the *Heliozoa* or sun-animalcules, a group of marine Radiolarians. **2.** *sb.* One of the *Heliozoa*. So **Heliozo·ic** *a.*

Helispherical (helisfe·rikăl), *a.* 1646. [irreg. f. HELIX + SPHERICAL.] Winding spirally upon a sphere.

H. line: the rhumb-line in Navigation (HUTTON).

Helium (hī·liə̆m). 1878. [f. Gr. ἥλιος sun; see -IUM.] *Chem.* One of the chemical elements, a transparent gas, first obtained by Prof. Ramsay in 1895, but previously inferred to exist from a line (D_3) in the solar spectrum. (Cf. CORONIUM.) Symbol He.

Helix (he·liks, hī·liks). Pl. **helices** (he·lisīz). 1563. [– L. *helix, helic-* – Gr. ἕλιξ (-ικ-) anything of spiral form.] **1.** Anything of a spiral or coiled form, whether in one plane (as a watch-spring), or advancing round an axis (like a corkscrew), but usually the latter; a coil, a spiral, as an electro-magnetic coil of wire, the thread of a screw, a tendril, etc. In *Geom.*, a curve on any developable surface (e.g. a cone) which becomes a straight line when the surface is unrolled into a plane; dist. from a *spiral*, which is applied only to plane curves 1643. **2.** *Arch.*, etc. A spiral ornament, a volute; *spec.* applied to the eight smaller volutes under the abacus of the Corinthian capital 1563. **3.** *Anat.* The curved fold which forms the rim of the external ear 1693. **4.** *Zool.* A genus of molluscs with spiral shells, of which the common snail is typical 1820.

Hell (hel), *sb.* [OE. *hel(l)* = OFris. *helle*, OS. *hell(j)a* (Du. *hel*), OHG. *hella* (G. *hölle*), ON. *hel*, Goth. *halja* :– Gmc. **χaljō*, f. **χal-* **χel-* **χul-* cover, conceal.] **1.** The abode of the dead; the place of departed spirits; the infernal regions regarded as a place of existence after death; the grave; HADES. (In N.T. (R.V.) *hell* is everywhere reserved for γέεννα.) **2.** The abode of devils and condemned spirits; the place or state of punishment of the wicked after death OE. **3.** The powers or inhabitants of hell; also, the kingdom or power of hell ME. **4. a.** A place or state of wickedness, suffering, or misery ME. **b.** A place of turmoil and discord 1818. **c.** *A hell of a* — 1778. †**5.** A part of a building, etc. compared to hell; the name of a part of the old law courts at Westminster, app. used as a record office; also, a place of confinement for debtors –1661. **6.** The 'den' to which captives are carried in Prisoner's Base, etc. 1557. **7.** A place into which a tailor throws his shreds, or a printer his refuse type, etc. 1592. **8.** A gambling-house 1794. **9.** In imprecations, etc., used like *devil* 1596.

1. His soul was not left in h. [*R.V.* Hades] *Acts* 2:31. **2.** *P.L.* x. 230. **3.** H. heard th' unsufferable noise MILT. A H. of ougly Deuills SHAKS. **4. a.** The prisons were hells on earth MACAULAY. **5.** One that before the Iudgment carries poore soules to hel SHAKS. **8.** The proprietor of a h. STEVENSON.

Phr. *Hell-for-leather*: at breakneck speed, orig. with reference to riding on horseback.

Comb.: **h.-bent** *a. U.S.*, 'fiendishly', doggedly, or recklessly determined; also as *adv.*; **-box,** a box for holding refuse type; **-broth,** a decoction of infernal character, or prepared for an infernal purpose; **-diver** *U.S.*, a grebe; **-driver** *U.S.*, the hellgrammite; **-hag,** a hell-cat; **-kite,** a kite of h., a person of hellish cruelty.

Hell, *v.* 1799. [– Ger. *hellen*, f. *hell* clear.] *trans.* To burnish (gold or silver).

Hellbender (he·lbe:ndəɹ). *U.S.* 1812. [f. HELL *sb.* + BENDER, one who or that which bends.] **1.** The menopome or American salamander, a repulsive amphibian, from one to two feet in length, of which two species (*Menopoma alleghaniensis, M. horrida*) are found in the Ohio and Mississippi valleys. **2.** A protracted and reckless debauch (Farmer).

He·ll-born, *a.* 1593. Born of or in hell.

He·ll-bred, *a.* 1590. Bred or engendered in hell.

He·ll-cat. 1605. [perh. suggested by *Heccat*, HECATE.] A furious vixen; a witch. Also applied to a man.

Hellebore (he·lĭboᵊɹ). [ME. *el(l)ebre, eleure* – OFr. *ellebre, elebore* or med.L. *eleborus*, L. *(h)elleborus* – Gr. ἐλλέβορος (ἐλλ-); refash. XVI after the prevailing Gr. form.] **1.** A name anciently given to species of *Helleborus* and *Veratrum*, reputed as specifics for mental disease; now, in *Bot.*, applied to the species of *Helleborus* (N.O. *Ranunculaceæ*), including the Christmas Rose and its congeners: **a.** the plant; **b.** the drug. ME. **2.** *attrib.*, as *h.-root* 1792.

1. b. Wretches fitter for a course of h. than for the stake SCOTT. *Comb.*: **Black H.,** (*a*) of the ancients, *Helleborus officinalis*; (*b*) of some moderns, the Christmas Rose, *H. niger*; **White H.** (of the ancients), *Veratrum album*; **Swamp H.,** *V. viride*, also called *American* or *Green H.*

Hence **Hellebore·in, Hellebo·resin, Hellebore·tin,** and **Helle·borin,** chemical principles derived from h.

Helleborine (he·lĭborəin). 1597. [– Fr. *helleborine* or L. *(h)elleborine* (Pliny) – Gr. ἐλλεβορίνη a plant like hellebore; see -INE[1].] *Bot.* An orchidaceous plant of the genus *Epipactis* (formerly called *Serapias*), or of the closely-allied genus *Cephalanthera*.

Helleborism (he·lĭboriz'm). 1621. [– late L. *(h)elleborismus* – Gr. ἐλλεβορισμός a curing by hellebore; see -ISM.] **a.** The treatment of diseases by hellebore. **b.** The symptoms of hellebore administered in excess. **c.** A purgative made from hellebore. So **He·lleborize** *v. trans.* to treat with hellebore, as for madness.

Hellene (helī·n, he·līn). 1662. [– Gr. Ἕλλην a Greek.] A Greek, ancient or modern.

Hellenian (helī·niăn), *a.* 1611. [f. Gr. Ἑλλήνιος HELLENIC + -AN.] Grecian; HELLENIC 1813.

Hellenic (helī·nik, -e·nik), *a.* (*sb.*) 1644. [– Gr. Ἑλληνικός; see HELLENE, -IC.] **1.** Of or pertaining to the Hellenes or Greeks, ancient or modern; Greek, Grecian. **2.** *sb.* **a.** The Greek language 1870. **b.** *pl.* Writings on Greek subjects 1847.

1. H. grace 1879. **2. b.** Hellenics LANDOR (*title*).

Hellenism (he·lėniz'm). 1609. [– Gr. Ἑλληνισμός, f. Ἑλληνίζειν to HELLENIZE; see -ISM.] **1.** A phrase, idiom, or construction used or formed in the Greek manner. **2.** Conformity to Hellenic speech and ideas; imitation of Greek characteristics, e.g. by the Jews of the Dispersion, the later Romans, etc.; the principle of hellenizing 1862. **3.** The national character or spirit of the Greeks; Grecian culture 1865. **b.** Applied by M. Arnold to that form of culture, or ideal of life, of which the ancient Greek is taken as the type. (Cf. HEBRAISM.) 1869. **4.** Greek nationality; the Hellenic 'world' as a political entity 1883.

3. b. The great movement which goes by the name of the Renascence, was an up-rising and re-instatement of man's intellectual impulses and of H. M. ARNOLD.

Hellenist (he·lėnist). 1613. [– Gr. Ἑλληνιστής, f. Ἑλληνίζειν; see -IST. Cf. Fr. *hellėniste*.] **1.** One who used the Greek language, though not a native Greek. Applied *esp.* to the Jews of the Dispersion. Also *attrib.* **2.** One skilled in the Greek language and literature; a Greek scholar 1680. **3.** One of the Byzantine Greeks who contributed to the revival of classical learning in Europe in the 15th c. (Mod. Dicts.)

1. There arose a murmuring of the Grecian Jews [*marg.* Hellenists] against the Hebrews R. V. *Acts* 6:1.

Hellenistic, -al (helėni·stik, -ăl), *a.* 1656. [f. prec. + -IC; see -ICAL.] Of or pertaining to the Hellenists.

The term H. was coined to denote the language of Greek-speaking Jews WESTCOTT & HORT. Hence **Helleni·sticism,** the H. condition or stage of history. **Helleni·stically** *adv.*

Hellenize (he·lėnize), *v.* 1613. [– Gr. Ἑλληνίζειν to speak Greek, to make Greek, f. Ἕλλην HELLENE.] **1.** *intr.* To use the Greek language; to become a Greek or Hellenist. **b.** To adopt Hellenism (sense 3 b.) M. ARNOLD. **2.** *trans.* To make Greek or Hellenistic in form or character 1799. Hence **He:lleniza·tion,** the action of hellenizing or condition of being hellenized. **He·llenizer.**

Hellespont (he·lėspǫnt). 1591. [– Gr. Ἑλλήσποντος; explained as sea (πόντος) of Helle (Ἕλλη), daughter of Athamas, said to have been drowned in it.] Ancient name for the Strait of the Dardanelles; hence *fig.* something that separates lovers. *Two Gent.* I. i. 22 & 26. Hence **Hellespo·ntine** *a.*

Hell-fire, hell fire. OE. [orig. two wds., *helle* being genitive case; now usu. hyphened. In N.T. rendering Gr. γέεννα τοῦ πυρός, fiery hell.] **1.** The fire of hell. **2.** A member of a Hell-fire club 1720.

attrib. **Hell-fire club,** name given to clubs of reckless young men, early in the 18th c. So **Hell-fired** *a.* 'set on fire of hell' (*Jas.* 3:6); 'damned'.

Hell-gate, *pl.* **hell-gates.** OE. [orig. two wds., *helle* being gen.] The portal or entrance of hell.

MILT. *P.L.* II. 246.

He·llgrammite, he·lgramite. *U.S.* 1877. [Of unkn. origin.] The larva of a neuropterous insect, *Corydalus cornutus*, the hellgrammite fly, much used as a bait for the black bass.

He·ll-hound. OE. [orig. two wds., *helle* in genitive case.] **1.** Hound or dog of hell; esp. Cerberus. **2.** A fiend; a fiendish person ME. **3.** *attrib.* 1719.

2. Tyrone with his Hell-hounds being not farre from Corke 1633.

He·llicat. *Sc.* 1815. [app. a fanciful alt. by Scott of (Sc. dial.) *halokit*, f. *halok* light, thoughtless girl; perh. with some notion of *hell-cat*.] **1.** *adj.* Light-headed, giddy. **2.** *sb.* A wicked creature 1816.

Hellier (he·lyəɹ). Now *dial.* [ME. *helyer*, f. HELE *v.*; cf. *sawyer*. See -IER.] A slater or tiler.

Hellish (he·liʃ), *a.* (*adv.*) 1530. [f. HELL *sb.* + -ISH[1].] **1.** Of or pertaining to hell; infernal. **2.** Of the nature of hell; worthy of hell; diabolical, fiendish 1569; as an intensive 1798. **3.** *adv.* Infernally, devilishly; execrably 1613.

1. Diabolical and h. magic DE FOE. **2.** H. noises SCOTT. Hence **He·llish-ly** *adv.*, **-ness.**

Hello (hĕlōᵘ·), *interj.* and *sb.* 1854. Var. of HALLO, q.v. Hence **Hello** *v.* to shout *hello!*

‖**Helluo** (he·liu,o). 1583. [L. *helluo, hēluo* gormandizer.] **1.** A glutton; Also *transf.* and *fig.* **2.** *Zool.* A genus of beetles belonging to the family *Carybidæ*.

1. *transf.* To let an H. loose upon the Revenue NORTH.

Hellward (he·lwǫɹd). ME. [f. HELL *sb.* + -WARD; orig. *to hellward*.] **1.** *adv.* Towards hell. **2.** *adj.* Directed or conducting to hell 1829.

†**He·lly,** *a.* (*adv.*) 1532. [f. HELL *sb.* + -Y[1] (or perh. -LY).] **1.** Hellish –1613. **2.** *adv.* Hellishly –1762.

Helm (helm), *sb.*[1] [OE. *helm* = OFris., OS., OHG. (Du., G.) *helm*, ON. *hjálmr*, Goth. *hilms* :– Gmc. **χelmaz* :– **kelmos*, f. IE. base **kel-* cover, conceal.] **1.** A helmet. Now *poet.* and *arch.* **2.** The crown or top of anything (*Obs.* exc. *dial.*) OE. †**3.** The head of an alembic or retort –1718. **4.** (Also *helm-cloud.*) The local name in the Lake District of a cloud which forms over a mountain top before and during a storm; esp. that which accompanies the *helm-wind*, a kind of cyclone, revolving on a horizontal axis parallel to the escarpment of the Pennines near Cross Fell 1696.

Helm (helm), *sb.*^{2} [OE. *helma*, corresp. to MLG. *helm* handle, OHG. *helmo*, *halmo*, ON. *hjalmvọlr* 'rudder-stick'; of doubtful origin, prob. rel. to HELVE.] **1.** The handle or tiller, in large ships the wheel, by which the rudder is managed; occas., the whole steering gear. **2. a.** *fig.* That by which affairs, etc. are guided OE. **b.** *transf.* Any part which is used like a helm 1660. †**3.** A handle, helve –1615.

1. Many times the ships will feele no helme SIR T. HERBERT. Phr. *Down with the helm, Down h.*, the order to place the h. so as to bring the rudder to windward. *Up with the h., Up h.*, the order to place the h. so as to bring the rudder to leeward. See also ALEE, EASE *v.*, FEEL *v.*, PORT *v.*^{2}, STARBOARD *v.*, WEATHER. **2. a.** You slander The Helmes o'th' State SHAKS. *Comb.*: **h. circle**, the smallest circle in which a ship can be turned; **h.-port**, 'that hole in the counter through which the head of the rudder passes'.

Helm, *sb.*^{3} *dial.* ME. [app. rel. to HAULM; cf. G. *halm*, Du. and LG. *helm*.] The stalk of corn; the stalks collectively, straw; *esp.* as made up for thatching. *Comb.* **h.-bote**, the right of cutting h. in a common field for thatching.

Helm, *v.*^{1} [OE. *helmian*, f. HELM *sb.*^{1}] *trans.* To furnish or cover with a helm. Chiefly *poet.*

Helm, *v.*^{2} 1603. [f. HELM *sb.*^{2}] *trans.* To guide with or as with a helm; to steer. Chiefly *fig.*

The businesse he hath helmed, must . . giue him a better proclamation SHAKS.

He·lmage. *rare.* 1864. [f. HELM *sb.*^{2} + -AGE.] Guidance, direction.

Helmed (helmd), *ppl. a.* ME. [f. HELM *v.*^{1} or *sb.*^{1} + -ED.] Wearing a helm; helmeted.

The h. Cherubim, And sworded Seraphim MILT.

Helmet (he·lmėt), *sb.* 1470. [– OFr. *helmet*, f. *helme*; see HELM *sb.*^{1}, -ET.] **1.** A defensive cover for the head; a piece of armour, usually made of, or strengthened with, metal, which covers the head wholly or in part. **b.** Extended to other defensive or protective head-gear, e.g. that worn by policemen, firemen, and divers, and the felt or pith hat worn in hot climates 1842. **2.** *Her.* The figure of a helmet placed above the escutcheon in an achievement and supporting the crest 1610. **3.** = HELM *sb.*^{1} 3. 1599. **4.** A kind of fancy pigeon; so named from the appearance of the head 1668. **5.** (in full *helmet-shell.*) The shell of a mollusc of the genus *Cassis* 1753. **6.** A fossil echinoderm, *Galerites albogalerus* 1887. **7.** *Bot.* The arched upper part of the corolla (or calyx) in labiates, orchids, etc. 1793. **8.** An appendage of the stipes of the maxilla of some insects, as the cockroach 1828.

Comb.: **h.-beetle**, a beetle of the family *Cassididæ*, having a dilated thorax forming a kind of h. covering the head; **-bird**, a turakoo; **-cockatoo**, *Callocephalon galeatum*, 'an iron-grey bird with a bright red head' (Newton); **-crab**, a species of King-crab, *Limulus longispinus*; **-flower**, a name for Monkshood or Aconite, and for orchids of the genus *Coryanthes*; **-hornbill**, *Buceros galeatus*; **-quail**, a quail of the American genus *Lophortyx*, having an elegant curled crest; **-shell** = sense 5; **-stone** (1681) = sense 6. Hence **He·lmet** *v.* to furnish with a h. **He·lmeted** *ppl. a.* wearing a h.; in *Bot.* h-shaped, galeate. †**Helmetie·r, Helmettier**, a soldier wearing a h.

Helmet-crest. 1509. **1.** (Also *helmet crest.*) The crest of a helmet. **2.** A crested humming-bird of the genus *Oxypogon* 1863.

Helminth (he·lminþ). 1852. [– Gr. ἕλμινς, ἑλμινθ- (comb. form ἑλμινθο-) maw-worm.] **1.** A worm, esp. an intestinal worm. **2.** *Min.* A variety of chlorite occurring in felspar and quartz 1861.

Helminthagogue (helmi·nþăgǫg). 1704. [f. Gr. ἑλμινθ- (see prec.) + ἀγωγός drawing forth.] **1.** *adj.* 'Having power to expel intestinal worms' (*Syd. Soc. Lex.*); anthelmintic 1854. **2.** *sb.* [sc. *medicine*.]

Helminthiasis (helminþəi·ăsis). 1811. [mod.L., f. Gr. ἑλμινθιᾶν suffer from worms; see HELMINTH and -ASIS.] *Path.* A diseased condition characterized by the presence of worms in the body.

Helminthic (helmi·nþik). 1704. [f. Gr. ἑλμινθ- HELMINTH + -IC.] **1.** *adj.* Pertaining to a helminth or intestinal worm 1755. **2.** *sb.* = HELMINTHAGOGUE 2.

Helmi·nthite. 1859. [f. as prec. + -ITE^1 2 b.] *Geol.* One of the long sinuous tracks on the surfaces of many sandstones, usually considered as worm-trails.

Helmi·nthoid, *a.* 1854. [f. as prec. + -OID.] Resembling a helminth; vermiform.

Helminthology (helminþǫ·lŏdʒi). 1819. [f. as prec. + -LOGY.] That branch of zoology, or of medical science, which treats of helminths. Hence **Helmintholo·gic, -al** *a.* pertaining to h. **Helmintho·logist**, one versed in h.

Helmless (he·lmlės), *a.*^{1} 1600. [f. HELM *sb.*^{1} + -LESS.] Without a helm or helmet.

He·lmless, *a.*^{2} 1824. [f. HELM *sb.*^{2} + -LESS.] Without steering gear; rudderless. Also *fig.*

He·lmsman. 1622. [f. as prec. + MAN.] A steersman.

Helm-wind: see HELM *sb.*^{1} 4.

Helot (he·lǫt, hī·lǫt). 1579. [– L. *Helotes* – Gr. Εἵλωτες (pl. of Εἵλως), also *Hilotæ* – Gr. Εἱλῶται (pl. of Εἱλώτης); usu. derived from Ἕλος Helos, a town in Laconia whose inhabitants were enslaved. (With capital H now only in the historical sense.)] *Gr. Antiq.* (*Helot*) One of a class of serfs in ancient Sparta intermediate in status between the ordinary slaves and the free Spartan citizens. **b.** *transf.* (*helot*) A serf, a bondsman 1823.

Drunken H.: in allusion to Plutarch's statement that Helots were, on certain occasions, compelled to appear in a state of intoxication, as a lesson to the Spartan youth. Hence **He·lotage, He·lotism**, the condition of a H. or h.; the Spartan system of serfage; a system under which a class of the community are treated as a permanently inferior order. **He·lotize** *v.* to reduce to the condition of a H. **He·lotry**, helots or serfs collectively; the condition of Helots; serfdom.

Help (help), *v.* Pa. t. **helped** (helpt), *arch.* **holp** (hōᵘlp); pa. pple. **helped**, *arch.* **holpen** (hōᵘ·lpĕn, -p'n). [OE. *helpan* = OFris. *helpa*, OS. *helpan* (Du. *helpen*), OHG. *helfan* (G. *helfen*), ON. *hjalpa*, Goth. *hilpan*, f. Gmc. base *xalp- *xelp- *xulp-.] **1.** *trans.* To furnish (a person, etc.) with what is serviceable to his efforts or his needs; to aid, assist. **b.** *absol.* or *intr.* To afford aid or assistance; often in *imper.* as a cry for assistance ME. †**2.** *trans.* To be of use or service to, to profit –1648. †**b.** *absol.* or *intr.* To be of use or service; to avail –1747. **3.** *trans.* To make more effectual; to further, promote 1559. **4.** With *infin.* or *clause* ME. **5.** Ellipt. with advs. and preps. = to help to proceed, go, come, get (*away, down, forward*, etc.; *to, into, out of*, etc.) ME. **b.** With adv., etc. followed by *with*: esp. in reference to clothing, e.g. *to help* a person *on* (or *off*) *with* his coat = to help him to get it on or off ME. **c.** *To h. out* or *through*: to assist in completing something; to eke out, supplement. Also *absol.* 1618. **6.** To serve (a person) with food at a meal. Const. *to*. 1688. **b.** *transf.* To distribute (food) at a meal 1805. **7.** To succour in some distress or misfortune; hence, to deliver, save, relieve (*from, of*); *spec.* to cure of a disease, or the like. *Obs.* or *arch.* ME. **8.** To relieve or cure (a malady); to remedy, amend. *Obs.* or *arch.* OE. **9.** To remedy, obviate, prevent, cause to be otherwise. (With *can, cannot*, etc.) 1589. **b.** To avoid, refrain from, forbear; to do otherwise than. (With *can, cannot.*) Usu. with *vbl. sb.* (occas. *infin.*), or *it* = doing it. 1697. **c.** Idiomatically with *can* instead of *cannot* after a negative expressed or implied 1804.

1. Fortune helpeth bothe the good and euylle folke CAXTON. Helpe me Cassius, or I sinke SHAKS. Phr. *So help me God*, the formula in a solemn oath. *God h. him* (*them*, etc.), a parenthetical exclam. of pity. **b.** Helpe, O king 2 *Sam.* 14:4. **3.** The troubles of the time helped . . the progress of the town GREEN. **4.** He help'd to bury whom he help'd to starve POPE. I would fain stay and h. thee tend him M. ARNOLD. **5.** A Hangman to helpe him to bed SHAKS. To h. on a work 1886. **b.** H. me up the hill with this load (*mod.*). **c.** To h. out a bad cause WOLLASTON. Phr. *H.* (a person) *to*: to aid in obtaining; to provide with. Helpe me to a Candle SHAKS. *H. oneself to*: to take for oneself; *euphem.* to steal. Also without *to*. **6.** He did not h. himself to any food SCOTT. **b.** A spoon to h. the gravy with 1889. **7.** H. us from famine TENNYSON. **8.** The jingling of the guinea helps the hurt that Honour feels TENNYSON. **9.** One thing there is . . which I fear will touch me; but I shall h. it, I hope PEPYS. **b.** Not one of us could h. laughing CARLYLE. **c.** I did not trouble myself more than I could h. SPURGEON.

Help (help), *sb.* [OE. *help* = OFris. *helpe*, OS. *helpa*, OHG. *helfa*, ON. *hjálp* :– Gmc. *xelpō, f. *xelp-; see prec.] **1.** The action of helping; the supplementing of action or resources by what makes them more efficient; aid, assistance, succour. Also with *a* and *pl.* (now *rare*). **2.** *transf.* Any thing or person that affords help; an aid OE. **3.** A person, or company of persons, whose office it is to render help ME. **b.** A person employed to give assistance in manual work; in *U.S.*, a hired labourer or servant, esp. a domestic servant 1645. **c.** The labour of hired persons; *collect.* the body of servants belonging to a farm or household (*U.S.*) 1817. **4.** Relief, cure, remedy; now only, means of obviating or avoiding something OE. **5.** A portion of food helped; a helping 1809.

1. Calling out for helpe SIR T. HERBERT. I am perfectly sensible of . . the weakness and fewness of the helps BURKE. †*At h.*: in (our) favour. *Haml.* IV. iii. 46. **2.** God is . . a very present helpe in trouble *Ps.* 46:1. Books are . . helps to knowledge BLACKIE. **3. b.** *Lady h.*, a lady engaged to assist and h. the mistress of a house. *Mother's h.*, a superior kind of nurse-maid. **4.** What's past helpe Should be past greefe SHAKS. It is their way and there is no h. for it MRS. CARLYLE.

Helper (he·lpəɹ). ME. [f. HELP *v.* + -ER^1.] **1.** One who (or that which) helps or assists; an auxiliary. **2.** An assistant in some kind of work; *spec.* a groom's assistant in a stable 1686.

1. My . . h. to a husband SHAKS. **2.** Two sleepy helpers put the wrong harness on the wrong horses DICKENS.

Helpful (he·lpfŭl), *a.* ME. [f. HELP *sb.* + -FUL.] Full of help; rendering help; useful, serviceable, profitable.

Heauens make our presence and our practises Pleasant and helpfull to him SHAKS. Hence **He·lpful-ly** *adv.*, **-ness.** So †**Helply** *a.* ME.

Helping (he·lpiŋ), *vbl. sb.* ME. [f. HELP *v.* + -ING^1.] **1.** The action of HELP *v.*; aid; †an aid; †an ally. **2.** *concr.* A portion of food served at one time; = HELP *sb.* 5. 1824.

Helping, *ppl. a.* ME. (*h. hand* 1450.)

Helpless (he·lplės), *a.* ME. [f. HELP *sb.* + -LESS.] **1.** Destitute of help; needy. **2.** Unable to help oneself; shiftless. (The current sense.) 1620. **3.** Affording no help; unavailing, unprofitable. Now *rare*. 1590. †**4.** That cannot be helped. SPENSER.

1. Helper of the H. . . be thou my Fortress 1694. H. of all that human wants require DRYDEN. **2.** H. infants CRABBE. **3.** A sharp accuser, but a h. friend POPE. Hence **He·lpless-ly** *adv.*, **-ness.**

Helpmate (he·lpmēᵗt). 1715. [f. HELP *sb.* or *v.* + MATE *sb.*^{2}, by assoc. with next.] A companion who is a help, or who renders help. Chiefly applied to a wife or husband.

In Minorca the ass and the hog are . . helpmates, and are yoked together in order to turn up the land PENNANT.

Helpmeet (he·lpmīt). 1673. [The two wds. *help meet* in Gen. 2:18, 20 ('an help meet for him'), first improp. hyphened, and then taken as one word.] A suitable helper; a helpmate; usu. of a wife or husband.

More passed . . between Selwyn and his h. 1805.

Helter-skelter (he·ltəɹ,ske·ltəɹ). 1593. [Rhyming jingle like *harum-scarum*, perh. based ult. on ME. *skelte* hasten (XIV).]

A. *adv.* In disordered haste; pell-mell. Helter-skelter haue I rode to thee SHAKS.

B. *attrib.* or *adj.* Characterized by disorderly haste or headlong confusion 1730.

C. *sb.* A helter-skelter run or flight 1713. **b.** A lighthouse-shaped structure down the outside of which pleasure-seekers slide seated on a mat 1906.

Such a helter-skelter of prayers and sins LONGF.

Helve (helv), *sb.* [OE. *helfe*, WS. *hielfe*, corresp. to OS. *helfi* (MDu. *helf, helve*), OHG. *halp*; f. WGmc. *xalb- (which appears also in HALTER). Cf. HELM *sb.*^{2}] **1.** A handle of an axe, chisel, hammer, etc. *To throw h. after hatchet*: to risk everything. **2.** (Also *helve-hammer.*) A tilt-hammer, the helve of which oscillates on bearings, so that it is raised by a cam carried by a revolving shaft, and falls by its own weight 1858. Hence **Helve** *v.* (ME., now *rare*), to furnish with a h.

Helvetian (helvī·ʃ'ăn). 1559. [f. *Helvetia* Switzerland (cf. *omnis civitas Helvetia* in

Cæsar), *Helvetius* pertaining to the *Helvetii*; see -IAN.] **A.** *adj.* **a.** Pertaining to the ancient Helvetii, a people of Gallia Lugdunensis. **b.** Swiss. **B.** *sb.* **a.** One of the ancient Helvetii. **b.** A Swiss. 1593.

Helvetic (helve·tik). 1708. [– L. *Helveticus* pertaining to the *Helvetii*; see prec., -IC.]

A. *adj.* Helvetian, Swiss.

B. *sb.* A Swiss Protestant; a Zwinglian.

Helvin, -ine (he·lvin). 1818. [f. L. *helvus* light bay; see -INE[5].] *Min.* A honey-yellow or greenish silicate of glucinum and manganese, occurring in regular tetrahedral crystals. var. **He·lvite.**

Hem (hem), *sb.*[1] [OE. *hem*, corresp. to OFris. *hemme* enclosed land, presumably rel. to HAM *sb.*[2]] **1.** The border or edging of a piece of cloth or a garment. **2.** *spec.* (in current use). A border made on a piece of cloth by doubling the edge itself, and sewing it down, to strengthen it and prevent ravelling 1665. †**3.** The edge, border, rim, margin of anything –1674. Also *fig.* **4. a.** The partition which divides the hearth from the fireplace in a reverberatory furnace; the fire-bridge 1693. **b.** *Arch.* The projecting and spiral parts of the Ionic capital 1823.

3. Entomb'd vpon the very hemme o' th' Sea SHAKS.

Hem (h'm, hem), *interj.* and *sb.*[2] 1526. [A vocalized representation of the sound made in clearing the throat with a slight effort; more closely *hm* or *h'm*.]

A. *int.* An utterance like a slight half cough, used to attract attention, give warning, or express doubt or hesitation.

H., syr, yet beware of Had I wyste SKELTON.

B. *sb.* The utterance of this sound; the sound itself 1547.

After every sygh make an h., or cough after it 1547.

†**Hem, 'em** (ĕm), *pers. pron., 3rd pl., dat.-acc.* [orig. OE. *him, hiom, heom*, dat. pl. in all genders of HE; subseq. supplanting the accus. *hi*; and finally itself displaced by *them*, exc. colloq. or dial.] **1.** *Dative.* (To) them –1599. **b.** Governed by *prep.* Them –1750. **2.** *Accusative.* Them –1868. **3.** *Refl.* and *Reciprocal Pron.* (*dat.* and *acc.*) Themselves, to themselves; (to) each other –1579.

Hem, *v.*[1] 1440. [f. HEM *sb.*[1]] **1.** *trans.* To edge or border; to decorate with a border, fringe, etc. **2.** To turn in and sew down the edge of. *intr.* To do the particular kind of sewing used in this operation. 1530. **3.** To confine or bound; to enclose, limit, restrain, imprison. Now usu. with *in*, also *about, round, up*; *hem out*, to shut out. 1538.

1. All the skirt about Was hemd with golden fringe SPENSER. **3.** Hemm'd with warlike Foes DRYDEN.

Hem, *v.*[2] 1470. [f. HEM *interj.*] **1.** *intr.* To utter the sound described under HEM *int.*; to stammer or hesitate in speaking. **2.** *trans.* To remove, clear *away* with a hem or cough. Also *fig.* 1600.

1. She speaks much of her father. . and hems and beats her heart SHAKS. *2. A. Y. L.* I. iii. 19.

Hema-, Hemato-, var. sp. of HÆMA-, etc.

He-man: see HE *pron.* V.

Hemelytrum: see HEMI-ELYTRUM.

‖**Hemeralopia** (he:mĕrălōᵘ·piă). 1706. [mod.L., f. Gr. ἡμεράλωψ, f. ἡμέρα day + ἀλαός blind + ὤψ eye; see -IA[1], and cf. NYCTALOPIA.] *Path.* 'Day-blindness'; a visual defect in which the eyes see indistinctly, or not at all by daylight, but fairly well by night or artificial light. (But others make the word = 'night-blindness', NYCTALOPIA.) Hence **Hemeralo·pic** *a.*

Hemerobian (hemĕrōᵘ·biăn). 1842. [f. mod.L. *Hemerobius* – Gr., f. ἡμέρα + -βιος living; see -IAN.] **1.** *adj.* Pertaining to the genus *Hemerobius* or the family *Hemerobiidæ* of neuropterous insects. **2.** *sb.* One of these; a day-fly.

‖**Hemeroca·llis.** 1656. [Gr. ἡμεροκαλλίς a kind of lily that blooms but for a day, f. ἡμέρα + κάλλος beauty.] The Day Lily, a genus of Liliaceous plants chiefly natives of temperate Asia and Eastern Europe.

Hemi- (he·mi, hĭ·mi), *prefix.* [repr. Gr. ἡμι-, comb. element = L. *sēmi-* SEMI-, Gmc. **sami-* half (OE. *sām-* (cf. SAND-BLIND), OS., OHG. *sāmi-*); used in many techn. terms in later L., e.g. *hemicrania* (see MEGRIM[1]), *hemicyclium* (whence, through Fr., HEMICYCLE).] Half-; one half, the half, pertaining to or affecting one half.

Hemialbu·min, *Chem.* a substance thought to be one of the two original constituents of ordinary albumin; it is converted on digestion into **Hemia·lbumose,** which is prob. an antecedent of *hemipeptone.* **Hemia·mb, -iambus,** *Pros.* an iambic dimeter catalectic. ‖**Hemianæsthe·sia,** *Path.* loss of sensation in one side of the body; hence **Hemianæsthe·sic** *a.* **Hemiana·tropous** *a., Bot.*, half-anatropous; = HEMITROPOUS. **Hemice·rebral** *a., Anat.* of or pertaining to either of the two CEREBRAL hemispheres. **Hemico·llin** [COLLIN], *Chem.* a peptone-like body formed along with semi-glutin, when a solution of gelatin is boiled a long time. **He·mide:mise·miqua:ver,** *Mus.* a note of half the length of a demisemiquaver, also its symbol. **Hemidiape·nte,** *Anc. Mus.* a diminished or imperfect fifth. **Hemidi·tone** [DITONE], *Anc. Mus.* a minor third. **Hemi-encepha·lic** *a., Anat.* of or pertaining to a *hemiencephalon*, or lateral half of the ENCEPHALON or brain. **Hemi·gamous** [Gr. γάμος] *a., Bot.* said of grasses having one of the two florets of a spicule neuter, and the other unisexual. **Hemigeo·meter,** *Entom.* a caterpillar of the *Noctuidæ*, which in its mode of progression resembles the true geometer caterpillars. **He·miglyph,** *Arch.* the half-glyph or -groove at the edge of the triglyph in the Doric entablature. **Hemiholohe·dral** *a., Cryst.* having half the number of planes in all the octants. **Hemimelli·tic,** *Chem.* a crystalline tribasic acid $C_9H_6O_6$. **Hemiocta·he·dron,** *Cryst.* a tetrahedron; hence **Hemiocta·he·dral** *a.* **He·mione** [Gr. ἡμίονος, f. ὄνος ass], *Zool.* the dziggetai. **Hemio·rthotype** *a., Cryst.* = monoclinic. ‖**Hemiparaple·gia** [Gr. παραπληγία stroke on one side], paralysis of one lower limb. **Hemipe·ptone,** *Chem.* a variety of peptone derived from hemialbumose by a continuance of the digestive process; see *Hemialbumin.* **Hemipro·tein,** *Chem.* a kind of syntonin, obtained by boiling albumin with dilute sulphuric acid for a few hours. **Hemirha·mphine** *a., Ichth.* (a fish) having the upper jaw very short in comparison with the lower, as in the genus *Hemirhamphus* or half-bills.

Hemiano·psia. 1885. [mod.L., f. HEMI- + Gr. ἀν- AN- 10 + ὄψις sight; see -IA[1].] *Path.* Half-blindness, being a loss of perception of one half the field of vision. Also **He:miano·pia, -o·psy.**

Hemibranch (he·mibræŋk). 1880. [f. HEMI- + Gr. βράγχια gills.] An incomplete gill; a fish of the order *Hemibranchii*, having the branchial apparatus incomplete. Hence **Hemibra·nchiate** *a.* half-gilled; *sb.* a h.

He·micarp. 1854. [f. HEMI- + Gr. καρπός fruit.] *Bot.* A half-fruit; one of the two carpels which constitute the fruit of the *Umbelliferæ.*

‖**Hemicrania** (hemikrēⁱ·niă). 1597. [Late L. *hemicrania* – Gr. ἡμικρανία, f. ἡμι- HEMI- + κρανίον skull; see -IA[1] and MEGRIM[1].] *Path.* Headache confined to one side of the head, megrim. So †**Hemicrane.** Hence **Hemicra·nic** *a.* pertaining or subject to h.

Hemicycle (he·misəik'l). 1603. [– Fr. *hémicycle* – L. *hemicyclium* – Gr. ἡμικύκλιον, f. ἡμι- HEMI- + κύκλος circle.] A half-circle; a semicircular structure, such as an apse-like recess, etc.

Forming themselves into a h. or half moon figure COWPER. Hence **Hemicy·clic** *a. Bot.* half-cyclic: said of flowers which have some parts arranged spirally (*acyclic*) and others in whorls (*cyclic*).

Hemida·ctyl. 1863. [f. HEMI- + Gr. δάκτυλος finger.] *Zool.* **1.** *adj.* Having an oval disc at the base of the toes, as in the saurian genus *Hemidactylus* (Webster). **2.** *sb.* A saurian of this genus; a gecko. Hence **Hemida·ctylous** *a.*

Hemidome (he·midōᵘm). 1868. [f. HEMI- + DOME *sb.*] *Cryst.* A pair of parallel and equal faces, parallel to the orthodiagonal in the monoclinic system (in which two such pairs constitute a dome). Hence **Hemidoma·tic** *a.* of or pertaining to a h.

‖**Hemi-elytrum** (hemi,e·litrŏm). *Pl.* **-a.** Also *erron.* **hemelytrum.** 1826. [mod.L., f. Gr. ἡμι- + ἔλυτρον ELYTRUM, sheath.] *Zool.* The fore wing of an insect, which is coriaceous at the base and membranous at the end, as in the *Hemiptera* and *Heteroptera.* Hence **Hemi-e·lytral** *a.*

Hemihedral (hemihī·drăl, -he·drăl), *a.* Also **hemiedral.** 1837. [f. HEMI- + Gr. ἕδρα seat, base + -AL[1].] Of a crystal: Having half the number of planes required by the highest degree of symmetry belonging to its system; thus, a tetrahedron is the hemihedral form corresponding to the holohedral octahedron. Hence **Hemihe·drally** *adv.*

Hemihedron (hemihī·drǒn, -he·drǒn). 1837. [f. as prec. after *hexahedron*, etc.] *Cryst.* A form or crystal of a hemihedral type. So **Hemihe·drism, Hemihe·dry,** the property of crystallization in hemihedral forms.

‖**Hemimetabola** (he:mi,mĭtæ·bŏlă), *sb. pl.* 1870. [mod.L., f. HEMI- + METABOLA.] *Entom.* A division of insects comprising those which undergo incomplete metamorphosis. Hence **Hemimeta·bolic, Hemimeta·bolous** *adjs.* of the nature of *Hemimetabola*; undergoing incomplete metamorphosis.

Hemimorphic (hemi,mǭ·ɹfik), *a.* 1864. [f. HEMI + Gr. μορφή + -IC.] *Cryst.* Of a crystal: Having unlike planes or modifications at the ends of the same axis. So **Hemimo·rphism,** the property of being h. **Hemimo·rphous** *a.* = HEMIMORPHIC.

‖**Hemina** (hĭməi·nă). Also **hemine.** 1601. [L. – Gr. ἡμίνα, f. ἡμι- half. Cf. Fr. *hémine* (XVIII).] A liquid measure (orig. ancient Sicilian) of about half a pint; also, a measure for corn, variously computed.

‖**Hemio·pia, Hemio·psia.** Also **-opy, -opsy.** 1811. [mod.L., f. HEMI- + Gr. ὤψ, ὠπ- eye, ὄψις sight; see -IA[1].] *Path.* = HEMIANOPSIA.

‖**Hemiplegia** (hemiplī·dʒiă). 1600. [mod. L. – Gr. ἡμιπληγία paralysis, f. ἡμι- HEMI- + πληγή stroke; see -IA[1]. Cf. DIPLEGIA, PARAPLEGIA.] *Path.* Paralysis of one side of the body. Hence **Hemiple·giac** *a.* affected with or subject to h.; *sb.* one so affected. **Hemiple·gian** *a.* **Hemiple·gic** *a.* pertaining to or characterized by h.; affected with or subject to h. vars. **He·miplegy.** †**He·miplexy.**

Hemipod, -pode (he·mipǫd, -pōᵘd). 1862. [– mod.L. *hemipodius* (generic name), f. Gr. ἡμι- HEMI- + πούς, ποδός foot. See -POD.] A member of the genus *Hemipodius*, or *Turnix*, of three-toed quail-like birds; a bush-quail, ortygan.

Hemiprism (he·mipriz'm). 1864. [HEMI-.] *Cryst.* A pair of parallel faces, parallel to the vertical axis of the crystal in the triclinic system (in which two such pairs constitute a prism). Hence **Hemiprisma·tic** *a.*

Hemipter (hĭmi·ptəɹ). 1828. [– Fr. *hémiptère* – mod.L. *hemipterus*; see next.] One of the *Hemiptera.*

‖**Hemiptera** (hĭmi·ptĕră), *sb. pl.* Rarely in *sing.* **Hemipteron.** 1816. [mod.L., neut. pl. of *hemipterus*, f. HEMI- + Gr. πτερόν wing, in reference to the structure of the wings.] *Entom.* A large order of Insects, characterized by a suctorial mouth, and in the HETEROPTERA by wings coriaceous at the base and membranous at the tip. Also called *Rhyncota.* Examples are bugs, lice, and plant-lice. Hence **Hemi·pteral** *a.* hemipterous. **Hemi·pteran** *a.* hemipterous; *sb.* one of the *Hemiptera.* **Hemi·pterist,** a student or collector of *H.*

Hemipterous (hĭmi·ptĕrəs), *a.* 1816. [f. prec. + -OUS.] *Entom.* Pertaining to or characteristic of the *Hemiptera.*

Hemisect, *v.* 1878. [f. HEMI- + *-sect* in BISECT.] *trans.* To bisect, esp. longitudinally. So **Hemise·ction.**

Hemisphere (he·misfīᵊɹ). ME. [In the form †*(h)emisperie, -sphery* (XIV) – L. *hemisphærium* – Gr. ἡμισφαίριον, f. ἡμι- HEMI- + σφαῖρα SPHERE; in the form *hemisphere* (XVI), †*-spere* (XV) = OFr. *emisp(h)ere* (mod. *hémisphère*).] **1.** *gen.* A half-sphere; one of the halves formed by a plane passing through the centre of a sphere 1585. **2.** *spec.* Half of the celestial sphere; in early use, esp. the sky above us; in *Astron.*, usually, one of the halves into which the celestial globe is divided by the equinoctial or by the ecliptic. (The earliest sense in Eng.) ME. **3.** One of the halves of the terrestrial globe 1551. **4.** A map or projection of half the (terrestrial or celestial) globe 1706. **5.** *Anat.* Each of the halves of the cerebrum of the brain 1804. **6.** *transf.* and *fig.* = 'sphere' of action, life, or thought 1503.

1. *Magdeburg hemispheres*, a contrivance invented by Otto von Guericke of Magdeburg to demonstrate the pressure of the air. It consists of two hemispheres, forming when fitted together a cavity from which the air can be withdrawn by an air-pump. When this has been done great force is required to separate the two parts. **6.** Beyond the h. of my knowledge 1856. Hence **He·misphered** *a.* (*rare*), formed as a h.; having a cerebral h. (of such a kind). **Hemisphe·ric, -al** *a.* of, pertaining to, or resembling a h.; extending over a h. **Hemisphe·rically** *adv.* **Hemisphe·rico-**, comb. f. *Hemispheric.*

Hemispheroid (hemisfīᵊroid). 1727. [f. HEMI- + SPHEROID, or f. prec. + -OID. Cf. Fr. *hémisphéroïde* (1732).] The half of a spheroid. Hence **Hemispheroi·dal** *a.* having the form of a h.

†**Hemisphe·rule.** 1696. [f. HEMI- + SPHERULE.] A half-spherule; a small hemispherical lens –1756.

Hemistich (he·mistik). 1575. [– late L. *hemistichium* – Gr. ἡμιστίχιον; see HEMI-, STICH.] *Pros.* The half or section of a line of verse; also, a line of less than the usual length. Hence **He·mistichal** *a.* pertaining to a h.

Hemisy·mmetry. 1881. [HEMI-.] *Cryst.* Same as HEMIHEDRISM. Hence **Hemisymme·trical** *a.* hemihedral.

Hemisystema·tic, *a.* 1878. [HEMI-.] *Cryst.* (See quot.)

A *hemi-systematic form* is a form in which only half the origin-planes or normals are extant STORY-MASKELYNE.

†**He·mitone.** 1603. [– L. *hemitonium* – Gr. ἡμιτόνιον, f. HEMI- + τόνος tone.] = SEMITONE –1760.

Hemi·tropal, *a.* 1864. [f. as next + -AL[1].] = HEMITROPOUS 2.

Hemitrope (he·mitroᵘp). 1805. [– Fr. *hémitrope* (Haüy, 1801), f. HEMI- + Gr. -τροπος turning.] *Cryst.* **1.** *adj.* = HEMITROPIC. **2.** *sb.* A hemitropic crystal 1805. So **He·mitropism, Hemi·tropy,** hemitropic crystallization.

Hemitropic (hemitrǫ·pik), *a.* 1886. [f. as prec. + -IC.] *Cryst.* Said of composite or twin crystals, which are united together in such a way that, if we conceive one of them as being turned through half a revolution round a particular axis, corresponding faces and edges in the two crystals would become parallel.

Hemi·tropous, *a.* 1860. [f. as prec. + -OUS.] **1.** *Cryst.* = prec. **2.** *Bot.* Said of an ovule so formed that the hilum lies half-way between the base and the apex.

Hemlock (he·mlǫk). [OE. *hymlice, hym-, hemlic*, of unkn. origin. The alt. of the final syll. to *-lock* (XV) is paralleled in CHARLOCK.] **1.** The common name of *Conium maculatum*, a poisonous umbelliferous plant, having finely divided leaves, and small white flowers; used as a powerful sedative. Also in rural use applied to the large *Umbelliferæ* generally. **2.** A North Amer. tree *Abies canadensis*, more fully *Hemlock Fir, H. Spruce* 1728. **b.** *Ground H.*: a Canadian species or variety of Yew 1866. **3.** A poisonous potion obtained from the Common Hemlock. (Believed to have been the poison administered to Socrates.) 1601.

2. The murmuring pines and the hemlocks, Bearded with moss LONGF. **3.** A drowsy numbness pains My sense, as though of h. I had drunk KEATS.

Comb.: **h. dropwort**, *Œnanthe crocata*; **h. parsley**, a N. Amer. umbelliferous plant resembling h., but not poisonous; there are two species, *Conioselinum canadense* and *C. fischeri*.

Hemmel. *dial.* 1717. [var. of HELM *sb.*[1] in sense 'roofed shelter for cattle, etc.'] Cow-shed.

Hemmer (he·məɹ). 1483. [f. HEM *v.*[1] + -ER[1].] One who hems. **b.** An 'attachment' to a sewing machine for doing hemming (Knight) 1875.

Hemo-, var. spelling of HÆMO-, usual in U.S., and occasional in Great Britain, as in *hemorrhage*, etc.

Hemp (hemp). *sb.* [OE. *henep, hænep* = OS. *hanap* (Du. *hennep*), OHG. *hanaf* (G. *hanf*), ON. *hampr* :- Gmc. **χanipiz*, rel. to Gr. κάνναβις (whence L. *cannabis*; cf. CANVAS).] **1.** An annual herbaceous plant, *Cannabis sativa*, N.O. *Urticaceæ*, cultivated for its valuable fibre. **2.** The cortical fibre of this plant, used for making cordage, and woven into stout fabrics ME. **3.** In allusion to a rope for hanging 1532. **4.** A narcotic drug obtained from the Indian hemp; bhang; hashish 1870. **5.** Applied to other plants yielding a useful fibre, or otherwise resembling hemp 1597.

3. Let not Hempe his Wind-pipe suffocate SHAKS. **5. African H.,** (*a*) = *bowstring hemp* (*a*); (*b*) *Sparmannia africana*. **Bastard H.,** Hemp-nettle and H.-agrimony. **Bowstring H.,** (*a*) a plant of the genus *Sanseviera*, esp. *S. guineensis*, a liliaceous plant of tropical Africa, the leaf-fibres of which are used for bowstrings and for making ropes; (*b*) in India, *S. Roxburghiana*; also *Calatropis gigantea* (N.O. *Asclepiadaceæ*). **Canada** or **Indian H.,** *Apocynum cannabinum*, a N. Amer. perennial. **Indian H.,** a tropical variety of common h., *Cannabis indica*. **Manilla H.,** the fibre of *Musa textilis*. **Sisal H.,** the fibre of species of *Agave*, esp. *A. sisalana*. **Water H.,** a name for *Eupatorium cannabinum* and *Bidens tripartita*, in U.S. for *Acnida cannabina*.

Comb.: **h.-cake**, the residue of crushed hempseed, after extraction of the oil; **-oil**, the oil pressed out of hempseed; **-palm**, a palm *Chamærops excelsa*, of China and Japan, the fibres of which are made into cordage.

Hemp-agrimony. 1778. *Herb.* A book-name for *Eupatorium cannabinum*; also for other species. **b.** *Water Hemp-agrimony*, Bur-Marigold or *Bidens*.

Hempen (he·mpĕn), *a.* (*sb.*) ME. [f. HEMP *sb.* + -EN[4].] **1.** Made of hemp; of or pertaining to hemp. **2.** Resembling hemp 1651. **3.** *sb.* Hempen cloth 1777.

1. *H. homespun*, homespun cloth made of hemp; hence, one clad in this, one of rustic manners. What h. home-spuns haue we swaggering here SHAKS.

He·mp-nettle. 1801. The genus *Galeopsis*.

Hempseed (he·mpsīd). ME. The seed of hemp. **b.** A gallows-bird. SHAKS. Also *attrib.*, as in **hempseed calculus** (*Path.*), a variety of the mulberry-calculus.

He·mpstring. 1566. *lit.* String made of hemp. Hence *transf.*, one who deserves the halter.

He·mpweed. 1796. A name of species of *Eupatorium*.

Hempy (he·mpi), *a.* 1440. [f. HEMP *sb.* + -Y[1].] Made of, like, or of the nature of hemp; producing hemp.

Hemself(e, -selve(n, themselves: see SELF.

He·m-stitch, *v.* 1839. [f. HEM *sb.*[1] + STITCH *v.*[1]] *trans.* To hem with an ornamental stitch of a particular kind, giving the effect of a row of stitching; to ornament with this stitch. Hence **He·m-stitch** *sb.* ornamental needlework of this kind.

†**Hemule, hemuse.** 1486. [perh. a perversion of L. *hinnuleus* young stag, roebuck.] *Venery.* A roebuck of the third year –1660.

Hen (hen), *sb.* [OE. *henn* = OFris., MLG. *henne*, OHG. *henna* (G. *henne*) :- WGmc. **χannja*, f. Gmc. **χanon* cock (OE. *hana*), rel. to L. *canere* sing.] **1.** The female of the common domestic fowl. (occas. = 'domestic fowls', including the males.) **2.** The female of various other birds; also, = *hen-bird* ME. **3.** A female fish or crustacean 1810. **4.** *fig.* Of persons 1626. **5.** A kind of bivalve shell-fish, *Venus mercenaria*. Also *locally*, A fresh-water mussel. 1603. **6.** *attrib.* in sense 'female' OE.

Comb.: **h.-blindness**, nyctalopia; **-driver**, the hen-harrier; †**-harm**, the hen-harrier; **-plant**, a name for *Plantago lanceolata* and *P. major*.

†**Hen, henne,** *adv.* [OE. **hio-*, *heonan(e)*, *-one*, = OS., OHG. *hinana, hinan* (G. *hinnen*); also OE. *hina, heona* = MLG., MDu. *hēne* (Du. *heen*), OHG. *hina* (G. *hin*); WGmc. formations on the pronominal base Gmc. **χi-* HE.] = HENCE: of time, place, or inference. OE. and ME. only.

†**He·nad.** 1678. [– Gr. ἑνάς, ἑνάδ- unit, f. ἕν one; see -AD.] A unit, monad (in the Platonic philosophy).

Hen and chickens. †**1.** The Pleiades 1613. **2.** A compound daisy 1794; London Pride, etc. **3.** A children's game 1894.

Henbane (he·nbēⁱn). ME. [f. HEN *sb.* + BANE.] **1.** Name of the annual plant *Hyoscyamus niger*, a viscid weed, growing on waste ground, having dull yellow flowers streaked with purple, and narcotic and poisonous properties; also, the genus as a whole. **2.** The drug extracted from this 1840. **3.** *attrib.* ME.

Henbit (he·nbit). 1578. [f. HEN *sb.* + BIT *sb.*[2]] Name of †**a.** Ivy-leaved Speedwell (*Veronica hederifolia*); also called *Small H.*; **b.** A species of Dead-nettle (*Lamium amplexicaule*); formerly known as *Greater H.* Also *H. Nettle, H. Dead-nettle.* 1597.

Hence (hens), *adv.* [ME. *hennes, hens*, f. HEN, HENNE *adv.* + *-es*, -S *suffix*. The sp. *-ce* is phonetic, to retain the unvoiced sound denoted in the earlier sp. by *-s*. See C (the letter). Cf. THENCE, WHENCE.]

I. Of place. **1.** (Away) from here; to or at a distance; away. Also with redundant *from*. **2.** *ellipt.* Chiefly as a command: *Hence!* go hence. *H. with*: go away with, take away 1573. **3.** *spec.* From this world ME.; †in the next world (SHAKS.).

1. High you hense 1440. Not past three quarters of a mile h. SHAKS. **2.** H. with her, out o' dore SHAKS. **3.** Before I goe h., and be no more *Ps.* 39:13.

II. Of time. From this time; onward ME. from now ME. Also with *from*.

Fro hennes in to domes day CHAUCER. Some houre h. SHAKS.

III. Of issue, etc. **1.** From this, as a source of origin 1597. **2.** (As a result) from this. Also with *from*. 1608. **3.** (As an inference) from this; therefore 1586.

1. My Flora was my Sun..All other faces borrowed h. Their light and grace SUCKLING. **2.** Learn courage h. POPE. **3.** It is so with men generally, and h. we assume it to be so with you 1898.

†**Hence,** *v. rare.* 1580. [f. prec.] *trans.* To order hence; *intr.* to go hence, depart –1614.

Henceforth (he·ns,fōᵊɹþ, hensfōᵊ·ɹþ), *adv.* ME. [f. as prec. + FORTH *adv.*] From this time forth. Also with *from* (arch.).

A power..with which the Monarchy was h. to reckon J. R. GREEN.

Hencefo·rward, *adv.* ME. [f. HENCE *adv.* + FORWARD.] From this time forward; henceforth. Also with *from* (*arch.*). So †**Hencefo·rwards** *adv.*

†**Hench-boy.** 1512. [f. *hench-* in HENCHMAN + BOY.] A page of honour, a boy attendant –1683.

Henchman (he·nʃmæ̆n). Also †**henxman.** *Pl.* **-men.** [ME. *hengest-, henxst-, henx-, hensman*, perh. horse-attendant (later with elevation of status, as in *groom, marshal*), f. OE. *heng(e)st*; see HENGEST.] **1. a.** ? A groom. **b.** A squire, or page of honour to a prince or great man. In later 16th c. use, app. = HENCH-BOY. *Obs.* (exc. *Hist.*) since 17th c. **2.** The chief gillie of a Highland chief; hence, generally, a trusty follower or attendant 1730. **b.** A stout political partisan; *esp.* in U.S. 'A mercenary adherent' (*Cent. Dict.*) 1839.

Hen-coop (he·n,kūp). 1697. A coop in which poultry are kept.

†**Hend, hende,** *a.* (*adv.*) [aphet. f. OE. *ġehende* adj. (and adv.), near, convenient, lit. at hand, handy.] **1.** Near, at hand –ME. **2.** Convenient, handy (*rare*) –1513. **3.** Ready with the hand, dexterous; skilful –1550. **4.** Courteous; kind, 'nice' –1765. **5.** Comely, fair –1450. **6.** *absol.* or as *sb.* Gentle, courteous, or gracious one or ones (see 4) –1549. **7.** *adv.* Near, at hand –1507; courteously, kindly, gently –1450.

Hendeca-, bef. a vowel **hendec-**; erron. **endeca-**. Comb. form of Gr. ἕνδεκα eleven, as in **Hende·cachord,** *Mus.* a series or scale of eleven notes; hence **Hendecacho·rdal** *a.*, relating to such a scale.

Hendecagon (hende·kăgǫ̆n). Also erron. **en-**. 1704. [f. HENDECA + -GON.] **a.** *Geom.* A plane figure having eleven sides and eleven angles. †**b.** *Fortif.* A fort with eleven bastions.

Hendecasyllabic (he:ndĭ-, hende:kăsilæ·bik). Also erron. **en-**. 1727. [f. as next + -IC; see also SYLLABIC.] *Pros.* **1.** *adj.* Of a verse: Consisting of eleven syllables. **2.** *sb.* A hendecasyllabic verse. (Usu. in *pl.*) 1836.

Hendecasyllable (he:ndi-, hende:kăsi·lă-b'l). Also erron. **en-**. 1603. [– L. *hendecasyllabus* (sc. *versus*) – Gr. ἑνδεκασύλλαβος (sc. στίχος), subst. use of the adj. 'eleven-syllabled'; see HENDECA-, SYLLABLE.] *Pros.* A verse or line of eleven syllables.

‖**Hendiadys** (hendəi·ădis). 1586. [med.L., f. Gr. phr. ἓν διὰ δυοῖν 'one through two' (Servius).] *Gram.* A figure of speech in which a single idea is expressed by two words connected by a conjunction; e.g. by two sbs. with *and* instead of an adj. and sb.

Law and heraldry, a kind of h., meaning 'heraldic law' 1887.

†**Hendy**, *a.* ME. only. [f. HEND *a.* + -Y¹.] = HEND *a.*

Hen-egg. [In OE. two wds., with *henne* in genitive; now usually *hen's egg*.] The egg of a hen.

Henen, obs. var. of HEN, hence.

Henequen (he·nĭken). Also **-quin, henne-quen.** 1880. [– Sp. *jeniquen, geniquen*, from native name.] The fibrous product known as *Sisal hemp*, obtained from the leaves of species of *Agave*; also, the plant itself.

Heng, ME. inflexion of HANG *v.*

†**He·ngest.** [OE. *heng(e)st* stallion, gelding = OFris. *hengst, hanxt*, MLG. *hengest*, OHG. *hengist*, Du., G. *hengst*, ON. *hestr*.] A male horse; usually a gelding –ME. (Also a proper name, and in various place-names.)

He·n-ha:rrier. 1565. [f. HEN *sb.* + HARRIER¹; in reference to its preying upon poultry.] *Ornith.* A European bird of prey, *Circus cyaneus*, also called Blue Hawk, Blue Kite.

He·n-hawk. 1855. *Ornith.* U.S. name for various species of Hawks and Buzzards, esp. *Buteo borealis* and *B. lineatus*. *Blue hen-hawk*, the adult Amer. goshawk.

He·n-hea:rted, *a.* 1522. Timorous; chicken-hearted.

He·n-house. 1512. A small house or shed in which poultry are shut up for the night.

He·nism. [f. Gr. εἷς, ἑν- one + -ISM. Cf. HENAD.] = MONISM. Max-Müller.

Henna (he·nă). 1600. [– Arab. *ḥinnā'*. Cf. ALCANNA, ALKANET.] The Egyptian Privet, *Lawsonia inermis* (N.O. *Lythraceæ*); the shoots and leaves of this plant used, esp. in the East, as a dye for parts of the body, or made into a cosmetic with catechu. Also *attrib.*

He·nnery, 1859. [f. HEN *sb.* + -ERY.] A place for rearing poultry.

Hennes, obs. f. HENCE.

Henny (he·ni). 1854. [f. HEN *sb.* + -Y¹.] **1.** *adj.* Of or pertaining to a hen; hen-like: said of some male fowls; so *h.-feathered* 1855. **2.** *sb.* A hen-like male fowl 1854.

Henotheism (he·noþī,iz'm). 1860. [f. Gr. ἑνο-, stem of εἷς one + θεός god + -ISM.] The belief in a single god without asserting that he is the only God: a stage of belief between polytheism and monotheism. So **He·no-theist, Henothei·stic** *a.*

Henotic (henǫ·tik), *a.* 1878. [– Gr. ἑνωτικός serving to unite, f. ἕνωσις unification, f. ἕν one; see -OTIC.] Unifying; reconciling. GLADSTONE.

He·n-peck, *v.* *colloq.* 1688. [Back-formation from HEN-PECKED.] *trans.* Of a wife: To domineer over or rule (the husband).

But—oh! ye lords of ladies intellectual..have they not hen-peck'd you all BYRON.

Hen-pecked (he·n,pekt), *ppl. a.* *colloq.* 1680. [lit. pecked by a hen or hens: alluding to the plucking of the domestic cock by his hens.] Domineered over or ruled by a wife.

A Step-dame..rules my hen-peck'd Sire DRYDEN.

Hen-roost. OE. [f. HEN *sb.* + ROOST *sb.*¹] A place where domestic fowls roost at night. **b.** *fig.* A source of plunder 1909.

Hen's-foot. 1578. [From the resemblance of the leaves to a hen's claws.] Name of: †**a.** [tr. L. *pes gallinaceus* (Pliny).] The Climbing Fumitory, *Corydalis claviculata* –1601. **b.** [L. *pes pulli*.] Bur-parsley, *Caucalis daucoides* 1597.

Hent, *v.* *Obs.* exc. *arch.* or *dial.* [OE. *hentan* :– Gmc. *χent-, wk. grade *χunt-, whence OE. *huntian* HUNT.] **1.** *trans.* To lay hold of, seize; to take or hold in one's hand; to catch (*arch.*). **2.** To get; to 'catch' (harm, etc.); to apprehend ME. Hence **Hent** *sb.* the act of seizing; *fig.* conception, intention, design. †**Henter**, one who seizes.

Henware (he·nwēᵊɹ). *Sc.* 1808. [app. f. HEN *sb.* + WARE *sb.*¹] The edible seaweed *Alaria esculenta*, also called *badderlocks*.

Heo, *dial* **hoo**, *pers. pron.*, *3rd sing. fem.*, *nom. Obs.* exc. *dial.* [OE. *hīu, hīo, hēo*, fem. of HE. Later, the north. and e.midl. dialects exchanged *hio, heo, hyo, ȝho, ȝhe* for the forms, north. *sco, scho, sho*, e.midl. *scæ, sȝe, sche*, SHE.] The original fem. pron. corresponding to *he*; now repl. by SHE. Used of women, and of things grammatically feminine.

Heortology (hiǫɹtǫ·lŏdʒi). 1900. [– G. *heortologie*, Fr. *héortologie*, f. Gr. ἑορτή feast; see -LOGY.] The department of ecclesiology which deals with festivals. Hence **-o·logist.**

Hep, var. form of HIP *sb.*²

‖**Hepar** (hī·paɹ). 1693. [Late L. *hepar* liver – Gr. ἧπαρ.] *Chem.* and *Med.* **1.** An old name for a metallic sulphide, having a reddish-brown or liver colour. Also, for compounds of sulphur with other substances. 1796. **2.** Also more fully, *hepar sulphuris* or *hepar sulphur*: **a.** (*H. s. kalinum*) Old name for *potassa sulphurata* 1693. **b.** (*H. s. calcareum*) Homœopathic name for calcium sulphide 1866.

Hepat-, bef. a vowel = HEPATO-, comb. f. Gr. ἧπαρ, ἡπατ- liver: as in **Hepata·lgia**, neuralgia of the liver; hence **Hepata·lgic** *a.* **Hepatemphra·xis** [Gr. ἔμφραξις], obstruction of the liver; hence **Hepatemphra·ctic** *a.*

Hepatic (hĭpæ·tik). ME. [– L. *hepaticus* – Gr. ἡπατικός, f. ἧπαρ, ἡπατ- liver; see -IC. Cf. Fr. *hépatique*.]

A. *adj.* **1.** Of or pertaining to the liver 1599. **2.** Acting on the liver 1671. **3.** Liver-coloured, dark brownish-red; as in *H. aloes* ME. **4.** Pertaining to a hepar; sulphurous 1651. †**5.** *H. moss*, a liverwort (see HEPATICA 2) 1824.

1. Phr. *H. artery, ducts*; *h. apoplexy, disease*. **3.** *H. pyrites*, decomposed liver-brown tessular crystals of iron pyrites. **4.** †*H. air* or *gas*, sulphuretted hydrogen 1786. So †**Hepa·tical** *a.* (in sense 1).

B. *sb.* A medicine that acts on the liver and increases the secretion of bile 1486.

‖**Hepatica** (hĭpæ·tikă). 1548. [med.L. *hepatica* (sc. *herba*), subst. use of fem. of L. *hepaticus*; see prec.] *Bot.* **1.** A subgenus or section of the genus *Anemone*; esp. *Anemone (Hepatica) triloba*, the three-lobed leaves of which were fancied to resemble the liver 1578. **2.** An old name for Common Liverwort, *Marchantia polymorpha*, a lichen-like plant which creeps over wet rocks and damp ground, rooting from the lower surface of the thallus. *Hepaticæ*, a group of Cryptogams allied to the Mosses, containing plants which have no operculum, and as a rule possess elaters; e.g. the Common Liverwort.

†**Hepatite**¹ (he·pătəit). ME. [– L. *hepatitis* – Gr. ἡπατῖτις.] A precious stone (*hepatitis gemma* Pliny) said to resemble the liver –1706.

Hepatite². 1802. [Named by Karsten, 1800 (*Hepatit*), from the older name *lapis hepaticus*.] *Min.* A name of varieties of Barytes emitting a fetid, sulphurous, or hepatic odour when rubbed or heated; liver-stone.

‖**Hepatitis** (hepătəi·tis). 1727. [mod.L., f. Gr. ἧπαρ, ἡπατ- liver + -ITIS.] *Path.* Inflammation of the substance of the liver.

Hepatization (hepătəizēⁱ·ʃən). 1796. [f. next + -ATION.] †**1.** *Chem.* Impregnation with sulphuretted hydrogen. KIRWAN. **2.** *Path.* Consolidation of the lung tissue, so that it becomes solid and friable somewhat like liver, being first of a red and afterwards of a grey colour 1822.

Hepatize (he·pătəiz), *v.* 1786. [f. Gr. ἧπαρ, ἡπατ- liver + -IZE.] *trans.* †**a.** *Chem.* To impregnate with sulphuretted hydrogen. **b.** *Path.* To convert (the lungs) by engorgement and effusion into a substance resembling liver.

a. Hepatized water 1786, ammonia 1834.

Hepato-, repr. Gr. ἡπατο-, comb. f. ἧπαρ liver; as in **He·patocele** [Gr. κήλη tumour], hernia of the liver. **Hepatocy·stic** [CYST] *a.*, pertaining to the liver and the gall-bladder, or uniting the two. **Hepatoga·stric** *a.*, pertaining to both the liver and the stomach. **Hepatoge·nic, Hepato·genous** *adjs.*, originating from the liver. **He·patolith** [Gr. λίθος], a gall-stone; hence **Hepatoli·thic** *a.* **Hepato·logy** [-LOGY], that part of medical science which treats of the liver; hence **Hepato·logist; Hepatolo·gical** *a.* **He:patopa·ncreas,** *Biol.* name for the glandular organ, called the liver in Invertebrates, in reference to its twofold function of secretion and digestion. **Hepato-re·nal** *a.*, relating to the liver and the kidneys. **Hepato·scopy** [Gr. -σκοπία], inspection of the liver; divination by means of this.

‖**Hephæstus** (hĭfī·stŏs). 1658. = Gr. Ἥφαιστος god of fire, identified by the Romans with Vulcan. Hence **Hephæ·stian** *a.* of, belonging to, or made by H. **Hephæ·stic** *a.* relating to fire, the forge, or use of the smith's hammer.

Hephthemimer (hefþĭmi·məɹ). Occas. **hephthemim.** 1706. [– late L. *hephthemimeres* (-*is*) – Gr. ἑφθημιμερής 'containing seven halves', f. ἑπτά seven + ἡμι- half + μέρος part, -μερης -partite.] *Anc. Pros.* A group or catalectic colon of seven half-feet; the part of a hexameter preceding the cæsura when this divides the fourth foot, as in

'Inferretque deos Latio · genus unde Latinum'. Hence **Hephthemi·meral** *a.*, as in *h. cæsura*.

Hepper. 1861. [Of unkn. origin.] Local name of a smolt, or young salmon of the second year.

Hepta-, bef. a vowel HEPT-, comb. f. Gr. ἑπτά seven. In *Chem.* it indicates the presence of seven atoms of an element, as *heptacarbon*, etc.

Heptaco·lic [Gr. κῶλον] *a.*, in ancient prosody: of seven cola or members, as 'a heptacolic period'. ‖**Hepta·meron** [Gr. ἡμέρα], a seven days' work; title of a collection of stories made by Queen Margaret of Navarre, *a*1549 (cf. DECAMERON). **Heptaphy·llous** *a.*, *Bot.* having seven leaves or calyx sepals. **Heptase·mic** [late L. *heptasemos* – Gr.] *a.*, in ancient prosody: containing seven units of time or moræ. **Heptaspe·rmous** [Gr. σπέρμα] *a.*, *Bot.* bearing seven seeds. **He·ptastich** [Gr. στίχος] *sb.*, a group of seven lines of verse: *a.*, seven lines long. **Hepta·valent** [L. *valentem*] *a.*, *Chem.* combining with or capable of replacing seven atoms of hydrogen or other univalent element or radical.

Heptachord (he·ptăkǭɹd). 1694. [– Gr. ἑπτάχορδος seven-stringed, f. ἑπτά seven + χορδή string. Cf. late L. *heptachordus* with seven strings; -*um* series of seven strings (Boethius).] *Mus.* †**1.** *adj.* Seven-stringed –1741. **2.** *sb.* **a.** A musical instrument of seven strings 1765. **b.** A series of seven notes, formed of two conjunct tetrachords 1774. **c.** The interval of a seventh 1694.

Heptad (he·ptæd). 1660. [– Gr. ἑπτάς, ἑπταδ-, f. ἑπτά seven; see -AD. Cf. late L. *heptas* the number seven (Mart. Cap.).] **1.** The sum or number of seven; a group of seven 1660. *spec.* = HEBDOMAD 1876. **2.** *Chem.* An atom or molecule whose equivalence is seven atoms of hydrogen. Hence **Hepta·dic** *a.*

He·ptaglot, *a.* and *sb.* 1684. [f. Gr. ἑπτά + γλῶττα tongue, -γλωττος -tongued, prob. after POLYGLOT.] **a.** *adj.* Using or written in seven languages. **b.** *sb.* A book in seven languages.

Heptagon (he·ptăgǫn). 1570. [– Fr. *heptagone* or med.L. *heptagonum*, subst. use of n. sing. of late L. *heptagonus* adj. (Boeth.) – Gr. ἑπτάγωνος seven-cornered; see HEPTA-, -GON.] **1.** *Geom.* A plane figure having seven angles and seven sides. **2.** *attrib.* or *adj.* 1775. Hence **Hepta·gonal** *a.* having seven angles and seven sides. *Heptagonal numbers*, the series of POLYGONAL numbers 1, 7, 18, 34, 55, 81, etc. formed by continuous summation of the arithmetical series 1, 6, 11, 16, 21, 26, etc.

‖**Heptagynia** (heptădʒi·niă). 1760. [mod. L. (Linnæus, 1735), f. HEPTA- + Gr. γυνή woman, wife, female, taken in the sense of female organ, pistil; see -IA¹.] *Bot.* An order in the Linnæan Sexual System, comprising plants having seven pistils. So **He·ptagyn**, a plant of this order. **Heptagy·nian, Heptagy·nious** *adjs.* of or pertaining to this order. **Hepta·gynous** *a.* having seven pistils.

Heptahedron (-hī·drǫn, -he·drǫn). 1658. [f. HEPTA- + *-hedron* in POLYHEDRON, TETRAHEDRON (Billingsley).] A solid figure having seven faces. So **Heptahe·dral** *a.* seven-sided, seven-faced.

Heptamerous (heptæ·mĕrəs), *a.* 1790. [f. HEPTA- + Gr. μέρος part + -OUS.] Consisting of seven members or parts.

‖**Hepta·ndria.** 1753. [mod.L. (Linnæus, 1735), f. *heptandrus*, f. HEPTA- + Gr. ἀνήρ, ἀνδρ- male, man; see -IA[1].] *Bot.* The seventh class in the Sexual System of Linnæus, containing plants having seven stamens. So **Hepta·nder,** a member of this class. **Hepta·ndrian** *a.* of or belonging to H. **Hepta·ndrous** *a.* having seven stamens.

Heptane (he·ptēⁱn). 1877. [f. HEPTA- + -ANE 2.] *Chem.* The paraffin of the heptacarbon series, having the formula C_7H_{16}. 'Of these hydrocarbons nine are possible and four are known' (*Fownes' Chem.*). So **Heptene** (he·ptīn) [see -ENE], the olefine of the heptacarbon series (C_7H_{14}) also called **He·ptylene,** homologous and polymeric with ethene (C_2H_4); it is known to exist in three isomeric forms. **Heptine** (he·ptəin) [see -INE], the hydrocarbon of the same series (C_7H_{12}), homologous with acetyline or ethine. **Hepto·ic** *a.*, applied to fatty acids, aldehydes, etc., belonging to the heptacarbon series, as *heptoic acid*, $C_7H_{14}O_2$. **Heptil** (he·ptil) [see -YL], the hydrocarbon radical (C_7H_{15}) of heptylic or oenanthylic alcohol and its derivatives; hence **Hepty·lic** *a.*; **He·ptylami·ne** (see AMINE).

Heptarch (he·ptaɹk). 1679. [f. HEPTA- + -ARCH, after TETRARCH.] A ruler of one division of a heptarchy 1822. †**b.** A seventh king (see Rev. 17: 9–11).

B. *adj. Bot.* Arising from seven distinct points of origin 1884.

So **Hepta·rchal, Hepta·rchic, -al** *adjs.* of or pertaining to a heptarchy.

Heptarchy (he·ptaɹki). 1576. [f. HEPTA- + -ARCHY, after *tetrarchy*. Cf. mod.L. *heptarchia* (Camden, 1586).] A government by seven rulers; an aggregate of seven petty kingdoms, each under its own ruler; *spec.* the seven kingdoms established by the Angles and Saxons in Britain. Also †**Heptarchate** 1650.

In that Heptarchie of our Saxons, vsually six of the Kings were but as subiects to the supreme SELDEN.

Heptasyllabic (heptăsilæ·bik), *a.* (*sb.*) 1771. [f. Gr. ἑπτασύλλαβος of seven syllables (see HEPTA-, SYLLABLE) + -IC.] (A verse) consisting of seven syllables.

Heptateuch (he·ptătiūk). 1678. [– late L. *heptateuchus* (Jerome) – Gr. ἑπτάτευχος, f. ἑπτά seven + τεῦχος book.] A volume consisting of seven books; *occas.* the first seven books of the Bible, after *Pentateuch*.

Her (hɔ̄ɹ, hɔ̆ɹ), *pers. pron. 3rd sing. fem., dat.-accus.* [OE. *hire*, dative case of *hīo*, HEO 'she'. The dative began in X to be used instead of the original accusative *hīe*, *hī*, *hīġ*, *hȳ*, and now as indirect and direct objective represents both cases, as in 'we met *her* and gave *her* the book to take with *her*'.] **1.** The female being in question: the objective case of SHE. **2.** For names of things feminine grammatically, or (later) by personification OE. **b.** Represented as used by Welsh or Gaelic speakers for *he, him*, or for the speaker himself 1526. **3.** *refl.* = herself; to herself. (Now *poetic.*) OE. **4.** Erron. for the *nominative* 1698.

Her (hɔ̄ɹ, hɔ̆ɹ), *poss. pron., 3rd sing. fem.* [OE. *hiere, hire*, gen. of *hīo*, HEO 'she'. In OE. used as both an objective and a possessive gen.; the former use became obs. in ME., and *hire* remained a possessive gen., indistinguishable in use from a possessive adj., and is thus included in the same class with *my, thy, his, our, your, their*. Like these, it has developed an absolute form HERS, for which HERN was also used in late ME., and still exists in some dialects.] **1.** as *gen. case* of *pers. pron.*: Of her. OE. and ME. only. **2.** *Poss. adj. pron.* (orig. *poss. gen.*): Of or belonging to her; that female's; also *refl.* her own OE. **b.** Used of things feminine †grammatically, or by personification OE. **c.** Of animals regarded as feminine, irrespectively of sex ME. **3.** After a *sb.*, a substitute for the gender inflexion OE.

2. Her hopes, her fears, her joys, were all Bounded within the cloister wall SCOTT. **b.** The prestes broughte the Arke..vnto hir place COVERDALE *2 Chr.* 5:7. The Shippe boaring the Moone with her maine Mast SHAKS. **c.** Go to the Emmet (thou slogarde) considre hir wayes COVERDALE *Prov.* 6:6. **3.** The wyf of bathe hire tale ME.

†**Her,** *poss. pron., 3rd pl.* [OE. *hiera, hira; hyra, hiora, hiara, heora*, gen. pl., in all genders, of HE. In ME. treated as a possessive adj. Early encroached upon by *þeȝȝre* from Old Norse, which, in the form *their*, prevailed before 1500. The form *her* has long disappeared.]

Heraclean (herăklī·ăn), *a.* 1883. [– L. *Heracleus*, also *-clius* – Gr. Ἡράκλειος, f. Ἡρακλῆς HERCULES; see -AN, -EAN.] Pertaining to Heracles.

H. stone (*lapis Heracleus*, λίθος Ἡρακλεία): the magnet, so called from its great attractive power.

Heracleid, -id (he·răkləid, -id). 1835. [– Gr. Ἡρακλείδης (pl. -αι), L. *Heracleides* (pl. *-æ*), a descendant of Ἡρακλῆς or Hercules.] One of the descendants of Heracles from whom the Dorian aristocracy of the Peloponnesus claimed descent. (Usu. in *pl.*) Hence **Heraclei·dan** *a.* pertaining to a H.

Heracleonite (heræ·kliŏnəit). 1555. [f. name *Heracleon* + -ITE[1] 1.] *Eccl. Hist.* One of a sect of Gnostics founded by Heracleon in the 2nd c.

Heraclitean (he:răkləitī·ăn), *a.* (*sb.*) 1864. [f. L. *Heracliteus*, Gr. Ἡρακλείτειος + -AN.] **1.** Of, pertaining to, or of the style of Heraclitus of Ephesus, of the 5th c. B.C. (called the 'weeping philosopher'), or his theories. **2.** *sb.* A disciple of Heraclitus 1882. So **Heracli·tic** *a.* and *sb.*

Herald (he·răld), *sb.* [ME. *heraud, herauld* – OFr. *herau(l)t* (mod. *héraut*) – Gmc. **χariwald-*, f. **χarjaz* army + **wald-* rule, WIELD.] **1.** An officer having the duty of making royal or state proclamations, and of bearing ceremonial messages between princes or sovereign powers. Also, **b.**, employed in the tourney to make proclamations, convey challenges, and marshal the combatants ME. Hence, **c.**, having the function of arranging public processions, funerals, etc.; of regulating the use of armorial bearings (cf. DISCLAIM *v.*); of settling questions of precedence; and later, of recording proved pedigrees ME. **2.** *transf.* and *fig.* **a.** A messenger, envoy. Hence, a title of newspapers. ME. **b.** A forerunner, precursor 1592. **3.** One skilled in heraldry 1821. **4.** (In full, *Herald-moth.*) One of the noctuid moths, *Gonoptera libatrix* 1832.

1. †*Herald of arms* ME., †*h. at arms* 1646. †*King h., Lyon h.*: ancient names of Garter king-of-arms and Lyon king-of-arms; see KING-OF-ARMS. *Heralds' College*, or *College of Arms*: a royal corporation, founded 1483, consisting of the Earl Marshal, kings-of-arms, heralds, and pursuivants, exercising jurisdiction in matters armorial, and now recording proved pedigrees and granting armorial bearings. *Heralds' Office*, the office of this corporation. **2. a.** His tongue, the H. of his imagination, is a busie Officer 1615. **b.** It was the Larke the Herauld of the Morne SHAKS. *Comb.*: **h.-crab** = *heraldic crab*; **-moth**: see sense 4. Hence †**He·raldize** *v.* to emblazon. **He·raldship,** the office or dignity of a h.

He·rald, *v.* ME. [– OFr. *herauder, heraulder*, etc., f. prec.] *trans.* To proclaim, to announce, as at hand or drawing nigh; to usher *in*.

Heraldic, -al (hĕræ·ldik, -ăl), *a.* 1610. [f. HERALD *sb.* + -IC, -ICAL. Cf. Fr. *héraldique* (XV).] Of or pertaining to heraldry. Also *fig.*

Heraldic crab: a Japanese crab, *Huenia heraldica*, one of the *Maiadæ*; so called because the shape of its carapace suggests the shield and mantle of coat armour. Hence **Hera·ldically** *adv.*

Heraldry (he·răldri). 1572. [f. HERALD *sb.* + -RY; cf. *poetry*.] **1.** The art or science of a herald; now esp. the art or science of blazoning armorial bearings, of tracing and recording pedigrees, and of deciding questions of precedence. †**b.** Heraldic practice. *Haml.* I. i. 87. †**c.** Heraldic title, rank, or precedence. *All's Well* II. iii. 280. **2.** A heraldic emblazonment or device; also *collect.*; armorial bearings; heraldic symbolism. Also *fig.* 1593. **3.** The office of herald 1594. **4.** Heraldic pomp 1630.

2. This Heraudry in Lucrece face was seene, Argued by Beauties red and Vertues white SHAKS. So †**He·raldy** (in senses 1, 2).

Heraud, -aut, etc., obs. ff. HERALD.

Herb (hɔ̄ɹb), *sb.* [ME. *erbe, herbe* – OFr. *erbe* (mod. *herbe*) :– L. *herba* grass, green crops, herb. The sp. with *h* is recorded from the earliest times, but the pronunc. without initial aspirate was regular till early XIX.] **1.** A plant of which the stem does not become woody and persistent, but dies down to the ground (or entirely) after flowering. **2.** Applied to plants of which the leaves, or stem and leaves, are used for food or medicine, or for their scent or flavour ME. **3.** *collect.* Herbage. Also *fig.* ME. **4.** The leafy part of a plant, as dist. from the root 1662.

2. Erbis of vertue þat growen in hem WYCLIF. *Combs.*: **h. beer,** a beverage prepared from herbs; **-tea, -water,** a medicinal infusion of herbs. **b.** In names of plants, as **h. Gerard,** Goutweed, *Ægopodium podagraria*; **h. Margaret,** 'the daisy, *Bellis perennis*' (Prior); **h.-royal** [Fr. *herbe royale*] southernwood. See also *H.* BENNET, *H.* CHRISTOPHER; also HERB-GRACE, H. PARIS, H. ROBERT, etc.

†‖**Herba.** 1585. [It.] A sort of grass-cloth imported formerly from India –1813.

Herbaceous (həɹbēⁱ·ʃəs), *a.* 1646. [f. L. *herbaceus* grassy, f. *herba* HERB; see -ACEOUS.] **1.** Of the nature of a herb; *esp.* not forming wood, but dying down every year; consisting of such plants, as *h. border*. **b.** Of the texture and colour of an ordinary leaf 1794. †**2.** Herbivorous. DERHAM.

1. Ginger is the root of neither tree nor shrub, but of an h. plant SIR T. BROWNE. **b.** Flowers.. only green, or what botanists call h. 1794. **Herba·ceously** *adv.*

Herbage (hɔ̄·ɹbėdʒ). [ME. also *erbage* – OFr. *erbage* (mod. *herbage*) :– med.L. *herbaticum, -us* (also *herbagium*) right of pasture, pasturage, f. L. *herba* HERB; see -AGE.] **1.** Herbs collectively; herbaceous growth or vegetation; esp. grass, etc., as used for pasture 1390. **2.** = HERB 4. 1701. **3.** *Law.* The natural herbage of any land as a distinct species of property; hence 'a liberty that a man hath to feede his catell in another mans ground, as in the forest' (Cowell) 1450.

1. Chalk hills, covered by a scanty h. SIR B. BRODIE. Hence **He·rbaged** *a.* covered with h.

Herbal (hɔ̄·ɹbăl), *sb.* 1516. [– med.L. *herbalis* (sc. *liber*), f. L. *herba*; see -AL[1].] **1.** A book containing the names and descriptions of herbs, or of plants in general. *Obs.* exc. *Hist.* †**2.** = HERBARIUM. –1847.

Herbal (hɔ̄·ɹbăl), *a.* 1612. [– Fr. †*herbal* or med.L. *herbalis*; see prec.] **1.** Belonging to, consisting of, or made from herbs. †**2.** Herbaceous 1682.

Herbalist (hɔ̄·ɹbălist). 1592. [f. HERBAL *sb.* + -IST.] **1.** One versed in the knowledge of herbs or plants; a botanist. Now used of the early botanical writers. 1594. **2.** A dealer in medicinal herbs or simples 1592. So †**He·rbalism** (*rare*), also †**He·rbarism,** the science of herbs or plants. **He·rbalize** *v.* (*arch.*), to collect (medicinal) herbs.

Herbar(e, obs. var. of ARBOUR.

†**Herba·rian.** 1577. [f. L. *herbaria* botany or *herbarius* botanist; see HERBARIUM, -AN.] A herbalist –1578.

†**Herbarist.** 1577. [f. L. *herbaria* botany (see HERBARIUM) + -IST.] A herbalist –1794.

Herbarium (həɹbēᵊ·riŏm). 1776. [– late L. *herbarium*, subst. use of n. of adj. repr. by L. *herbarius* botanist, *herbaria* (sc. *ars*) botany (Pliny); see -ARIUM.] A collection of dried plants systematically arranged; a *hortus siccus*. Also, a book or case for such a collection.

He·rbarize, *v. arch.* 1670. [f. HERBARIST + -IZE.] = HERBORIZE.

Herbary (hɔ̄·ɹbări), *sb.* 1548. [Three words :– L. *herbarius* botanist; late L. *herbarium* HERBARIUM; med.L. *herbarius, -um* kitchen garden; see -ARY[1].] †**1.** A herbalist –1568. **2.** A herbarium 1591. **3.** A garden of herbs or vegetables 1634. †**4.** The science of herbs. HAKEWILL.

Herbergage, var of HARBERGAGE.

Herberger(e, -geour, -jour, etc., obs. ff. HARBINGER.

Herbescent (həɹbe·sěnt), *a.* 1727. [– *herbescent-*, pres. ppl. stem of L. *herbescere*, f. *herba*; see HERB, -ESCENT.] Growing like a herb; becoming herbaceous.

Herb-grace, herb of grace. 1548. [app. of English origin; supposed to have arisen like the synonym, *Herb of Repentance*, out of the formal coincidence of the name *rue* with RUE *v.* and *sb.* repent, repentance.] **1.** The herb Rue, *Ruta graveolens*. Now *Obs.* or *dial.* **2.** A herb of virtue 1866. Also *fig.*

1. Ther's Rew for you, and heere's some for me. Wee may call it Herbe-Grace a Sundaies SHAKS.

Herbid (hǝ̄·ɹbid), *a.* ? *Obs.* 1657. [– L. *herbidus*, f. *herba* HERB; see -ID[1].] Grassy, grass-like.

Herbiferous (həɹbi·fĕrəs), *a.* 1656. [f. L. *herbifer* (f. *herba* HERB) + -OUS; see -FEROUS.] Bearing herbs.

†**Herbist.** 1611. [– Fr. †*herbiste*, f. *herbe* HERB + *-iste* -IST.] = HERBALIST. –1656.

‖**Herbivora** (həɹbi·vŏră), *sb. pl.* 1830. [n. pl. of mod.L. *herbivorus*, f. *herba* HERB; see -VOROUS. Cf. Fr. *herbivore* (XVIII).] *Zool.* A general name for animals, esp. Mammals, that feed on herbage or plants. *spec.* A division of Marsupials, including the kangaroos; also a division of Cetacea. So **He·rbivore,** one of the H. **Herbi·vorous** *a.* herb-eating; of or pertaining to the H.

†**Herb John.** 1440. [tr. med.L. *herba Johannis*, OFr. *herbe Johan* (mod. *herbe de Saint-Jean*).] **1.** St. John's-wort, *Hypericum perforatum* –1460. **2.** App. some tasteless neutral herb; hence, something inert or indifferent –1679.

2. Like Herb-John in the pot, that does neither much good nor hurt GURNALL.

He·rbless, *a.* 1682. [f. HERB + -LESS.] Destitute of herbs or herbage.

He·rblet. [f. HERB + -LET.] A little herb. SHAKS.

Herborist (hǝ̄·ɹbŏrist). 1578. [– Fr. *herboriste*, f. *herbe* HERB by assoc. with L. *arbor* tree; cf. next and ARBOUR.] A herbalist.

Herborize (hǝ̄·ɹbŏrəiz), *v.* 1664. [– Fr. *herboriser*, f. as prec. by assoc. with *arboriser* collect plants.] **1.** *intr.* To garden (*rare*). **2.** To gather herbs; to botanize 1749. Hence **He:rboriza·tion,** the action of herborizing; also, by confusion, for ARBORIZATION.

Herborized, *ppl. a.* 1788. Used by confusion for *arborized*.

Herbose (həɹbōᵘ·s), *a.* 1721. [– L. *herbosus* f. *herba* HERB; see -OSE[1].] Abounding in herbs or herbage.

Herbous (hǝ̄·ɹbəs), *a.* 1712. [– L. *herbosus*; see prec., -OUS.] Of the nature of a herb; herbaceous.

Herb Paris. 1578. [– med.L. *herba Paris*; in Fr. *herbe à Paris, parisette*.] A book-name for *Paris quadrifolia* (N.O. *Trilliaceæ*), also called True-love, a dictyogenous plant, bearing a single greenish flower at the top of the stem, and just beneath it four large ovate leaves in the form of a cross.

Herb Robert. ME. [– med.L. *herba Roberti*. Variously referred to Robert Duke of Normandy, to St. Robert, and to St. Rupert.] A common wild species of Crane's-bill or Geranium (*G. robertianum*).

Herbrough, obs. f. HARBOUR *sb.*[1] and *v.*

He·rb-woman. 1608. A woman who sells herbs.

Herby (hǝ̄·ɹbi), *a.* 1552. [f. HERB + -Y[1].] **1.** Full of herbs; grassy. **2.** Herbaceous; pertaining to herbs 1552.

1. An h. seat on broad Scamander's shore CHAPMAN.

Hercogamy (həɹkǫ·gămi). Also **herk-.** 1880. [f. Gr. ἕρκος fence + γάμος, -γαμια marriage.] *Bot.* The prevention of self-fertilization in flowers by means of structural obstacles. Hence **Hercoga·mic, -o·gamous** *adjs.* unable to be self-fertilized.

Herculanean (hǝ̄ɹkiulēⁱ·niăn), *a.* 1780. [f. L. *Herculaneus* + -AN; see -EAN.] Of or pertaining to Herculaneum, a town in Campania, which was buried with Pompeii in the eruption of Vesuvius 79 A.D.

Herculean (həɹkiū·liăn), *a.* 1596. [f. L. *Herculeus*, (f. *Hercules*, see next) + -AN; see -EAN.] **1.** Of or pertaining to Hercules 1610. **2.** Like Hercules, esp. in strength, courage, or labours 1596. **b.** *transf.* Of things: Strong, powerful, violent 1602. **3.** Requiring the strength of a Hercules; difficult to accomplish; excessive, immense 1617.

1. *H. pillars, straits*: see HERCULES. **2.** The Danite strong, H. Samson MILT. **3.** An h. task 1875.

Hercules (hǝ̄·ɹkiulīz). ME. [L. *Hercules*, alt. of Gr. Ἡρακλῆς, f. Ἥρα wife of Zeus + κλέος glory, lit. 'having or showing the glory of Hera'.] **1.** A hero of Greek and Roman mythology, celebrated for his great strength, and for the accomplishment of the twelve extraordinary tasks or 'labours' imposed upon him by Hera. After death he was ranked among the gods. **b.** A representation of Hercules 1638. **2.** One who resembles Hercules in strength; a strong man 1567. **3.** A name given to powerful machines; esp. a machine for cleansing the streets 1890. **4.** *Entom.* (In full, *H. Beetle*.) A gigantic lamellicorn beetle, *Dynastes* (or *Megasoma*) *hercules* 1816. **5.** *Astron.* One of the northern constellations 1551.

1. 'Not H. against two' the proverb is GREENE. *Pillars of H., Hercules' Pillars*: the rocks Calpé (now Gibraltar) and Abyla (Ceuta), on either side of the Strait of Gibraltar, fabled to have been set up by H.; so *Straits of H.* Hence *fig.* an ultimate limit.

Comb.: **H. braid,** a thick corded worsted braid; **H. knot,** a kind of knot very difficult to undo; **H. powder,** a powerful explosive used in mining operations.

Hercules' club. [From the club which Hercules bore.] **a.** A big and formidable stick 1657. **b.** A kind of firework 1688. **c.** A plant, *Xanthoxylon clava-herculis*; also *Aralia spinosa* 1882.

Hercynian (həɹsi·niăn), *a.* 1598. [f. L. *Hercynia* (sc. *silva*), = Gr. Ἑρκύνιος δρυμός the Hercynian forest; see -AN.] Applied to the wooded mountain-system of Middle Germany, or to portions of it; esp. to the Erzgebirge, whence *H. gneiss*.

Herd (hǝ̄ɹd), *sb.*[1] [OE. *heord* = MLG. *herde*, OHG. *herta* (G. *herde*), ON. *hjǫrð*, Goth. *hairda* :– Gmc. **χerðō*.] **1.** A company of domestic animals of one kind, kept together by a keeper. (The notion of a keeper is now little present.) **b.** As contrasted with *flock*, *herd* is restricted to bovine domestic animals 1587. **2.** A company of animals of any kind feeding or travelling together; a school (of whales, etc.) ME. **3.** A multitude of people. (Now always disparaging.) ME. **b.** Of things: A great number 1618.

1. The lowing h. winds slowly o'er the lea GRAY. **b.** *Lev.* 27:32. **2.** The grisly Boar is singled from his H. SOMERVILLE. **3.** A h. of parasites JAS. MILL. Phr. *The herd*: the multitude, the rabble.

Herd, *sb.*[2] [OE. *hirdi*, WS. *hierde* = OS. *hirdi, herdi*, OHG. *hirti* (G. *hirte*), ON. *hirðir*, Goth. *hairdeis* :– Gmc. **χerðjaz*, f. **χerðō* (see prec.).] **1.** A keeper of a herd or flock of domestic animals; a herdsman. Now usu. in comb., but in the north a common word for *shepherd*. †**2.** *fig.* A pastor –1562.

Herd (hǝ̄ɹd), *v.*[1] ME. [f. HERD *sb.*[1]] **1.** *intr.* To go in a herd; to form a herd or herds. Said also contemptuously of men. **b.** Of things: To come together 1704. **2.** To join oneself to any band or company, faction or party; to go in company *with* ME. **3.** *trans.* To place in or among a herd. Also *fig.* 1592. **4.** To collect into a herd. Also *fig.* To amass. 1615.

1. They are but sheep which alwaies heard together SIDNEY. **3.** The rest, However great we are, honest, and valiant, Are hearded with the vulgar B. JONS.

Herd, *v.*[2] ME. [f. HERD *sb.*[2]] **1.** *trans.* To tend (sheep or cattle). Also *fig.* Also *intr.* †**2.** *fig.* (*trans.*) To keep safe –1560.

1. *fig.* God, who herds the stars of heaven As sheep within his sheepfold SWINBURNE.

He·rd-book. 1822. [f. HERD *sb.*[1] + BOOK.] A book containing the pedigree, etc. of a breed of cattle or pigs.

Herd-boy. 1637. [orig. f. HERD *sb.*[2] + BOY; but later erron. referred to HERD *sb.*[1], whence *herd's-boy*. See HERDSMAN.] **1.** A boy who acts as a herd or assists a herd. **2.** A cow-boy. *U.S.* and *colonial Eng.* 1878.

Herder (hǝ̄·ɹdəɹ). Chiefly *U.S.* 1635. [f. HERD *v.*[2] + -ER[1].] A herdsman. Also *fig.*

Herderite (hǝ̄·ɹdərəit). 1828. [f. name of Baron S. A. W. von *Herder* + -ITE[1] 2b.] *Min.* A fluo-phosphate of glucinum and calcium, found in brilliant transparent crystals.

He·rdess. ME. [f. HERD *sb.*[2] + -ESS[1].] A shepherdess.

Herd-grass, herd's-grass. *U.S.* 1747. [f. HERD *sb.*[1] + GRASS.] Any grass grown for hay or pasture; esp. Timothy, *Phleum pratense*, and Redtop, *Agrostis vulgaris*.

†**Herd-groom.** ME. [f. HERD *sb.*[2] + GROOM.] A shepherd-lad –1633.

Herdic (hǝ̄·ɹdik). *U.S.* 1882. [f. name of Peter *Herdic*, of Pennsylvania, the inventor.] A cab with a low-hung body, entered at the back.

†**He·rdman.** [OE. *hierdemann*; f. HERD *sb.*[2] + MAN.] A herdsman; *fig.* and *transf.* esp. a spiritual pastor –1656.

Herdsman (hǝ̄·ɹdz,mæ̆n). 1603. [Altered f. HERDMAN (after *craftsman*, etc.), introduced when HERD *sb.*[2] went out of English use; thus = man of a herd. In the north HERD *sb.*[2] remains in use.] **1.** A keeper of domestic animals which go in herds. **2.** *Orkney.* The Common Skua 1885. So **He·rdswoman,** a woman who tends cattle SCOTT.

Herdwick (hǝ̄·ɹdwik). OE. [f. HERD *sb.*[2] + -WICK.] †**1.** The tract of land under the charge of a 'herd' employed by the owner; a pasture-ground –1564. **2.** (In full *H. sheep*): A hardy breed of mountain sheep, supposed to have originated on the herdwicks of the Abbey of Furness 1837.

†**Here,** *sb.* [OE. *here* = OFris., OS., OHG. *heri* (Du., G. *heer*), ON. *herr*, Goth. *harjis* :– Gmc. **χarjaz*. See HARRY *v.*, HARBOUR *sb.*[1] HERIOT.] An armed host, an army. Also: A host; a great company –1470.

Here (hīᵊɹ), *adv.* [OE. *hēr* = OFris., OS. *hēr*, OHG. *hiar* (Du., G. *hier*), ON. *hér*, Goth. *her* (beside OFris., OS. *hir*); obscurely f. Gmc. pronominal base **χi-* this (see HE *pron.*).] **1.** In this place; in the place where the speaker is, or places himself. **b.** *ellipt.* = Present, *adsum* OE. **c.** = Whom or which you see here 1596. **d.** Used for emphasis 1460. **2.** *Here is* = there is here, see or behold here. (Fr. *voici*.) 1460. **b.** *Here's to*: ellipt. for *Here's a health to* 1592. **3.** In this world; in this life; on earth OE. **4.** At this point in action, speech, or thought; in this passage OE. **5.** In this matter; in this case; in this particular ME. **6.** In ordinary use, taking the place of HITHER OE. **7.** Used ellipt. in calling an attendant, etc. Hence, to call attention to or introduce a command. 1632.

1. He is not h.: for he is risen *Matt.* 28:6. **b.** *Mids. N.* I. ii. 45. **c.** My brother, h., is ready to give information (*mod.*). **2.** Heere's a change indeed in the Commonwealth SHAKS. **b.** Heere's to my Loue SHAKS. **3.** Man wants but little h. below GOLDSM. **4.** H. followeth the Anthem *Bk. Com. Prayer.* **5.** H. was his sin; An over-reaching of his commission BP. HALL. **6.** Call Pedro h. BYRON. **7.** H., take away the Tea-table SWIFT.

Phrases. **Here and there. a.** In this place and in that; at intervals of space (or time). **b.** To this place and to that; to and fro. **Here, there, and everywhere.** In every place, indicated or not. **Neither here nor there.** Of no account either one way or the other. **Here below.** On this earth, in this world. **Here goes!** An exclam. declaring one's resolution or resignation to perform some (bold or rash) act. **He we (you) are.** Here is what we (you) want. *colloq.* **Here-** in comb. with adverbs and preps. These originated in the juxtaposition of *here* and another adv. qualifying the same vb., but later the adv. came to be felt as a prep., governing *here*.

B. as *sb.*: = This place; also, the present; the present life (*Lear* I. i. 264).

Hereabout (hīᵊrăbau·t), *adv.* ME. [f. HERE *adv.* + ABOUT.] †**1.** About or concerning this –1644. **2.** About or near this place ME. So **Hereabou·ts** *adv.*

Hereafter (hīᵊrɑ·ftəɹ), *adv.* (*a.*, *sb.*) [OE. *hēræfter*, f. *hēr* HERE *adv.* + AFTER.] **1.** After, in this writing, book, or place; occas. = immediately after. **2.** After this in time; in time to come OE. **3.** In a future state 1618. **4.** *adj.* To come, future (now *rare*) 1591.

2. More of this h. SHAKS. 4. H. Ages SHAKS.
B. *sb.* 1. Time to come; the future 1546. 2. A future life; the world to come 1702.
2. What, if there be an h., a judgment to come? WESLEY.

†**Herea·fterward,** *adv.* Also **-wards.** ME. [f. HERE *adv.* + AFTERWARD.] = prec. adv. –1674.

Hereane·nt, *adv.* ME. [f. HERE *adv.* + ANENT.] Concerning this.

Hereat (hīᵊræ·t), *adv.* ME. [f. HERE *adv.* + AT.] †1. At this place; here –1650. 2. At this; as a result of this 1557.
2. All admired h. FULLER.

Hereaway (hīᵊ·răwēⁱ:), *adv.* Now *dial.* and *U.S.* ME. [f. as prec. + AWAY *adv.*] 1. Away in this direction; hereabouts. 2. Hither 1549.

Hereby (hīᵊɹbəi·, hīᵊ·ɹbəi), *adv.* ME. [f. HERE *adv.* + BY *prep.*] †1. (*hereby·*) By or near this place; close by –1655. 2. By, through, or from this ME.
1. *L.L.L.* IV. i. 9. 2. And h. wee doe knowe that we know him, if we keepe his commandements 1 *John* 2:3.

Hereditable (hĭre·dităb'l), *a.* 1494. [– Fr. †*héréditable* or med.L. *hereditabilis*, f. eccl. L. *hereditare*; see next, -ABLE.] 1. Of things: That may be inherited; heritable. †2. Of persons: Capable of inheriting; having a right of inheritance –1655. **Here:ditabi·lity** = *Heritability.* **Here·ditably** *adv.* by way of inheritance.

Hereditament (herĭdi·tămĕnt, hĭre·dită-). 1475. [– med.L. *hereditamentum*, f. late L. *hereditare* inherit, f. *heres, hered-* HEIR; see -MENT.] 1. *Law.* Any property that can be inherited; any thing, corporeal or incorporeal, that in the absence of a will descended to the heir at common law, and now to the 'real representative'; real property. 2. Heirship, inheritance 1509.

Here·ditarily, *adv.* 1603. [f. HEREDITARY *a.* + -LY².] In a hereditary manner; by way of (an) inheritance.

Here·ditariness. 1640. [f. as prec. + -NESS.] The quality of being hereditary.

Hereditary (hĭre·ditări), *a.* 1577. [– L. *hereditarius*, f. *hereditas* HEREDITY; see -ARY¹. Cf. Fr. *héréditaire*.] 1. *Law* and *Hist.* Descending by inheritance from generation to generation; that has been or may be transmitted according to definite rules of descent; legally vesting, upon the death of the holder, in his heir 1601. 2. Transmitted in a line of progeny; passing naturally from parents to offspring 1577. 3. Of persons: Holding their position by inheritance 1651. 4. Of or pertaining to inheritance 1790.
1. A h. priesthood..in the family of Aaron STANLEY. 2. An h. gout 1699. The h. instincts of forest life 1862. 3. H. bondsmen BYRON. 4. H. transmission 1879.

Heredity (hĭre·dĭti). 1540. [– (O)Fr. *hérédité*, or L. *hereditas*, f. *heres, hered-* HEIR; see -ITY.] †1. Hereditary succession; inheritance; an inheritance. 2. *Law.* Hereditary character, quality, or condition; the fact of being hereditary or heritable 1784. 3. *Biol.* The property in virtue of which offspring inherit the nature and characteristics of parents and ancestors; the tendency of like to beget like. (Often called a law of nature.) 1863.

Heregeld (he·rĕgeld). *Obs.* exc. *Hist.* [OE. *heregield*, f. *here* host (see HERE *sb.*), the (Danish) army + *gield*, etc., payment. See GUILD.] *OE. Hist.* The tribute paid to the Danish host; Danegeld.

Here-hence, *adv.* *Obs.* or *dial.* 1526. [f. HERE *adv.* + HENCE.] †1. As a result of this –1695. †2. From henceforth –1616. 3. From here 1669.

Herein (hīᵊri·n), *adv.* OE. [orig. *hēr inne*, f. *hēr* HERE *adv.* + *innan, inne*, adv., subseq. IN, *adv.* and *prep.*] 1. Here within, in here; in, also into, this place. 2. In this ME.
2. Heare in is my father glorified TINDALE *John* 15:8. **Herein above, h. after, h. before** = above, after, before, in this document, etc., are often written as one word.

Heremeit, -mit, -myt(e, obs. ff. HERMIT.

Hereness (hīᵊ·ɹnės). 1674. [f. HERE *adv.* + -NESS.] The being here.

Hereof (hīᵊrǫ·v), *adv.* OE. [f. HERE *adv.* + OF *prep.*] 1. Of this; concerning this. †2. From this; from here –1587.
I. Upon the Receipt h. STEELE. 2. H... began [etc.] 1568.

Hereon (hīᵊrǫ·n), *adv.* Now *rare.* OE. [f. HERE *adv.* + ON *prep.*] †1. Herein –1573. 2. On this subject, matter, etc.; on this basis ME. 3. = HEREUPON 2. 1602.

Hereout (hīᵊrau·t), *adv.* ME. [f. HERE *adv.* + OUT *adv.*] Out of this place; †from this source –1568.

Hereri·ght. *s.w. dial.* ME. [f. HERE *adv.* + RIGHT *adv.*] Straightway.

Heresiarch (he·rėsi,ā:ɹk, hĭrī·si,aɹk). Also **hær-.** 1624. [– eccl. L. *hæresiarcha* – Gr. αἱρεσιάρχης leader of a school, (eccl. Gr.) leader of a sect (Justinian), f. αἵρεσις see HERESY, -ARCH.] A leader or founder of a heresy. Also *transf.* Hence †**Heresiarchy,** the founding of a heresy; *erron.*, an arch-heresy (SIR T. HERBERT).

Heresiography (he:rėsi,ǫ·grăfi). 1645. [f. Gr. αἵρεσις HERESY + -GRAPHY.] A treatise on heresy or heresies. So **Heresio·grapher,** one who treats of heresies.

Heresiologist (he:rėsi,ǫ·lŏdʒist). 1710. [f. as prec. + -LOGIST.] One who treats of heresy or heresies. So **Heresio·loger. Heresio·logy.**

Heresy (he·rėsi). [ME. (*h*)*eresie* – OFr. (*h*)*eresie* (mod. *hérésie*) – Rom. *heresia, for L. *hæresis* school of thought, in eccl L. heretical religious doctrine – Gr. αἵρεσις school of thought, in eccl. Gr. heretical sect (Josephus); orig. 'choice', etc., f. αἱρεῖσθαι choose, f. αἱρεῖν take.] 1. Theological opinion or doctrine held in opposition to the 'catholic' or orthodox doctrine of the Christian Church. Also *transf.* b. with *a* and *pl.* A heretical opinion or doctrine ME. 2. Hence, Opinion or doctrine in philosophy, politics, science, art, etc. at variance with what is orthodox. Also with *a* and *pl.* ME. 3. In sense of Gr. αἵρεσις: A school of thought; a sect ME.
1. Deluded people! that do not consider that the greatest heresie in the world is a wicked life TILLOTSON. b. False teachers..shal brynge in damnable heresies N.T. (Genev.) 2 *Pet.* 2:1. 2. The doctrine of Evolution..which it is intellectual h...to question 1877. 3. It bihoueth heresies for to be WYCLIF 1 *Cor.* 11:19. *Comb.* **h.-hunt, -hunter** (1765), **-ing.**

Heretic (he·rėtik), *sb.* (*a.*) ME. [– (O)Fr. *hérétique* – eccl. L. *hæreticus* adj. and sb. – Gr. αἱρετικός able to choose, in eccl. use heretic(al), f. αἱρεῖσθαι; see prec., -IC.] 1. One who maintains a heresy or heresies (see HERESY 1). 2. Hence, One who maintains opinions on any subject at variance with those generally received 1599. 3. *adj.* = next (*rare*) ME.
1. When a papist uses the word heretics, he generally means the protestants WATTS. 2. Thou wast euer an obstinate heretique in the despight of Beautie SHAKS. 3. Obedience to an h. prince DRYDEN.

Heretical (hĭre·tikăl), *a.* 1532. [– med.L. *hereticalis*, f. *hereticus*; see prec., -ICAL. Cf. OFr. *heretical*.] Of or pertaining to heresy or heretics; of the nature of heresy. Hence **Here·tical-ly** *adv.*, **-ness.**

Hereticate (hĭre·tikeⁱt), *v.* 1629. [– *hereticat-*, pa. ppl. stem of med.L. *hereticare*, f. *hereticus*; see HERETIC, -ATE³.] 1. *trans.* To pronounce heretical. 2. To make a heretic of 1731.
1. Arbitrary and hereticating anathemas C. MATHER. 2. Could Peter Auterius really believe that he saved the souls of those whom he hereticated? S. R. MAITLAND. Hence **Heretica·tion.**

Here·ticide. [erron. f. HERETIC + -CIDE 2.] The putting of a heretic to death. C. MATHER.

Hereto (hīᵊɹtū·), *adv.* ME. [f. HERE *adv.* + TO *prep.*] †1. To this place –1598. 2. To this; with reference to this ME. 3. (Annexed) to this 1559. †4. Hitherto –1607.

Heretofore (hīᵊɹtŭfōᵊ·ɹ), *adv.* (*a., sb.*) ME. [f. HERE *adv.* + TOFORE.] 1. Before this; formerly. 2. *adj.* Former 1491. 3. *sb.* Time past 1824.

Heretoga (he·rėtōᵘgă), **heretoch, -togh.** [OE. *heretoga* = OFris. *hertoga*, OS. *heritogo* (Du. *hertog*), OHG. *herizogo* (G. *herzog*), ON. *hertogi*; f. *here* army, HERE *sb.* + *-toga*, f. *tēon* lead; see TEE *v.*¹] *OE. Hist.* The leader of an army; the commander of the militia of a shire. Taken in 17th and 18th c. as = DUKE.

Hereunder (hīᵊrɒ·ndəɹ), *adv.* ME. [f. HERE *adv.* + UNDER *prep.*] Under this.

Hereunto (hīᵊrɒntū·, -ɒ·ntu), *adv.* 1509. [f. as prec. + UNTO *prep.*] Unto or to this; to this document.

Hereupon (hīᵊrŏpǫ·n), *adv.* ME. [f. as prec. + UPON *prep.*] 1. Upon this matter, etc. 2. Immediately following upon this (in time or consequence) ME.

Herewith (hīᵊɹwi·ð), *adv.* OE. [f. as prec. + WITH *prep.*] With this; †at the same time with this –1546. So **Herewitha·l** *adv.* (*arch.*).

†**Herigaut.** ME. [– OFr. *herigaut, hargaut*, med.L. *herigaldus, -um, -gaudum.*] An upper garment or cloak of 13th and 14th c.

Heriot (he·riǫt). [OE. *heregeatwa, -we* (whence med.L. *herietum, -otum* XII, AFr. *heriet*), f. *here* army (see HERE *sb.*) + *geatwa* (= ON. *gǫtvar* pl.) trappings.] 1. *Eng. Law* A feudal service, orig. consisting of weapons, horses, or other military equipments, restored to a lord on the death of his tenant; afterwards a render of the best live beast or dead chattel of a deceased tenant due by legal custom to the lord of whom he held. Now an incident of manorial tenures only. Also *transf.* and *fig.* OE. 2. *attrib.*, as *h.-land* OE.
Comb.: **h. custom,** a h. depending merely upon immemorial usage; **h. service,** one due upon a special reservation in a grant or lease of lands. BLACKSTONE.
Hence **He·riotable** *a.* subject to the payment of heriots.

Herisson (he·risən). 1594. [– Fr. *hérisson*; see URCHIN.] †1. A hedgehog –1600. ‖2. *Fortif.* A barrier, consisting of a revolving beam, armed with spikes 1704.

Heritable (he·rităb'l), *a.* (*sb.*) ME. [– (O)Fr. *héritable*, f. *heriter* :– eccl. L. *hereditare*; see HEREDITABLE.] 1. Capable of being inherited, inheritable. 2. Naturally transmissible from parent to offspring; hereditary 1570. 3. Of persons: Capable of inheriting; succeeding by right of inheritance 1575. 4. *sb. pl.* (*Sc. Law.*) Heritable possessions; lands and other property that passes to the heir-at-law 1801.
2. No h. disease in the family 1879. Hence **He·ritably** *adv.* by way or right of inheritance c1440. **Heritabi·lity,** h. quality.

Heritage (he·ritĕdʒ). ME. [– OFr. (*h*)*eritage* (mod. *hé-*), f. *heriter*, etc. – eccl. L. *hereditare*, f. *heres, hered-* HEIR; see -AGE.] 1. That which has been or may be inherited. b. *transf.* and *fig.* The 'portion' allotted to or reserved for any one ME. †2. The fact of inheriting; hereditary succession –1556. 3. Anything given or received to be a proper possession ME. b. The ancient Israelites, as the peculiar possession of God; the Church of God ME. 4. An inherited lot or portion 1621.
1. It was..part of my h., Which my dead father did bequeath to me SHAKS. b. Which hath his h. in helle GOWER. 3. Loe, children are an h. of the Lord *Ps.* 127:3. b. O Lorde..blesse thyne h. *Bk. Com. Prayer.* 4. Lord of himself;—that h. of woe BYRON.

Heritance (he·rităns). *arch.* ME. [– OFr. *heritance*, f. *heriter* (see prec.) + -ANCE.] Inheritance; heirship. Also *fig.*

Heritor (he·ritǫɹ). 1475. [In XV *heriter* – AFr. *heriter* = (O)Fr. *heritier* :– *hæreditarius* (see HEREDITARY); conformed to -OR 2 (cf. *bachelor*).] 1. An heir or heiress. 2. *Sc. Law.* The proprietor of a heritable subject 1597. Hence **He·ritress,** †**-trice, trix.**

Herl, *sb.* ME. [See HARL.] = HARL *sb.*

Herling, hirling. *Sc.* 1684. [Of unkn. origin.] The name, on the Solway Firth, for the fish *Salmo albus.*

†**Herm,** ‖**Herma** (hō·ɹmă). 1579. [L. *Herma*, pl. *-æ*, a latinized form of *Hermes* – Gr. Ἑρμῆς Mercury.] A statue, consisting of a four-cornered pillar surmounted by a head or bust, usually that of Hermes. Such statues were numerous in ancient Athens, and were used as boundary-marks, milestones, sign-posts, etc. So **Hermæ·an** *a.* of Hermes.

Hermaic (həɹmē·ik), *a.* (*sb.*) 1678. [– Gr. Ἑρμαϊκός of or like Hermes.] **1.** = HERMETIC *a.* 1. **b.** as *sb.* (*pl.*) The writings attributed to Hermes Trismegistus 1678. **2.** = HERMÆAN. 1820.

‖**Hermanda·d.** 1760. [Sp. = brotherhood.] In Spain, orig. a league against the oppression of the nobles; a voluntary organization becoming afterwards regular national police.

†**Hermaphrode·ity.** [irreg. f. HERMAPHRODITE.] The state of being hermaphrodite. B. JONS.

Herma·phrodism. 1828. [– Fr. *hermaphrodisme*, irreg. f. *hermaphrodite*, see -ISM.] *Biol.* = HERMAPHRODITISM.

Hermaphrodite (həɹmæ·frŏdəit). ME. [– L. *hermaphroditus* – Gr. ἑρμαφρόδιτος, orig. proper name of the son of Hermes and Aphrodite, who, according to the myth, grew together with the nymph Salmacis and thus combined male and female characters.]

A. *sb.* **1.** A human being, or animal, in which parts characteristic of both sexes are combined. **b.** A catamite. ADDISON. **2.** *Zool.* An animal in which the male and female organs are (normally) present in the same individual, as in some molluscs and worms 1727. **3.** *Bot.* A plant or flower in which the stamens and pistils are present in the same flower 1727. **4.** *fig.* A person or thing in which two opposites are combined 1659.

1. The monstrosity known as h. does exist, but is excessively rare VAN BUREN. **4.** Henry the Eighth, was a kind of H. in Religion 1687. A very taught-rigged h., or brig forward and schooner aft 1833.

B. *adj.* **1.** Having parts belonging to both sexes combined in the same individual. Also applied to organs which combine the characters of both sexes. 1607. **2.** *transf.* and *fig.* Combining two opposites 1593.

1. Nero did shew certain H. Mares TOPSELL. This worm is h. 1797. This plant is occasionally h. in Sikkim HOOKER. **2.** H. Convents, wherein Monks and Nuns lived together FULLER. A small h. brig R. H. DANA. Hence **Hermaphrodi·tic, -al** *a.* belonging to or of the nature of a h. (*lit.* and *fig.*); combining two opposites. **Hermaphrodi·tically** *adv.* **Herma·phroditism,** the condition of a h.

Hermeneut (hɔ̄·ɹmĭniūt). *rare.* [– Gr. ἑρμηνευτής, agent-noun f. ἑρμηνεύειν interpret, f. ἑρμηνεύς interpreter.] An interpreter, esp. in the early church.

Hermeneutic, -al (hɔ̄ɹmĭniū·tik, -ăl), *a.* 1798. [– Gr. ἑρμηνευτικός, f. ἑρμηνευτής; see prec., -IC, -ICAL.] Pertaining to interpretation; esp. as dist. from exegesis. **Hermeneu·tically** *adv.*

Hermeneu·tics. 1737. [– mod.L. *hermeneutica* – Gr. ἑρμηνευτική, subst. use (sc. τέχνη art) of fem. sing. of adj. ἑρμηνευτικός; see prec., -IC, -ICS.] The art or science of interpretation, esp. of Scripture. Commonly dist. from *exegesis* or practical exposition.

Hermes (hɔ̄·ɹmīz). 1605. [L., Gr. Ἑρμῆς.] **1.** *Gr. Myth.* A deity, the son of Zeus and Maia, the messenger of the gods, the god of science, commerce, eloquence, and many of the arts of life; commonly figured as a youth, with the *caduceus* or rod, *petasus* or brimmed hat, and *talaria* or winged shoes. Identified with Mercury. Hence **b.** = HERMA. 1727. †**2.** The metal Mercury. MILT. *P. L.* III. 603. **3.** *Hermes Trismegistus* (Gr. Ἑρμῆς τρὶς μέγιστος, Hermes thrice-greatest) the Egyptian god Thoth, as identified with the Grecian Hermes, and as the founder of occult science, esp. alchemy 1605.

3. Phr. †*Hermes' seal* = Hermetic seal (see HERMETIC A). †*Hermes' fire*: = CORPOSANT; also, a will-o'-the-wisp.

Hermetic (həɹme·tik). 1637. [– mod.L. *hermeticus*, f. (prob. after *magnes, magneticus*) *Hermes Trismegistus*; see prec. 3, -IC.]

A. *adj.* **1.** Pertaining to Hermes Trismegistus, and the writings ascribed to him 1676. **2.** Hence, Relating to or dealing with occult science, esp. alchemy; magical; alchemical 1637. **3.** Pertaining to the god Hermes, or to a HERMA (*mod.*).

2. Phr. *H. art, philosophy, science*: names for alchemy or chemistry. *H. seal, sealing*: air-tight closure of a vessel by fusion, soldering, or welding; also *Surg.* a method of dressing wounds by closing them externally. Also *fig.* Hence *hermetic* = 'hermetically sealed'.

B. *sb.* An alchemist or chemist 1684. **2.** *pl.* Alchemy 1865. So **Herme·tical** *a.* = HERMETIC *a.* 1, 2. **He·rmetist,** a H. philosopher.

Hermetically (həɹme·tikăli), *adv.* 1605. [f. as prec. + -AL¹, -LY²; see -ICAL, -ICALLY.] **1.** By fusion; hence, by any mode which forms an air-tight closure. **b.** *Surg.* See HERMETIC *a.* 2 (quots.) 1870. **c.** *fig.* Tightly; absolutely (closed) 1698. †**2.** By alchemy 1664.

Hermit (hɔ̄·ɹmit), *sb.* See also EREMITE. [ME. *armite, (h)ermite, (h)eremite* – OFr. *(h)ermite* (mod. *ermite*) or Chr. L. *eremita* (med.L. *her-*) – Gr. ἐρημίτης, f. ἐρημία desert, f. ἔρημος solitary, deserted. Cf. EREMITE.] **1.** = EREMITE 1. Hence, A person living in solitude 1799. Hence, **2.** A vagabond 1495; †a beadsman (also *fig.*) –1688.

1. A withered Hermite, fivescore winters worne SHAKS. **2.** For those [honours] of old..we rest your Ermites SHAKS.

Comb.: **h.-bird,** (*a*) a humming-bird of genus *Phaëthornis*; (*b*) a nun-bird; **-crab,** †**-fish, -lobster,** a crab of the family *Paguridæ*, which usually occupies a cast-off molluscan shell; **-crow,** the chough; **-thrush,** a N. American thrush, *Turdus solitarius*, celebrated for its song; **-warbler,** the western warbler, *Dendrœca occidentalis*, of the Pacific slope of N. America.

Hermitage (hɔ̄·ɹmitėdʒ). ME. [– OFr. *(h)ermitage* (mod. *ermitage*), f. *(h)ermite*; see prec., -AGE.] **1.** The habitation of a hermit; a solitary dwelling-place 1648. **2.** A French wine produced from vineyards on a hill near Valence 1680.

1. The peaceful h., The hairy gown and mossy cell MILT.

Hermitary. *rare.* 1754. [– med.L. *heremitarium* (also *-orium*); see HERMIT, -ARY¹.] A hermit's cell; a hermitage. Also **Hermitory** ME.

He·rmitess. 1633. [f. HERMIT + -ESS¹.] A female hermit. So †**Hermitress.**

Hermitic, -al (həɹmi·tik, -ăl), *a.* 1586. [alt., after *hermit*, from *(h)eremitic, -al*; see EREMITIC, -AL¹.] Of or pertaining to a hermit.

Hermo-, comb. f. HERMES, as in **Hermokopid,** a mutilator of Hermæ; etc.

Hermodactyl (hɔ̄ɹmodæ·ktil). *Obs.* exc. *Hist.* ME. [– med.L. *hermodactylus* – Gr. ἑρμοδάκτυλος, lit. Hermes' finger. Cf. OFr. *hermodactile*.] **1.** A bulbous root, prob. of a species of *Colchicum*, brought from the East, and formerly used in medicine. Also, the plant. **2.** Applied by Lyte to the Meadow Saffron, *Colchicum autumnale*; and later to the Snake's-head Iris, *Hermodactylus tuberosus* 1578.

Hern, hirn (hɔ̄ɹn), *sb. dial.* [OE. *hyrne* = OFris. *herne*, ON. *hyrna* corner, angle, nook :– Gmc. **χurnjōn*, f. stem of HORN.] A corner.

Lurkynge in hernes and in lanes blynde CHAUCER.

Hern, herne, *arch.* and *dial.* ff. HERON, freq. in lit. use.

Hern, *poss. pron.* ME. [f. HER *poss. pron.* (*sing.*), app. by form-assoc. with the ME. pairs *mī, mīn, thī, thīn* (where the deriv. form arose not by adding, but by dropping *n*). Cf. *hisn, ourn, yourn*.] *Obs.* exc. *s.* and *midl. dial.* = HERS.

‖**Hernia** (hɔ̄·ɹniă). *Pl.* **-æ, -as.** ME. [L. *hernia* (med.L. also *hirnia*).] *Path.* A tumour formed by the displacement and resulting protrusion of a part of an organ through an aperture, natural or accidental, in the walls of its containing cavity; a rupture. Also *attrib.*, as *h. truss*, etc. Hence **He·rnial** *a.* of or pertaining to h.; chiefly in *hernial sac*. **He·rniary** *a.* of or pertaining to h. or its surgical treatment. **He·rniated,** †**He·rnious** *adjs.* affected with h.

Hernio-, comb. f. HERNIA, as in **Hernio·logy,** that part of pathology which treats of hernia, a treatise on hernia; etc.

Herniotomy (hɔ̄ɹniǫ·tŏmi). 1811. [f. HERNIO- + -TOMY.] *Surg.* The operation of cutting for strangulated hernia. So **Hernio·tomist,** one who practises h.

Hernsew, -shaw, -shew: see HERONSEW.

Hero (hīᵊ·ro). Pl. **heroes** (hīᵊ·roᵘz). ME. [In earliest use chiefly pl. *heroes*, with sing. *heroe* (both of 3 syll.) and *heros* – L. *hērōs*, pl. *hērōēs* – Gr. ἥρως, pl. ἥρωες. The common *heroe* (XVI–XVIII) was superseded by *hero* (XVII), with pl. *heroes* (2 syll.).] **1.** *Antiq.* A name given to men of superhuman strength, courage, or ability, favoured by the gods; regarded later as demigods, and immortal. **2.** One who does brave or noble deeds; an illustrious warrior 1586. **3.** A man who exhibits extraordinary bravery, firmness, or greatness of soul, in connection with any pursuit, work, or enterprise; a man admired and venerated for his achievements and noble qualities 1661. **4.** The man who forms the subject of an epic; the chief male personage in a poem, play, or story 1697. **5.** *attrib.* 1670.

1. My young Ulyssean heroë CHAPMAN. A Chief sings some great Action of a God or Heroe 1763. **2.** See, the conquering h. comes MORELL. **3.** Who would not be the h. of an age? DRYDEN. No man is a h. to his *valet de chambre* FOOTE. *Comb.* **h.-worship,** the worship of heroes, and of great men generally.

Hence **Heroo·logist,** one who discourses on heroes. **He·roship,** the state, position, or character of a h.

Herodian (hĭrōᵘ·diăn), *a.* and *sb.*¹ ME. [– eccl. L. (Vulg.) *Herodianus* – eccl. Gr. Ἡρωδιανός pertaining to Herod, *sb. pl.* followers of Herod (Mark 3:6); see -IAN.]

A. *adj.* **1.** Of or pertaining to Herod, king of Judæa (B.C. 38–4), or to members of his family of the same name; built by Herod 1633. **2.** Blustering, magniloquent 1886.

1. *Herodian disease*: phthiriasis or some like disease (see *Acts* 12:23).

B. *sb. pl.* A Jewish party, mainly political, who were partisans of the H. dynasty, and lax in their Judaism. Hence, a term of reproach. ME.

They jumpe with Caesar, like the Herodians 1592.

Herodian (hĭrōᵘ·diăn), *sb.*² 1609. [In sense 1 f. eccl. L., med.L. *herodius* heron (irreg. – Gr. ἐρωδιός heron) + -AN. In sense 2 – mod.L. *herodius*, repr. Gr. ἐρωδιός.] †**1.** A heron. **2.** *Ornith.* One of an order of birds, *Herodii* or *Herodiones*, comprising the herons, storks, ibises, and spoonbills.

†**He·roess.** 1612. [f. HERO + -ESS¹.] = HEROINE. –1715.

Heroic (hĭrōᵘ·ik). 1549. [– Fr. *héroïque* (XV) or L. *heroicus* – Gr. ἡρωικός pertaining to heroes, f. ἥρως HERO; see -IC.]

A. *adj.* **1.** Of or pertaining to a hero or heroes; characteristic of a hero; of the nature of a hero. **2.** Of or pertaining to the heroes of antiquity 1667. **3.** Relating to the deeds of heroes; epic 1581; (of verse) used in heroic poetry 1617; (of language) magniloquent; hence, high-flown 1591. **4.** Having recourse to bold, daring, or extreme measures; attempting great things 1664. **5.** In statuary: Of a size between life and colossal 1794.

1. A life h. MILT. Their heroick deliverer BURKE. The choir..rich in h. dust 1834. **2.** Th' H. Race.. That fought at Theb's and Ilium MILT. **3.** This Subject for H. Song MILT. The English Verse, which we call Heroique, consists of no more than Ten Syllables DRYDEN. (So in German and Italian; in Gr. and L. poetry it was the hexameter; in French, the Alexandrine of twelve syllables.) **4.** Commonplace reforms, which h. legislation has overlooked GOLDWIN SMITH.

B. *sb.* †**1.** A hero; *esp.* a personage of the heroic age –1667. **2.** Heroic verse: chiefly in pl. 1596. **b.** *pl.* High-flown or bombastic language or sentiments 1700. †**3.** A heroic poet. S. BUTLER.

2. b. He [Cæsar] had..no Byronic mock heroics FROUDE. Hence **Hero·icness,** h. character or quality = HEROISM.

Heroical (hĭrōᵘ·ikăl), *a.* 1513. [f. as prec.; see -ICAL.] = HEROIC *a.* Hence **Hero·ical-ly** *adv.*, **-ness.**

Heroi-co·mic, -al, *a.* 1712. [– Fr. *héroï-comique*; see HEROIC, COMIC.] That combines the heroic with the comic; of the nature of a burlesque on the heroic.

The Rape of the Lock. An Heroi-comical Poem. POPE.

Heroin (he·ro,in). *Chem.* 1899. [– G. *heroin*, said to be f. Gr. ἥρως HERO because of the inflated notion of the personality which follows its use; see -IN¹.] A drug derived from morphine used as an anodyne and sedative.

Heroine (he·ro,in), *sb.* (*a.*) 1659. [– Fr. *héroïne* or L. *heroina* – Gr. ἡρωΐνη; see HERO,

-INE[3].] **1.** A female hero; a demi-goddess. **2.** A woman of exalted spirit or achievements 1662. **3.** The principal female character in a poem, story, or play 1715.

1. He sees the shades of the ancient heroines POPE. **2.** That famous H. [Queen Elizabeth] EVELYN.

Heroism (he·roˌiz'm). 1717. [– Fr. *héroïsme*, f. *héros* HERO + *-isme* -ISM.] The action and qualities of a hero; exalted courage or boldness; heroic conduct; (with *pl.*) a heroic action or trait.

No way has been found for making h. easy EMERSON.

Heroize (hīᵊ·roᵘəiz), *v.* 1738. [f. HERO + -IZE.] To make a hero of; to play the hero BROWNING.

Heron (he·rən). Also *arch.*, *poet.*, *dial.* **hern** (həɹn). [ME. *heiroun*, *heroun*, *herne* – OFr. *hairon* (mod. *héron*) – Gmc. **χaizaron* (whence OHG. *heigaro*; cf. ON. *hegri*).] **1.** The name of a large natural group of long-necked long-legged wading birds, belonging to the genus *Ardea* or family *Ardeidæ*; esp. the Common or Grey Heron of Europe, *A. cinerea*. **b.** With defining epithet, applied to other species of *Ardea*, etc. 1577. **2.** *attrib.*, as *h.-hawking* 1709, *h.-plume* SCOTT.

1. I come from haunts of coot and hern TENNYSON. **b.** Night H., *Nycticorax Gardeni* RAY. The Great White H. (*Ardea alba*) YARRELL. The Great Blue H. of America, *Ardea herodias*, The Purple H., *A. purpurea* NEWTON.

†**He·roner.** ME. [– AFr. *heroner* = (O)Fr. *héronnier* adj., in *faucon héronnier*, f. *héron* HERON; see -ER[2].] A falcon trained to fly at the heron; also, *falcon heroner* –1611.

Heronry, hernery (he·rənri, hə̄·ɹnəri). 1603. [f. HERON + -RY.] A place where herons breed.

Heron's-bill. ? *Obs.* 1578. A book-name for the British species of *Erodium* and *Geranium*; usu. called Stork's-bill and Crane's-bill.

He·ronsew, -shew, -shaw. Now somewhat *arch.* or *dial.* ME. [– OFr. *heronceau*, earlier *-cel*, dim. of *heron* HERON.] *lit.* A little or young heron; but in use = HERON.

Phr. *To know a hawk from a heronshaw*, conjectural emendation of 'I know a Hawke from a Handsaw' (Shaks.); see HANDSAW.

‖**Herpes** (hə̄·ɹpīz). ME. [L. – Gr. ἕρπης shingles, lit. 'creeping', f. ἕρπειν creep.] **1.** A disease of the skin (or occas. of a mucous membrane) characterized by the appearance of patches of distinct vesicles. (Applied to many cutaneous affections.) **2.** *Entom.* A genus of Coleoptera of the family *Curculionidæ* (weevils). Hence **Herpe·tic** *a.* pertaining to or of the nature of h.; affected with h. **Herpe·tiform** *a.* presenting the form of h. **He·rpetism,** a constitutional tendency to h., or the like.

Herpetology[1] (hə̄ɹpètǫ·lŏdʒi). 1824. [f. Gr. ἑρπετόν creeping thing + -LOGY. Cf. Fr. *herpétologie*.] That part of zoology which treats of reptiles. Hence **He:rpetolo·gic, -al** *a.* pertaining to h. **He:rpetolo·gically** *adv.* **Herpeto·logist.**

Herpeto·logy[2]. 1857. [f. Gr. ἕρπης, ἑρπητ- HERPES + -LOGY.] That part of pathology which treats of herpes; a description of herpes.

Herpeto·tomy. [f. Gr. ἑρπετόν reptile + -TOMY.] The dissection or anatomy of reptiles. So **Herpeto·tomist,** a dissector of reptiles.

Herring (he·riŋ). [OE. *hǣring*, *hēring* = OFris. *hēreng*, MLG. *hērink*, *harink* (Du. *haring*), OHG. *hāring* (G. *hering*) :– WGmc. **χǣriŋʒa*.] A sea-fish, *Clupea harengus*, inhabiting the North Atlantic Ocean, and coming near the coast at certain seasons in vast shoals to spawn. Also other species of *Clupea*.

Comb.: **h.-drift**: see DRIFT *sb.* II. 5 b; **-gull,** a species of gull, *Larus argentatus*, which follows herring-shoals and preys upon them; **-hog** (*dial.*), the grampus; **-king,** also **King of the h-s,** *Chimæra monstrosa*; also a species of ribbon-fish, *Regalecus glesne*.

Herring-bone, *sb.* (*a.*) 1652. **1.** The bone of a herring. **2.** *attrib.* or *adj.* Resembling in appearance the bones of a herring; applied *spec.* in *Arch.* to a kind of masonry and of paving in which the stones or tiles are set obliquely in alternate rows so as to form a zig-zag pattern; as *herring-bone ashlar, balk, bond, work*, etc. 1659.

2. Herring-bone stitch (*Sewing*), a kind of cross-stitch, chiefly used in flannel; hence *herring-bone seam, thread*, etc. **Herring-bone bridging** (*Carpentry*), strutting pieces between thin joists, laid diagonally, to prevent lateral deflexion. Hence **Herring-bone** *v. trans.* to work with a herring-bone stitch or pattern. Also *absol.* or *intr.*

Herring-pond. 1686. The sea, esp. the N. Atlantic Ocean (*joc.*).

‖**Herrnhuter** (he·rnhūtər). 1748. [f. *Herrnhut* (lit. the Lord's keeping), the name of their first German settlement on the estate of Count von Zinzendorf in Saxony.] One of the sect of 'United Brethren' or Moravians.

Hers (hə̄ɹz), *poss. pron.* ME. [A double possessive, f. poss. pron. *hire*, HER, thus *hires*, *her's*, *hers*. Of northern origin, the midl. and southern equivalent being HERN.] The absol. form of HER, used when no noun follows: = Her one, her ones; that or those pertaining to her. **b.** *Of hers* = belonging to her 1478.

As mine on hers, so hers is set on mine *Rom. & Jul.* II. iii. 59. Hers and mine Adultery *Cymb.* V. v. 186.

†**Hersall.** Short for REHEARSAL. Spenser.

Herschel (hə̄·ɹʃĕl). 1819. *Astron.* A name proposed for the planet Uranus, discovered by Sir W. Herschel in 1781.

Herschelian (həɹʃe·liăn), *a.* (*sb.*) 1792. [f. *Herschel* + -IAN.] Of or pertaining to Sir W. Herschel (1738–1822), or Sir John Herschel (1792–1871). *Herschelian (telescope)*, a form of reflecting telescope with a concave mirror slightly inclined to the axis.

Herse (hə̄ɹs). 1480. [– (O)Fr. *herse* harrow; see HEARSE.] †**1.** A harrow. **b.** A portcullis grated and spiked. *Hist.* 1704. **c.** *Her.* A charge representing a portcullis or a harrow 1525. **2.** *Mil.* A form of battle array. *Hist.* 1523. **3.** A frame on which skins are dried 1839. Hence **Hersed** *a.* drawn up in a h. (sense 2).

Herself (həɹse·lf), *pron.* [OE. *hire self*, *selfre*, f. *hire* HER, *dat.-acc. pers. pron.* + SELF. *Self* was in OE. an adj. which could be inflected in concord with any case of the pronoun; e.g. *hēo self, hire selfre, hīe selfe*; the dat. form is the source of the modern use. For the history of the constructions see SELF.] **1.** Emphatic use. Very her, very she, that very woman, etc. = L. *ipsa* ME. **2.** Reflexive use. OE. **3.** From the 14th c., *her* has often been treated as the possessive pron., and *self* as sb., whence *her sweet self*, and the like.

1. Seke Vertu for hir selfe 1559. Iulia her selfe did giue it me SHAKS. The..Widdow, and her selfe..Are mighty Gossips SHAKS. *To be herself* to be in her normal condition. Also used alone in predicate after *be, become*, etc. = by herself, alone. Also as HER *pers. pron.* 2 b. **2.** To talk to her self 1690. To forget herself TENNYSON.

Hership (hə̄·ɹʃip). *Sc. arch.* or *Hist.* ME. [f. HERE army, host, or stem of OE. *herġan* to HARRY + -SHIP. Cf. ON. *herskapr* 'warfare, harrying', which may be the actual source.] **1.** Harrying; a foray. **2.** A harried condition; hence, ruin, distress, famine, caused by a foray, etc. 1536. **3.** Cattle, etc., forcibly driven off 1535.

Hert(e, obs. ff. HART, HEART, HURT *v.*

Hertfordshire (hā·ɹfǒɹdʃəɹ). 1661. [Name of an Eng. county.] In phr. *H. kindness*: drinking to the person who immediately before drank to one.

Hertzian (hə̄·ɹtsiăn), *a.* 1890. (f. the name H. R. *Hertz* (1857–94), German physicist + -IAN.] Of or pertaining to Hertz or to the type of experiments, apparatus, etc., used by him. Also **Hertz** (hə̄ɹts, ‖hḗrts) used attrib.

H. telegraphy: wireless telegraphy. *H. waves*: see WAVE *sb.* I. 5a.

†**Hery,** *v.* [OE. *herian* = Goth. *hazjan* praise :– Gmc. **χasjan*, of unkn. origin.] *trans.* To praise, exalt, worship –1622.

Hesitancy (he·zităn̆si). 1617. [– L. *hæsitantia*, (in late L. 'hesitation, delay'), f. *hæsitant-*; see next, -ANCY.] The quality or condition of hesitating; indecision, vacillation. So **He·sitance.**

Hesitant (he·zităn̆t), *a.* 1647. [– *hæsitant-*, pres. ppl. stem of L. *hæsitare*; see next, -ANT.] Hesitating; undecided; stammering Hence **He·sitantly** *adv.*

Hesitate (he·ziteⁱt), *v.* 1623. [– *hæsitat-*, pa. ppl. stem of L. *hæsitare* stick fast, be undecided, stammer, f. *hæs-* pa. ppl. stem of *hærēre* stick, hold fast; see -ATE[3].] **1.** *intr.* To hold back in doubt; to show, or speak with, indecision; to find difficulty in deciding; to scruple. **2.** To stammer 1706. **3.** *trans.* To express or say with hesitation 1735.

1. He may pause, but he must not h. RUSKIN. **3.** Just hint a fault, and h. dislike POPE. Hence **He·sitater, -or. He·sitating-ly** *adv.*, **-ness.**

Hesitation (hezitēⁱ·ʃən). 1622. [– L. *hæsitatio*, f. as prec.; see -ION. Cf. (O)Fr. *hésitation*.] **1.** The action of hesitating; a pausing or delaying due to irresolution; the condition of doubt in relation to action. Also with *pl.* **2.** Stammering 1709.

Hesitative (he·ziteⁱtiv), *a.* 1795. [f. HESITATE + -IVE.] Showing, or given to, hesitation.

His h. manner of speaking MOZLEY. So **He·sitatory** *a.* NORTH.

Hesper (he·spəɹ). *poet.* 1623. [– L. HESPERUS.] = HESPERUS.

A Phospher 'mongst the Living, late wert thou, But Shin'st among the Dead a H. now 1656.

Hesper-, stem of HESPERUS, used in the same sense as HESPERID-, as in **Hespe·ric, Hespere·tic, Hesperi·nic, Hesperi·sic** *adjs.*, denominating acids.

Hesperian (hespīᵊ·riăn). 1547. [f. L. *hesperius*, Gr. ἑσπέριος, f. *Hesperia*, Gr. Ἑσπερία (poet.) land of the west, f. Ἕσπερος; see HESPERUS, -IAN.]

A. *adj.* **1.** Western, of or pertaining to the land where the sun sets (*poet.*). **2.** Of or pertaining to the HESPERIDES (*poet.*) 1622. **3.** *Entom.* Of or pertaining to the family of butterflies called *Hesperidæ* or Skippers 1840.

2. Happy Iles, Like those H. Gardens fam'd of old MILT.

B. *sb.* **1.** An inhabitant of a western land 1601. **2.** A Hesperian butterfly; a Skipper.

Hesperid-, Gr. ἑσπεριδ- stem of Ἑσπερίδες Hesperides, with sense 'of or derived from the orange or its congeners'; see HESPERIDES 2.

Hence **a.** *Bot.* **Hespe·ridate, Hesperi·deous** *adjs.*, of the orange structure or kind. ‖**Hespe·ri·dium,** a fruit of the structure of the orange, pulpy within and covered by a separable rind. **b.** *Chem.* **Hespe·ridene, Hespe·ridin, Hespe·ridine,** chemical products obtained from the hesperideous fruits.

‖**Hesperides** (hespe·ridīz), *sb. pl.* 1590. [L. – Gr. Ἑσπερίδες, pl. of ἑσπερίς 'western', 'a daughter of the west', 'land of the sunset', f. ἕσπερος; see HESPERUS.] **1.** *Gr. Myth.* The nymphs, daughters of Hesperus, who were fabled to guard, with the aid of a dragon, the garden in which the golden apples grew in the Isles of the Blest, at the western extremity of the earth 1656. Also *transf.* **b.** Hence, the garden itself; also, the 'Fortunate Islands' or 'Isles of the Blest' (αἱ Μακάρων νῆσοι), in which the garden was situated 1590. **2.** *Bot.* Name for a class of plants, containing the orange family (*Aurantiaceæ*) and related orders 1857.

Hence **Hesperi·dian, -ean** *a.* of or pertaining to the gardens of the Hesperides.

‖**Hesperornis** (hespěrǭ·ɹnis). 1871. [f. Gr. ἕσπερος western + ὄρνις bird.] *Palæont.* A genus of fossil birds of the western hemisphere.

‖**Hesperus** (he·spěrŏs). ME. [L. – Gr. ἕσπερος adj. western; sb. the evening star.] The evening star.

Þe eue sterre hesperus CHAUCER.

Hessian (he·siăn), *a.* and *sb.*[1] 1677. [f. *Hesse*, a grand duchy of Germany + -IAN.]

A. *adj.* Of or pertaining to Hesse in Germany.

Hessian boot, a kind of high boot, with tassels in front at the top, first worn by the H. troops. **H. crucible,** a crucible made of the best fire-clay and coarse sand: used in U.S. in all experiments where fluxes are needed. **H. fly,** a fly or midge (*Cecidomyia destructor*), of which the larva is very destructive to wheat; so named, because erron. supposed to have been carried into America by the H. troops, during the War of Independence.

B. *sb.* **1.** A native of Hesse; a soldier of or from Hesse 1742. **2.** In U.S., A mercenary

1877. **3.** (*hessians.*) Short for *Hessian boots* (see A) 1801. **4.** A strong coarse cloth, used for packing bales 1881.

Hessian (he·siăn), *sb.*[2] 1856. [f. Dr. Otto *Hesse* of Königsberg.] *Math.* The Jacobian of the first derivatives of a function.

Hessite (he·səit). 1849. [Named 1843 after G. H. *Hess* of St. Petersburg; see -ITE[1] 2 b.] *Min.* Telluride of silver, occurring in grey, sectile masses.

Hest (hest), *sb. arch.* [ME. *heste*, f. (on the model of abstr. sbs. in *-te*, e.g. *ishefte* creation) *hes*, OE. *hǽs* :– *χaittiz, f. *χaitan call (see HIGHT *v.*[1]).] **1.** Bidding, command, injunction, behest (*arch.*). †**2.** Vow, promise. Cf. BEHEST. –1599. †**3.** Will, determination –1845.

1. O my Father, I haue broke your h. to say so SHAKS. Hence †**Hest** *v.* to promise; to command.

†**He·stern,** *a.* 1577. [– L. *hesternus.*] Yester-. –1708.

Hesternal (hestə̄·ɹnăl), *a.* 1649. [f. L. *hesternus* + -AL[1].] Of yesterday.

Hesychast (he·sikæst). 1797. [– late Gr. ἡσυχαστής hermit (Justinian, *Nov.* 5:3), f. ἡσυχάζειν be still, f. ἥσυχος still, quiet.] *Eccl. Hist.* One of a school of quietists which arose among the monks of Mt. Athos in the 14th c. Also *attrib.* Hence **Hesycha·stic** *a.* appeasing; in *Eccl. Hist.* pertaining to the Hesychasts.

‖**Hetæra** (hĭtī³·ră), **hetaira** (hĭtai·ră). Pl. **hetæræ** (-rī), **hetairai** (-rai). 1820. [Gr. ἑταίρα, fem. of ἑταῖρος companion.] (In ancient Greece, and hence *transf.*) A female companion; a mistress, concubine; a courtesan.

Hetærism (hĭtī³·riz'm), **hetairism** (hĭtai·riz'm). 1860. [– Gr. ἑταιρισμός harlotry, f. ἑταιρίζειν be a courtesan, f. ἑταίρα; see prec., -ISM.] **1.** Open concubinage. **2.** *Anthropol.* Name for a supposed primitive form of the sexual relations: communal marriage in a tribe 1870. Hence **Hetairist, -istic** *a.*

Hetchel, early form of HATCHEL.

Hete: see HIGHT *v.*[1]

Hetero- (hetĕro), bef. a vowel **heter-,** comb. f. Gr. ἕτερος the other of two, other, different; often opp. to *homo-*, sometimes to *auto-*, *homœo-*, *iso-*, *ortho-*, *syn-*.

He·teracanth [Gr. ἄκανθα] *a.*, *Ichth.* having the spines of the dorsal and anal fins alternately broader on one side than the other; opp. to *homacanth.* †**He·terarchy,** the rule of an alien. **Heteroca·rpian, -ca·rpous** [Gr. καρπός] *adjs., Bot.* producing fruit of different kinds; so **Hetero-ca·rpism. Heteroce·phalous** [Gr. κεφαλή] *a., Bot.* applied to a composite plant producing flower-heads of different kinds, male and female. **Heterochi·ral** [Gr. χείρ] *a.*, of identical form but with lateral inversion, as the right and left hands; opp. to *homochiral*; hence **Heterochi·r-ally** *adv.* **Heterochro·mous** [Gr. χρῶμα colour] *a.*, of different colours, as the flowers of some *Compositæ*, e.g. the daisy and asters. **He·te-rocyst** [Gr. κύστις bladder], *Biol.* a cell of exceptional structure or form found in certain algæ and fungi. **Heteroda·ctyl, -da·ctylous** [Gr. δάκτυλος] *adjs., Zool.* having the toes, or one of them, irregular or abnormal, as certain families of birds. **Heteroga·ngliate** *a., Zool.* having the ganglia of the nervous system unsymmetrically arranged, as most molluscs; opp. to *homogangliate.* **Hetero·gynal, Hetero·gynous** [Gr. γυνή female] *adjs., Zool.* applied to species of animals in which the females are of two kinds, fertile and neuter, as in bees, ants, etc. **Hetero·lobous** [Gr. λοβός lobe] *a.*, having unequal lobes. **Heteropo·lar** *a.*, having polar correspondence to something different from itself; having dissimilar poles. **Hetero·ptics** *nonce-wd.*, irregularity in vision. **Heteroso·matous** [Gr. σῶμα] *a., Zool.* having a body deviating from the normal type; said esp. of flat fishes; so **He·terosome; Heteroso·mous** *a.* **Hetero·sporous** [Gr. σπόρος seed] *a., Bot.* producing two different kinds of spores; opp.to *homosporous* or *isosporous.* **Heterothe·rmal** [Gr. θερμός hot] *a., Biol.* having a temperature other than that of the surroundings, as plants and cold-blooded animals; opp. to *homothermal* or *homothermous.* **Hetero·trichal, Hetero·trichous** [Gr. θρίξ, τριχ- hair] *adjs., Biol.* belonging to the order *Heterotricha* of ciliate infusorians, in which the cilia of the oral region differ in size and arrangement from those of the rest of the body; also said of the cilia. **Heterozo·nal** *a., Cryst.* said of faces (or poles) of a crystallographic system which lie in different zones (or zone-systems); opp. to *tautozonal.*

Heterocercal (hetĕrosə̄·ɹkăl), *a.* 1838. [f. HETERO- + Gr. κέρκος tail + -AL[1].] Having the lobes of the tail unequal. Opp to *homocercal.* Hence **Heterocerca·lity, He·terocercy,** the condition of being h.

Heterocerous (hetĕrǫ·sĕrəs), *a.* 1881. [f. mod.L. *Heterocera* n. pl. (f. HETERO- + Gr. κέρας horn) + -OUS.] *Entom.* Belonging to the sub-order of lepidopterous insects *Heterocera* (Moths); so called from the diversified forms of the antennæ.

Heterochronic (-krǫ·nik), *a.* 1854. [f. HETERO- + Gr. χρόνος time + -IC.] *Biol.* and *Path.* **a.** Occurring at irregular times; intermittent: applied to the pulse. **b.** Occurring or developed at an abnormal time 1876. So ‖**Heterochro·nia, Hetero·chronism, Hetero·chrony,** occurrence or development at an abnormal time.

Heteroclite (he·tĕrokləit). 1580. [– late L. *heteroclitus* – Gr. ἑτερόκλιτος, f. ἑτερο- HETERO- + -κλιτος, f. κλίνειν bend, inflect.]

A. *adj.* **1.** *Gram.* Irregularly or anomalously declined or inflected: chiefly of nouns 1656. **2.** *fig.* Irregular, abnormal, eccentric. Said of persons and things. Now *rare.* 1598.

2. This h. animal [the bat] BOYLE. So †**Hetero·clital,** †**Heterocli·tic, -al,** †**Hetero·clitous** *adjs.*

B. *sb.* **1.** *Gram.* A word irregularly inflected; *esp.* a noun which deviates from the regular declension 1580. **2.** *fig.* A person or thing that deviates from the ordinary rule; an anomaly. Now *rare* or *Obs.* 1605.

2. Ther are strange Heteroclites in Religion now adaies HOWELL.

He·terodont. 1877. [f. HETER- + Gr. ὀδούς, ὀδοντ- tooth.] **A.** *adj.* Having teeth of different kinds (incisors, canines, and molars), as most mammals. **B.** *sb.* A h. animal.

Heterodox (he·tĕrŏdǫks). 1619. [– late L. *heterodoxus, -os* – Gr. ἑτερόδοξος, f. ἑτερο- HETERO- + δόξα opinion.]

A. *adj.* **1.** Of doctrines, opinions, etc.: Not in accordance with established doctrines or opinions, or those generally recognized as orthodox. Orig. in religion and theology. 1637. **2.** Of persons: Holding unorthodox opinions 1657.

1. Some of the h. opinions which he avows.. particularly his Arianism MACAULAY. So †**He·terodoxal** *a.*

†**B.** *sb.* A heterodox opinion or person –1691.

Heterodoxy (he·tĕrŏdǫksi). 1652. [– Gr. ἑτεροδοξία, f. as prec. + -ια -Y[3].] **1.** The quality or character of being heterodox; deviation from orthodoxy 1659. **2.** with *a* and *pl.* A heterodox opinion 1652.

Heterodromous (hetĕrǫ·drŏməs), *a.* 1710. [f. mod.L. *heterodromus* (f. Gr. ἑτερο- HETERO- + -δρομος running) + -OUS.] Running in different directions; opp. to *homodromous.* †**a.** *Mech.* Applied to levers of the first order, in which the power and the weight move in opposite directions –1751. **b.** *Bot.* Turning in opposite directions on the main stem and on a branch, as the generating spiral of a phyllotaxis 1870. So **He·terodrome** 1849; **Hetero·dromy,** h. condition.

Heterodyne (he·tĕrodəin). 1908. [f. HETERO- + DYNE.] *Wireless Telegr.* and *Telephony.* A method by which incoming oscillations are combined with other oscillations of a slightly different frequency, so that a 'beat' is set up. Also = *h. receiver*, etc. Also as vb.

Heterogamous (hetĕrǫ·găməs), *a.* 1842. [f. Gr. ἑτερο- HETERO- + γάμος marriage + -OUS, after Fr. *hétérogame* (De Candolle).] **1.** *Bot.* Applied to conditions in which stamens and pistils are not regularly present in each flower or floret. **2.** *Biol.* Characterized by the alternation of differently organized generations, as of a parthenogenetic and a sexual generation 1897. **3.** Pertaining to irregular marriage 1862.

Heterogamy (hetĕrǫ·gămi). 1874. [f. as prec. + -Y[3].] **1.** *Bot.* Mediate or indirect fertilization of plants. **2.** *Biol.* The quality of being HETEROGAMOUS (sense 2) 1884.

Heterogene (he·tĕrŏdʒīn), *a.* ? *Obs.* 1541. [– Gr. ἑτερογενής of different kinds, f. ἑτερο- HETERO- + γένος, γενε- kind.] = HETEROGENEOUS.

Heterogeneal (he:tĕrŏdʒī·niăl). 1602. [– med.L. *heterogeneus* (f. Gr. ἑτερογενής, f. as prec.) + -AL[1].] **1.** *adj.* = HETEROGENEOUS. **2.** *sb.* A heterogeneous person or thing 1602. So †**Heteroge·nean** *a.* = sense 1.

Heterogeneity (he:tĕro,dʒĭnī·ĭti). 1641. [– med.L. *heterogeneitas*, f. as prec.; see -ITY.] The quality or condition of being heterogeneous. **b.** with *a* and *pl.* A heterogeneous element or constituent 1651.

Heterogeneous (hetĕrŏdʒī·niəs), *a.* 1624. [f. as HETEROGENEAL + -OUS.] The opposite of *homogeneous.* **1.** Diverse in kind or nature; of completely different characters; incongruous; foreign. **2.** Composed of diverse elements or constituents; not homogeneous 1630. **3.** *Math.* **a.** Of different kinds, so as to be incommensurable. **b.** Non-homogeneous. *H. Surds:* such as have different radical signs. 1656.

Phr. *H. nouns*, nouns of different genders in the singular and plural. *H. numbers*, mixed numbers consisting of integers and fractions.

Hence **Heteroge·neous-ly** *adv.*, **-ness.**

Heterogenesis (he:tĕro,dʒe·nĭsis). 1854. [f. HETERO- + GENESIS.] *Biol.* †**1.** Abnormal organic development. †**2.** Sexual reproduction from two different germs, male and female. CARPENTER. **3.** The origination of a living being otherwise than from a parent of the same kind 1864. **b.** *esp.* Abiogenesis; spontaneous generation 1878. **c.** Alternation of generations 1863. Hence **Heterogene·tic** *a.* of, pertaining to, or characterized by h. **Hetero·genist,** an upholder of the doctrine of spontaneous generation.

†**Hetero·genous,** *a.* Less correct f. HETEROGENEOUS.

Heterogeny (hetĕrǫ·dʒĭni). 1647. [In sense 1 app. f. HETEROGENE + -Y[3]; in senses 2, 3 f. HETERO- + -GENY.] †**1.** Heterogeneousness. **2.** *concr.* A heterogeneous collection. HAWTHORNE. **3.** *Biol.* Spontaneous generation 1863. Hence **-genist.**

Heterogonous (hetĕrǫ·gŏnəs), *a.* 1877. [f. Gr. ἑτερο- HETERO- + γόνος offspring + -OUS.] **1.** *Bot.* Having incongruous reproductive organs; applied to flowers in which cross-fertilization is secured by the stamens and pistils being dimorphic or trimorphic. Also **He·terogone** *a.* 1877. **2.** *Biol.* Producing offspring dissimilar to the parent 1883. So **Hetero·gonism, Hetero·gony,** the condition of being h.

Heterography (-ǫ·grăfi). 1783. [f. HETERO- + -GRAPHY, after ORTHOGRAPHY.] **1.** Incorrect spelling. **2.** Inconsistent spelling (as the current spelling of English). DE QUINCEY. So **Hetero·grapher,** one who practises h. **Heterogra·phic** *a.* pertaining to or characterized by h.

Heterologous (-ǫ·lŏgəs), *a.* 1822. [f. Gr. ἑτερο- + λόγος ratio, etc. + -OUS.] Having a different relation, or consisting of different elements; not corresponding. Opp. to HOMOLOGOUS. **a.** *Path.* Of a different formation from that of the normal tissue of the part. **b.** *Chem.* Gerhardt's term for bodies derived from each other by definite chemical metamorphoses 1880.

Heterology (-ǫ·lŏdʒi). 1854. [f. as prec. + -Y[3].] The condition of being heterologous; opp. to HOMOLOGY.

Hetero·meran. 1842. [f. mod.L. *Heteromera* n. pl. (f. Gr. ἑτερο- HETERO- + μέρος part) + -AN.] *Entom.* A beetle belonging to the *Heteromera*, a division of *Coleoptera* in which the two anterior pairs of legs have five tarsal joints, but the third pair only four.

Heteromerous (hetĕrǫ·mĕrəs), *a.* 1826. [f. as prec. + -OUS.] **1.** *Entom.* Having legs differing in the number of their tarsal joints; *spec.* belonging to the division *Heteromera* of coleopterous insects (see prec.). **2.** *Bot.* Having parts differing in arrangement, or in number 1875. **3.** *Chem.* Unrelated as to chemical composition, as in certain cases of isomorphism 1864.

Heteromorphic (hetĕromǭ·ɹfik), *a.* 1864. [f. Gr. ἑτερο- HETERO- + μορφή form + -IC.] **1.** Of different or dissimilar forms. **a.** *Entom.* Existing in different forms at different stages of life: said of insects which undergo complete metamorphosis (*Heteromorpha*). **b.** *Bot.* Applied to flowers or plants differing in the relative length of the stamens and pistils (including *dimorphic* and *trimorphic*) 1874. **2.** Of abnormal form (*mod.*). So **Heteromo·rphism, Heteromo·rphy,** h. condition or property.

Heteromorphous (hetĕrǫmǭ·ɹfəs), *a.* 1826. [f. as prec. + -OUS.] **1.** Of abnormal or irregular form. **2.** *Entom.* = HETEROMORPHIC 1 a.

Heteronomic (-nǫ·mik), *a.* 1864. [f. Gr. ἑτερο- HETERO- + νόμος law + -IC.] Showing a different mode of operation or arrangement.

Heteronomous (-ǫ·nŏməs), *a.* 1824. [f. as prec. + -OUS.] **1.** Subject to different laws. **2.** *Biol.* Having different laws or modes of growth; applied to parts differentiated from the same primitive type 1870. **3.** Subject to an external law; opp. to *autonomous* 1894.

Heteronomy (-ǫ·nŏmi). 1824. [f. as prec. + -Y[3]; see -NOMY.] **1.** Presence of a different law. **2.** *Moral Phil.* Subjection to the rule of another being or power (e.g. of the will to the passions); subjection to external law. Opp. to *autonomy*. 1855. **3.** *Biol.* Heteronomous condition; differentiation from a common primitive type 1870.

Heteronym (he·tĕrŏnim). 1697. [f. Gr. ἑτερ- HETERO- + ὄνυμα name, after *synonym*.] †**1.** One or other of two heteronymous terms. **2.** A word spelt like another, but having a different sound and meaning; opp. to *homonym* and *synonym* 1889. **3.** A name of a thing in one language which is a translation of the name in another language 1885.

Heteronymous (hetĕrǫ·niməs), *a.* 1697. [f. Gr. ἑτερώνυμος (f. as prec.) + -OUS.] **1.** Having different names, as two correlatives, e.g. *husband, wife*; opp. to *synonymous*. **2.** *Optics.* Applied to the two images of one object seen in looking at a point beyond it, when the left image is that seen by the right eye and *vice versa*; opp. to *homonymous* 1881. **3.** Pertaining to, of the nature of, or having a heteronym. Hence **Hetero·nymously** *adv.*

Heteroousian, heterousian (he:tĕro,au·siăn, hetĕrau·siăn, -ū·siăn). 1678. [f. Patristic Gr. ἑτεροούσιος, ἑτερούσιος (f. ἑτερο- HETERO- + οὐσία essence, substance) + -AN. Opp. to *homoousian* and *homoiousian*.] *Theol.* **1.** *adj.* Of different essence or substance. **2.** *sb.* One who held the Father and the Son to be different in essence or substance; an Arian 1874. Hence **Heteroou·sious** *a.* = 1.

Heteropathic (-pæ·þik), *a.* 1830. [f. as next + -IC.] **1.** *Med.* = ALLOPATHIC. **2.** Differing in their effect 1843.

Heteropathy (-ǫ·păþi). 1847. [f. HETERO- + -PATHY.] **1.** *Med.* = ALLOPATHY; opp. to *homœopathy*. **2.** *Path.* A state of abnormal organic susceptibility in the presence of any irritation 1886. **3.** Antipathy excited by suffering; opp. to *sympathy* 1874.

‖**Heterophasia** (-fē[i]·ziă). 1877. [mod.L., f. HETERO- + Gr. -φασια, f. φάσις speech; see -IA[1].] *Path.* = HETEROPHEMY (as a result of mental disease).

He·terophemy (-fīmi). 1875. [f. as prec. + -φημια, φήμη, φῆμις voice, speech; see -IA[1].] The saying or writing of one word or phrase when another is meant. Hence **Heterophe·mism,** an instance of h. **Heterophe·mist,** one who says something else than he means to say.

Heterophyllous (-fi·ləs), *a.* 1828. [f. HETERO- + Gr. φύλλον leaf + -OUS.] **1.** *Bot.* Bearing leaves of different form. **2.** *Zool.* Belonging to the group *Heterophylli* of cephalopods. So **He·terophy:lly,** the condition of being h.

He·teroplasm. 1878. [f. as prec. + Gr. πλάσμα anything moulded. Cf. HOMOPLAST.] *Path.* A tissue formed in a part where it does not normally occur. So **Heteropla·stic** *a.* of or belonging to the formation of a h.; of the nature of a h.; in *Biol.* dissimilar in formation or structure, as the different tissues of the body.

Heteroplasty (he·tĕroplæsti). *Surg.* 1874. [See prec. and -PLASTY.] Removal or grafting of tissue from an individual.

Heteropod (he·tĕrŏpǫd). 1835. [f. next; see -POD.] *Zool.* **1.** *adj.* Of or belonging to the *Heteropoda* 1882. **2.** *sb.* One of the *Heteropoda*.

‖**Heteropoda** (hetĕrǫ·pŏdă), *sb. pl.* 1835. [mod.L., f. HETERO-; see -POD, -A 4.] **a.** A group of Crustacea including forms with 14 feet, some adapted for swimming. **b.** An order or subclass of Gastropods, having the feet modified into a swimming organ. **c.** A group of Echinoderms. Hence **Hetero·podan** = HETEROPOD *sb.* **Hetero·podous** *a.* = HETEROPOD *a.*

Hetero·pter. *Entom.* 1864. One of the *Heteroptera*.

‖**Heteroptera** (hetĕrǫ·ptĕră), *sb. pl.* 1826. [mod.L., f. HETERO- + Gr. πτερόν wing; see -A 4.] *Entom.* A suborder of HEMIPTERA, comprising those insects whose wings are coriaceous at the base and membranous at the tip; the true bugs. Opp. to HOMOPTERA. Hence **Hetero·pteran** = HETEROPTER. **Hetero·pterous** *a.* belonging to or like the *H.*

Heteroscian (hetĕrǫ·ʃiăn). 1616. [f. late L. *heteroscius* (usually in nom. pl. used subst.) – Gr. ἑτερόσκιος throwing a shadow only one way (f. ἕτερος one or other of two + σκία shadow) + -AN.] **1.** *sb.* A name applied to people of the two temperate zones in reference to the fact that, in the two zones, noon-shadows always fall in opposite directions. (Cf. *Amphiscian*.) Usu. in *pl.*; the L. pl. **heteroscii** is also used. **2.** *adj.* Of, pertaining to, or of the nature of noon-shadows, in the temperate zones 1646.

Heterostatic (-stæ·tik), *a.* 1867. [f. HETERO- + STATIC.] *Electr.* Applied to electrostatic instruments in which there is electrification independent of that to be tested.

Heterostrophic (-strǫ·fik), *a.* [f. HETERO- + Gr. -στροφος turning + -IC.] Turning or winding in another direction; in *Conch.* applied *spec.* to certain univalve shells. So **Hetero·strophe, Hetero·strophy,** the condition of being h.

Heterostyled (he·tĕro,stəild), *a.* 1876. [f. HETERO- + STYLE + -ED[2].] *Bot.* = HETEROMORPHIC 1 b. So **Heterosty·lism, He·terostyly,** heteromorphism. **Heterosty·lous** *a.* = HETEROSTYLED.

He·terotaxy (-tæksi). 1854. [f. HETERO- + Gr. -ταξια, f. τάξις arrangement.] **1.** *Anat.* and *Bot.* Aberrant or abnormal disposition of organs or parts. **2.** *Geol.* Want of regularity in stratification 1889. So **Heterota·ctous** *a.* characterized by h.

Heterotopy (hetĕrǫ·tŏpi). 1876. [– mod.L. *heterotopia* (also used), f. HETERO- + Gr. -τοπια, f. τόπος place; see -Y[3].] Displacement in position, misplacement: **a.** *Path.* The occurrence of a tumour in a part where its elements do not normally exist. **b.** *Biol.* Gradual displacement of cells or parts by adaptation to the changed conditions of embryonic existence 1879. Hence **Hetero·to·pic, Hetero·topous** *adjs.* of, pertaining to, or of the nature of h. **Hetero·topism** = HETEROTOPY.

Heterotropic (-trǫ·pik), *a.* 1885. [f. HETERO- + Gr. -τροπος turning + -IC.] *Physics.* = ÆOLOTROPIC, ANISOTROPIC.

Heterotropous (-ǫ·trŏpəs), *a.* 1819. [f. as prec. + -OUS.] = HEMITROPOUS 2. So **Hetero·tropal** *a.*

Heterozygote (he:tĕrozəi·go[u]t). 1902. [f. HETERO- + ZYGOTE.] *Biol.* A zygote formed by the union of two unlike gametes. **Heterozygo·sis, -zygo·sity, -zy·goted** *a.*, **-zy·gous** *a.*

†**Hething,** *vbl. sb.* ME. [– ON. *hæðing* scoffing, derision, f. *hæða* mock, scoff at.] Derision; scorn, contempt; dishonour –1540.

‖**Hetman** (he·tmăn). Also **attaman.** 1710. [Pol. *hetman*, prob. – G. *hauptmann* 'head man', captain, earlier *heubtmann*.] A Polish captain or military commander.

Heugh, heuch (hiux). *Sc.* and *n. dial.* ME. [repr. of ME. *hōȝ*, OE. *hōh*, f. ablaut grade **xanx*- of HANG *v.* Cf. HOE *sb.*[1]] **1.** A hanging descent; a precipice, cliff, or scaur; usu., one overhanging a river or the sea. **2.** A glen with steep overhanging sides 1450. **3.** The steep face of a quarry or the like (*quarry h.*); a coal-pit; *fig.* a pit 1592.

Heuk, var. of HUKE *Obs.*

Heulandite (hiū·lændəit). 1822. [f. H. *Heuland*, English mineralogist; see -ITE[1] 2 b.] *Min.* A mineral of the Zeolite group; a hydrated silicate of aluminium and calcium; found in crystals of various colours with pearly lustre.

Heureka, the proper sp. of EUREKA, q.v.

Heuretic (hiure·tik), *sb. rare.* [– Gr. εὑρετικός inventive, f. εὑρίσκειν find; see -IC.] The branch of logic which treats of the art of discovery or invention. SIR W. HAMILTON.

Heuristic (hiuri·stik), *a.* (*sb.*) 1860. [irreg. f. Gr. εὑρίσκειν find, after words in -ISTIC from vbs. in -ίζειν -IZE. Cf. EUREKA.] **1.** Serving to find out; *spec.* applied to a system of education under which the pupil is trained to find out things for himself. **2.** *sb.* = prec. ABP. THOMSON.

Heved, obs. f. HEAD.

Hew (hiū), *v.* Pa. t. **hewed** (hiūd); pa. pple. **hewn** (hiūn), **hewed.** [OE. *hēawan* = OFris. *hawa, howa*, OS. *hauwan* (Du. *houwen*), OHG. *houwan* (G. *hauen*), ON. *hǫggva* :– Gmc. **xauwan*.] **1.** *intr.* To deal blows with a cutting weapon. **2.** *trans.* To strike forcibly with a cutting instrument; to chop, hack, gash OE. **3.** To shape with cutting blows OE. **4.** To cut with an axe or the like so as to fell or bring down; *esp.* with *down*, etc. OE. **5.** To sever by a cutting blow; now with *away, off, out, from*, etc. OE. **6.** To chop into pieces; esp. with *asunder, to pieces*, etc. ME. **7.** To make, form, or produce by hewing OE.

1. Hewe not to hye, lest the chips fall in thine iye J. HEYWOOD. **3.** When a rude and Unpolish'd Stone is hewen into a beautiful Statue CUDWORTH. *Rough hew*: see ROUGH-HEW *v.* **4.** Command thou, that they h. me Cedar trees out of Lebanon 1 *Kings* 5:6. **5.** The fragment of rock left when the rest is hewn away FREEMAN. **6.** He tooke a yoke of oxen, and hewed them in pieces 1 *Sam.* 11:7. **7.** Phr. *To h. one's way.* Their Canoes..are hued out of one tree SIR T. HERBERT.

†**Hew,** *sb.* 1596. [f. HEW *v.*] An act of hewing; hacking, slaughter; a cut or gash produced by hewing –1618.

Hew, obs. f. EWE, HUE, YEW.

†**Hewe.** [OE. *hīwan* pl. (of **hīwa*), domestics, ME. *hiwen, heowen, hewen, heowes* and *hewes* pl.; also (later) *hewe* sing.; deriv. of root of Goth. *heiwa*- household. Cf. HIND *sb.*[2]] A domestic, a servant. OE. and ME. only.

Hewer (hiū·əɹ). ME. [f. HEW *v.* + -ER[1].] One who hews; in a colliery, the man who cuts coal from the seam 1708.

H. of wood and drawer of water (*Joshua* 9:21), a labourer of the lowest kind, drudge.

Hewgh, *int.* = WHEW. *Lear* IV. vi. 93.

Hew-hole, var. of HICKWALL.

Hewn (hiūn), *ppl. a.* ME. [pa. pple. of HEW *v.*] **1.** Fashioned by hewing with a chisel, axe, etc.; made by or resulting from hewing. **2.** Excavated or hollowed out by hewing ME.

†**Hewt.** 1575. [prob. :– OE. *hiewet* hewing; cf. OFr. *copeiz* COPSE.] ? A copse; a grove –1688.

Hex- (heks), Gr. ἕξ six, a comb. form, used chiefly in *Chem.*, in sense 'containing six atoms or molecules of the radical or substance'; as *hexdecyl* (= HEXADECYL), etc.

Hexa- (heksă), bef. a vowel **hex-**, comb. f. Gr. ἕξ six. In *Chem.* it indicates the presence of six atoms of some element, as in *hexacarbon*.

Hexaba·sic *a.*, *Chem.* having six atoms of a base, or of replaceable hydrogen. **Hexaca·psular** *a.*, *Bot.* having six capsules. **He·xace** (he·ksăsi) [Gr. ἀκή point], *Cryst.* the summit of a polyhedron formed by the concurrence of six faces. **Hexaco·lic** [Gr. κῶλον] *a.*, *Pros.* consisting of six cola. **Hexacora·llan, -co·ralline** [CORAL] *Zool.*, *adjs.* pertaining to the *Hexacoralla*, a chief division of the *Coralligena* or corals in which the fundamental number of intermesenteric chambers of the body cavity and of the tentacles is six; *sb.* one of these corals. **Hexa·ctine, Hexa·ctinal, -acti·nal** [Gr. ἀκτίς, ἀκτῖνος ray] *adjs.*, *Zool.* having six rays, as a sponge spicule. **Hexacti·nian** *a.*, *Zool.* pertaining to the *Hexactiniæ*, a group of *Actiniaria* having septa in pairs, in number six or a multiple of six. **Hexadacty·lic, Hexada·ctylous** [Gr. δάκτυλος] *adjs.*, *Anat.* having six fingers or six toes; so **Hexada·ctylism,** hexadactylous condition. **He·xaglot** [Gr. γλῶττα] *a.*, written or composed in six languages. **Hexa-**

pe·talous *a.*, *Bot.* having six petals. **Hexaphy·llous** [Gr. φύλλον] *a.*, *Bot.* applied to a calyx having six sepals or to a leaf consisting of six leaflets. **Hexapro·style** [PROSTYLE] *a.*, *Arch.* having a portico of six columns in front. **Hexa·pterous** [Gr. πτερόν] *a.*, provided with six wings or wing-like appendages. **He·xarchy** [Gr. -αρχία], a group of six states. **Hexase·mic** [Gr. ἑξάσημος] *a.*, *Pros.* containing six units of time or moræ. **Hexa·stichous** *a.*, *Bot.* arranged in six rows. **Hexastigm** [Gr. στίγμα], a figure determined by six points.

Hexachord (he·ksăkǭɹd). 1694. [app. f. (after Gr. τετράχορδον scale of four notes) Gr. ἑξα- HEXA- + χορδή CHORD *sb.*[2]; but the chronology is obscure.] *Mus.* A diatonic series or scale of six notes, having a semitone between the third and fourth. See GAMUT. 1730. †**2.** The interval of a sixth –1741. **3.** A musical instrument with six strings 1858.

Hexactinellid (he:ksæktine·lid). 1865. [f. mod.L. *Hexactinellidæ*, (f. Gr. ἕξ + ἀκτίς, ἀκτῖν- ray + L. dim. *-ell-*); see -ID[3].] **1.** *adj.* Of or belonging to the *Hexactinellidæ*, a family of siliceous sponges. **2.** *sb.* A sponge of this family 1879.

Hexad (he·ksæd). 1660. [– Gr. ἑξάς, -αδ- a group of six.] **1.** The number six (in the Pythagorean System); a series of six numbers. **2.** A group of six 1879. **3.** *Chem.* An element or radical that has the combining power of six units, i.e. of six atoms of hydrogen. Chiefly *attrib.* 1869. Hence **Hexa·dic** *a.* of the nature of a h. (sense 3).

Hexadecane (he·ksădīkēⁱn). 1872. [f. Gr. ἑξα- + δέκα ten (for ἑκκαίδεκα sixteen) + -ANE.] *Chem.* The paraffin of the 16-carbon series, also called CETANE. So **Hexadeco·ic** *a.* **Hexade·cyl,** the radical $C_{16}H_{33}$, also called CETYL.

‖**Hexaëmeron** (heksă,ī·mĕrǫn). Also **hexameron.** 1593. [Late L. *hexaemeron* (the title of a work by Ambrose) = Gr. ἑξαήμερον, subst. use of n. of adj. -ος, f. ἕξ six + ἡμέρα day; ἡ ἑξαήμερος was the title of a work by Basil.] The six days of the creation; a history of the creation as contained in Genesis; or a treatise thereon.

Hexagon (he·ksăgǫn). 1570. [– late L. *hexagonum* – Gr. ἑξάγωνον, subst. use of n. of adj. ἑξάγωνος six-cornered; see HEXA-, -GON. Cf. Fr. *hexagone.*] **1.** *Geom.* A plane figure having six sides and six angles. Also *attrib.* **2.** *Fortif.* A fort with six bastions 1669.

1. Bees..make their cells regular hexagons REID.

Hexagonal (heksæ·gŏnăl), *a.* (*sb.*) 1571. [f. prec. + -AL[1].] **1.** Of or pertaining to a hexagon; having six sides and six angles. **2.** Of solids: Whose section or base is a hexagon 1646. **3.** *Cryst.* Denominating a system of crystallization, which is referred to three lateral axes, normally inclined to each other at 60°, and a vertical axis at right angles to these and differing from them in length. Also, Of or belonging to this system. 1837. **4.** *Geom.* and *Cryst.* Having a relation to six angles, as *h. symmetry* 1878. **5.** *sb.* A hexagonal number 1796.

1. Phr. *Hexagonal numbers*, the series of POLYGONAL numbers 1, 6, 15, 28, 45, etc., formed by continuous summation of the arithmetical series 1, 5, 9, 13, 17, etc. Hence **Hexa·gonally** *adv.* **Hexa·gonalize** *v. trans.* to form into hexagons. vars. †**Hexago·nial,** †**Hexago·nical.**

Hexagonous (heksæ·gŏnəs), *a.* 1870. [f. HEXAGON + -OUS.] *Bot.* Having six edges; hexagonal in section. (Often written 6-*gonous.*)

Hexagram (he·ksăgræm). 1863. [f. HEXA- + Gr. γράμμα line.] **1.** A figure formed by two intersecting equilateral triangles, each side of the one being parallel to a side of the other, and the six angular points coinciding with those of a hexagon 1871. **2.** *Geom.* A figure of six lines 1863.

‖**Hexagynia** (heksădʒi·niă). 1778. [Bot. L., f. HEXA- + Gr. γυνή in sense 'female organ, pistil'. See -IA[1].] *Bot.* A Linnæan order of plants having six pistils. Hence **He·xagyn,** a plant of this order. **Hexagy·nian, Hexagy·nious** *adjs.* belonging to this order. **Hexa·gynous** *a.* having six pistils.

Hexahedral (heksăhī·drăl, -he·drăl), *a.* 1800. [f. next + -AL[1].] Of the form of a hexahedron; having six sides or faces. So †**Hexahe·drical** *a.* BOYLE.

Hexahedron (heksăhī·drǫn, -he·drǫn). 1571. [– Gr. ἑξάεδρον, subst. use of n. of adj. ἑξάεδρος with six surfaces; see HEXA-, -HEDRON.] *Geom.*, etc. A solid figure having six faces; *esp.* the *regular hexahedron* or cube.

Hexakis-, Gr. ἑξάκις six times, comb. form. **He:xakisoctahe·dron,** a solid figure contained by forty-eight scalene triangles. **He:xakistetrahe·dron,** a solid figure contained by twenty-four scalene triangles, being the hemihedral form of the hexakisoctahedron.

Hexamerous (heksæ·mĕrəs), *a.* 1857. [f. HEXA- + Gr. μέρος part + -OUS.] Having the parts six in number. (In *Bot.* often written 6-*merous.*)

Hexameter (heksæ·mĭtəɹ). ME. [– L. *hexameter* adj. and (sc. *versus* verse) sb. – Gr. ἑξάμετρος of six measures, f. ἑξα- HEXA- + μέτρον measure, metre.]

A. *adj.* (Now only sb. used attrib.) *Pros.* Consisting of six metrical feet; *esp.* dactyls and spondees 1546.

B. *sb.* A verse or line of six metrical feet; *esp.* the *dactylic hexameter* (*catalectic*), consisting of five dactyls and a trochee, or (in Latin poets) oftener a spondee; for any or all of the first four dactyls a spondee may be substituted, but in the fifth foot a spondee is admitted only for special effect ME.

These lame Hexameters the strong-wing'd music of Homer! No—but a most burlesque, barbarous experiment TENNYSON. Hence **Hexa·metral** *a.* of or pertaining to the h. **Hexame·tric, -al** *a.* of or pertaining to a h.; consisting of six metrical feet; composed in hexameters. **Hexa·metrist,** one who writes hexameters. **Hexa·metrize** *v. intr.* to write hexameters; *trans.* to celebrate in hexameters.

‖**Hexandria** (heksæ·ndriă). 1753. [mod.L. (Linn.), f. Gr. ἕξ six + ἀνήρ, ἀνδρ- man, male, in sense of 'male organ, stamen'; see -IA[1].] *Bot.* A Linnæan class of plants having six (equal) stamens. Hence **Hexa·nder,** a plant of this class. **Hexa·ndrian, -ious** *adjs.* of or pertaining to this class. **Hexa·ndric, Hexa·ndrous** *adjs.* having six (equal) stamens.

Hexane (he·ksēⁱn). 1877. [f. HEX- + -ANE.] *Chem.* The paraffin of the hexacarbon series, C_6H_{14}; of this there are five forms. So **He·xene,** the olefine of the hexacarbon series (C_6H_{12}), also called *hexylene*, homologous and polymeric with ethene; it exists in many metameric forms. **He·xine,** the hydrocarbon C_6H_{10} of the same series. **Hexoic acid,** $C_6H_{12}O_2$, the same as caproic acid. **Hexo·ylene,** one of the isomeric forms of hexine.

†**He·xangle.** 1657. [f. HEXA- + ANGLE *sb.*[2]] = HEXAGON.

Hexangular (heksæ·ŋgiŭlăɹ), *a.* 1665. [f. prec., after *angular.*] Having six angles; hexagonal.

‖**Hexapla** (he·ksăplă). Also **hexaple.** 1613. [– Gr. (τὰ) ἑξαπλᾶ (title of Origen's work), n. pl. of ἑξαπλοῦς sixfold.] A sixfold text in parallel arrangement, as that made by Origen of the O.T. Hence **He·xaplar, Hexapla·rian** *adjs.* of the form or character of a h.

Hexapod (he·ksăpǫd), *sb.* (*a.*) 1668. [– Gr. ἑξάπους, -ποδ- six-footed; see HEXA-, -POD, on which the mod. use is based.] **1.** An animal having six feet, an insect. **2.** *adj.* Having six feet; belonging to the class *Hexapoda* or *Insecta*, hexapodous 1815. Hence **Hexa·podal, Hexa·podous** *adjs.* having six feet, belonging to this class. **Hexa·podan** *a.* and *sb.* = HEXAPOD *a.* and *sb.*

Hexapody (heksæ·pŏdi). 1844. [f. Gr. ἑξάπους, -ποδ- of six feet, after *dipody, tetrapody*; see -Y[3].] *Pros.* A line or verse consisting of six feet.

Hexastich (he·ksăstik). 1577. [– mod.L. *hexastichon* – Gr. ἑξάστιχον, subst. use of n. sing. adj. -ος of six rows or lines; see HEXA-, STICH.] A group of six lines of verse.

Hexastyle (he·ksăstəil), *a.* (*sb.*) 1704. [– Gr. ἑξάστυλος, f. ἕξ (HEXA-) + στῦλος pillar. Cf. Fr. *hexastyle.*] **1.** Having six columns; applied to a portico or temple 1748. **2.** *sb.* A portico or temple having six columns.

Hexateuch (he·ksătiūk). 1878. [f. Gr. ἕξ (HEXA-) + τεῦχος book, after *pentateuch.*] The first six books of the O.T.

Hexatomic (heksătǫ·mik), *a.* 1873. [f. HEXA- + ATOMIC.] *Chem.* Containing or consisting of six atoms; having six replaceable hydrogen atoms; also = next.

Hexavalent (heksæ·vălĕnt), *a.* 1886. [f. HEXA- + -VALENT.] *Chem.* Combining with or capable of replacing six atoms of hydrogen or other univalent element or radical.

Hexene, Hexine: see under HEXANE.

Hexoctahe·dron. 1570. [f. HEX(A)- + OCTAHEDRON.] *Geom.* etc. †**a.** The critical form of the CUBO-*octahedron.* DANA. **b.** = HEXAKISOCTAHEDRON.

Hexode (he·ksoᵘd), *a.* 1894. [f. HEXA- + Gr. ὁδός way, path.] *Electr. Telegr. lit.* Of six ways: applied to a mode of multiplex telegraphy, whereby six messages can be transmitted simultaneously.

Hexoic acid, Hexoylene: see under HEXANE.

Hexpa·rtite, *a.* 1842. [f. Gr. ἕξ six, or HEX(A)-, + *-partite* in *quadripartite, sexpartite.*] Sexpartite, sextipartite.

Hexyl (he·ksil). 1869. [f. HEX- + -YL.] *Chem.* The hydrocarbon radical C_6H_{13}. It may exist in various forms. Also *attrib.*, as in *h. alcohol*, etc. Hence **He·xylene** = HEXENE. **Hexy·lic** *a.* of or pertaining to h., as *hexylic acid*, etc.

Hey (hēⁱ, hē), *int.* (*sb.*) [ME. *hei, hay*; cf. OFr. *hai, hay*, Du., G. *hei*, Sw. *hej*. See HEIGH.] A call to attract attention; also, an exclam. of exultation, incitement, surprise, etc.; sometimes an interrogative (= *eh ?*). As *sb.* A cry of 'hey!' ME.

Phr. *Hey for* —: an utterance of applause or exultant appreciation of some person or thing, or of some place which one resolves to reach 1661. **Hey-go-mad** (*dial.*), as *adj.* = boisterously excited. **Hey-pass, Hey presto:** exclams. of command by conjurors and jugglers; also as *sbs.*

Hey-day (hēⁱ·dēⁱ·), *int. arch.* 1526. [The earliest form *heyda* (XVI) agrees with LG. *heida*, also *heidi* hurrah!] An exclamation of gaiety or surprise.

Hey-day, heyday (hēⁱ·dēⁱ), *sb.* 1590. [f. prec.] **1.** State of exaltation or excitement. **2.** The stage or period when excited feeling is at its height. Often associated with *day*, and taken as the most flourishing or exalted time 1751. Also *attrib.*

1. At your age, The hey-day in the blood is tame *Haml.* III. iv. 69. **2.** In the hey-day of youth 1807, of his powers 1877.

Hey-day guise, -de-gay: see HAY *sb.*[4]

‖**Heyduck** (hai·duk, hēⁱ·dʊk). 1615. [– Czech, Pol., Serb. *hajduk*, in Magyar *hajdú*, pl. *-dúk* – Turk. *haydud* robber, brigand.] A term, app. meaning orig. 'robber, brigand' (as still in Serbia, etc.), which in Hungary became the name of a special body of foot-soldiers, and in Poland of the liveried personal followers and attendants of the nobles.

Heygh, obs. f. HIGH.

Hey-ho, hey ho (hēⁱ·hōᵘ·), *int.* 1471. An utterance marking the rhythm of movement in heaving and hauling (cf. HEAVE HO); often used in the burdens of songs, etc.

Heynne, var. of HYNE *adv.*, hence.

Heyþen, obs. f. HEATHEN.

†**Hi,** *pron.*[1] OE., ME. Her.

†**Hi,** *pron.*[2] OE., ME. They; them.

Hi (həi), *int.* 1475. [A parallel form to HEY.] An exclam. used to call attention.

Hiant (həi·ănt), *a.* 1800. [– *hiant-*, pres. ppl. stem of L. *hiare* gape; see -ANT.] Gaping.

Hiate (həi·eⁱt), *v. rare.* 1646. [– *hiat-*, pa. ppl. stem of L. *hiare* gape; see -ATE[3].] *intr.* To gape; to cause a hiatus. **Hia·tion,** gaping.

Hiatus (həi,ēⁱ·tɒs). *Pl.* **hiatus, hiatuses.** 1563. [– L. *hiatus* gaping, opening, f. *hiare* gape.] **1.** A break in continuity; a gaping chasm; an opening or aperture. Now *rare.* ‖**b.** *Anat.* A foramen 1886. **2.** A gap in a series; a lacuna in a writing, etc.; a missing link in a chain of events, etc. 1613. **3.** *Gram.* and *Pros.* The break between two vowels coming together without an intervening consonant in successive words or syllables 1706.

Hibernacle (həi·bəɹnĕk'l). Also **hy-**. 1708. [f. L. *hibernaculum*; see next.] A winter retreat; a hibernaculum.

‖**Hibernaculum** (həibəɹnæ·kiulŏm). Also **hy-**. Pl. **-a**. 1699. [L., usu. in pl., f. *hibernare* HIBERNATE; see -CULE.] †**1.** A greenhouse for wintering plants. EVELYN. **2.** *Zool.* The winter quarters of a hibernating animal 1789. **3.** *Bot.* A part of a plant that protects the embryo during the winter, as a bulb or bud 1760. **4.** *Zool.* **a.** An encysted winter-bud of a polyzoan 1885. **b.** The false operculum of a snail 1888. Hence **Hiberna·cular** *a.*

Hibernal (həibɔ̄·ɹnăl), *a.* Also **hy-**. 1626. [– late L. *hibernalis*, f. *hibernus* wintry; see -AL[1].] Of, pertaining to, or proper to winter; appearing in winter. Also *fig.*

Hibernate (həi·bəɹne[i]t), *v.* Also **hy-**. 1802. [– *hibernat-*, pa. ppl. stem of L. *hibernare*, f. *hiberna* winter quarters, n. pl. of *hibernus* of winter; see -ATE[3].] *intr.* To winter; to spend the winter in some special state suited to resist it; said esp. of animals that pass the winter in a state of torpor. Also *transf.* of persons. Also *fig.*

fig. Inclination would lead me to h. during half the year SOUTHEY. Hence **Hi·berna:tor**, an animal that hibernates. **Hiberna·tion**, the action, condition, or period of hibernating; also *fig.*

Hibernian (həibɔ̄·ɹniăn), *a.* (*sb.*) Also **hy-**. 1632. [f. L. *Hibernia*, alteration of *Iverna*, *Iuverna*, *Iuberna* – Gr. Ἰϝέρνη, Ἰέρνη – OCelt. **Iveriu*, acc. **Iverionem* (Ir. *Eriu*, acc. *Eirinn* Erin, later MIr. *Eri*, whence OE. *Iraland* Ireland.] **1.** Of or belonging to Ireland; Irish. **2.** *sb.* A native of Ireland; an Irishman 1709.

1. The truly H. predicament of being notoriously unknown F. HALL. Hence **Hibe·rnianism,** Irish character or nationality; an Irish characteristic, trait, or idiom.

Hibernicism (həibɔ̄·ɹnisiz'm). 1758. [prob. f. L. *Hibernia* Ireland, after *Anglicism*.] **1.** An idiom or expression characteristic of Irish speech; esp. an Irish bull (see BULL *sb.*[4]). **2.** Irish nationality 1807. So **Hibe·rnicize** *v.* to make Irish in form or character.

Hiberno-, formative element f. med.L. *Hibernus* (Bede) Irish, as in **Hiberno-Celtic,** Celtic of Ireland.

‖**Hibiscus** (hibi·skŏs). 1706. [L. – Gr. ἱβίσκος, identified by Dioscorides with ἀλθαία marsh-mallow, ALTHÆA.] *Bot.* A large genus of malvaceous plants (herbs, shrubs, and trees), mostly from tropical countries; the Rose-mallows.

Hiccius doccius (hi·kʃiŏs dǫ·kʃiŏs). 1676. [A corruption of L. *hicce est doctus* 'here is the learned man', if not merely a nonsense formula simulating Latin.] A formula used by jugglers; hence, 'a cant word for a juggler; one that plays fast and loose' (J.). Also *attrib.*

Hiccup (hi·kŏp), *sb.* Also **hiccough.** 1580. [imit.; early forms *hickop*, *hi(c)kup*, which superseded earlier †*hicket*, †*hickock*, of imit. origin; cf. ON. *hixti* sb., *hixta* v., Du. *hik*, *hikken*, Sw. *hicka*, Da. *hik(ke)*, Russ. *ikát'*, and Fr. *hoquet*. The form *hiccough* (XVII) is due to assim. to *cough*, but the pronunc. has not been affected.] An involuntary spasm of the respiratory organs, consisting in a quick inspiratory movement of the diaphragm checked suddenly by closure of the glottis, and accompanied by a characteristic sound. Also, a succession of such spasms. *fig.* 1669. Hence **Hi·ccup** *v. intr.* to make the sound of a h.; *trans.* to utter with hiccups, as a drunken person.

‖**Hic jacet** (hik dʒē[i]·set). 1601. [L. = 'here lies'.] The first two words of a Latin epitaph; hence, an epitaph.

The cold Hic Jacets of the dead TENNYSON.

Hick, *sb.*[1] 1565. [A familiar by-form of *Richard*; cf. *Dick*, and *Hob* = Robert, *Hodge* = Roger.] An ignorant countryman; a booby (now *U.S.*).

Hick, *sb.*[2] *rare.* Also **hic.** 1607. [See next.] A hiccup; a hesitation in speech. Hence **Hick** *v. intr.* to hiccup.

†**Hicket,** *sb.* 1544. [One of the earlier forms of *hiccup*, the other being *hickock*, both with a dim. formative *-et*, *-ock*. The stem *hick* is echoic.] Early form of HICCUP *sb.* –1684. So †**Hicket** *v.* Also †**Hickock** *sb.* and *v.*

Hickory (hi·kəri). 1676. [Shortening of *pohickery*, the native Virginian form of which is cited as *paw-* or *powcohiccora* for milk or oil extracted from the nuts.] **1.** A N. American tree of the genus *Carya*, with tough heavy wood, and bearing drupes enclosing nuts, the kernels of which in several species are edible. Also **h.-tree.** 1682.

There are about a dozen species, all natives of N. America, the commonest being the Shell-bark, Scaly-bark, or Shag-bark H. (*C. alba*); others are the Bitter-nut or Swamp H. (*C. amara*), and the Pig-nut, Hog-nut, or Broom H. (*C. porcina*).

2. The wood of the American hickory, or a stick, or the like, made of it 1676. **3.** The nut of the American hickory 1866. **4.** *attrib.* 1741.

2. *Old Hickory*, a nickname of Andrew Jackson, President of U.S. 1829–1837.

Comb.: **h.-elm**, an American elm (*Ulmus racemosa*); **-eucalyptus**, an Australian tree, *Eucalyptus punctata*, with very hard tough wood; **-girdler**, a longicorn beetle, *Oncideres cingulatus*, of U.S.; **-horned** *a.*, having very tough or hard horns; **-pine**, N. American species of pine, *Pinus balfouriana*, var. *aristata*, and *P. pungens*; **-shirt** (*U.S.*), a coarse and durable shirt, made of heavy twilled cotton with a narrow blue stripe or a check; **-tree** (see 1).

†**Hicksco·rner.** 1530. [See HICK *sb.*[1]] A character in an interlude of the same name repr. a travelled libertine who scoffs at religion; hence, a scoffer –1622. Hence **-scorning** *a.* 1601.

Hicksite (hi·ksəit). 1839. [f. the name *Hicks* + -ITE[1] 1.] A member of a seceding body of American Quakers, founded by Elias Hicks in 1827, and holding Socinian doctrines.

Hickwall (hi·kwǭl). *local.* Also **hyghwhele, highaw(e, hickle,** etc. 14.. [prob. echoic, in the early form *hyghwhele*, whence other forms modified by popular etymology. Cf. HECCO, HIGH-HOLE, WITWALL, YAFFLE.] The Green Woodpecker.

Hid (hid), *ppl. a.* ME. [pa. pple. of HIDE *v.*[1]] Hidden, concealed, secret.

Hidage (həi·dėdʒ). *Obs.* exc. *Hist.* ME. [– AL. *hidagium*, f. *hida* HIDE *sb.*[2]; see -AGE.] **1.** A tax payable to the royal exchequer for each hide of land. **2.** The assessed value or measurement of lands, on which the tax was levied 1862.

‖**Hidalgo** (hidæ·lgo). 1594. [Sp., formerly also *hijo dalgo*, i.e. *hijo* (*filho*) *de algo*, son of something. Cf. FIDALGO.] In Spain: One of the lower nobility; a gentleman by birth. Also *transf.*

Hidden (hi·d'n), *ppl. a.* 1547. [See HIDE *v.*[1]] **1.** Concealed, secret, occult, etc.; see HIDE *v.*[1] **2.** *Mus.* Applied to the consecutive fifths or octaves suggested between two parts when they move in similar motion to the interval of a fifth or octave 1869.

1. Who..wil lighten the hidden things of darkenes N.T. (Rhem.) 1 *Cor.* 4:5.

Hi·ddenly, *adv.* 1580. [f. prec. + -LY[2].] In a hidden manner.

Hide (həid), *sb.*[1] [OE. *hȳd* = OFris. *hēd*, OS. *hūd* (Du. *huid*), OHG. *hūt* (G. *haut*), ON. *húð* :– Gmc. **χūðiz* :– IE. **kūtis*, repr. by L. *cutis*, Gr. κύτος.] **1.** The skin of an animal, raw or dressed; esp. applied to the skins of the larger beasts and such as may be tanned into leather. **2.** The human skin. (Now contemptuous or joc.) OE. **3.** A whip made of hide 1851.

1. Phr. (*In*) *hide and hair*: wholly, entirely. **2.** Who could have beleevd so much insolence durst vent it self from out the h. of a varlet? MILT.

Comb.: **h.-drogher,** a coasting vessel trading in hides; the master of such a vessel; **-money** [tr. Gr. δερματικόν), the money arising from the hides of the victims sacrificed at Athens; **-scraper, -stretcher, -worker.**

Hide, *sb.*[2] *Obs.* exc. *Hist.* [OE. *hīd*, earlier *hīģid*, f. *hīģ-*, *hīw-* (in comb.) = OHG. *hī-*, ON. *hý-*, Goth. *heiwa-*, rel. to L. *civis* citizen, and to a Gmc. *n*-stem in OE. *hīwan* (pl.), OFris. *hīuna* members of a household, OHG. *hī(w)un*, ON. *hjún* man and wife. See HIND *sb.*[2]] **1.** A measure of land in OE. times, and later; primarily, the amount required by one free family with its dependants; defined as being as much land as could be tilled with one plough in a year. See CARUCATE. The *hide* was normally = 100 acres, but the size of the acre itself varied. **2.** *nonce-use.* (Assoc. with HIDE *sb.*[1]) As much land as could be measured by a thong cut out of a hide. MARLOWE & NASHE.

1. Phr. *Hide and gaine* [OFr. *gaigne*], orig. synonyms of arable land; later, taken as a phrase.

Hide, *sb.*[3] ME. [f. HIDE *v.*[1]] †**1.** Concealment. ME. only. **2.** A cache 1649.

Hide (həid), *v.*[1] Pa. t. **hid**; pa. pple. **hid, hidden** (hi·d'n). [OE. *hȳdan* = OFris. *hēda*, MDu. *hūden*, LG. (*ver*)*hüen* :– WGmc. **χūdjan*.] **1.** *trans.* To put or keep out of sight; to conceal from the notice of others; to secrete. **2. a.** *refl.* To put or keep oneself out of sight OE. **b.** *intr.* To conceal oneself ME. **3.** *trans.* To keep from the knowledge of others; to keep secret ME. **4.** To prevent from being seen; to obstruct the view of; to cover up ME.

1. She hidded the swerde CAXTON. Phr. *To h. one's face*: (*a*) to turn away one's eyes, take no heed (Biblical); (*b*) to keep out of sight. Thou didst h. thy face, and I was troubled *Ps.* 30:7. *To hide one's head*: (*a*) to take shelter; (*b*) to keep out of sight. †*All hid*: the cry in hide-and-seek; hence, the game itself. *L.L.L.* IV. iii. 78. **2. b.** *Hide fox and all after*: an old cry in hide-and-seek. *Haml.* IV. ii. 32. **3.** He that has a secret should not only h. it, but h. that he has it to h. CARLYLE. **4.** A few seconds before the sun was totally hid 1810.

Hide, *v.*[2] 1757. [f. HIDE *sb.*[1]] **1.** *trans.* To remove the hide from; to flay. **2.** To beat the hide of; to thrash (*slang* or *colloq.*) 1825.

Hide-and-seek. 1672. A children's game, in which one or more hide, and the rest, at a given signal, try to find them. Also *transf.*

The ragged boys..played..hide-and-seek among the tombstones DICKENS. Also **Hide-and-go-seek.**

Hidebound (həi·dbaund), *a.* (*sb.*) 1559. [f. HIDE *sb.*[1] + BOUND *ppl. a.*[2]; cf. *tongue-tied.*] **1.** Of cattle: Having the skin clinging closely to the back and ribs so that it cannot be loosened or raised with the fingers, as a result of bad feeding and emaciation. Also *transf.* and *fig.* **2.** Of trees: Having the bark so close and unyielding as to impede growth 1626; (of soil) starved and unproductive 1778. **3.** *transf.* and *fig.* Of persons, etc.: Restricted in view or scope; hence, bigoted 1603. †**b.** Close-fisted –1683. **4.** Bound with or in leather 1858

3. The h. humor which he calls his judgement MILT.

†**B.** *sb.* The diseases affecting cattle and trees described above in 1, 2. –1778.

Hence **Hi·debind** *v.* to render h.; to confine, constrict 1642.

Hided (həi·dėd), *a.* ME. [f. HIDE *sb.*[1] + -ED[2].] **1.** Having a hide (esp. of a specified kind). **2.** Made of hide 1798.

†**Hidegeld, -gild.** [OE. *hīdģield*, *-ģeld* hide-payment; see HIDE *sb.*[2], GUILD.] *OE. Law.* = HIDAGE. –1706.

Hi·deland. *Hist.* 1577. [f. HIDE *sb.*[2] + LAND.] = HIDE *sb.*[2] 1.

†**Hi·del(s.** [OE. *hȳdels*, f. HIDE *v.*[1] + -ELS. Cf. RIDDLE *sb.*[1]] Hiding-place.

Hideous (hi·diəs), *a.* (*adv.*) [ME. *hidous* – AFr. *hidous*, OFr. *hidos*, *-eus* (mod. *hideux*), earlier *hisdos*, f. *hide*, *hisde* fear, of unkn. origin. The ending was assim. to -EOUS XVI.] **1.** Frightful, dreadful, horrible; hence, horribly ugly or unpleasing, revolting. †**b.** Terrific on account of size; huge, immense. ME. **2.** Revolting to the moral sense; abominable; odious ME. †**3.** *adv.* Hideously. MILT. *P. L.* vi. 206.

1. Hurld headlong..With h. ruine and combustion down To bottomless perdition MILT. *P. L.* I. 46. H. alleys KINGSLEY, noises 1896. **b.** Of stature huge and h. he was SPENSER. **2.** This h. rashnesse SHAKS. Hence **Hi·deous-ly** *adv.* ME., **-ness** ME., **Hideo·sity** 1856.

Hider (həi·dəɹ). ME. [f. HIDE *v.*[1] + -ER[1].] One who hides.

Hiding (həi·diŋ), *vbl. sb.*[1] ME. [f. HIDE *v.*[1] + -ING[1].] **1.** The action of HIDE *v.*[1] (*lit.* and *fig.*); the condition of being hidden. **2.** Something that hides; a hiding-place ME.

1. A gentleman who was 'in h.' after..Culloden SCOTT.

Hi·ding, *vbl. sb.*[2] *slang* or *colloq.* 1809. [f. HIDE *v.*[2] + -ING[1].] A thrashing.

Hi·dlings, *adv.*, *sb.*, and *a.* *dial.* ME. [f. HID *ppl. a.* + -LING[2].] **1.** *In h.*, secretly. **2.**

sb. (*pl.*) Hiding-places 1597. **3.** *adj.* Secret, clandestine 1810.

Hidro-, var. of HYDRO-.

Hidrotic (hidrǫ·tik). 1705. [– Gr. ἱδρωτικός sudorific, apt to perspire, f. ἱδρώς, -ωτ- sweat; see -IC.] *Med.* **1.** *adj.* Of or pertaining to sweat; sudorific; diaphoretic 1727. **2.** *sb.* A medicinal agent causing sweat.

Hie (həi), *v.* Now *arch.* or *poet.* [OE. *hīġian*, of unkn. origin.] †**1.** *intr.* To strive, pant –ME. **2.** To hasten, go quickly ME. †**b.** To hasten on; to make progress; to speed –1608. **3.** *refl.* = sense 2. ME. **4.** *trans.* To cause to hasten. Now U.S., of urging *on* a hound. ME. **5.** with advb. accus.; usu. *to hie one's way* ME.

2. Thither..Accurst..he [Satan] hies MILT. *P. L.* II. 1055. **b.** The night higheth fast SPENSER. **3.** The Bees..high them home as fast as they can 1713. Hence †**Hie, hy** *sb.* haste, speed.

Hieland, obs. and Sc. var. of HIGHLAND.

Hield, heald, *v. Obs.* exc. *dial.* [OE. *hieldan* = OS. *ofheldian*, MDu. *helden* (Du. *hellen*) :- WGmc. **χalþjan*, f. **χalþa* inclined (OE. *heald* inclined, OHG. *halda* (G. *halde*), ON. *hallr* slope). See HEEL *v.*[2]] *trans.* and *intr.* To bend, incline. So †**Hield** *sb.*

Hiemal (həi·ĭmăl), *a.* Now *rare.* Also **hy-.** 1560. [– L. *hiemalis*, f. *hiems* winter; see -AL[1]. Cf. Fr. *hiémal*.] Of or belonging to winter; winter-.

Hiemate (həi·ĭmēit), *v. rare.* 1623. [– *hiemat-*, pa. ppl. stem of L. *hiemare*, f. *hiems* winter; see -ATE[3].] *intr.* To winter. Hence †**Hiema·tion.**

‖**Hiems** (həi·emz). 1450. [L. = winter.] Winter.

Hieracite (həi·ĕrăsəit). 1585. [– late L. *hieracita* (Rufinus), f. *Hierax*; see -ITE[1] 1.] *Eccl. Hist.* A follower of Hierax, an Egyptian ascetic (*c* 300 A.D.), who denied the resurrection of the body, and taught celibacy, etc.

‖**Hieracium** (həiĕrēi·ʃiŏm). 1565. [L. – Gr. ἱεράκιον hawkweed, f. ἱέραξ hawk; see -IUM.] *Bot.* A large genus of Composite plants, mostly with yellow flowers; Hawkweed.

‖**Hiera picra** (həi·ĕră pi·kră). ME. [med. L., f. Gr. ἱερά πικρά (Galen), i.e. ἱερά a name of many medicines, πικρά, fem. of πικρός bitter.] *Pharmacy.* A purgative drug composed of aloes and canella bark, sometimes mixed with honey, etc. Also corruptly *hickery-pickery*, etc.

Hierarch (həi·ĕrāɹk). 1574. [– med.L. *hierarcha* – Gr. ἱεράρχης high priest, f. ἱερός sacred + -αρχης -ARCH.] **1.** One who has rule or authority in holy things; an ecclesiastical potentate; a chief priest; an archbishop. **2.** Applied to an archangel 1667.

1. Their great H. the Pope MILT. **2.** The winged H. [Raphael] MILT. *P. L.* v. 468. Hence **Hiera·rchal, Hiera·rchic** *adjs.* of or belonging to a h. or a hierarchy.

Hiera·rchical, *a.* 1561. [f. med.L. *hierarchicus* – eccl. Gr. ἱεραρχικός, f. ἱεράχης (prec.); see -IC, -AL[1].] **1.** Belonging to a priestly hierarchy. **2.** Belonging to a regular gradation of orders, classes, or ranks (see HIERARCHY 4) 1832. Hence **Hiera·rchically** *adv.*

Hi·erarchism. 1846. [f. HIERARCH (or HIERARCHY) + -ISM.] Hierarchical practice and principles. So **Hi·erarchist,** an adherent of a hierarchy.

Hierarchy (həi·ĕrāɹki). [ME. *ierarchie, gerarchie* (superseded by latinized forms in XVI) – OFr. *ierarchie, gerarchie* (mod. *hiérarchie*) – med.L. (*h*)*ierarchia* – Gr. ἱεραρχία, f. ἱεράρχης; see HIERARCH, -Y[3].] **1.** Each of the three divisions of angels, every one comprising three orders, in the system of Dionysius the Areopagite; see CHERUB. Also, the angelic host. **b.** *transf.* of other beings ME. **2.** Rule or dominion in holy things; priestly government 1563. **3.** *concr.* An organized body of priests or clergy in successive orders or grades 1619. **4.** A body of persons or things ranked in grades, orders, or classes, one above another; *spec.* in *Nat. Science* and *Logic* 1643.

1. So sang the Hierarchies MILT. *P. L.* VII. 192. **b.** Olympus' faded h. KEATS. **4.** A h. of Concepts 1864.

Hieratic, -al (həiĕræ·tik, -ăl), *a.* 1656. [– L. *hieraticus* – Gr. ἱερατικός priestly, sacerdotal, f. ἱερᾶσθαι be a priest, f. ἱερεύς priest, ἱερός sacred; see -IC, -ICAL.] **1.** Pertaining to or used by the priestly class; used in connection with sacred subjects. *spec.* **a.** Applied to a style of ancient Egyptian writing, which consisted of abridged forms of hieroglyphics 1669. **b.** *Hieratic paper* = next. 1656. **c.** Applied to a style of art (esp. Egyptian or Greek), in which earlier types or methods, fixed by religious tradition, are conventionally adhered to. Also *fig.* 1841. **2.** *gen.* Priestly, sacerdotal 1859.

1. a. This mode of writing..has been called without much reason 'the hieratic' RAWLINSON. **2.** The Law and the Prophets..constituted..the h. Hebrew books 1893.

Hieratica (həiĕræ·tikă). 1832. [L. *hieratica* (sc. *charta*, Pliny), fem. of *hieraticus*; see prec.] Papyrus of the finest quality, anciently appropriated to sacred writings. (Now, a trade name of a special quality of paper.)

Hiero-, bef. a vowel **hier-**, comb. f. Gr. ἱερός sacred, holy.

Hierocracy (həiĕrǫ·krăsi). 1794. [f. HIERO- + -CRACY.] **1.** = HIERARCHY 2. **2.** = HIERARCHY 3. SOUTHEY. Hence **Hierocra·tic, -al** *a.* of or pertaining to a h.

Hierodule (həi·ĕrodiūl). 1835. [– late L. *hierodulus* – Gr. ἱερόδουλος (masc. and fem.), f. ἱερόν (n. of ἱερός used subst.) temple + δοῦλος slave.] A slave (of either sex) dwelling in a temple, and dedicated to the service of a god.

Hieroglyph (həi·ĕroglif), *sb.* 1598. [Back-formation from HIEROGLYPHIC or after Fr. *hiéroglyphe* (XVI).] **1.** A hieroglyphic character; a figure of a tree, animal, etc., standing for a word, syllable, or sound, and forming an element of a species of writing found on ancient Egyptian monuments or records; thence extended to the like in the writing of other races. Also, a writing of this kind. **2.** *transf.* and *fig.* A secret or enigmatical figure; an emblem 1646. Also *joc.* **3.** One who makes hieroglyphic inscriptions (*rare*) 1863.

2. On your brows..An h. of sorrow, a fiery sign SWINBURNE. So **Hi·eroglyph** *v.* to represent by a h.; to write in hieroglyphs. **Hiero·glypher** (*rare*).

Hieroglyphic (həiĕroˌgli·fik). Also †**gie-.** 1585. [– Fr. *hiéroglyphique* or late L. *hieroglyphicus* – Gr. ἱερογλυφικός, f. ἱερός sacred + γλυφή carving. The adj. was used subst. by Plutarch, τὰ ἱερογλυφικά (sc. γράμματα) letters, writing, whence *hieroglyphics*.]

A. *adj.* **1.** Of the nature of a hieroglyph (sense 1); written in or consisting of hieroglyphics. **2.** *transf.* and *fig.* Having a hidden meaning; symbolical, emblematic 1647. **3.** Containing or inscribed with hieroglyphs 1663. **4.** *joc.* Difficult to decipher 1856.

1. The Chinese..was in its origin a h. system MAX-MÜLLER. **2.** So that all fair Species be Hieroglyphick marks of Thee COWLEY. **4.** A h. scrawl 1856.

B. *sb.* **1.** *orig.* in *pl.* = Gr. τὰ ἱερογλυφικά. The character or mode of writing used by the ancient Egyptians (or others), consisting of figures of objects directly or figuratively representing words (*picture-writing*), or, in certain cases, syllables or letters. The sing. is rarely used. 1586. **2.** A picture standing for a word or notion; hence, a figure, device, or sign, having some hidden meaning; an enigmatical symbol, an emblem; a hieroglyph 1596. **b.** pl. *joc.* Characters difficult to make out 1734.

2. A silken string circles both their bodies as the Hyeroglific or bond of Wedlock SIR T. HERBERT. **b.** The hieroglyphics of Bradshaw 1862.

Hence †**Hierogly·phic** *v.* to represent by, or as by, a h.; to interpret or express, as a h. **Hierogly·phical** *a.* = HIEROGLYPHIC *a.* **Hierogly·phically** *adv.*

Hiero·glyphist. 1829. [f. HIEROGLYPH + -IST.] A writer of hieroglyphs; one versed in hieroglyphs. So **Hiero·glyphize** *v.* to write or express by hieroglyphics.

Hierogram (həi·ĕrogræm). 1656. [f. HIERO- + -GRAM.] A sacred symbol; a hieroglyph (*lit.* and *fig.*).

Hierogra·mmate, -at. 1864. [– Gr. ἱερογραμματεύς sacred scribe, f. ἱερός sacred + γραμματεύς clerk, scribe.] A writer of sacred records, *spec.* of hieroglyphics.

Hierogramma·tic, *a.* 1641. [f. HIEROGRAM on Gr. analogies; cf. GRAMMATIC.] Of the nature of a hierogram, relating to or consisting of hierograms. So **Hierogramma·tical** *a.* **Hierogra·mmatist** = prec.

Hierograph (həi·ĕrograf). 1835. [f. HIERO- + -GRAPH.] A sacred inscription or symbol; a hieroglyph. So **Hiero·grapher,** a sacred scribe. **Hierogra·phic, -al** *a.* of the nature of, or relating to, sacred writing or symbols. **Hiero·graphy,** a description of sacred things; †writing by hierograms.

Hiero·latry. 1814. [See HIERO-, -LATRY.] Worship of saints; hagiolatry. COLERIDGE.

Hierology (həiĕrǫ·lŏdʒi). 1828. [f. HIERO- + -LOGY.] †**1.** 'A discourse on sacred things' (Webster). †**2.** Hieroglyphic lore –1859. **3.** Sacred literature or lore; e.g. that of the Egyptians, Greeks, Jews, etc. 1854. **4.** = HAGIOLOGY. 1890. So **Hierolo·gic, -al** *a.* belonging to h. **Hiero·logist,** one versed in h.

Hi·eromancy. 1775. [See HIERO-, -MANCY.] Divination from observation of objects offered in sacrifice, or from sacred things.

Hieroma·rtyr. 1864. [f. HIERO- + MARTYR.] *Gr. Ch.* A martyr who was in holy orders.

‖**Hieromnemon** (həiĕrǫmnī·mǫn). 1727. [Gr. ἱερομνήμων adj. and sb., f. ἱερός + μνήμων mindful.] A sacred recorder. **1.** *Gr. Antiq.* The title of one of the two deputies sent by each tribe to the Amphictyonic council, whose office was concerned with religious matters 1753. **2.** *Gr. Ch.* An officer who stood behind the patriarch, and showed him the prayers, psalms, etc., he was to rehearse.

Hieromonach (həiĕromǫ·năk). 1882. [– Gr. ἱερομόναχος (see HIERO-, MONK).] *Gr. Ch.* A monk who is also a priest; opp. to a 'secular' cleric.

Hieronymian (həiĕroni·miăn). 1656. [f. *Hieronymus* (St. Jerome, d.420), one of the four great Latin Fathers of the Church; see -IAN.] **1.** *adj.* Of or belonging to St. Jerome, the author of the Latin Vulgate translation of the Bible 1884. **2.** *sb.* = HIERONYMITE *sb.* So **Hierony·mic** *a.* = 1.

Hieronymite (həiĕrǫ·niməit). 1550. [f. as prec. + -ITE[1] 1.] **1.** *sb.* A hermit of any of the orders of St. Jerome. **2.** *adj.* Belonging to any of these orders 1843.

Hierophant (həi·ĕrofænt). 1677. [– late L. *hierophanta, -es* – Gr. ἱεροφάντης, f. ἱερός sacred + -φαν-, base of φαίνειν reveal.] **1.** *Antiq.* An official expounder of sacred mysteries or ceremonies, esp. in ancient Greece; an initiating or presiding priest. **2.** *gen.* The minister of any 'revelation'; the interpreter of any esoteric principle 1822. So **Hi·erophancy,** the function of a h. **Hieropha·ntic** *a.* of or belonging to a h. or hierophants; resembling a h.

Hieroscopy (həiĕrǫ·skŏpi). 1727. [– Gr. ἱεροσκοπία, f. ἱερά sacrifices, victims + -σκοπία view.] = HIEROMANCY.

Hierosolymitan (həiĕrosǫ·liməităn). 1538. [– late L. *Hierosolymitanus* (Augustine), f. *Hierosolyma* = Gr. Ἱεροσόλυμα Jerusalem; see -AN.] **1.** *adj.* Belonging to Jerusalem 1721. **2.** *sb.* A native or inhabitant of Jerusalem. So **Hieroso·lymite** *sb.* and *a.*

Hierurgy (həi·ĕrɒɹdʒi). Also †**-ourgy.** 1678. [– Gr. ἱερουργία religious service, f. ἱερουργός sacrificing priest. Cf. LITURGY.] A sacred work; a religious observance or rite.

Hifalutin, var. of HIGHFALUTIN.

Higgle (hi·g'l), *v.* 1633. [var. of HAGGLE, expressive of niggling.] **1.** *intr.* To cavil as to terms; *esp.* to stickle for petty advantages in bargaining; to chaffer. **2.** 'To go selling provisions from door to door' (J.) 1790.

1. We will not h. with so frank a chapman for a few months under or over FULLER. To h. over an argument JOWETT. Also **Higgle-haggle.**

Higgledy-piggledy (hi·g'ldi pi·g'ldi), *adv.*, *sb.*, *a.* 1598. [Rhyming jingle prob. based on PIG with ref. to swine herding together.] **1.**

adv. Without any order of position or direction; in jumbled confusion. Usu. *contemptuous.* **2.** *sb.* A confusion; a disorderly jumble 1659. **3.** *adj.* Confused; topsy-turvy 1832.

Higgler (hi·gləɹ). 1637. [f. HIGGLE *v.* + -ER[1].] **1.** One who higgles in bargaining. **2.** An itinerant dealer; esp. a carrier or huckster who buys up poultry and dairy produce, and supplies in exchange petty commodities from the shops in town 1637.

High (həi), *a.* [OE. *hēah* (*hēaġ-*) = OFris. *hach*, OS., OHG. *hōh* (Du. *hoog*, G. *hoch*), ON. *hár*, Goth. *hauhs* :- Gmc. **χauχaz.* For the phonology cf. DIE *v.*[1], EYE *sb.*[1] THIGH.]

I. 1. Of considerable upward extent or magnitude; 'long upwards' (J.); lofty, tall. *High relief*: see RELIEF[2]. **2.** Having a (specified) upward extent OE. **3.** Situated far above the ground or some base. Formerly, as in *High Asia*, etc. denoting the upper (or inland) part. OE. **4.** Of physical actions: Extending to or from a height; performed at a height 1596. **b.** Of a vowel-sound: Produced with the tongue or part of it in a raised position. SWEET.

1. The trees so straight and hy SPENSER. **2.** The snow was..halfe legge h. 1633. **3.** Up above the world so h. 1836. She lay in the Garret four Story h. DE FOE. **4.** The bound and h. curuet Of Marses fierie steed *All's Well* II. iii. 299.

II. Fig. senses. **1.** Of exalted rank, station, dignity, position, or estimation OE. **2.** Of exalted quality, character, or style; high-class OE.; weighty, grave, serious ME.; advanced, abstruse ME. **3.** Chief, principal, main; special. Now only in certain collocations. ME. **4.** Rich in flavour or quality; luxurious ME. **5.** Of meat, esp. game: Slightly tainted; usu. as a desirable condition 1816. **6.** Of qualities, conditions, and actions: Of great amount, degree, force, or value ME. †**b.** Of the voice: Raised, loud –1776. **c.** *Geog.* Of latitude: At a great distance from the equator 1748. **d.** High-priced 1727. **e.** Played for high stakes 1828. **7.** Of a time or season: Well-advanced; fully come. (In *high noon, high day*, often with the notion that the sun is high in the heavens.) ME. **8.** 'Far advanced into antiquity' (J.); ancient 1601. **9.** Of or in reference to musical sounds: Acute in pitch; shrill ME. **10.** Showing pride, self-exaltation, resentment, or the like; haughty, pretentious, overbearing; wrathful ME. †**b.** Eager, keen –1709. **11.** Extreme in opinion (esp. political or religious); carrying an opinion or doctrine to an extreme 1675. **12.** Emotionally exalted; hilarious; chiefly in *high spirits* 1738; intoxicated (*slang*) 1627.

1. Princes and lordes of hie estate CAXTON. Phr. *High God, h. heaven*: emphatic for *God, heaven. The Most High*: the Supreme Being; God. How doth God know? and is there knowledge in the most H.? *Ps.* 73:11. **2.** A man of hye merite CAXTON. H. resolves POPE, thinking WORDSW., crimes and misdemeanours H. COX. H. Mathematics 1898. **3.** A place..where the hie market is holden 1553. H. altar, HIGH ROAD, etc. **4.** Like a Horse Full of h. Feeding SHAKS. **6.** An heigh folye CHAUCER. H. speed SHAKS. The Exchange is H. LOCKE. H. Duties 1714, temperature SCORESBY, explosives (see below) 1897. **d.** I suppose now stocks are h. SWIFT. **e.** H. play 1889. **7.** Tyle it was past hye none LD. BERNERS. H. summer 1860. **8.** Poems of h. antiquity WARTON. **10.** H. words 1592. Indeed the Bishops are so h., that very few do love them PEPYS. **11.** H. and Low, Watch-words of Party, on all tongues are rife WORDSW. **12.** A h. old time 1897.

Phrases. *H. and dry*: said of a vessel on shore out of the water; hence *fig.* out of the current of events or progress, 'stranded'. *With a h. hand*: imperiously. *On the h. horse*: see HORSE. *H. and low*: (people) of all conditions. *H. and mighty*: (*a*) formerly an epithet of dignity; (*b*) *colloq.* Imperious, arrogant. *High priori*: a burlesque alteration of A PRIORI. *On the h. ropes* (colloq.): in an elated, disdainful or enraged mood. **On h.** (rarely *upon, of h.*) [orig. *an high*; see AN *prep.*]. **a.** In or to a height, above, aloft; *spec.* up to or in heaven. †**b.** Aloud. **c.** *From on h.* (rarely *from h.*): from a h. place or position; *spec.* from heaven.

Combs., etc. **1.** In OE. *hēah* was often combined with a sb.; in ME. these combs. were often written *divisim*, and, when adjective inflexions were lost, they were indistinguishable from the ordinary use of the adj. bef. a sb. Thus: **a.** in lit. sense 'lofty', as *hēah-lond* HIGHLAND. **b.** High in degree, rank, or dignity, as *hēah-mæsse* high MASS; *hēah-stræt* HIGH STREET; *hēah-tīd* HIGH TIDE. **c.** *esp.* in names of offices and dignities, with sense 'chief, principal, head, arch-', sometimes 'exalted, lofty': e.g. *hēah-diacon* archdeacon; *hēah-ȝerēfa* high REEVE; *hēah-god* high God, the Most High; etc. **d.** On the analogy of these, frequently used with later official titles, implying the supreme officer or dignitary, or the like; e.g. *High Admiral, Bailiff, Master* (of St. Paul's School, etc.), *Sheriff, Steward*, etc. See these wds.

2. Special combs.: **h. Change,** the time of greatest activity on 'Change, or the Exchange at such a time (cf. II. 7); **h. cross,** a cross set on a pedestal in a market-place, or in the centre of a town or village; **h. explosive,** an explosive, such as dynamite, which is more rapid and powerful than gunpowder; †**h. Mall,** the time of greatest resort in the Mall (cf. II. 7); **h. place,** in Scripture, a place of worship or sacrifice (usually idolatrous) on a hill or high ground; **h. table,** a table raised above the rest at a public dinner; *spec.* in colleges, the table at which the head and the fellows sit; **h. tea,** a tea at which meat or fish is served. **b.** With agent-noun, denoting a high degree of performance; as *h.-bidder, -jumper, -liver*, etc.

3. a. With nouns forming *attrib.* phrases: as *h.-action, -speed, -pressure*, etc. **b.** Parasynthetic combs.: as *h.-angled, -arched, -coloured*, etc.; **h.-blooded,** of high blood, race, or descent, **-kilted,** wearing the kilt or petticoat high, or tucked up; *fig.* indecorous; **-necked.** See also Main words.

B. *sb.* [The adj. used absol.] **1.** A high place or region; a height. *Obs.* exc. *Sc.* ME. **b.** A high level or figure. †**2.** Height, altitude; *fig.* acme –1557. **3.** *Cards.* The ace or highest trump out. Also, the highest card in cutting for deal. See also ALL FOURS 1. 1680.

High (həi), *adv.* Compared HIGHER, HIGHEST. [OE. *hēah*, later *hēaġe*; thence early ME. *hēȝe, heȝ*, blending in form with the adj.] **1.** At or to a great distance upward; far up; aloft. **b.** *Horsemanship.* With high action 1686. **2.** *fig.* In or to a high position, degree, estimation, amount, price, etc. ME.; †loudly –1648; richly; to excess 1628. **3.** In or into a high latitude 1662. **4.** †**a.** Far on, late (in time). **b.** Far back, early. 1523. **5.** At or to a high pitch, shrilly 1601. †**6.** In a high manner (see HIGH *a.* II. 10) –1844.

1. Such as clymbe to hye 1559. **2.** Where it seems people do drink h. PEPYS. **5.** *Twel. N.* II. iii. 42. **6.** Others..reason'd h. Of Providence MILT. *P.L.* II. 558.

Phrases. *H. and low*: †Wholly, entirely; up and down; in every place or part (1694). *To play h.*: to play for h. stakes; to play a h. card. *To run h.*: *lit.* said of the sea when there is a strong current with a h. tide, or with h. waves; hence *fig.* of feelings or conditions 1711.

Combs. **a.** In syntactic comb. with pres. or pa. pple. of any vb. which can be qualified in the active or passive by *high* or *highly*: e.g. *to aim h.*, hence *h.-aiming, h.-aimed*; **h.-descended,** of lofty descent; **-finished,** of high finish; highly accomplished; **-grown,** grown to a height; overgrown with tall vegetation; **-strung,** strung to a high tension or pitch; *fig.* in a h. state of vigour or sensitiveness. **b.** With an adj. = Highly as *h. fantasticall* 1601. **c.** Occas. hyphened to a vb. 1632.

†**High,** *v.* [OE. *hēan*, f. *hēah* HIGH *a.*; cf. OHG. *hōhen*, Goth. *hauhjan.*] To make, or become, high or higher (*lit.* and *fig.*) –1633.

The tydes doe h. about some 6 Foot 1633.

Highball. 1894. **1.** A species of poker played with numbered balls. **2.** *slang.* A drink of whisky in a tall glass 1899.

Hi·gh-bi:nder. *U.S. slang.* 1806. [f. HIGH *a.* II. 10; cf. HELLBENDER.] **1.** A rough. **2.** One of a secret society of blackmailers said to exist among the Chinese in California and other parts 1887.

Hi·gh-blow:er. 1831. A horse that makes a blowing noise by flapping the nostrils at each expiration in galloping; a roarer.

Hi·gh-born, *a.* ME. Of noble birth.

High-bred, *a.* 1674. **1.** Of high breed, stock, or descent. **2.** Of, pertaining to, or characteristic of high breeding 1796.

Hi·gh-browed, *a.* 1875. [f. HIGH *a.* + BROW *sb.*[1] + -ED[2].] **1.** Lofty-browed. **2.** Intellectually superior. orig. *U.S.* 1908. So **Hi·gh-brow,** *a.*; *sb.* a person so characterized 1911.

High Church. 1702. [From *High-Churchman*, and used attrib. as in *High Church party*, and then subst.]

A. *adj.* or *attrib. phr.* Of, belonging to, or characteristic of High-Churchmen, or their principles and practices 1704.

B. *sb.* [orig. short for *H. C. party, H. C. principles.*] The party or principles of the High-Churchmen (see next). Hence **High-Chu·rchism,** High Church principles, doctrine, or practice. **High-Chu·rchist, -ite,** an adherent to High Church principles.

High-Chu·rchman. 1687. [orig. *high Churchman*; cf. *good Churchman*, etc.] A member of the Church of England holding opinions which give a high place to the authority and claims of the Episcopate and the priesthood, the saving grace of the sacraments, and, generally, to those points of doctrine, discipline, and ritual by which the Anglican Church is distinguished from the Calvinistic and the Protestant Nonconformist churches. Hence **High-Chu·rchmanship,** the doctrine or practice of High-Churchmen; adherence to the High Church party.

High court. 1450. A supreme court. Without qualification *High Court* now means 'High Court of Justice'. Also *attrib.*

High day, hi·gh-day, hi·ghday. ME. [f. HIGH *a.*; in 3, for *hey-day.*] **1.** A day of high celebration. †**2.** Full day, when the sun is high –1647. **3.** Perversion of HEY-DAY *sb.* 2, 1771. **4.** *attrib.* 1596.

4. Thou spend'st such high-day wit in praising him SHAKS.

Higher (həi·əɹ), *a.* (*sb.*) and *adv.* [OE. (WS.) *hīerra, hīera*; subseq. conformed to the positive as *hīehra, hēahra*, whence ME. *heȝer, hegher*, later *higher*; see HIGH *a.*, -ER[3].] **A.** *adj.* **1.** The comparative of HIGH *a.*, q.v. **2.** *spec.* Superior to the common sort; passing or lying beyond the ordinary limits 1836. **3.** quasi-*sb.* One higher; a superior ME.

2. Phr. *The h. classes, the h. education of women, h. mathematics. H. criticism*: see CRITICISM.

B. *adv.* Comparative of HIGH *adv.*, q.v. OE.

Higher, *v. rare.* 1715. [f. prec. adj.; cf. *lower* vb.] **1.** *trans.* To make higher, raise. **2.** *intr.* To become higher, mount 1872.

2. In ever-highering eagle-circles up To the great Sun of Glory TENNYSON.

Highermost (həi·əɹmōᵘst), *a.* (*adv.*) *rare.* 1629. [-MOST.] = HIGHEST.

Highest (həi·ėst), *a.* (*sb.*) and *adv.* [OE. *hīehst, hȳhst, hēhst*, and *hēahst, hēagost*, ME. *heȝest*; see HIGH *a.*, -EST.] **A.** *adj.* The superlative of HIGH *a.*, q.v. **B.** *absol.* or as *sb.* **1.** *absol. The Highest* (also *the most Highest*): the Supreme Being, God OE. †**2.** The highest part –1634. **3.** Highest position or pitch; usu. with *at* ME. **4.** That which is highest (in *fig.* sense) 1861. **b.** *In the highest* (Biblical): tr. L. *in excelsis*, Gr. ἐν ὑψίστοις = in the loftiest places, in the heavens; now *occas.*, 'in the highest degree' 1526.

3. Whan the sonne is in the hyest 1526. **4.** We needs must love the h. when we see it TENNYSON. **b.** Glory to God in the h. *Luke* 2:14.

C. *adv.* The superlative of HIGH *adv.* OE.

Highfalutin, -ing (həifălū·tin). orig. *U.S. slang.* 1848. [f. HIGH *a.* + obscurely formed element, which was perh. a whimsical pronunc. of *fluting*, pr. pple. of FLUTE *v.*] **1.** *sb.* Absurdly pompous speech or writing; bombast. **2.** *adj.* Absurdly pompous or bombastic in style 1857.

Hi·gh-flown, *a.* 1647. [orig. f. HIGH *adv.* + old str. pa. pple, of FLOW *v.*, from the sense 'in flood', 'swollen'; later assoc. with pa. pple. of FLY *v.*[1]; cf. next.] †**1.** Soaring high; elevated; elated –1842. **2.** Extravagant, hyperbolical; bombastic 1665. †**3.** Of persons: Extreme in opinion or party feeling. Cf. *High-flyer* 3. –1705.

2. Such are the high-flown expressions of Prudentius GIBBON. **3.** He was a high-flone Cavalier WOOD.

Hi·gh-flyer, -flier. 1589. [f. HIGH *adv.* + FLYER.] **1.** *lit.* One who or that which flies high. **b.** Pop. name of the Purple Emperor butterfly, and of the genus *Ypsipetes* of moths 1773. **2.** One who soars high in his ambitions, notions, etc. 1663. **3.** One who has lofty or high-flown notions on some question of polity, esp. ecclesiastical; *spec.* in 17–18th c. a High-Churchman; a Tory 1680. †**4.** A fast stage-coach –1868. **5.** *slang.*

A fashionable strumpet; a 'swell' beggar; a begging-letter writer 1700.

Hi·gh-flying, *a.* 1581. **1.** *lit.* That flies high, as a bird 1622. **2.** Soaring high in notions, aims, etc. 1581. **3.** Holding the principles of the HIGH-FLYERS; extreme 1695.

3. A high-flying monarchy man 1792.

Hi·gh-ha:nded, *a.* 1631. [See HIGH *a.*, Phrases.] Acting or done with a high hand, or in an overbearing or arbitrary manner. **High-ha·ndedly, -ness.**

Hi·gh(-)hat. *U.S.* 1899. A tall hat; *fig.* a person of affected superiority. Also *attrib.* or as *adj.*, and as *vb. intr.*

Hi·gh-hea:rted, *a.* ME. Courageous, high-spirited; in early use occas., Haughty. Hence **High-hea·rtedness.**

High-hoe. = HICKWALL.

Hi·gh-hole. *U.S.* 1860. [Etymologizing var. of *hyghwhele, highwale, hewhole,* early ff. HICKWALL.] The Flicker, *Colaptes auratus.* So **High-holder.**

Highland (həi·lænd). [OE. *hēahlond* promontory.] **A.** *sb.* **1.** High or elevated land; a lofty headland or cliff. **2.** *spec.* (Now always *pl.*, Sc. pronunc. hī·lănts.) A mountainous district; *spec.* The territory in Scotland formerly occupied by the Celtic clans ME.

1. Off the h. of Valparaiso 1748.

B. *attrib.* or *adj.* **1.** Of, pertaining to, or inhabiting high land or a mountainous district 1595. **2.** *spec.* Of, belonging to, or characteristic of the Highlands of Scotland ME.

1. Merely the h. clouds over the mountains KANE. **2.** *H. dress,* the kilt, etc., worn by the H. clansmen and soldiers. A generation of H. Thieves and Red-shanks MILT.

Highlander (həi·lændəɹ). 1632. [f. prec. + -ER^1 1.] **1.** An inhabitant of high land. **2.** *spec.* A native of the Highlands of Scotland. Also, a soldier of a Highland regiment. 1642. **b.** Highland cattle 1787. **Hi·ghlandman** 1425.

High light, hi·gh-light. 1658. [HIGH *a.* II. 6, LIGHT *sb.* 12.] **1.** In painting, photography, and cinematography, any of the brightest parts of a subject or a representation of it; often *pl.* Also *transf.* and *fig.* **2.** A moment or detail of vivid interest. Chiefly *pl.* 1905.

†High-lone, *adv.* 1597. [alt. of *alone,* of obscure origin. *High* prob. expresses degree or intensity. Cf. LONE *a.*] Quite alone, without support –1760.

High-low (həi·lōᵘ). 1801. [f. HIGH *a.* + LOW *a.*; in contrast with 'top' boots and 'low' shoes.] (Usu. *pl.*) A laced boot reaching up over the ankle.

Highly (həi·li), *adv.* [OE. *hēalīće*; see HIGH *a.*, -LY^2.] **1.** *lit.* In a high place or situation; aloft. **2.** In or to a high position or rank OE. **3.** In or to a high degree; very, much OE. **4.** With honour, appreciation, or praise ME. **5.** Proudly, arrogantly; ambitiously; with indignation or anger. *Obs.* or *arch.* ME. **6.** Hyphened to a ppl. adj., when this is used *attrib.* 1711.

Hi·ghman, high-man. 1598. [f. HIGH *a.* + MAN. Cf. LOWMAN.] Usu. *pl.* Dice loaded so as to turn up high numbers.

Hi·gh-me:ttled, *a.* 1626. Of high mettle; high-spirited, high-couraged.

A military and high-mettled nation BACON.

Hi·gh-mi:nded, *a.* 1503. **1.** Haughty, proud, or arrogant in spirit (*arch.*). **2.** Having a morally lofty character; magnanimous 1556.

1. Lord, I am not hye mynded, I haue no proude lokes COVERDALE *Ps.* 130[131]:1. **2.** Well-bred, and high-minded youths W. IRVING. Hence **High-mi·nded-ly** *adv.*, **-ness.**

Hi·ghmost, *a.* *Obs.* or *dial.* 1592. [-MOST.] = HIGHEST.

Highness (həi·nės), *sb.* [OE. *hēanes, -nis,* later *hēahnes,* f. *hēah* HIGH *a.*; see -NESS.] **1.** The quality or condition of being high; loftiness, tallness. In *lit.* sense now usu. HEIGHT. **†b.** *concr.* A height; top, summit –1491. **2.** With possessive (e.g. the King's Highness; His, Her, Your Highness), as a title of honour given to princes ME. **†3.** Haughtiness; overbearingness –1658. **4.** Greatness of degree, amount, force, etc. 1659.

4. The h. of the wind 1659, of the rates 1884.

Hi·gh-pitched, *a.* 1593. **1.** Of high pitch acoustically 1748. **2.** Of lofty tone or character 1593. **3.** Steep 1615.

2. High-pitch'd thoughts SHAKS., language 1875.

High priest, hi·gh-priest. ME. [See HIGH *a.* II. 3.] **1.** A chief priest; esp. the Jewish chief priest. Applied to Christ (*Heb.* 4:14). **2.** *transf.* The head of any 'cult' 1767.

2. Ricardo, the high-priest of the bullionists 1878. So **High-prie·stess. High-prie·sthood,** the office of high priest (also *fig.*). **High-prie·stly** *a.*

Hi·gh-rea:ching, *a.* 1594. *lit.* That reaches high; *fig.* aspiring.

H. Buckingham growes circumspect SHAKS.

High road, hi·gh-roa:d. 1709. [After HIGHWAY.] A highway. Also *fig.*

†Hi·gh-ru:nner. 1670. A false die loaded so as to run on the high numbers; cf. HIGHMAN. –1721.

High school: see SCHOOL *sb*^{1}. I. 1 g.

Hi·gh-se:t, *a.* ME. **1.** Set in a high position. **2.** High-pitched 1631.

†Hi·gh-shoe. 1650. **1.** One who wears high shoes, as rustics did in the 17th c.; hence, a rustic, plain man –1695. **2.** *pl.* **High shoon** used *attrib.* = Rustic, boorish –1676. Hence **†Hi·gh-shod, -shoed** *a.*

Hi·gh-sou:nding, *a.* 1560. **1.** Highly sonorous. **2.** Having an imposing or pretentious sound 1784.

1. Tinkling cymbal and high-sounding brass COWPER.

Hi:gh-spi·rited, *a.* 1631. Possessing or marked by a lofty, courageous, or bold spirit; mettlesome.

Hi·gh-ste:pper. 1860. A horse which lifts its feet high from the ground in moving; *transf.* a person of stately walk or bearing. So **Hi·gh-ste:pping** *a.* 1855.

Hi·gh-sto:mached, *a.* *Obs.* or *arch.* 1548. [See STOMACH.] Of high courage or spirit; haughty.

High stomack'd are they both, and full of ire *Rich. II,* I. i. 18.

High street. OE. [See HIGH *a.* II. 3, STREET.] Often down to 17th c., A highway, a main road, in country or town; now, usually, the proper name (*Hi·gh Street*) of that street of a town which is built upon a great highway, and is (or was orig.) the principal one in the town.

In OE. times often applied to one of the Roman Roads or 'Streets'; it remains as the name of one of these in Westmorland.

Hight, *v.*^{1} *arch.* [OE. *hātan* = OFris. *hēta,* OS. *hētan,* OHG. *heizzan* (G. *heissen* call, bid, be called; *es heisst* it is said), ON. *heita,* Goth. *haitan*; f. a base which has been related to L. *ciēre* summon, CITE. The only parts still in literary use are the pa. pple. *hight* 'called' and the kindred pa. t. *hight* 'was called', both conscious archaisms.]

I. *trans.* **†1.** To command, bid; to order, ordain; to bid come (*arch.* in Spenser) –1591. **2.** To promise, to vow. *Obs.* exc. *Sc.* OE. **†3.** *parenthetical.* To assure (one that it is as one says) –1515. **4.** To call, to name. (Now only in *pa. pple.*) OE.

2. Oon auow to grete god I heete CHAUCER. **4.** A little pest, hight Tommy Moore W. IRVING.

II. *intr.*; in origin *medio-passive.* To call oneself, be called, have or bear the name. (Now only in the archaic pa. t. *hight.*) OE.

Already in OE. the passive infinitive had to be supplied by the active **hátan,** ME. **hôten,** *north.* **hāte;** and from an early date in ME., the passive forms began to yield to the corresponding active ones: (*a*) in Pres. t. **hátan, hote(n.** (By Spenser also erron. in pa. t.) (*b*) in Pa. t. **het, hete;** later also in pres. t. (*c*) in Pa. t. **highte** (etc.), later **hight.** (*d*) From 14th c. to 18th c. *hight* was extended to the pres. t., and to the infinitive.

This gentil hostelrye That highte the Tabard CHAUCER. Lowder (for so his dog hote) SPENSER. It rightly hot The well of life — *F. Q.* I. xi. 29.

¶III. Used by Spenser as a *pseudo-archaism* in senses: **a.** to direct; **b.** to commit; **c.** to name, designate, mention; **d.** to mean.

Hence **†Hi·ghting (heting, hetting, hoting)** *vbl. sb.* bidding or promising; *concr.* a promise, a vow.

†Hight, *v.*^{2} [Early ME. *huihten, hihten,* of doubtful origin.] *trans.* To adorn, embellish, set off –1633.

Hight(h, obs. ff. or vars. of HEIGHT.

High-tide. [OE. *hēahtīd,* f. HIGH *a.* + TIDE *sb.* I. In mod. Eng. repr. G. *hochzeit* in obs. sense 'festival, festivity'.] A high time, high day, festival.

Hight tide: see TIDE.

Hi·gh-toned, *a.* 1779. [f. *high tone* + -ED^2.] **1.** High in pitch (vocal or musical). **2.** High-strung, tense 1804. **3.** High-principled; expressing lofty sentiments; having dignified manners 1814. **b.** *U.S. colloq.* Excellent, tasteful.

2. His temper was naturally irritable and high-toned 1814. **3.** In whose high-toned impartial mind Degrees of mortal rank and state Seem objects of indifferent weight SCOTT.

Highty-tighty, var. of HOITY-TOITY, q.v.

High water. 1626. The state of the tide when the water is highest; the time when the tide is at the full.

High-water mark. a. *lit.* The mark left by the tide at high water; esp. the highest line ever so reached 1553. Also, the highest line touched by a flooded river or lake. **b.** *fig.* The highest point of intensity, excellence, prosperity, etc. attained.

Highway (həi·wēⁱ:). [From HIGH *a.* II. 3 + WAY. In OE. a true compound; but in XV–XVII often two wds. Freq. antithetic to BY-WAY.] **1.** A public road open to all passengers, a high road; esp. a main or principal road. **2.** *transf.* **a.** The ordinary or main route by land or water ME. **b.** Any well-beaten track 1579. **3.** *fig.* A course of conduct leading directly to some end or result 1598; the ordinary or direct course (of conduct, thought, speech, etc.) 1637. **4.** *attrib.* 1600.

1. Phr. *The King's Highway*: an expression dating from the time when the king's h. was in a special manner under his protection. *To take* (*to*) *the h.,* to become a highwayman, footpad, etc. **2.** The Platte has become a h. for the fur traders W. IRVING. **3.** On the h. to ruin JOWETT. *Comb.* **h. rate, tax,** one imposed for the maintenance of highways.

Highwayman (həi·wēⁱmæn). 1649. [f. prec.] **1.** One who frequents the highway for the purpose of robbing passengers; esp. one who is mounted, as dist. from a *foot-pad.* **2.** *local.* A surveyor of highways 1888.

Hi·gh-wrought, *a.* 1604. **1.** Agitated to a high degree. **2.** Wrought with great art or skill; accurately finished 1728.

1. It is a high wrought Flood *Oth.* II. i. 2.

Higra, higre, obs. ff. EAGRE.

Hijacker (həi·dʒæ:kəɹ). *U.S. slang.* 1924. [Of unkn. origin.] An armed person who preys on bootleggers.

‖Hijra(h. See HEGIRA. Hence **‖Hijri** *a.*

Hike (həik), *v. colloq.* orig. *dial.* 1809. [Of dial. origin.] **1.** *intr.* To tramp (now esp. for pleasure). **2.** *trans.* To pull, drag 1867.

Hilar (həi·lăɹ), *a.* 1864. [f. HILUM + -AR^1.] Of or pertaining to a HILUM or HILUS.

Hilarious (hilēᵊ·riəs), *a.* 1823. [f. L. *hilaris* + -OUS; see next.] **1.** Cheerful, cheery. **2.** Boisterously merry; rollicking 1835. Hence **Hila·rious-ly** *adv.*, **-ness.**

Hilarity (hilæ·rĭti). 1500. [– Fr. *hilarité* – L. *hilaritas,* f. *hilaris* (*-us*) – Gr. ἱλαρός cheerful, gay; see -ITY.] **1.** Cheerfulness, gladsomeness. **2.** Boisterous merriment 1840.

1. No, Sir; wine gives not light, gay, ideal h.; but tumultuous, noisy, clamorous merriment JOHNSON.

Hilary (hi·lări). 1577. [f. *Hilarius,* bishop of Poitiers (died 367), whose festival is on Jan. 13.] Name of a term or session of the High Court of Justice in England; also of one of the University terms at Oxford and Dublin. (At Oxford now usu. called *Lent term.*)

Hildebra·ndic, *a.* 1837. [f. *Hildebrand* + -IC.] Of, pertaining to, or resembling the policy of Hildebrand, who as Gregory VII was Pope 1073–85, and was distinguished by his unbending assertion of the power of the papacy and hierarchy, and of the celibacy of the clergy. So **Hi·ldebra:ndine** *a.*, **Hi·ldebrandism, -ist.**

Hilding (hi·ldiŋ). *Obs.* or *arch.* 1582. [Of unkn. origin.] **†1.** A worthless or vicious beast, esp. a horse –1719. **2.** A good-for-nothing (man or woman) 1592. **3.** *attrib.* (in apposition) 1582.

Hile: see HILL *v.*[1], HILUM.

Hill (hil), *sb.* [OE. *hyll* = OFris. *hel*, LG. *hull*, MDu. *hille, hil, hul* :- WGmc. (of the LG. area) **χulni*, f. IE. base **kl-* **kel-* **kol-*, whence also L. *collis*, Gr. *κολωνός, -νή* hill.] **1.** A natural elevation of the earth's surface rising more or less steeply above the level of the surrounding land. Formerly the general term, including mountains; but now restricted; e.g. in Great Britain, confined to heights under 2,000 feet. **b.** After *up, down*, used without the article 1667. **2.** *fig.* Something not easily mounted or overcome 1440. **3.** A heap or mound of earth, sand, etc., raised or formed by human or other agency. Cf. ANT-HILL, etc. ME. **b.** A heap formed round a plant by banking up or hoeing 1572. **4.** *attrib.*, as *h.-country*, etc. ME.

1. Fast besyde salysbury upon an hull CAXTON. **b.** Up h. and down dale 1879. *The Hills*: in India, mountain districts of less altitude than the Himalayas, favoured as health resorts. **2.** Those.. That labour up the h. of heavenly Truth MILT.

Comb.: **h.-ant**, a species that forms ant-hills; **-bird**, (*a*) the fieldfare; (*b*) the upland plover or Bartramian sandpiper of N. America; **-fever**, a kind of remittent fever prevalent in the h. country of India; **-folk, -people**, hillmen; *spec.* (*a*) the Cameronians; (*b*) the elves or fairies of the hills; **-fox**, the Indian *Canis himalaicus*; **-oat**, *Avena strigosa*; **-partridge**, a gallinaceous bird of India, *Galloperdix lunulatus*; **-tit**, a bird of the family *Liotrichidæ*; **-wren**, a bird of the genus *Pnoepyga*.

Hill, *v.*[1] *Obs.* exc. *dial.* [ME. *hulen* (ü), *hilen, hyllen, hillen*, corresp. to OE. **hyllan*, *behylian*, corresp. to OS. *bihullean*, OHG. *hullen* (G. *hüllen*), ON. *hylja*, Goth. *huljan*, f. Gmc. **hul-*, weak grade of **hel-* HELE *v.*] **1.** *trans.* To cover, cover up, protect. Now *dial.* †**2.** To cover from sight; to hide, conceal. ME. only.

Hill, *v.*[2] 1577. [f. HILL *sb.*] **1.** *trans.* To form into a hill or heap; to heap up; also *fig.* 1581. **2.** *Agric.* To earth up the roots of (growing plants). Also *absol.* [App. a use of HILL *v.*[1] to cover, assoc. with HILL, *sb.* 3b.] 1577. †**3.** *intr.* To rise in or on a slope. LELAND. **4.** To assemble on rising ground, as ruffs 1768.

1. Mr. Lloyd is much against hilling of manure A. YOUNG. **2.** At Midsummer they h. them [hops] A. YOUNG. **4.** During spring, when the ruffs h. FOLKARD.

Hill-altar. 1539. An altar on a hill of height.

Hi·llet. *rare.* 1538. [f. HILL *sb.* + -ET.] A hillock.

Hill-fort. 1833. A fort constructed on a hill; *esp.* a hill-top fortification of prehistoric age.

That class of towns which, out of Gaulish hill-forts, grew into Roman and mediæval cities FREEMAN.

Hilliness (hi·linės). 1629. [f. HILLY *a.* + -NESS.] The quality or state of being hilly.

Hi·lling, *vbl. sb.*[1] Now *dial.* ME. [f. HILL *v.*[1] + -ING[1].] **1.** Covering, hiding, protection. **2.** *concr.* A covering; e.g. clothing, a bed-quilt, a roof, etc. ME.

Hi·lling, *vbl. sb.*[2] 1627. [f. HILL *v.*[2] + -ING[1].] The action of forming hills or heaps; *esp.* the earthing-up of plants.

Hill-man, hillman. 1830. **1.** One who frequents the hills; *spec.* applied to the Scottish Covenanters. **b.** An inhabitant of a hill-country: applied to the hill-tribes of India 1859. **2.** An elf or troll 1882. **3.** *spec.* A miner, a slate quarryman 1865; a hill-climber 1885.

1. a. The religious sect called Hill-men, or Cameronians 1830.

Hillo, hilloa (hi·lo, hilō^u·), *interj.* (*sb.*) 1602. [var. of HOLLO, with altered quality of the unstressed syll.] **1.** A call used to hail a distant or occupied person, or, now, to express surprise at an unexpected meeting. **2.** *sb.* A name for this call 1823.

Hillock (hi·lək), *sb.* ME. [f. HILL *sb.* + -OCK.] **1.** A little HILL (senses 1, 3). †**2.** A protuberance or prominence on any surface –1668. Hence **Hi·llocky** *a.*

Hill-side. ME. The slope of a hill. Also *attrib.*

Hill-top. 1530. The top of a hill. Also *attrib.*

Hilly (hi·li), *a.* ME. [f. HILL *sb.* + -Y[1].] **1.** Characterized by or abounding in hills. **2.** Elevated, steep ME.; hill-like 1658. †**3.** Hill-dwelling –1698.

1. The hillier regions 1872. **2.** A bay formed by h. promontories 1768. A h. Heap of Stones DRYDEN.

Hilt (hilt), *sb.* [OE. *hilt, hilte*, corresp. to OS. *hilte, helta*, MLG. *hilte*, MDu. *helte*, OHG. *helza*, ON. *hjalt* :- Gmc. **χeltaz*, **χeltiz*, **χeltjōn*, of unkn. origin.] **1.** The handle of a sword or dagger. Formerly often in *pl.* with same sense. **2.** The handle or haft of any other weapon or tool 1573.

2. The h. of his pistol KINGLAKE. Phr. *Up to the h.* (†*hilts*): completely. Hence **Hilt** *v.* to furnish or fit with a h.

Hi·lted, *a.* OE. [f. HILT *sb.* and *v.* + -ED.] Furnished with a hilt; in *Her.*, having a hilt of a different tincture from the blade.

‖**Hilum** (həi·lŏm). 1659. [L. *hilum* little thing, trifle; orig. 'that which adheres to a bean' (Festus); hence in Bot. use.] †**1.** Something very minute. D. PELL. **2.** *Bot.* The point of attachment of a seed to its seed-vessel; the scar on the ripe seed 1753. (Anglicized **hile** 1857.) **3.** *Anat.* = HILUS 2. 'Applied also to certain small apertures and depressions' (*Syd. Soc. Lex.*).

‖**Hilus** (həi·lŏs). 1700. [mod.L., altered from prec.] †**1.** = HILUM 2. **2.** *Anat.* The point at which any one of the viscera has its junction with the vascular system; a notch or fissure where a vessel enters an organ 1840.

Him (him, *enclitic* -im), *pers. pron.*, *3rd sing. masc.* (and †*neut.*), *dat.-accus.* [OE. *him* = OFris. *him*, MDu. *hem(e, him* (Du. *hem*), f. base of HE, with inflexion parallel to OS., OHG. *imu, imo* (G. *ihm*), which are f. base **i-* (L. *is* he, *id* it, Goth. *is, ita*, OHG. *er, ez*, G. *er, es*). OE. *hine*, which survives dial. as *en, un* was superseded by *him* in north. and midl. areas before 1200. In the neuter the acc. *hit, it* prevailed, so that *him* is now dat. and acc. masc. only.] **1.** As proper masc. pron. of the 3rd pers. sing., dat. and accus. (objective indirect and direct) of HE. Also as antecedent pron. Used of persons and animals of male sex. **2.** Formerly put also for other than male beings (see quots.) OE. **3.** For the *nominative*; esp. after *than, as*, and in predicate after *be* ME. **4.** *refl.* = himself, to himself. [= L. *sibi, se*, G. *sich.*) OE. **5.** quasi-*sb.* Male person, man 1880.

1. Wel is hym that wyth pacience can indure BARCLAY. H. did you leaue..vn-seconded by you 2 *Hen. IV*, II. iii. 32. For Ialousie and fere of hym Arcite CHAUCER. **2.** The Fire conteyneth in him the Aëre 1559. The Sun was sunk, and after h. the Starr Of Hesperus MILT. (*personif.*) Winter had wrapped his mantle about h. 1898. **3.** But sure it can't be h. VANBRUGH. Is it h.? BURKE. **4.** He put the thought from h. 1898. Then lies h. meekly down MILT. He who hath bent him o'er the dead BYRON.

Himalayan (himā·lăyăn, *erron.* himălē[i]·ăn), *a.* 1866. [f. *Himālaya* (Skr. f. *hima* snow + *ālaya* abode) + -AN. The erron. pronunc. is still frequent.] Of or pertaining to the Himalayas, the mountain chain forming the northern boundary of India; *fig.* enormous.

‖**Hima·ntopus.** 1753. [L. – Gr. *ἱμαντόπους* stilt, f. *ἱμάς, ἱμαντ-* thong, strap + *πούς* foot.] *Ornith.* A genus of wading-birds; the stilts.

‖**Himation** (himæ·tiŏn). 1850. [Gr. *ἱμάτιον*.] The outer garment worn by the ancient Greeks; 'an oblong piece of cloth thrown over the left shoulder, and fastened either over or under the right' (Liddell & Scott).

Himne, obs. f. HYMN.

Himself (himse·lf), *pron.* OE. [f. HIM *dat.-acc. pers. pron.* + SELF. *Self* was orig. an adj.] **1.** Emphatic use. = Very him, very he, that very man, etc. = L. *ipse*. **2.** Reflexive use. = L. *sibi, se*; G. *sich* OE. **3.** quasi-*sb.* 1622. **4.** With *self* treated as a sb. (= person, personality), and the possessive *his* substituted for *him*. Prevalent in the dialects, but in standard English used only where an adj., etc. intervenes, as *his own, true*, etc. *self.* ME.

1. They toke him self alyue COVERDALE 1 *Macc.* 8:7. (*In apposition*) Sanctified by saint Peter himselfe MORE. (*In substitution* for the nom. pron.) The dagger which h. Gave Edith TENNYSON. Phr. *To be himself*: to be in his normal condition (see SELF). **2.** Euery man for him self, and god for vs all HEYWOOD. [He] bad him with good heart sustain h. TENNYSON.

Himyarite (hi·myărəit), *sb.* 1842. [f. *Ḥimyar*, name of a traditional king of Yemen in Southern Arabia + -ITE[1] 1.] One of an ancient people of Southern Arabia (formerly called HOMERITE). Also *attrib.* = **Himyari·tic** *a.* of or pertaining to the Himyarites, their civilization, etc.; commonly applied to their language (a distinct dialect of Arabic akin to Ethiopic), and to its alphabet, and the inscriptions preserved in it. So **Himya·ric** *a.*

‖**Hin** (hin), *sb.* ME. [– bibl. Heb. *hîn*.] A Hebrew measure for liquids, containing a little over a gallon.

Hin, hine, *pers. pron.*, *3rd sing. masc.*, *accus. Obs.* exc. *dial.* [OE. *hine, hiene*, accus. of HE; superseded by the dative *him*. In the reduced form *ĕn, ŭn, 'n* (ən, 'n), still the ordinary accus. in s.w. dialects.] = HIM, *direct objective*. Also *reflexive*.

Hind (həind), *sb.*[1] [OE. *hind*, corresp. to OS. *hind*, (M)Du. *hinde*, OHG. *hinta* (G. *hinde*), ON. *hind* :- Gmc. **χinþjō* :- IE. **kemti-*, f. **kem-* hornless, repr. by Gr. *κεμάς* young deer.] **1.** The female of the (red) deer; *spec.* a female deer in and after its third year. **2.** (In full *h.-fish.*) One of various fishes of the family *Serranidæ* and genus *Epinephalus* 1734.

Comb. **hind's foot** (tr. Fr. *pied de biche*), a kind of crossbow.

Hind (həind). *sb.*[2] [ME. *hine* (orig. pl.), presumably developed from OE. *hīna*, *hīġna*, gen. pl. of *hīġan, hīwan* (cf. HIDE *sb.*[2]), as in *hīna fæder* 'paterfamilias'. For the parasitic *d* cf. SOUND *sb.*[2]] **1.** A (farm) servant ME.; *Sc.* and *north. dial.* a married farm-servant, for whom a cottage is provided 1596. **b.** A bailiff or steward on a farm (*local*) 1495. **2.** *transf.* A rustic, a boor 1570. †**3.** A lad; hence, Person, fellow, chap –1550.

1. Laborious hinds That had survived the father, served the son COWPER.

Hind (həind), *a.* ME. [This and the synon. HINDER *a.* appear to be abstracted from OE. *hindeweard* and *hinderweard* backward, back-, *bihindan* BEHIND.] Situated behind, in the rear, or at the back; posterior. Usu. opp. to *fore*, and often hyphened to its sb. **b.** Hence applied to the back part of (anything) 1870.

The fore-hoofs were upright and shapely, the h. flat and splayed G. WHITE. The hind-spring of your carriage MARRYAT.

Hi·ndberry. *Obs.* exc. *n. dial.* [OE. *hindberie*, corresp. to OS. *hindberi*, OHG. *hintberi* (G. *himbeere*); see HIND *sb.*[1], BERRY *sb.*[1] So called as growing in woods, and assumed to be eaten by hinds.] The raspberry.

Hind-calf. [OE. *hindċealf*; see HIND *sb.*[1] and CALF[1].] The young of a hind; a fawn.

Hinder (həi·ndəɹ), *a.* ME. [See HIND *a.*] **1.** Situated behind, at the back, or in the rear; posterior. (More frequently used than *hind.*) Last. †**2.** Latter (as opp. to *former*) –1669.

1. As I was standing in the h. Part of the Box ADDISON. Hence †**Hi·nderest, Hi·ndermost** *adjs.* hindmost. So **Hinderland** = HINTERLAND.

Hinder (hi·ndəɹ), *v.* [OE. *hindrian* = MLG., MDu. *hinderen*, OHG. *hintarōn* (G. *hindern*), ON. *hindra* :- Gmc. **χindarōjan*, f. **χindar*, repr. by OE. *hinder* below, OS. *hindiro*, OHG. *hintar*, Goth. *hindar* prep. beyond.] †**1.** *trans.* To do harm to –1639; to speak to the injury of –1580. **2.** To keep back; to impede, deter, obstruct, prevent. Often with *from* or *in*. ME. **3.** *absol.* or *intr.* To delay or frustrate action; to be an obstacle or impediment ME.

1. To hindre and empaire the name, and memorialle of the dead 1555. **2.** Not able..to helpe hym..in this his iourney..but rather to hynder and let hym 1526. These pleasures do h. me in my business PEPYS. That hinders not but that they are generally less doubtful LOCKE. **3.** It is not the dark place that hinders, but the dim eye CARLYLE. Hence **Hi·nderer**, one who (or that which) hinders.

Hi·nd-head. *Obs.* or *arch.* 1666. [f. HIND *a.* + HEAD.] The back of the head; the occiput.

‖**Hindi** (hi·ndī). 1800. [– Urdu *hindī*, f. *Hind* India.]
A. *adj.* Of or belonging to Northern India or its language 1825.
B. *sb.* The great Aryan vernacular language of Northern India, spoken from the frontiers of Bengal to those of the Punjab and Sindh, and from the Himalaya Mountains to the Nerbudda.

Hindmost (həi·ndmoᵘst, -məst), *a.* ME. [f. HIND *a.* + -MOST.] Furthest behind; last come to; most remote.
The hynmost of them were slayne COVERDALE 1 *Macc.* 4:15.

Hindoo: see HINDU.

Hindrance (hi·ndrăns), *sb.* ME. [f. HINDER *v.* + -ANCE.] †**1.** Injury, hurt, disadvantage –1597. **2.** Obstruction; an obstruction 1526.
2. Full liberty to speak without hinderance BAXTER. They become..hindrances rather than helps 1877. Hence †**Hi·ndrance** *v. trans.* to hinder.

Hind-sight, hi·ndsight. 1851. **1.** (*hind-sight*) The backsight of a rifle. **2.** (*hi·ndsight*). Perception after the event; opp. to *foresight* 1883. Hence **Hi·ndsighted** *a.*

Hindu, Hindoo (hi·ndu, hindū·). 1662. [– Urdu – Pers. *hindū*, formerly *hindō*, f. *Hind* India.]
A. *sb.* An Aryan of Northern India (Hindustan), who retains the native religion (Hinduism); hence, any one who professes Hinduism.
B. *adj.* Of, pertaining to, or characteristic of the Hindus or their religion; Indian 1698.
Hence **Hi·nduism, Hindooism,** the religion of the Hindus, a development of Brahmanism. **Hi·nduize, Hindooize** *v.* to render H.

Hindustani, Hindoostanee (hindustā·nī). 1800. [– Urdu – Pers. *hindūstānī*, f. *hindū*, formerly *hindō*, + *-stān* country + adj. suff. *-ī*.]
A. *adj.* Of or pertaining to Hindustan (in the stricter sense, i.e. 'India north of the Nerbudda, exclusive of Bengal and Behar'), or its people or language (see B.2).
B. *sb.* A native of Hindustan; a Hindu or Moslem of Upper India 1829. **2.** The language of the Moslem conquerors of Hindustan, being Hindi with a large admixture of Arabic, Persian, etc.; also called *Urdu*, i.e. *zabān-i-urdū* language of the camp. It is now a kind of *lingua franca* over all India. 1808.

Hine, obs. or dial. f. HIND *sb.*[1] and [2].

‖**Hing** (hiŋ). 1586. [Hindi *hīng* :- Skr. *hingu*.] The drug asafœtida.

Hinge (hindʒ), *sb.* [Of obscure origin; ME. *heng, heeng, hing*, with deriv. *hengle, heengle, hingle* (see -LE), which survived dial., corresp. to MLG., MHG. *hengel* (G. *hängel*), f. base of HANG *v.*; cf. (M)LG. *henge* hinge, Du. *hengel* fishing-rod, handle, *hengsel* hinge, handle. The pronunc. with dʒ (XVI) is of obscure development.] **1.** The joint or mechanism by which a gate or door is hung upon the side-post, so as to be opened or shut by being turned upon it. **b.** The similar mechanism of a lid, valve, etc. 1562. **2.** A natural movable joint; e.g. that of a bivalve shell 1702. **3.** *transf.* The axis of the earth; the two poles, and, by extension, the four cardinal points ME. **4.** *fig.* That on which something hangs or turns; a pivot, prop 1604; the cardinal point 1638; a turning-point, crisis 1727.
1. The door upon its hinges groans KEATS. **3.** The winds..rushed abroad From the four hinges of the world MILT. *P. R.* IV. 413. **4.** Say, on what h. does his obedience move COWPER. Phr. *Off the hinges*: unhinged; out of order; in (or into) disorder, physical or moral.
Comb.: **h.-joint** (*Anat.*), a joint whose movement can only be in one plane (e.g. that of the elbow or knee); a GINGLYMUS; **-pin,** a pin which fastens together the parts of a h.

Hinge, *v.* 1607. [f. HINGE *sb.*] **1.** *trans.* To bend (anything) as a hinge. **2.** To hang with or as with a hinge 1758. **3.** *intr.* To hang and turn *on*, as a door on its post 1719.
1. Be thou a Flatterer now..hindge thy knee *Timon* IV. iii. 211. **3.** The point on which the decision must..h. THIRLWALL.

Hinged (hindʒd), *a.* 1672. [f. HINGE *sb.* + -ED[2].] Having a hinge or hinges. So **Hi·ngeless** *a.* without a hinge 1614.

Hinnible (hi·nib'l), *a.* 1656. [f. L. *hinnibilis*, f. *hinnire* HINNY *v.*] Able to neigh or whinny.

Hinny (hi·ni), *sb.* 1688. [f. L. *hinnus* – Gr. ἴννος, γίννος; assim. to next.] The offspring of a she-ass by a stallion.

Hinny (hi·ni), *v.* ME. [In XV *henny* – (O)Fr. *hennir* :- L. *hinnire*, to which the word was finally assim.] *intr.* To neigh as a horse, to whinny.

Hinny, hinnie, Sc. and north. f. of HONEY.

Hint (hint), *sb.* 1604. [Of obscure origin; presumably var. of rare †*hent* (XVI–XVII) grasp, intention, f. HENT *v.*] †**1.** An occasion; an opportunity –1818. **2.** A slight indication; a suggestion or implication conveyed covertly but intelligibly 1604.
1. It is my h. to speak SCOTT. **2.** A sharp girl that can take a h. JOHNSON.

Hint (hint), *v.* 1648. [f. HINT *sb.*, sense 2.] **1.** *trans.* To give a hint of; to suggest or indicate slightly but intelligibly; †to give a hint to (a person) SIR T. BROWNE. **2.** *intr.* *Hint at*: to make a slight, but intelligible suggestion of 1697.
1. Just h. a fault, and hesitate dislike POPE. **2.** The spectator's imagination completes what the artist merely hints at HAWTHORNE. Hence **Hi·ntedly** *adv.* **Hi·nter. Hi·ntingly** *adv.*

‖**Hinterland** (hi·ntəɹlænd). 1890. [G., f. *hinter-* behind + *land* land.] The district behind that lying along the coast (or along the shore of a river); the back country.

Hip (hip), *sb.*[1] [OE. *hype* = MDu. *höpe*, *hüpe* (Du. *heup*), OHG. *huf*, pl. *huffi* (G. *hüfte*), Goth. *hups*, pl. *hupeis* :- Gmc. *χupiz, rel. to HOP *v.*[1]] **1.** The projecting part of the body on each side formed by the lateral expansions of the pelvis and upper part of the thigh-bone; the haunch. Also used for the hip-joint. **b.** *Zool.* = COXA 2. 1834. **2.** *Arch.* **a.** A projecting inclined edge on a roof, extending from the ridge or apex to the eaves, and having a slope on each side; the rafter at this edge 1690. **b.** A spandrel 1726.
1. Phr. *Down in the hip(s*: said of a horse when the haunch-bone is injured; hence *fig.*, out of spirits. *On* or *upon the h.* (usu. *to take, get, have* one on the h., phrases taken from wrestling): at a disadvantage. *H. and thigh*: with overwhelming blows; unsparingly. Usu. with *smite*, etc. (Biblical.)
a. *Comb.* in sense 1, as **h.-bath,** a bath in which a person can sit immersed up to the hips; **-belt,** a belt worn diagonally about the left h. and right side of the waist, a part of mediæval armour; **-disease,** a disease of the h.-joint, characterized by inflammation, fungous growth, and caries of the bones; **-pocket,** a pocket in a pair of trousers, just behind the h.; **-revolver,** one carried in the h.-pocket.
b. *Comb.* in sense 2, as **h.-knob,** a knob or ornament surmounting the h. of a roof; **-mould, -moulding,** (*a*) the mould or templet by which the h. of a roof is set out; (*b*) the 'back' or outer angle of the h.; **-pole,** a pole supporting the h.-rafter; **-rafter,** the rafter extending along the h. of a roof; **-tile,** a tile of special shape used at the h. of a roof; **-truss,** a combination of timbers supporting the h.-rafter.

Hip (hip), **hep** (hep), *sb.*[2] [OE. *hēope, hīope*, corresp. to OS. *hiopo* (Du. *joop*), OHG. *hiufa* (G. *hiefe*) :- WGmc. *χeup-.] The fruit of the wild rose, or of roses in general.
I fed on scarlet hips and stony haws COWPER.

Hip (hip), *sb.*[3] Also *pl.* **hipps.** 1710. [var. of HYP, abbrev. of *hypochondria*. Usu. spelt with *y* in the sb., but with *i* in the vb., etc.] Morbid depression of spirits; the 'blues'.

Hip *v.*[1] [ME. *hüppe, hyppe*, corresp. to MLG., Du. *huppen*, LG. *hüppen*, (M)HG. *hüpfen*, vars. of corresponding forms of HOP *v.*[1]] To hop.

Hip, *v.*[2] 1610. [f. HIP *sb.*[1]] **1.** *trans.* To dislocate or injure the hip of; to lame in the hip. **2.** To give a cross-buttock in wrestling; to throw over the hip 1675. **3.** To form with a hip, as a roof 1669.

Hip, *v.*[3] *colloq.* 1842. [f. HIP *sb.*[3]; perh. back-formation from HIPPED *a.*[2]] *trans.* To affect with hypochondria.

Hip, *interj.* (*sb.*[4]) Also **hep.** 1752. **1.** 'An exclamation or calling to one' (J.). **2.** An exclam. used to introduce a united cheer; hence as *sb.* 1827.
2. To..huzza after the 'hip! hip! hip!' of the toast giver HONE.

Hip-bone. ME. [HIP *sb.*[1]] The bone of the hip; i.e. either the *ilium*, or the *ischium*, or the *os innominatum* as a whole, or the upper part of the thigh-bone.

Hipe (həip), *v.* 18.. [perh. a deriv. of HIP *sb.*[1], but the phonology is obscure.] *Wrestling.* To throw (an antagonist) by lifting him from the ground, and rapidly placing one of the knees between his thighs.

Hip-girdle. [HIP *sb.*[1]] **1.** *Anat.* The pelvic girdle or arch, consisting of the ilium, ischium, and pubis. **2.** = *Hip-belt*: see HIP *sb.*[1]

Hip-gout. 1598. [f. HIP *sb.*[1] + GOUT *sb.*[1]] = SCIATICA.

Hip-joint. 1794. [HIP *sb.*[1]] The joint of the hip, the articulation of the head of the thigh-bone with the ilium.

Hip-joint disease = *hip-disease* (HIP *sb.*[1]).

Hipo-: obs. spelling of HYPO-.

Hipparch (hi·pāɹk). 1656. [– Gr. ἵππαρχος, f. ἵππος horse + -αρχος -ARCH.] *Gr. Antiq.* Commander of the horse.

‖**Hipparion** (hipēᵊ·riǫn). 1859. [mod.L. – Gr. ἱππάριον pony.] *Palæont.* An extinct genus of small quadrupeds, of Miocene and Pliocene age, regarded as ancestrally related to the horse.

Hipped, hipt (hipt), *a.*[1] 1508. [f. HIP *sb.*[1] and *v.*[2] + -ED.] **1.** Having hips, as *large-hipped*. **2.** *Arch.* Of a roof: Having hips (see HIP *sb.*[1] 2) 1771. **3.** Having the hip injured or dislocated 1565.

Hipped (hipt), *a.*[2] *colloq.* 1710. [orig. *hypt, hypp'd*, f. HIP *sb.*[3], HYP (XVIII), short for HYPOCHONDRIA; see -ED[2].] Morbidly depressed.

Hippiatric (hipiæ·trik). *rare.* 1646. [– Gr. ἱππιατρικός, f. ἱππιατρός veterinary surgeon, f. ἵππος horse + ἰατρός healer, physician; see -IC.]
A. *adj.* Relating to the treatment of diseases of horses 1674.
B. *sb.* One who treats diseases of horses. *pl.* Farriery; a treatise on this. So **Hippia·trical** *a.* **Hippia·trist. Hippia·try.**

Hippic (hi·pik), *a. rare.* 1846. [– Gr. ἱππικός, f. ἵππος horse; see -IC.] Pertaining to horses, esp. to horse-racing.

Hippish (hi·piʃ), *a. colloq.* 1706. [f. HIP *sb.*[3] + -ISH[1]. Cf. *hyppish* (see HYPPED).] Low-spirited.

Hippo (hi·po). Colloq. abbrev. of HIPPOPOTAMUS.

Hippo- (hipo), bef. a vowel **hipp-,** comb. f. Gr. ἵππος horse; as in: **Hippo·machy** [Gr. -μαχία], a fight on horseback. **Hipponoso·logy, Hippopatho·logy,** 'the doctrine of the diseases of the horse' (*Syd. Soc. Lex.*).

Hippocamp (hi·pokæmp). 1613. [f. next.] = HIPPOCAMPUS 1.

Hippocampus (hipokæ·mpǒs). *Pl.* **-i.** 1576. [– L. *hippocampus* – Gr. ἱππόκαμπος, f. ἵππος horse + κάμπος sea-monster.] **1.** *Myth.* A sea-horse, having two fore-feet, and the tail of a dolphin or fish, represented as drawing the car of Neptune 1606. **2.** *Ichth.* A genus of small fishes, having a head suggesting that of a horse; the sea-horse 1576. **3.** *Anat.* Each of two elongated eminences (*h. major* and *minor*) on the floor of each lateral ventricle of the brain; so called from their supposed resemblance to the fish (sense 2) 1706.

Hippocentaur (hipose·ntǭɹ). 1533. [– L. *hippocentaurus* – Gr. ἱπποκένταυρος, f. ἵππος horse + κένταυρος CENTAUR.] A fabulous creature, half man, half horse; a centaur. Hence **Hippocentau·ric** *a.* of the nature of a h.

Hippocras (hi·pokræs). *Obs.* exc. *Hist.* [ME. *ypocras* – OFr. *ipo-, ypocras*, forms of the name *Hippocrates* (see next) used for med.L. *vinum Hippocraticum*, i.e. wine filtered through 'Hippocrates' sleeve' or 'bag'; see next.] **1.** A cordial drink made of wine flavoured with spices, formerly much in vogue. †**2. Hippocras bag.** A conical bag of cotton, linen, or flannel, used as a filter –1674.
1. He drynketh Ypocras Clarree and Vernage Of spices hoote tencreessen his corage CHAUCER.

Hippocrates (hipǫ·krătīz). 1626. A famous ancient Greek physician born about 460 B.C.
†**Hippocrates' bag, sleeve** [tr. L. *manica Hippocratis*] = prec. 2.

Hippocratic (hipokræ·tik), *a.* 1620. [– med.L. *Hippocraticus*; see prec., -IC.] **1.** Of or belonging to Hippocrates. **2.** Applied to the shrunken and livid aspect of the countenance immediately before death; so called because described by Hippocrates. Also *fig.* 1713.

1. †*H. wine*, spiced wine, hippocras. **2.** Succeeded by..Lethargy, a dismal H. Face, staring Eyes 1713. So **Hippocra·tian, Hippocra·tical** *adjs.* = prec. **Hippo·cratism,** the doctrine of Hippocrates.

Hippocrene (hi·pokrīn). 1634. [– L. *Hippocrēnē*, Gr. Ἱπποκρήνη or Ἵππου κρήνη 'fountain of the horse', fabled to have been produced by a stroke of Pegasus' hoof.] A fountain on Mount Helicon, sacred to the Muses; hence used allusively in reference to poetic inspiration.

O for a beaker..Full of the true, the blushful H. KEATS.

Hippocrepian (hipokrī·piăn), *a.* (*sb.*) 1877. [f. HIPPO- + Gr. κρηπίς shoe + -IAN.] *Zool.* and *Bot.* **1.** Resembling a horseshoe; *spec.* applied to the lophophore of certain polyzoans, and so to these polyzoans themselves. **2.** *sb.* A hippocrepian polyzoan. So **Hippocre·piform** *a. Bot.* shaped like a horseshoe.

†**Hippodame.** 1590. [– Gr. ἱππόδαμος horse-tamer, but in 1 app. confused with *hippotame* HIPPOPOTAMUS.] **1.** *erron.* for HIPPOCAMP. SPENSER *F. Q.* III. xi. 40. **2.** A horse-tamer 1623.

Hippodrome (hi·pŏdrōᵘm), *sb.* 1585. [– (O)Fr. *hippodrome* or L. *hippodromus* – Gr. ἱππόδρομος, f. ἵππος horse + δρόμος race, course.] **1.** *Gr.* and *Rom. Antiq.* A course or circus for horse-races and chariot-races. Sometimes a name for a modern circus. **2.** *U.S. Sporting slang.* A race, etc., in which the result is fraudulently prearranged 1889.

Hippogriff, -gryph (hi·pogrif). 1656. [– Fr. *hippogriffe* – It. *ippogrifo*, f. Gr. ἵππος horse + It. *grifo* :– L. *gryphus* GRIFFIN¹.] A fabulous creature, like a griffin with the body and hind-quarters of a horse. Also *fig.*

Tell us no more of Icarus, Of Hypogryph, or Pegasus 1659.

Hippoid (hi·poid). 1880. [f. Gr. ἵππος + -OID.] *Zool.* An animal resembling, or allied to, the horse.

Hippolith (hi·poliþ). 1828. [– mod.L. *hippolithus*, f. Gr. ἵππος horse + λίθος stone.] A concretion or calculus found in the intestines of a horse.

‖**Hippomanes** (hipǫ·mănīz). 1601. [Gr. ἱππομανές, n. of ἱππομανής, f. ἵππος horse + μαν-, base of μαίνεσθαι be mad.] **a.** 'A small black fleshy substance said to occur on the forehead of a new-born foal.' **b.** 'A mucous humour that runs from mares a-horsing' (Liddell & Scott). Both reputed aphrodisiacs.

Hippophagy (hipǫ·fădʒi). 1828. [f. HIPPO- + -PHAGY.] The practice of eating horseflesh. So **Hippo·phagism** = prec. **Hippo·phagist,** an eater of horseflesh. **Hippo·phagous** *a.* eating horseflesh.

Hippopotamus (hipopǫ·tămŏs). *Pl.* **-muses, -mi.** ME. [– L. *hippopotamus* – late Gr. ἱπποπόταμος (Galen), for earlier ἵππος ὁ ποτάμιος the horse of the river (ποταμός). Earlier forms (from XIV) were *ypotam(e, hippotame, ypotamos, -anus* – OFr. *ypotame*, med.L. *ypotamus*.] A pachydermatous quadruped, the African river-horse, *Hippopotamus amphibius*, a very large beast with a thick heavy hairless body, large muzzle and tusks, and short legs, inhabiting the African rivers, etc. Hence **Hi:ppopo·tamic** *a.* belonging to or like a h.; huge, unwieldy. **Hippopo·tamid** (*Zool.*), an animal of the family *Hippopotamidæ*.

Hippotomy (hipǫ·tŏmi), *rare.* 1854. [f. HIPPO- + -TOMY.] The anatomy or dissection of the horse. So **Hippo·tomist** 1737.

Hippurate (hipiū̆ᵊ·rĕt). 1854. [f. HIPPURIC + -ATE⁴.] *Chem.* A salt of hippuric acid.

‖**Hippuria** (hipiū̆ᵊ·riă). 1857. [mod.L., f. prec. and next. See -URIA.] *Path.* 'Bouchardat's term for the presence in excess of hippuric acid or hippurates in the urine' (*Syd. Soc. Lex.*).

Hippuric (hipiū̆ᵊ·rik), *a.* 1838. [f. Gr. ἵππος horse + οὖρον urine + -IC.] *Chem.* In *Hippuric acid*, an acid ($C_9H_9NO_3$) found in the urine of horses and other herbivora.

Hippurite (hi·piurəit). 1842. [– mod.L. *Hippurites*, f. Gr. ἵππουρος horse-tailed. See -ITE¹ 2 a.] **1.** A fossil bivalve mollusc of the genus *Hippurites* or family *Hippuritidæ*. Also *attrib.* **2.** 'A kind of fossil cup-coral, *Cyathophyllum ceratites* of Goldfuss' (*Cent. Dict.*). Hence **Hippuri·tic** *a.* pertaining to, or containing, hippurites (sense 1).

Hip-roof. 1727. [f. HIP *sb.*¹ 2.] A roof having hips or sloping edges, the ends being inclined as well as the sides; a hipped roof. Hence **Hip-roofed** *a.*

Hip-shot, *a.* (*sb.*) Also **-shotten.** 1639. [f. HIP *sb.*¹ + *shot* pa. pple. of SHOOT *v.*] **1.** Having a dislocated hip-joint. **2.** *fig.* Lame, clumsy; disabled 1642. **3.** *sb.* Dislocation of the hip-joint 1720.

2. This hipshot grammarian MILT.

Hir, obs. ME. form of HER *pron.*

‖**Hircarra, -ah, hurcaru** (hɒɹkā·ră). *E. Ind.* 1747. [Hindi, Urdu, etc. *harkāra* messenger.] An E. Indian spy, messenger, or courier.

Hircic (hɔ̄·ɹsik), *a.* 1836. [f. L. *hircus* he-goat + -IC.] *Chem.* Of or pertaining to a goat. *Hircic acid*, a liquid fatty substance believed by Chevreul to be the odorous principle of mutton suet; now held to be a mixture of fatty acids.

Hircin (hɔ̄·ɹsin). 1836. [f. as prec. + -IN¹.] *Chem.* A substance existing in the fat of the goat (and sheep), on which its strong odour depends.

Hircine (hɔ̄·ɹsəin). 1656. [– L. *hircinus*, f. *hircus* he-goat; see -INE¹.]

A. *adj.* Of, belonging to, or resembling a goat; *spec.* Having a goatish smell. So **Hi·rcinous** *a.*

B. *sb.* A fossil amorphous resin which burns with a strong animal odour. Also called **Hircite.**

‖**Hircocervus** (hɔ̄ɹkosɔ̄·ɹvŏs). ME. [Late L. *hircocervus* (Boethius), f. *hircus* he-goat + *cervus* stag.] A fabulous creature, half goat, half stag.

Hire (həiᵊɹ), *sb.* [OE. *hȳr* = OFris. *hēre*, OS. *hūria*, MLG., MDu. *hūre* (Du. *huur*) :– WGmc. **χūrja*.] **1.** Payment contracted to be made for the temporary use of anything. (In OE., *esp.* usury, interest.) **2.** Payment contracted to be made for personal service; wages ME. Also *fig.* **3.** The action of hiring or fact of being hired 1615.

1. Bote hyre from Lambeth 1587. Bicycles on h. 1898. **2.** Their testimony against preaching for h. MORSE. *fig.* Treuli the hyris of synne, deeth WYCLIF *Rom.* 6:22. **3.** The h. of a horse 1898. *Comb.* **h.-system,** a system by which a hired article becomes the property of the hirer after a stipulated number of payments; so **h.-purchase.**

Hire (həiᵊɹ), *v.* [f. prec.; OE. *hȳrian* = OFris. *hēra*, MLG., MDu. *hūren* (Du. *huren*).] **1.** *trans.* To engage the services of (a person) for a stipulated reward; to employ for wages. **b.** *transf.* To engage to do something by a payment or reward; to bribe ME. **2.** To procure the temporary use of (any thing) for stipulated payment ME. **3.** To grant the temporary use of for stipulated payment; to let *out* on hire; to lease ME.

1. He hir'd the workers by the day COWLEY. **b.** Cullin..was hired..to kill the Queene 1631. **2.** I hired an ass LADY M. W. MONTAGU. **3.** They that were full, haue hired out themselues for bread 1 *Sam.* 2:5. Phr. *To h. out* (*intr.* for *refl.*), to engage oneself as a servant for payment. *U.S.* and *Colonial.* Hence **Hi·reable, hirable** *a.* capable of being hired. **Hired** *ppl. a.*, applied *spec.* in U.S. to free men or women engaged as servants.

Hi·reless, *a.* 1651. [f. HIRE *sb.* + -LESS.] Without hire or pay.

Hireling (həiᵊ·ɹliŋ). [OE. *hȳrling* (rare), f. *hȳr* HIRE *sb.* + -LING¹. Formed afresh in XVI (Coverdale), prob. after Du. *huurling*.]

A. *sb.* **1.** One who serves for hire or wages. **2.** One who makes material gain the motive of his actions; a mercenary. (Opprobrious.) 1574.

2. As an h., that loves the work for the wages BACON.

B. *adj.* Characteristic of or pertaining to a hireling; serving for hire or wages; mercenary. (Usu. opprobrious.) 1587.

The plot by h. witnesses improv'd DRYDEN.

†**Hiren** (həiᵊ·rĕn). 1597. [Corruption of *Irene*, Fr. *Irène*.] Name of a character in Peele's play of 'The Turkish Mahamet and Hyrin the fair Greek'; used subseq. as meaning 'a seductive woman', a harlot. 2 *Hen. IV*, II. iv. 173.

Hiren, obs. f. HERN, hers.

Hirer (həiᵊ·rəɹ). 1500. [f. HIRE *v.* + -ER¹.] **1.** One who hires. **2.** One who lets out something on hire. *Obs.* or *Sc.* 1591.

Hirondelle. *Obs.* exc. *Her.* 1600. [– Fr. *hirondelle*.] A swallow.

The Swallow, or h., forms the very early coat of the Arundells 1880.

Hi·rple, *v. Sc.* and *north. dial.* 1450. [Of unkn. origin.] To move with a gait between walking and crawling; to walk lame.

Hirrient (hi·riĕnt), *a.* (*sb.*) *rare.* 1832. [– *hirrient-*, pres. ppl. stem of L. *hirrire* snarl; see -ENT.] **1.** Snarling; trilled. **2.** *sb.* A trilled sound. (Cf. *litera canina*, Latin name for *r*.) 1860.

Hirsute (hɔ̄·ɹsiūt), *a.* 1621. [– L. *hirsutus*, rel. to synon. *hirtus*.] **1.** Having rough hair; hairy, shaggy. **2.** *Bot.* and *Zool.* Covered with long and stiffish hairs 1626. **3.** Of or pertaining to hair; consisting of hair 1823. Also *transf.* and *fig.* 1621.

1. A rugged attire, h. head, horrid beard BURTON. Hence **Hi·rsuteness,** h. quality or condition. **Hirsuto-,** comb. f. L. *hirsutus*, HIRSUTE, as *hirsuto-atrous*, with black hairs.

†**Hirudinal** (hirū·dināl), *a.* 1651. [f. L. *hirudo, -din-* + -AL¹.] Of or pertaining to a leech. So **Hiru·dinid,** a member of the *Hirudinidæ* or Leech family. **Hirudi·nean,** a member of the *Hirudinea* or order of annelids containing the leeches.

His (hiz, -iz), *poss. pron., 3rd sing. masc.* and †*neut.* [OE. *his*, gen. of HE and IT, to which there are parallel forms from the base **i-* (cf. HER *poss. pron.*) in OS., Goth. *is*, OHG. *es* (cf. HIM). About XI the gen. *his* began to be treated as an adj. (with pl. *hise*, occurring till XV). See next.] †**1.** as *gen. case* of *pers. pron.*: **a.** *masc.* Of him; of the male being or thing in question, L. *ejus*; **b.** *neut.* of it; **c.** *refl.* of himself, of itself, L. *sui* –ME. **2.** *Poss. adj. pron. masc.* (orig. *poss. gen.*, and then, like L. *ejus*, following its sb.). **a.** Of or belonging to him, that man's, the male being's; also *refl.* his own (L. *suus*) OE. **b.** Also used with objects which one ought to have, or has specially to deal with (e.g. to kill *his man*, to gain *his blue*), or in which every one is assumed to have his share (e.g. he knows *his Bible, his arithmetic*, etc.) 1709. **c.** In reference to inferior animals *his* (or *her*) varies with *its*; see HE, IT. OE. **3.** Referring to neuter nouns or things inanimate. (Now superseded by ITS, exc. where personification is implied.) OE. **4.** After a sb., used instead of the genitive inflexion. Chiefly with proper nouns. Archaically retained in Book-keeping and for some technical purposes. OE.

2. a. His bold defence of me ROWE. His friends retained his panoply GROTE. **c.** The owl, for all his feathers, was a-cold KEATS. **3.** And thou hearest his sounde TINDALE *John* 3:8 [(Great Bible) the sounde therof]. The Sun Had first his precept so to move MILT. *P. L.* X. 652. **4.** King Edward the Fourth his death H. WALPOLE. Phr. *His own*: see OWN. *His self*: see HIMSELF 4 and SELF.

His (hiz), *absol. poss. pron.* OE. [In ME. a form HISIS was tried for the absolute pron., but did not take root. Thus HIS remains for the absol. as well as for the simple possessive. See HISIS, HISN.] The absolute form of prec., used when no noun follows: = His one, his ones.

My beloued is mine, and I am his *S. of S.* 2:16.

His, obs. spelling of *is*.

Hish, *v.* ME. By-form of HISS *v.*

†**Hi·sis,** *absolute poss. pron.* [f. HIS *poss. pron.*, after *hir-is, hir-es, hers*, etc., from *her*, etc. As the simple possessive itself ended in *s*, this form did not take root.] = next. WYCLIF.

Hisn, his'n (hi·z'n), *absol. poss. pron. dial.* Late ME. [f. HIS; cf. *hern*, etc. App. due to form-association with *my, mine*, etc., in which the *-n* distinguishes the absolute from the adjective form. These forms in *-n* are midl. and southern.] = HIS *absol. poss. pron.*

Hispanic (hispæ·nik), *a. rare.* [f. L. *Hispanicus*, f. *Hispania* Spain; see -IC.] Pertaining to Spain or its people. So †**Hispa·nian** *a.* 1550, †**Hispa·nical** *a.* 1584, **Hispa·nically** *adv.* **Hispa·nicism,** a Spanish idiom or mode of speech. **Hispa·nicize** *v.* to render Spanish.

Hispaniolate (hispæ·niŏleˡt), *v. rare.* 1860. [f. Sp. *españolar* make Spanish + -ATE³, with assim. to L. *Hispania* Spain.] *trans.* To make Spanish. So **Hispa·niolize** 1583, **Hi·spanize** 1600 *vbs.*

Hispa·no-, comb. f. L. *Hispanus* Spanish; as in **H.-Gallican,** belonging in common to Spain and Gaul.

Hispid (hi·spid), *a.* 1646. [– L. *hispidus*; see -ID¹. Cf. (O)Fr. *hispide.*] Rough with stiff hairs or bristles; shaggy; bristly: in *Bot.* and *Zool.* Clothed with short stiff hairs or bristles; rough with minute spines. So **Hispi·dulous** *a.* slightly h.

Hiss (his), *sb.* 1513. [f. HISS *v.*] **1.** A sharp continuous spirant sound such as is emitted by geese and serpents, and in the pronunciation of 's'. **b.** *Phonetics.* A consonant produced with a hiss; a sibilant. Also *attrib.* 1890. **2.** This sound uttered in disapproval or scorn 1602.

1. The h. of russling wings MILT. *P. L.* I. 768. **2.** A dismal universal h., the sound Of public scorn—X. 508.

Hiss (his), *v.* ME. [imit., with an early by-form *hish.*] **1.** *intr.* To make the sharp spirant sound emitted by geese, serpents, etc., or caused (e.g.) by the escape of steam through a narrow aperture, or uttered in the pronunciation of 's'. (L. *sibilare.*) ME. **2.** To make this sound by way of disapproval or derision. (Usu. with *at.*) ME. **3.** *trans.* To express disapproval of by making this sound 1599. **4.** To utter or express by hissing or with a hiss 1775.

1. But þei hissen, as serpentes don MAUNDEV. **2.** Thou art disgraced and hissed at JER. TAYLOR. **3.** They have hissed me LAMB. Phr. *To h. out, away, down.* **4.** One of the threats hissed out by the Congress JOHNSON. Hence **Hi·sser.**

Hissing (hi·siŋ), *vbl. sb.* ME. [f. HISS *v.* + -ING¹.] **1.** The action of HISS *v.* **2.** *concr.* An occasion or object of expressed opprobrium (*arch.*) ME.

2. I will make this citie desolate and an h. (Genev.) *Jer.* 19:8. So **Hi·ssingly** *adv.*

Hist (hist), *interj.* SHAKS. [A natural exclam. Cf. ST, WHISHT.] A sibilant exclam. used to enjoin silence, attract attention, or call on people to listen.

Hist (hist), *v.* Now *poet.* 1604. [f. prec.] †**1.** *trans.* To summon with the exclam. 'hist!'; to summon without noise –1778. **2.** To incite. MIDDLETON.

1. And the mute Silence h. along MILT. *Pens.* 55.

Histioid (hi·stioid), *a.* 1854. [f. Gr. ἱστίον, dim. of ἱστός web, tissue + -OID.] *Phys.* and *Path.* = HISTOID. So **Histio·logy** = HISTOLOGY.

Histo-, comb. f. Gr. ἱστός, with sense 'tissue'.

Hi·stoblast [Gr. βλαστός], the primary element or unit of a tissue. **Histoche·mical** *a.*, relating to **Histoche·mistry,** the chemistry of organic tissues. **Histogra·phic, -al** *a.*, belonging to **Histo·graphy,** description of the tissues. **Histo·lysis** [Gr. λύσις], disintegration or dissolution of organic tissue; hence **Histoly·tic** *a.*, belonging to histolysis. **Histo·phyly** [Gr. φυλή], the history of tissues within a particular tribe of organisms. **Histo·tomy** [Gr. -τομία], 'the dissection of the organic tissues' (Mayne). **Hi·stozyme** [Gr. ζύμη], Schmiedeberg's term for a substance that causes fermentation in the tissues.

Histogenesis (histoˌdʒe·nésis). 1854. [f. HISTO- + -GENESIS.] *Biol.* The production or development of organic tissues. So **Histogene·tic** *a.* having the quality of producing tissue; relating to the formation of tissues. **Histogene·tically** *adv.* in relation to h. **Histo·geny,** in same sense.

Histoid (hi·stoid), *a.* 1872. [f. Gr. ἱστός web + -OID.] *Phys.* and *Path.* Like or of the nature of tissue, esp. connective tissue; spec. said of tumours.

Histology (histǫ·lŏdʒi). 1847. [f. HISTO- + -LOGY. Cf. Fr. *histologie.*] The science of organic tissues; that branch of anatomy, or of biology, which is concerned with the minute structure of the tissues of animals and plants. Hence **Histolo·gic, -al** *a.* belonging to h.; relating to organic tissues. **Histolo·gically** *adv.* **Histo·logist,** one versed in h.

†**Histo·rial,** *a.* (*sb.*) ME. [– (O)Fr. *historial* – late L. *historialis*, f. *historia* HISTORY *sb.*; see -AL¹.] **1.** Historical –1649. **2.** *sb.* History 1595. Hence †**Histo·rially** *adv.*

Historian (histōᵊ·riăn). 1531. [– (O)Fr. *historien*, f. L. *historia*, after *logicien*, etc.; see -AN, -IAN.] **1.** A writer or author of a history; esp. as dist. from the simple annalist or compiler. †**2.** A story-teller –1667. **3.** One versed in history (*rare*) 1645.

1. The H. [sayth] what men haue done SIDNEY. **3.** Great captains should be good historians SOUTH. Hence **Histo·rianess** SCOTT.

Historiated (histōᵊ·rieˡtėd), *ppl. a.* 1886. [repr. Fr. *historié* in same sense, pa. pple. of (O)Fr. *historier* †illustrate – med.L. *historiare.*] Decorated (as illuminated capitals) with figures of men or animals.

Historic (histǫ·rik), *a.* (*sb.*) 1669. [– L. *historicus* – Gr. ἱστορικός, f. ἱστορία HISTORY *sb.*; see -IC.] **1.** Of or belonging to history; of the nature of history as opp. to fiction or legend; historical. **2.** Dealing with or treating of history; = HISTORICAL 3. 1675. **3.** *esp.* Noted or celebrated in history. (The prevailing current sense.) 1794. **4.** Applied, in L. and Gr. Grammar, to those tenses of the vb. which are used in narration of past events; also, in L., to the infinitive mood when used instead of the indicative; and, generally, to the present tense, when used instead of the past in vivid narration 1845.

2. John Freeman, an h. painter H. WALPOLE. **3.** My first introduction to the h. scenes, which have since engaged so many years of my life GIBBON.

B. *sb. rare.* A historic work, picture, subject, etc. 1830.

Historical (histǫ·rikăl), *a.* 1513. [f. as prec.; see -ICAL.] **1.** = HISTORIC 1. 1561. **2.** Relating to or concerned with history or historical events 1513. **3.** Dealing with history, treating of history, as a *h. treatise* or *writer*; based upon history, as a *h. play, novel*, etc. 1590; representing history, as a *h. painting* 1658. **4.** = HISTORIC 3 (now the usual word) 1834. **5.** *Gram.* = HISTORIC 4. 1867.

2. *H. Method*, a method of investigation in which the history of the object is studied. **4.** This h. and gallant little ship [the May Flower] LONGF. Hence **Histo·rical-ly** *adv.*, **-ness.**

Historicity (histŏri·sĭti). 1880. [f. HISTORIC + -ITY, after *authenticity.*] Historical quality or character.

Historicize (histǫ·risəiz), *v.* 1846. [f. as prec. + -IZE.] **1.** *trans.* To make, or represent as, historic. **2.** *intr.* To recount historical events (*nonce-use*) 1887.

Historico-, comb. f. Gr. ἱστορικός: = historically.., historical and.., as in *h.-critical, -geographical*, etc.

Historied (hi·stŏrid), *a. rare.* 1585. [f. HISTORY *sb.* and *v.* + -ED.] **1.** Adorned with historical scenes. **2.** Having a history; storied 1818.

2. He sees, in some great-historied land [etc.] M. ARNOLD.

†**Histo·rier.** 1449. [– OFr. *historieur*, f. (O)Fr. *historier* HISTORY *v.*; see -ER².] A historian –1581.

‖**Historiette** (histōᵊriˌe·t). 1704. [Fr. – It. *istorietta*, f. *istoria* story; see *-ette.*] A short history or story.

Historify (histǫ·rifəi), *v.* 1586. [f. HISTORY *sb.* + -FY. Cf. HISTORIZE.] **1.** *trans.* To relate the history of; to record in history. **2.** *absol.* To write history; to narrate 1614.

1. That Church which you have so worthily historified LAMB.

Historiographer (histōᵊriǫ·grăfəɹ). 1494. [f. (O)Fr. *historiographe* or late L. *historiographus* (Jerome) – Gr. ἱστοριογράφος, f. ἱστορία HISTORY *sb.*; see -GRAPHER, -ER¹ 4. Cf. Fr. †*historiographeur.*] **1.** A chronicler or historian. **2.** *esp.* An official historian appointed in connection with a court 1555. Also *transf.* **3.** A writer of natural history (see HISTORY *sb.* 4) 1579.

2. *transf.* Scott became the h. royal of feudalism M. ARNOLD. So †**Histo·riograph,** in same sense. Hence **Historio·graphership.**

Historiography (histōᵊriǫ·grăfi). 1569. [– med.L. *historiographia* – Gr. ἱστοριογραφία, f. as prec.; see -GRAPHY.] The writing of history; written history. Hence **Histo:riogra·phic, -al** *a.* pertaining to h.

Historiology (histōᵊriǫ·lŏdʒi). 1616. [f. HISTORY *sb.* + -LOGY.] The knowledge or study of history. Hence **Historiolo·gical** *a.* pertaining to h.

Historio·nomer. *nonce-wd.* [f. HISTORY *sb.* after *astronomer.*] One versed in the laws which regulate the course of history. LOWELL.

Historize (hi·stŏrəiz), *v.* ? *Obs.* 1599. [f. HISTORY *sb.* + -IZE.] **1.** *trans.* To tell the history of; to narrate as history. †**2.** To represent EVELYN. **3.** *intr.* or *absol.* To act the historian 1632.

History (hi·stŏri), *sb.* ME. [– L. *historia* – Gr. ἱστορία learning or knowing by inquiry, narrative, history, f. ἵστωρ knowing, learned, wise man, judge :– *Ϝίδτωρ, f. *Ϝιδ- know (see WIT *v.*¹).] †**1.** A relation of incidents (in later use, only of those professedly true); a narrative, tale, story –1834. **2.** *spec.* A written narrative constituting a continuous methodical record, in order of time, of important or public events, esp. those connected with a particular country, people, individual, etc. 1485. **3.** (Without *a* or *pl.*) The formal record of the past, esp. of human affairs or actions 1482. Also *transf.*; esp. in pregnant sense, A career worthy of record 1654. **4.** A systematic account (without reference to time) of a set of natural phenomena. Now *rare*, exc. in NATURAL HISTORY. [Cf. the use of ἱστορία by Aristotle.] 1567. **5.** †A drama; *spec.* a historical play 1596. †**6.** A picture of an event or series of incidents –1776. ¶**7.** *Eccl.* = L. *historia*, liturgically applied (*a*) to a series of lessons from Scripture, named from the first words of the Respond to the first lesson; (*b*) to the general order of a particular Office.

1. A Mountebank on the Stage..gave them a H. of his Cures T. BROWN. **2.** *Chronicles, Annals*, are simpler forms of h., in which the year or period is the primary division; whereas in a *history*, each movement, action, or chain of events is dealt with as a whole. (See O.E.D.) How can there be a true H., when we see no Man living is able to write truly the H. of the last Week? SHADWELL. **3.** Phr. *Ancient H.*, history down to the fall of the Western Roman Empire in A.D. 476; also used *joc.* of 'matters which are out of date'. If fame were not an accident, and H. a distillation of Rumour CARLYLE. *transf.* The happiest women, like the happiest nations, have no h. GEO. ELIOT. **4.** H. of British Birds (*title*) 1797. **5.** The H. of Henrie the Fovrth (*title*) SHAKS. Last Scene of all, That ends this strange euentfull historie *A.Y.L.* II. vii. 164.

Comb.: **h.-maker,** (*a*) a writer of a h.; (*b*) one who 'makes history', i.e. performs actions which shape the course of h.; **-painter,** one who paints 'histories' (sense 6); so **-painting, -piece.**

†**History,** *v.* 1475. [– (O)Fr. *historier* – med.L. *historiare* (in both senses), f. L. *historia* HISTORY *sb.* In sense 2 partly through It. *istoriare, -ato.*] **1.** *trans.* To relate in a history; to recount –1597. **2.** To inscribe or adorn with 'histories' (sense 6) –1698.

‖**Histrio** (hi·strio). 1658. [L.] = next.

Histrion (hi·striŏn). 1566. [– Fr. *histrion* or L. *histrio, -ōn-* stage-player.] A stage-player. (Now usu. contemptuous.)

Histrionic (histriǫ·nik). 1648. [– late L. *histrionicus*, f. L. *histrio, -ōn-* stage-player; see -IC.]

A. *adj.* **1.** Of or relating to stage-players, or to play-acting; theatrical 1759. **2.** 'Stagey'; also *fig.* 'acting a part', hypocritical 1648.

2. H. mumm'ry, that let down The pulpit to the level of the stage COWPER. Phr. *H. paralysis* (Path.), facial palsy. *H. spasm*, spasm of the facial muscles.

B. *sb.* **1.** A stage-player. Also *fig.* 1859. **2.** *pl.* Theatricals; theatrical arts; acting, pretence 1864.

Hence **Histrio·nical** *a.* = HISTRIONIC *a.* 1, 2. **Histrio·nically** *adv.* **Histrio·nicism,** h. action.

Histrionism (hi·striŏniz'm). 1682. [f. HISTRION or L. *histrio* (see prec.) + -ISM.] Theatrical practice, action, or style; 'acting'.

Hit, *sb.* 1450. [f. HIT *v.*] **1.** A blow given to something aimed at; a stroke (at cricket, etc.); the collision of one body with another. **2.** A stroke of sarcasm, censure, etc. 1668. **3.** A fortunate chance 1666. **4.** A successful stroke of any kind 1815. **b.** A saying that goes to the point; a telling phrase 1836. **5.** *Back-gammon.* **a.** A game won by a player after the opponent has removed one or more men from the board, as dist. from a *gammon* or a *back-gammon.* **b.** The act of hitting a 'blot': see HIT *v.* I. 8. 1766.

1. A h., a very palpable h. *Haml.* v. ii. 292. **4.** The noble speaker had made the h. of the evening 1884.

Hit (hit), *v.* Pa. t. and pple. **hit.** [Late OE. (*ge*)*hittan* – ON. *hitta* light upon, meet with (Sw. *hitta*, Da. *hitte*), of unkn. origin; has taken over the orig. use 'strike' of SLAY *v.*]

I. 1. To reach or get at with a blow or a missile; to strike ME. **b.** *Cricket.* To strike (the ball) with the bat: hence with the bowler as object 1857. **2.** *absol.* or *intr.* To give a blow or blows ME. **3.** Of a missile, etc.: To come upon with force; to strike ME. **4.** *absol.* or *intr.* To come with forcible impact (*against, upon*, etc.) ME. **5.** *trans.* To deliver (a blow, stroke, etc.) ME. **6.** *trans.* To knock (a part of the body) *against* or *on* something 1639. **7.** *fig.* To smite, wound, hurt ME. **8.** *Backgammon.* To 'take up' (a man) 1599.

1. *Twel. N.* II. v. 51. **b.** Dr. Grace hit Hill square for 4 1883. **3.** *fig.* The sun, that now..hit the Northern hills TENNYSON. **4. b.** To strike exactly or at the proper point; usu. in phr. *to be hitting on all four* or *six cylinders*: (of an internal combustion engine) to be running or working perfectly; also *fig.* **5.** Phr. *To h. any one a blow*: to strike him with a blow. **6.** He hit his foot against the step 1898. **7.** Phr. *To h. home*: cf. HOME *adv. To be hard hit*: to be severely or deeply affected by something. This Objection hitteth not us at all 1678. **8.** Phr. *To h. a blot*: to throw a number which enables a player to take up an unguarded man. Hence *fig.* to discover a weak point.

II. 1. *trans.* To come upon, light upon, get at, reach, find, esp. something aimed at OE. Also *intr.* with *upon, on,* †*of*, in same sense. **2.** *intr.* To attain the object aimed at; to succeed; to come off as intended. *Obs.* or *dial.* ME. **3.** *trans.* To imitate to a nicety 1602. **4.** To fall in with exactly 1580. †**5.** To fall in suitably or exactly; to square *with*, agree *with* –1722. **6.** *intr.* To agree together. *Obs.* or *dial.* 1605.

1. You have hit my meaning right 1581. Egad, I can't h. the Joint SWIFT. *intr.* To h. upon the right hypothesis SAYCE. **3.** O, could he but haue drawne his wit As well in brasse, as he hath hit His face B. JONS. **4.** [I] sought with deedes thy will to hitt SIDNEY. **5.** The Scheme hit so exactly with my Temper DE FOE.

III. *intr.* To direct one's course; to pass, turn; to strike *out, in*, in a particular direction. ? Now *dial.* ME.

Phrases. *To h. it.* **a.** To guess the right thing. **b.** (Now usu. *to h. it off.*) To agree. **c.** To attain exactly to the point wanted; to strike the scent in hunting. *To h. the mark, the nail upon the head*, etc., usu. *fig. H. or miss*: Whether one hits or misses; happy-go-lucky. Also *attrib.* and *subst.*

Comb. with advs. **H. off. a.** To produce with success. **b.** To succeed in getting at or upon (e.g. the scent in hunting). **c.** To reproduce to a nicety. **H. out.** †**a.** *trans.* To knock out. **b.** To strike out, elicit. **c.** *intr.* To strike out with the fist. Also *fig.* **H. up** (*Cricket*): to make or score (runs).

Hit, obs. f. HIGHT *v.*, HEIGHT; obs. and dial. f. IT.

Hitch (hitʃ), *sb.* 1664. [f. HITCH *v.*] **1.** A short abrupt movement, pull, or push; a jerk 1674. **2.** *Mining.* A slight fault or dislocation of strata 1708. **3.** A limp, a hobble; an interference in a horse's pace 1664. **4.** The action of catching, as on a hook, etc. WEBSTER. **5.** Chiefly *Naut.* A noose or knot by which a rope is caught round or temporarily made fast to some object 1769. **6.** *fig.* An accidental or temporary stoppage; an impediment, obstruction 1748.

1. Ben..gives his trousers one h., and calls for a quartern MARRYAT. **5.** CLOVE-*hitch*, HALF-HITCH, etc. (see these wds.). **6.** There was some h. in the execution of our treaty 1794.

Hitch (hitʃ), *v.* 1440. [In *Promp. Parv.*, 1440, *hytchen*; also, later, without *h*; see ITCH *v.*[2] Of obscure origin. Cf. Sc. and north. *hotch* in same sense.] **1.** *trans.* To move as with a jerk; to shift a little away or aside; *esp.* to raise or lift with a jerk (orig. *Naut.*) 1833. Also *fig.* Also *intr.* for *pass.* **2.** *intr.* To shift one's position a little; to move with a jerk or succession of jerks 1629. **3.** To hobble; also (*dial.*) to hop 1513. **4.** *trans.* To catch as with a loop, noose, or hook; to fasten, esp. in a temporary way. Also *fig.* 1627. **b.** with *up*: To harness, yoke 1870. *To hitch horses together* (U.S.), to get on well, in harmony 1837; *pass.* (U.S.), to be married 1857. **5.** *intr.* To become fastened or caught, esp. by hooking on; to catch on something. Also *fig.* 1578. **6.** Of a horse: To strike the feet together in going; to interfere 1686.

1. Hitching his chair nearer the fire C. BRONTË. And then he hitch'd his trousers up BARHAM. *fig.* Now we must appear..affectionate, or Sneer will h. us into a story SHERIDAN. *intr.* for *pass.* Whoe'er offends, at some unlucky time Slides into verse, and hitches in a rhyme POPE. **4.** Hitching our shawls in a bramble MISS MITFORD. **b.** Now that is the wisdom of a man..to h. his waggon to a star EMERSON. **5.** The lariat hitched on one of his ears W. IRVING.

Hitchel, obs. and dial. f. HATCHEL.

Hithe, hythe (həið). [OE. *hȳþ*, OS. *hūth*, MLG. *-hude* (in place-names); of unkn. origin. Preserved in the place-names *Hythe, Rotherhithe, Lambeth* (orig. *Lambhithe*), *Chelsea* (OE. *ċealchȳþ*), *Bablockhithe, Hythe* Bridge in Oxford.] A port or haven; *esp.* a small landing-place on a river. Now *Obs.* exc. *Hist.*, and in place-names.

Hither (hi·ðəɹ). [OE. *hider*, corresp. to ON. *heðra* here, hither, Goth. *hidrē* hither, f. demonstr. base **χi-* (see HE, HENCE, HERE) + suffix appearing in L. *citra* on this side. For the change of *d* to *ð* cf. *father, mother, together.*]

A. *adv.* **1.** With vbs. of motion, etc.: To or towards this place. (Now only literary; see HERE.] †**2.** Up to this point (of time, etc.) –1607. †**3.** To this end or aim; to this subject or category; hereto –1694.

1. Come h. unto me 1550. **3.** Hyther tendyth al prudence and pollycy 1538. Phr. **Hither and thither:** to this place and that; to and fro; in various directions.

B. *adj.* Situated on this side, or in this direction; the nearer. Also *fig.* of time. ME.

On this h. side of the riuer HOLINSHED.

Hence **Hi·thermost** *a.* most in this direction; nearest.

Hitherto (hiðəɹtū·, hi·ðəɹtu), *adv.* (*a.*) ME. [f. HITHER *adv.* + TO *prep.*] **1.** Up to this time, until now, as yet. †**2.** Up to this point (in writing, etc.) –1762. **3.** To this place; thus far (*arch.*) 1535. †**4.** = HITHER 3. –1656. **5.** quasi-*adj.* [attrib. use of adv.] 1787.

1. The Lord hath blessed me h. *Josh.* 17:14. **3.** H. shalt thou come, but no further *Job* 38:11. **5.** All his h. offences MME. D'ARBLAY. So †**Hither-toward(s,** †**Hitherunto·, -u·nto,** *advs.*

Hitherward (hi·ðəɹwǫ̈ɹd), *adv. arch.* [OE. *hiderweard*, f. *hider* HITHER + *-weard* -WARD. (In OE. also adj.)] **1.** Towards this place; hither. **2.** On this side (*of*). Also *fig.* 1864. †**3.** Until now; hitherto –1513.

1. Marching h. SHAKS. **2.** H. of Sohr CARLYLE. So **Hi·therwards** *adv.*

Hitter (hi·təɹ). 1813. [f. HIT *v.* + -ER[1].] One who hits or strikes, as a *hard hitter.*

Hitty-missy (hi·ti mi·si), *adv.* (*a.*) 1553. [perh. f. **hit I, miss I*; cf. WILLY-NILLY.] **1.** Hit or miss; at random, at haphazard. **2.** *adj.* Random, haphazard 1885.

Hive (həiv), *sb.* [OE. *hȳf*, f. Gmc. **χūf-*, whence also ON. *húfr* ship's hull; cf. L. *cūpa* barrel. The present form depends upon OE. obl. forms.] **1.** An artificial receptacle for the habitation of a swarm of bees; a beehive. Also *fig.* **2.** *transf.* **a.** A place swarming with busy occupants 1634. **b.** A place whence swarms of people issue 1788. **3.** A hiveful of bees, a hived swarm ME.; *transf.* a teeming multitude 1832. **4.** Anything of the shape or structure of a beehive 1597.

2. a. This great H., the City COWLEY. **b.** The h. whence the Pelasgian people issued 1835. **3.** *transf.* There the h. of Roman liars worship a gluttonous emperor-idiot TENNYSON. *Comb.* **h.-bee**, the common honey-bee. Hence **Hi·veless** *a.* destitute of a h.

Hive (həiv), *v.* late ME. [f. HIVE *sb.*] **1.** *trans.* To gather (bees) into a hive; to locate (a swarm) in a hive. Also *transf.* and *fig.* **2.** To hoard, as honey, in the hive 1580. **3.** *intr.* To take to the hive, as bees. **b.** To live together as bees in a hive; also *transf.* 1577.

1. Your Gardner must..watch his Bees, and h. them 1615. **2.** Hiving wisdom with each studious year BYRON. **3.** Drones hiue not with me, Therefore I part with him *Merch. V.* II. v. 48. Hence **Hiver,** one who hives bees.

Hives (həivz), *sb. pl.* 1500. [Of unkn. origin.] 'Any eruption on the skin, when the disorder is supposed to proceed from an internal cause' (Jamieson); applied to chicken-pox; also, croup.

Hizz (hiz), *v.* Now *rare.* 1583. [imit.; cf. HISS.] *intr.* To hiss.

H'm, hm, *int.* See HEM *int.*, HUM *int.*

Ho (hō^{u}), *int.*[1] (and *sb.*[1]) ME. [A natural exclam. Not recorded in OE.; cf. ON. *hó* 'int., also a shepherd's call'.] **1.** An exclam. of surprise, admiration, exultation (often ironical), triumph, taunting. **2.** An exclam. to attract attention; often after the name of a thing or place ME. **3.** *sb.* A cry of 'ho' ME.

1. Phr. *ho! ho! ho!*, an expression of derision or derisive laughter. **2.** Then Westward-hoe *Twel. N.* III. i. 146. **3.** With a hey, and a ho, and a hey nonino *A. Y. L.* V. iii. 18.

Ho, *int.*[2] (and *sb.*[2]) Also †**hoa,** †**hoe.** ME. [– OFr. *ho* halt! stop!] **1.** †A cry to stop or to cease what one is doing –1631. **b.** A call to an animal to stop or stand still 1828. **2.** *sb.* Cessation, halt, intermission; limit. *Obs.* or *dial.* ME.

2. *Withouten ho, Out of all ho*, without stopping, unceasingly. *No ho*, no limit.

Ho, *int.*[3] A sailor's cry in heaving or hauling.

Ho, obs. f. HE, HEO, HI *prons.*, HOW, WHO; var. of O *adv.*

‖**Hoactzin, hoatzin** (hō^{u},æ·ktsin, hō^{u},æ·t-sin). Also **hoazin.** 1661. [Native name, derived from the bird's 'harsh grating hiss'.] A bird, *Opisthocomus hoazin*, or *O. cristatus*, native of tropical America, type and sole member of a group named by Huxley *Heteromorphæ.*

Hoaming, *ppl. a. Obs.* or *dial.* 1670. Origin and meaning uncertain.

What a Sea comes in. A h. Sea! we shall have foul weather DRYDEN & DAVENANT. [*Cf.* A great huminge sea NARBROUGH 1672.]

Hoar (hō^{ə}ɹ). [OE. *hār* = OS., OHG. *hēr* old, venerable (G. *hehr* august, stately, sacred), ON. *hárr* hoary, old :– Gmc. **χairaz*, f. base **χai-* :– IE. **koi-* shine.]

A. *adj.* **1.** Grey-haired with age; venerable. **2.** Of colour: Grey, greyish white OE. †**3.** Used as an attribute of stones, etc. marking a boundary line. Hence in place-names. –ME. **4.** Mouldy, musty. Also *fig. Obs.* exc. *dial.* 1544.

1. Youth and h. age POPE. **2.** Hoare haires *Isa.* 46:4. Haire frost 1644. Some h. hill MILT. H. cliffs THOMSON. **4.** An old Hare hoare is very good meat in Lent *Rom. & Jul.* II. iv. 141.

Comb.: **h.-leprosy,** elephantiasis; **-rime** = HOAR-FROST; **h. withy,** the White-beam, *Pyrus Aria.*

B. *sb.* **1.** Hoariness from age 1500. **2.** A hoary coating or appearance; esp. hoar-frost, rime 1567; †mould –1686.

2. The candy'd rhime and scattered h. 1731.

†**Hoar,** *v.* [OE. *hārian*, f. *hār* HOAR *a.*] To make or become hoary or musty –1750.

Hoard (hō^{ə}ɹd), *sb.* [OE. *hord* = OS. *hord*, *horth* treasure, secret place, OHG. *hort*, ON. *hodd*, Goth. *huzd* :– Gmc. **χuzdam.* For the sp. (rare before XVIII) cf. *board.*] **1.** A stock, store, esp. of money, hidden away or laid by; a treasure. Also *fig.* †**2.** A repository; a hiding-place, store; a treasury. Also *fig.* –1663. †**3.** Hoarding up. CHAUCER.

1. The Squirrels h. *Mids. N.* IV. i. 40. A..h of coins 1851.

Hoard (hō^{ə}ɹd), *v.* [OE. *hordian*, f. *hord* HOARD *sb.*] *trans.* To amass and put away for preservation or future use; to treasure *up*: esp. money or wealth. Also *absol.* Also *fig.* and *transf.*

The Granaries of Joseph: wherein he hoorded corne 1615. *absol.* A savage race, That h., and sleep, and feed TENNYSON. *fig.* Revenge will be smothered and hoarded BURKE. Hence **Hoa·rder,** †a steward; one who hoards up.

Hoarding (hō^{ə}·ɹdiŋ), *sb.* 1823. [f. *hoard*, earlier *hord, hourd* (XVIII), which seems to be based ult. on AFr. *hourdis, hurdis*, f. OFr.

hourd, hort (– Frankish **hurð* = OHG. *hurd* HURDLE) + *-is* :– L. *-itius* (see -ICE); see -ING[1].] 1. A temporary fence of boards enclosing a building while in course of erection or repair; hence, any hoarding on which bills are posted. 2. *Mil.* An overhanging gallery, protected by boarding in front, thrown out from the surface of a wall, to enable the defenders to protect the foot of the wall 1865.

†**Hoared** (hōᵊɹd), *ppl. a.* 1496. [f. HOAR *v.* + -ED[1].] Made or grown hoary or mouldy –1643.

Hoa·r-frost. ME. [Often two wds. See HOAR *a.* and FROST *sb.*] The white deposit formed by the freezing of dew, white frost.

He..scatereth yᵉ horefrost like ashes COVERDALE *Ps.* 147:16.

Hoa·rhead. ME. [f. HOAR *a.* + HEAD *sb.*] A hoary head; an old grey-haired man. Also *attrib.* Hence **Hoar-headed** *a.*

Hoarhound, var. of HOREHOUND.

Hoariness (hōᵊ·rinės). 1573. [f. HOARY *a.* + -NESS.] The quality or state of being hoary. So †**Hoa·rness.**

Hoarse (hōᵊɹs), *a.* OE. [In XV *hors(e*, later *hoorse, hoarse* (XVI–XVII) – ON. **hars* (:– **hairsaR*), *hás*; this superseded ME. *ho(o)s*, OE. *hās* (Sc. and north. *ha(a)s, hais*) = OFris. *hās*, MLG. *hēs, hēsch* (Du. *heesch*), OHG. *heis(i*, (M)HG. *heiser* :– Gmc. **χais(r)az*, **χairsaz*, of unkn. origin.] 1. Rough and deep-sounding, as the voice when affected with a cold, or the voice of a raven or frog; husky, croaking, raucous. 2. *transf.* Having a hoarse voice or sound OE. 3. quasi-*adv.* 1709.

1. His voice was h. and lowe 1584. The Tides with their h. Murmurs DRYDEN. 2. The h. Raven..croaking DRYDEN. The h. storm 1765. Hence **Hoa·rsely** *adv.* with a h. voice or sound. **Hoa·rsen** *v.* to make or become h. **Hoa·rseness**, the quality or condition of being h.

Hoar-stone. [In OE. two wds.: see HOAR *a.* and STONE.] 1. *lit.* A hoar, i.e. grey or ancient stone. OE. only. 2. *spec.* a. An ancient boundary stone OE. b. A stone of memorial; a standing stone 1666.

Hoary (hōᵊ·ri), *a.* 1530. [f. HOAR *a.* or *sb.* + -Y[1]. Cf. *dusky, haughty, vasty.*] 1. Grey or white with age; grey-haired 1573; ancient 1609. 2. Grey, greyish white 1573. †3. Mouldy, musty; corrupt –1693. 4. *Bot.* and *Entom.* Covered with short dense white or whitish hairs; canescent 1597.

1. Thou shalt rise vp before the h. head *Lev.* 19:32. The h. sinner FREEMAN. Windsor's h. towers COWPER. 2. The h. poplars HEBER.

Hoast (hōᵘst), *sb.* Chiefly *n. dial.* [ME. *host* – ON. *hóste* cough = MLG. *hōste*, MDu. *hoeste*, OHG. *huosto* (G. *husten*) :– Gmc. **χwōston*. Continuity with OE. *hwōsta* cannot be made out.] A cough. So **Hoast** *v.* to cough.

Hoatzin: see HOACTZIN.

Hoax (hōᵘks), *v.* 1796. [prob. contr. f. HOCUS.] *trans.* To deceive by an amusing or mischievous fabrication or fiction; to play upon the credulity of. Also *absol.* Hence **Hoax** *sb.* an act of hoaxing; a humorous or mischievous deception with which the credulity of the victim is imposed upon. **Hoa·xer,** one who hoaxes.

Hoazin: see HOACTZIN.

Hob (hǫb), *sb.*[1] ME. [By-form of *Rob*, short for *Robin, Robert*; now dial. except as in HOBGOBLIN; cf. HICK *sb.*[1], HODGE.] 1. Formerly a generic name for: A rustic, a clown. 2. = Robin Goodfellow or Puck; a hobgoblin, sprite, elf 1460.

2. From elves, hobs, and fairies..Defend us, good Heaven FLETCHER.

Hob, *sb.*[2] 1511. [Earliest form *hubbe* (XVI), prob. identical with HUB.] 1. In a fire-place, the part of the casing having a surface level with the top of the grate. Formerly also *hub.* 2. A (rounded) peg or pin used as a mark in games, *esp.* in quoits 1589. 3. (Also *hub.*) 'A hardened, threaded spindle, by which a comb or chasing-tool may be cut' (Knight) 1873. 4. Short for HOBNAIL. 1828.

Hob, in *hob a nob, hob and nob, hob or nob*: see HOB-NOB.

Hobbesian (hǫ·bziăn), *a.* 1776. [f. Thomas *Hobbes* (1588–1679); see -IAN.] Of or relating to Hobbes or his philosophy. Hence **Ho·bbesianism** = HOBBISM.

†**Hobbinoll, hobinoll.** 1579. [app. f. *Hob, Hobby*, or *Hobbin* = 'rustic' + NOLL noddle.] The name of a shepherd in Spenser's *Shepherd's Calendar*; hence, A countryman, rustic, boor –1652.

Hobbism (hǫ·biz'm). 1691. [f. *Hobb(es* (see HOBBESIAN) + -ISM.] The philosophy or principles of Thomas Hobbes. So **Ho·bbist,** an advocate of H., a disciple of Hobbes 1681.

Hobble (hǫ·b'l), *sb.* 1727. [f. HOBBLE *v.*] 1. The action of hobbling; an uneven, clumsy, infirm gait. Also *fig.* of utterance. 2. An awkward or perplexing situation (*dial.* and *colloq.*) 1775. 3. Anything used for hobbling horses, etc.; *transf.* a fetter 1831. 4. (In full *h.-skirt*) A close-fitting skirt so narrow at the bottom as to impede the wearer in walking 1911.

Hobble (hǫ·b'l), *v.* ME. [prob. of LG. origin (cf. early Du. *hobbelen* toss, rock from side to side, halt, stammer), frequent. of *hobben*. In sense 6 a var. of earlier HOPPLE.] 1. *intr.* To move unsteadily up and down in riding, floating, etc. 2. To walk lamely and with difficulty; to limp ME. 3. *fig.* To proceed irregularly and haltingly in action or speech; (of verse) to 'limp' 1522. 4. To cause to limp (*lit.* and *fig.*) 1870. 5. *trans.* To nonplus 1762. 6. = HOPPLE *v.* 1831.

2. I now h. about the garden with a stick MME. D'ARBLAY. 3. She hobbles in alternate verse M. PRIOR. 6. The horses were hobbled, by a cord from the fore to the hind foot 1835. Hence **Ho·bblingly** *adv.* lamely.

Ho·bble-bush. 1842. [Of unkn. origin.] The N. American Wayfaring-tree, *Viburnum lantanoides*, a small shrub with cymes of white flowers and purple berries.

Hobbledehoy (hǫ·b'ldĭhoi:), **hobbadehoy** (hǫ·bă-), **hobbedehoy** (hǫ·bĭ-). *colloq.* 1540. [Of unkn. origin.] A youth between boyhood and manhood, a stripling; *esp.* a clumsy or awkward youth. Also *transf.* Also *attrib.*

Why he's a mere hobbledehoy, neither a man nor a boy SWIFT. Hence **Hobbledehoy·dom, Hobbledehoy·hood,** the age or condition of a h. var. **Hob(b)letehoy.**

Hobbler[1] (hǫ·blǝɹ). *Obs.* exc. *Hist.* ME. [– AFr. *hobeleor, -lour* = AL. *hobellarius* (XIII), obscurely derived from late ME. *hobyn* HOBBY *sb.*[1] whence AL. *hobinus* (XIII).] A retainer bound to maintain a hobby for military service; a soldier who rode a hobby, a light horseman. ¶Erron. used by Scott for *hobby.*

Hobbler[2] (hǫ·blǝɹ). 1594. [f. HOBBLE *v.* + -ER[1].] 1. A person that hobbles in his gait 1665. †2. A child's top that spins unsteadily –1878. 3. An unlicensed pilot; also, a man on land employed in towing vessels by a rope 1800.

Hobby (hǫ·bi), *sb.*[1] [Earliest forms *hobyn, hoby*, i.e. *Hobin, Hobby* by-forms of the Christian name *Robin* (cf. HOB *sb.*[1]). See also HOBBLER[1], DOBBIN.] 1. A small or middle-sized horse; an ambling or pacing horse; a pony. Now *Hist., arch.,* or *dial.* †2. = HOBBY-HORSE 2. –1820. 3. = HOBBY-HORSE 4. 1689. 4. A favourite occupation or topic, pursued for amusement, and which is compared to the riding of a toy horse (sense 3); an individual pursuit to which a person is unduly devoted. Formerly HOBBY-HORSE (sense 5). 1816.

4. I quarrel with no man's h. SCOTT.

Hobby (hǫ·bi), *sb.*[2] 1440. [– OFr. *hobé, hobet*, dim. of *hobe* small bird of prey, rel. to Fr. *hobereau*, OFr. *hobel, hober(e)t*; cf. med.L. *hobetus, hobelus, oberus* (XIII); of unkn. origin.] A small species of falcon, *Falco subbuteo*, formerly flown at larks and other small birds. Hence †**Hobby** *v.* to hawk with a h. SKELTON.

Hobby-horse. 1557. [f. HOBBY *sb.*[1] + HORSE.] †1. = HOBBY *sb.*[1] 1. –1614. 2. A figure of a horse, made of wickerwork, or the like, fastened about the waist of one of the performers in a morris-dance, or on the stage, who executed various antics in the character of a horse; also, the name of this performer. †3. *transf.* a. A foolish person, jester, buffoon. b. A lustful person; a prostitute. –1616. 4. A stick with a horse's head which children bestride as a horse 1589; a wooden horse 1741. 5. A favourite pursuit or pastime; = HOBBY *sb.*[1] 4. Now *rare.* 1676.

1. Prov. *The hobby-horse is forgot*: app. a phrase from some old ballad. *L. L. L.* III. i. 30. 3. *L. L. L.* III. i. 31. 5. Almost every person hath some hobby horse or other HALE. Hence **Hobby-ho·rsical** *a.* (*joc.*), belonging or devoted to a hobby, crotchety, whimsical.

Hobgoblin (hǫ·bgǫblin), *sb.* (*a.*) 1530. [f. HOB *sb.*[1] 2 + GOBLIN.] 1. A mischievous, tricksy imp or sprite; another name for Robin Goodfellow; hence, a terrifying apparition, a bogy 1530. 2. *fig.* A bugbear 1709. 3. *attrib.* and *adj.* 1622.

2. A foolish consistency is the h. of little minds EMERSON. 3. H. terrors 1628.

Hobiler, var. of HOBBLER[1].

Hobits, Hobitzer, vars. of HOWITZ, HOWITZER.

Hobnail (hǫ·bnēⁱl), *sb.* 1594. [f. HOB *sb.*[2] + NAIL.] 1. A nail with a massive head and short tang, used for protecting the soles of heavy boots and shoes. 2. *transf.* A man who wears hobnailed boots; a rustic, clodhopper 1645. 3. *attrib.* or *adj.* Clownish, boorish 1624.

Comb. **h. liver**, a cirrhotic liver, studded with small prominences resembling hobnails. Hence **Ho·bnail** *v.* to set with hobnails; to trample down as with hobnailed shoes. **Ho·bnailed** *a.* set with hobnails; *transf.* rustic, boorish.

Ho·b-nob, *phr.* and *adv.* 1601. [orig. *hob or nob, hob-a-nob, hob and nob*, f. phr. (drink) *hob or nob*, etc. (see sense 3); continuing *hab-nab, hab or nab* (XVI); see HAB.] 1. phr. *Hob, nob*: have or have not; in Shaks., app. = 'give or take'. 2. *adv.* = *Hab nab* (HAB *adv.* 1); hit or miss; at random 1660. 3. **Hob or nob, hob a nob, hob and nob** (prob. = give or (and) take): used by two persons drinking to each other alternately 1756. b. quasi-*adj.* On terms of good-fellowship 1851.

1. Hob, nob, is his word: giu't or take't *Twel. N.* III. iv. 262.

Ho·b-nob, *v.* 1763. [From the adv. phr.; see prec. 3.] 1. *intr.* To drink to each other, drink together. 2. To hold familiar intercourse, be on familiar terms *with* 1828.

Ho·b-nob, *sb.* 1761. [f. as prec.] †1. A 'sentiment' used in hob-nobbing –1770. 2. A drinking to each other or together 1825.

Hobo (hōᵘ·bo). *U.S.* 1891. [Of unkn. origin.] A tramp.

Hoboe, hoboy, vars. of HAUTBOY.

Hobson's choice: see CHOICE *sb.*

Hob-thrush, Hob-thrust. *Obs.* exc. *dial.* 1590. [f. HOB *sb.*[1] + OE. *þyrs*, ON. *þurs* giant, goblin.] 1. A goblin. 2. (In full *h.-l. louse.*) A wood-louse (*dial.*) 1828.

‖**Hocco** (hǫ·ko). 1834. [Native name in Guiana.] A bird of the family *Cracidæ* (Curassows).

Hochheimer: see HOCKAMORE.

†**Hock** (hǫk), *sb.*[1] *Obs.* [OE. *hoc*, now only in HOLLYHOCK.] A name for malvaceous plants, esp. the Common and Marsh Mallow and the Hollyhock –1611.

Hock (hǫk), *sb.*[2] 1540. [Short for †*hockshin* (*hokschyne* XIV), OE. *hōhsinu*; see HOUGH.] 1. The joint in the hinder leg of a quadruped between the true knee and the fetlock, the angle of which points backward. 2. The knuckle end of a gammon of bacon 1706. 3. *attrib.*, as *h. action*, etc. 1641.

Hock (hǫk), *sb.*[3] 1625. [Shortened f. HOCKAMORE.] The wine called in German *Hochheimer*, produced at Hochheim on the Main; hence, commercially extended to other white German wines. Also *attrib.*

Hock, *sb.*[4] 1530. [perh. shortened from *hōk* HOOK.] A rod, stick, or chain, with a hook at the end. EVELYN.

Hock, *v.* 1563. [f. HOCK *sb.*[2]; cf. HOUGH *v.*] *trans.* To disable by cutting the tendons of the hock; to hough, hamstring.

†**Hockamore** (hǫ·kămōᵊɹ). 1673. [Anglicized f. G. *Hochheimer* (*wein*) wine of *Hochheim* on the Main, Germany.] = HOCK *sb.*[3] –1747.

Hock-cart. Now only *Hist.* 1648. [Cf. HOCKEY[1].] The cart which carried home the last load of the harvest.

Hock-day. Now only *Hist.* ME. [Of unkn. origin.] The second Tuesday after Easter Sunday (or, according to some,

Easter week): an important term-day, and, from the 14th c., a popular festival; also *pl.* including the preceding Monday.

†**Hocket.** 1601. [– Fr. *hoquet* hiccup, in OFr. shock, sudden interruption, hitch, f. *hoqueter* (XII).] **1.** = HICKET, HICCUP –1617. **2.** *Mediæval Mus.* An interruption of a voice-part by rests, so as to produce a broken or spasmodic effect. Now *Hist.* 1776.

Hockey[1] (hǫ·ki), **hawkey** (hǭ·ki), **horkey.** 1555. [Origin and etymological form unknown; cf. HOCK-CART.] The feast at harvest-home (*local*). Also *attrib.*

Hockey[2] (hǫ·ki). 1527. [Earliest form *hockie* (XVI), of unkn. origin.] **1.** An outdoor game of ball played with sticks hooked or curved at one end, with which the players of each side drive the ball towards their opponents' goal. **2.** (*U.S.*) The stick used in this game 1839. **3.** *attrib.* (*h.-stick* 1527).

†**Hockle,** *v.*[1] 1668. [app. f. HOCK *sb.*[2], or iterative of HOCK *v.*[1]; see -LE.] To hough, to hamstring.

Hockle, *v.*[2] *local.* ? *Obs.* 1746. [Of unkn. origin.] To cut up (stubble).

Hockmoney. Also *hocking-*. 1484. [f. *hock* in HOCK-DAY + MONEY.] The money collected at hocktide.

Hocktide. *Obs.* exc. *Hist.* 1484. [f. as prec + TIDE *sb.*] The season of the hock days: Hock Monday and Tuesday (the second Monday and Tuesday after Easter-day), long kept as a festival with various traditional customs.

Hocus (hōᵘ·kəs), *sb.* 1640. [Short for *Hocus Pocus,* HOCUS-POCUS.] †**1.** A conjuror –1699; †*transf.* an impostor (SOUTH). **2.** Jugglery, deception. *Obs.* or *arch.* 1652. **3.** Drugged liquor (*mod.*).

Hocus (hōᵘ·kəs), *v.* 1675. [f. prec.; see HOAX.] **1.** *trans.* To 'hoax'. **2.** To stupefy with drugs, esp. for a criminal purpose; hence, to drug (liquor) 1831.

Hocus-pocus (hōᵘ·kəs pōᵘ·kəs), *sb.* (*a.*) 1624. [Based ult. on *hax pax max Deus adimax* (XVI), pseudo-L. magical formula coined by vagrant students.] †**1.** A conjuror, juggler. Also *transf.* a trickster. –17... **2.** Used as a formula (sometimes with allusion to an assumed derivation from *hoc est corpus*) 1632. **3.** A juggler's trick; jugglery; sleight of hand; trickery, deception 1647. **4.** *attrib.* or *adj.* Juggling; cheating, tricky 1668.
1. He opens as Hokus Pocus do's his fists HY. MORE. **2.** The *hocus pocus* of a popish priest cannot turn bread into flesh 1772. Hence **Hocus-pocus** *v. intr.* to juggle; to practise deception; *trans.* to play tricks upon.

Hod (hǫd), *sb.* 1481. [app. a var. of HOT *sb.*[1] in same sense.] **1.** An open receptacle for carrying mortar, bricks, etc.; also the quantity carried in it. **2.** A receptacle for carrying or holding coal. Orig. *dial.* and *U.S.* 1825.
Comb. **h.-bearer, -carrier** = HODMAN, q.v.

Hod, early ME. f. *Had,* -HOOD, condition, etc.

Hodden (hǫ·d'n). *Sc.* 1591. [Of unkn. origin.] **1.** Coarse woollen cloth, as made formerly by country weavers on their hand-looms. Also *attrib.* **2. Hodden grey.** Grey hodden, made without dyeing, by a mixture of fleeces. Applied to cloth having the natural colour of the wool. Hence typical of rusticity. 1724.

Hoddy-doddy. *Obs.* exc. *dial.* 1553. [perh. a nursery reduplication; f. *dod* in DODMAN a shell-snail. The element *hoddy-* also seems to mean 'snail' (or perh. horned).]
A. *sb.* **1.** A small shell-snail (*dial.*). †**2.** A short dumpy person –1723. †**3.** A cuckold, with ref. to the 'horns' (cf. sense 1) –1656.
B. *adj.* **1.** Short and dumpy 1824. **2.** *dial.* Confused, in a whirl 1809.

†**Ho·ddypeak.** 1500. [f. *hoddy* (see prec.) + PEAK *sb.*[3], but the sense is obscure.] A fool, noddle, blockhead –1589.

Hodge (hǫdʒ). ME. [Pet-form of the Christian name *Roger*; cf. HICK *sb.*[1], HOB *sb.*[1]] **1.** As a typical name for the English rustic. **2.** *Jolly Hodge* (also *Jolly Roger*), the pirate's flag bearing the Death's Head and Cross-bones 1822.
Comb. **H.-razor,** a razor made to sell to Hodge; hence, in Carlyle, a sham.

Hodge-podge (hǫ·dʒ,pǫdʒ), *sb.* ME. [Also †*hogpoch* (XV), *hodge-potch* (XVI–XVII), var. of HOTCHPOTCH.] **1.** = HOTCHPOTCH 1. 1622. **2.** *contemptuous.* A clumsy mixture of ingredients 1615. **3.** = HOTCHPOTCH 2. ME. **4.** *attrib.*, as **hodge-podge act,** a legislative act embracing incongruous matters 1602. Hence **Hodge-podge** *v. trans.* to make a hodge-podge of; also *intr.* So †**Ho·dgepot** = HODGE-PODGE 1.

Hodgkin's disease. 1877. [f. Dr. Thomas *Hodgkin* (1798–1866), who first described it.] A disease marked by enlargement of the lymphatic glands and spleen, with progressive anæmia; also called *lymphadenoma.*

Hodiernal (hōᵘdiǝ·ɹnăl), *a.* 1656. [f. L. *hodiernus,* f. *hodie* to-day + -AL[1].] Of or belonging to the present day. So †**Ho·diern** *a.*

Hodman (hǫ·dmæ̆n). 1587. [f. HOD *sb.* + MAN.] **1.** A man who carries the hod; a bricklayer's labourer. Also *fig.* **2.** A term of contempt applied by undergraduates of Christ Church, Oxford, who were King's Scholars of Westminster School, to those who were not, and hence to other undergraduates 1677.

Hodmandod (hǫ·dmæ̆ndǫ:d), *sb.* (*a.*) 1626. [Redupl. var. of DODMAN; cf. HODDY-DODDY.] **1.** A shell-snail, a dodman. Also *fig.* †**2.** Corrupt for HOTTENTOT –1729. **3.** *adj.* Short and clumsy 1825.

Hodograph (hǫ·dograf). 1846. [f. Gr. ὁδός way + -GRAPH.] **1.** *Math.* A curve, of which the radius vector represents in magnitude and direction the velocity of a moving particle. Also *attrib.* **2.** A machine for registering the paces of a horse, etc. (Commonly, but erron., spelt *odograph.*) 1883. Hence **Hodogra·phic** *a.* **Hodogra·phically** *adv.* by means of a h.

Hodometer (hodǫ·mĭtəɹ), **odometer.** 1791. [– Fr. *odomètre,* f. Gr. ὁδός way + *-mètre* -METER.] An instrument attached to the wheel of a vehicle, which records the distance traversed; also a wheel used by surveyors, having a recording apparatus in the centre, and trundled along by a handle. Also applied to a pedometer. So **Hodome·trical** *a.* relating to the measurement of a ship's way, or to a h. **Hodo·metry, odo·metry,** measurement, as by a h., of distances traversed.

Hoe (hōᵘ), *sb.*[1] *Obs.* exc. *dial.* [OE. *hōh, hō,* the same word as the north. HEUGH.] 'A projecting ridge of land, a promontory' (Sweet); a height ending abruptly or steeply. Now only in place-names, etc.
That loftie place at Plimmouth call'd the Hoe DRAYTON.

Hoe (hōᵘ), *sb.*[2] [ME. *howe* – (O)Fr. *houe* – OFrank. **hauwa* = OHG. *houwa* (G. *haue*), rel. to *houwan* HEW *v.* The present form, repl. the normal *how,* was established by XVIII.] **1.** A tool used chiefly for breaking up or loosening the surface of the ground, hoeing up weeds, covering plants with soil, etc. It consists of a thin iron blade fixed transversely at the end of a long handle. **2.** A dentist's excavating instrument, shaped like a hoe 1875.
Dutch h., Scuffle h., kinds of *thrust-hoes,* as dist. from *draw-hoes* (the original type).

Hoe, *sb.*[3] *local.* 1804. [– ON. *hár* (Da. *haa*) dog-fish, shark.] In Orkney and Shetland the Picked Dog-fish, *Squalus acanthias.* Comb. **h.-mother** (contracted *homer*), the Basking Shark, *Selachus maximus.*

Hoe, *v.* ME. [f. HOE *sb.*[2]] **1.** *intr.* To use a hoe; to work with a hoe. **2.** *trans.* To weed (crops), thin *out* (plants), 'cultivate', with a hoe 1693. **3.** To break or stir up (the ground) with a hoe 1712. **4.** with adv. To dig *up,* raise *up,* take *away,* cut *down,* cover *in,* with a hoe 1699.

Hoe-cake (hōᵘ·kēⁱk). *U.S.* 1793. [orig. cake baked on the broad thin blade of a cotton-field hoe (*Cent. Dict.*).] Coarse bread, made of Indian meal, water, and salt, usu. in the form of a thin cake.

Hoe·-plough, *sb.* ? *Obs.* 1733. = HORSE-HOE. Hence as *v.*

‖**Hoey.** 1865. [Chinese (Mandarin dial.) *hūy* (*hūi*), society, club, guild.] A society of Chinese; esp. a secret society.

Hog (hǫg), *sb.*[1] [Late OE. *hogg, hocg*; perh. of Celtic origin (cf. W. *hwch* pig, sow = Cornish *hoch*).] **1.** A swine reared for slaughter; *spec.* a castrated male swine; hence, a swine generally. **b.** *U.S.* Pork 1860. **2.** Used as the name of the species: = SWINE. **b.** Formerly spec. a wild boar of the second year. 1483. **3.** Applied to different species of the family *Suidæ* 1732. **4.** A young sheep that has not yet been shorn ME. **b.** Specialized as *chilver-* or *ewe-h., tup-h.,* etc. 1607. **c.** Short for *h.-fleece, -wool* 1854. **d.** Applied to domestic animals of a year old 1775. **5.** *fig.* A coarse, self-indulgent, gluttonous, or filthy person ME. **b.** *spec.* A road hog (ROAD *sb.*) 1906. **6.** *slang.* A shilling 1673. **7. a.** A sort of broom or brush for cleaning a ship's bottom 1769. **b.** *Paper-making.* A device for agitating the pulp so as to keep it of uniform consistence 1807.
Phrase. *To go the whole h.*: to go all the way, to do the thing thoroughly (*slang*); hence, in derivative uses.
attrib. and *Comb.* **a. h.-cholera,** the swine-fever; **-constable** = HOG-REEVE; **hog('s)-flesh,** pork; **hog('s)-grease,** the lard or fat of a h.; **h.-pen, -pound,** a pigsty; **-ring,** a ring put into the snout of a pig to prevent grubbing; **-wallow,** a hollow in which pigs wallow; also, *spec.* in U.S., a natural depression having this appearance; **-ward,** a swineherd; **hog('s)-yoke,** a frame of wood put round a hog's neck to prevent its getting through hedges.
b. From sense 4 **h.-bull,** a yearling bull; **-colt,** a yearling colt; **-fence,** pasture fenced off for feeding young sheep or 'hogs' during the winter; **-fleece,** the fleece obtained from a 'hog'; **-lamb,** a castrated wether lamb; **-sheep** = sense 4; **-wool** = sense 4 c.
c. In names of animals resembling the hog, or infesting swine, as **h.-ape,** the mandrill baboon, *Simia porcaria*; **-beetle,** a beetle of the family *Curculionidæ*; **-caterpillar,** 'the larva of a Sphinx-moth, *Darapsa myron,* so called from the swollen thoracic joints' (*Cent. Dict.*); **-choke, -choker** (*U.S.*), an American sole, *Achirus lineatus,* of no market value; **-mouse,** the shrew-mouse; **-sucker,** a N. American fish, the Hammer-head, *Hypentelium nigricans*; **-tapir,** the Mexican tapir; **-tick,** a tick parasitic on swine, *Hæmatopinus suis.*
d. In names of plants devoured by, fit for, or left to hogs or swine, as **hog('s)-grass,** Swine's Cress, *Senebiera coronopus*; **hog('s)-meat,** (*a*) *Aristolochia grandiflora,* (*b*) *Boerhaavia decumbens* of Jamaica; **h.-peanut,** a twining plant of U.S., *Amphicarpæa monoica* (N.O. *Leguminosæ*), having purplish flowers and fleshy pea-shaped fruits; **hog's bane,** Goosefoot or Sowbane; **hog's bread,** Sowbread, *Cyclamen*; also = *hog-meat* b; **hog's garlic,** *Allium ursinum*; **hog's madder,** Ragwort, *Senecio jacobæa*; **h.-wort,** *Heptalon graveolens* (N.O. *Euphorbiaçeæ*) of U.S.

Hog, *sb.*[2] *local.* 1790. [Of obscure origin; it varies locally with *hod.*] A heap of potatoes or turnips covered with straw and soil; a 'pit'.

Hog (hǫg), *v.*[1] 1769. [f. HOG *sb.*[1]] **1.** *trans.* **a.** To arch (the back) upward like that of a hog. **b.** To cause (a ship, her keel, etc.) to arch upwards in the centre, as the result of a strain. 1798. **2.** *intr.* To rise arch-wise in the centre, as a ship when the ends droop 1818. **3.** *trans.* To cut (a horse's mane) short, so that it stands up like a hog's bristles 1769. **4.** To make a 'hog' of (a lamb) 1853. **5.** To appropriate greedily (*U.S. slang*) 1887. **b.** *intr.* To behave as a road hog 1925. **6.** To clean a ship's bottom with a 'hog' 1651.

Hog, *v.*[2] 1730. [f. HOG *sb.*[2]] To store (potatoes, etc.) in a hog (see HOG *sb.*[2]).

Hogarthian (hogā·ɹþiăn), *a.* 1798. [f. William *Hogarth* (1697–1764), satirical painter and caricaturist + -IAN.] Of or pertaining to Hogarth, or like his style of painting.

Ho·gback, hog-back. Also **hog's back.** 1661. **1.** A back like that of a hog. **2.** Anything shaped like a hog's back; *esp.* a sharply crested hill-ridge, steep on each side and sloping gradually at each end; a steep ridge of upheaval 1834. **3.** = HOG-FRAME 1886. Hence **Ho·g-backed** *a.* having a back like a hog's; having a rise in the middle like a hog's back.

Hog-brace: = HOG-FRAME.

†**Ho·g-cote.** Also **hog's-cote.** ME. [See COTE *sb.*[1]] A pigsty –1707.

Ho·g-deer. 1771. **1.** Name of two small Indian deer, *Axis porcinus* and *A. maculatus*. **2.** The Babiroussa or Indian hog 1777.

†**Hogen, hogan** (hǭᵘ·gĕn). 1657. [abbrev. of next.]

A. *adj.* **1.** High and mighty; superlatively fine –1733. **2.** Dutch 1710. **B.** *sb.* **1.** A Dutchman; *pl.* the Dutch, the States-General –1672. **2.** Strong drink –1737.

Hogen Mogen (hǭᵘ·gĕn mǭᵘ·gĕn). Also **Hogan Mogan.** 1638. [Perversion of Du. *Hoogmogendheiden*, 'High Mightinesses', the title of the States-General. In transf. senses occ. with small initial letters.]

A. *sb.* †**1.** 'Their High Mightinesses', the States-General of the United Provinces of the Netherlands –1685. **2.** Hence, the Dutch; a Dutchman: contemptuous 1672. †**3.** *transf.* Any high and mighty person. (*joc.* or *contemptuous.*) –1713.

3. White-hall..where our Hogens Mogens or Councell of State sit 1649.

B. *attrib.* and *adj.* **1.** Dutch. (*contemptuous.*) 1658. †**2.** High and mighty. (Often *contemptuous.*) –1705. †**3.** Strong, heady (of drink) –1663.

Hog-fish. 1597. [f. HOG *sb.*^{1} + FISH *sb.*^{1} Cf. G. *meerschwein*, It. †*pesce porco*, Sp. *puerco marino*, OFr. *porpeis*; see PORPOISE.] †**1.** The porpoise or Sea-hog –1686. †**2.** The West African Manatee –1613. **3.** A fish of the genus *Scorpæna*, having bristles on the head 1608. **4.** Also applied to the W. Indian *Lachnolæmus maximus* or *suillus*, having 14 dorsal spines, and the log-perch, *Percina caprodes*, of N. American rivers 1734.

Hog-frame. 1864. *Shipbuilding*, etc. A fore-and-aft frame, usually above deck and forming together with the frame of the vessel a truss to prevent hogging. Also called *hog-brace, hogging-frame.*

†**Ho·ggaster.** [ME. *hogaster* (also AFr. *hogastre*) – med.L. *hogaster, hocgaster* (XII), f. OE. *hogg, hocg* HOG *sb.*^{1} + L. suff. -ASTER as in late L. *porcastra* young pig (Oribasius), med.L. *porcaster* (VIII) piglet.] **1.** A boar in its third year –1831. **2.** A young sheep, a hog or hogget –1706.

Hogged (hǫgd), *ppl. a.* 1764. [f. HOG *v.*^{1} + -ED^1.] **1. a.** Of a ship: Drooping at stem and stern; hog-backed. **b.** Of a road: Raised in the centre. 1769. **2.** Of a horse's mane: Cut off short 1764.

Hogger (hǫ·gəɹ). *Sc.* and *n. dial.* 1681. [Of unkn. origin.] **1.** A stocking without a foot used as a gaiter. **2.** A short piece of pipe used as a connection. Hence *h.-pipe, -pump.* 1851.

Hoggerel, hogrel (hǫ·gərĕl, hǫ·grĕl). 1530. [f. HOG *sb.*^{1} + *-erel* -REL, in AL. *hogerellus* (XIII).] **1.** A young sheep of the second year. †**2.** = HOGGET 1. 1786.

Hoggery (hǫ·gəri). 1819. [f. HOG *sb.*^{1} + -ERY.] **1.** A hog-yard. **2.** Hogs or swine collectively 1856. **3.** Hoggishness (*rare*) 1864.

2. Crime and shame And all their h. trample your smooth world E. B. BROWNING.

Hogget (hǫ·gėt). Also **-it.** 1538. [f. HOG *sb.*^{1} + -ET; in AL. *hogettus* (XIV).] **1.** A young boar of the second year. ? *Obs.* 1786. **2.** A yearling sheep 1538. **3.** A year-old colt (*dial.*) 1787. **4.** *attrib.* 1841.

Ho·ggin. 1852. [Of unkn. origin.] Screened or sifted gravel.

Hogging-frame: = HOG-FRAME.

Hoggish (hǫ·giʃ), *a.* 1548. [f. HOG *sb.*^{1} + -ISH^1.] Of, belonging to, or characteristic of a hog; swinish, piggish; gluttonous; filthy; mean, selfish.

Is not a h. Life the height of some Mens Wishes SHAFTESB. Hence **Ho·ggish-ly** *adv.*, **-ness.**

Hog gum. 1756. [f. HOG *sb.*^{1} + GUM *sb.*^{2}] A kind of gum or resin obtained from various trees in the W. Indies, etc. Hence **Hog-gum tree.**

†**Ho·gherd.** ME. [f. HOG *sb.*^{1} + HERD *sb.*^{2}] A swineherd –1704.

Hog in armour. 1660. **1.** An awkward or clumsy person, stiff and ill at ease in his attire. (Hence Thackeray's 'Count Hogginarmo'.) **2.** The nine-banded armadillo, *Dasypus* or *Tatusia novemcinctus* 1729.

Ho·g-louse. 1587. [f. HOG *sb.*^{1} + LOUSE.] The woodlouse.

Hogmanay (hǫgmăně^i·, -ne^i). *Sc.* and *n.* 1680. [corresp. in meaning and use to OFr. *aguillanneuf* last day of the year, new-year's gift (given and asked for with the cry '*aguillanneuf*') of which the Norman form *hoguinané* may be the immed. source of the Eng. word.] The name given, in Scotland, etc., to the last day of the year, also called 'Cake-day'; the gift of an oatmeal cake, or the like, expected by children on that day; the word shouted by children calling at friend's houses and soliciting this customary gift. Also *attrib.*

Hog mane. 1804. [See HOG *v.*^{1} 3.] The mane of a horse when cut short. Hence **Ho·g-maned** *a.*

Ho·g-nose. 1736. A name given to some N. American species of ugly but harmless snakes of the genus *Heterodon*. More fully *Hog-nose snake.*

Ho·g-nut. 1771. **1.** *U.S.* The Broom Hickory, *Carya porcina*; also its fruit 1829. **2.** The Earth-nut or Pig-nut, *Bunium flexuosum.*

†**Hogo** (hǭᵘ·go). See also HAUT-GOÛT. 1649. [prop. *hogoo*, anglicized sp. of Fr. *haut goût* high flavour.] **1.** = HAUT-GOÛT 1. –1688. **b.** A high or putrescent flavour; a taint; a stench, stink. Also *fig.* –1852. **2.** = HAUT-GOÛT 3. –1736. Hence †**Hogo'd** *a.* 1663.

Ho·g-plum. 1697. **1.** The fruit of the species *Spondias*, esp. *S. lutea*, a common food for hogs in the W. Indies, etc. Also the tree, more fully called *Hog-plum tree.* **b.** In N. America applied to the wild-lime of Florida (*Ximenia*), the Chickasaw plum (*Prunus angustifolia*), etc. 1889.

Ho·g-reeve. *U.S.* 1689. [f. HOG *sb.*^{1} + REEVE *sb.*^{1}] An officer charged with the prevention or appraising of damages by stray swine. Formerly a town officer in New England.

Ho·g's bean, ho·g-bean. 1866. *Herb.* A tr. of the word *Hyoscyamus.*

Ho·g-score. Also **hog's score.** 1787. *Curling.* A distance-line drawn across the rink at about one-sixth of the rink's length from the tee, which a stone must cross in order to count. Also *fig.*

Hog's fennel. 1585. A name for some weeds with fennel-like leaves: **a.** Sow-fennel, *Peucedanum officinale*; **b.** Mayweed, *Anthemis cotula.*

Hogshead (hǫ·gzhed). ME. [f. *hog's* poss. of HOG *sb.*^{1} + HEAD. The reason for the name is unkn.] **1.** A large cask for liquids, etc.; *spec.* one of a definite capacity, which varied for different liquids and commodities. **2.** Hence, Such a caskful of liquor; a liquid measure containing 63 old wine-gallons (= 52½ imperial gallons). Abbrev. hhd. 1483. **b.** Of other commodities: A cask of varying capacity, in later use holding from 100 to 140 gallons 1491. **3.** Applied allusively to a person 1515.

3. His jabberment in Law, the flashiest and the fustiest that ever corrupted in such an unswill'd h. MILT.

Ho·g-skin, ho·gskin. 1700. **1.** The skin of a hog; leather made of this, pigskin; chiefly *attrib.* 1705. **2.** The skin of a hog used as a wine-bottle.

Hog's pudding. 1614. The entrail of a hog, variously stuffed with oatmeal, suet, tripe, etc., or with flour, currants, and spice.

Ho·gsty. Also **hog's sty.** 1475. A pigsty.

Ho·g-tie, *v.* *U.S.* 1894. [f. HOG *sb.*^{1} 1.] *trans.* To secure by tying the four feet, or the hands and feet, together.

Hog-trough (hǫ·gtrǫ̀f). Also **hog's trough.** 1530. A trough for hogs to feed out of. **b.** = *hog-wallow* (see HOG *sb.*^{1}) 1807.

Ho·g-wash. Also **hog's wash.** 1440. [See WASH *sb.* III. 3.] Swill given to pigs.

Ho·gweed. 1707. A name given to herbs pleasing to, or fit only for, hogs; e.g. in England, to Cow-parsnip, *Heracleum sphondylium*; in *U.S.*, to *Ambrosia artemisiæfolia.*

Hohl-flute (hǭᵘ·lflūt). 1660. [– G. *hohlflöte*, lit. hollow flute.] An open 8-ft. flute-stop on an organ, having a soft hollow tone.

Hoi, *int.* **Hoiden:** see HOY, HOYDEN.

Hoick (hoik), *v.* *slang* or *colloq.* 1907. [perh. var. HIKE *v.* (sense 2).] **1.** *trans.* To lift up or hoist, esp. with a jerk. **2.** To force (an aeroplane) to climb up steeply 1918.

Hoicks (hoiks), **hoick** (hoik), *interj.* 1607. [Earlier *hoika, hoic a* (with the hound's name), app. var. of *hyke a* (Turberville). Cf. YOICKS.] A call used in hunting to incite the hounds. Also *transf.* Hence **Hoicks (hoick)** *v. trans.* to incite with 'hoicks!'; *intr.* to 'hark *back*'.

‖**Hoi polloi** (hoi pǫ·loi). 1837. [Gr. οἱ πολλοί the many.] The masses, the rabble.

Hoise (hoiz), *v.* *Obs.* exc. *dial.* 1450. [Early forms were *hyse, hysse* (XV), Sc. *heis* (XVI), prob. – Du. *hijschen* or LG. *hissen, hiesen* (whence also Fr. *hisser*), but the Eng. forms are earlier than any cited from elsewhere. The word appears early as an int. used in hauling: Eng. *hissa, heisau*, Sp. *hiza*, etc. The change in the stem-vowel from *ī* to *oi* is paralleled by *foist, joist.* Cf. HEEZE.] **1.** *trans.* To raise by means of tackle or other mechanical appliance. Orig. *nautical*; often with *up.* 1490. **2.** To raise aloft, lift up; cf. HEEZE *v.* 1548. †**3.** To exalt, elevate; to raise in amount or price –1730. †**4.** To lift and remove –1750. †**5.** *intr.* (for *pass.*) To rise –1570.

1. We..hoissed sailes for Sidon 1615. The kettle to the top was hoist SWIFT. **2.** Phr. *Hoist with his own petard* (Shaks.): blown into the air with his own bomb; hence, injured or destroyed by his own device for the ruin of others. Hence **Hoi·ser,** one who or that which hoises. **Hoise** *sb.* a lift.

Hoist, *sb.* 1654. [f. HOIST *v.*] **1.** An act of hoisting; a lift. **2.** Something hoisted; *Naut.* a number of flags hoisted together as a signal 1805. **3.** An elevator, a lift, etc. 1835. **4.** *Naut.* **a.** The middle part of a mast. **b.** The perpendicular height of a sail or a flag. **c.** The fore edge of a staysail. 1764.

2. As the last h. was handed down Nelson turned to Captain Blackwood..with 'Now I can do no more' 1805.

Hoist (hoist), *v.* 1548. [alt. of HOISE *v.*, perh. through taking the pa. t. and pa. pple. as the stem-form (cf. *hoist*, SHAKS. Haml. III. iv. 207, *hoised*, Acts 27:40).] **1.** *trans.* To raise aloft; to set or put up. (Also with *up.*) **b.** *spec.* To lift up on the back of another in order to receive a flogging 1719. **2.** = HOISE *v.* 1. 1578. †**3.** = HOISE *v.* 4. –1762. †**4.** To overtax –1611. **5.** = HOISE *v.* 5. 1647.

1. *Ant. & Cl.* IV. xii. 34. We saw the two forts h. their colours 1748. **2.** Phr. *To h. down*: to lower.

Hoist-, in comb.: **hoistaway** (*U.S.*), a mechanical lift or elevator; **h.-bridge,** a form of drawbridge, in which the leaf or platform is raised; **-hole,** an opening through which things are hoisted; **-rope; -way** (*U.S.*) = *hoist-hole*, the shaft of a lift or elevator.

Hoit, *v.* *Obs.* or *dial.* Also **hoyt.** 1594. [Of unkn. origin. The two senses are unconnected.] **1.** *intr.* 'To indulge in riotous and noisy mirth' (Nares); to act the hoyden. **2.** To limp. *Sc.* 1693.

Hoity-toity (hoi·ti toi·ti), *sb., adj., adv., interj.* 1657. [Rhyming jingle f. prec. Also HIGHTY-TIGHTY (*a* 1700).] **A.** *sb.* **1.** Riotous or giddy behaviour; disturbance; flightiness. Also **b.** Assumption of superiority, huffiness. **2.** A hoyden, romp (*dial.*) 1719. **B.** *adj.* Frolicsome, giddy. Also **b.** 'Assuming, haughty, huffy. 1690. †**C.** *adv.* In a frolicsome or giddy manner –1763. **D.** *interj.* An exclam. of surprise or contempt, esp. at flighty or unduly assuming speech or action 1695.

†**Hoker,** *sb.* [OE. *hocor*; perh. related to OE. *hux, husc* 'mockery', root *huc-, hoc-*.] Mockery, derision; scorn; abuse –ME. Hence †**Hoker** *v.* to mock, scorn, revile. †**Ho·kerful** *a.*, scornful. †**Ho·kerly** *adv.* scornfully, mockingly, contemptuously.

Hoker moker, obs. f. HUGGER-MUGGER.

Hokum (hǭᵘ·kəm). orig. *U.S. Theatrical slang.* 1922. [perh. a blending of HOCUS-POCUS and BUNKUM.] Theatrical speech, action, etc., designed to make a sentimental or melodramatic appeal to an audience; hence, bunkum.

Hol, obs. var. of WHOLE.

Holarctic (holā·ɹktik), *a.* 1883. [f. Gr.

ὅλος whole (HOLO-) + ARCTIC.] In the Geographical Distribution of Animals: Of or pertaining to the entire northern or arctic region, as the H. region, or H. family of birds.

Hold, *sb.*[1] OE. [f. HOLD *v.*, and partly – ON. *hald* hold, fastening, support, custody.] **I. 1.** The action or an act of holding, keeping in hand, or grasping; grasp. Also, an opportunity of holding, occas. almost *concr.*, something to hold by. (The main current sense.) **2.** *fig.* A grasp which is not physical ME. **3.** Confinement, custody, imprisonment (*arch.*) ME. †**4.** Contention, struggle; resistance –1654.

1. Phr. *To catch, get, lay, lose, take h. In holds* (Wrestling, etc.), at grips. Let go thy h. *Lear* II. iv. 73. **2.** Tarry Iew, The Law hath yet another h. on you *Merch. V.* IV. i. 347. Phr. *Keep a good h. of the land*, i.e. keep as near it as can be done with safety.

II. *concr.* †**1.** Property held; a holding; *spec.* a tenement. Cf. COPYHOLD, etc. –1590. **2.** A place of refuge or shelter; a lurking-place ME. **3.** A fort or fortress; a STRONGHOLD (*arch.*) ME. **4.** Something which is laid hold of, or by or with which anything is laid hold of 1578; a thing that holds something 1517. †**5.** *Mus.* The sign now called a pause 1674. **6.** A prison-cell 1717.

2. *Cymb.* III. iii. 20. **3.** Some greater Roman h. LYTTON. **4.** *John* III. iv. 138. Locks, or Holds for water PLOT.

Hold (hō^{u}ld), *sb.*[2] 1591. [alt., by assim. to HOLD *v.*, of HOLL *sb.*, HOLE *sb.*] The interior cavity in a ship or vessel below the deck (or lower deck), where the cargo is stored.

Sixe foote water in h. RALEGH.

Hold, *sb.*[3] Now only *Hist.* [– ON. *hǫldr*, identified with OE. *hæleð*, G. *held*, in Norse law 'a kind of higher yeoman, the owner of allodial land', *poet.* a 'man'.] In OE. times, an officer of rank in the Danelaw, corresponding to the High Reeve among the English.

Hold (hō^{u}ld), *v.* Pa. t. **held;** pa. pple. **held,** *arch.* **holden** (hō^{u}·ld'n). [OE. *haldan* (*healdan*) = OFris. *halda*, OS. *haldan* (Du. *houden*), OHG. *haltan* (G. *halten*), ON. *halda*, Goth. *haldan*; Gmc. orig. redupl. str. vb. with the primitive sense 'watch (cf. BEHOLD), look after', 'pasture (cattle)', as in Gothic (tr. βόσκειν, ποιμαίνειν, retained in the sense of keeping flocks in OE. *heorde, scēp healdan*.] **I.** *trans.* †**1.** To keep watch over, keep in charge, herd, 'keep' (sheep, etc.); to rule (men). Only in OE. and early ME. **2.** To keep from getting away; to keep fast, grasp OE. **3.** To keep from falling, to sustain or support OE. **b.** In pregnant sense: To hold so as to keep in position, guide, control, or manage 1577. †**c.** To endure, 'stand' –1664. **4.** To carry, sustain, bear (the body, or a member) ME. **5.** To have or keep within it; to retain (fluid, etc.); *esp.* to contain (so much); to have capacity for OE. **6.** To have or keep as one's own; to own, as property; to be in possession or enjoyment of OE. **b.** To occupy (a position, office, quality, etc.) ME. **c.** *Mil.* To keep forcibly against an adversary, defend; to occupy OE. **d.** To occupy, be in (a place); to retain possession or occupation of ME. **e.** *fig.* Of disease, error, etc.: To possess, affect, occupy ME. **7.** To keep, preserve, retain; not to let go; to rivet the attention of. Also with complement. OE. †**b.** To continue to occupy; to 'keep' –1795. **8.** To keep together, to carry on; to perform (any function); to keep (company, silence, etc.); to use (language) habitually and constantly OE. †**9.** To keep unbroken or inviolate; to observe, abide by; the opposite of *to break* or *violate* –1625. **10.** To oblige, bind, constrain. *Obs.* or *arch.* ME. **11.** To keep back from action, hinder, prevent, restrain. *Obs.* or *arch.* exc. in special phrases. OE. **12.** To have or keep in the mind, entertain OE. **b.** With objective clause: To think, consider, believe (*that*) ME. **c.** To think, consider, esteem. Const. with simple compl. or (*arch.*) with *as, for*, or with infin. ME. **d.** Of a judge or court of law: To decide 1642. **e.** To have in a specified relation to the mind or thought; e.g. *to hold in esteem* ME. †**13.** To offer as a wager; to 'lay' –1768. †**b.** To accept as a wager –1626. ¶**14.** *Billiards.* = HOLE *v.* II. 2. [A corruption of *hole*, by association of *holed* and *hold*.] 1869.

2. *Tr. & Cr.* V. iii. 59. A..boy rushed up..to h. the rector's horse 1892. **b.** *U.S.* To keep back, detain (in custody), keep under arrest 1891. **3.** Ten brode arowis hilde he there CHAUCER. To h. good trumps 1879, the baby 1898. **b.** To h. the Plow B. GOOGE, a musket 1631. **c.** To h. compare WALLER. **5.** More diuels then vaste hell can h. *Mids. N.* V. i. 9. This jug holds two pints (*mod.*). **6.** Phr. *To have and to h.*: see HAVE *v.* Farms are held on a variety of tenure 1844. **b.** To h. a place during good behaviour 1809, land of a superior lord CRUISE, a title by diploma SCOTT. **7.** To h. the breath PURCHAS. She..found herself held by his eyes 1885. To h. to a Promise SHAKS., at bay 1892. **b.** She halt hire chambre CHAUCER. **8.** To h. converse CARY, a meeting 1840. **10.** So we..turned back, being holden (= BEHOLDEN) to the gentleman PEPYS. **11.** Phr. *To h. one's* TONGUE. **12.** The Church of England holds the three creeds as well as we 1667. **d.** The Court..held that the plea to its jurisdiction was insufficient 1863.

II. *intr.* and *absol.* **1.** To do the act of holding; to keep hold; to cling ME. †**b.** In the imper., used in offering; = Here! take it! [= Fr. *tiens*.] –1605. **c.** *Comm.* To retain goods, etc.; not to sell 1890. **d.** Of a female animal: To retain the seed; to conceive. Also *to h. to* (the male). 1614. **2.** Of things: To maintain connection; not to give way or become loose ME. **3.** To remain attached; to adhere, keep, 'stick' *to*; to abide *by* ME. **4.** To have capacity or contents; *spec.* Of a covert: To contain game 1581. **5.** To derive title to something (*of* or *from*) ME. †**b.** To be held (*of* or *from*) –1665. **6.** To depend; to belong or pertain. Now only as *fig.* from prec. ME. **7.** To maintain one's position; of a place, to be held or occupied; to hold out OE. **8.** To continue in a state or course; to last, endure ME.; to be or remain valid; to subsist; to apply ME. **9.** To continue to go, keep going, go on, or make one's way 1450. **10.** To take place, be held; to occur, prevail 1461. **11.** (for *refl.*) To restrain oneself, refrain (*from*); to stop. Often in *imper.* as an exclam.: = Stop! *arch.* 1589. **12.** In shooting: To aim 1881.

1. There was no anchor, none, To h. by TENNYSON. **b.** Hold, there's money for thee SHAKS. **2.** The lashings held bravely 1891. **3.** Hee will holde to the one, and despise the other *Matt.* 6:24. **5.** As thou doest h. of thy kyng, so doth thy tenaunt holde of the 1550. **b.** My crown is absolute, and holds of none DRYDEN. **7.** Our force by Land Hath Nobly held *Ant. & Cl.* III. xiii. 170. Phr. *To h. with* (arch. *of*, †*on*, *for*): to maintain allegiance to; to side with; *mod. colloq.* to agree with or approve of. **8.** The frost still held 1888. Phr. *To h. good, true.* **9.** Phr. *To h. on one's way, course.* **10.** Stormy weather again holds in north of Scotland 1892. **11.** Hold..a thought has struck me! SHERIDAN.

Phrases. *To h. at* BAY (*sb.*[4] 4), *to h. one's* BREATH, *to h. a* CANDLE *to, to* HAVE *and to h., to h. the* FIELD, *to h. one's* GROUND, *to h. with the* HARE *and run with the hounds, to h. one's* JAW, *to h. one's* NOSE, *to h. one's* PEACE, *to h. (in)* PLAY, *to h.* SHORT, *to h.* TACK, *to h. one's* TONGUE, etc.: see these words.

Hold..hand. a. *To h. one's hand*: to stay one's hand in the act of doing something; hence *gen.* to refrain. †**b.** *To h. hand*: (*a*) to bear a hand, co-operate; (*b*) to be on an equality *with*, to match. †**c.** *To h. in hand*: to assure (one); to pay attention to; to keep in suspense. **Hold..head. a.** *To h. one's head high*: to behave proudly or arrogantly. **b.** *To h. up one's head* (fig.): to maintain one's dignity, self-respect, or cheerfulness. **Hold one's own.** To maintain one's position, stand one's ground. **Hold water. a.** To stop a boat by holding the blades of the oars flat against the boat's way. **b.** *fig.* To be sound, valid, or tenable; to hold good when put to the test. **Hold wind.** *Naut.* To keep near the wind without making leeway; to keep well to windward; usu. *to hold a good wind.*

With adverbs. **Hold back. a.** *trans.* To keep back. **b.** *intr.* To refrain; to hesitate. **Hold down.** *trans.* to keep down (*lit.* and *fig.*) to keep under, repress, oppress. **Hold forth.** †**a.** *trans.* To offer, propound, set forth, exhibit. ? *Obs.* **b.** *intr.* [from *Phil.* 2:16.] To preach; to discourse, harangue. (Usu. somewhat contemptuous.) **Hold hard.** *intr.* (orig. a sporting phrase): To pull hard at the reins in order to stop the horse; hence *gen.* to 'pull up', halt, stop. Usu. in *imper.* (*colloq.*). **Hold in. a.** *trans.* To keep in, confine; to keep in check. **b.** *intr.* To 'keep in'; to restrain oneself, refrain, keep silence; to 'keep in' *with.* **Hold off. a.** *trans.* To keep off, away, or at a distance: to put off. **b.** *intr.* To keep oneself off, away, or at a distance; to refrain from action; to delay. **Hold on. a.** *trans.* To keep (something) on; to retain in its place on something. **b.** *intr.* To keep one's hold on something; to cling on; also *fig.* **c.** To keep on, continue, go on (rarely *refl.*) **d.** *imper.* Stop! wait! (*colloq.*). **e.** In shooting: To aim directly at. **Hold out. a.** *trans.* To extend (the hand, etc.). †**b.** To exhibit. **c.** *fig.* To proffer. **d.** To represent. **e.** To keep out. Now *rare.* **f.** To keep up. †**g.** To bear to the end. **h.** To occupy or defend to the end. **i.** To maintain resistance; to continue, endure, persist, last. **Hold over. a.** *intr.* (*Law*) To remain in occupation or in office beyond the regular term. **b.** *trans.* To reserve till a later time; to postpone. **Hold together. a.** *trans.* To keep together. *lit.* and *fig.* **b.** *intr.* To continue in union or connection; to remain entire; to cohere. *lit.* and *fig.* **Hold up. a.** *trans.* To keep raised or erect, support, sustain. **b.** *fig.* To support, sustain, keep up. **c.** To offer or present to notice; to exhibit; to present in a particular aspect. **d.** To keep back; in *Cards*, to keep in one's hand. **e.** (orig. *U.S.*) To stop by force and rob on the highway. (From the robbers' 'Hands up or I'll shoot!'). Also, to arrest the progress of (*lit.* and *fig.*). **f.** *intr.* (for *refl.*) To keep up, not to fall: usu. addressed to a horse. **g.** To endure, hold out; in *Hunting*, to keep up the pace. **h.** †To give in; to 'pull up' (*U.S. colloq.*). **i.** To keep from raining; rarely, to cease from raining. (Of the weather, the day, etc.).

Ho·ld-all. 1851. [f. HOLD *v.* + ALL.] A portable case for holding clothes and other articles required by soldiers, travellers, etc.

Ho·ld-back. 1581. [f. *hold back*.] **1.** Something that holds one back; a hindrance. **2.** The iron or strap on the shaft of a vehicle to which the breeching of the harness is attached. Also *hold-back hook*. 1864.

Holder[1] (hō^{u}·ldəɹ). ME. [f. HOLD *v.* + -ER[1].] **1.** One who holds or grasps. **2.** A tenant, occupier, possessor, owner. Often in comb., as *freeholder*, etc. ME. **3.** A contrivance for holding 1833. **4. a.** A canine tooth 1672. **b.** A prehensile organ in some animals 1774. **5.** With adverbs, as **holder-forth,** a preacher, orator (somewhat *contemptuous*); **holder-up,** a supporter; *spec.* a workman who supports a rivet with a hand-anvil or sledge-hammer in riveting 1661. **6.** That of which hold is taken; e.g. the strap by which a carriage window is drawn up 1794.

Holder[2]. 1495. [f. HOLD *sb.*[2] + -ER[1].] A workman employed in a ship's hold.

Holdfast (hō^{u}·ldfɑst). 1560. [f. *hold fast*: see HOLD *v.* I. 2 + FAST *adv.*]

A. *adj.* **1.** That holds fast (*lit.* and *fig.*) 1567. †**2.** Tenacious of what one has 1560.

B. *sb.* **1.** The action or fact of holding fast (*lit.* and *fig.*) 1578. **2.** Something to which one may hold fast 1566. **3.** One that holds fast: †**a.** A miser –1706; **b.** As name for a dog 1599. **4.** Something that holds fast; *spec.* a staple, hook, clamp, or bolt 1576.

Holding (hō^{u}·ldiŋ), *vbl. sb.* ME. [f. HOLD *v.* + -ING[1].] **I. 1.** The action of HOLD *v.* **b.** *spec.* The tenure of land ME. †**c.** Consistency. SHAKS. **2.** That which holds or lays hold 1770. **II. 1.** That which is held: a tenement 1640; property, esp. stocks or shares 1573. †**2.** A tenet –1851. †**3.** The burden of a song –1606.

attrib. and *Comb.* Of or for holding; as **holding-ground,** a bottom in which an anchor will hold, anchorage; also *fig.*; **-note** (*Mus.*), a note sustained in one part while the others are in motion. **H. company,** a trading company having the whole of, or a controlling interest in, the share capital of one or more other companies 1912.

Holding, *ppl. a.* ME. [f. as prec. + -ING[2].] **1.** That holds; retentive; grasping; tenacious. **2.** Applied to animals kept for breeding 1547.

Hold-up. orig. *U.S.* 1837. [See *hold up*, HOLD *v.*] **a.** A check in the progress of a person or thing; a temporary stoppage of traffic. **b.** Detention by force for robbery. Also (for *h. man*), one who robs by 'holding up'. 1885.

Hole (hō^{u}l), *sb.* [OE. *hol*, inflected *hole, holes*, etc. = ON. *hol*, orig. n. sing. of *hol* HOLL *a.*, = OFris., OS., (M)Du., OHG. *hol* (G. *hohl*), ON. *holr*, Gmc. **χulaz* (cf. OHG. *huli*, G. *höhle*, OE. *hylu*, ON. *hola* hollow, hole, *hylr* deep place, pool); ult. f. var. of IE. **kel-* cover, conceal; cf. HELE *v.*, HELL *sb.*, HELM *sb.*[1], HOLLOW *sb.*]

I. 1. A hollow place or cavity in a solid

body; a pit; an excavation made in the ground for an animal to live in; a hollow in the surface of the body, as *arm-hole*. **2.** *transf.* †**a.** A secret place –1688. **b.** A dungeon or prison-cell. Cf. BLACK-HOLE. 1535. **c.** A small dingy lodging or abode; a dirty, untidy, or shabby place 1616. **3.** *fig.* A scrape, 'mess' 1760. **4.** A cavity or receptacle into which a ball or marbles are to be got in various games; hence, in *Golf*, a point scored by the player who holes his ball in the fewest strokes from the tee 1583. **5.** = HOLL, HOLD (*sb.*[2]) of a ship 1483.

1. Hoole, or pyt yn an hylle, or other lyke ME. The foxes have holes *Luke* 9:58. **2. b.** He was clapped up in the H. PEPYS. **3.** I'm in a h. – no end of a h. OUIDA. **4.** *Golf.* Also, the distance between the teeing-ground and the hole to be played 1891.

II. 1. An aperture passing through anything; a perforation, opening, orifice OE. **2.** *fig.* A flaw, fault, ground for blame 1553.

1. Holes to look out to see thy enemyes 1529. **2.** If I finde a h. in his Coat, I will tell him my minde SHAKS. Phr. *To pick a h.* or *holes in* something.

Phrases. *To make a h.* (*in* anything): to use it up largely. *To make a h.* or *holes in*: to shoot. *To make a h. in the water*: see WATER *sb.* 6. *A round peg* (or *man*) *in a square h.*: see PEG *sb.*[1]

Hole (hō^{u}l), *v.* [OE. *holian* = OHG. *holōn*, Goth. *-hulōn*; f. Gmc. *hol-* HOLL *a.*] **I. 1.** *trans.* To make a hole or cavity in; to perforate, pierce. **2.** To sink (a shaft), drive (a tunnel) through 1708. **3.** *Mining.* To undercut (the coal) in a seam so as to release it from the other strata 1829. **4.** *intr.* To make a hole or holes; to dig ME.

1. She [the ship] has holed her bottom 1864.

II. 1. *trans.* To put into or plant in a hole or holes; to put in prison 1608. **2.** *spec.* in *Golf*, etc. To drive (the ball) into a hole or pocket. Also *to h. out.* 1803. **3.** *intr.* To go into a hole 1614.

1. So their prodigal sons are holed in some loathsome jail 1618. **2.** The..accuracy with which they..'h. out' 1867. **3.** The fox..has run to earth, or, as we have it, 'has holed' 1878. Hence **Ho·leable** *a.* (*Golf*).

Hole, -ful, -ly, -some, etc., the early (and etym.) spelling of WHOLE, etc.

Hole: see HOLL *a.*, HULL *sb.*[1]

Ho·le-and-co·rner, *adj. phr.* 1835. Done or happening in a 'hole and corner', or place which is not public; secret, clandestine, underhand. (*Contemptuous.*)

Holed (hō^{u}ld), *ppl. a.* 1481. [f. HOLE *v.* or *sb.* + -ED.] Having a hole or holes.

H. stone, a perforated stone considered to be a monument of prehistoric times 1769.

Holer (hō^{u}·ləɹ). 1829. [f. HOLE *v.* + -ER[1].] *spec.* The collier who holes or undercuts a coal-seam.

Holethnic: see HOLO-.

Holey (hō^{u}·li), *a.* ME. [f. HOLE *sb.* + -Y[1].] Full of holes.

H. dollar, a Spanish dollar out of which a 'dump' had been cut, formerly current in Australia.

Holibut: = HALIBUT.

Holidam(e, early f. HALIDOM.

Holiday (hǫ·lide^{i}), *sb.* [OE. *hāliġdæġ*, late OE. *hālidæġ*, found beside *hāliġ dæġ* as two wds. The uncombined forms are treated under HOLY-DAY.] **1.** A consecrated day, a religious festival. Now usu. HOLY-DAY, q.v. **2.** A day on which work is suspended; a day of recreation or amusement. (In early use not separable from 1.) ME. **b.** *collect. pl.* or *sing.* A vacation ME. **c.** Cessation from work; recreation 1526. **3.** *colloq. Naut.* A spot carelessly left uncoated in tarring or painting 1785. **4.** *attrib.* or as *adj.* Of, belonging to, or used on a holiday; festive; superior to the workaday sort, as *h. clothes, terms, English.* Sometimes: Suited only for a holiday; dainty, idle; trifling. 1440.

2. It is holliday, a day to dance in, and make mery at the Ale house 1577. **b.** At home for the holidays 1806. **c.** Phr. *To make h.*, to cease from work. †*To speak h.*, to use choice language. **4.** A Holy-day Wife, all play and no work 1695. Hence **Holiday** *v. intr.* to take a holiday.

Holily (hō^{u}·lili), *adv.* [OE. *hāliġlīċe*, f. HOLY *a.* + -LY[2].] **1.** In a holy manner; with sanctity or devoutness. **2.** Sacredly, scrupulously; solemnly. Now *rare* or *Obs.* ME.

Holiness (hō^{u}·linės). [OE. *hāliġnes, -nys*, f. *hāliġ* HOLY *a.* + -NESS.] **1.** The quality of being holy; spiritual perfection or purity; sanctity; saintliness; sacredness. **2.** *His Holiness*: a title of the Pope, given orig. to all bishops 1450.

1. Hir herte is verray chambre of hoolynesse CHAUCER. **2.** His H. [Pope Leo] 1858.

Holing (hō^{u}·liŋ), *vbl. sb.* ME. See HOLE *v.*

Holinight (hǫ·linəit). [Nonce-use, after HOLIDAY 2.] A night of pleasure. KEATS.

Holism (hǫ·liz'm, hō^{u}·liz'm). 1926 (J. C. Smuts). [f. Gr. ὅλος whole + -ISM.] The tendency in nature to produce wholes from the ordered grouping of units.

Holk, howk (hō^{u}k, hauk), *v.* Now *dial.* [north. ME. *holk*, cogn. w. MLG. *holken*, LG. *holken, hölken* hollow; f. base of HOLL *a.* + dim. formative *-k*, as in *talk*, etc.] **1.** *trans.* To excavate; to dig out or up. **2.** *intr.* To dig, turn things up 1513.

Holl, *sb. Obs.* exc. *dial.* [OE. *hol*, late OE. and ME. *holl*, n. sing. of *hol* adj. (see next) used subst. Retained chiefly in the north (pronounced hōul, houl); in Sc., *holl* has regularly become *how, howe.* Cf. HOLD *sb.*[2], HOLE *sb.*] **1.** A HOLE OE.; an excavation; a ditch 1701. †**2.** The HOLD of a ship –1627.

Holl (hō^{u}l), *a. Obs.* or *dial.* [OE. *hol* = OFris., OS., OHG. *hol* (Du. *hol*, G. *hohl*), ON. *holr* hollow, concave; cf. Goth. *hulundi* cave, *ushulōn* hollow out; f. Gmc. **χulaz*; see HOLE *sb.*] **1.** Hollow, concave; empty. **2.** Deeply excavated or depressed; lying in a hollow OE.

Holla (hǫ·lă, *rarely* hǫlā·), *interj.* (*sb.*) 1523. [– Fr. *holà*, i.e. *ho* Ho *int.*[2], *là* there. Cf. HALLO, HOLLO.] †**1.** An exclam. meaning Stop! **2.** A shout to excite attention 1588. **3.** A shout of exultation 1727. **4.** Also *holla ho!* [Fr. *holà ho!*] 1596. **5.** *sb.* A shout of *holla!* 1592.

1. Phr. *To cry h.* **2.** H., approach *L. L. L.* v. ii. 900. **4.** H. hoa, Curtis *Tam. Shr.* IV. i. 12. **5.** I thought I heard a h. M. SCOTT.

Holla *v.*: see HOLLO *v.*

Holland (hǫ·lănd). ME. [Du. *Holland*, in earliest sources *Holtlant*, f. *holt* wood + *-lant* land, describing the district about Dordrecht, the nucleus of Holland.] **1.** The name of a province of the Netherlands, now usually extended by foreigners to the kingdom of the Netherlands. **2.** A linen fabric, originally called, from the province of Holland in the Netherlands, *H. cloth.* When unbleached called *Brown H.* ME. **3.** *attrib.* or in *Comb.*: of holland 1554. Hence **Ho·llander,** a Dutchman 1547; also a Dutch ship. **Ho·llandish** *a.* (now *rare*), of or belonging to Holland (province or country); Dutch 1611.

Hollands (hǫ·lăndz), *sb.* 1788. [– Du. *hollandsch* (*ch* mute), in *hollandsch genever*, Hollands gin; see GENEVA[1].] A grain spirit manufactured in Holland: more fully *Hollands gin*, formerly *Hollands geneva.*

Ho·llantide, short for *All-hollantide*, Allhallowtide. 1560.

Holler, dial. and U.S. var. HOLLO.

Hollin, hollen (hǫ·lin, -ėn). Now *arch.* or *dial.* [OE. *holen, holeġn*, ME. *holin*, later *hollen*, Sc. *-in*, rel. to OS., OHG. *hulis* (MHG. *huls*, G. *hulst*), OFrank. **huls* (whence Fr. *houx*), and further to W. *celyn*, Ir. *cuilenn*, Gael. *cuilionn.*] = HOLLY.

Hollo, hollow (hǫ·lō). 1588. [Akin to *holla* and *hallo.*] **A.** *interj.* = HOLLA 2, 3. **B.** *sb.* A shout of *hollo! esp.* in hunting 1598.

Hollo, hollow (hǫ·lō), **holla** (hǫ·lă), *v.* 1542. [conn. w. HOLLA *int.*, HOLLO *int.*; also w. HALLO *int.* and HALLOW *v.*[2]] **1.** *intr.* To shout; to halloo; to call to the hounds in hunting. **2.** *trans.* **a.** With the thing shouted as object 1593. **b.** To call after (in hunting); to shout to 1605.

Phr. *Hollo away*, to drive away by holloing; *h. in, off*, to call in or off (dogs, etc.) by shouting; *h. out*, to shout out.

Holloa (hǫlō^{u}·), *interj., sb., v.* 1666. A form of HOLLO leading on to HALLOA, q.v.

Hollow (hǫ·lo^{u}), *sb.* [OE. *holh* hole, cave, obscurely rel. to *hol* HOLE *sb.*, HOLL *sb.* The *sb.* was formed anew XVI.] **1.** A hollow or concave formation or place, which is, or might have been, dug out; †a hole; †a bore; an excavation; an internal cavity; a void space. **2.** *spec.* A depression on the earth's surface; a valley, a basin 1553. **3.** The middle or depth (of night or of winter) 1865. **4.** Short for *h. moulding, h. plane, h. square*: see HOLLOW *a.* 1726.

1. The h. of a Tree SHAKS., of a Rock 1687. Who hath measured the waters in the h. of his hand? *Isa.* 40:12. **2.** Within the inner compasse and h. of Africke P. HOLLAND.

Hollow (hǫ·lo^{u}), *a.* and *adv.* [ME. *holȝ, holu*, inflected *hol(e)we*, attrib. use of OE. *holh* (see prec.). The origin of B. 2 is unknown.] **A.** *adj.* **1.** Having a hole or cavity inside; empty in the interior; opp. to *solid.* **2.** Having a hole, depression, or groove on the surface; sunken, indented; excavated, concave ME. **b.** Of the sea: Having the troughs between the crests of the waves very deep 1726. **3.** Empty, vacant, void; hence, hungry; lean ME. **4.** *transf.* Of sound: Wanting body; sepulchral 1563. **5.** *fig.* Wanting soundness, solidity, or substance; empty; insincere, false 1529. **6.** [f. the adv.] Complete, thorough, out-and-out (*colloq.*) 1750.

1. A h. tooth 1577, tree 1817. **2.** Our way to it was up a h. lane HAWTHORNE. H. and haggard faces LONGF. **3.** H. Pouerty, and Emptinesse 2 *Hen. IV*, I. iii. 75. **4.** My voice as h. as a ghost's 1798. **5.** Flattering and h. words GIBBON. A h. truce MOTLEY. Hence **Ho·llow-ly** *adv.*, **-ness.**

Comb., etc.: **h.-adz, -auger,** tools with concave face, for curved work; **-bastion,** that which has only a rampart and a parapet, ranging about its flanks and faces, leaving a void space towards the centre; **h. fowl,** 'poultry, rabbits, etc., any meat not sold by butchers' (Halliwell); **h.-ground** *a.*, ground so as to have a concave surface, as a *h.-g. razor*; **h. spar** [tr. Ger. *hohlspat*], CHIASTOLITE; †**h. vein,** the *vena cava*; **h.-way,** a way, road, or path, through a defile or cutting. Also *Hollow* SQUARE, HOLLOW-WARE.

B. *adv.* **1.** In a hollow manner; with a hollow sound. *Obs.* exc. in comb. 1500. **2.** Thoroughly, completely, out-and-out; also (*U.S.*) *all h.* (*colloq.*) 1668.

2. Local opinion would carry it h. J. H. NEWMAN.

Hollow (hǫ·lo^{u}), *v.*[1] late ME. [f. HOLLOW *a.*] **1.** *trans.* To render hollow or concave. Also with *out.* **2.** To form by making a hollow (*in* something); to excavate. Often with *out.* 1648. **3.** *intr.* To become hollow or concave 1860.

1. A rock hollowed out like the entrance to a church 1727. Hollowing one hand against his ear TENNYSON. **2.** A Grotto hollowed in the Rock 1687.

Hollow, *v.*[2]: see HOLLO *v.*

Ho·llow-ey·ed, *a.* 1529. Having the eyes deep sunk in their orbits.

Ho·llow-hea·rted, *a.* 1549. Insincere, false. Hence **Ho·llow-hea·rtedness.**

Ho·llow-root. 1578. [tr. G. *hol-, hohlwurtz*, applied to *Aristolachia*, also to *Corydalis tuberosa.*] **a.** A name for *Corydalis tuberosa* (*C. cava*); also for other species of *Corydalis.* **b.** *erron.* A name for *Adoxa moschatellina.*

Ho·llow-ware. 1416. Bowl- or tube-shaped ware of earthenware, wood, or (now esp.) metal. Also *attrib.*

Holly (hǫ·li). [Reduced form of OE. *holen, holeġn*, ME. *holin*; see HOLLIN.] A plant of the genus *Ilex*; *orig.* and *esp.* the common European holly, *I. aquifolium*, an evergreen shrub or small tree with dark-green tough glossy leaves, having indented edges set with sharp stiff prickles at the points, and bearing clusters of small green flowers succeeded by red berries; much used for Christmas decorations. The American holly, *I. opaca*, is found in the United States from Massachusetts southwards. Also *attrib.*

Comb.: **h.-fern,** *Aspidium* (or *Polystichum*) *lonchitis*, so named from its stiff prickly fronds; **-laurel,** 'the islay, *Prunus ilicifolia*, of California' (*Cent. Dict.*); **-oak,** the holm oak, *Quercus ilex*; **-rose,** †(*a*) an old name for species of *Cistus*; (*b*) *Turnera ulmifolia*, a W. Indian shrub with yellow flowers.

Holly, obs. f. WHOLLY.

Hollyhock (hǫ·lihǫk). ME. [f. HOLY *a.* + HOCK *sb.*[1] mallow; cf. the Welsh name *hocys bendigaid*, app. a transl. of a med.L. **malva benedicta.*] †**1.** *orig.* The Marsh Mallow, *Althæa officinalis* –1614. **2.** Now, The plant *Althæa rosea*, of the same genus as the prec., a native of China and southern Europe; many varieties, with flowers of different tints of red, purple, yellow, and white, are cultivated in gardens 1548. *Comb.* **h.-rose,** an American species of club-moss, *Selaginella lepidophylla,* also called *resurrection-plant.*

Holm¹, holme (hōᵘm). [In sense 1, OE. (poet.) *holm* billow, wave, sea; in sense 2 – ON. *holmr* islet in a bay, lake, or river, meadow on the shore; corresp. to OS. *holm* hill.] †**1.** The sea, the wave. OE. only. **2.** An islet; esp. in a river. Freq. in place-names. OE. **3.** A piece of flat low-lying ground by a river or stream ME.

3. 'Oh! green', said I, 'are Yarrow's holms' WORDSW.

Holm² (hōᵘm). ME. [alt. of *holin* HOLLIN.] **1.** The common holly. Now only *dial.* **2.** The HOLM-OAK 1552.

Comb., as **h.-cock, -screech, -thrush,** local names of the missel-thrush, which feeds on holly-berries.

‖**Ho·lmgang.** 1847. [– ON. *holmganga,* going to the holm' (or islet) on which a duel was fought.] A duel to the death.

Holm-oak (hōᵘ·m,ōᵘk). 1597. [f. HOLM² + OAK.] The evergreen oak (*Quercus ilex*); its foliage resembles that of the holly.

Holm-tree. ME. [f. HOLM².] = HOLM².

Holo- (hǫlo), bef. a vowel **hol-,** comb. f. Gr. ὅλος 'whole, entire; sometimes opp. to *hemi-* or *mero-*. In *Cryst.,* denoting that a crystal or crystalline form has the full number of faces (HOLOHEDRAL, HOLOSYMMETRICAL), or the full number of normals (HOLOSYSTEMATIC), belonging to its system.

‖**Hole·thnos** [Gr. ἔθνος primitives], an undivided stock or race; hence **Hole·thnic** *a.* (less correctly *holo-ethnic*), pertaining or relating to a holethnos. **Holobra·nchiate, -ious** *adjs., Ichthyol.* having complete branchial apparatus: opp. to *hemibranchiate*. **Holoce·phalous** [Gr. κεφαλή] *a.,* having an entire or undivided skull, as the group *Holocephali* of fishes, in which the hyomandibular bone is continuous with the cranium; so **Holoce·phal,** a fish belonging to this group. **Holocry·ptic** *a.,* wholly hidden; *spec.* of a cipher incapable of being read except by those who have the key. **Holocry·stalline** *a.,* wholly crystalline in structure; opp. to *hemicrystalline.* **Holohemihe·dral** *a., Cryst.* having the full number of planes in half the octants. **Holophanerous** (-fæ·nĕrəs) [Gr. φανερός] *a., Entom.* wholly discernible; applied to the metamorphosis of insects when complete. **Holophy·tic** [Gr. φυτόν] *a., Biol.* wholly plant-like; used in reference to the nutrition of certain Protozoa. **Holorhi·nal** [Gr. ῥίν-nose] *a., Ornith.* having the nasal bones slightly or not at all cleft. **Holosiderite** (-si·dĕrəit) [Gr. σίδηρος: see -ITE], a meteorite consisting wholly or almost wholly of iron. **Holo·stean** [Gr. ὀστέον] *a.,* entirely bony; having a wholly osseous skeleton, as the group *Holostei* of ganoid fishes; *sb.* a fish of this group; so **Holo·steous** *a.* = prec. **Holoste·ric** [irreg. f. Gr. στερεός] *a.,* wholly solid; applied to a barometric instrument in which no liquid is employed, as an aneroid. **Holothe·cal** [Gr. θήκη case] *a., Ornith.* having the tarsal envelope entire or undivided. **Holo·trichous** [Gr. θρίξ, τριχ-] *a., Biol.* belonging to the order *Holotricha* of infusorians, which have similar cilia all over the body. **Holozo·ic** [Gr. ζῷον] *a., Biol.* wholly like an animal in mode of nutrition: said of certain Protozoa, in opposition to *holophytic.*

Holoblastic (hǫloblæ·stik), *a.* 1872. [f. HOLO- + -BLAST + -IC; cf. *hypo-, mesoblastic.*] *Biol.* Of an ovum: Wholly germinal; undergoing total segmentation. Opp to. *meroblastic.* So **Ho·loblast,** a h. ovum.

Holocaust (hǫ·lokǭst). ME. [– (O)Fr. *holocauste* – late L. *holocaustum* – Gr. ὁλόκαυστον, f. ὅλος whole + καυστός, var. of καυτός burnt, f. καυ-, base of καίειν burn.] **1.** A sacrifice wholly consumed by fire; a whole burnt offering. **2.** *transf.* and *fig.* **a.** A complete sacrifice or offering. **b.** A sacrifice on a large scale. 1497. **c.** Complete destruction by fire, or that which is so consumed; complete destruction, esp. of a large number of persons; a great slaughter or massacre 1671.

2. c. Like that self-begotten bird..That..lay erewhile a Holocaust MILT. *Sams.* 1702. Louis VII..once made a h. of thirteen hundred persons in a church 1833.

Holograph (hǫ·lograf). 1623. [– Fr. *holographe* or late L. *holographus* – Gr. ὁλόγραφος; see HOLO-, -GRAPH.]

A. *adj.* Of a document: Wholly written by the person in whose name it appears 1669.

B. *sb.* **1.** A letter or other document written wholly by the person in whose name it appears 1623. **2.** *In h.*: wholly in the author's handwriting 1817.

2. Bequeathed..by testament In h. BROWNING. Hence **Holographic, -al** *a.* = A. **Holo·graphy,** writing wholly by one's own hand.

Holohedral (hǫlohī·drăl, -he·drăl), *a.* 1837. [f. HOLO- + Gr. ἕδρα seat, base + -AL¹.] *Cryst.* Having the full number of planes required by the highest degree of symmetry belonging to its system. So **Holohe·drism,** the quality of being h. **Holohe·dron,** a h. crystal or form.

‖**Holometabola** (hǫ·lomĭtæ·bŏlă), *sb. pl.* [mod.L., neut. pl. (sc. *insecta*), f. Gr. ὁλο- HOLO- + μεταβόλος changeable.] *Entom.* The insects which undergo complete metamorphosis. (Usu. called *Metabola.*) Hence **Holometabo·lic, Holometa·bolous** *adjs.*

Holometer (hǫlǫ·mĭtəɹ). 1696. [f. HOLO- + -METER.] A mathematical instrument for making all kinds of measurements.

Holomorphic (hǫlomǭ·ɹfik), *a.* 1880. [f. HOLO- + Gr. μορφή form + -IC.] **1.** *Cryst.* = HOLOHEDRAL. **2.** *Math.* Said of a function which is monogenic, uniform, and continuous 1880.

Holophote (hǫ·lofōᵘt). 1859. [f. HOLO- + Gr. φῶς, φωτός. (The adj. *holophotal* was earlier.)] An optical apparatus, used in light-houses, etc., by which practically the whole of the light from a lamp or other source is collected and made available for illumination. So **Holopho·tal** *a.* reflecting or refracting all, or nearly all, the light 1850. Hence **Holopho·tally** *adv.* **Holophoto·meter,** an apparatus for measuring the whole light emitted from a source.

Holophrastic (hǫlofræ·stik), *a.* 1860. [f. HOLO- + Gr. φραστικός, f. φράζειν tell.] Expressing a whole phrase or combination of ideas by a single word.

Holostomatous (hǫlo,stǫ·mătəs), *a.* 1855. [f. HOLO- + Gr. στόμα, στοματ- mouth + -OUS.] *Zool.* Having the mouth entire; as the division *Holostomata* of gastropod molluscs, having shells of which the mouth is not notched or prolonged into a siphon; or the group *Holostomi* of eel-like fishes, which have all the bones of the mouth fully developed. So **Holo·stomate, Holo·stomous** *adjs.* = prec. **Ho·lostòme,** one of the *Holostomata* or *Holostomi* (see above).

Holosy·mmetry. 1895. [f. HOLO- + SYMMETRY.] *Cryst.* = HOLOHEDRISM. Also **-ic(al** *adjs.*

Ho:losystema·tic, *a.* 1878. *Cryst.* [f. HOLO- + SYSTEMATIC.] Having the full number of normals required by the complete symmetry of its system.

Holothurian (hǫloþiū³·riăn). 1842. [f. mod.L. generic name *Holothuria,* f. *holothuria* (Pliny) – neut. pl. of Gr. ὁλοθούριον, a kind of zoophyte; see -IA², -AN.] **A.** *adj.* Of or pertaining to the genus *Holothuria* or division *Holothurioidea* of Echinoderms: see B. 1878.

B. *sb.* An animal belonging to the division of Echinoderms, of which *Holothuria* is the typical genus; they have an elongated form, a tough leathery integument, and a ring of tentacles around the mouth; a sea-slug, sea-cucumber, or trepang. So **Ho·lothure,** a holothurian. **Holothu·rid, Holothu·rioid** *adjs.* holothurian; *sbs.* a holothurian.

†**Holour.** ME. [– OFr. *holier, holer, huler,* var. of *horier, hourier, hurier* – OHG. *huorari, huareri* whorer, fornicator.] A fornicator; a debauchee –1460.

Holp(e, holpen: see HELP *v.*

Hols (hǫlz), *sb. pl.* 1906. Colloq. (esp. school-children's) abbrev. of *holidays.*

Holsom(e, obs. ff. WHOLESOME.

Holster (hōᵘ·lstəɹ). 1663. [corresp. to and contemp. with Du. *holster,* but the earlier history of neither word is apparent; the base may be Gmc. **χul-* **χel-*; see HELE *v.*] A leather case for a pistol fixed to the pommel of a horseman's saddle or worn on the belt. Hence **Ho·lstered** *a.* bearing holsters BYRON.

Holt¹ (hōᵘlt). [OE. *holt* = OFris., OS., ON. *holt,* (M)Du. *hout,* (O)HG. *holz* :– Gmc. **χultam* :– IE. **kl̥dos,* repr. by Gr. κλάδος twig.] †**1.** Wood, timber. OE. only. **2.** A wood; a copse. Now *poet.* and *dial.* (In many place-names.) OE. **3.** A wooded hill 1567.

2. These holtes and these hayes That han in wynter ded ben and dreye CHAUCER. Wither'd h. or tilth or pasturage TENNYSON.

Holt². ME. [Unexplained var. of HOLD *sb.*¹] **1.** Hold, grasp, grip; support. †**2.** A stronghold –1600. **3.** A place of refuge or abode; an animal's lair or den, esp. that of an otter 1590.

3. An old otter going for a strong h. 1885.

Holus-bolus (hōᵘ·lŏs bōᵘ·lŏs). 1847. [Of dial. origin; presumably burlesque latinization of *whole bolus* or repr. assumed Gr. *ὅλος βῶλος 'whole lump' (see BOLUS).] All in a lump: all at once.

Holw(e, obs. ff. HOLLOW.

Holy (hōᵘ·li), *a.* (*sb.*) [OE. *hāliġ, -eġ* = OFris. *hēlich,* OS. *hēlag, -eg,* OHG. *heilag* (Du., G. *heilig*), ON. *heilagr* :– Gmc. **χailaʒaz,* f. **χailaz* WHOLE.] **1.** Kept or regarded as inviolate from ordinary use, and set apart for religious use or observance; consecrated, dedicated, sacred. **b.** Dedicated or devoted *to.* **2.** Free from sin and evil, morally and spiritually perfect and unsullied OE. **3.** Hence, **a.** Of persons: Specially belonging to, commissioned by, or devoted to God OE. **b.** Of things: Pertaining to God or the Divine Persons; having their origin or sanction from God, or partaking of a Divine quality or character OE. **4.** Conformed to the will of God, entirely devoted to God; of godly character and life; sanctified, saintly; sinless OE.

1. Giue not that which is h. vnto the dogs *Matt.* 7:6. All is h. where devotion kneels O. W. HOLMES. **b.** [The Nazarite] is h. vnto the Lord *Num.* 6:8. H. to your businesse *Meas. for M.* v. i. 388. **2.** For I the Lord am h. *Lev.* 20:26. **3. a.** A h. Prophetesse SHAKS. The holly Bishops 1626. Matthew and Mark and Luke and h. John CLOUGH. **b.** H. scripture ELYOT. **4.** H., faire, and wise is she *Two Gent.* IV. ii. 41. So h., and so perfect is my loue *A. Y. L.* III. v. 99.

Combs., etc.: **H. Alliance:** an alliance formed in 1815, after the fall of Napoleon, between the sovereigns of Russia, Austria, and Prussia, with the professed object of uniting their respective governments in Christian brotherhood 1821. †**H. bone** [tr. L. *os sacrum*]: the SACRUM. **H. brotherhood** [tr. Sp. *Santa Hermandad*]: = HERMANDAD. **H. doors:** in the Greek Church, the doors in the screen which separates the altar and sanctuary from the main body of the church. †**H. oak:** an oak marking a parish boundary, at which a stop-page was made for the reading of the gospel in the 'beating of the bounds' during the Rogation days; called also *gospel-oak, gospel-tree* HERRICK. **H. One:** a holy person; a title of God or Christ; one dedicated to or consecrated by God COVERDALE. **Holy souls:** the souls of the faithful departed, the blessed dead OE. Also *Holy* CHURCH, *H.* CITY, *H.* FAMILY, *H.* FATHER, *H.* GRAIL, *H.* INQUISITION, *H.* LEAGUE, *H.* OFFICE, *H.* OIL, *H.* ORDER, *H.* PASSION, *H.* SATURDAY, *H.* SEE, *H.* SEPULCHRE, *H.* SPIRIT, *H.* SYNOD, *H.* TABLE, *H.* THURSDAY, *H.* WAR: see these words.

b. In names of plants: **h. grass,** a grass of genus *Hierochloe,* esp. *Northern Holy grass, H. borealis,* which is strewn about Catholic churches on festival days; **h. hay,** Sainfoin; **h. tree,** an Indian tree, *Melia azedarach,* also called Pride of India; †**h. wood,** the W. Indian *Guaiacum sanctum.* See also Main Words.

B. *absol.* or as *sb.* **1.** That which is holy OE. †**2.** A holy person: = HALLOW *sb.*¹ –1648. †**3.** *pl.* Devotions. PURCHAS. **4. Holy of holies.** [A Hebraism, rendered in Exod. 26:34 'most holy place', but literally reproduced in LXX and Vulgate, whence in Wyclif, etc.] The 'most holy place', the inner chamber of the sanctuary in the Jewish tabernacle and temple. Also *transf.* and *fig.* 1641. **5.** superl. *Holiest,* used *absol.* **a.** As a title of God or Christ ME. **b.** = Holy of holies: see 4. *Heb.* 10:19.

5. a. Praise to the Holiest in the height J. H. NEWMAN.

†**Ho·ly,** *v.* 1578. [f. HOLY *a.,* instead of the historical HALLOW *v.*¹] To sanctify, consecrate; to canonize –1622.

Holy bread. ME. The (ordinary leavened) bread which was blessed after the Eucharist and distributed to those who had not communicated (Fr. *pain bénit*). In post-Reformation times, The bread provided for the Eucharist.

Holy cross. ME. [tr. med.L. *sancta crux.*] The cross upon which Jesus Christ suffered death (see CROSS *sb.*). Hence in the titles of certain religious societies. **b.** *attrib.* **Holy Cross day,** the festival of the Exaltation of the Cross, September 14th.

Holy-day (hōᵘ·liˌdēⁱ). [OE. *hāliġ dæġ*, two wds.; revived in XIX. See also HOLIDAY, now usu. restricted to the sense 'day of recreation'.] A day set apart for religious observance, usually in commemoration of some sacred person or event; a religious festival. Also *attrib.*

Holy fire. *arch.* ME. [tr. L. *sacer ignis* (Celsus, Vergil).] Erysipelas, St. Anthony's fire; see FIRE *sb.*

Holy Ghost (hōᵘ·li gōᵘ·st). [prop. two words; in OE. *se hālga gāst, hāliġ gāst* tr. eccl. L. *spiritus sanctus*; in ME. often as comb. *haligast, holigost.*] **1.** The Divine Spirit; the Third Person of the God-head, the Holy Spirit. **2. a.** The figure of a dove as a symbol of the Holy Spirit. **b.** The Cross of the Order of the Holy Ghost. 1520. **3.** (Also *Holy Ghost's Root.*) The plant Angelica, *Archangelica officinalis* 1585. **4.** *attrib.*, as in **Holy Ghost flower, plant,** an orchid, *Peristeria elata*, also called *dove-plant*, from the resemblance of part of the flower to a dove 1866.

1. *Order of the Holy Ghost*, a French order of Knighthood (*ordre du Saint-Esprit*), instituted by Henry III in 1578. *Cross of the Holy Ghost*, a cross worn by the knights of this order, having a circle in the middle and on it the Holy Ghost in the form of a dove.

Holy Land. ME. [tr. med.L. *terra sancta*, Fr. *la Terre sainte.*] (with *the*) Western Palestine, or, more particularly, Judæa; so called as being the scene of the life and death of Jesus Christ, and as containing the Holy Sepulchre.

Holy place. 1526. A place that is holy; a sanctuary. *spec.* **a.** The outer chamber of the sanctuary in the Jewish tabernacle and temple. **b.** *pl.* Localities which are objects of pilgrimage in the Greek or Latin Church.

Holy rood (day). *arch.* [OE. *sēo hālige rōd*, tr. med.L. *Sancta Crux*; cf. HOLY CROSS.] = HOLY CROSS (DAY).

Holy stone, holy-stone, *sb.* 1777. [The stones (sense 1) were called *bibles* and *prayer-books* (large and small); cf. Du. *bijbel* (so used) and vb. *psalmzingen* sing psalms, for the operation; said to be so named because the work is done kneeling.] **1.** A soft sandstone used for scouring the decks of ships. **2.** [perh. for *holey stone.*] A stone with a natural hole it it, used as a charm 1825. Hence **Ho·lystone** *v.* to scour with a h.

Holy tide, holy-tide. OE. [See TIDE *sb.* I. 4.] A day or season of religious observance.

Holy water. [OE. *hāliġwæter*, ME. *haliwater*; tr. eccl. L. *aqua benedicta* 'blessed water', in Fr. *eau bénite.*] **1.** Water blessed by a priest and used in various rites. **2.** *attrib.* ME.

1. Provb. *As the devil loves holy water*, i.e. not at all. **2. Holy water sprinkle, †springle,** (*a*) an aspergillum, (*b*) a club armed with spikes, (*c*) a fox's brush. **Holy water †stick, †stock, †stop,** mod. (1793) **stoup,** a stoup or basin for holding holy water, placed near the entrance of a church.

Holy Week. 1710. [After It. *la settimana santa*, Fr. *la semaine sainte.*] The week immediately preceding Easter Sunday.

Holy well. OE. [A combined form occurs in the proper names *Holywell, Hollywell, Halliwell.*] A well or spring reputed to possess miraculous healing properties.

Holy Writ. OE. See WRIT 1 c.

‖**Hom** (hōᵘm). Also **homa.** 1855. [– Pers. *hūm*, also pronounced *hōm* = Skr. *sōma* SOMA¹.] The sacred plant of the ancient Persians and Parsees; also its juice; orig. the same as the SOMA of the Vedas.

Homacanth: see HOMO-.

Homage (hǫ·mėdʒ), *sb.* [ME. *(h)omage* – OFr. *(h)omage* (mod. *hommage*) :– med.L. *hominaticum*, f. L. *homo, homin-* man; see -AGE. Cf. MANRED.] **1.** In *Feudal Law*, Formal and public acknowledgement of allegiance, wherein a tenant or vassal declared himself the man of the king or the lord of whom he held, and bound himself to his service. **b.** An act of homage; a render or money payment made as an acknowledgement of vassalage 1599. **2.** A body of persons owning allegiance; *spec.* in *Eng. Law*, the body of tenants attending a manorial court, or the jury at such a court ME. **3.** *fig.* Acknowledgement of superiority; dutiful respect or honour shown ME.

1. Phr. *To do* (†*make*), *render h.*; *to resign h.*, formally to renounce allegiance. *Feudal h.*, h. paid to the lord. *Liege h.*, h. paid to the king. **2.** With the consent of the 'homage', i.e. of his copyholders 1865. **3.** To do h. and honour to almyghty god 1526. A reluctant h. to the justice of English principles MACKINTOSH. Hence †**Ho·mageable** *a.* bound to render h.

Ho·mage, *v.* 1592. [f. prec. sb.] †**1.** *trans.* To render or pay as a token of homage –1662. †**2.** *intr.* To pay homage –1636. **3.** *trans.* To do homage or allegiance to 1632.

Homager (hǫ·mėdʒəɹ). ME. [– OFr. *homager, -ier*, f. *homage* HOMAGE; see -ER².] One who owes homage or fealty; one who holds lands by homage. Also *fig.* **b.** *spec.* in *Eng. Law*, A manorial tenant 1598.

Thou blushest Anthony, and that blood of thine Is Cæsars h. *Ant. & Cl.* I. i. 31.

Homalographic (hǫ:măloˌgræ·fik), *a.* (*erron.* **homolo-**.) 1864. [f. Gr. ὁμαλός even, level + GRAPHIC.] *Geog.* Delineating in equal proportion; applied to a method of projection in which equal areas on the earth's surface are represented by equal areas on the map.

Homaloid (hǫ·măloid). 1876. [f. as prec. + -OID.] *Geom.* A homaloidal space of any number of dimensions; a flat. So **Homaloi·dal** *a.* of the nature of a plane; flat.

Homarine (hǫ·mărəin). 1880. [f. mod.L. *Homarus*, generic name of the lobster, f. Fr. *homard*; see -INE¹.] **1.** *adj.* Related to or having the characteristics of a lobster. **2.** *sb.* A crustacean of the genus *Homarus*; a lobster.

Homaxonial: see HOMO-.

Homburg (hǫ·mbɒɹg). 1901. [Name of a town in Prussia, where first worn.] In full *Homburg hat:* A man's soft felt hat with narrow brim and dented crown.

Home (hōᵘm), *sb.*¹ and *a.* [OE. *hām*, corresp. to OFris. *hām, hēm*, OS. *hēm* (Du. *heem*), (O)HG. *heim*, ON. *heimr*, Goth. *haims* :– Gmc. *χaim-, of disputed relations.]

A. *sb.* †**1.** A village or town; a vill with its cottages. OE. and early ME. **2.** A dwelling-place, house, abode; the fixed residence of a family or household; one's own house; the dwelling in which one habitually lives, or which one regards as one's proper abode. Occas., the home-circle or household. Also *transf.* OE. **3.** (Without qualifying word or pl.) The place of one's dwelling and nurturing, with its associations 1460. **4.** *fig.* With reference to the grave, or future state ME. **5.** A place, region, or state to which one properly belongs, in which one's affections centre, or where one finds rest, refuge, or satisfaction 1548. **6.** One's own country, one's native land; the place where one's ancestors dwelt 1595. **7.** The seat, centre, or native habitat 1706. **8.** An institution providing refuge or rest 1851. **9.** In games: The place in which one is free from attack; the goal 1855. **10.** *attrib.* and *Comb.*

3. *A h. from h.*, a place away from home which provides home-like accommodation or amenities. **4.** Man goeth to his longe h. *Eccl.* 12:5. **5.** Wherever woman has a tongue, there Mrs. Grundy has a h. LYTTON. **6.** Till then.. Will I not thinke of h., but follow Armes *John* II. i. 31. H. always means England; nobody calls India h. 1837. **7.** Sicily.. was the real h. of bucolic poetry 1886. **8.** The H. for Confirmed Invalids 1863. **9.** Not till the line for h. did he let the great horse [Persimmon] go 1897. **10.** (Freq. in comb. from 16th c.) *h.-ache*, home-sickness 1762.

Phrases. **At home. a.** At or in one's own house. Also *fig.* **b.** In one's own neighbourhood; in one's native land. (Opp. to *abroad.*) In the mother-country. **c.** At one's ease, as if in one's own h.; in one's element. Hence, Unconstrained; familiar *with*, well versed *in*. **d.** = Accessible to visitors. Hence, a formula inviting company to an informal reception. Hence '*not-at-home*'. **From home.** Not at home; abroad. †**Nearer home. a.** *lit.* Nearer one's own dwelling-place or country. **b.** *fig.* In or into closer relation or connection with oneself.

B. *attrib.* or *adj.* **1.** Of, relating to, or connected with, home or one's home; reared, fostered, or carried on at home; proceeding from home; domestic, family 1552. **2.** Near, or surrounding one's home, or the mansion on an estate. Hence, belonging to headquarters, principal; as *h. station.* 1662. **b.** Belonging to a locality in which a sporting contest or match takes place 1886. **3.** Domestic; opp. to *foreign* 1591. **b.** Treating of domestic affairs 1797. **4.** In games: Of, pertaining to, or situated at or near home (see A. 9); reaching or enabling a player to reach home. (Also hyphened.) 1857. **5.** That strikes home; searching, poignant, pointed; effective; to the point, close, direct. Now chiefly in *h. question, h. truth.* (Orig. adverbial (*h.-speaking* = *speaking h.*): see HOME *adv.* 4, 5; separation from the vbl. sb. caused it to be treated as an adj.; hence its extension to other sbs. as in *h. truth.*) 1625.

1. A h. pastime THACKERAY. Family or h. life SMILES. **2.** The h. covers were shot on Friday 1886. Phr. *H. Counties*, the counties nearest London, sometimes including Hertford and Sussex. *H. Circuit*: the assize circuit which has London as its centre; its area has been often changed. **b.** Phr. *H.-and-h. matches*: applied to two matches, one of which is played at the h. or locality of each side. **3.** The h. market 1794, trade 1842. H. politics 1885. **b.** *H. Office*: in Great Britain, the department of the 'Secretary of State for Home Affairs' (abbrev. *H. Secretary*); the building in which its business is carried on. **4.** *The last or h. hole* (Golf). **5.** People who pique themselves on telling h. truths 1843.

Home, *sb.*² *rare.* 1836. = HOMELYN.

Home (hōᵘm), *adv.* OE. [orig. accus. of HOME *sb.*¹, as the case of destination after a vb. of motion; cf. L. *ire domum* go home.] **1.** To one's home (see HOME, *sb.*¹ 2–6, 9). **2.** = Come home, at home after absence 1587. **3.** *Naut.* Towards or into the ship. Hence, of an anchor, away from its hold. 1603. **4.** To the point aimed at; as far as it will go; into or in close contact; closely, directly 1548. **b.** *Naut.* Full in (from the sea), full to the shore 1793. **5.** *fig.* To the very heart or root of a matter; closely, directly, thoroughly 1542. **6.** To 'oneself'; hence, †to one's normal condition 1526.

1. I lugged the money h. DE FOE. The Regent Bedford.. wrote h. to the government in England 1874. **2.** My son will be h. soon 1870. **3.** A sudden gust of wind brought h. our anchor 1748. **4.** Time is precious,..strike quick and h. NELSON. †*To come short h.*: to come to grief. **5.** The charge is.. not brought h. to William FREEMAN. Phr. *To come (go) h. to*: to touch intimately. †*To speak h.*, i.e. plainly and to the point. **b.** *To bring oneself h.*, *to be brought, come, get h.*: to recover oneself (financially), regain one's position. **c.** *Nothing to write h. about*: nothing to boast of. *Comb., as h-going*, etc.; *h-driven*; *h-push*, etc.

Home (hōᵘm), *v.* 1765. [f. HOME *sb.*¹] **1.** *intr.* To go home. **2.** To have one's home, dwell 1832. **3.** *trans.* To establish in a home 1802.

1. One bird [swallow] homed from Paris in ninety minutes 1889.

Home-born, *a.* 1587. [f. HOME *sb.*¹] Born or produced at home; native.

Home-bred, *a.* 1587. [f. HOME *sb.*¹] **1.** Bred or reared at home; native, indigenous; domestic. **2.** Of homely breeding 1602.

1. Foreign invaders or home-bred rebels FREEMAN.

Home-brew. 1853. [f. HOME *sb.*¹ + BREW *sb.*] Home-brewed ale, beer, or other beverage. Also *fig.*

Home-brewed, *a.* 1754. [f. as prec.] Brewed at home or for home consumption. *absol.* = prec. Also *fig.*

Ho·me-coming, *sb.* ME. [f. HOME *adv.* (Replacing ME. *home come.*)] A coming home, arrival at home. So **Ho·me-comer.**

At myn homcomyng CHAUCER.

Home-felt, *a.* 1634. [f. as prec.] Felt 'at home', intimately or in one's heart.

A sacred and home-felt delight MILT.

Ho·me-keeping, *a.* 1591. [f. HOME *sb.*¹] That keeps or takes care of a home; that remains at home.

Home-keeping youth, haue euer homely wits SHAKS. So **Ho·me-keeping** *sb.*

Homeland (hōᵘ·mlænd). 1670. The land which is one's home or where one's home is. Orig. *attrib.* **b.** = HOME *sb.*[1] 6. 1892.

Homeless (hōᵘ·mlės), *a.* 1615. [f. HOME *sb.*[1] + -LESS.] **1.** Having no home or permanent abode. Usu. of persons; hence *transf.* of their condition, etc. **2.** Affording no home 1797. Hence **Ho·meless-ly** *adv.*, **-ness.**

Ho·melike, *a.* 1817. [f. HOME *sb.*[1] + -LIKE.] Like home; suggestive of home; homely.

†**Ho·meling.** 1577. [f. HOME *sb.*[1] + -LING[1].] A home-born inhabitant; a native. Also *attrib.* or *adj.* –1649.

Homely (hōᵘ·mli), *a.* ME. [f. as prec. + -LY[1].] †**1.** Of or belonging to the home; domestic, family –1577. **2.** Familiar, intimate; at home *with.* Now *rare* or *arch.* ME. **3.** Such as belongs to home or is produced or practised at home (esp. a humble home); simple; plain; everyday; unpolished, rough, rude. (Sometimes approbative; but often apologetic, depreciative, or euphemistic for 'wanting refinement, or polish'.) ME. **4.** Of persons, their features, etc.: Plain, uncomely 1590.

2. This goode emperoure was..h. with euery man LD. BERNERS. **3.** Plain h. Terms ADDISON. The garden's homeliest roots BYRON. A dear little h. woman 1863. **4.** Some parts of Man be.. comely, some h. 1619. Hence **Ho·melily** *adv.* **Ho·meliness.**

†**Homely,** *adv.* ME. [f. HOME *sb.*[1] + -LY[2].] **1.** Familiarly –1650. **2.** Kindly –1596. **3.** Plainly, simply; without adornment; rudely, roughly –1697. **4.** Directly home; straight to the point; plainly –1688.

Homelyn (hōᵘ·mlin). 1666. [Of unkn. origin.] A fish, the Spotted Ray, *Raia maculata.*

Home-made, *a.* 1659. [f. HOME *sb.*[1]] Made at home or for home consumption; of domestic manufacture. Also *absol.*

Homeo-: see HOMŒO-.

Homer[1] (hōᵘ·məɹ). 1880. [f. HOME *v.* + -ER[1].] A homing pigeon.

‖**Homer**[2] (hōᵘ·məɹ). Also **chomer.** 1535. [– Heb. *ḥōmer* 'heap'.] A Hebrew measure of capacity, containing 10 ephahs, or 10 baths (liquid measure). Its content was prob. about 80 gallons. ¶Also erron. used for OMER, q.v.

Homer, contr. of *hoe-mother*; see HOE *sb.*[3]

Homeric (home·rik), *a.* 1771. [– L. *Homericus* – Gr. Ὁμηρικός, f. Ὅμηρος Homer; see -IC.] Of, pertaining to, or characteristic of Homer, his poems, or the age with which they deal; like, or of the style of, Homer.

Phr. *The H. question*: the question of the authorship, date, and construction of the *Iliad* and the *Odyssey.* So †**Home·rical** *a.*, **-ly** *adv.* †**Home·rican** *a.*

Homerid (hōᵘ·mĕrid). 1846. [– Gr. Ὁμηρίδης, usu. in pl. Ὁμηρίδαι, Lat. *Homeridæ*, a guild of poets in Chios who claimed descent from Homer and a hereditary property in the Homeric poems, which they recited publicly.] **1.** One of the *Homeridæ* (see above.) **2.** A Homeric scholar. BLACKIE.

Homerite (hōᵘ·mĕrəit). 1613. [– Gr. Ὁμηρῖται *pl.*] = HIMYARITE.

Homerology (hōᵘmĕrǫ·lǒdʒi). 1876. [f. *Homer* (see HOMERIC) + -LOGY.] The study of Homer and of the Homeric poems, their authorship, date, etc. Hence **Homero·logist.**

Home Rule. 1860 (but not in general use before 1871). [HOME *sb.*[1] B. 3.] Government of a country, colony, province, etc., by its own citizens; the political principle or theory, according to which a country or province manages its own affairs; used *spec.* in British politics with reference to the movement, begun about 1870, to obtain for Ireland self-government through the agency of a national parliament. Also *attrib.* (also **home-rule**). Hence **Home-ru·ler,** one who advocates or practises Home Rule.

Home-sick, homesick (hōᵘ·msik), *a.* 1798. [f. HOME *sb.*[1] + SICK *a.*, after next.] Affected with home-sickness.

Ho·me-sickness, homesickness. 1756. [f. HOME *sb.*[1] + SICKNESS, app. at first a rendering of G. (Swiss) *heimweh.*] A depressed state of mind and body caused by a longing for home when away from it; nostalgia.

Homespun (hōᵘ·mspɒn). 1590. [HOME *sb.*[1]] **A.** *adj.* **1.** Spun at home; of home manufacture; made of the material mentioned in B. 1. 1591. **2.** *fig.* Simple, unsophisticated; plain, homely; unpolished, rude 1600.

1. Plain, decent, h. cloth 1796. **2.** The plainest h. morality 1874. Simple, h. characters STEPHEN.

B. *sb.* **1.** Cloth made of yarn spun at home; hodden; also, a material made in imitation of this 1607. Also *fig.* **2.** *transf.* One who wears homespun; hence, a rustic, a clown 1590.

1. Homespuns are still much worn 1883. **2.** What hempen home-spuns haue we swaggering here? SHAKS.

Homestall (hōᵘ·mstǭl). [OE. *hāmsteall*, f. *hām* HOME + *steall* position, place.] †**1.** = HOMESTEAD –1814. **2.** A farm-yard (*dial.*) 1661.

Homestead (hōᵘ·mstėd). [OE. *hāmstede*, f. *hām* HOME + *stede* place, STEAD.] **1.** *gen.* The place of one's home: †**a.** The town, village, etc. in which one's dwelling is. **b.** A dwelling. **2.** A house with its dependent buildings and offices; esp. a farm-stead 1700. **3.** *U.S.* A farm occupied by the owner and his family; esp. the lot of 160 acres granted to a settler by the Homestead Act of Congress, 1862. Also *attrib.* 1693.

2. Twilight..Brought back..the herds to the h. LONGF. **3.** *H. exemption*, in U.S., the exemption of a h. from forced sale under execution for general debts. Hence **Ho·mestea:der,** the holder of a h.; *spec.* in *U.S.*, one who holds lands acquired under the Homestead Act of Congress.

Ho·mester. 1847. [f. HOME *sb.*[1] + -STER.] **1.** A stay-at-home (*rare*). **2.** *pl.* The home team in a sporting match 1891.

Ho·me-thrust. 1622. [f. HOME *adv.*] A thrust which goes home to the party aimed at.

Homeward (hōᵘ·mwǭɹd). [OE. *hāmweard*, f. *hām* HOME + *-weard* -WARD.] **A.** *adv.* Towards one's home, dwelling-place, or native land. **B.** *adj.* Directed or going homeward; leading home 1566.

Homeward-bound, *a.* 1602. [BOUND *ppl. a.*[1]] Bound homeward; esp. of a ship.

Homewards (hōᵘ·mwǭɹdz), *adv.* [OE. *hāmweardes*: see -WARDS.] = HOMEWARD *adv.*

Ho·me-work. 1856. [HOME *sb.*[1] B. 1.] **a.** Work done at home, esp. as dist. from work done in a shop or factory. **b.** Lessons to be done by a school-child at home 1889.

Hom(e)y (hōᵘ·mi), *a.* 1856. [f. HOME *sb.* + -Y[1].] Resembling or having a feeling of home.

Homicidal (hǫmisəi·dăl), *a.* 1725. [f. HOMICIDE[1, 2] + -AL[1].] Of, pertaining to, or characterized by homicide; tending to homicide; murderous.

H. mania: a state of partial insanity, accompanied by an impulse to the perpetration of murder. Hence **Homici·dally** *adv.*

Homicide (hǫ·misəid), *sb.*[1] ME. [– (O)Fr. *homicide* – L. *homicida*, f. shortened stem of *homo, homin-* + *-cida* -CIDE 1.] A manslayer; in earlier use often = murderer. Also *attrib.*

attrib. This regicide and h. government BURKE.

Ho·micide, *sb.*[2] ME. [– (O)Fr. *homicide* – L. *homicidium*; see prec., -CIDE 2.] The action, by a human being, of killing a human being.

In *Law*, usually classed as *justifiable, excusable*, or *felonious. Justifiable h.*, the killing of a man in obedience to law, or by unavoidable necessity, or for the prevention of an atrocious crime. *Excusable h.*, h. committed by misadventure, also in cases of self-defence, where the assailant did not originally intend murder, rape, or robbery. *Felonious h.* comprehends the wilful killing of a man through malice aforethought (murder); the unlawful killing of a man without such malice, either in a sudden heat, or involuntarily while committing an unlawful action not amounting to felony; also self-murder, suicide. Hence **Ho·micide** *v.* to kill or murder. var. †**Homicidy, -ie** (Chaucer).

Homiform, erron. f. HOMINIFORM.

Homilete (hǫ·milīt). *U.S.* 1875. [– Gr. ὁμιλητής disciple, scholar, f. ὁμιλεῖν; see next.] A HOMILIST.

Homiletic (hǫmile·tik). 1644. [– late L. *homileticus* – Gr. ὁμιλητικός, f. ὁμιλητός, vbl. adj. of ὁμιλεῖν consort or hold converse with, f. ὅμιλος crowd.]

A. *adj.* Of the nature of or characteristic of a homily; by way of a homily.

H. divinity or *theology* = Homiletics: see B. 1.

B. *sb.* usu. in pl. **Homiletics** [see -ICS]. **1.** The art of preaching; sacred rhetoric 1830. **2.** *pl.* Homilies. CARLYLE.

1. If the teaching of H. were confined to the multiplication of methods for laying out a discourse [etc.] PUSEY.

So **Homile·tical** *a.* †conversable, sociable; homiletic. **Homile·tically** *adv.* after the manner of a homily.

Homiliary (hǫmi·liări). 1844. [– med.L. *homiliarium, homiliarius* (sc. *liber*), f. eccl. L. *homilia* HOMILY; see -ARY[1]. Cf. OFr. *omiliaire.*] A book of homilies.

Homilist (hǫ·milist). 1616. [f. HOMILY + -IST, after next.] One who writes or delivers homilies. Hence **Homili·stical** *a.* characteristic of a h.

Homilize (hǫ·miləiz), *v.* 1624. [– med.L. *homilizare* (XII), f. eccl. L. *homilia* HOMILY + *-izare* -IZE.] *intr.* To discourse, preach, sermonize.

Homily (hǫ·mĭli). ME. [In XIV *omelie* – OFr. *omelie* (mod. *homélie*) – eccl. L. *homilia* – Gr. ὁμιλία intercourse, converse, discourse, (eccl.) sermon, f. ὅμιλος crowd; see -Y[3]. Finally assim. to the L. form in XVI.] A religious discourse addressed to a congregation; esp. a practical discourse with a view to spiritual edification. Applied *spec.* to the discourses contained in the *Books of Homilies* published in 1547 and 1563 for use in parish churches. **b.** *transf.* A serious admonition; a lecture; a tedious moralizing discourse 1600.

b. What tedious homilie of Loue haue you wearied your parishioners withall *A. Y. L.* III. ii. 164.

Hominal (hǫ·minăl), *a.* 1861. [– Fr. *hominal*, f. L. *homo, homin-* + *-al* -AL[1].] Of or relating to man (in Nat. Hist.).

Homing (hōᵘ·miŋ), *vbl. sb.* 1622. [f. HOME *sb.*[1] and *v.*] †**1.** *Naut.* (with *in*) The curving inwards of the sides of a vessel above its extreme breadth; 'falling' or 'tumbling' home. **2.** The action of going home; return home; the faculty of returning home from a distance. Also *attrib.*, esp. in reference to pigeons. 1765. So **Ho·ming** *ppl. a.* that goes home; as *homing pigeon.*

Hominid (hǫ·minid). 1889. [– mod.L. *Hominidæ*, a family of mammals represented by the single genus *Homo*, f. L. *homo, homin-*; see -ID[3].] A member of the *Hominidæ*; a man (zoologically considered).

†**Ho·miniform,** *a.* [f. L. *homo, homin-* man + -FORM.] Of human shape. CUDWORTH.

Ho·minify, *v.* 1579. [f. as prec. + -FY.] To make human.

Hominivorous (hǫmini·vŏrəs), *a.* 1859. [f. as prec. + -VOROUS.] Man-eating.

Hominy (hǫ·mĭni). 1629. [According to J. H. Trumbull, from *appumiunéonash* parched corn, f. *appwóon* he bakes or roasts + *min*, pl. *minneash* fruit, grain, berry.] Maize hulled and ground coarsely and prepared for food by being boiled with water or milk. Also *attrib.*

Homish (hōᵘ·miʃ), *a.* Also **homeish.** 1561. [f. HOME *sb.*[1] + -ISH[1].] †**1.** Belonging to home; domestic –1577. **2.** Suggestive of home; homelike 1789. Hence **Ho·mishness.**

Hommack, var. of HUMMOCK.

‖**Homo** (hōᵘ·mo). 1596. The Latin word for *man.* **a.** = 'human being'. **b.** *Zool.* The genus of which Man is the single species. **Homo sapiens** (sēᵘ·pienz): the human species.

Homo is a common name to all men SHAKS.

Homo-, bef. a vowel **hom-,** comb. f. Gr. ὁμός same; often in opposition to *hetero-.*

Ho·macanth [Gr. ἄκανθα spine] *a.*, *Ichth.* having the spines of the dorsal and anal fins symmetrical; opp. to *heteracanth.* **Homaxo·nial, Homaxo·nic** *adjs.*, in *Morphology*, having all the axes equal. **Ho:mocatego·ric** [CATEGORIC] *a.*, belonging to the same category. **Homochiral** [Gr. χείρ], of identical form and turned in the same direction, as two right or two left hands. **Homochro·mic, -chro·mous** [Gr. χρῶμα] *adjs.*, of the same colour, as the florets of most *Compositæ*; opp. to *heterochromous.* **Homode·mic** [Gr. δῆμος] *a.* = *homophylic.* **Homode·rmic** *a.*, *Biol.* derived from, or relating to derivation from, the same primary blastoderm of the embryo. **Homody·namous** [Gr. δύναμις] *a.*, *Comp. Anat.* having the same force or value; applied to parts serially homologous; so **Homody·namy,** the condition of being homodynamous. **Homoga·ngliate** *a.*, *Zool.* having the ganglia of the nervous system symmetrically arranged, as in the *Articulata*; opp. to heterogangliate. **Homo·malous** [Gr. ὁμαλός even] *a.*, *Bot.* applied to leaves or branches (esp. of mosses) which turn in the same direction; opp. to *heteromalous.* **Homo-organ,** *Biol.* = HOMOPLAST 2. **Homophy·lic** *a.*, *Biol.* belonging to the same race; relating to homophyly. **Homo·phyly** [Gr. ὁμοφυλία], the condition of being of the same race. **Homopo·lar, -po·lic** *adjs.*, having equal poles; opp. to *heteropolar.* **Homo·rgan** *Biol.* = *homoorgan.* **Homorga·nic** *a.*, 'having the same, or a uniform, organization; applied to plants' (*Syd. Soc. Lex.*); in *Phonetics*, produced by the same vocal organ. **Homosyste·mic** *a.*, belonging to the same system. **Homothe·rmous** [Gr. θερμός] *a.*, *Biol.* having a uniform temperature, as warm-blooded animals; opp. to *heterothermal.* **Homo·tonous** [Gr. τόνος] *a.*, having the same tone or sound.

b. In *Chemistry*, denoting a compound homologous with that whose name follows, as in *homatropine, homocuminic*, etc.

Homocentric (hǫmose·ntrik). 1621. [– mod.L. *homocentricus* (Fracastoro, 1535), f. Gr. ὁμο- HOMO- + κεντρικός CENTRIC. Cf. Fr. *homocentrique* (XVII).] **1.** *adj.* Having the same centre 1696. †**2.** *sb.* (In old Astronomy.) A sphere or circle concentric with another or with the earth; opp. to ECCENTRIC *sb.* BURTON.

Homocercal (hǫmosə̄·ɹkăl), *a.* 1838. [f. HOMO- + Gr. κέρκος tail + -AL¹.] *Ichthyol.* Having the lobes of the tail equal, having a symmetrical tail. Also said of the tail. Opp. to *heterocercal.* So **Ho·mocercy,** h. condition.

Homodont (hǫ·modǫnt). 1877. [f. HOMO- + Gr. ὀδούς, ὀδοντ- tooth.] **1.** *adj.* Having teeth all of the same kind. Also said of the teeth. Opp. to *heterodont.* 1888. **2.** *sb.* A homodont animal.

Homodromous (homǫ·drŏməs), *a.* 1710. [f. mod.L. *homodromus*, f. Gr. ὁμο- HOMO- + -δρομος running + -OUS.] Running in the same direction; opp. to *heterodromous.* †**a.** *Mech.* Applied to levers of the second and third orders, in which the power and the weight run in the same direction. **b.** *Bot.* Turning in the same direction, as two generating spirals of a phyllotaxis (e.g. on the main stem and on a branch.) So **Homo·dromal, Ho·modrome** *adjs.* = prec. b.; **Homo·dromy,** h. condition.

Homœo-, comb. f. Gr. ὅμοιος like, similar (also occas. written **homoio-,** in fully anglicized words, **homeo-**); sometimes opposed to *hetero-*.

Homœothe·rmal [Gr. θερμός] *a.*, *Biol.* = *Homothermous* (see HOMO-). **Homœo·topy** [Gr. τόπος], similarity of words or parts of words, as a cause of mistakes in copying. **Ho:mœozo·ic** [Gr. ζωή] *a.*, containing similar forms of life.

Homœoid (hǫ·mi₁oid). 1883. [f. Gr. ὅμοιος like + -OID.] *Math.* A shell bounded by two surfaces similar and similarly situated with regard to each other; sometimes restricted to a shell bounded by concentric ellipsoids. Hence **Homœoi·dal** *a.*

Homœomeral (hǫmiǫ·mĕrăl), *a.* [f. HOMŒO- + Gr. μέρος part + -AL¹.] *Pros.* Consisting of (metrically) similar parts.

Homœomeric (hǫmiome·rik), *a.* 1836. [f. as prec. + -IC.] **a.** Relating to homœomery; of the nature of homœomeries. **b.** Homogeneous 1865. So **Homœome·rical** *a.* = prec. a.

Homœomerous (hǫmi₁ǫ·mĕrəs), *a.* 1875. [f. as prec. + -OUS.] Having or consisting of similar parts. **1.** *Bot.* Applied to lichens in which the gonidia and hyphæ are distributed uniformly through the thallus; opp. to *heteromerous.* **2.** = HOMŒOMERIC *a.* 1892.

Homœomery (hǫmi₁ǫ·mĕri). Also **homoio-,** and in L. form **homœomeria.** 1660. [– L. *homœomeria* (Lucretius) – Gr. ὁμοιομέρεια, n. of quality f. ὁμοιομερής consisting of like parts, f. ὅμοιος like + μέρος part; see -Y³.] **a.** The theory (propounded by Anaxagoras) that the ultimate particles of matter are homogeneous. **b.** *pl.* The ultimate particles of matter, regarded as homogeneous.

Homœomorphous (hǫmiomǭ·ɹfəs), *a.* 1832. [f. HOMŒO- + Gr. μορφή form + -OUS.] Of similar form or structure. *spec.* in *Cryst.* Having similar crystalline forms; said esp. of substances differing in chemical composition or atomic proportions. Hence **Homœomo·rphism,** h. condition.

Homœopath (hǫ·m-, hōᵘ·miopæþ). Also **homeo-.** 1830. [– G. *homöopath* (Hahnemann, 1824); see next.] One who practises or advocates homœopathy. So **Homœo·pathist.**

Homœopathic (hǫm-, hōᵘmiopæ·þik), *a.* 1830. [– G. *homöopathisch* (Hahnemann, 1824); see HOMŒOPATHY, -IC.] **1.** Of or pertaining to homœopathy; practising or advocating homœopathy; **2.** *fig.* Very small or minute, like the doses in homœopathy. (Often *joc.*) 1838.

2. The chapel was h. in its dimensions 1876. Hence **Homœopa·thically** *adv.*

Homœopathy (hǫm-, hōᵘmi₁ǫ·păþi). Also **homeo-,** and formerly erron. **homöo-.** 1826. [– G. *homöopathie* (S. Hahnemann, 1755–1843), f. Gr. ὅμοιος like + -πάθεια -PATHY.] A system of medical practice founded by Hahnemann of Leipzig about 1796, according to which diseases are treated by the administration (usu. in very small doses) of drugs which would produce in a healthy person symptoms like those of the disease treated. The principle is expressed in the Latin adage 'Similia similibus curantur'.

‖**Homœoteleuton** (homī:o₁tīlᵝū·tǫn). Also **homoio-.** 1586. [Late L. – Gr. ὁμοιοτέλευτον (sc. ῥῆμα), f. ὅμοιος like + τελευτή ending.] **1.** *Rhet.* A figure consisting of a series of words with the same or similar endings. **2.** The occurrence of similar endings in two neighbouring words, clauses, or lines of writing, as a source of error in copying 1861. So **Homœ:oteleu·tic** *a.* having similar endings.

Homogamous (homǫ·găməs), *a.* 1842. [f. Gr. ὁμο- HOMO- + -γαμος married + -OUS.] *Bot.* **a.** Having all the florets hermaphrodite, or all of the same sex: said of certain grasses and composites. **b.** Applied to flowers in which the stamens and pistils ripen together 1854. **c.** *Evolution.* Of or pertaining to assortative mating 1903. So **Homo·gamy,** h. condition.

Homogen (hǫ·mŏdʒen). 1870. [f. HOMO- + -GEN.] *Biol.* A part or organ homogenetic with another; see HOMOGENETIC 1.

Homogene (hǫ·mŏdʒīn). Now *rare* or *Obs.* 1607. [– Gr. ὁμογενής of the same kind, f. ὁμο- HOMO- + γένος kind. Cf. HETEROGENE.] **1.** *adj.* = HOMOGENEOUS. **2.** *sb.* That which is homogeneous 1725.

2. Cold and rain congregate homogenes; for they gather together you [Sheridan] and your crew, at whist, punch, and claret SWIFT.

Homogeneal (hǫmo₁dʒī·niăl). Now *rare.* Also *erron.* **-ial.** 1603. [f. schol. L. *homogenealis*, f. *homogeneus* (f. Gr. ὁμογενής; see prec.) + *-alis* -AL¹. Cf. HETEROGENEAL.] **1.** *adj.* = HOMOGENEOUS. **2.** *sb.* A homogeneous substance or person 1651. Hence **Homoge·nealness,** homogeneity.

Homoge·neate, *v. rare.* 1648. [f. schol. L. *homogeneus* (see prec.) + -ATE³.] *trans.* To make homogeneous.

Homogeneity (hǫmo₁dʒīnī·Iti). 1625. [– schol. L. *homogeneitas*, f. as prec.; see -ITY. Cf. HETEROGENEITY.] The quality or condition of being homogeneous: **a.** Identity of kind with something else; **b.** Uniformity of composition or nature. **c.** *concr.* Something homogeneous 1638.

Homogeneous (hǫmo₁dʒī·niəs), *a.* 1641. [f. schol. L. *homogeneus* (see HOMOGENEAL) + -OUS. Cf. HETEROGENEOUS.] **1.** Of the same kind or nature; alike, similar, congruous. **2.** Of uniform nature or character throughout 1645. **3.** *Math.* **a.** Of the same kind, so as to be commensurable. **b.** Consisting of terms of the same dimensions. 1695.

1. The world and mind..are not h. BAIN. **2.** Ice is a..h. concretion SIR T. BROWNE. Hence **Homoge·neous-ly** *adv.*, **-ness.**

Homogenesis (hǫmo₁dʒe·nĕsis). 1858. [f. HOMO- + -GENESIS.] *Biol.* †**1.** Applied to asexual reproduction. CARPENTER. **2.** The ordinary form of sexual reproduction, in which the offspring resembles the parent and passes through the same course of development.

Homogenetic (-dʒĭne·tik), *a.* 1870. [f. HOMO- + -GENETIC.] *Biol.* **1.** Having a common descent or origin; applied to organs or parts of different organisms which show a correspondence of structure due to derivation from a common ancestor. **2.** Relating to HOMOGENESIS (sense 2) 1889. So **Homogene·tical** *a.* of, relating to, or having reference to, homogeny or community of descent.

Homogenous (homǫ·dʒĭnəs), *a.* 1870. [f. next, sense 2, + -OUS.] *Biol.* = HOMOGENETIC 1.

Homogeny (homǫ·dʒĭni). 1626. [orig. – mod.L. *homogenia* (Bacon) – Gr. ὁμογένεια; in mod. scientific use f. HOMO- + -GENY.] †**1.** Homogeneity. BACON. **2.** *Biol.* The quality of being homogenous; correspondence of structure due to common descent 1870.

Homogonous (homǫ·gŏnəs), *a.* 1877. [f. HOMO- + Gr. -γονος generating or γόνος offspring + -OUS.] **1.** *Bot.* Having similar reproductive organs; applied to flowers in which there is no difference in length in the stamens and pistils of different individuals; opp. to HETEROGONOUS 1. **2.** *Biol.* Producing offspring similar to the parent; opp. to HETEROGONOUS 2. 1883.

Homograph (hǫ·mŏgrɑf). 1873. [f. HOMO- + -GRAPH.] *Philol.* A word of the same spelling as another, but of different origin and meaning.

Homographic (hǫmogræ·fik), *a.* 1859. [In sense 1 – Fr. *homographique* (Chasles), f. *homo-* HOMO- + -GRAPHIC. In senses 2 and 3, f. HOMO- + -GRAPHIC.] **1.** *Geom.* Having the same anharmonic ratio or system of anharmonic ratios, as two figures of the same thing in different perspective; belonging or relating to such figures. **2.** *Gram.* Said of spelling in which each sound is always represented by the same character, which stands for that sound and no other; strictly phonetic; opp. to *heterographic* 1864. **3.** *Philol.* Of, belonging to, or consisting of homographs 1880.

Homography (homǫ·grăfi). 1859. [In sense 1, f. prec.; in sense 2, f. as senses 2 and 3 in prec.; see -GRAPHY.] **1.** *Geom.* = HOMOLOGY 4. **2.** *Gram.* Homographic spelling; see prec. (sense 2) 1864.

Homoio-: see HOMŒO-.

Homoiousian (hǫmoi₁ɑu·siăn, -ū·siăn). 1732. [f. eccl. L. *homoeousius* (Hilary, Jerome) – Gr. ὁμοιούσιος of like essence, f. ὅμοιος like, similar + οὐσία essence; see -AN.]

A. *adj.* **a.** Of like essence or substance. **b.** Relating to or maintaining likeness (as dist. from *identity* and from *difference*) of substance between the Father and the Son; see B. (Dist. from *heteroousian* and *homoousian.*) 1854.

B. *sb.* One who held the Father and the Son, in the Godhead, to be of like, but not the same, essence or substance; a Semi-Arian.

†**Homo·logal,** *a.* 1570. [f. mod.L. *homologus* HOMOLOGOUS + -AL¹.] = HOMOLOGOUS.

Homologate (homǫ·lŏgeⁱt), *v.* Chiefly *Sc.* 1644. [– *homologat-*, pa. ppl. stem of med.L. *homologare* agree, after Gr. ὁμολογεῖν; see -ATE³.] **1.** *trans.* To express agreement with; to assent to; to countenance; to confirm, ratify. **2.** *intr.* or *absol.* To agree; to express assent 1649. **3.** *trans.* To identify (*with* something else). HUTTON. Hence **Homologa·tion,** the action of homologating; *spec.* in *Sc. Law*, the action of confirming or ratifying (a defective or informal deed) by some subsequent act.

Homological (hǫmŏlǫ·dʒikăl), *a.* 1849. [f. as HOMOLOGY + -ICAL.] Involving or characterized by, or relating to, homology; homologous.

Homologize (homǫ·lŏdʒəiz), *v.* 1733. [f. as prec. + -IZE.] **1.** *intr.* To be homologous, to correspond. **2.** *trans.* To make, or show to be, homologous 1811. Hence **Homo·logizer** 1716.

‖**Homologon** (homǫ·lŏgǫn). 1871. [Gr.,

subst. use of n. of adj. ὁμόλογος agreeing, consonant, f. ὁμός same + λόγος ratio, proportion, analogy.] A homologue.

Homologous (hǫmǫ·lŏgəs), *a.* 1660. [f. med.L. *homologus* (– Gr. ὁμόλογος; see prec.) + -OUS.] Having the same relation, proportion, relative position, etc.; corresponding. **1.** *Math.* Having the same ratio or relative value as the two antecedents or the two consequents in a proportion, or the corresponding sides in similar figures. **b.** *Mod. Geom.* Having a relation of homology, as two plane figures; homological 1879. **2.** *Biol.* Having the same relation to a fundamental type; corresponding in type of structure. (Dist. from *analogous.*) 1846. **b.** *Path.* Of the same formation as the normal tissue of the part; said of morbid growths. (Opp. to HETEROLOGOUS.) 1871. **3.** *Chem.* Applied to series of compounds differing in composition successively by a constant amount of certain constituents, and showing a gradation of chemical and physical properties 1850.

2. In the vertebrata the front and hind limbs are h. DARWIN. **3.** Four classes of h. bodies namely alcohols, ethers, aldehydes, and acids DAUBENY.

Homologue (hǫ·mǫlǫg). 1848. [– Fr. *homologue* – Gr. ὁμόλογον HOMOLOGON.] That which is homologous; a homologous organ, etc.: see above.

Homology (hǫmǫ·lŏdʒi). 1656. [f. after HOMOLOGOUS; see -LOGY. Cf. Fr. *homologie.*] **1.** Homologous quality or condition; sameness of relation; correspondence. **2.** *Biol.* Correspondence in type of structure; see HOMOLOGOUS 2. Also that branch of Biology or Comparative Anatomy which deals with such correspondences. 1835. **3.** *Chem.* The relation of the compounds forming a homologous series; see HOMOLOGOUS 3. 1876. **4.** *Mod. Geom.* The relation of two figures, such that every point in each corresponds to a point in the other, and collinear points in one correspond to collinear points in the other; every straight line joining a pair of corresponding points passes through a fixed point called the *centre of h.*, and every pair of corresponding straight lines in the two figures intersect on a fixed straight line called the *axis of h.* 1879.

2. *General h.*, the relation of an organ or organism to the general type. *Serial h.*, the relation of corresponding parts forming a series in the same organism (e.g. legs, vertebræ, leaves). *Special h.*, the correspondence of a part or organ in one organism with a homologous part in another (e.g. of a horse's knee with a man's wrist).

Homomorph (hǫ·momǭɹf). 1886. [f. HOMO- + Gr. μορφή form.] A thing of the same form as another; applied to letters having the same form and to different words having the same spelling.

Homomorphic (hǫmomǭ·ɹfik), *a.* 1872. [f. as prec. + -IC.] Of the same or similar form. *spec.* **a.** *Entom.* Said of insects in which the larva more or less resembles the imago (*Homomorpha*); hemimetabolous or ametabolous. **b.** *Bot.* Applied to flowers or plants in which the relative length of the stamens and pistils does not differ; also to the self-fertilization of such flowers. **c.** *Biol.* Applied to organs or organisms showing an external resemblance, but not really related in structure or origin. So **Homomo·rphism, Ho·momo:rphy,** h. condition; resemblance of form, *esp.* without structural affinity. **Homomo·rphous** *a.* of the same form.

Homonomous (homǫ·nŏməs), *a.* 1854. [f. Gr. ὁμόνομος (f. ὁμός same + νόμος law) + -OUS.] Subject to the same or a constant law; *spec.* in *Biol.* Having the same law or mode of growth.

Homonomy (-ǫ·nŏmi). 1643. [f. as prec. + -Y[3]; see -NOMY.] Homonomous condition (see prec.).

Homonym (hǫ·mŏnim). 1697. [– L. *homonymum* – Gr. ὁμώνυμον, n. of ὁμώνυμος HOMONYMOUS; cf. med.L. *homonymus* namesake.] **1. a.** The same word used to denote different things. **b.** *Philol.* Applied to words having the same sound, but different meanings. **2.** A namesake 1851.

Homonymous (hǫmǫ·niməs), *a.* 1621. [f. L. *homonymus* (Quintilian) – Gr. ὁμώνυμος, f. ὁμός same + ὄνομα (Æol. ὄνυμα) name; see -OUS.] †**1.** Denoting different things by the same name; equivocal, ambiguous –1801. **2.** Having, or called by, the same name 1658. Hence **Homo·nymously** *adv.* So **Homony·mic** *a.* relating to homonyms, or homonymy 1862. **Homo·nymy,** the quality of being h. 1597.

Homoousian, homousian (hǫ·moˌau·siăn, homau·siăn, -ū·siăn). 1565. [– eccl.L. *homoousianus* (Augustine), f. *hom(o)ousius* (Jerome) – Gr. ὁμ(ο)ούσιος of the same essence, f. ὁμός same + οὐσία essence; see -IAN.]

Theol. **A.** *adj.* **a.** Of the same essence or substance. **b.** Relating to or maintaining the consubstantiality of the persons of the Trinity; see B. 1678.

The council of Nice established the homousian or consubstantial doctrine LARDNER.

B. *sb. Eccl. Hist.* One who holds the three persons of the Trinity to be of the same essence or substance 1565.

The Arrians called the Catholikes Homoousians 1565.

Homophene (hǫ·mofīn). 1883. [irreg. f. HOMO- + Gr. φαίνειν show, appear. (The regular form would be *homophane.*)] A word having the same form to the eye as another; used esp. in reference to the reading of deaf-mutes.

Homophone (hǫ·mofōᵘn). 1623. [– Gr. ὁμόφωνος of the same sound; see HOMO-, -PHONE.]

A. *adj.* Having the same sound (*rare*).

B. *sb. Philol.* (Usu. in *pl.*) Applied to words having the same sound, but differing in meaning or derivation; also to different symbols denoting the same group of sounds 1843.

Homophonic (hǫmofǫ·nik), *a.* 1879. [f. as prec. + -IC.] *Mus.* **1.** Producing, or consisting of, sounds of the same pitch; unisonous. Opp. to *antiphonic.* 1881. **2.** *loosely.* Said of music characterized by the predominance of one part or melody, to which the rest merely furnish harmonies; more correctly called *monophonic* or *monodic.* Opp. to *polyphonic.* 1879.

Homophonous (homǫ·fŏnəs), *a.* 1753. [f. as prec. + -OUS.] **1.** *Mus.* = HOMOPHONIC 1. **2.** Of the character of homophones 1826.

Homophony (homǫ·fŏni). 1776. [– Gr. ὁμοφωνία, f. ὁμόφωνος; see HOMOPHONE, -Y[3].] **1.** *Mus.* Homophonic music or style. **a.** Unison, or music performed in unison; opp. to *antiphony.* **b.** Monophony, monody; opp. to *polyphony.* **3.** *Philol.* Homophonous quality; identity of sound (of words) 1842.

Homoplast (hǫ·moplæst). 1870. [f. HOMO- + -PLAST.] *Biol.* **1.** An organ or part homoplastic with another; opp. to HOMOGEN. **2.** An aggregate or fusion of plastids all of the same structure; opp. to *alloplast* 1883.

Homoplastic (-plæ·stik), *a.* 1870. [f. as prec. + -IC.] *Biol.* Having a similarity of structure without community of origin. Opp. to HOMOGENETIC.

Homoplasy (homǫ·plăsi). 1870. [f. as prec. + Gr. -πλασια, f. πλάσις moulding.] *Biol.* Homoplastic condition; similarity of structure produced independently by similar external circumstances. Opp. to HOMOGENY 2.

‖**Homoptera** (homǫ·ptĕră), *sb. pl.* 1826. [mod.L. (Latreille, 1817), f. Gr. ὁμο- HOMO- + πτερόν wing.] *Entom.* A suborder of HEMIPTERA, comprising insects of various forms, with wings of uniform texture; contrasted with HETEROPTERA. Hence **Homo·pter, Homo·pteran,** a member of the *H.* **Homo·pterous** *a.*

Homosexual (hǫmoˌse·ksiuăl), *a.* (*sb.*). 1897. [f. HOMO- + SEXUAL.] Having a sexual propensity for persons of one's own sex. Also as *sb.* Hence **Ho:mose·xualism, -se·xualist, -sexua·lity, -se·xualize** *v.*

Homostyled (hǫ·moˌstəild), *a.* 1877. [f. HOMO- + STYLE + -ED[2].] *Bot.* = HOMOGONOUS 1; opp. to *heterostyled.* Also **Homosty·lic, -sty·lous** *adjs.* **Homosty·ly.**

Homotaxial (-tæ·ksiăl), *a.* 1870. [f. HOMO- + Gr. -ταξια (f. τάξις arrangement) + -AL[1].] *Geol.* Applied to strata in different regions, having the same relative position with respect to those underlying and overlying them, but not necessarily contemporaneous; also to the fossil remains found in such strata. **Homota·xially** *adv.* **Homota·xeous, Homota·xic** *adjs.* = HOMOTAXIAL. **Ho·motaxy.**

Homo·tropal, *a.* 1844. [f. as next + -AL[1].] *Bot.* = next.

Homotropous (-ǫ·trŏpəs), *a.* 1819. [f. Gr. ὁμο- HOMO- + -τροπος turning + -OUS, after Fr. *homotrope* (A. Richard, 1819).] *Bot.* Of the embryo of a seed: Having the radicle directed towards the hilum. Opp. to *antitropous* or *heterotropous.* Also· **-trope** *a.* 1831.

Homotype (hǫ·motəip). 1840. [f. HOMO- + -TYPE.] *Biol.* A part or organ having the same type of structure as another, a homologue.

The femur, the h. of the humerus OWEN. Hence **Ho·motypal, Homoty·pic, -al** *adjs.* of the character of, or relating to, a h.; homologous. **Homotypy** (hǫ·motəipi, homǫ·tipi), relation of homotypes; homology.

Homousian: see HOMOOUSIAN.

Homozygote (hǫmozəi·goᵘt). 1902. [f. HOMO- + ZYGOTE.] A zygote formed by the union of two like gametes. Hence **Ho:mozygo·sis, -zygo·sity, -zy·gous** *a.*

‖**Homuncio** (homʌ·nsio). 1643. [L., dim. of *homo, homin-* man.] = HOMUNCULE.

Homuncule, -uncle (homʌ·ŋkiul, -ʌ·ŋk'l). 1656. [– L. *homunculus* (also in Eng. use), dim. of *homo* man; see -CULE.] A diminutive man; a manikin. Hence **Homu·ncular** *a.* pigmy.

Homy: see HOMEY.

Hond, obs. f. HAND.

Hone (hōᵘn), *sb.*[1] [Specific use of OE. *hān* stone (often one serving as a landmark) = ON. *hein* :– Gmc. *χainō.] †**1.** A stone, a rock. OE. only. **2.** A whetstone used for giving a fine edge to cutting tools, esp. razors ME. **3.** Stone of which whetstones are made. (Various kinds of stone are used for this purpose.) 1793. *Comb.* **h.-stone** = senses 2 and 3; *spec.* a very siliceous clay slate having a conchoidal fracture across the grain of the rock; also called *novaculite.*

†**Hone,** *sb.*[2] [Known only from Gerarde's *Herbal* (1633).] A swelling or tumour.

Hone, *v.*[1] *dial.* and *U.S.* 1600. [– OFr. *hogner, -ier* grumble.] *intr.* To grumble, murmur, whine, moan. Also with *for, after.*

He lies..honing and moaning to himself LAMB.

Hone, *v.*[2] 1788. [f. HONE *sb.*[1]] *trans.* To sharpen on a hone. Hence **Honer.**

On beuks to h. my rhymin' razor 1788.

Hone: see OHONE. Hence as *vb.* BORROW.

Honest (ǫ·nėst), *a.* ME. [– OFr. *(h)oneste* (mod. *honnête*) – L. *honestus,* f. *honos,* **hones-* HONOUR *sb.*] †**1.** Of persons: Holding an honourable position; respectable –1692. **b.** As a vague epithet of appreciation. (Cf. *worthy.*) 1551. †**2.** Honourable; creditable –1720; respectable, decent, befitting –1674; decent in appearance; comely; neat, tidy –1566. **3.** Of persons: †Of good moral character, virtuous, upright –1702; *spec.* chaste, 'virtuous'; usu. of a woman (*arch.*) ME. **b.** Sincere, truthful, candid; that will not lie, cheat, or steal. (The prevailing modern sense.) ME. **c.** Ingenuous; open, frank 1634. **4.** Of actions, feelings, etc.: Fair, straightforward; free from fraud ME. **b.** Of money, gain, etc.: Legitimate 1700. **c.** Of a thing: Genuine 1598. **5.** *adv.* = Honestly; or (*poet.*) in comb. with another adj. = 'honest and ——' 1592.

1. Houses, wherein liue the honester sort of people, as Farmers in England 1624. Phr. *To make an h. woman of*: to marry (a woman) after seduction (*dial.* or *vulgar*) 1562. **b.** Your name h. Gentleman? *Mids. N.* III. i. 187. **2.** Many a manly wound All h., all before DRYDEN. H. mirth 1674. **3.** Wives may be merry, and yet h. too *Merry W.* IV. ii. 103. **b.** An h. man's the noblest work of God POPE. **4.** Their h. and reasonable excuses could not be heard GRAFTON. **b.** He turns an h. penny 1887. **c.** *Merry W.* IV. ii. 126. **5.** As I haue euer found thee h. true SHAKS.

So †**Honest** *v.* to honour; to justify, defend, excuse; to 'make an honest woman of'.

†**Hone·stete.** ME. only. [– OFr. *honesteté* (mod. *honnêteté*) = Pr. *honestetat,* Sp. *honestidad,* Pg. *honestidade* :– Rom. **honestitas, -tat-* for L. *honestas*; see -ITY.] HONESTY.

Honestly (ǫ·néstli), *adv.* ME. [f. HONEST *a.* + -LY².] †**1.** In a respectful manner; decently –1645. **2.** With upright conduct; esp. without fraud or falsehood; sincerely, fairly, frankly ME. †**3.** Chastely –1691.

2. I can h. say [etc.] BERKELEY. I came h. by it SWIFT. **3.** The married Women live h. PURCHAS.

Honesty (ǫ·nésti). ME. [– OFr. *(h)onesté* – L. *honestas, -at-*, f. *honestus* HONEST; see -TY¹.]

I. †**1.** Honourable position or estate; respectability –1520; respect –1613; reputation, credit –1548. †**2.** Decency, decorum; comeliness –1652. †**3.** Honourable character (in a wide sense) –1611; *spec.* chastity –1634; liberality –1607. **4.** Uprightness of disposition and conduct; straightforwardness; the quality opposed to lying, cheating, or stealing. (The prevailing modern sense.) 1579. Also *transf.* of things.

3. Let not . . wicked friendship force What h. and vertue cannot work B. JONS. A Venus (like in honestie, though not in beautie) SIR T. HERBERT. **4.** What other Oath, Then H. to H. ingag'd *Jul. C.* II. i. 127.

II. a. Pop. name of *Lunaria biennis*, a cruciferous plant with large purple (or occas. white) flowers and flat round semi-transparent pods (whence the name); also other species of *Lunaria*. 1597. **b.** (In full, *Maiden's H.*) A local name of wild Clematis (*C. vitalba*) 1640.

Honewort (hōᵘ·nwɒɹt). 1633. [f. HONE *sb.*² + WORT¹.] A name for Corn Parsley (*Petroselinum segetum*); also extended to *Sison amomum*, and other umbelliferous plants.

Honey (hɒ·ni), *sb.* (*a.*) [OE. *huniġ* = OFris. *hunig*, OS. *honeg, -ig*, OHG. *honag, -ang* (Du., G. *honig*), ON. *hunang* :- Gmc. **χuna(ŋ)am*.] **1.** A sweet viscid fluid, being the nectar of flowers collected and worked up for food by certain insects, esp. the honey-bee. **2.** Applied to products of the nature of, or resembling honey; esp. the nectar of flowers 1732. **3.** *fig.* Sweetness 1592. **4.** A term of endearment: Sweet one. (Now chiefly Irish, and, in form *hinnie, hinny* Sc., and North.) ME. **5.** *attrib.* Of, for, pertaining to, or connected with honey 1460.

1. A lande flowing with milke and hony *Exod.* 3:8. **2.** The h. of poison-flowers TENNYSON. **3.** Death that hath suckt the h. of thy breath *Rom. & Jul.* V. iii. 92.

Comb.: **h.-ant**, an ant of the genus *Myrmecocystus*, the workers of which in summer have the abdomen distended with h., which the others feed upon when food becomes scarce; **-badger**, the ratel; **-bag**, the enlargement of the alimentary canal in which the bee carries h.; †**-beer**, ? mead; **-creeper**, a bird of the neo-tropical family *Cœrebidæ* or *Dacnididæ*; **-fall** = HONEY-DEW 1; also *fig.* good luck; **-gland**, a nectary; **-kite** = HONEY-BUZZARD; **-moth**, the honeycomb moth; **-tube**, one of the two setiform tubes on the upper side of the abdomen of an aphis, which secrete a sweet fluid; **-words**, words of sweetness.

b. In names of plants and fruits: **h.-balm**, a labiate plant, *Melittis melissophyllum*; **-berry**, the sweet berry of a W. Indian tree, *Melicocca bijuga*; **-blob** *Sc.*, a sweet yellow gooseberry; **-bottle** (*local*), the bloom of *Erica tetralix*; **-bread**, the Carob (*Ceratonia siliqua*); **-garlic**, *Allium siculum*; **-locust**, the N. Amer. genus *Gleditschia*; **-stalks** *sb. pl.*, the stalks or flowers of clover (Shaks.); **-wood**, the Tasmanian tree *Bedfordia salicina*.

B. *adj.* Resembling, or of the nature of, honey; sweet, honeyed LYDGATE.

A thousand honie secrets shalt thou know SHAKS.

Honey, *v. arch.* ME. [f. prec. sb.] †**1.** *trans.* To make sweet with or as with honey –1645. †**2.** To use endearing terms to –1631. **b.** *absol.* or *intr.* To talk fondly or sweetly. *arch.* and *U.S.* 1602. †**3.** *trans.* To coax, flatter –1622.

2. b. The king came honeying about her TENNYSON.

Ho·ney-bear. 1838. **1.** The potto or kinkajou, *Cercoleptes caudivolvulus*, a native of tropical America. **2.** The sloth-bear, *Melursus labiatus*, of India 1875.

Ho·ney-bee. 1566. A bee that gathers and stores honey, esp. the common hive-bee.

Ho·ney-bird. 1605. †**1.** Fanciful name for a bee. **2.** A bird that feeds on honey or the nectar of flowers. Cf. HONEY-EATER, -SUCKER 1870. **3.** = HONEY-GUIDE 1. 1850.

Ho·ney-bu:zzard. 1674. A bird of prey of the genus *Pernis*, esp. the European species *P. apivorus*, which feeds chiefly on the larvæ of bees and wasps.

Honeycomb (hɒ·nikōᵘm), *sb.* [OE. *huniġcamb*, f. *huniġ* + *camb* COMB *sb.*¹] **1.** A structure of wax containing two series of hexagonal cells separated by thin partitions, formed by bees for the reception of honey and their eggs. Also *fig.* †**2.** A term of endearment –1552. **3.** A cavernous flaw in metal work, esp. in guns 1530. **4.** The reticulum or second stomach of ruminants, so called from its appearance 1658. **5.** Honeycomb work 1838. **6.** *attrib.* Of or pertaining to a honeycomb; like a honeycomb; having a surface hexagonally marked; as *h. cell, coil* (Wireless), *decoration, work*, etc. 1721.

1. Swetter abouen huny and huny kambe HAMPOLE. **5.** A large white quilt, real h. 1882.

Comb.: **h. bag** = sense 4; **h. coral**, a coral of the genus FAVOSITES; **h. moth**, a tineid moth of the genus *Galleria* which infests beehives; **h. ringworm, scall**, species of the disease FAVUS; **h. stitch**, a stitch used to draw together the gathers upon the neck and sleeves of smock-frocks, etc.; **h. stomach** = sense 4; so **h. tripe.**

Hence **Honeycomb** *v.*, to fill with cavities, undermine (*lit.* and *fig.*); to mark with honeycomb pattern 1768.

Honeycombed (hɒ·nikoᵘmd), *a.* 1627. [f. HONEYCOMB *v.* or *sb.* + -ED.] Formed or perforated like a honeycomb; as *h. lava*, etc.

Ho·ney-dew. 1577. **1.** A sweet sticky substance found on the leaves and stems of trees and plants, held to be excreted by aphides; formerly imagined to be in origin akin to dew. **2.** An ideally sweet or luscious substance 1608. **3.** A kind of tobacco sweetened with molasses 1857.

2. Sweet, as the Hony-deaw, which Hybla hath G. DANIEL.

Ho·ney-drop. ME. A drop of honey; occas. taken as a type of what is sweet and delicious.

Ho·ney-ea:ter. 1731. An animal that feeds on honey; *spec.* = HONEYSUCKER.

Honeyed, honied (hɒ·nid), *a.* ME. [f. HONEY *sb.* + -ED².] **1.** Abounding in or laden with honey; sweetened as with honey; consisting of or containing honey. **2.** *fig.* Sweet ME.

1. Wyne lyke vnto honyed wyne TURNER. **2.** H. nothings 1852.

Ho·ney-flower. 1712. **1.** A flowering shrub of the Cape of Good Hope, of the genus *Melianthus*. **2.** An Australian flower, *Lambertia formosa* 1802.

Ho·ney-guide. 1786. **1.** A small African bird of the genus *Indicator* which guides men and animals to the nests of bees. **2.** A marking in a flower, which serves to insects as a guide to the honey 1879.

Ho·neyless, *a.* 1601. [f. HONEY *sb.* + -LESS.] Destitute of honey. *Jul. C.* V. i. 35.

†**Honey-month.** 1696. [After next.] The first month after marriage –1710.

Honeymoon (hɒ·nimūːn), *sb.* 1546. The first month after marriage. Now, usually, the holiday spent together by a newly-married couple, before settling down at home. Also *transf.*

And now their honey-moon, that late was clear, Doth pale, obscure, and tenebrous appear BRETON. *transf.* In the Honey-moon of his Accession BOLINGBROKE. Hence **Ho·neymoon** *v. intr.* to spend the h.

Ho·ney-mouthed, *a.* 1539. Sweet or soft in speech; often implying insincerity.

If I proue hony-mouth'd, let my tongue blister SHAKS.

Ho·ney-pot. ME. **1.** A pot in which honey is stored. **2.** *pl.* A children's game. Also *attrib.* in reference to the posture 1821.

2. To squat low down on his haunches, like a political 'honey-pot' 1886.

Ho·ney-stone. 1795. = MELLITE.

Ho·neysu:cker. 1772. An animal that feeds on honey; *spec.* applied to various small birds, esp. the *Meliphagidæ, Cœrebidæ* etc.; a nectar-bird; a HONEY-EATER.

Honeysuckle (hɒ·nisɒk'l). [ME. *hunisuccle, -soukel*, extension of *hunisūce, -sūge, -souke* (surviving dial.), OE. *huniġsūce, -sūge* (f. *sūcan, sūgan* SUCK *v.*).] **1.** A name for the flowers of clover, and other flowers yielding honey. *Obs.* exc. *dial.* **2.** The common name of *Lonicera periclymenum*, also called Woodbine, a climbing shrub with fragrant yellowish trumpet-shaped flowers; thence extended to the whole genus. *Fly-honeysuckle*, the species *L. xylosteum* and *L. ciliata*. *Trumpet* or *Coral H.*, a N. American species, *L. sempervirens*, with evergreen foliage and scarlet flowers. 1548. **3.** Applied to shrubs or plants of other genera, in some way resembling the common honeysuckle; e.g. in Australia to species of *Banksia* 1592. **4.** A figure or ornament somewhat resembling a sprig or flower of honeysuckle; *esp.* in *Arch.* 1548.

1. As Honey-Suckles (both the Woodbine and the Trifoile) BACON. **2.** *Mids. N.* IV. i. 47. **3. False H.**, 'the genus *Azalea*' (Miller). **French H.**, name given to *Hedysarum coronarium*, a native of Italy, a leguminous plant, with flowers resembling those of the red clover. **White H.**, *Rhododendron viscosum* (*Azalea viscosa*); also white clover (see 1). *Comb.*: **h.-grass** (*dial.*), **-trefoil**, clover. **Ho·neysuckled** *a.* overgrown, or scented, with h.

Ho·ney-swee:t, *a.* OE. Sweet as honey, often a term of endearment.

Ho·ney-tongued, *a.* 1588. Speaking sweetly or winningly; using honeyed words.

Honeywort (hɒ·niwɒɹt). 1597. [See WORT¹.] A plant of the genus *Cerinthe* of boraginaceous plants, much frequented by bees.

‖**Hong** (hǫŋ). 1726. [– Chinese *hang* row, rank.] In China, a series of rooms used as a warehouse, factory, etc.; *spec.* (*a*) one of the foreign factories formerly maintained at Canton; (*b*) the corporation of Chinese merchants at Canton, who before 1842 had the monopoly of trade with Europeans; (*c*) a foreign trading establishing in China or Japan.

Hong(e, obs. inf., pa. t., etc. of HANG *v.*

Honied: see HONEYED.

Honiton (hǫ·nitən). 1851. The name of a town in Devonshire used attrib. to designate kinds of bobbin-lace.

Honk (hǫŋk), *sb.* 1843. [imit.] The snort of a pig; *U.S.* and *Canada*, the cry of the wild goose or swan. **b.** The harsh hoot of a motor-horn 1906. Hence **Honk** *v.*

Honor, Honorable: see HONOUR, etc.

†**Honorance.** ME. [– OFr. *honorance*, f. *honorer* HONOUR *v.*; see -ANCE.] The action of honouring or doing homage; honour –1716.

Honorarium (hǫn-, ǫnǒrēᵊ·riǒm). *Pl.* **-ums, -a.** 1658. [– L. *honorarium*, gift made on being admitted to a post of honour, subst. use (sc. *donum*) of n. of *honorarius* HONORARY; see -ARIUM.] An honorary reward; a fee for (professional) services rendered.

The emoluments and honoraria of physicians 1895. So **Ho·norary** *sb.* (now *rare* or *Obs.*).

Honorary (ǫ·nǒrări), *a.* 1614. [– L. *honorarius*, f. *honor*; see HONOUR *sb.*, -ARY¹.] **1.** Denoting or bringing honour; conferred or rendered in honour. **2.** *spec.* Conferred or rendered merely for the sake of honour, without the usual adjuncts 1661. **3.** Holding a title or position conferred as an honour, without emolument, or without the usual duties, privileges, etc.; titulary. Also, giving services (as secretary, treasurer, etc.) without emolument. 1705. **4.** Depending on honour; said of an obligation which cannot be legally enforced 1794.

1. The simple crown of olive, an h. reward GROTE. **2.** H. titles or degrees 1813. *H. monument*, a cenotaph. **3.** H. colonel of the 13th Infantry Regiment 1873. Phr. *H. feud* (Law): a title of nobility descendible to the eldest son.

Honorific (ǫnǒri·fik), *a.* (*sb.*) 1650. [– L. *honorificus* (Cicero), f. *honor*; see -FIC.] **1.** Doing or conferring honour; importing honour or respect; *spec.* applied to phrases, words, forms of speech, used, esp. in certain Oriental languages, to express respect. **2.** *sb.* An honorific word or phrase 1879.

1. The epithet Abu, father, is h. KEATINGE.

Honour, honor (ǫ·nəɹ), *sb.* [ME. *(h)onur, (h)onour, an(o)ur* – AFr. *anur, anour*, OFr. *(h)onor, (h)onur*, earlier *enor* (mod. *honneur*) :- L. *honor, honor-*.] **1.** High respect, esteem, or reverence, accorded to exalted worth or rank; deferential admiration or approbation, as felt, rendered, or received. **2.** Personal title to high respect or esteem; honourableness; elevation of character; a fine sense of and strict allegiance to what is due or right

1548. **b.** Word of honour (*arch.*) 1658. **3.** (Of a woman) Chastity, purity; good name ME. **4.** Exalted rank or position; dignity, distinction ME. **b.** With poss. pron., = 'honourable personality': now a formal title, esp. for County Court judges 1553. **5.** (Usu. in *pl.*) Something conferred or done as a token of respect or distinction; a mark of high regard; *esp.* a position or title of rank, a dignity ME. †**b.** A bow or curtsy –1805. **c.** *pl.* Courtesies rendered, as at an entertainment 1659. **d.** *pl.* Special distinction gained, in an examination, for proficiency beyond that required for a pass 1782. **6.** A source or cause of honour; one who or that which does credit (*to*) 1568. **b.** (Usu. in *pl.*) A decoration, adornment, ornament (*poet.*) 1613. **7.** *Law.* A seigniory of several manors held under one baron or lord paramount ME. **8. a.** *Cards.* (Chiefly *pl.*) *Whist.* The ace, king, queen, and knave of trumps (*Bridge*, the ten also). *Ombre* and *Quadrille.* The aces of spades and clubs, and the lowest card of the trump suit. 1674. **b.** *Golf.* The privilege of playing first from the tee 1896.

1. To shew my h. for them STEELE. Deie we raþer wiþ onour R. GLOUC. **2.** I could not love thee, dear, so much, Lov'd I not H. more LOVELACE. Say, what is H.? 'Tis the finest sense Of justice which the human mind can frame WORDSW. **3.** So as she may..Her h. and her name save GOWER. **4.** The king is likewise the fountain of h. BLACKSTONE. **5.** Weare it for an Honor in thy Cappe SHAKS. Papists were admitted in crowds to offices and honors MACAULAY. **c.** Phr. *To do the honours. Honours of war*: the privileges granted to a capitulating force, as of marching out under arms with colours flying and drums beating. **6.** Erasmus the honor of learning of all oure time ASCHAM. **b.** He..beares his blushing Honors thicke vpon him *Hen. VIII*, III. ii. 354.

Phrases. **a.** *Comm. For (the) h. (of..)*: said of the acceptance or payment of a bill of exchange (which has been refused by the drawee and duly protested) by a third party to protect the credit of the drawer or indorser. **b.** *In h.*: as a moral duty: sometimes implying that there is no legal obligation. **c.** *On* or *upon one's h.*: a phrase staking the personal credit of the speaker on the truth of his statement; used formally by members of the House of Lords in their judicial capacity; hence, an expression of strong assurance. **d.** *To do h. to*: to treat with h., confer h. upon; to do credit to. **e.** *H. bright* (colloq.): a protestation of (or interrog. an appeal to) one's h. or sincerity 1819. **f.** *Code* or *law of h.*: the set of rules or customs which regulate the conduct of a class of persons according to a conventional standard of h. **g.** *Court of h.*: a court or tribunal for determining questions concerning the laws or principles of h., as the courts of chivalry in former days. See also AFFAIR, DEBT, LEGION, MAID, POINT, WORD *of h.*

Comb.: **h.-court,** a court held within an h. or seigniory (sense 7); **-man** (also *honours-man*), one who has taken, or studies for, academical honours (sense 5 d); so **honours degree, honour(s) school;** **-point** (*Her.*), the point just above the fess-point of an escutcheon; **-policy,** a policy wherein it is stipulated that the policy should be deemed sufficient proof of interest.

Honour, honor (ǫ·nəɹ), *v.* ME. [– OFr. *onorer, onurer* (mod. *honorer*) :– L. *honorare*, f. *honor*- HONOUR *sb.*] †**1.** *trans.* To do honour to, pay worthy respect to; to worship, perform one's devotions to; to do obeisance or homage to; to venerate –1697. **2.** To hold in honour, respect highly; to reverence, worship; to regard or treat with honour ME. **3.** To confer honour or dignity upon; to do honour or credit to; to grace ME. **4.** *Comm.* To accept or pay (a bill of exchange, etc.) when due. Also *fig.* 1706.

1. They..h. with full Bowls their friendly Guest DRYDEN. **2.** H. thy father and thy mother *Exod.* 20:12. **3.** Thus shal ben honoured, whom euere the king wile honoure WYCLIF *Esther* 6:9. A Custome More honour'd in the breach, then the obseruance *Haml.* I. iv. 16. **4.** Nature has written a letter of credit upon some men's faces, which is honoured almost wherever presented THACKERAY.

Honourable, honor- (ǫ·nərăb'l), *a.* (*sb.*) ME. [– (O)Fr. *honorable* – L. *honorabilis*, f. *honorare*; see prec., -BLE.] **1.** Worthy of being honoured; entitled to respect, esteem, reverence. †**b.** Respectable in quality or amount; decent –1666. **2.** Of distinguished rank; noble, illustrious ME. **b.** Applied as an official or courtesy title 1450. **3.** Characterized by or accompanied with honour ME.; consistent with honour or reputation 1548. **4.** Showing or doing honour ME. **5.** Upright, honest; the reverse of base 1592.

1. He [Crist] is honurabile till all HAMPOLE. Marriage is h., but House-keeping is a Shrew SWIFT. **b.** Dined with Lord Cornbury..who kept a very honorable table EVELYN. **2.** Descended from an honorable family MACAULAY. **b.** The prefix 'Honourable' (Hon.) is given to younger sons of Earls and sons and daughters of peers below the rank of Marquess, to all present or past Maids of Honour, all Justices of the High Court (not being *Lords* Justices nor Lords of Appeal), to Lords of Session, the Lord Provost of Glasgow (during office), and especially to members of Governments or of Executive Councils in India and the Colonies. In the U.S. it is given to members of both Houses of Congress, and of State Legislatures, to judges, justices, etc. *Honourable* is also applied to the House of Commons collectively; 'honourable member' or 'gentleman' is applied to members individually; also formerly to members of the East India Company, etc. *Most Honourable* is applied to Marquesses; also to the Order of the Bath and H.M. Privy Council (collectively). *Right Honourable* is applied to peers below the rank of Marquess, to Privy Councillors, and to certain civil functionaries, as the Lord Mayors of London, York, and Belfast, and the Lord Provosts of Edinburgh and Glasgow; sometimes, also, in courtesy, to the sons and daughters of persons holding courtesy titles. **3.** Sure the Match Were rich and h. *Two Gent.* III. i. 64. To effect an h. peace LYTTON. **4.** An h. monument to his memory BOSWELL. **5.** For Brutus is an H. man *Jul. C.* III. ii. 87–8. The best and most h. course RALEGH.

B. *sb.* **a.** An honourable or distinguished person. **b.** One who has the title of Honourable. So *right h.* (colloq.) ME.

Six bear courtesy titles or are Honourables WARREN. Hence **Ho·nourableness, honor-. Ho·nourably, honor-** *adv.* in an h. manner.

Honourer, honorer (ǫ·nərəɹ). ME. [f. HONOUR *v.* + -ER[1].] One who honours; †a worshipper.

Ho·nourless, *a.* 1560. [f. HONOUR *sb.* + -LESS.] Destitute of honour; unhonoured, or unworthy of honour.

Hont, etc., obs. f. HUNT, etc.

Hoo (hū), *int.* and *sb.* 1606. A natural exclam., used as a call to attract attention, etc. Also imitative of the sound of an owl, the wind, etc. (Cf. WHOO.) So **Hoo-oo.** Hence **Hoo** *v. intr.* to make the sound 'hoo!'.

Hoo, ME. sp. of HO *int.* and *v.*

Hooch (hūtʃ). *U.S. slang.* 1903. Also **hootch.** [abbrev. of Alaskan *hoochinoo*, name of a tribe that made such liquor.] Alcoholic liquor, spirits.

Hood (hud), *sb.* [OE. *hōd* = OFris. *hōd*, MDu. *hoet* (Du. *hoed*), OHG. *huot* (G. *hut* hat) :– WGmc. *χ*ōda*, rel. to HAT.] **1.** A covering for the head and neck (and sometimes the shoulders), either forming part of a larger garment (as the hood of a cowl or cloak) or separate; in the latter sense applied in 14–16th c. to a soft covering for the head worn under the hat. **b.** A soft covering for the head worn by women; also, the close-fitting head-covering of an infant ME. **c.** *fig.* A cap of foam, mist, or cloud 1814. **2.** As a mark of official, or professional dignity; now *spec.* the badge worn over the gown (or surplice) by university graduates as indicating their degrees ME. †**3.** The part of a suit of armour that covers the head –1874. **4.** A covering put over the head of a hawk to keep her quiet 1575. **5.** Anything serving for a covering, capping, or protection, or resembling a hood in shape or use:

a. The straw covering of a beehive. **b.** The head or cover of a carriage; the cover of a pump; *Naut.* 'a covering for a companion-hatch, skylight, etc.' (Smyth). **c.** A dome-shaped projection over a fireplace, chimney, or ventilator; the 'cowl' of a chimney. **d.** The leathern shield in front of a wooden stirrup. **e.** *Shipbuilding* (*pl.*) The foremost and aftermost planks, within and without, of a ship's bottom. **f.** In plants, any hood-like part serving as a covering, esp. the vaulted upper part of the corolla or calyx in some flowers. **g.** In animals (e.g. the cobra and the hooded seal), a conformation of parts, or an arrangement of colour, suggesting a hood. **h.** The waterproof folding top or cover of a perambulator, motor car, etc.; (*U.S.*) = BONNET *sb.* 5 f.

6. The hooded seal; = HOOD-CAP 2. 1854.

Comb.: **h.-end** (*Shipbuilding*), the end of any of the planks which fit into the rabbets of the stem and stern posts; **-gastrula,** a form of secondary gastrula resulting from unequal segmentation, an amphigastrula; **-sheaf,** each of two sheaves placed slantwise on the top of a shock of corn so as to carry off the rain. Hence **Hood** *v. trans.* to cover with or as with a h.; sometimes for protection or concealment.

-hood (hud), *suffix.* [OE. *-hād* = OS. *-hēd*, (O)HG. *-heit*, orig. a Gmc. independent sb. meaning 'person, sex, condition, rank, quality', OE. *hād*, OS. *hēd*, OHG. *heit*, ON. *heiðr* (honour, worth), Goth. *haidus* (kind, manner).]

Hood-cap (hu·dˌkæp). 1842. [f. HOOD *sb.* + CAP *sb.*[1]] **1.** A close cap or bonnet covering the sides of the face, formerly worn by women. **2.** The hooded or bladder-nosed seal, *Cystophora cristata*; so called from having a piece of loose skin over its head, which it inflates when menaced 1864.

Hooded (hu·dėd), *a.* 1440. [f. HOOD *sb.* and *v.* + -ED.] **1.** Wearing or covered with a hood. **b.** Of a garment: Having a hood attached to it 1590. **2.** Of animals: Having a conformation of parts or an arrangement of colour suggesting a hood 1500. **3.** *Bot.* Hood-shaped, cucullate 1597. **4.** Having a protective covering 1847. **5.** *transf.* and *fig.* Covered; blind-folded; concealed 1652.

1. A h. hawk 1621. †*H. man*: (*a*) a Lollard; (*b*) a native Irishman. **2. Hooded crow,** *Corvus cornix.* **H. seal:** see HOOD-CAP 2. **H. serpent** or **snake,** a snake of the family *Elapidæ* or *Najidæ*, having the skin of the neck distensible, so as to resemble a hood; esp. the Indian cobra, *Naja tripudians.*

Hoodie, hoody (hu·di). 1789. [f. as prec. (sense 2) + *-ie* -Y[6].] The Hooded or Royston Crow, *Corvus cornix.* Also **hoodie-crow.**

Hoo·dless, *a.* ME. [f. HOOD *sb.* + -LESS.] Without a hood.

Hoodlum (hu·dlŏm). *U.S. slang.* 1872. [Of unkn. origin.] A youthful street rowdy; a dangerous rough.

†**Hoo·dman.** 1565. A hooded man; the blindfolded player in BLIND-MAN'S-BUFF –1601. So †**Hoo·dman-bli·nd,** blind-man's-buff.

Hoo·d-mould. 1840. A moulding over the head of a window, door, etc.; a label or dripstone. So **Hoo·d-moulding** 1838.

Hoodoo (hū·dū), *sb.* (*a.*) *U.S.* 1885. [unexpl. alt. of VOODOO.] **1.** = VOODOO. **2.** A person or thing whose presence causes bad luck 1889.

B. *adj.* Unlucky, bringing bad luck 1889.

Hoodwink (hu·dwiŋk), *v.* 1562. [f. HOOD *sb.* + WINK *v.*] **1.** *trans.* To cover the eyes with a hood or the like; to blindfold. **2.** *fig.* To cover up from sight 1600. **3.** *fig.* To blindfold mentally; to 'throw dust in the eyes of', humbug 1610. †**4.** *intr.* To wink. MILT.

1. Hawthorne's face was hoodwinked with a cloake 1631. **2.** *Temp.* IV. i. 206. **3.** The public..is easily hoodwinked 1756. Hence **Hoo·dwink** *sb.* †the act of hoodwinking; †the game of blind-man's-buff; a blind. †**Hoo·dwink** *a.* blindfold.

Hoodwort (hu·dwɒɹt). [f. HOOD *sb.* + WORT[1].] An American species of *Scutellaria* or Skull-cap, *S. laterifolia.*

Hoody: see HOODIE.

Hoof (hūf), *sb.* Pl. **hoofs,** occas. **hooves.** [OE. *hōf* = OFris., OS. *hōf* (Du. *hoef*), OHG. *huof* (G. *huf*), ON. *hófr* :– Gmc. **χōfaz*, rel. to synon. Skr. *śaphás*, Avestic *safa.*] **1.** The horny sheath which encases the ends of the digits or the foot of quadrupeds forming the order *Ungulata*, primarily that of the horse and other equine animals. Also *fig.* **2.** A hoofed animal, as the smallest unit of a herd or drove 1535; hence, †a fragment, particle 1655. **3.** The human foot (*joc.* or *derogative*) 1598.

1. Clattering flints batter'd with clanging hoofs TENNYSON. Phr. *To show the cloven h.* (see CLOVEN). **2.** There shal not one hooffe be left behynde COVERDALE *Exod.* 10:26. **3.** Phr. *To beat, pad, be upon the h.*: to be on the move. *To see a person's h. in anything*, to detect his influence in it. *Under the h.*: downtrodden.

Comb.: **h.-cushion, -pad,** a pad or cushion to prevent a horse's foot or shoe from striking or cutting the fellow foot; **-pick.**

Hence **Hoof** *v. intr.* to go on foot; *trans.* to strike with the h. **Hoo·fy** *a.* having a h. or hoofs.

Hoo·f-bound, *a.* (*sb.*) 1598. *Farriery.* Affected with a painful dryness and contraction of the hoof; lamed by having the shoe put on too tight. *sb.* A name for this affection.

Hoofed (hŭft, hū·fėd), *a.* and *ppl. a.* Also **hooved** (hūvd). 1513. [f. HOOF *sb.* and *v.* + -ED.] **1.** Having hoofs, ungulate; as *broad-h.* **2.** Beaten with hoofs 1860.

Hooflet (hū·flėt). 1834. [f. HOOF *sb.* + -LET.] One of the divisions of a cloven hoof.

Hook (huk), *sb.* [OE. *hōc* = OFris., MLG., MDu. *hōk* (Du. *hoek*) corner, angle, point of land, rel. to OE. *haca* bolt, OS. *haco* (MDu. *hake*, Du. *haak*), OHG. *hāko* (G. *haken*) hook, ON. *haki* (whence, or from MDu., dial. *hake* XV).] **1.** A length of metal, or piece of other material, bent back, or fashioned with a sharp angle, adapted for catching hold, dragging, sustaining suspended objects, or the like. (Often qualified to indicate shape or use, as *boat-*, *chain-*, *chimney-h.*, etc.) **b.** *Zool.* and *Bot.* A recurved and pointed organ or appendage of an animal or plant 1666. **2.** A slender bent piece of wire, usually armed with a barb, which is attached to a fishing-line and carries the bait; an angle; *fig.* a snare, a catch OE. **3.** A curved instrument with a cutting edge, as a *weed-hook*, a *reaping-hook* OE. **4.** The crook or pin on which a door or gate is hung; forming the fixed part of the hinge ME. †**5.** A shepherd's crook –1697. **6.** *Shipbuilding.* A bent piece of timber used to strengthen an angular framework. Cf. FUTTOCK. 1611. **7.** A sharp bend or angle, esp. in a river (now in proper names) 1563. **8. a.** A hook-shaped character or symbol; a 'pot-hook' 1668. †**b.** *pl.* Brackets (in printing); also, inverted commas –1806. **c.** *Mus.* One of the lines or marks at the end of the stem of a quaver (♪), etc. 1782. **9.** A projecting corner, point, or spit of land. [app. – Du. *hoek.*] 1855. **10.** *Cricket*, etc. The act of hooking 1897.

2. Farewell, Loue.. Thy bayted hokes shall tangle me no more WYATT. **3.** *Prov.* Ill shearer ne'er a good h. had. **7.** The very straight way that hath neither H. ne crook FOXE.

Phrases. *By h. and* (*or*) *by crook*: by any means, fair or foul. *Off the hooks*: †out of order; †to excess; †out of humour or spirits; at once, summarily. *To drop* (etc.) *off the hooks*, to die (*slang*). *On one's own h.*: on one's own account, at one's own risk (*colloq.*). *To sling* or *take one's hook*: to make off, decamp (*colloq.*).

Comb.: **h. and butt, h.-butt,** 'a mode of scarfing timber so that the parts resist tensile strain to part them' (Knight); **-climber,** a plant that climbs by means of its own hooklets, as members of the genera *Galium* and *Rubus*; **-pin,** a draw-pin; **-scarf, -scarf-joint** = *hook-butt*; **-squid,** a decapodous cephalopod of the family *Onychoteuthididæ*, having long tentacles armed with hooks, the bases of which are furnished with suckers; **-tip,** a moth of the genus *Platypteryx*, having the tips of the wings hook-shaped; **-wrench,** a spanner with a bent end adapted to grasp and turn a nut or coupling piece.

Hook (huk), *v.* ME. [f. prec. sb.] **1.** *trans.* To make hook-like or hooked (*rare*). **2.** *intr.* To bend as a hook ME. **3.** *intr.* To move with a sudden twist or jerk. Now *slang* or *dial.* To make off. Also *hook it.* ME. **4.** *trans.* to lay hold of with a hook; to make fast, attach, or secure with or as with a hook or hooks; to fasten together with hooks, or hooks and eyes 1611. **5.** *intr.* (for *refl.*) To attach oneself or be attached with or as with a hook. *H. on* (fig.): to join on. 1597. **6.** *trans.* To snatch with a hook; to steal 1615. **7.** To catch (a fish) with a hook 1771. Also *fig.* **8.** *transf.* and *fig.* **a.** To drag. **b.** To attach as with a hook. 1577. **c.** *Golf.* To drive (the ball) widely to the left hand. *Cricket.* = DRAW *v.* I. 12. 1857. **d.** *Boxing.* To strike (one's opponent) a swinging blow with the elbow bent 1898. **e.** *Rugby Football.* To secure and pass (the ball) backward with the foot in a scrummage 1906. **9.** To link by a hook or bent part 1823. **10.** To catch with the horns, attack with the horns, as a cow. Also *absol.* *U.S.* 1837.

3. He slipped from her and hooked it MAYHEW. **4.** *To h. on, in, up*, to attach by means of a hook. **5.** Go with her, with her: hooke-on, hooke-on SHAKS. **6.** To h. the money and hide it MARK TWAIN. **7.** *fig.* The first woman who fishes for him, hooks him THACKERAY. **9.** He hooked his arm into Tom's HUGHES.

Hookah (hu·kă). 1763. [– Urdu – Arab. *ḥuḳḳah* casket, vase, cup, etc.] A pipe for smoking, of Eastern origin, having a long flexible tube, the smoke being drawn through water contained in a vase; the narghile of India.

Hook and eye, hook-and-eye. 1578. A metallic fastening, esp. for a dress, consisting of a hook of flattened wire, and an eye or wire loop on which the hook catches. Also *fig.*

Hook-bill. 1613. [See BILL *sb.*^{1} and ^{2}.] **1.** A billhook. **2.** 'The curved beak of a bird' (Ogilvie). **Hoo·k-billed** *a.* having a curved bill.

Hooked (hukt, hu·kėd), *a.* OE. [f. HOOK *sb.* or *v.* + -ED.] **1.** Hook-shaped; hamate. **2.** Having a hook or hooks ME.

Hooker^{1} (hu·kəɹ). 1567. [f. HOOK *v.* + -ER^{1}.] One who or that which hooks.

Hooker^{2} (hu·kəɹ). 1641. [– Du. *hoeker*, f. *hoek* HOOK (in earlier *hoekboot*); see -ER^{1}.] **1.** A two-masted Dutch coasting or fishing vessel. **2.** A one-masted fishing smack on the Irish coast, similar to a hoy in build. Also *attrib.* 1801. **3.** Applied depreciatively or fondly to a ship 1823.

Hooklet (hu·klėt). 1816. [f. HOOK *sb.*, -LET.] A minute hook; esp. in *Nat. Hist.*

Hook-nose. 1681. A nose of a hooked shape with a downward curve; an aquiline nose. So **Hook-nosed** *a.* 1519.

Hooky (hu·ki), *a.* 1552. [f. HOOK *sb.* + -Y^{1}.] Hook-shaped; hooked.

Hool, obs. f. WHOLE.

Hoolee, holī (hū·lī, hōᵘ·lī). *E. Indies.* 1687. [Hindi *hōlī.*] The great carnival of the Hindus, held at the approach of the vernal equinox, in honour of Krishna and the Gopīs or milkmaids.

Hooligan (hū·ligăn). *slang.* 1898. [app. orig. the name of an Irish family in S.E. London conspicuous for ruffianism.] A (young) street rowdy or ruffian.

It is no wonder.. that H. gangs are bred in these vile.. byways *Daily News*, 26 July 1898. Hence **Hoo·liganism.**

‖**Hoolock** (hū·lǫk). 1809. [– *hulluk*, native name.] The black Gibbon, *Hylobates hoolock*, native of Assam.

Hoom(e, obs. ff. HOME.

Hoop (hūp), *sb.*^{1} [Late OE. *hōp* = OFris. *hōp*, MDu. *hoop* (Du. *hoep*) :- WGmc. **xōpa*, rel. to ON. *hóp* small land-locked bay.] **1.** A circular band or ring of metal, wood, etc.; esp. a circle of wood or flattened metal for binding together the staves of casks, tubs, etc. Also *fig.* **2.** Applied to rings, bands, or loops, having similar uses 1867. **2.** A circle of wood or iron (orig. a barrel-hoop) which is trundled along by children 1792. †**4.** One of the bands at equal intervals on a quart pot; hence, the quantity of liquor contained between two of these –1609. **5.** A measure of corn, etc. of varying capacity. Now *local.* ME. **6.** A circle of whalebone, steel, or other elastic material, used to expand the skirt of a woman's dress; hence, a hoop-petticoat or -skirt 1548. **7.** A finger-ring 1500. **8.** Any hoop-like structure or figure; a circle, ring, arc 1530. **9.** One of the iron arches used in croquet 1872.

1. *fig.* The friends thou hast, and their adoption tride, Grapple them to thy Soule, with hoopes of Steele *Haml.* I. iii. 63. **4.** 2 *Hen. VI*, IV. ii. 72. **6.** The swelling h. sustains The rich brocade PRIOR. **7.** A hoope of Gold, a paltry Ring *Merch. V.* V. i. 147.

Comb.: **h.-ash,** *Fraxinus sambucifolia*; also, the American Hackberry, *Celtis occidentalis*; **-bee,** a burrowing bee of the genus *Eucera*; **-cramp,** a ring-clutch for holding the ends of a hoop which are lapped over each other' (Knight); **-iron,** (*a*) thin flat bar-iron of which hoops are made; (*b*) the iron rod with which a child's h. is trundled; **-net,** a fishing-net, butterfly-net, etc. held open by a ring at its mouth; **-ring,** a ring consisting of a plain band; also, a finger-ring encircled with stones in a cut-down setting; **-shell,** a shell of the genus *Trochus*, a top-shell; **-skirt** = HOOP-PETTICOAT; **-snake,** a snake fabled to take its tail in its mouth and roll along like a h., *spec.* the harmless *Abastor erythrogrammus* of U.S.; **-tree,** *Melia sempervirens*; **-wood,** a tree yielding wood for hoops; in Jamaica *Calliandra latifolia*; in U.S. the Hoop-ash.

Hoop, *sb.*^{2} ME. [f. HOOP *v.*^{2} Cf. WHOOP *sb.* and *int.*, Fr. *houp* int.] **1.** A cry or call of 'hoop'. **2.** The sound attending hooping-cough 1811.

Hoop, *sb.*^{3} 1481. [– (O)Fr. *huppe* – pop.L. **ūpupa* for L. *ŭpupa* HOOPOE.] †**1.** The HOOPOE –1708. **2.** A local name for the Bullfinch. [? a different wd.] 1798.

Hoop, *v.*^{1} 1440. [f. HOOP *sb.*^{1}] **1.** To bind or fasten round with a hoop or hoops. **2.** *transf.* and *fig.* To encircle; to bind together, as the staves of a tub 1541.

Hoop, *v.*^{2} [Late ME. *houpe*, *howpe* – (O)Fr. *houper*, f. *houp*; see HOOP *sb.*^{2}] **1.** *intr.* To utter a hoop. †**2.** To shout with astonishment. SHAKS. **3.** To make the sound characteristic of hooping-cough 1822.

1. Ther-with-al they shriked and they howped CHAUCER. **2.** *A.Y.L.* III. ii. 203.

Hoop, *int.* = WHOOP.

Hooper^{1} (hū·pəɹ). ME. [f. HOOP *v.*^{1} + -ER^{1}.] One who fits hoops on casks, barrels, etc.; a cooper.

Hoo·per^{2}. 1556. [f. HOOP *v.*^{2} + -ER^{1}.] **1.** One who hoops or cries 'hoop'; only in *hoopers hide* = hide-and-seek 1719. **2.** The Whooping, Whistling, or Wild Swan, *Cygnus musicus* (*ferus*); so called from its cry.

Hoo·ping-cough. 1747. [f. HOOP *v.*^{2}] A contagious disease chiefly affecting children, and characterized by short, violent, and convulsive coughs, followed by a long sonorous inspiration called the hoop (whoop); the chin-cough. Also WHOOPING-COUGH.

Hoop-la (hū·plā). 1909. [f. HOOP *sb.*^{1} + LA *int.*] A game in which rings are thrown at objects that are won if encircled.

Hoopoe (hū·pū). 1668. [Alteration of HOOP *sb.*^{3}, after L. *upupa*, f. the cry (*up, up*) of the bird.] A bird of the family *Upupidæ*, esp. the typical *Upupa epops*, conspicuous by its variegated plumage and large erectile crest.

Hoo:p-pe·tticoat. 1711. **1.** A petticoat or skirt stiffened and expanded by hoops. **2.** A name for plants of the genus *Corbularia*; from the shape of the flower 1840.

Hoo·p-stick. 1703. **1.** A thin pliable stick or sapling suitable for making cask-hoops. **2.** One of the arched rails forming the framework of a carriage-head 1794.

Hoosh (hūʃ). *slang.* 1905. [Of unkn. origin.] Thick soup.

Hoosier (hū·ʒəɹ). *U.S.* 1832. [Of unkn. origin.] A nick-name for a native of Indiana.

Hoot (hūt), *sb.* 1600. [f. HOOT *v.*] **1.** A loud inarticulate shout, outcry; *spec.* a shout of disapprobation or obloquy; the sound of a motor-horn. **2.** The cry of an owl 1795. **3.** **Hoot owl,** the Tawny Owl, *Syrinium aluco* 1885.

Phr. *Not to care a hoot* or *two hoots* (orig. U.S.).

Hoot (hūt), *v.* [ME. *hūten*, perh. echoic, gave later *hout*, *howt*, altered in XVII to *hoot.*] **1.** *intr.* To shout, call out, make an inarticulate vocal noise; now, esp., to utter loud sounds of disapproval or obloquy. Also with *at* or *after.* **2.** *trans.* To assail with shouts of disapproval or contempt ME. **3.** *intr.* Applied to the cry of some birds, esp. the owl 1500; also to the sounds produced by a siren, fog-signal, etc. 1883.

Hoot (hūt), *int.* *Sc.* and *n. dial.* 1681. A natural exclam. of objection or repulsion; nearly synonymous with *tut!* with which it is combined in the more emphatic *hoot toot.* So **Hoots** *int.* [with advb. *-s.*] 1824.

Hooter (hū·təɹ). 1674. [f. HOOT *v.* + -ER^{1}.] One who or that which hoots; e.g. an owl; a steam whistle or siren 1878; a motor-horn 1908.

Hoove (hūv). 1840. [unexpl. var. of *heaves*; see HEAVE *sb.* 3, HOVEN *ppl. a.*] A disease of cattle, characterized by inflation of the stomach, usually due to eating too much green fodder.

Hop (hǫp), *sb.*^{1} [In XV *hoppe* – MLG., MDu. *hoppe* (Du. *hop*), in OS. *feldhoppo* = late OHG. *hopfo* (G. *hopfen*). The OE. word was *hymele.*] **1.** (Usu. in *pl.*) The ripened cones of the female hop-plant, used for giving a bitter flavour to malt liquors, etc. **2.** A climbing perennial diœcious plant (*Humulus lupulus*, N.O. *Urticaceæ*, suborder *Cannabineæ*), with rough lobed leaves like those of the vine. Much cultivated for the green cones of the female plant. 1538.

Comb.: **h.-back**, a vessel with a perforated bottom for straining off the hops from the liquor in making beer; **-bind, -bine**, the climbing stem of the hop-plant; **-clover** = *hop-trefoil*; **-flea**, a very small beetle (*Phyllotreta* or *Haltica concinna*), destructive to the hop-plant; **-fly**, a species of aphis (*Phorodon humuli*), destructive to the hop-plant; **h. frog-fly h. froth-fly**, a species of froth-fly (*Aphrophora interrupta* or *Amblycephalus interruptus*), destructive to the hop-plant; **h. hornbeam** (see HORNBEAM); **-jack** = *hop-back*; **-mildew**, a parasitic fungus of genus *Sphærotheca*, infesting the h.; **-oast**, a kiln for drying hops; **-pillow**, a pillow stuffed with hops to produce sleep; **-pocket** (see POCKET); **-pole**, a tall pole on which h.-plants are trained; **-tree**, a N. Amer. shrub, *Ptelea trifoliata*, N.O. *Rutaceæ*, with bitter fruit which has been used as a substitute for hops; **-trefoil**, a name for yellow clover (*Trifolium procumbens*); also applied to the hop medick, *Medicago lupulina*; **-vine**, the trailing stem or bine of the hop-plant, or the whole plant. See also Main Words.

Hop (hǫp), *sb.*² 1508. [f. HOP *v.*¹] **1.** An act, or the action, of hopping; a short spring, esp. on one foot. **b.** One stage of a long-distance flight in a flying machine 1909. **2.** *slang* or *colloq.* An informal dance 1731.

1. To take the ball on the h. 1888. Phr. **Hop, step, and jump** (also *h., skip, and jump*, etc.): the action of making these three movements in succession; an athletic exercise in which the players try who can cover most ground with these movements. Also *transf.* and *fig.* Also *attrib.*, and as *vb. intr.*

Hop (hǫp), *v.*¹ Pa. t. and pple. **hopped, hopt** (hǫpt). [OE. *hoppian*, corresp. to MHG. (G. dial.) *hopfen*, ON. *hoppa*, from a base repr. also in OE. *hoppetan*, G. *hopsen*, a var. of which appears in HIP *v.*¹] **1.** *intr.* To spring a short way with a leap, or a succession of leaps; said of persons, animals, and things. Now implying a short or undignified leap. **b.** *spec.* Of animals: To move by leaps with both or all the feet at once 1440. **c.** Of a person: To leap on one foot, or move onwards by a succession of such leaps 1700. **2.** To dance (only playful) ME. **3.** To limp 1700. **4.** *trans.* To hop or jump on to or over 1900.

1. Why hoppe ye so, ye greate hilles? COVERDALE *Ps.* 67(68):16. **b.** H. as light as bird from brier SHAKS. **3.** Away he hops with his crutch DE FOE. **Hop the twig, hop it** (*slang*): to go away quickly, 'be off'.

Hop (hǫp), *v.*² 1572. [f. HOP *sb.*¹] **1.** *trans.* To impregnate or flavour with hops. (Chiefly in *pass.*) **2.** *intr.* Of the plant: To produce hops 1848. **3.** To gather or pick hops 1717.

Hope (hōᵘp), *sb.*¹ [Late OE. *hopa*, also *tōhopa*, corresp. to OLG. *tōhopa*, OFris., MLG., MDu. *hope* (Du. *hoop*); orig. belonging to LG. areas; whence it spread to HG. (MHG. *hoffe*) and Scand. (Sw. *hopp*, Da. *haab*); of unkn. origin.] **1.** Expectation of something desired; desire combined with expectation. Also in pl., in sing. sense. **b.** Personified; esp. as one of the three heavenly graces (1 *Cor.* 13:13.) ME. †**2.** Expectation, prospect –1535. **3.** *transf.* Ground of hope; promise; a person or thing that gives hope for the future; that which is hoped for ME. ¶See also FORLORN HOPE.

1. H. springs eternal in the human breast POPE. Great hopes were entertained at Whitehall that [etc.] MACAULAY. **b.** Fair H., with smiling face but ling'ring foot HAN. MORE. **3.** A Child of great hopes 1676. Ihesu Crist oure h. WYCLIF 1 *Tim.* 1:1. Their brave h. SHAKS. Staking his very life on some dark h. SHELLEY.

Hope (hōᵘp), *sb.*² [Late OE. *hop* = MLG. *hop* (in place-names), MDu. *hop* bay; ult. origin disputed.] **1.** A piece of enclosed land, e.g. in the midst of fens or marshes. **2.** A small enclosed valley, esp. the upland part of a mountain valley ME. **3.** An inlet, small bay, haven ME.

Hope (hōᵘp), *v.* [Late OE. *hopian* = OFris. *hopia*, (M)Du. *hopen* (orig., like HOPE *sb.*¹, belonging to LG. areas), whence MHG., G. *hoffen*.] **1.** *intr.* To entertain expectation of something desired; to look (mentally) with expectation. **2.** *intr.* To trust, have confidence. (Now only a strong case of sense 1.) OE. **3.** *trans.* To expect with desire, or to desire with expectation; to look forward to OE. †**4.** To anticipate; to suppose, think, expect –1632.

1. H. for the best 1726. I hoped for better things from him 1899. **3.** None would live past years again; Yet all h. pleasure in what yet remain DRYDEN. When may we h. to see you SWIFT. **4.** Our Manciple I h. he wil be deed CHAUCER.

Hopeful (hōᵘpfŭl), *a.* (*sb.*) 1568. [f. HOPE *sb.*¹ + -FUL.] **1.** Full of hope; feeling hope; expectant of that which is desired 1594; expressive of hope 1607. **2.** Causing or inspiring hope; promising; sometimes ironical 1568. **3.** *sb.* A 'hopeful' boy or girl; chiefly ironical 1720.

1. H. of some reward 1665. **2.** Money to maintain h. students at the University WOOD. Here comes his h. nephew GOLDSM. **3.** Hoards diminish'd by young Hopeful's debts BYRON. Hence **Ho·peful-ly** *adv.*, **-ness**.

Hopeless (hōᵘ·plės), *a.* 1566. [f. as prec. + -LESS.] **1.** Destitute of hope; having no hope; despairing 1590. **2.** Of or concerning which there is no hope; despaired of, desperate 1566. †**3.** Unexpected –1624.

1. On this [ice-floe] they spent a dismal and h. night SCORESBY. **2.** H. depravity JOHNSON, maladies MACAULAY. Hence **Ho·peless-ly** *adv.*, **-ness**.

Ho·per. ME. [f. HOPE *v.* + -ER¹.] One who hopes.

Ho·p-gar:den. 1573. [f. HOP *sb*¹.] A piece of land devoted to the cultivation of hops.

Hoplite (hǫ·plait). 1727. [– Gr. ὁπλίτης, f. ὅπλον weapon, ὅπλα arms: see -ITE¹ 1.] A heavy-armed foot-soldier of ancient Greece.

Hoplo- (hǫplo), bef. a vowel **hopl-**, comb. f. Gr. ὅπλον weapon, piece of armour, or of ὁπλή hoof, as in **Hoplognathous** (-ǫ·gnăþəs) [Gr. γνάθος] *a.*, 'having the jaw armed' (*Syd. Soc. Lex.*). **Hoplo·podous** [Gr. ὁπλή hoof, πούς, ποδ- foot] *a.*, *Zool.* having the feet protected by hoofs.

Hop-o'-my-thumb (hǫ·pŏmiþʊ:m). Also **Hopthumb.** 1530. [orig. *hop on my thombe*, from HOP *v.*¹ (in imperative mood), applied hyperbolically to a very small person.] A dwarf, a pygmy. Cf. *Tom Thumb*.

Hopped (hǫpt), *a.* 1669. [f. HOP *sb.*¹ or *v.*² + -ED.] Furnished, mixed, or flavoured with hops.

Hopper¹ (hǫ·pəɹ). ME. [f. HOP *v.*¹ + -ER¹. The origin of sense 5 is not clear.] **1.** One who hops; in *pl.* a kind of game: see HOPSCOTCH. **2.** That which hops, esp. an insect or insect-larva that hops. Applied to a grasshopper, a froth-hopper, a cheese-hopper, etc. ME. **3.** A receiver like an inverted pyramid or cone, through which grain or anything to be ground passes into the mill; so called because it had originally a hopping or shaking motion ME. **4.** Any article resembling a mill hopper in shape or use 1763. **5.** A basket; *esp.* that in which the sower carries his seed. Now *dial.* ME. **6.** A barge in attendance on a dredging machine, which carries the mud or gravel out to sea and discharges it through an opening in its bottom. Also *h.-barge*. 1759. **7.** *Pianoforte.* A piece attached at the back part of a key to raise the hammer and regulate the distance to which it falls back from the string after striking it. Also called *grasshopper*. 1840. **8.** *attrib.*, as *hopper feed*, etc. 1500.

Comb.: **h.-boy**, 'a name given in mills to a rake which moves in a circle, drawing the meal over an opening through which it falls' (Craig); **-car**, a kind of truck for carrying coal, gravel, etc., shaped like a h., and emptying through an opening at the bottom; **-cock**, a valve for water-closets, etc.; **-hood**, a hooded seal in its second year. Hence **Ho·pperings** *sb. pl.*, gravel retained in the hopper of a gold-washing cradle 1893.

Hopper² (hǫ·pəɹ). 1719. [f. HOP *v.*² + -ER¹.] **1.** A hop-picker. **2.** A brewer's vat in which the infusion of hops is prepared to be added to the wort (*Cent. Dict.*). **3.** *attrib.*, as *h.-house* 1883.

†**Hoppestere.** [OE. *hoppystre*, f. *hoppian* to hop; see -STER.] A female dancer. In Chaucer used attrib. = 'dancing'. –ME.

Hoppet (hǫ·pėt). Chiefly *n. dial.* 1671. [perh. HOPPER¹ + -ET. Also in form *hobbet*.] **1.** A basket, esp. a small hand-basket. **2.** A large bucket, for lowering and raising men and materials in a mine shaft, etc. 1865. **3.** A beehive. *dial.*

Hop-picker. 1760. A labourer who picks the ripe hops from the bines; also, a machine for picking, cleaning, and sorting hops.

Hopping (hǫ·piŋ), *vbl. sb.*¹ ME. [f. HOP *v.*¹ + -ING¹.] **1.** The action of HOP *v.*¹ **2.** A dance; a rural festival ME.

Hopping, *vbl. sb.*² 1717. [f. HOP *sb.*¹ or *v.*² + -ING¹.] **1.** Hop-picking. **2.** The flavouring of malt liquor with hops 1816.

Hopping, *ppl. a.* 1785. [f. HOP *v.*¹ + -ING².] That hops (see HOP *v.*¹). **Hopping-dick,** name for a species of thrush (*Merula leucogenys*) common in Jamaica, resembling the blackbird. Hence **Ho·ppingly** *adv.*

Hopple (hǫ·p'l), *v.* 1586. [prob. of LG. origin; cf. early Flem. *hoppelen* (Kilian) = MDu. *hobelen* jump, dance; see HOBBLE *v.*] *trans.* To fasten together the legs of (a horse, etc.) to prevent it from straying; also *transf.* to fetter (a human being); cf. HOBBLE *v.* 6. Hence **Ho·pple** *sb.* an apparatus for hoppling horses, etc.; *transf.* a fetter.

‖**Hoppo** (hǫ·po). 1711. [Chinese *hoopoo*.] In China: The board of revenue or customs. Also (short for **h.-man**) an officer of the customs.

Hop-sack, hopsack (hǫ·psæk). 1481. [f. HOP *sb.*¹] **1.** A sack in which hops are packed. **2.** = next, b. 1892.

Hop-sacking. 1884. **a.** A coarse fabric of hemp and jute, of which hop-sacks are made. **b.** Applied to a woollen dress-fabric made with a roughened surface.

Hopscotch (hǫ·pskǫtʃ). 1801. [f. HOP *sb.*¹ + SCOTCH *sb.*¹ a line or scratch.] A children's game, consisting in hopping on one foot and driving forward with it a flat stone from one compartment to another of an oblong figure traced out on the ground, so as always to clear each scotch or line. Also *Hop-score*, *Hop-scot*, and (earlier) *Scotch-hoppers*.

Hopthumb: see HOP-O'-MY-THUMB.

Hop-yard. 1533. = HOP-GARDEN.

Horal (hōᵊ·răl), *a.* 1717. [– late L. *horalis*, f. L. *hora* HOUR; see -AL¹.] Of or pertaining to an hour or hours. Hence **Ho·rally** *adv.* hourly.

Horary, *sb. rare.* 1631. [– mod.L. *horarium* book of hours, subst. use of n. sing. of med.L. *horarius*; see next.] †**1.** *Eccl.* A book of offices for the canonical hours –1789. **2.** An hourly narrative 1864.

Horary (hōᵊ·rări), *a.* 1620. [– med.L. *horarius*, f. *hora* HOUR; see -ARY¹. Cf. Fr. *horaire* adj. (XVII).] **1.** Of, relating to, or indicating the hours 1664. **2.** Occurring every hour 1632. †**3.** Lasting only for an hour, or a short time.

1. *H. angle* = HOUR-ANGLE. *H. circle*: see CIRCLE *sb.*; also, the circle of hours on a dial-plate. **2.** H. shifts Of shirts and waste-coats B. JONS. **3.** Melons, Cucumbers, and other H. Fruits 1698.

H. question (Astrol.): a question the answer to which is obtained by erecting a figure of the heavens for the moment at which it is propounded 1647.

Horatian (horēⁱ·ʃ'ăn), *a.* (*sb.*) 1851. [– L. *Horatianus* (Gellius), f. *Horatius*, gentile name of the poet *Horace*; see -AN.] **1.** Belonging to or characteristic of the Latin poet Horace, or his poetry. **2.** *sb.* The language of Horace.

Horde (hōᵊɹd), *sb.* 1555. [– Pol. *horda* (whence Fr., G., Du. *horde*, Sw. *hord*), corresp. to Russ. *ordá*, It., Rum. *orda*; all ult. – Turki *ordī*, *ordū* camp. See URDU.] **1.** A tribe or troop of nomads, dwelling in tents or wagons, and migrating from place to place for pasturage, or for war or plunder. **2.** *transf.* A great company, esp. of the savage, uncivilized, or uncultivated 1613. **b.** Of animals: A moving swarm or pack 1834.

1. *Golden H.*, a tribe who possessed the khanate of Kiptchak, in Eastern Russia and western and central Asia, from the 13th c. till 1480. **2.** The h. of regicides BURKE. Hence **Horde** *v. intr.* to form a h.; to live as in a h.

Hordein (hǭ·ɹdiˌin). 1826. [f. L. *hordeum* barley + -IN¹.] *Chem.* A pulverulent substance obtained from barley-meal; a mixture of starch, cellular tissue, and an azotized body.

Hore, obs. f. HOAR.

Horehound, hoarhound (hōᵊ·ɹhaund). [OE. *hāre hūne*, f. *hār* HOAR + *hūne* 'marrubium', name of a plant, of unkn. origin. For the parasitic *d* cf. BOUND *ppl. a.*¹, SOUND *sb.*²] **1.** A labiate herb, *Marrubium vulgare*, having stem and leaves covered with white cottony pubescence; its aromatic bitter juice is much used as a remedy for coughs, etc. Hence extended to allied herbs, horehound proper being then distinguished as *Common* or *White H.* **2.** An extract of the plant *Marrubium vulgare*, used as a remedy for coughs 1562. **3.** *attrib.* 1855.

1. Black, Fetid, or **Stinking H.,** *Ballota nigra*, a common weed with dull purple flowers; **Water H.,** species of *Lycopus*.

Horizon (horəi·zən, -z'n), *sb.* [ME. *orizont(e, orizon* – OFr. *orizonte, orizon* (mod. *horizon*) – late L. *horizon, -ont-* – Gr. ὁρίζων, subst. use (sc. κύκλος circle) of pres. pple. of ὁρίζειν bound, limit, define, f. ὅρος boundary.] **1.** The boundary-line of that part of the earth's surface visible from a given point; the line at which earth and sky appear to meet. In strict use, the circle bounding the part of the earth's surface which would be visible if no irregularities or obstructions were present (called the *apparent, natural, sensible, physical* or *visible h.*, as dist. from 3), being the circle of contact with the earth's surface of a cone whose vertex is at the observer's eye. On the open sea or a great plain these coincide. **2.** *fig.* The boundary or limit of any circle or sphere of view, thought, action, etc.; limit or range of one's knowledge, experience, or interest; occas. = the region so bounded 1607. **3.** *Astron.* A great circle of the celestial sphere, the plane of which passes through the centre of the earth and is parallel to that of the sensible horizon of a given place; dist. as the *astronomical, celestial, mathematical, rational, real*, or *true h.* ME. **b.** *transf.* The celestial hemisphere within the horizon of any place 1577. **4. a.** The broad ring (usu. of wood) in which an artificial globe is fixed, the upper surface of which represents the plane of the rational horizon 1592. **b.** *Artificial* or *false h.*: a level reflecting surface, usu. of mercury, used in taking altitudes 1812. **5.** *Geol.* A plane of stratification assumed to have been once horizontal and continuous; a stratum characterized by particular fossils 1856. **6.** *Zool.* and *Anat.* A level line or surface, as the horizon of the teeth, that of the diaphragm. **7.** *attrib.* 1774.

1. And whiten gan the Orisonte shene CHAUCER. Nights Hemisphere had veild the H. round MILT. *P.L.* IX. 52. **2.** The Minister, who then began to climb the H. of favour 1659. **3. b.** When the Morning Sunne shall rayse his Carre Aboue the Border of this Ho·rizon 3 *Hen. VI*, IV. vii. 81. Hence **Hori·zon** *v.* to furnish with a h.; chiefly in *pa. pple.*; **Hori·zonless** *a.*, visually boundless.

Horizontal (hǫrizǫ·ntăl), *a.* (*sb.*) 1555. [– Fr. *horizontal* or mod.L. *horizontalis*, f. late L. *horizont-*; see prec., -AL¹.] **1.** Of or belonging to the horizon; on or occurring at the horizon. **2.** Parallel to the plane of the horizon; level, flat; measured in a line or plane parallel to the horizon 1638. **b.** *Bot.* Applied to parts or organs having a position at right angles to the stem or axis 1753. **c.** *Zool.* and *Anat.* Applied to parts, organs, or markings parallel to a plane supposed to extend from end to end and from side to side of the body 1881.

1. *H. parallax*, the geocentric parallax of a heavenly body when on the horizon. **2.** *H. plane* in *Perspective*, a plane at the level of the eye, intersecting the perspective plane at right angles, the line of intersection being the *h. line. H. (steam) engine*, one in which the piston moves horizontally. *H. wheel*, a wheel the plane of which is h., the axis being vertical; in a carriage, the wheel-plate or 'fifth wheel'.

B. *sb.* (the adj. used *ellipt.*) †**1.** = HORIZON 1555. **2.** *ellipt.* A horizontal line, bar, member, etc. 1674.

Hence **Horizo·ntalism,** the quality of being, or of having some part, h. **Ho:rizonta·lity,** h. condition, quality, or position. **Horizo·ntalize** *v.* to place in a h. position; whence **Horizo·ntaliza·tion,** the action of making h.; in *Craniometry*, the placing of the skull with the datum-plane truly h. **Horizo·ntally** *adv.*

†**Horme·tic,** *a. rare.* 1666. [– Gr. ὁρμητικός, f. ὁρμᾶν urge on; see -IC.] Having the property of urging on or impelling –1678.

Hormone (hǭ·ɹmoᵘn). *Physiol. Chem.* 1906. [f. Gr. ὁρμῶν, pres. pple. of ὁρμᾶν urge on.] A substance formed in an organ and serving to excite some vital process, as secretion. Hence **Hormo·nic** *a.*

Horn (hǭɹn), *sb.* [OE. *horn*, corresp. to OFris., OS., OHG., ON. *horn* (Du., G. *horn*), Goth. *haurn* :– Gmc. **χornaz, -am*, rel. to L. *cornu*, Gr. κέρας.]

I. 1. A non-deciduous excrescence, often curved and pointed, consisting of an epidermal sheath growing about a bony core, on the head of certain mammals, as cattle, sheep, goats, antelopes, etc. Also *fig.* **b.** That borne by the Ram (Aries) and Bull (Taurus) as figured among the constellations; etc.; the stars situated in those parts of the constellations ME. **c.** Put for 'horned animal' 1588. **2.** Each of the two branched appendages on the head of a deer. (These are osseous, deciduous, and (usually) borne only by the male.) OE. **3.** †The tusk of an elephant; the tusk of a narwhal 1607. **4.** A projection or process on the head of other animals; e.g. the excrescence on the beak of the HORNBILL, the antennæ or feelers of insects and crustaceans, the tentacles of gastropods, esp. of the snail and slug; also, loosely, a crest of feathers, a plumicorn, as in the horned owl, etc. ME. **5.** Horns have been attributed to deities, demons, to Moses, etc., and are represented in images, pictures, etc. ME. †**6.** Cuckolds were said to wear horns on the brow –1822. **7.** In Biblical uses: An emblem of power; a means of defence or resistance; hence *h. of salvation* used of God or Christ.

1. c. My Lady goes to kill hornes *L.L.L.* IV. i. 113. **3.** Hornes of Iuorie, and Ebenie *Ezek.* 27 : 15. **4.** Phr. *To draw in* (*pull in*, etc.) *one's horns*: to lower one's pretensions: in allusion to the snail's habit of drawing in its retractile tentacles (which bear the eyes), when disturbed. **6.** *Much Ado*, II. i. 28. **7.** Phr. *To lift up the h.*: to exalt oneself; to show fight.

II. 1. The substance of which the horns of animals are made, as a material for manufacturing purposes, etc. 1545. **2.** A structure of the nature of horn; the epidermis or cuticle of which hoofs, nails, corns, the callosities on the camel's legs, etc. consist ME. **3.** An article made of horn; the side of a lantern; a horn spoon or scoop, a SHOE-HORN 1483.

1. H. is a still more powerful manure than bone 1843.

III. 1. A vessel formed from, or shaped after, the horn of a cow or other beast, for holding liquid, powder, etc.; a drinking-horn; a powder-flask; etc. Hence a hornful. OE. **2.** A wind instrument more or less resembling a horn in shape. Often qualified, as *bugle h., hunting-h.*, etc. OE. **b.** (More fully *French h.*) An orchestral wind instrument of the trumpet class, developed from the hunting-horn, and consisting of a continuous tube some 17 feet in length, curved for convenience in holding, and having a wide bell and a conoidal mouthpiece 1742. **c.** An 8-foot reed-stop on an organ 1722. **d.** An instrument on motor vehicles, etc., sounded as a warning signal 1901. **3.** The wind instrument as used in legal process ME.

1. A penne and ink-horne 1583. Phr. *H. of plenty* or *abundance* = CORNUCOPIA. **2.** Ther's a Post come from my Master, with his horne full of good newes *Merch. V.* V. i. 47. Phr. *To wind the h.*, to sound the h.; also *fig.* of insects piping or humming. What time the grey-fly winds her sultry h. MILT. *Lycidas* 28. **b.** The voice was drown'd By the French h. POPE. *English h.* (Fr. *cor anglais*), a wind instrument of the oboe kind, the tenor oboe in F. **3.** Phr. *To put* (*denounce*) *to the h.*, to proclaim an outlaw.

IV. 1. A horn-like appendage or ornament worn on the head. (Cf. sense I. 5.) ME. **2.** A horn-like projection at each corner of the altar in the Jewish temple; one of the two outer corners of the altar in some churches OE. **3.** Each end of a crescent; each extremity of the moon in her first and last quarters; a cusp OE. **b.** Each tip or end of a bow 1611. **4.** Each of the two wings of an army (L. *cornu*) 1533. **5.** Each of two (or more) lateral projections, arms, or branches ME. **6. a.** The awns of barley (*dial.*) 1825. **b.** *fig.* Rigid branches of leafless trees 1850. **7.** A pointed or tapering projection (see below) ME. **8.** *Arch.* Each of the Ionic volutes (likened to rams' horns); the projections of an abacus, etc. OE. **9.** *Naut.* One of the jaws, or semicircular ends of booms and gaffs; also, the outer end of a cross-tree 1794. **10.** *Fortif.* = HORNWORK 1709. **11.** Each of the alternatives of a dilemma (schol. L. *argumentum cornutum*), on which one is figured as liable to be impaled 1548.

1. High head attire piked with horns CAMDEN. **2.** *Exod.* 27 : 2. **3.** The Idol Isis, bearing two hornes of the Moone MORYSON. **5.** Within the long horns of a sandy bay MORRIS. **7. a.** The beak of an anvil. **b.** Each of the crutches on a side-saddle; also the high pommel of a Spanish saddle. **c.** A promontory. **d.** A mountain peak (occas. *fig.*, or = Swiss-Ger. *horn*). **e.** A part of a plant shaped like a horn, beak, or spur. **f.** The minute apex of a Hebrew letter. **11.** Both the Horns of Fates Dilemma wound COWLEY.

attrib. and *Comb.* **1.** General: as *h.-blower*; *h. bow, cup, lantern*; *h. measurement, shavings*, etc. **2.** Special: †**h. ABC** = HORN-BOOK; †**-beast,** a horned beast; **-beech** = HORNBEAM; †**-coot** = HORN-OWL; **-core,** the central bony part of the h. of quadrupeds, a process of the frontal bone; **-distemper,** a disease of cattle, affecting the internal substance of the horn; **-drum** (*Hydraulics*), a water-raising wheel divided into sections by curved partitions (Knight); **-eyed** *a.*, having a horny film over the eye, dull-eyed; **-fly,** a dipterous insect, *Hæmatobia serrata*, which clusters on the horns of cattle; **-frog,** the horned frog; **h. grass,** a grass of the genus *Ceratochloa*; **-lead,** chloride of lead, which assumes a horny appearance on fusing; **-maker,** †one who cuckolds; **-mercury,** chloride of mercury; **-nose,** a rhinoceros; †**-penny** = HORNGELD; **-pike,** the garfish; **-pith,** the soft porous bone which fills the cavity of a h.; **-plant,** a seaweed, *Ecklonia buccinalis*; **-pock, -pox,** a mild form of small-pox or chicken-pox; **-poppy,** the Horned Poppy, *Glaucium luteum*; **-pout** (*U.S.*), a name of fishes of the genus *Amiurus*, esp. *A. catus*; **-quicksilver,** = *horn-mercury*; **-rimmed** *a.*, (wearing spectacles) having rims made of horn; **-snake,** the Pine Snake or Bull Snake, *Coluber melanoleucus*; **-tail,** an insect of the family *Uroceridæ*, having a prominent h. on the abdomen of the male; **-weed,** (*a*) = HORNWORT; (*b*) = *horn-plant*.

Horn (hǭɹn), *v.* ME. [f. prec.] **1.** To furnish with horns or horn. †**2.** To cuckold –1823. **3.** To butt or gore with the horns 1599. **b.** *To h. in*: to 'butt in' (*U.S.*) 1912. **4.** To adjust (the frame of a ship) so as to be at right angles to the line of the keel 1850. †**5.** *Sc. Law.* To 'put to the horn' –1705.

Hornbeak (hǭ·ɹnbīk). Now *dial.* 1565. = HORN-FISH 1.

Hornbeam (hǭ·ɹnbīm). 1568. [f. HORN *sb.* + BEAM.] A tree, *Carpinus betulus*, indigenous in England; so called from its hard, tough, close-grained wood. Also *C. americana*, the Blue Beech. (Earlier called *hard-beam.*)

Hop Hornbeam, the genus *Ostrya*, so called from the hop-like appearance of the ripe catkins; it has two species, *O. vulgaris* of Southern Europe, and *O. virginica* of America.

Hornbill (hǭ·ɹnbil). 1773. [f. HORN *sb.* + BILL *sb.*²] A bird of the family *Bucerotidæ*, so called from the horn-like excrescence surmounting the bill.

H. Cuckoo, the keel-billed Cuckoo, *Crotophaga*, of N. America.

Hornblende (hǭ·ɹnblend). Also **-blend.** 1770. [– G. *hornblende*, f. *horn* horn + BLENDE.] *Min.* A mineral closely allied to augite, and composed chiefly of silica, magnesia, and lime. It is a constituent of many rocks, as granite, syenite, etc., and has numerous varieties, which are sometimes all included under the name AMPHIBOLE¹. It is usually of a dark brown, black, or greenish-black colour. Also *attrib.*, as in **hornblende schist, slate,** hornblende rock of a schistose nature. Hence **Hornble·ndic** *a.* of the nature of, or containing h.

Horn-book (hǭ·ɹnbuk). 1588. A leaf of paper containing the alphabet (often, also, the ten digits, some elements of spelling, and the Lord's Prayer) protected by a thin plate of translucent horn, and mounted on a tablet of wood with a handle. See also BATTLEDORE 3. Also *transf.* a primer.

Yes, yes, he teaches boyes the Horne-booke *L.L.L.* V. i. 49.

Horned (hǭ·ɹnĕd, hǭɹnd), *a.* ME. [f. HORN *sb.* + -ED².] **1.** Having horns. **2.** Having, bearing, or wearing an appendage, ornament, etc., called a horn; having horn-like projections or excrescences ME. †**3.** Applied to bishops with reference to the shape of the mitre –1651. **4.** Furnished or fitted with horn 1590.

1. Cerastes hornd, Hydrus, and Ellops drear MILT. *P.L.* x. 525. *H. syllogism* (*argument*, etc.): the dilemma 1548. **2.** One side of a Silver Medal we find Moses h. SIR T. BROWNE. **Horned crow** or **pie**, old name of the Hornbill. **H. frog, toad,** a lizard of the genus *Phrynosoma*, having the head and back covered with spikes (*U.S.*). **H. hog,** (*a*) the Babiroussa; †(*b*) a kind of fish with a horn on its head. **H. horse,** the Gnu. †**H.-snout,** the rhinoceros. Also *Horned* LARK (*sb.*[1]), OWL, POPPY, etc. Hence **Ho·rnedness.**

Horner (hǭ·ɹnəɹ). ME. [f. HORN *sb.* or *v.* + -ED[1].] **1.** A worker in horn. **2.** One who blows or winds a horn ME. †**3.** One who cuckolds –1717. †**4.** *Sc. Law.* One who has been 'put to the horn' 1568.

Hornet (hǭ·ɹnėt). OE. [The forms *hornet* (XVI), and earlier *harnette* (XIV), *hernet* (XV) are prob. – MLG. *hornte*, MDu. *hornte*, *hornete*, corresp. to OE. *hyrnet*, OS. *hornut*, OHG. *hornuz* (G. *hornisse*), which have the appearance of derivs. of HORN; see -ET.] **1.** An insect of the wasp family, esp. the European *Vespa crabro* and the American *V. maculata*, much larger and stronger than other wasps, and inflicting a more serious sting. Also *transf.* and *fig.* †**2.** The horned beetle or stag-beetle –1598. **3.** An artificial fly for salmon-fishing 1867.

1. Phr. *To bring a hornet's nest about one's ears, arouse a nest of hornets*: to stir up a host of virulent enemies around one. *Comb.*: **h.-clearwing, -hawk, -moth,** names for certain moths of the genus *Sesia*; **-fly,** a dipterous insect of the family *Asilidæ*, a hawk-fly or robber-fly.

Horn-fish. OE. **1.** The garfish, *Belone vulgaris*, so called from its long projecting beak. **2.** The sauger or sand-pike, *Stizostedium canadense* 1885. **3.** A fish of the family *Syngnathidæ*; a pipe-fish.

†**Horngeld.** 12th c. [f. HORN *sb.* + GELD *sb.*] *Old Law.* = CORNAGE –1628.

Hornify (hǭ·ɹnifəi), *v.* 1607. [f. HORNY *a.* + -FY.] **1.** *trans.* To make horny or horn-like 1670. †**2.** To cuckold –1769.

Horning (hǭ·ɹniŋ), *vbl. sb.* ME. [f. HORN *sb.* or *v.* + -ING[1].] †**1.** Covering or furnishing with horn. †**2.** Cuckolding, cuckoldry –1762. **3.** *Sc. Law.* 'Putting to the horn'; proclaiming an outlaw 1536. **4.** The fact of becoming a crescent 1646. **5.** *Shipbuilding*: see HORN *v.* 4. 1879.

3. *Letters of h.*: a process of execution issued under the signet directing a messenger to charge a debtor to pay or perform in terms of the letters, under pain of being 'put to the horn', i.e. declared rebel. (Not quite obsolete.)

Hornish (hǭ·ɹniʃ), *a.* 1634. [f. HORN *sb.* + -ISH[1].] Of or pertaining to a horn; of the nature of horn.

‖**Hornito** (hornī·to). 1830. [Sp., dim. of *horno* (:– L. *furnus*) oven, furnace.] A low oven-shaped mound of volcanic origin, usually emitting smoke and vapour.

Hornless (hǭ·ɹnlės), *a.* ME. [f. HORN *sb.* + -LESS.] Without horns.

Horn-mad, *a. arch.* 1579. App. orig. of horned beasts: Enraged so as to be ready to horn any one. Hence of persons: Stark mad; furious. †**b.** Sometimes by word-play: Furious because cuckolded –1822.

b. Why Mistresse, sure my Master is horne mad. ..I meane not Cuckold mad, But sure he is starke mad *Com. Err.* II. i. 57.

Horn-owl. 1601. A horned owl, or one having plumicorns on the head, as some species of *Asio* and *Otus*; †a name for the Eagle-owl.

Hornpipe (hǭ·ɹnpəip). ME. **1.** An obsolete wind instrument. So called from having the bell and mouthpiece made of horn. **2.** A lively dance, usually performed by a single person, orig. to the accompaniment of the wind instrument, and associated with the merrymaking of sailors 1485. **3.** A piece of music for such a dance 1789. **4.** *attrib.* 1797.

1. A..Tabrere That..a Horne pype playd SPENSER.

Horn-plate. 1856. An iron frame attached to the lower part of a carriage or truck and having two guides in which the journal-box of the axle moves; an axle-guard, pedestal.

Horn-silver. 1770. [tr. G. *hornsilber.*] *Min.* Native chloride of silver; cerargyrite.

†**Hornslate.** 1791. [tr. G. *hornschiefer.*] *Min.* A schistous form of hornstone.

Hornstone (hǭ·ɹnˌstōᵘn). 1668. [tr. G. *hornstein*; so named from its appearance.] *Min.* Chert.

Ho·rnswo:ggle, *v. U.S. slang.* 1829. [Of unkn. origin.] *trans.* To best, swindle, humbug, bamboozle.

†**Horn-wood,** *a.* 1500. [f. HORN *sb.* + WOOD *a.* mad.] = HORN-MAD –1600.

Hornwork (hǭ·ɹnwɒɹk). 1641. [f. HORN *sb.* + WORK.] **1.** *Fortif.* An outwork, consisting of two demi-bastions connected by a curtain and joined to the main work by two parallel wings. **2.** Work done in horn 1642. †**3.** Cuckoldry –1813.

Hornwort (hǭ·ɹnwɒɹt). 1805. [f. HORN *sb.* + WORT[1], after Gr. κερατόφυλλον, i.e. horn-leaf.] An aquatic plant, *Ceratophyllum demersum*, with dense whorls of finely divided leaves; also called *Horned Pondweed*.

Hornwrack (hǭ·ɹnræk). 1819. [f. HORN *sb.* + WRACK *sb.*[2]] A polyzoon of the genus *Flustra*, resembling a seaweed, and of somewhat horny consistency.

Horny (hǭ·ɹni), *a.* ME. [f. HORN *sb.* + -Y[1].] **1.** Consisting of horn; resembling horn; corneous. **2.** *transf.* Callous and hardened so as to be horn-like in texture 1693; hence *h.-handed* 1859. **3.** Semi-opaque 1652. **4.** Having or abounding in horns or horn-like projections 1530.

1. The Ravens with their h. beaks Food to Elijah bringing MILT. *P.R.* II. 267. **2.** Till his hard h. Fingers ake with Pain DRYDEN. **3.** The dim and h. spectacle of senses BP. HALL.

Horography (horǫ·grăfi). 1727. [– Fr. *horographie*, f. Gr. ὥρα time, season + -γραφία -GRAPHY.] **1.** The art of making or constructing dials. **2.** 'An account of the hours' (J.) 1755. So **Horo·grapher.**

Horologe (hǫ·rǫlǫdʒ). [ME. *orloge* – OFr. *orloge, oriloge* (mod. *horloge*) :– L. *horologium* time-piece – Gr. ὡρολόγιον, dim. of ὡρολόγος, f. ὥρα time, hour + -λογος telling (see -LOGUE). Refash. later after L.] An instrument for telling the hour; a timepiece; a dial, hourglass, or clock. Also *transf.* and *fig.* (see quot.).

A Clokke or an abbey Orlogge CHAUCER. Many other flowers close and open their petals at certain hours of the day; and thus constitute, what Linneus calls the H., or Watch of Flora E. DARWIN. So **Horo·loger,** a clock- or watch-maker; a proclaimer of the hours. **Horo·logist,** a horologer.

Horologic (hǫrolǫ·dʒik), *a.* 1665. [– late L. *horologicus* – Gr. ὡρολογικός; see prec., -IC.] Of or pertaining to horology. So **Horolo·gical** *a.* of or pertaining to a horologe or to horology; measuring time.

†**Horologiography** (hǫ:rolǫdʒiǫ·grăfi). 1639. [– mod.L. *horologiographia* (Dee); see HOROLOGE, -GRAPHY.] **a.** A description of horologes or timepieces. **b.** The art of constructing them. –1696. Hence †**Horologio·grapher,** a maker of timepieces. †**Horologiogra·phic** *a.* relating to dialling.

‖**Horologium** (hǫrolǫ·dʒiŏm, -lōᵘ·dʒiŏm). 1661. [L., see HOROLOGE.] **1.** = HOROLOGE. **2.** *Astrol.* A southern constellation 1819. **3.** *Gr. Ch.* A book containing the offices for the canonical hours 1724.

Horology[1] (horǫ·lŏdʒi). ME. [– L. *horologium*; see HOROLOGE.] †**1.** = HOROLOGE –1836. **2.** = HOROLOGIUM 3. 1890.

Horo·logy[2]. 1819. [f. Gr. ὥρα time, hour + -LOGY.] The art or science of measuring time; the construction of horologes. So **Horo·logist** 1798.

Horometer (horǫ·mĭtəɹ). 1775. [f. as prec. + -METER.] An instrument for measuring the time. Hence **Horome·trical** *a.* of or pertaining to the measurement of time.

Horometry (horǫ·mĭtri). 1570. [f. as prec. + -METRY.] The measurement of time; also, 'the determination of the exact error of a time-piece by observation'.

Account of the Hindustanee H. 1798.

Horopter (horǫ·ptəɹ). 1704. [f. Gr. ὅρος limit + ὀπτήρ one who looks. Cf. Fr. *horoptère.*] *Optics.* A line or surface containing all those points in space, of which images fall on corresponding points of the two retinæ; the aggregate of points which are seen single in any given position of the eyes. Hence **Horopte·ric, Horo·ptery** *adjs.* pertaining to or forming a h.; *horopteric circle*, the h.

Horoscopal (horǫ·skŏpăl), *a.* 1649. [f. L *horoscopus* HOROSCOPE + -AL[1].] Of or pertaining to a horoscope.

Horoscope (hǫ·rŏskoᵘp), *sb.* OE. [In current form (XVI) – (O)Fr. *horoscope* – L. *horoscopus* (also used) – Gr. ὡροσκόπος nativity, horoscope, etc., f. ὥρα time, hour + σκοπός observer (cf. SCOPE).] **1.** *Astrol.* An observation of the sky and of the configuration of the planets at a certain moment, e.g. the instant of a person's birth; hence, a plan of the twelve houses or twelve signs of the zodiac, showing the disposition of the heavens at a particular moment. In early use, spec. = ASCENDANT, or *house of the ascendant.* Also *fig.* †**2.** A figure or table on which the hours are marked: **a.** a dial; **b.** a table showing the length of the days and nights at different places and seasons; **c.** the planisphere invented by John of Padua. –1696.

1. Phr. *To cast a h.* (see CAST *v.*), to calculate the degree of the ecliptic which is on the eastern horizon at a given moment, e.g. at the birth of a child, and thence to erect an astrological figure of the heavens, so as to discover the influence of the planets upon his life and fortunes. *fig.* The h. of the Church MILT., of nations LONGF. Hence **Ho·roscope** *v. intr.* to form a h.; *trans.* to cast the nativity of. **Ho·roscoper,** one who casts horoscopes. **Horosco·pic, -al,** *adjs.* of or pertaining to a h.

Horoscopy (horǫ·skŏpi). 1651. [f. HOROSCOPE + -Y[3].] **a.** The casting of horoscopes. **b.** The aspect of the heavens at a given moment, esp. that of a nativity.

Horrendous (hǫre·ndəs), *a. rare.* 1659. [f. L. *horrendus* (gerundive of *horrēre*) + -OUS; cf. *tremendous, stupendous.*] Fitted to excite horror; frightful, horrible.

Horrent (hǫ·rĕnt), *a.* Chiefly *poet.* 1667. [– *horrent-*, pres. ppl. stem of *horrēre*; see -ENT.] **1.** Bristling; standing up as bristles; rough with bristling points. **2.** Shuddering 1721.

1. Inclos'd With bright imblazonrie, and h. Arms MILT. *P.L.* II. 513. **2.** H. they heard SOUTHEY.

Horribility (hǫrĭbi·lĭti). Now *rare.* [ME. *horriblete* – OFr. *horribleté*, f. *horrible*; see next, -ITY. Cf. med.L. *horribilitas.* In mod. use f. HORRIBLE.] The quality of being horrible; †something horrible.

The h. of 'committing' puns DISRAELI.

Horrible (hǫ·rĭb'l), *a.* (*sb. adv.*) ME. [– OFr. *orrible*, (also mod.) *horrible* – L. *horribilis*, f. *horrēre* stand on end (of hair), tremble, shudder; see -IBLE.] Exciting or fitted to excite horror; tending to make one shudder; extremely repulsive; dreadful, hideous, shocking, frightful, awful. **b.** as a strong intensive (now *colloq.*): Excessive, immoderate 1460.

A Dungeon h., on all sides round As one great Furnace flam'd MILT. *P.L.* I. 61. A h. monster DE FOE. **b.** [Solomon] multiplying wiues to an h. number SIR T. MORE. My h. cold 1676.

B. as *sb.* A horrible person or thing ME.; a story of horrible crime or the like.

'Penny-dreadfuls' and 'halfpenny horribles' 1890.

C. as *adv.* Horribly, terribly; as an intensive, Exceedingly ME.

Hence **Ho·rribleness. Ho·rribly** *adv.*

Horrid (hǫ·rid), *a.* (*adv.*) 1590. [– L. *horridus*, f. *horrēre* (see prec.); see -ID[1].] **1.** Bristling, shaggy, rough. (Chiefly *poet.*) **2.** Causing horror or aversion; revolting; dreadful, frightful, abominable, detestable. (In mod. use, somewhat less strong than *horrible.*) 1601. **3.** *colloq.* Offensive, disagreeable, detested; very bad or objectionable. (Often a feminine term of strong aversion.) 1666. **4.** *adv.* Horridly, abominably, very objectionably (*colloq.* or *vulgar*) 1615.

1. A rugged attire, hirsute head, h. beard BURTON. This h. Alp EVELYN. **2.** They set up the horridest yell DE FOE. **3.** A h. shame PEPYS. I should not wear those h. dresses LYTTON. H. weather 1864. **4.** Went to bed h. soon 1753. Hence **Ho·rrid-ly** *adv.*, **-ness.**

Horrific (hǫri·fik), *a.* 1653. [– Fr. *horrifique* or L. *horrificus*, f. *horrēre* (see HORRIBLE); see -FIC.] Causing horror, horrifying. Hence **Horri·fically** *adv.*

Horrification (hǫrifikē[i]·ʃən). 1800. [f. HORRIFY + -FICATION, after similar pairs, as *magnify, magnification.*] The action of horrifying; the being horrified; *concr.* something horrifying.

Horrify (hǫ·rifəi), *v.* 1791. [– L. *horrificare* cause horror, f. *horrificus*; see HORRIFIC, -FY.] *trans.* To cause or excite horror in; to move to horror.

In a way horrifying to Quakers 1866.

Horripilation (hǫripilē¹·ʃən). 1656. [– late L. (Vulgate) *horripilatio, -iōn-*, f. *horripilare*, f. *horrēre* (see HORRIBLE) + *pilus* hair; see -ATION.] Erection of the hairs on the skin by contraction of the cutaneous muscles (caused by cold, fear, etc.); creeping of the flesh. So **Horri·pilant** *a.* causing h.

Horrisonant (hǫri·sŏnănt), *a.* 1656. [var. of †*horrisonous* (L. *horrisonus*, Cicero) by substitution of suffix -ANT.] Sounding horribly. So †**Horri·sonous** *a.* = prec.

Horror (hǫ·rəɹ), *sb.* late ME. [– OFr. (*h*)*orrour* (mod. *horreur*) :– L. *horror, -ōr-*, f. *horrēre*; see HORRIBLE, -OR 1.] **1.** Roughness, ruggedness. (Now *poet.* or *rhet.*) **2.** A shuddering or shivering; now *esp.* (*Med.*) as a symptom of disease 1533. †**b.** Ruffling of surface –1765. **3.** A painful emotion compounded of loathing and fear; a shuddering with terror and repugnance; the feeling excited by something shocking or frightful. Also in weaker sense, Intense dislike or repugnance. (The prevalent use always.) ME. †**4.** A feeling of awe or reverent fear; a thrill of awe, or of imaginative fear –1720. **5.** *transf.* The quality of exciting repugnance and dread; horribleness; something horrifying ME.

1. Which thick with Shades, and a brown H., stood DRYDEN. **2. b.** Such fresh h. as you see driven through the wrinkled waves CHAPMAN. **3.** Ther shal horrour and grisly drede dwellen withouten ende CHAUCER. Nature's h. of a vacuum 1833. Phr. *The horrors* (colloq.): a fit of horror; *spec.* such as occurs in delirium tremens. **4.** A reverend h. silenced all the sky POPE. **5.** *Chamber of Horrors*, the name of a room in Madame Tussaud's waxworks exhibition, containing effigies of noted criminals and the like; hence *transf.* a place full of horrors. *Comb.*, as *h.-stricken, -struck* adjs.

‖**Hors**, *adv.* and *prep.* 1714. [Fr., doublet of *fors* :– L. *foris* out of doors, abroad.] Out, out of: in the following phrases:

‖**Hors de combat** (hordəkoṅba), *adv.*, out of fight, disabled from fighting; also *transf.* and *fig.* 1745.

‖**Hors d'œuvre** (hordōvr), *adv.* and *sb.*

A. *adv.* Out of the ordinary course of things. ADDISON.

B. *sb.* [The Eng. pl. usually has *-s*.] **1.** Something out of the ordinary course. H. WALPOLE. **2.** An extra dish served as a relish at the beginning or between the courses of a meal. Also *fig.* 1742.

Horse (hǭɹs), *sb.* [OE. *hors* = OFris. *hors, hars, hers*, OS. *hros, hers* (MLG. *ros, ors*, MDu. *ors*, Du. *ros*), OHG. (*h*)*ros* (MHG. *ros, ors*, G. *ross*), ON. *hróss* :– Gmc. **χorsam*, **χorsaz*, of unkn. origin.]

I. The animal, etc. **1.** A solid-hoofed perissodactyl quadruped (*Equus caballus*), having a flowing mane and tail; its voice is a neigh. In the domestic state used as a beast of burden and draught, and esp. for riding upon. (The pl. was in OE. the same as the sing.; *horses* appears c1205, and is now usual in literary language, though *horse* sometimes appears as the collective pl.) **b.** *spec.* The stallion or gelding, as dist. from a mare or colt 1485. **c.** In *Zool.* sometimes extended to all species of the genus *Equus*, or even of the family *Equidæ*. **2.** A representation, figure, or model of a horse ME. **3.** *Mil.* A horse and its rider; hence a cavalry soldier 1548. **4.** *fig.* Applied contemptuously or playfully to a man, with reference to qualities of the quadruped 1500.

1. Come on, then, horse and Chariots let vs haue *Tit. A.* II. ii. 18. **b.** Phr. *To take the h.*: (of the mare) to conceive. **3.** Fifteene hundred Foot, fiue hundred Horse Are march'd vp 2 *Hen. IV*, II. i. 186. Phr. *H. and foot*: both divisions of an army; hence, whole forces; †*advb.* with all one's might. **4.** If I tell thee a Lye, spit in my face, call me H. SHAKS.

II. Things resembling the quadruped. **1.** A contrivance on which a man rides, sits astride, or is carried, as on horseback 1597. **2.** A frame or structure on which something is mounted or supported 1703. **3.** An instrument, appliance, or device for some service suggesting that of a horse ME. **4.** *Naut.* See quots. 1626. †**5.** A lottery-ticket hired out by the day –1731. **6.** A mass of rock or earthy matter enclosed within a lode or vein; a fault or obstruction in the course of a vein; hence *to take h.* 1778. **7.** A 'crib' for students in preparing their work. *U.S.* **8.** *slang.* Among workmen, work charged for before it is executed. Also *dead h.* 1638.

1. I saw the iron horses of the steam Toss to the morning air their plumes of smoke LONGF. A kind of rack called the h. 1895. **2.** Horses, or Trussels 1703. Drying horses for their clothes 1826. **3.** The engine to batter wals (called sometime the h., and now is named the ram) P. HOLLAND. **4.** Horses for the Yards; a Conveniency for the Men to tread on, in going out to furl the Sails 1711. *Horse*, a thick iron rod. for the main sheet to travel on 1794. Horses are also called jack-stays, on which sails are hauled out, as gaff-sails SMYTH.

Phrases. **To horse. a.** To horseback; used absol. as an order to mount. **b.** Of a mare: To the stallion. *To take h.*, to mount, start, or proceed on horseback; see also I. 1. b. and II. 6. *To talk h.*, to talk big or boastfully. **Dead h.** Taken as typical of that which has ceased to be of use, and which it is vain to attempt to revive. *To work*, etc. *for a dead h.*: to do work which has been paid for in advance, and so brings in nothing. *To flog a dead h.*: to engage in fruitless effort. **Flying h.** Pegasus; hence *Astron.* the constellation Pegasus. **Gift h.** (Earlier *given h.*) A horse bestowed as a gift. *To look a gift horse in the mouth*: to criticize a gift. **Great h.** (now *Hist.*) The horse used in battle or tournament. **High h. a.** *lit.* The war-horse or charger. **b.** *To mount* or *ride the high h.* (colloq.): to give oneself airs; to behave pretentiously or arrogantly. **White H. a.** The figure of a white h., reputed as the ensign of the Saxons when they invaded Britain, and the heraldic ensign of Brunswick, Hanover, and Kent; also, the figure of a h. cut on the face of chalk downs near Uffington in Berkshire, and elsewhere. **b.** A high white-crested racing wave. †**Wooden h.** The scaffold, the gallows; an instrument of torture. FULLER. *A h. that was foaled of an acorn*, the scaffold, the gibbet.

attrib. and *Comb.* **1.** General: as *h.-foal*, etc.; *h.-beef, -craft, -factor*, etc.; *h.-ball, -feed, -ferry, -path, -transport, -yard*, etc.; *h.-barge, -drill, -harrow, -rake, -tram*, etc.; *h.-artillery, -soldier, -troop, -trooper*, etc.; *h.-exercise*; *h.-breeder, -dealer*, etc.; *h.-towing*; *h.-face, joke, mouth, vein*, etc.

2. Special: **a. h. aloes,** caballine, or fetid aloes; **-boot,** a leather covering for the hoof and pastern of a h., to protect them from interfering; **-bridge; -butcher; -doctor; -drench,** a draught of medicine administered to a h.; also, a horn, etc., by which it is administered; **-furniture,** the trappings of horses; **-iron** (see HORSE *v.* 9); **-knacker,** one who buys up old or worn-out horses, and slaughters them for their commercial products; **-monger; -pick, -picker,** a hooked instrument for removing a stone from a horse's foot; **-piece,** a large piece of whale's blubber; **h. pistol,** a large pistol carried at the pommel of the saddle when on horseback; †**-plea,** a special plea for delaying the cause and carrying it over the term; **-rough,** a calk fitted to a horse's shoe to prevent slipping in frosty weather; **-run,** a contrivance for drawing up loaded wheelbarrows from the deep cuttings by the help of a h., which goes backwards and forwards; **-towel,** a coarse towel, hung on a roller, for general use; **-tree,** the beam on which timber is placed previous to sawing; **-walk,** the path of a h. in working a gin, whim, etc.

b. In names of animals (sometimes denoting a large or coarse kind, sometimes with the sense 'infesting horses'): **h.-ant,** a large species of ant; **-bot,** the larva of the **horse-bee** or bot-fly (*Œstrus equi*); **-conch,** a large shell-fish (*Strombus gigas*); **-crab** = HORSESHOE-*crab*; **-emmet** = *horse-ant*; **-finch,** the chaffinch (*local*); **-lark,** the corn bunting (Cornwall); **-masher, -musher** = next (*a*); **-match, -matcher,** (*a*) the Stonechat or Wheatear (*Saxicola œnanthe*); (*b*) the Red-backed Shrike (*Lanius collurio*); **-mussel,** a large coarse kind of mussel of the genus *Modiola*; also a freshwater mussel, *Unio* or *Anodonta*; **-sponge,** the commercial bath-sponge (*Spongia equina*); **-stinger,** the Dragon-fly; **-tick** = HORSE-FLY; †**-whale,** the walrus; **-worm,** a maggot infesting horses, as the larva of the common bot-fly.

c. In names of plants, fruits, etc. (often denoting a large, strong, or coarse kind): **h.-balm,** a strong-scented labiate plant of the N. Amer. genus *Collinsonia*, with yellowish flowers; **-bane,** name for species of *Œnanthe*, supposed to cause palsy in horses; **-bean,** a coarse variety of the common bean, used for feeding horses; **-beech,** the Hornbeam (see BEECH 2); **-brier,** 'the common green-brier or catbrier of N. America, *Smilax rotundifolia*' (*Cent. Dict.*); **-cane,** the Great Ragweed of N. America; **-cassia,** a leguminous tree (*Cassia marginata*), bearing long pods containing a purgative pulp used in the E. Indies as a medicine for horses; **-daisy,** the Ox-eye Daisy (see DAISY 2); †**-elder,** elecampane; **-eye, -eye bean,** the seed of the Cowage (*Mucuna pruriens*), a W. Indian leguminous plant; also that of *Dolichos lablab*; **-fennel** (see FENNEL); **-gentian, -ginseng,** a N. American caprifoliaceous plant of the genus *Triosteum*, having a bitter root; **-parsley,** a large-leaved umbelliferous plant, *Smyrnium olusatrum*; **-purslane,** a W. Indian plant, *Trianthema monogyna*; **-sorrel,** *Rumex hydrolapatham*; **-sugar,** a shrub (*Symplocos tinctoria*), found in the southern U.S., also called *sweetleaf*, the leaves of which are used as fodder; **-thistle,** †(*a*) Wild Lettuce; (*b*) a thistle of the genus *Cirsium*; **-tongue,** (*a*) = DOUBLE-TONGUE 2; (*b*) the Hart's-tongue Fern; **-vetch** = HORSE-SHOE-*vetch*; **-weed,** name for two N. Amer. plants, *Erigeron canadensis*, also called *butter-weed* (now frequent in England), and *Collinsonia canadensis*, also called *horse-mint*; **-wood,** name for various W. Indian shrubs of the genus *Calliandra*.

Horse, *v.* OE. [f. prec. sb.] **1.** *trans.* To provide with a horse or horses; to set on horseback. Also *transf.* **2.** *intr.* To mount or go on horseback ME. **3.** *trans.* To raise or hoist up. Now *technical.* 1460. **4.** To elevate on a man's back, e.g. for flogging 1563. †**5.** *Naut.* Of a current, etc.: To carry with force –1726. **6.** Of a stallion: To cover (a mare) ME. **7.** To bestride. SHAKS. **8.** *Horse away*: to spend in a lottery. See HORSE *sb.* II. 5. FIELDING. **9.** *Horse up*: to drive (oakum) between the planks of a ship 1850.

1. Maron of Turin, who horsed oure Company from Lyons to Turin CORYAT. Guns horsed for service 1888. **4.** The biggest boy. .horsed me—and I was flogged THACKERAY. **9.** *Horse iron*, an iron. .used. .by caulkers, to *horse-up* or harden in the oakum 1850.

Horse-back, horseback, *sb.* (*adv.*) ME. †**1.** (hǭ·ɹsˌbæ·k). The back of a horse –1704. **2.** (hǭ·ɹsbæk). See quots. ME. **3.** *Geol.* (hǭ·ɹsbæk) A low and somewhat sharp ridge of gravel or sand; a hog-back. *U.S.* 1857. **4.** *Coal-mining.* 'A portion of the roof or floor which bulges or intrudes into the coal' 1855. **5.** *adv.* Short for *on horseback* 1727.

2. Phr. *On h.* (†*a h.*): sitting or riding on a horse; (mounting) upon a horse. A couple of robbers a-horseback suddenly appeared SMOLLETT. Set a beggar on horse-back, and he'll ride to the devil COBBETT.

Ho·rse-block. 1753. **1.** A small platform, ascended by 3 or 4 steps, used in mounting a horse. **2.** 'A square frame of strong boards, used by excavators to elevate the ends of their wheeling-planks' (Gwilt) 1825.

Ho·rse-boat. 1591. **1.** A ferry-boat for conveying horses or carriages. **2.** (*U.S.*) A boat drawn by horses 1828.

Ho·rse-box. 1846. **1.** A closed carriage for transporting horses by railway. **2.** Applied joc. to large pews with high sides, formerly common 1884.

Ho·rse-boy. 1537. A stable-boy. (Often contemptuous.)

Ho·rse-bread. 1467. Bread made of beans, bran, etc. for food for horses.

Ho·rse-breaker. 1550. One who breaks in horses for use.

Ho·rse-car. *U.S.* 1864. **1.** A car drawn by a horse or horses. Also *attrib.* **2.** A railway car for the transport of horses. (*Cent. Dict.*)

Ho·rse-che·stnut. 1597. [tr. obs. Bot. L. *Castanea equina*. Cf. G. *rosskastanie*.] **1.** The hard smooth shining brown seed or nut of the tree described in 2. 1611. **2.** A large ornamental tree, *Æsculus hippocastanum* (N.O. *Sapindaceæ*), introduced into England c1550. Also, the allied genus *Pavia*, usu. called *buck-eye*.

Ho·rse-coper (-kōᵘ:pəɹ), **-couper** (-kau:-pəɹ). 1681. [f. HORSE + COPER¹, *couper* (see COUP *v.*¹).] A horse-dealer.

†**Ho·rse-corser, -courser.** 1552. [See CORSE *v.*, SCORSE.] A jobbing dealer in horses –1818. So †**Ho·rse-corsing, -coursing,** horse-jobbing.

Ho·rse-course. 1715. **1.** A horse-race. **2.** A race-course 1766.

Ho·rse-fai·r. ME. A fair or annual market for the sale of horses.

Ho·rse-fish. 1582. Any fish with a head more or less like that of a horse. **a.** The fish *Vomer setipinnis*, and the allied *Selene vomer*. **b.** The *Hippocampus* or sea-horse.

Ho·rse-flesh, horseflesh. ME. **1.** The flesh of a horse, esp. as food 1532. **2.** Living horses collectively ME. †**3.** = HORSE *sb.* II. 8. 1688. **4.** *attrib.* usu. in reference to the colour, a peculiar reddish bronze. **Horse-flesh ore,** an ore of copper, bornite.

2. Profoundly learned in Horse-flesh STEELE.

Ho·rse-fly. ME. [f. FLY *sb.*[1] 2.] One of various dipterous insects troublesome to horses, as the horse-tick (family *Hippoboscidæ*), the breeze or gadfly (*Tabanidæ*), the bot-fly (*Œstridæ*).

attrib. **Horse-fly-weed,** *Baptisia tinctoria*, also called *wild indigo*.

Horse-foot. ME. †**1.** A horse's foot –1597. †**2.** The plant Coltsfoot –1633. **3.** A crustacean of the genus *Limulus*, called *horseshoe-crab* 1672.

Ho·rsegate. 1619. [f. GATE *sb.*[2] going.] A right of pasturage for a horse, e.g. in a common field.

Ho:rse-go·dmother. *dial.* and *vulgar.* 1569. A large coarse-looking woman.

Horse guard (hǭ·ɹsgā:ɹd). 1645. **1.** One of a body of picked cavalry for special service as a guard; formerly also *collective* 1647. **b.** *pl.* The cavalry brigade of the English Household troops; *spec.* the third regiment of this body, the *Royal Horse Guards* 1661. **2.** *pl.* The barracks, head-quarters or guard-house of such cavalry; *spec.* a building in London, opposite Whitehall, bearing this name 1645. **3.** *pl.* The personnel of the office of the Commander-in-Chief and the military authorities at the head of the army 1826.

2. News that White Hall was on fire; and presently more particulars, that the Horse-guard was on fire PEPYS. **3.** I can't say that I owe my successes to any favour or confidence from the Horse Guards WELLINGTON.

Horsehair (hǭ·ɹshēᵊɹ). ME. **a.** A hair from the mane or tail of a horse. **b.** A mass of such hair ME. **c.** *attrib.* and *Comb.*, as *h. chair*; **h.-worm,** a hairworm or Gordius.

Ho·rse-head. ME. **1.** The head of a horse, or a head like that of a horse. **2.** The stony inner cast of the fossil Trigonia 1708. **3.** *Zool.* = HORSE-FISH. †**4.** *Mining.* A kind of ventilator –1802.

Ho·rse-hoe, *sb.* 1731. [f. HORSE *sb.* + HOE *sb.*[2]] A frame mounted on wheels and furnished with ranges of shares, each of which acts like a hoe. Hence **Horse-hoe** *v.* to work with a horse-hoe.

Ho·rse-hoof. ME. [f. HORSE *sb.* + HOOF.] **1.** The hoof of a horse 1539. **2.** The plant Coltsfoot ME. **3.** = HORSE-FOOT 3. 1699.

Ho·rse-jo:ckey. 1782. One hired to ride a horse in a race. (Now simply *jockey.*)

Horse latitudes, *sb. pl.* 1777. [The origin of the name is uncertain.] The belt of calms and light airs which borders the northern edge of the N.E. trade-winds.

Horse-laugh (hǭ·ɹs,lɑf). 1713. A loud coarse laugh.

Horse-leech (hǭ·ɹs,lītʃ), *sb.* ME. [f. HORSE *sb.* + LEECH *sb.*[1]] †**1.** A farrier, a veterinary surgeon –1653. **2.** A large aquatic sucking worm (*Hæmopsis sanguisorba*) ME. **3.** *fig.* A rapacious insatiable person 1546. Hence †**Ho·rse-lee:chery, -leechcraft,** veterinary medicine.

Ho·rse-li:tter. ME. **1.** A litter hung on poles, carried between two horses, one in front and the other behind. **2.** A bed of straw or hay for horses. **b.** The manure consisting of such straw mixed with the excrements of horses. 1624.

Ho·rse-load. ME. A load for a horse; sometimes, a determinate weight; cf. LOAD. Also *fig.* a large quantity.

†**Ho·rsely,** *a.* Also **horsly(e.** [f. HORSE *sb.* + -LY[1]; cf. *manly.*] Of the nature of a good horse. CHAUCER.

Ho·rse-ma·ckerel. 1705. A name for several fishes allied to the mackerel; *esp.* the Cavally or Scad (*Caranx vulgaris*).

Horseman (hǭ·ɹs,mæ̆n). *Pl.* **-men.** ME. **1.** One who rides on horseback; one skilled in riding and managing a horse. *spec.* a mounted soldier. **2.** A man who attends to horses 1882. **3.** An inferior variety of the carrier pigeon 1693. **4.** *Ichthyol.* A sciænoid fish of the genus *Eques* found on the coasts of Central America. Hence **Ho·rsemanship,** the art of riding on horseback, and (formerly) of breeding, rearing, and managing horses; the duties of the *manège*.

Horse-marine (hǭ·ɹs,mărī·n). 1824. [f. HORSE *sb.* + MARINE *sb.*] **1.** A marine mounted on horseback, or a cavalryman doing a marine's work 1878. **2.** *joc.* (*pl.*) An imaginary corps of mounted marine soldiers, as a type of men out of their element 1824.

Ho·rse-master. 1523. One who owns or manages horses; also, a horse-breaker.

Ho·rse-mill. 1467. A mill driven by a horse; usually, by one walking in a circle; *fig.* a monotonous round.

Ho·rse-mint. ME. [See HORSE *sb. attrib.* 2 c.] **1.** A name of the wild mints, esp. *Mentha sylvestris* and *M. aquatica.* **2.** Applied in N. America to species of *Monarda*, etc.

Ho·rse-nail. ME. **1.** A horseshoe-nail. **2.** A tadpole (*local*) 1608.

Ho·rse-play. 1589. †**1.** Play in which a horse takes part; theatrical horsemanship. Also *transf.* –1668. **2.** Rough, coarse, or boisterous play 1589.

2. He [Collier] is too much given to horse-play in his raillery DRYDEN.

Ho·rse-plum. 1530. **1.** A small red variety of plum. **2.** (*U.S.*) The common wild plum of N. America (*Prunus americana*) 1797.

Ho·rse-pond. 1701. A pond for watering and washing horses; also, for ducking obnoxious persons.

Ho·rse-power. 1806. **1.** The power or rate of work of a horse in drawing; hence in *Mech.*, a unit for measuring the work of a prime motor, taken as = 550 foot-pounds per second (about 1⅓ times the actual power of a horse). Abbrev. H.P. **2.** *transf.* Power or rate of work as estimated by this unit. Also *fig.* 1860. **3.** A machine worked by a horse, by which the pull or weight of a horse is converted into power for driving other machinery 1853.

1. Nominal horse-power. .has no fixed relation to indicated horse-power 1881. The term 'horse-power' has probably seen its best days 1897. One 25 horse-power engine 1872. **2.** What is the horse-power of the Niagara? MAURY. **3.** An ordinary horse-power, such as is used for thrashing-machines [etc.] KNIGHT.

Ho·rse-pox. 1656. [See POX.] †**1.** A severe or virulent pox. (Used in coarse execrations.) –1694. **2.** A pustular disease of horses 1884.

Ho·rse-race. 1581. [RACE *sb.*[1]] A race between mounted horses. Hence **Horse-racer, -racing.**

Ho·rse-radish. 1561. [See HORSE *sb. attrib.* 2 c.] **1.** A cruciferous plant (*Cochlearia armoracia*), a native of middle Europe and western Asia; the thick rootstock of this plant, which has a pungent flavour, and is scraped or grated as a condiment. **2.** *attrib.* and *Comb.*, as **horse-radish tree,** a tree (*Moringa pterygosperma*), a native of India, cultivated for its pod-like capsules, and for its winged seeds (*ben-nuts*), from which oil of ben is obtained; the root resembles horse-radish in flavour.

Horse-scorser, -scourser: see HORSE-CORSER.

Ho·rse-se·nse. *U.S. colloq.* 1870. Strong common sense, often found in ignorant and rude persons.

Horseshoe, horse-shoe (hǭ·ɹs,ʃū), *sb.* ME. **1.** A shoe for a horse, now usually formed of a narrow iron plate bent to the outline of the horse's hoof and nailed to the foot. **2.** Anything shaped like a horseshoe, or a circular arc larger than a semicircle 1489. **3.** *Bot.* = *horseshoe-vetch* 1578. **4.** *Zool.* A horseshoe-crab 1775. **5.** *attrib.*, as *h. arch, bend, table*, etc. 1796.

1. A Tradition, that 'tis a lucky thing to find a Horse-shoe BOYLE. **2.** The river making a kind of a double horse-shoe DE FOE.

Comb.: **h.-bat,** any species of bat having a nose-leaf more or less horseshoe-shaped; **-crab,** a crab-like animal of the genus *Limulus*, so called from the shape of its shell; a king-crab; **h. head,** a disease in infants, in which the sutures of the skull are too open; **h. magnet,** one bent so that the two ends almost meet; **h.-nail,** a nail of soft iron for fastening on horseshoes; **-vetch,** a leguminous plant (*Hippocrepis comosa*) bearing umbels of yellow flowers, and jointed pods each division of which resembles a h. Hence **Ho·rseshoe** *v.* to provide with horseshoes; *Arch.* to make (an arch) horseshoe-shaped. **Ho·rse-sho:er. Ho·rse-shoeing,** the art or craft of shoeing horses.

Horse-tail, ho·rsetail. ME. **1.** A horse's tail. **b.** Used in Turkey as the symbol of war, and as an ensign denoting the rank of a pasha; see TAIL *sb.*[1] 1613. **2.** Name of the genus *Equisetum*, a cryptogamous plant with leafless jointed branches 1538. **b. Tree horse-tail** = *horsetail-tree* 1884. **3.** A hippurite. **4.** *Anat.* The leash of nerves in which the spinal cord ends (in mod.L. *cauda equina*). **5.** *attrib.* and *Comb.*, as **horsetail-tree,** a tree of the genus *Casuarina*, esp. the Australian *C. equisetifolia*.

1. b. While all Christendom trembled at the sight of the horse-tails, Soliman died 1840.

Horsewhip (hǭ·ɹs,hwip), *sb.* 1694. A whip for driving or controlling a horse. Hence **Ho·rsewhip** *v.* to chastise with a h.

Horsewoman (hǭ·ɹs,wu:măn). 1564. A woman who rides on horseback.

Ho·rsing, *vbl. sb.* ME. [f. HORSE *v.* + -ING[1].] **1.** Provision of horses. **2.** The covering of a mare 1523. **3.** A mounting as on a horse; a flogging inflicted while on another's back 1688. *Comb.*: **h.-block, -stone** = HORSE-BLOCK.

Horst (hǭɹst). 1893. [G.] *Geol.* A term introduced by E. Suess for tracts of the earth's surface which have become immobile and formed buttresses against which surrounding tracts have been pressed.

Horsy (hǭ·ɹsi), *a.* 1591. [f. HORSE *sb.* + -Y[1].] **1.** Of, pertaining to, or of the nature of a horse or horses. **2.** Having to do with horses; devoted to horses or horse-racing; affecting the dress and language of a groom or jockey 1852. Hence **Ho·rsiness** (esp. in sense 2).

Hortation (hǫɹtēⁱ·ʃən). 1536. [– L. *hortatio*, f. *hortat-*, pa. ppl. stem of *hortari* exhort; see -ION.] The action of exhorting or inciting; exhortation.

Hortative (hǭ·ɹtătiv). 1607. [– L. *hortativus*, f. as prec.; see -IVE.]

A. *adj.* Characterized by exhortation; serving to exhort 1623.

B. *sb.* A hortatory speech.

Hortatory (hǭ·ɹtătəri), *a.* 1576. [– late L. *hortatorius*, f. as prec.; see -ORY[2].] Of, pertaining to, or characterized by exhortation or encouragement; hortative.

Horte·nsial, *a.* ? *Obs.* 1655. [f. L. *hortensis* (f. *hortus* garden) + -AL[1].] Of or belonging to a garden. So **Horte·nsian** *a.* ? *Obs.*

†**Ho·rticultor.** *rare.* 1760. [prob. f. next by substitution of L. *cultor* cultivator for *-culture.*] = HORTICULTURIST.

Horticulture (hǭ·ɹtikɒ:ltiŭɹ, -tʃəɹ). 1678. [f. L. *hortus* garden, after AGRICULTURE.] The cultivation of a garden; the art or science of cultivating or managing gardens, including the growing of flowers, fruit, and vegetables. So **Horticu·ltural** *a.* of or pertaining to h. **Horticu·lturist,** one who practises h.; esp. one who practises it scientifically as a profession.

Hortulan (hǭ·ɹtiŭlăn), *a.* 1664. [– L. *hortulanus*, f. *hortulus*, dim. of *hortus* garden; see -ULE, -AN. Cf. ORTOLAN.] Of or belonging to a garden or gardening.

‖**Hortus siccus** (hǭ·ɹtɒ̆s si·kɒ̆s). 1687. [L., = dry garden.] An arranged collection of dried plants; a herbarium.

fig. The *hortus siccus* of dissent BURKE.

†**Ho·rtyard.** 1555. [An affected alteration of *orchard*, frequent in XVI–XVII, infl. by L. *hortus* garden.] An ORCHARD; occas. a garden generally –1699.

Hory, horry, *a.* *Obs.* exc. *dial.* Also **howry.** [OE. *horiġ*, f. *horh* filth + *-iġ* -Y[1].] Foul, dirty, filthy; slanderous. TENNYSON.

Hosanna (hozæ·nă). [In OE. and ME. *osanna*, later *hosanna* (Tindale) – late L. (*h*)*osanna* – Gr. ὡσαννά – Mishnaic Heb. *hôša'nā*, abbrev. of bibl. *hôšī'a-nnā.*]

A. *interj.* An exclam., meaning 'Save now!' or 'Save, pray!', occurring in Ps. 118:25. Used by the Jews as an appeal for deliverance, and an ascription of praise to God, and in the Christian Church as an ascription of praise.

And the multitudes..cried, saying, H. to the sonne of David *Matt.* 21:9. H. to the living Lord HEBER.

B. *sb.* A cry of 'hosanna'; a shout of praise 1641.

Hose (hōᵘz), *sb.* Pl. **hosen** (*arch.* or *dial.*), †**hoses**; *collect. pl.* **hose.** [Late OE. *hosa, -e,* = OS., OHG., ON. *hosa* (Du. *hoos* stocking, water-hose, G. *hose(n)* trousers) :- Gmc. **χuson, -ōn.* Sense 3 is prob. f. Du.] **1.** An article of clothing for the leg, sometimes also covering the foot. *collect. pl.* **hose.** In mod. use = Stockings reaching to the knee. *Half-hose,* short stockings or socks. ME. †**2.** Occas. = breeches, drawers; esp. in DOUBLET *and h.*, as the typical male apparel 1460. **3.** A flexible tube or pipe for conveying water or other liquid where it is wanted 1495. **4.** A sheath; *spec.* the sheath enclosing the ear or straw of corn; the sheath or spathe of an Arum 1450. **5.** A socket; in a printing press, a case connected by hooks with the platen to keep it in place. 1611.

1. Hir hosen weren of fyn scarlet reed CHAUCER. Hee beeing in loue, could not see to garter his h. *Two Gent.* II. i. 83. **2.** 1 *Hen. IV*, II. iv. 239. †*Shipman's hose,* wide trousers worn by sailors.

Comb.: **h.-bridge, -jumper, -protector, -shield,** devices for the protection of firemen's h. lying across a street or road; **-hook,** a hook for raising the h. of a fire-engine.

Hose (hōᵘz), *v.* ME. [f. HOSE *sb.*] **1.** *trans.* To provide with hose. **2.** To drench with a hose 1889.

Hosed (hōᵘzd), *a.* ME. [f. HOSE *v.* or *sb.* + -ED.] **1.** Wearing hose. **2.** Of a horse: Having the lower part of the legs covered with white hair 1720.

Hose-in-hose, *a.* and *sb.* 1629. [See HOSE *sb.* 4.] Said of flowers which appear to have one corolla within another, esp. a variety of *Primula* or Polyanthus.

Ho·se-net. Chiefly *Sc.* 1552. A small net resembling a stocking, affixed to a pole (Jam.); *fig.* a position from which escape is difficult.

Hosier (hōᵘ·ʒiəɹ, hōᵘ·ziəɹ). ME. [f. HOSE *sb.* + -IER.] One who makes or deals in hose (stockings and socks) and underclothing generally.

Hosiery (hōᵘ·ʒiəri, hōᵘ·ziəri). 1789. [f. prec.; see -ERY.] **1.** Hose collectively; extended to the whole class of goods in which a hosier deals 1790. **2.** The business of a hosier. **3.** A factory where hose is woven.

Hospice (hǫ·spis). 1818. [- (O)Fr. *hospice* - L. *hospitium* hospitality, lodging, f. *hospes, hospit-* HOST *sb.*[2]] **1.** A house of rest and entertainment for pilgrims, travellers, or strangers, esp. that belonging to the monks of St. Bernard on the Alps; also, a home for the destitute. **2.** A hostel for students 1895.

Hospitable (hǫ·spităb'l), *a.* 1570. [- Fr. †*hospitable,* f. *hospiter* receive as a guest, in med.L. *hospitare*; see -ABLE.] **1.** Offering or affording welcome and entertainment to strangers; extending a generous hospitality to guests and visitors. **2.** *transf.* Disposed to receive or welcome kindly; open and generous in disposition 1655.

1. The savages in America are extremely h. KEATINGE. His h. gate DRAYTON. **2.** The religion of the Greeks was h. to novelties 1887. Hence **Ho·spitableness. Ho·spitably** *adv.*

Hospitage (hǫ·spitėdʒ). *Obs.* or *arch.* 1590. [- med.L. *hospitagium,* f. *hospes, hospit-* HOST *sb.*[2]; see -AGE.] †**1.** Guestship. SPENSER. †**2.** Lodging. SPEED. **3.** A hospice 1855.

Hospital (hǫ·spităl), *sb.* ME. [- OFr. *hospital* (mod. *hôpital*) - med.L. *hospitale,* subst. use of n. of L. *hospitalis*; see next. Cf. HOSTEL.] **1.** A place of rest and entertainment; a hospice. Hence, one of the establishments of the Knights Hospitallers. **2.** A charitable institution for the housing and maintenance of the needy, infirm, or aged. *Obs.* exc. in Eng. legal use and in proper names. ME. **b.** A university hall or hostel 1536. **c.** A charitable institution for the education and maintenance of the young 1552. **3.** *spec.* An institution for the care of the sick and wounded, or of those who require medical treatment. (The current use.) ME. †**4.** A place of lodging -1590.

3. *fig.* For the world, I count it not an Inne, but an Hospitall, and a place, not to live, but to die in SIR T. BROWNE.

Comb.: **h.-boy,** a charity-boy; **h. fever,** a kind of typhus fever arising in crowded hospitals from the poisonous atmosphere; **h. gangrene,** a spreading, sloughing, gangrenous inflammation starting from a wound and arising in crowded hospitals; **H. Saturday,** a particular Saturday in the year on which collections of money for the local hospitals are organized in the streets and elsewhere; **h.-ship,** a vessel fitted up as a floating h. for seamen; **H. Sunday,** a particular Sunday in the year on which collections of money are made in places of worship for the local hospitals; **h. ulcer** = *hospital gangrene.*

†**Ho·spital,** *a.* ME. [- L. *hospitalis* hospitable, f. *hospes, hospit-* HOST *sb.*[2]; see -AL[1]. Cf. OFr. *hospital* in same sense.] **1.** = HOSPITABLE -1697. **2.** Used as tr. L. *hospitalis* or Gr. ξένιος 'protector of the rights of hospitality', as in *h. Jove,* etc. -1807.

Hospitalism (hǫ·spităliz'm). 1869. [f. HOSPITAL *sb.* + -ISM.] The hospital system; used esp. with reference to its hygienic evils.

Hospitality (hǫspitæ·lĭti). ME. [- (O)Fr. *hospitalité* - L. *hospitalitas, -tat-,* f. *hospitalis*; see HOSPITAL *a.*, -ITY.] **1.** The act or practice of being hospitable; the reception and entertainment of guests or strangers with liberality and goodwill. **b.** with *pl.* †**2.** Hospitableness -1711. †**3.** A HOSPITAL (sense 2) -1761.

1. 'Old English hospitality' SMOLLETT. **b.** In convivial and domestic hospitalities EMERSON. **3.** The h. of St. Leonard's near York HUME.

Hospitaller, -aler (hǫ·spităləɹ). ME. [OFr. *hospitalier* - med.L. *hospitalarius* (also *-aris*), f. *hospitale*; see HOSPITAL *sb.*, -ER[2], 1, 2. HOSTELER, OSTLER are doublets.] **1.** = HOSTELER 1. 1483. **2.** *spec.* A member of a religious order formed for the care of the sick and infirm in hospitals. Such were orig. the *Knights Hospitallers* (see 3) ME. **3.** More fully, *Knights Hospitallers,* an order of military monks, which took its origin from a hospital founded at Jerusalem, *c*1048, by merchants of Amalfi, for the benefit of poor pilgrims, but subsequently received a military organization, and became a bulwark of Christendom in the East. They were known as *Knights of the Hospital of St. John of Jerusalem,* etc., and, after the removal of the chief seat of the order to Malta, as *Knights of Malta.* ME. **4.** In St. Bartholomew's Hospital and St. Thomas's Hospital (orig. religious foundations): The title of the chaplain 1552.

†**Hospitate** (hǫ·spiteⁱt), *v. rare.* 1623. [- *hospitat-,* pa. ppl. stem of L. *hospitari* be a guest, and med.L. *hospitare* receive as a guest, f. L. *hospes, hospit-* HOST *sb.*[2]; see -ATE[3].] †**1.** *trans.* To lodge or entertain. (Dicts.) †**2.** To lodge, take up one's abode. GREW. So **Ho·spitator.**

†**Hospi·tious,** *a.* 1588. [f. L. *hospitium* (see HOSPICE) + -OUS.] Hospitable -1784.

‖**Hospitium** (hǫspi·ʃiǒm). 1650. [L; see HOSPICE.] **1.** = HOSPICE 1. **2.** A hall or hostel for students in a university 1895.

‖**Hospodar** (hǫ·spodāɹ). 1684. [- Rum. *hospodár* - Ukr. *hospodár'* = Russ. *gospodár',* f. *gospód'* lord.] A word meaning 'lord', a title formerly borne by the governors of the provinces of Wallachia and Moldavia.

Hoss (hǫs), dial. and U.S. var. HORSE.

Host (hōᵘst), *sb.*[1] ME. [- OFr. *(h)ost, (h)oost* :- L. *hostis* stranger, enemy, in med.L. army; see GUEST.] **1.** An armed multitude of men; an army. Now *arch.* and *poet.* Also *fig.* and *transf.* **2.** *transf.* A great company; a multitude 1613. **3.** In Biblical uses (see below.) ME.

1. The sight of the armed h. which surrounded her 1840. *fig.* He was a h. of debaters in himself BURKE. **2.** A h. of thoughts M. PATTISON, of books JOWETT. **3.** *H.* or *hosts of heaven,* (*a*) the multitude of angels that attend on God; (*b*) the sun, moon, and stars. *Lord* (*God*) *of Hosts* (*Jehovah Ts'bāōth*): an O.T. title of Jehovah; app. referring sometimes to the heavenly hosts, sometimes to the armies of Israel, and hence in mod. use with the sense 'God of armies' or 'of battles'. Lord God of Hosts, be with us yet KIPLING. Hence **Ho·sted** *a.* in hosts.

Host (hōᵘst), *sb.*[2] ME. [- OFr. *(h)oste* (mod *hôte*) :- L. *hospis, hospit-* host, prob. f. *hostis* (see prec.).] **1.** A man who lodges and entertains another in his house; the correl. of *guest.* **2.** *spec.* A man who lodges and entertains for payment; the landlord of an inn ME. **3.** *Biol.* An animal or plant having a parasite or commensal habitually living in or upon it 1857. †**4.** A guest -1559.

1. Conduct me to mine H., we loue him highly *Macb.* I. vi. 29. **2.** Mine H. of the Garter SHAKS. Phr. *To reckon without one's h.*: to calculate one's score without consulting one's h.; to come to conclusions without complete data.

†**Host,** *sb.*[3] ME. [perh. - OFr. *osté, hosté,* var. of *ostel, hostel* HOSTEL. The pl. of the latter was often *ostez, ostes,* whence by reaction the sing. *osté*; mod. Fr. dialects have *hôté, ôté.* For the loss of final *-e* in Eng. cf. ASSIGN *sb.*[2]] A hostel, inn -1590.

Phr. *To be* (or *lie*) *at h.*: to be put up at an inn; *fig.* to be at home *with.*

Host (hōᵘst), *sb.*[4] ME. [- OFr. *(h)oiste* :- L. *hostia* victim, sacrifice.] †**1.** A victim for sacrifice; a sacrifice (*lit.* and *fig.*); often said of Christ -1653. **2.** *Eccl.* The bread consecrated in the Eucharist, regarded as the body of Christ sacrificially offered; a wafer used in celebrating Mass ME.

†**Host,** *v.* ME. [f. HOST *sb.*[2]] **1.** *trans.* To receive and entertain as a guest -1613. **2.** *intr.* To be a guest; to put up -1656.

Hostage (hǫ·stėdʒ), *sb.*[1] ME. [- (O)Fr. *ostage, hostage* (mod. *otage*) :- Rom. **obsidiaticum,* f. late L. *obsidiatus* hostageship, f. *obses, obsid-* hostage, f. *ob* OB- + **sed-* SIT; see -AGE. The initial *h* was induced by assim. to the words connected with HOST *sb.*[2]] †**1.** Pledge or security given to enemies or allies for the fulfilment of any undertaking by the handing over of one or more persons into their power; the state or condition of the persons thus handed over. (No pl.) -1731. **2.** (with *pl.*) A person thus given and held in pledge ME. **3.** *gen.* A pledge or security ME. †**4.** A treaty (*rare*). MALORY.

1. To give the young King..in H. to the Queen TINDAL. **2.** To solicit the exchange of hostages GIBBON. **3.** He that hath wife and children, hath given hostages to fortune BACON. Hence **Ho·stageship** = sense 1.

†**Ho·stage,** *sb.*[2] ME. [- OFr. *(h)ostage,* f. *(h)oste* HOST *sb.*[2] + *-age* -AGE. From OFr. are med.L. *hostagium, hospitagium.*] **1.** Entertainment; lodging, residence. **2.** A hostel, hostelry, inn. Also *attrib.* -1852.

Hostel (hǫ·stĕl), *sb.* ME. [- OFr. *(h)ostel* (mod. *hôtel* HOTEL) :- med.L. *hospitale* HOSPITAL.] †**1.** A place of sojourn; a lodging. Also *transf.* and *fig.* -1610. **2.** *spec.* An inn, a hotel. (Revived in 19th c. by Scott.) ME. **3.** A house of residence for students; esp. (in recent times) for students connected with a non-resident college; = HALL *sb.* 4 a. 1536. †**4.** A town mansion; = HOTEL 1. -1670. **5.** *attrib.* 1610.

2. The h., or inn SCOTT. **4.** His H. at Paris..was then the best House next to the Queen Mothers COTTON.

Hosteler (hǫ·stĕləɹ). Now *arch.* or *Hist.* ME. [- AFr. *hosteler,* OFr. *(h)ostelier* (mod. *hôtelier*), f. *hostel*; see prec., -ER[2] 2. Also in form HOSTLER; now more usually OSTLER.] **1.** One who receives, lodges, or entertains guests or strangers; *spec.* in a monastery, one whose office was to attend to guests or strangers. *Obs.* exc. *Hist.* **2.** An innkeeper (*arch.*) ME. †**3.** A student who lives in a hostel (sense 3) -1655.

Hostelry (hǫ·stĕlri). Now *arch.* ME. [- OFr. *(h)ostelerie* (mod. *hôtellerie*), f. *hostelier*; see prec., -ERY.] **1.** An inn, a hostel. **2.** Hostel business (*nonce-use*) 1855.

1. A bashful child, homely brought up, In a rude hostelrie B. JONS.

Hostess (hōᵘ·stės). ME. [- OFr. *(h)ostesse* (mod. *hôtesse*), f. *(h)oste* HOST *sb.*[2]; see -ESS[1].] **1.** A woman that lodges and entertains guests. **2.** *spec.* The mistress of an inn ME. Hence **Ho·stessship,** the office of h.

Hostie (hǫ·sti). *Obs.* or *arch.* 1483. [- (O)Fr. *hostie* - late (eccl.) L. *hostia* (see HOST *sb.*[4]), in cl. L. 'animal sacrificed'.] **1.** = HOST *sb.*[4] 1. **2.** = HOST *sb.*[4] 2. 1641.

Hostile (hǫ·stəil), *a.* (*sb.*) 1487. [- Fr. *hostile* or L. *hostilis,* f. *hostis* enemy; see HOST *sb.*[1], -ILE.] **1.** Of, pertaining to, or characteristic of an enemy; pertaining to or engaged in hostilities. **b.** Unfriendly 1782. **2.** Contrary, adverse, antagonistic 1791. **3.** *sb.* A hostile person; *spec.* (*U.S.*) a N. American Indian unfriendly to the Whites 1860.

1. The operations of h. armies WELLINGTON. Men of different and h. races FREEMAN. **2.** Princes, h. to the established faith MACAULAY. Hence **Ho·stilely** *adv.*, **Ho·stileness.**

Hostility (hǫsti·lĭti). 1473. [– Fr. *hostilité* or late L. *hostilitas*, f. *hostilis*; see prec., -ITY.] **1.** The state or fact of being hostile; hostile action; *esp.* such as involves war; *pl.* acts of warfare, war 1613. **2.** Opposition or antagonism 1632.

1. Open acts of sedition and h. 1706. A suspension of hostilities was agreed on PRESCOTT.

Hosting (hōᵘ·stiŋ), *vbl. sb. Obs.* exc. *arch.* or *Hist.* ME. [f. †*host* gather into a host, assemble in battle array (f. HOST *sb.*[1]) + -ING[1].] The raising of a host or armed multitude; hostile encounter or array; †a military expedition. Also *attrib.*

That Angel should with Angel warr, And in fierce h. meet MILT. *P.L.* VI. 93.

Ho·stler. ME. [A syncopated form of *hosteler*. The form OSTLER is now more prevalent.] A man who attends to horses at an inn; a stableman, a groom. **b.** *U.S.* The keeper of the round-house for sheltering locomotives 1890.

Ho·stless, *a. rare.* 1590. [f. HOST *sb.*[2] + -LESS.] Without a host; †inhospitable.

Hostry (hōᵘ·stri). *Obs.* or *arch.* ME. [– OFr. *host(e)rie*, f. *(h)oste* HOST *sb.*[2]; see -ERY.] = HOSTELRY.

Hot, hott (hǫt), *sb.*[1] *Obs.* exc. *dial.* ME. [– (O)Fr. *hotte* creel, panier, prob. of Gmc. origin. See HOD.] **1.** A kind of basket or pannier for carrying earth, sand, lime, manure, etc. *n. dial.* †**2.** (Also **hut(t.**) A padded sheath for the spur of a fighting cock –1806.

Hot (hǫt), *a.* (*sb.*[2]) [OE. *hāt* = OFris., OS. *het* (Du. *heet*), OHG. *heiʒ* (G. *heiss*), ON. *heitr* :- Gmc. **χaitaz.*] **1.** Having or communicating much heat; of or at a high temperature; the opposite of *cold*. (Differing from *warm* in degree.) **2.** Having or producing the sensation of heat (in a high degree). Usu. in predicate. ME. †**3.** In the physiology of the Middle Ages, expressing one of the fundamental qualities of humours, elements, planets, and bodies in general; see COLD *a.* –1670. **4.** Pungent, acrid, biting; corrosive; ardent 1548. **5.** *transf.* Excited; fervent OE.; angry, wrathful ME.; lustful; 'in heat' 1500. **6.** Intense, violent; raging, keen. (Chiefly of conflict or the like.) OE. **b.** *transf.* Uncomfortable 1611. **7.** *Hunting.* Of the scent: Strong, intense 1648. **b.** Of colour: Disagreeably intense 1896. **c.** Of a Treasury bill: Newly issued (*colloq.*) 1928. **d.** Of dance music; Highly elaborated 1928. **8.** That has not had time to cool down; said *esp.* of acts, and of a person fresh from an act ME. †**9.** *absol.* or as *sb.* Hot condition, heat –1667.

1. The wether was hoat HALL. Three h. dishes WOOD. **2.** I am h. with haste SHAKS. Violent H. Pains 1702. **4.** The Mustard is too h. a little *Tam. Shr.* IV. iii. 25. **5.** Hotter wex his loue CHAUCER. She is so h. because the meate is colde *Com. Err.* I. ii. 47. **6.** In the hottest of the fight 1845. **b.** A h. corner 1896.

Phrases. *To blow h. and cold*: see BLOW *v.*[1] *Hot and hot*: said of dishes served in succession as soon as cooked; also *absol.* as *sb.* food thus served. Also *fig. To give it* (a person) *h.*: to administer a severe chastisement. So *to get* or *catch it h.* (colloq.). *To make it h. for*: to make the position uncomfortable for. *Too h. for* or *too h. to hold* (a person): said of a place, etc. which is made too disagreeable for him.

Comb.: **h. air,** vaporous or pretentious talk; also *attrib.*; **-drawn** *a.*, extracted with the application of heat (opp. to *cold-drawn*); **-plate,** a heated flat surface on a stove, etc., for cooking or the like; **h. spot** *spec.*, (*a*) a spot in the intake manifold of an internal-combustion engine specially heated from the exhaust; (*b*) a spot in the combustion chamber which becomes overheated and causes pre-ignition; **h. with** (*colloq.*), h. spirits and water with sugar 1837.

Hot, *adv.* [OE. *hāte* = OS. *hēto*, OHG. *heizo*; afterwards levelled with the adj.] **1.** At a high temperature; pungently. **2.** *fig.* Ardently, violently, angrily, etc.; see the adj. ME.

Hot (hǫt), *v.* [OE. *hātian*, f. *hāt* HOT *a.*; later formed afresh from the adj.] †**1.** *intr.* To be or become hot. (Only in OE.) **2.** *trans.* To heat. (Now *colloq.*) late ME.

Hot, obs. pa. t. and pple. of HIGHT *v.*[1].

Ho·tbed, ho·t-bed. 1626. **1.** A bed of earth heated by fermenting manure, for raising or forcing plants. **2.** *fig.* A place that favours the rapid growth or development of any condition, e.g. of corruption 1768. **3.** 'A platform in a rolling-mill on which rolled bars lie to cool' (Raymond) 1881. **4.** *attrib.* 1810.

2. Hotbeds of fever and ague KINGSLEY.

Hot blast. 1836. A blast of heated air forced into a furnace. Also *attrib.*, and short for *hot-blast process*, etc.

Hot-bloo·ded, *a.* 1598. Having hot blood; ardent or excitable; passionate.

Ho·t-brain. 1605. = HOT-HEAD. So **Ho·t-brained,** *a.* having an excitable brain.

Hotchkiss (hǫ·tʃkis). 1880. [From the inventor's name, B. B. *Hotchkiss* (1826–85).] A kind of machine gun and of rifle.

Hotchpot, hotch-pot (hǫ·tʃ,pǫt). ME. [– AFr., (O)Fr. *hochepot*, f. *hocher* shake, prob. of LG. origin, + *pot* POT *sb.*[1]] **1.** = HOTCHPOTCH 1. **2.** *Eng. Law.* The blending or gathering together of properties for the purpose of securing equality of division, *esp.* in the distribution of the property of an intestate parent; cf. COLLATION *sb.* 1. 1552. Also *fig.* **3.** *transf.* = HOTCHPOTCH 2. ME.

2. Bring the amount of their advancement into h. 1848. **3.** A h. of true religion and poperye J. UDALL.

Hotchpotch, hotch-potch (hǫ·tʃ,pǫtʃ). ME. [Alteration, by rhyming assim., of prec.] **1.** *Cookery.* A dish containing a mixture of many ingredients 1583. **2.** *fig.* A confused assemblage, a medley, jumble, farrago ME. **3.** *Eng. Law.* = HOTCHPOT 2. 1602. **4.** *adj.* Like a hotchpot, confused 1599.

2. A hotch-potch of errors 1728. **4.** This h. Religion PURCHAS.

Hot cockles. *Obs.* exc. *Hist.* 1580. [The origin of the name is unknown.] A rustic game in which one player covers his eyes and being struck by the others in turn guesses who struck him. Also *attrib.*

Hot dog. *U.S. colloq.* 1908. A hot sausage enclosed as a sandwich in a roll of bread.

Hote: see HIGHT *v.*[1]

Hotel (hote·l, ote·l). 1644. [– Fr. *hôtel*, later form of *hostel*; see HOSTEL.] **1.** (In Fr. use.) **a.** A town mansion. ‖**b.** A public official residence, *Hôtel de ville*, a town hall. ‖**c.** *Hôtel-Dieu*, a hospital. †**2.** A HOSTEL in a university 1748. **3.** An inn; esp. one of a superior kind 1765.

1. A few great men still retained their hereditary hotels between the Strand and the river MACAULAY.

Ho·t-foot. *adv.* ME. [f. HOT *a.* + FOOT *sb.* Cf. FOOT-HOT.] With eager pace; in hot haste; hastily. Also as *adj.* 1582, as *sb.* 1869, and as *vb.* 1896.

Ho·t(-)head. 1660. A hot-headed person.

Hot-headed (hǫ·t,he:dėd, -he·dėd), *a.* 1641. **1.** Having a hot head (in *lit.* sense) 1693. **2.** *fig.* Excitable; impetuous, headstrong, rash 1641.

2. Too hot-headed and violent for a diplomatist 1887. Hence **Hot-hea·ded-ly** *adv.*, **-ness.**

Hot-house, hothouse (hǫ·thaus). 1451. †**1.** = BAGNIO 1. –1759. †**2.** A brothel –1699. **3.** A structure kept artificially heated for the growth of plants of warmer climates, or of flowers and fruits out of season. Also *attrib.* Also *fig.* 1749. **4.** A heated room or building for drying something 1555.

3. The technical system is a h. of mendacity BENTHAM.

‖**Hoti** (hǫ·ti). *Pl.* **hoties** (hǫ·tiz). 1638. [Gr. ὅτι conj., that, because.] A statement introduced by 'that', an assertion, or fact asserted (opp. to DIOTI).

Poor sciolists who scarce know the Hoties of things HOWELL.

Hotly (hǫ·tli), *adv.* 1525. [f. HOT *a.* + -LY[2].] **1.** With great heat; so as to be hot or pungent 1592. **2.** *fig.* With fervour; ardently, passionately, keenly; excitedly.

2. The King h. retorted [etc.] J. R. GREEN. So **Ho·tness,** heat.

Ho·t-pot, hot pot. 1700. **1.** A hot drink of ale, etc. *local.* **2.** A dish composed of mutton or beef with potatoes, or potatoes and onions, cooked in an oven in an earthenware pot with a tight-fitting cover 1854. Also *attrib.*

Ho·t-press, *sb.* 1631. A contrivance for pressing paper or cloth between glazed boards and hot metal plates, to make the surface smooth and glossy. Also *attrib.* = *hot-pressed.* So **Hot-press** *v.* to subject to pressure in a hot-press; to make smooth and glossy by so doing. Usu. in pa. pple., or vbl. sb. **Hot-presser,** one whose occupation is hot-pressing paper or cloth.

Ho·t-short, *a.* 1798. [f. HOT *a.* + *short*, after the earlier RED-SHORT; cf. COLD-SHORT.] Of iron: Brittle in its hot state; opp. to *cold-short.*

Hotspur (hǫ·tspɒɹ). 1460. **1.** One whose spur is hot with impetuous riding; hence, a heady or rash person. **2.** *attrib.* or *adj.* Fiery-spirited, hasty, rash 1596. **3.** An early pea 1700.

1. Herry Percy the yonger, whom the Scottis clepid Herry Hatspore CAPGRAVE. Hence **Ho·t-spurred** *a.* = 2.

Hottentot (hǫ·t'ntǫt). 1677. [– S.Afr. Du. *Hottentot*, also †*Ottentot*, †*Hottentoo*, according to an early account an imit. word to denote stammering or stuttering, with ref. to the abrupt pronunc. and 'clicks' of the language; see also HODMANDOD 2.] **1.** A member of a native S. African race of low stature and dark yellowish-brown complexion, who formerly occupied the region near the Cape of Good Hope. **b.** *transf.* A person of inferior intellect or culture 1726. **2.** *attrib.* Of or belonging to this race 1718.

1. b. The utmost I can do for him, is to consider him a respectable H. CHESTERF. *Comb.*: **Hottentot('s) bread,** *Testudinaria elephantipes*; **H. cherry,** *Cassine maurocenia.* Hence **Ho·ttentotism,** a practice characteristic of Hottentots, a species of stammering.

Hot water. ME. **1.** Water at a high temperature. Also *attrib.* **2.** *fig.* A state of ferment, trouble, or great discomfort; a scrape (*colloq.*) 1537.

2. Always getting into hot water R. H. DANA.

Hot well, hot-well. ME. **1.** A spring of naturally hot water. **2.** A reservoir in a condensing steam-engine, into which the hot water passes from the condenser 1766.

Houdah: see HOWDAH.

Hough (hǫk), *sb.* [ME. *hoȝ*, *houȝ*, prob. f. shortened first element of OE. *hōhsinu* hamstring, tendon of Achilles (corresp. to ON. *hásin*), f. *hōh* heel + *sinu* sinew. Cf. HOCK *sb.*[2]] **1.** = HOCK *sb.*[2] 1. **2.** The hollow part behind the knee-joint in man; the adjacent back part of the thigh. Chiefly *Sc.* 1508. **3.** A joint of beef, venison, etc., consisting of the part extending from the hough (sense 1) some distance up the leg; the 'leg' of beef ME. Hence **Hough** *v.* to disable by cutting the sinew or tendons of the h.; to hamstring. **Hou·gher,** one who houghs or hamstrings; in Ireland, one of the Whiteboys.

Hough, var. spelling of HOE *sb.*[2] and *v.*

Hough-sinew, *sb.* (OE.) and *v.* (1472). [OE. *hōhsinu*; see HOUGH *sb.*, HOX *v.*] = HOUGH *sb.*, *v.*

Houlet, obs. f. HOWLET.

Hoult, var. of HOLT.

Hound (haund), *sb.*[1] [OE. *hund* = OFris., OS. *hund* (Du. *hond*), OHG. *hunt* (G. *hund*), ON. *hundr*, Goth. *hunds* :- Gmc. **χundaz* :- **kwntós*, f. IE. **kwn-*, repr. by (O)Ir. *cú* (gen. *con*), Gr. κύων (gen. κυνός).] **1.** A dog, generally. (Now only *arch.* or *poet.*) **2.** *spec.* A dog kept or used for the chase, usu. one hunting by scent. Now esp. applied to a foxhound; also to a harrier; (*the*) *hounds*, a pack of foxhounds. ME. Also *fig.* and *transf.* **3. a.** Applied opprobriously or contemptuously to a man; cf. DOG *sb.* OE. **b.** *transf.* A player who follows the 'scent' in *hare and hounds* 1857. **4.** Short for HOUND-FISH 1603. **5.** *attrib.* 1483.

2. Phr. *To ride to hounds, To follow the hounds. To hold with the hare and run with the hounds*: see HARE. *transf.* or *fig. The h. of hell*, Cerberus; *Orion's h.*, the dog-star. **3.** Boy, false H. *Cor.* V. vi. 113. *Comb.* **h.-shark,** a small species of shark, *Galeus canis*, common on the Atlantic coast of N. America.

Hound (haund), *sb.*[2] 1495. [*Hound(e*, recorded since 1495, is an alteration (with excrescent *-d*, as in SOUND *sb.*[2]) of earlier *houne, hune* (Laȝamon), whence AFr. *houne* (XIV) – ON. *húnn* knob at the top of the mast-head. Mod. use shows infl. of HOUND *sb.*[1]] **1.** *Naut.* A truck (TRUCK *sb.*[2] 2); also, one of the projections on each side of the mast on which the trestle-trees rest, a cheek. **2.** One of the wooden bars connecting the fore-carriage of a springless wagon, etc., with the splinter-bar or shaft. *U.S.* and *local Eng.* 1860.

Hound (haund), *v.* 1528. [f. HOUND *sb.*[1]] **1.** *trans.* To hunt, chase, or pursue with hounds, or as a dog does. Also *absol.* Also *fig.* and *transf.* **2.** To set (a hound, etc.) *at* a quarry; to incite or urge *on* to attack or chase anything 1652. **3.** *transf.* To incite or set (a person) *at* or *on* another; also *Sc.* with *out* 1570.

1. *transf.* To h. the fugitives from place to place 1897. **3.** To h. the rabble upon them as tyrants MOTLEY.

Hou·nd-fish, hou·ndfish. ME. †**1.** = DOG-FISH. **2.** Applied to: **a.** species of garfish of genus *Tylosurus*; **b.** *Blue hound-fish*, a former name in Massachusetts of *Pomatomus saltatrix*, now called the Blue-fish; **c.** *Speckled hound-fish*, a former name of the Spanish Mackerel 1672.

Hou·nding, *sb.* 1860. [f. HOUND *sb.*[2] + -ING[3], perh. after BUNTING *sb.*[2], COAMING.] *Naut.* The lower part of the mast, below the hounds.

Hounding (hau·ndiŋ), *vbl. sb.* 1854. [f. HOUND *v.* + -ING[1].] The action of HOUND *v.*; *spec.* the tracking and driving of a deer, etc., by a hound or hounds, until it is brought under the hunter's gun. Also *fig.*

†**Hou·nds-berry.** ME. **1.** The Black Bryony, *Tamus communis*. **2.** The Black Nightshade, *Solanum nigrum* –1597. **3.** The Wild Cornel or Dogwood. LYTE.

†**Hou·ndsfoot.** 1710. [– Du. *hondsvot*, G. *hundsfott* scoundrel, lit. *cunnus canis*.] A scoundrel, a rascal. Also *attrib.* –1814.

Hound's-tongue. OE. [tr. late L. *lingua canis*, repr. L. *cynoglossos*, Gr. κυνόγλωσσον.] Any plant of the genus *Cynoglossum* of boraginaceous plants, esp. *C. officinale*.

Hour (auᵊɹ). [ME. *ure, our(e*, later *hour(e* – AFr. *ure*, OFr. *ore, eure* (mod. *heure*) :– L. *hora* – Gr. ὥρα season, time of day, hour; repl. OE. *tīd* TIDE and *stund*.] **1.** The twenty-fourth part of a civil day; sixty minutes. **2.** A short or limited space of time, more or less than an hour ME.; *pl.* stated time of occupation or duty 1857. **3.** Each of those points of time at which the twelve successive divisions after noon or midnight, as shown by a dial, are completed; hence, any definite 'time of day' ME. **b.** *pl.* Habitual time of getting up and (esp.) going to bed 1556. **4.** A definite time in general; an appointed time; an occasion ME. **5.** *Eccl. pl.* In full *canonical hours* (see also CANONICAL): The seven offices of mattins (with lauds), prime, terce, sext, none, vespers, and compline; a book containing these; *sing.* any of these. (The earliest recorded use.) ME. **6.** *Mythol.* (*pl.* with capital H, = L. *Horæ*, Gr. Ὧραι.) Female divinities supposed to preside over the changes of the seasons 1634. **7.** *Astr.* and *Geog.* An angular measure of right ascension or longitude, being the 24th part of a great circle of the sphere, or 15 degrees 1777.

1. *Sidereal, solar hour*, 24th part of a sidereal, solar day. Thus this battaile continued .III. long houres HALL. **2.** Sad houres seeme long *Rom. & Jul.* I. i. 167. A reduction of hours without any diminution of wages MILL. **3.** Watchmen.. called the hours of the night SERJT. BALLANTINE. *The eleventh h.*: see ELEVENTH. *Small hours*: the hours after midnight numbered one, two, etc. **b.** I keep early hours 1891. **4.** Myne houre is not yett come TINDALE *John* 2:4. Phr. *Of the h.*: of the present hour; as in 'the question of the h.' *In a good* (*happy*, etc.) *h.*: at a fortunate time; happily; so *in an evil* (*ill*, etc.) *h.* **6.** The rosy-bosomed Hours MILT. *Comus* 986.

Comb.: **h.-angle,** *Astr.* the angular distance between the meridian and the declination-circle passing through a heavenly body, which is the measure of the sidereal time elapsed since its culmination; **-bell,** a bell rung every h., or that sounds the hours; **-book,** *Eccl.* a book of hours (sense 5); **-hand,** the short hand of a clock or watch which indicates the hours; **-plate,** the dial-plate of a clock or watch, inscribed with figures denoting the hours.

Ho·ur-circle. 1674. **1.** Any great circle of the celestial sphere passing through the poles; a meridian or declination-circle. Twenty-four of these are commonly marked on the globe, each distant from the next by one hour of right ascension. 1690. **2.** A small brass circle at the north pole of an artificial globe, graduated into hours and divisions of an hour 1674. **3.** A graduated circle upon an equatorial telescope, parallel to the plane of the equator, by means of which the hour-angle of a star is observed 1837.

Hou·r-glass. 1515. A contrivance for measuring time, consisting of a glass vessel with obconical ends connected by a constricted neck, through which a quantity of sand (or sometimes mercury) runs in exactly an hour. Often *fig.* Also *attrib.* referring to the shape of an hour-glass.

The figure of Time with an Hour-glass in one hand, and a Scythe in the other ADDISON.

‖**Houri** (hūᵊ·ri, hauᵊ·ri). 1737. [– Fr. *houri* – Pers. *ḥūrī*, f. Arab. *ḥūr*, pl. of *ḥawra*; in *ḥūr-al-ʻayūn* (females) gazelle-like in the eyes.] A nymph of the Moslem Paradise. Hence, a voluptuously beautiful woman.

Hourly (auᵊ·ɹli), *a.* 1513. [f. HOUR + -LY[1].] **1.** Of or belonging to an hour; of an hour's age or duration. **2.** Occurring every hour; done, etc. hour by hour; frequent, continual 1530.

2. This is an accident of hourely proofe SHAKS.

Hourly (auᵊ·ɹli), *adv.* 1470. [f. HOUR + -LY[2].] **1.** Every hour; continually, very frequently. †**2.** For a short time –1549.

1. Two spoonfuls h. BYRON.

Housage (hau·zėdʒ). 1617. [f. HOUSE *v.*[1] + -AGE.] **1.** A fee paid for housing goods. **2.** The condition of being housed. COLERIDGE.

House (haus), *sb.*[1] Pl. **houses** (hau·zėz). [OE. *hūs* = OFris., OS., OHG. *hūs* (Du. *huis*, G. *haus*), ON. *hús*, Goth. *hūs* (only in *gudhūs* temple) :– Gmc. **χūsam*, of unkn. origin.] **1.** A building for human habitation; *esp.* a dwelling-place. **b.** The portion of a building occupied by one tenant or family. *Sc.* **2.** A place of worship; a temple; a church. (Usu. *h. of God, of prayer*, etc.) OE. **b.** An inn, tavern 1550. **3.** A building for the keeping of cattle, birds, plants, goods, etc. 1503. **4. a.** A religious house, a convent; *transf.* the religious fraternity abiding there ME. **b.** A college in a university (i.e. either the building or the fellows and students collectively) 1536. **c.** A boarding-house attached to a public school; the boys lodged there 1857. **d.** The building in which a legislative or deliberative assembly meets; *transf.* the assembly itself; a quorum of such an assembly 1541. **e.** Applied also to other deliberative assemblies; formerly also to a municipal corporation 1562. **f.** A place of business; *transf.* a mercantile firm. *The H.* (colloq.): the Stock Exchange. **g.** A theatre, PLAYHOUSE; *transf.* the audience or attendance 1662. **5.** The persons living in one dwelling; a household, family OE. **6.** A family including ancestors and descendants; a lineage, a race OE. **7. a.** *fig.* Dwelling-place; place of abode, rest, deposit, etc. OE. **b.** *transf.* The habitation of any animal OE. **8.** *Astrol.* **a.** A twelfth part of the heavens as divided by great circles through the north and south points of the horizon; the whole sky, excluding those parts that never rise and that never set, being thus divided into twelve houses, numbered eastwards, beginning with the *house of the ascendant* (see ASCENDANT B. 1), each having its special signification. **b.** A sign of the zodiac considered as the seat of the greatest influence of a particular planet; each of the seven planets, except the sun and moon, having two such houses, a *day house* and a *night house*. ME. †**9.** Each square of a chess-board –1829.

1. His h. is his castle MULCASTER. *The H.*, a euphemism for the workhouse. **2.** When my master goeth into the h. of Rimmon to worship there 2 *Kings* 5:18. On to God's h. the people prest TENNYSON. **b.** To drink freely..for the good of the h. GOLDSM. A tied house..is one.. owned by a brewer for the sale of his goods 1891. **3.** Doues with noysome stench Are from their.. Houses driven away 1 *Hen. VI*, I. v. 24. **4. b.** Heads of Houses 1856. *The H.*, Christ Church, Oxford. *Peterhouse*, St. Peter's College, Cambridge. **d.** Phr. *To make a h., keep a h.* (i.e. a quorum). **f.** The Rule of the House is sometimes a great bugbear to compositors 1892. **g.** Acted..to constantly crowded houses CIBBER. **5.** The whole h. was down with influenza 1899. **6.** A plague a both your houses! *Rom. & Jul.* III. i. 111. **7. a.** Yet if some voice that man could trust Should murmur from the narrow h. TENNYSON. **b.** The swallow..to build his hanging h. Intent THOMSON.

Phrases. *H. of call*: **a.** a h. where journeymen of a particular trade assemble, where carriers call for commissions, or where various persons may be heard of; **b.** a h. where one is wont to call. *H. of ill* (*evil*) *fame* (*repute*): a disreputable h.; *esp.* a brothel. *H. and home*: an alliterative strengthening of 'home'. *H. of office*: domestic apartment; †pantry; privy 1419. †*H. of religion* (also *h. of piety*): a religious house, a convent. *Keep h.* **a.** To maintain and preside over a household; also *fig.* **b.** To manage the affairs of a household. (See also HOUSEKEEPER, -KEEPING.) **c.** (Usu. *to keep the h.*) To stay indoors; to be confined to the h.; also *fig.* *Like a h. on fire* (*afire*): as fast as a h. would burn. *As safe as houses*: perfectly safe.

attrib. and *Comb.* **1.** General: as *h.-drain, -rent, -room, -wall, -window*, etc.; *h.-broom, -clock, -flannel*, etc.; *h. affairs, h. work*; *h.-chaplain, -folk*, etc.; *h.-hunter, -hunting, -owner*, etc.; *h.-proud* adj., etc.

2. Special: as **h.-agent,** an agent employed in the sale and letting of houses, the collection of rents, etc.; **-barge** = HOUSE-BOAT; **-book,** a book for household accounts; **-boy**; **-car** (*U.S.*), 'a box-car; a closed railroad-car for carrying freight'; **-chambermaid,** a servant who is both chambermaid and housemaid; **-cricket,** the common species of cricket (*Acheta domestica*) frequenting houses (as dist. from the *field-cricket*); **-dinner, -supper,** (held at a club, school, boarding-house, etc., for members and their guests); **-duty,** a tax imposed on inhabited houses in England; **-engine** (*Mech.*), a steam-engine structurally dependent on the building in which it is contained; **-factor** = *house-agent*; **-flag,** the distinguishing flag of a shipping house; **-fly,** the common fly (*Musca domestica*); **-line** *Naut.*, a small line of three strands, used for seizings, etc. (also called *housing*); **-martin,** the common martin (*Chelidon urbica*); **-parlour-maid** (cf. *house-chambermaid*); **-party,** the guests staying in a h.; **-physician,** a resident physician in a hospital; **-shrew,** the common shrew-mouse (*Crocidura* (*Sorex*) *aranea*); **-snake,** *Ophibolus getulus*, found in N. America, also called *chain-snake*; **-sparrow,** the common sparrow (*Passer domesticus*); **-spider,** any species of spider infesting houses; **-surgeon,** a resident surgeon in a hospital; **-swallow,** the common swallow (*Hirundo rustica*); **-tablemaid** (cf. *house-chambermaid*); **-tax** = *house-duty*; **-waiting-maid** (cf. *house-chambermaid*); †**-wood,** wood for housebote.

House (haus), *sb.*[2] [ME. *house* XIV (in AL. *hu(s)cia* XIII) – OFr. *houce* (mod. *housse*) – med.L. *hultia* for **hulftia* – Gmc. **χulfti* (MDu. *hulfte* pocket for bow and arrow, MHG. *hulft* covering). Cf. HOUSING *sb.*[2]] A covering of textile material; usu. one attached to a saddle, so as to cover the back and flanks of a horse; a housing.

House (hauz), *v.*[1] [OE. *hūsian* (in sense 1) = MLG., MDu. *hūsen*, OHG. *hūsōn* (Du. *huizen*, G. *hausen*), ON. *húsa*; f. HOUSE *sb.*[1]] **I.** *trans.* **1.** To receive or put into a house; to provide with a house to dwell in; to keep or store in a house or building. †**b.** To drive or pursue into a house –1715. **2.** To receive, as a house does; to give shelter to 1610. **3.** *transf.* and *fig.* To cover as with a roof; to harbour, lodge 1577. **4. a.** *Naut.* To place in a secure or unexposed position; to lower and fasten 1769; to cover or protect with a roof 1821. **b.** *Carpentry.* To fix in a socket, mortice, or the like 1833. **c.** *pass.* Of hops: To become massed with bines at the top of the poles.

1. To h. plants BACON, an oat-rick G. WHITE, children 1832. **b.** *Com. Err.* V. i. 188. **2.** Caves That h. the cold-crowned snake TENNYSON. **4. a.** A large ship, with her top-gallant-masts housed R. H. DANA.

II. *intr.* †**1.** To erect a house; to build –1496. **2.** To dwell in (or as in) a house; to harbour 1591. †**3.** *House in* (also in *pass.*):

said of a ship of which the upper works are built narrower than the lower –1711.

2. Graze where you will, you shall not h. with me SHAKS. Where Saturn houses DRYDEN.

House (hauz), *v.*² 1500. [f. HOUSE *sb.*²; cf. (O)Fr. *housser.*] *trans.* To cover (a horse) with a house or housing.

Hou·se-boat. 1790. A boat roofed over and fitted up as a house, for living in.

Hou·sebote. [OE. *hūsbōt*, f. *hūs* HOUSE *sb.*¹ + *bōt* BOOT *sb.*¹] *Law.* The repair of a house; wood for this purpose; the right of a tenant to take this from the landlord's estate.

Housebreaker (hau·sˌbrēⁱkəɹ). ME. **1.** One who breaks open and enters a house with intent to commit a felony. **2.** One whose business it is to demolish houses 1875. Hence **Hou·se-break** *v.* to break into a house with felonious intent. So **Hou·sebreaking,** the crime of breaking open and entering a house with felonious intent. Also *attrib.*

Hou·se-builder. 1769. One whose business is the building of houses; a builder.

House-builder Moth: a W. Indian insect (*Oiketicus sandersii*).

Housecarl (hau·sˌkāɹl). [Late OE. *hūscarl* – ON. *húskarl* manservant, f. *hús* house + *karl* man. See CARL *sb.*¹] *Hist.* A member of the bodyguard or household troops of a (Danish or late Old English) king or noble.

Hou·se-dog. 1711. A watch-dog; a domestic dog.

Hou·se-dove. 1530. **1.** A tame dove or pigeon. **2.** *fig.* A stay-at-home 1579.

Hou·se-father. 1552. [tr. L. *paterfamilias*; in mod. use tr. G. *hausvater.*] The father of a household or family; the male head of a collection of persons living together as a family.

Household (hau·sˌhōᵘld). ME. [f. HOUSE *sb.*¹ + HOLD *sb.*¹ Cf. MDu. *huushoud, huysholt.*]

I. †**1.** The maintaining of a house or family; housekeeping –1576. †**2.** The contents of a house collectively; household goods –1709. **3.** The inmates of a house collectively; a domestic establishment ME. **4.** Ellipt. for *h. bread, coal,* etc. 1638.

3. The master of the h. should be up early and before all his servants JOWETT. The housholde of fayth TINDALE *Gal.* 6:10. *The Household* = the royal or imperial h.

II. *attrib.* (and *adj.*) **a.** Of or belonging to a household, domestic ME. **b.** Of or belonging to the royal household, as **h. troops,** troops specially appointed to guard the person of the sovereign 1711. **c.** *fig.* Familiar, intimate, homely (*arch.*) 1450.

c. Good plain houshold judgment STERNE.

Comb.: **h. bread,** bread for ordinary household use; now, white bread made of inferior flour; **h. franchise, suffrage,** the right of voting in parliamentary or other elections, consequent on being a householder (see HOUSEHOLDER); **h. gods** (*Rom. Antiq.*), the *Lares* and *Penates*, divinities supposed to preside over the h., whose images were kept in the *atrium* or central room of the house; *fig.* the essentials of home life; **h. loaf,** a loaf of h. bread; **h. servant**; **h. word,** a saying in familiar use; a name known to everybody.

Householder (hau·sˌhōᵘldəɹ). ME. [f. HOUSE *sb.*¹ + HOLDER¹ 2.] The person who holds or occupies a house as his own dwelling and that of his household; esp., one qualified to exercise the franchise by the occupancy of a house or tenement. Hence, The head of a household or family.

With your head full of ten-pound householders MACAULAY. So **Hou·seholding** *sb.* †housekeeping; occupation of a house; also *attrib.*

Household-stuff. *arch.* 1511. The goods, utensils, vessels, etc. belonging to a household.

Housekeeper (hau·sˌkīpəɹ). 1440. [f. HOUSE *sb.*¹ + KEEPER, i.e. keeper of a house.] **1.** = HOUSEHOLDER. Now *rare* or *Obs.* †**2.** One who keeps a (good, bountiful, etc.) house; a hospitable person –1707. **3. a.** A person in charge of a house, office, place of business, etc. 1632. †**b.** A watch-dog –1688. **4.** A woman engaged in housekeeping; *esp.* the woman in control of the female servants of a household 1607. **5.** One who 'keeps the house', or stays at home 1710.

2. John Barnston..a bountiful house keeper FULLER. **3. b.** *Macb.* III. i. 97. **4.** *Cor.* I. iii. 55.

Housekeeping (hau·sˌkīpiŋ), *sb.* 1538. [f. HOUSE *sb.*¹ + KEEPING *vbl. sb.*] **1.** The maintenance of a household; the management of household affairs 1550. †**2.** The keeping of a good (or other) table; hospitality –1849. **b.** *concr.* Provisions for household use (*pseudo-arch.*) 1826.

2. b. 'Tell me..what is in the pantry?' 'Small h. enough,' said Phoebe SCOTT.

Housel (hau·z'l), *sb. Obs.* exc. *Hist.* [OE. *hūsl* (whence ON. *húsl*) = Goth. *hunsl* sacrifice, θυσία; of unkn. origin.] The consecrated elements at the Eucharist; the administration or reception of the Holy Communion.

Housel (hau·z'l), *v. Obs.* exc. *Hist.* [OE. *hūslian*, f. *hūsl* (prec.). Cf. Goth. *hunsljan* sacrifice, σπένδειν.] *trans.* To administer, *pass.* (and *refl.*) to receive, the Holy Communion.

Houseleek (hau·sˌlīk). 1440. [f. HOUSE *sb.*¹ + LEEK.] The plant *Sempervivum tectorum*, a succulent herb with pink flowers, thick stem, and leaves forming a dense rosette close to the root, which grows commonly on walls and roofs. Hence, any species of the genus *Sempervivum*, N.O. *Crassulaceæ*.

Houseless (hau·slės), *a.* ME. [f. HOUSE *sb.*¹ + -LESS.] **1.** Not having a house; having no shelter; homeless. **2.** Destitute of houses to shelter 1586.

1. Your House-lesse heads SHAKS. **2.** The h. woods WORDSW. Hence **Hou·selessness,** h. condition.

Houseling (hau·sliŋ), *sb. Obs.* or *dial.* 1598. [f. HOUSE *sb.*¹ + -LING¹.] A stay-at-home; also, an animal bred up by hand (*dial.*).

Houseling, -lling (hau·z'liŋ). *vbl. sb. Obs.* exc. *Hist.* OE. [f. HOUSEL *v.* + -ING¹.] **1.** Administration of the Eucharist; communion. **2.** *attrib.* Sacramental 1474.

2. Phr. **Houseling people**: communicants.

Housemaid (hau·sˌmēⁱd). 1694. A female domestic servant, having charge esp. of the reception-rooms and bed-rooms. Also *attrib.*

Housemaid's knee: an inflammation of the bursa over the knee-cap, induced by kneeling on hard floors.

Housemaster (hau·sˌmaːstəɹ). 1878. **1.** The master of a house or household (*rare*). **2.** (*Hou·se-ma·ster.*) The master of a boarding-house at a public school 1884.

Housemate (hau·sˌmēⁱt). 1809. One who lives in the same house with another. Also *fig.*

Hou·se-mother. 1837. [orig. tr. Ger. *hausmutter* (Carlyle).] The mother of a household or family; the female head of a community living together as a family.

Hou·se-place, houseplace. 1812. The common living-room in a farm-house or cottage (*local*).

Hou·se-room. 1586. Room in a house for a person or thing; lodging. Also *fig.*

Hou·se-top. 1526. The top or roof of a house. **b.** *fig.* A public place (cf. Luke 12:3).

Hou·se-warming. 1577. The action of celebrating the entrance into the occupation of a new house or home with an entertainment; also, the entertainment.

I dined at Chiffinch's house-warming EVELYN. Hence **House-warm** *v.* to give, to take part in, a h.

Housewife (hau·sˌwəif, hɒ·zwif, hɒ·zif), *sb.* Pl. **housewives** (hau·sˌwəivz, hɒ·z(w)ivz). [ME. *hus(e)wif* (XIII), f. HOUSE *sb.*¹ + WIFE. Elision of *w* (cf. *Chiswick*, etc.) gave the forms HUSSY, HUZZY, dial. *hussif.*] **1.** The mistress of a family; the wife of a householder. Often, A woman who manages her household with skill and thrift, a domestic economist. †**2.** A light, worthless, or pert woman or girl. Usu. *huswife*; now HUSSY, q.v. –1705. **3.** (Usu. hɒ·zif). A pocket-case for needles, pins, thread, scissors, etc. (Still often spelt *huswife, hussive.*) 1749.

1. There is..but An Hour in one whole Day between A H. and a Slut 1710.

Hou·sewife (see prec.), *v.* Now *rare.* Also **-wive.** 1566. [f. prec. sb.] **1.** *intr.* To act the housewife; to manage a household with skill and thrift; to practise economy. **2.** *trans.* To manage with skill and thrift; to economize, make the most of. (Cf. *to husband.*) 1632.

2. The vndrest Hearth, and the ill house-wif'd roome 1649. I must h. the money DE FOE.

Housewifely (hau·sˌwəifli, hɒ·z(w)ifli), *a.* 1526. [f. as prec. + -LY¹.] **1.** Of the character of a housewife; skilful and thrifty in the management of a house. **2.** Belonging to or befitting a housewife 1560.

2. A most h. bunch of keys C. BRONTE.

Housewifery (hau·sˌwəifri, hɒ·z(w)ifri). 1440. [f. as prec. + -RY.] **1.** The function or province of a housewife; domestic economy; housekeeping. **2.** *concr.* Articles of household use. ?*Obs.* 1552.

Housewright (hau·sˌrəit). Now *rare.* 1549, [f. HOUSE *sb.*¹ + WRIGHT.] A builder of houses; a house-carpenter.

Housing (hau·ziŋ), *sb.*¹ ME. [f. HOUSE *v.*¹ or *sb.*¹ + -ING¹.] **1.** The action of HOUSE *v.*¹ **2. a.** Shelter of or as of a house; lodging ME. **b.** Houses collectively; house-property; *spec.* outhouses or outbuildings ME. †**c.** A house –1831. **d.** Provision of houses 1899. †**3.** *Arch.* A canopied niche for a statue, etc.; also *collect.* tabernacle-work –1521. (*Hist.*) **4.** *Naut.* **a.** A covering or roofing for a ship when laid up, or under stress of weather. **b.** The part of a lower mast between the heel and the upper deck, or of the bowsprit between the stem and the knight-heads. **c.** = *house-line* (see HOUSE *sb.*¹). 1821. **5.** *Carpentry.* A space excavated out of one body for the insertion of the extremity of another 1823. **6.** *Mech.* **a.** 'One of the plates or guards on the railway-carriage or truck, which form a lateral support for the axle-boxes.' **b.** 'The framing holding a journal-box.' **c.** 'The uprights supporting the cross-slide of a planer.' (KNIGHT.) 1875. *Comb.* **h.-box** = JOURNAL-BOX.

Housing (hau·ziŋ), *sb.*² ME. [f. HOUSE *sb.*² and *v.*² + -ING¹.] **1.** A covering. (Often in *pl.*) Rare in gen. sense. **2.** *spec.* A cloth covering put on a horse, etc., for defence or ornament; caparison, trappings 1645. **b.** 'The leather fastened at a horse's collar to turn over the back when it rains' (Halliwell). **3.** *attrib.*, as in **h.-cloth,** a cloth used for a housing 1607.

Housling: = HOUSELING.

Houss, var. of HOUSE *sb.*²

‖**Houstonia** (hustōᵘ·niă). 1838. [mod.L., f. Dr. W. *Houston*, a botanist (died 1733); see -IA¹.] *Bot.* A N. American genus of plants (N.O. *Rubiaceæ*), with delicate four-parted flowers of various colours; the best known is *H. cærulea*, the Bluet.

Hout, var. of HOOT.

Houting (hau·tiŋ). 1880. [Of unkn. origin.] A species of whitefish, *Coregonus oxyrhynchus*, found in some freshwater lakes.

Houve, hoove. *Obs.* or *Sc.* [OE. *hūfe* = MLG., MDu. *hūve* (Du. *huif*), OHG. *hūba* (G. *haube*) :– Gmc. **χūbōn*, f. **χūb-*, repr. also by OE. *hȳf* (:– **hūb-*) HIVE.] A covering for the head; a turban, a coif; a cap, a skull-cap; in Sc. (*how, hoo*) a night-cap.

Houyhnhnm (hwi·hn'm, hwi·n'm). 1727. [A combination of letters to suggest the neigh of a horse.] Swift's name in *Gulliver's Travels* for one of a race of beings described as horses endowed with reason and bearing rule over a degraded brutish race of men, called the Yahoos. Hence *transf.*

†**Hove,** *v.*¹ ME. [Of unkn. origin; of great frequency in ME. from XIII; in XVI largely superseded by HOVER *v.*] **1.** *intr.* To HOVER –1590. **2.** To wait, linger, stay, remain –1595. **3.** To come or go floating or soaring; to be borne, move, or pass away –1650.

Hove, *v.*² *Obs.* or *dial.* ME. [app. f. HEAVE *v.* (pa. t. *hove*, pa. pple. *hoven*).] †**1.** *trans.* To lift –1570. **2.** *trans.* To swell, inflate, puff up or out. Chiefly in pa. pple. **Hoved** = HOVEN. 1601. **3.** *intr.* (for *refl.*) To rise; to swell up 1590.

Hove, *v.*³ Abbrev. for BEHOVE.

Hove, pa. t. and pple. of HEAVE (see also HOVEN).

Hovel (hǫ·v'l, hɒ·v'l), *sb.* ME. [The earliest exx. are from easterly areas; perh. of LG. origin, but no corresp. form is known.] **1.** An open shed; an outhouse used as a shelter for cattle, a receptacle for grain or tools. **2.** A rude or miserable dwelling-place; a wretched cabin 1625. **3.** The conical building enclosing a porcelain oven or kiln 1825. **4.** A stack of corn, etc. 1591.

Hovel, *v.*¹ 1583. [f. HOVEL *sb.*] **a.** *trans.* To shelter as in a hovel or shed. **b.** (*Archit.*) To form like an open hovel or shed; as 'to hovel a chimney' 1823.

a. To houell thee with Swine and Rogues forlorne *Lear* IV. vii. 39.

Hovel, *v.*² 1880. [perh. back-formation from HOVELLER.] **a.** *intr.* To pursue the occupation of a hoveller. **b.** *trans.* To bring (a vessel) into harbour, moor and unload it, etc. Hence **Hovelling** *vbl. sb.* the business of a hoveller, piloting.

Hoveller (hǫ·v'ləɹ, hɒ·v'ləɹ). Also **-eler.** 1769. [Of unkn. origin. Cf. local *hobbler* in same sense.] **1.** An unlicensed pilot or boatman, esp. on the Kentish coast; often applied to a boatman who goes out to wrecks, occas. with a view to plunder. **2.** The craft used by these boatmen 1880.

Hoven (hōᵘ·v'n), *ppl. a.* Now *dial.* Also **hove.** 1555. [pa. pple. of HEAVE *v.* (esp. in sense I. 5); see also HEAVE *sb.* 3 and cf. HOOVE.] Swollen, bloated, puffed out; as cattle with over-feeding. Also *fig.*

Hover (hǫ·vəɹ, hɒ·vəɹ), *sb.* 1513. [f. HOVER *v.*] **1.** An act of hovering 1893. **2.** The action or condition of remaining in suspense 1513. **3.** Any overhanging stone or bank under which a fish, otter, etc., can hide. Chiefly *s. dial.* 1602.

Comb. **H.-fly,** a dipterous insect of the order *Bombyliidæ*, which hovers over flowers without settling.

Hover (hǫ·vəɹ, hɒ·vəɹ), *v.* ME. [f. HOVE *v.*¹ + -ER⁵.] **1.** *intr.* To hang or remain suspended in the air *over* or *about* a particular spot. **2.** *transf.* and *fig.* To keep hanging or lingering *about* (a person or place), to wait near at hand, move to and fro near or around 1581. **3.** †To hesitate before taking action; to waver in indecision; hence, to hang *on the verge of* 1440. †**4.** *trans.* Of a bird: To flap or flutter (the wings) –1687. **5.** To brood over; to cover (the young) with wings and body 1776.

1. This hauke hovereth to longe above PALSGR. Cloudes alwaies hovering about the tops thereof 1600. **2.** Pestilence was hovering in the track of famine GEO. ELIOT. **3.** A mind hovering on the verge of madness 1899. **5.** Capons..h. chickens like hens G. WHITE. Hence **Ho·verer,** an animal or thing that hovers. **Ho·veringly** *adv.*

How (hau), *sb.*¹ *north.* ME. [– ON. *haugr*, f. Gmc. **χauχ*- HIGH.] **1.** A hill, hillock; as in Great H., Silver H., etc. **2.** An artificial mound, tumulus, or barrow 1669.

How (hau), *adv.* (*sb.*²) [OE. *hū* = OFris. *hū*, *hō*, OS. (*h*)*wō*, *hwuo* (MLG. *woe*, Du. *hoe*), OHG. *wuo* :– WGmc. **χwō*, adv. formation on **χwa*- WHO, WHAT.] An adverb primarily interrog., used also in exclams., and in conjunctive and relative constructions.

I. In direct questions. **1.** In what way or manner? By what means? **2.** In what condition or state? ME. **3.** To what effect? With what meaning? Also, By what name? *arch.* (Repl. by 'What?') ME. **4.** *ellipt.* for 'How is it?' or 'How say you?' and used interjectionally. (Now 'What?' or 'What!') *arch.* (exc. in *how about*..?) OE. **5.** To what extent? In what degree? OE. **6.** At what rate or price? 1597.

1. How schulen deede men ryse aȝen? WYCLIF 1 *Cor.* 15:35. How saidst thou, She is my sister? *Gen.* 26:9. *As how* (ellipt.): see AS *adv.* *How if*..? ='How will (would) it be if..?' **2.** Phr. *How are you? How do you do?* (formerly *How do you?*). How's little Miss Sharp? THACKERAY. *How's that?* in *Cricket*, an appeal to the umpire to say whether a batsman is 'out' or not. **3.** How art thou call'd? SHAKS. **4.** How! signior..have you not authority? DE FOE. Don't say 'How?' for 'What?' O. W. HOLMES. **5.** How old..are you? 1573. **6.** How do you sell the plums? 1899.

II. In direct exclams. In what a way! to what an extent or degree! OE.

How are the mightie fallen! 2 *Sam.* 1:19.

III. In dependent questions and exclams. **1.** In what way, manner, condition, etc.; by what means OE. **2.** Followed by an infinitive: In what way; by what means ME. **3.** After verbs of saying, perceiving, and the like: = That OE. **4.** To what extent; in what degree OE.

1. Shakespeare has taught us how great men should speak and act JOWETT. Be wary how you engage THACKERAY. **2.** There is no better lesson how not to do it 1897. **3.** Shee had heard..how that the Lord had visited his people *Ruth* 1:6.

IV. Introducing a relative clause. **1.** In what way, manner, condition, etc.; by what means; in the way that; however; as ME. †**2.** To what extent, in what degree (that); HOWEVER –1602. †**b.** Correlative to *so*: To what extent; in what degree; as.. as –1879. †**3.** With sb. as antecedent: In which (way); by which (name) –1690.

1. Be that how it will 1695. **2. b.** Phr. *By how much..by so much* = L. *quantum..tantum.* (A Latinism.)

V. With indef. adj. or adv.: In (some, any) way or manner (*rare*) OE.

He found means, some how or other, to go DE FOE.

Phrase. **How so.** ME. **a.** *interrog.*: How is it so? How is that? †**b.** *relative*: Howsoever. †**c.** However much; although.

B. *sb.*² (often in collocation with *why*.) **1.** A question or query as to the way or manner 1533. **2.** The way or manner (in which) 1551.

1. Bother your hows and whys! 1899. **2.** Must we in all things look for the how, and the why, and the wherefore? LONGF.

How, howe, *int.* (*sb.*³) *Obs.* or *dial.* ME. [A natural utterance.] **1.** = Ho *int.*¹ Also *sb.* as name for this. **2.** A cry of sailors in heaving the anchor up, etc.: usu. with *hale, heave.* Also *sb.* as name for this. 1450.

Howbeit (hau,bī·it). ME. [orig. three wds. *how be it*, with pa. t. *how were it* (= however it were).]

A. *adv.* However it may be; be that as it may; nevertheless; however (*arch.*) 1470.

†**B.** *conj.* or *conj. adv.* (orig. with *that*). Though, although –1634.

‖**Howdah** (hau·dă). *E. Indies.* Also **houda(h.** 1774. [– Urdu *hawda* – Arab. *hawdaj* litter carried by camel or elephant.] A seat to contain two or more persons, usually fitted with a railing and a canopy, erected on the back of an elephant.

How-do-ye, how-d'ye, howdy. *phr.* and *sb.* Now *Obs.* or *dial.* 1563. **1.** The phr. *how do ye? how do you?* = how are you? **2.** *sb.* = next 2. 1575. **3.** *attrib.* or *adj.* 1600.

How-do-you-do, how-d'ye-do, *phr.* and *sb.* 1632. **1.** A phrase inquiring after the health of the person addressed; see Do *v.* 1697. **2.** *sb.* Used as a name for the inquiry 1632. **3.** A 'business'; an awkward state of things 1835. Hence **How-d'ye-do** *v.* to say 'How d'ye do?' to.

Howdy, -ie (hau·di). *Sc.* and *n. dial.*, *vulgar.* 1725. [Of unkn. origin.] A midwife.

Howel (hau·ĕl), *sb.* 1846. [prob. of LG. origin; cf. MLG. *hövel*, LG. *höwel* plane.] A plane with a convex sole, used by coopers for smoothing the insides of casks, etc. Hence **How·el** *v.* to plane or smooth with a h.

However (hau,e·vəɹ); contr. **howe'er** (hauēᵊ·ɹ), *adv.* late ME. [f. How *adv.* + EVER *adv.* Superseded earlier †*how so.*] **1.** In whatever manner; by whatever means; to whatever extent. **b.** However much; although. *Obs.* or *arch.* 1591. †**2.** In any case, at all events, at any rate. (Now merged in 3.) –1790. **3.** For all that, nevertheless, notwithstanding; yet; = *but* at the beginning of the sentence 1613. **4.** Interrog. (and conjunctive): How, in any circumstances or way whatever? (See EVER *adv.*) *colloq.* 1871.

1. I coniure you..(How ere you come to know it) answer me *Macb.* IV. i. 51. His innocence, h. manifest, could not save him M. PATTISON. **3.** I, h., Must not omit [etc.] MILTON. **4.** H. did you manage it? 1899.

†**Howish** (hau·iʃ), *a. colloq.* 1694. [f. How *adv.* + -ISH¹.] Having a vague sense of indisposition; 'all-overish' –1802.

†**Howitz, haubitz.** 1687. [– G. *haubitze*, †*hau(f)enitz*, introduced into German during the Hussite wars (cf. PISTOL), – Czech *houfnice* stone-sling, catapult.] = next. (Usu. unchanged in pl.) –1781.

Howitzer (hau·itsəɹ). 1695. [– Du. *houwitser*, f. G. *haubitze* (see prec., -ER¹.); superseding HOWITZ.] A short, comparatively light gun, which fires a heavy projectile at a high angle of elevation and low velocity. *Comb.*, as *h.-boat.*

Howker, var. of HOOKER².

Howl (haul), *sb.* 1599. [f. HOWL *v.*] **1.** The prolonged and mournful cry of a dog, wolf, etc., which dwells upon the vowel *u*; the similar sound of the wind, etc. 1605; or in a wireless receiver during tuning-in 1921. **2.** A loud wail of pain or anguish; a savage yell of rage or disappointment. (Often *contempt.*)

1. The Wolfe, Whose howle's his Watch *Macb.* II. i. 54.

Howl (haul), *v.* [ME. *houle*, corresp. to MLG., MDu. *hūlen* (Du. *huilen*), MHG. *hiulen, hiuweln*, rel. to OHG. *hūwila* (MHG. *hiuwel*) owl; perh. immed. f. ME. *hūle* (XIII), later *howle* OWL (cf. also L. *ululare* howl, *ulula* owl, Gr. ὑλᾶν bark).] **1.** *intr.* To utter a prolonged, loud, and doleful cry, in which the sound of *u* (*ū*) prevails. Said of dogs, wolves, etc.; formerly also of the owl. **2.** Of a human being: To utter a similar sound; to wail, lament, esp. with pain. Now often used contemptuously. ME. **3.** *trans.* To utter with howling. Also *h. out.* 1530. **4.** *intr.* To make a prolonged wailing noise. Of an organ: To cipher. 1687. **b.** Of a wireless receiver (see prec.) 1920.

1. They heard Dogges howle on the shore PURCHAS. **2.** Goo to nowe ye Ryche men. Wepe and howle TINDALE *Jas.* 5:1. He still howls about the expense of printing SCOTT. **3.** Howling certaine Psalmes PURCHAS. **4.** The wind was howling 1875.

Howler (hau·ləɹ). 1840. [f. HOWL *v.* + -ER¹.] **1.** An animal that howls; *spec.* a S. American Monkey of the genus *Mycetes*. **2.** A person hired to howl at a funeral 1844. **3.** *slang.* Something 'crying'; *spec.* a glaring blunder 1872.

Howlet (hau·lĕt, *Sc.* hu·lĕt). *dial.* See also OWLET. 1450. [In XV *howlott, -att*, app. dim. of OWL (see -ET) with assim. to HOWL *v.* Cf. OWLET (XVI). Connection with Fr. *hulotte* (XVI) cannot be made out.] An owl, owlet.

How·ling, *ppl. a.* 1605. [f. HOWL *v.* + -ING².] **1.** That howls. **2.** Filled with howling; dreary. In the Biblical phr. *h. wilderness*, etc., merely intensive. 1611. **3.** *fig.* (chiefly *slang.*) Glaring, 'screaming' 1865.

3. A h. swell SALA. Hence **How·lingly** *adv.*

Howsoever (hau:soᵘ,e·vəɹ). *arch.* late ME. [f. *how so* (see How *adv.*, HOWEVER) + EVER *adv.* Superseded next.] **1.** = HOWEVER 1. (Sometimes with ellipsis.) **2.** With adj. or adv.: To what extent or in what degree soever 1557. †**3.** = HOWEVER 2. –1663. †**4.** = HOWEVER 3. –1709.

2. How low soeuer the matter SHAKS. H. well instructed he might be BOLINGBROKE.

Howsomever (hau:sɒ̆me·vəɹ), *adv.* Now *dial.* or *vulgar.* ME. [A parallel formation with *howsoever*, with the conj. *sum, som* (= Da., Sw. *som* as, that) instead of *so*. Superseded by prec.] †**1.** = HOWEVER 1, 1 b. –1601. **2.** = HOWEVER 3. 1562.

†**Hox,** *v. Obs.* or *dial.* ME. [Shortened f. †*hoxen* v. (XIV), rel. to HOUGH-SINEW.] *trans.* To hough, to hamstring –1756.

Hoy (hoi), *sb.*¹ 1495. [– MDu. *hoei*, var. of *hoede, heude* (mod. *heu*), of unkn. origin.] 'A small vessel, usually rigged as a sloop, and employed in carrying passengers and goods, particularly in short distances on the seacoast' (Smyth).

Hoy (hoi), *interj.* (*sb.*²) ME. [A natural exclam. Cf. AHOY.] **1.** A cry used to call attention; also to incite or drive hogs, etc. In naut. language used in hailing or calling aloft. **2.** *sb.* A call of 'hoy!' 1641. Hence **Hoy** *v.* to urge on with cries of 'hoy!'; to drive with shouts; *intr.* to call 'hoy!'

‖**Hoya** (hoi·ă). 1851. [mod. Bot. L., f. Thomas *Hoy*, an English gardener (died 1821); see -A².] *Bot.* A large genus of climbing evergreen plants (N.O. *Asclepiadaceæ*), bearing dense umbels of showy flowers; commonly known as *honey-plants, wax-plants*, or *wax-flowers*. They are cultivated in greenhouses for their beauty.

Hoyden (hoi·dĕn), *sb.* (*a.*) 1593. [prob. – (M)Du. *heiden* HEATHEN, gipsy.] †**1.** A clown, boor –1708. **2.** A rude, or ill-bred girl (or woman); a romp 1676. **3.** *attrib.* or *adj.* Belonging to, or of the character of a hoyden; inelegant in deportment, roystering 1728. Hence **Hoy·denhood,** the condition of a h. **Hoy·denish** *a.* having the character or manners of a h.; characteristic of a h. **Hoy·denishness.**

Hoy·den, *v.* 1709. [f. prec. sb.] *intr.* To play the hoyden.

†**Hoyle.** 1614. [Of unkn. origin.] *Archery.* A mark when shooting at ROVERS –1835.

Hoyman (hoi·mǣn). 1666. [f. HOY *sb.*[1] + MAN.] A man in charge of a hoy.

Hr-, a frequent combination in OE. [:- Gmc. *hr-* :- IE. *kr-*.] In initial *hr-*, the *h* was lost in the transition to ME.: e.g. OE. *hræfn, hróf*, etc., now RAVEN, ROOF, etc.

Huanaco, var. of GUANACO.

Hub (hɒb). 1511. [prob. identical with HOB *sb.*[2], of which *hub(be* is the earliest form, the basic meaning being perh. 'lump, mass'.] †**1.** The HOB of a fire-place –1825. **2.** The central solid part of a wheel; the nave 1649. **3.** *transf.* and *fig.* A central point of revolution, activity, life, interest, etc. 1858. **4.** Techn., etc. uses:

a. *Die-sinking.* A cylindrical piece of steel on which the design for a coin is engraved in relief 1851. **b.** An abruptly raised piece of ground, a stumbling-block 1669. **c.** A thick sod 1828. **d.** A block for stopping the wheel of a vehicle 1856.

2. Phr. *Up to the h.* (U.S.): as far as possible; deeply or inextricably involved, as a wheel in mud. **3.** Boston State-House is the hub of the solar system O. W. HOLMES. *Comb.* **h.-band,** a metal band to reinforce a wooden h. of a wheel.

Hub a dub. [imit.; cf. RUB-A-DUB.] The noise of beating a drum. MME. D'ARBLAY.

Hubble bubble (hɒ·b'lˌbɒ·b'l). 1634. [Reduplication of BUBBLE, as suggestive of the sound.] **1.** A rudimentary form of hookah in which the smoke bubbles through a coco-nut shell, or the like, half-filled with water. **2.** A representation of a bubbling sound; also of confused talk 1740. **3.** *attrib.* Of confused ideas, speech, etc. 1754.

2. There was a considerable roll and hubble-bubble of the tides as we rounded the point LADY BRASSEY.

Hubbub (hɒ·bɒb). 1555. [In XVI *hoo boube, -boobe*, often referred to as an Irish cry. Cf. Ir. *abú* used in battle-cries, and Gael. *ub! ub! ubub!* int. of aversion or contempt, *ubh ubh!* int. of disgust or amazement.] **1.** A confused noise of a multitude shouting or yelling. **b.** The din of a crowd, or of a multitude of speakers heard at once 1779. **2.** Noisy turmoil; confusion, disturbance; a riot, row 1619.

1. b. The h...of Parliamentary discussion SEELEY. So **Hu·bbuboo:, -aboo:,** a confused yelling; esp. as a savage war-cry; hence, a tumult, turmoil.

Hubby, *a. U.S.* 1860. [f. HUB 4 b + -Y[1].] 'Full of hubs or projecting protuberances; as, a road that has been frozen while muddy is hubby' (Webster).

Hübnerite (hü·bnərəit). 1867. [Named 1865, after Adolph *Hübner*, who analysed it; see -ITE[1] 2 b.] *Min.* Tungstate of manganese, found in reddish-brown bladed crystals.

Hubristic (hiubri·stik), *a.* 1831. [irreg. (for *hybristic*) – Gr. ὑβριστικός, f. ὕβρις outrage, contempt; see -IC.] Insolent, contemptuous.

Huck (hɒk), *sb.*[1] *Obs.* exc. *dial.* 1788. (In comb. ME.) [perh. to be referred ult. to *hŭk- be bent, as repr. in MLG., MDu. *hūken, hukken* sit bent, crouch.] The hip, the haunch. *Comb.*: **H.-bone** = HUCKLE-BONE 1. **H.-backed, h.-shouldered** *adjs.* hump-backed, crump-shouldered.

Huck, *sb.*[2] 1851. Short for HUCKABACK.

Huck (hɒk), *v. Obs.* exc. *dial.* ME. [The base of HUCKSTER, q.v.] *intr.* To higgle in trading; to chaffer, bargain. Also *fig.*

Huckaback (hɒ·kăbæk). 1690. [Also †*hugaback*, †*hag-a-bag*; of unkn. origin.] A stout linen fabric, with the weft threads thrown alternately up so as to form a rough surface, used for towelling, etc. Also *attrib.* or as *adj.*

Huckle (hɒ·k'l), *sb.* 1529. [dim. of HUCK *sb.*[1] (see -LE); see HUCKLE-BONE.] **1.** The hip or haunch. †**2.** ? The hock of a quadruped TOPSELL. *Comb.*: **H.-back,** a hump-back; **h.-backed** *a.*

†**Huckle,** *v.* 1620. [f. HUCK *v.* + -LE.] *intr.* To haggle in bargaining –1655.

Huckleberry (hɒ·k'lˌberi). *U.S.* 1670. [prob. alt. of HURTLEBERRY, WHORTLEBERRY.] The fruit and plant of species of *Gaylussacia* (N.O. *Vacciniaceæ*), low berry-bearing shrubs common in N. America. Also applied to N. American species of the closely allied *Vaccinium*, more properly called *blueberry*. Also *attrib.*

Huckle-bone (hɒ·k'lˌbōᵘn). 1529. [f. HUCKLE *sb.*; parallel with *huck-bone*, late ME. *hoke-bone* (XV), Sc. *hukebane* (DUNBAR); see HUCK *sb.*[1]] **1.** The hip- or haunch-bone; the ischium or whole *os innominatum*. **2.** The astragalus in the hock-joint of a quadruped; the knuckle-bone 1542.

Huckster (hɒ·kstəɹ), *sb.* ME. [The earliest repr. (XII) of a group based on **huk-*, prob. of LG. origin (but MDu. *hoeker, hoekster* hawker, retailer, are not recorded so early), other members being *huckstery* (XIV), HUCK *v.* (XV), †*hukker* sb. (XIII), *hucker* v. (XVI); see -STER.] **1.** A retailer of small goods, in a petty shop or booth, or at a stall; a pedlar, a hawker. **b.** As term of reproach: A regrater of corn, etc.; a broker, a middleman 1573. **2.** *transf.* and *fig.* A person ready to make his profit of anything in a mean and petty way 1553.

Phr. †*In huckster's hands (handling)*: where it is likely to be roughly used or lost; unlikely to be recovered. Hence †**Hu·cksterage,** huckstering, haggling. **Hu·cksteress, -tress,** a female h. **Hu·ckstery,** the business, or place of business, of a h.; *pl.* the goods dealt in by a h.

Hu·ckster, *v.* 1592. [f. HUCKSTER *sb.*] **1.** *intr.* To bargain, haggle (*lit.* and *fig.*). **2.** *trans.* To traffic in, in a petty way; to retail; to bargain over (*lit.* and *fig.*) 1642. Hence **Hu·cksterer.**

Hud (hɒd). *Obs.* exc. *dial.* ME. [perh. f. Gmc. **xūd-*, base of HIDE *v.*[1]; see also HUDDLE *v.*] The husk of a seed, the hull or shell of a fruit; a pod or seed-vessel.

†**Hudder-mudder,** *sb.* 1461. [A reduplicated compound of which the first element appears to be rel. to ME. *hoder* huddle, wrap up. Cf. the later HUGGER-MUGGER.] Concealment –1583.

Huddle (hɒ·d'l), *sb.* 1579. [app. f. HUDDLE *v.*] **1.** A mass of things crowded together in hurried confusion 1586; a confused crowd of persons or animals 1642. **2. a.** Confusion, disorder; confused utterance. **b.** Disorderly haste, hurry, bustle. 1606. †**3.** A miserly old hunks –1604.

1. The women..were all got in a h. together, out of their wits 1742.

Huddle (hɒ·d'l), *v.* 1579. [perh. of LG. origin and ult. f. **xūd-*; see HIDE *v.*[1], HUD.] **I.** *trans.* †**1.** To put or keep out of sight; to hush *up* –1795. **2.** To jumble; to pile or heap up confusedly 1579. **b.** To draw (oneself) together 'all of a heap' 1755. **3.** To push or thrust in a disorderly mass or heap *into, out of* (etc.) 1655. **b.** with *on*: To put on (clothes) 'all of a heap' 1697. **4.** To drive or push hurriedly; to hurry (a person or thing). ? *Obs.* 1649. Also with *over, through, up.*

1. The matter was hudled up, and little spoken of it 1653. **2.** Hudling iest vpon iest *Much Ado* II. i. 252. Huddled together in a flock GOLDSM. **3.** They huddled the king's body into a postchaise THACKERAY. **b.** His clothes seem to be huddled on anyhow HELPS. **4.** Let him forecast his Work with timely care, Which else is huddled DRYDEN. To h. up a compromise MACAULAY.

II. *intr.* **1.** To gather or flock in a congested mass; to crowd together unceremoniously; to nestle closely in a heap. Also with *together, up.* 1596. †**2.** To hurry in disorder or confusion –1766.

1. The cattle huddled on the lea TENNYSON. **2.** Fools h. on, and always are in haste ROWE.

†**Hu·ddle,** *a.* and *adv.* 1564. [Goes with contemp. HUDDLE *v.*]

A. *adj.* Huddled, confused, congested –1713. **B.** *adv.* Confusedly; in a crowding mass; in disorderly haste –1606.

Hudibrastic (hiūdibræ·stik), *a.* (*sb*). 1712. [f. *Hudibras*, after *fantastic*, etc.] In the metre or after the manner of *Hudibras*, by Samuel Butler, 1663–78; burlesque-heroic. *sb.* Hudibrastic verse or language 1739. Hence **Hudibra·stically** *adv.*

Hu·dsonite. 1842. [Named from the *Hudson* River, near which it is found. See -ITE[1] 2 b.] *Min.* A variety of pyroxene, containing much iron.

Hue (hiū), *sb.*[1] [OE. *hēw, hēow, hīw, hīew* form, shape, appearance, colour, beauty = ON. *hý* down on plants (Sw. *hy* skin, complexion), Goth. *hiwi* form, appearance :- Gmc. **xiujam*, of unkn. origin.] †**1.** Form; appearance; species –1653. **2.** External appearance of the face and skin; complexion. Also *transf.* ME. **3.** Colour OE. **b.** *Chromatics.* Variety of any colour; tint or quality of a particular colour 1857.

2. She was not broun ne dun of hewe CHAUCER. **3.** The ashen h. of age SCOTT. **b.** The first [crimson] is a red with a violet h. 1861.

Hue, *sb.*[2] ME. [– OFr. *hu*, etc. outcry, noise, hunting-cry, war-cry, f. *huer* HUE *v.*[2]] Outcry, shouting, clamour, esp. that raised by a multitude in war or the chase. *Obs.* exc. in HUE AND CRY, q. v.

Hue (hiū), *v.*[1] [OE. *hīwian*, f. *hīw* HUE *sb.*[1]] *trans.* To form, fashion, figure; esp. (in later use) to colour. Chiefly in pa. pple. Also *fig.*

Hue, *v.*[2] Now *local.* ME. [– (O)Fr. *huer* shout as in war, or the chase; of imit. origin.] **1.** *intr.* To shout, make an outcry; *spec.* in hunting, and now in the Cornish sea fisheries. **2.** *trans.* To assail, drive, or guide with shouts 1590.

Hue and cry, *sb.* (Often hyphened.) 1502. [– legal AFr. *hu e cri*, i.e. *hu* outcry, HUE *sb.*[2], *e* and, *cri* CRY *sb.*] **1.** *Law.* Outcry calling for the pursuit of a felon, raised by the party aggrieved, by a constable, etc. **b.** A proclamation for the capture of a criminal or the finding of stolen goods 1601. **2.** The pursuit of a felon with such outcry 1648. **3.** *gen.* A cry of alarm or opposition; outcry 1584. Hence **Hue-and-cry** *v.* to raise the hue and cry; to pursue with hue and cry.

Hued (hiūd), *ppl. a.* OE. [f. HUE *v.*[1] or *sb.*[1] + -ED.] Having a hue, coloured.

Hueless (hiū·lės), *a.* [f. HUE *sb.*[1] + -LESS.] †**1.** (In OE. and ME.) Formless. **2.** Colourless, pallid OE.

Huer (hiū·əɹ). Now *local.* 1530. [f. HUE *v.*[2] + -ER[1].] †**1.** One employed to drive deer with noise and shouting –1674. **2.** *Fishing.* One who directs seine-fishing from high ground by the sea, as in the Cornish pilchard fishery. Cf. BALKER[2]. 1602.

Huff (hɒf), *sb.* 1599. [f. HUFF *v.*] †**1.** A puff of wind; a slight blast –1725. **2.** A gust *of* anger or annoyance 1599; a fit of petulance or offended dignity caused by an affront 1757. †**3.** Inflated opinion of oneself; arrogance, bluster, bounce –1697. †**4.** One who swaggers; a hector, a bully –1713. **5.** *Draughts.* An act of huffing 1860.

2. She went out of the room quite in a h. MISS BURNEY. **4.** Every Silly Huff [is call'd] a Captain T. BROWN.

Huff (hɒf), *v.* 1583. [imit. of the sound of blowing or puffing.] **1.** *intr.* To blow, puff. *Obs.* exc. *dial.* †**2.** *trans.* To blow; esp. to blow or puff *up*. Also *fig.* –1719. **3.** *intr.* To swell, swell up. *Obs.* exc. *dial.* 1656. †**4.** *intr.* To puff or swell with pride or arrogance; to storm, bluster, talk big; to bluff –1734. **5.** *intr.* To swell with anger or irritation; to take offence 1598. **6.** *trans.* To hector, bully; to chide, storm at. (Cf. 'to blow up'.) 1674. **b.** To treat with arrogance or contempt 1676. **7.** To offend the dignity of; to put in a huff. Chiefly in *passive.* 1814. **8.** *Draughts.* To remove (an opponent's man) from the board as a forfeit for failing to take a piece that is *en prise*. The removal was marked by blowing on the piece. 1688.

5. The..woman has huffed, and won't trust me MARRYAT. Hence †**Hu·ffer,** a swaggering, hectoring person. **Hu·ffingly** *adv.*

Huff-cap (hɒ·fˌkæp). *Obs.* or *arch.* 1577. [f. HUFF *v.* + CAP *sb.*, i.e. 'that huffs or raises the cap'.] **A.** *adj.* **1.** Of liquor: Heady. *Obs.* exc. *Hist.* 1599. **2.** Blustering, swaggering (*arch.*) 1597. **B.** *sb.* **1.** Strong and heady ale 1577. †**2.** A swashbuckler –1706.

Hu·ffish, *a.* 1755. [f. HUFF *sb.* + -ISH[1].] Arrogant; petulant. **Hu·ffish-ly** *adv.*, **-ness.**

Huffle (hɒ·f'l), *v. Obs.* exc. *dial.* 1583. [dim. and frequent. of HUFF *v.*: see -LE.] *trans.* To blow, inflate (*lit.* and *fig.*); also *intr.* to bluster; of the wind: to make a sound as of blowing in gusts (hence as *sb.*).

†**Huff-snuff,** *sb.* 1583. [f. HUFF *v.* +

SNUFF, in the sense 'offence, resentment'.] A conceited fellow who is quick to take offence; a hector, bully –1653. Also *attrib.*

Huffy (hʊ·fi), *a.* 1677. [f. HUFF *sb.* + -Y[1].] **1.** Windy, effervescent, puffy. *Obs.* or *dial.* †**2.** *fig.* Airy, unsubstantial –1681. †**3.** Puffed up; haughty; blustering –1691. **4.** †**a.** Arrogant. **b.** Ready to take offence 1680.

1. Champaign, and other h. liquors 1765. **4.** She is very apt to be h. 1890. Hence **Hu·ffily** *adv.* **Hu·ffiness.**

Hug (hʊg), *sb.* 1617. [f. HUG *v.*] **1.** A strong clasp with the arms; an embrace of affection; the squeeze of a bear 1659. **2.** A squeezing grip in wrestling; esp. *Cornish h.*; hence *fig.* 1617.

Hug (hʊg), *v.* 1567. [prob. of Scand. origin; cf. ON. (Norw.) *hugga* comfort, console, rel. to *hugr* thought, feeling, interest, *hugða* interest, affection, *hugsa* think.] **1.** *trans.* To clasp or squeeze tightly in the arms; usu. = embrace; but also said of a bear squeezing a man, etc., between its forelegs. Also *transf.* and *fig.* **b.** *fig.* To caress or court, *esp.* in order to get favour or patronage 1622. **c.** To cherish (an opinion, belief, etc.) with fervour 1649. **2.** *refl.* †To make oneself snug –1757; *fig.* to felicitate oneself 1622. **3.** *intr.* To lie close, cuddle 1595. **4.** *trans.* (orig. *Naut.*) To cling to (the shore, etc.) 1824.

1. He bewept my Fortune, And hugg'd me in his armes SHAKS. *To h. one's chains* (fig.): to delight in bondage. **b.** The sordid practice of hugging or caressing attorneys 1832. **4.** Hugging the Spanish coast MARRYAT. Hence **Hu·ggingly** *adv.*

Huge (hiūdʒ), *a.* [ME. *huge, hoge, howge*, aphetic – OFr. *ahuge, ahoge, ahoege*, of unkn. origin.] Very great, large, or big; immense, enormous, vast; *transf.* of very great power, rank, capabilities, etc.

He..made an hughe fire GOWER. A matter of.. h. moment 1680. Hugest Heiress now going CARLYLE. Hence **Hu·ge-ly** *adv.*, **-ness.** var. **Hu·geous, -ly, -ness.**

Hugger (hʊ·gəɹ), *sb.*[1] 1682. [f. HUG *v.* + -ER[1].] One who hugs.

†**Hu·gger,** *sb.*[2] 1576. [Cf. HUGGER *v.*] Concealment.

Hugger (hʊ·gəɹ), *v.* *Obs.* exc. *dial.* 1520. [perh. short for HUGGER-MUGGER *v.*] †**1.** *intr.* To lie concealed. **2.** *trans.* To conceal 1600. †**3.** *intr.* To get into confusion. SKELTON.

Hugger-mugger (hʊ·gəɹ,mʊ·gəɹ). 1526. [Preceded by *hucker mucker* or *moker* (XVI) and *hoder moder* XV (see HUDDER-MUDDER); prob. based on (dial.) *mucker*, ME. *mokere* hoard, and ME. *hoder* huddle, wrap up; ult. origin unkn.]

A. *sb.* **1.** Concealment, secrecy; esp. in phr. *in h.* Now *arch.* or *vulgar.* 1529. **2.** Disorder; a muddle 1674.

1. To clap up the marriage in hugger-mugger FORD.

B. *adj.* **1.** Secret, clandestine 1692. **2.** Disorderly, confused, makeshift 1840.

C. *adv.* **1.** Secretly, clandestinely 1526. **2.** In a muddle 1880.

Hugger-mugger, *v.* late ME. [f. prec.] **1.** *trans.* To keep secret; to hush *up.* **2.** *intr.* To proceed in a clandestine manner; to go *on* in a muddled way 1805.

Huggery (hʊ·gəri). 1804. [f. HUG *v.*, HUGGER *sb.*[1]; see -ERY.] The action or practice of hugging (see HUG *v.* 1 b.)

Huggle (hʊ·g'l), *v.* Now *dial.* 1583. [perh. iterative of HUG *v.*; see -LE.] To hug.

†**Hugmatee.** 1699. [perh. f. phr. *hug-me-t'ye.*] Cant name of a kind of ale –1704.

Huguenot (hiū·gĕnǫt), *sb.* (*a.*) 1562. [– Fr. *huguenot*, alt., by assim. to the name of a Geneva burgomaster, Besançon *Hugues*, of †*eiguenot*, pl. †*aignos*, †*hugenaulx* – Du. *eedgenot* – Swiss G. *eidgenoss* confederate, f. *eid* OATH + *genoss* associate.] **1.** A French Protestant in the 16th and 17th c. In French, orig. a nick-name, said to have been imported from Geneva. **2.** *adj.* Of or belonging to the Huguenots 1682. Hence **Hu·guenotism,** the religious system of the Huguenots; Calvinism.

†**Hu·gy,** *a.* ME. [f. HUGE *a.* + -Y[1].] = HUGE –1728.

Huh (hʊ), *interj.* 1608. An exclam. of suppressed feeling.

Huia (hū·iă). Also **hui** (hū·i). 1845. [Native Maori; from the bird's whistle.] A New Zealand bird, *Heteralocha acutirostris*, the tail feathers of which are prized by the Maoris as ornaments.

†**Huisher, husher,** now as Fr. ‖**huissier** (wisye), *sb.* ME. [– (O)Fr. *huissier* :– med.L. *ustiarius* (VI) for L. *ostiarius* door-keeper, f. *ostium* door + *-arius* -ER[2]. See USHER.] = USHER. Hence †**Huisher** *v. trans.* to usher, precede.

‖**Huitain** (witē[i]·n). 1589. [Fr., f. *huit* eight.] A set of eight lines of verse.

Huke (hiūk), *sb.* *Obs.* exc. *Hist.* [ME. *huke, hewk(e, huyke* – OFr. *huque, heuque*, in med.L. *huca* (XIII), corresp. to MDu. *hūke, heuke* (Du. *huik*), MLG. *hoike*, etc.; of unkn. origin.] A kind of cape or cloak with a hood worn by women and afterwards by men. Applied also to the Arab *haïk*; see HAIK.

†**Hulch,** *sb.* (*a.*) 1611. [Of unkn. origin.] **1.** A hump. COTGR. **2.** *adj.* Hunched. Also in comb. **h.-backed** *a.* hunch-backed; also *transf.* of round-backed tools. –1708. Hence **Hu·lchy** *a.* humpy, hump-backed. (*Obs.* or *dial.*)

‖**Huldee, huldi** (hʊ·ldī). *E. Ind.* 1832. [Hindi, etc.] Vernacular name of the plant *Curcuma longa*, the tubers of which yield turmeric; also of the powdered turmeric.

Hulk (hʊlk), *sb.* [Late OE. *hulc* (in AL. *hulcus* XII), prob. reinforced in ME. from MLG. *hulk, holk(e*, MDu. *hulke, hulc* (Du. *hulk*) = late OHG. *holko* (G. *hulk, holk*), whence OFr. *hulque*; prob. a Mediterranean word (cf. Gr. ὁλκάς cargo ship).] **1.** A ship. Usually, in ME. and later, A large ship of burden or transport, often associated with the carrack. Now *arch.* = 'big, unwieldy vessel'. †**2.** The HULL of a ship –1829. **3.** The body of a dismantled ship (worn out and unfit for sea service), retained in use as a store-vessel, etc. (See also SHEER-HULK.) 1671. **b.** A vessel of this kind formerly used as a prison. Usu. *pl.* 1797. **4.** *transf.* and *fig.* A big, unwieldy person, or mass 1597.

1. The sooty h. Steered sluggish on THOMSON. **3.** Like Drake's old H. at Deptford COTTON. **b.** The sentence of death..would be commuted for—the hulks MEDWIN.

Hulk (hʊlk), *v.*[1] 1575. [var. of HOLK *v.* hollow out.] **1.** *trans.* To disembowel. *dial.* **2.** *Mining.* To remove the 'gouge' or softer part of a lode before blasting 1881.

Hulk (hʊlk), *v.*[2] 1793. [f. HULK *sb.*] **1.** *trans.* †**a.** To condemn to the hulks (see HULK *sb.* 3 b). **b.** To lodge (sailors, etc.) temporarily in a hulk. 1827. **2.** *intr.* To act, hang about, or go in a hulking manner (*dial.*) 1793. **3.** (With *up.*) To rise bulkily 1880.

Hulking (hʊ·lkiŋ), *a.* *colloq.* 1698. [f. HULK *sb.* 4 + -ING[2].] Bulky, unwieldy; ungainly on account of bulk.

A great h. son JOWETT. So **Hu·lky** *a. colloq.*

Hull (hʊl), *sb.*[1] [Late OE. *hulu*, f. wk. grade of *helan* cover (cf. HELE *v.*, HELL, HELM *sb.*[1]), whence also OE. *hylma*, OHG. *hulla* mantle, head-covering (G. *hülle*) :– **χuljō*, and Du. *huls*, OHG. *hulsa* (G. *hülse* husk, pod) :– **χulisō.*] **1.** The shell, pod, or husk of pease and beans; the outer covering of any fruit or seed. **2.** *transf.* and *fig.* A covering, envelope; the case of a chrysalis; *pl.* clothes, garments 1718.

2. Blankets, and bibs, and other nameless hulls CARLYLE.

Hull (hʊl), *sb.*[2] late ME. [XV *hulle*, also *hoole, holle*, perh. subst. use of *hol* HOLL *a.* but the transference from the interior to the exterior of the vessel is a difficulty.] The body or frame of a ship, apart from the masts, sails, and rigging. Also of a flying boat or rigid airship. †**b.** = HULK *sb.* 3. –1666.

We discovered by her H. she was a Christian Frigot 1676. Phr. *To lie at h.* = HULL *v.*[2] 1 (see AHULL). *H. down*: so far away that the h. is below the horizon and invisible. So *H. out*: with the h. above the horizon.

Hull (hʊl), *v.*[1] ME. [f. HULL *sb.*[1]] *trans.* To remove the hull, shell, or husk of. Also *transf.* Hence **Hu·ller,** *spec.* a hulling-machine.

Hull (hʊl), *v.*[2] 1545. [f. HULL *sb.*[2]] †**1.** *intr.* *Naut.* Of a ship: To float or be driven on the hull alone; to lie a-hull –1708. Also *transf.* and *fig.* **2.** *trans.* To strike (a ship) in the hull with cannon shot 1726.

2. The Phœnix was thrice hulled by our shot 1776.

Hullabaloo (hʊ:lăbălū·), *sb.* (*int.*) 1762. [First recorded from northerly sources; occurs with a great variety of forms in the first element, viz. *hollo-, halloo-, hallo-, holli, hulla-*, corresp. to those of HALLOO, HOLLA, HULLO; the addition of the jingle may have been suggested by *hurly-burly*.] **a.** Tumultuous noise; uproar; clamorous confusion. Also *fig.* **b.** as *int.* 1845.

Hulled (hʊld), *a.* 1577. [f. HULL *sb.*[1] and [2] + -ED[2].] Having a hull (of a particular kind.)

Hulled (hʊld), *ppl. a.* ME. [f. HULL *v.*[1] + -ED[1].] Stripped of the hull or husk.

Hullo, hulloa (hŏlō[u]·), *interj.* 1857. [var. of HALLO, HALLOA, HILLO, HILLOA, HOLLO, HOLLOA.] A call used to hail a person or to excite his attention.

Huloist, Hulotheism: see HYLOIST, -THEISM.

Hulver (hʊ·lvəɹ). *Obs.* exc. *dial.* [In XV *hulfere*, = ON. *hulfr*, explained as 'holly' (Craigie).] Holly. *Knee h.*, Butcher's Broom. *Sea h.*, Sea Holly, Eryngo. Also *attrib.*

Hum (hʊm), *sb.*[1] 1469. [Goes with HUM *v.*[1] It is doubtful whether sense 3 belongs here.] **1.** A low continuous sound made by a bee, etc., also by a spinning top, machinery in motion, etc. (Dist. from a *buzz* by not being sibilant.) 1601. **b.** A murmur of many distant voices or noises 1599. **2. a.** An inarticulate vocal murmur uttered with closed lips in a pause of speaking, from hesitation, embarrassment, affectation 1469. **b.** A like sound uttered in approbation, mild surprise, dissent, etc. 1653. †**3.** Strong or double ale –1719.

1. The h. of the mill EMERSON. **b.** The h. of expectation FROUDE. **2. a.** These Shrugs, these Hum's, and Ha's *Wint. T.* II. i. 74. **3.** Would I had some h. FLETCHER.

Hum, *sb.*[2] 1751. [Short for HUMBUG *sb.*] An imposition, a hoax (*slang* or *colloq.*).

Hum (hʊm), *v.*[1] [In XIV, XV *humme*, imit.; cf. BUM *v.*[1], also MHG. (G. dial.) *hummen*, and G. *summen, brummen*, Du. *brommen.*] **1.** *intr.* To make a low continuous murmuring sound or note, as a bee, etc.; also said of a spinning top, etc.; to sing with closed lips (cf. 4). **2.** *intr.* To make a low inarticulate vocal sound; *esp.* in expression of dissatisfaction, or †of approbation or applause ME. **b.** To make an inarticulate murmur in a pause of speaking, from hesitation, embarrassment, etc. Usu. in phr. *to h. and ha* (*haw*) ME. **3.** To give forth an indistinct sound by the blending of many voices, etc.; hence (*colloq.*) to be all astir 1726. **4.** *trans.* To sing with closed lips and without articulation 1602. †**5.** To greet with a hum (of applause) –1733.

1. Bees cluster and h. BOWEN. **2.** Upon which the Rabble hummed 1687. **b.** H. and stroke thy Beard *Tr. & Cr.* I. iii. 165. **3.** The whole country was humming with dacoits KIPLING. Phr. (colloq.) *To make things hum*: to keep in activity. **4.** Low humming..Some ancient Border gathering song SCOTT.

Hum, *v.*[2] *arch.* 1751. [Short for HUMBUG *v.*] To hoax, take in, humbug (*slang* or *colloq.*).

Hum, *v.*[3] *colloq.* or *slang.* 1909. [Of unkn. origin.] *intr.* To smell disagreeably. Hence as *sb.*

Hum (həm), *interj.* 1596. An inarticulate exclam. uttered with the lips closed, either in a pause of hesitation, etc., or as expressing slight dissatisfaction, dissent, etc.

Human (hiū·măn), *a.* (*sb.*) late ME. [In earliest use *humain(e, -ayn(e* – (O)Fr. *humain*, fem. *-aine* :– L. *humanus*, rel. to *homo* man; see -AN. Orig. stressed and spelt *huma·ne* (see HUMANE), but the form *human* (based directly on Latin) occurs in late XVII (Dryden).] **1.** Of, belonging to, or characteristic of man. **2.** Of the nature of man; that is a man; consisting of men 1484. **b.** *Astrol.* Applied to signs of the zodiac, or constellations, figured in the form of men or women 1658. **3.** Mundane, secular. (Often opp. to *divine.*) 1533. **4.** Having the qualities or attributes proper to man 1727. **5.** *sb.* A human being, a man. (Now chiefly *joc.* or *affected.*) 1533. With *the*: The human race 1841.

1. The Structure of the h. Body JOS. BUTLER. **2.** Humane Sacrifices were offered to Diana PURCHAS. **3.** To err is humane, to forgive divine POPE. In all h. probability 1712. **4.** He was very h., and sent the poor Seamen Presents 1727.

†**Hu·manate,** *a.* [– late and med.L. *humanatus*, pa. pple. of *humanare* invest with human nature, incarnate, f. *humanus*; see HUMAN, -ATE[3].] Made human; converted into human flesh. CRANMER. So †**Humana·tion,** incarnation.

Humane (hiumē·n), *a.* 1500. [Earlier spelling of HUMAN, restricted after 1700 to particular senses, and assoc. w. L. *humanus.*] **1.** Characterized by such behaviour or disposition towards others as befits a man: †civil, courteous, obliging –1784; kind, benevolent 1603. **b.** Applied to certain implements, etc. which inflict less pain than others of their kind 1904. **2.** Applied to those branches of literature (*literæ humaniores*) which tend to humanize or refine, as the ancient classics, rhetoric, and poetry; hence, elegant, polite. (See HUMANITY.) 1691.

1. H. civility MARVELL. To be h. is human TRENCH. *H. Society*: a society for the rescue of drowning persons 1776. **2.** The more h. and polite Part of Letters 1712. Hence **Huma·ne-ly** *adv.*, **-ness.**

Humaniform (hiumæ·nifǫɹm), *a.* 1889. [Latinizing calque on *anthropomorphic*; see HUMAN, -FORM. Not continuous with *Humaniformian* (see below) – late L. *Humaniformiani* (Cassiodorus), repr. Gr. ἀνθρωπομορφιανοί; cf. ANTHROPOMORPHITE.] Of human form; anthropomorphous. So †**Humanifo·rmian,** an anthropomorphite 1550–1624.

Humanify (hiumæ·nifəi), *v.* 1629. [f. HUMAN *a.* + -FY.] To make human. Hence **Huma:nifica·tion.**

Humanism (hiū·măniz'm). 1812. [In sense 1 f. HUMAN *a.* + -ISM; in senses 2–4 based on next, with change of suffix.] †**1.** Belief in the mere humanity of Christ. COLERIDGE. **2.** The quality of being human; devotion to human interests 1836. **3.** Any system of thought or action which is concerned with merely human interests, or with those of the human race in general; the 'Religion of Humanity' 1860. **4.** Devotion to those studies which promote human culture; literary culture; *esp.* the system of the Humanists 1832.

3. Comtism or Positivism, or, as it might be called, H. 1876. **4.** The h. of Erasmus and More 1885.

Humanist (hiū·mănist). 1589. [– Fr. *humaniste* (XVI) – It. *umanista*; see HUMAN, -IST.] **1.** A student of human affairs, or of human nature 1617. **2.** One versed in the 'humanities'; a classical scholar; *esp.* a Latinist (*arch.*) 1589. **3.** *Literary Hist.* One of the scholars who, at the Renaissance, devoted themselves to the study of Roman, and afterwards of Greek, antiquity; hence, applied to later disciples of the same culture 1670. Also *attrib.*

2. I might repute him as a good h., but I should ever doubt him for a good devine HARINGTON. **3.** Milton was born a h., but the Puritan temper mastered him M. ARNOLD.

Humani·stic, -al, *a.* 1716. [f. prec. + -IC, -ICAL.] Pertaining to the humanists; pertaining to classical studies; classical.

Humanitarian (hiumænitēə·riăn). 1819. [f. HUMANITY, after *unitarian, trinitarian*; see -ARIAN.]

A. *sb.* **1.** *Theol.* One who affirms the mere humanity of Christ. **2.** One who professes the 'Religion of Humanity', holding that man's duty is chiefly or wholly comprised in the advancement of the welfare of the human race 1831. **3.** A philanthropist; *esp.* one who goes to excess in his humane principles 1844.

3. A man cannot be too really humane, but the typical h. is only sentimental 1891.

B. *adj.* **1.** Holding the views or doctrines of humanitarians; held or practised by humanitarians 1846. **2.** Having regard to the interests of humanity or mankind at large. Often *contemptuous* or *hostile.* 1855.

2. The nonsense of h. sentimentalists 1897. Hence **Humanita·rianism,** the system, principles, or practice of humanitarians.

†**Humanitian** (-i·ʃăn). 1577. [irreg. f. HUMANITY + -AN, after *logician*, etc. Superseded by HUMANIST.] One versed in the humanities; a classical scholar –1691.

Humanity (hiumæ·nĭti). ME. [– (O)Fr. *humanité* – L. *humanitas, -tat-*, f. *humanus*; see HUMAN *a.*, -ITY.]

I. Conn. w. *human.* **1.** The quality or condition of being human, manhood; human nature; man in the abstract. **b.** *pl.* Human attributes; traits or touches of human nature or feeling; points that appeal to man 1800. **2.** The human race; mankind 1579.

1. I would change my H. with a Baboone *Oth.* I. iii. 317. **b.** The fair humanities of old religion COLERIDGE. **2.** Their Services to h. are very great 1874.

II. Conn. w. *humane.* **1.** The character or quality of being humane: †civility, courtesy; obligingness –1794; kindness, benevolence ME. **b.** *pl.* Instances or acts of humanity 1577. **2.** Learning or literature concerned with human culture, as grammar, rhetoric, poetry, and esp. the ancient Latin and Greek classics. **a.** *sing.* (Still used in the Scottish Universities = 'the study of the Latin language and literature'.) 1483. **b.** *pl.* (Usu. with *the*; = Fr. *les humanités.*) 1702. Also *attrib.* **c.** One of the classes in a Jesuit school.

1. Great tenderness of heart, and h. of disposition BURKE. **b.** The courtesies and humanities of generous warfare SOUTHEY. **2. b.** An Eton captain. . critically learned in all the humanities EMERSON.

Humanize (hiū·mănəiz), *v.* 1603. [– Fr. *humaniser*, f. L. *humanus*; see HUMAN, -IZE.] **1.** *trans.* To make or render human; to give a human character or form to; to conform to human nature or use; *spec.* to modify (lymph, milk) by communicating to it human characteristics. **2.** To make humane; to civilize, soften, refine 1647. **3.** *intr.* for *pass.* To grow humane 1790.

1. The Fijians humanized their gods 1895. **2.** To h. the way in which war is carried on FREEMAN. **3.** Humanizing by degrees, it [the law of nations] admitted slavery instead of death [as a punishment] FRANKLIN. Hence **Humaniza·tion; Hu·manizer,** one who or that which humanizes.

Humankind (hiū·măn,kəi·nd). 1645. [prop. two wds.; written as one, after *mankind.*] The human race; mankind.

Humanly (hiū·mănli), *adv.* 1485. [f. HUMAN *a.* + -LY[2].] **1.** After the manner of man, in accordance with human nature; by human means 1613. **2.** From the standpoint of man 1581. **3.** With the feelings distinctive of man; with human kindness 1485.

2. [The deed] was thought humanely impossible 1707. **3.** Modestly bold, and h. severe POPE.

Hu·manness. 1727. [f. as prec. + -NESS.] Human quality.

Humate (hiū·mĕt), *sb.* 1844. [f. HUMIC + -ATE[4].] *Chem.* A salt of humic acid.

†**Huma·tion.** 1635. [– L. *humatio*, f. *humat-*, pa. ppl. stem of *humare* bury; see -ION.] Burial; inhumation –1661.

†**Hum-bird.** 1634. [f. HUM *sb.*[1] or vb.-stem + BIRD.] = HUMMING-BIRD –1819.

Humble (hɒ·mb'l), *a.*[1] [ME. (*h*)*umble* – OFr. *umble*, (also mod.) *humble* – L. *humilis* low, lowly, mean, base, f. *humus* ground, earth, rel. to *homo* man. The pronunc. ɒ·mb'l, repr. the original, is still used by some old-fashioned speakers.] **1.** Having a low estimate of oneself; not self-asserting or assuming; lowly; the opposite of *proud.* **2.** Of lowly condition, rank, or estate; modest, unpretentious ME.; †low-lying –1729; low-growing 1658.

1. Christ was h., they are proud 1640. Your faithful h. servant, Wm. Pinkney 1808. **2.** I am from h., he from honored name SHAKS. The h. Plains below 1729. *H. plant*: the common Sensitive plant.

Humble, *a.*[2]: see HUMMEL *a.*

Humble, *v.*[1] ME. [f. HUMBLE *a.*[1]] **1.** *trans.* To render humble or meek; to cause to think more lowly of oneself 1591. **2.** To lower in dignity, position, condition, or degree; to bring low, abase 1484. **3.** *refl.* To render oneself humble; to do obeisance, bow (*arch.*) ME.

1. Loue's a mighty Lord, And hath so humbled me *Two Gent.* II. iv. 137. **2.** The prowde shall be allway humbled CAXTON. **3.** The army . . humbled them selfes mekely before the crosse HALL. Hence **Hu·mblingly** *adv.*

†**Humble,** *v.*[2] ME. [app. of same origin as MHG., LG., G. *hummel(e)n*, Du. *hommelen* hum, buzz; cf. HUMBLE-BEE.] *intr.* To rumble; to mumble; to hum or buzz as a bee –1617.

Humble, *v.*[3]: see HUMMEL *v.*

Humble-bee (hɒ·mb'lbī:). 1450. [prob. – MLG. *hummelbē, homelbē*, f. *hummel* = (M)Du. *hommel*, OHG. *humbal* (G. *hummel*) + *bē* BEE[1]. Cf. HUMBLE *v.*[2], and BUMBLE-BEE.] A large wild bee, of the genus *Bombus*, which makes a loud humming sound; a bumble-bee.

Humbleness (hɒ·mb'lnės). ME. [f. HUMBLE *a.* + -NESS.] The quality of being humble; meekness, lowliness; unpretentiousness.

With bated breath, and whispring humblenesse SHAKS.

Humble pie. 1648. [For sense 1 see HUMBLES.]

†**1.** = UMBLE PIE, a pie made of the umbles of a deer. **2.** *To eat humble pie*: to be very submissive; to submit to humiliation 1830.

Humbler (hɒ·mbləɹ). 1611. [f. HUMBLE *v.*[1] + -ER[1].] One who or that which humbles.

†**Humbles,** *sb. pl.* 1460. Occas. sp. of UMBLES, the inwards of a deer, etc. –1709.

†**Humblesse.** ME. [– OFr. (*h*)*umblesse*, f. (*h*)*umble*; see HUMBLE *a.*[1], -ESS[2].] Humbleness, humility –1736.

Humbly (hɒ·mbli), *adv.* ME. [f. HUMBLE *a.*[1] + -LY[2].] **1.** In a humble manner; with humility. **2.** Modestly; unpretentiously 1746.

Humbug (hɒ·mbɒg), *sb.* (*a.*) *colloq.* 1751. [Of unkn. origin; its vogue is commented upon in *The Student*, 1751 ('Of the Superlative Advantages arising from the use of the new-invented Science, called the Humbug').] †**1.** A hoax; an imposition –1799. **2.** An imposture, fraud, sham 1751. **3.** Deception, pretence; used interjectionally = 'stuff and nonsense!' 1825. **4.** An impostor, a 'fraud' 1804. **5.** A kind of sweetmeat (*dial.*) 1825. **6.** *attrib.* Humbugging 1812.

Humbug (hɒ·mbɒg), *v.* 1751. [f. HUMBUG *sb.* In XVIII stressed *humbu·g.*] **1.** *trans.* To practise humbug upon; to impose upon, hoax, delude. **b.** To change or transfer by trickery 1821. **2.** *intr.* To practise humbug; to be a humbug; 'to fool *about*' 1753. Hence **Humbugger,** a humbug, impostor. **Humbu·ggery,** humbug, imposture.

Humdrum (hɒ·m,drɒ·m, hɒ·mdrɒm). 1553. [Not common before XVIII; of unkn. origin, but app. based on HUM *v.*[1]]

A. *adj.* **1.** Lacking variety; commonplace; monotonous, dull. †**2.** (*adj.* or *adv.*) Without distinction; undecided –1710.

1. A plain h. Sermon J. H. NEWMAN.

B. *sb.* **1.** A dull, monotonous, commonplace fellow 1598. **2.** Dullness, commonplaceness, monotony. Also with *a* and *pl.* 1727. Hence **Hu:mdru·m** *v.* to proceed in a h. fashion.

Humdudgeon (hɒ:mdɒ·dʒən). 1785. [Cf. HUM *sb.*[2] and DUDGEON *sb.*[2]] An imaginary illness.

Humect (hiume·kt), *v.* Now *rare.* 1531. [– (*h*)*umect-*, pa. ppl. stem of L. (*h*)*umectare*, f. (*h*)*umectus* moist, wet, f. (*h*)*umēre* be moist. Cf. Fr. *humecter* (XVI).] **1.** *trans.* To moisten, wet. **2.** *intr.* To become moist 1686.

Humectant (hiume·ktănt). ? *Obs.* 1659. [– (*h*)*umectant-*, pres. ppl. stem of L. (*h*)*umectare*; see prec., -ANT. Cf. Fr. *humectant* (XVI).] **a.** *adj.* Moistening, wetting. **b.** *sb.* *Med.* A diluent 1822.

Humectate (hiume·ktēt), *v.* Now *rare.* 1640. [– (*h*)*umectat-*, pa. ppl. stem of L. (*h*)*umectare*; see prec., -ATE[3].] = HUMECT 1. So **Humecta·tion,** the action of moistening; the condition of being moistened; †liquefaction 1425. †**Hume·ctative** *a.* tending to moisten.

Hume·ctive. *rare.* 1633. [f. HUMECT *v.* + -IVE; cf. *adaptive, selective.*] **a.** *adj.* Humectative. **b.** *sb.* = HUMECTANT *sb.* 1828.

Humeral (hiū·mĕrăl). 1615. [In A. – Fr. *huméral* or mod.L. *humeralis*, f. *humerus*; see HUMERUS, -AL[1]. In B. – late (eccl.) L. (*h*)*umeralis* adj., (*h*)*umerale* sb.]

A. *adj.* **1.** *Anat.* Of or pertaining to the HUMERUS. **2.** Of or pertaining to the shoulder or shoulders 1853.

2. *H. veil* (Eccl.): an oblong vestment of silk worn round the shoulders in various rites and enveloping the hands when holding sacred vessels.

B. *sb.* **1.** *Eccl.* †**a.** A part of the Jewish sacerdotal vestment, worn on the shoulder. TRAPP. **b.** = *Humeral veil* (A. 2).

Humero- (hiū·mĕro), comb. f. L. *humerus* shoulder, in the sense of 'pertaining to the humerus and . .', as *humero-cubital*, etc.

‖**Humerus** (hiū·mĕrŏs). Pl. **-i.** 1666. [L. (more correctly *umerus*), = shoulder, (rarely) upper arm.] *Anat.* The bone of the upper arm, extending from the shoulder-joint to the elbow-joint; the homogenetic bone in other vertebrates.

†**Humet,** *sb.* 1500. [– OFr. **heaumet*, dim. of *heaume* tiller of a rudder; see -ET.] *Her.* A fess or bar so couped that its extremities do not touch the sides of the shield –1592. Hence **Hume·tty** *a.* said of an ordinary of which the extremities are couped so as not to reach the sides of the escutcheon.

Humic (hiū·mik), *a.* 1844. [f. HUMUS + -IC.] *Chem.* Of or pertaining to humus or mould. *H. acid*, an acid found in humus or derived from it by boiling with an alkali.

Humicubation (hiūmi,kiubē[i]·ʃən). 1656. [– mod.L. *humicubatio*, f. *humi* on the ground + L. *cubatio* lying, f. *cubare* lie down; see -ATION.] Lying down on the ground, esp. by way of penitence or humiliation.

Humid (hiū·mid), *a.* 1549. [– Fr. *humide* or L. *humidus*, var. of *umidus*, f. *umēre* be moist; see -ID[1].] Slightly wet as with steam, vapour, or mist; moist, damp. **b.** Of diseases: Marked by a moist discharge 1813.

The h. Flours, that breathd Thir morning Incense MILT. Mouldering walls and h. floor GOLDSM. Hence **Humi·dify** *v.* to render h. **Hu·mid-ly** *adv.*, **-ness.**

Humidity (hiumi·dĭti). ME. [– (O)Fr. *humidité* or L. *humiditas*, f. *humidus*; see prec., -ITY.] **1.** The quality of being humid; moistness, dampness 1450. **2.** *concr.* Moisture; damp; *pl.* the humours and juices of animals and plants ME.

1. *Relative H.* (of the atmosphere) in *Meteorol.*, the amount of moisture which it contains as compared with that of complete saturation at the given temperature.

Humifuse (hiū·mifiūs), *a.* 1854. [– mod.L. *humifusus*, f. *humi* on the ground + *fusus*, pa. pple. of *fundere* pour, extend, spread.] *Bot.* Applied to the stalk of vegetables when it stretches over the surface of the ground, but without sending out roots.

Humify (hiū·mifəi), *v. rare.* Also **humefy.** 1651. [– late L. (*h*)*umificare*, f. L. (*h*)*umificus*, f. *humidus*; see HUMID, -FY.] *trans.* To render humid; to moisten.

Humiliant (hiumi·liănt), *a. rare.* 1844. [f. HUMILIATE on the anal. of *conciliate, conciliant, hesitate, hesitant*, etc.; see -ANT.] Humiliating. E. B. BROWNING.

Humiliate (hiumi·lie[i]t), *v.* 1533. [– *humiliat-*, pa. ppl. stem of late L. *humiliare*, f. *humilis* HUMBLE *a.*[1]; see -ATE[3].] †**1.** *trans.* To make low or humble in position, condition, or feeling; to humble. Also *refl.* **2.** To subject to humiliation; to mortify 1757.

2. The country was humiliated by defeat GREEN. Hence **Humi·liatingly** *adv.* **Humi·liator.**

Humiliation (hiū:mili,ē[i]·ʃən). ME. [– (O)Fr. *humiliation* – late L. *humiliatio*, f. as prec.; see -ION.] The action of humiliating or condition of being humiliated; humbling, abasement. Formerly often = humility. Also with *a* and *pl.*

Where will the h. of this country end? 'JUNIUS' Incensed by multiplied wrongs and humiliations MACAULAY.

Humility (hiumi·lĭti). ME. [– (O)Fr. *humilité* – L. *humilitas*, f. *humilis* HUMBLE *a.*[1]; see -ITY.] **1.** The quality of being humble or having a lowly opinion of oneself; meekness, lowliness, humbleness; the opposite of *pride* or *haughtiness*. **b.** With *pl.* An act of self-abasement 1612. **2.** Humble or low condition, rank, or estate; unpretentiousness 1623. **3.** A local name of several N. American birds of the family *Scolopacidæ* 1634.

1. b. With these humilities. .they satisfied the young king 1612. **2.** The h. of the fare LAMB.

Humin (hiū·min). 1844. [f. HUMUS + -IN[1].] *Chem.* A neutral substance said to exist in black humus.

Humite (hiū·məit). 1814. [Named after Sir Abraham *Hume*, of London. See -ITE[1] 2 b.] *Min.* A fluo-silicate of magnesium, long considered a variety of chondrodite, but now made a distinct species.

Hummel (hʊ·m'l), **humble** (hʊ·mb'l), *a. Sc.* 1474. [In XV, *hommyl*, later *humble* (XVI), corresp. to LG. *hummel, hommel* hornless beast; prob. radically connected with HAMBLE *v.*] **1.** Of cattle: Hornless 1536. **2.** Of corn or grain: Awnless 1474. †**3.** Chapped. P. HOLLAND.

Hummel, humble, *v. Sc.* and *n. dial.* 1788. [f. prec.] **1.** *trans.* To deprive of the horns. **2.** To remove the awns from (barley) 1800. Hence **Hu·mmelled, -eled, hu·mbled** *a.* **Hu·mmeller, -eler,** one who, or a machine which, hummels.

Hummer (hʊ·məɹ). 1605. [f. HUM *v.*[1] + -ER[1].] A thing or person that hums. **1.** An insect that hums; also a humming-bird. **2.** A person or thing marked by extreme energy, activity, etc. (*colloq.* or *slang*) 1681.

Humming (hʊ·miŋ), *vbl. sb.* 1440. [f. HUM *v.*[1] + -ING[1].] The action of HUM *v.*[1]

Humming, *ppl. a.* 1578. [f. as prec. + -ING[2].] **1.** That hums; †that hums approbation. Sometimes hyphened to its noun, as *h.-bee, -top*, etc. **2.** Of extraordinary activity, intensity, or magnitude; brisk, 'booming'; 'thumping', 'stunning' (*slang* or *colloq.*) 1654. **b.** Of liquor: Strong; ? frothing (*colloq.*) 1675.

2. b. A Tub of h. stuff would make a Cat speak 1675.

Hu·mming-bird. 1637. Any bird of the large family *Trochilidæ*, the species of which make a humming sound by the rapid vibration of their wings.

They are all of very small size, and are usually brilliantly coloured. They are peculiar to America, and most frequent within the tropics. *attrib.* **Humming-bird hawk-moth (sphinx),** a species of hawk-moth (*Macroglossa stellatarum*), whose flight resembles that of a humming-bird.

Hummock (hʊ·mək). 1555. [orig. and predominantly in naut. use; of unkn. origin.] **1.** A boss-like protuberance, rising above the general level of a surface; a low hillock or knoll. **b.** A sand hill on the seashore 1793. **c.** *Geol.* An elevated or detached boss of rock 1808. **d.** A protuberance on an ice field or floe 1818. **2.** In southern U.S., an elevation rising above a plain or swamp and often densely covered with hardwood trees; a clump of such trees on a knoll. (The local form in Florida, etc. is *hammock.*) 1636. Hence **Hu·mmocked** *ppl. a.* thrown into hummocks; hummocky. **Hu·mmocking,** the forming of hummocks on an ice field.

Hummocky (hʊ·məki), *a.* 1766. [f. prec. + -Y[1].] **1.** Abounding in or characterized by hummocks. **2.** Of the form or nature of a hummock 1791.

‖**Hummum** (hʊ·mʊm). 1634. [– Turk. – Arab. *ḥammām* bath, HAMMAM.] An Oriental bathing establishment; a Turkish bath; a HAMMAM.

Humoral (hiū·mŏrăl), *a.* 1543. [– (O)Fr. *humoral* or med.L. *humoralis*, f. L. *humor* HUMOUR; see -AL[1].] **1.** *Med.* Of or belonging to, consisting of, or containing any of the humours or fluids of the body; caused by a disordered state of the humours 1547. **b.** Relating to the bodily humours; applied esp. to the ancient doctrine that all diseases were due to disorder in the humours; as, *humoral pathology* 1793. †**2.** *gen.* Humid, fluid. TIMME. Hence **Hu·moralism,** h. pathology. **Hu·moralist,** a believer in h. pathology. **Humorali·stic** *a.* of or belonging to the humoralists.

Humoresque (hiūmŏre·sk), *sb.* 1889. [– G. *humoreske*, f. *humor* – Eng. HUMOUR *sb.* + *-eske*; see -ESQUE.] *Mus.* A humorous or capricious composition.

Humorism (hiū·mŏriz'm). 1831. [f. HUMOUR *sb.* + -ISM, after next.] **1.** *Med.* The doctrine of the four bodily humours (see HUMOUR *sb.*), and their relation to temperaments and to diseases 1832. **2.** The characteristics of a humorist (see HUMORIST 2). COLERIDGE.

Humorist, humourist (hiū·mŏrist). 1596. [In sense 1 f. HUMOUR *sb.* 2 b, perh. through synon. Fr. *humoriste* (f. *humeur* HUMOUR); in sense 2 (whence synon. Fr. *humoriste*), f. HUMOUR *sb.* II. 4; see -IST.] †**1.** A fantastical or whimsical person; a faddist –1830. **2.** A facetious or comical person, a wag; now *esp.* one skilled in the literary or artistic expression of humour. Also *fig.* 1599. **3.** = HUMORALIST 1846.

1. A humourist is one that is greatly pleased, or greatly displeased with little things WATTS. **2.** Men. .prefer the Conversation of Humourists before that of the Serious 1707. Hence **Humori·stic** *a.* belonging to, characteristic of, or of the nature of a humorist; (*occas.*) humorous.

Humorize (hiū·mŏrəiz), *v.* 1598. [f. HUMOUR + -IZE.] †**1.** *intr.* To comply with the humour of a person or thing. MARSTON. **2.** To speak or think humorously 1609.

Humorous (hiū·mŏrəs), *a.* 1578. [f. HUMOUR + -OUS. In sense 1 cf. Fr. †*humoreux* (XVI) damp, full of sap, and late L. *humorosus.*] †**1.** Moist, humid, damp –1612. †**2.** = HUMORAL 1. –1831. †**3.** Full of, or subject to, humours; capricious, whimsical; odd, fantastic –1823; moody, peevish –1842. **4.** Full of, characterized by, or showing humour or drollery; facetious, comical 1705.

1. The hum'rous Fogges, night DRAYTON. **3.** Pall'd Appetite is h., and must be gratify'd with Sauces rather than Food STEELE. He is h. to his Wife, he beats his Children PENN. **4.** The Western American is always h. BESANT & RICE. Hence **Hu·morous-ly** *adv.*, **-ness.**

Humour, humor (hiū·məɹ, yū·məɹ), *sb.* ME. [– AFr. (*h*)*umour*, OFr. (*h*)*umor, -ur* (mod. *humeur*) :– L. (*h*)*umor*, f. (*h*)*ūm-*, as in HUMID; see -OUR.]

I. Physical senses. †**1.** Moisture; damp exhalation –1697. **2.** Any fluid or juice of an animal or plant, either natural or morbid. Now *rare* or *arch.* ME. **b.** *spec.* One of the four chief fluids (*cardinal humours*) of the body (blood, phlegm, choler, and melancholy or black choler), by the relative proportions of which a person's physical and mental qualities and disposition were formerly held to be determined (see TEMPERAMENT). *Obs.* exc. *Hist.* ME. **3.** One of the transparent fluid or semifluid parts of the eye, viz. the *aqueous humour* in front of the iris, and the *vitreous humour*, which fills most of the space between the iris and the retina; formerly including also the denser *crystalline lens* ME.

1. To. .sucke vp the humours Of the danke Morning *Jul. C.* II. i. 262. **2. b.** He answered me that choler was the cause of my sicknes 1581. †*Black h.*, black choler or melancholy.

II. 1. Mental disposition (orig. as determined by the proportion of the bodily humours; see I. 2 b); temperament 1475. †**b.** *transf.* Character, style; sentiment, spirit (of a writing, musical composition, etc.) –1717. **2.** Temporary state of mind; mood, temper 1525; †habitual frame of mind –1676. **3.** A state of mind having no apparent ground or reason; mere fancy, whim, caprice, freak, vagary 1565. **4. a.** That quality of action, speech, or writing, which excites amusement; oddity, comicality. **b.** The faculty of perceiving what is ludicrous or amusing, or of expressing it; jocose imagination or treatment of a subject. (Less purely intellectual than *wit*, and often allied to pathos.) 1682.

1. Thus Ile curbe her mad and headstrong humor *Tam. Shr.* IV. i. 212. **2.** Was euer woman in this humour woo'd? SHAKS. Every Man in his Humour B. JONS. (*title*). **3.** These are complements, these are humours *L.L.L.* III. i. 23. I haue an humour to knocke you indifferently well . .and that's the humour of it *Hen. V*, II. i. 63. The humors of Election Day HAWTHORNE. **4.** The happy compound of pathos and playfulness, which we style. h. 1854. Phrase. *Out of h.*: displeased; out of conceit *with.*

Humour, humor, *v.* 1588. [f. HUMOUR *sb.*] **1.** *trans.* To comply with the humour of;

to indulge. **2.** *fig.* To comply with the peculiar nature or exigencies of; to adapt oneself to; to act in compliance with; to fit, suit (*with* something) 1588. †**3.** *trans.* To give a particular style to. WALTON.

1. To h. the ignorant *L.L.L.* IV. ii. 52. **2.** The man That with smooth air couldst humour best our tongue MILT. (In wood-carving) to h. the wood. **3.** This Song was well humor'd by the maker 1653.

Humoured, humored (hiū·məɹd, yū·məɹd), *a.* 1598. [f. HUMOUR *sb.* and *v.* + -ED.] **1.** Having a (specified) disposition, as GOOD-HUMOURED, etc. †**2.** Imaginary. PURCHAS. **3.** Indulged 1649.

Hu·mourless, -orless, *a.* 1847. [f. HUMOUR *sb.* + -LESS.] Devoid of humour.

Humoursome, humorsome (hiū·məɹsɒ̆m), *a.* 1656. [f. HUMOUR *sb.* + -SOME[1].] **1.** = HUMOROUS 3. **2.** Indulgent 1876.

1. The Divine Will..not a meer arbitrary, H... thing CUDWORTH. Hence **Hu·moursome-ly** *adv.*, **-ness.**

Hump (hɒmp), *sb.* 1708. [First exemplified, 1681, in *hump-back(ed*, repl. earlier synon. *crump-backed*, and perh. a blending of this with synon. *hunch-backed*; the similar LG. *humpe*, Du. *homp* lump, hunk (whence G. *humpe*) may be related.] **1.** A protuberance; esp. a protuberance on the back occurring as a normal feature in the camel, bison, etc., or as a deformity in man. **2.** *transf.* A hummock 1838. **3.** A fit of ill humour; sulks (*slang*) 1727. **4.** *attrib.* 1807.

Hump, *v.* 1673. [f. prec.] †**1.** *intr.* To have a fit of ill humour, sulk. **2.** *trans.* To give (one) 'the hump'. THACKERAY. **3.** *trans.* To make hump-shaped; to hunch. Also *absol.* 1840. **4.** To hoist or carry (a bundle) upon the back (*Austral. slang*) 1853. **5.** *refl.* To exert oneself, make an effort (*U.S. slang*) 1835.

Humpback, hump-back, *sb.* (*a.*) 1697. [See HUMP *sb.*] **1.** (*hu·mp-ba·ck.*) A back having a hump. **2.** (*hu·mpback.*) A person with a humped back 1712. **3.** = *h. whale* 1725. **4.** *adj.* Having a hump on the back 1725.

4. Humpback whale, a whale of the genus *Megaptera*, so called because the low dorsal fin forms a characteristic hump on the back.

Hump-backed, *a.* 1681. [See HUMP *sb.*, -ED[2].] Having a humped or crooked back; hunched. Also *transf.*

Humped (hɒmpt), *a.* 1713. [f. HUMP *sb.* + -ED[2].] Having a hump (or humps); having the back rounded.

Humph (hɒmf), *interj.* (and *sb.*) 1681. The syllable 'h'mf!' used as an expression of doubt or dissatisfaction. Also *sb.*, as a name for this utterance. Hence **Humph** *v.* to utter the syllable 'h'mf!'.

Hu·mpless, *a.* 1868. [f. HUMP *sb.* + -LESS.] Having no hump.

†**Hump-shoulder.** 1704. [See HUMP *sb.*] A shoulder raised into a hump. Hence †**Hump-shouldered** *a.* having a hump-shoulder.

Humpty (hɒ·m^{p}ti), *a.* 1825. [app. f. HUMP *sb.*, or *humpt* HUMPED, but the formation is anomalous, and may have arisen out of the next word.] Humped, hump-backed. Also as *sb.*, a low padded cushion seat 1924.

Humpty-dumpty (hɒ·m^{p}ti dɒ·m^{p}ti). 1698. [With sense 1 cf. HUM *sb.*[1] 3; sense 2 is perh. f. HUMPY *a.* + DUMPY *a.*[2], with unexpl. intrusive *t*.]

A. *sb.* **1.** A drink, 'ale boiled with brandy'. **2.** A short, dumpy, hump-shouldered person; in the nursery rime explained as an egg (in reference to its shape); also allusively 1785.

B. *adj.* Short and fat 1785.

Humpy (hɒ·mpi), *sb.* 1873. [Native *oompi*, infl. by *hump*.] A native Australian hut.

Humpy (hɒ·mpi), *a.* 1708. [f. HUMP *sb.* + -Y[1].] Having humps; marked by protuberances; humped; hump-like.

Humstrum (hɒ·mstrɒm). 1739. [f. HUM *v.*[1] + STRUM *v.*] **1.** A musical instrument of rude construction or out of tune. **2.** Indifferently played music 1882.

‖**Humus** (hiū·mɒ̆s). 1796. [L. 'mould, ground, soil'.] Vegetable mould; the dark-brown or black substance resulting from the slow decomposition of organic matter. It is a valuable constituent of soils. Also *attrib.*

Hun (hɒn). [OE. (pl.) *Hūne, Hūnas*, corresp. to MHG. *Hiunen* (G. *Hunnen*), ON. *Húnar*, also *Hýnar* – late L. *Hunni, Hūni*, also *Chunni, Chūni*, med.L. also *Hun(n)ones*, Gr. Οὖννοι – Turki *Hun-yü*.] **1.** One of an Asiatic race of warlike nomads, who invaded Europe *c* A.D. 375, and later, under their king Attila (styled *Flagellum Dei*, the scourge of God), overran and ravaged a great part of it. **2.** *transf.* A reckless destroyer of the beauties of nature or art; cf. 'Goth', 'Vandal' 1806. **b.** During the war of 1914–18, applied generally to the Germans, in allusion to their methods of warfare.

2. Where furious Frank, and fiery H., Shout in their sulphurous canopy CAMPBELL.

Hunch (hɒnʃ), *sb.* 1630. [In sense 1 from next; in sense 2 deduced from *hunch-backed*.] **1.** The act of hunching; a push, thrust, shove. *Obs.* exc. *dial.* **2.** A hump 1804. **3.** A lump, a hunk 1790. **4.** *U.S.* A presentiment 1904.

Hunch (hɒnʃ), *v.* 1581. [This and prec. go with HUNCH-BACK, -ED.] **1.** *intr.* To push, thrust, shove. Also *fig. dial.* **2.** *trans.* To push, shove, thrust. *dial.* 1659. **3.** *trans.* To compress, bend, or arch convexly 1678.

2. Hunching and Justling one another 1668. **3.** He sat..hunched up, with his knees and his chin together 1892.

Hunchback, hunch-back. 1712. [Back-formation from earlier *hunch-backed* (SHAKS.), synon. with †*bunch-backed*, †*hulch-backed* (XVI); of unkn. origin.] **1.** (hɒ·nʃ,bæ·k) A hunched back 1718. **2.** (hɒ·nʃ,bæk) = HUMP-BACK *sb.* 2. 1712. **3.** *attrib.* Hump-backed 1850. So **Hu·nchbacked** *a.* having a protuberant or crooked back.

Hundred (hɒ·ndrĕd), *sb.* and *a.* [Late OE. *hundred* = OFris. *hundred*, OS. *hunderod* (Du. *honderd*), MHG., G. *hundert*, ON. *hundrað* (whence *hundrað, -eð* in late Northumb., surviving dial. in *hunderth*); Gmc., f. **χundam* hundred + **raþ* = number (cf. Goth. *raþjō* number, account).] **1.** The cardinal number equal to ten times ten, or five score. Symbols 100 or C. **a.** As sb. or quasi-sb. In sing., usually *a* (arch. *an*) *h.*, emphatically *one h.*; in expressing rate, *the h.* In pl., *hundreds*. After a numeral adj., *hundred* is generally used as a collective pl. (Cf. *dozen*.) OE. **b.** As adj. or quasi-adj., followed immediately by a pl. (or collective) noun OE. **c.** The cardinal form *hundred* is also used as an ordinal when followed by other numbers, the last of which alone takes the ordinal form; e.g. 'the hundred-and-first', etc. **2.** Often used indef. for a large number ME.; also, for a definite number more than five score 1469. **3.** In England, etc.: A subdivision of a county or shire, having its own court; also formerly the court. *Chiltern Hundreds*: see CHILTERN. OE. **b.** A division of a county in Delaware 1621. **4.** = HUNDREDWEIGHT 1542.

1. Add one round h. POPE. Tickets fabricated by the h. 1885. Some hundreds of men were present (*mod.*). Eight h. of the brave COWPER. **b.** The h. and one odd chances (*mod.*). Phr. *The Hundred Days*, the period of the restoration of Napoleon Bonaparte, after his escape from Elba, ending June 22, 1815. **2.** Phr. *Great* or *long h.*: usu. = 120. **3.** It is certain that in some instances the h. was deemed to contain exactly 100 hides of land F. W. MAITLAND. *Comb.* **Hundred-court,** in *Eng. Hist.* the court having civil and criminal jurisdiction within a territorial hundred.

Hundredal (hɒ·ndrĕdăl), *a.* 1862. [f. HUNDRED 3 + -AL[1].] Of or pertaining to a territorial hundred.

Hu·ndredary. 1700. [– med.L. *hundredarius*; see next and -ARY.] = HUNDREDER 1.

Hundreder, -or (hɒ·ndrĕdəɹ, -ǫɹ). 1455. [f. HUNDRED 3 + -ER[2], -OR 2; in med.L. *hundredarius*.] **1.** The bailiff or chief officer of a hundred. **2.** An inhabitant of a hundred, esp. one liable to serve on a jury 1501.

Hundredfold (hɒ·ndrĕdfō^{u}ld). ME. [f. HUNDRED + -FOLD.] **1.** *adj.* A hundred times as much or as many. **2.** *adv.* A hundred times (in amount). Now always *a* (*an*) *h.* ME. **3.** *sb.* A hundred times the amount or number ME.

2. Armies which outnumbered them a h. MACAULAY. **3.** Some [brought forth] an h. *Matt.* 13:8.

Hundredth (hɒ·ndrĕdþ), *a.* (*sb.*) ME. [f. HUNDRED + -TH[2].] **1.** Coming last in order of a hundred successive individuals. **2.** *sb.* A hundredth part 1774.

1. *Hundredth part*: one of a hundred equal parts into which a whole is, or may be, divided.

Hundredweight (hɒ·ndrĕdwē^{i}t). 1474. [f. HUNDRED + WEIGHT. The pl. is unchanged after a numeral or an adj. expressing plurality, as *many*.] An avoirdupois weight equal to 112 pounds; prob. orig. to 100 pounds, whence the name. Abbrev. cwt. (formerly C.).

Locally it has varied from 100 to 120 lb.; in U.S. it is now usu. 100 lb.

Hung (hɒŋ), *ppl. a.* 1641. [pa. pple. of HANG *v.*] **1.** Suspended; (of meat) suspended in the air to be cured by drying, or to become high 1655. **2.** Furnished *with* hanging things 1648; †having pendent organs –1785. **3.** *U.S.* Of a jury: see HANG *v.* I. 6 b.

Hung, pa. t. and pple. of HANG *v.*

†**Hu·ngar.** 1565. [– G. *Ungar*, med.L. *Hungarus* Hungarian.] **1.** A Hungarian –1606. **2.** A gold coin of Hungary, worth about 5*s.* –1756.

Hungarian (hɒŋgē^{ə}·riăn). 1553. [f. med.L. *Hungaria* HUNGARY + -AN.] **A.** *adj.* **1.** Of, belonging to, or native of Hungary 1600. †**2.** Thievish; needy, beggarly (with play on *hungry*) –1608.

1. H. horse, H. leather. **2.** *Merry W.* I. iii. 23.

B. *sb.* **1.** A native or inhabitant of Hungary; a Hungarian horse; the language of Hungary 1553. †**2.** (With play on *hunger*.) A hungry person, a great eater –1632.

†**Hunga·ric,** *a.* 1661. [– med.L. *Hungaricus*.] = HUNGARIAN *a.* 1. –1694.

H. fever: an old name for typhus fever.

Hungary (hɒ·ŋgări). 1450. [– med.L. *Hungaria* (Fr. *Hongrie*), f. *(H)ungari, Ungri, Ugri* (cf. UGRIAN), med. Gr. Οὔγγροι, G. *Ungarn*, foreign name of the people called by themselves MAGYAR.] **1.** A country of central Europe, formerly a part of the Austro-Hungarian monarchy. †**2.** A Hungarian 1502.

H. water: a distilled water, made of rosemary flowers infused in rectified spirit of wine 1698.

Hunger (hɒ·ŋgəɹ), *sb.* [OE. *hungor, -ur* = OS., OHG. *hungar* (Du. *honger*, G. *hunger*), ON. *hungr* :– Gmc. **χuŋʒruz* (Gothic has *hūhrus* :– **χuŋχruz*).] **1.** The uneasy or painful sensation caused by want of food; craving appetite. Also, the exhausted condition caused by want of food. Often personified. **2.** Dearth; famine. *Obs.* or *arch.* OE. **3.** *transf.* and *fig.* Strong desire or craving 1548.

1. For strong hounguer he criede loude ME. The parent of all industries is H. DRUMMOND.

Comb. **h.-march,** a march undertaken esp. by unemployed to call attention to their condition; **h.-rot,** a disease in corn or †cattle due to deficient nourishment; **h.-strike** *sb.*, refusal by a prisoner to take food, in order to obtain release; also *vb.*

Hunger (hɒ·ŋgəɹ), *v.* [OE. *hyngran, -ian* (= OS. *gihungrian*, Goth. *huggrjan*) was superseded in ME. by *hungeren* through assim. to the sb.] †**1.** *impers.* as in *it hungers me*: 'there is hunger to me', I am hungry –ME. **2.** *intr.* To feel or suffer hunger, be hungry OE. **3.** *transf.* and *fig.* To long *for*, to hanker *after* 1440. †**4.** *trans.* To have a hunger or craving for; to desire with longing –1563. **5.** To subject to hunger; to starve, famish 1575.

2. I hungerd and yhe me fedde HAMPOLE. **3.** Blessed are they which doe h. and thirst after righteousnesse *Matt.* 5:6.

Hu·nger-bit, *a.* ME. = next.

Hu·nger-bitten, *a.* [OE. *hungerbiten*.] Pinched with hunger; famished, starved.

Hungered (hɒ·ŋgəɹd), *a. arch.* ME. [Partly aphet. f. A-HUNGERED, partly pa. pple. of HUNGER *v.* 5.] Hungry; famished, starved.

Hu·ngerer. ME. [f. HUNGER *v.* + -ER[1].] One who suffers hunger; one who longs.

Hu·ngerly, *a. Obs.* or *arch.* ME. [f. HUNGER *sb.* + -LY[1].] Hungry-looking; having a famished look. So **Hu·ngerly** *adv.* hungrily, greedily. *Obs.* or *arch.* 1557.

†**Hu·nger-starve,** *v.* ME. [f. HUNGER *sb.* + STARVE *v.*] *trans.* To starve with hunger; to starve –1879.

Hungry (hɒ·ŋgri), *a.* [OE. *hungriġ* = OFris. *hungerig*, OHG. *hung(a)rag* (G. *hungrig*); see -Y¹.] **1.** Having the sensation of hunger; feeling pain or uneasiness from want of food; having a keen appetite. Also *transf.* **2. a.** Famine-stricken. ? *Obs.* ME. **b.** Of food: Eaten with keen appetite. Now *rare* or *Obs.* 1552. **3. a.** Of food, etc.: That leaves one hungry. Hence *fig.* Unsatisfying. Now *rare.* 1561. **b.** Inducing hunger (*rare*) 1611. **4.** *transf.* and *fig.* Eager, greedy, avaricious ME. **5.** 'More disposed to draw from other substances than to impart to them' (J.); esp. of land, etc.: Not rich or fertile, poor; of rivers: Not supplying food for fish. †Applied formerly also to hard waters, acrid wines, etc. 1420.

1. Hee hath filled the h. with good things *Luke* 1:53. *transf.* Yond Cassius has a leane and h. looke *Jul. C.* I. ii. 194. **2. a.** In the sowre h. tyme CHAUCER. **3. b.** A h. sermon THACKERAY. **4.** The h. flame devours the silent dead POPE. **5.** Flat tracts of h. pasture ground KEATINGE. Hence **Hu·ngrily** *adv.* **Hu·ngriness.**

Hunk (hɒŋk), *sb.* 1813. [prob. of LDu. origin; cf. WFlem. *een hunke brood* a hunk of bread.] A large piece cut off; a thick or clumsy piece, a lump; a hunch.

Hunker (hɒ·ŋkəɹ), *sb.* *U.S.* ? *Obs.* 1849. [app. f. HUNKS *sb.* + -ER¹.] In U.S. politics: A conservative, one opposed to innovation or change; a nickname first used in the State of New York about 1845. Hence **Hu·nkerism.**

Hunkers (hɒ·ŋkəɹz), *sb. pl.* *Sc.* 1785. [Connected with Sc. *hunker* squat; cf. synon. MDu. *hucken*, MLG. *hūken* (Du. *huiken*, G. *hocken*), ON. *húka*.] In the phr. *on one's hunkers*, in a squatting position, with the haunches, knees, and ankles acutely bent.

Hunks (hɒŋks), *sb.* Also **hunx.** 1602. [Of unkn. origin.] A surly, crusty old person; now usu., a close-fisted, stingy man; a miser. They all think me a close old h. EARL ORRERY.

Hunnish (hɒ·niʃ), *a.* [f. HUN + -ISH¹.] Of, pertaining to, or like the Huns BYRON.

†Hunt, *sb.*¹ [OE. *hunta*, superseded by HUNTER; survives in the surname *Hunt*.] A hunter; a huntsman –1807.

Hunt (hɒnt), *sb.*² ME. [f. HUNT *v.*] **1.** The act of hunting; the act of chasing wild animals for sport or for food; the chase. **b.** *fig.* and *gen.* Pursuit, as of a wild animal; a search, esp. a diligent search 1605. **2. a.** A body of persons engaged in, or associated for the purpose of, hunting with a pack of hounds 1579. **†b.** Game killed in hunting. *Cymb.* III. vi. 90. **c.** The district hunted 1857. **3.** *Change-ringing.* (Cf. HUNT *v.* 7.) 1684.

1. The h. is vp, the morne is bright and gray *Tit. A.* II. ii. 1. **b.** On a h. for lodgings 1852. **2. c.** Within the Heythrop h. (*mod.*).

Hunt (hɒnt), *v.* [OE. *huntian*, f. weak grade of stem of *hentan* seize; see HENT *v.*] **1.** *intr.* To go in pursuit of wild animals or game; to engage in the chase. Also of animals: to pursue their prey. **2.** *trans.* To pursue (wild animals or game) for the purpose of catching or killing; to chase for food or sport; often *spec.* to pursue with hounds. Also said of animals. OE. **3.** (*fig.* and *gen.*) *intr.* To search (*after* or *for* anything), esp. with eagerness ME.; *trans.* to search for (esp. with desire or diligence); to endeavour to capture, obtain, or find ME.; to track 1579. **4.** *trans.* To pursue with force, violence, or hostility; to chase or drive *away* or *out* ME. Also *fig.* **5.** To scour (a district) in pursuit of game; *spec.* to make (a district) the field of fox-hunting; *fig.* to examine every corner of 1440. **6.** To use in hunting 1607. **7.** *Change-ringing.* To alter the position of a bell in successive changes so as to shift it by degrees from the first place to the last (*hunting up*), or from the last to the first (*h. down*) 1684.

1. The dog kinds..love to h. in company GOLDSM. **2.** The King he is hunting the Deare *L.L.L.* IV. iii. 1. **3.** Sathanas..dayly hunteth to take thy soule 1526. He neuer huntit benefice 1573. I hunted the seams still farther up the glacier TYNDALL. **4.** He might lay his account with being hunted out of society SCOTT. **5.** He hunted the Cottesmore country 1875. **6.** To rear, feed, hunt, and discipline the pack SOMERVILLE.

Phrase. *To h. counter*: see COUNTER *adv.* 1; **h. the slipper,** a parlour game in which a ring of players passes a slipper covertly while a player in the middle tries to get hold of it 1766.

Hunter (hɒ·ntəɹ). ME. [f. HUNT *v.* + -ER¹. Superseded HUNT *sb.*¹] **1.** A man who hunts; one engaged in the chase of wild animals; a huntsman. **b.** *fig.* and *gen.* One who searches eagerly for something. (Usu. in comb., as *fortune-h.*, etc.) ME. **2.** A horse used, or adapted for use, in hunting 1655. **b.** A dog used in or adapted for hunting 1591. **3.** An animal that hunts its prey; *spec.* = *hunting-spider* 1658. **4.** = *Hunting-watch* 1851. **5.** *attrib.* 1483.

Comb. **hunter's mass,** a shortened mass for hunters eager for the chase 1595; **hunter's moon,** a name for the full moon next after the HARVEST MOON.

Hunterian (hɒntīᵊ·riăn), *a.* 1807. [f. *Hunter* + -IAN.] Of or belonging to John Hunter (1728–1793), or his brother William Hunter (1718–1783), famous Scottish surgeons.

Hu·nting, *vbl. sb.* OE. [f. HUNT *v.* + -ING¹.] The action of HUNT *v.* Also *Comb.* So **Hu·nting** *ppl. a.*

Comb.: **h.-box,** a small country-house for h.; **-case,** a watch-case with a hinged cover to protect the glass; **-crop,** a straight whipstock with a leather loop for insertion of a thong or lash; **-dog,** a dog used for hunting; also, the Hyena-dog of S. Africa, which hunts in packs; **-field,** the ground on which a hunt is going on; also, the body of mounted huntsmen following the hounds; **-flask; -horn,** a horn on which signals are blown in hunting; on a side-saddle, the second pommel on the near side; **h. leopard,** the Cheetah (*Felis jubata*); **-piece,** a picture representing a hunting scene; **-seat,** a country-house occupied only during the hunting season; **-shirt** *U.S.*, a trapper's shirt, orig. made of deerskin and ornamented; **-song,** a song sung during a hunt, or relating to hunting; **-watch,** a watch having a *hunting-case* to protect the glass.

Hu·nting-ground. 1777. [f. HUNTING *vbl. sb.*] A district or tract of country adapted for hunting, or in which hunting is practised. Also *fig.*

Happy hunting-ground(s: those expected by the American Indians in the world to come; hence, the future state. Also *fig.* a favourable place for hunting, collecting, etc.

Huntress (hɒ·ntrės). ME. [f. HUNTER + -ESS¹.] **1.** A woman (or goddess) who follows the chase. Also *transf.* and *fig.* **2.** A mare used for hunting 1858.

Huntsman (hɒ·ntsmæ̆n). 1567. [f. *hunt's*, genitive of HUNT *sb.* + MAN.] **1.** A man who hunts, a hunter. **2.** *spec.* The manager of a hunt, who takes charge of the hounds and directs the pursuit of game 1596.

Comb. **h.'s cup,** *Sarracenia purpurea*, a N. Amer. plant so called from its pitcher-shaped leaves.

Hu·ntsmanship. 1631. [f. prec. + -SHIP.] The position, office, or business of a huntsman; the art of hunting.

Hunt's-up. 1537. Orig. *the hunt is up*, an old song or tune sung or played to awaken huntsmen in the morning, and also used as a dance. Hence: **a.** An early morning song; **†b.** a disturbance, uproar. *Obs.* or *dial.*

a. Hunting thee hence, with Hunts vp to the day SHAKS.

Hup, hupp (hɒp), *interj.* 1733. [Cf. Du. *hop!* gee-up.] A call to a horse to quicken his pace. Hence **Hup** *v. intr.* to shout *hup*, to urge on a horse.

Hu·rcheon. *Sc.* and *north.* ME. [– ONFr. *herichon*; see URCHIN.] A hedgehog.

Hurden: see HARDEN.

Hu·rdies, *sb. pl.* *Sc.* 1535. [Of unkn. origin.] The buttocks, the hips. Also *fig.*

Hurdle (hɒ̄·ɹd'l), *sb.* [OE. *hyrdel* :– **χurðilaz*, f. Gmc. **χurðiz*, repr. by OS. *hurth*, MLG, *hurt, hort*, (M)Du. *horde*, OHG. *hurt* (G. *hürde*) hurdle, ON. *hurð*, Goth. *haurds* door; based on IE. **krt-* (cf. Gr. κάρταλος basket, L. *cratis* hurdle); see -LE; for the vocalism cf. *bundle*, etc.] **1.** A portable rectangular frame, orig. having horizontal bars interwoven or wattled with withes of hazel, willow, etc.; = wattle; but now often an open frame, like a field gate; used chiefly to form temporary fences, sheep-pens, etc. **b.** A kind of frame or sledge on which traitors used to be drawn through the streets to execution ME. **c.** *Fortif.*, etc. A wattled hurdle, used to lay upon marshy ground or across a ditch to provide a firm passage, or for other purposes ME. **2.** Anything formed, like a hurdle, of crossing bars or grating ME.

Comb. **h.-race,** a race in which the contestants have to jump over hurdles; also *the hurdles*. **Hu·rdler,** one who makes hurdles or runs in hurdle-races.

Hu·rdle, *v.* 1598. [f. prec. sb.] **†1.** *trans.* To construct like a hurdle; to wattle. **2.** To enclose or mark *off* with hurdles 1632. **†3.** To bush-harrow 1733. **4.** *intr.* To compete in a hurdle-race 1896.

Hurds: see HARDS.

Hurdy-gurdy (hɒ̄·ɹdi,gɒ̄:ɹdi). 1749. [Rhyming comp. suggested by the sound of the instrument; cf. Sc. and north. *hirdy-girdy* uproar, disorderly noise (XV).] **1.** A lute-like instrument, having strings (two or more of which are tuned as drones); the strings are sounded by the revolution of a rosined wheel turned by the left hand, the notes being obtained by the action of keys which stop the strings. Now applied pop. to the barrel-organ. **2.** (More fully *hurdy-gurdy wheel*.) An impact wheel driven by a tangential jet of water which strikes a series of buckets on the periphery. *U.S.* 1872.

Hure. ME. [– (O)Fr. *hure*, in OFr. hair of the head, head of man or beast, in mod. Fr. head of certain animals; in med.L. *hura* rough cap, with which cf. OFr. *hurepel* hat; of unkn. origin.] **†1.** A cap –1482. **2.** The head of a boar, wolf, or bear 1844.

Hurkaru, var. of HIRCARRA.

Hurl (hɒ̄ɹl), *sb.* ME. [f. HURL *v.*] **1.** The action or an act of hurling 1530. **2.** The stick or club used in the game of hurling 1791. **3.** Swirl (*rare*) ME. **†4.** Strife, contention; tumult –1653.

Hurl (hɒ̄ɹl), *v.* [corresp. in form and sense to LG. *hurreln* toss, throw, push, dash, but no chronological contact has been established; they are prob. independent imit. formations.] **1.** *intr.* To move with violence or impetuosity; to rush; to dash. *Obs.* or *arch.* **2.** *trans.* To drive or impel with impetuous force or violence ME. **3.** *trans.* To precipitate, throw down, overthrow (*lit.* and *fig.*) ME. **4.** To throw or cast; to fling; †to 'throw' in wrestling ME. **b.** *spec.* To play the game of hurling 1766. **5.** *transf.* and *fig.* To throw out or forth (words, threats, rays, etc.) with force 1590. **†6.** *intr.* To roar or bluster as the wind; to howl –1598.

2. Amr hurled his troops..in vain against the solid walls of Babylon 1884. **3.** Raised to power and hurled from it MACAULAY. **4.** Hector and Ajax h. their lances at each other 1874. **5.** Hurling defiance toward the vault of Heav'n MILT. *P. L.* I. 669.

Hu·rlbat. 1440. [app. f. HURL *v.* + BAT *sb.*²] **†1.** ? Some form of club; rendering L. *aclys* a small javelin –1656. **†2.** Used to render L. *cæstus* CESTUS² –1791. **3.** = HURL *sb.* 2. 1820.

Hurl-bone, late var. of WHIRL-BONE.

†Hurled, *a.* 1460. [Also as *hurl-footed* (XVIII); cf. Du. *horrel* (*-voet*) club-foot.] Deformed or distorted, as a club-foot –1647.

†Hurlement. 1585. [f. HURL *v.* + -MENT.] Rush, violence; confusion –1618.

Hurler (hɒ̄·ɹləɹ). 1440. [f. HURL *v.* + -ER¹.] **1.** One who throws with violence 1532. **2.** *spec.* One who plays either game of HURLING 1602. **3.** One who contends or strives 1440.

Hurley (hɒ̄·ɹli). Also **hurly.** 1825. [f. HURL *v.*] **1.** The Irish game of hurling 1841. **2.** The stick or club used in this game; a club or cudgel of the same shape 1825. **3.** The ball used in hurling 1856.

†Hurley-hacket. *Sc.* 1529. [Cf. HURL *v.*] **1.** A sport consisting in sliding down a steep place in a trough or sledge, as in tobogganing –1810. **2.** An ill-hung carriage. SCOTT.

Hurling (hɒ̄·ɹliŋ), *vbl. sb.* ME. [f. HURL *v.* + -ING¹.] **1.** Throwing; esp. with violence. **2. a.** A game, closely akin to hand-ball, once popular in Cornwall 1600. **b.** In Ireland, a game resembling hockey 1366. **†3.** Strife; commotion –1576. **†4.** The violent rushing of wind; the sound of this; rolling of thunder –1668.

2. a. H. taketh his denomination from throwing of the ball CAREW.

†**Hurlpit, -pool,** var. ff. WHIRLPIT *Obs.*, WHIRLPOOL.

†**Hurlwind.** 1509. [From a confusion of HURL *v.* and WHIRL *v.*; cf. prec.] = WHIRLWIND –1640.

Hurly (hŏ·ɹli). 1596. [f. HURL *v.*; cf. HURLING *vbl. sb.* 3; see -Y⁶.] Commotion; strife.

Hurly-burly (hŏ·ɹli,bŏ·ɹli), *sb.*, *a.*, and *adv.* 1539. [Preceded by †*hurling and burling*, a jingling collocation based on HURLING 3 (XIV), HURL *sb.* 4. The simple HURLY is later.] **1.** *sb.* Commotion, strife, uproar, confusion. (Formerly a dignified word.) **2.** *adj.* Attended with commotion or disturbance; tumultuous 1596. †**3.** *adv.* Tumultuously; confusedly –1704.

1. When the Hurley-burley's done, When the Battaile's lost, and wonne *Macb.* I. i. 3. Hence **Hurly-burly** *v.* to throw into, or make, a hurly-burly. *Obs.* or *arch.*

Huronian (hiurōᵘ·niăn), *a.* 1862. [f. *Huron* + -IAN.] *Geol.* Of or belonging to Lake Huron; a term at one time applied to a division of the archæan series of rocks as found in Canada.

Hurr (hŏɹ, hɒrr), *v.* *Obs.* exc. *dial.* ME. [imit.] *intr.* To make a dull sound of vibration or trilling.

R is the Dogs Letter, and hurreth in the sound B. JONS.

Hurrah (hurā·, hŏrā·), **hurray** (hurēⁱ·, hŏrēⁱ·), *int.* and *sb.* 1686. [A later substitute for HUZZA. The form *hurrah* is literary and dignified; the popular form is *hooray*.]

A. *int.* A shout expressive of approbation, encouragement, or exultation; used esp. as a 'cheer' at public meetings, etc. 1716.

Hurrah for brown Autumn! hurrah! hurrah! 1845.

B. *sb.* **1.** A name for this shout 1686. ‖**2.** Repr. Fr. *hourra*, Russian *urá*: The shout of attack of the Cossacks; hence, an attack 1841.

Hurrah's nest: a disorderly mass: a state of confusion or disorder. *U.S.*

Hurrah·, hurray·, *v.* 1798. [f. prec.] **1.** *intr.* To shout 'hurrah!' **2.** *trans.* To encourage with shouts of 'hurrah!'; to 'cheer' 1832.

†**Hurrer.** ME. [f. HURE + -ER¹; cf. AL. *hurarius* cap-maker.] A maker of, or dealer in, hats and caps –1766.

Hurricane (hɒ·rikeⁱn, -kĕn), *sb.* 1555. Also †**furicane.** [Earliest forms include *furacan(e, hurricano, uracan* – Sp. *huracan* and Pg. *furacão* – Carib *hura-*, *furacan*. The present form (XVII) has perh. been infl. by *hurry* in the sense 'disturbance'.] **1.** Primarily, one of the violent wind-storms or cyclones of the W. Indies; hence, any storm in which the wind blows with terrific violence. Also *transf.* and *fig.* †**2.** A crowded fashionable assembly at a private house –1805.

1. The winds are..stark mad in an herricano FULLER. *fig.* A h. of cheers 1882.

Comb.: **h.-bird,** the frigate-bird; **-deck,** a light upper deck or platform in some steamers; so **-decked** *a.*, having a h.-deck; **-house,** a shelter at the mast-head for the look-out man; also, a kind of round-house on deck; **-lamp,** a lamp so constructed as not to be extinguished by violent wind.

Hence **Hurricane** *v. intr.* to make a commotion; *trans.* to blow upon as a h.

†**Hurrica·no,** *sb.* 1605. Also †**furicano.** **1.** An early form of HURRICANE. **2.** Applied to a waterspout –1627.

2. The dreadfull spout, Which Shipmen doe the H. call *Tr. & Cr.* V. ii. 172. Hence **Hurrica·no** *v.* (*rare*), to whirl or drive as a hurricane.

Hurried (hɒ·rid), *ppl. a.* 1667. [f. HURRY *v.* + -ED¹.] Driven along, done or performed, with a rapidity due to pressure or want of time; characterized by hurry; full of haste; hasty.

1. Haste Of midnight march, and h. meeting here MILT. *P.L.* V. 778. A h. moment 1829, embrace 1855. Hence **Hu·rried-ly** *adv.*, **-ness.**

Hurrier (hɒ·riəɹ). 1611. [f. HURRY *v.* + -ER¹.] One who hurries (see the vb.).

Hurry (hɒ·ri), *sb.* 1600. [orig. the sb. is identical in sense with HURLY. Senses 2 and 3, together with the earliest uses of the vb., based on the element *hurr*, have a more immediately imitative origin.] †**1.** Commotion, agitation; tumult –1843; excitement, perturbation –1789. **2.** Excited, hasty, or impetuous motion; rush. Now *rare* or *Obs.* 1659. **3.** Action accelerated by pressure or want of time; undue haste; the condition of being obliged to act quickly; eagerness to get something done quickly 1692. **b.** Qualified by *no* or *any* (with neg. implication): Need for hurry 1849. **4.** *advb.* 1796.

1. Too much h. of spirits MME. D'ARBLAY. **2.** A h. of hoofs in a village street LONGF. **3.** There is no h. in the designs of God 1879. **b.** Is there any h.? (*mod.*). **5.** as *adj.* (U.S.), hurried.

Hurry (hɒ·ri), *v.* 1590. [Of imit. origin; *whirry* carry along swiftly (cf. WHIRR *v.*) is of equal date; similar formations are (MH)G. *hurren* move quickly, Du. *herrie* agitation.] **1.** *trans.* To carry, convey, or cause to go with excessive haste 1592; to carry or drive with impetuosity or without deliberation to some action, conduct, or condition of mind 1595; †to drive with impetuous motion –1696. **2.** *intr.* To move or act with excited haste, or effort at speed. *Hurry up!* make haste (*colloq.*) 1590. †**3.** *trans.* To agitate; to harass, worry. *Obs.* exc. *dial.* –1848. **4.** To urge to greater speed; to hasten unduly 1713.

1. A second fear..Which madly hurries her she knows not whither SHAKS. To h. you into an act of unjust aggression THIRLWALL. **2.** Nature never hurries, never takes leaps 1871. **3.** Her form wasted, her spirits were hurried HT. MARTINEAU. **4.** H. up the tea 1889. Hence **Hu·rryingly** *adv.*

Hurrygraph (hɒ·rigrɑf). *U.S.* 1861. [f. HURRY *sb.* + GRAPH.] A hurried sketch or impression.

Hurry-scurry (hɒ·ri,skɒ·ri), *adv.*, *adj.*, and *sb.* *colloq.* 1732. [Jingling extension of HURRY *v.*, perh. infl. by *scud* or *scuttle*.] **1.** *adv.* In disorderly haste, pell-mell 1750. **2.** *adj.* Characterized by hurry and commotion 1732. **3.** *sb.* The hurrying and disorderly rushing of a number; a rush 1754. Hence **Hu·rry-scu·rry** *v. intr.* to run or rush in confused and undignified haste.

Hurst (hŏɹst). Also **hirst,** etc. [OE. *hyrst*, f. base repr. by OS., OHG. *hurst*, (also mod. G.) *horst*.]

I. 1. An eminence, hillock, knoll, or bank, esp. one of a sandy nature; a ford made by a bed of sand or shingle. **2.** A grove of trees; a copse; a wood; a wooded eminence OE.

1. We are bound to drive the bullocks All by hollows, hirsts, and hillocks SCOTT. **2.** Hursts that house the boar 1871.

II. Techn. senses. (Connection with prec. is doubtful.) **1.** The frame of a pair of millstones 1710. **2.** The ring of the helve of a trip- or tilt-hammer, which bears the trunnions 1825.

Comb.: **h.beech,** the Hornbeam; **-frame** = sense II. 2.

Hurt (hŏɹt), *sb.*¹ ME. [– OFr. *hurt*, f. *hurter*; see HURT *v.*] †**1.** A knock, blow, or stroke causing a wound or damage –1844. **2.** Bodily injury so caused; a wound; a lesion; damage ME. **3.** *gen.* Harm, wrong, damage, detriment ME.

1. Of the great disordering of horses with the hurts of our English arrowes 1590. **2.** Herbes.. To heele with youre hurtes hastily CHAUCER. A mortall h. SHAKS. **3.** What h. can it do you? DICKENS.

Hurt (hŏɹt), *sb.*² 1562. [– Fr. †*heurte* (XVI).] *Her.* A roundel azure; usu. held to represent a hurtleberry.

Hurt (hŏɹt), *sb.*³ Now *dial.* 1542. [Of unkn. origin; cf. the s.w. dial. var. WHORT.] = HURTLEBERRY.

Hurt (hŏɹt), *v.* Pa. t. and pple. **hurt.** ME. [– OFr. *hurter* (mod. *heurter*) :– Gallo-Rom. **hurtare*, perh. of Gmc. origin.]

I. Trans. uses. †**1.** To knock, strike, dash (a thing against another, or two things together) –1634. †**2.** To knock, strike, give a blow to (so as to wound or injure) –1662. **3.** To cause bodily or physical injury or pain to ME. **4.** *gen.* To injure, do harm to; to wrong ME. **5.** To give mental pain to; to distress, vex, offend 1526.

2. Whan þurgh þe body hurte was Diomede CHAUCER. **3.** I haue foughten with a knyght..I am sore hurte and he bothe MALORY. **4.** Tressilian..had much hurt his interest with her SCOTT. **5.** I own I was hurt to hear it SHERIDAN.

II. Intr. and absol. uses. †**1.** *intr.* To strike, dash (*on* or *against* something); to come into collision –1622. **2.** *absol.* To cause injury, do harm; to cause or inflict pain ME. **3.** *intr.* for *pass.* To suffer injury or pain. (Now only *colloq.*) ME.

2. They shall not h. nor destroy in all my holy mountaine *Isa.* 11:9. **3.** Does your hand still h.? 1898.

Hurter¹ (hŏ·ɹtəɹ). 1472. [f. prec. + -ER¹.] One who or that which hurts or injures.

I shall not be a h. if no helper BEAUM. & FL.

Hurter² (hŏ·ɹtəɹ). ME. [– AFr. *hurtur*, *hurtour* (in AL. *hurturum*, *-ium* XIII), f. *hurter*; see HURT *v.*, -OUR, -ER². Cf. mod. Fr. *heurtoir*.] **1.** The shoulder of an axle, against which the nave of the wheel strikes; also, a strengthening piece on the shoulder of an axle. **2. a.** A beam fixed on a gun-platform, to stop the wheels of the gun-carriage from injuring the parapet. **b.** A wooden or iron piece fastened to the top-rails of the lower gun-carriage or chassis, to check the motion of the gun. 1828.

Hurtful (hŏ·ɹtfŭl), *a.* 1526. [f. HURT *sb.*¹ + -FUL.] Causing hurt or injury; harmful, noxious, noisome. Hence **Hu·rtful-ly** *adv.*, **-ness.**

Hurtle (hŏ·ɹt'l), *sb.* *poet.* and *rhet.* 1773. [f. next.] The action or an act of hurtling; dashing together, collision, conflict; clashing sound.

Hurtle (hŏ·ɹt'l), *v.* Now only *lit.* or *arch.* ME. [f. HURT *v.* 'strike with a shock' + -LE.]

I. *trans.* **1.** = HURT *v.* I. 1. **2.** To strike or dash against; to come into collision with. Also *fig.* ME. **3.** To drive violently or swiftly; to dash, dart, shoot, fling, cast. Often confounded with *hurl*. By Spenser, *erron.*, To brandish. 1590.

2. The ragged cindery masses hurtling one another in the atmosphere 1881. **3.** An arrow, hurtel'd ere so high MARVELL.

II. *intr.* **1.** To strike *together* or *against* something, esp. with violence or noise; to dash, clash, impinge; to meet in shock and encounter. Also *fig.* ME. **2.** To emit a sound of collision; to clatter; hence, to move with clattering; to come with a crash 1509. **3.** To dash, rush, hurry; esp. with noise 1509.

1. Together hurtled both their steedes FAIRFAX. **2.** The noise of Battel hurtled in the Ayre *Jul. C.* II. ii. 22. **3.** Pell mell the men came hurtling out 1873.

Hurtleberry (hŏ·ɹt'lberi). 1460. [Earlier than synon. HURT *sb.*³ and WHORT, WHORTLEBERRY (Lyte); of unkn. origin.] The fruit of *Vaccinium myrtillus*, or the shrub itself; the whortleberry or bilberry; also applied to other species of *Vaccinium*, and to the HUCKLEBERRY.

Hurtless (hŏ·ɹtlĕs), *a.* ME. [f. HURT *sb.*¹ + -LESS.] **1.** Free from hurt; unhurt. **2.** Causing no hurt; harmless 1549.

1. On lionet shalt hurtlesse soe, And on the dragon tread 1586. **2.** H. blows DRYDEN. Hence **Hu·rtless-ly** *adv.*, **-ness.**

Husband (hɒ·zbănd), *sb.* [Late OE. *hūsbonda* – ON. *húsbóndi* master of a house, husband, f. *hús* HOUSE *sb.*¹ + *bóndi*, contr. of **bóandi*, **búandi*, subst. use of pres. pple. of *bóa*, *búa* dwell, have a household = OE., OS., OHG. *búan*, Goth. *bauan*. Cf. BOND *sb.*²]

I. †**1.** The master of a house, the male head of a household –ME. **2.** A man joined to a woman by marriage. Correl. of *wife*. ME. Also *transf.* of animals and †plants 1553.

2. Thou hast no h. yet, nor I no wife: Giue me thy hand *Com. Err.* III. ii. 68. By marriage, the h. and wife are one person in law BLACKSTONE.

II. †**1.** One who tills and cultivates the soil; a cultivator, farmer, husbandman. In early north. use, a manorial tenant. –1697. **2.** The manager of a household or establishment; a housekeeper; a steward. *Obs.* exc. in spec. applications. 1450. **3.** With qualifying epithet. A saving, frugal, or provident man; an economist. (Cf. HOUSEWIFE.) Now *rare* or *arch.* 1510.

1. He was accounted..the greatest H., and most excellent Manager of Bees in Cornwall 1723. **2.** *Ship's husband*: an agent appointed by the owners to attend to the business of a ship while in port; esp. to see that the ship is in all respects well found. Now little used. **3.** I had been so good a h. of my rum, that I had a great deal left DE FOE.

Husband (hʌ·zbănd), *v.* ME. [f. prec. sb.] **I. 1.** *trans.* To till (the ground), to dress or tend (trees); to cultivate. Also *fig.* **2.** To administer as a good householder or steward; to manage with thrift and prudence; to economize; also, to save 1440.

1. Husbanding the Vallies which lie nearest to them HEYLIN. 2. We were obliged to h. our ammunition 1748.

II. 1. *trans.* To provide or match with a husband; to mate 1565. **2.** To act the part of a husband to; to become the husband of, to marry 1601. **b.** *fig.* To espouse (an opinion) 1883.

1. I am husbanded with such a Clowne 1602. 2. Husbanding his means, with the hope of ultimately husbanding a wife 1843. Hence **Hu·sbandable** *a.* (*rare*), capable of being economically used; fit for cultivation.

Hu·sbandage. 1809. [f. HUSBAND *sb.* + -AGE.] The commission or allowance paid to a ship's husband.

Hu·sbandland. ME. [f. HUSBAND *sb.* or ON. *húsbóndi* in its sense of 'freeholder' + LAND.] An old northern term for the holding of a husband or manorial tenant, = yardland, virgate; the land occupied and tilled by the tenants of a manor, in contradistinction to the demesne lands.

Hu·sbandless, *a.* 1546. [f. HUSBAND *sb.* + -LESS.] Unwedded; widowed.

Hu·sbandlike, *a.* and *adv.* 1542. [f. as prec. + -LIKE.] After the manner of a husband.

Husbandly (hʌ·zbăndli), *a.* 1573. [f. as prec. + -LY[1].] **1.** Belonging to or befitting a husband; marital 1581. **2.** Pertaining to a husbandman or to husbandry. ? *Obs.* 1573. †**3.** Thrifty, saving, economical –1734. So **Hu·sbandly** *adv.* thriftily, frugally, economically.

Husbandman (hʌ·zbăndmæ̆n). *Pl.* **-men.** ME. [f. HUSBAND *sb.* + MAN. In early use often two wds.] **1.** A man who tills and cultivates the soil; a farmer. Also *fig.* †**2.** = HUSBAND *sb.* I. 1. ME. only. †**3.** = HUSBAND *sb.* II. 3. STEELE.

Husbandry (hʌ·zbăndri). ME. [f. as prec. + -RY.] †**1.** Domestic economy. †**b.** *transf.* and *fig.* Management (as of a household) –1658. **2.** The business of a husbandman; agriculture, farming ME.; †industrial occupation generally –1639. †**3.** *concr.* Household goods; agricultural produce; land under cultivation; the body of husbandmen on an estate –1628. **4.** (Good or bad) economy; *absol.* economy, thrift, profit ME.

1. The h. and mannage of my house *Merch. V.* III. iv. 25. 2. The chief branch of h. is the rearing of sheep 1806. 3. Spoones and stooles, and al swich housbondrye CHAUCER. Ye are goddis husbandrye TINDALE 1 *Cor.* 3:9. 4. Good h. and frugality are quite out of fashion 1745.

Hush (hʌʃ), *sb.* 1601. [f. HUSH *v.*[1] Rare bef. XIX.] Suppression of sound; silence; stillness, quiet.

It is the h. of night BYRON.

Hush (hʌʃ), *a. arch.* 1602. [A later modification of HUSHT *a.*; preceded by *hust* a. (XIV) (see HUST *int.*). Cf. ST, SH, WHISHT.] Silent, still, hushed. *Haml.* II. ii. 508.

Hush (hʌʃ), *v.*[1] 1546. [The earliest recorded word of this form, prob. orig. a back-formation from HUSHT *a.* regarded as a pa. pple.; cf. prec.] **1.** *trans.* To make silent, still, or quiet; to silence. **2.** *transf.* and *fig.* To suppress; to allay, lull, pacify. Also with *up.* 1632. **3.** *intr.* To become or be silent, quiet, or still. Also *colloq.* with *up.* 1561.

2. Phr. *H. up*: to suppress mention of; to keep from getting known.

Hush *v.*[2] *dial.* 1613. [A modification of the natural utterance SH!; cf. SHOO. Cf. G. *huschen* in same sense.] To shoo.

Hush, *v.*[3] *n. dial.* 1750. [imit.] *trans.* To send or let forth (water) with a rush; *spec.* in *Lead Mining,* to send a rush of water over a sloping surface, in order to uncover ore, and separate it from earth and stones.

Hush (hʌʃ), *int.* 1604. [Later form of HUSHT *int.*, or imper. of HUSH *v.*[1]] A command to be quiet; silence!

Hu·sh-boat, -ship. [HUSH *int.*, *v.*[1]] An armed ship disguised as a peaceful vessel to lure German submarines in the war of 1914–18.

Hushed (hʌʃt), *ppl. a.* 1602. [Historically for HUSHT, but treated later as pa. pple. of HUSH *v.*[1]] Silenced, stilled, quieted.

No more; but hush'd as Midnight Silence go DRYDEN.

Husher = *usher*: see HUISHER.

Hush-hush. 1919. Reduplic. of HUSH *int.*, used attrib. to denote anything to be kept specially secret.

Hush-money. 1709. [See HUSH *v.*[1] 2.] Money paid to prevent disclosure or exposure, or to hush up a crime, etc.

Husht, *int.* Now **dial.** ME. [app. a var. of HUST *int.*; see next, and HUSH *a.*] = HUSH *int.*

Husht (hʌʃt), *a. arch.* ME. [In XV *hussht, hushte* varies with *hust* and *whist,* derived from the corresp. interjectional forms (see HUST *int.*, WHIST *a.*, *int.*). It was at length felt as a pa. pple., as if *hush-t,* whence a new vb. HUSH *v.*[1] Now treated as a var. sp. of *hush'd,* HUSHED.] Silent, still, quiet; later, Rendered silent.

Euen as the wind is h. before it raineth SHAKS.

Husk (hʌsk), *sb.*[1] late ME. [prob. – LG. *hūske* little house, core of fruit, sheath = MDu. *hūskjin* (Du. *huisken*), dim. of *hūs* HOUSE *sb.*[1]] **1.** The dry outer integument of certain fruits and seeds; a glume or rind; *spec.* in *U.S.*, the outer covering of an ear of maize or Indian corn. **2.** †**a.** The coriaceous wing-case of an insect; an elytron. **b.** The shell or case of a chrysalis; a cocoon (? *arch.*). 1552. **3.** *techn.* 'The supporting frame of a run of millstones' (Knight) 1875. **4.** *transf.* and *fig.* The (usually worthless) outside or exterior of anything 1547.

1. The huskes that the swine did eate *Luke* 15:16. 2. The dragon-fly..An inner impulse rent the veil Of his old h. TENNYSON. 4. A few huskes of reason 1644.

Husk (hʌsk), *sb.*[2] 1722. [In sense 1 perh. f. prec.; in sense 2 app. f. HUSKY *a.*] **1.** A disease affecting cattle; a short dry cough. **2.** Huskiness 1816.

Husk (hʌsk), *v.*[1] 1562. [f. HUSK *sb.*[1]] *trans.* To remove the husk from.

Husk (hʌsk), *v.*[2] *local.* 1577. [Goes with HUSK *sb.*[2]] *intr.* Of cattle: To cough as when suffering from the husk.

Husked (hʌskt), *a.* 1583. [f. HUSK *sb.*[1] and *v.*[1] + -ED.] †**1.** Furnished or covered with a husk –1686. **2.** Stripped of the husk 1607.

Husking (hʌ·skiŋ), *vbl. sb.* 1721. [f. HUSK *v.*[1] + -ING[1].] The action of HUSK *v.*[1] *spec.* in *U.S.* The removal of the husk from Indian corn; hence, a gathering of neighbours and friends to assist a farmer in husking his corn; called also *h.-bee.*

Fair day; h. at Colo's 1712.

Husky (hʌ·ski), *sb.* 1864. [Supposed to be from ESKIMO.] An Eskimo; the Eskimo language; an Eskimo dog.

Husky (hʌ·ski), *a.* 1552. [f. HUSK *sb.*[1] + -Y[1].] **1.** Full of, containing, or consisting of husks; of the nature of a husk. **2.** Dry as a husk; arid (*lit.* and *fig.*) 1599. **3.** Of persons and their voice: Dry in the throat, so that the sound of the voice becomes more or less a hoarse whisper 1722. **4.** *U.S.* and *Canadian colloq.* Tough, strong, hefty; also as *sb.* 1884.

3. His voice was h. with anger LONGF. Hence **Hu·skily** *adv.* **Hu·skiness** (in sense 3).

‖**Hu·so.** Also **huse.** 1706. [med.L. – OHG. *hūso*; cf. HAUSEN.] The great sturgeon, *Acipenser huso,* of the Black and Caspian Seas.

Huss, *sb. dial.* Also **hurse.** 1440. [First recorded as *husk(e*; of unkn. origin.] The dog-fish. Also *attrib.*

Hussar (huzā·ɹ). 1532. [– Magyar *huszár* †freebooter, (later) light horseman – OSerb. *husar, gusar, hursar* – It. *corsaro* CORSAIR.] **1.** One of a body of light horsemen organized in Hungary in the 15th c.; hence, the name of light cavalry regiments formed elsewhere in Europe in imitation of these. **2.** *transf.* and *fig.* A skirmisher; a free-lance in literature or debate 1768.

1. *Black* or *Death H.*, one of the 'Black Brunswickers' (hussars with black uniform) who, in the war with France, 1809–13, neither gave nor received quarter; hence *fig.* I belong to the Black Hussars of Literature, who neither give nor receive criticism SCOTT.

Hussite (hʌ·səit, hu·səit). 1532. [– mod.L. *Hussita* (usu. pl.), f. John *Huss* or *Hus,* orig. of *Husinec,* in Bohemia. See -ITE[1] 1.] A follower of John Huss, the Bohemian religious reformer of the 15th c. Also *attrib.* or *adj.*

Hussy, huzzy (hʌ·zi), *sb.* 1530. [Reduction of *huswif,* HOUSEWIFE; cf. GOODY *sb.*[1]] †**1.** = HOUSEWIFE 1. –1800. **2.** A rustic, rude, opprobrious, or playfully rude mode of addressing a woman 1650. **3.** In some rural districts = Woman, lass; hence, A light or worthless woman; an ill-behaved or mischievous girl; a jade, minx. Also *joc.* and in raillery. 1647. †**4.** = HOUSEWIFE 3. –1824.

†**Hust,** *interj.* [A natural utterance, enjoining silence.] A sharp whispered sound enjoining silence: = HIST! ST! HUSH! (Chaucer.) So †**Hust** *a.* silent, quiet, hushed.

Husting (hʌ·stiŋ). Usu. in pl. **hustings.** [Late OE. *hūsting* – ON. *hūsþing* 'house of assembly', one held by a king, etc., with his immediate followers, as opp. to the ordinary *þing* (see THING *sb.*[2]) or general assembly.] **1.** (In form *husting.*) An assembly for deliberative purposes, esp. one summoned by a king or other leader; a council. *Obs.* exc. *Hist.* **2.** (In form *husting,* pl. *hustings.*) A court held in the Guildhall of London by the Lord Mayor, Recorder, and Sheriffs (or Aldermen), long the supreme court of the city OE. †**3.** (In form *hustings,* const. as *sing.*) The upper end of the Guildhall, where this court was held; the platform on which the Lord Mayor and Aldermen took their seats –1761. **4.** The temporary platform on which candidates for Parliament formerly stood for nomination, and while addressing the electors. Hence, the proceedings at a parliamentary election. 1719. Now *U.S.*, any place where political campaign speeches are made.

4. When the rotten hustings shake TENNYSON.

Hustle (hʌ·s'l), *v.* 1684. [– (M)Du. *husselen, hutselen* shake, e.g. in the game of hustle-cap, frequent. of *hutsen* = MHG. *hutzen* (cf. *hussen* run, *hutschen* push); f. Gmc. imit. base **xut-*. The second sense is of Eng. development.] †**1.** *trans.* To shake to and fro, toss (money in a hat, etc.). Also *absol.* –1801. **2.** To push or knock about unceremoniously; to jostle in a rough or violent fashion. Also *fig.* Also with *into, out of, through.* 1751. **b.** To urge forward in a rough unfastidious fashion 1887. **3.** *intr.* To push roughly *against.* Also *absol.* 1823. **b.** *intr.* To push or elbow one's way 1855. **4.** *intr.* To hurry, to bustle; to make a push 1821.

2. Dearling..was hustled by a gang of pick-pockets 1798. b. He hustles the cob into a canter 1887. 4. The King. had hustled along the floor SCOTT. Hence **Hu·stle** *sb.* the act of hustling (*pitch and h.*, pitch-and-toss 1688); in *U.S.*, 'push'.

Hustle-cap (hʌ·s'l,kæ:p). ? *Obs.* 1709. [f. HUSTLE *v.* (sense 1) + CAP *sb.*] A form of pitch-and-toss, in which the coins were shaken in a cap before being tossed.

Hustlement (hʌ·s'lmĕnt). *Obs.* exc. *dial.* ME. [– OFr. *(h)ostillement,* etc. furniture, f. *hostiller* furnish, equip, f. *(h)ostil,* *(h)ostille* tool (mod. *outil*).] Household furniture; chiefly *pl.* household goods.

Hustler (hʌ·sləɹ). 1825. [f. HUSTLE *v.* + -ER[1].] **1.** One who hustles; one of a gang of pickpockets who work on this plan. **2.** orig. *U.S.* One who works with impatient energy. 1886.

Huswife, etc.: see HOUSEWIFE, etc.

Hut (hʌt), *sb.* 1545. [– Fr. *hutte* – (M)HG. *hütte*; a HG. word which has been adopted elsewhere, prob. through military use.] **1. a.** *Mil.* A wooden structure for the temporary housing of troops. Also *transf.* **b.** A small dwelling of rude and mean construction, often of branches, turf, or mud. In Australia, a stockman's cottage 1658. **2.** The back end or body of the breech-pin of a musket 1853.

1. Dining off black bread..in a Swiss peasant's h. 1893.

Hut (hʌt), *v.* 1652. [– Fr. *(se) hutter* (XVI)

make a hut for one's lodging, f. *hutte*; see prec.] **1.** *trans.* To place in a hut or huts; to furnish with a hut or huts. **2.** *intr.* To lodge or take shelter in a hut or huts; to go into winter quarters, as troops 1807.

1. Some of the men are hutted, but the officers are still in tents 1879.

Hutch (hɒtʃ), *sb.* ME. [– (O)Fr. *huche*, (dial.) *huge* :– med.L. *hūtica* (AL. *hugia* XII) of unkn. origin.] **1.** A chest or coffer, in which things are stored. **2.** A box or box-like pen or house in which an animal is confined, as a *rabbit-hutch* 1607. **b.** Applied contemptuously to a hut or cabin, or *joc.* to a small house 1607. **3.** Techn. **a.** Short for bolting-hutch 1619. **b.** A box for washing ore 1881. **c.** A box-like carriage, wagon, truck, etc. for use in agriculture, mining, etc. 1744. **d.** As a measure = about 2 cwt. 1802.

2. b. I cannot express what a satisfaction it was to me to come into my old h. DE FOE.

†**Hutch,** *a.* 1624. [app. a var. of HULCH *a.*; but cf. HUCK *sb.*[1], HUCKLE *sb.*] Hunched, humped, gibbous; chiefly in *h. back* –1668.

Hutch, *v.* 1574. [f. HUTCH *sb.*] **1.** *trans.* To put or lay up in a hutch or chest. Also *fig.* **2.** To wash (ore) in a hutch. (Recent Dicts.)

†**Hutchet.** 1572. [– Fr. *huchet* (XV) – (O)Fr. *hucher* shout or whistle for.] *Her.* A bugle –1661.

Hutchinsonian (hɒtʃinsōᵘ·niăn). 1753. [See -IAN.]

A. *adj.* Of or pertaining to John Hutchinson (died 1737), a writer on natural philosophy, who interpreted the Bible mystically, and opposed the Newtonian philosophy 1765.

B. *sb.* An adherent of the above.

‖**Hutia** (hutī·ă). [Sp.] Any rodent of the West Indian genus *Capromys*.

Hutment (hɒ·tmĕnt). 1889. [f. HUT *v.* + -MENT.] Accommodation in huts; an encampment of huts.

Huttonian (hɒtōᵘ·niăn), *a.* 1802. [See -IAN.] **A.** *adj.* Of or relating to James Hutton the geologist (1726–1796), who maintained against Werner the igneous or plutonic origin of basalt, granite, etc. **B.** *sb.* An adherent of Hutton's geological principles 1802.

Huxter, etc., obs. ff. HUCKSTER, etc.

Huyghenian (həigī·niăn), *a.* 1704. [f. *Huyghens* + -IAN.] Of or pertaining to Christian Huyghens, a Dutch mathematician and astronomer (1629–95).

H. eyepiece, a negative eyepiece invented by Huyghens, consisting of two plano-convex lenses, with their plane sides towards the eye.

Huzz (hɒz), *v.* 1555. [imit.; cf. *whizz.*] *intr.* (rarely *trans.*) To buzz.

Wi' 'is kittle o' steam Huzzin' an' maäzin' the blessed feälds TENNYSON.

Huzza (hɒzā·, huzā·), *int.* and *sb.* 1573. [Said by writers of XVII–XVIII to have been orig. a sailor's cheer or salute; as such it may be identical with the old hauling-cry †*heisau*, †*hissa* (see HOISE), but G. has *hussa* as a cry of pursuit and exultation. Cf. HURRAH.] **1.** *int.* A shout of exultation, encouragement, or applause; a hurrah 1682. **2.** *sb.* The shout of huzza 1573.

2. They made a great h. or shout at our approch EVELYN.

Huzza (hɒzā·, huzā·), *v.* Also **-ah, -ay** (hɒzēⁱ·), *v.* 1683. [f. prec.] **1.** *intr.* To shout huzza. **2.** *trans.* To acclaim with huzzas 1688.

2. The way of the world, which huzzays all prosperity THACKERAY.

Hw-, a freq. OE. initial element (:– Gmc. *χw-, IE. *qʷ-), later WH-, q.v.

Hy, obs. f. HIGH.

Hyacine, corrupt f. HYACINTH (sense 1).

Hyacinth (hai·ăsinþ). See also JACINTH. 1553. [– Fr. *hyacinthe* – L. *hyacinthus* – Gr. ὑάκινθος purple or dark-red flower (fabled to have sprung from the blood of Hyacinthus and to bear the initials AI or the int. AIAI), precious stone, a word of pre-Hellenic origin.] **1.** A precious stone. **a.** Repr. Gr. ὑάκινθος, L. *hyacinthus*, a stone of a blue colour, prob. the sapphire. **b.** In mod. use, a reddish-orange variety of zircon; also applied to varieties of garnet and topaz of similar colour. **c.** *Her.* The name for the colour *tenné* or tawny 1704. **2.** A plant. **a.** Repr. Gr. ὑάκινθος, L. *hyacinthus*, a name for some flower; according to Ovid a deep red or purple lily. It was said to have sprung up from the blood of the slain youth Hyacinthus, and to have the letters AI, or AIAI, on its petals. Now only *Hist.* or *poet.* 1578. **b.** Eng. name of the genus *Hyacinthus* (N.O. *Liliaceæ*), bulbous plants with spikes of bell-shaped six-parted flowers, of various colours; esp. *H. Orientalis*, a native of the Levant. Also applied to allied plants of similar habit. **3.** A bird; a kind of water-hen with purple plumage, as the genera *Ionornis* and *Porphyrio*. **4.** *attrib.*, esp. in reference to the reddish-orange colour of the gem, or the blue and purple colour of the flower 1694.

2. O hyacinths! for ay your AI keep still, Nay, with more marks of woe your leaves now fill DRUMM. OF HAWTH. **b. Wild** or **Wood H.** (of Britain), *Scilla nutans* (= BLUEBELL 2); (of N. America), *Scilla* or *Camassia Fraseri*. **4.** The h.-hued hills OUIDA. Hence **Hyaci·nthian** *a.* of or pertaining to the h.: hyacinthine.

Hyacinthine (həi,ăsi·nþin, -əin), *a.* 1656. [– L. *hyacinthinus* – Gr. ὑακίνθινος applied to hair; see -INE².] **1.** Of the colour of a hyacinth (gem or flower). (Chiefly as a poetic epithet of hair, after Hom. *Od.* VI. 231.) **2.** Of, made of, or adorned with hyacinths 1675. **3.** Like the boy Hyacinthus 1847.

1. Hyacinthin locks Round from his parted forelock manly hung Clustring MILT *P. L.* IV. 301. 3. The h. boy, for whom Morn well might break and April bloom EMERSON.

‖**Hyades** (həi·ădīz), *sb. pl.* Rarely **Hyads.** ME. [– Gr. Ὑάδες fem. pl., popularly connected with ὕειν rain, their heliacal rising being supposed to prognosticate rain, but perh. from ὗς SWINE, the L. name being *suculæ* little pigs.] *Astron.* A group of stars near the Pleiades, the chief of which is the bright red star Aldebaran.

Thro' scudding drifts the rainy Hyades Vext the dim sea TENNYSON.

Hyæna, var. of HYENA.

Hyalescent (həi,ăle·sĕnt), *a.* [f. Gr. ὕαλος glass + -ESCENT.] Becoming hyaline or glassy. So **Hyale·scence,** the process of becoming or condition of being hyaline. 1864.

Hyaline (həi·ălin, -əin), *a.* and *sb.* 1661. [– L. *hyalinus* – late Gr. ὑάλινος, f. ὕαλος glass; see -INE².]

A. *adj.* Resembling glass, transparent as glass, crystalline, vitreous. (Chiefy *techn.*)

B. *sb.* **1.** 'A sea of glass like unto crystal' (Rev. 4:6); hence poet. for the smooth sea, the clear sky, or anything transparent 1667. **2.** *Anat.* and *Biol.* **a.** The HYALOID membrane of the eye. **b.** Hyaline cartilage, i.e. ordinary cartilage, as dist. from fibro-cartilage, etc. **c.** = *Hyaloplasm* (see HYALO-) 1864.

1. On the cleer H., the Glassie Sea MILT. *P. L.* VII. 619.

Hyalite (həi·ăləit). 1794. [f. Gr. ὕαλος glass + -ITE¹ 2 b.] *Min.* A colourless variety of opal, occurring in globular concretions.

‖**Hyalitis** (həi,ăləi·tis). 1847. [f. as prec. + -ITIS.] *Path.* Inflammation of the vitreous humour of the eye.

Hyalo- (həi,ălo), comb. f. Gr. ὕαλος glass. **Hy·alograph** [Gr. -γραφος that writes], 'an instrument for etching on a transparent surface'; so **Hyalo·graphy,** 'the art of writing or engraving on glass' (Webster). **Hy·alophane** [Gr. -φανης], *Min.* a barium feldspar, found in transparent crystals. **Hy·aloplasm** [Gr. πλάσμα], *Biol.* transparent homogeneous protoplasm; hence **Hyalopla·smic** *a.* †**Hy·alotype,** a positive picture, copied on glass from a negative on glass.

Hyaloid (həi·ăloid). 1835. [– Fr. *hyaloïde* or late L. *hyaloïdes* – Gr. ὑαλοειδής like glass, f. ὕαλος glass; see -OID.]

A. *adj.* (Chiefly *Anat.*) **a.** Glassy, hyaline. **b.** Connected with the hyaloid membrane.

a. *H. coat* or *membrane*, a thin transparent membrane enveloping the vitreous humour of the eye. **b.** *H. artery, canal, vein* (*Syd. Soc. Lex.*).

B. *sb.* **1.** *Anat.* The hyaloid membrane; see A. a. 1838. **2.** = HYALINE B. 1. 1844.

‖**Hyalonema** (həi,ălonī·mă). 1855. [mod. L., f. Gr. ὕαλος glass + νῆμα thread.] The glass-rope sponge, which roots itself to the sea-bed by a long stem twisted of fine siliceous threads.

Hybern-, obs. var. of HIBERN-.

Hyblæan (həiblī·ăn), *a.* Also **Hyblaen.** 1614. [f. L. *Hyblæus* (f. *Hybla*, Gr. Ὕβλη) + -AN; see -EAN.] Of or pertaining to the town of Hybla in Sicily celebrated for its bees; hence *poet.* honied, sweet, mellifluous.

Busy as H. swarms 1682. So **Hy·blan** *a.*

Hybodont (hi·bodǫnt). 1836. [f. Gr. ὕβος hump, ὑβός hump-backed + ὀδούς, ὀδοντ- tooth.]

A. *sb.* A shark of the extinct genus *Hybodon* or family *Hybodontidæ*, with conical compressed teeth.

B. *adj.* Belonging to the *Hybodontidæ* 1872.

Hybrid (həi·brid). 1601. [– L. *hybrida*, (*h*)*ibrida* offspring of a tame sow and a wild boar, one born of a Roman father and a foreign mother or of a freeman and a slave.]

A. *sb.* **1.** The offspring of two animals or plants of different species, or (less strictly) varieties; a half-breed, cross-breed, mongrel. **2.** *transf.* and *fig.* Anything derived from heterogeneous sources; in *Philol.* a composite word formed of elements belonging to different languages 1850.

1. Grotesque hybrids, half-bird, half-beast 1851. At the best we [English] are but hybrids 1861. The common Oxlip. . is certainly a h. between the primrose and the cowslip DARWIN.

B. *adj.* **1.** Produced by the interbreeding of two different species or varieties; mongrel, cross-bred, half-bred 1775. **2.** *transf.* and *fig.* Derived from heterogeneous sources; composed of incongruous elements; mongrel 1716.

2. *H. bill*, a bill in Parliament combining the characteristics of a public and private bill, which is referred to a *h. committee*, i.e. a committee nominated partly (as in a public bill) by the House of Commons, and partly (as in a private bill) by the Committee of Selection.

Hence **Hybri·dity,** h. condition.

Hybridism (həi·bridiz'm, hi·b-). 1845. [f. prec. + -ISM.] **1.** The fact or condition of being hybrid; also, the production of hybrids; cross-breeding. **2.** *Philol.* The formation of a word from elements belonging to two different languages 1862. So **Hy·bridist,** a hybridizer.

Hybridize (həi·bridəiz, hi·b-), *v.* 1845. [f. HYBRID + -IZE.] **1.** *trans.* To cause to interbreed and thus to produce hybrids. **2.** *intr.* **a.** To produce a hybrid or hybrids between two distinct species or varieties 1853. **b.** To cross or interbreed 1862. Hence **Hy·bridi:zable** *a.* capable of hybridization. **Hy:bridiza·tion,** the formation of hybrids; cross-breeding. **Hy·bridizer,** one who produces hybrids by cross-breeding.

Hy·bridous, *a.* Now *rare* or *Obs.* 1691. [f. HYBRID *sb.* + -OUS. (The only word of the group in Johnson.)] = HYBRID *a.*

Hydage, obs. f. HIDAGE.

Hydatic (həidæ·tik), *a.* 1710. [– Gr. ὑδατικός watery; see next and -IC.] Pertaining to or of the nature of a hydatid; watery. So †**Hyda·tical** *a.*

Hydatid (həi·dătid, hi·d-), *sb.* (*a.*) Chiefly in *pl.*; formerly in L. form **hydatides** (hidæ·tidīz). 1683. [– mod.L. *hydatis*, *-id-* – Gr. ὑδατίς, -ιδ- drop of water, etc., f. ὕδωρ, ὑδατ- water; see -ID². Cf. Fr. *hydatide* (XVII).] *Path.* **1.** A cyst containing a clear watery fluid, occurring as a morbid formation in the tissues of animal bodies; *esp.* one formed by and containing the larva of a tapeworm (esp. of *Tænia echinococcus*) in its encysted state. **2.** *attrib.* or *adj.* Of or belonging to hydatids; of the nature of a hydatid; containing or affected with hydatids 1807.

Hence **Hydati·diform** (also contr. **Hy·datiform**) *a.* having the form or character of a h.

Hydr-, the usual form of HYDRO- bef. a vowel.

Hydra (həi·dră). ME. [Earliest in OFr. or anglicized forms *ydre*, *idre*, *hydre*; – L. *hydra* – Gr. ὕδρα water-serpent.]

I. 1. *Gr. Myth.* The fabulous many-headed snake of the marshes of Lerna, whose heads grew again as fast as they were cut off; at length killed by Hercules. **2.** *transf.* and *fig.* An evil resembling the Lernæan hydra, *esp.* in the difficulty of its extirpation 1494. **3.** *rhet.* Any terrific serpent or reptile 1546. **4.** A water-snake 1608. **5.** *Astron.* An ancient southern constellation, represented as a water-snake or sea-serpent. Its chief star is Alphard or Cor Hydræ. 1559.

1. Worse Then Fables yet have feign'd, or fear conceiv'd, Gorgons and Hydra's, and Chimera's dire MILT. *P. L.* II. 628. **2.** The h. of revolt lay stunned and prostrate MERIVALE.

II. *Zool.* (pl. usu. **hydræ.**) A genus of Hydrozoa, consisting of freshwater polyps of very simple structure, the body forming a cylindrical tube, with a mouth surrounded by a ring of tentacles with stinging thread-cells. (So named by Linnæus (1756), because cutting it in pieces only multiplies its numbers.) **b.** The sexual bud or medusa of any hydroid hydrozoan; so called from its resemblance to an individual of the genus Hydra 1865. **c.** *Hydra tuba*: a larval or non-sexual form of hydroid in certain Hydrozoa, of a trumpet-like form 1847.

Hydracid (həidræ·sid). 1826. [f. HYDRO- d + ACID.] *Chem.* An acid containing hydrogen, as dist. from an *oxyacid*, or *oxacid*, containing oxygen; now applied esp. to the halogen acids, or simple compounds of hydrogen with chlorine, bromine, iodine, etc.

‖**Hydræmia** (həidrī·miă). Also **hydremia.** 1845. [f. HYDR(O- b + Gr. -αιμία, f. αἷμα blood.] *Path.* A watery condition of the blood. Hence **Hydræ·mic, -emic** *a.* of the nature of or affected with h.

Hydragogue (həi·drăgǫg). 1638. [– late L. *hydragogus* adj. (Cælius Aurelianus) – Gr. ὑδραγωγός conveying water, f. ὑδρ- HYDRO- + ἄγειν lead; ὑδραγωγὰ φάρμακα (Galen) medicines which remove water from the body. Cf. Fr. *hydragogue.*]

A. *adj.* Of medicines: Having the property of removing water or serum, or of causing watery evacuations.

B. *sb.* [sc. *medicine* or *drug.*] 1658.

Hydramide (həi·drămə̆id). 1865. [f. HYDR(O- d + AMIDE.] *Chem.* A tertiary diamide formed by the action of ammonia on certain aldehydes.

Hydramine (həi·drămə̆in). 1877. [f. HYDR(O- d + AMINE.] *Chem.* An oxethene base; an amine containing hydroxyl substitution compounds of ethyl.

‖**Hydrangea** (həidrēⁱ·ndʒiă). 1753. [mod. L. *Hydrangēa* (Linn.), f. Gr. ὑδρ- HYDRO- + ἄγγος vessel (in allusion to the cup-like form of the seed-capsule). Cf. Fr. *hydrangée.*] A genus of shrubs (N.O. *Saxifragaceæ*), with white, blue, or pink flowers in large globular clusters; esp. the Chinese species *H. hortensis*, commonly cultivated in Great Britain.

Hydrant (həi·drănt). 1828. [irreg. f. Gr. ὕδρο, ὑδρ- HYDRO- + -ANT. Of U.S. origin.] An apparatus for drawing water directly from a main, consisting of a pipe with one or more nozzles, or with a spout or the like.

Hydranth (həi·drænþ). 1874. [f. HYDRA II + Gr. ἄνθος flower.] *Zool.* One of the non-sexual zooids occurring in colonial Hydrozoa. Sometimes extended to any hydroid (free or colonial).

‖**Hydrargyrum** (həidrā·ɹdʒirǒm). 1563. [mod.L. *hydrargyrum*, altered from L. *hydrargyrus* – Gr. ὑδράργυρος artificial quick-silver, f. ὑδρ- HYDRO- + ἄργυρος silver.] Quick-silver, mercury. Symbol Hg. Hence **Hydra·rgyral, -ate, -ic, -ous** *adjs.* mercurial. **Hydra·rgyrism,** ‖**Hydrargyro·sis,** mercurial poisoning.

‖**Hydrarthrosis** (həidraɹþrōᵘ·sis). 1861. [f. HYDR(O- b + ARTHROSIS.] *Path.* Dropsy of the joints.

Hydrastine (həidræ·stə̆in). 1876. [f. mod. L. *Hydrastis* + -INE⁵.] **a.** An alkaloid obtained from the root of *Hydrastis canadensis*, a N. American ranunculaceous plant. **b.** A medicine consisting of this alkaloid mixed with berberine and resin.

Hydrate (həi·drĕt), *sb.* 1802. [– Fr. *hydrate*, f. Gr. ὕδωρ, ὑδρ- water; see -ATE⁴.] *Chem.* A compound of water with another compound or an element, e.g. hydrate of chlorine. Formerly, and still by some, applied also to a HYDROXIDE, e.g. KOH, potassium hydrate; NH_4OH, ammonium hydrate. Hence **Hy·drate** *v. trans.* to combine chemically with water; to convert into a h. **Hy·drated** *a.* chemically combined with water or its elements; formed into a h. **Hydra·tion,** the action of hydrating or condition of being hydrated; as *water of h.*, as contrasted with *water of constitution.*

Hydraulic (həidrǭ·lik). 1626. [– L. *hydraulicus* – Gr. ὑδραυλικός, f. ὕδωρ, ὑδρ- water + αὐλός pipe; see -IC. Cf. Fr. *hydraulique* (XV).]

A. *adj.* **1.** Pertaining to water (or other liquid) as conveyed through pipes or channels, esp. by mechanical means; belonging to hydraulics 1661. **2.** Applied to various mechanical contrivances operated by water-power, or in which water is conveyed through pipes; e.g. a *h. crane, engine, machine, motor* 1656. **3.** Applied to substances which harden under water and so become impervious to it; as *h. cement, lime, mortar* 1851.

1. *H. mining*: a method of mining in which the force of a powerful jet of water is used to wear down a bed of auriferous gravel or earth, and to carry the debris to the sluices where the particles of gold are separated. **2.** *H. belt*, an endless woollen band passing over rollers for raising water by absorption and compression. *H. block* (*Ship-building*), a hydraulic lifting-press made to occupy the place of a building-block beneath the keel of a vessel in a repairing-dock, so as to raise the vessel when needed. *H. elevator, lift*, a lift or hoist worked by h. power. *H. main*, in gas-works, a large pipe containing water, and receiving the pipes from the several retorts, which dip below the surface of the water so that the raw gas is partly purified on its way to the condenser. *H. press* = HYDROSTATIC *press*. *H. ram*, an automatic pump in which the kinetic energy of a descending column of water in a pipe is used to raise some of the water to a height above that of its original source; also applied to the lifting piston of a hydrostatic press. *H. valve*, a valve formed by an inverted cup with its edge under water over the upturned open end of a pipe, so as to close the pipe against the passage of air.

B. *sb.* **a.** Short for *h. engine, press*, etc. **b.** Applied hydraulic force. 1729.

Hence †**Hydrau·lical** *a.* = prec. A. **Hydrau·lically** *adv.* by means of h. power or appliances. **Hydrau·licking** *vbl. sb.* h. mining.

Hydraulico-, comb. f. Gr. ὑδραυλικός HYDRAULIC.

‖**Hydrau·licon.** *Pl.* **-a.** 1570. [Gr. ὑδραυλικόν (ὄργανον): see HYDRAULIC.] An ancient musical instrument in which water was used, prob. to regulate the pressure of the air; a water-organ.

Hydraulics (həidrǭ·liks). 1671. [pl. of HYDRAULIC; see -ICS.] The department of science which deals with the conveyance of water or other liquids through pipes, etc., and with the mechanical applications of the force exerted by moving liquids. Often used more widely, as = *hydrokinetics* or *hydrodynamics.*

Hydrazine (həi·drăzə̆in). 1887. [mod. f. HYDR(OGEN + AZO- (for AZOTE) + -INE⁵.] *Chem.* A colourless stable gas, with strong alkaline reaction, N_2H_4. Also extended to a class of compounds in which one or more of the hydrogen atoms in this are replaced by a univalent radical, as *Ethyl h.* $N_2H_3.C_2H_5$.

Hydremia, -ic: see HYDRÆMIA, -IC.

‖**Hydria** (həi·driă, hi·driă). *Pl.* **-æ.** 1850. [L. – Gr. ὑδρία water-pot.] A water-pot; in *Archæol.* a large Greek jar or pitcher for carrying water, with two or three handles.

Hydriad (həi·driæd). 1864. [– Gr. ὑδριάς, -αδ- (νύμφη), f. ὕδωρ, ὑδρ- water.] A water-nymph.

Hydric (həi·drik), *a.* 1854. [f. HYDR(OGEN + -IC.] *Chem.* Of hydrogen, containing hydrogen in chemical combination; as in *h. chloride* = *hydrogen chloride* or *hydrochloric acid.*

Hydride (həi·drə̆id). 1849. [f. HYDR(O- d + -IDE.] *Chem.* †**a.** = HYDRATE in the earlier sense. **b.** Now, a substance formed by the union of hydrogen with an element or a radical.

Hydriform (həi·drifǭɹm), *a.* 1822. [f. HYDRA and -FORM.] Hydra-shaped; having the form of the hydra polyp.

†**Hydriodate** (həidrəi·odĕt). 1823. [f. as next + -ATE⁴.] *Chem.* A hydriodide –1851.

Hydriodic (həidrəi,ǫ·dik), *a.* 1819. [f. HYDR(OGEN + IOD(INE + -IC.] *Chem.* Containing hydrogen and iodine in chemical combination. **H. acid,** the simple combination of hydrogen and iodine, also called *hydrogen iodide* (HI), a colourless very soluble gas, of strongly acid properties and suffocating odour. So **Hydriodide** (həidrəi·odə̆id), a compound of h. acid with an organic radical (or, formerly, with an element).

Hydro- (həidro), bef. a vowel also **hydr-,** = Gr. ὑδρ(ο-, comb. f. ὕδωρ water. Hence:

a. Miscellaneous terms, in which *hydro-* has the sense of 'water', as in *hydrography*, etc.; or is loosely combined, as in *hydrogeology*, etc.

b. In medical and pathological terminology, *hydro-* is prefixed (*a*) to names of parts of the body, to denote that such part is dropsical or affected with an accumulation of serous fluid, as *hydrocardia*, etc.; also, in the combination *hydropneumo-*, to express the presence of water and air, as in *hydropneumopericardium*, etc.; (*b*) to names of diseases or diseased formations, denoting the accompaniment of dropsy or of an accumulation of serous fluid, as *hydrocachexia, -y, -diarrhœa*, etc.

c. Prefixed to names of minerals, *hydro-* denotes a hydrous compound.

d. In mod. chemical terms, the prefix *hydro-* originally meant combination with water. Hence, as this often implies combination with the hydrogen of the water, *hydr(o-* has become the regular combining form of *hydrogen*, like *oxy-* for *oxygen*, etc. Prefixed to the name of a compound substance *hydro-* usually means the addition or substitution of hydrogen in its constitution, e.g. *benzoin* $C_{14}H_{12}O_2$, *hydrobenzoin* $C_{14}H_{14}O_2$, etc.

e. In mod. zoological terminology, *hydro-* is used in the nomenclature relating to members of the class HYDROZOA and their organs or parts.

f. Derivs. of Gr. ἱδρώς 'sweat' have been erron. written *hydro-* instead of *hidro-*, e.g. *hydroadenitis* inflammation of the sweat glands.

Hydrobaro·meter, an instrument for determining the depth of the ocean from the pressure of the super-incumbent water. **Hy·drobranch** [Gr. βράγχια gills], *Zool.* a member of the *Hydrobranchiata*, a division of gastropods containing species which breathe water only; so **Hydrobra·nchiate** *a.*, pertaining to the *Hydrobranchiata.* **Hydrocau·line** [Gr. καυλός stem] *a.*, *Zool.* pertaining to or characteristic of the ‖**Hydrocau·lus** or main stem of the cœnosarc of a hydrozoan. ‖**Hydroce·phalis** [Gr. κεφαλή], the oral and stomachal regions of a hydroid. **Hydroco·ralline** [CORALLINE] *a.*, *Zool.* pertaining to the *Hydrocorallinæ*, an order or sub-order of *Hydroidea*, the coral-making hydroid hydrozoa; *sb.* one of this order. **Hy·drocycle** [CYCLE *sb.*], a velocipede adapted for propulsion on the surface of water. **Hy·drocyst** [Gr. κύστις CYST], *Zool.* one of the tentacles or feelers, resembling immature polypites, attached to the cœnosarc in certain Hydrozoa, as in the family *Physophoridæ*; hence **Hydrocy·stic** *a.* **Hydrœ·cial** *a.*, pertaining to the ‖**Hydrœ·cium** [Gr. οἰκίον, f. οἶκος], a sac into which the cœnosarc can be retracted in certain Hydrozoa, as the *Calycophoridæ.* **Hydro-extractor,** a centrifugal machine for drying clothes, etc. **Hydroferricya·nic, -ferridcyanic** *a.*, *Chem.* in *h. acid* = hydrogen ferricyanide, $H_6Fe_2Cy_{12}$; hence **Hydroferri(d)cy·anate,** a salt of this acid. **Hydroferrocya·nic** *a.*, *Chem.* in *h. acid* = hydrogen ferrocyanide, H_4FeCy_6; hence **Hydroferrocy·anate,** a salt of this acid. **Hydrogalva·nic** [GALVANIC] *a.*, pertaining to the production of galvanic electricity by means of liquids. †**Hydro·gnosy** [Gr. -γνωσια], a history and description of the waters of the earth. **Hydro,io·dic** = HYDRIODIC. **Hydroma·gnesite,** *Min.* hydrous carbonate of magnesium, found in white silky crystals or earthy crusts. **Hydromedu·san** [MEDUSA] *a.*, belonging or related to the *Hydromedusæ*, now a subclass of Hydrozoa (called also *Craspedota*), formerly a synonym of Hydrozoa; *sb.* a member of this subclass. **Hydrome·tallurgy** [METALLURGY], 'the act or process of assaying or reducing ores in the wet way, or by means of liquid re-agents' (Webster). **Hydrome·teor,** an atmospheric phenomenon which depends on the vapour of water, as rain, hail, and snow; hence **Hy:drometeorolo·gical** *a.*, pertaining to **Hy:drometeoro·logy,** that part of meteorology which deals with atmospheric phenomena depending on the vapour of water. **Hydromi·ca,** *Min.* a variety of potash mica containing more water than ordinary muscovite; hence **Hydromica·ceous** *a.* **Hydroperitonæ·um,** *Path.* same as ASCITES. **Hy·drophid** [Gr. ὄφις serpent], *Zool.* a venomous sea-snake of the genus *Hydrophis* or family *Hydrophidæ*, found in the Indian Ocean. **Hy·drophyll,** *Bot.* Lindley's name for plants of N.O. *Hydrophyllaceæ*, of which the typical genus is *Hydrophyllum*, the Waterleaf of N. America. **Hydrophyllia·ceous** *a.*, having the characters of the ‖**Hydrophy·llium** [Gr. φύλλιον] = BRACT 2. **Hy·dropult** [-*pult* in CATAPULT], a force-pump worked by hand; a garden-pump. ‖**Hydro·rachis, -o·rrhachis,** *Path.* extensive serous accumulation within the spinal canal. ‖**Hydrorhi·za**

[Gr. ῥίζα root], the root-stock or rooting fibres by which a colony of Hydrozoa is attached to some foreign object; hence **Hydrorhi·zal** *a.* **Hy·dro-spire** [Gr. σπεῖρα coil, SPIRE], one of the system of lamellar tubes lying between and below the ambulacra in blastoids, supposed to have been respiratory in function. **Hydrota·lcite** [TALC], *Min.* a hydrous oxide of aluminium and magnesium, a fibrous white mineral of pearly lustre and greasy feel. **Hydrotellu·ric** *a., Chem.* formed by hydrogen and tellurium in chemical combination; *h. acid*, telluretted hydrogen, H_2Te, an offensive gas; its salts are **Hydrote·llurates.** ‖**Hydrothe·ca** [L. *theca*, Gr. θήκη receptacle], *Zool.* one of the perisarcal cups or calycles in which the polypites in certain Hydrozoa (as the *Sertularidæ*) are lodged; hence **Hydrothe·cal** *a.*

Hy:dro-ae·roplane. 1914. [See HYDRO-. Cf. Fr. *hydroaéroplane.*] An aeroplane adapted for rising from and landing on water.

†**Hydrobro·mate.** 1836. [f. as next + -ATE[4].] *Chem.* A bromide, viewed as a salt of hydrobromic acid; also, a hydrobromide –1876.

Hydrobromic (həidroˌbrōᵘ·mik), *a.* 1836. [f. HYDRO- d + BROMIC.] *Chem.* Containing hydrogen and bromine in combination.

H. acid, also called *hydrogen bromide* (HBr), a colourless gas with a pungent odour and strongly acid taste, fuming in the atmosphere and very soluble in water. So **Hydrobro·mide,** a compound of h. acid with an organic radical.

Hydrocarbon (həidroˌkā·ɹbǫ̆n). 1826. [f. as prec. + CARBON.] *Chem.* A chemical compound of hydrogen and carbon. (These compounds, the *paraffins, olefines, acetylenes, benzenes*, etc., are very numerous, and constitute the subject-matter of organic chemistry.) **b.** *attrib.*, as *h. radical, series*, etc. **H. gas:** any gaseous h. Hence **Hy:drocarbona·ceous** *a.* pertaining to, of the nature of, or containing a h. **Hydrocarbo·nic, Hydroca·rbonous** *adjs.* of the nature of a h.

Hydrocarbonate (-kā·ɹbŏnĕt). 1800. [f. HYDRO- d + CARBONATE.] *Chem.* A hydrocarbon; †formerly, carburetted hydrogen (CH_4).

†**Hydroca·rburet.** 1815. [f. HYDRO- d + CARBURET.] *Chem.* A hydrocarbon; *spec.* carburetted hydrogen gas –1850.

Hydrocele (həi·drosīl). 1597. [– Fr. *hydrocèle* (Paré, XVI) or L. *hydrocele* – Gr. ὑδροκήλη (Galen), f. ὑδρο- HYDRO- + κήλη tumour.] *Path.* A tumour with a collection of serous fluid; *spec.* a tumour of this kind in the cavity of the *tunica vaginalis* of the testis; dropsy of the testicle or of the scrotum. Hence **-ce·lous** *a.*

‖**Hydrocephalus** (həidrose·fălŏs). 1670. [Medical L. – Gr. ὑδροκέφαλον (Galen) water in the head, f. ὑδρο- HYDRO- b + κεφαλή head.] *Path.* An accumulation of serous fluid in the cavity of the cranium, resulting in gradual expansion of the skull, and finally inducing general weakness, with mental failure; water on the brain.

Children are more liable to hydrocephali than adults CHAMBERS. Hence **Hydrocepha·lic** *a.* pertaining to, or characteristic of, h.; affected with h. **Hydroce·phaloid** *a.*, resembling h., as in *hydrocephaloid disease*, a condition of coma incident to young children and resulting apparently from cerebral anæmia. **Hydroce·phalous** *a.* affected with h. var. **Hydroce·phaly.**

†**Hydrochlo·rate.** 1819. [f. as next + -ate[4].] *Chem.* An old name for a chloride; also for a hydrochloride –1880.

Hydrochloric (həidroˌklōᵊ·rik), *a.* 1817. [f. HYDRO- d + CHLORIC.] *Chem.* Containing hydrogen and chlorine in chemical combination.

H. acid, called also *hydrogen chloride* (HCl), a colourless gas of strongly acid taste and pungent odour, extremely soluble in water. (Earlier names were *muriatic acid, spirit of salt, chlorhydric acid.*)

Hydrochloride (həidroˌklōᵊ·rəid). 1826. [f. HYDRO- d + CHLORIDE.] *Chem.* A compound of hydrochloric acid with an organic radical (formerly, also, with an element).

†**Hydrocyanate** (həidroˌsəi·ănĕt). 1818. [f. as next + -ATE.[4]] *Chem.* An old name for a cyanide, considered as a salt of hydrocyanic acid –1854.

Hydrocyanic (həidroˌsəiˌæ·nik), *a.* 1818. [f. HYDRO- d + CYANIC.] *Chem.* Containing hydrogen and cyanogen in chemical combination.

H. acid, or *hydrogen cyanide* (HCN or HCy), the combination of hydrogen with cyanogen (CN or Cy), an extremely poisonous volatile liquid with an odour like that of bitter almonds, the solution in water being known as *prussic acid.*

Hydrodynamic, -al (həi:droˌdəi-, -dinæ·-mik, -ăl), *a.* 1828. [– mod.L. *hydrodynamicus*; see next and DYNAMIC. See -ICAL.] Pertaining to the forces acted upon or exerted by water or other liquids; belonging to HYDRODYNAMICS.

Hydrodynamics (həi:droˌdəi-, -dinæ·-miks). 1779. [– mod.L. *hydrodynamica* (Daniel Bernoulli, 1738); see HYDRO- a and DYNAMICS.] The branch of Physics which treats of the forces acting upon or exerted by liquids. Orig. = HYDROKINETICS; now usually including Hydrokinetics and Hydrostatics.

Hydrodynamometer (-dəinămǫ·mĭtəɹ). 1890. [f. HYDRO- a + DYNAMOMETER.] An instrument for measuring the force exerted by a liquid in motion.

Hydro-ele·ctric, *a.* 1832. [f. HYDRO- a + ELECTRIC.] †**1.** Of or pertaining to hydro-electricity; galvanic –1855. **2.** Effecting the development of electricity by the friction of water or steam 1863. **3.** Producing electricity by utilizing the motive power of water 1905. So **Hy:dro-electricity.**

†**Hydroflu·ate.** 1841. [f. HYDRO- d + FLUATE.] *Chem.* An old name for a fluoride viewed as a salt of hydrofluoric acid; also for a hydrofluoride.

Hydrofluoric (həidrofluˌǫ·rik), *a.* 1822. [f. HYDRO- d + FLUORIC.] *Chem.* Containing hydrogen and fluorine in chemical combination.

H. acid, or *hydrogen fluoride* (HF), a colourless gas, fuming in moist air and rapidly absorbed by water.

Hydrofluosilicic (həi:droˌflūˌosili·sik), *a.* 1842. [f. HYDRO- d + FLUO- + SILICIC.] *Chem.* Containing hydrogen, fluorine, and silicon in chemical combination.

H. acid (H_2SiF_6), or *hydrogen silicofluoride*, a fuming liquid which gradually attacks glass, esp. on heating. So **Hydrofluosi·licate,** a salt of h. acid; a silico-fluoride.

Hydrogen (həi·drŏdʒĕn). Also †**hydrogene.** 1791. [– Fr. *hydrogène* (G. de Morveau, 1787), f. Gr. ὕδωρ, ὑδρ- water; see -GEN.] *Chem.* **1.** One of the elements; a colourless, invisible, odourless gas; it burns with a pale-blue flame, whence its former name of *inflammable air.* It is the lightest substance known, having a specific gravity of about one-fourteenth of that of air. Symbol H; atomic weight 1.

It occurs free in nature in small quantities in certain volcanic gases, and is an essential constituent of all animal and vegetable matter. On combustion in oxygen (or air) it yields water (H_2O). It is a constituent of all acids, in which it can be replaced by bases to form salts.

2. *attrib.* **a.** *h. lamp*, etc.; **h. acid** = HYDRACID; †**h. air, gas,** old names for h. **b.** In systematic names of chemical compounds of h. with an element or radical = 'of hydrogen'; as *h. bromide* HBr; *h. dioxide* H_2O_2 (oxygenated water); *h. sulphide* H_2S (also sulphuretted h.); etc. On the analogy of h. chloride, etc., acids are often named as salts of h., e.g. *h. chlorate* $HClO_3$ (= chloric acid), etc.

Hydrogenate (həi·drodʒĕneⁱt, həidrǫ·dʒĕneⁱt), *v.* 1809. [f. prec. + -ATE[3].] *Chem.* To charge, or cause to combine, with hydrogen; to hydrogenize. Hence **Hydrogena·tion.**

Hydrogenium (həidroˌdʒī·niŏm). 1868. [f. as prec. + -IUM.] *Chem.* Hydrogen regarded as a metal.

Hydrogenize (həi·drodʒĕnəi:z), *v.* 1802. [f. as prec. + -IZE.] *Chem.* To charge, or combine with hydrogen.

Hydrogenous (həidrǫ·dʒĕnəs), *a.* 1791. [f. HYDROGEN + -OUS.] *Chem.* Of, pertaining to, or consisting of hydrogen.

Hydrogeology (həi:droˌdʒiˌǫ·lŏdʒi). 1824. [f. HYDRO- a + GEOLOGY.] That part of geology which treats of the relations of water on or below the earth's surface. Hence **Hydrogeolo·gical** *a.* relating to this.

Hydrographer (həidrǫ·grăfəɹ). 1559. [f. HYDRO- + -GRAPHER, after GEOGRAPHER.] One skilled in hydrography; *spec.* one who makes hydrographic surveys and constructs charts of the sea, its currents, etc. So **Hydrogra·phic, -al** *a.* pertaining or relating to hydrography. **Hydrogra·phically** *adv. rare.*

Hydrography (həidrǫ·grăfi). 1559. [f. as prec. + -GRAPHY.] **1.** The science which has for its object the description of the waters of the earth's surface, comprising the study and mapping of their forms and physical features, of the contour of the sea-bottom, shallows, etc., and of winds, tides, currents, and the like. (In earlier use, including the principles of Navigation.) Also, a treatise on this science. **2.** The subject-matter of this science 1852. †**3.** [Gr. γραφή, -γραφία.] Writing with water. Also *fig.* –1659.

3. *fig.* In Grief's Hydrography CLEVELAND.

†**Hydro·guret.** 1819. [f. HYDROGEN + -URET (after *sulphuret*).] *Chem.* A hydruret or hydride. Hence †**Hydro·guretted** *a.* chemically combined with hydrogen.

Hydroid (həi·droid). 1864. [f. HYDRA II + -OID.]

A. *adj. Zool.* Resembling or allied to the genus *Hydra* of Hydrozoa; belonging to the order or subclass *Hydroidea*, of which *Hydra* is the typical genus.

B. *sb. Zool.* **a.** One of the *Hydroidea.* **b.** One of the two forms of zooids occurring in Hydrozoa, resembling *Hydra* in structure, but typically asexual; opp. to *Medusa.* 1865. So **Hydroi·dean** = B. a.

Hydrokinetic, -al (-kəine·tik, -ăl). *a.* 1873. [f. HYDRO- a + KINETIC + -AL[1]. See -ICAL.] Relating to the motion of liquids. So **Hydrokine·tics,** the kinetics of liquids; that branch of hydrodynamics which deals with the motion of liquids.

Hydrology (həidrǫ·lŏdʒi). 1762. [– mod.L. *hydrologia*, f. *hydro-* HYDRO- a; see -LOGY. Cf. Fr. *hydrologie* (XVIII).] The science which treats of water, its properties and laws, its distribution over the earth's surface, etc. Hence **Hydrolo·gic, -al** *a.* pertaining or relating to h. **Hydro·logist,** one skilled in h.

Hydrolysis (həidrǫ·lisis). 1880. [f. HYDRO- + -LYSIS.] A decomposition of water in which the two constituents (H and OH) are separated and fixed in distinct compounds. So **Hydroly·tic** *a.* of or pertaining to h.

Hydromancy (həi·dromænsi). ME. [– (O)Fr. *hydromancie* or late L. *hydromantia*, f. Gr. ὑδρο- HYDRO- + *-mantia* -MANCY.] Divination by means of water, or the pretended appearance of spirits therein.

Hydromania (həidromēⁱ·niă). 1793. [f. HYDRO- + MANIA.] A mania for water; *Path.* an excessive craving for liquids.

Hydromantic (həidromæ·ntik). 1590. [– med.L. *hydromanticus*, f. late L. *hydromantia* HYDROMANCY + *-icus* -IC; see -MANTIC, -MANCY.]

A. *adj.* Of or pertaining to hydromancy 1651.

†**B.** *sb.* **1.** = HYDROMANCY 1590. **2.** One skilled in hydromancy 1638.

Hydromechanics (həi:droˌmĭkæ·niks). 1851. [f. HYDRO- a + MECHANICS.] The mechanics of liquids; hydrodynamics (in its wider sense); esp. in relation to its application to mechanical contrivances.

Hydromel (həi·dromel). ME. [– L. *hydromeli*, (-*mel*) – Gr. ὑδρόμελι, f. ὑδρο- HYDRO- a + μέλι honey.] A liquor consisting of honey and water, which when fermented is called *vinous h.* or *mead.*

Hydrometer (həidrǫ·mĭtəɹ). 1675. [f. HYDRO- a + -METER. Fr. *hydromètre* has commonly the sense 'rain-gauge'.] **1.** An instrument for determining the specific gravity of liquids, or, in some forms, of either liquids or solids.

The common type consists of a graduated stem having a hollow bulb and a weight at its lower end, so as to float with the stem upright in a liquid, the specific gravity of which is indicated by the depth to which the stem is immersed.

2. An instrument used to determine the velocity or force of a current; a current-gauge 1727.

Hydrometry (həidrǫ·mĕtri). 1727. [– mod.L. *hydrometria*, f. *hydro-* HYDRO- + *-metria* -METRY.] The determination of specific gravity by means of the hydrometer; hence, that part of hydrostatics which deals with this. (In early use app. co-extensive with 'hydrodynamics' in the mod. sense.) So **Hydrome·tric, -al** *a.* of or pertaining to h.; relating to the measurement of the velocity and force of currents.

‖**Hydronephrosis** (həi:droˌnĭfrōᵘ·sis). 1847. [mod.L., f. HYDRO- + Gr. νεφρός kidney + -OSIS.] *Path.* A distended condition of the ureter, the pelvis, and the renal calices, caused by an obstruction of the outflow of urine; dropsy of the kidney. So **Hydronephro·tic** *a.* relating to, characteristic of, or affected with h.

Hy·dropath. 1842. [f. HYDROPATHY, after *allopath*, etc.; cf. G. *hydropath*, Fr. *hydropathe.*] = HYDROPATHIST.

Hydropathy (həidrǫ·păþi). 1843. [f. HYDRO- after *allopathy, homœopathy*; see -PATHY. Cf. G. *hydropathie.*] A kind of medical treatment, consisting in the external and internal application of water; the water-cure. Hence **Hydropa·thic, -al** *a.* of, pertaining to, or of the nature of h.; practising h. **Hydro·pathist,** one who practises or advocates h. **Hydro·pathize** *v* to practise h.

Hydrophane (həi·drŏfeⁱn). 1784. [f. Gr. ὑδρο- HYDRO- + -φανής apparent, φανός bright, clear, f. φαίνειν show.] *Min.* A variety of opaque or partly translucent opal which absorbs water upon immersion and becomes transparent. Hence **Hydro·phanous** *a.* having the property of becoming transparent by immersion in water.

Hydrophobe (həi·drŏfoᵘb). [– Fr. *hydrophobe* – L. *hydrophobus* (Pliny), Gr. ὑδροφόβος having a horror of water; see HYDRO- a, -PHOBE.] One affected with hydrophobia.

Hydrophobia (həidrŏfōᵘ·biă). Also 7–8 **hydrophoby** (həidrǫ·fŏbi). 1547. [– late L. *hydrophobia* (Cælius Aurelianus) – Gr. ὑδροφοβία horror of water, f. ὑδροφόβος; see prec., -PHOBIA.] **1.** *Path.* A symptom of rabies or canine madness when transmitted to man, consisting in an aversion to liquids, and difficulty in swallowing them; hence, rabies, esp. in human beings. **2.** In etym. sense: Horror of water; *fig.* Madness 1759.

2. I am mortally sick at sea, and regard with..a kind of h. the great gulf that lies between us HUME. Hence **Hydropho·bial, Hydropho·bic, Hydro·phobous** *adjs.* of or pertaining to h.; affected with h. **Hydro·phobist,** one who treats cases of h.

Hydrophoran (həidrǫ·fŏrăn). [f. mod.L. *Hydrophora* (f. HYDRA + Gr. -φόρος bearing) + -AN.] **a.** *adj.* Belonging to the *Hydrophora,* one of the three subclasses of Hydrozoa, comprising *Hydra* and compound forms bearing zooids similar to *Hydra*. **b.** *sb.* One of the *Hydrophora.* So **Hydro·phorous** *a.*

Hydrophore (həi·drofōᵊɹ). 1842. [– Gr. ὑδροφόρος water-carrying; see HYDRO-, -PHORE.] An instrument for procuring specimens of water from any desired depth, in a river, lake, or ocean.

Hydrophyte (həi·drŏfəit). 1832. [f. HYDRO- a + -PHYTE.] *Bot.* An aquatic plant; applied esp. to the *Algæ*. Hence **Hydrophyto·graphy,** the description of aquatic plants. **Hydrophyto·logy,** the branch of botany which deals with aquatic plants.

‖**Hydrophyton** (həidrǫ·fitǫn). 1885. [Latinized form of prec. (Gr. φυτόν plant).] *Zool.* The branched plant-like structure supporting the zooids in certain colonial Hydrozoa. Hence **Hydro·phytous** *a.* having the character of a h.

Hydropic (həidrǫ·pik). [ME. *ydropike* – OFr. *ydropique, -ike* – L. *hydropicus* – Gr. ὑδρωπικός, f. ὕδρωψ HYDROPS; see -IC. In XVI conformed to the L., with Fr. *hydropique.*]

A. *adj.* **1.** = DROPSICAL 1, 2. 1483. †**2.** Having an insatiable thirst, like a dropsical person; hence *fig.* –1763. **3.** Charged with water; swollen 1651. †**4.** Curing dropsy –1710.

3. It..swels like an hydropick cloud JER. TAYLOR.

B. *sb.* **1.** A dropsical person. Now *rare.* 1549. **2.** A medicine for the dropsy 1694.

So **Hydro·pical** *a.* (now *rare*) = prec. A. 1–3; of thirst, unquenchable. **Hydro·pically** *adv.* with or as with dropsy.

Hydroplane (həi·droplēⁱn). 1907. [f. HYDRO- + PLANE *sb.*³] **1.** A plane for lifting a boat above the surface of the water; a boat designed to skim upon the surface. **2.** The bow-rudder of a submarine. 1911. **3.** = HYDRO-AEROPLANE. 1914.

Hydro-pneumatic (həi:droˌniumæ·tik), *a.* (*sb.*) 1794. [f. HYDRO- a + PNEUMATIC.] Pertaining to water and air or gas; applied to apparatus involving the combined action of water and air.

‖**Hydrops** (həi·drǫps). Now only *Path.* ME. (**ydrope**) [L. – Gr. ὕδρωψ dropsy, f. ὕδωρ, ὑδρ- water.] Dropsy.

Hydropsy (həi·drǫpsi). [ME. *id-, ydropesie* – OFr. *idropesie* – med.L. (*h*)*ydropisia*, for L. *hydropisis* – Gr. *ὑδρώπισις, repl. ὕδρωψ HYDROPS. See DROPSY.] Dropsy. Hence †**Hydro·psic, -ical** *adjs.* hydropic.

Hydroptic (həidrǫ·ptik), *a. Obs.* exc. *arch.* 1631. [erron. f. HYDROPSY, after *epilepsy, epileptic.*] = HYDROPIC. So †**Hydro·ptical** *a.*

Hydroquinone (həidroˌkwəi·noᵘn). Also **-chinon(e, -kinone.** 1865. [f. HYDRO(GEN + QUINONE.] *Chem.* A diatomic phenol, $C_6H_4(OH)_2$, prepared from quinone, $C_6H_4O_2$, by reduction with sulphurous acid, crystallizing from water in colourless rhombic prisms. Now used as a developer in photography.

Hydroscope (həi·droˌskoᵘp). 1678. [– Gr. ὑδροσκόπος (see HYDRO- a, -SCOPE) water-seeker, well-sinker, and ὑδροσκόπιον water-clock (Synezius). In sense 3 f. HYDRO- a + -SCOPE.] †**1.** A hygroscope. **2.** A kind of water-clock; a cylindrical graduated tube, filled with water, which measured time by trickling through an aperture in the bottom. *Hist.* 1727. **3.** A telescope for use under water 1909.

Hydrosome (həi·drosōᵘm). 1861. [– mod.L. *hydrosoma* (also used), f. HYDRA + Gr. σῶμα body.] *Zool.* The entire body of any hydrozoan, esp. that of a colonial hydrozoan consisting of a number of zooids connected by a cœnosarc. Hence **Hydroso·mal, Hydroso·matous** *adjs.* of or belonging to a h.

Hydrosphere (həi·drosfīᵊɹ). 1887. [f. HYDRO- a + SPHERE, after *atmosphere.*] The waters of the earth's surface collectively.

Hydrostat (həi·drostæt). 1858. [f. HYDRO- a + -STAT.] **1.** An apparatus for preventing the explosion of steam-boilers. **2.** An electrical device for detecting the presence of water 1871.

Hydrostatic (həidroˌstæ·tik); *a.* 1671. [ult. f. Gr. ὑδρο- HYDRO- a + στατικός making to stand, balancing, weighing; but prob. proximately f. Gr. ὑδροστάτης hydrostatic balance, in med.Gr. a fire-engine, which prob. originated mod.L. *hydrostaticus*, Fr. *hydrostatique.*] **1.** Relating to the equilibrium of liquids, and the pressure exerted by liquids at rest; belonging to hydrostatics. **2.** Used to denominate various instruments and appliances involving the pressure of water or other liquid as a source of power or otherwise 1681. **3.** Used in reference to certain aquatic animals having air-bladders which enable them to float upon the surface of the water 1840.

1. *H. paradox*: the principle (depending on the law of uniform pressure of liquids) that any quantity of a perfect liquid, however small, may be made to balance any quantity (or any weight), however great. **2.** *H. balance*: a balance for ascertaining the specific gravity of substances by weighing them in water. *H. bed*: a water-bed. *H. bellows*: a contrivance for illustrating the law of uniform distribution of pressure in liquids; it consists of a bellows-like chamber, into which water, being introduced by a narrow vertical tube, supports a weight placed on the upper board of the bellows. *H. press*: a machine in which the pressure of a body of water is transmitted from a cylinder of small sectional area to one of greater, and thus multiplied in accordance with the law of h. pressure. Also called *hydraulic press* or *Bramah's press.*

So **Hydrosta·tical** *a.* dealing with or referring to hydrostatics; also = prec. **Hydrosta·tically** *adv.* in accordance with, or by means of hydrostatics. **Hy:drostati·cian,** one versed in hydrostatics.

Hydrostatics (həidroˌstæ·tiks). 1660. [In form pl. of HYDROSTATIC; cf. STATICS, and see -IC 2. In Fr. *hydrostatique* (1695).] That department of Physics which treats of the pressure and equilibrium of liquids at rest; the statics of liquids; a branch of *Hydrodynamics* in the wide sense.

†**Hydrosulphate** (həidrosɒ·lfĕt). 1828. [f. HYDRO(GEN + SULPHATE.] *Chem.* Now called a *hydrosulphide* or *sulphydrate* –1872.

Hydrosulphide (həidrosɒ·lfəid). 1849. [f. HYDRO(GEN + SULPHIDE.] *Chem.* A compound obtained by the union of hydrogen sulphide (sulphuretted hydrogen) with a metal or radical; a sulphydrate.

†**Hydrosulphuret** (-sɒ·lfiuret). 1800. [f. HYDRO(GEN + SULPHURET.] *Chem.* An old name for a hydrosulphide –1826. So **Hydrosu·lphuretted** *a.* charged or combined with sulphuretted hydrogen.

†**Hydrosulphuric** (-sɒlfiūᵊ·rik), *a.* 1823. [f. HYDRO(GEN + SULPHURIC.] *Chem.* Containing or consisting of hydrogen and sulphur only; as *h. acid*, an old name for hydrogen sulphide (H_2S), also called sulphydric acid –1872.

†**Hydrosulphurous** (-sɒ·lfiurəs), *a.* 1855. [f. as prec. + SULPHUROUS.] In *h. acid,* a name given first to dithionic acid; afterwards to hydrogen hyposulphite, $H_2S_2O_4$.

Hydrotherapeutic (həi:droˌþerăpiū·tik), *a.* 1885. [f. HYDRO- b + THERAPEUTIC.] Hydropathic. So **Hy:drotherapeu·tics** *pl.* [see -ICS], that part of medicine which treats of the therapeutical application of water; water-cure.

Hydrotherapy (həidroˌþe·răpi). 1876. [f. HYDRO- b + THERAPY.] Hydrotherapeutics.

Hydrothermal (həidroþə̄·ɹmăl), *a.* 1849. [f. Gr. ὑδρο- + θερμός; see THERMAL.] *Geol.* Of or relating to heated water; *spec.* applied to its action in bringing about changes in the earth's crust.

‖**Hydrothorax** (həidroþōᵊ·ræks). 1793. [Medical L., f. HYDRO- b + THORAX.] *Path.* A disease characterized by an effusion of serous fluid into one or both of the pleural cavities; dropsy of the chest.

Hydrotic (həidrǫ·tik). 1671. [erron. for HIDROTIC, through confusion with derivs. of ὑδρο- HYDRO-.] **a.** *adj.* Sudorific; also sometimes, Causing a discharge of water. **b.** *sb.* A sudorific medicine, or in wider sense, a hydragogue. So **Hydro·tical** *a.* 1616, **-ly** *adv.*

Hydrotropic (həidroˌtrǫ·pik), *a.* [f. Gr. ὑδρο- + -τροπος turning + -IC. Cf. HELIOTROPIC.] *Bot.* Turning towards or under the influence of water. So **Hydro·tropism,** the property, exhibited esp. by roots, of bending or turning under the influence of moisture.

Hydrous (həi·drəs), *a.* 1826. [f. Gr. ὕδωρ, ὑδρο- water + -OUS.] *Chem.* and *Min.* Containing water, as an additional chemical or mineral constituent.

Hydroxide (həidrǫ·ksəid). 1851. [f. HYDRO- d + OXIDE.] *Chem.* A compound of an element or radical with oxygen and hydrogen, not with water; by some restricted to compounds whose reactions indicate the presence of the group hydroxyl (OH). (Formerly used interchangeably with HYDRATE.)

Hydro·xy-. *Chem.* Bef. a vowel **hydrox-.** 1872. [f. HYDRO(GEN + OXY(GEN.] An element signifying the addition or substitution of oxygen and hydrogen or the radical hydroxyl.

Hydroxyl (həidrǫ·ksil). 1866. [f. prec. + -YL.] *Chem.* The monad radical HO or OH, consisting of an atom of hydrogen in combination with an atom of oxygen, which is a constituent of many chemical compounds. Also *attrib.* **b.** in *Comb.* indicating the addition or substitution of the group OH in the compound, as *h.-benzol*, etc. 1872.

Hydroxylamine (həidrǫ·ksilăməin). 1869. [f. prec. + AMINE.] *Chem.* A basic substance, NH_2OH, allied to ammonia, which combines with acids to form a well-defined series of salts.

‖**Hydrozoa** (həidrŏzōᵘ·ă), *sb. pl.* 1843. [mod.L., f. HYDRO- e, as comb. f. HYDRA II

+ Gr. ζῷον. See -A 4.] *Zool.* A class of Cœlenterate animals, chiefly marine. Familiar examples are the freshwater Hydra, and the various organisms called Acalephs, Medusæ, or Jelly-fishes. Also in sing. **Hydrozo·on,** one of these. Hence **Hydrozo·al, -an, -ic** *adjs.* of or belonging to this class. **Hydrozo·an** *sb.* an animal of this class.

†**Hydruret** (həi·druret). 1812. [f. HYDR(O-GEN + -URET (taken from *sulphuret*).] *Chem.* A compound of hydrogen with a metal or organic radical; a hydride. Hence **Hy·druretted** *a.* combined with hydrogen.

‖**Hydrus** (həi·drŏs). 1667. [L. – Gr. ὕδρος water-snake; cf. HYDRA.] **1.** A fabulous sea-serpent. **b.** A former name for the genus *Hydrophis* of venomous sea-snakes 1838. **2.** *Astron.* One of the southern constellations 1796.

1. Cerastes hornd, H., and Ellops drear MILT. *P.L.* X. 525.

Hye, obs. f. HIE.

Hyemal, etc., var. of HIEMAL, etc.

Hyena, hyæna (həi,ī·nă). ME. [Earliest (XIV) as *hyane, hyene* – OFr. *hyene*; later – L. *hyæna* – Gr. ὕαινα, prop. fem. of ὗς SWINE, with suffix as in λέαινα lioness, etc.] **1.** A carnivorous quadruped of a family *Hyænidæ* allied to the Dog-tribe, though in the skull approaching the *Felidæ* or Cat-kind; having powerful jaws, neck, and shoulders, but poor hind quarters.

There are three extant species, the Striped H. (*Hyæna striata*), inhabiting northern Africa and much of Asia; the Brown H. (*H. brunnea*), and Spotted H. or Tiger-wolf (*H. crocuta*), natives of southern Africa. The extinct Cave H. (*H. spelæa*) inhabited many parts of the Old World. The name *Laughing H.*, orig. applied to the Striped H., is considered by some to be more appropriate to the Spotted H.

2. *transf.* Applied to a cruel, treacherous, and rapacious person 1671. **3.** A name of the Thylacine or Tasmanian Tiger 1832. †**4.** A fabulous stone said to be taken from the eye of the hyena; also called *hyæneum* –1855. **5.** *attrib.*, as *h. foeman, laughter* 1818.

2. Out, out, Hyæna MILT. *Sams.* 748.

Hye·na-dog. 1837. **1.** A S. African quadruped (*Lycaon pictus*), superficially resembling the hyenas. †**2.** The AARD-WOLF of S. Africa 1838.

Hyetal (həi·ĕtăl), *a. rare.* 1864. [f. Gr. ὑετός rain + -AL¹.] Of or belonging to rain.

Hyeto- (həi,ĕto), comb. f. Gr. ὑετός rain, as in:

Hy·etograph, a chart showing the rainfall (*Syd. Soc. Lex.*); hence **Hyetogra·phic, -al** *a.*; **Hyetogra·phically** *adv.*; **Hyeto·graphy,** the branch of meteorology that deals with the distribution and mapping of the rainfall. **Hyetolo·gical** *a.*, of or pertaining to **Hyeto·logy,** the branch of meteorology that treats of rain. **Hyeto·meter,** a rain-gauge 1730. **Hyetome·trograph,** an automatic instrument for registering the amount of rainfall during successive periods.

‖**Hygeia** (həidʒī·ă). 1737. [– Gr. ὑγεία, late form of ὑγίεια health, 'Υγίεια the goddess of health, f. ὑγιής sound, healthy. A rare variant *Hygiea* represents Gr. ὑγίεια.] **1.** In *Gr. Myth.* the goddess of health, daughter of Æsculapius; health personified; *transf.* a system of sanitation or medical practice. **2.** *Astron.* The 10th asteroid. Hence **Hygei·an** *a.* pertaining to Hygeia, or to health; healthy; sanitary. **Hy·geist,** one versed in hygiene.

Hygiene (həi·dʒīn, həi·dʒi,īn). 1796. [– Fr. *hygiène* – mod.L. *hygieina* – Gr. ὑγιεινή (sc. τέχνη art), subst. use of fem. of ὑγιεινός healthful, f. ὑγιής healthful.] Knowledge or practice as relating to the maintenance of health; a system of principles or rules for preserving or promoting health; sanitary science. Hence **Hygie·nic** *a.* belonging or relating to h.; sanitary. **Hygie·nically** *adv.* **Hygie·nics** *pl.* [see -ICS] = HYGIENE. **Hy·gienist,** one versed in h.

Hygiology (həidʒi,ǫ·lŏdʒi). 1855. [f. Gr. ὑγεία (see HYGEIA) + -LOGY.] The science of health; hygiene.

Hygrine (həi·grəin). 1865. [f. Gr. ὑγρός moist + -INE⁵.] *Chem.* An alkaloid obtained from coca-leaves in the form of a thick pale yellow oil of a burning taste.

Hygro- (həi·gro), bef. a vowel **hygr-,** repr. Gr. ὑγρο-, ὑγρ-, comb. f. ὑγρός wet, moist, fluid.

Hy·grodeik [Gr. δεικνύναι], a form of hygrometer consisting of a wet-bulb and a dry-bulb thermometer together with a scale on which the degree of humidity is shown by an index whose position depends on the height of the mercurial column in each. **Hy·grograph** [Gr. -γραφος], an instrument for registering automatically the variations in the humidity of the air. **Hygro·phanous** [Gr. ὑγροφανής] *a.*, *Bot.* of moist appearance; also, appearing translucent when moist and opaque when dry (*Syd. Soc. Lex.*). **Hygro·philous** [Gr. φίλος] *a.*, *Bot.* affecting moist places. **Hy·groplasm** [Gr. πλάσμα a thing moulded], a term for the fluid part of protoplasm. †**Hygrosta·tics,** 'the art of finding the specific weights of moist bodies' (Bailey).

Hygrology (həigrǫ·lŏdʒi). 1790. [f. HYGRO- + -LOGY.] That department of physics which relates to the humidity of the atmosphere or other bodies. ¶Erron. explained in mod. Dicts.

Hygrometer (həigrǫ·mĭtəɹ). 1670. [f. HYGRO- + -METER; prob. – Fr. *hygromètre* (1666).] An instrument for measuring the humidity of the air or a gas, or the ratio of the amount of moisture actually present in it to that required for saturation. (Formerly often applied to a contrivance to which the name HYGROSCOPE is more properly given.)

Hygrometric (həigrome·trik), *a.* 1794. [f. as prec. + -IC.] **1.** Belonging to hygrometry; measuring, or relating to, the degree of humidity of the atmosphere or other bodies 1819. **2.** = HYGROSCOPIC 2. 1794. **3.** Said of water, etc. so diffused as to be apparent only by the humidity it imparts 1835. So **Hygrome·trical** *a.*, **-ly** *adv.*

Hygrometry (həigrǫ·mĕtri). 1783. [f. as prec.; see -METRY.] That branch of physics which relates to the measurement of the humidity of the air.

Hygroscope (həi·grŏskoᵘp). 1665. [f. as prec. + -SCOPE.] An instrument which indicates (without accurately measuring) the degree of humidity of the air.

Hygroscopic (həigro,skǫ·pik). *a.* 1775. [f. as prec. + -IC.] **1.** Pertaining to the hygroscope or hygroscopy; hygrometric. **2.** *spec.* Said of bodies which are sensitive to moisture, and thus indicate roughly the presence or absence of humidity 1790. **3.** = HYGROMETRIC 3. 1862. So **Hygrosco·pical,** *a.*, **-ly** *adv.* **Hy:groscopi·city,** h. quality.

Hygroscopy (həigrǫ·skŏpi). 1855. [f. as prec. + -Y³.] The observation of the humidity of the air or other substance.

Hyke (həik), *int.* ? *Obs.* 1764. [Cf. HEY and HI, used in same sense.] A call to incite dogs to the chase SCOTT. Hence **Hyke** *v.*

‖**Hyla** (həi·lă). 1842. [mod.L., adopted as generic name by Laurenti (1768), – Gr. ὕλη wood, forest.] A tree-frog or tree-toad, as *Hyla pickeringi* of the U.S.

Hyla, var. of HYLE.

Hylactic (hilæ·ktik), *a. rare.* 1861. [– Gr. ὑλακτικός given to barking.] Of the nature of barking. So **Hyla·ctism,** barking.

‖**Hylæosaurus** (həiliosǭ·rŏs). Also **hylæ·osaur.** 1833. [mod.L. (Mantell, 1832), f. Gr. ὑλαῖος belonging to forests, (f. ὕλη wood) + σαῦρος lizard.] *Palæont.* A gigantic fossil saurian, found in the Wealden formation of Tilgate forest, chiefly characterized by a dermal ridge of large bony spines.

†**Hyla·rchic,** †**-al,** *a.* 1676. [f. HYLE + -ARCH + -IC.] Ruling over matter –1713.

†‖**Hyla·smus.** [mod.L., f. med.L. *hyle* (see next) + quasi-Gr. suffix -ασμος.] Materialization. H. MORE. So †**Hyla·stic** *a.*, **-ally** *adv.* 1639.

†‖**Hyle** (həi·lĭ). ME. [med.L. *hyle* – Gr. ὕλη wood, timber, material, used by Aristotle and in later Gr. as = 'matter'. Cf. OFr. *hyle.*] Matter, substance; the first matter of the universe –1774. So **Hy·lic,** †**-al** *a.* material. (In Gnostic theology opp. to *psychic* and *pneumatic.*) **Hy·licism,** materialism. **Hy·licist,** a materialist.

Hyleg (həi·leg). 1625. [– Pers. *hailāj* calculation of a nativity.] *Astrol.* Ruling planet of a nativity; apheta. Hence †**Hylegi·acal** *a.* of or pertaining to the h.; *sb.* = hylegiacal place.

Hylo- (həilo) = Gr. ὑλο- (ῡ), comb. f. ὕλη wood, material, matter (see HYLE).

Hy·lobate [– mod.L. *Hylobates* – Gr. ὑλοβάτης wood-walker], a long-armed ape or gibbon. **Hy:lo-ide·al** *a.*, pertaining to **Hy:lo-ide·alism,** the doctrine that reality belongs to the immediate object of belief as such; material or somatic idealism; hence **Hy:lo-ide·alist. Hylomo·rphic, -al** *a.*, pertaining to **Hylomo·rphism** [Gr. μορφή], (*a*) the doctrine that primordial matter is the First Cause of the universe; (*b*) the scholastic theory of matter and form; so **Hylomo·rphist.** †**Hylopa·thian** *a.*, pertaining to, or holding the view that all things are affections of matter; *sb.* one who holds this view. †**Hylo-pa·thic** *a.*, capable of affecting or being affected by matter. **Hylo·pathism,** the doctrine that matter is sentient; hence **Hylo·pathist.** †**Hylo·pathy** [Gr. πάθος, -πάθεια affection], a spirit's power of affecting matter. **Hylo·phagous** [Gr. -φαγος] *a.*, wood-eating (said of certain beetles). †**Hylosta·tic, -al** [Gr. στατικός STATIC] *a.*, that places or arranges matter. **Hylo·theism** [THEISM], the doctrine that God and matter are identical; material pantheism; hence **Hylo·theist; Hy:lothei·stic** *a.*

‖**Hylodes** (həilōᵘ·dīz). 1858. [mod.L. – Gr. ὑλώδης woody.] *Zool.* A genus of American toads; one of these.

Hyloist (həi·lo,ist). 1818. [erron. for *hylist*, f. Gr. ὕλη matter.] One who affirms that matter is God.

Hylozoic (həilozōᵘ·ik), *a.* 1678. [f. HYLO- + Gr. ζωή life + -IC.] Of or pertaining to hylozoism; materialistic.

Hylozoism (həilozōᵘ·iz'm). 1678. [f. as prec. + -ISM.] The theory that matter has life, or that life is merely a property of matter. Hence **Hylozo·ist,** a believer in h. **Hylozo·istic** *a.*

Hymen¹ (həi·mĕn). 1590. [– L. *Hymen*, – Gr. 'Υμήν.] **1.** In *Gr.* and *Rom. Myth.*: The god of marriage, represented as a young man carrying a torch and veil. **2.** Marriage; wedlock; nuptials. Now *rare.* 1608. **3.** A hymeneal song (*rare*) 1613.

1. Would..That..at the marriage-day The cup of H. had been full of poison MARLOWE. *Hymen's fane, temple*, etc., the church at which a marriage is solemnized.

Hymen² (həi·mĕn). 1615. [– late L. *hymen* (Donatus, Servius) – Gr. ὑμήν, ὑμεν- membrane. Cf. Fr. *hymen* (Paré XVI).] **1.** *Anat.* The virginal membrane, stretched across and partially closing the external orifice of the vagina. **2.** *Conch.* The ligament between the opposite valves of a bivalve shell.

Hymenaic (həimĕnēⁱ·ik), *a. rare.* [– late L. *hymenaicus* (Servius) = Gr. ὑμεναϊκός, f. ὑμέναιος, f. 'Υμήν HYMEN¹; see -IC.] *lit.* Of or pertaining to Hymen; used to invoke Hymen.

H. dimeter, a dactylic dimeter acatalectic (—◡◡—◡◡).

Hymeneal (həimĕnī·ăl). 1602. [f. L. *hymenæus* (– Gr. ὑμέναιος belonging to wedlock) + -AL¹.]

A. *adj.* Pertaining to marriage.

Views of h. connections MME. D'ARBLAY.

B. *sb.* **1.** A wedding-hymn 1717. **3.** *pl.* Nuptials 1655.

2. I will not talk any more politically but turn to hymeneals H. WALPOLE. Hence **Hymene·ally** *adv.* So **Hymene·an** *a.* and †*sb.* (in sense B. 1).

Hymenial (həimī·niăl), *a.* 1874. [f. HYMENIUM + -AL¹.] *Bot.* Pertaining to the hymenium.

‖**Hymenium** (həimī·niŏm). Pl. **-ia.** 1830. [mod.L. – Gr. ὑμένιον, dim. of ὑμήν membrane, capsule or seed-vessel of plants; see HYMEN², -IUM.] *Bot.* The spore-bearing surface in fungi. In the common mushroom it covers the gills. Also *attrib.*

Hymeno- (həi:mĕno), repr. Gr. ὑμενο-, comb. f. ὑμήν, ὑμένος membrane, HYMEN², as in HYMENOPTEROUS.

Hymeno·geny [-GENY], the production of membranes by the simple contact of two liquids. **Hy:menomyce·te** [– mod.L. *hymenomycetes* pl., f. Gr. μύκητες mushrooms], one of the *Hymenomycetes*, an order of fungi in which the hymenium is on the exposed surface of the sporophore; hence **Hy:menomyce·tal, -tous** *adjs.*, belonging to or having the nature of a hymenomycete; **Hy:menomyce·toid** *a.*, resembling a hymenomycete. **Hy·menophore,** ‖**Hymeno·phorum** [Gr. -φορος carrying], the part of a fungus which supports the hymenium. **Hymeno·tomy** [Gr. -τομία, τομή], incision of the hymen.

Hymenopter (hǝimĕnǫ·ptǝɹ). 1828. [– Fr. *hymenoptère*; see next.] A hymenopterous insect.

‖**Hymenoptera** (hǝimĕnǫ·ptĕră), *sb. pl.* 1773. [mod.L. (LINN., 1748), n. pl. of *hymenopterus* – Gr. ὑμενόπτερος membrane-winged, f. ὑμήν, ὑμεν- HYMEN² + πτερόν wing; see -A 4.] *Zool.* An extensive order of insects (including the ants, wasps, bees, etc.), having four membranous wings (sometimes caducous or absent); the females have an ovipositor, which may also serve as a sting. Hence **Hymeno·pteral** *a.* hymenopterous. **Hymeno·pteran**, one of this order. **Hymeno·pterist**, an entomologist whose special study is H.

Hymenopterology (hǝi:mĕnǫptĕrǫ·lŏdʒi). 1855. [f. prec. + -LOGY.] The branch of Entomology which deals with Hymenoptera. Hence **Hymenoptero·logist. Hymenopterolo·gical** *a.*

Hymenopterous (hǝimĕnǫ·ptĕrǝs), *a.* 1813. [f. mod.L. *hymenopterus* (see HYMENOPTERA) + -OUS.] Having membranous wings; belonging to the Hymenoptera.

Hymn (him), *sb.* [ME. *imne, ymne* – OFr. *ymne* – L. *hymnus* (whence OE. *ymen*) – Gr. ὕμνος song in praise of a god or hero, in LXX rendering various Heb. words meaning a song of praise to God, and hence in N.T. and other Christian writings. The later form was refash. after Latin; the loss of final n in pronunc. is shown in XVI (*hymme, imme*).] **1.** A song of praise to God; *spec.* a metrical composition adapted to be sung in a religious service; sometimes dist. from *psalm* or *anthem*, as not being part of the text of the Bible. **2.** An ode or song of praise in honour of a deity, a country, etc. 1513. **3.** *attrib.*, as in **h.-book.**

1. The earliest h. of Christian devotion.. Hosanna to the Son of David STANLEY. **2.** Every noone-tide they sing Hymnes to the Sunne PURCHAS.

Hymn (him), *v.* 1667. [f. prec. sb.] **1.** *trans.* To worship or praise in song; to sing hymns to. **2.** To sing as a hymn; to express in a song of praise 1727. **3.** *absol.* To sing hymns 1715.

1. Hymning th' Eternal Father MILT. *P.L.* VI. 96. **2.** They h. their praises JOWETT. **3.** The lark that hymned on high 1827. Hence **Hymner** (hi·mǝɹ, hi·mnǝɹ), a singer of hymns 1816.

Hymnal (hi·mnăl), *a.* (*sb.*). ME. [f. L. *hymnus* + -AL¹. The sb. use repr. a med.L. *hymnale*.] **1.** Of or pertaining to a hymn or hymns 1644. **2.** *sb.* A collection of hymns; a hymn-book. So **Hy·mnary** 1888.

Hymnic (hi·mnik), *a.* (*sb.*). 1589. [f. HYMN *sb.* + -IC.] **1.** Of, pertaining to, of the nature of, a hymn or hymns. **2.** *sb.* A composition of the nature of a hymn. LAMB.

Hymnist (hi·mnist). 1621. [f. HYMN *sb.* + -IST, after *psalmist*. Cf. med.L. *hymnista* (Aldhelm), after late L. *psalmista*.] A composer of hymns.

Hymnody (hi·mnŏdi). 1711. [– med.L. *hymnodia* – Gr. ὑμνῳδία singing of hymns; cf. PSALMODY.] **1.** The singing, or composition, of hymns. **2.** Hymns collectively; the body of hymns belonging to any age, country, church, etc. 1864.

1. The Moravians being great in h. 1876. **2.** The jewels of German h. SCHAFF.

Hymno·grapher. 1619. [f. Gr. ὑμνογράφος hymn-writer + -ER¹ 4; see -GRAPHER.] A composer of hymns. So **Hymno·graphy**, the history and bibliography of hymns 1864.

Hymnology (himnǫ·lŏdʒi). 1638. [orig. – Gr. ὑμνολογία hymn-singing, med.L. *hymnologia* praise in song (IX), but in mod. usage f. HYMN *sb.* + -LOGY.] †**1.** The singing of hymns –1855. **2.** The composition of hymns 1839. **3.** The study of hymns, their history, use, etc.; also, hymns collectively 1818.

3. A handbook of h. 1880. Hence **Hymnolo·gic, -al** *a.* of or pertaining to h.; **-ly** *adv.* in relation to h. **Hymno·logist**, a composer or student of hymns.

Hynd, hyne, obs. ff. HIND.

Hynder, obs. f. HINDER *a.*, *v.*

Hyne (hǝin), *adv. dial.* ME. (Sc.) [contr. form of *hethen*; cf. SYNE.] Hence.

Hyo- (hǝiˌo). 1811. [f. Gr. ὑο- in ὑοειδής; see HYOID.] A formative element referring to the hyoid bone in connection with adjoining parts of the body.

Hyobra·nchial *a.*, pertaining to the hyoid bone and the branchiæ. **Hy:o-epiglo·ttic, Hy:o-epiglotti·dean** *adjs.*, connecting the hyoid bone with the epiglottis. **Hyoga·noid, Hy:oganoi·dean** [GANOID] *adjs.*, belonging to, or characteristic of, the *Hyoganoidei*, a subclass of ganoid fishes, having the hyoid apparatus like those of the teleosts. **Hyoglo·ssal, Hyoglo·ssian** [Gr. γλῶσσα] *adjs.*, connected with the hyoid bone and the tongue. ‖**Hyoglo·ssus,** a muscle of the hyoid bone and tongue. **Hyome·ntal** [L. *mentum*] *a.*, pertaining to the hyoid bone and the chin. ‖**Hyopla·stron** [PLASTRON] = HYOSTERNAL *sb.*; hence **Hyopla·stral** *a.* **Hyosca·pular** *a.*, pertaining to the hyoid bone and the scapula. **Hyothy·roid** *a.*, pertaining to the hyoid bone and the thyroid cartilage: as *sb.* = hyothyroid muscle.

Hyoid (hǝi·oid). 1811. [– Fr. *hyoïde* – mod.L. *hyoïdes*, f. ῦ name of the letter υ; see -OID.] *Anat.*

A. *adj.* **1.** *H. bone*: the tongue-bone or *os linguæ*, situated between the chin and the thyroid cartilage. In man it is a horseshoe- or U-shaped bone (whence the name) embedded horizontally in the root of the tongue, with its convexity pointing forwards. **2.** Pertaining to the hyoid bone 1842.

2. *H. arch, h. apparatus*, the second visceral arch in Vertebrates, lying between the hyomandibular and hyobranchial clefts.

B. *sb.* **1.** The hyoid bone; see A. 1. 1872. **2.** The hyoid artery 1883.

Hence **Hyoi·dal, Hyoi·dan** *adjs.* = next.

Hyoidean (hǝiˌoi·dǐˌăn), *a.* 1835. [f. mod. L. *hyoideus* (f. *hyoides* HYOID B) + -AN.] *Anat.* Of or belonging to the hyoid (bone).

Hyomandibular (hǝi:oˌmændi·biŭlăɹ). 1872. [f. HYO- + MANDIBULAR.] *Anat.*

A. *adj.* Pertaining to the hyoid bone and the mandible or lower jaw 1875.

H. bone, in fishes, the bone of the suspensorium which articulates with the cranium. *H. cleft*, the cleft between the mandibular and hyoid arches in the embryo of Vertebrates.

B. *sb.* The hyomandibular bone.

Hyoscine (hǝi·osǝin). 1872. [Arbitrarily f. HYOS(CYAMUS + -INE⁵.] *Chem.* An amorphous alkaloid isomerous with hyoscyamine.

Hyoscyamine (hǝiˌosǝi·ămǝin). 1836. [f. next + -INE⁵.] *Chem.* An extremely poisonous alkaloid ($C_{17}H_{23}NO_3$), obtained from the seeds of *Hyoscyamus niger* and some other *Solanaceæ*, isomerous with atropine; used in medicine as a sedative. So ‖**Hy:oscya·mia.**

‖**Hyoscyamus** (hǝiˌosǝi·ămŏs). 1799. [mod.L. – Gr. ὑοσκύαμος, f. ὑός, gen. of ὗς swine + κύαμος bean.] A genus of plants belonging to the N.O. *Solanaceæ*; the British species is *Hyoscyamus niger*, HENBANE. Also, the tincture of henbane.

Hyosternal (hǝiˌostǝ·ɹnăl), *a.* (*sb.*) 1835. [f. HYO- + STERNAL.] **1.** Pertaining to the hyoid apparatus and the sternum or breastbone 1870. **2.** *sb.* Each of the second pair of plates in the plastron of a turtle, also called the hypoplastron.

‖**Hyosternum** (hǝiˌostǝ·ɹnŏm). [f. HYO- + STERNUM.] = prec. 2.

Hyostylic (hǝiˌostǝi·lik), *a.* 1880. [f. HYO- + Gr. στῦλος pillar + -IC.] *Anat.* Having the lower jaw suspended from the cranium by a hyomandibular bone (opp. to *autostylic* and *amphistylic*). Also said of the lower jaw itself.

Hyp (hip). Also *pl.* **hyps.** *colloq.* ? *Obs.* 1705. [abbrev. of HYPOCHONDRIA. Cf. HIP *sb.*³, *v.*³] Usu. *the h.*, *the hyps*: hypochondria. Heav'n send thou hast not got the hyps! SWIFT.

Hyp-, the form of HYPO- used bef. a vowel.

Hypæthral, -ethral (hǝip-, hipī·prăl), *a.* 1794. [– L. *hypæthrus* – Gr. ὕπαιθρος, f. ὑπό under, HYPO- + αἰθήρ air, ETHER; see -AL¹.] **1.** Open to the sky; having no roof. **2.** Open-air 1879.

1. The internal colonnade to the hypaethral temple is a peristyle 1794.

‖**Hypallage** (hǝipæ·lădʒi, hip-). 1577. [Late L. – Gr. ὑπαλλαγή, f. ὑπό HYPO- + ἀλλαγ-, stem of ἀλλάσσειν exchange, f. ἄλλος other.] A figure of speech in which there is an interchange of two elements of a proposition, their natural relations being reversed. (In Quintillian VIII. vi. 23 = METONYMY.)

The phrase 'you also are become dead to the law',..is a h. for 'the law has become dead to you' 1874.

‖**Hypanthium** (h(ǝ)ipæ·nþiŏm). 1855. [mod.L., f. HYPO- 2 + Gr. ἄνθος flower; see -IUM.] *Bot.* An enlargement or other development of the torus under the calyx. GRAY. Hence **Hypa·nthial** *a.*

Hypapophysis (hǝipăpǫ·fisis, hip-). *Pl.* **-ses.** 1854. [f. HYPO- 2 (*b*) + APOPHYSIS.] *Anat.* An APOPHYSIS or spinous process on the lower or ventral side of a vertebral centrum. Hence **Hypapophy·sial** *a.*

Hyparterial (-aɹtīᵊ·riăl), *a.* [f. HYP(O- 2 + ARTERIAL.] *Anat.* Situated beneath the artery or trachea. (Mod. Dicts.)

Hypaspist (hǝipæ·spist, hip-). 1827. [– Gr. ὑπασπιστής shield-bearer, f. ὑπό HYPO- 1 + ἀσπίς shield.] A shield-bearer; one of a picked body of troops in the Macedonian army.

‖**Hypate** (hi·pătí). 1603. [L. – Gr. ὑπάτη (sc. χορδή CHORD) uppermost string.] The name of the lowest tone in the lowest two tetrachords of ancient Greek music.

Hypaxial (hǝipæ·ksiăl, hip-), *a.* 1872. [f. HYPO- 2 + AXIS + -AL¹.] *Compar. Anat.* Lying beneath, or on the ventral side of, the vertebral axis.

Hyper (hǝi·pǝɹ), joc. or colloq. abbrev. (*a*) of *hypercritic*, (*b*) of *hyper-Calvinist*.

Hyper- (hǝipǝɹ), *prefix*, repr. Gr. ὑπερ- (ὑπέρ prep. and adv., 'over, beyond, over much, above measure').

I. Formations with prepositional force of 'over, beyond, or above' (what is denoted by the second element). **1.** General formations: **a.** adjs., as *hyperangelical*, etc. **b.** Rarely in sbs. and vbs.; e.g. *hypergoddess, hyperdeify*. **2.** *Mus.* In *hyperæolian*, etc., denoting either (*a*) the acute modes in ancient Greek music, which began at a definite interval above the ordinary *Æolian*, etc., or (*b*) the 'authentic' modes in mediaeval music (the same as *Æolian, Dorian*, etc.) as contrasted with the 'plagal' modes *hypoæolian*, etc. **3.** In *Math.*, as in *hyperconic, hyper-elliptic*, etc. See also HYPERDETERMINANT.

II. Formations with adverbial sense of 'over much, to excess, exceedingly'. **1.** General formations: as *hyperacid*, etc.; *hyperacidity*, etc.; *hypervitalize*. **2.** Spec. and techn. terms, as *hyperalbuminosis*, etc.

III. 1. Formations in which *hyper-* qualifies the second element adverbially or attributively; as in HYPERAPOPHYSIS, etc. **2.** In *Chem.*, *hyper-* denotes the highest in a series of oxygen compounds (cf. HYPO- 5); e.g. *hyperoxide*; now usually expressed by PER-.

Some words belonging to the above groups follow here: for the more important see in their alphabetical places.

‖**Hyperalbumino·sis,** *Path.* excess of albumen in the blood. **Hyperbra:chycepha·lic** *a.*, *Craniol.* extremely brachycephalic; applied to a skull of which the cranial index is over 85; so **Hyperbrachyce·phaly,** h. condition. **Hyperbra·nchial** *a.*, *Zool.* situated above the gills or branchiæ. ‖**Hyperca·rdia** [Gr. καρδία], *Path.* hypertrophy of the heart. **Hyperchro·matism,** abnormally intense coloration. **Hyperco·nic** *a.*, *Geom.* relating to the intersection of two conicoids or surfaces of the second order. ‖**Hyperge·nesis,** excessive production or growth. **Hyperhidro·sis, -idro·sis** (erron. *-hydrosis*), *Path.* excessive sweating. **Hyperidea·tion,** excessive mental activity or restlessness. **Hypermne·sia** [Gr. μνῆσις], unusual power of memory. **Hypernutri·tion** = HYPERTROPHY. **Hyperorga·nic** *a.*, beyond or independent of the organism. **Hyperorthogna·thic** *a.*, *Craniol.* excessively orthognathic; applied to a skull in which the cranial index is over 91; so **Hyperortho·gnathy,** h. condition. **Hyperpyre·tic** [Gr. πυρετός] *a.*, *Path.* pertaining to or affected with ‖**Hyperpyre·xia,** a high or excessive degree of fever; whence ‖**Hyperpyre·xial, Hyperpyre·xic** *adjs.* = *hyperpyretic*. ‖**Hypersarco·ma, Hypersarco·sis,** *Path.* proud or fungous flesh. **Hy·perspace,** *Geom.* space of more than three dimensions. ‖**Hypertricho·sis** [Gr. τρίχωσις, f. τριχ-, θρίξ], excessive growth of hair.

‖**Hyperæmia** (hǝipǝrī·miă). Also **-hæmia -emia.** 1836. [mod.L., f. HYPER- II. 2 + Gr. -αιμια (cf. *anæmia*), f. αἷμα blood.] *Path.* An excessive accumulation of blood in a particular part; congestion.

Active or *arterial h.*, congestion arising from increased flow through the arteries. *Passive* or *venous h.*, congestion due to obstruction in a vein. Hence **Hyperæ·mic, -e·mic** *a.* of, pertaining to, or affected with h.

‖**Hyperæsthesia** (es-, -isþī·siă). 1849. [mod.L., f. HYPER- II. 2 + Gr. -αισθησία, αἰσθησις perception, feeling.] *Path.* Excessive and morbid sensitiveness of the nerves or nerve-centres. Also *transf.* So **Hyperæsthe·tic** *a.* affected with h.

Hyperapophysis (-ăpǫ·fisis). 1872. [f. HYPER- III. 1. + APOPHYSIS.] *Anat.* A process of bone extending backward from the neural spine of one vertebra to that of another, or developed from the postzygapophysis. Hence **Hyperapophy·sial** *a.*

†**Hyperaspist** (-æ·spist). 1638. [– Gr. ὑπερασπιστής, f. ὑπερασπίζειν hold a shield over, f. ἀσπίς shield.] A defender, champion –1747.

‖**Hyperbaton** (həipə̄·ɹbătǫn). 1579. [L. – Gr. ὑπέρβατον, lit. 'overstepping', f. ὑπερβαίνειν.] *Gram.* and *Rhet.* A figure of speech in which the natural order of words or phrases is inverted, esp. for the sake of emphasis. Also, an instance of this.

The sence..ys 'the fende makethe this' for whiche Chaucer vsethe..(accordinge to the rethoricall figure Hiperbatone), 'This makethe the fende' THYNNE. Hence **Hyperba·tic** *a.* pertaining to or of the nature of h.; inverted. **Hyperba·tically** *adv.*

Hyperbola (həipə̄·ɹbŏlă). 1668. [– mod.L. *hyperbola* – Gr. ὑπερβολή, lit. 'excess', f. ὑπερβάλλειν (ὑπέρ over + βάλλειν throw). So named because the inclination of its plane to the base of the cone exceeds that of the side of the cone (see ELLIPSE).] *Geom.* One of the conic sections; a plane curve consisting of two separate, equal and similar, infinite branches, formed by the intersection of a plane with both branches of a double cone (i.e. two similar cones on opposite sides of the same vertex). It may also be defined as a curve in which the focal distance of any point bears to its distance from the directrix a constant ratio greater than unity. It has two foci, one for each branch, and two asymptotes, which intersect in the centre of the curve, midway between the vertices of its two branches. (Often applied to one branch of the curve.) **b.** Extended (after Newton) to algebraic curves of higher degrees denoted by equations analogous to that of the common hyperbola 1727. Hence †**Hyperboliform** *a.* of the form of, or resembling, a h. (Dicts.)

Hyperbole (həipə̄·ɹbŏli). 1529. [L. – Gr. ὑπερβολή excess, exaggeration; cf. prec.] **1.** *Rhet.* A figure of speech consisting in exaggerated statement, used to express strong feeling or produce a strong impression, and not intended to be taken literally. Also, an instance of this. **b.** *gen.* Excess, extravagance (*rare*) 1652. †**2.** *Geom.* = HYPERBOLA –1716.

1. Scriptural Examples of H...Deut. 9.1, Cities fenced up to heaven..Joh. 21.25, The whole world could not contain the books 1657. var. †**Hype·rboly** (in sense 1) 1598.

Hyperbolic (həipəɹbǫ·lik), *a.* 1646. [– late L. *hyperbolicus* (Jerome) – Gr. ὑπερβολικός, f. ὑπερβολή HYPERBOLE; see -IC.] **1.** *Rhet.* = HYPERBOLICAL 1. **2.** *Geom.* Of, belonging to, or of the form or nature of a hyperbola; having some relation to the hyperbola 1676.

2. *H. curvature*, the same as ANTICLASTIC curvature. *H. function*; a function having a relation to a rectangular hyperbola similar to that of the ordinary trigonometrical functions to a circle; as the *h. sine, cosine, tangent*, etc. (abbrev. *sinh, cosh, tanh*, etc.). *H. logarithm*: a logarithm to the base *e* (2·71828..), a natural or Napierian logarithm; so called because proportional to a segment of the area between a hyperbola and its asymptote. *H. spiral*: a spiral in which the radius vector varies inversely as the angle turned through by it.

Hyperbolical (həipəɹbǫ·likăl), *a.* ME. [f. as prec. + -AL[1]; see -ICAL.] **1.** *Rhet.* Of the nature of, involving, or using hyperbole; exaggerated, extravagant. †**b.** *gen.* Excessive, enormous –1859. **2.** *Geom.* = HYPERBOLIC 2. 1571. Hence **Hyperbo·lically** *adv.*

Hyperbolism (həipə̄·ɹbŏliz'm). 1653. **1.** *Rhet.* [f. HYPERBOLE + -ISM.] Use of or addiction to hyperbole; exaggerated style, or an instance of this. **2.** *Geom.* [– mod.L. *hyperbolismus* (Newton).] A curve whose equation is derived from that of another curve by substituting *xy* for *y*, as that of the hyperbola is from that of the straight line 1861. So **Hype·rbolist,** one given to the use of hyperbole 1661. **Hype·rbolize** *v.* to exaggerate (*trans.* and *intr.*) 1594.

Hyperboloid (həipə̄·ɹbŏloid). 1684. [f. HYPERBOLA + -OID. Cf. Fr. *hyperboloïde.*] †**1.** = HYPERBOLA b. –1796. **2.** A solid or surface of the second degree, some of whose plane sections are hyperbolas, the others being ellipses or circles. Formerly restricted to those of circular section, generated by the revolution of a hyperbola about one of its axes; now called *hyperboloids of revolution* 1743.

There are two kinds of h.: *the h. of one sheet* and *of two sheets*, e.g. those generated by revolution about the conjugate and transverse axes respectively.

Hyperborean (həipəɹbōᵊ·riăn). 1591. [– late L. *hyperboreanus* = cl. L. *hyperboreus* – Gr. ὑπερβόρεος, -βόρειος, f. ὑπερ- HYPER- I + βόρειος northern, βορέας BOREAS.] **A.** *adj.* Of, pertaining to, or characterizing the extreme north of the earth, or (*colloq.* or *joc.*) of a particular country; in ethnological use, cf. B. **b.** Of or pertaining to the fabled Hyperboreans 1613.

Even to the h. or frozen sea 1633.

B. *sb.* An inhabitant of the extreme north of the earth; in *pl.* members of an ethnological group of Arctic races. *loosely* and *fig.* One who lives in a northerly clime. 1601.

In Greek legend the Hyperboreans were a happy people who lived in sunshine and plenty beyond the north wind.

Hypercatalectic (-kætăle·ktik), *a.* 1704. [– late L. *hypercatalecticus* (Servius, Priscian), f. Gr. ὑπερκατάληκτος; see HYPER- I, CATALECTIC.] *Pros.* Of a verse or colon: Having an extra syllable after the last complete dipody. Also applied to the syllable. †Formerly also = HYPERMETRIC.

Hypercritic (həipəɹkri·tik), *sb.* (*a.*) 1618. [– mod.L. (XVI) *hypercriticus* (see HYPER- II. 1, CRITIC *sb.*), applied vituperatively to the younger Scaliger by the Italian R. Titius in 1589, and by Debrio in 1609. Cf. Fr. *hypercritique* (Boileau, 1703).] **1.** †A master critic; a severe critic; an over-critical person 1633. †**2.** Hypercriticism; also, a critique –1757. **3.** *adj.* = next. KEATS.

Hypercri·tical, *a.* 1605. [orig. f. prec. + -AL[1]; in later use formed anew from HYPER- II. 1 + CRITICAL.] Unduly critical; addicted to hypercriticism; as *h. carpers*. Hence **Hypercri·tically** *adv.*

Hypercriticism (-kri·tisiz'm). 1678. [HYPER- II. 1 + CRITICISM.] Excessive, unduly severe, or minute criticism. So **Hypercri·ticize** *v.*

Hyperdete·rminant. 1845. [HYPER- I. 3.] *Math.* **a.** *sb.* A determinant of operative symbols; a symbolic expression for an invariant or covariant; invented by Cayley. **b.** *adj.* Of the nature of a hyperdeterminant.

‖**Hyperdulia** (həipəɹdulәi·ă). 1530. [med. L.; see HYPER- II. 1. Cf. Fr. *hyperdulie.*] The superior DULIA or veneration paid by Roman Catholics to the Virgin Mary. Hence **Hyperdu·lic, -al** *a.* of the nature of h.

Hypergamy (həipə̄·ɹgămi). 1881. [f. HYPER- III. 1 + Gr. γάμος marriage.] Marriage with one of equal or superior caste: in reference to Hindu customs.

‖**Hypericum** (həipe·rikŏm, *etym.* hipərəi·kŏm). 1471. [L. *hypericum, hypericon* – Gr. ὑπέρεικον, f. ὑπέρ over + ἐρείκη heath.] **1.** *Bot.* A large genus of plants (herbs or shrubs), the type of the N.O. *Hypericaceæ*, having pentamerous yellow flowers, and leaves usually marked with pellucid dots; commonly known as St. John's-worts. †**2.** *Pharm.* (in form *hypericon*). A drug prepared from a plant of this genus –1691.

‖**Hyperinosis** (həi:pərinōᵘ·sis). 1845. [f. HYPER- II. 2 + Gr. ἴς, ἰνός fibre + -OSIS.] *Path.* A diseased state of the blood in which it contains an excessive amount of fibrin. Hence **Hyperino·sed, -o·tic** *adjs.* having excess of fibrin.

Hypermetamorphosis (həi:pəɹ,metămǭ·ɹfŏsis). 1875. [HYPER- II. 2.] *Entom.* An extreme form of metamorphosis occurring in certain insects, in which the animal passes through two or more different larval stages. So **Hypermetamo·rphism,** the character of undergoing h. **Hypermetamo·rphic, -morpho·tic** *adjs.* characterized by h.

Hypermeter (həipə̄·ɹmĭtəɹ). 1656. [– Gr. ὑπέρμετρος, -ον beyond measure, beyond metre, f. μέτρον measure.] **1.** *Pros.* A hypermetric verse. **2.** *joc.* A person taller than ordinary. ADDISON. Hence **Hyperme·tric, -ical** *a.*

Hypermetrope (həipəɹme·troᵘp). 1864. [f. Gr. ὑπέρμετρος beyond measure + ὤψ, ὠπ- eye.] *Path.* A person affected with hypermetropia.

‖**Hypermetropia** (həi:pəɹmĭtrōᵘ·piă). Also **-metropy** (-me·trŏpi). 1868. [mod.L., f. as prec. + *-ia* -IA[1].] *Path.* An affection of the eye, usually due to a flattened form of the eyeball, in which the focus of parallel rays lies behind instead of on the retina; long-sightedness. Hence **Hypermetro·pic** *a.*

‖**Hyperoödon** (həipərōᵘ·ŏdǫn). 1843. [mod. L., f. Gr. ὑπερῷος superior, or ὑπερῴη palate + ὀδούς, ὀδον(τ- tooth.] *Zool.* A genus of Cetacea, containing the bottle-nosed whales.

‖**Hyperopia** (-ōᵘ·piă). 1884. [f. HYPER- II. 2 + Gr. ὤψ, ὠπ- eye + *-ia* -IA[1].] *Path.* = HYPERMETROPIA. So **Hypero·pic** *a.*

‖**Hyperostosis** (həi:pəɹǫstōᵘ·sis). *Pl.* **-oses.** 1835. [f. as prec. + Gr. ὀστέον, ὀστο- bone; see -OSIS.] *Path.*, etc. An overgrowth of bony tissue; hypertrophy of bone; exostosis.

Hyperoxida·tion. 1876. [HYPER- II. 1.] Excessive oxidation. HARLEY.

Hyperoxide (-ǫ·ksəid). 1855. [HYPER- III. 2.] *Chem.* = PEROXIDE.

Hyperoxygenate (-ǫ·ksidʒĕneⁱt), *v.* 1793. [f. HYPER- II. 1 + OXYGENATE.] *trans.* To supersaturate with oxygen. (Chiefly in pa. pple.) **b.** *joc.* To impart excess of sourness to 1811.

b. An old huckstering grocer..whose natural sourness..is hyperoxygenated by Methodism SOUTHEY. So **Hyperoxygena·tion,** the action of hyperoxygenating; hyperoxygenated condition. **Hypero·xygenize** *v.* = HYPEROXYGENATE (chiefly in pa. pple.).

†**Hyperoxymuriate** (həi:pərǫksimiūᵊ·riĕt). 1794. [HYPER- III. 2.] *Chem.* A salt of 'hyperoxymuriatic' (now called chloric) acid; a chlorate –1854.

†**Hyperoxymuria·tic,** *a.* 1794. [HYPER- III. 2 + OXYMURIATIC.] *Chem.* In *H. acid*, the old name of chloric acid $HClO_3$ –1807.

Hyperper (həipə̄·ɹpəɹ). 1598. [– med.L. *hyperperum, -pyrum* – Gr. ὑπέρπυρον, f. ὑπέρ HYPER- + πῦρ fire; applied to gold highly refined by fire.] *Numism.* A Byzantine coin; the gold solidus.

Hyperphysical (həipəɹfi·zikăl), *a.* 1600. [HYPER- I. 1.] Above or beyond what is physical; supernatural. Hence **Hyperphy·sically** *adv.* So **Hyperphy·sics,** the science or subject of the supernatural.

‖**Hyperplasia** (həipəɹplēⁱ·ziă). 1861. [mod. L., f. HYPER- II. 2 + Gr. πλάσις formation; see -IA[1].] *Path.* A form of hypertrophy consisting in abnormal multiplication of the cellular elements of a part or organ; excessive cell-formation. So **Hy·perplasm** = prec. **Hyperpla·sic, -pla·stic** *adjs.* of, pertaining to, or exhibiting h.

Hypersthene (həi·pəɹsþīn). 1808. [– Fr. *hypersthène* (Haüy, 1803), f. HYPER- II. 1 + Gr. σθένος strength; from its superior hardness as compared with hornblende.] *Min.* A silicate of iron and magnesium, of the pyroxene group, a greenish-black or greenish-grey mineral, closely allied to hornblende, often exhibiting a peculiar metalloidal lustre. Also *attrib.* Hence **Hypersthe·nic** *a.*[1] related to or containing h. **Hypersthe·nite,** a dark granite-like aggregate of h. and labradorite.

‖**Hypersthenia** (həipəɹsþī·niă). 1855. [mod. L., f. HYPER- II. 2 + Gr. σθένος strength; see -IA[1].] *Path.* Extreme or morbid excitement of the vital powers; the opposite of *asthenia*. Hence **Hypersthe·nic** *a.*[2] relating to, characterized by, or producing h.

Hyperthesis (həipə̄·ɹþĭsis). 1882. [– Gr. ὑπέρθεσις, f. ὑπέρ HYPER- + θέσις placing.] Transposition, metathesis. So **Hyperthe·tic** *a.* pertaining to or exhibiting h. †**Hyperthe·tical** *a.* superlative. CHAPMAN.

Hypertrophy (həipə̄·ɹtrŏfi), *sb.* 1834. [– mod.L. *hypertrophia* (after late L. *atrophia*),

f. Gr. ὑπέρ HYPER- II. 2 + -τροφία, τροφή nourishment; cf. ATROPHY.] *Physiol.* and *Path.* Excessive growth or development of a part or organ, produced by excessive nutrition. The opposite of ATROPHY. *fig.* Overgrowth. Hence **Hypertro·phic, -al** *a.* of the nature of, affected with, or producing h. **Hype·rtrophous** *a.* characterized by h. **Hype·rtrophy** *v.* to affect with or undergo h.

||**Hypha** (həi·fă). *Pl.* **-phæ** (-fī). 1866. [mod.L. (C. L. Willdenow, 1810) – Gr. ὑφή web.] *Bot.* The structural element of the thallome of Fungi, consisting of long slender branched filaments, usually having transverse septa, and together constituting the *mycelium*. Hence **Hy·phal** *a.*

Hyphæresis, -eresis (hi-, həifīə·rĭsis). 1890. [– Gr. ὑφαίρεσις taking away from under, omission; cf. *aphæresis*.] *Gram.* The omission of a letter or syllable in the body of a word.

Hyphen (həi·fĕn), *sb.* 1620. [– late L. *hyphen* – late Gr. ὑφέν the sign ‿, subst. use of ὑφέν together, f. ὑφ-, ὑπό HYPO- 1 + ἕν, n. of εἷς one.] **1.** A short dash or line (-) used to connect two words together as a compound; also, to join the separated syllables of a word, as at the end of a line; or to divide a word into parts. **b.** Applied to the 'plus' sign (+). DAUBENY. **2.** *transf.* A short pause between two syllables in speaking 1868; a connecting link 1868. Hence **Hy·phen** *v.* to join by a h.; to write (a compound) with a h. So **Hy·phenate** *v.*

Hy·phenated *ppl. a.* (orig. *U.S.*), applied to persons whose nationality is designated by a hyphened form; hence, to a person whose patriotic allegiance is assumed to be divided 1893. So **Hy·phenate** *sb.*

Hyphomycetous (hi:f-, həi:fo,məisī·təs), *a.* 1887. [f. mod.L. *Hyphomycetes* (f. Gr. ὑφή web + μύκητες fungi) + -OUS.] *Bot.* Of or belonging to the *Hyphomycetes*, a group of fungi consisting simply of hyphæ.

Hypinosis (hipinōᵘ·sis). 1845. [f. HYPO- 4 + Gr. ἴς, ἰνός tissue + -OSIS.] *Path.* A diseased state of the blood in which the quantity of fibrin is below the normal. Hence **Hypino·tic** *a.*

Hypnagogic (hipnăgǫ·dʒik), *a.* 1886. [– Fr. *hypnagogique*, f. Gr. ὕπνος sleep + ἀγωγός leading, f. ἄγειν lead; see -IC.] *Properly*, Inducing sleep; in use = that accompanies falling asleep.

Hypno- (hi·pno), bef. a vowel **hypn-**, comb. f. Gr. ὕπνος sleep. Used chiefly in new pathological terms.

Hy·pnobate [Gr. -βατης walker], a sleep-walker. **Hy·pnocyst,** *Biol.* an encysted protozoan which remains quiescent and does not develop spores. **Hypnoge·nesis, Hypno·geny,** induction of the hypnotic state; so **Hypnogene·tic, -ge·nic, Hypno·genous** *adjs.*, producing the hypnotic state; *rarely*, producing sleep. **Hypnogene·tically** *adv.*, by hypnogenesis. **Hypno·logy,** the science of the phenomena of sleep; hence **Hypnolo·gic, -al** *a.* **Hypno·logist,** one versed in hypnology. **Hy·pnosperm, -spore,** *Bot.* an oospore or zygospore (in the *Algæ*) which, after fertilization, passes through a period of rest before germinating; a resting cell or spore; so **Hy·pnospora:nge, Hy·pnospora·ngium,** *Bot.* a sporangium containing hypnospores; **Hypnospo·ric** *a.*, of the nature of a hypnospore.

Hypnoid, *a.*[1]: see under HYPNUM.

Hypnoid (hi·pnoid), *a.*[2], **hypnoidal** (hipnoi·dăl), *a.* *U.S.* 1904. [f. Gr. ὕπνος sleep + -OID.] Resembling hypnosis; hypnotic.

Hypnosis (hipnōᵘ·sis). 1876. [mod.L., f. Gr. ὕπνος sleep + -OSIS.] *Phys.* **1.** The inducement or the gradual approach of sleep. **2.** Artificially produced sleep; esp. the hypnotic state 1882.

Hypnotic (hipnǫ·tik). 1625. [– Fr. *hypnotique* (Paré) – late L. *hypnoticus* – Gr. ὑπνωτικός putting to sleep, narcotic, f. ὑπνοῦν put to sleep, f. ὕπνος sleep; see -IC.]

A. *adj.* **1.** Inducing sleep; soporific. **2.** Pertaining to or of the nature of hypnotism or 'nervous sleep'; accompanied by or producing hypnotism 1843. **3.** Susceptible to hypnotism 1881.

1. H. Draughts 1758. **2.** The h. or so-called mesmeric state MAUDSLEY. **3.** The trained h. subject 1892.

B. *sb.* **1.** An agent that produces sleep; a sedative or soporific drug 1681. **2.** A person under the influence of hypnotism 1888.

†**Hypno·tical** *a.* = A. 1. **Hypno·tically** *adv.*

Hypnotism (hi·pnŏtiz'm). 1842. [f. HYPNOTIC + -ISM. First used as a shortened form of *neuro-hypnotism* by Dr. James Braid of Manchester, who introduced the term.] **1.** The process of hypnotizing, or artificially producing a state in which the subject appears to be in a deep sleep, without any power of changing his mental or physical condition, except under the influence of some external suggestion or direction. On recovering from this condition, the person has usually no remembrance of what he has said or done during the hypnotic state. Also, the branch of science which deals with the production of this state. See BRAIDISM, MESMERISM.

The usual way of inducing the state consists in causing a person to look fixedly, for several minutes, with complete concentration, at a bright object placed above and in front of the eyes at so short a distance that the convergence of the optic axes can only be accomplished with effort.

2. The hypnotized or hypnotic condition 1843. **3.** Sleepiness or sleep artificially induced by any means; also *fig.* 1860.

So **Hy·pnotist,** a hypnotizer. **Hy·pnotize** *v.* to put into a hypnotic state; to mesmerize; also *absol.* **Hypnotiza·tion,** the action of hypnotizing; hypnotized condition. **Hy·pnotizer,** one who hypnotizes.

||**Hypnum** (hi·pnŏm). *Pl.* **-nums, -na.** 1753. [mod.L. – Gr. ὕπνον 'moss growing on trees'.] *Bot.* A large genus of pleurocarpous mosses; feather-moss. Hence **Hy·pnoid** *a.*[1] belonging or akin to the genus *H.* **Hypno·philous** *a.* growing among the mosses.

Hypo[1] (hi·po). ? *Obs.* 1711. [abbrev. of HYPOCHONDRIA; cf. HYP.] Morbid depression of spirits.

Hypo[2] (həi·po). 1861. [abbrev. of HYPOSULPHITE.] *Photogr.* The salt formerly called hyposulphite, now thiosulphate, of soda, used for fixing photographic pictures. Also *attrib.*

Hypo- (həipo, hipo), bef. vowels also **hyp-,** *prefix*, repr. Gr. ὑπο-, ὑπ- (f. ὑπό prep. and adv. 'under' = L. *sub.*) The first vowel in Gr. ὑπο-, L. *hypo-*, is short, but *y* is now usually treated in all positions except before two consonants as (əi), against both etymology and history.

1. In words from Greek; as *hypochondria, hypocrisy, hypotenuse*, etc.

2. In modern formations, with sense 'under, beneath, below'; as (*a*) *hypobasal*, HYPODERMIC, etc.; (*b*) HYPOBLAST, *hypozoa* (animals low in the scale).

3. *Mus.* In *hypoæolian, -dorian*, etc., used to denote either (*a*) the grave modes in ancient Greek music, beginning at a definite interval below the ordinary *Æolian, Dorian*, etc., or (*b*) the 'plagal' modes in mediæval music, each of which has a compass a fourth below that of the corresponding 'authentic' mode.

4. 'To some extent', 'slightly', 'somewhat' in adjs.; 'slight' or 'deficient' in sbs.; the opposite of HYPER- II.

5. In Chemistry, *hypo-* (in contrast with HYPER- III. 2) is used to name an oxygen compound lower in the series than that having the simple name without *hypo-*; thus *sulphurous acid* = H_2SO_3, *hyposulphurous acid* = H_2SO_2.

Some words belonging to the above groups follow here: for the more important see in their alphabetical places.

||**Hypoa·ria** *pl.* [Gr. ᾠάριον little egg], *Ichthyol.* a pair of protuberant oval ganglia developed beneath the optic lobes of osseous fishes; hence **Hypoa·rian** *a.* **Hypoba·sal** *a.*, *Bot.* applied to the lower of the two cells or portions of the oospore of vascular cryptogams (cf. EPIBASAL). ||**Hypo·bole** [Gr. ὑποβολή suggestion], *Rhet.* the mentioning and refuting of objections which might be brought against the speaker's case by an opponent. ||**Hypocatha·rsis,** *Med.* a slight purging; so **Hypocatha·rtic** *a.* ||**Hypocli·dium** [Gr. κλείς, κλειδ- key], *Ornith.* the interclavicular element of the clavicles of a bird, seen in the merry-thought of a fowl; hence **Hypocli·dian** *a.* **Hy·pocone,** *Zool.* the sixth cusp of the upper molar tooth of mammals of the group *Bunodonta*. **Hypocry·stalline** *a.*, *Min.* consisting of crystals contained in a non-crystalline or massive mineral substance. ||**Hypoda·ctylum** [Gr. δάκτυλος], *Ornith.* the lower surface of a bird's toe. **Hy:poderma·tomy** [Gr. δέρμα skin + τομή cutting], *Med.* incision of a subcutaneous part. **Hypodermo·clysis** [Gr. κλύσις a drenching], *Med.* the injection of nutrient fluids under the skin in the collapse from cholera, etc. ||**Hypodia·stole** [Gr. ὑποδιαστολή], *Gr. Gram.* = DIASTOLE 3. **Hypodi·crotous** *a.*, *Phys.* having a slight secondary wave in each pulse-beat. **Hypo-elli·psoid,** *Geom.* a curve traced by a point in the circumference of a circle or ellipse rolling along the inside of an ellipse. **Hypogæ·ate,** *Chem.* a salt of hypogæic acid. **Hypogæ·ic** [f. mod.L. (*Arachis*) *hypogæa* the earth-nut] *a.*, in *h. acid*, $C_{16}H_{30}O_2$, discovered in oil of earth-nut. **Hypo·genous** [Gr. -γενής produced] *a. Bot.*, (*a*) growing upon the under surface of leaves; (*b*) growing beneath the surface. **Hypo·gnathism,** hypognathous conformation. **Hypo·gnathous** [Gr. γνάθος jaw] *a.*, *Ornith.* having the under mandible longer than the upper. **Hypophy·al** [see HYO-, HYOID] *a.*, *Anat.* forming the base of the hyoid arch; *sb.*, that part of the hyoid arch which lies between the stylohyal and basibranchial. **Hypo·menous** [Gr. μένειν] *a.*, *Bot.* arising from below an organ, without adhering to it. **Hy·pomere** [Gr. μέρος], *Biol.* the lower half of certain sponges; hence **Hypo·meral** *a.*, pertaining to a h. **Hypopho·nic** [Gr. φωνή] *a.*, serving as an accompaniment or response; so **Hypo·phonous** *a.* ||**Hypophy·llium** [Gr. φύλλιον little leaf], *Bot.* a small abortive leaf, like a scale, placed below a cluster of leaf-like branches or leaves. **Hypophy·llous** [Gr. φύλλον] *a.*, *Bot.* growing under, or on the under side of, a leaf. **Hypophy·sics,** matters that lie beneath physics. ||**Hypopla·stron,** *Zool.* the third lateral piece of the plastron of Chelonia: = *hyposternal*; hence **Hypopla·stral** *a.* ||**Hypo·ptilum** [Gr. πτίλον feather], *Ornith.* the subsidiary shaft or plume of a feather, which springs from the main stem at the junction of quill and rachis; the after-shaft, the hyporachis; hence **Hypo·ptilar** *a.* ||**Hy·popus** [Gr. ὑπόπους having feet beneath], *Zool.* a heteromorphous nymphal form of certain acaroids; hence **Hypo·pial** *a.* ||**Hypopy·gium** [Gr. ὑποπύγιον rump, tail, πυγή buttocks], *Entom.*, (*a*) the last ventral segment of the abdomen; (*b*) the clasping organ at the end of the abdomen of many male dipterous insects. ||**Hypo·rachis (-rrhachis)** [Gr. ῥάχις spine], *Ornith.* the accessory rachis or shaft of a bird's feather, the hypoptilum; hence **Hyporachi·dian (hyporrh-)** *a.* ||**Hypora·dius,** *Ornith.* one of the barbs of the hyporachis of a feather; hence **Hypora·dial** *a.* **Hyporrhy·thmic** *a.*, deficient in rhythm; said of a heroic hexameter when the cæsura is not observed. **Hyposke·letal** *a.*, *Anat.* = HYPAXIAL (cf. EPISKELETAL). **Hyposte·rnal** [Gr. ὑπόστερνος: see STERNUM] *a.*, *Anat.*, in *h. bone*, also *hyposternal* as *sb.*, the hypoplastron of a chelonian; also called ||**Hyposte·rnum.** **Hyposti·gma** [Gr. ὑποστιγμή a comma], *Palæogr.* the comma, which anciently had the form of a modern full stop. **Hyposto·matous, hypo·stomous** [Gr. στόμα, στοματ-] *a.*, *Zool.* having the mouth inferior, as certain fishes and infusoria (*Hypostomata*). ||**Hypo·strophe** [Gr. ὑποστροφή turning back], (*a*) *Path.* a turning or tossing as of the sick in bed; a relapse; a falling back, as of the womb; (*b*) *Rhet.* reversion to a subject after a parenthesis. **Hy·postyle** [Gr. ὑπόστυλος: see STYLE] *a.*, *Arch.* having the roof supported on pillars. **Hyposyllogi·stic** *a.*, having the value, but not the strict form, of a syllogism. **Hypota·ctic** [Gr. ὑποτακτικός] *a.*, *Gram.* dependent, subordinate in construction. ||**Hypota·rsus,** *Ornith.* a process of the hinder part of the tarso-metatarsus of most birds; the talus or so-called calcaneum; hence **Hypota·rsal** *a.* **Hypota·xis** [Gr. ὑπόταξις], *Gram.* subordination, subordinate construction. ||**Hypothe·cium** [Gr. θηκίον, dim. of θήκη case], *Bot.* the mass of fibres lying beneath the sub-hymenial layer; hence **Hypothe·cial** *a.* **Hypo·thenar** [Gr. ὑποθέναρ, f. θέναρ palm of the hand] *a.*, *Anat.* of or pertaining to the eminence on the inner side of the palm, over the metacarpal bone of the little finger. **Hypo·trichous** [Gr. θρίξ, τριχ-] *a.*, *Zool.* of or pertaining to the *Hypotricha*, an order of the class *Ciliata* of *Protozoa*, having the locomotive cilia confined to the ventral surface. **Hypotympa·nic** *a.*, *Anat.* situated beneath the tympanum; applied esp. to the lower bone of the jaw-pier in osseous fishes; *sb.* the quadrate. ||**Hypozeu·gma,** *Gram.* the combination of several subjects with a single verb or predicate. ||**Hypozeu·xis,** *Gram.* the use of several parallel clauses, each having its own subject and verb. ||**Hypozo·a** [Gr. ζῷον], *Zool.* = PROTOZOA; hence **Hypozo·an** *a.* **Hypozo·ic** *a.*, *Geol.* lying beneath the strata which contain remains of living organisms; *Zool.* of or pertaining to the *Hypozoa*.

Hypoblast (həi·po-, hi·poblæst). 1875. [– mod.L. *hypoblastus*; see HYPO- 2 (b), -BLAST.] **1.** *Bot.* The flat dorsal cotyledon of a grass. ? *Obs.* 1882. **2.** *Biol.* The inner layer of cells in the BLASTODERM 1875. Hence **Hypobla·stic** *a.*

Hypobranchial (həipo-, hipobræ·ŋkiăl), *a.* 1848. [f. HYPO- 2 + BRANCHIAL.] *Anat.* **a.** *adj.* Situated under the branchiæ or gills.

b. *sb. pl.* The lower portion of the branchial arch.

Hypobromite (həipo-, hipobrōᵘ·məit). 1877. [HYPO- 5.] *Chem.* A salt of hypobromous acid.

Hypobromous (həipo- hipobrōᵘ·məs), *a.* 1865. [f. HYPO- 5 + *bromous* (acid).] *Chem.* In *h. acid*, an acid (HBrO) derived from bromine, having strong oxidizing and bleaching properties.

Hypocaust (həi·pǒkǭst, hi·po-). 1678. [– L. *hypocaustum* (Pliny) – Gr. ὑπόκαυστον, lit. room or place 'heated from below', f. ὑπό HYPO- 1 + καυ-, καίειν burn.] *Rom. Antiq.* A hollow space extending under the floor of the *calidarium*, in which the heat from the furnace (*hypocausis*) was accumulated for the heating of the house or of a bath. **b.** *transf.* A stove. SCOTT.

Hypochlorite (həipo-, hipoklōᵊ·rəit). 1835. [HYPO- 5.] *Chem.* A salt of hypochlorous acid.

Hypochlorous (həipo, hipoklōᵊ·rəs), *a.* 1841. [f. HYPO- 5 + CHLOROUS.] *Chem. H. acid*, an oxy-acid of chlorine (HClO), which possesses strong oxidizing and bleaching qualities.

Hypochonder, -chondre (hipokǫ·ndəɹ). ? *Obs.* 1547. [– (O)Fr. *hypocondre* (XIV) – med.L. **hypochondrium*, n. sing., for late L. *hypochondria*; see next.] = HYPOCHONDRIUM. Also *pl.* = HYPOCHONDRIA 1.

Hypochondria (həipokǫ·ndriă, hipo-). 1563. [– late L. *hypoc(h)ondria* n. pl. – Gr. τὰ ὑποχόνδρια (also n. sing. τὸ ὑποχόνδριον), n. pl. used subst. of ὑποχόνδριος adj., f. ὑπό HYPO- 1 + χόνδρος gristle, cartilage, esp. that of the breast-bone.] ||**1.** as pl. of HYPOCHONDRIUM. Those parts of the human abdomen which lie immediately under the ribs on each side of the epigastric region. **†b.** The viscera situated in the hypochondria; the liver, gall-bladder, spleen, etc., formerly supposed to be the seat of melancholy and 'vapours' –1652. **†c.** Erron. as *sing.* –1727. **2.** as *sing.* General depression, melancholy, or low spirits, for which there is no real cause 1668.

2. Will Hazard was cured of his h. by three glasses 1710. Hence **Hypocho·ndrial** *a.*

Hypochondriac (həipokǫ·ndriæ̆k, hipo-). 1615. [– Fr. *hypocondriaque* (XVI) – Gr. ὑποχονδριακός affected in the hypochondria, f. (τὰ) ὑποχόνδρια; see prec., -AC, and cf. med.L. *hypochondriaca*.]

A. *adj.* **1.** Of states: Proceeding from the hypochondria, regarded as the seat of melancholy; hence, consisting in a settled depression of spirits. ? *Obs.* **b.** Of persons, their dispositions, etc.: Affected by hypochondria 1641. **2.** *Anat.* Situated in the hypochondria 1727. *H. region*, the part of the abdomen occupied by the hypochondria. 1727.

1. b. Complaints founded only in an h. imagination 1782.

B. *sb.* **1.** A person affected with or subject to hypochondria 1639. **†2.** = HYPOCHONDRIA 2. –1796.

2. Abbreviations exquisitely refined: as . . Hypps, or Hippo, for Hypochondriacks SWIFT.

So **Hypochondri·acal** *a.* = prec. A. **Hypochondri·acally,** *adv.* **Hypochondri·acism** = HYPOCHONDRIA 2.

Hypochondriasis (həi:poˌkǫndrəi·ăsis, hi:po-). 1766. [f. HYPOCHONDRIA + -ASIS. But the suffix *-asis* is almost entirely limited to names of cutaneous diseases.] *Path.* A disorder of the nervous system, generally accompanied by indigestion, but chiefly characterized by the patient's unfounded belief that he is suffering from some serious bodily disease. So **Hypocho·ndriasm** (in same sense). **Hypocho·ndriast** = HYPOCHONDRIAC *sb.* 1.

Hypocho·ndric, *a. rare.* 1681. [f. as prec. + -IC.] = HYPOCHONDRIAC *a.*

||**Hypochondrium** (həipokǫ·ndriə̆m, hi·po-). 1696. [med. and mod.L. *hypochondrium*; see HYPOCHONDER.] Each of the two hypochondriac regions which are distinguished as 'right' and 'left'.

†Hypocho·ndry. 1621. [– med.L. *hypochondrium*, late L. *-ia*; see HYPOCHONDRIA.] **1.** = HYPOCHONDRIUM. Chiefly *pl.* –1685. **2.** = HYPOCHONDRIA 2. –1874.

†Hy·pocist. 1751. [Cf. Fr. *hypociste*.] = next.

†Hypocistis. 1425. [– L. *hypocistis* (Pliny) – Gr. ὑποκιστίς, f. ὑπό under + κίστος the plant Cistus.] *Med.* The solidified juice of *Cytinus hypocistis*, a parasitic plant of the South of Europe, growing on the roots of Cistus; it contains gallic acid, and was formerly used as a tonic and astringent –1751.

Hypocorism (həip-, hipǫ·kǒriz'm). *rare.* 1850. [– Gr. ὑποκόρισμα, -κορισμος pet-name, f. ὑποκορίζεσθαι play the child, f. ὑπό HYPO- 4 + κόρη child; see ISM.] A pet-name.

Hypocoristic (həi:po-, hi:pokǒri·stik), *a.* 1796. [– Gr. ὑποκοριστικός; see prec., -ISTIC.] Of the nature of a pet-name; pertaining to the habit of using endearing or euphemistic terms.

Harry . . is the free or h. name for Henry PEGGE. So **†Hypocori·stical** *a.* 1609, **-ly** *adv.* 1652.

Hypocotyl (həipo-, hipoˌkǫ·til). 1880. *Bot.* Name for the hypocotyledonous stem. Hence **Hypoco·tylous** *a.*

Hypocotyledonary (həi:po-, hi:poˌkǫtilī·dǒnări), *a.* 1875. [f. HYPO- 2 + COTYLEDON + -ARY¹.] Placed under, or supporting, the cotyledons. So **Hypocotyle·donous** *a.*

Hypocrateriform (həi:po-, hi:poˌkrătīᵊ·rifǭɹm), *a.* 1760. [– mod.L. *hypocrateriformis*, f. Gr. ὑποκρατήριον stand of a large mixing-bowl (f. ὑπό HYPO- 1 + κρατήρ CRATER); see -FORM.] *Bot.* Having the form of a salver raised on a support: said of a corolla in which the tube is long and cylindrical, with a flat spreading limb at right angles to it, as the periwinkle and phlox. So **Hypocrate·rimorphous** *a.*

||**Hypo·crisis.** ME. [eccl. L.; see next.] Hypocrisy.

Hypocrisy (hipǫ·krĭsi). [ME. *ipocrisie*, etc. – OFr. *ypocrisie* (mod. *hypo-*), irreg. – eccl. L. *hypocrisis* – Gr. ὑπόκρισις, f. ὑποκρίνεσθαι answer, play a part, pretend, f. ὑπό HYPO- 1 + κρίνειν decide, determine, judge. The etymol. sp. with *h-* became current (as in French) in XVI.] The assuming of a false appearance of virtue or goodness, with dissimulation of real character or inclinations, esp. in respect of religious life or belief; hence, dissimulation, pretence, sham. Also, an instance of this.

It is the law of goodness to produce h. MOZLEY.

Hypocrite (hi·pǒkrit). [ME. *ypocrite*, etc. – OFr. *ypo-*, *ipocrite* (mod. *hypo-*) – eccl. L. *hypocrita* – Gr. ὑποκριτής actor, dissembler, pretender, f. ὑποκρίνεσθαι; see prec.] One who falsely professes to be virtuously or religiously inclined; one who pretends to be other and better than he is; hence, a dissembler, pretender. Also *attrib.* or *adj.*

Woe vnto you, Scribes and Pharisees, hypocrites *Matt.* 23:13. Her cousins, seeing her with red eyes, set her down as a h. JANE AUSTEN. *attrib.* H. fanatics SWIFT. Hence **Hypo·crital** *a.* (now *rare*), hypocritical. **†Hy·pocritely** *a.* and *adv.*

Hypocritic (hipǫkri·tik). 1540. [– med.L. *hypocriticus* – Gr. ὑποκριτικός; see HYPOCRISY, -IC.]

A. *adj.* = HYPOCRITICAL.

His silken smiles, his h. air CHURCHILL.

B. *sb. rare.* **1.** = HYPOCRITE 1818. **†2.** The art of declamation with appropriate gesture. BURNEY.

Hypocritical (hipǒkri·tikăl), *a.* 1538. [f. as prec.; see -ICAL.] Of the nature of, characterized by, hypocrisy; (of persons) addicted to hypocrisy.

They are exceedingly subtill, hypocriticall and double-dealing PURCHAS. Formal or h. professions FREEMAN. Hence **Hypocri·tically** *adv.* 1548.

Hypocycloid (həipo-, hiposəi·kloid). 1843. [f. HYPO- 2 + CYCLOID.] *Geom.* A curve traced by a point in the circumference of a circle which rolls round the interior circumference of another circle (cf. EPICYCLOID). Hence **Hypocycloi·dal** *a.*

Hypoderm (həi·po-, hi·podə̄ɹm). 1855. [Anglicized f. next. Cf. Fr. *hypoderme* (Bot.).] = HYPODERMA 1.

||**Hypoderma** (həipo-, hipodə̄·ɹmă). *Pl.* **-dermata.** 1826. [mod.L., f. Gr. ὑπό under + δέρμα skin; cf. HYPODERMIS.] **1.** *Zool.* A tissue or layer lying beneath the skin or outer integument in Arthropoda and other invertebrates; 'the subcutaneous areolar tissue of the skin of mammals' (*Syd. Soc. Lex.*). **2.** *Bot.* A layer of cells lying immediately under the epidermis of a leaf or stem 1877. Hence **Hypode·rmal** *a.*

Hypodermatic (həi:po-, hi:poˌdəɹmæ·tik), *a.* 1855. [HYPO- 2.] = HYPODERMIC. Also as *sb.* = hypodermic injection. Hence **Hypoderma·tically** *adv.*

Hypodermic (həipo-, hipodə̄·ɹmik), *a.* 1865. [f. HYPODERMA + -IC. Cf. DERMIC.] **1.** *Med.* Pertaining to the use of medical remedies introduced beneath the skin of the patient; esp. in *h. injection*, the introduction of drugs into the system in this manner. **b.** as *sb.*: A hypodermic remedy 1875. **2.** *Anat.* Lying under the skin: pertaining to the hypoderm 1877. Hence **Hypode·rmically** *adv.* subcutaneously.

||**Hypodermis** (həipo-, hipodə̄·ɹmis). 1866. [f. HYPO- 2 + Gr. -δερμις, *-dermis* as in EPIDERMIS.] **1.** *Bot.* The inner layer of the spore-case of an urn-moss. **2.** *Zool.* = HYPODERMA 1. 1874.

Hypogæic, etc.: see HYPO-.

Hypogastric (həipo-, hipogæ·strik). 1656. [– Fr. *hypogastrique* (Paré), f. *hypogastre*, f. mod.L. *hypogastrium*; see next, -IC.]

A. *adj.* Pertaining to, or situated in, the hypogastrium.

H. region = HYPOGASTRIUM. So **†Hypoga·strical** *a.* 1615.

†B. *sb. pl.* The hypogastric arteries (*rare*) 1722–1797.

||**Hypogastrium** (həipo-, hipogæ·striə̆m). 1681. [mod.L. – Gr. ὑπογάστριον, f. ὑπό HYPO- 1 + γαστήρ, γαστρ- belly; see -IUM.] The lowest region of the abdomen; *spec.* the central part of this, lying between the iliac regions. So **Hypoga·strocele** (*Path.*), a hernia in the hypogastric region.

Hypoge·al, *a.* 1686. [f. as next + -AL¹.] = next.

Hypogean (həipo-, hipodʒī·ăn), *a.* 1852. [f. late L. *hypogeus* – Gr. ὑπόγειος underground (f. γῆ earth) + -AN.] Existing or growing underground; subterranean.

Hypogene (həi·po-, hi·podʒīn), *a.* 1833. [f. HYPO- 2 + Gr. γεν- produce, γίγνεσθαι be born, originate. Cf. Fr. *hypogène*.] *Geol.* Formed under the surface; applied to rocks otherwise called primary and metamorphic; also, subterranean, hypogean. Hence **Hypoge·nic** *a.*

Hypogeous (həipo-, hipodʒī·əs), *a.* Also **-gæous.** 1847. [f. as HYPOGEAN + -OUS.] = HYPOGEAN.

||**Hypogeum** (həipodʒī·ə̆m, hipo-). Also **-gæum.** *Pl.* **-gea** (-ʒī·ă). 1706. [L. *hypogeum, hypogæum* – Gr. ὑπόγειον, ὑπόγαιον adj. n. sing. used subst.; see HYPOGEAN.] An underground chamber or vault. var. **Hy·pogee** (*rare*) 1656.

Hypoglossal (həipo-, hipoglǫ·săl), *a.* 1831. [f. mod.L. HYPOGLOSSUS + -AL¹.] *H. nerve*, the motor nerve of the tongue proceeding from the medulla oblongata and forming the twelfth or last pair of cranial nerves. Also *absol.* = HYPOGLOSSUS.

||**Hypoglossus** (həi·po-, hipoglǫ·sə̆s). 1811. [mod.L., f. Gr. ὑπό under + γλῶσσα tongue.] *Anat.* The hypoglossal nerve.

Hypogyn (həi·po-, hi·podʒin). 1847. [perh. extracted f. next.] *Bot.* A hypogynous plant. So **Hypogy·nic** *a.* = next.

Hypogynous (həip-, hipǫ·dʒinəs), *a.* 1821. [f. mod.L. *hypogynus* (1789), f. Gr. ὑπό under + γυνή woman taken as = 'pistil' + -OUS.] *Bot.* Situated below the pistils or ovary; said of stamens when these grow on the receptacle and are not united to any other organ; also of plants having the stamens so placed. So **Hypo·gyny,** h. state.

Hyponasty (həi·po-, hi·ponæsti). 1875. [f. HYPO- 2 + Gr. ναστός pressed + -Y³. Cf. EPINASTY.] *Bot.* A tendency in plant-organs to grow more rapidly on the under or dorsal side than on the upper or ventral. Hence **Hypona·stic** *a.* pertaining to or characterized by h.

†Hyponitric (həipo-, hiponəi·trik), *a.* 1854. [f. HYPO- 5 + NITRIC.] *Chem.* In *h. acid*, an old name for tetroxide (or peroxide) of nitrogen, pernitric acid, NO_2 or N_2O_4 –1876.

Hyponitrite (həipo-, hiponəi·trəit). 1836. [HYPO- 5.] *Chem.* A salt of hyponitrous acid.

Hyponitrous (həipo-, hiponəi·trəs), *a.* 1826. [f. HYPO- 5 + NITROUS.] *Chem.* In *h. acid*, an unstable acid $(HNO)_2$, obtained in combination as a potassium salt.

Hypopharynx (həipo-, hipofæ·riŋks). 1826. [– Fr. *hypopharynx*, f. *hypo-* HYPO- 2 + *pharynx* PHARYNX.] *Entom.* A median projection from the internal surface of the lower lip in insects. Hence **Hy:popharyn·geal** *a.* situated beneath, or in the lower part of, the pharynx; belonging to the h.

Hypophosphate (həipo-, hipofǫ·sfĕt). 1864. [HYPO- 5.] *Chem.* A salt of hypophosphoric acid.

Hypophosphite (həipo-, hipofǫ·sfəit). 1818. [HYPO- 5.] *Chem.* A salt of hypophosphorous acid.

Hypophosphoric (həipo-, hipofǭsfǫ·rik), *a.* 1854. [f. HYPO- 5 + PHOSPHORIC.] In *h. acid*, $P_2O_2(OH)_4$, a tetrabasic acid, obtained as an odourless liquid.

Hypophosphorous (həipo-, hipofǫ·sfǭrəs), *a.* 1818. [f. HYPO- 5 + PHOSPHOROUS.] In *h. acid*, a monobasic acid of phosphorus, PH_3O_2.

‖**Hypophysis** (həip-, hipǫ·fisis). 1706. [mod.L. – Gr. ὑπόφυσις offshoot, outgrowth, f. ὑπό HYPO- 2 + φύσις growth. Cf. APOPHYSIS, EPIPHYSIS.] †1. *Path.* Cataract in the eye. 2. *Bot.* A part of the embryo in angiosperms, from which the root and root-cap are developed 1875. 3. *Anat.* (In full *H. cerebri*) The pituitary body of the brain 1864. Hence **Hypophy·sial** *a.* of or pertaining to the h. of the brain.

‖**Hyposcenium** (həiposī·niəm, hipo-). 1753. [mod.L., based, after *proscenium*, on Gr. τὰ ὑποσκήνια parts beneath the stage, f. ὑπό beneath + σκήνη stage; see -IUM.] *Gr. Antiq.* The low wall supporting the front of the stage in a Greek theatre.

‖**Hypospadias** (həipospē·diæs, hipo-). 1855. [– Gr. ὑποσπαδίας (Galen, also in late L.) one affected with hypospadias, app. f. ὑπό HYPO- 1 + σπᾶν draw.] *Path.* A congenital malformation consisting in a fissure of the lower wall of the male urethra, the result of arrested development. Hence **Hypospa·diac, -dial, Hyospa·dic** *adjs.* of the nature of, pertaining to, or affected with h.

Hypostasis (həip-, hipǫ·stăsis). *Pl.* **-ses** (-sīz). 1529. [– eccl.L. *hypostasis* (Jerome) – Gr. ὑπόστασις (f. ὑπό HYPO- 1 + στάσις standing, position, state), lit. that which stands under, hence, sediment; also, groundwork, foundation, subject-matter; later, substance, subsistence, existence, reality, essence, personality.] 1. *Med.* **a.** Sediment, deposit; *spec.* that of urine 1590. **b.** Hyperæmia in dependent organs of the body, caused by subsidence of the blood into these parts 1855. †2. Base, foundation, support –1621. 3. *Metaph.* That which subsists, or underlies anything; substance: (*a*) as opp. to attributes or 'accidents'; (*b*) as dist. from what is unsubstantial 1605. 4. Essence, principle, essential principle 1678. 5. *Theol.* Personality, personal existence, person: (*a*) dist. from *nature*, as in the one h. of Christ as dist. from his two *natures* (human and divine), (*b*) dist. from *substance*, as in the three 'hypostases' of the Godhead, which are said to be the same in 'substance' 1529. 6. *Bot.* The suspensor of an embryo 1866.

3. Either as a property or attribute or as an h. or self-subsistence COLERIDGE. 5. That two natures could be concentred into one h. (or person) JER. TAYLOR. So †**Hypo·stasy** = HYPOSTASIS 1, 5.

Hypostasize (həip-, hipǫ·stăsəiz), *v.* 1809. [f. prec. + -IZE.] *trans.* = HYPOSTATIZE *v.* Hence **Hypostasiza·tion.**

Hypostatic (həipo-, hipostæ·tik), *a.* 1678. [– med.L. *hypostaticus* – Gr. ὑποστατικός pertaining to substance, substantial, personal, f. ὑποστατός set under, supporting. Cf. Fr. *hypostatique* (XV).] 1. *Theol.* Of or pertaining to substance, essence, or personality (see HYPOSTASIS). 2. *Path.* Of the nature of hypostasis or excess of blood in the dependent parts of the body 1866.

1. *H. union*: (*a*) the union of the divine and human natures in the 'hypostasis' of Christ; (*b*) the consubstantial union of the three 'hypostases' in the Godhead. So **Hyposta·tical** *a.* = prec. sense 1 1561; †of or pertaining to the essential principles or elements of bodies; hence **-a·lity** 1545. **Hyposta·tically** *adv.* 1593.

Hypostatize (həip-, hi·pǫstătəiz), *v.* 1829. [f. Gr. ὑποστατός (see prec.) + -IZE.] *trans.* To make into or treat as a substance. Hence **Hypostatiza·tion.**

Hypostome (həi·postōᵘm, hi·po-). 1862. [– Fr. *hypostome*, mod.L. *hypostoma* (also used), f. HYPO- 2 + Gr. στόμα mouth.] A part of the mouth in some invertebrates; e.g. the clypeus of dipterous insects, the labium or under lip of trilobites, the proboscis of Hydrozoa.

†**Hyposu·lphate.** 1819. [HYPO- 5.] *Chem.* A salt of hyposulphuric acid. (Now called a DITHIONATE.)

Hyposulphite (həipo-, hiposʊ·lfəit). 1826. [– Fr. *hyposulfite*; see HYPO- 5 and SULPHITE.] *Chem.* A salt of hyposulphurous acid. **a.** Orig. (and still commercially) applied to the salts now called by chemists *thiosulphates.* **b.** Now, a salt of the acid $H_2S_2O_4$, formerly called a *hydrosulphite* 1872.

†**Hyposulphu·ric,** *a.* 1819. [– Fr. *hyposulphurique*; see HYPO- 5, SULPHURIC.] *Chem.* In *h. acid*, an old name of DITHIONIC acid.

Hyposulphurous (həipo-, hiposʊ·lfiŭrəs), *a.* 1817. [f. HYPO- 5 + SULPHUROUS.] In *h. acid*: †**a.** The orig. name for *thiosulphuric acid.* **b.** Now, the acid $H_2S_2O_4$; formerly called *hydrosulphurous acid* 1872.

Hypotenusal (həip-, hipǫtĕniū·săl). Also **hypothenusal.** 1571. [– late L. *hypotenusalis*, f. L. *hypotenusa*; see next, -AL¹.]

A. *adj.* Pertaining to, of the nature of, or forming a hypotenuse. Now *rare.*

†**B.** *sb.* (sc. *line*) = HYPOTENUSE –1661.

Hypotenuse (həip-, hipǫ·tĕniūs). Also **hypothenuse.** 1571. [– L. *hypotenusa* – Gr. ὑποτείνουσα, pres. pple. fem. of ὑποτείνειν stretch under, the full expression being ἡ τὴν ὀρθὴν γωνίαν ὑποτείνουσα (sc. γραμμή or πλευρά). The erron. sp. with *th* was formerly the more usual.] The side of a right-angled triangle which subtends, or is opposite to, the right angle.

‖**Hypothallus** (həipo-, hipoþæ·lǒs). 1855. [mod.L., f. HYPO- 2 + THALLUS.] *Bot.* The fibrous or filamentary substratum on which the thallus of lichens is developed. Hence **Hypotha·lline** *a.*

Hypothec (həip-, hipǫ·þĕk). Also **hypotheca** (h(ə)ipoþī·kă). 1592. [– Fr. *hypothèque* – late L. *hypotheca* – Gr. ὑποθήκη deposit, pledge, f. ὑποτιθέναι deposit as a pledge, f. ὑπο down + τιθέναι put, place.] 'A security established by law in favour of a creditor over a subject belonging to his debtor, while the subject continues in the debtor's possession' (*Bell's Dict. Law Scot.*). **a.** *Rom. Law.* 'An agreement without delivery' (Poste). **b.** *Scots Law.* The lien or prior claim of a landlord for his rent over the crop and stock of a tenant farmer (but see now *Act* 43 *Vict.* c. 12 § 1), and over the furniture and other effects of a tenant in urban property 1730. So **Hypo·thecal** (? *Obs.*), **Hypo·thecary** *adjs.*, of, pertaining to, of the nature of, an h. or mortgage.

Hypothecate (həip-, hipǫ·þĭkēᵗt), *v.* 1681. [f. *hypothecat-*, pa. ppl. stem of med.L. *hypothecare*, f. *hypotheca*; see prec., -ATE³.] *trans.* To give or pledge as security; to pawn, mortgage.

He had no power to h. any part of the public revenue MACAULAY. Hence **Hypo·thecator,** one who hypothecates or pledges something as security.

Hypothecation (həip-, hipǫþĭkē¹·ʃən). 1681. [f. prec.; see -ATION.] The act of pledging as security; pledging or pawning. In some legal systems applied only to a lien upon immovable property; in others to a lien on any kind of property.

Hypothenusal, hypothenuse, erron. ff. HYPOTENUSAL, HYPOTENUSE.

Hypothesis (həip-, hipǫ·þĭsis). Pl. **-ses** (-sīz). 1596. [– late L. *hypothesis* – Gr. ὑπόθεσις foundation, base, f. ὑπό under + θέσις placing.] †1. A subordinate thesis; a particular case of a general proposition –1721. 2. A proposition or principle put forth or stated merely as a basis for reasoning or argument, or as a premiss from which to draw a conclusion. In *Logic*, The antecedent or protasis of a conjunctive or conditional proposition. 1656. **b.** A case or alternative considered or dealt with as a basis for action 1794. 3. A supposition or conjecture put forth to account for known facts; *esp.* in the sciences, a provisional supposition which accounts for known facts, and serves as a starting-point for further investigation by which it may be proved or disproved 1646. 4. A supposition in general; something assumed to be true without proof; an assumption 1654. **b.** Hence *spec.* A mere assumption or guess 1625.

1. If the thesis be true, the h. will follow FILMER. 2. Collusion being, by h., out of the question BABBAGE. **b.** In each of these last hypotheses, you will observe the necessity that we should be within reach of each other WELLINGTON. 3. The celebrated nebular hypotheses of Herschel and of Laplace 1893. 4. **b.** Your reasoning..seems plausible; but still it is only h. SCOTT. Hence **Hypo·thesize** *v. intr.* to frame a h.; *trans.* to assume 1738.

Hypothetic (həip-, hipǫþe·tik), *a.* (*sb.*) 1680. [– L. *hypotheticus* – Gr. ὑποθετικός pertaining to ὑπόθεσις; see prec., -IC.] = next.

Hypothetical (həipoþe·tikăl, hipo-), *a.* (*sb.*) 1588. [f. as prec. + -AL¹; see -ICAL.] 1. Involving hypothesis; conjectural 1617. **b.** *Logic*, Of a proposition: Conditional; opp. to CATEGORICAL. Of a syllogism: Having a hypothetical proposition for one of its premisses. 1588. 2. Depending on hypothesis; supposed, assumed 1665. 3. *sb.* A hypothetical proposition or syllogism 1654.

2. It would be..impossible..to declare..what would be our conduct upon any h. case WELLINGTON. Phr. †*H. necessity*: that kind of necessity which exists only on the supposition that something is or is to be; repr. Aristotle's ἀναγκαῖον ἐξ ὑποθέσεως. Hence **Hypothe·tically** *adv.*

Hypothetico-disjunctive, *a.* 1837. *Logic.* Combining the 'hypothetical' (conjunctive) and disjunctive forms of statement; applied to a conditional proposition of which the consequent is disjunctive (e.g. If A is B, C is either D or E); also to the DILEMMA. **b.** as *sb.* A proposition or syllogism of this kind.

Hypo·thetize, *v. rare.* 1852. [f. Gr. ὑπόθετος, base of ὑποθετικός HYPOTHETIC, + -IZE]. = HYPOTHESIZE.

‖**Hypotrachelium** (h(ə)ipotrăkī·liəm). 1563. [L. – Gr. ὑποτραχήλιον, f. ὑπό HYPO- 1 + τράχηλος neck; see -IUM.] *Arch.* The lower part or neck of the capital of a column; in the Doric order, the groove between the neck of the capital and the shaft.

Hypotrochoid (h(ə)ipotrōᵘ·koid, h(ə)ipǫ·trokoid). 1843. [f. HYPO- 2 + TROCHOID.] *Geom.* The curve described by a point rigidly connected with the centre of a circle which rolls on the inside of another circle. Hence **Hypotrochoi·dal** *a.* of the form of, or pertaining to, a h.

‖**Hypotyposis** (h(ə)ipot(ə)ipōᵘ·sis). 1583. [– Gr. ὑποτύπωσις sketch, outline, pattern, f. ὑποτυποῦν sketch, f. τύπος TYPE; see -OSIS.] *Rhet.* Vivid description of a scene, event, or situation.

Hypoxanthine (həip-, hipǫksæ·nþəin). 1850. [f. HYPO- 5 + XANTHINE.] *Chem.* A nitrogenous substance, $C_5H_4N_4O$, found in the muscle, spleen, heart, etc. of vertebrates, and forming a white crystalline powder; also called *sarcine.* Hence **Hypoxa·nthic** *a.* derived from, or of the nature of, h.

Hypped (hipt), *ppl. a.* 1710. Now HIPPED *a.²*, q.v. So **Hy·ppish** *a.*

Hypsi- (hi·psi), repr. Gr. ὕψι *adv.* on high, aloft, in comb. also = high, lofty. See also HYPSO-.

Hypsiloid (hipsəi·loid, hi·psiloid), *a.* 1886. [– Gr. ὖ ψιλόν 'simple u' + -ειδής -OID, with assim. to prec.] V-shaped or U-shaped.

Hypsistarian (hipsistē³·riăn). 1705. [f. Gr. Ὑψιστάριος (f. ὕψιστος highest) + -AN.] *Eccl. Hist.* **a.** *adj.* Belonging to an eclectic sect (4th c.), so called from worshipping God under the name of the Most High (ὕψιστος). **b.** *sb.* A member of this sect.

Hypso- (hi·pso), repr. rare Gr. ὑψο-, used with same force as ὑψι- HYPSI-; in mod. use, occas. as comb. f. ὕψος 'height'.

Hypsometer (hipsǫ·mĭtəɹ). 1840. [f. prec. + -METER.] An instrument for measuring altitudes, esp. one consisting essentially of a delicate thermometer, by which the boiling-point of water is observed at particular elevations. Hence **Hypsome·tric, -al** *a.* pertaining to hypsometry or the h. **Hypsome·trically** *adv.* **Hypso·metry,** the measuring of altitudes; the science which treats of this; also, the condition of a part of the earth's surface in reference to height above (or depth below) the level of the sea.

Hypt, variant of HYPPED.

Hypural (həip-, hipiūə·răl), *a.* (*sb.*) 1871. [f. Gr. ὑπ(ό HYPO- 2 + οὐρά tail + -AL¹.] Situated beneath the tail; *spec.* in *Ichthyol.* applied to the bones beneath the axis of the tail, which support fin-rays. Also *absol.* as *sb.*

Hyraci-, hyraco- (bef. a vowel **hyrac-**), L. and Gr. comb. forms respectively of HYRAX.

Hyracoid (həiə·răkoid), *a.* [f. L. *hyrac-*, stem of HYRAX + -OID.] Resembling a hyrax; pertaining to or characteristic of the order or sub-order *Hyracoidea*, containing the Hyrax and its congeners.

‖**Hyrax** (həiə·ræks). 1832. [mod.L. – Gr. ὕραξ, ὑρακ- shrew-mouse.] *Zool.* A genus of small rabbit-like quadrupeds, containing the DAMAN, cony, or rock-rabbit of Syria, an Abyssinian species or sub-species, and the Cape Hyrax or rock-badger (*klipdas*) of S. Africa. It is now made the type of an order or sub-order *Hyracoidea*. So **Hyra·cid** *a.* belonging to the family *Hyracidæ*, or its sole genus *Hyrax*.

Hyrse, obs. f. HIRSE.

Hyrst: see HURST.

Hyson (həi·sən). 1740. [– Chinese *hsi-ch'un*, in Cantonese *hei-ch'un*, 'bright spring', the name of coarse green tea. *Young Hyson* is *yü-ch'ien* = 'before the rains' (when picked).] A species of green tea from China. *Young H.*, a fine green tea (see above).

Hy-spy (həi spəi). Also **I spy.** 1777. A boy's game played by hiders and seekers, in which a seeker cries 'hy spy!', on discovering one of the hiders.

Hyssop (hi·sǫp). [OE. (*h*)*ysope*, reinforced in ME. by OFr. *ysope, isope*, later assim. to the source, L. *hyssopus, -um* – Gr. ὕσσωπος, -ον, of Semitic origin (cf. Heb. *'ēzōḇ*).] **1.** A small bushy aromatic herb of the genus *Hyssopus* (N. O. *Labiatæ*); esp. *H. officinalis*. **2.** In Biblical use: A plant, prob. the Thorny Caper (*Capparis spinosa*), the twigs of which were used for sprinkling in Jewish rites; hence, a bunch of this used in ceremonial purification, and allusively OE. **b.** As the type of a lowly plant (1 Kings 4:33); whence *fig.* ME. **3.** Applied in the western U.S. to species of *Artemisia* 1807.

2. Purge me with hyssope, and I shalbe cleane *Ps.* 51:7. **b.** And hee spake of trees, from the Cedar tree that is in Lebanon, euen vnto the Hyssope that springeth out of the wall 1 *Kings* 4:33.

Hyst-: see HIST-.

Hysteranthous (histĕræ·nþəs), *a.* 1835. [f. Gr. ὕστερος later + ἄνθος flower + -OUS.] *Bot.* Of plants: Having the flowers appearing before the leaves. (The word should mean the reverse of this.)

Hysterectomy (histĕre·ktŏmi). 1881. [f. HYSTERO- + -ECTOMY.] Excision of the uterus.

‖**Hysteresis** (histĕrī·sis). 1881. [– Gr. ὑστέρησις short-coming, deficiency, f. ὑστερεῖν be behind, come late, f. ὕστερος late.] *Electr.* The lagging of magnetic effects behind their causes. So **Hystere·sial** *a.*

‖**Hysteria** (histiə·riă). 1801. [mod.L., f. L. *hystericus*; see next, -IA¹.] **1.** *Path.* A functional disturbance of the nervous system, characterized by anæsthesia, hyperæsthesia, convulsions, etc., and usually attended with emotional disturbances or perversion of the moral and intellectual faculties. (Colloq. called *hysterics*.) Women being more liable than men to this disorder, it was originally thought to be due to a disturbance of the uterus. **2.** *transf.* and *fig.* Unhealthy emotion or excitement 1839.

2. A wave of humanitarian h. 1897.

Hysteric (histe·rik). 1657. [– L. *hystericus* – Gr. ὑστερικός belonging to, suffering in, the womb, hysterical, f. ὑστέρα womb, esp. in ὑστερικὰ πάθη, ὑστερικὴ πνίξ (in mod.L. *hysterica passio*). Cf. Fr. *hystérique* (XVI).]

A. *adj.* **1.** = HYSTERICAL A. 1. **2.** = HYSTERICAL A. 2. 1751. †**3.** Of medicines: Good for diseases of the uterus –1732.

2. The united pangs..produced a sort of h. laugh SMOLLETT.

B. *sb.* †**1.** A remedy for uterine disorders –1757. **2.** One subject to hysteria 1751. **3.** *pl.* **Hysterics** (also *sing.*). An equivalent of HYSTERIA, but chiefly = hysterical fits or convulsions; hence in sing.: A convulsive fit of laughter or weeping 1727.

3. Sobs, And indications of hysterics BYRON. Hence **Hyste·ricism,** h. state; hysteria.

Hysterical (histe·rikăl). 1615. [f. as prec. + -AL¹; see -ICAL.]

A. *adj.* **1.** Of, pertaining to, or characteristic of hysteria; affected with hysteria. **2.** *transf.* and *fig.* Morbidly emotional or excited 1704.

B. *sb.* †**1.** = HYSTERIC B. 1. –1671. **2.** *pl.* = HYSTERIC B. 3 (*rare*) 1834.

Hence **Hyste·rically** *adv.*

Hystero-¹ (hi·stĕro), bef. a vowel **hyster-,** comb. f. Gr. ὑστέρα womb. Used in recent formations with the senses: **a.** Of the womb, uterine, as in *h.-paralysis*, etc. **b.** Accompanied or associated with hysteria, hysterical, as *h.-catalepsy*, etc.

Hy·sterocele [Gr. κήλη tumour], *Path.* a hernia containing the uterus or part of it. ‖**Hysterody·nia** [Gr. ὀδύνη pain], *Path.* pain of the womb. **Hy:stero-e·pilepsy,** a form of hysteria characterized by the occurrence of epileptiform convulsions; occurring chiefly among females; hence **Hy:stero-epile·ptic** *a.* and *sb.* **Hy·sterophore** [Gr. -φορος], *Surg.* a pessary for supporting the uterus.

Hy·stero-², comb. f. Gr. ὕστερος later.

Hysteroge·nic, *a.* 1886. [f. HYSTERO-¹ + *-genic* as in PHOTOGENIC; see -GEN, -IC.] *Path.* Producing hysteria; relating to the production of hysteria. So **Hystero·genous** *a.* **Hystero·geny,** the production of hysteria.

Hysteroid, -al (hi·stĕroid, -ăl), *a.* 1855. [irreg. f. HYSTERIA + -OID + -AL¹.] Resembling or having the form of hysteria.

†**Hystero·logy**¹. 1623. [– late L *hysterologia* – Gr. ὑστερολογία; see HYSTERO-², -LOGY.] *Gram.*, etc. = HYSTERON PROTERON –1842.

Hystero·logy². 1855. [f. HYSTERO-¹ + -LOGY.] *Med.* A treatise on the uterus.

‖**Hysteron proteron** (hi·stĕrǫn, prǫ·tĕrǫn), *sb.* (*a.* and *adv.*) 1565. [Late L. (Servius) – Gr. ὕστερον πρότερον latter [put as] former.] **1.** *Gram.* and *Rhet.* A figure of speech in which what should come last is put first. **2.** *gen.* The position or arrangement of things in the reverse of their natural or rational order 1589. **3.** as *adj.* 1646. †**4.** as *adv.* By or with an inversion of the natural order of things –1617.

1. In these woordes..'Take ye: Eate ye: This is my Bodie', They have founde a Figure called Hysteron Proteron JEWEL. **3.** This *hysteron proteron* Stuff NORTH.

Hysterophyte (hi·stĕrŏfəit). 1855. [– mod.L. *hysterophytum*, pl. *-phyta* (Fries, 1821), f. Gr. ὑστέρα womb + φυτόν plant.] *Bot.* A plant of the class *Hysterophyta* or *Fungi*; any fungus growing upon, and deriving its nourishment from, organic matter. Hence **Hy:stero·phytal** *a.* fungal.

‖**Hysterosis** (histĕrōᵘ·sis). 1620. [mod.L.; see HYSTERO-², -OSIS.] = HYSTERON PROTERON.

Hysterotomy (histĕrǫ·tŏmi). 1801. [– mod.L. *hysterotomia*; see HYSTERO-¹, -TOMY. Cf. Fr. *hystérotomie* (XVIII).] *Surg.* The operation of cutting into the uterus; the Cæsarean section; also = HYSTERECTOMY. So **Hy·sterotome,** a knife for performing h.

Hystricid (hi·strisid). [– mod.L. *Hystricidæ*, f. *hystrix, hystric-* – Gr. ὕστριξ, ὑστριχ- porcupine; see -ID³.] *Zool.* A rodent of the family *Hystricidæ*; a porcupine. So **Hy·stricine** *a.* pertaining to the sub-family *Hystricinæ* 1883.

Hystricomorph (hi·strikomǭɹf). 1882. [– mod.L. *Hystricomorpha*, f. as prec. + Gr. -μορφος shaped (μορφή form); see -A 4.] *Zool.* A member of the *Hystricomorpha*, a primary division of Rodents including the porcupine and its congeners. So **Hy:stricomo·rphic, -phine** *adjs.* of, belonging to, or having the characters of the *Hystricomorpha*.

I

I (əi), the ninth letter and third vowel of the Roman alphabet, going back through the Greek *Iota* to the Semitic *Yod*. The Semitic letter represents a consonant (= English *y* in *yellow, yoke*, etc.); by the Greeks, who had no *y* consonant, it was adopted as the symbol of the *i* vowel. In the Latin alphabet, on the other hand, it was used with both values, viz. that of *i* vowel (long and short), and *y* consonant, as in *ibīdem, ibis*; *iacui, Iouis*. When the consonant sound (y) passed in Romanic into the 'soft g' sound (dʒ), it continued to be symbolized by I until the early part of the 17th century, when it came to be denoted by J j, a differentiated form of I i, which was then confined to the vowel-sounds.

The original value of the Græco-Roman **I** vowel when long was that of the 'high-front-narrow' vowel of Bell's scale, as in French *machine*, etc. In Teutonic, the short *i* has prob. always been the corresponding 'wide' vowel (i), as in Eng. f*i*nny, m*i*ssing. Long *i*, on the other hand, has changed into a diphthong with *i* as its second element. The English diphthong is here symbolized by (əi), the first element being taken as the 'mid-mixed-wide' vowel of Bell's scale, the general 'obscure vowel' of English; but it varies locally. Cf. OE., OHG., OLG. *mīn* with Eng. *mine*, Ger. *mein*, Du. *mijn*.

For other values of the letter *i* see the key to the pronunciation.

The dot surmounting the minuscule or 'small letter' i is derived from a diacritic mark, like an acute accent, used in Latin MSS. to indicate the *i* in positions in which it might have been mistaken for part of another letter. The same cause led finally to the growth in English of a kind of scribal canon that *i* must not be used as a final letter, but must in this position be changed to *y*; though in inflected forms, where the *i* was not final, it was retained; hence *city, cities*; *holy, holier, holiest*, etc.

I. The letter and its name. (Pl. *Is, I's, is, i's*.) *I per se*, or *I per se I*, the letter *I* forming a syllable by itself, esp. the pronoun *I*. Also *fig.* esp. in *To dot the* i's, etc.; see DOT *v.*¹

II. I. Used to denote serial order; marking, e.g., the ninth sheet of a book, etc. **2.** In *Logic*, a particular affirmative. **3.** The Roman numeral symbol for ONE. (This was not originally the letter, but a single line denoting unity.) **4.** *Math.* In Higher Algebra, *i* or ι often stands for $\sqrt{-1}$. In Quaternions, *i, j, k*, are symbols of vectors.

III. *Abbreviations.* I (*Chem.*) = Iodine. I (*Zool.*) = incisor. I.D.B. = illicit diamond buyer. *i.h.p.* (*Mech.*) = indicated horse-power. I.L.P. = Independent Labour Party. See also IHS, and IOU.

I (əi), *pers. pron.*, 1*st sing. nom.* [OE. *ić* = OFris., OS. (Du.) *ik*, OHG. *ih* (G. *ich*), ON. *ek(a)*, Goth. *ik* (:– Gmc. **eka* :– **egō*), corresp. basically, but with variation of vowel, consonant, and ending to L. *egŏ*, Rom. **eo* (whence Fr. *je*, etc.), Gr. ἐγώ(ν), Skr. *ahám*, Av. *azem*, OSl. (*j*)*azŭ* (Russ. *ya*), Lith. *eo*, Lett., OPruss., Arm. *es*. The oblique cases of the singular are applied from a stem *me*- common to the whole Aryan family. The plural nom. *we* has a Germanic form **wi-z* from a primitive stem *wei-*, Skr. *vay-ám*; its oblique cases are from a stem *uns-* (:– **n̥s*), co-radicate with L. *nos*, Skr. *nas*. The paradigm of the pronoun in modern English is:

		SINGULAR.	PLURAL.
Nom.		I	we
Dat. Acc.		me	us
Poss. Pron.	*absol.*	mine	ours.
	adj.	my	our.]

I. As pronoun. **1.** The pronoun by which a speaker or writer denotes himself, in the nominative case. **2.** Sometimes used for the objective after a verb or preposition. (This is now considered ungrammatical.) 1596.

1. I care not, I, to fish in seas 1653. Poor I to be a nun DRYDEN. **2.** My father hath no childe but I SHAKS.

II. As substantive. **1.** The pronoun as a word 1599. **2.** *Metaph.* The subject or object of self-consciousness; the *ego* 1710.

1. Phr. *Another I* = a second self. **2.** A Manifestation of Power from something which is *not I* CARLYLE.

Phrase. I AM, the Lord Jehovah, the Self-existent (*Exod.* 3:14).

I, obs. f. AYE yes, and of EYE; var. of †HI, they.

I', i, weakened f. IN *prep.* bef. a cons., as in *i'faith*; now *dial.* or *arch.*

†**I-**[1], *prefix*, also written Y-, OE. *ȝe-*, forming collective sbs., deriv. adjs., advbs., and vbs.; esp. used with the pa. pple. of verbs.

I-[2], reduced f. IN-[3] (q.v.), occurring in words of L. origin bef. *gn-* (later *n*), as *ignoble, ignominy*, etc.

-i, *suffix*: pron. əi in L. words, i in It. words; pl. inflexion of L. masc. sbs. in *-us* and *-er*, and of It. sbs. in *-o* and *-e*, retained in Eng. in learned and techn. use, e.g. *cirri, foci, radii*; *banditti, dilettanti*; *illuminati, literati*.

-i-, connective or quasi-connective L. *-i-*, being the stem-vowel, as in *omni-vorus*, or a weakened representative thereof, as in *herbi-vorus* (*herba-*), or merely connective, as in *gramin-i-vorus* (*gramin-*). So in many English words.

Ia-: obs. sp. of JA-.

-ia, *suffix*[1], a termination of L. and Gr. sbs. [= *-i-*, -ι-, stem or connective vowel + -A *suffix* 2]. Examples in Eng. use are *hydrophobia, mania, militia*, etc.; hence frequent in mod.L. terms of Pathology, of Botany, in names of countries, and in names of alkaloids (after *ammonia*), as *aconitia, atropia*, etc., in which the ending *-ine* is now preferred.

-ia, *suffix*[2] [f. *-i-* stem or connective vowel + -A *suffix* 4], forming plurals of L. and Gr. sbs. in *-ium, -e* (*-i*), -ιον, some of which are in Eng. use, as *paraphernalia, regalia*, etc.; hence freq. in mod.L. names of classes, etc. in Zoology, as *Mammalia*, etc.

-ial, *suffix*, repr. L. *-ialis, -iale*, in adjs. formed from sb. stems in *-io-, -ia-*, as *curialis, tibialis*; extensively used in med.L., Fr., and Eng. to form derivative adjs. from L. adjs. in *-is, -ius*, as *cælestis, celestial, terrestris, terrestrial, dictatorius, dictatorial*. Formally, a comp. prefix f. -I- + -AL[1].

Iamb (əi·æmb). 1842. [Anglicized form of IAMBUS. Cf. Fr. *ïambe* (XVI).] *Pros.* = IAMBUS.

Iambic (əi,æ·mbik). 1575. [– Fr. *ïambique* – late L. *iambicus* – Gr. ἰαμβικός; see IAMBUS, -IC.]

A. *adj.* Of a verse, rhythm, etc.: Consisting of, characterized by, or based on iambuses. Of a foot: Consisting of, or of the nature of, an iambus. 1586. **2.** Of a poet: Employing iambic metres 1581.

1. The feet of our verses are either iambick, as 'aloft, create'; or trochaick, as 'holy, lofty' JOHNSON. **2.** Th' Iambick Muse P. FLETCHER. So **Ia·mbical** *a.*, **-ly** *adv.*

B. *sb.* (Usu. *pl.*) An iambic foot or verse. Also *transf.* a piece of invective or satire in verse (cf. IAMBUS) 1575.

Ĭămbĭcs mārch frŏm shōrt tŏ lōng COLERIDGE.

Iambist (əi,æ·mbist). 1839. [– Gr. ἰαμβιστής libeller, f. ἰαμβίζειν assail in iambics, lampoon; see IAMBUS, -IST.] A writer of iambics. So **Ia·mbize** *v.* (*rare*), to attack in iambic verse; to satirize.

Iambographer (əi,æmbǫ·grăfəɹ). 1625. [f. Gr. ἰαμβογράφος + -ER[1] 4; see next, -GRAPHER.] A writer of iambics.

‖**Iambus** (əi,æ·mbŏs). 1586. [L. – Gr. ἴαμβος, f. ἰάπτειν assail (in words); the iambic trimeter being first used by Greek satiric writers.] A metrical foot consisting of a short followed by a long syllable; in accentual verse, of an unaccented followed by an accented syllable.

-ian, *suffix*, repr. L. *-ianus*, i.e. an original or connective vowel *-i-*, with suffix *-anus*; see -AN 1, 'of or belonging to'. In mod. formations, esp. from proper names, the number of which is without limit, as *Addisonian, Bodleian, Gladstonian, Wordsworthian*; *Aberdonian, Oxonian*, etc. In sbs. like *theologian*, *-ian* is a refashioning of Fr. *-ien*.

Ianthine (əi,æ·nþin), *a.* 1609. [– L. *ianthinus* – Gr. ἰάνθινος.] Violet-coloured.

Iatraliptic (əi,ætrăli·ptik). *rare.* 1656. [– L. *iatralipticus* – Gr. ἰατραλειπτικός, f. ἰατραλείπτης, f. ἰατρός physician + ἀλείπτης anointer.] **a.** *adj.* Relating to the cure of diseases by the use of unguents. **b.** *sb.* A physician who follows this method.

Iatric (əi,æ·trik), *a. rare.* 1851. [– Gr. ἰατρικός, f. ἰατρός healer, physician, f. ἰᾶσθαι heal; see -IC.] Medical; medicinal. So **Ia·trical** *a.* medical 1688; **Ia:trico-scri·ptural** *a.* 1716.

I..am..still under Iatrical advice BYRON.

Iatro- (əi,ē^i·tro, əi,æ·tro), comb. form of ἰατρός physician.

Iatro-che·mical *a.* = CHEMIATRIC; so **Iatroche·mist,** one belonging to the iatro-chemical school; also *gen.* one who applies chemistry to medical practice. **Ia:tromathema·tical** *a.*, †practising medicine in conjunction with astrology; relating to or holding a mathematical theory of medicine; hence **Ia:tromathema·tically** *adv.* 1603; so **Ia:tromathemati·cian,** one belonging to the iatromathematical school.

Iberian (əibī^ə·riăn). 1601. [f. L. *Iberia*, the country of the *Iberi* or *Iberes* – Gr. Ἴβηρες the Spaniards; also an Asiatic people near the Caucasus. See -AN, -IAN.]

A. *adj.* **1.** Of or pertaining to ancient Iberia in Europe, or its inhabitants; hence **a.** Basque; **b.** Of Spain and Portugal unitedly. 1618. **2.** Of or pertaining to ancient Iberia in Asia, corresp. to modern Georgia 1671.

2. The Hyrcanian cliffs Of Caucasus, and dark I. dales MILT. *P.R.* III. 318.

B. *sb.* **1. a.** A Basque; a Spaniard 1623. **b.** The Basque language. **2.** An inhabitant of ancient Iberia in Asia 1601.

Ibex (əi·beks). Pl. **ibexes**, rarely **ibices** (əi·bisīz). 1607. [L. *ibex, ibic-*.] A species of wild goat (*Capra ibex* or *Ibex ibex*) inhabiting the Alps and Apennines, the male of which has very large strongly ridged recurved horns, and brownish or reddish grey hair; the female, shorter horns and grey hair; also called *bouquetin* and *steinbock*.

‖**Ibidem** (ibəi·dem). 1663. [L., f. *ibi* there + *-dem*, as in *idem, tandem*, etc.] In the same place. Abbrev. *ibid.* or *ib.*

Ibis (əi·bis). *Pl.* **ibises**; also (now rarely) **ibides** (əi·bidīz), **ibes** (əi·bīz). ME. [– L. *ibis* (gen. *ibis, ibidis*, pl. *ibes*) – Gr. ἶβις the ibis, an Egyptian bird.] A genus of large grallatorial birds of the family *Ibididæ*, allied to the stork and heron, comprising many species with long legs and slender decurved bill; a bird of this genus, esp. (and originally) the Sacred Ibis of Egypt (*Ibis religiosa*), with white and black plumage, venerated by the ancient Egyptians.

Other species are the Glossy, Scarlet, and White I.

-ible, the form of the suffix -BLE, repr. L. *-ĭbilis*, and *-ībilis*; as *legible, visible, audible*, etc. Often displaced by *-able* in words that have come through Fr., or are formed on an Eng. verb, as *referable, tenable, dividable*, etc.

Ibsenism (i·bsəniz'm). 1891. [f. the name of Henrik *Ibsen* (1828–1906), Norwegian dramatist and poet + -ISM.] The dramatic principles and aims characteristic of the writings of Ibsen and the Ibsenites, which expose conventional hypocrisies. Hence **Ibse·nian** *a.* and *sb.* **I·bsenite,** an admirer or imitator of Ibsen.

Ic, obs. f. I *pron.*

-ic (formerly **-ick, -ik(e, -ique**) *suffix*, primarily forming adjs., many of which are used as sbs. having also the form **-ics**; see 2.

1. In adjs., immediately repr. Fr.*-ique* – L. *-ic-us*, occurring in words of L. formation, as *civicus, classicus*, or in L. words adopted from Gr., as *comicus* κωμικός. This suffix in Gr. formed adjs. with the sense 'after the manner of', 'of the nature of', 'pertaining to', 'of'. In L. it was used chiefly in the compound suffix *-aticus* (-ATIC, -AGE), and in wds. formed from Gr., or on Gr. types. **b.** In *Chem.*, the suffix is used to form the names of oxygen acids and other compounds having a higher degree of oxidation than those whose names end in *-ous*; e.g. *chloric acid* HO_3Cl, *chlorous acid* HO_2Cl.

2. Already in Gr., adjs. in -ικός were used absol. as sbs., e.g. in sing. masc., as Στωικός (man) of the porch, Stoic, hence in L. *Stoicus*; also, in sing. fem., in names of arts (sc. τέχνη), or systems of thought, knowledge, or action (sc. θεωρία, φιλοσοφία), e.g. ἡ μουσική music, ἡ ἠθική ethics, etc.; and in neut. pl., as τὰ οἰκονομικά things pertaining to domestic economy, a treatise on this, economics.

In English, words of this class in use bef. 1500 had the singular form, as *arsmetike, magike, logike* (*-ique*), etc.; this form is retained in *arithmetic, logic, magic, music, rhetoric.* Subseq., forms in **-ics** (*-iques*) occur as names of treatises, e.g. *etiques* = τὰ ἠθικά; and towards 1600 this form is applied to the subject-matter of such treatises, in *mathematics, economics*, etc. From 1600 onward this has been the accepted form with names of sciences, as *acoustics*, etc., or matters of practice, as *æsthetics, politics, tactics*, etc. The names of sciences, even though ending in *-ics*, are construed as singular; while names of practical matters, as *gymnastics, politics, tactics*, remain plural, in construction as well as in form.

3. Besides the preceding, there are many other sbs. formed directly from adjs. in *-ic* taken absol., as *emetic, cosmetic* (pl. *emetics*, etc.); *epic, lyric, Anacreontics, iambics; domestic, rustic, classic, mechanic, lunatic.*

-ical, a compound suffix, f. -IC + -AL[1], forming an adj. from a sb. in *-ic*, as *music, musical*, or a secondary adj., as *comic, comical.* Many adjs. have a form both in *-ic* and *-ical*, that in *-ical* being usually the earlier and the more commonly used. Often also the form in *-ic* is restricted to the sense 'of' or 'of the nature of' the subject in question, while that in *-ical* has wider or more transferred senses.

-ically, advb. ending, f. -ICAL + -LY[2], forming advs. from adjs. in *-ical*, which are used also as the advs. from the corresponding adjs. in -IC. Thus *poetic, poetical*, adv. *poetically.*

Icarian (əikē^ə·riăn), *a.* 1595. [f. L. *Icarius* = Gr. Ἰκάριος, f. *Icarus*, Ἴκαρος the son of Daedalus, in Gr. Myth. See -AN, -IAN.] Of, pertaining to, or characteristic of Icarus, who, in escaping from Crete, flew so high that the sun melted the wax with which his wings were fastened on, so that he fell into the sea; hence, applied to ambitious acts which end in ruin.

With I. winge 1639.

†**Icasm.** [– Gr. εἴκασμα comparison, simile, f. εἰκάζειν make like, depict.] A figurative expression. HY. MORE.

Ice (əis), *sb.* [OE. *īs* = OFris., OS., OHG. *īs* (Du. *ijs*, G. *eis*), ON. *iss* :– Gmc. **īsam*, **īsaz*, having analogues elsewhere in the Iranian languages.] **1.** Frozen water; water rendered solid by cold. **b.** With *pl.*: A mass or piece of ice OE. **2.** *The ice*: the layer of ice on a river, lake, sea, etc. ME. **3.** *fig.* ME. **4.** A congeiation resembling ice. BACON. **5. a.** A frozen confection. Now with *an* and *pl.* An ice-cream or water-ice 1773. **b.** = ICING 1725. **6.** *attrib.*, as *ice-beach, -chart, -cutter*, etc. 1591.

2. Phr. *To break the ice*: to make a passage for boats, etc. by breaking the frozen surface of a river, lake, etc.; *fig.* to make a beginning; in mod. usage, to break through cold reserve. *To cut no ice*: to effect nothing. **3.** Tut, tut, thou art all Ice SHAKS.

Comb.: **i.-action,** the action of ice upon the surface of the earth, esp. during the ice-age; **-age,** the glacial period (see GLACIAL); **-anchor,** a grapnel for holding a ship to an ice-floe; **-apron,** a pointed structure for protecting a bridge-pier from ice carried down by the stream; **-axe,** an axe used by Alpine climbers, for cutting steps; **-bag,** an india-rubber bag filled with ice for application to some part of the body; **-beam,** a beam placed at the stern or bow of a ship to resist the pressure of ice; **-bearer,** a CRYOPHORUS; **-bed,** a stratified glacial deposit; **-belt** = ICE-FOOT; **-boulder,** a boulder conveyed by glacial action; **-box,** a box for holding ice, an ice-chest; **-calk** = CALK *sb.* 2; **-canoe,** a canoe with iron runners for use on frozen lakes or rivers; **-chair,** a sledge-chair; **-chamber,** a compartment containing, or cooled by, ice; a refrigerating chamber; **-chest,** a refrigerator; **-claw,** an iron claw for grappling and lifting blocks of ice; **-closet,** an ice-chamber or ice-chest; **-creeper** = *ice-calk*; **-drift,** drifted ice in the mass; **-escape,** an apparatus for rescuing persons who have fallen through the ice; **-fender,** a fender or guard to protect a vessel from injury by ice; **-ferns,** the fern-like formations produced on glass by the action of frost; **-fish,** the capelin; **-flow,** an ice-stream; **-fox,** the Arctic fox; **-glass** = *crackle-glass* (CRACKLE *sb.*): **-gull,** U.S. name for the glaucous gull and the ivory gull; **-ladder** = *ice-escape*; **-ledge** = ICE-FOOT; **-machine,** a machine for making ice artificially; **-mark,** a mark, scratch, or groove produced by ice-action, esp. during the ice-age; **-mill,** a glacier-mill; **-pack,** a body of separate pieces of drift-ice closely packed so as to form one great ice-field; **-pail,** a pail for holding ice, in which bottles of wine, etc. are cooled; **-paper,** transparent gelatine in thin sheets used in copying drawings; **-period,** the ice-age; **-pit,** a pit in which ice is stored for preservation; **-pitcher,** a pitcher with double sides, or the like, for holding broken ice or iced water; **-plane,** an instrument for smoothing ice; an instrument for shaving off fragments of ice for cooling drinks; **-poultice,** a bag or bladder filled with pounded ice for application to parts of the body; **-pudding,** a frozen confection in the form of a pudding; **-pulse,** the throbbing movement which precedes an ice-quake; **-quake,** a convulsion which accompanies the break-up of an ice-field or ice-floe; **-raft,** a floating sheet of ice; **-river** = ICE-STREAM; **-saw,** a large saw employed by Arctic voyagers and in ice harvesting for cutting ice; **-ship,** one specially built to resist ice-pressure; **-shoe,** a spiked shoe for walking on ice; **-striæ,** thin lines of scoring made in rocks by ice passing over them; **-system,** a connected system or group of glaciers; **-whale,** the great polar whale; **-yacht** = ICE-BOAT 1; hence **-yachting, -yachtsman.**

Ice (əis), *v.* ME. [f. the sb.] **1.** *trans.* To cover with ice; to convert into ice. Also *fig.* **2.** To cover or garnish (cakes, etc.) with a concretion of sugar (cf. ICING). Also *fig.* 1602. **3.** To refrigerate with ice; to cool (esp. wine) by placing it among ice 1825. **4.** To make cold; to freeze, chill. Chiefly *fig.* 1804. **5.** *intr.* To turn to ice; to freeze. Also *fig.* 1839.

-ice, *suffix,* in ME. also **-is(e, -ys(e,** etc. **1.** – OFr. *-ice (-ise),* of non-popular origin, - L. *-itia,* or *-itius,* or *-itium.* Thus *avarice,* etc. (– L. *avaritia,* etc.), the later *police* (– L. *politia*), *novice, precipice, service* (= L. *novitius, precipitium, servitium*). Cf. -ISE[2].

2. The ending *-ice* has various other origins, partly through assimilation to the preceding; as in *(ac)complice, (ap)prentice, bodice, poultice.*

Iceberg (əi·sbɔ̄ɹg). 1774. [prob. – (M)Du. *ijsberg,* whence also G. *eisberg,* Sw. *isberg,* Da. *isbjerg.*] †**1.** An Arctic glacier, which comes close to the coast, and is seen from the sea as a hill or 'hummock' –1821. **2.** A detached portion of a glacier carried out to sea; a huge floating mass of ice, often rising to a great height above the water 1820. Also *fig.*

2. Ice-berg. [*Note*] This term..I restrict..to detached ice, in contradistinction to the glacier or ice *in situ* KANE. *fig.* Captain Thelwal is a perfect i. 1840.

I·ce-bird. 1620. *Ornith.* **1.** The little auk or sea-dove. **2.** The Indian night-jar 1862.

Iceblink (əi·sbliŋk). 1817. [= Du. *ijsblink,* G. *eisblink,* Da. *iisblink, -blik,* Sw. *isblink.* The question of the orig. lang., and history, is obscure. See ICE *sb.,* BLINK *sb.*[2]] **1.** A luminous appearance on the horizon, caused by the reflection of light from ice. See BLINK *sb.*[2] 4. **2.** The name of a range of ice-cliffs in Greenland. Also generally: An ice-cliff. ?*Obs.* 1819.

I·ce-boat. 1819. **1.** A boat mounted on runners for propulsion on the ice. **2.** A boat or barge for breaking the ice in a river or canal 1838.

I·ce-bolt. 1789. [f. BOLT *sb.*[1]] **a.** A sudden deadly chill. **b.** An avalanche.

Ice-bound (əi·sˌbaund), *ppl. a.* 1659. [f. ICE *sb.* + BOUND *ppl. a.*[2]] Held fast by ice; frozen in; hemmed in by ice.

I·ce-brea:ker. 1838. [f. ICE *sb.* + BREAKER[1].] **1.** Anything that breaks up moving ice; *spec.* an ice-apron. **2.** A vessel for breaking a channel through ice 1875. **3.** A whaler's name for the Greenland whale.

I·ce-cap. 1854. **1.** A permanent cap or covering of ice over a tract of country, as e.g. at either pole 1875. **2.** *Med.* A bladder or bag containing pounded ice, for application to the head in congestion of the brain, etc. 1854.

I:ce-crea·m. 1769. [Earlier *iced cream,* 1688.] Cream or custard, flavoured, sweetened, and congealed. Also *attrib.*

Iced (əist), *ppl. a.* 1688. [f. ICE *sb.* or *v.* + -ED.] Covered with ice; cooled by means of ice. Of a cake, etc.: Covered with icing.

I·ce-fall. 1817. [After *waterfall.*] **1.** A cataract of ice; a part of a glacier resembling a frozen waterfall. **2.** The fall of a mass of ice 1861.

I·ce-field. 1694. A wide flat expanse of ice.

Ice-floe (əi·sˌflōᵘ). 1819. [See FLOE.] A large sheet of floating ice, smaller than an ice-field.

I·ce-foot. 1856. [– Da. *isfod,* in same sense.] **a.** A belt or ledge of ice extending along the coast in Arctic regions. **b.** Also, the margin of an ice-floe 1897.

I·ce-hill. 1694. A hill or mound of ice; an elevated glacier; a slope covered with ice, for tobogganing, etc. †Also, a floating iceberg.

I·ce-hook. 1694. †**a.** A kind of boat-hook, used to push large flakes of ice away from a ship. †**b.** An ice-anchor. **c.** A hook used in hoisting ice for storage.

I·ce-house. 1687. A structure, often underground, and with non-conducting walls, in which ice is stored for use during the year.

Ice-island. 1777. = ICEBERG 2. So **I·ce-isle** 1808.

Iceland[1] (əi·sˌlænd). 1842. [f. ICE *sb.* + LAND *sb.*] A country covered with ice; the region of perpetual ice.

Iceland[2] (əi·slănd). [ME. *Island, Islond* (XIII) – ON. *Ísland,* f. *íss* ICE + *land* LAND.] The name of a large island lying on the border of the Arctic Ocean, between Norway and Greenland; used *attrib.* in names of articles imported from or peculiar to that country, as **I. cur, I. dog** (also short **I.**), a shaggy sharp-eared white dog, formerly in favour as a lapdog in England; **I. lichen, I. moss,** a species of edible lichen, *Cetraria islandica,* having medicinal properties; **I. poppy,** a variety of *Papaver nudicaule,* the yellow Arctic poppy; **I. spar,** a transparent variety of calcite, used in demonstrating the polarization of light.

Icelander (əi·slăndəɹ). 1613. [f. prec. + -ER[1].] An inhabitant or native of Iceland.

Icelandic (əislæ·ndik). 1674. [f. prec. + -IC.]

A. *adj.* Pertaining to Iceland, or to Icelandic (see B.).

B. *sb.* The language of Iceland, which in all essential points retains the form of Old Norse 1833.

Iceman, ice-man (əi·smæn). 1855. **1.** A man skilled in traversing ice. **2.** A man appointed to look after the ice on a skating-pond and assist in cases of accident 1860. **3.** One engaged in the ice trade, or in harvesting ice (*U.S.*) 1864. Hence **I·cemanship,** ice-craft.

I·ce-ma:ster. 1853. A pilot skilled in navigating vessels among ice-floes.

I·ce-mou:nt(ain. 1694. = ICEBERG.

I·ce-plant. 1753. A plant (*Mesembryanthemum crystallinum*), having leaves covered with pellucid watery vesicles looking like ice; a native of the Canary Islands, S. Africa, etc.

I·ce-plough. 1858. An instrument used in America for cutting grooves in ice, for the purpose of removing large blocks which are stored for summer use.

I·ce-sheet. 1873. A sheet or layer of ice covering an extensive tract of land; as e.g. during the ice-age.

I·cespar. 1816. [alt. of G. *eisspath* (Werner, 1812, from its appearance); cf. FELDSPAR.] *Min.* Glassy orthoclase, first found in the lava of Vesuvius.

I·ce-stream. 1853. **1.** A stream of ice-floes carried in a particular course; esp. that which sweeps round Cape Farewell in Greenland 1878. **2.** A valley glacier.

I·ce-work. 1729. **1.** Frosted work. **2.** *Geol.* Work done by glaciers or icebergs 1843.

Ich, obs. f. I *pron.,* EACH.

Ichneumon (ikniū·mǫn). 1572. [– L. *ichneumon* – Gr. ἰχνεύμων lit. tracker, f. ἰχνεύειν track, f. ἴχνος track, footstep.] **1.** A small brownish-coloured slender-bodied carnivorous quadruped, *Herpestes* (formerly *Viverra*) *ichneumon,* closely allied to the mongoose, and resembling the weasel tribe in form and habits. It is found in Egypt, and is noted for destroying the eggs of the crocodile, on which account it was venerated by the ancient Egyptians. (Called also *Pharaoh's Rat,* and formerly *Indian Mouse*). Cf. COCKATRICE. **2.** A small parasitic hymenopterous insect (family *Ichneumonidæ*), which deposits its eggs in or on the larva of another insect, upon which its larvae feed when hatched; an ichneumon-fly 1658.

1. I., a beaste of Egypte..who creepeth into the body of a Crocodyle, when in sleape he gapeth and eating his bowels, sleaeth him 1572.

Comb.: **I.-fly** = 2; †**i. maggot,** the larva of the i.-fly.

Ichneumon-, comb. stem of prec. (in sense 2), as in **Ichneumo·nidan** *a.,* pertaining to the family *Ichneumonidæ* of hymenopterous insects; *sb.,* an insect of this family 1815. **Ichneumo·niform** *a.,* having the form or characters of an ichneumon-fly.

Ichnite (i·knəit). 1854. [f. Gr. ἴχνος track + -ITE[1] 2 a.] *Geol.* A fossil footprint.

Ichnography (iknǫ·grăfi). 1598. [– Fr. *ichnographie* or L. *ichnographia* – Gr. ἰχνογραφία, f. ἴχνος track, trace; see -GRAPHY.] A ground-plan; a horizontal section of a building or part of it; also, the plan or map of a place. Also *transf.* and *fig.* Hence **Ichnogra·phic, -al,** *a.* pertaining or relating to i. **Ichnogra·phically** *adv.*

Ichnolite (i·knŏləit). 1846. [f. Gr. ἴχνος track, trace + -LITE.] = ICHNITE.

Ichnolithology (i:knoˌliþǫ·lŏdʒi). 1882. [f. as prec. + LITHOLOGY.] = ICHNOLOGY. Hence **I:chnolitholo·gical** *a.*

Ichnology (iknǫ·lŏdʒi). 1851. [f. as prec. + -LOGY.] **a.** That part of palæontology which treats of fossil footprints. **b.** The ichnological features of a district collectively. Hence **Ichnolo·gical** *a.*

‖**Ichoglan** (i·tʃoglæn). 1677. [obs. Turk., f. *īch* interior + *oğlān* young man.] A page in waiting in the palace of the Sultan.

Ichor (əi·kǫɹ). 1638. [– Gr. ἰχώρ.] **1.** *Gr. Myth.* The ethereal fluid, not blood, supposed to flow in the veins of the gods 1676. **2.** *transf.* and *fig.* Blood; a fluid likened to the blood of animals 1638. **3.** *Path.* A watery acrid discharge from certain wounds and sores 1651.

2. The azure i. of this élite of the earth R. FORD. Hence **Ichorous** (əi·kŏrəs), *a.* of the nature of i.; containing or discharging i.

‖**Ichorrhæmia** (əikŏrī·miă). Also **-emia.** 1854. [f. Gr. ἰχώρ ICHOR + -αιμία, f. αἷμα blood.] *Path.* Poisoning of the blood from the absorption of sanious matter.

Ichthyic (i·kþiˌik), *a.* 1844. [– Gr. ἰχθυϊκός fishy, f. ἰχθύς fish; see -IC.] Of, pertaining to, or characteristic of fishes; piscine. So **I·chthyal, I·chthyan** *adjs.*

Ichthyo- (i·kþiˌo), bef. a vowel **ichthy-,** comb. f. Gr. ἰχθύς, ἰχθύος fish.

I·chthydin, I·chthyin (-thin), I·chthylin (-ulin), *Chem.* names of albuminoid substances got from the egg-yolk of various fishes. **Ichthyo-co·prolite** [COPROLITE], *Palæont.* the fossilized excrement of a fish; also *ichthyocoprus.* **I·chthyodo:nt** [Gr. ὀδοντ-], *Palæont.* a fossil tooth of a fish. **Ichthyo·latry** [-LATRY], the worship of fishes, or of a fish-god, as Dagon. **I·chthyoma:ncy** [-MANCY], divination by means of the head or entrails of fishes; so **Ichthyoma·ntic** *a.* **Ichthyophthi·ran** [Gr. φθείρ louse] *a., Zool.* belonging to the crustacean order *Ichthyophthira,* parasites upon fishes; *sb.* a fish-louse. **Ichthyo·tomist** [Gr. -τομος cutting], an anatomist of fishes; so **Ichthyo·tomy. I:chthyta·xidermy,** the taxidermy or stuffing of the skins of fishes as zoological specimens.

‖**Ichthyocolla** (ikþiˌokǫ·lă). 1601. [L. – Gr. ἰχθυόκολλα, f. ἰχθυο- (prec.) + κόλλα glue.] Fish-glue, isinglass. Also *attrib.*

Ichthyodorylite, -dorulite (i:kþiˌodǫ·riləit, -dǫ·rˈŭləit). 1837. [f. ICHTHYO- + Gr. δόρυ spear + -LITE.] *Palæont.* A fossil spine of a fish or fish-like vertebrate.

Ichthyo·grapher. 1677. [f. ICHTHYO- + -GRAPHER.] A writer on fishes. So **Ichthyo·graphy. Ichthyogra·phic** *a.*

Ichthyoid (i·kþiˌoid). 1855. [f. as prec. + -OID.]
A. *adj.* Fish-like. So **Ichthyoi·dal** *a.*
B. *sb.* A vertebrate of the fish type; *spec.* = ICHTHYOPSID 1863.

Ichthyol (i·kþiˌǫl). 1885. [f. as prec. + -OL 3.] *Med.* A brownish-yellow syrupy liquid obtained by the dry distillation of bituminous rocks containing remains of fossil fishes; used as a remedy in skin diseases. (Proprietary term.) Hence **Ichthyo·lic** *a.*

Ichthyolite (i·kþiˌǒləit). 1828. [f. as prec. + -LITE.] *Palæont.* A fossil fish; any fossil of ichthyic origin. Hence **Ichthyoli·tic** *a.*

Ichthyology (ikþiˌǫ·lŏdʒi). 1646. [f. as prec. + -LOGY.] The natural history of fishes as a branch of zoology. **b.** The ichthyological features (*of* a district), the fishes (*of* a region) as subjects of scientific study. Hence **Ichthyolo·gic, -al** *a.* of or pertaining to i. **Ichthyolo·gically** *adv.* **Ichthyo·logist,** an expert, or student, in i.

Ichthyomorphic (i:kþiˌomǭ·ɹfik), *a.* 1879. [f. as prec. + Gr. μορφή form + -IC.] **a.** Having the form of a fish, as the fish-god Dagon. **b.** Possessing the zoological characters of fishes; ichthyoid.

‖**Ichthyophagi** (ikþiˌǫ·fădʒəi), *sb. pl.* 1555. [L. *Ichthyophagi* (pl.) – Gr. Ἰχθυοφάγοι, name of fish-eating races, f. ἰχθυο- ICHTHYO- + -φαγος eating; see -PHAGOUS, -PHAGY.] Fish-eaters. (Rarely in *sing.*) So †**Ichthyo·phagan** (*rare*), **Ichthyo·phagist, -gite,** a fish-eater. **Ichthyo·phagous** *a.* fish-eating. **Ichthyo·phagy,** the practice of eating fish.

Ichthyophthalmite (ikþiˌǫfþæ·lməit). 1805. [– Gr. ἰχθύς fish + ὀφθαλμός eye + -ITE[1] 2 b, in ref. to its appearance.] *Min.* = APOPHYLLITE.

‖**Ichthyopsida** (ikþiˌǫ·psidă), *sb. pl.* 1871. [mod.L., f. ICHTHYO- + Gr. ὄψις appearance; see -ID[3], -A[4].] *Zool.* The lowest of the three primary groups of *Vertebrata* in Huxley's classification, comprising the amphibians, the fishes, and fish-like vertebrates. Hence **Ichthyo·psid, -o·psidan, -opsi·dian** *adjs.* of or belonging to the *I.*; *sbs.* a vertebrate of this group.

Ichthyopterygian (i:kþiˌoptĕri·dʒiăn). [f. Gr. ἰχθυο- see ICHTHYO- + πτέρυξ, πτερυγ- wing, πτερύγιον wing, fin + -AN.] *Palæont.* **a.** *adj.* Belonging to the *Ichthyopterygia*, an order of extinct marine reptiles, so named from the paddle- or fin-like character of the digits of the fore and hind limbs, the type of which is the ichthyosaurus. **b.** *sb.* An ichthyosaurian.

Ichthyornis (ikþiˌǭ·ɹnis). 1872. [mod.L. (Marsh, 1872), f. ἰχθύς fish + ὄρνις, -ιθ- bird.] *Palæont.* An extinct order of toothed birds (*Odontornithes*) belonging to the sub-class *Odontotormæ*, having socketed teeth and biconcave vertebræ, the remains of which occur in the cretaceous rocks of N. America. Hence **Ichthyorni·thic** *a.* **Ichthyorni·thid,** a bird of the family *Ichthyornithidæ*.

Ichthyosaur (i·kþiˌosǭɹ). 1830. [Anglicized form of next.] = next, b.

Ichthyosaurus (i:kþiˌosǭ·rŏs). *Pl.* **i.-** 1832. [mod.L., f. ICHTHYO- + Gr. σαῦρος (= σαύρα) lizard.] *Palæont.* A genus of extinct marine animals, combining the characters of saurian reptiles and of fishes with some features of whales, and having an enormous head, a tapering body, four paddles, and a long tail. (Found chiefly in the Lias). **b.** An animal of this genus. Hence **Ichthyosau·rian** *a.* of or pertaining to the i.; belonging to the order *Ichthyosauria*; *sb.* an animal of this order. **Ichthyosau·rid,** an animal of the I. family, *Ichthyosauridæ*. **Ichthyosau·roid** *a.* having the form or characters of an i.

‖**Ichthyosis** (ikþiˌōᵘ·sis). 1815. [mod.L., f. Gr. ἰχθύς fish + -OSIS.] *Path.* A congenital disease of the skin in which the epidermis assumes a dry and horny appearance. (Also called *fish-skin disease* and *porcupine disease*.) Hence **Ichthyo·tic** *a.* subject to or affected with i.

-ician (i·ʃăn), a compound suffix, in Fr. *-icien*, consisting of -IAN (ME. and Fr. *-ien*) added to names of arts or sciences in L. *-ica*, Fr. *-ique*, Eng. -IC, -ICS, to denote a person skilled in the art or science; e.g. *arithmetician, politician, statistician*; occas. formed by analogy on names not ending in -IC, as *academician*, etc.; cf. also *patrician*, f. L. *patricius*.

‖**Icica** (i·sikă). 1865. [Native name in Guiana.] *Bot.* Name of a genus of S. American trees (N.O. *Burseraceæ*), of which *I. altissima* is the Cedar-wood and *I. heptaphylla* the Incense-wood of Guiana. **I. resin,** a fragrant resin obtained from the Incense-wood; hence **I·cican, I·cacin,** a crystalline resin, obtained from this.

Icicle (əi·sik'l). [Late ME. *iisse* (*ysse*) *ikkle, ysekele, iseyokel*, f. ICE + ICKLE, after MSw. *isikil* (= MDa. *isegel*); cf. Norw. *isjøkel, -jokkel*; repl. OE. **isġiċel* (whence ME. *isechele*), for which *ises ġiċel* 'icicle of ice' is attested.] **1.** A pendent rod-like ice-formation, produced by the freezing of falling or dripping water. Also *transf.* **2.** *Her.* (See quot.) 1830.
1. Eaves of snow, from which long icicles depended TYNDALL. *transf.* Saltpeter in long icicles 1644. **2.** *Icicles*, depicted in shape as guttées, but reversed ROBSON. Hence **I·cicled** *a.* overhung with icicles; also, †frozen.

Icily (əi·sili), *adv.* 1848. [f. ICY *a.* + -LY[2].] Freezingly. Also *fig.* So **I·ciness,** the quality of being icy. Chiefly *fig.*

Icing (əi·siŋ), *vbl. sb.* 1769. [f. ICE *v.* + -ING[1].] **1.** The process of encrusting or adorning with crystallizations of sugar; *concr.* an incrustation of sugar. **2.** The process of cooling or preserving by means of ice 1837.

-icity (i·sĭti), a compound suffix – Fr. *-icité* – L. *-icitate-* (nom. *-icitas*), formed by the addition of *-tāt-* (see -TY[1]) to adj. stems in *-ic(i)-*, as *rusticitas*, f. *rusticus*. On the analogy of these, abstract sbs. in *-icité* in Fr. and *-icity* in Eng. are formed upon adjs. of any origin in *-ic*; e.g. *atomicity, electricity, publicity*, etc.

Icker (i·kəɹ). 1513. Sc. form of EAR *sb.*[2]

Ickle (i·k'l). *Obs.* exc. *dial.* [ME. *ikyl* var. of *ychele* – OE. *ġiċel, ġiċela* :– **jakilaz, -on*, cogn. with ON. *jǫkull* icicle, glacier :– **jakulaz* (cf. ON. *jaki* ice floe).] = ICICLE. Also *transf.*

†**Icod** (ikǫ·d), *int.* 1697. Var. of ECOD, q.v. –1790.

I-come(n, ME. pa. pple. of COME *v.*

Icon (əi·kǫn). Also **ikon, eikon.** 1572. [– L. *icon* (Pliny) – Gr. εἰκών likeness, image, similitude.] †**1.** An image, figure, or representation; a portrait; an illustration in a book –1727. **b.** An image in the solid; a statue 1577. **2.** *Eastern Ch.* A representation of some sacred personage, itself regarded as sacred, and honoured with a relative worship 1833. †**3.** *Rhet.* A simile –1676.
1. b. The I. of an Elephant SIR T. HERBERT. **2.** Behind them were carried. .six censers, and six sacred ikons 1833.

Iconic (əikǫ·nik), *a.* Also **eiconic.** 1656. [– L. *iconicus* – Gr. εἰκονικός, f. εἰκών ICON; see -IC.] Of or pertaining to an icon; of the nature of a portrait; *spec.* in *Art*, applied to the ancient portrait statues of victorious athletes, and hence to memorial statues and busts of a fixed type. So **Ico·nical** *a. rare* 1652.

†**I·conism.** 1656. [– L. *iconismus* – Gr. εἰκονισμός delineation, f. εἰκονίζειν; see next, -ISM.] A representation of some image or figure; imagery; metaphor –1680.

†**I·conize,** *v.* [– Gr. εἰκονίζειν, f. εἰκών ICON; see -IZE.] *trans.* To form into an image; to figure, to represent. CUDWORTH.

Icono-, Gr. εἰκονο-, comb. f. εἰκών ICON.
Iconodu·ly [see DULIA], the veneration of images; so **I:conodu·lic** (*-doulic*) *a.*; **I·conodule, Iconodu·list,** a venerator of images. **I:conoma·nia,** an infatuated devotion to images; a mania for collecting icons or portraits. **I·conophile, Icono·philist** [Gr. φίλος], a connoisseur of pictures, engravings, book illustrations, and the like; hence **Icono·philism, -phily,** the taste for these.

Iconoclasm (əikǫ·nŏklæz'm). 1756. [f. *iconoclast*, after Gr. analogies, e.g. πλάσμα moulding, πλάστης moulder.] The breaking or destroying of images; *esp.* of images and pictures set up as objects of veneration; hence *transf.* and *fig.*

Iconoclast (əikǫ·nŏklæst), *sb.* (*a.*) 1641. [– med.L. *iconoclastes* – eccl. Gr. εἰκονοκλάστης, f. εἰκών image, κλᾶν break.] **1.** A breaker or destroyer of images; *spec.* one who took part in the movement in the 8th and 9th centuries to put down the use of these in religious worship in the Christian churches of the East; hence, applied analogously to Protestants in the 16th and 17th centuries. **2.** *transf.* and *fig.* One who assails cherished beliefs or venerated institutions on the ground that they are erroneous or pernicious 1842. **3.** *attrib.* or *adj.* Iconoclastic 1685.
1. The Puritans. .seem mere savage Iconoclasts CARLYLE. **2.** Kant was the great i. J. MARTINEAU. **3.** An i. riot 1845. Hence **Iconocla·stic** *a.* of or pertaining to iconoclasts or iconoclasm. **Iconocla·stically** *adv.* **Iconocla·sticism,** the principles or practice of iconoclasts.

Ico·nograph. 1884. [– Gr. εἰκονογράφος portrait-painter; see ICON, -GRAPH.] A drawing, engraving, or illustration for a book; = ICON 1.

Iconography (əikŏnǫ·grăfi). 1628. [– Gr. εἰκονογραφία sketch, description (Strabo); see ICONO-, -GRAPHY.] †**1.** *concr.* A pictorial representation; a drawing or plan –1678. **2.** The description of any subject by means of drawings or figures; any book in which this is done; also, the branch of knowledge which deals with representative art in general 1678.
2. The i. of the altar-canopy 1874. Hence **Icono·grapher,** one who makes figures or drawings of objects. **Iconogra·phic, -al** *a.* of or pertaining to i.

Iconolater (əikŏnǫ·lătəɹ). 1654. [– eccl. Gr. εἰκονολάτρης; see ICONO-, -LATER. Cf. mod.L. *iconolatres* (XVII).] A worshipper of images. So **Icono·latry,** image-worship.

Iconology (əikŏnǫ·lŏdʒi). 1730. [f. as prec. + -LOGY. Cf. Fr. *iconologie* in same sense (XVII).] **1.** That branch of knowledge which deals with the subject of icons; also icons collectively, or as objects of investigation, etc. **2.** Symbolical representation; symbolism 1849. Hence **Iconolo·gical** *a.*, **-lo·gically** *adv.* 1730. **Icono·logist.**

Iconomachy (əikŏnǫ·măki). 1581. [f. eccl. Gr. εἰκονομαχεῖν war against images, on Gr. analogies; see ICONO-, -MACHY.] A war against images; hostility to images in connection with worship. So †**Icono·machal** (*erron.* **-mical**) *a.* hostile to images.

‖**Iconostas** (əikǫ·nostæs). 1833. [Russ., f. Gr. εἰκονόστασις; see next.] = next.

‖**Iconostasis** (əikŏnǫ·stăsis). 1833. [mod. eccl. Gr. εἰκονόστασις, f. εἰκονο- ICONO- + στάσις position, station.] *Eastern Ch.* The screen separating the sanctuary or 'bema' from the main body of the church, and on which the icons are placed.

Icos-, icosa-, icosi-, repr. Gr. comb. forms of εἴκοσι twenty.
Icosaco·lic [Gr. κῶλον member, COLON[2]] *a.*, *Anc. Pros.* consisting of twenty cola or members. **Icosase·mic** [Gr. σῆμα mark, σημεῖον mark, mora] *a.*, *Anc. Pros.* consisting of or containing twenty moræ or units of time, i.e. the equivalent of twenty short syllables. **Ico·sian** *a.*, of or pertaining to twenty.

Icosahedron (əi:kosăhī·drǫn, -he·drǫn). 1570. [– late L. *icosahedrum*, med.L. also *-hedron* – Gr. εἰκοσάεδρον, n. of adj. used subst., (sc. σχῆμα figure), f. εἴκοσι twenty + ἕδρα seat, base.] *Geom.* A solid contained by twenty plane faces; *spec.* the *regular icosahedron*, contained by twenty equilateral triangles. Hence **Icosahe·dral** *a.* having twenty faces.

‖**Icosandria** (əikosæ·ndriă). 1753. [mod.L. (Linn.), f. Gr. εἴκοσι twenty + ἀνήρ, ἀνδρ- taken as = 'stamen'. See -IA.] *Bot.* A Linnæan class, containing plants with twenty or more stamens inserted on the calyx. Hence **Icosa·nder,** a plant of this class. **Icosa·ndrian, Icosa·ndrous** *adjs.* belonging to this class.

I:cosite:trahe·dron. 1831. [f. Gr. εἴκοσι + τετρα- four + ἕδρα base. Cf. TETRAHEDRON.] *Geom.* and *Cryst.* A solid figure contained by twenty-four plane faces; *esp.* a *deltohedron* or *trapezohedron*.

I-cried, ME. pa. pple. of CRY *v.*

-ics *suffix*: see -IC 2.

Icteric (ikte·rik). 1600. [– L. *ictericus* – Gr. ἰκτερικός, f. ἴκτερος jaundice; see -IC. Cf. (O)Fr. *ictérique*.]

A. *adj.* Belonging to, of the nature of, or affected with jaundice. So **Icte·rical** *a.* **b.** Used for the cure of jaundice 1710.

I. Oriole: a N. American bird (*Icterus vulgaris*), having black and yellow plumage; also called *troopial*.

B. *sb.* **1.** A person affected with jaundice 1634. **2.** A remedy for jaundice 1727.

Icterine (i·ktĕrəin), *a.* 1855. [f. ICTERUS + -INE[1].] *Zool.* **a.** Yellowish. **b.** Belonging to the family *Icteridæ* or sub-family *Icterinæ* of American passerine birds (typical genus *Icterus*) 1884.

Icteritious (-i·ʃəs), *a.* 1609. [f. late L. *icteritia* jaundice (see ICTERUS, -IA[1]) + -OUS; see -ITIOUS[1].] Jaundiced; also *fig.*

Icteroid (i·ktĕroid), *a.* 1855. [f. next + -OID.] Resembling or characteristic of jaundice.

‖**Icterus** (i·ktĕrŏs). 1706. [L. – Gr. ἴκτερος jaundice; also, a certain yellowish-green bird.] **1.** *Path.* Jaundice. **b.** *Bot.* A disease of plants in which the leaves turn yellow 1866. **2.** *Zool.* A genus of American passerine birds, now restricted to the American orioles 1713.

Ictic (i·ktik), *a. rare.* 1847. [irreg. f. L. *ictus* (*u*-stem); see -IC.] **1.** Of the nature of a blow or stroke; abrupt and sudden. **2.** *Pros.* Pertaining or due to the ictus 1898.

‖**Ictus** (i·ktŏs). 1707. [L., f. *ict-*, pa. ppl. stem of *icere* strike.] **1.** *Pros.* Stress on a particular syllable of a foot or verse 1752. **2.** *Med.* **a.** The beat of the pulse. **b.** *Ictus solis* (L.): sunstroke 1811.

Icy (əi·si), *a.* [OE. *īsiġ*. Formed anew in XV f. ICE + -Y[1].] **1.** Abounding in ice; covered or overlaid with ice. **2.** Consisting of ice 1600. **3.** Resembling ice; extremely cold, frosty; slippery 1590. Also *fig.*

1. The flowers of the I. Zones 1796. 2. Greenland's i. mountains HEBER. 3. An i. current 1886. *fig.* If he be leaden, ycie, cold, vnwilling, Be thou so too SHAKS. *Comb.*, as *icy-pearled* (having pearls or sparkling drops of ice), *-wheeled*, etc.

Id (id). 1893. [G. (Weissmann, 1893), the first syll. of *idioplasm* (see IDIO-, PLASM).] *Biol.* In Weissmann's theory of heredity: A unit of germ-plasm or idioplasm.

-id, *suffix*[1], repr. Fr. *-ide*, L. *-idus*, used to form adjs., chiefly from verbs with *ē*-stems, as *acidus* from *acēre*, etc.; occas. from verbs with *i*- or consonant stems, and from sbs., as *fluidus*, f. *fluere*, *morbidus*, f. *morbus*, etc. Not a living formative in Eng.

-id, *suffix*[2], corresp. to Fr. *-ide*, in sbs. derived from L. sbs. in *-is*, *-id-*, adopted from Gr. sbs. in -ις, -ιδα; as *chrysalid*, *pyramid*, etc. In botanical terms, as *orchid*, etc., this formative denotes a member of the family *Orchidaceæ*, etc.

-id, *suffix*[3]. (*a*) In zoological appellatives, sb. and adj.: (i) formed from L. names of Families in *-idæ*, pl. of *-ides*, repr. Gr. -ίδης = son of'; as *Araneid*, a member of the Family *Araneidæ*. (ii) formed from L. names of Classes, etc., in *-ida*, taken as neut. pl. of *-ides* = Gr. -ίδης; as *Arachnid*, a member of the Class *Arachnida*. See -IDAN. (*b*) *Astron.* Applied to groups or showers of meteors radiating from a constellation, after which they are named, as *Leonid*, *Quadrantid*.

-id, *suffix*[4], early spelling of the chemical suffix -IDE, still used by some, esp. in U.S.

-idan, in zoological appellatives, sb. and adj., formed on -ID[3] with suffix -AN, meaning 'of or pertaining to', or 'a member of' the group designated by the suffix *-ida* or *-idæ*; as *arachnidan* (f. *Arachnida*) = *arachnid*, etc.

Idant (əi·dănt). 1893. [Arbitrarily f. ID + -ANT.] *Biol.* One of the chromatin bodies in the nucleus of a reproductive or other cell, regarded as consisting of 'ids' (see ID).

Ide[1] (əid). 1839. [– mod.L. *idus* (Linnæus) – Sw. *id*. So Fr. *ide*.] A freshwater cyprinoid fish (*Leuciscus idus* or *I. melanotus*), of northern Europe.

Ide[2]: see IDES.

-ide, *Chem.*, a suffix used to form names of simple compounds of an element with another element or a radical. It is added to the stem or an abbreviated form of the word, and was first used in *ox-ide* from *oxygen*. It sometimes displaced other derivs. in *-et*, *-uret*.

Idea (əidī·ă), *sb.* Also *erron.* †**idæa.** Pl. **ideas**; formerly sometimes **ideæ**. 1531. [– L. *idea* (in Platonic sense) – Gr. ἰδέα look, semblance, form, kind, nature, ideal form, model, f. base of ἰδεῖν see. Cf. the earlier IDEE.]

I. Archetype, pattern, plan, standard. **1.** In Platonic philosophy: An eternally existing pattern of any class of things, of which the individual things are imperfect copies, and from which they derive their existence 1563. **2.** A standard of perfection; an ideal. *Obs.* or *arch.* 1586. **3.** The conception of a standard or principle to be realized or aimed at; the plan or design according to which something is created or constructed 1581. **4.** In weaker sense: A notion of something to be done; an intention, plan of action 1617. †**5.** A pattern, type; a preliminary sketch or draft; an outline; something in an undeveloped state –1702. **6.** *Mus.* A musical theme, phrase, or figure as sketched 1880.

2. How widely we are fallen from the pure Exemplar and I. of our Nature SIR T. BROWNE. 3. This new created World..how good, how faire, Answering his great I. MILT. *P.L.* VII. 557. 4. The i. of short parliaments is..plausible enough BURKE.

†**II.** A figure, representation, image, symbol (*of* something) 1531–1714; form, figure (as a quality or attribute); shape; aspect; nature or character –1737.

III. 1. †**a.** The mental image of something previously seen or known, and recalled by the memory –1764. **b.** More generally: A conception 1612. **c.** Something merely imagined 1588. **2.** More widely: Any product of mental apprehension or activity, existing in the mind as an object of knowledge or thought; a thought, conception, notion; an item of knowledge or belief; a way of thinking 1645. **b.** A vague belief, opinion, or estimate; a supposition, impression, fancy 1712.

1. Th' I. of her life shal sweetly creepe Into his study of imagination SHAKS. **b.** Then gay Ideas crowd the vacant brain POPE. **c.** Which make.. Predestination a meere Idæa PRYNNE. Phr. *In idea* (= Fr. *en idée*), in mind, in thought; opp. to *in reality*. 2. To teach the young i. how to shoot THOMSON. **b.** I had no i. you would be flooded 1866.

IV. Mod. Philosophy. **1.** [from III.] With Descartes and Locke: The immediate object of thought or mental perception 1666. **2.** [from I. 1.] **a.** In the Kantian and transcendental schools: One of the *noumena* or ultimate principles apprehended by reason. **b.** In Hegelianism: The absolute truth of which all phenomenal existence is the expression; *the Idea*, the Absolute. 1838.

1. The leading doctrine of Locke, as is well known, is the derivation of all our ideas from sensation and from reflection HALLAM.

Idea'd, ideaed (əidī·ăd), *a.* 1753. [f. IDEA *sb.* + -ED[2].] Having an idea or ideas, *esp.* of a specified kind.

Ideal (əidī·ăl). 1611. [– Fr. *idéal* – late L. *idealis* (Martianus Capella), f. L. *idea*; see IDEA, -AL[1].]

A. *adj.* **1.** Existing as an idea or archetype; relating to or consisting of ideas (see IDEA *sb.* I. 1) 1647. **2.** Conceived as perfect in its kind. Cf. IDEA *sb.* I. 2, 3. 1613. **3.** Of, pertaining to, or of the nature of an idea or conception 1611; representing an idea 1846. **4.** Existing only in idea; opp. to *real* or *actual*. Hence sometimes, Not real or practical; visionary 1611. **5.** *Philos.* Idealistic 1764. **6.** *Math.* Applied to a number or quantity which has no actual existence, but is assumed in a system of complex numbers 1860.

1. The Natural existence of things is founded upon their I. existence 1691. 2. I. perfection BOLINGBROKE, beauty RUSKIN, enjoyment 1861. 3. The crucifix..is an i., not a realistic representation 1874. 4. They despised the i. terrors of a foreign superstition GIBBON.

B. *sb.* **1.** A conception of something, or a thing conceived, as perfect in its kind; a perfect type; a standard of excellence 1798. **2.** An imaginary thing 1884.

1. The Chinese i. of making all people alike MILL. [Confucius] as the i. of a sage MAX-MÜLLER.

¶See also BEAU-IDEAL.

Idealess (əidī·ă,lės), *a.* 1818. [f. IDEA *sb.* + -LESS.] Destitute of ideas; conveying no idea.

Idealism (əidī·ăliz'm). 1796. [– Fr. *idéalisme* or G. *idealismus*, f. as IDEAL + -ISM.] **1.** *Philos.* Any system in which the object of external perception is held to consist, either in itself, or as perceived, of ideas (see IDEA *sb.*).

Subjective Idealism is the opinion that the object of external perception consists, whether in itself or as known to us, in ideas of the perceiving mind; *Critical* or *Transcendental I.*, the opinion (of Kant) that it consists, as known to us, but not necessarily in itself, of such ideas; *Objective I.*, the opinion (of Schelling) that while, as known to us, it consists of such ideas, it consists also, as it is in itself, of ideas identical with these; *Absolute I.*, (*a*) the opinion (of Hegel) that it consists, not only as known to us, but in itself, of ideas, not however ours, but those of the universal mind; (*b*) also applied more generally to other forms of idealism which do not suppose an independent reality underlying our ideas of external objects.

2. The practice of idealizing; imaginative treatment in art or literature; ideal style or character; opp. to *realism*. Also, aspiration after an ideal. 1829. **b.** (with *pl.*) An act or product of idealizing 1822.

2. The perfected i. which reigns in his [Titian's] greatest works 1841.

Idealist (əidī·ălist). 1701. [f. IDEAL + -IST. Cf. Fr. *idéaliste* (XVIII).] **1.** *Philos.* One who holds a doctrine of idealism; see prec. 1. **2.** One who idealizes; an artist or writer who treats a subject imaginatively. Opp. to *realist*. 1805. **3.** One who conceives, or follows after ideals. Sometimes *depreciatively*, A visionary. 1829. **4.** *attrib.* or *adj.* = next 1875.

Idealistic (əidi,ăli·stik), *a.* 1829. [f. prec. + -IC.] Pertaining to or characteristic of an idealist; belonging to or having the character of idealism. Hence **Ideali·stical** *a.*, **-ly** *adv.*

Ideality (əidi,æ·lĭti). 1701. [f. IDEAL + -ITY.] †**1.** The faculty of forming ideas (see IDEA *sb.* I. 1). NORRIS. **2.** The imaginative faculty. (Orig. a term of *Phrenology*) 1828. **3.** The quality of being ideal 1817. **4.** with *pl.*: Something ideal or imaginary 1844.

4. Amiable idealities about 'love in a cottage' 1844.

Idealize (əidī·ăləiz), *v.* 1786. [f. IDEAL + -IZE.] *trans.* To make ideal; to represent in an ideal form or character; to exalt to an ideal perfection 1795. **b.** *absol.* or *intr.* To conceive an ideal or ideals 1786.

b. [Men's] natural propensity to i. 1786. Hence **Idealiza·tion. Ide·alizer.**

Ideally (əidī·ăli), *adv.* 1598. [f. IDEAL *a.* + -LY[2].] †**1.** In 'idea' or archetype –1701. **2.** Imaginarily 1598. **3.** In conformity with the ideal 1840. **4.** *Biol.* In relation to a general plan or archetype (of a class) 1859.

Idealogical, etc. erron. ff. IDEOLOGICAL, etc.

Ideate (əidī·eit), *v.* 1610. [– *ideat-*, pa. ppl. stem of med.L. *ideare* form an idea or conception (of), f. *idea* IDEA; see -ATE[3].] **1.** *trans.* To form the idea of; to imagine, conceive. **2.** *absol.* or *intr.* **a.** To form ideas, to think. **b.** To devise something imaginary. 1862.

1. A State which Plato Ideated DONNE. Hence **Idea·tion**, the formation of ideas of things not present to the senses. **Idea·tional, Ide·ative** (*rare*) *adjs.* of or pertaining to ideation.

Ide·ate, *a.* and *sb.* 1677. [f. as prec. + -ATE[2], -ATE[1]. Cf. med.L. *ideatus* mentally conceived.]

A. *sb.* Produced by or deriving its existence from a (Platonic) idea; see IDEA *sb.* I. 1.

B. *sb.* The external object of which an idea is formed 1677.

Idee (əidī·). *Obs.* exc. in vulgar use. ME. (LYDGATE). [– (O)Fr. *idée* – L. *idea* IDEA.] = IDEA.

‖**Idée fixe** (idefīks). 1836. [Fr.] A fixed idea.

‖**Idem** (əi·dem, i·dem). ME. [L. *īdem* masc., *ĭdem* neut. 'the same'.] The same word, name, title, author, etc. Abbrev. *id.*

I·dent, -ant, *a. Sc.* 1567. [Later form of ITHAND *a.*; cf. EIDENT.] Diligent, persistent. Hence **I·dently** *adv.* 1438.

Identic (əide·ntik), *a.* 1649. [– med.L. *identicus*, f. *ident-* as in *identitas*; see IDENTITY, -IC.] **1.** = IDENTICAL 1, 2. **2.** In diplomacy, applied to action or language in which two or more governments agree to use precisely the same form, in their relations with some other power; esp. in *identic note* 1863.

Identical (əide·ntikăl), *a.* 1620. [f. as prec. + -AL[1]; see -ICAL.] **1.** The same; the very same. (Often emphasized by *same, very*.) 1633. **2.** Agreeing entirely in material, constitution, properties, qualities, or meaning 1677. **3.** *Logic.* Said of a proposition, the terms of which denote the same thing; as *man is a human being* 1620. **4.** *Alg.* Expressing or effecting identity, as *i. equation, i. operation* 1875.

1. In the same identicall path 1633. **2.** Crystals.. are cases of..cohesion of i. particles 1896. Hence **Ide·ntical-ly** *adv.*, **-ness.**

†**Identi·fic**, *a.* 1678. [– med.L. *identificus*, f. *identificare*; see IDENTIFY, -FIC.] Doing the same; concurring in action. GALE. So †**Identi·fically** *adv.*, identically 1475; †**Identifica·lity** 1716.

Identification (əide:ntifikeⁱ·ʃən). 1644. [orig. – med.L. *identificatio*, later f. IDENTIFY; see -FICATION.] The action of identifying or fact of being identified.

The i. of Serbâl with Sinai STANLEY, of habitual offenders 1887.

Identify (əide·ntifəi), *v.* 1644. [– med.L. *identificare*, f. *ident-* (see IDENTITY) + *-ficare* -FY.] **1.** *trans.* To make identical (*with*, †*to* something); to regard or treat as the same. **b.** To make one *with*; to associate inseparably. Chiefly *refl.* and *pass.* 1780. †**c.** *intr.* To be made, become, or prove to be the same –1834. **2.** To determine the identity of; in *Nat. Hist.* to refer a specimen to its proper species 1769.

1. Osiris, whom he identifies with Serapis GIBBON. **b.** Let us i...ourselves with the people BURKE. **c.** Your taste and mine do not always..i. LAMB. **2.** To i. stolen goods 1828. Hence **Ide·ntifiable** *a.* able to be identified.

Identism (əide·ntiz'm). 1857. [f. *ident-* (see IDENTITY) + -ISM.] The system or doctrine of (absolute) identity (see IDENTITY 1).

Identity (əide·ntĭti). 1570. [– late L. *identitas*, f. L. *idem* same, prob. after *entitas* ENTITY, but poss. assoc. with *identidem* over and over again, repeatedly; thus *ident-* was established as the comb. form of *idem*; see IDENTIFY.] **1.** The quality or condition of being the same; absolute or essential sameness; oneness. Also with *an* and *pl.* **2.** Individuality, personality 1638; individual existence (?*Obs.*) 1683. **3.** *Alg.* An identical equation, i.e. one which is true for all values of the literal quantities 1859. **4.** The condition of being identified in feeling, interest, etc. (*rare*) 1868. **5.** *attrib.* = 'that serves to identify the holder', as *identity card, disc,* etc. 1900.

1. *Absolute identity*, that asserted in the doctrine of Schelling that mind and matter are phenomenal modifications of the same substance. I. of conviction FROUDE. **2.** *Personal i.*: continuity of the personality. **4.** He is..in visible i. with the age GLADSTONE. Phr. *Law* or *Principle of I.*: the so-called principle that 'Every A is A'.

Ideo- (əi·di,o), combining f. Gr. ἰδέα IDEA, as in **Ideo-motor** [MOTOR] *a.*, applied by W. B. Carpenter to automatic muscular movements arising from complete occupation of the mind by an idea, and to the cerebral centres controlling such movements; so **Ideo-mo·tion,** ideo-motor movement. **I·deophone** [Gr. φωνή], a sound or group of sounds denoting an idea, i.e. a spoken word (A. J. Ellis). **Ideopra·xist** [Gr. πρᾶξις; see -IST], one whose practice is actuated by an idea.

Ideogram (əi·dio,græm). 1838. [f. IDEO- + -GRAM.] = next.

Ideograph (əi·dio,grɑf). Also *erron.* **idea-.** 1835. [f. IDEO- + -GRAPH.] A character or figure symbolizing the idea of a thing without expressing the name of it, as the Chinese characters, etc.

Thus in English, the i. + may be pronounced 'plus', 'added to', or 'more' according to the pleasure of the reader SAYCE. Hence **I:deogra·phic** *a.* of the nature of an i.; relating to or composed of ideographs; *sb.* an ideographic character; *pl.* a method of writing in ideographic characters. **Ideogra·phical** *a.*, **-ly** *adv.*

Ideography (əidi,ǫ·grăfi). Also *erron.* **idea-.** 1836. [f. IDEO- + -GRAPHY.] The representation of ideas by graphic signs; writing consisting of ideographs.

Ideolo·gic, -ical, *a.* 1797. [f. IDEOLOGY + -IC, -ICAL.] Belonging or relating to ideology.

Ideologist (əidi,ǫ·lŏdʒist). Also *erron.* **idea-.** 1798. [– Fr. *idéologiste*; see next and -IST.] **1.** One versed in ideology (sense 1). **2.** A person occupied with an idea or ideas; esp. a visionary, a mere theorist 1818. So **Ide·ologue** 1815.

Ideology (əidi,ǫ·lŏdʒi). 1796. [– Fr. *idéologie* (Destutt de Tracy, 1796); see IDEO-, -LOGY.] **1.** The science of ideas; the study of the origin and nature of ideas. **b.** *spec.* The system of Condillac, which derived all ideas from sensations. **2.** Ideal or abstract speculation; visionary theorizing 1813. **3.** A system of ideas concerning phenomena, esp. those of social life; the manner of thinking characteristic of a class or an individual.

Ides (əidz), *sb. pl.* Rarely in sing. **ide.** ME. [– (O)Fr. *ides* – L. *idūs* (pl.), said by Varro to be an Etruscan word.] In the ancient Roman calendar, the eighth day after the nones, i.e. the 15th of March, May, July, October, and the 13th of the other months.

The days after the nones were reckoned forward to the ides; hence 'the sixth of the ides' (or 'the sixth ide') 'of June', loosely rendering L. *ante diem sextum Idus Junias* = June 8.

Cæsar..Beware the Ides of March *Jul. C.* I. ii. 17.

‖**Id est.** 1598. [L., = 'that is'.] Two Latin words, used in Eng. in the sense 'that is to say'. Abbrev. *i.e.* (formerly often *i.*).

Idiasm (i·di,æz'm). 1868. [– Gr. ἰδιασμός peculiarity, f. ἴδιος peculiar.] A peculiarity, mannerism.

Idic (i·dik), *a.* 1893. [f. ID + -IC.] Pertaining to an id or ids.

Idio- (i·dio), repr. Gr. ἰδιο-, comb. f. ἴδιος own, personal, private, peculiar, separate, distinct.

I·dioblast [-BLAST], *Bot.* an individual plant-cell of different nature or content from the surrounding tissue. **Idiocyclo·phanous** [CYCLO-] *a.*, = *idiophanous*. **Idiodi·nic** [Gr. ὠδίς, ὠδιν- birth-pains] *a.*, *Zool.* having a special opening for the extrusion of genital products. †**Idio-ele·ctric** *a.*, capable of being electrified by friction. **Idiogo·naduct**, the gonaduct of an idiodinic animal. **I·diograph**, one's private mark or signature; hence **Idiogra·phic** *a.* **Idio·meter** [-METER], an instrument for measuring the personal equation of an observer, by observation of the transit of an artificial star whose actual motion is exactly known. **Idiomu·scular** *a.*, *Path.* a term for the local contraction, under physical stimulus, of a muscle which is fatigued or dying. **Idio·phanism** idiophanous nature or property. **Idio·phanous** [Gr. -φανής] *a.*, exhibiting axial interference figures without the use of polarizing apparatus. **I·dioplasm** *Biol.* a term for the special portion of protoplasm in a germ or cell which is supposed to determine the character of the resulting organism; hence **Idioplasma·tic** *a.* **Idiopsycho·logy**, the psychology of one's own mind; hence **Idiopsycholo·gical** *a.* **Idiorepu·lsive** *a.*, self-repelling. **Idiosta·tic** [STATIC] *a.*, not employing any auxiliary electrification in the measurement of electricity (opp. to HETEROSTATIC).

Idio·crasy. 1654. Now *rare.* [– Gr. ἰδιοκρασία, f. ἰδιο- IDIO- + -κρασία, κρᾶσις mixing.] = IDIOSYNCRASY –1755. Hence **Idiocra·tic, -al** *a.* idiosyncratic.

Idiocy (i·diŏsi). 1487. [f. IDIOT, prob. after *lunatic, lunacy*; but cf. Gr. ἰδιωτεία uncouthness, want of education.] The state or condition of being an idiot; extreme mental imbecility.

I. is a defect of mind which is either congenital, or due to causes operating during the first few years of life MAUDSLEY.

Idiom (i·diəm). 1588. [– Fr. *idiome* or late L. *idioma* – Gr. ἰδίωμα property, peculiar phraseology, f. ἰδιοῦσθαι make one's own, f. ἴδιος own, private.] **1.** The form of speech peculiar to a people or country. **b.** A dialect 1598. **2.** = IDIOTISM I. 2. 1598. **3.** A form of expression, construction, phrase, etc. peculiar to a language; a peculiarity of phraseology approved by usage, and often having a meaning other than its grammatical or logical one 1628. **4.** Specific form or property; peculiar nature; peculiarity. *Obs.* exc. as *fig.* of 1 or 2. 1644.

1. Our Vernacular I. ADDISON. The classics of the Tuscan i. GIBBON. **2.** The I. of it, as to the main, appears to be Teutonick 1683. **3.** Every speech hath certaine Idiomes, and customary Phrases of its own HOWELL. **4.** The idioms of national opinion and feeling MACAULAY.

Idiomatic (idiŏmæ·tik), *a.* 1712. [– Gr. ἰδιωματικός peculiar, characteristic, f. ἰδίωμα, -ατ- IDIOM.] **1.** Peculiar to or characteristic of a particular language; vernacular; colloquial. **2.** Given to or marked by the use of idioms 1839.

2. Like most i...writers, he [Dryden] knew very little about the language historically or critically LOWELL. So **Idioma·tical** *a.* Hence **Idioma·tical-ly** *adv.*, **-ness.**

Idiomorphic (idiomǭ·ɹfik), *a.* 1887. [f. IDIO- + Gr. μορφή form + -IC.] *Min.* Having its own characteristic form; *spec.* having its characteristic crystallographic faces: said of one of the constituent minerals of a rock. Hence **Idiomo·rphically** *adv.*

Idiopathic, -al (idiopæ·þik, -ăl), *a.* 1669. [f. IDIOPATHY + -IC; see -ICAL.] **1.** *Path.* Of a disease: Of the nature of a primary morbid state; not consequent upon another disease. **2.** Of the nature of a particular affection or susceptibility 1846. Hence **Idiopa·thically** *adv.* So **I:diopathe·tic, -al** *a. rare.*

Idiopathy (idi,ǫ·păþi). 1640. [– mod.L. *idiopathia* – Gr. ἰδιοπάθεια (Galen); see IDIO- and -PATHY.] †**1.** A feeling or sensation peculiar to an individual or class –1688. **2.** *Path.* A disease not preceded or occasioned by any other; a primary disease 1640.

2. This moral i...this itch for seeing memorable places..is peculiarly English 1833.

Idiosyncrasy (idiosi·ŋkrăsi). 1604. [– Gr. ἰδιοσυγκρασία, -κρασις, f. ἴδιος IDIO- + σύγκρασις commixture, tempering, f. σύν SYN- + κρᾶσις mixture (CRASIS). Cf. Fr. *idiosyncrasie* (XVIII).] A peculiarity of constitution or temperament. **1.** The physical constitution of an individual or †class. Now only *Med.* **2.** The mental constitution peculiar to a person or class; individual bent of mind or inclination 1665. **3.** A mode of expression peculiar to an author 1837.

1. Something in the i. of the patient that puzzles the physician BERKELEY. **2.** The pertinacious i. of the Gallic genius STUBBS. **3.** The style of Bacon has an i. 1837. Hence **Idiosyncra·tic, -al** *a.* pertaining to, or of the nature of, i. **Idiosyncra·tically** *adv.* by peculiarity of constitution.

Idiot (i·diət), *sb.* ME. [– (O)Fr. *idiot* – L. *idiota* ignorant person – Gr. ἰδιώτης private person, plebeian, ignorant, lay(man), f. ἴδιος private, peculiar.] †**1.** An ignorant, uneducated man; a simple man; a clown –1722. †**b.** *spec.* A layman –1660. †**c.** One not professionally learned; also, a private man –1663. **2.** A person so deficient mentally as to be incapable of ordinary reasoning or rational conduct. Applied to one permanently so afflicted. ME. **b.** A term of reprobation: A blockhead, an utter fool ME. †**c.** A man of weak intellect maintained as a professional fool or jester –1711. **3.** *attrib.* or quasi-*adj.*, as *i. boy, laugh,* etc. ME.

1. The bisshop repreuyd hym sore as unconnyng and an ydeote CAXTON. **b.** For he would not Take orders but remaine an Idiote 1611. **2.** Idiots make very few or no Propositions, and reason scarce at all LOCKE. **b.** You i., do you know what peril you stand in? DICKENS. Hence **Idiot** *v. trans.* to call (any one) i. TENNYSON. **I·diotcy** = IDIOCY. **Idio·tic** *a.* devoid of intellect; utterly stupid, senseless, foolish. †**Idiotish** *a.* idiotic.

Idio·tical, *a.* 1646. [f. late L. *idioticus* – Gr. ἰδιωτικός (in form, not in sense); see prec., -IC, -ICAL.] †**1.** Uneducated, plain, ignorant –1725. †**2.** Private, personal (*rare*) –1660. **3.** = IDIOTIC 1656. Hence **Idio·tical-ly** *adv.*, **-ness.**

‖**Idioticon** (idi,ǭᵘ·tikǫn). 1842. [– Gr. ἰδιωτικόν, subst. use of n. sing. of ἰδιωτικός; see prec.] A dictionary confined to a particular dialect, or containing words and phrases peculiar to one part of a country.

Idiotism (i·diŏtiz'm). 1588. [– Fr. *idiotisme* idiom, idiomatic expression or phrase (XVI); idiocy (XVII) – L. *idiotismus* common or vulgar manner of speaking – Gr. ἰδιωτισμός. In II, partly f. IDIOT + -ISM.]

I. †**1.** = IDIOM 1. –1716. †**2.** The peculiar character or genius of a language –1731. **3.** = IDIOM 3. 1615. †**b.** *transf.* A peculiarity of action, manner, or habit –1639.

II. 1. Ignorance; lack of knowledge or culture 1635. **2.** = IDIOCY (now *rare*) 1611. **b.** Extreme folly, senselessness, or stupidity 1592.

2. Direct Lunacie and Ideotism 1632. **b.** What i. it would be in me to trust myself to a ministry capable of such baseness WILKES.

Idiotize (i·diŏtəiz), *v.* 1716. [f. IDIOT + -IZE.] †**1.** *intr.* To act in a way peculiar to themselves. **2.** *intr.* To become idiotic or stupid 1800. **3.** *trans.* To make idiotic; to befool 1831.

I·diotry. 1494. [f. IDIOT + -RY.] **a.** *Sc. Law.* = IDIOCY. **b.** Idiotic conduct, madness 1757.

Idle (əid'l), *a.* (*sb.*) [OE. *idel* = OFris. *idel*, OS. *idal* empty, worthless (Du. *ijdel* vain, useless, frivolous, trifling, conceited), OHG. *ītal* empty, useless (G. *eitel* bare, mere, worthless, vain); WGmc., of unkn. origin.] †**1.** Empty; void (*of*) –ME. **2.** Void of any real worth, usefulness, or significance; hence, ineffective, vain, frivolous, trifling OE. †**b.** Void of meaning or sense; also (of persons) light-headed –1658. **c.** Groundless 1590. **3.** Of things: Useless OE. **4.** Doing nothing, unemployed OE. **b.** Of things, esp. time: Unoccupied ME. **5.** Of things: Inactive, not moving or in operation 1522. **6.** Lazy, indolent ME. †**7.** quasi-*adv.* = IDLY –1663.

1. I am idel erþe & voide, til þou illumyne me 1450. **2.** He is no i. talker 1576. I. conjectures 1802. **c.** I. or malicious reports MACAULAY, hopes BROWNING. **3.** Vsurping Iuie, Brier, or i. Mosse SHAKS. **4.** Vacaboundes and ydell persones 1530. **b.** *I. bread* = bread of idleness (IDLENESS). Dozing out all his i. noons COWPER. Phr. *I. worms*, worms said joc. to breed in the fingers of the idle (*Rom & Jul.* I. iv. 65, Qo. 1597). **5.** We don't keep the pits i. for the fun of the thing 1898. **I. wheel, i.-wheel,** an intermediate wheel used for connecting two geared wheels when they cannot be brought sufficiently near to gear directly, or when it is necessary that the follower should revolve in the same direction as the leader, which it would not do if they geared directly. *I. pulley*, the loose pulley of the 'fast-and-loose-pulley' arrangement. **6.** †*I. bellies*, indolent sluggards or gluttons (cf. *Titus* 1:12).

Comb. **i.-tongs** = LAZY-TONGS.

B. *sb.* (the *adj.* used *absol.*). †**1.** *In* (earlier *on, an*) *i.*: in vain –1500. †**2.** Idleness –1606. †**3.** An idler –1709.

1. Euery man that taketh goddes name in ydel CHAUCER.

Idle (əid'l), *v.* 1592. [f. prec. adj.] **1.** *intr.* To move idly. **2.** To be idle 1668. **b.** quasi-*trans.* *To i.* (time) *away*, to pass in idleness 1652. **3.** *trans.* To cause to be idle 1826.

†**I·dle-hea:ded,** *a.* 1598. [Parasynthetic f. *idle head.*] **1.** Of little understanding; silly; crazy –1631. **2.** Off one's head; distracted, delirious –1694.

1. The superstitious idle-headed-Eld SHAKS.

I·dleman. *rare.* ME. **1.** One who has no occupation; †formerly, in Ireland, a gentleman. **2.** One employed to do odd jobs 1845.

Idleness (əi·d'lnės). [OE. *idelnes*; see -NESS.] †**1.** Vanity –ME. **2.** Groundlessness, worthlessness; triviality; ineptitude, futility 1645. †**3.** Light-headedness; delirium; also folly (*rare*) –1645. **4.** The condition of being idle; want of occupation; habitual indolence; an instance of this. (Now the ordinary sense.) OE.

2. The i. of the proceedings 1885. **4.** *Bread of i.*, bread not earned by labour; [She] eateth not the bread of i. *Prov.* 31:27.

Idler (əi·dləɹ). 1534. [f. IDLE *v.* + -ER[1].] **1.** One who idles or is idle; one who spends his time in idleness; an indolent person. **2.** *Naut.* One of those who, being liable to constant day duty on board a ship-of-war, are not subjected to keep the night-watch 1794. **3.** *Machinery.* An idle wheel (see IDLE *a.* 5) 1875.

Idlesse (əi·dlės). *arch.* Also **idless.** 1596. [Pseudo-antique f. IDLE *a.*; see -ESS[2].] Idleness; *dolce far niente.*

Idly (əi·dli), *adv.* OE. [f. IDLE *a.* + -LY[2]. (Formerly *idlely*.)] **1.** Vainly, in vain; uselessly; carelessly, frivolously, ineffectively. †**b.** Incoherently, deliriously –1632. **2.** In an idle or lazy way; indolently, inactively ME.

Ido (ī·do). 1907. [In this language, = offspring.] An artificial language, based on Esperanto. Hence **I·doist.**

Idocrase (əi·dokrēⁱs). 1804. [– Fr. *idocrase* (Haüy, 1796), f. Gr. εἶδος form + κρᾶσις mixture.] *Min.* = VESUVIANITE.

Idol (əi·dəl, əi·d'l), *sb.* [ME. *ydel, ydol* – (O)Fr. †*id(e)le, idole* – L. *idolum* image, form, apparition, (eccl.) idol – Gr. εἴδωλον (same meanings), f. εἶδος form, shape.] **I.** From Jewish and Christian use. **1.** An image or similitude of a deity or divinity, used as an object of worship; applied to those used by pagans, whence, in scriptural language, = 'false god' (1 Cor. 8:4). **b.** Applied polemically to any material object of adoration in a Christian Church 1545. **2.** *fig.* Any thing or person that is the object of excessive or supreme devotion 1562.

1. Their dumb idols, whom they called by the name of the holy gods DE FOE. **b.** This mischievous i. the mass 1554. **2.** Money, the I. of other People, was the least of his Care 1737. A hero who was the i. of his army THIRLWALL.

II. From classical Greek (and Latin) use. †**1.** An image, effigy, or figure of a person or thing; esp. a statue –1605. †**b.** A counterpart, likeness –1667. **2.** An incorporeal phantom 1563. **3.** A mental fiction; a fantasy 1577. **b.** *Logic.* = IDOLUM 2. 1678. †**4.** A fictitious personation; a sham; a pretender –1660. **5.** *attrib.* 1585.

1. b. Th' Apostat in his Sun-bright Chariot sate, I. of Majestie Divine MILT. *P.L.* VI. 101. **3.** Vain idols and phantoms of blessedness 1899. **b.** This is but another i. of the Atheists den CUDWORTH. **5.** I. shapes KEBLE.

Phr. *Idol shepherd* (Zech. 11:17): used in 17th c. polemics, sometimes with allusion to idolatry, sometimes with *idol* taken as 'counterfeit' or 'sham', sometimes associated with *idle*, 'neglectful of duty'. *Comb.* **i.-shell,** a tropical mollusc of the family *Ampullariidæ.*

Hence †**I·dol** *v.* (*rare*), to make an i. of; to idolize.

†**Idola·ster.** ME. [– OFr. *idolastre* (mod. *idolâtre*), var. (by confusion with *-astre* -ASTER) of *idolatre*; see next.] = IDOLATER 1. –1616.

Idolater (əidǫ·lătəɹ). ME. [Earliest †*idolatrer*, †*-trour*, either f. (O)Fr. *idolâtre* + -ER[1], -OUR, -OR 2, or f. IDOLATRY, after *astronomer/astronomy*; the present form (XVI) was either a phonetic reduction of *idolatrer* or – Fr. *idolâtre* – Rom. (med.L.) *idolatra*, for *idololatra, -tres* – Gr. εἰδωλολάτρης see IDOLATRY, -LATER.] **1.** A worshipper of idols; one who pays divine honours to an image or representation of a god, or to any natural object as a deity. **2.** An adorer, devoted admirer (*of*) 1566.

2. Old covetous men, ydolaters of their treasures 1566. var. †**Ido·latrer.** Hence **Ido·latress,** a female i. Also *fig.*

Idolatric, †-al (əidolæ·trik, -ăl), *a.* 1550. [– med.L. *idolatricus* (cf. *idololatricus*, Tertullian) – med.L. *idolatria* IDOLATRY; see -IC, -ICAL. Cf. Fr. *idolâtrique.*] Idolatrous.

Idolatrize (əidǫ·lătrəiz), *v.* 1592. [f. IDOLATRY + -IZE.] †**1.** *intr.* To worship idols; to commit idolatry –1706. **2.** *trans.* To make an idol of; to worship idolatrously. Chiefly in *fig.* use. 1615. †**3.** To render idolatrous. CUDWORTH. Hence **Ido·latrizer.**

Idolatrous (əidǫ·lătrəs), *a.* 1550. [f. †*idolatrer* (see IDOLATER) + -OUS; superseded IDOLATRIC, -AL.] **1.** Of, pertaining to, or of the nature of idolatry. **2.** Used in idol-worship. ?*Obs.* 1613. **3.** Given to the worship of idols or false gods 1600.

1. I. veneration for the state 1863. **2.** He saw an i. altar at Damascus FULLER. **3.** The Philistines I., uncircumcised, unclean MILT. *Samson* 1364. Hence **Ido·latrous-ly** *adv.*, **-ness.**

Idolatry (əidǫ·lătri). ME. [– (O)Fr. *idolâtrie* – Rom. (med.L.) *idolatria*, for eccl.L. *idololatria* (Tertullian) – Gr. (N.T.) εἰδωλολατρεία, f. εἴδωλον IDOL; see -LATRY.] **1.** The worship of idols or images 'made with hands', or of any created object. †**b.** *pl.* Idolatrous objects. MILT. **2.** Immoderate attachment to or veneration for any person or thing; admiration savouring of adoration ME.

1. b. To worship Calves, the Deities of Egypt.. And all the Idolatries of Heathen round MILT. *P.R.* III. 418.

†**I·dolish,** *a.* 1530. [f. IDOL *sb.* + -ISH[1].] Heathenish; idolatrous –1641.

Idolism (əi·dŏliz'm). 1608. [f. IDOL *sb.* + -ISM.] **1.** The practice of idolatry. **2.** The action of idolizing; an idolization 1825. **3.** A false mental image or notion; cf. EIDOLON 1671.

Idolist (əi·dŏlist). 1614. [f. as prec. + -IST.] A worshipper of idols. Also *attrib.*

Idolize (əi·dŏləiz), *v.* 1598. [f. IDOL *sb.* + -IZE.] **1.** *trans.* To make an idol of. to render idolatrous worship to; hence, to adore, or love to excess. **b.** To make into an idol. ?*Obs.* 1669. **2.** *intr.* To practise idolatry 1631.

1. They [my soldiers] do not i. me, but look upon the Cause they fight for CROMWELL. **2.** To i. after the manner of Egypt 1864. Hence **I:doliza·tion. I·dolizer.**

Idolo-, comb. f. Gr. εἴδωλον IDOL, as in ‖**Idolodouli·a** [Gr. δουλεία DULIA], veneration of an inferior kind given to idols or images. **Idolo-gra·phical** *a.* descriptive of idols. **Ido·lomancy** [Gr. μαντεία], divination by idols. **Idoloma·nia** †**Idolo·many,** zealous idolatry.

Idoloclast (əidǫ·lŏklæst). 1843. [f. IDOLO- + Gr. -κλάστης breaker, after *iconoclast.*] A breaker of idols; an iconoclast. Hence **Idolocla·stic** *a.*

†**Idolo·later.** 1608. [– eccl.L. *idololatra, -tres*; see IDOLATER.] = IDOLATER. Hence †**Idolola·tric, †-al** *a.* idolatrous. So †**Idolo·latry** [eccl.L. *idololatria*, Gr. εἰδωλολατρεία] = IDOLATRY 1550.

Idolothyte (əidǫ·lŏþəit). ?*Obs.* 1562. [– eccl.L. *idolothytus* (Tertullian) – Gr. εἰδωλόθυτος offered to idols, f. εἴδωλον IDOL + θυτός sacrificed.] **A.** *adj.* Offered to an idol. **B.** *sb.* A thing offered to an idol. Chiefly *pl.* 1579.

Hence **Idolothy·tic** *a.* of or characterized by the eating of meats offered to idols. HUXLEY.

†**Idolous,** *a.* 1546. [f. IDOL *sb.* + -OUS.] **a.** Of the nature of an idol. **b.** Idolatrous. –1617.

‖**Idolum, -on** (əidōᵘ·lǒm, -ǫn). *Pl.* **idola** (†**-aes,** †**-ums**). 1619. [L. – Gr. εἴδωλον IDOL.] **1.** An image or unsubstantial appearance; a phantom; a mental image or idea. **2.** A false mental image; a fallacy 1640.

2. What Bacon expressively termed Idola, empty assumptions and misconceptions SAYCE.

Idoneous (əidōᵘ·niəs), *a.* Now *rare.* 1615. [f. L. *idoneus* fit, suitable + -OUS.] Apt, fit, suitable.

An Ecclesiastical Benefice..ought to be conferr'd on an I. Person AYLIFFE. So **Idone·ity,** fitness, suitableness, aptitude. **Ido·neousness.**

Idorgan (i·dǭ:ɹgăn). 1883. [Arbitrarily f. ID(EAL + ORGAN.] *Biol.* An ideal or potential organism.

Idrialin (i·driălin). 1838. [irreg. f. *Idria* in Austria where the mineral is found in the quicksilver mines; see -INE[5].] **1.** *Min.* Original name of IDRIALITE 1844. **2.** *Chem.* The essential constituent of idrialite, $C_{42}H_{28}O$, forming colourless scales which melt at a very high temperature.

Idrialite (i·driăləit). 1849. [f. prec., with substitution of the now regular suffix -ITE[1] 2 b.] *Min.* A mineral hydrocarbon, called also inflammable cinnabar.

Idyll, idyl (i·dil, əi·-). 1601. [– L. *idyllium* – Gr. εἰδύλλιον, dim. of εἶδος form, picture; see -IUM.] **1.** A short poem, descriptive of some picturesque scene or incident, chiefly in rustic life. **2.** *transf.* An episode or a series of events or circumstances suitable for an idyll 1841. **3.** *Mus.* A pastoral or sentimental composition.

1. Phr. *Prose idyll*, an idyllic composition in prose. Those amatorious eidyls and eclogues of Theocritus P. HOLLAND. Auld Licht Idylls (*title*) BARRIE. [in prose.] **2.** The pairing of the birds is an i. EMERSON. Hence **Idy·llian** (*rare*), **Idy·llic, -al** *adjs.* of, belonging to, or of the nature of an i.; forming a suitable theme for an i. **Idy·llically** *adv.* **I·dyllist. I·dyllize** *v.* to make into an i.; to render idyllic.

‖**Idy·llium, -on.** *Pl.* **idyllia** (**-ums, -ons**). 1579. [L. – Gr.; see prec.] = IDYLL.

Ie-, former sp. of JE-, as in *Iesus*, etc.; see I, the letter.

-ie, earlier form of -Y[6] suffix; in mod. use chiefly known as the Sc. spelling now also often adopted in Eng., as in *birdie, doggie*, etc.

-ier, a suffix forming nouns designating position, employment, or profession, derived from sbs., rarely agent-nouns from vbs., (1) in words dating from ME., in which the suffix is unstressed, and varies with *-yer*, as *collier, bowyer*, (2) in words of later date, in which the suffix is stressed, and varies with -EER, as *bombardier, cashier*, etc.

1. In words of ME. date, the suffix is of obscure and app. of diverse origin. Cf. *cottier* (*cotier* = med.L. *cotarius*), *tilier, bowyer*, etc. In other words, as *carrier, courtier, currier, soldier*, the suffix is really *-er* (or earlier *-our*), the *i* belonging to the vb. stem.

2. In words of later introduction, the suffix is the Fr. *-ier* (:– L. *-arius*: see -ARY[1]). Many of these also occur with *-eer*, expressing the Eng. pronunciation; in some of these -EER has been established, and from them has become a living Eng. suffix, as in *auctioneer, charioteer*, etc.

‖**Ier-oe** (ĭĕrōᵘ·). *Sc.* 1701. [Gael. *iar-ogha*, f. *iar* after + *ogha* grandchild.] A great-grandchild.

If (if), *conj.* (*sb.*) [OE. *ġif, ġyf*, corresp. (with variation due to stress conditions) to OFris. *jef, ef, jof, of*, OS. *ef, of* (Du. *of*), OHG. *ibu, oba, ube*, also *niba, noba, nube* if not (G. *ob* whether, if), ON. *ef* if, Goth. *ibai, iba* whether, lest, *niba(i* if not, *jabai* if, although; by some regarded as case-forms of a sb. repr. by OHG. *iba* condition, ON. *if, ef, efan, ifan*, etc. doubt, whence *efa, ifa* vb.; ult. etym. unkn.]

I. Introducing a clause of condition or supposition (the protasis of a conditional sentence).

On condition that; given or granted that; in (the) case that; supposing that; on the supposition that.

1. *With the protasis in the indicative.* The indicative after *if* implies that the speaker expresses no adverse opinion as to the truth of the statement in the clause; he may accept it. **2.** *With the protasis in the subjunctive, and the apodosis in the indicative or imperative.* The subjunctive after *if* implies that the speaker guards himself against endorsing the truth of the statement; he may doubt it OE. **3.** *With both protasis and apodosis in the subjunctive.* Expressing a mere hypothesis. OE. **4.** The conditional clause is often elliptical; thus *if not* (= if a thing is, be, or were not), formerly sometimes = 'unless, except' ME. **5.** The conditional clause alone is sometimes used as an exclam. to express (*a*) a wish or determination, e.g. *If I had only known!* (sc. I would have done so-and-so); (*b*) surprise or indignation, e.g. *If ever I heard the like of that!* OE.

1. She's six and fifty if she's a day SHERIDAN. Declare if thou knowest it all *Job* 38:18. **2.** If thou be the sonne of God, command that these stones bee made bread *Matt.* 4:3. If euer I were Traitor, My name be blotted from the booke of Life *Rich. II*, I. iii. 201. **3.** If I were you, I would not do it (*mod.*). **4.** He weighed eighteen stone, if a pound 1884.

Phrases. **An if, and if** (see AN *conj.* 2) = If. *arch.* **As if,** followed by a clause containing a past subj. (sometimes ellipt.), or an infinitive expressing purpose or destination: As the case would be if; as though.

If so be (that), if it happen that, supposing that. *arch.* and *dial.*

II. Introducing a noun-clause depending on the verb *see, ask, learn, doubt, know*, or the like: Whether OE.

Hee sent foorth a doue from him, to see if the waters were abated *Gen.* 8:8.

B. *sb.* The conditional conjunction used as a name for itself; hence, a condition, a supposition 1513.

Thou seruest me, I wene, with iffes and with andes SIR T. MORE.

I'faith. 1420. = in faith: see FAITH *sb.* III. 2.

Ife·cks, I'fe·gs, *int. Obs.* exc. *dial.* 1610. [Perversion of prec.] Used as a trivial oath: In faith, by my faith.

I-fere: see YFERE *sb.* and *adv.*

-iferous, -ific, -ification, -ify, comb. ff. -FEROUS, -FIC, -FICATION, -FY, q.v.

†**Igad, i'gad** (igæ·d), *int.* 1671. Var. of EGAD –1728.

Igasuric (igăsiūᵊ·rik), *a.* 1830. [– Fr. *igasurique*, f. *igasur*, Malay name for St. Ignatius' Bean; see -IC.] *Chem.* In *i. acid*, an acid contained in small quantities in St. Ignatius' bean, *nux vomica*, and the root of *Strychnos colubrina.* So **Igasu·rate,** a salt of i. acid. **Igasu·rine,** a poisonous alkaloid found in *nux vomica.*

Igdrasil: see YGGDRASIL.

‖**Igloo** (i·glu). 1856. [Eskimo, = house.] **1.** An Eskimo dome-shaped hut, esp. one built of snow. **2.** The cavity in the snow above a seal's breathing-hole 1882.

†**Igna·ro.** 1620. [– It. *ignaro* adj.] An ignoramus –1686.

Ignatian (ignēⁱ·ʃiăn), *a.* (*sb.*) 1605. [f. *Ignatius* (see def.) + -AN.] **1.** Pertaining to Ignatius Loyola (1491–1556), or to the Society of Jesus founded by him. **2.** Of or belonging to St. Ignatius, bishop of Antioch, martyred at Rome in the 2nd century; esp. in *I. Epistles*, letters doubtfully attributed to him 1832. **3.** *sb.* A follower of Ignatius Loyola; a JESUIT 1613.

Ignatius' Bean. 1751. = Bean of St. Ignatius, the poisonous seed of *Strychnos ignatii.*

Igneous (i·gni,əs), *a.* 1664. [f. L. *igneus* (f. *ignis* fire) + -OUS; see -EOUS.] **1.** Of, pertaining to, or of the nature of fire; fiery. **2.** Resulting from, or produced by, the action of fire; *esp.* in *Geol.* Produced by volcanic agency (opp. to AQUEOUS) 1665.

1. I. exhalations LYELL. **2.** The i. origin of basalts 1796.

Ignescent (igne·sĕnt). 1828. [– *ignescent-*, pr. ppl. stem of L. *ignescere* take fire, become inflamed, f. *ignis* fire; see -ESCENT.] **A.** *adj.* Kindling, bursting into flame; firing up. **B.** *sb.* An ignescent body or substance 1828.

Ignicolist (igni·kŏlist). 1816. [f. L. *ignis* + *-cola* (f. *colere* to worship) + -IST.] A fire-worshipper.

Igniferous (igni·fĕrəs), *a.* 1618. [f. L. *ignifer* fire-bearing (f. *ignis* fire) + -OUS; see -FEROUS.] Producing fire. Also *fig.*

†**Igni·fluous,** *a. rare.* 1623. [f. late L. *ignifluus* (f. *ignis* fire + *-fluus* flowing) + -OUS.] Flowing with fire –1659.

Igniform (i·gnifǭɹm), *a. rare.* 1744. [f. L. *ignis* fire + -FORM.] Of the form of fire.

Ignify (i·gnifəi), *v. rare.* 1586. [f. L. *ignis* fire + -FY.] *trans.* To cause to burn.

Ignigenous (igni·dʒĕnəs), *a. rare.* 1727. [f. L. *ignis* fire + -GENOUS.] Produced by the action of fire.

Ignipotent (igni·pŏtĕnt), *a.* 1656. [– L. *ignipotens, -ent-* (Vergilian epithet of Vulcan), f. *ignis* fire + *potens* POTENT.] Ruling or having power over fire.

Th' pow'r i. her word obeys POPE.

Ignipuncture (ignipɒ·ŋktiŭɹ). 1886. [f. L. *ignis* fire + PUNCTURE; cf. AQUAPUNCTURE.] *Surg.* Puncture with a white-hot styliform cautery.

‖**Ignis fatuus** (i·gnis fæ·tiu,ŏs). 1563. [mod.L., 'foolish fire', so named from its erratic flitting from place to place.] A phosphorescent light seen hovering or flitting over marshy ground, supposed to be due to the spontaneous combustion of an inflammable gas (phosphuretted hydrogen) derived from decaying organic matter; pop. called *Will-o'-the-wisp, Jack-a-lantern*, etc. **b.** *fig.* Any delusive guiding principle, hope, aim, etc. 1599.

An *Ignis Fatuus* that bewitches And leads Men into Pools and Ditches BUTLER *Hud.* I. i. 509.

†**Ignite,** *a.* 1560. [– L. *ignitus*, pa. pple. of *ignire*; see next.] In a white or red heat; glowing with heat, fiery –1704.

Ignite (ignəi·t), *v.* 1666. [– *ignit-*, pa. ppl. stem of L. *ignire* set on fire, f. *ignis* fire.] **1.** *trans.* To subject to the action of fire, to make intensely hot; in chemical use, to heat to the point of combustion or chemical change. **2.** To set fire to, to kindle; also *fig.* 1823. **3.** *intr.* To take fire; to begin to burn 1818.

1. A piece of the substance was ignited to whiteness 1795. **2.** To i. a lamp TYNDALL. **3.** The gas ignited 1885. Hence **Igni·table, -ible** *a.* capable of being ignited. **Igni·ter,** one who or that which ignites.

Ignition (igni·ʃən). 1612. [– Fr. *ignition* or med.L. *ignitio*, f. as prec.; see -ION.] **1.** The action of igniting; *esp.* Heating to the point of combustion, or of chemical change; the condition of being so heated or on fire. **2.** The action of setting fire to anything; the process of taking fire; also, *loosely*, burning 1816. **b.** A means of igniting 1881. **c.** The process or the means of igniting the mixture in the cylinder of an internal combustion engine 1894.

Ignivomous (igni·vŏməs), *a.* 1603. [f. late L. *ignivomus* (Lactantius), f. *ignis* fire + *-vomus* vomiting; see -OUS.] Vomiting fire; also *fig.*

Ignobility (ignobi·lĭti). 1483. [– L. *ignobilitas* want of fame, low birth, f. *ignobilis* IGNOBLE; see -ITY.] The quality of being ignoble.

Ignoble (ignōᵘ·b'l), *a.* 1494. [– Fr. *ignoble* or L. *ignobilis*, f. *in-* (= I-[2]) IN-[3] + *gnobilis* NOBLE; see -BLE.] **1.** Of persons: Not noble in respect of birth, position, or reputation; of low birth or humble station. Also of animals, things, places, etc. **2.** Not noble in disposition, nature, or quality; dishonourable 1592.

1. I was not i. of Descent SHAKS. Any i. occupation JOWETT. The old division of noble and i. hawks 1833. (*Note.* The term 'ignoble' was applied to the short-winged hawks, e.g. the goshawk and the sparrow-hawk, which rake after the quarry, as dist. from the long-winged falcons, which stoop to the quarry at a single swoop.) This Clermont is a meane and i. place CORYAT. **2.** Thus Belial..Counsel'd i. ease MILT. *P.L.* II. 227. Hence **Igno·bleness. Igno·bly** *adv.*

Ignoble (ignōᵘ·b'l), *v. rare.* 1590. [f. prec., as the opposite to ENNOBLE.] *trans.* To make ignoble or infamous. Also *fig.*

Ignominious (ignŏmi·niəs), *a.* 1450. [– (O)Fr. *ignominieux* or L. *ignominiosus*, f. *ignominia*; see next, -OUS.] **1.** Full of ignominy; involving shame, disgrace, or obloquy; discreditable. Also sometimes: Lowering to one's dignity or self-respect. **2.** Of persons: Covered with, or deserving, ignominy; infamous 1577.

1. The i. terms of peace were rejected with disdain GIBBON. **2.** Then first with fear surpris'd and sense of paine, Fled i. MILT. *P.L.* VI. 395. Hence **Ignomi·nious-ly** *adv.*, **-ness.** So †**Igno·mious** *a.* 1574.

Ignominy (i·gnŏmini). 1540. [– Fr. *ignominie* or L. *ignominia*, f. *in-* (= I-[2]) IN-[3] + **gnomen, nomen* name, reputation; see -Y[3].]] **1.** Dishonour, disgrace, infamy; the condition of being in disgrace, etc. **2.** Ignominious or base quality or conduct; that which entails disgrace 1564.

1. Even his successes had been purchased with i. THIRLWALL. **2.** [Death is] the very disgrace and i. of our natures SIR T. BROWNE. So †**I·gnomy** 1534.

Igno·rable, *a.* [f. IGNORE *v.* + -ABLE. Cf. Fr. *ignorable* in same sense.] Capable of being ignored; of which one may be ignorant. FERRIER.

Ignoramus (ignŏrēⁱ·mŏs). *Pl.* **-uses** (-ŏsĕz), also †**-us.** 1577. [L., = 'we do not know', (in legal use) 'we take no notice of (it)'.] †**1.** The endorsement formerly made by a Grand Jury upon a bill or indictment, when they considered the evidence insufficient to warrant the case going to a petty jury. Hence quasi-*sb.*, or *ellipt.* Also *transf.* an answer which admits ignorance of the point in question; *fig.* a state of ignorance. (The endorsement now used is 'not a true bill', or 'not found', or 'no bill'.) **b.** *attrib.* as in *i. jury, crew, Whig* (alluding to the Grand Jury which rejected the bill against the Earl of Shaftesbury, 1681). **2.** An ignorant person. [f. *Ignoramus*, used as a name for a lawyer. See O.E.D.] 1616.

1. As for Medusa's brother I return i. 1658. **2.** I. and Dulman his Clearke 1634. Hence †**Ignora·mus'd** *ppl. a.* freed from prosecution by the *ignoramus* of the Grand Jury 1734.

Ignorance (i·gnŏrăns). ME. [– (O)Fr. *ignorance* – L. *ignorantia*, f. *ignorant-*; see next, -ANCE.] **1.** The fact or condition of being ignorant; want of knowledge (general or special). Also with *an* and *pl.* (*rare*) 1749. †**2.** With *an* and *pl.* An act due to want of knowledge; an offence or sin caused by ignorance –1611.

1. Marvell is the daughter of ignoraunce 1573. National i. of decent art RUSKIN. **2.** Our ignorances haue reached vp vnto heauen 1 *Esd.* 8 : 75. So †**I·gnorancy** (in sense 1) 1526.

Ignorant (i·gnŏrănt), *a.* (*sb.*) ME. [– (O)Fr. *ignorant* – *ignorant-*, pr. ppl. stem of L. *ignorare*; see IGNORE, -ANT.] **1.** Destitute of knowledge; unknowing, unlearned. Also *fig.* or *transf.* of things. **2.** with *of*: Having no knowledge of; hence †unconscious of, innocent of, having no share in 1483. **3.** *transf.* Resulting from ignorance 1509. †**b.** That keeps one in ignorance. SHAKS. †4. Of things: Unknown –1634. **5.** *sb.* An ignorant person (now *rare*) 1480.

1. There were..none so i. as not to know his deeds MOTLEY. *fig. Cymb.* III. i. 27. **2.** Of cards and dice they are happily i. 1615. **3.** Alas, what i. sin haue I committed *Oth.* IV. ii. 70. **b.** *Wint. T.* I. ii. 397. **4.** Whence he is, tis i. to vs CHAPMAN. **5.** Church authorities..too often entrust their buildings to ignorants 1874.

Ignorantine (ignŏræ·ntin), *a.* and *sb.* 1861. [– Fr. *ignorantin*, f. *ignorant* IGNORANT, after *capucin*, etc.; see -INE[1].] *I. friars, Ignorantines*: a name taken by the Brethren of Saint-Jean-de-Dieu, an order founded in 1495 to minister to the sick poor; they subsequently devoted themselves to the instruction of the poor. Hence, the name is given in France to the 'Brethren of the Christian Schools' or 'Christian Brothers', a community founded *c*1680, for the education of the poor.

I·gnorantism. *rare.* 1856. [f. IGNORANT + -ISM; cf. Fr. *ignorantisme.*] = OBSCURANTISM. So **I·gnorantist.**

Ignorantly (i·gnŏrăntli), *adv.* 1495. [f. as prec. + -LY[2].] In an ignorant manner; without knowledge.

Whom ye then i. worship, hym shewe I vnto you TINDALE *Acts* 17:23.

Ignoratio elenchi. [Scholastic L., tr. Gr. ἡ τοῦ ἐλέγχου ἄγνοια (Aristotle) ignorance of the conditions of a valid proof.] See next, 3.

Ignoration (ignorēⁱ·ʃən). 1588. [– L. *ignoratio*, f. *ignorat-*, pa. ppl. stem of *ignorare*; see IGNORE, -ION.] †**1.** The fact or condition of being ignorant 1612. **2.** The action of ignoring; the being ignored 1865. **3.** *Ignoration of the Elench*, repr. scholastic L. **Ignoratio elenchi** (ignǒrēⁱ·ʃio ile·ŋkəi), a logical fallacy consisting in disproving some statement different from that advanced by an opponent; also extended to any argument irrelevant to the object in view 1588.

Ignore (ignōᵊ·ɹ), *v.* 1611. [– (O)Fr. *ignorer* or L. *ignorare*, f. *in-* (= I-[2]) IN-[3] + base *gno-* know.] **1.** *trans.* To be ignorant of. *Obs.* or *rare.* **2.** Said of a Grand Jury: To return (a bill) with the endorsement 'not found' (see IGNORAMUS 1); to refuse acceptance of 1830. **3.** To refuse to take notice of; to leave out of consideration, shut one's eyes to 1801.

1. The little that I know, and they i. BOYLE. **3.** To i. an invitation 1832, an important feature of necessary evidence FROUDE.

†**Ignote.** 1623. [– L. *ignotus*, f. *in-* (= I-[2]) IN-[3] + (*g*)*notus* known.] **a.** *adj.* Unknown. **b.** *sb.* A person unknown 1639.

a. Th' i. are better than ill known COWLEY.

Iguana (igwā·nă). 1555. [– Sp. *iguana*, repr. Carib name *iwana.*] A large arboreal lizard of the W. Indies and S. America, *I. tuberculata*, which attains to a length of five feet or more; also, in Zool., the name of the genus, which includes the *horned i.* of San Domingo, and other species; loosely applied to lizards of allied genera. Hence **Igua·nian** *a.* resembling an i., belonging to the i. family *Iguanidæ*; *sb.* one of this family; also **Igua·nid. Igua·noid** *a.* and *sb.* = *iguanian.*

Iguanodon (igwæ·nŏdǫn). 1830. [f. prec., after *mastodon*, etc.] *Palæont.* A large herbivorous saurian found fossil in the Wealden formation; it was from 25 to 30 feet long, and its teeth and bones resembled those of the iguana; whence the name. So **Igua·nodont** *a.* having teeth like those of the iguana; *sb.* a saurian so characterized; one of the family *Iguanodontidæ* of extinct dinosaurs, typified by the i.

‖**Ihram** (irā·m, iχrā·m). Also †**hir(r)awem.** 1704. [– Arab. *'iḥrām*, f. *ḥarama* forbid. See HAREM.] **1.** The dress worn by Moslem pilgrims, consisting of two pieces of white cotton. **2.** The state in which a pilgrim is held to be while he wears this garb, during which many acts are unlawful 1704.

IHS, in ME., late and med.L., etc., repr. a Greek MS. abbrev. of the word *IH(ΣΟΥ)Σ*, Jesus; also used as a symbol or monogram of the sacred name.

Often looked upon as a Latin contraction, and explained variously as standing for *Iesus Hominum Salvator*, Jesus Saviour of men, *In Hoc Signo* (*vinces*), in this sign (thou shalt conquer), or *In Hac Salus*, in this (cross) is salvation.

Ik, ME. form of I *pron.*

Il-[1], assim. form of the prefix IN-[2] before initial *l*, as in *il-lation*, etc. See IN-[2].

Il-[2], assim. form of the neg. prefix IN-[3] before initial *l*, as in *il-legal*, etc.; also ILLOGICAL.

-il, -ile, *suffixes*, repr. L. *-ilis* and *-īlis*, forming adjs., and occas. sbs., as in *fossilis* fossil, *agilis* agile. These suffixes are in origin the same, viz. *-lis* with connective *-i-*, which with *-i-* stems as *civi-s*, etc. gave *-īlis*. The mod. tendency is to pronounce (-əil), with some exceptions, in all cases.

†**Ile**[1]. 1601 [– L. *ile* or *ileum*; see ILEUM, ILIUM. Cf. (O)Fr. (pl.) *iles* (XIII).] = ILEUM –1656.

Ile[2], var. of AIL *sb.*[2], awn of barley, etc.

Ile, obs. f. ILL, I'LL, ISLE, AISLE.

I·leac, *a.* 1822. A refash. of ILIAC *a.* after L. *ileus*, or ILEUM.

Ileitis (ili,əi·tis). 1855. [f. ILEUM + -ITIS]. *Path.* Inflammation of the ileum.

Ileo-, comb. f. ILEUM; as,

Ileo-cæ·cal *a.*, relating to or connected with the ileum and the cæcum; as in *ileo-cæcal valve*, a valve consisting of two semilunar folds at the opening of the ileum into the cæcum; the name is occas. restricted to the lower of these. **Ileo-co·lic** *a.*, relating to or connected with the ileum and the colon; *ileo-colic valve* = *ileo-cæcal valve* (sometimes restricted to the upper fold of this). **Ileo-coli·tis**, inflammation of the ileum and colon.

†**I·leon.** 1495. [med.L. (in Gr. form). Cf. (O)Fr. *iléon.*] = ILEUM –1767.

‖**Ileum** (i·li,ŏm, əi·-). 1682. [var. of L. *ilium* ILIUM. Cl. L. had usually *ilia* (pl. of *ile* or *ilium*). The form *ileum* (*ileon, -os*) is app. due to a confusion of this with *ileus* (see next).] *Anat.* The third portion of the small intestine, succeeding the jejunum and opening into the cæcum.

‖**Ileus** (i·li,ŏs, əi·-). 1706. [L. *ileus, ileos* – Gr. ἰλεός or εἰλεός colic, app. f. εἴλειν to roll.] **1.** *Path.* A painful affection due to intestinal obstruction, esp. in the ileum; also called *iliac passion.* **2.** *Anat.* = ILEUM 1706.

Ilex (əi·leks). ME. [– L. *ilex*, perh. a Mediterranean word.] **1.** The holm-oak or evergreen oak (*Quercus ilex*). Also *attrib.* ‖**2.** In mod. Botany, a genus of *Aquifoliaceæ*, including the common holly (*I. aquifolium*), and numerous other trees 1565.

Iliac (i·liæk), *a.* (*sb.*) 1519. [– late L. *iliacus*, in form a derivative of *ilia* (i) flanks, (ii) entrails, but the suffix is Gr. and sense 1 goes with L. *ileus* ILEUS.] **1.** Properly, Of the nature of the disease called ILEUS; but taken as = Pertaining to or affecting the ILEUM. **2.** Pertaining to the flank, or to the ilium or flank-bone 1541. **3.** *sb.* Short for *i. passion* (*Obs.*); also for *i. artery*, etc. 1782.

1. *Iliac passion* [late L. *passio iliaca*] = ILEUS 1. **2.** *I. artery*, each of the two arteries, right and left, into which the abdominal aorta divides. *I. bone*, the ilium. So †**Ili·acal** *a.* = ILIAC *a.*

Iliad (i·liæd). 1579. [– L. *Ilias, Iliad-* – Gr. Ἰλιάς, Ἰλιαδ-; subst. use of adj. (sc. ποίησις, poem) 'pertaining to Ilium'.] **1.** A great epic poem of ancient Greece traditionally attributed to Homer, describing the ten years' siege of Ilium or Troy by the Greeks. **2.** *transf.* and *fig.* **a.** An epic poem like that of Homer 1619. **b.** A long series of disasters or the like (Gr. Ἰλιὰς κακῶν, Demosthenes); a long story 1609.

2. b. It opens another I. of woes to Europe BURKE. Hence **I·liadist**, a rhapsodist; a writer of Iliads.

Ilicic (əili·sik), *a.* 1861. [f. L. *ilex, ilic-* (see ILEX 2) + -IC.] *Chem.* Of or pertaining to the holly; in *i. acid*, an acid contained in the leaves of the holly. So **I·licate**, a salt of i. acid. **I·licin**, the non-nitrogenous bitter principle of the holly.

Ilio- (i:lio), comb. f. ILIUM 3; as,

Ilio-do·rsal *a.*, relating to the dorsum of the ilium. ‖**Iliopso·as**, the iliac and psoas muscles regarded as one muscle. Esp. in comb. with adjs. relating to other parts of the body with sense 'relating to or connecting the ilium and..', as **ilio-fe·moral, -lu·mbar, -perone·al** [Gr. περόνη fibula] (applied to muscles connecting the ilium and the fibula; also as *sb.*), etc.

Ilion, obs. var. of ILIUM.

-ility, compound suffix (Fr. *-ilité*, L. *-ilitas*), consisting of -ITY added to adjs. in *-il* (*civility*), *-ile* (*servility*), or *-le* (*ability*).

Ilium (i·liŏm). *Pl.* **ilia.** Also formerly **ilion**, *pl.* **ilia.** ME. [L. *ilium*; in cl. L. only in pl. *ilia* flanks, sides, also entrails. See also ILEUM.] *Anat.* †**1.** The ILEUM –1827. †**2.** *pl.* The flanks (L. *ilia*) –1706. **3.** The anterior or superior bone of the pelvis, the hip-bone; usually (as in man) articulating with the sacrum, and anchylosing with the ischium and pubis, forming together with these latter the *os innominatum* 1706.

Ilixanthin (əiliksæ·nþin). 1865. [f. ILEX holly + ξανθός yellow + -IN[1].] *Chem.* A yellow colouring matter obtained from the holly.

Ilk (ilk), *a.*[1] (*pron.*) Now *Sc.* [OE. *ilca* m., *ilce* fem. and n., f. **ĭ-* that, the same (as in Goth. *is* he, OHG. *ir*, also mod. *er*, L. *is* that, *īdem, idem* same) + **līk-* form (see LIKE and cf. the formation of SUCH, WHICH).] †**1.** Same, identical –1556. †**2.** *absol. The, that ilk*: the same (person or persons, or thing) –1650.

Phr. *Of that ilk*, of the same place, territorial designation, or name; as *Wemyss of that i.* = Wemyss of Wemyss. *Sc.* Hence *ilk* is erron. used for 'family, class, set'; any member of that ilk 1845.

Ilk, *a.*[2] (*pron.*). Now *Sc.* OE. [ME. *ilk a(n)* XII (*illc an* Orm), i.e. *ilk* :– OE. *ylc* EACH + A *adj.*[2]] = EACH 1 a; every.

Ill (il), *a.* and *sb.* ME. [– ON. *illr* adj.; *illa* adv., *ilt* n. of adj. as sb.; ult. origin unknown.]

A. *adj.* **1.** Morally evil; wicked, vicious, blameworthy. **b.** Imputing or implying evil 1483. **2.** Malevolent, unfriendly, unkind, harsh, cruel ME. **3.** Doing or tending to do harm; hurtful; dangerous ME. **4.** Causing pain, discomfort, or inconvenience; offensive, objectionable ME. **5.** Of conditions, fortune, etc.: Wretched, unlucky; unfavourable, disastrous ME. **6.** Difficult, troublesome. (Usu. with *dative inf.* as 'ill to please'.) ME. **7.** In privative sense: Not good ME. **8.** Of health, etc.: Unsound, disordered. Hence, of persons, etc.: Out of health, not well; almost always used predicatively. (The prevailing mod. sense.) 1460.

1. I. company 1680, actions BUTLER, habits LANDOR. **b.** He that hath an yll name, is halfe hangd 1546. **2.** I. tongues SHELLEY, offices MACAULAY. **3.** There's some i. Planet raignes SHAKS. *I. weeds grow apace* Provb. **4.** Great raine and yll wether HALL. **5.** Woe vnto the wicked, it shall be i. with him *Isa.* 3:11. *It's an i. wind that blows nobody good* Provb. **7.** I am i. at these Numbers SHAKS. I. Manners occasion Good laws FULLER. **8.** My eye was very red and i., in the morning PEPYS. Children are well and i. in a day 1849.

Phrases (often unnecessarily hyphened): **i. desert**, demerit, blameworthiness (so *i. deserving*); **i. ease**, discomfort; **i. fame** (see 1 b.); esp. in *house of i. fame*; **i. grace** (see GRACE *sb.*); **i. part** (see PART *sb.*); **i. success**, imperfect success (sense 6); often = failure (cf. 5); **i. temper** (see TEMPER *sb.*). See also Main Words.

B. *sb.* [the adj. used absol.] **1.** = EVIL *sb.* 1; the opposite of good ME. **2.** Moral evil; wickedness, sin, wrong-doing (*arch.*) ME. †**b.** A wicked act –1741. **3.** Something blameful, unfavourable, unfriendly, or injurious. (Perh. orig. the adv.) ME. **4.** Evil as caused; harm, injury, mischief ME. **5.** Evil as suffered; misfortune, disaster, trouble, distress; (with *pl.*) a calamity, etc. ME. **6.** Bodily disorder. (Chiefly *Sc.*) ME.

1. Great good must have great i. as opposite 1605. **2.** Forgive..The i. that I this day have done KEN. **3.** I can think no i. of him 1899. **4.** Loue worketh no i. to his neighbour *Rom.* 13:10. **5.** To know if good or i. shall befall them 1660. No sense have they of ills to come GRAY. **6.** An i. no doctor could unravel SHELLEY.

Ill (il), *adv.* [Early ME. *ille*, f. ILL *a.*; cf. ON. *illa* adv.] In an ill manner; badly.

Phr. *To speak, think*, etc. *i.* (*of*); *to like i., to take i. I. at ease* (see EASE *sb.*). *I.-to-do*: in poor circumstances. *I.-off*: badly off (the opposite of *well-off*: see OFF). My youth i.-spent 1601. I. fares the land..Where wealth accumulates, and men decay GOLDSM. He..behaved extremely i. 1793. We can i. spare him 1832.

Ill (il), *v.* Now *dial.* ME. [f. ILL *a.*] †**1.** *trans.* To harm, wrong –1614. **2.** To speak ill of 1530.

I'll, formerly †**Ile**, abbrev. of *I will.* 1591.

Ill-, in comb.

A. General uses. **I.** From ILL *a.* See ILL BLOOD, ILL BREEDING, etc.

II. From ILL *sb.* See ILL-WILLER, -WILLING, -WISH, -WISHER, etc.; also *ill-deceived* (deceived by evil).
III. From ILL *adv.* **1.** With verbs, as ILL-TREAT, ILL-USE. **2.** With adjs. derived from verbs, as *ill-manageable*, etc. **3.** With pres. pples., or adjs. of ppl. form, forming adjs., as *ill-according*; ILL-FARING, -JUDGING, -LOOKING, etc. **4.** With pa. pples., or adjs. of the same form, forming adjs., as ILL-AFFECTED, -DISPOSED, -GOT, -GOTTEN, etc.; ILL-ADVISED, -BRED, -SORTED, etc.
IV. Parasynthetic combs., in which *ill-* is sometimes of adverbial, sometimes of adjectival origin. See ILL-CONDITIONED, -FAVOURED, -HUMOURED, -MANNERED, -NATURED, -STARRED, -TEMPERED, -TONGUED, etc.
B. Special Combs.: **ill-accu·stomed** *a.*, (*a*) little habituated to something; (*b*) little frequented by customers; **ill-born** *a.*, of evil birth or origin; **ill-content, -contented** *adjs.*, discontented, †displeased; **ill-fashioned** *a.*, of an i. fashion, or badly fashioned; **ill-friended** *a.*, ill provided with friends; **ill-lived** (-ləivd) *a.*, leading a bad or immoral life; etc.

†Illa·bile, *a. rare.* 1740. [f. IL-² + LABILE.] Not liable to slip, fall, or err; infallible. CHEYNE.

†Illa·borate, *a. rare.* 1631. [– L. *illaboratus*; see IL-² and cf. ELABORATE.] Unlaboured; unfinished –1751.

†Illa·chrymable, *a. rare.* 1623. [– L. *illacrimabilis*, f. *il-* IL-² + *lacrimare* weep + *-bilis* -BLE.] Unmoved by tears; incapable of weeping. (Dicts.)

Ill-advi·sed, *a.* 1592. [ILL- III. 4.] Done without wise consideration, injudicious; *occas.*, ill-counselled, following bad advice. Hence **Ill-advi·sedly** *adv.*

Ill-affe·cted, *a.* 1596. [ILL- III. 4.] **†1.** Affected with illness; diseased –1727. **2.** Unfriendly, disaffected 1596. Hence **Ill-affe·ctedness.**

†Illa·psable, *a.* [f. IL-² + LAPSABLE.] Not liable to fall. GLANVILL.

Illapse (ilæ·ps, ill-), *sb.* Now *rare.* 1614. [– L. *illapsus*, f. *illabi* slip, etc. in; see IL-¹ and LAPSE.] **1.** The act of gliding, slipping, or falling in, of gently sinking into or permeating something. **2.** A gentle gliding movement (*rare*) 1835.

1. Praying for the i. of the Holy Ghost 1881.

Illapse (ilæ·ps, ill-), *v.* Now *rare.* 1666. [– *illaps-*, pa. ppl. stem of L. *illabi*; see IL-², LAPSE.] *intr.* To fall, glide, or slip in.

The illapsing of Souls into prepared Matter HALE.

†Illa·queable, *a.* [f. next + -ABLE.] Capable of being ensnared. CUDWORTH.

Illaqueate (ilæ·kwi,eᶦt), *v.* ?*Obs.* 1548. [– *illaqueat-*, pa. ppl. stem of L. *illaqueare*, f. *in-* IL-¹ + *laqueare*, f. *laqueus* noose, snare; see -ATE³.] *trans.* To catch as in a noose; to ensnare, entangle.

Let not..his scholastic retiary versatility of logic i. your good sense COLERIDGE. So **†Illa·queate** *ppl. a.* ensnared. **Illaquea·tion,** the action of catching or entangling in a noose; the being ensnared; also, 'a snare' (J.).

Illation (ilēᶦ·ʃən). 1533. [– L. *illatio*, f. as next; see -ION.] **1.** The action of drawing a conclusion from premisses; hence, an inference, deduction, or conclusion. **2.** *Eccl.* The Eucharistic Preface to the *Ter-sanctus.* 1863.

1. In the process of syllogising there is not really an i. or inference 1832.

Illative (ilēᶦ·tiv). 1591. [– L. *illativus*, f. *illatus*, used as pa. pple. of *inferre* INFER; see -IVE.]

A. *adj.* **1.** Of words: Introducing or stating an inference; esp. in *illative particle* 1611. **2.** Of the nature of an illation; inferential 1637. **3.** Of, pertaining to, or characterized by illation 1870.

3. The Ratiocinative or I. Sense J. H. NEWMAN.
†B. *sb.* An illative particle –1659; an illative clause –1651. Hence **Illa·tively** *adv.*

Illaudable (ilǭ·dăb'l), *a.* 1589. [– L. *illaudabilis*; see IL-², LAUDABLE.] Not laudable; unworthy of praise or commendation. Hence **Illau·dably** *adv. rare.*

I·ll-being. 1840. [f. ILL *adv.* + BEING *vbl. sb.*] The antithesis of *well-being.* CARLYLE.

Ill blood, i·ll-bloo·d. 1624. [See ILL *a.* 2, and BLOOD *sb.* II. 2.] Unfriendly feeling, animosity; strife.

I·ll-bo·ding, *a.* [ILL- II.] That bodes evil; of evil omen. 1 *Hen. VI*, IV. v. 6.

Ill-bred, *a.* 1622. [f. ILL- III. 4 + BRED *ppl. a.*] **1.** Badly brought up; unmannerly, rude. **†2.** Of a bad breed. *rare.* 1796. So **Ill breeding, i·ll-bree·ding,** bad bringing up; hence, bad manners, rudeness.

Ill-condi·tioned, *a.* 1614. [f. *ill condition* + -ED².] Having bad qualities; in a bad condition or state; now usually, of an evil disposition, malignant. In Geometry, applied to a triangle which has very unequal angles.

I:ll-dee·dy, *a.* Now *Sc.* 1460. [f. *ill deed* + -Y¹. Cf. DEEDY.] Given to evil deeds; mischievous.

Ill-dispo·sed, *a.* ME. [f. ILL- III. 4.] **1.** Having a bad disposition; wicked; malignant, malevolent; unpropitious. **†2.** Unwell, indisposed –1645. **3.** Badly arranged 1726. **4.** Disinclined (*to do* something). GOLDSM.

†Illecebra·tion. *rare.* 1624. [f. late L. *illecebrare*, f. *illecebra* charm, lure. See -ATION.] The action of alluring; enticement –1704. So **†Ille·cebrous** *a.* alluring, enticing 1531.

†Ille·ct, *v. rare.* 1529. [– *illect-*, pa. ppl. stem of L. *illicere* allure, entice.] *trans.* To allure, entice –1534.

Illegal (ilī·găl), *a.* 1626. [– (O)Fr. *illégal* or med.L. *illegalis*; see IL-², LEGAL.] Not legal; contrary to, or forbidden by, law.

They have set aside a return as i. 'JUNIUS'. I. commerce 1817. Hence **Ille·gal-ly** *adv.*, **-ness.**

Illegality (iligæ·lĭti). 1639. [– (O)Fr. *illégalité* or med.L. *illegalitas*; see prec., -ITY.] **1.** The quality or condition of being illegal; also, an instance of this. **†2.** = ILLEGITIMACY. Fielding.

1. The I. of Ship-money CLARENDON.

Illegible (ile·dʒib'l), *a.* 1640. [f. IL-² + LEGIBLE.] Not legible; undecipherable. **†b.** Unreadable, because of language or matter –1828.

I. writing RUSKIN. **b.** Sir Michael Scott, again—being all magic, witchcraft, and mystery—is absolutely i. 1828. Hence **Illegibi·lity. Ille·gibly** *adv.*

Illegitimacy (ilĭdʒi·timăsi). 1680. [f. next; see -ACY.] The quality or state of not being legitimate; *spec.* bastardy.

Illegitimate (ilĭdʒi·timĕt), *a.* (*sb.*) 1536. [f. late L. *illegitimus*, after LEGITIMATE *a.*] **1.** Not legitimate, not in accordance with law; unauthorized; spurious; irregular, improper 1645. **2.** *spec.* **a.** Not born in lawful wedlock; spurious, bastard. (The earliest sense in Eng.) 1536. **b.** Not correctly deduced or inferred; illogical 1599. **c.** Naturally or physiologically abnormal 1615. **3.** *sb.* A bastard 1583.

1. I. government BURKE, curiosity 1876. **2. a.** I am a Bastard..in euery thing i. SHAKS. **b.** O i. construction SHAKS. **c.** These i. plants, as they may be called, are not fully fertile DARWIN. Hence **Illegi·timately** *adv.* 1633. **Illegitima·tion,** the action, or an act, of declaring i.; † = ILLEGITIMACY 1553.

Illegitimate (ilĭdʒi·timeᶦt), *v.* 1611. [f. prec. Cf. LEGITIMATE *v.*] *trans.* To declare or pronounce illegitimate; to bastardize. So **Illegi·timatize** *v.*, **Illegi·timize** *v.*

Illeism (i·lī,iz'm). 1809. [f. L. *ille* he; after *egoism.*] Excessive use of the pronoun *he.* COLERIDGE. So **I·lleist.**

†Ille·viable, *a. rare.* 1642. [f. IL-² + LEVIABLE; cf. AL. *illevabilis* (XV), *illeviabilis* (XVI).] That cannot be levied –1706.

Illfare (i·l,fēᵊɹ). ME. [f. ILL *a.* + FARE *sb.*¹] The condition of getting on badly; the opposite of *welfare.*

Ill-faring, *a.* 1400. [f. ILL *adv.* + *faring* (FARE *v.*¹ 6).] Faring badly.

Ill-fa·ted, *a.* 1710. [ILL- III. 4.] **1.** Having or destined to an evil fate. **2.** Fraught with bad fortune 1715.

Ill-fa·voured, -ored, *a.* 1530. *Sc.* **ill-fa(u)rd,** etc. [f. ILL *a.* + FAVOUR *sb.* + -ED².] Having an unpleasing appearance; ill-looking, uncomely; *transf.* offensive; objectionable.

The seuen thin and ill fauoured kine *Gen.* 41: 27. Democracy is an ill-favoured word to English ears 1865. Hence **Ill-fa·voured-ly** *adv.*, **-ness.**

Ill-got, *a.* 1593. [f. ILL- III. 4 + *got*, pa. pple. of GET *v.*] = next.

Things ill got had ever bad success SHAKS.

Ill-go·tten, *a.* 1552. [f. as prec. + GOTTEN.] Gained by evil means; *esp.* in *i. goods.*

Ill humour, i·ll-hu·mour. 1568. [prop. two wds.: ILL *a.* + HUMOUR *sb.*] **†1.** A disordered bodily humour (see HUMOUR *sb.* I. 2) –1665. **2.** A disagreeable mood; crossness, sullenness, bad temper. (Often hyphened.) 1748. Hence **I·ll-hu·moured** *a.*, **-ly** *adv.*

Illiberal (ili·bĕrăl, ill-), *a.* (*sb.*) 1535. [– (O)Fr. *illibéral* in same sense – L. *illiberalis* mean, sordid, f. *in-* IL-² + *liberalis* LIBERAL.] **1.** Not befitting a free man; not pertaining to or acquainted with the liberal arts (see LIBERAL), unscholarly; ill-bred, ungentlemanly; base, mean, vulgar, rude. **2.** Not generous in respect to the opinions, rights, or liberty of others; narrow-minded, bigoted; opposed to liberal principles 1649. **3.** Not free in giving; stingy 1623. **4.** *sb.* One who is not liberal; one opposed to Liberalism in politics 1818.

1. I. Latin CHESTERF., occupation JOWETT. **2.** Popery..of the most..i. kind ROBERTSON. **3.** An oversparing or i. Hand 1695. **4.** I am a violent I.; but it does not follow that I must be a Conservative RUSKIN. Hence **Illi·beralism, Illi·beralness,** illiberality, i. principles. **Illibera·lity,** the quality of being i. **Illi·beralize** *v.* to render i. **Illi·berally** *adv.*

Illicit (ili·sit, ill-), *a.* 1652. [– (O)Fr. *illicite* or L. *illicitus*; see IL-², LICIT.] Not authorized or allowed; improper, irregular; *esp.* not sanctioned by law, rule, or custom; unlawful, forbidden.

I. commerce 1748, love 1806, distillation MCCULLOCH. *Illicit process* (Logic): the fallacy in which a term not distributed in the premisses of a syllogism is distributed in the conclusion 1827. Hence **Illi·cit-ly** *adv.*, **-ness.** So **†Illi·citous** *a.* 1611.

†Illiga·tion. [– late L. *illigatio*, f. *illigat-*, pa. ppl. stem of L. *illigare* fetter, entangle, f. *in-* IL-¹ + *ligare* bind; see -ION.] Entanglement. FELTHAM.

†Illi·ghten, *v.* 1555. [app. altered f. *alighten* (see ALIGHT *v.*³), after *illuminate* etc. Cf. ENLIGHTEN.] *trans.* To illuminate, enlighten (*lit.* and *fig.*) –1693.

Illimitable (ili·mităb'l, ill-), *a.* (*sb.*) 1596. [– late L. *illimitatus*; see IL-², LIMITATE. Cf. Fr. *illimitable.*] **1.** That cannot be limited; having no determinable limits; boundless. **2.** *sb.* That which is illimitable 1884.

1. The heauens i. hight SPENSER. Hence **Illi:mitabi·lity, Illi·mitableness,** boundlessness. **Illi·mitably** *adv.*

†Illi·mitate, *a.* 1602. [– late L. *illimitatus*; see prec.] Unlimited, unbounded –1640.

Illimitation (ilimitēᶦ·ʃən). *rare.* 1610. [f. IL-² + LIMITATION. Cf. med.L. *illimitatio.*] The condition or fact of being free from limitation.

Illimited (ili·mitėd, ill-), *a.* 1602. [f. IL-² + LIMITED.] Not limited; unrestrained.

Some plead for an i. toleration of all Religions 1645. Hence **Illi·mited-ly** *adv.*, **-ness.**

Illinition (ilini·ʃən). Also *erron.* **-ation.** 1678. [– late and med.L. *illinitio*, f. *illinīre*, var. of L. *illinere*, f. *in-* IL-¹ + *linere* smear; see -ION.] **1.** A smearing or rubbing in or on, of ointment, liniment, etc.; *concr.* that which is smeared or rubbed in 1684. **2.** *transf.* **†a.** A calcining process, in which metals were anointed with certain solutions –1683. **b.** *concr.* A thin crust or coating of extraneous matter on the surface of metals, etc. 1796.

2. b. A thin crust or i. of black manganese KIRWAN.

†Illiqua·tion. 1612. [– med.L. **illiquatio*, f. *in-* IL-¹ + *liquatio* melting, melting-point (XIII); see LIQUATION.] *Chem.* The melting or infusing of one substance into another –1678.

Illiquid (ili·kwid, ill-), *a.* 1694. [f. IL-² + LIQUID *a.* (II. 3. b), or – med.L. **illiquidus*, f. *in-* IL-² + *liquidus* clear of debts (XIII). Cf. Fr. *†illiquide.*] *Law.* Of a right, debt, or claim: Not clear or manifest; not ascertained or legally constituted. Of an asset, etc.: Not easily realizable. Hence **Illiqui·dity.**

I·llish, *a. rare.* 1637. [f. ILL *a.* + -ISH¹.] Somewhat unwell.

Illision (ili·ʒən, ill-). Now *rare.* 1603. [– late L. *illisio*, f. *illis-*, pa. ppl. stem of L. *illidere* strike or dash against; see -ION.] The action of striking against something.

Illiteracy (ili·tĕrăsi). 1660. [f. ILLITERATE; see -ACY.] The quality or condition of being illiterate; ignorance of letters; absence of education; *esp.* inability to read and write. **b.** An error due to want of learning. POPE.

To reform the i. of the clergy WARTON. Comparative i., as tested by marks instead of names 1888.

Illiteral (ili·tĕrăl, ill-), *a.* 1765. [f. IL-[2] + LITERAL.] Not literal.

Illiterate (ili·tĕrĕt), *a.* (*sb.*) 1556. [– L. *illitteratus*, f. *in-* IL-[2] + *litteratus* liberally educated, LITERATE.] **1. a.** Of persons: Ignorant of letters or literature; without education; *spec.* (in reference to census returns, voting by ballot, etc.) Unable to read, i.e. totally illiterate. **b.** Of things: Characterized by ignorance of letters, or absence of learning or education 1597. **2.** In L. sense: Not written upon; not expressed in words (*rare*) 1645. **3.** *sb.* An illiterate, unlearned, or uneducated person; *spec.* one unable to read 1628.

1. a. The i. fishermen of Galilee E. IRVING. **b.** Bookless or i. religions MAX-MÜLLER. **3.** In Ireland the illiterates were 21 per cent. of the electors 1893. So †**Illi·terated** *a.* = prec. 1. Hence **Illi·terate-ly** *adv.*, **-ness**. **Illi·terature**, illiteracy; want of learning 1592.

Ill-judged, *a.* 1717. [f. ILL- III. 4 + *judged.*] Done without judgement, injudicious.

An ill-judged economy 1828. So **I·ll-ju·dging** *a.* judging malevolently, judging mistakenly; uncritical; injudicious.

†**Ill·looked,** *a.* 1636. [f. ILL *a.* + LOOK *sb.* + -ED[2].] Having evil looks; ill-looking, ugly –1821. So **I·ll-loo·king** *a.* of evil or repulsive appearance, ugly 1633.

Ill luck, i·ll-lu·ck. 1548. [f. ILL *a.* 5 + LUCK *sb.*] Unfavourable luck; bad fortune, misfortune. Also *attrib.* MILT.

Ill-ma·nnered, *a.* ME. [f. ILL *a.* + MANNER *sb.*[1] + -ED[2].] Unmannerly, rude. Hence **I:ll-ma·nneredly** *adv.* Also **I:ll-ma·nnerly** *a.*

Ill nature, i·ll-na·ture. 1691. [f. ILL *a.* + NATURE.] Malevolent disposition or character; unkindly feeling.

Ill-na·tured, *a.* 1635. [f. prec. + -ED[2].] †**1.** Of evil or bad nature or character; malignant –1788. **2.** Of evil disposition; unkindly, churlish, spiteful 1635.

1. Must the earth..be sad, because some ill-natured star is sullen? FULLER. **2.** People say such ill-natured things 1869. Hence **I:ll-na·tured-ly** *adv.*, **-ness** (*rare*).

Illness (i·lnės). 1500. [f. ILL *a.* + -NESS.] †**1.** Bad moral quality; badness –1718. †**2.** Unpleasantness; troublesomeness; noxiousness; badness –1718. **3.** Bad or unhealthy condition of the body (or, formerly, of a part); the condition of being ill (ILL *a.* 8); disease, ailment, sickness. Also with *an* and *pl.* (The only current mod. sense.) 1689.

1. Ambition..without The illnesse should attend it *Macb.* I. v. 21. **2.** The i. of the Weather LOCKE. **3.** In the family circle Sir Walter Scott seldom spoke of his i. LOCKHART.

Illocal (ilōᵘ·kăl, ill-), *a.* 1601. [– late L. *illocalis*, f. *in-* IL-[2] + *localis* LOCAL.] **1.** Not local, having no location in space. †**2.** Out of place, *nonce-use.* 1804. Hence **Illoca·lity,** the condition of being i. 1678. **Illo·cally** *adv.* 1678.

Illogic (ilǫ·dʒik, ill-). 1856. [f. IL-[2] + LOGIC, after next.] The opposite of logic; illogicalness.

Illogical (ilǫ·dʒikăl, ill-), *a.* 1588. [f. IL-[2] + LOGICAL.] Not logical; devoid of or contrary to logic; ignorant or negligent of the principles of sound reasoning.

A foolish and i. antipathy 1850. Hence **Illogica·lity,** i. quality or character; unreasonableness; an instance of this. **Illo·gically** *adv.* **Illo·gicalness,** illogicality.

Ill-o·mened, *a.* 1685. [f. *ill omen* + -ED[2].] Having bad omens; ill-starred; inauspicious.

Illoricated (ilǫrikeⁱtėd, ill-), *a.* 1861. [f. IL-[2] + LORICATED.] *Zool.* Without a lorica or hard shell-like covering. So **Illo·ricate** *a.*

Ill-placed, *a.* 1655. [ILL- III. 4.] Badly placed; also, misplaced, inopportune.

Ill-so·rted, *a.* 1691. [f. ILL- III. 4 + *sorted.*] Badly assorted; ill-matched.

He and his wife were an ill-sorted pair BYRON.

Ill-starred, *a.* 1604. [f. ILL *a.* + STAR *sb.*[1] + -ED[2].] Born under an evil star (according to astrology); unfortunate, unlucky, ill-fated. *transf.* Disastrous 1704.

How dost thou looke now? Oh ill-Starr'd wench *Oth.* V. ii. 272.

Ill-te·mpered, *a.* 1601. [Partly f. ILL- III. 4 + *tempered*; partly f. *ill temper* + -ED[2].] †**1.** Having the 'humours' badly tempered or mixed; unhealthy, distempered –1685. **2.** Having a bad temper; morose, cross, peevish 1601.

1. *Jul. C.* IV. iii. 115. **2.** You cross-grained, ill-tempered, good for nothing whelp 1825.

Illth (ilþ). 1860. [f. ILL *a.* + -TH[1].] The reverse of *wealth* or 'well-being'. Coined by RUSKIN.

Ill-timed, *a.* 1692. [ILL- III. 4.] Badly timed; unseasonable.

Ill-tongued, *a.* 1300. [f. ILL *a.* + TONGUE *sb.* + -ED[2].] Having an evil tongue.

Ill-treat (i:l'trī·t), *v.* 1794. [f. ILL *adv.* + TREAT *v.*, after the phrases *ill treated, ill treatment.* Cf. ILL-USE.] *trans.* To treat badly; to ill-use, maltreat. So **Ill-trea·tment** 1825.

†**Ill-turned,** *a.* 1637. [f. ILL- III. 4 + *turned.*] Badly turned, shaped, or expressed; also, ill-disposed –1774.

Illucidate (il^{i}ū·sideⁱt), *v. rare.* 1545. [– late and med.L. *illucidat-*, pa. ppl. stem of *illucidare* give light to (v), explain (xv), f. after L. *elucidare* ELUCIDATE, with substitution of prefix *il-* IL-[1] to impart the force of 'on, upon', as in *illucēre, illuminare* shine on.] *trans.* To shed light upon; to clear up, elucidate. Hence **Illu·cidative** *a.*

Illude (il^{i}ū·d), *v.* Now *rare.* 1420. [– L. *illudere* make sport of, f. *in-* IL-[1] + *ludere* play.] †**1.** *trans.* To mock, deride –1704. **2.** To trick, deceive with false hopes 1447. †**3.** To evade, elude –1820.

Illume (il^{i}ū·m), *v.* 1602. [Short for ILLUMINE.] = ILLUMINE; almost exclusively *poetic.*

A second sun array'd in flame, To burn, to kindle, to i. SHELLEY. Thou camest Thy Disciples to i. NEALE.

Illuminable (il^{i}ū·minăb'l), *a.* 1730. [f. ILLUMINE *v.* + -ABLE.] Capable of being illuminated.

Illuminant (il^{i}ū·minănt). 1644. [– *illuminant-*, pres. ppl. stem of L. *illuminare*; see next, -ANT.] **a.** *adj.* Lighting up, enlightening 1677. **b.** *sb.* That which illumines or illuminates; an illuminating agent; a source of illumination.

Illuminate (il^{i}ū·minĕt), *ppl. a.* and *sb.* ME. [– L. *illuminatus*, pa. pple. of *illuminare*; see next, -ATE[2].]

A. *pa. pple.* and *adj.* **1.** Lighted up; made bright by light (*arch.*) **2.** Enlightened †spiritually or intellectually 1563.

2. Speaking to the i. or Baptized 1672. I. by learning BACON.

B. *sb.* A spiritually or intellectually enlightened person, or one claiming to be so or to have the inner light (*arch.*) 1600.

Illuminate (il^{i}ū·mineⁱt), *v.* 1535. [– *illuminat-*, pa. ppl. stem of L. *illuminare*, f. IL-[1] + *lumen, lumin-* light; see -ATE[3].] **1.** *trans.* To light up, give light to. (*lit.* and *fig.*) **2.** To throw light upon (a subject); to elucidate. Also *absol.* 1586. **3.** To make resplendent; to shed a lustre upon 1601. **4.** To decorate profusely with lights, as a sign of festivity or rejoicing 1702. **5.** To set alight (*rare*) 1658. Also *intr.* (for *refl.*) **6.** To decorate (an initial letter, word, or text) with gold, silver, and colours, or with tracery and miniature designs, executed in colours; to adorn (a manuscript, inscription, text, etc.) with such decorative letters and miniatures. (Repl. ENLUMINE.) 1706.

1. Two great lights..To i. the Earth MILT. *P.L.* VII. 350. *fig.* I. mine eies..O good Lord T. BENTLEY. Disciplines i. the intellect 1635. **3.** *Jul. C.* I. iii. 110. **4.** The whole City being..illuminated 1702. Hence **Illu·minated** *ppl. a.* in senses of the vb.; *spec.* of or belonging to the ILLUMINATI (see next). **Illu·minatingly** *adv.*

‖**Illuminati** (il^{i}ūminēⁱ·tai, ilūminā·tī), *sb. pl.* Also *sing.* **-ato** (-ā·to); †pl. **-oes.** 1599. [L., pl. of *illuminatus*, pa. pple. of *illuminare* (see prec.), or pl. of It. *illuminato.*] Persons claiming special enlightenment in religious, or (later) intellectual matters. **a.** A sect of Spanish heretics which existed in the 16th c. under the name of *Alumbrados* or 'enlightened'; also, a similar but obscure sect of French Familists in Louis XIII's reign. **b.** As tr. Ger. *Illuminaten*, the name of a secret society, founded at Ingolstadt in Bavaria, in 1776, by Prof. Adam Weishaupt, holding deistic and republican principles; hence applied to other thinkers regarded as atheistic or free-thinking, e.g. the French Encyclopædists 1797. **c.** *gen.* Persons affecting to possess special enlightenment on any subject; often used satirically 1816.

Illumination (il^{i}ūminēⁱ·ʃən). ME. [–(O)Fr. *illumination* – late L. *illuminatio*, f. *illuminat-*; see ILLUMINATE *v.*, -ION.] **1.** The action of illuminating; the being illuminated; a lighting up, a supplying of light 1563. Also *fig.* **b.** *Optics.* Degree of lighting up 1863. **2.** Spiritual enlightenment; divine inspiration; †*spec.* baptism. (The earliest sense in Eng.) ME. **3.** Intellectual enlightenment; information, learning; †occas. in *pl.*, intellectual gifts. Also, the doctrines of the *Illuminati.* 1634. **4.** The lighting up of a building, town, etc., in token of festivity or rejoicing. Also with *an* and *pl.* An instance of this; also *pl.* the lights themselves. 1691. †**5.** Elucidation (*rare*) –1658. **6.** The embellishment of a letter or writing with colours, etc.: see ILLUMINATE *v.* 6. **b.** with *pl.* The designs, etc., employed in such embellishment. †**c.** The colouring of maps or prints. 1678.

2. A praier for illuminacion of mynde 1450. **4.** When London had a grand i. BYRON. **6.** I. admits no shadows, but only gradations of pure colour RUSKIN.

Illuminatism (il^{i}ū·minĕtiz'm). 1798. [f. ILLUMINATI or G. *illuminaten* + -ISM.] = ILLUMINISM. So **Illu·minatist** = ILLUMINIST.

Illuminative (il^{i}ū·mineⁱtiv, -ĕtiv), *a.* 1644. [– Fr. *illuminatif, -ive* or med.L. *illuminativus*; see ILLUMINATE *v.*, -IVE.] **1.** Having the property of illuminating or affording light. Also *fig.* **2.** Pertaining to the illumination of writing 1870.

1. Ordinary i. gas 1870. *fig.* The purgative, i., and unitive stages of devotion SOUTHEY. **2.** I. art 1870. Hence **Illu·minatively** *adv.* NASHE.

Illuminator (il^{i}ū·mineⁱtəɹ). 1485. [– eccl.L. *illuminator*, in med.L. also 'adorner, limner' (sense 4), f. *illuminat-*; see ILLUMINATE *v.*, -OR 2.] **1.** He who or that which illuminates, an illuminant 1598; *techn.* an instrument or device for concentrating or reflecting the light 1837. **2.** One who illuminates spiritually. (The earliest sense in Eng.) 1485. **3.** One who illuminates intellectually; applied contemptuously to the 18th c. Illuminati 1777. **4.** One who embellishes letters or manuscripts with gold and colours: see ILLUMINATE *v.* 6. 1699.

Illu·minatory, *a. rare.* 1762. [f. ILLUMINATE *v.* + -ORY[2].] Illuminative; explanatory.

Illumine (il^{i}ū·min), *v.* ME. [– (O)Fr. *illuminer* – late L. *illuminare* ILLUMINATE.] = ILLUMINATE *v.*

The long-illumined cities TENNYSON. What in me is dark I. MILT. *P.L.* I. 23. Sonnets..illumined with letters of gold POPE.

Illuminee·. 1800. [– Fr. *illuminé*; see -EE[1].] One of the Illuminati.

Illuminer (il^{i}ū·minəɹ). Also **-or.** 1450. [f. ILLUMINE *v.* + -ER[1].] **1.** An illuminator; an enlightener (*lit.* and *fig.*). †**2.** A source of light; a luminary –1686. †**3.** One who illuminates manuscripts, etc. –1824.

Illuminism (il^{i}ū·miniz'm). 1798. [– Fr. *illuminisme* (Dict. Acad. 1835), f. *illuminer* ILLUMINE; see -ISM.] The doctrines or principles of the ILLUMINATI, or of any sect so called; also *gen.*

In Spain, I. associated itself with freemasonry 1840. So **Illu·minist,** one who holds the doctrine of i. Aslo *attrib.* **Illumini·stic** *a.*, pertaining to i., or the illuminists.

Illuminize (il^{i}ū·minəiz), *v.* 1800. [f. ILLUMINE *v.* + -IZE.] **1.** *intr.* To be an illuminist. COLERIDGE. **2.** *trans.* 'To initiate into the doctrine or principles of the Illuminati' (Webster).

†**Illu·minous,** *a.*[1] 1485. [f. IL-[1] + LUMINOUS, after *illumine* etc.] Bright –1745.

Illuminous (il^{i}ū·minəs, ill-), *a.*[2] *rare.* 1656. [f. IL-[2] + LUMINOUS.] Non-luminous, dark.

‖**Illupi** (i·lupi). *East-Ind.* 1832. [Tamil *iluppai* or *iruppai*, Malayalam *iruppa.*] An evergreen tree, *Bassia longifolia* (N.O. *Sapotaceæ*), a native of Southern India. *I. oil*, a fixed solid oil obtained from i. seeds.

†**Illu·re, Illu·rement.** Alterations of ALLURE, ALLUREMENT, after words having prefix *il-*. –1661.

Ill usage, i·ll-u·sage. 1621. [prop. two wds., but commonly hyphened after *ill-used.*] The action of using ill; bad or unkind treatment.

Ill-use (i:l,yū·z), *v.* 1841. [prop. two wds.; see prec.] *trans.* To use badly; to treat cruelly, unkindly, or inconsiderately.

Ill-used (i·l,yū·zd), *pa. pple.* and *ppl. a.* 1594. [orig. two wds., hyphened when used attrib.; now taken as pa. pple. of prec. vb.] Badly used; ill-treated.

Illusion (il'ū·ʒən). ME. [– (O)Fr. *illusion* – L. *illusio*, f. *illudere* mock, jest at, f. *in-* IL-¹ + *ludere* play, sport; see -ION.] †**1.** The action of deriding or mocking; derision, mockery –1567. **2.** †**a.** The action, or an act, of deceiving the bodily or the mental eye by what is unreal or false; deception, delusion, befooling –1695. **b.** The fact or condition of being deceived by false appearances; a false conception or idea; a deception, delusion, fancy 1571. **3.** A deceptive or illusive appearance, statement, belief, etc.; in early use often *spec.* An apparition, phantom ME. **4.** Sensuous perception of an external object, involving a false belief or conception; often including *hallucination.* Also (with *pl.*) an instance of this. 1774. **5.** Name of a thin transparent kind of tulle 1887.

2. a. *Hen. VIII*, I. ii. 178. **b.** A sense of universal i. . follows the reading of metaphysics H. SPENCER. **3.** Stay I.: If thou hast any sound, or vse of Voyce, Speake to me *Haml.* I. i. 127. **4.** As distinguished from hallucinations, illusions 'must always have a starting-point in some actual impression, whereas a hallucination has no such basis' 1881. Hence **Illu·sionable** *a.* (*rare*) liable to illusions. **Illu·sionary** *a.* illusory.

Illusionism (il'ū·ʒəniz'm). 1843. [f. ILLUSION + -ISM.] The theory that the material world is an illusion.

Illusionist (il'ū·ʒənist). 1843. [f. as prec. + -IST.] **1.** One who holds the theory of illusionism. **2.** A sleight-of-hand performer 1864. **3.** One given to illusion. WEBSTER.

Illusive (il'ū·siv), *a.* 1679. [– med.L. *illusivus*, f. *illus-*, pa. ppl. stem of L. *illudere*; see ILLUDE, -IVE.] That tends to illude; productive of illusion or false impression; deceptive, illusory.

A vain i. show, That melts whene'er the sunbeams glow SCOTT. Hence **Illu·sive-ly** *adv.*, **-ness.**

Illusor (il'ū·səɹ). *rare.* ME. [– eccl. L. *illusor*, f. as prec.; see -OR 2.] A deceiver, deluder.

Illusory (il'ū·səri), *a.* 1599. [– eccl.L. *illusorius*, f. as prec. + *-orius* -ORY².] Tending to deceive by unreal prospects; of the nature of an illusion; illusive. In first quot. as *sb.* = an illusion.

To trust him uppon pledges is a meare illusorye Q. ELIZ. The price given . is i. ROGERS. Hence **Illu·sorily** *adv.* **Illu·soriness.**

†**Illu·strable**, *a.* 1658. [f. L. *illustrare*; see -BLE.] = next –1668.

Illustratable (ilŏstre'·tăb'l, -lɒ·strĕtăb'l), *a.* 1850. [f. ILLUSTRATE *v.* + -ABLE.] Capable of being illustrated.

Illustrate (i·lŏstre'ᵗt, ilɒ·stre'ᵗt), *v.* 1526. [– *illustrat-*, pa. ppl. stem of L. *illustrare*, f. *in-* IL-¹ + *lustrare* illuminate; see -ATE³.] †**1.** *trans.* To light up, illumine –1717. **b.** *fig.* (*Obs.* or *arch.*) 1526. †**2.** To make lustrous, luminous, or bright; *gen.* to beautify, adorn –1748. **3.** To set in a good light. Now *rare.* **4.** To shed lustre upon; to make illustrious; to confer honour or distinction upon. Now *rare* or *Obs.* 1530. **5.** To elucidate, clear up, explain 1538. **6.** To make clear by means of examples; to exemplify 1612. **7.** To elucidate by means of pictures; to ornament (a book, etc.) with elucidatory designs. Said also of the pictures. 1638.

3. Pitt . . apt enough to take any step to i. his own measures H. WALPOLE. **4.** Mr. Wedderburne . . who now illustrates the title of Lord Loughborough GIBBON. **5.** You have . . illustrated it by quotations and metaphors 1874. **6.** To i. the advantages of vigilance and foresight 1786. **7.** To i. the results of an expedition with photographs 1873. So †**Illu·strate** *ppl. a.* illustrated, illuminated, enlightened, etc.; *adj.* illuminated, resplendent, clear; lustrous, illustrious. **I·llustrated** *ppl. a.* †made bright; having pictorial illustrations; *sb.* an illustrated newspaper or magazine.

Illustration (ilŏstrē'·ʃən). ME. [– (O)Fr. *illustration* – L. *illustratio*, f. as prec.; see -ION.] †**1.** Illumination (spiritual, intellectual, or physical) –1764. **2.** The action of making or fact of being made illustrious; distinction. Also, an example, means or cause of distinction. 1616. **3.** The action or fact of making clear or evident; elucidation; exemplification 1581. Also with *an* and *pl.* **4.** The pictorial elucidation of any subject 1813; an illustrative picture, drawing, cut, or the like 1817.

Illustrative (ilɒ·strĕtiv, i·lŏstre'tiv), *a.* 1643. [f. ILLUSTRATE + -IVE.] Serving or tending to illustrate; explanatory; exemplificatory. Const. *of.* Hence **Illu·stratively** *adv.*

Illustrator (i·lŏstrē'təɹ). 1598. [– eccl.L. *illustrator* (Lactantius), f. as prec.; see -OR 2. Later directly f. ILLUSTRATE.] One who or that which illustrates (see the vb.). So **I·llustratress.**

Illu·stratory, *a.* 1734. [f. ILLUSTRATE *v.* + -ORY².] Illustrative.

†**Illustre**, *a.* 1500. [– Fr. *illustre* (XV) or L. *illustris.*] Illustrious –1653.

†**Illustre**, *v.* 1490. [– L. *illustrare* and Fr. *illustrer* (XVI); see ILLUSTRATE, prec.] **1.** *trans.* To illumine –1606. **2.** To render illustrious –1657.

2. As ye valew your places, i. them 1657.

Illustrious (ilɒ·striəs), *a.* 1566. [f. L. *illustris* + -OUS.] †**1.** Lighted up, having lustre; luminous, shining, bright –1886. †**2.** Clearly manifest –1792. **3.** Possessing lustre; distinguished; renowned, famous 1566. †¶ Not lustrous (IL-²). *Cymb.* I. vi. 109. (Some read *illustrous.*)

2. The final cause of uniformity is i. KAMES. **3.** This high i. Prince *Lear* V. iii. 135. One leaf of the i. folio LAMB. Hence **Illu·strious-ly** *adv.*, **-ness.**

‖**Illustrissimo** (ilŏstri·simo, It. *ilustri·simo*), *a.* and *sb.* 1623. Also anglicized **-issim(e** 1609. [It. – L. *illustrissimus*, superlative of *illustris* illustrious.] **a.** *adj.* Most illustrious; used as a title of courtesy in speaking to or of Italian nobles (and others). **b.** *sb.* A man of noble rank.

Illustrous: see under ILLUSTRIOUS.

Ill will, i·ll-wi·ll, *sb.* ME. [In early use northern, corresp. to ON. *illvili.*] Evil feeling or intention towards another; malevolence, enmity, dislike. Hence †**Ill-will** *v. trans.* to wish evil to. **I·ll-wi·lled** *a.* (*Obs.* exc. *dial.*) malevolent; †reluctant. **I·ll-wi·ller**, an ill-wisher. **Ill-wi·lling** *a.* wishing ill.

Ill-wisher (i:l wi·ʃəɹ). 1607. [f. ILL *adv.* (or *sb.*) + WISHER.] One who wishes evil to another. So **I:ll-wi·sh** *v.* to wish evil to 1865.

Illy (i·l,li), *adv.* Now chiefly *U.S.* 1549. [f. ILL *a.* + -LY².] Badly; ill.

Ilmenite (i·lmĕnəit). 1827. [f. the *Ilmen* mountains (in southern Urals), where found + -ITE¹ 2 b.] *Min.* Oxide of iron and titanium found in brilliant black crystals.

Ilvaite (i·lvă,əit). 1816. [f. *Ilva* Elba, where found + -ITE¹ 2 b.] *Min.* A black crystalline silicate of iron and calcium, called also lievrite.

Im-¹, assim. form of the suffix IN-², before *b, m, p.* Many words taken into ME. from Fr. have both *em-* and *im-*, and in some, as *empanel, impanel*, the variation still continues; see EM- and IN-². In words more recently derived from Latin (or from Italian) *im-* is the regular form.

Im-², assim. form in L. of the neg. prefix IN-³ before *b, m, p*, which retains the same form in English, as *immemorial, impossible.*

I'm (əim), colloq. contr. of *I am.*

Image (i·mĕdʒ), *sb.* ME. [– (O)Fr. *image* – L. *imago, imagin-*, rel. to *imitari* IMITATE.] **1.** An artificial imitation or representation of the external form of any object, esp. of a person. **a.** A statue, effigy, sculptured figure. (Often applied to figures as objects of worship). **b.** (Less usually) A likeness, portrait, picture, carving, or the like. (Now *rare* or *Obs.* exc. in allusions to Matt. 22:20) ME. †**c.** Applied to the constellations, as figures, etc. –1674. **d.** *fig.* 1548. **2.** An optical appearance or counterpart of an object, such as is produced by rays of light either reflected as from a mirror, refracted as through a lens, or falling on a surface after passing through a small aperture ME. **b.** *transf.* (*a*) A collection of heat-rays concentrated at a particular point or portion of space, analogous to an image formed by light-rays. (*b*) *Electr.* (See quot.) 1873. **3.** *abstractly.* Appearance, form; semblance, likeness. (Now only with reference to biblical language, esp. Gen. 1:26, 27.) ME. Also *concr.* (*Obs.* or *arch.*) 1530. **4.** A counterpart, copy ME.; a symbol, emblem, representation 1566; a type, typical example, embodiment 1548. **5.** A mental representation of something (esp. a visible object); a mental picture or impression; an idea, conception ME. **6.** A vivid or graphic description 1522. **7.** *Rhet.* A simile, metaphor, or figure of speech 1676.

1. a. An ymage, þat haþ .iiij. hedes MAUNDEV. The ymage of godde Hamone 1450. **b.** Whos is this ymage, and the wrytyng aboue? WYCLIF *Matt.* 22:20. **2.** *Negative* or *accidental i.*: that seen after looking intently at a bright-coloured object, and having a colour complementary to that of the object. (See also AFTER-IMAGE.) *Real i.* in *Optics*, an image produced by reflection or refraction, when the rays from each point of the object actually meet at a point; when they diverge as if from a point beyond the reflecting or refracting body, it is called a *virtual i.* **b.** (*b*) An imaginary electrified point, which has no physical existence . . but which may be called an electrical i., because the action of the surface on external points is the same as that which would be produced by the imaginary electrified point if the spherical surface were removed MAXWELL. **3.** God created man in his owne I. *Gen.* 1:27. *concr.* Diverse ymages lyke terrible develles HALL. **4.** Sleepe is the i. of death 1620. This Play is the I. of a murder done in Vienna *Haml.* III. ii. 248. An awful i. of calm power SHELLEY. **5.** She endeavoured to dismiss his i. from her mind 1797. **6.** Theocritus . . has only given a plain i. of the way of life amongst the peasants 1717.

Comb., as *i.-graver, -monger*, etc.

Image (i·mĕdʒ), *v.* 1440. [f. IMAGE *sb.*; earlier – (O)Fr. *imager.*] **1.** *trans.* To make an image of; to represent by an image; to figure, portray, delineate. Also *fig.* 1790. **2.** To reflect, mirror 1792. **3.** To copy (*rare*) 1611; to resemble (*rare*) 1701. **4.** †**a.** To devise, plan –1460. **b.** To imagine, represent *to onself* 1708. **5.** To describe (esp. vividly or graphically) 1628. **6.** To symbolize, typify 1816.

1. Shrines of imag'd saints WARTON. **2.** Structures imaged in the wave ROGERS. **4. b.** We i. to ourselves the Tarpeian Rock as a tremendous precipice 1781. **6.** O stream! . . Thou imagest my life SHELLEY. Hence **I·mageable** *a.* capable of being imaged, esp. in the mind.

I·mage-brea:ker. 1596. One who destroys images; an iconoclast. So **I·mage-brea:king** *sb.* and *a.*

Imaged (i·mĕdʒd), *a.* 1718. [f. IMAGE *sb.* and *v.* + -ED.] **1.** [f. the vb.] Represented by an image (physical or mental). **2.** [f. the sb.] Of porcelain: Decorated with human figures 1797.

I·mageless, *a.* 1821. [f. IMAGE *sb.* + -LESS.] Without an image or images.

I·mage-ma:ker. 1500. A maker of images (usu. in sense 1 a).

Imager (i·mĕdʒəɹ). [ME. *imageour* – OFr. *imageur*, also *imager* (mod. *imagier*), f. *image* IMAGE; for the suffix, see -ER² 3, -OUR.] †A sculptor, carver –1603; †a painter (*rare*) 1591.

Imagery (i·mĕdʒəri, i·mĕdʒ,ri). ME. [– OFr. *imagerie*, f. *imageur, imager* (see prec.); see -ERY.] **1.** Images collectively; imagework. Rarely including pictures. Also in *pl.* †**b.** Figured work on a textile fabric; embroidery –1777. **c.** *transf.* Scenery; nature's imagework 1647. †**2.** Idolatry –1624. †**3.** The art of statuary or carving; *rarely*, of painting –1611. †**4.** Workmanship, make, figure, form, fashion –1667. †**5.** = IMAGE *sb.* 4 –1649. **6.** †**a.** Imagination, fancy, groundless belief. **b.** The result of this; mental images collectively or generally. 1611. **7.** The use of rhetorical images, or such images collectively;

figurative illustration, esp. of an ornate character 1589.

1. His cup embost with I. SPENSER. **b.** A counterpoynt of arras silk with ymagery 1480. **c.** The visible scene. . With all its solemn i., its rocks, Its woods WORDSW. **4.** Dress your people unto the i. of Christ JER. TAYLOR. **6. b.** Like a dream's dim i. SHELLEY. **7.** The glowing i. of prophets 1858.

I·mage-wo:rship. 1628. The worship of images; idolatry. So **I·mage-wo:rshipper. I·mage-wo:rshipping** *sb.* and *a.*

†**Imagilet.** [perh. for *imagelet*; see -LET.] A statuette. FULLER.

Imaginable (imæ·dʒinăb'l), *a.* ME. [– late L. *imaginabilis* (Boethius), f. *imaginare*; see IMAGINE, -BLE.] Capable of being imagined; conceivable.

Such a dreadfull noyse, as is scarce i. SIR T. HERBERT. Guilty of the greatest crimes i. 1692. So **Imaginabi·lity** (*rare*), **Ima·ginableness,** quality of being i. **Ima·ginably** *adv.*

†**Ima·ginal,** *a.*[1] *rare.* 1647. [app. f. IMAGINE *v.* + -AL[1].] Of or pertaining to the imagination; imaginable –1658.

Imaginal (imæ·dʒinăl), *a.*[2] 1877. [f. L. *imagin-*, stem of IMAGO + -AL[1].] *Entom.* Of or pertaining to an insect imago.

Imaginal discs: certain regularly arranged discoidal masses of indifferent tissue, which the apodal maggot carries in the interior of its body when it leaves the egg. These undergo little or no change until the larva encloses itself in its hardened last-shed cuticle, and becomes a pupa.

†**Ima·ginant.** 1605. [– *imaginant-*, pres. ppl. stem of L. *imaginari*; see IMAGINE, -ANT.] **A.** *ppl. a.* That imagines. BACON. **B.** *sb.* One who i magines –1663.

Imaginary (imæ·dʒĭnări), *a.* (*sb.*) ME. [– L. *imaginarius*, f. *imago, imagin-*; see IMAGE, -ARY[1].] **1.** Existing only in imagination or fancy; not really existing. (Opp. to *real, actual.*) **b.** Said of lines, etc. assumed to be drawn through or between certain points 1601. **c.** *Math.* Applied to quantities or loci having no real existence, but assumed to exist; e.g. the square root of a negative quantity, or any expression involving this, or any point, curve, etc. denoted algebraically by such an expression. Also *transf.* Relating to imaginary quantities or loci, as *i. geometry, projection*, etc. (Opp. to *real.*) 1706. †**2.** Imaginative –1677. †**3.** Of the nature of an image –1669. †**4.** Putative. DONNE. †**5.** Imaginable –1687. †**6.** *sb.* An imagination; a fancy –1748. **7.** *sb.* (*Math.*) An imaginary quantity or expression; see 1 c above 1864.

1. After giving me i. wit and beauty, you give me i. passions, and you tell me I'm in love LADY M. W. MONTAGU. **2.** SHAKS. *Sonn.* xxvii. **3.** SHAKS. *Lucr.* 1422. Hence **Ima·ginarily** *adv.* 1593.

†**Ima·ginate,** *ppl. a.* Chiefly *Sc.* 1533. [– L. *imaginatus*, pa. pple. of *imaginari*; see IMAGINE, -ATE[2].] Imagined; imaginary –1601.

Imagination (imædʒinē^i·ʃən). ME. [– (O)Fr. *imagination* – L. *imaginatio*, f. *imaginat-*, pa. ppl. stem of *imaginari*; see prec., -ION.] **1.** The action of imagining, or forming a mental concept of what is not actually present to the senses (cf. sense 3); the result of this, a mental image or idea (freq. characterized as *vain, false*, etc.). †**2.** The mental consideration of actions or events not yet in existence. **a.** Scheming or devising; a device, scheme, plot; a fanciful project. *Obs.* exc. as a biblical archaism. ME. **b.** Expectation, anticipation –1654. **3.** That faculty of the mind by which we conceive the absent as if it were present (freq. including memory); the 'reproductive imagination' ME. **4.** The power which the mind has of forming concepts beyond those derived from external objects; the 'productive imagination'. **a.** Fancy ME. **b.** The creative faculty; poetic genius 1509. **5.** The operation of the mind; thinking; thought, opinion. Now *rare* or *Obs.* ME.

1. They. . accounted his undoubted divinations, madde immaginations 1576. Could such an i. ever have been entertained by him? HUME. **2. a.** I., or Compassing. . was punishable by our Law 1660. **b.** To tell you truly mine own i., I thought [etc.] MARVELL. **3.** The beauty of her countenance haunting his i. 1797. **4. a.** Looke how i. blowes him SHAKS. **b.** And as i. bodies forth the forms of things vnknowne; the Poet's pen Turnes them to shapes, and giues to aire nothing, A locall habitation, and a name SHAKS. Hence **Imagina·tional** *a.*

Imaginative (imæ·dʒĭnē^{i}tiv, -ĕtiv), *a.* (*sb.*) ME. [– (O)Fr. *imaginatif, -ive* – med.L. *imaginativus*, f. as prec.; see -IVE.] **1.** Of persons: Given to imagining. †**a.** Full of thoughts, plans, or devices. **b.** Full of idle fancies. **c.** Having inventive genius. **2.** Of, pertaining to, or concerned in the exercise of imagination as a mental faculty ME. †**3.** Existing only in imagination; imaginary –1646. **4.** Characterized by, or resulting from, the productive imagination; bearing evidence of high creative fancy 1829. †**5.** *sb.* Imagination –1641.

1. The Witches themselues are I., and beleeue oft-times, they doe that, which they doe not BACON. **2.** Milton had a highly i., Cowley a very fanciful mind COLERIDGE. **4.** The i. tale of Sintram and his Companions SCOTT. Hence **Ima·ginative-ly** *adv.* 1430, **-ness** 1664.

Imagine (imæ·dʒin), *v.* ME. [– (O)Fr. *imaginer* – L. *imaginare* form an image of, represent, fashion, (medio-pass.) *imaginari* picture to oneself, fancy, f. *imago, imagin-*; see IMAGE.]

I. *trans.* **1.** To form a mental image of, to represent to oneself in imagination, to picture to oneself. **2.** To create as a mental conception, to conceive; to assume, suppose (a mathematical line, etc.) ME. **3.** To devise, plot, plan, compass. Now a biblical or legal archaism. ME. †**4.** To ponder, meditate –1582. **5.** To conjecture, suspect, suppose ME. **6.** To form an idea or notion with regard to something not known with certainty, to suppose, 'take into one's head' (*that*) 1548.

1. A thing. . that is not possible for man to ymagine the like without seeing 1566. **2.** I. your self in the same case MORE. **3.** Why do. . the people i. a vaine thing? *Ps.* 2:1. To i. the Death of the Prince. . is made High Treason 1707.

II. *intr.* †**1.** To meditate; to form designs –1589. **2.** To exercise the imagination 1631. **3.** *Imagine of*: = sense I. 1. 1586.

2. Women may be trained to reason and i. as well as men 1809. Hence **Ima·giner,** one who imagines.

Imagist (i·mĕdʒist). 1919. [f. IMAGE *sb.* + -IST.] One of a group of modern poets who, in revolt against romanticism, seek clarity of expression through the use of precise images. Also *attrib.* Hence **I·magism,** the practices and work of the imagists.

Imago (imē^i·go). *Pl.* **imagines** (-ē^i·dʒiniz) and **imagos.** 1797. [An application of L. *imago* IMAGE (Linn.).] *Entom.* The final and perfect stage or form of an insect after its metamorphoses; the 'perfect insect'.

‖**Imam, imaum** (imā·m). 1613. [– Arab. *'imām* leader, f. *'amma* precede.] **1.** The officiating priest of a Moslem mosque. **2.** A title given to various Moslem leaders and chiefs; as, the Caliph, or other independent princes, etc. 1662.

‖**Imaret** (imā·ret, i·măret). 1613. [– Turk. – Arab. *'imāra* building, edifice, hence 'hospice'.] A hospice for pilgrims and travellers in Turkey.

Imb-: see EMB-.

Imba·n, *v.* [See IM-[1] and BAN *v.*] To put under a ban. J. BARLOW.

Imba·nd, *v.* [f. IM-[1] + BAND *sb.*[3]] To form into a band. J. BARLOW.

†**Imba·rge,** *v.* 1596. [f. IM-[1] + BARGE *sb.*] *trans.* To embark –1627.

Imbarge, -bargo: see EMBARGE, etc.

Imbark (imbā·ɹk), *v.* 1647. [f. IM-[1] + BARK *sb.*[1]] *trans.* To enclose in or clothe with bark. Also *fig.*

Imbark, -ation, etc.: see EMBARK, etc.

†**Imba·rn,** *v.* 1610. [f. IM-[1] + BARN *sb.*] *trans.* To gather into a barn or barns; to garner. Also *fig.* –1796.

Imbase: see EMBASE.

†**Imba·stardize,** *v.* [f. IM-[1] + BASTARDIZE, perh. after It. *imbastardire.*] *trans.* To render bastard or degenerate. MILTON.

Imbathe, -battle, -bay: see EMB-.

Imbecile (i·mbĭsil, i·mbĭsīl), *a.* (*sb.*) 1549. [– Fr. †*imbécille* (now -*ile*) – L. *imbecillus, -is*, f. *in-* IM-[2] + *bĕcillum*, var. of *baculum* stick, staff, the etymol. meaning being 'without support' (*sine baculo*).] **1.** Weak, feeble; esp. of body. **2.** Mentally weak; of weak character or will through want of mental power; hence, Fatuous, idiotic. (The chief current sense.) 1804. **b.** Of actions: Stupid, absurd, idiotic 1861. **3.** *sb.* A person of weak intellect 1802.

2. But he had the misfortune to be 'imbecile'. . in fact, he was partially an idiot DE QUINCEY. Hence **I·mbecilely** *adv.* stupidly, idiotically.

†**Imbe·cile,** *v.* 1539. [Confused with EMBEZZLE *v.*, q.v.] **1.** *trans.* To make imbecile, weak, or impotent –1651. **2.** In senses of EMBEZZLE *v.*, q.v. 1546.

1. To i. and hinder health 1574. **2.** The dede of the foundation was lost or imbecilled away 1546.

Imbecilitate (imbĭsi·lite^{i}t), *v.* 1653. [f. IMBECILITY, after *debilitate, facilitate*, etc.; see -ATE[3].] *trans.* = IMBECILE *v.* 1.

Imbecility (imbĭsi·lĭti). 1533. [– (O)Fr. *imbécillité* – L. *imbecillitas, -tat-*, f. *imbecillus*; see IMBECILE, -ITY, and cf. EMBEZZLE.] **1.** Weakness, feebleness, impotence. Also with *an* and *pl.* **b.** Incompetency or incapacity (*to do* something) 1767. **2.** Weakness of mind, esp. as characterizing action; hence, silliness, absurdity, folly; an example of this. (Pathologically, *imbecility* is a defect of mental power of less degree than idiocy, and not congenital.) 1624.

1. The i. of the Irish administration MACAULAY. **2.** I. is. . weakness of mind owing to defective mental development MAUDSLEY.

Imbed, Imbellish: see EMBED, etc.

†**Imbellic,** *a.* [f. IM-[2] + BELLIC, or L. *imbellis* + -IC.] Unwarlike. FELTHAM.

Imber, obs. and var. f. EMBER.

Inbesel(l, etc., obs. ff. EMBEZZLE.

Imbibe (imbəi·b), *v.* ME. [In I – Fr. *imbiber* (not recorded before XVI); in II – its source L. *imbibere*, f. *in-* IM-[1] + *bibere* drink.]

†**I.** *trans.* To soak, imbue, or saturate, with moisture; to steep. Also *fig.* –1804. †**b.** With inverted construction: To instil *into* –1812.

II. 1. *trans.* To take into one's mind or moral system 1555. **2.** To drink in (liquid), absorb (moisture) 1621. **3.** To take up, absorb, or assimilate (a gas, etc.); to take (solids) into solution or suspension 1626. †**4.** *transf.* To absorb, swallow up –1712.

1. They may also herewith i. trewe religion EDEN. **2.** So barren sands i. the shower COWPER. To i. brandy-and-water 1859, fresh air HELPS. **3.** Such salts are readily imbibed by water BP. BERKELEY. The heat of the sun's rays, which the earth imbibes 1834. Hence **Imbi·ber,** one who or that which imbibes or drinks.

Imbibition (imbibi·ʃən). 1471. [– med.L. *imbibitio* absorption, infusion, f. *imbibit-*, pa. ppl. stem of *imbibere*; see prec., -ION. Cf. (O)Fr. *imbibition.*] The action of imbibing (see the vb.).

Phr. †*To lie in i.*: to lie a-soak or a-steep. When wood distends on i. 1875. The i. of truth HOLLAND.

Imbitter, Imblaze: see EMBITTER, etc.

Imbody, -bog, -boil, -bolden: see EMBODY, etc.

†**Imbo·nity.** [– late L. *imbonitas* (Tertullian), f. *in-* IM-[2] + *bonitas* goodness; see BOUNTY.] The reverse of goodness; unkindness. BURTON.

Imborder, var. of EMBORDER.

†**Imbo·rdure,** *v.* 1486. [f. IM-[1] + BORDURE.] *trans.* To encompass with a border; *spec.* in *Her.* to furnish with a bordure of the same tincture –1658.

†‖**Imboscata** (imboskā·ta). Also **em-.** 1595. [It. See next.] = AMBUSH, q.v. –1820.

†**Imbosk,** *v.* 1562. [– It. *imboscare*, f. *in-* IM-[1] + *bosco* wood. Cf. EMBOSS *v.*[2]] *refl.* To hide or conceal oneself –1657. Also *intr.* for *refl.* 1641.

Imbosom, -boss(e, -bosture, -bound, -bow, -bowel, -bower, -box, -brace, -braid, etc.: see EMBOSOM, etc.

†**Imbra·nch,** *v.* Also **en-, in-.** 1577. [f. IM-[1] + BRANCH *sb.*] To graft on the stock –1598.

Imbrangle, Imbrase: see EMB-.

Imbreathe (imbrī·ð), *v.* 1574. [f. IM-[1] + BREATHE *v.*; cf. EMBREATHE, INBREATHE.] **1.** *trans.* To breathe in, inhale. Also *fig.* **2.** To inspire, instil; to inspire *with* 1601.

Imbred, -breed: see INBRED, INBREED.

Imbreviate (imbrī·vi,e^{i}t), *v.* 1609. [– *imbreviat-*, pa. ppl. stem of med.L. *imbreviare*, f. *in-* IM-[1] + late L. *brevis, breve* summary, med.L. writ, letter; see BRIEF *sb.*, -ATE[3].] *trans.* To put into the form of a brief; to enrol, register.

‖**Imbrex** (i·mbreks). *Pl.* **imbrices** (i·mbrisīz). 1857. [L., f. *imber* rain-shower.] **1.** *Archæol.* A curved roof-tile. **2.** One of the scales of an imbrication 1890.

Imbricate (i·mbrikĕt), *a.* (*sb.*) 1656. [– L. *imbricatus*, pa. pple. of *imbricare* cover with rain-tiles, f. *imbrex, imbric-* roof-tile; see prec., -ATE^2.] †**1.** Formed like a gutter-tile or pantile –1661. **2.** Covered with or composed of scales or scale-like parts overlapping like roof-tiles; e.g. said of the scaly covering of reptiles and fishes, of leaf-buds, the involucre of *Compositæ*, etc. 1656. **b.** Of leaves, scales, etc.: Overlapping like tiles 1796. **3.** = IMBRICATED 3. 1890. **4.** *sb.* A reptile, fish, etc. covered with imbricated scales 1862. Hence **I·mbricately** *adv.* in an imbricated manner or order.

Imbricate (i·mbrikeᶦt), *v.* 1784. [– *imbricat-*, pa. ppl. stem of L. *imbricare*; see prec., -ATE^3.] **1.** *trans.* To place so as to overlap like roof-tiles. **2.** *trans.* and *absol.* To overlap like tiles 1820. Hence **I·mbricative** *a.* = IMBRICATE *a.* 2.

Imbricated (i·mbrikeᶦtĕd), *ppl. a.* 1704. [f. prec. + -ED^1.] †**1.** Of leaves: Hollowed in like a gutter-tile –1741. **2.** = IMBRICATE *a.* 2, 2 b. 1753. **3.** Resembling in pattern a surface of overlapping tiles 1875.

2. I. like the cone of the Scotch fir GEIKIE. **3.** [Majolica] ornamented..with..i. patterns 1875.

Imbrication (imbrikēᶦ·ʃən). 1650. [f. IMBRICATE *v.* and *a.* + -ION.] †**1.** ?The dropping of water from roof-tiles. BULWER. †**2.** 'A covering with tile' –1658. **3.** An overlapping as of tiles; a decorative pattern imitative of this 1713.

Imbrica·to-. Comb. f. L. *imbricatus*, = imbricately-, imbricated and —; as *i.-granulous.*

†**Imbri·er,** *v.* 1605. [f. IM-^{1} + BRIER *sb.*^{1}] To entangle as among briers –1690.

†**Imbroca·do^1.** 1600. [Altered f. It. *imbroccata*; see -ADO.] = IMBROCCATA –1657.

†**Imbroca·do^2.** 1656. [Altered f. It. *imbroccato.*] = BROCADE. (Dicts.)

†**Imbrocca·ta.** 1595. [– It., f. *imbroccare* 'to giue a thrust at fence ouer the dagger', f. *brocco*, †*brocca* stud, nail (cf. BROACH *sb.*).] A pass or thrust in fencing.

Imbroglio (imbrōᵘ·lyo). Also **em-.** 1750. [– It. *imbroglio*, f. *imbrogliare* confuse, corresp. to Fr. *embrouiller* EMBROIL; see IM-^{1}, BROIL *sb.*^{1}, *v.*^{2}] **1.** A confused heap. **2.** A state of confused entanglement; a complicated or difficult situation; a serious misunderstanding, embroilment 1818. **3.** *Mus.* 'A passage in which the vocal or instrumental parts are made to sing, or play, against each other, in such a manner as to produce the effect of..confusion' (Grove) 1880.

1. Papers and books, a huge i. GRAY. **2.** A financial i. 1833.

Imbrown, obs. f. EMBROWN.

Imbrue (imbrū·), *v.* ME. [Early forms *enbrewe, enbrower* – OFr. *embruer, embrouer* bedaub, bedabble, f. *en-* IM-^{1} + OFr. *breu, bro* (cf. mod. *brouet* broth) – Rom. **brodum* (cf. It. *imbrodolare* dirty, bedabble) – Gmc. **broþam* BROTH.] †**1.** *trans.* To stain, dirty, defile –1593. **2.** To stain, dye (*in* or *with*) 1529. **b.** Said of blood, etc. Now *rare.* 1597. †**3.** In pregnant sense (*with blood* understood) –1749. †**4.** To soak *in*, saturate *with.* Also *absol.* –1634. †**5.** *fig.* To steep *in*; to imbue *with*; to infect –1674. ¶**6.** To pour, to emit moisture. SPENSER *F.Q.* II. v. 33.

2. Wretches, who have imbrued their hands in so much innocent blood CROMWELL. **3.** *absol.* What? shall wee haue Incision? Shall wee embrew? SHAKS. **5.** Imbrued with Heresies 1565. Hence **Imbrue·d** *ppl. a.*; *spec.* in *Her.* stained with blood. **Imbrue·ment** (*rare*).

Imbrute (imbrū·t), *v.* Also **em-.** 1634. [f. IM-^{1} + BRUTE *sb.*^{1}] **1.** *trans.* To degrade to the level of a brute; to make bestial 1640. **2.** *intr.* To sink to the level of a brute 1634.

1. MILT. *P.L.* IX. 166. **2.** The soul grows clotted by contagion, Embodies, and embrutes MILT. *Comus* 468. Hence **Imbru·tement,** brutalization.

Imbue (imbiū·), *v.* 1555. [In the earliest exx. in pa. pple. f. Fr. *imbu*, †*imbu(i)t*, or its source L. *imbutus*, pa. pple. of *imbuere* moisten, stain, imbue.] **1.** *trans.* To saturate; to dye, tinge, impregnate (*with*) 1594. **b.** To imbrue (with blood) 1850. **2.** To impregnate, permeate, pervade, or inspire (*with* opinions, etc.) 1555.

1. Cere-cloth, imbued with unguents and spices 1878. **2.** Thy words with Grace divine Imbu'd MILT. *P.L.* VIII. 216. Hence **Imbue·ment,** imbuing; the fact of being imbued.

Imburse (imbɒ̄·ɹs), *v.* Now *rare.* 1530. [– med.L. *imbursare* put in one's purse, appropriate, f. *in-* IM-^{1} + late L. *bursa* purse. Cf. *reimburse.*] **1.** *trans.* To put into one's (or a) purse; to store up. **2.** †**a.** To enrich 1646. **b.** To pay, refund 1721. Hence **Imbu·rsement** (*rare*), supplying with money; payment 1665.

†**Imbu·te,** *v.* 1657. [– *imbut-*, pa. ppl. stem of L. *imbuere* IMBUE.] *trans.* To steep, soak. TOMLINSON. Hence †**Imbu·tion,** steeping, soaking.

Imide (i·məid, iməi·d). 1850. [Arbitrary alteration of AMIDE.] *Chem.* A name for derivatives of ammonia (NH_3), in which two atoms of hydrogen are exchanged for a metal or organic radical; these being viewed as compounds of the metal, etc., with a hypothetical radical **Imidogen** (iməi·doˌdʒen), NH. Often in comb., as in *succinimide* NH.CO. Hence **Imi·do-,** comb. form.

Imitable (i·mităb'l), *a.* 1550. [– Fr. *imitable* (XVI) or L. (late L.) *imitabilis*, f. *imitari* IMITATE; see -ABLE.] **1.** Capable of being imitated 1598. †**2.** Deserving of imitation –1781.

1. Pindar is i. by none COWLEY. **2.** The worst of times afford i. examples of virtue SIR T. BROWNE. Hence **I:mitabi·lity, I·mitableness,** i. quality. †**I·mitably** *adv.*

I·mitancy. 1832. [Nonce-word f. IMITATE; see -ANCY.] The quality or property of imitating; imitativeness. CARLYLE.

Imitate (i·miteᶦt), *v.* 1534. [– *imitat-*, pa. ppl. stem of L. *imitari* copy, rel. to *imago* IMAGE; see -ATE^3.] **1.** *trans.* To do or try to do after the manner of; to follow the example of; to copy in action. **b.** *occas.*, To mimic, counterfeit 1613. **2.** To copy, reproduce 1590. **3.** To be, become, or make oneself like; to assume the aspect of; to simulate 1588. †**4.** To make in imitation of.

1. The Children imitating their Parents DAMPIER. **b.** Of Apes and Monkies there are..that will i. all they see 1660. **2.** To i. the workes of others 1638, an ode GAY. **3.** In habite they i. the Italians 1615. **4.** The counterfet Is poorely imitated after you SHAKS. *Sonn.* liii.

Imitation (imitēᶦ·ʃən). 1502. [– (O)Fr. *imitation* or L. *imitatio*, f. as prec.; see -ION.] **1.** The action or practice of imitating. **2.** The product of imitating; a copy, an artificial likeness; a counterfeit 1601. **3.** *Literature.* 'A method of translating looser than paraphrase, in which modern examples and illustrations are used for ancient, or domestick for foreign' (J.); an example of this 1656. **4.** *Mus.* The repetition of a phrase or melody, usually at a different pitch, either with the same intervals, rhythm, motion, etc. (*exact i.*), or with these more or less modified (*free i.*) 1727. **5.** *attrib.* Made (of cheaper material) in imitation of a real or genuine article or substance 1858.

1. I. is the sincerest of flattery 1820. Phr. *In i. of.* **2.** Modern imitations of ancient coins 1876. **3.** In i. of Horace his second Ode, B. 4. COWLEY. **5.** I. tortoise-shell 1895. Hence **Imita·tional** *a.* of, pertaining to, or characterized by i. **Imita·tionist,** one who practises i., or gives imitations.

Imitative (i·miteᶦtiv), *a.* (*sb.*) 1584. [– late L. *imitativus*, f. as prec.; see -IVE.] **1.** Characterized by or consisting in imitation. **2.** Given to imitation; prone to copy or mimic 1752. **3.** Simulative; fictitious; counterfeit 1838. †**4.** *sb.* A verb expressing any kind of imitation. PHILLIPS.

1. *Imitative arts*, the arts of painting and sculpture. *I. word*, a word which reproduces a natural sound. Walking..in a manner feebly i. of the human gait 1867. **2.** Human beings are very i. SYD. SMITH. Hence **I·mitative-ly** *adv.*, **-ness.**

Imitator (i·mitēᶦtəɹ). 1523. [– L. *imitator*, orig. partly through Fr. *imitateur*; see IMITATE, -OR 2 b.] One who imitates another; one who produces an imitation of anything. Also *transf.* of things. Hence **I·mita:torship,** the office of an i. So **I·mitatress, Imita·trix,** a female i.

Immaculacy (imæ·kiŭlăsi). 1799. [f. IMMACULATE; see -ACY.] Immaculate condition or quality.

Immaculate (imæ·kiŭlĕt), *a.* ME. [– L. *immaculatus*; see IM-^{2}, MACULATE *ppl. a.*] **1.** Free from spot or stain; pure, unblemished, undefiled. **2.** Free from fault or flaw. (Chiefly in neg. or ironical use.) 1832. **3. a.** Spotlessly clean or neat 1735. **b.** *Nat. Hist.* Without coloured spots or marks 1797.

1. *Immaculate Conception*, the conception of the Virgin Mary, as held to have been free from the taint of original sin. *I. lamb*, applied to Christ, after L. *agnus immaculatus* (Gr. ἀμνὸς ἄμωμος 1 *Pet.* 1:19. **2.** The Sceptical philosophy is by no means so i. 1856. **3. a.** A white-glov'd Chaplain..in immac'late trim POPE. Hence **Imma·culate-ly** *adv.*, **-ness.**

†**Immai·led,** *a.* [f. IM-^{1} + MAIL *sb.*^{1} + -ED^1.] Clad in mail. W. BROWNE.

Imma·lleable, *a. rare.* 1675. [f. IM-^{2} + MALLEABLE.] Not malleable.

Imma·nacle, *v. rare.* 1634. [f. IM-^{1} + MANACLE *sb.*] *trans.* To put manacles on; to handcuff; to fetter. MILT. *Comus* 665.

Immana·tion. [IM-^{1}, after EMANATION.] A flowing in. LAMB.

Immane (imēᶦ·n), *a. arch.* 1602. [– L. *immanis* monstrous, huge, savage, (earlier) wicked, cruel, f. *in-* IM-^{2} + *mānis, mānus* good.] **1.** Monstrous in size or strength; huge, tremendous 1615. **2.** Inhumanly cruel or savage.

1. A man in shape i., and monsterous CHAPMAN. Hence **Imma·ne-ly** *adv.*, **-ness.**

Immanence (i·mănĕns). 1816. [f. IMMANENT *a.*; see -ENCE.] The fact or condition of being immanent; indwelling. So **I·mmanency,** indwellingness 1659.

Immanent (i·mănĕnt), *a.* 1535. [– *immanent-*, pr. ppl. stem of late L. *immanēre* (Augustine), f. *in-* IM-^{1} + L. *manēre* remain, dwell; see -ENT. Cf. Fr. *immanent.*] **1.** Indwelling, inherent; actually present or abiding *in*; remaining within. (Opp. to *transcendent.*) **2.** *I. act* (*action*): an act which is performed entirely within the mind of the subject, and produces no external effect; opp. to a *transient* or *transitive act.* Now *rare.* 1613.

1. They have not cared to recognize it [the external world] as the shrine of i. Deity J. MARTINEAU. **2.** A cognition is an i. act of mind SIR W. HAMILTON. Hence **I·mmanently** *adv.* Also **Immanental** (imăne·ntăl), *a.* pertaining to the doctrine of immanence 1885; **I·mmanentism,** the doctrine of immanence 1907; **I·mmanentist** *a.* 1917.

Imma·nifest, *a. rare.* 1646. [– late and med.L. *immanifestus* obscure, f. *in-* IM-^{2} + L. *manifestus* MANIFEST *a.* Cf. OFr. *immanifeste.*] Not manifest or evident.

†**Imma·nity.** 1557. [– Fr. †*immanité* or L. *immanitas*, f. *immanis*; see IMMANE, -ITY.] The quality of being immane; enormity –1667; monstrous cruelty –1669.

Immantle (imæ·nt'l, imm-), *v.* 1601. [f. IM-^{1} + MANTLE *sb.*] **1.** *trans.* To cover or enwrap with, or as with, a mantle. †**2.** To place round as a fortification. P. HOLLAND.

Imma·rble, *v. rare.* 1642. [f. IM-^{1} + MARBLE *sb.* Cf. EMMARBLE.] *trans.* To convert into marble; to make cold, hard, etc., as marble.

Immarcescible (imaɹse·sib'l), *a.* Now *rare.* 1432. [– late L. *immarcescibilis*, f. *in-* IM-^{2} + *marcescere, marcēre* fade; see -IBLE. Cf. Fr. *immarcescible.*] Unfading; imperishable; esp. in *i. crown* (*of glory*). Hence **Immarce·scibly** *adv.*

Immarginate (imā·ɹdʒinĕt, imm-), *a.* 1826. [f. IM-^{2} + MARGINATE *a.*] *Entom.* Having no distinct or separate margin.

Imma·rtial, *a. rare.* [f. IM-^{2} + MARTIAL.] Unwarlike. CHAPMAN.

†**Imma·sk,** *v.* [f. IM-^{1} + MASK *sb.* or *v.*] *trans.* To cover as with a mask; to disguise. SHAKS.

†**Imma·tchable,** *a.* 1596. [f. IM-^{2} + MATCHABLE.] Unmatchable –1630.

Immaterial (imătīᵊ·riăl), *a.* (*sb.*) ME. [– late L. *immaterialis* (Ambrose, Jerome); see IM-^{2}, MATERIAL. Cf. OFr. *immatériel.*] **1.** Not consisting of matter; incorporeal; spiritual. **b.** *pl.* as *sb.* Non-material things 1661. **2.** Having little substance. *Tr. & Cr.* V. i. 35. †**3.** Not pertinent to the matter –1632. **4.** Of little or no importance 1698.

1. That strange i. Power of the Loadstone 1641. 4. The question of notice becomes i. after my finding that there was no agreement CHITTY. Hence **Immate·riality**, the quality or character of being i.; an i. thing, existence, or essence. **Immate·rial-ly** *adv.*, **-ness.**

Immaterialism (imătīᵊ·riăliz'm). 1713. [f. prec. + -ISM, after *materialism.*] **1.** The doctrine that matter does not exist in itself as a substance or cause, but that all things have existence only as the ideas or perceptions of a mind. **2.** = *Immateriality.* BYRON. So **Immate·rialist,** one who holds the doctrine of i.

Immaterialize (imătīᵊ·riăləiz), *v.* 1661. [f. as prec. + -IZE.] *trans.* To render immaterial or incorporeal.

†**Immate·riate,** *a.* 1626. [f. IM-¹ + MATERIATE *a.*] = IMMATERIAL –1653.

Immature (imătiūᵊ·ɹ), *a.* 1548. [– L. *immaturus* untimely, unripe, f. *in-* IM-² + *maturus* MATURE. Cf. Fr. †*immature.*] **1.** Untimely, premature. (Mostly of death.) *Obs.* or *arch.* **2.** Not mature; not perfect or complete; unripe 1599.

2. I. Fruit BRADLEY, polypi DARWIN, student 1823. Hence **Immatu·re-ly** *adv.*, **-ness. Immatu·rity,** the quality or condition of being i.

Immeability (imī,ăbi·lĭti). 1731. [f. med.L. *immeabilis* impassable, f. *in-* IM-² + L. *meabilis* (f. *meare* pass, see -BLE); see -ITY.] Inability to pass or flow through a channel.

Immeasurable (ime·ʒ¹ŭrăb'l, imm-), *a.* 1440. [f. IM-² + MEASURABLE. Cf. Fr. *immésurable* (XVI).] That cannot be measured; immense.

The vast i. Abyss MILT. *P. L.* VII. 211. Hence **Immea:surabi·lity, Immea·surableness,** incapability of being measured. **Immea·surably** *adv.*

Immeasured (ime·ʒ¹ŭɹd, imm-), *a.* 1456. [var., with prefix-substitution, of earlier UNMEASURED, both reflecting L. *immensus.* Cf. Fr. †*immesuré.*] Not measured; immense, vast.

†**Immecha·nical,** *a.* 1715. [Later var. of UNMECHANICAL (Boyle, 1674), with substitution of prefix.] Not mechanical –1796. Hence **Immecha·nically** *adv.* So †**Imme·chanism,** non-mechanical property; inertia.

Immediacy (imī·diăsi). 1605. [f. next; see -ACY.] **1.** Freedom from intermediate agency; direct relation or connection; directness. **b.** *Logic,* etc. (See IMMEDIATE 2, quots.) 1834. **2.** The condition of being the immediate lord or vassal (see IMMEDIATE 1 b.) 1762. **3.** The condition of being immediate in time 1856.

1. *Lear* V. iii. 65. 2. Varel lost its i. or independency, and stands at present under the superiority of Oldenburg 1762. 3. I. of enjoyment 1856.

Immediate (imī·diĕt), *a.* (*adv.*) 1508. [– (O)Fr. *immédiat* or late L. *immediatus,* f. *in-* IM-² + *mediatus* MEDIATE *a.*] **1.** That has no intermediary or intervening member, medium, or agent; that is in actual contact or direct relation 1548. **b.** *spec.* In *Feudal* language, said of the relation between two persons, one of whom holds of the other directly, as in *i. lord, tenant, tenure*; also ellipt. = Holding directly of the sovereign or lord paramount, *spec.* in Germany, of the Emperor 1543. **2.** Acting or existing without any intervening medium or agency; involving actual contact or direct relation; opp. to *mediate* and *remote* 1533. **3.** Having no person, thing, or space intervening, in place, order, or succession; proximate, nearest, next; close, near; often used *loosely,* of a distance which is of no account 1602. **4.** Of time: Present or next adjacent; of things: Pertaining to the time current or instant 1605. **b.** Taking effect without delay; instant 1568. **5.** Having a direct bearing 1725. †**6.** *adv.* [partly L. *immediātē.*] Immediately –1626.

1. His [the Emperor's] more i. servants GIBBON. The i. object of all art is either pleasure or utility BUCKLE. 2. By Our owne ymmediate commaunde 1625. Phr. *Immediate inference* (Logic): an inference drawn from a single premiss, without the intervention of a middle term. *I. knowledge* (Philos.): knowledge of self-evident truth; intuitive knowledge. *I. auscultation* (Med.): auscultation performed without the stethoscope. 3. You are the most i. to our throne *Haml.* I. ii. 109. In the i. neighbourhood (*mod.*). 4. The i. future FROUDE. An i. reply will oblige (*mod.*). 5. Destitute of obvious or i. utility 1896. Hence **Imme·diateness.**

Immediately (imī·diĕtli), *adv.* (*conj.*) ME. [Rendering med.L. adv. *immediatē* (see prec. 6).] **1.** In an immediate way; by direct agency; directly. **2.** With no person, thing, or distance intervening in time, space, order, or succession; closely; proximately; directly 1466. **3.** Without any delay; instantly ME. **b.** as *conj.* (ellipt. for *immediately that*). The moment that 1839.

1. Canow..was immediately vnder the dominion of the Tartars HAKLUYT. I. holden of the Crown 1647. 3. He bade me goe immeadiatlye 1500.

Immediatism (imī·diĕtiz'm). 1825. [f. IMMEDIATE *a.* + -ISM.] **1.** Immediateness. *rare.* **2.** The principle of immediate action; in *U.S. Hist.* the policy of the immediate abolition of slavery 1835; hence **Imme·diatist** 1835.

Immedicable (ime·dikăb'l), *a.* 1533. [– L. *immedicabilis,* f. *in-* IM-² + *medicabilis* curable, MEDICABLE. Cf. Fr. †*immédicable.*] Incapable of being healed, incurable. Also *transf.* and *fig.*

I. wounds 1596, disaffection MILT. **Imme·dicably** *adv.*

Immelodious (imĭlōᵘ·diəs, imm-), *a.* 1601. [f. IM-² + MELODIOUS.] Unmelodious.

Immemorable (ime·mŏrăb'l), *a.* 1552. [– L. *immemorabilis,* f. *in-* IM-² + *memorabilis* MEMORABLE. Cf. Fr. *immémorable* (XVI).] **1.** Not memorable; not worth remembering. †**2.** = IMMEMORIAL –1796.

Immemorial (imĭmōᵊ·riăl), *a.* 1602. [– med.L. *immemorialis,* f. *in-* IM-² + L. *memorialis* (Suetonius) MEMORIAL. Cf. Fr. *immémorial* (XVI).] That is beyond memory or out of mind; ancient beyond memory or record; extremely old.

The moan of doves in i. elms TENNYSON. *I. usage* (Law): a practice which has existed time out of mind; custom; prescription. Hence **Immemo·rially** *adv.*

Immense (ime·ns), *a.* (*sb.*) 1490. [– (O)Fr. *immense* – L. *immensus* immeasurable, f. (after Gr. ἄμετρος) *in-* IM-² + *mensus,* pa. pple. of *metiri* measure.] **1.** Unmeasured; hence, immeasurably large; boundless; infinite. ?*Obs.* 1599. **2.** Extremely great or large; vast, huge 1490. **3.** *slang.* Splendid 1762. **4.** *sb.* Immensity 1791.

1. That i. and boundless ocean Of nature's riches DANIEL. 2. I. Armies 1660. At i. length 1895. An i. eater 1899. Hence **Imme·nse-ly** *adv.*, **-ness.**

†**Imme·nsible,** *a.* 1579. [– Fr. †*immensible* or late L. *immensibilis,* f. *in-* IM-² + *mens-* pa. ppl. stem of L. *metiri* measure; see -IBLE.] Immeasurable; immense –1630.

Immensity (ime·nsĭti). 1450. [– (O)Fr. *immensité* or L. *immensitas,* f. *immensus* IMMENSE; see -ITY.] **1.** The quality or condition of being immense; boundlessness, infinity. **2.** Vast magnitude; hugeness 1652; an immense deal 1778. **3.** That which is immense 1631.

1. The i. of God STILLINGFL. Thou whose exterior semblance doth belie Thy Soul's i. WORDSW. 2. The i. of the disaster 1883. 3. Thou..shutt'st in little room I. DONNE. Yon blue i. BYRON.

†**Imme·nsive,** *a.* 1604. [– Fr. †*immensif, -ive* (XVI), f. *immense* IMMENSE; see -IVE.] Immeasurable, immense –1648.

Immensurable (ime·nsiŭrăb'l, -ʃŭr-), *a.* 1535. [– Fr. *immensurable* (XV) or late L. *immensurabilis,* f. *in-* IM-² + *mensurabilis* MENSURABLE.] Immeasurable.

What an i. space is the Firmament DERHAM. Hence **Immensurabi·lity, Imme·nsurableness.**

†**Imme·nsurate,** *a.* 1654. [– late L. *immensuratus,* f. *in-* IM-² + *mensuratus,* pa. pple. of L. *mensurare* MEASURE *v.*; see -ATE².] Unmeasured, immense –1766.

Immerd (imə̄·ɹd), *v. rare.* 1635. [– med.L. **immerdare* (whence (O)Fr. *emmerder*), f. *in-* IM-¹ + L. *merda* dung, ordure.] *trans.* To bury in or cover with ordure.

Immerge (imə̄·ɹdʒ, imm-), *v.* Now *rare.* 1611. [– L. *immergere*; see IMMERSE.] **1.** *trans.* To dip, plunge, put under the surface of a liquid; to immerse 1624. Also *transf.* and *fig.* **2.** *intr.* (for *refl.*) To plunge or dip oneself in a liquid; to sink. Also *transf.* and *fig.* 1706. †**b.** *spec.* of a celestial body: To enter the shadow of another in an eclipse, or to disappear behind another in an occultation; to sink below the horizon –1787.

1. To i. birds in spirits 1770. *fig.* We..i. ourselves in luxury JOHNSON. 2. I. up to the Breast in a warm Bath WESLEY. Hence **Imme·rgence,** the action of immerging.

†**Immergent,** *a.* Erron. sp. of EMERGENT, in sense 'urgent' –1792.

†**Imme·rit,** *sb.* 1628. [f. IM-² + MERIT *sb.*, after earlier DEMERIT *sb.* with substitution of prefix.] Demerit –1750.

†**Imme·rited,** *ppl. a.* 1600. [f. IM-² + *merited* (MERIT *v.*).] Unmerited. Hence †**Imme·rit** *v.* not to deserve or merit (only in *pres. pple.* and *ppl. a.*).

†**Imme·ritous,** *a.* [f. IMMERIT *sb.* + -OUS.] Undeserving, without merit. MILTON.

Immerse (imə̄·ɹs), *v.* 1605. [– *immers-*, pa. ppl. stem of L. *immergere,* f. *in-* IM-¹ + *mergere* dip, MERGE.] **1.** *trans.* To dip or plunge into a liquid; to put overhead in water, etc.; *spec.* to baptize by immersion. Also *transf.* and †*fig.* **2.** *transf.* and *fig.* To plunge or sink into a (particular) state of body or mind; to steep, absorb in some action or activity. Chiefly *pass.* or *refl.* 1664. **3.** *intr.* for *refl.* To plunge oneself, sink, become absorbed (*lit.* and *fig.*). Now *rare* or *Obs.* 1667.

1. To i. meat in a solution of salt 1879. *transf.* More than a mile immers'd within the wood DRYDEN. *fig.* Other formes..are more immersed into matter BACON. 2. A youth immersed in Mathematics COWPER.

†**Imme·rse,** *ppl. a.* 1626. [– L. *immersus,* pa. pple. of *immergere* IMMERGE.] Immersed –1647.

After long Inquiry of Things, I. in Matter BACON.

Immersed (imə̄·ɹst), *ppl. a.* 1667. [f. IMMERSE *v.* + -ED¹.] Dipped, plunged, or sunk in, or as in, a liquid 1678. **b.** Growing wholly under water. GRAY. **c.** *Biol.* Sunken or embedded in a surface 1826. †**d.** *Astron.* Plunged in darkness, eclipsed –1854.

†**Immersible** (imə̄·ɹsĭb'l), *a.*¹ *rare.* 1693. [f. IMMERSE *v.* + -IBLE, after (or as a refash. of) L. *immersabilis* (Horace).] That cannot sink in water. Hence **Immersibi·lity.**

Imme·rsible, *a.*² *rare.* 1846. [f. IMMERSE *v.* + -IBLE.] Capable of being immersed.

Immersion (imə̄·ɹʃən). 1450. [– late L. *immersio,* f. *immers-*; see IMMERSE, -ION.] The action of immerging or immersing. **1.** Dipping or plunging into water or other liquid, and *transf.* into other things 1658. **b.** The administration of Christian baptism by dipping the whole person in water; dist. from *affusion* or *aspersion* 1629. **c.** *Alch.* Reduction of a metal in some solvent 1683. **2.** *transf.* and *fig.* Absorption in some condition, action, interest, etc. 1647. **3.** *Astron.* The disappearance of a celestial body behind another or in its shadow, as in an occultation or eclipse; opp. to *emersion* 1690. **4.** *Microscopy.* The introduction of a liquid between the object-glass and the object 1875. **5.** *attrib.*, as (sense 1) *i. bath,* (4) *i. fluid, lens, objective,* etc. 1875.

1. Two or Three total Emersions in the Cold Bath ADDISON. 2. His i. in the Peninsular War ALISON. 5. *I. lens,* an achromatic objective for the microscope, which is used with a drop of water between the front lens and the slide, to prevent the extreme refraction of the luminous pencils if air is present. Hence **Imme·rsionism,** the doctrine or practice of i. in baptism. **Imme·rsionist,** one who adheres to immersionism.

Immesh, var. of ENMESH *v.*

Immethodic, -al (imeþǫ·dik, -ăl, imm-), *a.* 1605. [f. IM-² + METHODIC.] Having no method; unmethodical. Hence **Immetho·dical-ly** *adv.*, **-ness.**

Immethodize (ime·þŏdəiz), *v.* 1811. [f. IM-² + METHOD + -IZE.] *trans.* To emancipate from method; to render unmethodical. LAMB.

Immetrical (ime·trikăl, imm-), *a.* 1598. [f. IM-² + METRICAL.] Not metrical; unmetrical. Hence **Imme·trical-ly** *adv.*, **-ness.**

Immigrant (i·migrănt). 1787. [– *immigrant-*, pres. ppl. stem of L. *immigrare,* after *emigrant*; see next.] **A.** *adj.* Immigrating 1805. **B.** *sb.* One who or that which immigrates; a person who migrates into a country as a settler. (orig. in N. Amer. use.)

Immigrate (i·migreⁱt), *v.* 1623. [– *immigrat-*, pa. ppl. stem of L. *immigrare,* f. *in-* IM-¹ + *migrare* MIGRATE.] **1.** *intr.* To come to settle in a country (which is not one's own);

to pass into a new habitat (*lit.* and *fig.*). **2.** *trans.* To bring in as settlers 1896.

2. The expense of immigrating coolie labour from the East Indies 1898. Hence **Immigra·tion,** entrance into a country for the purpose of settling there. **I·mmigrator,** an immigrant. **I·mmigratory** *a.* of or pertaining to immigration.

†**Immi·nd, inmi·nd,** *v.* 1647. [f. IM-¹ + MIND *sb.*; cf. to put (a person) in mind.] *trans.* To remind –1660.

Imminence (i·minĕns). 1606. [– L. *imminentia*, f. as next; see -ENCE.] **1.** The fact or condition of being imminent or impending 1655. **2.** That which is imminent; impending evil or peril 1606.

1. The i. of any danger or distress FULLER. **2.** I.. dare all i. that gods and men Addresse their dangers in SHAKS. So **I·mminency,** imminent quality or character.

Imminent (i·minĕnt), *a.* 1528. [– *imminent-*, pr. ppl. stem of L. *imminēre* project, be impending, f. *in-* IM-¹ + **min-*; see EMINENT, PROMINENT. Cf. (O)Fr. *imminent.*] **1.** Of an event, etc. (usu. of evil or danger): Impending threateningly, hanging over one's head; ready to overtake one; coming on shortly. †**2.** Remaining intent (*upon* something) 1641. **3.** In lit. sense: Overhanging 1727. †**4.** Confused with IMMANENT –1856.

1. Haire-breadth scapes i' th' i. deadly breach SHAKS. Invasion was i. STUBBS. **2.** Their eyes ever I. upon worldly matters MILT. Hence **I·mminently** *adv.*

Immingle (imi·ŋg'l, imm-), *v.* 1606. [f. IM-¹ + MINGLE *v.*] *trans.* To mix or blend intimately; to mingle. Also *intr.* for *refl.*

intr. Where.. with the chestnut the oak-trees i. CLOUGH.

†**I·mminute,** *a.* 1681. [– L. *imminutus*, pa. pple. of *imminuere*, f. *in-* IM-¹ + *minuere* lessen.] Lessened. So †**Imminu·tion,** lessening, decrease.

Immiscible (imi·sĭb'l), *a.* 1671. [– late L. *immiscibilis*; see IM-², MISCIBLE.] That cannot be mixed; incapable of mixture.

Like water and oil, they are i. 1833. Hence **Immiscibi·lity,** i. quality. **Immi·scibly** *adv.*

Immission (imi·ʃən, imm-). Now *rare*. 1526. [– L. *immissio*, f. *immiss-*, pa. ppl. stem of *immittere*; see next, -ION.] The action of immitting; insertion, injection, admission, introduction. The opposite of *emission*. **b.** That which is immitted 1526.

Immit (imi·t), *v.* Now *rare* or *Obs.* 1578. [– L. *immittere* send in, introduce, f. *in-* IM-¹ + *mittere* send.] *trans.* To put in, inject, infuse; to introduce; the opposite of *emit*.

Immitigable (imi·tigăb'l), *a.* 1576. [– late L. *immitigabilis* (Cælius Aurelianus); see IM-², MITIGABLE.] That cannot be mitigated, softened, or appeased. Hence **Immi·tigably** *adv.*

Immix (imi·ks), *v.* Now *rare*. ME. [f. *immixt* pa. pple., analysed as implying a present *immix*. See MIX *v.*, ADMIX, COMMIX, which had a like origin.] *trans.* To mix in (*with* something else); to mix intimately, mix up, commingle. Also *refl.* and *intr.*

Samson with these immixt, inevitably Pulled down the same destruction on himself MILT. *Sams.* 1657.

†**Immi·xable,** *a.* 1641. [f. IM-² + *mixable.*] Immiscible.

†**Immixt, immixed** (imi·kst), *a.* 1622. [– L. *immixtus*, f. *in-* IM-² + *mixtus* MIXED. Cf. ADMIXT, COMMIXT.] Not mixed, pure, simple –1659.

They [the Chinese] are the most ancient and i. people in the Universe SIR T. HERBERT. Hence **Immi·xtness, -edness.** So †**Immi·xt** *v.* (*rare*) = IMMIX.

†**Immi·xture**¹. *rare.* 1648. [f. IM-² + MIXTURE, after prec.] The condition of being unmixed; purity; simplicity.

Immixture² (imi·kstiŭɹ). 1859. [f. IM-¹ + MIXTURE.] The action of immixing or mixing up; commingling; the fact of being mixed up (*in* something).

To avoid an i. in political strife BRYCE.

Immobile (imōᵘ·bil), *a.* ME. [– (O)Fr. *immobile* – L. *immobilis*; see IM-², MOBILE.] Incapable of moving or being moved; immovable (*lit.* and *fig.*); fixed, stable. Also loosely: That does not move; motionless, stationary. var. †**Immoble.**

Immobility (imobi·lĭti). 1483. [– (O)Fr. *immobilité* or late L. *immobilitas, -tat-*, f. *immobilis*; see prec., -ITY.] The quality or condition of being immobile; fixedness, stability; motionlessness (*lit.* and *fig.*). **b.** *concr.* = IMMOVABLE B. Browning.

Immobilize (imōᵘ·biləiz), *v.* 1871. [– Fr. *immobiliser*, f. *immobile*, see IMMOBILE, -IZE. Cf. MOBILIZE.] *trans.* To render immobile; to keep (a joint or limb) without motion for surgical purposes; to render (troops) incapable of being mobilized; to withdraw (specie) from circulation, holding it against bank-notes.

To oblige the enemy to i. around us considerable forces 1871. Hence **Immobiliza·tion,** the action or process of immobilizing; *concr.* specie withdrawn from circulation.

†**Immo·deracy.** *rare.* 1682. [f. IMMODERATE; see -ACY.] Want of moderation; excess –1686. So †**Immoderancy.** SIR T. BROWNE.

Immoderate (imǫ·dĕrĕt), *a.* ME. [– L. *immoderatus*; see IM-² and MODERATE.] **1.** Not moderate; exceeding usual or proper limits; excessive, extravagant; unreasonable; extreme. †**2.** Unrestrained; intemperate –1696. †**3.** Boundless; very great (*rare*) –1656.

1. I. slepe ELYOT, expenses 1601. Pindarus was i. in the ornaments of his poesie 1638. Hence **Immo·derate-ly** *adv.*, **-ness.**

Immoderation (imǫdĕrēⁱ·ʃən). 1541. [– Fr. *immodération* or L. *immoderatio*; see IM-², MODERATION.] The opposite of moderation; immoderateness, excess. †**b.** *pl.* Excesses –1679.

Immodest (imǫ·dĕst), *a.* 1570. [– Fr. *immodeste* or L. *immodestus*; see IM-², MODEST.] Not modest, void of modesty. **1.** Arrogant, forward, impudent. **2.** Improper, indelicate, indecent, lewd, unchaste 1590.

1. With this i. clamorous outrage SHAKS. **2.** To speak lewd words and sing i. songs DE FOE. **Immo·destly** *adv.*

Immodesty (imǫ·dĕsti). 1597. [– Fr. *immodestie* or L. *immodestia*; see IM-², MODESTY.] Want of modesty; arrogance; impudence 1605; impropriety, indelicacy; unchastity 1597.

She shames to think that ought within her face Should breed th' opinion of i. DANIEL.

†**Immo·dish,** *a.* 1649. [f. IM-² + MODISH.] Unfashionable –1690.

Immo·dulated, *ppl. a. rare.* 1765. [f. IM-² + *modulated.*] Not modulated; without vocal modulation.

†**Immolate,** *ppl. a. Obs.* or *arch.* 1534. [– L. *immolatus*, pa. pple. of *immolare*; see next, -ATE².] Sacrificed, immolated –1830.

Immolate (i·moleⁱt), *v.* 1548. [– *immolat-*, pa. ppl. stem of L. *immolare* (orig.) sprinkle with sacrificial meal, f. *in-* IM-¹ + *mola* MEAL *sb.*¹; see -ATE³.] **1.** *trans.* To sacrifice, offer in sacrifice; to kill as a victim. (Now only of sacrifices in which life is taken.) †Also *absol.* or *intr.* **2.** *transf.* and *fig.* To give up to destruction or severe loss for the sake of something else; to sacrifice 1634.

1. Human victims were immolated to the Thunderer 1851. **2.** To i. their own inclinations.. to their Vanity BOYLE.

Immolation (imolēⁱ·ʃən). 1533. [– L. *immolatio*, f. as prec.; see -ION. Cf. (O)Fr. *immolation.*] **1.** The action of immolating; sacrificial slaughter of a victim; sacrifice. **b.** Applied to the sacrifice of the mass 1548. **c.** *concr.* That which is immolated; a sacrifice, an oblation 1589. **2.** *fig.* Sacrifice 1690.

1. The I. of Isaac SIR T. BROWNE. **2.** This i. of genius and fame at the shrine of conscience EMERSON.

I·mmolator. 1652. [– L. *immolator*, f. as prec.; see -OR 2.] One who immolates or offers in sacrifice.

†**Immo·ment,** *a.* [Arbitrary f. IM-² + MOMENT *sb.*] Of no moment; trifling. *Ant. & Cl.* V. ii. 166. So **Immome·ntous** *a.* (*rare*), unimportant 1726.

Immoral (imǫ·răl), *a.* (*sb.*) 1660. [f. IM-² + MORAL *a.*] The opposite of *moral*. **1.** Not consistent with, or not conforming to, moral law; opposed to or violating morality: now often, morally evil or impure; vicious, dissolute. †**2.** Non-moral. SHERLOCK.

1. The same dissolute i. temper of mind BUTLER.

B. *sb.* An immoral lesson; *pl.* bad morals; also, an immoral person 1863.

Hence **Immo·rally** *adv.* in an i. manner. Also **Immo·ralism,** i. practice 1918; **Immo·ralist,** one who practises immorality 1691.

Immorality (imoræ·lĭti). 1566. [– med.L. *immoralitas* (XIII), f. *in-* IM-² + eccl.L. *moralitas* (Tertullian) MORALITY.] **1.** Immoral quality, character, or conduct; wickedness, viciousness. (Now often used spec. of sexual impurity.) **2.** An immoral act or practice; a vice 1631.

1. The educated Greeks.. had no horror of i. as such FROUDE. **2.** Deceit and falsehood are not regarded as immoralities in the eyes of Asiatics 1859.

Immo·ralize, *v. rare.* 1754. [f. IMMORAL + -IZE.] *trans.* To render immoral.

†**Immorigerous,** *a.* 1623. [f. IM-² + MORIGEROUS.] Unyielding; rebellious; uncivil –1732. Hence †**Immori·gerousness,** uncomplying obstinacy 1649.

Immortal (imǭ·ɹtăl). ME. [– L. *immortalis* undying (as pl. sb., the gods), f. *in-* IM-² + *mortalis* MORTAL. Cf. (O)Fr. *immortel.*]

A. *adj.* **1.** Not mortal; not subject to death; undying; living for ever. **b.** *transf.* Pertaining to immortal beings or immortality; heavenly, divine 1535. **2.** In wider sense: Everlasting, unfading, incorruptible 1630. **b.** *spec.* Of fame, etc.: Lasting through all time 1514. **3.** In hyperbolical use: Lasting, perpetual, constant 1538; †*colloq.* excessive –1627.

1. Lyke a þyng inmortal semede sche CHAUCER. Now vnto yᵉ king eternal, i., inuisible.. be honour and glory for euer & euer TINDALE 1 *Tim.* 1:17. **b.** I haue Immortall longings in me *Ant. & Cl.* V. ii. 283. **2.** The race, where that immortall garland is to be run for MILT. **b.** Airs, Married to i. verse MILT. †*I. herb* = IMMORTELLE. **3.** I have made myself an i. enemy by it PEPYS.

B. *sb.* **1.** An immortal being; one not subject to death. In *pl.*, a title for the gods of mythology. 16.. **2.** *fig.* **a.** In *pl.* a title for the royal bodyguard of ancient Persia; also, for other troops 1803. **b.** A person, esp. an author, of enduring fame. Usu. in *pl.* 1882. **3.** That which is immortal; immortality 1841.

1. Under yon great city fight no few Sprung from Immortals COWPER.

Hence **Immo·rtalism,** a doctrine of or belief in immortality. **Immo·rtalist,** one who believes in immortality. **Immo·rtally** *adv.* eternally; perpetually; *colloq.* infinitely.

Immortality (imǫɹtæ·lĭti). ME. [– L. *immortalitas*, f. *immortalis*; see prec., -ITY. Cf. (O)Fr. *immortalité.*] **1.** The quality or condition of being immortal; exemption from death or annihilation; endless existence; eternity; perpetuity. **2.** Enduring fame or remembrance 1535.

1. Phr. *Conditional i.*: the theological doctrine that human i. is conditional upon faith in Christ. This mortall must put on immortalite TINDALE 1 *Cor.* 15:53. The Sadducees denied.. the i. of the Soul BAXTER. **2.** Shakespeare's i. is secure 1866.

Immortalization (imǭ:ɹtăləizēⁱ·ʃən). 1603. [f. next + -ATION. Cf. Fr. *immortalisation.*] The action of immortalizing, or fact of being immortalized.

Immortalize (imǭ·ɹtăləiz), *v.* 1566. [f. IMMORTAL + -IZE. Cf. Fr. *immortaliser.*] **1.** *trans.* To render immortal; to exempt from death 1633; to perpetuate 1566; to confer enduring fame upon (the prevailing sense); also *absol.* 1589. **2.** *intr.* To become immortal (*rare*) 1737.

1. A genius.. who has immortalized Edinburgh,—Walter Scott LD. COCKBURN. Hence **Immo·rtalizer.**

‖**Immortelle** (imǫɹte·l, ‖Fr. immortęl). 1832. [Fr. (short for *fleur immortelle*).] A name for various composite flowers of papery texture (esp. species of *Helichrysum*, *Xeranthemum*, etc.) which retain their colour after being dried; = EVERLASTING.

Immortification (imǭ:ɹtifikēⁱ·ʃən). 1626. [– med. (eccl.) L. *immortificatio* (cf. *immortificatus* in A Kempis *De Imitatione*), f. *in-* IM-² + *mortificatio* MORTIFICATION. Cf. Fr. *immortification* (XVI).] Want of mortification; a condition of the soul in which the passions are not mortified.

†**Immo·te,** *a.* 1601. [– L. *immotus*, f. *in-* IM-² + *motus* moved, pa. pple. of *movēre* MOVE.] Unmoved –1685.

Immotile (imōᵘ·til, -əil), *a.* 1872. [f. IM-² + MOTILE.] Not motile; incapable of movement. So **Immo·tive** *a.* 1627.

Immovable (imū·văb'l), *a.* (and *sb.*) ME. [f. IM-² + MOVABLE. Cf. Fr. †*immo(u)vable.*] **A.** *adj.* **1.** *lit.* That cannot be moved physically; firmly fixed; incapable of movement. Often loosely: Motionless, stationary, fixed. **2.** *fig.* Not subject to change; unalterable, fixed ME.; steadfast, unyielding 1534; emotionless, impassive 1639. **3.** *Law.* Not liable to be removed; permanent; opp. to *movable* 1449.

1. I. as Statues 1662. **2.** *Immovable feast*: see FEAST *sb.* Resting immooveable in his counsels 1600. His features were i. DICKENS. **3.** All commodities, Moveable, and Immoveable HOBBES.

B. *sb.* (*Law.*) A piece or article of property that is immovable (see A. 3); usu. in *pl.* Immovable property, as land and things adherent thereto, as trees, buildings, servitudes 1588.

Hence **Immovabi·lity, Immo·vableness,** i. quality or condition. **Immo·vably** *adv.* in an i. manner (*lit.* and *fig.*).

Immund (imʋ·nd), *a. rare.* 1621. [– L. *immundus*, f. *in-* IM-² + *mundus* clean, pure.] Unclean, foul.

†**Immundi·city.** 1530. [– Fr. †*immondicité*, irreg. f. *immondice* impurity – L. *immunditia.*] Uncleanness, impurity; filthiness; in *pl.* impurities –1660.

Immune (imiū·n), *a.* ME. [– L. *immunis* exempt from a service or charge, f. *in-* IM-² + *munis* ready for service; in sense 2 after Fr. *immune* (c1880).] **1.** Free (*from* some liability); exempt. *Obs.* exc. *fig.* from 2. **2.** *spec.* Having immunity *from* poison, contagion, etc., esp. through inoculation, etc. 1881; serving to develop immunity 1902.

Immunity (imiū·nĭti). ME. [– L. *immunitas*, f. *immunis*; see prec., -ITY. Cf. (O)Fr. *immunité*. In sense 5 after Fr. *immunité* (cf. prec.).] **1.** *Law.* Exemption from a service, obligation, or duty; freedom from liability to taxation, jurisdiction, etc.; privilege granted to an individual or a corporation conferring particular exemptions. Also less strictly: Non-liability, privilege. Also with *pl.* **2.** *spec.* (*Eccl.*) Exemption of eccl. persons and things from secular or civil liabilities, burdens, or duties. Chiefly with *an* and *pl.* 1513. †**3.** Undue freedom, licence –1680. **4.** Exemption *from* any usual liability, or from anything injurious 1592. **5.** The condition of being immune; immunization; see IMMUNE *a.* 2. 1879.

1. I. from taxation without consent of parliament HALLAM. **2.** The immunite..of that sacred Sanctuarie MORE. **4.** I. from Trouble HALE, from snakes 1894. **5.** The i. of vipers from their own poison 1887.

Immunize (i·miunəiz), *v.* 1892. [f. IMMUNE + -IZE.] *trans.* To render immune from poison or infection. Hence **Immuniza·tion,** immunizing or being immunized.

Immure (imiūᵊ·ɹ), *v.* 1583. [– med.L. *immurare* (perh. through Fr. *emmurer*), f. L. *in-* IM-¹ + *murus* wall.] †**1.** *trans.* To wallin, to surround with walls; to fortify –1746. **2.** To enclose within walls; to imprison; to confine as in a prison 1588. Also *transf.* and *fig.* (now *rare*). **3.** To build into a wall; to entomb in a wall. Also *transf.* 1675.

1. An Altar..immured by a Square Wall 1698. **2.** Immur'd (in the Fleet) HOWELL, in the walls of a cloister 1791. *fig.* Loue..Liues not alone emured in the braine SHAKS. *refl.* To i. himself..in a German University 1826. Hence †**Immu·re** *sb.* something that immures; a wall SHAKS. **Immu·rement,** imprisonment, confinement.

Immu·sical, *a.* Now *rare.* 1626. [f. IM-² + MUSICAL. Cf. earlier UNMUSICAL.] Not musical or harmonious.

Immutable (imiū·tăb'l), *a.* ME. [– L. *immutabilis*, f. *in-* IM-² + *mutabilis* MUTABLE.] Not mutable; not subject to or susceptible of change; unalterable. **b.** *techn.* Invariable; used e.g. of the markings of a species 1621.

We speak of eternal and i. justice JOWETT. Hence **Immutabi·lity, Immu·tableness. Immu·tably** *adv.*

Immutate (i·miutĕt), *a. rare.* 1788. [– L. *immutatus*, f. *in-* IM-² + *mutatus*, pa. pple. of *mutare* change; see -ATE².] Unchanged. So †**Immu·te** *a.* 1639.

†**Immuta·tion.** 1540. [– L. *immutatio*, f. *immutat-*, pa. ppl. stem of *immutare*; see next, -ION.] Mutation, change, alteration, transformation –1704.

†**Immu·te,** *v.* 1613. [– L. *immutare*, f. *in-* IM-¹ + *mutare* change.] *trans.* To produce a change in; to alter, transform –1661.

Imp (imp), *sb.* [OE. *impa* or *impe*; see next.] †**1.** A young shoot; a sapling; a sucker, slip, scion –1672. †**2.** A graft –1706. **3.** Scion (esp. of a noble house); offspring, child (usu. male). *Obs.* since 17th c., exc. as a literary archaism, or as in 5. ME. **b.** = 'Child' (*fig.* and *transf.*). *Obs.* or *arch.* ME. **4.** *spec.* A child of the devil or of hell 1526; hence, a little devil or demon, an evil spirit 1584. **5.** A mischievous child; a young urchin; often used playfully 1642. †**6.** A youth; fellow, lad, boy –1889. **7.** A piece added on, to eke out, lengthen out, or enlarge something; e.g. †an additional tag to a bell-rope; an addition to a beehive to increase its height (*dial.*); a length of twisted hair in a fishing line (*dial.*) 1595.

3. Prince Edward, that goodly ympe HALL. **b.** Art thou..that Impe of Glory? QUARLES. **4.** The Devil's Impe the Pope 1648. A scoffing man.. shows more of the i. than of the angel CARLYLE. Small i. of blackness, off at once LOCKER *To Printer's Devil.* **5.** I was..an incorrigibly idle i. SCOTT.

Imp (imp), *v.* [OE. *impian* (f. prec.), corresp. to OHG. *impfōn* (G. *impfen*), shortened analogues of OHG. *impitōn* (MHG. *impfeten*) – Rom. **impotare*, f. med.L. *impotus* graft (Salic Law) – Gr. ἔμφυτος implanted, engrafted, vbl. adj. of ἐμφύειν implant, f. ἐν IN¹, IM-¹, EM- + φύειν.] †**1.** *trans.* To graft, engraft –1681. **2.** *transf.* and *fig.* To engraft, implant; to inlay, set or fix in (*arch.*) ME. **3.** *Falconry.* To engraft feathers in a damaged wing, so as to restore or improve the powers of flight; hence, allusively 1477. **4.** To extend, lengthen, enlarge, add to; to eke *out*; to repair; to add on a piece to 1592.

2. They were imped in the wicked family of Ahab TRAPP. **3.** Ymping a fether to make me flye LYLY. Phr. *To i. the wings of*: to strengthen the flight of; Their Buzzard-wings, imp'd with our Eagles Plumes DRAYTON. If I imp my wing on thine, Affliction shall advance the flight in me G. HERBERT. Imp'd with Wings, The Grubs proceed to Bees with pointed Stings DRYDEN. **4.** To i. out..unavoidable defects with [etc.] CLARENDON.

Imp. Abbrev. of *imperator, imperial, imprimatur*, etc.

†**Impa·cable,** *a.* 1571. [f. IM-² + L. *pacare* pacify, appease + -ABLE. Cf. AL. *pacabilis*, placable, *impacabilis* not payable, not current.] That cannot be appeased; implacable –1602. Hence †**Impacabi·lity.**

Impack (impæ·k), *v. rare.* 1590. [– AL. *impaccare* pack (XIII), f. *in-* IM-¹ + *paccare* pack (wool, etc.); see PACK *v.*] *trans.* To pack in; to press closely together into a mass. Hence **Impa·ckment,** impacking or being impacked.

Impact (i·mpækt), *sb.* 1781. [– *impact-*, pa. ppl. stem of L. *impingere* IMPINGE.] The act of impinging; the striking of one body against another; collision. Chiefly in *Dynamics*, in reference to momentum. Also *fig.*

The i. of the vibrations of the luminous ether on the retina HUXLEY. *fig.* The i. of barbarian conquest STUBBS.

†**Impa·ct,** *ppl. a.* 1563. [– L. *impactus*, pa. pple. of *impingere* IMPINGE.] = IMPACTED. Const. as *pple.* or *adj.* –1652.

Impact (impæ·kt), *v.* 1601. [orig. and usu. in pa. pple. *impacted*, f. L. *impactus* + -ED¹; the vb. is from this.] **1.** *trans.* To press closely into or in something; to fix firmly in; to pack in. **2.** To stamp or impress (*on* something). GALE. **3.** To make impact *with* 1916.

Impa·cted, *ppl. a.* 1683. [See prec.] Pressed closely in, firmly fixed.

Impaction (impæ·kʃən). 1739. [f. IMPACT *v.* + -ION.] The action of becoming, or condition of being, impacted or firmly fixed in. So **Impa·ctment.**

Impaint (impē¹·nt), *v.* 1596. [f. IM-¹ + PAINT *v.*] *trans.* To paint upon something, depict. 1 *Hen. IV*, v. i. 80.

Impair (impēᵊ·ɹ), *sb.*¹ *Obs.* or *arch.* 1568. [f. IMPAIR *v.*] An act of impairing; the being impaired; impairement.

I·mpair, *a.* (and *sb.*²). 1606. [Cf. Fr. *impair* unequal (XV), and *pair* equal.] †**1.** (?) 'Unsuitable' (T.), unfit; inferior. (But the reading is disputed.) *Tr. & Cr.* IV. v. 103. **2.** Not paired; odd 1839. **b.** *sb.* An unpaired or odd one 1880.

Impair (impēᵊ·ɹ), *v.* [ME. *empaire, -peire* – OFr. *empeirier* (mod. *empirer*) :- Rom. **impejorare* make worse, f. *in-* IM-¹ + late L. *pejorare.*] **1.** *trans.* To make worse, less valuable, or weaker; to lessen injuriously; to damage, injure. **2.** *intr.* (for *refl.*) To grow or become worse; to suffer injury or loss; to deteriorate ME.

1. It never wastes nor empairs an Estate FULLER. Truth No years i. YOUNG. **2.** Flesh may empaire ..but reason can repaire SPENSER. Hence **Impai·rable** *a.* (*rare*) that can be impaired. **Impai·rer. Impai·rment,** the action of impairing; the being impaired; deterioration ME.

Impalace (impæ·lės), *v.* 1611. [IM-¹.] *trans.* To place or install in a palace.

†**Impa·latable,** *a. rare.* 1787. [IM-².] Not palatable –1814.

Impale (impē¹·l), *v.* 1530. Also †**em-.** [– Fr. *empaler* or med.L. *impalare*, f. *in-* IM-¹ + *palus* stake, PALE *sb.*¹] **1.** *trans.* To enclose with pales or stakes; to surround with a palisade; to fence in. Also *transf.* and *fig.* Now *rare.* †**b.** *Mil.* To enclose or surround (troops) for defence, as with other troops, or with wagons, etc. (Improp., To set in array.) –1670. **2.** To surround for adornment; to encircle, as with a crown or garland; to border, edge. *Obs.* or *arch.* 1553. **3.** *Her.* To marshal (two coats of arms) side by side on one shield, divided palewise 1605. †**b.** *fig.* To place side by side –1659. **4.** To thrust a pointed stake through the body of; to fix upon a stake thrust up through the body 1613. Also *transf.*

1. Their country goeth under the tearme of *The English Pale*, because the first Englishmen..did empale for themselves certaine limits in the East part of the Iland *Camden's Brit.* II. 73 (Ireland). **b.** The Legionaries stood..impal'd with light armed MILTON. **3. b.** The Admission of St. Patrick..to be match'd and impaled with the Blessed Virgin in the Honour thereof FULLER. **4.** Let them..be..empal'd and left To writhe at leisure round the bloody stake ADDISON. *transf.* The falcon often impales himself on the long and sharp beak [of the heron] 1807.

Impalement (impē¹·lmĕnt). 1598. Also †**em-.** [– Fr. *empalement*, f. *empaler*; see prec., -MENT. In later use direct f. the verb.] **1.** The action of enclosing with pales; *concr.* an enclosing fence or palisade 1611. Also *transf.* and *fig.* †**2.** *Bot.* Applied to the calyx, and, in composite flowers, to the involucre –1799. **3.** *Her.* The marshalling of two coats of arms side by side on one shield divided palewise; the arms so marshalled 1774. **4.** The torture or punishment of impaling (see IMPALE *v.* 4) 1630. **5.** The act or fact of being impaled upon the spikes of a gate, etc. 1887.

†**Impa·ler.** 1671. [f. IMPALE *v.* + -ER¹.] Applied by Grew to each of the calyx-leaves or sepals of a single flower, and the bracts of a composite.

†**Impa·llid,** *v. rare.* [f. IM-¹ + PALLID.] *trans.* To render pallid or pale. FELTHAM.

Impalm (impā·m), *v. rare.* 1611. [f. IM-¹ + PALM *sb.*²] *trans.* To take or grasp in the palm of the hand; also *fig.*

†**Impa·lmed,** *a.* [f. IM-¹ + *palmed*, repr. L. *palmatus*, as in *tunica palmata.*] Embroidered with palm-branches: said of the tunica worn by Roman generals in their triumphal processions. FELTHAM.

Impalpable (impæ·lpăb'l), *a.* 1509. [– Fr. *impalpable* or late L. *impalpabilis*; see IM-² and PALPABLE.] **1.** Incapable of being felt; imperceptible to the touch; intangible. Said of things immaterial; also, of very fine powder, in which no grit is felt. **2.** *fig.* Not (readily) apprehensible by the mind; producing no definite impression; 'intangible' 1774.

1. A thing i., A shadow COWPER. An i. transparent gas 1873. **2.** The almost i. beauties of style and expression 1838. Hence **Impalpabi·lity,** i. quality. **Impa·lpably** *adv.*

Impalsy (impǭ·lzi), *v.* 1750. [f. IM-¹ + PALSY *sb.*] To affect with or as with palsy, to paralyse.

Impaludism (impæ·liudiz'm). 1881. [f. IM-¹ + L. *palus, palud-* marsh + -ISM.]

The general morbid state occurring in inhabitants of marshy districts.

Impanate (impēⁱ·nět, i·mpǎnět), *ppl. a.* 1550. [– med.L. *impanatus*, pa. pple. of *impanare*; see IMPANE, -ATE².] Contained or embodied in bread; see IMPANATION. So **Impanate** *v.* (*rare*), to embody in bread.

Impanation (impǎnēⁱ·ʃən). 1548. [– med. L. *impanatio*, f. *impanat-*, pa. ppl. stem of *impanare*; see IMPANE, -ION. Cf. Fr. *impanation* (XVI).] In Eucharistic theory: A local presence or inclusion of the body of Christ in the bread after consecration: one of the modifications of the doctrine of the real presence.

Impanator (i·mpǎnēⁱtəɹ). 1855. [– med.L. *impanator*, f. as prec.; see -OR 2, -ATOR.] One who holds the doctrine of impanation.

†**Impa·ne**, *v.* 1547. [– med.L. *impanare*, f. *in-* IN-¹ + *panis* bread.] *trans.* To embody in bread; see IMPANATION –1548.

Impa·nel, impa·nnel, *v.* 1514. Var. of EMPANEL *v.*

Imparadise, em- (impæ·rǎdəis, em-), *v.* 1586. [See IM-¹ and PARADISE.] **1.** *trans.* To place in, or as in, Paradise; to transport, ravish 1592. **2.** To make a paradise of (a place or state).

1. Imparadis't in one anothers arms MILT.

†**Imparalleled** (impæ·răleld), *a.* 1604. [f. IM-² + *paralleled.*] Without parallel, matchless –1680.

†**Impa·rdonable**, *a.* 1523. [f. IM-² + PARDONABLE.] Not to be pardoned, unpardonable –1797. Hence †**Impa·rdonably** *adv.*

Imparidigitate (impæ:ridi·dʒitět), *a.* 1864. [f. L. *impar* unequal, uneven + DIGITATE; opp. PARIDIGITATE.] *Zool.* Having an odd number of fingers or toes on each limb; perissodactyl.

Imparipinnate (-pi·nět), *a.* Also **-pennate.** 1847. [– mod.L. *imparipinnatus* (Linnæus, 1751); cf. prec. and PINNATE; opp. PARIPINNATE.] *Bot.* Pinnate (as a leaf) with an odd terminal leaflet.

Imparisyllabic (impæ:risilæ·bik), *a.* 1730. [f. L. *impar* unequal + SYLLABIC. Cf. PARISYLLABIC.] *Gram.* Applied to Greek and Latin nouns which have not the same number of syllables in all the cases: e.g. nom. *lapis*, gen. *lapidis*; etc. Also †**-ical** 1671.

Imparity (impæ·riti). Now *rare* or *Obs.* 1563. [– late L. *imparitas* (Boethius), f. *impar* unequal, uneven; see IM-², PARITY. Cf. (O)Fr. *imparité.*] **1.** = DISPARITY 1. †**2.** = DISPARITY 2. –1687. †**3.** Of numbers: The quality of not being divisible into two equal (integral) parts; unevenness; an uneven or odd number –1659.

1. That there might be no imparitie nor inequality at all among his citizens HOLLAND. **3.** By two and three, the first parity and i. SIR T. BROWNE.

Impark (impā·ɹk), *v.* Also †**em-.** ME. [– AFr. *enparker*, OFr. *emparquer* (in AL. *imparcare*), f. *en-* IM-¹ + *parc* PARK.] **1.** *trans.* To enclose in a park, as beasts of the chase; hence *gen.* to confine, shut up. **2.** To enclose (land) for a park 1535.

1. Their Deer are no where imparked 1665. Hence **Imparka·tion**, enclosure of land for a park (also *gen.*).

Imparl (impā·ɹl), *v.* Also **em-.** *Obs.* exc. *Hist.* 1461. [– AFr. *enparler*, OFr. *emparler* speak, plead, f. *em-* EM-, IM-¹ + *parler* speak.] †**1.** *intr.* To speak *together*, or *with* another, upon a matter; to parley –1600. **2.** *Law.* 'To have license to settle a litigation amicably; to obtain delay by adjustment' (Wharton). *Obs.* in practice; see next, 2. 1461. †**3.** *trans.* To talk over (*rare*) –1805.

Imparlance (impā·ɹlǎns). *Obs.* exc. *Hist.* 1579. [– OFr. *emparlance*, f. *emparler*; see prec., -ANCE.] †**1.** Conference, discussion, parleying –1828. **2.** *Law.* An extension of time to put in a response in pleading a case, on the (real or fictitious) ground of a desire to negotiate for an amicable settlement; a continuance of the case to another day; a petition for, or leave granted for, such delay. (Abolished in 1853.) Also *fig.*

2. But with rejoinders and replies..Demur, i., and essoign, The parties ne'er could issue join SWIFT.

Imparsonee (impāɹsǒnī·), *a.* 1607. [repr. med.L. (*persona*) *impersonata*, pa. ppl. fem. of AL. *personare* induct, institute, f. *persona*, after words like APPELLEE; see PARSON, -EE¹.] *Eccl. Law.* In phr. *Parson imparsonee*, a clergyman duly presented, instituted, and inducted into a parsonage or rectory.

Impart (impā·ɹt), *v.* 1471. [– OFr. *impartir* – L. *impartire* (usu. *impertire*), f. *in-* IM-¹ + *pars, part-* share, PART.] **1.** *trans.* To give a part or share of; to make another a partaker of; to bestow, communicate. (Usu. (now only) with immaterial object.) Also *absol.* 1477. **2.** To communicate as knowledge or information; to make known, tell, relate (*arch.*) 1547. †**b.** *refl.* To make known one's mind –1653. †**3.** To give a share of to each of several persons; to distribute –1601. †**4.** To have or get a share of; to partake –1655. †**b.** *intr.* To partake *in* –1615.

1. Thee stars imparted no light 1583. *absol.* He that hath two coats, let him i. to him that hath none *Luke* 3:11. **2.** When I did first i. my loue to you SHAKS. **b.** Imparting himself equally to all Men CLARENDON. Hence **Impa·rtance** (*rare*; not on L. analogies), **Imparta·tion**, the action of imparting; communication. **Impa·rter**, one who or that which imparts.

Impartial (impā·ɹʃǎl), *a.* 1593. [f. IM-² + PARTIAL.] **1.** Not partial; not favouring one more than another; unprejudiced, unbiased, fair, just, equitable. †**2.** Not fragmentary; entire, complete (*rare*) 1716. ¶**3.** Misused for *partial. Rom. & Jul.* Qo. 1, l. 1856.

1. An i. Conscience SOUTH, Sovereign 'JUNIUS', tribunal 1838. **2.** An i. and universal Obedience 1716. Hence **Impa·rtialist** (*rare*), one who professes impartiality. **Impa·rtial-ly** *adv.*, **-ness** (*rare*).

Impartiality (impāɹʃi,æ·lǐti). 1611. [f. prec. + -ITY.] **1.** The quality of being impartial; freedom from prejudice or bias; fairness. †**2.** Completeness. 1716.

1. I. to children FIELDING. A tone of historic i. 1836.

Impartible (impā·ɹtib'l), *a.*¹ (*sb.*) 1398. [– late and med.L. *impartibilis*, f. *in-* IM-² + *partibilis* PARTIBLE.] **1.** Incapable of being parted or divided; not subject to partition; indivisible. Now chiefly legal. **2.** *sb.* Something that is indivisible 1788.

1. The question..whether the estate..was partible or i. 1890. Hence **Impartibi·lity**¹, i. quality 1656. **Impa·rtibly** *adv.* 1631.

†**Impartible**, *a.*² *rare.* 1631. [f. L. *impartiri*; see -IBLE.] Capable of being imparted. Hence **Impartibility**², communicability.

Imparticipable (impaɹti·sipǎb'l), *a.* (*sb.*) 1789. [f. IM-² + PARTICIPABLE.] **1.** Incapable of being participated or shared. **2.** *sb.* An imparticipable thing 1789.

Impartment (impā·ɹtměnt). 1602. [f. IMPART *v.* + -MENT.] The fact of imparting, or that which is imparted; communication; a communication.

It beckons you to go away with it, As if it some i. did desire To you alone *Haml.* I. iv. 59.

Impassable (impɑ·sǎb'l), *a.* 1568. [f. IM-² + PASSABLE, perh. through Fr. *impassable.*] **1.** That cannot be passed along, through or across. †**2.** That cannot pass (away or through) –1832. **3.** That cannot be made to pass (*rare*) 1865.

1. I. Woods DAMPIER, bounds 1844. **3.** To make half-sovereigns practically i. 1887. Hence **Impassabi·lity, Impa·ssableness**, i. quality or condition. **Impa·ssably** *adv.*

‖**Impasse** (ę̃pā·s, impɑ·s). 1851. [Fr. (Voltaire), f. *im-* IM-² + stem of *passer.*] A road or way having no outlet; a blind alley, 'cul-de-sac'. Also *fig.*

Impassible (impæ·sib'l), *a.* ME. [– (O)Fr. *impassible* – eccl.L. *impassibilis*; see IM-², PASSIBLE.] **1.** Incapable of suffering; not subject to pain. **2.** Incapable of suffering injury or detriment 1491. **3.** Incapable of feeling or emotion; impassive, insensible, unimpressible 1592. †**4.** Insufferable (*rare*) –1665.

1. That i. state, where all tears shall be wiped from our eyes 1667. **2.** I. as air 1839. **3.** He was i. before victory, before danger, before defeat THACKERAY. Hence **Impassibi·lity, Impa·ssibleness**, the quality of being i. **Impa·ssibly** *adv.*

Impassion (impæ·ʃən), *v.* Also †**em-.** 1591. [– It. *impassionare*, f. *in-* IM-¹ + *passione* PASSION.] *trans.* To fill or inflame with passion; to excite deeply or strongly. Also *absol.* Hence **Impa·ssionable** *a.* easily roused to passion. (Dicts.)

Impassionate (impæ·ʃənět), *a.*¹ Now *rare.* 1590. [– It. *impassionato*, pa. pple. of *impassionare*; see prec., -ATE².] = IMPASSIONED. Hence **Impa·ssionately** *adv.*

Impassionate, *a.*² Now *rare.* 1621. [f. IM-² + PASSIONATE.] Free from passion; dispassionate.

Impassionate (impæ·ʃəneⁱt), *v.* 1639. [f. IMPASSIONATE *a.*¹; see -ATE³.] **1.** *trans.* = IMPASSION 1641. †**2.** *intr.* To be or become impassioned –1646.

Impassioned (impæ·ʃənd), *ppl. a.* Also †**em-.** 1603. [f. IMPASSION *v.* + -ED¹.] Filled or inflamed with passion; deeply moved; passionate, ardent.

The Tempter all impassioned thus began MILT. *P.L.* IX. 678. Hence **Impa·ssioned-ly** *adv.*, **-ness.**

Impassive (impæ·siv), *a.* 1667. [IM-² + PASSIVE.] **1.** = IMPASSIBLE 1. **2.** Naturally without sensation; not susceptible of physical impression or injury, invulnerable 1687; insensible, unconscious 1848. **3.** Deficient in, or void of, mental feeling or emotion; unimpressionable, apathetic; also, in good sense, imperturbable, serene 1699. **4.** Intolerable (*rare*) 1828.

1. MILT. *P. L.* VI. 455. **2.** On the i. Ice the light'nings play POPE. **3.** An attitude of i. reserve FROUDE. Hence **Impa·ssive-ly** *adv.* 1828, **-ness** 1648. **Impassi·vity** 1794.

Impastation (impæsteⁱ·ʃən). 1727. [f. IMPASTE *v.* + -ATION, perh. through Fr. *impastation.*] The formation of a paste; also *concr.* a sort of mason's work, made of stucco, or stone ground small, and wrought up again in manner of a paste.

Impaste (impēⁱ·st), *v.* 1548. [– It. *impastare*, f. *in-* IM-¹ + *pasta* PASTE.] **1.** *trans.* To enclose in or encrust with or as with a paste. **2.** To make into a paste or crust 1576. **3.** *Painting.* To paint by laying on colour thickly 1727.

2. *Haml.* II. ii. 481. **3.** Heavily impasted pictures 1865.

‖**Impasto** (impɑ·sto). 1784. [It., f. *impastare*; see prec.] *Painting.* The laying on of colour thickly; impasting, as a characteristic of style; see prec. 3. Also *attrib.*

attrib. It is impossible to clean i. work 1880.

†**Impa·sture**, *v.* 1612. [f. IM-¹ + PASTURE *sb.*] **1.** *trans.* To place in a pasture; to turn out to graze –1614. **2.** To enclose for pasture. BLITH.

†**Impa·tible**, *v.* 1541. [– L. *impatibilis*, *-pet-*, insufferable, f. *in-* IM-² + *patibilis* PATIBLE. Sense 1 is late (eccl.) L.] **1.** = IMPASSIBLE 1, 2. **2.** Intolerable –1659.

1. The Devil..is a Spirit, and so i. of materiall Fire FULLER.

Impatience (impēⁱ·ʃěns). ME. [– (O)Fr. *impatience* – L. *impatientia*; see IM-², PATIENCE.] The fact or quality of being impatient. **1.** Want of endurance; failure to bear suffering, annoyance, etc. with equanimity; irascibility. Often with *of*, or *inf.* **2.** *esp.* Intolerance of delay; restlessness of desire or expectation; restless eagerness 1581.

1. [Thou] makest fortune wroth and Aspere by thine in-pacience CHAUCER. I. of cold and wet TOPSELL, of contradiction D'ISRAELI. **2.** I wait with i. for..your return 1712. So †**Impa·tiency** (esp. as a quality or disposition).

Impatient (impēⁱ·ʃěnt), *a.* (*sb.*) ME. [– (O)Fr. *impatient* – L. *impatiens, -ent-*; see IM-², PATIENT.] **1.** Not patient; not bearing or enduring (pain, etc.) with composure; easily provoked. Also *transf.* of action or speech: Indicating impatience. Often with *of, inf.*, or *dependent clause.* **2.** That does not willingly endure delay; restless in desire or expectation. Const. *for*, or *inf.* 1588. **b.** *transf.* and *fig.* Characterized by or attended with, impatience of delay 1703. †**3.** 'Not to be borne' (J.) –1646. **4.** *sb.* An impatient person 1502.

1. An i. Spirit is never without Woe STEELE. I. of Advice STEELE, of heat 1893. **2.** I. for the day POPE. *transf.* This one i. Minute 1703. **3.** SPENSER *F. Q.* II. i. 44. Hence **Impa·tient-ly** *adv.*, †**-ness** (*rare*).

†**Impa·tronize**, *v.* 1577. [– Fr. *impatroniser*, alt. f. OFr. *empatroner*, *-ir* – It. *impatronire, impadronire*, f. *im-* IM-¹ +

(O)Fr. *patron*, It. *padrone* PATRON; see -IZE.] **1.** *trans.* To put in possession *of*; usu. *refl.* –1681. **b.** *transf.* To take possession of –1799. **2.** To patronize 1629.

1. To i. themselves of many Cities and Strongholds 1681. Hence †**Impa:troniza·tion,** absolute seigniory or possession; the act of impatronizing.

Impave (impēⁱ·v), *v. rare.* 1833. [f. IM-¹ + PAVE *v.*] To pave in; to set in a pavement.

Impaved with rude fidelity Of art Mosaic WORDSW.

Impavid (impæ·vid), *a. rare.* 1857. [– L. *impavidus*, f. *in-* IM-² + *pavidus* fearful.] Fearless, undaunted. Hence **Impa·vidly** *adv.*

Impawn (impǭ·n), *v.* 1596. [f. IM-¹ + PAWN *v.* or *sb.*] **1.** *trans.* To put in pawn; to pledge. Also *fig.* **2.** *fig.* To risk the safety of 1613.

‖**Impayable** (impēⁱ·ăb'l, Fr. ęṅpęyabl'), *a.* ME. [Fr., f. *im-* (IM-²) + *payer*. Now often treated as Fr.] †**1.** Unappeasable. HAMPOLE. **2.** That cannot be paid or discharged 1797. ‖**3.** Beyond price. **b.** *colloq.* 'Beyond anything'. 1818.

3. The cheese, the fruits, the salad..were *impayables* SCOTT.

Impeach (impī·tʃ), *v.* [ME. *empeche, empesche* – OFr. *empecher, empescher* (mod. *empêcher* prevent) :– late L. *impedicare* catch, entangle, f. *in-* IM-¹ + *pedica* FETTER.] †**1.** *trans.* To impede, hinder, prevent –1690. †**2.** To hinder the action, progress, or well-being of; to affect prejudicially; to hurt, endamage, impair –1691. **3.** To challenge, call in question, attack; to discredit, disparage 1590. **4.** *gen.* To bring a charge against; to accuse *of*, charge *with* ME.; to 'peach' upon 1617; to find fault with, to censure 1813. **5.** *spec.* To accuse of treason or other high crime or misdemeanour (usu. against the state) before a competent tribunal 1568. Also applied transf. to analogous judicial processes 1734.

1. A Ditch..to i. the Assaults of an Enemy 1690. **3.** To i one's credit 1600, a general rule FIELDING, a contract BLACKSTONE. **4.** Nothing..that might i. me either with error or vntrueth 1590. **5.** Latimer was impeached and accused by the voice of the Commons 1863. Hence **Impea·ch** *sb.* †hindrance, impediment 1551; †detriment 1575; challenge, impeachment 1590. **Impea·chable** *a.* capable of being impeached; liable to impeachment; chargeable 1503. **Impea·cher,** one who impeaches 1552.

Impeachment (impī·tʃmĕnt). ME. [-OFr. *empe(s)chement* (mod. *empêchement*); see prec., -MENT.] The action of impeaching. †**1.** Hindrance, obstruction; impediment –1674. †**2.** Detriment –1648. **3.** A calling in question or discrediting; disparagement 1478. **4.** Accusation, charge. *Obs.* exc. in *the soft i.* ME. **5.** The accusation and prosecution of a person for treason or other high crime or misdemeanour before a competent tribunal; in Great Britain, 'the judicial process by which any man, from the rank of a peer downwards, may be tried before the House of Lords at the instance of the House of Commons'; in U.S., a similar process in which the accusers are the House of Representatives and the court is the Senate 1640.

1. Boris..without i. now ascended the throne MILT. **3.** Without an i. to their honour 1658. **4.** A considerable i. of heresy 1865. Phr. *Without impeachment of waste* (= law L. *absque impetitione vasti*): 'a reservation frequently made to a tenant for life, that no man shall proceed against him for waste committed' (Wharton). **5.** The articles of Strafford's i. HALLAM.

Impearl (impə̄·ɹl), *v.* 1586. [– Fr. *emperler* or It. *imperlare*; see IM-¹, PEARL.] **1.** *trans.* To deck with or as with pearls 1591. **2.** To make pearly or pearl-like 1639. **3.** To form into pearl-like drops 1586.

1. The flowry Meads, Impearl'd with tears SYLVESTER. **3.** Dew-drops, which the Sun Impearls on every leaf and every flouer MILT *P. L.* v. 747.

Impeccable (impe·kăb'l), *a.* (*sb.*) 1531. [– L. *impeccabilis*, f. *in-* IM-² + *peccare* sin; see -ABLE.] **1.** Of persons: Not liable to sin; exempt from the possibility of doing wrong. **2.** Of things: Faultless, unerring 1620. **3.** *sb.* One who is impeccable 1748.

1. The Pope is not only infallible, but also i. 1670. Hence **Impeccabi·lity,** the quality or character of being i. **Impe·ccably** *adv.* without liability to sin.

Impeccancy (impe·kănsi). 1614. [– eccl.L. *impeccantia* (Tertullian), f. *in-* IM-² + *peccantia* (Tertullian); see PECCANCY.] Sinlessness; inerrancy.

Impeccant (impe·kănt), *a.* 1763. [f. IM-² + L. *peccare* sin + -ANT; or direct f. earlier PECCANT.] Not sinning; unerring.

Impectinate (impe·ktinĕt), *a.* [f. IM-² + PECTINATE.] *Entom.* Not pectinate; not comb-toothed: said of antennæ, etc. (Recent Dicts.)

Impecunious (impīkiū·niəs), *a.* 1596. [f. IM-² + PECUNIOUS.] Having no money, penniless; in want of money.

A poore i. creature NASHE. var. **Impecu·niary.** Hence **Impecunio·sity,** lack of money; pennilessness.

Impedance (impī·dăns). 1886. [f. IMPEDE *v.* + -ANCE.] *Electr.* The ratio of the root mean square voltage applied to an electric circuit, to the current flowing in the circuit.

Impede (impī·d), *v.* 1605. [– L. *impedire*, f. *in-* IM-¹ + *pes, ped-* foot.] *trans.* To obstruct in progress or action; to hinder; to stand in the way of.

My load, light as it was, impeded me TYNDALL. Hence †**Impe·dible** *a.* that can be impeded or hindered.

Impedient (impī·diĕnt), *a.* (*sb.*) 1596. [f. IMPEDE *v.* + -ENT, after EXPEDIENT.] **1.** Obstructive, hindering. **2.** *sb.* [sc. *agent*] 1661.

Impediment (impe·dimĕnt), *sb.* ME. [– L. *impedimentum* hindrance, pl. *-menta* baggage, f. *impedire* IMPEDE, see -MENT.] **1.** The fact of impeding or condition of being impeded; *concr.* something that impedes; a hindrance, an obstruction. **2.** †A (physical) defect –1657; *esp.* a stammer or stutter 1494. **3.** (Chiefly *pl.*) Baggage, esp. of an army; IMPEDIMENTA 1540. **4.** The impedited conditions of a planet; see IMPEDITE *v.* 2. 1819.

1. Thus farre..Haue we marcht on without i. SHAKS. Hence †**Impe·diment** *v.* to obstruct. **Impedime·ntal** *a.* obstructive; impeditive.

‖**Impedimenta** (impedime·ntă), *sb. pl.* 1600. [L.; see prec.] Things which encumber progress; baggage; travelling equipment (of an army, etc.).

†**I·mpedite,** *ppl. a.* 1544. [– L. *impeditus*, pa. pple. of *impedire*; see next.] Impeded, obstructed, hindered; having an impediment. *Astrol.*: see IMPEDITE *v.* 2. –1671.

Impedite (i·mpĭdəit), *v.* Now *rare* or *Obs.* 1535. [– *impedit-* pa. ppl. stem of L. *impedire*; see IMPEDE.] **1.** = IMPEDE. **2.** *Astrol.* Said of a planet when its influence is hindered by the position of another 1647. So †**Impedi·tion,** hindering; being hindered. **Impe·ditive,** *a.* of the nature of an impediment; obstructive.

Impel (impe·l), *v.* 1490. [– L. *impellere*, f. *in-* IM-¹ + *pellere* drive. Cf. Fr. †*impeller* (XVI).] **1.** *trans.* To drive, force, or constrain (a person) *to* some action, or *to do* something; to urge on, incite. **2.** *lit.* To drive or cause to move onward; to impart motion to; to propel 1611.

1. Human nature will i. him to seek pleasure instead of virtue JOWETT. **2.** The heart..impels the blood through the arteries 1793. Hence **Impe·ller,** one who, or that which, impels.

Impellent (impe·lĕnt). 1620. [f. IMPEL *v.* + -ENT.] **a.** *adj.* That impels; impelling. **b.** *sb.* A thing which impels 1644.

†**Impe·n,** *v.* 1627. [f. IM-¹ + PEN *sb.*¹ or *v.*¹] *trans.* To shut up in a pen or fold –1661. Hence †**Impe·nt** *pa. pple.* 1633.

†**Impe·nd,** *v.*¹ 1486. [– L. *impendĕre* lay out, expend, f. *in-* IM-¹ + *pendĕre* weigh, pay out.] *trans.* To pay; to expend; to apply (money); to bestow –1690.

Impend (impe·nd), *v.*² 1599. [– L. *impendēre*, f. *in-* IM-¹ + *pendēre* hang.] **1.** *intr.* To hang or be suspended (*over*) 1780. **2.** *transf.* and *fig.* Of evil or danger: To hang threateningly (*over*) as about to fall 1599. **3.** Hence *gen.* To be about to happen; to be imminent 1674. **4.** *trans.* To overhang, hover over (*rare*). 1652.

2. Barbarism is ever impending over the civilized world J. H. NEWMAN. **3.** A war which was.. impending THIRLWALL.

Impendent (impe·ndĕnt), *a.* Now *rare.* 1592. [– *impendent-*, pr. ppl. stem of L. *impendēre*; see prec., -ENT; partly (esp. later) f. IMPEND *v.* Cf. Fr. †*impendent* imminent.] **1.** Overhanging 1611. **2.** Imminent; near at hand.

2. If..I. horrors, threatning hideous fall One day upon our heads MILT. *P. L.* II. 177. So **Impe·nding** *ppl. a.* Hence **Impe·ndence,** imminence. **Impe·ndency,** imminent or threatening character; an impending circumstance.

Impenetrability (impe:nĭtrăbi·lĭti). 1665. [f. next; see -ILITY.] **1.** The quality or condition of being impenetrable; inscrutability; unfathomableness; 'unsusceptibility of intellectual impression' (J.) 1706. **2.** *Nat. Philos.* That property of matter in virtue of which two bodies cannot occupy the same place at the same time 1665.

Impenetrable (impe·nĭtrăb'l), *a.* 1460. [– (O)Fr. *impénétrable* – L. *impenetrabilis*, f. *in-* IM-² + *penetrabilis* PENETRABLE.] **1.** That cannot be penetrated or pierced; impossible to get into or through. Const. *to, by.* **2.** *transf.* and *fig.* Inscrutable; unfathomable 1531. **3.** Impervious to intellectual or moral influences, impressions, or ideas 1596. **4.** *Nat. Philos.* Possessing impenetrability (see prec. 2) 1666.

1. Woods i. To Starr or Sun-light MILT. *P. L.* IX 1086, I. mist WORDSW. **2.** An i. secret LINGARD, countenance 1800. **3.** It is the most i. curre That euer kept with men SHAKS. Hence **Impe·netrableness,** impenetrability. **Impe·netrably** *adv.*

Impe·netrate, *v.* 1859. [f. IM-¹ + PENETRATE.] *trans.* To penetrate intimately.

Impenitence (impe·nitĕns). 1624. [– late (eccl.) L. *impænitentia* (Jerome), f. *in-* IM-² + *pænitentia* PENITENCE. Cf. Fr. *impénitence.*] The fact or condition of being impenitent; want of repentance; hardness of heart; obduracy.

Denouncing wrauth to come On thir i. MILT. *P. L.* XI. 816. So **Impe·nitency,** the quality or state of being impenitent.

Impenitent (impe·nitĕnt). 1532. [– eccl. L. *impænitens, -ent-* (Cyprian), f. *in-* IM-² + *pænitens* PENITENT. Cf. Fr. *impénitent.*]

A. *adj.* Not penitent; having no contrition or sorrow for sin; unrepentant, obdurate.

After thy hardnesse, and i. heart N.T. (Rhem.) *Rom.* 2:5. I. Criminals and Malefactors STEELE. Hence **Impe·nitently** *adv.*

B. *sb.* An impenitent person 1532.

†**Impe·nitible,** *a.* 1614. [– eccl. L. *impænitibilis*, f. *in-* IM-² + stem of L. *pænitēre* repent + *-ibilis* -IBLE.] Incapable of repentance –1637.

Impennate (impe·nĕt), *a.* and *sb.* 1842. [f. IM-² + PENNATE.] **a.** *adj.* Featherless, wingless; *spec.* applied to the *Impennes*, certain swimming birds which have small wings covered with scale-like feathers, as the penguins. **b.** *sb.* A bird of this kind.

†**Impe·nnous,** *a.* [f. IM-² + med. L. *pennosus*, f. L. *penna* feather; see -OUS.] Wingless. SIR T. BROWNE.

Impeople (impī·p'l) *v.*, var. of EMPEOPLE.

†**I·mperance.** [f. IMPERATE *v.* and *ppl. a.*; see -ANCE.] Commandingness. CHAPMAN. So †**I·mperant** *a.* commanding, ruling 1617.

†**I·mperate,** *ppl. a.* 1470. [– L. *imperatus*, pa. pple. of *imperare*; see next, -ATE².] **a.** as *pa. pple.* Commanded, ruled –1677. **b.** as *adj.* 'Commanded' *sc.* by the will; opp. to ELICIT *a.*, q.v. –1710.

b. All the actions elicite or i., which a sinner must performe..that God may be pacified 1624.

†**Imperate,** *v.* 1599. [– *imperat-*, pa. ppl. stem of L. *imperare*; see next, -ATE³.] *trans.* To command, rule, govern –1660. **Impera·tion,** the action of commanding (*rare*). BENTHAM.

Imperative (impe·rătiv). 1530. [– late L. *imperativus* specially ordered (Macrobius), *Gram.* (Martianus Capella), tr. Gr. προστακτική (sc. ἔγκλισις), f. *imperat-*, pa. ppl. stem of L. *imperare* command; see -IVE.]

A. *adj.* **1.** *Gram.* Expressing command: applied to the verbal mood or forms which express a command, request, or exhortation. **2.** Having the quality or property of commanding; commanding, peremptory 1598. **3.** Demanding obedience; that must be done or performed; urgent; of the nature of a duty; obligatory 1823.

2. The suits of kings are i. BP. HALL. **3.** The condition of our sick men made it i. that I should return at once KANE.

B. *sb.* **1.** *Gram.* The imperative mood or a verbal form belonging to it 1530. **2.** An imperative action, speech, condition, etc.; a command 1606.

2. The unconditional i. of the moral law SIR W. HAMILTON. Hence **Imperati·val** *a.*, **Impe·ratively** *adv.*, **-ness.**

‖**Imperator** (impĕrēⁱ·tǫɹ). 1579. [L., f. *imperare* (see prec.) + *-or* -OR 2.] **a.** In Roman History, a word orig. meaning 'commander', under the Republic, conferred by salutation of the soldiers on a victorious general; afterwards, under the Empire, confined to the head of the state, in whose name all victories were won, and thus = EMPEROR, q.v. **b.** *gen.* Absolute ruler, emperor; commander, ruler 1588.

a. Pompeyes souldiers saluted him by the name of I. NORTH. Hence **Impera·torship,** the office of i.

Imperatorial (imperătōᵊ·riăl), *a.* 1660. [f. L. *imperatorius* + -AL¹.] **1.** Of or pertaining to an imperator, emperor, or commander; imperial. †**2.** Imperative 1690.

1. A speech of i. grandeur DE QUINCEY. Hence **Imperato·rially** *adv.* vars. †**Imperato·rian** 1640, †**Imperato·rious** 1625, †**Impe·ratory** 1616.

Imperatorin (imperătōᵊ·rin). Also **imperatrin.** 1838. [f. Bot. L. *Imperatoria* + -IN¹.] *Chem.* A neutral substance discovered in the root of masterwort, *Imperatoria ostruthium*; the same as peucedanin.

†**Impe·ratrice.** 1460. [– Fr. *impératrice* (XVI) – L. *imperatrix, -tric-*, fem. of IMPERATOR; see -TRIX.] Empress –1542. So ‖**Impera·trix.**

Imperceivable (impəɹsī·văb'l), *a.* Now *rare.* 1617. [f. IM-² + PERCEIVABLE.] Imperceptible. Hence **Impercei·vableness. Impercei·vably** *adv.*

†**Imperceived,** *a. rare.* 1624. [f. IM-² + *perceived*, pa. pple. of PERCEIVE.] Not perceived –1691.

†**Impercei·verant,** *a.* [Cf. †*perceiverant* (c1509), f. ONFr. **perceivre;* see IM-², PERCEIVE *v.*, -ANT.] Not perceiving, undiscerning. *Cymb.* IV. i. 15.

Imperceptible (impəɹse·ptĭb'l), *a.* (*sb.*) 1526. [– Fr. *imperceptible* or med.L. *imperceptibilis*, f. *in-* IM-² + late L. *perceptibilis* PERCEPTIBLE.] Not perceptible. **a.** Naturally incapable of affecting the perceptive faculties. **b.** So slight, gradual, subtle, or indistinct as not to be perceptible 1635.

a. As for the soule, it is..i. to all the naturall senses P. HOLLAND. **b.** I. gradations 1853.

B. *sb.* An imperceptible thing or creature; with *the*: that which is imperceptible 1709.

Hence **I:mperceptibi·lity,** incapability of being perceived. **Imperce·ptibleness. Imperce·ptibly** *adv.*

Imperception (impəɹse·pʃən). 1662. [f. IM-² + PERCEPTION.] Absence or want of perception.

Imperceptive (impəɹse·ptiv), *a.* 1661. [f. IM-² + PERCEPTIVE.] **1.** Not perceptive; impercipient. **2.** In pass. sense: Imperceptible (*rare*). MOZLEY.

Hence **Imperce·ptiveness. Impercepti·vity.**

Impercipient (impəɹsi·piĕnt), *a.* (*sb.*) 1813. [f. IM-² + PERCIPIENT.] Not perceiving; lacking perception. **b.** *sb.* One who lacks perception 1898. So **Imperci·pience,** lack of perception.

†**Impe·rdible,** *a. rare.* [– med.L. *imperdibilis* imperishable, f. *in-* IM-² + late L. *perdibilis* perishable, f. L. *perdere* destroy; see -IBLE.] That cannot be lost or destroyed. FELTHAM. Hence †**Imperdibi·lity,** i. quality.

Imperence (i·mpĕrĕns). 1766. A vulgar corruption of IMPUDENCE. So **I·mperent** *a.*

Imperfect (impɔ̄·ɹfĕkt), *a.* (*sb.*) [ME. *inperfit* – (O)Fr. *imparfait* – L. *imperfectus*; see IM-², PERFECT.]

I. 1. Wanting some part; not fully formed, made, or done; unfinished, incomplete; deficient. **2.** Not coming up to the standard; defective, faulty ME. †**3.** Vicious, evil –1630. **4.** Not fully instructed or accomplished *in* 1570.

1. Inperfit cercles CHAUCER. **2.** Your other Senses grow i. By your eyes anguish *Lear* IV. vi. 5. **4.** I. in the Doctrine of Meteors SIR T. BROWNE.

II. Techn. senses. **1.** *Gram.* Applied to a tense which denotes action going on but not completed; usually to the past tense of incomplete or progressive action ('past imperfect'), as *I was writing* 1530. †**2.** *Arith.* **a.** Applied to a number which is not equal to the sum of its aliquot parts; opp. to *perfect.* **b.** Applied to a power (square, cube, etc.) whose root is an incommensurable quantity; opp. to a *perfect square, cube,* etc. –1706. **3.** *Mus.* †**a.** In mediæval music, applied to a note when reckoned as twice (not three times) the length of a note of the next lower denomination; and hence to 'modes', etc. characterized by such relative value of the notes. **b.** Applied to Plain Chant melodies which do not extend through the entire compass of the mode in which they are written (Grove). **c.** Sometimes applied to a diminished fourth, fifth, or triad; see DIMINISHED. 1597. **4.** *Bot.* Applied to flowers in which any normal part is wanting 1704. **5.** *Law.* (See quots.) 1832.

3. *Imperfect cadence*: one ending not on the direct chord of the tonic, but usually on that of the dominant, and having the effect of a partial close or stop; a *half-close. I. concords* or *consonances*: a name for the thirds and sixths, major and minor. **5.** An i. law..is a law which wants a sanction and which therefore is not binding 1832. *I. obligations*, moral duties, which cannot be enforced by law. *I. trusts*: executory trusts (EXECUTORY *a.* 3).

B. as *sb.* **1.** *Gram.* The imperfect (i.e. past imperfect) tense 1871. †**2.** *Mus.* An imperfect concord 1667.

Hence **Impe·rfect-ly** *adv.*, **-ness.**

†**Impe·rfect,** *v.* 1555. [f. prec. adj.] *trans.* To render imperfect; to destroy the perfection of –1682.

Imperfe·ctible, *a.* 1869. [f. IM-² + PERFECTIBLE.] Incapable of being made perfect. Hence **Imperfectibi·lity,** incapability of being made perfect 1836.

Imperfection (impəɹfe·kʃən). ME. [– (O)Fr. *imperfection* or late L. *imperfectio*, f. L. *imperfectus* IMPERFECT; see -ION.] **1.** The condition or quality of being imperfect; incompleteness; defectiveness, faultiness. **2.** (with *pl.*) A defect, fault, blemish ME. †**3.** *Mus.* The making of a note imperfect, or the condition of its being imperfect –1880.

1. The necessary i. of language JOWETT. **2.** Sent to my account With all my imperfections on my head SHAKS.

Imperfective (impəɹfe·ktiv), *a.* 1677. [f. IMPERFECT *a.* + -IVE.] †**1.** Characterized by imperfection –1684. **2.** *Slavonic Grammar.* Applied to a form or 'aspect' of the verb expressing action not completed (either continuous, or repeated); opp. to *perfective* 1844.

Imperforable (impɔ̄·ɹfŏrăb'l), *a.* 1658. [– med.L. *imperforabilis*, f. *in-* IM-² + *perforare* PERFORATE + *-bilis* -BLE. Cf. late and med.L. *perforabilis* vulnerable.] That cannot be perforated.

Imperforate (impɔ̄·ɹfŏrĕt), *a.* 1673. [f. IM-² + PERFORATE *ppl. a.*] Not perforated; having no perforation, foramen, or opening. Chiefly in scientific and technical use. So **Impe·rforated** *a.* 1650.

Imperforation (impɔ̄ɹfŏrēⁱ·ʃən). 1656. [f. IM-² + PERFORATION. Cf. Fr. *imperforation* (XVII).] The condition of being imperforate; a case of this.

Imperial (impīᵊ·riăl). ME. [– (O)Fr. *impérial* – L. *imperialis*, f. *imperium* rule, EMPIRE; see -AL¹, -IAL.]

A. *adj.* Pertaining to an empire or emperor.

I. 1. Of or pertaining to the (or an) empire. **2.** Of or pertaining to a sovereign state, which in its independence and importance ranks with an empire 1532. **3.** Of or pertaining to the (or an) emperor ME.; *spec.* belonging to the party of the (Romano-German) Emperor 1470. **4.** *fig.* and *transf.* Of the nature or rank of an emperor; commanding, supreme in authority ME. **5.** Majestic, august, exalted ME.; domineering, imperious 1581. **6.** Befitting an emperor; of special excellence; magnificent 1731.

1. *Imperial chamber*, is a sovereign court, established for the affairs of the immediate states of the empire E. CHAMBERS. The I. double eagle 1861. **2.** The imperiall lawes of the Realme of Englande 1556. The United Kingdom is an 'Imperial' State—a State exercising 'imperium', or dominion over the colonies and other dependencies 1888. **3.** The I. titles and I. pretensions of the English Kings in the tenth and eleventh centuries FREEMAN. A series of i. coins from Augustus to Diocletian D. WILSON. **4.** And the imperiall Votresse passed on, In maiden meditation, fancy free SHAKS. **5.** The Lily's height bespoke command, A fair i. flower COWPER. **6.** These are I. Works, and worthy Kings POPE.

II. *spec.* **1.** Applied to those weights and measures appointed by statute to be used throughout the United Kingdom 1838. **2.** In names of products and commodities of special size and quality, as *I. tea* 1664. **b.** Name of a size of paper: of printing-paper usually 22 by 32 inches, of writing-paper 22 by 30. 1668.

Phrases. *I. blue*: an aniline blue dye, also called *spirit-blue. I. city*: (*a*) a city that is the seat of empire, or that is itself a sovereign state; (*b*) any city of the old German Empire which owned allegiance to the Emperor alone. †*I. crown*: = CROWN IMPERIAL (*Fritillaria imperialis*). *I. drink* (formerly †*i. water*): a drink made of cream of tartar flavoured with lemons and sweetened. *I. yellow*: name of a kind of porcelain made in China, having a uniform yellow glaze, reserved for the use of the i. court; hence transf.

B. *sb.* **1.** = IMPERIALIST 1. 1524. **b.** An imperial personage 1588. **2.** A Russian gold coin, formerly worth 10 silver roubles, now 15. 1839. **3.** A case or trunk for luggage, adapted for the roof of a coach or carriage. Also the roof itself (Fr. *impériale*). 1794. **4.** A trade name for articles of special size or quality; as, a large decanter 1858; a size of paper (see A. II. 2 b) 1712; etc. †**5.** Short for *cloth imperial*, a textile fabric in use in the Middle Ages, with figures woven in gold; app. so called as being made at Constantinople –1876. **6.** A small tuft of hair left growing beneath the lower lip; so called because the Emperor Napoleon III wore such a tuft 1839.

Imperialism (impīᵊ·riăliz'm). 1858. [f. prec. + -ISM, after next.] **1.** The rule of an emperor, esp. when despotic. **2.** The principle or spirit of empire; advocacy of imperial interests 1881.

1. I., or, indeed, any worse form of despotism 1869. **2.** I mean the greater pride in Empire which is called I...a larger patriotism 1899.

Imperialist (impīᵊ·riălist). 1603. [f. IMPERIAL + -IST, after Fr. *impérialiste.*] **1.** An adherent of the (or an) emperor (usu., 1600–1800, of the German Emperor); one of the emperor's party. **2.** An advocate of imperialism 1800. **3.** *attrib.* or *adj.* Adhering or pertaining to imperialism 1868. Hence **Imperiali·stic** *a.* = prec. 3. **Imperiali·stically** *adv.*

Imperiality (impīᵊri,æ·lĭti). 1534. [f. as prec. + -ITY.] †**1.** Imperial rank, power, or authority –1629. **2.** A joc. title for an imperial personage; also *collect.* = imperial personages (cf. *royalty*) 1870. ¶*Erron.* An imperial right or privilege (Dicts.). (Based on a misprinted quot. from Tooke; see IMPERIALTY 2.)

Imperialize (impīᵊ·riăləiz), *v.* 1634. [f. as prec. + -IZE.] †**1.** *intr.* To act imperially. SIR T. HERBERT. †**2.** *trans.* To attach to the party of the Emperor (e.g. against the Papacy). FULLER. **3.** To render imperial 1805.

Imperially (impīᵊ·riăli), *adv.* 1550. [f. IMPERIAL *a.* + -LY².] **1.** In an imperial manner. **2.** *Her. I. crowned*: said of charges represented with an imperial crown 1823.

Imperialty (impīᵊ·riălti). *rare.* 1600. [f. IMPERIAL + -TY¹, after *royalty.*] †**1.** Imperial state or government –1616. **2.** An imperial right or privilege; a tax levied by an emperor or empress. (Cf. *royalty*) 1799.

2. The late empress having..relinquished her imperialties on the private mines 1799.

Imperil (impe·ril), *v.* Also **em-.** 1596. [f. EM-, IM-¹ + PERIL, prob. after ENDANGER.] *trans.* To bring into or put in peril; to endanger. Hence **Impe·rilled, -iled** *ppl. a.*; also **Impe·rilment,** imperilling, or being imperilled.

Imperious (impīᵊ·riəs), *a.* 1541. [– L. *imperiosus*, f. *imperium* command, EMPIRE; see -OUS, -IOUS. Cf. Fr. *impérieux.*] †**1.** Imperial –1703. **2.** Ruling, sovereign, dominant; commanding; majestic, stately. *Obs.* (or merged in 3 or 4.) –1819. **3.** Overbearing, dictatorial, domineering. (The prevailing mod. sense.) 1555. **4.** Urgent, overmastering, imperative 1541.

1. King, be thy thoughts I. like thy name SHAKS. **2.** It is Emperious, both o'r Love and Hate DRAY-

TON. The i. Mountaine Taurus SIR T. HERBERT. **3.** A proud, i. aristocrat, contemptuous..of popular rights FROUDE. **4.** The i. necessity which urges us 1877. Hence **Imperious-ly** *adv.*, **-ness.**

†**Impe·rish,** *v.* var. of EMPERISH, q.v.

Imperishable (impe·riʃăb'l), *a.* 1648. [f. IM-² + PERISHABLE. Cf. Fr. *impérissable* (XVII).] That cannot perish; not subject to decay; indestructible, immortal, enduring.

Goods deeds Do no i. record find Save in the rolls of heaven WORDSW. Hence **Impe:rishabi·lity, Impe·rishableness,** the quality of being i. **Impe·rishably** *adv.* indestructibly.

‖**Imperium** (impĭ°·riŏm). 1651. [L.] Command; absolute power; supreme or imperial power; EMPIRE.

L. phr. *Imperium in imperio*, an empire within an empire, an independent authority exercised or claimed within the jurisdiction of another authority.

Impermanent (impə̄·ɹmănĕnt), *a.* 1653. [f. IM-² + PERMANENT. Cf. med.L. *impermanentia.*] Not permanent or lasting. Hence **Impe·rmanence,** the fact or condition of being i. **Impe·rmanency,** the quality or state of being i.

Impermeable (impə̄·ɹmĭăb'l), *a.* 1697. [– Fr. *imperméable* or late L. *impermeabilis*, f. *in-* IM-² + late L. *permeabilis* PERMEABLE.] Not permeable; that cannot be passed through or traversed; *spec.* in *Physics*, that does not permit the passage of water or any fluid, liquid or gaseous.

A bed of hard and i. clay 1827. Hence **Impermeabi·lity, Impe·rmeableness,** i. quality. **Impe·rmeably** *adv.*

Impermi·ssible, *a.* 1858. [f. IM-² + PERMISSIBLE.] Not permissible.

†**Impermi·xt,** *a.* Also **in-.** 1500. [– L. *impermixtus*, f. *in-* IM-² + *permixtus* PERMIXED, PERMIXT.] Unmixed, unmingled –1677.

Imperscri·ptible *a.* 1832. [f. L. *in-* IM-² + *perscript-*, pa. ppl. stem of *perscribere* write at length, register, f. *per* PER- + *scribere* write; see SCRIBE, -IBLE.] For which no written authority can be adduced; unrecorded; as, an *imperscriptible right.*

†**Imperscru·table,** *a.* 1526. [– late and med.L. *imperscrutabilis*, f. L. *in-* IM-² + *perscrutari* search through; see -ABLE.] Not to be searched out; inscrutable –1681.

†**Imperse·verant,** *a.* [f. IM-² + PERSEVERANT.] Not persevering. BP. ANDREWES.

Impersonal (impə̄·ɹsənăl). 1520. [– late L. *impersonalis*; see IM-², PERSONAL. Cf. Fr. *impersonel*, †*-onal.*]

A. *adj.* **1.** *Gram.* A term applied to verbs when used only in the third person singular, as *it rains, methinks*, etc. (Many ordinary verbs have impersonal constructions.) **2.** Having no personal reference or connection; said of things 1630. **3.** Not possessing personality 1842.

3. Slaves being regarded as i. men 1875.

B. *sb.* **1.** *Gram.* An impersonal verb 1509. **2.** An impersonal thing or creature (*rare*) 1796.

Hence **Impersona·lity,** i. quality; an impersonal being or creation. **Impe·rsonalize** *v.* to render i: **Impe:rsonaliza·tion,** the action of rendering i.; an impersonalized condition or form. **Impe·rsonally** *adv.* in an i. manner.

Impersonate (impə̄·ɹsəne¹t), *v.* 1624. [f. L. *in-* IM-¹ + *persona* PERSON + -ATE³, after *incorporate.*] †**1.** *trans.* To embody in a person. **2.** To invest with a supposed personality; to personify 1624; to embody in one's own person; to typify 1855. **3.** To act (a character); to personate 1715.

2. His position was dignified and important, as impersonating the unity of the race STUBBS. **3.** To i. his [Shakespeare's] characters 1863. Hence **Impe·rsonator,** one who plays a part.

Impersonate (impə̄·ɹsənĕt), *ppl. a.* 1820. [Short for *impersonated*; see -ATE².] Embodied in a person; impersonated.

Impersonation (impə̄ɹsənē¹·ʃən). 1800. [f. IMPERSONATE *v.* + -ION.] **1.** The action of impersonating or fact of being impersonated; personification; *concr.* an instance of this. **2.** The dramatic representation of a character 1825.

1. The very i. of good-humour DICKENS.

Impersonify (impəɹsǫ·nifəi), *v.* 1804. [f. IM-¹ + PERSONIFY, after IMPERSONATE *v.*] *trans.* To represent in personal form; to personify. Hence **Imperso:nifica·tion** 1799.

†**Impe·rspicable** *a.* 1665. [– late L. *imperspicabilis*; see IM-², PERSPICABLE.] Not to be discerned; invisible.

Imperspicu·ity. 1659. [f. IM-² + PERSPICUITY. Cf. med.L. *imperspicuitas.*] The reverse of perspicuity; obscurity. So **Imperspi·cuous** *a.* (*rare*), obscure.

Imperspi·rable, *a.* Now *rare.* 1684. [f. IM-² + PERSPIRABLE.] Incapable of perspiration. Hence **Imperspirabi·lity.**

Impersua·dable, *a.* 1704. [f. IM-² + PERSUADABLE.] Not persuadable. Hence **Impersua·dableness.**

†**Impersua·sible,** *a.* 1576. [– OFr. *impersuasible* or med.L. *impersuasibilis*; see IM-², PERSUASIBLE.] = prec. Hence †**Impersuasibi·lity** 1549. †**Impersua·sibly** *adv.* 1659.

†**Impe·rtinacy,** erron. f. IMPERTINENCY.

Impertinence (impə̄·ɹtinĕns), *sb.* 1603. [– (O)Fr. *impertinence*, or f. next; see -ENCE.] **1.** The fact or character of not pertaining to the matter in hand; want of pertinence; irrelevance 1626; (with *pl.*) an irrelevance 1612. **2.** Inappropriateness, incongruity; triviality, trifling, folly, absurdity 1629; (with *pl.*) something which is inappropriate, etc. 1603. **3.** Interference with what lies beyond one's province; presumptuous or forward behaviour or speech, esp. to a superior; insolence. (The chief current sense in colloq. use.) 1712. **b.** (with *pl.*) An instance of this; a piece of impertinence 1822.

2. Unacquainted with the vain i. of forms 'JUNIUS'. **3.** Masters and mistresses sometimes provoke i. from their servants MRS. CHAPONE. **b.** We resent wholesome counsels as an i. HAZLITT. Hence **Impe·rtinence** *v.* to treat with i. (H. WALPOLE). So **Impe·rtinency** (in all senses) 1589.

Impertinent (impə̄·ɹtinĕnt), *a.* (*sb.*) ME. [– (O)Fr. *impertinent* or late L. *impertinens, -ent-* not pertinent, in med.L. inept; see IM-², PERTINENT.] †**1.** Not appertaining (*to*); unconnected; inconsonant –1810. **2.** Not pertaining to the matter in hand; not pertinent; not to the point; irrelevant. Now *rare* exc. in *Law.* ME. **3.** Not suitable to the circumstances; not consonant with reason; absurd, trivial, silly 1590. **4.** Const. *to* (*unto*): in senses 2 and 3. 1532. **5.** Of persons, etc.: Meddling beyond one's province; intrusive, presumptuous; insolent or saucy in speech or behaviour. (The chief current sense in colloq. use.) 1681. **6.** *sb.* An impertinent †matter, or person 1628.

1. I. to each other and to any common purpose COLERIDGE. **2.** *Temp.* I. ii. 138. **3.** In comparison of this, all other Knowledge is vain, light and i. HALE. **4.** I thynke it not impartinent vnto this matter 1564. **5.** I have been i. in interrupting you 1681. **6.** An inquistive i...medling where he has nothing to do 1710. Hence **Impe·rtinently** *adv.*

†**Impertra·nsible,** *a.* 1677. [– med.L. *impertransibilis*, f. *in-* IM-² + *pertransibilis* (Isidore), f. L. *per* PER- + *transire* go or pass through. See TRANSIT, -IBLE.] That cannot be passed through or crossed. Hence †**Impertransibi·lity.**

Imperturbable (impəɹtō·ɹbăb'l), *a.* 1450. [– late L. *imperturbabilis* (Augustine); see IM-², PERTURB *v.*, -ABLE. Cf. Fr. *imperturbable.*] Not liable to be mentally perturbed, agitated, or excited; serene, calm.

Great was the embarrassment..even of the i. Burleigh MOTLEY. Hence **Imperturbabi·lity, Impertu·rbableness,** i. quality or condition. **Impertu·rbably** *adv.* in an i. manner; calmly.

Imperturba·tion. 1648. [– late (eccl.) L. *imperturbatio* impassibility (Jerome, tr. Gr. ἀπάθεια); see IM-², PERTURBATION.] Freedom from perturbation; calmness.

Impertu·rbed, *a.* 1721. [f. IM-² + *perturbed.*] Not perturbed; undisturbed, unmoved.

Imperviable (impə̄·ɹviăb'l), *a.* 1816. [alt. of IMPERVIOUS with substitution of the more expressive suffix.] Impervious; impermeable. Hence **Imperviabi·lity. Impe·rviableness.**

Impervious (impə̄·ɹviəs), *a.* 1650. [f. L. *impervius* + -OUS; see IM-², PERVIOUS.] Through which there is no way; not affording passage (*to*); impermeable. Also *fig.*

1. The western channel into it is i., by reason of rocks PENNANT. *fig.* To deal with men i. to argument BUCKLE. Hence **Impe·rvious-ly** *adv.*, **-ness.**

†**I·mpery.** ME. Var. of EMPERY –1657.

Impest (impe·st), *v.* Also †**em-.** 1618. [– Fr. *empester*, f. *em-* EM-¹, IM-¹ + *peste* plague; see PEST.] *trans.* To infect with a plague or pestilence. Hence **Impesta·tion,** the action of impesting.

†**Impe·ster,** *v.* Also †**em-.** 1601. [– OFr. *empestrer* (mod. *empêtrer*) – pop.L. **impastoriare*, f. *in-* IM-¹ + L. *pastoria* (sc. *catena* chain) hobble for a horse.] *trans.* To hobble (a horse); to entangle, embarrass, encumber –1807.

Impeticos, *v.* A burlesque word; cf. *impocket* and *petticoat. Twel. N.* II. iii. 27.

‖**Impetigo** (impĭtəi·go). Pl. **-igines** (-i·dʒiniz). ME. [L., f. *impetere* assail, f. *in-* IM-¹ + *petere* seek.] A name for various pustular diseases of the skin, and in *pl.* for such diseases in general.

The leprosy of the Romans before the time of Cicero was the i. 1803. Hence **Impeti·ginous** *a.* pertaining to or of the nature of i.; 'scurfy; covered with small scabs' (J.).

†**I·mpetrable,** *a.* 1599. [– L. *impetrabilis*, f. *impetrare*; see next, -BLE. Cf. Fr. *impétrable.*] **1.** That may be obtained by request. HOBBES. **2.** Capable of effecting something, successful. NASHE.

†**I·mpetrate,** *ppl. a.* 1528. [– L. *impetratus*, pa. pple. of *impetrare*; see next, -ATE².] Obtained by request; impetrated –1722.

Impetrate (i·mpĕtrē¹t), *v.* 1533. [– *impetrat-*, pa. ppl. stem of L. *impetrare*, f. *in-* IM-¹ + *patrare* bring to an end; see -ATE³ and cf. PERPETRATE.] **1.** *trans.* To obtain by request or entreaty; to procure. Now chiefly *Theol.* (also in *Rom. Law*). **2.** To request, beseech, ask for. Now *rare.* 1565. Hence **I·mpetrative** (*rare*), **I·mpetratory** *adjs.* having the quality of obtaining by or as by request. var. †**Impetre** ME.

Impetration (impĕtrē¹·ʃən). 1484. [– AFr. *impetracioun* and L. *impetratio*, f. as prec.; see -ION.] **1.** The action of procuring by request or entreaty. (Chiefly *Theol.*) 1518. **b.** *Law.* The obtaining (of a writ) 1648. **c.** 'The pre-obtaining of church benefices in England from the court of Rome, which belonged to the gift and disposition of the king, and other lay-patrons of this realm' (Tomlins) 1484. **2.** Petition, supplication, request 1618.

1. c. That..penalties..should be attached to all i. of benefices from Rome by purchase or otherwise FROUDE.

Impetuosity (impe:tiu,ǫ·sĭti). 1585. [– (O)Fr. *impétuosité* – late L. *impetuositas*, f. *impetuosus*; see next, -ITY.] The quality or character of being impetuous; sudden or violent energy of movement, action, etc.; vehemence; (with *pl.*) an impetuous movement, action, or feeling.

You know the i. of my brother's temper FIELDING. Flames..issued forth with great i. 1811.

Impetuous (impe·tiu,əs), *a.* ME. [– (O)Fr. *impétueux* – late L. *impetuosus*, f. *impetus*; see next, -OUS, -UOUS.] **1.** Of physical things or actions: Having much impetus; moving with great force or violence; very rapid, forcibly rushing, violent 1489. **2.** Of feelings, etc., and hence of persons: Acting with or marked by great, sudden, or rash energy; vehement, violent, passionate ME.

1. Impietouse wyndes 1547; impittious haste SHAKS. That great and i. River RAY. **2.** The i. vivacity of youth JOHNSON. The i., ready to go at that which others are afraid to approach JOWETT. Hence **Impe·tuous-ly** *adv.*, **-ness.**

Impetus (i·mpĭtŏs). 1641. [– L. *impetus* assault, violent impulse, vehemence, f. *impetere* rush upon, assail, f. *in-* IM-¹ + *petere* seek.] **1.** The force with which a body moves and overcomes resistance; energy of motion; impulse, impulsion 1656. **b.** *Gunnery.* The altitude due to the initial velocity of a projectile, i.e..the space through which it must fall to attain an equal velocity; the force of projection as measured by this 1807. **2.** In ref. to feelings, actions, etc.: Moving force, impulse, stimulus 1641.

2. Fugitive Huguenots gave a fresh i. to weaving 1872.

Impeyan (i·mpiăn), *a.* (*sb.*) Also **Impeian.** 1870. [Named in 1787, after Sir Elijah and Lady *Impey*, who tried to naturalize the bird in England.] *Impeyan pheasant*: a kind of E. Indian pheasant (*Lophophorus impeyanus*), with crested head; the male has plumage of metallic hues. Also other species of *Lophophorus*. **b.** Of or belonging to this pheasant. **c.** *sb.* = I. pheasant.

‖**Imphee** (i·mfi). 1857. [*imfe*, native name in Natal.] A species of sugar-cane, *Holcus saccharatus* (Linn.), also called African or Chinese Sugar-cane, Broom Corn, Sorgho, and Planter's Friend.

‖**I·mpi.** 1879. [Zulu, = body or company, esp. of armed men.] A body of Kaffir warriors; a force, detachment, army.

Impicture (impi·ktiŭɹ), *v.* 1520. Also †**en-, em-.** [f. IM-[1] + PICTURE.] **1.** *trans.* To portray. †**2.** To impress as with a picture. SPENSER.

Impie·rce, var. of EMPIERCE *v.*

†**Impie·rceable,** *a.* ME. [f. IM-[2] + PIERCEABLE. In earliest use (XIV) perh. repr. an OFr. *imperceable.] Not pierceable; that cannot be pierced –1691.

Impiety (impəi·eti). ME. [– (O)Fr. *impiété* or L. *impietas, -tat-*, f. *impius*; see IMPIOUS, -ITY.] **1.** Want of reverence for God or religion; ungodliness; unrighteousness, wickedness. Also with *an* and *pl.* **2.** Absence of natural piety, as of child to parent; want of dutifulness; hence, want of reverence generally 1588.

1. The impietie of Arrius and other heretikes 1600. When I..had seene impieties without number 2 *Esd.* 3:29. **2.** An instance of filial i. 1899.

†**Impi·gnorate,** *pa. pple.* 1548. [– med.L. *impignoratus*, pa. pple of *impignorare* pledge, mortgage, f. *in-* IM-[1] + L. *pignus, pignor-* pledge; see -ATE[2].] Pledged, pawned, mortgaged –1684. So **Impi·gnorate** *v.* (chiefly *Sc.*) to place in pawn; to pledge, mortgage. **Impi:gnora·tion,** pledging, pawning, mortgage.

Imping (i·mpiŋ), *vbl. sb.* ME. [f. IMP *v.* + -ING[1].] The action of IMP *v.*; grafting, engrafting; the repairing of a hawk's wing with adscititious feathers. Also *attrib.*

Impinge (impi·ndʒ), *v.* 1535. [– L. *impingere*, f. *in-* IM-[1] + *pangere* fix, drive in.] **1.** *trans.* To fasten or fix on forcibly (*rare*). **2.** To strike, dash, hurl a thing *upon* something else; *refl.* = 4. 1660. **3.** To strike; to collide with. Now *rare.* 1777. **4.** *intr.* To strike or dash; to come into (violent) contact; to collide 1605. Also *fig.* **5.** To encroach or infringe *on* or *upon* 1758.

4. A ship that is void of a Pilot, must needs i. upon the next rock or sands BURTON. Rays of light impinging on the retina give rise to sensory impulses 1878. Hence **Impi·ngement,** impact, collision (*lit.* and *fig.*); encroachment. So **Impi·ngent** *a.* (*rare*), impinging.

†**Impi·nguate,** *v.* 1620. [– *impinguat-*, pa. ppl. stem of L. *impinguare*, f. *in-* IM-[1] + *pinguis* fat; see -ATE[3].] *trans.* To make fat; to fatten –1693. Hence †**Impingua·tion.**

Impious (i·mpiəs), *a.* 1575. [f. L. *impius* (see IM-[2], PIOUS) + -OUS.] **1.** Not pious; without piety or reverence for God and his ordinances; presumptuously irreligious, wicked, or profane. **2.** Wanting in natural reverence and dutifulness, esp. to parents (*rare*) 1613.

1. Canst thou with i. obloquie condemne The just Decree of God? MILT. *P. L.* v. 813. E'er i. plow to wound the earth began T. BROWN. Hence **I·mpious-ly** *adv.*, **-ness.**

Impish (i·mpiʃ), *a.* 1652. [f. IMP *sb.* + -ISH[1].] Having the characteristics of an imp. Hence **I·mpish-ly** *adv.*, **-ness.**

Impiteous (impi·tiəs), *a.* 1877. [f. IM-[2] + PITEOUS.] Pitiless.

Implacable (implæ·kăb'l, -plēⁱ·kăb'l), *a.* 1450. [– Fr. *implacable* or L. *implacabilis*; see IM-[2], PLACABLE.] **1.** That cannot be appeased; irreconcilable; inexorable. †**2.** That cannot be assauged or mitigated –1862.

1. The i. enemy of Bourbon 1769. Sectaries..i. of those who differed from them 1785. **2.** O how I burne with i. fire SPENSER *F.Q.* II. vi. 44. Hence **Implacabi·lity,** the condition of being i. **Impla·cableness. Impla·cably** *adv.*

Impla·cement, var. of EMPLACEMENT.

Implacental (implăse·ntăl). 1839. [f. IM-[2] + PLACENTAL. Cf. mod.L. *Implacentalia* (name of the group) and PLACENTALIA.] *Zool.* **a.** *adj.* Having no placenta, a term applied to the group of mammals consisting of the marsupials and monotremes (*Implacentalia*). **b.** *sb.* A mammal having no placenta 1864. So **Implace·ntate** *a.* (Dicts.)

Implant (implɑ·nt), *v.* 1541. Also †**em-.** [– Fr. *implanter* or late L. *implantare* engraft; see IM-[1], PLANT *v.*] **1.** *trans.* To plant in, insert, infix. Chiefly *pass.* 1545. **2.** To fix or instil (a principle, etc.) *in* one. Chiefly *pass.* (The ordinary use.) 1541. †**b.** To engraft (a bud). Also *fig. rare.* –1675. **3.** To plant. Also *fig.* 1610.

2. They are both inclinations of nature, implanted of God 1541. **3.** Those [herbs] which the gardiner implanteth 1753. *fig.* Minds well implanted with solid and elaborate breeding MILT. Hence **Impla·nter.**

Implantation (implɑntēⁱ·ʃən). 1578. [– Fr. *implantation*, f. *implanter*; see prec., -ATION.] The action or process of implanting; the fact or manner of being implanted. Also *attrib.*

Implate (implēⁱ·t), *v. rare.* [f. IM-[1] + PLATE *sb.*] *trans.* To cover with plates; to sheathe (Dicts.).

Implausible (implǭ·zib'l), *a.* 1602. [f. IM-[2] + PLAUSIBLE.] †**1.** Not worthy of applause; unacceptable. WARNER. **2.** Not having the appearance of truth, probability, or acceptability; not plausible 1677.

2. The art of making plausible or i. harangues SWIFT. Hence **Implausibi·lity, Implau·sibleness,** want of plausibility. **Implau·sibly** *adv.*

Impleach (implī·tʃ), *v. poet.* 1597. Also †**em-.** [f. IM-[1] + PLEACH.] To entwine, interweave.

Implead (implī·d), *v.* [ME. *en-, emplede* – AFr. *en-, empleder* = OFr. *empleidier*, etc.; see EM-, IM-[1], PLEAD.] **1.** *trans.* To sue (a person, etc.) in a court of justice, raise an action against. Now only *arch.* or *Hist.* †**2.** To arraign, accuse, impeach. Const. *of.* –1846. **3.** *nonce-use.* To plead *with* 1839.

1. To sue or be sued, i. or be impleaded BLACKSTONE. Hence †**Implea·dable** *a.*[1] that may be sued (as a person) or prosecuted (as a suit) 1570; capable of being pleaded 1648. †**Implea·der,** a prosecutor, accuser, or impeacher 1577.

†**Implea·dable,** *a.*[2] 1607. [f. IM-[2] + PLEADABLE.] Not to be pleaded against, or met by any plea –1614.

†**Implea·sing,** *a. rare.* 1602. [f. IM-[2] + PLEASING *ppl. a.*] Unpleasing –1613.

Impledge (imple·dʒ), *v.* 1548. Also †**em-.** [f. IM-[1] + PLEDGE *sb.*] *trans.* To pledge, pawn; to give as security; to engage.

Implement (i·mplĭmĕnt), *sb.* 1454. [– med.L. *implementa* (pl.) noun of instrument corresp. to med.L. *implēre* employ, spend, extended use (by assoc. with *implicare*, EMPLOY) of L. *implēre* fill up, fulfil, discharge, f. *in-* IM-[1] + *plēre* fill.]

I. 1. *pl.* Things that serve as equipment or outfit, as household furniture, ecclesiastical vestments, etc. In *sing.* An article of furniture, dress, etc. †**b.** *gen.* Requisites –1752. **2.** *pl.* The apparatus, instruments, etc. employed in any trade or in executing any piece of work; as *agricultural implements, flint implements*, etc. In *sing.* A tool, instrument. 1538. Also *fig.*

2. *fig.* Those Sciential rules, which are the implements of instruction MILTON.

II. †**1.** Something necessary to make a thing complete (*rare*) –1650. **2.** *Sc. Law.* Full performance 1678.

Hence **Impleme·ntal** *a.* of the nature of an i. or implements 1676.

Implement (i·mplĭmĕnt), *v.* Chiefly *Sc.* 1806. [f. IMPLEMENT *sb.* II., which repr. late L. *implementum* filling up, noun of action of L. *implēre* (prec.).] **1.** *trans.* To complete, perform; to fulfil. **2.** To complete, supplement 1843. **3.** To provide with implements 1886.

1. To i. an obligation 1806, an order of court 1833. The chief mechanical requisites of the barometer are implemented in such an instrument as the following NICHOL. **2.** To i. wages by pauper relief 1843.

Implete (implī·t), *v. U.S.* 1862. [– *implet-*, pa. ppl. stem of L. *implēre* fill up, f. *in-* IM-[1] + *plēre* fill.] *trans.* To fill.

Impletion (implī·ʃən). 1583. [– late and med. eccl. L. *impletio*, f. as prec.; see -ION.] **1.** The action of filling; the being filled; fullness. †**2.** Fulfilment (of prophecy) –1716.

†**Imple·tive,** *a. rare.* 1647. [f. *implet-*, pa. ppl. stem of L. *implēre* fill up, + -IVE.] Having the quality of filling –1677.

†**I·mplex,** *a. rare.* 1710. [– L. *implexus*, pa. pple. of *implectere* entwine, f. *in-* IM-[1] + *plectere* twist, plait. Perh. through Fr. *implexe*, in same sense as Eng.] Involved; having a complicated plot. ADDISON *Spect.* No. 297 ¶ 2. So †**Implexed** *ppl. a.* 1619. **Imple·xion,** complication, intertwining 1678.

Impliable (impləi·ăb'l), *a.*[1] *rare.* 1734. [f. IM-[2] + PLIABLE.] Not pliable; inflexible.

Impli·able, *a.*[2] 1865. [f. IMPLY *v.* + -ABLE.] Capable of being implied.

Implicate (i·mplikĕt), *a.* and *sb.* 1450. [– L. *implicatus*, pa. pple. of *implicare*; see next, -ATE[1, 2].]

A. *adj.* **1.** Intertwined, twisted together; also, wrapped up *with*, entangled *in.* †**2.** Intricate –1637. Hence †**I·mplicateness.**

B. *sb.* †**1.** Entanglement, confusion. SANDERSON. **2.** That which is implied 1881.

Implicate (i·mplikeⁱt), *v.* 1600. [– *implicat-*, pa. ppl. stem of L. *implicare*, f. *in-* IM-[1] + *plicare* fold; see -ATE[3].] **1.** *trans.* To intertwine; to entwine, entangle 1610. **2.** To involve; to bring into connection *with* 1600.

1. [They] i., and intangle themselves together so, as to make, as it were, little knots BOYLE. **2.** It implicates a contradiction 1600. In no conspiracy against the government had a Quaker been implicated MACAULAY. The brain is pathologically implicated in insanity 1887. Hence **I·mplicative** *a.* Having the quality of implying 1602; †*sb.* a statement or writing implying more than it expressly states 1589. **I·mplicatively** *adv.* ?*Obs.* 1579.

Implication (implikēⁱ·ʃən). ME. [– L. *implicatio*, f. as prec.; see -ION.] **1.** The action of implicating; the condition of being implicated. Also *fig.* **2.** The action of implying; the fact of being implied or involved, without being plainly expressed; that which is involved or implied in something else 1581. **3.** The process of involving or fact of being involved in some condition, etc. 1873.

1. The implications of the sinewes of the arme 1578. The mystic i. of his nature with ours J. MARTINEAU. **2.** Phr. *By i.*: by what is implied, by natural inference. Either expressly or by i. 1793.

Implicit (impli·sit), *a.* 1599. [– Fr. *implicite* (Calvin) or L. *implicitus*, later form of *implicatus*, pa. pple. of *implicere* IMPLICATE *v.*] †**1.** Entangled, entwined; involved –1803; involved in each other; overlapping, as, *i. years* –1704. **2.** Implied though not plainly expressed; naturally or necessarily involved in something else 1599. **3.** Resting on the authority of another without doubt or inquiry; unquestioning, absolute; as, *i. faith, belief, confidence, obedience, submission*, etc. 1610. †**b.** Hence, *erron.*: Absolute, unmitigated –1651. **c.** *transf.* Of persons: Characterized by implicit faith, credulity, or obedience ?*Obs.* 1694.

1. The..bush with frizl'd hair i. MILT. *P. L.* VII. 323. **2.** I. threats 1665, Atheists 1633, desires GEO. ELIOT. The undeveloped conceptions that lay i. in it SAYCE. **3. b.** When the Peace is grounded, but vpon an implicite ignorance BACON. Hence **Impli·cit-ly** *adv.*, **-ness.** So †**Impli·city,** entanglement, complication, involution.

Implied (impləi·d), *ppl. a.* 1529. [f. IMPLY *v.* + -ED[1].] Contained or stated by implication; involved in what is expressed; necessarily intended though not expressed; see IMPLY *v.*

Phr. *I. contract, warranty*, etc.: see these wds. So **Impli·edly** *adv.* by implication, implicitly 1400.

Implode (implōᵘ·d), *v.* 1881. [f. IM-[1] + L. *plodere, plaudere* to clap, after EXPLODE.] **1.** *intr.* and *trans.* To burst inwards. **2.** *trans.* To utter or pronounce by implosion. Hence **Implo·dent,** an implosive sound.

Imploration (implorēⁱ·ʃən). 1577. [– Fr. †*imploration* or L. *imploratio*, f. *implorat-*, pa. ppl. stem of *implorare*; see IMPLORE, -ION.] The action of imploring; earnest supplication.

†**Implora·tor.** 1602. [– med.L. *implorator*, f. as prec.; see -OR 2. Cf. Fr. †*implorateur* (XVI).] One who implores.

Meere implorators of vnholy Sutes *Haml.* I. iii. 129. So **Implo·ratory** *a.* (*rare*), of imploring or beseeching nature 1832.

Implore (implōᵊ·ɹ), *v.* 1500. [– Fr. *implorer*

or L. *implorare* invoke with tears, f. *in-* IM-[1] + *plorare* weep.] **1.** *trans.* **a.** To beg or pray for (aid, pardon, etc.) with touching entreaties; to ask for in supplication; to beseech. †Formerly sometimes with two objects. 1540. **b.** To beseech (a person) with deep emotion (to do something) 1603. **2.** *intr.* To utter touching supplications 1500.

1. a. Hee might plainely discerne her dolorous gesture in the act of imploring his succour 1632. Hence †**Implo·re,** *sb.* imploration, entreaty. **Implo·rer** (*rare*). **Implo·ring-ly** *adv.*, **-ness.**

Implosion (implōᵘ·ʒən). 1877. [f. IM-[1] + *-plosion*; of EXPLOSION.] **1.** The bursting inwards of a vessel from external pressure 1880. **2.** *Phonetics.* (See quot.) 1877.

2. The i. consists in closing the glottis simultaneously with the stop position, and then compressing the air between the glottis stoppage and the mouth one SWEET. So **Implo·sive** *a.* and *sb.* (a sound) formed by implosion.

Implume (impl[i]ū·m), *v. rare.* 1612. [var. of contemp. EMPLUME; see EM- *prefix.*] = EMPLUME *v.*

Implu·med, *a. rare.* 1604. [See prec., -ED[1].] Unfeathered, unfledged; deprived of feathers.

Implunge (implʊ·ndʒ), *v.* 1590. [f. IM-[1] + PLUNGE *v.*] *trans.* To plunge *in* or *into.* Now *rare.*

‖**Impluvium** (impl[i]ū·viŏm). 1811. [L., f. *impluere* rain into.] In ancient Roman houses, the square basin situated in the middle of the atrium or hall, which received the rainwater from the COMPLUVIUM or open space in the roof. (But occas. = *compluvium.*)

Imply (impləi·), *v.* ME. [– OFr. *emplier* :– L. *implicare* IMPLICATE. See also EMPLOY.] †**1.** *trans.* To enfold, enwrap, entangle, involve; in *lit.* and *fig.* senses –1823. **2.** To involve or comprise logically; to involve the truth or existence of (something not expressly asserted or maintained) 1529. **b.** Of a word or name: To involve by signification; to import, mean 1630. **3.** To express indirectly; to insinuate 1581. †**4.** = EMPLOY *v.* –1659. ¶**5.** To refer, ascribe; = APPLY *v.* I. 9. *Obs.* 1655.

1. Phœbus. .His blushing face in foggy cloud implyes SPENSER. **2.** In Job. .mention is made of fish-hooks, which must i. Anglers in those times WALTON. There are situations in which despair does not i. inactivity BURKE. **5.** Whence might this distaste arise?. .Is it. .your perverse and peevish will, To which I most i. it? WEBSTER & ROWLEY.

Impo·cket, *v.* Also **em-.** 1728. [IM-[1].] *trans.* To put into one's pocket; to pocket.

Impoison, obs. f. EMPOISON.

†**Impo·larily,** *adv.* 1646. [f. IM-[2] + POLARILY (Sir Thomas Browne).] Not according to polarity.

Impolder (impōᵘ·ldəɹ), *v.* 1899. [– Du. *inpolderen*: see IM-[1] and POLDER.] *trans.* To make a polder of; to reclaim from the sea.

Impolicy (impǫ·lisi). 1747. [f. IM-[2] + POLICY *sb.*[1], after *impolitic.*] The quality of being impolitic; bad policy; inexpediency.

An act of such flagrant i. and injustice 1798.

Impolite (impoləi·t), *a.* 1612. [– L. *impolitus*, f. *in-* IM-[2] + *politus* POLITE.] Not polished; wanting polish; rude, rough; discourteous. **Impoli·te-ly** *adv.*, **-ness.**

Impolitic (impǫ·litik), *a.* 1600. [f. IM-[2] + POLITIC.] Not politic; not according to good policy; unsuitable for the end desired; inexpedient.

The most unjust and i. of all things, unequal taxation BURKE. So †**Impoli·tical** *a.* Hence **Impoli·tically, Impo·liticly** *advs.* in an i. manner. **Impo·liticness,** impolicy.

Imponderable (impǫ·ndĕrăb'l). 1794. [f. IM-[2] + PONDERABLE (Sir Thomas Browne).] **A.** *adj.* Not ponderable; *spec.* in *Physics*, having no weight, as the luminiferous ether. **b.** Having no appreciable weight 1846. **B.** *sb.* An imponderable substance, etc. 1842.

Hence **Imponderabi·lity,** i. quality. **Impo·nderableness. Impo·nderably** *adv.* without any weight.

Imponderous (impǫ·ndĕrəs), *a. rare.* 1646. [f. IM-[2] + PONDEROUS.] Without weight; imponderable; *loosely*, extremely light. Hence **Impo·nderousness.**

†**Impo·ne,** *v.* 1529. [– L. *imponere*, f. *in-* IM-[1] + *ponere* place.] *trans.* To place upon something; to impose –1729. **b.** To 'lay', stake, wager. (Doubtful. Cf. IMPAWN.) *Haml.* V. ii. 155 (1623).

Imponent (impōᵘ·nĕnt). 1842. [Formally a variant, with the senses of IMPOSE *v.*, of IMPOSER, after pairs like *opponent, opposer.*] **A.** *adj.* That imposes T. H. GREEN. **B.** *sb.* One who imposes 1842.

†**Impoo·r,** *v.* 1613. [f. IM-[1] + POOR; cf. *enrich.*] To impoverish.

†**Impo·pular,** *a.* 1721. [f. IM-[2] + POPULAR.] Unpopular. Hence †**Impo·pularly** *adv.*

Imporous (impǭ[ə]·rəs), *a.* ? *Obs.* 1646. [f. IM-[2] + POROUS.] Not porous; having no pores. var. †**Imporo·se.**

Hence †**Imporo·sity** (rare) 1626.

Import (i·mpoɹt, *formerly* impōᵊ·ɹt), *sb.* 1588. [f. IMPORT *v.*]

I. 1. The fact of importing or signifying something; that which a thing imports; purport, meaning 1601. **2.** Consequence, importance 1588.

1. Words of dubious i. BYRON. **2.** Most serious designes, and of great i. indeed too *L. L. L.* V. i. 106.

II. 1. That which is imported or brought in from abroad. (Usu. in *pl.*) Opp. to *export.* Also *attrib.* 1690. **2.** The action of importing; importation 1797.

1. The Imports exceed the Exports CHILD. **2.** It is an error. .to look on the balance of trade as a mere question of i. and export GOSCHEN.

Import (impōᵊ·ɹt), *v.* ME. [– L. *importare* carry or bring in, f. *in-* IM-[1] + *portare* carry. In sense 5 in its med.L. sense of 'imply, mean' (so Fr. *importer*).]

I. From cl. L. *importare.* **1.** *trans.* To bring in; to introduce from abroad, or from one use or connection to another 1508. **2.** *spec.* To bring in (goods or merchandise) from a foreign country, in international commerce. Opp. to *export.* 1548. **3.** To convey to another, communicate (information). Merged in I. 1 and 5. 1565. †**4.** To bring about; to carry with it as a consequence or result –1705. **5.** To involve; to imply 1529; to convey in its meaning; to signify, denote 1533; to bear as its purport; to express, state, make known ME.; to portend 1591.

1. They imported with them into England the old Runic language and letters WARTON. **2.** We i. things of great value, and, in return, export little or nothing BURKE. **5.** Release. .by deed under seal. .imports valuable consideration and creates an estoppel 1884. The levee was exactly what the word imports MACAULAY. They. .passed a resolution importing [etc.] MACAULAY. Comets importing change of Times and States SHAKS.

II. From med.L., It. *importare*, Fr. *importer.* **1.** *intr.* To involve a considerable result (actual or possible); to be important, signify, matter. (Only in 3rd person.) *arch.* 1588. **2.** *trans.* To concern. (Only in 3rd person.) 1561.

1. Neither imported it where we lodged MORYSON. **2.** A question that imports us nearly 1865. Let me say. .what it imports thee to know SCOTT.

III. From Fr. *emporter.* †**1. a.** To lead (a person *to do* something). EVELYN. †**b.** To influence in feeling, carry away. EVELYN. †**2.** To gain, win (victory). **b.** *intr.* To gain the victory, prevail. **c.** *trans.* To overcome. –1624.

2. b. But Scipio imported and prevailed in the end P. HOLLAND.

†**Importable,** *a.*[1] ME. [– OFr. *importable* – late L. *importabilis* unbearable, f. *in-* IM-[2] + *portabilis* bearable, PORTABLE.] That cannot be carried or borne; usu. *fig.* unendurable –1651. Hence †**Impo·rtableness.** †**Impo·rtably** *adv.*

Importable (impōᵊ·ɹtăb'l), *a.*[2] 1533. [f. IMPORT *v.* + -ABLE.] Capable of being imported or introduced. Hence **Importabi·lity,** capability of being imported or introduced.

Importance (impǭ·ɹtăns, -pōᵊ·ɹ-). 1505. [– Fr. *importance* – med.L. *importantia* significance, consequence; see next, -ANCE.]

I. 1. The fact or quality of being important; moment, significance, gravity, consequence 1508. **b.** Personal consequence 1678. †**2.** An affair of consequence –1670. †**3.** Urgency; importunity –1781.

1. Emploienge treasour. .on thynges. .of small importaunce ELYOT. **b.** A family. .of some i. 1874. **2.** *Cymb.* I. iv. 45. **3.** *John* II. 1. 7.

†**II. 1.** Income, revenue. *Sc. Obs.* 1505–33. **2.** = IMPORT *sb.* 1. –1709. **b.** Bearing 1691.

2. The wisest beholder. .could not say if th' i. were Ioy or Sorrow SHAKS. So †**Impo·rtancy** = prec. I.

Important (impǭ·ɹtănt, -pōᵊ·ɹ-), *a.* 1586. [– Fr. *important* – med.L. *importans, -ant-*, f. *importare* 'be of consequence, weight, or force' (cf. IMPORT *v.*); see -ANT.] **1.** Having much import or significance; weighty, grave, significant. **2.** Having an air of importance; consequential 1713. †**3.** Urgent, pressing, importunate –1630.

1. How. .i. is it to every man to be frequented with learning 1586. **2.** Discoursing, with i. face, On ribbons, fans, and gloves and lace SWIFT. **3.** *Much Ado* II. i. 74. Hence **Impo·rtantly** *adv.* weightily; consequentially.

Importation (impoɹtēⁱ·ʃən). 1601. [f. IMPORT *v.* + -ATION. (Hence in Fr.)] **1. a.** *Commerce.* The action of importing goods, etc. from abroad; opp. to *exportation.* **b.** *gen.* Bringing in, introduction 1666. **2.** *concr.* †Imports collectively; an imported article 1664.

2. Solomon's i., Gold and apes POPE.

Importer (impōᵊ·ɹtəɹ). 1700. [f. IMPORT *v.* + -ER[1].] One who or that which imports or introduces; *esp.* a merchant who imports goods from abroad.

Impo·rting, *ppl. a.* 1579. [f. as prec. + -ING[2].] †**1.** That imports or signifies; important –1654. **2.** That imports merchandise 1812.

†**Impo·rtless,** *a.* [f. IMPORT *sb.* I. + -LESS.] Without import; trivial. *Tr. & Cr.* I. iii. 71.

†**Impo·rtunable,** *a.* 1482. [In sense 1 f. IMPORTUNITY, after *discomfort/discomfortable.* In sense 2 f. IMPORTUNATE *a.*; see -ABLE.] **1.** Burdensome, heavy –1611. **2.** Troublesome 1566.

Importunacy (impǭ·ɹtiunăsi). 1548. [f. IMPORTUNATE *a.*; see -ACY.] IMPORTUNITY 3.

Importunate (impǭ·ɹtiunĕt), *a.* 1477. [f. L. *importunus* (see IMPORTUNE *a.*) + -ATE[2], perh. on the model of *obstinate.*] †**1.** Inopportune, untimely –1659. †**2.** Burdensome; grave –1824; troublesome –1691. **3.** Pressing, urgent; busy. *Obs.* or *arch.* 1542. **4.** Persistent in solicitation; pertinacious 1477.

3. I. busines 1542. **4.** I. creditors 1863. Hence **Impo·rtunate-ly** *adv.*, **-ness.**

Importunate (impǭ·ɹtiuneⁱt), *v.* 1598. [f. prec.; see -ATE[3].] = IMPORTUNE *v.* 3. Hence **Impo·rtunator,** one who importunes.

Importune (impǫɹtiū·n, impǭ·ɹtiun), *a.* (*sb.*) ME. [– Fr. *importun, -une* or L. *importunus* applied to waves and storms, opp. to *opportunus* OPPORTUNE, f. *in-* IM-[2] + *Portunus* the protecting god of harbours.] †**1.** Inopportune, untimely; unfit –1704. †**2.** Troublesome, burdensome; vexatious; heavy, exacting –1864. †**3.** = IMPORTUNATE *a.* 3. –1647. **4.** Persistent in solicitation; pertinacious; irksome through importunity 1447. †**5.** *sb.* One who is importune. [= Fr. *importun.*] –1734.

1. A Wild Ass, with Brayings I. SWIFT. **4.** Yet seynge this weddowe is so i. vpon me I will delyuer her COVERDALE *Luke* 18:5. Hence **Importu·nely** *adv.* (now *rare*).

Importune (impǫɹtiū·n, impǭ·ɹtiun), *v.* 1530. [– Fr. *importuner* or med.L. *importunari*, f. L. *importunus*; see prec.] †**1.** *trans.* To burden; to trouble, worry, pester, annoy –1788. †**2.** To press, urge. Also *absol.* –1615. **3.** To solicit pressingly or persistently; to beset with petitions 1530. **4.** To ask for (a thing) urgently and persistently 1588. **5.** *intr.* To be importunate 1548. ¶**6.** To import, portend. (A Spenserian misuse.) 1590.

2. *Meas. for M.* I. i. 57. **3.** Ye were importun'd the passing it MILT. **5.** Too poor for a bribe, and too proud to i.; He had not the method of making a fortune GRAY. Hence **Importuner.**

Importunity (impǫɹtiū·nĭti). 1450. [– (O)Fr. *importunité* – L. *importunitas*, f. *importunus*; see prec., -ITY.] †**1.** The condition of being inopportune; unseasonableness; an unsuitable time –1589. †**2.** Burdensomeness, trouble –1739. **3.** Troublesome pertinacity in solicitation 1460.

3. Because of hys importunite he woll ryse and geve hym as many as he nedeth TINDALE *Luke* 11:8.

Imposable (impōᵘ·zăb'l), *a. rare.* 1660. [f.

IMPOSE *v.* + -ABLE.] **1.** That may be imposed or laid on. **2.** That may be imposed upon; gullible 1734. Hence **Impo·sableness.**

Impose (impōu·z), *v.* 1484. Also †**em-.** [– (O)Fr. *imposer*, †*emposer*, f. *em-*, *im-* IM-[1] + *poser*, to repr. L. *imponere* place on or into, inflict, set over, lay as a burden, deceive, trick; see POSE *v.*[1]]

I. *trans.* **1.** To lay on or set on; to put, place, or deposit (*arch.*) 1597. **b.** *Eccl.* To lay on hands in blessing, or in ordination, confirmation, etc. 1582. **c.** *Printing.* To lay pages of type or stereotype plates in proper order on the imposing-stone or the bed of a press, and secure them in a chase 1652. **2.** *fig.* **a.** *gen.* To put, place; to place authoritatively 1681. **b.** To bestow (a name or title) *upon, on*, †*to* 1500. †**c.** To put authoritatively (an end, conclusion, etc.) to –1611. †**3.** To lay (a crime) to the account of; to impute. (The earliest use.) –1663. **4.** To lay on; to inflict (something) *on* or *upon* 1581. **5.** To 'put' (a thing) *upon* (a person) by false representations; to palm off 1650.

1. She impos'd a stone Close to the cauernes mouth CHAPMAN. **2. b.** The name was imposed antecedent to his birth 1774. **4.** What Fates i., that men must needs abide SHAKS. Minos..imposed upon the Athenians a cruel tribute JOWETT. To i. duties on foreign merchandise 1863. **5.** To i. such a Cheat upon the World 1681.

II. *intr.* **1.** To put oneself *upon* (in various senses) 1625. **2.** To put a tax, to levy an impost (*upon*). ?*Obs.* 1618. **3.** To practise imposture; also with *on, upon* 1662.

1. When it [Truth] is found, it imposeth vpon mens Thoughts BACON. To i. upon a generous person 1694, on the good nature of others 1883. **2.** To restraine the Crowne from imposing upon the people without their consent 1642. **3.** To be imposed upon by fine Things and false Addresses STEELE.

Hence †**Impo·se** *sb.* (*rare*), the imposition of a charge, duty, or task 1591–1605. **Impo·sement** (*rare*), imposition 1664. **Impo·ser** 1597.

Imposing (impōu·ziŋ), *vbl. sb.* 1610. [f. IMPOSE *v.* + -ING[1].] The action of imposing; imposition. **b.** *Printing.* The arrangement of pages of type in a forme 1727.

attrib. **i.-stone, -table,** a slab of stone or metal on which pages of type or stereotype plates are imposed.

Imposing (impōu·ziŋ), *ppl. a.* 1651. [f. as prec. + -ING[2].] **1.** That peremptorily enjoins; exacting. **2.** That impresses by appearance or manner 1786. **3.** Using deception; practising imposture 1754.

2. Mountains..of i. magnitude TYNDALL. Hence **Impo·sing-ly** *adv.*, **-ness.**

Imposition (impŏzi·ʃən). ME. [– (O)Fr. *imposition* or L. *impositio*; see IM-[1], POSITION.] **1.** The action of putting, placing, or laying on 1597. **b.** *spec.* The laying on of hands in blessing, ordination, confirmation, etc. ME. **c.** *Printing.* The imposing or arranging of pages of type in the forme 1824. **2.** The action of attaching, affixing, or ascribing; bestowal (of a name, etc.) ME. †**3.** Accusation. *Wint. T.* I. ii. 74. **4.** The action of imposing; the action of inflicting, levying, or enjoining 1593; †taxation –1628. **5.** Anything imposed, levied, or enjoined; an impost; tax, duty 1460; †an injunction –1664; an exercise or task imposed as a punishment at school or college 1746; †in 17th c. Puritanical use, a dogma or ceremony imposed without scriptural warrant. **6.** The action of deceiving by palming off what is false or unreal; an instance of this, an imposture 1632.

1. The i. of my hand on his forehead, instantly put a stop to his spasms MEDWIN. **b.** Thus..the grace of God is given by the i. of hands JER. TAYLOR. **4.** The superstitious impositions of fasts BURTON. **6.** The predictions..were mere impositions on the people SWIFT.

Impossibilist (impǫ·sibilist). 1900. [f. IMPOSSIBLE + -IST.] One who advocates a policy which is impossible of realization. So **Impo·ssibilism.**

Impossibi·litate, *v. rare.* 1633. [In XVII = med.L. *impossibilitare* (XIV), f. L. *impossibilitas* IMPOSSIBILITY. Cf. Sp. *imposibilitar*, It. *impossibilitare*.] *trans.* To render impossible.

Impossibility (impǫsibi·lĭti). ME. [–(O)Fr. *impossibilité* or L. *impossibilitas*, f. *impossibilis*; see next, -ITY.] **1.** The quality of being impossible; (with *an* and *pl.*) an impossible thing. †**2.** Impotence, inability –1796.

1. The i. that his Intelligence could be true CLARENDON. Is not every genius an i. till he appear? CARLYLE.

Impossible (impǫ·sĭb'l). ME. [– (O)Fr. *impossible* or L. *impossibilis*; see IM-[2], POSSIBLE.]

A. *adj.* **1.** Not possible; that cannot be done, exist, or come into being; that cannot be, in existing or specified circumstances. Const. *to* or *for*. **2.** *Math.* Having no possible or real value, imaginary 1673. **3.** In recent use, with ellipsis of some qualification implied by the context; as, impossible to deal with or recognize, etc.; 'out of the question' 1858.

1. They..laughed therat as at an i. lye MORE. Craggie cliff..i. to climbe MILT. *P. L.* IV. 548. **3.** Oxford..home of..i. loyalties! M. ARNOLD. The ..ghosts..made the place absolutely i. 1884.

B. *sb.* = IMPOSSIBILITY (*rare* in *sing.*) ME. With *the*: That which is or seems impossible 1845. Hence **Impo·ssibleness** (*rare*). **Impo·ssibly** *adv.*

Impost[1] (i·mpōust). 1568. [– Fr. †*impost* (now *impôt*) – med.L. *impostus, -um*, subst. use of *impostus, impositus*, pa. pple. of L. *imponere* IMPOSE.] **1.** A tax, duty, imposition, tribute; *spec.* a customs-duty levied on merchandise. Now chiefly *Hist.* (Dicts., following Cowell, make *impost* a duty on *imported* goods; but this limitation wants evidence.) **2.** *Racing slang.* The weight which a horse has to carry in a handicap race 1883.

1. A bench of Judges..declared the new i. [shipmoney] to be legal J. R. GREEN.

Impost[2] (i·mpōust). 1664. [– Fr. *imposte* or its source It. *imposta*, subst. use of fem. pa. pple. of *imporre* :– L. *imponere* IMPOSE.] *Arch.* **1.** The upper course of a pillar or abutment, frequently projecting in the form of an ornamental moulding or capital, on which the foot of an arch rests. (Where there is no projection, the impost is called *continuous*.) **2.** A horizontal block supported by upright stones, as at Stonehenge. Also *attrib.* 1768.

†**Impo·sterous,** *a.* 1562. [f. *imposter* IMPOSTOR, or perh. f. IMPOSTURE + -OUS.] **1.** Of the nature of an imposture; false –1665. **2.** Having the character of an impostor –1652.

Imposthume: see IMPOSTUME.

Impostor (impǫ·stəɹ). 1586. [– Fr. *imposteur* – late L. *impostor*, contr. of *impositor* (cf. IMPOST[1]), f. pa. ppl. stem of L. *imponere* IMPOSE; see -OR 2.] One who imposes on others; a deceiver, swindler, cheat; now chiefly one who passes himself off as some one other than he is. Also *attrib.*

Being found a meere I., he dyed most miserably 1624. So †**Imposto·rious** 1623, **Impo·storous** 1548 *adjs.* having the character of an i. or imposture. Hence **Impo·storship,** the office or character of an i. 1620. †**Impo·story** (*rare*) = IMPOSTURE 1653. **Impo·stress** 1614, †**Impo·strix** 1655 (both *rare*), a female i.

Impostrous (impǫ·strəs), *a.* 1612. [abbrev. of IMPOSTEROUS or -OROUS; cf. *monster, -trous*.] **1.** Having the character of an impostor. **2.** Of the nature of an imposture 1635.

1. An i. pretender to knowledge GROTE. **2.** I. lies 1635.

†**Impo·stumate, -thumate,** *ppl. a.* 1601. [Altered f. *apostumate* APOSTEMATE *ppl. a.*, after IMPOSTUME.] Affected with impostumes; of the nature of an impostume. Also *fig.* –1764.

†**Impo·stumate, -thumate** *v.* 1592. [Altered f. *apostumate* APOSTEMATE *v.*, after IMPOSTUME; cf. prec.] **1.** *trans.* To affect with an impostume –1758. **2.** *intr.* To swell into an impostume; to fester, gather –1762. So **Impostuma·tion, -thuma·tion** (now *rare*), suppuration; = IMPOSTUME *sb.* 1524.

Impostume, -thume (impǫ·stiŭm), *sb.* Now *rare.* ME. [– OFr. *empostume*, alt. of *apostume*, later form of *aposteme*; see APOSTEM(E).] **1.** A purulent swelling or cyst in any part of the body; an abscess. **2.** *fig.* **a.** A moral or political festering sore; the swelling of pride, etc. 1565. †**b.** Applied to a gathering cloud DRAYTON.

1. An Error in the judgment, is like an impostem in the Head SOUTH. **2.** The imposthume I prick to relieve thee of,—Vanity BROWNING. Hence †**Impo·stume, -thume** *v.* = IMPOSTUMATE *v.* ME.

†**Impo·sturage.** *rare.* 1654. [f. next + -AGE.] Imposture –1656.

Imposture (impǫ·stiŭɹ). 1537. [– Fr. *imposture* – late L. *impostura*, f. *impost-*, pa. ppl. stem of L. *imponere*; see IMPOST[1], -URE.] **1.** The action or practice of imposing on others; wilful and fraudulent deception. †**b.** Illusion –1794. **2.** A cheat, a fraud 1548; a thing (or person) which is pretended to be what it is not 1699.

1. There's a sure market for i. BYRON. **2.** Many of the Bones which were carried about by Monks, were none of their Bones but Impostures BURNET.

Imposturous (impǫ·stiŭrəs), *a.* 1608. [f. IMPOSTURE + -OUS.] **1.** Of the nature of imposture (now *rare*). †**2.** Given to imposture; having the character of an impostor –1697.

2. The shamefull vntruth of those i. liers SPEED.

†**Impo·stury.** [f. as prec. + -Y[3].] Imposture. G. SANDYS.

Imposure (impōu·ʒiŭɹ). *rare.* 1682. [f. IMPOSE *v.* + -URE.] An imposing, a laying on.

Impot (i·mpǫt). Schoolboys' abbreviation of IMPOSITION (sense 5).

Impotable, *a.* 1608. [In XVII –late L. *impotabilis* (Jerome); later f. IM-[2] + POTABLE.] Undrinkable.

Impotence (i·mpŏtĕns). ME. [–(O)Fr. *impotence* –L. *impotentia*; see IM-[2], POTENCE[1].] **1.** Want of strength or power; utter inability or weakness; helplessness. **2.** Want of physical power; feebleness of body, as through illness, etc. ME. **b.** *Path.* Want of sexual power; usu. said of the male 1655. †**3.** Lack of self-restraint, violent passion –1720.

1. O i. of mind, in body strong! MILT. *Sams.* 52. **2.** A condition of i. and dotage 1836. **3.** MILT. *P.L.* II. 156. So **I·mpotency** ME.

Impotent (i·mpŏtĕnt), *a.* (*sb.*) ME. [– (O)Fr. *impotent* – L. *impotens, -ent-*; see IM-[2], POTENT.] **1.** Having no power or ability to do anything; helpless; ineffective 1444. **2.** Physically weak; without bodily strength; helpless, decrepit ME. **b.** Wanting in sexual power; incapable of reproduction 1615. †**3.** Not master of oneself; unrestrained, headlong, passionate. Also with *of*. 1596. **4.** *sb.* An impotent person 1425.

1. The works of man are i. against the assaults of nature GIBBON. **2.** He was feble and Oold, And inpotent LYDG. **3.** But Juno, i. of passion, broke Her sullen silence POPE. **4.** Impotents of all sorts PETTY. Hence **I·mpotently** *adv.*

†**Impo·tionate,** *v.* [– *impotionat-*, pa. ppl. stem of med.L. *impotionare*, f. *in-* IM-[1] + *potio* POISON, *potionare*.] *trans.* To poison. FOXE.

Impound (impau·nd), *v.* 1554. Also †**em-.** [f. IM-[1] + POUND *sb.*[2]] **1.** *trans.* To shut up in or as in a pound. **2.** To seize or secure by legal right; to take possession of (a document or the like) to be held in custody of the law 1651.

1. Some cattle..had been impounded for tithe-payment HT. MARTINEAU. How to i. the Rebels, that none of them might escape BACON. Hence †**Impou·ndage, Impou·ndment,** the act of impounding. **Impou·nder,** one who impounds.

Impoverish (impǫ·vĕriʃ), *v.* 1440. [f. *empoveriss-*, lengthened stem of OFr. *empov(e)rir* (mod. *empauvrir*), f. *em-* (*im-*), IM-[1] + *povre* POOR; see -ISH[2].] **1.** *trans.* To make poor; to reduce to poverty. †**b.** To make bare *of* (some form of wealth) –1726. **2.** To make weak or poor in quality; to exhaust the strength or native quality of 1631.

1. Corruption..impoverishes and enslaves the country 'JUNIUS'. **2.** To i. the blood ALLBUTT. Hence **Impo·verisher. Impo·verishment,** the fact or process of impoverishing; impoverished condition; loss of wealth or means.

Impower, obs. var. of EMPOWER.

Impracticability (impræ:ktikăbi·lĭti). 1747. [f. IMPRACTICABLE; see -ITY.] **1.** The quality or condition of being impracticable; practical impossibility. **b.** Intractability, stubbornness 1764. **2.** with *an* and *pl.* Something impracticable 1797.

Impracticable (impræ·ktikăb'l), *a.* (*sb.*) 1653. [f. IM-[2] + PRACTICABLE.] **1.** Not practicable; that cannot be carried out or done; practically impossible 1677. **2.** That cannot be put to use or practically dealt with; unmanageable, intractable, unserviceable 1653. **3.** *sb.* An impracticable person 1829.

1. An i. design 1696. **2.** Idle and i. wastes W. IRVING. An i. way CROMWELL, pass GROTE. A poor i. creature! GOLDSM. **3.** An utter i. 1829. Hence **Impra·cticableness. Impra·cticably** *adv.*

Impra·ctical, *a. rare.* [IM-[2] + PRACTICAL.] **1.** Impracticable (now *U.S.*) 1774. **2.** Unpractical 1865.

Imprecate (i·mprĭkeⁱt), *v.* 1613. [– *imprecat-*, pa. ppl. stem of L. *imprecari*, f. (in senses 1 and 2) *in-* IM-[1] + *precari* PRAY; see -ATE[3].] **1.** *trans.* To pray for, invoke. **b.** To beg for (*rare*) 1636. **2.** To pray (a deity), supplicate. Now *rare* or *Obs.* 1643. †**3.** *absol.* or *intr.* To pray; to invoke evil –1673. **4.** *trans.* To invoke evil upon; to curse. Now *rare.* 1616.

1. She..imprecated a thousand curses upon his head SMOLLETT. **b.** He..would only i. patience till [etc.] LOWELL. **4.** His co-religionists were imprecating him as the man who had brought this persecution upon them 1879. Hence **I·mprecatingly** *adv.* in the way of a curse 1652.

Imprecation (imprĭkēⁱ·ʃən). 1585. [– L. *imprecatio*, f. as prec.; see -ION. Cf. Fr. *imprécation.*] **1.** The action of imprecating, or invoking evil upon any one, in an oath or adjuration; cursing 1589; (with *pl.*) a curse 1603. †**2.** A prayer, invocation, entreaty –1631.

1. At each fierce i. he quenched a light, and dashed down a candle FROUDE.

Imprecatory (i·mprĭkeⁱ:təri, -kĕtəri, imprĭkēⁱ·təri), *a.* 1587. [– med.L. *imprecatorius* invoking a curse, appropriate to prayer (XIII), f. as prec.; see -ORY[2].] Expressing or involving imprecation; invoking evil; cursing.

The i. Psalms 1881. **I·mprecatorily** *adv.*

Imprecise (imprĭsəi·s), *a. rare.* 1805. [f. IM-[2] + PRECISE.] Not precise. So **Impreci·sion** (*rare*), want of precision; inexactness 1803.

Impredicable (impre·dikăb'l), *a. rare.* 1623. [f. IM-[2] + PREDICABLE.] That cannot be predicated.

Impregn (imprī·n), *v.* Now only *poet.* 1425. [– late L. *impregnare*; see IMPREGNATE *v.*] = IMPREGNATE *v.* (in all senses).

Impregnable (impre·gnăb'l), *a.* ME. [In XV *imprenable* – OFr. *imprenable*, f. *in-* IM-[2] + *prenable* takeable, f. *pren-*, stem of *prendre* take :– L. *prehendere*; see COMPREHEND, -ABLE. The later forms *impre(i)gnable*, which depend on OFr. vars. (cf. PREGNANT *a.*[1]), induced the pronunc. with g.] Of a fortress, etc.: That cannot be taken by arms; incapable of being reduced by force; able to hold out against all attacks. Also *fig.*

1. The Seas, Which he hath giu'n for fence i. 3 *Hen. VI*, IV. i. 44. *fig.* A man politely i. to the intrusion of human curiosity CARLYLE. Hence **Impregnabi·lity,** i. condition or quality. **Impre·gnableness** (*rare*). **Impre·gnably** *adv.*

Impregnant (impre·gnănt), *a.*[1] (*sb.*) 1641. [In sense 1 f. IM-[1] + PREGNANT[2]; in sense 2 f. *impregnant-*, pr. ppl. stem of late L. *impregnare*; see IMPREGNATE *v.*, -ANT.] †**1.** Impregnated, pregnant. Also *fig.* –1712. **2.** Impregnating. Also as *sb.* That which impregnates 1661.

†**Impregnant,** *a.*[2] *rare.* [f. IM-[2] + PREGNANT *a.*[2]] Sterile. OSBORNE.

Impregnate (impre·gnĕt), *ppl. a.* 1545. [– late L. *impregnatus*, pa. pple. of *imprægnare*; see next, -ATE[2].] **1.** Impregnated (*lit.* and *fig.*). ¶**2.** Erron. for IMPREGNABLE 1632.

Impregnate (impre·gneⁱt), *v.* 1605. [– *impregnat-* pa. ppl. stem of late L. *imprægnare*, f. *in-* IM-[1] + *prægnare* be PREGNANT; see -ATE[3]. Perh. directly f. prec.] **1.** *trans.* To make pregnant; to cause to conceive; to fertilize; in *Biol.*, also, to fecundate the female reproductive cell or ovum 1646. Also *fig.* **b.** *intr.* for *pass.* To become pregnant. ADDISON. **2.** To fill *with* some active principle, element, or ingredient, diffused through it or mixed intimately with it; to imbue, saturate. Earlier = to fill. (Usu. in *pass.*) 1605. Also *fig.* **3.** Said of the active principle or influence: To be diffused through (something); to permeate, interpenetrate, fill, saturate 1664.

2. Water impregnated with some penetrating Salt ARBUTHNOT. *fig.* To i. his colleagues with the same loftiness of principle LYTTON. **3.** Light impregnates air, air impregnates vapour BERKELEY. Hence **Impre·gnatory** *a.* having the function of impregnating.

Impregnation (impregnēⁱ·ʃən). 1605. [f. prec. + -ATION, or – (O)Fr. *impregnation.*] **1.** The action or process of making pregnant; fecundation, fertilization. **2.** The action of imbuing or fact of being imbued with something; diffusion of an active element through a substance; saturation. Also *fig.* 1641. **3.** *concr.* That with which something is impregnated 1713; in *Geol.*, a mineral deposit consisting of a rock impregnated with ore, not forming a true vein 1881.

2. The I. of the Blood with Air RAY.

†**Impreju·dicate,** *ppl. a.* 1640. [f. IM-[2] + PREJUDICATE *ppl. a.*] Unprejudiced –1677.

Impren(i)able, etc., obs. ff. IMPREGNABLE.

Imprepara·tion. 1597. [f. IM-[2] + PREPARATION.] Unpreparedness.

†**Impre·sa.** 1589. [– It. *impresa* (imprē·za) undertaking, device, etc. :– Rom. *imprensa*; see EMPRISE.] **1.** An emblem or device, usu. with a motto –1653. **2.** The sentence accompanying an emblem; hence, a motto, maxim, proverb –1641.

1. In an i., the figures express and illustrate the one part of the author's intention, and the word the other DRUMM. OF HAWTH. var. †**Impre·so.**

‖**Impresario** (imprezā·rio). Also erron. **impress-.** 1746. [It. *impresario* undertaker, contractor, f. *impresa*; see prec.; -ARY[1].] One who organizes public entertainments; *esp.* the manager of an operatic or concert company.

Imprescriptible (imprĭskri·ptib'l), *a.* 1563. [– med.L. *imprescriptibilis*, f. *in-* IM-[2] + *prescriptibilis* prescriptible. Cf. Fr. *imprescriptible* (XVI).] Not subject to prescription; that cannot in any circumstances be taken away or abandoned; esp. in *i. right(s.*

The author of an ideal creation..has an i. property in the fame of his work 1884. Hence **Imprescriptibi·lity** (*rare*), the quality of being i. **Imprescri·ptibly** *adv.*

†**Impre·se, i·mprese.** 1588. [– Fr. †*imprese* – It.; see IMPRESA.] = IMPRESA. –1811.

Emblazon'd Shields, Impreses quaint MILT.

Impress (i·mpres), *sb.*[1] 1590. [f. IMPRESS *v.*[1] Formerly also stressed *impre·ss.*] **1.** The act of impressing or stamping; the 'stamp' (*of* anything); *concr.* a mark or indentation made by pressure, e.g. of a seal or stamp 1592. †**b.** A cast, mould (*rare*) 1695. **c.** = IMPRINT; impression 1877. **2.** *fig.* **a.** Characteristic or distinctive mark; stamp 1590. **b.** An impression upon the mind or senses. Now *rare.* 1591. **3.** *Comb.*, as *i. copy*, a press-copy 1885.

1. The..I. of thy Feet WATTS. **b.** Having taken the Impresses of the Insides of these Shells WOODWARD. **2.** Lucerne bears most strongly the i. of the middle ages 1832. **b.** *Two Gent.* III. ii. 6.

Impress (i·mpres), *sb.*[2] Now *rare.* 1602. [f. IMPRESS *v.*[2] Formerly stressed *impre·ss.*] Impressment; enforced service in the army or navy. Also *attrib.*, as **i.-gang** = PRESS-GANG.

We are all much alarmed.. with a military i. 1803.

Impress (i·mpres), *sb.*[3] *Obs.* exc. *Hist.* 1611. [var. of IMPRESE. In XVI–XVII also *impre·ss.*] = IMPRESA.

Their shields broken, their impresses defaced BURKE.

†**Impress,** *sb.*[4] 1569. [var. of IMPREST *sb.*[1]] **1.** = IMPREST *sb.*[1] –1633. Also *attrib.* **2.** A charge made upon the pay of a naval officer who has not satisfactorily accounted for public money advanced to him 1803.

Impress (impre·s), *v.*[1] ME. [– (O)Fr. *em-, impresser*, f. *im-* IM-[1] + *presser* PRESS *v.*[1], after L. *imprimere.*]

I. *trans.* **1.** To apply with pressure; to produce by pressure (a mark *on*, †*in*); to imprint, stamp. **2. a.** *fig.* To stamp (a character or quality) *upon* anything ME. **b.** *transf.* To produce or communicate (motion), exert (force) by pressure. Const. *on, upon.* 1717. **3.** *fig.* To imprint (an idea, etc.) *on* (†*in, to*) the mind; to enforce, urge (a rule of conduct, etc.) *on* another ME. †**4.** To print –1781.

1. He did i. On the green moss his tremulous step SHELLEY. **2.** The image of virtue, which Nature had impressed upon his heart 1791. **b.** The force impressed upon a ship by the wind 1765. **3.** A few such examples impressed a salutary consternation GIBBON.

II. *trans.* **1.** To exert pressure upon; to press; to mark by means of pressure, esp. with a stamp, seal, etc. Const. *with.* 1588. Also *fig.* **2.** To affect or influence strongly. Usu. said of the instrument. 1736.

1. His hart like an Agot with your print impressed *L. L. L.* II. i. 236. *fig.* Real property..impressed.. with an implied trust for sale 1884. **2.** The letter.. does not i. me favourably DICKENS. He tried to i. me with his importance (*mod.*).

†**III.** *intr.* To press in; to throng about –1480.

Impress (impre·s), *v.*[2] 1596. [f. IM-[1] + PRESS *v.*[2]] *trans.* To levy or furnish (a force) for military or naval service, to enlist; *spec.* to compel (men) to serve in the army or navy (in recent use, only the latter); to force authoritatively into service. **b.** To take by authority for royal or public service 1749. **c.** *fig.* or *transf.* 1657.

Yesterday sailed the Diamond..to i. men 1803. **b.** I impressed his wagons WASHINGTON. **c.** Hypotheses into the service of which Philology was impressed 1869.

†**Impre·ss,** *v.*[3] *rare* 1665. [erron. for IMPREST *v.*[1]; cf. IMPRESS *sb.*[4]] **1.** *trans.* = IMPREST *v.*[1] 1 –1819. **2.** To charge with a deduction (the pay of an officer) in respect to public moneys or stores not accounted for by him 1803.

†**Impre·ssa**[1]. 1586. Erron. form of IMPRESA (cf. IMPRESS *sb.*[3]) –1656.

†**Impre·ssa**[2]. 1628. Erron. form of IMPRESS *sb.*[1] (2 a) –1647.

Impre·ssed, *ppl. a.* ME. [f. IMPRESS *v.*[1] + -ED[1].] In the senses of IMPRESS *v.*[1] I; in *Zool.* and *Bot.*, having an appearance of being stamped in; sunk in, depressed.

Impressible (impre·sib'l), *a.* 1626. [f. as prec. + -IBLE.] Capable of being impressed (on something); susceptible, impressionable. Hence **Impressibi·lity,** also **-ability,** the quality of being i. **Impre·ssibleness. Impre·ssibly** *adv.*

Impression (impre·ʃən), *sb.* ME. [– (O)Fr. *impression* – L. *impressio* onset, attack, (in Cicero) emphasis, mental impression, f. *impress-*, pa. ppl. stem of *imprimere*, f. *in-* IM-[1] + *premere* PRESS.] **1.** The action or process of impressing: *esp.* **a.** The action involved in the pressure of one thing upon or into the surface of another; also, the effect of this 1444. †**b.** A charge, onset –1799. **c.** The impact of any atmospheric or physical force. ?*Obs.* 1694. †**d.** A stress, emphasis –1824. **2.** A mark produced upon any surface by pressure. Hence, a depression, indentation; also, a mould, cast, copy. Also *fig.* ME. †**b.** A mark, trace, indication –1658. **3.** The process of printing. Now *rare.* 1509. **b.** The result of printing; a print; a printed copy 1559. **c.** The printing of one issue (of a book, etc.); hence, the aggregate of copies thus printed; see EDITION 3 b. 1570. **4.** The effective action of one thing upon another; influence; the effect of such action ME. †**5.** *spec.* An atmospheric influence, condition, or phenomenon –1684. **6.** The effect produced by external force or influence on the senses or the mind; a sensation 1632; an effect produced on the intellect, conscience, or feelings ME. **7.** A notion, remembrance, or belief, impressed upon the mind; *esp.*, in mod. use, a vague or indistinct survival from more distinct knowledge 1613. **8.** *Painting.* **a.** 'The ground-colour'. **b.** A stratum of a single colour laid upon a wall or surface for ornament, or for protection from humidity. 1864.

1. a. The i. of order on..chaos 1875. **2.** As..a seal [is said] to make an i. upon wax BERKELEY. *fig.* The stamp and clear i. of good sense COWPER. **3.** The i. of the fourth volume had consumed three months GIBBON. **b.** Very early impressions of Dürer's engravings 1869. **c.** Of this translation there were six impressions before the year 1601 WARTON. **4.** One of the hardest of the metals; a file can scarcely make any i. on it IMISON. **5.** *Fiery impression*, a comet, meteor, or the like. **6.** Those perceptions, which enter with most force and violence, we may name *impressions* HUME. An i. of sound..is carried to the brain BAIN. His Sermons made no I. on his English Auditory FULLER. **7.** I have an i. that I have met him before (*mod.*). Phr. *Under the impression.*

Hence **Impre·ssion** *v.* (*rare*), to stamp; to affect with an impression; (in *pass.*) to be affected 1612.

Impressionable (impre·ʃənăb'l), *a.* 1836. [– Fr. *impressionnable*; f. *impressionner*; see prec., -ABLE.] **1.** Easily susceptible of impressions; sensitive. **2.** Capable of being impressed 1878.

1. She had a pretty face and an i. disposition T. HOOK. **2.** Tinfoil thin enough to be i. by the metal style 1878. Hence **Impressionabi·lity,** susceptibility to impressions 1835. So **Impre·ssional** *a.* = IMPRESSIONABLE.

Impre·ssionary, *a.* 1889. [f. IMPRESSION + -ARY[1].] = IMPRESSIONISTIC.

Impressionism (impre·ʃəniz'm). 1839. [f. IMPRESSION *sb.* + -ISM.] †**1.** Applied to the philosophy of Hume. *nonce-use.* **2.** [after Fr. *impressionnisme*, 1876] The theory or practice of the impressionist school of painting (see next) 1882. **3.** The literary presentation of salient features, done in a few strokes 1883.

Impressionist (impre·ʃənist). 1881. [– Fr. *impressionniste* (1874), applied in an unfavourable sense with ref. to a picture by Claude Monet entitled *Impression*. See -IST.] A painter who endeavours to express the general impression produced by a scene or object, to the exclusion of minute details or elaborate finish; also, a writer who practises a similar method. Hence **Impressioni·stic** *a.* of or pertaining to impressionism; in the style of the impressionists. **Impressioni·stically** *adv.*

Impre·ssionless, *a. rare.* 1864. [-LESS.] Without impression; unimpressible.

Impressive (impre·siv), *a.* 1593. [f. IMPRESS *v.*[1] + -IVE. Cf. med.L. *impressivus.*] †**1.** Capable of being easily impressed; impressible –1665. **2.** Characterized by making a deep impression on the mind or senses; able to excite deep feeling. Rarely said of persons. 1775.

1. Men..of..i. tempers, and weak intellectuals 1665. **2.** An i. actress LAMB, scene TYNDALL. Hence **Impre·ssive-ly** *adv.*, **-ness.**

Impre·ssment[1]. *rare.* 1854. [f. IMPRESS *v*[1]. + -MENT. In sense 2 for Fr. *empressement.*] **1.** Exertion of pressure 1865. **2.** Earnestness, ardour 1854.

Impressment[2] (impre·smĕnt). 1796. [f. IMPRESS *v.*[2] + -MENT.] The act or practice of impressing or forcibly taking for the public service. Also *fig.*

†**Impre·ssor.** *rare.* 1631. [f. IMPRESS *v.*[1] + -OR 2.] One who, or that which, makes impressions –1663.

Impressure (impre·ʃ'ŭɹ). Now *rare.* 1600. [f. IMPRESS *v.*[1] + -URE, after *pressure.*] **1.** The action of exerting pressure upon 1649. **2.** An impression; an indentation 1600. **3.** A mental or sensuous impression 1607.

Imprest (i·mprest), *a.* and *sb.*[1] 1568. [For the earlier PREST *a.* and *sb.* The *im-* may be partly due to the phr. *in prest* (*money*); see PREST *a.* Cf. IMPRESS *sb.*[4]]

†**A.** *adj.* Of money: Lent, or advanced, esp. to soldiers, sailors, and public officials –1755.

B. *sb.* An advance (of money) made to one who is charged with some business by the state. †Formerly, also, advance-pay of soldiers or sailors. 1568. †**b.** *gen.* An advance, a loan –1704.

Vpon euery Contract we make, we giue the Victualers an i. before hand MORYSON. *Bill of I.*, an order authorizing a person to draw money in advance; so *i.-bill.*

†**Imprest,** *sb.*[2] 1610. [f. IMPREST *v.*[2]] = IMPRESSMENT[2]. –1651.

†**Impre·st,** *v.*[1] 1565. [– med.L. *imprestare* (whence It. *imprestare*) lend, advance as an imprest; see IMPREST *sb.*[1] and the earlier PREST *v.*[1]] **1.** *trans.* To advance, lend (money) –1810. **b.** To furnish (a person) with an advance of money –1613. **2.** To draw (a bill or money by a bill) –1661.

†**Impre·st,** *v.*[2] 1589. [f. *imprest, impressed,* pa. pple. of IMPRESS *v.*[2], perh. confused with IMPREST *v.*[1]] *trans.* To impress for the army or navy –1708.

†**Impre·valency.** [f. IM-[2] + PREVALENCY.] Want of prevailing power. BP. HALL. So †**Impre·valence.**

Impreve·ntable, *a. rare.* 1864. [IM-[2].] That cannot be prevented. Hence **Impreventabi·lity,** i. state or quality.

Imprimatur (imprimē[i]·tŏɹ). 1640. [L. = 'let it be printed', 3rd. sing. pres. subj. pass. of *imprimere*; see IMPRINT *v.*] **1.** The formula, signed by an official licenser of the press, authorizing the printing of a book; hence as *sb.* an official licence to print. **2.** *fig.* Sanction 1672.

†**Imprime,** *v.* 1575. Also **em-.** [f. IM-[1] + PRIME *a.* or *sb.*, or L. *primus.*] **1.** *trans. Hunting.* (See quot.) –1775. **2.** To begin. WOTTON.

1. When he is hunted and doth first leave the herde we say that he is syngled or emprymed TURBERVILLE. Hence †**Impri·me** *sb.* the act of impriming a deer. †**Impri·ming** *vbl. sb.* beginning, commencement.

†**I·mpriment.** [– *impriment-*, pr. ppl. stem of L. *imprimere*; see IMPRINT *v.*] Something that impresses or imprints. STERNE.

†**Impri·mery.** Also **-ie.** 1663. [– Fr. *imprimerie* printing, printing-house, f. *imprimer* print, *imprimeur* printer; see -ERY.] **1.** A printing-office or printing-house –1696. **2.** Printing. WOOD. **3.** A print or impression. BLOUNT.

‖**Imprimis** (imprəi·mis), *adv.* or *adv. phr.* 1465. [L., assim. form of *in primis* 'among the first things', i.e. *in* IN *prep.* and *primis*, abl. pl. of *primus* first (PRIME).] In the first place, first. Now unusual.

Imprint (i·mprint), *sb.* 1480. [In XV (Caxton) *empreynte, -printe* – (O)Fr. *empreinte*, subst. use of pa. pple. fem. of *empreindre* :– pop. L. **impremere* for cl. L. *imprimere*, f. *in-* IM-[1] + *premere* PRESS. See PRINT *sb.*] **1.** A figure impressed or imprinted on something; a mark produced by pressure; an impression, stamp 1483. Also *fig.* **2.** †**a.** The condition of being printed (in phr. *in enprinte*) –1485. **b.** The printing of a book, etc. 1899. **c.** An impression *of* a writing 1882. **3.** The name of the publisher, place of publication, and date, printed in a book, usually at the foot of the title-page (*publisher's i.*); also, the name of printer and place of printing, printed at the end of a book, or on the back of the title-page (*printer's i.*) 1790. †**4.** An onset. CAXTON.

3. The i... 'At the Clarendon Press' 1790.

Imprint (impri·nt), *v.* [Earliest forms *em-* (XIV) – OFr. *empreinter*, f. *empreint*, pa. pple. of *empreindre*; see prec. and cf. PRINT *v.*] **1.** *trans.* To mark by pressure; to impress, stamp. †**2.** To impress (letters or characters) on paper or the like by means of type; to PRINT –1822. **3.** *fig.* **a.** To impress *on* or *in* the mind, memory, etc. ME. **b.** To impress (a quality, etc.) *on* or *in* a person or thing; to communicate. In *pass.* of a quality: To exist strongly marked *in* or *on* a person, etc. 1526. **4.** *transf.* To stamp or impress (something) *with* a figure, etc. ME. **b.** *fig.* To impress *with* some feeling, quality, etc. 1765.

1. The Volto Santo or print of our Saviour's face, which he imprinted in the handkerchief of St. Veronica 1670. **2.** Imprinted at London by Robert Barker BIBLE (1611) *title-p.* **3. a.** I. this in thy memorie 1576. **b.** That wisedome which the Divine hand hath imprinted in his workes G. SANDYS. Hence **Impri·nter,** one who or that which imprints; †a printer 1548.

Imprison (impri·z'n), *v.* ME. [– OFr. *emprisoner* (mod. *-onner*); see IM-[1], PRISON.] **1.** *trans.* To put in prison; to detain in custody; to confine. **2.** *transf.* and *fig.* To confine, shut up; in various connections 1533.

1. Lord, they know that I imprisoned..them that beleeued on thee *Acts* 22:19. Since imprison'd in my mother Thou me freed'st C'TESS PEMBROKE. **2.** Try to i. the resistless wind DRYDEN. Hence **Impri·sonable** *a.* capable of or liable to imprisonment. **Impri·soner,** one who imprisons.

Imprisonment (impri·z'nmĕnt). ME. [– AFr. *enprisounement*, OFr. *-one-*, f. *enprisoner*; see prec., -MENT.] The action of imprisoning, or fact or condition of being imprisoned; confinement; incarceration. Also *transf.* and *fig.*

Imprisonment, is when a man is by publique Authority deprived of liberty HOBBES. *fig.* Into the slavishe i. of vices most detestable FLEMING.

Improbability (imprǫbăbi·lIti). 1598. [f. next + -ITY.] The quality of being improbable; unlikelihood; (with *an* and *pl.*) something unlikely.

Improbable (imprǫ·băb'l), *a.* 1598. [– Fr. *improbable* or L. *improbabilis* in the med.L. sense 'hard to prove, improbable'; see IM-[2], PROBABLE.] **1.** Not probable; not likely to be true; not easy to believe; unlikely. **2.** In pregnant sense: Unlikely to 'do', suit, etc. 1659.

1. If this were plaid vpon a stage now, I could condemne it as an i. fiction SHAKS. I. of success 1654. **2.** In the most i. soile HAMMOND. Hence **Impro·bableness. Impro·bably** *adv.*

†**Improbate,** *v.* [– *improbat-*, pa. ppl. stem of L. *improbare* disapprove, f. *in-* IM-[2] + *probare* approve; see -ATE[3].] *trans.* To disapprove, disallow. BLOUNT.

Improbation (imprǫbē[i]·ʃən). 1551. [In sense 1 – Fr. *improbation* or L. *improbatio*, f. as prec.; see -ION; in senses 2 and 3 – AL. *improbatio* disproof, refutation (XIII).] †**1.** Disapprobation, disapproval –1789. †**2.** Disproof, confutation (*rare*) –1657. **3.** *Sc. Law.* Disproof of a writ; an action brought to prove a document to be false or forged 1575.

Improbative (imprǫ·bătiv), *a.* 1677. [– AL. *improbativus* tending to refute, f. as prec.; see -IVE, -ATIVE. Cf. PROBATIVE.] **1.** Liable to improbation or disproof. **2.** = IMPROBATORY 1876.

Improbatory (imprǫ·bătəri), *a.* 1828. [f. IM-[2] + PROBATORY.] Having the function of disproving; in *Sc. Law*, made in improbation of a writ.

Improbity (imprō[u]·bIti, imprǫ·bIti). ME. [– L. *improbitas* wickedness; see IM-[2], PROBITY. Cf. (O)Fr. *improbité.*] **1.** Persistency, perseverance. *Obs.* or *nonce-use.* **2.** Wickedness, want of principle or integrity 1594.

2. The exuberant I. of ill Men 1695.

†**Improdu·ction.** *rare.* 1662. [f. IM-[2] + PRODUCTION.] The condition of not having been produced from anything else –1678.

†**Improfi·cience.** *rare.* 1605. [f. IM-[2] + PROFICIENCE.] Lack of proficiency. So **Improfi·ciency** (now *rare*).

†**Impro·fitable,** *a.* ME. [f. IM-[2] + PROFITABLE.] Unprofitable –1725.

Improgressive (improgre·siv), *a.* 1809. [f. IM-[2] + PROGRESSIVE.] Not progressive; unprogressive. **Improgre·ssive-ly** *adv.*, **-ness.**

†**Improli·fic,** †**-al,** *a.* 1646. [f. IM-[2] + PROLIFIC, -AL[1].] Not prolific –1686.

†**Improli·ficate,** *v.* [f. IM-[1] + PROLIFICATE.] To render prolific, to fertilize. SIR T. BROWNE.

†**Impro·mpt,** *a.* [f. IM-[2] + PROMPT *a.*] Not ready; unready. STERNE.

Impromptu (imprǫ·m[p]tiū). 1669. [– Fr. *impromptu* (Molière, 1659) – L. phr. *in promptu* at hand, in readiness; see PROMPT *a.*]

A. *adv.* Without preparation, off-hand.

This was made almost *impromptu* BOSWELL.

B. *sb.* Something composed or uttered without preparation; an extemporaneous composition or performance; an improvisation. Also, a musical composition having the character of an improvisation. 1683.

C. *adj.* **1.** Composed or uttered without premeditation; improvised 1789. **2.** Made or done on the spur of the moment; extemporized, makeshift 1764.

1. I. poems 1789, replies D'ISRAELI. **2.** An i. visit 1856. Hence **Impro·mptuary** *a.* = C. 1 (BENTHAM).

Improper (imprǫ·pəɹ), *a.* 1531. [– (O)Fr. *impropre* or L. *improprius*; see IM-[2], PROPER *a.*] Not proper; the opposite of proper. **1.** Not strictly belonging to the thing under consideration; not in accordance with truth, fact, reason, or rule; abnormal; incorrect, wrong. **b.** Not properly so called 1575. **2.** Not in accordance with the circumstances or the end in view; unsuitable, ill-adapted 1570. **3.** Unbecoming; indecorous, indecent. Also *transf.* of a person. 1739. †**4.** ?Not peculiar to an individual; general, common (*rare*) 1610.

1. To eate Christs flesh—to pluck out our right eye..We cannot read any of these literally and properly..therefore we must seek for a spiritual and i. sense 1649. **b.** *Improper fraction*: a fraction whose numerator is greater than (or equal to) its denominator. *I. diphthong*: see DIPHTHONG. They are not to be adorned with any art but such improper ones as nature is said to bestow, as singing and poetry FLETCHER. [This quot. is taken in sense 4 in recent Dicts.] **2.** As i. to be approached as a rocky lee shore 1774. **3.** I am too old to be i. H. WALPOLE. Hence †**Impro·perty,** impropriety 1555–1663.

†**Improper**, *v.* ME. [– AL. *impropriare*; see IMPROPRIATE *v.*] = IMPROPRIATE *v.* 1, 2. –1642.
If he would..i., and inclose the Sun beames, to comfort the rich JEWEL.

†**Impropera·tion**[1]. 1502. [– late L. *improperatio* – pa. ppl. stem of L. *improperare* (Petronius).] The action of unbraiding or reviling; a reproach, taunt –1643.

†**Impropera·tion**[2]. 1536. Erron. f. IMPROPRIATION –1624.

Improperly (imprǫ·pəɹli), *adv.* ME. [f. IMPROPER + -LY[2]; isolated instance in Gower perh. after OFr. *improprement.*] In an improper manner; wrongly, incorrectly, unsuitably, unbecomingly.

†**Impropi·tious**, *a.* [IM-[2].] Not propitious; unfavourable. WOTTON.

†**Impropo·rtion.** 1450. [f. IM-[2] + PROPORTION *sb.*] Want of proportion, disproportion –1675. Hence †**Impropo·rtionable**, †**Impropo·rtionate** *adjs.* disproportionate.

Impropriate (imprōᵘ·priˌeⁱt), *v.* 1538. [– *impropriat-*, pa. ppl. stem of AL. *impropriare*, f. *in-* IM-[1] + *proprius* PROPER; see -ATE[3].] †**1.** *trans.* To make one's (or some one's) own; to appropriate –1703. **2.** *spec.* To annex (an ecclesiastical benefice) to a corporation or person, as their corporate or private property 1538; esp. **b.** (in later use) to place tithes or ecclesiastical property in lay hands 1613.

1. They i. the Preaching of the Gospell to one certain Order of men HOBBES. Hence **Impro·priator**, one to whom a benefice is impropriated; esp. = *lay impropriator*; †also *gen.* **Impro:pria·trix**, a female i.

Impropriate (imprōᵘ·priˌĕt), *ppl. a.* 1538. [– AL. *impropriatus*, pa. pple. of *impropriare*; see prec., -ATE[2].] **1.** Appropriated to some person or persons. ? *Obs.* 1600. **2.** Of a benefice or tithes: Impropriated.

Impropriation (imprōᵘpriˌēⁱ·ʃən). 1535 [– mod.L. (AL.) *impropriatio*, f. as prec.; see -ION.] **1.** The action of impropriating (see IMPROPRIATE *v.* 2). **b.** The proprietorship thus conveyed 1631. **c.** An impropriated benefice 1578. †**2.** *gen.* The action of making proper to some person or thing; appropriation –1728. †**b.** Something appropriated; a property –1651.

1. c. An i. which the Lord Gray of Wilton..restored to the Church FULLER.

Impropriety (improˌprəi·ĕti). 1611. [– Fr. *impropriété* or L. *improprietas*, f. *improprius* IMPROPER; see -ITY.] **1.** The quality of being improper; incorrectness; inappropriateness 1697; unseemliness; morally improper conduct 1751. **2.** With *an* and *pl.* An instance of improper language, conduct, etc.; a breach of propriety 1674.

1. We may..say, without i., that [etc.] MILL. The i. of holding a public discussion with such men JOWETT. The i. of my conduct JOHNSON. **2.** Every language has likewise its improprieties and absurdities JOHNSON.

†**Impro·pry, -rie**, *v.* 1526. [– AL. *impropriare*; see IMPROPER *v.*] *trans.* To appropriate, impropriate –1571.

†**Improspe·rity.** 1528. [f. IM-[2] + PROSPERITY.] Want of, or the opposite of, prosperity; unprosperousness –1722.

†**Impro·sperous**, *a.* 1598. [f. IM-[2] + PROSPEROUS.] **1.** Not prosperous; unsuccessful –1829. **2.** Of fortune, etc.: Unpropitious –1656. Hence †**Impro·sperous-ly** *adv.* 1594, †**-ness** 1647.

Improvable (imprū·văb'l), *a.* Also **improveable.** 1646. [f. IMPROVE *v.*[2] + -ABLE.] **1.** Capable of being turned to profit; that may be taken advantage of; serviceable. Now *rare.* **2.** Of land: Capable of being profitably cultivated; capable of being made more productive 1659. **3.** Capable of being made better 1677.

1. Finding this project of a penny-post..apparently i. NORTH. **2.** A fine spread of improveable lands ADDISON. **3.** With Moral principles..i. by the exercise of his Faculties HALE. Hence **Improvabi·lity, Improv·ableness**, the quality of being i. **Impro·vably** *adv.*

†**Improve**, *v.*[1] 1449. [– OFr. *improver* (mod. *improuver*) – L. *improbare* disapprove; see IMPROBATE *v.*] **1.** *trans.* To disprove, refute, confute –1678. **2.** To disapprove as bad; to disallow; to reprove; to censure, condemn –1642.

1. We..will in due place i. their error therein 1606. **2.** When they had improued and disallowed my sayinges 1551.

Improve (imprū·v), *v.*[2] 1509. [Early forms *em-, improwe* – AFr. *emprower, emprouer* (in AL. *appro(w)are, appruare*), f. OFr. *em-* IM-[1] + *prou* profit (:– late L. *prode*, evolved from L. *prodest* is of advantage), later infl. by PROVE. Cf. APPROVE *v.*[2]] †**1.** *refl. To i. oneself (of)*: to make one's profit (of) –1655. **2.** *trans.* To make good use of, turn to profit or good account; *spec.* to enlarge upon for spiritual edification 1539. †**b.** To invest (money); in N. America, to enclose and cultivate (land). **c.** To employ to advantage, as a means or instrument 1529; later American: *spec.* to occupy (a place). †**3.** To enhance in monetary value –1750. †**4.** To make greater in amount or degree; to advance. (Now merged in 5.) –1771. †**b.** To augment (what is evil), to make worse –1800. **5.** To advance or raise to a better quality or condition; to make better; to ameliorate. (The prevailing mod. sense.) 1617. **6.** *absol.* To make improvements 1699. **7.** *intr.* To increase, augment, advance, develop. *Obs.* (exc. as merged in 8). 1650. **8.** *intr.* To increase in value or excellence; to become better 1727.

1. The Townsmen..unconscionably improving themselves on the Scholars necessities FULLER. **2.** How doth the little busy bee I. each shining hour! WATTS. To i. an opportunity LINGARD, the occasion FREEMAN. **b.** To I...Lands for the proffit thereof 1653. To i., and put it [his Talent] out BUTLER. **c.** Places..improved for Trading and Fishing 1677. Every Corner is improved for Cupboards CELIA FIENNES. **3.** They i. their commodities to a treble price MORYSON. **4. b.** As wholesome Medicines the Disease i., There where they work not well COWLEY. **5.** The habit of attention may be improved by exercise SIR B. BRODIE. **6.** Phr. *To i. on* or *upon*: to make something better than. We cannot i. upon nature 1867. **8.** Trade..has..improved 1885.

†**Improve**, *v.*[3] 1612. [var. of *aprove*, APPROVE *v.*[1]] **1.** *trans.* To prove, establish, show to be true or real –1670; *intr.* to prove or turn out to be (*rare*) 1612. **2.** *trans.* To approve, countenance. C. MATHER.

Improvement (imprū·vmĕnt). 1453. [– AFr. *emprowement*, f. *emprower*; see IMPROVE *v.*[2], -MENT.] **1.** The turning of a thing to profit or good account; making the most of a thing; realization of the profits of anything; *concr.* profit. *Obs.* in *lit.* sense. **2.** *spec.* †The turning of land to better account; cultivation and occupation of land; merged at length in sense 5. 1549. **b.** *concr.* A piece of land improved by inclosure, building, etc. *Obs.* exc. in *U.S. dial.* 1473. **c.** *fig.* Bodily or mental cultivation or culture; an accomplishment. *Obs.* exc. as merged in 5, 6. 1711. **3.** The turning to account of any person or thing (now *Obs.* or *U.S. dial.*), or of any event or season 1611. **b.** *spec.* The profitable spiritual application of a text or incident 1655. †**4.** The action or process of enhancing, or an instance of this 1548–1788. †**b.** quasi-*concr.* An advanced stage, development (*of* something) –1716. †**c.** *concr.* Increase, produce –1719. **5.** The action or process of making or becoming better; betterment, amelioration 1647. **6.** With *an* and *pl.*: **a.** An act of making or becoming better; that by which anything is made better 1697. **b.** With *on* or *upon*: An advance upon (something previous); hence, a thing that is an advance upon (the former thing) 1712.

2. b. My aunt's bell rings for our afternoon's walk round the improvements GOLDSM. **c.** I look upon your city as the best place of i. SOUTH. **3.** Prompt i. of the opportunity 1899. **4.** This was nothing but..an improuement of his griefe 1617. **5.** The i. of Trade 1662, of body and mind JOWETT. **6.** It is a great i. to add the juice of two Seville oranges MRS. GLASSE. **b.** The sons are no great i. upon the sires SPURGEON.

Improver (imprū·vəɹ). 1647. [f. IMPROVE *v.*[2] + -ER[1].] **1.** One who or that which improves; †a cultivator, occupier. **2.** Short for *dress-improver* 1884. **3.** A person who works at a trade, and accepts the opportunity of improvement wholly or in part instead of wages 1858; in the Civil Service, applied to a grade of clerks intermediate between boy clerks and assistant clerks.

2. Her 'improver' was found to be so arranged as to hold 6 lb. of smuggled tobacco 1884.

†**Improvi·ded**, *a.* 1548. [f. IM-[2] + PROVIDED.] **1.** Unprovided; unprepared –1622. **2.** Unforeseen. SPENSER.

Improvidence (imprǫ·vidĕns). 1425. [– Fr. †*improvidence* or late L. *improvidentia*; see IM-[2], PROVIDENCE.] The fact or quality of being improvident; want of foresight; thriftlessness.

Shee'le lift thee to i., And breake thy neck from steepe securite MARSTON.

Improvident (imprǫ·vidĕnt), *a.* 1514. [– Fr. †*improvident*; see IM-[2], PROVIDENT.] **1.** Unforeseeing; that does not forecast the future. **2.** Not circumspect; heedless; unwary 1591. **3.** Thriftless 1624.

1. The i...conduct of the German powers 1795. **2.** Improuident Souldiors, had your Watch been good, This sudden Mischiefe neuer could haue falne SHAKS.

†**Improvide·ntially**, *adv.* 1797. [f. IM-[2] + PROVIDENTIALLY.] = next –1819.

Impro·vidently, *adv.* 1607. [f. IMPROVIDENT *a.* + -LY[2].] **1.** In an improvident manner; without providing for the future. **2.** In an unforeseen manner (*rare*) 1885.

1. Agricultural labourers marry early and i. 1868.

Improving (imprū·viŋ), *vbl. sb.* 1602. [f. IMPROVE *v.*[2] + -ING[1].] The action of IMPROVE *v.*[2]; improvement.

Improving lease (Sc. Law): a lease granted to a tenant for a longer period than the usual one, with the object of encouraging him to make permanent improvements on the holding.

Improvisate (imprǫ·vizeⁱt), *v.* 1832. [f. Fr. *improviser* or It. *improvvisare*; see IMPROVISE, -ATE[3].] = IMPROVISE (*trans.* and *intr.*). So **Impro·visate** *ppl. a.* (*rare*), improvised; impromptu.

Improvisation (i:mprŏvəizēⁱ·ʃən, imprǫvizēⁱ·ʃən). 1786. [f. IMPROVISE + -ATION or IMPROVISATE + -ION; prob. after the earlier IMPROVISATORE.] **1.** The action of improvising; also *concr.* verse, music, etc. so improvised. **2.** The production or execution of anything off-hand; anything so produced or executed 1874.

1. The thrush-like i... that charm[s] us in our Elizabethan drama LOWELL.

Impro·visatize, *v. rare.* 1847. [irreg. f. IMPROVISATE + -IZE] = IMPROVISATE.

Improvisator (imprǫ·vizēⁱtəɹ). 1795. [f. IMPROVISE + -ATOR or IMPROVISATE + -OR 2, after It. *improvvisatore*, Fr. *improvisateur.*] One who composes extempore; an improviser.

‖**Improvisatore, -provvisatore** (*improv-(v)īzatō·re*). Pl. **-ori** (-*ō·ri*), also **-ores.** 1765. [It., f. *improvvisare* IMPROVISE.] An improvisator (Italian or of the Italian type).

Improvisatorial (imprǫvizătōᵊ·riăl), *a.* 1822. [f. *improvisatory* + -AL[1]; see -ORIAL.] Of, pertaining to, or having the nature of an improvisator; relating to or having the power of improvisation. Hence **Improvisato·rially** *adv.* So **Improvi·satory** *a.* 1806.

‖**Improvisatrice, -provvisa-** (*improv(v)īzatrī·tʃe*). Pl. **-trici** (-*trī·tʃi*). 1804. [It., fem. of *improvvisatore*; see -TRICE.] A woman who improvises.

Improvise (i·mprŏvəiz), *v.* 1826. [– Fr. *improviser* or its source, It. *improvvisare*, f. *improvviso* extempore – L. *improvisus* unforeseen, f. *in-* IM-[2] + *provisus*, pa. pple. of *providere* PROVIDE.] **1.** *trans.* To compose, utter, or perform extempore. **2.** To get up on the spur of the moment; to provide for the occasion 1854. **3.** *intr.* To compose, utter, or perform verse or music impromptu; to speak extemporaneously; to do anything on the spur of the moment 1830.

1. The singular faculty of being able to i. quotations DISRAELI. **2.** To i. a dance 1854, a tent DICKENS. Hence **Improvi·se** *sb.* an improvisation 1820. **Improvi·sedly** *adv.* **Improvi·ser.**

†**Improvi·sion.** 1646. [– med.L. *improvisio*, f. L. *in-* IM-[2] + *provisio* PROVISION.] Want of provision or forethought –1649.

†**Improviso** (improvəi·zo), *a.* 1786. [It., = L. *improvisus*; see IMPROVISE.] Improvised, extempore –1789.

Improvvisatore, -trice: see IMPROVIS-.

Imprudence (imprū·dĕns). 1445. [– (O)Fr. *imprudence* or L. *imprudentia*, f. *imprudens, -ent-*; see next, -ENCE.] The quality or fact of being imprudent; want of prudence, rashness; (with *an* and *pl.*) an imprudent act.

Not taking those precautions against the weather. . I soon suffered for my i. 1831. Love at first sight sounds like an i. LUBBOCK. So †**Impru·dency** 1576.

Imprudent (imprū·dĕnt), *a.* (*sb.*) ME. [– L. *imprudens, -ent-*, f. *in-* IM-[2] + *prudens* PRUDENT. Later perh. after Fr. *imprudent* (XV–XVI).] **1.** Not prudent, wanting in prudence or discretion; rash, heedless, indiscreet, incautious. †**2.** *sb.* An imprudent person –1767.

1. I. men are call'd Fools 1710. Loss for the folly of i. actions R. COKE. Hence **Impru·dently** *adv.*

†**Imprude·ntial,** *a.* [f. IM-[2] + PRUDENTIAL.] Not prudential. MILT.

Impuberal (impiū·bĕrăl), *a. rare.* 1836. [f. IM-[2] + PUBERAL.] Not come to puberty or maturity; immature. So **Impu·berate, Impu·bic** *adjs.* (*rare*).

Impuberty (impiū·bəɹti). 1785. [f. IM-[2] + PUBERTY, but cf. med.L. *impubertas* youth (XV).] The condition of not having reached the state or age of puberty.

Impudence (i·mpiŭdĕns). ME. [– L. *impudentia*, f. *impudens*; see next, -ENCE.] The quality or fact of being impudent. †**1.** Shamelessness; immodesty –1712. **2.** Shameless effrontery; insolence; unabashed presumption 1611. **b.** Applied to an impudent person. DRYDEN. **3.** In a neutral sense: Freedom from shamefastness 1619.

1. *All's Well*, II. i. 173. **2.** Some with I. invade the Court DRYDEN. 'Confound his impudence!' muttered Squeers DICKENS. **3.** I had not enterprise nor i. enough to venture from my concealment W. IRVING. So **I·mpudency** (now *rare*), in all senses 1529.

Impudent (i·mpiŭdĕnt), *a.* (*sb.*) ME. [– L. *impudens, -ent-*, f. *in-* IM-[2] + *pudens* ashamed, modest, orig. pr. pple. of *pudēre* feel ashamed; see -ENT.] †**1.** Wanting in modesty; shameless, unblushing; indelicate –1732. **2.** Possessed of unblushing effrontery; shamelessly forward, insolently disrespectful 1563. **3.** *sb.* A person of unblushing effrontery or insolence 1586.

1. Inpudent is he that. .hath no shame of hise synnes CHAUCER. **2.** A wicked, i., bold-faced hussy DICKENS. An i. reply 1873. Hence **I·mpudently** *adv.*

Impudicity (impiudi·sĭti). 1528. [– Fr. *impudicité*, irreg. f. L. *impudicitia*, f. *impudicus* shameless; see -ICITY.] Shamelessness, immodesty.

Impugn (impiū·n), *v.* ME. [– L. *impugnare*, f. *in-* IM-[1] + *pugnare* fight.] †**1.** *trans.* To fight against; to attack, assail, assault (a person, city, etc.) –1651. †**b.** To withstand, resist, oppose –1660. **2.** To assail by word or argument; to call in question; to oppose as false or erroneous ME. **b.** To find fault with, accuse (now *rare*) ME.

2. The saint was scarcely canonised, before his claims to beatitude were impugned DISRAELI. Hence **Impu·gnable** *a.*[1] (*rare*), **Impu·gnant** *a.*, opposed *to*, **Impugna·tion** ME., **Impu·gner, Impu·gnment.**

Impugnable (impɒ·gnăb'l), *a.*[2] ? *Obs.* 1570. [f. IM-[2] + L. *pugnare* + -ABLE.] That cannot be assailed or overcome.

Impuissance (impiū·isăns). 1483. [–(O)Fr. *impuissance*; see IM-[2], PUISSANCE.] Impotence, powerlessness, weakness.

An i. to conserve himself 1602.

Impuissant (impiū·isănt), *a.* 1629. [– Fr. *impuissant*; see IM-[2], PUISSANT.] Impotent, powerless, weak.

Impulse (i·mpɒls), *sb.* 1647. [– L. *impulsus*, f. pa. ppl. stem of L. *impellere* IMPEL; cf. PULSE *sb.*[1]] **1.** An act of impelling; an application of sudden force causing motion; a thrust, a push 1650. Also *fig.* **2.** *Dynamics.* **a.** An indefinitely large force enduring for an inappreciably short time but producing a finite momentum; such as the blow of a hammer, etc. 1796. **b.** The product of the average value *of* any force multiplied by the time during which it acts (CLERK-MAXWELL) 1875. **3. a.** Force or influence exerted upon the mind by some external stimulus; suggestion, incitement 1660. **b.** Incitement arising from some state of mind or feeling 1647. **c.** Sudden inclination to act without premeditation 1763. **4.** The effect produced by impulsion; momentum, impetus 1715. Also *fig.* **b.** *Path.* 'The wave of change which travels through nerve and muscle in passing from rest into action' (*Syd. Soc. Lex.*) 1886. **5.** *attrib.* 1825.

1. We cannot conceive how any thing but i. of body can move body LOCKE. *fig.* The blind impulses of Fatality and Fortune BENTLEY. **3. a.** A. . Divine I. and Impression 1674. **b.** Under an i. of curiosity 1833. **c.** Guided by i. rather than by judgement FREEMAN. **4.** *fig.* Orseolo gave a new i. to navigation YEATS.

Impu·lse, *v.* Now *rare.* 1611. [f. the sb., or as prec. Cf. Fr. †*impulser.*] *trans.* To give an impulse to; to impel; to instigate.

Impulsion (impɒ·lʃən). ME. [– (O)Fr. *impulsion* or L. *impulsio*, f. as prec.; see -ION.] **1.** The action of impelling or forcing onward; also of striking upon, pushing, or pressing against without producing motion; the condition of being impelled. Also *transf.* and *fig.* †**b.** An impelling cause or occasion. BACON. **2. a.** Instigation, incitement 1533. **b.** Determination to action from natural tendency or temporary excitement; impulse 1530. **3.** Impetus 1795.

1. The centrifugal force, or force of i., is still unknown 1794. **2. a.** Atreus and Thyestes. .at the i. of their mother slew this Chrysippus HOBBES. **b.** The like i. from which a drowning man catches at a twig 1793. **3.** The i. which Kant had given to philosophy SIR W. HAMILTON.

Impulsive (impɒ·lsiv), *a.* (*sb.*) ME. [– (O)Fr. *impulsif, -ive* (rare before XVIII) or late L. *impulsivus*, f. as prec.; see -IVE.] **1.** Having the property of impelling; characterized by impulsion or impetus 1604. **2.** Impelling or determining to action 1555. **3.** Of persons, etc.: Actuated or characterized by impulse; apt to be moved by sudden impulse or swayed by emotion 1847. †**4.** *sb.* An impelling agent or cause –1659.

1. The force Of the i. chariot CHAPMAN. When a force produces it's effect instantaneously, it is said to be i. 1803. **2.** The love of God was the i. (= originating) cause HORNECK. Hence **Impu·lsive-ly** *adv.*, **-ness. Impu·lsivist,** one who acts on impulse. **Impulsi·vity,** impulsiveness.

†**Impu·lsor.** 1653. [– L. *impulsor*, f. as prec.; see -OR 2.] One who, or that which, impels –1700. So **Impu·lsory** *a.* (*rare*), that tends to impel 1659.

Impu·nctate, *ppl. a.* 1819. [f. IM-[2] + PUNCTATE.] Not punctate; not marked with points or dots.

Impu·nctual, *a.* 1864. [f. IM-[2] + PUNCTUAL.] Not punctual; behind time. So **Impunctua·lity,** want of punctuality 1790.

†**Impune** (impiū·n), *a.* [– L. *impunis* unpunished, f. *in-* IM-[2] + *pœna* penalty, punishment, f. *punire* PUNISH.] Unpunished; enjoying impunity. T. ADAMS.

Impunible (impiū·nĭb'l), *a. rare.* 1660. [f. IM-[2] + med.L. *punibilis*, f. *punire* punish; see -BLE.] Not punishable; unpunishable. Hence **Impu·nibly** *adv.*

Impunity (impiū·nĭti). 1532. [– L. *impunitas*, f. *impunis*; see IMPUNE, -ITY.] Exemption from punishment or penalty; exemption from injury or loss.

Delay of punishment is no sort nor degree of presumption of final i. BUTLER. The venom of the most deadly snakes may be swallowed with i. PRINGLE.

†**Impura·tion.** [f. IMPURE *v.* + -ATION.] Pollution (*lit.* and *fig.*). BP. HALL.

Impure (impiūᵊ·ɹ), *a.* 1536. [– L. *impurus*, f. *in-* IM-[2] + *purus* PURE. Cf. (O)Fr. *impur.*] **I. 1.** Containing some defiling or offensive matter; dirty, unclean 1597; not pure ceremonially; unhallowed 1612. **2.** Not pure morally; defiled by sin; unchaste; filthy 1536.

1. An i. atmosphere 1807. The invader, who had touched the hallowed soil with i. feet THIRLWALL. **2.** Defaming as i. what God declares Pure MILT.

II. Mixed with some extraneous matter; contaminated, adulterated 1626. **b.** Of a language, style, etc.: Containing foreign idioms or grammatical blemishes 1613. **c.** Of a colour: Containing an admixture of some other colour or colours; also said of a spectrum when the colours overlap 1860.

I. mercury 1816, thought 1704. **c.** The rainbow is an imperfect or i. spectrum TYNDALL. Hence †**Impu·re** *v.* to make, or become, i. 1597. **Impu·re-ly** *adv.*, **-ness.**

Impu·ritan. 1617. [f. IMPURE *a.*, after PURITAN.] One who practises impurity; also, a dyslogistic term for one opposed to Puritanism.

Impurity (impiūᵊ·rĭti). 1450. [– Fr. †*impurité* (now *impureté*) or L. *impuritas*, f. *impurus*; see IMPURE, -ITY.] **1.** The quality or condition of being impure, in any sense; foulness; defilement 1548. **2.** That which is or makes impure; dirt; corruption; foreign matter 1450.

1. The i. of the ayr 1660, of thought 1704. I. or beastlinesse is not hard to be defined HEALEY. **2.** Novels. .full of impurities, impieties 1639. Ashes or other impurities 1799.

Impurple, obs. f. EMPURPLE *v.*

Imputable (impiū·tăb'l), *a.* 1626. [– med.L. *imputabilis*, f. L. *imputare*; see IMPUTE, -ABLE. Cf. (O)Fr. *imputable.*] **1.** That may be imputed *to* or assigned to the account of; chargeable, attributable. †**2.** Liable to imputation; open to accusation or censure; culpable –1784.

1. The errour is i. onely to the Transcriber 1626. **2.** Some justly blameable and i. Act SHAFTESB. Hence **Imputabi·lity, Impu·tableness,** the quality of being i. **Impu·tably** *adv.*

Imputation (impiutēⁱ·ʃən). 1545. [– Fr. *imputation* or late L. *imputatio*, f. *imputat-*, pa. ppl. stem of L. *imputare*; see next, -ION.] **1.** The action of imputing or charging; the fact of being charged with a crime, fault, etc.; (with *pl.*) accusation, charge 1581. **2.** *Theol.* The attributing to believers of the righteousness of Christ, and to Christ of human sin, by vicarious substitution; also, the imputing of the guilt of Adam's sin to all his descendants 1545. †**3.** The making a merit of a thing. EARLE.

1. I would humour his men, with the i. of beeing neere their Mayster SHAKS. The i. of a new violation of faith BURKE. **2.** I. is the attributing of a character to a person which he does not really possess HOOK.

Imputative (impiū·tătiv), *a.* 1579. [– late L. *imputativus* (Tertullian), f. as prec.; see -IVE; perh. infl. by PUTATIVE.] Characterized by being imputed; existing or arising by imputation.

A man would think we need no i. wickedness 1691. Hence **Impu·tative-ly** *adv.*, **-ness.**

Impute (impiū·t), *v.* ME. [–(O)Fr. *imputer* – L. *imputare* bring into the reckoning or charge, f. *in-* IM-[1] + *putare* reckon.] **1.** *trans.* To bring (a fault, etc.) into the reckoning against; to lay to the charge of; to attribute or assign *to.* **b.** Occas. in a good sense: To set to the credit of; to ascribe or reckon *to* 1574. **2.** *Theol.* To attribute or ascribe (righteousness, guilt, etc.) *to* a person by vicarious substitution 1583. **3.** To arraign or tax *with* fault; to accuse. ? *Obs.* 1596. †**4.** To reckon or take into account; to consider –1794. †**5.** To impart –1675.

1. We usually ascribe good, but i. evil JOHNSON. **b.** It was imputed to him for righteousness *Rom.* 4 : 22. **2.** Thy merit Imputed shall absolve them who renounce Thir own both righteous and unrighteous deeds MILT. *P.L.* III. 291. **4.** [K. Henry VI] for his holy life was imputed a Saint SPEED. Hence **Impu·tedly** *adv.* by imputation.

Imputrescence (impiutre·sĕns). 1658. [f. IM-[2] + PUTRESCENCE.] Absence of decomposition.

Imputre·scible, *a.* 1656. [f. IM-[2] + PUTRESCIBLE.] Not subject to decomposition. **Imputrescibi·lity.**

†**Imputrid** (impiū·trid), *a.* 1684. [f. IM-[2] + PUTRID.] Not putrid; applied to a fever –1824.

In, *sb.* 1764. [f. IN *adv.*] **1.** *pl.* **a.** The party that is in office, usu. in phr. (*the*) *ins and outs.* **b.** In games: The side whose turn it is to play 1862. **2. Ins and outs.** Windings or turnings in and out in a road, a course of action, etc.; sinuous ramifications 1670. **b.** Those who are constantly entering and leaving the workhouse 1884.

1. a. Everything the Ins do the Outs denounce SPURGEON. **2.** The ins and outs of legal method 1878.

In, *a.* 1599. [In *adv.* used *attrib.*, or as positive of INNER, INMOST.] That is in; that lies, remains, lives, is situated, or is used in or within; internal. (Usu. hyphened to the sb.)

In (in), *v.* OE. [The OE. (*ge*)*innian* (cf. OHG. (*ge*)*innōn* take up) appear to attach themselves in part to *inn* IN *adv.* and partly to be more immediately assoc. with the derivative INN *sb.*] **1.** *trans.* †To give or put in; to take in, include, enclose; *esp.* to take in or reclaim (waste land). Now *dial.* **2.** To gather into the barn, stackyard, etc.; to harvest or house ME. **3.** To get in, gather in, collect 1615. †**4.** To take in mentally. FLORIO. †**5.** *intr.* To go in, to enter; in 17th c. to begin –1639.

2. He taryed tyll they had inned all their corne 1525. **5.** We inne diversely, but end alike 1639.

In (in), *prep.* [OE. *in* = OFris., OS., OHG. (Du., G.), Goth. *in*, ON. *í*, rel. to L. *in* (older *en*), Gr. ἐν, ἐνί, OIr. *in*, W. *yn*, Lith. *ĩ*, OPruss. *en*, OSl. *vŭ(n-)*, Russ. *v* (*vo*, *vn-*) :– IE **en*, **n*. Reduced to *i* before cons. by 1200, and so retained arch. and dial., as in *i'th'* in the, and *i'faith*; cf. HANDICAP.] *General sense*:—The preposition expressing the relation of inclusion, situation, position, existence, or action within limits of space, time, condition, circumstances, etc. In ancient times, expressing also (like L. *in*) motion or direction from a point outside to one within limits (now ordinarily *in-to*, INTO).

I. Of position or location. **1.** Within the limits or bounds of, within (any place or thing). †**2.** = ON (of position) –1730. †**b.** = AT –1671. **3.** *In* is now regular with collectives thought of as singular (*in an army*, *a crowd*) OE. **4.** With numerals, nouns of quantity, etc. expressing ratio or rate 1436. **5.** Defining the particular part of anything in which it is affected ME. **6.** Expressing relation to that which covers, clothes, or envelopes, its material, its colour, etc., = clothed in, wearing, bound in, etc. OE. **7.** With non-physical realms, regions of thought, departments or faculties of the mind, spheres of action, etc., treated as having extension or content OE.

1. Summe in þe Eir, and summe in þe Eorþe, and summe in helle deope LANGL. In the green woods SHELLEY; in the East DICKENS. *With the article omitted: *In bed*, *in chancery*, *in church*, *in school*, *in town*; in Capernaum 1526 in Europe 1686. **2. b.** Ere in the head of nations he appear MILT. *P. R.* I. 98. **4.** A debtor..offered 6*s.* 8*d.* in the pound 1892. **5.** A masked battery took them in flank 1795. **6.** Martirs clothed alle in purpul ME. A lady in a Gainsborough hat 1899. **7.** I discover an arrant laziness in my soul FULLER. Opposed in politics MACAULAY.

II. 1. Of situation, i.e. kind or nature of position OE. **b.** Situation within the range of sensuous observation or the sphere of action of another ME. **2.** Of condition or state, physical, mental, or moral OE. **3.** Of occupation or engagement ME. **b.** In the process or act of, in case of ME. **4.** Of manner (way, mode, style, fashion) ME. **b.** Of form, shape, conformation, arrangement, order OE. **c.** Of manner of speech or writing OE. **d.** *colloq.* Within the sphere of (a particular class or order of things) 1866. **5.** Of means or instrumentality (now usually *with*) OE. **6.** Of material, constituents, and the like ME. **7.** Of degree, extent, measure ME. **8.** Expressing object, aim, or purpose ME. **9.** In reference to; in the case, matter, or province of ME.

1. *In the dust*, *in hot water*, etc.; *in chains*, *in a leash*, etc.; *in the sunshine*, *in all weathers*, etc. **b.** In sight of God's high Throne MILT. **2.** *In a blaze*, *in debt*, *doubt*, *sickness*, etc.; *in cash*, *in liquor*, *in tears*. **3.** In search of plunder DICKENS. **b.** Drowned in crossing the river 1899. **4.** *In confidence*, *in piteous terms*, etc. **b.** Did he..begin in rogue, and end in enthusiast? SOUTHEY. **d.** The newest..thing in pinnacles RUSKIN. **5.** A French Ship..ballasted in mahogany 1804. Progne, with her Bosom stain'd in Blood DRYDEN. I drinke to you in a Cup of Sack SHAKS. **6.** Half-length portraits, in crayons DICKENS. **7.** Differing but in degree MILT. **8.** *In affirmation*, *memory*, *recompense*, *scorn*, *witness*, etc.

III. Of time. **1.** Within the limits of a period or space of time OE. **2.** In the course of ME. **3.** Before or at the expiration of; within the space of ME. **4.** Formerly (and still occas.) used, where *at*, *on*, *during*, *for* are now in use, or where the prep. is omitted OE.

1. Between..Twelve and Four in the Morning STEELE. The prince in his childhood THIRLWALL. The..houses you see in a railway excursion 1859. **2.** In a moment and in the twincklynge of an eye TINDALE 1 *Cor.* 15:52. **3.** I rallied in a day or two 1843. **4.** The Duke in Counsell? In (= *at*) this time of the night? SHAKS. Looke you..that our Armies ioyn not in (= *on*) a hot day SHAKS. To Westminster Hall, where I have not been..in (= *for*) some months PEPYS. This engine..set out in (*in* now omitted) four hours after my landing SWIFT.

IV. Pregnant uses: sometimes due to ellipsis. **1.** With reflexive pronouns: *In himself*, *in itself*, etc.: in his or its own person, essence, or nature; absolutely ME. **2.** In spiritual or mystical union with ME. **3.** In the person or case of ME. **4.** Belonging to, as a quality, attribute, faculty, or capacity; hence, within the ability, capacity, thought, etc. of ME. **5.** In the hands of; legally vested in 1460. **6.** Partaking, sharing, associated, or actually engaged in 1728. **7.** Of representative character or capacity, as *in* NAME *of*, *in* RIGHT *of*; see the sbs. **8.** Ellipt. for 'in the character of' 1831.

1. Of things absolutely or in themselves MILL. **2.** Blessed are the dead which die in the Lord *Rev.* 14:13. **3.** Good against fits in women 1707. **4.** To prefer evil to good is not in human nature JOWETT. **5.** The minerals, therefore, are in the trustees 1884. **6.** Phr. *To be in it*, to be an actual competitor, partner, etc.; to be in the running, to count for something. **8.** I am to come out in Bianca F. A. KEMBLE.

V. Of motion or direction. See also II. 8. **1.** = INTO OE. †**2.** Hence formerly used where *upon*, *on*, *towards*, *unto*, *to* are now in use –1557.

1. And broghte hire hoom with hym in his contree CHAUCER. He..in the Billows plung'd his hoary Head DRYDEN.

Phrases. **In so far**: in such measure or degree (as); to such extent (that). **In that**: in the fact that; in its being the case that; seeing that; as, because. See also INASMUCH, INSOMUCH, etc.

In (in), *adv.* (*a.*) [Distinct in origin from IN *prep.* Repr. (i) OE. *in(n)* used with verbs of motion (cf. INTO) = OFris., OS., Du. *in*, OHG. *in* (with secondary lengthening), G. *ein*, ON., Goth. *inn*; (ii) OE. *inne*, used with verbs of position = OFris., OS. *inna*, OHG. *inna*, *-i*, *-e*, ON. *inni*, Goth. *inna*, orig. locative. Cf. OE. *hērinne* HEREIN, *þǣrin*, *-inne* THEREIN.]

I. Of motion or direction. [OE. *inn*, *in*.] **1.** Expressing motion from a point without to a place within certain limits (see also under COME, GO, PASS, PUT, etc.). **b.** Used after *may*, *must*, *shall*, etc., or absol. with imperative force, with omission of 'go', 'enter', etc. (cf. IN *v.* 5). Now chiefly *poet.* or *rhet.* OE. **2.** Expressing motion in the direction of some central point; hence, in proximity to some point specified or implied; into or in close quarters 1702. **3.** Into the bargain; in addition (to the legal amount); over and above, besides; as in to *get*, *give*, *throw in* 1634.

1. In comes my nephew DE FOE. **b.** The door is open! I'll in, and take my leave of her 1668. Phr. *Day in*, *day out*; continually. **2.** About five yards in, it [the path] took a turn 1888. **3.** And so you have the fight in gratis DICKENS.

II. Of position. **1.** Within a certain space; esp. inside a house ME. **b.** On the inside, within ME. **2.** In various special senses (see quots.) 1588.

1. Dame, art thow in? 1475. **b.** A sheepskin coat with the woolly side in 1873. 2. †**a.** = Engaged, involved; All my plots Turn back upon myself; but I am in, And must go on MASSINGER. **b.** = In office, in power; Who's in, who's out *Lear* v. iii. 15. **c.** = In possession of the field, etc.; having the turn or right to play; He scored 33..while he was in in 1884. **d.** In legal possession of (an estate); In by descent CRUISE. **e.** Of fire or light: Burning, lighted; The law..which orders the Fire to be always kept in ADDISON. **f.** Of a train, coach, mail, etc.: Come in, arrived. **g.** = In the market, in season; Savoys are in 1891.

Phrases. **In for. a.** Engaged or involved *in* some business, etc. *for* a specified time; finally committed or destined to do or suffer something. **b.** *esp.* in phr. *in for it*: Committed to a course of action; also, certain to meet with punishment, etc. **c.** In the competition for something. **d.** *In for a penny*, *in for a pound*; see PENNY. **In with. a.** In agreement with; on friendly terms with. **b.** *Naut.* Close in to, near (the land). **c.** †*To come in with*, to overtake; also = *to fall in with* (see FALL *v.*).

Combs. **1.** Pples. and vbl. sbs., nouns of action, and agent-nouns, from vbs. qualified by *in*, are formed by prefixing *in-*, when used as adjs. or sbs. Their number is practically unlimited. See IN- *pref.*[1]

2. With sbs. Usu. opp. to *out-*. (Cf. IN *a.*) Thus **i·n-brother,** a resident brother of a fraternity or guild; **i·n-burgess,** one resident in the burgh; **i·n-case,** a case of an in-patient; **i·n-patient,** one who remains in a hospital while under treatment; **i·n-pensioner,** one resident in a charitable institution.

3. With verbs: see IN- *pref.*[1]

4. With advs. and prepositions; as IN-BETWEEN.

In (in). The Latin prep. *in* (with the ablative case) 'in' (with accusative) 'into', occurs in many phrases, of which the chief are given below.

1. in ca·pite, in chief (see CHIEF *sb.*), holding directly from the crown 1558. **2. in exte·nso,** at full length 1826. **3. in extre·mis,** in the last agonies 1530. **4. in fo·rma pau·peris,** in the form of a poor person (exempted from liability to pay the costs of an action; see PAUPER *sb.*); hence, in a humble or abject manner 1592. **5. in infini·tum,** to infinity, without end 1564. **6. in li·mine,** on the threshold, at the very outset 1804. **7. in lo·co,** in the place of; esp. **in loco pare·ntis,** in the place or position of a parent 1710. **8. in me·dias re·s,** into the midst of affairs, into the middle of a narrative 1786. **9. in memo·riam,** to the memory of. Hence as *sb.* = A memorial poem or writing. 1850. **10. in nu·bibus,** in the clouds; not yet settled; also, incapable of being carried out 1583. **11. in pa·rtibus (infide·lium),** in parts inhabited by unbelievers. In *R.C.Ch.* describing a titular bishop in an uncivilized or a heretical country 1687. **12. in perpe·tuum,** to all time 1642. **13. in pontifica·libus,** in pontificals, in the proper vestments of a pope, cardinal, etc. 1494. **14. in pro·pria perso·na,** in his (her, etc.) own person 1654. **15. in si·tu,** in its (original) place; in position 1817. **16. in sta·tu quo (ante, prius,** or **nunc),** in the same state (as formerly or now) 1602. **17. in terro·rem,** as a warning, in order to terrify others 1612. **18. in to·to,** as a whole, absolutely, completely 1798. **19. in tra·nsitu,** in passing, on the way. **20. in va·cuo,** in a vacuum or empty space 1660.

In-, *pref.*[1], the prep. and adv. IN, in comb. with vbs., vbl. derivs., and other words. In OE. the adv. *inn*, *in*, was freely used in collocation with vbs. of motion or change of state. In the infinitive the adv. generally stood before the vb., and in derived vbl. sbs. and adjs. always so. In this position the adv. came at length to be written in comb. with the vb.; hence, many regular compounds with stress on *in-*, thus *incoming*, *income*, *incomer*, *indweller*, *inlet*, *insight*, etc. Other formations, in which the prefix usually has the sense 'in, within, internal', are *inborn*, *inside*, *inward*, etc.

In- *pref.*[2], repr. L. *in-* adv. and prep., used in comb. with vbs. or their derivatives, less commonly with other parts of speech, with the senses 'into, in, within; on, upon; towards, against', sometimes expressing onward motion or continuance, sometimes intensive, sometimes transitive, and in other cases with no appreciable force. For *Form-history*, see EN-, IL-[1], IM-[1], IR-[1].

In-, *pref.*[3], the L. *in-*, cogn. w. Gr. ἀ-, ἀν-, Gmc. *un-*, prefixed to adjs. and their derivatives, rarely to other wds., to express negation or privation. In Eng. the modern tendency is to restrict *in-* to words obviously answering to Latin types, and to prefer the OE. negative *un-* in other cases, as *unavailing*, *uncertain*, *undevout*. Writers in XVII, however, made extensive use of this prefix, and many words were formed from their positive congeners, as *inorganity* from *organity*; so *inobservation*, *inoppressive*, *inordinance*, and such is prob. the derivation of many words for which a Latin parallel can be discovered, as in *ingustable*, *inseparate*, *innubilous*, *inornate*, etc.

In-, *pref.*[4], of Gmc. origin, prefixed to OE. and ME. adjs., with the sense 'inly', 'intimately', 'thoroughly', and hence 'exceedingly', 'very'.

-in, *suffix*[1]. *Chem.* A modification of the chemical suffix -INE[5], used for the names of neutral substances, such as glycerides, glucosides, bitter principles, colouring matters, which are thus distinguished from names of alkaloids and basic substances in -INE. Some of these were formerly spelt with *-ine*, esp. *dextrine*, *gelatine*, *margarine*, and are still so spelt in non-scientific use.

-in, *suffix*[2], obs. var. of -INE[1] in adjs., as *feminin*, *genuin*, etc.; also occas. var. of -INE[4] :—L. *-ina*, as in *ruin*.

-ina, *suffix*[1], L. fem. suffix found in *regina* queen, extended in It. or Sp., and thence in Eng. use, to form feminine titles, *as czarina*, and female Christian names, as *Alexandrina*, etc. It occurs also in *concertina, seraphina*, etc., names of musical instruments.

-ina, *suffix*[2], in wds. which are the n. pl. of L. adjs. in *-inus*, and in mod.L. wds. formed after them, used (in agreement with *animalia*, understood) to form names of groups of animals related to some typical genus, as *Bombycina* (genus *Bombyx*), etc.

Inability (inăbi·lĭti). ME. [f. IN-[3] + ABILITY. Cf. (O)Fr. *inhabilité*, med.L. *inhabilitas*.] The condition of being unable; want of ability, physical, mental, or moral; lack of power, capacity, or means. †**b.** *spec.* Bodily infirmity –1834.

My distressing i. to sleep at night DICKENS.

Inable-, -ment, obs. ff. ENABLE, -MENT.

Ina·bstinence. 1667. [IN-[3].] Want of abstinence; failure to abstain. MILT. *P. L.* XI. 476.

†**Inabstra·cted,** *ppl. a. rare.* 16.. [IN-[3].] Not abstracted.

†**Inabu·sively,** *adv.* 1677. [IN-[3].] Not abusively, properly. LD. NORTH.

Inaccessible (inække·sĭb'l), *a.* †Also *erron.* **-able.** 1555. [– (O)Fr. *inaccessible* or late L. *inaccessibilis* (Tertullian); see IN-[3], ACCESSIBLE.] **1.** That cannot be reached, entered, or got to; that cannot be scaled or penetrated. **2.** *fig.* Unapproachable 1583. †**3.** (tr. Gr. ἄαπτος.) 'Not to be touched, resistless, invincible'. CHAPMAN.

1. Its i. acropolis defied them GROTE. **2.** This savage hero was not i. to pity GIBBON. Hence **I:naccessibi·lity,** quality or condition of being i.; unapproachableness. **Inacce·ssibleness. Inacce·ssibly** *adv.*

Inacco·rdant, *a.* 1822. [IN-[3].] Not accordant; inharmonious. So **Inacco·rdance, -ancy,** i. quality. **Inacco·rdantly** *adv.*

Inaccuracy (inæ·kiŭrăsi). 1757. [f. next; see -ACY, and cf. *accuracy*.] The quality or condition of being inaccurate; want of accuracy; also with *an* and *pl.*

An appearance of i. in the use of terms 1772. Historical inaccuracies 1883.

Inaccurate (inæ·kiŭrĕt), *a.* 1738. [f. IN-[3] + ACCURATE.] Not accurate; inexact, incorrect, erroneous.

I. modes of expression JOWETT. **Ina·ccurate-ly** *adv.* 1669, **-ness.**

Inacquai·ntance. 1607. [IN-[3].] The being unacquainted; want of acquaintance.

Inacquie·scent, *a.* [IN-[3].] Not acquiescent. SCOTT. So †**Inacquie·scency** 1647.

†**Inact** (inæ·kt), *v.*[1] 1647. [f. IN-[2] + ACT *v.*] *trans.* To actuate –1662.

Inact, *v.*[2], obs. f. ENACT.

Inaction (inæ·kʃən). 1707. [f. IN-[3] + ACTION *sb.*] Absence of action or activity; inertness, supineness.

Inactive (inæ·ktiv), *a.* 1725. [IN-[3].] Not active; not disposed to act; inert, indolent, sluggish; passive, quiescent.

The seeming Charms of an idle and i. life POPE. A converter of i. or free, into active or combined oxygen 1866. An i. market 1883. Hence **Ina·ctively** *adv.* So **Ina·ctiveness** 1678.

Inactivity (inækti·vĭti). 1646. [IN-[3].] The quality or state of being inactive; want of activity; inertness, sluggishness; passiveness, quiescence.

Poor Fenton..died..of Indolence and I. POPE. The Government should be taught that the highest wisdom of a state is a wise and masterly i. CALHOUN.

†**Inactuate** (inæ·ktiu,eᶦt), *v.* 1651. [f. IN-[2] + ACTUATE.] *trans.* To make active, put in action –1662. Hence **Inactua·tion.**

Inadaptabi·lity. 1840. [IN-[3].] Want of adaptability.

So **Inada·ptable** *a.*, **Inadapta·tion, Inada·ptive** *a.*

Inadequate (inæ·dĭkwĕt), *a.* 1675. [IN-[3].] Not adequate; not equal to requirement; insufficient.

I. conceptions BOYLE, terms 1792, remuneration 1880. Resources..i. to meet the expenses of war GREEN. Hence **Ina·dequacy,** insufficiency. **Ina·dequate-ly** *adv.*, **-ness. Inadequa·tion** *arch.* 1630.

Inadhe·rent, *a.* 1855. [IN-[3].] Not adherent; free. So **Inadhe·sion,** non-adhesion 1796. **Inadhe·sive** *a.* not adhesive 1811.

Inadmissible (inădmi·sĭb'l), *a.* 1776. [f. IN-[3] + ADMISSIBLE. Cf. Fr. *inadmissible.*] Not admissible; not to be admitted, entertained, or allowed.

Tea, coffee, and alcohol are i. ALLBUTT. Hence **Inadmissibi·lity,** the fact or quality of being i.

†**Inadu·lterate,** *a.* [f. IN-[3] + ADULTERATE *ppl. a.*] Unadulterated. HERRICK.

Inadventurous (inădve·ntiŭrəs), *a.* 1853. [IN-[3].] Not adventurous; unenterprising.

Inadvertence (inădvɔ̄·ɹtĕns). 1568. [– med.L. *inadvertentia*, see IN-[3], ADVERTENCE.] The fact or habit of being inadvertent; failure to observe or pay attention; inattention; also = next. **b.** with *an* and *pl.* An act or fault of inattention; an oversight 1725.

The said letter..was, through i., laid before the board BURKE. Marriage is one of those inadvertences which can hardly go for nothing even in the easiest life 1876.

Inadvertency (inădvɔ̄·ɹtĕnsi). 1592. [– med.L. *inadvertentia* (see -ENCY); see IN-[3], ADVERTENCY.] The quality or character of being inadvertent; also = prec.

Inadvertent (inădvɔ̄·ɹtĕnt), *a.* 1653. [f. IN-[3] + ADVERTENT.] **1.** Not properly attentive; inobservant, negligent; heedless. **2.** Of actions, etc.: Characterized by want of attention; hence, unintentional 1724.

2. An i. step may crush the snail, That crawls at evening in the public path COWPER. Hence **Inadve·rtently** *adv.*

†**Inadve·rtisement.** [f. IN-[3] + ADVERTISEMENT 1.] Want of attention; inadvertence. SIR T. BROWNE.

Inadvisable (inădvəi·zăb'l), *a. rare.* 1870. [IN-[3].] Unadvisable. Hence **Inadvisabi·lity,** unadvisableness 1864.

Inadvisedly (inădvəi·zĕdli), *adv. rare.* 1894. [IN-[3].] Unadvisedly. So **Inadvi·sedness** 1652.

-inæ, *suffix*, in wds. which are the fem. pl. of L. adjs. in *-inus* -INE[1], used (in agreement with *bestiæ*, understood) to form names of sub-families of animals. as *Caninæ* (L. *caninus* canine), *Felinæ* (L. *felinus* feline).

Inæsthetic (inĭspe·tik), *a.* 1846. [IN-[3].] Not æsthetic; void of taste.

†**Ina·ffable,** *a.* 1656. [IN-[3].] Not affable. So †**Inaffabi·lity** 1611.

†**Inaffe·cted,** *ppl. a. rare.* 1617. [IN-[3].] = UNAFFECTED. Hence †**Inaffe·cted-ly** *adv.*, †**-ness.**

†**Inai·dible,** *a.* [IN-[3].] That cannot be assisted; helpless. *All's Well* II. i. 122.

Inalienable (inēᶦ·liĕnăb'l), *a.* 1645. [f. IN-[3] + ALIENABLE. Cf. Fr. *inaliénable.*] Not alienable; that cannot be transferred from its present ownership or relation.

The i. character of alimony 1884. Hence **Ina:lienabi·lity,** i. quality. **Ina·lienably** *adv.*

Inalime·ntal, *a. rare.* 1626. [IN-[3].] Not affording aliment or nourishment.

Inalterable (inǭ·ltərăb'l), *a.* 1533. [– med.L. *inalterabilis*, see IN-[3], ALTERABLE.] Not alterable; unchangeable, immutable; unalterable. Hence **Inalterabi·lity,** unchangeableness. **Ina·lterably** *adv.*

Inamissible (inămi·sĭb'l), *a.* Now *rare.* 1649. [– Fr. *inamissible* or med.L. *inamissibilis*; see IN-[3], AMISSIBLE.] Not liable to be lost. Hence **Inamissibi·lity. Inami·ssibleness.**

Inamorata (inæmorā·tă). Also **en-.** 1651. [– It. *inamorata* (now *innam-*), fem. of INAMORATO.] A female lover, mistress, sweetheart.

The faire I. who from farre Had spy'd the Ship which her hearts treasure bare 1651.

Ina·morate, *a.* and *sb.* 1602. [Anglicized form of prec. and next; see -ATE[2].] **a.** *adj.* Enamoured, in love. †**b.** *sb.* One in love, a lover –1612. Hence †**Ina·morately** *adv.* lovingly 1599.

Inamorato (inæmorā·to). Also **en-.** 1592. [– It. *inamorato* (now *innam-*), pa. pple. of *inam(m)orare* = OFr. *enamourer* ENAMOUR *v.*] A lover.

Inamour, -ed, obs. ff. ENAMOUR, -ED.

Inamo·vable, *a. rare.* 1851. [f. IN-[3] + AMOVABLE. Cf. Fr. *inamovible.*] Not removable. Hence **Inamovabi·lity,** the quality of being i. 1849.

In and in, in-and-in. 1630. [IN *adv.*]

A. *adv.* Further and further in; continually inwards. Also *attrib.* (in quasi-*adj.* use).

Phr. *To breed in and in*, to breed always within a limited stock 1765. So *to marry in and in.*

B. *sb.* †**1.** The name given to a throw made with four dice, when these fell all alike or as two doublets –1668. †**b.** A gambling game played with four dice; the player who threw *in and in* (see above) took all the stake –1674. **2.** A space which opens up and ever discloses something further in 1890.

In and out, in-and-out, *adv.* ME. [Cf. also *ins and outs*, IN *sb.* 2.] **1.** Alternately in and out; now in, now out. †**2.** Inside out –1591. **3.** Both in and out 1895. **4.** *attrib.* (quasi-*adj.*) in various senses 1640.

1. Her feet beneath her petticoat Like little mice stole in and out SUCKLING. He was much in and out 1855. **3.** To know a man in and out 1895. **4.** *In-and-out cottage*, a cottage of irregular plan. *In-and-out running*, alternate winning and losing of races.

Inane (inēᶦ·n). 1662. [– L. *inanis* empty, vain.]

A. *adj.* **1.** Empty, void. **2.** Of persons, etc.: Destitute of sense; silly; empty-headed.

1. Vast i. infinities KINGSLEY. **2.** Some i. and vacant smile SHELLEY.

B. *sb.* **1.** That which is inane; void or empty space; vacuity; the 'formless void' 1677. **2.** An empty-headed person. POPE.

1. Atoms..dispers'd and dancing in the great I. 1700. Hence **Ina·nely** *adv.* emptily, senselessly.

†**Ina·ngular,** *a.* 1646. [IN-[3].] Not angular.

Inanimate (inæ·nimĕt), *a.* (*sb.*) 1563. [– late L. *inanimatus* lifeless (Boethius); see IN-[3], ANIMATE *ppl. a.* Cf. Fr. *inanimé.*] **1.** Not animated; lifeless; *spec.* not endowed with animal life, as in *inanimate nature*, i.e. all outside the animal world. **2.** Without the activity of life (*lit.* and *fig.*); spiritless, dull 1704. **3.** *sb.* An inanimate thing 1652.

1. And Ardennes waves above them her green leaves, Dewy with nature's tear-drops, as they pass, Grieving, if aught i. e'er grieves, Over the unreturning brave BYRON. **2.** The stock markets were quite i. 1893. So †**Ina·nimated** *a.* 1646–1826. Hence **Ina·nimate-ly** *adv.*, **-ness.**

†**Ina·nimate,** *v.* 1600. [– *inanimat-*, pa. ppl. stem of late L. *inanimare* inspire, fire; see IN-[2], ANIMATE *v.*] *trans.* To put life into (*lit.* and *fig.*) –1689. Hence †**Inanima·tion**[1], infusion of life, spirit, or vitality 1614–1647.

Inanima·tion[2]. 1784. [f. IN-[3] + ANIMATION.] Inanimate condition; absence of life or liveliness.

Inanition (inăni·ʃən). ME. [– late L. *inanitio*, f. L. *inanire*, f. *inanis*; see INANE, -ITION. Cf. (O)Fr. *inanition.*] The action or process of emptying; the condition of being empty, or (*spec.*) exhausted from want of nourishment. Also *fig.*

Hunger and thirst are inanitions of the body JOWETT, *fig.* Anarchy..usually..perishes of i. FROUDE.

Inanity (inæ·nĭti). 1501. [– L. *inanitas*, f. *inanis*; see INANE, -ITY. Cf. (O)Fr. *inanité.*] **1.** The quality or condition of being empty or void; emptiness 1607. **2.** *fig.* **a.** Want of substance or solidity; unsatisfactoriness; vanity; hollowness 1603. **b.** Lack of ideas or sense; frivolity, senselessness, silliness 1753. **c.** Vacuity of existence; idleness, inaction 1782. **3.** with *an* and *pl.* An inane remark or practice 1661.

1. What shall fill..the I. and Vacuity of the heart of man? 1631. **2. b.** To treat a topic with i. 1803. **3.** The vanities and inanities of fashion HOLLAND.

Ina·pathy. *rare.* 1846. [IN-[3].] The opposite of apathy.

†**Inapo·state,** *a.* [IN-[3].] Not apostate; loyal. HERRICK.

†**Inappa·rent,** *a.* 1626. [IN-[3].] Not apparent; invisible; latent –1753.

†**Inappea·lable,** *a.* 1651. [IN-[3].] = INAPPELLABLE.

Inappea·sable, *a.* 1840. [IN-[3].] Not to be appeased.

Inappellable (inăpe·lăb'l), *a.* 1825. [– Fr. †*inappelable*, f. *appeler* APPEAL *v.*] From which there is no appeal. Hence **Inappellabi·lity.**

Inappetent (inæ·pĭtĕnt), *a.* 1796. [IN-[3].] Not appetent; without desire or longing. So **Ina·ppetence** 1691, **-ency** 1611, lack of appetence.

Inapplicable (inæ·plikăb'l), *a.* 1656. [IN-[3].] Not applicable; incapable of being applied (*to* some case); unsuitable (*to* the purpose).

Döppler's method was practically i. LUBBOCK.

Hence **Ina:pplicabi·lity,** the quality of being i. **Ina·pplicably** *adv.*

Inapplication (inæplikēⁱ·ʃən). 1721. [IN-³.] **1.** Want of application, e.g. to one's duties. **2.** Inapplicability 1784.

Inapposite (inæ·pŏzit), *a.* 1661. [IN-³.] Not apposite, not to the point, out of place; impertinent. Hence **Ina·ppositely** *adv.*

Inappreciable (inăprī·ʃiăb'l), *a.* Also **-tiable.** 1787. [f. IN-³ + *appreciable.* Cf. Fr. *inappréciable* (XV) in both senses.] Not appreciable; †priceless –1868; too inconsiderable to be estimated; imperceptible 1802.

A barrier of i. value SCOTT. An inappretiable quantity 1802. Hence **Inappre·ciably** *adv.*

Inappreciation (inăprīʃiₑēⁱ·ʃən). 1864. [IN-³.] Want of appreciation; failure to estimate duly.

Inappreciative (inăprī·ʃiĕtiv), *a.* 1868. [IN-³.] Wanting in appreciation. Hence **Inappre·ciative-ly** *adv.*, **-ness.**

Inapprehensible (inæprĭhe·nsib'l), *a.* 1641. [f. IN-³ + APPREHENSIBLE. In XVII prob. – late L. *inapprehensibilis.*] Not apprehensible; that cannot be grasped by the senses or intellect.

Inapprehension (inæprĭhe·nʃən). 1744. [IN-³.] Want of apprehension.

Inapprehe·nsive, *a.* 1651. [IN-³.] Not apprehensive; without apprehension; unconcerned. Hence **Inapprehe·nsiveness.**

Inapproachable (inăprōᵘ·tʃăb'l), *a.* 1828. [IN-³.] That cannot be approached; inaccessible, unapproachable. Hence **Inapproa·chably** *adv.*

Inappropriate (inăprōᵘ·priĕt), *a.* 1804. [IN-³.] Not appropriate; not suitable to the case; unfitting, improper. Hence **Inappro·priate-ly** *adv.*, **-ness.**

Inapt (inæ·pt), *a.* 1744. [f. IN-³ + APT *a.* Cf. INEPT.] **1.** Unsuitable, inappropriate, inapposite. **2.** Not apt; unskilful, awkward 1860. Hence **Ina·pt-ly** *adv.*, **-ness.**

Inaptitude (inæ·ptitiūd). 1620. [f. IN-³ + APTITUDE. Cf. INEPTITUDE.] Want of aptitude.

†**Ina·quate,** *ppl. a.* 1550. [– late L. *inaquatus,* pa. pple. of *inaquare* turn into water, f. *in-* IN-² + *aqua* water; see -ATE².] Converted into water. Hence †**Inaqua·tion,** conversion into water.

Inarable (inæ·răb'l), *a.* 1656. [f. IN-³ + ARABLE; in XVII from med.L. *inarabilis.*] Not arable.

Inarch (inā·ɹtʃ), *v.*¹ 1629. [f. IN-² + ARCH *v.*] *trans.* To graft by connecting a growing branch without separating it from its parent stock; to graft by approach; see APPROACH *sb.* 7. Hence **Ina·rching** *vbl. sb.* grafting by approach; *transf.* = ANAPLASTY (*rare*).

Ina·rch, *v.*² *rare.* 1882. [f. IN-¹ + ARCH *v.*] To arch in, encompass like an arch.

†**Ina·rk,** *v. rare.* 1595. [f. IN-¹ or ² + ARK *sb.*] *trans.* To put or enclose in an ark –1646.

Inarm (inā·ɹm), *v.* Also **en-.** 1612. [f. as prec. + ARM *sb.*¹; cf. Fr. *embrasser.*] *trans.* To clasp within or as with the arms; to embrace; to throw the arms round.

Inarticulate (inaɹti·kiŭlĕt), *a.* 1603. [In sense 1, f. IN-³ + ARTICULATE; with sense 2 cf. late L. *inarticulatus* in same sense.] Not articulate; the opposite of ARTICULATE. **1.** Not jointed or hinged; esp. in *Zool.* and *Bot.* Not composed of segments united by joints 1607. **b.** Of or belonging to the division *Inarticulata* of Brachiopods, now called *Ecardines* (*mod.*). **2.** Of sound or voice: Not of the nature of articulate speech; not uttered with intelligible modulations. Also, indistinctly pronounced. 1603. **b.** Not able to use articulate speech; dumb 1754. **c.** *transf.* Having no distinct meaning 1855.

2. Solemn Musick, which is i. Poesie DRYDEN. **b.** The poor Earl, who is i. with the palsy H. WALPOLE. **c.** I. gibberish 1855. So **Inarti·culated** *ppl. a.* Hence **Inarti·culate-ly** *adv.*, **-ness.**

†**Inarticula·tion**¹. 1578. [f. IN-² + ARTICULATION (sense 1).] = ENARTHROSIS –1634.

Inarticula·tion². *rare.* 1765. [f. IN-³ + ARTICULATION (sense 4).] Absence of distinct articulation; inarticulate utterance.

Inartificial (ināɹtifi·ʃăl), *a.* 1588. [f. IN-³ + ARTIFICIAL; in sense 3 – L. *inartificialis* (Quintilian, rendering Gr. ἄτεχνος) not according to the rules of art (i.e. of logic).] Not artificial. **1.** Not produced by art or constructive skill; natural. Now *rare.* 1656. **2.** Rude, clumsy; inartistic 1613. †**3.** Of an argument: Not according to the art of Logic, but derived from testimony or authority –1725. **4.** Artless, unaffected, natural 1664. **5.** Plain, simple, straightforward 1823.

2. Unskilfull and i. buildings 1671. An i. classification HERSCHEL. **3.** An i. Argument is the Testimony of another WATTS. Hence **Inartifi·cia·lity. Inartifi·cial-ly** *adv.*, **-ness.**

Inartistic, -al (inaɹti·stik, -ăl), *a.* 1849. [IN-³.] Not in accordance with the principles of art; also, having no appreciation for art. **Inarti·stically** *adv.*

Inasmuch (inæ̆zmɒ·tʃ), *adv.* ME. [orig. *in as much,* occas. later *in asmuch,* now written as one wd.; tr. OFr. *en tant* (*que*), repr. L. *in tantum* (*ut*), i.e. *in* IN *prep.*, *tantum* so much.]

I. In phr. *Inasmuch as.* **1.** In so far as, to such a degree as, according as. **2.** In that; seeing that; considering that; since, because.

1. In as much as ye haue done it vnto one of the least of these my brethren, ye haue done it vnto me *Matt.* 25:40. **2.** I. as 'he was delivered for our sins' WESLEY.

†**II.** Without *as*: In an equal degree, likewise. SWIFT.

Inattention (inăte·nʃən). 1710. [f. IN-³ + ATTENTION. Cf. Fr. *inattention.*] Want of attention; failure to attend; want of observant care or notice; heedlessness, negligence. **b.** Want of courteous personal attention 1792.

The universal Indolence and I. among us 1710.

Inattentive (inăte·ntiv), *a.* 1741. [f. IN-³ + ATTENTIVE. Cf. Fr. *inattentif.*] Not attentive; not applying the mind steadily; not observant; negligent.

An unsteady and i. habit of mind WATTS. Hence **Inatte·ntive-ly** *adv.*, **-ness.**

Inaudible (inǭ·dĭb'l), *a.* 1601. [f. IN-³ + AUDIBLE; cf. late L. *inaudibilis.*] Not audible; not capable of being heard.

Th'i., and noiselesse foot of time SHAKS. Hence **Inaudibi·lity,** the quality or condition of being i. **Inau·dibly** *adv.*

Inaugur (inǭ·gɒɹ), *v.* Now *rare.* 1555. Also **-ure.** [– (O)Fr. *inaugurer* or L. *inaugurare*; see INAUGURATE *v.*] †**1.** *trans.* = INAUGURATE *v.* 1. –1706. **2.** = INAUGURATE *v.* 5. 1890.

Inaugural (inǭ·giŭrăl), *a.* (*sb.*) 1689. [– Fr. *inaugural,* f. *inaugurer* inaugurate, after L. *auguralis*; see AUGURAL.] **1.** Of or pertaining to inauguration; forming part of the formal commencement of any course or career. **2.** *sb.* An inaugural speech or address. *U.S.* 1860.

1. Mr. Thwaites Greek Professor made his I. Speech 1708.

†**Inau·gurate,** *a.* 1600. [– L. *inauguratus,* pa. pple. of *inaugurare*; see next, -ATE².] Inaugurated, formally installed into office –1681.

Inaugurate (inǭ·giŭreⁱt), *v.* 1606. [– *inaugurat-*, pa. ppl. stem of L. *inaugurare* take omens from the flight of birds, f. *in-* IN-¹ + *augurare* AUGUR *v.*; see -ATE³.] **1.** *trans.* To admit or induct to an office or dignity by a formal ceremony; to consecrate, install, invest. †**2.** To invest with a sacred character, etc. F. JUNIUS. **3.** To make auspicious; to sanctify, consecrate (*rare*) 1639. **4.** 'To begin with good omens' (J.); to begin with some formal ceremony or notable act; to enter upon; to usher in; to initiate. (Sometimes merely grandiose for 'begin'.) 1755. **5.** To introduce into public use by a formal opening ceremony 1852.

1. To i. a King DRAYTON, a bishop 1637, a Caliph 1708. **4.** To i. the revolution 1851, a new era 1865, the daily work of a school GRANT. **5.** To i. a statue 1852. Hence **Inau·gurator,** one who inaugurates; an initiator. **Inau·guratory** *a.* = INAUGURAL.

Inauguration (inǭgiŭrēⁱ·ʃən). 1569. [– (O)Fr. *inauguration* or late L. *inauguratio,* f. as prec.; see -ION.] The action of inaugurating. **1.** Formal induction, institution, or ushering in with auspicious ceremonies. **2.** The formal commencement or introduction of a course of action, an important era or period of time, etc. 1856. **3.** *attrib.* = INAUGURAL 1686.

1. The King's Anniversary I. 1627. **2.** The i. of privateering 1872. **3.** An i.-speech 1772.

Inaunter, var. of ENAUNTER, in case (that).

Inaurate (inǭ·rĕt), *a. rare.* 1826. [– L. *inauratus,* pa. pple. of *inaurare,* f. *in-* IN-² + *aurare* gild, f. *aurum* gold; see -ATE².] **a.** Gilded, covered with gold. **b.** *Entom.* Applied to parts having a metallic lustre.

†**Inau·rate,** *v. rare.* 1623. [– *inaurat-*, pa. ppl. stem of L. *inaurare*; see prec., -ATE³.] *trans.* To gild. Hence †**Inaura·tion,** gilding.

†**Inau·spicate,** *a.* 1632. [– L. *inauspicatus* at which no auspices were taken; see IN-³, AUSPICATE *a.*] Ill-omened, inauspicious –1668.

Inauspicious (inǭspi·ʃəs), *a.* 1592. [f. IN-³ + AUSPICIOUS.] Not auspicious; ill-omened, unlucky, unfortunate.

The yoke of i. starres SHAKS. A tardy and i. season KANE. Hence **Inauspi·cious-ly** *adv.*, **-ness.**

Inauthe·ntic, *a. rare.* 1860. [f. IN-³ + AUTHENTIC.] Not authentic. Hence **Inauthenti·city.**

Inautho·ritative, *a.* 1659. [IN-³.] Not authoritative; having no authority.

In banco: see BANCO *sb.*

Inbardge, var. of IMBARGE *v.*

I·n-beaming, *vbl. sb.* 1662. [f. IN *adv.* + BEAMING *vbl. sb.*] A beaming or shining in.

In-being, inbeing (i·nbī:iŋ). 1587. [f. IN *adv.* + BEING *vbl. sb.*] **1.** Inherence, immanence 1617. **2.** Inward or essential nature 1661. †**3.** An indwelling being: applied to the 'persons' of the Trinity –1643.

3. In the same most single essence are three Persons or In-beings GOLDING.

I·nbe:nt, *ppl. a.* 1586. [f. IN *adv.* + BENT *ppl. a.*] Bent or curved inwards; turned or directed inwards.

In-between. 1815. [phr. *in between,* used subst. or attrib.] **a.** quasi-*sb.* An interval; also, a person who intervenes. **b.** quasi-*adj.* Placed between.

†**Inblow·,** *v.* [OE. *inblāwan,* f. IN-¹ + BLOW *v.*, tr. L. *inflare, inspirare.*] *trans.* To blow or breathe into; to inflate; to inspire –1678. Hence †**Inblown** *ppl. a.*

Inboard (i·nbōᵊɹd). 1850. [prop. a phr., IN *prep.* + BOARD *sb.* V.]

Naut. **A.** *adv.* Within the sides of a ship or vessel 1853.

Luckily, those who were upset managed to fall i. 1863.

B. *prep.* Inside, within (a vessel) 1864.

C. *adj.* Situated within or towards the centre of the vessel 1850.

Inbond (i·nbǫnd), *a.* 1842. [f. IN-¹ + BOND *sb.*¹] *Building.* Said of a brick or stone laid with its length across a wall (also called a *header*); also of a wall built of these. Opp. to *outbond.*

Inborn (i·nbǭ·ɹn, i·nbǫɹn), *ppl. a.* OE. [OE. *inboren,* after late L. *innatus* INNATE; cf. Du. *ingeboren,* G. *eingeboren*; see IN-¹, BORN.] †**1.** Born in a place; aboriginal –1875. **2.** Of a quality, etc.: Born in a person; innate 1513. **b.** *transf.* Of a person: That was born such (*rare*) 1818.

2. Some i. sense Of courtesy PALGRAVE. **b.** The Arab is..an i. gentleman BOSW. SMITH.

†**Inbow·,** *v.* ME. [f. IN-¹ + Bow *v.*¹] **1.** *trans.* To bend into a curved or arched form; to incurve, arch –1625. **2.** To bow or bend (towards); to incline. WYCLIF.

†**I·nbowed, in-bowed,** *a.* 1586. [f. IN *adv.* + *bowed.*] Bowed or bent inwards or concavely; as, an *inbowed bone* –1658.

Inbreak (i·nbrēⁱk). *rare.* 1837. [f. IN *adv.* + BREAK *sb.*¹, after *outbreak.*] A breaking in, invasion, forcible incursion. So **I·nbrea:king** *vbl. sb.* 1652.

Inbreathe (inbrī·ð), *v.* ME. [f. IN-¹ + BREATHE *v.* after L. *inspirare.*) **1.** *trans.* To breathe (something) in (*lit.* and *fig.*) **2.** To inspire (a person) 1851. Hebce **Inbrea·ther.**

Inbred (i·nbre·d, i·nbred), *ppl. a.* Also †**im-.** 1592. [f. IN *adv.* + BRED.] **1.** Bred within; innate. †**2.** Bred in a place, native 1638. **3.** (Prop. *in-bred.*) Bred in-and-in 1892.

1. Your i. Curiosity, and love of Experimental Learning BOYLE.

Inbreed (inbrī·d), *v.* Also **im-**. 1599. [f. IN-¹ + BREED *v.*] **1.** *trans.* To engender or produce within. †**2.** To breed or bring up *in* a course of action. HOLLAND.

1. To i. and cherish in a great people the seeds of vertu MILT.

In-breeding (i·nbrī:diŋ), *vbl. sb.* 1842. [f. IN *adv.* + BREEDING *vbl. sb.*] Breeding in-and-in.

In-breeding..generally results mischievously 1881.

Inbri·ng, i:n-bri·ng, *v.* Now *rare* or *Obs.* Chiefly *Sc.* [OE. *inbringan*, f. IN-¹ + BRING; tr. L. *offerre*, etc.] *trans.* To bring in; to introduce; *esp.* in *Sc. Law*, to bring in by legal authority. So **I·nbri:nging** *vbl. sb.*

Inburning (i·nbǒ:ɹniŋ), *ppl. a.* [f. IN *adv.* + BURNING *ppl. a.*] Burning internally. SPENSER.

Inburst (i·nbǒɹst), *sb. rare.* 1837. [f. IN *adv.* + BURST *sb.*; cf. *outburst.*] A bursting in, irruption. So **Inbu·rst** *v.* (*rare*), to burst in 1540.

||**Inca** (i·ŋkă). 1594. [Peruvian, 'lord, king, emperor', also, 'man of the blood royal'. Early form *Inga*, Sp. alt. of *Inca*, the native form.] The title of the emperor or king of Peru before its conquest by the Spaniards; also, one of the royal race of Peru.

attrib. **I. Cockatoo,** an adaptation of G. *Inka Kakadu*, name of the Pink or Leadbetter's Cockatoo of Australia. **I. tern,** a species of tern (*Nænia inca*), the Bearded Tern.

Inca·ge, etc., obs. var. of ENCAGE, etc.

Incalculable (inkæ·lkiŭlăb'l), *a.* 1795. [f. IN-³ + CALCULABLE. Cf. Fr. *incalculable.*] **1.** That cannot be calculated, computed, or forecast. **2.** Of a person, etc.: That cannot be reckoned upon 1876.

1. I. mischiefs BURKE. An i. course BURKE. **2.** An i. temper 1879. Hence **Inca:lculabi·lity,** i. quality. **Inca·lculableness. Inca·lculably** *adv.*

†**Inca·lendared,** *pa. pple.* 1622. [f. IN-² + CALENDAR *v.* or *sb.* + -ED.] Canonized.

Incalescent (inkăle·sĕnt), *a.* Now *rare.* 1680. [– *incalesc-*, pr. ppl. stem of L. *incalescere*, f. *in-* IN-² + *calescere* grow warm; see -ENT.] Becoming hot or warm; increasing in warmth (*lit.* and *fig.*). Hence **Incale·scence** 1646, †**Incale·scency** 1658, the action or process of becoming i.; rise of temperature; heating.

In-calf (in,kā·f), *a.* 1556. [phr. *in calf* used *attrib.*] Of a cow: That is in calf. So **Inca·lver,** a cow in calf.

†**Incameration** (inkæmĕrē¹·ʃən). 1670. [– Fr. *incamération*, f. *incamérer* – It. *incamerare*, f. *in-* IN-² + *camera* chamber, the papal treasury.] Annexation to the papal domain –1741.

Incamp, -ment: see ENCAMP, -MENT.

Incan (i·ŋkăn), *a.* 1885. [f. INCA + -AN.] Pertaining to the Incas of Peru.

Incandesce (inkænde·s), *v.* 1874. [Back-formation, through earlier *incandescing* (by suffix-substitution for *incandescent*), from INCANDESCENT.] **1.** *intr.* To be or become incandescent; to glow with heat. Chiefly in pres. pple. **2.** *trans.* To render incandescent 1883.

Incandescent (inkænde·sĕnt), *a.* 1794. [– Fr. *incandescent* – *incandescent-*, pres. ppl. stem of L. *incandescere* glow, f. *in-* IN-² + *candescere* become white, f. *candidus*; see CANDID, -ESCENT.] **1.** Luminous or glowing with heat. **b.** *gen.* Glowing, brilliantly luminous 1867. **c.** *techn.* Applied to that form of electric light produced by the incandescence of a filament or strip of carbon; the *glow-lamp* as dist. from the *arc light*. Hence *transf.* of gas and other lamps. 1881. **2.** *fig.* Ardent, fiery; 'flaming up' 1859.

1. The hypothesis of an originally i. globe PAGE. **b.** The i. snow 1872. **2.** The 'incandescent passions' of the Anti-Semites 1894. Hence **Incande·scence,** the state of being i. (*lit.* and *fig.*). **Incande·scency,** the quality or state of being i.

Incanescent (inkăne·sĕnt), *a. rare.* 1866. [– *incanescent-*, pres. ppl. stem of L. *incanescere*, f. *in-* IN-² + *canescere* grow white; see -ESCENT.] = CANESCENT.

Incanous (inkē¹·nəs), *a.* 1864. [f. L. *incanus* hoary + -OUS.] *Bot.* Hoary with white pubescence.

†**Inca·nt,** *v.* 1546. [– L. *incantare* chant, etc., f. *in-* IN-² + *cantare* sing.] **a.** *intr.* To use incantation or enchantment. **b.** *trans.* To enchant, charm. –1665.

Incantation (inkæntē¹·ʃən). ME. [– (O)Fr. *incantation* – late L. *incantatio*, f. *incantat-*, pa. ppl. stem of L. *incantare*; see prec., -ION.] The use of a formula of words spoken or chanted to produce a magical effect; the utterance of a spell or charm; more widely, The use of magical ceremonies or arts; sorcery, enchantment. **b.** with *pl.* An instance of this; *concr.* a spell, charm ME.

Like the demons of old summoned by i. BURTON. So **I·ncanta:tor** (*rare*), one who uses i. **Inca·ntatory** *a.* (*rare*), using, or of the nature of, i.

Incanton (inkæ·ntǫn), *v.* 1705. [f. IN-² + CANTON *sb.*¹] *trans.* To make into or admit as a canton.

Incapable (inkē¹·păb'l), *a.* (*sb*). 1591. [– Fr. *incapable* or late L. *incapabilis* incomprehensible, later 'that cannot be taken in'; see IN-³, CAPABLE.]

I. Not capable; the opposite of capable. †**1.** Unable to take in, contain, hold, or keep –1841. †**b.** Unable to put up with; impatient *of* –1712. **2.** Not open to or susceptible of; insensible to. Const. *of*. *Obs.* or *arch.* 1601. **3.** Of such a nature, or in such a condition, as not to allow or admit of; not susceptible of. Const. *of*, or (formerly) with *inf.* 1712. **4.** Not having the capacity, power, or fitness for; unable. Const. *of*, or (formerly) with *inf.* 1610. **b.** In a good sense: Not having the depravity, moral weakness, etc. for 1755. **5.** *absol.* Incompetent; without ordinary capacity 1594. **6.** Not (legally) qualified or entitled; disqualified. Const. *of*, or (formerly) with *inf.* 1651.

1. I. of more SHAKS. *Sonn.* cxiii. **2.** As one i. of her owne distresse *Haml.* IV. vii. 179. **3.** Not i. to be beloved 1712. **4.** Growne incapeable Of reasonable affayres SHAKS. I. of much exertion 1842. **b.** My foes..have laid things to my charge whereof I am i., even in thought SCOTT. **5.** Phr. *Drunk and i.*, i.e. so drunk as to be incapable of taking care of himself. **6.** I. of holding any public employment MACAULAY.

†**II.** In passive sense: That cannot be received or apprehended (*rare*). Const. *to*. –1625.

B. *sb.* A thoroughly incompetent person 1809.

Hence **Incapabi·lity,** the quality or condition of being i. **Inca·pableness. Inca·pably** *adv.*

Incapacious (inkăpē¹·ʃəs), *a.* 1617. [f. late L. *incapax*, *-ac-* + -OUS; see IN-³, CAPACIOUS.] **1.** Not of sufficient size to take in something. **b.** Not able to contain much; narrow, limited. (*lit.* and *fig.*) 1635. **2.** Not having mental capacity for something. Const. *of*, or (formerly) with *inf.* Also *absol.* 1617.

2. Buzzing them into popular eares and capacities, i. of them BP. MOUNTAGU.

Incapacitate (inkăpæ·site¹t), *v.* 1657. [f. INCAPACITY + -ATE³. Cf. CAPACITATE.] **1.** *trans.* To deprive of capacity; to disqualify, unfit 1661. **2.** To disqualify in law.

1. My lameness does not i. me..for the work of the day school 1882. **2.** You have incapacitated public Preachers from sitting in Parliament CROMWELL. Hence **Incapacita·tion,** the action of incapacitating or fact of being incapacitated; disqualification.

Incapacity (inkăpæ·sĭti). 1611. [– Fr. *incapacité* or late L. *incapacitas*; see IN-³, CAPACITY.] **1.** Want of capacity; inability, powerlessness; incompetence; (with *an* and *pl.*) an instance of this. **b.** Inability to take, receive, or deal with in some way. Const. *of*, *for*. 1655. **2.** Legal disqualification, disability; an instance of this 1648.

1. His i. and ignorance were equal to his presumption GIBBON. **2.** Persons..lying..under an I. *c*1680.

Incapsulate (inkæ·psiŭle¹t), *v.* Also **en-**. 1874. [f. IN-² + L. *capsula* capsule + -ATE³.] *trans.* To enclose in a capsule. Hence **Inca·psulating** *ppl. a.*; applied *fig.* to certain languages in which modifying elements are inserted in the body of a word 1868. Hence **Incapsula·tion,** the action or process of incapsulating 1860.

Incarcerate (inkā·ɹsĕrĕt), *ppl. a. arch.* *a* 1500. [– med.L. *incarceratus*, pa. pple. of *incarcerare*; see next, -ATE².] Incarcerated; confined, shut in.

Incarcerate (inkā·ɹsĕre¹t), *v.* 1560. [– *incarcerat-*, pa. ppl. stem of med.L. *incarcerare*, f. *in-* IN-² + *carcer* prison; see -ATE³.] *trans.* To shut up in, or as in, prison; to confine.

What is it..to i. the Liberty of the Subject under the Iron and weighty Chains of an Arbitrary Government? 1640. Hence **Inca·rcerated** *ppl. a.*; *spec.* in *Path.*, variously used of a strangulated, obstructed, or otherwise irreducible hernia and of a retained placenta. **Incarcera·tion,** imprisonment 1536. **Inca·rcerator,** one who incarcerates or imprisons.

†**Inca·rdinate,** *a.* Used joc. for *incarnate.* Hee's the verie diuell i. *Twel. N.* v. i. 185.

Incardinate (inkā·ɹdine¹t), *v.* 1609. [– *incardinat-* (see -ATE³), pa. ppl. stem of late L. *incardinare* (Gregory the Great) ordain to the first rank in a church, f. *in-* IN-² + *cardo*, *cardin-* hinge, *cardinalis* chief presbyter; see CARDINAL.] *trans.* **a.** To institute as principal priest, deacon, etc. at a particular church or place. **b.** To institute to a cardinalship. So **Incardina·tion.**

Incardinated..that is Mortized or riueted to a Church, as a hinge to a dore 1609.

Incarn (inkā·ɹn), *v.* Also †**en-**. ME. [– late L. *incarnare* make flesh, make fleshy; cf. INCARNATE *v.*, INCARNATIVE.] **1.** *trans.* To cover with flesh, heal over (a wound, etc.); *absol.* to cause flesh to grow 1541. **b.** *intr.* To become covered with flesh, to heal 1689. **2.** To incarnate (*rare*) 1563.

Incarnadine (inkā·ɹnădin, -əin). 1591. [– Fr. *incarnadin*, *-ine* – It. *incarnadino*, var. of *incarnatino* flesh-colour, deriv. of *incarnato* INCARNATE.]

A. *adj.* Prop., Flesh-coloured, carnation, pale red or pink; also, crimson of blood-red (cf. CARNATION²); in mod. use occas. = Blood-stained (from Shaks.; see INCARNADINE *v.*)

You'll..calmly wash those hands i. BYRON.

B. *sb.* Flesh-colour, blush colour; also, a crimson or blood-red colour 1622.

Inca·rnadine, *v. arch.* 1605. [– Fr. *incarnadin*, *-ine* – It. *incarnadino*, north. var. of *incarnatino* carnation, flesh-colour, f. *incarnato*; see INCARNATE *a.*, -INE¹.] *trans.* To dye or tinge with incarnadine; to redden. (From Shaks. onward associated with the colour of blood.)

This my Hand will rather The multitudinous Seas i., Making the Greene, one Red *Macb.* II. ii. 62.

Incarnate (inkā·ɹnĕt), *a.* ME. [– eccl.L. *incarnatus*, pa. pple. of *incarnari* be made flesh, f. *in-* IN-² + *caro*, *carn-* flesh; see -ATE². Sense 2 is – Fr. *incarnat* or mod.L. *incarnatus.*] **1.** Clothed or invested with flesh; embodied in flesh; in a human (or animal) bodily form. **b.** Of a quality, etc.: Impersonated 1532. **2.** Flesh-coloured; light pink or crimson. *Obs.* exc. in *Bot.* 1533.

1. And slay th' i. Deity WESLEY. Phr. *Devil incarnate*: applied hyperbolically to a person, but the adj. often becomes nearly = 'out-and-out', 'arrant'. **b.** The quack is a Falsehood. I. 1839. **2.** The common red and i. clovers DARWIN.

Incarnate (inkā·ɹne¹t), *v.* 1533. [– *incarnat-*, pa. ppl. stem of late (eccl.) L. *incarnare*, *-ari* (Novatian III); see INCARNATE *a.*, -ATE³.] **1.** *trans.* To render incarnate; to embody in flesh. **2.** *transf.* and *fig.* **a.** To actualize, embody (an abstraction) 1591. **b.** To impersonate (a quality, etc.) 1806. †**3.** = INCARN 1. –1725. †**b.** *intr.* for *refl.* = INCARN 1 b. –1759. †**4.** To make carnal; to despiritualize –1683. **5.** To convert (vegetable matter) into flesh. PLAYFAIR.

1. I must not ask why God took this way to i. his Son DONNE. **2. b.** This friar incarnated the Venetian spirit SYMONDS. **3. b.** My uncle Toby's wound was near well..'twas just beginning to i. STERNE. **5.** To 'i.' Indian corn [i.e. by feeding cattle with it] 1882.

Incarnation (inkaɹnē¹·ʃən). ME. [– (O)Fr. *incarnation* – eccl. L. *incarnatio*, f. as prec.; see -ION.] **1.** The action of incarnating or fact of being incarnated or 'made flesh'; assumption of, or existence in, a bodily (esp. human) form. **a.** *spec.* of Christ, or of God in Christ. Often absol. *The Incarnation.* (The earliest sense. In early use often in reference to the date of the incarnation or birth of Christ.) **b.** *fig.* Embodiment. ? *Obs.* 1615. **2.** *concr.* **a.** An incarnate or embodied form (*of*) 1742. **b.** A living type or embodiment (*of* a quality, etc.) 1833. **c.** Loosely: A thing which is an embodiment (*of*) 1821. **3.** The formation of new flesh upon or in a wound or sore; healing up; granulation; *concr.* a growth of new flesh

1544. **4.** Flesh-colour, carnation; a pigment or dye of this colour. *Obs.* or *arch.* 1485. **b.** *attrib.* or as *adj.* = INCARNATE *a.* 2. 1562.

1. He was borne after the Incarnation of oure lord ij. c. yeres 1477. **2. a.** His [Vishnu's] first i. was that of a fish 1843. **b.** William Rufus..a foul i. of selfishness STUBBS.

†**Incarnative** (inkā·ɹnătiv). ME. [– Fr. †*incarnatif, -ive* or med.L. *incarnativus*, f. *incarnare* make flesh grow; see INCARN, -ATIVE.]

A. *adj.* **1.** Promoting the growth of flesh in a wound or sore –1694. **2.** Used joc. for *incarnate* (= 'arrant'). GREENE & LODGE.

B. *sb.* [sc. *medicine, application*] 1568–1720.

Inca·rve, *v. rare.* Also **en-.** 1596. [IN-[2] = EN-[1] B. 3 + CARVE *v.*] *trans.* To carve or engrave in or upon something –1615.

Incase, -ment, vars. of ENCASE, -MENT.

†**Inca·sk,** *v.* 1611. [f. IN-[1] + CASK *sb.*] *trans.* **a.** To put into a cask. **b.** To cover with, or as with, a casque or helmet. SHELTON.

†**Inca·stellate, en-,** *v.* 1538. [– *incastellat-*, pa. ppl. stem of med.L. *incastellare* (= It. *incastellare*), f. *in-* IN-[2] + L. *castellum*; see CASTLE, -ATE[3]. Cf. OFr. *enchasteler.*] *trans.* To make into a castle; to fortify; to enclose with masonry –1601. So †**Inca·stle** *v.*

†**Inca·stellated,** *ppl. a.* 1611. [– It. *incastellato* 'hoof-bound' (Florio). Cf. Fr. *encastelé.*] Hoof-bound (as a horse). (Dicts.) So †**Inca·stled, inca·stelled** *ppl. a.* in same sense.

Incatenation (inkætĭnē·ʃən). 1762. [– med.L. *incatenatio*, f. *incatenat-*, pa. ppl. stem of *incatenare* enchain, f. *in-* IN-[2] + L. *catenare* bind with chains; see -ION.] Putting in or fastening with chains; harnessing; a linking or being linked together. So **Inca·tenate** *v.* 1839.

†**Incau·telous,** *a.* 1610. [f. IN-[3] + CAUTELOUS.] Incautious –1734.

Incaution (inkǭ·ʃən). 1715. [f. IN-[3] + CAUTION.] Want of caution.

Incautious (inkǭ·ʃəs), *a.* 1703. [f. IN-[3] + CAUTIOUS, after L. *incautus.*] Not cautious; wanting in caution; heedless, unwary, rash.

An i. moment 1800, employment of language 1832. Hence **Incau·tious-ly** *adv.*, **-ness.**

Incavate (i·nkăvĕt), *a. rare.* [var. of EXCAVATE *ppl. a.* by prefix-substitution.] Hollowed, bent inwards. (Dicts.)

Incavation (inkăvē·ʃən). 1799. [var. of EXCAVATION by prefix-substitution.] The action of making hollow; also, a hollow on a surface; a hollowed place.

†**Inca·ve,** *v.*[1] [var. of EXCAVE *v.* by prefix-substitution.] To make hollow; to bend inwards. SIDNEY.

Incave, encave (inkē·v, en-), *v.*[2] 1604. [f. IN-[2], EN-[1] + CAVE *sb.* Cf. (O)Fr. *encaver.*] *trans.* To enclose or shut up in, or as in, a cave. So **Inca·vern, encavern** *v.* 1611.

Incede (insī·d), *v. rare.* 1669. [– L. *incēdere* go on, f. *in-* IN-[2] + *cēdere* go; see CEDE.] *intr.* To move on, advance; to move with measured or stately pace. Hence **Ince·dingly** *adv.* (often with allusion to Virgil, *Æn.* I. 46).

Incele·brity. 1803. [IN-[3].] Want of celebrity.

Incend (inse·nd), *v.* *Obs.* (exc. as *nonce-wd.*) 1502. [– L. *incendere* set on fire; see INCENSE *sb.* and *v.*[2]] **1.** *trans.* To set alight 1597. †**2.** To engender (bodily heat); to heat, inflame –1621. †**3.** To inflame, excite (the mind, passions, etc.); to incite to action –1684.

Incendiarism (inse·ndiăriz'm). 1674. [f. INCENDIARY + -ISM.] The practice or commission of arson. *fig.* Inflammatory agitation.

Incendiary (inse·ndiări). 1606. [– L. *incendiarius*, f. *incendium* burning fire; see INCENSE *sb.*, -ARY[1].]

A. *adj.* **1.** Consisting in, or pertaining to, the malicious setting on fire of buildings or other property 1611. **b.** *Mil.* Adapted for setting on fire an enemy's buildings, ships, etc. 1871. **2.** *fig.* Tending to stir up strife, violence, or sedition; inflammatory 1614.

1. An i. outrage at Norwich SPEED. **b.** A shower of i. shells 1871. **2.** I. publications 1853.

B. *sb.* **1.** One who wilfully or criminally causes a conflagration; one who commits arson 1606. **2.** *fig.* One who stirs up civil strife or violence; an inflammatory agitator; a firebrand 1631. †**b.** An incentive to evil –1726.

2. The Jesuits had been the incendiaries of the late insurrection H. WALPOLE.

†**Ince·ndious,** *a.* 1823. [f. prec., by suffix-substitution; cf. *compendiary, compendious.*] = INCENDIARY *a.* Hence †**Ince·ndiously** *adv.*

Incensation (insensē·ʃən). 1853. [f. INCENSE *v.*[1] + -ATION.] The action of censing.

Incense (i·nsens), *sb.* [ME. *ansens, encens* – (O)Fr. *encens* – eccl.L. *incensum*, subst. use of n. of *incensus*, pa. pple. of *incendere* set fire to, f. *in-* IN-[2] + **candere* cause to glow (*candēre* glow; see CANDLE).] **1.** An aromatic gum, etc., or a mixture of fragrant gums or spices, used for producing a sweet smell when burned. **2.** The smoke or perfume of incense, esp. when burned as an oblation or in religious ceremonial ME. **3.** *transf.* and *fig.* ME.

1. And moore encens in to the fyr he caste CHAUCER. **2.** A thicke cloud of i. went vp *Ezek.* 8:11. **3.** *transf.* The humid Flours, that breathd Thir morning I. MILT. *P. L.* IX. 194. *fig.* Offer pure i. to so pure a shrine SHAKS. *Lucr.* 194.

Comb.: **i.-boat,** a boat-shaped vessel used to hold i. for transfer to a censer; †**-brass,** tr. Gr. χαλκολίβανον in *Rev.* 1:15 (1611 'fine brass', but also explained as 'yellow frankincense'); **-breathing** *a.*, exhaling fragrance; **-cedar,** the genus *Libocedrus*; esp. the White Cedar (*L. decurrens*); **-tree,** a name for various trees yielding i., esp. of the genera *Boswellia* and *Icica*; also applied to a species of *Pittosporum*, from its fragrant flowers; **-wood,** the wood of *Icica heptaphylla.*

Incense (i·nsens), *v.*[1] ME. [–(O)Fr. *encenser*, f. *encense* (see prec.) or eccl.L. *incensare.*] **1.** *trans.* To fumigate or perfume with incense, esp. in connection with a religious ceremony; to burn or offer incense before, or to; to cense. Also *transf.* and *fig.* **2.** To burn or offer as incense (*lit.* and *fig.*) 1605. **3.** *intr.* To burn of offer incense ME.

1. To i. Idols 1709. *transf.* Wild roses incensed the fresh air 1861. **3.** To i. unto Idols 1638.

Incense (inse·ns), *v.*[2] ME. [– OFr. *incenser*, f. *incens-*, pa. ppl. stem of L. *incendere* (see INCENSE *sb.*).] †**1.** *trans.* To set on fire, kindle; to consume with fire, burn –1700. †**2.** To inflame (passion, etc.) –1809. **3.** †To fire (a person *with* passion, etc.) –1664. **b.** *spec.* To inflame with wrath, excite to anger, enrage, exasperate. (The current sense.) 1494. Also *fig.* †**4.** To incite to some action; to stir up, set on –1639.

1. Like pretious Odours, most fragrant, when they are incensed, or crushed BACON. **2.** Will God i. his ire For such a petty Trespass? MILT. *P. L.* IX. 692. **3. b.** This so incensed her father, that [etc.] FIELDING. *fig.* Winds wrastling with great fires, i. the flames DEKKER. Hence **Incensed** (inse·nst. *poet.* inse·nsĕd) *ppl. a.* kindled (*lit.* and *fig.*); inflamed with wrath; in *Her.* said of an animal depicted with fire issuing from mouth and ears. **Ince·nsement** (now *rare*), anger, exasperation.

Incenser[1] (i·nsensəɹ). 1555. [– Fr. *encenseur*, f. *encenser*; see INCENSE *v.*[1], -ER[2] 2.] One who burns or offers incense; also *fig.*

Incenser[2]: see INCENSOR.

†**Ince·nsion.** ME. [– L. *incensio* burning, f. *incens-*, pa. ppl. stem of *incendere* set on fire; see INCENSE *sb.*, -ION. Cf. OFr. *incension.*] **1.** Burning; setting on fire; conflagration –1656. **2.** Bodily inflammation –1745. **3.** Incensement. BAXTER.

†**Ince·nsive,** *a.* (*sb.*) *rare.* 1563. [– Fr. †*incensif, -ive* or med.L. *incensivus* inflammatory, f. as prec.; see -IVE.] **1.** Of inflamed disposition, full of rage. FOXE. **2.** Inflammatory –1677. **3.** *sb.* = INCENTIVE *sb.* RALEGH.

†**Ince·nsor, -er.** 1555. [– Fr. †*incenseur* in same senses, or L. *incensor* one who kindles, in late L. 'instigator'; f. as prec.; see -OR 2, -ER[2] 3.] One who kindles, inflames, or incites; an instigator –1627.

Incensory (i·nsensŏri). 1611. [– med.L. *incensorium*, f. *incensum* INCENSE *sb.*; see CENSER, -ORY[1].] †**1.** ? A burnt offering. CHAPMAN. **2.** A censer 1645.

Incensurable (inse·nsiŭrăb'l, -ʃiŭr-), *a. rare.* 1846. [IN-[3].] Not censurable. Hence **Ince·nsurably** *adv. rare.*

Incentive (inse·ntiv). ME. [– L. *incentivus* that sets the tune, that provokes or incites (sb. *-ivum*), f. *incent-*, var. of *incant-*; see INCANTATION, -IVE. In sense 2 app. confounded with INCENSIVE.]

A. *adj.* **1.** Having the quality of inciting; provocative 1603. †**2.** Having the property of kindling –1708.

1. An i. speech in the House of Lords NORTH. **2.** Part i. reed Provide, pernicious with one touch to fire MILT. *P. L.* VI. 519. Hence **Ince·ntively** *adv.*

B. *sb.* [L. *incentivum.*] Something that arouses feeling, or incites to action; an exciting cause or motive; an incitement, provocation, spur ME.

An I. to the Love of our Country STEELE.

Incentor (inse·ntəɹ). Now *rare.* 1563. [– late L. *incentor* setter of a tune, inciter, f. *incent-*; see prec., -OR 2.] **1.** One who excites (strife, etc.); one who incites *to* action. †**2.** 'He that singeth the descant'. BLOUNT.

Incentre, en- (in-, ense·ntəɹ), *v. rare.* 1611. [f. IN-[2], EN-[1] + CENTRE.] *trans.* To centre *in* something; to fix in the centre.

Incept (inse·pt), *v.* 1569. [– *incept-*, pa. ppl. stem of L. *incipere* begin, in med.L. in sense 2, f. *in-* IN-[2] + *capere* take; see INCIPIENT.] **1.** *trans.* To undertake; to begin, enter upon. **2.** *intr.* = COMMENCE *v.* 4. (Retained in the University of Cambridge until 1926.) Hence *gen.* to enter upon one's career or office 1852. **3.** *trans.* (*Biol.*) To take in, as an organism or cell 1863.

2. The 'Licentiate' was not regarded as a full 'Master' or 'Doctor' till he had 'incepted' 1895.

Inception (inse·pʃən). 1483. [– (O)Fr. *inception* or L. *inceptio* beginning, in med.L. admission to teach, f. *incept-*, pa. ppl. stem of *incipere* commence; see prec., -ION.] **1.** Origination, beginning, commencement. **2.** In Univ. use: The action of incepting (cf. COMMENCEMENT 2) 1680. **3.** The action of taking in, as an organism 1849.

1. Between the i. and the execution of the project LECKY.

Inceptive (inse·ptiv). 1612. [– med.L. *inceptivus* (late L. (IV) in sense 2), f. as prec.; see -IVE. Cf. Fr. †*inceptif, -ive.*]

A. *adj.* **1.** Beginning, incipient; initial 1662. **2.** *Gram.* and *Logic.* Expressing the beginning of action, as *i. verb, proposition*, etc. 1656. Hence **Ince·ptively** *adv.* in an i. way.

2. Verbs I., the same as Inchoatives 1706.

B. *sb.* **1.** An inceptive verb or proposition 1612. †**2.** (*pl.*) Initial circumstances; beginnings –1734.

Inceptor (inse·ptəɹ, -ǭɹ). 1479. [– med.L. *inceptor* (in sense 1), in cl.L. 'beginner', f. as prec.; see -OR 2.] **1.** One who incepts at a University. **2.** *gen.* A beginner (*rare*) 1706.

†**I·ncerate,** *v. rare.* 1623. [– *incerat-*, pa. ppl. stem of L. *incerare* spread wax on, f. *in-* IN-[2] + *cera* wax; see -ATE[3].] To cover with wax –1727. Hence †**Incera·tion,** the action of covering with wax, or of making a substance like moist wax.

†**Ince·rtain.** 1491. [– (O)Fr. *incertain*; see IN-[3], CERTAIN.] **A.** *adj.* = UNCERTAIN –1741. **B.** *sb.* **1.** Uncertainty 1502. **2.** An obs. game at cards. SHADWELL. So †**Ince·rtainly** *adv.*

†**Ince·rtainty.** 1484. [– Fr. †*incertaineté*; see prec., -TY[1].] = UNCERTAINTY –1792.

Incertitude (insǭ·ɹtitiūd). 1601. [– (O)Fr. *incertitude* or late L. *incertitudo*; see IN-[3], CERTITUDE.] **1.** Subjective uncertainty. **2.** Objective uncertainty; insecurity 1603.

1. Thus we were brought back to our old i. BURKE. **2.** The i. and instabilitie of this life HOLLAND.

Incessable (inse·săb'l), *a.* Now *rare.* 1545. [– Fr. †*incessable* or late L. *incessabilis*, f. *cessare* CEASE; see -ABLE. In XV–XVII sometimes assim. in form to *cease.*] Ceaseless, incessant. Hence **Ince·ssably** *adv.* ME.

Incessancy (inse·sănsi). 1615. [f. next; see -ANCY.] The quality of being incessant or unceasing; unbroken continuance.

Incessant (inse·sănt), *a.* 1532. [– Fr. *incessant* or late L. *incessans, -ant-*, f. *in-* IN-[3] + *cessans*, pr. pple. of L. *cessare* CEASE; see -ANT.] **1.** That does not cease; unceasing, ceaseless, continual, either in duration or repetition. †**2.** Unending, endless, everlasting –1564. **3.** quasi-*adv.* Without intermission or pause 1557.

1. The i. weepings of my wife SHAKS. The rude flint Yields to the i. drop SMOLLETT. **3.** Do they not..call I. on his tardy Vengeance? ROWE.

Hence **Ince·ssantly** *adv.* unceasingly; instantly ME. **Ince·ssantness.**

†**Ince·ssion.** *rare.* 1651. [– late L. *incessio* (cl.L. *incessus*), f. *incess-*, pa. ppl. stem of *incedere*; see INCEDE, -ION. Cf. Fr. †*incession.*] Onward motion; progression –1845.

The i. or locall motion of animals SIR T. BROWNE

Incest (i·nsest). ME. [– L. *incestus* sb., or *incestum*, subst. use of n. of *incestus* impure, unchaste, f. *in-* IN-^{3} + *castus* CHASTE.] The crime of sexual intercourse or cohabitation between persons related within the degrees within which marriage is prohibited by law.

Spiritual i. (in *R. C. Ch.*): (*a*) Marriage or sexual connection between persons related by spiritual affinity, or with a person under a vow of chastity, etc. (*b*) The holding by the same person of two benefices, one of which depends on the collation of the other.

Incestuous (inse·stiu,əs), *a.* 1532. [– late L. *incestuosus*, f. L. *incestus*; see prec., -OUS.] **1.** Guilty of incest 1552. †**b.** Loosely: Adulterous –1681. **2.** Of the nature of or involving incest 1532. †3. Begotten of incest –1621.

1. Caius Caligula, that wicked and i. emperor 1592. **2.** He had even trampled on the laws of Persia by an i. union with his sisters THIRLWALL. Hence **Ince·stuous-ly** *adv.*, **-ness.**

Inch (in^{t}ʃ), *sb.*^{1} [Late OE. *ynće*, corresp. to OHG. *unza*, Goth. *unkja* :- **uŋkja* – L. *uncia* twelfth part. See OUNCE *sb.*^{1}] **1.** A measure of length, the twelfth part of a foot. Hence, a measure of surface and of solidity (explicitly *square* or *superficial*, *cubic* or *solid inch*). Used also as the unit of measurement of rainfall, of atmospheric pressure, and of the flow of water. **2.** *transf.* and *fig.* The least amount or part (of space, time, material or immaterial things); a very little; a bit ME. **3.** *attrib.* See quots. 1646.

1. The gill contains 8·665 cubic inches 1900. *Inch of rain*: that quantity which would cover a surface to the depth of an i.; = 3,630 cubic feet on an acre. *I. of pressure*: that amount which balances the weight of a column of mercury, an inch high, in the mercurial barometer. *Miner's i. of water*: that amount that will pass in 24 hours through an opening of 1 square inch under a constant pressure of 6 inches. **2.** I'll flog you within an i. of your life DICKENS. **3.** (*a*) Of the length, thickness, etc. of an inch; as *i.-board* (board an inch thick); of the focal length of an inch, as *i. object-glass.* (*b*) With prefixed numeral (*two-i.*, etc.); Of the length, diameter, etc. of (so many) inches.

Phrases. *By inches, i. by i.*: by small degrees, very gradually. *Inches* = stature; I would I had thy inches SHAKS. *Give him an i. and he'll take an ell*: undue advantage will be taken of slight concessions.

Comb.: **i.-measure,** etc., one divided into inches; **-pound** (*Dynamics*), the work done in raising a pound weight vertically through an i. (cf. *foot-pound* s.v. FOOT *sb.*); **-worm,** a geometer caterpillar.

Inch (inʃ), *sb.*^{2} ME. [– Gael. *innis* (i·niʃ) = (O)Ir. *inis*, W. *ynys*, prob. rel. (obscurely) to L. *insula* ISLE.] A small island; also, locally, a meadow by a river (as the Inches of Perth).

Inch (in^{t}ʃ), *v.* 1599. [f. INCH *sb.*^{1}] **1.** *intr.* To move, advance, or retreat by inches or small degrees. **2.** *trans.* To drive by inches or small degrees 1667. **3.** To measure or compute the number of inches in 1673.

1. With slow paces measures back the field, And inches to the walls DRYDEN. **2.** And so i. him and shove him out of the world DRYDEN.

Phr. *I. out*: to eke out by small amounts; †to deal out sparingly.

Incha·mber, *v. rare.* 1611. [f. IN-^{2} + CHAMBER.] *trans.* To lodge in or as in a chamber.

†**Incha·ngeable,** *a. rare.* 1583. [IN-^{3}.] Unchangeable –1654. So †**Inchangeabi·lity,** unchangeableness.

Inchant, etc.: see ENCHANT, etc.

†**Incha·ritable,** *a.* 1496. [IN-^{3}.] Not charitable; uncharitable –1670.

†**Incha·rity.** 1589. [f. IN-^{3} + CHARITY; cf. prec.] Want of charity –1679.

Inchase: see ENCHASE *v.*^{2}

†**Incha·stity.** 1586. [f. IN-^{3} + CHASTITY.] Unchastity –1671.

Inched (inʃt), *a.* 1605. [f. INCH *sb.*^{1} or *v.* + -ED.] Containing (so many) inches in length or other dimension.

Inchest, var. of ENCHEST *v.*

Inchmeal (i·n^{t}ʃ,mīl), *adv.* (*sb.*) 1530. [f. INCH *sb.*^{1} + -MEAL.] By inches; little by little. Also with *by*.

To die, as it were, by inch-meal FLAVEL.

Inchoate (i·nko,ĕt), *a.* 1534. [– L. *inchoatus*, pa. pple. of *inchoare*, less correct form of *incohare* begin; see -ATE^2.] Just begun, incipient; in an initial or early stage; hence elementary, imperfect, undeveloped, immature.

It was a Church i., beginning, not perfect 1581. Hence **I·nchoate-ly** *adv.*, **-ness.**

Inchoate (i·nko,e^{i}t), *v.* 1612. [– *inchoat-*, pa. ppl. stem of L. *inchoare*; see prec., -ATE^3.] **1.** *trans.* To begin; also, to cause to begin, bring about. **2.** *intr.* To make a beginning 1654.

Inchoation (inko,ē^i·ʃən). 1530. [– late L. *inchoatio*, f. as prec.; see -ION.] Beginning, commencement; origination; early stage. †**b.** *pl.* Beginnings –1660. †**c.** A prefix 1661.

But the i. of those graces, the consummation whereof dependeth on mysteries ensuing HOOKER.

Inchoative (inkō^u·ătiv, i·nko,e^{i}tiv). 1530. [Sense 1 in med.L., sense 2 in late L. (Charisius) *inchoativus*, f. as prec.; see -IVE.] **A.** *adj.* **1.** That is in an incipient stage; rudimentary, inchoate; initial 1631. **2.** *Gram.* Of verbs: Inceptive 1530. Hence **Incho·atively** *adv.* in an i. manner.

1. The solution. .is still in its i. stages CARLYLE. **B.** *sb.* (*Gram.*) An inchoative verb 1530.

†**I·nchpin.** 1571 [app. f. INCH *sb.*^{1} + PIN *sb.*; in sense 1 perh. a corruption of some other word.] **1.** The sweetbread of a deer; also explained as 'the lower gut', etc. –1688. **2.** ? A pin an inch long. GOLDING.

Inchu·rch, obs. var. of ENCHURCH *v.*

†**Inci·curable,** *a. rare.* 1657. [f. IN-^{3} + L. *cicurare* CICURATE + -ABLE.] That cannot be tamed; hence, of plants, that cannot be naturalized –1776.

Incide (insəi·d), *v.*^{1} ? *Obs.* 1597. [– L. *incīdere* cut into, f. *in-* IN-^{2} + *cædere* cut. Cf. INCISE.] **1.** *Surg.* To cut into, make incision (*trans.* or *intr.*). †**2.** *Med.* To sever, loosen, disperse, resolve (a viscid humour, phlegm, etc.); = CUT *v.* II. 4. –1797.

Incide (insəi·d), *v.*^{2} *rare.* 1774. [– L. *incidere* fall upon, f. *in-* IN-^{2} + *cadere* fall. Cf. INCIDENT *a.*] *intr.* To fall *upon*; to have incidence.

Incidence (i·nsidĕns). ME. [– (O)Fr. *incidence*, or med.L. *incidentia* (sb. fem.); see INCIDENT *a.*, -ENCE.] †**1.** = INCIDENT *sb.* 1. –1651. **2.** The act or fact of falling upon, or coming in contact with 1656. **3.** *Physics.* The falling of a line, or anything moving in a line (as a ray of light, etc.), upon a surface; the manner of such falling 1626. **4.** *Astron.* = IMMERSION 3. 1727. **5.** The range or scope of a thing, the extent of its influence or effects 1825.

1. Many operations have been invented sometimes by a casual i. and occurrence BACON. **2.** The i. of a heavy gale KANE. **3.** *Angle of Incidence*, the angle which the incident line, ray, etc. makes with the perpendicular to the surface at the point of i. *Axis of i.*, the perpendicular to the surface at the point of i. **5.** The i. and effect of taxes and regulations MCCULLOCH.

†**I·ncidency.** 1611. [See prec., -ENCY.] **1.** An incident –1701. **2.** The quality of being liable to fall *to*; (with *pl.*) a thing incident *to* –1683. **3.** *Physics.* = INCIDENCE 3. –1704. **4.** The meeting of lines. MORSE.

Incident (i·nsidĕnt), *sb.* ME. [– (O)Fr. *incident*, subst. use of adj.; see next.] **1.** Something that occurs casually in connection with something else; an event of accessory or subordinate character. **2.** An occurrence viewed as a separate circumstance 1462. †**b.** A matter, an affair (*rare*) –1761. **3.** A distinct piece of action in a play or poem 1695; a single feature in a picture 1705. **4.** †An accessory circumstance –1755; in *Law*, a privilege, burden, custom, etc. commonly or invariably attaching to an office, estate, or the like 1628. †**b.** An incidental expense –1776.

3. No person, no i. in the play, but must be of use to carry on the main design DRYDEN. A sweet piece of rock i. RUSKIN. **4.** The 'incidents' of tenure by knight-service 1876.

Incident (i·nsidĕnt), *a.* 1488. [– Fr. *incident* or L. *incidens*, *-ent-*, pr. pple. of *incidere* fall upon, happen to, f. *in-* IN-^{2} + *cadere* fall; see. -ENT.] **1.** Liable to befall or occur *to*; likely to happen; hence, naturally attaching. **2.** *Law.* Attaching itself, as a privilege, burden, or custom, *to* an office, position, etc. 1491. †**3.** Relating or pertinent *to* –1614. †**4.** Apt to fall into; liable *to*; subject *to* –1767. **5.** = INCIDENTAL 1. Now *rare* or *Obs.* 1523. **6.** Subordinate, subsidiary, accessory 1725. **7.** Falling or striking upon or against, as light upon a surface. Const. *upon.* 1667.

1. The fallacies i. to categorical syllogisms REID. **2.** Fealtie is incydent to everye manner of Service 1574. **5.** By occasion i. there was talke of a text of Scripture 1581. With all the Charges i. BUTLER. **6.** Phr. †*Incident proposition*, a proposition inserted in a principal one, and introduced by a relative pronoun; a subordinate relative clause.

Incidental (inside·ntăl), *a.* (*sb.*) 1616. [orig. – med.L. *incidentalis* (cf. *angulus incidentalis* angle of incidence), f. as prec.; see -AL^1. In mod. use f. INCIDENT *a.* + -AL^1.] **1.** Occurring or liable to occur in fortuitous or subordinate conjunction with something else; casual 1644. **b.** Of a charge or expense: Such as is incurred apart from the primary disbursements 1739. **2.** Casually met with (*rare*) 1856. **3.** *sb.* An incidental circumstance, event, charge, etc. 1707.

1. Those i. discourses which we have wandered into MILT. **b.** The house rent, and the i. charges of a family 1804. Phr. *Incidental images, colours*: such as are perceived by the eye as a consequence of visual impressions no longer present. *Incidental music*, marches, dances, songs, etc. introduced during the action of a play. Hence **Incide·ntal-ly** *adv.*, **-ness.**

†**I·ncidently,** *adv.* 1529. [f. INCIDENT *a.* + -LY^2.] Incidentally –1824.

Incinerable (insi·nĕrăb'l), *a. rare.* [f. med.L. *incinerare*, or direct from INCINERATE *v.* + -ABLE.] Capable of being burnt to ashes. SIR T. BROWNE.

†**Inci·nerate,** *ppl. a.* 1471. [– med.L. *incineratus*, pa. pple. of *incinerare*; see next, -ATE^2.] Incinerated –1626.

Incinerate (insi·nĕre^{i}t), *v.* 1555. [– *incinerat-*, pa. ppl. stem of med.L. *incinerare*, f. *in-* IN-^{2} + *cinis, ciner-* ashes; see -ATE^3.] **1.** *trans.* To reduce to ashes, consume by fire. **2.** *intr.* To become reduced to ashes 1800.

1. It is the Fire only that Incinerates Bodies BOYLE. Hence **Incinera·tion,** reduction to ashes 1529; *spec.* (esp. in U.S.) the cremation of the dead.

Incipience (insi·piĕns). 1864. [f. INCIPIENT; see -ENCE.] Beginning, commencement; the fact or condition of being incipient; with *pl.* A beginning. So **Inci·piency,** the quality or state of being incipient 1817.

Incipient (insi·piĕnt). 1589. [– *incipient-*, pr. ppl. stem of L. *incipere* undertake, begin, f. *in-* IN-^{2} + *capere* take; see -ENT.]

A. *adj.* Beginning; coming into, or in an early stage of, existence; in an initial stage 1669. Hence **Inci·piently** *adv.*

I. madness JOHNSON, fermentation SIR H. DAVY. **B.** *sb.* †**1.** = INCEPTOR –1598. **2.** *Heb. Gram.* The verbal 'tense' or form with prefixed servile letters, variously called Future, Present, and Imperfect 1866.

‖**Incipit** (i·nsipit). [L., 3rd pers. sing. pres. ind. of *incipere* (see prec.): used, as in old MSS., to introduce the title of a literary work.] The opening words of a poem or other piece. Cf. EXPLICIT.

Incircle, obs. f. ENCIRCLE *v.*

†**Inci·rclet.** [f. IN-^{1} or ^{2} + CIRCLET.] A little circular curl or spiral. SIDNEY.

†**Incircumscri·ptible,** *a.* 1550. [– late (eccl.) L. *incircumscriptibilis*; see IN-^{3}, CIRCUMSCRIPTIBLE. Cf. Fr. †*-ible.*] Incapable of being circumscribed or limited –1652.

Incircumscri·ption. *rare.* 1651. [– late L. *incircumscriptio* (Gregory the Great, tr. τὸ ἀπερίγραφον); see IN-^{3}, CIRCUMSCRIPTION.] The condition of being uncircumscribed; boundlessness.

†**Incircumspe·ct,** *a.* 1531. [IN-^{3}.] Not circumspect; incautious, heedless –1651.

†**Incircumspe·ction.** 1646. [IN-^{3}.] Want of circumspection; heedlessness, unwariness –1683.

Incise (insəi·z), *v.* 1541. [– Fr. *inciser*, f. *incis-*, pa. ppl. stem of L. *incīdere*, f. *in-* IN-^{2} + *cædere* cut.] **1.** *trans.* To cut into, make an incision in; to cut marks upon, engrave *with* figures. Also *absol.* **2.** To form by cutting; to carve, engrave 1631.

2. I on thy Tombe this Epitaph i. CAREW.

Incised (insəi·zd), *ppl. a.* 1597. [f. INCISE *v.* + -ED[1].] **1.** Cut into; marked by cutting. **b.** *Bot. and Zool.* Having marginal notches; as a leaf or an insect's wing 1826. **2.** Produced by incision; engraved 1807.

Incision (insi·ʒən). ME. [– (O)Fr. *incision* or late L. *incisio*, f. *incis-*; see INCISE *v.*, -ION.] **1.** The action of cutting into something 1474. **2.** The effect of cutting into something; a division produced by cutting; a cut, a gash ME. **b.** *Bot.* and *Zool.* A deep indentation or notch 1578. †**3.** *Med.* The loosening and removal of viscid humours; cf. INCIDE *v.*[1] 2. BACON. **4.** *fig.* Incisiveness 1862. ¶**5.** Used erron. for INSITION, engrafting 1601.

Incisive (insəi·siv), *a.* (*sb.*) 1528. [– med.L. *incisivus*, f. as prec.; see -IVE. Cf. (O)Fr. *incisif, -ive.*] **1.** Having the quality of cutting into something; cutting, penetrating with a sharp edge 1597. **2.** *Anat.* Applied to the incisor teeth; and hence to the *incisive bones* = the premaxillary bones 1804. †**3.** Cutting, piercing; 'cutting' viscid humours (see INCIDE *v.*[1] 2) –1694. **4.** *fig.* Sharp or keen in mental qualities; penetrating, acute, trenchant 1850. **5.** *sb.* An incisor tooth 1804.

4. Her i. smile E.B. BROWNING. An i. and pungent style 1880. Hence **Inci·sively** *adv.*, **-ness.**

Inciso- (insəi·so), comb. advb. f. L. *incisus*, used in the sense 'incisedly—', 'incised and —', as *i.-dentate*, etc.

Incisor (insəi·səɹ, -ǫɹ). 1672. [– med.L. *incisor*, in *dens incisor* incisor tooth, f. L. *incisor* lit. 'cutter', f. *incis-* (see INCISE) + *-or* -OR 2.] *Anat.* and *Zool.* A tooth adapted for cutting; any one of the front teeth in either jaw, situated between the canine teeth on each side. **b.** *attrib.* Adapted for cutting, as *i. forceps, tooth*; connected with the incisor teeth, as *i. artery*, etc. 1837.

Incisory (insəi·sŏri), *a.* 1594. [f. as prec.; see -ORY[2].] Having the property of cutting, incisive; applied to the incisor teeth.

Incisure (insi·ʒ[i]ŭɹ). 1597. [– L. *incisura*, f. *incis-*; see INCISE *v.*, -URE. Cf. OFr. *enciseüre.*] A cut, notch, slit, cleft.

Incitable (insəi·tăb'l), *a. rare.* 1800. [f. INCITE *v.* + -ABLE. Cf. Fr. *incitable.*] Capable of being incited or urged to action. Hence **Incitabi·lity.**

Incitant (i·nsitănt, insəi·tănt). 1802. [f. INCITE + -ANT, after Fr. *incitant.*] **A.** *adj.* That incites, stimulating 1886. **B.** *sb.* That which incites.

†**I·ncitate**, *v.* 1597. [– *incitat-*, pa. ppl. stem of L. *incitare*; see INCITE, -ATE[3].] *trans.* To incite –1623. So †**I·ncitate** *ppl. a.* 1568.

Incitation (insəitē[i]·ʃən, insitē[i]·ʃən). 1477. [– (O)Fr. *incitation* or L. *incitatio*, f. as prec.; see -ION.] **1.** The action of inciting; incitement, stimulation. †**2.** That which incites; a stimulus, incitement –1709. †**3.** Power of inciting –1684.

2. This passion..the..noblest I. to honest Attempts STEELE.

†**Inci·tative**, *a.* and *sb. rare.* 1490. [– Fr. †*incitatif, -ive* exciting; cf. med.L. *incitativum* incentive; see next, -IVE.] = INCITANT *a.* and *sb.* –1620.

Incite (insəi·t), *v.* 1483. [– (O)Fr. *inciter* – L. *incitare*, f. *in-* IN-[2] + *citare* set in rapid motion, rouse; see CITE.] *trans.* To urge or spur on; to stir up, instigate, stimulate. Const. *to, unto*; *to do* something.

The Pope incited the King of Spain to make war against the Republick BRAMHALL. Manufactures were incited 1812. Hence **Inci·ter. Inci·tingly** *adv.*

Incitement (insəi·tmĕnt). 1594. [f. INCITE + -MENT. Cf. Fr. †*incitement* (XVI), L. *incitamentum.*] **1.** The action of inciting. †Also, the condition of being incited. **2.** That which incites or rouses to action; an exciting cause; a stimulus, incentive, spur 1600.

1. Chiefly by the i. of the Cardinal 1647. **2.** Pleasure, the greatest i. of evil JOWETT.

Incito-motor (insəi:tomō[u]·təɹ, -ǫɹ), *a. rare.* 1886. [f. INCITE *v.* + MOTOR, after EXCITO-MOTOR, q.v. Cf. Fr. *incito-moteur.*] Inciting to motion or muscular action; applied to the action of the nervous centres which determine the contraction of the muscles through the intermediation of the motor nerves. Also erron. identified with *excito-motor*. So **Inci:tomo·tory** *a.* 1884.

†**Inci·vil**, *a.* 1586. [– (O)Fr. *incivil* or L. *incivilis* unmannerly (in med.L. also in sense 1); see IN-[3], CIVIL.] **1.** Not according to civil law. DANIEL. **2.** Savage, barbarous. MARLOWE. **3.** Rude, clownish –1707.

Incivility (insivi·lĭti). 1584. [– Fr. *incivilité* or late L. *incivilitas*; see prec., -ITY.] The quality or condition of being incivil or uncivil. †**1.** Want of civilization; savageness, barbarism –1811. †**2.** Want of good manners or good breeding –1673. **3.** Want of civility or politeness; discourtesy, rudeness. Also with *an* and *pl.* 1612.

1. That barbarous relic of feudal i., duelling 1811. **3.** [Guildford] was treated by Jeffreys with marked i. MACAULAY. No person offered me the least i. LUDLOW.

Incivilization (insi·vilizē[i]·ʃən, -əiz-). 1823. [IN-[3].] Uncivilized condition; want of civilization. So †**Inci·vilize** *v.* 1603.

Incivism (i·nsiviz'm). 1794. [– Fr. *incivisme*; see IN-[3] and CIVISM.] The opposite of CIVISM; want of good citizenship; *orig.*, want of loyalty to the principles of the French Revolution: regarded as a crime against the Republic.

Socrates is to be..exculpated from the charge of i. GROTE.

†**Inclama·tion.** *rare.* 1612. [– late L. *inclamatio*, f. *inclamat-*, pa. ppl. stem of L. *inclamare* call out, exclaim against, f. *in-* IN-[2] + *clamare* call.] A calling upon, invocation. Also, a cry, a loud call. –1613.

Inclasp, obs. f. ENCLASP *v.*

Inclau·dent, *a.* [f. IN-[3] + *claudent.*] *Bot.* Not closing. PAXTON.

†**Incla·vate**, *v. rare.* 1666. [– *inclavat-*, pa. ppl. stem of med.L. *inclavare*, f. *in-* IN-[2] + L. *clavus* nail; see -ATE[3].] *trans.* To nail or bolt in, fix firmly.

Inclave, obs. f. ENCLAVE *a. Her.*

Incle, var. of INKLE *sb.* and *v.*

I·n-clea:ring. 1872. [IN *adv.*] The cheques, bills of exchange, etc., collectively, payable by a bank, and received through the Clearing-house for settlement; also *attrib.*

Inclemency (inkle·mĕnsi). 1559. [– L. *inclementia*, f. *inclement-*; see next, -ENCY.] The quality or condition of being inclement. **1.** Severity of weather; (with *pl.*) an instance of this 1699. †**2.** Want of kindliness of disposition; pitilessness, unmercifulness –1658.

1. The I. of the weather 1725. The inclemencies of a cold climate 1748. **2.** The inclemencie of the late Pope laboring to forestall him in his just throne BP. HALL.

Inclement (inkle·mĕnt), *a.* 1621. [– Fr. *inclément* or L. *inclemens, -ent-*; see IN-[3], CLEMENT.] Not clement. **1.** Of climate, etc.: Not temperate; extreme; severe 1667. †**2.** Not kindly; pitiless, harsh, severe, cruel –1725.

1. To shun Th' i. Seasons, Rain, Ice, Hail and Snow MILT. *P. L.* x. 1063. **2.** Pope Clement the fift, was i. and cruell 1621. Hence **Incle·ment-ly** *adv.*, **-ness.**

Inclinable (inkləi·năb'l), *a.* 1449. [Late ME. *enclinable* – OFr. *enclinable* (mod. *in-*), f. *encliner* (*in-*); see INCLINE *v.*, -ABLE.] **1.** Having a (mental) leaning in some direction; inclined, disposed 1494. **2.** Favourably disposed; favourable; amenable 1449. **3.** Having a tendency to some physical quality, character, condition, or action 1607. **4.** Capable of being inclined 1766.

1. Of a Noble Nature, and i. to mercy FELTHAM. Too i. for factions 1654. **2.** An argument that the nabob is i. to the French 1759. **3.** His Hair i. to Red 1683. Hence †**Incli·nableness.** †**Incli·nably** *adv.*

Inclination (inklinē[i]·ʃən). 1483. [– (O)Fr. *inclination* or L. *inclinatio*, f. *inclinat-*, pa. ppl. stem of *inclinare*; see INCLINE *v.*, -ION.] **I. 1.** The action or an act of inclining. †**b.** Decantation, or tilting a vessel for pouring –1758. **2.** The fact or condition of being inclined; deviation from the normal vertical or horizontal position or direction; leaning or slanting position; slope, slant 1530. **b.** The amount of slope or deviation from the horizontal position 1799. **c.** *Dialling.* The amount by which the plane of an inclining dial deviates from the vertical 1593. **d.** The dip of the magnetic needle. Hence *attrib.* in *i.-chart*, etc. 1678. **3.** *gen.* (chiefly in *Geom.*) The direction of a line, surface, or body, with respect to another line, surface, or body which has a different direction; the difference of direction of two lines, etc. regarded as tending towards each other; usually, the amount of such difference measured by the *angle of inclination*. In *Astron.* occas. *spec.* the position of the plane of a planet's orbit in relation to that of the ecliptic, measured by the angle between them 1570.

1. A courteous i. of the head 1850. **2. b.** The drain has an i. of one foot in 100 yards 1799.

II. 1. The action of inclining, bending, or directing the mind to something. ? *Obs.* 1509. **2.** Disposition, propensity ME.; liking, affection 1647; †natural disposition; nature, character –1713. **3.** Formerly, the general character or nature (of a thing); now only as *fig.* from prec. 1593. **4.** *transf.* An action or practice to which one is inclined 1526; †a person for whom one has a liking –1712.

2. Each his several way Pursues, as i. or sad choice Leads him perplext MILT. *P. L.* II. 524. **3.** The whole i. of the War depending on him 1653. **4.** Thieving is a very prevalent i. among them MORSE. Jack had, of late, been her i. ARBUTHNOT.

III. *Gr.* and *L. Gram.* The throwing of the accent of an enclitic upon the last syllable of the word to which it is attached 1842.

Inclina·tional, *a. rare.* 1821. [f. prec. + -AL[1].] **a.** Relating to inclination to the horizon 1879. **b.** Of or pertaining to mental disposition.

Inclinatory (inkləi·nătəri), *a.* ? *Obs.* 1613. [f. *inclinat-* (see INCLINATION) + -ORY[2].] Relating to or characterized by inclination or dip. *I. needle* = DIPPING-NEEDLE. Hence **Incli·natorily** *adv.*

Incline (inkləi·n, i·n,kləin), *sb.* 1600. [f. the vb.] †**1.** = INCLINATION II. 2. **2.** An inclined plane or surface; a slope, declivity; an inclined roadway along which mineral is conveyed 1846.

Incline (inkləi·n), *v.* [ME. *encline* – OFr. *encliner*, later assim. to L. source *inclinare*, f. *in-* IN-[2] + *clinare* bend.]

I. *trans.* **1.** To bend or bow (the head, the body, etc.) towards a person or thing, and hence forward or downward. †Also *fig.* **2.** To give a tendency to (a person, the mind, will, etc.); to dispose ME. **3.** To cause to lean; to slope, tilt 1590; †to direct (something immaterial) towards a particular object –1626. **4.** *Gr.* and *L. Gram.* To cause (a dependent word) to lean its accent upon the preceding word (see ENCLITIC *a.*) 1751.

1. Thou oughtest to enclyne and bowe thy kne CAXTON. Enclyne thine eares to me COVERDALE *Ps.* 16[17]: 6. **2.** Such advice as God shall i. him.. to propound MILT. **3.** Just as the Twig is bent, the Trẹe's inclin'd POPE. Oure God..hath enclyned mercy vnto vs COVERDALE *Ezra* 9: 9.

II. *intr.* **1.** To bend the head or body forward or downward; to bow. ? *Obs.* ME. **2.** *fig.* To bow, submit, yield *to*; to condescend; to accede (*to*) 1440. **3.** To turn in mind, etc. in a given direction; to apply oneself (*to*). (Now mostly with mixture of next.) ME. **4.** To have a mental leaning towards something; to be disposed or inclined ME. **5.** To slope, slant, bend downwards. Const. *to, towards.* 1568. **b.** *Dialling.* Said of a dial the plane of which leans forwards; opp. to *recline* 1593. **6.** *gen.* To have an oblique position or direction, so as to make angles with something else 1553. **b.** *Mil.* To move in a direction at angles with the front, so as to gain ground to the flank while advancing 1796. **7.** *fig.* To have a tendency, tend (*to*) 1509; to have some quality in an incipient degree 1589.

2. To enclyne to theyr desyre MORE. **3.** To..i. to virtue 1580. **4.** Their hearts inclined to follow Abimelech: for they said, He is our brother *Judg.* 9: 3. **6.** A course directly East, or inclining to the South PURCHAS. **7.** Victory inclined to the side of the allies GIBBON. He was stout and well-built, inclining to corpulence MARRYAT.

Inclined (inkləi·nd), *ppl. a.* ME. [f. INCLINE *v.* + -ED[1].] **1.** Leaning or falling away from the vertical or horizontal; sloping, slanting 1541; making an angle with something else (const. *to*) 1813. **2.** Disposed; in the mood or mind for something ME. †**3.**

Having a particular disposition, character, or nature -1616.

1. Phr. *Inclined plane*, a material plane surface inclined at an acute angle to the horizon, constituting one of the mechanical powers. **2.** Every Ryver to the see Enclyned ys to goo by kynde CHAUCER. *Dishonestly i.*, *well-inclined*.

Incliner (inklәi·nәɹ). 1609. [f. as prec. + -ER¹.] One who or that which inclines; an inclining dial.

Inclining (inklәi·niŋ), *vbl. sb.* ME. [f. as prec. + -ING¹.] **1.** A bending forward or downward; a bowing of the head or body; a slope, declivity. †Also *fig.* **2.** Tendency, bent ME.; party, following (*Obs.* or *arch.*) 1604.

2. Hold your hands Both you of my i. and the rest SHAKS.

Inclinometer (inkliṇǫ·mītәɹ). 1842. [irreg. f. L. *inclinare* + -METER; cf. DECLINOMETER. Cf. Fr. *inclinomètre*.] An instrument for measuring the vertical intensity of the earth's magnetic force, as shown by the inclination or dip of the magnetic needle.

Inclip (inkli·p), *v. arch.* 1608. [f. IN-¹ + CLIP *v.*¹] *trans.* To clasp, enclose.

What ere the Ocean pales, or skie inclippes SHAKS.

Incloister, var. of ENCLOISTER *v.*

Inclose (inklōᵘ·z), *v.* ME. Var. form of ENCLOSE, being the legal and statutory form, in reference to the inclosing of common and waste lands; still occas. in other senses; see ENCLOSE.

Inclosure (inklōᵘ·ʒ¹ŭɹ, -ʒәɹ). 1517. Var. form of ENCLOSURE, being the statutory form in reference to the inclosing of waste lands, commons, etc. Formerly also in other senses.

Your letter..with the i., was duly received 1776. The I. Commissioners for England and Wales 1845.

Incloude, -owd, obs. ff. ENCLOUD.

Include (inklū·d), *v.* ME. [- L. *includere*, f. *in-* IN-² + *claudere* shut.] **1.** *trans.* To shut or close in; †to shut up, confine. Now only in *pass.* Also *fig.* **b.** To enclose (in an area) 1662. **2.** To contain, comprise, embrace: **a.** as a member of an aggregate, or a constituent part of a whole ME.; **b.** as a subordinate element, corollary, or secondary feature 1526. **3.** To place in a class or category; to embrace in a general survey; to reckon in a calculation, etc. 1560. †**4.** To bring to a close. SHAKS.

1. He [Ashmole] shew'd me a toade included in amber EVELYN. **b.** It was after included in its circuit STILLINGFL. **2. a.** Dispersed are the glories it included SHAKS. It includes..the Pie, Jay, Nutcracker, etc. BEWICK. **b.** The losse of such a Lord, includes all harmes SHAKS. **3.** Men of feeble parts..are not to be included in this number 1794. **4.** *Two Gent.* V. iv. 160. Hence **Inclu·dible, -able** *a.* capable of being included.

Included (inklū·dėd), *ppl. a.* 1552. [f. prec. + -ED¹.] Shut in, enclosed, contained, comprised. **b.** *Bot.* Said of parts (esp. the style or stamens) which do not protrude beyond the corolla 1847.

Including (inklū·diŋ), *ppl. a.* 1670. [f. as prec. + -ING².] **1.** That includes (see the vb.). **2.** Often = Inclusive of. (Syntactically, it agrees sometimes with the word for the group previously (or afterwards) mentioned, but oftener with an indef. pron. *one*, *we*, *you* understood.) 1853.

2. These premises..were..in the occupation of several other warehousemen, i. Mr. T. Tapling 1864. Hence **Inclu·dingly** *adv.* 1449.

Inclu·se. *Obs.* exc. *Hist.* ME. [- L. *inclusus*, pa. pple. of *includere* INCLUDE.] **A.** *adj.* Enclosed. **B.** *sb.* An anchorite. So †**Inclu·se** *v. trans.* to enclose, shut up.

Inclusion (inklū·ʒәn). 1600. [- L. *inclusio*, f. *inclus-*, pa. ppl. stem of *includere*; see INCLUDE, -ION.] **1.** The action of including; the fact or condition of being included; an instance of this. **2.** *concr.* That which is included; *spec.* in *Min.*, A gaseous or liquid substance, or a small body, contained in a crystal or a mineral mass 1839.

1. In this Kingdome the name of Frenchman hath by i. comprehended all kind of Aliens SELDEN.

Inclusive (inklū·siv), *a.* (*sb.*) 1515. [- med.L. *inclusivus*, f. as prec.; see -IVE. Cf. Fr. *inclusif*, *-ive*. Sense 3 as in med.L. *inclusivē*.] **1.** Including, enclosing, comprehending 1594; comprehensive 1601; characterized by including or taking in, as opp. to excluding or leaving out 1651. †**2.** Characterized by being included in something else -1735. **3.** quasi-*adv.* = INCLUSIVELY 2. 1515. **4.** *sb.* An inclusive proposition or particle 1533.

1. The inclusiue Verge of Golden Mettall, that must round my Brow SHAKS. Phr. *I. terms*, *payment*, etc.: such as include all accessory payments. *I. of*, including or embracing. **3.** From Monday till Saturday i. 1873. Hence **Inclu·siveness.**

Inclusively (inklū·sivli), *adv.* 1578. [f. prec. + -LY².] **1.** In a way that includes; so as to include or be included. **2.** With inclusion of the term or limit mentioned; one or both extremes being included 1597.

†**Incoa·ched,** *ppl. a.* Also **en-**. 1599. [f. IN-² + COACH + -ED¹.] Conveyed in a coach or carriage -1618.

†**Inco,a·cted,** *a. rare.* [f. L. *incoactus*, or f. IN-³ + COACT *v.* + -ED¹.] Uncompelled, unconstrained. HALE.

Incoagulable (inko,æ·giŭlăb'l), *a.* 1667. [- med.L. *incoagulabilis*; see IN-³, COAGULABLE.] Not coagulable; incapable of coagulation.

Inco,ale·scence. *rare.* 1846. [IN-³.] Non-coalescence.

†**Inco·cted,** *a.* 1645. [f. L. *incoctus* + -ED¹ 2.] Uncooked, raw; hence, indigestible -1657. So †**Inco·ctible** *a.* 1684.

Incoercible (inko,ә·ɹsīb'l), *a.* 1710. [f. IN-³ + COERCIBLE. Cf. Fr. *incoercible* (XVIII).] **1.** That cannot be coerced, restrained, or overpowered by force 1756. **2.** That cannot be confined; volatile 1710. †**b.** Incapable of being liquefied by pressure; formerly said of some gases 1861.

Incoexistence (in,kōᵒ,ėgzi·stēns). [IN-³.] Absence of coexistence; the fact of not existing together. LOCKE.

Incoffin (inkǫ·fin), *v.* 1570. [f. IN-² + COFFIN *v.*] To enclose in, as in, or like, a coffin.

Incog (inkǫ·g). 1700. [colloq. abbrev. of INCOGNITO, INCOGNITA.] **A.** *adj.* = INCOGNITO, INCOGNITA *adjs.* 1705. **B.** *adv.* = INCOGNITO *adv.* **C.** *sb.* = INCOGNITO *sb.* INCOGNITA *sb.*¹

Incogitable (inkǫ·dʒităb'l), *a.* 1522. [- L. *incogitabilis* (in later use 'inconceivable'); see IN-³, COGITABLE.] Unthinkable, inconceivable. Hence **Incogitabi·lity** (*rare*), the quality of being i.

†**Inco·gitance.** *rare.* 1637. [f. as next; see -ANCE.] = next -1659.

†**Inco·gitancy.** 1612. [- L. *incogitantia*, f. *incogitans*, *-ant-*; see next, -ANCY.] **1.** Want of thought or reflection; thoughtlessness; inadvertence -1759. **2.** Want of the faculty of thought -1673.

1. Infirmities..are, vsually, sins of incogitancie 1612.

Incogitant (inkǫ·dʒitănt), *a.* 1628. [- L. *incogitans*, *-ant-*; see IN-³, COGITANT.] That does not think; thoughtless; without the faculty of thought.

A light i. young man 1679. Hence **Inco·gitantly** *adv.*

Incogitative (inkǫ·dʒiteⁱtiv), *a. rare.* 1690. [f. IN-³ + COGITATIVE.] Unthinking; without the faculty of thought.

A mere, bare, pure, i. Matter 1706. Hence **Inco:gitati·vity** (*rare*), the quality of being i.

‖**Incognita** (inkǫ·gnită), *a.* and *sb.*¹ 1668. [It., fem. of *incognito* unknown.]

A. *adj.* Of a female: Unknown or disguised; having one's identity unavowed.

She would go to Naples *incognita* 1884.

B. *sb.* **1.** An unknown or disguised woman; one whose identity is not made known 1718. **2.** Unknown or unavowed character (of a woman) 1882.

2. The Queen will not assume her i. until [etc.] 1882.

‖**Inco·gnita,** *sb.*² *pl.* 1846. [L., n. pl. of L. *incognitus* unknown; see next.] Unknown things or places.

†**Inco·gnite,** *a.* 1609. [- L. *incognitus* unknown, f. *in-* IN-³ + *cognitus*, pa. pple. of *cognoscere* know.] Unknown -1678.

Inco·gnitive, *a.* [f. IN-³ + COGNITIVE.] Destitute of the faculty of cognition. F. HALL.

‖**Incognito** (inkǫ·gnito), *a.*, *adv.*, *sb.* Pl. **-ti** (-tī). 1638. [- It. *incognito* - L. *incognitus*; see INCOGNITE.]

A. *adj.* Unknown; whose identity is concealed or unavowed; concealed under a disguised or assumed character 1649.

A Fool is very troublesome, when he Presumes he is I. 1676.

B. *adv.* With one's real name, title, or character undisclosed or disguised; used esp. in reference to royal or dignified personages who wish not to be openly recognized 1649.

'Twas long ago Since Gods came down *Incognito* PRIOR.

C. *sb.* **1.** An unknown man; one who conceals his identity 1638. **2.** The condition of being unknown, anonymity; fictituous character; disguise.

2. Few writers would have preserved their i. so long 1874.

Incognizable, -isable (inkǫ·gni-, -kǫ·nizăb'l), *a.* 1767. [f. IN-³ + COGNIZABLE.] Not cognizable; incapable of being known, perceived, or apprehended; incapable of recognition.

On life's incognisable sea M. ARNOLD.

Incognizance (inkǫ·gni-, -kǫ·nizăns). 1856. [f. IN-³ + COGNIZANCE.] Want of knowledge or recognition.

Incognizant (inkǫ·gni-, -kǫ·nizănt), *a.* 1837. [f. IN-³ + COGNIZANT.] Not cognizant; without knowledge or apprehension *of*; unaware, unconscious *of*.

A man..is never altogether incognisant..of himself FERRIER.

Incognoscible (inkǫgnǫ·sīb'l), *a.* 1691. [- late L. *incognoscibilis*; see IN-³, COGNOSCIBLE.] Unknowable, beyond cognizance. Hence **Incognoscibi·lity,** the quality or condition of being i.

Incoherence (inkohīᵊ·rēns). 1611. [f. IN-³ + COHERENCE.] **1.** *lit.* Want of cohesion 1672. **2.** Want of connection; incompatibility, incongruity of subjects or matters 1665. **3.** Want of coherence in thought or language, incongruity, inconsistency. Also with *an* and *pl.* 1611.

1. The..shale..from its i. has been denuded for the most part MURCHISON. **3.** A Petition fraught with Nonsense and I., Confusion and Impertinence SOUTH. This mythic theory is a mass of incoherences 1859. So **Incohe·rency** (in senses 2, 3).

Incoherent (inkohīᵊ·rēnt), *a.* 1626. [f. IN-³ + COHERENT.] **1.** Without physical coherence or cohesion; unconnected, disjoined, loose 1695. Also *transf.* and *fig.* **2.** Of abstract things, actions, thought, language, etc.: Consisting of incongruous parts; not logically connected or unified; inconsistent, uncoordinated; disjointed 1626. **3.** Incapable of cohering or coalescing; naturally different: incongruous 1643.

2. An i. fortuitous system, governed by chance BERKELEY. She muttered an i. sentence 1791. **3.** His armour was patched up of a thousand i. pieces SWIFT. Hence **Incohe·rent-ly** *adv.*, **-ness** (*rare*).

Incohesive (inkohī·siv), *a.* 1846. [IN-³.] Not cohesive.

Incoincident (inko,i·nsidēnt), *a.* 1636. [f. IN-³ + COINCIDENT.] Not coinciding; not necessarily existing together; not identical. Hence **Inco,i·ncidence,** want of coincidence or agreement.

†**Incolu·mity.** 1533. [- L. *incolumitas* safety, soundness, f. *incolumis* safe, sound; see -ITY. Cf. OFr. *incolumité* good health, good condition.] Safety, soundness, freedom from danger -1672.

Incomber, obs. var. of ENCUMBER.

†**Incombi·ning,** *a.* [IN-³.] Not combining; incompatible. MILT.

Incombustible (inkǫ̆mbʊ·stīb'l), *a.* (*sb.*) 1460. [- med.L. *incombustibilis*; see IN-³, COMBUSTIBLE. Cf. (O)Fr. *incombustible*.] **1.** Incapable of being burnt or consumed by fire. **2.** *sb.* That which is incombustible 1807.

1. An infusible and i. substance, as chalk or magnesia 1874. Hence **Incombustibi·lity, Incombu·stibleness.**

Income (i·nkǒm), *sb.*¹ ME. [In ME. use prob. - ON. *innkoma* arrival; later, a new formation on phr. *come in* (cf. OUTCOME); in sense 5 preceded by (dial.) *incoming(s*; see INCOMING *vbl. sb.*] **1.** Coming in, entrance, arrival, advent; beginning. Now *rare.* **b.**

spec. Spiritual influx or communication. (Now *Obs.* or *rare.*) 1647. †**2.** A fee paid on coming in; entrance-money –1712. †**3.** A new-comer, immigrant –1804. †**4.** Something added or incidental –1602. **5.** *spec.* That which comes in as the periodical produce of one's work, business, lands, or investments (commonly expressed in terms of money); annual or periodical receipts accruing to a person or corporation; revenue. Formerly also in *pl.* = Receipts, profits 1601. *National income*, the income of a nation as a whole.

1. Pain pays the i. of each precious thing SHAKS. **b.** The pure Incomes of his holy Life..flow in upon them 1678. **5.** No Fields afford So large an I. to the Village Lord DRYDEN. The incomes of the poor clergy GEO. ELIOT. *attrib.* **Income bonds,** bonds of a corporation or company, the interest of which is not cumulative, secured by a lien upon the net income of each year, after payment of prior charges.

Income (i·nkɒm), *sb.*[2] *Sc.* and *n. dial.* 1808. [f. IN *adv.* + COME. Cf. ANCOME.] A morbid affection of any part of the body, a swelling, impostume, or the like.

†**Inco·me,** *v.* [OE. *incuman*; a collocation of IN *adv.* + COME *v.* Now repl. by *come in.*] *intr.* To come in, enter –1565.

Incomer (i·nkɒ:mə). 1514. [f. IN *adv.* + COMER.] One who comes in; opp. to *outgoer*; also *spec.* **a.** a visitor, immigrant, or foreign resident; **b.** an intruder; an invader; **c.** a successor; **d.** *Sport.* a bird that flies towards the sportsman.

I·ncome-tax. 1799. [INCOME *sb.*[1] 5.) A tax levied in some countries on incomes.

In Great Britain first introduced as a war-tax in 1799; re-introduced in 1842, and maintained since. Assessed at a rate annually fixed by Parliament. The existing income-tax..certainly is a tax that should not be retained a moment after it can be dispensed with McCULLOCH.

Incoming (i·nkɒ:miŋ), *vbl. sb.* ME. [f. IN *adv.* + COMING *vbl. sb.*] **1.** The action or fact of coming in; entrance; arrival. (Opp. to *outgoing.*) **2.** = INCOME *sb.*[1] 5. (Usu. in *pl.*) 1596.

1. The i. of spring 1825. **2.** The nominal incomings are 900 *l.* 1881.

I·ncoming, *ppl. a.* 1753. [f. IN *adv.* + COMING *ppl. a.*] That comes in or enters; also *spec.* **a.** succeeding; **b.** immigrant; **c.** coming in as profit; **d.** (of a period of time) about to begin.

†**Incomm·end,** *v.* 1574. [f. IN-[2] + COMMEND (sense 1) after *intrust*, obs. var. of ENTRUST.] = COMMEND *v.* 1 –1621.

In commendam: see COMMENDAM.

Incommensurable (inkǫme·nsiŭrăb'l, -ʃŭr-), *a.* (*sb.*) 1557. [– late L. *incommensurabilis* (Boethius); see IN-[3], COMMENSURABLE. Cf. (O)Fr. *incommensurable.*] **1.** *Math.* Not commensurable; having no common measure (integral or fractional). Said of two or more quantities or magnitudes, or of one in relation to another; also sometimes *absol.* = incommensurable with ordinary or rational quantities, as the natural numbers 1570. **b.** (in *Arith.*) Having no (integral) common measure except unity 1557. **2.** *gen.* Having no common standard of measurement 1660. **b.** *spec.* Not worthy to be measured *with*; utterly disproportioned to 1799. **3.** *sb.* An incommensurable quantity, etc.; usu. in *pl.* 1741.

1. That the Diameter of every Square is I. with the Sides CUDWORTH. **2. b.** Solutions, which I still dismissed as i. with the facts 1892. Hence **Incomme:nsurabi·lity, Incomme·nsurableness** (*rare*) i. quality. **Incomme·nsurably** *adv.*

Incommensurate (inkǫme·nsiŭrĕt, -ʃŭr-), *a.* 1650. [IN-[3].] **1.** Not commensurate; not of corresponding measure or degree; out of proportion, inadequate. Const. *with, to.* 1684. †**b.** Disproportioned. BULWER. **2.** = INCOMMENSURABLE 1687.

1. Power, unfortunately, i. with good will 1856. **2.** Difficulty and doubt are i. J. H. NEWMAN. Hence **Incomme·nsurate-ly** *adv.*, **-ness.**

Incommiscible (inkǫmi·sib'l), *a. rare.* 1620. [– late L. *incommiscibilis* (Tertullian); see IN-[3], COM-, MISCIBLE.] Incapable of being mixed together. Hence **Incommiscibi·lity.**

†**Incommi·xed, -mi·xt,** *a.* 1513, [– late L. *incommixtus*; see IN-[3], COMMIX.] Not mixed together, or with something –1660. So †**Incommi·xture,** unmixed condition.

†**Inco·mmodate,** *v.* 1555. [– *incommodat-*, pa. ppl. stem of L. *incommodare*, f. *incommodus* inconvenient; see -ATE[3].] = INCOMMODE *v.* –1693. So †**Inco·mmodate** *ppl. a.* incommoded. **Incommoda·tion** (now *rare*), inconvenience.

†**Incommo·de,** *a.* (*sb.*) 1518. [– Fr. *incommode* – L. *incommodus*; see IN-[3], COMMODE *a.*] **1.** = INCOMMODIOUS 1, 4. –1771. **2.** *sb.* An inconvenience. WOLSEY.

Incommode (inkǫmōᵘ·d), *v.* 1598. [– Fr. *incommoder* or L. *incommodare*, f. *incommodus* inconvenient; see prec.] **1.** *trans.* To subject to inconvenience or discomfort; to trouble, annoy, molest, embarrass. **2.** To hinder, impede, obstruct (an action, etc.) 1702.

1. At first, the confinement of a chamber incommoded us W. IRVING. So †**Incommo·dement,** condition of being incommoded.

Incommodious (inkǫmōᵘ·diəs), *a.* 1551. [f. IN-[3] + COMMODIOUS.] **1.** Causing inconvenience or discomfort; troublesome, disagreeable. †**2.** Hurtful, injurious –1655. †**3.** Unprofitable, unfit, unsuitable; unbefitting –1714. **4.** Of places, etc.: Not convenient for shelter, travelling, etc.; inconveniently small, narrow, etc.; uncomfortable 1615.

1. Their life is nothing hard or i. 1551. **4.** An i. port POPE, prison HOWARD. Hence **Incommo·dious-ly** *adv.*, **-ness.**

Incommodity (inkǫmǫ·dĭti). ME. [– (O)Fr. *incommodité* – L. *incommoditas*, f. *incommodus*; see INCOMMODE *a.*, -ITY.] **1.** Incommodious quality, condition, or state of things; inconvenience, disadvantage, discomfort. **2.** With *pl.* An incommodious thing or circumstance ME.

1. Moche teene and incommodité Foloweth age 1500. **2.** The Incommodities and Commodities of Vsury BACON.

Incommunicable (inkǫmiū·nikăb'l), *a.* 1568. [– late L. *incommunicabilis* not to be imparted; see IN-[3], COMMUNICABLE. Cf. Fr. *incommunicable* (XVI).] **1.** Not communicable; incapable of being imparted or shared 1577. **2.** Incapable of being told or uttered; ineffable, unspeakable 1664. **3.** Not communicative 1568. **4.** Not in communication (with others or with each other); without intercourse 1646.

1. The i. power of the crown 1760. **3.** Terrible iudges, seuere, intractable, collerick, i. NORTH. **4.** The two worlds..were not i. GROTE. Hence **Incommu:nicabi·lity, Incommu·nicableness,** the quality of being i. **Incommu·nicably** *adv.*

†**Incommu·nicated,** *ppl. a.* 1646. [f. IN-[3] + COMMUNICATE *v.* (senses 1–5) + -ED[1].] Not communicated; that is without communication –1664. So **Incommu·nicating** *a.* not communicating, without communication. †**Incommunica·tion,** absence of communication or imparting 1611.

Incommunicative (inkǫmiū·nikĕtiv), *a.* 1670. [IN-[3].] Not communicative; not disposed for intercourse or conversation; uncommunicative.

A silent and i. sort of character HAWTHORNE. Hence **Incommu·nicative-ly** *adv.*, **-ness.**

Incommutable (inkǫmiū·tăb'l), *a.* 1450. [– L. *incommutabilis* not changeable. In sense 2 f. IN-[3] + COMMUTABLE.] **1.** Not changeable; not liable to alteration; immutable. **2.** Not commutable; unexchangeable 1775.

1. The giver of a perfect and i. law CHALMERS. Hence **Incommutabi·lity, Incommu·tableness. Incommu·tably** *adv.*

Incompact (inkǫmpæ·kt), *a.* 1616. [IN-[3].] Not compact; loosely put together; of loose consistency. Also *transf.* and *fig.*

transf. The empire of the Czars being already i. and vast LANDOR. Hence **Incompa·ct-ly** *adv.*, **-ness.**

Incompa·cted, *a.* 1680. [IN-[3].] Incompact.

Incomparable (inkǫ·mpărăb'l), *a.* (*adv.*, *sb.*) ME. [– (O)Fr. *incomparable* – L. *incomparabilis*; see IN-[3], COMPARABLE.] **1.** With which there is no comparison; matchless, peerless, transcendent. **2.** Not to be compared (*with* or *to*) 1614.

1. She was afterwards his i. wife FULLER.

†**B.** *adv.* Incomparably –1664.

C. *sb.* An incomparable person or thing 1704.

Such a succession of incomparables PENN. Hence **Inco:mparabi·lity, Inco·mparableness,** the quality of being i. **Inco·mparably** *adv.* ME.

†**Incompa·red,** *a.* [IN-[3].] Unmatched. SPENSER.

†**Incompa·ssion.** 1625. [IN-[3].] Absence of compassion or pity –1675.

†**Incompa·ssionate,** *a.* 1611. [IN-[3].] Not compassionate; void of compassion or pity –1679. Hence †**Incompa·ssionate-ly** *adv.*, †**-ness.**

Incompatible (inkǫmpæ·tĭb'l), *a.* (*sb.*) 1563. [– med.L. *incompatibilis* (said of benefices); see IN-[3] and COMPATIBLE.] Not compatible. **1.** Of benefices, etc.: Incapable of being held together. **2.** Mutually intolerant; incapable of existing together in the same subject; discordant, incongruous, inconsistent 1592. †**3.** Unable to 'get on' together; at variance –1722. †**4.** Irreconcilable –1635. **5.** *sb.* An incompatible person or thing 1711.

2. The use of the shield is i. with that of the bow GIBBON. He felt that to be a politician and a preacher of righteousness was to combine two vocations practically i. 1871. Hence **Incompatibi·lity, Incompa·tibleness. Incompa·tibly** *adv.*

Incompetence (inkǫ·mpĭtĕns). 1663. [– Fr. *incompétence*; after INCOMPETENT.] †**1.** Inadequacy. **2.** The fact or condition of being incompetent; want of the requisite ability, power, or qualification; incapacity 1716. **3.** Of a logical conclusion: Want of legitimacy; faultiness 1837.

2. I. of the aortic and mitral valves 1876. **3.** The competence or i. of any Conclusion SIR W. HAMILTON.

Incompetency (inkǫ·mpĭtĕnsi). 1611. [f. prec. or next; see -ENCY.] **1.** The quality of being incompetent; = INCOMPETENCE 2. Also, with *pl.*, an instance of this. **2.** Legal incapacity or disqualification 1650. **3.** Logical illegitimacy 1837.

1. [The] utter i. of the bishops PRIESTLEY. **2.** The testator's alleged i. to enter into the agreement 1833.

Incompetent (inkǫ·mpĭtĕnt), *a.* (*sb.*) 1597. [– Fr. *incompétent* or late L. *incompetens, -ent-*; see IN-[3], COMPETENT.] †**1.** Inadequate –1823. **2.** Of inadequate ability or fitness; not having the requisite capacity or qualification; incapable. Rarely of things. 1635. **3.** Not legally competent or qualified 1597. **4.** Logically illegitimate 1835. **5.** *sb.* An incompetent person 1866.

1. A purse i. to this demand LAMB. **2.** The Nabob, who was totally i. to his own defence JAS. MILL. **3.** Subjects..judges i. To judge their king DANIEL. **5.** A dauber, an i., not fit to be a sign-painter STEVENSON. Hence **Inco·mpetent-ly** *adv.*, **-ness.**

†**Incompe·tible,** *a.* 1513. [f. IN-[3] + COMPETIBLE.] **1.** Incompetent. **2.** Not competible; not within one's competence or capacity; not properly applicable *to*; inappropriate. 1533. Occas. confused with *incompatible.* –1684.

Puffed vp with incomparable and i. Titles of Learning BP. MOUNTAGU. Hence †**Incompetibi·lity,** incompetency, incapacity.

Incomplete (inkǫmplī·t), *a.* ME. [– late L. *incompletus*; see IN-[3], COMPLETE. Cf. (O)Fr. *incomplet.*] Not complete; not fully formed, made, or done; not whole or thorough; wanting some part; unfinished, defective.

It pleaseth him in mercy to account himself i. and maimed without us HOOKER. *Incomplete flower*, a flower wanting one or more of the normal parts (calyx, corolla, stamens, or pistils). *I. metamorphosis* (in insects, etc.), imperfect metamorphosis. Hence **Incomple·te-ly** *adv.*, **-ness.**

Incomple·tion. 1804. [IN-[3].] Incomplete condition.

Incomplex (inkǫ·mpleks, *formerly* inkǫmple·ks), *a.* 1658. [– late and med.L. *incomplexus*; see IN-[3], COMPLEX *a.*] Not complex; not involved; simple. Hence †**Incomple·xly** *adv.*

†**Incompli·able,** *a.* 1625. [f. IN-[3] + COMPLIABLE.] Not able or ready to comply or act in concord; unconformable –1664.

Incompliance (inkǫmplai·ăns). Now *rare.* 1655. [IN-[3].] †**1.** Want of conformity. †**2.** Unaccommodating disposition; want of complaisance –1805. **3.** Failure to comply; non-compliance 1708.

2. A martial man..is apt to have a tincture of sowerness and incomplyance in his behaviour COLLIER.

Incompliant (inkǒmpləi·ănt), *a.* Now *rare.* 1647. [IN-[3].] Not compliant. **1.** Not yielding to the desires or requests of others; unaccommodating 1707. **2.** Of things: **a.** Incompatible. **b.** Unpliant, unyielding. 1647. Hence **Incompli·ancy** (*rare*), i. character. **Incompli·antly** *adv.*

†**Incompo·rtable,** *a.* [f. IN-[3] + COMPORTABLE.] Not to be borne. NORTH.

†**Incomposed** (inkǒmpōᵘ·zd), *a.* 1608. [f. IN-[3] + COMPOSED. Cf. Fr. *incomposé.*] **1.** Not composite; simple, uncompounded –1683. **2.** Wanting in composure or orderly arrangement; disordered; agitated, discomposed 1608. **3.** Indisposed (*to*) 1660.

2. The Anarch old With faultring speech and visage incompos'd MILT. *P. L.* II. 989. †**Incompo·sed-ly** *adv.* 1612, †**-ness**.

Incomposite (inkǫ·mpǒzit), *a.* (*sb.*) 1677. [– L. *incompositus*; see IN-[3] and COMPOSITE.] **1.** Not composite; simple, uncompounded. As *sb.* Something uncompounded. **2.** Not properly composed or put together 1879.

1. *Incomposite number* (Arith.): a prime number. ? *Obs.*

Incompossible (inkǒmpǫ·sĭb'l), *a.* Now *rare.* 1605. [– schol.L. *incompossibilis*; see IN-[3] and COMPOSSIBLE.] Not possible together; that cannot exist or be true together; wholly incompatible or inconsistent.

To adopt the Hamiltonian word, the two Judgments are i. BOWEN. Hence **Incompossibi·lity,** i. quality; also, with *pl.*, an instance of this.

†**Incompo·sure.** 1644. [IN-[3].] Discomposure, disorder –1706.

†**Incomprehe·nse,** *a.* [– late L. *incomprehensus*, f. *in-* IN-[3] + *comprehensus*, pa. pple. of *comprehendere* COMPREHEND.] Not comprehended within limits; boundless. MARSTON.

Incomprehensible (i:nkǫmprĭhe·nsĭb'l), *a.* (*sb.*) ME. [– L. *incomprehensibilis*; see IN-[3] and COMPREHENSIBLE. Cf. (O)Fr. *incompréhensible.*] **1.** That cannot be contained within limits. (Chiefly *Theol.*) *arch.* **2.** That cannot be grasped by the understanding; beyond the reach of intellect. *Obs.* or *arch.* exc. as in b. ME. **b.** That cannot be understood; inconceivable, unintelligible 1604. †**3.** That cannot be grasped (physically); impalpable (*rare*) –1745. **4.** *sb.* An incomprehensible being or thing (in sense 1 or 2) 1548.

1. The father i., the sonne i.: and the holy ghost i. *Athan. Creed.* The Firmament..And all her numberd Starrs, that seem to rowle Spaces i. MILT. *P. L.* VIII. 20. **2. b.** She was perfectly i. to me DICKENS. **4.** That notion..is nothing but a bundle of incomprehensibles CUDWORTH. Hence **Incomprehensibi·lity, Incomprehe·nsibleness. Incomprehe·nsibly** *adv.*

Incomprehension (i:nkǫmprĭhe·nʃən). 1605. [f. IN-[3] + COMPREHENSION.] The fact of not grasping with the mind; want of comprehension; failure to understand.

Our ignorance and i. of the least things in Nature GALE.

Incomprehensive (i:nkǫmprĭhe·nsiv), *a.* 1652. [f. IN-[3] + COMPREHENSIVE, in early use perh. – med.L. *comprehensivus* (XII).] **1.** Not comprehensive; not understanding. **2.** Not inclusive 1774. †**3.** Incomprehensible –1791. Hence **Incomprehe·nsive·ly** *adv.*, **-ness.**

Incompressible (inkǒmpre·sĭb'l), *a.* 1730. [f. IN-[3] + COMPRESSIBLE. Cf. Fr. *incompressible.*] That cannot be compressed or squeezed into smaller compass; incapable of compression. Also *fig.*

Liquids in general are treated in hydrostatics as i. bodies LARDNER. Hence **Incompressibi·lity,** the quality of being i.

†**Inco·mpt,** *a.* 1631. [– L. *incom(p)tus* unadorned, rough; see IN-[3], COMPT *a.*] Void of neatness; inelegant –1669. Hence †**Inco·mptness.**

Incomputable (inkǒmpiū·tăb'l, inkǫ·mpiutăb'l), *a.* 1606. [f. IN-[3] + COMPUTABLE.] That cannot be computed.

†**Inconcea·lable,** *a.* [IN-[3].] That cannot be concealed. SIR T. BROWNE.

Inconceivable (inkǒnsī·văb'l), *a.* (*sb.*) 1631. [f. IN-[3] + CONCEIVABLE.] **1.** That cannot be conceived or realized in the imagination; unthinkable. Often merely = 'hardly credible', 'extraordinary'. **2.** *spec.* As a philosophical term.

(*a*) Opposed to the fundamental laws of thought, self-contradictory. (*b*) Repugnant to recognized axioms or laws of nature. (*c*) Involving a combination of facts which appears incredible. (*d*) Incapable of being represented by a mental image 1655.

1. With an i. dexterity 1646. **2.** What is i. or contradictious, is nothing at all to us H. MORE. Power without substance is inconceivable REID. The i. qualities of space 1875. Hence **Inconceivabi·lity,** the quality of being i; something that is i. **Inconcei·vableness. Inconcei·vably** *adv.*

B. *sb.* A thing or quality that cannot be conceived 1706.

†**Inconce·ptible,** *a.* [f. IN-[3] + CONCEPTIBLE.] Inconceivable. HALE.

†**Inconce·rning,** *a. rare.* 1642. [f. IN-[3] + CONCERNING.] That does not matter; unimportant –1650.

†**Inconci·liable,** *a. rare.* Also **-cilable, -cileable.** 1643. [f. IN-[3] + CONCILIABLE.] Incapable of being conciliated; irreconcilable –1694.

†**Inconci·nn, -e,** *a. rare.* 1660. [– L. *inconcinnus* or f. IN-[3] + CONCINNE.] Not adjusted or adapted; incongruous –1678. So †**Inconci·nnate** *a.* awkward; not adapted; unsuitable 1533. †**Inconci·nnately** *adv.* inelegantly.

Inconci·nnity. *Obs.* or *arch.* 1616. [– L. *inconcinnitas* or f. IN-[3] + CONCINNITY.] Want of concinnity; inelegance; impropriety, unsuitableness.

†**Inconci·nnous,** *a.* 1662. [f. L. *inconcinnus* + -OUS or f. IN-[3] + CONCINNOUS.] **1.** Incongruous. **2.** *Mus.* Inharmonious –1811.

†**Inconclu·dent,** *a.* 1671. [f. IN-[3] + CONCLUDENT.] = next. So †**Inconclu·dency** 1654.

†**Inconclu·ding,** *a.* 1644. [f. IN-[3] + CONCLUDING *ppl. a.*] Inconclusive –1677.

Inconclu·sion. 1847. [f. IN-[3] + CONCLUSION.] The condition of reaching no conclusion; an inconclusive result.

Inconclusive (inkǒnklū·siv), *a.* 1690. [f. IN-[3] + CONCLUSIVE.] **1.** Not conclusive in argument or evidence; that does not bring to an end (a doubt, dispute, etc.); not decisive. **b.** Given to inconclusion. SIR H. TAYLOR. **2.** Not conclusive in action 1841.

1. Long and i. debates..on the legality of a Papal abdication MILMAN. **2.** The i. nature of his Indian operations 1841. Hence **Inconclu·sive·ly** *adv.*, **-ness.**

†**Inconco·ct,** *a.* 1596. [f. IN-[3] + CONCOCT *a.*] = next –1626.

†**Inconco·cted,** *a.* 1605. [f. IN-[3] + CONCOCTED.] Not concocted; not fully digested or matured; not softened by ripening; raw –1677.

†**Inconco·ction.** 1626. [f. IN-[3] + CONCOCTION.] The fact or condition of being unconcocted or undigested.

Inconcre·te, *a.* Now *rare.* 1626. [– late (eccl.) L. *inconcretus* incorporeal; see IN-[3], CONCRETE *a.*] Not concrete; abstract; immaterial.

†**Inconcu·rrent,** *a.* 1651. [IN-[3].] Not concurrent. So †**Inconcu·rring** *a.* 1646.

†**Inconcu·ssible,** *a.* Also **-able.** 1589. [– Fr. †*inconcussible*; see IN-[3], CONCUSS *v.*, -IBLE.] That cannot be shaken; firmly fixed, stable –1715.

Incondensable (inkǒnde·nsăb'l), *a.* Also *erron.* **-ible.** 1736. [f. IN-[3] + CONDENSABLE.] That cannot be condensed; incapable of being made more dense or compact; *spec.* incapable of being reduced to the liquid or solid condition. Hence **Incondensabi·lity** (*erron.* **-ibility**), i. quality.

Incondite (inkǫ·ndit), *a.* 1539. [– L. *inconditus*, f. *in-* IN-[3] + *conditus*, pa. pple. of *condere* put together.] **1.** Ill constructed, ill composed: said esp. of literary and artistic compositions 1634. **2.** Unformed; rude, unpolished, unrefined 1539.

1. An i. collection..of..rules AUSTIN. **2.** The Negresses..forgot themselves..and were altogether i. KINGSLEY. Hence **Inco·nditely** *adv.*

†**Incondi·tional,** *a.* [f. IN-[3] + CONDITIONAL[1].] Unconditional. SIR T. BROWNE.

Inconditionate (inkǒndi·ʃənĕt), *a.* (*sb.*) 1654. [f. IN-[3] + CONDITIONATE *a.*] **1.** Not limited by conditions; unconditioned. **2.** *sb.* (*Philos.*) An entity which is unconditioned; a form under which the Unconditioned is conceived 1829.

1. The power of Government.. i. 1654. not..is **2.** The Unconditioned and the species, or Inconditionates which it contains—viz., Absolute and Infinite VEITCH.

†**Inconfi·rmed,** *a.* [f. IN-[3] + CONFIRMED.] Not become firm or strong. SIR T. BROWNE.

†**Inconfo·rm,** *a.* 1659. [f. IN-[3] + CONFORM *a.*] Not conformed *to* –1663. So **Inconfo·rmable** *a.* not conformable; unconformable 1612. †**Inconfo·rmist** = NONCONFORMIST.

Inconformity (inkǒnfǭ·ɹmĭti). 1594. [f. IN-[3] + CONFORMITY.] Want of conformity. **b.** *spec.* = NONCONFORMITY 1633.

Inconfused (inkǒnfiū·zd), *a.* 1626. [f. IN-[3] + CONFUSED, after L. *inconfusus.*] Not confused; free from mixture of the elements.

†**Inconfu·sion.** [f. IN-[3] + CONFUSION, after L. *inconfusus.* Cf. prec.] Unconfused condition. BACON.

†**Inconfu·table,** *a.* [IN-[3].] Not confutable. PENN. Hence †**Inconfu·tably** *adv.* 1664.

Incongealable (inkǒndʒī·lăb'l), *a.* ? *Obs.* 1623. [f. IN-[3] + CONGEALABLE.] Incapable of being congealed.

†**Incong·nerous,** *a.* [f. IN-[3] + CONGENEROUS.] Not of the same kind; the opposite of CONGENEROUS. SIR T. BROWNE.

Incongenial (inkǒndʒī·niăl), *a.* 1797. [IN-[3].] Not congenial; uncongenial. Hence **Incongenia·lity.**

Incongruent (inkǫ·ŋgruˌĕnt), *a.* 1531. [–L. *incongruens, -ent-*; see IN-[3], CONGRUENT.] Not congruent; disagreeing, unsuitable, incongruous. Hence **Inco·ngruence, Inco·ngruency** (? *Obs.*), want of congruence; incongruity. **Inco·ngruently** *adv.*

Incongruity (inkǒnˌgrū·ĭti). 1532. [– late L. *incongruitas*; see IN-[3], CONGRUITY. Cf. Fr. *incongruité.*] **1.** The quality, condition, or fact of being incongruous; want of accordance or harmony; inconsistency. Also with *an* and *pl.* 1610. **2.** Want of accordance with what is reasonable or fitting; unsuitableness, inappropriateness, absurdity. Also with *an* and *pl.* 1597. **3.** Want of harmony of parts or elements; incoherence. Also with *an* and *pl.* 1532. †**4.** *Gram.* Grammatical incorrectness; solecism –1612.

1. Such I. and Nonconformity in their furniture MARVELL. **2.** Without i...we cannot speak of geometrical beauty JOHNSON. **3.** The i. of the clerk's apparel SCOTT.

Incongruous (inkǫ·ŋgruˌəs), *a.* 1611. [– L. *incongruus* (f. *in-* IN-[3] + *congruus*) + -OUS. See CONGRUOUS.] Not congruous. **1.** Disagreeing in character, or qualities; not in keeping; disaccordant, inconsistent, inharmonious, unsuited. Const. *with, to.* (Often with a mixture of sense 2.) **2.** Unbecoming, unsuitable, inappropriate, absurd, out of place 1623. **3.** Not self-consistent; incoherent 1658. †**4.** *Gram.* Grammatically incorrect –1678. **5.** *Theory of Numbers.* Of two numbers: Not congruent; giving different remainders when divided by the modulus (see CONGRUENCE 3) 1864.

1. The cart way of the village divides..two very i. soils G. WHITE. **2.** How i. and irrational the common Temper of Mankind is DE FOE. **3.** Of all human characters a fanatic philosopher is the most i. H. WALPOLE. Hence **Inco·ngruous-ly** *adv.*, **-ness.**

†**Inconjunct** (inkǒndʒɒ·ŋkt), *a.* 1603. [f. IN-[3] + CONJUNCT.] Not in conjunction; *spec.* in *Astrol.*, said of two planets or their positions when neither affects the operation of the other –1819.

Inconne·cted, *a. rare.* 1732. [IN-[3].] Not connected; disconnected. Hence **Inconne·ctedness.**

Inconnection, -exion (inkǒne·kʃən). ? *Obs.* 1620. [IN-[3].] Want of connection; unconnectedness; an instance of this.

Inconscient (inkǫ·nʃiĕnt), *a. rare.* 1885. [f. IN-[3] + CONSCIENT.] Unconscious.

Whether you believe that Creation was the work of design or of i. law. LD. SALISBURY.

†**Inco·nscionable,** *a.* 1596. [f. IN-[3] + CONSCIONABLE.] Not having, or not regarding, conscience; unconscionable –1800. Hence †**Inco·nscionableness.** †**Inco·nscionably** *adv.*

Inconscious (inkǫ·nʃəs), *a.* Now *rare.* 1670. [f. late L. *inconscius* unaware, ignorant + -OUS. In later use f. IN-[3] + CONSCIOUS.] †**1.** Not privy to some deed. MILT.

2. Not conscious; unconscious 1678. Hence **Inco·nsciously** *adv.*

Inconsecutive (inkǫnse·kiŭtiv), *a.* 1836. [IN-³.] Not consecutive; inconsequent. Hence **Inconse·cutive-ly** *adv.*, **-ness.**

Inconsequence (inkǫ·nsĭkwĕns). 1588. [– L. *inconsequentia* (Quintilian), f. *inconsequens, -ent-*; see next, -ENCE.] **1.** Want of logical sequence; inconclusiveness, illogicalness; an instance of this. **2.** Want of natural connection of ideas, actions, or events; an irrelevant action or circumstance 1842. **3.** The practice or habit of drawing inconsequent inferences, or of speaking or acting disconnectedly 1817. †**4.** The being of no consequence –1812.

1. Mr. S. himself could not but see the i. of his own argument GATAKER. **3.** That mingling of i. which belongs to us all, and not unhappily GEO. ELIOT. So †**Inco·nsequency.**

Inconsequent (inkǫ·nsĭkwĕnt), *a.* (*sb.*) 1579. [– L. *inconsequens, -ent-* not logically consequent; see IN-³, CONSEQUENT.] **1.** Not following as a logical conclusion; falsely inferred 1627. **b.** Not following in the natural order of events; irrelevant 1881. **2.** Wanting in logical reasoning; involving erroneous inference 1579; disconnected, inconsecutive; irrelevant 1869. **3.** *transf.* Of a person: Characterized by inconsequence 1794. **4.** Of no consequence (*rare*). STERNE. †**5.** *sb.* An illogical inference; a *non sequitur.* PRYNNE.

1. His illation from thence deduced [is] i. HAKEWILL. **2.** Confused thought and i. reasoning 1877. **5.** A meer i. 1643. Hence **Inco·nsequent-ly** *adv.*, **-ness** (*rare*).

Inconsequential (inkǫnsĭkwe·nʃăl), *a.* 1621. [f. IN-³ + CONSEQUENTIAL.] = INCONSEQUENT. Hence **Inconsequentia·lity,** i. quality or character. **Inconsequentially** *adv.*

Inconsiderable (inkǫnsi·dərăb'l), *a.* 1598. [– Fr. †*inconsidérable* or late L. *inconsiderabilis*; see IN-³, CONSIDERABLE.] Not considerable. †**1.** Incalculable (*rare*) –1631. **2.** Not to be considered; beneath notice; insignificant 1637. **b.** Hence, of very small value, amount, or size 1648. †**3.** Inconsiderate, thoughtless (*rare*) –1726.

2. I never heard of the fellow. He is i. 1658. **b.** I. sums 1654. An i. stream MORSE. I. in numbers 1812. Hence **Inconsi·derableness,** i. quality. **Inconsi·derably** *adv.*

†**Inconsi·deracy.** *rare.* 1748. [f. INCONSIDERATE: see -ACY.] Inconsiderateness –1847. So †**Inconsi·derance** (*rare*) 1549.

Inconsiderate (inkǫnsi·dərĕt), *a.* (*sb.*) 1450. [– L. *inconsideratus*; see IN-³ and CONSIDERATE.] **1.** Not properly considered; thoughtless, unadvised, precipitate, rash. **2.** Of persons, etc.: Acting without deliberation; thoughtless, imprudent, indiscreet 1595. **3.** Without consideration for others 1842. †**4.** Of no importance –1703. **5.** *sb.* An inconsiderate or thoughtless person 1588.

1. Sauls i. and rash oath 1612. **2.** The i. multitude MILT. They are younger and more i. JOWETT. **3.** Of an i. temper 1842. So **Inconsi·derate-ly** *adv.* 1460, **-ness. Inconsi·dered** *a.* (in sense 1).

Inconsideration (inkǫnsidərē̍·ʃən). 1526. [– Fr. *inconsidération* or late L. *inconsideratio*; see IN-³, CONSIDERATION.] **1.** Want of consideration; indiscretion. **2.** Absence of consideration for others 1872.

1. Faults of i. and thoughtlessness JANE AUSTEN. **2.** [Nature's] merciless i. for the individual where the interests of the Race are in question W. R. GREG.

Inconsistence (inkǫnsi·stĕns). Now *rare* or *Obs.* 1643. [f. INCONSISTENT (after *consistence*); see -ENCE.] = INCONSISTENCY.

Inconsistency (inkǫnsi·stĕnsi). 1647. [f. as prec. (after *consistency*); see -ENCY.] **1.** Want of consistency; lack of accordance or harmony (*with* something, or *between* things); incompatibility, contrariety, opposition 1699. **2.** Want of agreement between two things or parts of a thing; a discrepancy, an incongruity 1647. **3.** Of persons: Want of consistency in thought or action; an inconsistent act 1665.

1. The i. of our Religion with Magic ADDISON. **2.** Nor is there any i. in wise and good fathers having foolish..sons JOWETT. **3.** I.—the only thing in which men are consistent HOR. SMITH. The inconsistencies of which Pitt had been guilty MACAULAY.

Inconsistent (inkǫnsi·stĕnt), *a.* (*sb.*) 1646. [f. IN-³ + CONSISTENT.] Not consistent. **1.** Of a substance: Without consistence; of incoherent nature (*rare*) 1677. **2.** Not consisting; not agreeing in substance, spirit, or form; not in keeping; at variance, discordant, incompatible, incongruous 1646. **3.** Wanting in harmony; self-contradictory; involving inconsistency 1651. **4.** Of a person: Not consistent in thought or action. Const. *with,* †*to,* or *absol.* 1709. **5.** *sb.* (*pl.*) Things, statements, etc. which are inconsistent with each other or with something else 1652.

1. The parts..of dust [are] i. RUSKIN. **2.** Resentment is not i. with good-will BUTLER. **4.** You.. are i. with your own principles 'JUNIUS'. *absol.* Thoughtless, thankless, i. man YOUNG. Hence **Inconsi·stent-ly** *adv.*, **-ness** (*rare*).

Inconsolable (inkǫnsōᵘ·lăb'l), *a.* 1596. [– Fr. *inconsolable* or L. *inconsolabilis*; see IN-³, CONSOLABLE.] Not admitting of consolation; that cannot be consoled, alleviated, or assuaged.

I. woe 1862. Still i. for his loss C. BRONTË. Hence **Inconso·labi·lity, Inconso·lableness,** i. condition. **Inconso·lably** *adv.*

Inconsolate (inkǫ·nsŏlĕt), *a. rare.* 1656. [f. IN-³ + CONSOLATE *a.*] Unconsoled, disconsolate. Hence **Inco·nsolately** *adv.*

Inconsonant (inkǫ·nsŏnănt), *a.* 1658. [f. IN-³ + CONSONANT *a.*] Not consonant or agreeable *to,* †*unto*; not agreeing *with.*

A Fiction utterly i. to the whole Method of Nature HALE. Hence **Inco·nsonance,** †**Inco·nsonancy** (*rare*) 1650, want of consonance or agreement. **Inco·nsonantly** *adv.*

Inconspicuous (inkǫnspi·kiuˌəs), *a.* 1624. [f. L. *inconspicuus* + -OUS; see IN-³, CONSPICUOUS.] †**1.** That cannot be seen or discerned –1793. **2.** Not readily seen; not prominent or striking 1828.

2. Small and i. flowers 1845. **Inconspi·cuous-ly** *adv.*, **-ness.**

†**Inco·nstance.** ME. [– (O)Fr. *inconstance* – L. *inconstantia,* f. *inconstant-*; see INCONSTANT, -ANCE.] = INCONSTANCY –1712.

Inconstancy (inkǫ·nstănsi). 1526. [– L. *inconstantia*; see prec. and -ANCY.] Want of constancy. **1.** Fickleness; changeableness; an instance of this. **2.** Mutability; irregularity; absence of uniformity 1613. †**3.** Inconsistency (in statements, etc.); an instance of this –1605.

1. Lightnesse and inconstancie in love SPENSER. **2.** The silent Moone..constant image of the worlds inconstancie PURCHAS.

Inconstant (inkǫ·nstănt), *a.* (*sb.*) ME. [– (O)Fr. *inconstant* – L. *inconstans, -ant-*; see IN-³, CONSTANT.] Not constant. **1.** Not steadfast; fickle, changeable. **2.** Of things: Frequently changing; variable, irregular 1526. **3.** *sb.* An inconstant person or thing 1647.

1. The fickle, i., volatile temper of the people 1844. **2.** Th' i. Moone, That monethly changes SHAKS. **3.** Let us eliminate the inconstants RUSKIN. Hence **Inco·nstant-ly** *adv.*, †**-ness.**

Inconsumable (inkǫnsiū·măb'l), *a.* 1646. [IN-³.] **1.** Not consumable by fire, etc. **2.** *Pol. Econ.* Not consumable in use 1785.

2. The i. things, like machinery, leather, coin 1884. Hence **Inconsu·mably** *adv.*

†**Inconsu·mmate,** *a. rare.* 1641. [– late L. *inconsummatus*; see IN-³, CONSUMMATE *a.*] Not consummated or completed; unfinished –1695.

†**Inconsu·mptible,** *a.* 1579. [– Fr. †*inconsomptible, -sumpt-,* or late L. *inconsumptibilis*; see IN-³, CONSUMPTIBLE.] Incapable of being consumed –1708. So †**Inconsu·mptive** 1513.

Inconta·minate, *a.* 1508. [– L. *incontaminatus*; see IN-³, CONTAMINATE *ppl. a.*] Uncontaminated, undefiled.

Incontestable (inkǫnte·stăb'l), *a.* Also *erron.* **-ible.** 1673. [– Fr. *incontestable* or med.L. *incontestabilis*; see IN-³, CONTESTABLE.] That cannot be contested or disputed; unquestionable, incontrovertible.

I. proof 1748, beauty SCOTT, evidence 1885. Hence **Inconte:stabi·lity,** i. quality. **Inconte·stableness. Incontestably** *adv.*

†**Inconte·sted,** *a.* 1712. [IN-³.] Undisputed –1794.

†**Inconti·guous,** *a. rare.* 1660. [f. IN-³ + CONTIGUOUS.] Not in contact; unconnected –1685. Hence †**Inconti·guously** *adv.*

Incontinence (inkǫ·ntinĕns). ME. [–(O)Fr. *incontinence* or L. *incontinentia*; see IN-³, CONTINENCE.] **1.** Want of continence or self-restraint; inability to contain or restrain: **a.** Unchastity. **b.** *gen.* (Const. *of.*) 1836. **2.** *Path.* Inability to retain a natural evacuation 1754.

1. b. [They] do not waste themselves by i. of tongue CARLYLE. So †**Inco·ntinency** 1485.

Incontinent (inkǫ·ntinĕnt), *a.* (*sb.*) ME. [– (O)Fr. *incontinent* or L. *incontinens, -ent-*; see IN-³, CONTINENT *a.*] **1.** Not continent; wanting in self-restraint, esp. with reference to sexual appetite. **2.** Unable to contain or retain. Usu. with *of.* 1641. **3.** Unable to retain natural evacuations 1828. **4.** *sb.* An unchaste person. B. JONS. Hence **Inco·ntinently** *adv.*[1] in an i. manner.

Incontinent (inkǫ·ntinĕnt), *adv. arch.* ME. [– OFr. *en-, incontenant* = Sp., It. *incontinente* – late L. *in continenti,* sc. *tempore* 'in CONTINUOUS time', without an interval. Cf. CONTINENT *a.* 6.] Straightway, at once, immediately.

The Lords will be here i. SCOTT. So **Inco·ntinently** *adv.*[2] 1484.

Inconti·nuous, *a. rare.* 1862. [IN-³.] Not continuous. So **Incontinu·ity.**

Incontrollable (inkǫntrōᵘ·lăb'l), *a.* 1599. [f. IN-³ + CONTROLLABLE.] **1.** That cannot be controlled; uncontrollable. †**2.** That cannot be interfered with; fixed, unchangeable –1646. †**3.** Incontrovertible –1646. Hence **Incontro·llably** *adv.*

Incontrovertible (inkǫntrǒvə̄·ɹtĭb'l), *a.* 1646. [IN-³.] That cannot be controverted; indisputable. Hence **Incontrovertibi·lity, Incontrove·rtibleness. Incontrove·rtibly** *adv.*

Inconvenience (inkǫnvī·niĕns), *sb.* ME. [– OFr. *inconvenience* (mod. *inconvenance*) – late L. *inconvenientia* incongruity, inconsistency; see IN-³, CONVENIENCE.] The fact or quality of being inconvenient. †**1.** Want of agreement; inconsistency with reason or rule, absurdity; an instance of this –1706. †**b.** Unsuitableness –1684. †**2.** Moral unsuitableness; unseemly behaviour; impropriety; also with *an* and *pl.* –1560. †**3.** Harm, injury, mischief; misfortune, trouble. †Also with *an* and *pl.* –1796. **4.** Want of adaptation to personal ease; discomfort; incommodity. Also with *an* and *pl.* 1578.

2. They fall..sometimes from hot words to further i. *Homilies.* **3.** Rapine, ruine, and a thousand inconveniences, follow 1608. **4.** She could have spared him without the smallest i. DICKENS. Hence **Inconve·nience** *v.* to cause i. to; to put to i.; to incommode. So **Inconve·niency** = INCONVENIENCE.

Inconvenient (inkǫnvī·niĕnt). ME. [–OFr. *inconvenient* adj. – L. *inconveniens, -ent-* not accordant; see IN-³, CONVENIENT. Branch B. is – (O)Fr. *inconvenient* sb.]

A. *adj.* †**1.** Not agreeing or consonant; incongruous; absurd –1674. †**2.** Unsuitable, inappropriate, out of place –1840. †**3.** Morally unsuitable; unseemly, improper –1694. **4.** Unfavourable to comfort; incommodious, embarrassing, disadvantageous, awkward 1651.

2. If it appeare not inconuenient to you *A. Y. L.* v. ii. 73. **4.** A good choice of i. lodgings DICKENS.

†**B.** *sb.* That which is inconvenient –1658.

Hence **Inconve·nient-ly** *adv.*, †**-ness** (*rare*).

Inconversable (inkǫnvə̄·ɹsăb'l), *a.* ? *Obs.* Also *erron.* **-ible.** 1577. [f. IN-³ + CONVERSABLE.] Not conversable; †unsociable; uncommunicative.

Inconversant (inkǫ·nvəɹsănt), *a. rare.* 1679. [IN-³.] Not conversant; not versed *in* or familiar *with.*

†**Inconve·rted,** *a.* [IN-³.] Not turned or changed; unconverted. SIR T. BROWNE.

Inconvertible (inkǫnvə̄·ɹtĭb'l), *a.* 1646. [– Fr. *inconvertible* or late L. *inconvertibilis*; see IN-³, CONVERTIBLE. In later use f. CONVERTIBLE.] **1.** Incapable of being changed into anything else; †*spec.* indigestible. **2.** Not interchangeable. Usu. of terms: Not equivalent. 1706. **b.** *Logic.* Of a proposition: That cannot be converted 1864. **3.** Not exchangeable for something else. *spec.* of paper money, That cannot be converted into specie. 1833.

3. I. bank paper would have been everywhere refused 1833. Hence **Inconvertibi·lity, Inconve·rtibleness. Inconve·rtibly** *adv.*

Inconvincible (inkǫnvi·nsĭb'l), *a.* 1674. [IN-³.] Incapable of being convinced; not open to conviction.

None are so i. as your half-witted people 1674. Hence **Inconvincibi·lity. Inconvi·ncibly** *adv.* 1646.

†**Inco·ny,** *a.* 1588. [A cant word that rimed with *money*. Origin unkn.] ? Rare, fine, delicate, pretty, nice. *L. L. L.* III. i. 136. –1633.

Incoordinate (inko,ǭ·ɹdinĕt), *a.* 1889. [IN-³.] Not co-ordinate. So **Incoo·rdinated. I:ncoordina·tion,** want of co-ordination; esp. in *Phys.* in reference to muscular action (see CO-ORDINATION) 1876.

†**Inco·rd,** *v. rare.* 1611. [– It. *incordare.*] *Incordare*..to incord or burst as a horse FLORIO. So †**Inco·rded** *ppl. a.* (of a horse) ruptured; suffering from hernia 1607. †**Inco·rding** *vbl. sb.* rupture or hernia in a horse 1598.

†**Inco·rnished,** *ppl. a. rare.* [f. IN-² + *cornish* CORNICE + -ED¹; after It. *incorniciare.*] Furnished with a cornice or cornices. EVELYN.

Incoronate (inkǫ·rŏnĕt), *a.* 1867. [– It. *incoronato*, pa. pple. of *incoronare* crown. In *Bot.*, var. (+ IN-²) of CORONATE *a.*] Wearing or having a crown; crowned. So **Incorona·tion,** coronation, crowning 1470.

Inco·rporable, *a.* 1607. [f. INCORPORATE *v.*; see -ABLE. Cf. Fr. *incorporable.*] Capable of being incorporated.

†**Inco·rporal,** *a.* (*sb.*) 1551. [– L. *incorporalis*; see IN-³, CORPORAL.] **1.** = INCORPOREAL; immaterial –1646. **2.** *sb.* An incorporeal thing or place. CUDWORTH. Hence †**Inco·rporality,** the quality of being incorporeal. †**Inco·rporally** *adv.* immaterially.

Inco·rporate, *a. rare.* 1540. [– late L. *incorporatus* not embodied, f. *in-* IN-³ + *corporatus* CORPORATE *ppl. a.*] Without body or material substance; unembodied.

Incorporate (inkǭ·ɹpŏrĕt), *ppl. a.* ME. [– late L. *incorporatus*, pa. pple. of *incorporare*; see next, -ATE².] **1.** United in one body (*lit.* and *fig.*). Now *rare.* **2.** Of a company, etc.: Formally constituted as a corporation. Also of persons; United in a corporation. 1480. †**b.** Associated with others, as members of the same corporation –1684. **3.** Having a bodily form ME.

1. It is Caska, one i. To our Attempts SHAKS. 2. b. The Welshmen our neighbours, or rather our i. countrimen CAMDEN. 3. Ideals never yet i. GEO. ELIOT.

Incorporate (inkǭ·ɹpŏreⁱt), *v.* ME. [– *incorporat-*, pa. ppl. stem of late L. *incorporare*; see IN-², CORPORATE *v.*]

I. *trans.* **1.** To combine or unite into one body or substance; to mix or blend thoroughly together (a number of things or one thing *with* another). Also *fig.* 1544. **2.** To put into or include in the body or substance of something else; to embody, include ME. **b.** To include as a part or parts of itself (*esp.* of literary material) 1824. **3.** To combine into a society or organization; *esp.* to constitute as a legal corporation 1460. **b.** To admit (a person) as member of a company or association 1530. **4.** To furnish with a body; to embody (*rare*) 1623.

1. A melted Cement, made of Pitch, Rosin and Wood-ashes, well incorporated BOYLE. *transf.* You shall not stay alone, Till holy Church i. two in one SHAKS. 2. b. The best edition, incorporating all the works of the author DIBDIN. 3. b. Yesterday was incorporated A. M. Mr. Stevens HEARNE.

II. *intr.* **1.** Of one thing; To unite or combine with something else so as to form one body. Const. *with*, occas. *into*. 1594. **2.** Of two or more things: To unite so as to form one body; to grow into each other; to form an intimate union (*lit.* and *fig.*). ? *Obs.* 1625.

1. Grace can no more i. with sin, than oyle with water FLAVEL. 2. Truth and Falshood..may Cleaue, but they will not I. BACON. Hence **Inco·rporated** *ppl. a.* in senses of the vb.; †embodied 1644; constituted as a legal or formal corporation 1677. **Inco·rporating** *ppl. a.*; as *I. union* (said orig. of the Union between England and Scotland in 1707).

Incorporation (inkǭɹpŏrēⁱ·ʃən). ME. [– late L. *incorporatio*, f. as prec.; see -ION.] **1.** The action of incorporating; the being incorporated. **b.** *Philol.* The combination of two or more parts of speech in one word. SAYCE. **2.** The action of forming into a community or (legal) corporation 1460. †**b.** The document creating or legalizing a corporation; a charter –1605. **3.** An incorporated society or company 1530. **4.** Embodiment (*rare*) 1645.

1. The i. of two independent legislatures 1812. 2. The Patent for the I. of the Parish Clerks 1640. 3. An eminent member of the Goldsmiths' I. SCOTT.

Incorporative (inkǭ·ɹpŏrĕtiv), *a.* 1592. [f. INCORPORATE *v.* + -IVE.] Characterized by or tending to incorporation.

Incorporator (inkǭ·ɹpŏreⁱtəɹ). 1670. [f. as prec. + -OR 2.] **1.** One who incorporates, or combines into one body or substance 1829. **2.** One who takes part in the formation of an incorporated company; one of the original members of an incorporated company 1670. **3.** A member of one University who is incorporated in another 1887.

Incorporeal (inkǫɹpōᵊ·riăl), *a.* (*sb.*) 1532. [f. L. *incorporeus* (Macrobius) + -AL¹.] Not corporeal. **1.** Having no material structure; not composed of matter; immaterial. **2.** Of, pertaining to, or characteristic of immaterial beings 1667. **3.** *Law.* Having no material existence in itself, but attaching as a right or profit to some actual thing; esp. *i. hereditament* 1628. **4.** *sb.* (*pl.*) Things incorporeal 1628.

1. Two active i. principles, heat and cold HALLAM. 2. MILT. *P. L.* VIII. 37. 3. Property called i., such as an annuity BENTHAM. Hence †**Incorpo·realism,** the doctrine that i. spirit or substance exists. †**Incorpo·realist,** one who holds this view. **Incorporea·lity. Incorpo·really** *adv.*

Incorporeity (inkǭɹpŏrī·ĭti). 1601. [– med.L. *incorporeitas*, f. L. *incorporeus* INCORPOREAL; see -ITY.] The quality of being incorporeal; immateriality; with *pl.*, an incorporeal quality.

Incorpsed (inkǭ·ɹpst), *a. rare.* 1602. [f. IN-² + CORPSE + -ED².] Made into one body (with something).

Incorrect (inkŏre·kt), *a.* 1432. [– Fr. *incorrect* or L. *incorrectus*; see IN-³ + CORRECT *a.*] †**1.** Uncorrected; unchastened –1602. **2.** Of a book: Containing many scribal or typographical errors 1484. **3.** Not in conformity with a recognized standard; faulty 1672. **4.** Not in accordance with fact; erroneous, inaccurate 1828.

1. *Haml.* I. ii. 95. 3. The Wit of the last Age was yet more i. than their Language DRYDEN. A practice that was considered i. 1883. 4. An i. statement, narration or calculation 1828. Hence **Incorre·ct-ly** *adv.*, **-ness.**

†**Incorre·ction.** *rare.* 1598. [f. IN-³ + CORRECTION.] **1.** The action of making incorrect. **2.** The condition of being uncorrected 1649. **3.** Incorrectness, faultiness. H. WALPOLE.

Incorrespo·ndence. *rare.* 1667. [IN-³.] Want of correspondence or harmony. So **Incorrespo·ndency** (*rare*).

†**Incorrespo·ndent,** *a. rare.* 1599. [IN-³.] Not in agreement or harmony –1667, So **Incorrespo·nding** *a.*

Incorrigible (inkǫ·ridʒĭb'l), *a.* (*sb.*) ME. [– (O)Fr. *incorrigible* or L. *incorrigibilis*; see IN-³, CORRIGIBLE.] **1.** Bad beyond correction or reform. †**2.** Of something faulty: That cannot be set right. Of disease: Incurable. –1804. **3.** *sb.* One who is incorrigible 1746.

1. An habituated, infatuated, i., cauterized Drunkard 1655. 2. An i. ulcer ABERNETHY. Hence **Inco:rrigibi·lity, Inco·rrigibleness. Inco·rrigibly** *adv.*

Incorro·dible, *a.* 1855. [IN-³.] Incapable of being corroded.

Incorro·sive, *a. rare.* 1871. [IN-³.] Having no tendency to corrosion.

Incorrupt (inkǫ̆rɒ·pt), *a.* Now *rare.* ME. [– L. *incorruptus*, f. *in-* IN-³ + *corruptus* CORRUPT *ppl. a.*] Not corrupt; free from corruption. **1.** Of organic matter: Free from decomposition or putrefaction; not decayed; not infected with decay. **2.** Not debased or perverted; pure, sound 1550. **b.** Of a text, etc.: Not affected by error or corruption. 1624. **3.** Morally uncorrupted; pure in life; *esp.* not to be bribed into wrong-doing 1545.

2. The first church of the Apostles..was moste pure and incorrupte CRANMER. 3. The most juste and i. juge 1545. So †**Incorru·pted** *a.* (in all senses). Hence **Incorru·pt-ly** *adv.*, **-ness.**

Incorruptible (inkǫ̆rɒ·ptĭb'l), *a.* (*sb.*) ME. [– (O)Fr. *incorruptible* or eccl. L. *incorruptibilis*; see IN-³, CORRUPTIBLE.] **1.** Not corruptible; that cannot decay or perish; everlasting, eternal. **2.** That cannot be perverted or bribed 1667. **3.** *sb.* (*pl.*) An ancient Christian sect, the Aphthartodocetæ, who maintained the incorruptibility of the body of Christ 1727.

1. The deed shall ryse i. TINDALE 1 *Cor.* 15:52. 2. Suppos'd Not i. of Faith, not prooff Against temptation MILT. *P. L.* IX. 298. Hence **Incorruptibi·lity, Incorru·ptibleness. Incorru·ptibly** *adv.*

Incorruption (inkǫ̆rɒ·pʃən). *arch.* 1526. [– (O)Fr. *incorruption* or eccl. L. *incorruptio* (Tertullian), f. *in-* IN-³ + *corruptio* CORRUPTION.] **1.** Freedom from physical corruption. Now *arch.* and only in reference to 1 Cor. 15: 42, etc. †**2.** Freedom from corrupt conduct –1677. †**3.** Of texts: Freedom from erroneous alterations –1662.

1. Hit is sowen in corrupcion and ryseth in incorrupcion TINDALE 1 *Cor.* 15:42.

†**Incorru·ptive,** *a.* [f. IN-³ + CORRUPTIVE.] Not liable to decay. AKENSIDE.

†**Incourse.** *rare.* 1440. [– L. *incursus* incursion, with assim. to *concourse*, etc.] Running in; inrush; assault, attack –1668.

Incrassate (inkræ·sĕt), *a.* 1608. [– late L. *incrassatus*, pa. pple. of *incrassare*; see next, -ATE².] †**1.** Thickened (in consistence); condensed –1685. †**2.** *fig.* Of the mind: Dulled –1660. **3.** *Zool.* and *Bot.* Of a thickened or swollen form 1760.

3. Peduncle..I., thickened towards the Flower 1760.

Incrassate (inkræ·seⁱt), *v.* 1601. [– *incrassat-*, pa. ppl. stem of late L. *incrassare*, f. *in-* IN-² + *crassare*, f. *crassus* CRASS; see -ATE³.] **1.** *trans.* To thicken in consistence; to condense, inspissate. Now *rare.* Also *absol.* and †*intr.* †**2.** *fig.* To make gross (the mind, etc.); to dull –1666. **3.** To thicken in †sound or form 1668.

1. Liquors which time hath incrassated into gellies SIR T. BROWNE. *intr.* These naturally subtile Parts..i. and grow clumsy CHEYNE.

Incrassated (inkræ·seⁱtĕd), *ppl. a.* 1657. [f. prec. + -ED¹.] Thickened. †**b.** Used as = aspirated –1691.

Incrassation (inkræsēⁱ·ʃən). 1633. [f. INCRASSATE *v.* + -ION.] **1.** The action of incrassating, or condition of being incrassated; thickening; *concr.* a thickened formation 1822. †**2.** Phonetic thickening; aspiration. WILKINS.

Incrassative (inkræ·sătiv). ? *Obs.* 1666. [f. as prec. + -IVE.] **A.** *adj.* Having the quality of incrassating the 'humours'. **B.** *sb.* [sc. *medicine*, etc.]

Increasable (inkrī·săb'l), *a.* 1534. [f. INCREASE *v.* + -ABLE.] Capable of being increased.

A low quit-rent, i. at definite periods 1806. Hence **Increa·sableness. Increa·sably** *adv.*

Increase (i·nkrīs, *formerly* inkrī·s), *sb.* [ME. *encres*, etc., f. the vb.]

I. The action of increasing. **1.** The action, process, or fact of becoming or making greater; augmentation, growth, enlargement, extension. †**b.** *spec.* The advance of daylight from sunrise to noon; the waxing of the moon –1665. **2.** The becoming numerous or more frequent; multiplication ME. **b.** *spec.* The multiplication of a family or race; the production of offspring; reproduction, procreation, propagation, breeding ME. †**3.** *spec.* Advancement, progress –1719.

1. As if encrease of Appetite had growne By what it fed on SHAKS. With i. of business came i. of expense 1870. b. Seeds will grow soonest..if they be Set..in the I. of the Moone BACON. 2. b. Drie vp in her the Organs of i. SHAKS. Phr. *On the increase*: becoming greater or more frequent.

II. †**1.** The result of increasing; an increased amount, addition, increment ME. **2.** Offspring, progeny, brood. Properly collective. 1552. **3.** Vegetable produce, crops (*arch.*). Also *transf.* and *fig.* 1535.

1. Thou wilt but adde encrease vnto my Wrath SHAKS. **2.** And all the i. of thine house shall die in the floure of their age 1 *Sam.* 23:3. **3.** The teeming autumn, big with rich i. SHAKS. *transf.* Behold..the Seas with her merveilous increse 1559. *fig.* Thou shalt not..lend him thy victuals for i. *Lev.* 25:37.

Increase (inkrī·s), *v.* [ME. *encres* – AFr. *encres-*, OFr. *encreis-*, stem of *encreistre* :– L. *incrēscere*, f. *in-* IN-[2] + *crēscere* grow; the pref. was assim. to L. XV.]

I. *intr.* **1.** To become greater in size, amount, duration, or degree; to wax, grow. Also with *in.* **2.** To grow in numbers, to multiply; *esp.* by propagation ME. **3.** To advance in wealth, fortune, power, influence, etc.; to thrive; to prosper. *Obs.* or *arch.* ME. **4.** *Lat. Gram.* Of a noun, etc.: To have one syllable more in the genitive 1612.

1. The Poo..That Estward ay encresseth in his cours CHAUCER. He..encreased in stature and in wisdom 1814. **2.** And bad euery creature in his kynde encrees LANGL. **3.** He must increace: and I muste decreace TINDALE *John* 3:30.

II. *trans.* **1.** To cause to wax or grow; to make greater in amount or degree. Also with *in.* ME. **2.** To make more numerous, multiply ME. †**b.** To cause to yield increase. DRYDEN. **3.** To make more wealthy, prosperous, or powerful; to cause to thrive; to promote. *Obs.* or *arch.* ME.

1. Thou shalt encrease the price thereof *Lev.* 25:16. **2.** Take ye wiues..that ye may bee increased there *Jer.* 29:6. **3.** Cicero..increased the latine tounge after another sorte ASCHAM. Hence **Increa·sedly** *adv.* (*rare*), in an increased degree. **Increa·singly** *adv.* more and more.

†**Increa·seful,** *a. rare.* 1593. [f. INCREASE *sb.* + -FUL.] Full of increase; productive, fruitful –1599.

Increasement (inkrī·smĕnt). Now *rare.* ME. [f. INCREASE *v.* + -MENT.] **1.** = INCREASE *sb.* I. 1, 2. 1509. **2.** = INCREASE *sb.* II. 1–3.

Increaser (inkrī·səɹ). 1528. [f. INCREASE *v.* + -ER[1].] One who or that which increases (see the vb.).

Increate (inkri,ē[i]·t), *a.* ME. [– eccl.L. *increatus* (IV), f. *in-* IN-[3] + *creatus*, pa. pple. of L. *creare* CREATE; see -ATE[2].] Not created, uncreated; said of divine beings or attributes.

Bright effluence of bright essence i. MILT. *P. L.* III. 6. So †**Increated** *ppl. a.* in same sense.

Incredible (inkre·dĭb'l), *a.* ME. [– L. *incredibilis*; see IN-[3], CREDIBLE.] **1.** Not credible; that cannot be believed. **b.** In weakened sense: Inconceivable 1482. **c.** Of a person (*rare*). BENTHAM. †**2.** Unbelieving (*rare*) –1761.

1. Why should it be thought a thing i. with you, that God should raise the dead? *Acts* 26:8. **b.** These stories do i. mischief BURKE. Hence **Incredibi·lity,** the quality or fact of being i.; that which is i. **Incre·dibleness. Incre·dibly** *adv.* in an i. manner or degree.

†**Incre·ditable,** *a.* 1695. [IN-[3].] Discreditable. –1732.

†**Incre·dited,** *a.* 1633. [IN-[3].] Disbelieved.

Incredulity (inkrĭdiū·lĭti). [– (O)Fr. *incrédulité* – L. *incredulitas* (in later eccl. use, religious disbelief), f. *incredulus*; see next, -ITY.] **1.** A disbelieving frame of mind; unwillingness to believe; disbelief. †**2.** Want of religious faith; unbelief –1619.

1. The i. of St. Thomas H. WALPOLE. **2.** Either in the faith of Christ or..in i. 1560.

Incredulous (inkre·diŭləs), *a.* 1579. [f. L. *incredulus* (see IN-[3], CREDULOUS) + -OUS.] **1.** Unbelieving; not ready to believe; sceptical. Not now used of religious unbelief. **b.** Of action, etc.: Indicating or prompted by incredulity 1613. †**2.** = INCREDIBLE –1750.

They call it philosophical to be i. on holy things LANDOR. **b.** I. smiles PURCHAS. **2.** Miracles.. will be thought i. in this age 1631. Hence **Incre·dulous-ly** *adv.*, **-ness.**

†**I·ncremable,** *a. rare.* [– med.L. *incremabilis*, f. *in-* IN-[3] + *cremabilis* combustible, f. L. *cremare* burn; see -ABLE. Cf. OFr. *incremable.*] That cannot be consumed by fire; incombustible. SIR T. BROWNE.

Incremation (inkrĭmē[i]·ʃən). Now *rare* or *Obs.* 1826. [f. IN-[2] + CREMATION.] = CREMATION (now the usual word).

Increment (i·nkrĭmĕnt). ME. [– L. *incrementum*, f. stem of *increscere*; see INCREASE *v.*, -MENT.] **1.** The action or process of becoming greater, or (with *pl.*) a case of this; increase, augmentation, growth. **b.** Advancement. *Obs.* or *arch.* 1609. **c.** The waxing of the moon; *spec.* in *Heraldry* 1610. **d.** *Rhet.* 'An ascending towards a climax' (= L. *incrementum* in Quintilian) 1753. **2.** Amount of increase; an addition; an amount gained, profit 1631. **b.** *Math.* and *Phys.* A small (or sometimes infinitesimal) amount by which a variable quantity increases (*e.g.* in a given small time); *spec.* the increase of a function due to a small increase in the variable, as in the *Method of Increments*, now called the Calculus of Finite Differences (see DIFFERENCE *sb.*) 1721. **3.** A quantity obtained from another by increase or addition. Const. *of.* (*rare.*) 1864.

1. We add daily increments to our knowledge and science KIRBY. **d.** *Increment*..4. (*Rhet.*) An amplification without strict climax, as in the following passage: 'Finally, brethren, whatsoever things are true..' *Phil.* 4:8. WEBSTER. **2.** *Unearned increment*: see UNEARNED. Hence **Increme·ntal** *a.*, of or relating to an i. or increments.

†**I·ncrepate,** *v.* 1570. [– *increpat-*, pa. ppl. stem of L. *increpare* make a noise at, scold, f. *in-* IN-[2] + *crepare* make a noise, creak; see -ATE[3].] *trans.* To chide, rebuke, reprove –1657. So **Increpa·tion** (*Obs.* or *arch.*), chiding, reproof, rebuke; with *pl.* a reproof 1502.

Increscent (inkre·sĕnt). 1572. [– *increscent-*, pr. ppl. stem of L. *increscere*; see INCREASE, -ENT.]

A. *adj.* Increasing, becoming greater. Chiefly of the moon: Waxing, in her increment 1658.

B. *sb.* (Chiefly *Her.*) The moon in her increment, represented as a crescent with the horns towards the dexter side. (Opp. to *decrescent.*) So †**Incre·scence,** increase 1533.

†**Incre·st,** *v. rare.* Also **en-.** 1611. [f. IN-[2] + CREST *sb.*] *trans.* To adorn with or as with a crest –1616.

Incriminate (inkri·mine[i]t), *v.* 1730. [– *incriminat-*, pa. ppl. stem of late L. *incriminare* accuse, f. *in-* IN-[2] + *crimen* charge; see CRIME, -ATE[3].] *trans.* To charge with a crime; to involve in an accusation or charge. So **Incrimina·tion** (*rare*), the action of incriminating; the fact or condition of being so incriminated 1651. **Incri·minator,** an accuser. LANDOR. **Incri·minatory** *a.* tending to i.

Incro·tchet, *v. rare.* Also **en-.** 1806. [f. IN-[2], EN-[1] + CROTCHET *sb.*] *trans.* To enclose within crotchets or brackets.

‖**Incroyable** (ẹṅkrwayab'l). 1797. [Fr. *incroyable* incredible.] Name for the French fop or dandy of the period of the Directory.

†**I·ncruent,** *a. rare.* 1624. [– L. *incruentus*, f. *in-* IN-[3] + *cruentus* bloody; in eccl.L. applied to the Eucharist.] Bloodless; not attended with shedding of blood –1660. So †**Incrue·ntal,** †**Incrue·ntous** *adjs.*

Incrust, etc., var. of ENCRUST, etc.

Incrustate (inkrɒ·stĕt), *ppl. a.* 1626. [– L. *incrustatus*, pa. pple. of *incrustare*; see next, -ATE[2].] †**1.** Formed or hardened into a crust –1731. **2.** Enveloped with a crust. *Obs.* exc. *Bot.* 1671. **3.** *Zool.* and *Bot.* Having the form of a crust, as a polyzoan or lichen; *spec.* of or pertaining to the *Incrustata*, a division of cyclostomatous Polyzoa.

Incrustate (i·nkrɒste[i]t), *v.* Now *rare.* Also **en-.** 1570. [– *incrustat-*, pa. ppl. stem of L. *incrustare*, f. *in-* IN-[2] + *crusta* CRUST.] **1.** = ENCRUST 2. †**2.** In the arts: **a.** = ENCRUST 1. **b.** To attach as or like an incrustation. –1764.

Incrustation (inkrɒstē[i]·ʃən). Also **en-.** 1607. [–Fr. *incrustation* or late L. *incrustatio*, f. as prec.; see -ION.] **1.** The action of encrusting; the formation of a crust, the fact or condition of being encrusted 1656. **2.** A facing of marble, mosaic, etc. on a building. †Also *fig.* 1607. **3.** A crust or hard coating formed naturally on an object; *esp.* a calcareous or crystalline concretion or deposit 1671. Also *fig.* **4.** A scab or eschar on the surface of a body 1656.

2. *fig.* The old popishe ceremonies..are, as it were, an I. both vnlawful and vnseemly 1607. **3.** *fig.* Hidden under the incrustations of sense and evil habit J. MARTINEAU.

†**Incry·stal,** *v.* 1611. [f. IN-[2] + CRYSTAL *sb.*] **1.** *trans.* (and *intr.*) To CRYSTALLIZE. **2.** To enclose in crystal 1648.

2. The humour was..But lovers tears inchristalled HERRICK.

Incry·stallizable, *a. rare.* 1807. [IN-[3].] Incapable of being crystallized; uncrystallizable.

Incubate (i·nkiube[i]t), *v.* 1641. [– *incubat-*, pa. ppl. stem of L. *incubare*, f. *in-* IN-[3] + *cubare* lie; see -ATE[3].] **1.** *trans.* To sit upon (eggs) in order to hatch them; to hatch (eggs) thus or by some equivalent process 1721. Also *fig.* **2.** *intr.* To sit upon eggs, to brood 1755. Also *fig.* **3. a.** *intr. Path.* Of a disease: To pass through the process of INCUBATION. **b.** *trans. Biol.* To place in an incubator (for developing bacteria). 1896.

Incubation (inkiubē[i]·ʃən). 1614. [– L. *incubatio* brooding, f. as prec.; see -ION.] **1.** The action of sitting on eggs in order to hatch them; the hatching of eggs by sitting on them 1646. Also *transf.* and *fig.* **2.** *Path.* The process or phase through which the germs of disease pass between contagion or inoculation and the development of the first symptoms 1835. **3.** *Gr. Antiq.* The practice of sleeping in a temple or sacred place for oracular purposes 1871. **4.** *attrib.*, as *i.-period*, etc. 1858.

1. *fig.* He who, by his i. upon the waters of the creation, hatched that rude mass into the beautiful form we now see GURNALL. Phr. *Period of i.*, the space of time occupied by this process, which varies greatly for different diseases. Hence **Incuba·tional** *a.*

Incubative (i·nkiube[i]tiv), *a.* 1835. [f. INCUBATE *v.* + -IVE.] Of or pertaining to incubation, esp. the incubation of disease; characterized by incubation.

Incubator (i·nkiube[i]təɹ). 1854. [f. INCUBATE *v.* + -OR 2.] **1.** A bird which incubates. Also *fig.* 1858. **2.** An apparatus for hatching birds by artificial heat 1854. **b.** An apparatus for rearing children born prematurely. **3.** An apparatus for the artificial development of bacteria 1896. **4.** *fig.* and *transf.* A breeder, author, source 1864.

Incubatory (i·nkiubə[i]təri), *a.* 1877. [f. INCUBATE *v.* + -ORY[2].] Incubative.

†**Incu·be,** *v.* [f. IN-[2] + CUBE *sb.*] To infix like a cube. MILT.

†**I·ncubee.** A distortion of INCUBUS. B. JONS.

†**Incu·biture.** 1653. [f. *incubit-* (pa. ppl. stem of L. *incubare* INCUBATE) + -URE.] = INCUBATION 1. –1743.

Incubous (i·nkiubəs), *a.* 1857. [f. L. *incubare* lie on (see INCUBATE *v.*) + -OUS.] *Bot.* Having the leaves so disposed that the tip of one leaf or other part lies flat over the base of the next above it.

‖**Incubus** (i·nkiubɒs). Pl. **-bi** (-bəi); also **-buses,** etc. ME. [– late L. *incubus* (Augustine), cl.L. *incubo* nightmare, f. *incubare* lie on; see INCUBATE *v.*] **1.** A feigned evil spirit or demon, supposed to descend upon persons in their sleep, and especially to seek carnal intercourse with women. In the Middle Ages, their existence was recognized by law. **2.** The nightmare 1561. **3.** A person or thing that weighs upon and oppresses like a nightmare 1648. **4.** *Entom.* Name of a parasitic genus of hymenopterous insects.

1. Belial the dissolutest Spirit that fell The sensuallest, and after Asmodai The fleshliest I. MILT. *P. R.* II. 152. **3.** The many years preaching of such an Incumbent, I may say, such an I. ofttimes MILT. The i. of evil habits 1875.

†**Incu·lcate,** *ppl. a.* 1608. [– L. *inculcatus*, pa. pple. of *inculcare*; see next, -ATE[2].] Inculcated, taught –1653.

Inculcate (i·nkɒlke[i]t, inkɒ·lke[i]t), *v.* 1550. [– *inculcat-*, pa. ppl. stem of L. *inculcare* stamp in with the heel, press in, f. *in-* IN-[2] + *calcare* tread, f. *calx, calc-* heel; see -ATE[3].] *trans.* To endeavour to force (a thing) into or impress (it) on the mind of another by emphatic admonition, or by persistent repetition; to urge on the mind; to teach forcibly.

That commandement which Christ did so often i. vnto Peter HOOKER. An opinion..difficult to i. upon the minds of others 1802. Hence †**Inculcatedly** *adv.* by impressive repetition. **Inculca·tion,** the action of impressing on the mind by forcible admonition or frequent repetition. †**Incu·lcative** *a.* (*rare*), tending to i.; impressive.

Inculcator (see the vb.). one who inculcates. **Incu·lcatory** *a.* (*rare*), fitted or tending to i.

†**Incu·lk,** *v.* 1528. [– Fr. *inculquer* or L. *inculcare* INCULCATE.] = INCULCATE *v.* –1576.

†**Incu·lp,** *v.* [– Fr. *inculper* or L. *inculpare* INCULPATE.] = INCULPATE *v.* SHELTON.

Inculpable (inkɒ·lpăb'l), *a.* Now *rare.* 1491. [– late L. *inculpabilis*, f. *in-* IN-[3] + *culpabilis* CULPABLE.] Not culpable; free from blame.

Suche personages..whose lyues be i. ELYOT. Hence **Inculpabi·lity, Incu·lpableness,** blamelessness. **Incu·lpably** *adv.*

†**Incu·lpate,** *a. rare.* 1612. [– late L. *inculpatus*, pa. pple. of *inculpare*; see next, -ATE[2].] Unblamed, inculpable –1647.

Inculpate (i·nkɒlpe[i]t, inkɒ·lpe[i]t), *v.* 1799. [– *inculpat-*, pa. ppl. stem of late L. *inculpare*, f. *in-* IN-[2] + *culpare* blame; see -ATE[3].] **1.** *trans.* To bring a charge against; to accuse; to blame. **2.** To involve in a charge; to incriminate 1839.

1. We should be slow to i. motives 1833. **2.** Attempting to exculpate himself and i. Dr. Nassau for [etc.] 1897. Hence **Inculpa·tion,** blame, censure, incrimination. **Incu·lpative, Incu·lpatory** *adjs.* tending to incriminate; attributing fault or blame.

Incult (inkɒ·lt), *a.* Now *rare.* 1599. [– L. *incultus*, f. *in-* IN-[3] + *cultus*, pa. pple. of *colere* cultivate. Cf. Fr. *inculte.*] **1.** Uncultivated, untilled 1621. **2.** Unpolished, untrimmed, inartistic, rude. **3.** Of persons, etc.: Wanting in culture; inelegant, rough, coarse 1621.

1. Germany then, saith Tacitus, was i. and horrid, now full of magnificent Cities BURTON. **2.** His style is diffuse and i. 1851. **3.** He is i., but clever 1862.

†**Incu·ltivated,** *a.* 1665. [IN-[3].] Uncultivated; unpolished, rude –1716. So **Incultiva·tion** 1784.

†**Incu·lture.** *rare.* 1627. [IN-[3].] Want of culture or cultivation –1867.

†**Incu·mbence.** 1677. [f. as next; see -ENCE.] **a.** The fact of being incumbent. **b.** A matter that is incumbent; a duty or obligation. –1768.

Incumbency (inkɒ·mbĕnsi). 1608. [– AL. *incumbentia* (XV), f. *incumbens, -ent-* INCUMBENT *sb.*; see -ENCY.] **1.** The condition of lying or pressing upon something; brooding; a spiritual overshadowing. Now *rare* or *Obs.* 1651. **b.** With *an* and *pl.*: An incumbent weight or mass 1679. **2.** The quality of being incumbent as a duty; an incumbent duty or obligation. Now *rare.* 1608. **3.** The position or office of an incumbent; now only *Eccl.* (or *transf.* from this). Also, the sphere, or period of tenure, of an incumbent. 1656.

2. All the incumbencies of a family DONNE. **3.** He has retired from his i. and given up his benefice 1886.

Incumbent (inkɒ·mbĕnt), *sb.* ME. [– AL. *incumbens, -ent-* (XIV), subst. use of pr. pple. of L. *incumbere* (see next). This use is peculiarly English.] The holder of an ecclesiastical benefice; hence *gen.*, of any office (now *rare*) 1672.

The I. lent me the Church WHITEFIELD. The i. of the coronership 1884.

Incumbent (inkɒ·mbĕnt), *a.* 1548. [– *incumbent-*, pr. ppl. stem of L. *incumbere* lie or lean upon, apply oneself to, f. *in-* IN-[2] + **cumbere*, f. nasalized stem corresp. to *cubare* (see INCUBATE); see -ENT.] **1.** That lies, leans, rests, or presses with its weight upon something else 1624. **2.** *spec.* **a.** *Physics.* Of air, fluid, or other weight, as exerting downward pressure 1660. **b.** *Geol.* Superincumbent, as a stratum 1789. **c.** *Bot.* Said of an *anther* when it lies flat against the inner side of the filament; of *cotyledons* when the back of one is applied to the radicle 1760. **d.** *Zool.* Of hairs, spines, etc.: Lying along the surface on which they grow. **e.** *Ornith.* Of the hind toe of a bird: Resting on the ground with its whole length, its insertion being on a level with the anterior toes. **3.** Resting or falling upon a person as a duty or obligation. Const. *on, upon,* 1567. †**4.** Impending, imminent, threatening –1793. †**5.** Bending one's energies to some work –1814. †**6.** In occupation of a benefice. Const. *on.* –1661.

1. He stears his flight Aloft, i. on the dusky Air MILT. *P. L.* I. 226. **3.** That there was a duty i. upon us CROMWELL. **5.** Habits of firm and i. application SCOTT. Hence **Incu·mbently** *adv.*

Incumber, Incumbrance, etc., var. ENCUMBER, ENCUMBRANCE, etc.

†**Incumbi·tion.** [irreg. f. L. *incumbere.* See -ITION.] The action of lying or pressing upon; also *fig.* STERNE.

‖**Incunabula** (inkiunæ·biŭlă), *sb. pl.* 1824. [– L. n. pl., swaddling-clothes, cradle, birthplace, infancy, origin, f. *in-* IN-[2] + *cunabula*, f. *cunæ* cradle.] **1.** The earliest stages in the development of anything. **2.** (With sing. *incunabulum*): Books produced in the infancy of printing; *spec.* those printed before 1501. var. **Incu·nable.** 1861. **3.** *Ornith.* The breeding-places of a species of bird. Hence **Incuna·bular** *a.* of or pertaining to early printed books. **Incuna·bulist,** one who collects or is interested in incunabula.

Incur (inkɒ̄·ɹ), *v.* ME. [– L. *incurrere*, f. *in-* IN-[2] + *currere* run. Cf. OFr. *encourre*, Fr. *encourir.*]

I. *intr.* †**1.** To run, flow, fall, or come *to* or *into* –1677. †**b.** To come in so as to meet the eye, etc. –1692. †**2.** To run *into* (danger, etc.); to render oneself liable *to* (damage) –1620.

1. b. They are Inuisible, and incurre not to the Eie BACON.

II. *trans.* †**1.** To run into; to come upon, meet with –1680. **2.** To run or fall into (some consequence, usu. undesirable); to bring upon oneself ME. †**3.** To cause to be incurred; to entail –1784.

2. I should haue..incurred the suspicion of fraud LYLY. **3.** This sickness has necessarily incurred expences 1784.

Incurable (inkiūə·răb'l), *a.* (*sb.*) ME. [– (O)Fr. *incurable* or late L. *incurabilis*; see IN-[3], CURABLE.] **1.** That cannot be cured; incapable of being healed by medicine or medical skill. **2.** *transf.* and *fig.* Not admitting of remedy or correction ME. **3.** *sb.* A person suffering from an incurable disease. Usu. in *pl.* 1652.

1. God..him..smoot With invisible wounde, ay i. CHAUCER. **2.** Ignorance is not so i. as error BERKELEY. Hence **Incurabi·lity, Incu·rableness. Incu·rably** *adv.* in an i. manner; to an i. degree.

Incurious (inkiūə·riəs), *a.* 1570. [– L. *incuriosus* careless, f. *in-* IN-[3] + *curiosus* careful. In sense II. 2 f. IN-[3] + CURIOUS.]

I. Subjectively. **1.** Without care or concern; negligent, heedless; untroubled (*arch.*). **2.** Devoid of curiosity 1613. **3.** Inattentive, careless 1691. †**4.** Not precise; uncritical; undiscriminating –1749.

1. In his Cloaths and Habit..he was not now only i., but too negligent CLARENDON. **2.** I. and indifferent about truth 1774. **3.** The more careless and i. Observer RAY.

II. Objectively. †**1.** Not carefully prepared, made, composed, or done –1824. **2.** Unworthy of careful notice; not curious. (Esp. in neg. forms of expression.) 1747.

2. The inscriptions..are not i. 1776. Hence **Incurio·sity, Incu·riousness,** want of care; want of curiosity or interest in things. **Incu·riously** *adv.*

Incurrent (inkɒ·rĕnt), *a.* 1563. [– *incurrent-*, pr. ppl. stem of L. *incurrere*; see INCUR, -ENT.] Running in; penetrating into the interior; †falling within (a period).

The most principal matters in his time i. FOXE. Hence **Incu·rrence,** the action or fact of incurring, e.g. liabilities; the entrance of sensations or impressions.

Incursion (inkɒ̄·ɹʃən). ME. [– L. *incursio*, f. *incurs-*, pa. ppl. stem of *incurrere* INCUR; see -ION. Cf. (O)Fr. *incursion.*] **1.** The action of running in or of running against 1615. **2.** A hostile inroad or invasion; esp. a sudden attack ME. Also *transf.* and *fig.* †**3.** The action of incurring (blame, etc.) HEALEY.

1. The inevitable i. of new images JOHNSON. **2.** Against the Scythian, whose incursions wild Have wasted Sogdiana MILT. *P. R.* III. 301. Phr. †*Sins of daily incursion*: the small sins which make daily inroads upon a holy life.

Incursive (inkɒ̄·ɹsiv), *a.* 1592. [– med.L. *incursivus*, f. as prec.; see -IVE. Partly f. INCURSION.] Given to making incursions; aggressive, invasive.

Incurtain, obs. var. of ENCURTAIN *v.*

Incurvate (inkɒ̄·ɹvĕt), *ppl. a.* 1647. [– L. *incurvatus*, pa. pple. of *incurvare*; see INCURVE, -ATE[2].] = INCURVED.

Incurvate (inkɒ̄·ɹve[i]t, i·n-), *v.* 1578. [– *incurvat-*, pa. ppl. stem of L. *incurvare*; see INCURVE, -ATE[3].] **1.** *trans.* To bring into a curved shape; to bend; to crook; now, *spec.*, to bend or curve inwards. †**2.** *intr.* To take or have a curved shape –1697.

Incurvation (inkɒɹvē[i]·ʃən). 1607. [– L. *incurvatio*, f. as prec.; see -ION.] **1.** The action or process of bending or curving; an instance of this 1608. †**b.** *spec.* Bowing in reverence or worship –1702. **2.** The condition of being bent; curvature; a curve or bend. Also *fig.* 1647. **3.** A curving inwards, or the condition of being curved inwards 1822.

1. b. Must i. towards the East be still continued? 1607. **2.** *fig.* The incurvations of practice..when compared with the rectitude of the rule BLACKSTONE. **3.** It [whitlow] is also occasioned by an i. of the nails 1822. So **Incu·rvature** (*rare*), in sense 3.

Incurve (inkɒ̄·ɹv), *v.* 1610. [– L. *incurvare*, f. *in-* IN-[2] + *curvare* to crook, bend, CURVE.] **1.** *trans.* = INCURVATE *v.* 1; in mod. use, To curve or bend (something) inwards. **2.** *intr.* To curve or bend inwards 1704.

2. Those fair open fields that i. to thy beautiful hollow CLOUGH.

Incurved (inkɒ̄·ɹvd), *ppl. a.* 1623. [f. prec. + -ED[1].] Bent into or having a curved form; in mod. use, Having an inward curvature. (Now chiefly in *Zool.* and *Bot.*)

†**Incu·rvity.** [f. IN-[2] + CURVITY.] The quality of being incurved; inward curvature. SIR T. BROWNE.

‖**Incus** (i·ŋkɒs). 1669. [L. = anvil.] *Anat.* and *Zool.* **1.** The middle one of the three small bones of the ear (*malleus, incus,* and *stapes*). **2.** A part of the mouth-apparatus in *Rotifera*, upon which the two mallei work 1877.

Incuse (inkiū·z). 1818. [– L. *incusus*, pa. pple. of *incudere*; see next. The subst. use corresp. to Fr. *incuse* (XVII).] *adj.* Hammered or stamped in; said of a figure or impression upon a coin or the like. *sb.* A figure stamped in; an impression in intaglio upon a coin, etc. 1818.

sb. The head of Proserpine in an i. surrounded by dolphins 1879.

Incuse (inkiū·z), *v.* 1864. [– *incus-*, pa. ppl. stem of L. *incudere* work on the anvil (*incus*).] *trans.* To impress by stamping; to mark with an impressed figure. Chiefly in pa. pple.

†**Incuss,** *v.* 1527. [– *incuss-*, pa. ppl. stem of L. *incutere* (see INCUTE), f. *in-* IN-[2] + *quatere* shake, strike, dash. Cf. CONCUSS, DISCUSS.] *trans.* To strike in, impress; to strike (terror, etc.) into the mind; to inspire a person with (some feeling) –1613.

Incut (i·nkɒt), *ppl. a.* 1888. [f. IN *adv.* + CUT *ppl. a.*] Set in by or as by cutting; *spec.* in *Printing*, inserted in a space left in the outside of the text, instead of in the margin; also called *cut-in.*

†**Incu·te,** *v.* 1542. [– L. *incutere* strike into; see INCUSS *v.*] = INCUSS.

Incysted, obs. f. ENCYSTED.

Ind (ind). ME. [– (O)Fr. *Inde* :– L. *India.*] **1.** = INDIA. Now *arch.* or *poet.* †**2.** *pl.* Indians –1526.

1. From the east to westerne Inde *A. Y. L.* III. ii. 93.

Ind-, *Chem.*: see INDI-, INDO-.

‖**Indaba** (indā·bă). 1894. [Zulu *in-daba* subject, topic, matter, business.] A communication or transaction of affairs, a conference between or with South African natives.

Indagate (i·ndăge[i]t), *v.* ? *Obs.* 1623. [– *indagat-*, pa. ppl. stem of L. *indagare* trace out, search into, investigate; see -ATE[3].] *trans.* To search into, investigate. So **Indaga·tion** (? *Obs.*), the action of tracking out; investigation 1589. †**Indagative** *a.* inclined to seek (JER. TAYLOR). **I·ndagator** (now *rare*), a searcher, investigator.

Indam(m)age, obs. var. ENDAMAGE.

Indart (indā·ɹt), *v.* 1598. [f. IN-[1] + DART *v.*] *trans.* To dart in.

†**Inde.** ME. [– OFr. *inde* adj. violet, also sb. (as in mod.Fr.) – L. *indicum*; see INDIGO.] A blue dye obtained from India, now called INDIGO; the colour of this, or a fabric dyed with it –1658. **b.** *attrib.* or as *adj.* Blue. ME. only.

Indear, obs. var. of ENDEAR.

Inde·bt, *v.* Now *rare.* 1565. [Inferred from INDEBTED, perh. after Fr. *endetter.* See next.] **1.** *trans.* To involve in debt. **2.** To bring under an obligation 1603.

2. Thy Fortune hath indebted thee to none DANIEL.

Indebted (inde·tėd), *ppl. a.* [ME. *an-, endetted* – (with suffix -ED[1]) OFr. *endetté,* pa. pple. of *endetter* involve in debt; assim. to L. in prefix and root (med.L. *indebitare*).] **1.** Owing money; in debt. **2.** Under obligation to another on account of some liability incurred or claim unsatisfied; bound. *Obs.* or *arch.* ME. **3.** Owing gratitude; beholden 1561.

1. He being..gretly endetted ME. **2.** When I have promised, I am i.; and debts may be claimed, must be paid BP. HALL. **3.** For this observation I am i. to an ingenious and worthy friend PRIESTLEY. Hence **Inde·btedness,** the condition of being indebted; the sum owed; debts collectively. **Inde·btment** (*rare*), indebtedness.

†Inde·cence. *rare.* 1714. [f. INDECENT (see -ENCE), perh. after Fr. *indécence.*] = INDECENCY 1. –1797.

Indecency (indī·sĕnsi). 1589. [– L. *indecentia,* f. *indecent-* (see next); see -ENCY.] **1.** Unseemliness; unbecoming or outrageous conduct; an instance of this. **†2.** Uncomeliness of form –1648. **3.** Immodesty; a quality savouring of obscenity; an indecent act 1692.

1. These Bishops..were fain to descend to many indecencies and indignities to support themselves FULLER. **3.** The hatred of i...is a modern virtue DARWIN.

Indecent (indī·sĕnt), *a.* 1563. [– (O)Fr. *indécent* or L. *indecens, -ent-*; see IN-[3], DECENT.] **1.** Unbecoming; in extremely bad taste; unseemly. **†2.** Uncomely –1743. **3.** Offending against propriety or delicacy; immodest; suggesting or tending to obscenity 1613.

1. With i. haste 1839. **3.** Their Dances were lascivious, their Gestures i., and their Songs immodest 1676. Hence **Inde·cent-ly** *adv.,* **-ness.**

Indeciduate (indĭsi·diu,ĕt), *a.* 1879. [IN-[3].] Not deciduate, as a placenta; not having a decidua; belonging to the *Indeciduata* (a division of mammals comprising the Ruminantia, Edentata, and Cetacea).

Indeciduous (indĭsi·diu,əs), *a.* 1646. [IN-[3].] **†1.** Not liable to fall off or be shed –1656. **2.** *Bot.* Of a leaf: Not deciduous. Of a tree or plant: Not losing the leaves annually; evergreen. 1755.

1. The indiciduous and unshaven locks of Apollo 1646.

†Inde·cimable, *a.* [= med.L. **indecimabilis* (cf. *indecimatus* untithed), f. *in-* IN-[3] + *decimabilis* tithable, f. L. *decimare* (in late (eccl.) L. exact tithes from); see -ABLE.] Not decimable; not liable to pay tithe. COKE.

Indecipherable (indĭsəi·fərăb'l), *a.* 1802. [IN-[3].] Incapable of being deciphered or made out. Hence **Indeci:pherabi·lity, Indeci·pherableness.**

Indecision (indĭsi·ʒən). 1763. [– Fr. *indécision*; see IN-[3], DECISION.] Want of decision; inability to make up one's mind; hesitation.

The term i...implies an idea very nicely different from that of irresolution; yet it has a tendency to produce it SHENSTONE.

Indecisive (indĭsəi·siv), *a.* 1726. [IN-[3].] **1.** Not decisive; not such as to settle (a question, contest, etc.); inconclusive. **2.** Characterized by indecision; undecided; hesitating; irresolute 1787. **3.** Uncertain; not definite, indistinct 1816.

1. An i. predatory war MACAULAY. **2.** Perplexed and i. whether to go forwards or backwards MOZLEY. Hence **Indeci·sive-ly** *adv.,* **-ness.**

Indeclinable (indĭkləi·năb'l), *a.* (*sb.*) ME. [– Fr. *indéclinable* – L. *indeclinabilis* (*Gram.,* late L.); see IN-[3], DECLINABLE.] **†1.** Incapable of declining, or being caused to decline; undeviating, fixed, constant –1637. **†2.** That cannot be turned aside from; inevitable –1660. **3.** *Gram.* Incapable of being declined grammatically; having no inflexions 1530. **4.** *sb.* An indeclinable word 1530.

3. Adjectives are i., having no variation either of Gender, Case, or Number 1748. Hence **Indecli·nably** *adv.*

Indecomposable (indĭkǫmpōᵘ·zăb'l), *a.* 1812. [IN-[3]; cf. Fr. *indécomposable* (Voltaire, 1738).] Incapable of being decomposed or resolved into constituent elements.

Indecorous (indĭkōᵊ·rəs, -de·kŏrəs), *a.* 1680. [– L. *indecorus* (see IN-[3], DECOROUS) + -OUS.] **†1.** Unbecoming –1692. **2.** Contrary to, or wanting, decorum or propriety of behaviour; in bad taste 1682; indecent (*rare*) 1829.

2. Among savages especially haste is i. KANE. I. statues MACAULAY. **Indecorous-ly** *adv.,* **-ness.**

Indecorum (indĭkōᵊ·rŏm). 1575. [– L. *indecorum,* subst. use of n. sing. of adj. *indecorus*; see prec.] **1.** An indecorous or unbecoming action or proceeding; an impropriety. **2.** The quality of being indecorous; impropriety, now esp. of behaviour 1664.

2. The charge is not..for *i.,* or indiscretion, but for *falsehood* BURKE.

Indeed (indī·d), *adv. phrase.* [ME. adv. phr. *in dede,* i.e. IN *prep.,* dat. of DEED; till *c*1600 as two words.] **1.** In actual fact, in reality, in truth. **b.** Freq. placed after a word in order to emphasize it 1575. **2.** In reality, in real nature or essence ME. **3.** With confirming and amplifying force: In point of fact, as a matter of fact 1535. **4.** With concessive force = It is true, it must be admitted 1563. **5.** In dialogue, used to emphasize the reply to a question or remark 1583; also in echoing the question asked by another speaker 1766. **6.** Interrogatively = 'Is it so?' 'Really?' 1598. **7.** As an exclam., expressing irony, contempt, amazement, incredulity, or the like 1710.

1. The lorde is risen in dede TINDALE *Luke* 24: 34. **b.** This is Musick i. WALTON. Marvellous i. 1742. **3.** I am..a cautious man, i. a timid one 1885. **4.** Latin, not classical i., but good of its kind 1894. **5.** Can you tell me? I. I cannot JOWETT. 'Who is this Mr. Grey?' 'Who, i.' DISRAELI. **6.** 'That's Jarsper's.' 'I.?' said Mr. Datchery DICKENS. **7.** 'O, i.', I said, 'what a wonderful thing' JOWETT. Phr. *Indeed and indeed,* really and truly (*colloq.*).

Indefatigable (indĭfæ·tigăb'l), *a.* 1586. [– Fr. †*indéfatigable* (mod. *infatigable*) or L. *indefatigabilis*; see IN-[3], DEFATIGABLE.] Incapable of being wearied; that cannot be tired out; unremitting in labour or effort.

Upborn with i. wings Over the vast abrupt MILT. *P. L.* II. 408. A man of industry i. SIR T. BROWNE. Hence **Indefa:tigabi·lity, Indefa·tigableness,** the quality of being i. **Indefa·tigably** *adv.*

Indefeasible (indĭfī·zĭb'l), *a.* 1548. [IN-[3].] Not defeasible; not liable to be made void, or done away with; that cannot be forfeited.

A good and indefeisible estate BLOUNT. The great writers..have mostly asserted freedom of conscience as an i. right MILL. Hence **Indefeasibi·lity, Indefea·sibleness. Indefea·sibly** *adv.*

Indefectible (indĭfe·ktĭb'l), *a.* 1659. [IN-[3].] Not defectible. **1.** Not liable to failure, defect, or decay; unfailing. **2.** Faultless 1833.

1. The burning, and not consuming bush, signifies the i. splendor of the church 1736. **2.** An i. wisdom 1852. Hence **Indefectibi·lity,** quality of being i. 1624. **Indefe·ctibly** *adv.*

Indefective (indĭfe·ktiv), *a.* ? *Obs.* 1641. [– med.L. *indefectivus*; see IN-[3], DEFECTIVE, and cf. Fr. †*indéfectif.*] Not defective; free from defect; faultless, flawless.

Upon Condition of absolute i. obedience SOUTH.

Indefensible (indĭfe·nsĭb'l), *a.* 1529. [f. IN-[3] + DEFENSIBLE. Cf. Fr. †*indéfensible.*] Not defensible; admitting of no defence.

I. small townes and villages 1569. An i. hypothesis 1799, quarrel FROUDE. Hence **Indefensibi·lity, Indefe·nsibleness. Indefe·nsibly** *adv.*

†Indefe·nsive, *a.* 1586. [IN-[3].] Defenceless –1634.

The sword awes the i. villager SIR T. HERBERT.

†Indeficient (indĭfi·ʃĕnt), *a.* 1508. [– Fr. †*indéficient* or late (eccl.) L. *indeficiens, -ent-*; see IN-[3], DEFICIENT.] Unfailing, exhaustless –1851.

The Lamb His people feeds from i. streams TRENCH. Hence **Indefi·ciency.** †**Indefi·ciently** *adv.*

Indefinable (indĭfəi·năb'l), *a.* 1810. [f. IN-[3] + DEFINABLE.] That cannot be defined or exactly described. Hence **Indefi·nableness. Indefi·nably** *adv.*

Indefinite (inde·finit), *a.* (*sb.*) 1530. [– L. *indefinitus*; see IN-[3], DEFINITE. Cf. Fr. *indéfini.*] Undefined, unlimited.

I. *gen.* **1.** Without distinct limitation of being or character; indeterminate, vague, undefined 1561. **2.** Of indetermined extent, amount, or number 1594. **†b.** Formerly *occas.,* Boundless, infinite –1745.

1. Some generall i. promises 1651. A fine, though i., emotion 1885. **2.** Commodities that admitted of i. multiplication 1884. **b.** I. and omnipresent God, Inhabiting eternity! 1745.

II. *spec.* **1.** *Gram.* Applied to various adjs., pronominal words, and advs.; as *any, other, some, such, anyhow,* etc.; esp. in *indefinite article,* the individualizing adj. *a, an* (A *adj.*[2]), or its equivalents in other langs. 1530. **2.** *Logic.* Applied to propositions in which the subject has no mark of quantity 1697. **3.** *Bot.* **a.** Said of inflorescence; also called CENTRIPETAL (q.v.), or *indeterminate* 1876. **b.** Said of the stamens or other parts of the flower when numerous and not clearly multiples of the number of the petals, etc. 1845.

B. *sb.* (the adj. used ellipt.) An indefinite thing, word, statement, etc.; something which cannot be definitely specified, described, or classed 1591.

So **Inde·finite-ly** *adv.* 1471, **-ness** 1589.

Indefinitive (indĭfi·nĭtiv), *a.* *rare.* 1580. [IN-[3].] Not definitive; not characterized by definition; indefinite.

A school of opinion..fixed in its principles, i. and progressive in their range J. H. NEWMAN. Hence **Indefi·nitive-ly** *adv.,* **-ness.**

Indefinitude (indĭfi·nitiud). 1677. [f. INDEFINITE after *infinite/infinitude.*] **†1.** The condition of having no known limit; undefined or undefinable number or amount. HALE. **2.** Indefiniteness, undefined state 1827. So **Indefi·nity** (*rare*), in both senses 1623.

Indehiscent (indĭhi·sĕnt), *a.* 1832. [IN-[3].] *Bot.* Not dehiscent; said of fruits which do not split open when mature, but liberate the seed by decay. Hence **Indehi·scence.**

Indele·ctable, *a.* *rare.* 1585. [IN-[3].] Unpleasant.

Indeliberate (indĭli·bĕrĕt), *a.* 1617. [f. IN-[3] + DELIBERATE *a.* Cf. med.L. *indeliberatus.*] **†1.** Of persons, etc.: Wanting in deliberation; hasty or rash –1677. **2.** Done without deliberation; unpremeditated. Now *rare.* 1655. So †**Indeli·berated** *a.* (in sense 2). Hence **Indeli·berate-ly** *adv.* (*rare*), **-ness** (*rare*). **Indelibera·tion,** want of deliberation or forethought 1614.

Indelible (inde·lĭb'l), *a.* 1529. [In XVI *indeleble* – Fr. *indélébile* or L. *indelebilis*; see IN-[3], DELIBLE.] That cannot be deleted, blotted out, or effaced; ineffaceable, permanent.

Phr. *Indelible ink,* ink which makes i. marks. An indeleble note of infamy SANDERSON. Man still bears in his bodily frame the i. stamp of his lowly origin DARWIN. An i. impression DISRAELI. The i. (= indefeasible) rights of mankind BLACKSTONE. Hence **Inde·libleness. Inde·libly** *adv.*

Indelicacy (inde·likăsi). 1712. [IN-[3].] Want of delicacy; want of a nice sense of propriety, refinement, or good taste; coarseness of character, manners, etc.

Your Papers would be chargeable with something worse than I., they would be Immoral STEELE. The i. of the Hindus 1818.

Indelicate (inde·likĕt), *a.* 1742. [IN-[3].] **1.** Wanting in, or offensive to, delicacy or propriety; coarse, unrefined. **2.** Wanting in fine tact 1800. **†3.** Of food: Coarse –1777.

1. The..most i. sarcasms 1804. **2.** She felt that ..it would be i. to attempt more 1800. Hence **Inde·licately** *adv.*

Indemnification (inde:mnifikēⁱ·ʃən). 1732. [f. INDEMNIFY; see -FICATION.] **1.** The action of compensating for actual loss or damage sustained; also the fact of being compensated; *concr.* the payment made with this object. **b.** The action of compensating for trouble, annoyance, etc.; *concr.* the recompense so rendered 1774. **†2.** Indemnity.

1. Giving him a full i. and equivalent for the injury thereby sustained BLACKSTONE.

Indemnify (inde·mnifəi), *v.*[1] 1611. [f. L. *indemnis* unhurt + -FY. Cf. med.L. *indemnificare.*] **1.** *trans.* To keep free *from,* secure *against* (any hurt, harm, or loss); to give an indemnity to. **2.** To compensate *for* loss suffered, expenses incurred, etc. 1693. **b.** To compensate *for* disadvantages, annoyances, hardships, etc. 1707.

1. The fact indemnified the peace officers..if they killed any of the mob in endeavouring to suppress..riot BLACKSTONE. **2. b.** The high price of provisions indemnifies the cultivator for the hard life 1836.

†**Inde·mnify,** *v.*[2] *rare.* 1583. [f. IN-[2] + DAMNIFY.] *trans.* To hurt, harm –1593.

Indemnity[1] (inde·mnĭti). 1467. [– (O)Fr. *indemnité* – late L. *indemnitas*, f. *indemnis* free from loss or hurt, f. *in-* IN-[3] + *damnum*; see DAMAGE, -ITY.] **1.** Security or protection against contingent hurt, damage, or loss; safety. **2.** A legal exemption from the penalties or liabilities incurred by any course of action 1670. **3.** Compensation for loss, etc.; indemnification 1793; a sum paid by way of compensation 1872. **4.** *attrib.*, as *i. bill*, etc. 1818.

1. Thei would prouide sufficiently for thindemnity of the wytnes in that behalfe MORE. Insurance ought to be a contract of i. LUBBOCK. **2.** Receiving beforehand an i. for every excess BUCKLE. *Act* (or *Bill*) *of Indemnity*, an act of Parliament or other authority granting exemption from the penalties attaching to any unconstitutional or illegal proceeding. Also *fig.* **3.** Within four years, France had to pay to Germany a war i. of £240,000,000 FAWCETT.

†**Inde·mnity**[2]. *rare.* 1556. [– Fr. †*indampnité* or med.L. *indem(p)nitas*, f. *indamnum* (for *damnum* DAMAGE) + *-itas* -ITY.] Damage, hurt –1629.

Indemonstrable (indĭmǫ·nstrăb'l), *a.* 1570. [f. IN-[3] + DEMONSTRABLE. Cf. Fr. †*indémonstrable*.] Incapable of being demonstrated or proved. (Said *esp.* of axiomatic truths, principles, etc.) Hence **Indemo:nstrabi·lity, Indemo·nstrableness. Indemo·nstrably** *adv.*

Indenize, etc.: see ENDENIZE, etc.

Indent (inde·nt, i·ndent), *sb.*[1] 1589. [– INDENT *v.*[1]] **1.** An incision in the edge of a thing; a deep recess; an indentation 1596. **2.** *Printing.* = INDENTION 2. 1884. **3.** = INDENTURE *sb.* 2. 1551. **b.** A certificate of a money claim; *spec.* an indented certificate issued by the U.S. Government, at the end of the War of Independence, for the principal or interest due on the public debt. *Obs.* exc. *Hist.* 1788. **4.** An official requisition for stores. (Orig. by a covenanted servant of the East India Company.) 1772. **5.** *Comm.* An order for goods, esp. one sent to England from abroad 1800.

Indent (i·ndent), *sb.*[2] 1690. [f. INDENT *v.*[2]] A dint or depression in the surface of anything; an indentation.

Indent (inde·nt), *v.*[1] [– AFr. *endenter*, AL. *indentare*, f. *in-* IN-[2] + *dens, dent-* tooth.] **1.** To make a tooth-like incision or incisions in the edge or border of; to notch or jag; now, chiefly, to give a strongly serrate outline to. **b.** To penetrate deeply (a coast-line, etc.). Also *transf.* 1555. **c.** *intr.* To form a recess 1784. **2.** *trans.* To sever the two halves of a document, drawn up in duplicate, by a toothed, zig-zag, or wavy line, so that the two parts exactly tally with each other; hence, to draw up (a document) in two or more exactly corresponding copies. See INDENTURE *sb.* 2. ME. †**3.** *intr.* To enter into an engagement by indenture; hence, to covenant; to engage. Also *fig.* –1759. †**4.** *trans.* **a.** To covenant, stipulate, agree about, promise –1631. †**b.** To engage (a person) as a servant, etc. by or as by indentures –1804. **5.** *intr.* To make out a written order with a duplicate or counterfoil; hence, to make a requisition *on* or *upon*. (Orig. Anglo-Indian.) Also, later, to draw *upon*. 1829. **6.** *trans.* To make an incision in (a board, etc.) for the purpose of dovetailing, etc.; to join or joint together by this method 1741. **7.** *Printing.* To set back (from the margin) the beginning of (one or more lines); to insert (notes) in the text 1676. †**8.** *intr.* To move in a zigzag or indented line; to double –1643. †**b.** *trans. To i. the way*: in same sense –1622.

1. b. Lochleven, an arm of the sea which deeply indents the western coast of Scotland MACAULAY. **3.** He indented not what reward he should have ABP. SANDYS. **5.** I have indented largely, (to use our Indian official term,) for the requisite books MACAULAY. **7.** You must i. your Line four Spaces at least MOXON.

Indent (inde·nt), *v.*[2] ME. [f. IN-[2] + DENT *v.* In actual use not regarded as distinct from prec.] †**1.** *trans.* To inlay, set, emboss –1730. **2.** *trans.* To form as a dint, dent, or depression; to impress ME. **3.** To make a dint or dints in (a thing) with or as with a blow; to dint or dent 1586. **4.** *intr.* To become indented or furrowed 1653.

2. Deep Scars were seen indented on his Breast DRYDEN. **3.** Shields indented deep in glorious wars POPE.

Indentation (indentēⁱ·ʃən). 1728. [f. INDENT *v.*[1] and [2]; see -ATION.]

I. f. INDENT *v.*[1] **1.** The action of indenting; the condition of being indented; denticulation; toothing 1836. **2.** A cut, notch, or angular incision in anything; a deep recess in a coastline, or the like 1728. **3.** *Printing.* = INDENTION I. 2. 1864.

2. The Greek coast is full of indentations BUCKLE.

II. f. INDENT *v.*[2] The action of impressing so as to form a dent or dint; the dent, hollow, or depression thus formed; any depression in a surface 1847.

Indented (inde·ntėd), *ppl. a.*[1] ME. [f. INDENT *v.*[1] + -ED[1].] **1.** Having the edge deeply cut with angular incisions; serrated 1440. **b.** Having a serrated or zigzag figure, direction, or course; constructed with salient and re-entrant angles, as a battery, parapet, etc. 1600. **2.** *Her.* Of an ordinary, etc.: Having a series of similar indentations or notches ME. **3.** Of a legal document: Cut zigzag or wavy at the top or edge; having counterparts severed by a zigzag line ME. **4.** Bound by an indenture 1758. **5.** *Printing.* Set in, so as to break the line of the margin 1840.

1. *Indented Line* (in *Fortif.*) a serrated line, forming several angles, so that one side defends another. **3.** Deeds are divided into two sorts; deeds poll, or cut in a straight line; and deeds indented CRUISE.

Indented (inde·ntėd), *ppl. a.*[2] 1635. [f. INDENT *v.*[2] + -ED[1].] Impressed, struck, or dinted in, so as to make a depression in a surface. **b.** Marked with sharp depressions on the surface, as if caused by blows. Hence **Inde·ntedly** *adv.*

Indentee (indentī·), *a.* 1727. [– Fr. *endenté* – med.L. *indentatus* (XIV in *Her.*); see INDENT *v.*[1], -EE[1].] *Her.* Having indents not joined to each other, but set apart.

Indenting (inde·ntiŋ), *vbl. sb.*[1] ME. [f. INDENT *v.*[1] + -ING[1].] The action of INDENT *v.*[1], or its result. **a.** = INDENTATION I. 1, 2. **b.** The making of an INDENTURE (I. 2) or INDENT (*sb.*[1] 3–5) 1472.

Indenting (inde·ntiŋ), *vbl. sb.*[2] 1580. [f. INDENT *v.*[2] + -ING[1].] = INDENTATION II.

Indention (inde·nʃən). 1733. [irreg. f. INDENT *v.*[1] and [2].]

I. f. INDENT *v.*[1] **1.** = INDENTATION I. 1, 2. **2.** *Printing.* The indenting of a line in printing or writing; the leaving of a blank space at the beginning of a line at the commencement of a new paragraph, etc.; the blank space so left 1824.

2. *Hanging* or *reverse i.*, the projection of the first line of a paragraph, etc., beyond the vertical line of those that follow.

II. f. INDENT *v.*[2] = INDENTATION II. 1839.

†**Inde·ntment.** 1597. [var. of INDENTURE with change of suffix. See next, -MENT.] **1.** Indentation –1713. **2.** An indenture, covenant –1611.

Indenture (inde·ntiŭɹ), *sb.* [Earliest in MSc. *en-*, *indenture* – AFr. *endenture* (OFr. *-ëure*), med.L. *indentura*, f. *indentatus*, pa. pple. of *indentare*. See INDENT *v.*, -URE.]

I. f. INDENT *v.*[1] **1.** The action of indenting; an indentation 1671. **2.** A deed between two or more parties with mutual covenants, executed in two or more copies, all having their tops or edges correspondingly indented for identification and security. Hence, any deed or sealed agreement between two or more parties. ME. **b.** *spec.* The contract by which an apprentice is bound to a master 1463. **c.** An official list, inventory, certificate, etc., prepared (orig. in duplicate) for purposes of control, as a voucher, etc. ME. **d.** *fig.* Contract, mutual engagement 1540. †**3.** A zigzag line or course; a doubling –1781.

2. And our Indentures Tripartite are drawne SHAKS. **b.** *To take up one's indentures*, to receive the i. back from the master in evidence of the completion of apprenticeship or service. **d.** My heart hath past Indentures with mine eye, Not to behold a Maid QUARLES.

II. f. INDENT *v.*[2] †**1.** An inlaying or embossing 1664. **2.** = INDENTATION II. 1793.

Inde·nture, *v.* 1631. [f. INDENTURE *sb.*] †**1.** *intr.* To enter into an indenture 1658. **2.** *trans.* To bind by indentures 1676. †**3.** *intr.* To move in a zigzag line –1635. **4.** *trans.* To indent, furrow 1770.

4. Age may creep on, and i. the brow *c* 1770.

I·ndentwise, *adv.* 1758. [f. INDENT *sb.*[1] + -WISE.] After the form of an indenture, with a counterpart.

Independence (indĭpe·ndĕns). Also †**-ance.** 1640. [f. INDEPENDENT, partly after Fr. *indépendance*; see -ENCE.] **1.** The condition or quality of being independent; the fact of not depending on another (see the adj.); exemption from external control or support; individual liberty of thought or action. Rarely in bad sense: Insubordination. **2.** *concr.* A competency; = INDEPENDENCY 3 c. 1815. **3.** *attrib.* 1860.

1. The charms of i. let us sing SHENSTONE. The dignified clergy..pretended to a total i. on the State HUME. **3.** *Independence Day*, July 4, the day on which, in 1776, the Declaration of I. was made; celebrated annually in U.S. as a national holiday.

Independency (indĭpe·ndĕnsi). Also †**-ancy.** 1611. [f. as prec. + -ENCY.] **1.** = prec. 1. Now *rare.* **2.** = CONGREGATIONALISM 1. 1642. **3.** *concr. pl.* Independent things 1659. **b.** An autonomous state 1818. **c.** A competency; a fortune on which the possessor can live without earning his bread 1748.

3. c. The deceased had something in the nature of an i., however modest 1886.

Independent (indĭpe·ndĕnt). Also †**-ant.** 1611. [f. IN-[3] + DEPENDENT, partly after Fr. *indépendant*.] Not dependent.

A. *adj.* **1.** Not depending upon the authority of another; not in a position of subordination; not subject to external control or rule; self-governing, free. **2.** (with capital *I.*) = CONGREGATIONAL 2. 1642. **3.** Not contingent on or conditioned by anything else 1614; not depending on the existence or action of others, or of each other 1790. **4.** Not dependent on another for support or supplies 1670. **b.** *simply.* (*a*) Not dependent on any one else for one's living; (*b*) not needing to earn one's living. 1732. **c.** *transf.* Constituting a competency 1790. **5.** Not influenced or biased by the opinions of others; thinking or acting for oneself 1735. **b.** (cf. 4), Refusing to be under obligation to others (*mod.*). **6.** *Math.* Not depending on another for its value. *I. variable*: a quantity whose variation does not depend on that of another. 1852.

1. An i. workman, such as a weaver or shoemaker A. SMITH. It has been said..that the church is i. on the state 1785. **3.** Beauty and Merit are Things real, and i. on Taste and Opinion STEELE. An i. inquiry has been instituted by the Local Board of Health 1900. Phr. *Independent of* (†*on*, †*from*): = Independently of, without regard to, irrespective of. **4. b.** *transf.* A dry but i. crust COWPER. **c.** A person of i. means 1885. **5.** A person capable of taking an i. stand HAWTHORNE. *I. Labour Party* (see LABOUR). **b.** The widow..is very i., and refuses all pecuniary aid 1900.

B. *sb.* **1.** An adherent of Independency; a member of an Independent church; a Congregationalist 1644. **2.** A person who acts independently of any organized party; also, a member of any organized party called *Independent* 1808.

Hence **Indepe·ndentism**: †**a.** = INDEPENDENCY 2; **b.** the principles of any party called *Independent.* **Indepe·ndently** *adv.*

†**Indepe·nding,** *a.* 1604. [var. of INDEPENDENT with substitution of suffix.] = INDEPENDENT *a.* –1675.

Indepo·sable, *a. rare.* [IN-[3].] That cannot be deposed. STILLINGFL.

†**Inde·pravate,** *a.* 1609. [f. IN-[3] + DEPRAVATE *ppl. a.* or – L. *indepravatus.*] Uncorrupted.

†**Indeprehe·nsible,** *a.* 1633. [f. IN-[3] + DEPREHENSIBLE. Cf. late L. *indeprehensibilis.*] Incapable of being mentally apprehended; undiscoverable –1652.

Indeprivable (indĭprai·văb'l), *a.* Now *rare.* 1585. [f. IN-[3] + DEPRIVABLE.] **1.** Incapable of being taken away. **2.** That cannot be deprived of something. WEBSTER.

Indescribable (indĭskrai·băb'l), *a.* (*sb.*) 1794. [IN-[3].] **A.** *adj.* That cannot be described; indefinite, vague; transcending description. **B.** *sb.* (*pl.*) Things which cannot be described; (*slang*) trousers 1794. Hence **Indescribabi·lity,** incapacity of being described; something that cannot be described. **Indescri·bably** *adv.*

Indescri·ptive, *a. rare.* 1828. [IN-[3].] Not descriptive.

Indesert (indĭzə̄·ɹt). Now *rare.* 1612. [f. IN-[3] + DESERT *sb.*[1]] Absence of desert 1646. *pl.* Demerits, faults.

Indesignate (inde·zignĕt), *a.* 1844. [f. IN-[3] + DESIGNATE *ppl. a.*] *Logic.* Not quantified, indefinite. Also as *sb.*

The I. is..often not thought in any relation of quantity at all MILL.

†**Inde·sinent,** *a.* 1601. [See IN-[3] and DESINENT.] Unceasing, perpetual –1799. Hence †**Inde·sinency.** †**Inde·sinently** *adv.*

†**Indesi·rable,** *a.* 1846. [IN-[3].] Undesirable.

Indestructible (indĭstrɒ·ktĭb'l), *a.* 1674. [IN-[3].] That cannot be destroyed; incapable of destruction. Hence **Indestructibi·lity, Indestru·ctibleness. Indestru·ctibly** *adv.*

Indeterminable (indĭtə̄·ɹminăb'l), *a.* (*sb.*) 1486. [– late L. *indeterminabilis* (Tertullian); see IN-[3], DETERMINABLE.] †**1.** Not capable of being limited in respect of range, number, etc. (*rare*) –1690. **2.** Of disputes, etc.: Incapable of being settled 1611. **3.** Incapable of being definitely fixed; *spec.* in *Nat. Hist.* 1646. **4.** *sb.* An indeterminable point or problem. SIR T. BROWNE. Hence **Indete·rminableness. Indete·rminably** *adv.*

Indeterminate (indĭtə̄·ɹminĕt), *a.* (*sb.*) ME. [– late L. *indeterminatus* (Tertullian); see IN-[3], DETERMINATE *ppl. a.*] Not determined; undetermined. †**1.** Not definitely set down. CHAUCER. **2.** Not fixed in extent, number, character, or nature; indefinite, indistinct, uncertain 1603. **b.** Of statements, words, etc.: Wanting in precision, vague 1774. **c.** *Math.* Of a quantity: Not limited to a fixed value or number of values. (Also as *sb.*) Of a problem: Having an unlimited number of solutions. 1706. **d.** *Bot.* (*a*) = INDEFINITE II. 3 a, 1731; (*b*) of æstivation; Having parts which do not come into contact in the bud 1842. **3.** Not established; uncertain 1626. **4.** Not decided; left doubtful 1656. **5.** Not determined by motives (regarded as external forces); acting freely 1836.

2. Empires of great extent but i. limits 1782. **b.** Some is an i. adjective JEVONS. **c.** *I. analysis*, the branch of analysis which deals with the solution of i. problems. *Method of i. coefficients* (more prop. of *undetermined coefficients*), a method of analysis invented by Descartes. *I. equation*, an equation in which the unknown quantities are i. *I. form*, a form consisting of two i. quantities. *I. series*, a series whose terms proceed by the powers of an i. quantity. **3.** An i. future GEO. ELIOT. **5.** In positive morality, the mandate is conceived as emanating from an i. superior GROTE. Hence **Indete·rminacy** (*rare*). **Indete·rminate-ly** *adv.*, **-ness.**

Indetermination (indĭtə̄ɹminē[i]·ʃən). 1619. [f. prec.; see -ATION. Cf. Fr. *indétermination.*] Absence of determination; the fact or condition of being undetermined or indeterminate 1649. †**b.** An indeterminate number or quantity. FOTHERBY.

Indetermined (indĭtə̄·ɹmind), *a.* Now *rare.* 1611. [f. IN-[3] + DETERMINED *ppl. a.*] Not determined, UNDETERMINED. †**b.** *Math.* = INDETERMINATE 2 c. –1743.

Indeterminism (indĭtə̄·ɹminiz'm). 1874. [f. IN-[3] + DETERMINISM.] The theory that human action is not necessarily determined by motives, but is in some sense free. So **Indete·rminist,** one who holds the doctrine of i.

†**Indevi·rginate,** *a. rare.* 1616. [f. IN-[3] + DEVIRGINATE *ppl. a.*] Undeflowered. Also *fig.* Unsullied. –1822.

†**Indevo·te,** *a. rare.* [– late L. *indevotus* impious; see IN-[3], DEVOTE *a.*] = INDEVOUT. Bentley.

†**Indevo·ted,** *a.* 1647. [f. IN-[3] + DEVOTED *ppl. a.*] Not devoted; disaffected or disloyal –1759.

Indevotion (indĭvō[u]·ʃən). 1526. [f. IN-[3] + DEVOTION. Cf. Fr. *indévotion*, late L. *indevotio.*] Want of devotion; indevout feeling or action.

The sloth and i. of the clergy 1866.

Indevout (indĭvau·t), *a.* 1450. [f. IN-[3] + DEVOUT. In XV tr. late L. *indevotus* (see INDEVOTE).] Not devout, irreverent, irreligious. Hence **Indevou·t-ly** *adv.*, **-ness.**

Indew, obs. f. ENDUE.

Index (i·ndeks), *sb.* Pl. **indexes** and **indices** (i·ndisīz). ME. [– L. *index*, pl. *indices*, forefinger, informer, sign, inscription, f. *in-* IN-[2] + *-dex, -dic-* as in *judex* JUDGE, f. **dik-* point out.] **1.** The forefinger; so called because used in pointing. Now chiefly *Anat.* **2.** A piece of wood, metal, etc., which serves as a pointer; *esp.* in scientific instruments, a pointer on a graduated scale, which indicates movements or measurements 1594. **b.** An alidade 1571. **3.** The hand of a clock or watch; also, the gnomon of a sundial. Now *rare.* 1594. **4.** That which serves to direct *to* a particular fact or conclusion; a guiding principle 1598. **b.** A sign, token, or indication *of* something 1607. **5.** †**a.** A table of contents prefixed to a book, an argument; also, a preface, prologue. **b.** An alphabetical list (usually) at the end of a book, of the names, subjects, etc. occurring in it, with indication of the places where they occur 1580. Also *fig.* **6.** *spec.* (short for *Index librorum prohibitorum*). The list, published by authority, of books which Roman Catholics are forbidden to read, or may read only in expurgated editions 1613. **b.** ‖*Index expurgatorius* (L.), *Expurgatory I.*, an authoritative specification of the passages to be expunged or altered in works otherwise permitted. Also *transf.* and *fig.* 1611. †**7. a.** *Mus.* = DIRECT *sb.* 2. –1869. **b.** *Printing.* = HAND *sb.* IV. 1. ? *Obs.* 1727. **8.** *Math.* **a.** *Alg.* = EXPONENT *sb.* 2. 1674. †**b.** The integral part, or characteristic, of a logarithm –1828. **9.** In various sciences, a number or formula expressing some property, form, ratio, etc. of the thing in question. See quots. 1829.

4. Lest when my lisping guiltie Tongue should hault, My Lookes might prove the I. to my Fault DRAYTON. **b.** That olde saying is vntrue 'the face Is i. of the heart' 1616. **9.** *I. of refraction* or *refractive i.* (of a medium), in *Optics*, the ratio between the sines of the angles of incidence and refraction of a ray of light passing from some medium (usually air) into the given medium. In *Craniometry*, a formula expressing the ratio of one diameter, etc. of the skull to another, as *alveolar* or *basilar, cephalic*, etc., *i.* In *Cryst.*, each of the three (or four) whole numbers which define the position of a face of a crystal. *I. of friction*, in *Dynamics*, the coefficient of friction; see COEFFICIENT.

Comb.: **i·-arm** = sense 2 b; **-correction,** a correction for i.-error; **-digit** = sense 1; **-error,** the constant error in the reading of a mathematical instrument, due to the zero of the i. not being exactly adjusted to that of the limb; **-finger,** (*a*) = sense 1, (*b*) = sense 2; **-gauge,** a measuring instrument in which the distance between the measuring-points is shown by an i.; **-glass,** a mirror at the fixed point of the i.-arm in an astronomical or surveying instrument, from which the light is reflected to the horizon-glass; **-hand** = senses 2 and 3; **i. machine,** a machine for fancy weaving, being a modification of the Jacquard loom.

Index (i·ndeks), *v.* 1720. [f. prec. sb.] **1.** *trans.* To furnish with an index. **2.** To enter (a word, name, etc.) in an index 1761. **3.** To place on the INDEX (*sb.* 6) 1791. **4.** To indicate 1788. Hence **I·ndexer,** one who compiles an index.

Indexical (inde·ksikăl), *a.* 1828. [irreg. f. INDEX *sb.* + -ICAL.] **a.** Arranged like an index. **b.** Relating or pertaining to, or of the nature of, an index. So **Inde·xically** *adv.* in the manner of an index, alphabetically 1728.

Indexte·rity. *rare.* 1611. [f. IN-[3] + DEXTERITY. Cf. Fr. †*indextérité.*] Want of dexterity; awkwardness.

Indi-. *Chem.* [f. L. *Indus*, as root of *indicum, indigo.*] A comb. element used in naming substances derived from or related to indigo, as *indifulvin*, etc.

India (i·ndiă). OE. [In OE. *India, Indea*, but the present use dates from XVI (prob. immed. after Sp. or Pg.), the ME. form being IND – L. *India* – Gr. Ἰνδία, f. Ἰνδός the river Indus – Pers. *hind* (OPers. *hindu*) = Av. *hendu*, Skr. *sindhu* river, spec. the Indus, hence the region of the Indus, Sindh (by extension, with Greeks and Persians) the country east of this (see HINDUSTAN), also the regions further east (*Further I.*).] **1.** A country of Southern Asia, lying east of the river Indus and south of the Himalaya mountains (also called *Hindustan*); also extended to include *Farther* or *Further India*, between this and China. See also EAST INDIA. †**2.** Formerly applied to America, or some parts of it; cf. INDIES, WEST INDIES –1772. †**3.** *pl.* = INDIES –1604. **4.** Short for *India silk, paper*, etc. 1712. **5.** *attrib.*, as *India cloth, muslin, silk*, etc.; also *India bonds, stock*, etc. 1658.

Comb.: **I. Docks,** docks in East London, formerly appropriated to vessels trading with the East and West Indies; †**I. House,** the office of the E. I. Company in London; **I. ink** (see INDIAN INK); **I. Office,** that department of the British Government which deals with Indian affairs; **I. proof** = *I. paper proof*: see INDIA PAPER I; **I. red** = *Indian red* (see INDIAN A.); †**I. wood,** logwood.

Indiademed (indəi·ădemd), *ppl. a.* [f. IN-[1] or [2]. Cf. ENDIADEM (EN- *prefix.*[1])] Set in a diadem. SOUTHEY.

Indiaman (i·ndiămæn). Pl. **-men.** 1709. [f. INDIA + MAN as in *man of war*, etc.] A large ship engaged in the trade with India.

Indian (i·ndiăn). 1390. [f. INDIA: cf. -AN.]

A. *adj.* **1.** Belonging or relating to India, or the East Indies, or to the British Indian Empire; native to India 1566. **b.** Of Indian manufacture, material, or pattern 1673. **2.** Belonging or relating to the original inhabitants of America and the West Indies 1618. **3.** Made of Indian corn or maize, as *I. bread, I. meal, I. dumpling* 1635.

1. Ganges or Hydaspes, I. streams MILT. *P. L.* III. 436. **2.** *I. house*, a wigwam.

Special collocations. **a.** of India or the East Indies (sense 1), or so originally supposed: **I. almond,** a large tree (*Terminalia catappa*), the seeds of which resemble almonds; **I. berry** = COCCULUS INDICUS, or the plant which yields this; **I. blue,** indigo; **I. cane,** the Bamboo; **I. club,** a club of varying weight, for use in gymnastic exercises; †**I. cock,** the turkey (but the bird is a native of N. America); **I. crocus,** a name for the dwarf orchids of the subgenus *Pleione* (genus *Cœlogyne*); **I. eye,** a species of pink (*Dianthus plumarius*), so called from the eye-shaped marking on the corolla; **I. fire,** a composition of sulphur, realgar, and nitre, burning with a brilliant white flame, used as a signal-light; **I. geranium,** a grass of the genus *Andropogon*, which yields a fragrant oil used in perfumery; †**I. grass,** an old name of silkworm gut used by anglers (see also in b below); **I. heart,** a plant of the genus *Cardiospermum*; **I. hemp**: see HEMP 5 (see also in b below); **I. hog,** the Babiroussa; **I. leaf,** the aromatic leaf of a species of *Cinnamomum*; **I. light** = BENGAL *light*; **I. oak,** the teak-tree; **I. Ocean; I. red,** a red pigment orig. obtained from the East Indies in the form of an earth containing oxide of iron; now prepared artificially by roasting iron sulphate; **I. reed** = next (see also in b below); **I. shot,** the plant *Canna indica* (N.O. *Marantaceæ*), so called from its round hard black seeds; **I. yellow,** a bright yellow pigment obtained from India, consisting mainly of euxanthate of magnesium.

b. of North America or the West Indies: **I. balm,** the purple Trillium or Birth-root (*Trillium erectum* or *T. pendulum*); **I. bean,** *Catalpa bignonioides*; **I. bread,** †(*a*) the Cassava; (*b*) bread made from I. corn; **I. cress, cresses,** the Nasturtium, so called from the flavour of the leaves; †**I. drug,** tobacco; **I. file,** th same as *single file*, so called because the N. Amer. Indians usually march in this order; **I. gift,** a gift for which an equivalent return is expected; **I. grass,** *Sorghum nutans* and *Molinia cœrulea*; **I. hemp.** *Apocynum cannabinum*, a plant having a fibrous integument used by the N. Amer. Indians for the same purposes as hemp; †**I. herb,** tobacco; **I. path,** a footpath through the woods, such as is made by N. Amer. Indians; **I. physic,** *Gillenia trifoliata*, a N. Amer. rosaceous plant with a medicinal root; **I. pipe,** *Monotropa uniflora*, a leafless plant with a solitary drooping flower, of a uniform pinkish-white throughout, parasitic on the roots of trees; **I. plantain,** the genus *Cacalia* of composite plants; **I. poke,** the White Hellebore of N. America, *Veratrum viride*; **I. pudding,** a pudding made with I. meal, molasses, and suet; also, the same as *hasty-pudding*; **I. reed,** a blow-pipe such as the N. Amer. Indians use for shooting arrows; **I. rice** = CANADA *rice*; **I. shoe,** (*a*) a mocassin; (*b*) an American name for the plant *Cypripedium* or Lady's Slipper; **I. tobacco,** *Lobelia inflata*; **I. turnip,** (*a*) the tuberous root of *Arisæma triphyllum* (N.O. *Araceæ*), or the plant itself; (*b*) the edible tuberous root of *Psoralea esculenta*; **I. weed,** tobacco; †**I. wheat,** an old name for Indian corn.

B. *sb.* **1.** A native of India or the East Indies; an East Indian. **b.** An Anglo-Indian

1751. **2.** A member of any of the aboriginal races of America or the West Indies; an American Indian 1553. **3.** Name of a constellation (*Indus*) lying between Sagittarius and the south pole 1674.

2. *Red Indian*: one of the aboriginal race of N. America; so called from the coppery colour of their skin.

Indian corn. 1621. [INDIAN *a.* 2.] The common name of *Zea Mays*, or of the grain produced by it; cultivated by the Americans at the time of the discovery of America. Also called MAIZE, and in U.S. simply CORN.

Indian fig. 1594. **1.** The Prickly Pear 1712. **2.** *Indian fig-tree.* **a.** The BANIAN tree 1594. †**b.** The BANANA 1613.

Indian ink. Also **India ink.** 1665. A black pigment made in China and Japan, sold in sticks; it consists of lampblack made into a paste with a solution of gum and dried. Called also *China ink* (CHINA[1] I).

Indianist (i·ndiănist). 1851. [f. INDIA + -IST, with connective *-n-*.] One versed in the languages, history, etc. of India.

Indian summer. 1794. [INDIAN *a.* 2.] A period of calm, dry, mild weather, with hazy atmosphere, occurring in the late autumn in the Northern U.S. Also *fig.*

India paper. 1768. (*Indian p.* 1750.) **1.** A soft absorbent paper of creamy-yellow or pale buff colour, imported from China, and used for the proofs of engravings. Also used loosely of similar papers. Hence *India paper proofs* (also *India proofs*). **2.** (*Oxford India paper.*) A very thin tough opaque printing-paper made by the Oxford University Press in imitation of paper from the East 1875.

I:ndia-ru·bber, India rubber. 1799. **1.** = CAOUTCHOUC, q.v. In later use shortened to *rubber*. **2.** *attrib.*, as *india-rubber ball, band,* etc.; *india-rubber plant, tree, vine*; *india-rubber works* 1833.

†**I·ndiary,** *a.* [f. INDIA + -ARY[2].] Relating to India. SIR T. BROWNE.

†**I·ndical,** *a.* 1661. [f. L. *index, indic-* INDEX + -AL[1].] Pertaining to an index or indexes.

Indican (i·ndikæ̆n). 1859. [f. L. *indicum* INDIGO + -AN I. 2; cf. ALLOXAN.] *Chem.* The natural glucoside ($C_{26}H_{31}NO_{17}$) formed in plants which yield indigo, by the decomposition of which indigo-blue is produced; it forms a light-brown syrup, of bitter taste, and slightly acid reaction. **b.** *Indican of urine*: an incorrect name for the potassium salt of indoxyl sulphuric acid, a normal constituent of the urine of animals.

Indicant (i·ndikănt). 1607. [– *indicant-*, pr. ppl. stem of L. *indicare*; see next, -ANT.] **A.** *adj.* That indicates; indicative. **B.** *sb.* (*Med.*) That which indicates the remedy or treatment suitable 1623.

Indicate (i·ndikeˡt), *v.* 1651. [– *indicat-*, pa. ppl. stem of L. *indicare*, f. *in-* IN-[2] + *dicare* proclaim; cf. INDEX and see -ATE[3].] **1.** *trans.* To point out, point to, make known, show (more or less distinctly). In *Med.* to point out as a remedy or treatment. **2.** To be a sign or symptom of; to betoken 1706. **3.** *trans.* Of persons: To point out, direct attention to. *Occas.*, To point to with the hand or by gesture. 1808. **4.** To state or express; *esp.* to express briefly, lightly, or without development; to give an indication of 1751.

1. Above the steeple shines a plate, That turns and turns, to i. From what point blows the weather COWPER. **2.** Large noses..were considered as indicating prudence 1798. **4.** The waves are indicated on the plinth 1846.

Indication (indikēˡ·ʃən). 1541. [– Fr. *indication* – L. *indicatio*, f. as prec.; see -ION.] **1.** The action of indicating; that in which this is embodied; a hint, suggestion, etc. 1626. **b.** *spec.* in *Med.* A suggestion or direction as to the treatment of a disease, derived from the symptoms 1541. **2.** A sign, token, or symptom; an expression by sign or token 1660.

1. The indications of the senses are always imperfect, and often misleading TAIT. **2.** Modesty is the certain I. of a great Spirit STEELE.

Indicative (indi·kătiv, i·ndikeˡtiv), *a.* (*sb.*) 1490. [– (O)Fr. *indicatif, -ive* – late L. *indicativus* (*Gram.*), tr. Gr. ὁριστική (sc. ἔγκλισις); f. as prec.; see -IVE.] **1.** *Gram.* That points out, states, or declares: applied to that mood of a verb which states a relation of objective fact between the subject and predicate 1530. **2.** That indicates, points out, or directs; that hints or suggests; also with *of* 1490. **3.** *sb. Gram.* The indicative mood; a verb in the indicative mood 1530.

1. The I. Mood sheweth or declareth, as *laudo* I praise MILT. **2.** I. Signs of any change in States and times 1663. Hence **Indicatively** *adv.*

Indicator (i·ndikeˡtəɹ). 1666. [f. INDICATE *v.* + -OR 2. In 1 b – late L. *indicator.*] **1.** One who or that which points out, or directs attention to, something 1831. **b.** *Anat.* The muscle which extends the index or forefinger; the *extensor indicis* 1696. **c.** In a microscope, A pointer which indicates the position of an object 1837. **2.** That which serves as an indication *of* something 1666. **b.** Anything used in a scientific experiment to indicate the presence of a substance or quality, change in a body, etc.; *esp.* a chemical reagent 1842. **3.** *techn.*:

a. An instrument which indicates the pressure of steam on the piston of a steam-engine at each portion of its stroke. **b.** In a blast-furnace, a gauge which indicates the proper height of a charge. **c.** The dial and mechanism by which messages are indicated in a dial-telegraph. **d.** An instrument which indicates at any moment the position of the cage in the shaft of a mine. **e.** A contrivance in a lending library for showing what books are out or in. 1839.

4. *Ornith.* A honey-guide, a bird of the genus *Indicator*, or family *Indicatoridæ* 1835.

1. Birds..were celestial indicators of the god's commands FROUDE.

Comb.: **i.-card,** the card on which an i.-diagram is traced; **-cylinder,** the cylinder of a steam-engine i.; **-diagram,** a figure traced by the i. of a steam-engine, showing the pressure at different points of the stroke; **-muscle** = sense 1 b; **-pointer,** the pointer in a telegraph i.; **-telegraph,** a form of telegraph in which the letters of a message are indicated by a pointer on a dial-plate.

Indicatory (i·ndikătəri, i·ndikeˡtəri), *a.* 1590. [f. INDICATE + -ORY[2].] †**1.** *Med.* Symptomatic; cf. INDICANT *a.* –1624. **2.** Serving to indicate or point out something. Also with *of.* 1734.

Indicatrix (indikēˡ·triks). 1841. [mod.L., fem. of INDICATOR; see -TRIX. Cf. DIRECTRIX.] **1.** *Geom.* The curve in which a given surface is cut by a plane indefinitely near and parallel to the tangent-plane at any point; so called because it indicates the nature of the curvature of the surface at that point. **2.** *Optical indicatrix*: L. Fletcher's name for a surface (sphere, spheroid, or ellipsoid) devised to indicate by its geometrical characters the optical characters of rays of light refracted through a crystal of any kind 1892.

‖**Indicavit** (indikēˡ·vit), *sb.* 1607. [L.; = 'he has pointed out'; 3rd sing. perf. ind. used subst.] *Law.* A writ of prohibition, by which, in certain cases, a suit might be removed from the eccl. court to the king's court at the instance of the patron of the defendant.

†**I·ndice.** *rare.* 1595. [– Fr. *indice* – L. INDICIUM.] An indication, sign –1645.

Indices, Indicia, pl. of INDEX, INDICIUM.

†**Indi·cible,** *a.* 1480. [– Fr. *indicible* or late L. *indicibilis* (Jerome), f. *in-* IN-[3] + *dicibilis* (in med.L.), f. L. *dicere* say; see -BLE.] Unspeakable, inexpressible –1685.

O vnparalell'd loss! O griefe i. EVELYN.

‖**Indicium** (indi·ʃiŏm). Pl. **indicia.** 1625. [L., f. *index, indic-* INDEX.] An indication, sign, token. Chiefly in *pl.*

Indicolite (indi·kŏləit). 1808. [f. L. *indicum* INDIGO + -LITE.] *Min.* An indigo-coloured variety of tourmaline.

Indict (indəi·t), *v.*[1] [ME. *endite*, later with latinized prefix *indite*, and finally *indict* (XVI), – legal AFr. *enditer* (XIII), corresp. in form but not in sense to OFr. *enditier* declare, dictate, compose, INDITE :– Rom. **indictare* (in AL. indict XIII), f. *indict-*, pa. ppl. stem of L. *indicere* proclaim, appoint, impose, f. *in-* IN-[2] + *dicere* pronounce, utter.] **1.** *trans.* To bring a charge against; to accuse (a person) *for* (†*of*) a crime, *as* (†*for*) a culprit. **2.** To make (it) matter of indictment (*rare*) 1670.

1. They indicted our friends as rioters ELLWOOD.

Hence **Indi·ctable** *a.* liable to be indicted; on account of which an indictment may be raised. **Indictee·**, a person indicted. **Indi·cter,** one who indicts.

†**Indi·ct,** *v.*[2] 1538. [– *indict-*, pa. ppl. stem of L. *indicere* proclaim; see prec.] To declare authoritatively, announce, proclaim –1720.

To i. a new Parliament 1648, a day for prayer with fasting C. MATHER, war EVELYN.

Indict, obs. erron. f. INDITE.

Indiction (indi·kʃən). ME. [– L. *indictio*, f. as INDICT *v.*[2]; see -ION.] **1.** The action of announcing authoritatively and publicly; an appointment, declaration, proclamation 1563. **2.** The decree of the Roman Emperors fixing the valuation on which the property-tax was assessed at the beginning of each period of fifteen years; hence, the amount paid on this basis. Also *transf.* 1586. **3.** The fiscal period of fifteen years, instituted by the Emperor Constantine in A.D. 313, and reckoned from the 1st of Sept. 312, which became a usual means of dating ordinary events, etc. Also called *Cycle* or *Era of i.* or *indictions.* ME. Also *transf.* **4.** A specified year in the cycle of fifteen years, counting from A.D. 312–13, indicated by its numerical position in the cycle; the number thus indicating a year ME. †**5.** An eccl. observance authoritatively enjoined, or the period of it; *esp.* a public fast –1685.

1. The cruell indictions of warres 1586. **5.** The frequency of our Theatrical pastimes during that I. [Lent] EVELYN. Hence **Indi·ctional** *a.* of or pertaining to an i. or cycle of years.

†**Indictive** (indi·ktiv), *a. rare.* 1656. [– L. *indictivus*, f. as prec.; see -IVE.] Proclaimed or appointed by authority –1741.

Indictment (indəi·tmĕnt). ME. [– AFr. *enditement* (in AL. *indictamentum* XIII), f. *enditer*; see INDICT *v.*[1], -MENT. The development of the AFr., AL., and ME. sense is not accounted for.] **1.** The action of indicting or accusing; spec. in *Eng. Law.* the legal process in which a formal accusation is preferred to and presented by a Grand Jury. **b.** The legal document containing the charge 1506. **2.** *Sc. Law.* A form of process by which a criminal is brought to trial at the instance of the Lord Advocate; the formal written charge 1773.

Phr. *Bill of i.*, the written accusation as preferred to the Grand Jury, before it has been by them either found a true bill or ignored.

Indies (i·ndiz), *sb. pl.* 1555. [Pl. of INDY, INDIE.] **1.** A name given to the lands and regions now distinguished as EAST and WEST INDIES, q.v. †**2.** Used allusively for a region or place yielding great wealth –1742.

2. They shall be my East and West Indies SHAKS.

Indifference (indi·fĕrĕns). late ME. [f. as next; see -ENCE.] †**1.** = INDIFFERENCY 1. –1754. **2.** Absence of feeling for or against; hence *esp.* Absence of care for or about a person or thing; unconcern, apathy. Const. *to, towards.* 1659. **3.** Indetermination of the will, or of a body to rest or motion; neutrality 1728. **4.** †The quality of being neither good nor bad (TILLOTSON); mediocrity 1864. **5.** = INDIFFERENCY II. 1. 1656. **6.** The fact of making no difference; unimportance; a thing or matter of no importance 1644. **7.** *Magnetism. I. point, point of i.*: the middle zone of a magnet where the attractive powers of the two ends neutralize each other 1886.

2. The human mind is often..in a state neither of pain nor pleasure, which I call a state of i. BURKE. **6.** The Necessity or I. of observing the Mosaic Rites 1708.

Indifferency (indi·fĕrĕnsi). late ME. [– L. *indifferentia*, f. *indifferens, -ent-*; see next, -ENCY.]

I. 1. Absence of bias, prejudice, or favour; impartiality, equity. Now *rare.* **2.** = INDIFFERENCE 2. Now *rare.* 1625. †**3.** Indetermination of the will; freedom of choice –1699. **4.** Of a word: Capability of being applied to different things; neutral or equivocal sense. Now *rare* or *Obs.* 1596. †**5.** Of a place: Neutrality in point of advantage –1645. †**6.** The condition of being neither good nor bad –1692.

2. How long will you halt in this I.? BP. HALL. **3.** This I. to do or not to do, cannot be the true Notion of Liberty BURNET.

II. 1. Want of difference in nature or character; substantial equivalence. Now *rare.* 1568. **2.** Absence of difference in respect of consequence, effect, meaning, or importance; the fact of its being of no consequence either way 1564. †**b.** A matter of indifference –1668.

1. You have arrived at a fine Pyrrhonism, at an equivalence and i. of all actions EMERSON. **2.** It is a matter of meere i. FULKE.

Indifferent (indi·fĕrĕnt), *a.* (*sb.* and *adv.*) ME. [– (O)Fr. *indifférent* or L. *indifferens, -ent-*; see IN-[3], DIFFERENT.]

I. 1. Without difference of inclination; unbiased, impartial, disinterested; fair, just, even-handed. *arch.* **2.** Having no inclination or feeling for or against a thing; hence, Unconcerned, apathetic, insensible. Const. *to.* 1519. †**3.** Of neutral disposition; equally disposed or indisposed *to* –1690. †**4.** Having a neutral relation *to* (two or more things); impartially pertinent or applicable –1678. †**5.** Not more advantageous to one person or party than to another –1655. **6.** †Of medium quality or character –1699; fairly large; tolerable (*Obs.* or *arch.*) 1546. **7.** Of neutral quality; neither good nor bad 1532. **b.** Hence, by euphemism: Not particularly good. (Often preceded by *but* or *very.*) 1638. **c.** In poor health. *Obs.* or *dial.* 1753. **8.** In scientific use: **a.** Neutral in chemical, electrical, or magnetic quality, as *i. point* **b.** Undifferentiated, as *i. cell, tissue,* etc. 1855.

1. I leave to all worthy and i. men to judge RALEGH. Phr. *I. justice*, impartial or even-handed justice. **2.** These mighty cliffs..I. to the sun or snow SCOTT. **6.** I. wealth to maintain his family..nothing superfluous LYLY. **7.** Bards and bardlings, good, bad, and i. 1821. **b.** After an ill supper, he was shewed an i. bed CLARENDON.

II. †**1.** Not different; equal, even; identical, the same –1721. **2.** Regarded as not mattering either way. Cf. I. 2. 1513. **b.** Of no consequence either way; immaterial 1611. **c.** *spec.* Of an observance, etc.: That may be equally well observed or neglected; non-essential 1563.

2. I am arm'd, And dangers are to me i. *Jul. C.* I. iii. 115. **b.** Many haue sinned for a smal matter [*marg.* thing i.] *Ecclus.* 27:1.

Hence **Indi·fferent-ly** *adv.* ME., **-ness.**

B. *sb.* †**1.** One who is disinterested –1602. **2.** One who is neutral or unconcerned, esp. in religion or politics 1556. **3.** *pl.* Things indifferent; non-essentials (*rare*) 1626.

†**C.** *adv.* To some extent; moderately, tolerably, fairly –1826.

You have seen me act my part i. well SCOTT.

Indiffere·ntiated, *a. rare.* 1878. [IN-[3].] Not differentiated; not specialized.

Indifferentism (indi·fĕrĕntiz'm). 1827. [f. INDIFFERENT *a.* + -ISM. Cf. Fr. *indifférentisme.*] **1.** A spirit of indifference professed and practised 1831. **b.** *esp.* Adiaphorism; absence of zeal or interest in religious matters 1827. **2.** *Philos.* A theory in which the characteristic differences of mind and matter are supposed to disappear 1866. Also, = ADIAPHORISM, IDENTISM.

1. b. His anxiety to promote Christian charity converted into i. PUSEY. So **Indi·fferentist,** one who professes or practises indifference, neutrality, or unconcern.

Indifulvin (indifʊ·lvin). 1865. [f. INDI- + L. *fulvus* yellow + -IN[1].] *Chem.* A brittle, friable, reddish-yellow resin ($C_{22}H_{20}N_2O_3$), obtained from indican.

Indifuscin (-fʊ·sin). 1859. [f. INDI- + L. *fuscus* dark + -IN[1].] *Chem.* A brown powder ($C_{24}H_{20}N_2O_9$) obtained from indican.

Indigen, var. of INDIGENE.

‖**Indi·gena.** Pl. **-næ.** 1591. [L.; see INDIGENE.] = INDIGENE *sb.* Hence **Indi·genal** *a.* = INDIGENOUS; *sb.* = INDIGENE *sb.*

Indigence (i·ndidʒĕns). ME. [– (O)Fr. *indigence* or L. *indigentia*, f. *indigent-*; see INDIGENT, -ENCE.] †**1.** The fact or condition of wanting or needing (a thing); lack, deficiency; requirement –1775. **2.** *spec.* Want of the means of subsistence; poverty, penury, destitution ME. †**3.** A want, a need –1694.

2. As they had before been reduced from affluence to i. BURKE. So **I·ndigency** (in all senses).

Indigene (i·ndidʒīn). 1598. [– Fr. *indigène* – L. *indigena* native (adj. and sb.), f. *indi-* strengthened form of *in-* IN-[2] + *-gena* (corresp. to Gr. *-γενής*), f. *gen-, base of *gignere* beget.] †**A.** *adj.* = INDIGENOUS –1697. **B.** *sb.* A native 1664.

Indigenous (indi·dʒĭnəs), *a.* 1646. [f. L. *indigena* + -OUS; see prec.] **1.** Born or produced naturally in a land or region; native *to* (the soil, region, etc.). **b.** *transf.* and *fig.* Inborn, innate 1864. **2.** Native, vernacular 1844.

1. Yet were they [Negroes] all transported from Africa..and are not i. or proper natives of America SIR T. BROWNE. **b.** Joy and hope are emotions i. to the human mind 1864. **2.** I. schools H. H. WILSON. Hence **Indi·genousl-y** *adv.*, **-ness.**

Indigent (i·ndidʒĕnt), *a.* (*sb.*) ME. [–(O)Fr. *indigent* – L. *indigens, -ent-*, pr. pple. of *indigēre* lack, f. *indi-* (see INDIGENE) + *egēre* be in want, need; see -ENT.] **1.** Lacking in what is requisite; wanting, deficient (*arch.*). Also with *of.* **2.** *spec.* Lacking the necessaries of life; needy, poor ME. **3.** *sb.* An indigent person 1563.

1. How low, how little are the Proud, How i. the Great GRAY. **2.** I. faint Soules, past corporall toyle SHAKS. Hence **I·ndigent-ly** *adv.*, **-ness.**

†**Indige·st,** *a.* (*sb.*) ME. [– L. *indigestus* unarranged, f. *in-* IN-[3] + *digestus*, pa. pple. of *digerere* DIGEST *v.* Cf. (O)Fr. *indigeste.*] **1.** Undigested; crude; shapeless, confused; unarranged –1806. **2.** *sb.* A shapeless mass 1595.

1. A chaos rude and i. W. BROWNE. **2.** *K. John* v. vii. 26.

Indigested (indidʒe·stĕd), *a.* 1587. [f. IN-[3] + DIGESTED *ppl. a.*] **1.** Not arranged; without form; shapeless, chaotic 1593. **b.** Not ordered in the mind; ill-considered 1587. **2.** Not digested in the stomach 1620. †**3.** Not purified or rectified by heat; crude, raw. WOTTON. †**4.** 'Not brought to suppuration' (J.) 1676.

1. A rude and i. Chaos, or confusion of matters PURCHAS. **b.** The wild and i. Notion of raising my Fortune DE FOE.

Indigestible (indidʒe·stĭb'l), *a.* 1528. (Earlier †*-able.*) [– Fr. *indigestible* or late L. *indigestibilis*; see IN-[3], DIGESTIBLE.] Incapable of being digested, or difficult to digest; not easily assimilated as food. Also *fig.* and *transf.*

fig. Indigestable malice PURCHAS. Hence **Indigestibi·lity, Indige·stibleness.**

Indigestion (indidʒe·styən). 1450. [–(O)Fr. *indigestion* or late L. *indigestio*; see IN-[3], DIGESTION.] **1.** Want of digestion; incapacity of or difficulty in digesting food. Also *fig.* **b.** with *pl.* A case or attack of indigestion 1702. **2.** Undigested condition; disorder, imperfection. Also, an instance of this. 1656.

1. I. is learnedly spoken of as dyspepsia BEALE.

Indigestive (indidʒe·stiv), *a.* 1632. [f. IN-[3] + DIGESTIVE. Cf. Fr. †*indigestif, -ive.*] **1.** Suffering from indigestion; tending to indigestion; dyspeptic. †**2.** Not ready to digest offences. COTTON.

Indigitate (indi·dʒiteⁱt), *v.* 1617. [– *indigitat-*, pa. ppl. stem of L. *indigitare* call upon, invoke (a deity), of obscure origin; in XVI erron. assoc. w. L. *digitus* finger; sense 3 is taken direct from *digitus.*] †**1.** *trans.* **a.** To call, to indicate by a name. **b.** To proclaim, declare. –1680. †**2.** To point out with or as with the finger; to indicate –1716. **3.** *intr.* To interlock like the fingers of two hands. 1835.

1. b. The Scriptures did i. he would rise again the third day HACKET. **2.** Their lines did seem to i. and point at our times SIR T. BROWNE. Hence **Indigita·tion,** †the action of indigitating; in *Anat.*, interlocking of the fingers of two hands; hence, the mode of junction of muscle and tendon.

Indiglucin (indiglū·sin). 1865. [f. INDI- + Gr. *γλυκύς* sweet + -IN[1].] *Chem.* A light yellow 'sugar', $C_6H_{10}O_6$, one of the constituents of indican.

Indign (indəi·n), *a.* Now only *poet.* 1450. [– (O)Fr. *indigne* or L. *indignus*, f. *in-* IN-[3] + *dignus* worthy.] **1.** Unworthy; undeserving (*arch.*). **2.** Unbecoming; fraught with shame or dishonour; disgraceful 1545.

1. A cursyd foole and Indygne hounde CAXTON. **2.** All indigne, and base aduersities, make head against my Estimation SHAKS. Hence †**Indi·gnly** *adv.*

Indi·gnance. *rare.* 1590. [f. INDIGNANT; see -ANCE.] Indignation; the being indignant. So **Indi·gnancy** (*rare*).

Indignant (indi·gnănt), *a.* 1590. [– L. *indignant-*, pres. ppl. stem of L. *indignari* regard as unworthy, f. *indignus*; see INDIGN, -ANT.] Affected with indignation; provoked to wrath by something unworthy, unjust, or ungrateful; 'inflamed at once with anger and disdain' (J.). Also *fig.* of things.

Full of fiers fury and i. hate To him he turned SPENSER. *fig.* His seat..I. spurns the cottage from the green GOLDSM. Hence **Indi·gnantly** *adv.*

Indignation (indignēⁱ·ʃən). ME. [– (O)Fr. *indignation* or L. *indignatio*, f. *indignat-*, pa. ppl. stem of *indignari*; see prec., -ION.] †**1.** The action of counting or treating as unworthy of regard; disdain, contempt –1530. **2.** Anger at what is unworthy or wrongful; wrath excited by a sense of wrong, or by meanness, injustice, wickedness, or misconduct; righteous or dignified anger ME. †**3.** The turning of the stomach against unwelcome food, etc. –1668.

2. Go, my puple..be hid a litil while, to the tyme that passe myn indignacioun WYCLIF *Isa.* 26:20. So great was the i. against Wolsey FROUDE. *fig.* Ready mounted are they to spit forth Their Iron i. 'gainst your walles SHAKS.

†**Indi·gnify,** *v.* 1595. [f. IN-[3] + DIGNIFY. Cf. med.L. *indignificare* render unworthy.] To treat with indignity; to dishonour; to represent as unworthy –1743.

Indignity (indi·gnĭti). 1584. [– Fr. *indignité* or L. *indignitas*, f. *indignus* INDIGN; see -ITY.] †**1.** The being unworthy; unworthiness. In *pl.*, Unworthy qualities. –1677. †**2.** The quality of being unbecoming, dishonourable, or disgraceful; want of dignity or honour. **b.** Disgraceful conduct; a disgraceful act. –1766. **3.** Unworthy treatment; contemptuous or insolent usage. With *an* and *pl.*: A slight; an insult or affront. 1584. †**4.** = INDIGNATION 2. –1784.

1. Accept my Zeale, and pardon mine Indignitie SYLVESTER. **2.** Oh, i.! oh, blot To honour and religion! MILT. *Sams.* 411. **3.** Their contempts and indignities offered to our Countrey and Prince HAKLUYT. **4.** God..took this their affront in high i. FULLER.

Indigo (i·ndigo), *sb.* (*a.*) 1555. [The usual form in XVI–XVII was *indico* – Sp. *indico* – L. *indicum* (Pliny) – Gr. *ἰνδικόν* (Dioscorides) the blue Indian dye, subst. use of n. of *Ἰνδικός* INDIAN. The form *indigo* (XVI) repr. Pg. *indigo*, which passed also into Fr., Du., G., and Russian.] **1.** A substance obtained in the form of a blue powder from plants of the genus *Indigofera*, N. O. *Leguminosæ*, and largely used as a dye.

It is produced by the decomposition of the glucoside INDICAN, which exists also in woad and various other plants. Its essential constituent is indigo-blue; besides which, however, *commercial* or *crude indigo* contains indigo-red, indigo-brown, and some earthy matters (indigo-gluten).

b. *pl.* Sorts or samples of indigo 1609. **2.** A plant from which indigo is obtained, INDIGO-PLANT, including several species of *Indigofera*; esp. *I. tinctoria*, *I. anil*, and *I. floribunda* 1600. **3.** The colour yielded by indigo, reckoned by Newton as one of the seven prismatic or primary colours 1622.

B. *adj.* (attrib. use of 3.) Of a deep violet-blue colour 1856.

A sky of..a streaky i. hue 1878.

Comb.: **i.-berry,** the fruit of *Randia latifolia* and *R. aculeata*, from which a blue dye is obtained; **-brown,** a brown resinous substance, a mixture of indihumin and indiretin, existing in all kinds of commercial i.; **-carmine,** indigo-disulphonate of sodium or potassium, used for dyeing silk and as a water-colour; **-copper,** the mineral COVELLINE; **-finch** = INDIGO-BIRD; **-gelatine, -gluten,** the glutinous matter found in commercial i.; **-green,** a green substance obtained from i. by adding potash to an alcoholic solution of an alkaline hyposulphindigotate; **-purple,** purple obtained from i. by the action of fused sodium sulphate; **-purpurin, -red,** synonyms of INDIRUBIN; **-snake** (*U.S.*), the gopher-snake; **-yellow,** 'a substance produced by heating hyposulphindigotate of calcium with lime-water in contact with air; it is a transparent yellow mass' (Watts).

I·ndigo-bi:rd. 1864. A N. American bird, a species of finch, *Cyanospiza cyanea*, family *Fringillidæ*, the male of which has the head and upper parts of rich indigo-blue.

Indigo-blue. 1712. **A.** *sb.* **1.** The blue-violet colour of indigo. **2.** The blue colouring matter of indigo, also called *indigotin*, crystallizing in fine right rhombic prisms of blue colour and metallic lustre; pure indigo 1838. **B.** *adj.* Of the blue colour of indigo 1836.

Indigogen (i·ndigo,dʒən). 1838. [f. INDIGO + -GEN 'producing'.] *Chem.* An obs. name for INDIGO-WHITE.

Indigometer (indigǫ·mǐtəɹ). 1828. [f. as prec. + -METER.] An instrument for ascertaining the strength of indigo. So **Indigo·metry,** the art or method of determining the colouring power of indigo.

Indigo-plant. 1757. A plant yielding indigo; *spec.* a plant of the genus *Indigofera.*

I·ndigotate. 1838. [f. as next + -ATE[4].] *Chem.* A salt of indigotic acid; a nitrosalicylate.

Indigotic (indigǫ·tik), *a.* 1838. [f. next + -IC.] Of, pertaining to, or produced from indigo.

I. acid, = ANILIC *acid.*

Indigotin (i·ndigotin). 1838. [– Fr. *indigotine* (also *indigoterie, -ier*), f. *indigo* INDIGO + *t* euphonic + *-ine*; see -IN[1], -INE[5].] *Chem.* = INDIGO-BLUE. Also *attrib.* and *Comb.*

Indigo-white. 1874. *Chem.* Reduced or deoxidized indigo, also called *leucindigo,* a white crystalline powder obtained by reduction from commercial indigo; it is reconverted by oxidation to indigo-blue.

Indihumin (indi,hiū·min). 1865. [f. INDI- + L. *humus* soil + -IN[1].] *Chem.* A product of the decomposition of indican, which occurs with indiretin in indigo-brown.

†**Indi·latory,** *a. rare.* 1654. [IN-[3].] Not dilatory.

†**Indi·ligence.** 1496. [– L. *indiligentia*; see IN-[3] and DILIGENCE.] **1.** Want of diligence –1658. **2.** Want of attention –1651. So †**Indi·ligent** *a.* idle, slothful; inattentive. †**Indi·ligently** *adv.*

Indime·nsional, *a.* 1875. [IN-[3].] Having no dimensions.

†**Indimi·nishable,** *a. rare.* 1641. [IN-[3].] That cannot be diminished or lessened –1799.

Indin (i·ndin). 1845. [f. IND- indigo- + -IN[1].] *Chem.* A crystalline substance of a beautiful rose-colour, isomeric with indigo-blue.

Indirect (indire·kt), *a.* 1474. [– (O)Fr. *indirect* or med.L. *indirectus*; see IN-[3], DIRECT *a.*] Not direct. **1.** Of a way, etc.: Not straight; crooked; devious; of a movement: Oblique. (Chiefly *fig.*) **b.** Of actions, etc.: Not straightforward; not fair and open; crooked, deceitful, corrupt 1570. **2.** Not taking the straight or nearest course to the end aimed at; roundabout 1584. **b.** *Logic.* 1727. **c.** *Pol. Econ.* Of taxation: Not levied directly upon the person on whom it ultimately falls 1801. **3.** *Gram.* Of speech or narration: Put in a reported form, not in the speaker's own words; oblique; opp. to *direct* 1866. **4.** Not directly aimed at or attained; not immediately resulting from an action or cause 1823.

1. Heauen knowes..By what by-pathes, and i. crook'd-ways I met this Crowne SHAKS. **b.** Livings..may not by corrupt and i. Dealings be transferred to other Uses 1570. **2.** Implicite or i. proofs WATERLAND. **b.** *I. Modes,* of syllogisms.. are the five last modes of the first figure..It is the conversion of the conclusion which renders the modes i. 1727. Showing that something impossible or absurd follows from contradicting our conclusion is called i. demonstration ABP. THOMSON. **c.** They [i. taxes] consist in the levy of imposts on articles of consumption [etc.] ROGERS. **4.** Happiness is not the direct aim, but the i. consequence of the good government JOWETT. Hence **Indire·ct-ly** *adv.*, **-ness.**

Indire·cted, *a. rare.* 1601. [IN-[3].] Not directed or guided –1819.

Indirection (indire·kʃən). 1595. [f. INDIRECT, after DIRECTION.] **1.** Indirect movement or action; roundabout means or method 1602. **2.** Want of straightforwardness in action; deceit; malpractice.

1. And thus doe we..By indirections finde directions out *Haml.* II. i. 65. **2.** *Jul. C.* IV. iii. 75.

Indiretin (indirī·tin). 1865. [f. INDI- + Gr. ῥητίνη resin + -IN[1].] *Chem.* A dark-brown shining resin, one of the components of indigo-brown, obtained from indican.

Indirubin (indirū·bin). 1859. [f. INDI- + L. *ruber* red + -IN[1].] *Chem.* A substance, isomeric with indigo-blue, obtained by decomposition of indican. Also called *indigopurpurin* and *indigo-red.*

Indiscernible (indizə̄·ɹnĭb'l). Also †**-able.** 1635. [f. IN-[3] + DISCERNIBLE; cf. Fr. *indiscernable.*] **A.** *adj.* **1.** Incapable of being discerned; imperceptible, undiscoverable. **2.** Indistinguishable. *Obs.* or *arch.* 1646.

1. A rapid look, i. by male eye READE.

B. *sb.* **1.** An animal, etc. that cannot be discerned by the senses. KIRBY. **2.** *Metaph.* A thing that cannot be distinguished from some other thing or things 1717.

2. Where there is no difference, there is no activity, and hence no substance or individuality. This is the meaning of the celebrated 'identity of indiscernibles' 1877. Hence **Indisce·rnibleness. Indisce·rnibly** *adv.*

†**Indisce·rpible,** *a.* 1659. [f. IN-[3] + †DISCERPIBLE.] = INDISCERPTIBLE –1839. Hence †**Indiscerpibi·lity,** †**Indisce·rpibleness.** †**Indisce·rpibly** *adv.*

Indiscerptible (indisə̄·ɹptĭb'l), *a.* 1736. [f. IN-[3] + DISCERPTIBLE.] Incapable of being divided into parts; not destructible by dissolution of parts.

The soul has no parts to be separated; in Butler's phrase, it is i. 1848. Hence **Indiscerptibi·lity, Indisce·rptibleness. Indisce·rptibly** *adv.*

Indisciplinable (indi·siplinăb'l), *a.* 1600. [f. IN-[3] + DISCIPLINABLE. Cf. Fr. *indisciplinable,* med.L. *indisciplinabilis.*] Incapable of being disciplined; intractable.

Indiscipline (indi·siplin). 1783. [f. IN-[3] + DISCIPLINE, or – Fr. *indiscipline.*] Absence or lack of discipline; want of the order and method acquired by training.

Indiscoverable (indiskɒ·vərăb'l), *a.* 1640. [IN-[3].] Not discoverable; undiscoverable.

†**Indiscovered,** *a.* [IN-[3].] Not discovered. COWLEY.

†**Indisco·very.** 1629. [IN-[3].] Non-discovery –1646.

Indiscreet (indiskrī·t), *a.* ME. [– L. *indiscretus* (see next), in med.L. sense careless, indiscreet. Cf. Fr. *indiscret* (XVI).] †**1.** Without sound judgement –1675. **2.** Imprudent in speech or action; inconsiderate; unadvised 1588.

1. I. chroniclers 1617. **2.** It would ill become me to be vaine, i., or a foole *L.L.L.* IV. ii. 31. Hence **Indiscree·t-ly** *adv.*, **-ness.**

Indiscrete (indiskrī·t), *a.* 1608. [– L. *indiscretus* unseparated, undistinguished, f. *in-* IN-[3] + *discretus* DISCRETE.] †**1.** Not distinctly distinguishable from contiguous objects or parts –1661. **2.** Not divided into distinct parts 1782.

2. Next all was water, all a chaos i. 1883. Hence **Indiscre·tely** *adv.* without separation or division.

Indiscretion (indiskre·ʃən). ME. [– (O)Fr. *indiscrétion* or late L. *indiscretio* lack of discernment (Jerome); see IN-[3], DISCRETION.] **1.** Want of discretion; in early use, chiefly, want of discernment or discrimination; in later, want of judgement; imprudence. **2.** An indiscreet act or step. (Sometimes *euphem.*, for an immoral act or practice.) 1601.

2. A youth, guilty only of an i. MACAULAY.

Indiscriminate (indiskri·minĕt), *a.* 1597. [f. IN-[3] + DISCRIMINATE *a.*] **1.** Of things: Not marked by discrimination or discernment; done without making distinctions; confused, promiscuous 1649. **2.** Of persons: Undiscriminating; making no distinctions 1792. **3.** quasi-*adv.* Indiscriminately 1597.

1. I. vengeance 1777, slaughter THIRLWALL, censure and applause STANLEY. **2.** An i. admirer 1840. Hence **Indiscri·minate-ly** *adv.*, **-ness.**

Indiscriminating (indiskri·mineᶦtiŋ), *a.* 1754. [IN-[3].] Not discriminating. Hence **Indiscri·minatingly** *adv.*

Indiscrimination (indiskriminē̆ᶦ·ʃən). 1649. [f. IN-[3] + DISCRIMINATION.] The fact of not discriminating; the condition of not being discriminated; absence of distinction; want of discernment.

Indiscriminative (indiskri·minĕtiv), *a.* 1854. [f. IN-[3] + DISCRIMINATIVE.] Not characterized by, or inclined to, discrimination. So †**Indiscri·minatively** *adv.* 1684.

†**Indiscu·ssed,** *a. rare.* 1534. [IN-[3].] Undiscussed –1631.

†**I·ndish,** *a.* 1548. [f. IND + -ISH[1].] = INDIAN *a.* –1601.

Indispensable (indispe·nsăb'l); *a.* (*sb.*) Also †**-ible.** 1533. [– med.L. *indispensabilis, -ibilis* in sense 1; see IN-[3], DISPENSABLE.] Not to be dispensed with. †**1.** Not subject to eccl. dispensation; not to be permitted, allowed, or condoned –1654. **2.** Of a law, duty, etc.: That cannot be remitted, set aside, or neglected 1649. **3.** That cannot be done without; absolutely necessary or requisite. Const. *to, for.* 1696. **4.** *sb.* An indispensable thing or person 1681. *pl.* (*colloq. euphemism*) Trousers 1841.

1. [He] absolutely condemnes this marriage as incestuous and i. BP. HALL. **2.** Our obligations to obey all God's commands..are absolute and i. BUTLER. **3.** The knowledge of anatomy is i. to him 1793. Hence **Indispensabi·lity, Indispe·nsableness. Indispe·nsably** *adv.*

†**Indispe·rsed,** *a. rare.* 1647. [IN-[3].] Undispersed –1686.

Indispose (indispō̆ᵘ·z), *v.* 1657. [f. IN-[3] + DISPOSE *v.*] **1.** To put out of the proper disposition for some action or result; to render unfit or incapable; to disqualify. **2.** To put out of health, disorder. (See INDISPOSED.) 1694. **3.** To affect with mental indisposition, disincline, render averse or unwilling 1692. **3.** To cause to be unfavourably disposed; to set at variance. (Now unusual.) 1748. **5.** To render not liable or subject (*to* something) 1822.

1. Not to get one's Sleep..indisposes one..for the Day 1863. **3.** Indisposing landlords to let long leases of farms MALTHUS. **4.** Polemical conversations..certainly do i., for a time, the contending parties towards each other CHESTERF. **5.** Inoculation indisposes the constitution to infection 1830.

Indisposed (indispō̆ᵘ·zd), *ppl. a.* late ME. [Partly – Fr. *indisposé* or L. *indispositus* disordered, unprepared; partly directly f. IN-[3] + DISPOSED *ppl. a.*] †**1.** Not put in order, out of order –1691. †**2.** Unfitted, unqualified –1646. †**3.** Evilly disposed, ill-conditioned 1464–1597. **4.** Out of health, unwell; not very well. (Mostly predicative.) 1598. **5.** Not disposed or inclined mentally or physically; unwilling, unfriendly (now *rare*) 1646. †**6.** Not disposed *of* –1694.

Hence **Indispo·sedness** (now *rare* or *Obs.*), the condition of being indisposed; indisposition.

Indisposition (i:ndispŏzi·ʃən). 1440. [– Fr. *indisposition* or f. IN-[3] + DISPOSITION, after prec.] The fact or condition of being indisposed. †**1.** Want of adaptation; unfitness; incapacity –1750. †**2.** Want of apt arrangement; displacement or misplacement; disorder –1677. †**3.** Evil disposition 1553. **4.** Disordered bodily condition; ailment; esp. of a slight character 1598. **5.** Disinclination, unwillingness 1594. **6.** The state of being unfavourably disposed *to* or *towards* 1647. **7.** The condition of not being liable or subject (*mod.*).

4. A long i. of Health hath much hindred..me HALE. **5.** A great i. to prayer 1628. **6.** An i. to the interests of Ireland BURKE. **7.** The two substances showed an i. to combine 1900.

Indisputable (indi·spiutăb'l, indispiū·tăb'l) *a.* 1551. [– late L. *indisputabilis*; see IN-[3], DISPUTABLE.] **1.** That cannot be disputed; unquestionable. †**2.** Undisputing. RICHARDSON. Hence **Indisputabi·lity, Indisputableness. Indisputably** *adv.*

†**Indispu·ted,** *a.* 1643. [IN-[3].] Not disputed –1804.

Indissociable (indisō̆ᵘ·ʃiăb'l), *a.* 1855. [IN-[3].] Incapable of being dissociated.

Indissoluble (indi·sǫliŭb'l, indisǫ·liŭb'l), *a.* 1542. [– L. *indissolubilis*; see IN-[3], DISSOLUBLE.] Not dissoluble. **1.** That cannot be dissolved or decomposed; that cannot be destroyed, put an end to, or abolished; indestructible 1568. †**2.** That cannot be dissolved in a liquid. (Repl. by INSOLUBLE.) –1794. **b.** That cannot be melted or liquefied. ?*Obs.* 1751. **3.** That cannot be dissolved, undone, or broken; firm, stable, lasting. (The prevailing sense.) 1542.

1. Well fenced with an i. wall P. HOLLAND. **2. b.** Some bodies, i. by heat, can set the furnace and crucible at defiance JOHNSON. **3.** An i. tye SHAKS., chain of circumstances PRIESTLEY. Hence **Indissolubility** (indi:sǫl-, indisǫ:liubi·liti), **Indissolubleness,** the quality of being i. **Indissolubly** *adv.*

†**Indisso·lvable,** *a.* Also †**-ible.** 1531. [IN-³.] = INDISSOLUBLE (in all senses) –1788. Hence †**Indissolvabi·lity,** †**Indisso·lvableness.** †**Indisso·lvably** *adv.*

†**Indi·stance.** 1624. [– med.L. *indistantia* nearness, f. as next; see IN-³, DISTANCE.] The quality or character of being 'indistant'. So †**Indi·stancy.** –1659.

†**Indi·stant,** *a.* 1644. [– *indistant-*, stem of med.L. *indistans*, contiguous, uninterrupted; see IN-³, DISTANT.] **1.** Not distant, not separated by an interval; continuous –1788. **2.** Without material extension. CUDWORTH. Hence †**Indi·stantly** *adv.*

Indistinct (indisti·ŋkt), *a.* late ME. [– L. *indistinctus*; see IN-³, DISTINCT. Cf. Fr. *indistinct* (XVI).] **1.** Not seen or heard clearly; confused, blurred; hence, faint, dim, obscure. Also *transf.* Also of the act of perception, or a perceiving faculty. **2.** Not distinct; not kept separate or apart in the mind or perception; not clearly defined or marked off 1604. **3.** Of judgement or action: Not distinguishing between different things; undiscriminating, indiscriminate. Now *rare* or *Obs.* 1650.

1. The public haunt. .Hums i. THOMSON. An i. recollection JOWETT. **2.** Three sacred persons in Trinitie, distinguished really, and yet i. essentially 1604. **3.** Some in an i. voracity eating almost any SIR T. BROWNE. So **Indisti·nctly** *adv.* 1420.

†**Indisti·nctible,** *a.* [app. f. IN-³ + †DISTINCT *v.* + -IBLE.] Undistinguishable. WARTON.

Indistinction (indisti·ŋkʃən). Now *rare.* 1624. [f. IN-³ + DISTINCTION, after *indistinct.*] **1.** The fact of not distinguishing. **2.** The condition or fact of not being distinct or different; undistinguishableness 1644. †**3.** Indistinctness, obscurity, dimness –1795.

1. That scandalous i. between the worthy and the worthless 1768. **2.** In a body there cannot be i. of parts, but each must possesse his own portion of parts JER. TAYLOR.

Indistinctive (indisti·ŋktiv), *a.* 1699. [f. IN-³ + DISTINCTIVE, after *indistinct.*] **1.** Not distinguishing; undiscriminating. **2.** Without distinctive character or features 1846. Hence **Indisti·nctive-ly** *adv.*, **-ness.**

Indisti·nctness. 1727. [f. INDISTINCT *a.* + -NESS.] The quality or condition of being indistinct; obscurity, dimness.

The ambiguity or i. of Terms WHATELY. I. of outline 1880.

Indistinguishable (indisti·ŋgwiʃăb'l), *a.* 1606. [IN-³.] **1.** Incapable of being discriminated or recognized as different *from* something else, or from each other 1658. **b.** *transf.* Of which the parts are not distinguishable 1606. **2.** That cannot be clearly perceived; not discernible; imperceptible 1642.

1. The true seeds of Cypresse and Rampions are i. by old eyes SIR T. BROWNE. **b.** You whorson i. Curre SHAKS. **2.** The. .i. lapse of time COLERIDGE. Hence **Indistinguishabi·lity, Indisti·nguishableness. Indisti·nguishably** *adv.*

Indisti·nguished, *a.* Now *rare.* 1605. [IN-³.] Not distinguished; undistinguished.

†**Indisti·nguishing,** *a.* 1828. [IN-³.] Undiscriminating; as, *i. liberalities.* (WEBSTER.)

Indistributable (indistri·biutăb'l), *a.* 1847. [IN-³.] That cannot be distributed.

Indisturbable (indistɔ̈·ɹbăb'l), *a.* 1660. [f. IN-³ + DISTURB + -ABLE.] Incapable of being disturbed.

Indisturbance (indistɔ̈·ɹbăns). Now *rare.* 1659. [IN-³.] Absence of disturbance; quietness, tranquillity.

†**Indi·tch,** *v.* 1597. [f. IN-¹ or ² + DITCH *sb.*] **1.** *trans.* To cast into or bury in (or as in) a ditch –1630. **2.** To surround with a ditch; to entrench –1610.

Indite (indəi·t), *v.* ME. [– OFr. *enditier* :– Rom. **indictare*; see INDICT *v.*¹] †**1.** *trans.* = DICTATE *v.* 1. Also *absol.* –1815. †**2.** = DICTATE *v.* 2. –1709. **3.** To put into words, compose (a poem, etc.); to express or describe in a literary composition ME. Also *absol.* or *intr.* **4.** *trans.* To put into written words, to pen; to set down in writing. In later use, passing into 3. ME. ¶**5.** *Catachr.* for *invite. Rom. & Jul.* II. iv. 135.

3. He hadde deuised his artycles so wysely, and endicted the[m] so well MORE. My heart is inditing a good matter *Ps.* 45:1. **4.** To endite Tickets for the Bear-garden MARVELL. Hence **Indi·tement,** composition in prose or verse. **Indi·ter,** one who indites, composes, or dictates, an author, writer, etc.

Indium (i·ndiɒ̆m). 1864. [f. radical of *ind-icum* INDIGO + *-ium*, after *sodium*, etc.; in reference to the two indigo lines which form the characteristic spectrum of the metal.] *Chem.* A soft silver-white metal of extreme rarity, occurring in association with zinc and other metals; discovered by means of spectrum analysis in the zinc-blende of Freiberg. Symbol In. Also *attrib.*

Indivertible (indivɔ̈·ɹtĭb'l), *a.* 1821. [f. IN-³ + DIVERTIBLE.] Incapable of being diverted or turned aside.

Indivi·dable, *a.* 1602. [IN-³.] Indivisible –1637.

†**Indivi·ded,** *a.* 1563. [IN-³.] Undivided –1695.

Individual (indivi·diu,ăl). ME. [– med.L. *individualis*, f. L. *individuus* indivisible, inseparable, f. *in-* IN-³ + *dividuus* divisible, f. *dividere* DIVIDE; see -AL¹.]

A. *adj.* †**1.** One in substance or essence; indivisible –1678. †**2.** Inseparable –1667. **3.** Existing as a separate indivisible entity; numerically one, single; particular, special 1613. †**b.** Identical, selfsame, very same –1804. **4.** Distinguished from others by attributes of its own 1646. **5.** Characteristic of an individual 1605.

1. The holy and indiuiduall Trinitie 1623. **2.** To have thee by my side Henceforth an i. solace dear MILT. *P.L.* IV. 486. **3.** Every man in his physical nature is one i. single agent BUTLER. A determination in each i. man to go his own way FROUDE. **b.** Which I do believe to be this i. Book 1701. **4.** He is so quaint and so i. in his views 1894. **5.** As touching the Manners of learned men, it is a thing personall and individuall BACON.

B. *sb.* †**1.** *pl.* Inseparable things; see A. 2. –1661. **2.** A single object or thing, or a group of things regarded as a unit; a single member of a class, group, or number 1605. **b.** *Logic* and *Metaph.* An object which is determined by properties peculiar to itself and cannot be sub-divided into others of the same kind; *spec.* in *Logic*, An object included in a species, as a species is in a genus 1628. **c.** *Zool.* and *Bot.* A single member of a species; a single specimen of an animal or plant 1859. **d.** *Biol.* An organism regarded as having a separate existence 1776. **3.** A single human being, as opp. to Society, the Family, etc. 1626. **b.** A human being, a person. (Now chiefly vulgar or disparaging.) 1742. †**4.** Short for *i. person*; person, personality, self –1800.

2. That individuals die, his will ordains DRYDEN. **3. b.** The i. whom I desired to meet KANE.

Individualism (indivi·diu,ăliz'm). 1835. [f. INDIVIDUAL + -ISM, after Fr. *individualisme.*] **1.** Self-centred feeling or conduct as a principle; free and independent individual action or thought; egoism. **2.** The social theory which advocates the free and independent action of the individual. Opp. to COLLECTIVISM and SOCIALISM. 1884. **3.** = INDIVIDUALITY 2, 3. 1854. **4.** *Philos.* **a.** The doctrine that reality is constituted of individual entities. **b.** The doctrine that the self is the only knowable existence; egoism. 1877.

Indivi·dualist. 1840. [f. as prec. + -IST, after Fr. *individualiste.*] An adherent of individualism. Also *attrib.* or as *adj.* Hence **Indivi:duali·stic** *a.* of or pertaining to individualism or individualists.

Individuality (individiu,æ·lĭti). 1614. [f. INDIVIDUAL *a.* + -ITY; in XVII – med.L. *individualitas.*] **1.** The state or quality of being indivisible or inseparable; an indivisible or inseparable entity 1645. **2.** The fact or condition of existing as an individual; separate and continuous existence 1658. **3.** The aggregate of properties peculiar to an individual; the sum of the attributes which distinguish an object from others of the same kind; individual character. **b.** Idiosyncrasy. 1614. **c.** *pl.* Individual characteristics 1647. **4.** An individual personality 1775.

1. There ought to be an i. in Mariage MILT. **3.** The Puritan i. is nowhere so overpowering as in Milton 1874. **4.** Here sit poor I, with nothing but my own solitary i. JOHNSON.

Individualize (indivi·diu,ălәiz), *v.* 1637. [f. as prec. + -IZE.] **1.** *trans.* To render individual; to characterize by distinctive marks or qualities; to mark out from other persons or things. Also *absol.* **2.** To specify, particularize. Also *absol.* 1656.

1. The peculiarities which i. and distinguish the humour of Addison 1805. Hence **I:ndividualiza·-tion.**

Individually (indivi·diu,ăli), *adv.* 1597. [f. as prec. + -LY².] †**1.** Indivisibly; inseparably, undividedly –1627. **2.** In individual identity. ? *Obs.* 1624. **3.** Personally; in an individual capacity 1660. **4.** In an individual or distinctive manner; as single persons or things; each by each, one by one; opp. to *collectively* 1641.

1. An attribute. .i. proper to the Godhead HAKEWILL. **2.** Phr. *I. the same*, identically the same. *I. different*, different as individuals (though possibly of the same species). **4.** The sacrifice which they collectively made was i. repaid to them JOWETT.

Indivi·duate, *ppl. a.* 1606. [– med.L. *individuatus*, pa. pple. of *individuare*; see next, -ATE².] †**1.** Undivided, indivisible, inseparable –1751. **2.** Rendered individual; individualized (*arch.*) 1606.

Individuate (indivi·diu,eᶦt), *v.* 1614. [– *individuat-*, pa. ppl. stem of med.L. *individuare* render individual, f. L. *individuus* INDIVIDUAL; see -ATE³.] **1.** *trans.* To form into an individual entity 1646. **2.** To give an individual character to; to distinguish from others of the same species; to individualize; to single out 1614. †**3.** To appropriate to an individual. TRAPP.

1. There was a seminality and contracted Adam in the rib, which. .was individuated into Eve SIR T. BROWNE. **2.** Circumstances i. actions 1641. Hence **Indivi·duator,** one who or that which individuates.

Individuation (i:ndividiu,ē̆ᶦ·ʃən). 1628. [– med.L. *individuatio*, f. as prec.; see -ION.] **1.** The action or process of individuating. *spec.* in Scholastic Philosophy, The process leading to individual existence, as distinct from that of the species. **2.** The condition of being an individual; individuality, personal identity 1642. **3. a.** *Biol.* The sum of the processes on which the life of the individual depends 1867. **b.** The unification of parts or forces necessary to constitute an individual or organic unity. MIVART.

†**Individu·ity.** 1605. [– med.L. *individuitas*, f. L. *individuus*; see INDIVIDUAL, -ITY. Cf. Fr. †*individuité* (XVI–XVII).] **1.** The quality of being indivisible –1695. **2.** The quality that constitutes an individual –1656.

†**Indivi·duous,** *a.* 1642. [f. L. *individuus* undivided, indivisible + -OUS.] Of undivided nature; indivisible. HY. MORE.

‖**Individuum** (indivi·diu,ɒ̆m). Pl. **-a, -ums.** 1555. [L. *individuum* indivisible particle, atom, in late L. an individual, subst. use of n. sing. of *individuus*; see prec. Treated as a Latin word in senses 1 and 2, but in 3 as naturalized, with pl. *-ums.*] **1.** The indivisible; an indivisible entity 1599; †an atom –1706. **2.** *Logic.* A member of a species 1555. **3.** An individual person or thing 1591.

2. Phr. *I. vagum*: something indicated as an individual, without specific identification: From particular propositions nothing can be concluded, because the *Individua vaga* are. .barren POPE.

†**Indivi·nity.** [IN-³.] Absence of divine character. SIR T. BROWNE.

Indivisible (indivi·zĭb'l). ME. [– late L. *indivisibilis*; see IN-³, DIVISIBLE. Cf. (O)Fr. *indivisibilité.*]

A. *adj.* Not divisible; incapable of being divided, distributed, or †separated.

Dominion (that is) supreme power is i., insomuch as no man can serve two Masters HOBBES.

B. *sb.* That which is indivisible; an infinitely small particle or quantity 1644.

One instant or i. or time DIGBY. *Method of indivisibles*: a method of calculating areas, volumes, etc., based on the conception of indivisibles, published by Bonaventura in 1635. Hence **Indivisibi·lity, Indivi·sibleness. Indivi·sibly** *adv.*

Indivision (indivi·ʒən). 1624. [– late L. *indivisio* (Boethius); see IN-³, DIVISION. Cf. Fr. *indivision* (XVI).] Absence of division; undivided condition.

Indo-¹ (i·ndo), comb. f. Gr. Ἰνδός, L. *Indus*, employed in modern compounds, in which it qualifies another word, sb. or adj., or denotes the combination of Indian with some other characteristic (chiefly ethnological); as *I.-British, -Briton, -English,* etc.; **I.-Chinese,** belonging to Further India, or the region between India and China; etc.

Indo-[2]. Bef. a vowel **ind-**. [f. Gr. Ἰνδός, L. *Indus,* as root of *indicum* INDIGO.] *Chem.* A formative of names of compound bodies relating to indigo, or belonging to the INDOLE group; see INDOGEN, etc.

†**Indo·cible,** *a.* 1555. [– Fr. †*indocible* or late L. *indocibilis,* or f. IN-[3] + DOCIBLE.] Incapable of being taught or instructed; unteachable –1774. Hence †**Indocibi·lity,** †**Indo·cibleness.**

Indocile (indō^u·səil, -dǫ·sil), *a.* 1603. [– Fr. *indocile* or L. *indocilis,* or f. IN-[3] + DOCILE.] Unwilling or unapt to be taught; not readily submitting to instruction or guidance; intractable. Hence **Indocility** (indosi·lĭti) 1648.

Indoctrinate (indǫ·ktrineˈt), *v.* Also †**en-.** 1578. [f. †*indoctrine* (see below), earlier *en-* (– OFr. *endoctriner*) + -ATE[3]; or f. IN-[2] + DOCTRINATE.] **1.** *trans.* To imbue with learning, to teach. **b.** To instruct *in* a subject, principle, etc. 1656. **c.** To imbue *with* a doctrine, idea, or opinion 1832. **d.** To bring *into* a knowledge of something 1841. **2.** To teach, inculcate (a subject, etc.) (*rare*) 1800.

1. They are altogether unlearned, even the Priests meanly indoctrinated HEYLIN. **c.** Fully indoctrinated with a sense of the magnitude of their office M. ARNOLD. Hence **Indo:ctrina·tion,** instruction; formal teaching. var. †**Indo·ctrine** *v.* 1450.

I:ndo-Europe·an. 1814. [f. INDO-[1] + EUROPEAN.]

A. *adj.* Common to India and Europe; applied to the great family or class of cognate languages (also called INDO-GERMANIC and ARYAN, q.v.) spoken over the greater part of Europe and extending into Asia as far as northern India, and to the race or its divisions using one or other of these languages. **b.** Pertaining or belonging to the Indo-European family of languages or peoples, as *Indo-European root, philology, culture,* etc.

B. *sb.* A member of the Indo-European race; an Aryan 1871.

Indogen (i·ndŏdʒĕn). 1886. [f. INDO-[2] + -GEN 1.] *Chem.* A name for the group $C_6H_4\langle{}^{CO}_{NH}\rangle C$, the double molecule of which (di-indogen) constitutes indigo-blue. **Indo·genide,** any compound of i. with another radical.

I:ndo-Ge·rman, *a. rare.* 1826. = next.

I:ndo-Germa·nic, *a.* 1835. [f. INDO-[1] + GERMANIC, after G. *indogermanisch* (Klaproth *Asia Polyglotta,* 1823, repr. the extreme terms of his *Indisch-Medisch-Sclavisch-Germanisch*).] = INDO-EUROPEAN *a.,* ARYAN *a.* (The term is faulty as not including Celtic.) Hence **I:ndo-Ge·rmanist,** a student of Indo-Germanic philology.

Indoin (i·ndoˌin). 1884. [f. INDO-[2] + -IN[1].] *Chem.* A blue dye-stuff, related to indigo.

Indole (i·ndō^u l). Also (*improp.*) **indol.** 1869. [f. INDO-[2] + *-ole* (from L. *oleum* oil); see -OL 3.] *Chem.* A crystalline substance, also called *ketole,* formed in large shining colourless laminæ, having a peculiar odour; it is obtained artificially by reduction of indigo-blue; *pl.* alkylated derivatives of indole.

I. group, the group including indole, isatin, indigo, and related compounds and derivatives.

Indolence (i·ndŏlĕns). 1603. [– Fr. *indolence* or L. *indolentia* freedom from pain, f. as next; see -ENCE.] †**1.** Insensibility to pain; want of feeling –1723. †**2.** Freedom from pain; a neutral state, in which neither pain nor pleasure is felt –1751. **3.** The disposition to avoid trouble; love of ease; laziness; sluggishness 1710.

2. I. is like the state of a sleeping Man STANLEY. **3.** Some men fail as preachers through intellectual i. 1878. So †**I·ndolency,** in all senses.

Indolent (i·ndŏlĕnt), *a.* (*sb.*) 1663. [– late L. *indolens, -ent-,* f. *in-* IN-[3] + pr. pple. of *dolēre* suffer pain, give pain; see -ENT. Cf. Fr. *indolent.*] **1.** *Path.* Causing no pain, painless; esp. in *i. tumour, ulcer.* **2.** Averse to toil or exertion; slothful, lazy, idle 1710. †**3.** *sb.* An indolent person –1810.

2. A good-natured i. Man STEELE. Hence **I·ndolent-ly** *adv.,* **-ness.**

‖**Indoles** (i·ndoliz). *rare.* 1673. [L., f. *indu-* in, within + **ol-* grow (cf. ADULT, etc.).] Innate quality or character.

Indoline (i·ndoləin). 1884. [f. INDOLE + -INE[5].] *Chem.* A polymer of indole, formed by heating leucindigo with barium hydrate, zinc-dust, and water, crystallizing in long bright yellow needles.

†**Indo·mable,** *a. rare.* 1450. [– Fr. †*indomable* or L. *indomabilis,* f. *in-* IN-[3] + *domabilis* tameable, f. *domare* tame; see -BLE.] Untameable –1728.

Indomitable (indǫ·mităb'l), *a.* 1634. [– late L. *indomitabilis,* f. *in-* IN-[3] + *domitare*; see DAUNT, -ABLE.] **1.** Untameable. ? *Obs.* **2.** That cannot be overcome or subdued by labour, difficulties, or opposition; unyielding. Usually approbative. (The ordinary use.) 1830.

1. I. pride SCOTT. **2.** I. strength 1830, energy 1865. Hence **Indomitabi·lity, Indo·mitableness,** the quality of being i. **Indo·mitably** *adv.*

Indonesian (indonī·ʃ^iăn). 1881. [f. INDO-[1] + Gr. νῆσος island + -IAN.] **a.** *adj.* Of or belonging to the East Indian islands. **b.** *sb.* An inhabitant of these islands.

Indoor, in-door (i·ndō^əɹ), *a.* (*adv.*) 1711. [For earlier *within-door* (Bacon).] **1.** Pertaining to the interior of a house, etc.; situated or done within doors or under cover. **b.** Within the workhouse or poorhouse 1864. **2.** *adv.* = next. TENNYSON.

1. b. I. and outdoor poor 1864. I. relief FAWCETT.

Indoors, in-doors (i:ndō^ə·ɹz), *adv.* 1799. [repr. earlier *within doors.*] Within or into a house, etc.; under cover. †**b.** *attrib.* = IN-DOOR *adj.* WASHINGTON.

Indophenol (-fī·nǫl). 1892. [f. INDO-[2] + PHENOL.] *Chem.* A coal-tar colour used in dyeing, produced by the simultaneous oxidation of a phenol and a paradiamine; one of its commercial forms is *naphthol blue.*

Indorsation (indǫɹsēˈ·ʃən). 1540. [f. *indorse,* ENDORSE *v.*; chiefly *Sc.*] Indorsement.

Indo·rse, etc., variant of ENDORSE, etc.

Indorse is the form found in legal and statutory use; it is also approved in all American Dicts.; but *Endorse* is now almost universal in Eng. commercial use.

Indow, -ment, obs. ff. ENDOW, -MENT.

Indoxyl (indǫ·ksil). 1886. [f. INDO-[2] + OX(Y- 2 + -YL.] *Chem.* A brownish oil, isomeric with oxindole, formed when indoxylic acid is heated above its melting-point. Hence **Indoxy·lic** *a.,* in *I. acid,* a white crystalline precipitate, slightly soluble in water; its salts are **Indo·xylates.**

†**Indrape,** *v.* 1622. [f. IN-[2] + DRAPE *v.*] *trans.* To make into cloth; to weave –1843.

Indraught, indraft (i·nˌdrɑft). 1570. [f. IN *adv.* + DRAUGHT; cf. OUTDRAUGHT.] **1.** The act of drawing in; inward attraction 1682. **2.** An inward flow, stream, or current, as of water or air; *esp.* a current setting towards the land or up an estuary, etc. Also *transf.* and *fig.* 1594. †**3.** A place where the water flows into the land; an inlet; inward passage. Also *fig.* –1706.

2. To avoid the I. of the Bay or Gulf of Mexico DE FOE.

Indraw·al. 1869. [f. IN *adv.* + DRAW *v.,* after *withdrawal.*] = prec.

I·ndraw:ing, *ppl. a.* 1598. [IN *adv.*] That draws in or inward.

Like some old wreck on some i. sea TENNYSON.

Indrawn, *ppl. a.* 1751. [IN *adv.*] Drawn in. **a.** as *adj.,* or bef. sb. (i·nˌdrǭn). **b.** as *pple.,* or after sb. (inˌdrǭ·n) 1865.

†**Indre·nch,** *v.* Also †**en-.** 1593. [f. IN-[2], EN-[1] + DRENCH *v.*] *trans.* To drench or drown in something; to immerse –1609.

‖**Indri** (i·ndri). Also **indris.** 1839. [A Malagasy exclam. *indry!* 'lo! behold!', or *indry izy* 'there he is', mistaken by Sonnerat for the name of the animal; the only Malagasy name is *babakoto,* lit. 'father-child'.] A name given to the BABACOOTE, a lemurine animal of Madagascar (*Indris* or *Lichanotus brevicaudatus*), living in trees, with soft woolly hair, very long hind legs, and very short tail.

Indubious (indiū·biəs), *a.* 1624. [f. L. *indubius* + -OUS, or f. IN-[3] + DUBIOUS.] **1.** Not admitting of doubt; indubitable. †**2.** Feeling no doubt; free from doubt 1665.

1. Am I not free to attend for the ripe and i. instinct? CLOUGH.

Indubitable (indiū·bităb'l), *a.* (*sb.*) 1625. [– Fr. *indubitable* or L. *indubitabilis,* or f. IN-[3] + DUBITABLE.] That cannot be doubted; perfectly certain or evident. As *sb.* An indubitable thing or fact. WATTS. Hence **Indu·bitableness. Indu·bitably** *adv.* unquestionably.

†**Indu·bitate,** *a.* 1475. [– L. *indubitatus,* f. *in-* IN-[3] + *dubitatus,* pa. pple. of *dubitare* DOUBT *v.*; see -ATE[2].] Undoubted –1678. So †**Indu·bitated** 1641.

†**Indu·bitate,** *v. rare.* 1646. [– *indubitat-,* pa. ppl. stem of L. *indubitare* doubt, f. *in-* IN-[2] + *dubitare* DOUBT *v.*; see -ATE[3].] *trans.* To render doubtful or uncertain; to call in question –1660.

To i. a thing of so constant credit 1660.

Induce (indiū·s), *v.* ME. [– L. *inducere,* f. *in-* IN-[2] + *ducere* lead; from XIV to XVIII often with *en-* after Fr. *enduire* (cf. ENDUE).] **1.** *trans.* To lead (a person) by persuasion or some influence *to* (†*into,* †*unto*) some action, condition, belief, etc.; to move, influence, prevail upon (any one) *to do* something. **2.** To bring in, introduce. *Obs.* or blended with 3. ME. **3.** To bring about, bring on, produce, cause, give rise to ME. **b.** *spec.* To produce (an electric current or magnetic state) by induction 1812. †**4.** To lead to (something) as a conclusion or inference; to suggest, imply –1646. **5.** To infer; *esp.* in recent use, to derive as an induction 1563. †**6.** To draw (something) on or over –1784.

1. If he coulde not by fayre and gentle speche i. them vnto his opinion 1551. These considerations i. me to believe [etc.] 1796. **2.** To i. peace HALL, doubt into a question PALEY. A thinge written by me to i. children to the latin tongue 1556. **3.** Gentle walking without inducing fatigue 1780. **5.** From a sufficient number of results a proposition or law is induced 1888. Hence **Indu·cer.**

Induced (indiū·st), *ppl. a.* 1585. [f. prec. + -ED[1].] In the senses of the vb. (see esp. INDUCE *v.* 3 b).

Induced current, an electric current excited by INDUCTION. *I. magnet,* a magnet affected by induction.

Inducement (indiū·smĕnt). 1594. [f. as prec. + -MENT.] †**1.** The action of inducing –1648. **2.** That which induces; something attractive by which a person is led on or persuaded to action 1594; †an incentive –1691. †**3.** A preamble or introduction to a book or subject –1617. **b.** *Law.* (See below.) 1792. †**4.** A leading to some conclusion or inference; that which leads to a conclusion. SIR T. BROWNE.

2. Inducements to foreign artisans to come over and settle in this country SMILES. **3. b.** *Matters of i.* (Law): introductory averments stating the circumstances, etc., leading up to the matter in dispute, but not stating such matter.

Indu·cible, *a. rare.* 1643. [f. INDUCE *v.* + -IBLE.] **1.** Capable of being brought on, brought about, or caused 1677. †**2.** Capable of being inferred. SIR T. BROWNE.

Induct (indɒ·kt), *v.* ME. [– *induct-,* pa. ppl. stem of L. *inducere* INDUCE.] **1.** *trans. Eccl.* To introduce formally into possession of a benefice or living. **b.** To introduce into office 1548. **c.** To install in a seat, room, etc. 1706. **2.** To lead, conduct *into* (*lit.* and *fig.*) (*rare*) 1600. **3.** To introduce (*to*); to initiate (*into*) 1603. **4.** *absol.* To form an induction WHEWELL. **5.** *Electr.* = INDUCE *v.* 3 b. 1839.

1. c. Inducting himself into the pulpit SCOTT.

Inductance (indɒ·ktăns). 1888. [f. prec. + -ANCE.] *Electr.* Capacity for magnetic induction; also, self-induction, or the coefficient of self-induction. *ellipt.* = i. coil.

attrib. **i. coil,** a coil of large inductance; *spec.* a wireless tuning coil.

Inductile (indɒ·ktil, -təil), *a.* 1736. [f. IN-[3] + DUCTILE. Cf. Fr. *inductile.*] Not ductile; not pliable; unyielding to influences. Hence **Inducti·lity.**

Induction (indɒ·kʃən). ME. [– (O)Fr. *induction* or L. *inductio,* f. *induct-,* pa. ppl. stem of *inducere* INDUCE; see -ION.] †**1.** The action of inducing by persuasion; inducement –1588. **2.** The action of initiating in the knowledge of something; the process of being initiated; introduction, initiation.

Now *rare*. 1526. **3.** An introduction; a preface, preamble (*arch.*) 1533. †**b.** An initial step in any undertaking. SHAKS. **4.** *Eccl.* The action of formally introducing a clergyman into a benefice, together with all rights, profits, etc. pertaining to it ME. **b.** *gen.* The formal introduction to an office, position, or possession; installation 1460. **5.** The action of introducing (a person, custom, etc.). *rare.* 1604. **6.** The adducing *of* a number of separate facts, particulars, etc., esp. for the purpose of proving a general statement 1551. **7.** *Logic.* The process of inferring a general law or principle from the observation of particular instances (opp. to DEDUCTION, q.v.) 1553; a conclusion derived from induction; formerly used in the wider sense of 'inference' 1440. **8.** *Math.* The process of proving that a theorem is true, because it *is* true in a certain case, and therefore in the next case, and hence in the next but one, and so on 1838. **9.** *Electr.* and *Magnetism.* The action of inducing or bringing about an electric or magnetic state in a body by the proximity (without contact) of an electrified or magnetized body 1812.

2. I have never yet seen any service, and must have my i. some time or other DE FOE. **3.** That which hee takes for the second Argument..is no argument, but an i. to those that follow MILT. **b.** These promises are faire, the parties sure, And our i. full of prosperous hope SHAKS. **7.** You must take up with I., and bid adieu to Demonstration BERKELEY. The contrast between his wide inductions and the apparently flimsy foundations on which they are made to rest 1868. **9.** Phr. *Electrodynamic* or *voltaic i.*, the production of an electric current (*induced current*) by the influence of another independent current. *Electromagnetic i.*, the production of a state of magnetic polarity in a body near or round which an electric or galvanic current passes, or the generation of an electric current by the action of a magnet (the latter called more properly *magneto-electric i.*). *Electrostatic i.*, the production of an electrical charge upon a body by the influence of a neighbouring body charged with statical electricity, as exemplified in Volta's electrophorus. *Magnetic i.*, the production of magnetic properties in iron or other substances when placed in a magnetic field. *Mutual i.*, the reaction of two electric circuits upon each other; *self-i.*, the reaction of different parts of the same circuit upon each other.

Comb.: (sense 9) **i.-balance,** an electrical apparatus so contrived that the currents induced in the secondary wires of two induction-coils balance each other; **-coil,** an apparatus for producing electric currents by induction, consisting of two separate coils of wire generally surrounding a soft-iron core, the primary coil being connected with an external source of electricity, and having an arrangement for causing the electric current to vary in intensity, the effect of which is to produce a current of different character in the secondary coil; (sense 3) **-pipe,** the pipe through which the live steam is introduced into the cylinder of a steam-engine; **-port,** the opening by which steam passes from the steam-chest into the cylinder; **-valve,** the valve which controls the passage of steam into the cylinder. Hence **Indu·ctional** *a.* of, pertaining to, or of the nature of i.

Inductive (indɒ·ktiv), *a.* 1607. [– late L. *inductivus* hypothetical (Priscian), in med.L. inducing, leading to, f. as prec.; see -IVE. Cf. (O)Fr. *inductif, -ive.*] **1.** Leading on (*to* some action, etc.); inducing. †**2.** Productive *of* –1772. **3.** *Logic.* Of the nature of, based upon, or using induction 1764. **4.** Of the nature of, pertaining to, or due to electric or magnetic induction 1849. **5.** Introductory 1868.

1. Ungovern'd appetite..a brutish vice, I. mainly to the sin of Eve MILT. *P.L.* XI. 519. **3.** The i. mind of a Davy or a Faraday 1842. **4.** I. retardation in long ocean cables 1879. Hence **Indu·ctive-ly** *adv.* by i. reasoning; by electric induction; **-ness.** **Inducti·vity,** inductive quality 1888.

Inducto- (indɒ·kto), comb. form of INDUCTION; as in:

Inducto·meter, an instrument for ascertaining the force of electrical induction 1839.

Inductor (indɒ·ktəɹ). 1652. [– late L. *inductor*, f. *induct-* INDUCT; see -OR 2. In senses 2 and 3 f. INDUCT + -OR 2.] **1.** One who introduces or initiates (*rare*). **2.** One who inducts a clergyman to a benefice 1726. **3.** Any part of an electric apparatus which acts inductively on another 1849.

Inductorium (indɒktōᵊ·riɒm). 1875. [f. INDUCT *v.* 5, or the stem of INDUCTION 9 + -ORIUM.] A name for the induction-coil as adapted for the display of the electric spark.

Indu·ctory, *a.* 1632. [var. of INDUCTIVE 1 by substitution of suffix, or f. INDUCT *v.*; see -ORY[2].] Introductory.

†**Indu·ctric,** *a.* 1849. [irreg. f. INDUCTION, after *electric.*] *Electr.* Operating by induction. So **Indu·ctrical** *a.*

Indue, etc., var. of ENDUE, etc.

Indulge (indɒ·ldʒ), *v.* 1638. [– L. *indulgēre* (perh. orig.) allow space or time for, (hence) give rein to.]

I. *trans.* **1.** To treat (a person) with complaisance; to gratify by compliance, or by absence of restraint or strictness; to humour. Const. *in.* 1660. Also *fig.* **b.** *refl.* To give free course to one's inclination; to take one's pleasure. Const. *in.* 1659. **c.** To gratify (a person) *with* something given or granted 1790. **2.** To grant an indulgence to; see INDULGENCE *sb.* II. 1662. **3.** To gratify (a desire or inclination); to give oneslf up to, yield to. Occas. merely: To entertain, cherish. 1656. **4.** To bestow or grant (something) as a favour, or as a matter of free grace; to concede as an indulgence. Now *rare.* 1638. **5.** *Comm.* To grant an indulgence on (a bill). Cf. INDULGENCE *sb.* II. 3. 1766.

1. b. Pleasing anticipations in which he indulged himself MAR. EDGEWORTH. **3.** To i. my own fancy, I began to compile this work BLOUNT. **4.** Scarce indulging himself necessary Relaxations 1648.

II. *intr.* (with prep.) †**1.** *Indulge to*: to grant indulgence *to*, to give way to, gratify (a propensity = I. 3; rarely a person = I. 1) –1790. **2.** *Indulge in* (ellipt. for *indulge oneself in*, I. 1 b): To give free course to one's inclination for; to take one's pleasure freely in 1706.

2. Any little amusement in which he could i. DICKENS. Hence †**Indu·lgement,** indulgence. **Indu·lger.** **Indu·lgingly** *adv.*

Indulgence (indɒ·ldʒĕns), *sb.* ME. [– (O)Fr. *indulgence* – L. *indulgentia*, f. *indulgent-*; see INDULGENT, -ENCE.]

I. *gen.* **1.** The action of indulging (a person), or the fact of being indulgent; favouring forbearance or relaxation of restraint. Sometimes dyslogistic: Over-lenient treatment **b.** With *an* and *pl.* An instance of this 1591. **2.** The action of indulging (desire, inclination, etc.); the yielding to some propensity (const. *of*, *in*, †*to*); the action of indulging *in* some practice, luxury, etc. 1638. Also *absol.*

1. Left to her self..Shee first his weak i. will accuse MILT. *P.L.* IX. 1186. **b.** He..supplied [them] with every i. MACAULAY. **2.** The i. of private malice 1769. I. in Sin 1843. *absol.* To grow Rich, that he may live in figure and i. LAW.

II. *spec.* (from I. 1 b). **1.** *R. C. Ch.* 'A remission of the punishment which is still due to sin after sacramental absolution, this remission being valid in the court of conscience and before God, and being made by an application of the treasure of the Church on the part of a lawful superior' ME. **2.** *Eng. Hist.* Applied to the grant or offer to Nonconformists, in the reigns of Charles II and James II, of certain religious liberties as special favours, but not as legal rights 1672. **3.** *Comm.* An extension, made as a favour, of the time within which a bill of exchange or a debt is to be paid 1827.

1. Among others he had recourse to a sale of Indulgences ROBERTSON. **2.** *Declaration of Indulgence*, a royal proclamation, e.g. that of Charles II in 1672, offering certain religious liberties.

Indu·lgence, *v.* 1599. [f. prec. sb.] †**1.** *trans.* = INDULGE *v.* I. 4. **2.** *R. C. Ch.* To attach an indulgence to (a particular act or object); see next 1866.

Indulgenced (indɒ·ldʒĕnst), *ppl. a.* 1841. [f. prec. sb. or vb. + -ED.] *R. C. Ch.* Having an indulgence attached to it; applied to prayers, material objects, etc., the use of which is declared to convey an indulgence.

Indulgency (indɒ·ldʒĕnsi). Now *rare.* 1547. [– L. *indulgentia*; see INDULGENCE, -ENCY.] = INDULGENCE *sb.* I. 1, 2, II. 1.

Indulgent (indɒ·ldʒĕnt), *a.* 1509. [– Fr. *indulgent* or L. *indulgentia*, f. *indulgent-*, pr. ppl. stem of *indulgēre*; see INDULGE, -ENT.] **1.** That indulges or tends to indulge; disposed to comply with desire or humour or to overlook faults or failings; not strict or severe; not exercising restraint. Often dyslogistically, Not exercising due restraint, weakly lenient. Also *fig.* of things. †**2.** SELF-INDULGENT –1705.

1. Such in thy behalf shall be Th' i. censure of posterity WALLER. The most i. of landlords 1839. *fig.* I. summer 1860. **2.** The feeble old, i. of their ease DRYDEN. Hence **Indu·lgent-ly** *adv.*, **-ness.**

†**Indulge·ntial,** *a.* [– med.L. *indulgentialis* in *littera indulgentialis* XIII), f. L. *indulgentia*; see INDULGENCE, -AL[1].] Of or pertaining to indulgences; see INDULGENCE *sb.* II. 1. BREVINT.

†**Indu·lgiate,** *v. rare.* 1615. [irreg. f. INDULGE *v.* + -ATE[3].] *trans.* = INDULGE *v.* –1628.

Induline (i·ndiŭləin). 1882. [f. IND(O-[2] + *-ul-* dim. + -INE[5].] *Chem.* A general name for a series of compounds related to aniline, yielding blue-black, blue, and greyish dyes, known in commerce as nigrosine, violaniline, Elberfeld blue, aniline grey, etc.

Indult (indɒ·lt). 1535. [– Fr. *indult* – late L. *indultum* grant, concession (med.L. spec. in eccl. use), subst. use of n. of *indultus*, pa. pple. of *indulgēre* INDULGE.] †**1.** A special privilege granted by authority –1625. **2.** *R. C. Ch.* 'A licence or permission granted by the Pope..authorising something to be done which the common law of the Church does not sanction' (*Cath. Dict.*) 1536. **3.** *Hist.* A duty paid to the king of Spain or Portugal on imported goods. (Dicts.) So ‖**Indulto** [Sp. and Pg.], in all senses 1645.

†**Indument.** 1494. [In I – L. *indumentum* garment; in II = ENDUEMENT, ENDOWMENT.]

I. 1. Clothing, investiture; a garment, robe, vesture. Also *fig.* –1684. **2.** *Nat. Hist.* A covering, as of hair, feathers, etc.; an integument; an investing membrane. (Also in L. form *indumentum.*) –1864.

II. 1. = ENDUEMENT –1659. **2.** = ENDOWMENT 1602.

‖**Induna** (indū·nă). 1875. [Zulu, f. nominal prefix *in-* + stem *duna* (cf. *iduna*, pl. *amaduna*) male, sire, lord.] An officer under the king or chief of the Zulus, Matabele, and other S. African tribes.

Induplicate (indiū·plikĕt), *a.* 1830. [IN-[2] + DUPLICATE *a.*] *Bot.* Folded or rolled in at the edges, without overlapping; said of leaves and petals in vernation or æstivation. So **Induplica·tion,** folding or doubling in; an example of this. **Induplica·tive** *a.* = INDUPLICATE.

Indurance, obs. f. ENDURANCE.

Indurate (i·ndiurĕt), *ppl. a.* Now *rare.* ME. [– L. *induratus*, pa. pple. of *indurare*; see next, -ATE[2].] **1.** Made hard, hardened 1530. **2.** Of persons, etc.: Morally hardened, rendered callous; also, stubborn, obstinate.

2. They are as indurat as Pharaoh 1667.

Indurate (i·ndiureᵗt), *v.* 1538. [– *indurat-*, pa. ppl. stem of L. *indurare* make hard, f. *in-* IN-[2] + *durus* hard; see -ATE[3].] **1.** *trans.* To make hard or hardy; to harden 1575. **2.** To harden (the heart, etc.); to render callous or unfeeling; to make stubborn 1538. **3.** *intr.* To become or grow hard; (of a custom) to become fixed 1626.

1. They [slaves] had been indurated to want, exposure and toil 1879. **2.** More like to i. than to mollify LATIMER. **3.** The prescription will soon grow, and began to i. 1881. Hence **I·ndurative** *a.* of hardening tendency or quality 1592.

Induration (indiurēⁱ·ʃən). ME. [– (O)Fr. *induration* or late L. *induratio*, f. as prec.; see -ION.] **1.** The action of hardening; the process of being hardened or becoming hard; also, hardened condition. Now chiefly in *Geol.* or *Path.* **2.** A hardening of character or feeling; stubbornness; callousness 1493.

2. To what a degree of i. and searedness must you have brought yourself 1873.

Indusial (indiū·ziăl), *a.* 1833. [f. INDUSIUM + -AL[1].] *Geol.* Containing, or composed of, indusia or larva-cases.

I. limestone, a form of freshwater limestone in Auvergne, so called from the cases of the larvæ of Phryganea, great heaps of which have been encrusted, as they lay, and formed into a rock. LYELL.

Indusiate (indiū·ziĕt), *ppl. a.* 1830. [f. INDUSIUM + -ATE[2].] *Bot.* Furnished with an indusium. So **Indu·siated.**

Indusiform (indiū·zifǭɹm), *a.* 1857. [f.

INDUSIUM + -FORM.] *Bot.* Having the shape of an indusium.

||**Indusium** (indiū·ziŏm). Pl. **-ia.** 1706. [L. 'tunic', f. *induere* put on (a garment).] **1.** *Anat.* The amnion of the fœtus. **2.** *Bot.* **a.** The membranous scale covering the sorus of a fern 1807. **b.** A collection of hairs united into a sort of cup, and enclosing the stigma in the *Goodeniaceæ*. LINDLEY. **3.** *Entom.* The case of a larva 1832.

Industrial (indɒ·striăl). 1590. [The first ex. (XVI) is of fruits produced by labour (so Fr. †*industrial*); later partly – Fr. *industriel*, partly f. INDUSTRY + -AL[1].]

A. *adj.* Pertaining to, or of the nature of, industry or productive labour; resulting from industry. Of persons: Engaged in or connected with an industry or industries. **b.** Of a quality suitable only for industrial use 1904.

Industrial school: a school for teaching one or more branches of industry; *spec.* a school established for the compulsory attendance of neglected children, where they are instructed in some industry or trade.

B. *sb.* **1.** One engaged in industrial pursuits 1865. **2.** *pl.* Shares in a joint-stock industrial enterprise 1894.

Hence **Indu·strialize** *v.*, **Indu·strially** *adv.*

Indu·strialism. 1831. [f. prec. + -ISM. Cf. Fr. *industrialisme.*] A system of things arising from or involving the existence of great industries; the organization of industrial occupations. So **Indu·strialist,** a worker or manufacturer.

Industrious (indɒ·striəs). *a.* 1523. [– Fr. *industrieux* or late L. *industriosus*, f. *industria*; see next, -OUS.] Characterized by industry. †**1.** Skilful, able, clever, ingenious –1687. **2.** Characterized by application; painstaking, zealous, attentive, careful 1552. †**3.** Intentional, designed, purposed, voluntary –1817. **4.** Characterized by or showing assiduous and steady work. (The prevailing sense.) 1591.

2. I. to seeke out the trueth of these thinges SPENSER. I. after wisdom MILT., of the common good DRYDEN. **4.** Solomon seeing the young man that he was i. 1 *Kings* 11:28. I. habits GOLDSM., toil COWPER. Hence **Indu·strious-ly** *adv.*, **-ness.**

Industry (i·ndŏstri). 1477. [– (O)Fr. *industrie* or L. *industria* diligence; see -Y[3].] †**1.** Intelligent or clever working; skill, ingenuity, dexterity –1613. †**2.** A device, contrivance; a crafty expedient –1621. **3.** Diligence or assiduity in any task or effort; close and steady application to the business in hand 1531. **4.** Systematic work or labour; habitual employment, now esp. in the productive arts or manufactures 1611. **5.** A particular branch of productive labour; a trade or manufacture 1566.

3. By industrie and diligence any perfection may be attained 1576. **4.** The Leaders of I...are virtually the Captains of the World CARLYLE. *House of i.*, a workhouse. *School of i.*, an industrial school. **5.** The rights and properties of our national industries DISRAELI.

Phr. †*Of industry*, on purpose (after L. *de* or *ex industria*) –1648.

Indutive (indiū·tiv), *a.* 1866. [– *indut-*, pa. ppl. stem of L. *induere* (see INDUSIUM) + -IVE.] *Bot.* Of seeds: Having the usual integument or covering.

||**Induviæ** (indiū·vi,ī), *sb. pl.* 1835. [L. *induviæ* clothing, f. *induere* put on (a garment).] *Bot.* Leaves which not being articulated with the stem cannot fall off but decay upon it. LINDLEY. Hence **Indu·viate** *a.* clothed with i.

Indwell (i:n,dwe·l), *v.* Pa. t. and pple. **indwelt.** ME. [f. IN-[1] + DWELL, in Wyclif rendering L. *inhabitare.*] **1.** *trans.* To dwell in, inhabit, occupy as a dwelling. Also *fig.* **2.** *intr.* To dwell, abide, have one's abode (*in*). Also *fig.*

1. *fig.* The Holy Ghost became a Dove, not as a symbol, but as a constantly indwelt form MILMAN. Hence **Indweller, in-dweller** (i·n,dwe:ləɹ), one who dwells in a place; an inhabitant; a sojourner.

Indwelling (i·ndwe:liŋ), *vbl. sb.* ME. [f. IN *adv.* + DWELLING *vbl. sb.*; cf. prec. In Wyclif rendering L. *inhabitatio.*] The action of dwelling in a place. Usu. *fig.* The abiding of God or the Divine Spirit in the heart or soul.

By the i. of God all objects are infused, and contained within TRAHERNE.

†**Indy, Indie.** 1509. [– L. *India*; cf. *Italy*, etc.] = INDIA –1647.

-ine, *suffix*[1], forming adjs., repr. L. *-īnus, -īna, -īnum*, with the sense 'of' or 'pertaining to', 'of the nature of'. Examples are L. *adulterinus* adulterine, *divinus* divine, *femininus* feminine, etc.; also, *Alpinus* Alpine, etc. The termination is now greatly used in *Nat. Hist.*, in forming adjs. on the names of genera, as *acarine, accipitrine*, etc. In these Nat. Hist. adjs. the pronunciation is (-əin), usually unstressed; but in other words it is very various; cf. *divine* (-əi·n), *marine* (-ī·n), *feminine* (-in), *leonine* (-əin). Also *riverine*.

-ine, *suffix*[2], forming adjs., repr. L. *-ĭnus*, – Gr. -ινος, as *adamantinus* adamantine, *pristinus* pristine, etc. The etym. and historical pronunciation is (-in), e.g. (pri·stin), (ædăma·ntin); but cf. *crystalline* (-əin), etc.

-ine, *suffix*[3], repr. Fr. *-ine*, L. *-ina*, Gr. -ινη, forming fem. titles, as in Gr. ἡρωΐνη, L. *heroina*, Fr. *héroïne* heroine. See also *landgravine, margravine*.

-ine, *suffix*[4], forming sbs., repr. Fr. *-ine* (*-in*), L. *-ina* (*-inus*), in origin identical with -INE[1]. The adjs. in *-inus, -ina* were also used subst., as in *concubinus, -ina* concubine, *Antoninus* Antonine, etc. The Eng. form of those in *-ina* is *-ine*, occas. *-in*; those in *-inus* give Fr. and Eng. *-in*, but in Eng. often *-ine*.

In Romanic, and hence in Eng. in the Fr. form *-ine* (-ī·n), this suffix is greatly used in forming names of derived substances, similative appellations, diminutives, etc.; e.g. *dentine, grenadine*, etc.

-ine, *suffix*[5], *Chem.*, in origin an offshoot of -INE[4], as occurring in the names of some derived substances; see GELATIN, -INE. At first the ending *-ine* was by some reduced to *-in*; but recently, in systematic nomenclature, *-ine* is now used (1) in forming names of alkaloids and basic substances, as *aconitine*, etc., which are thus distinguished from names of neutral substances, proteids, etc., in *-in* (see -IN[1]); and (2) in Hofmann's systematic names of hydrocarbons of the form C_nH_{2n-2}, as *ethine* or acetylene, C_2H_2, etc. In the names of the elements, etc., *-ine* is retained. In pop. and commercial use, *-ine* is still current in some cases where systematic nomenclature requires *-in*; see -IN[1].

-ine, as used to form the names of minerals, has in later use been changed, in the names of species, to *-ite*; thus *chalcosine, erythrine* are in Dana *chalcocite, erythrite*.

Inearth (inə̄·ɹþ), *v.* 1801. [f. IN-[1] + EARTH *sb.*] To inter. Chiefly *poet.*

Inebriant (inī·briănt). 1819. [f. INEBRIATE *v.*, after *intoxicate/intoxicant*; see -ANT.] **a.** *adj.* Intoxicating. **b.** *sb.* An intoxicant.

Inebriate (inī·briĕt), *ppl. a.* and *sb.* 1497. [– L. *inebriatus*, pa. pple. of *inebriare*; see next, -ATE[2].] **1.** *ppl. a.* Inebriated; intoxicated (*lit.* and *fig.*). **2.** *sb.* An intoxicated person; now only, a habitual drunkard 1794.

1. Thus spake Peter as a man i. and made drounken with the swetenesse of this vision UDALL. **2.** An Asylum for Inebriates 1864.

Inebriate (inī·brie[i]t), *v.* 1497. [– *inebriat-*, pa. ppl. stem of L. *inebriare*, f. *in-* IN-[2] + *ebriare* intoxicate, f. *ebrius* drunk; see -ATE[3].] **1.** *trans.* To make drunk; to intoxicate. Also *absol.* 1555. **2.** *transf.* and *fig.* **a.** To excite or stupefy, as with liquor 1497. †**b.** To refresh as with drink; to drench –1649. †**3.** *intr.* To become intoxicated. BACON.

1. The cups That cheer but not i. COWPER. **2. a.** A sophistical rhetorician, inebriated with the exuberance of his own verbosity DISRAELI.

Inebriation (inībri,ē[i]·ʃən). 1526. [– late L. *inebriatio*, f. as prec.; see -ION. Cf. Fr. †*inébriation.*] The action of inebriating, or condition of being inebriated; intoxication 1646. **b.** *fig.* Intoxication of the mind or feelings; excitement or emotion such as to cause loss of mental or moral balance.

b. They did not preserve him from the i. of prosperity 1828.

†**Ine·briative,** *a.* 1615. [f. INEBRIATE *v.* + -IVE. Cf. OFr. *inébriatif, -ive.*] Intoxicating; of or pertaining to inebriation –1628.

Inebriety (inībrəi·ĕti). 1775. [f. IN-[2] + EBRIETY.] The state or habit of being inebriated; drunkenness; esp. habitual drunkenness, regarded as a disease. Also *fig.*

Inebrious (inī·briəs), *a. rare.* 1450. [In XV – OFr. **inebrieus* or med.L. **inebriosus*, f. *in-* IN-[2] + L. *ebriosus* (after *inebriare*); in later use f. IN-[2] + EBRIOUS.] †**1.** Inebriating, intoxicating –1704. **2.** Drunken; addicted to drunkenness 1837.

Inedible (ine·dib'l), *a.* 1822. [IN-[3].] Not edible; unfit to be eaten. Hence **Inedibi·lity.**

Inedited (ine·ditėd), *a.* 1760. [IN-[3].] Not edited; unpublished; not described in any published work.

Her letters, still extant although i. 1855.

Ineffable (ine·făb'l), *a.* (*sb.*) 1450. [– (O)Fr. *ineffable* or L. *ineffabilis*, f. *in-* IN-[3] + *effabilis*, f. *effari* speak out, f. *ex-* EF- + *fari* speak; see -ABLE.] **1.** That cannot be expressed in words; unspeakable, unutterable, inexpressible. **2.** That must not be uttered 1597. †**3.** *Math.* Irrational, surd –1729. **4.** *sb. pl.* (*colloq.*) Trousers 1823.

1. Thankes be vnto God for his i. gyfte TINDALE 2 *Cor.* 9:15. **2.** To thee, the i. Name BROWNING. Hence **Ineffabi·lity, Ine·ffableness. Ine·ffably** *adv.* in an i. manner, or to an i. extent or degree.

Ineffaceable (inėfē[i]·săb'l), *a.* 1804. [f. IN-[3] + EFFACEABLE. Cf. Fr. *ineffaçable.*] That cannot be effaced or obliterated; indelible (*lit.* and *fig.*). Hence **Ineffaceabi·lity,** i. quality. **Ineffa·ceably** *adv.*

Ineffectible (inėfe·ktĭb'l), *a. rare.* Also **-able.** 1649. [– med.L. *ineffectibilis* incapable of having an efficient cause. In sense 3 f. IN-[3] + EFFECTIBLE.] †**1.** Ineffectual, ineffective. BP. HALL. †**2.** Not to be effected by ordinary means; supernatural BP. HALL. **3.** Impracticable 1806.

Ineffective (inėfe·ktiv), *a.* (*sb.*) 1651. [f. IN-[3] + EFFECTIVE.] **1.** Insufficient to produce any, or the intended, effect; hence, ineffectual; inoperative. **2.** Of a person: Inefficient 1653. **3.** *sb.* A person unfit for work or service 1856.

1. I. remedies 1651. I. architecture 1858. An i. appeal 1898. **2.** I. age SOUTHEY. Hence **Ineffe·ctive-ly** *adv.*, **-ness.**

Ineffectual (inėfe·ktiŭăl), *a.* ME. [orig. – med.L. *ineffectualis*; later f. IN-[3] + EFFECTUAL.] Not effectual; without any, or the intended, effect; unavailing. **b.** Of things: Not producing the usual effect; weak or tame in effect 1784. **c.** Of a person: That is a failure 1865.

All his efforts were i. 1704. **b.** A white face,—shivering, i. lips E.B. BROWNING. **c.** Pope Stephen III...a weak and i. man 1897. Hence **Ineffectua·lity, Ineffe·ctualness. Ineffe·ctually** *adv.*

Ineffervescence (inefəɹve·sĕns). *rare.* 1794. [IN-[3].] The fact of not effervescing; absecence of effervescence. So **Inefferve·scent** *a.* (*rare*), having the quality of not effervescing. **Ineffervescibi·lity,** incapability of effervescing.

Inefficacious (inefikē[i]·ʃəs), *a.* 1658. [f. IN-[3] + EFFICACIOUS.] Of a remedy, treatment, etc. Not efficacious; without efficacy.

The precaution..is quite i. DICKENS. Hence **Ineffica·cious-ly** *adv.*, **-ness** 1646.

Ineffica·city. 1721. [– Fr. *inefficacité*; see IN-[3], EFFICACITY.] = next.

Inefficacy (ine·fikăsi). 1612. [– late L. *inefficacia*; in later use, f. IN-[3] + EFFICACY.] Want of efficacy; incapacity to produce the desired effect.

The i. of advice is usually the fault of the counsellor 1751.

Inefficiency (inėfi·ʃĕnsi). 1749. [f. IN-[3] + EFFICIENCY.] Want of efficiency; inability to effect something; ineffectiveness, inefficient character.

The scandalous i. of the Government 1878.

Inefficient (inėfi·ʃĕnt), *a.* (*sb.*) 1750. [IN-[3].] **1.** Not efficient; failing to produce, or incapable of producing, the desired effect; ineffective. Of a person: Not effecting something; not having the ability or industry required for what one has to do; not fully capable. **2.** *sb.* An inefficient person 1898.

1. Ploughs of an i. structure 1804. He..rarely promoted an i. person KEIGHTLEY. **2.** 'Inefficients' by birth 1898. Hence **Ineffi·ciently** *adv.*

Inelaborate (inĭlæ·bŏrĕt), *a.* 1650. [IN-[3].

Cf. Fr. †*inélaboré*.] Not elaborate; not having much labour expended on it; simple or slight in workmanship. Hence **Inela·borately** *adv*.

Inelaborated (inĭlæ·bŏrēⁱtĕd), *a*. 1623. [IN-³.] Not laboriously worked out; not thoroughly formed by natural or chemical process.

Inelastic (inĭlæ·stik), *a*. 1748. [IN-³.] Not elastic; void of elasticity or springiness.

I. fluids, a name for liquids, as being void of 'elasticity' in the older sense (see ELASTIC A. 2). So **I:nelasti·city**, absence of elasticity; rigidity.

Inelegant (ine·lĭgănt), *a*. 1509. [– Fr. *inélégant* – L. *inelegans, -ant-*; see IN-³, ELEGANT.] **1.** Wanting in grace of form or manner; unrefined; clumsy, coarse, unpolished. Used *esp.* of language and literary style. **2.** Wanting in æsthetic refinement or delicacy 1667. **3.** (*nonce-use* from late L.) Not in harmony with the main body of the Law 1832.

1. When the forms..are i., that is, when they are composed of unvaried lines HOGARTH. His imitation of Horace on Lucilius is not i. JOHNSON. **2.** Order, so contriv'd as not to mix Tastes, not well joyned, i. MILT. *P.L.* v. 335. Hence **Ine·legance, Ine·legancy. Ine·legantly** *adv*.

Ineligible (ine·lidʒĭb'l), *a*. 1770. [f. IN-³ + ELIGIBLE. Cf. Fr. *inéligible* (XVIII), med.L. *ineligibilis* (XIII).] **1.** Incapable of being elected; disqualified for election to an office or position. **b.** Hence, Unfit to be chosen 1828. †**2.** Of actions: Such as one would not choose to do; inexpedient; undesirable –1797. **3.** *absol.* with *pl.* as *sb.* One not eligible as a suitor or husband 1896.

1. b. As a son-in-law he was quite i. TROLLOPE. Hence **Ine:ligibi·lity, Ine·ligibleness,** the quality or fact of being i. **Ine·ligibly** *adv.* in an i. manner.

Ineloquent (ine·lŏkwĕnt), *a*. 1530. [f. IN-³ + ELOQUENT. Cf. Fr. †*inéloquent*.] Not eloquent; void of eloquence.

The i. Brindley, behold he has chained seas together CARLYLE. Hence **Ine·loquence. Ine·loquently** *adv*.

Ineluctable (inĭlɒ·ktăb'l), *a*. 1623. [– L. *ineluctabilis*, f. *in-* IN-³ + *eluctari* struggle out; see -ABLE. Cf. RELUCTANT.] From which one cannot escape by struggling; inescapable.

Struggling in the grip of some force outside themselves, inexorable, i. MRS. H. WARD. Hence **Inelu·ctably** *adv*.

Ineludible (inĭlⁱū·dĭb'l), *a*. Also **-able.** 1662. [IN-³.] That cannot be eluded or escaped. Hence **Inelu·dibly** *adv*.

Inembryonate (ine·mbri,ŏnĕt), *a*. 1846. [f. IN-³ + EMBRYONATE *a*.] *Biol.* Not embryonate; having no embryo.

†**Ine·narrable,** *a*. 1450. [– (O)Fr. *inénarrable* – L. *inenarrabilis*, f. *in-* IN-³ + *ennarrare* narrate; see -BLE.] That cannot be narrated, told, or described; unspeakable –1716.

Earth's i. continent CHAPMAN.

Inept (ine·pt), *a*. 1561. [– L. *ineptus*, f. *in-* IN-³ + *aptus* APT *a*.] **1.** Not adapted or adaptable; without aptitude; unsuitable, unfit (*arch.*) 1603. **b.** Inappropriate 1675. **2.** Absurd; silly, foolish 1604. **3.** *Law.* Void, of no effect 1561.

1. The differences between *apt* and *inept* Counsellours HOBBES. **b.** I. words, which do not affect the..absolute gift 1883. **2.** She look'd on you as an I. Animal 1710. So **Ine·pt-ly** *adv.* 1523. **Ine·ptness.**

Ineptitude (ine·ptitiud). 1615. [– L. *ineptitudo*, f. *ineptus* INEPT; see -TUDE. Cf. Fr. †*ineptitude*.] **1.** Want of aptitude; inaptness, unfitness; incapacity. **2.** Want of mental capacity; silliness; a silly act or remark 1656.

1. That I. for Society, which is frequently the Fault of us Scholars STEELE. **2.** The i. of statesmen 1885.

Inequable (inī·k-, -e·kwăb'l), *a*. *rare.* 1717. [– L. *inæquabilis*; see IN-³ and EQUABLE.] Uneven; not uniform. So †**Inequabi·lity** (*rare*) 1581.

Inequal (inī·kwăl), *a*. ME. [– L. *inæqualis*, f. *in-* IN-³ + *æqualis* EQUAL. Cf. OFr. *inequal* (mod. *inégal*).] = UNEQUAL. **b.** Of a surface: Uneven 1661. Hence **Ine·qual-ly** *adv.*, **-ness.**

Inequality (inĭkwǫ·lĭti). 1484. [– OFr. *inequalité* (mod. *inégalité*) or L. *inæqualitas*, f. *inæqualis*; see prec., -ITY.] The condition of being unequal; want of equality. **1.** Want of equality between persons or things; disparity; as in physical qualities; in dignity, rank, or circumstances, etc. **b.** A condition of superiority or inferiority in relation to something, *esp.* the being unequal *to* a task, insufficiency 1553. **2.** †**a.** Of persons: Unequal treatment of others; partiality. **b.** Of things: Want of due proportion, uneven distribution. 1538. **3.** Want of uniformity: **a.** in surface or outline 1607; **b.** in motion, action, or condition; in duration or recurrence; in rate or proportion; in manner, quality, degree, etc. 1626. **4.** *Astron.* A deviation from uniformity in the motion of a heavenly body 1690. **5.** *Math.* **a.** The relation between quantities that are unequal in value or magnitude. *Sign of i.*, either > ('is greater than') or < ('is less than'). **b.** An expression of this relation; dist. from *equation*. 1875.

1. Inequalities in the wages of labour and profits of stock ADAM SMITH. The i. between the rich and the poor 1802. **b.** Conscious of the I. of a Female Pen to so Masculine an Attempt MRS. CENTLIVRE. **2.** Inequalities in the pressure of the income-tax 1858. **3. a.** Fine inequalities of hill and dale 1801. **b.** The i. of the Pulse W. SALMON, of our climate HANWAY. In Wordsworth there are no inequalities COLERIDGE.

Inequation (inĭkwēⁱ·ʃən). 1855. [f. IN-³ + EQUATION.] A formula expressing inequality; = INEQUALITY 5 b.

Ine·qui-, combining element, in sense 'unequal', 'unequally', not of L. formation, but f. IN-³ + EQUI-: e.g.

Ine:quia·xed, ine:quia·xial *a.* having unequal axes; **ine:quidi·stant** *a.* not equidistant; **ine:quilo·bate, ine·quilobed** *a.* having unequal lobes.

Inequilateral (inĭkwilæ·tĕrăl), *a*. 1662. [f. IN-³ + EQUILATERAL.] Having unequal sides.

I. shell: one in which a transverse line drawn through the apex of the umbo divides the valve into two unequal and unsymmetrical parts.

In equilibrio: see EQUILIBRIUM.

Inequitable (ine·kwităb'l), *a*. 1667. [f. IN-³ + EQUITABLE.] Not equitable; unfair, unjust. Hence **Ine·quitably** *adv*.

†**Ine·quitate,** *v*. [– *inequitat-*, pa. ppl. stem of L. *inequitare* ride on or over, f. *in-* IN-² + *equitare* ride.] *trans.* To ride over or through; hence, to pervade, permeate. HY. MORE.

Inequity (ine·kwĭti). 1556. [IN-³.] Want of equity or justice; the fact or quality of being unfair; unfairness, partiality. **b.** with *pl.* An unfair or unjust matter or action 1857.

Many of her statesmen confess its i. and inexpediency 1876.

Inequivalve (inī·kwivalv), *a*. 1776. [f. INEQUI- + VALVE.] *Conch.* Having valves of unequal size. So **Ine·quivalved, Ine:quiva·lvular** *a*.

Ineradicable (inĭræ·dikăb'l), *a*. 1818. [IN-³.] Incapable of being eradicated or lroted out. Also *fig.*

This i. taint of sin BYRON. Hence **Inera·dicably** *adv*.

Inerasable (inĭrēⁱ·săb'l), *a*. Also **-ible.** 1811. [IN-³.] That cannot be erased. Hence **Inera·sably, -ibly** *adv*.

†**Inerge·tic,** †**-al,** *a*. 1691. [f. IN-³ + (EN)-ERGETIC(AL).] Without energy; inactive, sluggish –1852.

Inerm (inə̄·ɹm), *a*. 1760. [– L. *inermis* unarmed, f. *in-* IN-³ + *arma* arms. Cf. Fr. *inerme* (XVIII) in same sense, perh. the source.] *Bot.* Destitute of prickles or thorns; unarmed. So **Ine·rmous** *a*. (Dicts.)

Inerrable (ine·răb'l), *a*. 1613. [– L. *inerrabilis*, f. *in-* IN-³ + *errare* err; see -BLE.] Incapable of erring; infallible.

Catholic Christianity rested on an i. Church as the teacher of truth 1879. Hence **Inerrabi·lity, Ine·rrableness,** infallibility. **Ine·rrably** *adv*.

Inerrant (ine·rănt), *a*. 1652. [– L. *inerrans*, *-ant-* fixed (of stars), f. *in-* IN-³ + *errans*, pr. pple. of *errare* wander; see -ANT.] †**1.** *Astron.* Of a star: Fixed; not planetary. GAULE. **2.** That does not err; unerring 1837. So **Ine·rrancy,** the quality of being i.

Inerratic (ineræ·tik), *a*. 1655. [IN-³.] Not erratic or wandering; fixed (as a star); following a fixed course.

†**Ine·rring,** *a*. [IN-³.] = UNERRING. Howell. So †**Ine·rringly** *adv.* unerringly.

Inert (inə̄·ɹt), *a*. 1647. [– L. *iners, inert-* unskilled, inactive, f. *in-* IN-³ + *ars, art-* skill, ART. Cf. Fr. *inerte*.] **1.** Having no inherent power of action, motion, or resistance; having the property of INERTIA. **b.** Without active chemical, physiological, or other properties; neutral 1800. **2.** Of persons, animals, and (*transf.*) moving things: Inactive, sluggish, not inclined for or capable of action. Also of mental faculties. 1774.

1. Matter is said to be passive and i. BERKELEY. *fig.* The i. mass of accumulated prejudices HAZLITT. **b.** Carbon..is totally i. at ordinary heats H. SPENCER. *I. gas* (Chem.), a gaseous element such as helium, argon, neon, krypton, and xenon which are chemically inactive; also *ellipt.* as *sb.* **2.** Timid as a Minister and i. as a statesman BRIGHT. An i. little town DICKENS. Hence **Ine·rtion,** i. condition; inactivity; sloth. **Ine·rtly** *adv.*, **-ness.**

Inertia (inə̄·ɹʃiă). 1713. [– L. *inertia* inactivity, f. *iners, inert-*; see prec., -IA¹.] **1.** *Physics.* That property of matter by virtue of which it continues in its existing state, whether of rest or of uniform motion in a straight line, unless that state is altered by external force. Also called *vis inertiæ*. Also *fig.* **2.** *transf.* Inactivity; disinclination to act; inertness, apathy 1822.

Ine·rtial *a.* of, pertaining to, or of the nature of i.

Inerudite (ine·rudəit), *a*. 1801. [– L. *ineruditus*; see IN-³ and ERUDITE.] Not erudite; unlearned, uninstructed. So †**Inerudi·tion,** want of erudition 1685.

Inescapable (inĕskēⁱ·păb'l), *a*. 1792. [IN-³.] That cannot be escaped or avoided; inevitable.

†**Ine·scate,** *v*. 1602. [– *inescat-*, pa. ppl. stem of L. *inescare* allure with bait, f. *in-* IN-² + *esca* food; see -ATE³.] *trans.* To allure with or as with a bait; to entice.

They i. and circumvent poore silly Soules 1602. So †**Inesca·tion,** alluring; an allurement.

Ine·sculent, *a*. 1831. [IN-³.] Inedible.

Inescutcheon (inĕskɒ·tʃən). 1610. [f. IN *adv.* + ESCUTCHEON.] *Her.* An escutcheon of pretence, or other small escutcheon, charged on a larger escutcheon.

In esse: see ESSE 1.

Inessential (inĕse·nʃăl), *a*. (*sb.*) 1677. [IN-³.] **1.** Devoid of essence; unsubstantial, immaterial. **2.** Not of the essence of a thing; not necessary to the constitution or existence of any thing 1836. **3.** *sb.* That which is inessential 1778.

1. His i. figure cast no shade Upon the golden floor SHELLEY. Hence **Inesse:ntia·lity,** i. quality.

Inestimable (ine·stimăb'l), *a*. ME. [– (O)Fr. *inestimable* – L. *inæstimabilis*; see IN-³, ESTIMABLE.] **1.** Incapable of being estimated; too great, profound, or intense to be computed. **b.** Priceless; invaluable 1579. †**2.** quasi-*adv.* Inestimably –1581.

1. The wealth consumed was i. DE FOE. **b.** This charter, the i. monument of English freedom BURKE. †**Ine:stimabi·lity, -ableness. Ine·stimably** *adv*.

Ineunt (i·ni,ɒnt). 1836. [– *ineunt-*, pr. ppl. stem of L. *inire* go in, enter, f. *in-* IN-² + *ire* go.] **A.** *adj.* Entering. **B.** *sb.* A point of a curve. Also *i-point*. 1859.

Ineva·sible, *a*. 1846. [IN-³.] Not evasible; that cannot be evaded.

Inevidence (ine·vidĕns). Now *rare.* 1654. [– med.L. *inevidentia* (XIV), f. next; see -ENCE.] Lack of evidence; obscurity (*rare*) 1671; †uncertainty –1677.

Inevident (ine·vidĕnt), *a*. Now *rare.* 1614. [– late L. *inevidens, -ent-* (Boethius); see IN-³, EVIDENT.] Not evident; not clear or obvious; obscure.

Inevitable (ine·vităb'l), *a*. ME. [– L. *inevitabilis*, f. *in-* IN-³ + *evitabilis*, f. *evitare*, f. *e-* EX-¹ + *vitare* avoid; see -ABLE.] That cannot be avoided; not admitting of escape or evasion; that cannot fail to occur, etc.

All..Await alike th' i. hour GRAY. *The i.* (absol.), what cannot be avoided or escaped; There is no good in arguing with the i. LOWELL. Hence **Ine:vitabi·lity, Ine·vitableness. Ine·vitably** *adv*.

Inexact (inegzæ·kt), *a*. 1828. [IN-³. Cf. Fr. *inexact*.] Not exact; not strictly correct or precise. **b.** Of a person: Characterized by inexactness 1849. Hence **Inexa·ct-ly** *adv.*, **-ness.**

Inexactitude (inegzæ·ktitiud). 1786. [IN-³. Cf. Fr. *inexactitude*.] The quality or character of being inexact; want of exactitude, accuracy, or precision; inexactness. Also, an instance of this.

The author's i. of thought and expression 1869.

Inexcitable (ineksəi·tăb'l), *a. rare.* 1616. [In sense 1 (stressed *ine·xcitable*) – L. *inexcitabilis*; in 2, f. IN-[3] + EXCITABLE.] †**1.** From which one cannot be roused –1651. **2.** Not excitable; not liable to excitement 1828.
1. In this i. sleepe CHAPMAN. Hence **Inexci:tabi·lity** (*rare*), the quality of being i.

Inexcommu·nicable, *a. rare.* 1610. [IN-[3].] That cannot be excommunicated.
A multitude is i. 1617.

Inexcusable (inekskiū·zăb'l), *a.* late ME. [– L. *inexcusabilis*; see IN-[3] and EXCUSABLE. Cf. Fr. *inexcusable* (XV).] Not excusable; incapable of being justified.
Therfore arte thou i. o man TINDALE *Rom.* 2:1. An i. affront LYTTON. Hence **Inexcu:sabi·lity, Inexcu·sableness. Inexcu·sably** *adv.*

†**Ine·xecrable,** *a.* A perversion of *inexorable*; cf. med.L. *inexecrabilis* unappeasable.
O be thou damn'd, i. dogge *Merch. V.* IV. i. 128.

Inexecutable (inekse·kiutăb'l), *a.* 1833. [IN-[3]. Cf. Fr. *inexécutable* (XVIII).] That cannot be executed.
The arbitrary..provisions of this edict made it i. M. ARNOLD.

Inexecution (ineksĭkiū·ʃən). 1681. [IN-[3]. Cf. Fr. *inexécution* (XVII).] Lack or neglect of execution; non-performance.
His i. of orders baffled that effort JEFFERSON.

Inexertion (inegzə̄·ɹʃən). 1794. [IN-[3].] Want of exertion; failure to exert (oneself) or exercise (a faculty); inactivity.

Inexha·lable, *a.* [IN-[3].] Not exhalable; that cannot be evaporated. SIR T. BROWNE.

†**Inexhau·st,** *a.* 1612. [– L. *inexhaustus*; see IN-[3] and EXHAUST *ppl. a.*] = next –1665.

Inexhausted (inegzǭ·stėd), *a.* 1626. [IN-[3].] Unexhausted.
I. Sources of Perfection ADDISON. Hence **Inexhau·stedly** *adv.* without exhaustion.

Inexhaustible (inegzǭ·stĭb'l), *a.* Also **-able.** 1601. [IN-[3]. Cf. Fr. †*inexhaustible* (XV–XVI).] Not exhaustible. **1.** Incapable of being consumed or spent; exhaustless 1631. **2.** Incapable of being emptied of contents 1601. **3.** Incapable of being worn out in strength or vigour 1762.
1. Our inexhaustable strata of coal PENNANT. **2.** An i. purse 1646. **3.** Almost i. by toil 1848. Hence **Inexhau:stibi·lity, Inexhau·stibleness. Inexhau·stibly** *adv.*

Inexhaustive (inegzǭ·stiv), *a.* 1728. [IN-[3].] Not exhaustive; exhaustless. Hence **Inexhau·stively** *adv.*

Inexhau·stless, *a.* 1739. [Confusion of *inexhaustible* and *exhaustless.*] Exhaustless.

Inexist (i:negzi·st), *v.* 1678. [f. IN *adv.* + EXIST. Cf. med.L. *inexistere* inhere, exist in. Cf. INEXISTENT[1].] *intr.* To exist or have its being *in* something else.
The roundness inexists in the clay, and the thought of it inexists in my understanding TUCKER.

Inexistence[1] (inegzi·stĕns). 1635. [f. IN-[2] + EXISTENCE. Cf. med.L. *inexistentia* inherence.] The fact or condition of existing in something; inherence.

Inexi·stence[2]. Now *rare.* 1623. [f. IN-[3] + EXISTENCE.] The fact or condition of not existing; non-existence.

†**Inexi·stency**[1]. 1674. [f. IN-[2] + EXISTENCY. Cf. med.L. *inexistentia* inherence.] = INEXISTENCE[1]; also (with *pl.*) something inexistent or inherent –1774.

†**Inexistency**[2]. 1659. [f. IN-[3] + EXISTENCY.] = INEXISTENCE[2].

Inexistent (i:negzi·stĕnt), *a.*[1] Also †**-ant.** 1553. [– late L. *inexistens, -ent-* (Boethius), pr. pple. of *inexistere* (recorded later); see INEXIST *v.*] Existing or having its being in something else; inherent.

Inexi·stent, *a.*[2] ?*Obs.* 1646. [f. IN-[3] + EXISTENT.] Not existing; not having existence.

Inexorable (ine·ksŏrăb'l), *a.* 1553. [– Fr. *inexorable* or L. *inexorabilis*; see IN-[3], EXORABLE.] Incapable of being persuaded by entreaty; not to be moved from one's purpose or determination; relentless, rigidly severe.
More i. farre, Then emptie Tygers, or the roaring Sea SHAKS. Lawes..are things deafe and i. P. HOLLAND. How entirely i. is the nature of facts 1858. Hence **Ine:xorabi·lity, Ine·xorableness,** the quality of being i. **Ine·xorably** *adv.* relentlessly.

Inexpansible (inekspæ·nsĭb'l), *a.* 1878. [IN-[3].] Not expansible; incapable of being expanded.

Inexpectable (inekspe·ktăb'l), *a.* [IN-[3].] Not to be expected. BP. HALL.

Inexpe·ctant, *a.* 1853. [IN-[3].] Devoid of expectation. So **Inexpe·ctancy,** absence of expectancy 1643. **Inexpecta·tion,** absence of expectation 1627.

†**Inexpe·cted,** *a.* 1586. [IN-[3].] Not expected; unlooked-for –1651. Hence †**Inexpe·cted-ly** *adv.*, †**-ness.**

Inexpedience (inekspī·diĕns). Now *rare.* 1608. [See next and -ENCE.] = next.

Inexpediency (inekspī·diĕnsi). 1641. [f. IN-[3] + EXPEDIENCY; or f. INEXPEDIENT; see -ENCY.] The quality of being inexpedient; disadvantageousness, impolicy.
The i. of attempting to raise any considerable revenue by means of income-taxes MCCULLOCH.

Inexpedient (inekspī·diĕnt), *a.* 1608. [IN-[3].] Not expedient; disadvantageous in the circumstances; unadvisable, impolitic.
Nothing could be more correctly lawful; but.. few things would be more manifestly i. BENTHAM. Hence **Inexpe·diently** *adv.*

Inexpensive (inekspe·nsiv), *a.* 1837. [IN-[3].] **1.** Not expensive or costly; cheap. **2.** Not given to expenditure 1859. Hence **Inexpe·nsive-ly** *adv.*, **-ness.**

Inexperience (inekspīə·riĕns). 1598. [– Fr. *inexpérience* – late L. *inexperientia*; see IN-[3], EXPERIENCE.] Want of experience; hence want of adequate knowledge or skill.
Those Failings which are incident to Youth and I. DRYDEN.

Inexperienced (inekspīə·riĕnst), *a.* 1626. [IN-[3].] Not experienced; having no (or little) experience; lacking the knowledge or skill derived from experience. Const. *in.*
We were not i. in sledging over the ice KANE.

Inexpert (inekspə̄·ɹt), *a.* 1450. [– OFr. *inexpert* – L. *inexpertus* untried, unexperienced; see IN-[3], EXPERT *a.*] †**1.** Not experienced; having no (or little) experience. Const. *in, of.* –1697. **2.** Wanting the aptitude or dexterity derived from experience; unskilled 1597. Hence **Inexpe·rt-ly** *adv.*, **-ness.**

Inexpiable (ine·kspiăb'l), *a.* 1570. [– L. *inexpiabilis*; see IN-[3], EXPIABLE. Cf. Fr. *inexpiable.*] **1.** Of an offence: That cannot be expiated or atoned for. **2.** Of a feeling, etc.: That cannot be appeased by expiation; irreconcilable. (Also *transf.* of an action.) 1598.
1. His mirth is an i. sin 1728. **2.** To raise in me i. hate MILT. *Sams.* 839. I. war BURKE. Hence **Ine·xpiableness, Ine·xpiably** *adv.*

Inexpiate (ine·kspiĕt), *a.* 1611. [– late L. *inexpiatus*; see IN-[3], EXPIATE *ppl.-a.*] **1.** Not expiated or atoned for 1819. †**2.** Unappeased.
2. To rest i. were much too rude a part 1611.

Inexplainable (inekplē̆i·năb'l), *a. rare.* 1623. [IN-[3].] That cannot be explained; inexplicable.

†**Ine·xpleble,** *a.* Also erron. **inexpleable.** 1569. [– L. *inexplebilis*, f. *in-* IN-[3] + *explēre* fill up; see -BLE.] That cannot be filled; insatiable –1788. Hence †**Ine·xplebly** *adv.* (erron. **inexpleably**), insatiably.

Inexplicable (ine·ksplikăb'l), *a.* (*adv.*) late ME. [– Fr. *inexplicable* or L. *inexplicabilis* that cannot be unfolded or loosened; see IN-[3], EXPLICABLE.] †**1.** That cannot be unfolded, untwisted, or disentangled; inextricable; very complex –1656. †**b.** as *adv.* Inexplicably. CAXTON. †**2.** That cannot be unfolded in words; inexpressible –1691. **3.** That cannot be explained; unintelligible; (in recent use) unaccountable 1546.
1. Mazes..of knottes i. EDEN. **2.** The i. benefite of knowledge 1551. **3.** I. dumbe shewes SHAKS., mysteries MAURY. Hence **Ine:xplicabi·lity, Ine·xplicableness. Ine·xplicably** *adv.*

Inexplicit (inekspli·sit), *a.* 1802. [IN-[3]. Cf. L. *inexplicitus* in same sense.] Not explicit; indefinite; not clear in terms or statement. So **Inexpli·cit-ly** *adv.* 1757, **-ness.**

Inexplo·rable, *a.* 1646. [IN-[3].] That cannot be explored; inscrutable.

Inexplo·sive, *a.* 1867. [IN-[3].] Not liable to or capable of explosion.

Inexpressible (inekspre·sĭb'l). 1625. [IN-[3].] **A.** *adj.* That cannot be expressed in words; unutterable, unspeakable, indescribable. (Often as an emotional intensive.)
Ere mid-day arriv'd In Eden, distance i. By Numbers that have name MILT. *P.L.* VIII. 113. Its seclusion gives it an i. charm TYNDALL.

B. *sb.* **1.** Something inexpressible 1652. **2.** *pl.* (*colloq.*) Breeches or trousers 1790.
Hence **Inexpressibi·lity, Inexpre·ssibleness. Inexpre·ssibly** *adv.* (as an emotional intensive).

Inexpressive (inekspre·siv), *a.* 1652. [IN-[3]. Cf. Fr. *inexpressif.*] **1.** = INEXPRESSIBLE *a.* (*arch.*). **2.** Not expressive; wanting in expression 1744.
2. His i. eye 1860. Hence **Inexpre·ssive-ly** *adv.*, **-ness.**

Inexpugnable (inekspɒ·gnăb'l), *a.* 1490. [– (O)Fr. *inexpugnable* – L. *inexpugnabilis*; see IN-[3], EXPUGNABLE.] That cannot be taken by assault or storm; incapable of being overthrown by force; impregnable, invincible. *lit.* and *fig.*
How the i. walles of Jerico were ouerthrown MORE. *fig.* An i. desire of sleeping 1590. Hence **Inexpu·gnably** *adv.*

†**Inexsu·perable,** *a.* 1623. [– L. *inexsuperabilis*, f. *in-* IN-[3] + *ex-* EX-[1] + *superabilis* SUPERABLE.] That cannot be overcome.

Inexte·nded, *a. rare.* 1739. [IN-[3].] Without extension.

Inextensible (inekste·nsĭb'l), *a.* 1840. [IN-[3]. Cf. Fr. *inextensible.*] Not capable of extension; that cannot be stretched or drawn out in length.
The assumption..that the ether is i. and incompressible 1881. Hence **Inextensibi·lity,** the quality of being i.

Inexte·nsion. 1827. [IN-[3].] Want of extension; unextended state.

In entenso: see IN *Lat. prep.*

Inexte·rminable, *a. rare.* 1586. [– late L. *inexterminabilis*; see IN-[3], EXTERMINABLE.] †**1.** Having no possible end; interminable –1668. **2.** That cannot be exterminated 1828.

Inexti·nct, *a. rare.* 1623. [– L. *inextinctus,* or f. IN-[3] + EXTINCT.] Unextinguished.

†**Inexti·nguible,** *a.* ME. [– Fr. *inextinguible* or L. *inex(s)tinguibilis*, f. *in-* IN-[3] + *ex(s)tinguere* EXTINGUISH; see -BLE.] = next –1677.

Inextinguishable (inieksti·ŋgwiʃăb'l), *a.* 1509. [IN-[3].] That cannot be extinguished (see the vb.); unquenchable, indestructible, etc.
I. rage MILT., laughter COWPER, hope SOUTHEY. Hence **Inexti·nguishably** *adv.*

Inexti·nguished, *a.* 1746. [IN-[3].] Not extinguished; still burning; unextinguished.

Inextirpable (inekstə̄·ɹpăb'l), *a.* 1623. [– L. *inex(s)tirpabilis*, f. *in-* IN-[3] + *ex(s)tirpare* EXTIRPATE; see -BLE.] That cannot be extirpated or rooted out.

In extremis: see IN *Lat. prep.*

Inextricable (ine·kstrikăb'l), *a.* late ME. [– L. *inextricabilis*, f. *in-* IN-[3] + *extricare* EXTRICATE; see -BLE.] **1.** From which one cannot extricate oneself (*lit.* and *fig.*). **2.** Of a knot, etc.: That cannot be disentangled or untied. Also *transf.* 1610. †**3.** Of a problem: That cannot be solved –1664. **4.** Intricately involved, confused, or perplexed; incapable of being put straight 1655. **4.** Intricate, elaborate, exquisitely wrought (*rare*) 1691.
1. We..lose our selves in i. Mazes 1720. Struggling with an i. trouble HAWTHORNE. **4.** The ecclesiastical polity of the realm was in i. confusion MACAULAY. **5.** The i. richness of the fully developed Gothic jamb and arch RUSKIN. Hence **Ine:xtricabi·lity, Ine·xtricableness. Ine·xtricably** *adv.*

†**Ineye** (in,əi·), *v.* ME. [f. IN-[2] + EYE, after L. *inoculare.*] *trans.* To put an eye or bud into (the bark of a tree); to inoculate –1708.

Infall (i·nfǭl). 1645. [f. IN *adv.* + FALL *sb.*, after Du. *inval* hostile incursion.] An inroad, attack, incursion, or descent (*upon* or *into*). Now *rare.*

Infallibilism (infæ·libiliz'm). 1870. [f. as next + -ISM.] The principle of the infallibility of some person or thing, esp. of the Pope.

Infallibilist (infæ·libilist). Also **-blist.** 1870. [– late L. *infallibilis* INFALLIBLE + -IST.] One who upholds the infallibility of some person or thing, esp. of the Pope. Also *attrib.*

Infallibility (infælĭbi·lĭti). 1611. [– Fr. †*infallibilité* or med.L. *infallibilitas*; see INFALLIBLE, -ITY.] **1.** The quality or fact of being infallible or exempt from liability to err. **2.** The quality of being unfailing; unfailing certainty 1631.

1. The Pope sitting in his Chaire,..may yet erre for all his i. GATAKER. *His I.*, a title given to the Pope; also, a mock title. **2.** The i. of a gun KANE.

Infallible (infæ·lĭb'l), *a.* (*sb.*) late ME. [– Fr. *infaillible* or late L. *infallibilis*; see IN-[3], FALLIBLE.] Not fallible. **1.** Not liable to be deceived or mistaken; incapable of erring. **2.** Not liable to fail; unfailing; sure; certain 1526. **3.** *sb.* One who or that which is infallible 1816.

1. Parliaments are not i. 'JUNIUS'. **2.** An i. Maxime 1654, ointment and plaister ARBUTHNOT, fruit of Unwisdom 1843. Hence **Infa·llibleness**, infallibility. **Infa·llibly** *adv.* indubitably; unerringly.

†**Infa·llid**, *a.* 1635. [alt. f. INFALLIBLE by suffix-substitution (-ID[1]), after *horrible*/*horrid*.] = INFALLIBLE 2.

†**Infama·tion.** 1533. [– (O)Fr. *infamation* or late L. *infamatio*, f. *infamat-*, pa. ppl. stem of L. *infamare*; see INFAME *v.*, -ION.] The action of holding up to infamy; defamation –1651.

Infa·matory, *a.* *rare.* 1612. [– med.L. *infamatorius*, f. as prec.; see -ORY[2].] †**a.** = DEFAMATORY. **b.** Bringing infamy.

†**Infa·me**, *sb.* ME. [– OFr. *infame*, *en-* masc. – late L. *infamium* for cl. L. *infamia* INFAMY.] = INFAMY –1616. So †**Infa·me** *a.* = INFAMOUS 1572.

Infame (infē[1]·m), *v. arch.* ME. [– OFr. *enfamer* – L. *infamare* render infamous, f. *infamis*, f. *in-* IN-[3] + *fama* FAME.] **1.** *trans.* To render infamous; to reprobate. †**2.** To defame –1604. †**3.** To accuse of something infamous –1797.

1. This inhuman Practice will i. your Government PENN.

Infamize (i·nfămaiz), *v.* 1596. [f. L. *infamis*; see prec., -IZE.] = INFAME *v.* 1, 2. Hence (by perversion) †**Infa·monize** *v.* (*L. L. L.* v. ii. 684).

Infamous (i·nfăməs), *a.* ME. [– med.L. *infamosus*, for L. *infamis*; see IN-[3], FAMOUS.] **1.** Of ill fame or repute; notorious *for* badness of any kind; held in infamy or public disgrace. **2.** Deserving of infamy; of shameful badness, vileness, or abominableness; of a character or quality deserving utter reprobation. (A strong adj. of detestation.) 1489. **3.** *Law.* Of a person: Deprived of civil rights, in consequence of conviction of certain crimes 1548. **b.** Of a crime or punishment: Involving or entailing infamy 1555.

1. Those that be neere..shall mocke thee which art i. *Ezek.* 22:5. The high-way betwixt Jericho and Jerusalem is i. for theeving FULLER. **2.** False erraunt knight, i., and foreswore SPENSER. Detest the very ground on which was acted such an i. Treachery 1703. **3.** They are condemned to lose the Franchise or Freedom of the Law, that is, become I., and of no Credit 1707. **b.** And so had two wives at once, which is by the civil law a thing i. 1555. Phr. *I. crime*, a term now chiefly applied to sodomy and kindred offences. Hence **I·nfamous-ly** *adv.*, **-ness.**

Infamy (i·nfămi). 1473. [– (O)Fr. *infamie* – L. *infamia*, f. *infamis*; see INFAME *v.*, -Y[3]. Replaced earlier INFAME *sb.*] **1.** Evil fame or reputation; public reproach, shame, or disgrace. Also with *an* and *pl.* **2.** The quality or character of being infamous or of shameful vileness; (with *pl.*) an infamous act. 1513. **3.** *Law.* The loss of all or certain of the rights of a citizen, consequent on conviction of certain crimes; see INFAMOUS 3. 1609.

1. Ye are taken vp in the lips of talkers, and are an i. [= an object of public reproach] of the people *Ezek.* 36:3. **2.** The i. of the peace was more deeply..felt GIBBON.

Infancy (i·nfănsi). 1494. [– L. *infantia* inability to speak, childhood, f. *infans*, *infant-*; see INFANT *sb.*[1], -ANCY.] **1.** The condition of being an infant; early childhood, babyhood. **2.** *Law.* The condition of being a minor; the period of life during which a person remains under guardianship (extending, in common law, to the end of the twenty-first year); minority, nonage 1658. **3.** *fig.* The earliest period in the history of anything; the rudimentary stage in any process of growth 1555. **4.** *concr.* (chiefly *rhet.*) Infants collectively 1598. †**5.** In etym. sense: Speechlessness; silence. MILT.

1. Heaven lies about us in our i. WORDSW. **2.** The defendant pleaded i., the goods having been supplied before he was of age 1900. **3.** Thrice happy was the worlds first infancie P. FLETCHER. **4.** Old age and i. Promiscuous perished SHELLEY.

Infa·nd, *a. Obs.* exc. as *nonce-wd.* 1608. [– L. *infandus* unspeakable, abominable, f. *in-* IN-[3] + *fandus*, gerundive of *fari* speak.] = next.

†**Infa·ndous**, *a.* 1644. [f. as prec. + -OUS.] Unspeakable, not to be spoken of; nefarious –1708.

I·nfangthief. [OE. *infangenþēof*, f. IN *adv.* + *fangen*, pa. pple. of *fōn* seize (see FANG *v.*[1]) + *þēof* thief; lit. 'thief seized within'.] *OE. Law.* The right of the lord of a manor to try and to amerce a thief caught within its limits.

Infant (i·nfănt), *sb.*[1] [Late ME. *enfaunt* (with early assim. to L.) – (O)Fr. *enfant* :– L. *infans*, *infant-*, subst. use of *infans* unable to speak, f. *in-* IN-[3] + pr. pple. of *fari* speak; see -ANT.] **1.** A child during the earliest period of life (or still unborn); esp. a child in arms; often, any child under seven years of age. Also *fig.* and *transf.* **2.** A person under (legal) age; a minor. In common law, a person under the age of twenty-one years; in the case of a ruler, one under the age at which he becomes constitutionally capable of exercising sovereignty 1513. †**3.** A youth of noble or gentle birth –1600. **4.** Applied joc. to various productions of exceptional size, strength, etc. 1832. **5.** *attrib.* (or *adj.*) **a.** That is an infant or like an infant, as *i. heir, martyr*, etc. 1595. **b.** In its earliest stage, undeveloped, nascent, incipient, as *i. blossom, civilization, navy*, etc. 1593. **c.** Of or belonging to an infant or infants, proper to or intended for infants; infantile; as *i. class, years*, etc. 1586.

1. An i. crying in the night: An i. crying for the light: And with no language but a cry TENNYSON. *transf.* The Canker Galls, the Infants of the Spring SHAKS. **3.** The noble I. [Rinaldo] stood a space Confused, speechless 1600. **4.** The heaviest gun..the Woolwich I..weighs 35 tons 1874. *Comb.* **i.-baptism,** the baptism of infants, pædobaptism.

Infant (i·nfănt), *sb.*[2] 1555. [– Sp., Pg. *infante*; see INFANTE.] A prince or princess of Spain or Portugal; = INFANTE, INFANTA.

†**I·nfant**, *v.* 1483. [– (O)Fr. *enfanter* (with assim. to L.), f. *enfant* INFANT *sb.*[1]] *trans.* To bring forth (a child). Also *fig.* –1642.

This worthy Motto, No Bishop, no King is of the same batch, and infanted out of the same feares MILT.

‖**Infanta** (infa·ntă). 1601. [Sp., Pg., fem. of INFANTE.] A daughter of the king and queen of Spain or Portugal; *spec.* the eldest daughter who is not heir to the throne. †Also *transf.* and *fig.* of other young ladies.

transf. Lady Catherine grew frightened, lest her i. [her daughter] should vex herself sick H. WALPOLE.

‖**Infante** (infa·nte). 1555. [Sp., Pg. *infante* :– L. *infans*, *infant-* INFANT *sb.*[1]] A son of the king and queen of Spain or Portugal other than the heir to the throne (who is called *principe*); *spec.* the second son.

I·nfanthood. 1862. [f. INFANT *sb.*[1] + -HOOD.] = INFANCY.

Infa·nticidal, *a.* 1835. [f. INFANTICIDE[2] + -AL.] Of or practising infanticide.

Infanticide[1] (infæ·ntisəid). 1680. [– Fr. *infanticide* – late L. *infanticida*; see INFANT *sb.*[1], -CIDE 1.] One who kills an infant.

Infanticide[2] (infæ·ntisəid). 1656. [– Fr. *infanticide* – late L. *infanticidium*; see INFANT *sb.*[1], -CIDE 2.] The killing of infants, *esp.* the killing of new-born infants, as a custom among primitive peoples, and in the ancient world. **b.** *spec.* The crime of murdering an infant after its birth, perpetrated by or with the consent of its parents, esp. the mother 1789.

Infantile (i·nfăntəil, -til), *a.* 1696. [– Fr. *infantile* or L. *infantilis*; see INFANT *sb.*[1], -ILE.] Of or pertaining to an infant, infants, or infancy; belonging to a person when an infant; existing in its infancy. **b.** Infant-like 1772.

I. diseases 1800, literature 1864.

Infantilism (infæ·ntiliz'm). 1895. [f. prec. + -ISM.] *Path.* The state of being mentally or physically undeveloped.

Infantine (i·nfăntəin), *a.* 1603. [– Fr. †*infantin*, var. of (O)Fr. *enfantin*, f. *enfant* INFANT *sb.*[1]; see -INE[1].] = INFANTILE.

A degree of credulity next to i. BURKE.

†**I·nfantly**, *a.* 1618. [-LY[1].] Infant-like.

Infantry (i·nfăntri). 1579. [– Fr. *infanterie* – It. *infanteria*, f. *infante* youth, foot-soldier; see INFANT *sb.*[1], -ERY.] **1.** The body of foot-soldiers; foot-soldiers collectively; that part of an army which consists of men who march and manœuvre on foot and carry, small arms, now a rifle. **2.** Infants collectively. Now *joc.* 1613. **3.** *attrib.*, as *i. brigade*, etc. 1813.

1. *Mounted I.*, soldiers mounted for the sake of transit, but who fight on foot.

I·nfantryman. 1883. A soldier of an infantry regiment.

I·nfant-schoo·l. 1833. A school for young children (usually under seven years of age).

Infarce, -se, var. of ENFARCE *v. Obs.*

Infarct (infā·ɹkt), *sb.* 1873. [– mod.L. *infarctus*, f. *infarct-*, pa. ppl. stem of L. *infarcire*, f. *in-* IN-[2] + *farcire* stuff.] *Path.* A portion of tissue that has become stuffed with extravasated blood, serum, or other matter; the substance of an infarction. So **Infa·rct** *v. trans.* to affect with infarction 1822.

Infarction (infā·ɹkʃən). 1689. [f. as prec. + -ION.] *Path.* The action of stuffing up or condition of being stuffed up, obstruction; *concr.* = INFARCT *sb.* Now usually restricted to morbid conditions of the tissues resulting from obstruction of the circulation, as by an embolus.

Infare (i·nfēᵊɹ). [OE. *innfær*, f. *inn* IN *adv.* + *fær* going, FARE *sb.*[1]] †**1.** (OE. and early ME.) The act of going in; an entrance, way in. **2.** *Sc.*, *n. dial.*, and *U.S.* A feast or entertainment given on entering a new house; *esp.* at the reception of a bride in her new home ME.

†**Infa·shionable**, *a. rare.* 1635. [IN-[3].] Unfashionable –1787.

†**Infa·tigable**, *a.* 1510. [– Fr. *infatigable* – L. *infatigabilis*; see IN-[3], FATIGABLE.] = INDEFATIGABLE –1713.

Infatuate (infæ·tiuĕt), *ppl. a.* 1471. [– L. *infatuatus*, pa. pple. of L. *infatuare*; see next, -ATE[2].] Infatuated.

Infatuate (infæ·tiueᶦt), *v.* 1533. [– *infatuat-*, pa. ppl. stem of L. *infatuare*, f. *in-* IN-[2] + *fatuus* FATUOUS; see -ATE[3].] †**1.** *trans.* To turn (counsels, etc.) into folly, to exhibit the foolishness of; to confound, frustrate, bring to nought –1724. **2.** To make (a person) utterly foolish or fatuous; to inspire with an extravagant passion 1567.

1. God hath infatuated your high subtle wisdom TINDALE. **2.** The short-lived joy that infatuated the public BOSWELL. Hence **Infa·tuatedly** *adv.*

Infatuation (infætiu,ēᶦ·ʃən). 1649. [f. INFATUATE *v.* + -ION. Cf. late L. *infatuatio* foolishness.] The action of infatuating or condition of being infatuated; an extravagantly foolish or unreasoning passion.

The I. of the Enthusiast, sets him above the Fear of Death 1718. Your i. about that girl blinds you 1815.

Infaust (infǭ·st), *a. rare.* 1658. [– L. *infaustus* unlucky, perh. through Fr. †*infauste*.] Unlucky, unfortunate, ill-omened. So †**Infau·sting**, a rendering i., a boding of ill-luck 1622.

Infeasible (infī·zĭb'l), *a.* Now *rare.* 1533. [f. IN-[3] + FEASIBLE.] Not capable of being accomplished or carried out; impracticable. So **Infeasibi·lity, Infea·sibleness,** the quality of being i.

†**Infect**, *ppl. a.* ME. [– L. *infectus*, pa. pple. of *inficere*; see next.] Infected. Often construed as pa. pple. of next. –1617.

Infect (infe·kt), *v.* ME. [– *infect-*, pa. ppl. stem of L. *inficere* dip in, stain, taint, spoil, f. *in-* IN-[2] + *facere* put, do.] **1.** *trans.* To affect, influence, or imbue with some quality or property by immersion or infusion. *Obs.* or *rare.* 1495. †**2.** To spoil or corrupt by noxious influence, admixture, or alloy; to adulterate –1693. **3.** To fill (the air, etc.) with noxious corruption or the germs of disease ME. **4.** To affect with disease; to act upon by infection or contagion. Also *absol.* ME. Also *transf.* and *fig.* **5.** To taint with moral corruption; to deprave ME. **6.** To taint with crime; to involve in crime or its penalties 1580. **b.** *Internat. Law.* To taint with illegality 1758. **7.** To imbue with an opinion or belief, esp. heresy or seditious views. Also said of the opinion. 1483. **8.** To affect (a person) with some feeling. Also of feelings: To take hold of. 1595. **9.** To affect or influence with some quality or by introducing something extraneous 1605. **b.** *spec.* Of a sound: To affect and alter the sound in a neighbouring syllable 1872. †**10.** To infest –1712.

3. If her breath were as terrible as [her] terminations,..she would i. to the north starre SHAKS. **4.** Persons infected with plague DE FOE. *fig.* With a Son's death t'i. a Father's sight DRYDEN. **7.** Whan the heresye of the arryans had enfected al Italye CAXTON. **8.** 'Twas a feare Which oft infects the wisest SHAKS. **10.** Much infected with serpents, moskittos [etc.] 1712. Hence **Infe·cter** (?*Obs.*), **-or,** one who infects. **Infe·ctible** *a.* (*rare*), capable of being infected.

Infection (infe·kʃən). ME. [– (O)Fr. *infection* or late L. *infectio*, f. as prec.; see -ION.] †**1.** The action or process of affecting injuriously, or the fact of being so affected; corrupt condition –1621. †**2.** Contamination of air or water, etc. –1801. **3.** The agency, substance, germ, or principle by which an infectious disease is communicated or transmitted ME. **b.** *pl.* Morbific influences, principles, or germs 1533. **4.** The communication of disease, esp. by the agency of the atmosphere or water (hence, strictly, dist. from *contagion*); the action or process of infecting; the fact of being infected 1548. **5.** Disease caused by infection; a plague, epidemic, pestilence; †*occas.*, A disease, a seizure with disease 1563. **6.** Moral contamination; an instance of this 1529. **7.** Communication of harmful opinions or beliefs 1529. **8.** *Internat. Law.* Contamination by illegality: see INFECTIOUS 6. 1879. **9.** The contagious or 'catching' influence or operation of example, sympathy, etc. 1616. †**10.** The process of moistening, colouring, etc. by immersion or infusion (*rare*) –1686. **11.** *Celt. Gram.* Alteration of a sound under the influence of a neighbouring sound 1872. ¶**12.** Misused *joc.* for *affection*, liking. SHAKS.

3. The i. may be in the very air DE FOE. **b.** All the infections that the Sunne suckes vp From Bogs, Fens, Flats, on Prosper fall *Temp.* II. ii. 1. **4.** As a man suspected of i. is refused admission into cities JOHNSON. **5.** He found himself shunned in public places as an i. THIRLWALL. **7.** A heart that..throws off the i. of these times YOUNG. **9.** The i. of his..enthusiasm 1873. Hence **Infe·ctionist** (*rare*), one who lays stress upon i. as a cause of disease.

Infectious (infe·kʃəs), *a.* 1542. [f. INFECTION + -OUS.] **1.** Having the quality or power of communicating disease by infection; infecting with disease; pestilential, unhealthy. **2.** Of diseases: Apt to be communicated by infection (dist. from CONTAGIOUS) 1592. **b.** *transf.* Of or for infectious diseases 1887. †**3.** Infected with disease –1727. **4.** Tending to contaminate character, morals, etc. Now *rare.* 1547. **5.** Of actions, emotions, etc.: 'Catching', contagious 1611. **6.** *Internat. Law.* Tainting with illegality (said of contraband or hostile goods in their effect on the rest of a cargo, or on the ship) 1878.

1. There is something i. in the atmosphere LYTTON. **2.** The fever was highly i. 1790. **b.** The i. hospital 1887. **3.** *Oth.* IV. i. 21 [*Qos.* infected]. **5.** An i. good humour and urbanity 1899. Hence **Infe·ctious-ly** *adv.*, **-ness.** var. †**Infe·ctuous** 1495.

Infective (infe·ktiv), *a.* ME. [– med.L. *infectivus* infective, poisonous, f. *infect-*; see INFECT *v.*, -IVE. In recent medical use f. INFECT *v.* + -IVE.] **1.** Infectious. **2.** Producing moral infection 1576. †**3.** Producing an amotion, feeling, etc. by infection –1703.

1. The i. matter shown to exist in the blood serum 1883. Hence **Infe·ctiveness, Infecti·vity.**

Infecund (infe·kɒnd), *a.* ME. [– L. *infecundus*; see IN-³, FECUND.] Not fecund; barren, unproductive. So †**Infecu·ndous** *a. rare.*

Infecundity (infǐkɒ·ndǐti). 1605. [– L. *infecunditas*; see IN-³, FECUNDITY.] Unfruitfulness, barrenness (*lit.* and *fig.*).

Infeeble, obs. f. ENFEEBLE *v.*

Infeft (infe·ft), *v. Sc. Law.* 1462. Var. of ENFEOFF with *t* from pa. tense and pa. pple. So **Infe·ftment** 1456 = ENFEOFFMENT.

Infelicific (infīlisi·fik), *a.* 1874. [f. IN-³ + FELICIFIC.] *Ethics.* Productive of unhappiness.

Infelicitous (infǐli·sitəs), *a.* 1835. [f. IN-³ + FELICITOUS.] Unhappy, unfortunate; *esp.* not apt or appropriate; the opposite of FELICITOUS.

An i. idea 1857, illustration 1884. **Infeli·citously** *adv.*

Infelicity (infǐli·sǐti). ME. [– L. *infelicitas*, f. *infelix*, *-ic-* unhappy; see -ITY. Cf. Fr. †*infélicité* (XV).] **1.** The state of being unhappy or unfortunate; an unhappy condition; unhappiness; bad fortune, ill luck, misfortune. **b.** An instance of bad fortune; a misfortune; a cause or source of unhappiness 1577. **2.** Unlucky inaptness or inappropriateness; with *pl.* an inapt expression or detail of style 1617.

1. That pure i. which accompanies some people in their walk through life LAMB. **2.** With how great i. or incongruity soever it be HALES.

Infelo·nious, *a.* [IN-³.] Not of the nature of felony. GEO. ELIOT.

Infelt, *ppl. a.* 1586. [f. IN *adv.* + FELT *ppl. a.*] Inwardly felt or experienced.

Infeodation: see INFEUDATION.

Infeof(f, -ment, obs. ff. ENFEOFF, -MENT.

Infer (infə̄·ɹ), *v.* Inflected **inferred,** etc. 1526. [– L. *inferre* bear or bring in, inflict, make (war), cause, in med.L. infer, f. *in-* IN-² + *ferre* BEAR *v.*¹] †**1.** *trans.* To bring on, bring about, induce, occasion, cause, procure –1754. †**b.** To confer –1614. †**c.** To cause to be. MILT. *P. L.* VII. 116. †**2.** To bring in, introduce; to mention, report; to adduce, allege –1710. **3.** To bring in or draw as a conclusion; in *Logic*, To derive by deduction or induction from something known or assumed; to accept from evidence or premisses; to conclude 1529. Also *absol.* **4.** To lead to as a conclusion; to involve as a consequence; to imply. (Said of a fact or statement.) 1530.

1. Inferre faire Englands peace by this Alliance SHAKS. **2.** Full well hath Clifford plaid the Orator, Inferring arguments of mighty force SHAKS. **3.** What I never meant Don't you i. PRIOR. *absol.* To *infer* is to be regarded as the proper office of the Philosopher;—to *prove*, of the Advocate WHATELY. **4.** Consider first, that Great or Bright inferrs not Excellence MILT. *P.L.* VIII. 91. Hence **Inferable, -ible** (infə̄·răb'l, i·nfĕrib'l) *a.* that may be inferred; deducible.

Inference (i·nfĕrĕns). 1594. [– med.L. *inferentia* (Abelard), f. pr. ppl. stem of L. *inferre*, repl. cl. L. *illatio* ILLATION.] **1.** The action or process of inferring; *esp.* in *Logic*, the forming of a conclusion from premisses, either by induction or deduction; = ILLATION 1. Also (with *pl.*), an act of inferring; the logical form in which this is expressed. **2.** That which is inferred, a conclusion drawn from data or premisses 1612.

1. Religion is..a matter of deduction and i. BUTLER. In any i., we argue either to something already implied in the premisses or not: if the latter, the i. is inductive, if the former, deductive. If the deductive i. contain only a single premiss, it is immediate; if it contain two premisses, and the conclusion be drawn from these jointly, it is mediate, and is called a syllogism FOWLER. **2.** To draw inferences has been said to be the great business of life MILL.

Inferential (infĕre·nʃăl), *a.* 1657. [– med.L. *inferentia* (see prec.) + -AL¹.] Of, pertaining to, or depending on, or of the nature of inference.

The belief was, probably, i. 1854. Hence **Infere·ntially** *adv.* in an i. manner; in the way of inference; *occas.* (qualifying the whole statement) = as may be inferred.

Inferior (infiᵊ·riəɹ). ME. [– L. *inferior*, compar. of *inferus* low.] Lower; opp. to *superior.*

A. *adj.* **1.** Lower in position; nether, subjacent. (Now chiefly techn.) **2.** Lower in degree, rank, importance, quality, amount, etc.; of less value or consideration; lesser; subordinate 1531. **3.** Of low degree, rank, etc.; in mod. use esp.: Of no great value or excellence; comparatively bad, poor, mean 1531. **4.** *Astron.* **a.** Applied to Venus and Mercury, whose orbits lie within that of the earth (orig., according to Ptolemaic astronomy, as having their spheres below that of the sun). **b.** *I. conjunction*: that of an inferior planet with the sun when between the earth and the sun. **c.** *I. meridian*: that part of the celestial meridian which lies below the pole; so *i. passage* (of the meridian), etc. 1658. **5.** *Bot.* Growing below some other part or organ; said of the calyx when growing below or free from the ovary, and of the ovary when adherent to the sides of the calyx so as to be below the lobes of it 1785. **6.** *Anat.* and *Zool.* Applied to parts or organs situated below others of the same kind, or below the usual or normal position. 1826. **7.** *Printing.* Applied to small letters or figures cast or made to range at the bottom of the ordinary letters in a line of type, as in H_2, C_nH_{2n-2}. 1888.

1. The old Glacial drift..being observed in several places as an i. deposit DANA. **2.** The labours of inferiour tenants 1607. The body, or, as some love to call it, our inferiour nature BURKE. I feel myself inferiour to the task BOSWELL. **3.** The country with which he shows so i. an acquaintance 1878.

B. *sb.* **1.** A person inferior to another (in rank, etc.); one of less consideration, attainments, etc.; a subordinate 1502. **2.** A thing inferior to another; †also formerly (in *pl.*), things of this lower world, sublunary affairs or events 1589. **3.** *Printing.* An inferior letter; see A. 7. 1884.

1. Love towards Inferiors is Courtesy and Condescension SHERLOCK.

Hence **Inferio·rity. Infe·riorly** *adv.*

Infernal (infə̄·ɹnăl). ME. [– (O)Fr. *infernal* – Chr. L. *infernalis* (Prudentius), f. *infernus*, parallel to *inferus* (prec.) as *supernus* SUPERNAL to *superus* SUPERIOR (*inferni* the shades, *inferna* the lower regions, in Christian use *infernus* hell); see -AL¹.]

A. *adj.* **1.** Of or relating to the world or regions below, i.e. to the realm of the dead in ancient mythology, or the abode of evil spirits in Jewish and Christian belief; of, pertaining or relating to, hell. **2.** Like that of hell; hellish 1562. **3.** Of the nature of the inhabitants of hell; diabolical, fiendish 1603. **4.** *colloq.* "Confounded'; execrable, detestable 1764.

1. The courte of i. Pluto EDEN. The flocking shadows pale, Troop to th' infernall jail MILT. **2.** The i. hiss and crackle of the flame KINGSLEY. **3.** Voltaire, With an i. sneer upon his lips 1827. Phr. †*I. stone*: an old name for lunar caustic 1706. *I. machine*: an apparatus (often harmless in appearance) contrived to produce an explosion and criminally destroy life or property; formerly, an explosive machine used in war 1810. **4.** An i. ass 1897.

B. *sb.* **1.** An inhabitant of the infernal regions or of hell. (Usu. in *pl.*) 1582. †**2.** *pl.* The infernal regions –1673.

Hence **Infernally** *adv.* (usu. *colloq.*)

‖**Inferno** (infə̄·ɹno). 1834. [It. :– Chr. L. *infernus* (see prec.).] Hell; a place compared to hell, or to Dante's *Inferno.*

Infero- (i·nfĕro), mod. comb. form of L. *inferus* low, used in *Zool.*, etc. to designate parts situated low down or on the under side; as:

Infero-ante·rior *a.*, situated below and in front; **-fro·ntal** *a.*, in the lower part of the forehead; **-la·teral** *a.*, below and on the side; **-me·dian** *a.*, in the middle of the under side; **-poste·rior** *a.*, below and behind.

Inferobranch (i·nfĕroˌbræːŋk). 1836. [f. INFERO- + L. *branchiæ* gills.] *Zool.* One of the order or sub-order *Inferobranchiata* of gastropod molluscs, originally comprising those in which the gills are situated under the projecting border of the mantle, now including also allied forms without gills. So **I:nferobra·nchian, -bra·nchiate** *adjs.* belonging to the *Inferobranchiata*; *sbs.* = INFEROBRANCH.

Inferrible, -able (infə̄·rīb'l, -ăb'l), *a.* 1646. [In XVII *inferrible* (Sir Thomas Browne) – med.L. *inferibilis* (XIV), with double *rr* on Eng. anal. as in *inferring*; for later *-able*, see -IBLE.] That may be inferred; deducible. Hence **Infe·rribly** *adv.*

Infertile (infə̄·ɹtəil, -til), *a.* 1597. [– Fr. *infertile* or late L. *infertilis*; see IN-³, FERTILE.] Not fertile; unproductive, barren, sterile.

To sowe the same in an infertille grownde 1597. Hence **Infe·rtilely** *adv.* **Inferti·lity.**

†**Infe·st,** *a.* 1513. [– L. *infestus*; see next.] Hostile –1641.

Infest (infe·st), *v.* 1477. [– (O)Fr. *infester* or L. *infestare*, f. *infestus* hostile, unsafe.] **1.** *trans.* To attack, annoy, or trouble in a persistent manner; to molest; to harass. **2.** To trouble (a country or place) with hostile attacks; to visit persistently or in large numbers (or even singly) with evil intent; to swarm in or about, so as to be troublesome 1602.

1. He sought all manner of ways to i. the Emperor FOXE. That complication of political diseases which infests the nation FIELDING. **2.** The Turkish Pyrats, which..infested al those Seas PURCHAS. Wasps i. the Camp with loud Alarms DRYDEN. Hence **Infe·ster** *sb.* (*rare*), one who, or that which, infests.

Infestation (infestēⁱ·ʃən). 1492. [– (O)Fr. *infestation* or late L. *infestatio*, f. *infestat-*, pa. ppl. stem of L. *infestare*; see prec., -ION.] The action of infesting; now used esp. of insects which attack plants, grain, etc., usu. in large swarms. Also, an attack or assault of this kind.

The i. did much harm in young Fir woods 1881.

†**Infe·ster,** *v. rare.* 1563. [f. IN-[2] + FESTER *v.*] *trans.* To render (a sore) festered, to cause to rankle. Also *fig.* –1611.

†**Infe·stious,** *a.* 1593. Also **-uous.** [irreg. f. L. *infestus* or INFEST *v.*, after adjs. in *-ious, -uous.* Cf. *infectious.*] Hostile –1709. So †**Infe·stive** *a.*[1]

†**Infe·stive,** *a.*[2] 1623. [– L. *infestivus*; see IN-[3] and FESTIVE.] 'Without mirth or pleasantness'. (Dicts.) So **Infesti·vity** (*rare*), absence of festivity; dullness 1727.

Infeudation (infiudēⁱ·ʃən). 1473. [– med.L. *infeudatio, infeodatio*, f. pa. ppl. stem of *infeudare, infeodare*, f. *feudum, feodum*; see FEUD[2], FEE *sb.*[2], -ION. Cf. (O)Fr. *inféodation*, formerly *infeudation.*] **1. a.** The granting of an estate to be held in fee; enfeoffment. **b.** *I. of tithes*, the granting of tithes to laymen. **2.** A deed of enfeoffment 1647.

Infibulate (infi·biuleⁱt), *v. rare.* 1623. [– *infibulat-*, pa. ppl. stem of L. *infibulare*; see IN-[2], FIBULA, -ATE[3].] *trans.* To fasten with a clasp or buckle. Hence **Infi:bula·tion,** the action of infibulating; *spec.* the fastening of the sexual organs with a fibula or clasp.

Infidel (i·nfidĕl). 1460. [– Fr. *infidèle* or L. *infidelis* unfaithful, (eccl.) unbelieving, f. *in-* IN-[3] + *fidelis* faithful, f. *fides* FAITH.]

A. *sb.* †**1.** An unbeliever 1526. **2.** *spec.* **a.** An adherent of a religion opposed to Christianity; esp. a Moslem, a Saracen (the earliest sense in Eng.); also, *occas.*, a Jew or a pagan. Now chiefly *Hist.* 1470. **b.** From a non-Christian point of view: = Gentile, Giaour, etc. 1534. **3.** A disbeliever in religion generally; esp. one in a Christian land who denies the divine origin and authority of Christianity; a professed unbeliever. Usu. a term of opprobrium. 1526. **4.** *gen.* One who does not believe in something specified. (Freq. *fig.* from 3.) 1606.

2. a. Two honderd sarasyns or Infydeles MALORY. **b.** I sought to wed The daughter of an I. MILT. *Sams.* 221. **4.** Spiritual communications, as regards which Mrs. Browning is a believer, and her husband an i. 1858.

B. *adj.* **1.** Unbelieving; pagan, heathen, etc. 1460; †incredulous, sceptical (*rare*) –1704. **2.** Of, pertaining to, or characteristic of, infidels or infidelity 1742.

Infidelity (infide·lĭti). ME. [– (O)Fr. *infidélité* or L. *infidelitas*, f. *infidelis*; see prec., -ITY.] **1.** Want of faith; unbelief, esp. disbelief in the truth or evidence of Christianity; the attitude of an infidel. †**b.** Islam; Heathenism (*rare*) –1613. **2.** *gen.* Disbelief, incredulity 1579. **3.** Unfaithfulness or disloyalty to a person; esp., in mod. use, to a husband or wife 1529; an act or instance of this 1714. †**4.** Untrustworthiness; an instance of this –1785.

1. I. is the proper opposite of faith MANNING. **3.** Mischiefs arising from conjugal i. and impunity 1700. **4.** The i. of that conveyance [the post] BURKE.

Infield, in-field (i·nˌfīld), *sb.* 1551. [f. IN *adv.* + FIELD *sb.*] **1.** The land of a farm which lies around or near the homestead; hence, arable land as opp. to pasture; land regularly manured and cropped 1733; orig. *attrib.*, in *i. land* 1551. **2.** *Base-ball.* The diamond. **b.** The four fielders placed on the boundaries of the in-field. **3.** *Cricket.* The part of the ground near the wicket, or the fieldsmen stationed there (hence **In-fieldsman**) 1910.

1. *Infield and outfield*, a system of husbandry which confines manuring and tillage to the infield land.

Infie·ld, *v.* 1856. [f. IN-[2] + FIELD *sb.*] To enclose, as a field.

I·n-fi:ghting, *vbl. sb.* 1812. [f. IN *adv.* + FIGHTING *vbl. sb.*] *Pugilism.* Fighting or boxing at close quarters; the practice of getting close up to an opponent.

Infi·gured, *ppl. a.* Also **en-.** 1611. [f. IN-[2], EN-[1] + FIGURED.] Marked or adorned with figures.

Infile, obs. var. of ENFILE *v.*

Infilm, *v.* 1864. [f. IN-[2] + FILM *v.*] To cover with a film; to coat thinly.

Infilter (infi·ltəɹ), *v.* 1846. [f. IN *adv.* + FILTER *v.*, or – Fr. *infiltrer* (Paré).] = next 1.

Infiltrate (infi·ltreⁱt), *v.* 1758. [f. IN-[2] + FILTRATE *v.*, after Fr. *infiltrer*; see prec.] **1.** *trans.* To introduce by filtration; to cause (a fluid) to permeate through pores or interstices. Also *fig.* **2.** To pass into or permeate by filtration 1758. **3.** *intr.* To pass through or into a substance by filtration; to percolate through pores or interstices 1828. Also *fig.*

2. Carbonized remains, often infiltrated with mineral matter HUXLEY. **3.** Education infiltrates from the upper and governing classes to the lower 1861.

Infiltration (infiltrēⁱ·ʃən). 1796. [f. INFILTRATE + -ION, prob. after Fr. *infiltration.*] **1.** The action or process of infiltrating; percolation. Also *fig.* **b.** The penetration by settlement, etc. of one people into another 1904. **2.** The action of infiltrating a substance with something; the process, fact, or condition of being infiltrated or permeated 1830. **3.** An infiltrated deposit 1812.

1. The i. of sea-water through lavas KIRWAN. *fig.* The i. of tribal ideas MAINE. **2.** Fatty I.—which is often described as 'fatty degeneration'—consists in the i. of the tissues with fat, which is deposited in them from the blood 1873. **3.** Calcareous infiltrations filling the cavities of other stones KIRWAN.

Infine, *adv. phr.*: see FINE *sb.*[1] I. 1.

Infinitary (infi·nitări), *a.* [= G. *infinitär*, as in *infinitärkalkul* (Du Bois Raymond); see -ARY[1].] *Math.* Relating to infinity, or to an infinite value of a quantity.

Infinitate (infi·niteⁱt), *v.* 1864. [– *infinitat-*, pa. ppl. stem of schol. L. *infinitare* (Abelard), f. *infinitus*; see next, -ATE[3].] *trans.* To render infinite; in *Logic*, to make (a term, or predicate) 'infinite' or indefinite in extent, by prefixing a negative. Hence **Infinita·tion,** the action of infinitating; the condition of being infinitated; hence, applied to *permutation* or *obversion* 1652.

Infinite (i·nfinit), *a.* (*adv.*) and *sb.* ME. [– L. *infinitus* unbounded, unlimited; see IN-[3], FINITE.]

A. *adj.* **1.** Having no limit or end; boundless; immeasurably great in extent, duration, etc. Chiefly of God or His attributes; also of space, time, etc. **b.** Loosely: Exceedingly great; immense, vast ME. †**c.** Immensely long, 'endless' –1638. **2.** with *sb. pl.* Unlimited in number; very many, 'no end of'. Now *arch.* or *rare* ME. †**3.** Indeterminate in nature, meaning, etc. –1663. **4.** *Math.* †**a.** Of indefinite length or magnitude. BARROW. **b.** Having no limit; opp. to *finite*, also to *closed* 1692. **5.** *Mus.* Of a canon: Made continually to recur to the beginning, so as never to come to a regular close; circular 1811. **6.** *Gram.* Applied to those parts of the verb which are not limited by person and number. Opp. to *finite*. 1871. **7.** *Logic.* Infinitated 1860.

1. Greate is our Lorde,..yee his wyszdome is i. COVERDALE *Ps.* 146[7]:5. No man can have in his mind an image of i. magnitude HOBBES. **b.** Gratiano speakes an i. deale of nothing SHAKS. **2.** I. other Instances of like nature may be given HALE. **4.** *I. series* (Math.): a series of quantities or expressions which may be indefinitely continued without ever coming to an end 1706. So **i. decimal** 1796.

†**B.** *adv.* Infinitely; in hyperbolical sense = very greatly –1673.

C. *absol.* or as *sb.* **1.** That which is infinite; an infinite being, thing, quantity, extent, etc. Now usu. in *sing.* with *the*, esp. as a designation of God 1587. **2.** In hyperbolical use: A very great amount or number; very much or many; 'no end' 1563. **3.** *Math.* An infinite quantity: see A. 4 b. 1656.

1. The Presence-chamber of the I. MARTINEAU. **2.** There was i. of new cakes placed PEPYS. That Calais tower has an i. of symbolism in it RUSKIN.

Infinitely (i·nfinitli), *adv.* ME. [f. prec. + -LY[2].] **1.** In an infinite degree, or to an infinite extent. **b.** *Loosely*, Exceedingly, immensely, vastly 1584. †**2.** To an indefinite distance or extent –1695. †**3.** In an indefinite manner or sense; generally –1591. **4.** *Math.* Without limit 1692.

1. Every particle of matter is i. divisible PRIESTLEY. **b.** Dear Prue—I have yours of the 14th, and am i. obliged to you for the length of it STEELE.

I·nfiniteness. Now *rare.* 1534. [f. INFINITE *a.* + -NESS.] The quality or condition of being infinite; infinity; immensity, vastness.

The Schools talk of the I. of Space 1700. The i. of her sensuality FORD.

Infinitesimal (infinite·simăl). 1655. [f. mod.L. *infinitesimus*, f. L. *infinitus* INFINITE, after *centesimus* hundredth; see -AL[1].] Orig. an *ordinal*, viz. the 'infiniteth' in order; but like other ordinals, also used to name fractions, thus *i. part* or *i.* came to mean unity divided by infinity ($\frac{1}{\infty}$), and thus an infinitely small part or quantity.

A. *sb.* (or *absol.*) †**1.** As ordinal: The 'infiniteth' member of a series. HY. MORE. **2.** (Chiefly *Math.*) As a fraction. The inverse or reciprocal of an infinite quantity; †an infinitely small fraction *of* anything. Hence **b.** (*Math.*) An infinitely small quantity, a quantity less than any assignable quantity. **3.** *Loosely.* An extremely small quantity or amount 1840.

B. *adj.* **1.** (Chiefly *Math.*) **a.** Infinitely or indefinitely small. (Correl. to *infinite*, and, with it, opp. to *finite.*) **b.** *transf.* Relating to infinitesimal quantities; esp. in *i. calculus*, a name for the differential and integral calculuses considered as one. 1710. **2.** *Loosely*, Too small to be measured or reckoned; extremely minute or insignificant 1733.

2. The i. Vessels of the Nervous System HARTLEY. Hence **Infinite·simally** *adv.* in an i. degree; use. qualifying *small.*

Infiniteth, *a. nonce-wd.* 1708. [f. INFINITE + -TH[2], termination of ordinal numerals.] *Math.* The ordinal numeral corresponding to *infinite*. E. HALLEY. (**Infinitieth,** from *infinity*, is now in oral use.)

Infinitival (infi:nitəi·văl), *a.* 1869. [f. L. *infinitivus* (see next) + -AL[1].] *Gram.* Of or belonging to the infinitive.

Infinitive (infi·nitiv). 1470. [– L. *infinitivus* unlimited, indefinite, infinitive, f. *in-* IN-[3] + *finitivus* definite. Cf. (O)Fr. *infinitif, -ive.*]

A. *adj.* **1.** *Gram.* The name of that form of a verb which expresses simply the notion of the verb without predicating it of any subject. Usu. classed as a *mood*, though strictly a substantive with certain verbal functions, esp. those of governing an object, and being qualified by an adv. 1520.

(Called by Quintilian and Priscian *infinitus modus*, by Diomedes *infinitivus* 'because it has not definite persons and numbers'.)

In mod. Eng., the infinitive has the simple uninflected form of the vb. In OE., the infinitive had (in the nom.-acc. case) the suffix *-an*, ME. *-en, -e*; it had also a dative form in *-anne*, ME. *-enne, -ene, -en, -e.* The latter is sometimes called by mod. grammarians the *gerundial* or *gerundive infinitive.* (It answers more to the L. supine.) The OE. nom.-acc. infinitive is the source of the simple infinitive, as in 'we saw him *come*', etc. The dative infinitive is formally the source of the infinitive with *to*; but *to* is now prefixed also to the nom.-acc. infinitive, where OE. had the simple form in *-an*, as in '*to see* is to believe', etc.

†**2.** Infinite, endless. Also as *adv.* 1470.

B. *sb.* **1.** *Gram.* The infinitive 'mood' or form of a verb 1530. †**2.** An infinite amount; an infinity. MARKHAM.

1. *Split* (or *cleft*) *i.*, an i. with an adv. between *to* and the verbal part. The following is an example:
To sit on rocks, to muse o'er flood and fell,
To slowly trace the forest's shady scene.
BYRON, *Ch. Harold* II. xxv.

Hence **Infi·nitively** *adv.* in the i. mood; †infinitely (*rare*).

Infinito- (infinəi·to), comb. f. L. *infinitus* INFINITE, with the sense 'infinitely, to an infinite degree', as in *i.-infinitesimal* (used by Hartley to describe an infinitesimal of the second degree). Also loosely with sense 'infinite and', as in *i.-absolute*.

Infinitude (infi·nitiud). 1641. [f. L. *infinitus* INFINITE, after *magnitudo, multitudo*.] **1.** The quality or attribute of being infinite; boundlessness. Also, *loosely*, Immensity, vastness. **2.** (with *pl.*) Something that is infinite (or, *loosely*, indefinitely great); a boundless (or vast) extent, space, amount, number, etc.; infinity 1667.

1. The universe fatigues with its i. 1890. **2.** I am who fill I. MILT. *P.L.* VII. 168. An i. of complex relations DARWIN.

‖**Infinitum** (infinəi·tǒm). 1682. [L., n. sing. of adj. *infinitus* INFINITE; also as sb.] = INFINITY; see AD INFINITUM, etc.

Infinituple (infi·nitiup'l), *a.* 1722. [f. L. *infinitus* INFINITE, after *centuple*, etc.] Infinitely as much or as many; an infinite number of times (something else). WOLLASTON.

Infinity (infi·nĭti). ME. [– (O)Fr. *infinité* – L. *infinitas*, f. *infinitus* INFINITE; see -ITY.] **1.** The quality of being infinite or having no limit; boundlessness (esp. as an attribute of Deity). **2.** Something that is infinite; infinite extent, amount, duration, etc.; a boundless space; an endless or unlimited time ME. **3.** Loosely (from 1 and 2): Immensity, vastness; a very great amount or number, 'no end' (*of*) ME. **4.** *Math.* **a.** Infinite quantity (see INFINITE A. 4 b): denoted by the symbol ∞. Also, an infinite number (*of* something) 1692. **b.** *Geom.* Infinite distance, or that region of space which is infinitely distant; usu. in phr. *at i.* 1873.

1. One whose..i. passeth all nombre, that is almightye God himself MORE. **2.** There cannot be more infinities than one; for one of them would limit the other RALEGH. Man's point of life 'between two infinities' (of that expression Marcus Aurelius is the real owner) M. ARNOLD. **3.** An i. of pains JOWETT. Phr. *To i.* (= L. *ad* or *in infinitum*): endlessly, without limit.

Infirm (infǝ̄·ɹm), *a.* ME. [– L. *infirmus*; see IN-[3], FIRM *a.*] **1.** Of things: Not firm or strong; weak, unsound; frail, shaky, feeble. Also *transf.* of arguments, titles, etc. Now *rare*. **2.** Of persons, etc.: Not strong and healthy; physically weak or feeble, esp. through age. Also *transf.* of age. 1605. **3.** Not firm or strong in character or purpose; weak, irresolute 1526.

1. Those that build on sandie or infirme ground 1624. The i. title of the House of Lancaster LD. BROUGHAM. **2.** A poore, infirme, weake, and dispis'd old man *Lear* III. ii. 20. What is infirme, from your sound parts shall flie SHAKS. **3.** Infirme of purpose: Giue me the Daggers SHAKS. Hence **Infi·rm-ly** *adv.*, **-ness** (now *rare*).

Infirm (infǝ̄·ɹm), *v.* Now *rare*. 1449. [– L. *infirmare* weaken, invalidate, f. *infirmus* (see prec.). Cf. (O)Fr. *infirmer*.] To make infirm; to weaken; to invalidate (a law, custom, etc.). The bad faith of the Habsburgs could not i. Magyar rights 1890.

Infirmarer (infǝ̄·ɹmărəɹ). ME. [– OFr. *enfermerier*, app. f. *enfermerie* INFIRMARY; but poss. f. †*enfermer* – OFr. *enfermier* (mod. *infirmier*) + -ER[1] 3. See also FERMERER.] *Hist.* In mediæval monasteries, the person who had charge of the infirmary. So **Infi·rmaress** [-ESS[1]]. **Infirma·rian**, in same sense.

Infirmary (infǝ̄·ɹmări). 1451. [– med.L. *infirmaria* (sc. *domus*), f. L. *infirmus* INFIRM; see -ARY[1]. See FERMERY.] **1.** A building or part of a building for the treatment of the sick or wounded; a hospital. Also *fig.* †**2.** A conservatory 1707.

Infirmation (infəɹmēⁱ·ʃən). [– L. *infirmatio*, f. *infirmat-*, pa. ppl. stem of *infirmare*; see INFIRM *v.*, -ION.] The action of weakening or invalidating (evidence).

Infirmative (infǝ̄·ɹmătiv), *a.* (*sb.*) *rare*. 1611. [f. INFIRM *v.* + -ATIVE. Cf. Fr. *infirmatif* (XVII) in same sense.] Tending to weaken or invalidate. As *sb.* That which tends to weaken.

†**Infi·rmatory.** *rare*. 1598. [– med.L. *infirmatorium*, f. *infirmat-* (see INFIRMATION) + *-orium* -ORY[1].] = INFIRMARY –1678. var. †**Infi·rmitory** 1538–1645.

Infirmity (infǝ̄·ɹmĭti). ME. [– L. *infirmitas*, f. *infirmus*; see INFIRM *a.*, -ITY. Cf. Fr. *infirmité*.] The condition of being infirm. **1.** Weakness or want of strength; inability; an instance or case of this. **b.** Of an argument or title: Want of validity 1614. **2.** Physical weakness, debility, frailty, feebleness of body, resulting from some defect, disease, or (now mostly) old age ME. **3.** A special form or variety of weakness; †an illness, disease; now esp. a falling in some faculty or sense ME. **4.** Weakness of character; moral weakness or frailty; also with *an* and *pl.* ME.

1. When I could no longer hurt them, the revolutionists have trampled on my i. BURKE. **2.** I. that decaies the wise *Twel. N.* I. v. 82. **3.** He is a little deaf and has a similar i. in sight JOWETT. **4.** The head of the house..was a byword for i. of purpose 1873. Fame..(That last i. of Noble mind) MILT. *Lycidas* 71.

Infix (i·nfiks), *sb.* 1881. [In XVII – *infix-* (see next); in mod. *Gram.* use, f. IN-[1] or [2] after *prefix, suffix* by substitution of prefix. Cf. next (sense 3).] *Gram.* A modifying element inserted in the body of a word.

Infix (infi·ks), *v.* Also **en-**. 1502. [Partly – *infix-*, pa. ppl. stem of L. *infigere* fix in; partly f. IN-[1] or [2] + FIX *v.*] **1.** *trans.* To fix or fasten *in*; to implant or insert firmly. Also *fig.* **b.** To fix or fasten on something 1601. **2.** To fix (a fact, etc.) *in* the mind or memory; to impress 1542. **3.** *Gram.* To insert (a formative element) in the body of a word (cf. prec.) 1868.

1. Infixing their Nailes in the Fronts of them, they claw off the skin 1650. *fig.* The vices which they introduced, and the habits they infixed LAMB. **2.** First soundly i. in thy mind what thou desirest to remember FULLER. Hence **Infi·xion** (*rare*), the action of infixing; the condition of being infixed.

Inflamable, obs. var. of INFLAMMABLE.

Inflame (inflēⁱ·m), *v.* Also **en-**. [ME. *inflaume, -flamme* – (O)Fr. *enflammer* :– L. *inflammare*, f. *in-* IN-[2] + *flamma* FLAME.]

I. *trans.* **1.** To cause to blaze; to set on fire; to kindle. **b.** *transf.* To light up or redden as if with flame 1477. **2.** *fig.* To fire with passion, strong feeling, or desire; to kindle (passion, etc.) ME. **3.** To heat, make hot; *esp.* to raise (the body or blood) to a feverish heat; to excite inflammation in 1530. **4.** To add heat or fuel to, to aggravate 1607; †to augment (a price, etc.) –1773.

1. Gardiner had inflamed many Martyrs, and hath now his body inflamed 1631. **b.** The red, reflected sky Inflames the river 1892. **2.** Having their minds enflamed with passion 1726. **3.** My father's face..Inflamed with wrath TENNYSON. **4.** To i. an animosity 1879, a reckoning GOLDSM.

II. *intr.* **1.** To burst into flame; to catch fire 1638. **2.** To become hot with passion; to glow with feeling 1559. **3.** To be affected with inflammation 1607.

Hence **Infla·med** *ppl. a.* set on fire, etc.; *Her.* depicted as in flames. **Infla·mer**, one who or that which inflames; an instigator.

Inflammable (inflæ·măb'l), *a.* (*sb.*) Also †**inflameable.** 1570. [In form *inflam(e)able* (XVII–XVIII) f. prec. + -ABLE; *inflammable* after Fr. *inflammable* (XVII).] **1.** Capable of being inflamed; susceptible of combustion; easily set on fire. **2.** Excitable, hasty-tempered, passionate 1800. **3.** *sb.* An inflammable substance 1770.

1. Alcohol is very i. ROSCOE. *I. air*, old name for hydrogen gas. **2.** A sanguine and i. disposition 1845. Hence **Inflammabi·lity, Infla·mmableness**, i. quality. **Infla·mmably** *adv.*

Inflammation (inflămēⁱ·ʃən). 1533. [– L. *inflammatio*, f. *inflammat-*, pa. ppl. stem of *inflammare*; see INFLAME *v.*, -ION. Cf. (O)Fr. *inflammation*, perh. partly the source.] **1.** The action of inflaming; setting on fire or catching fire; the condition of being in flames 1563. †**b.** *concr.* Something in flames –1772. **2.** The action of inflaming mentally; the condition of being so inflamed; excitement, fervour. Also, an instance of this. 1597. **3.** *Path.* A morbid process affecting some part of the body, characterized by excessive heat, swelling, pain, and redness; also, an instance of this 1533. †**4.** Augmentation of charge 1821.

1. The i. of the Cities of the Plain 1650. **2.** The means of calming a people in a state of extreme i. BURKE. **4.** The i. of his weekly bills BYRON.

Inflammative (inflæ·mătiv), *a.* and *sb.* *rare*. 1685. [– med.L. *inflammativus*, f. as prec.; see -IVE. Cf. Fr. †*inflammatif* (XV–XVI).] = INFLAMMATORY *a.* and *sb.*

Inflammatory (inflæ·mătəri), *a.* and *sb.* 1681. [f. stem of *inflammation* + -ORY[1] and [2].] †**1.** Of, pertaining to, characterized by, or causing a blazing condition –1796. **2.** Tending to excite desire, passion, anger, or animosity. (Now usu. in a bad sense.) 1711. **3.** That tends to inflame the blood; exciting the brain or senses; stimulating 1733. **4.** *Path.* Of the nature of, pertaining to, indicative of, or characterized by inflammation 1732. **5.** *sb.* That which inflames, excites, or rouses feeling or passion 1681.

2. I. libels 1767, powers of art GIBBON, speeches 1834. **4.** I. Distempers ARBUTHNOT. Hence **Infla·mmatorily** *adv.*

†**Inflate**, *ppl. a.* late ME. [– L. *inflatus*, pa. pple. of *inflare*; see next, -ATE[2].] = INFLATED.

Inflate (inflēⁱ·t), *v.* 1502. [– *inflat-*, pa. ppl. stem of L. *inflare*, f. *in-* IN-[2] + *flare* blow; see -ATE[3].] **1.** *trans.* To blow out or distend with wind or air; to fill with air or gas; also *absol.* to cause flatulence 1533. **2.** To puff up (a person) *with* high spirits, pride, etc.; to elate. Also *absol.* 1502. **3.** To dilate, distend, or swell; to enlarge 1705. **4.** To swell or expand artificially or unduly 1843.

1. To i. the lungs 1834, a balloon ROSCOE, (*fig.*) vanity 1870. **2.** Character that prosperity could not i. 1803. **3.** When Passion's tumults in the bosom rise, I. the features, and enrage the eyes 1782. **4.** We i. our paper currency EMERSON. Hence **Infla·table** *a.* that can be inflated. **Infla·tingly** *adv.* **Infla·ter, -or**, one who or that which inflates.

Inflated (inflēⁱ·tėd), *ppl. a.* 1652. [f. prec. + -ED[1].] **1.** Puffed out or swollen by air or gas 1681. **2.** Of language: Turgid, bombastic 1652. **3.** Expanded, as if by inflation 1726. **4.** Elated with vanity or false notions 1784. **5.** Raised in price artificially 1881.

1. Bridges on..i. skins 1853. **2.** The account..is long and i. GOLDSM. **4.** I. and astrut with self-conceit, He gulps the windy diet COWPER. **5.** An i. state of prices that could not possibly be maintained GLADSTONE.

Inflation (inflēⁱ·ʃən). ME. [– L. *inflatio*, f. *inflat-*; see INFLATE *v.*, -ION.] **1.** The action of inflating with air or gas 1601. **2.** The condition of being inflated with air or gas, or of being distended as if with air ME. **3.** The condition of being puffed up with vanity, pride, or false notions 1526. **4.** Turgidity, bombast 1603. **5.** Increase beyond proper limits; esp. of prices, the issue of inconvertible paper money, etc. 1864. Hence **Infla·tionary** *a.*, marked by inflation of prices; **Infla·tionist**, one who advocates an increase of the paper currency; also *attrib.*; so **Infla·tionism.**

‖**Inflatus** (inflēⁱ·tǒs). [L. *inflatus*; see IN-[2], FLATUS.] A blowing or breathing into; inflation; inspiration. E. B. BROWNING.

Inflect (infle·kt), *v.* ME. [– L. *inflectere*, f. *in-* IN-[2] + *flectere* bend.] **1.** *trans.* To bend inwards; to bend into a curve or angle; hence, to bend, to curve. Also *fig.* †**2.** *Optics.* = DIFFRACT *v.* –1811. **3.** *Gram.* To vary the termination of (a word) in order to express different grammatical relations 1668. **4.** To modulate (the voice); spec. in *Music*, to flatten or sharpen (a note) by a chromatic semitone 1828.

2. Are they [rays of light] not reflected, refracted, and inflected by one and the same principle? NEWTON.

Inflected (infle·ktėd), *ppl. a.* 1646. [f. prec. + -ED[1].] **1.** Bent or curved; bent inwards. **2.** *Gram.* Having inflexions; characterized by grammatical inflexion 1775.

Inflection: see INFLEXION.

Inflective (infle·ktiv), *a.* 1666. [f. INFLECT *v.* + -IVE.] **1.** Inflecting; tending to inflect. **2.** Pertaining to or characterized by grammatical inflexion 1799.

2. The glories of a completely i. language 1875.

Inflesh, obs. f. ENFLESH *v.*

†**Infle·x**, *a.* 1753. [– L. *inflexus*, pa. pple. of *inflectere* INFLECT.] *Bot.* = INFLEXED –1794.

Inflexed (infle·kst). *ppl. a.* 1661. [f. as prec. + -ED[1].] Bent inwards; incurved.

Inflexibility[1] (infleksĭbi·lĭti). 1611. [f. INFLEXIBLE[1] + -ITY. Cf. Fr. *inflexibilité*.] The quality or condition of being inflexible;

incapability of being bent; unyielding stiffness, rigidity; firmness of purpose, obstinacy.
Features arranged into the utmost i. of expression SCOTT. Bone..cannot swell, in consequence of its i. 1876.

Inflexibility[2]: see INFLEXIBLE[2].

Inflexible (infle·ksĭb'l), *a.*[1] ME. [– L. *inflexibilis*; see IN-[3], FLEXIBLE. Cf. (O)Fr. *inflexible.*] Not flexible. **1.** Incapable of being bent; not pliant; rigid, stiff. **2.** Unbending in temper or purpose; immovable, inexorable ME. **3.** Unalterable, rigidly fixed 1693.
2. He is i., stedfast, and faileþ not TREVISA. **3.** Nature's laws are more i. than iron 1871. Hence **Infle·xibleness** (*rare*). **Infle·xibly** *adv.* 1534.

†**Infle·xible,** *a.*[2] *rare.* ME. [f. L. *inflex-* (see INFLEX *a.*) + -IBLE.] Capable of being inflected; in *Optics*, diffrangible –1857. Hence †**Inflexibi·lity**[2].

Inflexion, inflection (infle·kʃən). 1531. [– (O)Fr. *inflexion* or L. *inflexio*, f. *inflex-*, pa. ppl. stem of *inflectere*; see INFLECT, -ION. As to the sp. cf. CONNECTION, etc.] **1.** The action of inflecting; the condition of being inflected; *concr.* a bending, bend, curvature, or angle. Also *fig.* †**2.** *Optics.* = DIFFRACTION –1831. **3.** *Geom.* Change of curvature from convex to concave at a particular point on a curve; *point of i.*, the point at which this takes place 1721. **4.** *Gram.* The modification of the form of a word to express different grammatical relations; including the declension of sbs., adjs., and pronouns, the conjugation of vbs., and the comparison of adjs. and advs. 1668. **b.** *concr.* An inflected form; also, the inflexional suffix 1668. **5.** Modulation of the voice; in speaking or singing, a change in the pitch or tone of the voice 1600.
Hence **Infle·xional, infle·ctional** *a.* pertaining to or characterized by grammatical inflexion.

Inflexive (infle·ksiv), *a.*[1] [f. *inflex-* (see prec.) + -IVE.] = INFLECTIVE. (Dicts.).

†**Inflexive,** *a.*[2] [f. IN-[3] + FLEXIVE.] Inflexible. CHAPMAN.

†**Infle·xure.** 1578. [f. IN-[2] + FLEXURE, after INFLEXION.] A bend, curve, or turn inwards –1658.

Inflict (infli·kt), *v.* 1566. [– *inflict-*, pa. ppl. stem of L. *infligere*, f. *in-* IN-[2] + *fligere* dash or strike, inflict.] **1.** *trans.* To lay on as a stroke, blow, or wound; to impose; to cause to be borne 1593. **2.** With inverted construction: To afflict (a person) *with* something painful or disagreeable. (Now *rare*). 1566.
1. To i. paine, lasting shame SHAKS., a penalty HOBBES. **2.** We should be inflicted with less.. twaddle 1883. Hence **Infli·ctable** *a.* that can or may be inflicted. **Infli·cter, -or,** one who inflicts. **Infli·ctive** *a.* tending to i.; pertaining to infliction.

Infliction (infli·kʃən). 1534. [– late L. *inflictio*, f. as prec.; see -ION. Cf. Fr. *infliction.*] The action of inflicting (pain, punishment, annoyance, etc.); the fact of being inflicted (*Meas. for M.* I. iii. 28). **b.** Something inflicted, as pain, punishment, etc.; an annoyance, a 'visitation' 1586.
b. Such Persecutions, as seem to be Divine Inflictions 1665.

Inflood (inflɒ·d), *v.* 1855. [f. IN-[1] or [2] + FLOOD *v.*] *intr.* To flow in, to enter as a flood.
The silent inflooding of the day STEVENSON.

Inflorescence (inflore·sĕns). 1760. [– mod.L. *inflorescentia* (Linnæus), f. late L. *inflorescere* come into flower; see IN-[2], FLORESCENCE.] *Bot.* **1.** The mode in which the flowers of a plant are arranged in relation to the axis and to each other; the flowering system. **b.** The collective flower or blossom of a plant 1851. **2.** The process of coming into flower; blossoming. Also *fig.* 1800.
1. I. affords the truest, and in most Genera the most elegant Distinction 1760.

Inflow (i·nflōᵘ), *sb.* 1839. [f. IN *adv.* + FLOW *sb.*[1]] = INFLUX.

Inflow (inflōᵘ·), *v.* 1651. [f. IN-[1] + FLOW *v.*] †**1.** *intr. Astrol.* = INFLUE *v.* –1670. **2.** To flow in 1882. †**3.** *trans.* To cause to flow in. HOBBES.

†**Influe,** *v. rare.* 1426. [–(O)Fr. *influer* or L. *influere* flow in; see next.] *intr.* To shed (heavenly) influence –1618.

Influence (i·nfluĕns), *sb.* ME. [– (O)Fr. *influence* or med.L. *influentia* (whence also Pr., Sp. *influencia*, It. *influenza*), f. *influent-*, pr. ppl. stem of L. *influere* flow in, f. *in-* IN-[2] + *fluere* flow; see -ENCE.] †**1.** The action or fact of flowing in; inflow, influx –1702. **2.** *spec.* in *Astrol.* The supposed flowing from the stars of an ethereal fluid acting upon the character and destiny of men, and affecting sublunary things generally. In later times taken as an exercise of occult power. ME. **b.** *transf.* The exercise of analogous power by human beings. Now only *poet.* ME. †**c.** Disposition, or temperament, as held to be due to astral influence –1663. †**3.** The inflowing or infusion (*into* a person or thing) of any kind of divine, moral, or other secret power or principle; that which thus flows in or is infused –1677. **4.** The exertion of action of which the operation is unseen, except in its effects, by one person or thing upon another; the action thus exercised. Orig. const. *into*; now *on*, *upon*, *in*. 1588. **5.** The capacity of producing effects by insensible or invisible means; ascendancy of a person or social group; control not formally or overtly expressed 1652. **6.** A thing or person that exercises influence 1736. **7.** *Electr.* = INDUCTION 9. 1870.
2. Canst thou bind the sweete influences of Pleiades? *Job* 38:31. What euill starre On you hath frownd, and pourd his i. bad? SPENSER *F.Q.* I. viii. 42. **b.** Ladies, whose bright eyes Rain i. MILT. **c.** Germans and Bohemians, nations by i. heavie, slowe 1601. **3.** MILT. *P.L.* V. 695. **4.** Before they had much i. on my thoughts JOHNSON. Phr. *Undue i.*: see UNDUE. **5.** To owe a position to i., not to merit 1900.

Influence (i·nfluĕns), *v.* 1658. [f. prec. Cf. Fr. *influencer.*] **1.** *trans.* To exert influence upon, to affect by influence. Sometimes esp. to move by undue influence; †formerly *spec.* of astral influence. **2.** *intr.* To exert influence 1670. †**3.** *trans.* To cause to flow in; to infuse, instil –1705.
1. The Sovereign can i. the conduct of public affairs LD. BROUGHAM. Expenditures to 'influence' city council 1891. Hence **I·nfluencer,** one who or that which influences. **I·nfluencive** *a.* (*rare*), having the quality of influencing.

Influent (i·nfluĕnt), *a.* (*sb.*) ME. [– *influent-*; see INFLUENCE *sb.*, -ENT.] **1.** Flowing in. Also *transf.* and *fig.* 1445. †**2.** Exercising astral influence or occult power –1856. †**3.** Influential –1657. **4.** *sb.* A tributary, an affluent 1859.
1. Thames, with i. tide COWPER. **2.** Multitudinous mountains .. panting .. Beneath the i. heavens E. B. BROWNING. [Humility] is more..i. upon others, then any other vertue 1654.

Influential (influe·nʃăl), *a.* 1570. [f. med.L. *influentia* INFLUENCE + -AL[1].] †**1.** *Astrol.* Possessing or exercising astral influence; of, pertaining to, or of the nature of such influence –1664. †**b.** *transf.* Working by hidden processes –1745. **2.** Having or exerting influence, power, or effect 1655. **3.** Having great influence; powerful 1734.
2. Hurtful errours, i. on practice BARROW. **3.** Very i. among the Citisens NORTH. I. precepts H. SPENCER. Hence **Influe·ntially** *adv.* with influence; in an i. manner; *Electr.* by induction.

Influenza (influ,e·nză). 1743. [– It. *influenza* INFLUENCE :– med.L. *influentia*.
It. *influenza* has the sense (developed, app., from the notion of 'astral' or 'occult influence') of 'visitation' of any epidemic disease; hence, absol., that of 'an epidemic'; applied spec. to the epidemic of 1743 (called also *la grippe*), for which it became the English specific name.]
A specific febrile zymotic disorder, highly contagious, and occurring usually in widespread epidemics. Its symptoms and sequelæ include rapid prostration and severe catarrh. Applied loosely to any severe catarrh of the respiratory mucous membrane, *esp.* to an *influenza-cold*.
attrib. and *Comb.*, as *i. bacillus*, etc.; **i.-cold,** a severe cold with symptoms resembling those of i.

Influx (i·nflɒks). 1626. [– Fr. *influx* or late L. *influxus*, f. L. *influere* flow in; see IN-[2], FLUX.] **1.** The act or fact of flowing in; an inflow. **b.** The mouth of a river 1652. **2.** *transf.* The continuous ingression of persons or things into some place or sphere 1652. †**3.** = INFLUENCE 2. –1650. †**4.** = INFLUENCE 3–5. –1703.
1. A strong i. of light 1823. **b.** The Kennet, near its I. into the Thames 1675. **2.** An i. of unruly people 1652, of new opinions 1775, of Greek EARLE, of settlers from the Slave States BRYCE.

Influxion (inflɒ·kʃən). Now *rare.* 1605. [– late L. *influxio*, f. *influx-*, pa. ppl. stem of *influere*; see IN-[2], FLUXION.] **1.** Inflow, influx. †**2.** = INFLUENCE 2. –1642.

†**Influ·xious,** *a.* [f. prec. + -OUS; see -IOUS.] Shedding (astral) influence. HOWELL.

†**Influ·xive,** *a.* 1624. [f. INFLUX (senses 3 and 4) + -IVE.] Infusing or communicating influence, influential –1657. Hence †**Influ·xively** *adv.* by influxion.

Info·ld, obs. var. of ENFOLD.

†**Info·liate,** *v. rare.* 1640. [f. IN-[2] + FOLIATE *v.* (cf. contemp. FOLIATE *a.* furnished with leaves).] *intr.* To put on leaves, to become leafy –1656.

Inform (infǭ·ɹm), *a.* 1555. [– Fr. *informe* or L. *informis*, f. *in-* IN-[3] + *forma* FORM.] **1.** Having no regular form; unshapen, misshapen (*arch.*). **2.** Without form; formless; of the nature of matter unendowed with 'form' 1654.

Inform (infǭ·ɹm), *v.* [ME. *enfo(u)rme* – OFr. *enfo(u)rmer* (mod. *informer*) – L. *informare* shape, form an idea of, describe, f. *in-* IN-[2] + *forma* FORM.]
I. †**1.** *trans.* To put into form or shape; to shape –1643; to arrange; to compose –1666. †**2.** *intr.* To take shape; to form –1652.
2. It is the bloody Businesse, which informes Thus to mine Eyes *Macb.* II. i. 48.
II. *trans.* To give 'form' or formative principle to; hence, to stamp, impress, or imbue *with* some specific quality or attribute; to inspire, animate ME.
The God of Souldiers..informe Thy thoughts with Noblenesse *Cor.* V. iii. 71. Long as Breath informs this fleeting Frame M. PRIOR.
III. 1. *trans.* To form (the mind, character, etc.), esp. by imparting learning or instruction; hence, To instruct, teach; †to advise. Now *rare.* ME. †**b.** To direct, guide –1846. **2.** To impart knowledge of some particular fact or occurrence to; to tell (one) of something; to apprise. The prevailing mod. sense. ME. Also *refl.* **3.** *absol.* or *intr.* †**a.** To give information; to report –1683. **b.** To lay or exhibit an information, bring a charge or complaint (*against*, rarely *on*) 1586.
1. Nor are we informed by nature, in future contingencies and accidents BUTLER. **b.** MILT. *Comus* 180. **2.** Some have enformed me that my realme was never so riche HALL. **3. a.** *Macb.* I. v. 34. **b.** You must not i. against him GOLDSM.
IV. †**1.** *trans.* To impart the knowledge of; to instruct in, to teach –1621. †**2.** To make known, report, relate, tell –1810.
1. To i. religion BACON. **2.** It is informed us that your young and ryotous people will ryse HALL. *All's Well* IV. i. 91.

Informal (infǭ·ɹmăl), *a.* 1584. [IN-[3].] Not formal. **1.** Not done or made according to a regular or prescribed form; not observing forms; not according to order; irregular; unofficial, disorderly. **b.** Unceremonious 1828. †**2.** ? Disordered in mind 1603.
1. An i. overture W. IRVING. **b.** An i. visit 1828. **2.** These poore informall women SHAKS. Hence **Informa·lity,** the quality or fact of being i.; absence of formality; an instance of this. **Info·rmally** *adv.*

Informant (infǭ·ɹmănt). 1661. [f. INFORM *v.* (in different senses of the verb) + -ANT.]
A. *adj. Metaph.* Informing; giving form; actuating; see INFORM *v.* II. 1890.
B. *sb.* †**1.** That which informs, animates, or actuates GLANVILL. **2.** One who gives information of some fact or occurrence 1693. **b.** *Law.* One who lays an information against a person; an informer 1783.
2. b. It was the last evidence of the kind. The i. was hanged BURKE.

In forma pauperis: see IN *Lat. prep.*

Information (infǫ̆ɹmē[i]·ʃən). [– (O)Fr. *information* – L. *informatio*, f. *informat-*, pa. ppl. stem of *informare*; see INFORM *v.*, -ION.]
I. 1. The action of informing (in sense III. 1 of the vb.); training, instruction; communication of instructive knowledge. Now *rare* or *Obs.* †Also with *an* and *pl.* An instruction –1760. **2.** The action of telling or fact of being told of something ME. **3.** That of which one is apprised or told; intelligence, news 1450. †Also with *an* and *pl.* 1527. **4.** The action of informing against, charging, or accusing (a person). Now *Obs.*, exc. as transf. from 5. 1480. **5.** *Law.* **a.** A complaint or

charge against a person lodged with or presented to a court or magistrate, in order to the institution of criminal proceedings without formal indictment. (The original object of this procedure was to dispense with the previous finding of a grand jury.) 1467. **b.** A complaint of the Crown in respect of some civil claim, in the form of a statement of the facts by the attorney-general or other proper officer, either *ex officio*, or on the relation of a private individual 1624.

1. For the i. of our judgment and the conduct of our lives BUTLER. **2.** This I have by credible informacion learned MORE. **3.** Some informations from an eminent person SWIFT. **4.** *Hen. VIII*, v. iii. 110.

†**II.** The action of informing with some active or essential quality (see INFORM *v.* II); inspiration, animation (e.g. of the body by the soul) –1870.

That..no i. of pride may enter into us CLARENDON. Hence **Informa·tional** *a.* of, pertaining to, or conveying i.

Informative (infǭ·ɹmătiv), *a.* 1626. [– med.L. *informativus*, f. as prec.; see -IVE.] Having the quality of informing; animative 1647; instructive 1655; of the nature of legal information. Hence **Info·rmatively** *adv.*

Informatory (infǭ·ɹmătŏri), *a.* 1881. [f. stem of INFORMAT(ION + -ORY².] Having the quality of instructing or communicating information.

†**Info·rmed,** *a.* 1526. [f. IN-³ + FORMED, after L. *informis*.] **1.** Of faith: Not vitalized or animated by charity. (An awkward use.) –1630. **2.** Unformed; imperfectly formed –1686.

Info·rmed, *ppl. a.* 1549. [f. INFORM *v.* + -ED¹.] Instructed; enlightened; now usu. *well-*, *ill-informed*.

Informer (infǭ·ɹməɹ). ME. [f. INFORM *v.* + -ER¹.] †**1.** An instructor, teacher –1662. **2.** One who communicates information ME. **3.** One who informs against another, or lays an information; *spec.* one who makes it his business to detect offenders against penal laws and to lay informations against them; a *common informer* 1503. **4.** An inspirer, animator, vitalizer (see INFORM *v.* II) 1727.

4. Nature! i. of the Poet's art POPE.

Informidable (infǭ·ɹmidăb'l), *a. rare.* 1667. [IN-³.] Not formidable; not to be dreaded.

Of limb Heroic built..Foe not i. MILT. *P.L.* IX. 486.

Informity (infǭ·ɹmĭti). Now *rare* or *Obs.* 1583. [–late L. *informitas, -tat-*, f. L. *informis*; see INFORM *a.*, -ITY.] Unformed condition, shapelessness; deformity. Also *fig.*

†**Info·rmous,** *a.* 1610. [– med.L. **informosus*, f. *in-* IN-³ + L. *formosus* beautiful, f. *forma* FORM; see -OUS. Cf. †*formous*, which may be the source.] Having no definite form, shapeless; unshapely –1701.

†**Info·rtunate,** *a.* ME. [– L. *infortunatus*; see IN-³, FORTUNATE.] Unfortunate –1682.

The day i. that I was bore 1440. An i. dream PURCHAS, Planet 1671. Hence †**Info·rtunate-ly** *adv.*, †**-ness.**

Infortune (infǭ·ɹtiŭn). ME. [–(O)Fr. *infortune*; see IN-³, FORTUNE.] †**1.** Want of good fortune; ill fortune, ill luck. †Also with *an* and *pl.* –1653. **2.** *Astrol.* A malevolent planet or aspect 1632. So †**Infortuned** *ppl. a.* unfortunate. CHAUCER.

†**Infortu·nity.** 1477. [– OFr. *infortunité*, f. *infortune*; see prec., -ITY. Cf. med.L. *infortunitas*.] Unfortunate condition; misfortune; a misfortune –1720.

†**Infou·nd,** *v.* ME. [– L. *infundere*, f. *in-* IN-² + *fundere* pour, see FOUND *v.*², to which the present word conforms. Cf. Fr. †*infondre*.] *trans.* To pour in; to infuse. (Usu. in *fig.* sense.) –1589.

Infra- (i·nfră), *prefix*, repr. L. *infra* adv. and prep. 'below, underneath, beneath'. Regularly opposed to *supra-* (or *super-*).

A. In prepositional relation to the sb. represented in second element. **1.** Denoting 'below', 'beneath' (i.e. 'lower down than') in respect of local situation or position. **2.** Denoting 'below' or 'beneath' in respect of status or condition, as *infrabestial*, etc. **3.** Denoting 'within' (as in med.L.), as *infraterritorial*, etc.

B. In attrib. or advb. relation to the second element: 'lower', 'inferior', 'under-', as *infraposition*, etc.

The use of the hyphen is practically optional, though it is usually omitted in recognized terms, except when the second element begins with a vowel. **Infra-axi·llary** *a.*, *Anat.* lying below the armpit; *Bot.* situated below the axil of a leaf or branch; **infra-bra·nchial** *a.*, *Zool.* situated below the branchiæ or gills; **infraclavi·cular** *a.*, *Anat.* situated below the clavicle or collar-bone as in *i. bone*; also as *sb.* = *infraclavicular bone*, **infrahu·man** *a.*; **infrahy·oid** *a.*, *Anat.* lying below the hyoid bone; **infrala·bial** *a.*, *Anat.* situated below the lips; **infrali·ttoral** *a.*, pertaining to the zone of the sea below the littoral region; **inframa·rginal** *a.*, situated beneath the margin or border, as in *i. convolution*, the superior temporal convolution; **inframaxi·llary** *a.*, situated below the jaw, as in *i. nerve*; *sb.* the lower jaw-bone; **inframe·dian** *a.*, applied to the zone of the ocean below the median zone; **infrana·tural** *a.*, below what is natural; hence **infrana·turalism; infra-o·rbital** *a.*, *Anat.* situated below the orbit of the eye; **infrapo·sed** *a.*, placed below something else (cf. *superposed*); so **infraposi·tion; infrasca·pular** *a.*, *Anat.* situated below the shoulder-blade; **infraspi·nal** *a.*, *Anat.* situated beneath the spine of the scapula; so **infraspi·nate, -spi·nous** *adjs.*; **infrastape·dial** *a.*, situated below the axis of the stapes of the middle ear in birds; **infraste·rnal** *a.*, *Anat.* situated below the sternum or breast-bone; **infrate·mporal** *a.*, *Anat.* situated below the temples; **infraterrito·rial** *a.*, lying within a territory; **infratro·chlear** *a.*, *Anat.* situated beneath the trochlea of the trochlearis muscle in the eye.

†**Infract,** *a.* 1566. [– L. *infractus*, pa. pple. of *infringere*; see INFRINGE *v.*] Unbroken; unweakened; whole –1613.

Infract (infræ·kt), *v.* 1798. [– *infract-*, pa. ppl. stem of L. *infringere*; see INFRINGE *v.*] *trans.* To break; to violate, infringe. Chiefly *U.S.* So **Infra·ctible** *a.* capable of being infracted or broken.

Infraction (infræ·kʃən). 1623. [– L. *infractio*, f. as prec.; see -ION. Cf. (O)Fr. *infraction*.] **1.** The action of fracturing; *concr.* a fracture. **2.** The action of infringing (a bond or obligation); breach, violation 1673. †**3.** *Optics.* = REFRACTION 1635.

Infractor (infræ·ktəɹ). 1524. [– med.L. *infractor*, f. as prec.; see -OR 2.] One who breaks or infringes; a violator, infringer.

‖**Infra dig.** (i·nfră di·g), *adj. phr.* 1824. [colloq. abbrev. of L. *infra dignitatem*.] Beneath one's dignity; unbecoming one's position; undignified.

Infragrant (infrēⁱ·grănt), *a.* 1813. [IN-³.] Malodorous.

Infralapsarian (i:nfrălæpsēᵊ·riăn). 1731. [f. L. *infra* under, beneath + *lapsus* fall, LAPSE + -ARIAN.] *Theol.* **A.** *sb.* A term applied in the 17th c. to Calvinists holding the view that God's election of some to everlasting life was consequent to his prescience of the Fall of man, or that it contemplated man as already fallen, and was thus a remedial measure; opp. to SUPRALAPSARIAN. **B.** *adj.* Of or pertaining to the Infralapsarians or their doctrine 1775. Hence **Infralapsa·rianism**, the doctrine of Infralapsarians.

SUBLAPSARIAN is, in English writers, more usual than *Infralapsarian*. But some distinguish the two, associating *Sublapsarian* with the view that the Fall was foreseen, and *Infralapsarian* with the view that it was permitted, by God.

Infranchise, etc. obs. ff. ENFRANCHISE, etc.

Infrangible (infræ·ndʒĭb'l), *a.* 1597. [– Fr. †*infrangible* or med.L. *infrangibilis*; partly f. IN-³ + FRANGIBLE.] **1.** That cannot be broken; unbreakable. Also *fig.* **2.** That cannot be infringed; inviolable 1834.

1. I. Atomes 1603. And link'd their fetlocks with a golden band, I., immortal POPE. Hence **Infrangibi·lity, Infra·ngibleness. Infra·ngibly** *adv.*

Infrequence (infrī·kwĕns). *rare.* 1644. [f. as next; see -ENCE.] = next.

Infrequency (infrī·kwĕnsi). 1600. [– L. *infrequentia*, f. *infrequens*; see next, -ENCY.] †**1.** The fact or state of being unfrequented; also, Small attendance; paucity, fewness –1658. **2.** The fact or state of rarely occurring; uncommonness, rarity 1677.

1. The solitude and i. of the place P. HOLLAND. **2.** The i. of marriage GIBBON.

Infrequent (infrī·kwĕnt), *a.* 1531. [– L. *infrequens, -ent-*; see IN-³, FREQUENT.] Not frequent: †little used (ELYOT); not occurring often 1612; (qualifying an agent-noun) that does something rarely 1722; not plentiful 1682.

Words of i. occurrence JOHNSON. A sparing and i. worshipper of the Deity WOLLASTON. Hence **Infre·quently** *adv.*

Infrigidate (infri·dʒideⁱt), *v.* Now *rare.* 1545. [– *infrigidat-*, pa. ppl. stem of late L. *infrigidare*, f. *in-* IN-² + *frigidus* cold, FRIGID; see -ATE³.] *trans.* To make cold; to chill, cool. Hence **Infrigida·tion,** the action of cooling or condition of being cooled; refrigeration.

Infringe (infri·ndʒ), *v.* 1533. [– L. *infringere*, f. *in-* IN-² + *frangere* break.] †**1.** *trans.* To break, shatter (*rare* in physical sense); to crush; to defeat, frustrate; to invalidate –1671. **2.** To violate or break (an oath, pledge, treaty, etc.); to contravene 1533. †**3.** To refute; to contradict –1660. †**4.** To weaken, impair; to mitigate –1694. **5.** *intr.* To break in or encroach *on* or *upon* 1760.

2. Ioue for your Loue would i. an oath SHAKS. **5.** They did not i. upon this boundary for some time COOK. Hence **Infri·ngement,** the act or fact of infringing; breach, violation; encroachment; †contradiction. **Infri·nger,** one who infringes.

†**Infri·ngible,** *a.* Also **-eable.** 1548. [–late and med.L. *infringibilis*, f. L. *infringere* INFRINGE *v.*; see -IBLE.] That cannot be infringed or broken; unbreakable –1642; irrefragable –1629.

Infructuose (infrʋ·ktiu,ōᵘs), *a.* 1727. [– L. *infructuosus*; see next, -OSE¹.] = next.

Infructuous (infrʋ·ktiu,əs), *a.* 1615. [– L. *infructuosus*; see IN-³, FRUCTUOUS.] Not producing fruit, unfruitful, unprofitable (*lit.* and *fig.*). Hence **Infru·ctuously** *adv.*

‖**Infula** (i·nfiulă). 1610. [L. (in sense 1).] **1.** *Rom. Antiq.* A sort of fillet of red and white wool, worn on the forehead by priests, worshippers, and suppliants, or similarly placed on victims for sacrifice, etc. 1727. **2.** *Eccl.* Each of the two lappets of a bishop's mitre. Also in *Her.* var. †**I·nfule** (in sense 1).

Infumate, *v. rare.* 1721. [– *infumat-*, pa. ppl. stem of L. *infumare*, f. *in-* IN-² + *fumare* smoke, f. *fumus* smoke; see -ATE³.] *trans.* To smoke, to dry by smoking. Hence **Infumated** *ppl. a.* **Infuma·tion.** (Dicts.)

†**Infu·me,** *v.* 1601. [– L. *infumare*; see prec.] = prec. –1623.

‖**Infundibulum** (infʋndi·biŭlŏm). 1706. [L., f. *infundere* pour in; see INFOUND *v.*] †**1.** A funnel (*rare*). **2.** *Anat.* Applied to various funnel-shaped cavities or structures of the body; as, *i. of the brain* (*i. cerebri*), a funnel-shaped prolongation downwards and forwards of the third ventricle of the brain, at the extremity of which is the pituitary body; *i. of the lungs*, the funnel-shaped sacs in which the air-passages terminate 1799. **b.** *Zool.* (*a*) A tubular organ in the Cephalopoda through which the water is driven from the gills. (*b*) The gastric cavity of Ctenophora with which the œsophageal tube communicates. (*c*) The dilated upper extremity of the oviduct of a bird. 1877. Hence **Infundi·bular** *a.* funnel-shaped. **Infundi·bulate** *a.* having an i.; funnel-shaped. **Infundi·buliform** *a.* funnel-shaped.

†**Infu·neral,** *v.* [f. IN-² + FUNERAL *sb.* or *v.*] *trans.* To entomb. G. FLETCHER.

Infuriate (infiūᵊ·riĕt), *a.* 1667. [– med.L. *infuriatus*, pa. pple. of *infuriare*; see next, -ATE².] Excited to fury; maddened; raging, frantic, furious. Also *fig.* of things.

Th' i. hil that shoots the pillar'd flame THOMSON.

Infuriate (infiūᵊ·rieⁱt), *v.* 1667. [– *infuriat-*, pa. ppl. stem of med.L. *infuriare*, f. *in-* IN-² + L. *furiare* madden, f. *furia* FURY; see -ATE³.] *trans.* To fill with fury; to render mad with anger; to enrage.

This insulting allusion to his dark skin infuriates Neville DICKENS. Hence **Infu·riatingly** *adv.*

†**Infu·scate,** *v.* 1650. [– *infuscat-*, pa. ppl. stem of L. *infuscare*, f. *in-* IN-² + *fuscare*, f. *fuscus* dark-brown, dusky; see -ATE³.] *trans.* To make dark-coloured or dusky; to darken –1727. Hence **Infusca·tion,** the action of darkening; darkened condition.

†**Infu·se,** *sb.* 1568. [– L. *infusus* pouring in, f. *infundere*; see next.] = INFUSION –1596.

Infuse (infiū·z), *v.* ME. [– *infus-*, pa. ppl. stem of L. *infundere*, f. *in-* IN-[2] + *fundere* pour. Cf. INFOUND.] **1.** *trans.* To pour in; †to pour *into*; to introduce (a liquid ingredient). **2.** *transf.* and *fig.* To introduce as by pouring; to instil, insinuate 1526. **†3.** To pour *on* or *upon*; to shed, diffuse –1672. **4.** To steep or drench in a liquid, so as to extract the soluble properties; to macerate 1533. **b.** *intr.* To undergo infusion or maceration 1615. **5.** With inverted construction: To affect (a liquid) by steeping some soluble substance in it; hence, to imbue or inspire (a person) *with* some infused quality. In wider use, to impregnate (*with* some quality, opinion, etc.). 1560.

1. 'Tis of great consequence, what is infus'd Into a Vessell when it first is vs'd HEYWOOD. **2.** These words, these lookes, I. new life in me SHAKS. He infused his own intrepid spirit into the troops GIBBON. **4.** While I am infusing my tea BARRIE. **5.** Thou didst smile, Infused with a fortitude from heauen *Temp.* I. ii. 154. Hence **Infu·ser,** one who or that which, infuses; †*spec.* a retort.

Infusible (infiū·zĭb'l), *a.*[1] 1555. [f. IN-[3] + FUSIBLE.] Not fusible; incapable of being fused or melted.

Pure lime, except placed in clay, is i. KIRWAN. Hence **Infusibi·lity**[1], **Infu·sibleness,** i. quality.

Infu·sible, *a.*[2] *rare.* 1660. [– med.L. *infusibilis* susceptible of imbuing (with grace), or f. INFUSE (sense 2) + -IBLE.] Capable of being infused.

The doctrines being i. into all HAMMOND. Hence **Infusibi·lity**[2]. (Dicts.)

Infu·sile, *a.* 1825. [f. IN-[3] + FUSILE.] Not fusile.

Infusion (infiū·ʒən). 1425. [– (O)Fr. *infusion* or L. *infusio*, f. *infus-*; see INFUSE *v.*, -ION.] **1.** The action of pouring in, or fact of being poured in; that which is poured in. Now chiefly *fig.* **b.** *spec.* in *Surg.* Injection 1601. **2.** The process of pouring water over a substance, or steeping the substance in water, in order to impregnate the liquid with its properties or virtues 1573. **b.** A dilute liquid extract obtained from a substance by soaking it with, or steeping it in, water; also any water containing dissolved organic (esp. vegetable) matter 1550. **3.** An infused element, admixture, tincture 1626. **4.** = AFFUSION 1751.

1. *fig.* I.—the doctrine which regarded our *a priori* Ideas as infused into the Intellect by an act of God 1857. The continual i. into it of new blood to perform its functions J. H. NEWMAN. **2.** Oil of Ivy-berries, made by expressions or i. WALTON. **b.** Spunges wetted in I. of Tobacco BOYLE. **3.** He..was a gentleman with a slight i. of the footman LAMB. **4.** Baptism by i. JORTIN. Hence **Infu·sionism,** the docrtine that the soul is a divine emanation, infused into the body at conception or birth. **Infu·sionist,** an adherent of this doctrine.

Infusive (infiū·siv), *a.* 1630. [f. INFUSE *v.* + -IVE.] **1.** Having the quality or power of infusing 1728. **†2.** Naturally or divinely infused; innate. BRATHWAIT.

1. Th' i. force of Spring on Man THOMSON.

‖**Infusoria** (infiusōᵊ·riă), *sb. pl.* 1787. [subst. use (sc. *animalcula*) of n. pl. of mod.L. *infusorius*, f. *infus-*; see INFUSE, -IA[2], -ORIOUS.] A class of Protozoa, comprising ciliated, tentaculate, and flagellate animalcula, essentially unicellular, free-swimming, or sedentary; so called because found in infusions of decaying animal or vegetable matter.

Orig. the *Infusoria* comprehended an assemblage of minute, usually microscopic, organisms, of many diverse kinds, including some now classed as vegetables, as the *Diatomaceæ* and the *Desmidiaceæ*. As now constituted, the *Infusoria* are Protozoa characterized by a half liquid endosarc, a firm cortical ectosarc, an outer membraneous cuticle, a mouth and anus, and a contractile vesicle which injects fluid.

Hence **Infuso·rial** *a.* of or pertaining to the I.; consisting of or formed by I. **Infuso·rian** *a.* of or pertaining to the I.; *sb.* a member of the I.

‖**Infuso·rium.** 1876. [mod.L., sing. of prec.] An individual animalcule of the Infusoria.

Infusory (infiū·səri). 1684. [Sense 1 f. INFUSE *v.* + -ORY[2]; sense 2 f. prec.]

A. *adj.* **†1.** Of or pertaining to (surgical) injection. **2.** = INFUSORIAL. 1826.

B. *sb.* A member of the Infusoria 1835.

Ing (iŋ). *local.* [In XV *enge, inge* – ON. *eng* fem., *eng, engi* n. meadow, meadow-land, coradicate with OHG., OS. *angar* (G. *anger*).] A meadow; esp. one by the side of a river and low-lying. Also *attrib.*

-ing[1], suffix forming verbal derivs., orig. abstract nouns of action: OE. *-ung, -ing* :– Gmc. type *-*uŋgā* (and ?*-*iŋgā*) str. fem.; not identified exc. in Gmc. In ME. *-ing* (*-inge*) became the regular form.

1. The original function of the suffix was to form nouns of action; as *ācsung* ASKING, *fēding* FEEDING. Originally abstract, these sbs., even in OE., came to express a completed action, a process, habit, or art, as *leornung* LEARNING, *tīdung* TIDINGS, etc., and sometimes became concrete, as in *bedding*, etc. By extension, similar formations have been made from sbs., as *ballooning*, etc., and, by ellipsis, from advs., as *outing*, etc.

2. The vbl. sb. in *-ing* came also to be used as a gerund; i.e. a sb. with certain verbal functions; e.g. tne habit of *speaking loosely* (= loose speaking); he practises *writing* (= the writing of) *leading articles*; etc. This use is peculiar to English; it was unknown to OE. and early ME.

3. In Wyclif, etc., the form in **-inge, -ynge** also appears for the Dative Infinitive, OE. *-enne*, ME. *-ene, -en*. This is a case of phonetic confusion. See O.E.D.

-ing[2], suffix of the pr. participle, and of adjs. thence derived, or so formed; an alteration of OE. *-ende* = L. *-ent-*, Gr. *-οντ-*, Skr. *-ant-*.

-ing[3], a suffix forming derivative masc. sbs., with the sense of 'one belonging to', or 'of the kind of', hence 'one possessed of the quality of', and also as a patronymic = 'one descended from, a son of', and as a diminutive. See also -LING[1] (= *-l* + *-ing*).

Ingan (i·ŋən). 1725. Dial. f. ONION.

†Inganna·tion. 1646. [– It. *ingannazione*, f. *ingannare*, f. *inganno* fraud, deceit; see -ATION.] Deceiving; deception –1658.

Ingate (i·ngeⁱt), *sb.*[1] *n. dial.* 1496. [f. IN *adv.* + GATE *sb.*[2]] **1.** The action or faculty of entering; ingress. **2.** An entrance 1591. **†3.** *concr.* That which enters. Usu. in *pl.*: Ingoings, incomings, imports; also import duties or dues –1714.

I·ngate, *sb.*[2] 1858. [f. IN *adv.* + GATE *sb.*[3]] *Founding.* An aperture in a mould for pouring in metal.

Ingather (i:ngæ·ðəɹ), *v.* 1575. [f. IN *adv.* + GATHER *v.*] *trans.* To gather in. *lit.* and *fig.*

Ingathering (i·ngæ:ðəriŋ), *vbl. sb.* 1535. [f. IN *adv.* + GATHERING *vbl. sb.*] The action of gathering in or collecting (esp. the harvest); a gathering in.

Feast of I. = Feast of Tabernacles.

Ingem (indʒe·m), *v.* 1611. [f. IN-[2] + GEM *sb.*, chiefly after It. *ingemmare.*] To set or adorn with gems.

†Inge·minate, *ppl. a. rare.* 1637. [– L. *ingeminatus*, pa. pple. of *ingeminare* (next); see IN-[2], GEMINATE *a.*] Doubled, redoubled; repeated –1676.

Ingeminate (indʒe·mineⁱt), *v.* 1594. [– *ingeminat-*, pa. ppl. stem of L. *ingeminare* redouble, repeat; see IN-[2], GEMINATE *v.*] **1.** *trans.* To repeat, reiterate; to emphasize by repetition. **†2.** To double (a thing); to repeat (an action) (*rare*) –1686.

1. [Falkland] often..would with a shrill and sad accent, i. the word, Peace, Peace CLARENDON. Hence **Ingemina·tion,** the action of ingeminating; a repetition (*arch.*); duplication (*rare*) 1576.

Ingender, obs. f. ENGENDER.

†Inge:nerabi·lity. 1598. [f. INGENERABLE; see -ITY.] The quality of being ingenerable –1691.

Ingenerable (indʒe·nĕrăb'l), *a.* Now *rare.* ME. [– late L. *ingenerabilis*; see IN-[3], GENERABLE.] Incapable of being generated. (Chiefly in 17th c. phr. *i. and incorruptible.*) Hence **Inge·nerably** *adv.*

Ingenerate (indʒe·nĕrĕt), *a.* 1656. [– eccl.L. *ingeneratus* (Ambrose); see IN-[3], GENERATE *ppl. a.*] Not generated; self-existent.

The Soul is Incorruptible, I., and Immortal 1656. Hence **†Inge·nerateness.** CUDWORTH.

Ingenerate (indʒe·nĕrĕt), *ppl. a.* 1531. [– L. *ingeneratus*; see next.] **1.** Inborn, innate; (of diseases) congenital (*rare*). **†2.** Engendered, begotten (*lit.* and *fig.*) (*rare*) –1611.

1. That gravitie and sternesse, whiche is in you as it were by nature i. ELYOT.

Ingenerate (indʒe·nĕreⁱt), *v.* Now *rare.* 1528. [– *ingenerat-*, pa. ppl. stem of L. *ingenerare*; see IN-[2], GENERATE *v.*] *trans.* To generate within, engender, produce.

To shew..how these opynyons were ingenerated FOX. Hence **Ingenera·tion** (*rare*), the action of ingenerating.

†Inge·niary, *a.* [app. f. L. *ingenium* after MANUARY.] Inventive. EVELYN.

†Inge·niate, *v. rare.* [– *ingeniat-*, pa. ppl. stem of med.L. *ingeniare* contrive, f. L. *ingenium* genius, etc.; see -ATE[3].] *trans.* To devise, contrive, plan, design. DANIEL.

Ingenie, var. of INGENY *Obs.*

†Ingenio (indʒī·nio). 1600. [– Sp. *ingenio* engine (*i. de azucar* sugar-mill).] A sugar-mill or -works in the West Indies –1722.

Ingeniosity (indʒīni,ǫ·sĭti). Now *Obs.* or *rare.* 1607. [– Fr. *ingéniosité* or med.L. *ingeniositas*, f. L. *ingeniosus*; see next, -ITY.] The quality of being ingenious; ingenuity.

Ingenious (indʒī·niəs), *a.* late ME. [– Fr. *ingénieux* or L. *ingeniosus*, f. *ingenium*; see ENGINE, -IOUS.]

I. †1. Having high intellectual capacity; able, talented, possessed of genius. *Obs.* in gen. sense. –1807. **†b.** Of a composition, etc.: Showing these qualities –1809. **†2.** Intelligent; sagacious –1824. **3.** Having an aptitude for invention or construction; skilful (now usually in a light sense) 1576; of things, actions, etc.: Showing cleverness of invention or construction. (The current sense.) 1548.

1. Wine gives all things, it makes the dull i. T. BROWN. **b.** A good i. Sermon HEARNE. **3.** I. in tormenting ourselves 1885. An i. contrivance MAURY.

II. Used by confusion for INGENUOUS –1776. *Tam. Shr.* I. i. 9.

Inge·niously *adv.* in an i. manner; with skilful contrivance; †INGENUOUSLY. **Inge·niousness.**

†Inge·nit, -ite, *a.*[1] 1604. [– L. *ingenitus* inborn, pa. pple. of *ingignere* engender, f. *in-* IN-[2] + *gignere* beget.] Inborn, innate; native –1728.

An ingenite ardor of Navigation GALE.

†Ingenit, -ite, *a.*[2] 1677. [– eccl.L. *ingenitus* not begotten, f. *in-* IN-[3] + L. *genitus* born, begotten, f. *gignere* beget.] Not born or begotten; not made or produced; uncreated –1678.

As the Monad is Ingenit or Unmade CUDWORTH.

‖**Ingénue** (æṅʒenü). 1848. [Fr., fem. of *ingénu* INGENUOUS.] An artless innocent girl, esp. of the type represented on the stage. Hence **Ingénueism.**

Ingenuity (indʒĭniū·ĭti). 1592. [– L. *ingenuitas*, f. *ingenuus*; see next, -ITY. Cf. Fr. *ingénuité*. The uses of branch B are peculiarly English for *ingeniosity* and depend on the confusion of INGENIOUS and INGENUOUS in XVI–XVII.]

I. †1. The condition of being free-born or well-born –1658. **†b.** Liberal quality (of education); hence, Liberal education –1662. **†2.** Nobility of character or disposition; high-mindedness, generosity –1716. **3.** Freedom from dissimulation; honourable dealing; openness, candour, frankness. (Now usu. *ingenuousness.*) 1614.

1. b. A seminary of religion and i. FULLER. **3.** Melchior Canus..for a Papist a man of singular i. JACKSON.

II. Senses conn. w. INGENIOUS. **†1.** High intellectual capacity; genius, talent, wit. *Obs.* in gen. sense. –1795. **†2.** Intellectual capacity; intelligence; (one's) senses or wits –1675. **†b.** *transf.* Wisdom –1660. **3.** Capacity for invention or construction. Also an attribute of the thing, action, etc.: Skilfulness of contrivance or design. (The current sense.) 1649. Also with *an* and *pl.* 1650.

3. The i. of his knavery 1664, of our weavers PENNANT. [A] kind-hearted schemer..rich in petty ingenuities 1829.

Ingenuous (indʒe·niu,əs), *a.* 1588. [f. L. *ingenuus* native, inborn, free-born, noble, frank, f. *in-* IN-[2] + **gen-*, base of *gignere* beget; see -OUS, -UOUS.] **1.** Of free or honourable birth. (Chiefly in references to Roman History.) 1638. **2.** Noble in nature, character or disposition; generous, high-minded. *Obs.* or *arch.* 1599. **†b.** Also of animals or things –1664. **†3.** Befitting a free-born or high-born person; liberal –1757. **4.** Honourably straightforward; open, candid, frank. (The current sense.) 1598. **b.** Guileless, innocent; artless. (= Fr. *ingénu, -ue.*) 1673. **¶5.** In 17th c. freq. misused for *ingenious. Obs.* –1795.

2. They scoffe him; an iniury hardly indured by any i. man 1631. **b.** An i. soil 1664. **3.** That great opener of the mind, i. science BURKE. **4.** An i. confession 1621. Language..well weighed and well guarded, but clear and i. MACAULAY. **5.** *Cymb.* IV. ii. 186. Hence **Inge·nuously** *adv.* in an i. manner; †liberally. **Inge·nuousness,** the condition or quality of being i.; †(by confusion) *ingeniousness.*

†**I·ngeny.** 1474. [– L. *ingenium*, f. *in-* IN-[2] + **gen-*; see prec.] **1.** Mind; mental tendency, disposition –1708. **2.** Mental ability, genius –1697.

Inge·rminate, *v.* 1860. [IN-[2].] To cause to germinate. (Dicts.)

Ingest (indʒe·st), *v.* 1617. [– *ingest-*, pa. ppl. stem of L. *ingerere* carry in, etc., f. *in-* IN-[2] + *gerere* carry, bear.] †**1.** *trans.* To put in, thrust in. **2.** *spec.* To introduce (aliment) into the stomach (or mouth); to take in (food) 1620. Hence **Inge·stive** *a.* having the function of taking in aliment.

‖**Ingesta** (indʒe·stă), *sb. pl.* 1727. [L., n. pl. of *ingestus*, pa. pple. of *ingerere*; see prec.] *Phys.* Substances introduced into the body as nourishment.

Ingestion (indʒe·styən). 1597. [– late L. *ingestio*, f. *ingest-*; see INGEST, -ION.] †**1.** Introduction. **2.** The action of ingesting or taking in aliment 1620.

Inghamite (i·ŋəməit). 1743. [f. name *Ingham* + -ITE[1] 1.] A member of the religious body founded in 1742 by Benjamin *Ingham*, on principles resembling those of Moravians and Methodists.

Ingine, Sc. f. ENGINE.

Ingirt, var. of ENGIRT *v.*

Ingle (i·ŋ'l), *sb.*[1] Orig. *Sc.* 1508. [perh. – Gael. *aingeal* fire, light.] **1.** Fire; a fire burning upon the hearth; a house-fire. ¶**2.** *erron.* An open fireplace 1841. **3.** *attrib.* 1853.

1. His wee bit i., blinkin bonilie BURNS. *Comb.*: **i.-bench,** a bench beside the fire; **-cheek** (*Sc.*), the jamb of a fireplace; **-nook** (orig. *Sc.*), the chimney-corner; **-side,** a fireside.

†**Ingle,** *sb.*[2] 1592. [Of unkn. origin.] A catamite –1878. ¶Misused for 'familiar friend'. SCOTT.

†**Ingle,** *v.* 1595. [f. prec.] **1.** *trans.* To fondle, caress –1631. **2.** To wheedle, coax –1602. **3.** *intr.* To fondle *with* 1611.

Inglobate (inglōᵘ·bĕt), *a. rare.* 1852. [f. IN-[2] + GLOBATE *a.*] Formed into a globe or globular mass.

Inglobe, obs. f. ENGLOBE.

Inglorious (inglōᵊ·riəs), *a.* 1573. [f. L. *inglorius* + -OUS, or f. IN-[3] + GLORIOUS.] **1.** Not glorious; not known to fame; humble, obscure. Now *rare.* 1591. †Also with *of.* GIBBON. **2.** Bringing no glory (to a person); hence, shameful, disgraceful, ignominious 1573.

1. I. may they liue, i.die, That suffer learning liue in misery 1602. Some mute i. Milton here may rest GRAY. **2.** The victory over the senate was easy and i. GIBBON. Hence **Inglo·rious-ly** *adv.*, **-ness.**

Inglut, -glutte, obs. ff. ENGLUT *v.*

‖**Ingluvies** (inglū·viˌīz). 1727. [L., = crop, maw.] *Anat.* The crop of a bird, the first stomach of a ruminating animal, an insect, etc. Hence **Inˌglu·vial** *a.* (*rare*), of or pertaining to the i. or crop.

†**Inˌglu·vious,** *a.* 1569. [– L. *ingluviosus*; see prec., -OUS.] Greedy, gluttonous –1659. Hence †**Inglu·viously** *adv.*

I·nˌgoːing, *vbl. sb.* Now *rare.* ME. [f. the phr. *go in* (see IN-[1]) + -ING[1].] A going in; entrance; way in. **b.** The sum paid by a tenant or purchaser for fixtures, etc. on taking over business or other premises 1905.

I·nˌgoːing, *ppl. a.* 1825. [f. as prec. + -ING[2].] That goes in or inwards; that enters; as, an *i. tenant.* **b.** Penetrating, thorough 1928.

Ingorge, Ingrace, etc. var. ENGORGE, etc.

Ingot (i·ŋgǫt). ME. [orig. obscure; form and meaning suggest deriv. from IN-[1] and OE. *goten*, pa. pple. of *ġeotan* pour, cast in metal.] †**1.** A mould in which metal is cast; an ingot-mould –1799. **2.** A mass (usu. oblong or brick-shaped) of cast metal, esp. of gold, silver, or (now) of steel 1547. **3.** *attrib.* 1558.

1. And fro the fir he took vp his mateere And in thyngot putte it CHAUCER. **2.** Not, like a Miser, to gaze only on his Ingots STEELE.

†**Ingra·cious,** *a.* 1600. [IN-[3].] Ungracious –1676.

I·ngrain, *a.* (*sb.*) 1766. [f. the phr. *in grain*; see GRAIN *sb.*[1] III. 1. Now usu. *i·ngrain* bef. a sb., *ingrai·n* after it or in the predicate.] **1.** Dyed in grain; dyed with fast colours before manufacture; dyed in the fibre; thoroughly dyed. **b.** (*U.S.*) *Ingrain carpet*, a two-ply carpet in which the pattern goes through and through and appears on both sides 1863. Also *ellipt.* as *sb.* **2.** Of qualities, habits, etc.: Inborn, firmly fixed, inveterate, ingrained 1852; thorough 1865.

Ingrain, obs. or arch. var. of ENGRAIN *v.*

Ingrained (ingrēⁱnd), *ppl. a.* 1548. [app. orig. a var. of *engrained* ppl. a.; but now taken as if from *in* adv. + *grained* (cf. AL. *ingranatus* XIV). Stressed *i·ngrained* bef. a sb., otherwise *ingrai·ned.*] †**1.** Dyed in grain. **2.** *fig.* Wrought in the inmost texture; deeply rooted, inveterate 1599. **b.** Of persons: Out-and-out 1630.

2. I. wickedness 1855. **b.** He is an i. sceptic LOWELL.

†**Inˌgra·pple,** *v.* 1597. [f. IN-[2] + GRAPPLE *v.*] To join in grappling; to grapple together (*intr.* and *trans.*) –1661.

Then shall young Hotspur..I. with thy sonne 1597.

Ingrate (ingrēⁱ·t), *a.* (*sb.*) ME. [– L. *ingratus* unpleasant, ungrateful, f. *in-* IN-[3] + *gratus* pleasing, grateful; perh. partly through (O)Fr. *ingrat.*] **1.** Not grateful; †unpleasant –1702; †unfriendly –1563; unthankful (*arch.*) 1528. **2.** *sb.* An ungrateful person 1570. Hence †**Inˌgra·tely** *adv.*

†**Inˌgra·teful,** *a.* 1547. [f. IN-[3] + GRATEFUL.] **1.** Displeasing, disagreeable –1754. **2.** Not feeling or showing gratitude –1759.

1. The Oil is of an i. Odor 1694. **2.** Desirous of pleasures, and ingratefull for benefits 1547. Hence †**Inˌgra·teful-ly** *adv.*, †**-ness.**

Ingratiate (ingrēⁱ·ʃiˌeⁱt), *v.* 1622. [f. L. phr. *in gratiam* into favour + -ATE[3], after It. †*ingratiare, ingraziare.*] †**1.** *trans.* To bring into favour *with*; to render agreeable *to* –1755. **2.** *refl.* To get oneself into favour *with*; to render oneself agreeable *to* 1622. †Also *intr.* for *refl.* †**3.** *trans.* To make (a thing) pleasant, agreeable, or acceptable (*to* or *with*) –1748.

1. All this would not i. this Usurper with them FULLER. **2.** If he did not do somewhat to i. himself to the People CLARENDON. **3.** Things, when wanted, are ingratiated to us, as warmth after cold 1656. Hence **Ingra·tia:tingly** *adv.* in an ingratiating manner. **Ingratia·tion,** the action or process of ingratiating oneself. **Ingra·tiatory** *a.* that tends to i.

Ingratitude (ingræ·titiūd). ME. [– (O)Fr. *ingratitude* or late L. *ingratitudo*, f. *ingratus* INGRATE; see IN-[3], GRATITUDE.] **1.** Want of gratitude; indisposition to acknowledge or reciprocate benefits received; ungratefulness. †**2.** Unfriendliness, unkindness –1566.

1. I. is monstrous *Cor.* II. iii. 10. I. to benefactors is the first of revolutionary virtues BURKE.

†**Inˌgra·ve,** *v.* Also †**en-.** 1535. [f. IN-[1] or [2] + GRAVE *sb.*[1] or *v.*[1]] *trans.* To put in a grave; to bury –1683.

Ingrave, etc. obs. f. ENGRAVE *v.*, etc.

Ingravescent (ingrăve·sĕnt), *a.* 1822. [– *ingravescent-*, pr. ppl. stem of L. *ingravescere* grow heavy or heavier, f. *in-* IN-[2] + *gravescere*, f. *gravis* heavy; see -ENT.] Increasing in gravity or severity. Hence **Ingrave·scence.**

Ingravidate (ingræ·videⁱt), *v.* 1642. [– *ingravidat-*, pa. ppl. stem of late L. *ingravidare* make heavy or pregnant, f. *in-* IN-[2] + *gravidus*; see GRAVID, -ATE[3].] **1.** *trans.* To load or weigh; to render gravid, to impregnate. **2.** *intr.* To become heavy. TOMLINSON. Hence **Ingravida·tion,** the action of ingravidating or state of being ingravidated; pregnancy 1615.

†**Ingrea·t,** *v.* Also †**en-.** 1619. [f. IN-[2] + GREAT *a.*; cf. ENGREATEN.] *trans.* To make great, to magnify –1627.

†**Ingre·dience.** 1526. [In sense 2 f. as next; see -ENCE. For sense 1 see INGREDIENT.] **1.** That which enters into a mixture. **a.** The ingredients, separately or collectively –1694. **b.** (with *pl.*) A single ingredient –1661. **2.** The fact or process of entering in –1677.

1. a. This euen-handed Iustice Commends th' I. of our poyson'd Challice To our owne lips SHAKS. **b.** Ale requireth two ingrediences COGAN. So †**Ingre·diency.**

Ingredient (ingrī·diĕnt). 1460. [– *ingredient-*, pr. ppl. stem of L. *ingredi* enter, f. *in-* IN-[2] + *gradi* step, go; see -ENT. Primarily in medical use; the pl. was spelt *ingredience* (see prec.); cf. ACCIDENCE[2].]

A. *adj.* That enters in; entering into a thing or place (*Obs.* or *arch.*) 1611.

The generosity that is i. in the temper of the soul 1713.

B. *sb.* †**1.** One who, or that which, enters in –1624. **2.** Something that enters into the formation of a compound or element; a component part, constituent, element. Primarily used of medical, etc. mixtures 1460. †**b.** Chief ingredient. *Oth.* II. iii. 311.

1. [The air] being a perpetual ambient and i. WOTTON. **2.** Stupidity, I told you, is no i. in piety GAUDEN.

Ingress (i·ngres), *sb.* ME. [– L. *ingressus*, f. *ingress-*, pa. ppl. stem of *ingredi*; see prec.] **1.** The action or fact of entering. Also, Capacity or right of entrance, esp. in legal phr. *i., egress, and regress* 1543. **b.** A place or means of entrance ME. **2.** The action of entering upon a thing; a beginning, an attempt; also, The beginning of an action, period, etc. (*arch.*) ME. **3. a.** *Astrol.* The arrival of a planet at that part of the heaven occupied by another planet, or at the ascendant, or the mid-heaven 1603. **b.** *Astron.* The entrance of the sun into a sign of the zodiac. ?*Obs.* 1652. **c.** The first contact of an inferior planet with the sun, or of a satellite with its planet, at a transit 1751.

†**Ingre·ss,** *v.* ME. [f. *ingress-*; see prec.] To enter (*trans.* and *intr.*) –1817.

Ingression (ingre·ʃən). 1470. [– Fr. †*ingression* or L. *ingressio*, f. as prec.; see -ION.] The action of going in; entrance; invasion.

Ingreve, -grieve, -groove, -gross(e, vars. ENGRIEVE, etc.

Ingrowing (i·ngrōᵘːiŋ), *ppl. a.* 1869. [IN *adv.*] Growing inwards or within something; *spec.* of a nail: Growing into the flesh.

Ingrown (i·ngrōᵘn), *ppl. a.* 1670. [IN *adv.*] That has or is grown within something; native, innate. **b.** Of a nail: That has grown into the flesh 1878.

Ingrowth (i·ngrōᵘþ). 1852. [IN *adv.*] **a.** The action of growing inwards. **b.** That which grows inwards. (Opp. to *outgrowth.*) 1877.

‖**Inguen** (i·ŋgwen). 1706. [L.] The groin.

Inguilty, erron. f. UNGUILTY.

Inguinal (i·ŋgwinăl), *a.* 1681. [– L. *inguinalis* (Pliny), f. *inguen, inguin-* groin; see -AL[1]. Cf. Fr. *inguinal* (Paré).] *Anat.*, etc. Of, belonging to, or situated in the groin.

Inguino- (i·ŋgwino), comb. f. L. *inguen, inguin-*; as in **i.-scro·tal** *a.*, belonging to the groin and the scrotum; etc.

Ingulf, etc., var. of ENGULF, etc.

Ingurgitate (ingŏ·ɹdʒiteⁱt), *v.* 1570. [– *ingurgitat-*, pa. ppl. stem of L. *ingurgitare*, f. *in-* IN-[2] + *gurges, gurgit-* whirlpool, gulf; see -ATE[3].] **1.** *trans.* To swallow greedily or immoderately. Also *fig.* Also *absol.* **b.** To gorge, to cram with food or drink 1583. **2.** *trans.* To swallow up as a gulf or whirlpool; to engulf (*lit.* and *fig.*) 1619.

2. Bankers who..do not absorb and i. your principal 1849.

Ingurgitation (ingŏɹdʒitēⁱ·ʃən). 1530. [– late L. *ingurgitatio*, f. as prec.; see -ION.] **1.** The action of ingurgitating; guzzling or swilling. **b.** Engulfment 1826. ¶**2.** *erron.* A gurgling noise. HAWTHORNE.

1. A large draught and i. of wine BACON.

†**Ingu·stable,** *a.* Also *erron.* **-ible.** 1623. [f. IN-[3] + GUSTABLE.] Tasteless; not perceptible by the sense of taste –1656.

†**Inhabile,** *a.* 1678. [– (O)Fr. *inhabile* or L. *inhabilis* incapable, unfit, unable, f. *in-* IN-[3] + *habilis*; see ABLE, HABILE.] Unfit, unable; unqualified –1830. So †**Inhabi·lity** (doublet of *inability*), incapacity, disability; INABILITY 1488.

Inhabit (inhæ·bit), *v. Pa. pple.* **inhabited,** †**inhabit.** [ME. *en-*, *inhabite* – OFr. *enhabiter* or L. *inhabitare*, f. *in-* IN-[2] + *habitare* (see HABIT *v.*).] **1.** *trans.* To dwell in, occupy as an abode. Said of men and animals. Also *transf.* and *fig.* **2.** *intr.* To dwell, live; to have one's abode; to abide, lodge (*arch.*) ME. Also *transf.* and *fig.* †**3.** *trans.* To occupy or people (a place) –1651. †**4.** To settle (a person) in a place; to locate, house; *refl.* to take up one's abode; *pass.* to be domiciled or resident –1600.

1. They shall build houses, and i. them *Isa.* 65:21. The..fishes..which i. the mid ocean 1881. *fig.* The High and loftie One that inhabiteth eternitie *Isa.* 57:15. 2. To learn What creatures there i. MILT. *P.L.* II. 355. *fig.* See, on the Shoar inhabits purple Spring DRYDEN. 4. O knowledge ill inhabited, worse then Ioue in a thatch'd house SHAKS.

Inha·bitable, *a.*[1] 1601. [f. prec. + -ABLE.] Capable of being inhabited.

Hence **Inha:bitabi·lity**[1], **Inha·bitableness.**

†Inha·bitable, *a.*[2] ME. [– (O)Fr. *inhabitable* – L. *inhabitabilis* not habitable; see IN-[3], HABITABLE.] Not habitable, uninhabitable –1742. **b.** Uninhabited 1529.

The frozen ridges of the Alpes, Or any other ground i. SHAKS. Hence **Inha:bitabi·lity**[2].

†Inha·bitance. 1482. [f. as INHABITANT + -ANCE.] **1.** An inhabiting; inhabitation; residence –1630. **2.** An abode, dwelling –1611.

1. The ruines yet resting in the wilde Moores, which testifie a former i. CAREW.

Inhabitancy (inhæ·bitănsi). 1681. [f. as prec. + -ANCY. Cf. HABITANCY.] **1.** The fact of inhabiting or of being an inhabitant; occupation by an inhabitant or inhabitants; residence as an inhabitant, *esp.* during a specified period, so as to gain the rights and privileges of an inhabitant. **2.** A place of habitation. GROTE.

Inhabitant (inhæ·bitănt). 1462. [– AFr., OFr. *en-*, *inhabitant* (mod. *habitant*), f. *en-*, *inhabiter*; see INHABIT *v.*, -ANT.]

A. *adj.* Inhabiting, dwelling, resident (*arch.* or *Obs.*) 1526.

Specially if he be there i. 1625.

B. *sb.* One who inhabits; a human being or animal dwelling in a place; a permanent resident. (In early use only in *pl.*)

Leopards, Bores, Iaccalls, and such like sauage inhabitants 1615. Without the good will of a single English-born i. of England FREEMAN.

†Inha·bitate, *v.* 1600. [– *inhabitat-*, pa. ppl. stem of L. *inhabitare*; see IN-[2], HABIT *v.*, -ATE[3].] To inhabit –1720.

Inhabitation (inhæ:bitēⁱ·ʃən). ME. [– late and med.L. *inhabitatio* habitation, dwelling, f. as prec.; see -ION. Cf. AFr. *enhabitacion.*] **1.** The action of inhabiting; the being or becoming inhabited. **b.** *fig.* Spiritual indwelling 1615. **†2.** A place of dwelling; an inhabited region or building; an abode –1639. **†3.** A collection of inhabitants; population; settlement (*rare*) –1818.

1. The first i. of the Realme GRAFTON. **b.** The i. of the Holy Spirit GALE. 3. Or universal groan As if the whole i. perish'd MILT. *Sams.* 1512.

Inhabita·tiveness. 1838. [f. INHABIT *v.* + -ATIVE + -NESS.] *Phrenology.* = INHABITIVENESS.

†Inha·bited, *a.* 1614. [f. IN-[3] + HABITED *ppl. a.*] Uninhabited –1621.

Inha·bited, *ppl. a.* 1570. [f. INHABIT *v.* + -ED[1].] Dwelt in; having inhabitants.

Inhabiter (inhæ·bitəɹ). *arch.* ME. [f. as prec. + -ER[1].] One who inhabits, an inhabitant; †a colonist.

Inhabitiveness (inhæ·bitivnės). 1815. [f. INHABIT *v.* + -IVE + -NESS.] *Phrenology.* The disposition to remain always in the same abode; attachment to country and home.

You know my (what the phrenologists call) i. LOWELL.

Inhalant (inhēⁱ·lănt), *a.* (*sb.*) 1822. [f. INHALE *v.* + -ANT.] **1.** Inhaling; serving for inhalation 1825. **2.** *sb.* An inhalant opening or pore 1822; an apparatus for inhaling; a medicinal preparation for inhalation (*mod.*).

Inhalation (inhălēⁱ·ʃən). 1623. [– med.L. *inhalatio*, f. *inhalat-*, pa. ppl. stem of L. *inhalare*; see next, -ION.] **1.** The action, or an act, of inhaling; *spec.* inhaling of medicines or anæsthetics in the form of gas or vapour. **2.** *Med.* A preparation to be inhaled 1882.

Inhale (inhēⁱ·l), *v.* 1725. [– L. *inhalare*, f. *in-* IN-[2] + *halare* (cf. EXHALE).] **1.** *trans.* To breathe in; to take into the lungs. Also *fig.* **2.** *loosely.* To absorb (fluid) 1841.

1. We are continually inhaling and exhaling atmospheric air TYNDALL.

Inhaler (inhēⁱ·ləɹ). 1778. [f. prec. + -ER[1].] **1.** One who inhales 1835. **2.** A contrivance for inhaling. **a.** An apparatus for administering a medicinal or anæsthetic gas or vapour by inhalation 1778. **b.** An appliance for enabling a person to breathe with safety in a deleterious atmosphere or under water 1864.

Inhance, inhanse, obs. ff. ENHANCE *v.*

Inharmonic, -al (inhaɹmǫ·nik, -ăl), *a.* 1674. [IN-[3].] Not harmonic; dissonant, inharmonious; not according to the principle of harmony.

Inharmonious (inhaɹmōᵘ·niəs), *a.* 1711. [IN-[3]. Cf. Fr. *inharmonieux.*] **1.** Of sound: Not in harmony; sounding disagreeably; discordant, untuneful. **2.** Not harmonious in relation, action, or sentiment; disagreeing; conflicting 1748.

1. Sounds i. in themselves and harsh COWPER. Hence **Inharmo·nious-ly** *adv.*, **-ness.**

Inharmony (inhā·ɹmŏni). *rare.* 1799. [f. IN-[3] + HARMONY. Cf. Fr. *inharmonie.*] Want of harmony; discord.

Inhaul (i·nhǭl). 1860. [f. IN *adv.* + HAUL *sb.*] *Naut.* = next.

Inhauler (i·nhǭ:ləɹ). 1793. [f. IN *adv.* + HAULER.] An appliance for hauling in; *spec.* (*Naut.*) 'the rope used for hauling in the clue of a boomsail, or jib-traveller' (Smyth).

Inhaust (inhǭ·st), *v. rare.* 1547. [f. IN-[2] + *haust-*, pa. ppl. stem of L. *haurire* draw, after EXHAUST.] *trans.* To draw or suck in; to inhale; to imbibe. So **Inhau·stion,** inhalation.

Inhearse, obs. f. ENHEARSE.

Inhell (inhe·l), *v.* 1607. [f. IN-[2] + HELL *sb.* Cf. ENHEAVEN.] *trans.* To put into or confine in hell.

†Inherce, obs. f. ENHEARSE *v.* 1 *Hen. VI*, IV. vii. 45.

Inhere (inhīᵊ·ɹ), *v.* Also **†inhære.** 1586. [– L. *inhærēre*, f. *in-* IN-[2] + *hærēre* stick. Cf. *adhere.*] **1.** *intr.* To stick *in*; to be or remain fixed or lodged *in* something (*rare* or *Obs.*). Also *fig.* 1608. **2.** To exist, abide, or have its being, as an attribute, quality, etc., *in* a subject or thing. (The current sense.) 1586. **b.** To be vested or inherent *in*, as a right, power, etc. 1840.

1. *fig.* So strongly does it i. in our constitution, that very few are able to conquer it BURKE. 2. Knowledge and perception i. in mind alone BAIN.

Inherence (inhīᵊ·rĕns). Also **†inhærence.** 1577. [– med.L. *inherentia*, f. *inherent-*; see next, -ENCE. Cf. (O)Fr. *inhérence.*] The fact or condition of inhering; the state or quality of being inherent; permanent existence (as of an attribute) *in* a subject; indwelling. So **Inhe·rency** (in mod. use chiefly as a quality.)

Inherent (inhīᵊ·rĕnt), *a.* Also **†inhærent.** 1578. [– *inhærent-*, pr. ppl. stem of L. *inhærēre*; see INHERE *v.*, -ENT. Cf. Fr. *inhérent* (XVI).] **1.** Sticking in; fixed, situated, or contained in something (in physical sense). Also *fig.* (Now *rare* or *Obs.*) **2.** Existing in something as a permanent attribute or quality; forming an element, esp. an essential element, of something; intrinsic, essential 1588. **3.** Vested *in* or attached to a person, office, etc., as a right or privilege 1628.

1. *fig.* Least I..teach my Minde A most i. Basenesse SHAKS. 2. The melancholy i. in his constitution BOSWELL. 3. The legislative authority was i. in the general assembly GIBBON. Hence **Inhe·rently** *adv.*

Inherit (inhe·rit), *v.* [ME. *en(h)erite* – OFr. *enheriter* make heir, f. *en-* IN-[2] + *heriter* :– late and med.L. *inhereditare*, appoint as heir, f. L. *heres, hered-* HEIR.] **†1.** *trans.* To make heir, put in possession. (Cf. *disinherit.*) –1593. **2.** *trans.* To take or receive (property, *esp.* realty or a right, title, etc.) as heir of the former possessor (usu. an ancestor) at his decease; to get by legal descent or succession ME. **b.** To derive (a quality, etc., physical or mental) from one's progenitors by natural descent; to possess by transmission from parents or ancestry 1597. **c.** To receive from a predecessor in office. Chiefly *fig.* 1847. **3.** *transf.* To receive, obtain, have, or hold as one's portion ME. **4.** To succeed as heir 1533. **5.** *absol.* or *intr.* To succeed as an heir; to come into or take possession of an inheritance. Also *fig.* 1533.

1. *Rich. II*, I. i. 85. 2. Lat him as ayre, quen I am erþed, enherit my landis ME. **b.** The cold blood hee did..inherite of his Father SHAKS. 3. Good master, what shall I doe to i. eternall life? *Luke* 18:18. 4. Our sons i. us TENNYSON. 5. His Issue [were] barred from Inheriting TYRRELL. Hence **Inhe·ritage** (*rare*), a heritage, inheritance. **Inhe·ritor,** one who inherits, in various senses; an heir. **Inhe·ritress, -†trice, †-trix,** an heiress.

Inheritable (inhe·rităb'l), *a.* Also **†en-.** 1470. [– AFr. *en-*, *inheritable*, able to be made heir, f. *enheriter*; see INHERIT and -ABLE.] **1.** Capable of inheriting (see the vb.). **2.** Capable of being inherited. **a.** *lit.* = HERITABLE 1. 1483. **b.** *fig.* = HERITABLE 2. 1828.

1. In England..upon deficiency of I. Blood, Lands escheat to the Crown 1774. 2. **a.** The British Crown was in those early days i. by females SYD. SMITH. **b.** I. deviations of structure DARWIN. Hence **Inhe:ritabi·lity, Inhe·ritableness,** i. quality. **Inhe·ritably** *adv.* so as to be i., by inheritance.

Inheritance (inhe·rităns). ME. [– AFr. *inheritaunce* being admitted as heir, etc., f. *enheriter*; see INHERIT, -ABLE.]

I. The action or fact of inheriting. **1.** *lit.* Hereditary succession to property, a title, etc.; 'a perpetual or continuing right to an estate, vested in a person and his heirs' (Wharton). **2.** *transf.* and *fig.* **a.** Possession, ownership, of something as one's birthright; right of possession 1535. **b.** Natural derivation of qualities or characters from parents or ancestry 1859.

1. The realme of Fraunce to him..by lyneall enheritaunce aperteyning HALL. 2. **a.** But you hath the Lorde taken..that ye shulde be the people of his enheritaunce COVERDALE *Deut.* 4:20. **b.** These characters may be attributed to i. from a common progenitor DARWIN.

II. That which is inherited. **1.** *lit.* Property, or an estate, which passes by law to the heir on the decease of the possessor 1473. Also *fig.* **2.** *transf.* and *fig.* Something that one comes into possession of by right or divine grant; birthright. In biblical use applied to persons, etc., as God's possession (κλῆρος), and to possessions or blessings as received or enjoyed by such persons. (Cf. HERITAGE *sb.*) 1535.

1. He [the minister] is the tenant of the day, and has no interest in the i. 'JUNIUS'. *fig.* His name, The sole i. he left BYRON. 2. O helpe thy people, geue thy blessynge vnto thy enheritaunce COVERDALE *Ps.* 27[28]:9.

Inhesion (inhī·ʒən). Also **†inhæsion.** 1631. [– late L. *inhæsio*, f. *inhæs-*, pa. ppl. stem of L. *inhærēre*; see INHERE, -ION.] The action or fact of inhering, esp. as a quality or attribute; inherence.

Phr. *Subject of i.*, that in which a quality or attribute inheres.

†Inhe·sive, *a. rare.* 1639. [f. as prec. + -IVE; for the meaning cf. INHERE 2.] Having the quality of inhering; inherent. Hence **†Inhe·sively,** *adv.* inherently 1600–1681.

Inhiate (i·nhai,eⁱt), *v.* 1543. [– *inhiat-*, pa. ppl. stem of L. *inhiare* gape at, f. *in-* IN-[2] + *hiare* gape; see -ATE[3], HIATE *v.*] *intr.* To gape, open the mouth wide. Hence **†Inhia·tion,** the act of gaping *after*.

Inhibit (inhi·bit), *v.* Pa. pple. **inhibited;** also **†inhibit(e.** 1460. [– *inhibit-*, pa. ppl. stem of L. *inhibēre* hold in, hinder, f. *in-* IN-[2] + *habēre* hold.] **1.** *trans.* To forbid, prohibit, interdict (a person); **b.** without constr.: *esp.* to forbid (an ecclesiastic) to exercise clerical functions 1531. **2.** To forbid, prohibit (a thing, action, etc.). Now *rare.* 1494. **3.** To restrain, check, hinder, prevent, stop 1535.

1. The said Peckam inhibited all from selling victuals to him or his family FULLER. **b.** He did never i. me in my life LATIMER. 2. Burial may not be inhibited or deny'd to any one AYLIFFE. Hence **Inhi·biter, -or,** one who inhibits.

Inhibition (inhibi·ʃən). ME. [– (O)Fr. *inhibition* or L. *inhibitio*, f. as prec.; see -ION.] **1.** The action of inhibiting or forbidding; a prohibition. **2.** *spec.* **†a.** In *Eng. Law*, formerly = PROHIBITION. **b.** In *Eccl. Law.* The order of an eccl. court, stopping proceedings in inferior courts; also, now *esp.*, the command of a bishop or eccl. judge, that a clergyman shall cease from exercising ministerial functions. 1532. **3.** The action of preventing, hindering, or checking. Now esp. in *Physiol.* 1621.

3. By i. we mean the arrest of the functions of a structure or organ, by the action upon it of another, while its power to execute those functions is still retained 1883.

Inhibitory (inhi·bitəri), *a.* 1490. [– med.L. *inhibitorius*; see INHIBIT *v.*, -ORY[2]. Sense 2 refers to INHIBITION 3.] **1.** Of the nature of an inhibition; prohibitory. **2.** *Physiol.* That restrains, checks, or hinders action 1855.

1. This Original Right of the Archbishop, I. of our Liberty..is the very Point in Question 1701. **2.** *I. nerve*, a nerve of which the stimulation represses or diminishes action; The hypothesis that alcohol narcotises the i. nerve of the heart 1882.

†**Inhi·ve,** *v. rare.* 1611. [IN-¹ or ².] *trans.* To put into a hive; to HIVE –1622.

†**Inho·ld,** *v.* 1614. [f. IN-¹ + HOLD *v.*] **1.** *trans.* To hold within; to contain, enclose –1628. **2.** *intr.* To contain oneself, keep *from.* FULLER.

†**Inho·lder.** 1599. [f. prec., or as prec.] **1.** A tenant. SPENSER. **2.** That which holds or contains –1674.

†**Inhoo·p,** *v.* [f. IN-¹ or ² + HOOP *sb.* or *v.*] *trans.* In *Cockfighting*: To place or enclose in a hoop, to surround with a hoop. *Ant. & Cl.* II. iii. 38.

Inhospitable (inhǫ·spităb'l), *a.* 1570. [– Fr. †*inhospitable*, f. *in-* IN-³ + *hospitable* HOSPITABLE.] Not hospitable. **1.** Not disposed to welcome and entertain strangers; withholding hospitality from guests or visitors. **2.** *transf.* Of a region or coast: Not offering shelter or entertainment 1616.

1. Jael, who, with i. guile Smote Sisera sleeping, through the Temples nail'd MILT. **2.** The Coast is i. as well as the People 1727. Hence **Inhospitabi·lity, Inho·spitableness. Inho·spitably** *adv.* var. †**Inho·spital** *a.*

Inhospitality (inhǫspitæ·lĭti). 1570. [– L. *inhospitalitas*, f. *inhospitalis* inhospitable; see -ITY. Perh. partly through Fr. *inhospitalité.*] The quality or practice of being inhospitable; want of hospitality.

Inhuman (inhiū·măn), *a.* 1481. [– L. *inhumanus*, f. *in-* IN-³ + *humanus* HUMAN. In earlier exx. – Fr. *inhumain*. The sp. was *inhumane* till after 1700. The stress was orig. on the final syllable.] **1.** Of persons: Not having the qualities proper or natural to a human being; *esp.* destitute of natural kindness or pity; brutal, unfeeling. Also *fig.* of things. **b.** Of actions, etc.: Brutal, barbarous, cruel 1489. **2.** Not of the ordinary human type 1568.

1. E'er sounding Hammers forg'd th' inhumane Sword DRYDEN. **b.** Inhumane Cruelties CLARENDON. **2.** The human and i. wonders painted thrice the size of life D. JERROLD. Hence **Inhu·man-ly** *adv.*, **-ness.**

Inhumane (inhiumē¹·n), *a.* 1598. [– L. *inhumanus*; see prec. In later use f. IN-³ + HUMANE.] †**1.** = INHUMAN 1. –1777. †**2.** Uncivilized, uncultured, impolite. BUTLER. **3.** Not humane; destitute of compassion for suffering 1822. Hence **Inhuma·nely** *adv.*

Inhumanity (inhiumæ·nĭti). 1477. [–(O)Fr. *inhumanité* or L. *inhumanitas*; see INHUMAN, -ITY.] **1.** The quality of being inhuman or inhumane; want of human feeling; brutality, barbarous cruelty. **b.** With *an* and *pl.* An inhuman or cruel deed 1647. †**2.** Want of politeness or courtesy –1648.

1. Man's i. to Man Makes countless thousands mourn BURNS.

Inhumate (inhiū·me¹t, i·nhiume¹t), *v. rare.* 1612. [f. *inhumat-*, pa. ppl. stem of L. *inhumare* INHUME.] *trans.* To inhume, bury.

Inhumation (inhiumē¹·ʃən). 1612. [f. INHUMATE or INHUME; see -ATION. Cf. Fr. *inhumation* (XV).] **1.** The action or practice of burying in the ground; the fact or condition of being buried; interment 1636. **2.** The burying of a thing under ground. Also *fig.* 1658. †**3.** An obsolete chemical process, in which vessels were buried in earth, within a circular fire, for purposes of distillation –1650.

Inhume (inhiū·m), *v.* Also †**en-.** 1610. [– L. *inhumare*, f. *in-* IN-² + *humus* ground.] **1.** *trans.* To inter, bury (the dead); to lay in the grave. Also *fig.* **b.** *transf.* Of the earth or tomb: To cover (the dead). ?*Obs.* 1621. **2.** To bury in the ground; to cover with soil. Now *rare.* 1621.

1. Here's a storm Able to wake all of our name inhumed MIDDLETON. **2.** By which the Cities were inhumed LYELL.

Inial (i·niăl), *a.* 1808. [f. INION + -AL¹.] *Anat.* Of or belonging to the inion. So **I·niad** *adv.*, towards the inial aspect 1803.

†**Inima·ginable,** *a.* 1533. [– mod.L. *inimaginabilis* (Erasmus) and Fr. *inimaginable* (Montaigne); see IN-³, IMAGINABLE.] Unimaginable –1759.

Inimical (ini·mikăl), *a.* 1513. [– late L. *inimicalis*, f. *inimicus*; see ENEMY, -AL¹.] **1.** Having the disposition or temper of an enemy; unfriendly, hostile. Const. *to.* **2.** Adverse or injurious in tendency or influence; harmful, hurtful. Const. *to.* 1643.

1. A prince i. to civil and religious liberty 1765. **2.** Practices i. to health JOWETT. Hence **Inimica·lity, Ini·micalness. Ini·mically** *adv.*

†**Inimici·tious,** *a.* Also †**en-.** 1641. [f. L. *inimicitia* enmity + -OUS.] = INIMICAL –1761. So †**Ini·micous** *a.* 1597; †**Inimicity,** hostility 1561.

Inimitable (ini·mităb'l), *a.* 1531. [– Fr. *inimitable* or L. *inimitabilis*; sense 2 f. IN-³ + IMITABLE.] **1.** Incapable of being imitated; surpassing or defying imitation; peerless. **2.** Not to be imitated. WASHINGTON.

1. I. eloquence ELYOT, stile P. HOLLAND. The i. chemistry of nature 1756. Hence **Ini:mitabi·lity, Ini·mitableness. Ini·mitably** *adv.*

Ini·mitative, *a.* 1836. [IN-³.] = prec.

In infinitum: see IN *Lat. prep.*

Inion (i·ni,ǫn). 1803. [– Gr. ἰνίον nape of the neck.] *Anat.* A ridge of the occiput; *spec.* the external occipital protuberance.

†**Inique,** *a.* 1521. [– L. *iniquus*, f. *in-* IN-³ + *æquus* equal, just.] Unjust; iniquitous. –1730.

†**Ini·quitable,** *a.* 1734. [alt. f. INEQUITABLE after *iniquity, iniquitous.*] Unjust; iniquitous.

Iniquitous (ini·kwitəs), *a.* 1726. [f. INIQUITY + -OUS; cf. *felicitous.*] Characterized by iniquity; grossly unjust; wicked.

I. opinions SWIFT, prosecutions 1770. I. in price RUSKIN. Hence **Ini·quitous-ly** *adv.*, **-ness.**

Iniquity (ini·kwĭti). ME. [– OFr. *iniquité* – L. *iniquitas*, f. *iniquus*, f. *in-* IN-³ + *æquus* just, righteous.] **1.** The quality of being unrighteous, or (more often) unrighteous action or conduct; wickedness, sin; *occas.*, esp. in early use, Injurious or wrongful action towards another; now generally connoting gross injustice or public wrong. **b.** *pl.* Sins; wrongful acts, injuries 1477. †**2.** Want of equity; injustice, unfairness. *Obs.* exc. as implied in 1. 1587. **3.** The name of a comic character in the old morality plays, also called the VICE, representing some particular vice, or vice in general 1594. †**4.** Unfavourableness, adverse operation. (A Latinism.) –1619.

1. Departe from me all ye workers off iniquytie TINDALE *Luke* 13:27. **b.** The oppressions and iniquities of the Oude government 1804. **3.** Thus like the formall Vice, Iniquitie, I morallize two meanings in one word SHAKS. **4.** They all were destroyed by the iniquitie of Fortune 1619.

†**Ini·quous,** *a.* 1654. [f. L. *iniquus* (see prec.) + -OUS.] Unjust, unfair; wicked, iniquitous –1724.

Inirritable (ini·rităb'l), *a.* 1794. [IN-³.] Not irritable or suscepitble of excitement. Hence **Ini:rritabi·lity.**

Ini·irritative, *a.* ?*Obs.* 1796. [IN-³.] Characterized by absence of irritation, as *i. debility.*

Inisle, var. of ENISLE *v.*

Initial (ini·ʃăl). 1526. [– L. *initialis*, f. *initium* beginning; see -AL¹.]

A. *adj.* **1.** Of or pertaining to a beginning; existing at, or constituting, the beginning; primary; occas. = elementary, rudimentary. **2.** Standing at the beginning of a word, etc., or of the alphabet; as *i. letter* SIR T. MORE.

1. The square of the i. velocity PLAYFAIR. The i. stage of mental disease 1880. The cells from which these..masses of nascent tissues arise are known as *i. cells* 1885.

B. *sb.* †**1.** A beginning *of* something –1839. **2.** An initial letter; *esp.* (in *pl.*) the initial letters of a person's name and surname 1627. **3.** *Mus.* Each of the prescribed notes (usu. called *absolute initials*) on which a Plain-song melody may begin in any given mode. GROVE.

Initial (ini·ʃăl), *v.* 1864. [f. prec. B. 2.] *trans.* To mark or sign with initials; to put one's initials to or upon. Hence **Ini·tialed (-alled)** *ppl. a.* **Ini·tialing (-alling)** *vbl. sb.* and *ppl. a.*

Initially (ini·ʃăli), *adv.* 1628. [f. INITIAL *a.* + -LY².] In relation to, or in the way of, a beginning; at the outset, at first.

Initiate (ini·ʃi,e¹t), *v.* 1603. [– *initiat-*, pa. ppl. stem of L. *initiare* begin, f. *initium* beginning; see -ATE³.] **1.** *trans.* To begin, commence, enter upon; to introduce, set going, originate 1604. **b.** *intr.* To commence. ?*Obs.* 1618. **2.** *trans.* To admit with proper introductory rites or forms into some society or office, or to knowledge of or participation in some principles or observances, esp. of an occult character; hence, To instruct in the elements of any subject or practice. Const. *into, in* (†*to*). 1603. **3.** *intr.* **a.** To perform the first rite. POPE. **b.** To undergo initiation 1896.

1. They feared (for the present) to i. their attempt SPEED. **2.** Our author in his old age..initiated himself in the sacred rites of Delphos DRYDEN. To i. young people in the elements of Physical Science HUXLEY. Hence **Ini·tiated** *ppl. a.* (often *absol.* in *pl.* sense; rarely as sb. sing.).

Initiate (ini·ʃi,ĕt), *ppl. a.* and *sb.* 1605. [– L. *initiatus*, pa. pple. of *initiare*; see prec., -ATE².]

A. *ppl. a.* Initiated. **1.** Admitted into some society, office, or position; instructed in some secret knowledge 1610. †**b.** *transf.* Pertaining to a novice. *Macb.* III. iv. 143. **2.** Begun, commenced, introduced 1767.

1. We..that are i. Divines BURTON. **2.** As soon.. as any child was born, the father began to have a permanent interest in the lands..and was called *tenant by the curtesy initiate* BLACKSTONE.

B. *sb.* A person who has been initiated; hence, a beginner 1811.

Initiation (iniʃi,ē¹·ʃən). 1583. [– L. *initiatio* (in sense 2), f. as prec.; see -ION, and cf. Fr. *initiation* in same sense. Sense 1 – med.L. 'beginning'.] **1.** The action of initiating, or fact of being initiated; beginning, origination 1641. **2.** Formal introduction by preliminary instruction or initial ceremony into some office, society, etc., or to participation in some principles or observances; hence, Instruction in the elements of any subject or practice 1583.

1. The Church of Germanie had its i. or beginning in Martin Luther 1641. The i. of Parliamentary measures 1863. **2.** A large school is a most valuable i. into actual life 1876.

Initiative (ini·ʃiĕtiv), *sb.* 1793. [– Fr. *initiative* sb. (XVI), f. as next.] **1.** That which initiates, begins, or originates; the first step; hence, the act, or action, of taking the first step or lead; beginning, origination. **2.** The power, right, or function of initiating something. Hence *to possess* or *have the i.* 1793. **b.** *spec. Pol. Sci.* The right of a citizen or defined number of citizens, outside the Legislature, to initiate legislation, as in some of the Swiss cantons, and in Switzerland as a Federal Republic 1889.

1. Phr. *On one's own i.*, by one's own origination. *To take the i.* (Fr. *prendre l'initiative*): to make the first step, originate some action. **2. b.** Both Referendum and I. are institutions which have grown up gradually in the Cantons, spreading from one to another 1889.

Initiative (ini·ʃiĕtiv), *a.* 1642. [f. INITIATE *v.* + -IVE.] Characterized by initiating; having the function, power, or faculty of beginning or originating something; initiatory.

Initiator (ini·ʃi,e¹təɹ). 1676. [f. INITIATE *v.* + -OR 2.] One who or that which initiates. So **Ini·tiatress, -atrix,** a female i.

Initiatory (ini·ʃiĕtəri), *a.* (*sb.*) 1612. [f. INITIATE *v.* + -ORY².] **1.** Such as pertains to the beginning or first steps; initial, introductory. **2.** Pertaining or tending to initiation; serving to initiate (see INITIATE *v.* 2) 1632. **3.** *sb.* An initiatory rite 1675.

1. The i. stage of legal proceedings STUBBS. **2.** The i. Rite of water-baptism WARBURTON.

Inition (ini·ʃən). *rare.* 1463. [– OFr. *inition* – med.L. *initio*, f. *init-*, pa. ppl. stem of L. *inire* go into, enter; see -ION.] Entrance, beginning, initiation.

Inject (indʒe·kt), *v.* 1599. [– *inject-*, pa. ppl. stem of L. *inicere* throw in, f. *in-* IN-² + *jacere* throw.] **1.** *trans.* To throw in. *Obs.* in general sense. –1646. **b.** *spec.* To drive or force (a fluid, etc.) into a passage or cavity; cf. INJECTION 1 b. 1601. **2.** *fig.* To throw in, as a thought or feeling into the mind, etc.; to suggest; to interject. Now *rare.* 1639. **3.** *transf.* To fill or charge (a cavity, etc., or an animal body) by injection. Const. *with.* 1731. †**4.** To throw *on* something –1725.

1. b. I..injected Barley Water up the Nose 1758. **2.** Our Adversary injects..bad motions into our hearts FULLER. **3.** To i. the bladder with warm water 1844. **4.** Iniect the same on hot coales, and sitt therover 1599. Hence **Inje·cted** *ppl. a.*; *spec.* in *Path.* having the capillaries or small vessels distended with blood, bloodshot.

Injection (indʒe·kʃən). 1541. [– Fr. *injection* or L. *injectio*, f. as prec.; see -ION.] **1.** The action of injecting. *Obs.* in general sense. –1686. **b.** *spec.* The action of forcing a fluid, etc. into a passage or cavity, as by means of a syringe, pump, etc.; *esp.* the introduction in this way of a liquid or other substances into the vessels or cavities of the body, either for medicinal, or (in a dead body) preservative purposes 1541. **2.** *Path.* The fact of being charged with injected matter; injected or bloodshot condition 1806. **3.** *concr.* That which is injected; *spec.* a liquid or solution injected into an animal body, for medicinal or other purposes, as an enema, etc. 1607. **4.** *fig.* The throwing in of something from without, as of an idea into the mind, etc.; a suggestion, a hint. Now *rare.* 1622. **5.** *attrib.*, as *i. powder, syringe, theory*; *i.-cock, -condenser, -engine, -pipe, -valve, -water*, etc. (in relation to condensing steam-engines in which the steam is condensed by the injection of a jet of cold water) 1752.

4. Satans Injections are like Weeds that fall Into thy Garden, darted or'e the Wall QUARLES.

Injector (indʒe·ktəɹ). 1744. [f. INJECT + -OR 2.] **1.** A contrivance for injecting; an apparatus for injecting water into the boiler of a steam-engine. **2.** A person who injects 1897.

Injelly (indʒe·li), *v. rare.* 1842. [IN-[1] or [2].] To set or enclose in jelly.

Injoin: see ENJOIN.

†Injoint, *v.*[1] [f. IN-[1] + JOINT *v.*] *intr.* To unite, join. *Oth.* I. iii. 35.

†Injoi·nt, *v.*[2] [f. IN-[3] + JOINT *v.*] *trans.* To unjoint, disjoint. P. HOLLAND.

Injucu·ndity. *rare.* 1623. [– L. *injucunditas*, f. *injucundus* unpleasant; partly f. IN-[3] + JUCUNDITY.] Unpleasantness, disagreeableness.

Injudi·cial, *a. rare.* 1607. [IN-[3].] Not judicial; †injudicious; not according to the forms of law; not becoming a judge. Hence **Injudi·cially** *adv.*

Injudicious (indʒudi·ʃəs), *a.* 1649. [IN-[3].] Not judicious. **†1.** Wanting sound judgement; deficient in the power of judging aright –1694. **2.** Not manifesting practical judgement or discretion; showing want of judgement; unwise, ill-advised, ill-judged 1710.

1. The hearts of the in-judicious multitude 1654. **2.** To vindicate a man..against an i. biographer 1792. Hence **Injudi·cious-ly** *adv.*, **-ness.**

Injunction (indʒɒ·ŋkʃən). 1480. [– late L. *injunctio*, f. *injunct-*, pa. ppl. stem of L. *injungere* ENJOIN; see -ION.] **1.** The action of enjoining or authoritatively directing; an authoritative or emphatic admonition or order. **2.** *Law.* A judicial process by which one who is threatening to invade or has invaded the legal or equitable rights of another is restrained from commencing or continuing such wrongful act, or is commanded to restore matters to the position in which they stood previously to his action 1533. **†3.** Conjunction, union. MILT.

1. The high I. not to taste that Fruit MILT *P.L.* x. 13. Forgetful of his Mother's parting injunctions 1898. **2.** He may with an I., out of the Chancery stop their proceedings FULLER.

Injure (i·ndʒŭɹ), *v.* 1583. [Back-formation from INJURY *sb.*, repl. INJURY *v.*] **1.** *trans.* To do injustice to; to wrong 1592. **†2.** To do outrage to in speech; to insult, revile, calumniate –1659. **3.** To do hurt or harm to; to damage; to impair 1586. Also *intr.* for *refl.* 1848.

1. When haue I iniur'd thee? when done thee wrong? SHAKS. **3.** He had..injured himself in crossing the Gemmi TYNDALL. Hence **I·njurer.**

Injurious (indʒūᵊ·riəs), *a.* 1480. [– Fr. *injurieux* or L. *injuriosus*, f. *injuria* INJURY; see -OUS.] **1.** Wrongful; hurtful to the rights of another; wilfully inflicting injury or wrong 1494. **2.** Wilfully hurtful or offensive in language; insulting; calumnious. (Now only of words or speech.) 1480. **3.** Tending to hurt or damage; harmful, detrimental, deleterious 1559.

1. A wronged servant shall have right..from his i.master 1634. **2.** Call me their Traitor, thou injurious Tribune SHAKS. **3.** It would be i. to the public trade of England 1817. Hence **Inju·rious-ly** *adv.*, **-ness.**

Injury (i·ndʒŭri), *sb.* ME. [– AFr. *injurie* (mod.Fr. *injure* insult) – L. *injuria*, subst. use of fem. of *injurius* unjust, wrongful, f. *in-* IN-[3] + *jus, jur-* right; see JURY, -Y[3].] **1.** Wrongful action or treatment; violation or infringement of another's rights; suffering or mischief wilfully or unjustly inflicted. Also, A wrongful act; a wrong inflicted or suffered. **†2.** Intentionally hurtful or offensive speech or words; insult, calumny; a taunt, an affront –1710. **3.** Hurt or loss caused to or sustained by a person or thing; harm, detriment, damage; an instance of this ME.

1. By [wholesome laws]..we are bridled..from doing of iniuries 1611. I., as distinct from harm, may raise sudden anger BUTLER. **2.** He began to raile upon them with a thousand injuries FLORIO. **3.** Having sustained a heavy blow without i. SCOTT.

†I·njury, *v.* 1484. [–(O)Fr. *injurier* – late L. *injuriare*, f. L. *injuria* INJURY *sb.* Partly f. the sb. Superseded *c*1600 by INJURE *v.*] = INJURE –1651.

†Inju·st, *a.* ME. [– (O)Fr. *injuste* – L. *injustus*; see IN-[3], JUST.] = UNJUST –1711. Hence **†Inju·stly** *adv.*

Injustice (indʒɒ·stis). ME. [– (O)Fr. *injustice* – L. *injusticia*, f. *injustus*; see IN-[3], JUSTICE.] The opposite of justice; unjust action; wrong; unfairness. Also, An unjust act.

The many iniustices of yoʳ last edict 1601. All briberie and iniustice shall be blotted out *Ecclus.* 40:12.

†Inju·stifiable, *a. rare.* 1646. [IN-[3].] Unjustifiable –1714.

Ink (iŋk), *sb.*[1] [ME. *enke*, later *inc(k, inke* – OFr. *enque* (mod. *encre*) :– late L. *e·ncautum, e·ncaustum* – Gr. ἔγκαυστον purple ink used by Greek and Roman emperors for their signatures, f. ἐγκαίειν burn in (see ENCAUSTIC.] The coloured (usually black) fluid ordinarily employed in writing with a pen on paper, parchment, etc. (*writing ink*), or the viscous paste used in printing (*printing* or *printer's ink*). Also *fig.* and *transf.*

The word *ink* without qualification commonly means black writing ink. Inks are distinguished by their colour, as *black, red, blue, gold ink*, etc.; by the purpose which they serve, as *copying, lithographic, marking, printing* (or *printer's*), *writing ink*; by some special quality, as *indelible, invisible, sympathetic ink*; by the place of manufacture, as *China, Indian ink*, q.v.

Deformed monsters, fowle, and blacke as inke SPENSER. Battles..fought only by i. CARLYLE.

b. The black inky liquid secreted by the cuttle-fish and allied cephalopods, and stored in a sac or bladder 1586.

Comb. **1.** General: as *i.-drop, -maker, -stained*, etc.; *i.-bottle, -case, -reservoir*, etc.

2. Special: **i.-bag**, the bladder-shaped sac in the cuttle-fish, etc. containing the 'ink'; **-ball**, (*a*) = BALL *sb.*[1] 12; (*b*) a kind of oak-gall used in making i.; **-eraser**; **-fish**, a cuttle-fish or squid; **-gland** = *ink-bag*; **-nut** = MYROBALAN; **-pad**; **-pencil**; **-plant**, the European shrub *Coriaria myrtifolia*, or N. Zealand species *C. thymifolia*; **-powder**, the powdered ingredients of i.; **-sac** = *ink-bag*; **-spot** (*a*) a stain of i.; (*b*) a dark spot on the skin; **-well**, an ink-cup adapted to occupy a hole in a desk; **-writer**, a telegraph instrument which records messages in i.

Ink, *sb.*[2] 1572. [Of unkn. origin.] **†1.** *orig.* A mill-rind. Used as a charge in *Her.* **2.** Now, 'The socket which holds the toe of a vertical shaft or spindle' (Knight) 1875.

Ink (iŋk), *v.* 1562. [f. INK *sb.*[1]] *trans.* To mark, stain, or smear with or as with ink. **b.** To cover types with ink 1727.

I·nk-be:rry. 1716. A name given, from their colour or juice, to various shrubs, and their berries; *esp.* **a.** A small shrub of the holly family (*Prinos glaber* or *Ilex glabra*), a native of the Atlantic coast of N. America. **b.** The W. Indian indigo-berry (*Randia aculeata*).

Inker (i·ŋkəɹ). 1882. [f. INK *v.* + -ER[1].] One who or that which inks. **1.** A telegraph-instrument which records the message in ink. **2.** *Printing.* An inking-roller 1884.

I·nk-horn. ME. [f. INK *sb.*[1] + HORN *sb.*] **1.** A small portable vessel (orig. made of a horn) for holding writing ink; now seldom used. **2.** *attrib.* **a. †ink-horn mate, varlet,** a mere scribbler. SHAKS. **b. ink-horn term,** a learned or bookish word (*arch.*) 1543.

1. The man that..hadde an enk-horn in his rigge WYCLIF. *Ezek.* 9:11. **2. b.** Soche are your Ynkehorne termes BALE. Hence **†I·nk-hornism** (*rare*), an ink-horn term.

Inking (i·ŋkiŋ), *vbl. sb.* 1818. [f. INK *v.* + -ING[1].] The action of INK *v.*; *spec.* the covering of type with ink. **b.** *attrib.*, chiefly in terms relating to printing or to inking the type, as *i.-roller*, etc. 1790.

Inkle (i·ŋk'l), *sb.* Now *rare.* 1532. [Of unkn. origin.] A kind of linen tape, or the thread or yarn from which it is made.

Inkle (i·ŋk'l), *v. rare.* ME. [Of unkn. origin. See next.] **1.** *trans.* To utter in an undertone, to hint. (In later use a back-formation from INKLING 2.) **2.** *dial.* To get an inkling of 1866.

2. She inkled what it was BLACKMORE.

Inkling (i·ŋkliŋ), *vbl. sb.* ME. [f. INKLE *v.* + -ING[1].] **1.** Mentioning in an undertone; a faint or slight report or rumour. *Obs.* exc. *dial.* **2.** A hint, a slight intimation 1513. **3.** A hint received; hence, a vague notion; a suspicion 1546. **4.** *dial.* An inclination 1787.

1. There was an ynkling, that it wold not be long er you came 1576. **2.** Geuyng an incklyng of his secound cummyng UDALL. **3.** If he gets but an i.,..our project is marr'd FOOTE.

In-kneed (in,nī·d, i·n,nīd), *a.* 1724. [f. IN *adv.* + KNEE *sb.* + -ED[2].] Having the legs bent inwards at the knees.

†In,knit, *v.* [f. IN-[1] + KNIT *v.*] *trans.* To knit up, draw close together. CHAUCER.

Inknot (in,nǫ·t), *v. rare.* 1611. [f. IN-[1] + KNOT *v.*] To include in or with a knot; to tie in; also, = INNODATE *v.*

Inkpot (i·ŋk,pǫt). 1553. [INK *sb.*[1]] **1.** A small pot for holding writing-ink. **2.** *attrib.* **inkpot term** = ink-horn term (see INK-HORN 2 b) 1553.

Inkshed (i·ŋk,ʃed). *joc.* 1672. [f. INK *sb.*[1] + *-shed*, after BLOODSHED.] The shedding or spilling of ink; consumption or waste of ink in writing.

With no bloodshed..but with immense beershed and i. CARLYLE.

Inkstand (i·ŋk,stænd). 1675. A stand for holding one or more ink-bottles or ink-glasses (often with a tray, etc.); occas. applied to an inkpot. So **†In·k-sta:ndish.**

I·nkster. [f. INK *v.* or *sb.*[1] + -STER.] A scribbler. READE.

Inky (i·ŋki), *a.* 1581. [f. INK *sb.*[1] + -Y[1].] **1.** Of or pertaining to, written with, using ink; literary. **2.** As black as ink; very black or dark 1593. **3.** Stained with ink, inked 1683.

1. England..is now bound in with shame, With I. blottes, and rotten Parchment bonds SHAKS. **2.** A little i. tarn 1880. **3.** I. fingers 1894.

Inlace, var. of ENLACE.

†Inla·gary. 1607. [– med.L. *inlagaria*, f. ME. *inlaȝe* INLAW; see -ARY[1]. (AFr. *inlagerie*).] The restitution of an outlaw to the benefit and protection of the law. So **†Inlag·ation,** in same sense.

Inlaid (i·nlēⁱd, inlēⁱ·d), pa. pple. of INLAY *v.*

Inland (i·nlănd, i·nlænd). OE. [f. IN *adv.* + LAND *sb.*]

A. *sb.* **1.** The inner part of an estate, feudal manor, or farm; in OE. and feudal tenure, the land around the house occupied or cultivated by the owner, not held by any tenant (cf. DEMESNE II. 1.). **2.** *sing.* and *pl.* The inland country, the interior. †Formerly, also, the inlying districts near the capital and centres of population. 1573.

B. *adj.* (attrib. use of sb.) **1.** Of or pertaining to the interior part of a country or region; remote from the sea or border 1456. **2.** Carried on or operating within the limits of a country. Opp. to *foreign.* 1546.

1. *I. sea*, a large body of salt water, entirely or nearly severed from the ocean; applied also to large lakes. The improvement of our i. navigation 1792. **2.** The i. trade of England 1745. Phr. *I. bill of exchange. I. duty*, a duty on i. trade, etc., as the excise and stamp duties. *I. revenue*, the part of the national revenue consisting of taxes and i. duties.

C. *adv.* In or towards the interior or heart of

a country, as opp. to the coast or border, or to wild outlying districts 1600.

Yet am I in-land bred, And know some nourture SHAKS.

Inlander (i·nlăndəɹ). 1610. [f. as prec. + -ER¹.] One who dwells in the interior of a country.

Inlandish (i:nlæ·ndiʃ), *a.* 1657. [f. as prec. + -ISH¹.] †**1.** Home, domestic, native; opp. to *outlandish.* **2.** Of an inland nature or character 1849.

†**Inla·pidate,** *v.* [f. IN-² + L. *lapis, lapid-* + -ATE³.] *trans.* To convert into stone, to petrify. BACON.

Inlard, var. of ENLARD *v.*

Inlaw (i·nlǭ), *sb.* [ME. *inlaȝe*, f. IN-¹ + *laȝe* LAW, after *ūtlaȝe* outlaw.] One who is within the domain and protection of the law; opp. to *outlaw.* Now *Hist.*

Inlaw (inlǭ·), *v.* [OE. *inlagian*, f. IN-¹ + *lagu* LAW; cf. *ūtlagian* to outlaw.] *trans.* To bring within the authority and protection of the law, to reverse the outlawry of (a person).

-in-law. [f. IN *prep.* + LAW *sb.* after AFr. *en ley*, OFr. *en loi* (*de mariage*) 'in law (of marriage)'.] A phrase appended to names of relationship, as *father, mother, son*, etc., to indicate that the relationship is not by nature, but in the eye of the Canon Law, with reference to the degrees of affinity within which marriage is prohibited. These forms can be traced back to the 14th c. Formerly *-in-law* was also used in the sense of *step-*. Hence **In-law,** a relation by marriage 1894.

I·nlawry. [f. INLAW *v.* + -RY; cf. INLAGARY.] = INLAGARY. Lytton.

Inlay (i·nlēⁱ, inlēⁱ·), *sb.* 1656. [f. next.] **1.** The process or art of inlaying (*rare*). **2.** Material inlaid or prepared for inlaying; inlaid work 1697. Also *fig.* †**3.** The layering of plants. SIR T. BROWNE.

2. With rich i. the various floor was graced POPE. *fig.* The violet, Crocus, and hyacinth with rich i. Broidered the ground MILT. *P.L.* IV. 701.

Inlay (inlēⁱ·), *v.* 1596. [f. IN-¹ + LAY *v.*] †**1.** *trans.* To lay in, or as in, a place of concealment or preservation. DONNE. **2.** To lay or embed (a thing) in the substance of something else so that its surface becomes continuous with that of the matrix 1598. **b.** To insert a page of a book, a plate, or a cut, in space cut in a larger and stouter page, for its preservation, or to enlarge the margin, and thus the whole size 1810. **3.** To furnish or fit *with* a substance of a different kind embedded in its surface; to diversify or ornament (a thing) by such insertion of another material disposed decoratively 1596. Also *fig.* **b.** *transf.* Said of the material embedded 1784.

2. The moorstone courses, inlaid into the frame of the building SMEATON. **3.** Looke how the floore of heauen Is thicke inlayed with pattens of bright gold SHAKS. *fig.* But these things are . . thence borrow'd by the Monks to i. thir story MILT. **b.** The stream, That, as with molten glass, inlays the vale COWPER.

Inlayer (i·nlēⁱ:əɹ). 1660. [f. INLAY *v.* + -ER¹.] One who inlays (see the vb.).

Inleague, obs. var. of ENLEAGUE *v.*

†**Inlea·guer,** *v.* [f. IN-¹ + LEAGUER *sb.*¹, camp.] *intr.* To encamp with a besieging or beleaguering force. P. HOLLAND.

Inlet (i·nlet), *sb.* ME. [f. phr. *let in* (IN *adv.*, LET *v.*¹).] **1.** Letting in, admission. Now *rare.* **2.** A way of admission; an entrance 1624. **3.** A narrow opening by which the water penetrates into the land; a small arm of the sea; an indentation in the sea-coast or the bank of a lake or river; a creek 1570. **4.** A piece let in or inserted 1798. **5.** *attrib.*, as *i. area, valve*, etc. 1882.

2. These In-lets of Men and of Light [i.e. doors and windows] WOTTON. *fig.* An increase of our possessions is but an i. to new disquietudes GOLDSM.

Inlet (in,le·t), *v.* ME. [f. IN-¹ + LET *v.*¹ Orig. two wds. = *let in.*] To let in. †**1.** *trans.* To allow to enter –1661. **2.** To let in or insert (one thing) in another 1860. So †**I·nle:tter** (*rare*), one who gives admittance.

Inlighten, -list, etc.: see ENLIGHTEN, etc.

In loco: see IN *Lat. prep.*

Inlook (i·nluk). 1869. [f. IN *adv.* + LOOK *sb.*, after OUTLOOK.] Looking within, introspection.

†**I·nly,** *a.* [OE. *in(n)lić*, f. *inn* IN *adv.* + *-lić* -LY¹.] Inward, interior; inwardly felt –1612.

Didst thou but know the i. touch of Loue SHAKS.

Inly, *adv.* [OE. *in(n)līće*, f. *inn* IN *adv.* + *-līće* -LY².] **a.** Inwardly; in the heart, spirit, or inner nature; in regard to the inner life. **b.** In a way that goes to the heart; heartily; thoroughly, extremely.

Friends year by year more i. known EMERSON.

I·nlying, *vbl. sb.* 1734. = LYING-IN. So **I·nlying** *ppl. a.*, lying inside 1844; lying in 1864.

Inmate (i·nmeⁱt), *sb.* (*a.*) 1589. [prob. orig. f. INN *sb.* 1 dwelling (later assoc. with IN *adv.*) + MATE *sb.*] **1.** One who dwells with others in the same house (now *rare*). In early use, A lodger or subtenant. **b.** Sometimes, A foreigner, stranger. Often *fig.* 1600. **2.** In relation to the house: An occupant along with others; hence, *occas.*, = Indweller, inhabitant, occupier. Const. *of.* (*lit.* and *fig.*) 1597. **3.** *attrib.* or *adj.* That is an inmate (*lit.* and *fig.*); dwelling in the same house with, or in the house of, another; indwelling. ?*Obs.* 1630.

1. Taking an i. in to his hous 1601. **b.** He is but a new fellow, An in-mate here in Rome B. JONS. **2.** So spake the Enemie of Mankind, enclos'd In Serpent, I. bad MILT. *P.L.* IX. 495. An i. of a lunatic asylum MEDWIN. **3.** I. guests MILT. Hence **I·nmatecy** [irreg.: see -CY], the position of an i. 1806.

Inmeat (i·nmīt); usu. in pl. **inmeats.** Now *rare* exc. *dial.* 1616. [f. IN *adv.* + MEAT *sb.*] Those internal viscera of an animal which are used for food; hence *gen.* Entrails, inwards.

In medias res, In memoriam: see IN *Lat. prep.*

Inme·sh, var. of ENMESH *v.*

†**Inmew·,** *v.* [perh. f. IN-¹ + MEW *v.*] *trans.* ?To mew or coop up. BEAUM. & FL.

†**In mid,** *prep.* ME. only. [Analytical var. of ME. *on middle, amiddle*, AMID.] Amid, in the middle or centre of.

Inmost (i·nmoᵘst, -mŏst), *a.* (*sb., adv.*) [Earlier ME. *inmest, in(ne)mast* :- OE. *innemest*, f. *in, inne* IN *adv.*; see -MOST.] **1.** *lit.* Situated farthest within, most inward, most remote from the outside. Also *fig.* **2.** *absol.* or *sb.* That which is inmost; the inmost part (*lit.* and *fig.*). Rarely in *pl.* OE. **3.** *adv.* Most inwardly (*rare*) OE.

1. Into thir i. bower Handed they went MILT. *P.L.* IV. 738. *fig.* In the inmoste affeccion of their hertes UDALL. **2.** Lodge it in the i. of thy bosom FORD. **3.** Thro' all their i.-winding caves POPE. So †**I·nmore** *a.* inner. P. HOLLAND.

Inn (in), *sb.* [OE. *inn* :- **innam* (cf. ON. *inni* :- **innjam*); f. *inne* IN *adv.*] †**1.** A dwelling-place, habitation, lodging; a house (in relation to its inhabitant). †**2.** 'Dwelling-place', 'abode', 'place of sojourn', in fig. uses –1615. **3.** A public house for the lodging and entertainment of travellers, wayfarers, etc.; a hostelry or hotel; occas., *erron.*, a tavern which does not provide lodging ME. **b.** *fig. esp.* A temporary lodging as opp. to a permanent abode 1529. **4.** A lodging-house or house of residence for students (cf. HOSTEL *sb.*); now *Obs.*, exc. as in b and c. †**a.** At the Universities. 1346. (Preserved till 19th c. in *New Inn Hall*, Oxford). **b.** *Inns of Chancery*: certain sets of buildings in London, orig. places of residence and study for students and apprentices of law; also the societies by which they were occupied 1458. **c.** *Inns of Court*: the four sets of buildings in London (the Inner Temple, the Middle Temple, Lincoln's Inn, and Gray's Inn) belonging to the four legal societies which have the exclusive right of admitting persons to practise at the bar; hence, these four societies themselves. (Formerly also colloq. *inns a court*). 1396. **d.** *Serjeants' Inn*: a collegiate building of the now extinct order of Serjeants-at-Law, esp. that in Chancery Lane, sold in 1877. 1646. **5.** *attrib.* as †**i.-house** = sense 3; etc. 1694.

1. To let the world wag, and take mine ease in mine in HEYWOOD. Phr. †*To take* (*up*) *one's i.* (or *inns*): to take up one's residence, quarters –1647; With me ye may take up your In For this same night SPENSER. **2.** My people shal dwel in the ynnes of peace COVERDALE *Isa.* 32:18. **3.** He still has found The warmest welcome at an i. SHENSTONE. **b.** To that dark i., the grave SCOTT.

Inn (in), *v.* Now *rare.* [f. INN *sb.* (In OE. and ME. inseparable in form from IN *v.*, q.v.)] **1.** *trans.* To lodge, house. Often *refl.* **2.** *intr.* (?for *refl.*) To lodge, sojourn; now, to put up (at an inn or hostel) ME. **b.** Of a coach: To stop or put up (at an inn) 1748. **c.** *fig.* and *transf.* 1591.

1. Whan he had broght hem in to his Citee And Inned hem euerich in his degree CHAUCER. **2. b.** You had better send for them where the machine inns H. WALPOLE.

Inn, obs. f. IN *prep., adv.*, and *v.*

Innascibility (inæsĭbi·lĭti, inn-). 1602. [– eccl.L. *innascibilitas* (Hilary), f. *innascibilis* (Tertullian) incapable of being born, f. *in-* IN-³ + *nascibilis* who can be born, f. *nasci* be born; see -BLE, -ITY.] The attribute of being independent of birth: said of God the Father.

Innate (i·nnēⁱt, innēⁱ·t, inēⁱ·t), *a.* ME. [– L. *innatus*, pa. pple. of *innasci*, f. *in-* IN-² + *nasci* be born.] **1.** Existing in a person (or organism) from birth; belonging to the original or essential constitution (of body or mind); inborn, native, natural. **a.** Of qualities, principles, etc. (esp. mental); opp. to *acquired*, esp. in *innate ideas.* **b.** Of a vegetable formation: Originating within the matrix or substance of the plant. Of a mineral: Originating within the matrix; native. 1887. **2.** *transf.* Inherent. ?*Obs.* 1600. **3.** *Bot.* Said of a part or organ borne on the apex of another; as, an *i. anther* 1830.

1. a. It is an establish'd Opinion amongst some Men, That there are in the Understanding certain I. Principles. . which the Soul receives in its very first Being, and brings into the World with it LOCKE. It has been disputed whether there be any i. ideas, or whether all ideas be derived from sensation and reflexion HUME. var. †**Inna·ted** *a.* Hence **Inna·te-ly** *adv.*, **-ness. Inna·tive** *a.* (now *rare* or *Obs.*), innate, native 1513.

†**Innate,** *v. rare.* 1602. [f. prec.] *trans.* **a.** To make innate; to produce within something. **b.** (In Fuller) To imbue or endow by nature (*with* something); usu. in *pass.*

Innato-, comb. f. L. *innatus* INNATE *a.*, forming adjs. in which it adverbially qualifies the second element, as **inna:to-se·ssile,** innately sessile; etc.

Innavigable (inæ·vigăb'l, inn-), *a.* 1527. [– Fr. *innavigable* or L. *innavigabilis*; see IN-³, NAVIGABLE.] Not navigable; that cannot be navigated.

There is no . . Sea innauigable 1527. When a Ship . . is rendered i. [etc.] 1755. Hence **Inna:vigabi·lity, Inna·vigableness. Inna·vigably** *adv.*

†**I·nne,** *adv.* and *prep.* OE. [ME. repr. of two derivatives from OE. *in(n* adv., viz. (1) OE. *innan* adv. and prep. (of motion and position) = OFris. *inna*, OS. *innan*, OHG. *innan(a* (G. *innen*), ON. *innan*, Goth. *innana*; (2) OE. *inne* adv. of position = OFris., OS. *inne*, OHG. *inne, inni*, ON. *inni*, Goth. *inna.*]

A. *adv.* **1.** Of position: In, within, inside, indoors –1470. **2.** Of motion: In (to a place). Not in OE. –1486.

B. *prep.* **1.** Of position: In, within. Not in OE. –1450. **2.** Of motion: Into. ME. only.

Inner (i·nəɹ), *a.* (*sb.*) [OE. *inner(r)a, in(n)ra* = OFris. *inra*, OHG. *innaro, -ero* (G. *innere*), ON. *innri, iðri*; compar. of *in(n* IN adv.; see -ER³.] **1.** Situated more within; more or further inward; interior. Often with a positive force, antithetical, not to *in*, but to *outer*: Situated within; inward; internal. Also *fig.* and *transf.* **b.** *Mus.* Applied to parts or voices intermediate between the highest and lowest of the harmony (also called *middle*). **2.** Mental or spiritual OE. **3.** *sb.* That division of a target next outside the bull's-eye, or, in some targets, the division immediately outside the centre; also, *ellipt.* a shot which strikes this 1887.

1. Into an I. chamber ME. An inner tube of india-rubber . . separate from the outer cover 1902. **2.** The sense By which thy i. nature was apprised Of outward shows SHELLEY. Phr. *The i. man*, the i. part of man; the soul or mind; *joc.* the stomach or inside, esp. in reference to food. *I. Temple*: see TEMPLE *sb.*¹

I·nnerly, *adv. Obs.* or *rare.* ME. [f. INNER *a.* + -LY².] †More within; inwardly, internally.

Innermost (i·nəɹmōᵘst, -mŏst). ME. [f. INNER *a.* + -MOST.] **A.** *adj.* Inmost. **B.** *sb.*

The inmost part 1674. Hence **I·nnermostly** *adv.* E. B. BROWNING.

Innerness (i·nəɹnės). 1880. [f. INNER *a.* + -NESS.] Inwardness.

Innervate (inɔ̄·ɹveⁱt, inn-), *v.* 1870. [f. IN-² + L. *nervus* NERVE + -ATE³; cf. *enervate.*] *Physiol.* To supply (some organ or part) with nerve-force, or with nerves.

The ganglionic mass, whence the jaws and foot-jaws are innervated ROLLESTON.

Innervation (inəɹvēⁱ·ʃən). 1832. [f. as prec. + -ATION.] The action or process of innervating; the fact of being innervated; supply of nerve-force from a nerve-centre to some organ or part by means of nerves; stimulation of some organ by its nerves.

Innerve (inɔ̄·rv, inn-), *v.* 1828. [f. IN-² + NERVE *sb.* or *v.*] = INNERVATE; also *fig.* to animate.

Inness (i·nˌnės). *rare.* 1866. [f. IN *adv.* or *a.* + -NESS.] **a.** The quality of being *in* (something). **b.** Inner quality or state.

Innholder (i·nhōᵘ:ldəɹ). Now *rare.* 1464. [f. INN *sb.* + HOLDER¹]. = INNKEEPER.

Inning (i·niŋ), *vbl. sb.* [OE. *innung*; f. IN *v.*, or INN *v.* + -ING¹. Sense 4 has no historical connection with senses 1–3.]

I. From IN *v.* †**1.** A putting or getting in; what is put or got in; contents; income. OE. only. **2.** The action of taking in, inclosing, etc.; *esp.* the reclaiming of marsh or flooded land 1530. **b.** *pl.* Lands taken in or reclaimed 1706. **3.** The action of getting in; ingathering, harvesting 1522. **4.** In *Cricket, Base-ball*, etc. (in Great Britain always in *pl.* form **innings**, whether in sing. or pl. sense): That portion of the game played by either side while 'in' or at the bat. In *Cricket* also used of the play of, or score of runs made by, any one batsman during his turn 1746. **b.** *transf.* (in Great Britain always in *pl.*) The time during which a person, party, principle, etc. is in power; a turn 1855.

4. b. The new ideas of 'peace, retrenchment and reform' got their innings 1878.

II. The action of INN *v.*; lodging, housing; *concr.* a lodging, house OE.

Innkeeper (i·nˌkī:pəɹ). 1548. [f. INN *sb.* 3 + KEEPER.] One who keeps an inn or public house; an innholder, taverner. Hence **I·nnkee:ping** *sb.* the keeping of an inn (also *attrib.*); *adj.* that keeps an inn.

Innocence (i·nŏsėns). ME. [– (O)Fr. *innocence* – L. *innocentia*, f. *innocent-*; see INNOCENT, -ENCE.] **1.** Freedom from sin, guilt, or moral wrong in general; moral purity. **2.** The fact of not being guilty of that with which one is charged; guiltlessness 1559. **3.** Freedom from cunning or artifice; guilelessness, simplicity; hence, ignorance, silliness ME. **4.** Of things: Innocuousness 1828. **5.** *concr.* An innocent person or thing ME. **6.** *U.S.* A popular name of *Houstonia cærula*, which has small blue flowers 1845.

1. How came our first Parents to sin, and to lose their Primitive I.? SOUTH. **2.** Where the guilt is doubtful, a presumption of it should in general be admitted 'JUNIUS'. **3.** The servants, who had traded on my i. 1883. **5.** Well said, I. SHERIDAN.

Innocency (i·nŏsėnsi). Now *rare* or *arch.* ME. [– L. *innocentia*; see prec., -ENCY.] = prec.

Innocent (i·nŏsėnt). ME. [– (O)Fr. *innocent* or L. *innocens, -ent-*, f. *in-* IN-³ + *nocens*, pr. pple. of *nocēre* hurt, injure; see -ENT.]

A. *adj.* **1.** Doing no evil; free from moral wrong, sin, or guilt; pure, unpolluted. Now always implying 'unacquainted with evil'; but formerly sometimes (*e.g.* of God or Christ), Sinless, holy. Also *transf.* and *fig.* **2.** Free from specific wrong or guilt; not deserving of the suffering inflicted; not guilty, guiltless, unoffending ME. **b.** *colloq.* with *of*: Free from; devoid of 1706. **3.** Simple, guileless, unsuspecting; hence, naïve, ingenuous ME. **b.** Silly, half-witted. Now *dial.* 1548. **4.** Of actions, etc.: Free from guilt or moral evil. (Often blending with 5.) 1514. **5.** Of things: Doing no harm; not injurious; harmless, innocuous. (In *Path.* opp. to *malignant.*) 1662. **b.** Lawful 1828.

1. When we say that God made man i., What do we mean? MAURICE. *fig.* She woos the gentle air To hide her guilty front with i. snow MILT. **2.** *I. blood*, the blood (or life) of the i.; I haue sinned, in that I haue betraied the i. blood *Matt.* 27:4. The Peasant, i. of all these Ills DRYDEN. **b.** The Sermon..was quite i. of meaning WESLEY. **3.** For all she looks so i. as it were, take my Word for it she is no Fool STEELE. **4.** I think no pleasure i., that is to man hurtful FRANKLIN. **5.** His Powder upon Examination being found very i. BUDGELL.

B. *sb.* **1. a.** An innocent person; one not disposed to do harm, or unacquainted with evil ME. †**b.** A guiltless person –1748. **2.** *esp.* A young child; *spec.* in *pl.* (with capital), the young children slain by Herod after the birth of Jesus (Matt. 2:16), reckoned from early times as Christian martyrs (also called *the Holy Innocents*) ME. **3.** A guileless, simple, or unsuspecting person; hence **b.** A simpleton; a half-wit, an idiot ME.

1. Thou hast kill'd the sweetest i., That ere did lift vp eye *Oth.* V. ii. 199. **2.** (*Holy*) *Innocents' Day*, the 28th of December, observed as a church festival in commemoration of the slaughter of the Innocents. (Formerly called CHILDERMAS). **3.** In Scotland..a natural fool [was called] an i. SCOTT. Hence **I·nnocently** *adv.* in an i. manner ME.

Innocuity (inokiū·īti). 1855. [f. L. *innocuus* + -ITY; cf. Fr. *innocuité.*] The quality of being innocuous.

Innocuous (inǫ·kiuˌəs), *a.* 1598. [f. L. *innocuus*, f. *in-* IN-³ + *nocuus*, f. *nocēre* hurt; see -OUS.] Not hurtful or injurious; harmless. In *Zool.* applied *spec.* to the non-venomous snakes (constituting the order *Innocua*).

But over Diomedes' left shoulder passed The point i. COWPER. Hence **Inno·cuous-ly** *adv.*, **-ness.**

†**I·nnodate**, *v.* 1635. [– *innodat-*, pa. ppl. stem of late L. *innodare*, f. *in-* IN-² + *nodare*, f. *nodus* knot; see -ATE³.] *trans.* To fasten in or with a knot; *spec.* to include or involve in an anathema or interdict –1655. Hence †**Innoda·tion.**

Inno·minable, *a. arch.* ME. [– L. *innominabilis*, f. *in-* IN-³ + *nominabilis* that may be named, f. *nominare* name; see -BLE.] Incapable of being or unfit to be named.

Innominate (in(n)ǫ·minĕt), *a.* 1638. [– late L. *innominatus*; see *in-* IN-³, NOMINATE *ppl. a.*] **1.** Not named, unnamed, anonymous. **2.** *Rom. Law.* Of a contract: Unclassified 1774. **3.** Anat. *I. bone* (*os innominatum*), the hip-bone, a union of three original bones, ilium, ischium, and pubis. *I. artery* (*arteria innominata*), a large artery given off from the arch of the aorta, just before the left carotid artery. *I. vein* (*vena innominata*), each of the two veins formed by the junction of the subclavian and the internal jugular veins behind the inner ends of the clavicle. 1866. **b.** *absol.* as *sb.* (also in L. form *innominatum, -ata*): = *i. bone, artery, or vein* 1879.

Innovate (i·nŏveⁱt), *v.* 1548. [– *innovat-*, pa. ppl. stem of L. *innovare* renew, alter, f. *in* IN-² + *novare* make new, f. *novus* new; see -ATE³.] †**1.** *trans.* To change into something new; to alter; to renew –1818. †**2.** To bring in (something new); to introduce as new –1738. **3.** *intr.* To bring in or introduce novelties; to make changes *in* something established; to introduce innovations. Occas. const. *on* or *upon.* 1597.

1. Attempts to i. the constitutional or habitual character JOHNSON. **2.** Some words which I have innovated..upon his Latin DRYDEN. **3.** To i. is not to reform BURKE. So †**Innovate** *a.* newly introduced 1600. Hence **I·nnovative** *a.* having the character of innovating; †revolutionary. **I·nnovator**, one who innovates; †a revolutionist 1598; **I·nnovatory** *a.* 1853.

Innovation (inŏvēⁱ·ʃən). 1548. [– L. *innovatio*, f. as prec.; see -ION.] **1.** The action of innovating; the introduction of novelties; the alteration of what is established. †Formerly const. *of.* 1553. †**b.** Revolution (= L. *novæ res*) –1633. **2.** A change made by innovating; something newly introduced; a novel practice, method, etc. 1548. †**b.** A rebellion or insurrection –1726. **3.** *Bot.* The formation of a new shoot at the apex of a stem or branch; *esp.* that which takes place at the apex of the thallus of mosses; also (with *pl.*) a new shoot thus formed 1835.

1. The innouation of new honors SELDEN. **2.** The tribute you demand from the Hindûs..is an i. and an infringement of the laws of Hindustân 1800. Hence **Innova·tional** *a.* of, pertaining to, or characterized by i. 1817. **Innova·tionist**, one who favours innovations.

Innoxious (in(n)ǫ·kʃəs), *a.* 1623. [f. L. *innoxius* + -OUS; see IN-³, NOXIOUS.] **1.** Not noxious; harmless, innocuous 1638. †**2.** Innocent, blameless.

1. Even lions, when surfeited, are i. 1831. **2.** The good man walk'd i. thro' his age POPE. Hence **Inno·xious-ly** *adv.*, **-ness.**

†**Innu·bilous**, *a. rare.* 1656. [f. L. *innubilus* or f. IN-³ + NUBILOUS.] Cloudless –1708.

Innuendo (iniuˌe·ndo). Also *erron.* **inuendo.** *Pl.* **-does** (†**-do's**, †**dos**). 1564. [L., = 'by nodding at, pointing to, intimating', abl. gerund of *innuere* nod to, signify, f. *in-* IN-² + *nuere* nod.] **1.** The med. L. formula used to introduce a parenthetical explanation; = meaning, to wit, that is to say. **2.** Hence, as sb. The parenthetical explanation itself; *esp.* the injurious meaning alleged to be conveyed by words not *per se* injurious or actionable, which, in an action for libel or slander, is usually introduced into the record and issue by the words 'meaning thereby', after the expressions alleged to have been used 1701. **b.** The words or expressions thus explained or needing explanation; a blank to be filled up with the name of the person to whom it is alleged to refer 1755. **3.** An oblique hint or suggestion; an insinuation, esp. one of a depreciatory kind 1678.

2. No *I.* can make such Words actionable SCROGGS. **b.** An indictment for a libel, with all the *inuendos* filled up 1802. **3.** [He] sought by nods and winks and inuendoes to intimate his authorship W. IRVING.

Innue·ndo, *v.* 1705. [f. prec. sb.] **1.** *intr.* To utter or make innuendoes. **2.** *Law.* To interpret or construe by attaching an innuendo 1851.

Innumerable (in(n)iū·mĕrăb'l), *a.* ME. [– L. *innumerabilis*; see IN-³ and NUMERABLE.] Incapable of being numbered or reckoned; not to be counted for multitude; numberless. Often with exaggerative force. **a.** With sing. sb.; now only with *host, multitude*, etc. **b.** Now usu. with pl. sb. 1450.

a. An i. company of Angels *Heb.* 12:22. An i. flight Of harmefull fowles SPENSER. **b.** Cedars, with i. boughs MILT. Murmuring of i. bees TENNYSON. Hence **Innu:merabi·lity, Innu·merableness**, the quality of being i. **Innu·merably** *adv.*

Innumerous (in(n)iū·mĕrəs), *a. arch.* 1536. [– late L. *innumerosus*; see IN-³ and NUMEROUS.] **1.** Without number; innumerable, countless. Now only *poet.* or *rhet.* **2.** Void of metrical or rhythmical number (*rare*) 1886.

Innutrient (in(n)iū·triĕnt), *a.* 1822. [IN-³.] Not nourishing.

Innutrition (in(n)iutri·ʃən). 1796. [IN-³.] Lack of nutrition, failure of nourishment. *I. of the bones* = RICKETS.

Innutritious (in(n)iutri·ʃəs), *a.* 1796. [IN-³.] Not nutritious.

Ino- (əi·no), comb. f. Gr. ἴς, ἰνός muscle, fibre, nerve, strength, as in INOGEN, q.v.

†**Inobe·dience.** ME. [– OFr. *inobediance* or late (eccl.) L. *inobedientia* (Augustine); see IN-³, OBEDIENCE.] = DISOBEDIENCE –1684.

†**Inobe·dient**, *a.* ME. [– OFr. *inobedient* or late (eccl.) L. *inobediens, -ent-*; see IN-³, OBEDIENT.] = DISOBEDIENT –1805. Hence **Inobe·diently** *adv.*

Inobno·xious, *a. rare.* 1659. [IN-³.] Not obnoxious; not exposed *to*; inoffensive.

Inobservable (inǒbzɔ̄·ɹvăb'l), *a.* Now *rare.* 1600. [– L. *inobservabilis*; see IN-³ and OBSERVABLE.] Incapable of being observed; not noticeable.

Inobservance (inǒbzɔ̄·ɹvăns). 1611. [– Fr. *inobservance* or L. *inobservantia*; see IN-³, OBSERVANCE.] **1.** Failure to observe or notice; inattention. **2.** The not keeping of a law, custom, bond, promise, etc. 1626. So **Inobse·rvancy** (*rare*).

Inobservant (inǒbzɔ̄·ɹvănt), *a.* 1663. [– late L. *inobservans, -ant-*; see IN-³, OBSERVANT.] That does not observe or notice. Hence **Inobse·rvantness**, inobservance 1659.

Inobservation (inǫbzəɹvēⁱ·ʃən). *rare.* 1579. [f. IN-³ + OBSERVATION. Cf. Fr. *inobservation.*] †**1.** The non-observance *of* a law, promise, etc. –1653. **2.** Want of observation or attention; inobservance 1727.

Inobtrusive (inǒbtrū·siv), *a. rare.* 1796. [IN-³.] Not obtrusive; modest, retiring. Hence **Inobtru·sive-ly** *adv.*, **-ness.**

Inoca·rpin. 1865. [f. mod.Bot.L. *Inocarpus* (f. INO- fibrous + Gr. καρπός fruit) + -IN[1].] *Chem.* A red colouring matter contained in the juice of *Inocarpus edulis*, a tree of Asia and the E. India islands.

Inoccupa·tion. 1786. [IN-[3].] Want of occupation; unoccupied condition.

Inoculable (inǫ·kiŭlăb'l), *a.* 1847. [f. INOCULATE + -ABLE, perh. after Fr. *inoculable.*] Of a person: Capable of being infected with a disease by inoculation. Of a disease: Capable of being communicated by inoculation. Of matter or virus: That may inoculate a person or transmit a disease. Hence **Ino:culabi·lity.**

Inocular (inǫ·kiŭlăɹ), *a.* 1826. [IN-[2].] *Entom.* Of an antenna: Inserted in a sinus in the inner margin of the compound eye, which thus partly surrounds its base.

Inoculate (inǫ·kiŭleˈt), *v.* ME. [– *inoculat-*, pa. ppl. stem of L. *inoculare* engraft, implant, f. *in-* IN-[2] + *oculus* eye, bud; see -ATE[3].] **1.** *trans.* (*Hort.*) To set or insert (an eye, bud, or scion) in a plant for propagation; to subject (a plant) to the operation of budding; to propagate by inoculation; to bud (one plant) *into, on,* or *upon* (another). Also *absol.* Also *fig.* †**2.** *transf.* To join or unite by insertion –1668. **b.** *intr.* To become joined or united with continuity of substance –1720. **3.** *trans.* (*Path.*) To engraft or implant (a disease, or the germ or virus) upon a person by INOCULATION, q.v. 1722. **b.** To impregnate (a person or animal) with the virus or germs of a disease; *spec.* for the purpose of inducing a milder form of the disease and rendering the subject immune 1722. **c.** *absol.* or *intr.* To perform inoculation 1765. **d.** *fig.* (*trans.*) To imbue (a person) *with* 1824.

1. *fig.* The Pelhams..always inoculated private quarrels on affairs of state H. WALPOLE. **3. d.** My parents had tried in vain to i. me with wisdom W. IRVING. Hence **Ino·culative** *a.* characterized by or pertaining to inoculation. **Ino·culator.**

Inoculation (inǫkiulēˈ·ʃən). late ME. [– L. *inoculatio*, f. as prec.; see -ION. Partly through Fr. *inoculation.*] **1.** *Hort.* Grafting by budding; an instance of this. Also *transf.* **2.** *Path.* The introduction into the body, by puncture of the skin, or through a wound, of the virus or germs of an infectious disease. (Orig. applied, after 1700, to the intentional introduction of the virus of small-pox, but now also to the introduction (accidentally or otherwise) of the virus or germs of any bacterial disease into the body through a wound.) 1714. **b.** *fig.* The imbuing of a person *with* feelings, opinions, etc. 1824.

2. b. The popular pursuit of natural beauty, the i. of the crowd with it MOZLEY.

†**Ino·diate,** *v.* 1657. [– *inodiat-*, pa. ppl. stem of late L. *inodiare*; see ANNOY *v.*, -ATE[3].] *trans.* To render odious or hateful –1721.

†**Ino·dorate,** *a.* [f. IN-[3] + ODORATE *a.*] Unscented. BACON.

Inodorous (inōᵘ·dŏrəs), *a.* 1666. [f. L. *inodorus* + -OUS, or f. IN-[3] + ODOROUS.] Destitute of odour; without smell or scent. Hence **Ino·dorous-ly** *adv.*, **-ness.**

Inoffensive (inŏfe·nsiv), *a.* 1598. [IN-[3].] **1.** Doing or causing no harm; harmless, unoffending. **2.** Not objectionable; not offending the senses; not a cause of offence 1622.

1. An i. man for life and conversation..nothing of viciousness could be charged upon him FULLER. Useful and i. animals 1790. **2.** An i. medicine 1744. Hence **Inoffe·nsive-ly** *adv.*, **-ness.**

Inofficial (inŏfi·ʃăl), *a. rare.* 1632. [IN-[3].] Not official; unofficial.

Inofficious (inŏfi·ʃəs), *a.* 1603. [– L. *inofficiosus*, or f. IN-[3] + OFFICIOUS.] †**1.** Not ready to do one's duty or office; not inclined to do good offices; disobliging –1706. **b.** *Law.* Not in accordance with moral duty 1663. **2.** Without office, function, or operation 1884.

1. Thow drown'st thy selfe in i. sleep 1603. **b.** *I. testament*, a will not in accordance with the testator's natural affection and moral duties WHARTON. **2.** Where the operative part and the recital are at variance, the recital must be treated as i. 1885. Hence **Inoffi·cious-ly** *adv.*, **-ness.**

Inogen (əi·nodʒen). 1889. [f. INO- + -GEN 1.] *Physiol.* Hermann's term for a hypothetical complex substance supposed to exist in muscular fibre and to be the energy-yielding substance of muscle. Hence **Inoge·nic** *a.* of or pertaining to i.

†**Inopera·tion.** 1620. [– eccl.L. *inoperatio*; see IN-[2], OPERATION.] A working within; in-working –1645.

Inoperative (inǫ·pĕrĕtiv), *a.* 1631. [IN-[3].] Not operative; not working; in *Law*, without practical force, invalid.

The resolutions..not having been so ratified, were i. 1885. Hence **Ino·perativeness.**

Inope·rcular, *a. rare.* 1864. [f. IN-[3] + OPERCULAR.] *Conch.* = next.

Inoperculate (inopə̄·ɹkiŭlĕt), *a.* 1835. [f. IN-[3] + OPERCULATE *a.*] Not having an operculum or lid; *spec.* in *Conch.*, of or belonging to the *Inoperculata*, a division of *Pulmonifera* containing those univalves, such as snails, whose shell has no operculum. So **Inope·rculated** *a.*

†**Ino·pinable,** *a.* ME. [– L. *inopinabilis*; see IN-[3], OPINABLE. Cf. OFr. *inopinable.*] Not opinable; unthinkable, inconceivable; not to be thought of –1581.

This..is inopynable, incredible and a very paradox 1555.

Ino·pinate, *a.* 1598. [– L. *inopinatus*, f. *in-* IN-[3] + *opinatus*, pa. pple. of *opinari* suppose, believe, think; see -ATE[2].] Not thought of; unlooked for; unexpected –1807.

Inopportune (inǫ:pǫɹtiū·n), *a.* 1533. [– late L. *inopportunus* unfitting; see IN-[3] and OPPORTUNE. Rare till XIX.] Not opportune; inappropriate or inconvenient, esp. with regard to time; unsuited to the occasion; unseasonable.

No visit could have been more i. T. HOOK. Turbulent and i. in their demands 1869. Hence **Ino:pportu·ne-ly** *adv.*, **-ness.**

Inopportunist (inǫ:pǫ̆ɹtiū·nist), *sb.* (*a.*) 1880. [f. INOPPORTUNE + -IST, after *opportunist.*] **1.** One who believes a policy or course of action to be inopportune; *esp.* one who, on that ground, opposed the doctrine of Papal Infallibility at the Vatican Council, 1870; one opposed to the OPPORTUNISTS. **2.** *adj.* Of or belonging to the inopportunists 1888.

Inopportunity (i:nǫpǫ̆ɹtiū·nĭti). 1500. [– late L. *inopportunitas*, or f. INOPPORTUNE + -ITY.] The quality or fact of being inopportune; unseasonableness.

Inoppressive (inǒpre·siv), *a. rare.* 1627. [IN-[3].] Not oppressive; unoppressive.

†**Ino·pulent,** *a.* 1613. [IN-[3].] Not opulent; poor.

Inorb (inǭ·ɹb), *v.* 1847. [IN-[2].] *trans.* To place in an orb or sphere; to surround with or as with an orb; to encircle.

Inordinacy (inǭ·ɹdinăsi). Now *rare.* 1617. [f. INORDINATE; see -ACY.] The quality or condition of being inordinate; inordinateness; also, an inordinate act.

That wantonness of power, and i. of ambition 1785.

†**Ino·rdinance.** 1638. [f. IN-[3] + ORDINANCE; assoc. with INORDINATE.] An inordinate action or practice; an excess –1799.

Inordinate (inǭ·ɹdinĕt), *a.* ME. [– L. *inordinatus*, f. *in-* IN-[3] + *ordinatus*, pa. pple. of *ordinare* ORDAIN; see -ATE[2].] **1.** Not ordered; irregular, disorderly; not controlled or restrained. **2.** Not kept within orderly limits, immoderate, excessive ME. **3.** Of persons: Not conforming or subject to law or order, disorderly; immoderate, intemperate 1450.

1. To keep i. hours 1625. A rude and i. heap RAY. **2.** I. drinking 1665, vanity BURKE, prices 1872. **3.** I. admirers of antiquity BUCKLE. Hence **Ino·rdinate-ly** *adv.*, **-ness.**

†**Inordina·tion.** 1612. [– L. and med.L. *inordinatio* disorder; see IN-[3], ORDINATION.] The condition of being inordinate (in conduct, etc.); an instance of this –1788.

That intrinsick I., and Deviation from right Reason inherent in .. it [a Lye] SOUTH.

Inorganic (inǫɹgæ·nik), *a.* 1794. [f. IN-[3] + ORGANIC.] **1.** Not characterized by having organs; not formed with the organs of life; destitute of organized physical structure; said of inanimate matter and bodies formed of it without vital action. **b.** *Chem.* Of elements, compounds, etc.: Not entering into the composition of organized bodies; not formed under the action of the vital forces 1831. **2.** = INORGANICAL 1. 1821. **3.** Not belonging to the organism or structure; that does not arise by natural growth; spec. in *Philol.* of sounds or forms not arising from regular phonetic development 1843; *Path.* of abnormal heart-sounds not due to disease of the heart substance 1884. **4.** Without systematic arrangement. CARLYLE.

1. *I. world, nature*, the material world outside the animal and vegetable kingdoms; the world of matter, with its forces. **b.** *I. Chemistry*, that branch which investigates i. compounds; the chemistry of mineral substances. **3.** The yoke of an i. and alien despotism MERIVALE. These languages will hardly ever agree in what is anomalous or i. MAX-MÜLLER.

†**Inorga·nical,** *a.* 1621. [f. IN-[3] + ORGANICAL.] **1.** Without organs or instruments; not having, or not acting by, organs. Said of the soul or mind. –1688. **2.** = INORGANIC 1. –1690. Hence **Inorga·nically** *adv.* without organs or organization.

†**Inorga·nity.** *rare.* 1643. [f. IN-[3] + †*organity* condition of being organic.] The condition of being without organs –1727.

The i. of the Soul SIR T. BROWNE.

Ino:rganiza·tion. 1839. [IN-[3].] Absence of organization; unorganized condition.

Ino·rganized, *a.* 1649. [IN-[3].] Not organized; not having organization.

Inornate (inǭ·ɹnĕt), *a.* 1510. [– L. *inornatus*, or f. IN-[3] + ORNATE *a.*] Not ornate; unadorned, plain.

†**Inortho·graphy.** 1779. [IN-[3].] Incorrect spelling.

Inosculate (inǫ·skiŭleˈt), *v.* 1671. [f. IN-[2] + L. *osculare* furnish with a mouth or outlet, f. *osculum*, dim. of *os* mouth after Gr. ἀναστομοῦν (see ANASTOMOSIS).] **1.** *intr.* Of blood-vessels, etc.: To open into each other; to have connection terminally; to anastomose 1683. **2.** Of solid parts: To unite by interpenetrating or fitting closely into each other 1713. **3.** *trans.* To cause (blood-vessels, or the like) to open into each other; to connect by anastomosis 1734. **4.** To cause (fibres, or the like) to pass into each other 1671. **5.** *transf.* and *fig.* **a.** *intr.* To join or unite so as to become continuous; to blend 1836. **b.** *trans.* To cause to grow together or unite so as to become continuous 1829.

Inosculation (inǫskiŭlēˈ·ʃən), 1672. [f. prec.; see -ATION.] The action of inosculating; the opening of two vessels of an animal body, or of a vegetable, into each other; anastomosis; junction by insertion; hence, applied generally to the passing of one thing into another.

The i. of veins 1672.

Inosite (əi·nosəit). 1857. [f. a potential **inose* (f. INO- muscle + -OSE[1]) + -ITE[1]4a.] *Chem.* A non-fermentable saccharine substance ($C_6H_{12}O_6 + 2H_2O$), isomeric with glucose, discovered by Scherer (1850) in the fluid contained in the cardiac muscular tissue of the ox, and since found in other parts of the body and in plants.

Inoxidizable (inǫksidəi·zăb'l), *a.* 1864. [IN-[3].] Not oxidizable; incapable of rusting.

Ino·xidize, *v.* 1881. [IN-[3].] *trans.* To render not liable to oxidize.

Inp-: see IMP- as in *inpale*, etc.

In partibus, etc.: see IN *Lat. prep.*

I·n-pa:tient. 1760. See IN *adv.* Combs. 2.

I·n-phase. 1916. [attrib. use of phr. *in phase.*] *Electr.* Of the same phase.

Input (i·nput), *sb.* 1753. [IN *adv.* Combs. 1.] **1.** A sum put in (*Sc.*). **2.** That which is put or taken in; esp. of electrical apparatus 1893.

†**Input,** *v.* late ME. [f. IN-[1] or IN *adv.* + PUT *v.*; in earliest use (XIV) after L. *imponere.*] **1.** *trans.* To put on, impose. **2.** *Sc.* To put in, set (in some position) 1557–1839.

Inquarta·tion. *rare.* 1881. [perh. – Fr. *inquartation*; see QUARTATION.] A process of separating gold and silver.

Inquest (i·nkwest). [ME. *enqueste* – OFr. *enqueste* (mod. *enquête*) :– Rom. **inquesta*, subst. use of fem. of pa. pple. of **inquærere*; see INQUIRE.] **1.** A legal or judicial inquiry to ascertain or decide a matter of fact, esp. one made by a jury in a civil or criminal case. Formerly, a general term for all formal or official inquiries. Now mostly = 'coroner's inquest' (see CORONER). Also *fig.* **2.** The body of men appointed to hold a legal inquiry; a jury; now *esp.* a coroner's jury ME.

3. *gen.* †An inquiry or question; a questioning –1853; †a pursuit, a research; †a quest –1667; inquiry or investigation (now *rare*) 1625.

1. *Great I.*, an occasional name for the Domesday inquiry and valuation. *I. of Office*, an inquiry made by the king's officer, or by commissioners appointed for the purpose, concerning any matter that entitles the king to the possession of lands or tenements, goods or chattels. *fig. Great, last, general i.*, the last Judgement. 2. *Grand* or *great i.* = Grand JURY. *Grand* (or *great*) *i. of the nation*, applied to the House of Commons. 3. This is the laborious and vexatious i., that the soul must make after science SOUTH.

Inquiet (inkwəi·ĕt), *a.* ME. [– L. *inquietus*; see IN-³, QUIET. Cf. Fr. *inquiet* (XVI).] Not quiet; †restless, troublesome –1552; uneasy, anxious (*rare*) 1502. Hence †**Inqui·etness.**

Inquiet (inkwəi·ĕt), *v.* Now *rare.* ME. [– (O)Fr. *inquiéter* – L. *inquietare*, f. *inquietus*; see prec.] *trans.* To destroy the quiet of; †to disquiet, disturb (in mind) –1828.

Inquietation (inkwəi,ĕtē¹·ʃən). *arch.* 1461. [– OFr. *inquietation* – med.L. *inquietatio*, f. L. *inquietare*; see prec., -ATION.] The action of disturbing or molesting; the condition of being disturbed or disquieted.

Inquietude (inkwəi·ĕtiūd). 1440. [– (O)Fr. *inquiétude* or late L. *inquietudo*, f. *inquietus*; see INQUIET *a.*, -TUDE.] †1. Disturbed condition; disturbance –1797. 2. *Med.* Restlessness (of the body), caused by pain, uneasiness, or debility 1597. 3. Disturbance of mind; disquietude 1658. **b.** *pl.* Anxieties 1652.

Inquiline (i·nkwiləin), *sb.* (*a.*) *rare.* 1641. [– L. *inquilinus* sojourner, f. *in-* IN-² + *colere* dwell.] †1. A sojourner, a lodger, an indweller. BP. MONTAGU. 2. *Zool.* An animal which lives in the nest or abode of another; a commensal or guest 1879. 3. *attrib.* or as *adj.* 1716.

2. There are several genera of gall-flies which.. are known as guest gall-flies or inquilines 1884.

†**I·nquinate,** *v.* 1542. [– *inquinat-*, pa. ppl. stem of L. *inquinare* pollute; see -ATE³.] *trans.* To pollute, defile, corrupt –1682. So **Inquina·tion** [– late L. *inquinatio*] (now *rare*), pollution; polluted condition; a defilement; a defiling agent (*lit.* and *fig.*) 1447.

Inquirable, enquirable (in-, ĕnkwəi³·răb'l), *a.* Now *rare.* 1485. [f. INQUIRE *v.* + -ABLE.] That calls for inquiry; open to inquiry. (Chiefly in legal use.) Also with *into.*

†**Inquirance, enquirance.** [ME. *enquerance* (– OFr. or AFr.), f. *enquerant* pr. pple. of *enquerre* INQUIRE; see -ANCE.] Inquiry –1567.

Inquire, enquire (in-, ĕnkwəi³·ɹ), *v.* [ME. *enquere* – OFr. *enquerre* (mod. new formation *enquérir*) :– Rom. **inquærere*, for L. *inquirere*, f. *in-* IN-² + L. *quærere* ask. Both prefix and stem-vowel were conformed to L. in XV, *inquere, enquire, inquire.*] †1. *trans.* To search into, seek knowledge concerning, investigate, examine –1787. 2. To seek knowledge of (a thing) by putting a question; to ask about; to ask (something) *of*, Sc. *at* (a person) ME. **b.** with interrog. clause as object: To ask ME. †3. To address a question to, question, interrogate; to ask (some one) –1682. 4. *intr.* To make investigation; to search, seek; to make inquisition. Const. *into*, †*of*, †*after.* ME. 5. *intr.* To seek information by questioning; to put a question or questions; to ask. Const. *of*, also (now Sc.) *at, about, after.* ME. **b.** To make request *for* a thing; to ask to see a person. Const. *for.* 1500. †6. *trans.* To seek, search for, try to find. With *out* (rarely *forth*): To seek till one finds; to seek out, find out by seeking (often including the notion of *asking*). –1790. †7. *trans.* (or *absol.*) To ask for, demand (*rare*) –1656. ¶8. *erron.* To name. SPENSER *F. Q.* II. x. 12.

1. A Probe..to enquire the depth of a wound 1612. 2. You must enquire your way *Cor.* III. i. 54. **b.** I will i...if he has gone out GALT. 3. Thou no more..Shalt be enquir'd at Delphos MILT. *P.R.* I. 458. 4. Of faery lond yet if he more inquyre..He may it fynd SPENSER. 5. Goe and i. diligently of the childe N.T. (Rhem.) *Matt.* 2:8. Dauid enquired of the Lord 1 *Sam.* 23:2. **b.** Hath any body enquir'd for mee here to day? SHAKS. 6. Enquire the Iewes house out SHAKS. Hence **Inqui·rer, en-,** one who inquires; a seeker, investigator; a questioner. **Inqui·ringly, en-,** *adv.* in an inquiring manner.

‖**Inquirendo** (inkwəire·ndo). 1607. [L., = 'by inquiring' abl. gerund of *inquirere*, INQUIRE.] *Law.* 'An authority given to some official person to institute an enquiry concerning the Crown's interests' (Wharton). **b.** An investigation 1846.

Inquiry, enquiry (in-, ĕnkwəi³·ri). 1440. [Earlier *enquery*, f. *enquere* INQUIRE *v.* + -Y³; subseq. refash. after the vb.] The action, or an act or course, of inquiring. 1. The action of seeking, esp. (now always) for truth, knowledge, or information concerning something; search, research, investigation, examination. **b.** (with *pl.*) A course of inquiry, an investigation 1512. 2. The action of asking or questioning; interrogation. (*Comm.* = DEMAND *sb.* 4.) 1565. **b.** A question; a query 1548.

1. To reject the christian religion without i. 1743. **b.** Enquiries into Antiquity STEELE. 2. We coulde learne nothinge therof by enquiry 1565. **b.** Our reply to this reasonable enquiry is simple SCRIVENER.

Phr. *Court of I.*, a court legally constituted to inquire into and investigate any charge against an officer or soldier of the army, or any transaction which may possibly be found to call for proceedings before a court-martial. *Writ of I.*, a writ directing an i. or inquest.

†**Inqui·sible,** *a.* *a*1676. [– mod.L. *inquisibilis*, irreg. f. *inquis-*, for *inquisit-*; see next, -IBLE.] Capable of being inquired into; subject to inquisition. HALE.

†**Inquisite,** *v.* 1639. [– *inquisit-* (see next); perh. back-formation from INQUISITION.] 1. *trans.* To inquire into, investigate, examine. Also *absol.* –1734. 2. To proceed against (a person) by inquisition or by the method of the Inquisition –1736.

1. *absol.* He inquisited with justice and decorum NORTH.

Inquisition (inkwizi·ʃən), *sb.* ME. [– (O)Fr. *inquisition* – L. *inquisitio* (legal) examination, f. *inquisit-*, pa. ppl. stem of L. *inquirere* INQUIRE; see -ION.] 1. The action or process of inquiring or searching into matters; search, investigation, examination; †scrutiny, inspection. Also with *an* and *pl.* 2. A judicial or official investigation or inquiry, an inquest; also the document recording such inquiry and its result ME. 3. *R. C. Ch.* (with capital *I.*) An ecclesiastical tribunal (officially styled the Holy Office) for the suppression of heresy and punishment of heretics, organized in the 13th c. under Innocent III, under a central governing body at Rome called the Congregation of the Holy Office 1502. 4. *attrib.* 1612.

1. To make i. of the truth 1570. The i. of the curious F. HALL. I heartily abhor an i. in faith BERKELEY. 2. R. became a lunatic, and was so found by i. 1896. 3. By Order of the Tribunal of the I. at Toledo..Eight Jews were burnt alive 1691. 4. If I left them..To these I. dogs and the devildoms of Spain TENNYSON. Hence **Inquisi·tional** *a.* of or pertaining to the I. or to inquiry; inquisitorial 1644. So **Inquisi·tionary** *a.* (*rare*).

Inquisi·tion, *v.* 1644. [f. prec. sb.] *intr.* To make an inquisition or investigation; *trans.* To proceed against by the Inquisition.

Inquisitive (inkwi·zĭtiv), *a.* (*sb.*) ME. [– OFr. *inquisitif, -ive* – late L. *inquisitivus* (Boethius), f. as prec.; see -IVE.] 1. Given to inquiry, questioning, or research; desirous of, or eager for, knowledge; curious ME. **b.** Now usu. in bad sense: Unduly or impertinently curious; prying 1529. 2. *sb.* An inquisitive person 1589.

1. So many learned, wise and i. men BERKELEY. **b.** I. Persons..who have a Mind to pry into the Thoughts and Actions of their Neighbour SOUTH. Hence **Inqui·sitive-ly** *adv.*, **-ness.**

Inquisitor (inkwi·zitəɹ). 1504. [– Fr. *inquisiteur* (AFr. *-itour*) – L. *inquisitor*, f. as prec.; see -OR 2.] 1. One who makes inquisition or inquiry; an investigator; an inquisitive person. Const. *of, into.* 2. One whose official duty it is to inquire, examine, or investigate, in matters of crime, taxation, etc. 1513. †**b.** A detective, informer, or spy –1797. **c.** *transf.* and *fig.* 1734. 3. An officer of the Inquisition; see INQUISITION 3. 1545.

1. Curious Inquisitors of the causes of all naturall things 1586. 2. **c.** What's that to you, brother? Who made you the i. of my actions? FIELDING.

Inquisitorial (inkwizitō³·riăl), *a.* 1761. [f. med.L. *inquisitorius* (f. as prec.; see -ORY²) + -AL¹. Cf. Fr. *inquisitorial* (XVI).] 1. Of or pertaining to an (official) inquisitor or inquisitors; having or exercising the function of an inquisitor. 2. Of the character of an inquisitor; prying 1796.

1. An i. tribunal..was erected in the kingdom HUME. The Cruel and Dangerous I. System of the Church of Rome in Ireland 1821. 2. The i. or secret system [of criminal procedure] 1900. Hence **Inquisito·rial-ly** *adv.*, **-ness.** So †**Inquisito·rious** *a.* (in sense 2). MILTON.

Inqui·sitory, *a.* 1639. [– med.L. *inquisitorius*; see prec., -ORY².] = INQUISITORIAL.

†**Inquisitu·rient,** *a.* [f. *inquisit-* (see above) + -URIENT.] Eager to play the inquisitor. MILTON.

Inra·cinate, *v.* *rare.* 1882. [f. IN-², after DERACINATE.] *trans.* To enroot, to implant.

†**Inrai·l,** *v.* 1594. [f. IN-¹ + RAIL *v.* Cf. ENRAIL.] *trans.* To rail in, inclose with a railing –1724.

‖**In re.** [See IN *Lat. prep.* and RE *prep.*] **a.** In fact, in reality 1602. **b.** In the matter or case of 1877.

Inregister, obs. f. ENREGISTER *v.*

Inroad (i·nrōᵘd), *sb.* 1548. [f. IN *adv.* + ROAD *sb.*, in sense 'riding'.] 1. A hostile incursion into a country; a raid or foray. 2. *transf.* or *fig.* A powerful or sudden incursion; a forcible encroachment 1637. †3. An opening or passage in –1697.

1. Aggressive war, as distinguished from mere plundering inroads FREEMAN. 2. Papal inroads on the liberties of the Church J. R. GREEN.

Inroad, *v.* Now *rare.* 1625. [f. prec. sb.] †*trans.* To invade; to make an inroad into –1656. Also *intr.*

The Saracens..inroded Aquitain FULLER.

Inrol(l, obs. ff. ENROL(L.

I·nro:lling, *ppl. a.* 1851. [IN *adv.*] That rolls in (like a wave).

I:nru·nning, *vbl. sb.* ME. [IN *adv.*] †**a.** Incursion, attack (tr. L. *incursus*). WYCLIF. **b.** Inflowing, the place of inflowing. TENNYSON.

Inruption (inrɒ·pʃən). 1809. [refash. of IRRUPTION, emphasizing *in-*.] A breaking or bursting in.

Inrush (i·nrɒʃ), *sb.* 1817. [IN *adv.*] A rushing or pouring in; inflow, influx (*lit.* and *fig.*). The..i. of tourists 1883. So †**I:nru·sh** *v.* to rush in 1610–1773.

†**Insa·bbatist.** *rare.* 1634. [f. Fr. *insabbaté*, or med.L. *insabbatus, -sab(b)atatus*; see -IST. But now referred to the peculiar shoe (*sabate* = Fr. *sabot, savate*) worn by the sect.] A member of the sect of the Waldenses.

They were supposed falsely to neglect the Sabbath, and called Insabbathists 1804.

†**Insa·fety.** 1635. [IN-³.] Unsafeness; risk.

Insalivate (insæ·live¹t), *v.* 1855. [f. IN-² + SALIVATE.] *trans.* To mix or impregnate (food) with saliva in the act of mastication. So **Insaliva·tion** 1833.

Insalubrious (insăl¹ū·briəs), *a.* 1638. [f. L. *insalubris* (f. *in-* IN-³ + *salubris* salubrious), or f. IN-³ + SALUBRIOUS.] Not salubrious; detrimental to health. (Now chiefly of climate or surroundings.)

Insalubrity (insăl¹ū·brĭti). 1663. [– Fr. *insalubrité* (XVI) or f. IN-³ + SALUBRITY.] Unhealthy character (of locality, climate, etc.); †unwholesomeness (of food).

Insalutary (insæ·liutări), *a.* 1694. [f. IN-³ + SALUTARY.] Not salutary. †1. Injurious to health; insalubrious –1773. 2. Not having a healthy mental or social influence or effect. LYTTON.

Insa·nable, *a.* *rare.* 1547. [– Fr. †*insanable* or L. *insanabilis*, f. *in-* IN-³ + *sanabilis*, f. *sanare* heal; see -BLE.] That cannot be healed, cured, or remedied; incurable. Hence †**Insanabi·lity,** †**Insa·nableness,** i. quality. †**Insa·nably** *adv.*

Insane (insē¹·n), *a.* (*sb.*) 1560. [– L. *insanus*, f. *in-* IN-³ + *sanus* SANE.] 1. Of persons: Not of sound mind, mad, mentally deranged. Also of the mind: Unsound. **b.** *absol.* An insane person. Hence (*attrib.* use of the *pl.*), Set apart for the insane, as *i. asylum, ward*, etc. 1786. 2. Of actions (also colloq. of things): Mad, idiotic, irrational 1842. †3. Causing insanity. SHAKS.

2. The i. and excessive passion for athletics 1869. 3. Haue we eaten on the i. Root, That takes the Reason Prisoner? SHAKS. Hence **Insa·ne-ly** *adv.* **-ness.**

†**Insa·niate,** *v.* [irreg. f. L. *insania* + -ATE³.] *trans.* To make unsound or insane. FELTHAM.

†**Insa·nie.** *rare.* 1572. [– Fr. †*insanie* – L. *insania*, f. *insanus* INSANE.] Madness –1594.

Insanitary (insæ·nitări), *a.* 1874. [IN-³.] Not sanitary or healthful; injurious to health. Hence **Insa·nitariness.**

Insanitation (insænitēⁱ·ʃən). 1884. [IN-³.] Want of sanitation; insanitary condition; absence of sanitary requirements.

Insanity (insæ·nĭti). 1590. [– L. *insanitas*, f. *insanus* INSANE; see -ITY.] **1.** The condition of being insane; unsoundness of mind as a consequence of brain-disease; madness, lunacy. Orig. called *i. of mind.* **2.** Extreme folly; an instance of this 1844.

1. D. Skae's..definition of i. as 'a disease of the brain affecting the mind' is not disputable 1897. **2.** The insanities of idealism H. SPENCER.

†**Insa·pory,** *a. rare.* [irreg. f. IN-³ + L. *sapor* taste + -Y¹.] Unsavoury. SIR T. HERBERT.

Insatiable (insēⁱ·ʃⁱăb'l), *a.* ME. [Earliest form *insaciable* – OFr. *insaciable* (mod. *insatiable*) or L. *insatiabilis*; see IN-³, SATIABLE.] Not satiable; that cannot be satiated, satisfied, or appeased; that always craves for more. Const. *of*, rarely *with.* Also *fig.* of things.

I. of antiquity MILT., with war COWPER. *fig.* Insaciable whyrlepoles MORE. Hence **Insatiabi·lity, Insa·tiableness. Insa·tiably** *adv.*

Insatiate (insēⁱ·ʃiĕt), *a.* 1509. [– L. *insatiatus*, f. *in-* IN-³ + *satiatus* SATIATE *ppl. a.*] That is not satiated or satisfied; never satisfied; insatiable. Const. *of*, †*for.*

Satan..i. to pursue Vain Warr with Heav'n MILT. *P.L.* II. 8. I. of battle 1848. *fig.* I. hell, still crying, More MARSTON. So **Insa·tiated** *a.* (*rare*). Hence **Insa·tiate-ly** *adv.*, **-ness.**

Insati·ety. *rare.* 1578. [– OFr. *insacieté*, (also mod.) †*insatieté* – L. *insatietas*; see IN-³, SATIETY.] The condition of being insatiate; unsatisfied desire or demand.

†**Insatisfa·ction.** 1568. [IN-³.] Absence of satisfaction; dissatisfaction –1682.

†**Insa·turable,** *a.* ME. [– L. *insaturabilis* insatiable, f. *in-* IN-³ + *saturare* SATURATE; see -BLE.] Insatiable –1755.

Inscience (i·nʃiĕns). Now *rare.* 1578. [– L. *inscientia* ignorance; see IN-³, SCIENCE. Cf. Fr. †*inscience.*] The condition of not knowing; want of knowledge; ignorance.

Inscient (i·nʃiĕnt), *a.*¹ Now *rare.* 1578. [– L. *insciens, inscient-* ignorant; see IN-³, SCIENT *a.* Cf. OFr. *inscient.*] Not knowing; lacking knowledge; nescient, ignorant. So †**I·nscious** *a.* 1633.

I·nscient, *a.*² [f. IN-¹ or ² perh. after PRESCIENT.] Having inward knowledge. E. B. BROWNING.

Insconce, obs. f. ENSCONCE.

Inscribable (inskrəi·băb'l), *a.* 1846. [f. next + -ABLE.] Capable of being inscribed.

No non-rectangular parallelogram is i. in a circle 1900.

Inscribe (inskrəi·b), *v.* 1552. [– L. *inscribere*, f. *in-* IN-² + *scribere* write.] **1.** *trans.* To write, mark, or delineate in or on something, e.g. on a monument, tablet, etc. Also *fig.* **b.** To enroll on an official document or list 1605. **c.** *Comm.* To issue a state (or other) loan in the form of shares with registered holders (see INSCRIBED) 1884. **2.** To mark (a surface, column, etc.) with writing or other characters 1637. **b.** To dedicate *to* a person by a short inscription less formal than an ordinary dedication 1645. **3.** *Geom.* To delineate or trace (a figure or line) within a figure, so that some particular points of it lie in the boundary or periphery of that figure 1570.

An angular figure (polygon or polyhedron) is said to be inscribed in another figure when the angular points of the former lie in the bounding line or lines, or surface or surfaces, of the latter. A curved figure (plane or solid) is said to be inscribed in an angular figure when the former touches each of the bounding lines or surfaces of the latter. More rarely, a line is said to be inscribed in a figure when its extremities lie in the boundary of that figure.

1. We raise the marble and i. the flattering epitaph 1864. **2.** Like to that sanguine flower inscrib'd with woe MILT. **b.** An author may with great propriety i. his work to him by whose encouragement it was undertaken JOHNSON. Hence **Inscri·ber,** one who inscribes; the writer of an inscription. So **I·nscript,** something inscribed; an inscription. **Inscri·ptible** *a.* (*rare*) = INSCRIBABLE.

Inscribed (inskrəi·bd), *ppl. a.* 1571. [f. prec. + -ED¹.] In the senses of INSCRIBE *v.* **b.** Of a state (or other) loan: Issued not in the form of bonds passing from hand to hand, but as shares of which the names of the holders are registered or entered in a list kept at the head office of the issuing state or company 1882.

Inscription (inskri·pʃən). ME. [– L. *inscriptio*, f. *inscript-*, pa. ppl. stem of L. *inscribere*; see INSCRIBE, -ION. Cf. Fr. *inscription* (XVI).] **1.** The action of inscribing. Also *fig. rare.* 1652. **2.** *concr.* That which is inscribed; a piece of writing or lettering upon something; *esp.* a legend, description, or record traced upon some hard substance for the sake of durability, as on a monument, building, stone, tablet, medal, coin, vase, etc. 1538. Also *fig.* **3.** *spec.* **a.** A title, heading, superscription. (Now *rare* or *Obs.* as dist. from 2.) ME. **b.** A brief dedication of a book or work of art to a person; the superscription of a letter 1742. **4.** *Anat.* A marking upon some organ or part produced by another in contact with it; *esp.* on the fleshy part of a muscle where a tendon crosses it 1578. **5.** *Comm.* The action of inscribing stock; in *pl.* inscribed stocks (see INSCRIBED) 1797. Hence **Inscri·ptional** *a.* †bearing an inscription; characteristic of, or of the nature of, an i. or inscriptions.

Inscriptive (inskri·ptiv), *a.* 1740. [f. stem of INSCRIPTION + -IVE.] **1.** Of the nature of an inscription; belonging to or used in inscriptions. †**2.** Bearing an inscription. DYER.

Inscroll (inskrōᵘ·l), *v.* 1596. [f. IN-¹ or ² + SCROLL.] *trans.* To inscribe or enter upon a scroll. *Merch. V.* II. vii. 72.

Inscrutable (inskrū·tăb'l), *a.* (*sb.*) 1450. [– eccl.L. *inscrutabilis*, f. *in-* IN-³ + *scrutari*; see SCRUTINY, -ABLE.] **1.** That cannot be searched into or found out by searching; impenetrable, unfathomable; entirely mysterious. Rarely of things physical, as an abyss. **2.** *sb. pl.* Inscrutable things 1663.

1. The herte of man is i., and onely god knoweth it 1526. As i. a mystery as the origin of Life 1894. Hence **Inscrutabi·lity, Inscru·tableness. Inscru·tably** *adv.*

Insculp (inskʊ·lp), *v.* Now *rare* or *Obs.* Pa. pple. **insculped, insculpt.** ME. [– L. *insculpere* carve or engrave on, f. *in-* IN-² + *sculpere* carve, or – Fr. †*insculper.* Used first in pa. ppl. form *insculpt* – L. *insculptus*; whence perh. the finite verb.] **1.** *trans.* To carve, engrave or sculpture (upon something). Also *fig.* **2. a.** To shape artistically by cutting. **b.** To sculpture (stone, etc.); to CARVE. Also *fig.* 1578.

1. Which he insculped in two likely stones DRAYTON. **2. b.** The sacred Tables..insculpt Of God's own hand 1830. So †**Inscu·lpt** *v.*1487. †**Inscu·lption,** the action of carving or sculpturing upon something; a carved figure or inscription. Also *fig.*

Inscu·lpture, *sb.* ?*Obs.* 1607. [– Fr. †*insculpture*, f. *in-* IN-² + *sculpture* SCULPTURE *sb.*] A figure or inscription carved or sculptured upon something.

On his Grauestone, this I. *Timon* V. iv. 67.

Inscu·lpture, *v.* Also **en-.** 1787. [f. IN-² = EN- + SCULPTURE *v.*] *trans.* To carve or sculpture upon something.

Shapes..That yet survive ensculptured on the walls WORDSW.

†**Inscutcheon.** 1562. = INESCUTCHEON.

Inseam, obs. f. ENSEAM *v.*¹

Insearch(e, -er, var. of ENSEARCH, -ER.

†**Insecable,** *a. rare.* 1623. [– L. *insecabilis*, f. *in-* IN-³ + *secabilis*, f. *secare* cut; see -BLE. Cf. Fr. *insécable* (XVI).] Incapable of being cut –17..

Insect (i·nsekt), *sb.* 1601. [– L. *insectum* (sc. *animal*), pl. *insecta* (Pliny), subst. use of n. of pa. pple. of *insecare* cut into or up, f. *in-* IN-² + *secare* cut; rendering Gr. ἔντομον, pl. ἔντομα (Aristotle), sc. ζῷον, ζῷα animal(s).] **1.** A small invertebrate animal, usually having a body divided into segments, and several pairs of legs, and often winged; in pop. use comprising, besides the animals scientifically so called (see 2), many other arthropods, as spiders, mites, centipedes, wood-lice, etc., and other invertebrates, as the 'coral-insect'; still applied by the uneducated to earthworms, snails, etc., and even some small vertebrates, as frogs and tortoises. **2.** *Zool.* An animal belonging to the class *Insecta* of *Arthropoda*; see INSECTA 2. 1601. **3.** *fig.* Applied to any insignificant or despicable person 1684.

3. He, the little I., was recommended to King William HEARNE.

attrib. and *Comb.* **1.** General: as *i. pest, vermin*, etc.; *i. quire, race*, etc.; *i. understanding*; *i. egg, larva*, etc.; *i.-box, -cabinet, -trap.*

2. Special: as **i.-beds,** the calcareous bands of the British Lias, in which the relics of i.-life are very abundant; **-feeder,** a creature that feeds on insects; **-powder,** a powder (usually prepared from the dried flowers of species of *Pyrethrum*) used to kill or drive away insects.

†**Insect,** *a.* 1589. [– L. *insectus*, pa. pple. of *insecare*; see prec.] Having the body divided into segments; chiefly in *i. animals* = L. *animalia insecta*; see INSECTA.

‖**Insecta** (inse·ktă), *sb. pl.* 1609. [L., pl. of *insectum*; see INSECT *sb.*] †**1.** Former pl. of INSECT, as used pop. –1651. †**b.** Also erron. *insectæ, insecta's.* Also *fig.* –1658. **2.** *Zool.* A class of invertebrate animals; formerly comprising the whole of the ARTHROPODA, or all these except the *Crustacea* and *Arachnida*; now restricted to the *Hexapoda*, having the body divided into three regions (head, thorax, and abdomen), with six legs (all borne upon the thorax), and usually two or four wings (but in some cases none); constituting the largest class of *Arthropoda* 1727.

Insectarium (insektēᵊ·riŏm). Also **Insectary** (i·nsektări). 1881. [f. INSECTA + -ARIUM.] A place for keeping and breeding insects; an entomological vivarium.

†**Insecta·tion.** *rare.* 1535. [– L. *insectatio*, f. *insectat-*, pa. ppl. stem of *insectari* pursue, rail at; see -ION.] Railing, calumniation –1658.

Insected (inse·ktĕd), *ppl. a. rare.* 1645. [f. L. *insectus* (see INSECT *a.*) + -ED¹.] Cut into; divided, as it were, into segments, as an insect.

Insecticide¹ (inse·ktisəid). 1865. [f. INSECT *sb.* + -CIDE 1.] One who or that which kills insects; *spec.* a preparation used for destroying insects. **b.** *attrib.* or as *adj.* Having the property of destroying insects. So **Insectici·dal** *a.* 1857.

Inse·cticide². 1865. [f. as prec. + -CIDE 2.] The killing of insects.

Insectile (inse·ktil, -təil), *a.*¹ and *sb.* 1615. [f. L. *insectum* INSECT *sb.* + -ILE.]

A. *adj.* Of, pertaining to, or of the nature of an insect; consisting of insects; also *fig.* infesting like insects. Now *rare.* 1626.

†**B.** *sb.* = INSECT *sb.* –1666.

†**Inse·ctile,** *a.*² *rare.* [f. IN-³ + SECTILE.] Incapable of being cut or divided –1683.

Insection (inse·kʃən). 1653. [– late and med.L. *insectio*, f. pa. ppl. stem of *insecare* (see INSECT *sb.*); see -ION; cf. *dissection.*] The action of cutting into, incision; division into sections; *concr.* an incision, division, indentation.

‖**Insectivora** (insekti·vŏră), *sb. pl.* 1836. [subst. use of n. pl. of mod.L. *insectivorus* insect-eating, after L. *carnivorus* CARNIVOROUS; see INSECT *sb.*, -VOROUS.] *Zool.* **1.** An order of *Mammalia*, comprising numerous small quadrupeds, as the mole, shrew and hedgehog, most of which feed on insects. **b.** A group of *Cheiroptera*; the insectivorous Bats. **2.** *Entom.** A group of *Hymenoptera* which feed on other insects (Westwood).

Insectivore (inse·ktivoᵊɹ). Also **-vor.** 1863. [– Fr. *insectivore* (Cuvier, 1817) – mod.L. *insectivorus*; see prec.] An insectivorous animal or plant; *spec.* one of the *Insectivora.*

Insectivorous (insekti·vŏrəs), *a.* 1661. [f. mod.L. *insectivorus* (see INSECTIVORA) + -OUS; see -VOROUS.] Feeding on insects; applied to the *Insectivora* among mammals, and various birds, such as swallows; also to those plants which capture and absorb insects, as the sundew, Venus's fly-trap, etc.

Insectology (insektǫ·lŏdʒi). 1766. [– Fr. *insectologie* (Bonnet, 1744); see INSECT *sb.*, -LOGY.] A term formerly used as = ENTOMOLOGY; but now usually applied to the study of insects in their economic relations to man, as producers of silk, cochineal, etc., and as agricultural pests or benefactors. Hence **Insecto·loger, Insecto·logist,** a student of i.

Insecure (insĭkiūᵊ·ɹ), *a.* 1649. [– med.L. *insecurus* unsafe, or f. IN-³ + SECURE *a.*] Not secure. †**1.** Wanting assurance, confidence, or certainty; uncertain; without certainty *of* –1807. **2.** Unsafe; exposed to danger; liable to give way, fail, or be overcome 1654.

1. Troubled with sorrow and i. apprehensions JER. TAYLOR **2.** So in-secure did overmuch security make them 1654. Hence †**Insecu·re** *v.* (*rare*), to render i. **Insecu·re-ly** *adv.*, **-ness.**

Insecurity (insĭkiūᵊ·rĭti). 1646. [– med.L. *insecuritas* or f. IN-³ + SECURITY.] †**1.** The condition of not being sure; want of confidence; (subjective) uncertainty. SIR T. BROWNE. **2.** The state or quality of being unsafe; liability to give way, fail, or suffer loss or damage; want of firmness; a condition of danger. With *pl.* An instance of this. 1649.

2. The i. of all human acquisitions JOHNSON, of titles 1822, of great prosperity J. H. NEWMAN.

†**Insecu·tion.** [– late and med.L. *insecutio* pursuit, onslaught, f. *insecut-*, pa. ppl. stem of L. *insequi* follow upon, pursue, f. *in-* IN-² + *sequi* follow; see -ION.] The action of following closely upon; close pursuit. CHAPMAN.

Inseminate (inse·mineᶦt), *v.* 1623. [– *inseminat-*, pa. ppl. stem of L. *inseminare*, f. *in-* IN-² + *seminare* sow; see -ATE³.] *trans.* To sow in; to cast in as seed. Also *fig.* Hence **Insemina·tion.**

Insensate (inse·nsĕt), *a.* (*sb.*) 1500. [– eccl.L. *insensatus* (Tertullian), f. *in-* IN-³ + *sensatus* gifted with sense; see SENSATE *a.*] **1.** Without sensation, senseless, inanimate. **2.** Wanting in mental or moral feeling; devoid of sensibility 1553. †**b.** With *of, to*: Not feeling; unconscious of; unaffected by –1813. **3.** Lacking sense or understanding; unintelligent, senseless, foolish 1529. **4.** *sb.* An insensate person. [= Fr. *insensé.*] 1877.

1. The silence and the calm, Of mute i. things WORDSW. **2. b.** The Suitors souls, i. of their doom POPE. **3.** Projects the most i. [were] formed ALISON. Hence **Inse·nsate-ly** *adv.*, **-ness.**

Insense (inse·ns), *v.* *Obs.* exc. *n. dial.* [ME. *ensens(e* – OFr. *ensenser* enlighten, f. *en-* in, into + *sens* SENSE.] *trans.* To cause (a person) to understand or know; to inform.

Insensibility (insensibi·lĭti). 1510. [– (O)Fr. *insensibilité* or late L. *insensibilitas*, and f. IN-³ + SENSIBILITY.] The quality or condition of being insensible.

I. In passive sense. The quality of being imperceptible, or not appreciable by the senses (*rare*) 1635.

II. In active sense. **1.** Incapability, or deprivation, of (physical) feeling or sensation; unconsciousness; a swoon 1510. **b.** Physical insensitiveness (*to* something) 1808. **2.** Incapacity of mental feeling or emotion; want of moral susceptibility; apathy, indifference 1691.

1. I fell from my horse in a state of i. 1841. **b.** I. to the changes of the seasons W. IRVING. **2.** I. to the goodness of the Creator PALEY.

Insensible (inse·nsĭb'l), *a.* (*sb.*) ME. [– (O)Fr. *insensible* or L. *insensibilis*, and f. IN-³ + SENSIBLE, the sense-development of which is reflected in the present word.]

I. Passively. **1. a.** Imperceptible by the senses; non-material (now *rare*) ME. **b.** So small, slight, etc. as to be inappreciable by the senses or by the mind. (The prevailing sense.) 1584. †**2.** Unintelligible; without sense or meaning. (Chiefly in legal use.) –1884.

1. a. The names which stand for i. actions and notions, are derived from sensible objects MANSEL. **b.** There is an i. transition H. SPENCER. **2.** The words are i. and uncertain words 1657.

II. Actively. **1. a.** Not having the faculty of sensation. Now *rare*. ME. **b.** Deprived of sensation; unconscious ME. **c.** Incapable of physically feeling or knowing (something specified). Const. *of, to.* 1526. **2. a.** Incapable of mentally feeling, perceiving, or being affected by (something specified); unconscious; unsusceptible, indifferent. Const. *of, to,* etc. 1612. **b.** Incapable of feeling or emotion; callous, apathetic 1617. †**3.** Destitute of sense or intelligence; irrational –1794.

1. a. The i. spot on the retina BREWSTER. **b.** He fell down in a fit, and remained long i. MACAULAY. **c.** I. to wounds GEO. ELIOT. **2. a.** I. of your kindness 1802. Hence †**Inse·nsibleness,** the quality or condition of being i. **Inse·nsibly** *adv.* 1425.

Insensitive (inse·nsĭtiv), *a.* 1610. [IN-³.] Not sensitive; destitute of feeling or sensation; not susceptible of impressions. Also *transf.*

One spot on the retina, not very far from the most sensitive portion, is entirely i. to light. HARLAN. Hence **Inse·nsitiveness.**

Insensuous (inse·nsiuˌəs), *a.* *rare.* 1861. [IN-³.] Not sensuous; that is not an object of sense. E. B. BROWNING.

Insentient (inse·nʃᶦĕnt), *a.* 1764. [IN-³.] Not sentient; destitute of sensation or consciousness; indifferent (*rare*).

An i. inert substance REID. Shall I return it [a stone] thanks, the i. thing? BROWNING. Hence **Inse·ntience.**

Inseparable (inse·părăb'l), *a.* (*sb.*) ME. [– L. *inseparabilis*; see IN-³, SEPARABLE. Cf. (O)Fr. *inséparable.*] **1.** Not separable; incapable of being separated or disjoined. **2.** *sb.* Usu. *pl.* Things or persons that cannot be separated; inseparable companions 1520.

1. An i. union 1662. My i. companion during eleven years MRS. CARLYLE. *I. accident, attribute, quality,* etc. (*Logic*), an accident, etc., that cannot be separated from its subject. *I. prefix* or *preposition* (*Gram.*), a prefix found only in combination, and incapable of being used as a separate word; e.g. *mis-, un-*. Hence **Inseparabi·lity, Inse·parableness. Inse·parably** *adv.*

Inseparate (inse·părĕt), *a.* 1550. [f. IN-³ + SEPARATE *pa. pple.*] Not separate *from*; undivided; hence often = INSEPARABLE.

We live linked, i.—heart in heart SWINBURNE. Hence **Inse·parately** *adv.*

Insert (i·nsəɹt), *sb.* 1890. [f. INSERT *v.*, or abbrev. of INSERTION.] An insertion; a rider on a proof; *U.S.* a circular or the like placed between the leaves of a magazine or the folds of a newspaper.

Insert (insə̄·ɹt), *v.* 1529. [– *insert-*, pa. ppl. stem of L. *inserere*, f. *in-* IN-² + *serere* plant, join, put into.] **1.** *trans.* To set, put, or place in; to push or thrust in; to fit or fix in; to introduce; to engraft. Said primarily of putting any solid object into a space which it fits, or fills up. **b.** To put in or introduce; to include 1533. **2.** *Anat., Zool., Bot.* To attach; to join at a specified point of attachment. Only in *pa. pple.* 1828.

1. It inserts its long tongue into the holes through which the ants issue BEWICK. To i. vaccine matter in the arm 1799, a key in a lock DICKENS. **b.** Something he had inserted into the Magazine J. H. NEWMAN. To i. an advertisement in a newspaper 1900. Hence **Inse·rter.**

Inse·rted, *ppl. a.* 1598. [f. INSERT *v.* + -ED¹.] Set or put in; fitted in, engrafted. **b.** *Entom.* Set deeply; not free 1826.

Insertion (insə̄·ɹʃən). 1578. [– late L. *insertio*, f. L. *insert-*; see INSERT *v.*, -ION.] **1.** The action of inserting; see INSERT *v.* 1598. **2.** That which is inserted; an inserted addition, piece, or part 1624. **b.** *Needlework.* Embroidery or ornamental needlework, made to be sewed into plain material, for decorative purposes; a piece of such work 1858. **3.** *Anat.,* etc. The attachment of a muscle, external organ, etc., as to place and manner 1578.

1. The i. of artificial teeth 1878, of trade notices, advertisements, etc. in a newspaper 1900. **2. b.** A white straw hat, trimmed with buff i. 1881. **3.** Anthers erect, i. basal J. D. HOOKER.

†**Inse·rve,** *v.* *rare.* 1683. [– L. *inservire* be serviceable, f. *in-* IN-² + *servire* serve.] *intr.* To be of service or use *to*; to conduce *to.*

†**Inse·rvient,** *a.* 1646. [– *inservient-*, pr. ppl. stem of L. *inservire*; see prec., -ENT. Cf. *subservient.*] **1.** Serving, servile. SIR T. BROWNE. **2.** Subservient *to* some end; serviceable, conducive, assisting –1802. Hence †**Inse·rvience** 1657.

1. The i. and brutall faculties 1646.

†**Inse·ssion.** 1559. [– late L. *insessio* (tr. ἐγκάθισμα) sitz-bath; f. *insess-*, pa. ppl. stem of L. *insedēre*, f. *in-* IN-² + *sedēre* sit; see -ION.] The action of sitting in a bath –1684. **b.** A hip- or sitz-bath 1559–1657.

b. *Insessions* be bathing tubs..wherein the patient may sit vp to the middle or aboue P. HOLLAND.

Insessor (inse·səɹ). *rare.* 1835. [– late L. *insessor* occupant, passenger, f. as prec.; see -OR 2.] One who sits in or on.

The I. of the chariot of the cherubim 1835.

‖**Insessores** (insesōᵊ·rīz), *sb. pl.* 1823. [mod.L. 'sitters-upon', pl. of late L. *insessor*; see prec.] *Ornith.* The Perchers or Perching birds, having feet with three toes in front and one behind, adapted for perching on trees. (The composite character of the group has caused the use of the name to be given up.) Hence **Insesso·rial** *a.* of or pertaining to the *Insessores*, or Perchers.

Inset (i·nset), *sb.* 1559. [f. IN *adv.* + SET *sb.*] **1.** A setting in, inflow, influx (of water); hence, †a channel. Also *attrib.* **2.** That which is set in or inserted. **a.** A folded section of paper placed within another, completing the sequence of pagination; an extra page or set of pages inserted in a sheet or book; an advertisement on a separate leaf inserted in a magazine, etc. 1875. **b.** A smaller map, picture, etc. inserted within the border of a larger one 1881. **c.** A piece of cloth let into a dress 1894.

1. There are tidal influences combined with the general insets from the Atlantic LYELL.

Inse·t, *v.* Pa. pple. **inset;** also **insetted.** ME. [f. IN-¹ or IN *adv.* + SET *v.*] †**1.** To insert, engraft. Const. *to.* ME. only. **2.** To set in, insert; *spec.* to insert as an inset (INSET *sb.* 2 a) 1890. Hence **Insetter,** one employed to inset sheets.

Inseverable (inse·vərăb'l), *a.* 1661. [IN-³.] Incapable of being severed or broken; inseparable. Hence **Inse·verably** *adv.* 1640.

†**Insha·de,** *v.* [f. IN-² + SHADE *v.*] *trans.* To shade; to tint or vary one colour with another. W. BROWNE.

Inshave (i·nˌʃeᶦv). 1875. [f. IN *adv.* + SHAVE *sb.*¹] A tool used by coopers for shaving or planing the inner face of staves.

Insheath, obs. f. ENSHEATH.

Inshell, enshell (inˌʃe·l, en-), *v.* *rare.* 1607. [f. IN-¹, EN-¹ + SHELL *sb.*] *trans.* To withdraw within the shell. Also *fig.*

†**Inship,** *v.* 1591. [f. IN-¹ + SHIP *sb.*] *trans.* To put into a ship; to embark –1615.

In shore, i·n-sho·re, *adv. phr.* (*adj.*) 1701. [f. IN *adv.* + SHORE *sb.*¹] **1.** *adv.* From seaward in towards the shore; close to the shore 1748. **2.** *attrib.* or *adj.* Lying, situated, or carried on near or close to the shore 1701. **b.** Moving in towards the shore 1882.

1. She was..driven inshore by some boats 1812. The Havilah passing in-shore of the Bombay 1859. **2.** The i. fishing 1855, waters 1885. **b.** An i. wind 1882.

Inshrine: see ENSHRINE.

Inside (i·nsəi·d, insəi·d, i·nsəid), *sb., adj., adv.,* and *prep.* 1504. [f. IN *adj.* (*adv.* used *attrib.*) + SIDE *sb.*¹ The opposite of *outside.*]

A. *sb.* **1.** The inner side or surface; that side which is within, or nearer to the centre, or farther from the outer edge or surface. **2.** The interior 1550. **b.** *spec.* (i:nˌsəi·d) The interior of the body; the internal organs, esp. the stomach and bowels; the entrails. (Also in *pl.* in same sense) *colloq.* and *dial.* 1741. **c.** Inward nature, mind, thought, or meaning 1599. **d.** The middle or main portion of a period of time, exclusive of the beginning and end 1890. **3.** (adj. or adv. used ellipt.) An inside passenger or place in a coach or other vehicle (*colloq.*) 1798. **4.** In advb. phr. *i:nside ou·t*: so that the inner side becomes the outer.

1. Look'd he o' th' i. of the Paper? SHAKS. The i. of the pavement 1894. **2.** Shew the in-side of your Purse to the out-side of his hand, and no more adoe SHAKS. **b.** My i. cries cupboard KINGSLEY. **c.** Here's none but friends here, we may speak Our insides freely MASSINGER. **d.** Home for the i. of a fortnight T. HARDY. **3.** The four insides of a Dover coach are taken for to-morrow morning SOUTHEY.

B. *adj.* (i·nsəid). Situated on or in the inside; of, belonging to, or used for the inside (*lit.* and *fig.*); interior, internal 1611. **b.** *U.S.* Of a person: Working indoors 1892. **c.** *fig.* Coming from 'the inside'; not generally available 1888.

Is whispering nothing?..Kissing with in-side Lip? SHAKS. *I. cylinder, framing, gear,* used techn. in reference to locomotive engines having the driving-gear within the main frame. *I. callipers*, etc., i.e. used for the interior of cylindrical or hollow work. (*To cut, do*) *the i. edge* (*Skating*): a particular form of fancy skating on the inner edge of the skate-iron. *I. track*: in *Racing,* the inner, and therefore shorter, side of a curved track; hence *fig.* a position of advantage. **c.** Inside information 1888.

C. *adv.* (insəi·d). On or in the inside. **1.** On the inner side 1803. **2.** In or into the inner part; internally 1851.

2. Full, i., sir 1851. Now then, ladies and gentlemen, walk i.! 1866.

Phr. *I. of* (in reference to time): Within the space of; before the end of. *U.S.* and *Colonial colloq.*

D. *prep.* Inside of; on the inner side, or in the inner part, of; within 1791.

To run i. the Bermudas R. H. DANA.

I:nsi·der. 1875. [f. INSIDE + -ER¹.] One who is inside; a person who is within the limits of some place, society, etc.; hence, one who is in possession of special information.

†Insi·diate, *v.* 1624. [– *insidiat-*, pa. ppl. stem of L. *insidiari* lie in ambush, f. *insidiæ*; cf. next.] **1.** *trans.* To lie in wait for; to plot against –1656. **2.** *intr.* To lie in wait; to plot –1639. So **†Insidia·tion** 1612. **†Insi·diator** 1539.

Insidious (insi·diəs), *a.* 1545. [– L. *insidiosus* cunning, deceitful, f. *insidiæ* ambush, trick; see -OUS.] Full of wiles or plots; lying in wait or seeking to entrap or ensnare; sly, treacherous, deceitful, underhand, artful, cunning. (Of persons and things.)

A false, i. Tongue, may whisper a Lye so close, and low SOUTH. A more powerful and i. enemy J. H. NEWMAN. A victim to an i. disease 1900. Hence **Insi·dious-ly** *adv.*, **-ness.**

Insight¹ (i·nsəit). ME. [prob. of Scand. and LG. origin; cf. Sw. *insiht*, Da. *insigt*, Du. *inzicht*; G. *einsicht* (XVIII); see IN-¹, SIGHT.] **†1.** Internal sight, mental vision or perception, discernment; in early use occas., Understanding, wisdom –1647. **2.** A glimpse or view beneath the surface; the faculty or power of thus seeing 1580. **†3.** A mental looking *to* or *upon* something; consideration; respect, regard –1491. **†4.** Sight (of the bodily eyes); looking; looking in, inspection; a look –1663.

1. Much better is..the i. of the mind than the light, or eyesight, of the body 1578. **2.** This thorough I. into the Man..makes me disesteem him 1718. Hence **†I·nsighted** *a.* having i. 1602.

†Insight². *north.* and *Sc. Obs.* 1522. [Of unkn. origin.] Goods, *esp.* household furniture.

‖**Insignia** (insi·gniă), *sb. pl.* Less freq. in sing. **insigne** (insi·gni). 1648. [L., pl. of *insigne* mark, sign, badge of office, subst. use of *insignis* distinguished (as by a mark), f. *in-* IN-² + *signum* sign; see -IA².] **1.** Badges or distinguishing marks of office or honour; emblems of a nation, person, etc. **b.** Erron. used as sing. with pl. *-as* 1774. **2.** (usu. *fig.*) Marks or tokens indicative of anything 1796.

1. The *insignia* of the Order of the Bath WELLINGTON. **b.** A slender white wand, the dreaded insignia of his office W. IRVING. **2.** The i. of immortality BREWSTER.

Insignificance (insigni·fikăns). 1699. [f. next (see -ANCE), or f. IN-³ + SIGNIFICANCE.] The fact or quality of being insignificant. **1.** Want of signification or meaning 1754. **2.** Want of significance; unimportance; contemptibility.

2. A sufficient apology for a whole life of i. SCOTT. So **Insigni·ficancy** 1651.

Insignificant (insigni·fikănt), *a.* (*sb.*) 1627. [f. IN-³ + SIGNIFICANT.] **1.** Devoid of signification; meaningless 1651. **2.** Devoid of significance, weight, or force; †ineffective; immaterial; trivial; contemptible 1627. **3.** Small in size; petty 1748. **4.** *sb.* **a.** A word or thing without signification. **b.** An unimportant or contemptible person. 1710.

1. The frequency of i. speech HOBBES. **2.** An i. blockhead 1751. The Roman loss was i. in this battle FROUDE. **3.** Thebes had sunk to an i. village THIRLWALL. Hence **Insigni·ficantly** *adv.*

†Insigni·ficative, *a.* 1660. [f. IN-³ + SIGNIFICATIVE.] Not significative, not denoting by external signs –1751.

Insignment, obs. f. ENSIGNMENT.

†Insi·mulate, *v.* 1532. [– *insimulat-*, pa. ppl. stem of L. *insimulare* bring a plausible charge against, accuse, f. *in-* IN-² + *simulare* SIMULATE.] *trans.* To charge, accuse –1663. So **†Insimula·tion,** accusation 1586–1604.

Insincere (insinsīᵊ·ɹ), *a.* 1634. [– L. *insincerus*, f. *in-* IN-³ + *sincerus* SINCERE.] Not sincere or genuine; assuming a false guise in speech or conduct; dissembling, disingenuous.

Things stand..but ticklish and i. betwixt us and Holland MARVELL. Hence **Insince·rely** *adv.* 1625.

Insincerity (insinse·rĭti). 1548. [– late L. *insinceritas*, f. *in-* IN-³ + *sinceritas* SINCERITY.] **†1.** Want of purity, corruption. UDALL. **2.** The opposite of sincerity; the quality of being insincere; dissimulation; an instance of this 1699.

2. Manfredi, a statesman of the Italian school, who takes i. for wisdom 1792. The fashionable insincerities of his day A. DOBSON.

†Insi·new, *v.* Also **en-.** 1597. [f. IN-² + SINEW.] *trans.* To furnish with sinews; to innerve; to inspire with vigour or strength –1611.

All members of our Cause..That are insinewed to his Action 2 *Hen. IV*, IV. i. 172.

Insinuant (insi·niuˌănt), *a.* *rare.* 1639. [f. INSINUATE *v.* + -ANT, perh. immed. through Fr. *insinuant* (XVII).] **1.** Insinuating; wheedling, ingratiating. **2.** That steals its way in 1877.

Insinuate (insi·niuˌeᶦt), *v.* 1529. [– *insinuat-*, pa. ppl. stem of L. *insinuare*, f. *in-* IN-² + *sinuare* curve; see -ATE³.] **1.** *trans.* To introduce tortuously, sinuously, indirectly, or by devious methods; to introduce by imperceptible degrees or subtle means 1647. Also *refl.* and †*intr.* (for *refl.*). **2.** *trans.* To introduce (a person) by sinuous, stealthy, or artful ways into some position or relation; esp. *refl.* to worm oneself into the favour, etc. of another 1579. †Also *intr.* (for *refl.*) **3.** *refl.* Of an immaterial thing: To instil itself subtly; to win its way *into* men's minds, favour, or notice 1594. **†4.** *trans.* To draw, win, or attract (a person, etc.) subtly or covertly *to* or *unto* something –1677. **5.** To introduce to the mind indirectly, covertly, or privily; to infuse or instil subtly or imperceptibly 1529. **6.** To convey indirectly; to hint obliquely; now generally with implication of cunning or underhand action 1561. Also *absol.* **7.** To signify indirectly; to suggest, imply. *Obs.* or *arch.* 1533. **8.** *Law.* To register (a deed or document); to lodge for registration 1529.

1. Trees, which i. their roots into the fissures KENDALL. **2.** *refl.* They insinuated themselves into families to betray them 1832. **3.** A pure and humble religion gently insinuated itself into the minds of men GIBBON. **5.** In which wisdom was to be insinuated not enforced MAURICE. **6.** Hints and allusions, expressing little, insinuating much BP. BERKELEY. **7.** He did i. with his eyes, unto me, I should depart and leave them 1641.

Insi·nuating, *ppl. a.* 1591. [f. prec. vb. + -ING².] **1.** That penetrates sinuously between the particles of a body; subtly penetrating 1615. **2.** That artfully works his way into company, position, favour, etc.; wily, wheedling, ingratiating.

1. Black smoak..of the most subtile and i. nature 1799. **2.** [An] i. Hypocrite HY. MORE. Englishmen of honourable name..and i. address MACAULAY. Hence **Insi·nuatingly** *adv.*

Insinuation (insiniuˌēᶦ·ʃən). 1526. [– L. *insinuatio*, f. as INSINUATE; see -ION. Cf. (O)Fr. *insinuation*.] The action of insinuating. **1.** A winding or twisting 1661. **2.** Introduction or entrance by winding, indirect, or stealthy motion; stealing in 1614. **3.** The action of stealing into the favour of any one by winning, persuasive, or subtle means; a winning or ingratiating action or speech 1553. **4.** The subtle or insensible instilling of anything into the mind 1526. **5.** The suggestion or hinting of anything indirectly or covertly; (with *pl.*) an indirect or covert suggestion 1532. **†6.** *Law.* The production or delivery of a will for official registration, as a step towards procuring probate –1726.

2. The resistance of adamant is insufficient to defeat the i. of a fibre 1806. **3.** I never advanced a Step by way of I., to curry Favour or Affection, as they say, on any Side 1728. **4.** The i. of divine truth CUDWORTH. **5.** A modest title should only informe the buyer what the book containes without furder i. MILT.

Insinuative (insi·niuˌeᶦtiv, -ĕtiv), *a.* 1592. [f. INSINUATE *v.*, INSINUATION + -IVE.] **1.** Having the property of stealing into favour or confidence; subtly ingratiating. **2.** Tending to insinuate into the mind 1786. **3.** Characterized by or involving insinuation or suggestion; given to insinuations; suggestive, hinting 1648.

1. His Discourse [was] plausible and i. 1683. Hence **Insi·nuative-ly** *adv.*, **-ness.**

Insinuator (insi·niuˌeᶦtəɹ). 1598. [f. INSINUATE *v.* + -OR 2.] **a.** One who artfully creeps into favour; **b.** One who hints subtly.

Insi·nuatory, *a.* 1871. [f. as prec. + -ORY².] Insinuative.

Insipid (insi·pid), *a.* (*sb.*) 1620. [– Fr. *insipide* or late L. *insipidus*, f. *in-* IN-³ + *sapidus* SAPID.] **1.** Without taste; having only a very slight taste; without perceptible flavour. **2.** *fig.* Wanting the qualities which excite interest or emotion. lifeless, dull, flat 16.. **†3.** Devoid of taste, intelligence, or judgement; stupid, foolish, dull –1784. **†4.** *sb.* An insipid person or thing –1834.

1. No water can be pure that is not quite i. 1756. *I. diabetes* (*diabetes insipidus*), a form of diabetes dist. from *saccharine diabetes* (*diabetes mellitus*); see DIABETES. **2.** I. compliments DISRAELI. **3.** To church, where a most i. young coxcomb preached PEPYS. Hence **Insipi·dity,** the quality of being i.; an i. person, remark, etc. **Insi·pid-ly** *adv.*, **-ness.**

Insipient (insi·piĕnt). 1494. [– L. *insipiens, -ent-*, f. *in-* IN-³ + *sapiens* SAPIENT.] **A.** *adj.* Void of wisdom; foolish. (Now mostly disused to avoid confusion with *incipient.*) 1528. **†B.** *sb.* An unwise or foolish person –1633. So **Insi·pience,** the quality of being i. 1422.

Insist (insi·st), *v.* 1586. [– L. *insistere* stand upon, persist, f. *in-* IN-² + *sistere* stand.] **1.** *intr.* To stand or rest *on* or *upon.* ?*Obs.* 1598. **2.** To continue steadfastly in a course of action, to follow steadfastly *in* (*on*) a person's steps, etc.; to continue with urgency; to persevere (*arch.*) 1586. **3.** To dwell at length or with emphasis *on* or *upon* (†*of*, †*in*) a matter; hence, *to i. on* = to assert or maintain persistently 1596. **4.** To make a demand with persistent urgency; to take a persistent or peremptory stand (*on, upon,* †*for,* †*against*, etc.) 1623.

1. Angles likewise which i. on the Diameter, are all Right Angles 1709. **2.** To caste our eyes upon Nature, and to i. in her steps 1638. **3.** I cannot now i. Upon particulars B. JONS. Protarchus.. insists that..all pleasures are good JOWETT. **4.** To i. on the..appointment being made 1896. Hence **Insi·ster,** one who insists. **Insi·stingly** *adv.*

Insistence (insi·stĕns). Also **†-ance.** 1611. [f. prec. + -ENCE. For the sp. in *-ance*, see -ANCE.] The action of insisting; the fact, or quality, of being insistent.

Insistency (insi·stĕnsi). Also **†-ancy.** 1859. [f. as prec.; see -ENCY.] The quality of being insistent; urgency, pertinacity; an instance of this.

Insistent (insi·stĕnt), *a.* (*sb.*) Also **†-ant.** 1624. [f. INSIST *v.* + -ENT (in sense of the Eng. verb).] **1.** Standing or resting on something (*rare*). **2.** Dwelling firmly on something asserted, demanded, etc.; persistent, urgent. Hence, Enforcing attention. 1868. **3.** *Ornith.* [Fr. *insistant.*] Applied to the hind toe of birds when it is inserted so high that it touches the ground only with its tip; opp. to *incumbent* 1886. **4.** *sb.* An insistent person 1868.

2. The i. facts of sin, suffering, and misery 1888. Hence **Insi·stently** *adv.* in an i. manner.

†Insi·sture. [f. INSIST *v.* + -URE.] Continuance, persistence. *Tr. & Cr.* I. iii. 87.

†Insi·tiency. 1701. [f. IN-³ + L. *sitiens, -ent-* thirsty + -ENCY.] Freedom from thirst.

†Insi·tion¹. 1589. [– L. *insitio*, f. *insit-*, pa. ppl. stem of *inserere* engraft, f. *in-* IN-² + *serere* sow, plant.] The action of engrafting, engraftment; *concr.* a graft. Also *transf.* and *fig.* –1855.

†Insition², obs. erron. f. INCISION.

Insititious (insiti·ʃəs), *a.* 1639. [f. L. *insiticius* (f. *insit-*, see INSITION) + -OUS; see -ITIOUS¹.] Of engrafted or inserted nature; introduced from without.

In situ (1803): see IN *Lat. prep.*

Insnare, Insnarl, obs. ff. ENSNARE, etc.

Insobriety (insobrəi·ĕti). 1611. [f. IN-³ + SOBRIETY.] Want of sobriety; intemperance (either generally, or *spec.* in drinking).

Insociable (insōᵘ·ʃ'ăb'l), *a.* Now *rare.* 1581. [– L. *insociabilis*; see IN-³ and SOCIABLE.]

†**1.** That cannot be associated or combined; incompatible –1678. **2.** Unsociable 1588.

1. Lime and wood are i. WOTTON. **2.** This austere i. life SHAKS. Hence **Insociabi·lity, Inso·ciableness,** i. disposition or state. **Inso·ciably** *adv.*

†**Inso·ciate,** *a.* [f. IN-^{3} + SOCIATE *ppl. a.*] Not associated; solitary. B. JONS.

Insolate (i·nsole^{i}t), *v.* 1623. [– *insolat-*, pa. ppl. stem of L. *insolare* place in the sun, f. *in-* IN-^{2} + *sol* sun; see -ATE^3.] *trans.* To place in, or expose to the rays of, the sun.

Insolation (insolē^i·ʃən). 1612. [– L. *insolatio*, f. as prec.; see -ION.] The action of placing in the sun; exposure to the sun's rays; *occas.*, the effect of this. **1.** *gen.* 1654. **2.** *spec.* **a.** Exposure of some substance to the sun's rays, as for the purpose of drying, bleaching, or maturing 1612. **b.** Exposure of the body to the sun's rays for medical treatment 1626. **c.** Injurious exposure to the sun's rays or to excessive heat; sunstroke 1758.

Insole (i·nsō^{u}l). 1851. [f. IN *a.* + SOLE *sb.*^{1}] **a.** The inner sole of a boot or shoe. **b.** A flat piece of warm or waterproof material laid inside the shoe.

Insolence (i·nsŏlĕns). ME. [– L. *insolentia*, f. *insolent-*; see INSOLENT, -ENCE. Cf. Fr. *insolence* (XV).] **1.** The quality of being insolent, esp. as manifested in action. †**a.** Pride; arrogance, contempt for inferiors. **b.** Offensive contemptuousness of action or speech due to presumption; sauciness 1668. **c.** An insolent act; a piece of insolence (now *rare*) 1491. †**2.** Exultation. SPENSER. †**3.** Inexperience –1500. †**4.** The quality or character of being unusual; unaccustomedness 1631.

1. a. I do wonder, his i. can brooke to be commanded vnder Cominius SHAKS. *Cor.* I. i. 266. The rich Man's I. ROWE. **b.** When their I. was such, as to make Kings the Instruments of their Ambition 1683. **c.** The Assaults and Insolences of Night Robbers 1680.

I·nsolency. Now *rare.* 1494. [f. as prec.; see -ENCY.] = prec.

Insolent (i·nsŏlĕnt), *a.* (*sb.*) ME. [– L. *insolens, -ent-* unusual, excessive, arrogant, f. *in-* IN-^{3} + pr. pple. of *solēre* be accustomed; see -ENT.]

A. *adj.* **I.** †**1.** Proud, disdainful, arrogant, overbearing; offensively contemptuous of the rights of others. **2.** Contemptuous of rightful authority; presumptuously contemptuous; impertinently insulting 1678. †**3.** Immoderate, going beyond the bounds of propriety –1712.

1. How i. is upstart pride GAY. **2.** God will not gratifie their i. demand BAXTER. An idle, drunken, i. fellow 1884. **3.** All the Extremities of Household Expence, Furniture, and i. Equipage STEELE.

II. †**1.** Unaccustomed, unusual –1665. †**2.** Unused to a thing; inexperienced –1598.

B. *sb.* An insolent person 1595.

Out, i. *John* II. i. 122.

Hence **I·nsolent-ly** *adv.*, †**-ness.**

Insolidity (insoli·dĭti). ?*Obs.* 1578. [f. IN-^{3} + SOLIDITY. Cf. Fr. †*insolidité* (XV).] Absence of solidity; want of firmness or stability; frailty, flimsiness, weakness.

Insolubility (insǫliubi·lĭti). 1620. [– late L. *insolubilitas*; partly f. IN-^{3} + SOLUBILITY.] The quality of being insoluble. †**1.** Indissolubility. BRENT. **2.** Incapability of being solved; also, an insoluble problem 1837. **3.** Incapability of being dissolved in a liquid 1791.

1. The i. of Marriage 1620. **2.** The i. of this problem 1837.

Insoluble (insǫ·liub'l), *a.* (*sb.*) ME. [– (O)Fr. *insoluble* or L. *insolubilis*; see IN-^{3}, SOLUBLE.] **1.** That cannot be dissolved, undone, or loosed; indissoluble. Now *rare.* †**b.** Of arguments: Irrefragable (*rare*) –1676. **2.** That cannot be solved or explained, as a difficulty, problem, etc.; unsolvable ME. **3.** Incapable of being dissolved in a liquid 1713. **4.** *sb.* Something insoluble; a difficulty or problem that cannot be solved or explained ME.

1. Like a strong and i. wall P. HOLLAND. **2.** An i. question concerning the origin of evil WARBURTON. **3.** The i. salts 1857. Hence **Inso·lubleness. Inso·lubly** *adv.*

Insolvable (insǫ·lvăb'l), *a.* 1652. [f. IN-^{3} + SOLVABLE. Cf. Fr. *insolvable* (XV).] **1.** = INSOLUBLE *a.* †**2.** Of a debt: 'That cannot be paid' (J.) 1755. Hence **Insolvabi·lity, Inso·lvableness. Inso·lvably** *adv.*

Insolvency (insǫ·lvĕnsi). 1660. [f. INSOLVENT *a.*; see -ENCY.] The condition of being insolvent; the fact of being unable to pay one's debts or discharge one's liabilities; an instance of this. Also *transf.* and *fig.*

Prisoners..who intended to take the Benefit of the Act of I. 1725.

Insolvent (insǫ·lvĕnt), *a.* (*sb.*) 1591. [f. IN-^{3} + SOLVENT *a.*] Not solvent. **1.** Unable to pay one's debts or discharge one's liabilities; bankrupt. †**2.** Not able to be cashed or realized –1728. **3.** Pertaining or relating to insolvents or insolvency 1837. **4.** *sb.* An insolvent debtor 1725.

1. The cruel treatment of the i. debtors of the state GIBBON. **3.** He had been through the I. Court THACKERAY. **4.** An i. as distinguished from a bankrupt, was an i. who was not a trader; for originally only a trader could be made bankrupt WHARTON.

‖**Insomnia** (insǫ·mniă). 1758. [– L. *insomnia*, f. *insomnis* sleepless, f. *in-* IN-^{3} + *somnus* sleep + -IA^1.] Inability to sleep; sleeplessness. Also †**Insomnie** 1623, †**Insomnium** 1694–1856.

Insomnious (insǫ·mniəs), *a.* *rare.* 1658. [f. *insomnia* (or earlier †*insomnie*) + -OUS.] Affected with insomnia; sleepless.

Insomnolence (insǫ·mnŏlĕns). 1822. [IN-^{3}.] Insomnia. So **Inso·mnolency** 1843, **Inso·mnolent** *a.* 1840. (All *rare*).

Insomuch (insŏmʊ·tʃ), *adv.* ME. [transl. OFr. *en tant* (*que*); at first alternative to INASMUCH, but later differentiated.] **1.** *absol.* So much, so far. **2.** *Insomuch as.* **a.** Inasmuch as, seeing that, since 1485. †**b.** = sense 3. –1658. **c.** To such an extent as, so as 1651. **3.** *Insomuch that*: To such an extent that, so that. (The most usual construction.) †**4.** With ellipsis of *as*: = 2 a. –1605.

2. a. In so much as I am not French by birth, but born..in the city of Marseilles CAXTON. **c.** In so much and in so far as they are susceptible of becoming [etc.] BENTHAM. **3.** The rain fell in torrents, i. that..the soldiers were often ankle-deep in water ALISON. **4.** *A.Y.L.* V. ii. 60.

Insonorous (insŏnō^ə·rəs), *a.* *rare.* 1795. [IN-^{3}.] Not sonorous; giving a dull or muffled sound.

Insooth, *adv.*, for *in sooth*; see SOOTH *sb.*

Insorb (insǭ·ɹb), *v.* *rare.* 1878. [app. alt. f. ABSORB by prefix-substitution; but cf. med.L. *insorbēre* imbibe (XIV).] *trans.* To absorb *into.* So **Inso·rbent** *a.* absorbent 1756.

‖**Insouciance** (ęn̄susya·n̄s, *occas.* insū·siăns). 1799. [Fr., f. next; see -ANCE.] Carelessness, indifference, unconcern.

‖**Insouciant** (insū·siănt, Fr. ęn̄susyan̄). 1829. [Fr., f. *in-* IN-^{3} + *souciant*, pr. pple. of *soucier* care.] Careless, indifferent, unconcerned.

Insoul, var. of ENSOUL *v.*

Inspan (inspæ·n), *v.* *S.Afr.* 1850. [– Du. *inspannen* put horses to, f. *in* IN-^{2} + *spannen* stretch, bend; cf. OUTSPAN *v.*] *trans.* To yoke (horses, oxen, etc.) in a team to a vehicle; to harness (a wagon).

†**I·nspect,** *sb.* 1489. [app. – L. *inspectus* looking at, inspection, examination, f. as next.] The act of looking into a matter; inspection, examination –1746.

Inspect (inspe·kt), *v.* 1623. [– *inspect-*, pa. ppl. stem of L. *inspicere*, f. *in-* IN-^{2} + *specere* look, or – L. frequent. *inspectare.*] **1.** *trans.* To look carefully into; to view closely and critically; to examine; now *spec.* to investigate or oversee officially. †**2.** *intr.* To look closely or carefully; to examine *into* or *among* –1799.

1. He inspected nature with the close eye of a naturalist D'ISRAELI. **2.** That..you would please to i. among your father's papers SWIFT.

Inspection (inspe·kʃən). ME. [– (O)Fr. *inspection* – L. *inspectio*, f. as prec.; see -ION.] **1.** The action of inspecting or looking narrowly into; careful scrutiny or survey; close examination; *spec.* official investigation or oversight. †**2.** Insight, perception –1709. †**3.** A plan of a piece of ground; etc. which has been inspected; a design, survey, view –1795.

1. The I. of the Intrails of Beasts, to learn the will of Heaven BOYLE. *Trial by I.*, a mode of trial in which some point or issue, being evidently the object of sense, was decided by the judges of the Court upon the evidence of their own senses. Hence **Inspe·ctional** *a.* of, pertaining or relating to i.; *spec.* that can be read or understood at sight.

Inspective (inspe·ktiv), *a.* 1609. [– late L. *inspectivus* (Jerome), f. as prec.; see -IVE.] **1.** Given to inspection; watchful, attentive 1684. †**2.** Concerned with investigation; theoretical –1660.

Inspector (inspe·ktəɹ). 1602. [– L. *inspector*, f. as prec.; see -OR 2.] **1.** One who inspects or looks carefully at or into; an overseer, a superintendent; *spec.* an officer appointed to examine into, and supervise or report upon, the working of some department or institution, or the due observance of certain laws and regulations, as *I. of schools, of weights and measures, of mines*, etc. **b.** One who looks *into* something for information, from curiosity, etc. 1667. **c.** An officer of police ranking next below a superintendent and above a sergeant 1840. **2.** *Gr. Antiq.* = EPOPT 1818. **3. Inspector-General:** An officer at the head of a system of inspection, having under him a body of inspectors 1702. Hence **Inspe·ctoral** *a.*

Inspectorate (inspe·ktŏrĕt). 1762. [f. prec.; see -ATE^1.] **1. a.** The office or function of an inspector; supervision by inspectors. **b.** A body or staff of inspectors. Also *attrib.* **2.** A district under official inspection 1853.

Inspectorial (inspektō^ə·riăl), *a.* 1753. [f. INSPECTOR + -IAL; see -ORIAL.] Of, pertaining or belonging to inspectors; having the rank or position of an inspector.

Inspectorship (inspe·ktəɹʃip). 1753. [f. as prec. + -SHIP.] The office or position of an inspector; inspectorate.

Inspectress (inspe·ktrĕs). 1785. [f. INSPECTOR + -ESS^1.] A female inspector.

†**Inspe·rge,** *v.* 1599. [– L. *inspergere* sprinkle on or in, f. *in-* IN-^{2} + *spargere* scatter, sprinkle.] *trans.* To sprinkle on; to scatter on or in –1683.

†**Inspe·rse,** *v.* *rare.* 1577. [– *inspers-*, pa. ppl. stem of L. *inspergere*; see prec.] = prec. –1721. So †**Inspe·rsion,** the action of sprinkling on; that which is sprinkled on 1568.

‖**Inspeximus** (inspe·ksimŏs). 1628. [L., 'we have inspected'; the first word in recital of the inspection of charters, etc.] *Law.* A charter in which the grantor avouches to have inspected an earlier charter which he recites and confirms. Also *attrib.*

Insphere, -spheare, var. of ENSPHERE *v.*

Inspinne, var. of INCHPIN (sense 1).

Inspirable (inspəi^ə·răb'l), *a.* 1656. [f. INSPIRE *v.* + -ABLE.] Capable of being inspired (see the vb.).

†**Inspirate** (i·nspire^{i}t), *v.* 1615. [– *inspirat-*, pa. ppl. stem of L. *inspirare*; see INSPIRE *v.*, -ATE^3.] = INSPIRE *v.* –1810.

Inspiration (inspirē^i·ʃən). ME. [– (O)Fr. *inspiration* – late L. *inspiratio*, f. as prec.; see -ION.]

I. Lit. senses. †**1.** The action of blowing on or into (*rare*) –1710. **2.** The action, or an act, of inhaling; the drawing in of the breath into the lungs in respiration. (Opp. to EXPIRATION.) 1564. Also *transf.*

2. In I. the lungs are passive 1849.

II. Fig. senses. **1.** The action of inspiring; the fact or condition of being inspired; a breathing or infusion into the mind or soul. **a.** *spec.* (*Theol.*, etc.) A special immediate action or influence of the Spirit of God (or of some divine or supernatural being) upon the human mind or soul; said *esp.* of that divine influence under which the books of the Bible are held to have been written ME. **b.** *gen.* A breathing in of some idea, purpose, etc. into the mind; the suggestion of some feeling or impulse, esp. of an exalted kind SHAKS. **c.** The prompting (from some influential quarter) of the utterance or publication of particular views or information on some public matter 1880. **2.** *transf.* Something inspired; an inspired utterance or product 1819; an inspiring principle 1865.

1. a. *Verbal i.* of the Bible, the view according to which every word written was dictated by the Spirit of God. *Plenary i.*, the view that the inspiration of the writers extends to all subjects treated of, so that all their statements are to be received as infallibly true. The Prophets who teach us by diuine i. BIBLE *Transl. Pref.* 3. **b.** There is i. in numbers, in men acting at once and together MOZLEY. **2.** Whatever motive your own souls supply As i. BROWNING. Hence **Inspira·tional** *a.* of or pertaining to i.; inspired; inspiring.

Inspira·tionist. 1846. [f. prec. + -IST.] A believer in a theory of inspiration; as *plenary i.*, a believer in plenary inspiration.

Inspirator (i·nspireⁱtəɹ). 1624. [– late L. *inspirator* (see INSPIRATE *v.*, -OR 2); in sense 2 f. INSPIRE + -ATOR; cf. *respirator.*] †**1.** One who or that which inspires –1848. **2. a.** A kind of injector in a steam-engine 1890. **b.** A kind of respirator 1898.

Inspiratory (inspəiᵊ·rătəri, i·nspireⁱtəri), *a.* 1773. [f. INSPIRATE *v.* + -ORY².] Belonging to inspiration or inhalation; serving to draw in the air in respiration.

Inspire (inspəiᵊ·ɹ), *v.* ME. [– (O)Fr. *inspirer* – L. *inspirare*, f. *in-* IN-² + *spirare* breathe.]

I. Lit. senses. **1.** *trans.* To breathe or blow upon or into. *Obs.* or *arch.* †Also *intr.* †**2.** *trans.* To blow or breathe (air, etc.) upon or into –1697. **b.** To breathe (life, a soul) *in* or *into*. In later use, *fig.* ME. **3.** *trans.* To take into the lungs by breathing, inhale. (Opp. to EXPIRE.) 1528. **b.** *intr.* or *absol.* To draw in the breath 1661.

1. Descend, ye Nine!..The breathing instruments i. POPE. **2.** MILT. *P.L.* IV. 804. **3.** The Air we walk in and i. 1761.

II. Fig. senses. **1.** *trans.* To infuse some thought or feeling into (a person, etc.), as if by breathing; to animate by some mental or spiritual influence. **a.** *spec.* (*Theol.*, etc.) To influence or actuate by special divine or supernatural agency; used esp. in reference to the prophets, apostles, and Scripture writers ME. **b.** *gen.* To influence, animate, or actuate (a person) *with* a feeling, idea, impulse, etc. Also said of the feeling, influence, etc. ME. **2.** To breathe in or infuse (a feeling, thought, principle, etc.) into the mind or soul ME. Also *absol.* **3.** *transf. trans.* To suggest or prompt the utterance of particular views or information on some public matter, or to prompt a speaker or writer to such utterance 1883.

1. a. As god inspired hir forth sho went 1450. **b.** Poverty inspires necessity with daring JOWETT. What zeale, what furie, hath inspir'd thee now? SHAKS. **2.** Al scripture of God ynspyrid is profitable to teche WYCLIF. He inspired terror to the enemy and a just confidence to the troops GIBBON. Hence **Inspi·rer**, one who or that which inspires. **Inspi·ringly** *adv.*

Inspired (inspəiᵊ·ɹd), *ppl. a.* 1450. [f. prec. + -ED¹.] **1.** Blown on or into; inflated. *Obs.* or *arch.* 1649. **2.** Breathed in; inhaled. (Opp. to *expired.*) 1649. **3.** Actuated or animated by divine or supernatural influence 1667. **4.** Infused or communicated by divine or supernatural power; having the character of inspiration 1450. **5.** *transf.* Prompted by, or emanating from, an influential (but unavowed) source 1887.

3. Th' inspir'd Castalian Spring MILT. *P.L.* IV. 273. **4.** These abilities, wheresoever they be found, are the i. guift of God MILT. **5.** An i. paragraph 1887, journal 1897. Hence **Inspi·redly** *adv.* by or as by inspiration.

Inspirit (inspi·rit), *v.* 1610. [f. IN-² + SPIRIT *sb.*] **1.** *trans.* To put spirit, life, or energy into; to animate; to encourage; to incite (*to*, or *to do* something). **2.** To fill with, or cause to be possessed by, a spirit or supernatural being 1675.

1. To i. the doubtful courage of his soldiers SCOTT.

†**Inspi·ssate**, *ppl. a.* 1603. [– late L. *inspissatus*, pa. pple. of *inspissare*; see next, -ATE².] Inspissated, thickened –1720.

Inspissate (inspi·seⁱt, i·nspiseⁱt), *v.* 1626. [– *inspissat-*, pa. ppl. stem of late L. *inspissare*, f. *in-* IN-² + *spissus* thick, dense; see -ATE³.] **1.** *trans.* To thicken, condense. Also *fig.* **2.** *intr.* To become thick or dense 1755.

1. Pitch is tar inspissated BP. BERKELEY.

Inspissation (inspiseⁱ·ʃən). 1603. [f. INSPISSATE *v.* + -ION. Cf. med.L. *inspissatio* thickening (XIII).] The action of making, or process of becoming, thick or dense; thickening, condensation; an instance of this. So **Inspissative** *a.*, producing inspissation 1425.

Instability (instăbi·lĭti). ME. [– Fr. *instabilité* – L. *instabilitas, -tat-*, f. *instabilis*; see next, -ITY.] The quality of being unstable; lack of stability in regard to position, condition, or moral qualities; want of steadiness, fixity, or firmness of purpose or character. With *an* and *pl.*, an instance of this.

Some lamentyng the instabilitee of the Englishe people, iudged theim to be spotted with perpetuall infamie HALL.

Instable (instēⁱ·b'l), *a.* Now *rare.* 1483. [– (O)Fr. *instable* or L. *instabilis*, f. *in-* IN-³ + *stabilis* STABLE *a.* In mod. use f. STABLE *a.*] Not stable; lacking in stability; unstable. Hence †**Insta·bleness**, instability 1460.

Install (instǭ·l), *v.* Also **instal.** 1483. [– med.L. *installare*, f. *in-* IN-² + *stallum* STALL *sb.*¹ Cf. (O)Fr. *installer.*] **1.** *trans.* To invest with an office or dignity by seating in a stall or official seat. Hence, To instate in an office, rank, etc. with the customary ceremonies or formalities. **b.** To place in any office or position, esp. one of dignity; to establish in any place or condition 1647. **2.** To place (an apparatus, a system of lighting, heating, or the like) in position for service or use 1867.

1. The Bishop of Ostia..consecrates and instals the Pope HOWELL. **b.** What station charms thee? I'll i. thee there YOUNG. Hence **Insta·llant, -er.**

Installation (instǫlēⁱ·ʃən). 1606. [– med.L. *installatio*, f. *installare*; see prec., -ION. Cf. (O)Fr. *installation.*] **1.** The action of installing or fact of being installed; the ceremony of formally inducting (a person) into an ecclesiastical dignity, an order of knighthood, or an official position; hence, formal establishment in any office or position. **2.** The action of setting up or fixing in position for service or use (machinery, apparatus, etc.); a mechanical apparatus set up or put in position for use; *spec.* used to include all the necessary plant, materials, and work required to equip rooms or buildings with electric light 1882.

1. The ceremony of his [the Nizam's] i. MACAULAY.

Instalment¹, installment (instǭ·lmĕnt). 1589. [f. INSTALL *v.* + -MENT.] **1.** The action of installing or fact of being installed; installation. **b.** Establishment in any position, seat, or place 1646. †**2.** A place or seat wherein some one is installed (*rare*) –1610.

1. The instalement of this noble Duke, In the seate royall of this famous Ile SHAKS. **2.** Each faire I., Coate, and seu'rall Crest, With loyall Blazon, euermore be blest SHAKS.

Instalment² (instǭ·lmĕnt). Also **install-.** 1732. [alt. (prob. by assoc. with prec.) of earlier †*estallment*, aphetic †*stallment* (XV) – AFr. *estalement* (AL. (*e*)*stallamentum*, in- XIII), f. *estaler* fix (AL. *installare* (XIII) pay by instalments); see ESTALL *v.*] †**1.** The arrangement of the payment of a sum of money by fixed portions at fixed times –1775. **2.** 'The payment, or the time appointed for payment, of different portions of a sum of money, which, by agreement..is to be paid in parts, at certain stated times' (Tomlins) 1776. **3.** Each of several parts into which a sum payable is divided, in order to be paid at different fixed times; a part of a sum due paid in advance of the remainder 1776. Also *attrib.* (freq. in recent use).

3. *fig.* His conclusion may be accepted as a large i. of the truth H. SPENSER.

Instamp, obs. f. ENSTAMP.

Instance (i·nstăns), *sb.* ME. [– (O)Fr. *instance* – L. *instantia*, in schol.L. objection, example to the contrary (tr. Gr. ἔνστασις objection), f. *instans, instant-*, see INSTANT *a.*]

I. 1. Urgency in speech or action; urgent entreaty; earnestness; persistence. (*arch.* exc. in phr. *at the i. of.*) †**b.** Chiefly *pl.* An urgent entreaty, repeated solicitation –1862. †**2.** Impelling motive; cause –1665.

2. Tell him his Feares are shallow, without i. SHAKS.

II. Instant time. †**1.** A being present, presence; the present time –1597. †**2.** An instant; a moment –1674.

1. 2 *Hen. IV*, IV. i. 83. **2.** Those continued instances of time which flow into thousand yeares SIR T. BROWNE.

III. In Scholastic Logic, etc. †**1.** A case adduced in objection to or disproof of a universal assertion (= med.L. *instantia*, Gr. ἔνστασις) –1696. **2.** A fact or example brought forward in support of a general assertion or an argument, or in illustration of a general truth. Hence, a case, an illustrative example. Also, in broader sense, a case occurring, a recurring occasion. 1586. †**b.** A detail, circumstance –1745. †**3.** Something which proves or indicates; a proof, evidence; a sign, token, mark –1791.

1. To conclude upon an enumeration of particulars, without i. contradictory, is no conclusion, but a conjecture BACON. **2.** Noy..is an i. that mere knowledge is not true wisdom D'ISRAELI. Phr. †*To make* or *give i.* (*in*): = INSTANCE *v.* 2. 1614. *For i.*: for example 1657. **3.** SHAKS. *Lucr.* 1511.

IV. In legal use, etc. [From L. *instantia* in Ulpian.] **1.** A process or proceeding in a court of justice, a suit 1661. **2.** Hence, *In the first i.*: as the first step in proceeding; in the first place 1676.

1. *Court of first i.*, court of primary jurisdiction; The loser is seldom satisfied with the decision of a Court of first i. 1865. *I. court*, a branch of the former Admiralty Court, having jurisdiction in cases of private injuries to private rights occurring at sea or closely connected with maritime subjects and in contracts of a maritime nature 1802. **2.** The penalty is in the first i., corrective not penal 1850.

Instance (i·nstăns), *v.* late ME. [f. prec. sb.] †**1.** *trans.* To urge, entreat urgently, importune –1736. **2.** *intr.* To cite an instance, to adduce an example in illustration or proof. Const. *in* (the example adduced). Now *rare.* 1601. †**b.** Of a thing: To be exemplified 1667. **3.** *trans.* To illustrate, prove, or show, by means of an instance; to exemplify. Now *rare.* 1608. **4.** To cite as an instance or example. In imper. = 'Take as an instance'; cf. WITNESS. 1622.

2. It would be needless to i. in sheep which constantly flock together G. WHITE. **b.** This story doth not only i. in kingdoms, but in families too JER. TAYLOR. **4.** I may i. olive oil, which is mischievous to all plants JOWETT.

Instancy (i·nstănsi). 1515. [– L. *instantia*; see INSTANCE *sb.*, -ANCY.] **1.** The quality of being instant; urgency, earnestness, solicitation; pressure, pressing nature. **2.** Imminence (*rare*) 1658. **3.** Instantaneity (*rare*) 1851. †**4.** = INSTANCE III. 2. JACKSON.

1. Those heauenly precepts, which our Lord and Sauiour with so great instancie gaue as concerning peace and vnitie HOOKER.

Instant (i·nstănt), *sb.* ME. [After med.L. *instans* (sc. *tempus*) present moment of time; see next.] **1.** The time now present, or regarded as present; hence, point of time, moment 1500. **2.** An infinitely short space of time; a moment ME. †**3.** = INSTANCE *sb.* III. 2. JEWEL. †**4.** = INSTANCE *sb.* I. 1. P. HOLLAND.

1. Of all the extent of time, onely the i. is that which we can call ours FULLER. **2.** He was not an i. too soon 1891. Phr. *In an i.*, *on* (†*upon*, †*in*) *the i.*, etc. *The i.*, ellipt. = 'the very moment that', 'as soon as ever'.

Instant (i·nstănt), *a.* (*adv.*) 1477. [– (O)Fr. *instant* assiduous, at hand – L. *instans, instant-*, pr. pple. of *instare* be present or at hand, apply oneself to, f. *in-* IN-² + STARE stand; see -ANT.] **1.** Pressing, urgent; importunate. *Obs.* or *arch.* **2.** Now (or then) present, existing, or happening (*arch.*) 1527. **b.** Said of the current calendar month; now ellipt. as in *the* 10*th instant.* Abbrev. *inst.* 1547. **3.** Close at hand, imminent 1520. **4.** Following immediately 1596. **5.** *adv.* (*poet.*) Instantly, at once 1602.

1. They were i. with loud voyces, and required that he might be crucified BIBLE (Genev.) *Luke* 23:23. He has i. need of you 1856. **2. b.** The 20 or 21 of that i. 1583. The 3d of this i. March 1796. **3.** The abrupt Fate's footstep i. now BROWNING. **4.** The shame it selfe doth speake For i. remedy *Lear* I. iv. 268. **5.** You my sinnewes, grow not i. Old *Haml.* I. v. 94.

Instantaneous (instăntēⁱ·niəs), *a.* 1651. [f. med.L. *instantaneus* (f. L. *instans, instant-* (see prec.), after eccl.L. *momentaneus*) + -OUS.] **1.** Occurring or operating in an instant; done without any perceptible lapse of time. **2.** Existing at or pertaining to some particular instant. Chiefly in *Dynamics*, as *i. axis*, *i. centre of rotation* 1837.

1. Justification is a continued Act, and not any I. Act BAXTER. The motion of electricity..appears to be i. IMISON. Hence **Instantane·ity, Instanta·neousness. Instanta·neously** *adv.* 1644.

‖**Instanter** (instæ·ntəɹ), *adv.* 1688. [L. adv.] Immediately, forthwith, at once. (Orig. a law term, but now chiefly emphatic for *instantly*.)

He was at your service *instanter* 1883.

Insta·ntial, *a. rare.* 1647. [f. L. *instantia* INSTANCE *sb.* + -AL¹.] Of, pertaining to, or furnishing an instance or instances.

Instantly (i·nstăntli), *adv.* 1477. [f. INSTANT *a.* + -LY².] **1.** Urgently, with importunity (*arch.*). †**2.** At this or that very moment; now, just now, just –1632. **3.** In a moment; forthwith, at once 1552. **b.** *conjunctively.* The moment that, as soon as 1793. **4.** Immediately (in position). RUSKIN.

1. They..besought him i. TINDALE *Luke* 7:4. **3. b.** He ran across the grass i. he perceived his mother THACKERAY.

Instar (instā·ɹ), *v.* 1592. [f. IN-¹, EN-¹ + STAR *sb.*¹ Cf. med.L. *instellare* ornament with stars.] **1.** *trans.* To set as a star; to make a star of. **2.** To set or adorn with or as with stars 1652.

1. Our heart is high instarr'd in brighter spheres FORD.

Instate (instēⁱ·t), *v.* Also †**en-.** 1603. [f. IN-¹ + STATE *sb.* Cf. earlier *reinstate.*] **1.** *trans.* To put (a person) into a certain state or condition; to install, establish. Const. *in* (*into, to*). 1613. †**2.** To endow or invest (a person) *with* –1659.

1. It will not be my fault if she is not at once instated in her rights 1864. **2.** *Meas. for M.* v. i. 429. Hence **Insta·tement** (now *rare*), instating; establishment.

†**Instau·rate,** *v.* 1583. [– *instaurat-*; see next, -ATE³.] *trans.* = INSTORE *v.* –1666.

Instauration (instǫrēⁱ·ʃən). 1603. [– L. *instauratio*, f. *instaurat-*, pa. ppl. stem of *instaurare* restore; see IN-¹, -ION.] **1.** The action of restoring or repairing; renovation, renewal. †**2.** Institution, founding, establishment –1778.

1. His [Bacon's] grand i. of the sciences 1761. **2.** The i. and advancement of states BP. LOWTH.

Instaurator (i·nstǫrēⁱtəɹ). 1660. [– late L. *instaurator*, f. as prec.; see -OR 2.] **a.** One who restores or renews. **b.** A founder.

The great i. of all knowledge, Bacon M. PATTISON.

Instead (inste·d), *phrasal comb.* ME. [The two words *in stead* = 'in place'; before 1620 usu. written separately, but after *c*1640 conjunctly. See STEAD *sb.* Phr. *in* (*the*) *stead of*, after OFr. *en* (now *au*) *lieu de*, which continued L. (*in*) *loco* with gen., 'in the condition or relation (of)'.] **1.** Phr. *Instead of*, †*in stead of*: In place of, in lieu of, in room of; for, in substitution for. Also used ellipt. bef. a prep., adv., adj., or phrase. **2.** Without *of*: In its stead, in place of the thing mentioned; as a substitute 1667.

1. Catholicon the drugge, that it is in stead of all purges BIBLE *Transl. Pref.* 3. I. of money he gave promises GOLDSM. *ellipt.* I found the patient worse i. of better (*mod.*). **2.** To rase Quite out thir Native Language, and i. To sow a jangling noise of words unknown MILT.

Insteep (instī·p), *v.* Now *rare.* 1599. [f. IN-¹ + STEEP *v.*, after L. *immergere.*] *trans.* To immerse; to steep or soak *in*; to imbrue.

Where in gore he lay insteeped *Hen. V*, IV. vi. 12.

Instep (i·nstep). 1530. [Earlier forms *instep(pe*, also *instoppe*, *-stup*, *-stip*, prob. pointing to adoption of a foreign word; cf. WFris. *ynstap* opening in a shoe for the insertion of the foot.] **1.** The upper surface of the human foot between the toes and the ankle. **2.** That part of the hind-leg of a horse which extends from the hock to the pastern-joint. Also the corresponding parts in birds, etc. 1720. **3.** That part of a shoe, stocking, etc. fitting or covering the instep 1599. **4.** A part of a hill, a tree trunk, etc., resembling the human instep in shape or position 1681.

Instigate (i·nstigeⁱt), *v.* Pa. pple. **-ated;** also †**-at.** 1542. [– *instigat-*, pa. ppl. stem of L. *instigare*, f. *in-* IN-² + *stigare* prick, incite; see -ATE³.] **1.** *trans.* To spur, urge on; to stir up, stimulate, incite (now mostly to something evil). **2.** To stir up, foment, provoke 1852.

1. To i. Princes to warre upon one another HOBBES. **2.** What he and they called levying war was, in truth, no better than instigating murder THACKERAY. Hence **I·nstigatingly** *adv.* **I·nstigative** *a.* tending to i.; stimulative 1642. **I·nstigator** 1598. **Instiga·trix** 1611.

Instigation (instigēⁱ·ʃən). ME. [– (O)Fr. *instigation* or L. *instigatio*, f. as prec.; see -ION.] The action of instigating or goading; incitement, stimulation; an incentive, stimulus, spur.

That this foul deed was done by the i...of his step-mother FREEMAN.

Instil, instill (insti·l), *v.* 1533. [– L. *instillare*, f. *in-* IN-² + *stillare*, f. *stilla* drop. Cf. DISTIL.] **1.** *trans.* To put in by drops; to introduce in small quantities 1547. **2.** To introduce little by little into the mind, soul, heart, etc.; to cause to enter by degrees; to infuse gradually; to insinuate 1533. †**b.** To teach or urge stealthily –1807. †**3.** To imbue *with.* MILT.

1. Michael..from the Well of Life three drops instill'd MILT. *P.L.* XI. 416. **2.** How hast thou instill'd Thy malice into thousands MILT. *P.L.* VI. 269. Hence **I·nstillator, Insti·ller,** one who instils or infuses. **Insti·lment,** the action of instilling.

Instillation (instilēⁱ·ʃən). 1540. [– L. *instillatio*, f. *instillat-*, pa. ppl. stem of *instillare*; see prec., -ION.] The action of instilling; that which is instilled.

†**Insti·mulate,** *v.* 1570. [– *instimulat-*, pa. ppl. stem of L. *instimulare*; see IN-², STIMULATE.] *trans.* To incite, instigate, stimulate –1670. Hence †**Instimula·tion.**

Instinct (i·nstiŋkt), *sb.* ME. [– L. *instinctus* instigation, impulse, f. pa. ppl. stem of *instinguere* incite, impel, f. *in-* IN-² + *stinguere* prick.] †**1.** Instigation; impulse; prompting –1730. **2.** Innate impulse; natural or spontaneous tendency or inclination. In mod. use assoc. w. sense 3. 1568. **3.** *spec.* An innate propensity in organized beings (esp. in the lower animals), varying with the species, and manifesting itself in acts which appear to be rational, but are performed without conscious adaptation of means to ends. Also, the faculty supposed to be involved in this operation. 1596. **b.** Any faculty acting like animal instinct; intuition; unconscious dexterity or skill 1597.

2. There is a natural i. in all heavy bodies to lean and press upon the lowest parts 1726. Our love of the Alps is..a Teutonic i. SYMONDS. Edward was by i. a lawgiver STUBBS. **3.** The operation of i. is more sure and simple than that of reason GIBBON. The very essence of an i. is that it is followed independently of reason DARWIN. **b.** The true i. of genius HAMERTON.

Instinct (insti·ŋkt), *ppl. a.* Usu. const. as *pa. pple.* 1538. [– L. *instinctus*, pa. pple. of *instinguere*; see prec.] †**1.** Implanted naturally; innate –1628. †**2.** Impelled, moved, excited, inflamed, animated –1720. **3.** In recent use: Imbued or charged *with* something, as a moving or animating force or principle 1797.

2. Forth rush'd..The Chariot..undrawn, It self i. with Spirit MILT. *P.L.* VI. 752. **3.** I. with life to its finger-ends CARLYLE.

†**Insti·nct,** *v.* 1538. [– *instinct-*, pa. ppl. stem of L. *instinguere*; see prec.] **1.** *trans.* To instigate, prompt; impel internally –1694. **2.** To implant naturally or as an instinct; to infuse as an animating principle –1732.

†**Insti·nction.** 1440. [– Fr. †*instinction* (XV) or late L. *instinctio*, f. as prec.; see -ION.] **1.** Instigation; prompting; inspiration –1670. **2.** Innate impulse; instinct –1753.

Instinctive (insti·ŋktiv), *a.* (*adv.*) 1649. [f. INSTINCT *sb.* + -IVE.] Of the nature of instinct; operating by or resulting from innate prompting. **b.** *poet.* as *adv.* 1715.

I. intimations of the death of some absent friends BP. HALL. The i. fondness natural to parents 1718. The alternation of the lower limbs is i. in man BAIN. Hence **Insti·nctively** *adv.* in an i. manner; by instinct 1610.

Instincti·vity. [f. prec. + -ITY.] The quality of being instinctive; proneness to instinctive action. COLERIDGE.

Instipulate (insti·piŭlĕt), *a.* 1847. [f. IN-³ + STIPULATE *a.*] *Bot.* Not stipulate, having no stipules, exstipulate.

Institor (i·nstitǫɹ). 1657. [– L. *institor*, f. *instit-*, pa. ppl. stem of *insistere* step upon, follow, pursue; see -OR 2.] A factor or agent; a broker; a retailer, huckster, vendor. (Chiefly in *Rom.* and *Sc. Law.*) So **Insti·torial** *a.* of or pertaining to an i.

Institute (i·nstitiūt), *sb.*¹ 1520. [– L. *institutum* design, ordinance, precept, subst. use of n. of pa. pple. of *instituere* establish, ordain, arrange, teach, f. *in-* IN-² + *statuere* set up. In sense 3 corresp. to Fr. *institute, -s*, – L. *instituta* pl., also *institutiones* (= INSTITUTION 5), both in Cicero.] †**1.** Purpose, design –1670. **2.** Something instituted; an established law, custom, usage, or organization; an institution 1546. †**b.** The act of instituting –1657. **3.** A principle or element of instruction; usu. in *pl.*, a digest of the elements of a subject, esp. of jurisprudence. (So in Fr.) 1579. **4.** A society or organization instituted to promote literature, science, art, education, or the like; also, the building in which such work is carried on. Often specialized as *Literary, Philosophical, Mechanics' I.* 1829.

2. The institutes and customs of civil life MILT. **b.** Water, sanctify'd by Christ's i. MILT. **3.** *Institutes of Justinian* (*Institutiones Justiniani*), an elementary treatise on Roman Law, compiled by order of the Emperor Justinian in A.D. 533. *Institutes of medicine*, the statement of the principles on which medicine is based. **4.** The title of Member of the I. is the highest distinction to which a Frenchman of culture can aspire 1889.

I·nstitute, *sb.*² 1681. [– L. *institutus*, pa. pple. of *instituere*; see prec. Cf. INSTITUTE *v.* 2 b.] *Rom.* and *Sc. Law.* The person to whom an estate is first given in a testament or destination.

†**I·nstitute,** *ppl. a.* ME. [– AFr. *institut* (Britton) – L. *institutus*; see prec.] Instituted –1671.

Institute (i·nstitiūt), *v.* ME. [– *institut-*, pa. ppl. stem of L. *instituere*; see INSTITUTE *sb.*¹] **1.** *trans.* **a.** To set up, establish, found, ordain; to introduce, bring into use or practice 1483. †**b.** To order, arrange, put into form, frame –1745. **c.** To set on foot, initiate, start (an inquiry, etc.) 1797. **2.** To establish in an office, charge, or position; to appoint; now only, to place in a spiritual charge. Const. *to, into* (*in*), or *absol.* ME. **b.** *Rom. Law.* To appoint as heir or executor 1590. †**3.** To ground or establish in principles; to train, educate, instruct –1831.

1. The artists have instituted a yearly exhibition of pictures and statues JOHNSON. **c.** Mythological comparisons instituted by scholars MAX-MÜLLER. **2.** Cosin of Yorke, we i. your Grace To be our Regent in these parts of France SHAKS. Young.. was instituted to the united vicarages of St. Peter and St. Mary MASSON. **3.** Instituted..in all the learning of Greece and Rome MIDDLETON. Hence **I·nstituter** = INSTITUTOR.

Institution (institiū·ʃən). late ME. [–(O)Fr. *institution* – L. *institutio*, f. as prec.; see -ION.] **1.** The action of instituting or establishing; foundation; ordainment; the fact of being instituted 1450. **b.** *spec.* The establishment or ordination of a sacrament of the Christian Church, esp. of the Eucharist, by Christ. Hence, that part of the office of Baptism, and of the prayer of consecration in the Eucharist, which consists in reciting the words used in institution (more fully *words, commemoration*, or *recital of i.*) 1538. †**2.** The giving of form or order to a thing; orderly arrangement; regulation. **b.** System; constitution. –1821. **3.** Establishment in a charge or position. **a.** *Eccl.* In Episcopal churches, the establishment of a clergyman in the office of the cure of souls, by the bishop or his commissary. In the Church of England, the investment of the presentee to a living with the spiritual part of his benefice. ME. **b.** *Rom. Law.* The appointment of an heir 1880. †**4.** Training, instruction, education, teaching –1790. †**5.** Usu. in *pl.* **a.** Elements of instruction; first principles. **b.** An elementary treatise; = INSTITUTE *sb.*¹ 3. –1800. **6.** An established law, custom, usage, practice, organization, or other element in the political or social life of a people 1551. **b.** *colloq.* A well-established or familiar practice or object 1839. **7.** An establishment, organization, or association, instituted for the promotion of some object, esp. one of public utility, religious, charitable, educational, etc. The name is often popularly applied to the building appropriated to the work of a benevolent or educational institution. 1707. **b.** Often = INSTITUTE *sb.*¹ 4. 1800.

1. The i. of coined money ADAM SMITH. **3. a.** The i. by the bishop enables the clerk..to enter into his parsonage-house and take his tithes or ecclesiastical dues; but previous to induction he cannot lease them 1845. **6.** The i. of property 1871. **b.** The pillory was a flourishing i. in those days THACKERAY. **7.** The testator leaves £10,000 in charitable legacies to various institutions 1900. **b.** The Royal I. of Great Britain (incorporated 1800); the Smithsonian I. at Washington, U.S. (1830), etc.

Institutional (institiū·ʃənăl), *a.* 1617. [f. prec. + -AL[1].] **1.** Of, pertaining to, or originated by institution; having the character of an institution; furnished with institutions. **b.** Of religion; Expressed by means of or taking shape in definite institutions, as a church, a hierarchy, sacramental ordinances. **2.** Dealing with or pertaining to legal institutes or the elements of a subject 1765. **3.** Of or pertaining to an organized society, or the building in which its work is carried on 1882.

3. The dull monotony of i. life 1896. Hence **Institu·tionalism,** the system of institutions; *spec.* the principles of institutional religion; the system of housing people in institutions. **Institu·tionalist,** one who writes on legal institutes, or on the elements of a science or art. **Institu·tionalize** *v.*, to render institutional; to bring up in an institution.

Institutionary (institiū·ʃənări), *a.* 1646. [f. as prec. + -ARY[1].] †**1.** Of or pertaining to instruction or elements of instruction; educational –1734. **2.** Of or pertaining to legal institutes 1734. **3.** Relating to ecclesiastical institution 1814. **4.** Of or pertaining to institutions 1882.

Institutive (i·nstitiūtiv), *a.* (*sb.*). 1627. [f. INSTITUTE *v.* + -IVE.] **1.** Having the quality of instituting; pertaining to the institution of something. †**2.** Characterized by being instituted –1651. †**3.** *sb.* A person or thing that institutes 1644.

2. An i. decencie MILT. Hence **I·nstitutively** *adv.*

Institutor (i·nstitiūtəɹ). 1546. [– L. *institutor*; see INSTITUTE *v.*, -OR 2.] **1.** One who institutes or establishes; a founder; an organizer. †**2.** An instructor –1822. **3.** *U.S.* In the American Episcopal Church: A bishop, or a presbyter acting for him, who institutes a minister into a parish or church 1804. So **I·nstitutress** 1786, **Institu·trix** 1706, a female i.

†**Insto·p,** *v.* [f. IN-[1] + STOP *v.* (sense 3 b). Cf. Du. *instoppen* cram, stuff in.] *trans.* To stop, close up. DRYDEN.

†**Insto·re,** *v.* Also **instaur(e.** ME. [– L. *instaurare*; see IN-[2], RESTORE. The form *instore*, general from earliest use, was assim. to the established *restore.*] **1.** *trans.* To restore, repair, renew –1563. **2.** To erect, establish, institute, commence –1450. **3.** To furnish, provide, supply; to store *with* (*of*) –1633.

Instra·tified, *ppl. a.* 1828. [IN *adv.*] 'Stratified within something else' (Webster).

†**Instru·ct,** *ppl. a.* 1440. [– L. *instructus*, pa. pple. of *instruere*; see next.] **1.** Educated, taught, informed –1671. **2.** Furnished or equipped *with* something –1615.

2. Neither ship i. with oars, Nor men CHAPMAN.

Instruct (instrɒ·kt), *v.* 1477. [– *instruct-*, pa. ppl. stem of L. *instruere* set up, furnish, fit out, teach, f. IN-[2] + *struere* pile up, build.]

I. 1. *trans.* To furnish with knowledge or information; to teach, educate 1526. †**b.** To teach (a thing) –1670. **2.** To apprise, inform concerning a particular fact or circumstance 1500; also †*absol.* **b.** *Eng. Law.* To give information as a client to a solicitor, or as a solicitor to a counsel; to authorize one to appear as advocate 1836. **3.** To furnish with authoritative directions as to action 1557. **b.** *U.S.* To direct (a representative) how to vote, etc. 1841.

1. If we be ignorant, they [the Scriptures] will i. vs BIBLE *Transl. Pref.* 3. A teacher to i. me in latin BORROW. **2.** Being instructed in the precise time of his Nativity, calculates his fortunes SIR T. HERBERT. **3.** And she, being before instructed of her mother, said, Giue me heere Iohn Baptists head in a charger *Matt.* 14:8. I instructed him to take two grains only of the Digitalis daily 1800.

II. †**1.** (Chiefly *poet.*) To put in order; to form; to 'inform'; to make ready, prepare, equip, furnish –1774. **2.** *Sc. Law.* To furnish (a statement) with evidence or proof; to vouch, verify; to prove clearly 1681.

Hence **Instru·cter,** one who instructs (now usu. INSTRUCTOR). **Instru·ctible** *a.*, (*rare*) open to instruction.

Instruction (instrɒ·kʃən). ME. [– (O)Fr. *instruction* – late L. *instructio*, f. as prec.; see -ION.] **1.** The action of instructing or teaching; the imparting of knowledge or skill; education; †information 1506. **2.** The knowledge or teaching imparted. With *an* and *pl.* An item of knowledge imparted; a precept, a lesson ME. †**3.** Information. With *an* and *pl.* An item of information imparted or acquired, an account, a narrative. –1655. **4.** A making known to a person what he is required to do; a direction, an order, a mandate. Now usu. *pl.* ME. **b.** Direction given to a solicitor or counsel 1734.

2. To profit by the instructions of the pulpit 1873. **4.** Some of the company had..secret i...to take hym MORE. Hence **Instru·ctional** *a.* of or pertaining to i. or teaching; conveying information.

Instructive (instrɒ·ktiv), *a.* 1611. [f. INSTRUCT *v.* + -IVE. Cf. (O)Fr. *instructif, -ive.*] Having the character or quality of instructing; conveying instruction.

Essays and Characters Ironicall and I. 1615 (*title*). Hence **Instru·ctive-ly** *adv.*, **-ness.**

Instructor (instrɒ·ktəɹ). 1460. [– L. *instructor* preparer, in med.L. teacher, f. *instruct-*; see INSTRUCT *v.*, -OR 2. The forms in *-our* (XV–XVI) may be after current contemp. analogies (see -OUR). In mod. use f. INSTRUCT *v.* + -OR 2.] One who instructs; a teacher. **b.** *spec.* In Amer. colleges: A college teacher inferior in rank to a professor. So **Instru·ctress,** †**-trice,** a female i.; also *fig.*

Instrument (i·nstrŭmĕnt), *sb.* ME. [– (O)Fr. *instrument* – L. *instrumentum*, f. *instruere*; see INSTRUCT *v.*, -MENT.] **1.** A thing with or through which something is done or effected; a means. **b.** A person made use of by another person or being, for the accomplishment of a purpose (cf. *tool*) ME. **2.** A tool, implement, weapon. (Now usu. dist. from a *tool*, as being used for more delicate work or for artistic or scientific purposes.) ME. †**b.** *collect.* Apparatus. (A Latinism.) MILT. **3.** *spec.* A contrivance for producing musical sounds ME. (in early 19th c. *spec.* the pianoforte). †**4.** A part of the body having a special function; an organ –1718. **5.** *Law.* A formal legal document whereby a right is created or confirmed, or a fact recorded; a formal writing of any kind, as an agreement, deed, charter, or record, drawn up and executed in technical form 1483.

1. The Gods are iust, and of our pleasant vices Make instruments to plague vs SHAKS. Among the Tartars..cattle are the instruments of commerce ADAM SMITH. **b.** God used him as an i. to reform his Church BRAMHALL. **2.** Threshing instruments 1611. Instruments of torture 1843. Mathematical instruments (*mod.*). **b.** Much i. of war MILT. *P.R.* III. 388. **3.** I am a mynstrell as thou seest here by myne instrumentes LD. BERNERS.

Instrument (i·nstrŭmĕnt), *v.* 1719. [f. prec. sb. Cf. Fr. *instrumenter.*] **1.** *Law.* **a.** To draw up an instrument (see prec. 5). **b.** *trans.* To petition by means of an instrument. **2.** *Mus.* To arrange or score (a piece of music) for instruments, esp. for an orchestra 1822.

Instrumental (instrŭme·ntăl). ME. [– (O)Fr. *instrumental* – med.L. *instrumentalis*; see INSTRUMENT *sb.*, -AL[1].]

A. *adj.* **1.** Of the nature of or serving as an instrument or means. **b.** Serving well for the purpose; useful; effective, efficient. Now *rare* or *Obs.* 1602. **2.** Of, pertaining to, performed with, or arising from a material instrument; due to the instrument (as *i. error*) 1644. **3.** Of music: Performed on, or composed for, an instrument or instruments. (Opp. to *vocal.*) 1509. **b.** Of the nature of, or belonging to, a musical instrument (*rare*) 1683. †**4.** *Old Physiol.* Serving for some special vital function; organic –1607. **5.** *Gram.* The name of a case in Sanskrit, Slavonic, etc., denoting that *with* or *by* which something is done 1806.

1. I. in bringing about revolutions BUTLER. **b.** The Head is not more Natiue to the Heart, The Hand more Instrumentall to the Mouth SHAKS. **2.** To have recourse to i. aids HERSCHEL. **3.** Rare music, vocal and i. EVELYN. **b.** The nightingale.. breathes such sweet loud music out of her little i. throat WALTON.

B. *sb.* †**1.** That which is instrumental; an instrument, means –1643. †**2.** A bodily organ –1564. **3.** *Gram.* The instrumental case, the 'ablative of the instrument' 1806.

Hence **Instrume·ntalist,** a performer of i. music (opp. to *vocalist*) 1823. **I:nstrumenta·lity,** the quality or condition of being i.; agency; (with *pl.*) a means, an agency. **Instrumentaliza·tion,** (mere) execution of music on an instrument 1872. †**Instrume·ntalize** *v.* to make i. to some end 1594; to make an instrument of; to measure by means of instruments. **Instrume·ntally** *adv.* in an i. manner; as an instrument or means 1581; by an instrument or means; with or upon a musical instrument 1716; in the instrumental case 1846. †**Instrume·ntalness,** instrumentality.

†**Instrumentary** (instrume·ntări), *a.* 1564. [f. INSTRUMENT *sb.* + -ARY[1]. Cf. Fr. *instrumentaire* (XV).] **1.** = INSTRUMENTAL *a.* 1. –1657. **2.** = INSTRUMENTAL *a.* 4. –1638.

Instrumentation (i:nstrumentē[i]·ʃən). 1845. [– Fr. *instrumentation* (1824 Stendhal), f. *instrumenter*; see INSTRUMENT *v.*, -ATION.] **1.** *Mus.* The composition or arrangement of music for instruments, esp. for an orchestra; orchestration. ¶**b.** Erron. used for: Playing on instruments (with reference to style) 1856. **2.** The use of a scientific, surgical, or other instrument 1874. **3.** Operation or provision, of instruments or means; instrumental agency, instrumentality 1858.

1. The cantatas..possess..an i. far more brilliant and spirited 1845. **2.** The first principle of i. in the urethra is to avoid the use of force 1874. **3.** If I am caught, whether by your i. or not [etc.] 1883.

Instrume·ntist. *rare.* [f. INSTRUMENT + -IST.] Instrumentalist. DOWLAND.

†**Insty·le,** *v.* 1596. [f. IN-[2] + STYLE *sb.* or *v.* See ENSTYLE.] *trans.* To style, denominate –1759.

Insuavity (inswæ·vĭti). *rare.* 1621. [– L. *insuavitas*; see IN-[3] and SUAVITY.] Lack of suavity or sweetness: unpleasantness.

Insubjection (insŏbdʒe·kʃən). *rare.* 1818. [IN-[3].] Want of subjection; the state of not being subject to authority or control.

Insubmergible (insŏbmə·ɹdʒĭb'l), *a.* 1808. [IN-[3].] That cannot be submerged or sunk under water. So **Insubme·rsible** *a.*

Insubmi·ssion. *rare.* 1828. [IN-[3].] Want of submission; insubordination. WEBSTER.

Insubmi·ssive, *a.* 1841. [IN-[3].] Not submissive; unyielding to power or authority; unsubmissive.

Insubordinate (insŏbǭ·ɹdinĕt), *a.* (*sb.*) 1849. [IN-[3].] **1.** Not subordinate; not obedient to the orders of superiors. **2.** *sb.* One who is insubordinate 1886. Hence **Insubo·rdinately** *adv.*

Insubordination (insŏbǭɹdinē[i]·ʃən). 1790. [f. IN-[3] + SUBORDINATION, perh. after Fr. *insubordination.*] The fact or condition of being insubordinate; resistance to or defiance of authority; disobedience.

Insubstantial (insŏbstæ·nʃăl), *a.* 1607. [– late and med.L. *insubstantialis*; see IN-[3], SUBSTANTIAL.] **1.** Not existing in substance; not real; non-substantial 1610. **2.** Void of substance; not of stout or solid substance. Also *fig.*

1. This insubstantiall Pageant *Temp.* IV. i. 155. Hence **Insubstantia·lity,** unsubstantiality.

†**Insu·ccate,** *v. rare.* 1623. [– *insuc(c)at-*, pa. ppl. stem of L. *insuc(c)are*, f. *in-* IN-[2] + *suc(c)us* juice; see -ATE[3].] *trans.* To soak, steep. (Dicts.) So †**Insucca·tion,** the action of soaking or steeping.

Insuccess (insŏkse·s). 1646. [IN-[3].] Want of success. So †**Insucce·ssful** *a.*

Insucken (i·nsɒk'n), *a. Sc. Law.* 1546. [f. IN *prep.* + SUCKEN.] Situated within a certain sucken or jurisdiction having its own mill; astricted to a certain mill.

Insue, obs. f. ENSUE.

Insuetude (i·nswĭtiūd). *rare.* [– late L. *insuetudo*, f. *insuetus* unaccustomed; see IN-[3] and cf. DESUETUDE.] The quality of not being in use. LANDOR.

Insufferable (insɒ·fərăb'l), *a.* 1533. [f. IN-[3] + SUFFERABLE, perh. through Fr. († and dial.) *insouffrable.*] Not sufferable; intolerable, unbearable.

A vain Person is the most i. Creature living in a well-bred Assembly STEELE. Hence **Insu·fferably** *adv.*

Insufficience (insŏfi·ʃĕns). Now *rare.* ME. [– OFr. *insufficience*, f. late L. *insufficientia*; see next, -ENCE.] = INSUFFICIENCY.

Insufficiency (insŏfi·ʃĕnsi). 1488. [– late L. *insufficientia* (Tertullian), f. *insufficient-*; see next, -ENCY.] **1.** Of a person: Inability to fulfil requirements; incapacity, incompetence. *Obs.* or *arch.* Also with *an* and *pl.* **2.** Of a thing: Deficiency, inadequacy 1488. **3.** Physical incapacity or impotence; inability of a bodily organ to do its work 1714.

1. A due sense of his own faults and insufficiencies 1773. **2.** An i. of data CHALMERS. **3.** The marriage afterwards being declared Null, by Reason of his I. STEELE.

Insufficient (insŏfi·ʃĕnt), *a.* ME. [– OFr. *insufficient* – late L. *insufficiens, -ent-*; see IN-³, SUFFICIENT.] Not sufficient. †**1.** Of a person: Of inadequate ability; unfit; incompetent –1657. **2.** Of a thing: Deficient in force, quality, or amount; inadequate 1494.

1. Some of those that were ministers were much i. BACON. Hee is i. in lands 1620. **2.** But a single hand is i. for such a harvest DRYDEN. Hence **Insuffi·cient-ly** *adv.*, †**-ness.**

Insufflate (i·nsɒflēⁱt), *v.* 1657. [– *insufflat-*, pa. ppl. stem of late L. *insufflare* (Tertullian), f. *in-* IN-² + *sufflare* blow upon; see SUFFLATE.] **1.** *trans.* To blow or breathe in. EVELYN. **b.** *spec.* To breathe upon catechumens, or on the water of baptism. **2.** *Med.* To blow (air, gas, etc.) into some opening of the body; to treat by insufflation 1670. Hence **Insuffla·tor,** a contrivance for insufflating.

Insufflation (insɒflēⁱ·ʃən). 1580. [– late L. *insufflatio*, f. as prec.; see -ION. Cf. (O)Fr. *insufflation.*] **1.** The action of blowing or breathing on or into 1621. **b.** *spec.* Blowing or breathing upon a person or thing to symbolize the influence of the Holy Spirit and the expulsion of evil spirits; a rite of exorcism used in some churches 1580. **2.** The blowing or breathing (*of* something) in; in *Med.* of air, etc. into the lungs, or of gas, vapour, or powder into or on some part of the body 1823. **3.** The condition of being inflated 1866.

†**Insui·table,** *a. rare.* 1612. [IN-³.] Unsuitable –1692. Hence †**Insuitabi·lity.**

‖**Insula** (i·nsiulă). Pl. **-æ.** 1832. [L., an island, etc.] **1.** *Rom. Antiq.* A block of buildings; a square or space mapped out or divided off. **2.** *Anat.* **a.** The central lobe of the cerebrum; the lobule of the corpus striatum or Sylvian fissure, the Island of Reil. **b.** A term applied to a clot of blood floating in serum. 1886.

Insular (i·nsiŭlăɹ), *a.* (*sb.*) 1611. [– late L. *insularis*, f. *insula* island; see -AR¹.] **1.** Of or pertaining to an island; inhabiting or situated on an island. **2.** Of the nature of an island; composing or forming an island 1662. Also *transf.* **3.** Having the characteristic traits of islanders; *esp.* isolated; self-contained; narrow or prejudiced in feelings, ideas, or manners 1775. **4.** *sb.* An inhabitant of an island 1744.

1. Our i. feuds BURKE. The west coasts of continents enjoy i...climates 1885. **3.** The penury of i. conversation JOHNSON. Without ceasing to be English, he has escaped from being i. LOWELL. Hence **I·nsulari:sm,** the quality of being i.; esp. narrowness of ideas, feelings, or outlook. **I·nsularly** *adv.* var. **I·nsulary** *a.* and *sb.* (now *rare* or *Obs.*) 1585.

Insularity (insiulæ·rĭti). 1755. [f. prec. + -ITY.] **1.** The state or condition of being an island, or of being surrounded by water 1790. **2.** The condition of living on an island; hence, narrowness of mind or feeling, contractedness of view 1755.

1. The i. of Britain was first shown by Agricola, who sent his fleet round it PINKERTON. **2.** The proverbial i. of the average Briton 1893.

Insulate (i·nsiŭlĕt), *a.* Now *rare.* 1712. [– L. *insulatus* made into an island, f. *insula* island; see -ATE²; cf. ISOLATED.] Detached, isolated, insulated.

Insulate (i·nsiŭleⁱt), *v.* 1538. [f. L. *insula* + -ATE³, or *insulatus* adj. See prec.] **1.** *trans.* To make into an island by surrounding with water; to convert into an island. **2.** *transf.* and *fig.* To cause (a thing, person, etc.) to stand detached from its surroundings; to separate from the rest; to place apart; to isolate 1785. **3.** *Electr.* and *Heat.* To cut off or isolate from conducting bodies by the interposition of non-conductors, so as to prevent the passage of electricity or heat 1755. †**4.** *Chem.* and *Phys.* To free from combination with other elements; to isolate –1834.

1. Trent..turneth aside his streame Northward.. and so almost insulateth or encompasseth Burton P. HOLLAND. Phr. *Insulating stool*, one with glass legs, or other non-conducting supports, to i. a body placed on it.

Insulated (i·nsiŭleⁱtĕd), *ppl. a.* 1727. [f. prec. + -ED¹.] **1.** Made into an island; surrounded by water 1776. **2.** *transf.* and *fig.* Placed or standing apart; separated from intercourse with others; solitary, isolated 1727. **3.** Electrically cut off from (the earth or other conducting bodies) by being surrounded with non-conductors 1791.

2. I. pyramidal hills PENNANT. An i. life COWPER.

Insulation (insiulēⁱ·ʃən). 1798. [f. INSULATE *v.*; see -ATION.] **1.** The action of insulating; the fact or condition of being insulated; *concr.* an insulated object. **2.** The action of insulating electrically or physically; the condition of being isolated by non-conductors so as to prevent the passage of electricity or heat 1822. **b.** *concr.* Insulating material 1870.

Insulator (i·nsiŭleⁱtəɹ). 1801. [f. INSULATE *v.* + -OR 2.] One who or that which insulates; *spec.* a contrivance, usu. of glass or porcelain, for supporting or carrying telegraph-wires without carrying off the current.

Insulin (i·nsiŭlin). 1922. [f. L. *insula* islet + -IN¹.] *Pharm.* A drug extracted from the islets of Langerhans in the pancreas, used in the treatment of diabetes.

Insu·lse, *a.* Now *rare.* 1609. [– L. *insulsus*, f. *in-* IN-³ + *salsus* witty, lit. 'salted', pa. pple. of *salere*, f. *sal* salt.] **1.** Lacking wit or sense; dull, stupid; absurd. **2.** *lit.* Tasteless, insipid 1675.

Insu·lsity. Now *rare.* 1623. [– L. *insulsitas*, f. *insulsus*; see prec., -ITY.] The quality of being insulse; stupidity, senselessness.

Insult (i·nsɒlt), *sb.* 1603. [– Fr. *insulte* or – eccl.L. *insultus*, f. *in-* IN-² + *saltus* leap. Cf. next.] **1.** An act, or the action, of attacking or assailing; attack, assault, onset (*lit.* and *fig.*). *arch.* †**b.** *Mil.* An open and sudden attack, without preparations. **2.** An act, or the action, of insulting (in sense 1 or 2 of vb.); injuriously contemptuous speech or action; an affront 1671. †**3.** The act of leaping upon; 'covering'. DRYDEN.

2. The ruthless sneer that i. adds to grief SAVAGE. *Phr.* To add insult to injury.

Insult (insɒ·lt), *v.* 1570. [– L. *insultare*, f. *in-* IN-² + *saltare*, iterative-intensive of *salire* leap, jump.] †**1.** *intr.* To manifest arrogant or scornful delight by speech or behaviour; to exult proudly or contemptuously; to vaunt, glory, triumph –1857. **2.** *trans.* To assail with scornful abuse or offensive disrespect; to offer indignity to; to affront, outrage 1620. †**3.** *intr.* To make an attack or assault (*lit.* and *fig.*) –1670. **4.** *trans.* To attack, assault, assail (now only *fig.* in general sense). †**b.** *spec.* (*Mil.*) To attack openly and suddenly without preparations. 1697. †**5.** *intr.* To leap wantonly. GAULE.

1. They know how, The Lyon being dead euen Hares i. DANIEL. The Dutch do mightily i. of their victory PEPYS. Whilst the infidel..insults over their credulous fears PALEY. **2.** Whatever the canting Roundhead had regarded with reverence was insulted MACAULAY. **4.** Having no Fleet at Sea, the Portugueze insulted his Sea-coasts 1727. Hence **Insu·ltable** *a.* (*rare*), capable of being insulted. **Insu·lter. Insu·ltingly** *adv.*

Insultation (insɒltēⁱ·ʃən). *Obs.* or *arch.* 1513. [– OFr. *insultation* or L. *insultatio*, f. *insultat-*, pa. ppl. stem of *insultare;* see prec., -ION. Very common in XVII.] **1.** The action, or an act, of insulting (in sense 1 or 2 of vb.); injuriously contemptuous speech or behaviour; insult. †**2.** Attack, assault –1657.

†**Insultment.** [f. INSULT *v.* + -MENT.] The action of insulting; contemptuous triumph; insult. *Cymb.* III. v. 145.

†**Insu·me,** *v.* 1675. [var., by substitution of prefix, of ASSUME *v.* 3.] *trans.* To take in, absorb –1733. So †**Insu·mption,** absorption.

†‖**Insuper, in super** (insⁱŭ·pəɹ), *adv.* 1624. [L., f. *in* in + *super* above.] Over; *to stand in super*, to stand over as a balance or unsettled claim.

Insuperable (insiŭ·pərăb'l), *a.* (*sb.*) ME. [– OFr. *insuperable* or L. *insuperabilis*; see IN-³, SUPERABLE.] **1.** That cannot be overcome; unconquerable, invincible. *Obs.* or merged in 3. **2.** That cannot be surmounted or passed over 1660. **3.** *fig.* Of difficulties, etc.: That cannot be got over or overcome; invincible; insurmountable 1657. **4.** Unsurpassable. RUSKIN.

1. Invincible soldiers, and appointed with armes i. HOLLAND. **2.** I. highth of loftiest shade, Cedar, and Pine, and Firr MILT. *P.L.* IV. 138. **3.** His i. disinclination to entering into holy orders 1744. Hence **Insu:perabi·lity, Insu·perableness,** the quality of being i. **Insu·perably** *adv.*

Insupportable (insŏpōᵊ·ɹtăb'l), *a.* 1530. [–(O)Fr. *insupportable*; see IN-³, SUPPORTABLE.] **1.** That cannot be supported; unendurable; unbearable. **b.** Unjustifiable, indefensible 1649. †**2.** That cannot be sustained; irresistible –1697.

1. I. Insolence COWLEY, distress 1791. **2.** He gan advaunce With huge force and i. mayne SPENSER. Hence **Insuppo·rtableness. Insuppo·rtably** *adv.*

Insupposable (insŏpōᵘ·zăb'l), *a.* 1668. [IN-³.] That cannot be supposed.

Insuppressible (insŏpre·sĭb'l), *a.* 1610. [IN-³.] That cannot be suppressed; irrepressible. Hence **Insuppre·ssibly** *adv.*

Insuppressive (insŏpre·siv), *a. rare.* 1601. [IN-³.] Insuppressible. *Jul. C.* II. i. 134.

Insurable (inʃūᵊ·răb'l), *a.* 1810. [f. INSURE *v.* + -ABLE.] Capable of being, or proper to be, insured; sufficient to form a ground for insurance. **Insurabi·lity.**

Insurance (inʃūᵊ·răns). 1553. [Variant of ENSURANCE, with change of prefix as in INSURE.] †**1.** The action or a means of insuring or making certain –1788. †**2.** = ASSURANCE 3. 1706. †**3.** Betrothal, engagement to marry. UDALL. **4.** *Comm.* The act or system of insuring property, life, etc.; a contract by which the one party undertakes, in consideration of a payment (called a *premium*), to secure the other against pecuniary loss, by payment of a sum of money in the event of destruction of or damage to property (as by disaster at sea, fire, etc.), or of the death or disablement of a person; the department of business which deals with such contracts. Also called ASSURANCE (and in 17th c. occas. *ensurance*). 1651.

Assurance, the earlier term, is now rarely used of marine, fire, or accident insurance, and is retained in Great Britain in the nomenclature and use of most life insurance companies. But in general popular use, *insurance* is the prevalent term.

b. The sum paid for insuring; the premium 1666. **c.** The amount for which property or life is insured 1838. **d.** The act or system of insuring employed persons, or all citizens, against sickness or unemployment, esp. in accordance with the National Insurance Acts of 1911 and 1946 and the Unemployment Act of 1920. **5.** *attrib.*, as *i. company, policy*, etc. 1651.

4. Money was taken up upon bottomary and i., and the ship left by the master and seamen upon rocks where..she must perish PEPYS. Hence †**Insu·rancer,** one who gives i. or assurance; one who insures or makes sure.

Insu·rant. 1858. [f. INSURE *v.* + -ANT.] One who effects or obtains an insurance.

Insure (inʃūᵊ·ɹ), *v.* 1440. [var. of ENSURE (with IN-² for EN-¹).] †**1.** *trans.* To make (a person) sure (*of* a thing) –1686. †**2.** = ENSURE 2, 3. –1560. **3.** *Comm.* To secure the payment of a sum of money in the event of loss of or damage to property (esp. by casualty at sea, by fire, etc.), or of the death or disablement of a person, in consideration of the payment of a premium and observance of certain conditions; to effect an insurance upon. Said either of the person who pays the premium, or of the office or underwriters who undertake the risk. For the latter many offices and writers prefer *assure* (esp. in reference to life insurance). 1635. **b.** *absol.* or *intr.* To undertake insurance risks; to effect an insurance 1651. **4.** *trans.* To make certain, to secure, to guarantee (some thing, event, etc.) 1681. **5.** To make safe, to secure (*against, from*) 1724.

3. As much more insured upon his ship and goods as they were worth PEPYS. To i. his House ADDISON, a life 1883. **c.** (Cf. INSURANCE 4 d). **4.** An ardour which could hardly fail to i. success BUCKLE. **5.** The evidence of trials past does not i. them against trials that may come 1864.

Insurer (inʃūᵊ·rəɹ). 1638. [f. INSURE + -ER¹.] One who or that which insures; *esp. Comm.* One who contracts, for a premium, to indemnify a person against losses; an underwriter. Also called *Assurer* (*Assuror*).

Insurge (insŏ·ɹdʒ), *v.* Now *rare.* 1523. [– L. *insurgere* rise up, f. *in-* IN-² + *surgere* rise. See SURGE.] †**1.** *intr.* To arise, spring up –1576. †**2.** To rise in opposition *against*; to make insurrection, revolt –1610. **3.** *trans.* To stir up; to raise in insurrection. *Obs.* exc. as *nonce-wd.* 1796.

Insurgent (insŏ·ɹdʒĕnt). 1765. [– Fr. †*insurgent* (XVIII in connection with the rising in N. America) – *insurgent-*, pr. ppl. stem of L. *insurgere*; see prec., -ENT.]

A. *adj.* **1.** Rising in active revolt. Also *fig.* 1814. **2.** Of the sea or a flood: Surging up or rushing in 1849.

1. The i. barons 1845. **2.** The broad volume of the i. Nile M. ARNOLD.

B. *sb.* One who rises in revolt against constituted authority; a rebel who is not recognized as a belligerent 1765.

The colonial insurgents 1812. Hence **Insu·rgence,** a rising, revolt. **Insu·rgency,** the quality or state of being i.

Insurmountable (insŏɹmau·ntăb'l), *a.* 1696. [IN-³; cf. Fr. *insurmontable* (XVI).] That cannot be surmounted, overcome, or passed over.

This difficulty is i. LOCKE. Hence **Insurmountabi·lity, Insurmou·ntableness. Insurmou·ntably** *adv.*

Insurrection (insŏre·kʃən). 1459. [– (O)Fr. *insurrection* – late L. *insurrectio*, f. *insurrect-*, pa. ppl. stem of L. *insurgere*; see INSURGE, -ION.] **1.** The action of rising in arms or open resistance against established authority or governmental restraint; with *pl.*, an armed rising, a revolt; an incipient or limited rebellion. Also *fig.* **2.** Upheaval. RUSKIN.

1. He [Jack Cade]..wrote letters to many Citees..to have made a comon i. 1459. Insurrections are generally wrong; revolutions are always right BUCKLE. *fig.* It is not the insurrections of ignorance that are dangerous, but the revolts of intelligence LOWELL. Hence **Insurre·ctional** *a.* of, pertaining to, or of the nature of i. **Insurre·ctionary** *a.* insurrectional; addicted to i. **Insurre·ctionist,** one who takes part in an i., or who advocates revolt against authority.

Insusceptible (insŏse·ptĭb'l), *a.* 1603. [IN-³; cf. Fr. *insusceptible* (XVI).] Not susceptible; not able or apt to receive impressions; not liable to be affected by something or in some way.

I. of mutation P. HOLLAND, to the infection of the smallpox 1808. I. or, as I may call them, not poisonable people 1880. Hence **Insusceptibi·lity.** So **Insusce·ptive** *a.*

†**Insuspe·ct(ed,** *a.* 1606. [IN-³.] Unsuspected –1646.

Insusurra·tion. *rare.* 1614. [– late L. *insusurratio*, f. *insusurrat-*, pa. ppl. stem of L. *insusurrare*; see IN-², SUSURRATION.] A whispering in the ear; an insinuation –1653.

Inswathe, var. of ENSWATHE *v.*

In't, arch. abbrev. of *in it.* **I'n't, i'nt,** obs. abbrev. of *isn't, is not.*

Intablature, obs. f. ENTABLATURE.

Intact (intæ·kt), *a.* 1450. [– L. *intactus*, f. *in-* IN-³ + *tactus*, pa. pple. of *tangere* touch.] Untouched; kept or left entire; unblemished; unimpaired.

†**Inta·ctible,** *a.* [IN-³.] = next. (Dicts.)

Inta·ctile, *a. rare.* 1659. [f. IN-³ + TACTILE. Cf. Fr. *intactile* (XVI).] Not tactile; intangible.

Intagliated (intæ·lyeⁱtĕd), *ppl. a.* 1782. [f. It. *intagliato*, pa. pple. of *intagliare* (see next) + -ED¹.] Carved on the surface; engraved in or as in intaglio.

‖**Intaglio** (intæ·lyo), *sb.* Pl. **intaglios,** rarely **intagli** (inta·lyi). Also *erron.* †**intaglia**; pl. **-as.** 1644. [It., f. *intagliare* engrave, f. *in-* IN-² + *tagliare* cut.] **1.** A figure or design incised or engraved; a cutting or engraving in stone or other hard material. Also *fig.* and *transf.* **b.** The process or art of carving or engraving in a hard material; incised carving; the condition or fact of being incised. Chiefly in phr. *in intaglio*, as opp. to *in relievo* or *in relief.* Also *fig.* 1762. **2.** Anything ornamented with incised work; esp. an incised gem. Opp. to *cameo.* 1654. **b.** A countersunk die 1825. Hence **Inta·glio** *v. trans.* to engrave with a sunk pattern or design; to execute in i.

Intail, obs. f. ENTAIL *sb.* and *v.*

Intake (i·nteⁱk). Chiefly *Sc.* and *n. dial.* 1523. [f. phr. *take in*; see IN *adv.*, TAKE *v.*] **1.** The act of taking in from outside; the quantity taken in 1808. **2.** (Chiefly *n. dial.*) An inclosure 1523. **3.** The place where water is taken into a channel or pipe 1559. **4.** *Mining.* The airway of a mine. Also *attrib.* 1851. **5.** A narrowing or abrupt contraction made in the width of a tube, a stocking, etc.; the point at which this is made 1808.

2. When horses in the sunburnt i. stood WORDSW.

†**Inta·minated,** *a.* [f. L. *intaminatus* unsullied (f. *contaminatus* after *intactus* INTACT) + -ED¹. See IN-³, CONTAMINATE.] Uncontaminated, uncorrupted, pure. WOOD.

Intangible (intæ·ndʒĭb'l), *a.* 1640. [– Fr. *intangible* or med.L. *intangibilis*, or f. IN-³ + TANGIBLE.] Not tangible; incapable of being touched; not cognizable by the sense of touch; impalpable. Also *fig.*

This wonderful i. aether TYNDALL. Hence **Inta:ngibi·lity, -ta·ngibleness. Inta·ngibly** *adv.*

†**Inta·ngle,** etc., obs. ff. ENTANGLE, etc.

†**Inta·stable,** *a.* [f. IN-³ + TAST(E)ABLE.] Incapable of being tasted. GREW.

Integer (i·ntĭdʒəɹ). 1509. [– L. *integer* intact, f. *in-* IN-³ + *tag-*, *teg-* root of *tangere* touch. Cf. ENTIRE.]

A. *adj.* (Now *rare* or *Obs.*) †**1.** Whole, entire 1509. †**2.** Marked by moral integrity; upright 1644. **3.** *Math.* = INTEGRAL A. 4 a. 1660.

3. A whole or i. number HUTTON.

B. *sb.* **1.** *Math.* A number or quantity denoting one or more whole things or units; a whole number or undivided quantity. Opp. to *fraction.* 1571. **2.** A particular quantity of any kind (as money, weight, etc.) taken as the unit of measurement. Now *rare* or *Obs.* 1822. **3.** *gen.* A whole or entire thing or entity 1848.

2. The Carat serves as the I. 1868.

Integrable (i·ntĭgrăb'l), *a.* 1727. [f. INTEGRATE *v.* + -ABLE.] Capable of being integrated (see INTEGRATE *v.* 2, 3). Hence **I:ntegrabi·lity.**

Integral (i·ntĭgrăl). 1551. [– late L. *integralis*, f. *integer*; see INTEGER, -AL¹. Cf. (O)Fr. *intégral.*]

A. *adj.* **1.** Of or pertaining to a whole. Said of a part or parts: Belonging to or making up an integral whole; constituent, component; *spec.* necessary to the completeness of the whole. **2.** Made up of component parts which together constitute a unity; in *Logic*, said of a whole consisting of or divisible into parts actually (not merely mentally) separable. *rare* or *Obs.* exc. in techn. use. 1588. **3.** Having no part or element lacking; unbroken, whole, entire, complete. Now somewhat *rare.* 1611. **4.** *Math.* **a.** Consisting of a whole number or undivided quantity; not fractional, or not involving a fraction 1658. **b.** Relating to, or involving integrals; obtained by, belonging to, or proceeding by integration 1727.

1. The arms, legs, etc. are *integral* parts; body and soul *essential* parts of a man E. CHAMBERS. **3.** Excerpta of Writers whose i. works are lost for ever 1794. Repent with an i...repentance JER. TAYLOR. **4. b.** *Integral calculus*: the calculus of integrals; that branch of the infinitesimal calculus which deals with the finding and properties of integrals of functions, also used to include the solution of differential equations, and parts of the theory of functions, etc.

B. *sb.* **1.** Something entire or undivided; a whole. *Obs.* exc. as *transf.* from 3 = total sum. 1620. †**2.** An integral part or element; a constituent, component –1685. **3.** *Math.* **a.** (of a function): That quantity of which the given function is the differential or differential coefficient; so called because it may be regarded as the whole sum of a series of consecutive values assumed by an infinitesimal function (differential) of the variable while the latter changes continuously from any one value to any other. When such limits of variation are fixed or determinate, it is called a *definite i.* An i. is denoted by the sign $\int$ (orig. a long *s*, for L. *summa* sum); in a definite i. the inferior and superior limits are indicated at the bottom and top of the sign, thus $\int_a^b$. **b.** (of a differential equation, or a system of such equations): An equation or system of equations from which the given equation or system can be derived by differentiation. 1727.

Integrality (intĭgræ·lĭti). 1611. [f. INTEGRAL + -ITY. Cf. Fr. *intégralité* (XVII).] The condition of being integral; wholeness, entirety, completeness.

Integrally (i·ntĭgrăli), *adv.* 1471. [f. as prec. + -LY².] In an integral manner; as a whole; entirely.

Integrant (i·ntĭgrănt), *a.* (*sb.*) 1637. [– Fr. *intégrant*, f. *intégrer*; see INTEGRATE *v.*, -ANT.] **1.** Of parts: = INTEGRAL A. 1. **2.** *sb.* That which integrates; a component 1824.

1. The Church consisteth of two i. parts, *viz.* Pastors and Sheepe 1637.

Integrate (i·ntĭgrĕt), *a.* 1485. [– L. *integratus*, pa. pple. of *integrare*; see next, -ATE².] = INTEGRAL A. 2, 3.

Integrate (i·ntĭgreⁱt), *v.* 1638. [– *integrat-*, pa. ppl. stem of L. *integrare*, f. *integer*; see INTEGER, -ATE³.] **1.** *trans.* To render entire or complete; to make up (a whole); said of the parts or elements. ?*Obs.* **b.** To complete (what is imperfect) by the addition of the necessary parts 1675. **2.** To combine (parts or elements) into a whole 1802. **3.** *Math.* To find or calculate the integral of; see INTEGRAL B. 3. Also *absol.* to perform the operation of integration. 1727. **b.** *transf.* and *fig.*; *spec.* to indicate or register the mean value, or the total sum of all the portions or elements, of some physical quantity 1864.

1. The particular doctrines which i. Christianity CHILLINGW. **b.** The fragmentary contribution of one being integrated by the fragmentary contributions of others DE QUINCEY. **3. b.** *Integrating spectroscope*, a spectroscope in which the slit receives light from all parts of a luminous object and blends it all together to form a single united spectrum; opp. to *analysing spectroscope.* Hence **I·ntegrative** *a.* integrating; tending to i.

Integration (intĭgrēⁱ·ʃən). 1620. [– L. *integratio*, f. as prec.; see -ION.] The action or process of integrating. **1.** The making up of a whole by adding together or combining the separate parts or elements; a making whole or entire. (Often opp. to *differentiation.*) **2.** *Math.* The operation of finding the integral of a given function or equation; the inverse of differentiation 1727.

2. *I. by parts*: i. by means of the formula $\int u dv = uv - \int v du$, where *u* and *v* are any functions of the same variable. *Constant of i.*: an arbitrary constant which must be added to get the complete expression for an integral. *Sign of i.*: the sign $\int$ denoting an integral (see INTEGRAL B. 3 a).

Integrator (i·ntĭgreⁱtəɹ). 1879. [f. INTEGRATE *v.* + -OR 2.] One who or that which integrates; *spec.* an instrument for indicating or registering the total amount or mean value of some physical quantity, as area, temperature, etc.; see INTEGRATE *v.* 3 b.

Integripallial (intĕgripæ·liăl), *a.* Also **integro-.** 1862. [f. *integri-*, comb. f. of L. *integer* entire + PALLIAL.] *Zool.* Having the pallial line not broken or indented; applied to a division of lamellibranchiate molluscs, in which the siphons are small or absent. Also **Integripa·lliate** *a.* (Opp. to *sinupallial*, *-ate.*)

Integrity (inte·grĭti). 1450. [– Fr. *intégrité* or L. *integritas*, f. *integer*; see INTEGER, -ITY.] **1.** The condition of having no part or element wanting; unbroken state; material wholeness, completeness, entirety. **2.** Unimpaired or uncorrupted state; original perfect condition; soundness 1450. **3.** †**a.** Innocence, sinlessness –1678. **b.** Soundness of moral principle; the character of uncorrupted virtue; uprightness, honesty, sincerity 1548.

1. The walls were standing..though not in their i. 1870. **2.** He did but restore the law to her integritie 1561. **3. b.** Better is the poore that walketh in his i., then he that is peruerse in his lippes, and is a foole *Prov.* 19:1.

†**Integuma·tion.** *rare.* 1803. [Shortened f. *integumentation.*] The formation of integuments –1828.

Integument (inte·giŭmĕnt). 1611. [– L. *integumentum*, f. *integere* cover; see IN-²,

TEGUMENT.] That with which anything is covered, enclosed, or clothed; *spec.* the natural covering or investment of the body, or of some part or organ, of an animal or plant; a skin, shell, husk, rind, etc. Hence **Integume·ntal** *a.* of or belonging to the i. **Integume·ntary** *a.* integumental, of the nature of an i.; cutaneous. **Integumenta·tion** (*rare*), the action of covering or condition of being covered with an i.

Intellect (i·ntělekt). ME. [– (O)Fr. *intellect* or L. *intellectus* perception, discernment, meaning, sense, f. *intellect-*, pa. ppl. stem of *intellegere.*] **1.** That faculty, or sum of faculties, of the mind or soul by which one knows and reasons (excluding sensation, and sometimes imagination; dist. from *feeling* and *will*); power of thought; understanding. Rarely in reference to the lower animals. **2.** *transf.* †**a.** An intellect embodied; an 'intelligence', a spirit. **b.** Intellect embodied; also, intellectual persons collectively. 1602. **3.** *pl.* Intellectual powers; 'wits', 'senses'. Now *arch.* or *vulgar.* 1698. **4.** That which one is to understand by something; the sense, purport (of a word or passage) –1588.

1. Hath Bullingbrooke Depos'd thine I.? SHAKS. **2.** It walked the town awhile, Numbering good intellects MILT. **3.** A man of sound intellects SMOLLETT. **4.** I will looke againe on the i. of the Letter *L.L.L.* IV. ii. 137.

I·ntellected, *a. rare.* 1791. [f. prec. + -ED².] Endowed with intellect.

Intelle·ctible, *a.* 1557. [– late and med.L. *intellectibilis*, f. L. *intellect-*; see INTELLECT, -IBLE.] †**a.** = INTELLECTIVE 1. **b.** = INTELLIGIBLE 3.

Intellection (intěle·kʃən). 1449. [– late and med.L. *intellectio* sense, understanding, f. as prec.; see -ION.] **1.** The action or process of understanding; *spec.* simple apprehension 1614. **b.** (with *pl.*) A particular act of understanding; *occas.*, the permanent result of such an act; a conception, notion, idea 1579. †**c.** The faculty of understanding; intellect –1797. †**d.** Understanding, information –1509. †**2.** *Gram.* and *Rhet.* The figure SYNECDOCHE –1553.

Intellective (intěle·ktiv), *a.* 1477. [– late L. *intellectivus*, f. as prec.; see -IVE. Cf. (O)Fr. *intellectif, -ive.*] **1.** Having the faculty of understanding; possessed of intellect. Applied, after Aristotle, to one of the parts of the soul (ψυχή). 1480. †**2.** = INTELLECTUAL A. 3 b –1632. **3.** = INTELLECTUAL A. 1. 1477. †**4.** = INTELLECTIBLE b –1656.

1. The Greek philosophers acknowledged several kinds of ψυχή, the nutritive, the sensitive, and the i. MILL. Hence **Intelle·ctively** *adv.*

Intellectual (intěle·ktiu,ăl). ME. [– L. *intellectualis*, f. *intellectus*; see INTELLECT, -AL¹. Cf. (O)Fr. *intellectuel.*]

A. *adj.* **1.** Of, or belonging to, the intellect or understanding. **b.** That appeals to or engages the intellect 1834. †**2.** Apprehensible or apprehended only by the intellect; non-material, spiritual; ideal –1711. †**3.** Characterized by or possessing intellection or understanding; intelligent –1797. **b.** Possessing a high degree of understanding; given to pursuits that exercise the intellect 1819.

1. Easy Credulity, which is the third cause of Intellectual slavery 1654. **b.** The more i. branches of warfare FREEMAN. **3.** Who would loose, Though full of pain, this i. being? MILT. *P. L.* II. 147. **b.** But—oh ye lords of ladies i., Inform us truly, have they not hen-peck'd you all? BYRON. Hence **Intelle·ctual-ly** *adv.*, **-ness.**

B. *sb.* †**1.** The intellectual faculty; the intellect, mind –1667. **2.** *pl.* = INTELLECT *sb.* 3. (*arch.*) 1615. **3.** *pl.* Things pertaining to the intellect 1650. **4.** An intellectual being; a person having superior powers of intellect 1652.

1. The Woman, opportune to all attempts, Her Husband..not nigh, Whose higher i. more I shun MILT. *P.L.* IX. 483. **2.** Your fear for Hartley's intellectuals is just and rational LAMB. **4.** A dinner of intellectuals 1884.

Intellectualism (intěle·ktiuăliz'm). 1829. [f. prec. + -ISM, in sense 1 after G. *intellectualismus.*] **1.** *Philos.* The doctrine that knowledge is wholly or mainly derived from the action of the intellect, i.e. from pure reason. **2.** Devotion to merely intellectual culture or pursuits 1838.

Intelle·ctualist. 1605. [– mod.L. *intellectualista* (Bacon), f. *intellectualis*; see INTELLECTUAL, -IST.] A devotee of the intellect or understanding; in *Philos.*, one who holds the doctrine of intellectualism.

Intellectuality (intělektiu,æ·lĭti). 1611. [– late L. *intellectualitas*; see INTELLECTUAL, -ITY.] The quality or state of being intellectual; intellectual power or ability.

Intellectualize (intěle·ktiu,ăləiz), *v.* 1819. [f. INTELLECTUAL *a.* + -IZE.] **1.** *trans.* To render intellectual; to give an intellectual character or quality to. Also *absol.* **2.** *intr.* [after *moralize.*] To exercise the intellect; to talk or write intellectually; to philosophize 1827.

1. It..refines and intellectualizes life 1821. Hence **Intelle:ctualiza·tion** 1821.

Intelligence (inte·lidʒĕns), *sb.* ME. [– (O)Fr. *intelligence* – L. *intelligentia*, f. *intelligens, -ent-*; see INTELLIGENT, -ENCE.] **1.** The faculty of understanding; intellect. **2.** Understanding as a quality admitting of degree; *spec.* superior understanding; quickness of mental apprehension, sagacity ME. **3.** The action or fact of mentally apprehending something; understanding, knowledge, comprehension (*of* something). Now *rare* or *Obs.* 1450. **4.** An impersonation of intelligence; an intelligent or rational being; esp. a spirit 1589. **5.** Mutual conveyance of information; communication, intercourse. Now *rare* or *Obs.* 1531. †**6.** A relation of intercourse between persons or parties. Also *fig.* –1827. **7.** Information, news, tidings 1450. †**b.** *pl.* A piece of information or news –1750. **c.** The obtaining of information; the agency for obtaining secret information; the secret service. 1697. (Revived in modern wars.)

1. He is led to the conception of a Power and an I. superior to his own HERSCHEL. **2.** Some learned Englisheman of good i. GRAFTON. **3.** I write, as he that none i. Of metres hath, ne floures of sentence 1530. **4.** How fully hast thou satisfi'd mee, pure I. of Heav'n, Angel serene MILT. *P. L.* VIII. 181. **5.** They took it into their heads..that he was of i. with the enemy 1717. **6.** He sent an embassy..to renew the good i. between them 1734. **7.** I. poured in from all quarters, that one place after another was assailed JAS. MILL. **c.** Comb., as *i. department, man, officer.*

†**Inte·lligence,** *v.* 1593. [f. prec.] **1.** *trans.* To bring intelligence of (an event, etc.); to inform (a person) –1642. **2.** *intr.* To convey intelligence; to tell tales 1616.

Intelligenced (-ĕnst, *poet.* -ĕnsĕd), *a.* 1602. [f. prec. sb. + -ED².] **a.** Having understanding. **b.** Informed.

Intelligencer (inte·lidʒĕnsəɹ). 1581. [f. INTELLIGENCE *sb.* + -ER¹, perh. after obs. Fr. *intelligencier* 'an *intelligencer*; an intelligence-giver; a spy' (Cotgrave).] One who conveys intelligence or information; an informer, a spy, a secret agent 1581; a bringer of news 1632. **b.** *fig.* Applied to things 1586; †as the title of a newspaper, etc. 1641–1801.

An I., which in real truth is no better than a Spie 1658.

†**Inte·lligencing,** *ppl. a.* 1608. [f. INTELLIGENCE *v.* or *sb.* + -ING².] Conveying intelligence or information; playing the spy –1711. *Wint. T.* II. iii. 68.

Intelligency (inte·lidʒĕnsi). Now *rare.* 1598. [– L. *intelligentia*; see INTELLIGENCE, -ENCY.] **1.** = INTELLIGENCE *sb.* 1. BROWNING. **2.** = INTELLIGENCE *sb.* 4. 1652. †**3.** = INTELLIGENCE *sb.* 5. –1711. †**4.** = INTELLIGENCE *sb.* 7 b. –1748.

Intelligent (inte·lidʒĕnt). 1509. [– *intellig-* (cl.L. *intelleg-*), pr. ppl. stem of L. *intellegere*, later *intelligere*, lit. choose among, f. *inter* INTER- + *legere* pick up, gather, choose, read; see -ENT.]

A. *adj.* **1.** Having the faculty of understanding; possessing intelligence or intellect 1598. **2.** Having or showing a high degree of intelligence; knowing, sensible, sagacious 1509. **3.** That understands (a particular thing, etc.); cognizant *of*; acquainted *with*; versed *in* 1546. †**4.** 'Bearing intelligence, giving information, communicative' (Schmidt *Shaks. Lex.*).

1. The work of an i. mind BUTLER. **2.** It is..in order of nature for him to govern that is the more i. BACON. **3.** I. of seasons MILT. **4.** Our Postes shall be swift, and i. betwixt vs SHAKS.

B. *sb.* **1.** An intelligent or rational being. **b.** A person of intelligence. Now *rare.* 1601. †**2.** An intelligencer, a spy –1751.

1. God..must of necessitie..be the first i. GALE.

Intelligential (intelidʒe·nʃăl), *a.* 1611. [f. L. *intelligentia* + -AL¹.] **1.** = INTELLECTUAL A. 1. **2.** Possessing, or of the nature of, intelligence 1646.

1. The Devil enterd, and his brutal sense..soon inspir'd With act i. MILT. *P. L.* IX. 190. **2.** An i. creature 1646.

†**Intellige·ntiary.** 1577. [f. as prec. + -ARY¹.] **1.** *adj.* Relating to or conveying intelligence or news. WOTTON. **2.** *sb.* = INTELLIGENCER.

Intelligently (inte·lidʒĕntli), *adv.* 1671. [f. INTELLIGENT *a.* + -LY².] In an intelligent manner; sagaciously, sensibly.

‖**Intelligentsia, -tzia** (intelidʒe·ntsiă). 1920. [– Russ. – Pol. *inteligiencja* – L. *intelligentia* INTELLIGENCE.] The class consisting of the educated portion of the population and regarded as capable of forming public opinion.

Intelligible (inte·lidʒĭb'l), *a.* (*sb.*) ME. [– L. *intellegi-, intelligibilis*, f. *intellegere* understand; see -IBLE.] †**1.** Capable of understanding; intelligent –1777. **2.** Capable of being understood; comprehensible 1509. **b.** Of a person in reference to his words 1655. **3.** *Philos.* Capable of being apprehended only by the understanding (not by the senses); objective to intellect. (Opp. to *sensible.*) ME. **4.** *sb.* That which is intelligible; an object of intellect or understanding; *spec.* in *Philos.* (see sense 3) 1601.

1. A meere Scholer is an i. Asse OVERBURY. **2.** What you say now is very i. BP. BERKELEY. **b.** He spoke so fast as to be hardly i. (*mod.*). **3.** The I. world..is..a world of a nature purely spiritual and intellectual 1701. Hence **Inte:lligibi·lity, Inte·lligibleness,** the quality of being i.; *transf.* an i. thing.

Inte·lligibly, *adv.* 1607. [f. prec. + -LY².] **1.** In an intelligible manner; comprehensibly. †**2.** In relation to the understanding; as an object of intellect. (Opp. to *sensibly.*) –1701.

Intemerate (inte·mĕrĕt), *a.* 1491. [– L. *intemeratus*, f. *in-* IN-³ + *temeratus*, pa. pple. of *temerare* violate; see -ATE².] Inviolate, undefiled, unblemished. So †**Inte·merated** *a.* Hence **Inte·merate-ly** *adv.*, **-ness.** †**Intemera·tion,** inviolate condition.

Intemperament (inte·mpĕrămĕnt). *rare.* 1698. [f. IN-³ + TEMPERAMENT.] An untempered or distempered condition (esp. of the body, blood, etc.).

Intemperance (inte·mpĕrăns). ME. [– (O)Fr. *intempérance* or L. *intemperantia*; see IN-³, TEMPERANCE.] Want of temperateness. †**1.** Intemperateness, inclemency, severity of the air, weather, or climate –1707. **2.** Lack of moderation or restraint; excess in any kind of action; *spec.* excessive indulgence of any passion or appetite 1547. **b.** with *pl.* An instance of this 1613. **3.** *spec.* Immoderate indulgence in intoxicating drink; addiction to drinking 1617.

2. Some..by violent stroke shall die,..by I. more In Meats and Drinks MILT. *P. L.* XI. 472. **3.** [Indifference] to the crying evils of *intemperance* 1841. So **Inte·mperancy** (in all senses) 1532.

†**Inte·mperant,** *a. rare.* 1542. [– Fr. *intempérant*, or f. IN-³ + †*temperant* adj.] Wanting moderation or self-restraint; incontinent, intemperate –1598.

Intemperate (inte·mpĕrĕt), *a.* ME. [– L. *intemperatus*; see IN-³, TEMPERATE *a.*] **1.** Not temperate, excessive, extreme; esp., of climate or weather, inclement, severe. Now *rare.* 1526. **2.** Of persons, etc. Without temperance or moderation; immoderate, unbridled; violent 1508. **3.** Characterized by excessive indulgence in a passion or appetite ME. **b.** *spec.* Given to an excessive use of intoxicating drink 1677.

1. *I. zone*, the Torrid or Frigid zone, as opp. to the Temperate zone. **2.** Many i. Speeches and passages happend 1688. The i. zeal of the reformers 1777. **3.** His concupiscible i. lust SHAKS. Hence **Inte·mperately** *adv.*

Inte·mperateness. Now *rare.* 1555. [f. prec. + -NESS.] The quality of being intemperate. **1.** = INTEMPERANCE 1. **2.** = INTEMPERANCE 2. 1571.

1. The intemperatenes of the ayer and region of Dariena EDEN. **2.** I. of language 1653.

†**Inte·mperature.** 1559. [f. IN-³ + TEMPERATURE (senses 4, 5, 6). Cf. Fr. †*intempérature* (XVII) in same senses.] **1.** = INTEMPERANCE 1. –1820. **2.** Abnormal or distempered condition of the body; intemperament –1799.

‖**Intemperies** (intempe·ri,īz). 1676. [L., f. *in-* (IN-³) + *temperies* temperature, temper.] Disordered condition of the body, dyscrasy; rarely, of the weather.

Intempestive (intempe·stiv), *a.* 1548. [– L. *intempestivus*; see IN-³, TEMPESTIVE. Cf. Fr. *intempestif, -ive* (XVI).] Untimely, unseasonable, inopportune.

Loud and i. laughter 1891. Hence **Intempe·stively** *adv.* So †**Intempesti·vity,** unseasonableness, untimeliness.

†**Inte·nable,** *a.* 1650. [IN-³.] That cannot be held or maintained; untenable –1752.

Intend (inte·nd), *v.* [ME. *entende, in-* – (O)Fr. *entendre,* †*intendre* – L. *intendere* extend, direct, intend, promote, f. *in-* IN-² + *tendere* stretch, TEND *v.*¹]

I. †**1.** *trans.* To stretch forth, extend; to point forwards –1633. †**2.** To stretch, strain, make tense; to expand, dilate (*lit.* and *fig.*) –1837. †**3.** To intensify (*trans.* and *intr.*) –1705.

2. As when a bow is successively intended and remitted CUDWORTH. **3.** The Church hath power to i. our Faith but not to extend it JER. TAYLOR.

II. 1. *trans.* To direct (the eyes, mind, etc.) *to, into, towards* something. Now a conscious Latinism. ME. **2.** *intr.* and *trans.* To direct one's course; to proceed on (a journey, etc.). (L. *intendere, intendere iter.*) *Obs.* or *arch.* ME. †**b.** *intr.* To start on a journey, to set out; *occas.*, ellipt. for 'intend to go or start' –1817. †**3.** *trans.* To refer, attribute, ascribe (a thing) *to* some one 1615.

1. I. thine eye Into the dim and undiscovered sky PATMORE. **2.** SHAKS. *Per.* I. ii. 116. **b.** I i. for England this spring, where I have some affairs to adjust BYRON.

III. [ult. f. L. *intendere* = *intendere animum.*] †**1.** *intr.* To direct the mind or attention; to pay heed; to apply oneself assiduously. Const. *to, unto,* rarely *about, on, at.* –1613. †**b.** *refl.* To devote oneself –1627. †**c.** *absol.* –1603. †**2.** To apply oneself *to do* something; to endeavour, strive –1674. †**3.** *intr.* To give ear, hearken –1568. †**b.** *trans.* To hearken to. LATIMER. †**4.** *intr.* To be in attendance or waiting; to attend –1644. †**b.** *trans.* To attend on or to –1633. †**5.** *trans.* To turn one's thoughts to; to occupy oneself with; to look after –1784.

1. Eche to his owene nede gan entende CHAUCER. **c.** But loe the eyes of God entend And watch to ayde the iust STERNHOLD & H. **4.** I wish that one of your number..may i. and appear at that Committee CROMWELL. **5.** I. at home..what best may ease The present misery MILT.

IV. †**1.** *trans.* To have understanding of (something); to apprehend *that* something is –1620. †**2.** *intr.* To have or come to an understanding; to agree; to be in accord. [Fr. *s'entendre.*] –1509. †**3.** To apprehend, conceive; to think; to judge –1638. †**4.** *trans.* To construe, interpret, or hold legally –1798.

4. The law will i. it to be so BLACKSTONE.

V. 1. *intr.* To have a purpose or design; to be minded. *Obs.*, exc. as absol. use of 2. ME. **2.** *trans.* To have in the mind as a fixed purpose; to purpose, design. (The chief current sense.) ME. **3.** To design (a thing) for some purpose; to destine (a thing or person) to a fate or use; to purpose to bestow; to mean (a thing) *to be* or *to do* something 1590. **4.** To design to express; to mean 1572. †**b.** To designate as something; to call (*rare*) –1605.

2. I know not Gentlemen what you i. SHAKS. He intended his son should have it in remainder for his life only CRUISE. **3.** A Play, Intended for great Theseus nuptiall day SHAKS. The second son is intended for the army 1900. **4.** By Profit I i. not here any Accession of Wealth HOBBES.

VI. Senses of uncertain position or origin. †**1.** *trans.* To expect. [OFr. *entendre* = Fr. *attendre.*] –1485. †**2.** To assert, maintain; to pretend; to claim –1634. †**3.** *intr.* To tend or incline –1640. **4.** *trans.* To superintend, direct. Cf. INTENDANT. 1791.

4. Nine arbiters, appointed to i. The whole arrangements of the public games COWPER.

Hence **Inte·nder,** one who intends or purposes; †a pretender.

†**Inte·ndance**¹. ME. [– OFr. *entendance* attention, etc., f. *entendre*; see prec., -ANCE.] Application of the mind; attention –1611.

Intendance² (inte·ndăns). 1739. [– Fr. *intendance* (XVI), f. *intendant* INTENDANT *sb.*; see -ANCE.] The function of an intendant; superintendence, direction; intendancy; *spec.* a department of the French public service, or the officials conducting it, as the war commissariat, etc. **b.** The official quarters or office of an intendant 1895.

Intendancy (inte·ndănsi). Also †**-ency.** 1598. [f. INTENDANT *sb.*; see prec. and -ANCY. In sense 2 – Sp. *intendencia.*] **1.** The office, position, or function of an intendant; a body of intendants. **b.** *fig.* Superintendence. WARBURTON. **2.** A district in Spanish America under an intendant (*intendente*) 1810.

Intendant (inte·ndănt), *sb.* Also †**-ent.** 1652. [– Fr. *intendant* – *intendent-*, pr. ppl. stem of L. *intendere*; see INTEND *v.*, -ANT.] One who has the charge, direction, or superintendence of a department of public business, the affairs of a town or province, the household of a prince or nobleman, etc.; a superintendent, a manager. Used orig. and chiefly as the title of certain public officers in France and elsewhere.

The Marquess..appointed him..I. of his household DISRAELI.

†**Inte·ndant,** *a.* Also †**en-.** ME. [– (O)Fr. *entendant* (whence earlier †*entendant*), pr. pple. of *entendre*; see INTEND, -ANT.] Attentive –1581.

Intended (inte·ndėd), *ppl. a.* (*sb.*) 1576. [f. INTEND *v.* + -ED¹.] **1.** Purposed; designed, meant; intentional 1586. †**2.** Stretched out or forth; extended; increased in force or intensity, strained –1667. †**3.** Minded, resolved –1657. **4.** *sb. colloq.* An intended husband or wife 1767.

1. Your entended iourney 1594. **2.** With sharpe i. sting SPENSER. Hence **Inte·ndedly** *adv.* designedly.

Intendence (inte·ndĕns). *arch.* 1687. [f. INTEND *v.*; see -ENCE.] The paying of attention, attendance.

Writ of i. and respondence, a writ under the Great Seal in favour of one who received an appointment from the king, ordering all persons to attend and respond to his requests.

Intendency, etc.: see INTENDANCY, etc.

†**Inte·ndiment.** 1528. [– med.L. *intendimentum* (XII); cf. INTENDMENT.] **1.** = INTENDMENT 1. –1590. **2.** Intention, purpose –1628. **3.** Attention. SPENSER.

Intending (inte·ndiŋ), *ppl. a.* 1660. [f. INTEND *v.* + -ING².] That intends. **b.** Qualifying an agent-noun: Purposing to be, that is (such) in intention 1788.

b. I. subscribers should communicate [etc.] 1884.

Intendment (inte·ndmĕnt). ME. [– (O)Fr. *entendement*, f. *entendre*; see INTEND, -MENT. Cf. INTENDIMENT.] †**1.** The faculty or action of understanding –1601. †**2.** Way of understanding (something); interpretation; view –1630. **3.** Signification; import. Now *rare* or *Obs.* ME. **4.** *Law.* The construction put upon anything by the common law; true meaning as fixed by law 1574. †**5.** The act or fact of intending; intent; that which is intended; a design, project –1804. †**b.** The purpose or object of anything –1732. †**6.** Tendency, inclination –1620. †**7.** An office of supervision. FORD.

1. Maister Chaucer..Mirour of fructuous entendement HOCCLEVE. **3.** A phrase of sinister and odious i. 1879. **4.** *Common i.*, customary or reasonable interpretation, as determined by the law. The Ordinary (which is the Bishop by common i.) 1577.

Intenerate (inte·nĕreⁱt), *v.* Now *rare.* 1595. [– *intenerat-*, pa. ppl. stem of mod.L. *intenerare*, f. *in-* IN-² + L. *tener* tender; see -ATE³.] *trans.* To make tender, soften, mollify (*lit.* and *fig.*).

Feare intenerates the heart, making it fit for all gracious impressions BP. HALL. So **Inte·nerate** *ppl. a.* intenerated. Hence **Intenera·tion,** the action of intenerating, or fact of being intenerated.

†**Inte·nible,** *a.* [perh. f. IN-³ + var. (with *-ible*) of *tenable*, with active meaning as in INCAPABLE 1 'unable to contain or hold'.] Incapable of holding or containing. *All's Well* I. iii. 208.

Intensate (inte·nseⁱt), *v. rare.* 1831. [f. INTENSE + -ATE³.] *trans.* To make intense; to intensify. Hence **Intensa·tion** 1826.

Intensative (inte·nsătiv). *rare.* 1853. [Expressive extension of INTENSIVE; see *-ative.* Cf. *preventive, preventative.*] **a.** *adj.* = INTENSIVE 4. 1870. **b.** *sb.* = INTENSIVE 7.

Intense (inte·ns), *a.* ME. [– (O)Fr. *intens(e* or L. *intensus* stretched, tight, violent, pa. pple. of *intendere* INTEND *v.*] *Etymologically,* Stretched, strained, high-strung. Hence: **1.** Of a quality or condition: Raised to or existing in a very high degree; violent, extreme, excessive; of colour, very deep; of a feeling, ardent. Also *transf.* of a thing. 1653. **2.** Of personal, esp. mental, action, etc.: Strenuously directed to some end; intent, eager, earnest, ardent 1645. **3.** Of a person: †**a.** Intent *upon* (*about*) something –1724. **b.** Feeling, or susceptible to, intense emotion 1830; often in trivial sense, highly sensitive or impressionable 1878. Also *transf.* of language, aspect, etc. 1684.

1. I. cold EVELYN. *transf.* The yellow stars grew more i. overhead W. BLACK. **2.** Somtime slackning the cords of i. thought and labour MILT. **3. b** 'The intense school' may be defined as always using the strongest possible word on every possible occasion MACKINTOSH. *transf.* The expression..i. and stern 1838. Hence **Inte·nsely** *adv.*, **Inte·nseness.**

Intensification (inte:nsifikēⁱ·ʃən). 1807. [f. INTENSIFY; see -FICATION.] The action of intensifying; intensified condition; *spec.* in *Photogr.*, the thickening or increasing of the opacity of the film of a negative.

Inte·nsifier (-fəi,əɹ). 1835. [f. next + -ER¹.] Something that intensifies; *spec.* in *Photogr.* (see next, 1 b).

Intensify (inte·nsifəi), *v.* 1817. [f. INTENSE + -FY.] **1.** *trans.* To render intense; to augment, strengthen, heighten, etc. **b.** *Photogr.* To make the chemically affected parts of (a negative) more dense or opaque, so as to produce a stronger contrast of light and shade 1861. **2.** *intr.* To grow in intensity 1853.

1. Her uneasiness will be greatly intensified DICKENS. **2.** There is no relief: the action intensifies 1896.

Intension (inte·nʃən). 1603. [– L. *intensio*, f. *intens-*, pa. ppl. stem of *intendere*; see INTENSE, -ION.] **1.** The action of stretching, tension; straining. ?*Obs.* **2.** Intentness; resolution, determination 1619. **3.** Intensification. (Opp. to *remission.*) 1610. **4.** Degree, esp. notable degree, of some quality, etc.; intensity, depth, strength, force. (Often contrasted with *extension.*) 1604. **5.** *Logic.* The COMPREHENSION of a notion or concept; the CONNOTATION of a term. (Opp. to EXTENSION.) 1836.

2. I found myself..listening with an agony of i. 1860. **3.** Brightness is the I. of Light 1658. **4.** The essence of farming on virgin soils is extension; on old land it is i. 1888.

Intensitive (inte·nsĭtiv), *a.* (*sb.*) *rare.* 1817. [irreg. f. INTENSITY + -IVE.] = INTENSATIVE, INTENSIVE.

Intensity (inte·nsĭti). 1665. [f. INTENSE + -ITY.] **1.** The quality of being intense; extreme force, strength, depth, brightness, etc. **2.** The degree or amount of some quality, condition, etc.; force, strength, energy, etc.; degree of some characteristic quality; *esp.* in *Physics*, as a measurable quantity 1794. **b.** *Photogr.* = DENSITY 4. 1855.

1. Such an i. of cold BOYLE. He..looked at the stranger for several seconds with a stern i. DICKENS. **2.** Denoting the degrees of i. of some particular qualities by figures 1796.

Intensive (inte·nsiv), *a.* (*sb.*) 1450. [– (O)Fr. *intensif, -ive* or med.L. *intensivus*; see INTENSE, -IVE.] †**1.** = INTENSE *a.* 1. –1687. †**2.** = INTENSE *a.* 2. –1669. **3.** Of, relating, or pertaining to intensity, as dist. from external spatial extent or amount; of or pertaining to logical intension 1604. **b.** Having the quality of intensity 1836. **4.** Having the property of making intense; intensifying; esp. in *Gram.*, expressing intensity; giving force or emphasis 1608. **5.** *Econ.* Applied to methods of cultivation, fishery, etc., which increase the productiveness of a given area; opp. to *extensive* 1832. **6.** Characterized by being intensified 1888. **7.** *sb.* Something that intensifies; *spec.* in *Gram.* an intensive word or prefix 1813.

2. I. thinking is tedious, and tires 1669. **3.** The

record of an i. as well as extensive development TRENCH. Hence **Inte·nsively** *adv.* intensely (now *rare*); †intently; in relation to intensity or to logical intension. **Inte·nsiveness.**

Intent (inte·nt), *sb.* [ME. *entent* – OFr. *entent* :– L. *intentus*, and *entente* – (O)Fr. *entente* :– Rom. **intenta*, f. pa. pple. of L. *intendere* INTEND.] **1.** The act or fact of intending or purposing; intention, purpose (formed in the mind); design. Formerly also, Will, inclination; that which is willed, pleasure, desire. Now chiefly in legal use. †**2.** Attention, heed –1704. †**3.** Intent effort, endeavour –1483. †**4.** Mind, or an act of the mind; understanding; frame of mind, spirit; perception; notion, opinion, or thought of any kind –1623. †**5.** Meaning; purport –1676. †**b.** *Law.* = INTENDMENT 4. –1767. **6.** An end purposed; aim, purpose. *rare* or *Obs.* exc. in phr. *To (for) all intents and purposes.* ME. †**7.** Intended subject or theme –1670.

1. The bare i. to commit treason is many times actual treason BLACKSTONE. **4.** She taketh in good entente The wyl of Crist CHAUCER. **6.** I highly recommend the end and i. of Pythagoras's injunction CHATHAM.

Intent (inte·nt), *a.* 1606. [– L. *intentus*, pa. pple. of *intendere*; see prec.] **1.** Having the mind strenuously bent upon something; eager, assiduous; bent, resolved 1610. **2.** Of the faculties, looks, etc.: Directed with strained attention; eager, keen; intense 1606. †**3.** Intensely active. SIR T. BROWNE.

1. I. our prayers to heare 1610, on high designs GOLDSM. **2.** The i. Application with which he pursues Trifles STEELE. Hence **Inte·ntly** *adv.* in an i. manner. **Inte·ntness.**

†**Intenta·tion.** *rare.* 1612. [– late and med. L. *intentatio* accusation, f. L. *intentare* attack, accuse (Cicero), f. *intendere*; see INTENT *sb.*, -ION.] An accusation; a threatening –1656.

Intention (inte·nʃən). [ME. *entencion* – OFr. *entencion* (mod. *intention*) – L. *intentio* stretching, etc., design, purpose, etc., f. *intent-*, pa. ppl. stem of *intendere*; see INTENT *sb.*, -ION.]

I. General senses. †**1.** The action of straining or directing the mind or attention to something –1749. †**2.** The action or faculty of understanding; way of understanding (something); notion. Also, the mind generally. –1526. †**3.** Meaning, import –1668. **4.** The action of intending; volition; purpose ME. **5.** That which is intended; a purpose, design ME. **b.** *pl.* (*colloq.*) Purposes in respect of a proposal of marriage 1796. **6.** Ultimate purpose; aim of an action ME. †**7.** = INTENSION 1. –1654. **b.** Forcible application or direction (*of* the mind, eye, thoughts, etc.). (With more of the notion of *tension* than in sense 1.) 1638. †**8.** = INTENSION 3. –1758.

4. You never open your mouth but with i. to give pain JOHNSON. **5.** Sir, Hell is paved with good intentions JOHNSON. **b.** Colonel Fitzwilliam had made it clear that he had no intentions at all, and..she did not mean to be unhappy about him JANE AUSTEN. **6.** To..loke wel to what entention the yeft is gyuen CAXTON. **7. b.** The toil and labour, and racking i. of the brain SOUTH.

II. Spec. uses. **1.** *Surg.* and *Med.* An aim or purpose in a healing process; hence, a plan or method of treatment (*arch.*) ME. **2.** *Logic.* The direction of the mind to an object; a conception formed by directing the mind to some object; a general concept 1532. **3.** *Theol.* One of the three things necessary, according to the Schoolmen, to the effectual administration and validity of a Sacrament, the others being *Matter* and *Form* 1690. **4.** (*Special*) *i.*, a special direction of prayer at mass, etc., to a certain object 1594.

1. *Healing by first intention*, the healing of a lesion or fracture by the immediate reunion of the severed parts, without granulation; *by second i.*, the healing of a wound by granulation after suppuration. **2.** *First intentions* (Logic), primary conceptions of things, formed by the direct application of the mind to the things themselves; e.g. the concepts of *a tree, an oak. Second intentions*, secondary conceptions formed by the application of thought to first intentions in their relations to each other; e.g. the concepts of *genus, species, difference*, etc. Logic was said [by Avicenna] to treat of *second intentions applied to first* MANSEL.

Intentional (inte·nʃənăl), *a.* 1530. [– Fr. *intentionnel* or med.L. *intentionalis*, f. *intentio*; see prec., -AL[1].] **1.** Of or pertaining to intention or purpose; existing (only) in intention. **2.** Done on purpose; intended 16.. **3.** *Schol. Philos.* Pertaining to the operations of the mind; mental; existing in or for the mind 1624.

2. An i. insult SCOTT. **3.** I. species HY. MORE. Hence **Inte·ntionally** *adv.* in an i. manner or relation.

Intentionality (inte:nʃənæ·lĭti). 1611. [– med.L. *intentionalitas*; see prec., -ITY.] The quality or fact of being intentional.

Intentioned (inte·nʃənd), *a.* 1647. [f. INTENTION + -ED[2].] Having intentions (of a specified kind); as, *equitably i.*

Intentive (inte·ntiv), *a.* *Obs.* or *arch.* [ME. *ententive*, later *in-* – OFr. *ententif, intentif, -ive* in same senses, f. *entent(e*; see INTENT *sb.*, -IVE.] **1.** Of persons: Attentive, heedful, intent. **2.** Of the faculties, etc.: Intently bent or directed ME.

2. His too i. trust to flatterers 1592. **Inte·ntively** *adv.*, **-ness.**

Inter (intə̄·ɹ), *v.* ME. [– (O)Fr. *enterrer* – Rom. **interrare*, f. *in-* IN-[2] + *terra* earth, repl. L. *inhumare* INHUME.] **1.** *trans.* To deposit (a corpse) in the earth; to inhume, bury. Also *transf.* and *fig.* †**2.** Said of a tomb: To enclose the corpse of 1631. †**3.** = BURY *v.* 3. –1741.

1. Dead and enterr'd DONNE. **2.** This rich marble doth i. The honoured wife of Winchester MILT.

‖**Inter** (i·ntəɹ), the L. prep. = 'between', 'among', occurs in L. phrases occasional in Eng., e.g. *inter alia*, amongst other things (less usu. *inter alios*, amongst other persons); *inter nos*, between ourselves; *inter se*, between or among themselves.

Inter-, *prefix.* The Latin prep. and adv., *inter* 'between, among, amid, in between, in the midst', used as an Eng. formative element.

I. In adverbial or adjectival relation to the second element.

1. Prefixed to vbs., pples., vbl. sbs., and ppl. adjs., to form verbs, etc.; as in: **a.** *interbreathe, -cloud, -dash, -distinguish, -lie, -mention, -receive, -set*, etc.; **b.** *interaccuse, -arch, -balance, -chase, grapple, -jangle, -oscillate, -talk, -vary, -wed, -wish*, etc. **2.** Prefixed in adjectival relation to sbs., or in adverbial relation to adjs.; as in: **a.** *inter-absorption, -colonization, -combat, -combination, -comparison, -mobility, -mutation; intercomparable, -repellent, -visible*, adjs., etc.; **b.** *intercalm* (an interval of calm), *-canal* (a canal connecting two others), etc.

II. In prepositional relation to the sb. expressed or implied in the second element.

1. Prefixed to *sbs.*, forming sbs.; as in: **a.** *interjoist, inter-modillion, interspiral*, etc.; also *interworld*; **b.** *interpapacy, inter-parliament*, INTERREGNUM. **2.** Prefixed to *adjs.*, in prepositional relation to the sb. implied (as interacinous, 'that is *inter acinos*, between the acini'); as in: **a.** INTERALVEOLAR, -ARTICULAR, -CELLULAR, *-epimeral, -mandibular, -peduncular, -sternal*, etc.; **b.** *interequinoctial, -sessional*, etc.; **c.** *interclerical* (between clergymen), *-collegiate, -departmental*, etc.; **d.** *intercranial* (prop. *intracranial*), *-imperial, -trinitarian*, etc. **3.** Prefixed to sbs., forming adjs.; as in *inter-club* (between different clubs), *-county, -empire, -school, -town, -university* (*-'varsity*), etc.

The main stress is on the radical word, exc. in I. 2 b; but, when this is a monosyllable, it tends to shift to *inter-*.

The following adjs., mostly belonging to II. 2, are given as being of subordinate importance, but not quite self-explanatory. **Intera·cinous,** situated or occurring between or among the acini of a gland. **Interauri·cular,** 'situated between the auricles of the heart' (*Syd. Soc. Lex.*). **Intercaro·tic, Intercaro·tid,** situated between the two carotid arteries. **Interca·rpal,** situated or occurring between the bones of the carpus. **Interco·smic, -al,** situated or existing between worlds. **Intercra·nial,** situated within the skull (prop. *intracranial*). **Interimpe·rial,** carried on between or connecting the various countries of the (British) Empire. **Interme·mbral,** subsisting (as a relation) between members or limbs, as *i. homology*. **Intermercu·rial** (prop. *intra-*), *Astron.* situated within the orbit of Mercury. **Intermetaca·rpal,** situated between the bones of the metacarpus; so also **Intermetata·rsal. Intermo·ntane,** situated between mountains. **Intero·cular,** situated or occurring between the eyes. **Interpe·talary,** *Bot.* situated between petals. **Interphala·ngeal,** situated between two successive phalanges of a finger or toe. **Interta·rsal,** *Anat.* situated between the bones of the tarsus. **Interti·dal,** inhabiting the sea-shore between the limits of high and low tide. **Intertrochante·ric,** situated between two trochanters; spec. applied to a line or ridge between the greater and lesser trochanter of the femur. **Intertu·bular,** situated between tubes or tubuli. **Interu·ngular, Interu·ngulate,** situated between the hoofs (e.g. in sheep).

Interact (i·ntərˌæ:kt), *sb.* 1750. [f. INTER- II. 1 + ACT *sb.*, after Fr. *entr'acte.*] The interval between two acts of a play; an interlude; hence, an intermediate employment.

Interact (intərˌæ·kt), *v.* 1839. [INTER- I. 1 b.] *intr.* To act reciprocally, to act on each other. Hence **Intera·ction,** reciprocal action; action or influence of persons or things on each other 1832. **Intera·ctive** *a.* reciprocally active.

Interadditive (intərˌæ·ditiv). 1819. [f. INTER- I. 2 a + ADDITIVE.] Something added or inserted between or among other things.

Inter-agent (intərˌēⁱ·dʒĕnt). 1728. [f. as prec. + AGENT.] An intermediate agent; a go-between. So **Inter-a·gency.**

Interall, obs. f. ENTRAIL.

Interalveolar (intərˌælvī·ŏlăr), *a.* 1834. [INTER- II. 2a.] *Anat.* **1.** Situated between the alveoli or air-cells of the lungs. **2.** Situated between the alveoli or sockets of the teeth of a sea-urchin 1877.

‖**Interambulacrum** (-ēⁱ·krŏm). *Pl.* **-acra.** 1870. [INTER- II. 1.] *Zool.* One of the imperforate plates occupying the intervals of the ambulacra or perforate plates in the shells of echinoderms. Hence **Interambula·cral** *a.* of or pertaining to interambulacra; situated between ambulacra.

Interamnian (intərˌæ·mniăn), *a.* 1774. [f. L. *interamnus* lying between two rivers (f. *inter* INTER- II. 2 a + *amnis*) + -IAN.] Lying between rivers, like Mesopotamia; enclosed by rivers.

Intera·nimate, *v. rare.* [INTER- I. 1 b.] *trans.* To animate mutually. DONNE.

†**Interarbora·tion.** [f. INTER- I. 2 a + L. *arbor* + -ATION.] Intermixture of the branches of trees on opposite sides. SIR T. BROWNE.

Interarticular (i:ntərˌaɹti·kiulăr), *a.* 1808. [INTER- II. 2 a.] Lying or prevailing between the contiguous surfaces in a joint.

Interatomic (i:ntərˌătǫ·mik), *a.* 1863. [INTER- II. 2 a.] Existing or acting between atoms.

Interaulic (intərˌǭ·lik), *a. nonce-wd.* 1864. [INTER- II. 2 a; see AULIC.] 'Existing between royal courts' (Webster).

Interauri·cular, etc.: see INTER- *pref.*

Interaxis (intərˌæ·ksis). *Pl.* **-axes** (-æ·ksīz). 1842. [INTER- II. 1.] *Arch.* The space between the axes. So **Intera·xal** *a.* pertaining to the i., situated between the axes.

†**Interba·state,** *v. rare.* 1657. [f. Fr. *interbaster* to quilt; see -ATE[3].] *trans.* To sew between (cotton, etc.) so as to keep in place; to quilt. Hence †**Interbasta·tion,** quilting. So †**Interba·ste** *v.* (rare) 1611.

Interbed (intəɹbe·d), *v.* 1858. [INTER- I. 1 a.] *trans.* To embed amongst or between, to interstratify.

Interbrachial (-brēⁱ·kiăl), *a.* (*sb.*) 1877. [INTER- II. 2 a.] **1.** *Zool.* = INTERAMBULACRAL, INTERRADIAL. **2.** *sb.* An interbrachial part or member.

I·nter-brain. 1887. [INTER- I. 2 b.] *Anat.* = DIENCEPHALON.

Interbranchial (-bræ·ŋkiăl), *a.* 1880. [INTER- II. 2 a.] *Zool.* Situated between the branchiæ or gills.

Interbreed (intəɹbrī·d), *v.* 1859. [INTER- I. 1 b.] **1.** *intr.* Of animals of different race or species: To breed with each other 1864. **2.** *intr.* or *absol.* To cause animals to interbreed 1859. **3.** *trans.* To cross-breed. Also *fig.* 1865.

†**Inte·rcalar,** *a.* 1533. [– L. *intercalaris*; see next; -AR[1].] = INTERCALARY 1. –1699.

Intercalary (intə̄·ɹkălări), *a.* 1614. [– L. *intercalarius* or *intercalaris*, f. *intercalare* INTERCALATE.] **1.** Of a day, days, or month: Inserted at intervals in the calendar in order to bring an inexact reckoning of the year into harmony with the solar year. **b.** Of a year: Having intercalated days or an additional month 1648. †**2.** Of a line or stanza: Inserted at intervals in a composition; of the nature of a refrain –1803. **3.** Of the nature of an insertion; interpolated, intervening 1798.

1. Since the reform of the calendar by Julius Cæsar (B.C. 46), an i. day (now Feb. 29) is required only once in four years; see BISSEXTILE and LEAP YEAR. 2. Having a double burthen or i. verse oft recurring HAMMOND. 3. I. spines OWEN. Last of the I. Kaisers CARLYLE.

Intercalate (intǭ·ɹkăleᶦt), *v.* 1614. [– *intercalat-*, pa. ppl. stem of L. *intercalare* proclaim the insertion of a day, etc., in the calendar, f. *inter* INTER- + *calare* proclaim solemnly; see -ATE³.] **1.** *trans.* To insert (an additional day, days, or month) in the calendar. Also *absol.* **2.** *transf.* To insert or interpose something additional, extraneous, etc. among other things; to interpolate. Chiefly in *pass.* 1824. **b.** *Geol.* in *pass. pple.* Interstratified, interbedded with the original series 1833.

2. b. Harder beds of rock, intercalated with the softer ones H. MILLER. var. †**Intercale** *v.* 1613.

Intercalation (intəɹkălēᶦ·ʃən). 1577. [– Fr. *intercalation* or L. *intercalatio*, f. as prec.; see -ION.] **1.** The insertion of an additional day, days, or month into the ordinary year; an intercalated day or space of time. **2.** *transf.* The insertion of any addition between the members of an existing or recognized series; the occurrence of a layer or bed of a different kind between the regular strata of a series; (with *an* and *pl.*) the thing or matter thus interjected 1648.

2. Successive intercalations indicative of more than one period of glaciation A. R. WALLACE.

Intercartilaginous (-kāɹtilæ·dʒinəs), *a.* 1872. [INTER- II. 2 a.] *Anat.* Situated between cartilages.

Intercede (intəɹsī·d), *v.* 1578. [– (O)Fr. *intercéder* or L. *intercedere*, f. *inter* INTER- + *cedere* go.] **1.** *intr. Rom. Hist.* Of the tribunes: To interpose a veto 1581. †**2.** To come *between* in time, space, or action; to intervene –1799. †**3.** *trans.* To come, pass, or lie between; to intervene between –1799. †**4.** *intr.* To come in the way –1673. **5.** *intr.* To interpose on behalf of another or others 1606.

4. Subjects are bound . . to obey the Magistrate Actively in all things where their Duty to God intercedes not MARVELL. **5.** I heare not one man open his mouth to i. for the offender BP. HALL. Hence **Interce·der.**

†**Interce·dent,** *a.* 1578. [f. INTERCEDE *v.* + -ENT. Cf. Fr. *intercédent* (obs. in same sense).] Coming between; intervening –1683. Hence †**Interce·dence** (*rare*), intervention 1640.

Intercellular (intəɹse·liŭlăɹ), *a.* 1835. [INTER- II. 2 a.] Situated between or among cells.

Only two cells form an i. passage, not three or four LINDLEY. So **I·nterce:ll, Interce·llulary** *adjs.*

Intercensal (intəɹse·nsăl), *a.* 1887. [improp. f. INTER- II. 2 b + L. *census* + -AL¹.; see CENSUAL.] Of or belonging to the interval between two censuses, occurring between two censuses.

Intercentral (intəɹse·ntrăl), *a.* 1870. [INTER- II. 2 a.] *Phys.* **a.** Situated between the centra of the vertebræ; see CENTRUM. **b.** Connecting, or relating to the connection of, nerve-centres.

‖**Interce·ntrum.** 1878. [f. INTER- II. 1 + CENTRUM.] *Comp. Anat.* A wedge- or chevron-shaped process, generally situated between the centra, occurring on the ventral aspect of the vertebral column in many Vertebrates, and esp. in Reptiles; = HYPAPOPHYSIS.

Intercept (i·ntəɹsept), *sb.* 1821. [f. INTERCEPT *v.*] **1.** An interception. **2.** *Math.* The part of a line lying between two points at which it is intersected by lines or planes 1864.

Intercept (intəɹse·pt), *v.* 1545. [– *intercept-*, pa. ppl. stem of L. *intercipere*, f. *inter* INTER- + *capere* take, seize.] **1.** *trans.* To seize, catch, or carry off on the way from one place to another; to cut off from the destination aimed at 1548. **b.** To stop the natural course of (light, heat, etc.); to cut off (light) *from* anything 1545. †**c.** To interrupt –1759. **d.** To check, cut off (passage or motion) from one place to another 1596. †**e.** *absol.* or *intr.* –1682. **2.** To prevent, check, stop, hinder 1576. **3.** To mark off or include (a certain space) between two points or lines; hence, to contain, enclose. *spec.* in *Math.* (see INTERCEPT *sb.* 2). 1571. **4.** To cut off (one thing) *from* another, or (*ellipt.*) from sight, access, etc. 1662.

1. I. . Marcht toward S. Albons, to i. the Queene SHAKS. To i. Ships STEELE, supplies 1847. **b.** God will shortely i. your brethe. . if ye repent not 1545. **d.** Vessels, sent out. . to i. his passage 1683. **2.** Causes less excusable also i. its influence J. MARTINEAU. **4.** The glass which now intercepts from the eye of the mind the realities of the future world CHALMERS. Hence †**Interce·pter** (*rare*), **-or,** one who or that which intercepts. **Interce·ption,** the action of intercepting; †*spec.* in *Med.* the interruption of the motion or passage of bodily humours. **Interce·ptive** *a.* having the quality of intercepting.

Intercession (intəɹse·ʃən). 1500. [– (O)Fr. *intercession* or L. *intercessio*, f. *intercess-*, pa. ppl. stem of *intercedere*; see INTERCEDE, -ION.] **1.** The action of interceding or pleading on behalf of (*rarely* against); entreaty, solicitation, or prayer for another; mediation 1534; †a petition or pleading on one's own behalf –1742. **2.** *Rom. Hist.* The action of interposing a veto 1573. †**3.** Interposition, intervention –1638. ¶**4.** Intermission –1683.

1. I will send to you the kyng, and make humble i. for your pardon HALL. Hee euer liueth to make i. for them *Heb.* 7:25. Hence **Interce·ssional** *a.* of or pertaining to i.

†**Interce·ssionate,** *v.* 1593. [f. prec. + -ATE³.] **1.** *intr.* = INTERCEDE *v.* –1598. **2.** *trans.* To entreat. NASHE.

Intercessor (intəɹse·səɹ). 1482. [– OFr. *intercessor* (mod. *-eur*) or L. *intercessor* (sense 2), f. *intercess-*; see INTERCESSION, -OR 2. In sense 1 spec. eccl. L.] **1.** One who intercedes on behalf of another; a mediator. **b.** In religious use: A Mediator 1526. †**2.** An intermediary; a go-between –1598. **3.** *Eccl.* A bishop, who, during a vacancy, administered the see, until a successor had been elected 1727.

Intercessorial (intəɹsesōᵊ·riăl), *a.* 1776. [f. next + -AL¹; see -ORIAL.] Of or pertaining to an intercessor.

Intercessory (intəɹse·səri), *a.* 1576. [– med.L. *intercessorius* (f. *intercessor*: see prec., -ORY²), esp. in *litteræ intercessoriæ* (XIII). Cf. OFr. *intercessoire.*] Having the function or purpose of intercession; that intercedes for others; as, an *i. prayer.*

†**Interchain,** *v. rare.* 1590. [INTER- I. 1 b.] *trans.* To chain or link one to another –1649. *Mids. N.* II. ii. 49.

Interchange (i·ntəɹtʃēᶦndʒ), *sb.* 1548. [In XVI also *enter-*, f. the verb; perh. partly – OFr. *entrechange.*] **1.** Giving and receiving with reciprocity; reciprocal exchange between two persons or parties. **2.** The change of each of two (or more) things, conditions, etc. for the other, or of one thing, etc. for another; the taking by each of the place or nature of the other 1581. **3.** Alternate or varied succession in time, order, or space; alternation, vicissitude 1559. **4.** *attrib.*, as in *i. service, station*, etc. (for the passage of traffic from one railway line to another) 1887.

1. Enter-change of Gifts, Letters, louing Embassies SHAKS. An i. of commodities betwixt two countries 1804. **2.** Enterchange of war for peace DRUMM. OF HAWTH. **3.** Sweet i. Of Hill and Vallie, Rivers, Wood and Plaines, Now Land, now Sea MILT.

Interchange (intəɹtʃēᶦ·ndʒ), *v.* Also †**enter-.** ME. [Earliest forms *enter-* – OFr. *entrechangier*; see INTER-, CHANGE *v.*] **1.** *trans.* To exchange mutually; to give and receive in reciprocity. **b.** Of one person or party: To exchange (something) *with* another person 1566. **2.** To put each of (two things) in the place of the other; †also, to exchange (one thing) *for* another; †to change (clothes) ME. **3.** To cause (things) to follow each other alternately or in succession 1561; *intr.* to alternate *with*; to become by turns 1483.

1. To i. presents 1624, opinions MACAULAY. **b.** I interchanged signals with His Majesty's Ship, L'Aimable 1805. **2.** Once more I shall enterchange My wained state, for Henries Regall Crowne SHAKS. **3.** *intr.* Those [Insecta] that Enterchange from Wormes to Flyes BACON.

Interchangeable (intəɹtʃēᶦ·ndʒăb'l), *a.* (*adv.*) 1450. [– OFr. *entrechangeable*, f. the verb (prec.); see -ABLE.] †**1.** Mutual, reciprocal –1665. †**b.** as *adv.* Mutually –1644. †**2. a.** Of two or more things: Coming or following in place of each other –1783. †**b.** Of one thing: Changeable –1749. **3.** Admitting an exchange of place or function 1569.

2. a. Darknesse and light hold i. dominions SIR T. BROWNE. **b.** I. Weather 1749. **3.** Not one. . recognizes it [*for the nonce*] as i. with 'for the occasion' F. HALL. Hence **Interchangeabi·lity, Intercha·ngeableness. Intercha·ngeably** *adv.* 1375.

†**Intercha·ngement.** 1601. [– OFr. *entrechangement*, f. the verb (cf. prec.); see -MENT.] = INTERCHANGE *sb.* 1. –1796.

†**Inte·rcident,** *a.* 1603. [– *intercident-*, pr. ppl. stem of L. *intercidere* fall between, occur meanwhile (the medical use is med. and mod.L.), f. *inter* INTER- + *cadere* fall; see -ENT.] **1.** *Med.* Of days in an illness: Falling between the critical and judicial days –1685. **2.** *Path.* Of the pulse: characterized by irregular rhythm. HARVEY. Hence †**Inte·rcidence,** the fact of being i. P. HOLLAND.

†**Interci·pient.** 1656. [– *intercipient-*, pr. ppl. stem of L. *intercipere*; see INTERCEPT *v.* -ENT.] **A.** *adj.* That intercepts or stops the flow of humours 1684. **B.** *sb.* An application which does this –1684.

†**Interci·sion.** 1578. [– Fr. †*intercision* or L. *intercisio* (sense 2 is med.L.), f. *inter* INTER-; see INCISION.] **1.** The action of cutting through; section, intersection. Also with *an*: A cross-section. –1726. **2.** The action of stopping or interrupting, esp. temporarily; the fact of being interrupted or ceasing for a time –1660. Also with *an* and *pl.* –1813. **3.** Falling away, failing –1651.

Interclavicle (intəɹ,klæ·vik'l). 1870. [INTER- II. 1.] *Anat.* A bone occurring between the clavicles in certain vertebrates. So **I:nterclavi·cular** *a.* lying between the clavicles; esp. in *i. bone, ligament, notch* 1831.

†**Interclo·se,** *v. rare.* 1457. [INTER- I. 1 a.] *trans.* To shut up; to enclose within –1680.

†**Interclu·de,** *v.* 1524. [– L. *intercludere*, f. *inter* INTER- + *claudere* CLOSE *v.*] **1.** *trans.* To close, shut up, block (a passage); to prevent the passage of –1683. **2.** To shut up, confine within bounds –1806. **3.** To shut off, cut off *from* –1621.

1. Like as the voice is sometimes intercluded by a hoarseness 1669. So †**Interclu·sion,** shutting up.

Intercolline (intəɹkǫ·ləin), *a.* 1858. [f. INTER- II. 2 a + L. *collis* a hill, *collinus* relating to a hill.] *Geol.* Lying between hills; applied by Sir Charles Lyell to the hollows lying between hills formed by accumulation of erupted volcanic matter.

Intercolonial (i:ntəɹkŏlōᵘ·niăl), *a.* 1855. [INTER- II. 2 c.] Existing, carried on, etc. between different colonies. Hence **Interco·lo·nially** *adv.*

I:nterco·lumn. ?*Obs.* 1665. [– L. *intercolumnium*, f. *inter* INTER- + *columna* COLUMN. Cf. Fr. *entrecolonne.*] *Arch.* The space between two columns.

Intercolumnar (i:ntəɹkŏlɒ·mnăɹ), *a.* 1842. [f. prec. + -AR¹. Cf. Fr. *intercolumnaire.*] **1.** *Arch.* Lying or placed between two columns 1862. **2.** *Anat.* Extending between the columns of the external abdominal rings. So **Intercolu·mniary** *a.* in sense 1. 1663.

†**Intercolumna·tion.** 1664. [var. of next, after COLUMNATION.] = next –1757.

Intercolumniation (i:ntəɹkŏlɒmniēᶦ·ʃən). 1624. [f. L. *intercolumnium* + -ATION.] **1.** = INTERCOLUMN. **2.** The placing of columns, with reference to the space between them 1847.

Interco·mmon, *v.* [ME. *entrecomon* – AFr. *entrecomuner*, f. *entre-* (INTER- I. 1 b) + *comuner* to COMMON, COMMUNE.] †**1.** *intr.* To have intercourse *with* others; to associate *with* or together –1675. **2.** *intr.* To share in the use of the same common 1598. †**3.** *intr.* To share or participate *with* others, or mutually –1661. †**4.** *trans. Sc. Law.* To denounce by 'letters of intercommuning'; hence, to outlaw –1717.

3. He and hogs did in some sort entercommon both in their diet and lodging FULLER. **4.** The numbers and desperate tempers of those who were intercommoned BURNET. Hence **Interco·mmonage,** the practice of sharing with others, esp. of using common pasture. **Interco·mmoner,** one who participates with others, esp. in the use of common pasture. Chiefly in *pl.*

Intercommune, *v.* Now *rare* or *Obs.* ME.

[– AFr. *entrecomuner*; see prec., and cf. COMMUNE *v.* Stressed at first *co·mmune*, later prob. *commu·ne*.] **1.** *intr.* To have mutual communion; to hold conversation with each other or with another. †**2.** To have intercourse, relations, or connection, esp. in *Sc. Law*, with rebels or denounced persons –1828. †**3.** To participate in the use of the same pasture or the like. HOLLAND. †**4.** *trans. Sc.* To denounce by letters or writ of intercommuning; to prohibit 'intercommuning with' –1730.

Interco·mmuner. 1620. [f. prec. (sense 4) + -ER^{1}.] *Sc. Law.* One who holds intercourse or correspondence with a person denounced by law. Now *Hist.*

Intercommu·nicable, *a.* 1822. [f. INTERCOMMUNICATE *v.*, after COMMUNICABLE.] Capable of or suitable for intercommunication.

Intercommunicate (i:ntəɹkǫmiū·nikeᶦt), *v.* 1586. [– *intercommunicat-*, pa. ppl. stem of AL. *intercommunicare* (XIV); see INTER- I. 1 b and COMMUNICATE *v.*] **1.** *intr.* To communicate mutually; to have mutual intercourse; to have free passage into each other. **2.** *trans.* To communicate, impart, or transmit to and from each other 1603.

1. The branchial chambers i. both above and below.

Intercommunication (-kǫmiūnikēᶦ·ʃən). 1586. [– AL. *intercommunicatio* (XIV), f. as prec.; see -ION.] **1.** Intercourse. **2.** Interchange of speech; mutual conference 1603. **3.** Passage to and fro by channels or lines of communication 1866.

Intercommunion (-kǫmiū·niən, -yen). 1761. [INTER- I. 2 a.] **1.** Communion with one another; intimate intercourse. **2.** The mutual action or relation between things in regard to functions 1817.

2. When all these studies reach the point of i. and connection with one another JOWETT.

Intercommunity (-kǫmiū·nĭti). 1587. [f. INTER- I. 2 a + COMMUNITY.] The quality of being common to various parties; the condition of having things in common.

Intercomparison, etc.: see INTER- *pref.*

Intercondylar (-kǫ·ndilăɹ), *a.* 1884. [INTER- II. 2 a.] Situated between condyles or rounded bone-ends. So **Interco·ndyloid** 1836.

Interconnect (-kǫne·kt), *v.* 1865. [INTER- I. 1 b.] *trans.* To connect each with the other. Chiefly in *pa. pple.*

Interconnection, -connexion (-kǫne·kʃən). 1822. [INTER- I. 2 a.] Mutual connection.

Intercontine·ntal, *a.* 1855. [INTER- II. 2 c.] Situated or subsisting between, or connecting, different continents; including persons of different continents; as *i. railways*.

Interconvertible (-kǫnvɔ̄·ɹtĭb'l), *a.* 1802. [INTER- I. 2 a.] Mutually convertible; interchangeable; as, *i. expressions*. Hence **Interconvertibi·lity. Interconve·rtibly** *adv.*

Intercostal (-kǫ·stăl). 1597. [f. INTER- II. 2 a + L. *costa* rib + -AL^{1}. Cf. Fr. *intercostal* (XVI).] **A.** *adj.* Situated between the ribs of the body; also *transf.*

transf. A keelson with i. plates 1869.

B. *sb. pl.* Intercostal parts 1681.

Two sets of muscles, called intercostals HUXLEY.

Intercourse (i·ntəɹkoᵊɹs). Also †**enter-.** 1467. [XV–XVII also *entercourse* – (O)Fr. *entrecours* exchange, commerce – L. *intercursus* (in med.L. senses), f. *intercurrere* intervene, f. *inter* between + *currere* run.] **1.** Communication to and fro between countries, etc.; mutual dealings between the inhabitants of different localities. In early use only with reference to trade. **2.** Social communication between individuals; dealings; discourse 1547. **b.** With *of* (= in respect of) 1613. **c.** Sexual connection 1798. **3.** Communion between man and that which is spiritual or unseen 1561. †**4.** Intercommunication between things or parts –1787. †**5.** Passage in; entrance –1658. **6.** Continuous interchange *of* (letters, etc.). Now *rare.* 1576. †**7.** Alternation –1655. †**8.** Intervention; an intervening course or space; an interval –1646.

1. They had free entercourse of trade one with another BINGHAM. **2.** Those with whom time and i. have made us familiar JOHNSON. **3.** A devout i. with God PUSEY. **6.** This sweet i. Of looks and smiles MILT.

Intercross (i·ntəɹkrǭs), *sb.* 1859. [INTER- I. 2 a.] An instance of cross-breeding or cross-fertilization.

Intercross (intəɹkrǭ·s), *v.* 1711. [INTER- I. 1 b.] **1.** *trans.* **a.** To cross each other (also *intr.* for *refl.*). **b.** To lay or place across each other. **2.** *intr.* Of plants or animals of different stocks or species: To breed or propagate with each other. Also *trans.* in *pass.* 1859.

2. The almost universal sterility of species when intercrossed DARWIN.

Intercrural (intəɹkrūᵊ·răl), *a.* 1693. [INTER- II. 2 a.] *Anat.* Situated between the crura, legs, or limbs, of the body, or of some part of it; see CRUS 2.

†**Intercu·r,** *v.* 1527. [– L. *intercurrere*; see INTERCOURSE. In earlier use through OFr. *entrecorre*.] **1.** *intr.* To run, come, or pass *between* persons or things –1625. **2.** To intervene, come in the way –1677.

Intercurrence (intəɹkɒ·rĕns). 1603. [f. next; see -ENCE.] Interwoven; an intervening occurrence.

Intercurrent (intəɹkɒ·rĕnt), *a.* (*sb.*) 1611. [– *intercurrent-*, pr. ppl. stem of L. *intercurrere*; see INTERCOURSE, -ENT.] That runs or comes between. **1.** †Lying or situated between –1685; intervening 1611. **2.** *spec.* in *Med.* **a.** Of a disease: Occurring during the progress of another disease. Also, Recurring at intervals. Formerly (of a fever), Happening at any period of the year. 1684. **b.** Of the pulse: Having an extra beat 1707. †**3.** *sb.* An incident. HOLLAND. Hence **Intercu·rrently** *adv.*

†**Intercuta·neous,** *a.* 1651. [– med.L. *intercutaneus* (see INTER-, CUTANEOUS) + -OUS.] Subcutaneous. Also, lying between the bark and stem of a tree –1664.

†**I·nterdeal,** *sb.* 1591. [f. INTER- I. 2 a + DEAL *sb.*^{2}] Mutual dealing, negotiation; intercourse; ado –1612.

Interdea·l, *v.* 1601. [f. INTER- I. 1 b + DEAL *v.*] *intr.* To deal or negotiate mutually.

I:nterdenomina·tional, *a.* 1877. [INTER- II. 2 c.] Common to several religious denominations.

Interdental (intəɹde·ntăl), *a.* 1874. [INTER- II. 2 a.] **1.** Situated or placed between the teeth (of a person or animal, or of a toothed wheel). **2.** *Phonology.* Pronounced by placing the tip of the tongue between the teeth 1877.

2. French (t) and (d) are dental, often also i. SWEET.

Interdepend (i:ntəɹdĭpe·nd), *v.* 1848. [INTER- I. 1 b.] *intr.* To depend upon each other mutually.

Interdependence (i:ntəɹdĭpe·ndĕns). Also **-ance.** 1822. [INTER- I. 2 a.] Mutual dependence. So **Interdepe·ndency** 1838.

Interdependent (i:ntəɹdĭpe·ndĕnt), *a.* 1817. [INTER- I. 2 a.] Dependent each upon the other. Hence **Interdepe·ndently** *adv.* in mutual dependence.

Interdict (i·ntəɹdikt), *sb.* [ME. *entredit* – OFr. *entredit* – L. *interdictum* (to which the Eng. word was assim. XVI), subst. use of n. of pa. pple. of *interdicere* interpose by speech, forbid by decree, f. *inter* INTER- + *dicere* say.] **1.** *gen.* An authoritative prohibition; an act of forbidding peremptorily 1626. **2.** *Law.* **a.** *Rom. Law.* A provisional decree of the prætor, in a dispute of private persons relating to possession, commanding or (more usually) forbidding something to be done 1611. **b.** *Sc. Law.* An order of the Court of Session, or of an inferior court, corresponding to an INJUNCTION in English Law 1810. **3.** *R. C. Ch.* An authoritative sentence debarring a particular place or person (esp. the former) from ecclesiastical functions and privileges ME.

1. These are not Fruits forbidden, no i. Defends the touching of these viands pure MILT. *P. R.* II. 369.

Interdict (intəɹdi·kt), *v.* [ME. *entredite*, etc., f. prec., after OFr. *entredire* – L. *interdicere*; see prec.]. **1.** *trans.* To declare authoritatively against the doing of (an action) or the use of (a thing); to forbid, prohibit; to debar by or as by a command 1502. **2.** To restrain (a person) by authority from the doing or use of something; to forbid to do something 1575. **3.** *Eccl.* To lay under an interdict (see INTERDICT *sb.* 3) ME.

1. Firm wisdom interdicts the soft'ning tear POPE. **2.** Who..will..i. thee his tabernacle ABP. SANDYS.

Interdiction (intəɹdi·kʃən). 1494. [– L. *interdictio*, f. *interdicere*; see prec., -ION.] The action of interdicting, or fact of being interdicted. **1.** Authoritative or peremptory prohibition 1579. **2.** *Eccl.* The issuing of an interdict; the action of laying, or condition of being laid, under an interdict 1494. **3. a.** *Sc. Law.* A restraint imposed upon a person incapable of managing his own affairs on account of unsoundness of mind, etc. **b.** *Law.* = INTERDICT *sb.* 2 a, b. 1575.

1. This I. of sepulchral Rites WARBURTON.

Interdi·ctive, *a. rare.* 1609. [– med.L. *interdictivus*, f. as prec.; see -IVE.] = INTERDICTORY.

Interdictor (intəɹdi·ktəɹ, -ǫɹ). 1681. [– late (eccl.) L. *interdictor* (Tertullian), f. as prec.; see -OR 2.] One who interdicts; esp. in *Sc. Law* (see INTERDICTION 3 a).

Interdictory (intəɹdi·ktəri), *a.* 1755. [– late L. *interdictorius*, f. as prec.; see -ORY^{2}.] Having the quality or effect of interdicting; prohibitory.

Interdiffuse (intəɹdifiū·z), *v.* 1882. [INTER- I. 1 a.] *trans.* To diffuse between or among other things. So **Interdiffu·sion,** mutual diffusion 1864. **Interdiffu·sive** *a.* tending to mutual diffusion 1859.

Interdigital (intəɹdi·dʒităl), *a.* 1836. [f. INTER- II. 2 a + DIGIT + -AL^{1}.] Situated between, or connecting, digits (fingers or toes).

Interdigitate (intəɹdi·dʒiteᶦt). *v.* 1847. [f. INTER- I. 1 b + DIGIT + -ATE^{3}.] **1.** *intr.* To interlock the fingers of the two hands when clasped; to inosculate by reciprocal serrations. **2.** *trans.* To cause to interlock or inosculate in this way (*rare*) 1864. Hence **I:nterdigita·tion,** the action or condition of interdigitating; *concr.* an interdigitating structure or process.

†**Intere·mption.** *rare.* 1656 [– late and med.L. *interemptio*, f. *interempt-*, pa. ppl. stem of L. *interimere* cut off, destroy; see -ION.] Destruction, slaughter –1664.

†**Interess,** *sb.* [ME. and AFr. *interesse* – med.L. *interesse* compensation for loss, interest on loan (XIII) – L. *interest*; see INTEREST *sb.*] = INTEREST *sb.* –1716.

†**Intere·ss,** *v. Pa. pple.* **interessed, -est.** 1570. [– Fr. *intéresser* †damage, concern, f. L. *interesse*; see INTEREST *sb.*] **1.** *trans.* = INTEREST *v.* 1. Chiefly in *pass.*, *to be interessed*, to have a right or share –1674. **2.** = INTEREST *v.* 2. Chiefly in *pass.* –1663. **3.** To affect injuriously; to endamage –1641. **4.** = INTEREST *v.* 4. –1711. **5.** To affect with a feeling of concern; *refl.* To concern oneself. –1697. Hence **Interessee·** (*rare*), an interested party.

‖**Intere·sse termini.** 1658. [med.L., = interest of term or end.] *Law.* A right of entry on a leasehold estate, acquired through a demise.

†**Intere·ssor.** [– med.L. (Du Cange), f. *interesse* be among.] A partner. PETTY.

Interest (i·ntĕrĕst), *sb.* 1450. [Late ME. alt. of INTERESS *sb.*, partly by addition of parasitic *t*, partly by assoc. with OFr. *interest* damage, loss (mod. *intérêt*), app. subst. use of L. *interest* it makes a difference, concerns, matters, 3rd. pers. sing. pres. ind. of *interesse* differ, be of importance, f. *inter* INTER- + *esse* be.]

I. 1. The relation of being objectively concerned in something, by having a right or title to, a claim upon, or a share in. **a.** Legal concern *in* a thing; esp. right or title to property, etc. Also *fig.* **b.** Right or title to spiritual privileges 1607. **c.** Share, part 1586. **d.** *esp.* A pecuniary share or stake in, or claim upon anything 1674. **2.** The relation of being concerned or affected in respect of advantage or detriment; esp. an advantageous relation of this kind 1533. **b.** Good, benefit, profit, advantage 1579. **3.** A thing in which one has an interest or concern 1618. **4.** A business, cause, or principle, in which a number of persons are interested; the party interested; a party having a common interest 1674. **5.** = SELF-INTEREST 1622. **6.** Influence due to personal connection; personal influence *with* (†*in*) a person or body of persons 1600. **7.** The feeling of one who is concerned or has a personal concern in any thing; hence, the state of feeling proper to such a relation; a feeling of concern for or curiosity about a person or thing 1771. **b.** *transf.* Power of exciting this feeling, interesting character or quality 1821. **8.** The fact or quality of mattering; concernment, importance 1809.

1. a. All your I. in those Territories Is vtterly bereft you SHAKS. **c.** Ah so much i. haue [I] in thy sorrow, As I had Title in thy Noble Husband SHAKS. **d.** Those fractional and volatile interests in trading adventures which go by the name of 'shares' KINGLAKE. **2.** To have an i. in the welfare of a country BURKE. **b.** One who has our i. at heart BURKE. *In the interest(s) of*: on the side of what is beneficial or advantageous to. SHAKS. *Lear* v. iii. 85. *Mod.* He represented Ipswich in the Liberal i. **4.** The notion of creating a new, that is, a moneyed i., in opposition to the landed i. BOLINGBROKE. **6.** To raise the people in the counties..where his i. lay HUME. **7.** A man with wide interests 1898. **b.** Questions of great i. JOWETT. **8.** Matters of subordinate i. 1845.

II. Senses related to med.L. *interesse*, as used in the phrase *damna et interesse*, Fr. *dommages et intérêts*, the indemnity due to any one for the damage done to him. Cf. OFr. *interest* in sense 'damage', also 'damages'. †**1.** Injury, detriment. **b.** Compensation for injury, damages (*rare*). –1607. **2.** Money paid for the use of money lent (the *principal*), or for forbearance of a debt, according to a fixed ratio (*rate per cent.*) 1545. **b.** *fig.* esp. in phr. *with interest*, with increase or augmentation 1589.

2. *Simple i.*, the i. paid on the principal as lent. *Compound* (†*compounded*) *i.* (*i. upon i.*), the i. eventually paid on a principal periodically increased by the addition of interest remaining unpaid. **b.** The latter..returned the blows with i. W. IRVING.

Interest (i·ntĕrĕst), *v.* 1608. [alt. of INTERESS *v.* after INTEREST *sb.*] **1.** *trans.* To invest with a share in or title to something, esp. a spiritual privilege. Const. *in.* 1610. **2.** To cause to have an objective interest or concern in the progress or fate of a matter; to involve; chiefly in *pass.* 1608. **3.** Of a thing: To concern; to affect; to relate to. *rare* or *Obsol.* 1638. **4.** To cause to take a personal interest, share, or part in; to engage *in.* *refl.* To take active part *in.* 1630. **5.** To affect with a feeling of concern; to excite the curiosity or attention of 1780.

1. By faith we become interested in the propitiation 1864. **3.** Their private opinions..doe not i. our beliefs 1638. **4.** They seek to i. in their design the City of London 1647. I am not called upon to i. myself in his behalf 1900. **5.** Your account of the first night interested me immensely DICKENS.

Interested (i·ntĕrĕstĕd), *ppl. a.* 1655. [f. prec. + -ED¹.] **1.** Concerned, affected; having an interest or share in something 1828. **2.** Self-seeking, self-interested. (The opposite of *disinterested.*) 1705. **3.** Characterized by a feeling of concern, sympathy, or curiosity 1665.

1. An i. witness 1828. **2.** The wretched consequences of i. marriages THACKERAY. **3.** An i. auditor 1900. Hence **I·nterested-ly** *adv.*, **-ness.**

Interesting (i·ntĕrĕstiŋ), *ppl. a.* 1711. [f. INTEREST *v.* + -ING².] Formerly (and still dial.) *intere·sting.*] †**1.** That concerns, touches, or affects; important –1813. **2.** Adapted to excite interest; of interest 1768.

1. In defence of what they thought most dear and i. to themselves 1769. **2.** An i. conversation 1843. All knowledge is i. to a wise man M. ARNOLD. *In an i. condition* (*situation*): pregnant 1748. Hence **I·nteresting-ly** *adv.*, **-ness.**

Interfacial (intəɹfē¹·ʃ¹ăl), *a.* 1837. [f. INTER- II. 2 a + L. *facies* face + -AL¹.] Included between two faces of a crystal or other solid; as in *i. angle.*

Interfascicular (-făsi·kiŭlăɹ), *a.* 1836. [f. INTER- II. 2 a + FASCICULE + -AR¹.] *Anat.* and *Bot.* Situated between fascicles or bundles of tissue.

Interfemoral (-fe·mŏrăl), *a.* 1828. [f. INTER- II. 2 a + *femur* (pl. *femora*) + -AL¹.] *Anat.* Extending between the femora or thighs; as, *the i. web of a bat.*

Interfenestration (i:ntəɹfenĕstrē¹·ʃən). 1823. [f. INTER- I. 2 a + FENESTRATION. Cf. *intercolumniation.*] *Archit.* The spacing of the windows of a building.

†**Interfe·re,** *v.*¹ late ME. [– obs. Fr. *interferer* introduce, app. f. L. *inter* + *ferre* carry.] *trans.* To interpose, intersperse; *intr.* to be intermingled *with.*

Interfere (intəɹfī³·ɹ), *v.*² 1530. [– OFr. *s'entreferir* strike each other, f. *entre* INTER- + *ferir* :– L. *ferire* strike.] **1.** *intr.* Of a horse: To strike the inside of the fetlock with the shoe or hoof of the opposite foot; to knock one leg against another. Said also of the feet. (Rarely of persons.) **2.** *intr.* Hence, of things generally: To strike against each other; to come into collision; to clash; to get in each other's way. Now chiefly in *Physics*, of waves of light, heat, sound, etc.: To exercise reciprocal action, so as to increase, diminish, or nullify the natural effect of each. †Also *fig.* 1613. †**3.** *intr.* To run into each other; to intercross, intersect –1725. **4. a.** Of things, actions, etc.: To come into collision or opposition, so as to affect the course of 1662. **b.** Of persons: To meddle *with*; to interpose in something, esp. without having the right to do so 1632. **5.** To interpose, so as to affect some action; to intervene. Const. *in.* 1743. **6.** *U.S. Football.* To interpose between the player with the ball and a would-be tackler so as to help the former 1920.

1. She [a mare] enterfears a little behind 1684. **2.** *fig.* When public duty and private feeling i... then justice calls for punishment 1836. **4. a.** No scruples of conscience to i. with his morality 'JUNIUS'. Hence **Interfe·rer.** **Interfe·ringly** *adv.*

Interference (intəɹfī³·rĕns). 1783. [irreg. f. prec. + -ENCE, after derivs. of L. *ferre*, e.g. *difference.*] **1.** The action or fact of interfering or intermeddling. **2.** *Physics.* The mutual action of two waves or systems of waves, in reinforcing or neutralizing each other, when their paths meet or cross 1830. Orig. introduced to designate phenomena observed in the mutual action of two rays of light, before the establishment of the undulatory theory; subseq. extended to sound-waves, the undulations on the surface of water, etc. **b.** *Wireless.* The intrusion of electrical disturbances which interfere with reception 1902. **3.** The action of interfering (of a horse). (Dicts.) **4.** *U.S.* The conflict of claims arising when two applications are made for a similar patent 1888. **5.** *U.S. Football*: see prec. 6.

1. Active i. in the struggles of the Continent 1874.

Comb.: **i. figure,** the figure produced when a section of crystal, appropriately cut, is viewed in converging polarized light; **i. fringe,** one of a series of alternate light and dark bands produced by a diffraction-grating. Hence **Interfere·ntial** *a.* of, pertaining to, or operating by, wave-interference.

Interferometer (i:ntəɹfī³rǫ·mĭtəɹ). 1899. [f. INTERFERE *v.*² + -METER.] An instrument for measuring lengths by means of the interference phenomena of two rays of light.

Interflow (intəɹflō^u·), *v.* 1610. [INTER- I. 1.] **1.** *intr.* To flow between (*rare*). **2.** *intr.* To flow into each other; to intermingle 1844. So **I·nterflow** *sb.* 1610.

Interfluent (intɔ̄·ɹflu,ĕnt), *a.* 1651. [INTER- I. 1.] **1.** Flowing between. Now *rare.* **2.** Intermingling; in which there is an interflow 1872. So **Inte·rfluence** 1817. **Inte·rfluous** *a.* 1656.

Interfold (intəɹfō^u·ld), *v.* 1579. [INTER- I. 1 b.] *trans.* (and *refl.*) To fold together or within each other; to involve in common folds.

Interfoliaceous (-fō^uliē¹·ʃəs), *a.* 1760. [f. INTER- II. 2 a + FOLIUM + -ACEOUS.] *Bot.* Situated alternately between a pair of opposite leaves.

Interfo·liate, *v.* 1696. [INTER- I. 1 a.] *trans.* To interleave.

Interfre·tted, *ppl. a.* 1828. [f. INTER- I. 1 b + FRETTED *ppl. a.*² 2.] *Her.* Interlaced.

Interfulgent (-fʊ·ldʒĕnt), *a.* *rare.* 1721. [f. INTER- I. 1 + FULGENT *a.*] Shining among or between.

Interfuse (intəɹfiū·z), *v.* 1593. [– *interfus-*, pa. ppl. stem of L. *interfundere*, f. *inter* INTER- + *fundere* pour; infl. by FUSE *v.*, INFUSE.] **1.** *trans.* To permeate or intersperse. **2.** To pour in, infuse 1667. **3.** To fuse or blend (*trans.* and *intr.*) 1851. **4.** *trans.* Of one thing: To penetrate or permeate and blend with 1876.

1. Abundantly interfused with Greek and Latin quotations HAWTHORNE. **2.** The ambient Aire wide interfus'd Imbracing round this florid Earth MILT. *P. L.* VII. 89. **4.** The genius which interfused the plays 1876.

Interfusion (-fiū·ʒən). 1817. [f. prec. + -ION, or f. INTER- + FUSION.] The action of interfusing or fact of being interfused.

Interganglio·nic, *a.* 1835. [f. INTER- II. 2 a + GANGLION + -IC.] *Anat.* Situated between or connecting ganglia, as the nerves of the sympathetic system.

†**Inte·rgatory.** Syncopated f. INTERROGATORY. *Merch. V.* v. i. 298.

Interglacial (-glē¹·ʃ¹ăl), *a.* 1867. [INTER- II. 2 b.] *Geol.* Lying between glacial periods; formed or occurring between two such periods.

Intergla·ndular, *a.* 1873. [f. INTER- II. 2 a + GLANDULE + -AR¹.] *Anat.* Lying between glands.

Interglobular (-glǫ·biŭlăɹ), *a.* 1859. [f. INTER- II. 2 a + GLOBULE + -AR¹.] *Anat.* Lying between globules (of dentine).

I·ntergrowth. 1844. [INTER- I. 2 a.] The growing (of things) into each other.

Interhæ·mal. 1846. [f. INTER- II. 2 a + Gr. αἷμα + -AL¹; cf. HÆMAL.] *Anat.* **A.** *adj.* Situated between hæmal spines. **B.** *sb.* An interhæmal bone or spine 1880.

Interhyal (-həi·ăl). 1884. [f. INTER- II. 2 a + HY(OID + -AL¹.] *Anat.* **A.** *adj.* Situated between two parts of the hyoid arch of a fish. **B.** *sb.* An intermediate bone or cartilage in the hyoid arch 1888.

Interim (i·ntərim). 1548. [L. *interim* adv., f. *inter* + advb. ending *-im.*]

‖**A.** *adv.* In the meantime, meanwhile 1580. I., take courage, and make your calculations anew 1804.

B. *sb.* **1.** An intervening time; the meantime; now usu. in phr. *in the i.* = A. 1563. †**2.** Something done in the interim; an interlude –1633. **3.** A provisional arrangement, adopted in the meanwhile 1558. **b.** *Ch. Hist.* (with capital *I.*) Each of three provisional arrangements for the adjustment of religious differences between the German Protestants and the Roman Catholic Church, promulgated, one in 1541 and two in 1548, pending a settlement by a General Council 1548.

1. Betweene the acting of a dreadfull thing, And the first motion, all the I. is Like a Phantasma, or a hideous Dreame *Jul. C.* II. i. 64. **2.** *L. L. L.* I. i. 172.

C. *adj.* Done, made, occurring, etc. in or for the meantime; provisional. Formerly also of time: Intervening. 1604.

I. orders for payment of alimony 1858. I. dividend 1882.

Hence **I·nterimist,** one who accepted or advocated one of the Interims (B. 3 b) 1560. **I:nterimi·stic** (†-ical 1643) *a.* = INTERIM C.; also, belonging to the Interimists; pertaining to or in accordance with the Interim 1859.

Interior (intī³·riəɹ). 1490. [– L. *interior*, compar. adj. from *inter* (superl. *intimus*).]

A. *adj.* **1.** Situated more within, or (simply) within something; internal. **b.** Inland; belonging to the interior 1777. **2.** Existing within limits figured as spatial: **a.** Internal, domestic; as opp. to *foreign* 1768; **b.** Inner, as distinct from what appears on the surface or is publicly declared 1775. **3.** Mental or spiritual; 'inward' 1513. **b.** Devoted to spiritual things; pious, devout 1756.

1. *I. angle* (Geom.): any one of the angles included between the sides of a rectilineal figure within the figure; also, an angle included between a straight line falling upon two other straight lines and either of the latter on the side towards the other. *I. planets*: Mercury and Venus, whose orbits are within that of the earth (more usu. called INFERIOR). *I. screw*, one cut on an i. or hollow surface, as of a nut, burr, or tap-hole. **b.** In the interiour parts of the empire SIR W. JONES. **2. a.** The i. trade, or that from place to place within the country JAS. MILL. **b.** There was to be no i. cabinet MACAULAY. **3. b.** Difference.. between the i. and the worldly man 1879.

B. *sb.* **1.** The interior part of anything; the inside 1828. **b.** The inland parts of a country, island, or continent; an inland region 1796. **c.** The inside of a building or room; also, a picture of this. (Usu. with *an* or in *pl.*) 1864. **2.** Inner nature or being; inward mind; soul, character 1596. **3.** The internal or home affairs of a country or state; the department concerned with these; in the titles *Secretary, Department of the I.* (U.S. and Canada), and *Minister of the I.*, used in reference to France, Germany, Italy, etc. 1838.

1. In the i. of the earth HUXLEY. **c.** A photographer noted for his interiors 1900. **2.** *Merch. V.* II. ix. 28. Hence **Inte·riorly** *adv.* internally; inwardly.

Interiority (intīᵊriǫ·rīti). *rare.* 1701. [– med. (theol.) L. *interioritas*; see INTERIOR, -ITY. Cf. Fr. †*intériorité*.] The quality or state of being interior; inner character or nature; an inner element.

Interja·cence. *rare.* 1864. [f. INTERJACENT; see -ENCE.] The fact of lying between.

Interjacency (intəɹdʒēⁱ·sĕnsi). 1646. [f. as prec. + -ENCY.] The quality or state of lying between; also, something lying between.

The I. of two Provinces between your Seat of Government and the Places to which you would now extend your Jurisdiction 1773.

Interjacent (intəɹdʒēⁱ·sĕnt), *a.* 1594. [– L. *interjacens, -ent-*, pr. pple. of *interjacēre*, f. *inter* INTER- + *jacēre* lie; see -ENT.] Lying or existing between; intervening; as, *i. nations.*

Interja·culate, *v.* [f. INTER- I. 1 a + (E)JACULATE.] To interject (an ejaculation). THACKERAY. Hence **Interja·culatory** *a.* expressed in parenthetical ejaculations 1827.

Interject (intəɹdʒe·kt), *v.* 1578. [– *interject-*, pa. ppl. stem of L. *intericere* interpose, f. *inter* INTER- + *jacere* throw, cast.] **1.** *trans.* To throw in between; to introduce abruptly; to insert, interpose. **b.** To remark parenthetically or as an interruption 1791. †**2.** *intr.* for *refl.* **a.** To cross one another, as two lines. **b.** To come between; to intervene, interpose –1676.

Interjection (intəɹdʒe·kʃən). ME. [– (O)Fr. *interjection* – L. *interjectio*, f. as prec.; see -ION.] **1.** The utterance of ejaculations expressive of emotion; an exclamation. **2.** *Gram.* A natural ejaculation expressing emotion, viewed as a Part of Speech 1530. **3.** The action of interjecting or interposing anything; also, that which is interjected 1598. †**4.** *Rhet.* = PARENTHESIS 1678.

1. The I. of Laughing BACON. **2.** How now! interiections? why then, some be of laughing, as ha, ha, he SHAKS. The i. may be defined as a form of speech which is articulate and symbolic but not grammatical EARLE. Hence **Interje·ctionary, Interje·ctory** *adjs.* characterized by i.

Interjectional (intəɹdʒe·kʃənăl), *a.* 1761. [f. prec. + -AL¹.] **1.** Of the nature of something thrown in between or among other remarks 1788. **2.** Of, belonging to, or of the nature of an interjection in language.

2. A number of i. sounds uttered with a strange variety of intonation SCOTT. Hence **Interje·ctionally** *adv.*

Interje·ctionalize, *v.* [-IZE.] *trans.* To make into an interjection. EARLE.

Interje·ctural, *a.* 1775. [var. of contemp. INTERJECTIONAL. Cf. †*interjecture* (XVI) interposition.] Of the nature of what is interjected; interjectional.

†**Interjoi·n,** *v.* [INTER- I. 1 b.] *trans.* To join reciprocally. *Cor.* IV. iv. 22.

Interju·nction. *rare.* 1836. [INTER- II. 1 a.] A mutual joining.

Interknit (intəɹni·t), *v.* 1805. [INTER- I. 1 b.] **1.** *trans.* To knit each into the other; to intertwine. **2.** *intr.* To intertwine. KEATS.

†**Interknow·,** *v.* Also **en-.** 1603. [INTER- I. 1 b.] To know mutually –1652. Hence †**Interknow·ledge,** mutual or reciprocal knowledge.

Interlace (intəɹlē·s), *v.* [– OFr. *entrelacier*, f. *entre* (ENTER-, INTER- I. 1) + *lacier* LACE *v.*] **1.** *trans.* To unite two (or more) things by intercrossing laces, strings, etc.; hence, to connect intricately; to entangle, involve. (*rare* in physical sense.) **2.** To intercross two series of threads, etc. with constant alternation 1523. **b.** *fig.* To alternate, to interweave 1576. †**3.** To interweave; to introduce as by interweaving; to insert, interpolate. Chiefly *fig.* or *transf.* –1677. **4.** To intersperse, vary, mingle, or mix *with.* Chiefly *transf.* and *fig.* 1531. **5.** *intr.* for *refl.* To cross each other intricately, as if woven together; to lie like the fingers of two interlaced hands 1596.

1. Ice..is built up of crystalline particles interlaced together HUXLEY. **2.** Trees..Now i. your trembling tops above DRUMM. OF HAWTH. *fig.* Interlacing of talke and communication 1576. **3.** SHAKS. *Lucr.* 1390. **5.** Through boughs that i. 1855. Hence **Interla·ced** *ppl. a.*; *spec.* in *Her.* applied to annulets, rings, etc. that are linked together as are the links of a chain.

Interlacement (intəɹlē·smĕnt). 1603. [f. prec. + -MENT. Cf. OFr. *entrelacement*.] **1.** The action of interlacing or condition of being interlaced; *concr.* an interlaced arrangement or structure. **2.** Intricate intermingling 1872.

Interlamellar (intəɹlæmĕ·lăɹ). *a.* 1846. [f. INTER- II. 2 a + LAMELLA + -AR¹.] *Zool.* Situated between or among lamellæ (*e.g.* of the gills).

Interlaminar (intəɹlæ·minăɹ), *a.* 1831. [f. INTER- II. 2 a + LAMINA + -AR¹.] *Anat.* Situated between laminæ or plates.

Interlaminate (intəɹlæ·minēⁱt), *v.* 1816. [f. INTER- I. 1 a + LAMINATE *v.*] *trans.* To insert in or between alternate laminae or plates. Hence **Interlamina·tion,** the action of interlaminating; an interlaminated formation 1833.

I·nterlapse. 1658. [INTER- I. 2 a.] The lapse of time between any two events.

Interlard (intəɹlā·ɹd), *v.* 1533. [Earlier *enter-* – (O)Fr. *entrelarder*, f. *entre-* (INTER- I. 1 a) + *larder* LARD *v.*] †**1.** *trans.* To mix with alternate layers of fat; in *Cookery*, to insert strips of fat, bacon, etc. into (lean meat) before cooking; to lard –1741. †Also *transf.* **2.** *fig.* To mix, mingle, or intersperse *with* 1563. †**3.** To interpose, interpolate –1755.

1. *transf.* Grey Marble, interlarded with white Alabaster 1632. **2.** To i. talk with oaths 1694, English composition with foreign words 1872. **3.** Speeches in which he often interlarded the words O tempora, O mores 1755.

Interlay (intəɹlēⁱ·), *v.* Pa. t. and pple. **-laid.** 1609. [INTER- I. 1 a.] *trans.* To lay or place between or among. Also *fig.*

Interleaf (i·ntəɹlīf). Pl. **-leaves.** 1741. [f. INTERLEAVE *v.*] A leaf inserted between the ordinary leaves of a book, usu. blank; also *transf.*

Interleague (intəɹlī·g), *v.* Now *rare.* 1590. [f. INTER- I. 1 b + LEAGUE *v.*, but perh. f. phr. (*to*) *enter league* (*with*).] *intr.* and *refl.* To enter into a league *with* another, or with each other.

Interleave (intəɹlī·v), *v.* 1668. [f. INTER- I. 1 a + LEAF *sb.* (pl. *leaves*).] *trans.* To insert leaves, usu. blank, between the ordinary leaves of (a book). Also *transf.* and *fig.*

fig. To i. days of hardship with days of ease DE QUINCEY.

†**Interli·bel,** *v. rare.* 1626. [INTER- I. 1 b.] *trans.* To libel (one another).

Interline (intəɹləi·n), *v.*¹ ME. [– med.L. *interlineare*; see INTER- I. 1 a, LINE *sb.*²] **1.** *trans.* To insert additional words between the lines of (a document). Chiefly *pass.*, const. *with.* Also *fig.* **2.** To insert (a word or words) between the lines in a written document 1589. **3.** *absol.* or *intr.* **a.** To make interlinear insertions 1576. †**b.** *fig.* To come between the lines –1655. †**4.** *trans.* To write or print in alternate lines. LOCKE. †**5.** To mark with lines, esp. of various colours –1661. †**6.** To place or insert something in lines between or among something else. Const. *with.* –1736.

1. The coopie..was interlined and sumwhear blotted 1563. **2.** Words accidentally omitted were also placed in the margin, or interlined 1882. **3. b.** As in night's gloomy page One silent star may i. H. VAUGHAN. **6.** I saw the foot..interlined among the horse DE FOE.

Interline (intəɹləi·n), *v.*² 1480. [f. INTER- I. 1 a + LINE *v.*¹] *trans.* To insert a second or inner lining between the stuff and ordinary lining of (a garment).

Interlineal (-li·niăl), *a.* 1526. [– Fr. †*interlinéal* or med.L. *interlinealis*; see INTER- II. 2 a, LINEAL.] †**1.** = INTERLINEAR 1. –1826. **2.** Disposed in alternate lines. RUSKIN.

Interlinear (-li·niăɹ), *a.* 1440. [– med.L. *interlinearis*; see INTER- II. 2 a, LINEAR.] **1.** Written or printed between the lines. **2.** Of a book: Having the same text in different languages printed in alternate lines. ? *Obs.* 1624.

1. *I. Gloss.* Anselm's gloss on the Vulgate, placed in MSS. between the lines of the Latin text. *I. system*: see HAMILTONIAN *a.* **2.** The I. Bible BEDELL. Hence **Interli·near-ly** *adv.*

Interlineary (intəɹli·niări). 1605. [– med.L. *interlinearis*; see prec., -ARY².]

A. *adj.* = INTERLINEAR.

B. *sb.* **1.** An interlinear version. Also *fig.* 1644. **2.** *ellipt.* for (a.) the Latin Interlinear version of the Bible by Arias Montanus (1568–72); (b.) the Interlinear Gloss on the Vulgate. 1659.

Hence **Interli·nearily** *adv.* between, or as between, the lines.

Interlineate (-li·niₗeⁱt), *v. rare.* 1693. [– *interlineat-*, pa. ppl. stem of med.L. *interlineare*; see INTERLINE, -ATE³. In mod. use, perh. back-formation from next.] *trans.* and *absol.* = INTERLINE *v.*¹ Also *fig.*

Interlineation (-liniₗē·ʃən). 1602. [– med.L. *interlineatio*, f. as prec.; see -ION.] The insertion of a word or words between the lines of a writing; that which is so inserted.

Interli·ning, *vbl. sb.* 1467. [f. INTERLINE *v.*¹ + -ING¹.] = INTERLINEATION.

Interlink (i·ntəɹliŋk), *sb.* 1634. [INTER- I. 2 b.] An intermediate or connecting link.

Interlink (intəɹli·ŋk), *v.* 1587. [INTER- I. 1 b.] *trans.* To link (two or more things) to one another, or (one thing) *with* something else. Often *fig.*

These are two Chains which are interlink'd DRYDEN.

Interlobate (-lōᵘ·bĕt), *a.* 1881. [f. INTER- II. 2 a + LOBE + -ATE².] Situated between loops or lobes, esp. in *Geol.* between the terminal lobes of a glacier-moraine.

Interlobular (-lǫ·biŭlăɹ), *a.* 1834. [f. INTER- II. 2 a + LOBULE + -AR¹.] *Anat.* and *Path.* Situated or occurring between the lobes of any organ.

Interlocation (-lokē·ʃən). *rare.* 1611. [f. INTER- I. 2 a. Cf. Fr. †*interlocation* (Cotgrave).] A placing between, interposition; also, something placed between.

Interlock (intəɹlǫ·k), *v.* 1632. [INTER- I. 1 b.] **1.** *intr.* To engage with each other by partial overlapping or interpenetration of alternate projections and recesses. Also *fig.* of immaterial things. **2.** *trans.* To lock or clasp within each other. Chiefly *pass.* 1807.

1. I felt my fingers work and my hand i. C. BRONTË. **2.** Fibres..inextricably interlocked 1879.

Interlocution (-lokiū·ʃən). 1534 [– L. *interlocutio*, f. *inter* between + *loqui* speak. Cf. Fr. *interlocution*.] **1.** The action (on the part of two or more persons) of talking or replying to each other. **a.** Talk, discourse, dialogue. †**b.** An alternate reading or speaking, as in making responses, etc. –1643. †**2.** The action of replying; a reply, response –1782. †**3.** The action of interrupting speech; an interruption; a parenthetical utterance –1683. †**4.** *Law.* An intermediate decree before final decision –1726.

Interlocutor¹ (-lǫ·kiŭtəɹ). 1514. [– mod.L., f. L. *interloqui, -locutio*; see prec.] One who takes part in a dialogue, conversation, or discussion. In *pl.* the persons who carry on a dialogue. **b.** With *poss. pron.* One who takes part in conversation with another 1848.

b. Your true rustic turns his back on his i. GEO. ELIOT.

Interlocutor² (-lǫ·kiŭtəɹ). 1533. [– med.L. **interlocutor* (whence Fr. *interlocuteur* XVI), = med.L. *interlocutorius* (also *interloquitorius*, from the verb), f. pa. ppl. stem of late L. *interloqui* pronounce an interlocutory sentence; see -OR 2.] *Sc. Law.* A judgement or order of a court or of the Lords Ordinary, signed by the pronouncing or presiding judge.

Interlocutory (-lǫ·kiŭtəri). 1590. [– med. L. *interlocutorius* (XIV), f. as prec.; see -ORY². Cf. (O)Fr. *interlocutoire*.]

A. *adj.* **1.** Of the nature of, pertaining to, or occurring in, dialogue or conversation 1597. **2.** Spoken intermediately 1821. **3.** *Law.* Pronounced during the course of an action; not finally decisive; esp. in *i. decree, injunction, judgement, order* 1590.

1. He knowes that interloquutory swearing is a sinne 1626. **2.** I. observations 1864.

B. *sb.* **1.** *Law.* An interlocutory decree. †**2.** A discussion. MOTTEUX.

Interlocutress (-lǫ·kiutrės). 1858. [f. INTERLOCUTOR[1] + -ESS[1].] A female interlocutor. So **Interlo·cutrice, -trix** 1848.

Interlope (intəɹlōu·p), *v.* 1603. [Back-formation from INTERLOPER.] **1.** *intr.* 'To run between parties and intercept the advantage that one should gain from the other; to traffic without a proper licence; to forestall; to anticipate irregularly' (J.); to intrude. †**2.** *trans.* To foist in; to intercalate –1659. †**3.** To intrude upon (*rare*) 1701.

2. Grotius interlopes the following passage HEYLIN.

Interloper (i·ntəɹlōupəɹ, intəɹlōu·pəɹ). 1590. [f. INTER- (as in *intermeddler*) + *loper* (as in LANDLOPER).] **1. a.** *orig.* An unauthorized trader; one who trespasses on the rights of a trade monopoly; †a ship engaged in unauthorized trading. **b.** *transf.* One who thrusts himself into any position or affair, which others consider as pertaining solely to themselves 1632. †**2.** An intercepter (*of* something). MILT.

1. b. He was a mere i., and we were entitled to use force to keep him out of our premises 1884.

†**Interlu·cate**, *v. rare.* 1623. [– *interlucat-*, pa. ppl. stem of L. *interlucare*, f. *inter* between + *lux*, *luc-* light; see -ATE[3].] To lop or thin a tree (Dicts.) So **Interluca·tion**, the action of thinning a tree or wood 1656.

Interlucent (-l'ū·sěnt), *a. rare.* 1727. [f. INTER- I. 2 a + LUCENT.] Shining between.

Interlude (i·ntəɹl'ūd), *sb.* ME. [– med.L. *interludium*, f. *inter* INTER- I. 2 + *ludus* play.] **1.** A dramatic or mimic representation, usually light or humorous, such as was commonly introduced between the acts of the long mystery-plays or moralities, etc.; hence, a stage-play, a comedy, a farce. Now (after Collier) applied as a specific name to the earliest form of the modern drama, as represented by the plays of J. Heywood. †Also *transf.* or *fig.* **2.** An interval in the performance of a play; the pause between the acts, or the means employed to fill this up. Also *fig.* 1660. **b.** *Mus.* An instrument piece played between the verses of a psalm or hymn, or in the intervals of a church-service, etc. 1838. **3.** *transf.* An interval in the course of some action or event; an intervening time or space of a different character 1751.

1. John Heywood's dramatic productions..are neither Miracle-plays nor Moral-plays, but what may be properly and strictly called Interludes J. P. COLLIER. **2.** Dreams are but interludes which fancy makes; When monarch reason sleeps, this mimic wakes DRYDEN. **3.** We were confined to the inn, except for the i. of the custom-house MME. D'ARBLAY.

Interlude (i·ntəɹl'ūd), *v.* 1608. [f. prec.] †**a.** *intr.* To perform a play. **b.** *intr.* To come between, as an interlude. **c.** *trans.* To interrupt, as with an interlude. Hence †**Interluder**, a player in an interlude.

†**Interlu·ency.** [f. *interluent-*, pr. ppl. stem of L. *interluere* flow between (see -ENCY), prob. after contemp. INTERFLUENT.] A flowing between. HALE.

Interlunar (intəɹl'ū·năɹ), *a.* 1598. [app. – Fr. †*interlunaire* (see -AR[2]), f. L. *interlunium*, after *lunaire* LUNAR.] Pertaining to the period between the old and new moon.

The moon..Hid in her vacant i. cave MILT. So †**Interlu·nary** *a.* 1594.

Interlunation (-l'unēi·ʃən). 1813. [See prec. and LUNATION.] The period between the old and the new moon; *fig.* a blank or dark interval. So **Interlune** (*rare*) 1561.

Intermarriage (intəɹmæ·rėdʒ). Also †**en-**. 1579. [INTER- I. 2 a.] **1.** The action or fact of intermarrying; union in or connection by marriage. **a.** Of two persons, or of one person *with* another. Now only in legal phraseology. **b.** Marriage between members of different families, castes, tribes, nations, or societies 1602. **2.** *loosely.* Marriage between persons (or interbreeding between animals) nearly related 1882.

Intermarry (intəɹmæ·ri), *v.* Also †**en-**. 1574. [INTER- I. 1 b.] **1.** *intr.* To contract matrimony, to marry. **a.** Said of couple; hence of one person (*with* another). Now only in legal phraseology. **b.** Of members of different families, castes, tribes, nations, or societies 1611. **2.** *trans.* To join in marriage; also *fig.* (*rare*) 1863.

1. b. The Hollanders obtaining a garrison there, intermarried with the Native Women 1665.

‖**Intermaxilla** (i:ntəɹmæksi·lă). *Pl.* **-æ.** 1882. [mod.L., f. INTER- II. 1 + MAXILLA.] *Anat.* Each of two bones situated between the maxillary bones of the upper jaw, in man small and soon fusing with these, but in most mammals large, distinct, and situated in front of them (thus usu. called *premaxilla*).

Intermaxillary (i:ntəɹmæ·ksilări, -mæksi·lări), *a.* (*sb.*) 1826. [f. INTER- II. 2 a + MAXILLA + -ARY[2].] *Anat.* and *Zool.* **1. a.** Situated between the maxillæ; as in *i. bone* (= prec.), *i. apodeme.* **b.** Belonging or attached to the intermaxilla; as *i. teeth.* **2.** *sb.* Short for *i. bone*, etc. 1834.

†**Intermea·n.** *rare.* 1599. [f. INTER- I. 2 b + MEAN *sb.*] An intermediate part, act, etc.; an interlude –1834.

Intermeddle (intəɹme·d'l), *v.* [– AFr. *intermedler* = OFr. *entremesler*; see INTER-, MEDDLE.] †**1.** *trans.* To meddle or mix together; to intermix. Const. *with.* –1733. †**2.** *refl.* = next –1594. **3.** *intr.* To concern oneself *with* or *in*; to have to do *with*; to meddle, interfere (esp. in what is none of one's business) 1477.

3. The see of Rome was alway ready to entermedle 1561. To i. in a business BURKE, with a department 1834.

Intermeddler (intəɹme·dləɹ). 1576. [f. prec. + -ER[1].] †**a.** One who concerns himself or has to do with something –1577. **b.** *spec.* One who meddles with what is none of his business; in early use = INTERLOPER 1601.

Intermediacy (intəɹmī·diăsi). *rare.* 1713. [f. INTERMEDIATE *a.*; see -ACY.] The state of being intermediate; intervention.

†**Interme·dial.** 1599. [f. INTER- I. 2 a + MEDIAL.] **A.** *adj.* **1.** = INTERMEDIATE *a.* –1852. **2.** = INTERMEDIARY *a.* 1. –1846. **B.** *sb.* = INTERMEDIATE *sb.* –1654.

Intermediary (intəɹmī·diări). 1788. [– Fr. *intermédiaire* – It. *intermediario*, f. L. *intermedius*; see next, -ARY[2].]

A. *adj.* **1.** Acting or of the nature of action between two parties; mediatory 1818. **2.** Situated or occurring between two things; intermediate 1788.

1. I. agents 1869. **2.** This i. stage of her life 1882.

B. *sb.* **1.** One who acts between others; a go-between, mediator 1791. **2.** Something acting between persons or things, a medium, means; also *abstr.* Agency (*of* something) 1859. **3.** An intermediate form or stage 1865.

Intermediate (intəɹmī·dièt), *a.* and *sb.* 1567. [– med.L. *intermediatus*, f. L. *intermedius*, f. *inter* INTER- + *medius* MID; see -ATE[2]. Cf. Fr. *intermédiat.*]

A. *adj.* Coming or occurring between two things, places, times, numbers, members of a series, etc.; 'holding the middle place or degree between two extremes' (J.); interposed, intervening.

I. points 1665, events HARTLEY, steps PALEY, stature 1823, agents MACAULAY. Phr. *I. state* (Theol.): the condition of souls between death and the resurrection or the last judgement 1777.

B. *sb.* Something intermediate or intervening; a middle term; a nexus between two things 1650. **2.** A person who intervenes between others 1879.

Intermediate (intəɹmī·dieit), *v.* 1610. [f. INTER- I. 1 + MEDIATE *v.*] †**1.** *intr.* To intervene. FRENCH. †**2.** To interfere, interpose –1716. **3.** To act between others; to mediate 1624. **4.** *trans.* To join by intermediate parts 1880.

Intermediately (intəɹmī·dietli), *adv.* 1730. [f. INTERMEDIATE *a.* + -LY[2].] **1.** In an intermediate position or relation. **2.** By intermediate agency; indirectly; opp. to *immediately* 1755.

Intermediation (intəɹmīdiēi·ʃən). 1602. [f. prec. vb., or f. INTER -I. 2 a + MEDIATION. Cf. med.L. *intermediatio* (XIII).] The action of intermediating; interposition, intervention.

Intermediator (intəɹmī·dieitəɹ). 1522. [f. INTERMEDIATE *v.* after *mediator.* Cf. med.L. *intermediator.*] One who or that which intermediates; a mediator.

†**Interme·dious**, *a. rare.* 1657. [f. L. *intermedius* intermediate + -OUS.] = INTERMEDIATE *a.* –1678.

Intermedium (intəɹmī·diŏm). *Pl.* **-ia, -iums.** 1589. [– late and med.L. *intermedium*, subst. use of n. sing. of L. *intermedius*; see INTERMEDIATE *a.*] **1.** Something intermediate in position; an interval of space. ? *Obs.* 1611. **2.** Something intermediate in time; †an interlude; an interval of time (? *Obs.*) 1589. **3.** An intermediate agent, intermediary, medium; also *abstr.* intermediate agency, mediation (*of*) 1660. **4.** *Comp. Anat.* [sc. *os.*] A bone of the carpus, situated between the ulnare and the radiale, or the corresponding bone of the tarsus between the tibiale and fibulare 1878.

†**Interme·ll**, *v. Obs.* (or rare archaism). [ME. *entremelle* – OFr. *entremeller*, *-mesler* (mod. *-mêler*); see INTER-, MELL *v.*] = INTERMEDDLE.

Intermembral, etc.: see INTER- *pref.*

Interment (intə̄·ɹmĕnt). ME. [f. INTER *v.* + -MENT.] The action of interring or burying in the earth.

‖**Intermezzo** (intəɹme·dzo). Pl. **-i** (*-i*), **-os** (*-oz*). 1834. [It. – L. *intermedium*; see INTERMEDIUM.] **1. a.** A short dramatic, musical, or other performance, of a light and pleasing character, introduced between the acts of a drama or opera. **b.** A short movement connecting the main divisions of a large musical work, instrumental or vocal. **2.** *transf.* An interval; an episode 1851.

2. The purgatorial i. of the Catholic Church 1875.

†**Intermi·ddle**, *a.* 1613. [f. INTER- I. 2 c + MIDDLE *a.*] = INTERMEDIATE.

Intermigration (-məigrēi·ʃən). 1677. [INTER- I. 2 a.] Interchange of abode or habitat; reciprocal migration.

Interminable (intə̄·ɹminăb'l), *a.* ME. [– (O)Fr. *interminable* or late L. *interminabilis*, f. *in-* IN-[3] + *terminare*; see TERMINATE, -ABLE.] That cannot be bounded or ended; boundless; endless. (In mod. use freq. implying impatience at the length of something.)

Possession..of lyf Intermynable CHAUCER. An i. controversy D'ISRAELI. Hence **Inte:rminabi·lity, Inte·rminableness. Inte·rminably** *adv.*

Interminate (intə̄·ɹminět), *a.* Now *rare.* 1533. [– L. *interminatus* boundless, f. *in-* IN-[3] + *terminatus*, pa. pple. of *terminare*; see TERMINATE *v.*, -ATE[2].] **1.** That is without end or limit; infinite. †**2.** quasi-*adv.* Without end, always. ABP. PARKER. So †**Inte·rminated** *a.*

†**Interminate**, *v.* 1631. [– *interminat-*, pa. ppl. stem of L. *interminari*, f. *inter* between + *minari* threaten; see -ATE[3].] *trans.* To threaten, menace (a thing) –1656.

†**I:ntermination.** 1526. [– late L. *interminatio* threatening, in med. L. commination, anathema, f. as prec.; see -ION.] Commination; a threat or menace –1684.

Intermi·ne, *v. rare.* 1622. [f. INTER- I. 1 + MINE *v.* or *sb.*] *trans.* To intersect with mines or veins.

Intermingle (intəɹmi·ŋg'l), *v.* 1470. [INTER- I. 1.] **1.** *trans.* To mingle (two or more things) together; also, to introduce and mix (an element) *with* or *among* other things. **2.** To intersperse *with*; †to variegate 1553. **3.** *intr.* To mingle together or *with* something 1626.

1. Fuller has intermingled a great deal of gossip and rubbish with his facts 1842. **3.** Shadow and sunshine intermingling quick COWPER.

‖**Interministerium** (-ministīə·riŏm). *rare.* [f. INTER- II. 1 + L. *ministerium* MINISTRY; formed by Walpole, after INTERREGNUM.] The period intervening between two ministries.

The I. still exists; no place is filled up H. WALPOLE.

†**Intermi·se.** 1612. [var. of ENTERMISE, with prefix in Latin form. Cf. INTERMIT *v.*[2]] Intervention, mediation, agency –1715.

Intermission[1] (intəɹmi·ʃən). 1426. [– Fr. *intermission* or L. *intermissio*, f. *intermiss-*, pa. ppl. stem of *intermittere*; see INTERMIT *v.*[1], -ION.] **1.** The fact of intermitting, giving over, or ceasing for a time; a temporary pause, cessation, etc. *spec.* in *Path.* of a fever or the pulse. **b.** Temporary cessation, respite, relief, rest, pause. Const. *from.* Now *rare.*

1576. **2.** The lapse of a space of time between events or periods of action; the time during which action temporarily ceases; interval; †vacation, recess 1563. **3.** An interruption or break of continuity in a wall, line of cliffs, or the like 1624.

1. I did laugh, sans i., An houre by his diall SHAKS. Phr. *Without i.* **b.** Rest or i. none I find MILT. *P. L.* II. 802. **2.** Chusing their Time in those Intermissions while the Preacher is at Ebb SWIFT.

†**Intermi·ssion**[2]. *rare.* 1628. [f. INTERMIT *v.*[2], after prec.] **1.** = INTERMISE –1670. **2.** Interposition, intervention (of a thing) –1667.

2. The third day that the Lords have, without i. of any other businesse, continued upon the question MARVELL.

Intermissive (intəɹmi·siv), *a.* 1586. [f. INTERMISSION (1 b) + -IVE.] Of the nature of, pertaining to, intermission; intermittent; coming at intervals.

Make Pleasure thy..i. Relaxation SIR T. BROWNE.

Intermit (intəɹmi·t), *v.*[1] 1542. [– L. *intermittere*, f. *inter* INTER- + *mittere* let go.] **1.** *trans.* To discontinue for a time; to suspend 1576. †**b.** To interrupt, cause intermission to –1704. †**c.** To omit, pass over –1692. **2.** *intr.* To cease or stop for a time; to be intermittent 1571. **b.** *spec.* in *Path.* of a fever (pain, etc.) or of the pulse 1626.

1. To i. it..for a year or two..and then to return to the use of it BOYLE. **2.** Let me know the exact time when your Courts i. JOHNSON.

†**Intermit**, *v.*[2] ME. [refash. of ENTERMETE, after L. *intermittere*; see prec.] **1.** *refl.* = ENTERMETE 1. –1548. **b.** *intr.* = INTROMIT 3. –1548. **2.** *trans.* = INTROMIT 1. –1676.

Intermittence (intəɹmi·tĕns). Also **-ance.** 1796. [– Fr. *intermittence*; see next, -ENCE.] **1.** The fact of intermitting; discontinuance for a time. **2.** Intermittent sequence. TYNDALL. So **Intermi·ttency,** intermission 1662.

Intermittent (intəɹmi·tĕnt), *a.* (*sb.*) 1603. [– *intermittent-*, pr. ppl. stem of L. *intermittere*; see INTERMIT *v.*[1], -ENT. Cf. Fr. *intermittent* (XVI).] **1.** That intermits or ceases for a time; coming or operating at intervals. *spec.* in *Path.* of the pulse, a fever, etc. **2.** *sb. Path.* An intermittent fever. Also *fig.* 1693.

1. This disorder was not in its nature i. BURKE. Hence **Intermi·ttently** *adv.* in an i. manner.

Intermittingly (-mi·tiŋli), *adv.* 1654. [f. *intermitting* ppl. a. + -LY[2].] In an intermitting manner; intermittently.

Intermix (intəɹmi·ks), *v.* 1562. [f. INTERMIXT, taken as pa. pple. of an Eng. vb.; see COMMIX, MIX.] **1.** *trans.* To mix together, intermingle. **2.** *intr.* To be or become mixed together; to blend or associate intimately 1722.

1. Hee, she knew would i. Grateful digressions, and solve high dispute With conjugal Caresses MILT.

Intermixed, intermixt (intəɹmi·kst), *ppl. a.* 1555. [orig. *intermixt*, – L. *intermixtus*, pa. pple. of *intermiscere*, f. *inter* + *miscere* mix. The form *intermixed* followed the formation of the vb. *intermix*.] Mixed together, intimately mixed. Hence **Intermi·xedly, intermi·xtly** *adv.* with intermixture, promiscuously. So †**Intermi·xtion** = next 1520.

Intermixture (intəɹmi·kstiŭɹ). 1586. [alt. of contemp. †*intermixtion* after MIXTURE.] **1.** The action of intermixing or fact of being intermixed; intimate mixture 1592. **2.** *concr.* or quasi-*concr.* Something, or a quantity or portion *of* something, intermixed with or added to something else.

1. From the i. of houses with trees, it [Norwich] is called a city in an orchard 1778.

Intermobility, etc.: see INTER- *pref.*

Intermolecular (intəɹmole·kiŭlăɹ), *a.* 1843. [f. INTER- II. 2 a + MOLECULE + -AR[1].] Existing, or occurring between the molecules of a body or substance.

Intermundane (intəɹmɒ·ndeⁱn), *a.* 1691. [f. INTER- II. 2 a + L. *mundus* world + -ANE, after MUNDANE.] **1.** Situated, or present, between different worlds. **2.** Existing between worlds reciprocally 1858.

1. The vast distance, between these great bodies, are call'd i. spaces LOCKE. So †**Intermu·ndial,** †**Intermu·ndian.**

‖**Intermu·ndium.** 1817. [A mod. sing. of L. *intermundia* (pl.) the spaces between the worlds.] A space between two worlds.

†**Intermu·re,** *v.* 1606. [alt. of contemp. IMMURE by substitution of prefix.] *trans.* To inclose between walls, to wall in –1628.

Intermuscular (intəɹmɒ·skiŭlăɹ), *a.* 1822. [f. INTER- II. 2 a + MUSCLE + -AR[1], after MUSCULAR.] *Anat.* Situated between muscles, or between muscular fibres.

Intermutation: see INTER- *pref.* I. 2 a.

Intermutual (intəɹmiū·tiuˌăl), *a.* 1595. [INTER- I. 2 a; pleonastic for *mutual*.] Mutual, reciprocal. Hence **Intermu·tually** *adv.*

Intern (intə̄·ɹn). Also †**interne.** 1578. [– (O)Fr. *interne* – L. *internus* inward, internal, f. *in* adv. + *-ternus* suffix; cf. EXTERN.]

A. *adj.* (Now *poet.* or *arch.*) = INTERNAL *a.*
B. *sb.* (Also *interne* after Fr.) An assistant resident physician or surgeon in a hospital 1891. *U.S.*

Intern (intə̄·ɹn), *v.* Also †**interne.** 1606. [– Fr. *interner*, f. *interne*; see prec.] †**1.** *intr.* To enter or pass in; to become incorporated or united with another being. **2.** *trans.* To confine within the limits of a country, district, or place; to oblige to reside within prescribed limits. Also *fig.* 1866. **3.** To send (goods, etc.) into the interior of a country. *U.S.*

2. To disarm troops crossing the neutral frontier and to i. them till the conclusion of peace 1874.

Internal (intə̄·ɹnăl). 1509. [– mod. L. *internalis*, f. L. *internus*; see INTERN, -AL[1]. Cf. Fr. †*internel* (XV–XVI).]

A. *adj.* **1.** Situated or existing within something; of or pertaining to the inside; inward 1590. **b.** *Anat.* Situated away from the surface of the body, or nearer the median line 1719. **2.** Pertaining to the inner nature or relations of anything; belonging to the thing or subject in itself; intrinsic 1607. **b.** Of or pertaining to the domestic (as dist. from the foreign) affairs of a country 1795. **3.** Of or belonging to the inner nature or life of man; mental or spiritual; inward; subjective 1509.

1. I. navigation 1804. *I. angle* (Geom.) = *interior angle* (see INTERIOR A. 1). *I. combustion* (*a*) see COMBUSTION 2 b; (*b*) applied to gas and oil engines, in which the energy necessary to produce motion is developed in the engine cylinder and not in a separate chamber 1888. **2.** The i. evidence for some statements renders them highly probable FREEMAN. **b.** The maintenance of i. peace STUBBS. **3.** Sensations and ideas are both i. 1869.

B. *sb.* **1.** *pl.* The inward parts or organs; inwards, entrails 1764. †**2.** *Med.* (usu. in *pl.*) A medicine or remedy to be taken internally –1704. **3.** Something belonging to the thing in itself. (Now always in *pl.*) 1652. †**4.** (Usu. in *pl.*) The inner nature, soul, spirit –17..

3. To Guard the Internals of Religion 1709. Hence **Interna·lity,** the quality or fact of being i.; also with *an* and *pl.*

Internally (intə̄·ɹnăli), *adv.* 1597. [f. prec. + -LY[2].] **1.** In, on, or with respect to, the inside or interior. **2.** With respect to the inner nature or relations of anything, esp. the internal affairs of a country, etc. 1791. **3.** Mentally, spiritually 1646.

Interna·sal, *a.* 1866. [f. INTER- II. 2 a + L. *nasus* nose + -AL[1], after NASAL.] = *intranasal* (see INTRA-).

International (intərnæ·ʃənăl). 1780. [f. INTER- II. 2 + NATION + -AL[1].] **A.** *adj.* Existing, constituted, or carried on between different nations; pertaining to the relations between nations. **b.** (with capital *I.*) Belonging to the International Working Men's Association, a society of working-men founded in London in 1864 (and dissolved in 1874), the objects of which were identified with those of the socialism of Marx.

The great science of i. law, the determining authority in questions of right between independent states HALLAM. An I. Exhibition 1861, yacht race 1888.

B. *sb.* **a.** A person belonging to two different nations (*e.g.* native of one and resident in another) 1870; one who takes part in an international contest 1895. **b.** (with capital *I*, and sometimes in Fr. form *-ale*) = International Working Men's Association (see A. b); also, a member or adherent of this. **b.** *First I.*, that of 1864–74; *Second I.*, formed in 1889 at Paris and having later its seat in Brussels; *Third I.*, formed in 1919 by the Russian communists (Bolsheviks) on a revolutionary basis.

‖**Internationale** (-næʃⁱŏnā·l, ‖æ̃ntęrnasyonal). [Fr. (sc. *chanson* song).] A revolutionary hymn composed by Eugène Pottier in 1871 and adopted by French socialists and later by others. (See also prec. B. b.)

Interna·tionalism. 1877. [f. INTERNATIONAL + -ISM.] International character or spirit; the principle of community of interests or action between different nations; *spec.* (with capital *I*) the doctrine or principles of the International Working Men's Association.

Interna·tionalist. 1864. [f. as prec. + -IST.] **a.** An advocate of or believer in internationalism; *spec.* a member of or a sympathizer with the International Working Men's Association. **b.** One versed in international law. **c.** One who takes part in an international contest.

Internationa·lity. 1864. [f. INTERNATIONAL + -ITY.] International quality, condition, or character.

Interna·tionalize, *v.* 1864. [f. as prec. + -IZE.] *trans.* To render international in character or use; *spec.* to bring (a country, territory, etc.) under the combined government or protection of two or more different nations. Hence **Interna:tionaliza·tion.**

Interna·tionally, *adv.* 1864. [f. as prec. + -LY[2].] In an international manner; between or among different nations.

Interne: see INTERN.

Internecine (intəɹnī·səin), *a.* 1663. [– L. *internecinus*, f. *internecio* general slaughter, massacre, extermination, f. *internecare* slaughter, exterminate, f. *inter-* (as in *interire* perish, *interficere* destroy) + *necare* kill.] **1.** *orig.* Deadly, destructive, characterized by great slaughter. **2.** *esp.* (In mod. use.) Mutually destructive, aiming at the slaughter or destruction of each other 1755.

1. *I. war*, war for the sake of slaughter, war to the death. **2.** Eight thousand Zealots, who stabbed each other in i. massacre FARRAR.

Internecion (intəɹnī·ʃən). *rare.* 1610. [– L. *internecio*; see prec., -ION.] Destruction, massacre.

Internecive (intəɹnī·siv), *a.* *rare.* 1819. [– L. *internecivus*, var. of *internecinus*; see INTERNECINE, -IVE.] = INTERNECINE 2.

†**Interne·ct,** *v.* 1694. [– L. *internectere* bind to each other, f. *inter* between + *nectere* tie, knot.] *trans.* To interconnect. So †**Interne·ction, -ne·xion,** mutual connection 1654.

Internee·. 1918. [f. INTERN *v.* 2 + -EE[1].] An interned person.

Interneural (intəɹniūᵊ·răl), *a.* (*sb.*) 1846. [f. INTER- II. 2 a + Gr. νεῦρον nerve + -AL[1].] *Anat.* and *Zool.* Situated between nerves, or between neural spines or arches; applied *spec.* to the dermal spines or bones supporting the dorsal fin-rays in fishes (cf. INTERSPINAL). **b.** as *sb.* (*pl.*) = Interneural spines 1880.

†**Inte·rnity.** *rare.* 1760. [f. INTERN *a.* + -ITY.] The quality of being internal, inwardness; something internal.

Internment (intə·ɹnmĕnt). 1870. [f. INTERN *v.* 2 + -MENT.] The action of interning; confining within prescribed limits.

Interno-, comb. advb. form of L. *internus* INTERNAL; as in **inte:rno-me·dial, -me·dian** *adjs.*, *Entom.* situated within the median line or nervure, or between the internal and median nervures, of the wing 1826.

Internodal (intəɹnōᵘ·dăl), *a.* 1835. [f. INTER- II. 2 a + NODE + -AL[1].] *Bot.* and *Zool.* Situated between nodes; belonging to or constituting an internode.

Internode (i·ntəɹnōᵘd). 1667. [– L. INTERNODIUM.] **1.** *Bot.* That part of a stem or branch intervening between two of the nodes or knots from which the leaves arise. **2.** *Zool.* and *Anat.* A slender part intervening between two nodes or joints; each bone of a finger or toe 1722.

†**Interno·dial,** *a.* [f. next + -AL[1].] = INTERNODAL. SIR T. BROWNE.

‖**Internodium** (intəɹnōᵘ·diŏm). Pl. **-ia.** Now *rare.* 1644. [L. (Pliny), f. *inter* (see

INTER- II. 1) + *nodus* knot; see -IUM.] = INTERNODE. (*erron.* A joint.)

†**I·nternunce.** Also **-nonce.** 1647. [– Fr. *internonce* – L. *internuntius* (*-nuncius*); see INTERNUNCIUS.] = INTERNUNCIO. –1847.

Internuncial (intəɹnɒ·nʃiăl), *a.* 1845. [f. L. *internuntius* (see below) + -AL¹.] Having the function of conveying messages between two parties, etc.; used *fig.* of the nerves.

†**Internu·nciess.** *rare.* [irreg. f. INTERNUNCIO + -ESS¹.] A female internuncio or messenger. CHAPMAN.

Internuncio (intəɹnɒ·nʃio). Also †**-tio.** 1641. [– It. *internunzio* – L. *internuntius* (*-nuncius*); see next.] **1.** A messenger between two parties. **2.** A representative or ambassador of the Pope at a foreign court while there is no nuncio, or at a minor court to which no nuncio is sent 1670. **3.** A minister representing a government, esp. that of Austria, at the Ottoman Porte 1700. Hence **Internu·ncioship,** the office or function of an i. or go-between.

‖**Internu·ncius.** 1675. [L. in med. spelling, for cl. L. *internuntius*, f. *inter* between + *nuntius* messenger.] = prec. 1.

Internuptial (intəɹnɒ·pʃăl), *a.* 1850. [f. INTER- I. 2 + NUPTIAL.] **1.** Pertaining to intermarriage. **2.** Intervening between two marriages or married states 1885.

Interoceanic (i:ntər,ōᵘʃi,æ·nik), *a.* 1855. [f. INTER- II. 2 a + OCEAN + -IC.] Situated between oceans; connecting two oceans, as a strait or canal.

Interocular, etc.: see INTER- *pref.*

Interopercular (i:ntər,opə·ɹkiŭlăɹ), *a.* 1854. [f. next + -AR¹.] *Ichthyol.* Belonging to, or of the nature of, an interoperculum; chiefly in *i. bone* = next.

‖**Interoperculum** (i:ntər,opə·ɹkiŭlŏm). 1834. [mod. L., f. INTER- I. 2 b + OPERCULUM.] *Ichthyol.* One of the bones forming the gill-cover; usually situated below the præoperculum, and partly between this and the operculum and suboperculum.

Interorbital (intər,ǫ·ɹbităl), *a.* 1852. [f. INTER- II. 2 a + ORBIT + AL¹.] *Anat.* Situated between the eye-sockets.

Interosculant (intər,ǫ·skiŭlănt), *a.* 1855. [f. INTER- I. 2 a + OSCULANT.] Interosculating; forming a connecting link.

An 'i.' group,—a party of genera and species which connect families scientifically far apart KINGSLEY.

Interosculate (intər,ǫ·skiŭleᶦt), *v.* 1882. [f. INTER- I. 1 b. + OSCULATE.] *intr.* **a.** To interpenetrate or inosculate with each other. **b.** To form a connecting link between two groups. Hence **I:nteroscula·tion.**

Intero·sseal, *a.* 1805. [f. as next + -AL¹.] = next.

Interosseous (intər,ǫ·siəs), *a.* 1745. [f. INTER- II. 2 a + L. *os, oss-* bone + -EOUS.] *Anat.* Situated between bones; said of various ligaments, muscles, nerves, and vessels.

†**Interpa·le,** *v.* 1553. [f. INTER- I. 1 + PALE *v.*] **1.** *trans.* To divide by pales, as in Heraldry; to alternate in vertical divisions. BRENDE. **2.** = IMPALE *v.* 2. LOVELACE.

Interparietal (-părəi·ĭtăl), *a.* (*sb.*) 1835. [f. INTER- II. 2 a + PARIETES + -AL¹.] *Anat.* **1.** Situated between the parietal bones of the skull. **2.** *sb.* The interparietal bone.

†**Interpau·se,** *v.* 1534. [f. INTER- I. 1 + PAUSE *v.*] *intr.* To pause in the midst of something. MORE. So †**I·nterpause** *sb.* a pause between or in the course of something 1599.

Interpel (intəɹpe·l), *v.* Now only in *Sc. Law.* ME. [– L. *interpellare* interrupt by speaking, f. *inter* INTER- + *-pellare* thrust or direct oneself (as in *appellare* APPEAL.] †**1.** *trans.* To appeal to; to petition –1591. †**2.** To interrupt (a person) in speaking; to break in on or disturb –1647. **3.** *Sc. Law.* To intercept, cut off, prevent 1722.

2. No more now, for I am interpell'd by many businesses HOWELL.

Interpellant (intəɹpe·lănt). 1869. [– Fr. *interpellant*, pr. pple. of *interpeller* – L. *interpellare*; see prec.] One who addresses an interpellation (e.g. in the French Chamber).

Interpellate (intəɹpe·leᶦt), *v.* 1599. [– *interpellat-*, pa. ppl. stem of L. *interpellare*; see INTERPEL, -ATE³.] †**1.** *trans.* To interrupt or break in upon. **2.** To address an interpellation to (a minister in the French or other Chamber) 1874.

Interpellation (i:ntəɹpelē¹·ʃən). 1526. [– L. *interpellatio*, f. as prec.; see -ION. Reintroduced f. Fr. in sense 5 in XIX.] †**1.** The action of appealing to or entreating; intercession –1670. †**2.** A summons, citation –1726. †**3.** The action of breaking in upon; interruption –1834. **4.** *Sc. Law.* Prevention, hindrance 1814. **5.** The action of interrupting the order of the day (in a foreign legislative Chamber) by asking from a minister an explanation of some matter belonging to his department 1837.

1. By the importunity of her i. BECON. **3.** Sophistic reasonings, and sarcastic interpellations LANDOR. **5.** An incessant fire of questions, interpellations, objurgations CARLYLE.

Interpenetrate (intəɹpe·nĭtreᶦt), *v.* 1809. [INTER- I. 1.] **1.** *trans.* To penetrate between the parts or particles of (anything); to pass through and through, permeate, pervade 1818. Also *intr.* **2.** *intr.* To penetrate each other; to unite or mingle by mutual penetration 1809. **b.** *trans.* To penetrate reciprocally 1843. **3.** *Arch.* (*trans.* and *intr.*) To appear as if penetrating or passing through a moulding, etc. 1840.

1. The water is everywhere interpenetrated by air, which the fishes breathe MEDWIN. **2.** Law and religion thus interpenetrating neutralized each other COLERIDGE. **3.** Their shafts interpenetrating the mouldings of the panels and tracery 1864.

Interpenetration (i:ntəɹpenĭtrē¹·ʃən). 1809. [INTER- I. 2 a.] **1.** The action of penetrating between or among; thorough penetration 1822. **2.** Mutual penetration 1809. **3.** *Arch.* The intersection of two forms; *spec.* an independent continuation of mouldings or other members past their intersection, so that the identity of a member is preserved after it has partly coincided with another or has been swallowed up in it 1840.

Interpe·netrative, *a.* 1860. [INTER- I. 2 a.] Intimately or reciprocally penetrative. Hence **Interpe·netratively** *adv.* 1834.

Interpetiolar (intəɹpe·tiŏlăɹ), *a.* 1830. [f. INTER- II. 2 a + PETIOLE + -AR¹.] *Bot.* Situated between petioles, or between a petiole and the axis. Also **Interpe·tiolary** *a.*

Interphalangeal: see INTER- *pref.*

Interpilaster (i:ntəɹpilæ·stəɹ). 1823. [INTER- II. 1.] *Arch.* The space between two pilasters.

†**Interpla·ce,** *v.* 1548. [INTER- I. 1 a, b.] *trans.* **a.** To place between or in the midst of. **b.** To place between each other or alternately. (Only in *pass.*) –1678.

Interplait (intəɹplæ·t), *v.* Also **-plat.** 1822. [INTER- I. 1 b.] *trans.* To plait together; to intertwine, interweave.

Interplanetary (-plæ·nĕtări), *a.* 1691. [f. INTER- II. 2 a + PLANET + -ARY².] Situated between the planets.

Interplay (i·ntəɹplē¹). 1862. [INTER- I. 2 a.] Reciprocal play, free interaction.

Interplead (intəɹplī·d), *v.* Also †**enterple(a)de.** 1473. [– AFr. *enterpleder*; see INTER- I. 1 a, b and PLEAD *v.*] **1.** *intr.* In *Law*: To litigate with each other in order to determine some point in dispute in which a third party is concerned. †**2.** *trans.* To raise as a plea –1716.

Interpleader (intəɹplī·dəɹ). Also †**enter-.** 1567. [– AFr. *enterpleder*, subst. use (see -ER⁴) of infin.; see prec.] *Law.* A suit pleaded between two parties to determine a matter of claim or right, on which the action of a third party depends, esp. to determine to which of them livery or payment ought to be made.

Interpleural (-plūᵊ·răl), *a.* 1879. [f. INTER- II. 2 a + PLEURA + -AL¹.] Situated between the pleuræ of the right and left lungs.

Interpoint (intəɹpoi·nt), *v.* 1595. [INTER- I. 1 a.] **a.** *trans.* To put a point or points between (words); to punctuate. **b.** *intr.* or *absol.* To insert a point or points.

Her sighes should i. her words DANIEL.

Interpolable (intɔ̄·ɹpŏlăb'l), *a.* [f. INTERPOLATE *v.*; see -ABLE.] That may be interpolated; suitable for interpolation. DE MORGAN.

Interpolar (-pōᵘ·lăɹ), *a.* (*sb.*) 1870. [f. INTER- II. 2 a + POLE *sb.*² + -AR¹.] Situated between the poles (of a galvanic battery, etc.). **b.** as *sb.* An interpolar wire 1882.

†**Inte·rpolate,** *ppl. a.* late ME. [– L. *interpolatus*, pa. pple. of *interpolare*; see next, -ATE².] Intermittent (esp. of fever); interpolated –1669.

Interpolate (intɔ̄·ɹpŏleᶦt), *v.* 1612. [– *interpolat-*, pa. ppl. stem of L. *interpolare*, furbish up, alter, f. *inter* INTER- + *-polare*, rel. to *polire* POLISH; see -ATE³.] †**1.** *trans.* To polish up; to put a fresh gloss on (*rare*) –1706. **2.** To alter or enlarge (a book or writing) by insertion of new matter; *esp.* to tamper with by inserting new or foreign matter 1612. Also *transf.* **3.** To introduce (words or passages) into a pre-existing writing; *esp.* to insert (spurious matter) in a genuine work without note or warning 1640. **b.** *transf.* To intercalate 1802. **4.** *intr.* or *absol.* To make insertions or interpolations 1720. †**5.** *trans.* To interrupt by an interval. (Only in *pass.*) HALE. **6.** *Math.* To insert an intermediate term or terms in a series 1796.

2. A Manuscript of Sir Ralph Hoptons..interpolated with his own hand FULLER. **3.** Words which no Vedelius can carp at as interpolated BP. HALL. **b.** By interpolating a month of 30 days WHEWELL.

Interpolation (intɔ̄:ɹpŏlē¹·ʃən). 1612. [– Fr. *interpolation* or L. *interpolatio* alteration, f. as prec.; see -ION.] †**1.** The action of furbishing or polishing up –1678. **2.** The action of interpolating a writing, or a word, etc. therein (cf. senses 2 and 3 of the vb.); the condition or fact of being interpolated 1612. **b.** With *pl.* An interpolated word or passage 1675. **3.** The action of introducing or inserting among other things or between the members of any series. Also with *an* and *pl.* An insertion. 1849. **b.** *Math.* The process of inserting in a series an intermediate number or quantity ascertained by calculation from those already known 1763. †**4.** Interposition of time; interval. 1615.

1. A Refinement and I. of Paganism CUDWORTH. **2.** This end was carried out by interpolations and falsification of ecclesiastical documents HUSSEY. **3.** The i. of fossiliferous..rocks MURCHISON.

Inte·rpolator. 1659. [– eccl.L. *interpolator*, f. as prec. + -OR 2. In Eng. use from senses 2, 3 of the verb.] One who interpolates.

Interpo·lish, *v. rare.* 1609. [INTER- I. 1 a.] To polish here and there or at intervals.

Interpone (intəɹpōᵘ·n), *v.* 1523. [– L. *interponere* place between, etc., f. *inter* between + *ponere* place.] *trans.* and *refl.* = INTERPOSE *v.* So †**Interpo·nent** (*rare*), one who or that which interposes 1592.

Interposal (intəɹpōᵘ·zăl). 1607. [f. next + -AL¹.] = INTERPOSITION 1, 2.

Interpose (intəɹpōᵘ·z), *v.* 1582. [– (O)Fr. *interposer*, based on L. *interponere*; see INTER-, POSE *v.*¹] **1.** *trans.* To place between, in space or time. Often with implication of obstruction or delay. 1599. **2.** †*refl.* To place oneself between; to stand in the way –1745. Also *intr.* (for *refl.*) **3.** *trans.* To put forth or introduce in the way of interference or intervention 1606. **4.** *intr.* (and †*refl.*) To put oneself forward or interfere in a matter; to intervene 1603. **5.** *trans.* To introduce, esp. in the midst of other matters as an interruption or digression 1582. **b.** *absol.* or *intr.* To interrupt, make a digression 1667. †**6.** *trans.* To come or be in the way of; to obstruct –1671.

1. Only a small part of the convexity of the globe is interposed between us and the sun MORSE. **2.** What watchfull Cares doe i. themselves Betwixt your Eyes, and Night? SHAKS. **3.** To i. arbitration 1798. **4.** I shall not i. in their Quarrel ADDISON. **5.** To i. a jocular, and perhaps ridiculous digression PETTY. Hence †**Interpose** *sb.* interposition. **Interpo·ser.**

Interposition (in:təɹpŏzi·ʃən). ME. [– (O)Fr. *interposition* or L. *interpositio*, f. pa. ppl. stem of *interponere*; see INTER-, POSITION.] **1.** The action of placing something or oneself between; the fact of being placed or situated between; intervention. **b.** An instance of this; *occas.*, that which is interposed 1650. **2.** Interference, mediation; also, an instance

of this 1461. †**3.** A parenthesis; a digression 1553.
2. By the immediate i. of Providence 'JUNIUS'.

†**Interpo·sure.** 1627. [f. INTERPOSE *v.* + -URE; cf. *composure*, etc.] Interposition –1733.

Interpret (intɔ̄·ɹprėt), *v.* ME. [– (O)Fr. *interpréter* or L. *interpretari* explain, translate, f. *interpres, -pret-* agent, broker, translator, interpreter, f. *inter* INTER- + unkn. element.] **1.** *trans.* To expound the meaning of; to render clear or explicit; to elucidate; to explain. †Formerly also, To translate. **b.** To explain to oneself 1795. **c.** In recent use: To give one's own interpretation of (a musical composition, a landscape, etc.); to render 1880. **2.** To expound or take in a specified manner ME. **3.** *absol.* or *intr.* To make an explanation; to give an exposition; *spec.* to act as an interpreter or dragoman. †Formerly also, To translate. ME. †**4.** *intr.* To signify, to mean. SELDEN.
1. And they shall call his name Emmanuel, which being interpreted is, God with vs *Matt.* 1:23. The law interprets..his wishes with regard to the disposal of his property FAWCETT. **2.** As thou wouldst be well interpreted by others i. others well DONNE. This transaction was interpreted into a bribe SMOLLETT. **3.** Unskilful with what words to pray, let mee I. for him MILT *P. L.* XI. 33.

Interpretable (intɔ̄·ɹprėtăb'l), *a.* 1611. [orig. – late (eccl.) and med.L. *interpretabilis* capable of translation, explicable; in later use, f. prec. + -ABLE.] Susceptible of interpretation, explicable.

†**Inte·rpretament.** *rare.* Also *erron.* **interpremenț.** 1645. [– L. *interpretamentum*, f. *interpretari*; see INTERPRET, -MENT.] Interpretation –1802.

Inte·rpretate, *v.* Now *rare* or *Obs.* 1522. [– *interpretat-*, pa. ppl. stem of L. *interpretari*; see INTERPRET, -ATE³.] = INTERPRET *v.*

Interpretation (intɔ̄:ɹprĭtēⁱ·ʃən). ME. [– (O)Fr. *interprétation* or L. *interpretatio*, f. as prec.; see -ION.] **1.** The action of interpreting; explanation, exposition. †**b.** The faculty or power of interpreting –1552. **2.** An explanation given; a way of explaining; †a comment ME. **b.** The representation of a part in a drama, or the rendering of a musical composition, according to one's conception of the author's idea 1880. **3.** The way in which a thing ought to be interpreted; proper explanation; hence, Signification, meaning ME. †**4.** The action of translating; a translation –1646.
1. *I. of Nature*, Bacon's phrase to denote the discovery of natural laws by means of induction. The just i. of geological phenomena HUXLEY. **b.** To another [is geven] the interpretacion off tonges TINDALE 1 *Cor.* 12:10. **2.** The ambiguity of oracles, and their ambodextrous interpretations 1651. They give mean Interpretations..to the worthiest Actions ADDISON. **4.** Cephas: which is by interpretacion, a stone TINDALE *John* 1:2.

Interpretative (intɔ̄·ɹprĭtēⁱtiv), *a.* 1569. [– med.L. *interpretativus* (XIII), f. as prec.; see -IVE.] **1.** Having the character, quality, or function of interpreting; explanatory, expository. **2.** Deduced or deducible by interpretation; inferential, constructive (*arch.* or *Obs.*) 1610.
1. I. lexicography JOHNSON. **2.** Constructive, or i. treasons 1798. Hence **Inte·rpretatively** *adv.* by way of interpretation (*rare*); †by inference, constructively.

Interpreter (intɔ̄·ɹprėtəɹ). [ME. *enter-, interpretour* – AFr., = OFr. *entre-, interpreteëur, -teur* – late L. *interpretator*, f. as prec.; in XVI conformed to agent-nouns in *-er*; see -ER² 3.] **1.** One who interprets or explains ME. **2.** One who translates languages ME. †**3.** One who makes known the will of another; a title of Mercury as messenger of the gods. (L. *interpres divum* Virgil.) –1678. †**4.** *Rhet.* = SYNONYMY 1589.
1. Then said Christian to the I., Expound this matter more fully to me BUNYAN. **2.** Hee [Joseph] spake vnto them by an i. *Gen.* 42:23. **3.** MILT. *P. L.* III. 657. Hence **Inte·rpretership.**

Interpretress (intɔ̄·ɹprėtrės). 1775. [f. INTERPRETER + -ESS¹.] A female interpreter. var. †**Inte·rpretess** 1717.

Interprovi·ncial, *a.* 1839. [f. INTER- II. 2 a + PROVINCE + -AL¹ as in *provincial*.] Lying, extending, or carried on, between different provinces; pertaining to the mutual relations of provinces.

Interpubic (intəɹpiū·bik), *a.* 1836. [f. INTER- II. 2 a + PUB(IS + -IC.] Situated between the pubic bones.

Interpunction (intəɹpɒ·ŋkʃən). 1617. [– L. *interpunctio*, f. *interpunct-*, pa. ppl. stem of *interpungere*, f. *inter* between + *pungere* prick, etc.; see -ION.] The insertion of points between words, clauses, or sentences; punctuation. *concr.* A point inserted.

Interpunctuate (intəɹpɒ·ŋktiu,eⁱt), *v.* 1850. [INTER- I. 1 a.] To insert the points between words and clauses; to punctuate. Also *fig.* So **Interpunctua·tion** = prec. sb. 1717.

Interradial (intəɹ,rēⁱ·diăl). 1870. [f. INTER- II. 2 a + RADIUS + -AL¹.] *Zool. adj.* Situated between radii or rays, as in an echinoderm. *sb.* An interradial part.

Interramal (intəɹ,rēⁱ·măl), *a.* 1874. [f. INTER- II. 2 a + RAMUS + -AL¹.] *Ornith.* Situated between the rami or branches of the lower jaw.

† **Inter,re·gency.** *rare.* 1600. [f. next; see -ENCY.] The tenure of an interrex or interregent –1674.

†**Inter,re·gent.** *rare.* 1600. [INTER- I. 2 b; after *interrex*.] = INTERREX.

‖**Interregnum** (intəɹ,re·gnɒ̆m). *Pl.* **-regna, -regnums.** 1579. [L., f. *inter* (INTER- II. 1) + *regnum* REIGN *sb.*; cf. next.] †**1.** Temporary authority or rule exercised during a vacancy of the throne or a suspension of the usual government –1770. **2.** The interval between the close of a king's reign and the accession of his successor 1590. **3.** A cessation or suspension of the usual ruling power. Also *fig.* 1648. **4.** A breach of continuity; an interval, pause, vacant space 1659. Hence **Inter,re·gnal** *a.*

Interreign (i·ntəɹ,rēⁱn). Now *rare.* 1533. [f. INTER- II. 1 + REIGN *sb.*, after prec.; partly – (O)Fr. *interrègne.*] †**1.** = INTERREGNUM 1. –1611. **2.** = INTERREGNUM 2. 1586.

Interrelated (i:ntəɹ,rĭlēⁱ·tėd), *ppl. a.* 1827. [INTER- I. 1 b.] Mutually related or connected.

Interrelation (i:ntəɹ,rĭlēⁱ·ʃən). 1848. [INTER- I. 2 a.] Mutual or reciprocal relation. So **I:nter,rela·tionship.**

Interrenal (intəɹ,rī·năl). 1893. [f. INTER- II. 2 a + L. *renes* kidneys + -AL¹.] *Anat.* **a.** *adj.* Situated between the kidneys. **b.** *sb.* An interrenal body.

Inte·rrer. 1611. [f. INTER *v.* + -ER¹.] One who inters.

‖**Interrex** (i·ntəɹ,reks). *Pl.* **-reges** (-rī·dʒīz). 1579. [L., f. *inter* (INTER- I. 2 b) + *rex* king.] One who holds the supreme authority in a state during an interregnum.
The regents at that time called *Interreges* NORTH.

†**Inte·rrogate,** *sb. rare.* Also **-rogat.** 1633. [– Fr. *interrogat* (XVI) or med.L. *interrogatum* interrogatory, f. as next; see -ATE¹.] A question; an interrogation –1661.

Interrogate (inte·rŏgeⁱt), *v.* 1483. [– *interrogat-*, pa. ppl. stem of L. *interrogare*, f. *inter* INTER- + *rogare* ask; see -ATE³.] **1.** *trans.* To ask questions of, to question, esp. formally; to examine by questions. Also *fig.* †**2.** To ask about (something) (*rare*) –1698. **3.** *absol.* or *intr.* To ask questions; *spec.* in *Law* (see INTERROGATORY B. 1) 1622.
1. *fig.* To i. Truth 1701, nature 1794, one's memory HELPS. **2.** Interrogating the State of Europe 1698. **3.** The leave of the court to i. must be obtained 1883. Hence **Inte:rrogatee·**, one who is interrogated. **Inte·rrogatingly** *adv.*

Interrogation (inte:rŏgēⁱ·ʃən). ME. [– (O)Fr. *interrogation* or L. *interrogatio*, f. as prec.; see -ION.] **1.** The action of interrogating; a questioning; †request 1551. **b.** With *an* and *pl.* A question ME. **2.** *Gram.* and *Rhet.* Questioning, or a question, as a form of speech 1532. **b.** *Point* (*mark, note*) *of interrogation*, also *i.-point* (and, formerly, *i.*): the symbol used in writing or printing to indicate a question, usually placed at the end of the sentence and having the form ? or ?.
A point of interrogation is also sometimes placed before a word or phrase, to query its correctness, existence, etc.
In Spanish, it is placed both before and after the question, in the former case inverted as in *¿Quien sabe?* who knows?
2. b. It is a mistake to be inquisitive. A walking i.-point is never a pleasant companion 1895. Hence **Interroga·tional** *a.* interrogative.

Interrogative (intərǫ·gătiv). 1520. [– late L. *interrogativus*, f. as prec.; see -IVE. Cf. Fr. *interrogatif, -ive* (XVI).]
A. *adj.* **1.** Of, pertaining to, or of the nature of questioning; having the form or force of a question 1597. **2.** *Rhet.* and *Gram.* Of a word or form: Employed in asking a question 1520. **3.** Given to asking questions; inquisitive (*rare*) 1709.
1. The i. method of Socrates JOWETT. **2.** *I. pronouns*, the pronouns *who? which? what? whether? I. adverbs*, such as *where? when? why? wherefore?* Hence **Interro·gatively** *adv.* in an i. manner.
B. *sb.* **1.** An interrogation 1581. **2.** *Gram.* A word or form employed in asking a question; esp. an interrogative pronoun 1530.

Interrogator (inte·rŏgeⁱtəɹ). 1751. [– late L. *interrogator*, f. as prec.; see -OR 2. Cf. Fr. *interrogateur* (XVI).] One who interrogates; a questioner.

Interrogatory (intərǫ·gătəri). 1533. [– late L. *interrogatorius*, f. as prec.; see -ORY². With B *sb.* cf. med.L. *interrogatorium* (pl. *-ia*), Fr. *interrogatoire*. See -ORY¹.] **A.** *adj.* = INTERROGATIVE *a.* 1576.
B. *sb.* **1.** An interrogation, a question; *spec.* in *Law*: A question formally put, or drawn up in writing to be put, to an accused person or a witness 1533. **2.** Examination (of an accused person) (*rare*). [= Fr. *interrogatoire.*] 1827.
1. A paper of interrogatories was laid before him by order of the Privy Council MACAULAY. Hence **Interro·gatorily** *adv.* interrogatively.

In terrorem: see IN *Lat. prep.*

†**Interru·pt,** *ppl. a.* ME. [– OFr. *interrupt* – L. *interruptus*, pa. pple. of *interrumpere*; see next.] Interrupted (see the vb.). In quot., Forming an interval or breach between two parts of something.
Our adversarie, whom no bounds Prescrib'd, no barrs of Hell..nor yet the main Abyss Wide i. can hold MILT.

Interrupt (intərɒ·pt), *v.* ME. [– *interrupt-*, pa. ppl. stem of L. *interrumpere*, f. *inter* INTER- + *rumpere* break.] **1.** *trans.* To break in upon (*esp.* speech or discourse); to break the continuity of; to break off, hinder the course of, cause to cease or stop (usu. temporarily). **2.** To break in upon (a person) while doing something, *esp.* speaking; to hinder or cause to stop (usu. temporarily) in what one is doing ME. **3.** *absol.* or *intr.*; also quasi-*trans.* = to say in interruption ME. †**4.** *trans.* To hinder, stop, prevent, thwart –1632. †**5.** To infringe, suspend (a law) –1587.
1. Not one of us but had his sleepe interrupted by fearfull dreames 1615. There being neither Tree nor Bush to i. his Charge CLARENDON. **2.** It were a grosse incivility to i. them in their conversation 1639. **3.** Please not to i., my good friend JOWETT.

Interrupted (intərɒ·ptėd), *ppl. a.* 1552. [f. prec. + -ED¹.] Broken in upon; broken off; having its course hindered or continuity broken; made discontinuous. **b.** *Bot.* (and *Zool.*) Having smaller, or otherwise differing, members (*e.g.* leaflets in a compound leaf) in the intervals between others in a series; also, discontinuous (as a linear marking) 1828.

Interru·ptedly, *adv.* 1663. [f. prec. + -LY².] With interruptions or void intervals; discontinuously. **b.** *Bot.* (and *Zool.*) With smaller or otherwise different members in the intervals between the others (see prec. b) 1753.
b. *Spiræa ulmaria*..leaves i. pinnate HOOKER.

Interrupter, -or (intərɒ·ptəɹ). 1511. [– late L. *interruptor*, f. *interrupt-*, see INTERRUPT *v.*, -OR 2. In later use f. INTERRUPT *v.* + -ER¹.] One who interrupts (see the vb.). **b.** A device for interrupting an electric current 1868.

Interruption (intərɒ·pʃən). ME. [– (O)Fr. *interruption* or L. *interruptio*, f. as prec.; see -ION.] The action of interrupting, or fact of being interrupted (see the vb.). **1.** Hindrance of course or continuance; temporary stoppage or cessation 1489. **2.** A breach of continuity in space or serial order; a break; the formation or existence of a gap ME. †**b.** Irruption. HALE. †**3.** The action, or an act, of hindering or thwarting –1595. **4.** *Sc. Law.* The step legally requisite to stop the currency of a period of prescription 1615.
1. I still go on with the work I have in hand, but with terrible interruptions BURKE. **2.** The Inter-

ruptions of the Strata WOODWARD. **b.** Places severed from the Continent by the i. of the Sea HALE. **3.** SHAKS. *John* III. iv. 9.

Interruptive (intərɒ·ptiv), *a.* 1643. [f. INTERRUPT *v.* + -IVE. Cf. med.L. *interruptivus.*] **1.** Having the quality of interrupting 1651. †**2.** Characterized by interruption; interrupted 1643.

Interscapular (intəɹskæ·piŭlăɹ), *a.* (*sb.*) 1721. [f. INTER- II. 2 a + SCAPULA + -AR[1].] **1.** *Anat.* and *Zool.* Situated between the scapulæ or shoulder-blades. **2.** *sb.* (in *pl.*) The interscapular feathers.

Interscendent (intəɹse·ndĕnt), *a. rare.* 1796. [– mod.L. *interscendens, -ent-* (Leibnitz), f. L. *inter* between, after *transcendens* TRANSCENDENT.] *Math.* Applied to expressions or equations involving incommensurable quantities in the exponents; regarded as being intermediate between *algebraic* and *transcendental.* Also **Interscende·ntal** *a.*

†**Interscri·be,** *v. rare.* 1656. [– L. *interscribere* write between, f. *inter* between + *scribere* write.] To write between, to interline.

Interseam (intəɹsī·m), *v. Obs.* or *arch.* 1589. [– Fr. *entresemer* sow among, f. *entre-* between + *semer* :– L. *seminare* to sow. But app. often assoc. w. SEAM *v.*] *trans.* To sprinkle or scatter between or amongst other things; to intersperse. Chiefly in *pa. pple.*

†**Intersecant,** *a.* (*sb.*) *rare.* 1658. [– *intersecant-*, pr. ppl. stem of L. *intersecare*; see next, -ANT.] Intersecting. As *sb.* (in *pl.*) Intersecting lines.

Intersect (intəɹse·kt), *v.* 1615. [– *intersect-*, pa. ppl. stem of L. *intersecare* cut asunder, intersect, f. *inter-* between + *secare* cut.] **1.** *trans.* To divide (something) in two by passing through or lying across it; to cross. Freq. in *pass.* (const. *with* or *by*). **b.** *Geom.* Of a line or surface: To cut (see CUT *v.* IV. 1) 1646. **c.** To divide (two things) by passing between them 1784. **2.** *intr.* (for *refl.*) To cross or cut each another; chiefly *Geom.* 1847.

1. Crevasses also i. the ice TYNDALL. **b.** Where these two Arches I., or cut each other, there is the Center MOXON. **c.** Lands intersected by a narrow frith Abhor each other COWPER. **2.** Straight streets intersecting at right angles GROTE.

Intersection (intəɹse·kʃən). 1559. [– L. *intersectio*, f. as prec.; see -ION. Cf. (O)Fr. *intersection.*] **1.** The action or fact of intersecting. **2.** The place where two things intersect; chiefly *Geom.*, the point (or line) common to two lines or surfaces which intersect 1559. Hence **Interse·ctional** *a.*, of, pertaining to, or characterized by i.

Interseptal (intəɹse·ptăl), *a.* 1847. [f. INTER II. 2 a + SEPTUM + -AL[1].] Situated between septa or partitions. (Chiefly *Anat.* and *Zool.*)

†**Interse·rt,** *v.* 1583. [– *intersert-*, pa. ppl. stem of L. *interserere*, f. *inter* between + *serere* put, place, insert.] *trans.* To insert between other things; to interpolate –1691. So †**Interse·rtion,** the action of interserting; that which is interserted.

Interset: see INTER- *pref.* I. 1 a.

Intershock (intəɹʃǫ·k), *v. rare.* 1603. [f. INTER- I. 1 b + SHOCK *v.* In sense 1 – Fr. *s'entrechoquer.*] †**1.** *trans.* To shock or attack mutually –1605. **2.** *intr.* To strike together, collide 1650.

Intershoot (intəɹʃū·t), *v.* 1845. [INTER- I. 1 a.] *intr.* To shoot or glance at intervals. *trans.* To variegate at intervals (chiefly in pa. pple. *intershot*, const. *with.*)

Hues..intershooting, and to sight Lost and recovered WORDSW.

Intersidereal (i:ntəɹsəidīə·riăl), *a.* 1656. [f. INTER- II. 2 a + SIDEREAL, after INTERSTELLAR.] = INTERSTELLAR.

Intersocial (intəɹsōu·ʃăl), *a.* 1852. [f. INTER- II. 2 a + L. *socius* companion + -AL[1].] Existing between associates; social.

Intersomnial (intəɹsǫ·mniăl), *a.* 1849. [f. INTER- II. 2 d + L. *somnium* dream + -AL[1]; prop. *intrasomnial.*] Occurring in the midst of a dream. So **Interso·mnious** *a.* 'between sleeping and waking' (Worcester).

Interspace (i·ntəɹspēˈs), *sb.* ME. [INTER- I. 2 b.] **1.** A space between two things; interval. **2.** An interval of time 1629. So **Interspa·tial** *a.* of or belonging to an i.

Interspace (intəɹspēˈ·s), *v.* 1847. [INTER- I. 1.] *trans.* To put a space or interval between; to occupy or fill the space or interval between.

†**I·nterspeech.** 1579. [INTER- I. 2 a.] Speech between or among a number of persons; colloquy –1656.

Intersperse (intəɹspə̄·ɹs), *v.* Also †**entersparse.** 1566. [– *interspers-*, pa. ppl. stem of L. *interspergere*, f. *inter* between + *spargere* scatter, sprinkle.] **1.** *trans.* To scatter or sprinkle between or among other things; to mingle dispersedly or at intervals 1645. **2.** To furnish, adorn, or diversify *with* things scattered about or mingled at intervals.

1. The way in which you have interspersed local traditions and stories KINGSLEY. **2.** The face of the country was interspersed with groves GIBBON.

Interspersion (intəɹspə̄·ɹʃən). 1658. [f. prec. + -ION, after *dispersion*, etc.] The action of interspersing or condition of being interspersed.

Interspinal (intəɹspəi·năl), *a.* 1831. [f. INTER- II. 2 a + SPINE + -AL[1].] = next.

Interspinous (intəɹspəi·nəs), *a.* 1839. [f. as prec. + -OUS.] *Anat.* Situated between the spines or spinous processes of vertebræ.

†**Interspira·tion.** 1623. [– L. *interspiratio*, f. *interspirat-*, pa. ppl. stem of *interspirare*; see next, -ION.] A taking breath between; a breathing space –1656.

†**Interspi·re,** *v.* 1647. [– L. *interspirare*, f. *inter* between + *spirare* breathe.] To take breath between; to pause, take rest. HY. MORE.

Interstate, inter-state (i·ntəɹ,stēˈ:t), *a. U.S.* 1845. [INTER- II. 3.] Lying, extending, or carried on between states; pertaining to the mutual relations of the States of the American Union.

Trusts are purely State, and not i. affairs 1899.

Interstellar (intəɹste·lăɹ), *a.* 1626. [f. INTER- II. 2 a + L. *stella* star + -AR[1]; in mod.L. *interstellaris* (Bacon).] Situated between the stars; occupying or passing through the spaces between the stars.

A comet arriving from remote i. space PROCTOR. So **Interste·llary** *a.* (Dicts.)

Intersternal: see INTER- II. 2 a.

Interstice (intə̄·ɹstis, i·ntəɹstis). 1603. [– late L. *interstitium*, f. **interstit-*, pa. ppl. stem of L. *intersistere*, f. *inter* between + *sistere* stand.] **1.** An intervening space (usu. empty); *esp.* a relatively small or narrow space between things or the parts of a body; a narrow opening, chink, or crevice. **2.** An intervening space of time; an interval between actions. Now *rare.* 1639. **b.** *spec.* in *Canon Law* (*pl.*) The intervals required between the reception of the various degrees of holy orders 1745.

1. The interstices of water are always found full of air 1756. **2.** Long inter-regnums or interstices in government 1639. Hence **Intersticed** *a.* having interstices; also, fitted at intervals *with* something.

†**Intersti·nctive,** *a.* 1696. [f. †*interstinct* divided – L. *interstinctus*, pa. pple. of *interstinguere* separate, f. *inter* between + *stinguere* (see DISTINCT).] Serving to divide or mark off. WALLIS.

Interstitial (intəɹsti·ʃăl), *a.* 1646. [f. L. *interstitium* INTERSTICE + -AL[1].] **1.** Of the nature of an interstice; forming interstices. **2.** Of a thing: Pertaining to, existing in, or occupying interstices 1665. **3.** Of a physical or morbid process: Taking place in the interstices of a body, and so affecting its internal structure 1807.

2. *I. tissue* (Anat.), the fine connective tissue lying between the cells of other tissue. *I. organs*, smaller organs of the body situated between larger ones. Hence **Intersti·tially** *adv.*

†**Intersti·tion.** ME. [– L. *interstitio* pause, f. as INTERSTICE; see -ION.] = INTERSTITIUM.

†‖**Interstitium** (intəɹsti·ʃiŏm). *Pl.* **-stitia,** (**†-a's**), **-stitiums.** 1597. [L.; see INTERSTICE.] = INTERSTICE –1706.

Interstratification (-stræ:tifikēˈ·ʃən). 1855. [INTER- I. 2 a.] The condition or fact of being interstratified; an interposed formation or deposit.

Interstratify (-stræ·tifəi), *v.* 1822. [INTER- I. 1 b.] **1.** *trans.* in *pass.* Of geological strata: To be alternated or interspersed *with* other strata. **2.** *intr.* To lie as strata between other strata 1880. Hence **Interstra·tified** *ppl. a.* placed as a stratum between other strata 1839.

Intertangle (intəɹtæ·ŋg'l), *v.* 1589. [INTER- I. 1 b.] *trans.* To tangle together; to intertwine confusedly. Hence **Interta·nglement,** intertangled state or condition.

Intertarsal: see INTER- *pref.*

†**Interte·x,** *v.* 1578. [– L. *intertexere*, f. *inter* between + *texere* weave.] *trans.* To weave together, intertwine –1666.

Intertexture (intəɹte·kstiŭɹ). 1649. [f. L. *intertext-*, pa. ppl. stem of *intertexere* (see prec.) + -URE.] **1.** The action of interweaving; the fact or condition of being interwoven. **2.** quasi-*concr.* An intertwined or interwoven structure 1651.

2. I. firm Of thorny boughs COWPER.

Intertie (i·ntəɹtəi). 1703. [INTER- I. 2 b; but orig. a var. of †*interdice* (in same sense), arising from viewing the forms *inter-ties, interties* as plural.] A horizontal piece of timber connecting two vertical pieces.

Intertissued (intəɹti·ʃ'ud), *ppl. a.* 1599. [f. OFr. *entretissu* interwoven + -ED[1].] Interwoven.

†**Intertra·ffic.** 1603. [INTER- I. 2 a.] Traffic between two or more persons or places; reciprocal commerce –1640.

Intertranspi·cuous, *a.* [INTER- I. 2 a.] Transpicuous between or through each other. SHELLEY.

Intertransve·rse, *a.* 1831. [INTER- II. 2 a.] *Anat.* Situated between the transverse processes of the vertebræ.

Intertribal (intəɹtrəi·băl), *a.* 1862. [f. INTER- II. 2 c + TRIBE + -AL[1].] Existing or carried on between different tribes.

‖**Intertrigo** (intəɹtrəi·go). 1706. [L. (for *interterigo*), f. **interterere* rub against each other.] *Path.* Inflammation caused by the rubbing of one part of the surface of the skin against another.

Intertrochanteric: see INTER-.

Intertrochlear (-trǫ·kliăɹ), *a.* 1870. [f. INTER- II. 2 a + TROCHLEA + -AR[1].] Situated in the middle of the trochlear surface of a joint.

Intertropical (intəɹtrǫ·pikăl), *a.* 1794. [f. INTER- II. 2 a + TROPIC + -AL[1].] Of or pertaining to regions between the tropics; tropical.

Intertubular: see INTER-.

Intertwine (intəɹtwəi·n), *v.* 1641. [INTER- I. 1 b.] **1.** *trans.* To twine (things) together; to interlace, intertwist, interweave. Also *intr.* for *refl.* **2.** *trans.* To twine round and involve (*rare*) 1717. Hence **I·ntertwine** *sb.*, **Intertwi·nement,** the fact of intertwining; intertwined state; an intertwined formation. **Intertwi·ningly** *adv.* so as to i.

Intertwist (intəɹtwi·st), *v.* 1659. [INTER- I. 1 b.] *trans.* To twist one within another; to intertwine, intertangle. Hence **Intertwi·stingly** *adv.*

Interungular, -ungulate: see INTER-.

Interurban (intər,ɒ̄·ɹbăn), *a.* 1883. [f. INTER- II. 2 b + L. *urb(s* city + -AN.] Carried on between, or connecting, cities.

Interval (i·ntəɹvăl), *sb.* ME. [ult. – L. *intervallum* orig. space between ramparts, f. *inter* INTER- + *vallum*, but the earliest forms, *entrewal, entervale, intervalle*, are – OFr. *entreval(e*, later *-valle* (mod. *intervalle*).] **1.** The period of time between two events, actions, etc., or between two parts of an action, etc.; a period of cessation; a pause, break. **b.** *spec.* The space of time intervening between two febrile paroxysms, or between any fits or periods of disease 1634. **2.** The space of time intervening between two points of time; any intervening time 1616. **3.** An open space lying between two things or two parts of one thing; a gap, opening 1489. **4.** In N. America: = INTERVALE 3. 1684. **5.** *Mus.* The difference of pitch between two musical sounds or notes 1609. **6.** *fig.* Distance between persons in respect of position, beliefs, etc., or between things in respect of their qualities 1849.

1. The intervals of the play PEPYS. **b.** The intervals or good dayes of a Tertian Ague 1634. Phr. *Lucid i.*: see LUCID. **2.** An i. of more than sixty years GROTE. Phr. *At (†by) intervals*, now and again, not continuously. **3.** 'Twixt Host and Host but narrow space was left, A dreadful i. MILT *P.L.* VI. 105. Short intervals of still water 1791. Phr. *At intervals*, here and there. Hence **Interva·llic** *a.* 1847.

Interval (i·ntəɹvăl), *v. rare.* 1630. [f. prec. sb.] †**1.** *intr.* To come between or in an interval; to form an interval –1632. **2.** *trans.* (in *pass.*) To break or interrupt at intervals 1883.

2. A march of infinite light..intervaled indeed with eddies of shadow RUSKIN.

Intervale (i·ntəɹvēl). Now *Amer.* ME. [In former Eng. use, a var. of INTERVAL. Later, esp. in New England, assoc. w. *vale* (see sense 3).] †**1.** Of time: = INTERVAL *sb.* 1. –1682. †**2.** Of space: = INTERVAL *sb.* 3. –1684. **3.** In N. America: A low level tract of land, esp. along a river; = INTERVAL *sb.* 4. Also *attrib.* 1653.

3. By intervales we mean those low lands which are adjacent to the rivers 1794.

†‖**Interva·llum,** *Pl.* **-valla, -vallums.** 1574. [L.; see INTERVAL *sb.*] = INTERVAL *sb.* 1, 2. –1647.

He shall laugh with Interuallums SHAKS.

Inter-'varsity, -vary: see INTER- *pref.*

Intervein (intəɹvēⁱ·n), *v.* 1615. [f. INTER- I. 1 a + VEIN *sb.* or *v.*] **1.** *trans.* To intersect with or as with veins. **2.** (In *pass.*) To place in alternate veins 1811.

1. White the rest With vermeil intervein'd CARY.

Intervene (intəɹvī·n), *v.* 1588. [– L. *intervenire*, f. *inter* INTER- + *venire* come.] **1.** *intr.* To come in as something extraneous 1605. **2.** To happen or take place between other events, or between points in time 1610. **3.** To come in or between; to interpose (*spec.* in *Law*, cf. next) 1646. **4.** To come, extend, or lie *between* 1621. †**5.** *trans.* To come between; to intercept; to prevent, hinder –1839.

1. What wonder if so near Looks i. and smiles MILT. *P.L.* IX. 222. **2.** Some argument had intervened between them LAMB. **3.** In all the Negotiations where he has intervened TEMPLE. **4.** No clouds, no vapours i. DYER. **5.** Woodlands of birch .. and hazel .. intervening the different estates with natural sylvan marches DE QUINCEY.

Intervener¹ (intəɹvī·nəɹ). Rarely **-or.** 1621. [f. prec. vb. + -ER¹.] One who intervenes; *spec.* in *Law*, one who intervenes in a suit to which he was not originally a party.

Interve·ner². 1847. [f. INTERVENE *v.*, after *interpleader*, etc. See -ER⁴.] *Law.* The interposition of a person in a suit in an ecclesiastical court in defence of his own interest.

Intervenient (intəɹvī·niĕnt), *a.* (*sb.*) 1605. [– *intervenient-*, pr. ppl. stem of L. *intervenire*; see INTERVENE, -ENT.] **1.** That intervenes; that comes in as something extraneous. **2.** Intervening in space, time, or action 1618. **3.** *sb.* One who intervenes 1620.

2. On the horizon's verge, O'er i. waste WORDSW. Hence †**Interve·nience,** †**-ency,** intervention.

†**Interve·nt,** *v. rare.* 1593. [– *intervent-*, pa. ppl. stem of L. *intervenire*; see INTERVENE, -ENT.] *trans.* To come between, obstruct, thwart –1647.

Intervention (intəɹve·nʃən). ME. [– Fr. *intervention* or L. *interventio*, f. as prec.; see -ION.] **1.** The action of intervening, 'stepping in', or interfering in any affair, so as to affect its course or issue. **2.** Intermediate agency; the fact of coming in as an intermediary 1659. **3.** The fact of coming or being situated between in space, time, or order 1645.

1. The i. of the allied powers between Greece and Turkey in 1827. 1866. **2.** Adam was framed immediately by God, without the i. of man or woman 1659. **3.** Trade Winds..are frequently impeded by the i. of Islands 1671. Hence **Interve·ntionist,** one who favours i., esp. in international affairs 1839.

Interventor (intəɹve·ntəɹ). 1727. [– L. *interventor*, in late L. = mediator, f. as prec.; see -OR 2.] **1.** *Eccl.* = INTERCESSOR 3. **2.** *U.S.* A mine-inspector.

Interventricular (i:ntəɹventri·kiŭlăɹ), *a.* 1836. [f. INTER- II. 2 a + VENTRICLE + -AR¹, after *ventricular.*] *Anat.* Situated between the ventricles (of the heart or brain).

†**Intervenue.** 1636. [– Fr. †*inter-, entrevenue*, f. *inter-, entrevenir*; see INTERVENE, and cf. *avenue.*] Intervention.

†**Interve·rt,** *v.* 1600. [– L. *intervertere*, f. *inter* INTER- + *vertere* turn. Cf. Fr. *intervertir* (XVII).] **1.** To divert another way; to alienate, misapply, misuse –1648. *esp.* to appropriate, embezzle –1850. **2.** To give a different turn to –1825.

1. Interverting, embezeling their masters estates TRAPP. Hence †**Interve·rsion,** embezzlement 1676.

Intervertebral (intəɹvə·ɹtĭbrăl), *a.* 1782. [f. INTER- II. 2 a + VERTEBRA + -AL¹.] *Anat.* Situated between vertebræ. Hence **Interve·rtebrally** *adv.* between vertebræ.

Interview (i·ntəɹviū), *sb.* 1514. [Earlier form *entervew(e* – Fr. †*entreveue, -vue*, f. *entrevoir* have a glimpse of, *s'entrevoir* see each other (f. *entre* INTER + *voir* see), after *vue* VIEW.] **1.** A meeting of persons face to face, esp. for the purpose of formal conference on some point. **b.** *spec.* A meeting between a representative of the press and some one from whom he seeks to obtain statements for publication 1869. †**2.** Mutual view (*of* each other) (*rare*) –1667. †**3.** Inspection –1586; a view, glance, glimpse (*of* a thing) –1719.

1. Of Ceremonies in the enterview of Kings FLORIO. **b.** It is claimed for him [Joseph M'Cullagh, of St. Louis] that he was the inventor of the modern newspaper i. 1897. **2.** At i. both stood A while MILT. *P.L.* VI. 555.

†**Interview,** *v.*¹ 1548. [– Fr. *entrevu*, pa. pple. of (*s'*)*entrevoir*, on anal. of prec.] **1. a.** *trans.* To have a personal meeting with (each other). **b.** *intr.* To meet together in person. HALL. **2.** *trans.* To get a view of; to glance at –1624.

Interview (i·ntəɹviū), *v.*² 1869. [f. INTERVIEW *sb.* (sense 1 b).] *trans.* To have an interview with (a person); *spec.* To talk with so as to elicit statements for publication.

A northwest newspaper, in which I have been 'interviewed', and private conversation reported to the public LONGF. Hence **I·nterviewing** *vbl. sb.* **Interviewee·**, one who is interviewed.

Interviewer (i·ntəɹviū͡əɹ). 1869. [f. prec. + -ER¹.] One who interviews; *spec.* a journalist who interviews a person with the object of obtaining matter for publication.

Intervisible: see INTER- *pref.* I. 2 a.

Intervisit (intəɹvi·zit), *v.* 1609. [– Fr. *entrevisiter*, f. *entre-* (INTER- I. 1 b) + *visiter* to visit.] *intr.* To exchange visits.

Intervital (intəɹvəi·tăl), *a. rare.* 1850. [f. INTER- II. 2 a + L. *vita* life + -AL¹.] Existing between two lives or stages of existence.

[There] comes no faintest whisper from the i. gloom FARRAR.

Intervocal (intəɹvōᵘ·kăl), *a. rare.* 1891. [f. INTER- II. 2 a + L. *vocalis* vocal, a vowel.] Occurring between vowels. So **Intervoca·lic** *a.* (more usual) 1887.

Intervolution (intəɹvolⁱū·ʃən). 1850. [f. next, after *involve/involution.*] Intervolved condition; a winding.

Intervolve (intəɹvǫ·lv), *v.* 1667. [f. INTER- I. 1 + L. *volvere* roll, after *involve*, etc.] *trans.* To wind or roll up (things) within each other; to wind or involve (something) within the coils of something else. Also *intr.*

Mazes intricate, Eccentric, intervolv'd MILT.

Interweave (intəɹwī·v), *v.* Pa. t. **-wove,** pa. pple. **-woven** (†**-wove**); also †**-weaved.** 1578. [f. INTER- I. 1 b + WEAVE *v.*] **1.** *trans.* To weave together, as the warp and woof of a fabric; to interlace; to intertwine. **2.** *transf.* and *fig.* To intermingle as if by weaving; to intertwine intricately; to blend intimately 1589.

1. Two Olives..With roots intwin'd, and branches interwove POPE. A..method of interweaving gold with wool or linen 1870. **2.** The moral law is.. interwoven into our very nature BUTLER.

Interwind (intəɹwəi·nd), *v.* Pa. t. and pple. **-wound** (waund). 1693. [INTER- I. 1 b.] *trans.* To wind (things) into or through each other; to wind together; to intertwine, intertwist. Also *fig.* Also *intr.* (for *refl.*)

Interwish, etc.: see INTER- *pref.*

Interwork (intəɹwɔ̄·ɹk), *v.* Pa. t. and pple. **-wrought** (-rǭ·t), **-worked** (-wɔ̄·ɹkt). 1603. [INTER- I. 1 b.] *trans.* To work one thing into and through another; to combine by interpenetration. **b.** *intr.* To interact 1855.

Interwoven (intəɹwōᵘ·v'n), *ppl. a.* 1647. [pa. pple. of INTERWEAVE *v.*] Woven together; interlaced; intricately entangled.

Interwreathe (-rī·ð), *v.* 1658. [INTER- I. 1 b.] *trans.* To wreathe together; to intertwine into, or as in, a wreath.

†**Inte·stable,** *a.* 1590. [– late L. *intestabilis* (in cl. L. = infamous), f. *in-* IN-³ + *testabilis*, f. *testari*; see INTESTATE. Cf. Fr. †*intestable.*] **1.** Legally incapable of making or of benefiting by a will –1767. **2.** Disqualified from being a witness or giving evidence –1656. Hence †**Intestabi·lity.**

Intestacy (inte·stăsi). 1767. [f. INTESTATE *a.*; see -ACY.] *Law.* The condition or fact of dying intestate or without having made a will.

Intestate (inte·stĕt). ME. [– L. *intestatus*, f. *in-* IN-³ + *testatus*, pa. pple. of *testari* bear witness, make a will, f. *testis* witness; see TESTIFY, -ATE².] **A.** *adj.* **1.** Of a person: Not having made a will. **2.** Of things: Not disposed of by will 1538.

1. He..died i. JOHNSON. *fig. Rich. III*, IV. iv. 128. **2.** The admynystratyon of i. godys 1538.

B. *sb.* One who dies intestate 1658.

Intestinal (inte·stinăl, intestəi·năl), *a.* 1599. [– Fr. *intestinal* (Paré); see next, -AL¹.] **1.** Of or pertaining to the intestines; found in or affecting the intestines. **b.** Having an intestine or enteron; opp. to ANENTEROUS. **2.** = INTESTINE *a.* 1. E. B. BROWNING.

1. I. worms 1797. The i. tube 1851.

Intestine (inte·stin), *sb.* 1533. [– L. *intestinum*, subst. use of n. of adj. *intestinus*; see next.] **1.** The lower part of the alimentary canal, from the pyloric end of the stomach to the anus, called pop. the bowels or guts. In ordinary use, commonly pl.; the singular is applied to each of the two distinct parts, the *small intestine* (comprising the duodenum, jejunum, and ileum), and the *large intestine* (comprising the cæcum, colon, and rectum), and also, in scientific use, to the canal as a whole; in biology, it often includes the whole alimentary canal from the mouth downward 1597. †**2.** *fig.* The inmost part or member. LD. BERNERS.

Intestine (inte·stin), *a.* 1535. [– L. *intestinus*, f. *intus* within. Cf. (O)Fr. *intestin.*] **1.** Internal with regard to a country or people; domestic, civil. Also *fig.* †**2.** Internal with regard to human nature or the nature of things; inward, innate (*rare*) –1678. †**3.** Seated in the bowels; intestinal –1727. **4.** Internal with reference to any thing or place. (*Obs.* exc. as *fig.* from 1 or 3) 1664.

1. The i. shocke, And furious cloze of ciuill Butchery SHAKS. I. feuds PRIOR, foes 1764, division 1869. **4.** All i. Works as Wainscot, floors [etc.] EVELYN. Phr. *I. motion*: motion entirely within, or among the molecules of, a body.

†**I·ntext.** [app. an expressive var. of *context*, quasi 'what is woven in'.] The text or matter of a book. HERRICK.

Intextine (inte·kstin). Also **intexine.** 1835. [f. L. *intus* + EXTINE.] *Bot.* An inner coating of the pollen grain within the extine.

Inte·xture, *v. rare.* 1856. [f. L. *intext-*, ppl. stem of *intexere* weave in + -URE.] *trans.* To weave or work in. Hence **Inte·xtured** *ppl. a.*

Inthral(l, etc.: see ENTHRAL(L, etc.

†**Inthro·ng,** *v.* 1600. [f. IN-¹ + THRONG *v.*] *intr.* To throng, press, or crowd in. FAIRFAX.

†**Inthro·nizate,** *ppl. a.* Also **-tron-.** 1470. [– *inthronizatus*, pa. pple. of late L. *inthronizare*, tr. Gr. ἐνθρονίζειν; see ENTHRONE, -ATE².] *trans.* To enthrone –1577. Hence †**Inthroniza·tion,** obs. var. of ENTHRONIZATION.

Intice, etc., obs. var. ENTICE, etc.

Intil(l (ME.), Sc. and n. dial. ff. INTO.

Intimacy (i·ntimăsi). 1641. [f. INTIMATE *a.*; see -ACY.] **1.** The quality or condition of being intimate; close familiarity; *euphem.* for illicit sexual intercourse 1676. **b.** Closeness of observation, knowledge, or the like 1714. **2.** Intimate connection or union (*rare*) 1720.

1. Sir Thomas, drawing back from intimacies in general JANE AUSTEN. **2.** The Union and I. between Father and Son WATERLAND.

†**Intimado** (intimā·do). 1682. [alt. f. INTIMATE *sb.*, after Sp. words in *-ado*; see -ADO.] = INTIMATE *sb.* –1823.

His *intimados*..were in the world's eye a ragged regiment LAMB.

Intimate (i·ntimĕt). 1632. [– late L. *intimatus*, pa. pple. of *intimare*, f. *intimus* inmost, f. *int-* of INTER + superl. suffix; see -ATE².]

A. *adj.* **1.** Inmost, most inward, deep-seated; hence, Essential, intrinsic. Now chiefly in scientific use. **2.** Pertaining to the inmost thoughts or feelings 1671. **3.** Close in acquaintance or association; characterized by familiarity; very familiar. Also *transf.* of things: Pertaining to or dealing with such close personal relations. 1635. **b.** *euphem.* of illicit sexual intercourse 1889. **4.** Of knowledge or acquaintance: Close 1680. **5.** Of a relation between things: Very close 1692.

1. The i. structure of matter and ether 1878. **2.** I knew From i. impulse MILT. *Sams.* 223. **3.** A Knight who was an i. friend of his 1635. **4.** An i. knowledge of his character 'JUNIUS'. **5.** Pride.. is of such I... Connexion with Ingratitude SOUTH. Hence **I·ntimate-ly** *adv.* 1637, **-ness** (*rare*) 1642.

B. *sb.* A person with whom one is intimate; a very close friend or associate 1659.

Intimate (i·ntime^{i}t), *v.* Pa. pple. **intimated**; also †**intimate.** 1538. [– *intimat-*, pa. ppl. stem of late L. *intimare* announce; see prec., -ATE^3.] **1.** *trans.* To make known formally, to notify, state; †formerly, to proclaim, to declare (war). **2.** To make known indirectly; hence, to signify, indicate; to imply, to hint at 1590. **b.** To mention indirectly 1634. †**3.** To make intimate, familiarize –1654.

1. He incontinente did proclaime and i. open warre HALL. This resolution she intimated to the leaders of both factions W. ROBERTSON. **2.** The Apostle expresses one duty and intimates another JER. TAYLOR.

Intimation (intimē^i·ʃən). 1442. [– (O)Fr. *intimation* or late L. *intimatio*, f. as prec.; see -ION.] **1.** The action of intimating; formal notification; †formerly, declaration (of war). **b.** *Law.* Notification of a requirement made by law, and of the penalty in case of default. ?*Obs.* 1632. **2.** An expression by sign or token; an indication; a suggestion, a hint 1531.

1. They made an edict, with an i., that whosoever killed a storke should be banished HOLLAND. **2.** I have often had intimations in dreams JOWETT.

†**I·ntime,** *a.* 1618. [– (O)Fr. *intime* or L. *intimus* inmost; see INTIMATE.] = INTIMATE *a.* –1678.

Intimidate (inti·mide^{i}t), *v.* 1646. [– *intimidat-*, pa. ppl. stem of med.L. *intimidare*, f. *in-* IN-^{2} + *timidus* TIMID; see -ATE^3.] *trans.* To render timid, inspire with fear; to overawe, cow; now, *esp.* to force to or deter from some action by threats or violence.

Unless you can find means to corrupt or i. the jury 'JUNIUS'. Hence **Inti·midator. Inti·midatory** *a.* of intimidating nature or tendency.

Intimidation (intimidē^i·ʃən). 1658. [f. prec. + -ION. Cf. Fr. *intimidation* (XVI).] The action of intimidating or making afraid; the fact or condition of being intimidated; now, *esp.* the use of threats or violence to force to or restrain from some action.

What was denied to reason and policy is surrendered to i. J. W. CROKER.

Intimity (inti·mĭti). 1617. [f. INTIME + -ITY. In sense 2 app. – Fr. *intimité* (XVIII).] †**1.** = INTIMACY 1. **2.** Intimate quality or nature; inwardness; privacy 1889.

†**I·ntimous,** *a.* 1619. [f. INTIME + -OUS.] = INTIMATE *a.* –1665.

Intinction (inti·ŋkʃən). 1559. [– late L. *intinctio*, f. *intinct-*, pa. ppl. stem of L. *intingere* dip in; see -ION.] †**1.** The action of dipping in; a dyeing; that in which something has been dipped, an infusion –1658. **2.** *Eccl.* The action of dipping the bread in the wine at the Eucharist, so that the two kinds may be administered conjointly 1872.

†**Intincti·vity.** 1794. [f. as prec. + -IVE + -ITY, prob. after *inactivity*.] The quality of not communicating colour.

Intine (i·ntin). 1835. [f. L. *intus* within + -INE^1.] *Bot.* The inner membrane of the pollen grain.

Intire, Intitle, obs. ff. ENTIRE, ENTITLE.

Intitulation (intitiulē^i·ʃən). Also †**en-.** 1456. [– Fr. †*intitulation* or med.L. *intitulatio*, f. *intitulat-*, pa. ppl. stem of late L. *intitulare*; see next, -ION.] **1.** The action of entitling; a superscription, title. **2.** The action of bestowing a title; a designation 1586.

Intitule (inti·tiul), *v.* Also †**en-.** 1483. [– (O)Fr. *intituler* – late L. *intitulare* entitle, f. *in-* IN-^{2} + L. *titulus* TITLE.] **1.** = ENTITLE *v.*, in various senses. †**2.** To prefix *to* a book the name of a person to whom it is dedicated –1691. †**3.** To dedicate *to* by name or title –1707.

2. I intituled Your Majesty to a Work EVELYN. **3.** The Society [of the Garter] is entituled to St. George 1707.

Into (i·ntŭ), *prep.* [OE. *in(n) tō*, i.e. IN *adv.*, TO *prep.*, in which the adv. expresses general direction, and the prep. has reference to a particular point or place.] *General sense* :– The prep. expressing the motion which results in the position expressed by IN, or which is directed towards that position.

I. Of motion or direction; ordinary uses. **1.** Expressing motion to a position within a space or thing. Regularly after verbs of going, coming, bringing, putting, and the like. **2.** In reference to non-physical things, treated as having extension or content OE. **3. a.** Introducing the substance or form into which anything turns or grows, or is changed, moulded, fashioned, or made ME. **b.** Introducing the condition or result brought about by some action 1540. **4.** Introducing the parts produced by division, breaking, folding, and the like ME. **5.** Used techn. with the vb. MULTIPLY. **6.** As an addition or accession to; as *into the bargain*. [Perh. = in, to the bargain; cf. IN *adv.* I. 3.] 1646. **7.** Expressing direction without actual motion, after *turn, look, search*, etc. 1605. **8.** Introducing a period of time to the midst of which anything advances or continues 1594.

1. Come into the garden, Maud TENNYSON. A.. limitation which can easily be read into deed or will 1895. *ellipt.* At dawn he is into Bonair KIPLING. **2.** These things.. beaing beaten into the Dukes minde MORE. To fall into errour 1551. What Measures the Allies must enter into STEELE. **3. a.** The twilight thickened into night W. IRVING. **b.** Persecuted into insurrection 1849. **7.** If you can looke into the Seedes of Time SHAKS. **8.** We had now got into the month of March DICKENS.

II. Obs. senses. †**1.** Unto, even to; to the very..–1548. †**2.** Towards –1652. †**3.** Until, on to, up to (a time or date) –1534. †**4.** Unto, to (a thing or person) –1611. †**5.** Defining the part of anything in which it is penetrated, pierced, etc. –1788.

4. That he enchants Societies into him *Cymb.* I. vi. 167. **5.** I..fired again, and shot him into the head DE FOE.

III. Of position: = IN. (After 1400, *Sc.*) To laugh wi' tears into its een RAMSAY.

In-toed (stress variable), *a.* 1824. [IN *adv.*] Having the toes turned inwards.

Intolerable (intǫ·lĕrăb'l), *a.* (*adv.*) ME. [– (O)Fr. *intolérable* or L. *intolerabilis*; see IN-^{3}, TOLERABLE.] **1.** That cannot be tolerated, borne, or put up with; unendurable, insupportable, insufferable. †**b.** Loosely, as a strong intensive: Excessive, extreme, very great. (Cf. *awful*.) –1725. **2.** That cannot be withstood ME. **3.** *adv.* Intolerably; also, Exceedingly, extremely –1716.

1. A cloudless, i. sun 1861. I. conduct FROUDE. **b.** But one halfe penny-worth of Bread to this intollerable deale of Sacke? SHAKS. **3.** Her onely fault..Is, that she is intollerable curst *Tam. Shr.* I. ii. 89. Hence **Into:lerab·lity, Into·lerableness. Into·lerably** *adv.*

Intolerance (intǫ·lĕrăns). 1765. [– L. *intolerantia*, f. *intolerant-*, see next, -ANCE. Cf. Fr. *intolérance* (XVII).] **1.** The fact or habit of not tolerating (something); inability, or unwillingness, to tolerate or endure some particular thing. Const. *of*. **2.** *spec.* Absence of tolerance for difference of opinion or practice, esp. in religious matters; denial of the right to differ 1790.

1. I. of official peculation 1844. **2.** The great antagonist of i. is not humanity, but Knowledge BUCKLE. So †**Into·lerancy** 1623.

Intolerant (intǫ·lĕrănt), *a.* (*sb.*) 1735. [– L. *intolerans, -ant-*, pr. pple. of *tolerare* bear; see IN-^{3}, TOLERATE.] **1.** Not having the habit or capacity of tolerating (something); unable, or unwilling, to endure (something specified). Const. *of*. **b.** *Forestry.* Incapable of enduring shade. *U.S.* 1898. **2.** *spec.* That does not tolerate opinions or practices different from one's own, esp. in religious matters; that denies the right to differ; disposed to persecute those who differ 1765. **3.** *sb.* An intolerant person 1765.

1. The powers of human bodies being limited and i. of excesses ARBUTHNOT (J.). Some patients are very i. of arsenic 1880. **2.** The national temper of the Jews was i. PALEY. Hence **Into·lerantly** *adv.* So †**Into·lerating** *a.* 1710.

Intoleration (intǫlĕrē^i·ʃən). *rare.* 1611. [IN-^{3}.] Want of toleration ; intolerance.

Intomb(e, obs. f. ENTOMB.

‖**Intonaco, -ico** (intō·năko, -iko). 1806. [It. *intonico*, †*-aco* plaster.] The final coating of plaster spread upon a wall or other surface, esp. for fresco painting.

†**I·ntonate,** *v.*^{1} *rare.* 1626. [– *intonat-*, pa. ppl. stem of L. *intonare* thunder (forth), f. *in-* IN-^{2} + *tonare* thunder; see -ATE^3.] *trans.* To thunder forth –1739.

Intonate (i·ntone^{i}t), *v.*^{2} 1795. [– *intonat-*, pa. ppl. stem of med.L. *intonare*; see INTONE, -ATE^3.] **1.** *trans.* To INTONE. **2.** To utter or pronounce with a particular tone 1823. **3.** *Phonetics.* To emit or pronounce with sonant vibration; to voice 1875.

1. Savonarola..intonating..the psalm *Exurgat Deus* 1795.

Intonation (intonē^i·ʃən). 1620. [– med.L. *intonatio*, f. as prec.; see -ION. Cf. (O)Fr. *intonation*.] **1.** In *Church Music.* The opening phrase of a plain-song melody, preceding the reciting-note, and usually sung either by the priest alone, or by one or a few of the choristers; the recitation of this. **2.** The action of intoning, or reciting in a singing voice 1788. **3.** The utterance or production of musical tones; in reference to manner or style, esp. to exactitude of pitch 1776. **4.** Manner of utterance of the tones of the voice in speaking; accent 1791.

4. That unfortunate i. of Aberdeenshire 1791.

Intonator (i·ntonē^{i}tər). 1875. [f. INTONE + -ATOR.] A monochord or single string stretched across a flat sound-board, for the study of musical intervals.

Intone (intō^u·n), *v.* Also **en-.** 1485. [– med.L. *intonare*, f. *in-* IN-^{2} + *tonus* TONE. In XV–XVI ENTONE – OFr. *entoner* (mod. *entonner*).] **1.** *trans.* To utter in musical tones; to chant; *spec.* To recite in a singing voice; usu. to recite in monotone. Also *absol.* or *intr.* **2.** To sing the opening phrase of a plain-song melody at the beginning of a chant, canticle, etc. 1880. **3.** = INTONATE *v.*^{2} 2. 1860. **4.** *intr.* 'To make a slow protracted noise' (J.) 1728.

1. The Clergy began to i. their Litany MILMAN. **4.** So swells each wind-pipe: Ass intones to Ass POPE. Hence **Into·nement, en-** (*rare*), intonation.

Intorsion (intǫ·ɹʃən). 1760. [– Fr. *intorsion* – late L. *intortio*, var. *intorsio*; see IN-^{2}, TORSION.] The action of twisting; *spec.* in *Bot.* the twisting of the stem of a plant.

Intort (intǫ·ɹt), *v.* Now *rare.* 1615. [– *intort-*, pa. ppl. stem of L. *intorquēre*, f. *in-* IN-^{2} + *torquēre* twist.] *trans.* To twist or curl inwards. Perh. only in the pa. pple. **Into·rted.**

In toto: see IN *Lat. prep.*

I·ntou:rist. 1930. [IN *adv.*] The name of the State Travel Bureau of the U.S.S.R.

Into·xicant. 1863. [f. INTOXICATE *v.*; see -ANT.] **a.** *adj.* Intoxicating 1882. **b.** *sb.* An intoxicating substance or liquor.

Intoxicate (intǫ·ksikĕt), *ppl. a.* (*sb.*) ME. [– med.L. *intoxicatus*, pa. pple. of *intoxicare*; see next, -ATE^2.] †**1.** Rendered poisonous; empoisoned –1637, killed by poison –1607. **2.** Intoxicated, inebriated (*lit.* and *fig.*) 1500. **3.** *sb.* One who is intoxicated. H. WALPOLE.

2. The mind i. With present objects WORDSW.

Intoxicate (intǫ·ksike^{i}t), *v.* 1529. [– *intoxicat-*, pa. ppl. stem of med.L. *intoxicare*, f. *in-* IN-^{2} + L. *toxicum* poison; see TOXIC, -ATE^3.] †**1.** *trans.* To poison –1684. **2.** To stupefy or render unconscious or delirious, madden with a drug or alcoholic liquor; to inebriate, make drunk 1598. Also *absol.* **3.** *fig.* †**a.** To 'poison'; to corrupt morally or spiritually –1860. **b.** To stupefy or excite as with a drug or alcoholic liquor 1591.

2. It..goeth downe very pleasantly, intoxicating weake braines HAKLUYT. *absol.* Cordials, which heat and i. BERKELEY. **3. b.** So new a Power will undoubtedly i. Persons who were not born to it

CHAS. I. Hence **Into·xicated** (with alcoholic liquor 1576, *fig.* 1692). **Into·xicating** *ppl. a.*, **-ly** *adv.*

Intoxication (intǫksikēⁱ·ʃən). late ME. [– Fr. *intoxication* or med.L. *intoxicatio*, f. as prec.; see -ION.] **1.** The action of poisoning; the state of being poisoned; an instance of this. *Obs.* exc. *Med.* **2.** The action of stupefying with a drug or alcoholic liquor; the making drunk or inebriated; the condition of being so stupefied or made drunk 1646. **3.** *fig.* †**a.** The poisoning of the moral or mental faculties; a cause of this –1728. **b.** The action or power of highly exciting the mind; elation beyond the bounds of sobriety 1712.

3. b. The i. of wealth and power THIRLWALL.

Intra- (intră), *prefix*, repr. L. *intra* 'on the inside, within'. Sometimes confused with INTER-. Chiefly used in adjs., in which it stands in prepositional relation to the sb. implied in the second element.

Intra-a·cinous, occurring within an acinus or racemose gland. **Intraca·rpellary,** *Bot.* situated within a carpel; also (*erron.*) between or among carpels (prop. *intercarpellary*). **Intra·ce·llular,** *Biol.* situated or occurring within the substance of a cell (as digestion in Protozoa); hence **Intra-ce·llularly** *adv.* **Intra-ecclesia·stical,** existing or occurring within a church. **Intralo·cular,** situated within the loculi or chambers of some structure. **Intrama·rginal,** situated on the inner side of the margin, *e.g.* of a leaf. **Intramercu·rial, -ian,** *Astron.* situated within the orbit of Mercury. **Intrana·sal,** situated or occurring within the nose. **Intranu·clear,** situated within the nucleus of a cell. **Intraparo·chial,** existing or occurring within a parish. **Intrastro·mal,** situated within the stroma or connective tissue of an organ or structure. **Intraterrito·rial,** situated or contained within a territory. **Intrathora·cic,** situated or occurring within the thorax. **Intra-u·rban,** carried on within a city. **Intrava·lvular,** situated within or between valves (prop. *intervalvular*). **Intravite·lline** [L. *vitellus* yolk], occurring within the yolk of an egg.

Intracranial (-krēⁱ·niăl), *a.* 1847. [f. INTRA- + CRANIUM + -AL¹.] Situated or occurring within the cranium or skull.

Intractable (intræ·ktăb'l), *a.* (*sb.*) 1545. [– L. *intractabilis*, or f. IN-³ + TRACTABLE.] **1.** Of persons, etc.: Not to be guided; uncontrollable, refractory, stubborn. **2.** Of things: Not easily treated or dealt with; resisting treatment or effort 1607. **3.** *sb.* An unmanageable person 1883.

1. An i. people 1548, animal 1837, will 1878. **2.** Lands..of a boggy, i. character 1861. Hence **Intra·ctabi·lity, Intra·ctableness,** the quality of being i. **Intra·ctably** *adv.*

Intractile (intræ·ktil, -əil), *a.* *rare.* 1626. [f. IN-³ + TRACTILE.] †**1.** Not tractile; incapable of being drawn out in length; not ductile. BACON. **2.** = INTRACTABLE *a.* 2. 1880.

†**Intra·do.** 1640. [– Sp. *entrada* entry; see ENTRADA, -ADO 2.] **1.** A formal entry –1716. **2.** Income; revenue –1672. **3.** An entering upon 1654.

2. Their *Intrado* would never support their ordinary charges 1672.

Intrados (intrēⁱ·dǫs). 1772. [– Fr. *intrados*, f. L. *intra* INTRA- + Fr. *dos* back.] *Arch.* The lower or interior curve of an arch; *spec.* the lower curve of the voussoirs or stones which immediately form the arch. Cf. EXTRADOS.

Intrafoliaceous (-fōᵘliˌēⁱ·ʃəs), *a.* 1760. [f. INTRA- + FOLIUM + -ACEOUS.] *Bot.* Situated on the inner side of a leaf.

Intralobular (intrălǫ·biŭlăɹ), *a.* 1839. [f. INTRA- + LOBULE + -AR¹.] *Anat.* Situated or occurring within the lobes of an organ or structure; as, the *i. bile-vessels*, the biliary capillaries.

Intramolecular (-mole·kiŭlăɹ),*a.* 1884. [f. INTRA- + MOLECULE + -AR¹.] Situated, existing, or occurring within a molecule or the molecules of a body or substance.

Intramundane (-mɒ·ndēⁱn), *a.* 1845. [f. INTRA- + L. *mundus* world + -ANE, after MUNDANE.] Situated or existing within the world (i.e. this world, or the material or created world).

Intramural (intrămiūᵊ·răl), *a.* 1846. [f. INTRA- + L. *murus* wall + -AL¹.] **1.** Situated, existing, or performed within the walls of a city or building. **2.** *Anat., Path.*, and *Biol.* Situated within the substance of the wall of a hollow organ, or of a cell 1879.

Intranscalent (intrɑnskēⁱ·lĕnt), *a.* 1846. [f. IN-³ + TRANSCALENT, after *transparent.*] Impervious to heat. Hence **Intransca·lency.**

Intransferable (intrɑ·nsfĕrăb'l, intrɑnsfɔ̄·răb'l), *a.* 1853. [IN-³.] Incapable of being transferred.

Intransgressible (intrɑnsgre·sĭb'l), *a.* 1603. [IN-³.] That cannot or may not be transgressed.

†**Intra·nsient,** *a.* 1650. [IN-³.] Not passing over; not passing to another by succession –1717.

Intransigent (intrɑ·nsidʒĕnt). Also **-eant.** 1879. [– Fr. *intransigeant* (1875), based on Sp. *los intransigentes* party of the extreme left in the Spanish Cortes, (in 1873–4) extreme republicans; ult. f. *in-* IN-³ + pr. pple. of L. *transigere* come to an understanding; see TRANSACT, -ENT.]

A. *adj.* That refuses to come to terms; uncompromising, irreconcilable 1881.

The advancing tide of *intransigeant* radicalism 1883.

B. *sb.* An irreconcilable (in politics); an uncompromising Republican 1879.

Certain of the Intransigents..are averse to a reconciliation between Italy and the Papal See 1899. So **Intra·nsigence, -eance** 1882.

Intransitive (intrɑ·nsitiv), *a.* (*sb.*) 1612. [– late L. *intransitivus* not passing over (Priscian); see IN-³, TRANSITIVE.] **1.** *Gram.* Of verbs and their construction: Expressing action which does not pass over to an object; not taking a direct object. (See TRANSITIVE, NEUTER.) **b.** as *sb.* An intransitive verb 1824. **2.** That does not pass on to another person, or beyond certain limits (*rare*) 1641. **3.** *Math.* In the theory of groups, opp. to TRANSITIVE 1902.

2. And then it is for the image sake, and so far is i.; but whatever is paid more to the image is transitive, and passes further JER. TAYLOR. Hence **Intra·nsitively** *adv.* in an i. manner.

In transitu: see IN *Lat. prep.*

Intransla·table, *a.* 1690. [IN-³.] Untranslatable.

Intransmi·ssible, *a.* 1656. [IN-³] Not transmissible.

Intransmu·table, *a.* 1691. [IN-³.] Not transmutable or changeable into something else. Hence **Intransmutabi·lity.**

Intrant (i·ntrănt). 1560. [– *intrant-*, pr. ppl. stem of L. *intrare* enter, in med.L. senses; see -ANT. Cf. Fr. *intrant* (XVI) in sense 2.] **A.** *sb.* **1.** One who enters; an incomer (*rare*). **b.** One who enters into holy orders 1637. **c.** One who makes legal entry 1592. †**2.** Formerly, in the University of St. Andrews, a student chosen by each nation for the election of the Rector –1819.

1. The school in which the i. had been previously educated is specified MASSON.

B. *adj.* Entering; that enters 1803.

Intra-ocular (intrăˌǫ·kiŭlăɹ), *a.* 1826. [f. INTRA- + L. *oculus* eye + -AR¹.] Situated or occurring within the eyeball. (Also erron. for *interocular.*)

Intrap, obs. f. ENTRAP *v.*

Intrapetiolar (intrăpe·tiŏlăɹ), *a.* 1864. [f. INTRA- + PETIOLE + -AR¹.] *Bot.* Situated within, or on the inner side of, the petiole or leaf-stalk; applied **a.** to an axillary bud formed immediately under the base of the petiole and surrounded by it so as not to appear until the leaf has fallen; **b.** to a stipule, or pair of confluent stipules, between the petiole and the axis.

Intratropical (-trǫ·pikăl), *a.* 1811. [f. INTRA- + TROPIC + -AL¹.] Situated or occurring within the tropics.

Intra-uterine (intrăˌyū·tĕrin, -əin), *a.* 1835. [f. INTRA- + UTERUS + -INE¹.] Situated, occurring, or passed within the uterus or womb; relating to this stage of an animal's life.

Intravenous (intrăvī·nəs), *a.* 1847. [f. INTRA- + L. *vena* vein + -OUS.] Existing or taking place within a vein or the veins.

Intraventricular (-ventri·kiŭlăɹ), *a.* 1882. [f. INTRA- + VENTRICLE + -AR¹, after *ventricular.*] *Anat.* Situated or contained within a ventricle of the brain or heart.

Intreasure, etc.: see ENTREASURE etc.

†**Intreatable,** *a.* 1509. [– Fr. *intraitable*, f. *traiter* treat, after L. *intractabilis*; see INTRACTABLE.] That cannot be treated with; inexorable –1598.

Intrench (intre·nʃ), *v.* 1754. [f. IN-¹ + TRENCH.] **1.** *trans.* To make a trench in; to furrow. **2.** Var. of ENTRENCH *v.*

†**Intre·nchant,** *a.* *rare.* [f. IN-³ + TRENCHANT *a.*] Used passively: Incapable of being cut. *Macb.* v. viii. 9.

Intrenchment: see ENTRENCHMENT.

Intrepid (intre·pid), *a.* 1627. [– Fr. *intrépide* or L. *intrepidus*, f. *in-* IN-³ + *trepidus* agitated, alarmed.] Fearless; undaunted; daring; brave.

Is there to be no pride in i. patriotism? 1833. Hence **Intre·pid-ly** *adv.*, **-ness.**

Intrepidity (intrĭpi·dĭti). 1704. [f. as prec. + -ITY. Cf. Fr. *intrépidité.*] The quality of being intrepid; fearlessness; firmness of mind in the presence of danger; courage.

I. in the discharge of professional duty MACKINTOSH.

†**I·ntricable,** *a.* 1540. [– OFr. *intricable* or med.L. *intricabilis*, f. L. *intricare*; see INTRICATE *a.*, -BLE.] Entangling, perplexing; entangled –1621.

Intricacy (i·ntrikăsi). 1602. [f. next; see -ACY.] **1.** The quality of being intricate; complexity; complicated condition. **2.** quasi-*concr.* A complication; a perplexing difficulty. 1611.

1. A buisines of much intricasie1619. The beauty of a composed i. of form HOGARTH. **1.** A long i. of passages SCOTT.

Intricate (i·ntrikĕt), *a.* 1470. [– L. *intricatus*, pa. pple. of *intricare* entangle, perplex, f. *in-* IN-² + *tricæ* trifles, tricks, perplexities, f. *tricari* make difficulties; see -ATE².] **1.** Perplexingly entangled or involved; complicated 1579. **2.** Of thoughts, statements, etc.: Perplexingly complicated in meaning; involved; obscure 1470. †**3.** Ensnared, entangled –1528.

1. Wrestling amongst i. paths of Rockes 1632. A..Face I. as the Law COWLEY. I. and narrow lanes SCOTT. **2.** He..could..make the intricat'st anigmas plain 1683. The i. and subtle rule which was then in force 1849. Hence **I·ntricate-ly** *adv.*, **-ness.**

Intricate (i·ntrikeⁱt), *v.* Now *rare.* 1548. [– *intricat-*, pa. ppl. stem of L. *intricare*; see prec., -ATE³.] **1.** *trans.* To render intricate; to make involved; to complicate 1564. **2.** To entangle or ensnare; to involve in toils; to perplex.

1. How ever the matter may be intricated by passing through many perhaps unknowing hands BP. HALL.

†**Intrica·tion.** ME. [– med.L. *intricatio*, f. as prec.; see -ION. Cf. OFr. *intrication.*] The action of intricating; intricated condition; complication, entanglement –1773.

†‖**Intri·go.** 1648. [It.] = INTRIGUE *sb.* –1676. **b.** *spec.* The plot of a play –1672.

Intriguant, -gant (i·ntrigănt, Fr. ęntrigaṅ). 1781. [– Fr. *intriguant*, pr. pple. of *intriguer*; see INTRIGUE *v.*, -ANT.] An intriguer. So ‖**Intriguante, -gante** (intrigɑ·nt, Fr. ęntrigaṅt), a female intriguer.

Intrigue (intrī·g), *sb.* 1647. [– Fr. *intrigue*, †*intrique* – It. *intrigo*, *-ico*, f. *intrigare* :– L. *intricare*; see INTRICATE *a.*] †**1.** Intricacy, complexity; something complicated; a maze, a labyrinth –1686. †Also *fig.* **2.** The exertion of tortuous or underhand influence to accomplish some purpose; underhand scheming 1668. **b.** (with *pl.*) A plot to accomplish a purpose by such influence 1647. †**3.** The plot of a play, poem, or romance –1725. **4.** Clandestine illicit intimacy between a man and a woman 1668. **b.** *transf.* The combination of queen and knave in certain games of cards 1830.

2. A complicated scene..of plotting and i. JAS. MILL. **b.** He was made Cardinal by Intrigues, Factions, and Tumults DRYDEN. **4.** I., Philotis!.. I have laid that word by; amour sounds better DRYDEN. Hence **Intri·guish** *a.* somewhat of the nature of i. NORTH.

Intrigue (intrī·g), *v.* 1612. [– Fr. *intriguer* – It. *intrigare*; see prec.] **1.** *trans.* To trick, deceive, cheat; to perplex. Now *rare.* **2.** To entangle, involve; to implicate. Now *rare.* 1677. **3.** *intr.* To carry on a secret amour or illicit intimacy; to have a liaison 1660. **4.** *intr.* To carry on underhand plotting or scheming; to employ secret influence for the accomplishment of designs 1714. **b.** To bring or get by intrigue 1673. **5.** To excite the interest or curiosity of; to interest so as to puzzle or fascinate 1894. (A gallicism.)

2. It doth not seem worth the while. .with more subtilty to i. the Point BARROW. **3.** He had intrigued with a Vestal virgin FROUDE. **4. b.** Rigby . .had already intrigued himself into a subordinate office DISRAELI. **5.** The story itself does not greatly i. us 1905. Hence **Intri·guer. Intri·guery,** the practice of intriguing. †**Intri·guess,** a female intriguer. **Intri·guingly** *adv.* with secret machinations.

†**Intri·nce,** *a.* Also **intrinse.** [perh. abbr. f. INTRINSICATE; cf. *reverb* for *reverberate* in *Lear* I. i. 155. Godef. has OFr. *intrincé*, var. of *intrinquer, intriqué* intricate.] Intricate, involved. *Lear* II. ii. 81.

Intrinsic (intri·nsik), *a.* (*sb.*) 1490. [– (O)Fr. *intrinsèque* – late L. *intrinsecus*, f. L. adv. *intrinsecus* inwardly, inwards; from the first the ending was assim. to -IC.] †**1.** Situated within; interior, inner –1665. **b.** *Anat.* Applied to a muscle of a member or organ which has its origin and insertion within that organ; so in *Path.* to a morbid growth arising in the part or tissue in which it is found 1839. †**2.** Inward, internal (in *fig.* sense); secret –1689. †**b.** Intimate –1651. **3.** Belonging to the thing in itself; inherent, essential, proper 1642. Const. *to.* †**4.** *sb.* (*ellipt.* for 'inmost part', 'intrinsic value', 'intrinsic quality') –1751.

3. The intrinsick Value of Silver consider'd as Money LOCKE. Confirmed. .by i. probability THIRLWALL. The flower has no beauty. .that is not i. and native to it 1873. *I. equation of a curve* (Math.): an equation expressing the relation between its length and curvature (and so involving no reference to external points, lines, etc., as in equations referred to co-ordinates). So **Intri·nsical,** †**-ecal** *a.* (*sb.*). Now *rare.* Hence **Intrinsica·lity, Intri·nsicalness** (*rare*). **Intri·nsically** *adv.*

†**Intri·nsicate,** *a.* Also **-secate.** 1560. [app. f. It. *intrinsecato, -sicato* familiar, confused in sense with *intricato.*] = INTRICATE, involved, entangled. *Ant. & Cl.* v. ii. 307.

Intro- (intro), *prefix.* L. *intro* adv. 'to the inside', used with vbs. and their derivatives, as *introducere* to lead in. Hence in English words derived from L. or formed of L. elements.

Intro-a·ctive *a.* internally active; also, *loosely*, mutually active. **Introce·ssion** (*rare*), a depression or sinking of any parts inwards. **Introfle·xed** *ppl. a.*, bent or curved inwards; so **Introfle·xion. Introgre·ssion,** a going or coming in, entrance, incoming. **Intromole·cular** *a.*, subsisting within a molecule, or between its constituent atoms (dist. from *intermolecular*). †**Intropre·ssion,** pressure inwards. **Intropu·lsive** *a.* [L. *puls-* ppl. stem], having the quality of driving inwards. **Introrece·ption,** the action of receiving within.

Introduce (intrŏdiū·s), *v.* 1475. [– L. *introducere*, f. *intro* INTRO- + *ducere* lead, bring.] **1.** *trans.* To lead or bring into a place, or into the inside or midst of something; to bring in, conduct inwards 1639. **b.** To put in from without; to insert 1695. **c.** To usher or bring (a person) into a society or body 1766. **2.** To bring (a thing) into some sphere of action or thought; to bring in in the course of some action or in a composition; to add or insert as a (new) feature or element 1559. **3.** To bring into use or practice, vogue, or fashion; to institute (a law, custom, etc.) 1603. †**4.** To bring on, bring about, give rise to, occasion, induce –1692. **5.** To usher in (a time, action, matter, etc.); to start, open, begin 1667. †**6.** To bring (a person) into the knowledge of something; to teach, instruct –1500. **7.** To bring into personal acquaintance; to make known to a person or to a circle 1659. **b.** To present formally, as at court, etc. 1685. **c.** To bring out into society 1708. **8.** To bring to the notice or cognizance of a person, etc.; to bring a bill or measure before parliament, etc. 1766.

1. Byron gave orders to Tita to i. the monkey and bulldog MEDWIN. **b.** To i. metals into a flame TYNDALL. **c.** On the same day. .Bute was. .introduced into the Cabinet MACAULAY. **2.** To i. amendments into a bill 1849. **3.** The Julian calendar was introduced in the year 44 B.C. LOCKYER. **4.** Whatsoever introduces habits in children deserves the care and attention of their governors LOCKE. **5.** This discussion served to i. the young soldier's experiences SCOTT. **7.** He introduced himself to my acquaintance STERNE. **b.** The Chevalier. .begged to i. us at court 1718. **8.** To i. to the company a ballad GOLDSM. Hence †**Introdu·cement, Introdu·cer, Introdu·cible, -eable** *a.*

†**Introdu·ct,** *v.* 1481. [– *introduct-*, pa. ppl. stem of L. *introducere*; see prec.] **1.** *trans.* To teach, instruct –1500. **2.** To introduce; to bring in –1670.

Introduction (intrŏdɒ·kʃən). ME. [– (O)Fr. *introduction* or L. *introductio*, f. as prec.; see -ION.] **1.** The action of introducing or bringing in, etc. 1651. **b.** Something introduced; a practice or thing newly brought in, etc. 1603. †**2.** The action or process of leading to something; a preliminary step or stage –1660. †**3.** Initiation in the knowledge of a subject; elementary instruction –1702. **4.** That which leads to the knowledge or understanding of something 1529. **5.** The action of introducing or making known personally; *esp.* formal presentation of one person to another, or of persons to each other, with communication of names, etc. 1711.

1. The i. of a digression JOWETT, of metal LUBBOCK. **b.** This fish was a late i. ROGERS. **4.** His introductions or first lesson SIR T. BROWNE. The I. to the Work FIELDING. An I. to the Study of Electricity PRIESTLEY (*title*). The study of Etruscan art is a necessary i. to that of Roman 1874. **5.** To you. .I owe my i. to a large circle of friends J. H. NEWMAN. Phr. *Letter of i.*

Introductive (intrŏdɒ·ktiv), *a.* 1631. [– med.L. *introductivus*, f. as prec.; see -IVE.] = INTRODUCTORY. Hence **Introdu·ctively** *adv.*

Introdu·ctor. *arch.* 1638. [– late and med.L. *introductor*, f. as prec.; see -OR 2. Cf. Fr. *introducteur des ambassadeurs.*] One who or that which introduces; an introducer; esp. *an i. of ambassadors.* Hence **Introdu·ctress** 1657.

Introductory (intrŏdɒ·ktəri). ME. [– late L. *introductorius*, f. as prec.; see -ORY[2].] **A.** *adj.* **1.** Serving to introduce; introductive *of* 1605. **2.** Leading up to or on to something; preliminary 1660. Hence **Introdu·ctorily** *adv.*

1. I. letters 1787. Testimony. .i. of fraud 1800. **2.** I place Schools before Colledges, because they are i. thereunto 1661.

B. *sb.* †**1.** An introductory treatise 1391–1552. **2.** A preliminary step 1646.

Introit (i·ntroᵘit, i·ntroit). 1481. [– (O)Fr. *introït* – L. *introitus* entrance, f. *introire* enter, f. *intro* INTRO- + *ire* go.] †**1.** A going in; entrance –1716. **2.** *Eccl.* A psalm, etc. sung by the choir as the priest approaches the altar to celebrate the Eucharist; a variable part of the Mass consisting of an antiphon with verses of a psalm and Gloria Patri, said by the priest before the Kyrie eleison 1483.

Intromission (intromi·ʃən). 1545. [– Fr. *intromission* or L. *intromissio*; see INTRO-, MISSION. Cf. ENTERMETE.] The action of intromitting. **1.** The action of sending, letting, or putting in; insertion; admission, admittance 1601. **2.** Intermeddling, interference; esp. in or from *Sc. Law*, intermeddling with the effects of another, either with or without legal authority; in the latter case called *vicious i.* 1545.

Intromit (intromi·t), *v.* ME. [– L. *intromittere* introduce, f. *intro* INTRO- + *mittere* send.] **1.** *trans.* To cause or allow to enter; to put in, insert, introduce; to send or let in, admit. Now *rare.* 1582. †**2.** *refl.* To interfere (*with* or *in*) –1657. **3.** *intr.* for *refl.* To interfere, intermeddle, have to do *with.* (Now only *Sc.*) ME. **b.** *Sc. Law.* To deal *with*; *esp.* to deal with property or effects; either *legally*, or *viciously* without legal right 1522.

1. Whether our reasons eye be clear enough To i. true light HY. MORE.

Intromittent (intromi·tĕnt), *a.* 1836. [– *intromittent-*, pr. ppl. stem of L. *intromittere*; see INTROMIT, -ENT.] That intromits or introduces; having the function of intromission.

Chiefly in *Zool.* and *Physiol.*: *i. apparatus, organ*, the male copulatory organ.

Intromitter (intromi·təɹ). 1507. [f. INTROMIT + -ER[1].] One who intromits; *spec.* in *Sc. Law*, one who interferes or deals with the property of another.

Introrsal (intrǭ·ɹsăl), *a.* 1831. [f. as next + -AL[1].] = next.

Introrse (intrǭ·ɹs), *a.* 1842. [– L. *introrsus*, from *introversus* (turned) inwards.] *Bot.* Turned or directed inwards; of an anther which opens towards the centre of the flower. Hence **Intro·rsely** *adv.*

Introspect (introspe·kt), *v.* 1683. [– *introspect-*, pa. ppl. stem of L. *introspicere* look into (or f. *introspectare*, frequent. of this).] *trans.* To look into, esp. with the mind; to examine narrowly or thoroughly. Now *rare.*

Introspection (introspe·kʃən). 1677. [app. f. prec. + -ION. Cf. Fr. *introspection.*] **1.** The action of looking into, or under the surface of, things, esp. with the mind. ? *Obs.* exc. as in 2. **2.** *spec.* (with no object expressed): The action of looking within, or into one's own mind; examination or observation of one's own thoughts, feelings, etc. 1807.

2. In Homer's time. .i. had not begun its work 1850. Hence **Introspe·ctionist,** one who practices i.; one who adopts the psychological method of i.

Introspective (introspe·ktiv), *a.* 1820. [f. INTROSPECT, INTROSPECTION + -IVE.] Having the quality of looking within; examining into one's own thoughts, feelings, etc., or expressing such examination; of, pertaining to, characterized by, or given to introspection.

Whom I. .remember as a mild, melancholy, i. man SOUTHEY. Hence **Introspe·ctive-ly** *adv.*, **-ness. Introspe·ctor.**

†**Introsu·me,** *v.* 1657. [f. INTRO- + L. *sumere* take, as a var. of INSUME, after *assume, consume.*] *trans.* To take in; to take (medicine) internally; to absorb (nutriment) –1664. So †**Introsu·mption,** †**Introsu·mptive** *a.*

Introsusception (i:ntrosɒ̆se·pʃən). 1794. [app. a var. of INTUSSUSCEPTION by prefix-substitution.] The action of taking up or receiving within; = INTUSSUSCEPTION. **Introsusce·pted** *ppl. a.*

†**Introve·nient,** *a.* [– *intravenient-*, pr. ppl. stem of L. *introvenire* come in, f. *intro* INTRO- + *venire* come; see -ENT.] Coming in. SIR T. BROWNE.

Introversible (introvɔ̄·ɹsĭb'l), *a.* 1883. [Formed by prefix-substitution as opposite of EVERSIBLE.] Capable of being introverted, as the finger of a glove.

Introversion (introvɔ̄·ɹʃən). 1654. [f. INTROVERT *v.*, after *evert/eversion*, etc.] **1.** The action of turning the thoughts inwards. **2.** The action of (physically) turning inwards, esp. of withdrawing an outer part into the interior; the condition of being so turned inwards 1794.

So **Introve·rsive** *a.* 1866.

I·ntrovert, *sb.* 1883. [f. next. Cf. CONVERT.] **1.** *Zool.* A part that is or can be introverted. **2.** *Psychol.* A person characterized by introversion 1916.

Introvert (introvɔ̄·ɹt), *v.* 1669. [– mod.L. *introvertere*, f. *intro* INTRO- + *vertere* turn.] **1.** *trans.* To turn (the mind, thought, etc.) inwards upon itself. **2.** To turn or bend inwards (physically); in *Zool.* to turn (a part or organ) inwards upon itself; to withdraw within its own tube or base 1784.

2. His awkward gait, his introverted toes COWPER. Hence **Introve·rtive** *a.* 1855.

Introvolution (i:ntroˌvolʹū·ʃən). *rare.* 1829. [f. INTRO- + *-volution* in *evolution*, etc.] The process of involving one thing within another.

Intrude (intrū·d), *v.* 1534. [– L. *intrudere*, f. *in-* IN-[2] + *trudere* thrust.] **1.** *trans.* To thrust, force, or drive (any thing) in 1563. **2.** *trans.* To thrust or bring in without leave; to force *on* or *upon* a person 1586. †**3.** *refl.* and *intr.* To thrust oneself into any benefice, possession, office, or dignity to which one has no title or claim; to usurp *on* or *upon* –1682. **4.** To thrust oneself in without warrant, leave, or welcome. Also *transf.* and *fig.* of things, etc. 1573. †**5.** *trans.* To enter forcibly. SHAKS. *Lucr.* 848.

1. Their parts are wedged and intruded one into another GREW. **2.** The tendency which intruded earthly Madonnas and saints between the worshipper and the spiritual Deity BRYCE. **4.** Thy wit wants edge And manners, to intru'd where I am grac'd SHAKS. To what end shouldst thou i. thy self unwarrantably into their companies? 1659. Hence **Intru·ded** *ppl. a.*; *spec.* in *Geol.* = INTRUSIVE 2 b.

Intruder (intrū·dəɹ). 1534. [f. prec. + -ER¹.] **1.** One who intrudes into an estate or benefice or usurps on the rights or privileges of another. Now only in legal use. **2.** One who thrusts himself in without right or welcome 1588.

2. Vnmannerly I. as thou art *Tit. A.* II. iii. 65.

Intru·dress. [f. prec. + -ESS¹.] A female intruder. FULLER.

†**Intru·nk,** *v.* [f. IN-¹ + TRUNK *sb.*] *trans.* To enclose in or as in a trunk. FORD.

Intruse (intrū·s), *a.* 1870. [– L. *intrusus*, pa. pple. of *intrudere* INTRUDE *v.*] *Bot.* Having a form as if pushed or thrust inwards.

Intrusion (intrū·ʒən). ME. [–(O)Fr. *intrusion* or med.L. *intrusio*; f. *intrus-*, pa. ppl. stem of L. *intrudere*; see INTRUDE *v.*, -ION.] **1.** The action of thrusting or forcing in, or fact of being thrust in; also *concr.* something thrust in 1639. **b.** *spec.* in *Geol.* The influx of rock in a state of fusion into fissures or between strata; a portion of intruded rock 1849. **2.** The action of thrusting oneself into a vacant estate or benefice to which one has no title or claim; *spec.* the entry of a stranger after the determination of a particular estate of freehold before the remainder-man or reversioner; also, a trespass on the lands of the crown. Hence, invasion; usurpation. (Now only in legal use.) ME. **b.** The settlement of a minister of the Church of Scotland without the consent of the congregation 1849. **3.** The action of thrusting oneself in without right or welcome; encroachment on something possessed or enjoyed by another 1592.

3. [George Fox's] i. of himself into assemblies where he was not wanted 1896. Hence **Intru·sional** *a.*

Intru·sionist. 1849. [f. prec. + -IST.] One who practises or supports intrusion (see INTRUSION 2 b). So **Intru·sionism** 1841.

Intrusive (intrū·siv), *a.* 1401. [f. *intrus-* (see INTRUSION) + -IVE.] **1.** Of intruding character; coming or entering without invitation or welcome. **2.** That has been intruded or thrust in 1847. **b.** *Geol.* Of an igneous rock: Forced, while in a state of fusion, into cavities or fissures of other rocks 1844.

1. Truth's i. voice severe SCOTT. Hence **Intru·sive-ly** *adv.*, **-ness.**

Intrust, var. f. ENTRUST.

Intubate (i·ntiubeᶦt), *v.* 1612. [f. IN-² + L. *tuba* TUBE + -ATE³.] †**1.** *trans.* To form into tubes 1612. **2.** *Med.* To treat by inserting a tube into an aperture, esp. into the larynx (see next). Also *absol.* 1889.

Intubation (intiubēᶦ·ʃən). 1887. [f. prec.; see -ATION.] The insertion of a tube; esp. *i. of the larynx*, the insertion of a tube into the glottis to keep it open, in diphtheria, etc.

Intuent (i·ntiuˌĕnt), *a.* 1865. [– *intuent-*, pr. ppl. stem of L. *intueri*; see INTUITION, -ENT.] That knows by intuition.

Intuit (i·ntiuˌit), *v.* Also **-ite.** 1776. [– *intuit-*, pa. ppl. stem of L. *intueri*; see next.] †**1.** *trans.* To instruct. **2. a.** *intr.* To receive knowledge by direct perception 1840. **b.** *trans.* To know by intuition 1858. Hence **Intu·itable** *a.*

2. b. He is a being..who by the eternal necessity even of his nature, intuits everything 1858.

Intuition (intiuˌi·ʃən). 1497. [– late L. *intuitio*, f. *intuit-*, pa. ppl. stem of L. *intueri* look upon, consider, contemplate, f. *in-* IN-² + *tueri* look. Cf. Fr. *intuition.*] †**1.** A looking upon or into; inspection; a sight or view. (= L. *intuitus.*) –1664. †**2.** The action of mentally looking at; contemplation; perception, recognition; mental view –1755. †**3.** Ulterior view; regard, respect, reference –1718. **4.** *Schol. Philos.* The immediate knowledge ascribed to angelic and spiritual beings, with whom vision and knowledge are identical 1652. **5.** *Mod. Philos.* The immediate apprehension of an object by the mind without the intervention of any reasoning process; a particular act of such apprehension 1600. **b.** Immediate apprehension by the intellect alone; an act of such apprehension 1659. **c.** Immediate apprehension by sense; an act of such apprehension 1819. **6.** Direct or immediate insight; an instance of this 1762.

3. Phr. *With i. to (of)*, with reference to. *In i. to*, in respect to, in view of. **4.** Our Superiors are guided by I., and our Inferiors by Instinct ADDISON. **5.** What we *feel*, and what we *do*, we may be said to know by i. PRIESTLEY. **b.** The truths known by i. are the original premises from which all others are inferred MILL. **c.** All our i. however takes place by means of the senses only 1819. **6.** The intuitions of genius unconscious of any process 1866.

Intuitional (intiuˌi·ʃənăl), *a.* 1860. [f. prec. + -AL¹.] **1.** Of, pertaining to, or derived from intuition; of the nature of intuition. **2.** Pertaining to that theory, or philosophical school, which bases certain elements of knowledge on intuition (see prec. 5 b) 1865.

Intui·tionalism. 1850. [f. prec. + -ISM.] The theory of the intuitional school; the doctrine that the perception of truth, or of certain truths, is by intuition. So **Intui·tionalist** = INTUITIONIST (in both senses).

Intuitionism (intiuˌi·ʃəniz'm). 1847. [f. INTUITION + -ISM.] **1.** The doctrine of Reid and others, that in perception, external objects are known immediately, without the intervention of a vicarious phenomenon. **2.** = INTUITIONALISM 1874. So **Intui·tionist,** one who holds the theory of i. (in either sense).

Intuitive (intiū·itiv), *a.* 1594. [– med.L. *intuitivus*, f. *intuit-*; see INTUITION, -IVE. Cf. Fr. *intuitif, -ive.*] †**1.** Beholding. BULWER. †**b.** Of sight or vision: That consists in immediate looking upon an object, and sees it as it is –1656. **2.** Of knowledge or mental perception: That consists in immediate apprehension, without the intervention of any reasoning process 1645. **b.** Of a truth: Apprehended by intuition 1872. **3.** Of the mind or reason, or a mental act, etc.: That acts by intuition or immediate apprehension; opp. to *discursive* 1667. **4.** Of persons: Possessing intuition 1652. **5.** Of or pertaining to the school of moral philosophy that holds the first principles of ethics to be apprehended by intuition 1861.

2. The i. vision comes like an inspiration 1849. **3.** Whence the soule Reason receives, and reason is her being, Discursive, or I. MILT. *P.L.* v. 488. **5.** The i. moralist..believes that the utilitarian theory is profoundly immoral LECKY. Hence **Intu·itive-ly** *adv.*, **-ness.**

Intuitivism (intiū·itiviz'm). 1874. [f. prec. + -ISM.] The doctrine that the fundamental principles of ethics are matters of intuition. So **Intu·itivist,** one who holds this doctrine; *attrib.* holding, or pertaining to, this doctrine.

Intumesce (intiume·s), *v.* 1796. [– L. *intumescere* swell up, f. *in-* IN-² + *tumescere*, inceptive of *tumēre* be tumid; see -ESCE.] *intr.* To swell up, become tumid; to bubble up.

Intumescence (intiume·sĕns). 1656. [– Fr. *intumescence*, f. L. *intumescere*; see prec., -ENCE.] **1.** The process of swelling up. Also *fig.* in reference to language. **2.** *Physiol.* A swelling of the tissue of any organ or part of the body, or of a plant. Also *concr.* 1822. **3.** The bubbling up of a fluid, etc. 1661. Also *fig.*

1. The i. of the tide JOHNSON. **3.** The mixture melted without i. 1796. *fig.* The i. of nations would have found its vent JOHNSON. So †**Intume·scency,** intumescent quality or condition 1650.

Intumescent (intiume·sĕnt), *a.* 1870. [f. INTUMESCE, INTUMESCENCE; see -ENT.] Swelling up; becoming tumid.

†**Intu·mulate,** *v.* Pa. pple. **-at(e** and **-ated.** 1535. [– *intumulat-*, pa. ppl. stem of med.L. *intumulare*, f. *in-* IN-² + *tumulus* burial mound; see -ATE³.] *trans.* To place in a tomb; to bury –1606.

Intune, var. of ENTUNE *v.*

†**Intu·rbidate,** *v. rare.* 1684. [f. IN-² + TURBID + -ATE³.] *trans.* To render turbid; to disturb, confuse –1834.

The confusion of ideas and conceptions under the same term painfully inturbidates his theology COLERIDGE.

Inturgescence (intɒɹdʒe·sĕns). 1755. [f. IN-² + TURGESCENCE.] The action of swelling up; a swollen condition. (Dicts.) So †**Inturge·scency** 1650.

Inturn (i·ntɒ̈ɹn). 1599. [IN *adv.*] †**1.** An inward turn, bend, or curve 1690. **2.** The turning in of the toes; also, a step in dancing 1599. †**3.** In wrestling: The act of putting a leg between the thighs of an opponent and lifting him up. Also *fig.* –1690.

†**I·ntuse.** [– L. *intusum*, subst. use of n. of pa. pple. of *intundere* bruise.] A bruise. SPENSER.

Intussuscept (iːntɒ̈sˌsɒ̈se·pt), *v.* 1835. [Back-formation from next.] *trans.* To take up within itself or some other part; to introvert, to invaginate; said spec. of part of a bowel. So **I:ntussusce·ptive** *a.* characterized by intussusception.

Intussusception (iːntɒ̈sˌsɒ̈se·pʃən). 1707. [– Fr. *intussusception* or mod.L. *intussusceptio*, f. L. *intus* within + *susceptio* SUSCEPTION. In sense 1 formed directly on SUSCEPTION.] **1.** A taking within; absorption into itself. Also *transf.* and *fig.* **2.** *Phys.* and *Biol.* The taking in of foreign matter by a living organism and its conversion into organic tissue. In *Veg. Phys.* opp. to *apposition.* 1764. **3.** *Path.* The inversion of one portion of intestine and its reception within an adjacent portion; invagination; introversion; an instance of this 1811.

1. A particle of dry gelatine may be swelled up by the i. of water HUXLEY. **2.** Some will have them [shells] increase by i., and others by juxtaposition 1771.

Intwine, etc., var. ENTWINE, etc.

Inula (i·niŭlă). 1822. [L., see ELECAMPANE.] A plant so called by Roman writers; identified by mediæval herbalists with Elecampane (*Inula helenium* Linn.); hence, in *Bot.*, the name of the genus of *Compositæ* to which Elecampane belongs.

Hence **I·nulin** [-IN¹] *Chem.*, a white starchy substance ($C_6H_{10}O_5$), obtained from the roots of Elecampane and other *Compositæ*. **I·nuloid,** a soluble modification of inulin, occurring in the roots of Jerusalem artichoke, dahlia, etc.

†**Inu·mbrate,** *v.* 1623. [– *inumbrat-*, pa. ppl. stem of L. *inumbrare*, f. *in-* IN-² + *umbra* shade, shadow; see -ATE³.] *trans.* To cast a shadow upon; to shade; to put in the shade –1822.

Inunct (inɒ·ŋkt), *v. rare.* 1513. [– *inunct-*, pa. ppl. stem of L. *inunguere*, f. *in-* IN-² + *unguere* smear, anoint.] *trans.* To anoint; to smear.

Inunction (inɒ·ŋkʃən). 1483. [– L. *inunctio*, f. as prec.; see -ION.] **1.** The action of anointing; smearing with, or rubbing in of, oil or ointment 1621. **b.** The anointing with oil in religious rites. Cf. UNCTION. 1483. **2.** *concr.* An ointment, liniment, or unguent 1601.

†**Inu·nctuous,** *a.* 1634. [IN-³.] Not unctuous; without oil or grease. So †**Inunctuo·sity** 1794.

Inundant (inɒ·ndănt), *a.* 1629. [f. *inundant-*, pr. ppl. stem of L. *inundare*; see next, -ANT. In XVII perh. infl. by †*inund* inundate.] Overflowing, inundating.

Inundate (i·nɒndeᶦt, inɒ·ndeᶦt), *v.* 1623. [– *inundat-*, pa. ppl. stem of L. *inundare*, f. *in-* IN-² + *undare* flow; see -ATE³.] The stress is now mostly on the first syllable.] **1.** *trans.* To overspread *with* a flood of water; to overflow, flood 1791. **2.** *transf.* and *fig.* To fill with an overflowing abundance or superfluity 1623.

1. The period when the Nile inundates Ægypt 1791. **2.** I was inundated with letters WASHINGTON.

Inundation (inɒndēᶦ·ʃən). ME. [– OFr. *inondacion* (mod. *-tion*) or L. *inundatio*, f. as prec.; see -ION.] **1.** The action of inundating; the fact of being inundated with water; an overflow of water; a flood. **2.** *transf.* and *fig.* An overspreading or overwhelming in superfluous abundance; overflowing, superabundance 1589.

1. This place hath a great pond caused by the i. of Nilus HAKLUYT. **2.** An I. of impertinent Visitors 1767.

†**Inundersta·nding,** *a.* [IN-³.] Not understanding; without apprehension. PEARSON.

Inurbane (inɒɹbēᶦ·n), *a.* 1623. [– L. *inurbanus*, f. *in-* IN-³ + *urbanus* URBANE.] Not urbane; unpolished; esp. impolite. Hence **Inurba·ne-ly** *adv.* 1610, **-ness** 1727.

Inurbanity (inɒɹbæ·nĭti). 1598. [– Fr. *inurbanité* or med.L. *inurbanitas* (XII), f. *in-* IN-³ + L. *urbanitas* URBANITY.] Lack of urbanity; unpolished manner or deportment; esp. incivility.

The proverbial i. of these official Cerberi 1825.

Inure, enure (iniūᵊ·ɹ, ėniūᵊ·ɹ), *v.*[1] 1489. [– AFr. *eneurer, f. phr. *en eure in use or practice, i.e. *en* IN-[2], EN-[1] + URE[1].] **1.** *trans.* To bring by use, habit, or continual exercise to a certain condition or state of mind; to accustom, habituate. †**2.** To put into exercise or operation; to exercise, to practise, to commit (a crime). (Chiefly in form *enure.*) 1549. **3.** *intr.* Chiefly *Law* and *U.S.* To come into operation; to operate; to take or have effect 1589.

1. We see to what easie satisfactions..he had inur'd his conscience MILT. The poor, inured to drudgery and distress COWPER. **2.** MILT. *P.L.* VIII. 239. **3.** This shall enure by force and way of grant COKE. A burial dress that shall i. for salvation in the realms of death KINGLAKE.

†**Inu·re**, *v.*[2] 1619. [– L. *inurere* burn in, f. *in-* IN-[2] + *urere* burn. Cf. INUST.] **1.** *trans.* To burn in, brand –1679. **2.** To burn in a flame 1709.

Inurement (iniūᵊ·ɹmĕnt). Also †**en-**. 1586. [f. INURE *v.*[1] + -MENT.] The action of inuring or state of being inured; habituation.

Inurn (inɔ̄·ɹn), *v.* Also †**en-**. 1602. [f. IN-[2] + URN.] *trans.* To put (the ashes of a cremated body) in an urn; (hence *transf.* to entomb, inter. Also *fig.*

The body was sometimes burnt and inurned, but sometimes buried 1861.

Inusitate (iniū·zitᵉit), *a.* Now *rare.* 1546. [– L. *inusitatus*, f. *in-* IN-[3] + *usitatus*, pa. pple. of *usitari* use often; see -ATE[2]] Unwonted, unusual, out of use. So **Inusita·tion** (*rare*), disuse.

†**Inu·st**, *a.* *rare.* 1634. [– L. *inustus*, pa. pple. of *inurere* INURE *v.*[2]] Burnt in, branded –1647.

†**Inu·stion.** 1618. [– late L. *inustio* branding, f. *inust-*; see prec., -ION.] **1.** Burning. T. ADAMS. **2.** The action of burning in or branding with fire. HY. MORE (1647). **3.** Cauterization –1834.

Inutile (iniū·til), *a.* 1484. [– (O)Fr. *inutile* – L. *inutilis*, f. *in-* IN-[3] + *utilis* useful. Cf. UTILE.] Useless, of no service, unprofitable.

Inutility (iniuti·lĭti). 1598. [– Fr. *inutilité* – L. *inutilitas*, f. *in-* IN-[3] + *utilitas*; see prec., -ITY.] The quality or state of being useless; want of utility; unprofitableness. **b.** A thing or person that is useless 1802.

To find nothing in knowledge but its i. LYTTON.

Inu·tterable, *a.* Now *rare.* 1603. [IN-[3].] That cannot be uttered; unutterable.

In vacuo: see IN *Lat. prep.*

Invade (invēⁱ·d), *v.* 1491. [– L. *invadere*, f. *in-* IN-[2] + *vadere* go.] **1.** *trans.* To enter in a hostile manner, or with armed force 1494. **2.** *transf.* and *fig.* To enter or penetrate after the manner of an invader 1548. **3.** *intr.* or *absol.* To make an invasion or attack 1491. **4.** *trans.* To intrude upon, infringe, encroach on, violate 1514. †**b.** To usurp, seize upon –1712. †**5.** To make an attack upon (a person). *lit.* and *fig.* –1753. †**6.** (Latinisms): **a.** To enter (*lit.* and *fig.*). SPENSER. **b.** To go; traverse 1598.

1. Asserhadon invades Babylon NEWTON. **2.** The deer i. the crops TENNANT. A sense of loss, of loneliness invades her M. ARNOLD. **4.** You did their Natural Rights i. COWLEY. Hence **Inva·der**, one who invades, intrudes, or seizes.

Inva·ginate, *a.* *rare.* 1887. [f. INVAGINATED on analogy of similar pairs; see -ATE[2].] Invaginated.

Invaginate (invæ·dʒineⁱt), *v.* 1656. [f. INVAGINATION; see -ATE[3]. In XVII dicts. f. med.L. *invaginare* sheathe.] **1.** *trans.* **a.** To put in a sheath. **b.** To turn (a tubular sheath) back within itself; to introvert. **2.** *intr.* To become invaginated 1887.

Invaginated (invæ·dʒineⁱted), *ppl. a.* 1835. [f. next (see -ATE[3], -ED[1]) on analogy of similar pairs.] Sheathed; turned into a sheath; introverted.

Invagination (invædʒinēⁱ·ʃən). 1658. [– mod.L. *invaginatio*; see IN-[2], VAGINA, -ATION. In XVII dicts. – med.L. (see INVAGINATE *v.*).] The action of sheathing or introverting; the condition of being sheathed or introverted; intussusception.

The Gastrula..was originated by an inversion or i. of the Blastula 1879.

Invalescence[1] (invăle·sĕns). *rare.* 1730. [f. IN-[3] + *-valescence* in *convalescence.*] Ill health.

Invalescence[2] (invăle·sĕns). *rare.* 1755. [f. L. *invalescere* grow strong, inceptive of *invalēre* be strong against; see -ENCE. Cf. med.L. *invalescentia* (XIII).] Strength; health; force (Dicts.).

†**Invaletu·dinary**, *a.* *rare.* 1661. [– med.L. *invaletudinarius*, f. L. *invaletudo, -din-* ill-health, f. *in-* IN-[3] + *valetudo* health; see -ARY[1].] Wanting health or strength; infirm, invalid –1661.

Invalid (invæ·lid), *a.*[1] 1635. [– L. *invalidus*; see IN-[3], VALID.] Not valid. †**1.** Without power or strength; weak, feeble –1834. **2.** Of no force; *esp.* without legal force, void 1635.

2. That which was i. from the beginning, cannot become valid by prescription or tract of time BRAMHALL.

Invalid (i·nvălīd, -lid, invălī·d), *a.*[2] and *sb.* Also **-ide.** 1642. [f. as prec., with pronunciation after Fr. *invalide.* Orig. only a special sense of prec.]

A. *adj.* Infirm from sickness or disease; enfeebled or disabled by illness or injury. Now only an attrib. use of the sb.

His invalide and suffering sister 1869.

B. *sb.* **1.** An infirm or sickly person 1709. **2.** A soldier or sailor disabled for active service 1704. **3.** *attrib.* **a.** (See A.) **b.** Of or for invalids. 1845.

2. *Invalides*, the *Hôtel des Invalides*, a hospital or home for old and disabled soldiers in Paris.

Hence **I·nvalidish** 1855, **I·nvalidy** 1894 *adjs. colloq.*, somewhat of an invalid.

Invalid (invæ·lid), *v.*[1] Now *rare.* 1626. [f. INVALID *a.*[1]; cf. INVALIDATE *v.* and Fr. *invalider* (XVI).] *trans.* To render invalid; to invalidate.

Invalid (i·nvălīd, invălī·d), *v.*[2] Also **-ide.** 1787. [f. INVALID *a.*[2]] **1.** *trans.* To make an invalid; to lay up or disable by illness or injury. (Chiefly in *pass.*) 1803. **2.** To enter on the sick-list; to report as unfit for active service 1787. **3.** *intr.* To become an invalid; of a soldier or sailor: To go on the sick-list; to leave the service on account of illness or injury 1829.

1. The Queen..was invalided at Windsor 1837. **2.** He was invalided home, sorely against his will 1882. **3.** The conscripts die first, they i. at an inexplicable rate 1885.

Invalidate (invæ·lideⁱt), *v.* 1649. [– *invalidat-*, pa. ppl. stem of med.L. *invalidare* invalidate, annul (XV), perh. partly after Fr. *invalider*; see -ATE[3].] *trans.* To render invalid; to render of no force or effect; *esp.* to deprive of legal efficacy.

To i. an Obligation 1651, an argument 1674, evidence 1801. Hence †**Inva·lidable** *a.* ineffective 1634.

Invalidation (invælidēⁱ·ʃən). 1771. [f. prec. + -ION. Cf. med.L. *invalidatio*, Fr. *invalidation.*] The action of invalidating or rendering invalid.

It is no i. of this high claim 1863.

Invalidism (i·nvălīdiz'm, invălī·diz'm). 1794. [f. INVALID *sb.* + -ISM.] The state of being an invalid; chronic infirmity or ill health that prevents activity.

Invalidity (invăli·dĭti). 1550. [– Fr. *invalidité* or med.L. *invaliditas*, f. L. *invalidus*; see INVALID *a.*[1], -ITY.] The quality of being invalid; *esp.* want of legal validity. †**2.** Want of strength or efficacy; weakness, incapacity –1698. **3.** [Related to INVALID *a.*[2]] Want of bodily strength or health; condition of being an invalid; bodily infirmity 1698.

1. The I. of their Passports 1711, of the evidence 1841. **3.** Allowances for both i. and old age 1891. So **Inva·lidness.**

Invalorous (invæ·lŏrəs), *a.* *rare.* 1846. [IN-[3].] Not valorous, cowardly.

Invaluable (invæ·liuˌăb'l), *a.* 1576. [IN-[3].] **1.** That cannot be valued; above and beyond valuation; inestimable. **2.** Without value, valueless 1640.

1. A free government..is an i. blessing BUTLER. Hence **Inva·luableness. Inva·luably** *adv.*

†**Inva·lued**, *a.* *poet.* *rare.* 1603. [IN-[3].] Invaluable –1806.

Invar (i·nvaɹ). 1902. [abbrev. of INVARIABLE.] An alloy of nickel and steel in which the coefficient of expansion is negligible.

Invariable (invēᵊ·riăb'l), *a.* (*sb.*) 1457. [– (O)Fr. *invariable* or late L. *invariabilis*; see IN-[3], VARIABLE.] **A.** *adj.* Not subject to variation or alteration; unchangeable; constant; unvarying. **b.** *Math.* Of a quantity: Constant. Of a point, line, etc.: Fixed. 1704. **B.** *sb.* *Math.* An invariable quantity, a constant 1864. Hence **Invariabi·lity, Inva·riableness,** unchangeableness. **Inva·riably** *adv.*

A. The value of gold and silver is certainly not i. MCCULLOCH.

Invariance (invēᵊriăns). 1878. [f. next; see -ANCE.] *Math.* The character of remaining unaltered after a linear transformation; the essential property of an invariant. So **Inva·riancy.**

Invariant (invēᵊ·riănt). 1851. [f. IN-[3] + VARIANT.]

A. *adj.* Unvarying 1874.

B. *sb.* *Math.* A function of the coefficients of a quantic, such that, if the quantic be linearly transformed, the same function of the new coefficients is equal to the first function multiplied by some power of the modulus of transformation. Hence **Inva·riantive** *a.* belonging to an i. **Inva·riantively** *adv.*

Invaried (invēᵊ·rid), *a.* *rare.* 1677. [IN-[3].] Unvaried.

Invasion (invēⁱ·ʒən). 1508. [– (O)Fr. *invasion* or late L. *invasio*, f. *invas-*, pa. ppl. stem of L. *invadere*; see INVADE, -ION.] **1.** The action of invading; an entrance or incursion with armed force; a hostile inroad. Also *fig.* **2.** Infringement by intrusion; encroachment upon the property, rights, privacy, etc. of any one 1650. †**3.** Assault, attack (upon a person, etc.) –1757.

1. *fig.* An i. of Disease BOYLE, of doubt 1847.

Invasive (invēⁱ·siv), *a.* 1456. [– Fr. †*invasif, -ive* or med.L. *invasivus*, f. as prec.; see -IVE.] **1.** Of, pertaining to, or of the nature of, invasion; †(of weapons) offensive. **2.** Characterized by invasion 1598. Also *transf.* and *fig.* **3.** Intrusive, encroaching 1670.

1. An i. war 1788. **2.** Th'i. foe's designs SHENSTONE.

Invecked (inve·kt), *ppl. a.* 1496. [Anglicized sp. of *invect- – L. *invectus*, pa. pple. of *invehere* carry in; see INVEIGH.] Bordered by or consisting (as an edge) of a series of small convex lobes. Chiefly in *Her.*

†**Inve·ct**, *v.* 1548. [– *invect-*; see prec., INVEIGH.] **1.** *trans.* To bring in, import, introduce. UDALL. **2.** *intr.* To inveigh –1625.

Invected (inve·ktėd), *ppl. a.* 1641. [f. as prec. + -ED[1].] Brought in, introduced; *spec.* in *Her.* = INVECKED.

†**Inve·ction.** 1450. [– L. *invectio* bringing in, importation; in late L. attacking with words; f. *invect-*; see next, -ION.] **1.** The action of inveighing; an invective –1651. **2.** Importation –1658.

Invective (inve·ktiv). ME. [– (O)Fr. *invectif, -ive* adj., *invective* sb. – late L. *invectivus, invectiva* (*oratio*) as sb., f. *invect-*, pa. ppl. stem of *invehere*; see next, -IVE.]

A. *adj.* **1.** Using or characterized by denunciatory or railing language; inclined to inveigh; vituperative, abusive. Now *rare.* †**2.** Carried or borne in (against something). FLORIO.

1. Divers i. speeches..had passed in the same 1576.

B. *sb.* **1.** A violent attack in words; a denunciatory or railing speech, writing, or expression 1523. **2.** (Without *pl.*) Vehement denunciation; vituperation 1602.

1. This it is that fills..Pamphlets with spightfull invectives BP. HALL. **2.** A torrent of i. 1839.

Hence **Inve·ctively** *adv.* (now *rare*).

Inveigh (invēⁱ·), *v.* 1486. [– L. *invehere* carry in, medio-pass. *invehi* be borne into, attack, assail with words, f. *in-* IN-[2] + *vehere* carry; for the sp. cf. †*conveigh* CONVEY.]

I. †**1.** *trans.* To introduce (*rare*) –1550. †**2.** To entice, inveigle –1680. †**3.** To carry away (*to* a place) 1878.

II. 1. *intr.* To utter vehement denunciation, reproach, or censure; to rail loudly. Const. *against* (†*at, of, on, upon*). (The current sense.) 1529. †**2.** *trans.* To attack or assail with words 1670.

1. Williams inveighed against Laud as a Papist

D'ISRAELI. Popular orators, who rose to power by inveighing against property FROUDE. Hence **Invei·gher.**

Inveigle (invī·g'l), *v.* 1494. [In XVI *envegle (-veugle)* – AFr. *envegler* alteration (cf. ENSAMPLE) of (O)Fr. *aveugler* blind, f. *aveugle* blind, prob. :– Rom. **ab oculis* 'without eyes'.] †**1.** *trans.* To blind in mind or judgement; to beguile, deceive –1709. **2.** To gain over by deceitful allurement; to entice, seduce 1540. †**b.** To entrap, ensnare, entangle –1707.

1. The subtiltie of Satan inueagling vs, as it did Eue HOOKER. **2.** Yet have they many baits, and guilefull spells To i. and invite th' unwary sense MILT. *Comus* 538. **b.** To enveigle and entangle his necessitous neighbour..till he have got a hank over his estate SANDERSON. Hence **Invei·glement,** cajolery, allurement, enticement. **Invei·gler.**

†**Invei·l,** *v.* 1592. [f. IN-[1] or [2] + VEIL *v.* Cf. ENVEIL.] To cover with or as with a veil –1763.

Invendible (inve·ndĭb'l), *a.* *rare.* 1706. [IN-[3].] Not vendible; unsaleable. Hence **Inve:ndibi·lity,** unsaleableness.

Inveneme, etc., obs. ff. ENVENOM, etc.

Invent (inve·nt), *v.* 1475. [– *invent-*, pa. ppl. stem of L. *invenire* come upon, discover, f. *in-* IN-[2] + *venire* come. Cf. Fr. *inventer* (XVI).] **1.** *trans.* To come upon, find; to discover. (*Obs.* exc. in reference to the *Invention of the Cross*: see INVENTION I. 1.) **2.** To find out or produce by mental activity; †to devise –1821; to fabricate, feign, 'make up' 1535. **3.** To find out in the way of original contrivance; to devise first, originate (a new method, instrument, etc.). The chief current sense. 1538. †**4.** To bring into use formally or by authority; to found, establish, institute, appoint –1692. †**5.** With *inf.*: To devise, contrive, find out how (*to do* something) –1729.

1. It was in a bed of this tender herb [sweet basil] that Our Lord's Cross was invented 1887. **2.** For laboured impiety, what apology can be invented? JOHNSON. The calumnies which..he had invented to blacken the fame of Anne Hyde MACAULAY. **3.** They invented the arte of printing 1601. Galileo invented the telescope 1783. I only said I invented the word 'agnostic' HUXLEY. **5.** They will i. to engage your attention BUTLER.

†**I·nventary, -arie.** 1459. [var. of INVENTORY *sb.*, after late L. *inventarium*; see -ARY[1].] = INVENTORY *sb.* –1763.

Inventer: see INVENTOR.

Inve·ntful, *a.* *rare.* 1797. [f. INVENT *v.* + -FUL.] Full of invention.

Inve·ntible, -able, *a.* *rare.* 1641. [f. INVENT *v.* + -IBLE (on L. analogy), -ABLE.] Capable of being invented. Hence **Inve·ntibleness.**

Invention (inve·nʃən). ME. [– L. *inventio*, f. *invent-*; see INVENT *v.*, -ION. Cf. (O)Fr. *invention* (XIV).]

I. 1. The action of coming upon or finding; discovery. *Obs.* or *arch.* **b.** *Rhet.* Selection of topics or arguments 1509. **2.** The action of devising, contriving, or making up; fabrication 1526. **3.** Contrivance or production of a new method, of an art, kind of instrument, etc. previously unknown; origination, introduction 1531. **b.** In art and literary composition: The devising of a subject, idea, or method of treatment, by exercise of the intellect or imagination 1638. **4.** The faculty of inventing or devising; inventiveness 1480. †**5.** Invented style, fashion, design –1715.

1. The i. and use of the four metals in Greece NEWTON. *Invention of the Cross*: the reputed finding of the Cross by Helena, mother of the Emperor Constantine, in A.D. 326; hence, the church festival observed on the 3rd of May in commemoration of this. **2.** This proceeding is not of my own i. SWIFT. **3.** The first inuention of Tobacco taking. JAS. I. **4.** He was not a man of much i. SMEATON. **5.** Guns of several Sizes and Inventions ADDISON.

II. 1. Something devised; a device, contrivance, design, plan, scheme 1513. †**2.** A literary composition –1601. **3.** A fabrication, fiction, figment 1500. **4.** An original contrivance or device 1546. **5.** *Mus.* A short piece of music in which a single idea is worked out in a simple manner. GROVE.

1. God hath made man vpright; but they haue sought out many inuentions *Eccl.* 7:29. **2.** *Twel. N.* v. i. 341. **3.** The story..was all meer I. 1748. **4.** Tyle and slate to couer houses were the inuencion of Sinyra 1546.

†**III.** Coming in, arrival. DRAYTON.

Hence **Inve·ntional** *a.* (*rare*), of, pertaining to, or of the nature of i. (Dicts.) †**Inve·ntious** *a.* = INVENTIVE 1, 2. 1591–1656.

Inventive (inve·ntiv), *a.* 1450. [– Fr. *inventif, -ive* or med.L. *inventivus* (XIII), f. as prec.; see -IVE.] **1.** Having the faculty of invention; original in contriving or devising. **2.** Produced by or showing original contrivance 1601. †**3.** Invented, fictitious –1673.

1. Those that haue ye inuentiuest heades ASCHAM. **2.** I. mockery and insult SCOTT. Hence **Inve·ntively** *adv.*, **-ness.**

Inventor (inve·ntəɹ). Also †**-er.** 1490. [– L. *inventor*, f. as prec.; see -OR 2. Cf. Fr. *inventeur*.] One who invents. †**1.** A discoverer. 1509–1744. **2.** One who devises something fictitious or false 1513. **3.** One who devises or produces something new (as an instrument, art, etc.) by original contrivance; 'the first finder-out'. (The prevailing sense.) 1490.

Inventorial (inventō°·riăl), *a.* *rare.* [f. next + -AL[1].] Pertaining to, or having the character of, an inventory; detailed. Hence **Invento·rially** *adv.* in detail 1604.

Inventory (i·nvĕntəri), *sb.* 1450. [– med.L. *inventorium*, for late L. *inventarium* (whence (O)Fr. *inventaire*, and INVENTARY), f. *invent-*; see INVENT *v.*, -ORY[1].] **1.** A detailed list of articles, such as goods and chattels, or parcels of land, found to have been in the possession of a person at his decease or conviction, sometimes with a statement of the nature and value of each; hence any such detailed statement of property, goods or furniture, or the like. **2.** *gen.* or *fig.* A list, catalogue; a detailed account 1589. **3.** *transf.* The lot of goods, etc., which are or may be made the subject of an inventory 1691. **4.** *U.S.* = STOCK-TAKING.

1. There take an Inuentory of all I haue SHAKS. **2.** What sects? What are their opinions? give us the I. MILTON.

Inventory (i·nvĕntəri), *v.* 1526. [f. prec. sb.] *trans.* To make an inventory or descriptive list of; to catalogue (goods, etc.). Also *gen.* or *fig.*

fig. It [my beauty] shal be inuentoried and euery particle and vtensile labell'd to my will SHAKS.

Inve·ntress. 1586. [-ESS[1].] A female inventor. So †**Inventri·ce** 1509–1546, **Inve·ntrix** 1604 (?*Obs.*).

Inveracious (invĕrē[i]·ʃəs), *a.* 1885. [IN-[3].] Untruthful. So **Invera·city** 1864.

Inverisimilitude (inve:risimi·litiūd). 1818. [IN-[3].] Lack of verisimilitude; unlikelihood; improbability.

Inverminate (invə̄·ɹminē[i]t), *v.* 1830. [app. f. IN-[2] + VERMIN + -ATE[3].] *trans.* To infest like worms; to swarm or burrow in. COLERIDGE. So **Inve:rmina·tion,** the condition of being infested with (intestinal) worms 1808.

Inverness (invərne·s). 1865. [– Gael. *Inbhir-nis* mouth of the (river) Ness.] A town in the Highlands of Scotland. Hence *I. cloak, overcoat,* name of an overcoat with a removable cape (*I. cape*).

Inverse (invə̄·ɹs, i·nvəɹs). 1658. [– L. *inversus*, pa. pple. of *invertere* INVERT *v.*]

A. *adj.* **1.** Turned upside down; inverted. **2.** Inverted in position, order, or relations 1831. **3.** *Math.* **a.** *Arith.* and *Alg.* Of such a nature in respect to another operation, relation, etc. that the starting-point of the one is the conclusion of the other, and *vice versa*; opposite in nature or effect. Opp. to *direct.* 1660. **b.** *Geom. Inverse point, line, curve,* etc., one related to another point, line, curve, etc., in the way of geometrical inversion (see INVERSION I. 3 b) 1873. **4.** *Cryst.* Opp. to *direct* 1878.

1. Make from these Piers i. Arches MOXON. **2.** Go on..Seeking, an i. Saul, a kingdom to find only asses CLOUGH. **3. a.** *Inverse ratio*: (*a*) a ratio in which the terms are reversed; (*b*) the ratio of two quantities which vary inversely, i.e. one of which increases in the proportion in which the other decreases, and *vice versa*; so *i. proportion. I. square*: often used for the relation of two quantities one of which varies inversely as the square of the other. *Rule of Three i.*: that case of the Rule of Three in which the antecedent of each of the ratios corresponds to the consequent of the other.

B. *sb.* **1.** An inverted state or condition; thus *CBA* is the inverse of *ABC* 1681. **2.** The result of inversion: **a.** *Math.* A ratio, proportion, or process in which the antecedents and consequents are interchanged. Also, short for *inverse function.* 1695. **b.** *Geom.* Short for *inverse curve, point,* etc. 1873. **c.** *Logic.* The proposition obtained by inversion 1896.

Inverse (invə̄·ɹs), *v.* Now *rare.* 1611. [f. prec.] *trans.* To turn upside down; to invert; to reverse in order or direction.

Inversely (invə̄·ɹsli), *adv.* 1660. [f. INVERSE *a.* + -LY[2].] In an inverse manner or order; as the inverse; by inversion. **b.** Invertedly; upside down 1776.

Inversion (invə̄·ɹʃən). 1551. [– L. *inversio*, f. *invers-*, pa. ppl. stem of *invertere*; see INVERT *v.*, -ION.]

I. 1. A turning upside down 1598. **b.** *Geol.* The folding back of stratified rocks upon each other, so that older strata overlie the newer 1849. **2.** A reversal of position, order, sequence, or relation 1599. †**b.** *Rhet.* = ANTISTROPHE 3 b. –1657. **c.** *Gram.* = ANASTROPHE 1586. **d.** *Mus.* The action of inverting an interval, chord, phrase, or subject (see INVERT *v.* I. 2. e); also, the interval, chord, etc. so produced 1806. **e.** *Logic.* An immediate inference in which the new subject is the negative of the original one 1896. **3.** *Math.* **a.** *Arith.* and *Alg.* The reversal of a ratio by interchanging the positions of the antecedent and consequent 1660. **b.** *Geom.* A transformation in which for each point of a given figure is substituted another point in the same straight line from a fixed point (called the *origin* or *centre of inversion*), and so situated that the product of the distances of the two points from the centre of inversion is constant (*cyclical* or *spherical inversion*). Also extended to similar transformations involving a more complex relation of corresponding points or lines, as *quadric inversion, tangential inversion.* 1873. **4.** *Mil.* An evolution by which ranks are converted into files 1635. **5.** *Chem.* A decomposition of certain carbohydrates into two different substances, as of cane-sugar into dextrose and lævulose, whereby the direction of the optical rotatory power is reversed 1864. †**6.** = METAPHOR –1589.

2. When we dress by a mirror we perform a series of inversions, very difficult at first BAIN. **b.** You maye confute the same by inuersion, that is to saie, tournyng his taile cleane contrary 1551.

II. 1. *Her.* See INVERTED II. 1. 1638. **2.** A turning outside in, introversion; a turning inside out. *spec.* in *Path.* 1598.

†**III.** Diversion to an improper purpose; perversion –1755.

Invert (i·nvəɹt), *sb.* 1838. [f. INVERT *v.*] **1.** An inverted arch. **2.** *Psychol.* One whose sex instincts are inverted 1897.

Invert (invə̄·ɹt), *v.* 1533. [– L. *invertere*, f. *in-* IN-[2] + *vertere* turn; lit. turn in, turn outside in, hence, turn the opposite way.]

I. 1. *trans.* To turn upside down 1613. †**b.** *fig.* To overthrow, upset; to subvert –1706. **2.** To reverse in position, order, or sequence; to turn in an opposite direction 1533. **b.** *fig.* 1552. †**c.** *Rhet.* To retort an argument upon an opponent –1796. †**d.** To use (words) in a non-literal sense. PUTTENHAM. **e.** *Mus.* To change the relative position of the notes of (an interval or chord) by placing the lowest note higher, usually an octave higher; also, to modify (a phrase or subject) by inverting the intervals between the successive notes, i.e. by reversing the direction of its motion 1838. **f.** *Logic.* To obtain the inverse of (a proposition) 1896. **g.** *Math.* To transform by inversion, obtain the inverse of. **3.** *Mil.* Cf. INVERSION I. 4. 1832. **4.** *Chem.* To break up (cane-sugar) into dextrose and lævulose 1864. †**5.** *intr.* To change to the opposite –1813.

1. Again the lab'ring hind inverts the soil SHENSTONE. **2.** The way is the same, but the order is inverted HOBBES. **b.** Thus is all inverted, many Kings, and few subjects PURCHAS. **c.** They inverted, and retaliated the impiety BURKE.

†**II.** *trans.* To divert from its proper purpose; to pervert to another use –1678.

III. †**1.** *trans.* To turn in or inward –1646. **2.** To turn outside in, or inside out; *spec.* in *Path.* 1615.

I·nvert, *a.* 1880. [Short for INVERTED.] In **I. sugar:** Sugar formed by the breaking up of cane-sugar into dextrose and lævulose.

Invertant (invə·ɹtǎnt), *a.* 1828. [f. INVERT *v.* + -ANT.] *Her.* = INVERTED II. 1.

Invertebral (invə·ɹtĭbrǎl), *a. rare.* 1816. [f. IN-^{3} + VERTEBRAL.] = INVERTEBRATE *a.*

‖**Invertebrata** (invəɹtĭbrē^{i}·tǎ), *sb. pl.* 1828. [mod.L. (sc. *animalia* animals), after Fr. *invertébrés* (Cuvier, 1805), f. *in-* IN-^{3} + *vertèbre* – L. *vertebra* VERTEBRA.] A name for all animals except the *Vertebrata* or backboned animals; now only a convenient negative term for all groups below the Vertebrata.

Invertebrate (invə·ɹtĭbrĕt). 1826. [Anglicized f. prec.; see -ATE^{1}, ^{2}.]

A. *adj.* Not having a backbone or spinal column. **b.** *fig.* Without 'backbone' 1879. **B.** *sb.* One of the Invertebrata 1826. Also *fig.*

Inverted (invə·ɹtėd), *ppl. a.* 1598. [f. INVERT *v.* + -ED^{1}.]

I. 1. Turned upside down. **b.** *Mus.* Of chords or intervals: Having the lowest note transposed an octave higher 1811. **2.** Reversed in position or order; turned in the opposite direction 1602. **3.** Reversed in relations 1702. **b.** Reversed in meaning 1646. **4.** *Mil.* Cf. INVERSION I. 4, INVERT *v.* I. 3. 1832. **5.** *Math.* = INVERSE *a.* I. 3. 1885. **6.** *Chem.* Of cane-sugar; Exhibiting lævorotatory power 1857.

1. They had no covering but an i. boat 1806. **2.** I live in an i. order. They who ought to have succeeded me are gone before me BURKE. **3.** This i. Idolatry, wherein the Image did Homage to the Man STEELE.

II. 1. *Her.* Turned inwards or towards the middle of the field: said of animals or their members 1610. **2.** *Path.* Introverted; turned inside out 1787. **i. commas:** ' ' or " ".

Hence **Inve·rtedly** *adv.* in an i. manner.

†**Invertible** (invə·ɹtib'l), *a.*^{1} 1534. [– late L. *invertibilis*, f. *in-* IN-^{3} + *vertere* turn; see -BLE.] That cannot be turned or reversed –1633.

An indurate and i. conscience CRANMER.

Inve·rtible, *a.*^{2} 1881. [f. INVERT *v.* + -IBLE.] **a.** That can be inverted. **b.** That tends to invert the usual order.

Invertin (invə·ɹtin, i·nvəɹtin). 1879. [f. INVERT *v.* + -IN^{1}.] *Chem.* A chemical ferment, obtained as a white powder from yeast desiccated in air; it is the constituent which produces the inversion of sugar.

Invertor (invə·ɹtəɹ). [f. INVERT *v.* + -OR 2.] An instrument for reversing an electric current; a commutator. (Mod. Dicts.)

Invest (inve·st), *v.* 1489. [– (O)Fr. *investir* or L. *investire* clothe, surround (extended in meaning in med.L.), f. *in-* IN-^{2} + *vestis* clothing. In II, after It. *investire.*]

I. 1. *trans.* To clothe; to dress or adorn 1583; to put on as clothes or ornaments 1596. **2.** *transf.* To cover or surround as with a garment. Const. *with.* 1548. **b.** To cover as a garment does 1632. **3.** *fig.* 1604. **4.** To clothe *with* or *in* the insignia of an office; hence, *with* the dignity itself; to install *in* an office or rank with proper rites 1489. **5.** To establish in the possession of any office, position, property, etc.; to endow with power, authority, or privilege. Const. *in, with.* 1564. **6.** To settle, secure, or vest (a right or power) in (a person) 1590. **7.** *Mil.* To enclose or hem in; to besiege, beleaguer; †to attack 1600.

1. Ile show you, how the Bride, faire Isis, they i. DRAYTON. So faire a crew. . Cannot find one this girdle to inuest SPENSER. **2. b.** Thread-like down which invests the plant 1861. **4.** The lord Thomas Stanley he inuested with the swoorde of the countie of Darby HALL. **5.** To i. a person with lands 1861. **6.** The powers invested in Congress 1794. **7.** Astorga is invested WELLINGTON.

II. To employ (money) in the purchase of anything from which interest or profit is expected 1613. **b.** *absol.* or *intr.* To make an investment; *colloq.* to lay out money 1864.

b. *colloq.* To i. in a penny time-table 1900.

†**Inve·stient,** *a.* 1695. [– *investient-*, pr. ppl. stem of L. *investire*; see prec., -ENT.] Investing, coating, enveloping –1762.

Investigable (inve·stigǎb'l), *a.*^{1} 1594. [– late L. *investigabilis*; see INVESTIGATE and -ABLE.] Capable of being investigated, traced out, or searched into; open to investigation.

†**Inve·stigable,** *a.*^{2} 1510. [– eccl.L. *investigabilis*, f. *in-* IN-^{3} + *vestigare* track, trace, + *-bilis* -BLE. Cf. OFr. *investigable.*] Incapable of being traced; unsearchable –1701.

Investigate (inve·stige^{i}t), *v.* 1510. [– *investigat-*, pa. ppl. stem of L. *investigare*, f. *in-* IN-^{2} + *vestigare* track, trace out; see -ATE^{3}.] **1.** *trans.* To search or inquire into; to examine systematically or in detail. **2.** *intr.* To make search; to reconnoitre, to scout; to inquire systematically, to make investigation 1510.

1. To i. a question of law 'JUNIUS'. **2.** To i. into the nature of Society MANDEVILLE. Hence **Inve·stigatingly** *adv.* **Inve·stigative** *a.* **Inve·stigator.**

Investigation (investigē^{i}·ʃən). late ME. [– (O)Fr. *investigation* or L. *investigatio*, f. as prec.; see -ION.] **1.** The action of investigating; search, inquiry; systematic examination; minute and careful research. Also with *an* and *pl.* **2.** The tracking of (a beast). T. TAYLOR.

1. I. of the truth 1602. Characters which require a long i. to unfold BURKE.

†**Inve·stion.** *rare.* 1586. [– med.L. *investio*, var. of *investitio*, f. L. *investire*; see INVEST *v.*, -ION.] The action of investing; investment –1632.

Investitive (inve·stitiv), *a.* 1780. [f. as next + -IVE.] Having the property or function of investing.

Investiture (inve·stitiŭɹ). ME. [– med.L. *investitura*, f. *investit-*, pa. ppl. stem of L. *investire*; see INVEST *v.*, -URE.] **1.** The action of clothing or robing; *concr.* that which clothes or covers. Chiefly *fig.* 1651. **2.** The action or ceremony of clothing in the insignia of an office; the formal investing of a person with an office or rank; the formal putting (a person) in possession of a fief or benefice. Often, spec., the livery and seizin of the temporalities of an eccl. dignity. ME. **3.** Clothing in attributes or qualities; establishment in any state of privilege or honour 1626. **4.** = INVESTMENT 4. Now *rare.* 1649. †**5.** = INVESTMENT 5. –1845.

1. The darkness of clouds is the accustomed i. of the Divine presence 1871. **2.** The king. . gave the bishop the i., or livery and seizin of his temporalities, by the delivery of a ring and staff BURKE. **3.** One incapable of i. with any grandeur LAMB.

Investment (inve·stmĕnt). 1597. [f. INVEST *v.* + -MENT.] **1.** The act of putting clothes or vestments on; *concr.* clothing; vestments. Also *fig.* **2.** *transf.* An envelope; a coating 1646. **3.** = INVESTITURE 2, 3. 1649. **4.** *Mil.* The surrounding or hemming in *of* a town or fort by a hostile force; beleaguerment; blockade. Also *attrib.* 1811. **5.** *Comm.* The investing of money or capital; an amount of money invested in some species of property. Also *attrib.* 1615. **b.** A form of property viewed as a vehicle in which money may be invested 1837.

1. You, Lord Arch-bishop. . Whose white Inuestments figure Innocence SHAKS. **3.** The i. of the powers of nature with personal life and consciousness 1885. **4.** To draw the i. closer KINGLAKE. **5.** Before the i. could be made, a change of the market might render it ineligible A. HAMILTON. **b.** 'I do not put myself in the way of hearing about profitable investments' 1837.

Investor (inve·stəɹ). Also †**-er.** 1586. [f. INVEST + -OR 2.] One who invests.

Investure (inve·stiŭɹ), *sb.* 1577. [f. INVEST + -URE. Not on L. analogies.] = INVESTITURE, INVESTMENT.

†**Inve·sture,** *v. rare.* 1552. [Partly f. prec.; partly f. IN-^{1} or ^{2} + VESTURE.] **1.** *trans.* To invest *in* an estate or dignity. ASCHAM. **2.** To clothe, to vest –1661.

2. Our monks investured in their copes FULLER.

Inveteracy (inve·tĕrǎsi). 1691. [f. next; see -ACY.] **1.** The quality of being inveterate; the state of being strong or deep-seated from long persistence 1719. **2.** Deep-rooted prejudice, hostility, or hatred; enmity of old standing 1691.

1. The i. of the people's prejudices ADDISON. **2.** The I. of the Jews against the Christians 1703.

Inveterate (inve·tĕrĕt), *a.* late ME. [– L. *inveteratus*, pa. pple. a. of *inveterare* make old, f. *in-* IN-^{2} + *vetus, veter-* old; see -ATE^{2}.] **1.** Of old standing; aged. **2.** Firmly established by long continuance; long-established; deep-rooted; obstinate. (Now mostly of things evil.) 1563. **3.** Full of obstinate prejudice or hatred; embittered, malignant; virulent. (Now *vulgar.*) 1528. **4.** Settled or confirmed in habit, condition, or practice; hardened, obstinate 1734.

1. An I. willow-tree EVELYN. **2.** An Extirpation of i., sinfull Habits SOUTH. I. disease COWLEY. His old and i. enemies ALISON. **3.** I felt i. against him DICKENS. **4.** An i. smoker 1859. Hence **Inve·terately** *adv.*, **-ness.**

Inveterate (inve·tĕre^{i}t), *v. Obs.* or *arch.* 1574. [f. prec. or – *inveterat-*, pa. ppl. stem of L. *inveterare*; see prec., -ATE^{3}.] **1.** To make old; to establish or confirm by age or long continuance; †also, to harden (the bowels). **2.** To render inveterate in enmity. J. HARRINGTON.

†**Inve·teration.** *rare.* 1631. [– L. *inveteratio*, f. *inveterat-*; see prec., -ION.] The action of rendering, or process of becoming, inveterate –1721.

†**Invi·ct,** *a.* 1494. [– L. *invictus*, f. *in-* IN-^{3} + *victus*, pa. pple. of *vincere* conquer. Cf. Fr. †*invicte.*] Unconquered –1678. So †**Invi·cted** *a.* 1600.

Invidious (invi·diəs), *a.* 1606. [– L. *invidiosus*, f. *invidia* ill will; see ENVY *sb.*, -IOUS.] **1.** Tending or fitted to excite ill will or envy. **2.** Of an action, duty, topic, etc.: Entailing odium or ill will upon the person performing, discharging, discussing, etc.; giving offence to others 1701; of a distinction, etc.: Offensively discriminating 1709. **3.** That looks with an evil eye; envious, grudging, jealous. Now *rare.* 1668. †**4.** Odious *to* a person (*rare*) –1720.

1. An i. Pamphlet 1755. His revenue. . was ample without being i. BURKE. **2.** The laws against the combinations of labourers. . were seen to be unjust and i. ROGERS. **4.** Joseph. . became i. to his elder Brethren STEELE. Hence **Invi·dious-ly** *adv.*, **-ness.**

Invigilancy (invi·dʒilǎnsi). *rare.* 1611. [f. IN-^{3} + VIGILANCY.] Absence of vigilance or watchfulness. So **Invi·gilance** (*rare*) 1828.

Invigilate (invi·dʒile^{i}t), *v.* 1553. [– *invigilat-*, pa. ppl. stem of L. *invigilare*, f. *in-* IN-^{2} + *vigilare* watch, f. *vigil* watchful; see -ATE^{3}.] **1.** *intr.* To keep watch. Now *spec.* To watch over students at examination. †**2.** *trans.* To arouse; to make watchful (*rare*) –16. . Hence **Invi·gilator. Invigila·tion.**

Invigorate (invi·gŏre^{i}t), *v.* 1646. [– *invigorat-*, pa. ppl. stem of med.L. **invigorare* (cf. Fr. †*envigorer* XV–XVI), f. *in-* IN-^{2} + L. *vigorare* make strong; see -ATE^{3}, and cf. next.] **1.** *trans.* To impart vigour to; to fill with life and energy; to strengthen, animate. **2.** *intr.* To become vigorous 1759.

1. Their minds and bodies were invigorated by exercise GIBBON. Hence **Invigora·tion. Invi·gorative** *a.* invigorating.

Invigour (invi·gəɹ), *v. rare.* Also †**en-.** 1611. [In form *envigour* – Fr. †*envigo(u)rer* (see prec.); subseq. assim. to IN-^{2}, VIGOUR.] *trans.* To invigorate.

†**Invi·le,** *v. rare.* [f. IN-^{2} + VILE *a.*] To render vile. DANIEL.

†**Invi·llage,** *v.* 1613. [f. IN-^{2} + VILLAGE.] *trans.* To make or reduce into a village.

Invincible (invi·nsĭb'l), *a.* (*sb.*) ME. [– (O)Fr. *invincible* – L. *invincibilis*, f. *in-* IN-^{3} + *vincibilis*, f. *vincere* conquer; see -IBLE.]

A. *adj.* **1.** That cannot be vanquished, overcome, or subdued; unconquerable. **b.** *transf.* and *fig.* 1482. †**2.** Unsurpassable –1617. **3.** Of or pertaining to the Invincibles (see B. b) 1885.

1. *I. Armada*: see ARMADA. The name 'Invincible', so commonly given to this fleet, was not official 1894. **b.** An i. reason and an argument infallible HALL.

B. *sb.* One who is invincible 1640. **b.** A member of an Irish assassination society so called, developed from the Fenians about 1881–2.

Hence **Invincibi·lity** 1601, **Invi·ncibleness. Invi·ncibly** *adv.*

Inviolable (invəi·ŏlǎb'l), *a.* 1530. [– (O)Fr. *inviolable* or L. *inviolabilis*; see IN-^{3}, VIOLABLE.] **1.** Not to be violated; not liable or allowed to suffer violence; to be kept sacredly free from profanation, infraction, or assault

1532. †**2.** That cannot be violated, broken, forced, or injured –1719.

1. Styx is the i. oath COWPER. Jove's i. altar POPE. A humble i. English home 1863. **2.** Th'i. Saints In Cubic Phalanx firm advanc't entire MILT. *P.L.* VI. 398. The strict and i. Harmony of the three Persons WATERLAND. Hence **Invi:olabi·lity, Invi·olableness** (now *rare*). **Invi·olably** *adv.*

Inviolacy (invəi·ŏlăsi). 1846. [f. next; see -ACY.] The condition of being inviolate; inviolateness.

Inviolate (invəi·ŏlĕt), *a.* ME. [– L. *inviolatus*, f. *in-* IN-³ + pa. pple. of *violare* VIOLATE; see -ATE².] Not violated; free from violation; unhurt, uninjured, unbroken; unprofaned, unmarred; intact.

With..fayth inuyolate LYDG. Clement VIII ordered that the relics should remain untouched, i. 1848. So **Invi·olated** *a.* 1548. Hence **Invi·olate-ly** *adv.*, **-ness.**

†**I·nvious,** *a.* 1622. [f. L. *invius* (f. *in-*, IN-³ + *via*) + -OUS.] Having no roads or ways; pathless, trackless –1681.

Invi·rile, *a.* [IN-³.] Unmanly, effeminate. LOWELL. So †**Inviri·lity,** effeminacy 1628.

Inviscate (invi·skeᵗt), *v.* ME. [– *inviscat-*, pa. ppl. stem of late L. *inviscare* smear with or snare with bird-lime, f. *in-* IN-² + *viscum* bird-lime.] **1.** *trans.* To render viscid or sticky; to mix or cover with a sticky substance. **2.** To catch in some sticky substance (*rare*) 1646.

2. A..clammy substance like tar, in which..insects are inviscated WITHERING. Hence **Invisca·tion.**

†**Invi·scerate,** *v.* 1626. [– *inviscerat-*, pa. ppl. stem of late L. *inviscerare*, f. *in-* IN-² + *viscera* entrails.] *trans.* To put into the 'bowels' or heart –1648. Hence †**Inviscera·tion.**

Invisible (invi·zĭb'l). ME. [– (O)Fr. *invisible* or L. *invisibilis*; see IN-³, VISIBLE.]

A. *adj.* **1.** That cannot be seen; that by its nature is not an object of sight. **2.** Not in sight; not to be seen 1555. **3.** Too small to be discerned; imperceptible 1665. **b.** *I. green*: a very dark shade of green, not easily distinguishable from black 1844.

1. *I. ink* (called also *sympathetic ink*), an ink which requires heat, vapour, or the like to make visible what is written in it. **2.** Langham called every day..but I was i. 1840.

B. *sb.* **1.** An invisible thing, person, or being 1646. **2.** One who denies the visible character of the Church; *spec.* in *pl.* certain German Protestants of the 16th c. 1818.

1. Swedenborg..with his invisibles LAMB. *The i.*, the unseen world; the Deity; The I. in things scarce seen reveal'd COWPER. Hence **Invisibi·lity, Invi·sibleness. Invi·sibly** *adv.*

†**Invi·sion.** [IN-³.] Want of vision; blindness of young animals. SIR T. BROWNE.

Invitation (invitēⁱ·ʃən). 1598. [– Fr. *invitation* or L. *invitatio*, f. *invitat-*, pa. ppl. stem of *invitare*; see INVITE *v.*, -ION.] **1.** The action of inviting to come, attend, or take part in something 1611. **b.** The spoken or written form in which a person is invited 1615. **c.** In the English Communion Service, the exhortation beginning 'Ye that do truly' 1883. **2.** *fig.* The presenting of attractions or inducements to come or advance; an instance of this; attraction; inducement 1598. **3.** *attrib.*, as *i.-performance*, one attended only by people invited 1808.

1. b. The invitations are out 1864. **2.** I spie entertainment in her;..she giues the leere of inuitation *Merry W.* I. iii. 50.

Invitatory (invəi·tătəri). ME. [– late L. *invitatorius* (esp. in med.L. senses), f. as prec.; see -ORY², ¹. Cf. (O)Fr. *invitatoire*.] **A.** *adj.* That invites or tends to invite; containing or conveying an invitation. **B.** *sb.* **1.** [= med.L. *invitatorium*.] An invitation 1666. **2.** *Eccl.* A form of invitation used in religious worship; *spec.* in the breviary, the antiphon to *Venite exultemus* at matins; in the Prayer Book, the invitatory psalm or *Venite* 1450.

I. psalm (*Eccl.*): the *Venite*, Psalm 95.

Invite (i·nvəit), *sb.* *colloq.* or *vulgar.* 1593. [f. next; cf. *request*, etc.] The act of inviting; an invitation.

Invite (invəi·t), *v.* 1533. [– Fr. *inviter* or L. *invitare*.] **1.** *trans.* Of a person: To ask (a person) graciously, kindly, or courteously, **a.** to come *to* (*into*, etc.) a place or proceeding 1553. **b.** *to do something* assumed to be agreeable 1583. **c.** To request 1854. †**d.** To try to attract or induce –1617. **e.** *fig.* Unintentionally to encourage (something) to come 1650. **2.** Of a thing: To present inducements to (a person) *to do* something or proceed *to* a place or action 1533. **b.** To tend to bring on 1599. †**c.** To attract physically –1800.

1. If thou be inuited of a mighty man, withdraw thy selfe, and so much the more will he inuite thee *Ecclus.* 13:9. **b.** She did not i. him to enter 1797. **c.** I never i. confidences W. BLACK. **e.** You threaten Peace, and you i. a War DRYDEN. **2.** The exemples of owre fathers..doo inuite vs hereunto EDEN. **b.** It seemed to i. discussion BURKE.

Invitee (invəitī·). 1837. [f. INVITE *v.* + -EE¹.] One who is invited.

Invitement (invəi·tmĕnt). Now *rare.* 1599. [– Fr. †*invitement* or L. *invitamentum*, f. *inviter*, *invitare*; see INVITE *v.*, -MENT.] †**1.** Inviting; an invitation –1639. **2.** Inducement; allurement 1627.

Inviter (invəi·təɹ). Also †**-or.** 1586. [f. INVITE *v.* + -ER¹.] One who invites. Hence **Invi·tress,** a female i. 1617.

Invitiate (invi·ʃiĕt), *a.* *rare.* 1590. [f. IN-³ + VITIATE *ppl. a.*] Without blemish.

Invi·ting, *ppl. a.* 1600. [f. INVITE *v.* + -ING².] **1.** That invites. **2.** Attractive; alluring; tempting 1604.

2. This Fruit Divine, Fair to the Eye, i. to the Taste MILT. *P.L.* IX. 777. Hence **Invi·ting-ly** *adv.*, **-ness.**

Invitrifiable (invi·trifəiᵢăb'l), *a.* 1796. [IN-³.] That cannot be vitrified or converted into glass.

Invocate (i·nvŏkeᵗt), *v.* Now *rare.* 1526. [– *invocat-*, pa. ppl. stem of L. *invocare*; see INVOKE, -ATE³.] **1.** *trans.* = INVOKE. †**2.** *intr.* To make invocation –1802.

1. Those old nine [Muses] which rimers inuocate SHAKS.

Invocation (invŏkēⁱ·ʃən). ME. [– (O)Fr. *invocation* – L. *invocatio*, f. as prec.; see -ION.] **1.** The action or an act of invoking or calling upon (God, a deity, etc.) in prayer or attestation; supplication for aid or protection. **b.** *Eccl.* A form of invocatory prayer. Also, The name or appellation used in invoking a divinity, etc. 1827. **2.** The action or an act of conjuring or summoning a devil or spirit by incantation; a charm, spell ME. **3.** *Admiralty Prize Procedure.* The calling in of papers or evidence from another case 1806.

1. I woll make i... Unto the god of sleepe anone CHAUCER. **2.** 'Tis a Greeke inuocation, to call fools into a circle SHAKS.

Invocatory (invǫ·kătəri, i·nvŏkēⁱtəri), *a.* 1691. [f. INVOCATION + -ORY², after *imprecation*, *imprecatory*.] Of the nature of, characterized by, or used in, invocation.

Invoice (i·nvois), *sb.* 1560. [orig. pl. of †INVOY (which is, however, recorded only later) – Fr. †*envoy*, *envoi*. See ENVOY *sb.*¹ For the sp. *-ce* cf. *dice*, *mice*, *pence*.] A list of the particular items of goods shipped or sent to a factor, consignee, or purchaser, with their value or prices, and charges. Also, *loosely*, A consignment of invoiced goods. Also *attrib.*

Invoice (i·nvois), *v.* 1619. [f. prec. sb.] *trans.* To make an invoice of, to enter in an invoice.

They should be invoiced at a reasonable and just price 1800.

Invoke (invōᵘ·k), *v.* 1490. [– (O)Fr. *invoquer*, – L. *invocare*, f. *in-* IN-² + *vocare* call.] **1.** *trans.* To call on (God, a deity, etc.) in prayer or as a witness; to appeal to for aid or protection; to summon or invite in prayer. **2.** To summon (a spirit) by charms or incantation; to conjure; also *fig.* 1602. **b.** To utter (a sacred *name*) in invocation 1698. **3.** To make supplication for, to implore 1617. **4.** *Admiralty Prize Procedure.* To call in evidence from a parallel case, or from the papers of a sister ship of the same owners, etc. 1802.

1. In witness of this our league, we i. the holy name of the living God 1777. **2.** Thou shalt stand by my side while I i. the phantom LYTTON. **3.** The spirits..who..i. the vengeance of Heaven on their destroyer 1832. Hence **Invo·ker,** one who invokes.

Involucel (invǫ·liusel). 1804. [– mod.L. *involucellum* (also used), dim. of INVOLUCRUM. Cf. Fr. *involucelle*.] *Bot.* A whorl of bracts surrounding one of the divisions in an inflorescence; a partial or secondary involucre. So **Involuce·llate** *a.* furnished with involucels.

Involucre (i·nvŏlᶦūkəɹ). 1578. [– Fr. *involucre* or L. *involucrum*; see next.] **1.** That which envelops or enwraps; a case, covering, envelope; *spec.* in *Anat.*, a membranous envelope, as the pericardium. Also *fig.* **2.** *Bot.* A whorl or rosette of bracts surrounding an inflorescence, or at the base of an umbel. **b.** In ferns, sometimes applied to the indusium. **c.** In fungi, the velum. 1787. **3.** *Zool.* = INVOLUCRUM 3. So **Involu·cral** *a.* of or pertaining to an i. 1845. **Involu·crate(d** 1830, **I·nvolucred** 1806 *adjs.* furnished with an i. **Involu·criform** *a.* having the form of an i. 1851.

‖**Involucrum** (invŏlᶦū·krŏm). Pl. **-a.** 1677. [L., f. *involvere* INVOLVE.] **1.** = INVOLUCRE 1. **2.** *Bot.* = INVOLUCRE 2. 1753. **3.** *Zool.* A kind of sheath about the base of the thread-cells of acalephs. HUXLEY.

Involuntary (invǫ·lŏntări), *a.* 1531. [– late L. *involuntarius*; see IN-³, VOLUNTARY. Cf. (O)Fr. *involontaire*.] **1.** Not voluntary; done or happening without exercise or without co-operation of the will; not done willingly or by choice; unintentional. **b.** *Physiol.* Concerned in bodily actions or processes which are independent of the will 1840. **2.** Unwilling 1597.

1. The i. closing of the eyelids when the surface of the eye is touched DARWIN. **2.** A vast i. throng POPE. Hence **Invo·luntarily** *adv.* **Invo·luntariness.**

Involute (i·nvŏlᶦut). 1661. [– L. *involutus*, pa. pple. of *involvere* INVOLVE.]

A. *adj.* **1.** Involved; intricate; †obscure 1669. **2.** Rolled or curled up spirally; spiral; *spec.* in *Conch.* Having the whorls wound closely round the axis, and nearly or wholly concealing it 1661. **3.** *Bot.* Rolled inwards at the edges 1760. **4.** *Geom.* †*I. figure* or *curve* = B. 2. –1796.

1. This most i. of Lies is finally winded off CARLYLE.

B. *sb.* **1.** Something involved or entangled (*rare*) 1845. **2.** *Geom.* A curve traced out by the end of a flexible inextensible string if unwound from a given curve in the plane of that curve, the locus of a point in a straight line which rolls without sliding on a given curve. Correl. to EVOLUTE. 1796.

Involuted (i·nvŏlᶦutĕd), *a.* 1797. [f. prec. + -ED¹.] **1.** = INVOLUTE *a.* 2, 3. **2.** *Phys.* That has passed through the process of involution (see INVOLUTION 4) 1898.

Involution (invŏlᶦū·ʃən). 1611. [– L. *involutio*, f. *involut-*, pa. ppl. stem of *involvere*; see INVOLVE *v.*, -ION. Cf. (O)Fr. *involution*.] **1.** The action of involving or fact of being involved; implication; also, quasi-*concr.*, that which is involved. **b.** *concr.* Something that involves or enwraps; a covering, etc. SIR T. BROWNE. **2.** An involved or entangled condition; complication; also *concr.*, something complicated; an intricate movement, etc. 1611. **3.** *Anat.* A rolling, curling, or turning inwards; *concr.* a part formed by this action 1851. **4.** *Phys.* The retrograde change which occurs in the body or in some organ in old age. Also *attrib.* 1860. **5.** *Math.* **a.** *Arith.* and *Alg.* The multiplication of a quantity into itself any number of times, so as to raise it to any assigned power 1706. **b.** *Geom.* A system of pairs of points on a straight line, so situated that the product of the distances of each pair from a fixed point on the line (the *centre of i.*) is constant 1847.

1. The i. or comprehension of Presbyter within Episcopus JER. TAYLOR. **2.** The style of the first act has..more i., than the general style of Fletcher HAZLITT. The involutions of an intricate dance 1858.

Involve (invǫ·lv), *v.* Also †**en-.** ME. [– L. *involvere*, f. *in*, IN-² + *volvere* roll.] **1.** *trans.* To roll or enwrap in anything; to enfold, envelop. Const. *in*, †*with*. ME. **2.** To wind in a spiral form; to wreath, coil, entwine 1555. **3.** *fig.* To envelop within the folds of some condition or circumstance ME.; to entangle, to render intricate 1533. **4.** To entangle (a person) in trouble, difficulties, perplexity, etc.; to embarrass. Const. *in*, †*with*, †*into*. ME. **5.** To implicate in a charge or crime 1655. **6.** To include; to contain, imply;

esp. to contain implicitly 1605. **7.** To roll up within itself; to overwhelm and swallow up 1605. **8.** *Math.* To multiply (a quantity) into itself any desired number of times; to raise to a power. Now *rare* or *Obs.* 1673.

1. I saw Fog only,..I. the passive city E. B. BROWNING. 2. Some of Serpent kinde,..involv'd Thir Snakie foulds MILT. *fig.* He knows His end with mine involvd MILT. 3. This passage is involved in great obscurity PALEY. 4. Involved in financial difficulties 1898. 5. Let not my Crime i. the Innocent 1695. 6. Mighty mysteries involved in numbers BERKELEY. Every argument involves some assumptions 1892. When the safety of the nation was involved U. S. GRANT. 7. The gathering number, as it moves along, Involves a vast involuntary throng POPE. 8. Let $a + x$ be involved to the 5th power HUTTON.

Involved (invǫ·lvd), *ppl. a.* 1607. [f. prec. + -ED¹.] **1.** In senses of prec. **†2.** Of persons, their actions, etc.; Not straightforward and open; underhand, reserved –1713.

Hence **Invo·lved-ly** *adv.*, **-ness.**

Involvement (invǫ·lvměnt). 1630. [f. as prec. + -MENT.] **1.** The action or process of involving; the fact of being involved 1706; that which is involved 1821. **†2.** A covering 1630.

†I·nvoy. [var. of ENVOY *sb.*¹ See INVOICE *sb.*] An INVOICE. MORYSON.

†Invu·lgar, *a.* 1604. [IN-³.] Not vulgar; refined; unusual –1627.

†Invu·lgar, *v.* 1599. [IN-².] *trans.* To divulge to the common people; to vulgarize.

Invu·lnerable, *a.* 1595. [– L. *invulnerabilis*; see IN-³, VULNERABLE.] Incapable of being wounded, hurt, or damaged (*lit.* and *fig.*).

Hence **Invu:lnerabi·lity, Invu·lnerableness. Invu·lnerably** *adv.*

†Invu·lnerate, *a.* 1680. [– L. *invulneratus*, f. *in-* IN-³ + *vulneratus*, pa. pple. of *vulnerare* wound.] Unwounded. So **†Invu·lnered** *a.* 1613–35.

Invultuation (invɒltiu,eⁱ·ʃən). 1856. Also **invultation.** [– med.L. *invultuatio* (XII) – *invultuare* (in OFr. *envouter* XIII) make a likeness, f. *in-* IN-² + *vultus* countenance, visage, likeness.] The making of a likeness, esp. the waxen effigy of a person for purposes of witchcraft.

Inwall (i·nwǭl), *sb.* 1611. [IN *adv.*] An inner or inside wall.

Inwall, *v.*, var. of ENWALL.

Inward (i·nwǫɹd). Comp. **†inwarder,** superl. **inwardest** (now *rare*). [OE. *innanweard, inneweard, inweard*, f. *innan, inne, inn* adv. and prep. + *-weard* (see -WARD).]

A. *adj.* **I. 1.** Situated within; that is the inner or inmost part; that is in or on the inside. **b.** Of the voice or a sound; Uttered without due opening of the mouth; muffled, indistinct. Also *transf.* of the utterer. 1774. **2.** Applied to the mind, thoughts, and mental faculties as located within the body; hence = mental or spiritual ME. **†b.** Deeply felt; hence, earnest, fervent –1627. **c.** Spiritually minded (?*Obs.*) 1450. **†3.** Intimate, familiar, confidential –1675. **†b.** Of a bird or beast: Domesticated, tame –1643. **†4.** Secret; private –1611. **5.** Domestic, intestine. *Obs.* or *arch.* 1513. **†6.** Intrinsic –1620.

1. b. The marten..when it sings, is so i. as scarce to be heard G. WHITE. 2. Behold, thou desirest trueth in the i. parts *Ps.* 51:6. *Inward man* = *inner man* (see INNER *a.* 2). 3. Friendly to all men, i. but with few QUARLES. 4. All i. grudges and open discordes HALL. 5. I. war amongst our selues MORE.

II. [From the adv.] Directed or proceeding towards the inside, as *i. postages* 1849.

B. *sb.* [absol. use of the adj.] **1.** The inward part, the inside; usu. *spec.* the internal parts or organs of the body, the entrails. (Now *rare* in *sing.*) OE. **2.** The inner nature or essence of a thing or person; that which is within; the interior character, qualities, thoughts, etc. (*rare* in *sing.*, *Obs.* in *pl.*) OE. **†3.** = INTIMATE *sb.* –1607. **4.** *pl.* Articles imported, or dues on such articles. Also *attrib.* 1761.

1. The intrailes or i. of beastes COGAN. The fat of the inwardes TINDALE. 3. Sir, I was an i. of his SHAKS.

Inward (i·nwǫɹd), *adv.* [OE. *innan-, inne-, inweard*; see prec.] **1.** Towards the inside or interior. **a.** Of motion OE. **b.** Of position ME. **2.** *fig.* Towards that which is within; into the mind or soul; into one's own thoughts ME. **b.** = INWARDLY *adv.* 3. OE.

1. a. Pathes..leading i. farr SPENSER. 2. Satiated with external pleasures, she turns i. 1766. b. We i. bled DRYDEN.

Inwardly (i·nwǫɹdli), *a. rare.* [OE. *inweardlić*, f. *inweard* + *-lić*, -LY¹.] **†a.** = INWARD *a.* –1504. **b.** Relating to what is inward or spiritual. COLERIDGE.

Inwardly (i·nwǫɹdli), *adv.* [OE. *inweardlīće*; see prec. and -LY².]

I. 1. In, on, or in reference to the inside or inner part; within 1483. **b.** With a voice that does not pass the lips; not aloud 1530. **2.** Intimately, thoroughly; closely ME. **3.** In heart; in mind or thought; in spirit ME. **†b.** In or from the inmost heart; fervently, earnestly –1632.

1. Therefore let Benedicke like couered fire.. waste i. *Much Ado* III. i. 78. b. Half i., half audibly she spoke TENNYSON. 3. They blesse with their mouth, but they curse i. *Ps.* 62:4.

II. Towards the inside or inner part; *fig.* towards that which is within; into the mind or soul (now *rare*) 1667.

Inwardness (i·nwǫɹdnės). ME. [f. INWARD *a.* + -NESS.] **†1.** The inner part or region; *pl.* Inward parts, entrails. Usu. *fig.* –1530. **2.** The inner nature, essence, or meaning 1605. **3.** The quality of being inward to something else (*lit.* or *fig.*) 1611. **†4.** Intimacy, familiarity –1715. **5.** Depth or intensity of feeling or thought 1836; spirituality 1859.

2. Sense cannot arrive to th' inwardnesse Of things HY. MORE. 4. In the..i. of conjugal conference STEELE. 5. This i. of the words of Christ JOWETT.

Inwards (i·nwǫɹdz), *adv.* [ME. *inwardes*, f. *inward* adv., with advb. gen. *-es, -s*, as in *besides*, etc; see -S *suffix*.] = INWARD *adv.*

Inweave (inwī·v), **enweave,** *v.* Pa. t. **-wove.** Pa. pple. **-woven** (also **†-weav'd, -wove**). 1578. [f. IN-¹ (or ²), EN-¹ + WEAVE *v.* Chiefly in pa. pple.] **1.** *trans.* To weave in; to weave (things) together; to interweave. Also *fig.* **2.** To insert (one thing) in or into another by weaving in or entwining. Const. *in, into* (*among, through*). 1596. Also *fig.* **3.** To combine *with* something inserted or entwined 1591. **4.** To form by weaving or plaiting 1667.

1. A living link in that Tissue of History, which inweaves all Being CARLYLE. 4. Down they cast Thir Crowns inwove with Amarant and Gold MILT.

Inwheel, var. of ENWHEEL *v. Obs.*

†Inwit. ME. [f. IN *adv.* + WIT *sb.* Not related to OE. *inwit, inwid* deceit.] **1.** Conscience; inward sense. Also *clean i.* = 'a clean heart'. ME. only. **2.** Reason, understanding; wisdom –1587. **3.** (tr. L. *animus*.) Heart, soul, mind; cheer, courage. WYCLIF.

Inwith (i·nwiþ). *Obs.* exc. *Sc.* ME. [f. IN *adv.* + WITH *prep.* Cf. WITHIN.] **A.** *prep.* Within, inside of. **†1.** Of place –1513. **†2.** Of time. ME. only.

1. This purs hath she i. her bosom hyd CHAUCER.

B. *adv.* **†1.** Denoting position: Within, inwardly –1565. **2.** Denoting direction: Inwards. *Sc.* 1768. **b.** Hence as *adj. Sc.* 1768.

Inwork (i:nwǒ·ɹk), *v. rare.* 1681. [IN-¹ or IN *adv.* See also INWROUGHT.] To work in or within (*trans.* and *intr.*).

Inworn, *ppl. a.* 1641. [IN *adv.*] **a.** as *pa. pple.* of *wear in*: Worn or pressed in. **b.** as *adj.* Inveterate.

Inwrap, -wreathe, etc.: see ENWRAP, etc.

Inwrought, *ppl. a.* Also **en-.** 1637. [f. IN *adv.* + *wrought*, pa. pple. of *work* vb.]

I. as *pa. pple.* (inrǭ·t). **1.** Of a fabric: Having something worked in by way of decoration (*lit.* and *fig.*). **2.** Of a pattern, etc. Worked into a fabric. Also *transf.* 1740. **3.** Worked together *with* something 1824; worked into anything as a constituent 1734.

1. His Mantle hairy, and his Bonnet sedge, I. with figures dim MILT. 2. Flowers enwrought On silken tissue WORDSW.

II. as *adj.* (i·nrǭt). (In senses as above.) 1830.

‖**Inyala** (inyā·lă). 1848. [Native name.] An antelope of S. Africa, *Tragelaphus angasi*, ranging from Nyasaland to Zululand.

Inyo·ke, *v. rare.* 1596. [IN-¹.] *trans.* **a.** To yoke or unite *to* something. **b.** To yoke in a wagon, etc.

Io (əi·o). 1593. [– L. *io*, Gr. ἰώ.] (Also *Io pæan.*) An exclam. of joy or triumph; occas. as *sb.*, an utterance of 'Io!', an exultant shout or song.

Io-, earlier spelling of JO-; see I, J, the letters.

Iod- (əi,od), comb. f. mod.L. *iodum* IODINE, used (chiefly before a vowel) in forming names of iodine compounds; as **iodhy·drin,** an iodine ether of glycerine; etc. Before a cons. usu. IODO-, q.v.

Iodal (əi·ǒdăl). 1838. [f. IOD- + AL(COHOL, after CHLORAL.] *Chem.* A compound of iodine, an oily liquid, analogous to chloral.

Iodate (əi·ǒdeⁱt), *sb.* 1826. [f. IODIC + -ATE⁴.] *Chem.* A salt of iodic acid. So **I·odate** *v.* to impregnate or treat with iodine.

†Iode. 1826. [– Fr. *iode* IODINE.] **1.** = IODINE 1830. **2.** = IODIDE.

Iodic (əi,ǫ·dik), *a.* 1826. [f. IOD- + -IC. Cf. Fr. *iodique* (Gay-Lussac, 1812).] Of or pertaining to iodine. **1.** *Chem.* Containing iodine in union with oxygen; as in *i. acid* (*hydrogen iodate*), an oxygen-acid of iodine. Also *Min.* in *i. silver* = IODYRITE. **2.** *Path.* Caused by administration of iodine 1887.

Iodide (əi·ǒdəid). 1822. [f. IOD- + -IDE.] *Chem.* A binary compound of iodine with a more positive element, or an organic radical.

Iodine (əi·ǒdin, -əin). 1814. [– Fr. *iode* (Gay-Lussac, 1812) – Gr. ἰώδης violet-coloured, f. ἴον violet + -ειδης like; see -OID, -INE⁵.] *Chem.* One of the non-metallic elements belonging to the halogen group; at ordinary temperatures a greyish-black soft brittle solid with a metallic lustre, volatilizing into a dense vapour of a deep violet colour; in chemical properties resembling chlorine and bromine, but less energetic. Symbol I; atomic weight 127. Also *attrib.*, as in *i. fluid, i. injection, i. poisoning.*

Iodine exists in sea-water and mineral springs, and in sea-weed and many marine animals, and is extensively obtained from the mother-liquor of Chilian sodium nitrate.

Iodism (əi·ǒdiz'm). 1832. [f. IOD- + -ISM.] *Path.* A morbid state induced by excessive or long-continued medicinal use of iodine (or its compounds).

Iodize (əi·ǒdəiz), *v.* 1841. [f. IOD- + -IZE.] *trans.* To treat or impregnate with iodine or an iodide. (Chiefly in *Photogr.* and *Med.*) Hence **I·odizer,** one who or that which iodizes.

Iodo- (əiǒdo), used as combining form of mod.L. *iodum* IODINE (chiefly bef. a cons.). Cf. IOD-.

Iodoform (əi,ōᵘ·dofǭɹm, əi·ǒdofǭɹm), *sb.* 1835. [f. IODO- + FORM(YL, after *chloroform*.] A compound of iodine (CHI_3), analogous to chloroform, obtained in light yellow scaly crystals, having an odour of saffron and a sweet taste; used medicinally, and as an antiseptic, esp. in surgical dressings. Hence **Io·doform, Iodofo·rmize** *vbs.* to treat or impregnate with i. **Iodofo·rmism,** poisoning by the medical use of iodoform.

I·odous, *a.* 1826. [f. IOD- + -OUS. Cf. Fr. *iodeux.*] **1.** *Chem.* Applied to compounds containing iodine in greater proportion to oxygen than those called *iodic*; e.g. a hypothetical *iodous acid*, HIO_2. **2.** Having the quality of, or resembling, iodine.

Iodyrite (əi,ǫ·dirəit). 1854. [f. IODINE, after *argyrite*; substituted by Dana for the earlier name *iodite*; see -ITE¹ 2 b.] *Min.* Native iodide of silver, a sectile mineral, usu. of a yellow colour.

Iolite (əi·ǒləit). 1810. [= G. *iolith* (Werner, 1808), f. Gr. ἴον violet + λίθος stone; see -LITE.] *Min.* A silicate of aluminium, iron, and magnesium, occurring in short orthorhombic crystals, or granular, of various shades of blue or violet-blue. Also called CORDIERITE or DICHROITE.

Ion (əi·ǫn). 1834. [– Gr. ἰόν, pr. pple. n. of ἰέναι go.] Either of the products (see ANION, CATION) which appear at the respective poles when a substance is subjected to electrolysis; hence, any of the electrically charged particles which are released by dissociation in an electrolyte; a molecule or atom considered electrically; a gaseous particle electrically charged by the action of Röntgen or other rays, etc.

-ion, *suffix*, repr. Fr. *-ion*, L. *-io, -ionem*, a suffix forming sbs. of condition or action from adjs. or sbs., occas. from the vb.-stem, but chiefly from the ppl. or supine stem in *t-, s-, x-*, e.g. *damnationem* condemning, *missionem*, sending, *co(n)nexionem* close union. Examples of all these occur in English, but chiefly those in *-tion* (*-sion, -xion*); the form in -ATION (q.v.) is the most frequent, and has become a living formative.

Ionian (əiˌōᵘ·niăn). 1563. [f. L. *Ionius* – Gr. Ἰώνιος + -AN.] **A.** *adj.* Of or pertaining to Ionia or to the Ionians; Ionic 1594.

Ionian mode (*Mus.*): **a.** A mode in ancient Greek music, characterized as soft and effeminate. **b.** The last of the 'authentic' ecclesiastical modes, having C for its final, and G for its dominant, corresp. to the modern major diatonic scale.

B. *sb.* A member of that division of the Hellenic race which occupied Attica and the northern coast of the Peloponnesus, and established colonies, esp. in Asia Minor, where a large district was named from them Ionia.

Ionic (əiˌǫ·nik), *a.*[1] and *sb.* 1579. [– L. *Ionicus* – Gr. Ἰωνικός; see -IC. Cf. Fr. *ionique* (XVI).] **A.** *adj.* **1.** = IONIAN *a.* **2.** *Arch.* Name of one of the three orders of Grecian architecture (Doric, Ionic, Corinthian), characterized by the two lateral volutes of the capital 1585. **3.** *Mus.* (See *Ionian mode*, a, above.) ?*Obs.* 1579. **4.** *Gr.* and *Lat. Pros.* Name of a foot consisting of two long syllables followed by two short ('ionic *a majore*'), or two short followed by two long ('ionic *a minore*'). *I. metre*, a metre consisting of Ionic feet. So †**Io·nical** *a.* 1624.

1. *I. dialect*, the most important of the three main branches of ancient Greek, of which also the Attic was a development. *I. School* or *Sect of philosophy*, that founded by Thales of Miletus in Asiatic Ionia.

B. *sb.* †**1.** = IONIAN *sb.*; a member of the Ionic School of philosophy –1613. **2.** The Ionic dialect of ancient Greece 1668. **3.** *Gr.* and *Lat. Pros.* An Ionic foot or verse; Ionic metre; see A. 4. 1612.

Hence **Io·nicize** *v. intr.* to use Ionic; *trans.* to render Ionic (in style or dialect).

Io·nic, *a.*[2] 1890. [f. ION + -IC.] *Physics.* Of or pertaining to ions.

I·onize, *v.* 1898. [f. ION + -IZE.] **1.** *intr.* Of an electrolyte; To split into ions 1899. **2.** *trans.* Of X rays, cathode rays, etc.: To produce ions in a gas and so make it a conductor. So **Ioniza·tion.**

-ior, *suffix*, repr. L. *-ior* of comparatives, as *inferior*, etc.; formerly *-iour* = Fr. *-ieur*.

Iota (əiˌōᵘ·tă). 1592. [– Gr. ἰῶτα, of Phœnician origin (cf. Heb. *yôḏ*). See JOT *sb.*[1]] **1.** The name of the Greek letter I, ι, corresp. to the Roman I, i, the smallest letter in the Greek alphabet 1607. **2.** *fig.* (after Matt. 5:18; see JOT): The least, or a very small, particle or quantity; an atom. (Usu. with negative.)

1. *Iota subscript*, a small iota written beneath a long vowel, forming the second element of a diphthong, as in ᾳ, ῃ, ῳ. **2.** Not an i. should be yielded of the principle of the bill BURKE.

Iotacism (əiˌōᵘ·tăsiz'm). 1656. [– late L. *iotacismus* – late Gr. ἰωτακισμός, f. ἰῶτα (see prec.) + -ισμός -ISM with hiatus-filling κ.] Excessive use or repetition of the letter *iota* or I; *spec.* the pronunciation of other Greek vowels like *iota* (i.e. as Latin *ī* or mod.Eng. *ee*), as in mod.Greek. So **Io·tacist.**

I O U (ǫi:ōᵘ:yū·). 1795. [= 'I owe you'. The abbreviation occurs 1618.] A document bearing these three letters followed by a specified sum, and signed, constituting a formal acknowledgement of a debt.

An I.O.U. is admissible evidence of a debt without a stamp 1795.

-iour, a compound suffix, viz. -OUR (OFr. *-ur, -or*, Fr. *-eur*), preceded by an *i* representing *i, ei, e*, of another element; as in *saviour*, ME. and AFr. *sauveour*, OFr. *sauve-ur, -e-or*, early Fr. *salvedur* :– L. *salvator-*; see also HAVIOUR and -OUR. Sometimes now written *-ior* (as *warrior*), *-ier* (as *soldier*).

-ious, a compound suffix, viz. -OUS, added to an *i* which is part of another suffix, repr. L. *-iosus*, Fr. *-ieux*, with sense 'characterized by, full of'. See -ITIOUS and -OUS.

Ipecac, shortened form of next. 1788.

Ipecacuanha (ipĭkækiuˌæ·nă). 1682. [– Pg. *ipecacuanha* (ipekakwa·nʸă) – Tupi-Guarani *ipe-kaa-guéne* 'low or creeping plant causing vomit' (Cavalcanti).] **1.** The root of *Cephaëlis ipecacuanha*, N.O. *Cinchonaceæ*, a S. Amer. small shrubby plant, which possesses emetic, diaphoretic, and purgative properties; also applied to the forms in which the drug is employed. **2.** The plant itself 1788. **3.** Transferred to other plants whose roots have emetic properties, e.g.

Bastard or **Wild I.** (*Asclepias curassavica*); **Peruvian, Striated,** or **Black I.** (*Psychotria emetica*); **White I.** (*Richardsonia scabra*)

4. *fig.* Something that produces nausea 1763. **5.** *attrib.*, as **i. wine,** the filtered infusion of the root in wine 1761.

4. An author, talking of his own works..is to me a dose of i. H. WALPOLE.

Ipocras, obs. f. HIPPOCRAS.

‖**Ipomœa** (əipomī·ă). Also **ipomæa, ipomea.** 1794. [mod.L. (Linn.), f. Gr. ἴψ ἰπο-, worm + ὅμοιος like.] *Bot.* A genus of twining or creeping plants, mostly tropical, N.O. *Convolvulaceæ*, with trumpet- or salver-shaped corolla; many of the species are cultivated as flowering plants, and one, *I. batatas*, furnishes the sweet potato. Hence **Ipomœ·ic** *a.* of Ipomœa, in *i. acid*, named from *Ipomœa jalapa*, jalap.

‖**Ipse dixit** (i·psi di·ksit). *Pl.* **ipse dixits.** 1572. [L., 'he himself said' (it); tr. Gr. αὐτὸς ἔφα, phr. used of Pythagoras by his followers.] An unproved assertion resting on the bare authority of some speaker; a dogmatic statement; a dictum.

The capricious *ipse dixit* of authority J. H. NEWMAN.

Ipseity (ipsī·ˌiti). 1659. [f. L. *ipse* self + -ITY, after EGOITY.] Personal identity and individuality; selfhood.

‖**Ipso facto** (i·psoᵘ fæ·ktoᵘ), *advb. phr.* 1548. [L.] By that very fact; by the fact itself.

Ir-[1], assimilated form in L. of IN-[2] bef. initial *r*, used in the same way in Eng., as in *ir-radiate*, etc.

Ir-[2], assimilated form in L. of IN-[3] bef. initial *r*, used in the same way in Eng., as in *ir-rational*, etc.

Iracund (əiᵊrăkɒnd), *a.* 1821. [– L. *iracundus*, f. *ira* + *-cundus* 'inclining to'.] Inclined to wrath; choleric, passionate. So †**Iracu·ndious** *a.* 1491–1662. **Iracu·ndity** 1840.

‖**Irade** (*ira·de*). 1883. [Turk. – Arab. *'irāda* will, decree.] A written decree issued by the Sultan of Turkey.

Iranian (əirē^i^niăn). 1789. [f. *īrān*, native name of Persia + -IAN.] **A.** *adj.* **1.** Of or pertaining to Iran or Persia; in *Compar. Philol.* applied to one of the two Asiatic families of the Indo-European languages, comprising Zend and Old Persian and their cognates. †**2. a.** Aryan. **b.** Indo-Iranian. –1850. So **Ira·nic** *a.*

B. *sb.* A member of the Iranian race; a speaker of an Iranian language 1789.

Irascible (əiræ·sĭb'l, iræ·s-), *a.* ME. [– (O)Fr. *irascible* – late L. *irascibilis*, f. *irasci* grow angry, f. *ira* IRE; see -IBLE.] Easily provoked to anger or resentment; prone to anger; irritable, choleric, passionate. **b.** Characterized by or arising from anger 1659.

A solitary and i. old gentleman 1873. **b.** I., and objurgatory speech 1659. Hence **Irascibi·lity, Ira·scibleness. Ira·scibly** *adv.*

Irate (əirē^i^·t), *a.* 1838. [– L. *iratus*, f. *ira* IRE; see -ATE[2].] Excited to ire; incensed, enraged, angry.

He was at once hauled up before the i. Commandant LIVINGSTONE. Hence **Ira·tely** *adv.*, in an i. manner.

Ire (əiᵊɹ). ME. [– (O)Fr. *ire* :– L. *ira* anger.] Anger; wrath. Now chiefly *poet.* and *rhet.*

Ireful (əiᵊ·ɹfŭl), *a.* ME. [f. IRE + -FUL.] **1.** Full of ire; angry, wrathful. **2.** Choleric, passionate ME. Hence **I·reful-ly** *adv.*, **-ness.**

Irenarch (əiᵊ·rĭnāɹk). 1702. [– late L. *irenarcha, -es* (Dig.) – Gr. εἰρηνάρχης; see EIRENARCH.] An Eastern provincial governor or keeper of the peace, under the Roman and Byzantine empires. Now *Hist.*

Irenic (əire·nik, əirī·nik). 1864. [– Gr. εἰρηνικός, f. εἰρήνη peace; see -IC. Cf. EIRENIC, Fr. *irénique*.] *adj.* Pacific, non-polemic. *sb. pl.* **Irenics:** irenical theology 1882.

Irenical (əire·nikăl, əirī·nikăl), *a.* 1660. [f. as prec. + -AL[1]; see -ICAL.] Peaceful, pacific; tending to promote peace, esp. in relation to theological or eccl. differences.

‖**Irenicon** (əirī·nikǫ̆n, əire·nikǫ̆n). 1618. [– Gr. εἰρηνικόν, subst. use of n. of εἰρηνικός adj.; see IRENIC, and cf. EIRENICON.] A proposal designed to promote peace; esp. in a church or between churches. So ‖**Ire·nicum.**

Irian (əiᵊ·riăn), *a.* 1857. [irreg. f. IRIS + -AN.] *Anat.* Belonging to the iris of the eye.

Iricism (əiᵊ·risiz'm). 1743. [irreg. f. IRISH, after *Scotticism*.] An Irishism.

Irid (əiᵊ·rid). *rare.* 1822. [– ἰριδ-, stem of Gr. ἶρις IRIS.] **1.** The iris of the eye. **2.** *Bot.* A plant of N.O. *Iridaceæ* 1866.

Iridaceous (əiᵊridē^i^·ʃəs, iri-), *a.* 1851. [f. mod.L. *iridaceus* (f. L. *iris, irid-* – Gr.; see prec.) + -OUS; cf. -ACEOUS.] *Bot.* Related to plants of the genus *Iris*; belonging to the N.O. *Iridaceæ*.

Iridal (əiᵊ·ridăl), *a. rare.* 1837. [f. L. *iris, irid-* Iris + -AL[1].] Of or belonging to the rainbow.

Iridectomy (əiᵊride·ktŏmi, iri-). 1855. [f. as prec. + Gr. ἐκτομή excision; see -TOMY.] *Surg.* Excision of a portion of the iris. Also *attrib.*

Iridescence (iride·sĕns). 1803. [f. IRIDESCENT; see -ENCE.] The quality of being iridescent; the interchange of colours as in the rainbow, mother-of-pearl, etc.; a play of glittering and changing colours. Also *fig.*

A rich metallic i. COUES. *fig.* Frequent iridescences of fancy 1803. So **Iride·scency** (?*Obs.*) 1799.

Iridescent (iride·sĕnt), *a.* 1796. [f. L. *iris, irid-* IRIS + -ESCENT.] Displaying colours like those of the rainbow, etc.; glittering or flashing with interchanging colours. Also *fig.*

The i. colours produced by heat on polished steel and copper MRS. SOMERVILLE. **Iride·scently** *adv.*

Iridian (əiri·diăn), *a.* 1864. [f. as prec. + -IAN.] **1.** Pertaining to the iris of the eye. **2.** Rainbow-like 1884.

Iridic (əiri·dik), *a.* 1845. [f. IRIDIUM + -IC.] *Chem.* Containing iridium; applied to compounds in which iridium is quadrivalent.

Iridious (əiri·diəs), *a.* 1865. [f. IRIDIUM + -OUS.] *Chem.* Containing iridium; applied to compounds in which iridium is trivalent.

Iridium (əiri·diŏm). 1804. [mod.L., f. L. *iris, irid-* IRIS + -IUM.] A white metal of the platinum group, resembling polished steel, and fusible with great difficulty, found (usu. with osmium) in native platinum, and in the native alloy IRIDOSMIUM. Chemical symbol Ir; atomic weight 193.

I should incline to call this metal *Iridium*, from the striking variety of colours which it gives, while dissolving in marine acid TENNANT.

Iridize (i·r-, əiᵊ·ridəiz), *v.* 1864. [f. L. *irid-* (see prec.) or IRIDIUM + -IZE.] **1.** *trans.* To make iridescent 1874. **2.** To cover or tip with iridium. Hence **I:ridiza·tion,** irisation; in *Path.*, the coloured halo seen round a light by persons affected with glaucoma.

Irido- (əiᵊ·rido, i·rido), – comb. form of ἶρις, ἰριδ- IRIS, used in forming pathological and surgical terms, chiefly denoting diseases of the iris and operations upon it; as **I:rido-dia·lysis,** the artificial separation of the iris from the ciliary ring; **I:ridodone·sis** [Gr. δονεῖν to shake], tremulousness of the iris; etc.

Iridodesis (əiᵊridǫ·dĭsis). 1858. [f. IRIDO- + δέσις binding.] *Surg.* An operation in which the iris is secured in a certain position by a ligature.

Iridoline (əiri·doləin). 1863. [f. L. *irid-* IRIS + *oleum* oil + -INE[5].] *Chem.* A base ($C_{10}H_9N$) occurring in coal-tar oil.

Iridosmine (əiᵊridǫ·sməin, iri-). 1827. [f. IRID(IUM + OSM(IUM + -INE[5].] A native alloy of the metals iridium and osmium, usually occurring in flattened grains with platinum. Also **Irido·smium,** and *osmiridium*.

Iridotomy (əiᵊridǫ·tŏmi, iri-). 1855. [f. IRIDO- + -TOMY.] Section of the iris.

Iris (əiᵊ·ris), *sb.* Pl. **irides** (əiᵊ·ridīz), **irises.** ME. [– L. *iris* – Gr. ἶρις, ἰριδ-. The pl. *irides* is chiefly used in sense 4.] **1.** *Gr. Myth.* The goddess who acted as the messenger of the gods, and displayed as her sign the rainbow; hence, allusively, a messenger 1593. **2.** A rainbow; a many-coloured refraction of light from drops of water 1490. **b.** *transf.* A rainbow-like appearance; a circle or halo of prismatic colours 1601. **c.** *fig.* 1821. **3. a.** A hexagonal prismatic crystal (Pliny *Nat. Hist.* XXXVII. ix. 52). **b.** A variety of rock crystal, having the property of reflecting the prismatic colours by means of natural flaws in its interior ME. **4.** *Anat.* A flat, circular, coloured membrane suspended vertically in the aqueous humour of the eye, and separating the anterior from the posterior chamber; in its centre is a circular opening called the pupil 1525. **b.** (*transf.*) *Entom.* The inner ring of an ocellated spot on an insect's wing 1826. **5.** *Bot.* A genus of plants, the type of the natural order *Iridaceæ*; most of the species have tuberous (less commonly bulbous or fibrous) roots, sword-shaped equitant leaves, and showy flowers; formerly often called Fleur-de-lis or Flower-de-luce. Also, a plant of this genus. 1578.

1. 2 *Hen. VI*, III. ii. 407. **2.** His Crest, that prouder then blew I. bends SHAKS. **b.** In the Spring a livelier i. changes on the burnish'd dove TENNYSON. **c.** Is Virtue but a shade? And Freedom but the i. of a storm? DISRAELI.

Comb.: **i.-diaphragm,** a contractile diaphragm for lenses, contrived so as to imitate the action of the i.; **-disease,** a form of herpes, generally affecting the back of the hands; **-root,** the root of *Iris florentina*, orris-root.

Iris (əiᵊ·ris), *v.* 1816. [f. prec.] *trans.* To make iridescent; to form into, or place as, a rainbow. Only in *pa. pple.*

Irisate (əiᵊ·riseᶦt), *v.* 1828. [irreg. f. IRIS *sb.* + -ATE³.] *trans.* To render iridescent. Hence **I·risated** *ppl. a.*, **Irisa·tion.**

Iriscope (əiᵊ·riskōᵘp). 1841. [irreg. f. IRIS *sb.* 2 + -SCOPE.] A device for exhibiting the primary colours by the action of the breath on a specially prepared plate of highly polished black glass.

Irised (əiᵊ·rist), *a.* 1816. [f. IRIS *sb.* or *v.* + -ED.] **1.** Having the colours of the rainbow. **2.** Having an iris or irises; as *large-irised* 1879.

Irish (əiᵊ·riʃ). ME. [f. OE. *Īras* inhabitants of *Īrland* Ireland (obscurely based on OIr. *Ériu*: see HIBERNIAN) + -ISH¹ (cf. ON. *Írskr*).]

A. *adj.* **1.** Of persons: Of, belonging to, or native to Ireland; orig. and esp. used of the Celtic inhabitants ME. †**b.** Belonging to the Scottish Highlands or the Gaelic inhabitants of them –1652. **2.** Of things: Of or pertaining to Ireland or its inhabitants (freq. denoting a species, variety, or quality peculiar to Ireland) ME. **3.** Epithet of the language of the Celtic inhabitants of Ireland. Hence applied to words, idioms, etc. belonging to that language, and to anything composed or written in it 1547. **4.** Having what are considered Irish characteristics 1589.

1. Irish Free State: see FREE STATE 3. **2.** *I. car, frieze, whisky*, etc.; also *I. elk, greyhound, wolf, wolf-hound*, etc. **I. daisy,** the dandelion. **I. moss,** the edible seaweed *Chondrus crispus*, also called carrageen. **I. blackguard, bull, stew** (see the sbs.). **I. diamond,** rock crystal. **4.** They laugh'd at such an i. blunder, To take the noise of brass for thunder SWIFT.

B. *sb.* (The adj. used ellipt.) **1. a.** as *pl.* The inhabitants of Ireland, or their descendants, esp. those of Celtic race ME. **b.** In *sing.* (with pl. *Irishes*). An Irishman. (Chiefly *Sc.*) 1613. **2.** The Irish language ME. †**b.** Scottish Gaelic; ERSE –1723. †**3.** An old game resembling backgammon –1664. **4.** *ellipt.*, e.g. for Irish linen, snuff, whisky, etc. 1799.

†*To weep I.*, to shed crocodile tears.

Irishism (əiᵊ·riʃiz'm). 1734. [f. IRISH + -ISM.] An Irish peculiarity, esp. of expression; a Hibernicism; an Irish bull.

Irishman (əiᵊ·riʃmæ̆n). *Pl.* **-men.** ME. [f. IRISH *a.* + MAN.] A native of Ireland; a man of Irish race. So **I·rishwoman** ME.

Irishry (əiᵊ·riʃri). *Hist.* or *arch.* ME. [f. IRISH *a.* + -RY.] **1.** *collect.* The native Irish. **2.** Irish character or nationality; an Irish trait 1834.

1. They that refuse to be under lawes..are tearmed the I., and commonly the Wilde Irish P. HOLLAND.

Iritis (əirəi·tis). 1818. [– G. *iritis* (1801), irreg. f. *iris* IRIS + -ITIS.] *Path.* Inflammation of the iris. Hence **Iri·tic** *a.* pertaining to or affected with i.; affecting the iris.

Irk (ɔ̄ɹk), *v. arch.* ME. [Of obsc. origin; its first appearance in Scandinavianized areas has suggested deriv. from ON. *yrkja* WORK, Sw. *yrka* claim, demand, insist.] †**1.** *intr.* To grow weary or tired; to feel disgusted; to be loath –1797. †**2.** *trans.* To be weary of or disgusted with; to loathe –1628. **3.** Of a thing: To affect with weariness, dislike, or disgust; to bore (*arch.*) 1513. **b.** impers. *It irks* (*me*), it wearies, annoys, troubles me; = L. *piget* 1483. *arch.*

3. Irks care the crop-full bird? BROWNING. **b.** It irk'd him to be here, he could not rest M. ARNOLD. †So **Irk** *a.*, weary, disgusted. ME.

Irksome (ɔ̄·ɹksŏm), *a.* ME. [f. IRK *v.* + -SOME¹.] †**1.** Tired; disgusted; bored. Const. *of*. –1590. **2.** Wearisome, tedious; burdensome, annoying. Formerly also, Distressing; in early use, Loathsome 1513.

2. Not to irksom toile, but to delight He made us MILT. *P.L.* IX. 242. **I·rksome-ly** *adv.*, **-ness.**

Iron (əi·əɹn), *sb.*¹ [OE. *īren*, perh. for **īrern*, alt. of *īsern* (by assoc. with the var. *īsen*) = OS., OHG. *īsarn* (Du. *ijzen*, G. *eisen*), ON. *ísarn*, Goth. *eisarn* :– Gmc. **īsarnam*, prob. – Celtic **īsarno-*, prob. rel. to L. *æs* (earlier *ais*) bronze, OE. *ār*, Goth. *aiz*, Skr. *áyas*.] **1.** A metal, the most abundant and useful of those used in the metallic state; very variously employed for tools, implements, machinery, constructions, and in many other applications.

Pure iron is soft and of a silver-white colour, but is scarcely known; the metal as commonly used has usually an admixture of carbon, and varies in colour from tin-white to dark grey. It is of three kinds, differing in the amount of carbon present: *malleable iron*, or WROUGHT *iron*, which is comparatively soft, very tenacious, fusible only at a very high temperature, and capable at a red heat of being hammered or rolled into any required shape; CAST IRON, which is hard and brittle, and fusible at a lower temperature; and STEEL, which partakes of the properties of both. Iron is very rarely found native, but is obtained from its ores, which are chiefly oxides or salts of the metal. Chemically, iron is a metallic element; symbol Fe (*ferrum*); atomic weight, 56. In alchemy it was represented by the sign for the planet Mars (♂).

b. With *an* and *pl.* A variety or sort of iron 1858. **c.** *Med.* A preparation of iron, used in medicine as a tonic 1803. **2.** With defining attribute; see also BAR (*sb.*¹), BOG (*sb.*¹), CAST-, PIG-IRON, WHITE, WROUGHT, etc. 1632. **3.** In fig. uses, as a type of extreme hardness or strength 1612. **4.** An instrument, utensil, or part of one, made of iron. (CURLING-*iron*, etc.) OE. **b.** *esp.* A brand-iron ME. †**c.** *pl.* Dies used in striking coins –1848. **d.** *Golf.* A golf-club having an iron head with an angle of loft between that of a mashie and that of a cleek 1857. **e.** *slang.* A portable fire-arm; a pistol 1836. **f.** *pl.* Iron supports for the legs. etc. **5.** *esp.* An implement of iron used when heated to smooth out linen, etc.; usu. defined, as BOX-*iron*, FLAT-IRON, etc. ME. **6.** †**a.** An iron weapon; a sword. **b.** Used (without *an* and *pl.*) with reference to warfare or slaughter. OE. **7.** An iron shackle or fetter; usu. in *pl.* OE. **8.** *attrib.* Of or pertaining to iron 1530.

3. Beare witnesse, all that haue not hearts of I. SHAKS. **4. b.** Hauing their conscience seared with a hote i. 1 *Tim.* 4:2. **6.** Meddle you must that's certain, or forsweare to weare i. about you SHAKS. Bismarck..is known throughout the world as 'the man of blood and iron' 1898. **7.** *In irons*, said of a person having the feet or hands fettered. Also *fig.* (*Naut.*) A square-rigged vessel is said to be *in irons* when, the yards being so braced that some sails are laid aback in coming up into the wind, she will not 'cast' or turn either way. Phr. *The i. entered into his soul*, Ps. 105[4]:18, a mistranslation of the Heb. (lit. 'his person entered into the iron', i.e. fetters, chains), now used fig. to express the impression made by captivity, affliction, or hard usage, upon the inmost being of the sufferer.

Phrases. *To strike while the i. is hot*: to act at the appropriate time. *To have* (or *put*) *many* (*too many*, etc.) *irons in the fire*: (*a*) to have or be engaged in (too) many occupations or undertakings; (*b*) to have or use several expedients to attain a purpose.

Combs. **1.** General: as in *i.-filings*, *-furnace*, etc.; *i.-using* adj.; *i.-smelling* sb.; *i.-branded* adj.; *i.-black*; *i.-brown*, *-red* adjs.

2. Special: **i.-cement,** a kind of very hard cement; **-clay** *a.*, of mixed iron and clay; **-cloth,** chain-mail; **i. cross** a Prussian order, conferred for bravery in war; **-fall,** a fall of meteoric i.; **-free** *a.*, free from i.; †proof against the force of i.; **i. period** (*Archæol.*) = IRON AGE 2; **-sponge,** i. in a loose state with little cohesion (see SPONGE); **-stain,** a stain produced by iron-rust or tincture of i., or on a plant by a fungus; **-yellow,** Mars yellow.

b. Esp. in names of chemical compounds and minerals; as **i.-clay,** same as *clay ironstone* (see CLAY *sb.*); **-flint,** ferruginous quartz; **-glance,** specular iron-ore (see GLANCE *sb.*²); **i. pyrites,** native bisulphuret of i. (see PYRITES).

†**Iron,** *sb.*² 1623. [app. a var. of *eren* ERNE, eagle.] In 17th c. dicts., A male eagle –1688.

Iron (əi·əɹn), *a.* [OE. *īsern*, *īsen*, *īren*, f. **īsern-en*, etc. In most mod. uses indistinguishable from the sb. used attrib.] **1.** Of iron; consisting or formed of iron. (L. *ferreus.*) **2.** Having the appearance of iron; of the colour of iron (or iron-rust) 1613. **3.** *fig.* Resembling iron in some quality, esp. hardness. **a.** Extremely hard or strong ME. **b.** Extremely hardy or robust; enduring 1617. **c.** Firm, inflexible; unyielding 1602. †**d.** Unimpressionable –1651. **e.** Harsh, cruel, merciless; severe 1591. **f.** Of or pertaining to the IRON AGE (q.v.); debased; wicked. (Sometimes mixed with prec. sense.) 1592. **g.** In phr. *i. sleep* or *slumber*, tr. L. *ferreus somnus* (Virg. *Æn.* X. 745). Chiefly *poet.* 1624.

1. Luke's i. crown, and Damien's bed of steel GOLDSM. **2.** A Knight of..i. hue 1632. **3. a.** Thy necke is an yron Sinew *Isa.* 48:4. **b.** The i. frame wasted by inward trouble 1864. **c.** Their ever-loyal i. leader TENNYSON. **e.** Her i. yoke BURKE. **f.** The bigots of the i. time SCOTT.

Phrases with specialized sense: **I. Crown,** the ancient crown of the kings of Lombardy, so called from having a circlet of i. inserted (reputed to have been made from one of the nails of the Cross); **i. horse,** a locomotive steam-engine; **i. walls,** the ironclad ships of the British navy, regarded as a defence to the country (cf. *wooden walls*).

Iron (əi·əɹn), *v.* ME. [f. IRON *sb.*¹] **1.** *trans.* To fit, furnish, cover, or arm with iron. (Chiefly in pa. pple.) **2.** To shackle with irons; to put in irons 1653. **3.** To smooth or press with a heated flat-iron, as cloth, etc. 1680. **b.** *fig.* esp. with *out* 1863.

2. The miserable victimes were imprisoned, ironed, scourged BURKE. **3.** The servants are all ironing 1789. **b.** The differences [are] amicably ironed out 1905.

Iron age. 1592. [See IRON *a.* 3 f.] **1.** *Gr. and Roman Mythol.* The last and worst age of the world, succeeding the Golden, Silver, and Brazen Ages. Hence *allusively*, An age or period of wickedness, debasement, etc. **2.** *Archæol.* That period, subsequent to the *stone age* and *bronze age*, in which iron weapons and implements were or are used by mankind. Hence *transf.*, a period characterized by the general use of iron. 1879.

I·ron-bark. 1802. [Austral-Eng., f. IRON *a.* or *sb.*¹ + BARK.] Any species of *Eucalyptus* having solid bark, as *E. resinifera*, *paniculata*, *Leucoxylon*, etc., trees valued for their timber. Also, the wood of any of these. Also *attrib.*

Iron-bound, *a.* ME. [f. IRON *sb.*¹ + pa. pple. of BIND *v.* (With shifting stress.)] **1.** Bound with iron; also, fettered. **2.** *transf.* Of a coast; Rock-bound 1769. **3.** *fig.* Rigorously confined or restricted; unimpressionable; hard and fast 1807.

1. Yren-bound coffres ME. **2.** An iron-bound coast 1852. **3.** The old iron-bound, feudal France EMERSON.

I·ron-cased (-kēᶦst), *a.* 1859. [f. IRON *sb.*¹ + *cased*, pa. pple. of CASE *v.*] Cased in iron; applied to ships of war, now called IRONCLAD.

I·ronclad, iron-clad. 1852. [See CLAD *ppl. a.*]

A. *adj.* **1.** Clad in iron; protected or covered with iron; *esp.* of a ship of war: Cased wholly or partly with thick plates of iron or steel, as a defence against shot, etc. **2.** *fig.* (Chiefly *U.S.*) Of an extremely strict or rigorous character, as a regulation, agreement, etc. 1884.

1. Two powerful iron-clad rams 1878. **2.** *I. oath*: an oath characterized by the severity of its requirements and penalties. Bills..full of the most arbitrary and 'iron-clad' provisions 1887.

B. *sb.* An ironclad ship: see A. 1. 1862.

Ironer (əi·əɹnəɹ). 1857. [f. IRON *v.* + -ER¹.] One who irons; *spec.* one whose occupation it is to iron clothes, etc.

I·ron-fou:nder. 1817. [f. IRON *sb.*[1] + FOUNDER *sb.*[2]] One who founds or casts iron. So **I·ron-fou:nding; I·ron-fou:ndry** 1784.

Iron-grey, -gray. [OE. *īsen-grǣġ.*] **A.** *adj.* Of the grey colour of freshly broken iron, or of dark hair when turning grey. **B.** *sb.* **1.** An iron-grey colour 1552. **2.** An iron-grey horse or dog 1523.

Iron-handed, *a.* 1768. [f. *iron hand* + -ED[2].] Having a 'hand of iron'; inflexible; severe, rigorous, despotic.
The iron-handed goddess, Necessity TUCKER.

I·ronheads (-hedz). 1863. A local name of the Knapweed (*Centaurea nigra*), from its hard involucre.

I·ron-hea:rted, *a.* 1618. [-ED[2].] Extremely hard-hearted; unfeeling; cruel.

Ironic (əirǫ·nik), *a.* 1614. [– Fr. *ironique* or late L. *ironicus* – Gr. εἰρωνικός dissembling, putting on a feigned ignorance; see IRONY, -IC.] Pertaining to irony; uttering or given to irony; of the nature of or containing irony.
An i. man..more especially an i. young man.. may be viewed as a pest to society CARLYLE.

Ironical (əirǫ·nikăl), *a.* 1576. [f. as prec.; see -ICAL.] **1.** Of the nature of irony; meaning the opposite of what is expressed. **2.** That uses or is given to irony 1589. †**3.** Dissembling; feigned, pretended (*rare*) –1727.
1. A bitterly i. compliment to Bentley's courtesy 1853. **2.** Socrates..got the name of..the i. philosopher 1793. Hence **Iro·nical-ly** *adv.*, **-ness.**

Ironing (əi·əɹniŋ), *vbl. sb.* 1710. [f. IRON *v.* + -ING[1].] **1.** The pressing and smoothing of clothes, etc., with a heated iron. Also *attrib.* **2.** The putting (*of* persons) in irons (*rare*) 1820.

I·ronish, *a.* Now *rare.* 1450. [f. IRON *sb.*[1] + -ISH[1].] †**1.** Of iron. **2.** Partaking of the qualities of iron; irony; ferruginous 1641.

Ironist (əiᵊ·rŏnist). 1727. [f. Gr. εἴρων dissembler, user of irony + -IST.] One who uses irony.

I·ronma:ster. 1674. The master of an iron-foundry or ironworks; a manufacturer of iron, esp. on a large scale.

I·ron-mine. 1601. **1.** A mine from which iron-ore is obtained. **2.** Iron-ore. Now *dial.* 1645.

Ironmonger (əi·əɹnmɒ:ŋgəɹ). ME. [f. IRON *sb.*[1] + MONGER.] A dealer in ironware; a hardware merchant.

Ironmongery (əi·əɹnmɒ:ŋgəri). 1711. [f. prec.; see -ERY.] **1.** Hardware; a general name for all articles made of iron. **b.** An ironmonger's shop 1841. **2.** Smith's work 1871. **3.** *attrib.* 1769.

Iron-mould, -mold (əi·əɹnmōᵘld), *sb.* 1601. [f. IRON *sb.*[1] + *mould*, earlier *mole* MOLE *sb.*[1]] A spot or discoloration on cloth, etc., caused by iron-rust or an ink-stain. Also *fig.* Hence **I·ron-mou:ld, -mold** *v.* to stain or become stained with iron-mould.

I·ron-o·re, iron ore. 1601. The ore of iron; any crude form in which iron is found in the earth. Also *attrib.*

I·ron-sa:nd. 1876. *Geol.* Sand containing particles of iron-ore, usually either magnetite or titaniferous oxide.

I·ron-si:ck, *a.* 1626. Said of a wooden ship when her bolts and nails are so corroded with rust that she has become leaky. Now *rare* or *Obs.*

Ironside (əi·əɹnsəid). Also (*sing.*) **Ironsides.** ME. **1.** *sing.* A man of great hardihood or bravery. **2.** *pl.* (*Ironsides.*) Applied to Cromwell's troopers in the Civil War; hence allusively. The sing. is sometimes used of one of these; a Puritan warrior. 1648. **3.** An ironclad 1861.
1. Is eldoste sone, Edmond yrene syde R. GLOUC. Lieutenant General Cromwell *alias* Ironside 1644. Hence he [Cromwell] acquired that terrible Name of Ironsides 1663.

I·ron-sided, *a.* 1825. [f. *iron side* + -ED[2].] Having sides made of or resembling iron; ironclad.

I·ronsmith. Now *rare* or *Obs.* ME. [f. IRON *sb.*[1] + SMITH.] **1.** An artificer in iron; a blacksmith. **2.** As a rendering of the native name of a bird, a species of barbet (*Megalæma faber*) 1885.

Ironstone, iron-stone (əi·əɹnstōᵘn, -stŏn). 1522. The name given to various hard iron-ores containing admixtures of silica, clay, etc. *attrib.* **Ironstone china, i. ware,** a hard kind of white pottery.

I·ron-tree. 1719. A name (more or less local) for various trees and shrubs with very hard wood, as *Ixora ferrea* of the W. Indies (also called *hardwood*), etc.

Ironware (əi·əɹnwēᵊɹ). 1477. [f. IRON *sb.*[1] + WARE *sb.*[2]] A general name for all light articles made of iron; hardware.

I·ronweed. 1827. [f. IRON *sb.*[1] + WEED *sb.*[1]; so called from the hard stem.] The Knapweed (*Centaurea nigra*), and the N. Amer. species of *Vernonia.*

Ironwood, iron-wood (əi·əɹnwud). 1657. A name (more or less local) for the extremely hard wood of various trees; also for the trees themselves.
Among these are the genus *Sideroxylon* (chiefly tropical); several species of *Diospyros* or Ebony; *Ostrya virginica, Bumelia lycioides, Carpinus americana,* etc. of N. America; *Erythroxylon areolatum,* etc. of the W. Indies; *Xylia dolabriformis, Mesua ferrea, Metrosideros vera,* etc. of the E. Indies; *Olea capensis* and *O. undulata* of S. Africa; *Notelæa ligustrina* of Tasmania and N.S. Wales; etc.

I·ronwork, iron-work (-wɒ̄ɹk). 1451. **1.** Work in iron; usu. *concr.* parts of things made of iron, or articles made of iron collectively. **2.** An establishment where iron is smelted, or where heavy iron goods are made. Now always in *pl.* form **ironworks** (sometimes construed as a *sing.*). 1581.

I·ronwort (-wɒ̄ɹt). 1562. [f. IRON *sb.*[1] + WORT[1], tr. L. *sideritis* (Pliny) – Gr. σιδηρῖτις, a herb that heals sword-wounds, f. σίδηρος iron.] Name for plants of the labiate genus *Sideritis*; also for species of *Galeopsis.*

Irony (əiᵊ·rŏni), *sb.* 1502. [– L. *ironia* (Cicero) – Gr. εἰρωνεία, f. εἴρων dissembler; see -Y[3].] **1.** A figure of speech in which the intended meaning is the opposite of that expressed by the words used; usually taking the form of sarcasm or ridicule in which laudatory expressions are used to imply condemnation or contempt. Also with *an* and *pl.* **2.** *fig.* A contradictory outcome of events as if in mockery of the promise and fitness of things. (In Fr. *ironie du sort.*) 1649. **3.** In etym. sense: Dissimulation, pretence; esp. in reference to the ignorance feigned by Socrates as a means of confuting an adversary (*Socratic i.*) 1502.
1. A drayman, in a passion, calls out, 'You are a pretty fellow', without suspecting that he is uttering i. MACAULAY. *Dramatic* or *tragic i.*, use of language having an inner meaning for a privileged audience, an outer for those immediately concerned. **2.** The i. of time 1884.

Irony (əi·əɹni), *a.* ME. [f. IRON *sb.*[1] + -Y[1].] Of iron; of the nature of iron; resembling, abounding in, or containing iron.
I. quartz 1843. Crystals of a clear i. brown 1875.

†**I·rous,** *a.* ME. [– AFr. *irous*, OFr. *iros* :– Rom. **irosus*, f. L. *ira*; see IRE, -OUS.] **1.** Given to anger, irascible –1574. **2.** Angry, enraged –1500. Hence †**I·rously** *adv.*

Irpe, *sb.* 1599. [Of unkn. origin.] Some kind of gesture: ? a toss of the head, the act of perking.
From Spanish shrugs, French faces, smirks, irpes, and all affected humours, Good Mercury defend us B. JONS. So †**Irpe** ?*a.*, ?perk, smart B. JONS.

Irradiance (irēⁱ·diăns). 1667. [f. IRRADIANT; see -ANCE.] The fact of irradiating; emitted radiance. Also *fig.* So **Irra·diancy,** the fact or quality of being irradiant 1646.

Irradiant (irēⁱ·diănt), *a.* 1526. [– *irradiant-*, pr. ppl. stem of L. *irradiare*; see IRRADIATE *v.*, -ANT.] Emitting rays of light; shining brightly. Also *fig.*
As Fire extinguish'd by th' I. Sun 1710.

Irradiate (irēⁱ·diĕt), *ppl. a.* 1526. [– L. *irradiatus*, pa. pple. of *irradiare*; see next, -ATE[2].] Illumined; made bright or brilliant. Const. as pple. or adj.
The sky Erewhile i. only with his beam CARY.

Irradiate (irēⁱ·dieⁱt), *v.* 1603. [– *irradiat-*, pa. ppl. stem of L. *irradiare* shine forth, f. *in-* IR-[1] + *radiare* shine, f. *radius* RAY; see -ATE[3].] **1.** *trans.* To direct rays of light upon; to shine upon; to illumine. †**b.** To influence with or as with rays of heat or anything radiant –1677. **2.** *fig.* and *transf.* To illumine with spiritual or intellectual light 1627; to brighten as with light 1651. **3.** To radiate; To send forth in or as in rays 1617. †**4.** *intr.* To radiate; to diverge in the form of rays –1794. **5.** *intr.* To emit rays, to shine (*on* or *upon*) 1642. **6.** *intr.* To become radiant 1800.
1. The midnight lightnings..That with their awful blaze, i. heaven SOUTHEY. **2.** The priest's jovial good humour irradiated his happy countenance LEVER. **6.** Lamb every now and then irradiates COLERIDGE. Hence **Irra·diative** *a.* of which the tendency or property is to i. **Irra·diator.**

Irradiation (irēⁱdi,ēⁱ·ʃən). 1589. [– (O)Fr. *irradiation* or late and med.L. *irradiatio*, f. as prec.; see -ION.]
I. 1. The action of irradiating; shining 1599. **b.** A ray of light, a beam 1643. **2.** *fig.* **a.** A beaming forth of spiritual light 1633. **b.** Intellectual illumination 1589. **3.** *Optics.* The apparent enlargement of the edges of an object strongly illuminated, when seen against a dark ground 1834.
3. People look larger in light clothes than in dark, which may also be explained as the effect of i. 1876.
II. 1. The emission of heat-rays 1794. †**2.** In older Physiology: The emission or emanation of any fluid, influence, principle, or virtue, from an active centre –1706. †**b.** The (fancied) emission of an immaterial fluid or influence from the eye –1696. **3.** *Physiol.* The transmission of excitation from a nerve-centre outwards 1847.

Irradicate (iræ·dikeⁱt), *v. rare.* [app. f. IR-[1] + L. *radicare* take root, f. *radix, radic-* root.] *trans.* To fix by the root, to enroot. SIR W. HAMILTON.

Irrationable (iræ·ʃənăb'l), *a. Obs.* or *arch.* 1583. [– L. *irrationabilis* unreasonable, f. *in-* IR-[2] + *rationabilis*; see REASONABLE.] = IRRATIONAL *a.* 1, 2. –1832. So †**Irrationabi·lity.**

Irrational (iræ·ʃənăl). 1470. [– L. *irrationalis*, f. *in-* IR-[2] + *rationalis* RATIONAL.]
A. *adj.* **1.** Not endowed with reason. **2.** Not in accordance with reason; illogical, absurd 1641. **3.** *Math.* Not rational; not commensurable with ordinary quantities such as the natural numbers; not expressible by an ordinary (finite) fraction, proper or improper. Usually applied to roots; the same as *surd.* 1551. **4.** *Gr. Pros.* Said of a syllable having a metrical value not corresponding to its actual time-value, or of a metrical foot containing such a syllable 1844.
1. The more i. kinds of animals SCOTT. **2.** Inconsiderate courage has given way to i. fear BURKE.
B. *sb.* **1.** A being not endowed with reason; one not guided by reason 1646. **2.** *Math.* An irrational number or quantity; a surd 1571.
Hence **Irra·tionalism,** a system of belief or action that disregards or contradicts rational principles. So **Irra·tionalist, Irrationali·stic** *a.* **Irra·tionally** *adv.*

Irrationality (iræʃənæ·lĭti). 1570. [f. prec. + -ITY.] **1.** The quality of being irrational (see IRRATIONAL *a.*) **2.** *Optics.* The inequality of the ratios of the dispersion of the various colours in spectra produced by refraction through different substances 1797.
1. Proof of the i. of mankind 1717.

Irrealizable (irī·ăləizăb'l), *a.* 1853. [IR-[2].] That cannot be realized; unrealizable.

Irrebuttable (irĭbɒ·tăb'l), *a.* 1834. [IR-[2].] That cannot be rebutted.

Irreceptive (irĭse·ptiv), *a.* 1846. [IR-[2].] Not receptive; incapable of receiving.

Irreciprocal (irĭsi·prŏkăl), *a.* 1886. [IR-[2].] Not reciprocal; as, *i. conduction* (Electr.), unipolar conduction. So **Irrecipro·city.**

Irreclaimable (irĭklēⁱ·măb'l), *a.* 1609. [IR-[2].] †**1.** Uncontrollable. P. HOLLAND. **2.** That cannot be reclaimed 1662; of land 1814. **3.** Irrevocable 1834. Hence **Irreclai·mably** *adv.*

Irrecognition (irekǫgni·ʃən). 1820. [IR-[2].] Absence of recognition; non-recognition.

Irrecognizable (ire·kǫgnəi:zăb'l), *a.* 1837. [IR-[2].] Incapable of being recognized; unrecognizable. Hence **Irrecognizabi·lity, -re·cognizably** *adv.*

Irreconcilable (ire·kǫnsəilăb'l, ire:kǫnsəi·lăb'l), *a.* (*sb.*) Also **-cileable.** 1599. [IR-[2].] **1.** That cannot be reconciled; implacably hostile. Const. *to.* **2.** Incompatible. Const. *to, with.* 1646. **3.** *sb.* A person who refuses to be reconciled; *esp.* One of a political party who refuses to come to any agreement or make any compromise 1748. **b.** *pl.* Principles, ideas, etc. which cannot be harmonized with each other 1895.

1. I. enemies GREEN. **2.** Creeds..i. with salvation 1866. **3.** From Oxford graduates down to Irish irreconcilables 1884. Hence **Irre:concilabi·lity, Irreconcilableness,** the quality of being i. **Irreconcilably** *adv.* 1598. var. **Irreconci·liable** *a. rare.*

†**Irre·concile,** *v.* 1647. [IR-².] *trans.* To render unreconciled; to make antagonistic; to estrange –1670. Hence **Irre·conci·lement.**

†**Irre·conciled,** *a.* 1599. [IR-².] Not reconciled; *spec.* in a state of variance with God –1750.

†**Irreconcilia·tion.** 1650. [IR-².] The fact or condition of being unreconciled –1678.

Irrecoverable (irĭkʊ·vərăb'l), *a.* 1533. [f. IR-² + RECOVERABLE. Cf. Fr. *irrécouvrable* (XVI).] That cannot be †revoked, got back, restored to health or life; *fig.* not capable of being remedied or rectified. †**b.** That cannot be recovered from –1674.

An i. sentence of death TUCKER. I. debts 1782, ill health 1809. *fig.* A final and i. fall 1679. Hence **Irreco·verableness. Irreco·verably** *adv.*

†**Irrecuperable** (irĭkiū·pərăb'l), *a.* ME. [– OFr. *irrecuperable* – late and med.L. *irrecuperabilis*, f. *in-* IR-² + L. *recuperare*; see RECUPERATE, -ABLE.] **1.** That cannot be recovered or regained –1644. **2.** That cannot be recovered from; incurable –1626.

1. Teares be lost upon a thing i. HACKET.

†**Irrecu·rable,** *a. rare.* 1548. [f. IR-² + †*recurable*; see RECURE *v.*] Incurable; irremediable –1579. So †**Irrecu·red** *a.* (*rare*), incurable 1598.

Irrecusable (irĭkiū·zăb'l), *a.* 1776. [– Fr. *irrécusable* or late L. *irrecusabilis*; see IR-², RECUSANT, -ABLE.] Incapable of being refused acceptance.

I will give him an i. proof H. WALPOLE. **Irrecu·sably** *adv.*

Irredeemable (irĭdī·măb'l), *a.* 1609. [f. IR-² + REDEEMABLE.] **1.** Incapable of being redeemed or bought back. **b.** Of paper currency: Not convertible into cash 1850. **2.** *fig.* That admits of no release or change of state; absolute, hopeless 1839. **3.** Beyond redemption; utterly depraved 1834.

1. The debt..for which annuities have been granted for a limited period is called the I. debt 1820. **2.** He..Wrought for his house an i. woe TENNYSON. Hence **Irredeemabi·lity, Irredee·mableness,** the quality of being not redeemable. **Irredee·mably** *adv.*

Irredentism (irĭde·ntiz'm). 1883. [See next and -ISM.] The policy or programme of the Irredentists.

Irredentist (irĭde·ntist). 1882. [– It. *irredentista*, f. (*Italia*) *irredenta* unredeemed or unrecovered (Italy); see IR-², REDEEM, -IST.] In Italian politics (since 1878), an adherent of the party which advocates the recovery and union to Italy of all Italian-speaking districts now subject to other countries. Also *attrib.* as *adj.*

Irreducible (irĭdiū·sĭb'l), *a.* 1633. [IR-².] **1.** That cannot be reduced to a desired form, state, condition, etc. **b.** *spec.* That cannot be reduced to a simpler or more intelligible form 1753. **2.** *Path.* That cannot be reduced by treatment to a desired form or condition 1836. **3.** Incapable of being reduced to a smaller number or amount 1860. **4.** Invincible, insuperable 1858.

1. Fashions..i. to rule HALLAM. **b.** *I. case* (Alg.): that case of cubic equations where the root.. appears under an impossible or imaginary form, and yet is real E. CHAMBERS. **2.** An i. tumour in the right groin 1859. Hence **Irreducibi·lity, Irredu·cibleness. Irredu·cibly** *adv.* var. **Irredu·ctible** *a.* (*rare*).

Irreflection, -flexion (irĭfle·kʃən). 1861. [f. IR-², perh. after Fr. *irréflexion*.] Want of reflection; unreflecting action or conduct.

Irreflective (irĭfle·ktiv), *a.* 1833. [f. IR-², perh. after Fr. *irréfléchi*.] Unreflecting. Hence **Irrefle·ctive-ly** *adv.*, **-ness.**

Irreformable (irĭfǭ·ɹmăb'l), *a.* 1609. [f. IR-² + REFORMABLE. Sense 2 prob. after Fr. *irréformable*.] **1.** Incapable of being reformed. **2.** Incapable of alteration 1812.

1. She was unteachable, i. 1892.

Irrefragable (ire·frăgăb'l), *a.* 1533. [– late L. *irrefragabilis*, f. *in-* IR-² + L. *refragari* oppose, contest, as opp. to *suffragari* (cf. SUFFRAGE); see -ABLE.] **1.** That cannot be refuted or disproved; incontrovertible, indisputable, undeniable. **2.** That cannot or must not be broken; indestructible; inviolable; irresistible. Now *rare.* 1562. †**3.** Of persons: Obstinate, inflexible –1621.

1. Alexander of Hales, the i. Doctor CAMDEN. An i. answer to the popular theories STUBBS. **3.** He is i. in his humour BURTON. Hence **Irre:fraga·bi·lity, Irre·fragableness. Irre·fragably** *adv.*

Irrefrangible (irĭfræ·ndʒib'l), *a.* 1719. [f. IR-² + REFRANGIBLE.] **1.** That cannot or must not be broken; inviolable. **2.** *Optics.* Not refrangible; incapable of being refracted.

Irrefutable (irĭfiū·tăb'l, ire·fiŭtăb'l), *a.* 1620. [– late L. *irrefutabilis*; see IR-², REFUTABLE.] That cannot be refuted or disproved; incontrovertible, irrefragable. Hence **Irrefutabi·lity,** the quality of being i. **Irrefutably** *adv.*

Irregenerate (irĭdʒe·nĕrĕt), *a. rare.* 1657. [IR-².] Not regenerate; unregenerate. Hence †**Irrege·neracy,** †**-genera·tion,** unregenerate state.

Irregular (ire·giŭlăɹ). [ME. *irreguler(e* – OFr. *irreguler* (later and mod. *irrégulier*, with change of suffix) – late L. and (esp.) med.L. *irregularis*; see IR-², REGULAR.]

A. *adj.* Not regular. **I. 1.** Of things: Not in conformity with rule or principle; contrary to rule; disorderly in action or conduct; anomalous, abnormal 1483. **b.** Unregulated; morally disorderly. ? *Obs.* 1608. **2.** Of persons: Not conforming to rule, law, or moral principle; lawless, disorderly ME. **3.** Not of regular or symmetrical form; unevenly placed 1584. **4.** In reference to time or motion: Unequal or uneven in continuance, occurrence, or succession. Hence of an agent: Doing something at irregular intervals or times. 1608.

1. The efforts of their i. valour GIBBON. An i. order 1894. **b.** I. appetite 1746, conduct 1804. **2.** The i. and wilde Glendower SHAKS. **3.** Two i. rows of tall meagre houses DICKENS. **4.** I. breathing 1791. An i. attendant (*mod.*).

II. Techn. senses. **1.** *Eccl.* Disqualified for ordination, or for exercise of clerical functions ME. **2.** *Gram.* Inflected not according to the normal method. Said also of the inflexion. 1611. **3.** *Math.* Having unequal sides 1700. **4.** *Bot.* and *Zool.* **a.** Abnormal in form. **b.** Not symmetrical or uniform in shape or arrangement; *spec.* of a flower, Having the members of the same cycle (esp. the petals) unlike in form or size. 1794. **5.** *Mil.* Of troops: Not belonging to the established army organization; not forming an organized military body 1856.

5. The Danes..put the i. English levies to flight FREEMAN.

B. *sb.* **1.** *Gram.* An irregular noun, verb, etc. (*rare*) 1611. **2.** One not belonging to the regular body; one not of the regular clergy; an irregular practitioner, attendant, etc. 1534. **b.** *Mil.* A soldier not of the regular army; usu. in *pl.* = irregular troops 1747.

2. b. With this small company of irregulars..we set out 1756. Hence **Irre·gular-ly** *adv.*, †**-ness.**

Irregularity (iregiŭlæ·rĭti). ME. [– (O)Fr. *irrégularité* – late (eccl.) and med.L. *irregularitas*; see IR-², REGULARITY.] The quality or state of being irregular; something that is irregular; *spec.* in *Eccl.* Infraction of the rules as to entrance into or exercise of holy orders; an impediment or disqualification by which a person is debarred from ordination, exercise of clerical functions, or ecclesiastical advancement.

†**Irregulate,** *a.* 1579. [– med.L. *irregulatus*; see IR-², REGULATE *ppl. a.*] Unregulated; irregular, disorderly –1650. So **Irre·gulated** *a. rare.* 1660.

Irre·gulate, *v.* 1600. [f. prec., or f. IR-² + REGULATE *v.*] *trans.* To render irregular; to disorder.

†**Irre·gulous,** *a.* [f. IRREGULAR (sense I. 2) by substitution of suffix -OUS.] Unruly, lawless. *Cymb.* IV. ii. 315.

†**Irreje·ctable,** *a.* [IR-².] That cannot be rejected. BOYLE.

†**Irrela·psable,** *a.* 1660. [IR-².] Not liable to relapse. HY. MORE.

Irrelate (irĭlē¹·t), *a. rare.* 1845. [f. next; see -ATE².] Not related, unrelated.

Irrelation (irĭlē¹·ʃən). 1848. [IR-².] Absence of relation, want of connection.

Irrelative (ire·lătiv), *a.* 1640. [f. IR-² + RELATIVE.] Not relative; unrelated, unconnected; hence, in *Metaph.*, without relations, absolute. **b.** Irrelevant 1649. **c.** *Mus.* (See quot.) 1811.

It seems evident, that they [colours, odours, etc.] have an absolute Being i. to Us BOYLE. **c.** *Irrelative*, a term applied to any two chords which do not contain some sound common to both 1811. Hence **Irre·lative-ly** *adv.*, **-ness.**

Irrelevance (ire·lĭvăns). 1561. [f. next; see -ANCE.] The fact or quality of being irrelevant; want of pertinence. Also with *an* and *pl.*

A second i. foisted in upon the back of the first 1872. So **Irre·levancy** 1592.

Irrelevant (ire·lĭvănt), *a.* 1558. (orig. Sc.). [f. IR-² + RELEVANT. Cf. Fr. †*irrelevant*.] Not relevant or pertinent to the case; that does not apply; said orig. of evidence or arguments.

No accumulation of facts can establish an i. conclusion 1877. Hence **Irre·levantly** *adv.*

Irrelievable (irĭlī·văb'l), *a.* 1670. [IR-².] Not relievable, that cannot be relieved.

Irreligion (irĭli·dʒən). 1592. [– Fr. *irréligion* or L. *irreligio*; see IR-², RELIGION.] **1.** Want of religion; hostility to or disregard of religious principles; irreligious conduct 1598. †**2.** A false or perverted religion –1655. Hence **Irreli·gionist,** one who supports or practices i.; a professed opponent of religion.

Irreligious (irĭli·dʒəs), *a.* 1561. [– L. (later esp. eccl. L.) *irreligiosus*; see IR-², RELIGIOUS. Cf. Fr. *irréligieux*.] **1.** Not religious; hostile to or without regard for religion; ungodly. Also *transf.* of things. †**2.** Believing in, practising, or pertaining to a false religion –1634.

1. I. men, whose short prospects are filled with earth, and sense, and mortal life BERKELEY. **2.** The issue of an I. Moore SHAKS. Hence **Irreli·gious-ly** *adv.*, **-ness.**

Irremeable (ire·mi,ăb'l, irĭ·mi,ăb'l), *a.* 1569. [– L. *irremeabilis*, f. *in-* IR-² + *remeare* go back, return, f. *re-* RE- + *meare* go, pass; see -ABLE. Cf. OFr. *irreméable*.] Admitting of no return.

The dark i. way POPE. Hence **Irre·meably** *adv.*

Irremediable (irĭmī·diăb'l), *a.* 1533. [– L. *irremediabilis*; see IR-², REMEDIABLE. Cf. Fr. *irrémédiable*.] Not remediable; that does not admit of remedy, cure, or correction; irreparable.

A person of a desperate fortune, i. and irrecoverable JER. TAYLOR. Hence **Irreme·diableness. Irreme·diably** *adv.* 1601.

Irremissible (irĭmi·sĭb'l), *a.* Also *erron.* †**-able.** ME. [– (O)Fr. *irrémissible* or eccl. L. *irremissibilis*; see IR-², REMISSIBLE.] Not remissible; for or of which there can be no remission.

An irremissable sin HALES, annual Tribute 1728. Hence **Irremissibi·lity, Irremi·ssibleness,** the quality or condition of being i. **Irrem·ssibly** *adv.*

†**Irremi·ssion.** 1631. [IR-².] Non-remission.

Irremi·ssive, *a.* 1817. [IR-².] Unremitting.

†**Irremi·ttable,** *a. rare.* 1587. [IR-².] = IRREMISSIBLE –1635.

Irremovable (irĭmū·văb'l), *a.* (*sb.*) 1597. [IR-².] **1.** Not removable; not subject to removal; permanent 1598. †**2.** Immovable, inflexible (*lit.* and *fig.*) –1822. **3.** *sb.* One whose position is permanent 1848. Hence **Irremovabi·lity, -mo·vableness, -mo·vably** *adv.*

Irremu·nerable, *a. rare.* 1623. [IR-². Cf. med.L. *irremunerabilis* (XII).] That cannot be remunerated or paid.

†**Irrenow·ned,** *a.* [IR-².] Unrenowned. SPENSER.

Irrepair (irĭpēᵊ·ɹ). *rare.* 1822. [IR-².] = DISREPAIR.

Irreparable (ire·părăb'l), *a.* ME. [– (O)Fr. *irréparable* – L. *irreparabilis*; see IR-², REPARABLE.] Not reparable; that cannot be rectified, remedied, or made good.

I. is the losse, and patience Saies, it is past her cure SHAKS. **Irre:parabi·lity, Irre·parableness. Irre·parably** *adv.* var. **Irrepai·rable** (now *rare*).

Irrepealable (irĭpī·lăb'l), *a.* 1633. [IR-².] Incapable of being repealed or annulled; irrevocable.

Let..this inhibitory Statute..stand..i. 1642. **Irrepealabi·lity, Irrepea·lableness. Irrepea·lably** *adv.*

Irrepe·ntant, *a. rare.* 1573. [IR-².] Not repentant; impenitent. So **Irrepe·ntance** (*rare*), non-repentance. **Irrepe·ntantly** *adv.*

Irreplaceable (iriplēⁱ·săb'l), *a.* 1807. [IR-².] Not replaceable; that cannot be replaced.

Irrepleviable (iri̊ple·viăb'l), *a.* 1543. [– med.L. *irrepleviabilis*, f. *in-* IR-² + *repleviabilis*, f. *repleviare*; see REPLEVIN, -ABLE.] *Law.* = next.

Irreplevisable (iri̊ple·vizăb'l), *a.* 1621. [f. IR-² + REPLEVISABLE.] *Law.* Not replevisable; that cannot be replevied or delivered on sureties.

Irreprehensible (irepri̊he·nsib'l), *a.* Now *rare.* ME. [– late L. *irreprehensibilis*; see IR-², REPREHENSIBLE. Cf. (O)Fr. *irrépréhensible.*] Not reprehensible or blameworthy; irreproachable. Hence **Irreprehe·nsibleness. Irreprehe·nsibly** *adv.*

Irrepresentable (irepri̊ze·ntăb'l), *a.* 1673. [IR-².] Incapable of representation.

Progressive actions, as such, are i. by painting DE QUINCEY. Hence **Irreprese·ntableness.**

Irrepressible (iri̊pre·sib'l), *a.* (*sb.*) 1818. [f. IR-² + REPRESS + -IBLE.] **1.** Not repressible; that cannot be repressed, restrained, or put down. (Of persons, often *joc.*) **2.** *sb.* An irrepressible person 1890.

1. The..uproar of the i. undergraduates 1879. **Irrepressibi·lity, -pre·ssibleness. Irrepre·ssibly** *adv.*

Irrepre·ssive, *a.* 1856. [IR-².] = prec.

Irreproachable (iri̊prōᵘ·tʃăb'l), *a.* 1634. [– Fr. *irréprochable*; see IR-², REPROACHABLE.] Not reproachable; free from blame, faultless.

An exact and i. Piece of Architecture EVELYN. Hence **Irreproachabi·lity, Irreproa·chableness,** the quality of being i. **Irreproa·chably** *adv.*

Irreprovable (iri̊prū·văb'l), *a.* 1504. [IR-².] **1.** Not reprovable; blameless, irreproachable. Now *rare.* †**2.** That cannot be disproved; irrefutable –1646. Hence **Irrepro·vableness. Irrepro·vably** *adv.*

Irreption (ire·pʃən). 1598. [– late L. *irreptio*, f. *irrept-*, pa. ppl. stem of L. *irrepere* creep in, f. *in-* IR-¹ + *repere* creep; see -ION.] Creeping or stealing in.

Irreptitious (irepti·ʃəs), *a.* 1673. [f. *irrept-* (see prec. and -ITIOUS), after *surreptitious.*] Characterized by creeping in or having crept in, esp. into a text.

†**Irre·putable,** *a.* 1709. [IR-².] Not reputable –1749.

Irresilient (iri̊z-, iri̊si·liĕnt), *a.* [IR-².] Non-resilient; that does not spring back or rebound. H. SPENCER.

Irresistance (iri̊zi·stăns). 1643. [IR-².] Absence of resistance; non-resistance.

Irresistible (iri̊zi·stib'l), *a.* (*sb.*) Also †**-able.** 1597. [– med.L. *irresistibilis* or f. IR-² + RESISTIBLE. In XVII–XVIII also *irresistable*, paralleled by Fr. †*irresistable*, med.L. *irresistabilis.*] **1.** Not resistible; too strong, weighty, or fascinating to be resisted. †**2.** Not to be resisted lawfully. PRYNNE. **3.** *sb.* An irresistible person 1774.

1. That Heroic, that Renown'd, Irresistible Samson MILT. The power of opinion is i. GIBBON. **Irresistibi·lity, Irresi·stibleness. Irresi·stibly** *adv.*

†**Irresi·stless,** *a.* 1669. [erron. blending of *irresistible* and *resistless.*] Resistless, irresistible –1796.

Irresoluble (ire·zŏlⁱub'l), *a.* 1646. [– L. *irresolubilis* indissoluble (Appuleius), infl. by *resoluble, soluble.* Cf. Fr. †*irrésoluble.*] **1.** Incapable of being resolved into elements; indissoluble; insoluble 1666. **2.** Incapable of being loosened and dispelled or relieved 1646. **3.** Incapable of being solved 1868.

2. With many moe almost i. scruples GAULE. Hence **Irre·solubleness,** the quality of being i.

Irresolute (ire·zŏlⁱut), *a.* 1573. [– L. *irresolutus* not loosened; in senses 2, 3, f. IR-² + RESOLUTE.] †**1.** Not resolved; left ambiguous or obscure –1603. **2.** Unresolved as to a course of action. Also *fig.* 1579. **3.** Wanting in resolution; infirm of purpose; vacillating 1600.

2. I. what part to take FRANKLIN. **3.** Cicero.. was i., timid and inconsistent J. H. NEWMAN. Hence **Irre·solute-ly** *adv.*, **-ness.**

Irresolution (irezŏlⁱū·ʃən). 1592. [f. IR-² + RESOLUTION. Cf. Fr. *irrésolution* (XVI) in same sense.] Want of resolution. †**1.** The condition of not having arrived at a settled opinion on some subject; uncertainty, doubt. With *pl.* An instance of this. –1813. **2.** The condition of being irresolute; indecision of character; vacillation. With *an* and *pl.* An instance of this. 1601.

2. His i. of mind..induced him to listen to the suggestions of the French ambassadors 1823.

Irresolvable (iri̊zǫ·lvăb'l), *a.* 1660. [IR-².] Not resolvable. **1.** Incapable of being solved. **2.** That cannot be resolved into elements or parts 1785. **3.** That cannot be disentangled 1886.

2. *I. nebulæ*, nebulæ that cannot be resolved into stars by telescopic examination. Hence **Irresolvabi·lity, Irreso·lvableness.**

†**Irreso·lved,** *a.* 1621. [IR-².] Not resolved; not settled in opinion; undecided; irresolute –1864. Hence **Irreso·lvedly** *adv.*

Irrespective (iri̊spe·ktiv), *a.* and *adv.* 1640. [IR-².] Not respective. †**1.** Disrespectful –1654. **2.** Characterized by disregard of particular persons or circumstances. Now *rare.* 1650. **3.** Existing or considered without respect or regard to something else; independent *of* 1694. **b.** Now chiefly advb.; = IRRESPECTIVELY. Const. *of.* 1839.

2. He..oversteps, in his i. zeal, every decency and every right opposed to his course COLERIDGE. **3.** A speculative interest, which is i. of all practical considerations BUCKLE.

Irrespectively (iri̊spe·ktivli), *adv.* 1624. [f. prec. + -LY².] †**1.** Disrespectfully. FEATLEY. †**2.** In a manner showing disregard of particular persons or circumstances –1716. **3.** Without regard to other things; independently 1648.

3. Prosperity, considered absolutely and i., is better and more desirable than adversity SOUTH.

Irrespirable (iri̊spəiᵊ·răb'l, ire·spiră̆b'l), *a.* 1822. [f. IR-² + RESPIRABLE, or – Fr. *irrespirable.*] Not respirable; unfit for respiration.

Irresponsible (iri̊spǫ·nsib'l), *a.* Also †**-able.** 1648. [f. IR-² + RESPONSIBLE. Cf. Fr. *irresponsable.*] **1.** Not responsible; not answerable for conduct or actions; not liable to be called to account; incapable of legal responsibility. Also, Acting or done without a sense of responsibility. **2.** Insolvent 1890.

They left the crown..perfectly i. BURKE. The prisoner was idiotic and i. 1890. **Irresponsibi·lity, Irrespo·nsibleness. Irrespo·nsibly** *adv.*

Irresponsive (iri̊spǫ·nsiv), *a.* 1846. [IR-².] Not responsive; not responding to a force or stimulus; giving no answer to a question or inquiry. Hence **Irrespo·nsiveness.**

Irrestrainable (iri̊strēⁱ·năb'l), *a.* 1643. [IR-².] Not restrainable; that cannot be held in check. Hence **Irrestrai·nably** *adv.*

Irresu·scitable, *a.* [IR-².] Not resuscitable; that cannot be restored to life. CARLYLE.

Irretention (iri̊te·nʃən). [IR-².] Lack of retention; irretentiveness. DE QUINCEY.

Irretentive (iri̊te·ntiv), *a.* 1749. [IR-².] Not retentive; lacking the power of retention. Hence **Irrete·ntiveness.**

Irretraceable (iri̊trēⁱ·săb'l), *a.* 1847. [IR-².] That cannot be retraced.

Irretractile (iri̊træ·ktil, -təil), *a.* [IR-².] Not retractile; incapable of being drawn back. H. SPENCER.

Irretrievable (iri̊trī·văb'l), *a.* 1695. [IR-².] That cannot be retrieved; irrecoverable; irreparable.

The i. decline of his brother's health GIBBON. **Irretrievabi·lity, Irretrie·vableness. Irretrie·vably** *adv.*

†**Irretu·rnable,** *a.* 1563. [f. IR-² + RETURNABLE.] That cannot be turned back; admitting of no return –1600.

Irrevea·lable, *a.* [IR-².] That cannot be revealed. So **Irrevea·lably** *adv.* (Dicts.)

Irreverence (ire·vĕrĕns). ME. [– L. *irreverentia*, f. *irreverent-*; see IRREVERENT, -ENCE. Cf. (O)Fr. *irrévérence.*] **1.** The fact or quality of being irreverent; disrespect to a person or thing held sacred or worthy of honour. **b.** with *an* and *pl.* An instance of this 1744. **2.** The condition of not being reverenced. CLARENDON.

Irreverend (ire·vĕrĕnd), *a.* 1576. [IR-².] **1.** Not reverend; unworthy of veneration 1748. ¶**2.** Formerly confused with IRREVERENT.

2. I. Gesture or Behaviour GRINDAL. **Irre·verendly** *adv.*

Irreverent (ire·vĕrĕnt), *a.* Also †**inr-.** 1494. [– L. *irreverens, -ent-*, f. *in-* IR-² + *reverens, -ent-*, pr. pple. of L. *reverēri* REVERE; see -ENT.] †**1.** = IRREVEREND. Fabyan. **2.** Not reverent; wanting in reverence; showing disrespect to a sacred or venerable person or thing 1550.

2. Th' i. Son Of him who built the Ark MILT. *P.L.* XII. 101. The i. irony of Mephistopheles B. TAYLOR. **Irre·verently** *adv.*

Irreversible (iri̊vǝ̄·ɹsib'l), *a.* Also †**-able.** 1625. [IR-².] That cannot be reversed. **1.** That cannot be undone, repealed, or annulled; irrevocable. **2.** That cannot be turned backwards, upside down, or in the opposite direction 1821.

1. The irreversable Decree of Fate 1728. **Irreversibi·lity, Irreve·rsibleness. Irreve·rsibly** *adv.*

Irrevocable (ire·vŏkăb'l), *a.* Also †**irrevo·kable.** ME. [– L. *irrevocabilis*; see IR-², REVOCABLE; in part through (O)Fr. *irrévocable.*] That cannot be recalled. **1.** That cannot be called, brought, fetched, or taken back; that is beyond recovery. **2.** That cannot be revoked, repealed, annulled, or undone; unalterable, irreversible. (The prevailing sense.) 1490.

1. The i. yesterday KINGSLEY. **2.** Bi the sentence irreuocable of theym [the gods] CAXTON. **Irre·vocabi·lity, Irre·vocableness. Irre·vocably** *adv.*

Irrevoluble (ire·vŏliub'l), *a. rare.* 1641. [f. IR-² + REVOLUBLE.] That has no finite period of revolution; of infinite circuit.

The datelesse and i. Circle of Eternity MILT.

Irrigable (i·rigăb'l), *a.* 1844. [f. next + -ABLE.] Capable of being irrigated.

Irrigate (i·rigeⁱt), *v.* 1615. [– *irrigat-*, pa. ppl. stem of L. *irrigare*, f. *in-* IR-¹ + *rigare* wet, water; see -ATE³.] **1.** *trans.* To supply with moisture; to moisten, wet. **2.** *spec.* To supply (land) with water by means of channels or streams passing through it; to water. (The prevailing sense.) 1623. **b.** *Med.* To supply (a part, a wound, etc.) with a constant flow or sprinkling of some liquid, for cooling, cleansing, or disinfecting 1876. **3.** *fig.* To refresh or make fruitful as with moisture 1686.

2. Country..artificially irrigated by a network of canals 1872.

Irrigation (irigēⁱ·ʃən). 1612. [– L. *irrigatio*, f. as prec.; see -ION. Cf. Fr. *irrigation* (XV).] The action of supplying or fact of being supplied with moisture; *spec.* the action of supplying land with water by means of channels or streams. Also *attrib.*

The Sixth Helpe of Ground is by..I. BACON.

Irrigator (i·rigeⁱtəɹ). 1829. [f. IRRIGATE + -OR 2.] **1.** One who or that which irrigates. **2.** *Med.* A contrivance for irrigating (sense 2 b) 1887.

Irriguous (iri·giu,əs), *a.* Now *rare.* 1651. [f. L. *irriguus* supplied with water, f. *in-* IR-¹ + *riguus* watered, f. *rigare*; see IRRIGATE, -OUS.] **1.** Irrigated; moistened, wet; *esp.* of a region or tract of land: well-watered, moist, watery. **2.** Having the quality of irrigating; watering, bedewing 1684.

1. The flourie lap Of som i. Valley MILT. *P.L.* IV. 255. **2.** A lordly river..Through the meadows sinuous, wandered i. CLOUGH. Hence **Irri·guousness.**

†**Irrisible** (iri·zib'l), *a.* 1767. [– late L. *irrisibilis*, f. *irris-*, pa. ppl. stem of L. *irridere*, f. *in-* IR-¹ + *ridere* laugh; see -IBLE.] Ridiculous.

Irrision (iri·ʒən). Now *rare* or *arch.* 1526. [– L. *irrisio*, f. as prec.; see -ION. Cf. Fr. †*irrision.*] The action of laughing at a person or thing in derision or contempt; mockery.

Appellatives of scorne, or i. JER. TAYLOR.

Irrisor (irəi·sǫɹ). *rare.* 1739. [– L. *irrisor* derider, f. as prec.; see -OR 2.] **1.** One who laughs at another; a mocker. **2.** *Zool.* A bird of the genus *Irrisor* or family *Irrisoridæ*, so called from their cry; a wood-hoopoe. Hence **Irri·sory** *a.*

Irritability (i:rităbi·liti). 1755. [– L. *irritabilitas*, f. *irritabilis*; see next, -ITY. Cf. Fr. *irritabilité.*] The quality or state of being irritable. **1.** The quality or state of being easily annoyed or excited to anger; proneness to vexation or annoyance; petulance 1791. **2.** *Path.* Of a bodily organ or part: The condition of being excessively or morbidly excitable or sensitive to the contact or action of anything 1785. **3.** *Physiol.* and *Biol.* The capacity of being excited to vital action (e.g. motion, contraction, nervous impulse, etc.) by the application of an external stimulus; a property of living matter or protoplasm in general, and esp. of certain organs or tissues of animals and plants, particularly muscles and nerves 1755.

1. The gloomy i. of his [Johnson's] existence BOSWELL.

Irritable (i·rităb'l), *a.* 1662. [– L. *irritabilis*, f. *irritare*; see IRRITATE *v.*[1], -BLE. Cf. Fr. *irritable* (XVI).] Capable of being irritated; susceptible of irritation. **1.** Readily excited to anger or impatience; easily ruffled or annoyed. **2.** Readily excited to action; highly responsive to stimulus; (of a bodily organ or part), Excessively or morbidly excitable or sensitive (see IRRITATE *v.*[1] 3) 1791. **3.** *Physiol.* and *Biol.* Capable of being excited to vital action by the application of some physical stimulus; said *esp.* of muscles and nerves, as subject respectively to contraction and to motor or sensory impulse under the influence of the proper external forces 1793.

1. His ill health made him more suspicious and i. than ever ELPHINSTONE. Hence **I·rritably** *adv.*

I·rritament. Now *rare* or *Obs.* 1634. [– L. *irritamentum* a provocative; see IRRITATE *v.*[1] and -MENT.] Something that excites or provokes an action, feeling, or state; a provocative, an incentive; an irritant.

Irritancy[1] (i·ritănsi). 1831. [f. IRRITANT *a.*[1]; see -ANCY.] Irritating quality or character; irritation.

I·rritancy[2]. 1681. [f. IRRITANT *a.*[2]; see -ANCY.] *Rom., Civil,* and *Sc. Law.* The fact of rendering, or condition of being rendered, null and void.

Irritant (i·ritănt), *a.*[1] and *sb.* 1636. [f. IRRITATE *v.*[1] + -ANT. Cf. Fr. *irritant* (XVII).]

A. *adj.* †**1.** That irritates or stirs up; exciting, provocative. **2.** Causing irritation, physical or (*rarely*) mental; irritating 1828.

2. I. poisons 1834. I. or factious opposition 1885.

B. *sb.* An irritant substance, body, or agency; in *Path.* a poison, etc. which produces irritation; in *Physiol.* and *Biol.* anything that stimulates an organ to its proper vital action. Also *fig.* 1802.

fig. A persecution which pinches, but does not suppress, is merely an i., and not an absorbent HELPS.

I·rritant, *a.*[2] 1592. [– late L. *irritans, -ant-*, pr. pple. of *irritare*; see IRRITATE *v.*[2], -ANT.] *Rom., Civil,* and *Sc. Law.* Rendering null and void.

The States elected Henry Duke of Anjowe for their king, with this clause i.; That if hee did violate any point of his oath, the people should owe him no allegeance HAYWARD.

Irritate (i·riteʲt), *v.*[1] 1531. [– *irritat-*, pa. ppl. stem of L. *irritare*; see -ATE[3].] †**1.** *trans.* To stir up, excite, provoke (a person, etc.) to some action. Const. *to, into,* or *inf.* –1841. †**b.** To stir up, give rise to (an action, feeling, etc.); to heighten, aggravate –1824. **2.** To exasperate, provoke; to vex, fret, annoy 1598. **3.** *Path.* To excite (a bodily organ or part) to morbid action, or to abnormal condition; to produce irritation in 1674. **4.** *Physiol.* and *Biol.* To stimulate (an organ of an animal or plant) to some characteristic action or condition, as motion, contraction, or nervous impulse 1803.

1. Cold maketh the Spirits vigorous, and irritateth them BACON. **b.** With us drink irritates quarrels SIR T. HERBERT. **2.** Dismiss the man, nor i. the god POPE. **4.** Irritating the soles, by tickling or otherwise CARPENTER. So †**I·rritate** *ppl. a.* irritated. **I·rritatedly, I·rritatingly** *advs.*

I·rritate, *v.*[2] 1605. [– *irritat-*, pa. ppl. stem of late L. *irritare* make void, f. L. *irritus* invalid; see IRRITE *a.*, -ATE[3].] *Rom., Civil,* and *Sc. Law.* *trans.* To render void, nullify; = DEFEAT *v.* 5.

Irritation (iritēʲ·ʃən). 1589. [– L. *irritatio*, f. *irritat-*; see IRRITATE *v.*[1], -ION. Cf. (O)Fr. *irritation.*] The action of irritating, or condition of being irritated. †**1.** The action of stirring up or provoking to activity; incitement –1859. **2.** Exasperation, provocation, vexation, annoyance 1703. **3.** *Path.* (and *Med.*) Excitement of a bodily part or organ to excessive sensitiveness or morbid action; the resulting condition 1685. **4.** *Physiol.* and *Biol.* The inducement of some vital action or condition (as motion, contraction, or nervous impulse) in an organ, tissue, etc. of an animal or plant by application of a stimulus 1794.

1. The whole body of the arts and sciences composes one vast machinery for the i. and development of the human intellect DE QUINCEY. **2.** Jacobinism which arises from penury and i. BURKE.

Irritative (i·riteʲtiv), *a.* 1686. [f. as IRRITATE *v.*[1] + -IVE. Cf. (O)Fr. *irritatif, -ive.*] **1.** Having the quality of stirring up or exciting to action; now in *Physiol.* or *Biol.* Having the property of stimulating to vital action. **2.** Tending to irritate; annoying 1878. **3.** *Path.* Characterized by or accompanied with irritation of the system or of some organ 1807.

3. I. fever 1807, conditions of the bone 1873.

Irritatory (i·riteʲtəri, -ătəri), *a.* [– med.L. *irritatorius*, f. *irritat-*; see IRRITATE *v.*[1], -ORY[2].] Irritative. HALES.

†**Irrite,** *a.* Also **irrit.** 1482. [– AFr., OFr. *irrit* or L. *irritus* invalid, f. *in-* IR-[2] + *ratus* established, valid.] Void, of no effect –1741.

†**Irrite,** *v.* 1450. [–(O)Fr. *irriter* – L. *irritare* IRRITATE *v.*[1]] = IRRITATE *v.*[1] –1661.

Irrorate (i·rŏrĕt), *a.* 1826. [– L. *irroratus*, pa. pple. of *irrorare*; see next, -ATE[2].] Irrorated (see next 2).

Irrorate (i·rŏreʲt), *v.* 1623. [– *irrorat-*, pa. ppl. stem of L. *irrorare* bedew, f. *in-* IR-[1] + *rorare* drop dew, f. *ros, ror-* dew; see -ATE[3].] †**1.** *trans.* To wet or sprinkle as with dew; to bedew, besprinkle; to moisten –1676. **2.** *Zool.*, esp. *Entom.* In *pa. pple.* = sprinkled minutely (*with* dots) 1843.

Irroration (irorēʲ·ʃən). 1623. [– late and med.L. *irroratio*, f. as prec.; see -ION.] †**1.** A sprinkling or wetting as with dew; a moistening –1784. **2.** *Zool.* A sprinkling of minute dots or spots of colour 1843.

Irrotational (iroᵘtēʲ·ʃənăl), *a.* 1875. [IR-[2].] *Dynamics.* Not rotational; characterized by absence of rotation; said of fluid motion.

Irrubrical (irū·brikăl), *a.* 1846. [IR-[2].] Not rubrical; contrary to the rubric.

†**I·rrugate,** *v.* 1566. [– *irrugat-*, pa. ppl. stem of L. *irrugare*, f. *in-* IR-[1] + *ruga* wrinkle; see -ATE[3].] *trans.* To wrinkle. So †**I·rrugation.**

Irrupt (irɒ·pt), *v. rare.* 1855. [– *irrupt-*, pa. ppl. stem of L. *irrumpere* break in, f. *in-* IR-[1] + *rumpere* break.] **1.** *trans.* To break into. **2.** *intr.* To burst in, break in, make an irruption 1886.

Irruption (irɒ·pʃən). 1533. [– L. *irruptio*, f. as prec.; see -ION. Cf. (O)Fr. *irruption.*] **1.** The action of bursting or breaking in; a violent entry, inroad, incursion, or invasion, esp. of a hostile force or tribe. ¶**2.** Confused with ERUPTION.

1. As if Nature made recompence for the irruptions of the seas P. HOLLAND. **2.** Vesuvius had lately made a terrible i. 1691. Feverish Irruptions ARBUTHNOT.

Irruptive (irɒ·ptiv), *a.* 1593. [f. as IRRUPT + -IVE.] Making or tending to irruption.

Irvingite (ə̄·ɹviŋəit). 1836. [f. the surname *Irving*; see -ITE[1] 1.] A member of a religious body founded about 1835 on the basis of principles promulgated by Edward Irving (1792–1834), a minister of the Church of Scotland, settled in London, and excommunicated in 1833. (The body itself assumes the title of *Catholic Apostolic Church.*) Also *attrib.* or *adj.* So **I·rvingism.**

Is (iz), *v.* 3 sing. pres. indic. of vb. BE, q.v.

Is-: see ISO-.

-is (-ys), ME. and esp. Sc. var. of the grammatical inflexion *-es, -s*, of the gen. sing., and the pl. of sbs., and of the 3rd pers. sing. of verbs. In MSS. sometimes treated as a separate word or element.

My Lord of Caunterbury is avis and agreement 1456.

Isabel (i·zăbel). 1828. [– Fr. *isabelle* = ISABELLA.] **1.** = ISABELLA 1. **2.** A small variety of the Pouter pigeon; so called from its colour 1867. **3.** A N. Amer. grape. LONGF.

Isabella (izăbe·lă), *a.* (*sb.*) 1600. [From the name *Isabella*, Fr. *Isabelle*, but the immed. ref. is unkn.] **1.** Greyish yellow; light buff. Also used as *sb.* (Not assoc. w. the Archduchess Isabella and the siege of Ostend, 1601–1604.) **2.** Applied to varieties of fruits: **a.** A kind of peach. **b.** A species of N. Amer. grape (*Vitis labrusca*) with large fruit, sometimes purple, often green and red. 1664.

Isabelline (izăbe·lin, -əin), *a.* 1859. [f. prec. + -INE[1].] Of an Isabella colour, greyish yellow.

Isagoge (əisăgōᵘ·dʒi, -gōᵘ·gi). 1652. [– L. *isagoge* – Gr. εἰσαγωγή introduction, f. εἰς into + ἄγειν lead.] An introduction.

Isagogic (əisăgǫ·dʒik), *a.* (*sb.*) 1828. [– L. *isagogicus* – Gr. εἰσαγωγικός, f. εἰσαγωγή; see prec., -IC.]

A. *adj.* Of or pertaining to isagoge; introductory to any branch of study.

The formal, introductory or i., studies 1887.

B. *sb.* (usu. in pl. *isagogics*). Introductory studies; *esp.* that part of theology which is introductory to exegesis 1864.

So †**Isago·gical** *a.* introductory 1529.

Isagonic, erron. form of ISOGONIC.

Isapostolic (əisæpǫstǫ·lik), *a.* 1860. [f. eccl. Gr. ἰσαπόστολος equal to an apostle + -IC.] Equal to, or contemporary with, the apostles; a name given in the Greek Church to bishops consecrated by the apostles, and to other persons eminent in the primitive church.

Isat-, an element derived from L. *isatis* (Gr. ἰσάτις) woad, used in *Chem.* to form the name of ISATIN, etc.

Isatic (əisæ·tik) *acid*, $C_8H_7NO_3$ (= isatin + H_2O); the salts of which are **Isatates** (əi·săteʲts). **I·satyde** (†**isathyd**), a substance bearing the same relation to isatin that indigo-white bears to indigo-blue, being formed from it by the addition of one atom of hydrogen.

Isatin (əi·sătin). Also **-ine.** 1845. [f. L. *isatis* – Gr. ἰσάτις woad + -IN[1].] *Chem.* A crystalline, reddish-orange substance ($C_8H_5NO_2$), of brilliant lustre, obtained from indigo by oxidation.

-isation, freq. var. of -IZATION.

Isatis (əi·sătis). 1774. [From some northern native name.] The white or Arctic fox, *Canis lagopus.*

Iscariot (iskæ·riǒt). 1581. [– L. *Iscariota* – Gr. Ἰσκαριώτης, understood to be Heb. *'îš-ḳ'rīyôṯ* man of Kerioth (a place in Palestine).] The surname of Judas, the disciple who betrayed Jesus Christ. Hence, = an accursed traitor. Also *attrib.* Hence **Iscario·tic, -ical** *a.* of or relating to Judas Iscariot.

Ischiadic (iski,æ·dik), *a.* 1727. [– L. *ischiadicus* – Gr. ἰσχιαδικός, f. ἰσχιάς, -αδ- pain in the hip, f. ἰσχίον hip-joint; see -IC.] Of or pertaining to the ischium; ischiatic. So **I·schial** *a.*

Ischiatic (iski,æ·tik), *a.* 1656. [– med.L. *ischiaticus* (after *rheumaticus*), for L. *ischiadicus*; see prec.] **1.** Of or pertaining to the ischium or hip; sciatic 1741. **2.** Affected with sciatica.

Ischio- (i:skio), – Gr. ἰσχιο-, comb. f. ἰσχίον ISCHIUM, with sense 'pertaining to or connecting the ischium and..', as **ischiore·ctal,** etc.

Hence also **Ischio-ca·psular** *a.* relating to or connected with the ischium and the capsular ligament of the hip-joint. **Ischio·cerite** [Gr. κέρας horn], *Zool.* the third joint of a fully developed antenna of a crustacean. **Ischio·podite** *sb.* [Gr. πούς, ποδ- foot], *Zool.* the third joint of a fully developed limb of a crustacean.

‖**Ischium** (i·skiɒ̆m). Pl. **ischia** (erron. †**-ias**). 1646. [L. – Gr. ἰσχίον hip-joint; later as now used.] The lowest of the three parts of the *os innominatum*, the bone on which the body rests when sitting.

Ischuretic (iskiure·tik). 1706. [f. Gr. ἰσχουρεῖν suffer from retention of urine; cf. next and *diuretic.*] **A.** *adj.* Having the property of curing ischuria. **B.** *sb.* A medicine that cures ischuria.

‖**Ischuria** (iskiūᵊ·riă). Also **ischury** (i·skiŭri). 1675. [late L. – Gr. ἰσχουρία retention of urine, f. ἴσχειν hold + οὖρον urine.] Difficulty in passing urine, due either to suppression or retention. Hence **Ischu·ric** *a.*

Ise, I'se, dial. or arch. abbrev. of *I shall* or *I is* (= I am).

-ise[1], freq. spelling of -IZE, q.v.
-ise[2], suffix of sbs., repr. OFr. *-ise*, properly :– L. *-ītia*, but also, in words of learned formation, put for L. *-icia, -itia, -icium, -itium*. Hence it became a living suffix, forming abstract sbs. of quality, state, or function, as in *couard-ise, gaillard-ise*, etc. In the words from L., *-ise* was subseq. changed in Fr. to *-ice*, as in *justice, service*, in which form the suffix mostly appears in Eng.
Isentropic: see Iso-.
Isethionic (əisīþi,ǫ·nik), *a*. 1838. [f. Iso- + ETHIONIC.] *Chem*. In *isethionic acid*, a monobasic acid, $C_2H_6SO_4$, formed by boiling ethionic acid with water. Hence **Ise·thionate.**
Ish (iʃ). *Sc*. 1375. [f. *ish* vb. (ME. and later Sc. – OFr. *issir* :– L. *exire* go out).] **a.** Exit, as in *ish and entry*. **b.** Expiry of a legal term.
-ish[1], a suffix forming adjs., of Com. Gmc. origin; cogn. w. Gr. *-ισκ-ος* dim. suffix of sbs. Sometimes syncopated to *-sh* (spelt also *-ch*); in Sc. *-ish* becomes *-is* and *-s*. Old formations have vowel-mutation, as *English* (cf. *Angle*), *French* (cf. *Frank*), *Welsh* (cf. *Wales*).
1. In OE. and the cognate langs., chiefly forming gentile adjs. from national names; e.g. *British* (OE. *Brittisc*), *English* (OE. *Englisc*, Sc. †*Inglis*), *Scottish, Scotch* (OE. *Scyttisc*; Sc. †*Scottis*, later *Scots*), etc. **2.** Added to other sbs., with the sense 'Of or belonging to a person or thing, of the nature or character of'. These were not numerous in OE., but in later times the ending is common, chiefly in a derogatory sense, 'Having the (objectionable) qualities of'; as in *apish, currish, womanish*, etc. Also from names of things, with sense 'Of the nature of, tending', as *bookish, freakish*, etc.; or from other parts of speech, as *stand-offish*, etc. **3.** Added to adjs. with the sense 'Of the nature of, approaching the quality of, somewhat'; e.g. *bluish* (*a*1400), *blackish* (*a*1500), etc. Now, in colloq. use, possible with nearly all monosyllabic adjs., and some others, e.g. *brightish, loudish, narrowish*, etc. **4.** Added to names of hours of the day or numbers of years to denote: Round about, somewhere near.
Hence advs. in **-ishly** and sbs. in **-ishness.**
-ish[2], a suffix of vbs., repr. Fr. *-iss-*, extended stem of vbs. in *-ir*, e.g. *périr, perissant*. The Fr. *-iss-* originated in the L. *-isc-* of inceptive vbs. Examples are *abolish, blemish, nourish, vanish*, etc. **b.** Irreg. extended in ADMONISH, DISTINGUISH, FAMISH etc.
Ishmael (i·ʃme,ĕl, i·ʃmė-). [Heb. proper name *Yišmā'ēl*; = 'God will hear'.] Proper name of the son of Abraham by Hagar; hence, An outcast; one 'whose land is against him' (Gen. 16:12), one at war with society 1899.
Hence **I·shmaelite** (a descendant of I., as the Arabs claim to be): *fig*. = ISHMAEL; **Ishmaelitic** (-i·tik), **I·shmaelitish** (-əi·tiʃ), *adjs*.
Isiac (əi·siæ̆k, i·siæ̆k). 1694. [– L. *Isiacus* – Gr. Ἰσιακός, f. Ἶσις.] **A.** *adj*. Of or relating to Isis, the principle goddess of ancient Egyptian mythology 1740. **B.** *sb*. A priest or worshipper of Isis.
I. table, a copper tablet, now in Turin, containing figures of Egyptian deities with Isis in the middle. Hence **Isiacal** (əisəi·ăkăl) *a*. 1613.
Isicle, isi(c)kle, obs. ff. ICICLE.
Isidorian (isidōᵊ·riăn), *a*. 1882. [f. *Isidorus* proper name; see -IAN.] Of or pertaining to Isidorus or Isidore; spec. to St. Isidore, archbishop of Seville 600–636, author of several historical and eccl. works, and of twenty books of *Origines* or Etymologies.
In the Middle Ages his name was attached to various other works, particularly to a collection of canons and decretals.
Isinglass (əi·ziŋglɑs). 1528. [Early forms *isomglas, ison-*, with assim. to *glass* – early Du. †*huysenblas*, f. †*huysen*, †*huys* sturgeon + †*blas* (mod. *blaas*) bladder (cf. G. *hausenblase*).] **1.** A whitish, semi-transparent, and very pure form of gelatin, obtained from the sounds or air-bladders of some freshwater fishes, esp. the sturgeon; used for making jellies, for clarifying liquors, etc. Also extended to similar substances made from hides, hoofs, etc. **2.** A name given to mica, from its resembling in appearance some kinds of isinglass 1747. **3.** *attrib*. and *Comb*., as *i. glue, size*; **i.-stone,** mica 1688.
Islam (i·slăm, i·z-, isla·m). 1613. [– Arab. *islām*, f. *aslama* he resigned himself (spec. to God), he became sincerely religious, 4th conjugation of *salama* he became or was safe. Cf. MOSLEM, SALAAM.] The religious system of Mohammed; the body of Moslems, the Moslem world 1818. †**b.** An orthodox Moslem –1814.
Poor faint smile Of dying I. SHELLEY. Hence **Islamic** (islæ·mic, islā·mik), **Islami·tic** *adjs*. Moslem. **I·slamism,** Islam. **I·slamite,** a Moslem; also *attrib*. **I·slamize** *v*. to convert or conform to Islam; also *intr*.
Island (əi·lænd), *sb*. [OE. (Anglian) *ēġland*, (WS.) *īeġland, īġland*, later *īland* = OFris. *eiland*, MDu., MLG. *eilant*, Du. *eiland*, ON. *eyland*; f. OE. *īeġ, īġ* island, in comp. water, sea + *land* LAND. The present sp. (XVI) is due to assim. to ISLE.] **1.** A piece of land completely surrounded by water. (Formerly including a peninsula, a place insulated at high water or during floods, or begirt by marshes.) **b.** = ISLE *sb*. 1 b. 1535. †**c.** In full, *island of ice*: an iceberg, or the like –1769. **2.** *transf*. Something resembling an island in position; an elevated piece of land surrounded by marsh land; a piece of woodland surrounded by prairie; a block of buildings [= L. *insula*] 1620. **b.** *Anat*. A detached or insulated portion of tissue or group of cells, entirely surrounded by parts of a different structure; *I. of Reil*, the central lobe of the cerebrum 1879. **c.** = REFUGE *sb*. 3 b. 1876. **3.** *attrib*. 1613.
1. The Iland was called Melita *Acts* 28:1. The i. [Britain] has produced two or three of the greatest men that ever existed EMERSON. **2.** A small hill, or iland, in the meddow on the west side of Charles Riuer 1650. **3.** The i.-fishing DRUMM. OF HAWTH. Our rough i.-story TENNYSON. The i.-home they won for us GEO. ELIOT. I.-belted shores 1884.
Comb.: **i.-continent,** an i. approaching the size of the continents, or containing several states, as Australia or Greenland; **-platform,** a platform at a railway station, with lines on each side of it.
Island (əi·lænd), *v*. 1661. [f. prec. sb.] **1.** *trans*. To make into or as into an island; to place as an island; to place or set on, or as on, an island; to insulate. **2.** To set or dot with or as with islands 1805.
1. Billowy mist . . islanding The peak whereon we stand SHELLEY. **2.** The waveless plain of Lombardy . . Islanded by cities fair SHELLEY.
Island, obs. f. ICELAND[2]. *Island crystal*, Iceland spar.
Islander (əi·lændəɹ). 1550. [f. ISLAND *sb*. + -ER[1].] A native or inhabitant of an island.
I·slandman. Now *rare* or *local*. 1577. = ISLANDER.
At Belfast applied to the ship-builders on Queen's Island, more fully *Queen's Islandmen*.
Isle (əil), *sb*. [ME. *ile*, later *isle* – OFr. *ile* (mod. *île*), (latinized) †*isle* :– L. *insula*.] **1.** An island; now more usually one of smaller size. Also *fig*. **b.** In O.T., after the equivalent Heb., applied to the lands beyond the sea; esp. in phr. *isles of the Gentiles* ME. **2.** A building or block of buildings, surrounded by streets. [L. *insula*.] 1670.
1. Great Ladie of the greatest I. SPENSER. **b.** The yles shall waite for his lawe *Isa*. 42:4.
Isle (əil), *v*. 1570. [f. prec. sb.] **1.** *trans*. = ISLAND *v*. 1. **2.** *intr*. To remain or lodge on an isle. TENNYSON.
1. Thank Him who isled us here TENNYSON.
I·sleman. *rare*. 1814. [f. ISLE + MAN.] = ISLESMAN, ISLANDER.
Islesman (əi·lz,mæ̆n). late ME. [Sc. (XV–XVI) *il(l)is, yl(l)is men*, (XVII) *ilsmen*.] An inhabitant or native of one of the Scottish groups of islands, esp. the Hebrides.
Islet (əi·lėt). 1538. [– OFr. *islet, -ete* (mod. *îlette*), dim. of *isle*; see ISLE, -ET.] **1.** A little island, an eyot or ait. **2.** *transf*. = ISLAND *sb*. 2. 1645. **b.** An isolated piece of animal or vegetable tissue 1851. **3.** *attrib*. 1810.
1. Where there is an i. in the stream GOLDSM. **2.** Islet . ., a spot of a different colour, included in a plaga or macula KIRBY & SP. **3.** That i. angle of the west 1871. Hence **I·sleted** *ppl. a*. placed like an i.; studded with islets.
Islot, ilot (əi·lǫt). 1772. [– Fr. *islot* (later *îlot*), dim. of *isle*; see ISLE, -OT[1].] An islet.
-ism, *suffix*, repr. Fr. *-isme*, L. *-ismus* – Gr. *-ισμός*, forming nouns of action from vbs. in *-ίζειν*, e.g. *βαπτίζειν, βαπτισμός* the action of dipping, baptism. An allied suffix was *-ισμα(τ-*, expressing the thing done, and which in some cases is the source of modern *-ism*. The following are the chief uses of the suffix:
1. Forming a simple noun of action, naming the process, or the completed action, or its result (rarely concrete); as in *agonism, aphorism, baptism, organism, syllogism*, etc. **b.** Expressing the action or conduct of a class of persons, as *heroism, patriotism, priggism, scoundrelism*, etc.; also the condition of a person or thing, as *barbarism, orphanism, parallelism*, etc.; also *Daltonism*.
2. Forming the name of a system of theory or practice, as *Arianism, Brahmanism, Chartism, Conservatism, Puseyism, Quietism*, etc. **b.** More of the nature of class-names or descriptive terms for doctrines or principles, are *agnosticism, altruism, bimetallism, jingoism, sansculottism, stoicism*, etc.
3. Forming a term denoting a peculiarity or characteristic, esp. of language, e.g. *Americanism, Græcism, Orientalism*, etc. To these add such as *archaism, colloquialism, modernism, solecism*.
Ism (i·z'm), *quasi-sb*. 1680. [The prec. suffix used generically.] A form of doctrine, theory, or practice having a distinctive character or relation; chiefly disparaging.
He is nothing,—no 'ist', professes no '-ism' but superbism and irrationalism SHELLEY.
Ismaelian, Ismaïlian (isme,ī·liăn, -i·liăn), *sb*. and *a*. 1839. [f. Arab proper name *'Ismā'īl*; see -IAN.] A member of a sect of the Shiite branch of Islam which held that, at the death of Djafar Madeck, the Imamship ought to have descended to the posterity of his deceased elder son Ismail, and not to the surviving younger son Mousa, to whom he left it. **b.** as *adj*.
I·smaelite, *sb*. (*a*.) Also (in sense c) **I·smailite.** 1571. [f. as prec. + -ITE[1] 1.] **a.** Another form of ISHMAELITE. **b.** A name formerly sometimes given (esp. by Jews) to the Arabs as descendants of Ishmael, and so to Moslems generally. **c.** *spec*. = ISMAELIAN.
Isn't, colloq. f. *is not*.
Iso- (əiso), bef. a vowel occas. **is-,** comb. f. Gr. *ἴσος* equal, used in numerous terms, nearly all scientific, the second element being properly and usually of Gr. origin, rarely of Latin (the proper prefix in the latter case being EQUI-). Some of the less important of these are:
Isentro·pic *a*. and *sb*. *Physics*, of equal entropy; (a line on a diagram) indicating successive states of a body in which the entropy remains constant. **I·sobath** (-bæþ) [Gr. *βάθος* depth], an inkstand with a float so contrived as to keep the ink in the dipping-well at a constant level. **Isobathytherm** (-bæ·piþəɹm) [Gr. *βαθύς* deep + *θέρμη* heat], a line connecting points having the same temperature in a vertical section of any part of the sea; so **Isobathythe·rmal, -the·rmic** *adjs*. **Isocephaly** (-se·fāli), **-kephaly** (-ke·fāli) [Gr. *κεφαλή* head], the principle observed in some ancient Greek reliefs, esp. in friezes, of representing the heads of all the figures at nearly the same level. **I·sochasm** (-kæz'm) [Gr. *χάσμα* gap], a line on a map, etc. connecting places having equal frequency of auroral displays; so **Isocha·smic** *a*. (lines or curves) bounding zones of equal auroral frequency. **Isochroous** (əisǫ·kro,əs) [Gr. *χρόα* colour] *a*., of the same colour throughout. **Isodimorphism** (əi:sodeimǭ·ɹfiz'm) [see DIMORPHISM], *Cryst*. 'isomorphism between the forms severally of two dimorphous substances' (Webster); so **I:sodimo·rphous** *a*., exhibiting isodimorphism. **Isohyetal** (-həi·ītăl), **-hy·etose** [Gr. *ὑετός* rain] *adjs*. (*sbs*.), (a line on a map, etc.) connecting places having equal annual or seasonal rainfall. **Isoneph** (əi·sonef) [Gr. *νέφος* cloud], a line on a map, etc. connecting places at which the amount of cloud for a given period (e.g. a year) is the same; so **Isonephelic** (-nīfe·lik) [Gr. *νεφέλη*] *a*., indicating equality in respect of cloudiness. **Isopiestic** (-pəi,e·stik) [Gr. *πιέζειν*] *a*., denoting equal pressure. **Isoseismal** (-səi·smăl) [Gr. *σεισμός* earthquake] *a*. and *sb*., (a line on a map, etc.) connecting points at which the intensity of an earthquake-shock is the same; so **Isosei·smic** *a*. **Isosporous** (əisǫ·spōrəs) [Gr. *σπόρος* seed] *a*., *Bot*. producing spores all of the same size or kind (opp. to *heterosporous*); so **Isospore** (əi·sospoᵊɹ), one of such spores. **Isostemonous** (-stī·mŏnəs) [Gr. *στήμων* in sense 'stamen'] *a*., *Bot*. having the stamens equal in number to the parts of the perianth; also said of the stamens; so **Isostemony** (-stī·mŏni), the condition of being isostemonous. **Isotrimorphism** (əi:sotrəim·ǭfiz'm), *Cryst*. 'isomorphism between the forms, severally, of two trimorphous substances' (Webster); so **I:sotrimo·rphous** *a*., exhibiting isotrimorphism.
b. In *Chem*. sometimes prefixed to the name of a compound substance to denote another substance isomeric with it. The number of such names is unlimited.

Isobar (əi·sobāɹ). Also **isobare.** 1864. [f. Gr. ἰσοβαρής of equal weight, f. ἰσο- Iso- + βαρε-, βάρος weight, βαρύς heavy.] *Phys. Geog.* and *Meteorol.* A line (drawn on a map, etc., or imaginary) connecting places on the earth's surface at which the barometric pressure is the same (at a given time, or on the average for a given period); an isobaric line.

Isobaric (əisobæ·rik), *a.* 1878. [f. prec. + -IC. (Not on Gr. analogies.)] Indicating equal barometric pressure; containing or relating to isobars.

Isobarism (əisǫ·bǎriz'm). 1882. [f. as prec. + -ISM.] Equality of weight. (Dicts.)

Isobarometric (əisobærome·trik), *a. rare.* 1864. [f. ISO- + BAROMETRIC.] = ISOBARIC.

Isocheim (əi·sokəim). Also **-chime.** 1864. [f. Gr. ἰσο- ISO- + χεῖμα winter-weather.] *Phys. Geog.* An isochimenal line.

Isocheimal (əisokəi·măl), *a.* and *sb.* Also **-chimal.** 1839. [f. prec. + -AL[1].] = ISOCHIMENAL.

Isochimenal (-kəi·mĭnăl). Also **-cheimenal.** 1846. [– Fr. *isochimène* (Humboldt, 1817), f. Gr. ἰσο- Iso- + χειμαίνειν be wintry, f. χεῖμα winter-weather, storm.] **A.** *adj.* Indicating equal mean winter temperatures; said of lines on a map, etc. **B.** *sb.* An isochimenal line, an isocheim.

Isochromatic (əi:so͵kromæ·tik), *a.* 1829. [f. ISO- + CHROMATIC.] **1.** *Optics.* Of the same colour or tint, as two lines or curves in an interference figure of a biaxial crystal. **2.** *Photogr.* = *orthochromatic.*

Isochronal (əisǫ·krŏnăl), *a.* †Also *erron.* **-cronal.** 1680. [f. mod.L. *isochronus* (Leibnitz) – Gr. ἰσόχρονος (f. ἰσο- ISO- + χρόνος time) + -AL[1].] = ISOCHRONOUS.
So **Isochro·nic, -al** *a.*

Isochronism (əisǫ·krŏniz'm). 1770. [f. as prec. + -ISM.] The character or property of being isochronous, or of oscillating or taking place in equal spaces of time.

Isochronous (əisǫ·krŏnəs), *a.* 1706. [f. as ISOCHRONAL + -OUS.] Taking place in or occupying equal times; equal in metrical length; equal in duration, or in intervals of occurrence; characterized by or relating to vibrations or motions of equal duration; vibrating uniformly, as a pendulum. **b.** Equal in duration (vibration-period, etc.) *to* or *with* something 1776. Hence **Iso·chronously** *adv.*

Isoclinal (əisokləi·năl), *a.* (*sb.*) 1839. [f. ISO- + Gr. κλίνειν bend, slope + -AL[1].] **1.** *Phys. Geog.* Indicating equal magnetic inclination; applied to lines connecting points of the earth's surface at which the magnetic inclination or dip is the same; relating to or containing such lines. **2.** *Geol.* Of strata: Dipping all in the same direction 1882. **3.** *sb.* An isoclinal line: see sense 1. 1889. So **Isocli·nic** *a.* and *sb.*

Isocracy (əisǫ·krăsi). 1652. [– Gr. ἰσοκρατία equality of power or political rights, f. ἰσο- ISO- + κράτος, κρατε- strength, power; see -CRACY.] Equality of power or rule; a system of government in which all the people possess equal political power.

A debasing i., which already views with suspicion the cultivation of the highest literature 1895.

Isocrymal (əisokrəi·măl). 1852. [f. Iso- + Gr. κρυμός cold + -AL[1].] *Phys. Geog.* **A.** *adj.* Applied to lines on a map, etc. connecting places at which the temperature is the same during a specified coldest part (*e.g.* the coldest 30 consecutive days) of the year. **B.** *sb.* An isocrymal line; also **I·socryme.**

Isodiabatic (əi:sodəi͵ăbæ·tik), *a.* 1859. [f. ISO- + Gr. διαβατικός able to pass through; cf. ADIABATIC.] *Physics.* Relating to or indicating the transmission of equal amounts of heat to and from a body or substance.

Isodiametric, -al (əisodəi͵ăme·trik, -ăl), *a.* 1884. [f. ISO- + DIAMETRIC.] Having equal diameters; *spec.* applied in *Bot.* to cells of rounded or polyhedral form; in *Cryst.* to crystals having equal lateral axes.

Isodynamic (əi:sodinæ·mik), *a.* (*sb.*) 1832. [f. Gr. ἰσοδύναμος + -IC; after *dynamic.*] Of or pertaining to equal force. **1.** *Phys. Geog.*, etc. Indicating equal (magnetic) force; applied to lines connecting points at which the intensity of the magnetic force is the same; or to a chart, etc. exhibiting these. Also as *sb.* An isodynamic line. **2.** Of equal force, value, or efficacy 1842. So **Isodyna·mical** *a.*, in sense 1.

Isodynamous (əisodi·nāməs), *a.* 1835. [f. as prec. + -OUS.] *Bot.* Growing with equal vigour on both sides.

Isogeotherm (əiso͵dʒī·oþə̄ɹm). 1864. [f. ISO- + Gr. γεω- earth + θέρμη heat, θερμός hot.] *Phys. Geog.* A line or surface (usu. imaginary) connecting points in the interior of the earth having the same temperature. Hence **Isogeothe·rmal, -the·rmic** *adjs.* of the nature of an i. 1832.

Isogonal (əisǫ·gŏnăl), *a.* (*sb.*) 1857. [f. Gr. ἰσογώνιος equiangular + -AL[1].] **1.** = ISOGONIC *a.*[1] and *sb.* **2.** Equiangular 1878.

Isogonic (əisogǫ·nik), *a.*[1] (*sb.*) 1851. [f. as prec. + -IC.] *Phys. Geog.* Indicating equal angles (of magnetic variation); applied to lines on a map, etc. connecting points of the earth's surface where the magnetic declination, or variation from the true north, is the same; or to a map, etc. exhibiting these. Also as *sb.* An isogonic line.

Isogo·nic, *a.*[2] [f. as next + -IC.] *Biol.* Characterized by isogonism. (Mod. Dicts.)

Isogonism (əisǫ·gŏniz'm). 1884. [f. ISO- + Gr. γόνος, γονή offspring + -ISM.] *Biol.* The production of sexual individuals of the same structure from different stocks, occurring in some *Hydrozoa.*

Isographic (əisogræ·fik), *a.* 1872. [f. Iso- + -GRAPHIC.] = HOMALOGRAPHIC. **Isogra·phically** *adv.* in the way of i. projection.

Isolable (əi·sŏlăb'l), *a.* 1855. [f. ISOLATE + -ABLE.] Capable of being isolated.

Isolate (əi·sŏleit), *v.* 1807. [Back-formation from ISOLATED (now regarded as pple. of the vb.); partly after Fr. *isoler.*] **1.** *trans.* To place apart or alone; to cause to stand alone; separate, detached, or unconnected with other things or persons; to insulate. **2.** *Chem.* To obtain as a separate substance 1836. **3.** *Electr.* = INSULATE *v.* 3. 1855. **4.** To cut off (an infected person or place) from all contact with others 1890.

1. Whatever isolates people from people is a mischievous partition wall 1845. High culture always isolates 1873.

Isolated (əi·sŏleitėd), *ppl. a.* 1763. [f. Fr. *isolé* – It. *isolato* :– late L. *insulatus* made into an island, f. *insula* ISLE; see -ATE[2], -ED[1].] Placed or standing apart or alone; detached or separate from other things or persons; unconnected with anything else; solitary.

Collective action is more efficacious than i. individual effort M. ARNOLD. Hence **I·solatedly** *adv.*

I·solating, *ppl. a.* 1861. [f. ISOLATE *v.* + -ING[2].] *Philol.* Applied to languages of which each element is an isolated or independent word, none being compounded or inflected.

Isolation (əisŏlēi·ʃən). 1833. [f. ISOLATE *v.*, partly after Fr. *isolation*; see -ATION.] The action of isolating; the fact or condition of being isolated; separation from other things or persons; solitariness. **b.** *attrib.* in *i. hospital, camp,* etc., one by which isolation is effected 1891.

I·solative, *a.* 1888. [f. ISOLATE *v.* + -IVE.] In *Phonetics,* said of sound-changes which take place without reference to neighbouring sounds.

I·solator. 1855. [f. ISOLATE *v.*; see -OR 2.] One who or that which isolates; an insulator.

Isologous (əisǫ·lŏgəs), *a.* 1857. [f. ISO- + Gr. λόγος relation, etc. + -OUS.] *Chem.* Having equality or parallelism of relations; applied to two or more hydrocarbon series, of each of which the members are related to each other in the same way.

The allylic, the benzoic, and the cinnamic series, are *i.* with that of alcohol 1857.

Isomer (əi·soməɹ). 1866. [– G. *isomer* (Berzelius, 1832), f. Gr. ἰσομερής sharing equally, f. ἰσο- ISO- + μέρος part, share; in Fr. *isomère.*] *Chem.* A substance isomeric with another; any one of a number of isomeric compounds.

Isomeric (əisome·rik), *a.* 1838. [f. as ISOMER + -IC; after G. *isomerisch* (Berzelius, 1832).] *Chem.* Composed of the same elements in the same proportions, and (ordinarily) having the same molecular weight, but forming different substances, with different properties (owing to the different grouping of the constituent atoms).

Isomeride (əisǫ·mĕrəid). 1857. [f. as ISOMER + -IDE.] *Chem.* = ISOMER.

Isomerism (əisǫ·mĕriz'm). 1838. [f. ISOMER + -ISM.] *Chem.* The fact or condition of being isomeric; identity of percentage composition in compounds differing in properties.

Bodies may conduct themselves chemically in exactly the same way, and yet differ in some of their physical properties, as in their action towards polarized light. To distinguish this kind of i...it is called *physical i.* 1896.

Isomeromorphism (əiso:mĕro͵mǭ·ɹfiz'm). 1864. [f. *isomero-*, comb. f. next + Gr. μορφή form + -ISM.] *Cryst.* Isomorphism between isomeric substances.

Isomerous (əisǫ·mĕrəs), *a.* 1857. [f. as ISOMER + -OUS.] **1.** *Bot.* Of a flower: Having the same number of parts in each whorl. (Said also of the whorls.) Opp. to HETEROMEROUS 2. **2.** *Chem.* = ISOMERIC 1864.

Isometric (əisome·trik), *a.* 1840. [f. Gr. ἰσομετρία (f. ἴσος + μέτρος) + -IC.] **1.** Of equal measure or dimensions 1855. **2.** Applied to a method of projection or perspective, in which the plane of projection is equally inclined to the three principal axes of the object, so that all dimensions parallel to these axes are represented in their actual proportions; used in drawing figures of machines, etc. 1840. **3.** *Cryst.* Applied to that system of crystalline forms characterized by three equal axes mutually at right angles (also called *cubic, tesseral,* etc.); belonging to this system 1868. So **Isome·trical** *a.* 1838. **Isome·trically** *adv.*

Isomorph (əi·somǭɹf). 1864. [f. ISO- + Gr. μορφή form.] *Chem.* and *Min.* A substance or organism isomorphous with another.

Isomorphic (əisomǭ·ɹfik), *a.* 1862. [f. as prec. + -IC.] **1.** *Chem.* and *Min.* Exhibiting isomorphism, isomorphous; pertaining to or involving isomorphism. **2.** *Math.* Of groups or other systems, exactly corresponding in form and in the relations between their elements 1897.

Isomorphism (əisomǭ·ɹfiz'm). 1828. [– G. *isomorphismus* (Mitscherlich, 1819), f. as prec. + -ISM.] The character of being isomorphous. **1.** *Chem.* and *Min.* The property of crystallizing in the same or closely related forms, esp. as exhibited by substances of analogous composition. **2.** *Math.* Identity of form and of operations between two or more groups.

1. The discovery by Professor Mitscherlich, of what is called the *isomorphism* of crystals, diminishes in some degree the value of crystalline form as a distinctive character TRIMMER.

Isomorphous (əisomǭ·ɹfəs), *a.* 1828. [f. as ISOMORPH + -OUS.] **1.** *Chem.* and *Min.* Having the property of crystallizing in the same or closely related geometric forms; said esp. of two compounds or groups of compounds of different elements, but of analogous composition. **2.** *Math.* = ISOMORPHIC 2.

-ison, suffix of sbs., repr. OFr. *-aison, -eison, -eson, -ison* :– L. *-ationem* (adopted later in the learned form *-ation*, which is thus a doublet of *-ison*), *-etionem, -itionem.* Examples *comparison, garrison, jettison, venison,* etc.

Isonomic (əisonǫ·mik), *a.* 1864. [– Gr. ἰσονομικός 'devoted to equality', f. ἰσονομία; see ISONOMY.] **1.** Having equal laws or rights (*rare*). **2.** *Chem.* Having the same or a similar arrangement of elements; involving analogy of composition, as *isomorphism* in the stricter sense 1864. **3.** Of the same or like polarity; applied to contact of parts of the body in experiments on animal magnetism; opp. to HETERONOMIC, q.v.

Isonomy (əisǫ·nŏmi). 1600. [– It. *isonomia* – Gr. ἰσονομία, f. (ult.) ἰσο- ISO- + νόμος law.] Equality of laws, or of people before the law.

Isopathy (əisǫ·păþi). *rare.* 1855. [f. ISO- + -PATHY.] *Med.* **a.** The theory that disease may be cured by a product of the disease, as small-pox by variolous matter. **b.** The popular notion that disease in a particular organ may be cured by eating the same organ of a healthy animal.

Isoperimeter (əi:sopĕri·mĭtəɹ). 1674. [– Gr. ἰσοπερίμετρος; see Iso- and PERIMETER.] *Geom.* A figure having a perimeter equal to that of another; usu. *pl.* Figures of equal perimeter.

Isoperimetrical (əi:soperime·trikăl), *a.* 1706. [f. as prec. + -ICAL.] *Geom.* **1.** Of figures: Having equal perimeters. **2.** Relating to or connected with isoperimetry 1743. So †**Isoperi·metral** *a.* 1625.

Isoperimetry (əisopĕri·mĕtri). 1811. [f. as ISOPERIMETER + -Y³.] *Geom.* That branch of geometry which deals with isoperimetrical figures and problems.

Isopleural (əisoplūə·răl), *a.* [f. as next + -AL¹.] Having equal sides, equilateral; *spec.* in *Zool.* belonging to the sub-class *Isopleura* of gastropods, which have the body bilaterally symmetrical, as in the chitons. **Isopleu·rous** *a.*

†**I·sopleure.** Also **isopleuron.** 1592. [– Gr. ἰσόπλευρος equilateral, f. ἰσο- Iso- + πλευρά rib, side.] An equilateral figure –1674.

Isopod (əi·sǒpǫd), *sb.* (*a.*) Also **isopode.** Pl. **isopods;** also freq. in L. form **iso·poda.** 1835. [– Fr. *isopode* – mod.L. *Isopoda* n. pl.; see Iso-, -POD.] *Zool.* An animal of the order *Isopoda* of sessile-eyed Crustaceans, characterized by seven pairs of equal and similarly placed thoracic legs; comprising marine, freshwater, and terrestrial species, some being parasitic. Also as *adj.*

So **Iso·podan** *a.* and *sb.* = prec. **Isopo·diform** *a.* having the form of an i., as certain insect larvæ. **Iso·podous** *a.* belonging to, or having the characters of, the *Isopoda* 1826.

Isopolity (əisopǫ·lĭti). 1836. [– Gr. ἰσοπολιτεία see Iso-, POLITY.] Chiefly *Anc. Hist.* Equality of rights of citizenship between different communities or states; reciprocity of civic rights.

Between America and England..one would be glad if there could exist some i. CLOUGH.

Isosceles (əisǫ·sĭlīz), *a.* (*sb.*) 1551. [– late L. *isosceles* – Gr. ἰσοσκελής, f. ἰσο Iso- + σκέλος leg.] *Geom.* Of a triangle: Having two of its sides equal.

Also **Isoscele** (əi·sosīl) *sb.* BROWNING.

Isospondylous (əisopǫ·ndiləs), *a.* [f. mod.L. *Isospondylus* (in pl. *-yli*) (f. Iso- + Gr. σπόνδυλος, σφόν- vertebra, joint) + -OUS.] *Ichthyol.* Belonging to, or having the characters of, the *Isospondyli*, an order of physostomous fishes.

Isostasy (əisǫ·stăsi). [f. Iso- + Gr. στάσις station + -Y³.] The equilibrium of the earth's crust; hydrostatic equilibrium. Hence **Isosta·tic** *a.* 1901.

‖**Isoteles** (əisǫ·tĭlīz). 1849. [– Gr. ἰσοτελής paying equal taxes, f. ἴσος equal + τέλος tax.] *Anc. Gr. Hist.* One of a class of *metœci* or resident aliens of Athens who enjoyed all civic (except political) rights. So **Iso·tely** the condition of an i.

Isotheral (əisǫ·þĕrăl, əi·soþĭᵊrăl). 1839. [f. next + -AL¹.] **A.** *adj.* Applied to lines on a map, etc. connecting places having the same mean summer temperature. **B.** *sb.* An isotheral line.

Isothere (əi·soþiᵊɹ). 1852. [– Fr. *isothère* sb. (= *ligne isothère*; Humboldt, 1817) – Gr. ἰσο- Iso- + θέρος summer.] *Phys. Geog.* An imaginary line passing through points on the earth's surface that have the same mean summer temperature.

Isotherm (əi·soþɔ̄ɹm). 1860. [– Fr. *isotherme* (Humboldt, 1817), f. Gr. ἰσο- Iso- + θέρμη heat, θερμός hot.] *Phys. Geog.* An imaginary line passing through points on the earth's surface that have the same mean temperature; an isothermal line.

Isothermal (əisoþɔ̄·ɹmăl). 1826. [f. Fr. *isotherme* (see prec.) + -AL¹.]

A. *adj.* Of, pertaining to, indicating, or corresponding to equal temperatures; **a.** *esp.* in *Phys. Geog.* applied to a line connecting places on the earth's surface at which the temperature for a particular period (e.g. a year) is the same; also to a map or chart exhibiting such lines. **b.** Applied to (imaginary) lines or surfaces of equal heat in a crystal or other body when heated 1854. **B.** *sb.* An isothermal line or surface; an isotherm 1852.

Hence **Isothe·rmobath** [Gr. βάθος depth], a line connecting points of equal temperature at various depths in a vertical section of the sea. **Isothe·rmous** *a.* = ISOTHERMAL *a.*

Isotope (əi·sotoᵘp). 1913. [f. Iso- + Gr. τόπος place.] *Chem.* A chemical element possessing the same chemical character as another element occupying the same place in the periodic table, but distinguished from it in other ways, as by its radio-activity or the differing mass of its atoms. SODDY. Hence **Isoto·pic** *a.*, **I·sotopism, Iso·topy.**

Isotopic was used by Cohen and Miller in a different sense in 1904.

Isotropic (əisotrǫ·pik), *a.* 1864. [f. Iso- + Gr. τρόπος turn, etc. + -IC.] *Physics.* Exhibiting equal physical properties or actions in all directions; opp. to *æolotropic* or *anisotropic*. So **I·sotrope, Iso·tropous** *adjs.* in same sense. **Iso·tropy,** the condition or quality of being i.

Israel (i·zre͵ĕl, i·zrė-). OE. [– eccl. L. *Isrāēl*, Gr. Ἰσραήλ – Heb. *yisrā'ēl* 'he that striveth with God', name conferred on Jacob (Gen. 32:28).] **1.** The people descended from Israel or Jacob, the 'children of Israel' collectively; the Jewish or Hebrew nation or people. **2.** In *fig.* uses; *esp.* the chosen people of God, the elect; the Christian Church, or true Christians collectively ME.

2. The greatest Troublers of our *Israel* 1692.

Israelite (i·zre͵ĕləit, i·zrė-). ME. [– late L. (Vulg.) *Isrāēlita* – Gr. Ἰσραηλίτης, Heb. *yisrā'ēlī*; see -ITE¹ 1.] **A.** *sb.* **1.** One of the people of Israel; a Hebrew; a Jew. **2.** *fig.* One of God's chosen people ME.

1. Behold an I. indeed in whom is no guile *John* 1:47.

B. *adj.* Pertaining to Israel; Jewish, Israelitish 1851.

So **I:sraeli·tic, †-al, I·sraeli:tish** *adjs.* belonging to the Israelites; Jewish.

Issuable (i·ʃ¹uăb'l, i·siu-), *a.* 1570. [f. ISSUE *sb.* and *v.* + -ABLE.] **1.** *Law.* In regard to which or during which issue may be joined. Also *transf.* **2.** That may be issued, as a writ or summons; authorized to be issued 1642. **3.** Liable to issue as the proceeds of any property, investment, or source of revenue 1674.

1. His Lordship held that there was no issueable matter in the paragraphs complained of 1890. Hence **I·ssuably** *adv.* so as to raise an issue.

Issuance (i·ʃ¹uăns, i·siu-). *U.S.* 1865. [f. next; see -ANCE.] The action of issuing; = ISSUE *sb.*

Issuant (i·ʃ¹u͵ănt, i·siu-), *a.* 1610. [f. ISSUE *v.* + -ANT, after Fr. pr. pples. in *-ant*. Superseding earlier *issant*.] **1.** Issuing or proceeding from a place or source. Now *rare.* 1634. **2.** *Her.* Emerging from the bottom of a chief, or (less usually) rising from another bearing or from the bottom of an escutcheon. Said esp. of a beast of which the upper half alone is visible.

Issue (i·ʃ¹u, i·siu), *sb.* ME. [– (O)Fr. *issue*, †*eissue* :– Rom. **exuta*, subst. use of fem. of pa. pple. **exutus*, for L. *exitus*, pa. pple. of *exire* go out or forth (see EXIT).]

I. 1. The action of going, passing, or flowing out; power of egress or exit; outgoing, outflow. Also *fig.* †**b.** A sortie –1685. **2.** Outgoing, termination, end, close 1483. **3.** *Med.* A discharge of blood or other matter from the body, either due to disease or produced surgically by counter-irritation 1526. **b.** An incision or artificial ulcer made for the purpose of causing such a discharge 1607.

1. The Lord kepe thin entre and thi issu WYCLIF *Ps.* 120[1]:8. To make i. HOLLAND. Place of i. TYNDALL. *fig.* Vnto God the Lord belong the issues from death *Ps.* 68:20. **3. b.** He had a blister, or i., upon his neck PEPYS.

II. A place or means of egress; outlet ME.

This Sea [the Caspian] is..without any i. to other Seas PURCHAS.

III. 1. Offspring; a child or children; a descendant or descendants. Now chiefly in legal use. †Formerly occas. with pl. *issues.* ME. Also *fig.* †**b.** A race, stock; also *fig.* –1680. **2.** Produce, proceeds; profits arising from lands, tenements, amerciaments, or fines. Now only in legal use. ME. †**b.** A fine, an amerciament; an order for levying such –1752. **3.** Outcome, product 1601. †**b.** An action, a deed (in relation to the doer). SHAKS.

1. No i. from this marriage survived 1850. **2.** Profytes and issues of the maners ME. **3. b.** *Jul. C.* III. i. 294.

IV. Event, result, consequence. Also in pl. *In the i.*, in the event ME. †**b.** Luck in an undertaking –1639. †**c.** Decision, conclusion –1719. **d.** The upshot of an argument, evidence, etc. 1604.

The i. of the combat GOUGE. **b.** *Ant. & Cl.* I. ii. 97. **d.** *Oth.* III. iii. 219.

V. *Law.* The point in question, at the conclusion of the pleadings in an action, when one side affirms and the other denies 1511. **b.** *transf.* A point on the decision of which something depends or is made to rest; a point or matter in contention; the point at which a matter becomes ripe for decision 1566. **c.** A matter or point which remains to be decided 1836.

Issue of law, an issue raised by a demurrer or analogous proceedings, conceding the fact alleged, but denying the application of the law as claimed. *General i.*, an issue raised by simply traversing the allegations in the declaration, as in the plea 'not guilty'. **b.** Phr. *To put to* (†*on, upon, an, the*) *i.*: to bring to a point admitting of decision. **c.** There is a mighty i. at stake..the good or evil of the human soul JOWETT.

Phrases. **At i. a.** In *Law*: The term used, when, in the course of pleading, the parties come to a point which one affirms and the other denies. Hence *gen.* of persons or parties: In controversy; at variance. **b.** Of a matter: In dispute; in question. **To join i. a.** *Law.* To submit an issue jointly for decision; also, of one party, To accept the issue tendered by the opposite party. **b.** *transf.* To accept or adopt a disputed point as the basis of argument in a controversy. **c.** To take up the opposite side of a case, or a contrary view *on* a question.

VI. From ISSUE *v.* The action of sending or giving out officially or publicly; an emission of bills of exchange, notes, bonds, shares, postage-stamps, etc. **b.** The set number or amount (of coins, notes, copies of a newspaper, etc.) issued at one time, or distinguished in pattern, etc., from those issued at another time. 1835. **c.** An item or amount given out 1861 (orig. *U.S.*).

Bank of issue: see BANK *sb.*³ The first small i. of the French assignats JEVONS.

Comb. **i. pea,** a pea or other small globular body placed in a surgical issue (I. 3 b), to keep up irritation.

Issue (i·ʃ¹u, i·siu), *v.* ME. [f. prec. sb.]

I. *intr.* **1.** To go or come out; to flow out; to come forth, sally out. **b.** To start forth, to branch out; †to stick out 1533. **c.** *transf.* and *fig.* To emerge 1481. **2.** To be born, or descended. Now only in legal use. 1450. **3.** To come as proceeds or revenue; to accrue 1443. **4.** To take origin, be derived, spring 1481. **b.** To result 1576. **5.** To turn out (in a specified way); to end or result *in* 1665. **6.** To be published or emitted 1640.

1. Let's..i. forth, and bid them Battaile straight SHAKS. **b.** From his head i. foure great hornes SIR T. HERBERT. **3.** A fee farme rent issuing out of white acre of ten shillings BACON. **4.** It issues from the rancour of a Villaine SHAKS. **5.** A philosophy which issues in such conclusions FROUDE. **6.** Before money can legally i. from the Treasury [etc.] 1795.

II. *trans.* **1.** To give exit to; to send forth, or allow to pass out; to let out; to emit; to discharge 1442. †**2.** To give birth to; to bear (offspring), have issue –1672. **3.** To give or send out authoritatively or officially; to send forth or deal out formally or publicly; to emit, put into circulation 1601. †**4.** To bring to an issue; to settle, terminate. Chiefly Amer. –1706. **b.** To cause to end *in* something (now *rare*) 1676. **5.** To supply (an army, etc.) *with* 1925.

1. A gaping wound Issuing life blood SHAKS. **2.** *Temp.* I. ii. 59. **3.** To i. process BLACKSTONE, writs BURKE, tickets DICKENS, parts of a Dictionary 1897.

Issueless (i·ʃ¹ulės, i·siulės), *a.* 1447. [-LESS.] Without issue; without offspring. **b.** Without result 1611.

Both their daughters i. 1791.

Issuer (i·ʃ¹u͵əɹ, i·siu͵əɹ). 1757. [f. ISSUE *v.* + -ER¹.] One who issues; see the vb.

I·ssuing, *vbl. sb.* 1481. [f. as prec. + -ING¹.] **1.** The action of ISSUE *v.* †**2.** *concr.* A place or point of issue; an outlet –1712.

-ist, *suffix*, corresp. to Fr. *-iste*, L. *-ista*, Gr. -ιστής, forming agent-nouns from verbs in -ίζειν (see -IZE), consisting of the agential -της added to the vb.-stem, as in βαπτίζειν, βαπτιστής, L. *baptista*, Fr. *baptiste* baptist. Cognate to the suffix -ισμός, -ISM.

In Eng. the suffix is used also in a multitude of terms having no corresponding words in *-ize* or *-ism*, which denominate the professed followers of some leader or school, the professional devotees of some principle, or the practisers of some art. In some cases the form in *-ist* is distinguished from the agent-noun in *-er* only by the more professional or systematic sense which it implies: cf. *copier, copyist*; *cycler, cyclist*; *philologer, philologist*.

Ist, quasi-*sb.* 1811. [The suffix *-ist* used generically.] A professor of some *ism*; a holder of some special doctrine, or adherent of some system; a votary of, or expert in, some science, art, or pursuit. Often disparaging or joc.

Is't (ist), arch., poet., colloq., or dial. abbrev. of *is it*.

-ister, †-istre, suffix repr. OFr. *-istre,* a by-form of *-iste*, -IST, said to have arisen through false analogy with words like *ministre*. Hence *evangelistre*, beside *evangeliste*; so *choristre*, etc. From OFr., these forms passed into English, where they were spelt first *-istre*, as in *queristre*, etc.; afterwards *-ister* as in *chorister*.

†Isthm(e. 1609. [– Fr. *isthme* (XVI) – L. *isthmus*.] = ISTHMUS –1646.

I·sthmian (see ISTHMUS), *a.* (*sb.*) 1601. [f. L. *isthmius* – Gr. ἴσθμιος + -AN.] **1.** Belonging to, situated upon, or forming, an isthmus or neck of land 1654. **2.** *spec.* Belonging to the Isthmus of Corinth; esp. in *Isthmian games*, one of the national festivals of ancient Greece, celebrated in the Isthmian sanctuary in the first and third years of each Olympiad 1603. **3.** *sb.* An inhabitant of an isthmus, e.g. of the Isthmus of Corinth 1601.

Isthmus (i·sþmŏs, i·stmŏs, i·smŏs). Pl. **isthmuses** (-ŏsėz), rarely **isthmi** (-əi). 1555. [– L. *isthmus* – Gr. ἰσθμός narrow passage, isthmus.] **1.** *Geog.* A narrow portion of land, enclosed on each side by water, and connecting two larger bodies of land; a neck of land. Also *fig.* **2.** *Anat., Zool.*, and *Bot.* A narrow part or organ connecting two larger parts; *esp.* the narrow passage connecting the cavity of the mouth with that of the pharynx (more fully *i. of the fauces* or *throat*) 1706.

-istic, double suffix of adjs. and sbs., corresp. to Fr. *-istique*, L. *-isticus*, Gr. -ιστικός, viz. the suffix -ικός -IC, added to sbs. in -ιστής -IST. In Eng., supplying a derivative adj. to sbs. in *-ist*; e.g. *altruistic, atheistic, realistic*, etc.

Words in *-istic* are essentially adjs., but like other adjs. in -IC, they are sometimes used as sbs. Sometimes also, like other adjs. in -IC, they have a secondary form in **-istical.**

Istle (i·stli, improp. i·st'l). Also **ixtle, ixtli.** 1883. [Commercial corruption of Mexican *ixtli*.] A valuable fibre obtained from *Bromelia sylvestris* and species of *Agave*, as *A. ixtli*, and used for cordage, nets, carpets, etc. *attrib.* **i.-grass,** a name for *Bromelia sylvestris*.

It (it), *pron.* [OE. *hit*, the neuter nom. and acc. of the stem *hi-*, the nom. masc. of which is HE, q.v. The dative and genitive were *him, his*, as in the masc. During the ME. period, *hit* lost its initial *h*, first when unemphatic, and at length in all positions, in standard English. In XVI the tendency arose to restrict the genitive *his* to the male sex. For the neuter was substituted at first *thereof* or *of it*, etc., and finally a new factitious genitive (possessive) *it's*, ITS.]

I. As nominative. **1.** The proper neuter pronoun of the third person sing. Used orig. of any neuter sb.; now only of things without life, and of animals when sex is not particularized; hence usually of all the lower animals, and sometimes of infants. **b.** *It* may refer to a matter expressed or implied in a statement, or occupying the mind of the speaker OE. Hence *mod. colloq.* predicatively, the supremely important or conventionally proper thing. **2.** As nom. of the vb. *to be*, *it* refers to the subject of thought, attention, or inquiry, whether impersonal or personal, in a sentence asking or stating what or who this is; as *What is it? It is I.* Often with a relative clause implied, as *Who is it* (that knocks)? So Fr. *ce*, Ger. *es*. **†b.** Used where *there* is now substituted. (Cf. Ger. *es ist, es sind.*) –1617. **c.** In archaic ballad style, the introductory *it* is sometimes = *there* 1603. **†d.** Used for *he, she*, or *that*. Cf. Fr. *c'est*, Ger. *es ist*. –1684. **3.** As the subject of an impersonal verb or impersonal statement, expressing action or a condition of things simply, without reference to any agent OE. **4.** When the logical subject of a verb is an infinitive phrase, a clause, or sentence, this usually follows the verb, and its place is taken by *it* as 'provisional' or 'anticipatory subject' OE. **b.** So also sometimes when the logical subject is a sb. OE. **c.** Also in a periphrastic construction; as *it was on a Monday that I met him* ME. **5.** The pronoun is also used pleonastically after the noun subject; now esp. in ballad poetry, or, in an interrog. sentence, in rhetorical prose, for the sake of emphasis ME.

1. And he was casting out a deuil, and it was dumbe *Luke* 11:14. It is a hearty child BAIN. **b.** Sir, you and I must part, but that's not it SHAKS. **c.** *slang.* The *ne plus ultra* 1900. **d.** Sex appeal 1927. **2. c.** It is an ancient mariner, And he stoppeth one of three COLERIDGE. **d.** 'Tis a Good Boy, said his Master BUNYAN. **3.** Phr. *It rains, it is very late, it is Christmas day.* It is a far cry to Lochow SCOTT. O heart, how fares it with thee now? TENNYSON. In a cronique it telleth thus GOWER. It tells in the Bible how David slew Goliath 1900. **4.** It was necessary to make a choice MACAULAY. It appears that you were present 1900. **b.** What may it be, the heavy sound? SCOTT. **c.** It was by him that money was coined MACAULAY. **5.** The deck it was their field of fame CAMPBELL.

II. As objective case (accus. and dat.). **1.** The neuter accusative or direct object after a verb; having the same range of reference as the nominative OE. **b.** Also used as an anticipatory object. Cf. I. 4. 1596. **2.** After a prep. (In OE. *hit* or *him*, according to the regimen of the prep.) ME. **3.** As simple dative = 'to it'. (In OE. *him*.) ME. **4.** Often used as an indef. object of a verb; so in imprecations. And in this way verbs are formed for the nonce upon nouns; e.g. *to king it, queen it, cab it*, etc. The use is now colloq. 1548.

1. Let it be neither mine nor thine, but diuide it 1 *Kings* 3:26. **b.** Publish it that she is dead *Much Ado* IV. i. 206. **2.** I to my office, and there hard at it till almost noon PEPYS. **3.** It grandame will Giue yt a plum SHAKS. **4.** Ile Queene it no inch farther SHAKS.

III. As possessive; = ITS. Now *dial.* ME. It's had it head bit off by it young SHAKS. That which with it owne glory can make them happy BP. HALL.

IV. As reflexive pron. **1.** In accus. and dative = ITSELF 1595. **2.** As possessive = ITS (L. *suus*) 1548.

1. My heart hath one poore string to stay it by SHAKS.

V. 1. As antecedent pron. followed by relative expressed or understood. (Rare; usu. *that which, the one that, what.*) ME. **2.** When the antecedent is the subject of a clause which precedes the relative, it may be used of persons as well as things 1596.

1. An if it please me which thou speak'st SHAKS. **2.** It is a good Diuine that followes his owne instructions SHAKS.

Itacism (ī·tăsiz'm). 1854. [– mod.L. *itacismus*, f. Gr. ἦτα, the name of the letter η, with ending as in *rhotacism*; cf. IOTACISM.] The giving to the Greek vowel η the sound-value ī, like Eng. *ee* (opp. to ETACISM, in which it has the original value ē); also, reduction in pronunciation of different Greek vowels and diphthongs to the sound ī (represented in ancient Greek by the letter ι, iota); hence the substitution in MSS. of ι for any of these vowels or diphthongs. So **I·tacist,** one who favours i. 1837.

Itacolumite (ităkǫ·liumait). 1862. [f. *Itacolumi*, a mountain in Brazil + -ITE[1] 2 b.] *Min.* A granular, quartzose, talcomicaceous slate.

Itaconic (ităkǫ·nik), *a.* 1865. [f. ACONITIC, by arbitrary transposition of letters.] *Chem.* Of, pertaining to, or derived from aconitin.

I. acid, $C_5H_6O_4$, an acid isomeric with citraconic and mesaconic acids, obtained in the dry distillation of citric acid. Its salts are **Ita·conates.**

Italian (itæ·liăn). ME. [– It. *italiano*, f. *Italia* Italy; see -AN.] **A.** *adj.* **1.** Of or pertaining to Italy or its people; native to or produced in Italy 1547. **†b.** Printing = ROMAN (type). STRYPE. **†c.** = ITALIC *a.* 3. –1723. **2.** As the designation of the modern language of Italy 1530. **3.** Applied to the form of handwriting developed in Italy, and now used in Great Britain, America, etc., which approaches in form to italic printing; opp. to the Gothic hand 1571.

1. Adde thus much more, that no I. Priest Shall tythe or toll in our dominions SHAKS. Phr. **I. cloth,** a kind of linen jean with satin face, largely used for linings. **I. roof,** a hip-roof. **I. sixth** (*Mus.*), a chord consisting of a note with its major third and augmented sixth. **I. warehouse,** a shop where I. groceries, fruits, olive oil, etc. are sold.

B. *sb.* **1.** A native of Italy ME. **2.** The Italian language 1485. **†3.** An Italian scholar. FLORIO.

1. The great merchants of Europe were the Italians 1818.

Italianate (itæ·liănĕt), *a.* 1572. [– It. *italianato*; see -ATE[2].] **1.** Rendered Italian; see ITALIANATE *v.* **2.** Of Italian character, form, or aspect 1592.

1. An Englishman Italionat is a Devill Incarnat HOWELL.

Italianate (itæ·liăneᶦt), *v.* 1567. [Found first in pa. pple. *Italianated*, f. It. *italianato*, whence the vb. was deduced; see -ATE[3].] *trans.* To render Italian; to give an Italian character to. (Usu. depreciatory.) **Ita·lianated** *ppl. a.* = ITALIANATE *a.* 1553.

Ita·lian i·ron, *sb.* 1833. A hollow cylindrical iron and heater, used for fluting and crimping lace, frills, etc. Hence as *vb.*

Italianism (itæ·liăniz'm). 1594. [f. ITALIAN + -ISM.] **1.** An Italian practice, feature, or trait; *esp.* an Italian expression or idiom. **2.** Italian quality, spirit, or taste; attachment to Italian ideas; sympathy with Italy 1824.

Italianize (itæ·liănəiz), *v.* 1611. [– Fr. *italianiser*; cf. ITALIAN and -IZE.] **1.** *intr.* To practise Italian fashions or habits; to become Italian (in character, etc.). **2.** *trans.* To make Italian in character or style 1673.

2. Nol's Latin clerks were somewhat Italianiz'd 1673. Hence **Ita·lianizer.**

Italic (itæ·lik). 1563. [– L. *Italicus* – Gr. Ἰταλικός, f. Ἰταλία, L. *Italia* Italy.]

A. *adj.* **1.** Of or pertaining to ancient Italy or its tribes; *spec.* in *Rom. Hist.* and *Law*, pertaining to parts of Italy other than Rome 1685. **b.** Pertaining to the Greek colonies in southern Italy; said of the school of philosophy founded in Magna Græcia by Pythagoras. (Occas. used to include the Eleatic school.) 1662. **c.** *Arch.* A name for the fifth of the classical orders, the COMPOSITE 1563. **†2.** = ITALIAN *a.* 1. –1734. **3.** (with small *i*) Applied to the species of printing type introduced by Aldus Manutius of Venice, in which the letters slope to the right. In early use also *Italica* (sc. *littera*). 1612.

2. The I. caution of the ambassador NORTH. **3.** Documents. . profusely underlined. . in which the *machinations of villains* are laid bare with i. fervour THACKERAY.

B. *sb.* **1.** A member of the Italic school (see A. 1 b) 1594. **2.** (with small *i*) *pl.* (rarely *sing.*) Italic letters: now usually employed for emphasis or distinction. See A. 3. 1676.

2. We quote the passage; the italics are ours 1900.

Hence **†Italic** *v.*, to italicize 1683.

Italicism (itæ·lisiz'm). *rare.* 1773. [f. ITALIC *a.* + -ISM.] An Italian expression or idiom; an Italianism.

Italicize (itæ·lisəiz), *v.* 1795. [f. ITALIC + -IZE.] *trans.* To print in italics.

The lines we have italicized are lines of very great beauty 1865.

Italiot, -ote (itæ·liǫt, -oᵘt). 1660. [– Gr. Ἰταλιώτης, f. Ἰταλία Italy. See -OT[2], -OTE.] **A.** *sb.* A person of Greek descent dwelling in ancient Italy; an inhabitant of Magna Græcia. **B.** *adj.* Of or pertaining to the Greek colonies in southern Italy.

Italo-, used as comb. f. *Italian*, as in **I:talo-Byza·ntine** *a.*, pertaining to Byzantine art as developed in Italy; **I:taloma·nia,** mania for things Italian.

Ita-palm (i·tă,pām). 1866. [f. *ita*, native Brazilian name + PALM *sb.*[1]] A palm-tree (*Mauritia flexuosa*) of tropical S. America.

Itch (itʃ), *sb.* [OE. *ġyċċe*, f. the vb.] **1.** An uneasy sensation of irritation in the skin;

spec. a contagious disease, in which the skin is covered with vesicles and pustules, accompanied by extreme irritation, now known to be produced by the itch-mite; scabies. **b.** Applied, with qualification, to forms of eczema and other skin diseases, as *bakers', bricklayers', grocers' i.* **2.** *fig.* An uneasy or restless hankering after something; usu. spoken contemptuously. Const. *of, for, after* (†*at*), or *inf.* 1532.

2. The i. of originality infects his thought and style LOWELL. *Comb.*: **i.-acarus, -insect, -mite, -tick,** a small parasitic arachnid (*Sarcoptes scabiei*) of the family *Acaridæ*, which burrows in the human skin, and gives rise to the disease called i. or scabies.

Itch (itʃ), *v.*[1] [OE. *ġiċċan, ġyċċan*, corresp. to OS. *jukkian*, (M)Du. *jeuken*, OHG. *jucchen* (G. *jucken*), f. WGmc. **juk-*. Initial *ġ* has disappeared as in *if* (OE. *ġif*), Ipswich (OE. *Gipeswić*).] **1.** *intr.* To have or feel irritation of the skin, such as causes an inclination to scratch the part affected; said of the part; also of the person affected. **2.** *fig.* To have an irritating desire or uneasy craving provoking to action. Const. with *inf.*; also *for.* ME.

1. Socrates dilates on the pleasures of itching and scratching JOWETT. **2.** His tongue itch't to be let loose 1622. Hence **I·tchingly** *adv.*

†**Itch,** *v.*[2] 1579. [app. identical with HITCH *v.* and early ME. *icche.*] = HITCH *v.* 2. –1621.

†**I·tchless,** *a.* 1635. [f. ITCH *sb.* + -LESS.] Free from itching or the itch; incorruptible –1648.

Itchy (i·tʃi), *a.* Now *colloq.* 1530. [f. as prec. + -Y[1].] Affected with itching or the itch; of the nature of the itch. Hence **I·tchiness** 1822.

-ite, *suffix*[1], corresp. to Fr. *-ite*, L. *-ita* (*-ites*) – Gr. *-ιτης*, forming adjs. and sbs. (of adj. origin) with the sense '(one) connected with or belonging to', 'a member of', as in *ὁπλίτης adj.* heavy-armed, *sb.* a heavy-armed soldier. In English:

1. Used to form names of persons (also adjectively), as in *Sybarite*; *Israelite, Sodomite*, etc.; *eremite, Monophysite*, etc.; also *Claphamite*, etc.; *Wycliffite, Puseyite*; *Shelleyite*; *Jacobite, Luddite, Peelite*, etc.

2. a. *Palæont.* Used to form the names of fossil organisms; as *ammonite, dendrite, lignite*, etc. **b.** *Min.* The systematic ending of the names of mineral species, as *anthracite*, etc.; *chlorite, hepatite*, etc.; *azurite, graphite, syenite, wernerite*, etc.

3. *Anat.* and *Zool.* Used to form terms denoting one of the constituent parts, segments, or joints of a body or organ; as in *somite* a segment of the body; so *pleurite, podite*, etc.

4. *Chem.* Used to form the names of some saccharine substances, glucoses, and other organic compounds, as *dulcite*, etc.; also of explosives, as *cordite, dynamite*, etc.; and of commercial products, as *vulcanite*, etc. **b.** In Inorganic Chemistry, *-ite* is the systematic termination of the salts of acids denominated by adjs. in *-ous*; e.g. *nitrite* a salt of *nitrous acid.*

A few of the words in *-ite* have derivative adjs. in **-itic,** as *Semitic*, etc.; many of those in group 1 have adjs. in **-itish,** as *Israelitish*, etc.

-ite, *suffix*[2], an ending of adjs. adapted from L. pa. pples. in *-itus* of vbs. in *-īre, -ēre, -ĕre*, as in *eruditus* erudite, *compositus* composite, etc.; of sbs. derived from the same or from the cognate L. sbs. in *-us*, as *appetitus* appetite; of verbs formed from the same ppl. stems, as *expedite, unite.*

Item (əi·tĕm), *adv.* and *sb.* ME. [– L. *item* adv., 'just so', 'in like manner', 'moreover', f. *ita* so, based on the pronominal stem **i-* (see HE, IT), with *-em* as in IDEM.]

‖**A.** *adv.* Likewise, also.

It shalbe Inuentoried. . As, I. two lippes indifferent redde, I. two grey eyes, with lids to them SHAKS.

B. *sb.* **1.** A statement, maxim, or admonition such as was commonly introduced by the word *item.* Hence, generally, an intimation, a hint. Now *U.S. local.* 1561. **2.** An article or unit of any kind; an entry in an account, a clause of a document, etc. 1578. **b.** A detail of information or news 1819.

1. Getting i. thereof, he departed to the sea HEARNE. **2.** Tauern items DEKKER. **b.** The items in a newspaper 1865.

Item (əi·tĕm), *v.* 1601. [f. prec.] *trans.* To set down by items; to enter as an item.

I have Item'd it in my memory ADDISON.

Itemize (əi·tĕməiz), *v.* Chiefly *U.S.* 1860. [f. ITEM *sb.* + -IZE.] *trans.* To set down by items or enter as an item; to specify the items of (an account, etc.).

Iter (i·təɹ, əi·təɹ). Pl. **iters,** ‖**iti·nera.** 1598. [– L. *iter* journey, way, road; in sense 1, AL. (XII).] **1.** *Hist.* = EYRE 1. Also *transf.* 1647. **b.** The record of proceedings during a circuit 1598. **2.** A Roman road or line of travel 1751. **3.** *Anat.* A way or passage; *spec.* the tubular cavity leading from the third to the fourth ventricle of the brain 1897.

†**Iterable** (i·tĕrăb'l), *a. rare.* 1561. [– late L. *iterabilis*, f. *iterare* ITERATE *v.*; see -ABLE.] Capable of being iterated or repeated –1682.

Iterance (i·tĕrăns). 1604. [f. ITERANT; see -ANCE.] Iteration. So **I·terancy** 1889.

Iterant (i·tĕrănt), *a.* 1626. [– L. *iterans, -ant-*, pr. pple. of *iterare*; see ITERATE *v.*, ANT.] That iterates; repeating, echoing.

A Reflexion I., which we call Eccho BACON.

†**I·terate,** *ppl. a.* 1471. [– L. *iteratus*, pa. pple. of *iterare*; see next, -ATE[2].] Iterated –1657. †**I·terately** *adv.* repeatedly.

Iterate (i·tĕre[i]t), *v.* 1533. [– *iterat-*, pa. ppl. stem of L. *iterare* repeat, f. *iterum* again, compar. f. the pronominal base **i-*; see ITEM, -ATE[3].] **1.** *trans.* To do over again; to perform a second time; to repeat; to renew. Now *rare.* **2.** To say or assert again or repeatedly; to repeat 1533.

1. To i. an experiment 1682. **2.** We i. the Psalms oftener then any other part of Scripture HOOKER.

Iteration (itĕrē[i]·ʃən). 1450. [– L. *iteratio*, f. as prec.; see -ION. Cf. Fr. *itération.*] **1.** Repetition of an action or process (now usu. implying frequency or long continuance); an instance of this. **2.** The repetition of something said 1530.

2. Tedius I. therof I let passe 1556.

Iterative (i·tĕrĕtiv), *a.* 1490. [– Fr. *itératif, -ive* (sense 1) and late L. *iterativus* (sense 2), f. as prec.; see -IVE.] **1.** Characterized by repeating or being repeated. **2.** *Gram.* Frequentative 1827. Hence **I·terative-ly** *adv.*, **-ness.**

†**Ithand,** *a. Sc.* and *north. dial.* ME. [– ON. *iðinn* assiduous, diligent. Cf. EIDENT, IDENT.] **1.** Assiduous, diligent –1570. **2.** Constant, continual –1536. Hence †**Ithandly** *adv.*

Ithyphallic (iþifæ·lik). 1614. [– late L. *ithyphallicus* – Gr. *ἰθυφαλλικός*, f. *ἰθύφαλλος*, f. *ἰθύς* straight + *φαλλός* PHALLUS; see -IC.]

A. *adj.* Pertaining to the phallus carried in procession at the Bacchic festivals; *spec.* composed in the metre of the Bacchic hymns (the trochaic dimeter brachycatalectic) 1795. **b.** Grossly indecent 1864. **B.** *sb.* A poem in ithyphallic metre; also, an indecent poem.

Itineracy (əiti·nĕrăsi, it-). 1827. [f. ITINERATE; see -ACY 3.] = ITINERANCY.

Itinerancy (əiti·nĕrănsi, it-). 1789. [f. next; see -ANCY.] **1.** The state or condition of being itinerant; the action of itinerating, esp. for a specific purpose, as preaching or public speaking; a journey from place to place 1802. **b.** A body of itinerants 1836. **2.** Itinerant preaching; *spec.* the system in practice in various Methodist churches, according to which the regular ministers are appointed not to a congregation, but to a circuit, which is changed triennially 1789. **b.** Itinerant ministry 1809.

Itinerant (əiti·nĕrănt, it-). 1570. [– *itinerans, -ant-*, pr. pple. of late L. *itinerari*, med.L. *-are*, f. L. *iter, itiner-* journey; see -ANT.]

A. *adj.* Journeying; travelling from place to place; not fixed or stationary; travelling on circuit. **b.** Journeying or travelling in connection with some employment or vocation; preaching in a circuit; of or pertaining to the regular Wesleyan ministry 1661. **c.** *fig.* and *transf.* 1634.

1. Such i. judges as go Oxford Circuit FULLER. **b.** To appoint to a Circuit as an I. Preacher 1829.

B. *sb.* One who travels from place to place, esp. in the pursuit of a trade or calling; a travelling preacher, etc. 1641.

Glad to turn i., To stroll and teach from town to town BUTLER. Hence **Iti·nerantly** *adv.*

‖**Itinerarium** (itinĕrē[ə]·riŏm). 1747. [Late L.; see next.] = ITINERARY *sb.* 2, 3.

Itinerary (əiti·nĕrări, it-), *sb.* 1450. [– late L. *itinerarium*, subst. use of n. of *itinerarius*; see next, -ARY[1]. Cf. (O)Fr. *itinéraire.*] **1.** A line or course of travel; a route. **2.** A journal of travel; an account of a journey 1483. **3.** A road-book, a guide-book 1538. **b.** *transf.* A sketch of a proposed route 1856. **4.** An itinerant (*rare*) 1709.

2. Many may rede the itineraryes of them that hath ben at Ierusalem 1526.

Itinerary (əiti·nĕrări, it-), *a.* 1552. [– late L. *itinerarius* of or pertaining to a journey, f. L. *iter, itiner-* journey, way, road; see -ARY[1]. Cf. (O)Fr. *itinéraire.*] **1.** Of or pertaining to a journey, travelling, or a route. **b.** Pertaining to roads (esp. Roman roads) or the description of roads. 1552. **2.** = ITINERANT *a.* 1617.

1. b. The i. system of the Romans was. . an effective instrument of centralization MERIVALE.

Itinerate (əiti·nĕre[i]t, it-), *v.* 1600. [– *itinerat-*, pa. ppl. stem of late L. *itinerare*; see ITINERANT, -ATE[3].] **1.** *intr.* To travel or journey from place to place. **b.** To travel from place to place preaching; *spec.* of a Methodist minister (cf. ITINERANCY 2) 1775. **2.** *trans.* To journey through, traverse 1830. Hence **Itinera·tion,** the action of itinerating; a preaching or lecturing tour 1623.

-ition, *suffix*, repr. Fr. *-ition*, L. *-ition-*, forming nouns of action from vbs. with ppl. stem in *-it-*, as in *position* from *positus, audition* from *auditus.* It is really a case of the suffix -ION, q.v.

-itious[1], compound suffix of adjs., f. L. *-ici-us* + -OUS. These L. endings, from the confusion of *c* and *t* in late and med.L. MSS., were formerly written *-itius*, whence the current Eng. spelling. Examples are *ascriptitious, factitious*, etc.

-itious[2], a combination of the suffix -OUS, repr. L. *-osus*, with derivs. containing *iti-*, chiefly sbs. in *-ition-*; e.g. *ambition, ambitious*, L. *ambitiosus*, etc.; see -IOUS, -OUS.

-itis, *suffix*, – Gr. *-ῖτις*, properly forming the fem. of adjs. in *-ιτης*; already in Gr. used to qualify *νόσος* disease, expressed or understood, e.g. *ἀρθρῖτις* (disease) of the joints, gout, *arthritis.* On the analogy of these, *-itis* has become in mod. medical L., and in Eng., the regular name for affections of particular parts and *spec.* (though not etymologically) for inflammatory diseases or inflammation of a part. Examples are *appendicitis, bronchitis, tonsillitis.*

Often jocularly used to denote something that is conceived as a disease; e.g. *suffragitis* = exaggerated advocacy of (woman's) suffrage.

-itous, compound suffix, containing the *-it-* of sbs. in -ITY, and the adj. ending -OUS; corresp. to Fr. *-iteux*, L. *-itosus*, contr. for *-itatosus*, as in *calamitosus* for *calamitatosus*; so *felicitous*, etc.

Its (its) *poss. pron.* [Formed *c*1600 from IT + *-s* of the possessive or genitive case, and at first commonly written *it's.* See IT III.]

A. As *adj. poss. pron.* Of or belonging to it, or that thing (L. *ejus*); also *refl.*, Of or belonging to itself, its own (L. *suus*) 1598.

From translation all Science had it's of-spring FLORIO. The Gospel has its mysteries J. H. NEWMAN.

B. As *absolute possessive.* Its own. *rare.*

It's, its, contraction of *it is.*

Itself (itse·lf), *pron.* OE. [orig. two words, IT *pron.* and SELF. In XVII–XVIII often treated as ITS + SELF; as still in *its own self*, and the like.]

I. Emphatic or limiting use. Usu. in apposition with a sb. in nom. or obj.: Very, the very, that very; alone (L. *ipsum*). Rarely alone as subject. **b.** Used alone in predicate, emphatically 1600.

The earth and tyme it selfe 1560. Or joy itself Without the touch of sorrow SHELLEY. **b.** An eye all pale Striving to be itself KEATS.

II. Reflexive use. = L. *sibi, se*; Ger. *sich.* OE.

Th' offence pardons it selfe SHAKS. His heart gathereth iniquitie to it selfe *Ps.* 41:6. The child will do itself a mischief 1900.

Ittria, Ittrium, *Chem.*: See YTTRIA, etc.

-ity [ME. *-ite* – Fr. *-ité*, L. *-itat-*, the usual form in which the suffix -TY[1] (L. *-tas, -tat-*, expressing state or condition) appears, the *-i-* being orig. either the stem vowel of the radical (e.g. L. *suavi-tas* suavity), or its weakened repr. (e.g. L. *puro-*, *puri-tas* purity), rarely a mere connective (e.g. L. *auctor-i-tas* authority). Hence many playful or pedantic nonce-wds., as *between-ity*, *woman-ity*. After *i* the suffix became *-etas*, as in *pietas*, *varietas*, f. *pius*, *varius*; hence *dubiety*, *piety*, *satiety*, etc. The termination was in L. often added to an adjectival suffix, e.g. *-aci-*, *-ali-*, *-bili-*, *-ili-*, *-ini-*, *-ui-*, *-uo-*, etc., whence the Eng. endings -ACITY, -ALITY, -BILITY, -ILITY, -INITY, -UITY.

‖**Itzebu, -boo** (itsibū·). 1616. [Japanese: two words, *itse*, *itche* one, *bû* division, quarter.] A Japanese phrase meaning 'one quarter', commonly applied to a silver coin in use before 1871; it is worth about 1*s.* 4*d.* sterling.

Iu-, earlier spelling of Iv-, and of Ju-.

Iulidan (əiyū·lidăn). 1885. [f. mod.L. *Iulida*, *-idæ*, f. *Iulus* (see next), -AN.] *Zool.* A myriapod of the family *Iulidæ* (see next 2).

‖**Iulus** (əiyū·lŏs). 1658. [L. (Pliny) – Gr. ἴουλος down, catkin, millepede.] †**1.** A catkin –1757. **2.** A genus of animals of the class Myriapoda, order *Chilognatha* (*Diplopoda*); a millepede.

-ium, *suffix*. *Chem.*, used to form the names of metallic elements, as *cadmium*, *iridium*.

I've, colloq. contr. of *I have*.

-ive, *suffix*, forming adjs. (and sbs.) Formerly also *-if*, *-ife*; – Fr. *-if*, fem. *-ive* :– L. *-ivus*. Largely used in Eng. to adapt L. words in *-ivus*, or form words on L. analogies, with the sense 'having a tendency to, having the nature, character, or quality of, given to (some action)'. Already in L. many of these adjs. were used subst.; hence in Eng.; e.g. *adjective*, *captive*, *derivative*, etc. Hence advs. in **-ively**, and abstr. sbs. in **-iveness**, **-ivity**.

In XVII *-ive* is sometimes synonymous with *-ible*, as *extensive* = extensible, *inexpressive* = inexpressible.

Ivied, ivyed (əi·vid), *a.* 1771. [f. Ivy + -ED[2].] Overgrown or clothed with ivy.

Ivorine (əi·vŏrīn). 1897. [f. Ivory + -INE[4].] Trade-name for a substance imitating ivory.

Ivory (əi·vŏri). [ME. *ivor*, *yvor(e*, *yvory* – OFr. *yvoire*, AFr. **ivorie* (mod. *ivoire*) – Rom.**eboreum*, f. L. *ebur*, *ebor-* ivory – a form rel. to Egyptian *āb*, *ābu*, Coptic *ebou*, *ebu* elephant, ivory (cf. Heb. *shenhabbīm* ivory, Skr. *ibhas* elephant.] **1.** The hard, white, elastic, and fine-grained substance (being dentine of exceptional hardness) composing the main part of the tusks of the elephant, mammoth (*fossil i.*), hippopotamus, walrus, and narwhal; it is employed as a material for many articles of use or ornament. **2.** A substance resembling ivory, or made in imitation of it 1842. **3.** *Black i.*: African negro slaves as an object of commerce. *slang.* 1873. **4.** The colour of ivory; ivory-white; *esp.* whiteness of the human skin 1590. **5.** An article made of ivory, esp. a carving in that material. **b.** *slang.* (usu. *pl.*) Dice; also billiard balls 1830; piano keys 1855. **6.** A tusk of an elephant, etc. 1894. **7.** *slang.* (*sing.* and *pl.*) The teeth 1782. **8.** *attrib.* **a.** Made or consisting of ivory ME. **b.** White or smooth as ivory 1586.

1. The tooth of an olyfaunt is yuorye CAXTON. **2.** *Vegetable i.*, the i.-like albumen of the seed of the S. Amer. palm *Phytelephas macrocarpa*. **5. b.** Suppose we adjourn to Fish Lane, and rattle the ivories LYTTON. **8. a.** *I. gate*; see GATE *sb.*[1] 4. *I. tower*, (fig.) a position of lofty seclusion (after Fr. *tour d'ivoire*, used by Sainte-Beuve of Vigny's seclusion in a turret room).

Comb.: **i.-bill**, a species of woodpecker, *Picus* or *Campephilus principalis*; **-gull**, a small white Arctic gull, *Pagophila eburnea*; **-nut**, the corozo-nut; hence **-(nut-)palm**, **-plant**; **-paper**, a thick paper or thin cardboard with a finely prepared polished surface, used by artists; **-shell**, a univalve of the genus *Eburna*, of an i. colour.

Ivory-black. 1634. A fine soft black pigment, obtained by calcining ivory in a closed vessel.

Ivory-type. 1875. *Photogr.* A picture produced by placing a photograph, light in colour, made translucent by varnish, tinted on the back, over a stronger picture, so as to give the effect of a photograph in natural colours.

Ivy (əi·vi). *Pl.* **ivies** (əi·viz). [OE. *ifiġ*, obscurely rel. to OHG. *ebah* (mod. G. dial. *efa*, *efai*, *ewich*) and the first element of MLG. *iflōf*, *iwlōf*, LG., Du. *eilof* (enlarged with the word LEAF), and OHG. *ebahewi*, MHG. *ebehöu*, *ephöu*, G. *efeu* (enlarged with the word HAY *sb.*[1]); of unkn. origin, unless referable to the base of L. IBEX, with the sense 'climber' (cf. Fris., Du. *klimop* ivy, lit. 'climb-up').] **1.** A climbing evergreen shrub (*Hedera helix*), indigenous to Europe and Asia, having dark-green shining leaves, usu. five-angled, and bearing umbels of greenish-yellow flowers, succeeded by dark berries; it is an ornamental covering of walls, ruins, etc. The plant was anciently sacred to Bacchus. **2.** Applied, with distinctive addition, to plants of other genera 1588. **3.** *attrib.* OE.

1. *Black*, *English i.*, the common i., also termed *H. nigra*, from its black berries. Here are cool mosses deep, And thro' the moss the ivies creep TENNYSON. **2. American** or **Five-leaved i.**, Virginia creeper, *Ampelopsis hederacea* or *quinquefolia*. **German i.**, *Senecio mikanoides*, a variety of Groundsel. **Japanese i.**, *Ampelopsis tricuspidata*. **West Indian i.**, *Marcgravia umbellata*. **3.** I.-crowned Bacchus MILT.

Comb.: **i.-garland**, a garland of i., formerly the sign of a house where wine was sold; **-leaf**, a leaf of i., †a thing of little value; †*To pipe in (with) an ivy-leaf* (fig.), to console oneself with some frivolous employment; **-tod** (*arch.*) = IVY-BUSH.

Ivy-bush. 1576. A bushy branch of ivy; *fig.* a place of concealment or retirement. †**b.** *spec.* A bush of ivy, or a picture of it, placed outside a tavern as a sign that wine was sold there; hence, the tavern itself. †Hence *fig.* A sign or display (of anything).

Iwis, ywis (iwi·s), *adj.*, *adv.*, and *sb. arch.* [ME. *ȝewis*, *iwis(se* :– OE. *ġewis* = OHG. *giwiss* (G. *gewiss*); f. Gmc. **ʒa-*, **ʒi-* + **wissa-* :– **widto-*, pa. ppl. formation on **wid-* know (see WIT *v.*[1]); freq. spelt *i wis*, *I wis*, and misinterpreted as 'I know'.] **A.** *adj.* (*ġewis*) Certain (subjectively and objectively). Only in OE. **B.** *adv.* (*ȝewis*, *iwis*, and *iwisse*) Certainly, assuredly, indeed. (The writing with capital I, and separation of the two elements, have led later authors to use it erron. as = *I wot*, *I know*, as if a present of *I wist.*) ME. †**C.** *sb.* [the adj. used absol.] Certainty –ME.

Ixia (i·ksiă). 1794. [mod. use of L. *ixia* – Gr. ἰξία kind of thistle.] *Bot.* A genus of S. African iridaceous plants, with large showy flowers.

Ixtle, ixtli: see ISTLE.

‖**Izar** (i·zăr). 1836. [Arab. *izār*, *izr'* veil, covering.] The outer garment of Moslem women, a long cotton mantle covering the whole figure.

Izard (i·zăɹd, ‖izā·r). Also **isard, izzard.** 1791. [– Fr. *isard*, Gascon *isart*, perh. of Iberian origin.] A capriform antelope allied to the chamois, found in the Pyrenees.

-ization (also **-isation**), suffix forming nouns of action from vbs. in -IZE: see next.

-ize (also written **-ise**), suffix forming vbs. = Fr. *-iser*, It. *-izzare*, Sp. *-izar*, – late L. *-izare*, f. Gr. -ίζειν, extensive formative of verbs. The suffix, whatever the element to which it is added, is in its origin the Gr. -ίζειν, L. *-izare*; and, as the pronunciation is also with *z*, there is no reason why in English the special French spelling in *-iser* should ever be followed. Hence here the termination is uniformly written *-ize*. In current English the following are the chief groups:

1. Words from Greek, or formed on Greek elements; **a.** with the trans. sense of 'make or conform to, or treat in the way of, the thing expressed by the basic word', as *baptize*, *anathematize*, *monopolize*, etc.; **b.** with the intrans. sense 'to act some person or character, do or follow some practice', as *apologize*, *philosophize*, etc.

2. Words formed on Latin adjs. or sbs., mostly with the trans. sense 'to make (that which is expressed by the derivation)', as *actualize*, *colonize*, *satirize*, etc.; trans. or intrans., as *cicatrize*, *moralize*, etc.; occas. only intrans., as *temporize*.

3. Words from later sources, as *bastardize*, *jeopardize* trans., *gormandize* intr.

4. Words formed on ethnic adjs., and the like, chiefly trans., as *Americanize*, *Anglicize*, etc.

5. Words formed on names of persons, sometimes with the intrans. Gr. sense of 'to act like, or in accordance with', as in *Calvinize*, but usu. in the trans. sense of 'to treat like, or after the method of, or according to the (chemical or other) process of'; as in *Boucherize*, *Bowdlerize*, *galvanize*, etc.; with other terms, and nonce-words such as *Gladstonize*, etc., without limit.

6. From names of substances, chemical and other; in the trans. sense of 'to charge, impregnate, treat, or affect with'; as *alcoholize*, *oxidize*, etc.; so in nonce-words, as *Londonize* to make like London, etc.

-izer, suffix of agent-n. from vbs. in -IZE.

Izzard (i·zăɹd). *arch.* or *dial.* Also **izzet, izzart, uzzard.** 1738. [Also dial. *uzzard* (XVII), EZOD (XVI), *izzat*, *izot*, *uzzit.*] The letter Z. Cf. EZOD.

Izzard, var. of IZARD.

J

J (dʒēi), the tenth letter of the English alphabet, is, in its origin, a comparatively late modification of the letter I. From the 11th to the 17th c., the letter I i represented both the vowel sound of *i*, and a consonant sound (dʒ). To keep the inconspicuous small i distinct, esp. in cursive writing, various scribal expedients were employed (see I). Among these, an initial i was often prolonged above or below the line, or both; a final i was generally prolonged below the line, and in both cases the 'tail' in cursive writing at length became a curve. The 'dot' was also used with the tailed form, and thus arose the modern j, *j*. But this was at first merely a final form of i, used in Latin in such forms as 'filij', and in numerals, as j, ij, xij. It was in the 17th c. that the differentiation of the two forms of the letter took place, i, *i* remaining for the vowel, and j, *j* being used for the consonant, and the capital forms of the latter, J, *J*, being introduced.

The sound regularly denoted by the letter J in English is the consonant (dʒ). In *hallelujah* it has the sound of the Roman i-consonant (y). So in proper names or alien terms from German and other languages in which the Roman value of *j* is retained, as *Jena* (yē·nă), *Jaeger*, etc. In a few French words, distinctly recognized as alien, *j* has the French sound (ʒ), as *déjeuner*, etc. In the transliteration of Oriental names, as *Jāt*, *Jenghiz*, etc., *j* is used with its English value.

I. 1. The letter. (pl. *Js*, J's, *js*, j's.) **2.** Short for **J-pen**, a broad-pointed pen, stamped with the letter J.

II. 1. Rarely used to express serial order. In the alphabetical designations of the batteries of the Royal Artillery, A, B, C, etc., J is used for the tenth. **2.** As a Roman numeral j was formerly used as a final form of i in j, ij, vj, etc.; this is retained in medical prescriptions. **3.** In *Math.* and *Physics*, *J* is used to denote the Jacobian; also Joule's mechanical equivalent of heat.

III. Abbrevs. J. stands for various proper names, as *John*, *Jane*, etc. J., Judge. J.P., Justice of Peace. Jr., jr., Junior. J.C.R., junior COMMON-ROOM.

‖**Jaal-goat** (dʒēi·ăl-, yā·ăl,gōu·t). 1838. [– Heb. *yā'ēl* mountain goat.] The wild goat of Mount Sinai, Upper Egypt, Abyssinia, etc. (*Capra jaala*).

Jab (dʒæb), *v. colloq.* and *dial.* 1825. [var., orig. Sc., of JOB *v.*[1]] *trans.* To thrust; to poke roughly; to stab. Also *absol.* or *intr.* Hence **Jab** *sb.* (*colloq.* or *dial.*), an act of jabbing with something pointed, or with the fist.

Jabber (dʒæ·bəɹ), *sb.* 1727. [f. next.] The act of jabbering; gabble, chatter; gibberish.

Jabber (dʒæ·bəɹ), *v.* 1499. [imit.; cf. GABBER *v.*] **1.** *intr.* To talk rapidly and indistinctly or unintelligibly; to speak volubly and with little sense. **2.** *trans.* To speak or utter rapidly and indistinctly; to express by jabbering. Often *contemptuously*. 1532.

2. To j. French ADDISON. Hence **Ja·bberer**, one who jabbers 1678. **Ja·bberingly** *adv.* in a jabbering manner. **Ja·bberment**, jabbering MILTON.

Jabbernowl, var. of JOBBERNOWL.

‖**Jabiru** (dʒæ·birū). Also **jaburu.** 1774. [Tupi-Guarani *jabirú*.] A large wading bird of tropical and subtropical America (*Mycteria americana*), of the stork family. Also applied to the allied *Xenorhynchus australis* and *indi-*

cus, and *Ephippiorhynchus senegalensis*, of the Old World.

‖**Jaborandi** (dʒæbŏræ·ndi, *prop.* dʒabŏrandī·). 1875. [Tupi-Guarani *jaburandi*, also *jaburandiba* (*iba* plant, tree).] The dried leaflets of a Brazilian plant *Pilocarpus pinnatifolius*. N.O. *Rutaceæ*, having diuretic and sudorific properties.

Jaborine (dʒæ·bŏrəin). 1887. [f. prec. + -INE[5].] *Chem.* An alkaloid contained, together with pilocarpine, in the leaves of jaborandi.

‖**Jabot** (ʒabo). 1823. [– Fr., 'bird's crop', 'shirt-frill', prob. f. a base **gab-* crop, maw, gullet, to which many Rom. words are referred.] **1.** A frill formerly worn by men on the front of a shirt, edging the opening. **2.** An ornamental frill on a woman's bodice 1881.

‖**Jacamar** (dʒæ·kămaɹ). 1825. [Fr. – Tupi-Guarani *jacamaciri* (Marcgrave, 1648).] Any bird of the family *Galbulidæ*, natives of South America, somewhat resembling the bee-eaters in appearance, and the kingfishers in habits.

‖**Jacana** (dʒæ·kănă). 1753. [prop. *jaçana* – Pg. *jaçaná* – Tupi-Guarani *jasaná*.] Any bird of the genus *Parra* (*Jacana*) or family *Parridæ* (*Jacanidæ*), consisting of grallatorial aquatic birds inhabiting the warmer regions of the world, having enormous straight claws, which enable them to walk on the floating leaves of aquatic plants.

‖**Jacaranda** (dʒækăræ·ndă, *prop.* dʒakărandă·). 1753. [Tupi-Guarani.] Name given to various trees of tropical America yielding fragrant and ornamental wood; esp. to those of the genus *Jacaranda* (N.O. *Bignoniaceæ*). **b.** The wood of any of these. **c.** A drug obtained from a tree of this genus.

‖**Jacare** (dʒæ·kăre). 1753. [Tupi-Guarani.] A South American alligator.

Jacent (dʒē^i·sĕnt), *a.* ? *Obs.* 1602. [– L. *jacens, jacent-*, pres. pple. of *jacēre* lie; see -ENT.] Lying; recumbent; *fig.* sluggish.

Jacinth (dʒæ·sinþ, dʒē^i·sinþ). [ME. *iacin(c)t* – OFr. *iacinte* (mod. *jacinthe*), or med.L. *iacintus*, L. *hyacinthus* HYACINTH.] **1. a.** Among the ancients, a gem of a blue colour, prob. sapphire. **b.** In mod. use, a reddish-orange gem, a variety of zircon. = HYACINTH 1. **c.** The colour of the gem (see b) 1572. †**2.** = HYACINTH 2. –1760. **3.** *attrib.* 1526.

Jack (dʒæk), *sb.*[1] [ME. *Iacke, Iakke* (disyll.) used from the first as familiar by-form of *John*, perh. through dim. *Jankin*; the resemblance to Fr. *Jacques* James (:– Rom. **Ja·cobus*, f. L. *Jacō·bus* JACOB) is a difficulty.]

I. Applied to a man, or the figure of one. **1.** (As proper noun.) A familiar by-form of *John*; hence, a generic proper name for a man of the common people. **b.** *Cousin Jack*: a familiar name for a Cornishman. †**2.** (As a common noun.) A man of the common people; a lad, fellow, chap; *esp.* an ill-mannered fellow, a 'knave' –1746. **3.** (As proper or common noun.) A familiar appellation for a sailor. Also JACK-TAR, q.v. 1659. **4.** Variously applied to a serving-man, a labourer, one who does odd jobs, etc. See also CHEAP *Jack*, STEEPLE *Jack*, etc. 1836. **5.** *Cards.* The knave of trumps in all-fours; hence *gen.* any one of the knaves 1674. **6.** A figure of a man which strikes the bell on the outside of a clock 1498.

1. And hee's now but Jacke Foord, that once were John HEYWOOD. A good J. makes a good Gill RAY. **2.** A mad-cap ruffian and a swearing Iacke SHAKS. Phr. †*To play the j.*: to play the knave. *Every man j.*: every individual man (*colloq.*). **6.** *Rich. III*, IV. ii. 117.

II. Applied to things which take the place of a lad or man, or save human labour; also more vaguely. **To separate contrivances, machines, utensils*, etc. **1.** A machine for turning the spit in roasting meat; a *bottle-jack* or a *smoke-jack* 1587. **2.** A name for various contrivances consisting (solely or mainly) of a roller or winch 1572. **3.** A wooden frame for sawing wood upon 1573. **4.** A machine, usually portable, for lifting heavy weights by force acting from below; in the commonest form, having a rack and a pinion wheel or screw and a handle turned by hand 1703. **5.** A contrivance for pulling off boots; a boot-jack. *rare* or *Obs.* (exc. in the compound). 1679. **6.** *Mining.* **a.** 'A kind of water-engine, turned by hand. *Staff.*' (Halliwell.) **b.** 'A wooden wedge or gad used in mining to assist in cleaving strata. 1858. ***To parts of instruments or machines.* **7.** In the virginal, spinet, and harpsichord: An upright piece of wood fixed to the back of the key-lever, and fitted with a quill which plucked the string as the jack rose on the key being pressed down. (By Shaks. and others erron. applied to the key.) 1598. **8.** In various machines.

a. An oscillating lever, e.g. in a stocking-frame or knitting-machine 1764. **b.** *Weaving* = Heck-box (see HECK) 1844. **c.** *Spinning.* A coarse bobbin and fly-frame operating on the sliver from the carding-machine 1875. **d.** *Telegr.*, etc. A terminal in a telegraph or telephone, consisting of a spring-clip by means of which instruments can be expeditiously introduced into the circuit.

9. In carriages: A small engine fixed to the bottom of the spring, and used to heighten or lower the body 1794. ****To things of smaller than the normal size.* **10.** The least bit; a whit. *Obs. colloq.* 1530. **11.** *Bowls.* A smaller bowl placed as a mark for the players to aim at 1611. **12.** *slang.* **a.** A farthing. **b.** A counter made to resemble a sovereign; so *half-j.* 1700. **13.** A quarter of a pint (*local*) 1736. **14.** *Naut.* Short for *jack cross-tree* (see IV. 1 b) 1840. *****To other things.* **15.** A post-chaise (*slang* or *colloq.*) 1812. **16.** A portable cresset or fire-basket used in hunting or fishing at night. *U.S.* 1895.

III. In names of animals. **1.** Applied to the male of various animals, chiefly in comb.; also simply: **a.** A male hawk, *esp.* merlin (= *jack-merlin*) 1623. **b.** (Short for JACKASS 1.) A male ass, *esp.* one kept for breeding mules. *U.S.* 1799. **2.** Name for various birds. **a.** Short for JACKDAW, *Jack-curlew, Cornish jack*, the Cornish chough, JACK SNIPE. **b.** In CURLEW-*jack*, JUMPING-*jack*, WHISKY JACK: see these wds. **3.** Name of various fishes, etc. **a.** A young or small pike 1587. **b.** Also applied to several American fishes; as the pike-perch, *Stizostedium vitreum*; a scorpænoid fish, *Sebastodes paucispinis*; several carangoid fishes, esp. *Caranx pisquetos* and *Seriola carolinensis*; and the pampano, *Trachynotus carolinus*. **c.** *Poor Jack* (also *dry* or *dried Jack*), dried hake; also called *Poor John* 1667.

IV. *Combs.*, etc. **1.** Combs. denoting things, etc.: **j.-back** [BACK *sb.*[2]], (*a*) in *Brewing*, a vessel with a perforated bottom for straining the wort from the hops (also called *hop-back*): (*b*) 'a tank which receives the cooled wort in a vinegar-factory' (Knight); **-engine** (*Coal-mining*), a donkey-engine; **-fishing,** (*a*) fishing for jack; (*b*) *U.S.*, fishing at night by means of a j. or cresset; **-hunting** *U.S.*, hunting by means of a jack-light (see II. 16); **-ladder** *Naut.*, 'one with wooden steps and side ropes' (Knight), = JACOB'S LADDER 2; **-lamp,** (*a*) a Davy-lamp with a glass cylinder outside the gauze; (*b*) *U.S.* = sense II. 16; **-pin** *Naut.*, a belaying-pin; **-pot,** in draw-poker, a pot or pool that has to accumulate until one of the players can open the betting with a pair of jacks or better; hence *fig.*; **-roll,** a winch or windlass turned directly by handles; **-sinker,** each of a series of thin metal plates suspended from the front end of the jacks in a stocking frame or knitting-machine, and serving, in conjunction with the *lead-sinkers*, to form loops upon the thread; **-towel,** a long towel with the ends sewed together, suspended from a roller.

b. In some uses *jack* has a diminutive force or meaning; as **j.-arch,** an arch whose thickness is only of one brick; **-block** *Naut.*, a small block seized to the topgallant-mast-head, for sending the topgallant-yards up and down; **-cross-tree** *Naut.*, an iron cross-tree at the head of a long topgallant mast, to support a royal or skysail mast; **-rafter, -rib, -timber,** one shorter than the full length.

2. Prefixed to another noun denoting a person, a thing personified, a trade, or a quality, so as to form a *quasi*-proper name or nickname; as *Jack Blunt* (a blunt fellow); *Jack boot(s* (the 'Boots' at an inn), *Jack Presbyter, Jack Priest*; **Jack Frost,** frost or frosty weather personified; †**Jack-sauce,** a saucy or impudent fellow; **Jack sprat,** a little fellow, a dwarf.

3. Substantive phrases with specific senses. *Jack at a pinch*, one who is ready for any emergency; 'a poor Hackney Parson'; *Jack in office*, a pretentious petty official; also *attrib.*; *Jack of (at) all trades*, a man who can turn his hand to any kind of business; *Jack of (on, o') both sides*, a person who sides first with one party and then with the other, a trimmer; †*Jack of the clock*, or *clock-house* = sense I. 6; also *transf.* of a person (*Rich. II*, v. v. 60); †*Jack out of office*, a person who has been dismissed from office; one whose 'occupation is gone'.

4. In names of animals (sometimes signifying *male*, sometimes *small, half-sized*). **a.** Denoting *male*, as *jack-hare*; esp. of falcons, as *jack-hobby, -kestrel, -merlin.* **b. Jack crow,** *Picathartes gymnocephalus*, a W. African corvine bird; **Jack curlew,** name for two small species of curlew: (*a*) the whimbrel, *Numenius phæopus*; (*b*) the *N. hudsonicus* of N. America; **Jack-fish,** the pike; also a name for other carangoid fishes; **Jack-salmon,** a pike-perch; **Jack-spaniard,** a large W. Indian species of wasp.

5. In popular names of plants. Sometimes denoting 'dwarf, undersized', as **Jack-by-the-hedge,** the hedge-garlic, *Sisymbrium Alliaria*; **Jack-in-the-bush,** local name for hedge-garlic; **Jack-in-the-pulpit** (*U.S.*), a N. American araceous plant, *Arisæma triphyllum*, so called from the appearance of the upright spadix partly surmounted by the enclosing spathe; **Jack oak,** a N. Amer. species of oak (*Quercus nigra*), also called *black jack.*

Jack, *sb.*[2] Now *arch.* ME. [– (O)Fr. *jaque*, of much disputed origin; perh. immed. – Sp., Pg. *jaco* (whence also It. *giaco*), of Arab. origin.] †**1. a.** A short and close-fitting jacket. ME. only. **b.** A coat of fence, usually of leather quilted, and in later times often plated with iron; *occas.*, a coat of mail (*arch.*) ME. **2.** A vessel for liquor; orig. of waxed leather coated outside with tar or pitch (= BLACK JACK 1); a (leathern) jug or tankard (*arch.*) 1573.

1. b. Like. . the yron plates of a iacke, one lying on an other 1578. Phr. †*To be on* (a person's) *j.*: to lay blows on him; to be down upon him.

Jack (dʒæk), *sb.*[3] 1633. [prob. a use of JACK *sb.*[1], as if short for 'jack-flag', i.e. small flag (as dist. from the ensign).] A ship's flag of smaller size than the ensign, used at sea as a signal, or as a mark of distinction; *spec.* the small flag, indicating nationality, which is flown from the jack-staff at the bow of a vessel, as in *British jack, Dutch jack*, etc.

In British use the jack has been since the 17th c. (except under the Commonwealth) a small-sized 'Union Flag' of the period (UNION JACK), which has also been, since 1707, inserted in the upper canton of the ensign; hence, the name 'union jack' is often improperly applied to the union flag itself, when this is not carried or used as a jack.

In the United States naval service the j. is a blue flag with a white five-pointed star for each State in the Union.

Jack, *sb.*[4] 1613. [– Pg. *jaca* – Malayalam *chakka.*] The fruit of an East Indian tree (*Artocarpus integrifolia*), a large and coarse kind of bread-fruit. Also the tree itself.

†**Jack,** *sb.*[5] 1695. Colloq. abbrev. of JACOBITE –1732.

Jack (dʒæk), *v.* 1873. [f. senses of JACK *sb.*[1]; in sense 3 of obscure origin.] **1.** *trans. To jack up*: To hoist with a jack (see JACK *sb.*[1] II. 4) 1885. **2.** *intr.* To hunt or fish at night with a jack (see JACK *sb.*[1] II. 16). *U.S.* 1881. **3.** *dial.* or *colloq. To jack up*: **a.** *trans.* (*a*) To do for, ruin 1873. (*b*) To throw up, give up, abandon 1880. **b.** *absol.* or *intr.* To give up suddenly or promptly 1873.

Jack-a-dandy (dʒæ:kădæ·ndi). 1632. [See JACK *sb.*[1] IV and cf. DANDY *sb.*[1]] A little pert or conceited fellow; a beau, fop, dandy.

Jackal (dʒæ·kǭl). 1603. [– (with assim. to JACK *sb.*[1]) Turk. *çakal* – Pers. *šaġāl, šagāl*, rel. to Skr. *sṛgāla.*] **1.** An animal of the dog kind, about the size of a fox; one of various species of *Canis*, as *C. aureus* or *C. anthus*, inhabiting Asia and Africa, hunting in packs by night with wailing cries, and feeding on dead carcases of small animals; formerly supposed to hunt up prey for the lion, hence termed 'the lion's provider'. **2.** *fig.* A person who acts like a jackal, *esp.* one who does mean work for another, or ministers to his requirements 1688.

1. I am a brother to jackals R.V. *Job* 30:29. Hence **Ja·ckal** *v. intr.*, to act as jackal (*for*).

Ja·ck-a-Le·nt. *arch.* Also **-o'-Lent, of Lent.** 1598. [See A *prep.*] **1.** A figure of a man, set up in Lent to be pelted. Hence *fig.* a butt for every one to throw at. **2.** *transf.* A puppet; an insignificant person 1598.

Jackanapes (dʒæ·kănē^{i}ps). *Pl.* **-apes,**

-apeses, (†-aps's). 1450. [orig. *Jack Napes*, perh. a playful name for a tame ape, with *n-* as in *Ned*, *Nell*, etc., and *-s* as in *Hobbes*, etc.] **1.** Name for a tame ape or monkey 1526. **2.** A ridiculous upstart; a pert, impertinent fellow; a coxcomb. (The current use.) 1555.

2. That Iacke an-apes with scarfes SHAKS. *attrib.* A scuruy Iack a-nape Priest SHAKS.

Jackaroo (dʒæ·kărū). *Austral.* 1880. [f. JACK *sb.*[1] + *kang)aroo.*] An inexperienced colonist.

Jackass (dʒæ·kˌæs). 1727. [f. JACK *sb.*[1] + ASS.] **1.** A male ass, a he-ass. **2.** = ASS 2. 1823. **3. Laughing Jackass:** the Giant Kingfisher of Australia (*Dacelo gigas*), so called from its cry 1798. **4.** *Naut.* a kind of heavy rough boat used in Newfoundland.

Comb.: **j.-copal,** the raw copal of Zanzibar; **-deer,** an African antelope, the sing-sing; **-fish,** an Australian fish (*Chilodactylus macropterus*), esteemed as food; **j. penguin,** a common species of penguin (*Spheniscus demersus*), so called from its cry; **j. rabbit** = JACK-RABBIT.

Jack-boot, ja·ckboot. 1686. [f. JACK *sb.*[1] (of unc. application) + BOOT *sb.*[3]] A large strong boot, the top of which came above the knee, orig. worn by cavalry soldiers; later, by fishermen and others.

†Ja·ck-boy. 1573. [f. JACK *sb.*[1] + BOY.] A boy employed in menial work; *spec.* a stableboy, groom, or postillion –1849.

Jack-chain. 1639. [f. JACK *sb.*[1] II. 1; because used in roasting-jacks.] A chain each link of which consists of a double loop of wire, resembling a figure of 8.

Jackdaw (dʒæ·kdǭ). 1543. [f. JACK *sb.*[1] + DAW.] **1.** The common name of the DAW (*Corvus monedula*), which frequents church towers, old buildings, etc.; noted for its loquacity and thievish propensities. **2.** *fig.* Applied *contempt.* a loquacious person 1605.

1. Iack dawes; the veriest theeves. .especially for silver and gold HOLLAND.

Jackeen (dʒækī·n). *Anglo-Irish.* 1840. [Irish dim. of JACK *sb.*[1]; see -EEN[2].] A self-assertive worthless fellow.

Jacket (dʒæ·kėt), *sb.* 1462. [– OFr. *ja(c)quet*, dim. of *jaque*; see JACK *sb.*[2], -ET.] **1.** An outer garment for the upper part of the body: the same as the jack; now, an outer garment with sleeves, reaching no lower than the waist; also a short coat without tails (as a *dinner jacket*). **b.** That worn by a jockey in horse-racing; now a loose-fitting blouse of silk or satin, of the owner's distinctive racing colours 1856. **c.** Applied to something worn round the body for other purposes than clothing; as a *strait jacket*, etc. **2.** An outer covering for anything, esp. one placed round a pipe, steam-cylinder, or boiler, to protect it, prevent escape or access of heat, etc. 1815. **b.** A paper wrapper in which a bound book is issued. 1894. **3. a.** The natural covering or coat of various animals; the fleece (of a sheep), hair (of a dog), fur (of a cat), etc.; also the skin (of a seal, fish, etc.) 1613. **b.** The skin of a potato (when cooked with the skin on) 1856.

1. Phr. *To dust, swinge, thrash, trim*, etc. (a person's) *j.*, to give him a beating. **b.** *To send in* (a jockey's) *j.*, *take away his j.*, etc.

Ja·cket, *v.* 1861. [f. prec. sb.] **1.** *trans.* To cover with or enclose in a jacket. **2.** *dial.* or *colloq.* To beat, thrash 1875.

Jacketed (dʒæ·kėtėd), *a.* 1552. [f. prec. sb. or v. + -ED.] Clothed, covered, or surrounded with a jacket.

Ja·cketing. 1851. [f. as prec. + -ING[1].] **1.** = JACKET *sb.* 2. 1881. **2.** Material for making jackets 1882. **3.** *colloq.* A beating. 1851.

Jack-frame. 1703. [f. JACK *sb.*[1] II. 2 + FRAME.] **1.** The frame in which a jack or winch is fixed. **2.** *Cotton Manuf.* A contrivance consisting of a rotating can containing a bobbin, formerly much used for giving a twist to the roving as delivered by the drawing rollers, and simultaneously winding it upon the bobbin. Also called *jack-in-a-box.* 1875.

Jack-fruit. 1830. = JACK *sb.*[4]

Jack-in-the-box, Jack-in-a-box. 1546. **†1.** A sharper or cheat –1725. **†2.** Applied contemptuously to the consecrated host 1546. **3.** A toy consisting of a box containing a figure with a spring, which leaps up when the lid is raised. Also *fig.* 1702. **4.** Techn.: **†a.** A self-acting valve for relieving watermains from accumulations of air. **b.** A screw-jack or lifting-jack, esp. one used in stowing cargo. **c.** A kind of screw-press. **d.** An instrument with a small but powerful screw, used by burglars to break open safes or doors. **e.** = JACK-FRAME 2.

Jack-in-the-green. 1801. **1.** A man or boy enclosed in a wooden or wicker pyramidal framework covered with leaves, in the May-day sports of chimney-sweepers, etc. **2.** A variety of primrose in which the calyx is transformed into leaves 1876.

Jack Johnson. 1914. Name of a Negro boxer (known as 'the Big Smoke'), applied in the war of 1914–18 to a German gun and shell.

Jack Ketch. 1705. [From the name of *John* or '*Jack*' *Ketch*, the common executioner 1663(?) –1686. He became notorious on account of his barbarity at the executions of William Lord Russell and others.] An appellation for the common executioner or hangman.

He is then a kind of jack-catch, an executioner-general WESLEY.

Jack-knife (dʒæ·kˌnəif), *sb.* 1776. [app. of U.S. origin; perh. assoc. with some sense of JACK *sb.*[1]] **1.** A large clasp-knife for the pocket; also, one with a lanyard, worn by seamen. **2.** In a telephone station = JACK *sb.*[1] II. 8 d. **Jack-knife** *v.* to cut with a j.-k. 1855.

Jack-line. 1615. [f. JACK *sb.*[1]; cf. JACK-CHAIN.] A kind of thin rope or line used for various purposes.

Jackman (dʒæ·kmæ̆n). *Sc.* 1567. [app. f. JACK *sb.*[1] I. 4 + MAN. Referred by Scott to JACK *sb.*[2]] An attendant or retainer kept by a nobleman or landowner. Now *Hist.*

Jack-o'-la·ntern, jack-a-lantern. 1663. **†1.** A man with a lantern; a night watchman –1704. **2.** An ignis fatuus or will-o'-the-wisp; *fig.* something misleading or elusive 1673. **3.** A lantern made of the rind of a large turnip or a pumpkin, with holes to represent eyes, nose, and mouth. *North Eng.*, *Sc.*, and *U.S.*

2. I have followed Cupid's Jack-a-lantern, and find myself in a quagmire SHERIDAN.

Ja·ck-pla:ne. 1763. [JACK *sb.*[1]] A long heavy plane used for coarse work.

Ja·ck-pu·dding. *arch.* 1648. [JACK *sb.*[1] IV. 2.] A buffoon, clown, or merry-andrew, *esp.* one attending on a mountebank.

Ja·ck-ra·bbit. *U.S.* 1882. [Short for *jackass-rabbit*; so called from its long ears.] One of several species of large prairie-hares with remarkably long ears and legs.

Ja·ck-screw. 1769. [JACK *sb.*[1] II. 4.] A lifting-jack with a screw.

Jack snipe, ja·ck-sni:pe. 1663. [See JACK *sb.*[1] III. 2.] A small species of snipe, *Scolopax* (*Gallinago*) *gallinula*; also called *half-snipe.* Also applied to the common American snipe, *Gallinago wilsoni*, the Dunlin, *Tringa alpina* (Shetland), and the pectoral sandpiper of N. America, *Tringa maculata.*

Ja·ck-staff. 1692. [f. JACK *sb.*[3] + STAFF.] *Naut.* A short staff, usually set upon the bowsprit or at the bow of a ship, on which the jack (JACK *sb.*[3]) is hoisted.

Jackstay (dʒæ·kˌstēⁱ). 1840. [JACK *sb.*[1] IV. 1.] *Naut.* **a.** A rope, rod, or batten placed along a yard or gaff to bend the sail to. **b.** A rod or rope running up and down on a mast, on which the square-sail yard travels.

Ja·ck-stone, ja·ckstone. 1814. [var. of CHECK-STONE; perh. assoc. w. JACK *v.*] A small round pebble or stone; esp., in *pl.*, a set of pebbles tossed up and caught in the game of dibs.

Ja·ck-straw·, ja·ckstraw. 1565. [See JACK *sb.*[1], in various senses. *Jack Straw* was a leader in the Rising of the Commons in 1381.] **1.** A 'man of straw'; a man of no substance or consideration. **2.** One of a set of straws, or strips of ivory, bone, wood, or the like, used in a game in which they are thrown on the table in a heap, and have to be picked up singly without disturbing the heap. Also, in *pl.*, the game thus played. 1801.

Jack-ta·r. 1781. [See JACK *sb.*[1] I. 3.] A familiar term for a common sailor.

Jacob (dʒēⁱ·kəb). 1662. [– Heb. *ya'ăḳōḇ* 'supplanter', whence Gr. Ἰάκωβος, eccl.L. *Jacōbus* (see JAMES).] A personal name and surname; used also in deriv. and transf. senses, partly referring to JACOB'S LADDER. **†1.** = JACOBUS. Pepys. **†2.** *slang.* **a.** A housebreaker carrying a ladder –1753. **b.** A ladder –1803. **c.** A simpleton –1812.

Phr. **Jacob's coat, membrane** (*Anat.*), the layer of rods and cones of the retina of the eye (named after Arthur Jacob, an Irish ophthalmic surgeon, died 1874); **Jacob's shell,** the scallop-shell *Pecten jacobæus*, the emblem of St. James the Greater; **Jacob's stone,** a name for the coronation stone of the Scottish kings at Scone, now in Westminster Abbey, fabled to be the stone of Jacob's pillow (*Gen.* 28:11); **Jacob's ulcer,** a term for *Lupus* or rodent ulcer of the eye (from Arthur Jacob).

Jacobean (dʒækŏbī·ăn), *a.* (*sb.*) Also **-æan.** 1770. [f. mod.L. *Jacobæus*, f. eccl.L. *Jacobus*, see prec., -EAN.] **1.** Of or pertaining to the reign or times of James I of England; *spec.* in *Arch.*, a term for the 17th-c. style in England, consisting of very late Gothic with a large Palladian admixture; also *transf.* in other arts 1844. **2.** Of or pertaining to St. James the Less, or the Epistle written by him 1883. **b.** *Jacobean lily*, a bulbous plant (*Sprekelia formosissima*), named after St. James 1770. **3.** *sb.* A statesman or writer of the time of James I. 1885.

Jacobian (dʒăkōᵘ·biăn). 1852. [f. *Jacobi* (see below) + -AN.] *Math.* **A.** *adj.* Pertaining to or named after K. G. J. Jacobi (1804–51), professor at Königsberg in Prussia; discovered, introduced, or investigated by Jacobi; as *J. function*, etc. **B.** *sb.* Short for *J. determinant*, an important functional determinant.

Jacobin (dʒæ·kŏbin), *sb.*[1] and *a.*[1] ME. [– (O)Fr. *Jacobin* – med.L. *Jacobinus*, f. eccl.L. *Jacobus*; see JACOB, -IN[2].]

A. *sb.* **1.** A Dominican friar. (Orig. applied to the French members of the order, from the church of *Saint-Jacques* (St. Jacobus) which was given to them, and near which they built their first convent.) Also *attrib.* or as *adj.* **2.** A member of a French political club established in 1789, at Paris, in the old convent of the Jacobins (sense 1), to maintain and propagate the principles of extreme democracy and absolute equality 1790. **b.** *transf.* An extreme radical in politics, etc. 1793. About 1800, a nickname for any political reformer.

2. b. With the Jacobins I shall keep no terms BURKE.

B. *adj.* **a.** Of or belonging to the Jacobins or Dominican friars. **b.** Pertaining to the Jacobins (sense 2 above); hence, ultra-democratic. 1795. Hence **Jacobi·nic, -al** *a.* of, pertaining to, or characteristic of the French Jacobins; ultrademocratic.

†Ja·cobin, *sb.*[2] and *a.*[2] 1517. [– OFr. *Jacobin* – med.L. *Jacobinus* (Du Cange), var. of *Jacobita* JACOBITE *sb.*[1]] **a.** *sb.* = JACOBITE *sb.*[1] **b.** *adj.* Of or pertaining to this sect. –1768.

Jacobin (dʒæ·kŏbin), *sb.*[3] Also **†Jacobine.** 1668. [– Fr. *jacobine*, fem. of *Jacobin*; see JACOBIN *sb.*[1]] An artificial breed of the domestic pigeon, with reversed feathers on the back of the neck, suggesting a cowl or hood.

Jacobinism (dʒæ·kŏbiniz'm). 1793. [– Fr. *Jacobinisme*; see JACOBIN *sb.*[1], -ISM.] The doctrine or practice of the French Jacobins; ultra-democratic principles. **b.** A Jacobinical trait or notion 1888.

Jacobinize (dʒæ̆·kŏbinəiz), *v.* 1793. [f. JACOBIN *sb.*[1] + -IZE.] *trans.* To render Jacobin, to imbue with revolutionary ideas. Hence **Ja:cobiniza·tion** 1798.

Jacobite (dʒæ·kŏbəit), *sb.*[1] and *a.*[1] ME. [– med.L. *Jacobita*, f. *Jacobus*; see JACOB, -ITE[1] 1.] A member of a Monophysite sect taking its name from Jacobus Baradæus, of Edessa, who revived the Eutychian heresy in the 6th c. Also *attrib.* or as *adj.*

†Ja·cobite, *sb.*[2] 1550. [– med.L. *Jacobita*, f. *Jacobus*; see JACOB, -ITE[1] 1.] = JACOBIN *sb.*[1] 1. –1818.

†Ja·cobite, *sb.*[3] 1658. [f. JACOB + -ITE[1] 1.] A descendant of Jacob, an Israelite; also applied to the 17th-c. Puritan refugees.

Jacobite (dʒæ·kŏbəit), *sb.*[4] and *a.*[2] 1611. [f. L. *Jacobus* JAMES + -ITE[1] 1.]

A. *sb.* An adherent of James II of England after his abdication, or of his own son the Pretender; a partisan of the Stuarts after the Revolution of 1688. 1689.

A private form of prayers..used amongst the Jacobites, for King James in his afflictions 1690.

B. *adj.* †**1.** In *Jacobite piece* = JACOBUS 1611. **2.** Of or pertaining to the adherents of James II and his family (see A.) 1692.

2. Atterbury was nothing more or less than a J. priest 1788. Hence **Jacobi·tic, -al** *a.* pertaining to the adherents of the Stuarts; holding Jacobite principles. **Jacobi·tically** *adv.* **Ja·cobitish** *a.* Jacobitical; **-ly** *adv.*

Jacobitism (dʒæ·kŏbəitiz'm). 1700. [f. JACOBITE *sb.*[4], *sb.*[1] + -ISM.] **1.** The principles of the Jacobites or adherents of James II and his family; adherence to the Stuart cause. **2.** The doctrines of the Jacobite sect of Christians 1882.

Ja·cob's la·dder. 1733. [In reference to Gen. 28:12.] **1.** A common garden plant, *Polemonium cæruleum*, having corymbs of blue (or white) flowers; so called from the ladder-like appearance of its leaves. **2.** *Naut.* A rope ladder with wooden steps for ascending the rigging from the deck 1840. **3.** *fig.* 1831.

Jacob's membrane, etc.: see JACOB.

Jacob's staff. 1548. [In sense 1 from St. James (*Jacobus*), whose symbols are a pilgrim's staff and a scallop shell. In other senses app. fanciful.] †**1.** A pilgrim's staff –1656. **2. a.** An instrument formerly used for taking the altitude of the sun; a cross-staff 1559. **b.** An instrument for measuring distances and heights, consisting of a square rod about three feet in length with a cursor which slips on the staff 1777. **c.** A straight rod shod with pointed iron, and having a socket-joint at the summit for supporting a surveyor's circumferentor instead of a tripod. †**3.** A staff containing a concealed sword or dagger –1656. **4.** A plant, the Great Mullein or Aaron's Rod 1879.

Jacobus (dʒăkōᵘ·bŏs). *Pl.* **-uses.** 1612. [– eccl.L. *Jacobus* JAMES; see JACOB.] The (unofficial) name of an English gold coin, struck in the reign of James I; it passed orig. for 20*s.*, later for 22*s.* or 24*s.*

Jaconet (dʒæ·kŏnĕt). 1769. [alt. of Urdu *jagannāthī*, f. *Jagannāth(pūrī)* 'Juggernaut town', in Cuttack, the place of origin.] A cotton fabric orig. imported, but now manufactured in England; now, A plain cotton cloth of medium thickness or weight, lighter than a shirting, and heavier than a mull.

†**Jacou·nce, jagou·nce.** ME. [– OFr. *jacunce, jagonce* :– pop.L. **iacuntius* for med.L. *iacintus*; see JACINTH.] The jacinth or hyacinth (precious stone) –1529.

Jacquard (dʒăkā·ɹd, dʒæ·kăɹd). 1835. Surname of Joseph Marie Jacquard of Lyons (died 1834), who invented an apparatus to facilitate the weaving of figured fabrics in the loom. Hence *J. apparatus, attachment, engine, machine, mechanism*; also **Jacquard loom,** a loom fitted with this apparatus, for the weaving of figured fabrics; *J. fabric, muslin, stripes*, etc. **b.** Also *ellipt.* as *sb.* = Jacquard apparatus, etc.

‖**Jacquerie** (ʒakəri·). 1523. [Fr., in OFr. *jaquerie*, peasants or villeins collectively, spec. as in Eng.; f. *Jacques*; cf. JACK *sb.*[1]] *Hist.* The rising of the villeins or peasants of northern France against the nobles in 1357–8; hence, Any rising of the peasantry.

Jactance (dʒæ·ktăns). *rare.* 1491. [– (O)Fr. *jactance* or L. *jactantia* boasting, f. *jactant-*, pres. ppl. stem of *jactare*; see next, -ANCE.] Boasting; vainglorious speaking. So **Ja·ctancy,** boastfulness, vainglory; boasting.

Jactation (dʒæktēⁱ·ʃən). 1576. [– L. *jactatio* in same senses, f. *jactat-*, pa. ppl. stem of *jactare*, frequent. of *jacere* throw; see -ION. Cf. Fr. *jactation* in sense 1.] **1.** = JACTITATION 2. 1680. **2.** Boasting, bragging, ostentatious display 1576.

Jactitation (dʒæktitēⁱ·ʃən). 1632. [– med.L *jactitatio* false declaration tending to someone's detriment, f. L. *jactitare* bring forward in public, utter, (later) boast, frequent. of *jactare*; see prec., -ION. In sense 2 app. an expressive extension of prec., sense 1.] **1.** Public or open declaration, esp. boasting, bragging. **2.** *Path.* A restless tossing of the body: a symptom of distress in severe diseases. **b.** A twitching or convulsive movement of a limb or muscle. 1665. †**3.** Bandying to and fro. STERNE.

1. *J. of marriage* (Law): a giving out or boasting falsely by a person that he or she is married to another whereby a reputation of their marriage may ensue.

Jaculate (dʒæ·kiŭleⁱt), *v. rare.* 1623. [– *jaculat-*, pa. ppl. stem of L. *jaculari* dart, hurl, f. *jaculum* dart, f. *jacere* throw; see -ATE[3].] *trans.* To dart, hurl; *intr.* (for *refl.*) to dart forward.

Jaculation (dʒækiŭlēⁱ·ʃən). *rare.* 1608. [– L. *jaculatio*, f. as prec.; see -ION.] The action of darting, hurling, or throwing; a hurl, a throw.

Hills Hurl'd to and fro with j. dire MILTON.

Jaculator (dʒæ·kiŭleⁱtəɹ). 1763. [– L. *jaculator*, f. as prec. + -OR 2.] **1.** One who throws or hurls (*rare*) 1796. **2.** A fish (*Toxotes jaculator*); :– ARCHER 5. Also *j. fish.*

Jaculatory (dʒæ·kiŭlătəri), *a. rare.* 1616. [– late L. *jaculatorius*, f. as prec.; see -ORY[2].] Pertaining to throwing or darting; that is thrown or darted; (of prayer) ejaculatory.

Jad (dʒæd). *local.* 1871. [Of unkn. origin.] In the Bath-stone quarries: 'A long deep holing or cutting made for the purpose of detaching large blocks of stone from their natural beds' (Gresley). Hence **Ja·dding** *vbl. sb.*, also *attrib.*

Jade (dʒēⁱd), *sb.*[1] ME. [Of unkn. origin.] **1.** A contemptuous name for a horse; a horse of inferior breed; a sorry worn-out horse; a vicious, worthless horse. **b.** *occas.* used without depreciatory sense: = Horse 1553. **c.** *fig.* 1577. **2.** A term of reprobation applied to a woman. Also used playfully, like *hussy.* 1560. **b.** Applied to Fortune, Nature, etc. personified 1594. **c.** Rarely to a man 1596.

1. Be blithe though thou ryde vp-on a Iade CHAUCER. **c.** You alwaies end with a Iades tricke SHAKS. **2.** An expensive J. of a Wife ADDISON. **b.** When Fortune, fickle jade's unkind 1812. **c.** A iolly Prater, but a I. to due SYLVESTER. Hence **Ja·dery,** behaviour of a j. 1612.

Jade (dʒēⁱd), *sb.*[2] 1727. [– Fr. *jade*; *le jade* was for earlier *l'ejade* – Sp. *ijada* (in *piedra de ijada* 'colic stone') :– Rom. **iliata*, f. L. *ilia* flanks.] **1.** A name given to **a.** NEPHRITE, a silicate of lime and magnesia, a hard translucent stone, in colour light green, bluish, or whitish; **b.** JADEITE, a silicate of sodium and aluminium, closely resembling nephrite in appearance. Sometimes also applied to SAUSSURITE. **2.** *attrib.* 1865.

Jade (dʒēⁱd), *v.* 1601. [f. JADE *sb.*[1]] **1.** *trans.* To make a jade of (a horse); to exhaust or wear out by driving or working hard; to fatigue, weary 1606. **2.** *intr.* To become tired or worn out; to grow dull or languid; to flag 1620. †**3.** *trans.* To befool; to jape –1679.

1. Our horses were jaded—perfectly 'done up' 1837. **2.** When I feel my Muse beginning to j., I retire to the solitary fireside of my study BURNS. **3.** I do not now foole my selfe, to let imagination iade mee SHAKS. Hence **Ja·ded** *ppl. a.* 1593; **Ja·ded-ly** *adv.*, **-ness.**

Jadeite (dʒēⁱ·dəit). 1865. [f. JADE *sb.*[2] + -ITE[1] 2b.] *Min.* See JADE *sb.*[2] The hardest and most highly prized variety of jade.

Jade-stone. 1775. [f. JADE *sb.*[2] + STONE.] = JADE *sb.*[2]

Jadish (dʒēⁱ·diʃ), *a.* 1573. [f. JADE *sb.*[1] + -ISH[1].] Of the nature of, or having the characteristics of, a jade; of or pertaining to a jade. **a.** Of a horse 1576. **b.** Of a person, *esp.* a woman 1573. **Ja·dish-ly** *adv.*, **-ness.**

Jag (dʒæg), *sb.*[1] Also **jagg.** [f. JAG *v.*[1]] **1.** A dag or pendant made by cutting the edge of a garment; also, a slash or cut in the surface of a garment to show a different colour underneath. †**b.** An attached pendant or fringe –1606. **2.** A shred of cloth; in *pl.* Rags, tatters. Also *transf.* and *fig.* A scrap, fragment. *Obs.* exc. *dial.* 1555. **3.** A hairy, bristly, or thread-like projection 1519. **4.** A sharp projection; a denticulation; a sharp or rugged point of rock, etc. 1578. **5.** A barb or dovetail which resists retraction 1875. **6.** *Sc.* A prick with anything sharp 1818.

Comb. **j.-bolt,** a bolt having a beard raised upon its angles with a chisel (hence **j.-bolt** *v.* to fasten with a jag-bolt).

Jag, *sb.*[2] *dial.* and *U.S.* 1597. [Of unkn. origin.] **1.** A load (usually a small cart-load) of hay, wood, etc. **b.** A pedlar's wallet. SCOTT. **c.** *slang.* A 'load' of drink; also, a drinking bout 1678. **2.** A portion or quantity; a 'lot'. *U.S.* 1834.

Jag (dʒæg), *v.*[1] ME. [First in w.midl., varying with *jogge*; prob. of symbolic formation; cf. RAG *v.*[1], TAG *sb.*[1], JOG *sb.*[2]] **1.** *trans.* To pierce with something sharp; †to stab; to prick (*Sc., north. Eng.*, and *U.S. dial.*) **2.** *trans.* To slash or pink (a garment, etc.) by way of ornament ME. **3.** To make indentations in the edge or surface of; to make ragged or uneven, rugged or bristling 1568. **4.** *Naut.* To lay in long bights, as a rope, and tie with stops. *U.S.*

Jag, *v.*[2] *dial.* 1747. [f. JAG *sb.*[2]] *trans.* To carry in a cart, or on a pack-horse.

Jagannāth, the better sp. of JUGGERNAUT.

‖**Jäger, jaeger** (yēⁱ·gəɹ). Also †**jager,** and YAGER, q.v. 1776. [G. *jäger* hunter, f. *jagen* hunt, chase.] **1.** A (German or Swiss) huntsman or hunter 1823. **2.** A rifleman or sharpshooter in the German and Austrian armies 1776. **3.** An attendant upon a person of rank or wealth, dressed in a huntsman's costume. Cf. CHASSEUR 3. 1831. **4.** A predatory sea-bird of the family *Laridæ*; a skua-gull 1838.

Jagg: see JAG.

Jagged (dʒæ·gĕd, dʒægd), *a.* 1440. [f. JAG *sb.*[1] and *v.*[1] + -ED. Now usu. disyllabic as adj., monosyllabic as pple.] **1.** Of a garment: Cut into jags: pinked, slashed. **2.** Having the edge irregularly cut, gashed, or torn 1577. **3.** Having deep irregular indentations and projecting points; laciniated; esp. of leaves, petals, etc. 1523. **b.** In names of plants: Having jagged leaves or flowers 1548. **4.** Irregularly and sharply pointed 1651.

2. A notched and j. knife DICKENS. **4.** Frowning cliffs and j. pinnacles MERIVALE. **Ja·gged-ly** *adv.*, **-ness.**

Jagger[1] (dʒæ·gəɹ). 1598. [f. JAG *v.*[1] + -ER[1].] One who or that which jags; *spec.* a jagging-iron, also a toothed chisel.

Ja·gger[2]. *dial.* 1514. [f. JAG *sb.*[2] or *v.*[2] + -ER[1].] **1.** A carrier; a hawker. **2.** *Mining.* A man who carries ore on pack-horses from a mine to the smelting-place 1747.

Jaggery (dʒæ·gəri). 1598. [– Indo-Pg. *jag(a)ra, jagre* – Canarese *sharkare* – Skr. *śarkarā* SUGAR.] A coarse dark brown sugar made in India by evaporation from palm sap. Also applied to any kind of crude sugar.

J. palm, a palm-tree that yields j., esp. *Caryota urens.*

Jaggy (dʒæ·gi), *a.* 1717. [f. JAG *sb.*[1] + -Y[1].] Having jags; jagged; in *Sc.*, prickly.

‖**Jaghire** (dʒagīᵊ·ɹ). *E. Indies.* Also **jaghir, jagir,** etc. 1622. [– Urdu *jāgīr*, f. Pers. *jā* place + *gīr* holding.] An assignment of the king's or government's share of the produce of a district to an individual or a body, as an annuity, either for private use or for the maintenance of a public (esp. military) establishment; also, the district, or the income, so assigned. Hence ‖**Jaghirdar** (dʒagīᵊ·ɹdaɹ) [Pers. *-dār* possessor], the holder of a j.

Jaguar (dʒæ·gwaɹ, dʒæ·giuˌăɹ). 1604. [– Tupi-Guarani *yaguara, jaguara* (ya-, ʒawara), orig. a class-name for all carnivorous beasts.] A large carnivorous feline quadruped, *Panthera onca*, yellowish-brown in colour and marked with ocellated spots, inhabiting wooded parts of America from Texas to Paraguay.

Of the large Spotted Cats, the largest is the J. 1875.

‖**Jaguarete.** 1753. [– Tupi-Guarani *jaguaretê*, f. as prec. + *-etê* 'true'; the specific name of the jaguar.] The Guarani name for the jaguar; long mistaken for a distinct species or variety, e.g. the Black Jaguar.

‖**Jaguarondi** (dʒægwărǫ·ndi, yægwa-). 1885. [Native name in Tupi-Guarani; cf. JAGUAR.] A large wild cat (*Felis yaguarundi*, Desmarest), dark brown or brownish grey in colour, with a long body and tail, inhabiting America from Texas to Paraguay.

‖**Jah** (dʒā). 1539. The form of the Heb. *Yah*, short for *Yahwe(h* (Jahveh) JEHOVAH, in the English Bible. See JEHOVAH.

Jahvism (yā·viz'm). Also **Jahveism, -ehism, Yahwism** (yā·veˌiz'm, yā·wiz'm). 1867. [f. *Jahveh, Jahve, Yahwe(h*, different transliterations of the Heb. (previously represented by JEHOVAH) + -ISM.] The religion of Jahveh; the system of doctrines and precepts connected with the worship of Jahveh. **b.** The use of *Jahve(h* as a name for God.

So **Jahvist** (yā·vist), **a.** a worshipper of Jahveh; **b.** = JEHOVIST 2. **Jahvi·stic** *a.* of or pertaining to Jahvism or the Jahvist.

Jail, gaol (dʒēⁱl), *sb.* [Two types: 1) ME. *gay(h)ole, -ol, gaill(e, gaile*, etc. – ONFr. *gaiole, gayolle, gaole*; 2) ME. *jaiole, jayle, jaile*, etc. – OFr. *jaiole, geole*, etc. (mod. *geôle*) prison :– Rom. and pop.Lat. **gaviola*, for **caveola*, dim. of *cavea* cavity, cage, coop; see CAGE. The Norman Fr. and ME. *gaiole, gaole* survives in the spelling *gaol* (chiefly due to statutory and official tradition); the current pronunciation corresponds to the form *jail*, which in U.S. is the official spelling.] **1.** A place or building for the confinement of persons accused or convicted of a crime or offence; a prison. Now, a public building for the confinement of persons committed by process of law. **b.** Without the article: = imprisonment 1447. **c.** *transf.* and *fig.* Place of confinement ME.

At that period the gaols were..depositories of pestilence MCCULLOCH. **b.** Having been sent to gaol by him twice KINGSLEY. **c.** [Love] is..A plesaunt gayl and esy prisoun ME.

Comb.: **†j. damp**, the noxious exhalation formerly common in jails; **j. distemper** = JAIL-FEVER; **j.-house** (*U.S.*), a jail; **j. money**, money paid for the maintenance of a jail.

Jail, gaol (dʒēⁱl), *v.* 1604. [f. prec.] *trans.* To confine in or as in a jail; to imprison.

One, whose bolts, That j. you from free life, bar you from death TENNYSON.

Jail-bird, gaol-bird (dʒēⁱ·lbɔ̄ɹd). 1603. [With allusion to a caged bird; see JAIL *sb.*] A prisoner in jail; esp. a habitual criminal; as a term of reproach, an incorrigible rogue.

Jai·l-deli:very, gaol-delivery. 1461. [See DELIVERY.] **1.** The clearing a jail of prisoners by bringing them to trial, esp. at the assizes; hence the judicial process by which every prisoner awaiting trial in a jail is either condemned or acquitted at the assizes. **2.** Deliverance from jail or imprisonment, whether by force or otherwise 1592.

1. [He] came before the Iustices of Gaole deliuery at Newegate HALL. **2.** The legislature has been obliged to make a general arbitrary jail-delivery BURKE.

Jailer, jailor, gaoler (dʒēⁱ·ləɹ). ME. [Two types corresp. to *gaol, jail*; see JAIL *sb.*, -ER² 2, -OR 2.] One who has charge of a jail or of the prisoners in it; a jail-keeper.

fig. His Iniury The Gaoler to his pitty SHAKS. Hence **Jai·leress, Jai·lership.**

Jail-fever, gaol-fever. 1753. [f. JAIL, GAOL *sb.* + FEVER *sb.*] A virulent type of typhus-fever, formerly endemic in crowded jails, and frequent in ships and other confined places.

Jain, ‖Jaina (dʒēⁱn, dʒēⁱ·nă). 1805. [Hindi *jain* :– Skr. *jainas* of or pertaining to a Buddha or saint, f. *jinas* a Buddha, a (Jain) saint, lit. 'overcomer', f. root *ji* conquer.] **A.** *sb.* A member of a non-Brahminical East Indian sect, holding doctrines closely resembling those of Buddhism. **B.** *adj.* Of or pertaining to the Jains or their religion. **Jai·nism**, the religious system of the Jains. **Jai·nist**, *sb.* and *a.* = JAIN.

Jakes (dʒēⁱks). Now *rare.* *c* 1530. [Of unkn. origin; perh. trivial use of the proper name *Jacques* (see JACK *sb.*¹) or of the gen. of *Jack*, quasi *Jak(k)es*.] A privy. Also *transf.* and *fig.*

Jalap (dʒæ·ləp, dʒǫ·ləp), *sb.* 1574. [– Fr. *jalap* – Sp. *jalapa*, in full *purga de Jalapa*, from *Jalapa* formerly *Xalapa*, a city of Mexico, in Aztec *Xalapan* (ʃalā·pan), lit. 'sand by the water', f. *xalli* sand + *atl* water + *pan* upon.] A purgative drug obtained from the tuberous roots of a Mexican climbing plant, *Exogonium* (*Ipomœa*) *purga* and some other convolvulaceous plants; the active principle is the resin contained in the tubers (*resin of j.*). Also applied to the plants themselves 1698. False or Garden J., *Mirabilis jalapa.* Hence **Ja·lap** *v.* to dose or purge with j.

Jalapin (dʒæ·lăpin). 1832. [f. mod.L. *jalāpa* (see prec.) + -IN¹.] *Chem.* A glucoside resin; the resin of jalap-stalks. It is a strong purgative. So **Jala·pic** *a.* in *jalapic acid*, $C_{68}H_{59}O_{35}$, an acid produced by dissolving j. in aqueous solutions of the alkalis or alkaline earths; hence **Ja·lapate**, a salt of this acid.

Jalouse (dʒălū·z), *v.* *Sc.* 1816. [– Fr. *jalouser* regard with jealousy, f. *jaloux, -ouse* JEALOUS.] **1.** *trans.* To be suspicious about. **2.** To suspect (that a thing is so); to surmise, guess 1816. ¶**3.** (*Misused by southern writers.*) To regard with jealousy; to begrudge jealously 1879.

‖Jalousie (ʒa·luzi). 1824. [Fr., = jealousy; also as here.] A blind or shutter made with slats which slope upwards from without, so as to exclude sun and rain, and admit air and some light. Hence **Ja·lousied** *a.* provided with a j. 1847.

Jam (dʒæm), *sb.*¹ Also **jamb.** 1806. [f. JAM *v.*] **a.** The action of jamming; a crush, a squeeze; a mass of things or persons tightly crowded or packed together; a block in a confined passage. **b.** The tight squeezing of one or more movable parts of a machine into or against another part so that they cannot move; the blocking of a machine from this cause 1890. Also *attrib.*

Comb.: **j.-nut**, an auxiliary nut screwed down upon the main nut to hold it; **-weld** (*Forging*), a weld in which the heated ends or edges of the parts are square butted against each other and welded.

Jam (dʒæm), *sb.*² 1730. [perh. identical with prec.] A conserve of fruit prepared by boiling it with sugar to a pulp. Also *transf.* and *fig.*

Without Real J.—cash and kisses—this world is a bitterish pill 1885.

‖Jam (dʒām), *sb.*³ ? *Obs.* 1793. [f. JAMA.] A kind of dress or frock for children.

‖Jam (dʒām), *sb.*⁴ Also **jám, jām.** 1843. ['Of obscure origin' (Yule).] An hereditary title of certain princes and noblemen in Sind, Kutch and Saurashtra.

Jam (dʒæm), *v.* Also **jamb.** 1706. [Of symbolic origin; cf. CHAM *v.*, CHAMP *v.*] **1.** *trans.* To press or squeeze (an object) tightly between two converging bodies or surfaces; to wedge or fix immovably in an opening 1719. **b.** To make fast by tightening 1726. **c.** To block (a passage, etc.) by crowding or crushing into it 1866. **d.** To bruise or crush by pressure 1832. **2.** *intr.* To become fixed, wedged, or held immovably; to stick fast 1706. **3.** *trans.* To cause the fixing or wedging of (some movable part of a machine) so that it cannot work; to render (a machine, gun, etc.) unworkable thus 1851; *intr.* to become unworkable thus 1885. **b.** Wireless. *trans.* To cause interference in (radio signals). Also *intr.* To be affected by such interference. 1914. **4.** *trans.* To press, squeeze, or crowd together in a compact mass; to force together 1768. **5.** To thrust or ram *into* a confined space 1793. Also with *against, down, in* 1836.

1. The Ship..stuck fast, jaum'd in between two Rocks DE FOE. **d.** He jamm'd his finger in the door 1840. **2.** The Ice jam'd 1706. **5.** Hats are jammed tightly on the head 1887. Hence **Jammed** *ppl. a.*

Jam, obs. f. JAMB.

‖Jama, jamah (dʒā·mă). *E. Ind.* 1776. [Urdu – Pers. *jāmah* clothing. Cf. PYJAMAS.] The long cotton gown worn by Hindus.

Jamadar, var. of JEMADAR.

Jamaica (dʒămēⁱ·kă). 1756. The name of a large West Indian island. Used *attrib.* of things native to or imported from that island, as *Jamaica bark, ebony*, etc. Also **J. pepper** = ALLSPICE; **J. rum,** often called simply **Jamaica; J. wood** = BRAZILETTO. Hence **Jamai·can** *a.* and *sb.* 1681.

Jamb (dʒæm). ME. [– (O)Fr. *jambe* leg, vertical supporting piece :– Rom. **gamba* (**camba*) leg, in late L. hoof, veterinary breeder's term – Gr. (cf. καμπή flexure, joint).] **1.** (also *jambe.*) *Her.* The leg of an animal represented on a coat of arms 1725. **b.** *Armour.* A leg-piece made of metal or cuir-bouilli 1834. **2.** *Arch.* Each of the side-posts of a doorway, window, or chimney-piece, upon which rests the lintel; a cheek; esp. in pop. use, (*pl.*) the stone cheeks of a fire-place ME. **3.** A projecting columnar part of a wall; a columnar mass or pillar in a quarry or mine 1687. **4.** *Mining.* A bed of clay or stone running across a mineral vein or seam 1721.

Jamb: see JAM *sb.*¹ and *v.*

Jambeau (dʒæ·mbo). *Hist.* Pl. **-eaux.** ME. [In form repr. AFr. **jambeau* deriv. of *jambe* leg.] A piece of armour for the leg; *pl.* leggings; a pair of jambes.

†Jambee. 1704. [f. *Jambi* a district, town, and large river of Sumatra.] A species of *Calamus* or *Dæmonorops* from the district of Jambi; a cane made of this, fashionable in Queen Anne's time –1709.

‖Jambo, jambu (dʒæ·mbo, -bū). *E. Ind.* 1598. [Vernacular forms repr. Skr. *jambu, jambū* 'rose-apple', and its derivs.] **a.** *Eugenia jambos* (*Jambosa vulgaris*), the Rose Apple. **b.** *Eugenia jambolana*, the Java Plum, also called *Jambolan* 1835. **c.** *Eugenia malaccensis*, the Malay Apple, and kindred species, native to the Malay archipelago 1727. So **Jambolan** = JAMBO b.

Jamboree·. [Of unkn. origin.] 1872. **1.** A noisy revel; a carousal or spree. *U.S. slang.* **2.** *Cards.* In railroad euchre, a hand containing the five highest trumps, which entitles the holder to score sixteen points. **3.** A rally of Boy Scouts; orig. applied to the international rally held at Olympia in Aug. 1920.

‖Jamdani (dʒāmdā·nī). *E. Ind.* Also **-danee.** 1858. [Pers.] A species of fine cotton cloth with spots or flowers woven in the loom.

James [– OFr. *James* = Pr., Cat. *Jaume, Jacme*, Sp. *Jaime*, It. *Giacomo* :– Rom. **Ja·comus* for L. *Ja·cobus*, alt. form of *Jacō·bus* JACOB.]

I. A Christian name; hence *transf.* **1.** A sovereign (*slang.*). (Cf. JACOBUS.) 1858. **2.** A burglar's crow-bar; = JEMMY *sb.* 4. 1812. **3.** A sheep's head 1827.

II. St. James, either apostle of the name; esp. St. James the Greater, whose shrine at Compostella was a centre of pilgrimage. *St. James's day, tide*, the 25th of July, dedicated to St. James the Greater ME. *St. James's shell*, a scallop-shell worn by pilgrims to the shrine at Compostella; also the scallop *Pecten jacobæus*. 1500. **b.** *St. James's wort*, Ragwort, *Senecio jacobæa* 1578.

III. Also, a surname; hence, **James's Powder,** a febrifuge, formerly very popular, prepared by Dr. Robert James (1703–1776).

Jamesonite (dʒēⁱ·msənəit). 1825. [f. Professor *Jameson*, of Edinburgh (1773–1854); see -ITE¹ 2b.] *Min.* Sulph-antimonide of lead, usually occurring in fibrous masses; feather-ore.

Jamestown-weed. *U.S.* Also **Jim(p)-son-weed.** 1687. [f. *Jamestown*, in Virginia.] The Thorn-apple, *Datura stramonium.*

Jammy (dʒæ·mi), *a.* 1895. [f. JAM *sb.*² + -Y¹.] Sticky with jam.

Jane (dʒēⁱn). ME. [f. OFr. *Janne(s*, Fr. *Gênes*.] **†1.** A small silver coin of Genoa –1671. **2.** = JEAN, the fabric, q.v.

†Jane-of-apes. *joc. nonce-wd.* [f. after *Jack-of-apes*.] A female Jackanapes. MASSINGER.

‖Jangada (dʒæŋgā·dă). 1598. [Pg. – Malayalam *changāḍam* – Skr. *saṃghāṭa* joining together.] A float or raft of logs joined together, and furnished with a lateen sail; used in parts of Brazil and Peru. **b.** *orig.* A raft used in the E. Indies.

Jangle (dʒæ·ŋg'l), *sb.* [In ME. – AFr. or OFr. *jangle* sb. from *jangler*; later, from next.] **†1.** Idle talk, chatter; an idle word. ME. only. **2.** Contention, altercation 1641. **3.** Discordant sound, ring, or clang 1795. **4.** Confused and noisy talk. (A blending of 1 and 3.) 1839.

1. Do manye goode werkes, and spek fewe Iangles CHAUCER. **3.** The mad j. of Matilda's lyre GIFFORD.

Jangle (dʒæ·ŋg'l), *v.* ME. [– OFr. *jangler, gengler* = Pr. *janglar*, prob. – Gmc. form repr. by (M)Du. *jangelen.*]

I. *intr.* **†1.** To chatter, babble, prate; said

also of birds –1774. **2.** To speak or sound harshly or discordantly ME.

1. Thy mynde is lorn, thou ianglest as a Iay CHAUCER. **2.** Thus they go on, wrangling and jangling 1797.

II. *trans.* **1.** To speak or utter in a noisy babbling, discordant, or contentious manner ME. **2.** To cause (a bell, etc.) to give forth a harsh discordant sound 1604.

2. Like sweet bells iangled out of time, and harsh SHAKS. Hence **Ja·ngler,** †a chatterer, a noisy disputant. †**Ja·ngleress.**

†**Ja·nglery.** ME. [– OFr. *janglerie,* f. *janglere, -eor;* see -ERY 1 b.] Idle talk; wrangling –1583.

Janitor (dʒæ·nitǫɹ). 1584. [– L. *janitor,* f. *janua* door; see -OR 2c.] **1.** A doorkeeper, porter, ostiary 1630. †**2.** An usher in a school –1876. **3.** *Sc.* and *U.S.* A caretaker of a building who has charge of the cleaning and heating of it 1878. Hence **Ja·nitoress, Ja·nitress, Ja·nitrix,** a female j.

Janizary, janissary (dʒæ·nizări, yæ·ni-). 1529. [Early forms represent various Rom. forms, the present prevailing sp. reflecting Fr. *janissaire;* ult. – Turk. *yeniçeri,* f. *yeni* new + *çeri* troops.] **1.** One of a former body of Turkish infantry, constituting the Sultan's guard and the main part of the standing army. The body was composed mainly of tributary children of Christians, and was abolished in 1826. **2.** Hence, any Turkish soldier; *esp.* one of an escort for travellers in the East 1615. **3.** *fig.,* etc. 1565. **4.** *attrib.* 1642. Hence **Janiza·rian** *a.*

3. The Romish Janizaries are the tribute Children of all Europe 1679.

Janker (dʒæ·ŋkəɹ). *Sc.* 1823. [Of unkn. origin.] A long pole on wheels, used for carrying logs and other heavy weights.

Jansenism (dʒæ·nsěniz'm). 1656. [f. as next + -ISM.] The doctrinal system of the Jansenists.

Jansenist (dʒæ·nsěnist), *sb.* (*a.*) 1664. [f. Cornelius *Jansen* (d. 1638), bishop of Ypres, Flanders + -IST.] A follower in the Roman Catholic Church of Cornelius Jansen, bishop of Ypres in Flanders (died 1638), who maintained after St. Augustine the perverseness and inability for good of the natural human will. Also *attrib.* or *adj.* Hence **Janseni·stic, -ical** *a.* 1711; †**Janse·nian** (*rare*).

Jant, etc.: see JAUNT, etc.

January (dʒæ·niuări). ME. [– L. *Januarius,* subst. use (sc. *mensis* month) of adj. of *Janus;* see next. The earliest Eng. forms are *Ieniuer, Ieneuer, Ianeuer* (XIII) – AFr., OFr. *Jeneuer, Geneuer* (mod. *janvier*).] The first month of the year according to modern reckoning. Abbrev. Jan.

Janus (dʒē̆·nǒs). 1508. An ancient Italian deity, regarded as having doors and entrances under his protection; represented with a face on the front and another on the back of his head; the doors of his temple in the Roman Forum were always open in time of war, and shut in time of peace. Often used *attrib.,* and allusively, referring to the two-faced figure.

Four faces each Had, like a double J. MILT *P.L.* XI. 29. *attrib.* A friend is Janus-faced: he looks to the past and the future EMERSON.

Jap. 1880. Colloq. abbrev. of JAPANESE.

Japan (dʒăpæ·n), *sb.* (*a.*) 1577. [ult. – Malay *Japang, Japung* – Chinese *jih pun* sunrise, orient (= Jap. *Nippon*), f. *jih* (Jap. *ni*) + *pun* (Jap. *pon, hon*).] **1.** A country of eastern Asia consisting of a long cluster of islands extending between Kamchatka in the north and the Philippines in the south. †**b.** *transf.* A Japanese 1588. **2.** A hard varnish of the kind used in work orig. imitating lacquer of Japan 1688. **3.** Japanese work, esp. with painted and varnished design 1742. **4. a.** Japanese porcelain. †**b.** Japanese silk 1729. **5.** *attrib.* Of, belonging to, native to, or produced in Japan; as **J. clover,** a leguminous annual introduced into southern U.S. in 1840 from China and Japan; **J. earth** = CATECHU; **J. ink,** a superior black writing ink, generally glossy when dry; **J. moth,** a moth of the genus *Adela* 1673. **6.** *attrib.,* in sense 2, as *j. cabinet, frame,* etc. 1681; *J. varnish* (*tree*) = AILANTO 1789.

Japan (dʒăpæ·n), *v.* 1688. [f. prec., sense 2.] **1.** *trans.* To lacquer with japan; to varnish with any material that gives a hard black gloss. **2.** *transf.* To make black and glossy as in japanning 1714. **3.** *slang.* To ordain. (With reference to the black coat.) 1756.

2. His gaiters, too, were fresh japann'd W. COMBE.

Japanese (dʒæpănī·z). 1604. [f. JAPAN + -ESE.] **A.** *adj.* Of or pertaining to Japan 1719. What more picturesque than the J. umbrellas? 1884.

B. *absol.* or as *sb.* **1.** A native of Japan. (Now only as adj. used absol. and unchanged for pl.) 1604. **2.** The Japanese language 1828.

Japanesery (dʒæpănī·zəri). 1885. Also in Fr. form **japonaiserie.** [f. prec. + -ERY, after Fr. (cf. CHINOISERIE).] Japanese conduct, art, decoration, etc.; an instance of this.

Japanned (dʒăpæ·nd), *ppl. a.* 1693. [f. JAPAN *v.* + -ED[1].] **1.** Varnished, lacquered, etc., with japan 1693. **b.** Polished with blacking 1750. **2.** Made or become Japanese 1889. So **Japa·nning** *vbl. sb.,* also *concr.* = JAPAN 2.

Japanner (dʒăpæ·nəɹ). 1614. [f. JAPAN *sb.* and *v.* + -ER[1].] †**1.** A Japanese; a Japanese ship –1764. **2.** One who japans, one who follows the trade of varnishing with japan 1695: †*joc.* a shoe-black –1734.

Jape (dʒē̆ip), *sb.* ME. [f. JAPE *v.*] †**1.** A trick, a device to deceive or cheat. *Obs.* since *c* 1515, but used by Scott. **2.** A device to amuse; a merry or idle tale; a jest, gibe. Revived in 19th c. ME. †**3.** A trifle, toy –1570. Hence **Ja·pish** *a.* 1745.

1. The japes and mockeries of evil spirits SCOTT.

Jape (dʒē̆ip), *v.* ME. [Appears to combine the form of OFr. *japer* (mod. *japper*) yelp, yap, with the sense of OFr. *gaber* mock, deride (cf. GAB *v.*[1]).] †**1.** *trans.* To trick, beguile, befool, deceive –1463. †**2.** To seduce; to know carnally. †Also *intr.* –1589. **3.** *trans.* To mock, deride, insult. Occas. used in 18–19th c. 1440. **4.** *intr.* To say or do something in jest or mockery ME. Hence **Ja·per,** one who japes; *esp.* a professional jester. †**Ja·pery,** ribaldry; a jest.

Japhetic (dʒăfe·tik), *a.* Also **Japetic.** 1828. [f. mod.L. *Japheti* descendants of *Japheth;* see -IC.] Of or belonging to Japheth, one of the sons of Noah; descended from Japheth: sometimes applied to the Indo-European family. So **Japhetite** (dʒē̆·fetəit), also **Japhethite,** a descendant of Japheth.

Japonic (dʒăpǫ·nik), *a.* 1673. [f. *Japon,* XVII var. of JAPAN + -IC.] Of or pertaining to Japan; Japanese. So †**Japo·nian** *a.* and *sb.* 1591.

J. earth: catechu, terra japonica.

Japonica (dʒăpǫ·nikă). 1819. [mod.L., fem. of *Japonicus* pertaining to Japan.] The name given to various ornamental plants orig. native to Japan, as the common camellia (*Camellia japonica*), the Japan quince (*Pyrus japonica*).

Jar (dʒāɹ), *sb.*[1] 1546. [Goes with JAR *v.*] **I. 1.** A harsh inharmonious sound; †*spec.* in *Mus.,* A discord 1553. †**2.** A vibration or tick of the clock. SHAKS. **3.** A quivering or grating sound 1669. **4.** A tremulous vibration resulting from concussion or physical shock 1815.

1. A little iarre in musick is not easily espied 1586. **2.** *Wint. T.* I. ii. 43.

II. 1. Discord, want of harmony; a divergence or conflict of opinions, etc.; †a discrepancy of statement 1548. **2.** Dissension, quarrelling 1546. **b.** A dissension; a petty (esp. domestic) broil 1583.

2. b. *Proverb.* Women's jars breed men's wars. Phr. *At* (*a*) j.: at discord (now *rare*).

III. A method of connecting the bit and the rods or cable in an apparatus for drilling rocks by impact, by means of which at each up-stroke a jar of the bit is produced which jerks it upwards 1864.

IV. A representation of the harsh vibratory sound made by certain birds and insects, whence their popular names, as JAR-BIRD, JAR-OWL; hence transf., as in NIGHTJAR.

Jar (dʒāɹ), *sb.*[2] 1592. [– Fr. *jarre* – Arab. *jarra* jar.] **1.** A vessel of earthenware, stoneware, or glass, without spout or handle (or two-handled), usu. more or less cylindrical in form. Orig. used only in its eastern sense of a large earthen vessel for holding water, oil, wine, etc. **2.** Such a vessel and its contents; hence a jarful. Formerly a measure of capacity. 1598.

1. *Leyden jar:* see LEYDEN. **2.** Sir, Spain has sent a thousand jars of oil POPE.

Jar, *sb.*[3] *arch.* or *colloq.* 1674. [Later form of *char* CHARE *sb.*[1], turn, turning; see AJAR *adv.*[1]] In *on* or *upon the* (or *a*) *j.,* on the turn, partly open, AJAR *adv.*[1]

Jar (dʒāɹ), *v.* Also †**gerre,** †**charre.** 1526. [This vb. and its sb., JAR[1], are in origin prob. echoic.]

I. 1. *intr.* To emit or make a harsh grating sound; to sound in discord with other sounds. Also *fig.* †**2.** *intr.* Of a clock (or, of minutes); To tick. Also in Shaks. *trans.* To cause to tick. 1593. **3.** *intr.* To strike against something with a grating sound, or so as to cause vibration; to clash 1665. **4.** *intr.* To sound harshly *in* (*obs.*), or fall with harsh effect *on,* the ear. Hence, To strike with discordant or painful effect *upon* the nerves, feelings, mind, conscience, etc. 1538. **5.** *intr.* To vibrate audibly; hence, to vibrate, shiver, or shake from an impact or shock 1735. **6.** *trans.* To cause to sound discordantly 1633. **7.** To cause to vibrate; to shake into vibration 1568. **8.** To injure by concussion or impact 1875.

1. Iarringe, and snarringe at me like dogs 1576, **2.** *Rich. II,* V. v. 51. **3.** As broadsword upon target jarred SCOTT. **4.** His laugh jars on one's ear THACKERAY. **7.** The five paved road. . jars the nerves terribly MRS. PIOZZI.

II. 1. *intr.* To be out of harmony or at discord in character or effect; to disagree; to conflict 1541. **b.** To clash 1621. **2.** *intr.* To be at strife; to quarrel; to dispute, wrangle 1550. †**3.** *trans.* To bring to discord –1628.

1. Orders and Degrees Jarr not with liberty, but well consist. MILT. *P.L.* V. 793.

‖**Jararaca** (dʒărără·kă). 1613. [Native name in Tupi-Guarani.] A venomous serpent of Brazil (*Bothrops jararaca*) of the family *Crotalidæ.*

Ja·r-bird [JAR *sb.*[1] IV.] Local name of the Nut-hatch. G. WHITE.

‖**Jarde.** 1727. [Fr. – It. *giarda.*] = JARDON.

‖**Jardinière** (ʒardinyę̄·r). 1841. [Fr.] **1.** An ornamental stand or receptacle for plants, flowers, etc. **2.** *Cookery.* A preparation of mixed vegetables stewed in a sauce; *j. soup,* vegetable soup 1846.

‖**Jardon.** 1720. [Fr. – It. *giardone,* augm. of *giarda* JARDE.] *Farriery.* A callous tumour on the leg of a horse, on the outside of the hock –1797.

Jarful (dʒā·ɹful). 1866. [f. JAR *sb.*[2] + -FUL.] As much as a jar will hold.

†**Ja·rgle,** *v.* 1549. [– OFr. *jar-, gargoillier* warble as a bird, murmur as a brook, chatter, prob. f. an imit. base; cf. JARGON *sb.*[1]] *intr.* To utter a harsh or shrill sound; to chatter, jar –1600.

†**Jargogle,** *v.* [Of unkn. origin.] *trans.* To confuse, jumble. LOCKE.

Jargon (dʒā·ɹgən), *sb.*[1] [Late ME. *iargo(u)n, girgoun, gargoun* – OFr. *jargoun, gergon, gargon;* ult. origin unkn.] **1.** Twittering, chattering. (Recently revived.) **2.** Unintelligible or meaningless talk or writing; nonsense, gibberish ME. †**3.** A cipher, or other system of characters or signs having an arbitrary meaning –1708. **4.** A barbarous, rude, or debased language or variety of speech; a 'lingo'; used esp. of a hybrid speech 1643. **5.** Applied contemptuously to the language of scholars, the terminology of a science or art, or the cant of a class, sect, trade, or profession 1651. **6.** A 'babel' of sounds 1711.

2. Alchymy. . is found to be mere J. and Imposture 1722. **4.** Others had the Levant J., which they call Lingua Frank DE FOE. **5.** The j. of the trade 1704, of the Law 1717. Metaphysical j. KAMES. Hence **Jargonee·r,** a jargon-monger. **Jargo·nic**[1].

Jargon, jargoon (dʒa·ɹgən, dʒaɹgū·n), *sb.*[2] 1769. [– Fr. *jargon* (XVIII) – It. *giargone,* usually identified (ult.) with ZIRCON.] A translucent, colourless, or smoky variety of the mineral zircon, found in Ceylon. Hence **Jargo·nic** *a.*[2] 1796.

Jargon (dʒā·ɹgən), *v.* ME. [– OFr. *jargonner* in same senses, f. *jargon* JARGON *sb.*[1]]

1. *intr.* To warble, twitter, chatter. *Obs.* from 15th to 19th c. **2.** *intr.* To utter jargon; to talk unintelligibly 1570.

2. Disappear, I say; away, and j. no more in that manner CARLYLE. Hence **Ja·rgoner.**

Jargonelle (dʒāɹgǒne·l). Also **-el.** 1693. [– Fr. *jargonelle*, dim. of *jargon*; see JARGON *sb.*[2], -EL.] An early-ripening variety of pear.

Ja·rgonist. *rare.* 1782. [f. JARGON *sb.*[1] + -IST.] One who affects or uses a jargon.

Jargonize (dʒā·ɹgŏnəiz), *v.* 1803. [f. as prec. + -IZE.] **a.** *intr.* To talk jargon or a jargon. **b.** *trans.* To bring (*into* a condition) by means of jargon; to translate into jargon.

†**Jark.** *Old Cant.* 1561. [Of unkn. origin.] A seal –1818.

‖**Jarl** (yāɹl). Also **yarl.** 1820. [ON. (= OE. *eorl* EARL), orig. 'a man of noble birth'.] An old Norse or Danish chieftain or under-king. *Hist.*

Jarosite (dʒæ·rosəit). 1854. [f. Barranco *Jaroso* in Spain; see -ITE[1] 2b.] *Min.* A hydrous sulphate of iron and potassium, occurring usually in yellowish rhombohedral crystals.

Jar-owl, jarr-owl. 1832. [f. JAR *sb.*[1] IV.] The goatsucker or nightjar (*local*).

Jarrah (dʒæ·rǎ). 1866. [– native name *djarryl, jerryhl.*] The mahogany gumtree (*Eucalyptus marginata*) of West Australia; the durable timber of this tree. Also *attrib.*

Jarring (dʒā·riŋ), *vbl. sb.* 1555. [f. JAR *v.* + -ING[1].] The action of JAR *v.* **1.** Harsh dissonance; discordant sound. **2.** Vibration caused by concussion 1775. **3.** Discordant action 1581. **4.** Disputing, wrangling 1574.

1. The j. of a distant door BYRON. **3.** A harsh j. of incongruent principles SIR J. REYNOLDS.

Ja·rring, *ppl. a.* 1552. [f. JAR *v.* + -ING[2].] That jars (see the vb.).

A violent j. Motion 1665. J. int'rests 1762, sectaries 1780. Hence **Ja·rring-ly** *adv.*, **-ness.**

Jarvey (dʒā·ɹvi). *colloq.* Also **jarvy, jarvie.** 1819. [By-form of *Jarvis* or *Jervis*, personal name.] **1.** A hackney-coachman 1820. †**2.** A hackney-coach –1868.

1. The old j. with his many-caped Benjamin SALA.

Jasey (dʒē[i]·zi). 1780. [perh. alt. of JERSEY, so called because made of Jersey yarn.] Humorous or familiar for a wig, esp. one made of worsted.

Jasmine, -in (dʒæ·smin), **jessamine, -in** (dʒe·sǎmin). 1548. [The two forms (of equal date) repr. Fr. *jasmin* and †*jessemin* – Arab. *yās(a)min* – Pers. *yāsamin* or *yāsaman.*] **1. a.** *orig.* The plant *Jasminum officinale*, a climbing shrub with fragrant white flowers, grown in England since the 16th c.; hence, **b.** Any species of plant of the botanical genus *Jasminum*, with white or yellow salver-shaped flowers. Also the flower of any of these.

Next to the Common or White Jasmine, the ordinary 'jessamine' of English literature, the best known is the Yellow-flowered, *J. fruticans*; the total number of species is about ninety.

c. Applied to plants of other genera 1760. **2.** A perfume derived from the flowers of the jasmine or jessamine 1670. **3.** *attrib.*, as *j. flower*, etc. 1644.

1. Where jasmine trails on either side the door CRABBE. **c. Cape J.**, *Gardenia florida* and *G. radicans*; **French J.**, *Calotropis procera*, a shrub found in Southern Asia and Africa; **Wild J.**, of Jamaica, a species of *Pavetta*; of the W. Indies, *Faramea odoratissima* and the genus *Ixora.*

Jasp (dʒɑsp). Now *rare* or *Obs.* ME. [– (O)Fr. *jaspe*; see JASPER.] = JASPER 1.

Ja·spachate (-ke[i]t), **ja·spagate.** 1681. [– Fr. *jaspagate* – L. *iaspachates* (Pliny), – Gr., f. ἴασπις jasper + ἀχάτης AGATE.] *Min.* The same as *agate jasper*; see JASPER *sb.* 1.

Jasper (dʒɑ·spəɹ), *sb.* [ME. *iaspre* – OFr. *jaspre*, var. of *jaspe* (also mod.) – L. *iaspis, -id-* – Gr. ἴασπις, -ιδ-, of oriental origin.] **1.** A kind of precious stone. **a.** As tr. Gr. ἴασπις or L. *iaspis*, any bright-coloured chalcedony except carnelian, the most esteemed being green. **b.** Now, an opaque cryptocrystalline variety of quartz, of various colours, usually red, yellow, or brown, due mostly to the presence of iron oxide.

Agate j., 'an agate consisting of j. with veinings and cloudings of chalcedony' (Dana). *Banded, striped*, or *ribbon j.*, a variety having the colours in broad stripes.

2. Short for *jasper-ware* 1825.

Comb.: **j.-opal,** an impure opal containing iron oxide and having the colour of yellow jasper; **j.-pottery, -ware,** a fine kind of porcelain invented by Wedgwood and used by him for his cameos, etc.

†**Ja·sper,** *v.* 1620. [f. JASPER *sb.*] **1.** *intr.* To have a clouding or speckling of various colours, like some kinds of jasper; to be variegated. **2.** *trans.* To marble, to speckle 1799. So **Ja·spered** *a.*, marbled, speckled 1620.

Ja·sperated, *ppl. a.* [f. JASPER *sb.* + -ATE[3] + -ED[2].] 'Mixed with jasper' (Webster).

Jasperize (dʒɑ·spərəiz), *v.* 1833. [f. as prec. + -IZE.] *trans.* To convert by petrifaction into jasper, or into a form of silica resembling jasper.

Jaspery (dʒɑ·spəri), *a.* 1797. [f. as prec. + -Y[1].] Of the nature of, resembling, or containing jasper.

†**Jaspi·dean,** *a.* 1796. [f. as next + -AN; see -EAN.] = next –1807.

Jaspideous (dʒæspi·dĭəs), *a.* 1804. [f. L. *iaspideus* (f. *iaspis*; see next) + -OUS.] Of the nature of jasper.

‖**Jaspis** (dʒæ·spis). ME. [L. *iaspis, -id-*; see JASPER.] = JASPER *sb.* 1 a; rarely 1 b.

Ja·spoid, *a.* 1855. [irreg. f. L. *jaspis* or Gr. ἴασπις JASP + -OID.] Resembling jasper.

†**Jaspo·nyx.** 1616. [– L. *iasponyx* – Gr. ἰασπόνυξ, f. ἴασπις JASPER + ὄνυξ ONYX.] An onyx partaking of the characters of jasper –1748.

‖**Jataka** (dʒæ·tăkă). 1861. [Skr., = nativity.] A narration of one of the incarnations of Buddha preceding Gautama.

Jauk (dʒǭk), *v. Sc.* 1568. [Of unkn. origin.] *intr.* To trifle, dawdle.

Jaunce, *v. Obs.* or *arch.* 1593. [perh. f. OFr.; cf. JAUNT *v.*] **a.** *trans.* ?To make (a horse) prance up and down. **b.** *intr.* ? To prance as a horse.

Spur-gall'd, and tyrd by iauncing Bullingbrooke SHAKS. So †**Jaunce** *sb.* = JAUNT *sb.* 1.

Jaundice (dʒǭ·ndis, dʒā·ndis), *sb.* [ME. *iaunes*, etc. – OFr. *jaunice* (mod. *-isse*) 'yellowness', f. *jaune* yellow; see -ICE. For the parasitic *d* cf. *sound, thunder.*] **1.** A morbid condition caused by obstruction of the bile, and marked by yellowness of the conjunctiva, skin, fluids, and tissues, and by constipation, loss of appetite, and weakness. (Called *yellow, black, green j.*, according to the colour of the skin.) **b.** *White j.* = CHLOROSIS; *blue j.* = CYANOSIS 1727. †**2.** A disease of trees in which there is discoloration of the leaves –1669. **3.** *transf.* and *fig.* 1629.

3. The Love of Gold, (That J. of the Soul, Which makes it look so Guilded and so Foul) COWLEY.

Jaundice (dʒǭ·ndis, dʒā·n-), *v.* 1791. [app. back-formation from next.] *trans.* To affect with jaundice; usually *fig.* To affect with envy or jealousy; to tinge the views of.

Her perceptions were jaundiced by passion 1791.

Jaundiced (dʒǭ·ndist, dʒā·n-), *a.* 1640. [f. JAUNDICE *sb.* + -ED[2].] **1.** Affected with jaundice. **2.** Yellow-coloured 1640. **3.** *fig.* 1699.

1. All looks yellow to the jaundic'd eye POPE. **3.** Here jealousy with jaundic'd look appears 1699.

Jaunt (dʒǭnt, dʒānt), *sb.* 1592. [Goes w. JAUNT *v.*, which appears a little earlier.] **1.** A fatiguing or troublesome journey. (Now only as an ironical use of 2.) **2.** An excursion, trip, journey, *esp.* one taken for pleasure 1678.

1. I arrived here, after a very troublesome j. 1752. **2.** I have been a j. to Oxford H. WALPOLE.

Jaunt (dʒǭnt, dʒānt), *v.* 1570. [Of unkn. origin. Cf. JAUNCE *v.*] †**1.** *trans.* (?) To make (a horse) prance up and down; to tire a horse by riding him up and down –1611. †**2.** To carry up and down on a prancing horse; to cart about (*rare*) –1818. **3.** *intr.* Of a person: To trot or trudge about. *Obs.* or *arch.* 1575. **4.** *intr.* To take a jaunt, now, esp., for pleasure 1647. **5.** *intr.* To move jauntily. R. BRIDGES.

Jau·nting-ca:r. 1801. [f. *jaunting* vbl. sb. + CAR.] A light, two-wheeled vehicle, popular in Ireland, now carrying four persons seated two on each side, either back to back (*outside jaunting-car*) or facing each other (*inside jaunting-car*), with a seat in front for the driver.

Jaunty (dʒā·nti, dʒǭ·nti), *a.* 1662. [In early use *jentee, juntee, ja(u)ntee* – Fr. *gentil* (ʒaṅti; see GENTLE, GENTEEL); assim. later to adjs. in -Y[1].] †**1.** Well-bred; gentlemanly; genteel –1830. **b.** Of things: Elegant, stylish (? *Obs.*) 1662. **2.** Easy and sprightly in manner; affecting airy self-satisfaction or unconcern 1672. **b.** Lively, brisk 1719.

2. This sort of Woman is usually a janty Slattern STEELE. Hence **Jau·ntily** *adv.* **Jau·ntiness.**

Java (dʒā·vǎ). 1842. Name of an island in the Malay archipelago. Used *attrib.* in names of things connected with it in origin, as **J. almond,** *Canarium commune*; **J. plum,** *Eugenia jambolana*; **J. sparrow,** a kind of weaver-bird (*Amadina oryzivora*). Also ellipt. **Java,** a variety of domestic fowl.

Javan (dʒā·văn). 1606. [f. JAVA + -AN.] *adj.* and *sb.* (A native) of Java. So **Javane·se.**

Javel[1] (dʒæ·v'l). ? *Obs.* ME. [Of unkn. origin.] A low fellow; a rascal.

†**Ja·vel**[2]. 1601. [– Fr. *javelle* = ONFr. *gavelle* GAVEL *sb.*[2]] = GAVEL *sb.*[2] –1611.

Javelin (dʒæ·v'lin), *sb.* 1513. [–(O)Fr. *javeline*, alt. of *javelot* JAVELOT.] **1.** A light spear thrown with the hand; a dart. Also *fig.* †**2.** A pike or half-pike; a lance –1839. **b.** = JAVELIN-MAN 1. 1849. †**3.** A fish; app. the pilchard or anchovy 1655. **4.** *attrib.* 1513.

1. *fig.* Where the grey rocks strike Their javelins up the azure E. B. BROWNING. Hence **Ja·velin** *v. trans.* to strike or pierce with or as with a j. **Javelinee·r,** a soldier armed with a j.; a javelin-man.

Javelin-man. 1705. [f. JAVELIN *sb.* + MAN.]. **1.** One of a body of men in the retinue of a sheriff who carried spears or pikes (JAVELIN *sb.* 2), and escorted the judges at assizes. **2.** A soldier armed with a javelin 1846.

†**Ja·velot.** 1489. [– (O)Fr. *javelot* – Gallo-Rom. *gabalottus.*] A small spear or javelin thrown with the hand or from a catapult –1708. Hence †**Javelotie·r,** a soldier armed with a j.

Jaw (dʒǭ), *sb.* late ME. [– OFr. *joe* cheek, jaw, in AFr. *jowe*, whence ME. *jow(e* (XIV–XVI), later *jawe* (XV–XVII), *jaw* (XVII–). The vocalism is parallel to that of PAW *sb.* The OFr. has been referred to a Gallo-Rom. **gauta* (cf. PAW – Rom. **pauta*).] **1.** One of the bones (or sets of bones) forming the framework of the mouth; in *sing.* more often the *lower* or *under jaw*, the inferior maxillary, than the *upper jaw* or superior maxillary. **2.** In *pl.* The bones and associated structures of the mouth including the teeth; hence, the cavity formed by these parts; the mouth, fauces, throat ME. **3.** *transf.* chiefly in *pl.* The two sides of a narrow pass, fissure, gorge, or channel; the narrow entrance into a valley, gulf, or sea; etc. ME. **4.** *pl.* Applied to the seizing or holding members of a machine, etc., arranged in pairs, and usually capable of an opening and closing movement; *spec. Naut.* the semicircular, concave, or forked end of a boom or gaff which clasps the mast with its projecting ends 1789. **5.** *fig.* (in *pl.*) The seizing action or capacity of any devouring agency, as death, time, etc. 1563. **6.** Vulgar loquacity; *esp.* cheeky or impudent talk; also, in vulgar language, A talk, a speech, a lecture, an address 1748.

1. The j. fell, and the eyes were fixed 1866. **2.** From his wide Jaws His Tongue unmoisten'd hangs SOMERVILLE. **5.** To winne renowne Euen in the iawes of danger, and of death SHAKS. **6.** Phr. *To hold* or *stop one's j.* (possibly at first literal).

Comb.: **j.-bit** (*U.S.*), a short bar placed beneath a journal box to unite the two pedestals in a car-truck; **-breaker,** a word hard to pronounce (colloq.); also, a machine with powerful jaws for crushing ore, etc.; **-rope** (*Naut.*), the rope which fastens the two horns or prongs of the boom or gaff round the mast; **-tooth,** a molar tooth; **-wedge** (*U.S.*), a wedge to tighten the axle-box in an axle-guard.

Jaw (dʒǭ), *v.* 1612. [f. prec.] †**1.** *trans.* To use the jaws upon. **2.** *slang.* **a.** *intr.* To use the vocal organs. (A vulgar or contemptuous equivalent for *speak.*) 1748. **b.** *trans.* To scold, lecture 1810. **3.** *To j. away*: to cut to the shape of jaws, or in a concave curve 1802.

Jawbation: see JOBATION.

Jaw-bone, jawbone (dʒǭ·bōun). 1489. [f. JAW *sb.* + BONE.] Any bone of the jaws; *spec.* each of the two forming the lower jaw.

Jawed (dʒǭd), *a.* 1529. [f. JAW *sb.* + -ED².] Having or furnished with jaws.

Jaw·-fall. 1660. **1.** Falling of the jaw; *fig.* dejection (*rare*). †**2.** Dislocation or subluxation of the lower jaw so that it cannot be shut. 1788.

Jaw·-fa:llen, *a.* 1603. [f. JAW *sb.* + *fallen* pa. pple.] Chop-fallen; dejected.

†**Jawn,** obs. var. of CHAWN *sb.* and *v.*

Jawy (dʒǭ·i), *a. rare.* 1654. [f. JAW *sb.* + -Y¹.] Of or pertaining to the jaw; forceful in language.

Jay (dʒēi). ME. [– OFr. *jay* (mod. *geai*) :– late L. *gaius*, beside *gaia*. The word has been identified with the L. proper name *Gaius* (cf. the uses of other personal names, as *jackdaw*, *robin*, Fr. *richard*, *jacques*, *colin*, Du. *wouter*).] **1.** A common European bird, *Garrulus glandarius*, in structure, etc. resembling the magpie, but in habits arboreal, and having a plumage in which vivid tints of blue are heightened by bars of jet-black and patches of white. **b.** Applied to birds of the sub-family *Garrulinæ* or family *Garrulidæ*, among which are the *Blue Jay* (*Cyanurus cristatus*) of N. America, the *Canada Jay* (*Periosoreus canadensis*), the *Grey Jay*, *Green Jay*, etc. 1688. **2.** Applied to: **a.** The Jackdaw; **b.** The Cornish chough, also called *Cornish jay*; **c.** The Missel thrush (*local*) 1484. **3.** *transf.* **a.** An impertinent chatterer. **b.** A showy, flashy, or light woman. **c.** A person absurdly dressed. **d.** A simpleton 1523.

3. Some Iay of Italy..hath betraid him SHAKS. **d. j.-walker** (orig. *U.S.*), one who crosses a street without regard to traffic regulations.

Jay·-bird. 1851. A jay: in parts of England, the Common Jay; in U.S., the Blue Jay.

Jay·-haw:ker. *U.S.* 1865. A name given to the irregular soldiers who fought in and around eastern Kansas, in the free soil conflict, and the early part of the American civil war; hence, a raiding guerrilla.

Jazerant, jesserant (dʒæ·zĕrănt, dʒe·s-). Now only *Hist.* ME. [– OFr. *jaseran(t*, *-enc*; orig. adj., in OFr. *osberc* (*hauberc*) *jazerant*, Sp. *cota jacerina*, f. Arab. *al-jazīra* the island (see AL-²), pl. *al-jazā'ir* Algiers.] 'A light coat of armour composed of splits or small plates of metal rivetted to each other or to a lining of some stout material' (Fairholt).

Jazz (dʒæz), *sb.* 1918. [Of unkn. origin.] A kind of music in syncopated time, as played by Negro bands in U.S. Hence, any syncopated dance music; also, a dance to this music; attrib. as *j.-band*, *-dance*, *-music*, *-step*. Also applied to fantastic designs or vivid patterns. Hence **Jazz** *v. intr.* to dance jazz; *trans.* to arrange as jazz; **Ja·zzy** *a.*, resembling jazz.

Jealous (dʒe·ləs), *a.* [ME *gelus*, *ielus* – OFr. *gelos* (mod. *jaloux*) :– med.L. *zelosus*, f. Chr.L. *zelus* – Gr. ζῆλος ZEAL; see -OUS.] †**1.** Vehement in wrath, desire, or devotion –1661. †**2.** Ardently amorous; fond, lustful –1555. **3.** Vigilant in guarding; suspiciously careful or watchful. Const. *of* (*for*, *over*). ME. **4.** Troubled by the belief, suspicion, or fear that the good which one desires to gain or keep for oneself has been or may be diverted to another; resentful towards another on account of known or suspected rivalry: **a.** in love or affection, esp. in sexual love ME.; **b.** in respect of success or advantage ME. **c.** in biblical language, said of God: Having a love which will tolerate no unfaithfulness in the beloved object ME. **5.** Suspicious; apprehensive of evil, fearful. Now *dial.* 1532. †**b.** Doubtful, mistrustful –1682. **6.** Suspiciously vigilant to prevent something (expressed or understood); vigilant in scrutinizing 1601. Also *transf.*

1. I haue been very iealous for the Lord God of hostes 1 *Kings* 19:10. **3.** The people, j. of their hardly-won liberties BRYCE. **4. a.** So young a husband's j. fears BYRON. **b.** Leading persons in the state were j. of his glory THIRLWALL. **c.** For I the Lorde thy God am a gelouse God COVERDALE *Exod.* 20:5. **5.** My master is very j. of the pestilence 1607. **b.** *Jul. C.* I. ii. 162. **6.** Measures [of weight, etc.] were subject to j. supervision ROGERS. Phr. †*Jealous glass*, an old name for glass which is translucent but not transparent. Hence **Jea·lous-ly** *adv.*, **-ness.**

†**Jealous-hood.** So printed in 4th Fol. Shaks. (1685), *Rom.* & *Jul.* IV. iv. 13, and taken by some as a single word = 'jealousy'.

Jealousy (dʒe·ləsi). ME. [– OFr. *gelosie* (mod. *jalousie*), f. *gelos*; see JEALOUS, -Y³.] The quality of being jealous. †**1.** Anger, wrath, indignation –1649. †**2.** Devotion, eagerness, anxiety to serve –1565. **3.** Solicitude or anxiety for the preservation or well-being of something ME. **4.** The state of mind arising from the suspicion, apprehension, or knowledge of rivalry: **a.** in love ME.; **b.** in respect of success or advantage ME.; **c.** see JEALOUS 4 c. ME. **5.** Suspicion; apprehension of evil; mistrust. Now *dial.* ME.

1. How long, Lord, wilt thou be angry, for euer? shall thy ielousie burne like fire? *Ps.* 79:5. **4. a.** Gelousy [is mightie] as the hell COVERDALE *Song Sol.* 8:6. **b.** Local jealousies FREEMAN. **c.** They prouoked him to iealousie with strange gods *Deut.* 32:16.

Jeames. 1600. †**a.** Obs. f. JAMES. **b.** (After Thackeray). A ludicrous name for a liveried footman (pron. dʒīmz).

Jean (dʒēin). 1488. [orig. *ie(a)ne*, *ge(a)ne fustian*; attrib. use of *Jene*, *Gene* – OFr. *Janne* (mod. *Gênes*) :– med.L. *Janua* Genoa. The Fr. form with *-s* is repr. by Eng. *geanes*, *jennes* (XVI), U.S. *jeans.*] †**1.** Genoa; *attrib.* = GENOESE –1607. **2.** A twilled cotton cloth; a kind of fustian. Orig. *jene fustian*, shortened to *jean*. In U.S. *jeans*. 1567. **b.** *attrib.* as *j. cap*, etc. 1801.

Jear(e, Jeat(e, obs. ff. JEER *sb.*¹, JET.

Jebusite (dʒe·biŭzəit). 1535. Name of a tribe of Canaanites, dispossessed of Jerusalem by David. In XVII a nickname for a Jesuit. Hence **Jebusite** *v.*, **Jebusi·tic, -i·tical, -itish** *a.*

Jedburgh, Jeddart staff: see STAFF *sb.* Whence **Jedwood-** (Scott) or **Jeddart-axe,** which is due to a misapprehension.

Jee (dʒī), *v. Sc.* 1722. [Of unkn. origin. Cf. GEE *v.*] **1.** *intr.* To move, to stir; to move to one side; to move to and fro 1727. **2.** *trans.* To cause to move; to move aside, shift, or displace slightly. Hence **Jee** *sb.* a move, motion 1829.

Jee, *adv.* and *int.* 1785. **a.** The verb-stem used advb. or as an exclam. **b.** = GEE *int.*, a word of command to a horse.

Jeer (dʒīᵊɹ), *sb.*¹ 1495. [Of unkn. origin.] *Naut.* Tackle for hoisting and lowering the lower yards. (Usu. in *pl.*) **b.** *Comb.*, as *j.-capstan*, etc.

Jeer (dʒīᵊɹ), *sb.*² 1579. [Goes with next.] **1.** An act of jeering; a scoff, flout, gibe, taunt 1625. †**b.** The action of jeering; mockery, scoffing –1753. †**2.** Phr. *In a jeer*, (?) in a huff. NORTH.

1. A blow is much sooner forgotten than a j. SPURGEON.

Jeer (dʒīᵊɹ), *v.* 1553. [Earliest forms are *gy(e)re*, *geere*. Of unkn. origin; *fleer* and *leer* have affinities of form and meaning.] **1.** *intr.* To speak in derision or mockery; to scoff derisively (*at*). **2.** *trans.* To address or treat with scornful derision; to deride, flout 1590.

1. Here Grub-street Geese presume to joke and j. GRAY. **2.** Yea, dost thou ieere & flowt me in the teeth? SHAKS. Hence **Jee·rer. Jee·ringly** *adv.*

Jeff (dʒef), *sb. Circus slang.* [Of unkn. origin.] A rope. DICKENS.

Jeffersonian (dʒefəɹsōu·niăn). *U.S.* 1856. [f. Thomas *Jefferson*, President of the U.S. 1801–1809; see -IAN.] *adj.* Pertaining to President Jefferson, or holding his political doctrines (now called DEMOCRATIC). *sb.* A supporter or follower of Jefferson; a Democrat 1880.

Jeffersonite (dʒe·fəɹsənəit). 1822. [Named after President *Jefferson*; see prec. and -ITE¹ 2b.] *Min.* A greenish-black variety of pyroxene, containing some zinc and manganese.

Jeg (dʒeg). 1875. [Cf. *jedge*, *jadge*, a Sc. form of GAUGE.] A templet or gauge for verifying shapes of parts in gun and gunstock making.

Jehad: see JIHAD.

‖**Jehovah** (dʒĭhōu·vă). 1530. [The Eng. and common European representation, since XVI, of the Hebrew divine name (YHWH, JHVH). This word (the 'sacred tetragrammaton'), as being too sacred for utterance, was pointed in the O.T. by the Masoretes with the vowels ᵃ, ō, ā, of ᵃdōnāy, as a direction to the reader to substitute ADONAI for the 'ineffable name'. Students of Hebrew at the Revival of Letters took these vowels as those of the sacred name itself, whence, in L. spelling, IeHoVa(H), i.e. *Iehoua(h)*. It is now held that the original name was YaHWe(H), i.e. *Jahve(h* = *Yahwe(h*, 'he that is', 'the self-existent', or 'the one ever coming into manifestation', but this meaning is conjectural.] The principal and personal name of God in the Old Testament; in English versions, 'the LORD'. Hence in mod. Christian use = God, the Almighty.

I appeared vnto Abraham Isaac and Iacob an allmightie God: but in my name Iehouah [*Wyclif* Adonay] was I not knowne vnto them TINDALE *Exod.* 6:3.

Jehovist (dʒĭhōu·vist). 1753. [f. JEHOV(AH + -IST.] †**1.** One who holds that the vowel-points annexed to the word Jehovah in Heb. represent the actual vowels of the word; opp. to ADONIST. **2.** A name applied to the author (or authors) of those non-Deuteronomic parts of the Hexateuch in which the divine name is rendered 'Jehovah'; opp. to ELOHIST. (Now usu. JAHVIST or *Yahwist.*) 1844.

Hence **Jehovi·stic** *a.* of or pertaining to the J. or Jehovists, characterized by the use of the name 'Jehovah'; also (rarely) pertaining to the religion of Jehovah. In both senses now usu. JAHVISTIC (or *Yahwistic*).

Jehu (dʒī·hiu). *joc.* 1682. [See 2 Kings 9:20.] **a.** A fast or furious driver. **b.** A driver, a coachman. Hence as *vb.*, to drive furiously 1779.

Jejunal (dʒĭdʒū·năl), *a.* 1878. [f. JEJUNUM + -AL¹.] Of or pertaining to the jejunum.

Jejune (dʒĭdʒū·n), *a.* 1615. [– L. *jejunus* fasting, barren, unproductive, meagre.] †**1.** Without food, fasting; hungry –1754. **2.** Deficient in nourishing or substantial qualities; thin, scanty; meagre, unsatisfying; (of land) poor, barren 1646. **3.** Unsatisfying to the mind or soul; dull, insipid, dry; thin, poor; wanting in substance. (The prevailing sense.) 1615.

3. Empty and j. speculations 1671. A very j. and unsatisfactory reason BLACKSTONE. Hence **Jeju·ne-ly** *adv.*, **-ness.**

Jejunity (dʒĭdʒū·nĭti). 1623. [– L. *jejunitas*, f. *jejunus*; see prec., -ITY.] The quality of being jejune; jejuneness.

‖**Jejunum** (dʒĭdʒū·nŏm). 1541. [Mediæval application of L. *jejunum*, neut. of *jejunus* fasting (sc. *intestinum*). So in Fr.] *Anat.* The second part of the small intestine, between the duodenum and ileum.

‖**Jelick** (dʒe·lik, *prop.* ye·lĕk). 1816. [Turk. *yelek* waistcoat.] A vest or bodice worn by Turkish women. Also YELEK.

Jell (dʒel), *v. U.S. colloq.* 1830. [Back-formation from JELLY *sb.*] *intr.* To congeal or jelly.

Jellied (dʒe·lid), *a.* 1593. [f. JELLY *sb.* and *v.* + -ED.] **1.** Turned into jelly; congealed, coagulated. †**2.** Flavoured with jelly, sweet. CLEVELAND.

Jelly (dʒe·li), *sb.* [ME. *geli*, *-y(e* – (O)Fr. *gelée* frost, jelly :– Rom. *gelata* (Reichenau Glosses), subst. use of fem. pa. pple. of *gelare* freeze, f. *gelu* frost.] **1.** An article of food, consisting chiefly of gelatin, obtained from various animal tissues by boiling and subsequent cooling, having a soft homogeneous consistence and usually semitransparent. Also, later, a preparation of the juice of fruit, etc., thickened into a similar consistence. †**b.** The substance GELATIN –1855. **2.** *gen.* Anything of the consistence of jelly 1600. **b.** *spec.* Applied to the alga *Nostoc*, which appears as a jelly-like mass on dry soil after rain, and was supposed to be the remains of a fallen star 1641. **c.** A mixture of gelatin and glycerin used for mounting microscopic objects 1856.

1. The J.. of Red Cabbage ARBUTHNOT. Thick j. made from chickens 1850. **2.** I could have beaten the Woman into a J. D'URFEY. **b.** Like that falling Meteor, there she lies, A J. cold on Earth SOMERVILLE.

Comb.: **j.-bag,** a bag for straining j. through; **-mould; -plant,** an Australian seaweed, *Eucheuma speciosum*, from which j., size, cement, etc. are made.

Jelly (dʒe·li), *v.* 1601. [f. JELLY *sb.*] **1.** *intr.* To come to the consistence of jelly; to congeal, coagulate. **2.** *trans.* To convert into jelly; to cause to 'set'; to reduce to the consistence of jelly 1601.

Je·lly-fish. 1707. †**1.** An oceanic fish of the genus *Plagyodus* or *Alepisaurus*, family *Scopelidæ*. **2.** Pop. name of various acalephs, medusas, or sea-nettles, from their gelatinous structure 1841. Also *fig.* Also *attrib.*

‖**Jemadar** (dʒe·mădaɹ). *E. Ind.* Also **jemi-, jamadar.** 1763. [– Urdu *jamaʻdār*, f. Pers. *jamaʻat* body of men (*jamaʻ* collection) + *dār* holder.] A native officer in a Sepoy regiment, corresponding to a lieutenant; also, a name for the head of a body of police, etc., or of servants. Hence **Jemadary,** the office of a j. 1863.

Jemima (dʒĕməi·mă). 1899. [Appellative use of the female name *Jemima*, eldest of the daughters of Job (*Job* 42:14).] **1.** A made-up tie. **2.** *pl.* Elastic-sided boots 1902.

Jemmy (dʒe·mi), *sb.* Also **jimmy.** 1753. [A pet-form and familiar equivalent of the name James: see -Y[6]. In sense 1 assoc. w., and in 2 and 3 prob. derived from, next.] †**1.** A dandy; a finical fellow –1764. †**2.** A kind of riding-boot; also *j. boot* –1771. **3.** A great-coat. DICKENS. **4.** A crow-bar used by burglars, generally made in sections 1811. **5.** A sheep's head as a dish 1836.

1. Phr. *Jemmy Jessamy* (*Jessamine*) attrib., dandified, foppish, effeminate. See JESSAMY. **5.** You're all jaw like a sheep's jimmy HENLEY & STEVENSON.

Jemmy (dʒe·mi), *a. Obs.* exc. *dial.* Also **gemmy, jimmy,** etc. 1750. [deriv. of *Jim*, GIM *a.*] Spruce, neat; dexterous.

A smart cock'd beaver and a j. cane LAMB. Hence **Je·mmily** *adv.* **Je·mminess.**

Jenequen, var. HENEQUEN [Sp. *jeniquen*].

‖**Je ne sais quoi** (ʒənsękwà). 1656. [Fr., = I know not what.] An inexpressible something.

Jennet (dʒe·nėt). 1463. [– Fr. *genet* (in sense 1) – Sp. *jinete* short-stirruped light horseman – N.Afr. Arab. *zenāta* Berber tribe famed for horsemanship. In Fr. and Eng. transferred from the horseman to the horse.] **1.** A small Spanish horse. **2.** A (Spanish) light horseman. *Obs.* exc. *Hist.* 1676.

1. Isabella, royally attired, rode on a Spanish j. PRESCOTT.

Jenneting (dʒe·nėtiŋ). 1601. [f. Fr. *Jeannet*, pet-form of *Jean* JOHN, as in Norman Fr. *pomme* (apple) *de Jeannet*; cf. †*perejonette* (Chaucer), and for the ending see -ING[3].] A kind of early apple.

Jenny (dʒe·ni). 1600. [A familiar or pet form of *Janet* (or of *Jane*), serving as a feminine of *Jack*, and hence used in similar applications.]

I. 1. The female name; hence, sometimes applied derisively to a man. (*Mod. Sc.*) **2.** Used as a prefix to denote a female animal, as *j.-ass, j.-hooper*, and occas. applied without reference to sex 1600. **b.** Short for *j. ass, j. wren* 1808. **3.** *Creeping J.*, the plant Moneywort 1882.

II. 1. Short for SPINNING-JENNY 1796. **2.** A locomotive crane which runs backwards and forwards, and moves heavy weights 1861. **3.** *Billiards.* A stroke made by a losing hazard into the middle or top pocket, from a ball lying near to the cushion 1856.

Jenny wren (dʒe·ni ˌ re·n). 1648. [See JENNY I. 2.] A pop. name for the wren; sometimes regarded in nursery lore as the wife, bride, or sweetheart of Robin Redbreast.

Jeofail (dʒe·fe[i]l), *sb.* 1541. [– AFr. *jeo fail* I am at fault, i.e. *jeo* (Fr. *je*) I, *fail* 1st. pers. pres. ind. sing. of *faillir* FAIL *v.*] *Law.* A mistake or oversight in pleading; also, an acknowledgement of such error. *Hist.* †**b.** *transf.* A mistake –1828. Hence †**Jeo·fail** *v. intr.* to fail to meet an obligation 1599.

Jeopard (dʒe·pǎɹd), *v.* ME. [Back-formation from JEOPARDY.] **1.** *trans.* To put in jeopardy; to expose to loss, injury, or death; to hazard. †**b.** *intr.* (for *refl.*) To run the risk; to venture –1598. †**2.** *trans.* To stake, bet –1580.

1. As ready to j. his life and fortune. . as ever his . . forefathers had been FREEMAN. Hence **Jeo·parder,** one who puts in jeopardy.

Jeopardize (dʒe·pǎɹdəiz), *v.* 1646. [f. prec. or JEOPARD(Y + -IZE.] *trans.* = prec. 1.

That he should j. his wilful head Only for spite at me SIR H. TAYLOR.

†**Jeo·pardous,** *a.* 1451. Also **-ious** (1502). [f. JEOPARD(Y + -OUS.] **1.** Fraught with risk –1661. **2.** Venturesome –1593.

1. Shippes sailyng into so jeoperdous and ferre parties HEN. VII. **2.** A lustye and iuperdous Knyght 1494. Hence †**Jeo·pardous-ly** *adv.*, **-ness.**

Jeopardy (dʒe·pǎɹdi), *sb.* [ME. *iuparti*, etc. – OFr. *iu parti*, later *ieu* (*geu*) *parti*, 'divided play', even game, hence uncertain chance; in med.L. *jocus partitus*. For the change of *t* to *d* cf. CARD *sb.*[2], DIAMOND; for the sp. *eo* cf. PEOPLE.] †**1.** *Chess*, etc. A problem –1500. †**b.** A device, trick, stratagem –1536. †**2.** A position in a game, undertaking, etc. in which the chances of winning and losing are even; uncertainty –1597. **3.** Risk of loss, harm, or death ME.

3. Why stand we in ieopardy euery houre? 1 *Cor.* 15:30. Hence **Jeo·pardy** *v.* = JEOPARD *v.* 1.

Jequirity (dʒĕkwi·rĭti). 1882. [– Fr. *jéqwirity* – Tupi-Guarani *jekiriti*.] A twining shrub, *Abrus precatorius*, the particoloured beans of which are used as ornaments, etc., and in medicine.

‖**Jerboa** (dʒəɹbō[u]·ă, dʒɔ̄·ɹboˌă). 1662. [– med.L. *jerbōa* – Arab. *yarbūʻ*, dial. *jarbūʻ* flesh of the loins, hence applied to the animal from the highly-developed muscles of its hind legs.] A small rodent quadruped, *Dipus sagitta*, found in the deserts of Africa; it is of the size of a rat, has very long hind legs and short fore legs, and a long tufted tail, and is a remarkable jumper. Hence, any Jumping-mouse of the genus *Dipus* or family *Dipodidæ*.

Comb. **J.-mouse,** a N. Amer. rodent of the genus *Dipodomys*, one of the pouched mice or kangaroo-rats of the South-western U.S. and Mexico.

Jere, in *good jere*, altered f. GOODYEAR, q.v. SCOTT.

Jereed: see JERID.

Jeremiad (dʒerĭməi·æ̆d). Also **-ade.** 1780. [– Fr. *jérémiade*, f. *Jérémie* – eccl.L. *Jeremias* Jeremiah, in allusion to the Lamentations of Jeremiah in the O.T.; see -AD.] A lamentation; a writing or speech in a strain of grief or distress; a doleful complaint; a complaining tirade.

I could sit down, and mourn, and utter doleful Jeremiads without end HELPS.

Jerfalcon, etc., obs. f. GERFALCON, etc.

Jericho (dʒe·riko). 1635. [A town in Palestine; see 2 Sam. 10:5.] Used in slang or colloq. phrases for a place of retirement or concealment, or a place far out of the way.

Let them all go to J., and ne're be seen againe 1648.

‖**Jerid, jereed** (dʒĕrī·d), *sb.* Also **jerreed, jerrid,** etc. 1662. [– Arab. *jarīd* palm-branch stripped of its leaves, lance, javelin.] A wooden javelin, about five feet long, used in games by Persian, Turkish, and Arabian horsemen. Also, a game in which this is used. Hence †**Jeri·d** *v. intr.*, to throw the jerid 1698.

Jerk (dʒɔ̄ɹk), *sb.*[1] 1555. [gen. synon. with JERT and the earlier YERK; all three forms may be phonetically symbolical in origin.] †**1.** A stripe, a lash –1796; *fig.* a lash of sarcasm –1741. **2.** A sharp sudden pull, throw, push, thrust, or twist 1575. **b.** (in pl. *the jerks*). Involuntary spasmodic movements of the limbs or features, esp. resulting from religious excitement 1805. **3.** *fig.* A short sharp witty speech; a sally 1588. †**4.** A short abrupt series of notes (of a bird) –1794.

2. His Jade gave him a Jerk B. JONS. **b.** These Methodis' sets people crazy with the jerks 1874. **3.** Sir, use your jerks and quillets at the bar BROME.

Jerk, *sb.*[2] 1799. [f. JERK *v.*[2]; see also JERKY *sb.*[2]] Jerked meat, charqui.

Jerk (dʒɔ̄ɹk), *v.*[1] 1550. [Goes with JERK *sb.*[1]] †**1.** *trans.* To strike with or as with a whip, switch, or wand –1709; †*fig.* to lash with satire or ridicule –1710. **2.** To move (anything) by a sharp suddenly arrested motion; to give a sudden thrust, push, pull, or twist to 1589. **b.** To throw or toss with a quick sharp motion 1786. **3.** *fig.* To utter (words or sounds) abruptly, or sharply and shortly 1602. **4.** *intr.* To give a jerk; to jerk a bow or nod; to move with a jerk 1606. **b.** To move the limbs or features spasmodically 1874. †**5.** *intr.* To sneer, carp, gird –1704. †**6.** *intr.* To utter a short sharp abrupt series of notes –1773.

2. He jerked the horse's mouth roughly 1875. **4.** The door jerked open 1833. **5.** You must be jerking at the times, forsooth 1643.

Jerk (dʒɔ̄ɹk), *v.*[2] 1707. Also †**jirk.** [repr. Amer. Sp. *charquear*, f. *charqui* – Quichua *echarqui* dried flesh in long strips, and *echarquini* prepare dried meat.] *trans.* To cure (meat, esp. beef) by cutting it into long thin slices and drying it in the sun.

Jerker (dʒɔ̄·ɹkəɹ). 1596. [f. JERK *v.*[1] + -ER[1].] **1.** One who jerks, esp. from religious excitement. **2.** *U.S.* A fish, the river-chub, *Hybopsis kentuckiensis*, also called *hornyhead* 1884.

Jerker, variant of JERQUER.

Jerkin[1] (dʒɔ̄·ɹkin). *arch.* or *Hist.* 1519. [Of unkn. origin.] A close-fitting jacket, jersey, or short coat, often made of leather. Still used *dial.* for a waistcoat, an under vest, or a loose jacket.

†**Je·rkin**[2]. 1539. [dim. deriv., perh. of *jer* in *jerfalcon*, GERFALCON.] The male of the gerfalcon.

†**Je·rkin**[3], *sb.* or *a.* 1612. In *j. beef* = jerked beef (see JERK *v.*[2]) –1657.

Jerkin-head. 1842. [perh. for *jerking-*, f. JERK *v.*[1] (as if the slope were jerkily interrupted).] *Arch.* (See quot.)

'A form of roofing which is half-gable, half-hip. The gable generally goes as high as the ties of the couples, above which the roof is hipped off' (*Chambers's Encycl.* V. 697).

Jerky (dʒɔ̄·ɹki), *a.* and *sb.*[1] 1858. [f. JERK *sb.*[1] + -Y 1.] **A.** *adj.* Characterized by jerks or sudden abrupt or twitching movements; often *fig.* spasmodic.

Talkers that have what may be called j. minds 1858. A j. style 1887. Hence **Je·rkily** *adv.*, **Je·rkiness.**

B. *sb.* A springless wagon. *U.S.* 1884.

Je·rky, *sb.*[2] *U.S.* 1890. [– American Sp. *charqui, charque*; see CHARQUI and JERK *v.*[2]] Jerked beef.

Jerm-, obs. sp. of GERM-, in various words.

Jeroboam (dʒerŏbō[u]·æ̆m). 1816. [So called in allusion to *Jeroboam* 'a mighty man of valour' (1 Kings 11:28), 'who made Israel to sin' (14:16).] A large bowl or goblet; a very large wine-bottle.

Jero·nymite, var. of HIERONYMITE.

Jeropiga, -pigia, var. of GEROPIGA.

Jerque (dʒɔ̄ɹk), *v.* Also †**jirk.** 1819. [Referred to It. *cercare* to search, but historical evidence is wanting.] *trans.* To search (a vessel) for unentered goods; to examine or search a ship's papers in order to ascertain whether the captain's and the customs officer's lists of cargo agree, and to see that all the cargo has been duly entered and described.

Jerquer (dʒɔ̄·ɹkəɹ). 1681. [See prec. vb.] A custom-house officer, a searcher; in the London Custom House, A clerical officer who examines and checks a ship's papers, to see that all the cargo has been duly entered and described.

Jerry (dʒe·ri), *sb.* 1834. [Familiar var. of *Jeremy* or *Jeremiah*.] **1.** A machine for shearing cloth 1883. **2.** Short for **j.-shop:** A low beer-house 1834. **3.** Short for **j. hat:** A round felt hat 1841. **4.** Short for JERRY-BUILDER 1890.

Je·rry, *a.* 1882. [prob. short for *jerry-built* (see next). Said to have arisen in Liverpool; recorded in Lancashire, Yorkshire, and Cheshire glossaries.] Constructed unsubstantially of bad materials.

Je·rry-bui:lder. 1881. [Of unkn. origin; see prec.] A speculating builder who 'runs up' unsubstantially built houses of inferior materials. So **Je·rry-bui:lding. Je·rry-bui:lt** *a.* built unsubstantially of bad materials; built to sell.

Jersey[1] (dʒɔ̄·ɹzi). 1583. The name of the largest of the Channel Islands; used *attrib.* and *ellipt.* **1.** *attrib.* Of Jersey; of Jersey worsted. **2.** *sb.* **a.** Jersey knitted work; Jersey worsted; worsted generally 1587. †**b.** Wool that has been combed and is ready for spinning –1790. **3.** A woollen knitted close-fitting tunic, with short or long sleeves, worn either as an outer tunic, or as an under-shirt or under-vest 1836. **4.** One of a breed of cattle of the Channel Islands; a cow of the island of Jersey 1881.

Je·rsey[2]. *U.S.* 1770. = New Jersey.

Jert, *sb., v.* Now *dial.* 1540. = JERK *sb.*[1], *v.*[1]

Jerusalem (dʒĕrū·sălĕm). 1615. [In A.V. *Jerusalem*, Vulg. (O.T.) *Jerusalem*, (N.T.) *Hierusalem*, the latter repr. a Hellenized form with initial aspirate and consequent assim. to ἱερός holy, the former deriving from Gr. Ἰερουσαλήμ, which prob. approximates to the earlier pronunc. *Yerūshālēm* of the Heb. name (interpreted as 'possession of peace'.)] The city of Palestine so named; the Holy City. Hence *attrib.* or *ellipt.* **J. letters,** letters or symbols tattooed on the arm or body in memory of a visit or pilgrimage to J.; **J. pony,** a donkey (in reference to Christ's riding into J. on an ass). See also ARTICHOKE, CROSS, etc.

Jervine (dʒə̄·ɹvəin). 1838. [Formerly also *jervina*; f. Sp. *jerva* the poisonous root of *Veratrum*. See -INE[5].] *Chem.* An alkaloid occurring, together with veratrine, in the roots of *Veratrum album* and *V. viride*. Also called *jervia*.

Jess (dʒes), *sb.*; in pl. **jesses** (dʒe·sėz). [ME. *ges* – OFr. *ges*, nom. sing. and acc. pl. of *get* (mod. *jet* cast) :– Rom. **jectus*, for L. *jactus* throw, f. *jacere* throw.] A short strap of leather, silk, etc., fastened round each of the legs of a hawk used in falconry; usually bearing on its free end a small ring or *varvel* to which the swivel of the leash is attached. Also *fig.*

Their talk was all of training, terms of art, Diet and seeling, jesses, leash and lure TENNYSON. Hence **Jess** *v. trans.* to put the jesses on (a hawk) 1860.

Jessamine, var. of JASMINE, q.v.

†**Jessamy.** 1633. [Corruption of *jessamine*.] **1.** = JASMINE 1. –1733. **2.** A dandy, fop. See JEMMY *sb.* –1802.

Jessant (dʒe·sănt), *a.* 1572. [In sense 1 – OFr. *gesant* (later *gisant*) lying, pr. pple. of *gésir* :– L. *jacēre* to lie. In sense 2 perh. a different word.] *Her.* **1.** Said of a charge represented as lying over another and partly covering it 1610. **2.** Said when an animal is represented with a branch, flower, etc. in its mouth or as if issuing from it.

2. *Jessant* stands between the names of the two charges, e.g. *a hart j. a branch of dittany*.

Jesse (dʒe·si). 1456. [Name of the father of David (1 Sam. 16:12).] A genealogical tree representing the genealogy of Christ from 'the root of Jesse' (cf. Isa. 11:1); used in churches as a decoration for a wall, window, vestment, etc., or in the form of a large branched candlestick; *attrib.* **J. window.**

Jessed (dʒest), *a.* 1610. [f. JESS *sb.* or *v.* + -ED.] Of a hawk: Furnished with or wearing jesses; in *Her.* having the jesses of a specified tincture.

Jest (dʒest), *sb.* [ME. *geste* – OFr. *geste*, *jeste* :– L. *gesta* doings, exploits, n. pl. of pa. pple. of *gerere* do, perform.] †**1.** A notable deed or action –1604. †**2.** A narrative of exploits; orig. in verse. ME. only. †**3.** An idle tale –1620. **4.** A mocking speech; a taunt, a jeer. Also, A piece of raillery or banter. 1548. **5.** A saying (or *transf.* recital) intended to excite laughter; a witticism, joke 1551. **6. a.** Trifling sport, fun 1551. **b.** Jesting, merriment; ridicule 1597. **c.** A jocular affair 1732. **7.** A sportive action, prank, or frolic; a practical joke. Now *rare.* 1566. †**8.** A pageant, masque, masquerade –1601. **9.** A laughing-stock 1598.

1. Settyng furthe the iestes, actes and deedes, of the nobilitie HALL. **4.** Too bitter is thy iest SHAKS. **5.** Let not thy laughter handsell thy owne J. QUARLES. **6. a.** His eyes do drop no teares: his prayres are in iest SHAKS. **b.** Alas poore Yorick,.. a fellow of infinite Iest SHAKS. **c.** Life is a j., and all things shew it GAY. **7.** Hold the sweete iest vp SHAKS. **8.** Why then make sport at me, then let me be your iest SHAKS.

Jest (dʒest), *v.* 1526. [f. prec.: = GEST *v.*[1], of which this is a var. sp.] **1.** *intr.* To utter gibes or taunts; to scoff, jeer, mock. **b.** *trans.* To jeer at; to ridicule; to banter 1721. **2.** *intr.* To trifle 1530. **3.** *intr.* To make witty or humorous remarks; to joke 1553. †**b.** *intr.* To disport oneself –1632.

2. Verily I do not iest with you; there came newes from him last night SHAKS. **3.** Because Mirth is agreeable, another thinks fit eternally to j. STEELE. **b.** As gentle, and as iocond, as to iest, Go I to fight SHAKS.

Jest-book (dʒe·stbuk). 1750. [f. JEST *sb.* + BOOK *sb.*] A book of jests or amusing stories.

Jester (dʒe·stəɹ). ME. [var. sp. of GESTER, or f. JEST *v.* + -ER[1].] **1.** A professional reciter of romances (*arch.*). **2.** A mimic, buffoon, or merry-andrew; esp. one maintained in a prince's court or nobleman's household 1510. **3.** One who jests, or speaks or acts in jest; a joker 1510.

2. A small whole length of Archee, the King's j. H. WALPOLE. **3.** Iesters do oft proue Prophets SHAKS.

Je·stful, *a.* 1831. [-FUL.] Full of jesting.

Jesting (dʒe·stiŋ), *vbl. sb.* 1526. [f. JEST *v.* + -ING[1].] The action of JEST *v.*; pleasantry; trifling; ridicule.

J., said Arcite, suits but ill with pain DRYDEN.

Je·sting, *ppl. a.* 1551. [f. as prec. + -ING[2].] That jests; jocose; trifling; †jeering.

What is Truth; said j. Pilate BACON. **Je·stingly** *adv.* 1568.

†**Je·suist.** *rare.* 1582. [– Fr. †*Jésuiste*; see next, -IST.] = next –1645.

Jesuit (dʒe·ziu,it), *sb.* Also †**-ite.** 1550. [– Fr. *jésuite* or mod.L. *Jesuita*, f. *Jesus* + *-ita* -ITE[1] 1.] **1.** A member of the 'Society of Jesus', a Roman Catholic order founded by Ignatius Loyola in 1534.

The object of the Society was to support and defend the Roman Church against the 16th-c. Reformers, and to propagate the faith among the heathen. The stringent organization of the order soon made it very powerful. Its secret power, and the casuistical principles maintained by many of its representatives, and generally ascribed to the body as a whole, have rendered its name odious not only in English, but in French and other languages, and have given rise to sense 2, and to the opprobrious sense attached to *Jesuitical*, *Jesuitry*, and other derivatives.

2. *transf.* A dissembling person; a prevaricator 1640. **3.** A dress worn by ladies in the 18th century, a kind of indoor morning gown 1767. **4.** *attrib.* or *adj.* That is a Jesuit; of or belonging to the Society of Jesus; Jesuitical 1660.

1. The diuels agents..by the name of Iesuites STUBBES. Teach Jesuits that have travell'd far, to Lye, Teach Fire to burn, and Winds to blow COWLEY. **2.** To humble the pride of some Jesuits, who call themselves Quakers 1777.

Comb. (genitival): **Jesuits' bark,** the bark of species of *Cinchona*, Peruvian bark (introduced into Europe from the Jesuit Missions in S. America); **Jesuits' drops,** 'name given to a preparation of garlic, Peruvian balsam, and sarsaparilla' (Mayne); **Jesuits' nut,** the seed of *Trapa natans*; †**Jesuits' powder,** an old name for powdered Peruvian bark; **Jesuits' tea,** an infusion of leaves of *Psoralea glandulosa*, a S. Amer. leguminous shrub.

†**Je·suit,** *v.* 1600. [f. prec. sb.] **1.** *intr.* To act the Jesuit (*rare*). **2.** *trans.* To make a Jesuit of –1645. **3.** To dose with Jesuits' bark (*nonce-use*). HARVEY.

†**Je·suited,** *a.* 1600. [f. JESUIT *sb.* or *v.* + -ED.] Made or become a Jesuit; imbued with the principles or character of the Jesuits; Jesuitical –1834.

Jesuitess (dʒe·ziu,itės). 1600. [f. JESUIT *sb.* + -ESS[1].] A female Jesuit; one of an order of nuns established on the principles of the Jesuits, but suppressed by Pope Urban VIII.

Jesuitic, -al (dʒeziu,i·tik, -ăl), *a.* 1600. [f. as prec.; see -IC, -ICAL.] **1.** Of or pertaining to the Jesuits; belonging to the Society of Jesus; Jesuit. **2.** Dissembling; practising equivocation or mental reservation of truth 1613. Hence **Jesui·tically** *adv.* 1600.

Jesuitism (dʒe·ziu,iti:z'm). 1609. [f. as prec. + -ISM. Cf. Fr. *jésuitisme*.] **1.** The principles or practice of the Jesuits. **2.** Principles or practice such as those ascribed to the Jesuits; Jesuitry 1613. **3.** A Jesuitical quibble or equivocation (*rare*) 1749.

Jesuitize (dʒe·ziu,itəiz), *v.* 1644. [f. as prec. + -IZE.] **1.** *intr.* To play the Jesuit; to propound Jesuitical doctrines. **2.** *trans.* To imbue with Jesuit principles 1679.

Jesuitry (dʒe·ziu,itri). 1832. [f. JESUIT *sb.* + -RY.] Subtle casuistry or prevarication; the doctrine that the end justifies the means.

Jesus (dʒī·zŏs). ME. [repr. Chr.L. *Iēsūs*, obl. cases *Iēsū* – Gr. Ἰησοῦς, Ἰησοῦ – late Heb. or Aramaic *yēšûʻa*, for earlier *yᵉhōšûʻa* Joshua, which is explained as 'Jah (or Jahveh) is salvation'.

During the ME. period regularly used in its OFr. (objective) form *Iesu* (*Jesu*). The (L. nom.) form *Iesus* (*Jesus*) was rare in ME., but became the regular Eng. form in XVI. In later use, *Jesu* occurs in hymns, rarely in nom. or obj., but frequently in the vocative.]

1. The name of the Founder of Christianity. **2.** A figure or representation of Jesus Christ, as a CRUCIFIX or ECCE HOMO, or an emblem or device such as the letters IHS, etc. 1487.

1. Euen soo: come lorde Iesu TINDALE *Rev.* 22:20 [so Cov., *Great B.*; *Geneva, Bps.*, etc. Iesus]. Jesu, lover of my soul C. WESLEY.

Jet (dʒet), *sb.*[1] and *a.* [ME. *geet, jeet*, later *jeat, jeit* – AFr. *geet*, **jeet*, OFr. *jaiet, jayet* (mod. *jais*) :– L. *gagates* GAGATE.]

A. *sb.* **1.** A hard compact black form of lignite, taking a brilliant polish. It is used in making toys, buttons, etc., and attracts light bodies when electrified by rubbing. †**b.** A piece of jet –1607. †**2.** Black marble –1648. **3.** The colour of jet; a deep glossy black 1450.

1. b. Your lustre too'll..Draw courtship to you, as a iet doth strawes B. JONS. **3.** The pansy freaked with jet MILT.

B. *attrib.* or *adj.* **1.** Made or consisting of jet 1444. **2.** Of the colour of jet 1716. **b.** *spec.* in **j. ant,** a kind of ant (*Formica fuliginosa*); †**-wood,** ebony 1607.

1. *fig.* J. memories (onely attracting straws and chaff unto them) FULLER. *Comb.* **j.-coal,** cannel coal.

†**Jet,** *sb.*[2] ME. [app. a substitution of *jet* = Fr. *jet* throw, cast, for certain senses of CAST *sb.*] **1.** A device, a contrivance. ME. only. **2.** Fashion, style, mode, manner –1526.

2. Phr. *Of the new j.*, *of the best j.*, etc.

Jet (dʒet), *sb.*[3] See also JUT *sb.*[2] 1610. [Partly from JET *v.*[2] (and *v.*[1]); partly from senses of Fr. *jet*, f. *jeter* throw, cast.] †**1.** = JETTY *sb.* 2. G. FLETCHER. †**2.** A dart, spring, 'sprint'. HY. MORE (1647). †**3.** An affected jerk of the body; a swagger –1719. **4.** A stream of water or other liquid shot forward or thrown upwards (either in a spurt or continuously), esp. from a small orifice; hence, any similar emission of steam, gas, or (rarely) of solid bodies 1696. Also *transf.* and *fig.* **5.** A spout or nozzle for emitting water, gas, etc. 1825. **6.** *Metal-casting.* **a.** A channel or tube for pouring melted metal into a mould. **b.** The projecting piece of metal left at the end of a type in casting, and subsequently broken off. 1875. **7.** A large ladle 1620.

Comb.: **j.-break,** the mark left, as on a metal type, by a jet or sprue when removed after casting; **-pump,** a pump in which fluid is impelled by a jet of air, steam, etc.

Jet, *sb.*[4] 1748. [By-form of GIST – Law Fr. *gist* (mod. *gît*), in the phr. *action gist* or *gît* 'action lies', taken subst.] = GIST *sb.*[3]

†**Jet,** *v.*[1] [ME. *gette, iett(e*, app. – Anglo-Fr. *gettre*, in XV Fr. *getter, jetter*, mod. *jeter* to throw, cast, etc.; but the senses are those of L. *jactare se*, *jactari* boast, brag, vaunt oneself, etc.]

I. 1. *intr.* To walk or move about in an ostentatious manner; to strut, swagger. Often with *up and down*. –1669. **b.** To caper, to trip –1700. **2.** *intr.* To stroll –1777. **3.** *trans.* To traverse ostentatiously 1530–1581.

1. The Pharisee, he goeth jetting bolt upright UDALL. Mistris Minx..iets its as gingerly as if she were dancing the Canaries NASHE.

II. 1. *intr.* To vaunt, to brag –1664. **2.** *intr.* To revel, roister, riot –1640.

Jet (dʒet), *v.*[2] 1588. [– OFr. *jeter* throw, cast, fling, dart :– Rom. **jectare*, for L. *jactare*.]

I. †**1.** *intr.* To project, protrude, jut. Const. *out, over* –1762. †**b.** *intr.* (*transf.*) To encroach *on* or *upon* –1636. †**2.** *trans.* To build *out* (part of a house, etc.); to cause to project –1714.

1. b. Insulting tyranny beginnes to iet Upon the innocent and lawlesse throane SHAKS.

II. 1. To throw, cast, toss. *Obs.* exc. *dial.* 1659. †**2.** *intr.* To spring, hop, bound, dart –1827. †**3.** *intr.* To jolt or jog –1676. †**4.** Of a bird: To jerk the tail up and down –1783.

2. Like as the haggard..Jets oft from perch to perch QUARLES.

III. 1. *intr.* To spout or spurt forth; to issue in a jet or jets 1692. **2.** *trans.* To emit in a jet or jets 1708.

2. Conflicting tides that..high their mingled billows j. SCOTT.

Je·t-bla·ck, *a.* 1475. Black like jet; glossy black.

‖**Jet d'eau** (ʒę₁do). Pl. **jets d'eau** (ʒę₁do). 1706. [Fr., = 'jet of water'.] An ornamental jet of water ascending from a fountain or pipe; the fountain or pipe from which this issues.

Jetsam (dʒe·tsăm). 1491. [Early forms *jetson, -sen,* later *-sam* (cf. FLOTSAM), contr. form of JETTISON *sb.*] Goods thrown overboard to lighten a ship in distress (and afterwards washed ashore).

The last clause is no part of the etymological meaning, which should be 'that which has been thrown overboard to save the ship', without reference to whether it sinks or floats. Recent Law-books take the word as 'that which is *thrown* or *cast ashore* by the sea'; Spelman and Blackstone, as 'merchandise thrown overboard and sunk in the sea'. Both explanations evidently arose in the attempt to distinguish *jetsam* from *flotsam.*

†**Jetteau** (dʒetō·). 1705. A form confusing It. *getto* (*d'acqua*) and Fr. *jet d'eau*: see JET D'EAU –1763.

†**Je·tter.** [ME. *gettour* – AFr. **getour* = (in form) OFr. *geteor,* etc., f. *geter* (see JET *v.*[1]); see -OUR, -ER[2] 3.] One who boasts, vaunts, or makes an ostentatious display; a braggadocio, bully, 'blade', 'spark' –1611.

Jettison (dʒe·tisən), *sb.* ME. [– AFr. *getteson,* OFr. *getaison* :– L. *jactatio, -ion-,* f. *jactare*; see JET *v.*[2], -ISON. See also JETSAM.] *Maritime Law.* The action of throwing goods overboard, esp. to lighten a ship in distress. **b.** *fig.* Throwing overboard 1887. Hence **Je·ttison** *v.* to throw overboard, esp. to lighten a ship in distress 1848.

Jetton (dʒe·tən). 1762. [– (O)Fr. *jeton,* f. *jeter* cast up (accounts), calculate (cf. med.L. *jactare valorem*); see JET *v.*[2]] A counter of metal, ivory, etc., formerly used in casting up accounts and in card-playing. Also applied to medals and tokens.

Jetty (dʒe·ti), *sb.* Also †**jettee.** See also JUTTY. ME. [– OFr. *jetee, getee* projecting part of a building, structure to protect a harbour, subst. use of fem. pa. pple. of *jeter* throw; see JET *v.*[2], -Y[5] and cf. JUT *v.*[2]] **1. a.** A mole, pier, or the like, constructed at the entrance of a harbour, or running out into the sea or a lake, so as to defend the harbour or coast; any similar structure. **b.** A projecting part of a wharf. Also *transf.* and *fig.* †**2.** A projecting part of a building; *esp.* an overhanging upper story –1677. †**3.** A bulwark or bastion –1867.

Comb. **j.-head,** that part of a wharf which projects beyond the rest; *esp.* the front of a wharf, whose side forms one of the cheeks of a wet or dry dock.

Jetty (dʒe·ti), *a.*[1] 1477. [f. JET *sb.*[1] + -Y[1].] **1.** Of the colour of jet; jet-black; also *advb.* **2.** Of the nature of jet 1875. Hence **Je·ttiness.**

†**Je·tty,** *a.*[2] [f. JET *sb.*[3] or *v.*[2] + -Y[1].] Swelling. CHAPMAN.

Jetty (dʒe·ti), *v.* 1449. [f. JETTY *sb.*] †**1.** *trans.* To cause to project, furnish with projections. †**2.** *intr.* To project, jut –1615. **3.** To furnish with a jetty 1889.

‖**Jeu** (ʒö). Pl. **jeux** (ʒo). [Fr., :– L. *jocus* pleasantry, jest; see JOKE *sb.*] The French for 'play' or 'game'; occurring in **jeu d'esprit** (ʒö dęspri), a play or playful action in which some cleverness is displayed; now usu., a witty or humorous trifle 1712; **jeu de mots** (ʒö də mo), a play on words, a pun 1823.

Jew (dʒ¹ū), *sb.* [ME. *Giw, Gyu, Iu, Iuw, Ieu* – OFr. *giu,* earlier *juiu* (mod. *juif*) :– L. *judæus* – Gr. Ἰουδαῖος, f. Aram. *yᵉhūḏāi,* Heb. *yᵉhûḏî,* f. *yᵉhûḏâh* Judah, name of a Jewish patriarch and the tribe descended from him.] **1.** One of the Hebrew or Jewish people, or one who professes Judaism. (Orig. a Hebrew of the kingdom of Judah; later, any Israelite who adhered to the worship of Jehovah as conducted at Jerusalem.)

In mediæval England, Jews, though honourably engaged in many pursuits, were particularly familiar as money-lenders, a profession closed by Canon Law to Christians. Thus the name of Jew came to be associated in the popular mind with usury and any extortionate practices that might be supposed to accompany it, and gained an opprobrious sense.

2. *transf.* As a name of opprobrium or reprobation, applied to a grasping or extortionate usurer, or a trader who drives hard bargains or deals craftily 1606. **3.** *attrib.* or as *adj.* That is a Jew, Jewish, as *Jew boy,* etc.; of or relating to Jews, as *Jew bill,* etc. 1613.

1. What is the reason? I am a Iewe; Hath not a Iew eyes? SHAKS. The same..abhorrence for idolatry which had distinguished the Jews from the other nations of the ancient world GIBBON. *Jew's eye*: something valued highly; Pictures.. Each 'worth a Jew's eye' 1844.

Comb.: **J.-baiting** *sb.* [= Ger. *Judenhetze*], systematic harrying of Jews; **-bush,** the Milk plant; **-lizard,** a large Australian lizard, *Amphibolurus barbatus.* **b.** Genitival Combs.: **Jews' frankincense,** a plant of the genus *Styrax* or the resin obtained from it (storax or benzoin); **Jews' houses,** remains of ancient tin-smelting furnaces in Cornwall; **Jews' thorn** = *Christ's thorn.*

Jew, *v.* 1824. [f. the sb. (sense 2).] *trans.* Used opprobriously: To cheat, overreach (*arch.*); to beat *down* in price.

Jewel (dʒ¹ū·ĕl), *sb.* [ME. *iuel, iowel, gewel* – AFr. *juel, jeuel,* OFr. *joel* (nom. sing. *joyaus,* mod. *joyau*); of doubtful formation, but ult. based on L. *jocus* jest, in Rom. game, sport.] **1.** An article of value used for adornment, usu. of the person; a costly ornament, *esp.* one made of gold, silver, or precious stones. *Obs.* in *gen.* sense. **b.** An ornament worn as the badge of an order, or as a mark of distinction or honour 1672. **2.** A precious stone, a gem; *esp.* one worn as an ornament. (The prevailing mod. sense.) 1590. **b.** *Watch-making.* A precious stone, usu. a ruby, used for a pivot-hole, on account of its resistance to wear 1825. **3.** *fig.* A precious thing or person; a 'treasure', a 'gem' ME. †**4.** *Naut.* A heavy ring, used to press together the two parts of a cable or rope which is laid round an article and then rove through the ring. Also *attrib.* –1755.

1. Heere, weare this Iewell for me, tis my picture SHAKS. **2.** A iewell rich he found That was a Ruby of right perfect hew SPENSER. *Comb.*: **j.-hole** (*Watch-making*), a hole drilled in a j. for a pivot. **3.** Oh, 'tis a j. of a husband DRYDEN.

Jew·el, *v.* 1601. [f. prec.] **1.** *trans.* To furnish or adorn with jewels. **b.** *Watch-making.* To fit with jewels for the pivot-holes. Usu. in *pa. pple.* 1804. **2.** *fig.* To bedeck as with jewels 1859.

1. b. A gold hunting watch..jewelled in four holes 1844.

Jew·el-block. 1769. *Naut.* The name given to each of two small blocks suspended at the extremities of the main and fore-top-sail yards, through which the halyards of the studding-sails are passed.

Jew·el-house. 1473. A house, building, or chamber in which jewels are kept. Now *rare.* **b.** *spec.* The room in the Tower of London in which the crown jewels are kept.

Jeweller, -eler (dʒ¹ū·ĕləɹ). ME. [– AFr. *jueler,* OFr. *juelier* (mod. *joaillier*); cf. JEWEL *sb.*, -ER[2] 2.] A maker of jewels; a dealer in jewels or jewellery.

Jewellery, jewelry (dʒ¹ū·ĕlri, dʒ¹ū·ĕləri). ME. [In ME. – OFr. *juelerie* (mod. *joaillerie* from *joaillier* jeweller); in mod. use (XVIII) a new formation from JEWEL, JEWELLER; see -ERY.] Jewellers' work; gems or ornaments made or sold by jewellers; jewels collectively, or as a form of adornment. Also *fig.*

In commercial use commonly spelt *jewellery.* The pronunc. with three syllables is usual with both forms.

Jewess (dʒ¹ū·ės). ME. [f. JEW *sb.* + -ESS[1].] A female Jew; a Jewish woman.

Jew-fish. 1697. [app. f. JEW *sb.* + FISH.] A name given to various fishes, chiefly of the family *Serranidæ.*

The Jew-fish..I judge so called by the English, because it hath Scales and Fins, therefore a clean Fish, according to the Levitical Law DAMPIER.

Jewis, -ise, var. JUISE *Obs.*, judgement.

Jewish (dʒ¹ū·iʃ), *a.* 1546. [f. JEW *sb.* + -ISH[1].] Of, belonging to, or characteristic of, the Jews; Israelitish, Hebrew. Also *fig.*

Hence **Jew·ish-ly** *adv.*, **-ness.**

†**Jew·ism.** 1579. [f. JEW *sb.* + -ISM.] The religious system of the Jews; Judaism –1800.

Jewry (dʒ¹ū³·ri). ME. [– AFr. *juerie,* OFr. *juierie* (mod. *juiverie*): see JEW, -ERY.] **1.** The land of the Jews, Judea; occas. = Palestine. *Obs.* or *arch.* **2.** The Jews' quarter in a town or city; the Ghetto. (Hence *Old Jewry* in London.) *Obs.* exc. *Hist.* ME. †**3.** The Jewish religion –1552. **4.** The Jewish people, race, nation, or community; the Jews collectively ME.

1. In Iewry is God knowne; his name is greate in Israel BIBLE (Great) *Ps.* 76:1.

Jew's-ear. 1544. [erron. tr. of med.L. *auricula Judæ* Judas's ear; so called from its shape, and from its being often found on the elder, on which tree Judas is said to have hanged himself.] An edible cup-shaped fungus (*Hirneola* or *Exidia auricula-judæ*), formerly in repute as a medicine.

Jews' harp, Jew's-harp. (Also occas. w. small j.) 1584. [var. of JEWS' TRUMP, q.v.] **1.** A musical instrument, consisting of an elastic steel tongue fixed at one end to a small lyre-shaped frame of brass or iron, and bent at the other end at right angles; it is played by holding the frame between the teeth and striking the free end of the metal tongue with the finger, variations of tone being produced by altering the size and shape of the cavity of the mouth. Called also *Jews' trump.* **2.** *Naut.* 'The shackle for joining a chain-cable to the anchor-ring' (Smyth) 1750.

Jews' stone, Jewstone. 1617. [tr. med.L. *lapis Judaicus.*] **1.** The fossil spine of a large sea-urchin, found in Syria, formerly used in medicine. ?*Obs.* 1633. **2.** A crystallized form of iron pyrites (also called *marcasite*), formerly used as a gem. ?*Obs.* 1617. **3.** A local name for hard unmanageable rocks 1803.

Jews' trump, Jew's-trump. Now *rare.* 1545. [Earlier than *Jews' harp.* In Scotland and N. of England called simply TRUMP, agreeing with the Fr. name *trompe,* now displaced by *guimbarde.* The first element was certainly *Jews* from the first. The attribution to the Jews occurs only in English.] = JEWS' HARP 1.

‖**Jezail** (dʒĕzai·l, -ē¹·l). *E. Ind.* 1838. [Urdu *jazāʼil.*] A long and heavy Afghan musket.

Jezebel (dʒe·zĕbĕl). 1558. Name of the infamous wife of Ahab, king of Israel (1 Kings 16:31, etc.); hence, a wicked abandoned woman, or a woman who paints her face.

Jib (dʒib), *sb.*[1] 1661. [Of unkn. origin.] **1.** *Naut.* A triangular stay-sail stretching from the outer end of the jib-boom to the fore-top-mast head in large ships, and from the bowsprit to the mast-head in smaller craft. **2.** *dial.* The under lip (in phr. *to hang the j.*) Also, the mouth, face, or nose. 1825.

1. *Flying j.*, a second sail of similar shape set before the jib on the *flying jib-boom*; in some large vessels as many as six jibs are carried, the outermost being the *jib of jibs.* Phr. *The cut of one's j.* (colloq.): one's personal appearance, countenance or look; If she disliked what the sailor calls the cut of their j. SCOTT.

Comb.: **j.-guy,** a stout rope which supports the jib-boom; **-halyard,** the halyard for raising and lowering the j.; **-header,** a topsail shaped like a j.; **-stay,** the stay on which the j. is set; **-traveller,** a circular iron hoop, with a hook and shackle, used to haul out the tack of the j.

Jib (dʒib), *sb.*[2] 1764. [perh. abbrev. of GIBBET.] The projecting arm of a crane; also, the boom of a derrick. *Comb.* **j.-crane,** a crane fitted with a j.

Jib (dʒib), *sb.*[3] 1801. [f. JIB *v.*[2]] **1.** The action of jibbing; a state of standstill. **2.** A jibbing horse, a jibber 1843.

Jib (dʒib), *v.*[1] Also **gibb, jibb;** see also GYBE *v.* 1691. [Of unkn. origin.] **1.** *trans.* To pull (a sail or yard) round from one side of a vessel to the other, as in tacking, etc. **2.** *intr.* Of a sail, etc.: GYBE *v.* 1. 1719. **b.** *transf.* Of other things: To swing round 1891.

Jib, *v.*[2] Also **jibb,** rare **gib.** 1811. [Of unkn. origin.] **1.** *intr.* Of a horse, etc.: To stop and refuse to go on; to move restively backwards or sideways. **2.** *fig.* To stop short, draw back, back out 1812. **b.** To start aside; to shy *at* 1882.

1. A backward swain is like a jibbing horse 1862. Hence **Ji·bber** *sb.* a horse that jibs.

Ji·bbah, Egyptian form of JUBBAH.

Jibber (dʒi·bəɹ), *v.* 1824. [Alternative spelling of GIBBER.] *intr.* To speak rapidly and inarticulately.

Jib-boom. 1748. [f. JIB *sb.*[1] + BOOM *sb.*[2]] *Naut.* A spar run out from the end of the bowsprit, to which the tack of the jib is lashed, and beyond which is sometimes extended the *flying jib-boom*.

Jib-door. 1800. [Of unkn. origin.] A door flush with the wall in which it stands, and usually made indistinguishable from it.

Jibe (dʒəib), *v. U.S.* Also **gibe.** 1813. [Of unkn. origin.] *intr.* To chime *in* (*with*); to agree.

Jibe, var. of GIBE *sb.* and *v.*, GYBE *v.*

Jiffy (dʒi·fi). *colloq.* 1785. [Of unkn. origin.] A very short space of time; e.g. *in a jiffy*. Also **Jiff** 1797.

Jig (dʒig), *sb.* 1560. [Of unkn. origin.] **1.** A lively, rapid, springy kind of dance. **2.** The music for such a dance; a rapid lively dance-tune; *spec.* one in triple rhythm (usually 6–8 or 12–8) 1588. †**3.** A song or ballad of lively, jocular, or mocking (often scurrilous) character –1673. †**4.** A light performance of a lively or comical character, given at the end, or in the interval, of a play –1728. **5.** A piece of sport, a joke; a trifle; a trick 1592. **6.** A name for various mechanical contrivances and simple machines, often merely with the sense 'dodge', 'device'. 'contrivance'. *spec.* **b.** A contrivance for jigging or dressing ore by shaking it up jerkily in a fluid medium (see JIG *v.* 5) 1877. **c.** *Coal-mining.* A steep tramway on which the loaded trucks as they descend draw up the empty trucks 1866. **7.** Applied joc. to a horse, a person, etc. 1706.

1. Wooing..is hot and hasty like a Scotch ijgge SHAKS. **2.** They sing to jigs, and dance to church music H. WALPOLE. **4.** He's for a Iigge, or a tale of Baudry SHAKS. **5.** Phr. *The j. is up* = the game is up (now *dial.* or *slang*). Her jigs, and her junketings, and her tears THACKERAY.

Comb.: **j.-pin,** a pin used by miners to hold the turn-beams, and prevent them from turning.

Jig (dʒig), *v.* Also †**gig.** 1588. [prob. f. JIG *sb.*] **1. a.** *trans.* To sing or play as a jig, or in the style of a jig (see JIG *sb.* 2, 3). ? *Obs.* **b.** *trans.* To dance (a jig or other lively dance) 1719. **c.** *intr.* To dance a jig; to dance in a rapid jerky fashion 1672. **2.** *intr.* To move up and down or to and fro with a rapid jerky motion 1604. **b.** *trans.* To jerk to and fro or up and down 1710. **3.** *intr.* To move in unison *with*; to agree, 'jump', chime *with* (*rare*) 1838. †**4.** *trans.* To put *off* with a trick. FORD. **5.** To dress (ore) by shaking it under water in a sieve or box with perforated bottom, or the like 1778. **6.** To shape an earthen vessel with a jigger (see JIGGER *sb.*[1] 4 a) 1865. **7.** In *Well-boring*, To bore with the aid of a spring-pole, which jerks up the rods and drill after the stroke (*U.S.*)

1. To Iigge off a tune at the tongues end SHAKS. **b.** While this brave Carmagnole-dance has hardly jigged itself out CARLYLE. **2.** *Haml.* III. i. 150.

Jigger (dʒi·gəɹ), *sb.*[1] 1675. [In some senses f. JIG *v.*; the relationship of others is obscure.] **1.** One who jigs or dances a jig. Also, A 'guy' (*dial.*). **2.** *Naut.* **a.** A small tackle consisting of a double and a single block and a fall; *esp.* one used to hold on the cable when it is heaved into the ship 1726. **b.** A small sail 1831. **c.** Short for *jigger-mast* 1880. **d.** A small vessel of the smack type furnished with a 'jigger' sail (see b) 1860. **3.** *Mining.* **a.** One who jigs ore (JIG *v.* 5). **b.** An apparatus for dressing ore, consisting of a sieve, or a box with holes, which is shaken up and down in water, or into which water is forced 1778. **4.** A name for various mechanical contrivances: e.g. **a.** *Pottery.* A horizontal lathe used in china-making 1825. **b.** A loose chain used as a warehouse crane. 1891. **c.** *Billiards.* A slang name for the rest 1847. **d.** A small roller or set of rollers fitted in a suspended oscillating frame, for graining leather 1883. **e.** *Printing.* A guide-mark used by compositors. **f.** *Wireless.* An oscillation transformer 1902. **g.** *Golf.* A short iron-headed club used for approaching 1893.

Comb.: **j.-mast** (*Naut.*), (*a*) a small mast at the stern, on which a j. (sense 2 b) is hoisted; (*b*) the aftermost mast of a four-masted merchant ship; **-tackle** (*Naut.*) = sense 2 a; **-yard** (*Naut.*), a yard on which the j. (sense 2 b) is extended.

Jigger (dʒi·gəɹ), *sb.*[2] 1781. [Later var. of CHIGOE.] **1.** = CHIGOE. **2.** Applied in U.S. to various harvest-ticks, e.g. *Leptus americanus* and *L. irritans*.

Jigger (dʒi·gəɹ), *v.*[1] *colloq.* 1867. [app. freq. of JIG *v.*; see -ER[5].] *intr.* To make a succession of rapid jerks; said of a fish struggling to free itself.

Ji·gger, *v.*[2] *slang* or *colloq.* 1837. A euphemistic substitute for a profane or indecent word, esp. in asseverations. (Only in *pass.*)

Ji·ggery-po·kery. *colloq.* 1896. [synon. with and perh. alt. of Sc. and north. dial. *jookery pawkery*, earlier *jawkry-pawkry* (XVII), jingling formation on JOUK *v.*[2]; see -ERY.] Humbug.

Jigget (dʒi·gėt), *v. colloq.* 1687. [dim. of JIG *v.*] *intr.* To jig; to hop or skip about; to shake up and down; to fidget.

Jigging (dʒi·giŋ), *vbl. sb.* 1641. [f. JIG *v.* + -ING[1].] The action of JIG *v.*; *spec.* in *Mining*, the method of dressing ore by the motion of a wire sieve in a vat of water, where the smallest particles pass through the sieve.

Comb.: **j.-machine,** a machine for jigging; = JIGGER *sb.*[1] 3 b; **-sieve,** a sieve for jigging ore.

Jiggish (dʒi·giʃ), *a.* 1624. [f. JIG *sb.* + -ISH[1].] **1.** Inclined to jigging; frivolous, frolicsome 1634. **2.** Of the nature of, or suitable for, a jig or light dance.

1. She is never sad, and yet not j. HABINGTON.

Jiggle (dʒi·g'l), *v.* 1836. [Partly f. JIG *v.* + -LE; partly modification of JOGGLE *v.*[1], to express smaller movements.] To move backwards and forwards, or up and down, with a light unsteady motion; to move in a rapid succession of slight jerks; to rock lightly (*trans.* and *intr.*). Hence **Ji·ggle** *sb.* a jiggling movement.

Jiggumbob (dʒi·gəmbǫb). *colloq.* ? *Obs.* 1613. [A humorous formation from JIG *sb.* or *v.*] = THINGUMBOB.

Ji·g-saw. 1873. [f. JIG *v.*] A vertically reciprocating saw used to cut irregular patterns. *J. puzzle*, a puzzle consisting of a picture mounted on board and cut into irregular pieces.

‖**Jihad, jehad** (dʒiha·d). 1869. [Arab. *jihād*.] A religious war of Moslems against unbelievers in Islam, inculcated as a duty by the Koran and traditions. **b.** *transf.* A war or crusade for or against some doctrine, opinion, etc.; a war to the death.

Jill, var. of GILL *sbs.*[3], [4].

Jillet (dʒi·lėt). *Sc.* 1755. [dim. of name *Jill* or GILL (*sb.*[4]); see -ET.] A giddy or flighty young woman; a jilt; a wench.

Jill-flirt, var. of GILL-FLIRT.

Jilt (dʒilt), *sb.* 1672. [Of unkn. origin.] †**1.** A harlot or strumpet; a kept mistress –1815. **2.** One who deceives or capriciously casts off a lover after giving him encouragement. (The current sense.) 1674. **3.** *Sc.* A wench 1816.

Jilt (dʒilt), *v.* 1660. [f. prec.] **1.** *trans.* To deceive after holding out hopes in love; to cast off (a lover) capriciously; to play the jilt towards. Orig. said only of a woman. 1673. Also *absol.* or *intr.* 1696. **2.** *gen.* To deceive, delude (*Obs.*); to prove false to (any one); to throw over for another. (Now chiefly *fig.* from 1.) 1660.

Jimcrack, obs. f. GIMCRACK.

Jim-crow (dʒi·m‚krōᵘ·). *U.S.* 1863. [app. f. *Jim*, var. of *Jem* (cf. JEMMY *sb.* 4).] An implement for bending or straightening iron rails by the pressure of a screw. Also *attrib.*, as *jim-crow planing-machine*, a planing-machine with a reversing tool, to plane both ways.

Jim-jam (dʒi·mdʒæm). 1550. [Fanciful reduplicated formation, with vowel-alternation as in *flim-flam, whim-wham*, but the basis is unknown.] †**1.** A gimcrack, a knick-knack (*colloq.*) –1592. **2.** *pl.* Delirium tremens (*slang*) 1885. **b.** *pl.* A fit of the creeps 1904.

Jimmy (dʒi·mi), variant of JEMMY (q.v.), in most senses.

Jimp (dʒimp), *a.* (*adv.*) *Sc.* and *n. dial.* 1508. [Of unkn. origin.] **1.** Slender, slim, delicate, graceful, neat. (A Sc. or northern word, introduced in 19th c. into English literature.) **2.** Scanty; bare (measure) 1768. **3.** *adv.* Barely 1814. Hence **Ji·mp-ly** *adv.*, **-ness.**

Jim(p)son-weed: see JAMESTOWN-WEED.

Jin: see GIN, JINN.

Jingall, var. of GINGALL.

Jingle (dʒi·ŋg'l), *sb.* Also †**gingle.** 1599. [f. JINGLE *v.*] **1.** A noise such as is made by small bells, or loose pieces of metal when struck, etc. **b.** Applied depreciatively to other sounds 1827. **2.** Something that jingles; a jingling bell, etc. 1615. **3.** Affected repetition of the same or similar sounds; a catching array of words, whether in prose or verse. Chiefly contemptuous. 1645. **4.** A covered two-wheeled car used in the south of Ireland and in Australia. Also *attrib.* 1806. **5.** U.S. name for the shell of the saddle-oyster, *Anomia*. Also *attrib.* 1887.

1. The continual j. of our sledge-bells SYMONDS. **b.** The scolding and the j. of the piano M. ARNOLD. **2.** The tambourine..and the Turkish j., used in the army HONE. **3.** Little gingles, and tinkling of words 1663.

Jingle (dʒi·ŋg'l), *v.* ME. [imit.; cf. JANGLE *v.*] **1.** *intr.* To give forth a mingling of ringing sounds, as by the striking together of coins, keys, etc. Also *transf.* and *fig.* **b.** To proceed or move with a jingling sound 1732. **2.** *trans.* To cause to emit a mingling of ringing sounds 1508. **3.** *intr.* **a.** Of prose or verse: To sound with alliteration, rhymes, or the like 1670. **b.** To play with words for the sake of sound; (*depreciatively*) to rhyme 1642.

1. The harness jingles, as it passes by 1871. **2.** Jingling his keys in one pocket 1874. **3. a.** A gingling verse,..*Ad mala patrata, sunt atra theatra parata* 1780. Hence **Ji·ngler,** one who or that which jingles; a rhymer. **Ji·nglingly** *adv.*

Jingo (dʒi·ŋgo), *int.*, *sb.*, and *a.* 1670. [orig. a piece of conjurer's gibberish. In 1694 *by jingo* is used by Motteux to render Fr. *par Dieu*; cf. *by Golly, Gosh, Jabers*, etc. In Scotland, *by jing* or *jings* is in common use.]

A. *int.* and *sb.* **I.** †**1.** (Usually *Hey* or *High Jingo!*) A conjurer's call for the appearance of something; the opposite of *Hey presto!* Hence, an exclam. of surprise at the appearance of something. –1730. **2.** *By jingo!* a strong form of asseveration (*colloq.* or *vulgar*) 1694.

2. By j., quoth Panurge, the Man talks somewhat like MOTTEUX *Rabelais* IV. lvi. 219. We don't want to fight, yet by Jingo! if we do, We've got the ships, we've got the men, and got the money too 1878.

II. [f. the expression 'by Jingo!' in the refrain of the music-hall song, quoted in sense 2 above.] A nickname for those who supported the policy of Lord Beaconsfield in sending a British fleet into Turkish waters to resist the advance of Russia in 1878; hence, a blatant 'patriot', a Chauvinist 1878.

B. *adj.* †**1.** Exhibiting vulgar dash. MILLAIS. **2.** Of or pertaining to the political jingo; characterized by jingoism 1879.

Jingoism (dʒi·ŋgo‚iz'm). 1878. [f. prec. + -ISM.] The policy or practices of the jingoes. So **Ji·ngoist** = JINGO A. II. 1884.

Jink (dʒink), *sb.* orig. *Sc.* 1700. [Goes with JINK *v.*] **1.** The act of eluding; a quick turn so as to give the slip to a pursuer or a guard 1786. **2.** *Cards.* The winning of a game of spoil-five, twenty-five, or forty-five, by taking all the tricks in one hand 1887. **3. High Jinks:** app. orig. high pranks. †**a.** A name for various frolics at drinking parties (*Sc.*) 1700. **b.** Lively or boisterous sport. (Also simply *jinks*.) 1842.

1. Our billie's gien us a' the j. An' owre the sea BURNS. **3. a.** The evening ended in the full jollity of *High Jinks* LOCKHART. **b.** A scene for romps and jinks 1851.

Jink (dʒink), *v.* Chiefly *Sc.* 1715. [Symbolic formation expressing nimble motion; of unkn. origin.] **1.** *intr.* To move with quick sudden action; to move jerkily to and fro 1785. **2.** *intr.* To make a quick elusive turn, so as to dodge a pursuer, etc. 1785. **3.** *trans.* To elude by dodging; to dodge 1774. **4.** To diddle 1785. **5.** *intr.* (*Cards*). To win a game of spoil-five, twenty-five, or forty-five by taking all the tricks in one hand 1887. Hence **Ji·nker,** one who or that which jinks.

‖**Jinn** (dʒin). Also **djin, ginn, jin.** 1684. [– Arab. *jinn*, collect., demons.] In Moslem demonology, an order of spirits lower than the angels, said to have the power of assuming human and animal forms, and to exercise supernatural influence over men. Oftener used as a *sing.* to denote one of these.

‖**Jinnee** (dʒinī·). Also GENIE. Also fem. **jinnee·yeh.** 1841. [– Arab. *jinnī*, fem. *jinnīyeh* demon or spirit.] The sing. of prec.

Jinny (dʒi·ni). 1797. Pet-form of JANE, used locally in transf. uses. *Mining.* A stationary engine used to let down or draw up trucks on an inclined plane; also = **jinny-road,** a self-acting inclined plane.

‖**Jinricksha, jinrikisha** (dʒinri·kʃă, -ri·kiʃă). 1874. [– Japanese *jin-riki-sha* (*j* = ʒ), f. *jin* man + *riki* power + *sha* vehicle.] A light two-wheeled hooded vehicle, drawn by one or more men. Shortened colloq. to *rickshaw.*

Jitney (dʒi·tni). *U.S.* 1915. [Of unkn. origin.] **a.** Five cents. **b.** An automobile that plies for a small fare.

Jiu-jitsu: see JU-JITSU.

Jo (dʒō). *Sc.* Also **joe.** 1529. [Sc. form of JOY *sb.*] †**1.** Joy, pleasure –1570. **2.** A sweetheart, darling, beloved one 1529.

2. John Anderson, my jo BURNS.

Joan (dʒōᵘn). 1588. [orig. *Joanna* or *Johanna*, fem. of *Jo(h)annes* John; hence transf.] **1.** Generic name for a female rustic. **2.** A close-fitting cap worn by women about 1750.

1. Some men must loue my Lady, and some Ione SHAKS.

Job (dʒǫb), *sb.*¹ 1557. [First (in Feuillerat, *Documents Relating to the Revels*..1547–1558) 'Iobbe of woorke'; of unkn. origin.] **1.** A piece of work; *esp.* a small definite piece of work in one's own calling. **2.** A piece of work, or transaction, done for hire, or with a special view to profit 1660. **3.** A public service or trust turned to private gain or party advantage 1667. †**b.** Personal profit; private interest –1785. **4.** Anything one has to do 1694. **5.** An affair, business, occurrence, state of things; esp. in *good j., bad j.* 1700. **6.** Short for *job-carriage, job-horse* –1863. **7.** *attrib.* Hired or used by the job or particular piece of work, or for a definite time, as *job-carriage -gardener, -horse*, etc. 1701.

1. He..never lack'd a j. for Giles to do BLOOMFIELD. Phr. *By the j.* I do not design to hire one [gardener]..but only employ him by the j. BERKELEY. **2.** Their Faith's a Dream, their Preaching but a J. 1778. **3.** Who makes a Trust or Charity a J., And gets an Act of Parliament to rob POPE. **4.** 'Tis an ugly j.: but soldiers obey commands BROWNING. Phr. *To do the j. for*, or *to do* (a person's) *j.*: (*a*) to do what is required by him; (*b*) *slang*, to 'do for', ruin, destroy. *To make a job of*: to manage successfully. *Bad j.*: a failure (see also sense 5).

Comb.: **j. lot,** a parcel of goods, of sundry kinds or qualities, bought as a speculation with a view to profit; hence (*depreciatively*) any miscellaneous lot of things, persons, etc.; **-price,** (*a*) a price paid for things hired or work done by the job.; (*b*) a price paid for things bought as a job lot; **-work,** piece-work.

Job (dʒǫb), *sb.*² 1560. [f. JOB *v.*¹] An act of 'jobbing'; an abrupt stabbing with the sharp end of anything; a peck, dab, thrust; a jerk or wrench of the bit in a horse's mouth.

Job (dʒōᵘb), *sb.*³ 1553. Name of an ancient patriarch, whose story forms a book of the Old Testament; a type (*a*) of destitution, (*b*) of patience.

Phrases. **Job's comforter,** one who, under the guise of comforting, aggravates distress (cf. *Job* 16:2). **Job's news,** news of disaster; so **Job's post,** a messenger who brings such news; see *Job* 1:13–19. **Job's tears** (also †*Job's drops*), a species of grass (*Coix lacryma*), having round shining grains resembling tears.

Job (dʒǫb), *v.*¹ 1490. [Of symbolic origin, expressive of a brief forcible action; cf. BOB *v.*³, DAB *v.*, JOB *v.*, STAB *v.* (†*stob*).] **1.** *trans.* To peck, dab, stab, prod, etc., as with the point of something; to hurt a horse's mouth with the bit; in pugilistic language, to strike with a sharp or cutting stroke. **2.** To thrust (something pointed) abruptly into something else 1573. **3.** *intr.* To peck (*at*) as a bird; to thrust (*at*) so as to stab or pierce; to penetrate *into* 1566.

1. He measured his distance accurately, and jobbed his adversary about the head 1818.

Job (dʒǫb), *v.*² 1670. [f. JOB *sb.*¹] **1.** *intr.* To do jobs; to work by the piece 1694. **2.** *trans.* To let out (a large piece of work) in separate portions to different contractors or workmen 1882. **3.** To hire (*occas.*, to let out on hire) for a particular job, or for a definite time (a horse, carriage, etc.). Also *absol.* 1786. **4.** To let or deal with for profit 1726. **5.** To buy and sell (stock or goods) as a broker; to deal with as a middleman 1670. **b.** *intr.* To buy and sell stock 1721. **6.** *intr.* To turn a public office or service, or a position of trust, improperly to private or party advantage; to practise jobbery 1732. **7.** *trans.* To make a job of (JOB *sb.*¹ 3, 4); to deal with in some way; *esp.* corruptly for private gain or advantage. Also with *away, into.* 1720. **8.** To put *off* by artifice 1876.

1. He had worked..and still jobbed about HONE. **3.** She went to the livery-man from whom she jobbed her carriage THACKERAY. **5.** The Essays are..jobb'd here by Scribners, New York WALT WHITMAN. **6.** I daresay he jobs, as all other people of consequence do, in elections and so forth SCOTT.

Jobation (dʒobē¹·ʃən). *colloq.* 1687. [f. JOBE *v.* + -ATION. Dialectally, usu. *jawbation*, as if from *jaw.*] The action of JOBE *v.*; a rebuke, reproof, *esp.* a long and tedious one; a 'lecture'.

Jobber¹ (dʒǫ·bəɹ). *dial.* 1580. [f. JOB *v.*¹ + -ER¹.] One who or that which jobs, pecks, pokes, thrusts, etc.

Jobber² (dʒǫ·bəɹ). 1670. [f. JOB *v.*² + -ER¹.] **1.** One who does jobs or is employed by the job; a hack; a piece-worker 1706. **2.** A job-master 1848. **3.** A broker, a middleman; a small trader or salesman 1670. **4.** A member of the Stock Exchange, who deals in stocks or shares on his own account; a STOCK-JOBBER; called, in the Stock Exchange itself, a *dealer* 1719. **5.** One who improperly uses a public office, trust, or service for private gain or party advantage 1739.

1. Our translators have usually been the jobbers of booksellers D'ISRAELI. **5.** He is an atrocious j. 1794.

Jobbernowl (dʒǫ·bəɹnōᵘl). *colloq.* 1592. [In XV *jobard* – Fr. *iobard* (XVI, but cf. *jobelot* XV), f. OFr. *jobe* stupid, silly + NOLL.] **1.** A blockish or stupid head 1599. **2.** A blockhead. Also *attrib.*

Jobbery (dʒǫ·bəri). 1832. [Cf. JOBBER² and -ERY.] **1.** Jobs collectively; job-work. Also *attrib.* **2.** The perpetration of corrupt jobs (see JOB *sb.*¹ 3) 1837.

Jo·bbing, *vbl. sb.* 1735. [f. JOB *v.*² + -ING¹.] The action of JOB *v.*² **1.** The doing of odd jobs 1800. **2.** The practice of a middleman or stock-jobber. (See also STOCK-JOBBING.) 1735. **3.** = JOBBERY 2. 1784. **4.** *attrib.* 1775.

2. The jobbing of the public funds BURKE. **3.** The system of Parliamentary jobbing ERSKINE MAY.

Jobbish (dʒǫ·biʃ), *a.* 1792. [f. JOB *sb.*¹ + -ISH¹.] Of the nature of a job (see JOB *sb.*¹ 3).

†**Jobe** (dʒōᵘb), *v. colloq.* Also **job.** 1670. [f. JOB *sb.*³, in allusion to the lengthy reproofs of Job's friends.] *trans.* To rebuke in a long and tedious harangue; to 'lecture' –1794.

A former president of St. John's college..would frequently Job his students for going constantly three or four times a day to chapel 1722.

Jobmaster, job-master (dʒǫ·b,mɑ:stəɹ). 1802. [f. JOB *sb.*¹ + MASTER *sb.*] A man who keeps a livery stable and lets out horses and carriages by the job.

†**Jo·cant,** *a.* 1440. [– L. *jocans, -ant-*, pr. pple. of *jocare* JOKE *v.*; perh. after JOCUND.] Mirthful, merry, jocund –1687. So †**Jo·cantry,** mirth, merriment.

Jockey (dʒǫ·ki), *sb.* 1529. [dim. or pet-form of *Jock*, Sc. by-form of John; orig. Sc. and n. Eng. See -Y⁶.] **1.** A diminutive of the name *Jock* or John, usu. = 'little Jock, Jacky, Johnny'; hence, applied to any man of the common people (chiefly Sc.); also, a lad; an under-strapper. (Cf. JACK *sb.*¹ 2.) **2.** A strolling minstrel or beggar; a vagabond. *Sc. Obs.* exc. *Hist.* 1683. **3.** One who manages or has to do with horses; a horse-dealer. *Obs.* or *dial.* 1638. **b.** Hence, A crafty or fraudulent bargainer; a cheat 1683. †**4.** One who rides or drives a horse; a postillion; a charioteer –1850. **5.** *spec.* A professional rider in horse-races. (The chief current sense.) 1641. **6.** *attrib.* 1670.

3. I, and W. Hewer, and a friend of his, a j., did go about to see several pairs of horses for my coach PEPYS. **5.** The jockies whipp'd, the horses ran COMBE.

Comb.: **j.-cap,** a peaked cap of the style worn by jockeys; **-club,** a club for the promotion and regulation of horse-racing; *spec.* the Jockey Club established at Newmarket, which is the supreme authority in England on these matters 1758; **-coat** a kind of great-coat (?formerly worn by horse-dealers); **-sleeve,** a sleeve like that of a jockey-coat.

So **Jo·ckeydom,** jockeys collectively. **Jo·ckeyism,** the style, phraseology, or practice of jockeys.

Jockey (dʒǫ·ki), *v.* 1659. [f. prec. sb.] **1.** *trans.* To play the jockey with (see prec. 3 b); to trick, take in, 'do'. **b.** To play tricks with; to manipulate in a tricky way 1890. **c.** *intr.* To play the jockey, act fraudulently; to aim at an advantage by adroit management 1835. **2.** *trans.* To ride (a horse) in a race, as a jockey 1825.

1. The way in which she jockied Jos, and which she described with infinite fun THACKERAY.

Jockeying (dʒǫ·ki,iŋ), *vbl. sb.* 1770. [f. JOCKEY *v.* + -ING¹.] The action of JOCKEY *v.* **1.** Horse-dealing; the riding and management of horses. Also *attrib.* **2.** Adroit management for the purpose of gaining an (unfair) advantage; trickery, cheating 1807.

Jockeyship (dʒǫ·kiʃip). 1763. [See -SHIP.] **1. a.** The art of a jockey; skill in horse-racing. **b.** The practice of jockeying (see prec. 2). **2.** A mock title for a jockey. COWPER.

1. b. To vie in j. or cunning at a bett SHENSTONE. **2.** Where can at last his j. retire? 1781.

Jocko (dʒǫ·ko). Also **jacko.** 1847. [– Fr. *jocko*, erroneously made by Buffon out of *engeco*, prop. *ncheko*, native name in the Gaboon country, W. Africa.] The chimpanzee; *occas.*, any ape.

Jockteleg (dʒǫ·ktĕleg). *Sc.* and *n. dial.* Also **jacklag, jackleg,** etc. 1672. [In earliest use Sc., in the form *Jock the leg*, later *jocteleg*; of unkn. origin.] A (large) clasp knife.

Jocose (dʒokōᵘ·s), *a.* 1673. [– L. *jocosus*, f. *jocus*; see JOKE *sb.*, -OSE¹.] **1.** Full of jokes; given to joking; playful, sportive, waggish. **2.** Of the nature of a joke, or characterized by jokes; playful in style or character 1699.

1. When they vouchsafe to..be j. and pleasant with an Adversary SHAFTESBURY. **2.** J. talk GEO. ELIOT. Hence **Joco·se-ly** *adv.*, **-ness.**

Jocoserious (dʒōᵘko,sīᵊ·riəs), *a.* 1661. [f. *joco-*, comb. f. L. *jocus* jest + SERIOUS.] Half jocular, half serious; blending jokes and serious matters.

Jocosity (dʒokǫ·sĭti). 1646. [f. JOCOSE + -ITY. Cf. mod.L. *jocositas* (Bacon).] Jocose quality or disposition; mirthfulness. **b.** A jocose saying or act 1859.

Jocular (dʒǫ·kiŭlăɹ), *a.* 1626. [– L. *jocularis*, f. *joculus*, dim. of *jocus*; see JOKE *sb.*, -ULAR.] **1.** Disposed to joking or jesting; mirthful, merry. **2.** Of the nature of, or containing, a joke; said or done in joke; comic, humorous 1674.

1. Pardon me for being j. ADDISON. **2.** Sheridan made some j. reply 1826. Hence **Jocula·rity,** the quality of being j. **Jo·cularly** *adv.*

‖**Joculator** (dʒǫ·kiŭlēⁱtəɹ). *Obs.* exc. *Hist.* 1500. [L., = jester; later, esp. med.L., professional jester, f. *joculari* jest; see JONGLEUR, JUGGLER.] A professional jester, minstrel, or jongleur. Hence †**Jo·culatory** *a.* characteristic of, or having the character of, a jester.

Jocund (dʒǫ·kŏnd, dʒōᵘ·kŏnd). *a.* ME. Now only literary. [– OFr. *jocond, jocund* – L. *jocundus*, late form of *jucundus* pleasant, agreeable, f. *juvare* help, delight.] Feeling, expressing, or communicating mirth or cheerfulness; merry, blithe, sprightly, light-hearted; pleasant, cheering. †**b.** Joyful, glad, well-pleased –1578.

Iocond day Stands tipto on the mistie Mountaines tops SHAKS. Hence **Jo·cund-ly** *adv.*, **-ness.** †**Jo·cundry,** j. action or disposition.

Jocundity (dʒokɒ·ndĭti). ME. [– late L. *jucunditas*, f. *jucundus*; see JOCUND, -ITY. Cf. OFr. *jocond-, jocundité.*] **1.** Jocund quality or condition; mirthfulness; mirth, merriment, glee. **b.** A pleasantry. NORTH. †**2.** Pleasure, joy, happiness (of a spiritual kind) –1628.

Jodel: see YODEL.

Joe (dʒōᵘ), *sb.*[1] 1772. Abbrev. of *Joannes* or JOHANNES, a Pg. gold coin.

Joe (dʒōᵘ), *sb.*[2] *colloq.* or *slang.* [Familiar abbrev. of *Joseph.*] **1.** Short for *Joe Miller* 1834. **2.** A fourpenny piece = JOEY[1] 1882. **3. Joe Manton,** a name given to fowling-pieces made by Joseph Manton, a London gunsmith 1816. **4. Joe Miller.** [From the name of Joseph Miller, a comedian (1684–1738), attached to a jest-book published after his death.] **a.** A jest-book 1789. **b.** A joke; *esp.* a stale joke, a 'chestnut' 1816. Hence **Joe-Millerism.** MEREDITH.

4. b. A fool and his money are soon parted, nephew: there is a Joe Miller for your Joe Manton SCOTT.

†**Joey**[1] (dʒōᵘ·i). *slang* or *colloq.* 1865. [dim. from prec.; see -Y[6]. Named from Joseph Hume.] A fourpenny piece.

Joey[2] (dʒōᵘ·i). 1839. [Native Austral. *joè.*] A young kangaroo; also *gen.* a young animal or child.

Jog (dʒǫg), *sb.*[1] 1611. [f. JOG *v.*] **1.** An act of jogging; a shake; a slight push; a nudge 1635. **2. a.** The act of moving mechanically up and down. **b.** The act of jogging along; also *transf.*, e.g. of the rhythm of verse. 1611.

1. A little breeze of wind..which..gave them a kind of a J. on their way towards the shore DE FOE. **2.** The familiar j. of a hack carriage 1889.

Jog, *sb.*[2] 1715. [In sense 1 var. of JAG *sb.*[1]; with sense 2 cf. JOGGLE *sb.*[2]] **1.** = JAG *sb.*[1] 4; also, a protuberance, swelling (*rare*). ? *Obs.* **2.** A right-angled notch, recess, or step, in a surface; any space cut out by such a notch (*U.S.*) 1881.

2. Her [Spain's] maritime advantages were indeed diminished by the j. which Portugal takes out of her territory 1893.

Jog (dʒǫg), *v.* [In late ME. in w. midl. texts, varying to some extent with JAG *v.*[1] and †*jug*, all symbolical of stabbing or jerking movement; not common in literature before XVI. Cf. SHOG *v.*] **1.** *trans.* To shake or move (a heavy body) with a push or jerk; also with *up.* Also *fig.* **2.** To give a slight push to; to nudge; esp. so as to arouse attention 1589. Also *fig.* **3.** *intr.* To move up and down or to and fro with a heavy unsteady motion; to move about as if shaken 1586. **4.** *intr.* To walk or ride with a jolting pace; to trudge; hence, to move on, go on, be off 1565. Also *fig.*

1. The Seamans needle which is jogged and troubled BP. REYNOLDS. **2.** Sudden I jogg'd Ulysses, who was laid Fast by my side POPE. *fig.* I jogged his memory by reverting to our water-party 1840. **3.** His sisters-elect, jigging and jogging in a mad polka 1852. **4.** The load jogg'd homeward down the lane CLARE. Iog-on, Iog-on the footpath way SHAKS. *fig.* My worldly matters j. on very well SCOTT. Hence **Jo·gger,** one who or that which jogs 1605.

Joggle (dʒǫ·g'l), *sb.*[1] 1727. [f. JOGGLE *v.*[1]] An act, or the action, of joggling.

Jo·ggle, *sb.*[2] 1703. [perh. f. JOG *sb.*[2] 1.] *Masonry* and *Carpentry.* A joint at the meeting of two adjacent pieces of stone or timber, to prevent them from sliding on one another; a notch in one piece, or a corresponding projection in the other, or a small piece let in between both, for this purpose. **b.** *Comb.*, as *j.-joint, -piece,* etc. 1703.

Joggle (dʒǫ·g'l), *v.*[1] 1513. [dim. or freq. of JOG *v.*; see -LE.] To jog continuously or repeatedly. **1.** *trans.* To shake to and fro, as by repeated jerks; to cause to move from side to side. **2.** *intr.* To move to and fro with repeated jerks; to shake or rock about, as something loose or unsteady; *dial.* to jog *along* 1683.

1. Something chanced to j. the magnets..and they instantly rushed together BREWSTER.

Joggle, *v.*[2] 1801. [f. JOGGLE *sb.*[2]] *Masonry* and *Carpentry. trans.* To join or fit together by means of a joggle; to fasten with a joggle.

Jo·g-jo:g, *adv.* and *adj.* 1780. [f. JOG *v.*] **1.** *adv.* With a jogging motion or pace. **2.** *adj.* = JOG-TROT B. 1837.

Jog-trot, *sb., adj., adv.* 1653. [f. JOG *v.* or *sb.*[1] + TROT *sb.*[1]] **A.** *sb.* (jo·g-tro·t). **1.** *lit.* A jogging trot; a slow regular jerky pace (usu. of a horse) 1796. **2.** *fig.* A slow, monotonous, or easy-going progression in any action 1756.

2. The monstrous jog-trot of daily life LEVER.

B. *adj.* (jo·g-trot). **1.** *lit.* Of the nature of a jog-trot, jogging; adapted for jogging along 1797. **2.** *fig.* Uniform and unhurried; according to routine; humdrum 1653. **b.** Acting in a jog-trot way 1766.

1. Pleasant jog-trot roads HUGHES.

C. *adv.* (jo·g-trot). At a jog-trot pace 1845. Hence **Jo·g-tro·t** *v.* to go or move at a jog-trot (*lit.* and *fig.*). **Jo·g-trotter.** SCOTT.

Johannean (dʒohæ·niăn), *a.* 1881. [f. eccl.L. *Johannes* + -AN.] = JOHANNINE.

Johannes, Joannes (dʒo(h)æ·nīz). 1756. [– late L. (Vulg.) *Joannes,* med.L. *Johannes*; see JOHN.] The name in the British colonies for the Pg. *dobra de quatro escudos* or *peça* of Joannes or João V (1703–1750), a gold coin valued at 6,400 reis, or about 36*s.* sterling (Also familiarly *jo,* or JOE.)

Johannine (dʒohæ·nəin), *a.* 1861. [f. as prec. + -INE[1].] Of, belonging to, or having the character of, the apostle John.

Johannisberger (dʒohæ·nisbɔ̄ɹgəɹ). 1822. [G.] A fine white wine produced at Johannisberg in the Rheingau.

John (dʒǫn). [ME. *Iohan, Ion,* later *Ihon, Iohn, John* – late L. (Vulg.) *Joannes* (med.L. *Johannes* – N.T. Gr. Ἰωάννης – Heb. *yôḥānān* for *yᵉhôḥānān,* expl. as 'God (Jah) is gracious'.] **1.** A masculine Christian name. **b.** Also used as a representative proper name for a footman, butler, waiter, messenger, or the like, and in other ways; cf. JACK, JOHNNY. †**2.** A plant; a variety of pink; usu. Sweet John –1597. †**3.** *Sir John*: familiar or contemptuous designation for a priest; from *Sir* as rendering L. *dominus* at the Universities. Cf. also MESS JOHN. –1653.

3. Com neer thou preest, com hyder thou sir Iohn CHAUCER.

Phr. etc. **J.-a-dreams,** a dreamy fellow; **J. Company,** joc. appellation of the East India Company, taken over from the name *Jan Kompanie,* by which the Dutch E.I.C., and now the Dutch government, are known to natives in the East; **J. Doe** (*Eng. Law*), the name given to the fictitious lessee of the plaintiff in the (now obsolete) action of ejectment; **J.-go-to-bed-at-noon,** pop. name for the Goat's-beard, *Tragopogon pratensis,* or other flowers which close about midday, as the Pimpernel and the Star-of-Bethlehem; †**J. Trot,** a bumpkin.

b. St. John's, in comp. **St. John's bread,** the fruit of the carob-tree; also, the tree 1568. **St. John's-wort,** name for plants of the genus *Hypericum* ME.

†**Jo·hn-a-no·kes.** 1531. [orig. *John atten Oke,* i.e. *John* (who dwells) *at the oak.*] A fictitious name for one of the parties in a legal action; hence, indefinitely, any one –1815.

Jo·hn-apple. 1609. = APPLE-JOHN.

†**Jo·hn-a-sti·les.** 1531. [orig. *John atte Stile,* i.e. *John* (who dwells) *at the stile.*] A fictitious name for a party in a legal action (usu. coupled with JOHN-A-NOKES) –1714.

John Bull. 1772. [Name of a character representing the English nation in Arbuthnot's satire (1712).] **1.** A personification of the English nation; Englishmen collectively, or the typical Englishman 1778. **b.** (with *a* and *pl.*) A typical Englishman 1772. **2.** A kind of game of chance. STRUTT.

1. b. Both, like true John Bulls, fought with better will than justice for Old England MME. D'ARBLAY. Hence **John-Bu·llism,** the typical English character; a typically English act, utterance, or characteristic.

John Dory (dʒǫn dōᵊ·ri). 1609. [In sense 2 from *John* added to *Dorée* or DORY, the name of the fish. No doubt a joc. formation.] **1.** As a proper name. **2.** A popular name of a fish, *Zeus faber,* formerly called simply the *dorée* or *dory* 1754.

Johnian (dʒōᵘ·niăn), *sb.* (*a.*) 1655. [f. JOHN + -IAN.] A member or student of St. John's College, Cambridge.

Johnny, Johnnie (dʒǫ·ni). 1673. [Familiar dim. of *John*; see -IE, -Y[6].] **1.** A fellow, chap; *spec.* a nickname given to Englishmen in the Mediterranean, to the Confederate soldiers in the American civil war, etc.; now chiefly, a fashionable young man of idle habits. **2.** Applied to a tiger 1815, a kind of penguin 1898, etc. **3.** *Johnny Raw*: nickname for a raw recruit, a novice 1813.

Jo·hnny-cake. Also **journey-cake.** 1775. [Of unc. origin.] **a.** *U.S.* A cake made of maize-meal, toasted before a fire, or baked in a pan. **b.** *Australia.* A cake made of wheatmeal, baked on the ashes or fried in a pan.

Johnsonese (dʒǫnsənī·z), *sb.* (*a*). 1843. [f. Samuel *Johnson* + -ESE.] The language or style of Dr. Johnson, or an imitation of it. **B.** *adj.* In the style of Dr. Johnson 1882.

Johnsonian (dʒǫnsōᵘ·niăn). 1791. [f. as prec. + -IAN.] **A.** *adj.* Of, belonging to, or characteristic of Dr. Samuel Johnson (1709–1784); applied esp. to a style of English abounding in words of Latin origin. **B.** *sb.* A student or admirer of Dr. Johnson 1887. Hence **Johnso·nianism,** J. style or J. phrase. So **Jo·hnsonize** *v. trans.* to clothe in or imbue with the style or language of Dr. Johnson.

Join, *sb.* 1825. [f. JOIN *v.*] An act of joining, or the fact of being joined; *concr.* a line of junction, a joining.

Join (dʒoin), *v.* [ME. *ioin, ioign* – *joign-,* pres. stem of (O)Fr. *joindre* :– L. *jungere,* f. IE. **jug-* (see YOKE *sb.*).]

I. *trans.* **1.** To put (things) together, so that they become physically united or continuous; to fasten, attach, connect, unite. †**b.** To harness (horses, etc. together, or to a vehicle); to yoke –1728. †**c.** To combine in a mixture –1626. **d.** *Geom.* To connect (two points) by a straight line 1660. **2.** To put or bring into close contact ME. **3.** To put together, combine, unite (immaterial things) ME. †**4.** To add, annex; to add in contribution –1709. **5.** To unite, combine (troops, etc.) into one body or company 1560. †**b.** *refl.* –1611. **6.** To link or unite in marriage, friendship, or any kind of association; to associate, ally ME.

1. Seas but j. the regions they divide POPE. **b.** He bade the light-foot Houres without delay To joyn his Steeds 1621. **3.** To j. Humanity and Policy together BACON. **4.** While expletives their feeble aid do j. POPE. **5.** *To j. forces* (fig.), to combine efforts. **b.** Then the Spirit saide vnto Philip, Goe neere, and ioyne thy selfe to this charet *Acts* 8:29. **6.** What therefore God hath joyned together, let not man put asunder *Matt.* 19:6.

II. *intr.* **1.** To come or be brought into material contact or connection; to combine, unite physically ME. **2.** To be in contact; to adjoin ME. **3.** †**a.** To come close together in time. **b.** To come together or exist together in operation ME. **4.** Of two or more: To come together, come into company ME. †**5.** *Astrol.* To come into conjunction –1697. **6.** To come together, meet, or engage in conflict. ? *Obs.* ME. **7.** To enter into association or alliance ME.

1. The ryver of Tames begynneth where Tame and Yse ioyne togyther PALSGR. **2.** Iustus.. whose house ioyned harde to the sinagoge TINDALE *Acts* 18:7. **3. b.** Tho' truths in manhood darkly j. TENNYSON. **6.** Looke you pray..that our Armies ioyn not in a hot day SHAKS. **7.** He makes it his business to j. in Conversation with Envious men STEELE.

III. *trans.* To form (a whole) by putting parts together, e.g. as a JOINER. *Obs.* exc. in phrases. ME.

IV. *trans.* To come into contact, contiguity, company, or union with; to associate oneself with; to become a member of; *ellipt.* for *join oneself to,* †*join to.* 1702.

The two hands that joyn one another are Emblems of Fidelity ADDISON. A young Fellow joyns us from t'other End of the Room STEELE. *absol.* When do you j.?—where is your regiment? LEVER. Phr. *To j. the* (*great* or *silent*) *majority,* to die. *To join up* (colloq.), to enlist.

Phrases. *To j. battle*: to come together and begin a battle; to enter upon a battle, or (*fig.*) a contest of any kind 1455. Also †*intr.* said of the battle 1650. *To j. hands* (from I. 2): **a.** *lit.* (*a*) To clasp one's hands together; (*b*) of two persons, To grasp each the hand of the other, in token of amity, or *spec.* of marriage; (*c*) of a third person (e.g. the priest at marriage), To cause two persons to grasp each other's hand. **b.** *fig.* (*j. hands, j. hand in hand*): To combine in some action or enterprise.

Join-, the vb.-stem used in comb., as in †**join-hand** *sb.* = JOINING-HAND.

Joinant (dʒoi·nănt), *a.* ME. [– (O)Fr. *joignant,* pr. pple. of *joindre*; see JOIN *v.,*

-ANT.] †1. Adjoining, adjacent. ME. only. 2. *Her.* = CONJOINED 1828.

Joinder (dʒoi·ndəɹ). 1601. [– legal AFr. *joinder*, subst. use of (O)Fr. *joindre*; see JOIN *v.*, -ER⁴.] The act of joining; conjunction, union; *spec.* in *Law* in various connections.

Joiner (dʒoi·nəɹ), *sb.* [ME. *ioynour* – AFr. *joignour*, OFr. *joigneor*, f. *joindre* JOIN *v.*; see -OUR, -ER² 3.] 1. One who joins (see JOIN *v.*¹) 1483. 2. A craftsman who constructs things by joining pieces of wood; a worker in wood who does lighter and more ornamental work than that of a *carpenter* ME. 3. *transf.* A machine for doing various kinds of work in wood 1875. 4. *colloq.*, *U.S.* One who joins many organizations. **Joi·ner** *v. intr.* to do the work of a j.; also *trans.* **Joi·nering** *vbl. sb.*

Joinery (dʒoi·nəri). 1672. [f. JOINER + -Y³; see -ERY.] 1. The art or occupation of a joiner; also *concr.* things made by a joiner. 2. *transf.* and *fig.* Work analogous to that of a joiner 1774.

2. That hideous piece of female j., a patch-work counterpane MISS MITFORD.

†**Joining-hand.** 1583. [f. *joining* + HAND *sb.*] Handwriting in which the successive letters of each word are joined, cursive hand –1812.

Joint (dʒoint), *sb.* ME. [– (O)Fr. *joint*, OFr. *jointe*, subst. use of *joint*, *jointe* pa. pple. of *joindre* JOIN.]

I. A junction. 1. A joining of two bones (or corresponding parts of an invertebrate animal), either rigidly, or (*esp.*) so as to move upon one another; an articulation. 2. A part of the stem of a plant from which a leaf or branch grows (esp. thickened, as in grasses); a node 1523. 3. That wherein or whereby two members or elements of an artificial structure or mechanism are joined or fitted together, either so as to be rigidly fixed (as *e.g.* bricks, stones, lengths of pipe, etc.), or as in a hinge, pivot, swivel ME. 4. *Geol.* A crack or fissure intersecting a mass of rock; usually occurring in sets of parallel planes, dividing the mass into blocks 1601.

1. Phr. *Out of j.* (ME.): *lit.* said of a dislocated bone; also of the part or member affected; *fig.* perverted, disordered, disorganized. The time is out of ioynt: Oh cursed spight, That euer I was borne to set it right *Haml.* I. v. 188. 3. *Universal j.*: see UNIVERSAL A. *adj.* 7. *To break j.*: see BREAK *v.* V. 2. 4. The partings which divide columnar basalt into prisms are joints LYELL.

II. 1. A part of an animal or plant body connected with another part by a joint or articution ME. 2. *spec.* One of the portions into which a carcass is divided by the butcher, consisting of one or more bones with the meat thereon 1576.

III. *slang* or *colloq.* (chiefly *U.S.*) A meeting-place, esp. for an illicit purpose; *spec.* an illicit opium-den or drinking-saloon 1883.

Comb.: **j.-bedded** *a.* (*Masonry*), of a stone; placed so that its natural bed (or horizontal surface) forms a vertical j. of the work; **-chair** (*Railways*), a chair (see CHAIR *sb.*) supporting the rails at a j.; **-coupling,** a form of universal joint for coupling sections of shafting; **-hinge,** the same as a strap-hinge; **-oil,** †**-water,** synovia; also in names of cattle diseases, as *joint-ill*, *-murrain*.

Joint (dʒoint), *a.* ME. [– (O)Fr. *joint*, pa. pple. of *joindre* JOIN.] 1. Put together, joined, combined, united. *spec.* Of two or more lives: Contemporaneous, concurrent 1606. 2. Of a person or persons: Having or doing (what is expressed by the noun) together or in common ME. 3. Of a thing, action, etc. (in *sing.*): Held, done, made, etc. by two or more persons, parties, or things, in conjunction; common to two or more ME. †4. Made up of parts joined or combined –1711.

1. By their joynt endeavours 1641. During the j. lives of the trustees 1883. 2. Ioynt heires with Christ *Rom.* 8:17. J.-owners of the Stockport and Woodley Junction 1878. 3. A ioynt burthen, laid vpon vs all SHAKS. J.-estates BLACKSTONE. A j. committee of the two Houses MACAULAY.

Joint (dʒoint), *v.* 1530. [f. JOINT *sb.*] 1. *trans.* To connect by a joint or joints; to fasten, fit together, unite. Also *fig.* 1547. b. To fill up the joints of stone, brickwork, etc. with mortar or the like; to point 1703. c. *Carpentry.* To prepare (a board, stave, etc.) for being joined to another 1864. 2. *intr.* for *refl.* To fit exactly into each other as in the joints of masonry, etc. 1695. 3. *trans.* To divide at a joint or into joints; to disjoint, to dismember 1530.

1. The fingers are..jointed together for motion RAY. b. They j. the paving with mortar SMEATON. 3. He joints the Neck: And with a stroke so strong The Helm flies off DRYDEN. To j. a piece of Meat 1709.

Jointed (dʒoi·ntėd), *a.* ME. [f. JOINT *sb.* + -ED².] Furnished with, constructed with, or having joints (see the sb.). b. In *comb.*: Having joints of a specified kind 1591.

In j. Armour MILT. b. Iron-j. TENNYSON. **Jo·intedly** *adv.*

†**Jointer**¹. 1566. [f. JOINT *a.*, or *joint-* in JOINTURE, + -ER¹.] A joint possessor; one who holds a jointure –1590.

Jointer² (dʒoi·ntəɹ). 1678. [f. JOINT *v.* + -ER¹.] 1. Name of various tools. a. *Carpentry*, etc. A long kind of plane used in dressing the edges of boards, staves, etc. for jointing; also a machine used in jointing staves. b. *Masonry.* A tool used for pointing the joints of brick or stone work 1703. c. A bent piece of iron inserted into a wall to strengthen a joint 1864. 2. A workman employed in jointing; *esp.* one who makes the junctions between parts of an electric wire, etc. 1876.

Comb. **j.-plane** = sense 1 a.

Jointing (dʒoi·ntiŋ), *vbl. sb.* 1591. [f. JOINT *v.* + -ING¹.] The action of JOINT *v.* Also *concr.* The structure of a joint or junction 1668.

Comb.: **j.-plane,** (*a*) a plane of fissure, as in a rock; (*b*) = JOINTER² 1 a; **-rule,** a long flat ruler used for guiding the jointer (JOINTER² 1 b) in marking the joints of brickwork.

Jointless (dʒoi·ntlės), *a.* 1559. [f. JOINT *sb.* + -LESS.] Without joints or the use of joints; stiff, rigid.

Jointly (dʒoi·ntli), *adv.* ME. [f. JOINT *a.* + -LY².] In a joint manner; so as to be joined; †together –1710; †continuously in space or time –1548; unitedly, conjunctly (the only current sense) ME.

A devise to two persons, to hold j. and severally 1767.

Jointress (dʒoi·ntrės). 1602. [f. JOINTER¹ + -ESS¹.] A widow who holds a jointure; a dowager.

Th' Imperiall Ioyntress of this Warlike State SHAKS.

†**Joint-ring.** 1604. A finger-ring made of two separable halves; = GEMEL 3. –1703.

Joint stock, joint-stock. 1615. [f. JOINT *a.* + STOCK.] 1. Stock or capital held by a number of persons jointly; capital divided into shares; a common fund. 2. *attrib.* (joi·ntstock). Holding a joint stock; formed or conducted on the basis of a joint stock; as *joint-stock bank, company, firm* 1797.

Joint-stool (dʒoi·nt,stūl). ME. [In sense 1 orig. *joined stool*; in 2 f. JOINT *sb.* I, 3.] 1. A stool made of parts joined or fitted together; a stool made by a joiner. *Obs.* exc. *Hist.* 2. *Mech.* A block holding up the ends of parts which belong in apposition, as railway rails, ways of vessels, etc. 1875.

Joint-tenant. 1531. [Law-Fr. *jointenant*: see JOINT *a.* and TENANT.] One who holds an undivided estate in the same right jointly with another or others, with right of survivorship, till the whole remains in a single hand. Also *fig.* So **Joint-te·nancy,** the holding of an estate by joint-tenants.

Jointure (dʒoi·ntiŭɹ), *sb.* ME. [– (O)Fr. *jointure* :– L. *junctura* JUNCTURE.] †1. Joining, union –1606. 2. *concr.* A joining, a joint (now *rare*) ME. †3. The holding of an estate by two or more persons in joint-tenancy –1767. 4. *spec.* a. *orig.* The holding of property to the joint use of husband and wife for life or in tail, as a provision for the latter during widowhood. Hence, b. A sole estate limited to the wife, to take effect upon the death of her husband for her own life at least 1451. †c. = *dowry*: see DOWRY 2. –1615.

4. He had married a widdow of 700 li. per annum joynter WOOD. Hence **Joi·nture** *v.* to settle a jointure upon; **Joi·ntureless** *a.*

Jointuress (dʒoi·ntiŭrės). 1693. [Altered f. JOINTRESS, after prec.] = JOINTRESS.

Jointweed (dʒoi·nt,wīd). 1866. Pop. name of various weeds with jointed stems. a. In U.S., *Polygonum articulatum.* b. Locally in Eng., various species of Horsetail (*Equisetum*); also the common Mare's-tail (*Hippuris vulgaris*).

Joi·nt-worm. 1706. 1. A tape-worm; as consisting of a series of joints. 2. *U.S.* The larva of various species of hymenopterous insects belonging to the genus *Isosoma*, which do great damage to grain.

Jointy (dʒoi·nti), *a.* 1578. [f. JOINT *sb.* + -Y¹.] Having numerous joints.

Joist (dʒoist), *sb.* [ME. *giste*, *gyste*, early mod. *just* – OFr. *giste* beam supporting a bridge (mod. *gîte*) :– subst. use of Rom. **jacitum*, n. pa. pple. of L. *jacēre* lie down. The development to *joist* is paralleled by *hoist*.] 1. One of the timbers, laid horizontally or nearly so, on which the boards of a floor or the laths of a ceiling are nailed; also, A timber which similarly supports the floor of a platform, a bridge, or other structure. †2. A mass of mineral in its natural bed. 1829.

Joist (dʒoist), *v.*¹ 1615. [f. prec.] *trans.* To furnish with, or fix on, joists.

Joist, *v.*² 1601. Obs. and dial. f. GIST *v.*

Joke (dʒōᵘk), *sb.* 1670. [orig. slang; perh. – L. *jocus* word-play, jest; cf. G. *jucks, jux* joke, spree, and Du. *jok* jest.] 1. Something said or done to excite laughter or amusement; a witticism, a jest; jesting, raillery; also, a ridiculous circumstance. 2. *transf.* A laughing-stock 1791. 3. Something not serious or earnest; a jesting matter 1726.

1. Phr. *Practical j.*, a trick played upon some person usually in order to have a laugh at his expense. *To crack a j.*; *to turn a matter into a j.* The simple j. that takes the shepherd's heart THOMSON. 2. I shall be the standing j. of the messtable 1823. Hence **Jo·ky** *a.*, jocular.

Joke (dʒōᵘk), *v.* 1670. [f. prec., or – L. *jocari* jest, joke.] 1. *intr.* To make a joke, to jest. 2. *trans.* To make the object of a joke or jokes; to chaff, banter, rally 1746.

1. Your Honour is pleas'd to j. with me STEELE. 2. Sir Joseph Banks joked her about Otoroo MRS. PIOZZI. Hence **Jo·kingly** *adv.* 1700.

Joker (dʒōᵘ·kəɹ). 1729. [f. JOKE *v.* + -ER¹.] 1. A jester; a merry fellow. 2. *slang.* Man, 'fellow', 'chap' 1811. 3. a. Something used in playing a trick 1858. b. An odd card in a pack, either left blank or ornamented, used in some games, counting usu. as a trump and sometimes as the highest trump 1885. 4. *U.S.* A clause unobtrusively inserted in a legislative enactment and affecting its operation in a way not immediately apparent 1904.

Jokesmith (dʒōᵘ·ksmiþ). 1813. [f. JOKE *sb.* + SMITH.] A manufacturer of jokes.

My j. Sidney, and all his kidney SOUTHEY.

‖**Jokul,** *prop.* **jökull** (yō·kul). Also **yokul.** 1780. [Icel. *jökull* icicle, hence ice, glacier; cf. ICICLE, ICKLE.] In reference to Iceland: A mountain permanently covered with ice and snow; a snow-mountain.

Jole, var. of JOWL. **Jolie, -if, -ife,** etc. obs. ff. JOLLY. **Joll(e,** obs. f. JOWL.

Jollification (dʒǫ:lifikēⁱ·ʃən). *colloq.* 1798. [f. JOLLY *a.* + -FICATION.] The action of jollifying; merrymaking, jollity.

We had a great j. here last week SCOTT.

Jollify (dʒǫ·lifəi), *v. colloq.* 1824. [f. as prec. + -FY.] To make merry; to make or become slightly intoxicated.

Jollily (dʒǫ·lili), *adv.* ME. [f. JOLLY *a.* + -LY².] In a jolly manner (see JOLLY *a.*) So †**Jo·lliment, Jo·lliness,** jollity, mirth.

Jollity (dʒǫ·lĭti). [ME. *jolivete*, *jolite*, etc. – OFr. *joliveté*, *jolité*, f. *jolif*, *joli*; see JOLLY *a.* -TY¹.] 1. The quality or condition of being jolly; exuberant mirth; †levity, giddiness. 2. Merrymaking, revelry; *pl.*, Festivities ME. †3. Pleasure,; esp. sexual pleasure, lust –1615. †4. Insolent presumption or self-confidence –1614. †5. Splendour, magnificence; finery –1698. †6. Pleasantry; joke, jest –1608.

1. Omnia fert ætas, both health and iolitie BARCLAY. 2. It comes, like an arrest of Treason in a J. FELTHAM. 4. In this iollitie of conceit, he determined to fight RALEGH. 5. Needie Nothing trimd in iollite SHAKS.

Jolloped (dʒǫ·ləpt), *a.* 1610. [f. *jollop* sb., wattle (app. f. JOWL *sb.*² + LAP *sb.*¹ 2) + -ED². Cf. *dewlapped* (see DEWLAP).] *Her.* = WATTLED.

Jolly (dʒǫ·li), *sb.*[1] *slang.* 1829. [JOLLY *a.* used as *sb.*] A royal marine.

I'm a J.—'Er Majesty's J.—Soldier and Sailor too KIPLING. *Tame j.*, a militiaman.

Jo·lly, *sb.*[2] 1829. Short for JOLLY-BOAT.

Jo·lly, *sb.*[3] *colloq.* [app. f. JOLLY *v.* 1.] = JOLLIFICATION.

Jolly (dʒǫ·li), *a.* and *adv.* [ME. *jolif* – OFr. *jolif,* (later and mod.) *joli* †gay, †pleasant, pretty, perh. f. ON. *jól* midwinter festival, feast, YULE. Final *f* was lost as in *hasty, tardy.*]

I. 1. Of gay disposition or character; lively; joyous; mirthful. Now *arch.* and chiefly of time. **†2.** Having the lively spirits of youth or health; fresh, sprightly –1586. **3.** In high spirits; exhilarated ME.; *euphem.* slightly intoxicated 1652. **4.** Indulging in, or fond of, conviviality; festive; jovial ME.

1. While the j. Hours lead on propitious May MILT. **3.** Young Churchill and a dozen more grew j., stayed till seven in the morning and drank thirty two bottles H. WALPOLE. **4.** The *j. god,* Bacchus. He became a viveur and j. dog about town THACKERAY.

II. †1. Of cheerful courage; high-hearted; brave –1642. **†2.** Overweeningly self-confident; arrogant, overbearing –1666.

†III. Amorous; wanton, lustful –1645.

In the Song of Songs, which is generally believed, even in the jolliest expressions, to figure the spousals of the church with Christ MILT.

IV. †1. Brilliant, showy, splendid –1688. **†2.** Finely dressed; = *Sc.* 'braw' –1593. **3.** Good-looking; fair, pretty. Now only *dial.* ME. **4.** Healthy and well developed; well-conditioned; plump (*dial.* and *colloq.*) 1661.

4. A dainty dame in her youth, and a j. woman in her age 1661.

V. 1. Splendid, fine, excellent; also *ironical* 1534. **2.** Exceedingly pleasant, agreeable, or 'nice'. Now *colloq.* 1549. **3.** As an admiring intensive: Admirably great, large, big, etc.; *ironically,* 'fine', 'nice'. Now *colloq.*

1. For he's a j. good fe-el-low FARRAR. **2.** This life is most jolly SHAKS. **3.** The king had four-and-twenty daughters, a j. number FULLER.

B. *adv.* **1.** In a jolly manner; merrily, pleasantly 1615. **2.** Qualifying an adj. or adv.; orig. appreciatively, later also ironically, with intensive force: Extremely, very. Now *colloq.* 1549.

2. 'Tis like you'll proue a iolly surly groome SHAKS.

Jolly (dʒǫ·li), *v.* 1610. [f. JOLLY *a.*] **1.** *intr.* To make merry, enjoy oneself (*rare*). **2.** *slang.* To treat (a person) in an agreeable manner, in order to keep him in good humour, or the like. Const. *up, along.* orig. *U.S.* 1893. **b.** = CHAFF *v.*[2].

Jolly-boat (dʒǫ·libōᵘt). 1727. [prob. alt. of app. synon. †*jolywat, gellywatte* (XV–XVII), of unkn. origin.] A clinker-built ship's boat, smaller than a cutter, used chiefly as a hack-boat for small work.

†Jo·llyhead [f. JOLLY *a.* + -HEAD.] Jollity. SPENSER.

Jolt (dʒōᵘlt), *sb.* 1599. [Goes with next; cf. JOT *sb.*[2]] **†1.** A knock (of the head, etc.) against something –1618. **2.** An abrupt shock or jerk which throws a person (or thing) up, to fall again by his (or its) own weight 1632; *fig.* a surprise 1905.

2. My daughter Evelyn going in the coach. .a j. (the doore being not fast shut) flung her quite out EVELYN.

Jolt (dʒōᵘlt), *v.* 1599. [synon. with somewhat earlier JOT *v.*[1], but the origin of both verbs is unknown, as also of the formally corresp. first element of JOLT-HEAD.] **†1.** *trans.* To butt or push; to give a knock to; to nudge –1778. **2.** To shake up from one's seat or place with a jerk or jerks; to carry or transport with jolts. (Chiefly in *pass.*) 1599. **3.** *intr.* To ride or move along with constant jolts 1703. **4.** *intr.* To move up and down or to and fro in a jerky manner 1788.

2. A Coach? I cannot abide to be iolted 1607. **3.** He whipped his horses, the coach jolted again JOHNSON. **4.** The shoulders. .jolting up and down in the convulsions of a hoarse laugh MME. D'ARBLAY. Hence **Jo·ltingly** *adv.*

Jolter (dʒōᵘ·ltəɹ), *sb.* 1611. [f. JOLT *v.* + -ER[1].] One who or that which jolts. So **Jo·lter** *v.* (*rare*) [-ER[5]], to jolt continuously (*trans.* and *intr.*).

Jolter-head, jolterhead. 1620. [An extension of JOLT HEAD.] **1.** (dʒōᵘ·ltəɹhe·d) = JOLT HEAD 1. 1700. **2.** (dʒōᵘ·ltəɹhed) = JOLT-HEAD 2. 1620. Hence **Jo·lter-hea:ded** *a.* So **Jolter-pate** (in sense 1). SCOTT.

Jolt head, jolt-head. ? *Obs.* 1533. [See JOLT *v.*] **†1.** *prop.* **jolt head** (dʒōᵘ·lt,he·d): A large, clumsy, or heavy head; a stupid head –1701. **2.** (dʒōᵘ·lt,hed) A heavy-headed or thick-headed person; a blockhead. Also *attrib.* 1573. Hence **Jo·lt-hea:ded** *a.* (now only fig.). ?*Obs.*

Jolty (dʒōᵘ·lti), *a.* 1834. [f. JOLT *sb.* + -Y[1].] Having or causing jolts, as *a j. coach.*

Jonah (dʒōᵘ·nă), *sb.* Also **Jonas.** 1612. **1.** A Hebrew prophet, the subject of the Book of Jonah; used allusively. **2. Jonah-crab,** a large crab (*Cancer borealis*) of the eastern coast of N. America 1893. Hence **Jonah** *v. trans.* to bring ill luck to.

Jonathan (dʒǫ·năpăn). 1816. [A personal name; orig. that of the son of Saul, king of Israel.] (esp. in phr. *Brother J.*) A generic name for the people of the United States, and also for a representative United States citizen.

The expression *Brother Jonathan* (cf. 2 *Sam.* 1:26) is said to have been applied to Jonathan Trumbull, Governor of Connecticut, by Washington; hence, to a New Englander, and at length as above.

‖**Jongleur** (ʒoṅglör). 1779. [– Fr. *jongleur,* alt. of *jougleur* (OFr. *jogleor*) :– L. *joculator,* *-or-* jester; see JUGGLER.] = JUGGLER 1.

The Jongleurs (the reciters of the merry and licentious fabliaux) MILMAN.

Jonquil (dʒɒ·ŋkwil, dʒǫ·n,kwil). Also **†iunquilia.** 1629. [– mod.L. *jonquilla* or Fr. *jonquille* – Sp. *junquillo,* dim. of *junco* :– L. *juncus* rush, reed. In early use *junquilia* – It. *giunchiglia.*] **1.** A species of Narcissus (*N. jonquilla*), having long linear leaves and spikes of fragrant white or yellow flowers; the rush-leaved Daffodil. **2.** A pale yellow colour like that of the jonquil. [Fr. *jonquille.*] 1791. **3.** A canary-bird of jonquil colour. Abbrev. *jonque.* 1865.

Joram: see JORUM.

Jordan (dʒǭ·ɹdăn). ME. [– med.L. *jurdanus,* of unkn. origin.] **†1.** A kind of pot or vessel formerly used by physicians and alchemists. ME. only. **2.** A chamber-pot. Now *vulgar* or *dial.* ME.

Jordan almond. 1440. [Late ME. *iardyne, jarden*; in med.L. *amigdalum jardinum* (*jardanum*); prob. – OFr. or Sp. *jardin* GARDEN; the present form (XVI) shows assim. to the river Jordan.] A fine variety of almond, now coming chiefly from Malaga. Also simply *jordan.*

Jorum (dʒōᵊ·rəm). 1730. [perh. f. name of *Joram,* who 'brought with him vessels of silver, and vessels of gold, and vessels of brass' (2 Sam. 8: 10).] A large drinking-bowl or vessel; also, its contents; *esp.* a bowl of punch. **b.** *fig.* A large quantity 1872.

Joseph (dʒōᵘ·zĕf). 1578. [repr. Heb. *yôsēp,* name of one of the twelve sons of Jacob, and esp. of the husband of Mary the mother of Jesus Christ; hence in derived uses.] **1.** In allusion to the patriarch Joseph 1849. **2.** A long cloak, worn chiefly by women in the eighteenth century when riding; it was buttoned down the front and had a small cape 1659. **3.** In names of flowers, as **Joseph's coat** (see Gen. 37:3), a cultivated variety of *Amarantus tricolor*; **Joseph's flower** (in ref. to the bearded figure of St. Joseph in art), Goat's-beard 1578.

Joskin (dʒǫ·skin). 1798. [Cf. *bumpkin,* and *joss* dial. to bump.] A country bumpkin, I hate the Joskins LAMB.

Joss (dʒǫs). 1711. [perh. ult. – Pg. †*deos, deus* :– L. *deus* god, through Javanese *dejos*; cf. Du. *joosje, josie.*] A Chinese figure of a deity, an idol. Also *transf.*

Comb.: **j.-house,** a Chinese temple or building for idol-worship; **-stick,** a thin cylinder or stick of fragrant tinder mixed with clay, used by the Chinese as incense, etc.

Josser (dʒǫ·səɹ). *slang.* 1886. [f. JOSS + -ER[1].] **1.** *Austral.* A padre. **2.** A simpleton; a fellow, chap.

Jostle, justle (dʒǫ·s'l, dʒɒ·s'l), *sb.* 1607. [f. next.] **†1.** A just or joust; a tussle –1609. **2.** A collision; a push or thrust that shakes; the action of a pushing crowd (*lit.* and *fig.*) 1611.

2. The jostle of South African nationalities 1881.

Jo·stle, ju·stle, *v.* ME. [f. JUST *v.* + -LE.] **I.** *intr.* **†1.** To just or tilt –1759. **2.** To knock or push *against,* to come into collision *with*; also *absol.* to push and shove 1546. Also *fig.* **b.** To contend for a place, etc. by pushing another away from it; hence, to vie *with* some one *for* some advantage 1614. **3.** To push one's way 1612.

2. They [the charets] shall iustle one against another in the broad wayes *Nahum* 2:4. **b.** None j. with him for the wall LAMB. **3.** It requires a strong man to j. through a crowd SCOTT.

II. *trans.* **1.** To shake or drive by pushing; to knock or push against; to elbow, hustle 1575. Also *fig.* **2.** *Racing.* To push against (a competitor) so as to retard him. Also *absol.* 1723. Also *fig.* **3.** To cause (one thing) to push against another (*lit.* and *fig.*) 1641.

1. Who standeth still i' the street Shall be hustled and justled about CLOUGH. One atom can jostle another out of its place TYNDALL.

Jo·stlement. 1859. [f. JOSTLE *v.* + -MENT.] Jostling.

Jot (dʒǫt), *sb.*[1] 1499. [– L. *iota* (pron. *yō·ta*), – Gr. ἰῶτα IOTA.] The least letter of any writing; hence *gen.* the least or a very little part, point, or amount; a whit. (Usu. with neg. expressed or implied.)

One iott or one tytle of the lawe shall not scape TINDALE *Matt.* 5:18. He. .never. .abated one j. of his claim 1868.

†Jot, *sb.*[2] [f. JOT *v.*[1] Cf. JOLTS *b.*] A jolt. HY. MORE (1647).

Jot, *v.*[1] Now *dial.* 1530. [Cf. JOLT *v.*] To jog, jolt, bump (*trans.* and *intr.*).

Jot, *v.*[2] 1721. [f. JOT *sb.*[1] In earliest use *Sc.*] *trans.* To write down in the briefest form, to make a short note of. Usu. *to j. down.* Hence **Jo·tter,** one who jots.

Jougs (dʒugz, dʒɒgz), *sb. pl.* 1595. [– Fr. *joug* or L. *jugum* yoke. The pl. form refers to its hinged halves.] An old Scottish instrument of punishment; it consisted of an iron collar, which was locked round the culprit's neck, and was attached by a chain to a wall or post.

He set an old woman in the j. (or Scottish pillory) SCOTT.

†Jouisance, -issance. 1483. [– Fr. *jouissance,* f. *jouir* enjoy; see -ANCE.] = ENJOYMENT –1750.

†Jouk, *v.*[1] ME. [– OFr. (Norman, Picard) *joquier,* etc., be at rest, also *jochier* (mod. *jucher*).] **1.** *intr.* Of birds: To perch, sit (upon branches); in *Falconry,* to roost, to sleep upon its perch –1672. **2.** *intr.* To lie asleep or at rest; to lie close; also, To abide, remain. ME. only.

Jouk, jook (dʒuk), *v.*[2] *Sc.* and *n. dial.* 1450. [Of uncertain origin; partly coincident with DUCK *v.*] **1.** *intr.* To dodge in order to avoid a missile or blow; to duck 1513. **2.** *intr.* To dart or spring out of the way or out of sight; to hide oneself by such action; to skulk 1510. **3.** *trans.* To dodge by ducking, bending, or springing aside 1812. **4.** *intr.* **†a.** To bend oneself supply as an acrobat 1450. **b.** To bow (jerkily) in salutation or obeisance 1567; *fig.* to cringe, fawn; to dissemble 1573.

1. But we must jouk and let the jaw gang by SCOTT. **4. b.** But why should we to nobles jouk? BURNS.

Joul(e, obs. f. JOWL.

Joule (dʒūl, dʒaul). 1882. [f. Dr. J. P. *Joule,* English physicist.] *Physics.* An electrical unit, the amount of work done or heat generated by a current of one ampère acting for one second against a resistance of one ohm.

Phr. **Joule's equivalent** = mechanical equivalent of heat: see EQUIVALENT *sb.* 3 c.

Jounce (dʒauns), *v.* 1440. [Of unkn. origin, like several other verbs in *-ounce,* viz. *bounce, flounce, pounce, trounce,* all of which are applied to kinds of abrupt or forcible movement.] **1.** *intr.* To move violently up and down; to bump, bounce, jolt. **2.** *trans.* To jolt, bump, or shake up and down, as by rough riding; to give (a person) a shaking 1581. Hence **Jounce** *sb.* a bump, a jolt; a jolting pace 1787.

Journal (dʒɔ̄·ɹnăl). ME. [– OFr. *jurnal, jornal* (mod. *journal*), subst. use of *journal* adj., for earlier *jornel* :– late L. *diurnalis* DIURNAL.]

A. *adj.* **1.** Daily, diurnal. Now *rare* or *Obs.* **2.** Ephemeral (*rare*) 1685.

B. *sb.* **I.** †**1.** *Eccl.* = DIURNAL *sb.* 1. –1549. †**2. a.** = ITINERARY –1613. †**b.** A record of travel –1792. **3.** A daily record of commercial transactions, entered as they occur, in order to the keeping of accounts 1500. **4. a.** A daily record of events or occurrences kept by any one for his own use. Now usually implying something more elaborate than a *diary*. 1610. **b.** A register of daily transactions kept by a public body or an association; *spec.* in pl. *Journals*, the record of the daily proceedings in one or other of the Houses of Parliament, kept by the Clerk of the House 1647. **c.** *Naut.* A daily register of the ship's course, the distance traversed, the winds and weather, etc. 1671. †**5.** A record of public events or transactions noted down as they occur, without historical discussion. Also in *pl.* –1687. **6.** A daily newspaper or other publication; hence, by extension, Any periodical publication containing news in any particular sphere 1728.

II. †**1.** A day's travel; a journey –1633. †**2.** Provision for a journey 1629. **3.** As much land as can be ploughed in a day. Prop. the Fr. word *journal* (ʒurnal). 1656. **4.** In *Machinery*. The part of a shaft or axle which rests on the bearings. (No explanation of the origin of this sense has been given.) 1814.

Comb.: **j.-bearing,** the support of a shaft or axle; **-box,** the box or structure enclosing the j. and its bearings; **-packing,** any mass of fibrous material saturated with oil or grease, and inserted in a journal-box to lubricate the j. Hence **Jou·rnal** *v.* to record in a j. 1803; in *Machinery*, to provide with or fix as a j. 1875.

Jou·rnal-book. 1603. [f. JOURNAL *a.* + BOOK *sb.*, after Fr. *livre journal*, but now taken as 'book consisting of a journal'.] A daybook of any kind; a diary of events; a book containing daily records.

Journalese (dʒɔ̄ɹnălī·z). *colloq.* 1882. [f. JOURNAL *sb.* + -ESE.] 'Newspaper' or 'penny-a-liner's' English.

Journalism (dʒɔ̄·ɹnăliz'm). 1833. [– Fr. *journalisme*, f. *journal*; see -ISM.] **1.** The occupation or profession of a journalist; journalistic writing; the public journals collectively. **2.** The practice of keeping a journal 1848.

Journalist (dʒɔ̄·ɹnălist). 1665. [f. JOURNAL + -IST. Cf. Fr. *journaliste*.] **1.** One who earns his living by editing or writing for a public journal or journals. **2.** One who keeps a journal 1712.

Journalistic (dʒɔ̄ɹnăli·stik), *a.* 1829. [f. prec. + -IC.] **1.** Of or pertaining to journals or journalism; connected with journalism. **2.** Addicted to journalism (*rare*) 1833.

Journalize (dʒɔ̄·ɹnăləiz), *v.* 1766. [f. JOURNAL + -IZE.] **1.** *trans.* To enter in a journal or book for daily accounts; *spec.* in *Book-keeping* (see JOURNAL *sb.* I. 3). **2.** To enter, record, or describe in or as in a private journal 1775. **3.** *intr.* To make entries in or keep a journal 1774. **4.** To do the work of a journalist 1864.

Journey (dʒɔ̄·ɹni), *sb.* ME. [– OFr. *jornee* (mod. *journée* day, day's work or travel) :– Rom. **diurnata*, f. L. *diurnum* daily portion, in late L. day, subst. use of n. of *diurnus*, f. *dies* day. Cf. DIURNAL.] †**I.** A day –1656.

†*Journeys accounts (Law)*, med.L. *diatæ computatæ* 'days counted', the number of days (usually fifteen) after the abatement of a writ within which a new writ might be obtained.

II. 1. A day's travel; the distance travelled in a day or a specified number of days ME. **2.** A spell of going or travelling, viewed as a distinct whole; an excursion or expedition to some distance; a round of travel. Usu. applied to land-travel, as dist. from a *voyage* by sea. Also *fig.* and *transf.* ME. †**3.** A military expedition, a campaign, etc. –1617.

1. Trent is. . thre dayes Iorney on this syde Venise 1560. We travelled onward by short journeys JOHNSON. **2.** Phr. *A j. by rail, on foot; j. to London, into the country*, etc. *To make* or *undertake a j.* And at parting. . they wish him a happy iourney MORYSON. *fig.* This life. . is a j., or rather one stage of our j. through matter TUCKER.

III. 1. A day's work; hence, a certain fixed amount of daily labour; a daily spell or turn of work. *Obs.* exc. *dial.* ME. †**2.** A day's doings; *gen.* business, affair –1672. †**3.** *esp.* A day's fighting; a battle, a fight –1617. **4.** A round or turn of work, such as is done at one time, in a day or a shorter space 1600; colloq. phr. *this journey*, on this occasion 1884.

Journey (dʒɔ̄·ɹni), *v.* ME. [– AFr. *journeyer*, OFr. *jo(u)rnoyer, -ier, -éer*, f. *jornee* JOURNEY *sb.*] **1.** *intr.* To make or proceed on a journey; to travel. Also *fig.* **2.** *trans.* To travel, traverse. ? *Obs.* 1531. †**3.** To ride or drive (a horse) –1607.

1. Satan had journied on, pensive and slow MILT. *P.L.* IV. 173. **2.** I journeyed many a land SCOTT. Hence **Jou·rneyer,** a traveller 1566.

Journeyman (dʒɔ̄·ɹnimæ̆n). 1424. [f. JOURNEY *sb.* III. 1 + MAN.] **1.** One who, having served his apprenticeship to a handicraft or trade, is qualified to work at it for days' wages; a qualified mechanic or artisan who works for another. Dist. on one side from *apprentice*, on the other from *master*. Also *fig.* a drudge, hireling. **2.** *Astron.* More fully, *journeyman clock*: a secondary clock in an observatory, used to compare with standard clocks 1764. **3.** *attrib.*, as *j. tailor*, etc. 1476.

1. *fig.* I haue thought some of Natures Iourneymen had made men, and not made them well SHAKS.

Journey-work (dʒɔ̄·ɹniwɔ̄ɹk). 1601. [f. as prec.] **1.** Work done for daily wages or for hire; the work of a journeyman. **2.** *fig.* Inferior or inefficient work; hackwork 1614.

Joust, *sb.* and *v.* **Jouster,** etc., common variant spellings of JUST, JUSTER, etc.

Jove (dʒōᵘv). ME. [– L. *Jovis, Jovem*, etc., obl. cases of OL. *Jovis*; see next.] **1.** = JUPITER 1. **2.** The planet Jupiter (*poet.*) ME. **b.** *Her.* = Azure 1562; **c.** *Alch.* Tin 1599.

1. Colloq. in the asseveration *By J.*; cf. L. *pro Juppiter, pro Jovem*.

Jovial (dʒōᵘ·viăl), *a.* 1590. [– Fr. *jovial* (XVI) – late L. *jovialis*, f. L. *Jovis, Jovem*, etc., obl. cases of OL. *Jovis* (for which cl. L. had JUPITER).] †**1.** Of or pertaining to Jove; Jove-like –1611. **2.** Of or belonging to the planet Jupiter 1665. †**3.** *Her.* Azure in colour. HOLLAND. †**4.** *Alchemy*. Of tin. SALMON. **5.** *Astrol.* Under the influence of the planet Jupiter, which made those born under it joyful and happy. Also *absol.* as *sb.* –1863. **6.** Merry, jolly; convivial 1592.

1. This princely j. fowl [the eagle] DRAYTON. **2.** Saturn. . hath several. . lesser Planets, like the J. Satellites 1690. **5.** According to that Star. . the Aspect of one is Saturnine, of another Jovial, etc. STANLEY. **6.** Be bright and Iouiall among your Guests to Night *Macb.* III. ii. 28. Hence **Jo·vially** *adv.*, **-ness.**

†**Jo·vialist.** 1569. [f. prec. + -IST.] **1.** A person born under the planet Jupiter –1653. **2.** A person of a jovial disposition –1656.

Joviality (dʒōᵘviæ·lĭti). 1626. [f. JOVIAL + -ITY. Cf. Fr. *jovialité* (XVII).] The quality of being jovial; good-fellowship; conviviality. var. **Jo·vialty** (now *rare*) 1621.

Jovialize (dʒōᵘ·viăləiz), *v.* 1614. [f. as prec. + -IZE.] To make or †be jovial.

Jovian (dʒōᵘ·viăn), *a.* (*sb.*) 1530. [f. L. *Jovis* JOVE + -AN. Cf. Fr. †*jovien* (XVI).] **1.** Of, belonging to, or of the nature of Jove. **2.** Of or belonging to the planet Jupiter 1794. **3.** *sb.* One who resembles or imitates Jove. MARSTON.

Jovice·ntric, *a.* 1864. [f. *Jovi-* as comb. form of JOVE + CENTRIC.] *Astron.* Referred to Jupiter as a centre; viewed as from the centre of Jupiter.

Jovinianist (dʒovi·niănist). 1449. [f. *Jovinianus* Jovinian + -IST. Cf. med.L. *Jovinianus* adj. (XIII), whence *Jovinian* (see below).] A follower or adherent of Jovinian, a monk of the 4th c., who denied the virginity of Mary, opposed certain forms of celibacy and asceticism, and maintained the equality of all sins, rewards, and punishments. Also *attrib.* So **Jovi·nian** = prec. 1585.

†**Jo·vy,** *a.* ME. [– late L. *Jovius*, f. *Jovis* JOVE.] Jovial –1667.

Jowl, jole (dʒōᵘl, dʒaul), *sb.*[1] [Later form of *chawle*, reduction of ME. *chavel*, OE. *ċeafl*, corresp. to OS. **kaɓal* (in dat. pl. *kaflun*), Flem. *kavel* gum, rel. to MHG. *kivel*, Du. *kevel*.] **1.** A jawbone, a 'chaft'; a jaw; esp. the under jaw; *pl.* Jaws. **2.** Idle or malicious talk; = JAW *sb.* 6. –1589. **3.** The cheek, a cheek 1668.

1. His mouth was too large and his jowl too heavy BESANT. **3.** *Cheek by jowl*, in earlier use *cheek by cheek*; see CHEEK *sb.*

Jowl, jole (dʒōᵘl, dʒaul), *sb.*[2] [Later form of ME. *cholle* (XIV), OE. *ċeole, -u* = OS., OHG. *kela* (G. *kehle*), throat, gullet, synon. with ME. *choller*, OE. *ċeolur* = OHG. *kelur* (cf. Skr. *gala*).] The external throat or neck when fat or prominent; the dewlap of cattle; the crop or the wattle of a bird, etc.

Jowl, jole (dʒōᵘl, dʒaul), *sb.*[3] [Later form of *cholle* (XIV), of unkn. origin; the *j*-forms appear earlier in this word than in JOWL *sb.*[1] and [2].] †**1.** The head of a man or beast –1825. **2.** *spec.* The head of a fish; hence (as a cut or dish) the head and shoulders of salmon, sturgeon, or ling ME.

Jowl, joll (dʒōᵘl), *sb.*[4] Now *dial.* 1520. [f. JOWL, JOLL *v.*] **1.** A bump; a blow, esp. on the head; a knock, a stroke. **2.** A single stroke of a bell. Chiefly *dial.* 1822.

Jowl, joll (dʒōᵘl), *v.* Now *dial.* ME. [perh. f. JOWL *sb.*[3], the notion app. being to knock a head or ball. Cf. JOLT *v.*] **1.** *trans.* To strike (a ball) with a stick. **2.** To bump; to strike, knock, or push; esp. to dash (the head) against something 1470. **3.** *trans.* To strike (the wall of a coal-pit), as a signal, etc. 1825. **4.** *intr.* and *trans.* To knell, or ring slowly, as a bell. Chiefly *dial.*

2. That Scull. . how the knaue iowles it to th' grownd *Haml.* V. i. 84.

Jowled (dʒōᵘld), *a.* 1614. [f. JOWL *sb.*[1] + -ED[2].] Having jowls or jaws (of a specified kind).

The crowd about the. . doors—blue-jowled Portuguese KIPLING.

Jowler (dʒōᵘ·ləɹ, dʒau·ləɹ). *Obs.* exc. *dial.* [f. as prec. + -ER[1].] A heavy-jawed dog. Also, a quasi-proper name for a dog.

Jowter (dʒau·təɹ). *dial.* 1463. [Of unkn. origin.] A fish-hawker. Also, A hawker of any kind.

Joy (dʒoi), *sb.* ME. [– OFr. *joie, joye* (mod. *joie*) :– Rom. **gaudia*, fem. for L. *gaudia*, pl. of *gaudium* joy, f. *gaudēre*.] **1.** Pleasurable emotion due to well-being or satisfaction; the feeling or state of being highly pleased; exultation of spirit; gladness, delight. Also with *a* and *pl.* **b.** The expression of glad feeling; mirth ME. **c.** Used interjectionally 1719. **2.** A pleasurable state or condition; a state of felicity; hence, the place of bliss, paradise. *Obs.* or *arch.* ME. **3.** A source or object of joy; a delight ME. **b.** As a term of endearment (esp. *dial.*) 1590. †**4.** = GLORY 4 –1483. †**5.** A jewel –1824.

1. They that sow in teares: shall reape in ioy *Ps.* 126:5. A j. in which I cannot rejoice TENNYSON. **b.** Breake foorth into ioy, sing together, yee waste places *Isa.* 52:9. **2.** So that at the last we may come to hys eternall ioye *Bk. Com. Prayer* 1552. **3.** The hyll of Sion is a fayre place, & the ioye of the whole earth BIBLE (Great) *Ps.* 48:2. **b.** His remembrance lay In Egypt with his joy SHAKS.

Comb.: **j.-bells, -fire, -gun,** bells rung, a bonfire lighted [Fr. *feu de joie*], or a gun fired to celebrate a joyful event; **-ride** (orig. *U.S.*), a ride in a motor-car without the owner's leave; hence *gen.*; **-stick,** the lever controlling the wing and tail planes of an aeroplane 1917; **-weed,** a plant of the genus *Alternanthera*.

Joy (dʒoi), *v.* ME. [– OFr. *joïr* (mod. *jouir*) :– Rom. **gaudire* for L. *gaudēre* rejoice.] †**1.** *refl.* To experience joy; to enjoy oneself; to rejoice –1712. **2.** *intr.* To feel or manifest joy; to be glad; to rejoice or delight ME. †**b.** *trans.* To rejoice at –1647. **3.** *trans.* To fill with joy; to gladden, delight ME. **4.** To derive enjoyment from; to enjoy. †Formerly, also, To have the use or benefit of. ME. †**5.** *trans.* To salute with expressions of joy, welcome, or honour; in early use, to glorify, extol –1725. †**b.** To wish joy *of*; to congratulate. Const. *of* (*in*). –1701.

1. He has never joyed himself since ADDISON. **2.** I shall neuer ioy in my herte vnto the tyme I haue slayne the LD. BERNERS. I j. to see you

1741. **3.** It joyes mee to heere thy soule prospereth CROMWELL. **4.** Who might have liv'd and joy'd immortal bliss MILT. *P.L.* IX. 1166. **5.** The faithful servant joy'd his unknown lord POPE. **b.** I come to j. you of a Crown ROWE.

Joyance (dʒoi·ăns). Chiefly *poet.* 1586. [f. JOY *v.* + -ANCE (Spenser).] **1.** Rejoicing; delight; enjoyment 1590. **2.** Festivity, merrymaking 1586. **3.** Joyous character or quality; delight, charm 1847.

1. Chearfull, fresh and full of ioyance glad SPENSER. **2.** His sports were faire, his ioyance innocent SPENSER. **3.** An illimitable distance of sylvan j. DISRAELI. So **Joy·ancy,** joyousness 1849. **Joy·ant** *a.* joyous 1670.

Joyful (dʒoi·fŭl), *a.* ME. [f. JOY *sb.* + -FUL.] **1.** Full of joy; having and showing joy; delighted. **2.** Expressing or manifesting joy; indicative of gladness ME. **3.** Fraught with or causing joy; delightful ME.

1. A ioyfull mother of two goodly sonnes SHAKS. **2.** Make a ioyfull noise vnto God *Ps.* 66:1. **3.** J. news 1592. Hence **Joy·ful-ly** *adv.*, **-ness.**

Joyless (dʒoi·lĕs), *a.* ME. [f. as prec. + -LESS.] **1.** Destitute of joy; sad, cheerless. **2.** Causing no joy; dismal, dreary ME.

1. A j. smile SHAKS. **2.** Doomed To eat his j. bread, lonely 1804. Hence **Joy·less-ly** *adv.*, **-ness.**

Joyous (dʒoi·əs), *a.* ME. [– AFr. *joyous*, OFr. *joios* (mod. *joyeux*), f. *joie* JOY *sb.*; see -OUS.] **1.** = JOYFUL 1, 2. **2.** = JOYFUL 3. 1450.

1. A citie full of bruit, a ioyous citie BIBLE (Genev.) *Isa.* 22:2. A j. laugh HARE. **2.** That j. season [harvest] 1796. Hence **Joy·ous-ly** *adv.*, **-ness.**

Joy·some, *a. rare.* 1613. [f. JOY *sb.* + -SOME¹.] Fraught with joy, gladsome.

Juba (dʒū·bă). *U.S.* 1834. [Negro.] A breakdown performed by plantation negroes of the Southern U.S., accompanied by repeated cries of *juba*.

Jubardy: see JEOPARDY.

Jubate (dʒū·bĕt), *a.* 1826. [– L. *jubatus*, f. *juba* mane; see -ATE².] *Zool.* Having a mane, or a fringe of hair like a mane.

‖**Jubbah** (dʒɒ·bă, dʒu·bbă). 1548. [– Arab. *jubba*, whence also Fr. *jupe*. Cf. JIBBAH.] An outer garment worn by Moslems and Parsees, consisting of a long cloth coat, open in front, with sleeves reaching nearly to the wrists.

‖**Jube** (dʒū·bi). 1725. [– Fr. *jubé* – L. *jube*, imper. of *jubēre* bid, order, first word of the formula *Jube, domine, benedicere* Sir, bid a blessing, addressed by the deacon to the celebrant before the reading of the Gospel, which, in some places, was done from the rood-loft.] **1.** A rood-loft or screen and gallery dividing the choir from the nave 1767. †**2.** A chair for the preacher, ordinarily placed within the enclosure of the choir 1725.

Jubilant (dʒū·bilănt), *a.* 1667. [– *jubilant-*, pr. ppl. stem of L. *jubilare*; see JUBILATE *v.*, -ANT.] Making a joyful noise; now generally, Making demonstrations of joy, exultingly glad. **b.** Expressing joy 1784.

Amid a mighty nation j. COLERIDGE. Hence **Ju·bilance, -ancy. Ju·bilantly** *adv.*

†**Ju·bilar,** *a.* 1613. [– med.L. *jubilarius*, prop. 'one that has continued 50 years in the same state'; see -AR².] = JUBILARY. **Jubila·rian** [f. as prec. + -AN.] *R.C.Ch.* a priest, monk, or nun who has been such for fifty years 1782. †**Ju·bilary** *a.* [f. as prec.; see -ARY.], of or pertaining to a jubilee, jubilar 1537.

‖**Jubilate** (dʒūbilēⁱ·ti, yūbilā·te), *sb.* ME. [L. *jubilate* 'shout (for joy)', imper. of *jubilare* (see next).] **1.** The hundredth psalm (*Jubilate Deo*, O be joyful in the Lord), used as a canticle in the Anglican service; also, the music to which this is set. **2.** *transf.* A call to rejoice; an outburst of triumph 1767. **3.** *R. C. Ch.* The third Sunday after Easter, so called because Ps. 66, which begins with *Jubilate*, is used as the introit on that day.

Jubilate (dʒū·bileⁱt), *v.* 1604. [– *jubilat-*, pa. ppl. stem of L. *jubilare* (rustic word) call, halloo, (in Chr. writers) shout for joy; see -ATE³.] †**1.** *trans.* To make glad. **2.** *intr.* To utter sounds of joy or exultation; to rejoice, exult 1641.

Jubilation (dʒūbilēⁱ·ʃən). ME. [– L. *jubilatio*, f. as prec.; see -ION.] The action of jubilating; exultation, gladness; public rejoicing. Also with *a* and *pl.*

Disconsolate amidst the publique Iubilations 1634.

†**Jubile·al,** *a. Obs.* 1588. [f. next + -AL¹.] Of jubilee. So **Jubile·an** *a.* 1624.

Jubilee (dʒū·bilī). Also †**jubile.** ME. [– (O)Fr. *jubilé* – Chr. L. *jubilæus* (sc. *annus* year) – (with assim. to *jubilare* JUBILATE *v.*) Chr. Gr. ἰωβηλαῖος, f. ἰώβηλος – Heb. *yōbēl* jubilee, orig. ram, (hence) ram's horn, with which the jubilee year was proclaimed.] **1.** *Jewish Hist.* (more fully *year of Jubilee*). A year of emancipation and restoration, which was to be kept every fifty years, and to be proclaimed by the blast of trumpets throughout the land; during it the fields were to be left untilled, Hebrew slaves were to be set free, and lands and houses in the open country or unwalled towns that had been sold were to revert to their former owners or their heirs. **b.** *fig.* or *transf.* A time of restitution, remission, or release 1584. **2.** *R. C. Ch.* A year of remission during which plenary indulgence may be obtained by a pilgrimage to Rome and certain pious works ME. **3.** The fiftieth anniversary of an event ME. †**b.** A period of fifty years –1726. **4.** A season or occasion of general rejoicing 1592. **5.** Exultant joy, jubilation 1526. **b.** Shouting; sound of jubilation 1526. **6.** *attrib.* ME.

1. And ye shall hallow the fiftieth yeere..It shalbe a Iubile vnto you *Lev.* 25:10. **b.** The first day of our J. is Death SIR T. BROWNE. **3.** *Silver J.* (after *Silver Wedding*), celebration of the twenty-fifth anniversary. *Diamond J.*, a name applied to the celebration of the sixtieth year of the reign of Queen Victoria. **5. b.** All along the crowded way Was j. and loud huzza SCOTT.

Jubilize (dʒū·biləiz), *v.* 1649. [In sense a, f. †*jubil* JUBILATE *v.*; in b, f. JUBILEE; see -IZE.] *intr.* **a.** To jubilate. **b.** To celebrate a jubilee.

Jucundity (dʒukɒ·ndĭti). ? *Obs.* 1536. [– L. *jucunditas*, f. *jucundus* JOCUND; see -ITY.] **1.** The quality of being pleasant; enjoyableness 1620. **2.** = JOCUNDITY 1536.

Judæo- (dʒiudī,o), used as comb. f. L. *judæus* Jewish, as in *Judæologist* (1858), *Judæo-Christian.*

Judaic (dʒudē·ik), *a.* 1611. [– L. *Judaicus* – Gr. Ἰουδαϊκός, f. Ἰουδαῖος JEW.] Of or pertaining to the Jews, Jewish. So **Juda·ical** *a.* 1470, **Juda·ically** *adv.* 1582.

Judaism (dʒū·dĕ,iz'm). 1494. [– Chr. L. *Judaismus* – Gr. Ἰουδαϊσμός (2 Macc. 2:21), f. Ἰουδαῖος JEW; see -ISM.] **1.** The profession or practice of the Jewish religion; the religious system or polity of the Jews. **2.** The act of Judaizing; a practice or style of thought like that of the Jews 1641. **3.** *Hist.* As tr. med.L. *Judaismus* = JEWRY 2; also, the revenue derived by the Crown from the Jews; the treasury which received the money 1782. Hence **Ju·daist,** a Judaizer. **Judai·stic** *a.* of, pertaining to, or characteristic of, Judaists.

Judaize (dʒū·dĕ,əiz), *v.* 1582. [– Chr. L. *judaizare* – Gr. ἰουδαΐζειν (Gal. 2:14); see -IZE.] **1.** *intr.* To play the Jew; to follow Jewish customs, religious rites, or practice. **2.** *trans.* To make Jewish; to imbue with Jewish doctrines or principles 1653.

1. That Vsurers should haue Orange-tawney Bonnets, because they doe Iudaize BACON. **2.** Error..in many other Points of Religion had miserably judaiz'd the Church MILTON. Hence **Judaiza·tion,** a becoming or making Jewish in character. **Ju·daizer,** one who adheres to Jewish ritual or practice.

Judas (dʒū·dăs). 1453. [– L. (Vulgate) *Judas, Juda* – Gr. Ἰούδας – Heb. *yᵉhūḏāh* Judah, one of the sons of Jacob, whence later a common Jewish name. In sense 3 – Fr. *judas.*] **1.** The name of the disciple who betrayed Jesus Christ; hence: One who betrays under the semblance of friendship; a traitor of the worst kind 1489. **2.** A painted socket of wood in which the paschal candle was set. *Hist.* 1453 (1310 in Anglo-Latin). **3.** A small lattice or aperture in a door, through which a person can look without being noticed from the other side 1865.

Comb.: **J.-blossom,** the blossom of the JUDAS-TREE; **-colour, -coloured** *a.* (of the hair or beard) red (from a mediæval belief that Judas Iscariot had red hair and beard); **-hole, -trap** = sense 3; **kiss; -like** *a.* and *adv.* Hence †**Judasly** *adv.*, treacherously 1508–1659.

Ju·das-tree. 1668. [From a popular belief that Judas hanged himself on a tree of this kind. So G. *Judasbaum*, Fr. *arbre de Judée.*] **1.** The common name of *Cercis siliquastrum*, a leguminous tree of Southern Europe and parts of Asia, with abundant purple flowers which appear in spring before the leaves. **2.** A local name for Elder (*Sambucus nigra*); see under JEW'S EAR.

Judcock (dʒɒ·dkǫk). 1621. [app. for *judge-cock* from its black crown compared to the judge's black cap.] The Jack Snipe.

Judge (dʒɒdʒ), *sb.* [ME. *juge* – (O)Fr. *juge* :– L. *judex, judic-*, f. *jus* right, law + *-dicus* speaking.] **1.** A public officer appointed to administer the law; one who has authority to hear and try cases in a court of justice. **2.** Used of God or Christ, as supreme arbiter, pronouncing sentence on men and moral beings ME. **3.** *Heb. Hist.* An officer (usually a leader in war) invested with temporary authority in ancient Israel in the period between Joshua and the kings. **b.** *pl.* (in full, *the Book of Judges*): the seventh book of the Old Testament, containing the history of this period. ME. **4.** A person appointed to decide in any contest, competition, or dispute; an arbiter, umpire ME. **5.** One who or that which judges of anything in question. Often in phr. *to be judge.* 1470. **6.** A person qualified to form or pronounce an opinion 1560. **7.** *Mining.* A staff used for gauging the depth of the holing 1875.

1. Ivdges ought to remember, that their office is *Ius dicere*, and not *Ius dare*; to interprete law, and not to make law, or giue Law BACON. *Circuit-j.*, a j. of a circuit court. *J. ordinary*, spec. the j. of the Court of Probate and Divorce, previous to 1875. *J.-advocate, j. in eyre, puisne j.*, etc: see ADVOCATE, etc. **2.** Shall not the Iudge of all the earth doe right? *Gen.* 18:25. **4.** He was one of the judges at a flower-show 1901. **5.** Well, thou shalt see: thy eyes shall be thy iudge SHAKS. **6.** I here disallow thee to be a competent j. WALTON. *Comb.* **j.-made** *a.* (of law), constituted by judicial decisions. Hence **Ju·dgeship,** the office of a j. 1677.

Judge (dʒɒdʒ), *v.* ME. [– OFr. *jugier*, later and mod. *juger* :– L. *judicare*, f. *judex*; see prec.]

I. *trans.* **1.** To try, or pronounce sentence upon (a person) in a court of justice; to sit in judgement upon. (Also said of God or Christ: cf. prec. 2.) †**2.** *spec.* To sentence, condemn –1675. **3.** To give sentence concerning (a matter); to try (a cause); to decide (a question) 1513. **4.** To decree, order ME. **5.** To assign or award by judgement. Now *rare* or *Obs.* ME. **6.** To govern or rule as an Israelitish judge (cf. prec. 3). Also *absol.* To hold the office of a judge. ME. **7.** To declare authoritatively (a person) to be (so-and-so). ? *Obs.* ME. **8.** To form an opinion about; to estimate; to appraise ME. **9.** To criticize; *esp.* to condemn, censure. Also *absol.* ME. **10.** To apprehend, think, consider, suppose; to conclude, suppose to be ME.

1. Then all thy Saints assembl'd, thou shalt j. Bad men and Angels MILT. *P.L.* III. 330. **3.** J. and defend my cause, O Lord TATE & BRADY. **5.** Ladies whose bright eyes..j. the prize Of wit or arms MILT. **6.** The example of Debora..when she judged Israel KNOX. **7.** Hee was iudged an vnprofitable seruant MORYSON. **8.** Men iudge by the complexion of the Skie The state and inclination of the day SHAKS. **9.** Iudge not lest ye be iudged. For as ye iudge so shal ye be iudged TINDALE *Matt.* 7:1, 2. **10.** Small townes I j. they were 1615. It was..judged better to begin the attack at once FREEMAN.

II. *intr.* **1.** To act as judge; to sit in judgement ME. **2.** To give a decision or opinion on any matter; *esp.* to arbitrate ME. **3.** To form an opinion; to arrive at a notion, esp. a sound or correct notion, about something; in *Logic*, To apprehend mentally the relation of two objects; to make a mental assertion or statement. Const. *of.* ME.

1. As for Civill matters they may j. without appeale 1639. **2.** God must j. 'twixt man and me BROWNING. **3.** When the mind assents to a proposition it judges MILL. From its form and colour he could..j. of its condition TYNDALL.

Judgement, judgment (dʒɒ·dʒmĕnt). ME. [– (O)Fr. *jugement*, f. *juger*; see prec., -MENT.] **1.** The action of trying a cause in a court of justice; trial. (Now *rare* or merged in 3.). **2.** The trial of moral beings by God (or Christ) as Judge; *spec.* the final trial at the end of the world. Often in *day of j.* ME. **3.** The sentence of a court of justice; a judicial decision or order in court ME. **b.** *Law.* (*ellipt.*) An assignment of chattels, etc. made by judgement or decree of court; the certificate of such judgement as a security 1677. **4.** Divine sentence or decision; *spec.* a misfortune or calamity regarded as a divine visitation or the like ME. **5.** Any formal or authoritative decision, as of an arbiter. (Now *rare*) ME. **6.** Criticism; censure ME. **7.** An opinion, estimate ME. †**b.** A form of religious opinion or belief; a 'persuasion' –1687. **8.** The faculty of judging; that function of the mind whereby it arrives at a notion of anything; the critical faculty; discernment 1535. **b.** Discernment, discretion, understanding, good sense 1576. †**c.** *transf.* A person having good judgement; a 'judge' –1682. **9.** *Logic.* The action of mentally apprehending the relation between two objects of thought; prediction, as an act of the mind. With *pl.* A mental assertion or statement. 1704. **10.** In biblical uses, chiefly as tr. Heb. *mišpāt.* **a.** Justice, righteousness, equity ME. **b.** A (divine) decree, ordinance, law, statute ME. **c.** (One's) right 1611. †**11.** The function of a judge or ruler (in ancient Israel). KNOX. **12.** *attrib.* 1526.

1. A Daniel come to iudgement, yea a Daniel SHAKS. Phr. *To sit in j.*: (*a*) *lit.* to preside as judge at a trial; (*b*) *fig.* to pass j. *upon* (see 6), to judge, criticize (with assumed superiority). **3.** He confessed the Inditement, and so had Iudgement to bee hanged HALL. **b.** Upon a marriage, a mother assigned an unregistered judgement to a trustee for her daughter for life 1858. **4.** Hence I tooke a thought, This was a Iudgement on me SHAKS. **5.** *Haml.* v. ii. 291. **6.** You have my designs, and I desire your judgment of them RAY. **7.** This waye in my iudgement doeth excell all the rest 1559. *Private j.*: formation of individual opinion (esp. in religious matters), as opp. to acceptance of a statement or doctrine on authority. **8. b.** A deed..owing more To want of judgment than to wrong design COWPER. **9.** A Judgment, then, is an expression that two notions can or cannot be reconciled ABP. THOMSON. **10. a.** *Isa.* 61:8. **b.** *Exod.* 21:1. **c.** *Deut.* 10:18.

Comb: **j. creditor,** a creditor in whose favour a j. has been given ordering the payment of the debt due to him; **j. debt,** a debt for the payment of which a j. has been given; **j. debtor,** a debtor against whom such a j. has been given; **j. summons,** a summons issued in a County Court against a *judgement debtor*, to show cause why he should not be imprisoned for default in payment. Hence †**Ju·dgemented** *a.* 1548–1821, **Ju·dgementless** *a.* 1590.

Ju·dg(e)ment-day. 1591. [= *day of judgement*; see prec. 2.] The day of God's final judgement; the last day; doomsday.

Ju·dg(e)ment-hall. 1534. A hall in which trials at law are held; a court of justice; a tribunal. (Chiefly *Hist.*)

Ju·dg(e)ment-seat. 1526. The seat on which a judge sits when trying a cause or pronouncing judgement; a tribunal.

He was driven from the judgement-seat with scorn FREEMAN.

Judger (dʒɒ·dʒəɹ). 1449. [f. JUDGE *v.* + -ER[1].] One who or that which judges.

Judgmatic, -al (dʒɒdʒmæ·tik, -ăl), *a. colloq.* 1774. [irreg. f. JUDGE + *-matic*, after *dogmatic.*] Judicious, discerning.

Judicable (dʒū·dikăb'l), *a.* Now *rare.* 1647. [– late L. *judicabilis*, f. *judicare* judge; see -ABLE.] Capable of being judged; liable to judgement.

Judica·tion. 1625. [– L. *judicatio*, f. *judicat-*, pa. ppl. stem of *judicare*, f. *judex, judic-* JUDGE; see -ION.] The action of judging, judgement.

Judicative (dʒū·dikĕtiv), *a.* 1641. [– med.L. *judicativus*, f. *judicat-*, pa. ppl. stem of L. *judicare*; see prec., -ATIVE.] Having the function of judging; judicial.

Appeals to their j. faculties 1678.

Judicatory (dʒū·dikătŏri, -di·kătŏri), *sb.* 1575. [– late L. *judicatorium* (glossing Gr. δικαστήριον), f. as prec.; see -ORY[1]. In sense 2 – med.L. in same sense (cf. Fr. †*judicatoire* sb.).] **1.** A court of judicature; a tribunal. Chiefly *Sc.* 1606. Also *transf.* and *fig.* **2.** Judicature; a system of judicature.

2. The Lords, as the Supreme Court of J. CLARENDON.

Ju·dicatory, *a.* ? *Obs.* 1603. [– late (eccl.)L. *judicatorius* pertaining to judgement, f. as prec.; see -ORY[2]. Cf. Fr. †*judicatoire* in same sense.] **1.** Having the function of judging or passing sentence; of or pertaining to judgement 1647. **2.** By which a judgement may be made; critical.

1. A great Share in the j. Power PENN.

Judicature (dʒū·dikătiŭɹ, -e[i]tiŭɹ). 1530. [f. med.L. *judicatura*, f. as prec.; see -URE. Cf. Fr. *judicature.*] **1.** The action of judging; administration of justice; judicial process. **2.** The office, function, or authority of a judge 1530. **b.** Extent of jurisdiction of a judge or court. BOUVIER. **3.** A body of judges; a legal tribunal, or such tribunals collectively 1593. †**4.** *fig.* Mental judgement; criticism –1758. †**5.** Judicial (as opp. to moral) quality. MILT. **6.** *attrib.* 1873.

1. We have demonstratively shewed..that J. is nothing else but an Interpretation of the Laws HOBBES. *Supreme Court of J. in England*, that constituted by Acts of Parliament in 1873 and 1875, in which were united the Courts of Chancery, King's Bench, Common Pleas, Exchequer, Admiralty, etc. **5.** Our Saviour disputes not here the J.,..but the morality of Divorce, whether it be Adultery or no 1643. **6. Judicature Acts,** a name given to the statutes establishing the Supreme Court of J., and regulating its practice.

Judicial (dʒudi·ʃăl). ME. [– L. *judicialis*, f. *judicium* judgement, f. *judex, judic-* judge; see -IAL.]

A. *adj.* **1.** Of or belonging to judgement in a court of law, or to a judge in relation to this function; pertaining to the administration of justice; proper to a legal tribunal; resulting from or fixed by a judgement in court. Also *fig.* **b.** Enforced by secular judges and tribunals; in *j. law*, opp. to *moral* and *ceremonial* ME. **c.** *Theol.* Inflicted by God as a judgement; of the nature of a divine judgement 1613. **2.** Having the function of judgement 1561. **3.** Of a judge; proper to a judge 1800. **4.** Giving judgement upon any matter; forming or expressing a judgement; critical 1589. **b.** *Astrol.* Relating to the judgement of the influence of stars· upon human affairs CHAUCER. †**5.** Judicious –1624.

1. J. separation is a new term introduced for the old divorce *a mensâ et thoro* 1858. *Judicial murder*, an unjust though legal death sentence. **c.** What is called a j. blindness BURKE. **2.** Parliaments were originally j. as well as legislative assemblies H. COX. *J. combat* (*duel*), one engaged in for formal decision of a controversy. *J. Committee of the Privy Council*: one of the two Appellate Tribunals in Great Britain, established in 1832 for the disposal of appeals made to the King in Council. **3.** Phr. *Purity of the j. ermine.* Hence **Judicia·lity** 1621. **Judi·cial-ly** *adv.*, **-ness.**

B. *sb.* [The adj. used ellipt.] †**1.** A judicial law or ordinance; see A. 1 b –1721. †**2.** Determination, decision, judgement –1631. †**b.** *Astrol.* A determination as to a future event from the positions of the heavenly bodies 1496–1652. †**3.** A legal judgement –1660.

Judiciary (dʒudi·ʃ[i]ări). Now *rare.* 1587. [– L. *judiciarius*, f. as prec.; see -ARY[1]. With B. *sb.* 1 cf. med.L. *judiciarius* adj. (XIV) judicial (*Astr.*) and Fr. (*astrologie*) *judiciaire.*] **A.** *adj.* = JUDICIAL A. 1604. **B.** *sb.* **1.** Judicial astrology; a judicial astrologer. 1587. **2.** = JUDICATURE 3. 1802.

Judicious (dʒudi·ʃəs), *a.* 1591. [– Fr. *judicieux*, f. L. *judicium* (whence Fr. †*judice*); see -OUS.] **1.** Having or exercising sound judgement; discreet, wise, sensible; *esp.* in relation to practical matters. **2.** Proceeding from or showing sound judgement; marked by discretion, wisdom, or good sense 1600. †**3.** = JUDICIAL A. 1. –1632.

1. Now this ouer-done..cannot but make the Iudicious greeue *Haml.* III. ii. 29. A j. pilot 1704. **2.** J. purchases 1833. A j. remark 1861. **3.** His last offences to vs Shall haue Iudicious hearing *Cor.* V. vi. 128. Hence **Judi·cious-ly** *adv.*, **-ness.**

Judy (dʒū·di). 1812. [Familiar form of *Judith.*] Name of the wife of Punch in 'Punch and Judy'; hence (*slang*) applied disparagingly, *esp.* to a woman of ridiculous appearance.

Jug (dʒɒg), *sb.*[1] 1569. A pet-name or familiar substitute for Joan, Joanna, and Jenny; applied as a common noun to a homely woman, maid-servant, sweetheart, or mistress; or in disparagement. Now *rare.*

Whoop Iugge I loue thee *Lear* I. iv. 245.

Jug (dʒɒg), *sb.*[2] 1538. [prob. spec. use of prec.] **1.** A deep vessel for holding liquids, usually with a swelling body, or one that tapers upward, having a handle on one side, and often a spout. Often differentiated, as *brown-, claret-, cream-jug*, etc. **b.** A jug with its contents; the liquid in a jug; *esp.* beer. Also, locally, A measure of capacity for ale or beer, usu. about a pint. 1635. **2.** *slang.* A prison, jail; more fully STONE-JUG 1834.

Comb. **j.-handled** *a. fig.* (*U.S.*), unilateral, one-sided, unbalanced.

Jug (dʒɒg), *sb.*[3] 1523. Imitation of one of the notes of a nightingale, etc.

Jug, *v.*[1] 1681. [f. JUG *sb.*[2]] †**1.** *intr.* To use a jug; to drink. **2.** *trans.* To stew or boil in a jug or jar (esp. a hare) 1747. **3.** *slang.* To shut up in jail. Also *transf.* To confine. 1841. **Jugged** (dʒɒgd) *ppl. a.*, esp. in *jugged hare.*

Jug, *v.*[2] 1598. [imit.; cf. JUG *sb.*[3]] *intr.* To utter a sound like 'jug', as a nightingale.

Jug, *v.*[3] 1600. [app. an altered by-form of JOUK *v.*[1] with specialized application.] *intr.* Of partridges, etc.: To crowd or nestle together on the ground; to collect in a covey. **b.** *trans.* To collect close together 1653.

Jugal (dʒū·găl), *a.* (*sb.*) 1598. [– L. *jugalis*, f. *jugum* YOKE; see -AL[1].] †**1.** Of or relating to a yoke; *esp.* conjugal –1656. **2.** *Anat.* Of or pertaining to the zygoma or bony arch of the cheek; malar, zygomatic 1578. **3.** *sb.* The jugal or malar bone 1854.

Jugate (dʒū·gĕt), *a.* 1887. [– L. *jugatus*, pa. pple. of *jugare* join together; see -ATE[2].] **1.** *Bot.* Of a pinnate leaf: Having leaflets in pairs; usu. in comb. (see BIJUGATE, etc.). Of the leaflets: Paired. **2.** *Numism.* = ACCOLLED 3. 1887.

Ju·gate, *v. rare.* 1623. [– *jugat-*, pa. ppl. stem of L. *jugare*; see prec., -ATE[3].] *trans.* To yoke or couple together. Hence **Ju·gated** *ppl. a.*; in *Bot.* = JUGATE *a.* 1; **Juga·tion,** (*a*) joining, linking 1701; (*b*) a system of land assessment based on the number of yokes of oxen employed 1883.

Juger (dʒū·dʒəɹ). 1853. [– L. *jugerum* (formerly used in Eng.).] An ancient Roman measure of land, containing 28,800 (Roman) square feet, or 240 by 120 (Roman) feet, i.e. about three-fifths of an acre.

Jugful (dʒɒ·gful). 1834. [f. JUG *sb.*[2] + -FUL.] As much as fills a jug.

Juggernaut, ‖**Jagannath** (dʒɒ·gənǫt). 1638. [– Hindi *Jagannath* – Skr. *Jagannātha*, f. *jagat-* world + *nāthás* lord, protector.] **1.** *Hindu Myth.* A title of Krishna, the eighth avater of Vishnu; *spec.* the image of this deity at Pūrī in Orissa, annually dragged in procession on an enormous car, under the wheels of which devotees are said to have thrown themselves to be crushed. Also *attrib.* **2.** *fig.* Anything to which persons blindly devote themselves, or are ruthlessly sacrificed.

2. That remorseless J.—'the needs of man' EDISON.

Juggins (dʒɒ·ginz). *slang.* 1882. [perh. a use of the surname *Juggins*, f. JUG *sb.*[1] + suffix as in *Dickens, Jenkins, Tomkins*; cf. earlier MUGGINS.] A simpleton.

Juggle (dʒɒ·g'l), *sb.*[1] 1657. [f. JUGGLE *v.*] A piece of juggling; a conjurer's trick; hence, an imposture, cheat, fraud.

Ju·ggle, *sb.*[2] 1875. [Of unkn origin.] A block of timber cut to a length, either in the round or split.

Juggle (dʒɒ·g'l), *v.* ME. [Back-formation from JUGGLER, or – OFr. *jogler, jugler* :– L. *joculari* jest, f. *joculus*, dim. of *jocus* JOKE.] †**1.** *intr.* To act as a JUGGLER (sense 1) –1608. **2.** To practise magic or legerdemain; to play conjuring tricks; to conjure 1440. **3.** *transf.* and *fig.* To play tricks so as to cheat or deceive 1528. **4.** *trans.* To deceive by jugglery; to trick, cheat, beguile 1531.

2. The conjurer juggles with two oranges 1885.

3. To j. with Scripture MILT. She never juggles or plays tricks with her understanding LAMB. 4. To j. men out of their Estates SELDEN. Hence **Ju·ggling** *vbl. sb.* and *ppl. a.* **Ju·gglingly** *adv.* (1647).

Juggler (dʒɒ·gləɹ). [ME. *iugelere, iugelour, iogeler* – OFr. *jog-, jug-, jouglere*, acc. *jogleor*, etc. (cf. JONGLEUR) :– L. *joculator, -ator-*, f. *joculari*; see prec., -ER³ 3; also OFr. *jogler* :– med.L. *jocularis* buffoon, subst. use of the adj. (see JOCULAR).] **1.** One who entertains people by stories, songs, buffoonery, tricks, etc.; a jester, buffoon. (Often contempt.) –1591. **2.** †A magician, wizard, sorcerer; a performer of legerdemain; a conjurer OE. **3.** *transf.* and *fig.* One who deceives by trickery ME.

2. After dinner comes in a jugleur, which showed us very pretty tricks PEPYS. 3. The Sophist..is proved to be a dissembler and j. with words JOWETT.

Jugglery (dʒɒ·gləri). ME. [– OFr. *jogle-, juglerie*, f. *jogler*, etc.; see JUGGLE *v.*, -ERY.] **1.** The art or practice of a juggler; conjuring, legerdemain. **2.** *transf.* Trickery, deception 1699.

2. An example of political j. and falsehood 1838.

Jugoslav (yūgoˌslaˑv). 1880. Also **Y-.** [Austrian German, f. Serb. *jugo-*, comb. form of *jug* south + SLAV.] A southern Slav; a member of the state of Jugoslavia, including the Serbs, Croats, and Slovenes. Also adj.

Jugular (dʒū·-, dʒɒ·giŭlăɹ). 1597. [– late L. *jugularis*, f. L. *jugulum* collar-bone, dim. of *jugum* yoke; see -AR¹.]

A. *adj.* **1.** *Anat.* Of, pertaining to, or situated in the neck or throat; *esp.* an epithet of the great veins of the neck, as the *external j. vein*, which conveys the blood from the superficial parts of the head, and the *internal j. vein*, which conveys it from the inside of the skull. **2.** *Ichthyol.* Of a fish: Having the ventral fins situated in front of the pectoral, i.e. in the region of the throat; said also of a ventral fin so situated 1766.

B. *sb.* **1.** *Anat.* Short for *jugular vein* 1614. **2.** *Ichthyol.* A jugular fish (see A. 2) 1835. So †**Ju·gulary** *a.*

Jugulate (dʒū·giŭlēᶦt), *v.* 1623. [– *jugulat-*, pa. ppl. stem of L. *jugulare*, cut the throat of, slay, f. *jugulum*; see next, -ATE³.] **1.** *trans.* To kill by cutting the throat; to put to death. **2.** *fig.* To 'strangle'; *spec.* to stop the course of (a disease) by a powerful remedy 1876.

2. Misplaced attempts to 'jugulate' the disease [pneumonia] ALLBUTT. So **Jugula·tion** (*rare*).

‖**Jugulum** (dʒū·giŭlɒm). 1706. [L., = collar-bone, also neck, throat, dim. formation from *jug-*, stem of *jungere* join.] *Anat.* and *Zool.* A name for the collar-bone; also for the throat or lower front part of the neck, esp. in birds; the analogous part in insects.

‖**Jugum** (dʒū·gɒm). *Pl.* **juga.** 1857. [L. (f. as prec.), = yoke.] *Bot.* **a.** A pair of leaflets in a pinnate leaf. **b.** Each of the ridges on the carpels of *Umbelliferæ*.

Juice (dʒūs), *sb.* ME. [– (O)Fr. *jus* :– L. *jus* broth, sauce, vegetable juice.] **1.** The watery or liquid part of vegetables or fruits, which can be expressed or extracted; *spec.* that of the grape. **2.** The fluid part of an animal body or substance; now usu. in *pl.* the bodily 'humours'; also used in *sing.* in the names of digestive secretions (*gastric j.*, etc.) ME. **3.** *gen.* The moisture naturally contained in or coming from anything ME. **4.** *fig.* Essence, spirit. ME. **5.** *slang.* **a.** Petrol 1909. **b.** Electricity 1903.

1. Wines we have of Grapes; and Drinkes of other Iuyce BACON. 2. Marrow and Fat and Blood, and other Nutritious Juices BENTLEY. 3. The mineral Juyces in the Earth WOODWARD. 4. A theory, pickled in the preserving juices of pulpit eloquence BURKE. Hence **Juice** *v.* (*rare*), to moisten or suffuse with j. **Juiced** *a.* having j. (of a specified quality). **Jui·celess** *a.* devoid of j.; dry (*lit.* and *fig.*).

Juicy (dʒū·si), *a.* ME. [f. prec. + -Y¹.] **1.** Full of juice; succulent. **b.** Of weather: Wet, rainy, soaking (*colloq.*) 1837. **2.** *fig.* Rich in wealth, etc.; the opposite of 'dry' (*colloq.*) 1621. **b.** *Artists' slang.* Characterized by rich liquid colouring 1820. Hence **Jui·cily** *adv.* (*slang*), excellently. **Jui·ciness** (*lit.* and *fig.*).

†**Juˌise.** ME. [– OFr. *juise*, by suffix-exchange for *juice* – L. *judicium* judgement; see -ICE.] Judgement, doom; penalty. Also *transf.* the gibbet. –1480.

Ju-jitsu (dʒūˌdʒi·tsu, dʒū·dʒitsu), *sb.* 1891. Also **jui-, jiu-jitsu, -jutsu.** [– Jap. *jūjutsu* (pron. dʒūdʒitsū), f. *jū* (Chinese *jeu* soft, yielding) + *jutsu, jutsz* (Chinese *shu, shut*) science.] The Japanese system of self-defence without weapons, now widely used as a form of physical training. Hence as *vb.* to overcome by ju-jitsu.

‖**Ju-ju, juju** (dʒū·dʒū). 1863. [gen. thought to be – Fr. *joujou* plaything, redupl. formation on *jouer* play :– L. *jocare*.] An object of any kind superstitiously venerated by W. African native tribes, and used as a charm or amulet; a fetish. Also, the supernatural power attributed to such objects, or the system of observances connected therewith; also, a ban or interdiction effected by means of such an object (cf. *taboo*). Also *attrib.* Hence **Ju·juism, -ist.**

Jujube (dʒū·dʒūb). 1550. [– Fr. *jujube* or med.L. *jujuba*, ult. – L. *zizyphum* – Gr. ζίζυφον.] **1.** An edible berry-like drupe, the fruit of various species of *Zizyphus* (N.O. *Rhamnaceæ*). **b.** Any species producing this fruit, as *Z. vulgaris* of the Mediterranean countries, *Z. jujuba* of China, *Z. lotus* of N. Africa 1562. **2.** A lozenge of gelatin, etc. flavoured with or imitating this fruit 1835.

1. The Lotus-eaters—whose favourite fruit still grows, under the name of the j., on the same coast THIRLWALL.

Comb.: **j. paste**, a jelly made from jujubes, or a confection flavoured with, or in imitation of, them; **-plum** = sense 1; **-tree** = sense 1 b.

Juke, obs. f. JOUK.

Julaceous (dʒulēᶦ·ʃəs), *a. rare.* 1880. [f. L. *julus*, prop. *iulus* IULUS + -ACEOUS.] *Bot.* Catkin-like, amentaceous. GRAY.

Julep (dʒū·lep). ME. [– (O)Fr. *julep*, med.L. *julapium* – Arab. *julāb* – Pers. *gulāb* rose-water, f. *gul* rose + *āb* water.] **1.** A sweet drink variously prepared; *esp.* a liquid sweetened with syrup or sugar, and used as a vehicle. **b.** *transf.* and *fig.* Something to cool or assuage the heat of passion, etc. 1624. **2.** *U.S.* A mixture of brandy, whisky, or other spirit, with sugar, ice, and some flavouring, usu. mint 1804.

1. Vse them with a iuleb of vyolettes 1543.

Julian (dʒū·liăn), *a.* 1592. [– L. *Julianus*, f. *Julius*; see -AN.] Pertaining to Julius Cæsar; used in *Chronol.* in connection with the calendar instituted by him in the year 46 B.C.

Julian account, = 'old style' (see STYLE); *J. calendar* (see CALENDAR *sb.*); *J. epoch, era*, the time from which the Julian calendar dates (46 B.C.); *J. period*, a period of 7,980 Julian years, proposed by Joseph Scaliger in 1582 as a universal standard of comparison of chronology, consisting of the product of the number of years in the solar and lunar cycles and the cycle of the indiction (28 × 19 × 15); *J. year*, a year of the Julian calendar, or the average year (= 365¼ days) of that calendar.

‖**Julienne** (ʒülye·n). 1810. [Fr. (XVIII), for *potage à la julienne*, f. proper name *Jules* or *Julien* (the reason is unknown).] A soup made of various vegetables, esp. carrots, chopped and cooked in meat broth. Also *attrib.*

Julius, †**Julio.** 1574. [– L. *Julius*, It. *giulio*.] A silver coin worth about sixpence, struck by Pope Julius II (1503–13).

July (dʒulǝi·). [– AFr. *julie* – L. *Julius* (sc. *mensis* month). The unexpl. stress on the second syll. has been established since Johnson's time.] The seventh month of the year, so named after Julius Cæsar.

Cæsar..was borne..vpon the fourth day before the Ides of Quintilis, which moneth, after his death, was..called for that cause, Iulie HOLLAND.

Julyflower, perversion of GILLYFLOWER.

Jumart (dʒū·maɹt). Also †**gimar.** 1690. [– Fr. *jumart*, formerly *jumare* – Pr. *gemerre, gemarre*.] An imaginary hybrid animal, said to be the offspring of a bull and a mare or she-ass, or of a horse or ass and a cow.

Jumbal, jumble (dʒɒ·mb'l). 1615. [perh. a use of GIMBAL 1, GIMMAL 1]. A kind of fine sweet cake or biscuit, formerly often made up in the form of rings or rolls; now in U.S., a thin crisp cake, composed of flour, sugar, butter, and eggs, flavoured with lemon-peel or sweet almonds.

Jumble (dʒɒ·mb'l), *sb.* 1661. [f. next.] **1.** A confused mixture, a medley; also, disorder, muddle. **2.** A shock, shaking, or jolting; *colloq.* a ride in a carriage 1674.

2. The j. of the sea made shooting uncertain 1851. *Comb.* **j.-sale**, a sale of miscellaneous cheap or second-hand articles at a charitable bazaar or the like.

Jumble (dʒɒ·mb'l), *v.* 1529. [Partly synon. with ME. †*jumpere*, †*jombre* (Chaucer), both app. being formed on a symbolic base with iterative or frequent. suffix.] **1.** *intr.* To move about in mingled disorder; to flounder about confusedly. **2.** *trans.* To muddle, confuse; often with *together* or *up* 1542. **3.** To stir up (a liquid, etc.) so as to mix the ingredients; to shake up; hence *colloq.* to take for a drive. ?*Obs.* 1616. **b.** *intr.* To travel with shaking or jolting 1748. **4.** *trans.* To put into mental confusion; to muddle 1668. †**5.** *intr.* To make a confused or rumbling noise; to strum on an instrument –1805.

1. In that fearfull Cave They [Furies] j., tumble, rumble, rage and rave SYLVESTER. 2. To j. the innocent and guilty into one mass, by a general indemnity BURKE. 3. That I might go abroad with my wife, who was not well, only to j. her PEPYS. Hence **Ju·mblement,** confused mixture 1707. **Ju·mbler.**

Jumble, var. of JUMBAL.

Jumbo (dʒɒ·mbo). 1823. [prob. the second element of MUMBO JUMBO.] A big clumsy person, animal, or thing; popularized, esp., as the name of an elephant, famous for its size, in the London Zoological Gardens; hence, anything big or great in its kind.

†**Ju·ment.** ME. [– L. *jumentum* (contr. of *jugimentum*) yoke-beast, f. *jug-*, stem of *jungere* join, *jugum* yoke.] A beast of burden; also a beast in general –1820.

Fit to fasten their Juments..unto them SIR T. BROWNE.

Jump (dʒɒmp), *sb.*¹ 1552. [f. JUMP *v.*] **1.** An act of jumping; a spring; a leap, a bound. **b.** esp. in reference to the distance cleared (*long j.*), or height jumped (*high j.*), as an athletic feat; also, a place to be jumped across, an obstacle to be cleared by jumping 1858. **2.** A sudden involuntary movement caused by a shock; a start. In *pl.* nervous starts; an affection marked by these, *spec.* (*a*) chorea, (*b*) delirium tremens (*slang*). 1879. **3.** Of things: A movement in which a thing is suddenly and abruptly thrown up or forward 1611. *spec.* in *Gunnery*: The vertical movement of the muzzle of a gun at the moment of discharge; the angle which measures this 1879. **4.** *fig.* A sudden abrupt rise, e.g. in price or the like; an abrupt change of level either upward or downward; a fault in stratification 1657. **5.** *fig.* A sudden and abrupt transition; an interval, gap, chasm, involving such sudden transition, *e.g.* in argument 1678. †**6.** Critical point, crisis –1641. †**b.** Venture, hazard –1606.

1. The hare..goeth by iumpes TOPSELL. 4. A j. up of 100 in the majority 1896. 5. Their nimble nonsense..gains remote conclusions at a j. COWPER. 6. b. Our fortune lyes Vpon this iumpe SHAKS. Phr. *From the j.*, from the start. *On the j.*, on the move (*colloq.*).

Jump, *sb.*² *Obs.* exc. *dial.* 1653. [perh. alt. of †*jup* JUPE.] **1.** A kind of short coat worn by men in the 17th and 18th centuries. **2.** A kind of under (or undress) bodice worn by women, esp. in the 18th c.; often used instead of stays. From *c*1740 usu. as pl. *jumps* (*a pair of jumps*). 1666. **3.** *attrib.*, as *j.-coat* 1660.

†**Jump,** *a.*, *adv.* 1539. [conn. w. JUMP *v.* I. 4.] **a.** *adj.* Coinciding; even; exact, precise –1637. **b.** *adv.* With exact coincidence; exactly, precisely –1656.

a. J. concord between our wit and will SIDNEY.

Jump (dʒɒmp), *v.* 1511. [prob. imit. of the sound of feet coming to the ground; cf. *bump, thump*.]

I. *intr.* **1.** To make a spring from the ground, etc. by flexion and sudden muscular extension of the legs, or the like; to throw oneself upward, forward, backward, or downward, from the point of support; to leap, spring, bound 1530. **b.** To move with a sudden involuntary jerk from excitement or shock; to start 1715. **2.** *transf.* Of things: To be moved or thrown up with a sudden jerk like a jump 1511. **3.** *fig.* To pass abruptly from one thing or state to another; to rise suddenly in amount, price, etc. 1579. **b.** To come *to* or arrive *at* (a conclusion, etc.) precipitately 1704. **4.** To act or come exactly *together*; to agree completely. Const. *with*. 1567.

1. Not the worst of the three, but iumpes twelue foote and a halfe by th' squire SHAKS. **b.** Phr. *To j. for joy*, said *lit.* of children, etc., also *fig.* to be joyfully excited 1775. **2.** The sea was beginning to j. HALL CAINE. **3.** Wool jumped up suddenly to 46*s.* per tod 1886. **b.** So given to jumping to conclusions is society 1884. **4.** Our humors j. together completely W. IRVING. Phr. *To j. at*: To spring as a beast at its prey; *fig.* to accept eagerly 1769. *To j. upon*: To pounce upon as a beast upon its victim; hence (*colloq.*) to come down crushingly upon 1868.

II. *trans.* **1.** To pass clear over with a leap; to clear 1600. †**2.** To effect or do as with a jump –1684. **3.** To cause to jump; to startle. Also *fig.* 1815. **4.** To pounce upon; to rob, to cheat; to 'steal a march' upon 1789. **5.** To skip over, pass by, evade 1749. †**6.** To hazard. SHAKS. †**7.** To make up hastily (a marriage, a match) –1615. **8. a.** *Iron-forging.* To flatten, 'upset', or shorten and thicken by endwise blows. Also *transf.* 1851. **b.** To join by welding the flattened ends 1864. **c.** To join (rails, etc.) end on end. 1884. **9.** *Quarrying.* To drill by means of a jumper 1851.

1. Jumping these crevices KANE. **3.** People.. whose nerves have been jumped by scorchers 1898. **4.** To j. the Transvaal 1899. Phr. *To j. a claim, etc.*; To take summary possession of a piece of land called a 'claim', on the ground that the former occupant has abandoned it, or has failed to comply with the legal requirements. Chiefly *U.S.* and *Colonial.* Also *transf.* **5.** Phr. *To j. one's bail*, to abscond, leaving one's sureties liable. *U.S. slang.* **6.** But heere..Wee'ld iumpe the life to come *Macb.* I. vii. 7.

Jump-, the vb.-stem used in *Comb.*: **j.-joint,** (*a*) a joint in which the parts are welded end to end together; (*b*) a flush-joint in which the edges of the plates or planking are laid close together and make a smooth surface; **-seat,** a movable carriage-seat; also *adj.* and *sb.* (ellipt.) (a carriage) provided with such a seat; **-weld,** a weld effected by hammering together the heated ends of two pieces of metal; hence **-weld** *v.*

Jumper (dʒɒ·mpəɹ), *sb.*[1] 1611. [f. JUMP *v.* + -ER[1].] **1.** One who or that which jumps. **2.** A name applied in the 18th c. to a body of Welsh Methodists who used to jump and dance as a part of religious worship; also to more recent sects 1774. **3.** One who jumps a claim 1855. **4.** Applied to tools, etc. having a jumping motion. **a.** *Quarrying.* A heavy drill, used in making blasting-holes in rock, etc. Also *attrib.* 1769. **b.** A spring or click controlling the star-wheel of a repeating clock 1850. **c.** *Telegraphy.* A wire used to cut out an instrument or part of a circuit, or to close temporarily a gap in a circuit. **5.** A rough kind of sledge, usu. consisting of two saplings with the ends turned up, fastened by cross-pieces. *U.S.* 1823. **6.** *Naut.* A preventer-rope made fast so as to prevent a yard, mast, etc. from jumping or springing up in rough weather. Also *attrib.* 1856.

Hence **Ju·mper** *v. trans.* to bore (a hole) with a j. (sense 4 a). **Ju·mperism,** the principles of the Jumpers (sense 2).

Ju·mper, *sb.*[2] 1853. [prob. f. JUMP *sb.*[2]] A loose outer jacket or shirt reaching to the hips, worn by sailors, truckmen, etc.; also, a hooded fur jacket worn by Eskimos, and the like. In recent use (also *jumper-blouse*), A loose-fitting blouse without fastenings, worn over the rest of the dress and not tucked in at the waist; also, an outer garment consisting of bodice and short legs, worn by young children as a protection to their clothing.

Jumping (dʒɒ·mpiŋ), *vbl. sb.* 1565. [f. JUMP *v.* + -ING[1].] The action of JUMP *v.* **b.** *attrib.*, as **j.-sheet,** a stout sheet into which persons may jump from a burning building.

Jumping (dʒɒ·mpiŋ), *ppl. a.* 1567. [f. as prec. + -ING[2].] That jumps. **b.** In names of animals characterized by jumping or springing: **j.-deer,** the black-tailed deer of N. America, *Cariacus macrotis*; **-hare,** a rodent quadruped of S. Africa, *Pedetes caffer* or *Helamys capensis*, resembling the jerboa; **-louse,** a flea-louse, a jumping plant-louse; **-mouse,** (*a*) the American deer-mouse, *Zapus hudsonius*; (*b*) = *jumping-rat*; **-mullet,** a gray mullet, *Mugil albula*; **-rat,** a rodent of the family *Dipodidæ*; **-shrew,** the elephant-shrew of Africa, an insectivorous quadruped of the family *Macroscelididæ*; **-spider,** one of the group of spiders which leap upon their prey. **c. j.-bean, -seed,** the seed of a Mexican euphorbiaceous plant, which jumps about by reason of the movements of the larva of a tortricid moth (*Carpocapsa saltitans*) enclosed within it; **-jack,** a child's toy made out of the merry-thought of a fowl; a toy figure of a man, which is made to jump by being pulled with strings; also *transf.*, the crested penguin. Hence **Ju·mpingly** *adv.*

Jumpy (dʒɒ·mpi), *a.* 1869. [f. JUMP *sb.*[1] + -Y[1].] Characterized by jumps (see JUMP *sb.*[1] 2, 5). **b.** Affected by nervous excitement 1879. Hence **Ju·mpiness.**

Juncaceous (dʒɒŋkēⁱ·ʃəs), *a.* 1855. [f. mod.L. *Juncaceæ* (f. *juncus* rush) + -OUS; see -ACEOUS.] *Bot.* Belonging to the N.O. *Juncaceæ* (the rush family).

Juncat, -cate, obs. ff. JUNKET.

Junco (dʒɒ·ŋko). 1706. [– Sp. *junco* – L. *juncus* rush.] †**a.** The Reed-sparrow or Reed-bunting (*Emberiza schœniclus*). **b.** A N. American genus of Finches, the Snow-birds; one of these.

Juncous (dʒɒ·ŋkəs), *a. rare.* 1755. [– L. *juncosus*, f. *juncus* rush; see -OUS.] Rushy.

Junction (dʒɒ·ŋkʃən). 1711. [– L. *junctio*, f. *junct-*, pa. ppl. stem of *jungere* JOIN; see -ION. Cf. Fr. *jonction.*] **1.** The action of joining or fact of being joined; union, combination; coalition. **2.** The point or place at which two things join or are joined; *spec.* the place or station on a railway where lines meet and unite 1841. **3.** (In full, *junction canal, j. line, j. railway*). A canal or railway forming a connection between two other lines or with a centre of commerce 1796. **4.** *attrib.* 1839.

1. The J. of the French and Bavarian Armies ADDISON. The j. of a talent for abstruse reasoning with much literary inexperience M. ARNOLD.

Comb. **j.-plate,** a break-joint plate riveted over the edges of boiler-plates, which make a butt-joint.

Juncture (dʒɒ·ŋktiŭɹ, -tʃəɹ). ME. [– L. *junctura* joint, f. as prec.; see -URE.] **1.** The action of joining together; joined condition; joining, junction 1589. **2.** The place at which, or structure by which, two things are joined; a joint, jointing, junction ME. †**b.** = JOINT *sb.* 1 –1717. **3.** Something that connects two things; a means of union (*rare*) 1677. **4.** A convergence of events or circumstances; a crisis, conjuncture 1656.

1. The j. with what precedes and follows 1821. **2.** It stands at the j. of that great river with another 1763. **4.** In the present critical j. of things BRIGHT.

June (dʒūn). [ME. *juyn, iun* – (O)Fr. *juin* :– L. *Junius* (sc. *mensis* month), var. of *Junonius* sacred to the goddess Juno; from XIV refash. after L.] The sixth month of the year, in which the summer solstice occurs in the northern hemisphere.

The month of Iune is begynnynge of Somer ME.

Comb.: *J.-apple* = JENNETING; **-berry,** the fruit (also called *service-berry*) of a small tree; the shad-bush (*Amelanchier canadensis*); also the tree; **-bug,** a name for various beetles which appear in June; (*a*) of the European genus *Rhinotrogus*; (*b*) of the genus *Lachnosterna* of the northern U.S. (*c*) *Allorhina nitida*, of the southern U.S.; **-grass** (*U.S.*), the Kentucky blue-grass, *Poa pratensis.*

Juneating, perverted f. JENNETING.

Jungle (dʒɒ·ŋg'l). 1776. [– Hindi, Marathi *jangal* :– Skr. *jangala*, dry, dry ground, desert.] **1.** In India, orig., Waste ground (= 'forest' in the original sense); hence, in Anglo-Indian use, **a.** Land overgrown with underwood, long grass, or tangled vegetation; also, the often impenetrable growth of vegetation covering such a tract 1776. **b.** with *a* and *pl.* A particular tract so covered; esp. as the dwelling-place of wild beasts 1783. **c.** Hence, used of similar tracts elsewhere 1849. **2.** *transf.* and *fig.* A wild, tangled mass 1850. **b.** *The Jungle* (*Stock Exch. slang*): the West African share market 1904. **3.** *attrib.* 1810.

1. a. Land Waste for Five Years..is called J. 1776. **c.** The Jordan..threading its tortuous way through its tropical j. STANLEY.

Comb.: **j.-bear,** the Sloth-bear of India, *Prochilus labiatus*; **-cat,** the Marsh-lynx, *Felis chaus*; **-cock,** the male jungle-fowl; **-fever**; **-fowl,** (*a*) an East Indian bird of the genus *Gallus*, esp. *G. ferrugineus* (*G. bankiva*); (*b*) a mound-bird of Australia, as *Megapodius tumulus*; **-hen,** the female jungle-fowl (*b*); **-market** (*Stock Exch.*), the market in shares of W. African Companies; **-ox,** the gayal; **-rice,** the millet-rice, *Panicum colonum*; **-sheep,** an Indian ruminant, *Kemas hypocrinus.* Hence **Ju·ngled** *a.*, covered with jungle 1842.

Jungly (dʒɒ·ŋgli), *a.* 1800. [f. JUNGLE + -Y[1].] Of the nature of or abounding in jungle; jungle-like.

Junior (dʒū·niəɹ), *a.* (*sb.*) 1526. [– L. *junior* (:– **juvenior*), compar. of *juvenis* young.] **1.** The younger: used to denote the younger of two bearing the same name in a family, esp. a son of the same name as his father; also the younger of two boys of the same surname in a school. Abbrev. *jun.*, *junr.*, or *jr.* 1623. **2.** Of less standing; of lower position, in a class, rank, profession, etc. 1766. †**3.** Belonging to youth or earlier life –1772. **4.** Of later date; more modern. Now rarely of persons. 1621. **5.** *sb.* [the adj. used *absol.*] A person who is younger than another, or of more recent entrance or lower standing in a class, profession, etc. 1526. **b.** With possessive 1548.

1. Tho. Crabb, Sen. and Tho. Crabb, Jun. of Malborrow..Wooll-men 1708. **2.** J. Sophisters 1766, flag-ship 1810, clerk 1870, partner 1871. **5.** In an American college the students are classed by years, those of the first year being called freshmen, of the second year sophomores, of the third year juniors BRYCE. **b.** His j. she by thirty years BYRON. Hence **Ju·niorate,** in the Society of Jesus, a two-years' course for junior members before entering the priesthood.

Juniority (dʒūni,ǫ·rĭti). 1554. [f. JUNIOR + -ITY, after earlier *seniority.*] The state or condition of being junior.

Juniper (dʒū·nipəɹ). ME. [– L. *juniperus.* Cf. GENEVA[1].] **1.** A genus of coniferous evergreen shrubs and trees; spec. and orig., the common European species *Juniperus communis*, a hardy spreading shrub or low tree, having awl-shaped prickly leaves and bluish-black or purple berries, with a pungent taste, yielding a volatile oil (*oil of juniper*) used in medicine as a stimulant and diuretic, also in the manufacture of gin. The wood is occas. used in joinery. **b.** Used loosely of coniferous trees of other genera, as the American Larch, and the White Cedar 1748. **c.** In translations of the Bible, used, after the Vulgate, to render Heb. *rethem* or *rōthem*, a white-flowered shrub, *Retama rætam* ME. †**2.** A name for the Fieldfare. FLORIO. **3.** *attrib.* 1382.

1. The coals of J. raked up will keep a glowing Fire for the space of a year SIR T. BROWNE.

Comb.: **j.-water,** a cordial drink made from or flavoured with j.; **-worm,** the larva of a N. Amer. geometrid moth (*Drepanodes varus*), which feeds on juniper-leaves.

Junk (dʒɒŋk), *sb.*[1] ME. [– OFr. *junc*, (also mod.) *jonc* :– L. *juncus* rush.] †**1.** A rush –1491. **2.** *Surg.* A form of splint, orig. stuffed with rushes or bents 1612.

Junk (dʒɒŋk), *sb.*[2] ME. [Of unkn. origin.] †**1.** *Naut.* An old or inferior cable or rope; usu. *old j.* –1769. **b.** Pieces of old cable used for making fenders, reef-points, gaskets, oakum, etc. 1666. **2.** *transf.* A piece or lump of anything; a CHUNK 1726. **3.** orig. *Naut.* The salt meat used as food on long voyages, compared to pieces of rope 1762. **4.** *Whale-fishery.* The mass of thick oily cellular tissue beneath the case and nostrils of a sperm-whale, containing spermaceti 1839. **5.** *attrib.* 1800.

1. c. Worthless stuff, rubbish (*colloq.*) 1913.

Comb.: **j.-dealer,** *U.S.*, a marine-store dealer; **-hook,** a hook used in handling the j. of a whale; **-ring,** (*a*) a metal ring confining the hemp packing of a piston; (*b*) a steam-tight metal packing round a piston; **-shop,** a marine store; **-vat,** in tanning, a large vat for holding weakened vat-liquor; **-wad,** a wad for a gun made of j. or oakum bound with spun-yarn.

Junk (dʒɒŋk), *sb.*[3] 1617. [– Fr. †*juncque* (mod. *jonque*), Pg. *junco*, or Du. *jonk* – Javanese *djong*, Malay *adjong.*] A name for the common type of native sailing vessel in the Chinese seas. It is flat-bottomed, has a square prow, prominent stem, full stern, the rudder suspended, and carries lug-sails.

Junk (dʒɒŋk), *v.* 1803. [f. JUNK *sb.*[2]] *trans.* To cut *off* in a lump; to cut into junks or chunks. **b.** To treat as junk; to 'scrap' 1916.

Junk-bottle. *U.S.* 1805. A thick strong bottle made of green or black glass, 'the ordinary black glass porter bottle' (Bartlett).

‖**Junker** (yu·ŋkəɹ). 1554. [G., for earlier *junkher(r*, f. MHG. *junc* YOUNG + *herre* (mod. *herr*) lord, compar. of *hēr* exalted, eminent. Cf. YOUNKER.] A young German noble; as a term of reproach, a narrow-minded, overbearing (younger) member of the aristocracy of Prussia, etc.; *spec.* a member of the reactionary party of the aristocracy, whose aim it is to maintain their own class privileges. Also *attrib.*

Bismarck is by instinct a J. 1891.

Junket (dʒɒ·ŋkėt), *sb.* ME. [– (O)Fr. *jonquette*, f. *jonc* rush :– L. *juncus*.] **1.** A basket (orig. made of rushes); *esp.* for carrying or catching fish. Now *dial.* **2.** A cream-cheese or the like (orig. made in a rush-basket or served on a rush-mat); now, a dish consisting of curds sweetened and flavoured, served with a layer of scalded cream on the top 1460. †**3.** Any dainty sweet-meat, cake, or confection; a kickshaw –1764. **4.** A feast or banquet; also (now only in U.S.), an outing at which eating and drinking are prominent; a picnic-party 1530.

2. Milke, crayme, and cruddes, and eke the Ioncate, þey close a mannes stomak . . þerfore ete hard chese aftir 1460. **4.** With these junkets and feasts they joyned the celebration of the Lords Supper 1655.

Junket (dʒɒ·ŋkėt), *v.* 1555. [f. prec. sb.] **1.** *intr.* To hold a banquet or feast; to make merry with good cheer; also (chiefly *U.S.*) to go on a pleasure excursion. **2.** *trans.* To entertain, feast. H. WALPOLE.

1. The Chancellor had intended to go junketting on the Rhine GREVILLE. Hence **Ju·nketer,** one who junkets; one who takes part in a junketing. **Ju·nketing** *vbl. sb.* feasting, merrymaking; also, picnicking; with *a* and *pl.* A feast, picnic, etc. †**Ju·nketry,** a sweetmeat 1599.

Juno (dʒū·no). 1606. [L. *Juno*, in L. mythology the wife of Jupiter; the goddess of marriage and childbirth.] **1.** A woman resembling the goddess Juno, e.g. in stately beauty, in jealousy, etc. **2.** *Astron.* Name of the third of the asteroids 1834.

1. His be yon J. of majestic size POPE. Hence **Juno,e·sque,** *a.* resembling J. in stately beauty. **Juno·nian** *a.* pertaining to J.

Junta (dʒɒ·ntă). 1623. [– Sp., Pg. *junta* (whence Fr. *junte*) = It. *giunta* :– Rom. subst. use of fem. pa. pple. *juncta* of *jungere* JOIN.] **1.** With reference to Spain or Italy: A deliberative or administrative council or committee. **2.** *gen.* = JUNTO 1. 1714.

Junto (dʒɒ·nto). Also †**juncto.** 1641. [erron. form of JUNTA, by assim. to Sp. sbs. in *o* (cf. -ADO 2).] **1.** A body of men who have combined for a common purpose, esp. a political purpose; a clique, faction, or cabal; a club or coterie. †**2.** = JUNTA 1. –1747.

1. The Juncto [the Rump] at Westminster have . . received more Money in one year than all the Kings of England 1680. As . . lately settled in a j. of the sex ADDISON.

Jupard(y(e, jupart(ye: see JEOPARD, -Y.

Jupe (dʒūp, Fr. ʒüp). Now only *Sc.* and *n. dial.* or as Fr. ME. [– Fr. *jupe* – Arab. *jubba* JUBBAH.] †**1.** A loose jacket, kirtle, or tunic worn by men –1837. **2.** *Sc.* A woman's jacket, kirtle, or bodice. Also *pl.* a kind of stays. 1810. ‖**3.** [from mod.Fr.] A woman's skirt 1825.

Jupiter (dʒū·pitəɹ). ME. [– L. *Juppiter, Jupiter*, for *Jovis-pater*, corresp. to Skr., *dyaús pitā* 'heaven father'. See JOVE.] **1.** The supreme deity of the ancient Romans, corresponding to the Greek Zeus; the ruler of gods and men, and the god of the heavens, whose weapon was the thunderbolt. Also in exclams., e.g. *by Jupiter.* **2.** *Astron.* The largest of the planets in the solar system, revolving in an orbit lying between those of Mars and Saturn ME. †**b.** *Alch.* The metal tin –1758. †**c.** *Her.* Name for the tincture AZURE in blazoning by the names of heavenly bodies –1766. **3.** In names of plants, as **Jupiter's staff,** Mullein, *Verbascum thapsus*, from its tall upright stem 1664.

1. [Adam] Smil'd . . as J. On Juno smiles MILT.

Jupiter's beard. 1567. [tr. L. *Barba Jovis.*] A name for various plants.

a. *Anthyllis barba-jovis*, the Silverbush, a S. European evergreen leguminous shrub, having leaves covered with silvery down. **b.** The common house-leek, *Sempervivum tectorum.* **c.** *Hydnum barba-jovis*, a hymenomycetous fungus with a white fibrous margin.

Jupon (dʒū·pǫn, dʒupǫ·n, Fr. ʒüpoṅ). ME. [– (O)Fr. *jupon*, deriv. of *jupe* JUPE.] **1.** A close-fitting tunic or doublet; esp. one worn by knights under the hauberk; later, a sleeveless surcoat worn outside the armour. *Obs.* exc. *Hist.* †**2.** A short kirtle worn by women –1595. ‖**3.** A woman's skirt 1851.

Jural (dʒūᵊ·răl), *a.* 1635. [f. L. *jus, jur-* law, right + -AL[1].] **1.** Of or relating to law or its administration. **2.** *Moral Philos.* Of or pertaining to rights and obligations 18 . .

2. By the adjective j. we shall denote that which has reference to the doctrine of rights and obligations WHEWELL. Hence **Ju·rally** *adv.*

Jurament (dʒūᵊ·rămĕnt). *Obs.* exc. *Hist.* 1575. [– late L. *juramentum*, f. L. *jurare* swear; see -MENT.] An oath.

Jurassic (dʒuræ·sik), *a.* 1833. [– Fr. *jurassique*, f. *Jura*, after *Liassic, Triassic.*] *Geol.* Of or pertaining to the Jura mountains: applied to formations belonging to the period between the Triassic and the Cretaceous, characterized by the prevalence of oolitic limestone, of which the Jura mountains between France and Switzerland are chiefly formed.

Jurat[1] (dʒūᵊ·ræ̆t, Fr. ʒüra). late ME. [– med.L. *juratus*, lit. 'sworn man', subst. use of masc. pa. pple. of L. *jurare* swear.] **1.** One who has taken an oath; *spec.* one sworn to give information about the crimes committed in his neighbourhood, and to assist the administration of justice. *Obs.* exc. *Hist.* 1450. **2.** A municipal officer (esp. of the Cinque Ports) holding a position similar to that of an alderman 1464. **3.** In the Channel Islands, one of a body of magistrates, chosen for life, who with the Bailiff form the Royal Court for administration of justice 1537. **4.** With reference to France, etc.: **a.** [= Fr. *jurat*] A municipal magistrate in certain towns 1432. **b.** A member of a company or corporation, sworn to see that nothing is done against its statutes 1714.

Jurat[2] (dʒūᵊ·ræ̆t). 1796. [– L. *juratum*, subst. use of pa. pple. n. of *jurare* swear.] *Law.* A memorandum as to when, where, and before whom an affidavit is sworn.

Juratory (dʒūᵊ·rătəri), *a.* 1553. [– late L. *juratorius* confirmed by oath; see JURAT[1], -ORY[2].] Of or pertaining to an oath or oaths; expressed or contained in an oath.

Freed from his j. obligation 1647.

Juridic, -al (dʒuri·dik, -ăl), *a.* 1502. [– L. *juridicus*, f. *jus, jur-* law + *-dicus* saying, f. *dicere* say; see -AL[1].] **1.** Of or pertaining to law or legal proceedings; occas. = legal. **2.** Assumed by law to exist; juristic 1892.

1. Judges or juridical writers SIR C. BOWEN. **2.** A Bill . . extending to juridical persons, that is, duly registered corporations or partnerships [etc.] 1900. Hence **Juri·dically** *adv.* in a juridical manner.

Jurisconsult (dʒūᵊ:ris,kǫ̆nsɒ·lt). 1605. [– L. *jurisconsultus*, f. *juris*, gen. of *jus* law + *consultus* skilled.] One learned in law, esp. in civil or international law; a jurist; a master of jurisprudence.

Jurisdiction (dʒūᵊrisdi·kʃən). ME. [Earliest forms *iure-, iuridiccioun* – OFr. *jure-* (also mod.) *juridiction*, later conformed to the original L. *jurisdictio*, f. *juris*, gen. sing. of *jus* law + *dictio* declaration; see JURY, DICTION.] **1.** Administration of justice; exercise of judicial authority, or of the functions of a judge or legal tribunal; legal authority or power. **2.** Power or authority in general; administration, rule, control ME. **3.** The range of judicial or administrative power; the territory over which such power extends. Also *fig.* ME. **4.** A judicial organization; a judicature; a court, or series of courts, of justice 1765.

1. To declare the Law, which is not Judgment, but J. HOBBES. **2.** To live exempt From Heav'n's high j. MILT. *P.L.* II. 319. **3.** Basil's care of the churches . . extended far beyond the limits of his own j. J. H. NEWMAN. **4.** The abolition of hereditary jurisdictions LECKY. Hence **Jurisdi·ctional** *a.*

Jurisdictive (dʒūᵊrisdi·ktiv), *a. rare.* 1640. [f. JURISDICTION, on anal. of *administration, administrative*, etc.] Of or pertaining to jurisdiction.

Jurisprudence (dʒūᵊris,prū·dĕns). 1628. [– late L. *jurisprudentia* (in Cicero *prudentia juris*), f. *juris* (see prec.) + *prudentia* knowledge of or skill in (a matter). Cf. Fr. *jurisprudence*, perh. the immediate source.] **1. a.** Knowledge of or skill in law. **b.** The science which treats of human laws (written or unwritten) in general; the philosophy of law 1756. **2.** A system or body of law 1656.

1. b. The domain of Comparative J., of which English Law forms a small province 1861. **2.** The history of our medical j. MACAULAY.

Jurispru·dent, *sb.* and *a.* 1628. [– Fr. †*jurisprudent*, back-formation from *jurisprudence*; see prec., -ENT. The L. expression was *juris-, jureperitus.*] **1.** *sb.* One versed in, or treating of, jurisprudence; a jurist. **2.** *adj.* Versed or skilled in jurisprudence 1737.

Jurisprudential (-de·nʃăl), *a.* 1651. [f. JURISPRUDENCE, after *prudence, prudential.*] Of or pertaining to jurisprudence; rarely of persons: JURISPRUDENT 2. Hence **Jurisprude·ntially** *adv.* in relation to jurisprudence.

Jurist (dʒūᵊ·rist). 1456. [– Fr *juriste* or med.L. *jurista*, f. L. *jus, jur-* law; see -IST.]

1. One who practises in law; a lawyer (now *U.S.*). **2.** One versed in the science of law; legal writer 1626. **3.** A student of law, or one who takes a degree in law 1691.

2. This is not to be measured by the principles of jurists BACON. Hence **Juri·stic, -al** *a.* of or pertaining to a j., or to the subject or study of law; legal; created by law. **Juri·stically** *adv.* in relation to law.

Juror (dʒūᵊ·rəɹ). ME. [– AFr. *jurour*, OFr. *jureor* (mod. *jureur*) :– L. *jurator*, f. *jurare* swear; see -OR 2.] **1.** A member of a jury; a juryman. †**2.** One who brings false witness or a false presentment; a slanderer; an oppressor; a covetous man –1550. **3.** One of a body of persons appointed to award prizes in a competition 1851. **4.** One who takes or has taken an oath; one who swears allegiance to some body or cause. (Cf. NON-JUROR.) 1592.

1. The false verdict of jurors, whether occasioned by embracery or not, was antiently considered as criminal BLACKSTONE. **2.** Sclaunderers, lyers, and iurours of the syse 1509.

Jury (dʒūᵊ·ri). [Late ME. *juree* – AFr. *juree* (in this sense) – OFr. *juree* oath, juridical inquiry, inquest – (AL. *jurata*) subst. use of pa. pple. fem. of L. *jurare* swear, f. *jus, jur-* an old term of law and religion; see -Y[5].]

I. A company of men sworn to render a 'verdict' or true answer upon some question or questions officially submitted to them; now, usually upon evidence delivered to them touching the issue; but orig. usually upon facts or matters within their own knowledge.

In England, juries in all criminal trials, in civil trials in the superior courts, and in writs of inquiry, consist of 12 men, who must be unanimous in their verdict. In Scotland, the number of the jury in a criminal trial is 15, and the verdict of a majority is accepted; in a civil trial the numberis 12, and their verdict must be unanimous.

Coroner's jury: see CORONER and INQUEST. *Grand j.*: a jury of inquiry, accusation, or presentment, consisting of from 12 to 23 'good and lawful men of a county', who are returned by the sheriff to every session of the peace, and of the assizes, to receive and inquire into indictments, before these are submitted to a trial jury, and to perform such other duties as may be committed to them. Grand juries were abolished by the Administration of Justice Act 1933 exc. for certain indictments in London and Middlesex. They have been done away with in many states of U.S.A. *Petty jury* or *trial jury*: a jury which tries the final issue of fact in civil or criminal proceedings. *Special jury*: a jury consisting of persons on the jurors' book who are of a certain station or occupy premises of a certain rateable value.

II. *transf.* **1.** Applied to the body of DICASTS (δικασταί) of ancient Athens, or the *judices* of ancient Rome 1856. **2.** A body of persons selected to award prizes in an exhibition or competition 1851. †**3.** A dozen –1650.

Jury-, Jury *a.* (*Naut.*): see JURY-MAST.

Juryman (dʒūᵊ·rimǣn). 1579. A man serving on a jury; a member of a jury.

Ju·ry-ma:st. 1616. [The first element is perh. identifiable with *iuerie, recorded as *i(u)were* 'remedium' in *Promptorium Parvulorum*, which may be an aphetic deriv. of OFr. *ajurie* aid, f. *aju-*, pres. stem of *aidier* AID + *-rie* -RY.] **1.** *Naut.* A temporary mast put up in place of one that has been broken or carried away. **b.** *transf.* An apparatus used in Pott's disease, to keep the spinal column straight, and prevent lateral curvature 1883. **2.** Hence *jury-* is used in comb. to designate other parts of a ship contrived for temporary use, as **j.-rig**, etc.; and joc. of other things, as **j.-leg**, a wooden leg 1666. **b.** Hence **Jury** *a.* = temporary, makeshift 1821.

2. b. I have..some j. chairs and tables BYRON.

Jussive (dʒɒ·siv), *a.* 1846. [f. *juss-*, pa. ppl. stem of L. *jubēre* command + -IVE.] *Grammar.* Expressing a command or order; as forms of the verb.

Just, joust (dʒɒst, dʒūst, dʒaust), *sb.* ME. [– OFr. *juste, jouste* (mod. *joute*), f. *juster*; see JUST *v.*] A combat in which two knights or men-at-arms on horseback encountered each other with lances; *spec.* a combat of this kind for exercise or sport; a tilt. Usu. in pl. *justs, jousts* (formerly construed as *sing.*), a series of these; a tournament.

For knightly giusts and fierce encounters fitt SPENSER.

Just (dʒɒst), *a.* ME. [– (O)Fr. *juste* – L. *justus*, f. *jus* law, right.] **1.** That does what is morally right, righteous. Now chiefly a Biblical archaism. **2.** Upright and impartial in one's dealings; equitable ME. †**b.** Faithful. Const. *of, to.* –1809. **3. a.** Consonant with the principles of moral right; equitable; fair. Of rewards, punishments, etc.: Merited. ME. **b.** Constituted by law or by equity, lawful, rightful; †legally valid ME. **4.** Well-founded ME. **5.** Conformable to the standard; right; proper; correct ME. **b.** *Mus.* in *just interval*, etc.: Harmonically pure; sounding perfectly in tune 1811. **6.** In accordance with reason, truth, or fact; right; true; correct 1490. †**b.** Of a copy, calculation, etc.: Exact, accurate, –1798. †**7.** Appropriate, suitable –1684. †**8.** Exact, as opp. to approximate. Also with defining word: = '(the) exact..'. –1759. †**b.** Exact or uniform in operation, regular, even –1769. †**9.** Equal; even, level –1725. †**10.** That is such properly, fully, or in all respects; complete in amount or character; full; proper, regular –1778.

1. *J. before (with) God* or simply, *j.*; Righteous in the sight of God; justified. Only the actions of the j. Smell sweet and blossom in the dust SHIRLEY. **2.** The Gods are iust SHAKS. **b.** He was my Friend, faithfull, and iust to me SHAKS. **3. a.** J. vengeance 1632. Is this fair, or reasonable, or j. to yourself? DICKENS. **b.** His country's j. liberties 1849. **4.** Alas! my fears were j. 1796. **5.** If they ffynd [the weights] not Iust: they breake them 1588. **6.** A j. picture of American public opinion BRYCE. **b.** Like a j. map SWIFT. **7.** Things to be done in their j. Season EVELYN. **8.** If thou tak'st more Or lesse then a iust pound SHAKS. **9.** The destin'd victim to dis-part In sev'n j. portions POPE. **10.** Before he come to j. yeares (*i.e.* full age) 1588.

Just, joust (dʒɒst, dʒūst, dʒaust), *v.* ME. [– OFr. *juster* (mod. *jouter*) bring together, unite, engage on horseback :– Rom. *juxtare come together, encounter, f. L. *juxta* near together, rel. to *jungere* JOIN, *jugum* YOKE.] †**1.** *intr.* To join battle, encounter, engage; *esp.* to fight on horseback as a knight or man-at-arms –1667. **2.** *spec.* To engage in a just or tournament; to tilt ME. **3.** *fig.* ME.

2. To Iust and Turney for her loue SHAKS. **3.** Auster and Boreas justing furiously Under hot Cancer SYLVESTER.

Just (dʒɒst), *adv.* ME. [f. JUST *a.*; cf. advb. use of Fr. *juste.*] **1.** Exactly, precisely; verily, actually; closely; of place, time, manner, degree, number, sameness, etc. †**2.** In an exact or accurate manner; with precision; punctually; correctly –1743. †**3.** In replies, etc.; = 'Exactly so', 'just so', 'right' –1698. **4.** *absol.* of time: Exactly at the moment spoken of; precisely now (or then) 1667. **5.** No more than; only, merely; barely. Often preceded by *but* or *only.* 1665. **6.** No less than; absolutely; actually, positively; really; quite; simply. Chiefly *Sc.*, *dial.*, and *U.S.* 1726. **b.** As an emphatic expletive 1855.

1. *J. at, in, over* (etc.) *the* = at, in, over (etc.) the very. *J. to the*, to the very. A parted eu'n iust betweene Twelue and One SHAKS. I will do j. as you advise 1891. Nor cut thou lesse nor more But iust a pound of flesh SHAKS. 'Tis iust the fashion SHAKS. **3.** *A.Y.L.* III. ii. 281. **4.** His only child was j. dead 1818. **5.** He can j. be said to live CHESTERF. J. a line to say that all goes well MRS. CARLYLE. I will j. walk on DISRAELI. **6.** Isn't it j. splendid? (*mod. colloq.*). Phr. *Just now.* **a.** At this exact moment. **b.** But now; only a moment ago. **c.** Directly, presently.

‖**Justaucorps** (ʒū·stokōr). 1656. [Fr., f. *juste* close-fitting + *au corps* to the body.] A close-fitting garment: *spec.* **a.** A body-coat reaching to the knees, worn in the 17th and 18th centuries. **b.** An outer garment worn by women in the 17th c. **c.** *Sc.* A jacket or waistcoat with sleeves.

Juster, jouster (dʒɒ·stəɹ, dʒū·stəɹ). ME. [– AFr. *justour*, OFr. *justeor, justeur*, f. *juster* JUST *v.*; see -ER² 3.] One who justs; a tilter; hence, †an antagonist.

Justice (dʒɒ·stis), *sb.* ME. [– (O)Fr. *justice* – L. *justitia* righteousness, equity, f. *justus* JUST; see -ICE.]

I. 1. The quality of being (morally) just or righteous; the principle of just dealing; just conduct; integrity, rectitude. (One of the four cardinal virtues.) ME. †**2.** *Theol.* Observance of the divine law; righteousness; the state of being 'just before God' –1622. **3.** = JUSTNESS 2, 3. 1588.

1. COMMUTATIVE, DISTRIBUTIVE *justice*: see these words. The path of j. was the path of wisdom MACAULAY. **3.** The j. of these observations 1885.

II. 1. Exercise of authority or power in maintenance of right; vindication of right by assignment of reward or punishment; requital of desert ME. **2.** The administration of law, or the forms and processes attending it; earlier, †Legal proceedings of any kind ME. †**b.** The persons administering the law; a judicial assembly, court of justice –1654. †**3.** Infliction of punishment, legal vengeance on an offender; *esp.* capital punishment; execution –1788. **4.** Personified, esp. in sense II. 1. 1599.

1. Phr. *Poetical j.*: the ideal justice in distribution of rewards and punishments supposed to befit a poem or the like. This rough j. of the world 1873. **2.** Assassins, and all flyers from the hand Of J. TENNYSON. Phr. *Jedwood* or *Jeddart* (= Jedburgh) *j.*, trial after execution. So †*Cupar j. Justices' j.*, the kind administered by petty magistrates, esp. when disproportionately severe. **3.** Phr. *To do j. on* or *upon (of)*, to punish, esp. by death. **4.** You are right Iustice, and you weigh this well: Therefore still beare the Ballance, and the Sword 2 *Hen. IV*, v. ii. 102.

III. 1. *gen.* A judicial officer; a judge; a magistrate ME. **2.** *spec.* In Great Britain and U.S.: A member of the judicature. **a.** A judge presiding over or belonging to one of the superior courts; since 1875, a member of the Supreme Court of Judicature ME. **b.** A justice of the peace, or other inferior magistrate; esp. in pl. *the Justices* 1586. **3. Justice of the Peace** (†*J. of peace*), an inferior magistrate appointed to preserve the peace in a county, town, or other district, and discharge other local magisterial functions ME.

2. a. *Chief J.* or *Lord Chief J.*, formerly, the title of the judges presiding over each of the courts of King's Bench and of Common Pleas; both offices are now merged under the title of *Lord Chief J. of England.* The judges of the Court of Appeal are called *Lords Justices*; a judge of the High Court of Justice is called *Mr. Justice.*

Phrase. *To do j. to* (a person or thing): **a.** to render (one) what is his due, or vindicate his just claims; hence, To treat (a subject or thing) in a manner showing due appreciation. *To do oneself j.*, to do something in a manner worthy of one's abilities. †**b.** To pledge in drinking (*Oth.* II. iii. 90).

Comb.: **j.-eyre (-air)**: see EYRE; **-seat**, seat of j., judgement-seat.

Justice (dʒɒ·stis), *v.* ME. [– AFr. *justicer* = OFr. *justicier* – med.L. *justitiare* exercise justice over, f. *justitia.*] †**1.** *trans.* To administer justice to; to rule, govern –1481. †**2.** To try in a court of law; to bring to trial; to punish judicially –1732. **3.** *intr.* To administer justice (as a justice of the peace) 1606.

Justicer (dʒɒ·stisəɹ). ME. [– AFr. *justicer*, OFr. *justicier* – med.L. *justitiarius*; see JUSTICIARY, -ER² 2.] **1.** One who maintains or executes justice (*arch.*). **2.** An administrator of justice; †a ruler or governor; a judge, magistrate (*arch.*) 1481. †**b.** *transf.* A judge, critic –1615. **3.** *spec.* = JUSTICE III. 2. 1535.

2. b. If some severe Censor and precise Iusticer blame this act HOLLAND.

Justiceship (dʒɒ·stisˌʃip). 1542. [f. JUSTICE *sb.* + -SHIP.] The office or dignity of a justice.

Justiciable (dʒɒsti·ʃiǎb'l), *a.* 1656. [– AFr. (O)Fr. *justiciable* amenable to a jurisdiction, also as sb., f. *justicier* JUSTICE *v.*; see -ABLE. So med.L. *justitiabilis.*] Liable to be tried in a court of justice; subject to jurisdiction. Hence **Justiciabi·lity.**

Justiciar (dʒɒsti·ʃiǎɹ). 1485. [– med.L. *justitiarius*; see next, -AR².] **1.** = JUSTICIARY *sb.* 1. 1579. **2.** = JUSTICE III. 2. a. *Obs.* exc. *Hist.* 1485. **3.** *gen.* = JUSTICER 1, 2. 1623.

Justiciary (dʒɒsti·ʃiǎri), *sb.*[1] 1532. [– med.L. *justitiarius, -ciarius* judge, f. L. *justitia* JUSTICE *sb.*; see -ARY¹.] **1.** *Eng. Hist.* The chief political and judicial officer under the Norman and early Plantagenet kings, acting as regent in the king's absence; more fully, *Chief J.* 1700. **2.** = JUSTICE III. 2. a, JUSTICIAR 2. *Obs.* exc. *Hist.* 1761. **3.** = JUSTICER 1, 2. 1548. **4.** Used to designate various foreign officers of state: = Fr. *justicier*, Sp. *justiciero*, It. *sindaco*, etc. 1763. †**5.** *Theol.* One who holds that man can of himself attain to righteousness –1716.

4. The j. of Arragon, a name dreadful to royal ears GIBBON.

Justiciary (dʒɒsti·ʃiǎri), *sb.*[2] *Sc.* 1473. [– med.L. *justitiaria* office of a judge or justiciar, f. *justitiarius* (prec.) + *-ia* -Y³; see -ARY¹.] The jurisdiction of a justiciar.

High Court of J., the supreme criminal tribunal of Scotland.

Justiciary (dʒɒsti·ʃiǎri), *a.* 1581. [– med.L. *justitiarius* judicial, f. L. *justitia* JUSTICE *sb.* + *-arius* -ARY¹.] **1.** Pertaining to or connected with the administration of justice or the office of a justice. †**2.** *Theol.* Self-righteous; see JUSTICIARY *sb.*[1] 5. –1665.

‖**Justicies** (dʒɒsti·ʃiˌīz). 1534. [AL., first word of the writ, 2nd pers. sing. pr. subj. of med.L. *justiciare* JUSTICE *v.*] *Law.* A writ, now abolished, directed to a sheriff, empowering him to hold plea of debt in his county court for sums exceeding forty shillings; so called from the opening words.

Justicing (dʒɒ·stisiŋ), *vbl. sb.* 1606. [f. JUSTICE *v.* + -ING¹.] The administration of justice. Chiefly *attrib.*, esp. in *j.-room*, e.g. in the house of a justice of the peace.

Justico, -coat, -core, ff. JUSTAUCORPS.

Justifiable (dʒɒ·stifəiˌǎb'l), *a.* 1523. [– (O)Fr. *justifiable*, f. *justifier* JUSTIFY; see -ABLE.] †**1.** = JUSTICIABLE –1643. **2.** Capable of being justified, or shown to be just 1561. †**b.** Of an assertion, etc.: Capable of being made good –1651. †**3.** Fitted to justify a claim or the like 1755.

2. *Justifiable homicide*: see HOMICIDE *sb.*² Emigration from one's own land seems hardly j. 1859. Hence **Ju:stifiabi·lity, Ju·stifiableness,** the quality of being j. **Ju·stifiably** *adv.*

Justification (dʒɒ:stifikēⁱ·ʃən). ME. [– (O)Fr. *justification* or Chr.L. *justificatio*, f. *justificat-*, pa. ppl. stem of Chr.L. *justificare*; see JUSTIFY, -ION, -FICATION.] †**1.** Administration of the law; execution of sentence; capital punishment –1480. †**2.** An ordinance; an ordained form –1609. **3.** The action of justifying or showing something to be just, right, or proper; vindication of oneself or another; exculpation; †verification. **b.** That which justifies; an apology, a defence. 1494. **4.** *Theol.* The action whereby man is justified, or freed from the penalty of sin, and accounted or made righteous by God; the fact or condition of being so justified 1526. **5.** *Law.* The showing in court that one had sufficient reason for doing that which he is called to answer; the ground for such a plea 1483. **b.** The justifying of bail: see JUSTIFY 7 b. **6.** The action of adjusting or arranging exactly, esp. in *Type-founding* and *Printing* 1672.

3. Nothing can with reason be urged in j. of revenge BUTLER. **4.** The plain Scriptural notion of j. is pardon, the forgiveness of sins WESLEY. **5.** If you have any thing of J., plead Not guilty 1660.

Justificative (dʒɒ·stifikeⁱtiv), *a.* 1611. [– Fr. *justificatif, -ive*, f. as prec.; see -IVE.] Serving to justify; justificatory.

Justificatory (dʒɒ·stifikeⁱtəri), *a.* 1579. [– med.L. *justificatorius* (XIV), f. as prec.; see -ORY².] Tending to justify; serving or intended to support a statement.

Justifier (dʒɒ·stifəiˌəɹ). 1526. [f. JUSTIFY + -ER¹.] **1.** One who or that which justifies (see JUSTIFY *v.*). **2.** *Type-founding* and *Printing*. **a.** A workman who 'justifies'; a wedge, etc. used in 'justifying' 1771.

1. Faith is the sole j. J. H. NEWMAN.

Justify (dʒɒ·stifəi), *v.* ME. [– (O)Fr. *justifier* – Chr.L. *justificare* do justice to, vindicate, f. L. *justus* JUST *a.*; see -FY.] †**1.** *trans.* To administer justice to; to try as a judge; to have jurisdiction over, rule, control; to treat justly. **b.** *absol.* To judge. –1620. †**2.** *trans.* To execute justice upon; to sentence; to punish, esp. (*Sc.*) to execute –1860. **3.** To show to be just or in the right; to vindicate (†*from* a charge) ME. **4.** To absolve, acquit, exculpate; *spec.* in *Theol.*, to declare free from the penalty of sin on the grounds of Christ's righteousness, or to make inherently righteous by the infusion of grace. Also *absol.* ME. **5.** To corroborate, prove, verify ME. †**b.** To affirm, aver –1781. **6.** To show or maintain the justice or reasonableness of; to defend as right or proper 1560. **b.** To furnish adequate grounds for, warrant 1658. †**c.** To render lawful –1725. **7.** *Law. intr.* and *trans.* **a.** To show adequate grounds for (that with which one is charged) 1529. **b.** *To j.* (†*oneself*) *as bail, to j. bail*: to show by oath, as a person furnishing bail, that after the payment of his debts he is of adequate pecuniary ability. †**8.** To approve of; to ratify –1729. **9.** To make exact; to fit or arrange exactly. Now only techn.; esp. (*Type-founding*), To adjust a 'strike' or 'drive', so as to form a correct matrix; (*Printing*) To adjust types together, so that they will exactly fill up the forme; to space out the line of type in the composing-stick properly; also *intr.* of type 1551.

2. Justified in the Grassmarket SCOTT. **3.** Iustifie not thy self before God COVERDALE *Ecclus.* 7:5. **4.** The innocent and righteous slay thou not: for I will not iustifie the wicked *Exod.* 23:7. **5.** The narratives of antiquity are justified by the experience of modern times GIBBON. **6.** That..I may assert th' eternal Providence, And justifie the wayes of God to men MILT. *P.L.* I. 26. **b.** This very necessity had..justified the Act 1658. **c.** Till..public nuptials j. the bride POPE.

Justle, var. of JOSTLE *v.*

Justly (dʒɒ·stli), *adv.* ME. [f. JUST *a.* + -LY².] In a just manner; righteously (*arch.*); rightfully, rightly; deservedly ME.; properly ME.; exactly, accurately (now *dial.*) ME.

To do iustly, and to loue mercy *Micah* 7:8. This I j. fear PENN. J. popular 1849.

Justness (dʒɒ·stnės). ME. [f. JUST *a.* + -NESS.] The quality of being just; = JUSTICE in its non-legal senses. †**1.** Righteousness; uprightness –1726. **2.** Rightfulness; fairness; validity, soundness 1559. **3.** Conformity to truth or to a standard; correctness; propriety; †exactness 1666.

2. The j. of a title KNOX, of a cause 1759. **3.** J. of perception to deal with facts M. ARNOLD.

Jut (dʒɒt), *sb.*¹ *Obs.* or *dial.* 1553. [Goes with JUT *v.*¹] A push, thrust, or shove against a resisting body; the shock of collision.

Jut (dʒɒt), *sb.*² 1709. [var. of JET *sb.*³; cf. JUT *v.*²] **1.** A jutting out; that which juts; a projection or protruding point 1786. †**2.** = JET *sb.*³ 3. CONGREVE.

Jut (dʒɒt), *v.*¹ *Obs.* or *dial.* 1548. [app. echoic; expressing both in sound and feeling the obstructed action in question.] †**1.** *intr.* To strike, knock, or push *against* something –1628. **2.** *trans.* To push, thrust, shove, jolt; to knock against something 1565.

1. One that would faine run an euen path..and iutt against no man 1628.

Jut (dʒɒt), *v.*² 1565. [var. of JET *v.*², by assim. to JUTTY *v.* (also JETTY *v.*), and JUTTY pier (also JETTY *sb.* 1.)] *intr.* To project or protrude. Often with *out* or *forth*. †**b.** *transf.* To encroach upon 1623.

Jute¹ (dʒūt). 1746. [– Bengali *jhōṭo, jhuṭo* :– Skr. *jūṭa*, var. of *jaṭā* braid of hair.] The fibre from the bark of the plants *Corchorus capsularis* and *C. olitorius* (N.O. *Tiliaceæ*), imported chiefly from Bengal, and used in the making of gunny, canvas, bagging, cordage, etc. **b.** The plant itself, or any plants of the same genus. Also *attrib.*

Jute² (dʒūt). [In XIV *Iutes* (Trevisa), repr. med.L. *Jutæ, Juti* pl. (Bede); in OE. *Eotas, Iotas* (cf. Icel. *Iótar* people of Jutland in Denmark).] In *pl.* One of the three Low German tribes which invaded and settled in Britain in the 5th and 6th centuries; they occupied parts of Kent and Hampshire.

†**Jutty,** *sb.* late ME. [Phonetic var. of JETTY *sb.*; cf. JUT *v.*²] **1.** = JETTY *sb.* 1 –1804. **2.** = JETTY *sb.* 2. –1703.

2. No Iutty frieze, Buttrice [etc.] *Macb.* I. vi. 6.

Jutty (dʒɒ·ti), *v.* *Obs.* or *arch.* ME. [Related to prec. sb.; cf. also JETTY *v.*] **1.** *intr.* To project, jut (*arch.*). †**2.** *trans.* To project beyond, overhang. SHAKS. †**3.** = JET *v.*² 2. 1611.

†**Ju·venal.** 1588. [– L. *juvenalis* (= *juvenilis*), f. *juvenis* young person; see -AL¹.] **1.** *adj.* Juvenile –1821. **2.** *sb.* A youth; a juvenile –1664.

Juvenescent (dʒūvĭne·sĕnt), *a.* 1821. [– *juvenescent-*, pr. ppl. stem of L. *juvenescere* reach the age of youth; see -ESCENT.] Becoming young or youthful. So **Juvene·scence,** the state of becoming young or youthful 1800.

Juvenile (dʒū·vĭnəil). 1625. [– L. *juvenilis*, f. *juvenis* young; see -ILE.]

A. *adj.* **1.** Young, youthful. **2.** Belonging to or characteristic of youth 1661.

1. Half a dozen j. messengers 1852. **2.** Dressed in a very j. manner DICKENS. Hence **Ju·venile-ly** *adv.*, **-ness.**

B. *sb.* A young person; a youth 1733; in booksellers' language, a children's book.

Some bashful j. LONGF.

‖**Juvenilia** (dʒūvĭni·liă). 1622. [L. neut. pl. of *juvenilis* (see prec.).] Achievements or works of a person's youth.

Juvenility (dʒūvĭni·lĭti). 1623. [– L. *juvenilitas*, f. *juvenilis* JUVENILE; see -ITY.] **1.** Juvenile condition; youthfulness; youthful manner, quality, character, or vigour. **2.** *concr.* Juveniles collectively 1823. **3.** *pl.* Juvenile characteristics, acts, or ideas 1661.

1. The Sallies of J. FOOTE. **3.** Juvenilities unbecoming the character of old age 1706.

Juwise, -ys(e, var. JUISE, judgement.

Juxta- (dʒɒkstă), *pref.*, repr. L. *juxta* adv. and prep. 'near, by the side of, according to'; as in **j.-ampu·llary** *a.*, situated by the side of an ampulla; **-spi·nal** *a.*, situated by the side of the (or a) spine; **-ta·bular** *a.* (*Rom. Law*), according to a testament or written document.

Juxtapose (dʒɒkstăpōᵘ·z), *v.* 1851. [– Fr. *juxtaposer*; see prec., POSE *v.*] *trans.* To place in juxtaposition. So **Juxtapo·sit** *v.* (*rare*) 1681.

Juxtaposition (dʒɒ:kstăpŏzi·ʃən). 1665. [– Fr. *juxtaposition*, f. as prec.; see POSITION.] The action of placing two or more things close together or side by side; the condition of being so placed.

Allah is great, no doubt, and J. his prophet CLOUGH.

Jymold, var. of GIMMALED.

Jynx (dʒiŋks). *Pl.* **jynges** (dʒi·ndʒīz). 1649. [– mod.L. *jynx*, for L. *iynx* – Gr. ἴυγξ, pl. ἴυγγες wryneck, bird made use of in witchcraft.] **1.** A bird, the wryneck (*Jynx* or *Iynx torquilla*); also called *yunx*. **2.** *transf.* A charm or spell. URQUHART.

K

K (kēⁱ), the eleventh letter of the alphabet in English, was an original letter of the Roman alphabet, taken from the Greek *Kappa* K, originally ꓘ, from Phœnician and general Semitic *Kaph* ꓘ. Its sound in Greek and Latin was, as in English, that of the back voiceless stop consonant, or guttural *tenuis*. But at an early period of Latin orthography, the letter C (orig. repr. Gr. *Gamma*) was employed for the k sound, and the letter K fell into disuse, except in a few archaic spellings.

In Old English, K is merely a supplemental symbol occasionally used instead of C for the guttural sound. But after the Conquest, in accordance with Norman usage, C was retained for the guttural only before *a, o, u, l, r*, and K was substituted for the same sound before *e, i, y*, and (later) *n*. Hence, in native words, initial K now appears only before *e, i, y*, and before *n* (:– OE. *cn-*), where it is no longer pronounced in Standard English. Medially and finally, *k* is used after a consonant (*ask, twinkle*), or long vowel (*make, like, week*); after a short vowel, *ck* is used instead of *cc* or *kk*, but the unstressed suffix, formerly *-ick* (*musick*), is now *-ic*, though, when a suffix in *e* or *i* follows, *k* reappears (*traffic, trafficker, trafficking*).

The native K words, being thus confined to Ke-, Ki-, Kn-, are few. But many foreign words of recent adoption, instead of being spelt with C before *a, o, u, l, r, h*, now take K in these positions; and in words from Greek also, many prefer to retain K, instead of latinizing it to C. In a very few words (not of English formation), K represents Gr. χ, esp. in the words in *kilo-*, as *kilogramme*, etc.

I. The letter. Pl. *Ks*, K's, *ks*, k's. (Now pronounced (kēⁱ); formerly (kī) was also current.)

II. In serial order K is the 11th or 10th number, according as J is or is not reckoned as a member.

III. In *Chem.* K is the symbol for Potassium (mod.L. *Kalium*). In *Meteorol.* K = cumulus. In *Assaying*, etc. K = carat. In *Astron.* *k* designates Gauss's Constant, the square of which is a measure of the mass of the sun.

IV. *Abbreviations.* **a.** K. = *Kate, Katherine, Kenneth*, etc. **b.** = *King, King's*: formerly used alone; now usu. in comb., as K.B., King's Bench; K.C., King's Counsel, King's College. **c.** = *Knight* (standing alone Kt.); in K.B., Knight Bachelor; K.B.E., Knight (Commander of the Order of the) British Empire; K.C.B., Knight Commander of the Bath; K.C.S.I., Knight Commander of the Star of India; K.G., Knight of the Garter; K.C.M.G., Knight Commander of the Order of St. Michael and St. George; K.P., Knight of the Order of St. Patrick; K.T., Knight of the Order of the Thistle; etc. **d.** *Electro-physiol.* = *Kathode* (also ka.), *Kathodic.* **e.** kg. = kilogramme; km. = kilometre.

Ka-, frequent var. of CA-, in ME., and in mod. representation of alien words; e.g. *kaaba, kadi, kaffeine*, etc.

‖**Kaama,** (kā·mă). Also **caama, kama, khama (kgama).** 1824. [Said by Burchell to be Hottentot, but current also in Sechuana.] The hartebeest, a S. Afr. antelope.

‖**Kabassou** (kăbæ·su). 1774. [Fr. (Buffon), – Galibi *capaçou*.] An armadillo of the genus *Xenerus*.

The K..with twelve bands GOLDSM.

Kabbala(h, -ism, -ize, var. CABBALA, etc.

Kabob, var. of CABOB.

Kad-: see also CAD-.

‖**Kaddish** (kæ·diʃ). 1613. [Aram. *ḳaddīš* holy.] A portion of the daily ritual of the synagogue, composed of thanksgiving and praise, concluding with a prayer for universal peace; specially recited also by orphan mourners.

‖**Kadi, kadee,** vars. of CADI.

Kaffir (kæ·fəɹ); prop. **Kafir** (kā·fīr). Also **kaffer, kaffre**; and see CAFFRE. 1801. [– Arab. *kāfir*, pr. pple. active of *kafara* be unbelieving.] **1.** = CAFFRE 1, 'infidel', Giaour 1814. **2.** = CAFFRE 2. Also *attrib.*, and as the name of their language 1801. **b.** *pl.* *Stock Exch.* The term for S. African mine shares. Also *attrib.* 1889. **3.** A native of Kafiristan in Asia 1854.

Kaffle, kafle, vars. of COFFLE, caravan.

Kafila, var. of CAFILA, caravan.

‖**Kaftan,** var. of CAFTAN.

‖**Kagu** (kā·gu). 1862. [Native name.] A grallatorial bird (*Rhinochetus jubatus*), of unusual type, peculiar to New Caledonia.

‖**Kahau** (kā·hau). 1840. [Malay, so called from its cry.] The proboscis-monkey of Borneo (*Nasalis larvatus*).

Kail, var. of KALE, colewort, broth.

‖**Kaimakam** (kaimăkā·m). 1645. [Osmanli Turkish *ḳāimaḳām* – Arab. *ḳā'im maḳām* one standing in the place (of another).] In the Turkish Empire: A lieutenant, deputy; a lieutenant-colonel; a deputy-governor; *spec.* the deputy of the Grand Vizier, and governor Constantinople.

Kaiman, Kain: see CAYMAN, CAIN.

Kainite (kai·nəit). 1868. [– G. *kainit*, f. Gr. καινός new + -ITE[1] 2 b; named by C. F. Zincken in 1865 with reference to its recent formation.] *Min.* Hydrous chlorosulphate of magnesium and potassium, found in Prussia and Galicia, largely used as a fertilizer.

Kainozoic, var. CAINOZOIC (*Geol.*).

Kairine (kai·rəin). 1883. [app. f. Gr. καιρός proper time + -INE[5].] *Chem.* A chinoline compound, *oxy-methyl-quinoline tetrahydride*, a strong antipyretic.

Kaiser (kai·zəɹ). ME. [– G. *kaiser* and Du. *keizer*, †*keiser*, †*keser*; a Gmc. adoption of L. *Cæsar* CÆSAR through Gr. καῖσαρ, repr. by OE. *cāsere*, OFris. *keisar*, OS. *kēsur*, *-ar*, ON. *keisari*, Goth. *kaisar*. ME. *caisere* (XII–XV) was – ON.; the mod. use is independent of the ME. currency of the word.] **a.** The Emperor; esp. the German Emperor (since 1871); cf. EMPEROR 1 and 2. **b.** An emperor, as a ruler superior to kings ME.

‖**Kajawah** (kădʒa·wă, ka·dʒāwă). 1634. [Urdu (Pers.) *kajāwah*.] A camel-litter for women; a kind of large pannier or wooden frame, a pair of which are carried by a camel.

‖**Kaka** (kā·kă). 1774. [Maori.] A New Zealand parrot of the genus *Nestor*, esp. *N. meridionalis*; its general colour is olive-brown, varied with red or yellow.

‖**Kakapo** (kā·kăpo). 1843. [Maori, f. *kaka* parrot + *po* night.] The ground-parrot or owl-parrot of New Zealand, *Strigops habroptilus*, with green plumage, marked with dark-brown and yellow.

‖**Kakaralli** (kăkăræ·li). Also **-ali.** 1858. [Native name.] The wood and bark of *Lecythis ollaria*, a tree of British Guiana, the timber of which is very durable in salt water.

‖**Kakemono** (kækĕmōᵘ·no). 1890. [Japanese, f. *kake-* hang + *mono* thing.] A Japanese wall-picture, painted on silk or paper, and mounted on rollers.

Kakistocracy (kækistǫ·krăsi). 1829. [f. Gr. κάκιστος worst + -CRACY, after *aristocracy*.] The government of a state by the worst citizens.

Kako-, var. sp. of CACO-, repr. Gr. κακο- bad, evil, favoured by many recent writers; e.g. *kakodaimon*, *kakogenesis*, etc., and esp. **kakodyl(e.** See the words under C.

‖**Kalan** (kala·n, kēⁱ·lăn). 1861. [Native name.] The sea-otter of the Northern Pacific (*Enhydris lutris*).

Kale, kail (kēⁱl, *Sc.* kēl). ME. [Northern var. of COLE[1].] **1.** A generic name for various edible plants of the genus *Brassica*; cole, colewort, cabbage; *spec.* the variety with wrinkled leaves not forming a compact head (*B. oleracea acephala*), borecole. **2.** Broth in which Scotch kale or cabbage forms a principal ingredient; hence *Sc.* Broth or soup made with various kinds of vegetables 1470.

2. I will be back here to my kail (= dinner) against ane o'clock SCOTT.

‖**Kaleege, kalij** (kălī·dʒ, kā·lidʒ). *E. Ind.* 1864. [– Hindi *kālij* (Yule).] An Asiatic pheasant of the genus *Euplocamus* or *Gallophasis*, found in the Himalayan region. (Corruptly *college-pheasant*.)

Kaleidophone (kăləi·dofoᵘn). 1827. [f. as next + -PHONE.] An instrument (invented by Wheatstone) for exhibiting the phenomena of sound-waves by means of a vibrating rod or plate with a reflector at the end.

Kaleidoscope (kăləi·dŏskoᵘp). 1817. [f. Gr. καλός beautiful + εἶδος form + -SCOPE. Named by its inventor, Sir David Brewster.] An optical instrument, consisting of from two to four reflecting surfaces placed in a tube, at one end of which is a small compartment containing pieces of coloured glass; on looking through the tube, numerous reflections of these are seen, producing brightly-coloured symmetrical figures, which may be constantly altered by rotation of the instrument. Also *fig.*

fig. This rainbow look'd like hope—Quite a celestial k. BYRON. Hence **Kaleidosco·pic, -al** *a.* of or belonging to the k.; exhibiting constantly changing, brightly coloured figures.

Kalend-: see CAL-.

Ka·le-, kai·l-yard. *Sc.* 1574. [f. KALE + YARD *sb.*[1]] **1.** A cabbage-garden, kitchen-garden, as commonly attached to a small cottage. **2.** Used with reference to a class of recent fiction, affecting to describe, with much use of the vernacular, common life in Scotland; hence *attrib.* as *Kailyard School*, *dialect*, etc. 1895 (W. H. Millar). Hence **Kai·lyarder, -ism.**

[The appellation is taken from the Scottish Jacobite song 'There grows a bonnie brier bush in our kail-yard', from which 'Ian Maclaren' took the title of his book 'Beside the Bonnie Brier Bush' (1894).]

Kali (kæ·li, kēⁱ·li, kēⁱ·ləi). 1578. [– N.Afr. Arab. *ḳalī*; see ALKALI.] **1.** = ALKALI 2. Also applied to Barilla (*Salsola Soda*), etc. †**2.** = ALKALI 1; hence, vegetable alkali, potash. (Latinized *kalium*, whence the symbol K for potassium.) –1819.

Hence **Kaliform** (kæ·lifǫɹm), *a.* having the appearance of Kali or Glasswort 1868. **Kaligenous** (kăli·dʒĭnəs), *a. Chem.* producing an alkali; said of metals that form alkalis with oxygen 1854.

‖**Kalmia** (kæ·lmiă). Also **calmia.** 1776. [mod.L. f. name of Peter *Kalm*, a pupil of Linnæus; see -IA[1].] *Bot.* A genus of American evergreen shrubs, N.O. *Ericaceæ*, with showy flowers, including the American Laurel, *K. latifolia*.

‖**Kalon** (kēⁱ·lǫn). 1749. [Gr. καλόν, adj. neut.] The (morally) beautiful; the 'summum bonum'; often *to kalon* (τὸ καλόν the beautiful).

‖**Kalpa** (kæ·lpă). 1794. [Skr.] In Hindu cosmology: A great age of the world, a period of 4,320,000,000 years; a day of Brahma; a thousand yugas.

Kam, var. of CAM *a.* and *adv.*

Kama, var. of KAAMA.

‖**Kamala** (kæ·mălă). 1820. [Skr.] A fine orange-coloured powder consisting of the glandular hairs from the fruit-capsules of an East Indian tree (*Mallotus philippinensis*), used for dyeing silks yellow, and as a vermifuge.

Kame, kaim (kēⁱm). 1862. *north.* and *Sc.* form of COMB *sb.* (q. v.), esp. in the sense of a steep and sharp hill ridge; hence in *Geol.* an esker or osar.

‖**Kami** (kā·mi). 1727. [Japanese, = 'superior, lord'.] **1.** A title given to daimios and governors, = 'lord'. **2.** In the Shinto or native religion of Japan: A divinity, a god (used by missionaries, etc. as = God).

‖**Kamichi** (ka·miʃi). 1834. [Brazilian, through Fr. *kamichi* (Buffon).] The horned screamer (*Palamedea cornuta*), a bird of Guiana and the Amazon.

Kampseen, Kamsin, vars. of KHAMSIN.

Kamptulicon (kæmptiū·likǫn). 1844. [f. Gr. ^ καμπτός flexible + οὖλος thick + -ικόν n. of -ικός -IC.] Floor-cloth composed of a mixture of india-rubber, gutta-percha, and cork, mounted on canvas.

Kan: see CAN, KHAN.

‖**Kanaka** (kæ·năkă, in Australia *improp.* kănæ·kă). 1840. [Hawaiian *kanaka* = 'man'.] A native of the South Sea Islands. Also *attrib*,

‖**Kanchil** (ka·ntʃil). 1820. [Malay *kanchil*, *kanchīl*.] The smallest known species of chevrotain (*Tragulus kanchil*), found in Borneo, Java, and Malacca.

Kand, var. of CAND, fluor-spar.

Kangaroo (kæŋgărū·). 1770. [Said by Capt. James Cook (1770) and Joseph Banks (1770) to have been a native Australian name (*kangooroo*), which is supported by some later writers, but denied by others.] **1.** A marsupial mammal of the family *Macropodidæ*, remarkable for its strong hind-quarters and leaping-power. The species are natives of Australia, Tasmania, Papua, and some neighbouring isles; the larger kinds being known as *kangaroos*, the smaller as *wallabies*. Also as *collect. sing.* **2.** With qualifying words, as **Brush K.** = WALLABY; **Giant, Great (†Sooty) K.,** *Macropus giganteus*; HARE-**K.**; RAT-**K.**; ROCK **K.**; **Tree K.**, an arboreal kangaroo (genus *Dendrolagus*). **3.** *fig.* esp. *joc.* A native of Australia 1827. **b.** *pl.* In Stock Exchange slang: West Australian mining shares; also, dealers in these shares 1896. **c.** Applied to a form of Parliamentary closure by which some amendments are selected for discussion and others excluded 1913. **4.** *attrib.* 1828.

Combs.: **k.-apple,** the edible fruit of the Australian plants *Solanum laciniatum* and *S.vescum*; also, the plants; **-bear,** the koala; **-grass,** a tall fodder-grass (*Anthistiria australis*), found in Australasia, Southern Asia, and Africa; **-mouse,** (*a*) the Australian pouched mouse; (*b*) a small American rodent of the genus *Perognathus*; etc.

Kangaroo-rat. 1788. A small Australian marsupial; a rat-kangaroo, potoroo, bettong.

‖**Kanoon.** (kănū·n). 1714. [– (Pers. –) Arab. *ḳānūn*.] A species of dulcimer, harp, or sackbut, with fifty to sixty strings.

Kant, obs. f. CANT *a.*, and CANT *sb.*[1]; also an oblique arm of a pier.

Kantian (kæ·ntiăn). 1803. [f. Immanuel *Kant*, German philosopher (1724–1804); see -IAN.]

A. *adj.* Of, pertaining to, or connected with Kant or his philosophy 1817. **B.** *sb.* One who holds the philosophical system of Kant. Hence **Ka·ntianism**; so **Ka·ntism, Ka·ntist, Ka·ntite** (*rare*).

Kantry, obs. f. CANTREF.

Kaolin (kā·ŏlin, kēⁱ·ŏlin). 1727. [– Fr. *kaolin* – Chinese *kao-*, *kau-ling* (f. *kao* high + *ling* hill), name of a mountain in North China whence first obtained.] A fine white clay produced by the decomposition of feldspar, used in the manufacture of porcelain; first employed by the Chinese, but subseq. found in many places.

Hence **Kaoli·nic** *a.* **Kaolinite** (kā-, kēⁱ·ŏlinəit), *Min.* a general name for those porcelain clays of which kaolin is the typical variety 1867. **Kaolinize** (kā-, kēⁱ·ŏlinəiz), *v. trans.* to convert into kaolin 1874. **Kaoliniza·tion.**

‖**Kapelle** (kape·lĕ). 1838. [G. (XVI) – It. *capella* (mod. *cappella*). Cf. CHAPEL *sb.* 7.] In Germany, a musical establishment consisting of a band or orchestra, with or without a choir, such as used to be maintained at most of the German courts. Hence ‖**Kapellmeister** (kape·lməi·ster), the leader or conductor of a kapelle or orchestra.

‖**Kapok** (kēⁱ·pǫk, kā·-). Also **capoc.** 1750. [– Malay *kāpoq*, through Fr. *capoc*, Du. *kapok*, or G. *kapock*.] A fine short-stapled cotton wool, known as silk cotton, surrounding the seeds of the tree *Eriodendron anfractuosum*; used for stuffing cushions, etc. Also *k.-tree*.

Kapp (kæp). 1891. [f. Gisbert *Kapp*, a designer of dynamos; cf. *Ampere*, etc.] A workshop unit of magnetic lines of force, = 6,000 times the centimetre-gramme-second unit.

Karacul: see CARACUL.

‖**Karagan** (kā·răgan). 1800. [Turki, f. *kara* black.] A species of fox, *Vulpes karagan*, inhabitating Tartary.

Karaite (kēᵊ·rā,əit). 1727. [f. Heb. *ḳ'rā'īm* scripturalists, f. *ḳārā* read; see -ITE[1] 1.] A member of a Jewish sect which rejects rabbinical tradition and bases its tenets on a literal interpretation of the Scriptures. So **Ka·raism, Ka·raitism,** the religious system of the Karaites.

‖**Karatas** (kărēⁱ·tăs). 1727. [perh. of Carib origin.] A West Indian and South American plant (*Bromelia karatas*), allied to the pine-apple, and yielding a valuable fibre; silk-grass.

‖**Karma** (kā·ɹmă). 1828. [Skr. *karma-n* action, effect, fate.] In Hinduism and Buddhism, the sum of a person's actions in one of his successive states of existence, regarded as determining his fate in the next; hence, necessary fate or destiny, following as effect from cause. Hence **Ka·rmic** *a.*

Karmathian, Car- (kaɹmēⁱ·þiăn), *sb.* (*adj.*). 1819. [After *Karmat*, founder of the sect.] One of a sect of Moslems founded in the 9th cent. As *adj.* Belonging to this sect.

Karn, -e, Karob, -e: see CAIRN, CAROB.

‖**Karoo, karroo** (kărū·). 1789. [Hottentot; of uncertain etym.] The name given to barren tracts in South Africa, consisting of extensive elevated plateaus, with a clayey soil, which during the dry season are entirely waterless and arid.

Kaross (kărọ·s). 1731. Also **kross(e, cross.** [S. Afr. Du. *karos*, perh. Hottentot, or corrupt. of Du. *kuras* cuirass.] A mantle (or sleeveless jacket) made of the skins of animals with the hair on, used by the Hottentots and other natives of South Africa.

‖**Karri** (kæ·ri). 1870. [Native name (West Australia).] An Australian tree (*Eucalyptus diversicolor*, one of the 'blue gums'); also, its hard red timber, used in street-paving.

Karstenite (kā·ɹstĕnəit). 1844. [– G. *karstenit*, named, 1813, after D. L. G. *Karsten*; see -ITE[1] 2 b.] *Min.* = ANHYDRITE.

‖**Kartel** (kā·ɹt'l). Also **cartle.** 1880. [S. Afr. Du.; app. – Pg. *catel, catle, catre* 'little bed' – Tamil *kaṭṭil* bedstead.] The wooden bed or hammock in a S. African ox-wagon.

Karval, -vel, obs. ff. CARVEL.

Karyo- (kæ·rio), occas. **caryo-,** comb. f. Gr. κάρυον nut, kernel, employed in biological terms referring to the nucleus of an animal or vegetable cell, esp. to changes which take place in its structure. The earliest of these were *karyolysis*, *-lytic* (Auerbach, 1874), *karyokinesis* (Schleicher).

†**Ka·ser.** [OE. *cāsere*; see KAISER.] = KAISER –1605.

‖**Kat.** 1858. [Arab. *ḳatt*.] A shrub, *Catha edulis*, N.O. *Celastraceæ*, a native of Arabia, where its leaves are used as tea.

Kat-: see also CAT-.

Kata-, *pref.*, a direct adoption of Gr. κατα-, in recent use often preferred to CATA- (q. v.).

‖**Katabasis** (kătæ·bāsis). 1837. [Gr. κατάβασις f. καταβαίνειν go down; cf. ANABASIS.] A going down; a military retreat.

Katabatic (kætăbæ·tik), *a.* 1918. [– Gr. καταβατικός, f. καταβαίνειν go down; see -IC.] *Meteorol.* Of a wind; Caused by the local gravitation of cold air down a steep slope.

Katabolism (kătæ·bŏliz'm). 1876. [f. Gr. καταβολή, f. καταβάλλειν throw down; see -ISM.] Destructive metabolism. So **Katabo·lic** *a.*

‖**Katabothron** (kætăbọ·þrǫn). Also **cata-.** Pl. **-a (-ons).** 1820. [– Gr. κατάβοθρον, f. κατά down + βόθρος hole.] A subterranean channel or deep chasm formed by water.

Katastate (kătæ·stēt). 1889. [f. Gr. κατά down + στατός placed.] *Biol.* One of the simpler products of katabolism.

Katheter, Kathetometer: see CATHET-.

Katydid (kēⁱ·tidid). *U.S.* 1784. [imit.] A large green orthopterous insect of the family *Locustidæ*, of arboreal habits, which produces by stridulation a noise to which its name is due; the common or broad-winged species (*Cyrtophyllum concavum*) abounds in the central and eastern states of America.

Kauri (kau·ri). Also **cowry, -ie, cowdi(e, kourie,** etc. 1823. [Maori *kauri*, also written *kaudi*, *r* and *d* interchanging in Maori.] A tall coniferous tree of New Zealand (*Agathis* or *Dammara australis*), which furnishes valuable timber and a resin called kauri-gum.

Comb. **k.-gum, -resin,** the fossil resin of kauri, used as a varnish (cf. DAMMAR).

‖**Kava** (kā·vă). Also **cava, kaava, kawa;** also AVA. 1777. [South-western Polynesian.] An intoxicating beverage prepared from the chewed, grated, or pounded roots of the Polynesian shrub *Piper methysticum* or *Macropiper latifolium* (N.O. *Piperaceæ*). Also, this plant, or its root. Also *attrib.* Hence **Ka·vain, Ka·wain,** a crystalline resin occurring in the kava root.

‖**Kavass** (kăvɑ·s). Also **cavass, kawass,** etc. 1819. [Turk. – Arab. *ḳawwās* archer, f. *ḳaws* bow.] An armed constable, an armed servant or courier (in Turkey).

Kaw, obs. f. CAW.

Kaw-: see CAW-, CAU-.

‖**Kayak** (kai·ăk). 1757. [Eskimo.] The canoe of the Greenlanders and other Eskimo, made of a framework of light wood covered with sealskins sewn together; the top has an opening in the middle to admit the single kayaker, who laces the covering round him to prevent the entrance of water. Hence **Kay·a-ker,** one who manages a k.

Kayan, see CAYENNE.

Kayles (kēⁱlz), *sb. pl.* Now *dial.* or *Hist.* ME. [– (M)Du. *kegel*, † *keyl-* (in *keylbane* skittle-alley) = OHG. *kegil* (G. *kegel*) tapering stick, cone, skittle.] *pl.* The set of pins used in a kind of ninepins or skittles; usu., the game played with these. **b.** *sing.* One of these pins (*rare*) 1652.

Kaynard, var. of CAYNARD *Obs.*, sluggard.

‖**Kazi** (kā·zī). 1625. [– Arab. *al-ḳāḍī* CADI.] A civil judge; = CADI.

‖**Kea** (kēⁱ·ă). 1862. [Maori; from its cry.] The Green Alpine Parrot of New Zealand (*Nestor notabilis*), which destroys sheep in order to prey upon their kidney-fat.

Kearn(e, obs. ff. KERN.

Keb (keb), *sb.* ME. [Of unkn. origin. Cf. AL. *kebba, kubba* XIV.] A ewe that has lost her lamb. Hence **Keb,** *v. dial. intr.* Of a ewe: **a.** To cast a lamb prematurely, or dead 1816. **b.** *To keb at*, to refuse to suckle (a lamb).

Bewitching the sheep, causing the ewes to 'keb' SCOTT.

Kebab, -ob, vars. of CABOB.

Kebbuck (ke·bək). *Sc.* 1470. [Of unkn. origin.] A cheese.

A huge kebbock—a cheese, that is, made with ewe-milk mixed with cow's milk SCOTT.

†**Ke·chel.** [OE. *cæ̆ćel* = MHG. *kuechel* (G. dial. *küchel*); dim f. **kōk-*, var. of **kak-*; see CAKE *sb.*] A little cake.

A God's k.: a cake given as alms in the name, or for the sake, of God. CHAUCER.

Keck, *sb.* Now *dial.* 1624. [A sing. of *kex* taken as a pl.] = KEX.

Keck (kek), *v.* 1601. [imit.] **1.** *intr.* To make a sound as if about to vomit; to retch; hence *to k. at*, to reject (food, etc.) with loathing. Also *fig.* **2.** *intr.* Of a bird: To utter a sound like *keck* 1844. Hence †**Ke·ck-ish** *a.* inclined to k.; squeamish 1603.

Keckle (ke·k'l), *sb. Sc.* 1820. [f. KECKLE v.[1]] A short spasmodic laugh; a chuckle.

Keckle (ke·k'l), *v.*[1] 1513. [var. (chiefly Sc.) of CACKLE *v.*[1], CHECKLE.] **1.** *intr.* To cackle. **2.** To chuckle, laugh, giggle; *trans.* to utter with or express by chuckling 1857.

2. 'Ah, you're a wag, Sir', keckled the old man KINGSLEY.

Keckle (ke·k'l), *v.*[2] 1627. [Of unkn. origin. Cf. CACKLE *v.*[2]] *Naut. trans.* To case a cable or hawser with rope in order to prevent chafing: cf. CACKLE *v.*[2] Hence **Ke·ckling** *vbl. sb.* old ropes which are wound about a cable.

Ke·ckle, *v.*[3] *dial.* 1619. [freq. of KECK *v.*; see -LE.] = KECK *v.* 1. Hence †**Ke·cklish** *a.* (*rare*), = KECKISH 1601.

Kecksy (ke·ksi). Chiefly *dial.* 1599. [f. *kexes* pl. of KEX, taken as = *kexies*.] = KEX, a hollow plant-stem.

Hateful Docks, rough Thistles, Keksyes, Burres SHAKS.

†**Ke·cky,** *a.* 1711. [f. KECK *sb.* + -Y[1].] = KEXY.

Ked, kade (ked, kēⁱd). 1570. [Of unkn. origin.] A sheep-tick or sheep-louse (*Melophagus ovinus*).

Kedge (kedʒ), *sb.* 1769. [app. short for KEDGE-ANCHOR.] = KEDGE-ANCHOR.

Kedge (kedʒ), *v.* 1627. [Earliest form *cagge* (XIV), dial. *cadge*; for the variation of *a* with *e* cf. CAG|KEG, CATCH|KETCH.] *intr.* **a.** To warp a ship, or move it from one position to another by winding in a hawser attached to a small anchor dropped at some distance; also *trans.* to warp. **b.** Of a ship: To move by means of kedging.

Kedge-anchor. Now *rare.* 1704. [f. KEDGE *v.*; cf. earlier *cagging-anker* (1497).] A small anchor with an iron stock used in mooring or warping.

†**Ke·dger.** 1497. [f. KEDGE *v.* = -ER[1].] = prec. –1751.

‖**Kedgeree** (ke·dʒərī). 1625. [Hindi *khichṛī*, Skr. *k'rsara* 'dish of rice and sesamum'.] An Indian dish of rice boiled with split pulse, onions, eggs, butter, and condiments; also, in European cookery, a dish made of cold fish, boiled rice, eggs, and condiments, served hot.

Kedlock (ke·dlǫk). *Obs.* exc. *dial.* ME. [app. repr. OE. *ćedelc* 'herb mercury', of unkn. origin.] **1.** = CHARLOCK. **2.** Identified with KEX 1694.

Keech (kītʃ). *Obs.* exc. *dial.* 1613. [Of unkn. origin.] A lump of congealed fat; the fat of a slaughtered animal rolled up into a lump.

Keek (kīk), *v.* Now only *Sc.* and *n. dial.* [ME. *kike*, corresp. in sense, and perh. form, to MDu. *kīken, kieken* (Du. *kijken*), LG. *kīken* look, peep.] *intr.* To peep. Also *fig.* of things. Hence **Keek** *sb.* a peep 1773.

Keel (kīl), *sb.*[1] [ME. *kele* – ON. *kjǫlr* :- **keluz*.] **1.** The lowest longitudinal timber of a ship or boat, on which the framework of the whole is built up; in boats and small vessels forming a prominent central ridge on the under surface; in iron vessels, a combination of iron plates taking the place of the keel of a wooden vessel. **2.** A ship, vessel. (*poet.*, after L. *carina*.) 1547. **3.** That part of anything which corresponds to a ship's keel; a keel-like lower part 1726; esp. in aircraft 1888. **4.** A central ridge along the back or convex surface of any organ or structure, as a leaf, a petal, a glume of grass, the lower mandible of a bird, etc. 1597. **5.** *spec.* in *Bot.* and *Zool.*

a. The two lowest petals of a papilionaceous corolla, more or less united and shaped like the prow of a boat; the carina 1776. **b.** A prominent ridge along the breastbone of birds of the class *Carinatæ* 1766.

6. *Arch.* A ridge or edge on a rounded moulding 1835.

1. The crooked k. the parting surge divides POPE. **False k.,** (*a*) an additional keel attached to the bottom of the true keel to protect it and increase the stability of the vessel; (*b*) an external keel subsequently added to a vessel. Phr. *On* (or *with*) *even k.*, with the keel level (see EVEN *a.*).

Comb.: **k.-block,** one of the short pieces of timber on which the keel of a vessel rests in building or in a dry dock; **-raking** = KEELHAULING; †**-rope,** a coarse rope formerly used for clearing the limber holes by drawing it backwards and forwards (Smyth).

Keel (kīl), *sb.*[2] [ME. *kele* – MLG. *kēl*, MDu. *kiel* ship, boat = OE. *ćēol*, OS., OHG. *kiol* (Du., G. *kiel*), ON. *kjóll* :- Gmc. **keulaz*. Since the 16th c. the Du. and G. *kiel* has lost its sense of 'ship' and taken that of KEEL *sb.*[1]] **1.** A flat-bottomed vessel, esp. a lighter as used on the Tyne and Wear for loading colliers. **b.** The quantity of coals carried in a keel, now = 8 Newcastle chaldrons or 21 tons 4 cwt. 1750. **2.** Used to render OE. *ćēol* in the passage of the Saxon Chronicle relating to the first coming of the Angles to Britain 1605.

Keel, *sb.*[3] Chiefly *Sc.* 1480. [Of unkn. origin.] Ruddle, or a mark made with this.

Keel (kīl), *v.*[1] *Obs.* exc. *dial.* [OE. *cēlan* = OFris. *kēla* (Du. *koelen*), OHG. *kuolen* (G. *kühlen*), ON. *kœla* :- Gmc. **kōljan*, f. **kōl-* COOL.] **1.** *trans.* To cool; *spec.* to cool (a hot liquid) by stirring, skimming, or pouring in something cold, in order to prevent it from boiling over. **2.** *intr.* To become cool or cold ME.

1. While greasie Ione doth keele the pot SHAKS. *fig.* Likely to lessen and k. the affections of the Subject MILT.

Keel (kīl), *v.*[2] 1808. [f. KEEL *sb.*[1]] **1.** *trans.* To plough (the sea) with a keel (*nonce-use*). **2.** *intr.* Of a ship: To roll on her keel 1867. **3.** Orig. *U.S. trans.* To turn up the keel of, show the bottom of. *K. over*, to turn over; to upset, capsize. 1828. **b.** *intr.* To turn or be turned over; to be upset; to fall over or be felled as if by a shock. 1860.

Keelage (kī·lėdʒ). *rare.* 1500. [f. KEEL *sb.*[1] + -AGE. Cf. med.L. *killagium* (XIII).] A toll or due payable by a ship on entering or anchoring in a harbour.

Keel-boat (kī·lbōᵘt). 1695. [f. KEEL *sb.*[1] and [2].] †**a.** ? A small keel –1746. **a.** A large flat boat used on American rivers 1822. **c.** A yacht with a keel instead of a centre-board 1893.

Keeled (kīld), *a.* 1787. [f. KEEL *sb.*[1] + -ED[2].] **a.** Having a keel 1847. **b.** Having a central dorsal ridge; carinate.

a. The boat was..k. and clinker-built MEDWIN. **b.** A k. leaf 1848, sternum 1865.

Keeler[1] (kī·ləɹ). *rare.* ME. [f. KEEL *sb.*[2] + -ER[1].] †**a.** A keelman. **b.** A man employed in managing coal-barges and colliers in the Newcastle district 1875.

Keeler[2]. *Obs.* exc. *dial.* ME. [f. KEEL *v.*[1] + -ER[1].] A vessel for cooling liquids; a shallow tub.

Keelhaul (kī·lhǫl), *v.* 1622. [– Du. *kielhalen.*] *trans.* To haul (a person) under the keel of a ship, either by lowering him on one side and hauling him across to the other side, or, in the case of smaller vessels, lowering him at the bows and drawing him along under the keel to the stern.

Keeling (kī·liŋ). *Sc.* and *n. dial.* ME. [Of unkn. origin.] A cod-fish.

Kee·livine, keelie vine. *Sc.* and *n. dial.* 1782. [Of unkn. origin.] A black-lead pencil, or more generally, any coloured pencil enclosed in wood (as a *red k.*); also, locally, black-lead, plumbago. Also *attrib.*, as *k. pen*, a pencil. Hence **Kee·livined** *a.* marked with a pencil.

Keelman (kī·lmǣn). ME. [f. KEEL *sb.*[2]] One who works on a keel or barge.

Keels, var. of KAYLES.

Keelson (also **Keelsale**), var. of KELSON.

Keen (kīn), *sb.* 1830. [– Ir. *caoine*; see KEEN *v.*[2]] An Irish funeral wail.

Keen (kīn), *a.* (*adv.*). [OE. *cēne* = OS. **kōni*, MLG. *kōne* (Du. *koen*), OHG. *kuoni* (G. *kühn*) bold, brave, ON. *kœnn* skilful, expert :– Gmc. **kōnjaz.*] †**1.** Wise, learned, clever –ME. †**2. a.** Brave, bold, daring –1605. †**b.** Of kings, etc.: Mighty, powerful, strong –1510. †**c.** Fierce, savage; cruel; harsh (*to* a person) –1622. †**d.** Bold, proud, insolent, heinous –1594. **3.** Having a very sharp edge or point; extremely sharp. (Now somewhat rhet., exc. in *keen edge.*) ME. **4.** *transf.* **a.** Operating on the touch or taste like a sharp instrument; acrid, pungent, stinging (now *unusual*) ME. **b.** Of cold, etc.: Piercing, intense. Of wind, air, etc.: Biting, piercing ME. **c.** Of sound, light, scent: Sharp, penetrating; shrill; vivid; clear; strong ME. **5.** Causing acute pain or deep distress; intense, bitter; sharp, cutting ME. **6.** Eager, ardent, fervid; intense ME.; const. *on, upon* 1714. **7.** Of the eyes, etc.: Sharp, penetrating. Hence, of other senses: Highly sensitive. 1720. **b.** Intellectually acute, shrewd; suggestive of mental sharpness 1704. †**8.** *adv.* Keenly –1667.

3. Out he caught a knyfe as A rasour kene CHAUCER. Plucke the keene teeth from the fierce Tygers jawes SHAKS. *fig.* Words K. to wound as sharpened swords SHELLEY. **4. a.** K. mustard 1658, hail SHELLEY. **b.** While the Winds Blow moist and k. MILT. **c.** One star..with k. beams SHELLEY. **5.** The keenest mental terrors DICKENS. K. speeches MACAULAY. **6.** A k. sportsman 1827. K. competition 1862, enjoyment 1865. K. about money KINGSLEY. **7.** Her glance is as the razor k. GAY. Dogs k. of scent 1875. **b.** A k. attorney CRABBE. His face was k. WORDSW. Hence **Kee·n-ly** *adv.*, **-ness.**

†**Keen,** *v.*[1] ME. [f. KEEN *a.*] †**a.** *intr.* To become keen. **b.** *trans.* To render keen; to sharpen 1599–1746.

Keen (kīn), *v.*[2] 1811. [– Ir. *caoinim* I wail.] **1.** *intr.* To utter the keen for the dead; to wail bitterly. **2.** *trans.* To bewail with Irish wailing 1830.

Hence **Keener,** a professional mourner at Irish wakes and funerals.

Keep (kīp), *sb.* ME. [f. KEEP *v.*] †**1.** Care, attention, heed, notice. Const. *of, infin.*, or *cl.* –1647. **2.** Charge; orig. only in phr. †*to take k.* ME. **3.** *Hist.* The innermost and strongest structure or central tower of a mediæval castle, serving as a last defence; a tower; a stronghold, donjon 1586. **4.** A contrivance which serves for containing or retaining something 1615; e.g. a stop in a door-frame 1833; a part of the axle-box in a locomotive engine, fitted beneath the axle and serving to hold an oiled pad against it 1881. **5.** The act of keeping or maintaining; the fact of being kept 1763. **b.** The food required to keep a person or animal; provender, pasture; maintenance 1825.

2. Take euer a besy kepe of thy selfe CAXTON. Often he vsed of hys keepe a sacrifice to bring SPENSER. **3.** Like the proud K. of Windsor rising in majesty of proportion, and girt [etc.] BURKE. Yon huge k. that hinders half the heaven TENNYSON. **5.** Phr. *Out at k.*, said of animals in hired pastures. *In good k.*, well kept. *For keeps*: to keep, for good; hence, altogether. *colloq. Comb.* **k.-tower** = sense 3.

Keep (kīp), *v.* Pa. t. and pa. pple. **kept.** [Late OE. *cēpan*, pa. t. *cēpte*, of which no cognates are known. Its sense-development has been infl. by its being used to render L. *servare*, with its comps. *conservare, observare, præservare, reservare.* Its meanings have close affinity with those of *hold*, but the meaning 'support, sustain' of the latter does not belong to *keep.*]

I. Early senses (with *genitive* in OE., afterwards with *simple object*). †**1.** To seize, lay hold of; to snatch, take –ME. †**2.** To try to catch or get –ME. †**3.** To take in, receive, contain, hold –ME. †**4.** To take in with the eyes, ears, or mind; to mark, observe; to watch –1697. †**5.** To watch for, await –1485. †**6.** To lie in wait for; to intercept on the way –ME. †**7.** To encounter –ME. †**8.** To meet in a friendly way; to greet, welcome –1460.

4. While the stars and course of heaven I k., My wearied eyes were seiz'd with fatal sleep DRYDEN.

II. *trans.* (in early use also *intr.*) †**1.** To have regard, to care, to reck –1589. †**2.** *intr.* To have care, take care; to give heed, look *to* –1450. **3.** *trans.* To pay attention or regard to; to observe, stand to OE. **4.** To celebrate, solemnize ME. **5.** To observe by attendance, etc., or in some prescribed or regular way 1450. **5.** To guard, defend, protect, preserve, save ME. **6.** To take care of; to look after, watch over, tend ME. **7.** To maintain in proper order ME. **8.** To maintain continuously in proper form and order (a diary, books, etc.) 1552. **9.** To provide for the sustenance of; to maintain, support. Also *refl.* ME. **10.** To maintain in one's service, or for one's use or enjoyment 1548. **b.** *To k. a woman* as a mistress 1530. **11.** To have habitually in stock 1706. †**12.** *refl.* To conduct oneself, behave –ME. **13.** To preserve in being or operation ME. **14.** With complement: To preserve, maintain, retain, or cause to continue, in some specified condition, state, place, position, action, or course ME. Also *refl.* **15.** To hold as a captive or prisoner; to hold in custody; to prevent from escaping ME. **16.** To cause or induce to remain; to detain. Also *fig.* 1653. **17.** To hold back; to restrain, control. Const. *from* (*off, out of*). ME. Also *refl.* **18.** To withhold from present use, to reserve; to lay up, store up. Also *refl.* ME. **19.** Actively to hold in possession; to continue to have, hold, or possess. Also *absol.* (The opposite of *to lose*; now a leading sense.) ME. Also *fig.* **20.** To withhold (*from*) 1461. **21.** To hide, conceal; not to divulge ME. **22.** To continue to follow (a way, path, course, etc.) so as not to lose it or get out of it ME. **23.** To stay or remain in, on, or at (a place); not to leave ME. **b.** To stay or retain one's place in or on, against opposition 1599. **24.** To carry on, conduct ME. **25.** To conduct as one's own 1513. **26.** To carry on, maintain (an action, war, disturbance, or the like) ME.

1. Ne how the grekes pleye The wake pleyes ne kepe I nat to seye CHAUCER. **3.** To kepe couenaunt LD. BERNERS. To. k. rules 1668, Faith STEELE, an oath FREEMAN, an appointment 1891. **4.** Phr. *To k. chapels, roll-call* (at college or school), *to k. terms, residence*, etc. *To k. regular* or *proper* (and so *late, early*) *hours.* **5.** His goode shelde kept hym CAXTON. The horsemen were left..to..kepe the passage 1560. To keepe him from stumbling *Tam. Shr.* III. ii. 59. **6.** Nor shall my Nel k. Lodgers SHAKS. Shall I keepe your hogs, and eat huskes with them? SHAKS. *To k. wicket* (see WICKET). Also *absol.* To act as wicket-keeper. **7.** This space is kept with the scythe 1827. **8.** No record was kept of the losses of the English 1869. **9.** The land would barely k. the cows 1858. He kept the younger ladies in gloves 1890. **10.** Because thou dost not keepe a dogge SHAKS. To k. pigs 1833, a gig 1853, a valet 1860. **13.** Phr. *To k. silence, company, stop, tune* (*with*); *to k. a look out, ward, watch*, etc. **14.** Phr. *To k. a prisoner, at arm's length, at it, in repair, out of mischief*, etc. **16.** Don't let me k. you 1885. **17.** Kepe thy tonge from euell BIBLE (Great) *Ps.* 34:13. **18.** To k. oneself for great occasions FREEMAN. **19.** To get and kepe not is but losse of payne 1559. **21.** Phr. *To k.* COUNSEL, a SECRET. **22.** We kept no path DE FOE. **23.** Phr. *To k. one's bed, one's room* (as in sickness); *to k. the house. To k. the deck, the saddle, one's ground*, etc. **25.** I k. a Coffee-house STEELE. **26.** What a catterwalling doe you keepe heere! SHAKS.

III. *intr.* **1.** To reside, dwell, live, lodge (now only *colloq.*, esp. at Cambridge and in U.S.) ME. **2.** To remain or stay for the time 1560. **3.** To remain or continue in a specified condition, state, position, etc. late ME. **4.** To continue, persevere, go on 1548. **5.** To remain in good condition; to last without spoiling. Also *fig.* 1586.

1. Where does Mr. Hollis 'keep'? inquired he of his bedmaker 1859. **2.** I kept..within doors DE FOE. The wind kept in the proper quarter 1891. **3.** Keepe in that minde, Ile deserue it *Merry W.* III. iii. 89. To k. friends 1883. **4.** Turn to the left and k. straight on 1889. She kept tumbling off her horse 1892. **5.** I had no hops to make it k. DE FOE. Your story..can k. 1889.

With preps. in specialized senses. **Keep at —.** To work persistently at. Also *to k. at it* (see AT *prep.* II. 2). **Keep from —.** To abstain from; to remain away from; to restrain oneself *from.* **Keep to —. a.** To stick to, abide by (a promise, etc.). **c.** To confine or restrict oneself to. **Keep with—.** To remain with; to keep company with; to keep up with.

With adverbs. **Keep away. a.** *trans.* To cause to remain absent or afar. **b.** *intr.* To remain absent or at a distance. **c.** *Naut. trans.* To cause to sail 'off the wind' or to leeward. *intr.* To sail off the wind or to leeward. **Keep back. a.** *trans.* To restrain; to detain; to hold back forcibly. **b.** To withhold; to reserve designedly; to conceal. **c.** *intr.* To hold oneself back. **Keep down. a.** *trans.* To hold down; to hold in subjection or under control; to repress. **b.** To keep low in amount or number; to prevent from growing or increasing. **c.** *Painting.* To keep low in tone. **d.** *Printing.* To set in lower-case type; to use capitals sparingly. **e.** *intr.* To remain subdued. **Keep in. a.** *trans.* To confine within; to hold in check; not to utter or give vent to; *spec.* to confine in school after hours. **b.** To keep (a fire) burning: see IN *adv.* II. 2 e. Also *intr.* of a fire. **c.** *Printing.* To set type closely spaced. **d.** *To keep one's hand in:* see HAND *sb.* **e.** *intr.* To remain indoors, or within a retreat, place, position, etc. **f.** To remain in favour or on good terms *with* (now *colloq.*). **Keep off. a.** *trans.* To hinder from coming near; to ward off; to avert. **b.** *intr.* To stay at a distance; not to come on. **Keep on. a.** *trans.* To maintain or retain in an existing condition or relation. **b.** To keep (a fire, etc.) going continuously. **c.** *intr.* To continue in a course or action; to go on with something. Now freq. with *pres. pple.* **d.** To remain fixed; to stay on. **Keep to.** *Naut. trans.* To cause (a ship) to sail close to the wind. **Keep together. a.** *trans.* To cause to remain in association or union. **b.** *intr.* To remain associated or united. **Keep under.** *trans.* To hold under control; to keep down. **Keep up. a.** *trans.* To keep shut up. †**b.** To keep undivulged. **c.** To support, sustain. Also *intr.* To bear up, so as not to break down. **b.** To maintain in proper condition; to support; to keep in repair; to keep burning. **e.** To maintain, retain, preserve (a quality, state of things, etc.). **f.** To maintain, go on with (an action). **g.** To cause to remain out of bed. **h.** *Printing.* To keep (type or matter) standing; also, to use capitals freely. **i.** *To k. up to*: to prevent from falling below (a level, standard, etc.); to keep informed of. Also *intr.* for *refl.* **j.** *intr.* To continue alongside; to proceed at an equal pace *with* (*lit.* and *fig.*). †**k.** To stay within doors; to put up *at.*

Keeper (kī·pəɹ). ME. [f. KEEP *v.* + -ER[1].] One who or that which keeps.

I. 1. One who has charge, care, or oversight of any person or thing. **b.** An officer who has charge of a forest, woods, or grounds; now *esp.* = GAMEKEEPER 1488. **2.** One who observes or keeps a law, promise, etc. ME. **3.** One who owns or carries on some establishment or business 1440. †**4.** One who keeps a mistress –1748. **5.** One who or that which keeps or retains 1548. **6.** Any mechanical device for keeping something in its place; a clasp, catch, etc. *spec.* (*a*) a loop securing the end of a buckled strap; (*b*) the mousing of a hook; (*c*) the box into which the bolt of a lock projects when shot; etc. 1575. **b.** A bar of soft iron placed across the poles of a horseshoe magnet to prevent loss of power; an armature; also, a shoe 1837. **c.** A ring that keeps another (esp. the wedding-ring) on the finger; a guard-ring 1851.

1. And hee [Cain] said, I know not: Am I my brothers keeper? *Gen.* 4: 9. *K. of the Exchange and Mint*: the Master of the Mint, an office held by the Chancellor of the Exchequer. *K. of the Great* (†*Broad*) *Seal*: an officer in England and Scotland who has the custody of the Great Seal; in England the office is now held by the Lord High Chancellor. *K. of the Privy Seal*: (*a*) in England an officer through whose hands pass charters, etc. before coming to the Great Seal, now called Lord Privy Seal; (*b*) a similar officer in Scotland and the Duchy of Cornwall. **3.** Isaac Beckett..Alehouse-keeper 1713.

II. 1. One who continues or remains *at* or *away from* a place 1611. **2.** A fruit, or other product, that keeps (well or ill) 1843.

Keepership (kī·pəɹʃip). 1485. [f. prec. + -SHIP.] The office or position of a keeper.

Keeping (kī·piŋ), *vbl. sb.* ME. [f. KEEP *v.* + -ING[1].] The action of KEEP *v.* **1.** Observance of a rule, institution, practice, promise, etc. **2.** Custody, charge, guardianship ME. **b.** Guard, defence. *Obs.* exc. *dial.* ME. **3.** The taking care of a thing or person; the state or condition in which a thing is kept ME. **4.** = KEEP *sb.* 5 b. 1644. †**b.** The maintaining of a mistress or lover; the fact or condition of being so maintained –1768. †**5.** Confinement; prison –1513. **6.** Retention; *pl.* things kept or retained ME. **7.** Reservation for future use 1560. **8. a.** In *Painting. orig.* The maintenance of the proper relation between the representations of nearer and more distant objects in a picture; hence, the maintenance of harmony of composition 1715. **b.** *gen.* Agreement, congruity, harmony 1819. **9.** Staying or remaining in a place or in a certain condition; remaining sound 1742.

1. The k. of Easter 1678. **2.** As upright as a new Chancellor, who has the k. of the King's Conscience 1735, **4. b.** Pray Madam were you ever in k.? GAY. **6.** Good prize and worth the k. SIR T. HERBERT. **7.** Fruits which spoil with k. JOWETT **8. b.** Phr. *In* or *out of k.* (*with*): in or out of harmony or agreement (with); Indications in k. with our view 1878.

Kee·ping-room. *local* and *U.S.* 1790. [KEEP *v.* III. 1.] The living room of a person or a family; a parlour.

Keepsake (kī·psēᵢk). 1790. [f. KEEP *v.* + SAKE; cf. *namesake.*] Anything kept or given to be kept for the sake of the giver. *spec.* The name for certain literary annuals; so called as being designed for gifts. Also *attrib.*

Keerie: see KERRIE.

Keeve, kive (kīv, kəiv). [OE. *cȳf*, perh. repr. Gmc. **kūbjō*, but with no exact quivalent in the cogn. languages.] A tub or vat; *spec.* a vat for holding liquid in brewing and bleaching; in *Mining*, a vessel in which tin or copper ore is washed.

‖**Kef, keif, kief** (kef, kəif, kīf). 1808. [Arab. *kayf* well-being, enjoyment (in Morocco, etc., Indian hemp).] **1.** A state of drowsiness or dreamy intoxication, such as is produced by the use of bhang, etc. **b.** The enjoyment of idleness; 'dolce far niente'. **2.** (In Morocco and Algeria, in form *kief*, *keef.*) Indian hemp or other substance smoked to produce this state. Also *attrib.* 1878.

1. I fell into *kef*, being incapable of sustained thought W. CORY.

‖**Keffiyeh** (kefī·ye). Also **keffiyeh, kefia,** etc. 1817. [Arab. *kūfiyya*, *kūfiyya*, in some parts pron. *kef(f)iya*, perh. – late L. *cofea*, *cuphia* COIF *sb.*] A kerchief worn as a head-dress by the Bedouin Arabs.

Keg (keg), *sb.* 1632. [Later form of CAG *sb.*[1] For the change of vowel cf. CATCH| KETCH.] A small barrel or cask, usu. of less than ten gallons. Also *attrib.*

‖**Kehaya** (kehăyā·). 1599. [Osmanli Turk. *kehya*, *kyāhya* – Pers. *katkudā*, f. *kad* house + *kudā* master.] A Turkish viceroy, deputy, etc.; a local governor.

Keilhauite (kəi·lhauˌəit). 1846. [Named, 1844, after Prof. B. M. *Keilhau*; see -ITE[1] 2 b.] *Min.* A titano-silicate of calcium, yttrium, and other metals.

Keir, var. of KIER.

‖**Keitloa** (kēᵢ·tloˌă). 1838. [Sechuana *kgetlwa*, *khetlwa.*] A species of S. African rhinoceros (*Rhinoceros keitloa*), having two horns of nearly equal length.

Keld (keld). *n. dial.* 1697. [– ON. *kelda.*] A well, fountain, spring. **b.** A deep, still, smooth part of a river. (Frequent in place-names e.g. *How Keld*, *Sal(t)keld*, etc.)

Kele, obs. f. KEEL.

Kell (kel). *Obs.* exc. *dial.* ME. [var. of *calle* CAUL *sb.*[1] For the change of vowel cf. CAG|KEG.] **1.** = CAUL *sb.*[1] 1. **2.** Gossamer threads forming a kind of film on grass 1523. **b.** The web or cocoon of a spinning caterpillar 1612. **3.** *Anat.* = CAUL 4. 1540. **4.** *spec.* = CAUL 5. 1530.

4. I'le have him cut to the k., then down the seames BEAUM. & FL. Hence **Kelled** (†**keld**) *a.* webbed DRAYTON.

Kell, obs. f. KALE, KILN.

Keloid (kī·loid). 1854. [– Fr. *kéloïde*, irreg. var. of *chéloïde* CHELOID.] *Path.* = CHELOID, q.v. Hence **Keloi·dal** *a.*

Kelp (kelp). [Late ME. *cülp(e*, of which *kelp* and rare †*kilpe* appear to be dial. vars.; this variation points to an OE. **cylp.*] **1.** A collective name for large seaweeds (chiefly *Fucaceæ* and *Laminariaceæ*) which are burnt for the sake of the substances found in the ashes. **b.** *spec.* The giant or great kelp (*Macrocystis pyrifera* or *Fucus giganteus*) of the Pacific coast of America, the largest of seaweeds 1834. **2.** The calcined ashes of seaweed used for the sake of the iodine, etc. they contain; formerly much used in the manufacture of soap and glass 1678. **3.** *attrib.* 1833.

Comb.: **k.-fish,** the name given to several fishes found on the Pacific coast of U.S.; **k.-pigeon,** the sheathbill, an Antarctic sea-bird; **k. raft,** a mass of kelp floating on the sea.

Kelpie, kelpy (ke·lpi). *Sc.* 1747. [Of unkn. origin.] The Lowland Scottish name of a fabled spirit or demon, usu. appearing in the shape of a horse, reputed to haunt lakes and rivers, and to take delight in, or bring about, the drowning of travellers and others. Also *water-kelpie.*

Kelpies' feet, impressions in the old red sandstone of Forfarshire.

Kelson, keelson (ke·lsən). [ME. *kelswayn*, *kelsweyn*, *kelsing*, mod. *kelsine*, perh. points to an original **kelswin*, the nearest parallel to which, and the prob. source, is LG *kielswin*, f. *kiel* KEEL *sb.*[1] + (prob.) *swin* SWINE, used, like *cat*, *dog*, *horse*, for a timber. The form *keelson* is due to assim. to KEEL *sb.*[1]] **1.** A line of timber placed inside a ship along the floor-timbers and parallel with the keel, to which it is bolted, so as to fasten the floor-timbers and the keel together; a similar bar or combination of iron plates in iron vessels. **2.** Used as = KEEL *sb.*[1] 1 (*rare*) 1831.

Comb. **cross-k.,** a beam placed across the kelson to support the boilers or engines of a steamer.

Kelt[1] (kelt). Now only *Sc.* ME. [Of unkn. origin.] A salmon, sea-trout, or herling after spawning. Hence **Ke·lted** *a.*, that has spawned 1847.

Kelt[2]. *Sc.* and *n. dial.* 1577. [Of unkn. origin. Cf. KELTER.] A kind of homespun cloth or frieze, usu. of black and white wool mixed. Also *attrib.* Also *fig.*

Kelt, var. of CELT[1].

†**Ke·lter**[1]. *north.* 1502. [Of unkn. origin. Cf. KELT[2].] A coarse cloth –1600.

Kelter[2], **kilter** (ke·ltəɹ, ki·ltəɹ). 1606. [Of unkn. origin.] Good condition, order. (Freq. in U.S., in form *kilter.*)

I must rest awhile. My brain is out of kilter LOWELL.

Keltic, Kelto-, var. CELTIC, CELTO-.

Kemb, *v. Obs.* exc. *dial.* Pa. t. and pa. pple. **kembed, kempt.** [OE. *cemban* :- **kambjan*, f. **kambaz* COMB *sb.* Repl. by COMB *v.*, but survives in *kempt* and *unkempt.*] **1.** *trans.* = COMB *v.* 1. Now *dial.* **b.** *fig.* To trim. CHAUCER. **c.** *joc.* To beat, thrash 1566. †**2.** = COMB *v.* 2. Also *absol.* –1715.

1. His longe heer was kembd bihynde his bak CHAUCER.

Kemelin(e, etc.: see KIMNEL.

Kemp, *sb.*[1] *Obs.* exc. *dial.* [OE. *cempa* = OFris. *kempa*, *kampa*, OS. *kempio*, OHG. *kempfo* :- WGmc. **kampjo.*] **1.** A big, strong, and brave warrior or athlete; a champion. **2.** *Sc.* A seed-stalk of the ribwort (*Plantago lanceolata*), used in a children's game 1825.

Kemp (kemp), *sb.*[2] ME. [– ON. *kamp-r* beard, moustache, etc.] †A coarse or stout hair, as those of the eyebrows; now, hair of this kind occurring among wool. Also in *comb.* **k.-hair**; **k.-haired** *a.* Hence **Ke·mpy** *a.* abounding in kemps.

Kemple. *Sc.* 1565. [– ON *kimbill* little trunk, bundle, f. *kimbla* truss up.] A measure of hay or straw.

Kempt (kemᵖt), *ppl. a. arch.* OE. [f. KEMB *v.*] Of hair or wool: Combed; esp. in comb., as *well-k.*, etc.

Ken (ken), *sb.*[1] 1545. [f. KEN *v.*] †**1.** = KENNING *vbl. sb.* 3 b –1625. **3.** Range of vision. Now *rare.* 1590. †**3.** Sight or view *of* a thing, place, etc.; possibility or capacity of seeing –1745. **4.** Power or exercise of vision; look, gaze 1666. **b.** Mental perception or recognition 1560.

1. *Cymb.* III. vi. 6. **2.** Beyond all K. by the best Telescopes RAY. The eye Is bounded in its k. to a stone's cast COWPER. **3.** To drown in k. of shore SHAKS.

Ken (ken), *sb.*[2] 1567. [Of cant origin.] A house; esp. one where thieves, beggars, or disreputable characters meet or lodge.

Ken (ken), *v.* [OE. *cennan* = OFris. *kenna*, *kanna*, OS. *kennian*, OHG. *kennen* (Du., G. *kennen*), ON. *kenna*, Goth. *kannjan*, f. **kann-* I know; see CAN *v.*[1] Properly causative, 'make known', which was the only use in OE. and Gothic, but in Gmc. langs. gen. it acquired the sense 'know' at an early period; in Eng. this use may be immed. due to Norse; in Sc. the word has displaced *knaw*, KNOW.]

I. In causative senses. (All *Obs.*) †**1.** *trans.* To make known –1567. †**2.** To direct, teach, or instruct (a person) –1529. †**3.** To direct, guide, show the way *to* (*unto*, *till*) a place or person –1560. †**4.** To consign, commend, deliver, bestow –1440.

II. In non-causative senses. **1.** To descry, see; to look at, scan. *arch.* ME. Also *absol.* (*Obs.* or *arch.*) 1577. **2.** To recognize; to identify. Now *north.* or *Sc.* ME. †**3.** To acknowledge, admit to be (genuine, valid, etc.) –1450. †**4.** To get to know –1586. **5.** To know (a person). Now *Sc.* ME. **6.** To know (a thing). Now chiefly *Sc.* ME. **7.** *intr.* or *absol.* To have knowledge (*of* or *about* something). Now *Sc.* ME.

1. As farre as I could k. thy Chalky Cliffes SHAKS. **2.** 'Tis he, I k. the manner of his gate, He rises on the toe SHAKS. **6.** He did k. the ambassador-craft as well as any in his age FULLER. **7.** It was his father then ye kent o' SCOTT.

Kendal (ke·ndăl). ME. [f. *Kendal* in Westmorland, place of manufacture.] †**1.** A species of green woollen cloth –1687. Also †*attrib.* **2. Kendal green. a.** = sense 1. Now only *arch.* or *Hist.* 1514. **b.** The green colour of Kendal cloth; also, the plant Dyer's Greenweed, with which it was dyed 1866.

2. a. Three mis-begotten Knaues, in Kendall Greene SHAKS.

Kennel (ke·nĕl), *sb.*[1] ME. [– AFr. **kenil* (cf. AL. *canillum* XII, *kenillum* XIII) = OFr. *chenil* :- med.L. **canile*, f. L. *canis* dog.] **1.** A house or cot for a house-dog; a house or range of buildings in which a pack of hounds are kept. **b.** The hole or lair of a fox 1735. Also *transf.* and *fig.* **2.** A pack of dogs or allied animals 1470. Also *transf.* and *fig.* **3.** *attrib.* ME.

1. First let the K. be the Huntsman's Care SOMERVILLE. *transf.* He got us a room—we were in a k. before DICKENS. **2.** *transf.* The howling of a k. of wolves 1765. *fig.* Hear the whole k. of Atheists come in with a full crie FULLER. *Comb.* **k.-book,** a book recording events of a kennel where dogs are bred.

Kennel (ke·nĕl), *sb.*[2] 1582. [Later form of CANNEL *sb.*[1]] The surface drain of a street; the gutter.

Kennel, *sb.*[3], obs. f. CANNEL *sb.*[2]

Kennel (ke·nĕl), *v.* 1552. [f. KENNEL *sb.*[1]] **1.** *intr.* To lie or dwell in a kennel; to retire into a kennel or lair. Of a person (*contemptuous*): To lodge or lurk. Also *fig.* **2.** *trans.* To put into, or keep in, a kennel 1592. Also *transf.* and *fig.*

1. Glad here to kennel in a Pad of Straw DRAYTON. **2.** Kennelling the Wolfe and the Lamb together 1641. Hence **Ke·nnelling** *vbl. sb.*, also *concr.* provision of kennels.

Kenning (ke·niŋ), *vbl. sb.* Now only *Sc.* and *n. dial.* (exc. sense 5). ME. [f. KEN *v.* + -ING[1].] †**1.** Teaching, instruction. ME. only. †**2.** = KEN *sb.*[1] 3. –1697. †**3.** Range of sight –1601. †**b.** The distance that bounds the range of ordinary vision, *esp.* at sea; hence, a marine measure of about 20 or 21 miles –1694. **4.** Mental cognition; knowledge, cognizance; recognition ME. **b.** A recognizable amount; a little 1786. **5.** One of the periphrastic expressions used instead of the simple name of a thing, esp. in Old Norse poetry 1883.

3. b. Scylley is a Kenning..from the very Westeste Point of Cornewaulle 1538. **4. b.** Tho' they may gang a kennin wrang, To step aside is human BURNS.

Keno, kino (kī·no). *U.S.* 1879. [Of unkn. origin.] A game of chance based on the drawing of numbers and covering of corresponding numbers on cards, in a manner similar to lotto.

Kenogenesis (kīnodʒe·nėsis). 1879. [irreg. for *cæno-* or *kainogenesis*, f. Gr. καινός new + γένεσις genesis.] Haeckel's term for the form of ontogenesis in which the true hereditary development of a germ is modified by features derived from its environment (opp. to *palingenesis*). Hence **Kenogene·tic** *a.*

‖**Kenosis** (kĭnōu·sis). 1873. [– Gr. κένωσις an emptying, with reference to *Phil.* 2: 7 ἑαυτὸν ἐκένωσε 'emptied himself'.] *Theol.* The self-limitation of the divine power and attributes by the Son of God in the Incarnation. Hence **Keno·tic** *a.* of or pertaining to k.; involving or accepting the doctrine of k.

Kenspeck (ke·nspek), *a. dial.* 1590. [Of Scand. origin, but the immed. source is uncertain; cf. ON. *kennispeki* faculty of recognition, MSw. *kännespaker*, Sw. *känspak*, Norw. *kjennespak* quick at recognizing, f. ON. *kenna* KEN *v.* + *spak-*, *spek-* wise, wisdom.] = next.

Kenspeckle (ke·nspek'l), *a. Sc.* and *n. dial.* 1714. [See prec. and -LE 1.] Easily recognizable; conspicuous.

Kentish (ke·ntiʃ), *a.* [OE. *Centisc*, f. *Cent* – L. *Cantium* (Cæsar), Κάντιον (Diodorus), Κάντιον ἄκρον (Ptolemy), f. OCelt. **kanto-* (i) rim, border, or (ii) white; see -ISH[1].] **1.** Of or belonging to Kent. Chiefly of the inhabitants or speech. **2.** *absol.* as *sb.* **a.** *pl.* The natives or inhabitants of Kent (*rare*). OE. **b.** The dialect of Kent. 1866.

Phr. **K. fire**, a prolonged and ordered salvo or volley of applause, or demonstration of impatience or dissent (said to have originated in reference to meetings held in Kent in 1828–9, in opposition to the Catholic Relief Bill); †**K. Knocker** [f. *K. Knock*, the sand-bank before the mouth of the Thames], a Kentish smuggler; **Kentish man, a** native of Kent born west of the Medway (opp. to *man of Kent*).

Kentle, obs. f. QUINTAL.

Kentledge (ke·ntlėdʒ). 1607. [– OFr. *quintelage* ballast, with assim. to prec.; see -AGE.] *Naut.* Pig-iron used as permanent ballast, usually laid upon the kelson-plates. Also *attrib.*

Kephalin (ke·fălin). 1878. [f. Gr. κεφαλή head + -IN[1].] *Chem.* Thudichum's term for a substance obtained from brain-matter.

Kephalo- (ke·fălo), var. f. CEPHALO-, preferred by some.

‖**Kepi** (kēi·pi, Fr. ke·pi). Also **képi.** 1861. [Fr. *képi* – Swiss G. *käppi*, dim. of *kappe* cap.] A French military cap, slightly tapering, with a flat top which slopes towards the front, and a horizontal peak.

Kept (kept), *ppl. a.* 1678. [f. KEEP *v.*] In senses of KEEP *v.*; *spec.* **a.** Maintained or supported by a paramour 1678. **b.** Financially supported and privately controlled by interested persons; as, *kept party*, *kept Press* 1888.

Kera- (ke·ră), from Gr. κέρας horn, occas. used in place of KERATO-, as **Ke·ralite** [-LITE], hornstone. **Ke·ratome** = *keratotome* (see KERATO-).

Keramic, -ist, vars. of CERAMIC, -IST.

Ke·rasine, *a.* 1864. [improp. f. Gr. κέρας horn + -INE[1].] Horny, corneous.

Keratin (ke·rătin). 1847. [f. Gr. κέρας, κερατ- horn + -IN[1].] An organic substance found in horn.

Keratitis (kerătəi·tis). 1858. [f. as prec. + -ITIS.] *Path.* Inflammation of the cornea.

Kerato-, bef. a vowel **kerat-**, var. of CERATO-, comb. f. Gr. κέρας, κερατ- horn, used in terms relating to horny substances, or to the cornea of the eye; as **Kerate·ctomy** [Gr. ἐκτομή], *Surg.* excision of part of the cornea. **Keratony·xis** [Gr. νύξις pricking], *Surg.* a method of operating for cataract. †**Ke·ratophyte** [Gr. φυτόν plant], *Zool.* a coral polyp with a horny axis. **Ke·ratotome** [Gr. -τομος cutting], *Surg.* a knife with triangular blade used for making incisions in the cornea. **Kerato·tomy**, incision of the cornea.

Keratode (ke·rătoud). 1872. [– Gr. κερατώδης horn-like, f. κέρας, κερατ- horn; see -ODE.] = KERATOSE *sb.*

Keratoid (ke·rătoid), *a.* 1873. [– Gr. κερατοειδής; see prec. and -OID.] **1.** *Math.* Resembling a horn in shape. *Keratoid cusp*: a cusp at which the two branches of the curve lie on opposite sides of the common tangent; a cusp of the first species. **2.** Resembling horn in substance 1885.

Keratose (ke·ratōus). 1851. [f. Gr. κέρας, κερατ- horn + -OSE[1].] **A.** *adj.* Of a horny substance; applied to the texture of certain sponges. **B.** *sb.* A substance resembling horn forming part of the skeleton of certain sponges 1865.

Kerb (kɔ̄ɹb), *sb.* 1664. [var. of CURB *sb.*, used in special senses.] **1.** See CURB III. **2.** *spec.* An edging of stone or the like, bordering a raised path, side-walk, or pavement.

2. *On the k.*: said of stock-exchange business done on the street-pavement, esp. after exchange hours.

Kerb (kɔ̄ɹb), *v.* 1861. [f. KERB *sb.*] *trans.* To furnish with a kerb. Hence **Ke·rbing** *vbl. sb.*, also *concr.* the stones forming a kerb.

Ke·rb-stone. Also **kirb-.** 1706. [KERB *sb.*] **a.** An edging of stone about the top of a well. **b.** One of the stones forming the kerb of a path; also, the kerb itself 1815.

attrib. **Kerb-stone broker** (*U.S.*), a broker, not a member of the stock exchange, who transacts business in the streets.

†**Kerch.** late ME. = CURCH.

Ke·rcher. *Obs.* exc. *dial.* [ME. *curcher*, *kercher*, by syncope from **cover-*, *kevercher* – OFr. *couvre-*, *cuevrechier*, erron. ff. *couvrechief*, etc.; see next.] = KERCHIEF. Hence **Ke·rchered** *a.* covered with a k.

Kerchief (kɔ̄·ɹtʃif), *sb.* [ME. *c(o)urchef*, *kerchif* – AFr. *courchef* = (O)Fr. *couvrechef*, *cuevrechef*, f. *couvrir* COVER *v.*[1] + *chief* head (see CHIEF). The form *kerchief*, for **keverchief*, is from the var. *cuevrechef* (cf. ME. *kever* cover, from *cuevr-*, stressed stem of *couvrir*).] **1.** A cloth used to cover the head, formerly a woman's head-dress. †**b.** An amice. †**c.** A woman who wears a kerchief. DRYDEN. **2.** A breast-kerchief or neckerchief ME. **3.** A handkerchief 1815.

1. Her goodly countenance..Set off with k. starchd and pinners clean GAY.

Ke·rchief, *v.* 1600. [f. prec.] To cover with a kerchief; in *pa. pple.* and *ppl. a.* **Kerchiefed.**

Morn..kercheft in a comely cloud MILT.

Kerf (kɔ̄ɹf). [OE. *cyrf* (ME. *kirf*, *kerf*) :- Gmc. **kurbiz*, f. **kurƀ-* **kerƀ-* CARVE; cf. ON. *kurfr* chip, *kyrfa* cut, and ME., mod. dial. CARF.] **1.** The act of cutting; a cut, stroke; †power of cutting. Now *rare.* **2.** The incision made by cutting, esp. by a saw 1523. **3.** The cut end or surface on a tree or branch ME. **4.** A cutting (of anything) 1678.

Kerite (kīə·rəit). 1875. [f. Gr. κηρός wax + -ITE[1] 4 a.] A kind of artificial caoutchouc for coating telegraph wires, made with tar or asphaltum, oils, and sulphur.

Kerl(e, obs. ff. CARL *sb.*[1]

Kermes (kɔ̄·ɹmīz, -mėz). 1598. [– Fr. *kermès* – Arab. (Pers.) *ķirmiz*. Cf. CRIMSON.] **1.** The pregnant female of the insect *Coccus ilicis*, formerly supposed to be a berry; gathered in large quantities from a species of evergreen oak in S. Europe and N. Africa, for use in dyeing, and formerly in medicine; the red dye-stuff consisting of the dried bodies of these insects; = ALKERMES 1. 1610. **2.** The species of oak (*Quercus coccifera*) on which this insect lives. More fully **kermes oak.** 1598. **3.** Amorphous trisulphide of antimony, of a brilliant red colour. More fully **kermes mineral.** 1753. **4.** *attrib.* 1671.

Kermesite (kɔ̄ɹ·mėzəit). 1843. [f. KERMES + -ITE[1] 2b.] *Min.* Native red antimony, a compound of the oxide and sulphide, occurring in cherry-red six-sided prismatic crystals.

‖**Kermis** (kɔ̄·ɹmis). Also **kermess(e. kirmess(e.** 1577. [– Du. *kermis*, †*-misse*, f. *kerk* CHURCH + *misse* MASS *sb.*[1]] In the Low Countries, etc.: A periodical (prop. annual) fair or carnival, characterized by much noisy merrymaking. *U.S.* a similar fair, usu. for charitable purposes.

Kern, kerne (kɔ̄ɹn), *sb.*[1] ME. [– Ir. *ceithern* (ke·hərn, ke·ərn) :- OIr. *ceitern* band of foot-soldiers. Cf. CATERAN.] **1.** *Hist.* A light-armed Irish foot-soldier; one of the poorer class among the 'wild Irish'. (Sometimes applied to Scottish Highlanders.) **b.** In collective sense; †*orig.* a band of Irish foot-soldiers ME. **2.** *transf.* A rustic, boor; †vagabond. Now *rare.* 1553.

1. Now for our Irish warres, We must supplant those rough rug-headed Kernes SHAKS.

Kern, *sb.*[2] *rare.* 1570. [rel. to KERN *v.*[1] and KERNEL *sb.*[1]; perh. repr. an OE. **cyrne*; cf. Norw. *kyrne* grain, and see CURN.] †**1.** Kernel (of a nut). **2.** A grain (of wheat, sand, etc.). Hence **Kern-stone,** ? coarse-grained sandstone, or perh. oolite. 1753.

Kern (kɔ̄ɹn), *sb.*[3] 1683. [perh. for **carn* – Fr. *carne* corner, salient angle, Norman-Picard var. of OFr. *charne* – L. *cardo*, *cardin-* hinge.] *Printing.* A part of a metal type projecting beyond the body or shank, as the curled head of f and tail of j, etc.

Kern (kɔ̄ɹn), *v.*[1] Now chiefly *dial.* [ME. *kerne*, *curne*, app. repr. OE. **cyrnan* :- Gmc. **kurnjan*, f. **kurnam* CORN *sb.*[1]] **1.** *intr.* Of corn: To form the hard grains in the ear; to seed. Also of fruit: To set. †**2.** *trans.* To cause to granulate; to make (salt) into grains –1726. **b.** To salt (meat). *Obs.* exc. *dial.* 1613. **c.** *intr.* To granulate. *Obs.* exc. *dial.* 1657.

2. Salt kerned on the rocks very white HAKLUYT.

Kern (kɔ̄ɹn), *v.*[2] 1683. [f. KERN *sb.*[3]] *Printing.* To furnish (a type) with a kern. Hence **Kerned** *ppl. a.*

Kernel (kɔ̄·ɹnĕl), *sb.*[1] [OE. *cyrnel*, dim. of *corn* seed; see CORN *sb.*[1], -EL. The present sp. appears XIV as a var. of northern and midl. *kirnel.*] **1.** A seed; esp. the seed contained within any fruit; a pip; a grape-stone. *Obs.* exc. *dial.* **2.** The softer (usu. edible) part within the hard shell of a nut or stone-fruit OE. **3.** The body of a seed (e.g. of wheat, etc.) within its husk, etc. ME. **4.** A morbid formation of rounded form in any part of the body; *esp.* an enlarged gland in the neck or groin. Usu. in *pl.* Now chiefly *dial.* OE. **5.** A gland; a tonsil; a lymphatic gland or ganglion; a rounded fatty mass. Now *rare* or *dial.* ME. **6.** A nucleus; a core; a centre of formation 1641. Also *fig.*

2. He..casts away the Kirnell, because hee hath lost the Shell QUARLES. **6.** This settlement, the k. of the great Norman Duchy FREEMAN. *fig.* The k. of Christianity—to be spiritually minded 1806.

†**Kernel,** *sb.*[2] ME. = CRENEL –1652.

Kernel (kɔ̄·ɹnĕl), *v.* 1483. [f. KERNEL *sb.*[1]] †**1.** *intr.* To form kernels or seed. Of land: To produce grain or corn. –1722. **2.** *trans.* To enclose as a kernel in its shell 1652.

Kernelled, -eled (kɔ̄·ɹnĕld), *a.* ME. [f. KERNEL *sb.*[1] + -ED[2].] †**a.** Of flesh: Full of kernels or glands. **b.** Of fruit: Having a kernel 1719.

Kernelly, -ely (kɔ̄·ɹnĕli), *a.* ME. [f. KERNEL *sb.*[1] + -Y[1].] †**1.** Of flesh: Glandular –1683. **2.** Of the nature of a kernel 1655.

†**Ke·rnish,** *a. rare.* 1581. [f. KERN *sb.*[1] + -ISH[1].] Of, or of the nature of, a kern –1641.

Kerolite, var. of CEROLITE.

Kerosene (ke·rŏsīn). 1854. [irreg. f. Gr. κηρός wax + -ENE.] A mixture of liquid hydrocarbons, obtained by the distillation of petroleum; also from coal and bituminous shale; extensively used as a lamp-oil. The usual name is *paraffin oil* or *paraffin.*

‖**Kerrie, keerie** (ke·ri, kīə·ri). 1731. [Hottentot or Bushman *kirri*; cf. KNOBKERRIE.] A short club or knobbed stick used as a weapon by natives of S. Africa.

Kers, -se, -ss, obs. or dial. ff. CRESS.

Kersey (kɔ̄·ɹzi). Now *rare.* ME. [prob. f. name of *Kersey* in Suffolk; cf. AL. *pannus cersegus* XIII, *carsea* XV, AFr. *drap de kersy* XIV.] **1.** A kind of coarse narrow cloth, woven from long wool, and usually ribbed. **2.** With *a* and *pl.* †A piece of kersey of a definite size; also, a make of kersey (chiefly in *pl.*) 1465. **3.** *pl.* Trousers made of kersey 1831. **4.** *attrib.* or *adj.* Made of kersey 1577; †*fig.* plain, homely 1588.

4. *fig.* Russet yeas and honest kersie noes SHAKS.

Kerseymere (kɔ̄·ɹzimīəɹ). 1798. [alt. of CASSIMERE, by assoc. with prec.] **1.** A twilled fine woollen cloth of a peculiar texture. **b.** *pl.* (rarely *sing*). Trousers made of kerseymere 1840. **2.** *attrib.* 1836.

Kerseynette, alt. f. CASSINETTE.

Kerve, obs. and dial. f. CARVE *v.*

Kesar, obs. f. KAISER.

Keslep, -lip, -lop, northern ff. CHEESELIP.

Kesse, obs. f. KISS *v.* **Kest, -e,** obs. ff. CAST *sb.* and *v.*

Kestrel (ke·strĕl). 14.. [Earliest form (XV) *castrell*, perh. for **casserell* – dial. var. *casserelle* of Fr. *crécerelle*, †*cresserelle* (dial. *cristel*), f. synon. *crécelle* rattle, kestrel, perh. f. imit. base **krek-* (the bird is supposed to be so called from its cry).] **1.** A species of small hawk (*Falcon tinnunculus*, or *Tinnunculus alaudarius*), also called *Stannel* or *Windhover*. **b.** *fig.* applied to persons, usually in contempt 1589. **2.** *attrib.* 1590.

1. b. Thou art thyself a kite, and k. to boot SCOTT.

Ket. Now *dial.* ME. [– ON. *kjǫt* (:– **ketwam*) flesh, in mod. Icel. *ket* (Sw. *kött*, Da. *kød*, *kjød*).] Raw flesh; carrion; *fig.* trash.

Ketch (ketʃ), *sb.*[1] 1655. [Later form of *cache* CATCH *sb.*[2]] A strongly-built two-masted vessel, usually from 100 to 250 tons burden, formerly much used as a bomb-vessel (see BOMB-KETCH); now a similarly rigged small coasting vessel. Also *attrib.*

Ketch, *sb.*[2] 1681. [See JACK KETCH.] The hangman. Hence **Ketch** *v. trans.* to hang.

Ketchup (ke·tʃɒ̆p). Also **Catchup.** 1711. [– Chinese (Amoy) *kōechiap*, *kê-tsiap* brine of pickled fish.] A sauce made from the juice of mushrooms, walnuts, tomatoes, etc. Often qualified, as *mushroom k.*, etc.

Ketine (kī·tain). 1892. [f. KET(ONE + -INE[5].] *Chem.* An oily liquid, $C_6H_8N_2$, or one of a series of homologous bases $C_nH_{2n-4}N_2$, formed by the reduction of nitrosoacetone and its homologues by sodium (or tin) and hydrochloric acid.

Keto- (kī·toᵘ), comb. form of KETONE, as in *keto-compound*, *-enol*, *-form*; *ketoge·nic* adj.

Ketone (kī·tōᵘn). 1851. [– G. *keton* (Gmelin, 1848), alt. of *aketon* ACETONE.] *Chem.* Name of a class of chemical compounds formed by oxidation of the secondary alcohols or carbinols, to which they stand in some respects in the relation of aldehydes. The lowest of the series, *dimethyl ketone*, is common ACETONE.

Hence **Keto·nic** *a.* of or pertaining to ketones, as in *ketonic acid.* So **Ke·tol,** a ketonic alcohol. **Ke·tose,** a sugar which is a ketonic alcohol, e.g. lævulose.

Kettle (ke·t'l). ME. [– ON. *ketill* = OE. *ćetel*, WS. *ćietel* (which gave ME. and dial. *chetel*), OS. (Du.) *ketel*, OHG. *kezzil* (G. *kessel*), Goth. *katils* :– Gme. **katilaz* – L. *catillus*, dim. of *catīnus* deep vessel for serving or cooking food.] **1.** A vessel, commonly of metal, for boiling water, etc.; now *esp.* a covered metal vessel with a spout, a TEA-KETTLE. **2.** *transf.* **a.** 'The brass or metal box of a compass' 1867. **b.** = POT-HOLE 1874. **†3.** Short for KETTLEDRUM. *Haml.* v. ii. 286.

Phr. *A k. of fish.* **a.** On the Tweed, etc. A picnic at which a kettle of fish cooked *al fresco* is the chief thing eaten; also simply *kettle* 1791. **b.** *fig.* A disagreeable or awkward state of things 1742.

Kettledrum (ke·t'lˌdrɒm). 1542. **1.** A musical instrument of percussion consisting of a hollow hemisphere of brass or copper, over the edge of which parchment is stretched and tuned to a definite note 1602. **†2.** = KETTLE-DRUMMER –1755. **3.** *colloq.* An afternoon tea-party on a large scale. Cf. DRUM *sb.*[1] 8. 1861.

2. Trumpets and Kettle-Drums in rich Liveries 1669. Hence **Ke·ttledru:mmer,** one who plays the k. 1683.

Ke·ttle-stitch. 1818. [– G. *kettelstich* chain-stitch, f. *kettel* small chain + *stich* stitch.] In bookbinding: A knot made at the head and tail of a book in sewing it, by which the thread holding one sheet is fastened to the thread in the next.

‖**Keuper** (koi·pəɹ). 1842. [A German miners' term.] *Geol.* The upper member of the Triassic system, consisting in Germany of marls, shales, sandstones, gypsum, and clays, in England chiefly of marls and sandstones.

Kevel (ke·v'l), *sb*,[1] Now *Sc.* and *n. dial.* ME. [– ON. *kefli* a round stick, small roller, gag, related to *kafli* a piece.] **1.** **†a.** A gag. **b.** A bit or twitch for a horse's mouth. **2.** A rounded piece of wood; a staff, cudgel 1807.

Kevel (ke·v'l), *sb.*[2] ME. [– ONFr. *keville* = (O)Fr. *cheville* pin, peg.] *Naut.* A peg or cleat, usually fixed in pairs, to which certain ropes are belayed.

Kevel (ke·v'l), *sb.*[3] *Sc.* and *n. dial.* ME. [Of unkn. origin.] A kind of hammer for rough-hewing or breaking stone; also *k.-hammer*, *-mell.* Hence **Ke·vel** *v.* to break (stones).

†Kevel, *sb.*[4] 1759. [Said to be the native name in Senegal.] A gazelle –1834.

Kever, common ME. f. COVER *v.*[1] and [2] in midl. and s. dial.; rare obs. f. COVER *sb.*[1]

Kex (keks). *Obs.* exc. *dial.* ME. [perh. of Celtic origin; cf. OCorn. *cegas* hemlock, W. *cegid*, Bret. *kegit* – L. *cicuta* hemlock; also Corn.-Eng. sing. *kager*, *kaiyer*.] **1.** The dry, usually hollow, stem of various herbaceous plants, *esp.* of large umbelliferous plants, such as Cow Parsnip, Wild Chervil, etc. **†b.** Without *a*: collectively, or as a material –1725. **2.** An umbelliferous plant with a hollow stalk 1578. **†3.** The husk, sheath, or hard case of a chrysalis –1688. **†4.** *fig.* A dried-up sapless person –1711.

1. I should be as dry as a k. wi' travelling so far T. HARDY. **2.** Tho' the rough k. break The starr'd mosaic TENNYSON. **3.** When the k., or husk, is broken, he proveth a fair flying butterfly HOLLAND. Hence **Ke·xy** *a.* (now *dial.*), like a k.; dry and brittle; withered, sapless.

Key (kī), *sb.*[1] [OE. *cǣġ* and *cǣġe* = OFris. *kei*, *kay*; not found elsewhere; of unkn. origin. The pronunc. kī is abnormal; *kē̆i* (cf. *grey*, *clay*, *whey*) prevailed till *c*1700, but evidence for forms anticipating the present pronunc. (which appears to be of north. origin) is as early as XV.]

I. 1. An instrument, usually of iron, for moving the bolt or bolts of a lock forwards or backwards, and so locking or unlocking what is fastened by it. **b.** The representation of a key, in painting, sculpture, etc. 1450. **2.** In pregnant sense, with reference to the powers implied by the possession of the keys of any place; hence as a symbol of office, and *fig.* the office itself. OE. *Gold k.*, the groom of the stole.

1. The k. turns, and the door upon its hinges groans KEATS. Phr. *To get* (*have*) *the k. of the street* (ironical), to be shut out for the night, or have no house to go to. **b.** *St. Peter's keys*, the cross keys borne in the Papal arms. *Greek key*, each of the key-like bends of which the Greek fret consists. **2.** All the townes in Acquitayne (except Bayon) delivered their keyes, and became vassals HALL.

II. *fig.* **1.** Something compared to a key, with its power of locking and unlocking; that which opens up, or closes, the way to something; that which gives opportunity for, or precludes, an action, state of things, etc. OE. **2.** *Theol.* (See *Matt.* 16:19.) Usu. *pl.*: The ecclesiastical authority held by Roman Catholics to be conferred by Christ on St. Peter and transmitted to the Popes as his successors. More widely: The disciplinary power of priests as successors of the Apostles. OE. **3.** A place which gives its possessor control over the passage into or from a certain district, territory, inland sea, etc. 1440. **4.** That which serves to open up, disclose, or explain what is unknown, mysterious, or obscure OE. *spec.* an explanatory scheme for the interpretation of a cipher, etc., a set of solutions of problems, a translation of a text, etc. in a foreign language for the use of learners, and the like. **5.** *Mus.* **†a.** [after Guido Aretino's use of *clavis*.] The lowest note or tone of a scale or sequence of notes; the key-note. Hence, **b.** A scheme or system of notes or tones definitely related to each other, according to (or *in*) which a piece of music is written; such scheme being based upon and named after some particular note (the *keynote*), as *the key of C.* Hence, **c.** The sum of melodic and harmonic relations existing between the tones of such a system; tonality. 1590. **6. a.** *transf.* (High or low) tone (of the voice); pitch 1599. **b.** *fig.* Intensity or force, 'pitch' (of feeling or action); tone or style (of thought or expression); sometimes, prevailing tone or idea, 'key-note' 1594. **c.** Tone or relative intensity (of colour) 1851.

1. Love, the k. of hearts, will open the closest coffers FULLER. *Golden* or *silver k.*, money, employed as a bribe to obtain the opening of a door or to gain a purpose. **3.** A very Important place, which is the K. of Sclavonia 1684. **4.** Poetry is the k. to the hieroglyphics of nature HARE. A K. to Henry's Exercises 1870. It was the k. to his success; he knew the value of time 1883. **5.** Both warbling of one song; both in one k. SHAKS. **6. a.** Men speak in a high or a low k. BERKELEY. **b.** Let peace and love exalt your K. of mirth QUARLES.

III. Applied to mechanical devices, in function or form, suggesting the key of a lock. **1.** A pin, bolt, wedge, etc., fitting into a hole or space contrived for it so as to lock various parts together; a cotter 1440. **2.** That which completes or holds together the parts of any fabric; *esp.* the key-stone of an arch, which holds the structure together ME. Also, the last board in a floor. Also †*fig.* **b.** That portion of a first coat of wall-plaster which passes between the laths and secures the rest; the roughness of a wall-surface which enables plaster to adhere to it 1825. **3.** In the organ, pianoforte, etc.: Each of the levers, which are pressed down by the fingers in playing, and actuate the internal mechanism so as to produce the notes 1500. Also, each of the small metal levers, actuated by the fingers, in the flute, oboe, clarinet, concertina, etc. 1688. **4.** Hence **a.** In telegraphy, A mechanical device for breaking and closing an electric circuit. **b.** In a type-writer, etc., each of a set of levers pressed by the fingers in the same manner as the keys of a pianoforte or organ 1837. **5.** An instrument for grasping a square or polygonal-headed screw, peg, or nut, and turning it by lever action 1610.

IV. A dry fruit with a thin membranous wing, usually growing in bunches, as in the ash and sycamore 1523.

Comb.: **k.-action,** the mechanism by which sounds are produced in musical instruments that have a key-board; **-bed** *Mech.*, the part of a shaft on or in which a key rests; **-bolt** *Mech.*, a bolt which is secured in its place by a key or cotter; **-bone,** (*a*) the collar-bone, clavicle (*nonce-use*); (*b*) a bone forming the key of a structure; **-groove** *Mech.* = *key-seat*; **-money,** a payment required from the tenant of a house before he is allowed to have the key; **-seat** *Mech.*, a key-bed or key-way; **-way** *Mech.*, a groove cut in a shaft, or in the boss of a wheel, to receive a key.

b. (in sense II. 4), as *key-map*, *-move*, *-sentence*, *-word*; passing into *adj.* in sense 'dominant', 'controlling', as **k. industry,** one which is essential to the carrying on of others; **k. man; k. position.**

Key (kī), *sb.*[2] Now written QUAY. ME. [– OFr. *kay*, *kai*, *cay*. For the ultimate etym. see CAY. In Eng., till XVIII, usually written *key* (less freq. *kay*), which latterly was pronounced as KEY *sb.*[1] The spelling *quay* is after later Fr. *quai*.] A wharf, a quay. **†b.** *transf.* A harbour, haven. QUARLES.

Key (kī), *sb.*[3] 1697. [var. of CAY – Sp. *cayo* shoal, reef. infl. in spelling and pronunc. by prec.] A low island, sand-bank, or reef, as in the W. Indies, etc. Cf. *Key West.*

Key (kī), *v.* [ME. *keize*, *keie*, etc., f. *keiȝe* KEY *sb.*[1]] **1.** *trans.* To lock with a key. Also *fig. rare.* **2. a,** To fasten by means of a pin, wedge, bolt, or cross-piece 1577. **b.** To cause (plaster) to adhere (to laths) 1881. **3.** To regulate the pitch of the strings of a musical instrument. Hence *fig.*: To give a certain tone or intensity to (feelings, thoughts); *to k. up*, to raise to a high pitch. 1636. **4.** To insert the keystone in (an arch). Also with *in.* 1735.

Keyage (kī·ėdʒ). Now written QUAYAGE. 1440. [– OFr. *kaiage*, *caiage*, in med.L. *caiagium* (XII); see KEY *sb.*[2], -AGE.] Quay-dues; quayage.

Keyboard (kī·bōᵊɹd). 1819. [KEY *sb.*[1] III. 3.] The set or row of keys in an organ, piano, type-writing machine, etc.

Key·-bu:gle. 1936. A bugle fitted with keys to increase the number of its sounds.

Key·-cold, *a.* Now *rare.* 1529. As cold as a key; very cold; *esp.* cold in death. Also *fig.*

Poore key-cold Figure of a holy King SHAKS.

Keyed (kīd), *a.* 1781. [f. KEY *sb.*[1] or *v.* + -ED.] **1.** Of a musical instrument: Furnished with keys. **2.** In carpentry, etc.: Secured by means of a key 1823. **3.** Of an arch: Constructed with a keystone 1841.

Keyhole (kī·hōᵘl). 1592. **1.** The hole by which the key is inserted into a lock. **2.** A hole made to receive a peg or key used in carpentry, etc. 1703.

attrib. and *Comb.*: **k. escutcheon,** an escutcheon-shaped plate of metal surrounding a keyhole; **k. limpet,** a gastropod of the family *Fissurellidæ*, having a shell with an aperture at the apex; **k. saw,** a narrow saw for cutting keyholes, etc.

Keyless (kī·lės), *a.* 1823. [f. KEY *sb.*[1] + -LESS.] Without a key; of a watch, etc.: wound up otherwise than by means of a key.

Key-note (kī·nōᵘt). 1752. *Mus.* The first, i.e. lowest, note of the scale of any key, which forms the basis of, and gives its name to, the key; the tonic. Also *transf.* and *fig.*

Keys (*kīz*). ME. [pl. of KEY *sb.*[1] in specialized use. Cf. AL. *claves legum* (XV).] The elective branch of the Legislature of the Isle of Man. More fully *House of Keys*. (The reason for the title is not clear.)

Keystone (kī·stōᵘn). 1637. [f. KEY *sb.*[1] III 2 + STONE *sb.* Cf. AL. (XII) *clavis* keystone or boss of vaulting.] **1.** The stone at the summit of an arch, which locks the whole together. Also *fig.* **2.** A bond-stone 1823. **3.** In chromolithography, the stone on which a general outline of the subject is made, serving as a guide in getting the colours in place 1875. **4.** A block of cast iron used to fill up spaces in a lead-smelting furnace 1839.

1. *fig.* The tenet of predestination was the k. of his religion MACAULAY. *Comb.* **K. State,** *U.S.*, popular appellation of Pennsylvania, as being the seventh or central one of the original thirteen states 1841.

Khaki (kā·ki). 1857. [Urdu *kākī* dust-coloured, f. *kāk* (– Pers.) dust.] **A.** *adj.* **a.** Dust-coloured; dull brownish yellow. **b.** (*attrib.* use of B.) Made of khaki cloth. 1863. **B.** *sb.* A fabric of this colour largely employed since 1899 for field-uniforms. Orig. of stout twilled cotton (*K. drill*), but now also of wool (*K. Bedford, K. serge*). 1857.

The Infantry were dressed in khakee 1859.

C. As *adj.*, *adv.*, or *sb.* in such constr. as *to vote k.*, *a k. election, the k. loan* (*khakis*), etc., used in reference to the S. African War of 1899–1902, and the war spirit of that time 1900.

‖**Khalifa** (kălī·fă), var. of CALIPH.

‖**Khalsa(h** (kā·lsă). *E. Ind.* 1776. [Urdu *ḵālṣa* – Pers. *ḵāliṣa* – Arab. (*'arḍ*) *ḵāliṣa* (land) exempt from tax, hence crown (land).] **1.** The state exchequer in Indian states. Also *attrib.*, as *k.-grain.* **2.** The Sikh community or sect 1790.

‖**Khamsin** (kæ·msin). 1685. [Arab. *ḵamsin*, mod. colloq. f. *ḵamsūn* fifty.] An oppressive hot wind from the south or south-east, which in Egypt blows at intervals for about 50 days in March, April, and May.

‖**Khan**[1] (kæn, kān). ME. [Early forms *caan, can(e, chan(e* – OFr. *chan* or med.L. *ca(a)nus, canis* – Turki (hence Arab., Pers.) *ḵān* lord, prince, altered form of *ḵāḵān*. Cf. CHAGAN, CHAM.] **a.** *Hist.* Specific title given to the successors of Chingīz Khan, who were supreme rulers over the Turkish, Tartar, and Mongol tribes, as well as emperors of China, during the Middle Ages. **b.** A title (now of slight import) commonly given to rulers, officials, or men of rank in Central Asia, Afghanistan, etc.

‖**Khan**[2] (kæn, kān). ME. [Arab. *ḵān* inn.] In the East: A caravanserai.

Khanate (kæ·n-, ka·neᵗt). Also **khanat.** 1799. [f. KHAN[1] + -ATE[1].] A district governed by a khan; the position of a khan.

‖**Khansamah, -saman** (kansā·ma(n). *E. Ind.* 1645. (Corruptly *consumah, consumer.*) [Urdu (Pers.) *ḵānsāmān*, f. *ḵān* KHAN[1] + *sāmān* household goods.] In India: A house-steward; the head of the kitchen and pantry department.

‖**Khedive** (kėdī·v). 1867. [– Fr. *khédive*, ult. – Pers. *ḵadīv, ḵedīv* prince, sovereign, var. of *ḵudaiv* petty god, f. *ḵudā* god.] The title of the viceroy of Egypt, accorded to Ismail Pasha by the Turkish government in 1867. Hence **Khedi·val, Khedi·vial** *a.* **Khedi·vate, Khedi·viate,** the office, authority, or government of the k.

‖**Khidmutgar** (ki·dmɒtgāɹ). 1765. [– Urdu – Pers. *ḵidmatgār*, f. Arab. *ḵidma(t* service + *-gār* agent-suffix.] In India: A male servant who waits at table.

‖**Khoja** (kōᵘ·dʒă). 1625. [Turk. and Pers. *ḵōjah*, prop. *ḵwājah*.] A professor or teacher in a Moslem school or college; a schoolmaster; a scribe, clerk.

‖**Khud** (kɒd). *E. Ind.* 1837. [Hindi *khaḍ*.] A deep ravine or chasm; a precipitous cleft in a hill-side.

‖**Khus-khus** (kɒ·skɒs). *E. Ind.* 1810. [Urdu (Pers.) *ḵas-ḵas*.] The sweet-scented root of an Indian grass, largely used in the manufacture of mats or screens ('tatties').

‖**Khutbah** (ku·tbă). 1800. [Arab. *ḵuṭba*, sermon, f. *ḵaṭaba* preach.] A form of sermon or oration used at meridian prayer on Fridays in Moslem mosques.

Kiang, var. KYANG, Tibetan wild horse.

Kibble (ki·b'l), *sb.*[1] 1671. [– G. *kübel* = OE. *cyfel* – med.L. *cupellus, -a* corn-measure, drinking-vessel, f. *cuppa* CUP. See also KEEVE, KIVE.] *Mining.* A large wooden or (later) iron bucket, for conveying ore or rubbish to the surface.

Ki·bble, *sb.*[2] 1891. [perh. alt. f. COBBLE *sb.*[1], or rel. to next.] = COBBLE *sb.*[1]

Kibble (ki·b'l), *v.*[1] 1790. [See prec.] *trans.* To bruise or grind coarsely; to crush into small pieces. Also *absol.* **Ki·bbler. Ki·bblerman.**

Kibble (ki·b'l), *v.*[2] 1891. [f. KIBBLE *sb.*[1]] To convey ore or rubbish in a kibble.

Kibe (kəib), *sb.* ME. [prob. – W. *cibi* (also *cibwst*).] **1.** A chapped or ulcerated chilblain, *esp.* one on the heel. Also *fig.* **2.** *transf.* **a.** A sore on a horse's foot. ? *Obs.* 1639. **b.** A breaking out at the top of the hoof in sheep. (So Welsh *cibi.*) 1846. †**c.** A hump or swelling. 1567.

1. *fig. To gall* or *tread on* (*one's*) *kibes*. to press upon closely so as to annoy. *To tread* or *follow on the kibes of*, to come closely at the heels of. Hence **Kibe** *v. rare*, to affect with kibes or chilblains; *erron.* to kick or gall 1757. **Kibed** *a.* affected with chilblains on the heels 1500.

‖**Kibitka** (kibi·tkă). 1799. [Russ., 'tent, tilt-wagon', f. Tartar *kibits*, with Russ. suffix *-ka*.] **1.** A circular tent covered with thick felt, used by the Tartars; *transf.* a Tartar household or family. **2.** A Russian wagon or sledge with a rounded cover or hood; a sledge with a tilt or covering 1806.

‖**Kiblah** (ki·blă). 1704. [Arab. *ḳibla*, that which is placed opposite.] The point (the temple at Mecca) to which Moslems turn at prayer. **b.** A niche in a Moslem building on the side towards Mecca 1775.

Kibosh (kəi·bǫʃ, kibǫ·ʃ). *slang.* 1836. [Of unkn. origin.] **1.** In phr. *To put the k. on*: to finish off, do for. **2.** Nonsense, 'rot' 1873.

Kiby (kəi·bi), *a.* Now *dial.* 1523. [f. KIBE *sb.* + -Y[1].] Affected with kibes.

†**Ki·chel.** *rare.* [OE. *ċiċel*, of obscure etym. Cf. KECHEL.] A small cake –ME.

Kick (kik), *sb.*[1] 1530. [f. KICK *v.*]

I. 1. An act of kicking. **b.** Ability or disposition to kick 1885. Also *fig.* **2.** *transf.* **a.** The recoil of a gun when discharged 1826. **b.** A jerk, jolt; jerking motion 1835. **3.** One who kicks. Usu. with adj. 1857.

1. *More kicks than halfpence*: more harshness than kindness 1824. **b.** He had not a k. in him 1898. **2. c.** *Electr.* A momentary high-voltage discharge in an inductive electric current 1910. **d.** *fig.* (orig. *U.S.*) A sharp stimulant effect, e.g. that of strong liquor or pungent seasoning; also, a thrill of excitement, fear, etc. 1903.

II. Slang senses. **1.** *The kick*: the fashion, the newest style 1700. **2.** A sixpence 1700. **3.** *pl.* Breeches. ? *Obs.* 1700. **4.** A pocket 1851. **5.** *The kick*: 'the sack' (SACK *sb.*[1] I. 3) 1844.

Kick (kik), *sb.*[2] 1861. [Of unkn. origin. Sense 1 may be humorously from prec.] **1.** An indentation in the bottom of a glass bottle, making it hold less. **2.** The projection on the tang of a pocket-knife blade, which prevents the edge of the blade from striking the spring 1864. **3.** The piece of wood fastened to the upper side of a 'stock-board' to make a depression in the lower face of a brick as moulded 1875.

Kick (kik), *v.* [Late ME. *kike*, of unkn. origin.]

I. 1. *intr.* To strike out with the foot. **b.** *slang.* To die 1725. **2.** *fig.* To show temper; to rebel, be recalcitrant ME. **3.** *transf.* **a.** Of firearms: To recoil when fired 1832. **b.** *Cricket.* Of the ground: To cause a ball to rebound in a more nearly vertical direction than usual 1882. **4.** *trans.* To strike (anything) with the foot 1590. **b.** *transf.* Of things: To strike (anything) with a violent impact. Of a gun: To strike in the recoil. 1667. **5.** With advs. or phrases: To impel, expel, eject, etc., with violence 1678. **6.** To accomplish, make, or do by kicking 1857.

1. They.., like galled camels, k. at every touch B. JONS. Phr. *To k. against the pricks* (*spur, goad*): to strike the foot against these; also *fig.* to be recalcitrant to one's own hurt ME. *To k. over the traces*: (of a horse) to get a leg over the traces so as to kick more freely; *fig.* to throw off the usual restraints 1861. **2.** *To k. against* or *at*, to object strongly to, rebel against; to spurn. **4.** I should kicke being kickt, and being at that passe, You would keepe from my heeles SHAKS. *To k. the bucket*, to die (*slang*); see BUCKET *sb.*[2]. *To k. one's heels*: see HEEL *sb.*[1] **b.** *To k. the beam*: see BEAM *sb.* 6. **5. b.** *intr.* (To be or lie) *kicking about*: i.e. in danger of being kicked or otherwise damaged 1867.

II. With advs. **Kick off. a.** *trans.* To throw off (shoes) by kicking or jerking the foot. **b.** *Football. intr.* To give the first kick. **Kick out. a.** *trans.* To turn out with a kick, or in an ignominious fashion. **b.** *Football. intr.* To re-start the game by kicking the ball towards the opposite goal from (or behind) the 25-yard line; also, to kick the ball over a side line. **c.** *intr.* To die (*slang*). **Kick up. a.** *trans.* To raise (dust, etc.) by or as by kicking; hence, to make (any disturbance or nuisance). **b.** *Cricket. intr.* Of a ball: To rebound more or less vertically.

Hence **Ki·ckable** *a.* **Ki·cker.**

†**Kickie-wickie.** [app. a joc. formation. Mod. editors usually adopt *kicksy-wicksy*, after the later folios.] A jocular or ludicrous term for a wife. *All's Well* II. iii. 297.

Kick-off (ki·k,ǫ̆f). 1857. The first kick to the ball in a football match. Also *fig.*

†**Kicksey-winsey.** 1599. [app. a whimsical formation, suggested by *kick* and *wince*; but the recorded senses seem to connect it with *kickshaws*.] **A.** *sb.* A fantastic device; a whim –1635. **B.** *adj.* Fantastic, whimsical, erratic –1652. **C.** *adv.* ? Topsy-turvy. J. TAYLOR.

Kickshaw, -shaws (ki·kʃǭ, -ʃǭz). 1597. [orig. *quelque chose, quelkchose, kickchose, kikeshawes* – Fr. *quelque chose* kękʃōz (formerly an elegant pronunc.) something.] **1.** A fancy dish in cookery. (Chiefly contemptuous: A 'something' French.) **2.** Something dainty or elegant, but unsubstantial; a toy, trifle, gewgaw 1601. **3.** A fantastical frivolous person. *Obs.* exc. *dial.* 1644. **4.** *attrib.* Frivolous, trifling 1658.

1. A ioynt of Mutton, and any pretty little tinie Kick-shawes SHAKS. **2.** Art thou good at these kickechawses [Maskes, etc.] Knight? SHAKS.

Kicksie-wicksie: see KICKIE-WICKIE.

Kick-up (ki·k,ɒp). 1793. [f. the phr. *kick up*.] **1.** The act of lifting the legs in, or as in, kicking 1861. **2.** A row; a great to-do 1793. **3.** A name given in Jamaica to two species of thrush, *Siurus noveboracensis* (Bessy Kick-up), and *S. aurocapillus* (Land Kick-up) 1847. **4.** = KICK *sb.*[2] 1. 1901.

Kid (kid), *sb.*[1] [ME. *kid(e, kede* – ON. *kið* :– **kiðjam*, rel. to OHG. *chizzī, kizzīn* (G. *kitze*) :– **kittīn*, **kiðnīn*, f. Gmc. **kið-*, of which no cognates are known.] **1.** The young of a goat. **2.** The flesh of a young goat ME. **3. a.** The skin of a kid. **b.** Leather made from kid-skins, or from substitutes; chiefly used for gloves and shoes; *pl.* gloves (or boots) made of this leather. 1677. **4.** *sing.* or *pl.* (Rendering L. *hædus* or *hædi*.) A pair of small stars in the constellation *Auriga*, represented as kids in the hand of the charioteer 1609. **5.** *slang.* A child, esp. a young child. (Orig. low slang.) 1690.

1. She koude skippe and make game As any kyde or calf folwynge his dame CHAUCER.

Kid (kid), *sb.*[2] Now *dial.* ME. [Of unkn. origin; W. *cedys* pl. is prob. from Eng.] A faggot or bundle of twigs, brushwood, gorse, etc., used either for burning, or for embedding in a bank, beach, etc.

Kid (kid), *sb.*[3] 1769. [perh. var. of KIT *sb.*[1]] A small wooden tub; esp. a sailor's mess-tub.

Kid (kid), *sb.*[4] *slang.* 1873. [f. KID *v.*[3]] Humbug, 'gammon'.

Kid (kid), *v.*[1] ME. [f. KID *sb.*[1]] **a.** *trans.* To give birth to (a kid). **b.** *intr.* To bring forth a kid or kids.

Kid (kid), *v.*[2] Now *dial.* 1504. [f. KID *sb.*[2]] *trans.* **a.** To bind up in kids or faggots; also *absol.* to make faggots. **b.** To secure (loose soil, etc.) by means of kids. Hence **Ki·dding** *vbl. sb.*; *concr.* kids used to secure loose soil, etc.; work in which kids are used.

Kid (kid), *v.*[3] *slang.* 1811. [perh. f. KID *sb.*[1] in sense 'to make a kid of'.] *trans.* To hoax, humbug, try to make (one) believe what is not true.

Kid, obs. f. KITH.

Kid, kidd(e, pa. t. and pple. of KITHE *v.*

Kidderminster (ki·dəɹminstəɹ). 1670. [Name of a town in Worcestershire.] **1.** *attrib.* Of or pertaining to Kidderminster; *spec.* a kind of carpet, originally manufactured there, in which the pattern is formed by the intersection of two cloths of different colours; also called *two-ply* and *ingrain* carpet. **2.** *absol.* = Kidderminster carpet or carpeting.

Kiddier. *Obs.* exc. *dial.* Also **kidder.** 1551. [Of unkn. origin.] = BADGER *sb.*[1] (q.v.).

Kiddle (ki·d'l). ME. [– AFr. *kidel* (whence AL. *kidellus*), OFr. *quidel, guidel* (mod. *guideau*).] **a.** A dam, weir, or barrier in a river, having an opening in it fitted with nets, etc. for catching fish. **b.** An arrangement of stake-nets on the sea-beach for the same purpose. Also *attrib.*

Kiddy (ki·di), *sb.* 1579. [f. KID *sb.*[1] + -Y[6].] **1.** A little kid (young goat). **2.** *slang* and *colloq.* A little child 1889. **3.** *Thieves' slang.* A professional thief of 'flashy' dress and manner; one who dresses in a similar style 1780. **4.** *attrib.* as *adj.*: Pertaining to, appropriate to, 'kiddies' 1805.

3. Poor Tom was once a k. upon town BYRON.

Kiddy (ki·di), *v. slang.* 1851. [Cf. prec. and KID *v.*[3]] *trans.* To hoax, humbug.

Kid glove. 1832. **1.** A glove made of kid-skin or similar leather. **2.** *attrib.* as *adj.* (*Kid-glove*) Characterized by wearing kid gloves;dainty or delicate in action or operation; avoiding real work; free from roughness or harshness 1856.

1. Phr. *With kid gloves*, in a gentle, delicate, or gingerly manner. Hence **Kid-gloved** *a.* wearing kid gloves; *fig.* refined, dainty, delicate, etc.

Kidling (ki·dliŋ). 1586. [f. KID *sb.*[1] + -LING[1].] A little kid.

Kidnap (ki·dnæp), *v.* 1682. [Back-formation from *kidnapper*, f. KID *sb.*[1] + *napper*, cant word (XVII) for 'thief', f. NAP *v.*[3], var. of NAB *v.* + -ER[1].] Orig., to steal or carry off (children or others) for service on the American plantations; hence, to steal (a child), to carry off (a person) by illegal force.

I will k. her and send her to Virginia DE FOE. So **Ki·dna:pper,** one who kidnaps children or others; also *fig.* 1678.

Kidney (ki·dni). [In ME. *kidnei*, pl. *kidneiren*, the second element is app. *ei* (see EGG *sb.*), pl. *eiren*, the first element being unascertained. But the var. ME. *kidneires*, the second element of which formally = ME. and dial. *nere(s)* kidney(s), suggests the possibility that the first element is (dial.) *kid* pod (see COD *sb.*[1]).] **1.** One of two glandular organs in the abdominal cavity of mammals, birds, and reptiles, which excrete urine and so remove effete nitrogenous matter from the blood. The kidneys of cattle, sheep, and pigs are eaten as food. **2.** *fig.* Temperament, nature; hence, class, stamp 1555. **3.** More fully *k. potato*; an oval variety of potato 1796. **4.** *attrib.*, as *k. disease, k. pie, k.-shaped*, etc. 1597.

1. Waiter, bring me a k. and some stout 1871. *fig.* A Youth, who officiates as the K. of the Coffee-house STEELE. **2.** Thinke of that, a man of my K.; ..that am as subject to heate as butter *Merry W.* III. v. 116. This fellow is not quite of a right k. FIELDING.

Phrase. †*Kidneys of wheat*, repr. 'fat of kidneys of wheat' *Deut.* 32:14; cf. *Ps.* 147:14 'the fat of wheat', the finest of the wheat, in allusion to the kidney-fat as the choicest part of an animal, which was offered in sacrifice.

Comb.: **k.-cotton,** a variety of *Gossypium barbadense*, a cotton plant of which the seeds are in kidney-shaped masses; **k. ore,** hæmatite occurring in kidney-shaped outline; **-piece,** a cam with a kidney-shaped outline; **-potato** = 3; **-vetch,** a leguminous herb (*Anthyllis vulneraria*), Lady's-fingers.

Kidney bean, kidney-bean. 1548. **1.** Name for the dwarf French bean (*Phaseolus vulgaris*), and for the Scarlet Runner (*P. multiflorus*). See BEAN. **2. Kidney-bean tree.** The American Wistaria (*Wistaria frutescens*), also the Chinese (*W. chinensis*), both grown as wall-climbers in Great Britain 1741.

Ki·dneywort. 1640. [See WORT[1].] *Herb.* The plant *Cotyledon umbilicus*, also called Navelwort; also *Saxifraga stellaris.*

Ki·d-skin. 1645. The skin of a kid, esp. as used for gloves; also skins of lambs, etc.

Kie, var. of *kye*, pl. of COW.

Kief, var. of KEF.

Kier (kīᵊɹ). 1573. [– ON. *ker* vessel, tub = OHG. *kar*, Goth. *kas.*] †**a.** A brewing-vat. **b.** A large vat in which cloth is boiled for bleaching, etc.

‖**Kieselguhr** (kī·z'lgūr). 1875. [G., f. *kiesel* gravel, CHESIL[1] + GUHR.] A diatomaceous earth, used as an absorbent of nitroglycerine in the manufacture of dynamite.

Kieserite (kī·zərəit). 1862. [Named (1861) after D. G. *Kieser*, of Jena; see -ITE[1] 2 b.] Hydrous magnesium sulphate, used in making Epsom salts, etc.

Kike, obs. f. KEEK *v.*, KICK *v.*

Kilderkin (ki·ldəɹkin). [Late ME. *kilderkyn*, alt. of *kyn(d)erkyn* – MDu. *kinderkin*, var. of *kin(n)eken, -kijn*, also *kyntken, -kijn, kindeken* (Du. *kinnetje*), dim. of *kintal, quintal*; see QUINTAL, -KIN.] **1.** A cask for liquids, fish, etc., holding 16 to 18 gallons. **2.** A cask of this size filled with some commodity; the quantity it contains; hence, a measure of capacity ME.

fig. A tun of man in thy large bulk is writ, But sure thow'rt but a k. of wit DRYDEN.

Kilkenny (kilke·ni). *K. cats*: two cats fabled to have fought until only their tails remained; used allusively. 1852.

Kill (kil), *sb.*[1] ME. [f. KILL *v.*] †**1.** A stroke, blow. ME. only. **2.** The act of killing an animal hunted as game 1852. **3.** A killed animal 1878. **4.** *Lawn Tennis* and *Rackets.* (Cf. KILL *v.* Phrases.) 1903.

Kill (kil), *sb.*[2] *U.S. local.* 1669. [– Du. *kil*, MDu. *kille* river-bed, channel.] A stream, 'creek', or tributary river; used esp. in place-names, as *Schuylkill.*

Kill, *sb.*[3] Also **kiln.** 1630. [Of unkn. origin.] On the Thames: An eel-trap or weel.

Kill (kil), *v.* Pa. t. and pa. pple. **killed** (kild). [ME. *cülle, külle, kille, kelle* point to an OE. **cyllan* :– Gmc. **kuljan*, rel. by gradation to **kwaljan* kill, QUELL.] †**1.** *trans.* To strike; to knock. Also *absol.* or *intr.* Also *fig.* ME. only. **2.** To put to death; to deprive of life; to slay. Also *fig.* ME. **b.** *absol.* To perform the act of killing, commit murder, cause death 1535. **c.** *intr.* in passive sense: To suffer killing; to yield (so much meat) when killed 1857. **d.** *trans.* To procure (meat) by killing animals 1560. **e.** To represent as killed or dead 1867. **3.** *transf.* To destroy the vitality or the activity of (an organism, a disease, etc.); to destroy, break up, or ruin. 1530. **4.** *fig.* To destroy, put an end to (a feeling, project, etc.) ME. **b.** To destroy (an appearance or quality) by contrast 1859. **5.** To consume (time), so as to bring it to an end 1728. **6.** In hyperbolic use: **a.** To overwhelm (a person) by a strong impression on the mind; to exhaust the strength of 1634. **b.** To injure seriously. (An Irishism.) 1800.

2. Yche other for to kylle With blody speris CHAUCER. What art thou, that telst of Nephews kilt? SPENSER. He was killing himself by late hours THACKERAY. Phr. *To k. out, off*, etc., to get rid of by killing. *To k. dead*, etc. **b.** They killed..near Blankney 1810. **c.** She [the cow] killed 34 stones 1888. **d.** To k. beefe and pork for 65 men of war 1689. **e.** He kills the hero in the last chapter (*mod.*). **3.** Potatoes have quite killed the land YOUNG. The lye will have lost its causticity, or, in technical language..it is killed 1875. **4.** [He] detected his wife..endeavouring to k. a laugh 1851. **6. c.** *intr.* (orig. *U.S.*) To make an irresistible impression; as *dressed to k.* 1848. **7.** *Printing.* To mark (matter) as not to be used.

Phrases. *To k. a ball*: (*a*) in tennis, to strike it so that it cannot be returned; (*b*) in football, to stop it dead. *To k. a bill* (in parliament): to prevent it from passing. *To k. with kindness*: to harm fatally by mistaken kindness. *K. or cure*, with reference to remedies which either cure or prove fatal.

Kill, obs. f. KILN.

Kill-, *vb. stem*, prefixed to sbs., forming *sbs.* with sense 'one who or that which kills ...', and *adjs.* = 'that kills..., -killing', as **kill-courtesy,** a boorish person; **kill-duck** *a.*, suitable for killing ducks; etc.

‖**Killadar** (ki·lădāɹ). *E. Ind.* 1778. [– Urdu (Pers.) *ķil'adār*, f. Arab. *ķal'a* (pl. *ķilā'*) fort + *-dār* holder.] The governor of a fort or castle.

Killas (ki·lăs). 1674. [Cornish.] Clay-slate; geologically, the clay-slate of Cornwall, of Devonian age, which rests on the granite.

Ki·ll-cow. *Obs.* exc. *dial.* 1581. [f. KILL *v.* + COW *sb.*[1]] **A.** *sb.* A bully, braggadocio; a terrible or great person; a man of importance 1589. **2.** *dial.* A serious affair. (Usu. in neg. phr.) 1825. **B.** *adj.* Bragging, bullying; terrifying 1581. Hence **Ki·llcow** *v.* to cow.

Ki·llcrop. *rare.* 1652. [– LG. *kilkrop* = G. *kielkropf* (the second element being CROP *sb.*).] An insatiate brat, popularly supposed to be a fairy changeling.

Killdee, Killdeer (ki·ldī, -dīᵊɹ). Also **kil-.** 1731. [Imitative of its note.] The largest species of Ring-plover (*Ægialitis vocifera*) of N. America.

Ki·ll-devil, *sb.* (*a.*) 1590. [f. KILL *v.* + DEVIL.] **1.** A recklessly daring fellow. MARLOWE. **2.** W. Indian name for rum. ? *Obs.* 1651. **3.** *Angling.* An artificial bait, made to spin in the water like a wounded fish 1833. **4.** *adj.* That would kill devils 1831.

Killer (ki·ləɹ). 1535. [f. KILL *v.* + -ER[1].] **1.** One who or that which kills. **b.** *Humane k.*: see HUMANE 1 b. **2.** (*k. whale*) A name of the grampus, *Orca gladiator*, and allied ferocious cetaceans 1725. **3.** An effective angler's bait 1681.

Ki·lles(s)e, var. CULLIS *sb.*[2], a groove or gutter; *spec.* in a cross-bow, or in a roof.

Killick, killock (ki·lik, -ək). 1630. [Of unkn. origin.] *Naut.* A heavy stone used on small vessels for an anchor; also a small anchor.

Killickinnick, var. of KINNIKINIC.

Killifish (ki·lifiʃ). Also **killy-.** 1836. [Commonly supposed to be f. KILL *sb.*[2] + FISH; but cf. KILLING *ppl. a.* 1 b.] Any of the small fish of several genera of *Cyprinodontidæ*, found in sheltered places on the east coast of N. America, and used as bait; esp. *Fundulus heteroclitus*, the *green k.*

Killing (ki·liŋ), *vbl. sb.* ME. [f. KILL *v.* + -ING[1].] **1.** Putting to death, murder. **2.** A dressing of slacked lime to 'kill' the grease in leather-dressing 1844.

Killing (ki·liŋ), *ppl. a.* ME. [f. KILL *v.* + -ING[2].] **1.** That kills (*lit.* and *fig.*). **b.** Of bait: Sure to kill 1681. **2.** In hyperbolic use: Able to kill. **a.** Fatal 1615. **b.** Overpoweringly attractive 1634. **c.** Exhausting 1850. **d.** That makes one 'die' with laughing (*colloq.*). **3.** As *adv.* Killingly 1670.

1. A Frost: a k. Frost SHAKS. Hence **Ki·lling-ly** *adv.*, **-ness.**

Ki·ll-joy, *sb.* and *a.* 1776. **A.** *sb.* One who or that which throws a gloom over social enjoyment. **B.** *adj.* That kills or puts an end to joy 1822.

Killock: see KILLICK.

†**Killow.** 1666. [Of unkn. origin. Cf. COLLOW.] A name given (orig. in Cumberland) to black-lead, plumbago, or graphite –1763.

Ki·ll-time, *sb.* (*a.*) 1748. [See KILL *v.* 5.] An occupation intended to 'kill time'. **b.** *adj.* Adapted to kill time 1759.

Kiln (kil, kiln), *sb.* [OE. *cylene* :– **cu·lina*, for L. *culī·na* kitchen, cooking-stove (for the shift in stress see KITCHEN). For the var. *kill* and pronunc. kil cf. ELL[1], MILL.] A furnace or oven for burning, baking, or drying; esp. (*a*) for calcining lime (LIME-KILN); (*b*) for baking bricks (BRICK-KILN), tiles, etc.; (*c*) for drying grain, hops, etc. or for making malt. Also *attrib.*

Phr. *To set the k. on fire, to fire the k.*, to cause a serious commotion; He has contrived to set the k. on fire as fast as I put it out SCOTT. *Comb.* **k.-hole,** the fire-hole of a k. Hence **Kiln** *v. trans*, to burn, bake, or dry in a k.; so **Ki·ln-dry** *v. trans.*

Kilo-. Arbitrary deriv. of Gr. χίλιοι a thousand, introduced in French in 1795, used in the Metric system to form names of weights and measures containing 1,000 times the unit. Also **Kilo** (ki·lo) *sb.*, abbrev. of KILOGRAMME.

Kilocycle (ki·lŏsəik'l). 1921. [f. KILO- + CYCLE *sb.*] One thousand cycles (see CYCLE *sb.* 10 b), esp. per second, as a unit in measuring frequency of electrical oscillations. (Abbrev. kc.)

Kilogramme, -gram (ki·lŏgræm). 1810. [– Fr. *kilogramme* (1795); see KILO- and GRAMME, GRAM.] A weight containing 1,000 grammes, or about 2·205 lb. avoirdupois.

Kilogrammetre, -meter (ki:lŏgræm,mī·-təɹ). 1866. [– Fr. *kilogrammètre*; see prec. and METRE.] *Physics.* The quantity of energy required to raise a weight of one kilogramme to the height of one metre.

Kilolitre, -liter (ki·lŏlītəɹ). 1810. [– Fr. *kilolitre* (1798); see KILO- and LITRE.] A measure of capacity containing 1,000 litres.

Kilometre, -meter (ki·lŏmītəɹ). 1810. [– Fr. *kilomètre* (1795); see KILO- and METRE.] A measure of length containing 1,000 metres, or 3280·89 feet, or nearly five-eighths of a mile. Hence **Kilome·tric, -al** *a.* of or pertaining to a k.; marking a k. on a road.

Kilowatt (ki·lŏwǫt). 1892. [f. KILO- + WATT.] *Electr.* A thousand watts.

Kilt (kilt), *sb.* 1730. [f. KILT *v.*] A part of the modern Highland dress, consisting of a skirt, usually of tartan cloth, deeply plaited, reaching from the waist to the knee; hence, any similar article of dress.

Hence **Ki·ltie**, a kilted Highland soldier.

Kilt (kilt), *v.* ME. [Of Scand. origin; cf. Sw. dial. *kilta* swathe, Da. *kilte* (*op*) tuck up, OIcel. *kilting, kjalta* skirt, lap.] **1.** *trans.* To tuck up (the skirts) round the body. Also with *up*. **2.** To fasten or tie up; to 'string up' 1697. **3.** *intr.* To go as with the loins girded 1816. **4.** *trans.* To gather in vertical pleats, as in a kilt 1887.

Kilt, obs. or dial. pa. pple. of KILL *v.*

Kilted (ki·ltėd), *a.* 1809. [f. KILT *sb.* + -ED[2].] Wearing a kilt.

Kilted (ki·ltėd), *ppl. a.* 1724. [f. KILT *v.* + -ED[1].] Tucked up or having the skirts tucked up; also, gathered in vertical pleats.

Kilter, var. of KELTER.

Kilting (ki·ltiŋ), *vbl. sb.* 1521. [f. KILT *v.* + -ING[1].] The action of KILT *v.*; the act of girding or tucking up, or of plaiting like a kilt; the result of this.

Kimberlite (ki·mbəɹləit). 1887. [f. *Kimberley* in Cape Colony + -ITE[1] 2 b.] *Min.* The eruptive rock, or 'blue ground', which is the matrix of the diamond at Kimberley and elsewhere.

†Ki·mbo, *a.* = AKIMBO. Dryden. So **†Ki·mbo** *v.* –1808.

Kim-kam, *a.* and *adv.* *dial.* 1582. [app. f. CAM *a.* and *adv.*, reduplicated as in contemp. *flim-flam, jim-jam.*] Crooked(ly); perverse(ly).

Kimmeridge (ki·məridʒ). 1832. A village on the Dorsetshire coast, where extensive beds of the Upper Oolite are developed. Hence *K. clay*, a bed of clay in the Upper Oolite, containing bituminous shales. *K. coal*, shale of the K. clay, containing so much bitumen that it may be burnt as coal.

Ki·mnel. *Obs.* exc. *dial.* [ME. *kem(b)elin, kim(e)lin, kim(e)nel*, app. rel. to OE. *cumb* COOMB[1].] A tub for household purposes.

‖**Kimono** (kimōᵘ·no). 1874. Earlier **kirimon** (1615). [Jap. Cf. KAKEMONO.] A long Japanese robe with sleeves. **b.** (Also **kimona.**) A European dressing-gown or wrap modelled on this 1902.

Kin (kin). [OE. *cyn(n* = OFris. *kin, ken, kon*, OS., OHG. *kunni* (Du. *kunne*), ON. *kyn*, Goth. *kuni* :– Gmc. **kunjam*, f. weak grade of **kin- *kan- *kun-* :– IE. **gen- *gon- *gn-* produce (whence Gr. γένος, L. *genus* race, GENUS).] **1.** A group of persons descended from a common ancestor, and so connected by blood-relationship; a family, stock, clan. Now *rare.* **2.** Ancestral stock or race; family; esp. in phr. (*come*) *of good* (*noble*, etc.) *k.* *Obs.* exc. *dial.* OE. **3.** One's kindred, kinsfolk, or relatives, collectively. (Now the chief sense.) OE. **b.** In predicative use, = Related 1597. **4.** Kinship, relationship. Now *rare.* 1548.

3. One of thy kin has a most weake *Pia-mater* SHAKS. One onely Daughter haue I, no Kin else SHAKS. **b.** One touch of nature makes the whole world kin SHAKS. **4.** Within Prohibited Degrees of Kin BUTLER.

Phrases. **Of kin** = AKIN; Related by blood-ties. Also, Related in character or qualities. *Near of k.*, closely related. *Next* (*†nearest*) *of k.*, most closely related; chiefly *absol.* the person (or persons) standing nearest in blood-relationship to another, and entitled to share in his personal estate in case of intestacy 1548.

-kin (kin), *suffix*, forming dims., corresp. to MDu. *-kijn, -ken* = G. *-chen*, as in MDu. *husekijn, huusken*, G. *häuschen* a little house. Used first in some familiar forms of personal (chiefly male) names adopted or adapted from names current in Flanders and Holland (e.g. MALKIN, *Perkin, Simkin*). Other words are either adopted from Du. (e.g. *kilderkin, manikin*) or are of obscure origin. The only English formations which have obtained permanent currency are *bootikin* (1727), *lambkin* (1579).

A variant *-kins* has in later times become current in certain endearing forms of address, as *babykins, boykins.*

Kinæsthesis (kəinėsþī·sis). Also **-thesia.** 1880. [f. Gr. κινεῖν move + αἴσθησις sensation.] The sense of muscular effort that accompanies a voluntary motion of the body. So **Kinæsthe·tic** *a.* belonging to k.

Kinchin (ki·ntʃin). *Cant.* 1561. [– G. *kindchen*, dim. (see -KIN) of *kind* child.] **1.** †**a.** *attrib.* in *k.-co(ve, -mort*, terms used by 16th c. tramps for a boy and girl respectively of their community. **b.** *absol.* A child, a 'kid'. (Now convicts' slang.) **2.** *attrib.* in **Kinchin-lay,** the practice of stealing money from children sent on errands. Also *fig.* 1838.

2. 'Ain't there any other line open?' 'Stop', said the Jew..'The kinchin lay' *O. Twist* xlii.

Kincob (ki·ŋkǫb). *E. Ind.* 1712. [– Urdu – Pers. *kamkāb*, f. *kamkā* damask silk – Chinese *kimsha* smooth satiny stuff, f. *kin* gold.] A rich Indian stuff, embroidered with gold or silver; a piece or variety of this. Also *attrib.*

Kind (kəind), *sb.* [OE. *cynd, -e*, earlier *ġecynd, ġecynde* :– **ʒakundiz, -jam*, f. Gmc. **ʒa-* Y- + **kunjam* KIN + **-diz* :– IE. *-tis* (abstr. suff.).]

I. Abstract senses. †**1.** Birth, origin, descent –1649. †**2.** The station, place, or property belonging to one by birth –ME. **3.** Natural disposition, nature (in later use *rare*) OE. **4.** Nature in general, or in the abstract, regarded as the established order (*rerum natura*). Rarely with *the*. *Obs.* (exc. as *arch.*) OE. †**5.** Gender; sex –1590. **6.** The manner natural to any one; hence, mode of action; manner, way, fashion. *arch.* OE. **7.** Generic or specific nature; esp. in phr. *in kind* (L. *in genere* or *in specie*), freq. contrasted with *in degree* 1628.

3. Sweet Grapes degen'rate there, and Fruits.. renounce their K. DRYDEN. †*To do one's kind*: to do what is natural; *spec.* to perform the sexual function. **5.** All they which be of the male k. [etc.] 1551. **6.** I have done Wonders in this K. STEELE. **7.** There are such wide differences in degree as to constitute almost differences in k. 1868.

II. A class of things. **1.** A race; a natural group of animals or plants having a common origin OE. †**b.** A class of the same sex; a sex (in collective sense) –1735. †**2.** = KIN 1, KINDRED 2 –1697. **3.** = KIN 2. *arch.* ME. **4.** A genus or species; also, A sort, variety, or description. (= L. *genus.*) Now the chief sense. OE.

1. As when the total k. Of birds..Came summond over Eden MILT. *P.L.* VI. 73. Poets were ever a careless k. 1739. **3.** [If she] came of a gentle k. SHAKS. **4.** Something of the k. had been done FREEMAN. They had haversacks of a kind with them, but very little in them 1895. *In* (*under*, †*with*) *one k.*, *both kinds* (Eccl.), referring to each of the elements (bread and wine) used in the Eucharist.

Phrases. **Kind of,** in *all kinds of trees* = 'trees of all kinds', *this k. of thing* = 'a thing of this kind'. As the original genitive phrase (see O.E.D. s.v. KIN *sb.*[1] 6 b) was in attrib. relation to the following sb., the natural tendency is still to treat *all kind of, no kind of*, etc., and hence also, *kind of*, as an attrib. or adj. phrase qualifying the sb. Hence the use of *all, many, other, those*, and the like, with a pl. verb and pronoun, when the sb. was pl., as in *these kind of men have their use*. *A kind of..*: A sort of..; a (person or thing) of a kind; what might be called a... *Kind of* (colloq.) is used adverbially: In a way, as it were, to some extent. *In kind* (tr. L. *in specie*: see SPECIE). **a.** In the very kind of thing in question; usually of payment: In goods or natural produce, as opp. to money. **b.** Of repayment: In something of the same kind as that received (chiefly *fig.*).

Kind (kəind), *a.* [OE. *ġecynde* :– **ʒakundjaz*, f. **ʒakundiz* KIND *sb.*; the prefix was dropped in early ME.]

I. Natural, native. †**1.** Of things, qualities, etc.: Natural; implanted by nature –1522; proper –1694. †**2.** Belonging to one by birth; lawful, rightful –1570. †**3.** Of persons: Rightful (heir, etc.) –ME.; natural –1589; related by kinship –1509.

1. What hay is kindest for sheep 1663.

II. 1. †**a.** Well-born, well-bred, gentle. **b.** Of a good kind; hence, good of its kind. Now only *dial.* ME. **2.** Of persons: Naturally well-disposed; sympathetic; considerate; †generous, liberal, courteous. Also of disposition. Also *fig.* (This (with b and c) is now the main sense.) ME. **b.** Exhibiting a friendly disposition by one's conduct *to* a person or animal. Also *fig.* ME. **c.** Of action, etc.: Arising from or displaying a kind disposition ME. **3.** Affectionate, loving, fond; on intimate terms. Also *euphem.* Now *rare* exc. *dial.* ME. †**4.** = KINDLY *a.* II. 3. –1774. **5.** Grateful, thankful. *Obs.* exc. *dial.* 1450. **6.** *dial.* or *techn.* Soft, tender; easy to work 1747.

1. b. A k. barley is one that malts well 1890. **2.** Who does a kindness, is not therefore k. POPE. *fig.* Your kinder Stars a Nobler Choice have giv'n DRYDEN. **b.** Be kinde and curteous to this Gentleman *Mids. N.* III. i. 167. **c.** Your k. letter gave me very sincere pleasure TENNYSON. **3.** Stiles where we stay'd to be k., Meadows in which we met TENNYSON. **5.** He should declare himself thankful and k., for all those benefits 1563. **6.** The importance of k. hair and good flesh in a feeding beast 1848.

III. As *adv.* = KINDLY. Now *colloq.* or *vulgar.* 1607.

He took it mighty k. H. WALPOLE.

Kindergarten (ki·ndəɹgā:ɹt'n). 1852. [– G. *kindergarten*, lit. 'children's garden'.] A school for developing the intelligence of young children by object-lessons, toys, games, singing, etc., according to a method devised by Friedrich Fröbel (1782–1852). Hence **Ki·nderga:rt(e)ner, -ing,** a teacher (teaching) in a k.

Kind-hearted, *a.* 1535. [KIND *a.*] Having naturally a kind disposition.

To thy selfe at least kind harted proue SHAKS. *Sonn.* X. Hence **Kindhea·rtedness.**

Kindle (ki·nd'l), *sb.* ME. [Appears in early ME. along with the cognate KINDLE *v.*[2]; app. a deriv. of *cynd* KIND *sb.*] †**1. a.** The young (of any animal), a young one. **b.** *collect.* A brood or litter (of kittens). –1486. **2.** *In k.* (of a hare): With young 1877.

Kindle (ki·nd'l), *v.*[1] [f. ON. *kynda* + -LE; suggested by ON. *kindill* candle, torch.] **1.** *trans.* To set fire to, light (a flame, fire, or combustible substance). **2.** *intr.* To begin to burn, catch fire, burst into flame ME. **3.** *fig. trans.* **a.** To inflame, inspire (a passion or feeling) ME. **b.** To fire, stir up (a person, the mind, etc.); to make ardent ME. **c.** To give rise to (†trouble, war, strife, etc.) ME. **4.** *intr.* **a.** Of passion, etc.: To rise, to be excited ME. **b.** To become inflamed or ardent; to glow; to become animated ME. **5.** *trans.* To light up as with fire 1715; *intr.* to become glowing or bright like fire 1797.

1. To k. wet straw into a flame BERKELEY. **2.** My eye..caught a light kindling in a window C. BRONTË. **3. a.** We kyndle Gods wrathe ouer vs 1547. **b.** Nothing remaines, but that I k. the boy thither *A. Y. L.* I. i. 179. **c.** He took measures for kindling a war with England HUME. **4. a.** As their fury kindled [etc.] 1845. **b.** The words began thus to k. in my spirit BUNYAN. **5.** The fires expanding .k. half the skies POPE. *intr.* Hereward's..eyes kindled KINGSLEY.

Kindle (ki·nd'l), *v.*[2] Now *dial.* [ME. *kündle, kindle, kendle*, perh. :– OE. **(ġe)-cyndlian*, f. *ġecynde*, ME. (*i*)*cünde*, *kind* birth, KIND *sb.*; see -LE.] *trans.* To bring forth, give birth to (young). Also *fig.* **b.** *absol.* (Of hares and rabbits.) ME.

As the Conie that you see dwell where shee is kindled SHAKS.

Kindler (ki·ndləɹ). 1450. [f. KINDLE *v.*[1] + -ER[1].] One who or that which kindles, sets on fire, incites, or stirs up.
Kindlers of riot, enemies of sleep GAY.

Kindless (kəi·ndlės), *a.* ME. [f. KIND *sb.* + -LESS.] †**1.** Without natural power, feeling, etc.; unnatural –1602. **2.** [As if f. KIND *a.*] Devoid of kindness (*rare*) 1847.
1. *Haml.* II. ii. 609. **2.** A sad, gloomy, k. November night 1881.

Kindlily (kəi·ndlili), *adv.* 1826. [f. KINDLY *a.* + -LY[2].] In a kindly manner.

Ki·ndliness. 1440. [f. as prec. + -NESS.] **1.** The quality or habit of being kindly; an instance of this. **2.** Mildness (of climate, etc.) favourable to vegetation 1654.
2. We ascribe..k. to dews 1794.

Kindling (ki·ndliŋ), *vbl. sb.*[1] ME. [f. KINDLE *v.*[1] + -ING[1].] **1.** The action of KINDLE *v.*[1] **2.** Material for lighting a fire. In *U.S.* usu. *pl.* 1513. Also **Kindling wood.**

Ki·ndling, *vbl. sb.*[2] ME. [f. KINDLE *v.*[2] + -ING[1].] **1.** The bringing forth of young 1440. **2. a.** *collect.* A brood or litter; issue. **b.** *sing.* One of a brood or litter; a young animal ME.

Kindly (kəi·ndli), *a.* [OE. *ġecyndelić*, f. *ġecynde* KIND *sb.* + *-lić* -LY[1].]
I. †**1.** Natural; = KIND *a.* 1. –1727. †**2.** = KIND *a.* 2. –1670. **3.** Having a right to one's position in virtue of birth or descent; rightful, lawful. Of children: Legitimate. Of a tenant (*Sc.*): Holding a lease of land which his ancestors have similarly held before him, and therefore usually on favourable terms. OE. **b.** Native-born (*arch.*) 1820.
1. Neither by lot of destiny Nor yet by k. death she perished SURREY. 'Tis lacke of kindely warmth, they are not kinde *Timon* II. ii. 226. **3.** Your service is not gratuitous—I trow ye hae land for it. Ye're k. tenants SCOTT. **b.** God keep the k. Scot from the cloth-yard shaft SCOTT.
II. 1. Of good natural qualities; of a good sort; in good condition; goodly (*arch.* or *dial.*) ME. **2.** Of persons: Kind-hearted, good-natured. Hence also of character, actions, etc. 1570. **b.** *transf.* and *fig.* Of things: Genial, benign; favourable to growth or *for* a particular crop 1655; also = KIND *a.* II. 6. **3.** Acceptable, agreeable, pleasant, genial. In later use blending with 2 b. ME.
1. A thick, k. grass COOK. **2.** The k. Force Of weeping Parents DRYDEN. **b.** A kind of white land..k. for hops 1789. The k. feel of skin 1766. **3.** As a lustie winter, Frostie, but kindely SHAKS.

Kindly (kəi·ndli), *adv.* [OE. *ġecyndeliċe*, f. as prec.; see -LY[2].] **1.** †Naturally –1586; fittingly (now esp. of processes which successfully follow their natural course) ME.; in an easy, natural way (now *dial.* or *colloq.*) ME.; †properly; exactly –1592. **2.** Affectionately; with sympathy, benevolence, or good nature ME. **3.** Agreeably, pleasantly 1596.
1. The Suppuration proceeding k., the Wound becomes a simple Wound 1758. Thou hast most k. hit it SHAKS. **2.** Tell him he is an ass,—but say so k. ABP. TAIT.
Phrases. *To take k.*, to accept pleasantly, or as a kindness. *To take k. to*, to be naturally attracted to. *To thank k.*, to thank heartily, as for kindness shown.

Kindness (kəi·ndnės). ME. [f. KIND *a.* + -NESS.] †**1.** Kinship; natural affection arising from this –1677. †**2.** *Sc.* Natural right or title derived from birth or descent; the status of a kindly tenant –1578. †**3.** Natural inclination or aptitude (*rare*) –1674. **4.** The quality or habit of being kind; an instance of this ME. **5.** Kind feeling; affection, love. Also, Good will, favour, friendship. Now *rare.* ME.
4. Yet doe I feare thy Nature, It is too full o' th' Milke of humane kindnesse, To catch the neerest way *Macb.* I. v. 18. **5.** It is not in my power..to hide a k. where I have one LADY M. W. MONTAGU.

Kindred (ki·ndrėd). [ME. *cün-*, *kinrede(n*, f. KIN + *-rēd(e* -RED condition.]
A. *sb.* **1.** The being of kin; relationship by blood (occas., but erron., by marriage); kinship. **b.** *fig.* Affinity in respect of qualities 1577. **2.** = KIN 1. Now *rare.* ME. †**3.** = KIN 2. –1513. **4.** = KIN 3. ME.
1. Wee plead not kinred Or neare propinquity HEYWOOD. **b.** Thy k. with the great of old TENNYSON. **4.** Her kindred's wishes, and her sire's commands POPE.
B. *attrib.* or *adj.* **1.** Of the same kin; related by birth or descent 1530. Also *fig.* **b.** Belonging to, existing between, or done by, relatives 1593. **2.** Allied in nature, character, or properties; having similar qualities ME.
1. *fig.* Carrick's k. shore SCOTT. **b.** K. bloud SHAKS. **2.** Some k. spirit GRAY. The formation of rain and k. phenomena HUXLEY.

Kine, arch. pl. of COW *sb.*[1]

Kinema: see CINEMA.

Kinematic (kəinĭmæ·tik, kin-). 1864. [f. Gr. κίνημα, -ματ- motion (f. κινεῖν move) + -IC.] **A.** *adj.* Relating to pure motion, i.e. to motion considered abstractly, without reference to force or mass. **B.** *sb.* = KINEMATICS 1873. So **Kinema·tical** *a.* of or pertaining to kinematics 1864.

Kinema·tics. 1840. [See prec. and -IC 2.] The science of pure motion, considered without reference to matter or force. (Cf. KINETICS.)

Kinematograph; see CINEMATOGRAPH.

Kinesi- (kəinī·si), bef. a vowel also **kines-,** comb. f. Gr. κίνησις motion, as in:
Kinesia·trics [-IC 2], treatment of diseases by means of gymnastics or muscular action. **Kinesio·logy** (Bentham), the science of motion. **Kinesi·pathy** 1855, **Kinesithe·rapy** [Gr. θεραπεία healing] = *Kinesiatrics.* **Kineso·dic** [Gr. ὁδός a path] *a. Physiol.* transmitting motor impulses, efferent.

Kinetic (kəine·tik), *a.* (*sb.*) 1855. [– Gr. κινητικός, f. κινεῖν move; see -IC.] **1.** Producing or causing motion. MAYNE. **2.** Of, pertaining or relating to, motion; due to or resulting from motion 1864. **3.** *sb.* = KINETICS 1873.
2. *K. energy*, the power of doing work possessed by a moving body by virtue of its motion. *K. theory of heat, of gases*: the theory that heat, or the gaseous state, is due to motion of particles of matter.

Kine·tics. 1864. [See prec. and -IC 2.] The branch of dynamics which investigates the relations between the motions of bodies and the forces acting upon them; opp. to *Statics*, which treats of bodies in equilibrium.

Kineto- (kəinī·to), repr. Gr. κινητο-, comb. f. κινητός movable, as in:
Kinetoge·nesis, the (theoretical) origination of animal structures in animal movements 1884. **Kine·tograph,** an apparatus for photographing a scene of action in every stage of its progress 1891. **Kine·toscope,** (*a*) a sort of movable panorama; (*b*) an apparatus for reproducing the scenes recorded by the kinetograph; (*c*) an instrument for illustrating the combination of circular movements of different radii in the production of curves.

King (kiŋ), *sb.* [OE. *cyning*, later *cyng*, *cing* = OFris. *kin-*, *kon-*, *kening*, OS., OHG. *kuning* (Du. *koning*, G. *könig*) :– Gmc. **kuniŋʒaz* (ON. *konungr* has a var. form of the suffix), prob. f. **kunjam* KIN + *-*iŋʒaz* -ING[3], as if 'scion of the (noble) race'; cf. Goth. *þiudans* king, f. *þiuda* people, nation.]
1. The usual title of the male sovereign ruler of an independent state, whose position may be either purely or partly hereditary, or elective. A King is held to rank below an Emperor. **2.** Applied to a woman (*rare*) ME. **3.** Applied to God or Christ. Freq. in phr. *K. of heaven, of glory, K. of kings*, etc. OE. **4.** A title given to one who holds a real or pretended authority or rank, or to one who plays the king 1656. **5.** One who has pre-eminence compared with that of a king, as a *railway-k.*, etc. ME. **b.** Applied to things personified, as *K. Caucus, K. Cotton, K. of terrors* (death), etc. 1592. **6.** *fig.* Something which has supremacy in its class ME. **7.** †**a.** The queen-bee. –1747. **b.** A fully developed male termite 1895. **8.** In games. **a.** In chess: The piece which each player has to protect against the moves made by the other, so as to avoid being finally check-mated ME. **b.** *Cards.* One card in each suit, bearing the representation of a king, and usually ranking highest except the ace 1563. **c.** *Draughts.* A crowned piece 1611. **9.** *ellipt.* **a.** A toast in which the king's health is drunk 1763. **b.** A king-post 1842.
1. *K. designate, possessive*: see the adjs. *Uncrowned k.*, one who has the power, but not the rank, of a king. *The Books of Kings*: certain books of the O.T. which contain the history of the kings of Israel and Judah. Also ellipt. *Kings. K. of Kings*, a king who has other kings under him, an emperor. *K. of men*, tr. Gr. ἄναξ ἀνδρῶν. *K. Charles*, short for *K. Charles's Spaniel* (see SPANIEL); *K. Harry*, the goldfinch. **2.** She [Maria Theresa] lived and died a K. BURKE. **4.** *K. of Heralds*, the King Herald or King-of-Arms. **5.** The old sugar kings of Jamaica 1894. **6.** *K. of beasts*, the lion. *K. of birds*, the eagle. *K. of the Mullets*, (*a*) a Mediterranean fish (*Mullus imberbis*); (*b*) the common bass. John Barleycorn, Thou K. o' grain BURNS.
Combs. **1.** General: as, *k.-bishop, -cardinal*, etc.; *k.-worship*, etc.; *k.-born*, etc.
2. Special: as, **k.-bee,** the queen-bee (see 7 a); **-card,** the best card left in a suit, e.g. the queen, if king and ace are out; **-cobra** = HAMADRYAD 2 a; **-conch, -conk,** a collector's name for a variety of conch; **-herald** (see HERALD); **-mullet,** the goat-fish (*Upeneus maculatus*) of the W. Indies; **-rod,** an iron rod used in place of a king-post; **-salmon,** the Californian Salmon (*Oncorhynchusquinnat*); **-snake,** a large N. Amer. snake (esp. *Ophibolus getulus*) which attacks other snakes; **-truss,** a roofing-truss which has a king-post; **-wood,** a Brazilian wood, prob. from a species of *Dalbergia*.
b. in names of birds, as **k.-auk** [tr. Norw. *alkekonge*], the little auk or rotche; **-crow,** the leader of a flock of crows; also the name of several species of drongo, esp. *Dicrurus ater*; **-duck, -eider,** *Somateria spectabilis*, allied to the eider-duck; **-hunter,** several species of African and Australian birds related to the kingfisher, but which do not feed on fish; **-lory, -parrakeet, -parrot,** several species of small parrots of the genus *Aprosmictus*, kept as cage-birds; **-penguin,** *Aptenodytes longirostris*; **-rail,** *Rallus elegans*; **-vulture,** *Gypagus* (*Cathartes*) *papa*, of tropical America, having a gaudy-coloured head.
c. in names of plants, as **k.-cob** = KING-CUP; **-fern,** the royal fern (*Osmunda regalis*); **-pine,** †(*a*) the pine-apple; (*b*) a large and stately Himalayan fir, *Picea webbiana*; etc.
3. Combs. with **king's. a.** With sense Of, belonging to, in the service of the king, as head of the State, royal; as *King's* COUNSEL, ENGLISH, EVIDENCE, HIGHWAY, PEACE, REMEMBRANCER, SHIP, THANE, etc., for which see these words; **King's Advocate,** the Scottish Attorney-General. **b. king's (bad) bargain,** a malingerer, a soldier or sailor who shirks his duty; **king's cushion,** a seat made by the crossed hands of two persons; **king's friends,** *Hist.*, a political party which supported George III and the power of the crown; **king's silver,** (*a*) silver blessed by the king, and intended for cramp-rings; (*b*) money paid into the Court of Common Pleas for licence to levy a fine; **king's yellow,** orpiment. **c.** in names of plants, as **king's bloom,** the peony; **king's spear,** a kind of asphodel; **king's taper,** the Great Mullein.
Phraseological comb.: **King Charles's Spaniel** (see SPANIEL).

King (kiŋ), *v.* ME. [f. prec.] **1.** *intr.* (usu. with *it*). To act the king; to rule, govern. **2.** *trans.* To make king 1593; †at *Draughts* 1679. **3.** To govern, as a king (*rare*) 1599.
2. Those traiterous Captains of Israel, who kinged themselves by slaying their masters SOUTH.

Ki·ng-bird. 1779. **1.** A species of bird of paradise, *Paradisea regia*. **2.** ? The eagle. BROWNING. **3.** An American tyrant fly-catcher, usually *Tyrannus carolinensis* (also called 'Bee-Martin'), remarkable for its intrepidity during the breeding season 1828. **4.** A sailor's name for species of tern (Newton).

Ki·ng-bolt. 1825. A main or large bolt in a mechanical structure; *esp.* a vertical bolt passing through the axle of a carriage or railway car, and forming a pivot on which the axle swings in taking curves.

Ki·ng-crab. 1698. [f. KING *sb.* + CRAB *sb.*[1]] A large arthropodous animal of the genus *Limulus*, having a convex carapace somewhat horseshoe-shaped; the horseshoe or Molucca crab. Now classed among the *Arachnida*.

Ki·ng-craft. 1643. The art of ruling as a king; *esp.* the use of crafty diplomacy in dealing with subjects.

Ki·ng-cup. 1538. The common buttercup; also, the Marsh Marigold.

Kingdom (ki·ŋdəm). [OE. *cyningdōm* = OS. *kuningdōm*, ON. *konungdómr*; see KING *sb.*, -DOM.] †**1.** Kingly function, authority, or power; sovereignty; kingship –1679. **2.** A monarchical state or government ME. **3.** The territory or country subject to a king; a realm ME. **b.** A familiar name for the Scottish county of Fife, which was one of the seven Pictish kingdoms 1710. **4.** *transf.* and *fig.* ME. **5.** A realm or province of nature; *esp.* the *animal, vegetable*, and *mineral kingdoms* 1691.
1. Monarchy..which Government, if he limit it

by Law, is called K.; if by his own will, Tyranny HOBBES. **2.** *United K.*, Great Britain and Ireland, so called since the Act of Union in 1800. A kingdom of the Just then let it be POPE. **3.** The utmost border of his K. MILT. **4.** *The k. of God*: the spiritual sovereignty of God or Christ, or the sphere over which this extends; the spiritual state of which God is the head. The Kingdome of perpetuall Night SHAKS. His mind his k., and his will his law COWPER.

Phrase. *Kingdom-come* (from *thy k. come* in the Lord's Prayer). **a.** The next world. *slang.* 1785. **b.** The millennial kingdom of Christ. Also *attrib.* 1848.

Kingdomed (ki·ŋdəmd), *a.* 1606. [f. prec. + -ED².] **1.** Furnished with, or constituted as, a kingdom. **2.** Consisting of (so many) kingdoms; as *ten-k.*, etc. 1854.

1. K. Achilles in commotion rages SHAKS.

Ki·ng-fish. 1750. A name given to fishes remarkable for their size, appearance, or value as food; esp. (*a*) the opah; (*b*) a scombroid fish of Florida (*Cybium regale*); (*c*) an American sciænoid fish (*Menticirrus nebulosus* or related species); (*d*) a sciænoid fish of S. Australia (*Sciæna antarctica*).

Kingfisher (ki·ŋfi:ʃəɹ). 1440. [First as *kyngys, kinges, king's fisher*; in present form from XVII.] **1.** A small European bird (*Alcedo ispida*) with a long cleft beak and brilliant plumage, feeding on fish, etc., which it captures by diving. Hence, extended to other birds of the family *Alcedinidæ* or *Halcyonidæ*. **2.** An artificial salmon-fly. ? *Obs.* 1787.

1. That a Kings fisher hanged by the bill sheweth where the winde is SIR T. BROWNE.

Kinghood (ki·ŋhud). ME. [f. KING *sb.* + -HOOD.] Kingship; the rank, authority, or office of king; kingly spirit or character.

Ki·ng-ki:ller. SHAKS. A regicide. So **Ki·ng-killing** *sb.* and *adj.*

Kingless (ki·ŋlės), *a.* ME. [f. KING *sb.* + -LESS.] Without a king; having no king.

Kinglet (ki·ŋlėt). 1603. [f. KING *sb.* + -LET.] **1.** A petty king; one ruling over a small territory. Usu. *contemptuous.* **2.** Pop. name of the Golden-crested Wren, *Regulus cristatus*; also of two allied N. Amer. species, *R. satrapa* and *R. calendula* 1839.

Kinglihood (ki·ŋlihud). [f. KINGLY *a.* + -HOOD.] Kingly state; royalty. TENNYSON.

Kinglike (ki·ŋləik). 1561. [f. KING *sb.* + -LIKE.] **A.** *adj.* Resembling a king; kingly; regal. **B.** *adv.* Like, or in a manner befitting, a king 1884.

Kingliness (ki·ŋlinės). 1548. [f. KINGLY *a.* + -NESS.] Kingly quality or character.

Kingling (ki·ŋliŋ). 1598. [f. KING *sb.* + -LING¹.] A little or petty king. (Less contemptuous than *kinglet.*)

Kingly (ki·ŋli), *a.* ME. [f. KING *sb.* + -LY¹.] **1.** Of the nature of a king or kings; royal; of royal rank. **2.** Of or belonging to a king; held, exercised, or issued by a king; suitable for a king; royal, regal ME. **b.** Of government: Monarchical 1658. **3.** Kinglike; dignified, majestic, noble 1593. Also *fig.*

1. Geue eare, o thou k. house COVERDALE *Hos.* 5:1. **2.** I thrice presented him a K. Crowne SHAKS. Leave k. backs to cope with k. cares COWPER. **b.** The k. form of government THIRLWALL. **3.** I am..More like a King, more K. in my thoughts SHAKS. *fig.* The kingliest Abbey in all Christian lands TENNYSON. So **Ki·ngly** *adv.* in a k. manner, royally, regally 1586.

Ki·ng-ma:ker. 1599. One who sets up kings; *spec.* an epithet of the Earl of Warwick, in the reigns of Henry VI and Edward IV.

King-of-Arms. Also (less correctly) **King-at-Arms.** 1449. [See ARM *sb.*² IV.] Title of the three chief heralds of the College of Arms, viz. Garter, the principal King of Arms, and Clarenceux and Norroy, provincial Kings of Arms, the former having jurisdiction south, and the other north, of the Trent. There are also the Lyon King of Arms of Scotland, and the Ulster King of Arms of Ireland; also Bath King of Arms.

King-piece. 1664. = KING-POST.

King-pin. 1895. = KING-BOLT. Also *transf.*

Ki·ng-post. 1776. *Carpentry.* An upright post in the centre of a roof-truss, extending from the ridge to the tie-beam.

King's Bench. ME. [See BENCH *sb.* 2 b.] A former court of record and the supreme court of common law in the kingdom; now represented by the King's Bench division of the High Court of Justice.

King's evil. ME. [tr. med.L. *regius morbus* (in cl. L. = jaundice); cf. OFr. *le mal le roy*, MDu. *conínces evel.*] Scrofula, which was formerly supposed to be curable by the king's (or queen's) touch. Also *fig.*

King's Highway: see HIGHWAY.

Kingship (ki·ŋʃip). ME. [f. KING *sb.* + -SHIP.] **1.** The office and dignity of a king; the fact of being king; reign. Also *fig.* **2.** Monarchical government 1648. **3.** With poss. pron.: (His) royal majesty. Also *fig.* 1648. **4.** The dominion of a king 1864.

King's man, ki·ngsman. 1639. **1.** A royalist. **2.** A custom-house officer 1814.

King's Peace: see PEACE.

Kingston (ki·ŋstən). 1666. The angel-fish or monk-fish (*Squatina angelus*).

Kinic, obs. f. QUINIC.

Kink (kiŋk), *sb.*¹ 1561. [– (M)LG. *kinke* (Du. *kink*), f. **kiŋk-* bend, var. of **kik-* (as in Icel. *kikna* bend at the knees).] †**1.** *pl.* Twist or wool prepared for weaving. **2.** A short twist or curl in a rope, thread, hair, etc., at which it is bent upon itself. (Orig. naut.) 1678. Also *transf.* of a crick in the neck, etc. 1851. **3.** *fig.* (orig. *U.S.*) A mental twist; a faddy notion or device 1803.

3. To bring up young people without kinks W. CORY.

Kink, *sb.*² *Sc.* and *n. dial.* 1788. [f. next; cf. synon. CHINK *sb.*¹] A fit or paroxysm, as of laughter or coughing.

Kink (kiŋk), *v.*¹ *Sc.* and *n. dial.* [north. form of CHINK *v.*¹, OE. *cincian*, app. a nasalized var. of Gmc. **kīkan*, whence MHG. *kīchen* gasp, etc. Cf. CHINCOUGH, KINKCOUGH, etc.] *intr.* To gasp convulsively for breath, as in hooping-cough or with laughing.

Kink (kiŋk), *v.*² 1697. [prob. – Du. *kinken*, f. *kink* KINK *sb.*¹] **1.** *intr.* To form a kink; to twist or curl stiffly, esp. at one point. **2.** *trans.* To cause to kink; to form a kink upon; to twist stiffly. Also *fig.* (Usu. in *pass.*) 1800.

‖**Kinkajou** (ki·ŋkădʒū). Also **kincajou.** 1796. [– Fr. *quincajou*, of N.-Amer. Indian origin; cf. Algonquin *kwingwaage*, Ojibway *gwingwaage* wolverine.] A carnivorous quadruped (*Cercoleptes caudivolvulus*) of Central and S. America, allied to the racoon; it is about the size of the common cat, has a prehensile tail, and is nocturnal in its habits. Also called *potto* or *honey-bear*.

Kinkcough (ki·ŋkkǫf). *n. dial.* 1568. [f. KINK *v.*¹ + COUGH *sb.* Cf. CHINCOUGH and next.] The hooping-cough.

Kinkhost (ki·ŋkhǫst). *Obs.* exc. *Sc.* [ME. *kinkehost* (XII), f. KINK *v.*¹ + HOAST, perh. through MLG. *kinkhōste.*] = prec.

Kinkle (ki·ŋk'l), *sb.* 1862. [f. KINK *sb.*¹ + -LE.] **1.** A little kink or twist. **2.** *fig.* A 'wrinkle', a hint. LYTTON. Hence **Ki·nkled** *a.* having kinkles; frizzed, crisped, as hair.

Kinky (ki·ŋki), *a.* 1860. [f. KINK *sb.*¹ + -Y.¹] **1.** Full of kinks; closely curled or twisted, as hair 1865. **2.** *fig.* (*U.S. colloq.*) Queer, crotchety 1860.

‖**Kinnikinic** (ki:nikini·k). Also **killickinnick, killikinik.** 1799. [Algonquin; lit. 'mixture'.] **1.** A mixture used by N. Amer. Indians as a substitute for tobacco, or for mixing with it; mostly dried sumach-leaves and the inner bark of dogwood or willow. **2.** Plants used for this, as the Silky Cornel, *Cornus sericea*, and esp. Bearberry, *Arctostaphylos uva-ursi* (also *trailing k., k.-vine*) 1839.

Kino (kī·no). 1788. [app. of W. African origin; cf. Mandingo *cano* = Gambia kino.] **1.** A substance resembling catechu, usually of a dark reddish-brown colour, consisting of the inspissated gum or juice of various tropical trees and shrubs; used in medicine and tanning as an astringent, and (in India) for dyeing cotton. Occas. called *Gum Kino*. **African** or **Gambia K.** (the kind first known in Europe, but now out of use) is the produce of *Pterocarpus erinaceus*; **Botany Bay K.** or **Australian K.**, of *Eucalyptus resinifera* and other species; **East India K., Malabar K.,** or **Amboyan K.** (the kind most used), of *Pterocarpus Marsupium*. **2.** Any of the plants which yield this 1876.

Kinology (kəinǫ·lŏdʒi). 1890. [irreg. f. Gr. κινεῖν move + -LOGY.] That branch of physics which treats of motion; kinematics.

Kinone, Kinoyl, Kinquina, etc.: see QUIN-.

-kins, *suffix*, variant of -KIN in certain mild oaths, as *bodikins, lakins, maskins, pittikins.* See also -KIN.

Kinsfolk(s (ki·nzfǭᵘk(s). Now *rare.* 1450. [f. KIN + FOLK, after *kinsman.*] Persons of the same kin; relations by blood; relatives.

They sought him among their kinsefolke and acquaintance *Luke* 2:44.

Kinship (ki·n,ʃip). 1833. [f. KIN + -SHIP.] Relationship by descent; consanguinity.

She was of k. with the queen 1880.

Kinsman (ki·nzmæ̆n). [Early ME. f. *cunnes, kinnes*, gen. of KIN + MAN.] A man of one's own kin; a relative by blood (or, loosely, by marriage). Now chiefly literary. Also *fig.* Hence **Ki·nsmanship,** kinship.

Ki·nswoman. ME. [f. as *kinsman* + WOMAN.] A woman of one's own kin; a female relative. Now only literary.

Kintlage, -ledge, -lidge, obs. ff. KENTLEDGE.

‖**Kiosk** (ki,ǫ·sk). 1625. [– Fr. *kiosque* (in It. *chiosco*) – Turk. *kiūshk* pavilion – Pers. *guš(a* pavilion.] **1.** A light open pavilion or summer-house, often supported by pillars; common in Turkey and Persia. **2.** A light structure resembling this, for the sale of newspapers, a band-stand, etc. 1865.

Kip (kip), *sb.*¹ 1525. [Of unkn. origin; sense 2 is synon. with MDu. *kip, kijp*, pack or bundle, esp. of hides.] **1.** The hide of a young or small beast (as a calf, a lamb, etc.) as used for leather 1530. **2.** A set or bundle of such hides, containing a definite number.

Kip, *sb.*² *slang.* 1766. [Cf. Da. *kippe* mean hut, *horekippe* brothel.] †**1.** A brothel. GOLDSM. **2.** A common lodging-house; a lodging in such a house; hence, a bed 1879. Hence **Kip** *v. intr.*, to go to bed, sleep.

Kipe (kəip). Now *dial.* [OE. *cȳpe*, app. = LG. *küpe* basket carried in the hand or on the back, also *kīpe* (XV). Cf. COOP *sb.*¹] A basket; †*spec.* an osier basket used for catching fish; a basket used as a measure (*dial.*).

Kippage (ki·pėdʒ). *Sc.* 1567. [Aphetic f. Fr. *équipage* equipage.] †**1.** A ship's crew or company. **2.** Disorder, confusion; a state of excitement or irritation 1814.

Kipper (ki·pəɹ), *sb.*¹ [Identical in form with OE. *cypera*, occurring once, in collocation with *leax* salmon, = OS. *kupiro*, ME. *kypre, kiper* (XIV), *kepper* (XVI), used app. in sense of KIPPER *sb.*²; perh. the most plausible conjecture is that of connection with OE. *copor*, etc., COPPER *sb.*¹ with allusion to the colour of the male salmon.] The male salmon (or sea trout) during the spawning season. Also *attrib.* or as *adj.* 1533. **b.** A (young) person, a child (*slang*) 1905.

Comb. †**k.-time,** the period of close time for salmon.

Kipper (ki·pəɹ), *sb.*² 1769. [Obscurely rel. to prec.] A kippered fish; now *esp.* a herring so cured (see KIPPER *v.*).

Ki·pper, *v.* 1773. [f. KIPPER *sb.*²] *trans.* To cure (fish) by cleaning, rubbing repeatedly with salt and pepper or other spice, and drying in the open air or in smoke.

Kipper-nut. 1597. [Of unkn. origin.] = EARTH-NUT.

Kirk (kōɹk, *Sc.* kėrk), *sb.* ME. [– ON. *kirkja* – OE. *ċir(i)ċe* CHURCH.] The Northern Eng. and Sc. form of CHURCH, in all its senses. **b.** In official use, the name 'Kirk of Scotland' gave place to 'Church of Scotland' at the date of the Westminster Assembly. But **(c)** in subsequent Eng. usage, 'kirk' often = the Church of Scotland, as dist. from the Church of England, or from the Episcopal Church in Scotland. So *Free K.* for the Free Church of Scotland 1674.

Comb. **Kirk-garth** ME. = CHURCHYARD. **Kirkman** ME. **1.** An ecclesiastic. **2.** A member of the 'kirk', i.e. the Church of Scotland 1650. **Kirk-session,** the lower court in the Established Church of Scotland and other Presbyterian

Churches, composed of the minister and elders 1717. **Kirkyard** ME., now *Sc.* = CHURCHYARD.

Kirk, *v.* Now *Sc.* ME. [f. KIRK *sb.*] *trans.* = CHURCH *v.*

Kirmess, -mish, var. of KERMIS.

Kirn[1], *sb.* and *v.* ME. [Cf. ON. *kirna* in same sense.] north. and Sc. f. CHURN.

Kirn[2]. *Sc.* and *n. dial.* 1777. [Of unkn. origin.] **1.** Harvest-home, harvest-supper. **2.** The cutting of the last handful of corn in the harvest-field 1808.

||**Kirschwasser** (ki·rʃvasər). Also **kirschen-.** 1819. [G., f. *kirsche* cherry + *wasser* water.] An alcoholic spirit distilled from a fermented liquor obtained by crushing wild cherries. Also abbrev. **Kirsch** (also **kirsh**) 1869.

Kirtle (kǭ·ɹt'l). [OE. *cyrtel* = ON. *kyrtill* tunic :- Gmc. **kurtilaz*, f. **kurt-*, usu. taken to be – L. *curtus* short; *see* CURT, -LE.] **1.** A man's tunic or coat, orig. a garment reaching to the knees or lower. **2.** A woman's gown. **b.** A skirt or outer petticoat. OE. **3.** *fig.* A covering of any sort; a coating of paint ME.

2. Ladies and gentlewomen were forbidden..to go abroad with wide hoop'd gowns or kirtles HOWELL.

Hence **Ki·rtled** *a.*, clothed in a kirtle 1634. Amid'st the flowry-kirtl'd Naiades MILT.

Kish[1] (kiʃ). 1776. [– Ir. *cis* (kiʃ), *ceis* (keʃ) basket, hamper.] A large wickerwork basket, used in Ireland for carrying turf, etc.

A k. of turf burns 2 barrels of lime A. YOUNG.

Kish[2] (kiʃ). 1812. [Of unkn. origin.] A form of impure graphite, which separates from certain kinds of iron in smelting. Also, A dross on the surface of melted lead.

||**Kismet** (ki·smet). 1849. [Turk. *kismet* – Arab. (Pers.) *ḳisma(t* portion, lot, fate, f. *ḳasama* divide.] Destiny, fate.

Kiss (kis), *sb.* [ME., f. KISS *v.*, superseding OE. *coss*; see next.] **1.** A touch or pressure given with the lips, in token of affection, greeting, or reverence; a salute or caress so given. **2.** *fig.* A light touch 1588. **b.** *Billiards.* Impact between balls both of which are in motion 1836. **3.** A sugar-plum 1825. **4.** A name for a drop of sealing-wax accidentally dropped beside the seal 1829.

1. Speake cosin, or..stop his mouth with a kisse SHAKS. Can danger lurk within a k.? COLERIDGE. **2.** *L. L. L.* IV. iii. 26. **4.** 'It's Peggy O'Dowd's fist', said George, laughing. 'I know it by the kisses on the seal' THACKERAY.

Kiss (kis), *v.* Pa. t. and pple. **kissed** (kist). [OE. *cyssan* = OFris. *kessa*, OS. *cussian* (Du. *cussen*), OHG. *kussen* (G. *küssen*), ON. *kyssa* :- Gmc. **kussjan*, f. **kussaz* kiss, whence OE. *coss* (to XVI).] **1.** *trans.* To press or touch with the lips, in token of affection, greeting, or reverence; to salute or caress with the lips; to give a kiss to. **2.** *intr.* or *absol.* ME. **b.** *trans.* with cognate obj.; also, to express by kissing 1830. **3.** *fig.* To touch lightly, as if in affection or greeting ME. Also *intr.* **b.** *spec.* in *Bowls*, *Billiards*, etc. said of a ball touching another ball lightly when both are in motion 1579. **4.** *trans.* with *adv.*, *prep.*, or *compl.* To put, get, or bring by kissing 1606.

1. With vs the wemen giue their mouth to be kissed, in other places their cheek, in many places their hand PUTTENHAM. **2.** K. and be friends, sirrah SWIFT. **b.** To k. good night 1883. **3.** When the sweet winde did gently kisse the trees SHAKS. *intr.* Like fire and powder; Which as they kisse consume SHAKS. **4.** We haue kist away Kingdomes, and Prouinces *Ant. & Cl.* III. x. 7.

Phrases. *To k. the book*, i.e. the Bible, New Testament, or Gospels, in taking an oath. *To k. the dust*, to be overthrown, humiliated, ruined, or slain; so *to k. the ground*. *To k. the hand* (*hands*) of a sovereign or superior, as a ceremonial greeting or leave-taking, or on appointment to an office of state; formerly, merely = to pay one's respects, to salute or bid farewell. *To k. the rod*, to accept correction submissively.

Kisser (ki·səɹ). 1537. [f. KISS *v.* + -ER[1].] One who kisses. **b.** The mouth (*vulgar*) 1860.

Kissing (ki·siŋ), *vbl. sb.* ME. [f. KISS *v.* + -ING[1].] The action of KISS *v.*

attrib. and *Comb.*, as †**k.-comfit,** a perfumed comfit for sweetening the breath; **k. dance** = CUSHION-*dance*; **-gate,** a small gate swinging in a U- or V-shaped enclosure, which allows only one person to pass at a time.

Kissing, *ppl. a.* 1590. [f. KISS *v.* + -ING[2].] That kisses.

Comb. **k.-crust** (*colloq.*), the soft part of the crust of a loaf where it has touched another in baking; **-kind,** *a.* on affectionate terms. **Ki·ssingly** *adv.*

Kist (kist), *sb.*[1] *Sc.* and *n. dial.* [ME. *ciste* – ON. *kista*; see CHEST *sb.*[1]] **1.** A chest, box, coffer. **2.** A chest in which money is kept; a treasury; also *transf.* the store of money itself 1619. **3.** A coffin ME. **b.** *Archæol.* = CIST 1, KISTVAEN 1853. Hence **Kist** *v.* to put into a k. or coffin.

||**Kist,** *sb.*[2] *E. Ind.* 1764. [Urdu (Pers., Arab.) *ḳisṭ* portion.] An instalment (of the yearly land revenue or other payment).

Kistvaen, cistvaen (ki·stvain). 1715. [– W. *cist faen*, i.e. *cist* CHEST *sb.*[1] and *faen* (*maen*) stone.] *Archæol.* = CIST 1.

Kit (kit), *sb.*[1] ME. [– MDu. *kitte* (Du. *kit* tankard), of unkn. origin.] **1.** A circular wooden vessel made of hooped staves; *esp.* a tub- or pail-shaped vessel, often with a lid, for carrying milk, butter, fish, etc.; hence, *occas.*, a square box for the same purpose. **b.** A basket of straw or rushes, for holding fish 1847. **2.** A collection of articles forming part of the equipment of a soldier, and carried in a valise or knapsack; also, the valise; occas. = outfit, 'turn-out', uniform 1785. **b.** A collection of personal effects, esp. as packed for travelling 1833. **c.** The outfit of tools required by a workman 1851. **3.** *colloq.* A set, lot, collection of things or persons 1785.

Comb. **k.-bag,** a stout bag in which to carry a soldier's or traveller's k.

Kit (kit), *sb.*[2] Now *rare.* 1519. [perh. deduced from the first syll. of L. *cithara*, Gr. κιθάρα CITHER.] A small fiddle, formerly much used by dancing masters.

Pray let me see you dance: I play upon the K. STEELE.

Kit (kit), *sb.*[3] 1562. Short f. KITTEN.

Kit (kit), *sb.*[4] 1533. **1.** Pet form of Catherine or Kate (cf. KITTY[1]). †**2.** A light woman –1639.

2. Kits of Cressides kinde GASCOIGNE.

Kit, *sb.*[5] 1584. [Pet form of *Christopher.*] In phr. *Kit with the canstick* or *candlestick* = JACK-O'-LANTERN.

Kit, *sb.*[6] 1740. [– G. *kitt.*] A composition of resin, pitch, and tallow applied to canvas.

Kit, *sb.*[7] 1885. [Of unkn. origin.] *Photogr.* A frame inserted in a plate-holder to adapt it to a smaller size of plate.

Kit (kit), *v.* 1725. [f. KIT *sb.*[1]] *trans.* To put into a kit or kits; esp. fish for market.

Kit, obs. inf., pa. t. and pa. pple., of CUT *v.*

Kit-cat[1] (ki·tkæt). Now *dial.* 1664. [redupl. from CAT *sb.*] The game of tip-cat.

Kit-cat[2] (ki·tkæt). Also **kit-kat.** 1704. [f. *Kit* (= Christopher) *Cat* or *Catling*, keeper of the pie-house where the club originally met, in Shire Lane by Temple Bar, London.] **1.** *attrib.* with *Club*: A club of Whig politicians and men of letters founded in James II' s time 1705. Also *absol.* **b.** A member of this club 1704. **2.** *attrib.* with *size*, *portrait*, etc.: A size of portrait, less than half-length, but including the hands. So called because the dining-room of the club was hung with portraits of the members, and was too low for half-size portraits. Also *absol.* Also *fig.* 1754.

Kitchen (ki·tʃėn), *sb.* [OE. *cyċene* = OS. **kukina* (MLG. *kökene*, MDu. *cokene*, Du. *keuken*), OHG. *chuhhina* (MHG. *küchen*, G. *küche*) :- WGmc. **ko·cina*, for **coci·na*, pop. var. of late L. *coquīna*, f. *coquere* cook.] **1.** That room or part of a house where food is cooked. Also *fig.* **b.** = CUISINE 1679. †**2.** A utensil in which food is prepared; e.g. a Dutch oven (*U.S.*) –1858. **3.** (Formerly also *k. meat.*) Food from the kitchen; hence, any kind of food eaten with bread, etc., as a relish. Chiefly *Sc.* and *north. Ir.* ME. **4.** *attrib.* ME.

1. The first foundation of a good House must be the K. 1616. **b.** The German k. is..execrable, and the French delicious CHESTERF. **3.** Hunger is the best k. *Mod. Sc. Prov.* **4.** *K.-fee*, dripping (so called as being a perquisite of the cook). *K.-garden*, a garden in which fruit and vegetables for the table are grown; also *attrib.* *K.-maid*, a girl employed in the k., usu. under the cook. *K.-physic* (joc.), nourishment for an invalid 1592. *K.-stuff*, requisites for the k., as vegetables, etc.; refuse of the kitchen, dripping, etc.; also *attrib.* of persons or things.

Kitchen (ki·tʃėn), *v.* 1590. [f. prec. sb.] †**1.** *trans.* To entertain in the kitchen. *Com. Err.* V. i. 415. **2.** *Sc.* To serve as 'kitchen' or relish; to season 1721.

Kitchener (ki·tʃėnəɹ). late ME. [f. as prec. + -ER[1].] **1.** One employed in a kitchen; *esp.* in a monastery. **2.** A cooking-range with its appliances 1851.

Kitchenette (kitʃėne·t). orig. *U.S.* 1922. [See -ETTE.] A small room, alcove, etc. in a house or flat, combining kitchen and pantry.

Kitchen-midden (ki·tʃėnmi:d'n). 1863. [tr. Da. *kjökken-* or *kökkenmödding*, f. *kökken* KITCHEN; see MIDDEN.] A refuse-heap of prehistoric date, consisting chiefly of the shells of edible molluscs and bones of animals, etc.

†**Ki·tchenry.** *rare.* 1609. [See -RY.] **1.** The body of servants employed in a kitchen –1658. **2.** The art of cooking. HOLLAND.

Kite (kəit), *sb.* [OE. *cȳta*; the name, corresp. to the base of MHG. *kūze* (G. *kauz*) screech-owl, and other words echoing various cries, may have been given from its shrill plaintive voice.] **1.** A bird of prey of the family *Falconidæ* and subfamily *Milvinæ*, with long wings, tail usually forked, and no tooth in the bill. **a.** *orig.* and *esp.* the European species *Milvus ictinus*, also called *Red K.* and *Glede*, formerly common in England. **b.** Also, other species of the genus, or of the subfamily; e.g. the **Brahminy K.,** *Haliastur indus* of Hindustan; **Indian** or **Pariah K.,** *Milvus govinda*; **Swallow-tailed K.,** *Elanoides forficatus* of N. America; etc. 1813. **2.** *fig.* One who preys upon others; a sharper; also vaguely, as a term of detestation 1553. **3.** [From its hovering in the air like the bird.] A toy consisting of a light frame, with paper or other thin material stretched upon it; mostly in the form of an isosceles triangle with a circular arc as base, or a quadrilateral; constructed to be *flown* in a strong wind by means of a string attached and a tail to balance it 1664. **4.** *Comm. slang.* A bill of exchange, etc., used for raising money on credit; an accommodation bill. A person thus raising money is said *to fly a k.* 1805. **5.** *Naut.* (*pl.*) The highest sails of a ship, which are set only in a light wind. Also *flying-kites.* 1856. **6.** *Geom.* A quadrilateral figure symmetrical about one diagonal 1893.

2. Ah you K. *Ant. & Cl.* III. xiii. 89. **3.** Phr. *To fly* (or *send up*) *a k.* (fig.): to try 'how the wind blows', i.e. in what direction things are tending. *Comb.* **k. balloon,** sausage-shaped captive balloon for military observations.

Kite, *v.* 1863. [f. prec. sb.] **1.** *intr.* To fly with a gliding motion like that of a kite; *trans.* to cause to fly high like a paper kite. **2.** *Comm. slang.* **a.** *intr.* To 'fly a kite'; see KITE *sb.* 4. **b.** *trans.* To convert into a kite or accommodation bill. 1864.

Kite, obs. f. KYTE, belly.

Kit-fox. 1812. [perh. f. KIT *sb.*[3], in ref. to its small size.] A small fox (*Vulpes velox*), of North-western America.

Kith (kiþ), *sb.* [OE. *cȳþ(þ*, earlier *cȳþþu* = OHG. *chundida* :- Gmc. **kunþiþō*, f. **kunþ-* known; see next, COUTH.] †**1.** Knowledge; information –1450. †**2.** One's native land; country –1513. **3.** The persons who are known, taken collectively; one's friends, fellow-countrymen, or neighbours; later, occas. confused with *kin*. *Obs.* or *arch.*, exc. in *Kith and kin*. OE.

Phr. *Kith and kin*: *orig.* Country and kinsfolk (see 2); in later use, Acquaintance and kinsfolk; now often taken as pleonastic for Kinsfolk, relatives.

Kithe, kythe (kəið). *v.* Now *Sc.* and *north.* [OE. *cȳþan* = OFris. *kētha*, OS. *kūðian*, OHG. *kunden*, ON. *kynna*, Goth. *kunþjan*, f. Gmc. **kunþ-*; see prec., COUTH.] **1.** *trans.* To make known; to manifest; *refl.* to show oneself, appear ME. **2.** *intr.* for *refl.* To come forth to sight; to become known; to appear ME. †**3.** *trans.* To manifest practically (a feeling, quality, etc.); hence, to practise, do –1724. †**4.** To own; to recognize –1613. Hence **Ki·thing, kything** *vbl. sb.* a making known, telling, showing, manifestation, etc.

Kitish (kəi·tiʃ), *a.* 1566. [f. KITE *sb.* + -ISH[1].] Like or of the nature of a kite; greedy.

Kitling (ki·tliŋ). Now *dial.* ME. [Commonly identified with ON. *ket(t)lingr* (Norw. *kjetling*) kitten.] †**1.** The young of any animal –1603. **2.** A young cat, a kitten (now *dial.*) 1530. †**3.** Applied to a person –1745. **4.** *attrib.* or *adj.* Resembling a kitten or that of a kitten; inexperienced; diminutive 1604.

2. Whether goe you, now?..to drowne kitlings? B. JONS.

Kitten (ki·t'n), *sb.* [Late ME. (XIV) *kitoun, ketoun* – AFr. **kitoun*, **ketoun*, var. of OFr. *chitoun, chetoun* (mod. *chaton*), dim. of *chat* CAT; the ending was assim. to -EN[1].] The young of the cat; a young cat. Also *transf.* and *fig.* Hence **Ki·ttenhood,** the state of being a k. **Ki·ttenish** *a.* like a k. or that of a k.

Ki·tten, *v.* 1495. [f. prec. sb.] Of a cat: To bring forth kittens; also of some other animals: To litter. *intr.* and *trans.*

†**Kittisol** (ki·tisǫl). 1588. [– Pg. and Sp. *quitasol*, f. *quitar* take away + *sol* sun. Cf. PARASOL.] A sunshade; *spec.* a Chinese umbrella made of bamboo and oiled paper –1875.

Kittiwake (ki·tiwēik). 1661. [Imitative of its cry.] Any sea-gull of the genus *Rissa*; esp. (and primarily) *R. tridactyla*, the common species of the North Atlantic and Arctic Oceans, a small gull having white plumage with black markings on the primaries, and the hind toe rudimentary. Also *k. gull.*

Kittle (ki·t'l), *a.* Orig. *Sc.* and *n. dial.* 1560. [f. KITTLE *v.*[1]] Ticklish; difficult to deal with; risky, precarious, nice, delicate. K. points of law 1728. *Kittle cattle*: people difficult to manage.

Kittle (ki·t'l), *v.*[1] Now *dial.* and chiefly *Sc.* [prob. of ON. origin, corresp. to late OE. *kitelung* '*titillatio*', noun of action from a verb repr. by OS. *kitilon* (Du. *kittelen*), OHG. *kizzilōn* (G. *kitzeln*), ON. *kitla*, f. Gmc. **kit-* **kut-*.] **1.** *trans.* To tickle (in physical sense). **2.** *fig.* To stir with feeling or emotion, usually pleasurable; to 'tickle' ME. **3.** To puzzle with question, etc. 1824.

1. *transf.* The best fiddler that ever kittled thairm with horse-hair SCOTT.

Ki·ttle, *v.*[2] Now *Sc.* and *n. dial.* 1530. [perh. back-formation from KITLING; but cf. Norw. *kjetla* in the same sense.] **1.** = KITTEN *v.* **2.** *fig.* (*intr.* and *pass.*) To come into being 1823.

Kitty[1] (ki·ti). 1500. [Pet form of Catherine.] †**1.** A young girl or woman; occas. a light woman (*Sc.*) –1572. **2.** Local name for the wren; also *kitty-wren* 1681.

Ki·tty[2]. 1719. [f. as KIT *sb.*[3] + -Y[6].] Pet name for a kitten.

Ki·tty[3]. 1825. [Of unkn. origin.] **1.** Prison, lock-up. *dial.* **2.** The pool at card games 1892. **b.** Applied to other kinds of pool or joint fund 1904. **3.** *Bowls.* The jack 1909.

Kitysol, Kive: see KITTISOL, KEEVE.

Kiver, obs. and dial. f. COVER *sb.* and *v.*

‖**Kiwi** (kī·wi). Also **kiwi-kiwi, kivi.** 1835. [Maori.] Native New Zealand name of the APTERYX, now used in English.

Kl-, occas. ME. spelling for *Cl-*, now only in words of foreign origin.

Klaxon (klæ·ksən). 1914. [Name of manufacturing company.] An (electric) motor-horn. Hence as *vb.*

‖**Kleenebok** (klē·nĕbǫk, klī·nbǫk). 1834. [S. Afr. Du., = little buck.] A small S. Afr. antelope (*Cephalophus monticola*), also called Blue Duiker.

Klepht (kleft). Also **kleft.** 1820. [– mod.Gr. κλέφτης, = Gr. κλέπτης thief.] One of those Greeks who after the conquest of Greece by the Turks in the 15th c. held out in the mountains. Hence, later, A brigand, bandit. Hence **Kle·phtism.**

Kleptomania (kleptomēi·niă). 1830. [f. *klepto-*, comb. form of Gr. κλέπτης thief, rel. to κλέπτειν steal; see -MANIA.] An irresistible tendency to theft in persons who are well-to-do, a supposed form of insanity. Hence **Kleptoma·niac,** one affected with k. (also *attrib.* or as *adj.*).

Klick, -er, -et, obs. ff. CLICK, etc.

Klino- (kləino), var. of CLINO-, as in *klinometer*, etc.; also **Klinocephalic** (-sĭfæ·lik), **-cephalous** (-se·făləs), *adjs.*, having a saddle-shaped depression at the vertex of the skull; hence **Klinoce·phalism, -ce·phaly.**

Klinostat (kləi·nostæt), a stand on which germinating seeds, etc. are placed, and which is made to revolve so as to counteract the influence of gravity on their growth.

‖**Klipdas** [S.Afr.Du. *klipdas* rock-badger.] See HYRAX.

‖**Klipspringer** (kli·pspri:ŋəɹ). 1785. [S. Afr. Du., f. *klip* rock + *springer* SPRINGER.] A small S. Afr. antelope (*Oreotragus saltatrix*).

Kloof (klūf). 1731. [– Du. *kloof* (klōf) cleft; see CLOVE *sb.*[4]] In S. Africa: A deep narrow valley; a ravine.

Kn-, an initial combination still retained by most Gmc. langs. In English the *k* is now silent.

Knab (næb), *v. Obs.* exc. *dial.* 1630. [imit.; cf. KNABBLE, KNAP *v.*[2]] To bite lightly, to nibble.

Knab: see NAB *sb.* and *v.*

†**Kna·bble,** *v.* 1567. [dim. or freq. of KNAB *v.*; cf. Du. *knabbelen*, LG. *knabbeln* (G. *knabbern*), also NIBBLE *v.*] To bite, gnaw, nibble. Usu. *intr.* or *absol.* with *at, upon.* –1684.

Knack (næk), *sb.*[1] [ME. *knak.* Of imit. origin. Cf. Du. *knak*, G. *knack, knacke*, etc.] †**1.** A sharp sounding blow, stroke, or rap. ME. only. **2.** A crack or snap such as is made by striking a stone with a hammer 1565.

Knack (næk), *sb.*[2] ME. [ult. of imit. origin, but perh. immed. – Du., LG. *knak* (prec.). Cf. KNAP *sb.*[2]] **1.** A trick; a device, artifice; formerly often, a crafty device, an underhand trick; later, a clever expedient, a dodge. **2.** The faculty of doing something cleverly, adroitly, and successfully. (Now the leading sense.) 1581. **b.** A trick of action, speech, etc. 1674. **3.** *concr.* An ingenious contrivance; a toy, trinket, KNICK-KNACK. ? *Obs.* 1540. †**b.** A choice dish; a dainty –1642. †**c.** A quaint device or conceit in writing –1660.

1. She ne used no suche knakkes smale CHAUCER. He has some k., or trick of the trade CARLYLE. **2.** Our Holland had the true k. of translating FULLER. **b.** The Lady..has..a K. of saying the commonest Things STEELE. **3.** Why 'tis..A knacke, a toy, a tricke, a babies cap SHAKS. **b.** As some teachers give to Boyes Junkets and Knacks, that they may learne apace MILT.

Knack (næk), *v.* ME. [Of imit. origin; with senses 2 and 3 cf. Du. *knakken*, MHG. *knacken* (also *gnacken*), etc. Cf. CLACK *v.*, CRACK.] †**1.** *intr.* To deal (sharp sounding) blows 1575. **2.** *trans.* To strike (things, etc.) together so as to produce a sharp abrupt noise; to gnash (the teeth); to snap (the fingers). Now *dial.* 1489. **3.** *intr.* To make a sharp abrupt noise, as when stones are struck together. Now *dial.* 1603. †**4.** *trans.* To 'break' (notes); to sing with trills or runs; to trill forth. ME. only. **b.** *intr.* To talk mincingly (*dial.*) 1674.

Knacker[1] (næ·kəɹ). Now *dial.* 16.. [f. KNACK *v.* + -ER[1].] Something that makes a sharp cracking noise; *spec.* a castanet.

Knacker[2] (næ·kəɹ). 1573. [In sense 1 perh. orig. maker of the smaller articles belonging to harness (f. KNACK *sb.*[2] + -ER[1]); the semantic relation of the senses is obscure.] **1.** A harness-maker, a saddler (*dial.*). **2.** One who buys worn-out horses, and slaughters them for their hides and hoofs, and for making dog's-meat, etc. 1812. **b.** One who buys old houses, ships, etc., for what he can make of them 1890. **3.** *transf.* An old worn-out horse (*dial.*) 1864. Hence **Kna·ckery,** a knacker's yard.

†**Kna·ckish,** *a. rare.* 1660. [f. KNACK *sb.*[2] + -ISH[1].] Artful, tricky; artificial –1694. Hence †**Kna·ckishness,** artificiality.

Knacky (næ·ki), *a.* 1710. [f. as prec. + -Y[1].] Having a knack; artful, clever, adroit, ingenious.

Knag (næg). 1440. [ME. *knag* or *knagge* = G. (orig. LG.) *knagge* knot, peg, etc.] **1.** A short or stiff projection from the trunk or branch of a tree; hence, a peg or hook for hanging anything on. †**2.** One of the knobs of a stag's horn; a tine –1657. **3.** A knot in wood, the base of a branch 1555. **4.** A pointed rock or crag 1552. Hence †**Kna·gged** *a.* furnished with protuberances, knobs, or knots; toothed, jagged 1400. **Kna·ggy** *a.* knotty, rough, rugged 1552. **Kna·gginess.**

Knap (næp), *sb.*[1] Chiefly *dial.* [OE. *cnæp(p* top, summit (of a hill); perh. cogn. w. ON. *knapp-r* knob, etc. (see KNOP *sb.*).] The summit of a hill; a hillock or knoll; a rising ground.

Knap, *sb.*[2] *Obs.* exc. *dial.* ME. [imit.; goes with KNAP *v.*[1]] **1.** An abrupt stroke or blow; a smart knock. **2.** The clapper of a mill 1622. †**3.** A cheating trick with dice –1680.

Knap, var. of KNOP *sb.*

Knap (næp), *v.*[1] Now *dial.* 1470. [imit., going with KNAP *sb.*[2]; cf. Du. and G. (orig. LG.) *knappen* crack, crackle, etc.] **1.** *trans.* To strike with a hard short sound; to knack, knock, rap. Also *absol.* or *intr.* **2.** *trans.* To snap or break by a smart blow. Now used *spec.* of the breaking of stones for the road. 1535. **b.** *intr.* To snap 1545. **3.** To utter smartly; to talk, chatter (a language). Also *intr. Sc.* and *n. dial.* 1581.

2. He hath knapped the speare in sonder COVERDALE *Ps.* 45[6]:9. 'Tis but silke that bindeth thee, K. the thread and thou art free HERRICK. **3.** He answered..that he could k. English with any one SCOTT.

Knap (næp), *v.*[2] Now *dial.* 1575. [Cf. KNAB *v.*; also Du. and G. (orig. LG.) *knappen* crack, snap, bite.] *intr.* and *trans.* To bite in a short or abrupt way; to snap; to nibble.

†**Kna·p-bottle.** 1640. [f. KNAP *v.*[1] + BOTTLE.] *Herb.* The Bladder-campion, *Silene inflata*, so called from its inflated calyx, which snaps when suddenly compressed.

Knapper (næ·pəɹ). *dial.* and *local.* 1787. [f. KNAP *v.*[1] + -ER[1].] One who or that which knaps; one who breaks stones, flints, or the like; *esp.* one who shapes flints with a hammer 1870. **b.** A knapping-hammer.

†**Kna·ppish,** *a. Obs.* exc. *dial.* 1513. [f. KNAP *v.*[2] + -ISH[1]. Cf. SNAPPISH.] Rudely abrupt or froward, testy –1629.

†**Kna·pple,** *v.* 1611. [frequent. of KNAP *v.*[2]; see -LE.] To bite shortly and repeatedly; to nibble –1878.

Kna·ppy, *a.* Now *dial.* 1552. [f. KNAP *sb.* and *v.* + -Y[1].] Full of knaps; lumpy; also, testy.

Knapsack (næ·psæk). 1603. [– MLG. *knapsack*, Du. *knapzak* (whence G. *knappsack*); the first element is held to be identical with G. *knappen* bite, eat (see KNAP *v.*[2]), and the second is SACK *sb.*[1]] A bag or case of canvas or leather for strapping to the back and carrying a soldier's necessaries; any similar receptacle used by travellers.

He packed up his k., and started for the train LYTTON.

Knapweed (næ·pwīd). ME. [orig. *knopweed* (XV), f. KNOP *sb.* + WEED *sb.*[1]; altered to *knap-* XVI; cf. *strop, strap.*] Common name of species of *Centaurea* (N.O. *Compositæ*), esp. *C. nigrā*, with a hard tough stem, and light purple flowers set on a rough dark-coloured globular involucre.

Knar (nāɹ). [ME. *knarre* (XIII), also late ME. *knor* (see KNUR) hard excrescence, corresp. to MLG., MDu., MHG. *knorre* (Du. *knorr*, G. *knorren*) knobby protuberance.] **1.** A rugged rock or stone. Now *dial.* **2.** A knot in wood; *spec.* a protuberance covered with bark on the trunk or root of a tree ME. †**3.** A knotted, thick-set fellow. CHAUCER. Hence **Knarred** *a.* knotted, gnarled. **Kna·rry** *a.* (*rare*), having knars; knotty ME.

†**Knarl** (nāɹl). *rare.* 1598. [Related to prec.; cf. KNURL.] A tangle, knot.

Knarle, Knarled, obs. ff. GNARL, -ED.

‖**Kna·ster,** G. sp. of CANASTER 2, a kind of tobacco.

Knave (nēiv), *sb.* [OE. *cnafa* = OHG. *knabo* (G. *knabe* boy) :– WGmc. **knabo*, obscurely rel. to synon. OE. *cnapa* = OS. *cnapo*, and OHG. *knappo* (G. *knappe* page, squire).] †**1.** A male child, a boy –1460. **2.** A boy or lad employed as a servant; hence, a menial; one of low condition. (Freq. opp. to *knight.*) *arch.* OE. **3.** An unprincipled man; a base and crafty rogue. (Now the main sense.) ME. **b.** *joc.* Now *rare.* 1553. **4.** *Cards.* The lowest court card of each suit, bearing the figure of a soldier or servant; the jack 1568.

2. Every Horseman hath two or thre horses, and to every horse a k. 1600. **3.** The veriest k. and bufflehead that ever he saw in his life PEPYS. **b.** How now, my pretty knaue, how dost thou? SHAKS. Hence **Knave** *v.* to call (any one) k.; to make a k. of; to steal like a k.; to force knavishly. (All nonce-uses.) 1545.

†**Kna·ve-child.** ME. only. A male child.

Knavery (nēi·vəri). 1528. [f. KNAVE *sb.* + -ERY.] **1.** Practices characteristic of a knave; dishonest and crafty dealing; trickery, roguery; an instance of this. †**2.** Roguishness, waggishness, playing of tricks –1646; tricks of dress (*Tam. Shr.* IV. iii. 58). †**3.** Pop. name for Bog Asphodel –1640.

1. The Sun sees much Knauery in a yere, and the Moone more in a quarter DEKKER. **2.** Full of iests, and gypes, and knaueries, and mockes SHAKS.

Knaveship (nēi·vʃip). 1550. [f. KNAVE *sb.* + -SHIP.] **1.** The condition of being a knave: used as a mock title 1589. †**2.** *Sc.* A small due, in meal, payable to the miller's servant, on each lot of corn ground at a thirlage mill –1818.

Kna·vess. [-ESS[1].] A she-knave. CARLYLE.

Knavish (nēi·viʃ), *a.* ME. [f. KNAVE *sb.* + -ISH[1].] Characteristic, or having the character, of a knave. †**1.** Low, vulgar; obscene –1529. †**2.** Roguish, rascally, impertinent –1603. **3.** Unprincipled, fraudulent 1570.

2. Cupid is a knauish lad, Thus to make poor females mad SHAKS. **3.** 'Tis a knauish peece of worke SHAKS. Hence **Kna·vish-ly** *adv.*, **-ness.**

Knaw(e, obs. ff. GNAW.

Knawel (nǫ·ėl). 1578. [– G. *knauel, kneuel* knot-grass.] A book-name of the German knot-grass, *Scleranthus.*

Knead (nīd), *v.* Pa. t. and pa. pple. **kneaded.** [OE. *cnedan* = OS. *knedan* (Du. *kneden*), OHG. *knetan* (G. *kneten*); WGmc. str. vb., f. **kned-* **knad-*, of which another grade appears in ON. *knoða.*] **1.** *trans.* To mix and work up into a homogeneous plastic mass, by drawing out, folding over, and pressing together; *esp.* to work up (moistened flour or clay) into dough or a paste; to make (bread, pottery, etc.) thus. **2.** *fig.* **a.** To reduce to a common mass, as if by kneading. **b.** To shape, as by kneading. ME. **3.** *transf.*, esp. in reference to massage 1606.

1. Take some flour and k. it with oil MRS. GLASSE. **2.** K. and shape her to your thought B. TAYLOR. **3.** I will knede him, Ile make him supple SHAKS. Hence **Knea·dable** *a.* capable of being kneaded. **Knea·der** one who, or that which, kneads **Knea·dingly** *adv.* in the manner of one who kneads.

Knea·ding-trough. ME. A wooden trough or tub in which to knead dough.

Knebelite (nēi·bėləit). 1818. [– G. *Knebelit*, named after Major von *Knebel*; see -ITE[1] 2 b.] *Min.* Hydrous silicate of iron and manganese.

Knee (nī), *sb.* [OE. *cnēo(w* = OFris. *kniu, knē, knī*, OS. *knio* (Du. *knie*), OHG. *kneo, kniu* (G. *knie*), ON. *kné*, Goth. *kniu* :– Gmc. **knewam* :– IE. **gneuom*, f. base **gneu* **geneu* **goneu* (cf. L. *genu*, Gr. γόνυ knee).] **1.** The joint, or region about the joint, between the thigh and the lower leg. **2.** A joint in an animal regarded as corresponding to the human knee; e.g. the carpal articulation of the foreleg of a horse, etc. 1450. **3.** The part of a garment covering the knee 1662. **4.** Anything resembling the knee in position or shape; e.g. a piece of timber or metal having a natural or artificial angular bend; *spec.* in *Shipbuilding* and *Mech.* ME. †**5.** *Bot.* A bent joint in some grasses –1878.

1. Stories learned at a mother's k. 1858. Phr. *To offer* or *give a k.*, to act as second in a pugilistic encounter, and give a principal the support of a knee between the rounds. *On the knees of the gods* (Gr. θεῶν ἐν γούνασι, Hom.), beyond human control 1879. **3.** My riding-cloth suit with close knees PEPYS. **4.** The sydes, knees, and feete of those hills 1640.

Comb.: **k.-bone,** the patella, knee-cap; **-boot,** a boot reaching to the k.; a leathern apron to draw over the knees in a carriage; **-breeches,** breeches reaching down to, or just below, the k.; **-brush,** (*a*) a tuft of long hair, immediately below the carpal joint, on the legs of some antelopes; (*b*) a hairy mass covering the legs of bees, on which they carry pollen; **-jerk,** a sudden extension of the leg occasioned by striking the tendon below the patella; **-piece,** a bent piece of timber used in shipbuilding; also = *knee-rafter*; **-rafter,** a rafter the lower end of which is bent downwards; **-reflex** = *knee-jerk*; **-roof** = CURB-ROOF; **-swell,** in the American organ a lever operated by the k., for crescendo and diminuendo effects.

Knee (nī), *v.* [In sense 1, OE. *cnēowian*, f. *cnēo(w* KNEE *sb.* Since XVI, f. KNEE *sb.*] **1.** *intr.* To go down on, or bend, the knee or knees. **b.** *trans.* with complement 1607. **2.** *trans.* To supplicate, or do obeisance to, by kneeling or bending the knee (*arch.*) 1592. **3.** To strike or touch with the knee 1892. **4.** *Carpentry.* To fasten with a knee or knees 1711.

1. b. K. The way into his mercy *Cor.* v. i. 5.

Knee-cap (nī·kæp). 1660. [f. KNEE *sb.* + CAP.] **1.** A cap or protective covering for the knee. **2.** The convex bone in front of the knee-joint; the patella, knee-pan 1869.

Kneed (nīd), *a.* 1597. [f. KNEE *sb.* and *v.* + -ED.] **1.** Furnished with knees; as *broken-, weak-*, KNOCK-KNEED 1652. **b.** *Bot.* Having joints like knees; bent like a knee; geniculate 1597. **c.** Having an angle like a knee; also *techn.*, Having a knee or knees 1775. **2.** Of trousers: Bulged at the knee 1887.

1. b *K. grass*, a name of *Setaria verticillata.*

Knee-deep, *a.* ME. **1.** So deep as to reach to the knee 1535. **2.** Sunk to the knee (*in* water, mud, etc.). Also *fig.*

1. Decks..almost constantly knee-deep in water 1748. **2.** Oxen..standing knee-deep in the cool water 1895.

Knee-hole. 1862. A hole or space between the pedestal drawers of a writing-table, to receive the knees. Also *attrib.* **b.** *ellipt.* A knee-hole table.

Knee-joint. 1648. **1.** The joint of the knee. **2.** *Mech.* A joint formed of two pieces hinged together endwise so as to resemble a knee, a toggle-joint. Also *attrib.* So **Knee·-joi:nted** *a.* geniculate.

Kneel (nīl), *v.* Pa. t. and pple. **kneeled** (nīld), **knelt** (nelt). [OE. *cnēowlian*, corresp. to (M)LG. *knēlen*, Du. *knielen.* The form *knelt*, which recalls *felt* and *dealt*, is of recent origin (XIX).] *intr.* To fall on the knees or a knee; to remain thus, as in supplication or homage. Const. *to*; also, with indirect passive. **b.** With *down*: To go down on the knees ME.

On these stones St. Peter kneeled 1756. *fig.* Who in heart not ever kneels HERBERT. **b.** But as for Cæsar, Kneele downe, kneele downe, and wonder SHAKS.

Kneeler (nī·ləɹ). ME. [f. prec. + -ER[1].] **1.** One who kneels; *spec.* in 16–17th c., one who received the Lord's Supper kneeling. **2.** *Ch. Hist.* **a.** One belonging to the third class of penitents in the early Eastern church, so called because they knelt during the whole of divine service. **b.** In the Apostolic Constitutions, one of the second class of catechumens, who received the bishop's blessing on bended knee. 1719. **3.** A board, stool, or hassock on which to kneel 1848.

Knee-pan (nī·pæn). ME. [f. KNEE *sb.* + PAN.] The bone in front of the knee-joint; the patella, knee-cap.

Knee·-ti:mber. 1607. Timber having a natural angular bend, suitable for making knees in shipbuilding or carpentry. Also *fig.* **b.** with *pl.* A bent piece of timber used in carpentry, etc. 1739.

Knell (nel), *sb.* [OE. *cnyll*, rel. to *cnyllan* (next).] The sound made by a bell when struck or rung, esp. when rung slowly and solemnly, as after a death or at a funeral. **b.** *fig.* A sound announcing a death or the passing away of something; an omen of death or extinction 1613. **c.** *transf.* A doleful cry, dirge, etc. 1647.

A K., That summons thee to Heauen, or to Hell SHAKS. The curfew tolls the k. of parting day GRAY. *fig.* Men whose names are a k. to all hope of progress EMERSON.

Knell (nel), *v.* Now chiefly *arch.* [OE. *cnyllan*, the normal midland repr. of which was *knyll(e* (XIV–XVI), of which there were ME. diál. vars. *knüll(e, knell(e*, but the present form appears to date from *c*1500 and may be due to assoc. with *bell.*] †**1.** *trans.* To knock; also *absol.* –ME. †**2.** *trans.* To ring (a bell); later, *esp.* to ring slowly and solemnly, as for a death etc., to toll; also *absol.* –1651. **3.** *intr.* **a.** Of a bell: To ring; now esp. for a death or at a funeral ME. **b.** *fig.* To sound ominously 1816. **4.** *trans.* To summon or call by or as by a knell (*into*, etc.) 1800. **b.** To proclaim by or as by a knell 1840.

3. a. Not worth a blessing, nor a bell to k. for thee FLETCHER. **b.** The words of the warlock are knelling in my ears SCOTT. **4.** Each matin bell, the Baron saith, Knells us back to a world of death COLERIDGE.

Knicker[1] (ni·kəɹ). 1694. [– Du. *knikker.*] **1.** A boy's marble of baked clay. **2.** (Also *nicker.*) A large flat button or disc of metal, used as a pitcher, in the boys' game 'on the line' 1899.

Knicker[2] (ni·kəɹ). 1881. In pl. *knickers*: *colloq.* contr. of KNICKERBOCKER II. Also *attrib.*, as *k. suit.*

Knickerbocker (ni·kəɹbǫkəɹ). 1848. [Pretended author, Diedrich *Knickerbocker*, of W. Irving's *History of New York.*]

I. (*with capital inital.*) **1.** A descendant of the original Dutch settlers of the New Netherlands in America; hence, a New Yorker. **2.** *attrib.* or as *adj.* Of or pertaining to the Knickerbockers of New York 1856.

2. The dreadful K. custom of calling on everybody LONGF.

II. (*with small initial*). *pl.* Loose-fitting breeches, gathered in at the knee; also extended to the whole costume worn with these. (Rarely in *sing.*) 1859.

The name is said to have been given to them from their resemblance to the knee-breeches of the Dutchmen in Cruikshank's illustrations to W. Irving's *History of New York.*

Knick-knack, nick-nack (ni·k,næk). 1618. [redupl. of KNACK *sb.*[2]] †**1.** A petty artifice –1673. **2.** Any curious or pleasing trifle of furniture, dress, or food; a trinket, gimcrack, kickshaw 1682. Hence **Knick-kna·ckatory, nick-n.,** a repository of knick-knacks. **Kni:ck-kna·ckery, nick-n.,** knick-knacks collectively; also = sense 2. **Kni·ck-kna:ckish** *a.* of the character of a knick-knack; trifling, flimsy. **Kni·ck-kna:cky** *a.* addicted to knick-knacks; affected, trifling.

Knife (nəif), *sb.* Pl. **knives** (nəivz). [Late OE. *cnīf* – ON. *knífr* = OFris., MLG. *knīf*, MDu. *cnijf* (Du. *knijf*) :– Gmc. **knībaz*, of unc. etym.] A cutting-instrument, consisting of a blade with a sharpened longitudinal edge fixed in a handle, either rigidly as in *table-* or *sheath-k.*, or with a joint as in *pocket-k.* **b.** A knife used as a weapon; applied to a short sword, cutlass, or hanger ME. **c.** A sharpened cutting-blade, as in a straw-cutter, turnip-cutter, etc. 1833.

Bought a large kitchen k., and half a dozen oyster knives PEPYS. **b.** Phr. *War to the k.*: war to the last extremity (*lit.* and *fig.*). *To get* or *have one's knife into* (a person): to exhibit a malicious or vindictive spirit towards; to persecute unrelentingly.

Comb.: **k.-boy,** a boy employed to clean table-knives; **-file,** a thin and tapering file, with a very sharp edge; **-grass,** a stout American sedge (*Scleria latifolia*) with sharp-edged leaves; **-rest,** a small metal or glass device on which to rest a carving-knife or -fork at table.

Knife (nəif), *v.* 1865. [f. KNIFE *sb.*] *trans.* To cut, strike, or stab with a knife. **b.** *U.S. slang.* To strike at secretly 1888.

Knife and fork. 1727. **1.** *lit.* as used in eating. Hence in phrases, as *to play a good knife and fork*, to eat heartily. Also *attrib.* **2.** A name of Herb Robert and the common club-moss 1879.

Knife-board. 1848. **1.** A board on which knives are cleaned. **2.** Pop. name for the original roof-seat on omnibuses, consisting of a double bench placed lengthways 1852.

Kni·fe-e:dge. 1818. **1.** The edge of a knife; also *transf.* Also *attrib.* = knife-edged. 1876. **2.** A wedge of hard steel, on which a pendulum, scale-beam, etc. is made to oscillate 1818. Also *transf.* and *fig.*

2. On a knife-edge of ice between two crevasses L. STEPHEN. Hence **Knife-edged** *a.*

Knife-grinder. 1611. **1.** One whose trade it is to grind knives, etc. **2.** A grindstone, emery-wheel, or the like for grinding tools 1875. **3. a.** A species of cicada. **b.** The night-jar or goatsucker. 1859.

Knight (nəit), *sb.* [OE. *cniht* boy, youth, man of arms, hero = OFris. *knecht, kniucht,* OS. *knecht,* OHG. *kneht* (Du., G. *knecht*) :– WGmc. **knehta,* of unkn. origin.] †**1.** A boy, youth, lad. OE. only. †**2.** A boy or lad as an attendant or servant; hence, any male servant or attendant –ME. **3.** With genitive, or poss. pron.: A military servant or follower; later, one devoted to the service of a lady as her attendant, or her champion in war or the tournament; hence also *fig.* OE. **4. a.** In the Middle Ages: A military servant of the king or other person of rank; a feudal tenant holding land from a superior on condition of serving in the field as a mounted and well-armed man. Later: One raised to honourable military rank by the king or other qualified person, usually only a person of noble birth who had served as page and squire. **b.** One upon whom corresponding rank is conferred by the sovereign in recognition of personal merit, or of services rendered to crown or country. OE.

The distinctive title of a knight is *Sir* prefixed to the name, as 'Sir John Falstaff'; *Knight* (*Knt.* or *Kt.*) may be added, but this is now unusual. The honour of knighthood is conferred by the accolade, by letters-patent, etc. Modern knights rank below baronets, and the dignity is not hereditary.

c. More fully *Knight of the Shire*: A gentleman representing a shire or county in parliament; orig. one of two of the rank of knight. Now only techn. or *Hist.* CHAUCER. †**5.** Applied to personages of ancient history or mythology –1606. **6. a.** *Rom. Antiq.* (tr. L. *eques* horseman). One of the class of *equites,* who originally formed the cavalry of the Roman army, and later were a wealthy and important class ME. **b.** *Gr. Antiq.* (tr. Gr. ἱππεύς horseman). A citizen of the second class at Athens in the constitution of Solon 1820. **7. a.** *Chess.* One of the pieces, now usually distinguished by the figure of a horse's head 1440. †**b.** The knave in cards 1585.

3. O find him, giue this Ring to my true K. SHAKS. In all your quarrels will I be your k. TENNYSON. **4.** She leaned against..The statue of the armed k. COLERIDGE. **5.** This Aiax..This blended k., halfe Troian, and halfe Greeke SHAKS.

Phrases. **a.** †*K. of the carpet* (see CARPET *sb.*). †*K. of the community* or *parliament* = Knight of the Shire (see 4 c). *K. of the Round Table,* one of King Arthur's knights (see ROUND TABLE).

b. *K. of the* BATH, GARTER, THISTLE, etc. (see these wds.). *K. of St. John, of Malta, of Rhodes* = HOSPITALLER 3. *K. of Windsor,* one of a small number of military officers who have pensions and apartments in Windsor Castle. A title of the higher classes of the Order of the British Empire: see G.B.E. (s.v. G), K.B.E. (s.v. K).

c. In jocular phr., e.g. *k. of the brush,* a painter, *k. of the pestle,* an apothecary, †*k. of industry* (Fr. *chevalier d'industrie*), a sharper, swindler.

d. *Knights of Labour,* an extensive association in the U.S., embracing many of the Trade Unions.

Knight (nəit), *v.* ME. [f. prec.] *trans.* To dub or create (one) a knight.

Knightage (nəi·tėdʒ). 1840. [f. KNIGHT *sb.* + -AGE.] The whole body of knights; a list and account of those who are knights.

Kni·ght-e·rrant. *Pl.* **knights-errant.** ME. [See ERRANT *a.* 1.] **1.** A mediæval knight who wandered in search of adventures. **2.** *transf.* A person of a chivalrous or adventurous spirit. Occas. in ridicule. 1751.

Knight-e·rrantry. 1654. [f. prec. + -RY.] **1.** The practice of a knight-errant; the action of knights who wandered in search of adventures. **2.** Readiness to engage in romantic adventure. Often depreciative: Quixotic behaviour. 1659. **3.** The body of knights-errant (*rare*) 1860.

2. It is a noble Piece of Knight-Errantry to enter the Lists against so many armed Pedagogues STEELE.

Knight-head (nəi·tˌhe:d). 1711. *Naut.* One of two large timbers in a vessel that rise obliquely from the keel behind the stem, one on each side, and support the bowsprit.

Knighthood (nəi·tˌhud). [OE. *cnihthād.* See -HOOD.] †**1.** Boyhood, youth. OE. only. **2.** The rank or dignity of a knight ME. **3.** The profession or vocation of a knight ME. †**b.** (tr. L. *militia.*) Military service –1552. **4.** Chivalrousness ME. **5.** The collective body of knights; a company of knights ME. †**b.** (tr. L. *militia.*) Military force, host. ME. only.

2. I would not take a K. for my Fortune SHAKS. **3.** The old virtues of k.—its truth and honour, its chastity and courage 1856. **4.** The noble knighthode that was in them reconforted them LD. BERNERS. **5.** The k. now-a-days are nothing like the k. of old time CHAPMAN.

†**Kni·ghtless,** *a. rare.* 1590. [f. KNIGHT *sb.* + -LESS.] Unbecoming a knight; unknightly –17..

Knightlike (nəi·tləik). ME. [f. as prec. + -LIKE.] **1.** *adj.* Like or befitting a knight; knightly. **2.** *adv.* = KNIGHTLY *adv.* ME.

2. If, knight-like, he despises fear SCOTT.

Knightly (nəi·tli), *a.* OE. [f. KNIGHT *sb.* + -LY¹.] †**1.** Boyish. OE. only. **2.** Having the rank or qualities of a knight; noble, chivalrous. Now *rare.* ME. **3.** Of, belonging to, suitable or appropriate to a knight ME. **4.** Consisting of knights (*rare*) 1845.

2. He was..k. in his attributes BYRON. **3.** As one for k. giusts and fierce encounters fitt SPENSER. K. deeds DRYDEN. The k. sword 1834. **4.** The k. order S. AUSTIN. Hence **Kni·ghtlihood, Kni·ghtliness,** k. condition or qualities.

Knightly (nəi·tli), *adv.* ME. [f. KNIGHT *sb.* + -LY².] In a manner befitting a knight; gallantly, chivalrously.

Say..why thou com'st thus k. clad in Armes? SHAKS.

Knight Marshal: see MARSHAL.

Knight of the post. 1580. [i.e. (perh.) of the whipping-post or pillory.] A notorious perjurer; one who got his living by giving false evidence; a false bail.

A knight of the post, whome in times past I haue seen as highly promoted as the pillory 1592.

Kni·ght-se:rvice. Also **knight's service.** ME. *Feudal System.* The military service which a knight was bound to render as a condition of holding his lands; hence, the tenure of land under condition of performing military service. Also *fig.*

Knight's fee. ME. *Feudal System.* The amount of land for which the services of an armed knight were due to the sovereign.

Knipperdolling (ni·pərdǫliŋ). 1594. *Ch. Hist.* An adherent of Bernhard Knipperdolling, a leader of the Münster Anabaptists in 1533–5; an Anabaptist; hence, a religious fanatic.

Knit (nit), *sb.* 1596. [f. KNIT *v.*] †**1.** The style or stitch in which anything is knitted; knitted work; texture –1603. **b.** The action or process of knitting 1924. **2.** *Mining.* A small particle of ore. RAYMOND.

1. Let..their garters [be] of an indifferent k. SHAKS.

Knit (nit), *v.* [OE. *cnyttan* = MLG., MDu. *knutten* (G. dial. *knütten*) :– WGmc. **knuttjan,* f. **knutto* KNOT *sb.*¹ The pa. pple. is *knitted,* contr. *knit,* but *knitten* has also been used.] **1.** *trans.* To tie in or with a knot; to fasten by or as by knotting. *arch.* and *dial.* **2.** *trans.* †**a.** To net –1687. **b.** To form (a close texture) by the interlooping of successive series of loops of yarn or thread. (Now the chief specific sense.) 1530. Also *absol.* or *intr.* **3.** *trans.* To interlock; to twine, weave, or plait together. *arch.* or *Obs.* 1470. **4.** To draw closely together; to contract in folds or wrinkles; †to clench (the fist) ME. **b.** *intr.* Said of the brows 1815. **5.** *trans.* To make close, dense, or hard; to compact; to concentrate ME. **b.** *intr.* (for *refl.*) To become consolidated 1605. **c.** *intr.* Of fruit: To form, set. Also of the tree or blossom: To form fruit. ME. †**d.** Of a female animal: To conceive 1732. **6.** *trans.* To conjoin or unite closely (contiguous members, broken parts) 1578. **b.** *intr.* To become closely united 1612. **c.** *intr.* Of bees: To cluster. Now *dial.* 1577. **7.** *fig.* To connect firmly; to unite or combine intimately ME. Also *intr.* (for *refl.*) **8.** *trans.* To constitute by joining (a covenant, etc.); to establish (a relation); to tie, cement ME. **9.** *intr.* To effervesce. [? A different word.] 1743.

1. A greate shete knytt at the iiij. corners TINDALE *Acts* 10:11. I knit my hand-kercher about your browes SHAKS. **2. b.** She can k. him a stocke SHAKS. **3.** Com, knit hands MILT. *Comus* 143. **4.** He knits his Brow, and shewes an angry Eye SHAKS. **5.** Knitting all his force, [he] got one hand free SPENSER. **6.** Nature cannot k. the bones while the parts are under a discharge WISEMAN. **7.** They [merchants] k. Mankind together in a mutual Intercourse of good Offices ADDISON. **8.** When peace was knit again HOLLAND.

Comb. **Knit up.** ME. **a.** *trans.* To tie up, to fasten up, to string up; to compose or repair by knitting (*lit.* and *fig.*). **b.** To close up; to conclude. †**c.** To sum up.

Hence **Knit** *ppl. a.,* made by knitting (as *knit stocking*).

Knitch (nitʃ). Now *dial.* [ME. *knücche, knycche* :– OE. *ġecnyċċe* 'bond'; f. same root as LG. *knuck(e,* G. *knocke,* a bundle of heckled flax.] A bundle (of wood, hay, corn, etc.) tied together; a sheaf or faggot.

If I dared break a hedge for a k. o' wood, they'd put me in prison KINGSLEY. Hence **Kni·tchel,** †**Knitchet,** a small k.; a handful (of reeds, etc.).

†**Kni·tster.** 1648. [f. KNIT *v.* + -STER.] = KNITTER 2.

Knitter (ni·təɹ). 1440. [f. KNIT *v.* + -ER¹.] **1.** One who or that which ties, knots, or closely joins together (*lit.* and *fig.*). **2.** One who knits yarn or thread for hosiery, etc. 1515. **b.** A knitting-machine 1890.

Knitting (ni·tiŋ), *vbl. sb.* ME. [f. KNIT *v.* + -ING¹.] **1.** The action of KNIT *v.* **2.** *spec.* The formation of a fabric by looping. *concr.* Knitted work. 1711.

attrib. and *Comb.,* as *k.-cotton, -machine,* etc.; **k.-needle,** a long straight blunt 'needle' or slender rod, used, two or more at a time, in knitting 1598; so **k.-pin** 1870; **-sheath,** a cylindrical sheath for holding a knitting-needle steady in knitting; etc.

Knittle (ni·t'l). ME. [A deriv. of KNIT *v.*; see -LE, -EL¹.] †**1.** A string for tying or fastening. ME. only. **2.** *spec.* **a.** *Naut.* A small line made of yarn, used on board ship. Also *attrib.* 1627. **b.** A string fastened to the neck of a bag to draw it together 1847.

Knive (nəiv), *v.* 1850. [f. KNIFE *sb.,* after *wife, wive,* etc.] = KNIFE *v.*

Knob (nǫb), *sb.* ME. [– MLG. *knobbe* knot, knob, bud; cf. Flem. *knobbe(n* lump of bread, etc., Du. *knobbel* bump, knot, and KNOP, NOB *sb.*³, KNUB, NUB.] **1.** A small rounded lump or mass, esp. at the end or on the surface of something; a rounded protuberance, boss, stud; a bump, hump, wart, pimple, etc. **b.** *Arch.* A boss of carved work 1730. **2.** A knoll; a hill in general; esp. in U.S. 1650. **3.** A small lump (of sugar, coal, etc.) 1676. **4.** *slang.* The head. Usually NOB, q.v. 1725. **5.** = KNOBSTICK 2. 1838.

1. The bolt is moved by..a fixed k. or handle, as in the common door catch 1833. *Hen. V,* III. vi. 108. The rocky k. called Whitemoss Howe 1872. **3.** A k. of sugar TUCKER. *Comb.* **k.-lock,** a lock which is opened with a k.

Knob (nǫb), *v.* 1566. [f. prec.] **1.** *trans.* To form knobs upon 1879. **2.** *intr.* To form a knob or knobs, to bunch 1566. **3.** *trans.* To free from knobs, to rough-dress (stone in the quarry) 1890.

Knobbed (nǫbd, nǫ·bėd), *a.* 1440. [f. KNOB *sb.* or *v.* + -ED.] Having a knob or knobs; formed into or ending in a knob.

Knobber (nǫ·bəɹ). ? *Obs.* 1700. [f. KNOB *sb.* + -ER¹.] *Venery.* A male deer in its second year; a brocket.

Knobble (nǫ·b'l). 1485. [dim. of KNOB *sb.* = Du., LG. *knobbel* knob, knot.] A small knob. Hence **Kno·bbly** *a.*

Knobbler (nǫ·bləɹ). 1686. [f. prec. + -ER¹.] **1.** = KNOBBER. **2.** *Metall.* A shingler; also *nobbler.*

Knobby (nǫ·bi), *a.* 1543. [f. KNOB *sb.* + -Y¹.] **1.** Full of, bearing, or covered with knobs or protuberances; knotty. **2.** Of the nature of a knob, knob-shaped 1764. Hence **Kno·bbiness** 1611.

Knobkerrie (nǫ·bke:ri). Also **-keerie, -kerry.** 1849. [f. KNOB *sb.* + KERRIE, after Cape Du. *knopkirie, -kieri.*] A short thick stick with a knobbed head, used as a weapon or missile by S. Afr. tribes. Also *transf.*

Knobstick (nǫ·bˌstik). 1824. **1.** A knobbed stick; a knobkerrie. **2.** = BLACK-LEG 3. Also *attrib.* 1826.

Knock, *sb.*¹ ME. [f. KNOCK *v.*] An act of knocking; a hard stroke or thump; *spec.* a rap at a door to gain admittance, etc.

Knock (nǫk), *sb.*² 1587. [In sense 1 – Gael., Ir. *cnoc* knoll, hillock. With 2 cf. Da. dial. *knock* little hillock.] **1.** A hill, a knoll 17... **2.** A Lincolnshire name for a sandbank. Cf. *Kentish K.*, a sandbank near the mouth of the Thames; also *K. Sand.*

Knock (nǫk), *v.* [OE. *cnocian* = MHG. *knochen*, ON. *knoka*; f. imit. base (cf. the similar and synon. OE. *cnucian*, MLG. *knaken*, Sw. *knaka*).] **1.** *intr.* To strike as with the fist or something hard; *esp.* to rap upon a door, etc., to gain admittance (const. *at*, †*on*, †*upon*). Also *fig.* **b.** *trans.* with indef. obj. *it*, To give knocks; also, with cognate obj. 1613. **2.** *trans.* To give a hard blow or blows to; to hit, strike, beat, hammer OE. **b.** To make a strong impression on; to 'fetch' (*slang*) 1883. **3.** *trans.* To drive or bring (a thing) violently against something else ME. **4.** *intr.* To come into violent collision with something; to strike, bump, clash 1530. **b.** Of mechanism: To rattle on account of parts being loose and striking each other 1869. Of a steam or internal combustion engine: To make a peculiar thumping noise 1904. **c.** with *adv.* or *advb. phr.*: To stir or move energetically, clumsily, and noisily, or at random, about a place 1825. **5.** *trans.* With extension: To drive by striking 1610. **b.** To rouse or summon by knocking at the door. *colloq.* 1706.

1. Knocke ȝe, and it shal be opnyd to ȝou WYCLIF *Matt.* 7:7. *fig. Temp.* I. ii. 8. **2.** I haue an humor to knocke you indifferently well SHAKS. **b.** Phr. *To k. on* (†*in*) *the head*: *esp.* to stun or kill by a blow on the head; often *loosely*, to kill in a summary way; *fig.* to put an end to. **c.** *U.S. colloq.* To speak ill or slightingly of, criticize captiously. Also *intr.* 1901. **3.** Phr. *To k. one's head against*: (*fig.*) to hurt oneself by coming into collision with resisting facts or conditions. **4. c.** A..Navy Captain.. who has knocked about Africa half his life 1839. **5.** He yeeld him thee asleepe, Where thou maist knocke a naile into his head SHAKS.

Phr. *To k. the bottom out of*: (*fig.*) to make of no effect (*colloq.*). *To k. into a* COCKED *hat, to k.* SPOTS *off* or *out of, to k. into the middle of next* WEEK, etc. (*slang.* or *colloq.*).

Comb. with advs. **Knock about. a.** *trans.* To treat roughly. **b.** *intr.* To move about in an irregular way; to lead an irregular life (*colloq.*). **Knock down. a.** *trans.* To fell to the ground with a blow or blows; also *fig.* **b.** To dispose of (an article) to a bidder at an auction sale by knock of hammer or mallet. **c.** To call upon (*for* a song, etc.) *colloq.* **d.** To lower effectively (prices, etc.). *colloq.* **e.** *U.S. slang.* To embezzle (passengers' fares) 1860. **Knock in. a.** *trans.* To drive in by or as by blows. **b.** *intr.* (*Univ. slang.*) To knock so as to get into college after the gate is closed. **Knock off. a.** *trans.* To strike off by or as by a blow; also *fig. To k. a person's head off*, to beat him easily. **b.** To cause to leave off work. **c.** *intr.* To leave off. **d.** *trans.* To stop, give up (work). **e.** To complete or do hastily. *colloq.* **f.** To strike off from an amount or sum. **Knock out. a.** *trans.* To resell by auction among themselves goods bought by confederates at a nominal price. **b.** *fig.* To vanquish, exhaust. *To k. out of time* (Pugilistic), to disable an opponent so that he is unable to respond to the call of 'Time'. **c.** To make roughly or hastily. *colloq.* **d.** *intr.* (*Univ. slang.*) To get out of college by knocking at the gate after it has been shut. **Knock together.** *trans.* To put together hastily or rudely. **Knock under.** *intr.* Short for *knock under board*, to succumb in a drinking-bout; to give in, knuckle under. **Knock up. a.** *trans.* To drive upwards by knocking. **b.** *intr.* To be driven up so as to strike something. *To k. up against*, to come into collision with; *fig.* to come across. **c.** To make up or arrange hastily. **d.** In *Cricket*, to make (so many runs) by striking the ball. *colloq.* **e.** To arouse by knocking at the door. **f.** To exhaust, tire out (esp. in *pass.*). **g.** *intr.* To become exhausted, to break down. **h.** *trans.* To put an end to.

Knock-, the vb.-stem or noun of action in Comb. **K.-bark** (*Mining*), ore that has been crushed. Also with advs., as **k.-under,** an act of knocking under; etc.

Kno·ck-about, knockabout, *a.* (*sb.*) 1876. [The phr. *knock about* used attrib. and as sb.] **A.** *adj.* **1.** Characterized by knocking about, or dealing blows 1885. **b.** *Theatr. slang.* Of noisy and violent character 1892. **2.** Characterized by wandering irregularly about 1886. **b.** Of clothes: Suitable for knocking about 1880. **c.** *Australia.* Applied to a labourer on a station who will turn his hand to anything 1876.

1. This k. sport [football] 1885. **b.** A k. entertainment 1897. **2. b.** Any make,..from k. suits to dress-clothes 1895.

B. *sb.* **1.** A knockabout performer or performance (see A. 1 b) 1887. **2.** *Australia.* A knockabout man (see A. 2 c) 1889.

Knock-down. 1690. [The phr. *knock down* used attrib. and as sb.]

A. *adj.* **1.** Such as to knock down; *fig.* overwhelming. **2.** *Knock-down price*, the price below which an article will not be knocked down at an auction 1895.

B. *sb.* **1.** Something overpowering; *e.g.* strong liquor (*slang*) 1698. **2.** A blow that knocks down; also *fig.* Also, A stand-up or free fight 1809.

Knocker (nǫ·kəɹ). ME. [f. KNOCK *v.* + -ER[1].] **1.** One who or that which knocks. **b.** A goblin imagined to dwell in mines, and to indicate the presence of ore by knocking 1747. **2.** An appendage, usually of iron or brass, fastened to a door, and hinged so that it may be made to strike against a metal plate, to attract attention. (The most usual sense.) 1598.

2. One could hardly find a K. at a Door in a whole Street after a Midnight Expedition of these *Beaux Esprits* STEELE. Phr. *Up to the k.*, in first-rate condition, in fine style (*slang*). **3.** *U.S. colloq.* A captious critic 1911.

Knocking (nǫ·kiŋ), *vbl. sb.* ME. [f. KNOCK *v.* + -ING[1].] **1.** The action of KNOCK *v.* **2.** *pl.* **a.** *Mining.* Ore that has been broken with a hammer before being crushed. **b.** Small pieces broken off from stone by hammering or chiselling. 1747.

Knock-knee (nǫ·kˌnī). 1827. [f. KNOCK *v.* + KNEE *sb.*] *pl.* Knees that knock together in walking from inward curvature of the legs. *sing.* Knock-kneed condition. Hence **Knock-kneed** *a.* having the legs bent inwards so that the knees knock together in walking; *fig.* halting 1806.

Kno·ck-me-dow·n. *colloq.* 1756.

A. *adj.* Such as to knock one down (*lit.* or *fig.*); riotous; overbearing; prostrating 1760. He's so positive, so knock-me-down J. H. NEWMAN.

B. *sb.* = KNOCK-DOWN B. 1.

Kno·ck-out. 1818. **A.** *adj.* Characterized by knocking out; *spec.* **a.** of, or in connection with, an auction sale; **b.** of a blow, etc.: Such as to knock out of the contest.

a. Combinations, by a set of men who attend real sales, and drive, by various means, respectable purchasers away, purchase at their own price, and afterwards privately sell the goods, under a form of public auction, termed 'Knock-out Sales' 1818.

B. *sb.* **1.** The practice of knocking out at auctions, etc.; a knock-out sale; also, one of the confederates who 'knock out' 1854. **2.** A knock-out blow 1894; hence, a defeat; also *slang*, something that excels or outdoes everything.

Knoll (nōᵘl), *sb.*[1] [OE. *cnoll*, corresp. to MDu. *knolle* clod, ball (Du. *knol* turnip, tuber), MHG. *knolle* clod (G. *knolle(n* clod, lump, tuber), ON. *knollr* mountain summit, Norw. *knoll* clod, tuber.] **1.** The rounded top of a mountain or hill. *Obs.* exc. *dial.* **2.** A small eminence of more or less rounded form; a hillock, a mound OE.

2. A Knole fitly placed..for a Cittadell 1628.

Knoll (nōᵘl), *sb.*[2] [Late ME., perh. imit. alteration of KNELL *sb.*] An act, or the action, of tolling a bell; the sound of a large bell (*arch.* and *dial.*).

Knoll (nōᵘl), *v.* 1440. [Goes with prec.] **1.** *trans.* To ring, toll (a bell); = KNELL *v.* 2. Also *fig.* Now *arch.* and *dial.* **2.** *intr.* = KNELL *v.* 3. Now chiefly *dial.* 1582. **b.** *trans.* To ring a knell for 1597. **c.** To ring or toll out. TENNYSON. **3.** *trans.* To summon by the sound of a bell 1600.

1. And so his Knell is knoll'd SHAKS. **2.** Where bels haue knoll'd to Church SHAKS. **b.** As a sullen Bell Remembred, knolling a departing Friend SHAKS. Hence **Kno·ller.**

Knop (nǫp), *sb.* late ME. [In XIV *knoppe*, *knappe* – MLG., MDu. *knoppe* (Du. *knop*) = OFris. *knop*, OHG. *knoph* (G. *knopf* knob, knot, button); cf. KNAP *sb.*[1]] **1.** A small rounded protuberance, a knob; a boss, stud, button, tassel, or the like; in *Arch.* = KNOB *sb.* 1 b. *Obs.* or *arch.* exc. *spec.* **2.** The bud of a flower (*arch.*) ME.

1. Sex silver spones with knopis of oure Ladie 1527. *Comb.* **k.-sedge,** the bur-reed, *Sparganium.*

†**Knop,** *v.* ME. [f. prec.] *trans.* To furnish or adorn with knops –1539.

Knopped (nǫpt), *a.* ? *Obs.* ME. [f. KNOP *sb.* or *v.* + -ED.] Having knops; knobbed; bearing buds; knob-shaped.

Knopweed, Knor, see KNAPWEED, KNUR.

Knosp (nǫsp). *rare.* 1808. [– G. *knospe* bud, boss, knob.] An ornament in the form of a bud, bunch, or rounded protuberance; a knob, boss. SCOTT. Hence **Knosped** *a.* furnished with knosps.

Knot (nǫt), *sb.*[1] [OE. *cnotta* = Du. *knot*, MLG. *knotte*, MHG. *knotze* knob, knot :– WGmc. **knutto* :– **knudn-*.]

I. 1. An intertwining of the parts of one or more ropes, cords, or the like, made for the purpose of fastening them together, or to something else, and drawn tight; a tie in a rope, necktie, etc.; also a tangle accidentally drawn tight. **2.** A tie worn as an ornament or adjunct to a dress; a bow of ribbon; a cockade or epaulette ME. **3.** *Naut.* A piece of knotted string fastened to the log-line, one of a series fixed at such intervals that the number of them that run out while the sand-glass is running indicates the ship's speed in nautical miles per hour; hence, each division so marked on the log-line, as a measure of the rate of motion. Also *attrib.* = 'running (so many) knots'. 1633. **b.** Hence, *loosely*, = 'nautical mile' 1748. **4.** A definite quantity of thread, yarn, etc., being so many coils tied by a knot 1398. **5.** Also *Porter's knot*: A kind of double shoulder-pad, with a loop passing round the forehead, used by London market-porters for carrying burdens 1719. **6.** A design or figure formed of crossing lines ME. **7.** A flower-bed laid out in an intricate design; any laid-out garden plot; a *flower-k.* Now chiefly *dial.* 1494. **8.** A central thickened meeting-point of lines, nerves, mountain-chains, etc. 1861. **9.** *Geom.* A unicursal curve in three-dimensional space, which, on being distorted so as to bring it into a plane without passing one part through another, will always have nodes 1877.

1. Mounsieur Parrolles..that had the whole theoricke of warre in the k. of his scarfe SHAKS. *Bowline k., diamond k., granny's k., loop-k., reef-k., running k., slip-k., surgeon's k.*, etc.; see the first element in these. **2.** The Officers to wear..a mourning K. on their left Arm 1708. **3.** A ten-knot breeze 1860. **b.** The ship went ten knots an hour 1748. **8.** The k. of Pasco, a great ganglion, as it were, of the system [of the Andes] HERSCHEL.

II. Fig. applications. **1.** A tangle or difficulty; a knotty point or problem OE. **b.** The main point in a problem; the complication in the plot of a story or drama, etc. ME. **2.** A bond of union; a tie, link ME. **b.** *spec.* The marriage tie ME. †**3.** A bond; a binding condition; a spell that binds –1813.

1. *Gordian k.*: see GORDIAN. The death of John cut the k. FREEMAN. **2. b.** Send for the Countie, ..He haue his k. knit vp to morrow morning *Rom. & Jul.* IV. ii. 24. **3.** This was the first K. upon their Liberty HOBBES.

III. *transf.* **1.** A hard lump in an animal body; a swelling or protuberance; a knob in a bone; a tumour, ganglion, wart, pimple, or the like ME. **2.** A thickened part in the tissue of a plant; an excrescence on a stem, branch, or root; a node on a stem; the hard mass formed in a trunk at the insertion of a branch, causing a rounded cross-grained piece in a board. Also, a bud. Also (*pl.*) a disease of plum and cherry trees. ME. **3.** A knob or embossed ornamentation in carved or hammered work; a stud; a boss ME. **4.** A hill of moderate height; esp. a rocky summit. Freq. in proper names in the north-west of England. ME. **5.** A mass formed by the aggregation and cohesion of particles; a lump, clot, concretion 1625. **6.** A small group, cluster, band, or company of persons or things ME.

1. Let grow thy Sinews till their knots be strong SHAKS. The Queen, who sat With lips severely placid, felt the k. Climb in her throat TENNYSON. **2.** Blunt wedges riue hard knots SHAKS. **6.** All do conclude Mr. Coventry, and Pett, and me, to be of a k. PEPYS.

Comb.: **k.-hole,** (*a*) a hole in a board, etc., caused by the falling out of a k.; (*b*) the hollow formed in the trunk of a tree by the decay of a branch; **-stitch,** a stitch by which ornamental knots are made; **-wood,** wood that is full of knots; *esp.* pine.

Knot (nǫt), *sb.*[2] 1452. [Of unkn. origin; later vars. were *knat*, GNAT[2].] A bird of the Snipe family (*Tringa canutus*), also called Red-breasted Sandpiper; it breeds within the Arctic Circle, but is common on the British coasts in late summer and autumn.

Knotts, i. *Canuti aves* vt opinor, e Dania enim aduolare creduntur CAMDEN.

Knot (nǫt), *v.* 1509. [f. KNOT *sb.*[1]] **1.** *trans.* To tie in a knot; to make knots in; to do up or secure with a knot 1547; *intr.* to form a knot or knots 1611. **2.** *intr.* To make or knit knots for fringes 1701; *trans.* to make or form (fringes) thus 1750. **3.** *trans.* To form protuberances, bosses, or knobs on or in; to make knotty; to knit (the brows) 1509. †**b.** *intr.* Of plants: To form knots or nodes; to bud; to form a close head; to 'set' –1660. **4.** *trans.* To combine firmly or intricately; to entangle, complicate 1611. †**b.** *intr.* To unite or gather together in a knot; to congregate; to concrete; to become knotted. **5.** *techn.* **a.** To cover the knots in (wood) before painting 1823. **b.** To remove knots from (cloth, etc.) 1875.

1. I wore The rope..Twisted as tight as I could k. the noose TENNYSON. **3.** The Gout had knotted all his Joynts 1697. **4. b.** A Cesterne, for foule Toades To k. and gender in *Oth.* IV. ii. 62. Hence **Kno·tting** *vbl. sb.* in all senses.

Knotberry. Also **knoutberry.** 1633. [perh. f. KNOT *sb.*[1] + BERRY.] Local name of the Cloudberry, *Rubus chamæmorus.*

Knot-grass. 1538. [f. KNOT *sb.*[1] + GRASS; from the knotted stem.] **1.** The plant *Polygonum aviculare*, a common weed in waste ground, with intricately-branched creeping stems, and small pink flowers; an infusion of it was formerly supposed to stunt the growth. Also *P. maritimum, P. virginianum*, etc. **2.** Applied to other plants with knotty stems, etc.; as Marsh Bent, Mare's-tail, etc. 1578.

1. You dwarfe You minimus, of hindring knot-grasse made SHAKS.

Knotless (nǫ·tlės), *a.* ME. [f. KNOT *sb.*[1] + -LESS.] Without a knot, free from knots; unknotted.

Ye'll slip frae me like a k. thread BURNS.

Knotted (nǫ·tėd), *a.* OE. [f. KNOT *sb.*[1] and *v.* + -ED.] **1.** Having knots; tied in a knot; fastened with a knot. **b.** *fig.* Entangled, intricate 1648. **2.** Formed or decorated with knots or bosses. **b.** Of a garden, laid out in knots. 1588. **3.** Characterized by knobs, protuberances, excrescences, or concretions; gnarled, as a trunk; having swollen joints, as a stem; knitted (as the brows) 1440. **b.** Forming a close head of blossom (*dial.*) 1744.

1. K. scourges COWPER. **b.** They're catch'd in k. law like nets BUTLER *Hud.* II. iii. 18. **2.** The West corner of thy curious k. garden SHAKS. **3.** The knees of k. Oakes *Tr. & Cr.* I. iii. 50. K. joints 1701, branches 1776.

Knotty (nǫ·ti), *a.* ME. [f. KNOT *sb.*[1] + -Y[1].] **1.** Having or full of knots. **2.** *fig.* Full of intellectual complications; hard to explain; puzzling ME. **3.** Hard and rough in character 1568.

1. She bare a skourge, with many a knottie string GASCOIGNE. Like knots in a k. board 1594. **2.** Auoid..Subtill and knottie Inquisitions BACON. **3.** To soften and dispell rooted and k. sorrowes MILT. *Comb.* **k.-pated** *a.* blockheaded. Hence **Kno·ttily** *adv.* **Kno·ttiness.**

Knotweed (nǫ·twīd). 1578. [f. KNOT *sb.*[1] + WEED *sb.*[1]] †**a.** Knawel. **b.** Name for species of *Centaurea* (Knapweed, etc.), from the knobby heads 1827. **c.** Name for species of *Polygonum* 1884.

Knotwork (nǫ·twɒ̄ɹk). 1851. **1.** Ornamental work consisting of, or representing, cords intertwined and knotted together. **2.** A kind of fancy needlework 1882.

Knotwort (nǫ·twɒ̄ɹt). 1845. [See WORT[1].] **a.** Knot-grass (*Polygonum aviculare*). **b.** *pl.* Lindley's name for the N.O. *Illecebraceæ.*

Knout (naut, nūt), *sb.* 1716. [– Fr. *knout* – Russ. *knut* – Icel. *knutr*, rel. to KNOT *sb.*[1]] A kind of scourge, often fatal in its effects, formerly used in Russia for flogging criminals. Hence **Knout** *v.* to flog with the k.

Know (nō^{u}), *sb.* 1592. [f. KNOW *v.*] The fact of knowing; knowledge. *In the k.* (colloq.), in possession of inside information.

Know (nō^{u}), *v.* Pa. t. **knew** (niū). Pa. pple. **known** (nō^{u}n). [Late OE. (rare) *cnāwan*, earlier *ġecnāwan*, corresp. to OHG. *-cnāen, -cnāhen*, ON. pr. ind. *knā*, pl. *knegum*. An original reduplicating vb. based on IE. **gn- *gnē- *gnō-*, repr. also by CAN *v.*[1], KEN *v.*, and L. (*g*)*noscere, cognoscere*, Gr. γιγνώσκειν.]

I. 1. *trans.* To recognize; to identify; to distinguish. †**2.** *trans.* To acknowledge the claims or authority of –1560.

1. Whether that in the life everlasting, we shal k. one an other 1560. We'll teach him to know Turtles from Iayes *Merry W.* III. iii. 44. **2.** I..k. the for my lorde 1450.

II. 1. To be acquainted with (a thing, place, person); to be familiar with (= Fr. *connaître*, Ger. *kennen*) ME. **b.** To have personal experience of (something) as affecting oneself. Also *fig.* Usu. with negatives. ME. **2.** To be personally acquainted or on familiar terms with (a person) ME. †**b.** *intr.* Of two persons: To be (mutually) acquainted (= Fr. *se connaître*) SHAKS. **3.** *trans.* To have carnal acquaintance with. (A Hebraism.) *arch.* ME.

1. He knew the Tauernes wel in al the toun CHAUCER. *refl.* K. thy selfe ELYOT. **b.** He has never known trouble 1877. **2.** They are neighbours of ours, but we do not k. them 1901. **b.** *Ant. & Cl.* II. vi. 86.

III. 1. To be aware or apprised of (= Fr. *savoir*, Ger. *wissen*); †to become cognizant of, ascertain ME. **2.** To be conversant with; *esp.* to be versed or skilled in; †to learn ME. **3.** To apprehend or comprehend as fact or truth. Formerly, *occas.*, †To get to understand ME. **b.** *absol.* or *intr.* To have understanding or knowledge ME. **4.** To be cognizant of (a fact); to apprehend (with the mind), to understand ME. **b.** *absol.* Often parenthetically, esp. in colloq. use, in *you k., we k., do you k.* ME.

1. Pray let me k. your mind in this POPE. I do not k. his age exactly 1776. **2.** Of course you k. your ABC. 'L. CARROLL'. Phr. *To k. better* (*than to do* something) *To k. by heart.* **3.** He did not k. his own mind MACAULAY. **b.** Large-brow'd Verulam, The first of those who k. TENNYSON. **4.** The Hollander..knows it right well, that there are none like English for Courage at Sea STURMY. When he knew himself insolvent 1817. He who does not k. what is true will not k. what is good JOWETT. **b.** Do you k., I saw the prettiest hat you can imagine JANE AUSTEN. Phr. *Not if I know it*, i.e. I will take care not to do the thing referred to.

IV. 1. *To k. how* (formerly also *to k.*): to understand the way, or be able (*to do* something) 1548. **b.** *ellipt.* in colloq. phr. *All one knows*, all one can; also *advb.*, to the utmost of one's ability 1872. †**2.** To make known –1450. **3.** In biblical language: To take notice of, care for; to look after, protect; to approve ME. **4.** Used (chiefly in sense III. 1) in colloq. and slang phrases expressing sagacity, cunning, or 'knowledge of the world', as *to k. what's what, to k. a thing or two, to k. the time of day*, etc. 1520.

1. I k. how to curse SHAKS. **b.** It cost him all he knew to restrain his anger 1883. **3.** Thou hast knowne my soule in aduersite COVERDALE *Ps.* 31:7. **4.** The foreigner who does not 'k. the ropes'—that is to say, who is crassly ignorant SALA.

Comb. (with prep.). **Know of—. a.** To be cognizant of (something as existing, an event as having occurred). **b.** *Colloq. phrase. Not that I k. of*, not so far as I k. †*Not that you k. of*, an expression of defiance 1742. Hence **Know·er,** one who knows.

Knowable (nō^{u}·ăb'l), *a.* (*sb.*) 1449. [f. KNOW *v.* + -ABLE.] **1.** That may be known; capable of being apprehended, understood, ascertained, or recognized. **2.** *sb.* A knowable thing; usu. in *pl.* 1661.

1. The k. Relations of unknown things HARTLEY. The body..was too much..disfigured to be k. 1806. Hence **Knowabi·lity, Know·ableness.**

Know-all. 1895. [f. KNOW *v.*] One who knows or professes to know everything.

Know(e (nau), Sc. and north. forms of KNOLL *sb.*[1]

Know-how (nō^{u}-hau). *slang* (orig. *U.S.*). 1857. Knowledge of how to do some particular thing.

Knowing (nō^{u}·iŋ), *vbl. sb.* ME. [f. KNOW *v.* + -ING[1].] The action or fact denoted by KNOW *v.* †**1.** Recognition. ME. only. †**2.** Personal acquaintance. ME. only. **3.** The action of getting to understand, or fact of understanding; knowledge ME. **4.** The fact of being aware of something; cognizance; intimation ME. †**b.** An experience. *Macb.* II. iv. 4.

3. K. is the acquiring and retaining knowledge and not forgetting JOWETT. **4.** There is no k. how young women will act 1794.

Knowing (nō^{u}·iŋ), *ppl. a.* ME. [f. KNOW *v.* + -ING[2].] **1.** That knows (see KNOW *v.*). **2.** Shrewd, cunning, acute, wide-awake. (Often implying the air of possessing information which one does not impart.) 1503. **3.** Showing knowledge of 'what is what' in fashion, dress, etc.; stylish, smart. *colloq. Obs.* or merged in 2. 1796.

1. Our ordinary k. faculties M. ARNOLD. A man who is k. about horses JOWETT. **2.** 'I believe you', replied George, with a k. jerk of his head 1852. Hence **Know·ing-ly** *adv.*, **-ness.**

Knowledge (nǫ·lėdʒ), *sb.* ME. [In earliest use north. (*knaulage*), later in gen. use *knowleche, -lache*; prob. f. next. The pronunc. nō^{u}·lėdʒ, used by some, is after *know.*]

I. †**1.** Acknowledgement, confession; recognition of the position or claims (of any one) –1548. †**2.** Recognition –1611. †**3.** Legal cognizance. Chiefly *Sc.* –1732. †**4.** *gen.* Cognizance, notice; in phr. *to take k. of* –1623.

4. Wherefore haue wee afflicted our soule, and thou takest no k.? *Isa.* 58:3.

II. 1. The fact of knowing a thing, state, etc., or person; acquaintance; familiarity ME. †**2.** Personal acquaintance, friendship, intimacy. **b.** One's acquaintances. –1600. **3.** Sexual intimacy. Now only in *carnal k.* (*arch.* and *legal*) ME. **4.** Acquaintance with a fact; state of being aware or informed; consciousness (of anything) ME. **b.** *absol.* Acquaintance with facts, range of information, ken 1542. **5.** Intellectual acquaintance with, or perception of, fact or truth; the fact, state, or condition of understanding. †Formerly, also, intelligence, intellect. ME. **b.** with *pl.* A mental apprehension; a cognition (*rare*) 1563. **6.** Theoretical or practical understanding *of* an art, science, language, etc. ME. **7.** The fact or condition of being instructed; information acquired by study; learning 1477. †**8.** Information; intelligence; intimation –1722. **9.** The sum of what is known 1534. **10.** (with *pl.*) A branch of learning; a science; an art. (Rarely in sing.) 1581. †**11.** A sign, mark, or token –1555.

1. His k. of human nature 1771. Phr. †*To grow out of k.*: to cease to be known. **4.** The k. that a person is poor 1901. **b.** Phr. *To one's k.*, so far as one is aware; also, as one is aware (in latter sense, also, *of one's k.*). *To come to one's k.* **5.** K... implies..firm belief,..of what is true..on sufficient grounds WHATELY. K. of nature JEVONS. **6.** Practical K. of Navigation at Sea STURMY. **7.** Hee that increaseth k. increaseth sorrow *Eccles.* 1:18. **9.** Abundance of emptie and unprofitable k. 1628.

Comb. **k.-box,** joc. name for the head.

†**Know·ledge,** *v.* [Early ME. *cnaw-, cnouleche* :– OE. **cnawlǣćan* implied in **cnāwlǣćung*, (a parallel *cnāwelǣćing* is recorded), f. (*ġe*)*cnāwan* know + *-lǣćan*, f. *lāc* (see -LOCK).] **1.** *trans.* = ACKNOWLEDGE *v.* 1. –1582. **b.** *absol.* or *intr.* To make acknowledgement –1526. †**c.** *intr.* with *to* (in biblical versions): To give thanks to, to praise –1535. **2.** *trans.* = ACKNOWLEDGE *v.* 2. –1643. **3.** = ACKNOWLEDGE *v.* 3. –1797. **4.** *trans.* To recognize and identify (a disease), to diagnose –1618.

2. They k. thee to be the Father of an infinite majesty 1535. Hence **Know·ledgement,** †formal acknowledgement; knowledge, cognizance (*arch.*). †**Know·ledging** *vbl. sb.* the action of the vb.; also, = KNOWLEDGE *sb.*

Knowledgeable (nǫ·lėdʒăb'l), *a.* 1607. [f. KNOWLEDGE *sb.* and *v.* + -ABLE.] †**1.** [f. the vb.] Capable of being perceived or recognized –1619. **2.** [f. the sb.] Possessing or showing knowledge or mental capacity. *colloq.* (orig. *dial.*). 1831. Hence **Know·ledgeableness. Know·ledgeably** *adv.*

Known (nō^{u}n), *ppl. a.* ME. [pa. pple. of KNOW *v.*] **1.** Become an object of knowledge; learned; familiar; often, familiar to all. †**2.** Possessed of knowledge; learned *in*; informed or aware *of* –1655.

1. Men of k. courage 1647. A k. Non-juror 1704.

Know-nothing (nō^{u}·nɒ:þiŋ), *sb.* and *a.*

1825. [KNOW v.] sb. **1. a.** An ignoramus. **b.** An agnostic. **2.** A member of a political party in U.S.A., called also the American party (1853–6). *adj.* Ignorant, agnostic. Hence **Know·no:thingism,** the profession of agnosticism 1866.

Knub (nɒb). Now *dial.* or *techn.* 1570. [– MLG. *knubbe,* var. of *knobbe* KNOB sb.] **1.** = KNOB sb. 1. **2.** The innermost wrapping of the chrysalis in a silk cocoon; usu. NUB 1812.

Knuckle (nɒ·k'l), *sb.* [Late ME. *knokel* – MLG. *knökel,* corresp. to OFris. *knok(e)le,* MDu. *knokel, knökel* (Du. *kneukel*), MHG. *knuchel, knüchel* (G. *knöchel*), dim. of the base of MLG. *knoke* (Du. *knok*), MHG. *knoche* (G. *knochen*) bone, perh. ult. rel. to KNEE.] †**1.** The end of a bone at a joint –1658. **2.** *spec.* The bone at a finger-joint; esp. applied to those at the roots of the fingers 1440. **3.** The projection of the carpal or tarsal joint of a quadruped; hence, a 'joint' of meat, *esp.* veal or ham, consisting of the knuckle-joint with the parts above and below it 1625. **4.** Something shaped or protruding like a knuckle of a bone. *spec.* †**a.** A thickened joint of a plant, a node. **b.** *Anat.* A projecting bend of the intestine. **c.** *Mech.* The projecting tubular part of a hinge through which the pintle runs. **d.** *Shipbuilding.* An acute angle in certain timbers. 1601. **5.** = KNUCKLE-DUSTER 1861.

2. Phr. *Near the knuckle* (colloq.): all but indecent. *Comb.*: **k.-bow, -guard,** a guard on a sword-hilt to cover the knuckles; **-end,** the small end of a leg of mutton or pork.

Knuckle (nɒ·k'l), *v.* 1740. [f. prec.] **1.** *intr.* To place one's knuckles on the ground in playing at marbles. Usu. *k. down.* **2.** *intr.* (*fig.*) To give in. Usu. *k. down* or *k. under.* 1740. **3.** *trans.* To tap, strike, press, or rub with the knuckles 1793.

2. He had to k. and comply in all points CARLYLE. Hence **Knuckle-down** as *sb.*: **a.** a game at marbles; **b.** submission; as *adv.* = submissively.

Knu·ckle-bo:ne. 1440. **1.** Any bone forming a knuckle 1577. **2.** In an animal: **a.** A limb-bone with a ball-like knob at the joint-end, or the rounded end of such a bone; also, = KNUCKLE sb. 3. 1440. **b.** One of the metacarpal or metatarsal bones of a sheep or the like; hence (usu. *pl.*) a game played with these; also called *huckle-bones* or *dibs* 1759.

Knuckled (nɒ·kl'd), *a.* ME. [f. KNUCKLE sb. + -ED².] †**1.** Knobbed, rugged; thick-jointed, as the stem of a plant –1626. **2.** Having (prominent) knuckles; protuberant like a knuckle 1842.

Knu·ckle-du:ster. 1858. [f. KNUCKLE sb. + DUSTER. (orig. criminals' slang, U.S.)] A metal instrument to protect the knuckles from injury in striking, and to add force to a blow.

Knu·ckle-jo:int. 1863. **1.** *lit.* Each joint of the knuckles (of the hands), or the joint of the leg of an animal called a knuckle. **2.** *Mech.* A joint in which a projection in one part is inserted into a corresponding recess in the other (like knuckles clasped together); also extended to universal joints, etc. 1863.

Knuffe, see GNOFF.

Knur, knurr (nɒ̄ɹ). [Late ME. (XV) *knor(re*; see KNAR.] †**1.** A hard excrescence or concretion in the flesh –1621. **2.** A knot or hardened excrescence on the trunk of a tree; a kernel in stone; any swollen formation 1545. **3.** A wooden ball used in the north country game of *Knur and spell,* resembling trap-ball. Also, A similar ball used in hockey, etc. 1852.

Knurl, nurl (nɒ̄ɹl), *sb.* 1608. [Derivative of KNUR; cf. KNARL.] **1.** A knot, knob, boss, nodule, etc.; a small bead or ridge on a metal surface. **2.** A thick-set stumpy person (*dial.*) 1674. Hence **Knurl, nurl** *v.* to make knurls, beadings, or ridges (on an edge or surface); to mill, to crenate. **Knurled, nurled** *a.* having knurls so wrought; crenated, milled 1611. **Knu·rly** *a.* having knurls; knurl-like, dwarfish 1602.

†**Knu·rry,** *a.* 1513. [f. KNUR + -Y¹.] **1.** Full of knurs, knotty, gnarled –1664. **2.** *fig.* Knotty, perplexing –1652.

Knut, joc. sp. and pron. of NUT (= dandy) 1911.

Koala (kouā·lă). *Australia.* 1808. [– native names *külla, kūla.* The current form *koala* perh. arose as a misreading of *koolah,* which was formerly current.] An arboreal marsupial mammal of Australia (*Phascolarctos cinereus*), of an ashen-grey colour, somewhat like a sloth in form. Also called the *Australian* or *Native Bear.*

‖**Kob** (kǫb). 1774. [Said to be the native name in Senegal.] An African water-antelope of the genus *Kobus.* So ‖**Ko·ba.**

‖**Kobold** (kōu·bǫld). 1830. [G. *kobold.* Cf. COBALT.] In German folklore: **a.** A familiar spirit, haunting houses and occas. helping the inmates; a brownie. **b.** An underground spirit haunting mines, etc.; a gnome.

Kobold, obs. f. COBALT.

Kodak (kōu·dæk), *sb.* 1888. [Arbitrary word invented by Mr. George Eastman as a trade-mark.] A kind of portable photographic camera with a continuous roll of sensitized film upon which successive negatives are made; also erroneously applied to any hand camera. **b.** *transf.* A photograph taken with a kodak 1895. Hence **Ko·dak** *v. intr.* to photograph with a kodak; *fig.* to catch or describe quickly or vividly.

‖**Koel** (kōu·ėl). 1826. [Hindi *kóïl,* f. Skr. *kokila.*] A cuckoo of the genus *Eudynamis,* esp. *E. honorata* of India, and *E. flindersi* of New Guinea and Australia.

‖**Koff** (kǫf). *rare.* 1794. [Du. *kof.*] *Naut.* A clumsy two-masted sailing-vessel, used by the Dutch, Danes, etc.

‖**Koftgari** (kǫftgărī·). *E. Indian.* 1874. [Urdu (Pers.) *kūft-, koftgarī* 'beaten-work'.] A kind of Indian damascene-work, in which a pattern traced on steel is inlaid with gold. Also abbrev. **Koft,** *attrib.* in *k.-work* 1880.

‖**Koh-i-noor** (kōu·hi,nūᵊɹ). 1849. [Pers. *kūh* mountain, *i* of, *nūr* light.] A famous Indian diamond, which became one of the British Crown jewels on the annexation of the Punjab in 1849; hence *fig.* anything superb of its kind.

‖**Kohl¹** (kō·h'l, kōul). 1799. [Arab. *kuḥl*; see ALCOHOL.] A powder (usu. of antimony) used in the East to darken the eyelids.

Kohl², abbrev. of next.

‖**Kohlrabi, kohl-rabi** (kōulrā·bi). Also erron. **khol-.** 1807. [– G. *kohlrabi* – (with assim. to *kohl* COLE¹) It. *cauli* or *cavoli rape,* pl. of *cavolo rapa* (whence Fr. *chou-rave*), repr. med.L. *caulorapa*; see COLE¹, RAPE sb.³] A cabbage with a turnip-shaped stem; the turnip-cabbage.

‖**Kokoon** (kokū·n), **kokong** (kokǫ·ŋ). 1806. [Sechuana *kgokoñ* or *khokong.*] A large antelope (*Antilope taurina*) of S. Africa.

Kon, kon(n)e, obs. ff. CAN *v.,* CON *v.*

Ko·nilite. 1821. [f. Gr. κόνις dust + -LITE.] *Min.* A powdered form of silica found in the cavities of trap.

Koodoo, kudu (kū·dū). 1777. [Xosa-Kaffir *iqudu.*] A large African antelope *Strepsiceros kudu*), having a brown coat marked with white stripes; the male has long spirally-twisted horns.

Koolah, obs. var. of KOALA.

Kopec(k, -peek, -pek, var. of COPECK.

‖**Kopje** (kǫ·pi). 1881. [Du. *kopje* (Afrikaans *koppie*), dim. of *kop* head; see COP sb.²] In S. Africa: A small hill.

Koran¹ (korā·n, kōᵊ·ræ̆n). 1625. [– Arab. *ḳur'ān* recitation, f. *ḳara'a* read. Cf. ALCORAN.] The sacred book of the Moslems, consisting of oral revelations by Mohammed collected in writing after his death; it is in Arabic. Hence **Kora·nic** *a.*

Koran² (kŏrā·n). 1775. [– S. Afr. Du. *kor-* or *knorhaan,* f. *kor-, knor-* the bird's cry + *haan* cock.] A S. Afr. bustard, of the genus *Eupodotes,* esp. *E. afra.*

‖**Kosher** (kǫ·ʃəɹ), *a.* (*sb.*) Also **cosher,** etc. 1851. [Heb. *kāšēr* fit, proper.] **1.** Applied to food prepared according to the Jewish law. Hence of shops, houses, etc., where this is sold or used. **2.** *sb.* (*ellipt.*) Kosher food; also, a kosher shop 1886.

‖**Kotal** (kōu·tæl). *E. Ind.* 1880. [Pushtu *kōtal* mountain pass.] The pass over a mountain; a col; the ridge or summit of a pass.

‖**Kotow** (kōtau·), *sb.* Also **kow-tow, -too,** etc. 1804. [Chinese *k'o-t'ou,* f. *k'o* knock + *t'ou* the head.] The Chinese custom of touching the ground with the forehead, as an expression of respect, submission, or worship. **b.** *fig.* An act of obsequious respect 1834. Hence **Kotow·,** *v. intr.* to perform the k.; *fig.* to act in an obsequious manner.

‖**Kotwal** (kǫ·twal). *E. Ind.* 1582. [Hindi *koṭwāl,* Urdu (Pers.) *kūtwāl.*] A chief officer of police for a city or town in India; a native town magistrate. Hence ‖**Kotwa·lee,** police station.

‖**Koulan, kulan** (kū·lăn). 1793. [Tartar *kulan.*] A species of equine quadruped (*Equus onager*), closely allied to the Dziggetai (with which it is united by some); the wild ass of Mesopotamia, Persia, and the banks of the Indus.

‖**Koumiss** (kū·mis). 1607. Cf. COSMOS². [=Fr. *koumis,* G. *kumiss,* Pol. *komis, kumys,* Russ. *kumýs*; – Tatar *kumiz.*] A fermented liquor prepared from mare's milk, used as a beverage by the Tartars; also, a spirituous liquor distilled from this. Imitations are also prepared from ass's milk and cow's milk.

‖**Kourbash, koorbash** (ku·rbaʃ), *sb.* Also **courbash,** etc. 1814. [– Arab. *kurbāj, kirbāj* – Turk. *kırbāç* whip.] A whip made of hippopotamus or other hide; an instrument of punishment in Turkey, Egypt, and the Sudan. Hence **Kou·rbash** *v. trans.* to flog with the k.

‖**Kousso** (ku·so). 1851. [Abyssinian.] The dried flowers of an Abyssinian plant, *Hagenia* (*Brayera*) *abyssinica,* used as an anthelmintic.

Kow-tow: see KOTOW.

Kraal (krāl), *sb.* 1731. [– S. Afr. Du. *kraal* – Pg. *curral*; see CORRAL.] **1.** A village of S. or Central African natives, consisting of a collection of huts surrounded by a fence or stockade. Also *transf.* the community of such a village. **b.** *loosely.* A hovel 1832. **2.** An enclosure for cattle or sheep; a stockade, pen, fold 1796. Hence **Kraal** *v. trans.* to enclose in a k.

‖**Krait** (krait). *E. Ind.* 1874. [Hindi *karait.*] A venomous snake of the genus *Bungarus,* esp. *B. cæruleus,* common in Bengal.

‖**Kraken** (krā·kĕn, krēi·kĕn). 1755. [– Norw. *kraken* (*n* is the suffixed def. art.).] A mythical sea-monster of enormous size, said to have been seen at times off the coast of Norway.

Far, far beneath in the abysmal sea,..The K. sleepeth TENNYSON.

‖**Krameria** (krămīᵊ·riă). 1855. [mod.L.; f. J. G. H. *Kramer,* an Austrian botanist. See -IA¹.] **a.** *Bot.* An anomalous genus of *Polygalaceae,* comprising branched spreading undershrubs, natives of America, having astringent properties. **b.** *Med.* The root of *K. triandra* (rhatany-root), or a drug made from this.

Krang, var. of KRENG.

‖**Krantz, kranz** (krænts). *S. Africa.* 1834. [S. Afr. Du. – Du. *krans* coronet, chaplet – OHG., (MH)G. *kranz* coronet, circle, encircling ring of mountains, f. a base meaning 'ring'.] A wall of rock encircling a mountain or summit; hence, any precipitous or overhanging wall of rocks.

Kreatic, Kreatine, etc., var. of CREATIC, CREATINE, etc.

Kreil, krele, obs. ff. CREEL.

Kremlin (kre·mlin). 1662. [– Fr. *kremlin,* f. Russ. *kreml'* citadel, of Tatar origin.] The citadel or fortified enclosure within a Russian town or city; *esp.* that of Moscow, which contains the imperial palace.

Kreng (kreŋ). Also **krang,** CRANG. 1820. [– Du. *kreng* carrion, carcass; etym. unkn.] The carcass of a whale from which the blubber has been removed. Hence **Kre·nging-hook,** an instrument for stripping the blubber from a dead whale; so **Kre·nger.**

Kreosote: see CREOSOTE.

‖**Kreutzer** (kroi·tsəɹ). Also **creutzer, kreuzer,** etc. 1547. [– G. *kreuzer,* f. *kreuz* CROSS, after med.L. *denarius crucigerus* 'cross-bearing penny'.] A small copper (orig. silver) coin formerly current in Germany and Austria.

‖**Kriegspiel** (krī·gˌspīl, ‖krī·kʃpīl). 1878. [G., 'war-game'.] A game in which blocks representing troops, guns, etc., are moved about on maps.

Kris, var. of CREESE, Malay dagger.

Krishnaism (kri·ʃnăˌiz'm). 1885. [f. *Krishna*, a great deity of later Hinduism, worshipped as an incarnation of Vishnu. See -ISM.] The worship of or belief in Krishna. So **Kri·shnaist, Kri·shnaite**, a worshipper of Krishna.

Kritarchy (kri·taɹki). [f. Gr. κριτής judge + *-archy*, after *monarchy*, etc.] The rule of the Judges in Israel. SOUTHEY.

Kroci-, krokydolite, var. CROCIDOLITE.

‖**Krone** (krō·nĕ). 1875. [G. *krone* (pl. *kronen*), Da. *krone* (pl. *kroner*), Sw. *krona* (pl. *kronor*) crown; cf. CROWN *sb.*] **1.** A silver coin of Denmark, Norway, and Sweden, worth 1*s*. 1$\frac{1}{2}$*d*. **2.** The German 10 mark gold piece 1898. **3.** An Austrian silver coin, = 10*d*. 1898.

Kroo, Krou, Kru (krū). 1835. [W. Afr.] *attrib.* or as *adj.* Of or pertaining to a Negro race so named on the coast of Liberia, skilful as seamen. Hence **Kru-man**, one of this race.

‖**Krummhorn** (kru·mhǭɹn). 1694. [G., f. *krumm* crooked + *horn* HORN.] *Mus.* **a.** An obsolete wind-instrument of a curved form. **b.** An organ reed-stop of 8 ft. pitch, resembling the clarinet in tone; called also corruptly CREMONA^2.

Kryo- (krəiˌo), var. sp. of *cryo-*, comb. f. Gr. κρύος frost.

Krypton (kri·ptǫn). 1898. [– Gr. κρυπτόν, n. of κρυπτός hidden.] *Chem.* A rare inert gaseous element discovered by Sir W. Ramsay. Symbol Kr; atomic number 36; atomic weight 83·7.

Ksar, obs. f. CZAR.

‖**Kshatriya, Kshatri** (kʃa·triˌya, -trī). *E. Ind.* 1782. [Skr. *kshatriya*, f. *kshatra* rule.] A member of the military caste, the second of the four great castes or classes among the Hindus.

‖**Kudos** (kiū·dǫs). 1793 (COLERIDGE). [– Gr. κῦδος.] Glory, fame, renown (*Univ. slang* and *colloq.*) Hence **Ku·dize** *v.*, **Ku·dos** *v.* (*nonce-wds.*), to praise, glorify.

Kufic, var. CUFIC.

‖**Kukang** (kū·kæŋ). 1861. [Malay *kūkang*.] The slow-paced lemur or loris.

Ku-Klux(-Klan) (kiū·klɒksˌklæ·n). 1868. [Fanciful invention said to be based on Gr. κύκλος circle, and CLAN.] A secret society formed in the Southern U.S. after the civil war of 1861–5 to protect the whites and to oppose Negro influence; its activities are associated with murder and outrage.

‖**Kukri** (ku·kri). 1811. [Hindi *kukrī*.] A curved knife, broadening towards the point, used by the Gurkhas.

Kulan, var. of KOULAN.

‖**Kultur** (kultū·r). [G. – L. *cultura* CULTURE.] Applied derisively to German civilization, esp. as exemplified by their method of warfare.

Kumis, -iss, -ys, var. of KOUMISS.

‖**Kümmel** (kü·mĕl). 1882. [G.; see CUMIN.] A liqueur, flavoured with cumin, made in North Germany.

‖**Kunkur** (kɒ·ŋkɒ̆ɹ). *E. Ind.* Also **concher, kankar**, etc. 1793. [– Hindi *kankar* – Prakrit *kakkaram*, Skr. *karkaram*.] A coarse kind of limestone found in India, in large tabular strata, or interspersed throughout the surface soil, in nodules of various sizes; used for lime, and also in road-making.

‖**Kupfernickel** (ku·pfərˌni:k'l). 1796. [G., f. *kupfer* copper + *nickel* NICKEL.] *Min.* = NICCOLITE.

‖**Kuphar** (ku·făɹ). 1800. [– Arab. *ḳuffa*.] A circular coracle of wicker-work covered with skins, used on the Euphrates.

‖**Kurgan** (kurga·n). 1889. [Russ., of Tartar origin.] A prehistoric sepulchral tumulus or barrow in Russia and Tartary.

‖**Kursaal** (kū·rˌzāl). 1849. [G., f. *kur*, *cur* CURE *sb.*^{1} + *saal* hall, room.] A public building at a German health resort, provided for the use of visitors.

‖**Kusima·nse.** 1861. [Native name.] A small burrowing carnivorous animal, *Crossarchus obscurus*, of W. Africa.

Kuskus, var. of KHUS-KHUS (= CUSCUS^2).

Kutch, Kutcha, var. of CUTCH^2, CUTCHA.

‖**Kuttar** (kɒtā·ɹ). *E. Ind.* 1696. [Hindi *kaṭṭār* :– Skr. *kaṭṭāra*.] A short Indian dagger, having a handle of two parallel bars, joined by a cross-piece.

‖**Kvass** (kvas). 1553. [Russ. *kvas*.] A fermented beverage in use in Russia; rye beer.

Ky, pl. of COW (now *Sc.* and *n. dial.*).

‖**Kyabuka, kiabooca** (kəiăbū·kă). 1831. [Malay *kayu-buku* knot-wood.] A Malaysian tree (*Pterospermum indicum*) furnishing an ornamental wood, also called *Amboyna wood*.

‖**Kyang** (kyæŋ *monosyll.*). Also **kiang.** 1882. [Tibetan *kyang*, *rkyang*.] A Tibetan species of wild horse or ass (*Equus kiang*).

Kyanite, var. CYANITE, now more usual.

Kyanize (kəi·ănəiz), *v.* 1837. [f. J. H. *Kyan*, inventor of the process (1832), + -IZE.] *trans.* To treat (wood) with a solution of corrosive sublimate, to prevent decay.

Kyano-, var. f. CYANO-; **Kyanophyll** (kəiˌæ·nofil) [Gr. φύλλον leaf], Kraus's name for a blue-green substance, supposed to be a constituent of chlorophyll.

Kyanol (kəi·ănǫl). 1855. [f. Gr. κύανος CYANO- + -OL.] A synonym of ANILINE.

†**Kyd, kydde**, *v.* (*pseudo-arch.*) 1530. [Evolved from ME. *kyd*, *i-kyd*, pa. pple. of KITHE *v.*, misused by Spenser.] *trans.* To know. *Sheph. Cal.* Dec. 92, 93.

Kye, pl. of COW (now *Sc.* and n. dial.).

Kyke, obs. f. KEEK.

Kyle (kəil). *Sc.* 1549. [– Gael. *caol* (kōl), gen. *caoil* (kōil) 'narrow strait or sound', sb. to *caol* narrow.] A narrow channel between two islands, or an island and the mainland; a sound, a strait.

‖**Kylie** (kəi·li). *W. Austral.* 1839. [Native name.] A boomerang.

‖**Kylin** (kī·li:n). Also **kilin.** 1857. [– Chinese *ch'i-lin* (Wade), f. *ch'i* male + *lin* female.] A fabulous animal of composite form, figured on Chinese and Japanese pottery.

Kylix: see CYLIX.

Kyloe (kəi·lŏ). *Sc.* 1727. [Also locally *kyley*, etc., repr. old vars. of the Northumb. place-name *Kyloe* (OE. *cȳ-lēah* cow pasture.] One of a small breed of cattle with long horns reared in the Highlands and Western Islands of Scotland.

Kymnel(l(e, etc · see KIMNEL.

Kymograph (kəi·mogrɑf). 1867. [f. Gr. κυμο-, comb. f. κῦμα wave + -GRAPH.] An instrument for graphically recording variations of pressure of a fluid, esp. in the vessels of a living animal. Also called *kymogra·phion*. Hence **Kymogra·phic** *a.*

Kymric, Kyphosis: see CYMRIC, etc.

‖**Kyrie** (kəiᵊ·ri, -iˌi, ki·rie). 1519. [Short for *Kyrie eleison*; see next.] **1.** = next. **b.** *esp.* A musical setting of the Kyrie eleison in the Ordinary of the Mass, or of the Responses to the Commandments in the Anglican Communion Service. †**2.** = next, 2. –1582.

‖**Kyrie eleison, eleëson** (ki·rie ėlē·isǫn). ME. [med.L. repr. of Gr. Κύριε ἐλέησον Lord, have mercy, as in the Gr. text of *Ps.* 122(1):3, *Matt.* 20:30, 31.] **1.** *Eccl.* The words of a short petition used in Eastern and Roman Churches, esp. at the beginning of the Mass; represented in the Anglican service by the words, 'Lord, have mercy upon us'. **b.** A musical setting of these words. †**2.** *transf.* A complaint; a scolding –1630.

‖**Kyrielle** (kirie·l). 1887. [– Fr. *kyrielle*, OFr. *kyriele*, in med.L. pl. *kirieles* (Du Cange); shortened form of *Kyrie eleison*.] A form of French poetry divided into little equal couplets, and ending with the same word which serves for the refrain.

Kyriologic, var. of CYRIOLOGIC.

Kyte (kəit). *Sc.* and *n. dial.* 1540. [Of unkn. origin.] The belly, stomach, paunch.

Kythe, var. sp. of KITHE *v.*

L

L (el), the twelfth letter of the modern and the eleventh of the ancient Roman alphabet, represents historically the Gr. *lambda* and ultimately the Semitic *lamed*.

The sound normally expressed by the letter is the 'point-side' consonant, i.e. a sound produced by the emission of breath at the sides, or one side, of the oral passage when it is partially closed by contact of the point of the tongue with the gums or palate.

I. 1. An object shaped like the letter L. (Also written *ell*.) **a.** An extention of a building at right angles to the main block. **b.** An elbow-joint of a pipe. **2.** *attrib.* and *Comb.*, as *L-shaped* adj.

II. Symbolical uses. **1.** Used to denote serial order; applied e.g. to the twelfth, or more usually the eleventh (I or J being omitted) group or section, the eleventh sheet of a book, etc. **2.** The Roman numeral for 50.

III. Abbrevs. L. = †Lord, Lordship (pl. LL.); in *Bot.* Linnæus; Latin; in Stage directions, etc., left; Licentiate, as L.D.S. = Licentiate of Dental Surgery; (*Chem.*) Lithium. L or l [L. *libra*] = pound of money, now often repr. by £; e.g. 100*l*. or £100; see also L.S.D. l = in ship's log-book, lightning; in references, line, as bk. 4, l. 8; in solmization, la. l.b.w. (*Cricket*), leg before wicket; *l.c.* (*Printing*), lower case. L.C.M. (*Arith.*), least common multiple. L.M. (*Prosody*), long metre. See also LL., LXX.

La (lā), *sb.* ME. [orig. first syllable of L. *labii*; see UT.] The sixth note in Guido d'Arezzo's hexachords, retained in solmization as the sixth note of the octave.

La (lā, la), *int.* 1598. [Cf. LO (OE. *lā* and early ME. *la*).] An exclam. formerly used to introduce or accompany a conventional phrase, an address, or an emphatic statement; in recent use, an expression of surprise. Now only *dial.*, *vulgar*, and *arch.* †**b.** Repeated as an expression of derision (*Timon* III. i. 22).

‖**Laager** (lā·gəɹ), *sb.* Also **lager.** 1850. [S. Afr. Du., = G. *lager*, Du. *leger*; see LEAGUER *sb.*^{1}] A camp, encampment; esp. one in the open marked out by a circle of wagons. Hence ‖**Laa·ger** *v. trans.* to form (wagons) into a l.; to encamp (persons) in a l. Also *absol.* or *intr.*

Lab (læb), *v. Obs.* or *dial.* ME. Also **labb.** [corresp. to Du. *labben* = *klappen* 'garrire, blaterare, fabulari' (Kilian). Cf. contemp. and synon. BLAB *v.*^{1}] *trans.* and *intr.* To blab –1475. So **Lab** *sb.*, a blab, tell-tale.

Lab. Abbrev. of LABORATORY (sense 1).

Labadist (læ·bădist). 1753. [– Fr. *Labadiste*, f. *Labadie*; see -IST.] *Eccl. Hist.* A follower of Jean de Labadie (1610–74), who seceded from the Roman Church and founded a sect holding Quietist views. So **La·badism.**

‖**Labarum** (læ·bărŏm). 1658. [Late L. (Tertullian), whence Byzantine Gr. λαβαρόν.] The imperial standard of Constantine the Great (306–337 A.D.), being the Roman military standard of the late Empire with Christian symbols added; hence *gen.*, a symbolical banner.

‖**Labba** (læ·bă). 1825. [perh. native name.] A cavy, *Cœlogenys paca*, native to Guiana.

Labby (læ·bi). 1901. [Of unkn. origin.] At Monte Carlo, a system in which the stakes are so arranged that a win cancels two previous losses.

‖**Labdanum** (læ·bdănŏm). Also †**lap-.** 1502. [med.L. form of L. LADANUM.] = LADANUM.

Heap cassia, sandal-buds, and stripes Of l. BROWNING.

Labefactation (læ:bĭfæktēi·ʃən). [– L. *labefactatio*, f. *labefactat-*, pa. ppl. stem of *labefactare*, freq. of *labefacere*; see next, -ATION.] = next. JOHNSON.

Labefaction (læbĭfæ·kʃən). 1620. [– *labefact-*, pa. ppl. stem of L. *labefacere* weaken, f. *labi* fall + *facere* make; see -ION.] A shaking, weakening; overthrow, downfall.

†**La·befy**, *v.* 1620. [– L. *labefacere*; see prec., -FY.] *trans.* To weaken, impair.

Label (lēi·bĕl), *sb.* ME. [– OFr. *label* ribbon, fillet (also *lambel*, mod. *lambeau* rag), prob. – Gmc. form rel. to LAP *sb.*[1], with dim. suffix.] **1.** A narrow band of linen, cloth etc.; the infula of a mitre. †**2.** A strip of paper or parchment attached to a document by way of supplement; hence, a supplementary note or clause, a codicil. Also *fig.* –1706. †**3.** *Astron.* and *Surveying.* In an astrolabe, etc., a narrow thin brass rule used chiefly in taking altitudes –1674. †**4.** *gen.* A slip or strip of anything; e.g. of land, of iron, etc. –1686. **5.** *Her.* A mark of cadency distinguishing the eldest son of a family and consisting in a band drawn across the upper part of the shield having (usu. three) dependent points (*label of three points*); cf. FILE *sb.*[2] I. 5. ME. **6.** A narrow strip of material attached to a document to carry the seal 1494. **7.** A slip of paper, cardboard, metal, etc. for attaching to an object and bearing its name, description, or destination. (The chief current sense.) Also *fig.* 1679. †**b.** An adhesive postage-stamp, etc. 1840–1900. **8.** *Arch.* (also *l.-mould, -ing*) A moulding over a door, window, etc.; a dripstone 1823.

1. A knit night-cap..With two long labels button'd to his chin BP. HALL. **2.** *Cymb.* V. v. 430. **7.** The hamper was directed by a l. on the cording DE FOE. **b.** Sheets of 1*d.* Labels containing 240 Stamps 1840.

Comb.: **l.-stop** *Arch.*, a boss or corbel supporting the end of a l.

Label (lēⁱ·bĕl), *v.* Also †**lable.** 1601. [f. prec.] *trans.* To attach a label to; *fig.* to designate as with a label, to set down in a category (*as* so-and-so).

fig. It would be most unjust to l. Byron..as a rhetorician only M. ARNOLD. Hence **La·beller.**

‖**Labellum** (lăbe·lŏm). 1826. [L., dim. of *labrum* lip.] **1.** *Bot.* The lower division or lip of an orchidaceous corolla 1830. **2.** *Entom.* One of a pair of tumid lobes terminating the proboscis of certain insects. Hence **Labe·lloid** *a. Bot.* lip-shaped.

Labial (lēⁱ·biăl). 1594. [– med.L. *labialis*, f. L. *labia* lips; see LIP, -AL[1].]

A. *adj.* **1.** Of or pertaining to the lips 1650. **b.** *Anat., Zool.*, etc. Pertaining to a lip, lip-like part, or LABIUM; like or serving as a lip 1656. **2.** *Phonetics.* Of a vocal sound: Formed by complete or partial closure of the lips, as p, b, m, f, v, w, and the 'rounded' vowels 1594.

1. The l. muscles that swelled with Vehement evolution of yesterday Marseillaises CLOUGH. *L. pipe*, an organ-pipe furnished with lips, a flue-pipe.

B. *sb.* **1.** A labial sound 1668. **2.** A labial part or organ, e.g. one of the labial palpi of insects, etc. 1885.

Hence **La·bialism,** tendency to labialize sounds. **La·bialize** *v.* to render (a sound) labial in character; to round (a vowel); hence **Labializa·tion.**

Labiate (lēⁱ·bi,ĕt). 1706. [– mod.L. *labiatus*, f. LABIUM; see -ATE[2].]

A. *adj.* **1.** *Bot.* **a.** Lipped; having the corolla or calyx divided into two parts which suggest lips; bilabiate. **b.** Belonging to the N.O. *Labiatæ*, consisting of plants usually having bilabiate flowers, opposite leaves, and square stalks, e.g. the mints, ground-ivy, etc. **2.** *Anat.* and *Zool.* Resembling a lip or labium (Dicts.). So **La·biated** *a.* 1707.

B. *sb. Bot.* A labiate plant 1845.

Labiatiflorous (lēⁱ:bi,eⁱtiflōᵊ·rəs), *a.* 1855. [f. mod.L. *labiatus* (see prec.) + *-florus* flowered + -OUS.] *Bot.* Having labiate flowers.

Labidometer (læbidǫ·mītəɹ). 1853. [f. Gr. λαβίς, λαβιδ- forceps + -METER Cf. Fr. *labidomètre*.] *Surg.* A pair of obstetric forceps with a scale attached for measuring the fœtal head.

Labile (lēⁱ·bil, læ·bil), *a.* 1447. [– late L. *labilis*, f. *labi* fall; see -ILE.] **1.** Liable or prone to lapse. †**2.** Slippery (*lit.* and *fig.*) –1654. **3.** Prone to undergo displacement or change; unstable. Now only in *Physics* and *Chemistry*. 1603. **4.** *Electr.* Said of the application of a current by moving an electrode over an affected region 1888.

3. A l. state of equilibrium LD. SALISBURY. Hence **Labi·lity,** proneness to lapse, instability.

Labio- (lēⁱ·bio), comb. f. L. *labium* lip, (*a*) *Phonetics*, 'formed with lips and —', as *labio-dental*, etc.; (*b*) *Path.*, 'having to do with lips and —', as *labio-alveolar*, etc.

‖**Labium** (lēⁱ·biŏm). 1597. [L., = 'lip'.] A lip or lip-like part. **1.** *Anat.* †**a.** One of the sides of the aperture of a vein. **b.** Chiefly in pl. **labia,** in full *labia pudendi*: The lips of the female pudendum 1722. **2.** In insects, crustaceans, etc., the floor of the mouth, which serves as an under lip 1828. **b.** *Conch.* The inner lip of a univalve shell 1839. **3.** *Bot.* The (lower) lip of a labiate corolla 1823.

Lablab (læ·blæb). 1823. [Arab. *lablāb*.] The Egyptian or black bean, a native of India, but naturalized in most warm countries.

†**Laborant.** 1665. [– med.L. *laborans, -ant-*, labourer, workman, pr. pple. of L. *laborare*; see LABOUR *v.*, -ANT. Cf. OFr. *laborant*.] A laboratory workman; chemist's assistant –1694.

Laboratory (læ·bŏrătəri). 1605. [– med.L. *laboratorium*, f. *laborat-*, pa. ppl. stem of L. *laborare*; see LABOUR *v.*, -ORY[1].] **1.** A building set apart for experiments in natural science, orig. and esp. in chemistry, and for the manufacture of chemicals, etc. Also *transf.* and *fig.* **2.** *Mil.* 'A department of an arsenal for the manufacture and examination of ammunition and combustible stores' (Voyle) 1716. **3.** *Metall.* 'The space between the fire and flue-bridges of a reverberatory furnace in which the work is performed; also called the *kitchen* and the *hearth*' (Raymond) 1839. **4.** *attrib.*, as *l.-work*, etc. 1769.

1. *fig.* A notion neatly turned out of the l. of the mind J. H. NEWMAN. Hence **La:borato·rial** *a.*

Laborious (lăbōᵊ·riəs), *a.* ME. [– (O)Fr. *laborieux* – L. *laboriosus*, f. *labor*; see LABOUR *sb.*, -IOUS.] **1.** Given to labour; hard-working. **b.** = LABOURING *ppl. a.* 1. 1777. **2.** Toilsome ME. **b.** Of concrete objects: Entailing labour in construction, execution, or working. **3.** *Midwifery.* Attended with severe labour 1637. †**4.** Pertaining to labour. QUARLES.

1. All..combine to drive The lazy Drones from the l. Hive DRYDEN. **b.** The l. classes BURKE. **2.** Hate not l. worke, neither husbandrie *Ecclus.* 7:15. **b.** L. orient ivory sphere in sphere TENNYSON. Hence **Labo·rious-ly** *adv.*, **-ness.** So †**La·borous** *a.* ME. –1782.

Labour, labor (lēⁱ·bəɹ), *sb.* ME. [– OFr. *labo(u)r* (mod. *labeur* ploughing) – L. *labor, labor-* labour, toil, exertion, trouble, suffering. In the British Isles the sp. with *-our* is usual, in U.S. *-or* is preferred.] **1.** Bodily or mental toil, esp. when painful or compulsory. **2.** *spec.* in mod. use: Physical exertion directed to the supply of the material wants of the community 1776. **b.** The general body of labourers and operatives who take this part in production. Chiefly *attrib.* 1880. **3.** An instance of bodily or mental toil ME. **4.** The product or result of toil. Also *pl. Obs.* exc. *arch.* ME. †**5.** Trouble taken. (Occas. *pl.*) –1656. **6.** The pains of childbirth; travail 1545. Also *fig.* †**7.** Eclipse. DRYDEN.

1. Man goeth forth vnto his worke: and to his l., vntill the euening *Ps.* 104:23. Pleasure is l. too, and tires as much COWPER. Phr. *Hard l.*: see HARD *a.* IV. 2. **2.** L., therefore, is the real measure of the exchangeable value of all commodities ADAM SMITH. **b.** The parliamentary representation of l. 1901. **3.** *A l. of Hercules*, a task requiring enormous strength. *L. of love*: see LOVE *sb.* **4.** The waxen L. of the Bees DRYDEN. **6.** The Queens in Labor They say in great Extremity SHAKS. *fig.* As if nature were..in l. to produce excellency BACON.

attrib. and *Comb.*, as *l. member, question*, etc.; *l.-saving* adj.; *l.-dimmed* adj.; also **l. exchange,** a State office where workers and employers of labour may be accommodated; **-market,** the supply of unemployed l. with reference to the demand for it; **-party** (also *Independent Labour Party*), a political party claiming to further the interests of the labouring or wage-earning classes; **-yard,** a yard in a workhouse or prison, where enforced l. is done by the inmates.

Hence **La·bourless, la·borless** *a.* without l.; requiring or doing no l.

Labour, labor (lēⁱ·bəɹ), *v.* ME. [– (O)Fr. *labourer* (now chiefly, plough) – L. *laborare*, f. *labor* labour, toil, exertion, trouble; see prec.]

I. *trans.* **1.** To spend labour upon (the ground, etc.); to cultivate (now *poet.* or *arch.*); to work (a mine). **2.** *gen.* To work upon; to produce or execute with labour. *Obs.* or *arch.* ME. †**3.** To use labour upon in rubbing, or the like; *hence*, to rub, pound, beat, etc. –1661. **4.** To belabour. *Obs.* exc. *dial.* 1594. **5.** To treat with great pains; to work out in detail, elaborate (a point, a question) 1449. **6.** To work with a view to (a result); to work hard for (a cause, etc.). *Obs.* or *arch.* ME. †**7.** To endeavour to influence or persuade –1633. †**8.** (with compl.) To bring into a specified condition or position by strenuous exertion –1697. †**9.** To work; to use in some work –1671; to cause to undergo fatigue. *arch.*

1. The English labourer..hazards much when he labours land for himself A. YOUNG. **2.** They..l. Honey to sustain their Lives DRYDEN. **5.** Though he labours this point, yet [etc.] BURKE. In a single figure, parts are often highly laboured 1846. **6.** How earnestly I laboured that re-union BURKE. **8.** Sisyphus that labours up the Hill The rowling Rock in vain DRYDEN.

II. *intr.* **1.** To exert oneself, toil; to work hard or against difficulties ME. **2.** To strive (*for* some end or *to* do something) ME. †**3.** To exert one's influence. Const. *to* (a person). –1587. **4.** To move, *esp.* with painful exertion (*lit.* and *fig.*) Now *rare.* ME. **5.** To be troubled or distressed, as by disease, want, etc.; to suffer from some impediment or defect. Const. *under* (†*of, with, on, in*). ME. †**6.** Of women: To travail. Also *fig.* –1711. **7.** Of a ship: To roll or pitch heavily 1627.

1. He that laboryth not, let him not eate 1542. **2.** I laboured for peace COVERDALE *Ps.* 120:7. L. not to comfort me *Isa.* 22:4. **4.** Make not all the people to l. thither *Josh.* 7:3. **5.** To l. under an entire misapprehension KINGSLEY. **6.** All women labouryng of chylde *Bk. Com. Prayer.* Hence †**La·bourable** *a.* capable of being laboured. **La·boured, la·bored** *ppl. a.* highly elaborated; showing indications of excessive labour; heavy, wanting in spontaneity.

Labourer, laborer (lēⁱ·bərəɹ). ME. [– (O)Fr. *laboureur*, f. *labourer*; see prec., -ER[2] 3.] One who labours. **1.** One who performs physical labour as a service or for a livelihood; *spec.* one who does work requiring chiefly bodily strength (often differentiated as *agricultural, dock, mason's l.*, etc.). **2.** *gen.* One who does work of any kind ME. **3.** A working insect, 'worker' 1601.

1. *Statute of Labourers*, mod. designation of the statute *De Servientibus* (23 Edw. III), regulating the rate of wages. An intelligent villager—not a labourer, but a man of the working-class 1891. **2.** The l. is worthy of his hire *Luke* 10:7.

Labouring, laboring (lēⁱ·bəriŋ), *vbl. sb.* ME. [f. LABOUR *v.* + -ING[1].] The action of LABOUR *v.* Also *attrib.*

Labouring, laboring (lēⁱ·bəriŋ), *ppl. a.* ME. [f. as prec. + -ING[2].] **1.** That labours; *esp.* performing unskilled labour, as in *l. man, population.* †**2.** Of a woman: Suffering the pangs of childbirth. Also *transf.* –1704. **3.** Striving against pressure or some obstacle; that is in trouble or distress; (of the heart) struggling under emotion or suppressed feeling, also heaving, palpitating; (of a ship) rolling or pitching heavily. (Often with some reference to 2.) ME. †**b.** Of the moon: Eclipsed. (A Latinism.) –1665.

1. I..oar'd with lab'ring arms along the flood POPE. Phr. *Labouring oar*: the oar which requires most labour to work it; hence *fig.* **2.** The l. mountain must bring forth a mouse DRYDEN. Hence **La·bouringly** *adv.*

Labourism (lēⁱ·bəriz'm). 1903. [f. LABOUR *sb.* + -ISM.] The principles and practice of the Labour Party. Hence **La·bourist, -ite.**

Laboursome, laborsome (lēⁱ·bəɹsŏm), *a.* 1551. [f. LABOUR *sb.* + -SOME[1].] †**1.** = LABORIOUS 1. –1620. **2.** = LABORIOUS 2. Now *rare* or *dial.* 1577. **3.** Of a ship: Liable to pitch and roll in a heavy sea 1691. Hence **La·boursome-ly** *adv.*, **-ness.**

Labrador (læ:brădǭ·ɹ), name of a large peninsula in British N. Amer.: **L. blue,** the blue of labradorite; **L. dog,** a variety of the Newfoundland dog; **L. duck,** a sea-duck of N. Amer.; **L. feldspar, spar, stone** (also simply *labrador*) = LABRADORITE; **L. tea,** *Ledum latifolium* and *L. palustre* of N. Amer., which have leaves that have been used for tea.

Labradorite (læbrădǭ·rəit). 1814. [f. prec. + -ITE[1] 2 b.] *Min.* A kind of feldspar from Labrador, which shows a brilliant variety of colour when turned in the light.

†**Labras.** Pistol's blunder for L. *labra*, pl. of *labrum* lip. *Merry W.* I. i. 166.

Labret (lēⁱ·brėt). 1857. [f. next. + -ET.] An ornament inserted in the lip.

‖**Labrum** (lēⁱ·brŏm). *Pl.* **labra.** 1816. [L., cogn. w. LABIUM.] A lip or lip-like part. **a.** In insects, etc.: The upper border or covering of the mouth. **b.** *Conch.* The outer lip of a univalve shell. Hence **La·bral** *a.*

Laburnum (lăbŏ·ɹnŏm). 1578. [– L. *laburnum* (Pliny), prob. of foreign origin.] A small leguminous tree, *Cytisus laburnum*, with profuse racemes of bright-yellow flowers. Applied also to similar plants.

Labyrinth (læ·bĭrinþ), *sb.* 1548. [– Fr. *labyrinthe* or L. *labyrinthus* – Gr. λαβύρινθος, of non-Hellenic origin.] **1.** An intricate structure of intercommunicating passages, through which it is difficult to find one's way without a clue; a maze 1549. **2.** *transf.* An intricate or tortuous arrangement (of physical features, buildings etc.) 1615. **b.** (*a*) *Metall.* A series of channels used for distributing and separating the ores in the order of the coarseness of grain 1839. (*b*) A chamber of many turnings for the condensation of fumes arising from dry distillation, etc. 1875. **3.** *Anat.* A complex cavity hollowed out of the temporal bone, consisting of a bony capsule (*osseous l.*) and a delicate membranous apparatus (*membranous l.*) contained by it; the internal ear 1696. **b.** Applied to other organs of intricate structure 1774. **4.** *fig.* An entanglement, maze of things, events, ideas, etc. 1548.

1. Crete will boast the L. SPENSER. Labyrinths are only proper for large gardens, and the finest in the world is said to be that of Versailles 1753. **2.** Leyden lies..in the midst of a l. of rivulets and canals 1777. **4.** The l. of the statutes under which London is governed 1883. *Comb.* **l. fret** *Arch.*, a fret, with many turnings, in the form of a l. Hence **La·byrinth** *v. trans.* to enclose in or as in a l.; to arrange in the form of a l. **Labyri·nthian, Labyri·nthic, -al, Labyri·nthine** *adjs.* pertaining to, of the nature or form of, a l.; *fig.* intricate, inextricable. So **Labyri·nthiform** *a.*

Labyrinthodon (læbĭri·nþŏdǫn). 1847. [mod.L., f. Gr. λαβύρινθος (prec.) + ὀδούς, ὀδοντ- tooth.] *Palæont.* Any large fossil amphibian of the genus *Labyrinthodon*, characterized by teeth of labyrinthine structure having the enamel folded and sunk inward. So **Labyri·nthodont. A.** *sb.* = prec. 1841. **B.** *adj.* Having labyrinthine teeth; *spec.* pertaining to the genus *Labyrinthodon* of fossil amphibians 1867.

Lac[1] (læk). 1553. [– (through Du. *lak*, Fr. *laque* (XV), or Sp., Pg. *laca*, It. *lacca*, med.L. *lac, lacca* XII/XIII), Hind. *lākh* :– Prakrit *lakkha* :– Skr. *lākshā*. Cf. LAKE *sb.*[4], SHELLAC.] **1.** Also (*gum-lac.*) The dark-red resinous incrustation produced on certain trees by the puncture of an insect (*Coccus lacca*), and used in the East as a scarlet dye. When melted, strained, and formed into irregular thin plates, it is known as *shell-lac* or SHELLAC. †**2.** The colour of lac; crimson; a pigment prepared from lac –1763. †**3.** = LACQUER 2 a, b. –1727. **4.** Ware coated with lac 1662.

attrib. and *Comb.*: **l.-cochineal,** the insect that produces l. (*Coccus lacca*); **-dye,** a scarlet dye prepared in India from l.; **-lake,** the purple pigment obtained from l. Hence †**Lac** *v.* to lacquer 1698–1727.

Lac[2], **lakh** (læk). *Anglo-Ind.* 1613. [– Hind. *lākh* :– Skr. *laksha* mark, sign, token, 100,000.] One hundred thousand; *occas.*, an indefinite number; *spec.* of coins, esp. in *a l. of rupees.*

Laccic (læ·ksik), *a.* 1794. [f. mod.L. *lacca* LAC[1] + -IC.] *Chem.* Only in *l. acid*, the acid procured from lac.

Laccin (læ·ksin). 1838. [f. as prec. + -IN[1].] The colouring principle in lac.

Laccolite (læ·kŏləit). 1877. [f. Gr. λάκκος a reservoir + -LITE.] *Geol.* A mass of igneous rock thrust up through the sedimentary beds, and giving a dome-like form to the overlying strata. var. **La·ccolith.**

Lace (lēⁱs), *sb.* [ME. *las, laas,* (later) *lace* – OFr. *laz, las* (mod. *lacs* noose) :– Rom. **lacium*, for L. *laqueus* noose.] †**1.** A net, noose, snare. Usu. *fig.* –1603. †**2.** A cord, line, string, thread, or tie. Also *transf.* and *fig.* –1650. **3.** *spec.* **a.** A string or cord serving to draw together opposite edges, e.g. of bodices, boots, etc., by being passed through eyelet-holes or over hooks, etc. and pulled tight ME. †**b.** A cord used to support a sword, etc.; a baldric, belt –1597. **4.** Braid for trimming men's coats, etc. Now only in *gold, silver l.* 1530. **5.** A delicate, open-work fabric of linen, cotton, silk, woollen, or metal threads, usually with inwrought or applied patterns 1555. **6.** A dash of spirits mixed with some beverage, esp. coffee 1704.

3. She was indeed a Pedler's daughter, and sold many Laces SHAKS. **4.** In a scarlet waistcoat, with rich gold l., and a gold-lace hat BOSWELL. **6.** He drinks his coffee without l. [perh. = 'sugar'] M. PRIOR.

Comb.: **l.-bark (tree),** (*a*) a W. Indian shrub (*Lagetta linteraia*), so called from the lace-like layers of its inner bark; (*b*) in New Zealand, *Plagianthus betulinus*, ribbon-wood; **-glass,** Venetian glass with lace-like designs; **-pillow,** the pillow or cushion which is laid on the lap of a woman making pillow-lace; **-woman,** one who works or deals in l.

Lace (lēⁱs), *v.* ME. [– OFr. *lacier* (mod. *lacer*) :– Rom. **laciare* ensnare, f. **lacium*; see prec.] †**1.** *trans.* To catch in, or as in, a noose or snare –1485. **2.** To fasten or tighten with, or as with, a lace or string. In mod. use *spec.* to fasten or tighten (boots, stays, etc.) with laces. Also with *down, on, together*. Also *transf.* and *fig.* ME. **b.** *intr.* (quasi-*pass.*) To admit of being fastened or tightened with laces 1792. **3.** To compress the waist of (a person) by drawing the laces tight. Also *fig.* 1566. **b.** *refl.*, and *intr.* for *refl.* 1650. **4.** *trans.* To thread or interlace (a fabric) *with* a lace, string, etc.; to embroider. Chiefly in *pa. pple.* 1483. **b.** To pass (a cord, etc.) in and out *through* a fabric, *through* holes, etc. Also *fig.* 1638. **5.** To trim with lace 1599. **6.** To diversify *with* streaks of colour 1592. **7.** To lash, beat, thrash 1599. †**8.** *Cookery.* To make incisions in (the breast of a bird) –1796. **9.** To mingle or dash (*with* spirits or †sugar) 1677.

2. Hir shoes were laced on hir legges hye CHAUCER. **3.** Rather straitly laced in her Presbyterian stays SCOTT. Phr. *To l. in*: to compress the waist by lacing. *intr.* I can..l. in to sixteen inches 1871. **4.** Oblong vellum binding laced with cat-gut 1880. **5.** Cloth a gold, and cuts, and lac'd with siluer SHAKS. **6.** Here lay Duncan, His Siluer skinne, lac'd with his Golden Blood SHAKS. **7.** If I meet thee, I will l. thee roundly 1615.

Comb., as *l.-boots* 1827; also *l.-up* adj. and sb. 1836.

Laced (lēⁱst), *ppl. a.*[1] 1533. [f. LACE *v.* + -ED[1].] In the senses of the vb.

Phr. †*L. mutton* (slang): a strumpet. *Two Gent.* I. i. 102.

†**Laced,** *ppl. a.*[2] 1486. [orig. *lassed*, for *lessed*, pa. pple. of LESS *v.*] *Her.* Lessened, diminished –1586.

Lacedæmonian (læ:sĭdimōᵘ·niăn). 1545. [f. L. *Lacedæmonius*, Gr. Λακεδαιμόνιος + -AN.] **A.** *adj.* **a.** Of or pertaining to Lacedæmon (Sparta) or its people. **b.** Of speech, etc. = LACONIC. **B.** *sb.* A Spartan.

La·ce-piece. 1874. [perh. f. LACE *sb.* 'tie-beam'.] The part of the prow of a wooden vessel above the cut-water and behind the figure-head.

Lacerable (læ·sĕrăb'l), *a.* 1656. [f. LACERATE *v.* + -ABLE.] Susceptible of laceration. Hence **Lacerabi·lity.**

Lacerate (læ·sĕrĕt), *ppl. a.* 1542. [– L. *laceratus*, pa. pple. of *lacerare*; see next, -ATE[2].] **1.** Mangled, torn, lacerated. Also *fig.* **2.** *Bot.* and *Zool.* Having the edge or point irregularly cut or cleft; jagged 1776. Hence **La·cerately** *adv.*

Lacerate (læ·sĕreⁱt), *v.* 1592. [– *lacerat-*, pa. ppl. stem of L. *lacerare*, f. *lacer* mangled, torn; see -ATE[3].] **1.** *trans.* To tear, mangle; to tear to pieces. **2.** *esp.* To afflict, distress, harrow (the heart) 1645.

1. Feet..lacerated by the thorns FARRAR. Hence **Lacera·tion, La·cerative** *a. rare.*

†**Lacert**[1]. *rare.* ME. [– L. *lacerta, lacertus* lizard.] A lizard –1696.

†**Lacert**[2]. ME. [– OFr. *lacerte* or L. *lacertus* muscle of the upper arm, pl. muscles in gen., similative use of *lacertus* lizard (see prec.); cf. MUSCLE (L. *musculus* 'little mouse').] A muscle –1696. So †**Lacertose, lacertous** *adjs.* muscular.

Lacertian (lăsō·ɹtiăn, -ʃ'iăn). 1822. [f. L. *lacerta, lacertus* lizard + -IAN.] **A.** *adj.* Of or pertaining to the lizards or *Lacertilia*; lizard-like, saurian 1843. **B.** *sb.* A lacertilian; a lizard. So **Lace·rtine** *a.*

Lacertilian (læ:səɹti·liăn). 1854. [f. mod.L. *Lacertilia* pl. the lizard tribe (see prec., -ILE, -IA[2]) + -AN.] **A.** *adj.* Belonging to the *Lacertilia*. **B.** *sb.* [sc. *animal*.].

Lacery, *sb.* (lēⁱ·səri). 1893. [f. LACE *sb.* + -ERY.] Lace-like work.

Lacet (leⁱse·t). 1862. [f. LACE *sb.* + -ET.] Applied to a kind of braid used with crochet work or lace stitches.

Laches (læ·tʃėz), *sb.* [ME. *lac(c)hesse* – AFr. *laches(se* = OFr. *laschesse* (mod. *lâchesse* cowardice), f. *lasche* (mod. *lâche*); see LASH *a.*, -ESS[2].] †**1.** Remissness, negligence; also, an act of neglect –1494. **2.** *Law.* Negligence in the performance of a legal duty; delay in asserting a right, claiming a privilege, or applying for redress 1574. **b.** *transf.* Culpable negligence in general 1844. Also †**Laches** *a.* remiss; whence †**Lachesness.**

2. b. The l. of this ministry DISRAELI.

‖**Lachesis** (læ·kĕsis). 1872. [mod.L. – Gr. Λάχεσις, one of the Fates.] *Zool.* A genus of venomous American snakes of the rattlesnake family (*Crotalidæ*).

†**Lachrymable, lacrymable,** *a.* 1490. [– L. *lacrimabilis* (in med.L. also *-ch-*), f. *lacrimare* shed tears; see -BLE.] **1.** Meet for tears; lamentable –1648. **2.** Expressive of mourning –1635.

‖**Lachryma Christi** (læ·krimă kri·stəi). Also †**lachrymæ Christi,** and *simply* **lacrima, -mæ.** 1670. [L., = Christ's tear(s); in Italian, *lagrima* (or *-e*) *di Cristo.*] A strong sweet red wine of southern Italy.

Lachrymal (læ·krimăl). 1541. [– med.L. *lachrymalis, lacrimalis*, f. L. *lacrima*, earlier *lacruma* tear, rel. to Gr. δάκρυ; see -AL[1]. The sp. with *ch* and *y* reflects med.L. practice; *y* is retained in Eng. by assoc. with the Greek word.]

A. *adj.* **1.** *Anat.* and *Phys.* Designating the organs concerned in the secretion of tears, and connected structures, etc. 1597. **2.** Of or pertaining to tears; *occas.*, given to, or indicative of, weeping. *L. vase*, one to hold tears. 1803.

2. The l. and suspirious clergy SYD. SMITH.

B. *sb.* **1.** *pl.* The lachrymal organs 1541. **b.** *Anat.* A lachrymal bone. MIVART. **2.** *pl.* Fits of weeping 1753. **3.** = LACHRYMATORY *sb.* 1769.

Lachrymation (lækrimēⁱ·ʃən). 1572. [– L. *lacrimatio*, f. *lacrimat-* pa. ppl. stem of *lacrimare*, f. *lacrima*; see prec., -ION.] The shedding of tears; weeping.

Lachrymatory (læ·krimătəri). 1658. [f. L. *lacrima* tear, after CHRISMATORY; see prec., -ORY[1,2].]

A. *adj.* Of or pertaining to tears; causing a flow of tears. *L. vase* = B. 1849.

B. *sb.* A vase to hold tears 1658.

No..Lachrymatories, or Tear-Bottles SIR T. BROWNE. So **La·chrymary** *a.* and *sb.* 1705.

La·chrymist. 1620. [f. L. *lacrima* tear + -IST.] A weeper.

Lachrymose (læ·krimōᵘs), *a.* 1661. [– L. *lacrimosus*, f. *lacrima* tear; see -OSE[1].] †**1.** Having the nature of tears. LOVELL. **2.** Given to tears; tearful 1727; mournful 1822. Hence **La·chrymosely** *adv.* var. **La·chrymous** 1490.

Lacing (lēⁱ·siŋ), *vbl. sb.* ME. [f. LACE *v.* + -ING[1].] **1.** The action of LACE *v.* **2.** *concr.* or quasi-*concr.* **a.** A fastening, tie; a shoe-string ME. **b.** Braiding for men's clothes 1593. **c.** The coloured border on the petal of a flower, etc. 1844. **d.** = LACE *sb.* 6. 1862. **3.** *techn.* **a.** *Bridge-building.* (see quot.) **b.** *Mining.* (*a*) Timbers placed across the tops of bars or caps to secure the roof between the gears. (*b*) Strips or light bars of wrought iron bent over at the ends and wedged in tight between the bars and the roof. 1883.

1. The sound l. which the young rascal should inevitably receive 1893. **3. a.** *Lacing*, a system of bars, not intersecting each other at the middle, used to connect the two channels of a strut in order to make them act as one member 1885.

‖**Lacinia** (lăsi·niă). Pl. **-iæ.** 1668. [L., lappet, flap, edge or corner of a garment.] **1.** *Bot.* A slash in a leaf, petal, etc.; the slender lobe thus produced. **2.** *Entom.* The apex of the maxilla, esp. when slender 1826.

Laciniate (lăsi·niĕt), *a.* Also *erron.* **lacinate.** 1760. [f. L. *lacinia*; see prec., -ATE². Cf. Fr. *lacinié.*] *Bot.* and *Zool.* Cut into deep and narrow irregular segments; jagged, slashed. So **Laci·niated** *ppl. a.* 1668. **Lacinia·tion,** a cutting into laciniæ or fringes 1846. **Laci·niolate** *a. Bot.* having minute laciniæ (Dicts.).

Lack (læk), *sb.*¹ [Early ME. *lac*; cf. OFris. *lek* blame, *lackia, leckia*, MLG., MDu. *lak* deficiency, fault, blame (Du. *lak* calumny); perh. pointing to a Gmc. **lak-*, orig. expressing 'deficiency', 'defect', which may have been actually repr. in OE. (whence AL. *lacca, laccum* X/XI); but some uses may be of Scand. or LG. origin.] †**1.** A defect; failing; a fault, offence, crime –1598. **2.** Deficiency, want, need (*of* something desirable or necessary); an instance of this ME. **3.** Indigence; also, famine, starvation 1555. †**4.** Absence –1605. **5.** quasi-*concr.* The thing wanting (*rare*) 1549.

1. The lacke is not in the law, but in vs LATIMER. **2.** L. of money 1753, of judgment RUSKIN. Phr. *No l.* (*of*): enough, plenty (of). *For* (*by, from, through*) *l. of*: for want (*rarely* loss) of. **5.** One great l. here and elsewhere is the green sod 1848.

†**Lack,** *sb.*² 1638. [See ALACK *int.* and GOOD *a.* II. 2.] Only in exclam. *Good l.!* –1807.

†**Lack,** *a.* 1479. [Cf. ON. *lakr* defective, and see LACK *sb.*¹] **1.** Of a quantity: Short, wanting –1644. **2.** Missing 1591.

1. *Little l. of*: not far short of: Sicke, sicke, alas, and little l. of dead SPENSER.

Lack (læk), *v.* ME. [Cf. MDu. *laken* be wanting, blame, ODa. *lakke* depreciate; see LACK *sb.*¹] **1.** *intr.* To be wanting or missing; to be deficient. Now only in *to be lacking.* **2.** *trans.* To be without; to be destitute of or deficient in ME. †**b.** with *cannot*: To do or go without –1592. †**c.** To perceive the absence of, miss. SHAKS. **3.** To stand in need of 1530. **4.** *intr.* To be short *of* something. Now *rare.* 1523.

1. In him lacked neither good will nor courage HALL. **2.** It withered away, because it lacked moisture *Luke* 8:6. Learning we l., not books CRABBE. **c.** I shall be lou'd when I am lack'd SHAKS. **3.** What do you lacke? what is't you buy? B. JONS. **4.** He that giueth vnto the poore, shall not lacke *Prov.* 28:27. *Comb.* **l.-all,** one who is in want of everything.

Lackadaisical (lækădē¹·zikăl), *a.* 1768. [f. next + -ICAL.] Like one who is given to crying 'Lackaday!'; full of vapid feeling or sentiment; affectedly languishing.

L. misses 1852, letters 1870. Hence **Lackadai·sical-ly** *adv.*, **-ness.**

Lackadaisy (læ·kăde¹·zi), *int.* (*sb, a.*) 1792. [Extended f. LACKADAY.] = LACKADAY, hence as *sb.* the utterance of the interjection; as *adj.* = prec.

La·ckaday, *int. Obs.* or *arch.* 1695. [aphet. f. ALACK-A-DAY.] = ALACK-A-DAY.

Lacker, var. of LACQUER *sb.* and *v.*

Lackey, lacquey (læ·ki), *sb.* 1529. [– Fr. *laquais*, †*alaquais* – Cat. *alacay* (whence also Sp. (*a*)*lacayo*, Pg. *lacayo*) = Sp., Pg. *alcaide* ALCAYDE.] **1.** A (liveried) footman or valet. Also *fig.* †**2.** A camp follower 1556.

1. He was not her lackey, and . . she might send some one else with her errands MOTLEY. **2.** The . . lackeys and dross of the camp LYTTON.

Comb.: **l.-caterpillar,** the caterpillar of the lackey-moth; **-moth,** a bombycid moth of the genus *Clisiocampa*, so called from the bright colours of the caterpillars, which are striped and decorated like footmen.

Lackey, lacquey (læ·ki), *v.* 1568. [f. prec.] †**1.** *intr.* To do service as a lackey, esp. as a running footman; to dance attendance, do menial service. Often *fig.* **2.** *trans.* To wait upon as a lackey; to dance attendance upon. Chiefly *transf.* and *fig.* 1596.

1. The Minutes (that lackey at the heeles of Time) run not faster away then do our joyes DEKKER. **2.** He had lacqueyed and flattered Walpole 1881.

Lackland (læ·klænd). 1594. [f. LACK *v.* + LAND *sb.*] **A.** *sb.* One who has no land. **B.** *adj.* Having no land.

John who inherited no territory . . was thence commonly denominated L. HUME.

Lack-Latin (stress variable). 1534. [f. LACK *v.* + LATIN *sb.*] †**A.** *sb.* One who knows little or no Latin; chiefly in *Sir John Lack-latin* = an ignorant priest. **B.** *adj.* Ignorant of Latin; unlearned.

Lack-lustre (stress variable). 1600. [f. LACK *v.* + LUSTRE *sb.*¹] **A.** *adj.* Wanting in brightness; orig. of the eye, after Shaks. **B.** *sb.* The absence of lustre (*rare*) 1788.

Lacmus (læ·kmŏs). 1794. [– Du. *lakmoes*, f. *lak* LAC¹ + *moes* pulp.] = LITMUS.

Laconian (lăkō^u·niăn). 1602. [f. L. *Laconia* (f. Gr. Λάκων Laconian) + -AN.] **A.** *adj.* Of or pertaining to Laconia or its inhabitants; Spartan. **B.** *sb.* An inhabitant of Laconia.

Laconic (lăkǫ·nik). 1583. [– L. *Laconicus* – Gr. Λακωνικός, f. Λάκων (prec.).] **A.** *adj.* **1.** = LACONIAN *a.* **2.** Laconian-like, esp. in speech and writing; brief, sententious 1589.

1. The severe L. Disciplin 1683. **2.** This l. fool makes brevity ridiculous DAVENANT.

B. *sb.* (The adj. used absol.) †**1.** A laconic speaker –1692. **2.** Laconic speech. *pl.* Brief or concise sentences. 1718.

2. Shall we never again talk together in l. ? ADDISON. So †**Laco·nical** *a.* 1576–1698, **-ly** *adv.* **Laco·nicism** = LACONISM 2 and 2 b.

Laconism (læ·kŏniz'm). 1570. [– Gr. λακωνισμός, f. λακωνίζειν LACONIZE.] **1.** Partiality for the Lacedæmonians (*rare*) 1655. **2.** The practice of imitating the Lacedæmonians, esp. in brevity of speech 1570. **b.** A laconic speech 1597.

2. His will was brief to l. 1858. **b.** The highway l. of 'your money or your life' D. JERROLD.

Laconize (læ·kŏnəiz), *v.* 1603. [– Gr. λακωνίζειν, f. Λάκων LACONIAN; see -IZE.] **1.** *intr.* To favour the Lacedæmonians, their customs, mode of speech, interests, etc. **2.** *trans.* To render Lacedæmonian 1873.

Lacquer, lacker (læ·kəɹ), *sb.* 1579. [In XVI *laker* – Fr. †*lacre* kind of sealing-wax, Sp., Pg. *lacre*, It. †*lacra*; app. unexpl. var. or extension of Sp., Pg. *laca* LAC¹. The later sp. *lacquer* is app. after Fr. *laque.*] †**1.** = LAC¹ 1. –1714. **2. a.** A gold-coloured varnish, chiefly, pale shellac dissolved in alcohol, and tinged with saffron, anatta, etc.; used esp. as a coating for brass 1673. **b.** Any of various kinds of resinous varnish, esp. the 'Japanese lacquer', capable of taking a hard polish, and used for coating articles of wood, etc. 1697. **3.** Articles of wood coated with lacquer (sense 2 b); chiefly made in Japan, China, and India 1895.

2. b. Japanese l. is the product of a tree, the *Rhus vernicifera* 1889.

Comb.: **l.-ware** = sense 3; **-work,** the making of lacquer-ware; also = *lacquer-ware.*

Lacquer, lacker (læ·kəɹ), *v.* 1688. [f. prec. sb.] *trans.* To coat with lacquer; hence *gen.* to varnish. Also *transf.* and *fig.* Also with *over.*

fig. Lackered over with an outer coating of fairseeming 1831. Hence **La·cquerer, la·ckerer.**

Lacquey, var. of LACKEY *sb.* and *v.*

Lacrim-, lacrym-: see LACHRYM-.

Lacrosse (lakrǫ·s). 1867. [f. Fr. (*le jeu de*) *la crosse* '(the game of) the hooked stick'.] A N. Amer. game resembling hockey, but the ball is driven and caught with a CROSSE.

Lactary (læ·ktări). *rare.* 1646. [– L. *lactarius*, f. *lac, lact-* milk; see -ARY¹.] **A.** *adj.* Of, pertaining to, or concerned with milk; milky. **B.** *sb.* A dairy 1669.

Lactate (læ·ktĕt). 1794. [f. LACT(IC + -ATE⁴.] *Chem.* A salt of lactic acid.

Lactation (lækté¹·ʃən). 1668. [– late L. *lactatio*, f. *lactat-*, pa. ppl. stem of L. *lactare* suckle, be in milk, f. *lac, lact-* milk; see -ION.] **1.** The action of suckling. **2.** The secretion of milk from the mammary glands 1857.

Lacteal (læ·ktiăl). 1633. [f. L. *lacteus* (f. *lac, lact-* milk) + -AL¹.]

A. *adj.* **1.** Of, pertaining to, or consisting of milk 1658; like milk 1633. **2.** *Anat.* Conveying a milky fluid, *sc.* chyle 1664.

2. They have l. vessels, or lymphatics 1843. Hence **La·cteally** *adv.* var. **La·ctean** *a.*

B. *sb. pl.* **1.** *Anat.* The lymphatic vessels of the mesentery, conveying the chyle from the small intestine to the thoracic duct 1680. †**2.** *Bot.* The lactiferous ducts. GREW.

Lacteous (læ·ktiəs), *a.* 1646. [f. L. *lacteus* (see prec.) + -OUS.] **1.** Of the nature of milk. **2.** Resembling milk, *esp.* in colour 1646. †**3.** = LACTEAL *a.* 2. BENTLEY.

2. †*L. circle*: the Milky Way. †*L. star*: one belonging to the Milky Way. **La·cteously** *adv.*

Lactescence (lækte·sĕns). 1684. [f. next; see -ENCE.] **1.** A milky appearance. **2.** *Bot.* Flow of sap from plants when wounded, usu. white, but occas. red 1760. So †**Lacte·scency** (in sense 1) 1756.

Lactescent (lækte·sĕnt), *a.* 1668. [– *lactescent-*, pr. ppl. stem of L. *lactescere*, inchoative vb. f. *lactēre* be milky; see -ESCENT.] **1.** Becoming milky in appearance. **2.** Of plants: Yielding a milky juice 1673. ¶**3.** Used for: Producing or secreting milk 1796.

Lactic (læ·ktik), *a.* 1790. [f. L. *lac, lact-* milk + -IC.] *Chem.* Of or pertaining to milk.

L. acid ($C_3H_6O_3$), the acid formed in sour milk. *L. fermentation*, the souring of milk, by the decomposition of the milk sugar.

Lactiferous (lækti·fĕrəs), *a.* 1673. [– late and med.L. *lactifer*, f. as prec.; see -FEROUS.] **1.** Producing, secreting, or conveying milk 1691. **2.** Conveying or yielding a milky fluid (in plants).

Lactifluous (lækti·fluəs), *a.* 1699. [f. as prec. + *-fluous*, after MELLIFLUOUS.] Flowing with milk.

Lacto- (læ·kto), used as comb. f. L. *lac, lact-*, milk (see -O-); as in **lacto·meter, la·ctoscope,** instruments for gauging the purity of milk; **la:cto-pro·tein,** an albuminous constituent of milk.

Lactose (læ·ktō^us). 1858. [f. L. *lac, lact-* milk + -OSE².] A saccharine substance in milk, commonly called sugar of milk.

Lacuna (lăkiū·nă). *Pl.* **-æ** (*-i*), **-as** (-ăz). 1663. [– L. *lacuna* pool, etc., f. *lacus* LAKE *sb.*²] **1.** A hiatus, blank, missing part. **2.** A gap, an empty space, spot, or cavity 1872. **b.** *Anat.* A mucous follicle; also, a space in the connective tissue giving origin to a lymphatic 1706. **c.** *Anat.* A small cavity in the bone substance 1845. **d.** *Bot.* An air-cell 1836. Hence **Lacu·nal** *a.* of, pertaining to, or like a l. **Lacu·nar** *a.* of or pertaining to a l. or lacunæ; characterized by lacunæ.

Lacunar (lăkiū·năɹ), *sb.* Pl. **-ars, -aria.** 1696. [– L. *lacunar*, f. *lacuna* (prec.).] **a.** A ceiling consisting of sunk or hollowed compartments. **b.** *pl.* The sunken panels in such a ceiling.

Lacunary (lăkiū·nări), *a.* 1716. [f. LACUNA + -ARY².] = LACUNAL *a.*, LACUNAR *a.*

Lacu·ne (1701), anglicized f. LACUNA.

Lacunose (lăkiū·nō^us), *a.* 1777. [– L. *lacunosus*, f. *lacuna*; see LACUNA, -OSE¹.] Full of lacunæ; *spec.* in *Nat. Hist.* Hence *lacunoso-*, comb. form.

Lacu·stral, *a. rare.* 1843. [f. next, with substitution of suffix, or f. Fr. *lacustre* + -AL¹.] = next.

Lacustrine (lăkʋ·strin), *a.* 1830. [f. L. *lacus* LAKE *sb.*², after PALUSTRINE.] Of or pertaining to a lake or lakes. Said *esp.* of plants or animals inhabiting lakes, and *Geol.* of strata, etc., which originated by deposition at the bottom of lakes; also with reference to 'lake dwellings'.

L. age, period, the period when lake-dwellings were common.

Lacy (lē¹·si), *a.* Also **lacey.** 1804. [f. LACE *sb.* + -Y¹.] Consisting of, or resembling, lace.

Lad (læd). [ME. *ladde*, of unkn. (perh. Scand.) origin.] †**1.** A serving-man; a man of low birth and position; a varlet –1721. **2.** A boy, youth; a young man, young fellow. Applied familiarly (occ. ironically) to a man of any age. 1535.

Lad, obs. pa. t. and pple. of LEAD *v.*

‖**Ladanum** (læ·dănŏm). 1551. [L. – Gr. λάδανον, λήδανον, f. λῆδον mastic.] **1.** A gum resin which exudes from plants of the genus *Cistus*, esp. *C. ladaniferus* and *C. creticus.* †**2.** = LAUDANUM 1627.

Ladder (læ·dəɹ), *sb.* [OE. *hlǣd(d)er* = OFris. *hlēdere*, MDu. *lēdere* (Du. *leer*), OHG. *leitara* (G. *leiter*) :– WGmc. **χlaidr-*, f. **χlai-* **χli-* (see LEAN *v.*¹).] **1.** An appliance made of wood, metal, or rope, usu. portable, consisting of a series of bars ('rungs') or steps fixed between two supports, for ascent and descent. †**b.** *esp.* The steps to a gallows –1655. **c.** *fig.* ME. **2.** Applied to things resembling a ladder ME.; recently, a ladder-like hole in a stocking.

1. [He] oft a lather tooke To gather fruit 1621. c. Northumberland, thou L. wherewithall The mounting Bullingbrooke ascends my Throne SHAKS. Phr. *To kick down the l.*: to repudiate the friends or means that have helped one to rise in the world. 2. *Cart-l.*, a rack or framework at the front, back, or sides of a cart, to increase its carrying capacity ME. *Fish-l.* (see FISH *sb.*[1]).

Comb.; **l.-dredge,** a dredge with buckets carried round on a ladder-like chain; **l. shell,** a marine shell of the genus *Scalaria*, a wentletrap; **l. way,** a way by which one ascends or descends by means of a l., (*a*) in the deck of a ship, (*b*) in the shaft of a mine.

Hence **La·dder** *v.* to furnish with a l. or ladders; (of a stocking) to be worn into 'ladders'.

Laddie (læ·di). Chiefly *Sc.* 1546. [f. LAD + -IE.] A young lad, a lad. (A term of endearment.)

Lade (lēid), *sb.* 1706. [app. a var. of LEAD *sb.*[2] (which occurs much earlier in the same sense); perh. confused with *lade*, the regular Sc. and north. form of LODE.] 1. A channel for leading water to a mill-wheel; a mill-race. Chiefly *Sc.* 1808. ¶2. Channel, water-course, mouth of a river (evolved from place-names in *-lade*, as Cricklade, etc.) 1706.

Lade (lēid), *v.* Pa. pple. **laden, laded.** [OE. *hladan*, corresp. to OFris. *hlada*, OS., OHG. *hladan* (Du., G. *laden*), ON. *hlaða*, Goth. *-hlaþan*. See LAST *sb.*[2]]

I. To load (pa. pple. *laden*). 1. *trans.* To put cargo on board (a ship). Also (now only in *pass.*) to load (a vehicle, an ass, etc.) **b.** To load *with*: To charge or fill abundantly. Now only in pa. pple. *laden.* 1481. **c.** To load oppressively. Now only (somewhat *arch.*) in pa. pple., burdened *with* sin, etc. 1538. 2. To put as a burden, freight, or cargo; now only, to ship (goods) as cargo OE. Also *absol.* or *intr.* †3. To load (a gun); also, to load (cartridges) in a gun -1690.

1. They laded their asses with the corne *Gen.* 42: 26. He..help'd At lading and unlading the tall barks TENNYSON. **b.** A tree wel laden and charged of fruyte 1484. ti L. him with irons 1602. Laden with the sinch **c.** whey had committed LANE. 2. It is impossible to l. or deliver Cargoes 1800. *absol.* A pier..at which vessels..l. and unlade MORSE.

II. To draw water (pa. pple *laded*). 1. *trans.* To draw (water); to take up or remove (water, etc.) from a river, a vessel, etc., with a ladle, scoop, or the like; to bale. (Now chiefly *techn.* and *dial.*) OE. Also *absol.* or *intr.* †2. To empty by 'lading' -1628.

1. To l. off the Whey clear from Curd 1784. 2. Like one that..chides the Sea..Saying hee'le l. it dry SHAKS.

Laden (lēi·d'n), *v.* 1514. [irreg. f. LADE *v.* + *-en*; but perh. partly a Sc. var. of LOADEN *v.*] = LADE *v.*

Lader (lēi·dəɹ). 1456. [f. as prec. + -ER[1].] One who lades; *esp.* one who freights a ship.

La-di-da (lādidā·). *slang.* 1883. [Imitative of 'swell' modes of utterance. The refrain of a comic song in 1880. Cf. LARDY-DARDY.] A derisive term for one who affects gentility; a 'swell'. Also *attrib.* or *adj.* and as *vb.*

Ladify: see LADYFY.

Lading (lēi·diŋ), *vbl. sb.* late ME. [f. LADE *v.* + -ING[1].] 1. The action of LADE *v.*; *esp.* the loading of a ship with its cargo. 2. *concr.* Freight, cargo 1526.

1. *Bill of l.* (see BILL *sb.*[3]).

Ladle (lēi·d'l), *sb.* [OE. *hlædel*, f. *hladan* LADE *v.*; see -EL[1].] 1. A large spoon with a cup-shaped bowl and long handle for lading liquids, etc. 2. *techn.* **a.** *Gunnery.* An instrument for charging with loose powder 1497. **b.** *Founding.* A pan with a handle, to hold molten metal for pouring. So in *Glass-making*, a similar instrument for conveying molten glass from the pot to the cuvette. 1483. 3. One of the float-boards of a water-wheel 1611.

1. Some stird the molten owre with ladles great SPENSER. *Comb.* **l.-board** = sense 3. Hence **La·dleful,** as much as fills a l.

Ladle (lēi·d'l), *v.* 1525. [f. prec.] *trans.* **a.** To fit up (a water-mill) with ladle-boards. **b.** To lift out with a ladle. Also with *out, up*; and *fig.* Hence **La·dler.**

b. He can l. you out Latin by the quart 1797.

Ladrone (lădrōu·n). 1745. [- Sp. *ladron* :- L. *latro, latron-* robber. See LARON.] Used *occas.* in books on Spain or Spanish America for: A highwayman. Also *attrib.*

La·d's-love. *dial.* 1825. [Cf. BOY'S LOVE.] The Southernwood (*Artemisia abrotanum*).

Lady (lēi·di), *sb.* [OE. *hlǣfdīġe*, f. *hlāf* LOAF *sb.*[1] + *-*dīġ*- knead (cf. OE. *dǣġe* kneader of bread: see DEY[1], also DOUGH); like LORD, peculiar to English. The OE. gen. *hlǣfdīġan* (ME. *ladie*) is repr. in LADY DAY (ME. *ure lefdi day* XIII, i.e. 'Our Lady's day'); so *Lady chapel* XV; also in plant-names, as *lady smock* XVI, etc.]

I. †1. The female head of a household -ME. 2. A woman who rules over subjects; the feminine corresp. to *lord.* Now *poet.* or *rhet.*, exc. in *lady of the manor.* OE. †**b.** *transf.* and *fig.* -1610. **c.** A woman who is the object of a man's devotion; a mistress, lady-love ME. 3. *spec.* The Virgin Mary. (Usu. *Our Lady* = L. *Domina Nostra*). OE. 4. A woman of superior social position; in mod. use, above a loosely-defined but not very high standard. Orig. the fem. analogue of *lord*; in mod. use, corresp. to *gentleman.* Often, merely a courteous synonym for 'woman', *esp.* in 'this lady'. See also YOUNG LADY. ME. **b.** *vocatively.* (*a*) In *sing.*, now only *poet.* or *rhet.* (*b*) In *pl.*, the usual term of address. ME. 5. A woman whose manners, habits, and sentiments are those characteristic of the higher ranks of society 1861. 6. As an honorific title (see below) ME. 7. Wife, consort. Now chiefly restricted to instances in which the formal title of 'Lady' is involved in the relationship; otherwise vulgar. ME. **b.** The female of an animal (cf. *Comb.* 1 a).

2. Great Ladie of the greatest Isle SPENSER. **b.** Rome, once the L. of the world 1601. **c.** Never a line from my l. yet! TENNYSON. 3. Phr. †*Our Lady's bands*: pregnancy. By Gods blessed Ladie (that was euer his othe) MORE. 4. What L. is that same? *L. L. L.* II. i. 192. This is giving the ladies reason, 'It is so because it is' TUCKER. Poor l. !.. But if she were a real l. she would never be an opera-singer 1886. **b.** Know you this paper, L.? SHELLEY. Phr. *L. of the lake*, the designation of a personage in the Arthurian legends, Nimue or Vivien. *L. of pleasure*, a courtesan. *L. of easy virtue*, a woman whose chastity is easily assailable. *L. of Babylon, of Rome*, abusive terms for the Roman Catholic Church, with reference to the 'scarlet woman' of the Apocalypse. *L. of the bedchamber, l.-in-waiting*, an attendant to a queen or princess. 6. (*a*) *Lady* is used as a less formal substitute for the designation of rank in speaking of a marchioness, countess, viscountess, or baroness; thus 'the Marchioness (of) A.' is spoken to, and of, as 'Lady A. (*b*) *Lady* (or more formally, *The Lady*) is prefixed to the Christian names of the daughters of dukes, marquises, and earls. (*c*) The wife of the holder of a courtesy title of *Lord* John B., etc., is known as '(The) Lady John B.' (*d*) The wife of a baronet or other knight ('Sir John C.') is commonly spoken of as 'Lady C.' *L. Mayoress*: see MAYORESS. (*e*) *Lady* is prefixed to designations of relationship, by way of respectful address or reference; Answer for yourself, l. cousin FIELDING. 7. About the end of May, Duke Lauderdale came down with his L. in great pomp BP. BURNET.

II. In transf. applications. 1. A kind of butterfly; now *painted l.* 1611. 2. The calcareous structure in the stomach of a lobster fancifully supposed to resemble the outline of a seated female figure 1653. 3. The smallest size of Welsh (and Cornish) roofing slates 1803.

Comb. 1. General: **a.** with sense 'female', as in *l. actor, clerk, doctor, farmer, friend, president*, etc.; also with names of animals, as *l.-dog, -pack*, etc. **b.** with sense 'claiming to be regarded as a lady', as in *l.-cook, -housekeeper*, etc.

2. Special (in many cases orig. uses of *lady* genitive, in sense I. 3): **L.-altar,** an altar in a Lady chapel; so †*lady-mass*, †-*priest*; **l.-clock** = LADY-BIRD; **(Our) L. eve, even,** the day before a Lady day; **l.-help,** a woman engaged to perform domestic service and treated as a lady; **-killer** *joc.*, a man who is credited with power of fascination over women; **L.-tide,** the time of the year about Lady day. **b.** In names of plants: **l.-bracken,** the brake, *Pteris aquilina*; **-fern,** an elegant fern, *Athyrium filix-femina*, etc.

3. With the genitive *lady's* (occas. *ladies*'): **ladies' gallery,** a gallery in the House of Commons reserved for ladies; **lady's maid,** a woman servant who attends to the toilet of a l.; **lady's** or **ladies' man,** a man who is devoted to female society; **ladies' school,** a school for the education of 'young ladies'. **b.** In names of plants, etc. (*Lady's* being here orig. a shortening of *Our Lady's*): **Lady's bedstraw** (see BEDSTRAW); **lady's bower,** clematis; **lady's comb,** the Shepherd's Needle, *Scandix pecten*; **lady's delight,** the violet; **(Our) Lady's hair,** (*a*) the grass *Briza media*; (*b*) *Adiantum capillus-veneris*, also called Venus' hair; **lady's thigh,** repr. Fr. *cuisse-madame*, a variety of pear; **lady's thimble,** (*a*) the Hare-bell; (*b*) the Foxglove; **lady's thumb** *U.S.*, *Polygonum persicaria.*

Lady (lēi·di), *v.* 1600. [f. LADY *sb.*] †1. *trans.* To make a lady of; to address as 'lady' -1614. 2. *intr. To l. it*: to play the lady or mistress (*rare*).

Lady-bird (lēi·diˌbəɹd). 1592. [In sense 1 f. LADY *sb.* I. 3 (genitive, as in LADY DAY).] 1. Name for the coleopterous insects of the genus *Coccinella* 1704. 2. A sweetheart, darling.

2. What Lamb: what Lady-bird *Rom. & Jul.* I. iii. 3.

Lady chapel. Orig. **Our Lady** (or **Lady's**) **chapel.** 1439. [See LADY *sb.*] A chapel dedicated to the Virgin, attached to large churches, often placed eastward of the high altar.

Lady-cow (lēi·diˌkau). 1606. [f. LADY *sb.* I. 3 (genitive).] = LADY-BIRD.

Lady day (lēi·diˌdēi). Orig. **Our Lady day.** [ME. *ure lefdi day*; see LADY *sb.*] Now only March 25th, the Feast of the Annunciation; formerly also Dec. 8th, the Conception of the Virgin, Sep. 8th, the Nativity, and Aug. 15th, the Assumption.

Lady-fish (lēi·diˌfiʃ). 1712. A name applied to many different species of fish, as *Albula vulpes, Harpe rufa, Scomberesox saurus, Sillago domina.*

Ladyfy, ladify (lēi·difəi), *v.* 1602. [f. LADY *sb.* + -FY.] *trans.* To make a lady of; to call 'Lady'.

Ladyhood (lēi·dihud). 1820. [f. LADY *sb.* + -HOOD.] 1. The condition of being a lady; the qualities pertaining to a lady. 2. Ladies collectively 1821.

Ladykin (lēi·dikin). 1853. [f. LADY *sb.* + -KIN.] A little lady; *occas.* used as a term of endearment.

Ladylike (lēi·diləik), *a.* 1586. [f. LADY *sb.* + -LIKE.] 1. Having the distinctive appearance or manner of a lady. Also *sarcastically* of men: Effeminate. 1601. 2. Befitting a lady; sometimes depreciatory, effeminately delicate or graceful.

1. He is a very lady-like poet HAZLITT. 2. You have not a very lady-like way of expressing yourself 1877. Hence **La·dylikeness.**

La·dy-love. Also pseudo-*arch.* **ladye-love.** 1733. [f. LADY *sb.*] 1. A sweetheart. 2. Love for ladies. BYRON.

Lady's cushion. Also †**Our Lady's cushion.** 1578. †**a.** The plant Thrift, *Armeria maritima.* **b.** The Mossy Saxifrage, *Saxifraga hypnoides.*

Lady's finger, lady-finger. *Pl. occas.* **ladies' fingers.** 1670. 1. *sing.* and *pl.* The plant *Anthyllis vulneraria*, the Kidney Vetch. 2. **a.** A kind of cake (cf. *finger-biscuit*). 1820. **b.** *Austral.* A kind of grape. Also, a banana. 1892. 3. *U.S.* (*a*) A variety of the potato; (*b*) One of the branchiæ of the lobster; (*c*) A variety of apple.

Lady's glove. 1538. [orig. LADY *sb.* I. 3.] The foxglove, *Digitalis purpurea.*

Ladyship (lēi·diʃip). ME. [See LADY and -SHIP.] 1. The condition of being a lady. 2. The personality of a lady ME. †3. Kindness befitting a mistress. GOWER. 4. A district governed by a lady. STEELE.

2. *Her, your l.*, a respectful substitute for *she, you*, referring to a lady; now only to one of the rank of 'Lady'. Also used *sarcastically.*

Lady's laces. 1597. The striped garden variety of *Phalaris arundinacea.*

Lady's mantle. 1548. [LADY *sb.* I. 3.] The rosaceous herb *Alchemilla vulgaris.* Also, with qualification, of other species.

Lady-smock. Also **lady's, ladies' smock.** 1588. The Cuckoo-flower, *Cardamine pratensis.* (Locally also, *Convolvulus sepium.*)

Ladie-smockes all siluer white SHAKS.

Lady's slipper. Also **ladies', lady slipper.** 1597. The orchidaceous plant *Cypripedium calceolus.* Also applied to the cultivated Calceolaria, and the Bird's-foot Trefoil.

Lady's traces, tresses. 1548. Name for orchids of the genus *Spiranthes*; also, locally, for grasses of the genus *Briza.*

Læn (lēin). [OE. *lǣn*; see LOAN *sb.*[1]] *OE. Law.* An estate held as a benefice. *Comb.*: **l.-land,** land held as 'læn'; **-right,** beneficiary right.

Læotropic (lī₁otrǫ·pik), *a.* Also *erron.* **leio-.** 1883. [f. Gr. λαιός left + τροπικός turning, f. τροπή turn; see -IC.] Turned or turning to the left; said of the whorls of a shell; opp. to *dexiotropic.*

Læt (lēᶦt). [OE. *læt* (once) = OFris. *lēt*, MDu. *lāt*, OHG. *lāʒ*; cf. Goth. *fralets* (tr. ἀπελεύθερος, *libertus*); f. Gmc. base of OE. *lǣtan* LET *v.*[1]] OE. term for a person of status intermediate between that of a freeman and a slave. *Hist.*

Lævigate, obs. erron. f. LEVIGATE.

Lævo-, levo- (lī·vo), used as comb. f. L. *lævus* (see -O-), in sense '(turning or turned) to the left', chiefly having reference to the property of causing the plane of a ray of polarized light to turn to the left: as in **a. lævo-gy·rate, -gy·rous** *adjs.*, characterized by turning the plane of polarization to the left; **-rota·tion,** rotation to the left; **b. lævo-co·mpound,** a chemical compound which causes lævo-rotation; **-glu·cose** = LÆVULOSE; etc.

Lævulin, levulin (lī·viŭlin). 1888. [f. LÆVUL(OSE + -IN[1].] *Chem.* A substance resembling dextrin, obtained from the roots of certain composite plants. Hence **Lævuli·nic,** only in *l. acid*, $C_5H_8O_3$.

Lævulose, levulose (lī·viŭlōᵘs). 1871. [f. L. *lævus* left + -ULE + -OSE[2].] *Chem.* The form of GLUCOSE which is lævo-rotatory to polarized light; fruit-sugar. Hence **Lævulosane** [+ -ANE], a substance into which l. is converted by heating.

Lafayette (lafeye·t). *U.S.* 1859. [f. General *Lafayette.*] **1.** A sciænoid fish of the Northern U.S. (*Liostomus xanthurus*). **2.** A stromateoid fish (*Stromateus triacanthus*) 1884.

Laft(e, obs. pa. t. and pa. pple. of LEAVE.

Lag (læg), *sb.*[1] and *a.* 1514. [perh. a perversion of LAST *a.* in the series *fog, seg, lag*, which is used dial. in children's games for 'first, second, last'. Cf. LAG *v.*[2]]

A. *sb.* **1.** The last or hindmost person (in a race, etc.). Now *rare* exc. in schoolboy use. †**2.** *pl.* Dregs, lees -1703. **3.** [f. the vb.] The condition of lagging 1837. **b.** *Physics.* Retardation in a current or movement of any kind; the amount of this 1855.

1. In threats the foremost, but the l. in fight DRYDEN. **3. b.** *L. of the tide*: the interval by which the tidewave falls behind the mean time in the first and third quarters of the moon. The l. of the steam valve of a steam-engine 1855.

B. *adj.* †Last, hindmost (*obs.*); belated, lagging, tardy (now *rare*) 1552.

Some tardie Cripple..That came too lagge to see him buried SHAKS. *Comb.*: **l.-end,** the fag end (now *rare*): †**-tooth,** a wisdom tooth.

Lag (læg), *sb.*[2] 1672. [prob. of Scand. origin; cf. Icel. *laggar*, Sw. *lagg* stave (*laggkärl* cask), ON. *lǫgg* rim of a barrel, f. Gmc. **laʒ-* LAY *v.*] **1.** A stave of a barrel. Now *dial.* **2.** One of the staves or laths forming the covering of a band-drum or a steam boiler or cylinder, or the upper casing of a carding machine 1847.

Comb. **l.-screw,** (*a*) a flat-headed screw used to secure lags to cylinders or drums; (*b*) U.S. = *coachscrew.*

Lag (læg), *sb.*[3] *Cant.* 1811. [f. LAG *v.*[3]] **1.** A convict under sentence of transportation or penal servitude. **2.** A term of transportation or penal servitude 1821.

Lag, *sb.*[4] *dial.* 1875. [Of unkn. origin. Cf. next.] A long, narrow, marshy meadow.

†**Lag,** *v.*[1] 1440. [Of unkn. origin; cf. DAG *v.*[1], CLAG *v.* and prec.] **1.** *trans.* To daggle, render wet or muddy. ME. only. **2.** *intr.* To become wet or muddy. BUNYAN.

Lag (læg), *v.*[2] 1530. [Goes with LAG *sb.*[1] and *a.*] **1.** *intr.* To progress too slowly; to fail to keep pace with others; to hang back, fall behind, remain in the rear. Also *fig.* **2.** *trans.* To cause to lag. *Obs.* exc. *dial.* 1570.

1. I shall not l. behinde, nor erre The way, thou leading MILT. *P. L.* x. 266. Hence **La·gger** *sb.*[1] 1523; **Lag-last** 1855.

Lag, *v.*[3] 1573. [Of unkn. origin.] †**1.** *trans.* To steal. **2. a.** To transport or send to penal servitude 1812. **b.** To catch, apprehend 1823.

Hence **La·gger** *sb.*[2] a convict undergoing or having undergone penal servitude.

Lag (læg), *v.*[4] 1887. [f. LAG *sb.*[2]] *trans.* To cover (a boiler, etc.) with wooden lags, strips of felt, etc.

Lagan (læ·găn). Also †**ligan.** 1491. [– OFr. *lagan* (whence med.L. *laganum*), perh. f. ON. *lagn-*, as in *lǫgn*, gen. *lagnar* drag-net, f. Gmc. **laʒ-* LAY *v.*] *Law.* Goods or wreckage lying on the bed of the sea.

†‖**Laga·rto.** 1577. [Sp.; see ALLIGATOR.] An alligator -1600.

Lagenian (lădʒī·niăn), *a.* 1890. [f. L. *lagena* flagon + -IAN.] *Zool.* Like or pertaining to the genus *Lagena* of *Foraminifera*, having a straight chambered shell.

Lageniform (ladʒī·nifǫɹm), *a.* 1826. [f. as prec. + -FORM.] *Zool.* and *Bot.* Shaped like a bottle or flask.

Lager beer (lā·gəɹ₁bīᵊɹ). Also simply **lager.** 1853. [– G. *lager bier* beer brewed for keeping, f. *lager* a store + *bier* beer.] A light beer, originally German.

Laggard (læ·gă̆ɹd). 1702. [f. LAG *v.*[1] + -ARD.] **A.** *adj.* Lagging, hanging back, slow. L. hounds SCOTT. A l. obedience MANNING. Hence **La·ggard-ly** *adv.*, **-ness.**

B. *sb.* One who lags behind; a lingerer, loiterer 1808.

A l. in love, and a dastard in war SCOTT.

Lagging (læ·giŋ), *vbl. sb.* 1837. [f. LAG *sb.*[2] and LAG *v.*[4] + -ING[1].] **1.** *pl.* and *coll. sing.* The strips of wood or felt with which a boiler, an arch, a wall, etc. are covered. Also the action of covering with these.

Lagging (læ·giŋ), *ppl. a.* 1593. [f. LAG *v.*[2] + -ING[2].] That lags; lingering, tardy.

Foure l. Winters, and foure wanton springs End in a word SHAKS. Hence **La·ggingly** *adv.*

†**La·gly,** *adv.* [f. LAG *a.* + -LY[2].] Lastly. FLORIO.

Lagomorph (læ·gŏmǫɹf). 1882. [f. Gr. λαγώς hare + μορφή form.] *Zool.* One of the *Lagomorpha*, a group of rodents of which the hares form one family. Hence **Lagomo·rphic** *a.*

Lagoon[1] (lăgū·n). 1612. [– It., Sp. *laguna* (partly through Fr. *lagune*) :– L. *lacuna* pool. See LACUNA.] **1.** An area of salt or brackish water separated from the sea by low sandbanks, *esp.* one of those near Venice. **2.** The lake-like stretch of water enclosed in an atoll 1769.

Comb. **l.-island,** an atoll.

Lagoon[2] (lăgū·n). *rare.* 1868. [Anglicized f. It. *lagone*, augm. of *lago* :– L. *lacus* LAKE *sb.*[2]] In Tuscany, the basin of a hot spring from which borax is obtained.

‖**Lagophthalmus** (læ:gǒfþæ·lmǒs). 1657. [mod.L. – Gr. λαγώφθαλμος adj. 'hare-eyed' (i.e. unable to close the eyes, as hares were supposed to be), f. λαγώς hare + ὀφθαλμός eye.] *Path.* A morbid condition in which the eye remains wide open. Also called ‖**Lagophtha·lmia,** and †**Lagophtha·lmy.** Hence **Lagophtha·lmic** *a.*

Lagune, var. of LAGOON[1].

Laic (lē·ik). 1491. [– late L. *laicus* – Gr. λαϊκός, f. λαός people; see -IC.] **A.** *adj.* = LAY *a.*

The prosecution [of Socrates] was truly laick 1736.

B. *sb.* One of the laity; a layman 1596.

No person, whether l. or priest 1847.

So **La·ical** *a.* **Laica·lity,** the state or condition of a layman. **La·ically** *adv.* in a laical manner.

Laicize (lē·isəiz), *v.* Also **-ise.** 1870. [f. LAIC + -IZE, perh. after Fr. *laïciser.*] *trans.* To make lay; to secularize; *esp.* to throw open (a head-mastership or other office) to laymen 1870. Hence **La:iciza·tion. La·icizer.**

Laid (lēᶦd), *ppl. a.* 1547. [pa. pple. of LAY *v.*] In senses of LAY *v.*

Laid paper, paper having a ribbed appearance, from parallel wires in the mould.

Laidly (lēᶦ·dli), *a.* *Sc.* and *arch.* ME. [north. var. of LOATHLY.] Hideous, repulsive.

Her l. wooer, whose income was better than his looks 1878.

Laigh (lēχ), *a.*, *adv.*, and *sb.* *Sc.* ME. [Sc. form of LOW *a.*] **1.** *adj.* = LOW *a.* **2.** *adv.* In a low position; to a low point; in a low tone 1583. **3.** *sb.* A hollow; a low-lying ground.

Lain, pa. pple. of LIE *v.*[1]

Lainer (lēᶦ·nəɹ). *Obs.* in literary use. ME. [– (O)Fr. *lanière*; see LANYARD.] A lace, strap, thong, lash.

Lair (lēᵊɹ), *sb.* [OE. *leġer* = OFris. *leger* situation, OS. *legar* bed (Du. *leger* bed, camp, LEAGUER *sb.*[1]), OHG. *leger* bed, camp (G. *lager*, infl. by *lage* situation), Goth. *ligrs*; f. Gmc. **leʒ-* (see LIE *v.*[1]).] †**1.** The action or fact of lying -1631. **2.** The resting place of a corpse; a grave, tomb. Now only *Sc.*, a plot in a graveyard. OE. **3.** That whereon one lies down to sleep; a bed, couch OE. **4.** A place for animals to lie down in; *esp.* for beasts of chase or of prey ME. **5.** *Agric.* Nature or kind of soil 1519.

4. Low of distant cattle..dropping down to l. CLARE.

Lair (lēᵊɹ), *v.* ME. [f. prec.] †**1.** *trans.* To prostrate. ME. only. **2. a.** *intr.* To lie (*on* a bed). **b.** Of cattle: To go to their lair. **c.** *trans.* To place in a lair. **d.** To serve as a lair for. 1607.

Lairage (lēᵊ·rėdʒ). 1866. [f. LAIR *sb.* or *v.* + -AGE.] The placing of cattle in a lair or lairs; space so occupied, or an establishment of such lairs.

Laird (lēᵊɹd). *Sc.* 1450. [Sc. form of LORD (repr. north. ME. *laverd*). For the vocalism cf. BAIRN.] A landed proprietor; orig. only one who held immediately from the king. Hence **Lai·rdship,** the condition, dignity, or estate of a l.; also, lairds as a whole 1649.

Laiser, obs. f. LEISURE.

‖**Laissez-aller** (lēᶦ·se æ·le; Fr. lęse ale). Also **laisser-aller.** 1818. [Fr.; as next + *aller* go, i.e. let (persons or things) go.] Absence of restraint; unconstrained freedom.

‖**Laissez-faire** (lēᶦ·se fēᵊɹ; Fr. lęse fęr). Also **laisser-faire.** 1825. [Fr.; *laissez* let + *faire* do, i.e. let (people) do (as they think best).] A phr. expressive of the principle of non-interference by government with the action of individuals, esp. in trade and in industrial affairs. Also *attrib.*

The 'orthodox' *laissez-faire* political economy 1887. Hence **Laissez-faireism.**

Laity (lēᶦ·ĭti). 1541. [f. LAY *a.* + -ITY; in AFr. *laité* (XIV) was used for 'lay property'.] **1.** The condition or state of a layman 1616. **2.** The body of the people not in orders as opp. to the clergy; laymen collectively 1541. **3.** Unprofessional people, as opp. to lawyers, doctors, artists, etc. 1832.

2. The clergy were now retrograding, while the l. were advancing HALLAM. **3.** Artists are wont to think the criticisms of the l. rather weak and superfluous HELPS.

†**Lake,** *sb.*[1] ME. [– ON. *leikr* play, corresp. to OHG. *leich* song, melody, Goth. *laiks* dance, f. Gmc. **laikan* play; see LAKE *v.*] **1.** Play, sport, fun. In *pl.* games, tricks. -1570. **2.** A fight, contest -1515.

Lake (lēᶦk), *sb.*[2] [Early ME. *lac* – (O)Fr. *lac* – L. *lacus* basin, tub, tank, lake, pool, pit. The present form, with long vowel, dating from late XIII, may be due to assim. to OE. *lacu* stream, or to independent adoption of L. *lacus.*] **1.** A large body of water surrounded by land; in recent use often applied to an ornamental piece of water in a park, etc. Also *transf.* and *fig.* †**2.** A pond, a pool -1609. †**3.** After L. *lacus* = a wine-vat -1657.

1. Never more Shall the l. glass her flying over it M. ARNOLD. *The Great L.* (a phrase borrowed from the N. Amer. Indians): the Atlantic Ocean. *The Great Lakes*: the five lakes Superior, Huron, Michigan, Erie, and Ontario, which form the boundary between Canada and the U.S. **2.** Ne noon so grey goos gooth in the l. CHAUCER.

attrib. and *Comb.* **1.** General: as *l.-fishery, -fowl, -shore*, etc.; *l.-trout*, etc.; *l.-reflected* adj.; *l.-diver.*

2. Special: **l.-basin,** a depression which contains or has contained, a l.; **-country** = LAKE-LAND; **-crater,** a crater which contains or has contained, a l.; **-fly,** a fly that frequents lakes; *U.S.*, an ephemerid (*Ephemera simulans*) which swarms in the Great Lakes in July; **-lawyer** *U.S.*, joc. name for the bow-fin and the burbot in allusion to their voracity; **-weed,** water-pepper (*Polygonum hydropiper*).

b. Lake poets, school, terms applied to Coleridge, Southey, and Wordsworth, who lived among the English lakes; **L. poetry,** their poetry.

c. lake-dweller, one who in prehistoric times lived in a **l.-dwelling** or **l.-habitation,** i.e. one built upon piles driven into the bed of a l.; **l.-hamlet, -settlement, -village,** a collection of such dwellings; **-man** = *lake-dweller.*

†**Lake,** *sb.*[3] ME. [prob. – Du. *laken*, corresp. to OE. *lacen* cloak, OFris. *leken*,

OS. *lakan*, OHG. *lahhan* (G. *laken* – LG.).] Fine linen –1603.

Lake (lēik), *sb.*[4] 1616. [unexpl. var. of LAC[1].] **1.** A pigment of a reddish hue, orig. obtained from lac (LAC[1]), and now from cochineal treated as in 2. **b.** *transf.* as the name of a colour 1660. **2.** A pigment obtained by the combination of some colouring matter with metallic oxide or earth. Often qualified, as *crimson*, *madder*, *yellow*, etc. *l. Indian l.*, a crimson pigment prepared from stick-lac treated with alum and alkali. 1684.

Lake (lēik), *v.* Now chiefly *dial.* [ME. *leyke*, *laike* – ON. *leika*, corresp. to OE. *lācan*, Goth. *laikan* :– Gmc. **laikan* play. Cf. LAKE *sb.*[1], LARK *v.*[2]] †**1.** *intr.* To exert oneself, leap, spring; hence, to fight –ME. **2.** To play, sport; *occas.* in amorous sense; *dial.* to take a holiday; to be out of work ME.

La·ke-land, la·keland. 1829. [f. LAKE *sb.*[2] + LAND.] The land of lakes; *spec.* the region of the English lakes, in Cumberland, Westmorland, and Lancashire.

Lakelet (lēi·klėt). 1796. [f. LAKE *sb.*[2] + -LET.] A small lake. Also *transf.*

Laker (lēi·kəɹ). 1798. [f. LAKE *sb.*[2] + -ER[1].] †**1.** A visitor to the English lakes. [A pun, with reference to LAKE *v.*] **2.** One of the Lake poets 1819.

2. The Lakers all..first despised, and then patronised 'Walter Scott' E. FITZGERALD.

Lakh: see LAC[2].

†**Lakin.** 1496. [Contr. f. LADY + -KIN.] Only in *By (our) l.*, a trivial form of *By Our Lady* –1625.

Lakke, obs. f. LACK.

Laky (lēi·ki), *a.*[1] 1611. [f. LAKE *sb.*[2] + -Y[1].] Of or pertaining to a lake; lake-like.

Laky (lēi·ki), *a.*[2] 1849. [f. LAKE *sb.*[4] + -Y[1].] Of the colour of lake; *spec.* of the blood, when the red corpuscles are acted upon by some solvent.

La-la (lā·lā·), *a.* 1785. [adj. use of *la la* interj.; see LA *int.* b.] So-so, poor.

Lallation (lælēi·ʃən). 1647. [f. L. *lallare* 'sing lalla or lullaby'; see -ATION.] †**a.** Childish utterance. **b.** An imperfect pronunciation of *r*, in which it sounds like *l*; lambdacism.

Lam (læm), *sb.* 1688. *local.* [– Fr. *lame* 'blade' in same sense. Cf. LAME *sb.*] *Weaving. pl.* Pieces of wood in a loom connected with the treadles and healds.

Lam (læm), *v.* 1595. [perh. of Scand. origin; cf. Norw., Da. *lamme* lame, paralyse, based on *lam-* of ON. *lamði* pa. t., *lamiðr* pa. pple. of *lemja* beat so as to cripple, LAME *v.*] **1.** *trans.* To beat soundly; to thrash; to whack. Now *colloq.* or *vulgar.* **2.** *intr.* Chiefly school-boy slang, as *to l. (it) into one, to l. out* 1875. Hence **La·mming** *vbl. sb.* a beating.

Lama (lā·mă). Also *erron.* **llama.** 1654. [Tibetan *blama*, the *b* being silent.] A Buddhist priest of Mongolia or Tibet.

Dalai (*dalae* or *delli*)*-l.*, title of the chief L. of Tibet; *Tesho-* or *Teshu-l.*, that of the chief L. of Mongolia. The former ranks highest, and is known to Europeans as the 'Grand Lama'. He receives almost divine honours.

Hence **La·maic,** *a.* of or pertaining to the lamas; believed or taught by the lamas. **La·maism** (also **la·mism**), the doctrine and observances inculcated by the lamas. **La·maist, La·maite,** one who professes lamaism; also *attrib.* **Lamai·stic, Lamai·tic** *adjs.*, of or pertaining to the lamaists.

Lama, erron. f. LLAMA.

Lamantin (lămæ·ntin). 1706. [– Fr. *lamantin*, *-entin*, alt. of Sp. *manaté*, perh. by assoc. with *lamenter*, with ref. to the animal's wailing cry.] The manatee.

Lamarckian (lămā·ɹkiăn). 1846. [f. *Lamarck*, French botanist and zoologist (1744–1829) + -IAN.] **A.** *adj.* Of or pertaining to Lamarck or to his theory ascribing organic evolution to inheritable modifications produced in the individual by habit, appetency, and the environment. **B.** *sb.* One who holds these views. So **Lama·rckianism, Lama·rckism,** Lamarck's doctrine of the origin of species. **Lama·rckite** = LAMARKIAN *sb.*

Lamasery (lamā·səri). 1867. [– Fr. *lamaserie* (P. E.-R. Huc, *c*1850), irreg. f. *lama* LAMA.] A Tibetan or Mongolian monastery of lamas.

Lamb (læm), *sb.* [OE. *lamb* = OFris., OS., OHG. *lamb* (Du. *lam*, G. *lamm*), ON., Goth. *lamb* (in Goth. 'sheep') :– Gmc. **lambaz.*] **1.** The young of the sheep. **2.** *fig.* **a.** A young member of a 'flock', esp. of the church OE. **b.** One who is as meek, gentle, innocent, or weak as a lamb OE. **c.** A simpleton 1668. **3.** *The Lamb*, †*God's Lamb*, *the Lamb of God*, a title of Christ. (After John 1:29, Rev. 5:6, etc.) OE. **b.** (*Her.*) *Holy Lamb* = AGNUS DEI b. 1823. **4.** *pl.* **a.** The name given to the ferocious soldiers of Col. Kirke's regiment in 1684–6, in ironical allusion to the device of the Paschal Lamb on their flag 1744. **b.** The name given to bodies of ruffians hired to commit acts of violence at elections 1844. **5.** The flesh of the lamb as food 1620. **b.** Short for LAMBSKIN 1527.

1. Ewes and their bleating Lambs MILT. *P. L.* XI. 645. As well be hanged for a sheep as a l. *Mod. Provb.* **3.** Worthy the L...for He was slain for us WATTS.

Comb.: **l.-ale,** an annual feast at lamb-shearing; **l.-florin** *Hist.*, a florin stamped with the 'Agnus Dei'; **lamb's fry,** the product of lambs' castration; **lamb's lettuce** = CORN-SALAD (*Valerianella olitoria*); **lambs' tails,** the catkins of the hazel.

Lamb (læm), *v.* 1456. [f. LAMB *sb.*] **1.** *trans.* (*pass.* only.) To bring forth; to drop (a lamb). **2.** *intr.* To bring forth a lamb; to yean 1611. **3.** Of a shepherd: To tend (ewes) at lambing-time. Also, *to l. down.* 1850.

Lamb, obs. f. LAM *v.*

†**Lamback,** *v.* 1589. [f. LAM *v.* + BACK *sb.*[1]] *trans.* To beat, thrash. Also *fig.* So **Lamba·ste** *v.* (*slang* and *dial.*) 1637.

Lambda (læ·mdă). ME. [Gr. λάμβδα (or λάβδα).] **1.** The 11th letter of the Greek alphabet, Λ, λ. **2.** *Anat.* The point of junction of the sagittal and lambdoidal sutures 1888.

L. moth, a moth marked with a l. on its wings.

Lambdacism (læ·mdăsiz'm), **labdacism** (læ·bd-). 1658. [– late L. *la(m)bdacismus* – Gr. λα(μ)βδακισμός (with interpolated κ), f. λά(μ)βδα; see -ISM.] **1.** A too frequent repetition of the letter *l* in speaking or writing. **2.** A confusion of *l* and *r* in pronunciation; lallation 1864.

Lambdoid (læ·mdoid), *a.* 1597. [– Fr. *lambdoïde* – mod.L. – Gr. λαμβδοειδής; see LAMBDA, -OID.] = next.

Lambdoidal (læmdoi·dăl), *a.* Also **lam-doidal.** 1653. [f. prec. + -AL[1].] Resembling the Gr. letter lambda (Λ) in form.

L. suture (*Anat.*), the suture connecting the two parietal bones with the occipital. *L. ridge*, the edge of the occipital bone forming the lambdoid suture.

Lambency (læ·mbĕnsi). 1817. [f. next; see -ENCY.] The state or quality of being lambent. Also *fig.*: *spec.* Brilliance and delicate play of wit or fancy 1871.

The soft l. of the streamlet RUSKIN.

Lambent (læ·mbĕnt), *a.* 1647. [– *lambent-*, pr. ppl. stem of L. *lambere* lick; see -ENT.] **1.** Of a flame (fire, light): Playing lightly upon a surface without burning it, like a tongue of fire; shining with a soft clear light and without fierce heat. **b.** Hence, of eyes, the sky, etc.: Softly radiant 1717. **c.** *fig.* Of wit, style, etc.: Playing lightly and brilliantly over its subjects 1871. **2.** In etym. sense: Licking, that licks 1706.

1. L. diffuse flashes of lightning without thunder 1834. *fig.* L. dulness played around his face DRYDEN. **b.** Eyes..l. with interior light 1867. **c.** The style so picturesque and l. DISRAELI. **La·mbently** *adv.*

Lambes, obs. f. LAMMAS.

†**La·mbitive.** 1646. [– med. L. **lambitivus*, **-um* ('linctus'), f. late L. *lambitare*, frequent. of L. *lambere* lick; see -IVE.] **A.** *adj.* Of medicines; Taken by licking up with the tongue. **B.** *sb.* A medicine so taken. –1710.

Lambkin (læ·mkin). 1579. [f. LAMB *sb.* + -KIN.] A little lamb. Also *transf.*, chiefly as a term of endearment.

Lamb-like, lamblike (læ·mləik), *a.* 1599. [f. LAMB *sb.* + -LIKE.] Like a lamb, or that of a lamb.

Lambling (læ·mliŋ). *rare.* 1591. [f. LAMB *sb.* + -LING[1].] A young or little lamb.

Lamboys (læ·mboiz). 1548. [In quot. (the source of the word) possibly a mistake for JAMBEAUX.] *Antiq.* An imitation in steel of the 'bases' or skirt, reaching from the waist to the knee; occas. found in Tudor armour.

The tasses, the l., the backpece HALL.

Lambrequin (læ·mbrėkin). 1725. [– Fr. *lambrequin* – Du. **lamperkin*, dim. of *lamper* veil; see -KIN.] **1.** A scarf or piece of stuff worn over the helmet as a covering: in *Her.* represented with one end (which is cut or jagged) pendent or floating. **2.** *U.S.* A short curtain or piece of drapery (with the lower edge scalloped or straight) placed over a door or window or suspended for ornament from a mantel-shelf 1883. **3.** *Ceramics.* Ornamentation consisting of solid colour with a lower edge of jagged or scalloped outline 1873.

Lambskin (læ·mˌskin), *sb.* Also **lamb's skin.** ME. **1.** **a.** The skin of a lamb with the wool on. **b.** The same dressed and used for clothing, for mats, etc. In *collect. sing.* fur so prepared. **2.** Leather made from the skin of lambs 1745. **3.** Woollen cloth made to resemble lambskin (Ogilvie). †**4.** *punningly.* A heavy blow. (Cf. LAM *v.*) –1622. **5.** *Mining.* Anthracite slack 1873.

1. He is wolf in lamskine hyd ME. Hence †**Lambskin** *v. trans.* to beat, to thrash.

Lamb's tongue. 1578. **1.** A name for species of plantain (tr. med.L. *arnoglossa*, Gr. ἀρνόγλωσσον), and other plants. **2.** A sort of plane with a deep narrow bit for making quirks; also, the moulding made by this 1858.

Lamb's-wool (læ·mzˌwul). 1429. **1.** The wool of lambs, used for hosiery, etc.; clothing-material made of this. Also *attrib.* **2.** A drink of hot ale mixed with the pulp of roasted apples, sugared and spiced 1592.

Lamda, -doidal: see LAMBDA, -DOIDAL.

Lame (lēim), *sb. techn.* 1586. [– (O)Fr. *lame* :– L. *lam(m)ina*, *lamna* thin plate or scale.] A thin plate, esp. of metal; a lamina; *spec.* applied to the small overlapping steel plates used in old armour.

Lame (lēim), *a.* [OE. *lama* = OFris. *lam*, *lom*, OS. *lamo* (Du. *lam*), OHG. *lam* (G. *lahm*), ON. *lami* :– Gmc. **lamaz*, orig. weak in the limbs, rel. to OHG. *luomi* dull, slack, gentle.] **1.** Crippled; weak, infirm; paralysed; unable to move. *Obs.* exc. *arch.* **b.** Crippled through injury to, or defect in, a limb, esp. in the foot or leg; limping, unable to walk OE. Also *transf.* of inanimate objects. **c.** Said of the limb; also of footsteps, etc. ME. **2.** *fig.* Maimed, halting; imperfect or defective. Said esp. of an argument, excuse, account, etc. ME. **b.** Of metrical feet, or verses composed of them: Halting, metrically defective 1600.

1. b. Another l. of a hande 1581. I was an eye unto the blynde, and a fote to the l. COVERDALE *Job* 29:15. **2.** Oh most l. and impotent conclusion SHAKS. A very l. story FREEMAN. **b.** The Prose is Fustian, and the Numbers l. DRYDEN.

Phr. *L. duck*: see DUCK *sb.*[1] 6. Hence **La·me-ly** *adv.*, **-ness.**

Lame (lēim), *v.* ME. [f. LAME *a.*; first in pa. pple. after ON. *lamiðr*; repl. OE. *lemian* = ON. *lemja* (pa. t. *lamða*, pa. pple. *lamiðr*).] *trans.* To make lame; to cripple.

Lamel (læ·mĕl). Now *rare.* 1676. [Anglicized f. next; cf. LAMIN.] = next.

‖**Lamella** (lăme·lă). Pl. **lamellæ** (lăme·lī). 1678. [L., dim. of LAMINA.] A thin plate, scale, layer, or film, esp. of bone or tissue; e.g. one of the thin plates or scales which compose some shells, one of the erect scales appended to the corollas of some flowers, etc. Hence **Lame·llar** *a.* (chiefly *scientific*), consisting of, characterized by, or arranged in lamellæ. **Lame·llarly** *adv.* in thin plates or scales.

Lamellate (læ·melĕt), *a.* 1826. [– mod.L. *lamellatus*; see LAMELLA, -ATE[2].] Furnished with or arranged in lamellæ; lamellar. Hence **Lame·llately** *adv.* **La·mellated** *a.* 1713.

Lamellibranch (lăme·libræŋk), *sb.* (*a.*) 1855. [– mod.L. *lamellibranchia* pl., f. LAMELLA + Gr. βράγχια gills.] *Zool.* A lamellibranchiate mollusc. **b.** *attrib.* or *adj.* = next 1867.

Lamellibranchiate (lămelibræ·ŋkiˌĕt), *a.*

(*sb.*) 1842. [– mod.L. *lamellibranchiatus*; see prec. and -ATE².] *Zool.* Belonging to the group *Lamellibranchiata* of molluscs (so called as having lamellate gills), including oysters, mussels, etc. 1855. **b.** *sb.* A lamellibranch.

Lamellicorn (lăme·likǭɹn). 1835. [– mod.L. *lamellicornis*, f. L. *lamella* thin plate + *cornu* horn.] *Entom.* **A.** *adj.* Belonging to the *Lamellicornes* or the group *Lamellicornia* of beetles, having antennæ characterized by a lamelliform club. **B.** *sb.* A lamellicorn beetle, as the dung-beetle, cockchafer, etc. So **Lamellico·rnate, -co·rnous** *adjs.* = A.

Lamelliferous (læmĕli·fĕrəs), *a.* 1832. [f. LAMELLA + -FEROUS.] Bearing or having lamellæ; lamellate.

Lamelliform (lăme·lifǭɹm), *a.* 1819. [f. LAMELLA + -FORM.] Having the form of a lamella or thin plate.

Lamellirostral (lămelirǫ·străl). 1835. [f. mod.L. *lamellirostris*, f. LAMELLA + L. *rostrum* beak + -AL¹.] *Ornith.* **A.** *adj.* Belonging to the family *Lamellirostres* of birds, so called as having lamellose bills. **B.** *sb.* A lamellirostral bird.

Lamellose (lăme·lōᵘs), *a.* 1752. [f. LAMELLA + -OSE¹.] = LAMELLATE.

Lament (lăme·nt), *sb.* 1591. [– L. *lamentum*, or from the verb.] **1.** An act of lamenting; a passionate expression of grief. Also *poet.* lamentation. **2.** A conventional form of mourning; an elegy; a dirge; also, the air to which a lamentation is sung or played 1698.

1. A voice of weeping heard, and loud l. MILTON.

Lament (lăme·nt), *v.* 1530. [– Fr. *lamenter* or L. *lamentari*, f. *lamentum* (prec.).] **1.** *trans.* To express or feel sorrow for or concerning; to mourn for; to bewail 1535. **2.** *intr.* To express or feel profound grief; to mourn passionately 1530. †**3.** *causative.* To distress –1704.

1. Samuel died, and all the Israelites..lamented him 1 *Sam.* 25:1. This stone laments the death of Andrea Pisano 1756. **2.** He loves not most that doth l. the most 1595. Hence **Lame·nter.** **Lame·ntingly** *adv.*

Lamentable (læ·mĕntăb'l), *a.* ME. [–(O)Fr. *lamentable* or L. *lamentabilis*, f. *lamentari*; see prec., -ABLE.] **1.** Full of or expressing sorrow; mournful, doleful. Now *rare* or *arch.* **2.** That is to be lamented; pitiable, deplorable ME. **b.** In joc. or trivial use: 'Pitiful, despicable' (J.); wretchedly bad 1699.

2. A l. change from that simplicity of manners STEELE. **b.** The result was something l. 1876. Hence **La·mentably** *adv.*

Lamentation (læmĕntē¹·ʃən). ME. [– (O)Fr. *lamentation* or L. *lamentatio*, f. *lamentat-*, pa. ppl. stem of *lamentari*; see LAMENT *v.*, -ION.] The action of lamenting; the passionate expression of grief; mourning; in weakened sense, regret. **b.** A lament ME.

They all made gret lămentasyon for his departyng LD. BERNERS. **b.** Take thou vp a l. for the princes of Israel *Ezek.* 19:1. *The Lamentations of Jeremiah*, or, shortly, *Lamentations*: a book of the O.T., ascribed to Jeremiah, and having for its subject the destruction of Jerusalem by the Chaldeans.

Lamented (lăme·ntĕd), *ppl. a.* 1611. [f. LAMENT *v.* + -ED¹.] Mourned for; bewailed; regretted.

Your late l. father 1864.

Lameter, lamiter (lē¹·mitəɹ). *Sc.* and *n. dial.* 1804. [Obscurely f. LAME *a.*] A lame person; a cripple.

‖**Lametta** (lăme·tă). 1858. [It., dim. of *lama* = LAME *sb.*] Brass, silver, or gold foil or wire.

‖**Lamia** (lē¹·miă). Pl. **-iæ, -ias.** ME. [L. *lamia* – Gr. Λαμία a fabulous monster, also, a fish of prey. Cf. Fr. *lamie.*] **1.** A fabulous monster with the body of a woman, who was said to prey upon human beings and suck children's blood. Also, a witch, she-demon. †**2.** *Ichth.* A genus of sharks –1776. **3.** *Entom.* A genus of longicorn beetles.

Lamin (læ·min). Also **lamen.** 1489. [Anglicized f. next; cf. LAMEL.] A lamina; a plate of metal used as an astrological instrument or as a charm.

‖**Lamina** (læ·mină). *Pl.* **laminæ** (læ·mini). 1656. [L. *lam(m)ina*. Cf. LAME *sb.*] A thin plate, scale, layer, or flake (of metal, etc.). **b.** *Anat.*, etc. A thin layer of bone, membrane, etc. 1706. **c.** *Geol.* The thinnest separable layer in stratified rock deposits 1794. **d.** *Bot.* (*a*) A thin plate of tissue. (*b*) The expanded portion of a leaf. (*c*) The (usually expanded) upper part of a petal. (*d*) The expanded part of the thallus or frond in algæ, etc. 1760.

Hence **La·minal, La·minar, La·minary, La·minose, La·minous** *adjs.* consisting of, arranged in, or formed into laminæ.

Laminable (læ·minăb'l), *a.* 1796. [f. LAMINATE *v.* + -ABLE.] Capable of being formed into thin plates or layers. Hence **Laminabi·lity,** l. quality.

Laminarian (læminēᵊ·riăn), *a.* 1851. [f. mod.L. *Laminaria*, name of a genus of seaweeds known as sea-tangle, f. L. *lamina*. See -ARIAN.] *L. zone*: the zone of the sea, extending from low-water mark to a depth of ninety feet, in which seaweeds of the genus *Laminaria* are found.

Laminarite (læ·minărəit). 1839. [f. as prec. + -ITE¹ 2a.] *Geol.* A fossil seaweed supposed to be allied to the genus *Laminaria*.

Laminate (læ·minĕt), *a.* 1668. [f. LAMINA + -ATE².] Having the form of or consisting of a lamina or thin plate; furnished with a lamina or laminæ.

Laminate (læ·mineⁱt), *v.* 1664. [f. LAMINA + -ATE³.] **1.** *trans.* To beat or roll (metal) into thin plates. **2.** To separate or split into layers or leaves. Also *intr.* for *refl.* 1668. **3.** To overlay with plates (of metal) 1697. **4.** To make by placing layer upon layer of material 1858.

Laminated (læ·mineⁱtĕd), *ppl. a.* 1668. [f. LAMINATE *v.* + -ED¹.] Consisting of, arranged in, or furnished with laminæ; made of a succession of layers of material.

Lamination (læminē¹·ʃən). 1676. [f. as prec.; see -ATION.] The action of laminating or condition of being laminated; also *concr.* in *pl.* laminæ.

Lamini- (læ·mini), comb. f. LAMINA, as in **Lamini·ferous** *a.*, having a structure consisting of laminæ or layers; **Laminipla·ntar** *a. Ornith.* having laminate tarsi, as the *Laminiplantares* of Sundevall's classification.

‖**Laminitis** (læminəi·tis). 1843. [f. LAMINA + -ITIS.] Inflammation of the sensitive laminæ of a horse's hoof.

La·mish, *a.* 1592. [f. LAME *a.* + -ISH¹.] Somewhat lame.

Lamm, obs. f. LAM *v.*

Lammas (læ·măs). [OE. *hlāfmæsse*, f. *hlāf* LOAF + *mæsse* MASS *sb.*¹; subseq. felt as if f. LAMB + MASS.] **1.** The 1st of August, in the early English church a harvest festival, at which loaves of bread were consecrated, made from the first ripe corn. (In Scotland, a usual quarter-day.) Also, the season of this festival. **2.** *Latter L.* (†*day*), (joc.) a day that will never come; *at Latter L.*, never. 1567.

1. Six years old last l. ADDISON.

attrib. and *Comb.*: chiefly with the sense of 'ripening at Lammas', as *L.-apple*, etc.: **L.-day,** August 1; **L.-land,** land that was private property till L. day (Aug. 1), but thereafter subject to common rights of pasturage till the spring; **L.-wheat** = *winter-wheat.*

Lammergeyer (læ·məɹgəiəɹ). 1817. [– G. *lämmergeier*, f. *lämmer*, pl. of *lamm* lamb + *geier* vulture, GEIR.] The Bearded Vulture, *Gypaetus barbatus*; it is the largest European bird of prey, and inhabits lofty mountains in Southern Europe, Asia, and Northern Africa.

Lamp (læmp), *sb.*¹ ME. [– (O)Fr. *lampe* :- late L. *lampada*, f. acc. of L. *lampas* – Gr. λαμπάς, λαμπαδ- torch, rel. to λάμπειν shine.] **1.** A vessel containing oil, which is burnt at a wick, for the purpose of illumination. Now also a vessel of glass or the like, enclosing a candle, oil, a gas-jet, or an incandescent wire. Often defined as *arc, Argand, Davy, electric, gas,* etc. *l.* **b.** Used for *torch*; (occas. with allusion to the Grecian torch-race: see LAMPADEDROMY) ME. **c.** = *safety-lamp* 1839. **2.** *transf.* **a.** *sing.* The sun, moon, a star or meteor; also, a flash (of lightning). *pl.* The stars or heavenly bodies in general. ME. **b.** *pl.* The eyes (formerly *poet.*; now *slang*) 1590. **3.** *fig.* A source or centre of light, spiritual or intellectual. Also, *l. of beauty, joy, life,* etc. 1500.

1. Darke Night strangles the trauailing Lampe SHAKS. Phr. *To smell of* (or †*taste*) *the l.* (said of a literary composition): to be manifestly the product of nocturnal or laborious study. **b.** Still the race of Hero-spirits pass the l. from hand to hand KINGSLEY. **2. a.** When they see Sun, we see the Lamps of night SIR T. HERBERT. **3.** Ages elapsed ere Homer's l. appeared COWPER. The Seven Lamps of Architecture (cf. *Exod.* 25:37, etc.) RUSKIN (*title*).

attrib. and *Comb.* **1.** General: as *l.-chimney, -shade, -wick,* etc.; *l.-bearer, -cleaner,* etc.; *l.-lighting,* adj. and sb.; *l.-lighted, -lit, -warmed* adjs., etc.

2. Special: **l.-fly,** ? a glow-worm; **-furnace,** a furnace in which a l. was used as the means of heating; **-jack** *U.S.*, a hood over a lamp chimney on the roof of a car; **-man,** (*a*) a maker of or dealer in lamps; (*b*) one who tends lamps; **-shell,** a brachiopod, esp. one of the genus *Terebratula* or family *Terebratulidæ*.

†**Lamp,** *sb.*² [perh. for *lampne – L. *lamina* (cf. LAME *sb.*).] ? A plate. CHAUCER.

Lamp (læmp), *v.* 1600. [f. LAMP *sb.*¹] **1.** *intr.* To shine. Also *fig.* 1609. **2.** *trans.* To supply with lamps 1600. **3.** *transf.* To light as with a lamp 1808.

2. To play with Luna or newe lampe the starres 1600.

Lampadedromy (læ:mpade·drŏmi). 1848. [– Gr. λαμπαδηδρομία, f. λαμπάς, λαμπαδ- torch + -δρομία running. Many Dicts. have the incorrect form *lampadrome*.] *Gr. Antiq.* A torch-race; a race (on foot or horseback) in which a lighted torch was passed from hand to hand. So ‖**La:mpadepho·ria, -dopho·ria.**

Lampadist (læ·mpădist). 1838. [– Gr. λαμπαδιστής, f. λαμπαδίζειν run a torch-race, f. λαμπάς, λαμπαδ- torch; see -IST.] *Gr. Antiq.* A competitor in a torch-race.

Lampads (læ·mpædz), *sb. pl. poet. rare.* 1796. [– Gr. λαμπάδες (Vulg. *lampades*), pl. of λαμπάς LAMP *sb.*¹] The seven 'lamps of fire' burning before the throne of God (Rev. 4:5).

Lampas (læ·mpăs), *sb.*¹ Also **lampers,** etc. 1523. [– (O)Fr. *lampas*, prob. f. dial. *lăpá* throat, *lăpé* gums, f. nasalized var. of Gmc. *lap- LAP *v.*¹] A disease of horses consisting in a swelling of the fleshy lining of the roof of the mouth behind the front teeth.

His horse..troubled with the Lampasse SHAKS.

Lampas (læ·mpăs), *sb.*² ME. [In sense 1 prob. – Du. †*lampers* (now *lamfer*); in 2 – Fr. *lampas, -asse*, which may be a different word.] †**1.** A kind of glossy crape –1559. **2.** A kind of flowered silk, orig. from China 1816.

†**La·mpate.** 1819. [f. LAMP(IC + -ATE⁴.] *Chem.* A salt of lampic acid; an aldehydate –1839.

Lamp-black (læ·mpblæ:k, læ:mpblæ·k), *sb.* 1598. A pigment consisting of almost pure, finely divided carbon; made by collecting the soot produced by burning oil or (now usually) gas. Also *attrib.* Hence **Lamp-bla·ck** *v.* to paint, smear, or coat with l.

Lamper-eel. 1824. [perh. f. *lampre*, var. of LAMPREY + EEL. Cf. LAMPREL.] **1.** = LAMPREY. **2.** *U.S.* The mutton-fish or eel-pout (*Zoarces anguillaris*) of N. America 1885.

Lampern (læ·mpəɹn). ME. [– OFr. *lampreion*, etc., dim. of *lampreie* LAMPREY. Cf. med.L. *lamprenus, lampronna* (XIV).] The river lamprey (*Petromyzon fluviatilis*).

Lampers, var. of LAMPAS *sb.*¹

†**La·mpic,** *a.* 1819. [f. LAMP *sb.*¹ + -IC.] *Chem.* In *l. acid*: an earlier name of aldehyde. (It was first prepared by burning ether in a lamp with a platinum wire twisted round the wick.) –1839.

Lamping (læ·mpiŋ), *ppl. a.* 1590. [f. LAMP *v.* + -ING².] Flashing, resplendent.

Emongst th' eternall spheres and l. sky SPENSER.

Lampion (læ·mpiən). 1848. [– Fr. *lampion* – It. *lampione*, augm. of *lampa* (– Fr. *lampe*) LAMP *sb.*¹; see -OON.] A pot or cup, often of coloured glass, containing oil with a wick, used in illuminations.

Lampless (læ·mplĕs), *a.* 1625. [f. LAMP *sb.*¹ + -LESS.] Destitute of lamps.

Your Ladies eyes are lamplesse to that vertue FLETCHER.

La·mplet. 1621. [f. LAMP *sb.*[1] + -LET.] A small lamp.

Lamplight (læ·mp,ləit). 1579. [f. LAMP *sb.*[1] + LIGHT *sb.*] The light given by a lamp or lamps.

Lamplighter (læ·mp,ləitəɹ). 1750. [f. as prec. + LIGHTER *sb.*[2]] **1.** One who lights lamps; one whose business it is to light the street lamps. **2.** *local U.S.* The calico bass 1888.

1. *Like a l.*, i.e. as quickly as the l. ran up his ladder: Skim up the rigging like a l. MARRYAT.

Lamp oil. 1581. Oil for burning in a lamp; also *fig.* nocturnal labour.

Lampoon (læmpū·n), *sb.* 1645. [– Fr. *lampon*, said to be f. *lampons* let us drink (used as a refrain), 1st pl. imper. of *lamper* gulp down, booze, nasalized form of *laper* LAP *v.*[1]; see -OON.] A virulent or scurrilous satire upon an individual.

The rancorous lampoons of Gregory Nazianzen against his sovereign DE QUINCEY. Hence **Lampoo·n** *v.* to make the subject of a l. **Lampoo·ner. Lampoo·nery,** the practice of writing lampoons; lampooning quality or spirit.

Lamp-post (læ·mp,pōᵘst). 1790. [f. LAMP *sb.*[1] + POST *sb.*[1]] A post, usu. of iron, used to support a street-lamp. In the French Revolution also for hanging a victim of popular fury.

†**Lamprel.** 1526. [f. *lampre* LAMPREY + -EL[2]. Cf. AL. *lamprilla* XIII.] Some fish like a lamprey –1688.

Lamprey (læ·mpri). ME. [– OFr. *lampreie* (mod. *lamproie*) :– med.L. *lampreda* (VIII), whence also OE. *lamprede*, OHG. *lampreta*, perh. alt. of *lampetra* (V), which is explained as f. L. *lambere* lick + *petra* stone (with allusion to the lamprey attaching itself to stones). Cf. LIMPET.] A pseudo-fish of the genus *Petromyzon*, resembling an eel in shape and in having no scales. It has a sucker-mouth, pouch-like gills, seven spiracles on each side of the head, and a fistula or opening on the top of the head.

Comb. **l.-eel**, the Sea-lamprey (*Petromyzon marinus*).

Lampro- (læ·mpro), repr. Gr. λαμπρο-, comb. f. λαμπρός bright, shining, as in **Lamprotype** [Gr. τύπος type], *Photogr.* a paper print glazed with collodion and gelatine; etc.

Lampron, -roon, etc., obs. ff. LAMPERN.

Lampyrine (læ·mpĭrin, -əin). 1842. [f. L. *lampyris* glow-worm – Gr. λαμπυρίς, f. λάμπειν shine. See -INE[1].] **A.** *adj.* Of or pertaining to the *Lampyrinæ* or fire-flies. **B.** *sb.* One of the *Lampyrinæ*.

Lanarkite (læ·nărkəit). 1835. [f. *Lanarkshire*, where first found, + -ITE[1] 2 b.] *Min.* Sulphocarbonate of lead, found in greenish-white, grey, or yellowish crystals.

Lanate (lē¹·nĕt), *a.* 1760. [– L. *lanatus*, f. *lana* wool; see -ATE[2].] *Bot.* and *Ent.* Having a woolly covering or surface. So **Lanated** *a.*

Lancashire (læ·ŋkăʃəɹ). 1834. [f. *Lancaster* name of the county town + SHIRE.] The name of an English county, used *attrib.* in *L. boiler*, a horizontal, cylindrical, internally fired boiler, having two flues; also (*ellipt.* as *sb.*) as the designation of a breed of cattle.

Lancaster (læ·ŋkæstəɹ). 1857. [f. C. W. *Lancaster*, the inventor (died 1878).] In full *L. gun, rifle*, the name of a cannon and rifle (respectively) having a slightly oval bore.

Lancasterian (læŋkæstīᵊ·riăn), *a.* Also **Lancastrian.** 1807. [f. proper name *Lancaster* + -IAN.] Of or pertaining to Joseph Lancaster (1778–1838) and the monitorial system which he established in schools.

Lancastrian (læŋkæ·striăn). 1548. [f. *Lancaster* + -IAN. Cf. YORKIST.]

A. *adj.* Pertaining to the English royal family which descended from John of Gaunt, Duke of Lancaster (died 1399), or to the party (whose emblem was the Red Rose) that supported this family in the Wars of the Roses.

B. *sb.* An adherent of the house of Lancaster; one of the Lancastrian faction in the Wars of the Roses.

Lance (lɑns), *sb.*[1] ME. [– (O)Fr. *lance* :– L. *lancea*, of alien (prob. Celtic) origin.] **1.** A weapon, consisting of a long wooden shaft and an iron or steel head, held by a horseman in charging at full speed. Also *transf.* and *fig.* **2.** A similar weapon, used for various purposes, e.g. for spearing fish 1727. **3.** = LANCET. Now *rare.* 1475. **4.** A horse-soldier armed with a lance; a lancer 1602. **b.** *Hist.* A man-at-arms with his attendant retinue. Cf. Fr. *lance fournie.* 1818. †**5.** A branch of a tree –1669. **6.** *techn.* **a.** *Carpentry.* A pointed blade, usually employed to sever the grain on each side of the intended path of a chipping-bit or router 1875. **b.** *Mil.* An instrument which conveys the charge of a piece of ordnance and forces it home into the bore 1802. **c.** *Pyrotechny.* A thin case containing compositions which burn with a white or coloured flame 1634.

1. The l. was the..peculiar weapon of the knight GIBBON. Phr. *To break a l.*: see BREAK *v.* I. 1. *L. in rest* (see REST). **2.** *Bomb-, gun-, hand-l.*, in *Whale-fishing*, an instrument for killing the whale after he has been harpooned and wearied out. **4.** A l., in other words, a belted knight, commands this party SCOTT.

Comb.: **l.-corporal** [after LANCEPESADE], one who acts as corporal, receiving pay as a private; **-fish** = LAUNCE[2]; **-head** = *lance-snake*; **-sergeant,** a corporal acting as a sergeant; **-snake,** a venomous snake of the American genus *Bothrops* (or *Craspedocephalus*), esp. *B. lanceolatus*, of the W. Indies; = FER-DE-LANCE 2.

†**Lance,** *sb.*[2] 1669. [f. LANCE *v.*] A cut, incision, slit. WORLIDGE.

Lance (lɑns), *v.* ME. [– (O)Fr. *lancer*, †*-ier*, f. *lance* LANCE *sb.*[1] Cf. LAUNCH *v.*]

I. 1. *trans.* To fling, launch, throw (a dart, also fire, etc.); to shoot out (the tongue). Now *rare* (chiefly *poet.*). **2.** *intr.* for *refl.* To spring, move quickly, rush. *Obs.* exc. *dial.* ME. †**3.** *intr.* To launch forth, push *out* –1595.

1. The torpedo-boat lances one of her horrid needles of steel 1898.

II. 1. To pierce with or as with a lance or a lancet; to cut, gash, slit. Also, To slit open. *Obs.* exc. *poet.* ME. **b.** *trans.* To wound or kill with a lance 1898. **2.** *Surg.* To make an incision in (the gums, a sore, etc.) with a lancet; to cut open. Occas. with person as object. Also, to fetch *out* or let out by lancing. 1474. Also *fig.* Also *absol.*

1. Then they Lanced his flesh with Knives BUNYAN. **2.** To l. and dress the..Tumours DE FOE.

Lancegay (lɑ·nsgē¹). *Obs.* exc. *Hist.* ME. [– OFr. *lancegaye*, perh. alt., by assoc. with *lance* LANCE *sb.*[1], of *l'archegaye* ASSAGAI.] A kind of lance.

La·nce-knight. *Hist.* 1523. [– G. *lanzknecht* (*lanz* = LANCE *sb.*[1]), perversion of *landsknecht*, f. *lands*, genitive of *land* LAND *sb.* + *knecht* in the sense of 'soldier' (see LANSQUENET). Orig. the G. word denoted the mercenary foot-soldiers belonging to the imperial territory, as dist. from the Swiss.] A mercenary foot-soldier, esp. one armed with a lance or pike.

Lancelet (lɑ·nslĕt). 1565. [f. LANCE *sb.*[1] + -LET.] †**1.** A lancet –1656. **2.** *Zool.* = AMPHIOXUS 1836.

†**La·ncely,** *a.* [f. LANCE *sb.*[1] + -LY[1].] Proper to a lance; lance-like. SIDNEY.

Lanceolar (lɑ·nsiŏlăɹ), *a.* 1810. [f. L. *lanceola* (dim. of *lancea* LANCE *sb.*[1]) + -AR[1].] = next.

Lanceolate (lɑ·nsiŏlĕt), *a.* 1760. [– late L. *lanceolatus*, f. as prec.; see -ATE[2].] Like a spear-head in shape; narrow and tapering to each end. ¶**b.** Lancet-shaped 1883.

Toadflax has linear leaves inclining to l. 1794. **b.** L. windows 1883. Hence **La·nceolately** *adv.* So **La·nceola:ted** *a.* 1752.

Lancepesade, lanceprisado (lɑns,pĕzā·d, lɑ:ns,prizā·do). *Hist.* 1578. [– Fr. †*lancepessade* (now *anspessade*) 'the meanest officer in a foot company' (COTGR.) – It. *lancia spezzata* soldier on a forlorn hope, devoted adherent, lit. broken lance, i.e. *lancia* LANCE *sb.*[1], *spezzata*, fem. pa. pple. of *spezzare* break; vars. with *-pres-*, *-pris-* (*-z-*) are due to assoc. with Sp., It. *presa* seizure, capture.] **a.** *pl.* Soldiers of a superior class not included in the ordinary companies. **b.** A non-commissioned officer of the lowest grade; a lance-corporal 1611. **c.** *transf.* 1605.

†**La·ncer**[1]. ME. [– OFr. *lanceor*, *lanceur*, f. *lancer* throw, or f. LANCE *v.* + -ER[2] 2.] **1.** One who lances or throws (a dart). ME. only. **2.** = LANCET –1688.

La·ncer[2] (lɑ·nsəɹ). 1590. [– Fr. *lancier*, f. *lance* LANCE *sb.*[1]; see -ER[2] 2. Cf. late L. *lancearius.*] **1.** A (cavalry) soldier armed with a lance; now only, one belonging to one of the regiments officially called Lancers. **2.** *pl.* A species of quadrille. Also the music for this. 1862. **3.** *attrib.* 1844.

1. The l. has sword [now carbine] and pistol besides his lance 1879.

Lancet (lɑ·nsĕt). ME. [– (O)Fr. *lancette*, dim. of *lance* LANCE *sb.*[1]; see -ET.] †**1.** ? A small lance. ME. only. **b.** In whale-fishing = LANCE *sb.*[1] 2. 1752. **2.** A surgical instrument usually with two edges and a point, used for bleeding, opening abscesses, etc. 1440. **3.** Short for *lancet arch, light, window* 1848.

2. Veins that seemed to invite the L. SHERIDAN.

Comb.: **l.-fish,** the doctor-fish (*Acanthurus*). **b.** *Arch.*, as **l. arch,** one with a pointed head like that of a l.; **l. window,** a high and narrow window terminating in a lancet arch; so, *l. Gothic, light, style.*

Lancewood (lɑ·ns,wud). 1697. [f. LANCE *sb.*[1] + WOOD *sb.*] **a.** A tough elastic wood imported chiefly from the W. Indies, used for carriage-shafts, fishing-rods, cabinet-work, etc. **b.** A tree yielding this wood; e.g. *Duguetia quitarensis* from Cuba, etc., and *Oxandra virgata* from Jamaica.

Lanch, obs. f. LAUNCH *sb.* and *v.*

Lanciform (lɑ·nsifǫɹm), *a.* 1855. [f. LANCE *sb.*[1] + -FORM.] Lance-shaped.

Lancinate (lɑ·nsinē¹t), *v. rare.* 1603. [– *lancinat-*, pa. ppl. stem of L. *lancinare* tear, rel. to *lacer*; see LACERATE and -ATE[3].] *trans.* To pierce, tear. Hence **La·ncinating** *ppl. a.*, (chiefly of pain) acute, shooting, piercing. **Lancina·tion,** cutting, lancing; *transf.* a cutting *into*; *fig.* acute agony.

Land (lænd), *sb.* [OE. *land* = OFris., OS., ON., Goth. *land*, OHG. *lant* (Du., G. *land*) :– Gmc. **landam.*] **1.** The solid portion of the earth's surface, as opp. to *sea, water.* Cf. *firm land* (see FIRM *a.*), DRY LAND. †**b.** A tract of land. Also *transf.* of ice. –1669. **2.** Ground or soil, esp. as having a particular use or particular properties. Often defined as *arable l., corn-l., plough-l., stubble l.* OE. **3.** A part of the earth's surface marked off by natural or political boundaries; a country, territory OE. **b.** *fig.* = Realm, domain OE. ¶**c.** *U.S.* Euphem. for *Lord*, in phrases *the land knows, good land!* 1849. **4.** Ground or territory as public or private property; landed property OE. **b.** *pl.* Territorial possessions OE. **c.** *Law.* (See quots.) 1628. †**5.** The country, as opp. to *the town* –1800. **6.** Expanse of country of undefined extent. *rare* exc. with qualifying word, as *down-l.*, HIGHLAND, etc. 1610. **7.** One of the strips into which a corn-field or a ploughed pasture-field is divided by water-furrows. Often taken as a measure of land-area and of length. OE. **8.** *Sc.* A building divided into flats or tenements for different households 1456. **9.** *techn.* **a.** [*transf.* from 7.] The space between the grooves of a rifle bore; also, the space between the furrows of a mill-stone 1854. **b.** In a steam-engine, the unperforated portion of the face-plate of a slide-valve 1875. **c.** The lap of the strakes in a clinker-built boat. Also called *landing* 1875.

1. Ye seken lond and see for yowre wynnynges CHAUCER. Naut. Phr. *L. to!* l. within sight. *L. ho!*: a cry of sailors when first sighting l. †*To set* (*the*) *land*: to take the bearings of l. *L. shut in*: a phrase used when another point of land hinders the sight of that which a ship came from. *How the land lies*: primarily *Naut.*; now chiefly *fig.* = what is the state of affairs. **2.** In England, the l. is rich, but coarse HUME. **3.** Phr. *The l. of Egypt, the l. of the midnight sun, the l. of the chrysanthemum*, etc. Go, view the l., euen Iericho *Josh.* 2:1. Ill fares the l., to hastening ills a prey, Where wealth accumulates, and men decay GOLDSM. *L. of promise, promised l.*: see PROMISE *sb.*, etc. *L. of cakes* (Sc.): applied to Scotland, or the Scottish Lowlands. Also HOLY LAND. **b.** *L. of the leal* (Sc.): the realm of the blessed departed, heaven. *L. of the living*: the present life. *In the l. of the living* (a Hebraism): alive. *L. of Nod*: see NOD. **4.** *Common, copyhold, debatable, demesne*, etc.: see the defining words. †*Concealed l.*: land privily held from the king by a person having no title thereto. This fellow might be in 's time a great buyer of L. *Haml.* v. i. 113. **b.** Messuages, lands, and tenements JARMAN. **c.** L. in the legall signification comprehendeth any ground, soile or earth whatsoeuer, as meadowes, pastures, woods, moores, waters, marishes, furses and heath...It legally includeth also all castles, houses, and other buildings COKE. *On Litt.* 4. L. hath also, in its legal signification, an indefinite extent, upwards as well as downwards BLACKSTONE. **6.** And sweet is all the l. about TENNYSON. **7.** Green balks and furrowed lands COWPER.

attrib. and *Comb.* **1.** General: **a.** *l.-boom, -development, -revenue, -tenure*, etc.; *l.-buyer, -monopolist, -nationalization*, etc.; *l.-surrounded* adj., etc.; *l.-army, -battle, -trade, -travel, -war*, etc. **b.** Prefixed to names of animals to indicate that they are terrestrial in their habits, and esp. to distinguish them from aquatic animals of the same name; as *l.-animal, -bird,* †*-cormorant, -fowl, -spaniel*, etc.; **l.-beetle,** a terrestrial predatory beetle, one of the group *Geadephaga;* **l. chelonian,** a tortoise; **-leech,** a leech of the genus *Hæmodipsa*, abounding in Ceylon; **-pike** = HELLBENDER 1; **-snail,** a snail of the family *Helicidæ*; **-sole,** the common red slug, *Arion rufus*; **-tortoise, -turtle,** any tortoise or turtle of terrestrial habits; †**-urchin,** the hedgehog; †**-winkle,** a snail.

2. Special: **l.-agency,** the occupation of a land-agent; **-agent,** a steward or manager of landed property; also, an agent for the sale of land; **-blink,** an atmospheric glow seen from a distance over snow-covered l. in the Arctic regions; **-boc,** *Hist.*, a charter of land; **-cast,** an orientation; **-chain,** a surveyor's chain; **-fish,** (*a*) ? a fresh-water fish; (*b*) a fish that lives on l.; hence, an unnatural creature; †**-frigate,** a strumpet; **-fyrd** *OE.* and *Hist.*, the land force; **-hunger,** keenness to acquire l.; hence **-hungry** *a.*; **-ice,** ice attached to the shore, as dist. from floe; **-lead,** a navigable opening in the ice along the shore; **-office** *U.S.* and *Colonial*, an office in which the sales of new l. are registered, warrants issued for the location of l., etc.; **-reeve,** a subordinate officer on an estate, who acts as assistant to the land-steward; **-score** *Hist.*, a division of l. [repr. OE. *landscoru*]; †**-scot,** a tax on l. formerly levied in some parishes for the maintenance of the church; **-scrip** *U.S.*, a negotiable certificate, entitling the holder to the possession of certain portions of public land: **-shark,** (*a*) one who lives by preying upon seamen when ashore; (*b*) *rarely*, a land-grabber; **-sick** *a.*, (*a*) sick for the sight of l.; (*b*) *Naut.*, (of a ship) impeded in its movements by being close to l.; **-steward,** one who manages a landed estate for the owner; **-stream,** a current in the sea due to river waters; **-swell,** the roll of the water near the shore; **-trash,** broken ice near the shore; **-valuer,** one whose profession is to value l. or landed estates; **-war,** (*a*) a war waged on l., opp. to a *naval war*; (*b*) a contention about l. or landed property; **-warrant** *U.S.*, a title to a lot of public l.; **-wash,** the wash of the tide near the shore.

Land (lænd), *v.* ME. [f. LAND *sb.*]

I. *trans.* **1.** To bring to land; to set on shore; to disembark. **2.** To bring into a specified place, e.g. on a journey; to bring into a certain position; usu. with advb. phr. Also *fig.* 1649. **b.** To set down from a vehicle 1851. **c.** *Naut.* To lower on to the deck or elsewhere by a rope or tackle 1867. **d.** *slang.* To get (a blow) home 1888. **e.** *Sporting colloq.* To bring (a horse) 'home', i.e. to the winning post. Also *intr.* to get in first, win. 1853. **f.** In uses corresponding to II. 2 c. 1918. **3.** *Angling.* To bring (a fish) to land. Also, *to l. the net.* 1613. **b.** *fig.* of a person, or a sum of money 1854. **4.** To fill or block *up* with earth; to silt up 1605.

1. He landed an Army in Apulia 1678. **2.** A jerk that nearly landed me on his [the horse's] back 1874. **e.** A shower of flukes at the latter end landed him the winner 1890.

II. *intr.* **1.** To come to land; to go ashore; to disembark ME. **2.** *lit.* and *fig.* To arrive at a place, a stage in a journey, etc.; to end *in* something 1679. **b.** To alight upon the ground, *e.g.* from a vehicle, after a jump, etc. 1693. **c.** Of aircraft: To come to earth from the air. Of a seaplane: To return to the water. 1899.

1. We..sailed into Syria, and landed at Tyre *Acts* 21: 3. **2. b.** The spot where the horse took off to where he landed is above eighteen feet 1814.

‖**Landamman(n** (la·ndaman). 1796. [Swiss G.; f. *land* LAND *sb.* + *amman(n* = G. *amtmann*, f. *amt* office + *mann* man.] In Switzerland, the chief magistrate or officer in certain cantons or certain smaller districts.

Landau (læ·ndǫ). 1743. [f. *Landau* in Germany, where first made.] A four-wheeled carriage, with a top in two parts, so that it may be closed or thrown half or entirely open. Also *l. carriage*.

Landaulet (læ:ndǫle·t). Also **-ette.** 1771. [f. prec. + -LET.] **a.** A small landau; a coupé with a folding top like a landau. **b.** A motor-car having a body the top back part of which may be opened or closed 1902. Also *demi-landau*.

La·nd-bank. 1696. A banking institution which issues notes on the security of landed property.

La·nd-breeze. 1667. A breeze blowing from land seawards.

La·nd-crab. 1638. Any species of crab that lives mostly on land but resorts to the sea for breeding.

†**Land-damn,** *v. trans.* ? To make a hell on earth for (a person). *Wint. T.* II. i. 143.

‖**Landdrost** (læ·nd,drōᵘst). Also *erron.* **landro(o)st.** 1731. [S. Afr. Du.; f. *land* LAND *sb.* + *drost* bailiff.] A kind of magistrate in S. Africa.

Landed (læ·ndėd), *a.* ME. [f. LAND *sb.* + -ED².] **1.** Possessed of land; having an estate in land. **2.** Consisting of land; consisting in the possession of land; (of revenue) derived from land 1711.

1. The old l. aristocracy ALISON. Phr. *L. interest*: interest in land as a possession; the class having such interest. **2.** A l. estate in Yorkshire TROLLOPE.

Lander (læ·ndəɹ). 1847. [f. LAND *v.* + -ER¹.] **1.** One who lands or goes ashore 1859. **2.** *Mining.* The man who lands the kibble at the mouth of the shaft 1847.

Landfall (læ·ndfǫl). 1627. **1.** *Naut.* An approach to or sighting of land, esp. for the first time on a sea-voyage. **b.** *concr.* The first land 'made' 1883. **2.** 'A sudden translation of property in land by the death of a rich man' (J.).

1. *To make a good* (or *bad*) *l.*: to meet with land in accordance with (or contrary to) one's reckoning.

La·nd-flood. ME. Overflowing of land by water from inland sources. Also *fig.*

Land-gavel (læ·ndgæ:vĕl). *Hist.* (Also †**langabull,** †**longable.**) [OE. *landgafol*, f. *land* LAND *sb.* + *gafol* GAVEL *sb.*¹] Land-tribute, land-tax; rent for land, ground-rent.

La·nd-grab:ber. 1872. One who grabs or seizes upon land, esp. in an unfair manner; *spec.* in Ireland, a man who takes a farm from which a tenant has been evicted.

Landgrave (læ·ndgrēⁱv). 1516. [– MLG. *landgrave* (= MHG. *lantgrâve*, G. *landgraf*); see LAND *sb.* and GRAVE *sb.*³] In Germany, a count having jurisdiction over a territory, and having under him several inferior counts; later, the title of certain German princes. Hence **La·ndgrave-ship** = next.

Landgraviate (lændgrēⁱ·vi,ĕt). Also **-gravate** (1761). 1656. [– med.L. *landgraviatus*, f. LANDGRAVE; see -ATE¹.] The office, jurisdiction, or province of a landgrave.

Landgravine (læ·ndgrăvīn). 1682. [– G. *landgräfin*, Du. *landgravin*.] The wife of a landgrave; a female ruler of a landgraviate.

La·ndho:lder. ME. [f. LAND *sb.* + HOLDER.] A holder, proprietor, or occupier of land; now occas. (opp. to *landowner*), a tenant holding land from a proprietor. So **La·ndhol:ding** *a.*

Landing (læ·ndiŋ), *vbl. sb.* 1440. [f. LAND *v.* + -ING¹.]

I. The action of LAND *v.* **1.** Disembarkation. **b.** Arrival at a stage or place of landing, e.g. on a staircase 1705. **c.** Coming to ground at the end of a jump 1881. **2.** *Angling.* (See LAND *v.* I. 3) late ME.; esp. in *l.-hook* 1847, *-net* 1837. **3.** *Mining.* Receiving the loaded skip at the mouth of a shaft 1860.

II. Concrete senses. **1.** A landing-place 1609. **2.** A platform at the top of a flight of stairs or between two flights of stairs 1789. **b.** Stone used for staircase landings 1837. **c.** *Mining.* A stopping-place for a cage in a shaft, etc., or for a train on an incline 1886.

2. The five bedrooms all opened on a square l. 1882.

Comb.: **l. charges, rates,** charges or fees paid on goods unloaded from a vessel; **l. floor** = sense II. 2; **l.-stage,** a platform, often a floating one, for the landing of passengers and goods from vessels; **-strake** *Boat-building*, 'the upper strake but one' (Weale); **-waiter,** a customs officer who superintends the landing of goods and examines them.

La·nding-place. 1512. **1.** A place where passengers and goods are or can be landed. **2.** = LANDING *vbl. sb.* II. 2 (now the usual word) 1611. **3.** *transf.* and *fig.* A place at which one arrives; a stopping- or resting-place 1727.

Landlady (læ·ndlēⁱdi). 1536. [f. LAND *sb.* + LADY *sb.*, after *landlord*.] **1.** 'A woman who has tenants holding from her' (J.); †*fig.* a mistress (*rare*). **2.** The mistress of an inn, lodging- or boarding-house 1654. †**b.** A gentleman's housekeeper 1618.

Land-law. [In sense 1 repr. OE. *landlagu*, f. *land* LAND *sb.* + *lagu* LAW *sb.*¹; otherwise modern.] **1.** (Also †*land's law.*) The law of a land or country; the 'law of the land'. **2.** Law, or a law, relating to land 1878.

Land league. 1880. An association of Irish tenant farmers and others, organized in 1879 under the name of 'The Irish National Land League' (and suppressed in 1881), having for its object primarily the reduction of rent, and ultimately the substitution of peasant proprietors for landlords. Hence **La·nd-leaguer, -leaguism.**

†**La·nd-leaper.** ME. [Earlier form of LAND-LOPER, with accommodation to Eng.] = LAND-LOPER –1706.

Landless (læ·ndlės), *a.* OE. [f. LAND *sb.* + -LESS.] **1.** Having no landed property. **2.** Without land 1605.

1. A list of Landlesse Resolutes *Haml.* I. i. 98. **2.** In an unknown l. sea MORRIS.

La·nd-line. 1875. **1.** The outline of the land against sky and sea. **2.** An overland telegraphic line, as opp. to a cable 1884.

Landlocked (læ·ndlǫkt), *pa. pple.* and *ppl. a.* 1622. [See LOCK *v.*] Shut in or enclosed by land; nearly surrounded by land. Also *transf.* of fish: Living in landlocked waters so as to be shut off from the sea.

The taking of..land-locked salmon 1868. Hence **La·nd-lock** *sb. rare*, †l. condition; l. country.

Land-loper, -louper (læ·ndlōᵘ:pəɹ, -lau:pəɹ). Now chiefly *Sc.* 15.. [– MDu. *landlooper*, f. *land* LAND *sb.* + *loopen* run; see LEAP *v.*] **1.** A vagabond; *fig.* †a renegade; an adventurer. †**2.** = LAND-LUBBER –1725.

1. This High-German land-louper, Dousterswivel SCOTT. Hence **La·nd-lo:ping, -lou:ping** *ppl. a.* Now *Sc.*

Landlord (læ·ndlǫɹd). ME. [OE. had *landhlāford*, but the mod. word is f. LAND *sb.* + LORD *sb.*] **1.** Orig., a lord or owner of land; in recorded use only *spec.* the person who lets land to a tenant. Hence (as correl. to *tenant*): A person of whom another person holds any tenement, whether a piece of land, a building, or part of a building. **2.** The keeper of a boarding house; an innkeeper 1674. **3.** A host (in private). Chiefly *Sc.* 1725.

1. L. of England art thou, and not King SHAKS. **3.** Persons still persist among us in calling the head of the family, or the host, the l. RAMSAY.

Landlordism (læ·ndlǫɹdiz'm). 1844. [f. prec. + -ISM.] The principles or practice of landlords; the system according to which land is owned by landlords to whom tenants pay a fixed rent (chiefly used with reference to Ireland); advocacy or practice of such a system.

†**La·ndlordry.** [f. as prec. + -RY.] Landlords as a class. BP. HALL.

La·ndlordship. 1828. [f. as prec. + -SHIP.] The position or condition of a landlord; the tenure of such a position.

Land-lubber (læ·ndlɒ:bəɹ). 1700. [f. LAND *sb.* + LUBBER.] A sailor's term of contempt for a landsman. Hence **La·ndlubberly** *a.*

Landman (læ·ndmæ̆n). [OE. *landmann*, f. *land* LAND *sb.* + MAN *sb.* Cf. LANDSMAN.] **1.** = COUNTRYMAN 1 (*rare*) –1641. **2.** A countryman, peasant (after G. *landmann*) ME. **3.** = LANDSMAN 2. Now *rare* or *Obs.* 1480. †**4.** A man having landed property –1708.

Landmark (læ·ndmāɹk). [OE. *landmearc* fem.; see LAND *sb.* and MARK *sb.*¹] **1.** The boundary of a country, estate, etc.; an object set up to mark a boundary line. Also *fig.* **2.** Any conspicuous object in the landscape, which serves as a guide (*orig.* and *esp.* to sailors in navigation); hence, any prominent object in a district, etc. 1570. **3.** (In mod. use) An object which is associated with some event or stage in a process; *esp.* an event which marks a period or turning-point in history 1859.

1. Cursed be he that remooueth his neighbours land-marke *Deut.* 27:17. **2.** Ith' midst an Altar as the Land-mark stood MILT. *P. L.* XI. 432.

La·nd-measure. 1611. †**a.** Measurement of land. **b.** Any of the denominations of measurement used in stating the area of land (e.g., the acre, the rood, etc.); also, a name for the system in current use. So **La·nd-measuring, -measurement,** the art or process of determining by measurement the area of lands, fields, farms, etc.; prop. a branch, but often used as a synonym, of land-surveying.

†**La·nd-meter.** 1582. [f. LAND *sb.* + METER *sb.*[1]] A surveyor –1693.

Landocracy (lændǫ·krăsi). *joc.* 1848. [f. LAND *sb.*; see -CRACY.] The class which owes its influence to its possession of land.

Landowner (læ·nd,ōⁿnəɹ). 1733. [f. LAND *sb.* + OWNER.] An owner or proprietor of land. Hence **La·ndownership.** So **La·nd-owning** *sb.* and *a.*

Landrail (læ·ndrēⁱl). 1766. [See RAIL *sb.*[3]; cf. *water-rail.*] The corn-crake, *Crex pratensis.*

La·nd-rat. 1596. [f. LAND *sb.* + RAT *sb.*] A rat that lives on land. †Also as a term of abuse (*Merch. V.* I. iii. 24).

Landscape (læ·ndskeⁱp). Also **landskip.** 1598. [– MDu. *lantscap*, mod. *landschap* landscape, province; see LAND *sb.*, -SHIP. Adopted from Du. as a painter's term, like *easel*; the form *landskip* (XVI) repr. the Du. pronunc. landsχəp.] **1.** A picture representing inland scenery, as dist. from a sea picture, a portrait, etc. †**b.** *spec.* A background of scenery in a portrait or figure-painting –1676. **2.** A prospect of inland scenery, such as can be taken in at a glance from one point of view; a piece of country scenery 1632. **3.** *gen.* Inland natural scenery, or its representation in painting 1602. †**4.** *transf.* and *fig.* **a.** A view *of* something –1711. **b.** A distant prospect; a vista –1698. **c.** A sketch outline; *occas.* a shadowy representation –1709. **d.** A compendium –1679. **e.** A bird's-eye view; a map –1723. **f.** The depiction of something in words –1712.

1. The landscapes exhibited on this occasion by Constable 1899. **2.** Streit mine eye hath caught new pleasures Whilst the Lantskip round it measures MILTON. **3.** The feeling for l. is often described as a modern one PATER. **4. d.** That Landskip of iniquity, that Sink of Sin, and that Compendium of baseness,..our Protector 1656.

Comb.: **l.-gardening,** the art of laying out grounds so as to produce the effect of natural scenery; so **l.-architecture** (*U.S.*); **l. marble,** a variety of marble which shows dendritic markings. Hence **La·ndscapist** (-skeⁱpist) a painter of l.

La·nd-se:rvice. 1586. Service performed on land; military, as opp. to naval, service.

La·nd-side. ME. †**1.** The shore –1533. **2.** The side towards the land; the landward side 1840. **3.** The flat side of a plough, which is turned towards the unploughed land 1765.

Landslide (læ·ndsləid). orig. *U.S.* 1856. = next. **b.** *fig.* A great majority of votes, an overwhelming victory, esp. in an election 1895.

Landslip (læ·ndslip). 1679. The sliding down of a mass of land on a mountain or cliff side; land which has so fallen. Also *fig.*

Landsman (læ·ndzmæ̆n). *Pl.* **landsmen.** OE. [f. genitive of LAND *sb.* + MAN *sb.*] †**1.** A native of a particular country –ME. **b.** One's fellow-countryman (*rare*) 1598. **2.** One who lives or works on land. **b.** *Naut.* 'The rating formerly of those on board a ship who had never been to sea' (Smyth). 1666.

La·nd-spring. 1642. A spring which comes into action through the overfulness of patches of soil. Also *fig.*

‖**Landsturm** (la·ntʃturm). 1814. [G.; lit. 'land-storm'.] In Germany, etc., a general levy in time of war; the forces so called out; the militia force consisting of those men not serving in the army or navy or in the *landwehr.*

La·nd-survey:ing. 1771. The process or art of making surveys of land. So **La·nd-survey:or.**

La·ndswoman. 1837. A woman who lives on land, or is skilled in land-work.

‖**Land-tag** (la·nt,tāχ). Also *anglicized* **land-day.** 1591. [G.] In Germany, the diet of a state; formerly, the Diet of Empire or of the German Confederation.

La·nd-tax. 1689. A tax on landed property.

La·nd-tie. 1715. [See TIE *sb.* 7.] A rod, beam, piece of masonry, etc. securing a face-wall, etc. to a bank.

La·nd-va:lue. 1880. The economic value of land, esp. as a basis of rating or taxation.

Landward (læ·ndwǭɹd), *adv.* and *a.* 1513. [f. LAND *sb.* + -WARD.] **A.** *adv.* Towards the land. 1610. **B.** *adj.* †**1.** Pertaining to the country (as opp. to town) 1513. **2.** Situated towards the land (as opp. to the sea); *occas.* belonging to the land 1845. So **La·ndwards** *adv.*

La·nd-wa:ter. 1531. **a.** Water that flows through or over land, as opp. to sea-water. **b.** A land-flood. **c.** Water free from ice along a frozen shore.

Landwehr (la·ndvēr). 1815. [G.; = 'land-defence'.] In Germany and elsewhere, that part of the organized land forces of which continuous service is required only in time of war. Also *transf.* Also *attrib.*

La·nd-wind. 1598. A wind blowing from the land seawards.

Lane (lēⁱn). [OE. *lane* = OFris. *lana, laen*, MDu. *lāne* (Du. *laan*), of unkn. origin.]

I. A narrow way between hedges or banks; a narrow road or street between houses or walls; a bye-way.

It is a long l. that has no turning *Proverb.* Phr. *Blind l.*: a cul-de-sac.

II. Transf. senses. **1.** A narrow passage or way, or something resembling this; *esp.* a channel of water in an ice-field (also called a *vein*); the course prescribed for ocean steamers ME. **2.** *slang.* The throat; chiefly in *the l., the narrow, red l.,* etc. 1542. **b.** Short for *Drury L.* (*Theatre*), *Petticoat L.,* etc. 1856.

1. The people..made a l. for hym to passe thorough 1525. A black l. of open water stopped our progress KANE.

Lane, Sc. f. LONE *a.*

Lang, Lang-: see LONG, LONG-.

Langate, obs. var. LANGUET.

Langobardic (læŋgŏbā·ɹdik), *a.* 1724. [– late L. *Langobardicus*, f. *Langobardi* the Lombards.] = LOMBARDIC.

Langrage (læ·ŋgrėdʒ). Also **langridge.** 1769. [Replacing †*langrel(l, -ill* (XVII, Capt. Smith); of unkn. origin.] Case-shot loaded with pieces of iron of irregular shape, formerly used to damage the rigging and sails of an enemy. Also *attrib.* So †**Langrel** *sb.*, in same sense 1595.

†**La·ngret.** 1550. [Of unkn. origin.] A kind of false die –1600.

Langshan (læ·ŋʃæn). 1871. [Name of a locality near Shanghai; in Chinese = 'wolf hill'.] A breed of black fowl, from China.

Langsyne (læ:ŋsəi·n), *adv.* (*sb.*) *Sc.* 1500. [prop. two words, i.e. Sc. *lang* LONG *adv.* + SYNE.] Long since, long ago. Also *sb.* esp. in *auld lang syne.*

Langteraloo, var. of LANTERLOO.

Language (læ·ŋgwėdʒ), *sb.* [ME. *langage*, later *language* – (O)Fr. *langage* (AFr. also *language*, after *langue* tongue, speech) :– Gallo-Roman **linguaticum*, f. L. *lingua* tongue, language; see -AGE.] **1.** The whole body of words and of methods of combining them used by a nation, people, or race; a 'tongue'. **b.** *transf.* Method of expression otherwise than by words 1606. **2.** *gen.* Words and the methods of combining them for the expression of thought 1599. **b.** Faculty of speech; ability to speak a foreign tongue. Now *rare.* 1526. **3.** Manner or style of expression ME. **b.** The phraseology or terms of a science, art, profession, etc., or of a class 1502. **c.** The style (of a composition); the wording (of a document, statute, etc.) 1712. **d.** *vulgar.* Short for *bad language* 1886. †**4.** The act of speaking; the use of speech –1514. †**b.** That which is said, words, talk, report –1636. **5.** A community having the same form of speech, a nation. *arch.* [A literalism of translation.] ME.

1. They haue beene at a great feast of Languages, and stolne the scraps *L.L.L.* V. i. 40. *Dead l.*: a language no longer in vernacular use. **b.** Ther's a l. in her eye, her cheeke, her lip SHAKS. *Finger l.* = DACTYLOLOGY. *L. of flowers*: a method of expressing sentiments by means of flowers. Choughs l., gabble enough, and good enough SHAKS. **2.** There is not chastitie enough in l., Without offence to vtter them SHAKS. **b.** Oh that those lips had l.! COWPER. **3.** *Bad l.*: oaths or coarse expressions. *Strong l.*: expressions indicative of excited feeling. Heretick is the best l. he affords me SIR T. BROWNE. **b.** I can drinke with any Tinker in his owne L. SHAKS. **d.** That rude eloquence which is known in Ivy Lane as 'language' BESANT. **5.** All people, nations, and languages trembled..before him *Dan.* 5:19.

Hence **La·nguage** *v. trans.* to express in l. **La·nguageless** *a.*

Languaged (læ·ŋgwėdʒd), *ppl. a.* ME. [f. prec. + -ED[2].] **1.** Skilled *in* a language or languages. Also *well l.* **b.** Provided with or having a language. Chiefly with qualifying word prefixed, as *many-, new-l.*, etc. 1605. **2.** Having (good, etc.) speech, (well or fair)-spoken. ? *Obs.* 1470. **3.** Worded 1646.

1. Well l. in the French and Italian 1593. **2.** Well-languag'd Daniel W. BROWNE.

‖**Langue** (lāṅg). ME. [Fr.] †**1.** A tongue or language –1665. **2.** A national division or branch of a religious and military Order, *e.g.* of the Hospitallers 1799.

Langued (læŋgd), *a.* 1572. [Anglicized f. Fr. *langué* (XV), f. *langue* tongue + pa. ppl. suffix *-é*; see -ATE[2], -Y[5].] *Her.* Of a charge; Represented with a tongue of a specified tincture.

†**Langue de bœuf.** ME. [Fr.; lit. 'ox tongue'.] **1.** Any of certain plants with rough leaves, now mostly called BUGLOSS, q.v. –1732. **2.** A spike or halberd, with a tongue-shaped head –1488.

‖**Languedoc** (lāṅgdok). 1664. Wine produced in the old French province of Languedoc.

Languescent (læŋgwe·sėnt), *a. rare.* 1837. [– *languescent-*, pr. ppl. stem of L. *languescere*, f. *languēre*; see LANGUISH *v.*, -ESCENT.] Growing faint or languid.

Languet (læ·ŋgwėt). Also **languette.** ME. [– OFr. *languete* (mod. *languette*), dim. of *langue* tongue; see -ETTE.] †**1.** The tongue of a balance. ME. only. †**2.** A tongue-shaped ornament; *esp.* a 'drop' of amber, jet, etc. –1548. †**3.** The latchet of a shoe –1787. **4.** Anything resembling a tongue in shape or use 1580; *spec.* in the flue-pipes of an organ, the flat plate fastened by its edge to the top of the foot, and opposite the mouth 1852. **5.** *Zool.* One of the row of little tongue-like processes along the dorsal edge of the branchial sac of an ascidian 1849.

4. At the point of a long L., or tongue of Rock HEYLIN.

Languid (læ·ŋgwid), *sb.* Also **language.** 1852. [Corruption of prec.] *Organ-building.* = LANGUET 4. (Also *attrib.*)

Languid (læ·ŋgwid), *a.* 1597. [– Fr. *languide* or L. *languidus*, f. *languēre*; see LANGUISH *v.*, -ID[1].] **1.** Faint; inert; wanting in vigour or vitality. **b.** Indisposed to physical exertion 1728. **2.** Spiritless, apathetic. Of interest, impressions: Faint, weak. 1713. **b.** Of ideas, style, language, a writer: Wanting in force, vividness, or interest 1677. **3.** Of business, etc.: Sluggish, dull 1832. **4.** Of inanimate things, physical motion, etc.: Weak, wanting in force; slow of movement. Of colour: Faint. 1646.

1. This recent illness had still left him l. 1876. *transf.* All round the coast the l. air did swoon TENNYSON. **2.** I'll hasten to my troops, And fire their l. souls with Cato's virtue ADDISON. In him dislike was a l. feeling MACAULAY. **3.** The market for exports was exceedingly l. ROGERS. **4.** The l. flames at length subside POPE. Hence **La·nguid-ly** *adv.*, **-ness.**

Languish (læ·ŋgwiʃ), *sb.* ME. [f. the vb.] **1.** The action or state of languishing. **2.** A tender look or glance 1715.

1. One desparate greefe cures with anothers l. SHAKS. **2.** A most bewitching l. carried all before it W. IRVING.

Languish (læ·ŋgwiʃ), *v.* ME. [– (O)Fr. *languiss-*, lengthened stem of *languir* :– Rom. **languire*, for L. *languēre* languish, rel. to *laxus* slack, LAX *a.*: see -ISH².] **1.** *intr.* To grow weak, faint, or feeble; to lose health or vitality; to continue in a state of feebleness and suffering. †In early use: To be sick (*of*). **b.** To live under lowering or depressing conditions 1489. **2.** To grow slack, lose vigour or intensity 1626. **3.** To droop in spirits; to pine with love or grief. Also with *for*. ME. of To put on a languid look, as an indication **b.** sentimental tenderness. Also quasi-*trans.* 1714. **4. a.** quasi-*trans.* (usu. with *out*): To pass (a period of time) in languishing 1611. †**b.** *causal.* To make to languish (*rare*) –1603.

1. What is it..the King languishes of? *Laf.* A Fistula, my Lord *All's Well* I. i. 37. He did not live, but languished through life MRS. JAMESON. **b.** To l. in poverty CARLYLE. **3.** The appetite languishes 1871. **3.** Languysshe no more, but plucke up thyne herte 1509. I l. for Relief WESLEY. **b.** When a visitor comes in, she smiles and languishes, you'd think that butter wouldn't melt in her mouth THACKERAY. Hence **La·nguisher.**

Languishment (læ·ŋgwiʃměnt). 1541. [f. prec. + -MENT.] **1.** Sickness, illness; physical weakness, pining, or suffering; *pl.* sufferings. ? *Obs.* 1596. **b.** Languor; inertness 1620. **c.** *fig.* of things 1617. **2.** Mental pain, distress, or pining; trouble, grief; depression of spirits, sadness 1591. **3.** *esp.* Amorous grief or pain 1541. **b.** Expression of sentimental emotion 1709.

3. Yet do I sometimes feel a l. For skies Italian KEATS. **b.** A look full of l. SMOLLETT.

Languor (læ·ŋgəɹ, læ·ŋgwǭɹ), *sb.* ME. [– OFr. *languor* (mod. *langueur*) – L. *languor*; reinforced later from Latin.] †**1.** Disease, sickness, illness –1609. †**2.** Sad case –1590. †**3.** Mental distress, pining, sorrow –1614. **4.** Faintness, lassitude 1656. **b.** Tenderness or softness (of mood, feeling, etc.); lassitude of spirit caused by sorrow, amorous longing, or the like 1751. **5.** Of immaterial things: Depressed condition, want of activity or interest; slackness, dullness 1748. **b.** Of the air, sky, etc.: Heaviness, oppressive stillness 1728.

3. My harts deepe l., and my soules sad teares SHAKS. **4.** Great Evacuations produce L. of Spirits 1707. **b.** Whene'er The languors of thy love-deep eyes Float on to me TENNYSON. **5.** Extreme l. now characterizes the trade for field seeds 1895. **b.** The l. of Rome—its weary pavements, its little life HAWTHORNE. So †**La·nguor** *v.* = LANGUISH *v.* (in various senses).

Languorous (læ·ŋg(w)ŏrəs), *a.* 1490. [– OFr. *langoros, langoureus*, f. *langor*; see prec., -OUS. In mod. use f. LANGUOR + -OUS.] †**1.** Distressful, sorrowful, mournful –1834. **2.** Full of, characterized by, or suggestive of languor 1821.

2. To wile the length from l. hours TENNYSON.

Laniard, var. of LANYARD.

Laniariform (læniē³·rifǭɹm), *a.* 1847. [f. LANIARY *sb.* + -FORM.] Shaped like laniary teeth.

Laniary (læ·niări). 1826. [– L. *laniarius* pertaining to a butcher, f. *lanius* butcher, f. *laniare* to tear; see -ARY¹.] **A.** *adj.* Of teeth: Adapted for tearing, canine. **B.** *sb.* A canine tooth.

Laniate (læ·niēⁱt), *v. rare.* 1721. [– *laniat-*, pa. ppl. stem of L. *laniare* tear, rend; see -ATE³.] *trans.* To tear to pieces.

Lanier, obs. f. LANNER.

Laniferous (lēⁱni·fěrəs), *a.* 1656. [f. L. *lanifer* (f. *lana* wool) + -OUS; see -FEROUS.] Wool-bearing.

Lanific (lēⁱni·fik), *a. rare.* 1693. [– L. *lanificus* (f. *lana* wool); see -FIC.] **a.** Wool-producing. **b.** Busied in spinning wool. So **Lani·fical** *a.* 1656.

†**La·nifice.** *rare.* 1626. [– Fr. †*lanifice* – L. *lanificium*, f. *lanificus*; see prec.] A spinning or weaving of wool; *concr.* wool-work –1633.

Lanigerous (lēⁱni·dʒěrəs), *a.* 1608. [f. L. *laniger* (f. *lana* wool) + -OUS; see -ATE³.] Wool-bearing; woolly.

‖**Lanista** (lăni·stă). 1834. [L.] A trainer of gladiators.

Lank (læŋk), *a.* (*sb.*) [OE. *hlanc*, f. Gmc. **χlaŋk-*, which appears in (M)HG. *lenken* bend, turn aside, OE. (*h*)*lanca* hip, loin, OHG. *lancha*; cf. FLANK, FLINCH, LINK *sb.*²] **1.** Loose from emptiness; not plump; shrunken, spare; flabby, hollow. Of grass: Long and flaccid 1634. Also *fig.* **2.** Of hair: Not wavy, straight and flat 1690. †**3.** *sb.* Leanness, scarcity, thinness –1727.

1. The bard was a l. bony figure, with short black hair BOSWELL. My Purse..is but l. D'URFEY. A poem l. and long COWPER. **2.** The extreme Puritan was at once known..by..his l. hair MACAULAY. Hence †**Lank** *v.* to make or become l. †**La·nk-ly** *adv.*, **-ness.**

Lanky (læ·ŋki), *a.* 1637. [f. LANK *a.* + -Y¹.] Awkwardly lean and long. †Also (of hair) somewhat lank. **La·nkily** *adv.*, **La·nkiness.**

Lanner (læ·nəɹ). ME. [– (O)Fr. *lanier*, perh. subst. use of *lanier* cowardly (cf. med.L. synonym *tardarius*), which was developed from a derogatory application of *lanier* weaver :– L. *lanarius* wool-merchant, f. *lana* wool; see -ER² 2.] A species of falcon, found in countries bordering on the Mediterranean, *Falco lanarius* or *F. feldeggi*. In *Falconry*, the female of this species. So **La·nneret** (†**lan(n)ard**), the male of the l.

Lanolin (læ·nŏlin). Also **lanoline.** 1882. [– G. *lanolin*, f. L. *lana* wool + *ol*(*eum* OIL + -IN¹.] *Chem.* The cholesterin-fatty matter extracted from sheep's wool, used as a basis for ointments.

Lansquenet (lɑ·nskěnet). Also **lamb-skin-it** (in sense 2 only). 1607. [– Fr. *lansquenet* – G. *landsknecht*, f. gen. of *land* LAND *sb.* + *knecht* in the sense of 'soldier'. Cf. LANCE-KNIGHT.] **1.** *Hist.* One of a class of mercenary soldiers in the German and other armies in the 16th and 17th centuries. **2.** A game at cards, of German origin 1687.

2. He..sits down to Macco and l. THACKERAY.

Lant (lænt), *sb.*¹ Now *rare.* [OE. *hland, hlond.* The form *lant* is app. n. w. dial.] Urine; chamber-lye. Hence †**Lant** *v.* to mingle with l. 1630.

Lant (lænt), *sb.*² 1620. [Cf. LAUNCE².] A fish; = LAUNCE².

Lant, *sb.*³ *dial.* 1706. Short for LANTERLOO.

Lantanium, var. of LANTHANUM.

†**La·nterloo.** 1668. [– Fr. *lantur*(*e*)*lu*, orig. the unmeaning refrain of a popular XVII song.] The older form of LOO *sb.*¹

Lantern (læ·ntəɹn), *sb.* Also **lanthorn.** ME. [– (O)Fr. *lanterne* :– L. *lanterna*, f. Gr. λαμπτήρ torch, lamp (f. λάμπειν shine; cf. LAMP *sb.*¹), after *lucerna* lamp.] **1.** A transparent case, e.g. of glass, horn, talc, enclosing and protecting a light. **b.** *spec.* = MAGIC LANTERN. Chiefly *attrib.* **c.** *transf.* and *fig.* ME. **2.** †A lighthouse –1705; the chamber at the top of a lighthouse, in which the light is placed 1796. **3.** *Arch.* An open erection, on the top of a dome or of a room, having the apertures glazed, to admit light; a similar structure for ventilation, etc. ME. **4.** A name of certain fishes; *esp.* the whiff, *Arnoglossus megastomus* 1674. **5. a.** The luminous appendage of the lantern-fly 1750. **b.** *Aristotle's Lantern*: a name for the masticating apparatus of *Echinus*, from its shape 1841. **6.** *techn.* **a.** *Calico-printing*, etc. A steam chamber in which the colours of printed fabrics are fixed 1839. **b.** *Electricity.* The part of the case of the quadrant electrometer which surrounds the mirror and suspension-fibres 1872. **c.** *Founding.* A perforated barrel to form a core upon 1839. **d.** *Mech.* A form of cog-wheel; 'a cylinder, in which the top and bottom are formed by circular plates or boards, connected by staves inserted at equal distances along their circumferences, serving as teeth' 1659.

1. By..the l. dimly burning 1816. †*L. and candle-light*: the old cry of the London bellman at night. **c.** Camden!..lanterne unto late succeeding age SPENSER.

Comb.: **l.-carrier** (also *-bearer*) = *lantern-fly*; **-fish,** the smooth sole; **-fly,** one of several species of insects of the family *Fulgoridæ*; **-jaws,** long thin jaws, giving a hollow appearance to the cheek; hence **-jawed** *a.*; **-light,** (*a*) the light from a l.; (*b*) a light (i.e. a glazed frame or sash) in the side of a l. (sense 3); (*c*) an arrangement for giving light through the roof of an apartment; **-pinion** = *lantern-wheel*; **-shell,** the bivalve genus *Anatina*, with a translucent shell; **-wheel** = sense 6 d.

Lantern (læ·ntəɹn), *v.* Also **lanthorn.** 1789. [f. the sb.] **1. a.** *trans.* To enclose as in a lantern. **b.** To furnish, or light, with a lantern. **2.** To put to death by hanging on a lamp-post. (= Fr. *lanterner.*) 1855.

Lanthanite (læ·nþănəit). 1849. [f. next + -ITE¹ 2 b.] *Min.* Hydrous carbonate of lanthanum, found in white tabular crystals.

Lanthanum (læ·nþănŏm). Also **lant(h)a-nium.** 1841. [f. Gr. λανθάνειν lie hid.] *Chem.* A rare element belonging to the group of earth metals, found in certain rare minerals, e.g. cerite; so called because it had lain concealed in oxide of cerium, etc. Symbol La.

Lanthopine (læ·nþŏpīn). 1880. [f. Gr. λανθάνειν (see prec.) + OP(IUM + -INE⁵.] *Chem.* An alkaloid found in opium.

Lanthorn, var. of LANTERN.

Lanuginous (lăniū·dʒinəs), *a.* 1575. [f. L. *lanuginosus*, f. *lanugo* down, f. *lana* wool; see -OUS.] Covered with down or fine soft hair; of the nature of down; downy. So **Lanu·ginose** 1693.

‖**Lanugo** (lăniū·go). 1677. [L.; see prec.] Fine soft hair or down, or a surface resembling this; *spec.* that covering the human fœtus.

Lanyard (læ·nyăɹd). 1425. [– (O)Fr. *lanière*, earlier *lasniere*, f. *lasne*, perh. due to crossing of *laz* LACE *sb.* and *nasle* – Gmc. **nastila-* (G. *nestel* string, lace); adopted earlier as LAINER. The final syll. was assoc. with YARD *sb.*²] **1.** = LAINER. Now *dial.* **2.** *Naut.* 'A short piece of rope or line made fast to anything to secure it, or as a handle' (Smyth). Used: **a.** to secure the shrouds and stays 1626; **b.** for firing a gun 1825; **c.** for various other purposes 1669. **d.** The material of lanyards 1862.

2. c. Four ladders (each of which to have a l. four fathoms long) NELSON.

Lanzknecht (Ger.): see LANSQUENET.

Laodicean (lēⁱ:ŏdisī·ăn). 1564. [f. L. *Laodicea* (– Gr. Λαοδίκεια) a city of Asia Minor + -AN. See -EAN.]

A. *adj.* **a.** Of or pertaining to Laodicea. **b.** 'Lukewarm, neither cold nor hot' (*Rev.* 3:16), *esp.* in religion, politics, etc. 1633.

b. This L. cant of tolerance MRS. H. WARD.

B. *sb.* **a.** An inhabitant of Laodicea 1611. **b.** One who is lukewarm in religion, politics, etc. 1625 (BACON). Hence **Laodice·anism,** indifference.

Lap (læp), *sb.*¹ [OE. *læppa*, corresp. to OFris. *lappa*, OS. *lappo*, OHG. *lappa*, with *pp* for *pf* from LG. (G. *lappen*); cf. ON. *leppr* clout, rag, lock of hair.] †**1.** A part (of a garment or the like) hanging down or projecting; a flap, lappet. In later use chiefly, a piece that hangs down at the bottom of a garment, one of the skirts of a coat, a portion of the skirt of a robe. Hence *pl.* (*colloq.*) a tail-coat. **2. a.** Of the ear, liver, lungs: = LOBE. *Obs.* exc. in *ear-lap*. OE. †**b.** A fold of flesh or skin –1615. †**3.** A cloth, clout –14.. **4.** The 'lap' (sense 1) used as a receptacle. †**a.** The fold of a robe over the breast; hence, the bosom –1643. **b.** The front portion of a skirt when held up ME. **5.** The front part from waist to knees of a person seated, as, with its covering garments, the place *in* or *on* which a child is nursed, or an object held ME. **b.** *transf.* A hollow among hills 1745.

1. When David had cut off the l. of Saul's Garment HALES. **4. b.** Girls with laps full of flowers LYTTON. **5.** A Saylors Wife had Chestnuts in her Lappe SHAKS. She lays me upon my Face in her L. STEELE. **b.** A little valley, or rather l. of land, among high hills W. IRVING. Phr. *In fortune's, pleasure's l.*: *in the l. of* (luxury, etc.): *in the l. of Providence, the future* (all *fig.*). †*To fall into the l.* or *laps of*: to come within the reach, or into the power, of. (*Lapse* is occas. written for *laps*, by confusion with LAPSE *sb.*) *Comb.* **l.-board,** a board to lay on the l., as a substitute for a table.

Lap (læp), *sb.*² ME. [f. LAP *v.*¹] **1.** Something that is lapped; *esp.* liquid food for dogs. Also, *slang* and *dial.*, any weak beverage. 1567. **b.** *slang.* Liquor in general 1618. **2.** The action or an act of lapping; also, so much as may be taken up thus. Also *fig.* ME. **3.** A sound resembling that of lapping; e.g. that of wavelets on the beach 1884.

Lap (læp), *sb.*³ 1673. [f. LAP *v.*²] †**1.** ? A bundle. **2.** The amount by which one thing overlaps another; hence *concr.* the overlapping part 1800. **b.** *Steam-engine.* The distance traversed by a slide-valve beyond what is needed to close the passage of steam to or from the cylinder 1869. **c.** *U.S.* Any portion of a railroad track used in common by the trains of more than one system 1895. **3.** *Euchre.* In a series of games: Counting upon the score of the ensuing game all the points made over and above the five of which the game consists 1886. **4.** A layer or sheet (usually wound upon a bobbin or roller) into which cotton, wool, or flax is formed in certain stages of its manufacture 1825. **5.** The act of encircling, or the length of rope required to encircle, a drum or wheel. Also, enough thread, etc., to go once round something. 1867. **b.** *Racing.* One circuit of the track 1861.

2. The hand-made cigarette..having a smaller 'l.' 1897. *Half-l.*: an arrangement, consisting in cutting away half the thickness of the two ends of rails, shafts, etc., to be joined, and fitting them together 1816. **5. b.** A running track, three laps to the mile 1884.

attrib. and *Comb.*, as (sense 2) *l.-dovetail, -jointed; l.-weld* sb. and vb. Also **l.-joint** = *half-l.* (see above).

Lap (læp), *sb.*⁴ 1812. [perh. a use of prec., as the original tool may have been a 'lap' or wrapping of cloth or leather.] A rotating disc of soft metal or wood, used to hold polishing powder in cutting or polishing gems or metal. **b.** *Gun-making.* An iron rod round which is secured a leaden plug of the exact size of the tube of the gun barrel to be polished 1881.

Lap (læp), *v.*¹ [OE. *lapian*, corresp. to MLG., MDu. *lapen*, OHG. *laffan*, f. Gmc. **lap-*, rel. to L. *lambere* lick, Gr. λάπτειν lick, lap. OE. *lapian* is repr. directly by ME., dial. *lape*, Sc. *laip*, the present *lap* being prob. due to (O)Fr. *laper*.] **1.** *intr.* To take up liquid with the tongue. **2.** *trans.* Of animals, *rarely* of human beings: To take up (liquid, *rarely* food) with the tongue; to drink greedily up. Also with *up*. **3.** *intr.* Of water: To move with a sound like that made in lapping 1823. **4.** *trans.* To beat upon (the shore, etc.) with a lapping sound 1854.

1. Vncouer Dogges, and l. *Timon* III. vi. 95. **2.** They'l take suggestion, as a Cat laps milke SHAKS. **3.** I heard the water lapping on the crag TENNYSON.

Lap (læp), *v.*² [ME., first in †*bilappe*, †*bileppe*, f. *bi-* BE- + *lappe*, **leppe* LAP *sb.*¹] **1.** *trans.* To coil, fold, wrap (a garment, etc.). Also *intr.* for *refl.* (now *dial.*). **2.** To fold, fold *up*, *together*; to roll *up* in successive layers. Const. *into*. Now only *dial.* ME. **3.** To enfold in a wrap or wraps, to enwrap, swathe; hence, to clothe, to bind up, tie round ME. Also *transf.* †**b.** To fold (*in the arms*); to embrace –1513. **4.** †**a.** To involve; to imply, include; to implicate; to wrap *up* in a disguise –1677. **b.** Of conditions, etc.: To enfold, surround, *esp.* with soothing, stupefying, or seductive effect. Often with *round*. ME. **5.** To enfold caressingly; to nurse, fondle; to surround with care. Now chiefly *pass.*, to be nursed *in* luxury, etc. ME. **6.** *trans.* **a.** To lay (something) *on*, *over* (another thing) so as partly to cover it. **b.** Of a slide-valve: To pass over and close (a port). Also, to cause (a slide-valve) to overlap the port. **c.** ? *U.S.* Of a boat, in racing: To come partly alongside (another). 1607. **7.** *Racing. trans.* To get one or more laps ahead of (a competitor) 1890. **b.** To travel over (a distance) as a lap 1923. **8.** [Prop. f. LAP *sb.*³ sense 4.] *trans.* To reduce raw cotton to a lap 1851.

3. The good old Prelate lies lapp'd in lead SCOTT. Phr. *To l. on*: to fix on with a lapping of thread or the like. **4. b.** And ever against eating Cares, L. me in soft Lydian Aires, Married to immortal verse MILTON. **5.** Lapped in idle luxury HAZLITT. Phr. *To l. into* (something): to project *into* (something). *To l. over* (with *over* adv.): to project beyond something else, forming a lap or flap; *fig.* to extend beyond some limit. *Comb.* **l.-work**, work in which one part is interchangeably lapped over another.

Lap (læp), *v.*³ 1881. [f. LAP *sb.*⁴] *trans.* To polish (steel, etc.) with a lap (see LAP *sb.*⁴).

Laparo- (læ·păro), rarely bef. a vowel **lapar-**, comb. f. Gr. λαπάρᾱ flank, f. λαπαρός soft, in terms of *Anat.*, *Surg.*, etc. **Lapare·ctomy** [Gr. ἐκτομ-, ἐκτέμνειν], an excision of a portion of the intestine at the side. **Laparo·tomy** [Gr. -τομία cutting], a cutting through the abdominal walls into the cavity of the abdomen.

La·p-dog. 1645. [f. LAP *sb.*¹ 5 + DOG.] A small dog, such as may lie in a lady's lap.

Lapel (lăpe·l). Also †**lapell(e, lappel.** 1789. [f. LAP *sb.*¹ + -EL.] That part of the front of a coat which is folded over towards either shoulder. Hence **Lape·lled** *a.* furnished with a l.; folded over so as to form a l. 1751.

Lapful (læ·pful). 1611. [f. LAP *sb.*¹ + -FUL.] So much as will fill a person's lap.

Lapicide (læ·pisəid). 1656. [– L. *lapicida* for *lapidicida*, f. *lapis*, *lapid-* stone; see -CIDE 1.] One who cuts stones, or inscriptions on stone.

Lapidarian (læpidēᵊ·riăn), *a. rare.* 1683. [f. L. *lapidarius* (see next) + -AN.] **a.** Versed in the knowledge of stones. **b.** Executed in, or inscribed on, stone.

Lapidary (læ·pidări). ME. [– L. *lapidarius* adj., in late L. as sb., = stonecutter, f. *lapis*, *lapid-* stone; see -ARY¹. With A 2. cf. med.L. *lapidarium* book of gems XIII.]

A. *sb.* **1. a.** An artificer who cuts, polishes, or engraves precious stones ME. †**b.** One skilled in gems or precious stones; a connoisseur of lapidary work –1796. **2.** A treatise on (precious) stones. *Obs.* exc. *Hist.* ME. †**3.** *collect.* Precious stones, jewellery –1609.

Comb. **lapidary('s-mill, -wheel,** the grinding and polishing apparatus of the l.

B. *adj.* **1. a.** Engraved on stone. **b.** Of style, etc.: Characteristic of or suitable for monumental inscriptions. 1724. **2.** Concerned with stones. *rare* exc. in *l. bee.* 1831.

1. In l. inscriptions a man is not upon oath JOHNSON. **2.** The l. red-tipped bees, that built.. in old dry stone walls H. MILLER.

Lapidate (læ·pidēⁱt), *v.* 1623. [– *lapidat-*, pa. ppl. stem of L. *lapidare* in same sense, f. *lapis*, *lapid-* stone; see -ATE³.] *trans.* To throw stones at; also, to stone to death. So **Lapida·tion,** stoning to death; pelting with stones 1611.

Lapideous (lăpi·dĭəs), *a.* Now *rare.* 1646. [f. L. *lapideus* (f. *lapis*, *lapid-* stone) + -OUS.] **1.** Of the nature of stone, stony. †**2.** Consisting of or inscribed on stone, as *l. records*. G. CHALMERS.

Lapidescent (læpide·sĕnt), *a.* (*sb.*) ? *Obs.* 1644. [– *lapidescent-*, pa. ppl. stem of L. *lapidescere* become stony, f. as prec.; see -ESCENT.] That is in process of becoming stone; having a tendency to solidify into stone. Said chiefly of petrifying waters and the salts dissolved or suspended in them. *sb.* [sc. *substance*]. Hence **Lapide·scence,** l. condition; petrifaction. **Lapide·scency.**

Lapidific, †-al (læpidi·fik, -ăl), *a.* 1646. [– Fr. *lapidifique* or med.L. **lapidificus*, f. *lapidificare*; see next, -ICAL.] Adapted to or concerned with the making of stones.

Lapidify (lăpi·difəi), *v.* 1657. [– Fr. *lapidifier* or med.L. *lapidificare*, f. L. *lapis*, *lapid-* stone; see -FY.] To †become or make into stone. Hence **Lapi:difica·tion** 1626.

†**La·pidist.** *rare.* 1647. [f. L. *lapis*, *lapid-* + -IST.] = LAPIDARY *sb.* 1 a or b –1691.

Lapidose (læ·pidōᵘs), *a.* ME. [– L. *lapidosus*, f. as prec; see -OSE¹.] **1.** Abounding in stones; of stony nature. **2.** Growing in stony ground 1866.

‖**Lapilli** (lăpi·ləi), *pl.* 1747. [L., pl. of *lapillus*, dim. of *lapis*. In the spec. sense orig. pl. of It. *lapillo*.] Small stones or pebbles; now only *spec.* of the fragments of stone ejected from volcanoes.

‖**Lapis** (læ·pis). 1641. The Latin word for 'stone'. **1.** Used in: **l. Armenus,** Armenian stone, a blue carbonate of copper; **l. calaminaris,** calamine; **l. causticus,** caustic potash; **l. infernalis,** lunar caustic; **l. judaicus** = JEW'S STONE 1; **l. ollaris,** potstone, or soapstone; etc. **2.** Short for: **a.** med.L. *lapis philosophicus*, philosophers' stone; **b.** LAPIS LAZULI. 1666.

‖**Lapis lazuli, lapis-lazuli** (læ·pis læ·ziŭləi). Also shortened LAZULI. ME. [f. L. *lapis* stone + *lazuli*, gen. of med.L. *lazulum*, varying with *lazur*, *lazurius*, f. Pers. *lāžhward* AZURE.] *Min.* A complex silicate containing sulphur, of bright blue colour, used as a pigment (see ULTRAMARINE). Also, the colour of this.

Some lump, ah God, of *lapis lazuli*,..Blue as a vein o'er the Madonna's breast BROWNING.

Lapland (læ·plænd). 1590. [– Sw. *Lappland*; see LAPP and LAND.] The most northerly portion of the Scandinavian peninsula; formerly, the fabled home of witches and magicians, who had power to send winds and tempests. Often *attrib.* †**b.** A native of this region; a Lapland witch –1635. Hence **La·plander,** an inhabitant of L.; a Lapp. So **Lapla·ndian, -ic, La·plandish** *adjs.* of or pertaining to L., its people, or their language.

†**La·pling.** 1627. [f. LAP *sb.*¹ + -LING¹.] One who loves to lie on a (lady's) lap –1658.

Lapp (læp). 1846. [– Sw. *Lapp*, perh. orig. a term of contempt (cf. MHG. *lappe* simpleton), in med.L. *Lappo, Lappon-*.]

A. *sb.* One of a Mongoloid race (called by themselves *Sabme*), of dwarfish stature, inhabiting the north of Scandinavia.

B. *adj.* Pertaining to this race, Lappish; also *absol.* the Lappish language.

Lappaceous (læpēⁱ·ʃəs), *a.* 1707. [f. L. *lappaceus* (f. *lappa* a bur) + -OUS.] *Bot.* Of, pertaining to, or resembling a bur.

Lapper¹ (læ·pəɹ). 1606. [f. LAP *v.*¹ + -ER¹.] One who laps, or takes up (liquid) with the tongue.

Lapper² (læ·pəɹ). 1732. [f. LAP *v.*² + -ER¹.] One who laps or folds up (linen).

Lapper³ (læ·pəɹ). 1877. [f. LAP *v.*³ + -ER¹.] One who uses a lap or lapidary's wheel.

Lappet (læ·pėt), *sb.* 1573. [f. LAP *sb.*¹ + -ET.] **1.** A loose or overlapping part of a garment; a flap, fold. **b.** *gen.* A part of anything that hangs loose 1677. **2. a.** A fold or pendent piece of flesh, skin, membrane, etc. 1605. **b.** A lobe of the ear, liver, lungs, etc. 1609. **3.** The flap or skirt (of a coat). Also, the lapel. 1726. **4.** One of the streamers attached to a lady's head-dress, or any appendage to headgear. In clerical attire, = BAND *sb.*² 4 b. 1720. **5.** Short for *lappet-moth* 1857.

4. A sealskin cap with ear lappets 1869.

Comb.: **l.-end,** the free end of a l. of lace, etc., often highly ornamented; **-moth,** one of several species of bombycid moths; **-weaving,** a method of weaving by which figures are produced on the surface of cloth by means of needles placed in a sliding frame; so **l.-muslin.**

Hence **La·ppet** *v. trans.* to cover with, or as with a l. 1864. **La·ppeted** *ppl. a.* wearing lappets; (of a head-dress) provided with lappets 1797.

Lappic (læ·pik), *a.* (*sb.*) [f. LAPP + -IC.] Pertaining to the Lapps. Also *absol.* the L. language.

Lapping (læ·piŋ), *vbl. sb.* ME. [f. LAP *v.*² + -ING¹.] †**1.** The action of LAP *v.*² Also *concr.* A wrapping; wraps, trappings. **2.** The process of forming into laps; *attrib.* in *l. cylinder, machine* 1825.

Lappish (læ·piʃ). 1875. [f. LAPP + -ISH¹.] **A.** *adj.* Of or pertaining to the Lapps or their language. **B.** *sb.* Their language.

Lapponian (læpōᵘ·niăn). 1607. [f. med.L. *Lappo, Lappon-* (see LAPP) + -IAN.] **A.** *adj.* = LAPPISH *a.* **B.** *sb.* A Lapp.

Lapsable, lapsible (læ·psăb'l, -ib'l), *a.* 1678. [f. LAPSE *v.* + -ABLE, -IBLE.] **1.** Liable to pass or change; liable to err or fall. Const. *into*. ? *Obs.* **2.** *Law.* Liable to lapse 1751. Hence **Lapsabi·lity, -ibi·lity** 1661.

Lapse (læps), *sb.* 1450. [– L. *lapsus*, f. *laps-*, pa. ppl. stem of *labi* glide, slip, fall, rel. to *labare* slip, *labor* LABOUR. Cf. Fr. *laps* (*de temps*).] †**1.** Utterance (of words). **2.** A slip of memory, tongue, pen, or †understanding; a slight error 1526. **3.** A weak or incautious falling from rectitude; a moral slip 1582. †**b.** *Theol.* The 'Fall' (of Adam) –1774. **c.** A lapsing *from* the faith, or *into* heresy; a deviation *from* one's rule of action 1660. **4.** A decline to a lower state or degree 1533. **5. a.** *Law.* The termination of a right or privilege through neglect to exercise it within the limited time, or through failure of some contingency 1570. **b.** *gen.* A falling into disuse 1838. **c.** A falling into ruin (*rare*) 1605. **6.** A gliding, flow (of water); a gliding flood. Also *occas.* a gentle downward motion. 1667. **b.** The gliding away (of life, time, etc.); a period elapsed 1758. **c.** *L. rate*, the rate of fall of temperature with height 1928.

3. The severe training which he had undergone made him less charitable for the lapses of others PRESCOTT. **c.** It is from their lapses and deviations from their principle, that alone we have any thing to hope BURKE. **5. a.** By the l. of some annuities on lives not so prolonged as her own, she found herself straitened H. WALPOLE. **6.** Sunnie Plaines, And liquid L. of murmuring Streams MILT. *P. L.* VIII. 263. **b.** Thou hast not felt the l. of hours M. ARNOLD.

Lapse (læps), *v.* 1611. [Partly – L. *lapsare* (f. *laps-*; see prec.), partly f. the *sb.*]

I. *intr.* **1.** To fall away by slow degrees; to sink gradually through want of effort or vigour. Also with *away, back*. Const. *from, into.* 1641. †**b.** *simply.* To fall into error, heresy, or sin –1667. †**2.** To fall into decay –1654. **3.** *Law.* Of a benefice, an estate, a right, etc.: To fall in, pass away, revert (*to* some one) by nonfulfilment of conditions or failure of persons entitled to possession. Of a devise or grant: To become void. 1726. **4.** To glide, pass with an effortless motion; to descend gradually, sink 1798. **b.** Of a stream: To glide, flow. Also with *along.* Occas. of a person, a vessel: To float, glide gently over the water. 1832. **c.** Of time: To glide past, pass *away* 1702.

1. Should the British constitution ultimately l. into a despotism MALTHUS. **b.** To l. in Fulnesse Is sorer, then to lye for Neede *Cymb.* III. vi. 12. **3.** The income..lapses and goes to the..next of kin 1884. **4. b.** I saw the river lapsing calmly onward HAWTHORNE.

II. *trans.* (causative). †**1.** To cause to slip or fall, to draw down. Const. *into.* –1681. †**2.** To let slip (time, a term); to let pass unused –1726. †**3.** To allow (a right) to lapse; to suffer the lapse of (a living); to forfeit, lose –1697. ¶**4.** ? Assoc. w. *Lapse* = *laps* pl. (LAP *sb.*[1] Phr.): ? To pounce upon as an offender 1601.

4. For which if I be lapsed in this place I shall pay deere *Twel. N.* III. iii. 36.

Lapsed (læpst), *ppl. a.* 1617. [f. LAPSE *v.* + -ED[1].] **1.** That has glided away, dropped out of use, disappeared, or fallen into decay 1667. **2.** Of a person: Fallen into a lower grade or condition; esp. fallen into sin, or from the faith; applied *Hist.* to Christians who denied the faith during persecution. Also *absol.* 1638. **3.** Said of a fief, devise, etc., the right to which has passed from the original holder, devisee, etc. 1617.

1. Once more I will renew His l. powers, though forfeit MILT. *P. L.* III. 176.

Lapser (læ·psəɹ). 1695. [f. LAPSE *v.* + -ER[1].] One who lapses (†esp. *from* the Christian faith).

Lapsible, etc.: see LAPSABLE, etc.

Lapsided, var. of LOP-SIDED.

La·pstone. 1778. [f. LAP *sb.*[1] + STONE.] A stone that shoemakers lay in their laps to beat leather upon.

La·p-streak. 1771. [f. LAP *sb.*[3] or *v.*[2] + *streak*, var. of STRAKE *sb.*[1]] A boat in which each strake overlaps the one below; a clinker-built boat.

‖**Lapsus** (læ·psŏs). 1667. [L.; see LAPSE *sb.*] A lapse, slip, or error. Chiefly in **l. linguæ,** a slip of the tongue, and **l. calami,** a slip of the pen.

Laputan (lăpiū·tăn). In Swift **Laputian.** 1726. [f. *Laputa*, the flying island in *Gulliver's Travels*, whose inhabitants were addicted to visionary projects; see -AN, -IAN.]

A. *adj.* Of or pertaining to Laputa; hence, chimerical, visionary, absurd.

B. *sb.* An inhabitant of Laputa.

Swift's idea of extracting sunbeams out of cucumbers, which he attributes to his L. philosophers HERSCHEL.

Lapwing (læ·pwiŋ). [OE. *hlēapewince*, the first element of which is formally identical with LEAP *v.*, and the second element contains the base (meaning 'move sideways or from side to side') of OE. *wincian* WINK *v.* Named from its manner of flight. The current form is connected in pop. etym. with LAP *v.*[2] and WING *sb.*] A bird of the plover family, *Vanellus vulgaris* or *cristatus*, common in the temperate parts of the Old World. Called also PEWIT, from its cry. Its eggs are the 'plovers' eggs' of the London markets. Also *attrib.* as *l. stratagem*, etc., in allusion to its habit of leading a stranger away from its nest.

This L. runs away with the shell on his head SHAKS. In the Spring the wanton l. gets himself another crest TENNYSON.

Laquais, -ay, obs. ff. LACKEY.

‖**Laquear** (læ·kwiaɹ). 1706. [f. L. *laqueus* noose, band; see LACE *sb.*] *Arch.* A ceiling consisting of compartments sunk or hollowed, with bands between the panels.

Laquearian (lækwiēᵊ·riăn), *a.* [f. late L. *laquearius* 'perh. some kind of gladiator' (f. prec.) + -IAN.] Of a gladiator: Armed with a noose to entangle his opponent. BYRON. So †**La·queary** *a.* SIR T. BROWNE.

‖**Lar** (lāɹ). *Pl.* ‖**lares** (lēᵊ·rīz), **lars** (lāɹz). Also †**larre.** 1586. [L. *lar*, pl. *lares.*] **1.** *Rom. Myth.* **a.** *pl.* The tutelary deities of a house; hence, the home. Often coupled with *Penates.* **b.** *sing.* A household or ancestral deity; also *fig.* **2.** *Zool.* The white-handed gibbon of Burma, *Hylobates lar* 1819.

1. On the holy Hearth, the Lars, and Lemures moan with midnight plaint MILTON. Build houses; joyne to ours anothers lares 1647. **b.** Thomas Pitt..the great *lar* of not fewer than five families in the English peerage 1889.

Larboard (lā·ɹbōᵊɹd, -bəɹd), *sb.* (*a.*) [ME. *lad(d)eborde, latheborde*, altered later to *ler-, leere-, larbord*, after *ster-, steere-, starbord*; f. *ladde-, lathe-* + OE. *bord* ship's side (BOARD *sb.* V. 1). Some connect the first component with LADE *v.*, taking it to mean 'the side on which cargo was received'.] *Naut.* **1.** The side of a ship which is to the left hand of a person looking from the stern to the bows. Opp. to STARBOARD. (Now repl. by *port*, to avoid confusion with *starboard*). †**b.** as *adv.* = To larboard –1667. **2.** *attrib.* or *adj.* Belonging to or situated on the left or port side of a vessel 1495. **b.** *joc.* for: Left 1781.

2. On the l. quarter FALCONER. **b.** My l. eye COWPER.

Larcener (lā·ɹsĕnəɹ). 1634. [f. LARCENY + -ER[1]. Cf. OFr. *larcineur.*] One who commits larceny. Also *fig.* So **La·rcenist** 1803.

Larcenous (lā·ɹsĕnəs), *a.* 1742. [f. LARCENY + -OUS. Cf. OFr. *larcineus, larrecinos.*] Pertaining to or characterized by larceny; thievish.

The l. and burglarious world SYD. SMITH. Hence **La·rcenously** *adv.* thievishly.

Larceny (lā·ɹsĕni). 1460. [– AFr. **larcenie*, f. (O)Fr. *larcin* :– L. *latrocinium*, f. *latro, latron-* brigand, robber, (earlier) mercenary soldier, f. Gr. λάτρον pay, λατρεύς mercenary, λατρεύειν serve. Cf. LATRIA, -LATRY.] *Law.* The felonious taking and carrying away of the personal goods of another with intent to convert them to the taker's use. Also *gen.* theft.

Distinction was formerly made between *grand* and *petty l.*, the former being larceny of property of more, the latter of less, than 12 pence in value. *Simple l.*, plain theft unaccompanied by any aggravating circumstance; *mixed* or *compound l.*, larceny including the aggravation of a taking from one's house or person.

Larch (lāɹtʃ). 1548. [Introduced by William Turner, – MHG. *larche*, var. of *lerche* (G. *lärche*) :– OHG. **larihha*, **lerihha* – L. *larix, laric-*, prob. of alien origin.] **1.** A well-known coniferous tree, *Abies larix* or *L. europæa*, a native of the Alps, largely cultivated. Its timber is tough. It yields Venetian turpentine, and the bark is used in tanning. **b.** Any tree of the genus *Larix*, e.g. the American Larch, *L. americana.* **2.** The wood of this tree 1867.

1. When rosy plumelets tuft the l. TENNYSON. *Comb.* **l.-bark,** the bark of the larch-tree; the *laricis cortex* of the British Pharmacopœia. Hence **La·rchen** *a.* consisting of larches, larch-.

†**La·rcin.** ME. [– AFr., (O)Fr. *larcin*; see LARCENY.] **1.** = LARCENY –1679. **2.** A larcener 1596–1656.

Lard (lāɹd), *sb.* ME. [– (O)Fr. *lard* bacon :– L. *lar(i)dum*, rel. to Gr. λαρινός fat.] †**1.** The fat of a swine; (fat) bacon or pork; *rarely*, other fat meat used for larding –1725. **2.** (Often *hog's lard*). The fat of a swine, esp. the internal fat of the abdomen, rendered and clarified, much used in cooking and in pharmacy ME. Also *transf.* **3.** *attrib.* 1555.

2. Fritters of flour fried in bear's l. W. IRVING. *Neutral l.*, l. made from the best internal fat. *Compound l.*, l. made from vegetable oils.

Comb.: **l.-oil,** an oil made from l., now used chiefly for lubricating machinery.

Lard (laɹd), *v.* ME. [– (O)Fr. *larder*, f. *lard* (see prec.).] **1.** *Cookery.* (*trans.*) To insert small strips of bacon, etc., in (meat, poultry, etc.) before cooking. Also *absol.* †**2.** To enrich with or as with fat; to fatten –1687. Also †*intr.* for *refl.* or *pass.* **3.** *transf.* To stick all over *with*; to cover, line, or strew *with.* *Obs.* or *arch.* 1543. Also †*fig.* **4.** To garnish (speech or writing) with particular words, expressions, ideas, etc.; to interlard 1549. **5.** To smear, cover, or mix with lard or fat; to grease (*rare*) ME. †**6.** *intr.* To ooze with lard. M. HANMER.

1. Nearly all lean meat may be larded with advantage 1884. **2.** Falstaffe sweates to death, and Lards the leane earth as he walkes along SHAKS. **3.** Their sides were altogether larded with arrowes SPEED. **4.** Monkes began to l. the lives of their Saints with lies FULLER. **5.** His Buff Doublet, larded o'er with Fat Of slaughter'd Brutes SOMERVILLE.

Lardacein (laɹdē[i]·si,in). 1873. [f. as next + -IN[1].] *Chem.* A nitrogenous substance found deposited under morbid conditions in certain minute arteries and tissues of the body.

Lardaceous (laɹdē[i]·ʃəs), *a.* 1822. [f. LARD *sb.* + -ACEOUS.] *Med.* Of the nature of or resembling lard; containing lardacein; *spec.* applied to amyloid degeneration; also said of the patient.

Larder[1] (lā·ɹdəɹ). ME. [– AFr. *larder*, OFr. *lardier*, med.L. *lardarium* (IX); see LARD *sb.*, -ER[2] 2.] **1.** A room or closet in which meat (? orig. bacon) and other provisions are stored. Also *transf.* and *fig.* †**2.** *fig.* Chiefly in phr. *to make l. of*: to turn into meat for the larder; hence, to slaughter; *to larder*, to the slaughterhouse. Also *occas.* simply = slaughter. –1450.

1. Dress drains our cellar dry, And keeps our larder lean COWPER. **2.** Than [in November] is the l. of the swine GOWER.

Comb.: **l.-beetle,** *Dermestes lardarius*, an insect which devours stored animal foods; **-house** = sense 1.

Larder[2]. [f. LARD *v.* + -ER[1].] One who lards. FLORIO.

Larderer (lā·ɹdĕrəɹ). 1483. [– AFr. **larderer*, in AL. *larderarius* (XI), f. *larder* LARDER + *-er* -ER[2] 2.] One who has charge of a larder.

Larderie, -ery, var. of LARDRY.

Lardiner (lā·ɹdinəɹ). ME. [– AFr. *lardiner*, alt. f. *larderer* (prec.); cf. AL. *lardinarius, lardinerius* (XII), perh. the source, after *gardin-, gardenarius* (XII/XIII).] †**1.** = LARDER[1] 1. *n.* and *Sc.* –1710. **2.** An official who has charge of a larder. *Obs.* exc. as the title of an honorary office. ME.

Lardon (lā·ɹdən), **lardoon** (laɹdū·n). 1450. [– (O)Fr. *lardon*, f. *lard* LARD *sb.*; see -OON.] *Cookery.* One of the pieces of bacon or pork used in larding meat.

†**La·rdry.** 1538. [– OFr. *larderie* larder, f. *lard* LARD *sb.*; see -ERY.] = LARDER[1] 1. –1661.

Lardy (lā·ɹdi), *a.* 1881. [f. LARD *sb.* + -Y[1].] Full of or containing lard; fat.

La·rdy-da·rdy, *a. slang.* 1861. [Cf. LA-DI-DA.] Affected and languidly foppish.

Lare: see LAIR, LAYER, LORE.

Lares: see LAR.

Large (lāɹdʒ), *a., adv.*, and *sb.* ME. [– (O)Fr. *large* (now 'broad, wide') :– L. *larga*, fem. of *largus* abundant, bountiful.]

A. *adj.* †**I.** Liberal in giving; munificent; open-handed. Also, liberal in expenditure, prodigal, lavish. –1688.

The poore King Reignier, whose l. style Agrees not with the leannesse of his purse SHAKS.

II. †**1.** Ample in quantity; copious, abundant –1667. †**2.** Ample in spatial extent; spacious, roomy, capacious –1697. **b.** *fig.* Of the heart: Capacious 1535. †**3.** = BROAD *a.* 1. Often in *long and l.* –1715. †**4.** With definite measures of space and time = GOOD *a.* V. 2. –1737. †**b.** Of the time of day: Full

–1470. **5.** Wide in range or capacity; comprehensive ME. **b.** With reference to artistic treatment: Broad 1782. **6.** Of discourse, etc.: Copious, lengthy. Now *rare.* 1477. †**b.** Of persons: Diffuse, prolix –1788. **7.** In mod. Eng., a general designation for considerable magnitude, without the emotional implication of *great.* The more colloq. synonym is *big.* ME. **8.** Of speech or manner: Pompous, 'big' 1605.

1. And we have yet l. day, for scarce the Sun Hath finisht half his journey MILT. *P. L.* v. 558. **2.** Two Golden Horns on his l. Front he wears DRYDEN. **3.** Southward through Eden went a River l. MILT. *P. L.* IV. 223. **4.** A l. League from Friburg 1678. **b.** It was l. mydnycht 1470. **5.** A l. memory SWIFT. The court had a l. discretion as to the joinder of parties 1886. L. in his offers of friendship 1883. **6.** Mr. Wyatt spake a l. speech by hart WOOD. **b.** I could be very l. upon this point PENN. **7.** A l. vpper roome 1611. Great Theron, l. of Limb DRYDEN. L. profits 1902. A l. lunch KIPLING. *Comb.* **l.-paper,** a size of paper used for a special edition of a book, having extra large margins; also *attrib.* **8.** Your l. speeches, may your deeds approue *Lear* I. i. 187.

III. [Developed from sense II. 2.] †**1.** Indulgent, lax; not strict or rigorous –1733. †**2.** Having few limitations or restrictions; allowing considerable freedom –1793. †**3.** Of language: Loose, inaccurate (*rare*). ME. only. **4.** Of speech, etc.: Free, unrestrained; lax, licentious, gross –1599. **5.** *Naut.* Said of a wind that crosses the line of the ship's course in a favourable direction, esp. on the beam or quarter 1591.

1. A l. conscience sticketh at nothing BIBLE (Douay) 1 *Sam.* 24. Comm. **4.** I neuer tempted her with word too l. *Much Ado* IV. i. 53. **5.** When the wind came larger we waied anchor and set saile 1591.

Comb.: **l.-eyed** *a.*, having a l. eye or l. eyes; characterized by wide open eyes; **-lunged** *a. Path.*, characterized by enlargement of the lungs; **-minded** *a.*, having a liberal mind; marked by breadth of ideas; taking a l. view of things; hence *large-mindedness.*

B. *adv.* †**1.** Amply; fully, quite, by a great deal; abundantly. Chiefly *n.* and *Sc.* –1667. †**2.** Generously –1667. †**3.** Of speech and writing: At length, fully –1676. †**4.** With ample gait –1695. **5.** *Naut.* **a.** With a large wind; with the wind on the quarter or abaft the beam; 'with the wind free when studding sails will draw' (Smyth); off the wind; chiefly in *to sail, go l.* 1627. **b.** ? Wide of a particular course 1670.

1. Provisions laid in l. For Man and Beast MILT. **2.** Well we may . l. bestow From l. bestowd MILT. *P. L.* v. 317. **3.** *New Presbyter* is but *Old Priest* writ L. MILT. **4.** A black Gelding . . Trotts l. 1695. **5.** *By and l.*: to the wind (within six points) and off it. †Also *fig.* All ways. *To go* or *lead l.*: in a manœuvre, to break off at a particular point from the course marked out, and proceed straight ahead.

C. *sb.* †**1.** Liberality, bounty; ? also = LARGESS 2 –1537. **2.** *Mus.* The longest note recognized in the early notation, equivalent to two or three 'longs', according to the rhythm employed; also, the character by which it was denoted, viz. ▀ or ⊓ 1547.

Phrases. **At large. a.** At liberty, free. †*At more l.*: at greater liberty. †*To set at l.* **b.** Unsettled; not limited or confined one way or another. ?*Obs.* **c.** Of speech, etc.: At length, fully. †**d.** In full size. *A.Y.L.* v. iv. 175. **e.** As a whole; in general; (taken) altogether. **f.** In a general sense; without particularizing. Now *rare.* **g.** In the open sea (*rare*). †**h.** Over a large area; abroad. **i.** *Naut.* = 'going large' (see LARGE B. 5 a). **j.** *Law.* In *Common at l.*: 'such as is neither appendant nor appurtenant to land, but is annexed to a man's person' (Blackstone). **k.** *U.S.* Said of electors or elected who represent the whole of a State and not merely a district of it. **l.** Without definite aim or application. †**At one's l.**: at liberty. **In l.**: on a l. scale; opp. to *in little.* †**With the largest:** in the most liberal fashion. LD. BERNERS.

Hence **La·rgely** *adv.* in a l. manner. **La·rgeness.**

Large (lāɹdʒ), *v.* ME. [f. LARGE *a.* Cf. OFr. *largir* and (with sense 2) Fr. *larguer* (XVII).] †**1.** *trans.* To enlarge, increase, widen –1647. **2.** *Naut.* Of the wind: To become 'large' 1622.

Large-handed, *a.* 1607. †**1.** *fig.* Rapacious. *Timon* IV. i. 11. **2.** *fig.* Open-handed 1628. **3.** *lit.* Having large hands 1896. Hence **Large-ha·ndedness.**

Large-hearted, *a.* 1640. Having a large heart (see LARGE *a.* II. 2. b); magnanimous, generous; having wide sympathies. Hence **Large-hea·rtedness.**

Largen (lā·ɹdʒ'n), *v. poet.* 1844. [f. LARGE *a.* + -EN[5].] To grow or make large or larger.

Eyes, large always, slowly l. PATMORE.

Largess, largesse (lā·ɹdʒes). *arch.* and *literary.* ME. [– (O)Fr. *largesse* :– Rom. **largitia*, f. L. *largus*; see LARGE *a.*, -ESS[2].] †**1.** Liberality, bountifulness, munificence. Also *personified.* –1623. **2.** Liberal or bountiful bestowal of gifts; *occas.* †lavish expenditure; *concr.* money or gifts freely bestowed ME. **b.** A free gift or dole 1561. **3.** *fig.* (from 2). A generous or plentiful bestowal; something freely bestowed 1533. †**4.** Freedom, liberty –1594.

2. Our Coffers, with too great a Court, And liberall Largesse, are growne somewhat light SHAKS. Your proposed largess to the Church BROWNING. *Largess!* or †*A largess!*: a call for a gift of money, addressed to a person of position on some special occasion. Only *Hist.*, except as surviving locally at 'harvest home'. **b.** A largess or bounty of five dollars a man DE FOE. **3.** He's like the sun, a largesse to the world CROWNE.

Larget (lā·ɹdʒėt). 1875. [– Fr. *larget*, f. *large* LARGE *a.*; see -ET.] A short piece of bar-iron for rolling into a sheet.

†**Largi·fical,** *a. rare.* 1656. [f. L. *largificus* (see LARGE *a.*, -FIC) + -AL[1]; see -ICAL.] Liberal, bountiful –1709.

Largish (lā·ɹdʒiʃ), *a.* 1754. [f. LARGE *a.* + -ISH[1].] Somewhat large.

Largition (laɹdʒi·ʃən). Now *rare.* 1533. [– L. *largitio*, f. *largit-*, pa. ppl. stem of *largiri* be bountiful, f. *largus*; see LARGE *a.*, -ION.] The bestowal of gifts or largess; bountiful giving.

‖**Largo** (lā·ɹgo). 1683. [It., = broad.] *Mus.* A direction: In slow time with a broad dignified treatment. Also as *sb.*

Lariat (læ·riăt), *sb.* 1835. [– Sp. *la reata*; see RIATA.] A rope used for picketing horses or mules; a cord or rope with a noose used in catching wild cattle; the lasso of Mexico and S. America. Hence **La·riat** *v. trans.* to secure with a l.

Larid (læ·rid). [– mod.L. *Laridæ*, f. *larus* (= Gr. λάρος) gull; see -ID[3].] *Ornith.* A bird of the *Laridæ* or gull family. Hence **La·ridine** *a.* having the characters of the gull family 1877.

Larigot (læ·rigǫt). 1811. [– Fr. *larigot.*] An organ stop.

Larikin, var. of LARRIKIN.

Lark (lāɹk), *sb.*[1], **laverock** (læ·vərək, *Sc.* lē·vrək). [OE. *lāferce*, older *læwerce, lāuricæ*, corresp. to MLG., MDu. *lēwer(i)ke* (Du. *leeuwerik*), OHG. *lērihha* (G. *lerche*), ON. *lævirki* (perh. f. Eng.); of unkn. origin.] **1.** A general name for any bird of the family *Alaudidæ*, but usu., when used without a prefix, the SKYLARK (*Alauda arvensis*). The lark has a sandy-brown plumage, and remarkably long hind-claws (cf. LARKSPUR). **2.** Applied with defining prefix to birds not belonging to the *Alaudidæ*; e.g. to certain buntings and pipits. Also TITLARK. 1766.

1. On þe morwe wan it was day, & þe larke bygan to synge ME. Rise with the Larke LYLY. With your Theame, I could O're-mount the Larke SHAKS. *Crested L., Horned L., Red L., Shore-l.*; also SKYLARK, *Woodlark* (members of the genus or family). **2.** The Mud-lark, Rock-Lark, Titlark and Tree-Lark are Pipits NEWTON.

Lark (lāɹk), *sb.*[2] *colloq.* (orig. *slang*). 1811. [f. LARK *v.*[2]] A frolic, a spree. Also *to go on, have, take a l.*

Lark (lāɹk), *v.*[1] [f. LARK *sb.*[1]] *intr.* To catch larks (*mod.*). So **La·rker**[1], one whose occupation it is to catch larks 1634.

Lark (lāɹk), *v.*[2] *colloq.* (orig. *slang.*) 1813. [perh. repr. dial. *laak, layke* LAKE *v.*] **1.** *intr.* To play tricks, frolic; to ride across country. **2.** *trans.* To tease sportively, 'gammon'; to ride (a horse) across country 1848.

1. Jumping the widest brooks, and larking over the newest gates in the country THACKERAY. Hence **La·rker**[2], one given to larking.

Lark-heel, lark's-heel. 1597. **1. a.** = LARKSPUR. **b.** The garden nasturtium (*Tropæolum*). **2.** The elongated heel common among negroes 1865. Hence **Lark-heeled** *a.*

Larkspur (lā·ɹkspɒɹ). 1578. [f. LARK *sb.*[1] + SPUR.] *Bot.* Any plant of the genus *Delphinium*; so called from the spur-shaped calyx. The common larkspur is *D. consolida.*

Larky (lā·ɹki), *a. colloq.* 1851. [f. LARK *sb.*[2] + -Y[1].] Inclined or ready for a lark.

Larmier (larmie). 1696. [– Fr. *larmier*, f. *larme* tear + *-ier* -ER[2] 2.] **1.** *Arch.* = CORONA 4, DRIP *sb.* 4. **2.** *Anat.* The 'tear-bag' in the lachrymal fossa 1848.

Larmoyant (laɹmoi·ănt), *a.* 1824. [– Fr. *larmoyant*, pr. pple. of *larmoyer* be tearful; see -ANT.] Given to tears, lachrymose.

†**Laron.** Also **laroone,** etc. ME. [– OFr. *laron* (mod. *larron*) :– L. *latro, latron-.* Cf. LADRONE.] A robber –1656.

Villanie, La-roone: Rugby, my Rapier SHAKS.

Larrikin (læ·rikin). Chiefly *Austral.* Also **larikin.** 1870. [Originated in Melbourne; perh. f. *Larry* (a dim. pet form of Lawrence, common in Ireland) + -KIN.] A (usu. juvenile) street rowdy; the Australian equivalent of the 'Hoodlum' or 'Hooligan'. Also *attrib.*

Larrup (læ·rɒ̆p), *v. dial.* and *colloq.* Also **larrop.** 1823. [Of dial. origin; perh. based on *lather* or *leather.*] *trans.* To beat, flog, thrash.

Is this a land of liberty, where a man can't l. his own nigger? FONBLANQUE.

Larry, var. of LORRY.

Larum (lēᵊ·rɒ̆m, læ·rɒ̆m), *sb.* 1533. [Aphetic f. ALARUM.] = ALARM *sb.* II. Also *attrib.*

†**Larum** (læ·rɒ̆m), *v. Obs.* exc. *dial.* 1595. [f. prec.] **1.** *trans.* **a.** To sound *forth* loudly. **b.** To alarm. –1758. **2.** *intr.* To rush *down* with loud cries. POPE.

La·rum-bell. *Obs.* exc. *poet.* 1568. [f. LARUM *sb.* + BELL.] = ALARM-BELL.

Larva (lā·ɹvă). *Pl.* **larvæ.** 1651. [L. *larva* a ghost; also, a mask.] **1.** A ghost, hob-goblin, spectre. *Obs.* exc. *Hist.* **2. a.** An insect in the grub state, i.e. from the time of leaving the egg till its transformation into a pupa. **b.** Applied to the immature form of other animals characterized by metamorphosis. 1768. Also *attrib.*

2. *fig.* The larvæ of future controversies 1854.

Larval (lā·ɹvăl), *a.* 1656. [– L. *larvalis*; see LARVA, -AL[1].] †**1.** Belonging to a ghost or goblin; ghastly. BLOUNT. **2.** Of or pertaining to a larva or grub 1848; in the condition of a larva 1864. **3.** *Path.* Of a disease: Latent, undeveloped 1897.

Larvate (lā·ɹveɪt), *a.* 1846. [– mod.L. *larvatus*, f. *larva*; see -ATE[2] 2.] Masked, covered as by a mask. So **La·rvated** *a.* 1623.

Larve (lāɹv). 1603. [– Fr. *larve* – L. *larva.*] **1.** = LARVA 1. †**2.** A mask (*lit.* and *fig.*) –1677. **3.** = LARVA 2. 1769.

Larvi- (lā·ɹvi), comb. f. L. *larva* LARVA. **La·rviform** *a.*, having the form of a larva. **Larvi·parous** [L. *parere*; see -OUS] *a.*, producing young in the condition of larvæ; produced in the form of larvæ.

Laryngeal (lări·ndʒiăl), *a.* Also †**laringeal.** 1795. [f. mod. L. *laryngeus*; see LARYNX, -EAL.] *Anat.* and *Surg.* Of or pertaining to, affecting or seated in, or used in dealing with, the larynx.

‖**Laryngismus** (lærindʒi·zmɒ̆s). 1822. [mod.L.; see LARYNX, -ISM.] *Path.* Spasm of the muscles closing the larynx; laryngeal suffocation.

‖**Laryngitis** (lærindʒəi·tis). 1822. [mod.L.; see LARYNX, -ITIS.] *Path.* Inflammation of the lining membrane of the larynx. Hence **Laryngi·tic** *a.*

Laryngo- (lări·ŋgo), bef. a vowel **laryng-,** comb. f. LARYNX. **Laryngo·logy,** that branch of medical science which treats of the larynx and its diseases; whence **Lary:ngolo·gical** *a.*, **Laryngo·logist. Laryngopha·rynx,** the larynx and the pharynx together; whence **Lary:ngo-phary·ngeal** *a.* **Laryngo·phony** (Gr. -φωνία sounding], the sound of the voice as heard through the stethoscope applied over the larynx. **Lary:ngotra·cheal** *a.*, pertaining both to the larynx and to the trachea or windpipe. **Lary:ngotracheo·tomy,** the operation of opening the larynx, and part of the trachea also. **Lary:ngo-ty·phus,** a form of typhus in which there is secondary ulceration of the larynx and necrosis of its cartilages.

Laryngoscope (lări·ŋgŏskōᵘp). 1860. [f. LARYNGO- + -SCOPE.] An apparatus which by a combination of mirrors enables an observer to inspect a patient's larynx. Hence **Lary:ngosco·pic, -al** *a.* of or pertaining to the l., or to inspection of the larynx. **Lary:ngo-sco·pically** *adv.* with respect to, or by the use of the l. **Laryngo·scopist,** one who uses, or is skilled in using, the l. **Laryngo·scopy,** inspection of the larynx; the use of the l.

Laryngotome (lări·ŋgotoᵘm). 1855. [f. LARYNGO- + Gr. -τόμος cutter.] *Surg.* An instrument for performing laryngotomy.

Laryngotomy (læriŋgǫ·tǒmi). 1661. [– Gr. λαρυγγοτομία; see LARYNGO-, -TOMY.] *Surg.* The operation of cutting into the larynx from without, esp. in order to provide an aperture for respiration. Hence **Lary:ngoto·mic** *a.*

Larynx (læ·riŋks). *Pl.* **larynges** (lări·ndʒīz). 1578. [mod.L. *larynx* – Gr. λάρυγξ, λαρυγγ-.] *Anat.* A cavity in the throat with cartilaginous walls, containing the vocal cords, by means of which sounds are produced. In man and most of the higher animals this cavity forms the upper part of the trachea or wind-pipe. In birds there are two larynges, one at each end of the trachea; the lower of these, called SYRINX, is the true organ of sound.

Las (lɑs), *int.* 1604. Aphetic f. ALAS.

Las, obs. form of LACE, LASS, LESS.

Lascar (læ·skăɹ, læskā·ɹ). 1625. [ult. based on Urdu (– Pers.) *laškar* army, camp, either as a misuse of this, or through early Pg. *laschar, lasquarin, -im* native (East Indian) soldier, the latter orig. – Urdu adj. *laškarī* military. Cf. LASHKAR.] **1.** An E. Indian sailor. Also *attrib.* **2.** *Anglo-Ind.* 'A tent-pitcher'; also, an inferior class of artilleryman (in full *gun-l.*) 1798.

†**Lascaree** (læskări·). 1712. [– Urdu (Pers.) *laškarī*; see prec.] = LASCAR 1.

†**Lascari·ne.** *Indian.* 1598. [– Pg. *lasquarin, -im*; see LASCAR.] An E. Indian soldier; also, one of the native police –1825.

†**Lasci·vient,** *a.* 1653. [– *lascivient-*, pr. ppl. stem of L. *lascivire* be wanton, f. *lascivia*; see next, -ENT.] Wantoning, lascivious –1703. Hence †**Lasci·viency.**

Lascivious (lăsi·viəs), *a.* ME. [– late L. *lasciviosus*, f. L. *lascivia* licentiousness, f. *lascivus* sportive, lustful, wanton; see -OUS.] Inclined to lust, lewd, wanton. **b.** Inciting to lust or wantonness; †voluptuous 1589.

Hee on Eve Began to cast l. Eyes MILT. *P. L.* IX. 1014. **b.** L. pictures 1602, meats BURTON. Hence **Lasci·vious-ly** *adv.*, **-ness.**

Laser (lēⁱ·səɹ, lēⁱ·zəɹ). *Hist.* 1578. [– L. *laser.*] A gum-resin mentioned by Roman writers, obtained from an umbelliferous plant called *laserpicium* or *silphium* (σίλφιον). *Comb.* **l.-wort,** any plant of the genus *Laserpitium*, esp. *L. latifolium.*

Lash (læʃ), *sb.*¹ ME. [f. LASH *v.*¹] **1.** †**a.** *gen.* A sudden or violent blow; a sweeping stroke. **b.** *spec.* A stroke with a thong or whip. Also *transf.* and *fig.* **2.** The flexible part of a whip; now occas., the piece of whipcord, etc. forming the extremity of this ME. **b.** *poet.* and *rhet.* = 'whip, scourge' (*lit.* and *fig.*) 1586. **c.** *The l.*: the punishment of flogging 1694. **3.** Short for EYE-LASH 1796.

1. *fig.* How smart a l. that speech doth giue my Conscience *Haml.* III. i. 50. **2. b.** With all this.. she has not escaped the l. of scandal MME. D'ARBLAY. **c.** He expired under the l. GIBBON.

Lash (læʃ), *sb.*² 1440. [perh. LASH *sb.*¹ substituted for other wds. of similar sound; or perh. var. of LATCH *sb.*] †**1.** A string, cord, thong. Cf. LACE *sb.* 2, LATCH *sb.* 1. †**2.** = LASSO *sb.* 1 (*rare*) 1748. **3.** *Weaving* = LEASE *sb.*⁴ or LEASH *sb.* 6. 1731.

Lash (læʃ), *a. Obs.* exc. *dial.* ME. [– OFr. *lasche* (mod. *lâche*) :– Rom. **lascus*, f. L. *laxus* lax. See LACHES.] †**1.** Culpably remiss –1694. †**2.** Loose, lax, relaxed –1546. **3. a.** Of food, fruits, grass, etc.: Soft, watery. **b.** Of weather: Raw, wet. **c.** Of a hide: Tender. 1440.

Lash (læʃ), *v.*¹ ME. [prob. imit. or symbolic, like the contemp. †*lush*; cf. the parallel *dash|dush, flash|flush, mash|mush, smash|* dial. *smush.*]

I. 1. To make a sudden movement; to dash, fly, rush, spring, start. Of light: To flash. Of tears, water: To pour, rush. Also with *about, away, back, down, out.* Const. *at, from, into, out of, to.* **2.** To let fly *at*, make a dash or rush *at*, aim a blow *at* ME. **3.** *trans.* To dash, throw, or move violently. Now only *techn.* ME. †**4.** To lavish, squander. Chiefly with *out.* –1657. †**b.** To pour *out* or forth impetuously (words, etc.) –1653. **5.** *intr.* with *out*: To rush, launch out, into excess 1560.

1. When it [sin] finds the least vent, it lashes out to the purpose SOUTH. **2.** To laugh at Follies, or to l. at Vice DRYDEN. Phr. *To l. out*: to strike out violently: (of a horse) to kick out. **5.** To l. out excessively in dress STRYPE.

II. Senses referring to LASH *sb.*¹ **1.** *trans.* To beat, strike with a lash, etc.; to flog, scourge ME. **b.** *transf.*, esp. of the action of waves upon the shore. Occas. *intr.* (*on* the shore). 1694. **c.** *fig.* esp. 'To scourge with satire' (J.); to castigate in words, rebuke 1590. **2.** With *adv.* or phr.: To urge or drive by, or as by, lashes 1594.

1. Lashing the pony until they reached their journey's end DICKENS. **b.** The rain lashed the panes C. BRONTË. **c.** Why, headstrong liberty is lasht with woe SHAKS. **2.** A glassy lake..Lashed into foaming waves COWPER.

Lash (læʃ), *v.*² 1440. [perh. of LG. origin; cf. MDu. *lasche* rag, patch, gusset, Du. *laschen* patch, sew together, scarf (timber).] †**1.** *trans.* To lace (a garment) –1611. **2.** Chiefly *Naut.* To fasten or make fast with a cord, rope, etc.; †to truss (clothes); to fasten *to* (something) 1624.

2. We had not a gun on board lashed 1748.

Lasher (læ·ʃəɹ). 1602. [f. LASH *v.*¹, ² + -ER¹.] One who or that which lashes. †**1.** One who beats or whips. Also *fig.* –1611. **2.** *Naut.* The cord, etc. used to fasten any object 1669. **3.** Chiefly *local* (on the Thames): The body of water that lashes or rushes over an opening in a barrier or weir; hence, the opening; a weir 1677. **b.** The pool into which this water falls 1851.

3. The huge rafts..shoot the lashers in safety 1884. **b.** Men who..To bathe in the abandon'd l. pass M. ARNOLD.

Lashing (læ·ʃiŋ), *vbl. sb.*¹ ME. [f. LASH *v.*¹ + -ING¹.] The action of LASH *v.*¹; beating, flogging. **b.** *pl.* (*Anglo-Irish*). 'Floods', abundance 1829.

†*L. out*, squandering. **b.** 'Lashings' of whiskey-punch LEVER.

Lashing (læ·ʃiŋ), *vbl. sb.*² 1669. [f. LASH *v.*² + -ING¹.] The action of LASH *v.*²; the action of fastening any movable body with a cord. Hence *concr.* the cord.

‖**Lashkar** (læ·ʃkaɹ). *Indian.* 1616. [Urdu (Pers.) *laškar* army, camp. See LASCAR.] †**a.** A camp of native Indian soldiers –1634. **b.** A body of Afridi soldiers 1897.

Lask (lɑsk), *sb.* 1542. [– ONFr. **lasque* (= OFr. *lasche*), f. **lasquer*; see next.] **1.** Diarrhœa; = LAX *sb.*² 2. Now only in veterinary use. †**2.** A laxative 1550.

Lask (lɑsk), *v.* ME. [– ONFr. **lasquer* = OFr. *lascher* (mod. *lâcher*) loosen :– Rom. *lascare* for L. *laxare*, f. *laxus* LAX *a.*] †**1.** *trans.* To lower in quality, quantity, or strength, relax. ME. only. †**2.** *intr.* To become loose in the bowels –1634. **3.** *Naut.* To 'go large', to sail neither 'by the wind' nor 'before the wind' 1622. Hence **La·sking** *vbl. sb.* and *ppl. a. Naut.* '(going) large'.

Lasket (lɑ·skėt). 1704. [perh. alt., after GASKET, of Fr. *lacet* (see LATCHET) which is used in the same sense.] One of the loops by which a bonnet is attached to the foot of a sail.

Laspring (læ·spriŋ). 1760. [perh. alt. of **laxpink*, †*lakspynk* (f. LAX *sb.*¹ + *pink* minnow, young salmon), and interpreted as a contr. of *last spring.*] Young salmon.

Lass (læs). [ME. *lasce, las(se*, north. development (cf. *ass* for **ask* ashes, *ass* for *ask* vb., *buss* for *busk* vb.) of **lask* :– ON. *laskwa*, fem. of **laskwar* unmarried, repr. by OSw. *løsk kona* unmarried woman.] **1.** A girl. (Not much used in the south.) **b.** *spec.* A maid-servant. *Sc.* and *n. dial.* **2.** A sweetheart 1596.

2. It was a Louer, and his lasse SHAKS. *Comb.* †**l.-lorn** *a.* forsaken by one's sweetheart. Hence **La·ssie,** a young l. **La·ssock,** a little girl.

Lass, freq. obs. f. LESS.

Lassitude (læ·sitiūd). 1533. [– Fr. *lassitude* or L. *lassitudo*, f. *lassus* weary; see -TUDE.] The condition of being weary; a flagging of the bodily or mental powers; indifference to exertion; weariness.

Periods of renewed enthusiasm after intervals of l. RUSKIN.

Lasso (læ·so), *sb.* 1808. [Sp. *lazo* (in America pronounced la·so) = OFr. *laz*; see LACE *sb.*] **1.** A long rope of untanned hide, having a noose at the end to catch cattle and wild horses; used chiefly in Spanish America. **2.** *Mil.* = *lasso-harness* 1847.

Comb.: **l.-cell,** one of the urticating cells of the *Cœlenterata*, which eject the contained thread in the manner of a l.; **-harness,** a kind of girth placed round a cavalry horse, with a l. or long rope attached, for use in helping to draw guns, etc.

Hence **La·sso** *v. trans.* to catch with a l.; *Mil.* to draw (guns, etc.) with lasso-harness.

Last (lɑst), *sb.*¹ [OE. *lāst* m. footprint, *lǣst* fem. boot, *lǣste* shoemaker's last = MLG. *lēst(e*, Du. *leest*, OHG. *leist* (G. *leisten*) last, ON. *leistr* foot, sock, Goth. *laists-* footprint, track; f. Gmc. **laist-* follow; see LAST *v.*¹] †**1.** A footstep, track, trace. After OE. only in Sc. *Not a l.*: nothing, not at all. –1500. **2.** A wooden model of the foot, on which shoemakers shape boots and shoes OE. **b.** *transf.* and *fig.* 1592–1647.

2. Great evil may arise from the cobbler leaving his l. and turning into..a legislator JOWETT. **b.** Here's gallants of all sizes, of all lasts 1607.

Last (lɑst), *sb.*² [OE. *hlæst* load, burden = OFris. *hlest*, (M)LG. (M)Du. *last*, OHG. *hlast* (G. *last*) :– WGmc. **hlatsta-*, *-sti-*, rel. to **hlatto-* (ON. *hlass* load), f. **hlaþ-* LADE *v.*] †**1.** A load, burden, weight carried –ME. **2.** A commercial denomination of weight, capacity, or quantity varying for different goods and localities. As a weight, it is estimated at 2 tons or 4,000 lb. In wool weight, it is 4,368 lb. (= 12 sacks). As a measure for grain and malt, it is now 10 quarters = 80 bushels. A last of cod and herrings is 12 barrels (but of red herrings and pilchards 10,000 to 13,200 fish). Cf. Ger. *last.* ME. †**b.** *transf.* A huge indefinite number –1712. †**3.** A unit in the measurement of a ship's burden = 2 tons (occas. 1 ton) –1796.

Last (lɑst), *sb.*³ ME. [f. LAST *v.*¹] **1.** Continuance, duration. Now *rare.* **2.** Staying power 1857.

1. Things memorable, of perpetuitie, fame, and l. 1587.

Last (lɑst), *sb.*⁴ *Obs.* exc. *Hist.* OE. [– AL. *lastum, lestum* (Domesday Book *lest*), used as = OE. *lǣþ* LATHE¹.] = LATHE¹. Also, the name for an administrative assembly; more fully *l.-court.*

Last (lɑst), *a.*, *adv.*, and *sb.*⁵ [OE. *latost*, Northumb. *lætest*, corresp. to OFris. *letast, lest*, OS. *latst, last, letist* (Du. *laatst, lest*), OHG. *lazzōst, lezzist* (G. *letzt*), ON. *latastr* :– Gmc. **latast-*, **latist-*; superl. of *læt* adj., *late* adv. LATE: see -EST. Latest is a new formation on *late.* For the reduction of the group *-tst-* cf. BEST.]

A. *adj.* **1.** Following all the others in a series, order, or enumeration; subsequent to all others in occurrence, existence, etc. ME. **b.** *ellipt.* The last day (of a month). Now *local.* **c.** Utmost ME. **2.** Belonging to the end, *esp.* of life or of the world ME. **3.** Next before a point of time expressed or implied; the present time or next before; most recent, latest ME. **b.** With ellipsis of *letter.* Now chiefly *commercial.* 1638. **c.** *ellipt.* (*colloq.*) (A person's) latest joke, freak, characteristic action or saying, etc. 1843. **4.** That comes after all others in rank or estimation; lowest. Chiefly *ellipt.* ME. **5.** The only remaining ME. **b.** Often = 'most unlikely', 'most unwilling', 'most unsuitable' 1450. **6.** Final, conclusive, definitive. ? Now only in *l. word.* 1654. **7.** Reaching its ultimate limit; utmost, extreme. Now chiefly in phr. *of the l. importance.* 1674.

1. Fairest of Starrs, l. in the train of Night MILT. *P. L.* v. 166. Phr. *The two* (*three*, etc.) *l.* (the more frequent form till 17th c.). *The l. two* (*three*, etc.): the form now preferred, exc. where *last* = 'last-mentioned'. *The second last*: the last but one. *The last sacraments*: those administered in preparation for death. In the l. two Columns STURMY. Though l., not least in loue SHAKS. **c.** The land's l. verge Holds him 1871. **2.** Phr. *The four l. things* (Theol. ; = L. *quatuor novissima*); Death, Judgement, Heaven, and Hell. Hosius.. with his l. breath, abjured the heresy J. H. NEWMAN. *The l. day*: the Day of Judgement, the end of the world. *The l. days*: the closing period of the life or history *of* (a person, etc.); also the days including and immediately preceding the Day of Judgement. **3.** Having writ to you l. post saves me [etc.] MARVELL. † *The last age*: the last century or so. *L. Wednesday, l. Christmas* (formerly †*Wednesday last was*, etc.); *l. evening*, yesterday evening; †*the l. day*, yesterday. **b.** I informed you in my l. FIELDING. **4.** The l. of nations now, though once the first COWPER. **5.** To the l. peny SHAKS. That l. infirmity of Noble mind MILTON. **b.** She was the l. person to be approached with undue familiarity PRESCOTT. **7.** Even shame, the l. of evils MILTON.

Special collocations: **l. brood, l. spring,** terms denoting a young salmon at a certain stage of growth. *L. cast, extremity, gasp, legs, post, will*, etc., see the sbs.

II. *absol.* (quasi-*sb.*) **a.** With a demonstrative or relative adj.: The last-mentioned person or thing 1560. **b.** The conclusion (now *rare*) 1607. **c.** The last day or last moments; the end of life, death. Chiefly with a possessive. ME. **d.** *One's l.*: the last thing a person does or can do; *esp.* in *to breathe one's l.* (sc. *breath*), *to look one's last* (sc. *look*), etc. ME. †**e.** The extremity 1633. **f.** *mod. colloq.* The end of one's dealings with something 1854. **g.** *U.S.* The end (of a week or month).

a. Which two l. were not agreed upon 1560. **b.** Heare the l. of our sea-sorrow *Temp.* I. ii. 107. **c.** As he drew nigh his l. 1860. **d.** Eyes looke your l. Armes take your l. embrace SHAKS. **e.** To endure the l. of misery 1633. **f.** I should never hear the l. of it DICKENS.

Phrases (with preps.) **At last** [ME. *attě laste*, for *at the* (earlier *than*) *laste*]: at the end, in the end, finally, ultimately. So *At* (*the*) *long l.*: at the end of all. **To the l.:** †(*a*) to the utmost; (*b*) up to or until the end, *esp.* of life, to the point of death; also *till the l.*

B. *adv.* **1.** After all others; at the latest time; at the end. (*Occas.* coupled with *least*). OE. **2.** On the occasion next before the present; in the last instance; most lately; latest ME. **3.** In the last place, lastly 1560. **4.** In the end, finally 1667.

1. Nor Man the least Though l. created MILT. *P.L.* III. 278. **2.** He came l. from Astracan DE FOE. †*L. past*: (with dates) said of the period next before the time of writing or speaking; also (of a period of time) extending to the present, (the) past (year, etc.). Sermons..preached in Lente l. past LATIMER. **3.** First, my Feare: then, my Curtsie: l., my Speech SHAKS. **4.** To fall In universal ruin l. MILTON.

Last (lɑst), *v.*[1] [OE. *lǣstan*, corresp. to OFris. *lāsta, lēsta* fulfil, OS. *lēstian* execute, OHG. (G.) *leisten* afford, yield, Goth. *laistjan* follow :– Gmc. **laistjan*, f. **laist-* LAST *sb.*[1]] †**1.** *trans.* **a.** In OE. only: To follow (a leader; with *dat.*), to follow, pursue (a course, etc.; with *accus.*). **b.** To carry out (a command, a promise); to pay (tribute), to abide by, maintain (peace) –1480. **2.** *intr.* To continue, endure; go on OE. † Also with complement –1667. **3.** To hold out, continue fresh, unexhausted, etc. ME. **b.** With indirect obj.: To suffice for a specified time 1530. **c.** quasi-*trans.* (*a*) To continue in vigour as long as or longer than (something else). Now only with *out.* †(*b*) To hold out under or against. 1500. **4.** To reach, stretch –1577.

2. While the civil war lasted MACAULAY. **3.** Dwelling-houses built to l. RUSKIN. **c.** Old Families l. not three Oakes SIR T. BROWNE.

Last (lɑst), *v.*[2] 1880. [f. LAST *sb.*[1]] *trans.* To put (a boot or shoe) on the last.

Lastage (lɑ·stėdʒ). ME. [In XIV *lestage* – AFr., (O)Fr. *lestage* (med.L. *lestagium* XI), f. *lest* = LAST *sb.*[2]] **1.** A toll payable by traders attending fairs and markets. *Obs.* exc. *Hist.* †**2.** The ballast of a ship –1736. **3.** A port duty for liberty to load a ship, levied at so much per last 1592. **4.** An impost levied on the catch of herrings at so much per last 1601. **5.** = TONNAGE 1858. †**6.** Garbage. BLOUNT.

Laster (lɑ·stəɹ). 1878. [f. LAST *sb.*[1] + -ER[1].] A workman who shapes a boot or shoe, by fixing the parts smoothly on a last.

Lasting (lɑ·stiŋ), *sb.* 1782. [ellipt. use of ppl. a.] A durable kind of cloth; = EVERLASTING B. 3 b. Also *attrib.*

Lasting (lɑ·stiŋ), *vbl. sb.*[1] ME. [f. LAST *v.*[1] + -ING[1].] The action of LAST *v.*[1]; continuance, duration, permanence. **b.** Staying power 1860. Also *attrib.*

Lasting (lɑ·stiŋ), *vbl. sb.*[2] 1875. [f. LAST *v.*[2] + -ING[1].] The action of shaping a boot or shoe on the last; chiefly *attrib.* as *l.-awl, -machine*, etc.

Lasting (lɑ·stiŋ), *ppl. a.* and *adj.* ME. [f. LAST *v.*[1] + -ING[2].] **1.** Continuing, enduring; permanent. **2.** Durable ME. **3.** *Sporting slang.* Having staying power 1811.

2. A l. colour STURMY, cloth BP. BERKELEY. Hence **La·sting-ly** *adv.*, **-ness.**

Lastly (lɑ·stli), *adv.* ME. [f. LAST *a.* + -LY[2].] **1.** At the end; in the last instance; ultimately. *Obs.* or *arch.*, exc. as used in a discourse or the like. †**2.** Conclusively, finally –1637. †**3.** Very lately, recently –1641.

2. As he pronounces l. on each deed MILT. *Lycidas* 83.

Lat, obs. f. LET *v.*

Latakia (lætākī·ă). 1833. [Short for *Latakia tobacco.*] A fine kind of Turkish tobacco produced near and shipped from Latakia (the ancient Laodicea), a sea-port of Syria.

Latch (lætʃ), *sb.* ME. [In sense 1 prob. a var. of LACE *sb.* (OFr. var. *lache* of *laz*; see LATCHET); in sense 2 prob. f. LATCH *v.*[1]] **1.** A loop or noose; a gin, snare; a tangle; a latchet, thong. *Obs.* exc. *dial.* and *techn.* **2.** A fastening for a door or gate, usu. consisting of a small bar which falls or slides into a catch, and is lifted or drawn by means of a thumb-lever, string, etc. from the outside. Now also, a kind of spring-lock (*drop-l., night-l.*) for a front door, which is opened from the outside by a key. ME. **3.** *Naut.* = LASKET 1710. †**4.** *Mil. Antiq.* A cross-bow with a trigger working like a door latch –1786.

Latch (lætʃ), *v.*[1] [OE. *læććan* seize, grasp, f. Gmc. **lakk-*, prob. :– **lagn-*, rel. to Gr. λάζεσθαι (:– **lagj-*), or **lagn-*, rel. to L. *laqueus* noose, LACE.] †**1.** *trans.* To take hold of, grasp, seize (esp. with the hand or claws); to clasp, embrace. Also *intr.* or *absol.* with *at, on, till.* –ME. †**2.** To take with force; to capture, seize upon –1535. **3.** To catch (something falling); to catch *in* (a receptacle). *Obs.* exc. *dial.* 1530. **4.** To be the recipient of; to receive (a name, gift; a blow, injury); to catch (a disease). *Obs.* exc. *dial.* ME. **5.** *intr.* To alight, settle (*dial.*) 1825.

3. Some l. the firebrands as they flew P. HOLLAND. **4.** *Macb.* IV. iii. 192.

Latch (lætʃ), *v.*[2] 1530. [f. LATCH *sb.*] *trans.* To fasten or secure with a latch.

The street door was to be latched, but not bolted 1882.

Latch(e, var. of LEACH *v.*

Latchet (læ·tʃėt). ME. [– OFr. *lachet*, var. of *lacet*, f. *laz* LACE *sb.*; see -ET.] †**1.** A loop; a narrow strip of anything, a thong –1709. †**b.** *Naut.* = LASKET –1627. **c.** A thong to fasten a shoe. Now only *dial.* exc. in Biblical allusions. 1440. **2.** A catch for a shutter-bar. [f. LATCH *sb.* + -ET.] 1842.

Latching (læ·tʃiŋ), *vbl. sb.* ME. [f. LATCH *v.*[1] + -ING[1].] †**1.** The action of LATCH *v.*[1] ME. only. **2.** *Naut.* = LASKET 1794.

Latch-key (læ·tʃ,kī). 1839. A key used to draw back the latch of an outer door.

Comb. *Latch-key vote*, the lodger-franchise.

La·tch-string. 1861. A string passed through a hole in a door so that the latch may be raised from the outside. Hence *fig.* in *U.S.* in colloq. phrases.

'Our latch string is out' has become a classic expression of cordial hospitality 1893.

Late (lēⁱt), *a.* (*sb.*) [OE. *læt* = OFris. *let*, OS. *lat*, OHG. *laz* (G. *lass*), ON. *latr*, Goth. *lats* :– Gmc. **lataz* slow, sluggish, f. **lat-* :– IE. **lad-* (repr. by L. *lassus* weary :– **ladtos*); see LET *v.*[2] The mod. f. *late* represents infl. forms of OE. *læt*, and OE. adv. *late.*] **1.** Slow, tardy; *dial.* slow in progress, tedious. Const. *to* with *inf.*; also with gen. or *of.* Now *dial.* **2.** After the due or customary time; delayed in time. Const. *to* with *inf.*, and *for.* OE. **b.** Of plants, fruit, etc.: Backward in flowering, ripening, etc. 1440. **3.** Far on in the day or night OE. Also *fig.* **4.** Belonging to an advanced stage in a period, development, etc. ME. **5.** Of a person: Recently deceased 1490. **b.** That was recently (what is implied by the sb.) but is not now (cf. LATE *adv.* 4 b) 1548. **6.** Recent in date; belonging to a recent period. Now *Obs.* of persons, and chiefly in phr. *of l. years.* 1513. **7.** Having to do with persons or things that arrive late (*colloq.*) 1862.

2. Phr. (impers.) *It is* (*too*) *l. to* do something. Don't be l. for the train 1884. L. learners BACON. My l. spring MILTON. **b.** The l. Narcissus DRYDEN. **3.** Phr. *It is l.* = the time is advanced. *L. hours*: hours after the proper time for sleep. Hence *colloq.* of persons 'keeping l. hours, rising or going to bed l.' *fig.* A sage reflection, But somewhat l. i' the day BYRON. **4.** The l. Latin hymn metres SWEET. **5.** Her..l. amyable husbonde CAXTON. **b.** Our late dwelling GOLDSM. His l. master 1842. **6.** The l. war 1817. During the l. reign MACAULAY. **7.** *L. fee* (earlier *l.-letter fee*), an increased fee paid to secure the dispatch of a letter posted after the advertised time of collection. Hence **La·te-ly** *adv.*, **-ness.**

B. *absol.* or quasi-*sb.* †**1.** Lateness. ME. only. **2. Of late:** during a comparatively short time extending to the present; recently, lately 1470.

Late (lēⁱt), *adv.* [OE. *late* = OHG. *laz*, *lazzo*, f. *lat-* infl. stem of OE. *læt* LATE *a.*] †**1.** Slowly. OE. only. **2.** After the proper or usual time; at an advanced period; after delay OE. Also *transf.* **3.** Of the time of day: At or till a late hour ME. **4.** Recently, of late, lately; but now; †not long (*ago, before*). Now only *poet.* ME. **b.** Not long since (but not now); recently (but no longer) 1474. **5.** Relatively near the end of a period, history, etc. 1849.

2. Better three houres too soone, than a mynute too l. SHAKS. A weight..which crushes soon or l. BYRON. **3.** After supper, her aunt sat l. 1794. **4.** Those climes where I have l. been straying BYRON. **b.** L. king, now captive SPENSER. **5.** So l. as the days of the Stuarts MACAULAY.

Comb. With a following ppl. adj., usu. hyphened, as (sense 2) *l.-born, -lamented*, etc.; (sense 4) *l.-lost, -transformed* adjs.

Lated (lēⁱ·tėd), *ppl. a. poet.* 1592. [As if f. **late* vb. (f. LATE *a.*) + -ED[1].] = BELATED.

Lateen (lætī·n), *a.* (*sb.*) 1727. [Phonetic sp. of Fr. *latine* (in *voile latine* 'Latin sail', so named as used in the Mediterranean), fem. of *latin* LATIN *a.*] *L. sail*: a triangular sail suspended by a long yard at an angle of about 45 degrees to the mast. Hence *attrib.*, belonging to or having such a rig, as *l. mizzen, vessel.*

Latency (lēⁱ·tĕnsi). 1638. [f. LATENT *a.*; see -ENCY.] The condition or quality of being latent; *spec.* in *Biol.* So **La·tence** (*rare*).

Latent (lēⁱ·tĕnt), *a.* 1616. [– *latent-*, pr. ppl. stem of L. *latēre* lie hid; see -ENT.] Hidden, concealed; present or existing but not manifest, exhibited, or developed; esp. in *Path.* of a disease. ?*Obs.* of material things. **b.** Disguised (*rare*) 1662.

The meaning l. under this specious phrase MACAULAY. *L. ambiguity*: in *Law*, a doubt as to the meaning of a document, not patent from the document itself, but raised by the evidence of some collateral or extrinsic matter. *L. heat* (Physics): see HEAT *sb.* 2. *L. buds* (Bot.): buds lying dormant till excited by some particular stimulus. Hence **La·tent-ly** *adv.*, **-ness.**

Later (lēⁱ·təɹ). 1450. [f. LATE *a.* + -ER[3].] **A.** *adj.* More late 1559.

B. *adv.* At a later time or period; subsequently. *L. on*: subsequently.

Later, obs. f. LATTER *a.*

-later: see -LATRY.

Laterad (læ·tĕræd), *adv.* 1803. [f. L. *latus, later-* side + -AD II. Cf. DEXTRAD.] *Anat.* Towards the side.

Lateral (læ·tĕrăl). 1600. [– L. *lateralis*, f. *latus, later-* side; see -AL[1]. Cf. (O)Fr. *latéral.*] **A.** *adj.* **1.** Of or pertaining to the side; at or from the side; side-. †**2.** Existing or moving side by side. Of winds: Coming from the same half (eastern or western) of the horizon –1667. **3.** *spec.* **a.** *Anat.* and *Zool.* Situated on one side or other of the mesial plane, as *l. eye, fin, lobe*, etc. 1722. **b.** *Bot.* Belonging to, situated or borne upon the side of an organ, as *l. bud, flower*, etc. 1764. **c.** *Path.* Of diseases: (*a*) Affecting the side or sides of the body; (*b*) confined to one side of the body; (*c*) (of curvature of the spine) directed sideways 1724. **d.** Surg. *L. operation*: a mode of cutting for the stone, in which the prostate gland and neck of the bladder are divided laterally. Also *l. lithotomy*. 1727. †**e.** *Math.* Of a quantity or equation: Of the first power or degree; linear –1706. **f.** *Cryst.* Applied to those axes of a crystal or crystalline form which are inclined to the vertical axis; also to edges, faces, or angles, connected with such axes 1805. **g.** *Physics* and *Mech.* Acting or placed at right angles to the line of motion or of strain 1803.

1. *L. branch* (of a family): a branch descended from a brother or sister of a person in the direct line of descent. *L. moraine*: see MORAINE. The river and its l. streams HUXLEY. **2.** Eurus and Zephir with thir l. noise, Sirocco, and Libecchio MILT. **3. g.** *L. pressure* or *stress*, a pressure or stress at right angles to the length, as of a beam or bridge. *L. strength*, strength which resists a tendency to fracture arising from l. pressure.

B. *sb.* A lateral or side part, member, or object (as a shoot, tooth, branch, etc.) 1635.

Hence **Latera·lity**, the quality of having (distinct) sides; (right- or left-) sidedness; excessive development on one side. **La·teralized** *ppl. a.* rendered l. in position. **La·terally** *adv.* 1561.

Lateran (læ·tĕrăn). ME. [– L. *Laterana, Lateranum.*] The name of a locality in Rome, orig. the site of the palace of the Plautii Laterani, afterwards of that of the popes of the same name, and the cathedral church known as St. John Lateran [L. *Sancti Joannis in Laterano*]. Also *attrib.* or as *adj.* (= Eccl. L. *Lateranensis*), esp. with reference to the five general councils of the Western Church held in the church of St. John Lateran.

Lateri- (læ·tĕri), comb. f. L. *latus later-*, side, in scientific terms; cf. LATERO-. **Laterifloral, -flo·rous** [L. *flos, flor-*] *adjs., Bot.* having lateral flowers. **Laterifo·lious** [L. *folium*] *a., Bot.* (of a flower) growing from the stem at the base of a leaf, axillary.

Laterite (læ·tĕrəit). 1807. [f. L. *later* brick + -ITE[1] 2 b.] *Min.* A red, porous, ferruginous rock, forming the surface covering in parts of India, etc. Hence **Lateri·tic** *a.* of the nature of or resembling l.

Lateritious (lætĕri·ʃ[i]əs), *a.* 1656. [f. L. *lateritius, -icius*, f. *later* brick; see -ITIOUS.] Pertaining to or resembling brick; brick-red; said chiefly of urinary deposits.

Latero- (læ·tĕro), used as comb. f. L. *latus, later-* side; cf. LATERI-, -O-. Usu. hyphened, (*a*) in sense 'pertaining to the side (and another part)', 'pertaining to the side of (a specified structure)', e.g. *l.-anterior, -nuchal* adjs.; (*b*) 'on or towards the side', e.g. *l.-flexion*, etc.

Latescent (le[i]te·sĕnt), *a.* 1836. [– *latescent-*, pr. ppl. stem of L. *latescere*, inceptive of *latēre* lie hid; see -ESCENT.] Becoming latent, hidden, or obscure. So **Late·scence**, l. condition or quality.

Latest (lē[i]·tĕst), *a.* (*adv.*) 1588. [mod. superl. f. LATE *a.* + -EST. Cf. LAST *a.*] **1.** = LAST. Now *arch.* and *poet.* **2.** Most late; most recent 1593. **b.** *The l.*, the most recent piece of news, fashion, etc. 1889. **3.** *adv.* 1667.

1. Now at the last gaspe of Loues l. Breath DRAYTON. **2.** The l. newes we heare SHAKS. Phr. *At (the) l.*: at the most advanced hour or date. **3.** My fairest, my espous'd, my l. found MILT.

Late-wake, corrupt f. LYKE-WAKE.

†**La·teward.** 1456. [f. LATE *a.* + -WARD.] **A.** *adj.* **1.** Late, slow, backward –1745. **2.** Pertaining to a late period 1577.

B. *adv.* **1.** Of late, recently –1649. **2.** Late, after the due time or season –1659. †**La·tewardly** *adv.* of late, lately; at a late date.

‖**Latex** (lē[i]·teks). 1662. [L., = liquid, fluid.] †**1.** *Old Phys.* The name for juice of any sort in the body; esp. the watery part of the blood, etc. –1766. **2.** *Bot.* A milky liquid found in many plants, which exudes when the plant is wounded, and coagulates on exposure to the air 1835; *spec.* that of rubber-trees 1909.

Lath (lɑþ), *sb.* [OE. *lætt* (corresp. to MDu. *latte*, Du. *lat*, G. dial. *latz*) survives in mod. dial. *lat*, but began to be replaced XIV in general use by *laþþe*, which appears to represent an OE. **læþþ-*, corresp. to OHG. *latta* (G. *latte*).] **1.** A thin narrow strip of wood used to form a groundwork for slates or tiles or plaster, and in the construction of lattice or trellis work and Venetian blinds. **b.** *collect.* Laths as a material used in building to form a wall or partition. Freq. in *l. and plaster* (usu. hyphened when used *attrib.* or quasi-*adj.*). 1490. **2.** *gen.* A thin, narrow, flat piece of wood. Also *transf.* 1592. **3.** The bending part of an arbalest or cross-bow 1545.

1. b. L.-and-plaster work ROGERS. **2.** A sword of l. SCOTT. *transf.* His ribs are laths QUARLES.

Comb.: **l.-brick,** a long narrow brick used for the floors of grain-kilns; **-nail,** a nail for fixing laths upon battens 1330.

Lath (lɑþ), *v.* 1532. [f. prec.] *trans.* To cover or furnish (a wall or ceiling) with laths for plastering. Also with *over*, and *absol.*

Lathe[1] (lē[i]ð). [irreg. repr. OE. *læþ*, corresp. to ON. *láð* landed possession, land, rel. to **lǣð-* in Goth. *unlēds* 'unlanded', poor, OE. *unlǣd(e* wretched.] One of the administrative districts (now five in number) into which Kent is divided, each containing several hundreds.

Comb.: †**l. reeve,** the official charged with the administration of a l.; †**l. silver,** the chief rent payable to the crown.

Lathe[2] (lē[i]ð). Now only *dial.* ME. [– ON. *hlaða*, conn. w. *hlaða* LADE *v.*] A barn.

Lathe[3] (lē[i]ð). Also †**lath.** 1476. [Varies in XVII with †*lare*; the two forms may represent parallel adoptions of ODa. *lad* (XV) stand, supporting frame-work, as in *drejelad* turning-lathe, *savelad* saw-bench, *væverlad* loom, perh. a special use of *lad* pile, heap :– ON. *hlað*, rel. to *hlaða* LADE *v.*] †**1.** ? *gen.* A supporting structure, stand, scaffold. **2.** *spec.* (In full *turning-l.*) A machine for turning wood, metal, ivory, etc., in which the article to be turned is held in a horizontal position by means of adjustable centres and rotated against cutting tools 1611. **b.** A machine for throwing and turning pottery-ware, the article being placed upon a revolving horizontal disc; a *potter's l.* 1727.

2. Could turn his Word and Oath and Faith As many ways as in a Lath BUTLER. *Engine-, foot-, hand-l.*, lathes driven by an engine, etc. *Centre-, chuck-, duplex-, mandrel-, pole-l.*, etc., special forms of lathes. *Chasing-, fluting-, oval-, screw-cutting-l.*, etc., lathes doing work of these kinds.

Lathe[4] (lē[i]ð). 1633. [cogn. w. synon. Sw. *lad*, and so ult. identical with LATHE[3]. Cf. LAY *sb.*[5]] The movable swing-frame or batten of a loom.

‖**Lathee** (latī·). 1850. [Hindi *lāṭhī*.] A long heavy stick, usu. of bamboo.

Lathen (lɑ·þ'n), *a. rare.* 1843. [f. LATH *sb.* + -EN[4].] Made of lath.

Lather (læ·ðəɹ), *sb.* [OE. *lēaðor* washing soda = ON. *lauðr* :– Gmc. **lauþram* :– IE. **loutrom*, whence Gr. λουτρόν bath. In its mod. sense f. LATHER *v.*] **1.** †**a.** Washing soda. OE. only. **b.** A froth or foam from soap and water. **c.** *transf.* Violent perspiration, esp. the frothy sweat of a horse 1660. **2.** The action of lathering 1626. Hence **La·thery** *a.* chiefly *fig.* frothy, unsubstantial.

Lather (læ·ðəɹ), *v.* [OE. *lēþran, līeþran* = ON. *leyðra* :– Gmc. **lauþrian* (cf. prec.); from XVI assim. in form to the sb.] **1.** *trans.* To cover with or as with a lather; to wash in or with a lather. **2.** *intr.* To become covered with foam; now chiefly of a horse ME. **3.** *intr.* To produce and form a lather or froth 1608. **4.** *trans.* To beat, thrash. Also *intr.* with *into*. Also *fig.* 1797.

1. Nello skipped round him, lathered him, seized him by the nose, and scraped him GEO. ELIOT.

Lathing (lɑ·þiŋ), *vbl. sb.* Also †**latting.** 1486. [f. LATH *v.* + -ING[1].] **1.** The action of LATH *v.* **2.** *concr.* Lath-work 1756.

Lathy (lɑ·þi), *a.* 1672. [f. LATH *sb.* + -Y[1].] **1.** Like a lath; thin, or long and thin. Said esp. of a very thin person. **2.** Made of lath (and plaster) 1804.

1. Duns Scotus his picture—a leane lathie man WOOD.

Lati- lē[i]ti, (læti,) comb. f. L. *latus* broad, as **Latico·state** *a., Zool.* having broad ribs. **Latide·ntate** *a., Zool.* having broad teeth. **Latifo·liate, -fo·lious** *adjs., Bot.* having broad leaves. †**Latiro·strous** [L. *rostrum* beak + -OUS] *a., Ornith.* having a broad beak: so **Latiro·stral, -ro·strate** *adjs.* **Latiste·rnal** *a.*, having a broad breast-bone.

Latian (lē[i]·ʃ[i]ăn), *a.* 1598. [f. L. *Latium* (see LATIN) + -AN.] Of or belonging to Latium; Latin.

†**Latibule.** *rare.* 1623. [– L. *latibulum*, f. *latēre* lie hidden.] A hiding-place.

Latibulize (lăti·biuləiz), *v. rare.* 1802. [f. as prec. + -IZE.] *intr.* To retire into a hiding-place or retreat (for the winter).

Laticiferous (lætisi·fĕrəs), *a.* 1835. [f. L. *latici-*, comb. form of LATEX; see -FEROUS.] *Bot.* Bearing or containing latex.

L. tissue, tissue containing l. tubes or vessels.

Laticlave (læ·tiklē[i]v). 1658. [– late L. *laticlavium, laticlavus*, f. *latus* broad + *clavus* purple stripe. (In cl. L. *latus clavus.*)] *Rom. Antiq.* A badge consisting of two broad purple stripes on the edge of the tunic, worn by senators and other persons of high rank.

‖**Latifundia** (lē[i]tifɒ·ndiă), *sb. pl.* 1630. [L. pl. of *latifundium*, f. *latus* broad + *fundus* estate.] Large estates. Hence **Latifu·ndian** *a.* possessing l. NORTH.

†**La·timer.** [Early ME. *latimer* – AFr. *latimer* (whence AL. *latimerus, -ius* XII/XIII, earlier *latimarius* 1086), = OFr. *latimier*, alt. of *latinier* (= AL. *latinarius* 1086) interpreter, etc.; see next, -ER[2] 2. For the OFr. var. *latimier, -nier*, cf. *loremier, -nier* LORIMER, LORINER.] An interpreter –1480.

Latin (læ·tin). [– (O)Fr. *latin* or L. *Latinus*, f. *Latium*, the part of Italy which included Rome. As sb. adopted in OE. as *lǣden*; see LEDEN.]

A. *adj.* **1.** Of or pertaining to Latium or the ancient Latins (or Romans) ME. **2.** Pertaining to, characteristic of, or composed in the language of the ancient Latins or Romans. Of a writer, etc.: Versed in the Latin language. OE. Also *transf.* (*joc.*). **3.** Distinctive epithet of that branch of the Catholic Church which acknowledges the primacy of the Bishop of Rome, and uses the Latin tongue in its rites, etc. Also applied to its rites, clergy, etc. 1560. **4. a.** Applied (in opposition to *Greek*) to what pertains to the peoples of Western Europe, viewed in their relations with the Eastern Empire and with the Saracens and Turks. **b.** Applied to the European peoples which speak languages derived from Latin (though not all of Roman descent). 1788.

1. Learned in the Latyne tongue *Bk. Com. Prayer* (1552). **2.** Remuneration, O, that's the Latine word for three-farthings *L. L. L.* III. i. 138. A L. Grammar 1668, translation 1777. *transf.* Hang-hog is latten for Bacon SHAKS. **4.** *L. union*: the monetary alliance formed in 1865 by France, Belgium, Italy, and Switzerland, and afterwards joined by Greece, for the adoption and maintenance of a uniform system of bimetallic coinage in each of these states, and the recognition by each state of the coins of the others as legal tender. Phr. *L. cross*: see CROSS *sb.* 13.

B. *absol.* and as *sb.* **1.** The language of the people of ancient Rome; the Latin language OE. **2.** An inhabitant or native of Latium; one who possessed the Latin right of citizenship ME. **3.** (Chiefly in *pl.*) **a.** *Hist.* = FRANK *sb.*[1] 2. **b.** A member or adherent of the Latin or Western Church; now *rare* or *obs.* exc. with reference to subjects of the Turkish Empire. ME. †**4.** A translation into Latin, as a school exercise. Chiefly *pl.* –1679.

1. And though thou hadst small Latine, and lesse Greeke B. JONS. *Dog-l.*: see DOG *sb.* 8. *False L.*: L. which is faulty in construction; hence *transf.*, a breach of manners. *Thieves' L.*, the secret language or cant of thieves. **3. b.** The Catholics (here [at Jerusalem] called 'Latins') 1867.

Hence †**La·tin** *v. trans.* to render or turn into L. 1553–1678. **La·tiner** (*colloq.*), a L. scholar; one who speaks L. 1691. **Lati·nic** *a.* of or pertaining to the ancient Latins or to the modern L. nations 1875. **Lati·nically** *adv.* 1784. **La·tinless** *a.* ignorant of L. 1599. †**La·tinly** *adv.* 1388–1656.

Latinism (læ·tiniz'm). 1570. [– med.L. *latinismus* (XIII); see prec., -ISM.] **1.** A Latin idiom, esp. one used by a writer in another language; conformity in style to Latin models. **2.** The influence or sphere of action of the Latin races, or the Latin Church 1920.

1. Milton's L. is so pronounced as to be un-English 1875.

Latinist (læ·tinist). 1538. [– med.L. *latinista*, f. as prec.; see -IST. Cf. Fr. *latiniste* (XV).] **1.** One versed in the Latin language; a Latin scholar; †*occas.* a writer of Latin. **2.** A theologian of the Latin Church. COVERDALE. Hence **Latini·stic** *a.* pertaining to or characterized by latinism; characteristic of a l. So **Latini·stical** *a.* 1723.

Latinity (lăti·nĭti). 1619. [– L. *latinitas, -tat-*, f. *Latinus*; see LATIN, -ITY. Cf. (O)Fr. *latinité*.] **1.** The manner of speaking or writing Latin; Latin (with reference to its construction or style). **2.** *Rom. Law.* The status of a Latin citizen 1880.

1. His l. is pure GIBBON.

Latinize (læ·tinəiz), *v.* 1589. [– late L. *latinizare*, f. as prec.; see -IZE. Cf. Fr. *latiniser*.] **1.** *trans.* To turn into Latin, to write in Latin, to give a Latin form to (a word, etc.). **2.** To make Latin or Latin-like; to make conformable to the ideas, customs, etc. of the Latins, or to the rites, etc. of the Latin Church 1603. **3.** *intr.* To use Latin forms, idioms, etc. 1642.

1. The tendency to l. our speech TRENCH. **2.** The Roman Catholic Church has..made great efforts to L. its Oriental branches 1882. **3.** One pretended crime..that I l. too much DRYDEN. Hence **Latiniza·tion, La·tinizer.**

†**Lation.** 1603. [– L. *latio*, in med.L. sense of carrying, locomotion, f. *lat-*, stem of *latus*, functioning as pa. pple. of *ferre* bear, carry; see -ION.] *Astrol.* The action of moving, or the motion of a body from one place to another; motion of translation –1690.

Latish (lēⁱ·tiʃ), *a.* Also **lateish.** 1611. [f. LATE *a.* + -ISH[1].] Somewhat late. Also as *adv.*

Latitancy (læ·titănsi). 1646. [f. next; see -ANCY.] The state of lying concealed or hid. Of an animal: Hibernation.

Latitant (læ·titănt), *a.* (*sb.*) 1646. [– *latitant-*, pr. ppl. stem of L. *latitare*, frequent. of *latēre* be hid; see -ANT.] That lies concealed; lurking, latent; (of an animal) hibernating. As *sb.* One who is in hiding 1887.

Latitat (læ·titæt). *Obs.* exc. *Hist.* 1523. [– L., 'he lies hid', 3rd sing. pres. ind. of *latitare*; see prec.] *Law.* A writ which supposed the defendant to lie concealed and which summoned him to answer in the King's Bench. So **Latita·tion** 1623.

Latitude (læ·titiūd). ME. [– L. *latitudo*, f. *latus* broad; see -TUDE. Cf. (O)Fr. *latitude*.] **I. 1.** Transverse dimension; breadth, width as opp. to length; also *occas.* spaciousness. Now only *joc.* †**b.** A wide compass or extent –1791. **2.** Extent, range, scope. Also, great or full extent. Now *rare*. 1605. †**b.** The range within which anything may vary –1796. †**c.** Local range –1638. **3.** Freedom from narrow restrictions; liberality of construction or interpretation; tolerated variety of action or opinion 1605. †**b.** Laxity –1702.

1. The l. and bredth of the Zodiack is .xij. degrees 1559. **b.** A chace with a vengeance all the l. of the land FULLER. **2.** His great learning and l. of knowledge SIR T. BROWNE. **3.** The l. which a court of equity allows itself in enforcing agreements against the letter 1858.

II. In Geography and Astronomy. **1.** *Geog.* **a.** Angular distance on a meridian; only in *degree, minute*, etc. *of l.* **b.** The angular distance on its meridian (of any place on the earth's surface) north or south from the equator. ME. **c.** A locality as defined by parallels of latitude; usu. in *pl.* = regions, climes, parts of the world. Also *fig.* 1632. **2.** *Astron.* The angular distance of a heavenly body from the ecliptic; called spec. *celestial l.* ME.

1. *Circle, parallel of l.*, see those words. A degree of l. measured on any meridian is about 69 miles everywhere 1867. **c.** Those latitudes and altitudes where no crops will grow 1882.

Hence **Latitu·dinal** *a.* relating to breadth or width (*rare*); relating to, connected with, or depending on geographical l.; corresponding with lines of l. **Latitu·dinally** *adv.*

Latitudinarian (læ:titiūdinēᵊ·riăn), *a.* and *sb.* 1662. [f. LATITUDE I. 3 (with assim. to *latitudin-*, stem of L. *latitudo*) + -ARIAN.] **A.** *adj.* Allowing, favouring, or characterized by latitude in opinion or action, esp. in religious matters; not insisting on strict adherence to any code, standard, formula, etc.; tolerating free thought on religious questions; characteristic of the latitudinarians 1672.

His opinions respecting ecclesiastical polity and modes of worship were l. MACAULAY.

B. *sb.* One who practises or favours latitude in thought, action, or conduct, esp. in religious matters; *spec.* one of the English divines of the 17th c., who, while attached to episcopal government and forms of worship, regarded them as things indifferent; hence, one who, though not a sceptic, is indifferent as to creeds and forms.

Dr. Wilkins, my friend, the Bishop of Chester.. is a mighty rising man, as being a L. PEPYS. *Latitudinarian*, one who fancies all religions are saving WESLEY *Eng. Dict.*

Hence **La:titudina·rianism,** l. doctrine, opinions, principles, or practice 1676. So †**Latitu·dinism** 1667–1685. **Latitu·dinous** *a.* characterized by latitude of interpretation. *U.S.* 1838.

Laton: see LATTEN.

Latonian (lătōᵘ·niăn), *a.* (*sb.*) 1591. [f. L. *Latonius*, f. *Latona* – Gr. (Æolic) Λάτων, (Attic) Λητώ; see -AN.] **A.** *adj.* Pertaining to Latona (= Gr. Leto), the mother of Apollo and Diana. **B.** *sb. The Latonian*: Apollo.

A. L. Twins..why hide you so your shining Fronts? SYLVESTER.

Latoun, obs. or arch. f. LATTEN.

Latrant (lēⁱ·trănt), *a.* 1702. [– *latrant-*, pr. ppl. stem of L. *latrare* bark; see -ANT.] Barking; also *fig.*

†**Latrate,** *v.* 1623. [– *latrat-*, pa. ppl. stem of L. *latrare* bark; see -ATE[3].] To bark like a dog; also *fig.*

Latration (lătrēⁱ·ʃən). 1623. [– med.L. *latratio*, f. as prec.; see -ION.] A barking; also *fig.*

†**Latrede,** *a. rare.* [OE. *lætrǣde*, f. *læt* LATE *a.* + *rǣd* counsel, REDE.] Slow, tardy. When a man is so l. or tarying CHAUCER.

Latreutic, -al (lătrū·tik, -ăl), *a. rare.* 1627. [– Gr. λατρευτικός pertaining to divine worship (f. λατρεύειν: see next) + -AL[1]; see -ICAL.] Of the nature of LATRIA.

‖**Latria** (lătrəi·ă). Also †**latreia.** 1526. [late L. – Gr. λατρεία, f. λατρεύειν serve, serve with prayer.] *Theol.* In R. C. language: The supreme worship which is due to God alone (dist. from DULIA and HYPERDULIA).

Latrine (lătrī·n). 1642. [– Fr. *latrine* – L. *latrina* bath, privy, contr. of *lavatrina*, f. *lavare* wash.] A privy.

†**Latrociny.** ME. [– L. *latrocinium*, f. *latro* robber. Cf. LARCENY.] **1.** Highway robbery, brigandage –1657. **2.** A band of robbers. Also *transf.* –1732.

-latry, -olatry, repr. Gr. -λατρεία worship, as in εἰδωλολατρεία IDOLATRY, *Mariolatry* etc. Hence, in joc. nonce-use, *babyolatry* (see BABY), etc. So -(*o*)*later*, repr. Gr. -λάτρης worshipper, as in *idolater, bibliolater*, etc.

Latten (læ·tĕn). [ME. *latoun, laton* – OFr. *laton, leiton* (mod. *laiton*), of unkn. origin.] **1.** A mixed metal of yellow colour, either identical with or very like brass; often hammered into thin sheets. Now only *arch.* and *Hist.* **2.** Iron tinned over, tin-plate; more explicitly *white l.* Also, any metal made in thin sheets. Now *dial.* 1611. **3.** *attrib.* or *adj.* Consisting or made of latten 1492. ¶**4.** Used with a pun on *Latin* 1607.

1. A dome of yellow laton from Andalusia R. F. BURTON. *Black l.* = latten-brass. *Shaven l.*, a thinner kind than black l. *Roll l.*, latten polished on both sides ready for use. **3. L.-brass,** milled brass in thin plates or sheets, used by braziers and for drawing into wire. **4.** I faith Ben: I'le e'en give him a douzen good Lattin Spoones, and thou shalt translate them 1655.

Latter (læ·təɹ), *a.* (*adv.*) [OE. *lætra* (fem. and neut. *-e*) adj., *lator* adv., compar. of *læt* LATE. The mod. LATER is a new formation on LATE *a.*]

A. *adj.* †**1.** Slower –ME. **2.** Later; *occas.* = 'second' (cf. LATTERMATH). Now only *poet.* or *arch.* ME. **3.** Pertaining to the end of life, of a period, the world, etc.; = LAST. *Obs.* exc. *arch.* in *l. days*. 1513. **4.** That has been mentioned second of two; opp. to *former* 1555. Also *absol.* or *ellipt.* 1608.

2. The opinion and practice of the l. Cato SWIFT. *L. Lammas*: see LAMMAS. **3.** *L. end*: the concluding part (of a period, etc.); the end of life, (one's) death. Also *joc.*, the posteriors. ME. Hence **La·tterly** *adv.*, at the l. end; lately. **La·ttermost** *a.* last.

†**B.** *adv.* **a.** More slowly. **b.** Later. –1590.

b. My wife, more carefull for the l. borne SHAKS.

La·tter-day, *adj. phr.* 1842. Belonging to 'the latter days'; modern.

Latter-day Saints, the name the Mormons give themselves.

Latterkin (læ·təɹkin). 1659. [Of unkn. origin.] A glazier's tool used in making lead-lights.

Lattermath (læ·təɹmaþ). *dial.* 1530. [f. LATTER *a.* + MATH.] The latter mowing; the aftermath. Also, the crops then reaped.

La·ttermint. [f. LATTER *a.* + MINT *sb.*[2]] ? A late kind of mint. KEATS.

Lattice (læ·tis), *sb.* ME. [– OFr. *lattis*, f. *latte* LATH *sb.* + *-is* -ICE.] **1.** A structure made of laths, or of wood or metal crossed and fastened together, with open spaces left between; used as a screen, e.g. in window openings; a window, gate, screen, etc. so constructed. Also *fig.* †**b.** A window of lattice-work (usu. painted red), or a pattern on the shutter or wall resembling this (see CHEQUER *sb.*[1] I. 4), formerly a sign of an alehouse or inn –1735. **c.** Lattices collectively; = LATTICE-WORK. Also *fig.* 1577. **2.** *transf.* 1657. †**3.** A part of the auditorium of a theatre 1818. **4.** *attrib.* ME.

1. Ahaziah fel downe thorow a lattesse in his vpper chamber 2 *Kings* 1:2. Thro' a l. on the soul Looks thy fair face and makes it still TENNYSON. **b.** If he draw not A L. to your doore, and hang a bush out 1639.

Comb.: **l.-bar** *Bridge-building*, a bar belonging to a system of latticing; **l. beam** = *lattice girder*; **l.-bridge,** a bridge consisting of a top and bottom flange connected by a number of flat iron bars forming a l.; **l. frame, girder,** a girder consisting of two horizontal bars connected by diagonal bars crossed so as to resemble lattice-work; **l. leaf (plant),** *Ouvirandra fenestralis* or lace-leaf of Madagascar; also **l. plant.**

Hence **Lattice** *v. trans.* to furnish with a l. or lattice-work. Also with *up, over*. 1428. **La·tticed** *a.*, *spec.* in *Nat. Hist.* having a conformation or marking resembling lattice-work; *Her.* of a pattern resembling fretty, but placed cross-ways.

Lattice-window. 1515. A window furnished with a lattice; also, now, one composed of small diamond-shaped panes set in lead-work.

Lattice-work. 1487. = LATTICE *sb.* 1. Also, something resembling this.

Latticing (læ·tisiŋ). 1885. [f. LATTICE *sb.* or *v.* + -ING[1].] The process of making a lattice or lattice-work; in *Bridge-building* (see quot).

Latticing, a system of bars crossing each other at the middle of their lengths, used to connect the two channels of a strut, in order to make them act as one member 1885.

‖**Latus** (lēⁱ·tɒ̆s). 1702. [L., = side.] *Math.* In *Conic sections*: **l. rectum,** a straight line drawn through the focus of a conic at right angles to the transverse diameter, the parameter.

Laud (lǫd), *sb.* ME. [– OFr. *laude*, pl. *laudes* – L. *laudes*, pl. of *laus* praise.] **1.** Praise, high commendation. Now *rare*, exc. in hymns. **2.** *pl.* The first of the day-hours of the Church, the Psalms of which always end with Pss. 148–150, sung as one psalm and technically called *laudes* ME. Also *transf.* **3.** A hymn or ascription of praise 1530.

1. Pursevantes and herauldes That crien ryche folkes laudes CHAUCER. **2.** Now midnight lauds were in Melrose sung SCOTT.

Laud (lǫd), *v.* ME. [– L. *laudare*, f. *laus, laud-* praise; see prec.] *trans.* To praise, to sing or speak the praises of; to celebrate. Often *to l. and bless* (*praise, magnify*). Orig. implying an act of worship.

So ye shal be happy, & your werkes lauded 1477. Hence **Lau·der** = LAUDATOR.

Laudable (lǫ·dăb'l), *a.* Also †**laudible.** ME. [– L. *laudabilis*, f. *laudare*; see prec. and -ABLE.] **1.** Praiseworthy, commendable. †Also, in early use, laudatory. **2.** Of satisfactory nature, quality, or operation; healthy, sound, wholesome. Now only *Path.* of secretions, *esp.* pus. 1514. †**3.** *sb.* in *pl.* Laudable qualities, good points 1715.

1. A l. ambition WALTON. L. curiosity RUSKIN. **2.** To promote a l. growth of flesh 1720. Healthy or l. pus 1878. Hence **Laudabi·lity** (*rare*), **Lau·dableness. Lau·dably** *adv.*

Laudanine (lǫ·dănəin). Also **-in.** 1888. [f. LAUDANUM + -INE[5].] *Chem.* A colourless to pale red crystalline alkaloid contained in opium.

Laudanum (lǫ·d'nɒ̆m). Also †**lodanum.** 1602. [– mod.L. *laudanum*, used by Paracelsus for a costly medicament, in which opium was early suspected to be the active ingredient. The wd. thus used may be a var. of LADANUM, or suggested by *laudare* to praise, or quite arbitrary.] **1.** In early use, any of various preparations in which opium was the main ingredient. Now: The simple alcoholic tincture of opium. †2. = LADANUM 1. –1702.

Laudation (lǫdēⁱ·ʃən). 1470. [– OFr. *laudacion* or L. *laudatio*, f. *laudat-*, pa. ppl. stem of *laudare*; see LAUD *v.*, -ION.] The action or an act of praising. Also, the condition of being praised.

As we read the long l. on the pedestal STANLEY.

Laudative (lǭ·dǎtiv). *rare*. 1605. [– L. *laudativus*, f. as prec.; see -IVE.] **A.** *adj.* Expressive of praise; laudatory. Const. *of*. 1609. †**B.** *sb.* A laudative expression or discourse; a eulogy, panegyric.

Laudator (lǫdēⁱ·təɹ). 1825. [– L. *laudator*, f. as prec; see -OR 2.] One who praises; a eulogist.

Laudatory (lǭ·dǎtəri). 1555. [– late L. *laudatorius*, f. as prec.; see -ORY².]

A. *adj.* Expressive of praise; eulogistic.

†**B.** *sb.* A laudatory discourse, a eulogy –1642.

B. A l. of itself obtruded in the very first word MILT. Hence **Lau·datorily** *adv.*

Laudian (lǭ·diǎn), *a.*, *sb.* Also †**Laudean.** 1691. [f. William *Laud*, archbishop of Canterbury 1633–45 + -IAN.] Of, pertaining to, or characteristic of Laud; favouring the tenets of Laud; instituted by Laud. As *sb.*, a follower of Laud. Hence **Lau·dianism,** the principles and practice of Laud and his followers; also **Lau·dism.**

Laugh (lɑf), *sb.* 1690. [f. next.] **1.** The action of laughing; laughing, or an inclination to laugh; laughter (*rare*). **2.** An act, or the manner, of laughing. Also *fig.* 1713. **3.** = LAUGHING-STOCK (*rare*) 1817.

1. Do you find jest, and I'll find l. GOLDSM. **2.** The heart's light l. pursued the circling jest S. ROGERS. Phr. *To have* or *get the l. on one's side*; *to have the l. of, to raise the l. against.*

Laugh (lɑf), *v.* [OE. *hlæhhan* (WS. *hliehhan*) = OFris. *hlakkia*, OS. **hlahhian*, OHG. *hlahhan*, *hlahhēn* (Du., G. *lachen*), ON. *hlæja*, Goth. *hlahjan*; Gmc. str. vb., but later in most of the langs. wholly or partially weak, f. **χlaχ-* **χlōχ-* **χlaʒ-* :– IE. imit. base **klak-* **klōk-* (cf. Gr. κλώσσειν cluck :– **klōkjein*).] **1.** *intr.* To manifest the spasmodic utterance, facial distortion, shaking of the sides, etc., which form the instinctive expression of mirth, amusement, sense of the ludicrous, scorn, etc. Also *transf.* to have the emotion which is expressed by laughing. **b.** Attributed *poet.* and *rhet.* to inanimate objects, chiefly with reference to movement or play of light and colour ME. **2.** quasi-*trans.* with cognate obj. Also, to utter laughingly or with laughter. 1470. **3.** With *dat.* of person, and *to* with sb., as in *to l. to scorn* (now *arch.* and *literary*) ME. **4.** With obj. and compl., adv., or advb. phr.: To produce a specified effect upon by laughing ME.

1. Then the whole quire hold their hips, and loffe SHAKS. Phr. *To l. in one's sleeve*: to l. to oneself. *To l. on the other, wrong side* (*of one's face, mouth*): to change to sadness and vexation from laughter and exultation. **b.** The heavens l. with you in your jubilee WORDSW. The wood fire..laughs broadly through the room HAWTHORNE. †*L. and lay* (or *lie*) *down*: an obsolete game at cards. **2.** The large Achilles..laughs out a loud applause SHAKS. **3.** All they that see me, l. me to scorne *Ps.* 22:7. †*To l. on, upon* (rarely *up, to*): to smile on. *To l. at*: to make fun of: to deride, ridicule. **4.** Will you l. me asleepe, for I am very heauy SHAKS. Whose whole life is to eat, and drink..and l. themselves fat TRAPP. *To l. away*: †(*a*) to let go with a laugh; (*b*) to get rid of with a laugh; (*c*) to while away (time) with laughter. *To l. down*: to subdue or silence with laughter. *To l. off, out* = *to laugh away* (*b*). *To l. over*: to recall or repeat with laughter or mirth.

Hence **Lau·ghable** *a.* that may be laughed at; to be laughed at. **Lau·ghably** *adv.* **Lau·ghableness.** **Laughee·**, the person laughed at (CARLYLE). **Lau·gher,** one who laughs; one addicted to laughing; also, a scoffer; also, a variety of pigeon (1735).

Laughing (lɑ·fiŋ), *vbl. sb.* ME. [f. LAUGH *v.* + -ING¹.] The action of LAUGH *v.*; laughter.

Comb.: **l.-matter,** a subject for laughter; **-muscle,** the *risorius*, or the muscle that produces the contortions attendant on laughter; †**-post, -stake** = LAUGHING-STOCK.

Laughing (lɑ·fiŋ), *ppl. a.* ME. [f. as prec. + -ING².] That laughs.

In names of animals, so called from their cry or aspect: **l. hyena, jackass** (see the sbs.); **l.-bird** *dial.*, the green woodpecker; **-crow,** any of various Asiatic birds; **-goose,** the white-fronted goose (*Anser albifrons*); **-thrush,** any of various Asiatic birds. Hence **Lau·ghingly** *adv.* 1530.

Laughing gas. 1842. Nitrous oxide, N_2O; used chiefly as anæsthetic, and so called from its exhilarating effects when inhaled.

Laughing-stock. 1519. [f. LAUGHING *vbl. sb.* + STOCK *sb.*¹] An object of laughter; a butt for ridicule.

You'll be a laughing stock to the whole bench, and a byword with all the pig-tailed lawyers SHERIDAN.

Laughsome (lɑ·fsɒm), *a. rare.* 1620. [f. LAUGH *sb.* + -SOME¹.] Addicted to laughing; (of things) laughable.

Laughter¹ (lɑ·ftəɹ). [OE. *hleahtor* = OHG. *hlahtar* (whence G. *gelächter*), ON. *hlátr* :– Gmc. **χlaχtraz*, f. **χlaχ-* LAUGH *v.*] The action of laughing; *occas.* a manner of laughing. **b.** A laugh (now *rare*) OE. **c.** Used for: A subject or matter for laughter 1596.

Homeric l. (see *Iliad* i. 599 ἄσβεστος γέλως, irrepressible laughter. Then shal oure mouth be fylled with l. COVERDALE *Ps.* 125:3. *Personified.* L. holding both his sides MILT. *L'Alleg.* 32. **b.** Exchanging quick low laughters BROWNING. **c.** L. for a Moneth, and a good iest for euer SHAKS. Hence **Lau·ghterless** *a.*

Laughter² (lɑ·ftəɹ). *dial.* 1601. [– ON. **lahtr, láttr* :– Gmc. **laχtram*, f. **laʒ-*, base of LAY *v.*] The whole number of eggs laid by a fowl before she is ready to sit.

Lau·ghworthy, *a. rare.* 1616. Deserving to be laughed at, ridiculous.

Laughy (lɑ·fi), *a. rare.* 1837. [f. LAUGH *sb.* or *v.* + -Y¹.] Inclined to laugh.

Laumontite (lǭ·mǫntəit). 1805. [Named (G. *lomonit*) by Werner, 1805, after Gillet de *Laumont*, its discoverer; see -ITE¹ 2 b.] *Min.* Hydrous silicate of aluminium and calcium.

†**Launce**¹. [– L. *lanx, lanc-*, It. *lance.*] A scale, balance. SPENSER.

Launce² (lɑns). 1623. [perh. an application of LANCE *sb.*¹] A fish of the genus *Ammodytes*; the sand-eel; = LANT *sb.*² Also called *sand-la(u)nce*. *Sable l.*: the capelin.

Launch (lǭnʃ, lānʃ), *sb.*¹ 1558. [f. LAUNCH *v.*] †**1.** The action or an act of lancing; a prick –1596. **2. a.** The action or process of launching a vessel. Also *fig.* with *out*. **b.** The starting off of a bird in flight. 1814. **3.** *concr.* in *Ship-building*. The slip or descent whereon the ship is built, including the machinery used in launching 1711. **4.** *dial.* An eel-trap 1847. **5.** *attrib.*, as **l.-block, -ways** = *launching-ways, launching-planks* 1720.

Launch (lǭnʃ, lānʃ), *sb.*² 1697. [– Sp. *lancha* pinnace, perh. of Malay origin; cf. Pg. *lanchara* – Malay *lancharan*, f. *lanchār* quick, nimble.] **1.** The largest boat of a man-of-war, for use in shallow water, usually sloop-rigged. **2.** A large boat propelled by electricity, steam, etc. (*electric l., steam-l.*), used for transporting passengers, or as a pleasure-craft 1865.

Launch (lǭnʃ, lānʃ), *v.* ME. [– AFr. *launcher*, ONFr. *lancher*, var. of *lancier* LANCE *v.*] †**1.** *trans.* = LANCE *v.* II. 1, 2. –1724. **2.** To hurl, shoot, discharge, send off (a missile, a blow, etc.). (Cf. LANCE *v.* I. 1.) ME. **b.** To dart forward (a weapon, a limb, etc.). Now only, to dart *out* (something long and flexible). ME. **3.** *intr.*, for *refl.* To rush, plunge, start or shoot forth; †to leap, vault; *transf.* to skip in reading ME. **b.** *fig.* (Now usually with *out.*) To enter boldly or freely into a course of action; to rush *into* expense; to burst *out* into (violent) speech 1608. **4.** *trans.* To cause (a vessel) to move or slide from the land, or the stocks, into the water; to set afloat; to lower (a boat) into the water ME. **b.** To send off, start upon a course, send adrift 1627. **c.** *fig.* To start (a person) *in, into,* or *on* a business, career, etc.; to set on foot (a project); to commence (an action). Also with *out*. 1602. **5.** *intr.* Of the ship: To be launched (now *rare*) 1665. **6.** To push *forth, out* from land, put to sea, advance seawards (*lit.* and *fig.*) 1534. **7.** *trans. Naut.* †**a.** To set up, hoist (a yard). **b.** To move (casks, etc.) by pushing. 1627.

1. Nine Bulls were launch'd by his victorious arm DRYDEN. *fig.* Thy Prophets..Rubb'd where they should haue launcht QUARLES. **2.** To l. a thunderbolt SCOTT, the censures of the church against offenders FREEMAN. **3. b.** I want time to l. into an ample discourse BOYLE. **4.** Was this the face that launch'd a thousand ships? MARLOWE. **c.** The Mississippi scheme launched by John Law 1872. *To l. into eternity*: rhet. for 'to put to death'. **6.** To l. out into an ocean of common-place HUME. *To l. into eternity*: rhet. for 'to die'.

Launching (lǭ·nʃiŋ, lā·nʃiŋ), *vbl. sb.* 1592. [f. prec. + -ING¹.] The action of LAUNCH *v.*

Comb. †**l.-knife,** a lancet; **l.-planks,** a set of planks mostly used to form the platform on each side of the ship, whereon the bilgeways slide for the purpose of launching; **l.-ways** = *launching-planks.*

Laund (lǭnd). *Obs.* exc. *arch.* See also LAWN *sb.*² ME. [– OFr. *launde* (mod. *lande*); see LAWN *sb.*²] An open space among woods, a glade (= L. *saltus*); untilled ground, pasture.

Through this L. anon the Deere will come SHAKS.

Launder (lǭ·ndəɹ, lā·ndəɹ), *sb.* ME. [Contr. f. LAVENDER *sb.*¹] †**1.** A man or woman who washes linen –1603. **2. a.** A trough for water, either cut in the earth, or formed of wood; *esp.* in *Mining*, one for washing the ore clean from dirt. **b.** A rain-water gutter. 1667. Now *local.*

Launder (lǭ·ndəɹ, lā·ndəɹ), *v.* 1597. [f. prec. sb.] **1.** *trans.* To wash and get up (linen). Also *transf.* and *fig.* †**2.** To sweat (gold or plate). B. JONS. **3.** Of a fabric: To bear laundering (well, etc.) 1909.

1. His linen [was] soft and badly laundered 1883. So **Lau·nderer,** one who launders (linen) (*Obs.* exc. *local* and *U.S.*) 1440; †one who sweats gold or plate.

Laundress (lǭ·ndrės, lā·ndrės), *sb.* 1524. [f. LAUNDER *sb.*, or *launderer*, + -ESS¹.] **1.** A woman who washes and gets up linen, etc. **2.** A caretaker of chambers in the Inns of Court 1592.

2. It's a curious circumstance, Sam, that they call the old women in these inns, laundresses DICKENS. Hence †**Lau·ndress** *v. trans.* to furnish with laundresses, act as l. to; *intr.* to act as a l. 1612–36.

Laundry (lǭ·ndri, lā·ndri). 1530. [Altered f. ME. *lavendry* (XIV) – OFr. *lavanderie* (cf. L. *lavandaria* things to be washed); see -RY. For vocalization of *v* cf. *auger, hawk, newt.*] †**1.** The action or process of washing –1626. **2.** An establishment for washing and getting up linen 1577. **b.** Articles washed and got up. *recent.* ¶**3.** Used for LAUNDRESS. *Merry W.* I. ii. 5. **4.** *attrib.*, as *l.-man*, etc. 1585.

‖**Laura** (lǭ·rǎ). 1727. [Gr. λαύρα lane, passage, alley.] *Christian Antiq.* An aggregation of detached cells, tenanted by recluse monks under a superior, in Egypt and elsewhere.

Lauraceous (lǭrēⁱ·ʃəs), *a.* [f. mod.L. *Lauraceæ* + -OUS.] *Bot.* Belonging to the N.O. *Lauraceæ* or laurel family. (Rec. Dicts.)

Laurate (lǭ·reⁱt). 1873. [f. LAURIC *a.* + -ATE⁴.] *Chem.* A salt of lauric acid.

†**Laure.** [OE. *laur* – L. *laurus* laurel. Cf. OFr. *laure*, perh. the source in ME.] The laurel or bay-tree; also, its leaves woven into a chaplet –1567.

Laureate (lǭ·riˌět). ME. [In senses 1, 2a – L. *laureatus*, f. *laurea* laurel-tree, laurel crown, subst. use of fem. of *laureus* adj., f. *laurus* LAUREL; see -ATE²; in 2b – *laureat-*, pa. ppl. stem of med.L. *laureare* (XIII) to crown with laurels.]

A. *adj.* **1.** Crowned with laurel (as a symbol of distinction) ME. **b.** Of a crown, wreath: Consisting of laurel, or imitating one composed of laurel. Hence (*poet.*) *l. shade*. ME. **2.** Worthy of special distinction or honour, pre-eminent in a sphere or faculty. **a.** *gen.* ? *Obs.* 1508. **b.** *spec.* Distinguished as a poet, worthy of the Muses' crown ME. **3.** *transf.* Of things: Worthy of the laurel-wreath. Also, Of or pertaining to poets, or to a poet laureate. late ME.

1. To strew the Laureat Herse where Lycid lies MILT. **b.** The l. wreath, that Cecil wore GRAY. †*L. letters* [tr. L. *litteræ laureatæ*], a letter or dispatch announcing a victory. **2. a.** No, Faustus, Thou art conjuror laureat, That canst command great Mephistophilis MARLOWE. **b.** *Poet Laureate*: in early use, a title given generally to eminent poets, and sometimes conferred by universities; in mod. use, the title given to a poet who receives a stipend as an officer of the Royal Household, writes court-odes, etc. The first recorded appointment by authority to the office of Poet Laureate was a 'warrant for a grant' to Dryden, on 13 April, 1668; confirmed by patent of 18 Aug., 1670. **3.** Langage l. LYDGATE. The laureat strain of Pindar GROTE.

B. *sb.* **1.** = *Poet laureate* 1529. **b.** A court panegyrist 1863. **2.** *U.S.* A degree title awarded in some institutions to women. BRYCE. **3.** *Numism.* = LAUREL *sb.* 4. 1727.

1. The courtly laureat pays His quit-rent ode, his pepper corn of praise COWPER. Hence **Lau·reate-ship.**

Laureate (lǫ·riˌeⁱt), *v.* *Obs.* exc. *Hist.* ME. [In sense 1 – med.L. *laureare* (see prec.); in sense 2 f. LAUREATE A 2.] **1.** *trans.* To crown with laurel as victor, poet, or the like; to confer honourable distinction upon. **2.** *spec.* **a.** To graduate or confer a University degree upon. **b.** To appoint (a poet) to the office of Laureate. 1637.

1. By his reygne is all Englonde lawreat 1509.

Laureation (lǭriˌēⁱ·ʃən). 1637. [– med.L. *laureatio* (XIII), f. *laureare* crown with laurels, f. L. *laureus* LAUREL *sb.*; see -ATION.] The action of crowning with laurel or making laureate; in the Sc. Universities, a term for graduation or admission to a degree; also, the creation of a poet laureate.

Laurel (lǫ·rĕl), *sb.* ME. **(lorer, laurer,** later, **lorel,** etc.) [– OFr. *lorier* (mod. *laurier*) – Pr. *laurier*, f. *laur* (= OFr. *lor*, Cat. *llor*, etc.) :– L. *laurus*, prob. of Mediterranean origin. The later form is due to dissimilation of *r..r* to *r..l*; cf. Sp. *laurel.*] **1.** The Bay-tree or Bay-laurel, *Laurus nobilis*; see BAY *sb.*¹ 2. Now *rare*, exc. as in 2. **b.** Any plant of the genus *Laurus* or the N.O. *Lauraceæ*. LINDLEY. **2.** The foliage of this tree as an emblem of victory or of distinction in poetry, etc. **a.** *collect. sing.* ME. **b.** *pl.* 1585. **c.** A branch or wreath of this tree (*lit.* and *fig.*) ME. †**d.** The dignity of Poet Laureate –1814. **3.** In mod. use, applied to *Cerasus laurocerasus* and other trees having leaves like those of the true laurel 1664. **4.** *Numism.* One of the English gold pieces (esp. those of 20s.), first coined in 1619, on which the monarch's head was figured with a wreath of laurel 1623. **5.** *attrib.* ME.

1. The victor palm, the laurer to deuyne CHAUCER. **2. a.** Gyff lawrelle to that lord of myght 1460. **b.** Phr. *To reap, win one's laurels, to repose, rest, retire, on one's laurels. To look to one's laurels*: to beware of losing one's pre-eminence. **c.** Fame flies after with a l. M. PRIOR. **3. Alexandrian Laurel,** *Ruscus racemosus*; **American Dwarf** or **Mountain L.** = KALMIA; **Cherry L.,** *Cerasus laurocerasus*; **Great L.,** U.S. name for *Rhododendron maximum*; **Japan L.** = AUCUBA; **Portugal L.,** *Cerasus lusitanica*; **Spurge L.,** *Daphne laureola*. For *Ground-, Rose-, Sheep-l.*, see the first element. *Comb.*: **l.-bay** = *Bay-laurel* (sense 1); **-thyme** = LAURUSTINUS; **-tree** = sense 1; **-water,** the water obtained by distillation from the leaves of the cherry laurel and containing a small proportion of prussic acid.

†**Lau·rel,** *a.* 1606. [f. LAUREL *sb.*] Crowned or wreathed with laurel; hence, renowned –1606.

Vpon your Sword Sit Laurell victory SHAKS.

Laurel (lǫ·rĕl), *v.* 1631. [f. as prec.] *trans.* To wreathe with laurel; to adorn with or as with laurel.

Laurelled (lǫ·rĕld), *ppl. a.* 1682. [f. LAUREL *sb.* or *v.* + -ED.] **a.** Crowned or wreathed with laurel. Hence *fig.* honoured, illustrious; cf. LAUREATE. **b.** Covered with a growth of laurel; also, made of laurel.

a. *L. letters*: cf. LAUREATE *a.* 1 (quot.). **b.** Here no sepulchre built In the laurell'd rock M. ARNOLD.

Laurentian (lǫre·nʃ'ăn), *a.* 1863. [f. L. *Laurentius* Laurence + -AN.] *Geol.* Epithet of certain sedimentary strata found in Canada near the river St. Lawrence. Also quasi-*sb.* in collective sense.

†**Laureole.** Also **lauriol(e.** ME. [– Fr. *lauréole* – L. *laureola*, lit. little garland of laurel.] Spurge Laurel –1596.

Laurestinus, erron. f. LAURUSTINUS.

Lauric (lǫ·rik), *a.* 1857. [f. L. *laurus* laurel + -IC.] *L. acid*, a white crystalline compound ($C_{12}H_{24}O_2$) obtained from the berries of *Laurus nobilis*. Hence in *L. aldehyde, ether*, compounds derived from this acid.

Laurin (lǫ·rin). 1838. [f. as prec. + -IN¹.] *Chem.* A crystalline substance ($C_{22}H_{30}O_3$) obtained from the berries of *Laurus nobilis*.

Laurite (lǫ·rəit). 1866. [Named by Wöhler, 1866, after Mrs. *Laura* Joy; see -ITE¹ 2 b.] *Min.* Sulphide of ruthenium, found with platinum in small brilliant crystals.

Laurustine (lǫ·rŏstəin). Also *erron.* †**lauri-, laure-.** 1683. [Englished form of next.] = next.

Laurustinus (lǫ:rŏstəi·nŏs). 1664. [– mod. L. *laurus tinus*, i.e. *laurus* laurel, *tinus* wild laurel.] An evergreen winter-flowering shrub, *Viburnum tinus*.

Laus(e, obs. ff. LOOSE *a.*

†**Lauti·tious,** *a.* [f. L. *lautitia* magnificence (f. *lautus* washed, sumptuous) + -OUS.] Sumptuous. HERRICK.

Lauwine (lǫ·win, G. lauvī·nə). Also **law-.** 1818. [– G. *lawine*, †*lauwin(e*, etc., of Swiss origin. Ult. origin unknown.] An avalanche.

Lava (lā·vă). 1750. [– It. *lava* †stream suddenly caused by rain, applied in Neapolitan dial. to a lava-stream from Vesuvius, f. *lavare* LAVE *v.*¹] †**1.** A stream of molten rock issuing from the crater of a volcano or from fissures in the earth. **2.** The fluid or semi-fluid matter flowing from a volcano 1760. Also *fig.* **3.** The substance that results from the cooling of the molten rock 1750. **b.** A kind of lava, a bed of lava 1796. **4.** *attrib.* 1802.

Comb.: **l.-millstone,** a hard and coarse basaltic millstone, obtained from quarries near Andernach on the Rhine; **-ware,** a kind of stoneware, manufactured and coloured to assume the semi-vitreous appearance of l.

‖**Lavabo** (lăvēⁱ·bo). 1740. [L., = 'I will wash'.] **1.** *Eccl.* **a.** The ritual washing of the celebrant's hands at the offertory, accompanied by the saying of Ps. 25[6]: 6–12, beginning *Lavabo inter innocentes manus meas.* **b.** The small towel, also the basin, used in this rite. **2.** A washing-trough used in some mediæval monasteries 1883.

Lavage (læ·vėdʒ). 1895. [– Fr. *lavage*, f. *laver* wash; see LAVE *v.*¹, -AGE.] *Med.* A cleansing of the stomach by means of emetics administered in large quantities of water.

Lavant (læ·vănt). *Sussex* and *Hants.* 1774. [Of unkn. origin.] A land-spring.

Lavatic (lăvæ·tik), *a.* 1830. [f. LAVA + -ATIC, app. after *aquatic*.] Consisting of or resembling lava.

Lavation (lăvēⁱ·ʃən). 1627. [– L. *lavatio* washing, f. *lavat-*, pa. ppl. stem of *lavare* wash; see -ION.] The action or an act of washing; *concr.* water for washing.

Lavatory (læ·vătŏri), *sb.* ME. [– late L. *lavatorium*, f. as prec.; see -ORY¹.] **1.** A vessel for washing, a laver, a bath. Also †*fig.* **2.** *Eccl.* The ritual washing of the celebrant's hands: (*a*) at the offertory (cf. LAVABO 1 a); †(*b*) at the taking of the ablutions. 1512. †**3.** A lotion –1694. **4.** An apartment with apparatus for washing the hands and face; now often combined with water-closets, etc. 1656. **5.** A laundry 1661. **6.** A place for washing gold 1727.

Lavatory (læ·vătŏri), *a.* 1846. [app. attrib. use of prec.] Of or pertaining to washing.

†**Lavature.** 1601. [– med.L. *lavatura* washing water, slops, f. as prec.; see -URE.] A lotion, a wash.

Lave (lēⁱv), *sb.* *Obs.* exc. *Sc.* [OE. *lāf* = OFris. *lāva*, OLG. *lēva*, OHG. *leiba*, ON. *leif*, Goth. *laiba* :– Gmc. **laibo*; see LEAVE *v.*¹] What is left over; the remainder, the rest.

†**Lave,** *a.* ME. [See LAVE *v.*²] Of ears (esp. a horse's ears): Drooping, hanging –1675. Hence **Lave-eared** (corruptly **leaf-eared**) *a.*, having lave ears.

Lave (lēⁱv), *v.*¹ Now chiefly *poet.* [– (O)Fr. *laver* :– L. *lavare* wash. Coalesced in ME. with OE. *lafian* wash by affusion, pour (water), if this verb survived (= (M)Du. *laven*, OHG, *labōn*, G. *laben* refresh – L. *lavare*).] **1.** *trans.* To wash, bathe. Also *fig.* Also *intr.* for *refl.* OE. **2.** *trans.* Of a body of water: To wash against, to flow along or past 1623. **3.** To pour out with or as with a ladle; to ladle. Also *absol.* OE. †**4.** *trans.* To draw (water) out or up with a bucket, ladle, or scoop; to bale. Also with *out, up,* and compl., and *absol.* –1708.

1. Basons, and ewers, to laue her dainty hands SHAKS. *intr.* In her chaste current oft the goddess laves POPE. **2.** Where Torridge laves its banks of green 1859. **3.** L. the water..in slight handfuls ..over the head and face 1862.

†**Lave,** *v.*² [Cf. ON. *lafa* to droop.] Of the ears: To droop, hang down. BP. HALL.

Laveer (lăvīᵊ·ɹ), *v.* *Obs.* exc. *literary.* 1598. [– Du. *laveeren*, earlier †*loveren* – Fr. †*loveer* (mod. *louvoyer*), f. *lof* windward, LUFF *sb.*; see -EER².] *intr.* To beat to windward; to tack. Hence **Lavee·rer,** one who laveers.

Lavement (lēⁱ·vˌmĕnt). 1650. [– (O)Fr. *lavement*, f. *laver* wash; see -MENT. Cf. med.L. *lavamentum*.] **1.** The action of washing or cleansing (*rare*). **2.** *Med.* An injection 1794.

†**La·vender,** *sb.*¹ ME. [– OFr. *lavandier* m., *-ière* fem. – Rom. **lavandarius*, f. L. *lavanda* things to be washed, n. pl. of gerundive of *lavare* wash; see -ER² 2.] A washer-woman, laundress. †Formerly also (*rarely*), a man who washes clothes. –1567.

Enuye..is lauender In the grete court alway CHAUCER.

Lavender (læ·vėndəɹ), *sb.*² and *a.* ME. [– AFr. *lavendre*, for **lavendle* – med.L. *lavendula*, etc. If the ult. source is L. *lavare* wash, the sense-development is obscure.]

A. *sb.* **1.** The plant *Lavandula vera* (N.O. *Labiatæ*), a small shrub with small pale bluish flowers, and narrow oblong or lanceolate leaves; cultivated extensively for its perfume. Also applied to *L. spica* (distinguished as *French L.* and †*L. spike*), and *L. stœchas* (formerly †*L. gentle*), and to certain other plants. **2.** The flowers and stalks of *Lavandula vera*, laid among linen or other clothes to preserve them from moths when stored 1584. **3.** The colour of lavender-flowers, a very pale blue with a trace of red 1882.

1. Here's flowers for you: Hot Lauender, Mints, Sauory, mariorum SHAKS. **Sea L.,** *Statice limonium*; also called †*Marsh L., L. Thrift.* †**L. of Spain** = LAVENDER COTTON. **2.** Phr. *To lay (up) in l.*: (*a*) to lay aside carefully for future use; (*b*) *slang*, to pawn; (*c*) to put out of the way of doing harm.

B. *adj.* Of the colour of lavender-flowers (see A. 3) 1882.

Too much of a lavender-kid-glove gentleman 1897. Hence **La·vender** *v. trans.* to perfume with l.; to put l. among (linen).

La·vender co·tton. 1530. Ground cypress (*Santolina chamæcyparissus*); formerly confused with *Artemisia abrotanum* or *maritima*.

La·vender-wa:ter. 1563. A perfume compounded, with alcohol and ambergris, from the distilled flowers of lavender.

Laver (lēⁱ·vəɹ), *sb.*¹ OE. [– L. *laver* (Pliny).] †**1.** A water-plant; = Gr. σίον –1601. **2.** A name for various marine algæ, esp., now, the edible species 1611. Also *attrib.*

2. Purple l., *Porphyra laciniata*. **Green l.,** *Ulva latissima* and *Ulva lactuca*.

Laver (lēⁱ·vəɹ), *sb.*² [ME. *lavo(u)r* – OFr. *laveor, laveoir* (mod. *lavoir*) – L. *lavatorium* LAVATORY.] **1.** A vessel, basin, or cistern for washing; in early use, chiefly a (metal) water-jug; *occas.* a pan or bowl for water. Now only *poet.* or *rhet.* **b.** The large brazen vessel for the ablutions of the Jewish priests (= Heb. *kiyyōr*, Vulg. *labrum*) 1535. **c.** The basin of a fountain. *Obs.* exc. *arch.* 1604. **2.** *transf.* and *fig.* The baptismal font; the spiritual 'washing' of baptism; any spiritually cleansing agency. After Gr. λουτρὸν παλιγγενεσίας Tit. 3:5. ME. †**3.** A process or mode of ablution –1684.

Laveroc(k, etc.: see LARK *sb.*¹

Lavic (lā·vik), *a.* 1835. [f. LAVA + -IC.] Of or pertaining to lava.

†**Lavish,** *sb.* 1483. [In XV, *lavas* – OFr. *lavasse* deluge of rain (cf. OFr. *lavis* 'torrent' of words), f. *laver* wash, pour; see LAVE *v.*¹, -ISH¹.] Profusion, excessive abundance; prodigality, lavishness. Phr. *To make l.* –1597.

Lavish (læ·viʃ), *a.* 1475. [f. LAVISH *sb.*] **1.** Effusive 1485; †unrestrained; loose, wild, licentious –1640. **2. a.** Expending or bestowing without stint; profuse; prodigal. Const. *of, in.* In early use often: Wasteful, extravagant. 1475. **b.** Expended, bestowed, or produced unstintedly; profuse, abundant 1576.

1. Phr. *L. of (one's) tongue.* When Meanes and lauish Manners meete together SHAKS. **2.** Your l. wasting servants..will be glad of a crust before they dye 1643. **b.** Let her haue needfull but not lauish meanes SHAKS. Hence **La·vish-ly** *adv.*, **-ness.**

Lavish (læ·viʃ), *v.* 1542. [f. LAVISH *a.*] **1.** *intr.* To be lavish, e.g. of words, etc. 1567. **2.** *trans.* To bestow, distribute, or spend profusely and recklessly; also with *away, out.*

2. They lauish gold out of the bagge *Isa.* 46:6. To l. pity on any one FULLER. Hence **La·visher. La·vishingly** *adv.* **La·vishment** (now *rare*), the action of lavishing.

Lavolta (lăvǫ·ltă), *sb.* *Obs.* exc. *arch.* *Englished* **lavolt.** 1580. [f. It. *la* the + *volta* turn.] 'A lively dance for two persons, consisting a good deal in high and active bounds' (Nares). Also *transf.* and *fig.*

Behold the sunne-beames.., Dancing Lauoltoes on the liquid floare 1600. Hence †**Lavo·lta** *v.* to dance a l.; to caper as in the l. †**Lavoltetee·r,** one who dances the l.

Lavrock, var. of LARK *sb.*[1]

Lavy (læ·vi). 1698. [Of unkn. origin.] A St. Kilda name for the guillemot.

Law (lǭ), *sb.*[1] [Late OE. *lagu* (pl. *laga*), whence ME. *laʒe, lawe*, repl. native *æ* (Æ *sb.*[2]); – ON. **lagu* (whence OIcel. *lǫg* collect., law); pl. of *lag* layer, stratum, share or partnership, fixed price, set tune :– **laʒam*, f. Gmc. **laʒ-* place; see LAY *v.*, LIE *v.*[1]]

I. **Human law.* **1.** The body of rules, whether formally enacted or customary, which a state or community recognizes as binding on its members or subjects. (In this sense usually *the law.*) †Also, in early use, a code or system of such rules. **b.** Often personified as an agent 1513. †**c.** What the law awards –1593. **2.** One of these rules. In early use only *pl.*, often with a collective sense (after L. *iura, leges*). OE. **3.** *gen.* **a.** Laws as obeyed or enforced; controlling influence of laws; the condition of society in which laws are observed ME. **b.** (*a*) Laws in general, as a human institution. (*b*) The science of which laws are the subject-matter; jurisprudence. ME. **c.** Rules or injunctions that must be obeyed ME. **4.** Often defined, according to the matter with which it is concerned, as *commercial, ecclesiastical*, etc. *l., the l. of evidence*, etc.; or according to the source from which it is derived, as *statute l., customary l., case-l.* (see CASE *sb.*[1]), etc. (*The*) *Canon l.*: see CANON[1]. Also CIVIL LAW, COMMON LAW, *Martial l.* (see MARTIAL). **b.** *Both laws* [after med.L. (*doctor*, etc.) *utriusque iuris*]: in mediæval use, the Civil and Canon Law; in modern Scotland, the Roman Civil Law and the municipal law of the country 1577. **c.** *International law, the l. of nations*, under which nations, as individual members of a common polity, are bound by a common rule of agreement or custom; opp. to *municipal l.*, the rules binding in local jurisdictions (see MUNICIPAL) 1548. **5.** In English technical use, the Statute and Common Law, in contradistinction to EQUITY 1591. **6.** Applied predicatively to legal decisions or opinions to denote that they are correct. Also *good* or *bad l.* 1593. **7.** (Usu. *the law.*) The legal profession. Orig. in *man of l.* (now somewhat *arch.*), a lawyer. ME. **b.** Legal knowledge 1630. **8.** The action of the courts of law, as a means of procuring redress of grievances, etc.; judicial remedy. *Occas.* = recourse to the courts, litigation. 1450.

1. The Venetian Law Cannot impugne you as you do proceed SHAKS. **b.** 'If the law supposes that,' said Mr. Bumble,..'the law is a ass—a idiot' DICKENS. Phr. *The l. of the Medes and Persians* (see Dan. 6:12): often used as a type of something unalterable. *Wager of L.*: see WAGER *sb.* **2.** A L. is the Command of him, or them that have the Soveraign Power HOBBES. **3. a.** Phr. *L. and order. Necessity knows* (or *has*) *no law.* **b.** Phr. *Court of l.* = COURT *sb.*[1] IV. 2. He consults men learned in the l. J. H. NEWMAN. **c.** Phr. *To give* (*the*) *l.* (*to*): to exercise undisputed sway; to impose one's will †*upon* (another). His father's wishes were l. 1853. **4. c.** The L. or Custom of Nations HOBBES. **7.** Three of his brothers are in the l. 1902. **8.** Phr. *To go to* (†*the*) *l., to have* or *take the l. of* or *on* (a person). *To take the l. into one's own hands* (transf.): to redress one's own grievance, or punish an offender, without judicial aid. *Halifax l., Lidford l.*: the summary procedure of certain local tribunals which acted on the maxim 'hang first, try afterwards'.

***Divine Law.* **9.** The body of commandments which express the will of God with regard to the conduct of His intelligent creatures. Also (with *a, the*, and *pl.*) a particular commandment. **a.** *gen.* OE. **b.** as revealed, esp. in the Bible. Hence *occas.* the Scriptures themselves. OE. **c.** as implanted in the mind by nature, or as demonstrable by reason ME. **10.** The precepts contained in the Pentateuch; esp. the ceremonial precepts considered separately OE. **b.** The Mosaic dispensation (as opp. to *the Gospel*); also, the system of Divine commands and of penalties contained in the Scriptures, considered apart from the offer of salvation by faith in Christ ME. **c.** The Pentateuch by itself ME. †**11.** A dispensation –1542. †**12.** A religious system; the Christian, Jewish, Moslem, or Pagan religion –1685.

9. a. Phr. *God's* (*Christ's*) *l., the l. of God.* **b.** His delight is in the L. of the Lord *Ps.* 1:2. **c.** Phr. †*L. of kind, natural l.* (now rarely *the l. of nature*), *l. of reason*, etc. **10.** Phr. *The l. of Moses, the Mosaic* or *Jewish l.*, etc. The Gentiles which haue not the L., doe by nature the things contained in the L. *Rom.* 2:14. **b.** Vain were all the deeds of the L. J. H. NEWMAN. **11.** *The old l.*, the Mosaic dispensation, the 'Old Covenant'; also, the books of the O.T. *The new l.*, the Gospel dispensation. **12.** Phr. *By my l.*: by my faith; By my lawe sire sayd Mopsius I see no way CAXTON.

****Combined applications.* **13.** Often used as the subject of propositions equally applying to human and divine law 1594.

My designe being not to shew what is L. here, and there, but what is L. HOBBES.

II. Without reference to an external commanding authority. †**1.** Custom, customary rule or usage; habit, practice, ways –15.. †**b.** *Old Cant.* A (specified) branch of the art of thieving –1591. †**2.** What is or is considered right or proper –ME. **3.** A rule of action or procedure, e.g. in an art or department of action, a game, etc. †Also, manner of life. ME. **b.** The code or body of rules recognized in a specified department of action ME.

1. *L. of* (*the*) *land*: custom of the country. **3.** These [the Gentiles] hauing not the L., are a L. vnto themselues *Rom.* 2:14. Self-protection is the first l. of life FROUDE. **b.** Phr. *L. of arms*: the settled custom of professional soldiers. *L. of honour* (see HONOUR *sb.*).

III. Scientific and philosophical uses. **1.** In the sciences of observation, a theoretical principle deduced from particular facts, expressible by the statement that a particular phenomenon always occurs if certain conditions be present. In the physical sciences, etc., called more explicitly *l. of nature* or *natural l.*, and in early use viewed as a command imposed by the Deity upon matter. 1665. **2.** Laws (of Nature) in general; the order and regularity in Nature expressed by laws 1853.

1. The conformity of individual cases to the general rule is that which constitutes a L. of Nature WHATELY. *Laws of motion*: chiefly used *spec.* for Newton's three propositions concerning motion and force. In certain sciences, particular laws are known by the names of their discoverers, as *Bode's law* concerning the distances of the planets, and *Kepler's laws* of planetary motions; *Avogadro's law* concerning the number of molecules in equal volumes of different gases, *Boyle's law* concerning the volume and pressure of gas, *Charles's law* concerning the volume and temperature of a gas, and *Dulong and Petit's law* of atomic heats; *Grimm's, Verner's, and Grassmann's laws* relating to certain sound changes in the Indo-European languages. **2.** In the argument against miracles the first objection is that they are against l. MOZLEY.

IV. *Sport.* An allowance in time or distance made to an animal that is to be hunted, or to a competitor in a race; a start 1600. **b.** Hence, Indulgence, mercy 1649.

So Huntsmen fair unto the Hares give L. DENHAM. **b.** The 'on dit' is that he has ten days more l. 1849.

attrib. and *Comb.* **1.** General: as in *l. dictionary, -faculty, -library, -system*, etc.; *l.-list*; *l.-charges, -costs, -reports*, etc.; *l.-binding, -calf, -sheep*, etc.

2. Special: **l.-bible,** Irish R.C. name for the Authorized Version; **-French,** the corrupt Norman French used in English law-books; **-Latin,** the barbarous Latin of early English statutes; **-lord,** one of the members of the House of Lords qualified to take part in its judicial business; **-neck-cloth,** joc. for a pillory; **-office** (*U.S.*) a lawyer's office; **-officer,** a public functionary employed in the administration of the l., or to advise the government in legal matters; *spec.* (in England) *law-officer* (*of the Crown*), either the Attorney or Solicitor General; †**prudent** *a.* [after *iuris prudentia*], marked by legal learning; **-term,** (*a*) a word or expression used in l.; (*b*) one of the periods appointed for the sitting of the law-courts; **-writer,** †(*a*) a legislator; (*b*) one who writes books on l.; (*c*) one who copies or engrosses legal documents.

Law (lǭ), *sb.*[2] *Sc.* and *north.* ME. [Northern repr. OE. *hlāw* LOW *sb.*[1]] **1.** A (more or less conical) hill, as *North Berwick L.*, etc. †**2.** A monumental tumulus of stones. CAMDEN.

Law (lǭ), *v.* [OE. *lagian*, f. *lagu* LAW *sb.*[1]] †**1.** *trans.* To ordain (laws); to render lawful –1651. **b.** *Sc.* To give the law to. BURNS. **2.** *intr.* To go to law, litigate. Also *to l. it.* Also quasi-*trans.* 1485. **b.** *trans.* To go to law with 1647. **3.** To mutilate (an animal) so as to make it incapable of doing mischief; usu. *spec.* to EXPEDITATE (a dog). *Obs.* exc. *Hist.* 1534.

Law (lǭ), *int.* Now *vulgar.* 1588. [Cf. LA, LO; in later use coalescing with *lor'* = LORD as an exclam.] An exclam. of astonishment; in early use chiefly asseverative.

Law-abi:ding, *a.* 1867. [f. LAW *sb.*[1] + pr. pple. of ABIDE *v.*] Abiding by, i.e. maintaining or submitting to the law.

Law·-book. ME. [f. LAW *sb.*[1] + BOOK. Cf. ON. *lǫg-bók.*] **1.** A book containing a code of laws. **2.** Chiefly *pl.* A book treating of law 1555.

Law·-breaker. ME. [Cf. OE. *lahbreca.*] One who violates the law.

Law·-day. *Obs.* exc. *Hist.* ME. [f. LAW *sb.*[1]] The day for the meeting of a court of law, esp. of a sheriff's court, or of the court leet; hence, the session of such a court, or the court itself.

Laweour, -er(e, -eyer(e, obs. ff. LAWYER.

Lawful (lǭ·fŭl), *a.* ME. [f. LAW *sb.*[1] + -FUL.] **1.** According or not contrary to law; permitted by law. †**b.** Permissible; justifiable –1717. **2.** Appointed, sanctioned, or recognized by law; legally qualified or entitled ME. **b.** Of offspring: Legitimate 1513. †**3.** Law-abiding, loyal –1642.

1. It is lawfull for all men, to saue themselues from violence 1560. **2.** Phr. *L. heir, king, money, succession, title*, etc.; also *l. captive, prey, prize,* (*to be*) *l. game*. Truly she must be giuen, or the marriage is not lawfull SHAKS. Phr. *L. age, years*: the age at which a person attains his legal majority. *L. day*, one on which it is lawful to transact business, or some particular kind of business. *L. money*, in certain American colonies, the local currency at the coin value upon which that which circulated in the colony was based before Queen Anne's proclamation of 1704. Hence **Law·ful-ly** *adv.*, **-ness.**

Lawgiver (lǭ·gi:vəɹ). ME. [f. LAW *sb.*[1] + GIVER.] One who gives, i.e. makes or promulgates, a law or code of laws; a legislator. So **Law·-giving** *ppl. a.* that gives or makes laws; also *occas.* that gives the law to.

Law·-hand. 1731. The style of handwriting used for legal documents. Also *occas.* matter written in this hand.

An immense desert of law-hand and parchment DICKENS.

Lawk, lawks (lǭk(s), *int.* 1768. [Deformation of LORD, perh. suggested by ALACK.] = Lord! Also *Lawk-a-mussy* = Lord have mercy! *Lawk-a-daisy* (*me*) = LACKADAISY.

Lawless (lǭ·lės), *a.* ME. [f. LAW *sb.*[1] + -LESS.] **1.** Without law; ignorant of, or not regulated by law. Of a law: Not based on right. Now *rare.* **b.** Exempt from law, above or beyond the reach of law ME. **2.** Regardless of, or disobedient to law. Of passions, etc.: Unbridled. ME.

1. A barbarous..people whose law is lawlesse HAKLUYT. **2.** Lawlesse desires are seas scorning all bounds DEKKER. L. violence 1855. Hence **Law·less-ly** *adv.*, **-ness.**

Law·-ma:ker. ME. [f. LAW *sb.*[1] + MAKER.] One who makes laws; a legislator.

Law·-me:rchant. 1622. [f. LAW *sb.*[1] + MERCHANT *a.*, after med.L. *lex mercatoria.*] A special system of rules for the regulation of trade and commerce, differing in some respects from the Common Law.

Lawn (lǫn), *sb.*[1] ME. [prob. f. *Laon*, name of a town in France, an important place of linen manufacture.] **1.** A kind of fine linen, resembling cambric; *pl.* pieces or sorts of this. Also *transf.* and *fig.* **2.** *spec.* This fabric used for the sleeves of a bishop. Hence, the dignity or office of a bishop. 1732. †**3.** An article of dress, etc., made of lawn –1812.

2. A Saint in Crape is twice a Saint in L. POPE. *Comb.* **l.-sieve,** a fine sieve, made of l. (or silk), used in cookery, porcelain-manufacture, etc.

Lawn (lǭn), *sb.*[2] 1548. [Later form of LAUND. For loss of *d* cf. GROIN *sb.*[2]] **1.** = LAUND. Now *arch.* and *dial.* **b.** A stretch of untilled or grass-covered ground 1674. **2.** A portion of a garden, etc., covered with grass, which is kept closely mown 1733. Also *attrib.*

1. The thistly l., the thick-entangled broom THOMSON. **2.** This L., a carpet all alive With shadows flung from leaves WORDSW.

Comb.: **l.-meet,** the meeting of a hunt in front of a gentleman's house; **-mower,** a machine provided with revolving spiral knives for cutting the grass on a l.; **-sprinkler,** a machine with revolving tubular arms from which water is sprinkled like rain. Hence **Lawn** *v. trans.* to turn into l. or grass-land; to make lawn-like.

Lawn sleeves, lawn-sleeves. 1640. Sleeves of lawn, as part of the episcopal dress. Hence, the dignity or office of a bishop; also, a bishop or bishops. **Lawn-sleeved** *a.*

Law·n-te·nnis. 1874. [LAWN *sb.*[2]] A modification of the game of tennis, played in the open air on a lawn or other prepared ground.

Lawny (lǭ·ni), *a.*[1] 1598. [f. LAWN *sb.*[1] + -Y[1].] **1.** Made of lawn. **b.** Dressed in lawn; also, pertaining to a wearer of lawn, i.e. a bishop 1647. **2.** Lawn-like 1615.

Lawny (lǭ·ni), *a.*[2] 1613. [f. LAWN *sb.*[2] + -Y[1].] †**a.** Containing lawns or glades. **b.** Resembling a lawn; covered with smooth grass.

b. There was a little l. islet SHELLEY.

Law·-sta:tioner. 1836. [f. LAW *sb.*[1] + STATIONER.] A tradesman who keeps in stock stationery and other things required by lawyers, and takes in manuscripts, etc. to be engrossed.

Lawsuit (lǭ·siūt). 1624. [f. LAW *sb.*[1] + SUIT *sb.*] A suit in law; a prosecution of a claim in a court of law.

Law·-wo:rthy, *a.* ? *Hist.* [f. LAW *sb.*[1] + WORTHY; a mod. rendering of OE. *þæra laga weorðe* (*þe*, etc.), 'worthy of (i.e. entitled to) the laws (which, etc.)'.] **a.** Of persons: Having a standing in the law-courts. **b.** Of things: Within the purview of the law; able to be dealt with by a court of law. 1818.

Lawyer (lǭ·yəɹ). [ME. *lawier, lawer,* f. LAW *sb.*[1]; see -ER[1], -IER 1, -YER.] **1.** One versed in the law; a member of the legal profession, one whose business it is to advise clients, or to conduct suits in the courts. Colloquially often limited to attorneys and solicitors. †**2.** A law-giver. MORE. **3.** *dial.* A long bramble 1857. **4.** *Penang lawyer* (see below) 1828. **5.** *Zool.* Local name in U.S. for: **a.** The Black-necked Stilt (*Himantopus nigricollis*); **b.** the Burbot (*Lota maculosa*), and the Bowfin or Mudfish (*Amia calva*). 1850.

1. A l. thus educated to the bar BLACKSTONE. **4.** *Penang l.*: a kind of walking-stick, made from the stem of a dwarf palm having prickly stalks, and much used in settling disputes at Penang.

Comb. **Lawyer-like** *a.* and *adv.* Hence **Law·-yerly** *a.*

Lax (læks), *sb.*[1] *Obs.* (revived as an alien wd. from the Continent.) [OE. *læx* (WS. *leax*) = LG. *las,* OHG. *lahs* (G. *lachs*), ON. (Sw., Da.) *lax* :– Gmc. **laxs-*.] A salmon; in later use, some particular kind of salmon.

Lax, *sb.*[2] 1526. [perh. f. LAX *v.*] †**1.** A laxative medicine –1544. **2.** = LASK *sb.* 1. *Obs.* exc. *dial.* 1540.

Lax (læks), *a.* ME. [– L. *laxus* loose. See SLACK *a.*] **1.** Of the bowels: Acting easily, loose. **2.** Slack; not tense, rigid, or tight. Hence of body or mind: Wanting in tone or tension. Now somewhat *rare.* 1660. **b.** Loose, relaxed 1782. **3. a.** Of organic tissue, stone, soils, etc.: Loose in texture; porous 1615. **b.** *Bot.* and *Zool.* Loosely or openly arranged, as an inflorescence, etc. 1796. **4.** Of clothes: Loose-fitting, worn loosely. Of persons: Negligent in attire and deportment. 1621. **5.** Loose, slack; vague, not precise 1450. **6.** quasi-*adv.* So as to have ample room. [A Latinism.] MILT. *P.L.* VII. 162.

1. The bowels l. ABERNETHY. **2.** Persons of weak l. fibre 1789. **4.** L. in their gaiters, laxer in their gait J. & H. SMITH. **5.** In a l. way of speaking BUTLER. L. metre 1847. L. in conduct 1874, in attendance 1884. Hence **La·x-ly** *adv.*, **-ness.**

†**Lax,** *v.* ME. [– L. *laxare,* f. *laxus* LAX *a.*] *trans.* To make lax; to loosen, relax; to purge. Also *absol.* –1685.

†**La·xate,** *v.* 1623. [– *laxat-,* pa. ppl. stem of L. *laxare* loosen; f. *laxus* LAX *a.*; see -ATE[3].] *trans.* To loosen, relax. Also *absol.* –1661.

Laxation (læksēi·ʃən). ME. [– late (medical) L. *laxatio,* f. as prec.; see -ION.] The action of loosening or relaxing; loosened or relaxed state; *occas.* an instance or means of relaxing.

Laxative (læ·ksătiv). ME. [– (O)Fr. *laxatif, -ive* or late (medical) L. *laxativus,* f. as prec.; see -IVE.]

A. *adj.* **1.** Having the property of relaxing. **2.** Of the bowels, or bodily constitution: Loose, subject to flux or free discharge of the fæces. Of a disease: Characterized by such discharge. Now *rare.* 1546. **b.** *transf.* Unable to contain one's speech or emotions. ? *Obs.* 1601.

2. b. Fellowes of practis'd and most laxatiue tongues B. JONS. Hence **La·xativeness.**

B. *sb.* **1.** A laxative medicine ME. †**2.** ? Relaxed condition of the bowels, flux –1527.

†‖**Laxator.** 1799. [mod.L. *laxator,* f. as prec.; see -OR 2.] *Anat.* A (supposed) muscle of the external ear –1808.

Laxist (læ·ksist). 1865. [f. LAX *a.* + -IST.] One who favours lax views or interpretation; *spec.* the designation given to the school of casuists in the Roman church who held that it was justifiable to follow any probability, however slight, in favour of liberty. Also *attrib.*

Laxity (læ·ksĭti). 1528. [– Fr. *laxité* or L. *laxitas,* f. *laxus*; see LAX *a.*, -ITY.] The quality of being lax: **a.** in physical senses; **b.** in moral and intellectual senses 1623.

b. Such tales..engender l. of morals among the young JOWETT.

†**Lay,** *sb.*[1] [Early ME. *lei, lai(e* – OFr. *lei* (mod. *loi*) :– *lex, leg-* law.] Law; *esp.* religious law; hence, a religion, a faith –1599.

Lay (lēi), *sb.*[2] ME. [– (O)Fr. *lai,* corresp. to Pr. *lais,* of unkn. origin.] **1.** A short lyric or narrative poem intended to be sung. Often *poet.* for 'song'. **b.** *poet.* Applied to the song of birds ME. †**2.** Strain, tune –1581.

1. The L. of the Last Minstrel SCOTT (*title*). These brief lays, of Sorrow born TENNYSON *In Mem.* **b.** The thrustelcok made eek his l. CHAUCER.

†**Lay,** *sb.*[3] ME. [perh. aphet. f. ALLAY *sb.*[1]] Alloy. Chiefly *attrib.* in *l. metal,* name of a kind of pewter. –1794.

Lay, *sb.*[4] 1558. [f. LAY *v.*] †**1.** A wager, stake –1769. **2.** A place of lying or lodging; lair, couch (of animals); an oyster- or mussel-bed 1590. †**3.** A layer; a course (of masonry) –1769. **4.** The act of imposing a tax; an impost, assessment, rate. Now *dial.* 1558. **5.** *slang.* A line or plan of business, occupation, adventure, etc.; a (particular) job, line, or tack 1707. **6.** The way, position, or direction in which anything is laid or lies (*esp.* said of country) 1819. **b.** *Naut.* Of a rope: The direction or amount of twist given to the strands. Also in *Spinning.* 1800. **c.** *Printing.* The relative position of the sheet of paper and the type or plate on the press 1871. **7.** A share in a venture; *esp.* in *Whaling,* the proportion of the proceeds of a voyage which is allotted to a man 1825. **8.** *In* (*full, good*) *l.*: laying eggs 1885.

1. It is an even laie, that an idiot shall conjecture right 1584. **3.** First they layed a l. of Brickes, then a Mat made of Canes, square as the Brickes HAKLUYT. **5.** He's not to be found on his old l. DICKENS. **6.** I..steered by the l. of the land THOREAU.

Lay (lēi), *sb.*[5] *dial.* 1789. [var. of LATHE[3] and [4].] **1.** *Weaving.* = LATHE[4]. **2.** Used for LATHE[3] 2. 1797.

Lay (lēi), *a.* (and *sb.*) ME. [– Fr. *lai* (now repl. by *laïque*) :– eccl. L. *laicus* – Gr. λαϊκός (cf. LAIC).] **1.** Of persons: Belonging to the 'people' as dist. from the clergy; non-clerical. (Often hyphened with official titles.) **2.** Characteristic of, connected with, occupied or performed by, laymen or the laity 1609. **3.** *transf.* †**a.** Unlearned (*rare*) –1535. **b.** Non-professional, *esp.* with reference to law and medicine 1810. †**c.** Unsanctified; secular, worldly, *esp.* in phr. *l. part.* –1668.

1. He expressed the most rooted prejudice against Lay-Preachers WESLEY. **2.** The bishop strove to get up a little l. conversation TROLLOPE. **3. b.** The prevention of disease..is too technical for l. interference 1897.

Special collocations. **L. abbot,** a layman in possession of abbey property. **L. baptism,** baptism administered by a layman. **L. brother,** a man who has taken the habit and vows of a religious order, but is employed mostly in manual labour. **L. clerk,** (*a*) a 'singing man' in a cathedral or collegiate church; (*b*) a parish clerk. **L. communion,** (*a*) the condition of being in communion with the Church as a layman; (*b*) the communicating of the laity in the Eucharist. **L. deacon,** a man in deacon's orders who follows a secular employment. **Lay-elder** (see ELDER *sb.*[2] 4). **L. lord,** a peer who is not a lawyer; opp. to *law lord.* †**L. presbyter,** ? = 'lay elder'. **L. reader,** a layman licensed to conduct religious services. **L. rector** (see RECTOR). **L. sister,** the analogue of 'lay brother'. **L. vicar** (see VICAR).

†**B.** *absol.* and *sb.* The lay people, laity; also, a layman –1680.

Lay (lēi), *v.* Pa. t. and pple. **laid** (lēid). [OE. *leċġan* = OFris. *ledza, leia,* OS. *leggian* (Du. *leggen*), OHG. *lecken, legen* (G. *legen*), ON. *legja,* Goth. *lagjan,* f. Gmc. **laȝjan,* f. **laȝ-,* var. of **leȝ-* LIE *v.*[1]] General sense: To cause to lie.

I. To prostrate. **1.** *trans.* To bring or cast down from an erect position; †*fig.* to cast down, abase. Now only with compl. **b.** Of wind or rain: To beat down (crops). Chiefly in *pass.* (In 16–17th c. spelt *ledge.*) 1590. **2.** To 'bring to bed' *of* a child; to deliver (a mother). *Obs.* exc. *dial.* 1460. **3.** To cause to subside (the sea, wind, dust, anxiety, anger, appetite, etc.). Now *arch.* or *dial.* exc. in *to l. the dust.* ME. **b.** To prevent (a spirit) from walking 1592. **4.** †To reduce (a swelling); to make to lie evenly 1579. **5.** *Naut.* To sail out so far as to bring (an object) to or below the horizon. (Opp. to *raise.*) 1574. **6.** *Gardening.* = LAYER *v.* 1 b. ? *Obs.* 1565.

1. One third of the town was laid in ashes 1890. *To l. low*: see the adj. **b.** Like flaws in summer laying lusty corn TENNYSON. **2.** The midwife that laid my mother of me BUNYAN. **3.** See how I l. the dust with my teares SHAKS. **b.** He faced the spectres of the mind And laid them TENNYSON.

II. To deposit. **1.** To place in a position of rest *on* the ground or other surface; to deposit OE. **2. a.** To place in a recumbent posture in a specified place ME. **b.** To deposit *in* the grave; to bury. Only with adv. or phr. indicating the place. OE. **3.** To produce and deposit (an egg). Also *absol.* OE. †**4.** With advb. phr. as compl., e.g. *to wed, in pawn*: To deposit as a pledge or in pawn; hence, to mortgage (lands) –1698. **5.** To deposit as a wager; to stake. Also *to l. a wager.* ME. **b.** *absol.* or *intr.* ME.

1. b. = *To lay on* or *upon the table* (see TABLE *sb.* II. 1. Phr.). **2. a.** The bent grass where I am laid M. ARNOLD. **b.** Part, in the Places where they fell, are laid DRYDEN. Phr. *To l. to sleep, asleep*: to put to rest; to bury; also *fig.* Also *to l. to rest.* **3.** There shall the great owle make her nest, and l. and hatch *Isa.* 34:15. **5.** Hee would l. ten to one, the king was dead 1632.

III. To place, set, apply. **1.** To place close *to*; to apply; sometimes const. *on, upon* OE. Also, †*To l. from, off* –1611. †**b.** To put *in* or commit *to* (prison) –1560. **c.** To put (dogs) *on* a scent. Also *to l. a trail on* (a quarry). 1781. **2.** To place (affection, hope, etc.) *on* or *in* a person or thing ME. **b.** *To l...before*: to bring to the sight of; hence, to submit to the consideration of OE. **3.** To set (a snare, a trap, an ambush); †to set (watch) ME. **b.** intr. *To l. for*: to set an ambush or a trap for; to waylay 1494. †**c.** *trans.* To set watch or guard in (a place); to beset; to search (a place) *for* –1645. †**4.** To post or station (soldiers, etc.); to station (post-horses) along a route. Also, to beset (a place) with soldiers. –1862. **b.** To place or locate (a scene) 1570. **5.** With object denoting a member of the body (see quots.) OE. **6.** *To l. hold* (*up*)*on, of*: to grasp, seize on; to avail oneself of (a pretext) 1535. **7.** *refl.* and *intr.* To apply oneself *to* 1535. **8.** *Mil.* To set (a gun, etc.) in the correct position for hitting a mark. Also *absol.* 1480. **9.** To put into a condition (usually one of subjection, passivity, or exposure), which is expressed by a complementary phrase ME.

1. Phr. *To l. to heart*: see HEART *sb.* And now also the axe is laid vnto the root of the trees *Luke* 3:9. He laid his robe from him *Jonah* 3:6. **2.** Phr. *To l. store upon*: to value (*arch.*). **b.** I shall this Day l. before my Reader a Letter ADDISON. **3.** Thou layd'st a Trap to take my Life SHAKS. **b.** Men in debt..layd for by their creditors MASSINGER. **c.** I..durst not peepe out, for all the Country is laid for me SHAKS. Phr. *To l. siege to*: to besiege; also *fig.* to attack. **4. b.** In faire Verona, where we l. our Scene SHAKS. **5.** Her arms across her breast she laid TENNYSON. Phr. †*To l. eyes on*: to look at. *To l. hands on* or *upon* a person or thing: (*a*) to place one's hands on or apply them to, esp. for purposes of appropriation or violence; hence (*b*) to seize, get hold of, appropriate; (*c*) to do violence to; now *to l. violent hands on* (with *oneself* = to commit suicide); (*d*) to perform the rite of imposition of hands in confirmation or ordination. *To l. a finger* or *one's finger(s upon*: see FINGER *sb.* 2. **6.** I laid hold of all Opportunities to exert it ADDISON. **9.** Phr. *To l. fallow, idle*: *to l.* (land) *dry, under water*: *l. under necessity, obligation, difficulty, a command*, etc. *To l. bare*: (*a*) to denude, remove the covering from; (*b*) to expose to view, reveal. *To l. under contribution*: see CONTRIBUTION 1. *To l. open, waste*: see the adjs. *To l. by the heels*: see HEEL *sb.*[1] *To l. alongside, by the lee*, etc. (*Naut.*). *To l. aback* (Naut.): to brace (a yard) in such a way that the wind will blow against the forward side of the sail. *To l....aboard* (Naut.): to run into or alongside (a ship), usually in order to board her. So *to l. close, to l. athwart the hawse.*

IV. To present, put forward. **1.** To put forward, allege (a claim, etc.) ME. **b.** To present (an information, indictment) in legal form 1798. **c.** *Law.* To state or describe *as*; to fix (damages) *at* a certain amount 1770. **2.** To bring forward as a charge, accusation, or imputation; to impute, attribute, ascribe. Const. *to, on.* ? *arch.* ME.

1. We muste not l. excuses LD. BERNERS. **c.** He laid his damages at 20,000*l*. 1891. **2.** There was leyde to him hye tresone 1473. E. G. with child, layd on the tapster WOOD. Phr. *To l. to* (a person's) *charge, at* or *to* (his) *door*: to charge upon. Also *to l. to one's credit*, etc.

V. To impose as a burden. **1.** To impose (a penalty, command, obligation, burden, tax, etc.). Const. *on, upon.* OE. **2.** To cast (blame, etc.) *on* or *upon* ME. **3.** *To l. stress, weight, emphasis on* or *upon*: to emphasize, attach importance to 1666. **4.** To bring (a stick, etc.) down *upon*; to inflict (blows). Also *to l. it on* (lit. and fig.) ME. **5.** *absol.* and *intr.* To deal blows; to make an attack. Chiefly in phrases with preps.; e.g. *to lay on* or *upon*; *to l. at* (now chiefly *dial.*); *to l. into* (slang or colloq.); *to l. about one*; occas. (trans.) *to l.* (a weapon) *about one*; whence *fig.* to act vigorously. ME. †**6.** To strike, beat, (a person) *on* the face, *over* the head, etc. (The personal obj. is prob. a dative.) –1712.

1. An additional duty..was laid on windows 1845. The burden of proof being laid on the accused person ROGERS. **3.** The great teachers laid all the stress on dogma 1890. **4.** I have laid it on Walpole..unsparingly MACAULAY. **5.** The sword of him that layeth at him cannot hold *Job* 41:26. They laid about them with their staves DISRAELI. **6.** Phr. †*To l. on the lips*: to kiss.

VI. To dispose or arrange properly over a surface. **1.** *trans.* To place in the proper horizontal position (a foundation (often *fig.*), a floor, stones or bricks) OE. **b.** To set out (a table), to spread (the cloth), place in order (plates, dishes, etc.); hence, in later use, to set out the table for (a meal). Also *absol.* †Also to prepare (a bed). ME. **c.** To trace (a ground-plan) 1594. **d.** *To l. a fire*: to place the fuel ready for lighting 1876. **e.** *Printing.* (*a*) To place and arrange (pages) for a forme upon the imposing stone; (*b*) to put (new type) in the cases. Also *to lay the case.* 1683. **2.** *Rope-making.* To twist yarn to form (a strand), or strands to form (a rope) 1486. **3.** *trans.* To fix the outlines of, arrange (a plan, plot, scheme); †to establish (a law), settle (a principle) OE. †**b.** *gen.* To contrive, arrange –1712. **c.** *intr.* †To make plans *for*; to plan, contrive, or intend *to do* something (now *dial.* and *U.S.*) 1450. **4.** *Naut. To l. one's* (or *a*) *course*: to be able to sail in the direction wished for, however barely the wind permits it (Smyth) 1669. †**5.** To set down *in* writing; to put into, express *in* (certain terms, or language) –1775. **6.** *Art.* **a.** To put upon a surface in layers; to put or arrange (colours, †a picture) on canvas 1570. **b.** *To l. a ground*: to spread a coating over a surface, as a basis for colours. So in Photogr., *to l. the grain.* 1762. **7.** To cover, spread, or coat (*with* something), esp. by way of ornament ME.

1. Thou Lord in the beginning hast layed the foundation of the earth *Heb.* 1:10. The first submarine cable was laid 1890. **b.** I found that the table was laid for three MARRYAT. **2.** The manner of laying the yarns into ropes 1853. **3.** His Design had been long laid W. WOTTON. **4.** The steamer's course was laid for Michipicoten 1890. **6.** Epithetes thick laid As varnish on a Harlot's cheek MILT. **7.** Black steel, Laid with gold tendrils 1879.

VII. In intr. uses, coinciding with or resembling those of LIE *v.*[1] (Now only an illiterate substitute for *lie.*) ME. **b.** *Naut.* To put oneself in a position indicated by the accompanying phr. or adv., e.g. *to l. at anchor, to l. by the wind*, etc. *To l. on the oars*, to cease rowing. 1530.

Thou..dashest him again to earth:—there let him l. BYRON. Phr. *To l. in wait*: see WAIT *sb.*

Comb. (with advs.) **Lay about.** †**a.** *trans.* To surround, beset. †**b.** *intr.* To contrive (*to do* something); to look out *for.* †**c.** To strike out with vigour. **L. abroad.** *trans.* To spread out (*arch.*). **L. aside.** *trans.* **a.** To put away from one's person; to put on one side. **b.** To dismiss from one's consideration or action; to abandon or postpone, to discontinue. †**c.** To get rid of. **d.** *pass.* To be incapacitated by illness. **L. away.** *trans.* = *lay aside*, a, b. **L. by.** **a.** *trans.* = *lay aside* a, b. **b.** To store up; to save (money). Also *absol.* **c.** To put away for future disposal or for safety. **d.** *pass.* To be 'laid aside' by illness. **e.** *intr.* (*Naut.*) = *lay to.* **L. down.** *trans.* **a.** To put down upon the ground, etc. *To l. down* (*one's*) *arms*: to surrender. **b.** To relinquish (office, hopes, etc.). **c.** To place in a recumbent or prostrate position. Often *refl.* **d.** To put down (money) as a wager or payment. **e.** To sacrifice (one's life). **f.** To construct (roads, railways, ships). Also *to l. down a keel.* **g.** To formulate definitely (a principle, rule, course of action, etc.). *To l. down the law*: to declare what the law is; hence *colloq.* to dogmatize. **h.** To set down on paper. **i.** *Agric.* To plant or sow (a field) with a certain crop, e.g. grass, etc. **j.** To store (wine) in cellars. **k.** *Sporting slang. To l. himself* (or simply *lay*) *down to his work*: of a horse, etc. to put all his strength into a race. **L. in.** **a.** *trans. To l. in the oars*: to unship them. **b.** To provide oneself with a stock of. Also said of 'taking in' food; hence *absol.* to feed vigorously (now *vulgar*). †**c.** To put in (a claim). Also *absol.* **d.** *Gardening.* To place in position (the new wood of a trained tree). **e.** To paint (a picture, etc.) in its first unfinished stage. **f.** To deliver (a blow). **g.** To discontinue working (a colliery). **L. off.** **a.** *trans.* To take off (now *U.S.*). †**b.** *Naut.* To steer (a ship) away from the shore. **c.** To mark off (plots of ground, etc.); to plot out land. **d.** To set off (distances) upon a surface. **e.** *Shipbuilding.* To transfer (plans) from the paper in the full size on the floor of the mould-loft. **f.** *dial.* and *U.S.* To discontinue; to discontinue the working of; to dismiss (a workman), usu. temporarily. Also *intr.*, to take a rest. **L. on.** **a.** *trans.* To impose (an injunction, penalty, tax). **b.** *intr.* To deal blows with vigour; to assail. **c.** *trans.* To inflict (blows); to ply (the lash). Also *to l. it on.* **d.** *To l.* (*it*) *on*: †(*a*) to be lavish in expense; (*b*) to pile on the charge for goods, etc. **e.** To apply a coat of (paint, etc.) to a surface. **f.** *Agric.* Of cattle: To put on (flesh); also *absol.* **g.** To put (dogs) on the scent. Also *transf.* in joc. use. **h.** To provide for the supply of (water, gas, etc.) through pipes from a reservoir. **L. out.** **a.** *trans.* To extend at length; to take out and expose to view, to the air, etc.; to spread out in order; to lay so as to project outwards. **b.** To stretch out and prepare (a body) for burial; hence (*slang*) to lay low, to 'do for'; (*fig.*) to put 'hors de combat'. **c.** To spend, expend (money). Also *absol.* †**d.** To exercise (powers, effort). **e.** *refl.* †To exert oneself *in, upon*; to take measures with a view to something. Const. *for, to* with *inf.* **f.** *intr.* With *for*: †To look out for; to take measures to win or get. Also, to scheme, plan *to* effect something. **g.** To display; to set forth, expound, demonstrate. ?Now *rare.* **h.** To apportion (land) for a purpose; to plot or plan out (grounds, streets, etc.). **i.** To map out; to set as a task or duty. **j.** *intr.* (*Naut.*). To go out towards the yard arms for the purpose of manipulating the sails. (Cf. *lie out.*) **L. over.** **a.** *trans.* To overlay. **b.** *U.S. colloq.* To allow to pass by; to postpone. **c.** ? *U.S. colloq.* To excel, put in the shade. **L. to.** *intr.* (*Naut.*) = *lie to* (see LIE *v.*[1]). **L. together.** **a.** *trans.* To place in juxtaposition; to add together. **b.** *To l....heads together*: to confer. **L. up.** **a.** *trans.* To put up and extend (one's limbs) on a couch. **b.** *Agric.* (*a*) To throw up (land) in ridges for sowing; often with *dry, rough, in ridges.* (*b*) To reserve for hay. **c.** To deposit in a place for safety; to store up; to put by. Often *absol.* to save money. Also *To l. up in lavender*: see LAVENDER *sb.*[2] 2. **d.** To cause to keep indoors or in bed through illness; often in *pass.* to be (taken) ill, to keep one's bed. **e.** To put away (a ship) in dock, etc. Also *intr.* for *pass.* or *refl.* **f.** *Rope-making* = sense VI. 2.

Lay, pa. t. of LIE *v.*[1]; dial. var. LEA *sb.*[2], *a.*

Lay-by (lē^{i}·bəi). 1879. [f. LAY *v.* + BY *adv.*] **1.** A slack part of a river in which barges are laid by out of use. **b.** A railway siding 1906. **2.** Something laid by; savings 1894.

Lay-day (lē^{i}·dē^{i}). 1845. [f. LAY *v.*; cf. G. *liegetage* pl. lay-days, (days of) demurrage.] *Comm.* One of a certain number of days allowed according to a charter-party for the loading and unloading of cargo.

Layer (lē^{i}·əɹ), *sb.* ME. [f. LAY *v.* + -ER[1].] **1.** One who or that which lays (see LAY *v.*). **2.** Something laid; a thickness of matter spread over a surface; *esp.* one of a series; a stratum, course, or bed ME. Also *fig.* **3.** *Gardening* and *Agric.* **a.** A shoot or twig of a plant fastened down and partly covered with earth, so that it may strike root while still attached to the parent stock 1664. **b.** *pl.* Patches of laid corn 1634. **c.** A field of grass or clover 1793.

Layer (lē^{i}·əɹ), *v.* 1796. [f. LAYER *sb.* 3.] **1.** *Gardening.* **a.** *intr.* To bend down layers to the ground and cover them partly with earth so that they may strike root and propagate the plant. **b.** *trans.* To propagate by layers. **c.** To make a layer of. **2.** Of crops: To be laid flat through weakness of growth 1882.

‖**Layette** (leye·t). 1874. [Fr., dim. of OFr. *laie* drawer, box – MDu. *laege*; see -ETTE.] Outfit of garments, toilet articles, and bedding for a new-born child.

Lay-fee. *Obs.* exc. *Hist.* ME. [– AFr. *lai fe*; see LAY *a.*, FEE *sb.*[2]] **1.** A fee or estate in land held by secular services, as dist. from an eccl. fee. †**2.** The laity. Orig. in phr. *of the lay fee.* –1641.

Lay figure (lē^{i}· fi·gəɹ). 1795. [f. *lay* (in LAY-MAN[2]) + FIGURE *sb.*] A jointed wooden figure of the human body, used by artists for the arrangement of draperies, posing, etc. **b.** *fig.* A person of no consequence, a nonentity; an unreal character in a novel 1835.

Laying (lē^{i}·iŋ), *vbl. sb.* ME. [f. LAY *v.* + -ING[1].] **1.** The action of LAY *v. Laying-on* = IMPOSITION (of hands). **2.** *concr.* **a.** What is laid. **b.** A layer, bed, stratum 1683. **c.** An oyster-bed 1846. **d.** *Building.* 'The first coat on lath of two-coat plaster, or set-work' 1823.

Lay-land: see LEA-LAND.

Layloc(k, obs. and dial. f. LILAC.

Layman[1] (lē^{i}·mæ̆n). ME. [orig. two wds.; see LAY *a.*] **1.** One of the laity. **2.** *transf.* An 'outsider' or non-expert (esp. in relation to law or medicine) 1477.

2. To declare and expresse to the lay men that be not learned in the law *Littleton's Tenures.* So **Lay·woman.**

†**Lay-man**[2]. 1688. [– Du. *leeman* for *ledenman, f. *led* (now *lid*) limb, joint (cf. LIMB).] = LAY FIGURE –1796.

Layner, obs. f. LAINER.

Lay·-off. 1904. [subst. use of phr. *lay off* (LAY *v.*).] A period during which a workman is temporarily discharged.

Lay·-out. 1869. Chiefly *U.S.* [See *lay out*, LAY *v.*] The act or process of laying out or planning in detail; that which is laid or spread out.

Lay-shaft. 1908. [prob. f. LAY *v.* VII.] A secondary shaft of a machine, driven by gearing from the main shaft.

†**Lay·ship.** [f. LAY *a.* + -SHIP.] The condition of a layman. MILT.

Laystall (lē^{i}·stǭl). 1527. [f. LAY *v.* + STALL *sb.*[1]] †**1.** A burial-place –1556. **2.** A place where refuse and dung are laid 1553.

2. The common Lay-stall of a Citie DRAYTON. So †**Laystow.**

Lazar (lē^{i}·zăɹ), *sb.* (*a.*) *arch.* ME. [– (partly through OFr. *lasdre*, mod. *ladre*) med.L. *lazarus*, an application of the proper name *Lazarus*, Luke 16:20.] **1.** A poor and diseased person, usu. one afflicted with a loathsome disease; *esp.* a leper. **2.** *adj.* Leprous 1483. Hence †**La·zarous** *a.* leprous.

Lazaret (læzăre·t). 1611. [– Fr. *lazaret* – It. *lazzaretto*; see next.] = next.

Lazaretto (læzăre·to). 1549. [– It. *lazzaretto*, f. †*lazzaro* LAZAR.] **1.** A house for the reception of the diseased poor, esp. lepers. (Chiefly with reference to foreign countries.) **2.** A building, occas. a ship, set apart for the performance of quarantine 1605. **3.** *Naut.* A space between decks, in some merchant vessels, used as a storeroom 1711.

La·zar-house. 1440. = prec., 1.

Lazarist (læ·zărist). 1747. [– Fr. *Lazariste*, f. *Lazare* Lazarus.] One of the Congregation of the Priests of the Mission founded by St. Vincent of Paul in 1624, and established in the College of St. Lazare at Paris.

Lazarus (læ·zărŏs). *rare.* 1508. [Proper name used allusively. See LAZAR.] A leper; a beggar.

Laze (lēⁱz), *sb. colloq.* 1862. [f. next.] The action of LAZE *v.*; an instance of this.

Laze (lēⁱz), *v.* 1592. [Back-formation from LAZY *a.*] **1.** *intr.* To lie, move, act, or enjoy oneself lazily. Also with advs. †Also *refl.* **2.** quasi-*trans.* To pass *away* in indolence 1627.

2. So the bloudless Tortoise..lazeth his life away FELTHAM.

La·zule. ? *Obs.* 1598. [– med.L. *lazulum* (XII); see LAPIS LAZULI.] = LAPIS LAZULI. Chiefly attrib. *l.-stone.*

Lazuli (læ·ziŭləi). 1789. Short for LAPIS LAZULI. Also *attrib.*, as **l.-finch,** a brilliant fringilloid bird (*Passerina amœna*) of western U.S.

Lazuline (læ·ziŭləin), *a.* 1877. [f. LAZULI + -INE¹.] Of the colour of lapis lazuli. PATMORE. Also *sb.* 1850.

Lazulite (læ·ziŭləit). 1801. [f. med.L. *lazulum* (see LAZULE) + -ITE¹ 2 b.] *Min.* Hydrous phosphate of aluminium and magnesium, found in blue monoclinic crystals; also the colour of this. ¶Occas. used = LAPIS LAZULI.

Lazurite (læ·ziŭrəit). 1892. [f. med.L. *lazur* (see AZURE) + -ITE¹ 2 b.] *Min.* The blue part of lapis lazuli.

Lazy (lēⁱ·zi). 1549. [Early forms *laysie, lasie, laesy*; perh. of LDu. origin (cf. LG. *lasich* languid, idle).]

A. *adj.* **1.** Averse to labour, indolent; idle; inactive, slothful. Also *transf.* of things, places, or conditions, favourable or appropriate to laziness. **2.** Of things: Sluggish, dull, slow-moving; now only *transf.* from sense 1. †Formerly of literary style, also of heat or chemical agents: Languid, having little energy. 1568. †**3.** *dial.* Bad –1787.

1. All..combine to drive The l. Drones from the laborious Hive DRYDEN. **2.** L. leaden-stepping Hours MILT.

Comb.: **l.-bed,** a bed for potato-growing, about six feet wide, with a trench on each side, from which earth is taken to cover the potatoes; also *attrib.*; **-boots, -bones** (*colloq.*), a l. person; **-pinion,** a pinion serving as a transmitter of motion between two other pinions or wheels; **scissors, -tongs,** a system of several pairs of levers crossing and pivoted at their centres in the manner of scissors, for picking up objects at a distance. Hence **La·zily** *adv.*, **La·ziness.**

†**B.** *sb.* A name for the SLOTH. SIR T. BROWNE.

‖**Lazzarone** (læzărōᵘ·ne, latsarō·ne). Chiefly *pl.* **lazzaroni** (-ī). 1792. [It., augm. of *lazzaro* LAZAR.] One of the lowest class at Naples, who lounge about the streets, living by odd jobs, or by begging.

About 30,000 lazaroni, or black guards MORSE.

lb. ME. Abbrev. of L. *libra* 'pound', *pl.* **lb., lbs.,** now only of weight, but formerly of sterling.

-le, *suffix*, pron. (′l), of various origin.

1. Mod. Eng. form of ME. *-el(e, -le*, repr. OE. *-el, -ela, -(e)le* in sbs. and *-ol, -ul, -el* in adjs. (The form -EL is retained after *ch, g* soft, *n, r, sh, th*, and *v*. After *m* the suffix becomes *-ble*.) The sbs. formed on noun-stems have occas. a dim. sense, as *bramble*, or that of 'appliance or tool', as in *thimble, handle*. In those formed on vb.-stems the suffix is agential as in *beadle*, instrumental as in *bridle, girdle*, or less definite as in *bundle*. Adjs. formed on vb.-stems have the sense 'apt or liable' (to do what the vb. expresses), as in *brittle, fickle, nimble*, etc.

2. Occas. representative of ME. *-el(l, -elle*, in sbs. adopted from Fr. This, in *castle, mantle*, is OFr. *-el* :– L. *-ellum* dim. suffix (see -EL); in *cattle* it is OFr. *-el* :– L. *-āle*, the neut. sing., and in *battle* it is OFr. *-aille* the neut. pl., of the adjective suffix *-ālis* (see -AL); in *bottle* it is OFr. *-eille* :– L. *-icula* dim. suffix.

3. A verbal formative, repr. ME. *-(e)len*, OE. *-lian* :– Gmc. type *-ilōjan*, with frequent. or dim. sense, as in *crackle, dazzle, gabble, sparkle, wriggle*, etc.

Lea (lī), *sb.*¹ [OE. *lēah, lēa*, corresp. to OHG. *lōh* 'lucus' (MHG. low brushwood, scrub-land) :– Gmc. **lauχ-* :– IE. **louq-*, repr. also by L. *lucus* grove, Lith. *laũkas* field, Skr. *lokás* open space.] A tract of open ground, either meadow, pasture, or arable land. After OE. chiefly poet. or rhet., ordinarily applied to grass land.

The lowing herd winds slowly o'er the l. GRAY.

Lea, ley, lay (lī, lēⁱ), *sb.*² Now *dial.* ME. [ellipt. use of LEA (*ley, lay*) adj. In AL., *lega* (XII), *leya* (XIII).] Land that has remained untilled for some time; arable land under grass; land 'laid down' for pasture, grassland. Also *attrib.*

The husbandman..had turned his acres into leyes, his syths and ploughs into swords DRUMM. OF HAWTH.

Lea (lī), *sb.*³ ME. [perh. a deriv. of Fr. *lier* (:– L. *ligare*) bind, tie. But cf. LEASE *sb.*⁴] A measure of yarn of varying quantity; in worsted 80 yards; in cotton and silk 120 yards.

Lea, ley, lay (lī, lēⁱ), *a.* Now *dial.* [perh. repr. OE. **lǣġe* (implied in comb. *lǣġhryċġ* LEA-RIG), f. base of LAY *v.*, LIE *v.*¹] Of land: Fallow, unploughed. Also *fig.*

Leach (lītʃ), *sb.* 1673. [app. f. LEACH *v.* In senses 1–3 prob. short for attributive combs.] **1.** A perforated vessel or trough used for making lye from wood ashes by pouring water over them. *Obs.* exc. *dial.* **2.** *Tanning.* The pit in which the tan-liquors are mixed 1777. **3.** *Salt-making.* The brine which drains from the salt, or is left in the pan when the salt is drawn out 1886. **4.** The action of leaching. **5.** 'A quantity of wood-ashes, through which water passes, and thus imbibes the alkali' (Webster) 1828.

Leach (lītʃ), *v.* Also **leech, latch, letch.** 1614. [prob. repr. OE. *leċċan* to water (tr. L. *rigare*) :– WGmc. **lakkjan*, f. **lak-*, repr. also by OE. *lacu* small stream, brook.] †**1.** *intr.* To soften, melt. *rare.* **2. a.** *trans.* To cause (a liquid) to percolate through some material 1796. **b.** To subject (bark, ores, etc.) to the action of percolating water, etc., with the view of removing the soluble constituents; to lixiviate 1840. **c.** *intr.* To pass through by percolation 1864. Also *intr.* for *refl.* Of ashes: To be subject to the action of percolating water 1883. **3.** *trans.* To take *away, out* by percolation 1860.

Leach(e, obs. ff. LEECH.

Leachy (lī·tʃi), *a.* ?*U.S.* 1879. [f. LEACH *v.* + -Y¹.] Of soil: Of a nature to let water percolate through; not capable of holding water; porous.

Lead (led), *sb.*¹ [OE. *lēad* = OFris. *lād*) MLG. *lōd* (Du. *lood*) lead, MHG. *lōt* (G. *lot*) plummet, solder :– WGmc. **lauda*.] **1.** The heaviest of the base metals, of a dull pale bluish-grey colour, easily fusible, soft and malleable. Chemical symbol Pb. Rarely *pl.* = kinds of lead. †**b.** Sometimes called *black lead* (= L. *plumbum nigrum*) in contradistinction to *white lead* (*plumbum album*), a name for tin –1753. **2.** See RED LEAD, WHITE *lead* 1450. **3.** Short for BLACK LEAD, graphite, or plumbago. Hence, a small stick of graphite for filling a pencil. 1840. **4.** The metal as fashioned into a leaden coffin, a bullet, etc.; the leaden part of anything ME. **5. a.** A large pot, cauldron, or kettle. (Orig. one made of lead.) Now only *dial.* OE. **b.** *dial.* A leaden milk-pan 1750. **6.** A sounding-lead 1440. **7.** *pl.* **a.** The strips of lead used to cover a roof; often *collect.* for a lead flat, a lead roof, †occas. construed as sing. 1578. **b.** The lead frames of the panes in lattice or stained glass windows 1705. **8.** *Printing.* A thin strip of type-metal, used in type-composition to separate lines 1808.

1. Phr. †*To lie, be wrapt in l.*: to be buried in a l. coffin. So †*to lay, lap in l.* **4.** Heauen keepe L. out of mee SHAKS. **6.** Phr. *To cast, heave the l. To arm the l.*: to fill the hollow in it with tallow in order to discover the nature of the bottom by the substances adhering (Smyth). **7. a.** A Goodly Leads upon the Top, railed with Statua's interposed BACON.

Combs.: **l.-arming,** the tallow used for arming a lead (see 6); **-ash, -ashes,** litharge; **-bath,** (*a*) the mass of melted l. in a lead-furnace; (*b*) the molten l. with which gold and silver ores are melted before cupellation: **l. glance** [= Du. *loodglans*], galena; **-light,** a window in which small panes are fixed in leaden cames, also *attrib.*; **-line,** (*a*) a sounding-lead or plumb-line; (*b*) a line loaded with leaden weights, running along the bottom of a net; (*c*) a bluish grey line along the gums at their junction with the teeth, indicating lead-poisoning; **-mill,** (*a*) an establishment for producing milled or sheet l.; (*b*) a circular plate of l. used by the lapidary for grinding or roughing; **-nail** (mostly *pl.*), a nail used to fasten a sheet of l. on a roof; **-ochre** = MASSICOT; **-paper,** a test-paper treated with a preparation of l.; **-pencil,** a pencil of graphite, often enclosed in cedar or other wood; **-plant** (*U.S.*), a shrub (*Amorpha canescens*) found in the west of the Mississippi valley, and believed to indicate the presence of l. ore; **-plaster** = DIACHYLON; **-poisoning,** poisoning by the introduction of l. into the system; **-spar** = ANGLESITE or CERUSSITE; **-tree,** (*a*) a W. Indian name for the tropical leguminous tree *Leucæna glauca*; (*b*) a crystal deposit of metallic l. or zinc that has been placed in a solution of acetate of l.; **-vitriol** = ANGLESITE; **-water** (= Ger. *bleiwasser*), dilute solution of acetate of l.; **-work,** plumbers' work and material; work in l., *esp.* glaziers' work; **-works** *pl.*, an establishment for smelting lead-ore; **-wort,** a herbaceous plant of southern Europe (*Plumbago europæa*); also any plant of the genus *Plumbago* or the order *Plumbaginaceæ*.

Lead (līd), *sb.*² ME. [f. LEAD *v.*¹] †**1.** The action of LEAD *v.*¹; leading –1510. **b.** Direction given by going in front; example; esp. in phr. *to follow the l. of* 1863. **c.** *spec.* in *Hunting*, etc., chiefly in phr. *to give a l.*, i.e. to go first in leaping a fence, etc. 1859. **d.** A guiding indication 1851. **2.** The front or leading place; the place in front *of* (something). Also, the position or function of leading (e.g. a party), leadership 1570. **3.** *concr.* Something that leads. **a.** An artificial watercourse: cf. MILL-LEAD 1541. **b.** A channel in an ice-field 1835. **c.** A path; a garden path; an alley. *Blind l.* = *blind alley* (see BLIND *a.* 10). 1590. **d.** A leash or string for leading a dog 1893. **4.** *Card-playing.* The action or right of playing the first card in a round or trick; also, the card so played, or proper to be played, or the suit to which it belongs 1742. **5.** *Curling.* The first player or the stone first played 1685. **6.** *Mining.* **a.** = LODE 5. 1812. **b.** *Gold-mining.* An alluvial deposit of gold along the bed of an ancient river 1855. **7.** *Theatr.* The principal part in a play; also, one who plays such a part 1874. **8.** *Friendly lead* (see FRIENDLY *a.* 2). Also simply *lead.* 1851. **9.** *techn.* **a.** *Electricity.* (*a*) The angle between the plane through the lines of contact of the brushes or collectors of a dynamo or electric motor with the commutator and the transverse plane bisecting the magnetic field. (*b*) A conductor conveying electricity from the source to the place where it is used. 1881. **b.** *Engineering*, etc. The distance to which ballast, coal, soil, etc. has to be conveyed (see LEAD *v.*¹ 1 b) to its destination 1841. **c.** *Horology.* The action of a tooth, as a tooth of a wheel, in impelling another tooth or pallet 1880. **d.** *Naut.* The direction in which running ropes lead fair, and come down to the deck (Smyth) 1860. **e.** *Steam-engine.* (See quots.) 1838.

2. Phr. *To take the* (or *a*) *l.*, to occupy the front place, to assume the function of leader. Each of our porters took the l. in turn TYNDALL. **4.** Phr. *To return one's partner's l.*: to play from the same suit on getting the l. **9. e.** *L. of the crank*, the setting of the crank of one engine a little in advance of the right angle to the other; namely at 100° or 110° in place of 90°. This assists in rendering the motion of the piston more uniform, by moderating its velocity at the end of the stroke. *L. of the valve*, the amount of opening which a valve has when the engine is on the centre 1881.

Comb.: **l.-off,** a commencement; also that which leads off, the first of a series; **-reins** *Coaching*, the leaders' reins; **-screw,** 'the main screw of a lathe, which gives the feed motion to the slide-rest' (Webster).

Lead (līd), *v.*¹ Pa. t. and pa. pple. **led.** [OE. *lǣdan* = OFris. *lēda*, OS. *lēdjan* (Du. *leiden*), OHG. (G.) *leiten*, ON. *leiða* :– Gmc. **laiðjan*, f. **laiðō* LOAD *sb.*]

I. To conduct. **1.** *trans.* To cause to go along with oneself. †**a.** To bring or take (a person or animal) to a place. (Phrases like *to l. captive* are now understood in sense 2.) –1704. **b.** To carry or convey, usu. in a cart, etc. Now only *n. dial.*: To cart (coal, corn, etc.). *To l. in* (grain): to house. OE. **c.** To bring forward, adduce (testimony); to bring (an action). Now only in *Sc. Law*. ME. **2.** To conduct, guide, esp. by going on in advance OE. **b.** Of motives, circumstances, etc.: To guide, direct to a place ME. **c.** Of a clue, light, sound, etc.: To serve (a person) as an indication of the way; to mark the course for. Also absol. *to l. in* (Naut.): to mark the course for entering port. 1697. **d.** *absol.* 1580. **e.** Phr. *To l. the way*: †(*a*) to guide, show the way to; (*b*) in later use, to take the lead in an expedition, etc. ME. **3.** Of a commander: To march at the head of and direct the movement of. Also with *on*. OE. **4.** To conduct (a person) by holding the hand, etc., (an animal) by means of a halter, bridle, etc. Const. *by* (the hand, etc.). OE. **b.** *fig.* (*a*) To guide by persuasion (in opposition to *drive*). (*b*) *To l. by the nose* (see quot.): to cause to obey submissively. ME. **5.** To guide with reference to action or opinion; to conduct by argument, etc., *to* a conclusion; to induce *to* do something ME. **6.** Of a way, road, etc.: To conduct (a person) *to* or *into* a place. Hence *absol.* or *intr.*: to have a specified direction. ME. **b.** *intr.* To form a channel *into*, a connecting link *to* (something) 1833. **c.** *intr. To l. to*: to have as a result 1770. **7.** *To l.* (a person) *a dance*: *transf.* and *fig.*, to put to the trouble of hurrying from place to place; hence, to compel to go through a course of irksome action. So *to l.* (a person) *a chase, a life*. 1529. **8. a.** To conduct (water, steam) through a channel or pipe ME. **b.** To guide the course or direction of (something flexible; e.g. a rope, etc. *over* a pulley, *through* a hole, etc.) OE. **c.** Naut. *intr.* Of a rope: To admit of being led 1860. †**9.** To conduct (affairs); to manage, govern –1579.

1. b. Faith, sir, ha's led the drumme before the English Tragedians SHAKS. **c.** No evidence has yet been led to show. SIR W. HAMILTON. **2.** Therefore shall not Moses..his people into Canaan l. MILT. *P.L.* XII. 309. **b.** Instinct early led him into the political arena 1892. **c.** L., Kindly Light, amid the encircling gloom, L. Thou me on J. H. NEWMAN. **d.** Pray you l. on *Oth.* I. i. 311. **3.** The Prince..led them on with great gallantry 1736. **4.** The captive soldier was led forth GOLDSM. Phr. *To l. apes (in hell)*: see APE *sb.* *To l. (a bride) to the altar, to church*: to marry. **b.** The Moore..will as tenderly be lead by th' Nose As Asses are *Oth.* I. iii. 407. **5.** Tintoret..may l. you wrong if you don't understand him RUSKIN. **6.** Broad steps l. down into a garden 1861. **c.** Several seizures of English cargoes led to reprisals on our part; reprisals led to a naval war M. PATTISON. **7.** She had led him the life of a dog 1892. **8. b.** Ropes..led through blocks fixed to stakes 1892.

II. To carry on. †**1.** To engage or take part in, to perform (dances, songs), to utter sounds. Cf. L. *ducere carmen, choros*. –1493. **2.** To go through, pass (life, †a portion of time). Cf. L. *ducere vitam*. Rarely, †To support life *by* (bread). OE.

2. Do l. your own life and let ours alone! BROWNING.

III. To precede, be foremost. (Cf. sense I. 2.) **1.** To have the first place in; *lit.* and *fig.* esp. in *to l. the dance, the van* ME. **b.** *absol.* To go first. Also with *off*. 1798. **2.** *trans.* To direct by one's example; to set (a fashion); to take the directing or principal part in (a proceeding, performance, etc.); to be chief of (a party, a movement); to have the official initiative in the proceedings of (a deliberative body) 1642. **3.** Of a barrister: *trans.* To act as leading counsel in (a cause); to act as leader to (another barrister); to take precedence of. Also *absol.* or *intr.* 1806. **4.** *Card-playing.* **a.** *intr.* To play the first card. Also with *off*. Said also of the card. Also in *indirect passive*. **b.** *trans.* As first player, to play (a specified card); to play one of (a suit or a specified suit). Also with *out*. 1731.

1. b. The Admiral's frigate led 1900. **2.** To l. an insurrection 1841, the singing 1859, the prayers 1866, the chorus 1883, the orchestra 1891. Disraeli still led the House of Commons 1891. **4. a.** *To l. to* or *l. up to*: to play a card in order to bring out (cards held by another player). **b.** I l. a heart SWIFT.

Combs. (with advs.). **Lead away. a.** *trans.* To induce to follow unthinkingly. Chiefly in *pass.* **b.** Naut. *To l. it away*: to take one's course. **Lead off.** *trans.* To open (a dance, a ball); hence *gen.* to begin. Also *intr.* or *absol.* **Lead on. a.** *trans.* To induce gradually to advance; to beguile into going to greater lengths. **b.** *intr.* To direct conversation *to* a subject. **Lead out.** *trans.* = *Lead off*. Also, to conduct (a partner) to the dance. **Lead up. a.** *trans.* = *Lead off*. ? *Obs.* **b.** intr. *To l. up to*: to form a gradual preparation for.

Lead (led), *v.*^{2} ME. [f. LEAD *sb.*^{1}] **1.** To cover with or enclose in lead. Also with *over*. **2.** To arm, load, or weight with lead 1481. **3.** To fix (glass of a window) with leaden cames 1530. †**4.** To line (pottery) with lead or lead-glaze; to glaze –1686. **5.** *Printing.* To separate lines of type with leads (see LEAD *sb.*^{1} 8) 1841. **6.** *passive* and *intr.* Of a gun-barrel: To become foul with a coating of lead 1875.

1. She leaded and paved the Friday Market Cross in Stamford FULLER. Hence **Lea·ded** *ppl. a.* (of panes of glass) fitted into leaden cames (1855); *Printing*, having the lines separated by leads (1805).

Leadage (lī·dėdʒ). 1891. [f. LEAD *v.*^{1} + -AGE.] Distance that coal has to be conveyed from the mine to a sea-board or railway.

Leaden (le·d'n), *a.* [OE. *lēaden*; see LEAD *sb.*^{1} and -EN^4.] **1.** Consisting or made of lead. Also *fig.* **2.** *transf.* and *fig.* **a.** Of base quality; opp. to *golden* 1577. **b.** Heavy as if made of lead 1579. **c.** Inert, depressing 1592. **d.** Dull grey, like lead ME.

1. What says this l. casket? *Merch. V.* II. vii. 15. *L. key, sceptre*, poet. for the powers of sleep or dullness. *L. sword*, type of a useless weapon. **2. a.** Base l. Earles, that glory in your birth MARLOWE. **b.** L. handes LYLY, feet 1585, slumbers 1725. **c.** Saturne, that l. planet 1647. **d.** Colour.. wan and of leden hewe CHAUCER. **Lea·den-ly** *adv.*, **-ness.**

Leaden (le·d'n), *v.* 1552. [f. LEAD *sb.*^{1} + -EN^5, or f. LEADEN *a.*] †**a.** *trans.* To fasten with molten lead. **b.** To make leaden or dull. **c.** *intr.* To press down like lead; only in **Leadening** *ppl. a.*

Leader (lī·dəɹ). OE. [f. LEAD *v.*^{1} + -ER^1.] **I.** One who leads. **1.** *gen.* in various senses of the vb.; †a carrier. *Follow my l.*: a game in which each player must do what the leader does, or pay forfeit; also *fig.* **2.** *esp.* **a.** *L. of the House of Commons*: the member of the government who has the official initiative in the proceedings of the House. **b.** A counsel who leads (see LEAD *v.*^{1} III. 3) in a case; a King's Counsel, whose status entitles him to lead. Also, the senior counsel of a circuit. 1856. **3.** One who leads a choir or band of dancers, musicians, or singers 1530. **4.** Among Methodists, the presiding member of a class (see CLASS *sb.* 7). Usu. *class-l.* 1743. **5.** One of the front horses in a team, or the front horse in a tandem 1700.

1. Ample Plains, Where oft the Flocks without a L. stray DRYDEN. All this day..they will gather to their leader's standard SCOTT. **3.** *Much Ado* II. i. 157.

II. A thing which leads. **1. a.** *gen.* ME. **b.** *colloq.* A remark or question intended to lead conversation (cf. FEELER 3) 1882. **2.** In a tree or shrub: The shoot which grows at the apex of the stem, or of a principal branch; also, a bine 1572. **3.** A tendon 1708. **4.** = LEADING ARTICLE 1. 1844. **5.** *Mining.* **a.** A drain or stream that by its colour indicates the presence of minerals 1809. **b.** A small and insignificant vein which leads to a larger and better 1670. **6.** *Fishing* (U.S.). The end portion of a reel-line, having the snells of the fly-hooks attached to it 1859. **7.** *Printing.* A line of dots or dashes to guide the eye 1824.

4. Give me a man who can write a l. DISRAELI. Hence **Lea·deress**, a female l. **Leaderette** (līdəre·t), a short editorial paragraph printed in the same type as the leaders in a newspaper 1880. **Lea·derless** *a.* without a l. **Lea·dership,** the dignity, office, or position of a l.; also, ability to lead.

Lea·dhillite. 1835. [f. *Leadhills* in Scotland, where found; see -ITE^1 2 b.] *Min.* A sulphato-carbonate of lead, found in whitish pearly crystals.

Lead-in. 1913. [LEAD *v.*^{1}] A conducting wire joining a wireless receiver with an external aerial.

Leading (lī·diŋ), *vbl. sb.*^{1} ME. [f. LEAD *v.*^{1} + -ING^1.] **1.** The action of LEAD *v.*^{1}; †carriage. **b.** *Light or l.* (Milton) = illumination or guidance 1644; hence Burke's phr., *men of light and l.* 1790. **2.** *Lead-mining.* One of the fine slender threads connecting the branches of a vein 1653. **3.** A directing influence or guidance; a term used by the Quakers 1889.

Comb.: **l.-block,** a fixed pulley, which alters the direction of the power, but does not increase it; **-business** (*Theatr.*), the parts usually taken by the leading actor; **-rein,** a rein to lead a horse, etc.; also *fig.*; **-staff,** †(*a*) a staff borne by a commanding officer; (*b*) a staff to lead a bull by means of a ring through its nose; **-string** (chiefly *pl.*), strings with which children used to be guided and supported when learning to walk 1677; hence in fig. phr.; a cord for leading an animal.

Leading (le·diŋ), *vbl. sb.*^{2} 1440. [f. LEAD *v.*^{2} + -ING^1.] The action of LEAD *v.*^{2}; esp. *concr.* = CAME; leadwork in general.

Leading (lī·diŋ), *ppl. a.* 1597. [f. LEAD *v.*^{1} + -ING^2.] That leads (see LEAD *v.*^{1}).

Special collocations: **l.-buoy,** one placed as a guide in sailing; **l. case** *Law*, one that serves as a precedent to decide other cases; **l. lady, man,** the chief actress or actor in a theatrical company; **l.-mark** *Naut.*, one of 'those objects which, kept in line or in transit, guide the pilot while working into port, as trees, spires, buoys, etc.' (Smyth). **l.-motive** *Mus.*, occas. tr. LEITMOTIV, q.v.; **l. note** *Mus.*, the seventh note of the scale, so called from its tendency to lead up to the tonic 1752; **l. question,** one that suggests the answer expected; **l. seventh** *Mus.*, the chord of the seventh on the leading note.

Hence **Lea·dingly** *adv.* in a l. manner.

Leading article. 1807. **1.** A large-type article in a newspaper, expressing at length editorial opinion on any subject. **2.** *Comm.* **a.** A principal article of trade 1818. **b.** An article which is sold at a low price in order to attract customers for other things.

Leadless (le·dlės), *a.* 1809. [f. LEAD *sb.*^{1} + -LESS.] Without lead.

L. pistol BYRON. L. glaze 1898.

Leadsman (le·dzmæn). 1857. [f. gen. of LEAD *sb.*^{1} + MAN.] The man who heaves the lead in taking soundings.

Leady (le·di), *a.* ME. [f. LEAD *sb.*^{1} + -Y^1.] Resembling lead, usu. in colour.

Leaf (līf), *sb.* Pl. **leaves.** [OE. *lēaf*, corresp. to OFris. *lāf*, OS. *lōf* (Du. *loof*), OHG. *loup* (G. *laub*), ON. *lauf*, Goth *laufs* :– Gmc. **laubaz, -am*, of which there are no certain cognates.]

I. 1. An expanded organ of a plant, usually green, produced laterally from a stem or branch, or springing from its root. When complete, it consists of a blade, footstalk, and stipules; pop., the word *leaf* denotes the blade alone. Some mod. botanists use the term to include also 'modified leaves', such as stamens, carpels, parts of the floral envelope, bracts, etc. **2.** *pop.* A petal; esp. in *rose-l.* 1565. **3.** *collect.* Foliage; leafage, leaves. Chiefly in *fall of the l.* *In (full) l.*: covered with foliage. 1537. **b.** Of wine: 'season', 'year' 1432. **4.** *spec.* The leaves: **a.** of the tobacco-plant 1618; **b.** of the tea-plant 1883. **5.** A representation of a leaf; esp. in *Archit.* 1459.

1. *fig.* This is the state of Man; to day he puts forth The tender Leaues of hopes, to morrow Blossomes SHAKS. **3.** *fig.* My way of life Is falne into the Seare, the yellow Leafe SHAKS. **4. a.** Tobacco in the leafe 1641.

II. Similative uses. **1.** A single fold of a folded sheet of paper, parchment, etc.; *esp.* in a book or manuscript (= two pages); hence, what is printed or written thereon OE. **2.** The layer of fat round the kidneys of a pig; also the inside fat of other animals. Now *dial.* and *U.S.* ME. **3.** A very thin sheet of metal, esp. gold or silver ME.; a lamina (of horn, marble, wood, etc.) 1601. **4. a.** A hinged part of a door, gate, or shutter ME. **b.** A hinged flap of a table; also *gen.* any movable addition to the top of a table 1558. **c.** The hinged part of a draw-bridge or bascule-bridge 1442. **d.** A hinged sight on a rifle barrel 1875. **5.** One of the teeth of a pinion 1706. **6.** The brim of a hat. Chiefly *Anglo-Irish*. 1767. **7.** Weaving. *L. of heddles*: all the heddles connected by the same two shafts of wood. *Twill of three, four*, etc. *leaves*: twill woven upon three, four, etc. leaves of heddles; hence *attrib.*, as *eight-leaf twill* 1831.

1. Phr. *To take a l. out of* (a person's) *book*: see BOOK *sb.* *To turn over a new l.*: to begin to mend one's ways; earlier, †*to turn the leaf* (1548).

Combs. **1.** General: as *l.-axil, -blade*, etc.; *l.-eater*; *l.-bearing* adj.; *l.-latticed, -strewn* adjs.; *l.-bladed* adj., etc.

2. Special: **l.-bearing** *a.*, having a leaf-like appendage; applied *spec.* to worms of the family *Phyllodocidæ*, which have gills in the form of leaves; **-beetle,** a beetle of the family *Chrysomelidæ*, which feed upon leaves only; **-bridge,** a bridge constructed with a leaf or leaves (sense II. 4 c); **-bud,** a bud from which leaves are produced (opp. to *flower-bud*); **-bundle,** the bundle of fibres running from the stem into the l. of a plant; **-butterfly,** one of the genus *Kallima*; **-climber,** a climber in which support is gained by the action, not of the stem, but of the leaves it bears; so **-climbing** *a.*; **-crumpler,** a moth, *Phycis indiginella*, of N. America, the caterpillars of which draw together and crumple the leaves on which they feed; **-cutting,** a l. used as a cutting in the propagation of certain plants; **-fat,** the fat round a pig's kidneys; **-flea,** an insect of the family *Psyllidæ* which lives on plants; **-folder,** a moth whose larvæ fold leaves together to form a protective covering; **-footed** *a.*, having leaf-like feet; **-frog,** a frog of the genus *Phyllomedusa*; **-gap** *Bot.*, a division in the fibre of a plant, caused by the protrusion of a leaf-bud; **-green** *a.*, of the colour of green leaves; also quasi-*sb.*; *sb.* = CHLOROPHYLL; **-hopper,** a name for insects of the family *Tettigoniadæ* which live mostly on the leaves of plants; **-insect,** a name for insects of the family *Phasmidæ*, esp. the genus *Phyllium*, in which the wings and sometimes the legs resemble leaves in shape and colour; **-lard,** lard from the flaky fat of the hog; **-lichen,** a lichen of the genus *Parmelia* or N.O. *Parmeliaceæ*; **-louse,** one of the aphides which infest the leaves of plants; a plant-louse; **-metal,** metal in thin leaves; **-miner,** a small caterpillar of a tineid moth which eats its way between the cuticles of leaves; so *leaf-mining caterpillar*; **-mould,** mould having a large proportion of decayed leaves in it; **-nosed** *a.*, having a leaf-like appendage on the snout; *spec.* applied to the phyllostomoid and rhinolophoid bats; **-opposed** *a. Bot.*, having opposite leaves; **-plant,** a plant cultivated for its leaves; **-red** = ERYTHROPHYLL; **-roller,** the caterpillar of certain (tortricid) moths, which rolls up the leaves of plants which it infests; so *leaf-rolling* adj.; **-rosette** *Bot.*, a cluster of leaves resembling a rosette; **-rust,** a mould which attacks trees, producing rusty spots on the leaves; **-scale,** a scale on a plant-stem which develops into a l.; **-scar,** the cicatrix left on the bark by the separation of the leaf-stalk of a fallen l.; **-sheath,** a sheath at the base of a leaf, embracing the stem, as in grasses; **-sight** (see II. 4 d); **-spine,** a l. which has developed into a long, conical, pointed, woody body; **-table,** a table with a leaf or flap; **-tendril,** a tendril consisting of a modified leaf or part of a leaf; **-thorn** = *leaf-spine*; **-tobacco,** the raw material as imported with the stalk on it; **-trace** *Bot.*, a 'vein' or fibrovascular bundle running down from a leaf into the stem; **-valve,** a valve which moves on a hinge; **-wasp,** a saw-fly; **-work** ornamental work consisting of leaf-forms.

Leaf (līf), *v.* See also LEAVE *v.*² 1611. [f. LEAF *sb.*] **1.** *intr.* To put forth leaves. Also *to l. out* (U.S.). **2. a.** To turn or turn *over* (the leaves of a book). Now *U.S.* **b.** To number (a leaf of a book). 1663.

Leaf, private soldier's form of LEAVE *sb.*

Leafage (lī·fėdʒ). 1599. [f. LEAF *sb.* + -AGE.] **1.** Leaves; foliage. **b.** The representation of these, *esp.* as an ornamentation 1703. **2.** Lamination (*rare*) 1833.

Lea·f-cutter. 1815. An insect that cuts or eats out portions of the leaves of trees; *spec.* in *leaf-cutter ant, bee.* So **leaf-cutting** *ppl. a.*, in *l.-cutting ant, bee* 1802.

Leaf-eared: see LAVE *a.*

Leafed (līft), *a.* See also LEAVED *a.* 1552. [f. LEAF *sb.* + -ED².] **1.** Having leaves; as *broad-, thick-, two-l.* **2.** (Broad-) brimmed 1841.

Leaf-gold. 1598. **1.** = GOLD-LEAF. Also *fig.* **2.** Native gold in the form of laminæ. RAYMOND.

†**Lea·fit.** 1787. [f. LEAF *sb.* + *-it*, perh. = -ET.] = LEAFLET 1. –1830.

Leafless (lī·flės), *a.* Also †LEAVELESS. 1590. [f. LEAF *sb.* + -LESS.] Without a leaf; destitute of leaves. Also *fig.*

L., yet soft as spring, The tender purple spray on copse and briers! M. ARNOLD. Hence **Lea·flessness.**

Leaflet (lī·flėt). 1787. [f. LEAF *sb.* + -LET.] **1.** †**a.** *Bot.* A sepal. **b.** *Bot.* One of the divisions of a compound leaf. **c.** *pop.* A young leaf; *rarely*, a petal. **2.** *Anat.* and *Zool.* An organ or part of one resembling a small leaf 1826. **3.** A small-sized leaf of paper or a sheet folded into leaves but not stitched, and containing printed matter, chiefly for gratuitous distribution 1867.

3. Leaflets (as Spurgeon and Co. have christened very young tracts) MISS BROUGHTON.

Leafy (lī·fi), *a.* (See also LEAVY.) 1552. [f. LEAF *sb.* + -Y¹.] **1.** Having, or abounding in, leaves; clothed with, made or consisting of, leaves. **b.** *spec.* in *Bot.* Foliate 1776. **2.** Of the nature of, or resembling, a leaf 1671; laminate 1754.

1. In the l. month of June COLERIDGE. Hence **Lea·finess.**

League (līg), *sb.*¹ late ME. [The earliest forms show two types, *leuge* and *leghe*, the first – late L. *leuca, leuga*, late Gr. λεύγη (of Gaulish origin), the second – the derived Pr. *lega* = (O)Fr. *lieue.*] An itinerary measure of distance, varying in different countries, but usu. estimated at about 3 miles; in Eng. use, only poet. or rhet. *Marine l.*: a unit of distance = 3 nautical miles or 3,041 fathoms. *Comb.* **l.-long** *a.* that extends the length of a l. 1860.

League (līg), *sb.*² Also †**le(a)ge,** †**ligue.** 1452. [Early forms (*ligg, ligue, leag(u)e, lege*) show deriv. (i) partly from Fr. *ligue* – It. *liga*, latinized form of *lega*, f. *legare* bind :– L. *ligare*; (ii) partly immed. f. It. *lega.*] **1.** A covenant or compact made between parties for their mutual protection and assistance, the prosecution of joint interests, and the like; a body of states or persons associated in such a covenant, a confederacy. **b.** In recent use, often adopted in the names of associations or societies having a common object 1846. **2.** *gen.* A covenant, compact, alliance. Now *rare.* 1509.

1. Yᵉ l. offensive and defensive wᵗʰ yᵉ States Genˡˡ 1678. *The League*, a l. formed in 1576 under the direction of the Guises, to prevent the accession of Henry IV to the French throne. *Holy L.*, a name given to several leagues, e.g. that formed by Pope Julius II against the French in 1511 and the Nuremberg L. of 1538. *Solemn L. and Covenant*: see COVENANT *sb.* 8. **b.** *Anti-Corn-Law L.*: a political association formed in 1838 to procure the abolition of the existing Corn Laws. *L. of Nations*, an association of self-governing states, dominions, etc. created by a covenant incorporated in the peace treaty of 1919 after the war of 1914–18, having as its object the maintenance of the peace of the world. ('The League of Nations Society' was formed in 1915.) **2.** Linkt in happie nuptial L. MILT. *P.L.* IV. 339.

League (līg), *v.* 1611. [f. LEAGUE *sb.*² Cf. Fr. *liguer.*] **1.** *trans.* To form or join into a league. †**2.** To bind, connect, join –1660. **3.** *intr.* To join in or form a league or alliance. Also *to l. against* in indirect pass. 1638.

1. Hotspur..leagued himself with the Scots J. R. GREEN. **3.** Where kings first leagued against the rights of men SHELLEY.

Leaguer (lī·gəɹ), *sb.*¹ 1577. [– Du. *leger* camp, corresp. to OE. *leġer* LAIR.] **1.** A military camp, esp. one engaged in a siege; an investing force. **2.** A siege 1598. ¶**3.** Occas. confused with *leager* LEDGER *a.* II. 1678.

1. I came into the imperial l. at the siege of Leipsic DE FOE. Phr. *In l.*: in camp; engaged in a siege. **2.** The l. of Lucknow SMILES.

Leaguer (lī·gəɹ), *sb.*² 1590. [f. LEAGUE *sb.*² + -ER¹.] A member of a league; e.g. of the League formed against the Huguenots in the reign of Henry III, the Anti-Corn-Law League, the Irish Land League, etc.

Leaguer (lī·gəɹ), *sb.*³ 1683. [perh. – Du. *ligger* tun, f. *liggen* LIE *v.*¹ Cf. G. *leger* (also *legger, wasserlegger*) fresh-water cask(s on board ship.] **a.** A measure of arrack 1712. **b.** A cask of wine or oil, ? of a certain size 1772. **c.** *Naut.* The longest water-cask, of 159 English imperial gallons 1683.

Lea·guer, *v.* 1596. [f. LEAGUER *sb.*¹] †**1.** *refl.* and *intr.* To set one's leaguer, to encamp; also, to lie, lodge –1676. **2.** *trans.* To besiege, beleaguer 1715.

2. Two mighty hosts a leaguer'd town embrace POPE.

†**Lea·guerer.** 1635. [f. LEAGUER *sb.*¹ + -ER¹.] A (Dutch) trooper –1654.

Leak (līk), *sb.* 1487. [See LEAK *v.*; the sb. is repr. by MDu. *lek*, ON. *leki.*] **1.** A hole or fissure in a vessel containing or immersed in a fluid, which lets the fluid pass into or out of the vessel; said orig. and esp. of ships; also in phr. *to spring a l.* Also *transf.* and *fig.* **2.** The action of leaking; leakage 1828.

1. Many little leaks may sink a ship FULLER. *transf.* A l. in the waistcoat-pocket in which you carry all your money 1806.

†**Leak,** *a.* [See LEAK *v.*; the adj. is repr. by MDu. *lek*, OE. *(h)lec*, G. dial. *lech*, ON. *lekr* (G. *leck* adj. (XVI) is from LG.).] = LEAKY. –1678.

Leak (līk), *v.* 1440. [prob. of LG. or Du. origin, with LEAK *sb.* and *a.*; the verb is repr. by MDu. *lēken*, OHG. *lechen*, MHG., G. dial. *lechen* crack, become leaky, ON. *leka*; f. Gmc. **lek-*, var. of **lak-* LACK *sb.*¹, *v.*] **1.** *intr.* To pass (*out, away, forth*) by a leak or leakage. Also *fig.* to pass *away* by gradual waste. **2.** To let fluid pass in or out through a leak 1513. †**b.** To 'make water' (*vulgar*) –1796. †**3.** *pass.* To have sprung a leak; to be emptied by leakage –1748. **4.** *trans.* To let (water, etc.) in or out through a leak. ? Now *U.S.* only. †Also *fig.* 1655. **5.** *Brewing.* To cause (liquor) to run *over, on, off*, in small quantities or gradually 1674.

1. A democracy that has allowed its chief political interests to l. away 1890. Phr. *To l. out* (fig.): to come to be known in spite of efforts at concealment 1840. **2.** The starboard boiler began to l. SIR J. ROSS. **4.** The pipe leaks gas; the roof leaks rain 1889.

Leakage (lī·kėdʒ). 1490. [f. LEAK *v.* + -AGE.] **1.** The action of leaking; loss of fluid by this means. **2.** *transf.* and *fig.* Diminution resulting from gradual waste or escape 1642. **3.** *concr.* That which leaks out. Also *fig.* 1661. **4.** Allowance for waste of fluid by leakage from the containing vessels 1591.

2. The Cabinet..was not famous for its power of preventing the l. of state matters KINGLAKE.

Leaky (lī·ki), *a.* 1606. [f. LEAK *sb.* + -Y¹.] Having a leak or leaks; full of leaks. **b.** Incontinent of urine 1727. **c.** *fig.* Not reticent, blabbing; not retentive 1692.

L. casks 1872. A l. gas pipe 1881. Hence **Lea·kiness.**

Leal (līl), *a.* Now *Sc.* and *n. dial.* ME. [– AFr. *leal*, OFr. *leel*, of which the var. *leial* became *loial* LOYAL.] **1.** Loyal, faithful, honest, true. **2.** True, genuine; real, actual; exact, accurate; very (truth). Of a blow or shot: Well-aimed. ME. †**3.** Lawful; also, just, fair –1727.

1. The leelest maid o them a' 1776. L. service 1884. *Land of the l.*: see LAND *sb.* Hence **Lea·lly** *adv.* **Le·alty** (now *arch.*) faithfulness, loyalty.

Lea-land, lay-land (lī·lænd, lēⁱ·lænd). ME. [f. LEA *a.* + LAND *sb.*] Fallow land; land 'laid down' to grass.

Leam (līm), *sb.*¹ Now *Sc.* and *n. dial.* [OE. *lēoma* = OS. *liomo*, ON. *ljómi* :– Gmc. **leuχmon* (cf. Goth. *lauhmuni* lightning), f. Gmc. **leuχ-* :– IE. **leuk-*, repr. also by L. *lūx, lūmen*; see LIGHT *sb.*] Light, flame; a flash, ray, or gleam of light; brightness, gleam. Also *fig.*

Leam (līm), *sb.*² *dial.* 1601. [Of unkn. origin.] A drain or watercourse in fen districts.

Leam (līm), *v.* Now *Sc.* and *n. dial.* ME. [f. LEAM *sb.*¹] *intr.* To shine, gleam; to light *up.*

Leamer, var. of LIMER¹, a hound.

Lean (līn), *sb.*¹ 1610. [f. LEAN *v.*] **1.** The act or condition of leaning; inclination. *On the l.*: inclining. 1776. †**2.** *concr.* Something to lean on; a support. HEALEY.

Lean (līn), *a.* and *sb.*² [OE. *hlǣne* :– Gmc. **χlainjaz*, perh. rel. to Lith. *klýnas* scrap, fragment, Lett. *kleins* feeble.] **1.** Wanting in flesh; not plump; thin. Also *transf.* **b.** *Ship-building.* 'Sharp', opp. to *bluff* 1769. **2.** *fig.* Poor in quantity or quality, meagre; slight, mean. Somewhat *arch.* Of diet: Poor, innutritious. ME. **3.** Of flesh or meat: Containing little or no fat ME. **4.** Wanting in rich elements or qualities. Now somewhat *rare.* ME. **5.** Scantily provided ME. **b.** Of seasons, etc.: Marked by scarcity 1670. **6.** *Printing.* (See quots.) 1676.

1. Yond Cassius has a leane and hungry looke, He thinkes too much SHAKS. *transf.* The l. Statue of a starv'd Renown 1693. **2.** My leane and low ability SHAKS. Their l. and flashy songs MILT. A l. diet 1890. **4.** A thick l. Mortar 1726. A country rough, l., and solitary 1817. L. fields 1899. **5.** Cash is very lene 1623. Dress..keeps our larder l. COWPER. **b.** L. times DRYDEN, years

1890. **6.** *L. strokes* are the narrow strokes in a Letter, as the Left Hand stroke in the letter A MOXON. *L. work*, the opposite of fat work—that is, poor unprofitable work 1871. Hence **Lea·n-ly** *adv.*, **-ness.**

B. *sb.* **1.** The lean part of anything; the muscular tissue of meat as dist. from the fat 1450. **2.** *Printing.* †**a.** A thin part or stroke of a letter 1683. **b.** Ill-paid work 1882.

1. Some fat to my leane 16..

Lean (līn), *v.*[1] Pa. t. and pa. pple. **leaned** (līnd), **leant** (lent). [OE. *hleonian, hlinian*, corresp. to OFris. *lena*, OS. *hlinon* (Du. *leunen*), OHG. *(h)linēn* (G. *lehnen*), f. Gmc. **χli-* (cf. Gr. κλῖμαξ ladder, CLIMAX, L. *clivus* declivity, Skr. *çri* lean), with *-n-* formative as in Gr. κλίνειν bend, L. *inclinare* INCLINE.] **1.** *intr.* To recline, lie down, rest. *Obs.* exc. *Sc.* in reflexive construction. **2.** To incline the body against an object for support; to support oneself *on, against* something. Also *transf.* of inanimate objects. ME. **b.** To press *upon*; to lay emphasis *upon* 1736. **3.** *fig.* To rely or depend *on* or *upon.* Also *refl.* ME. **4.** To bend or incline *from, over, towards, back, out,* †*up* OE. **b.** To move or be situated obliquely; to swerve (*aside*); *U.S.* to 'make tracks' ME. **5.** To incline *towards, to* some quality, etc. Also, to have a tendency favourable *to.* ME. **6.** To be somewhat partial or favourable; to be inclined or disposed *to* or *towards* 1530. †**b.** To defer *to* an opinion –1611. **7.** (causal) *trans.* **a.** To cause to lean or rest, to prop *against*, etc. ME. **b.** To cause to bend or incline ME.

1. Lenynge on myn elbowe and my syde CHAUCER. **2.** I leaned with my backe against an oke to rest me 1530. *transf.* Where the broad ocean leans against the land GOLDSM. Phr. *To l. upon* (*Mil.*): to be close up to something serving as a protection. **3.** Trust in the Lord..and leane not vnto thine owne vnderstanding *Prov.* 3:5. **4.** A cone of ice forty feet high leaned quite over our track TYNDALL. *fig.* Ev'n his failings lean'd to virtue's side GOLDSM. **5.** The Government leans towards Democracy BROUGHAM. **6.** Aristotle leanes to the contrary opinion 1604. Phr. *To l. against*: to be unfavourable to. Chiefly *legal.* **b.** *Cymb.* I. i. 78. **7. a.** Leane thine aged Back against mine Arme SHAKS. **b.** I..l. mine ear to the sounds of the air BOWEN.

†**Lean,** *v.*[2] [OE. *hlǣnian*, f. *hlǣne* LEAN *a.*] To become or to make lean –1616.

Leaning (lī·niŋ), *vbl. sb.* OE. [f. LEAN *v.*[1] + -ING[1].] **1.** The action of LEAN *v.*[1]; inclination; reclining. **2.** *fig.* Inclination, bias; tendency, 'penchant' 1587.

2. A l. towards Rome 1849.

Comb.: **l.-note** *Mus.* = APPOGGIATURA; **-stock,** (*a*) a support (*lit.* and *fig.*); (*b*) in an organ, the ledge on which a pipe rests.

Lean-to (lī·ntu), *sb.* (*a.*) 1461. [f. LEAN *v.*[1] + TO *adv.*] **1.** A building with rafters resting against the side of another; a penthouse. **2.** *attrib.* (or *adj.*) Belonging to or of the nature of such a building. Also, placed so as to lean against something. 1649.

2. They had set fire to the lean-to outhouse 1882.

†**Lea·ny,** *a.* ME. [f. LEAN *a.* + -Y[1].] Lean –1602.

Leap (līp), *sb.*[1] [OE. **hliep, hlȳp* :– **χlaupiz*; cf. OFris. *hlēp*, Du. *loop*, OHG. *hlouf* (G. *lauf*), ON. *hlaup.*] **1.** An act of leaping; a bound, jump, spring. **b.** *transf.* and *fig.* An abrupt movement or change OE. **2.** A leaping-place; something to be leaped over or from. Also, the place or distance leaped. (Freq. in place-names, as *Deerleap, Hindlip*, etc.) ME. **3.** Of animals: The action of leaping (the female) 1607. Also *transf.* **4.** The sudden fall of a river to a lower level 1796. **5.** *Mining.* A fault 1747. **6.** *Mus.* A passing from one note to another by an interval greater than a degree of the scale 1674.

1. Our elders took leaps, now they are all jumps 1825. Phr. *A l. in the dark*: a hazardous action of which the consequences are unforeseen. *By leaps, by leaps and bounds*: with startling rapidity of advance or increase. **2.** This Place was therefore called *The Lover's L.* ADDISON. *Salmon l.*, a precipitous fall in a river over which salmon leap in going up river to breed. **4.** The quiet stream is a succession of leaps and pools RUSKIN.

Comb.: **l.-day,** an intercalary day in the calendar, esp. February 29th.

Leap (līp), *sb.*[2] [OE. *lēap*, = ON. *laupr.*] **1.** A basket. Now *dial.* **2.** A basket in which to catch or keep fish OE.

Leap (līp), *v.* Pa. t. and pa. pple. **leaped** (līpt), **leapt** (lept). [OE. *hlēapan* = OFris. *(h)lāpa*, OS. *-hlōpan* (Du. *loopen*), OHG. *loufan* (G. *laufen* run), ON. *hlaupa* (whence Sc. LOUP *v.*), Goth. *-hlaupan* :– Gmc. **χlaupan*, without cognates elsewhere.] †**1.** *intr.* To run, rush, 'throw oneself' –1716. **2.** To rise with both (or all) feet suddenly from a standing-place and pass through the air to some other position; to jump, spring OE. **b.** To spring *upon* a horse, *into* the saddle OE. **c.** Of a fish: To spring from the water ME. **3.** To spring or jump (with joy, mirth, etc.) OE. **4.** To spring suddenly *to* or *upon* one's feet, *from* a sitting or recumbent position, or *up* ME. **5.** *transf.* of a thing: To move with a leap or bound ME. **b.** Of the heart (or pulse): To beat vigorously, throb 1526. **6.** *fig.* To pass abruptly (from one condition or position to another) ME. **b.** *Mus.* To pass from one note to another by an interval greater than a degree of the scale. **7.** *trans.* To pass from one side of (a thing) to the other by leaping. late ME. **8.** Of a male animal: To spring upon (the female) in copulation 1530.

1. Hameward with clever strides he lap RAMSAY. **2.** His hors for fere gan to turne, And leepe aside CHAUCER. He leaped up the stone steps by two at a time GEO. ELIOT. *Prov.* Look before you leap. **c.** Whenever a salmon leaps you must keep a slack line 1867. **3.** Reioice yee in that day, and leape for ioy *Luke* 6:23. **4.** Arethusa leaping from her Bed DRYDEN. **5.** I thought ten thousand swords must have leaped from their scabbards BURKE. The echos..leaped from cliff to cliff TYNDALL. **b.** His heart leapt high as he look'd PALGRAVE. **7.** The Nimrod..Leaps every fence but one COWPER.

Leaper (lī·pəɹ). [OE. *hlēapere*; see LEAP *v.* and -ER[1].] One who or that which leaps.

Lea·p-frog. 1599. [f. LEAP *v.* + FROG[1].] A boys' game in which one player places his hands upon the bent back or shoulders of another and leaps or vaults over him. Also, a jump or leap of this description. Hence **Leap-frog** *v.* to leap or vault as at leap-frog (*intr.* and *trans.*).

†**Lea·pful.** OE. [f. LEAP *sb.*[2] + -FUL.] A basketful –ME.

Leaping (lī·piŋ), *vbl. sb.* OE. [f. LEAP *v.* + -ING[1].] The action of LEAP *v.*

attrib. and *Comb.*: **l.-head** 1862, **l.-horn** 1859, the lower pommel on a side-saddle; †**l.-house,** a brothel; **l.-time,** the time of activity, youth.

Leaping (lī·piŋ), *ppl. a.* OE. [f. LEAP *v.* + -ING[2].] That leaps, etc.; see the vb.

l. spider, a jumping spider, one of the *Saltigradæ.* Hence **Lea·pingly** *adv.* by leaps.

Lea·p year. [Late ME. (XIV), f. LEAP *sb.*[1]; prob. of much older formation, as the ON. *hlaupár* is presumably, like other terms of the Roman calendar, imitated from Eng.] A year having one day (now Feb. 29) more than the common year; a bissextile year.

(Perhaps so called because in the bissextile year any fixed festival after Feb. falls on the next week-day but one to that on which it fell in the preceding year, not on the next week-day as usual.)

Lear[1] (līᵊɹ). Now *Sc.* and *n. dial.* ME. [f. LERE *v.*; in mod.Sc. a var. of *lair, lare*; see LORE *sb.*[1]] Instruction, learning; in early use, †a lesson; †also, a doctrine, religion.

†**Lear**[2]. ME. [– OFr. *loiure, lieure*, (also mod.) *liure* :– L. *ligatura* LIGATURE.] **1.** Tape; binding –1736. **2.** *Cookery.* A thickening for sauces, soups, etc.; a thickened sauce –1837.

Lear[3] (līᵊɹ). 1601. [perh. a developed use of *lear* LAIR *sb.* 5.] Colour (of sheep or cattle), due to the nature of the soil.

Lear: see LAIR, LEER, LERE, LIAR.

Lea·-rig. *dial.* [f. LEA *a.* + RIG *sb.*[1]; in OE. *lǣġhryċġ.*] A ridge left in grass at the end of a ploughed field.

Learn (lɔ̄ɹn), *v.* Pa. t. and pa. pple. **learned** (lɔ̄ɹnd), **learnt** (lɔ̄ɹnt). [OE. *leornian* = OFris. *lernia, lirnia*, OS. *līnon* (:– **liznōn*), OHG. *lernēn, lirnēn* (G. *lernen*) :– WGmc. **liznōjan*, **liznējan*, f. **lis-*, weak grade of **lais-*; see LORE *sb.*[1]]

I. 1. *trans.* To get knowledge of (a subject) or skill in (an art, etc.) by study, experience, or teaching. Also, to commit to memory, esp. in phrases *to l. by heart, by rote*, for which see the sbs. **2.** *intr.* To acquire knowledge of a subject or matter; to receive instruction OE. **3.** *trans.* To become informed of; to hear of, ascertain ME. **b.** *intr.* To be informed, ascertain, hear (*of*) 1756.

1. To l. True patience MILT. Henceforth I learne, that to obey is best MILT. L. to labour and to wait LONGF. Phr. *I am* (*yet*) *to l.*: I do not yet know. **2.** Sir, I am too old to learne *Lear* II. ii. 134. **3.** This good newes I have learned by a letter of yours 1638. Phr. *To l. out*: to discover (now *dial.*).

II. To impart knowledge. Now *vulgar.* **1.** *trans.* To teach ME. †**2.** To inform (a person) of something –1697.

1. No doubt the chickens crowed as the cocks had learned them FULLER. L. to know the House; l. the House to know you DISRAELI. To l. him a lesson 1889. **2.** Learne me the Proclamation *Tr. & Cr.* II. i. 22.

Hence **Lea·rnable** *a.* that may be learnt. **Lea·rner,** one who receives instruction; †a teacher.

Learned (lɔ̄·ɹnėd), *ppl. a.* ME. [f. LEARN *v.* + -ED[1].] **1.** Of a person: In early use, that has been taught; educated. Later, deeply-read, erudite. Const. *in*, †*of*. **b.** *absol.* Chiefly in pl. *the l.* 1568. **c.** Said of one 'learned in the law'; hence by courtesy of any lawyer 1485. **d.** *transf.* of a trained pig, etc. 1833. **2.** Of things: Pertaining to, manifesting, or characterized by, profound knowledge gained by study 1613. **b.** In art-criticism, with reference to draughtmanship, colouring, etc.: Exhibiting thorough knowledge of method 1748. **c.** Of a language, profession, or science: Pursued or studied chiefly by men of learning. Of words: Introduced or used by men of learning. 1581.

1. And Moyses was lernd in al the wysdom of Egipcians WYCLIF *Acts* 7:22. That dreaded phenomenon, a l. lady SCOTT. **2.** If Jonson's l. Sock be on MILT. A l. sermon FULLER, education 1763. **c.** The l. languages L. MURRAY, professions 1850, words 1869. Hence **Lea·rned-ly** *adv.*, **-ness.**

Learning (lɔ̄·ɹniŋ), *vbl. sb.* [OE. *leornung, -ing*, f. *leornian*; see LEARN *v.* and -ING[1].] **1.** The action of LEARN *v.* †**2.** What is learnt or taught: **a.** a lesson –1611; **b.** information –1606; **c.** a doctrine, *esp.* a maxim in law –1626; **d.** a science –1613; **e.** an acquirement SHAKS. **3.** Knowledge, esp. of language or literary or historical science, got by study; also, learnedness ME.

1. There's nothing so good for l., as teaching R. OWEN. **2. e.** *Haml.* V. ii. 35. **3.** Oxenford..a norishe of l., and a famous universitie 1559. What we want is not l., but knowledge LOWELL. *The new l.*: the studies, esp. that of Greek, introduced into England in the 16th c.; also applied to the doctrines of the Reformation 1530.

Leary: see LEERY *a.*

Leasable (lī·săb'l), *a.* 1611. [f. LEASE *v.* + -ABLE.] That may be leased.

Lease, *sb.*[1], **leaze** (līz). Now *dial.* [OE. *lǣs* :– Gmc. **lǣswō.* Occas. confused with the pl. of LEA *sb.*[1] Orig. meaning prob. land 'let alone', not tilled.] Pasture; pasturage; meadow-land; common.

Lease *sb.*[2]: see LEASE *a.*

Lease (līs), *sb.*[3] 1450. [– AFr. *les* = OFr. *lais, leis*, f. specific use of *lesser, laissier* (mod. *laisser*) let, leave :– L. *laxare*, f. *laxus* loose, LAX *a.*] **1.** A contract between parties, by which the one conveys lands or tenements to the other for life, for a term of years, or at will, usually in consideration of rent or other periodical compensation. **b.** The instrument by which the conveyance is made. **c.** The period of time for which the contract is made. **2.** *fig.*; esp. in phr. *a* (*new*) *l. of life* 1586. **3.** *Austral.* 'A piece of land leased for mining purposes' (Morris) 1890.

1. He got possession, on easy leases, of the revenues of Bath, Worcester and Hereford HUME. **b.** The l...had been lent..to the plaintiff..for perusal 1893. **2.** Our high plac'd Macbeth Shall liue the L. of Nature *Macb.* IV. i. 99.

Lease (līs), *sb.*[4] ME. [app. a var. of LEASH *sb.*, perh. confused with an adoption of Fr. *lisse, lice* = sense 2.] †**1.** A certain quantity of thread –1457. **2.** The crossing of the warp-threads in a loom; the place at which they cross 1839. **3.** = LEASH *sb.* 6 a. 1824.

†**Lease,** *a.* and *sb.*[2] [OE. *lēas* = OFris. *lās*, OS., OHG. *lōs* (Du., G. *los*), ON. *lauss*, Goth. *laus* :– Gmc. **lausaz*, f. **laus-* **leus-* **lus-*; see LOOSE *a.*] **A.** *adj.* Untrue, false, lying –1450.

An Authour..That halt not dremes false ne lees CHAUCER.

B. *sb.* Untruth, falsehood, lying –1598.

Thus seyt the bok withoutyn ony les CHAUCER.

Lease (līz), *v.*[1] Now *dial.* [OE. *lesan* gather, glean = OFris. *lesa* read, OS., OHG. *lesan* (Du. *lezen*, G. *lesen* gather, read), ON. *lesa*, Goth. *ga|lisan* gather.] **1.** *trans.* and *intr.* To glean. (In OE. used in wider sense: To gather, collect.) **2.** To pick ME.

†**Lease,** *v.*[2] [OE. *lēasian*, f. *lēas* LEASE *a.*; perh. partly a back-formation from LEASING *sb.*] *intr.* To tell lies –1594.

Lease (līs), *v.*[3] 1570. [– AFr. *lesser*; see LEASE *sb.*[3]] **1.** *trans.* To grant the possession or use of (lands, etc.) by a lease; to let *out* on lease. Also *transf.* and *fig.* **2.** To take a lease of; to hold by a lease 1877.

1. This land..Is now Leas'd out SHAKS. **2.** Angling..is hardly to be obtained unless by leasing a rod 1898.

Leasehold (lī·shōuld). 1720. [f. LEASE *sb.*[3] after *freehold.*] A tenure by lease; real estate so held. **b.** *attrib.* or *adj.* Held by lease 1731. Hence **Lea·seholder,** one who possesses l. property.

†**Lease-parole.** 1592. [f. LEASE *sb.*[3] + PAROLE.] A lease by word of mouth, not in writing –1672.

Leaser[1] (lī·zəɹ). Now *dial.* ME. [f. LEASE *v.*[1] + -ER[1].] A gleaner.

†**Lea·ser**[2]. *rare.* [OE. *lēasere*; see LEASE *v.*[2], -ER[1].] A liar –1641.

Leaser[3] (lī·səɹ). 1607. [f. LEASE *v.*[3] + -ER[1].] One who leases; a leaseholder.

Leash (līʃ), *sb.* ME. [– OFr. *lesse*, (also mod.) *laisse*, f. specific use of *laisser* let (a dog) run on a slack lead; see LEASE *sb.*[3] The development of Fr. s to Eng. ʃ is paralleled in *crush, cushion, frush.*] **1.** The thong in which hounds or coursing-dogs are held. **2.** A set of three hounds, hawks, hares, etc.; hence *gen.* (*a leash of* = three) ME. **3.** *Hawking.* The thong or string which is passed through the varvels of the jesses to secure the hawk 1497. **4.** *fig.*; esp. in phr. *To hold* or *have in l.*, to have control over, keep in bondage ME. †**5.** A snare, noose –1814. **6.** *Weaving.* **a.** One of the cords (having an eye in the middle to receive the warp-thread) which extend between the parallel laths of the heddle of a loom. Also *leish.* 1731. **b.** = LEASE *sb.*[4] 2. 1888.

1. The hounds, hunted on the l. 1888. Phr. *The l.*: †(*a*) the department concerned with the keeping of the king's hounds; (*b*) the art or practice of coursing. **2.** I contrived to bag a l. of trout 1882. **3.** Terms of art, Diet and seeling, jesses, l. and lure TENNYSON. **4.** For God hathe them in lease. Yea..they are his slaues BECON.

Leash (līʃ), *v.* 1503. [f. prec.] **1.** *trans.* To attach or connect by a leash 1599. **b.** *fig.* To link *together*, esp. in threes 1854. **2.** †To lash with a leash; to whip (*dial.*) 1503.

1. And, at his heeles, (Leasht in, like Hounds), should Famine, Sword, and Fire, Crouch for employment *Hen. V*, Prol. 7.

Leasing (lī·ziŋ), *sb. Obs.* or *arch.* exc. *dial.* (*Sc.* and *n.*) [OE. *lēasung*, f. *lēasian*; see LEASE *v.*[2] and -ING[1].] Lying, falsehood; a lie.

Comb.: **l.-maker,** a liar; *spec.* in *Sc. Law* (now *Hist.*), one who utters untrue and slanderous statements such as may prejudice the relations between the king and his subjects; so **l.-making,** verbal sedition.

Leasow (lī·so, le·zə), *sb.* Now *dial.* (*Sc. lizzure*, etc.) [OE. *lǣswe*, obl. form of *lǣs*. See LEASE *sb.*[1]] Pasture; pasturage; meadow-land.

Lea·sow, *v. Obs.* or *dial.* [OE. *lǣswian* (also *lǣsian*), f. *lǣsw-*, *lǣs* LEASOW *sb.*, LEASE *sb.*[1]] *trans.* and *intr.* To pasture, graze.

Least (līst). *a.* (*sb.*) and *adv.* [OE. *lǣst*, contr. of *lǣsest* :– **laisistaz*, f. **laisiz* LESS *a.*; see -EST.] Used as the superl. of LITTLE. **A.** *adj.* **I.** In concord with *sb.* expressed or understood. **1.** Smallest; slightest; †fewest. Often coupled with *last.* **2.** Lowest in power or position; meanest. *arch.* OE.

1. Nor l. in Number, nor in Name the last DRYDEN. Phr. *The l.*: often used, esp. after negs., for 'Any, however small'. *L. common multiple*: see MULTIPLE. **2.** Thou..art not the l. among the Princes of Iuda *Matt.* 2: 6.

II. Absol. uses (quasi-*sb.*). **1.** That which is least; the least quantity, amount, or †part *of* something ME. †**2.** as *sb.* A most minute quantity or part; a minimum –1813.

1. The very l. I can do is to apologize for the mistake 1902. Phr. *To say the l.* (*of it*). *At l., at the l.*: qualifying an expression of amount or number: = '(so much or many) at any rate, if not more'; hence, characterizing a statement as certainly valid, even if a wider one be not allowable; = 'at any rate', 'at all events'. *In the l.* †(*a*) At the lowest estimate. (*b*) In the smallest or slightest degree. **2.** There being in Nature no l. which cannot be divided STANLEY.

B. *adv.* In the least degree ME.

Mammon, the least erected Spirit that fell From heav'n MILT. Phr. *The l.*: in the least degree.

Least, obs. form of LEST.

Leastways (lī·stˌweiz), *adv.* ME. [See -WAYS.] †**a.** Orig. two wds. in the phr. *at* (*the*) *least way*(*s* = 'at least'. **b.** As one word, in the same sense. *dial.* and *vulgar.*

Leastwise (lī·stˌwəiz), *adv.* 1534. [See -WISE, and cf. prec.] †**a.** As two wds. in certain phrases: *at* (*the*) *least wise* = 'at least'; *in the least wise* = 'in the least'. **b.** As one word = 'at least'. Now *dial.* or *vulgar.*

Leat (līt). Chiefly *s.w. dial.* 1642. [OE., in *wætergelǣt* water channel; f. base of *lǣtan* LET *v.*[1]] An open water-course to conduct water for mills, mining works, etc.

Leather (le·ðəɹ), *sb.* [OE. *leþer* (only in compounds) = OFris. *lether*, OS. *leðar* (Du. *leer*), OHG. *ledar* (G. *leder*), ON. *leðr* :– Gmc. **leþram* :– IE. **letrom*, whence also OIr. *lethar*, W. *lledr*, Breton *ler.*] **1.** Skin prepared for use by tanning, etc. ME. **b.** *pl.* Kinds of leather 1853. **2.** Something made of leather, e.g. a strap, a thong; a piece of leather for a plaster or to tighten a tap; the leathern portion of a bellows, or of a pump-sucker ME. **b.** *pl.* Articles for wear made of leather, e.g. shoes, slippers, leggings, breeches 1837. **c.** *Cricket* and *Football.* The ball 1868. **3.** Skin. Now only *slang.* ME. **4.** *attrib.* or *adj.* Consisting or made of leather, or of a material resembling it OE.

1. *American l.*, a kind of oil-cloth; *patent l.*, l. having a fine black varnished surface. *Morocco, russia, Spanish, Turkey l.*: see those wds. Phr. *L. and prunella*: indifferent stuff. (A misinterpretation of Pope, *Essay on Man* IV. 204.) *Prov. phr.* A Currier, being present, said..If you have a Mind to have the Town well fortified and secure, take my Word, there is Nothing like L. 1767. **2.** *Upper l.*: see UPPER. **3.** Phr. *To lose l.*: to suffer abrasion of the skin. **4.** Where is thy L. Apron, and thy Rule? *Jul. C.* I. i. 7.

Comb.: **l.-back,** a large soft-shelled turtle, *Sphargis coriacea*; **-bark,** a tree of the genus *Thymelæa*; **-board,** a composition of leather scraps, paper, etc., glued together and rolled into sheets, used in shoe-making; **-carp,** a scaleless variety of the carp; **-coat,** a name for a russet apple, from the roughness of its skin; **-flower,** a N. American climbing plant (*Clematis viorna*) with thick leathery purplish sepals; **-head,** (*a*) *slang*, a blockhead; (*b*) *Austral.*, the friar-bird; **-leaf,** a low evergreen shrub of the northern U.S. (*Cassandra calyculata*), with coriaceous leaves; **-mouthed,** hard-mouthed, as fishes, horses, etc.; **-neck,** a sailor's name for a soldier, from the l. stock he used to wear; **-plant,** a composite plant of the genus *Celmisia*, a native of New Zealand; **-turtle** = *leather-back*; **-wing,** a bat; **-wood,** (*a*) a N. American shrub of the genus *Dirca*, with a very tough bark; (*b*) a Tasmanian tree with wood of a pale reddish mahogany colour, *Eucryphia billardieri* (Morris).

Leather (le·ðəɹ), *v.* ME. [f. LEATHER *sb.*] **1.** *trans.* To cover or arm with leather. **2.** To beat with a leathern thong; hence *gen.* to beat, thrash 1625. **b.** *fig. intr.* To work hard; with *away, on* 1869.

2. I'd like to l. 'im black and blue TENNYSON.

Leatherette (leðəre·t). 1880. [f. LEATHER *sb.* + -ETTE.] A fabric made of paper and cloth, in imitation of leather.

Lea·ther-ja·cket. 1770. [f. LEATHER *sb.* + JACKET.] **1.** Any of various fishes having a thick skin; e.g. *Balistes capriscus, Oligoplites saurus*, and species of *Monacanthus.* **2.** *Austral.* A kind of pancake 1846. **3.** *Austral.* Any of various trees having a tough bark; e.g. *Eucalyptus punctata* 1874. **4.** The grub of the crane-fly 1881.

Leathern (le·ðəɹn), *a.* [OE. *leþeren*, f. *leþer* LEATHER *sb.* + -EN[4].] **1.** Consisting or made of leather. **b.** Used of the skin of living animals ME. **2.** Leather-like. Said esp. of the bat's wings, hence of its flight, and of the bat itself. 1513.

1. *L. convenience, -ency*: a Quakers' term for a coach; hence used joc. At the duly appointed hour, creaked forth the l. convenience SCOTT. **b.** *A. Y. L.* II. i. 37. **2.** The weak-eyed bat..flits by on l. wing COLLINS.

Leatheroid (le·ðəroid). 1882. [f. LEATHER *sb.* + -OID.] Cotton paper chemically treated so as to resemble raw-hide.

Leathery (le·ðəri), *a.* 1552. [f. LEATHER *sb.* + -Y[1].] Resembling leather in appearance or texture; in botanical use = CORIACEOUS.

L. leaves of Conifers 1884.

Leave (līv), *sb.* [OE. *lēaf* = OHG. **louba* (MHG. *loube*, G. †*laube*) :– WGmc. **lauba*, whence **laubjan* permit; see LEVE *v.*[1]] **1.** Permission *to do* something. †**2.** Leave-taking; in phr. *audience of l.* –1734. **3.** [f. LEAVE *v.*[1]] *Billiards.* The position in which the balls are left for the following play 1901.

1. Phr. *To ask, beg, get, give, grant, have, obtain l.*; *by, with, without* (*the*) *l.* (*of*). *By your l.*: an apology for taking a liberty; often *ironical*, to introduce an unwelcome remark. †*To give l.* (*fig.* of conditions or circumstances): to allow, permit. *L. of absence*, or simply *l.*, permission to be absent from a post of duty. (See also *sick-leave.*) *On l.*: absent from duty by permission. Hence, the period of such absence. *To take* (*one's*) *l.*: orig. †to obtain permission to depart (*rare*); hence, to bid farewell. (See also FRENCH LEAVE.)

Leave (līv), *v.*[1] [OE. *lǣfan* = OFris. *lēva*, OS. *-lēbian*, OHG. *leiban* (cf. OHG. *bilīban*, G. *bleiben* remain), ON. *leifa*, Goth. *-laibjan* :– Gmc. **laibjan* remain, continue, f. **laibō* remainder; see LAVE *sb.*]

I. To have a remainder; to cause or allow to remain. **1.** *trans.* Of a deceased person: To have remaining after one (a widow, property, etc.). **b.** Of things or conditions: To have remaining as a trace, etc. after removal or cessation 1756. **2.** To transmit at one's death *to* heirs or successors. Hence, to bequeath or devise. OE. **b.** In passive: *To be* (*well*, etc.) *left*: to be well provided for by legacy, etc. 1606. **3.** To allow to remain in a certain place or condition; to abstain from taking or dealing with. *To be left*: to remain. OE. †**b.** *absol.*; also with *over* –1642. **c.** To have as a remainder (in subtraction); to yield as a remainder when deducted from some larger amount ME. **4.** †**a.** To neglect or omit to perform (some action, etc.); also to omit *to do* something –1624. **b.** To allow (an action, etc.) to stand over 1559. **5.** To commit, refer to another person or agent instead of oneself. Const. *to* or *dat.*; also *with.* ME. **b.** To allow (a person or thing) *to do* something, *to be* done or dealt with, without interference. 1456. **c.** *To l.* (*something*, etc.) *to be desired*: to be (more or less) unsatisfactory. **6.** To deposit or give in charge (some object) or station (a person) to remain after one's departure; to give (instructions, orders, information, e.g. one's name or address) for use during one's absence. Phr. *To l. a card on* (a person). ME.

1. In case he should..l. no lawful heir CRUISE **2.** Poore cosin Brooks hath left me 10 *l.* 1676. **3.** For, what place is left now for honestie? where lodgeth goodnes? FLEMING. Persons who..have ..very little liver left 1845. *To l. undone, unsaid*, etc. = to abstain from doing, saying, etc. To l. the argument without proofs, is to l. it without effect PALEY. **c.** Three from eleven leaves eight (*mod.*). **4. b.** Hee leaues repentance for gray hayres 1628. **5.** I..leave such theories to those that study Meteors SIR T. HERBERT. **b.** He left him to shift for himself COBBETT. **6.** He left word that he would soon be home DICKENS.

II. To depart from, quit, relinquish. **1.** To quit (a place, person, or thing); to deviate from (a line of road, etc.) ME. **b.** *colloq.* (orig. *U.S.*) *To get* (or *be*) *left*: to be left in the lurch 1891. **2.** To go away from permanently; to cease to reside at (a place), to belong to (a society, etc.); to quit the service of (a person) ME. **3.** To abandon, forsake (a habit, etc.); to lay aside (a dress). Now *rare* exc. in *l. off.* ME. **4.** To cease, desist from, stop. Now only *arch.* = *l. off.* ME. †**b.** *intr.* –1633. †**5.** To cease speaking of –1604. †**b.** *intr.* To stop, break off in a narrative –1614.

1. We..steered.., leaving those isles on the east DE FOE. Pray, sir, l. the room BYRON. They left him dead 1883. *absol.* (*colloq.*) We left about eleven 1867. **3.** The confession of a faulte is a profession to leaue the same BP. WATSON.

†**III.** *intr.* To remain; to remain *behind, over*; to continue or stay in one place –1541.

Phrases. *To l...alone*: = 'to let alone' (see ALONE 1 and LET *v.*[1]). *To l. go (of)* 1810, *to l. hold (of), to l. loose (of)* colloq.: to cease holding, to let go. *To l. it at that*: to proceed no farther with a matter 1902.

Combined with *advs.* **Leave behind.** †(*a*) To leave undone. (*b*) To go away without. (*c*) To have remaining after departure or removal, as a trace or consequence. **Leave off.** (*a*) *trans.* To cease from (an action, a habit). Also, to cease to wear or use (something). †(*b*) To give up; to forsake the society of. (*c*) *absol.* and *intr.* To cease doing; to make an end or interruption; to stop. Of a narrative: To end. Also *Comm.* of shares, etc.: To end (*at* a certain price) on the closing of the market. **Leave out.** To omit, not to insert or include. **Leave over.** To let 'stand over' for future consideration.

Leave (līv), *v.*[2] [ME. *lēve*, f. *lēf* LEAF *sb.*] *intr.* = LEAF *v.* 1.

†**Leave,** *v.*[3] [– (O)Fr. *lever*; see LEVY *v.*] *trans.* To raise (an army). SPENSER *F. Q.* II. x. 31.

Leaved (līvd), *a.* ME. [f. LEAF *sb.* or LEAVE *v.*[2] + -ED.] **1.** Having leaves; 'in leaf'. *lit.* and *fig.* Also *Her.* **b.** Having leaves (of a specified number or kind) ME. **2.** Resembling a (plant-) leaf 1841. †**3.** Laminate –1658. **4.** Of a door: Having (two) leaves 1610. **5.** Furnished with leaves (of paper) 1629.

1. A foursquare stem..leaued like vnto an Oke P. HOLLAND. **b.** Thick-leaved platans TENNYSON. **2.** L. forms 1865.

†**Lea·veless,** *a.* 1581. [var. of LEAFLESS.] Without leaves –1638.

Leaven (le·v'n), *sb.* [ME. *levain* – (O)Fr. *levain* – Gallo-Rom. use of L. *levamen* lit. 'means of raising', only in sense 'alleviation, relief', f. *levare* lighten, relieve, raise.] **1.** A substance which is added to dough to produce fermentation; *spec.* fermenting dough reserved from a previous batch. **b.** In wider sense; = FERMENT *sb.* 1. 1658. **2.** *fig.* **a.** An agency which transforms by progressive inward operation (cf. Matt. 13:33, etc.) ME. **b.** Used for: A tempering or modifying element 1576.

1. b. The l. of typhus 1822. **2. a.** There is a very sour l. of malevolence in many English and in many American minds against each other 1799. **b.** Pleasure with pain for l. SWINBURNE.

Phrases. *Of the same l.*: of the same sort or character. *The old l.*: after 1 *Cor.* 5:6, 7, the traces of the unregenerate condition.

Leaven (le·v'n), *v.* ME. [f. LEAVEN *sb.*] **1.** *trans.* To cause (dough) to ferment by means of leaven. **2.** *fig.* To permeate with a transforming influence; to imbue *with* some modifying element; †*rarely*, to corrupt by admixture 1550.

1. Know ye not that a little leauen leaueneth the whole lumpe? 1 *Cor.* 5:6. **2.** The indolent, evil thought would still insinuate itself until it leavened their entire character 1862.

Leavenous (le·v'nəs), *a.* 1649. [f. LEAVEN *sb.* + -OUS.] Having the properties of leaven.

Leaver (lī·vəɹ). 1548. [f. LEAVE *v.*[1] + -ER[1].] One who leaves (see LEAVE *v.*[1]). *Ant. & Cl.* IV. ix. 22.

Leave-taking (lī·vtē[i]:kiŋ), *vbl. sb.* ME. [f. LEAVE *sb.*] The taking leave of a person; saying farewell; †parting speech. So **Lea·ve-ta:ker** KIPLING.

Leaving (lī·viŋ), *vbl. sb.* ME. [f. LEAVE *v.*[1] + -ING[1].] **1.** The action of LEAVE *v.*[1] Also in Comb., as *leaving-off*. **2.** *concr.* †**a.** *sing.* What is left; remainder –1596. **b.** *pl.* in same sense. (Cf. L. *reliquiæ*.) ME. **3.** *attrib.* 1865.

2. b. The poorer sort..carried the leavings or fragments home 1686. **3.** *L. certificate, examination, exhibition*, in connection with leaving school or college. **L.-book** (at Eton), a book presented by friends on the occasion of one's 'leaving'. **L.-shop** (*slang*), an unlicensed pawn-shop.

Leavy (lī·vi), *a.* ME. [Earlier and more normal f. LEAFY.] **1.** Having leaves. *Obs.* exc. *poet.* **b.** Consisting of or made of leaves (natural or ornamental) 1610. †**2.** Of a gate: Having leaves. CHAPMAN. Hence †**Lea·viness.**

‖**Leban** (le·băn). Also **lebban, leben.** 1698. [Arab. *laban* milk, coagulated sour milk.] Coagulated sour milk, used as a drink among the Arabs.

Lecanomancy (le·kănomænsi). 1610. [– Gr. λεκανομαντεία, f. λεκάνη dish, pan, pot; see -MANCY.] Divination by the inspection of water in a basin.

Lecanoric (lekănǫ·rik), *a.* 1852. [f. *Lecanora*, name of a genus of lichens, + -IC.] *Chem.* In *l. acid*: a crystalline substance obtained by Schunck from certain lichens of the genus *Lecanora*. So **Lecanorate** (-ō[ə]·rĕt), a salt of l. acid; **Lecano·rin** = *lecanoric acid* 1844.

Lech (lek). 1768. [– W. *llech* (flat) stone. Cf. CROMLECH.] A Celtic monumental stone.

Leche (lī·tʃī). 1857. [Sechuana; cf. Sesuto *letsa* antelope.] A S. African water-buck, *Kobus leche*.

Lecher (le·tʃəɹ), *sb. arch.* ME. [– OFr. *lichiere* (nom.), *lecheor, -ur* (acc.), f. *lechier* live in debauchery or gluttony (mod. *lécher* lick) – Frankish **likkōn* :– Gmc. **likkōjan* LICK.] A lewd or grossly unchaste man, a debauchee. Hence †**Le·cher** *a.* lecherous; also, base, vile. †**Le·cher** *v. intr.* to play the l. †**Le·cherer,** a l. [AFr. *lecheryer*.]

Lecherous (le·tʃərəs), *a. arch.* ME. [– OFr. *lecheros*, f. *lecheor*; see prec., -OUS.] **1.** Addicted to lechery; consisting in, characterized by, or inciting to lechery. †**2.** = LICKEROUS –1535.

1. A leccherous thing win WYCLIF *Prov.* 20:1. Hence **Le·cherous-ly** *adv.*, **-ness.**

Lechery (le·tʃəri). ME. [– OFr. *lecherie*, f. as prec.; see -Y[3].] Habitual indulgence of lust; lewdness of living. Also *fig.* †**b.** *transf.* Inordinate pleasure. MASSINGER.

Lecithin (le·siþin). Also **-ine.** 1861. [f. Gr. λέκιθος yolk of egg + -IN[1].] *Chem.* A nitrogenous fatty substance found in the nerve tissues, the yolk of eggs, blood, and other fluids of the body.

Lectern (le·ktəɹn). Also †**lettern, lecturn,** etc. [ME. *lettorne, let(t)ron* – OFr. *letrun, lettrun* – med.L. *lectrum* (pseudo-Isidor), f. L. *legere* read.] A reading- or singing-desk in a church, esp. that from which the lessons are read; often in the form of an eagle with outspread wings supported on a column.

Lection (le·kʃən). ME. [– L. *lectio, lection-*, f. *lect-*, pa. ppl. stem of *legere* read; see -ION. Cf. OFr. *lection*.]

†**I.** = ELECTION. ME. –1535.

II. †**1.** The act of reading (*rare*); a particular way of reading or interpreting a passage –1702. **b.** *concr.* A reading of a text found in a particular copy or edition 1649. **2.** *Eccl.* A 'lesson' 1608.

Lectionary (le·kʃənări). 1491. [– med.L. *lectionarius* (XII), *-arium*, f. as prec.; see -ARY[1].] A book containing (the list of) 'lessons' or portions of Scripture appointed to be read at divine service.

‖**Lectisternium** (lektistə̄·ɹniŏm). 1597. [L., f. *lectus* couch, bed + *sternere* spread.] *Rom. Antiq.* A sacrifice of the nature of a feast, in which images of the gods were placed on couches with food before them.

Lector (le·ktǭɹ). 1483. [– L. *lector*, f. *lect-*, pa. ppl. stem of *legere* read; see -OR 2.] **1.** *Eccl.* An ecclesiastic belonging to one of the minor orders, who read the lessons. **2.** A reader; *spec.* a reader or lecturer in a college or university (now chiefly *Hist.* and with reference to foreign use) 1563.

†**Le·ctuary.** ME. [– med.L. *lectuarium*, aphetic f. *electuarium* ELECTUARY. Cf. OFr. *letuaire*.] An electuary –1578.

Lecture (le·ktiŭɹ, -tʃəɹ), *sb.* ME. [– (O)Fr. *lecture* or med.L. *lectura*, f. *lect-*, pa. ppl. stem of L. *legere* read; see -URE.] †**1.** The action of reading. Also *fig.* Also, that which is read. –1835. †**2.** The way in which a text reads; a lection –1680. **3.** The action of reading aloud. Also, a lection or lesson. *arch.* 1526. **4.** A discourse before an audience or class (e.g. in a university) upon a given subject, usu. for the purpose of instruction 1536. **b.** A discourse of the nature of a sermon, delivered on an occasion outside the regular order of services 1556. **c.** A lecture or course or series of lectures, given at stated periods; a foundation for a lecturer, a lectureship 1615. †**5.** A lesson given by a teacher to a pupil –1765. †Also *fig.* **6.** An admonition, esp. by way of reproof. Phr. *To read* (a person) *a l.* 1600.

4. The Common Law School, where the Vinerian Professor reads his Lectures 1827. **c.** The L. founded by the late rev. and pious John Bampton M.A. 1780. **6.** Our young bridegroom receiv'd a terrible l. 1732.

Le·cture, *v.* 1590. [f. LECTURE *sb.*] **1.** *intr.* To deliver a lecture or lectures. **2.** *trans.* To deliver lectures to or before (an audience) 1681. **3.** To admonish, rebuke, reprimand 1706.

Le·cturer. 1570. [f. LECTURE *v.* + -ER[1].] †**1.** = LECTOR 1. –1797. **2.** An assistant preacher in the Church of England, who delivers afternoon or evening lectures 1583. **3.** One who gives a lecture or lectures; *spec.* one appointed to deliver a course of lectures in a university or college, esp. as subordinate to a professor 1615. Hence **Le·cturership** 1891.

Le·ctureship. 1634. [f. LECTURE *sb.* (sense 4 c) + -SHIP; commonly used in place of the more regular *lecturership*.] The office of a lecturer.

Lecturn: see LECTERN.

Lecyth (le·siþ). 1846. [– mod.L. *Lecythis*, deduced from *Lecythidaceæ*; see -ID[2].] *Bot.* A plant of the order *Lecythidaceæ* (typical genus *Lecythis*). So **Le·cythid** *a.* 1871.

‖**Lecythus** (le·siþŏs). *Pl.* **lecythi** (-þəi). 1857. [– Gr. λήκυθος.] *Gr. Antiq.* A vase or flask with a narrow neck. Hence **Le·cythoid** *a.* resembling a l.

Led (led), *ppl. a.* 1553. [pa. pple. of LEAD *v.*[1]] In various uses (see the vb.).

Phrases. *Led horse*, a spare horse, led by an attendant or groom; also a sumpter-horse. *L.-captain*, a hanger-on, dependent, parasite.

†**Lede.** *Obs.* [repr. OE. *lēod* nation, people, *lēode, lēoda* men, people (= G. *leute*), *lēod* man.] A people, nation; persons collectively; (one's own) people; a man –1650.

Le·den. *Obs.* exc. *dial.* [OE. *lǣden*, repr. a Celtic or early Rom. pronunc. of L. *Latinum* Latin, confused with *lēden* language, f. *lēode* people.] †**1.** Latin. Only OE. †**2.** The language of a nation, etc.; a 'tongue' –ME. †**b.** Form of speech; way of speaking –1596. †**c.** *poet.* Applied to the 'language' of birds –1612.

Ledge (ledʒ), *sb.* [perh. f. ME. *legge* (ledʒə) LAY *v.*] **1.** A transverse bar or strip of wood, etc. fixed upon a door, gate, piece of furniture or the like. Now *dial.* and *techn.* **b.** *Naut.* A name for the small pieces of timber placed athwartships, under the decks of a ship, in the intervals between the beams ME. **c.** *Arch.* A small moulding; a string-course 1828. †**2.** A raised edging running along the extremity of a board or the like –1802. **3.** A narrow horizontal surface, formed by the top of some projection in the vertical face of a wall, etc. 1558. **b.** A shelf-like projection on the side of a rock or mountain 1732. **c.** *Fortif.* = BERM 1729. **4.** A ridge of rocks, esp. such as are near the shore beneath the surface of the sea; †a range of hills; a ridge of earth 1555. **5.** †A course or layer (WOTTON); *Mining*, a stratum of metal-bearing rock; a quartz-vein 1847. **6.** *attrib.* **l.-door** = *ledged door* 1825.

3. b. We clung to the crannies and ledges of the rock STEPHEN. **4.** Three of the ships on invisible ledges the South winds drave BOWEN. Hence **Ledged** *ppl. a.* having or furnished with a l. or ledges; as, *ledged door*, one in which vertical boards are held together by three horizontal ledges.

Ledge, *v.*[1] *Obs.* exc. *dial.* ME. Also †**lage,** etc. Aphet. f. *alegge, aledge* ALLEGE *v.*[2]

Nay 'tis no matter sir, what he leges in Latine SHAKS.

Ledge, *v.*[2] *rare.* 1598. [f. LEDGE *sb.*] **1.** *intr.* To form a ledge. **2.** *trans.* To furnish with a ledge; to form as a ledge 1599.

Ledgement, ledgment (le·dʒmĕnt). *Arch.* ME. [app. f. LEDGE *sb.* + -MENT.] **1.** A string-course or horizontal suit of mouldings, such as the base-mouldings, etc., of a building. **2.** The development of a surface, or the surface of a body stretched out on a plane, so that the dimensions of the different sides may be easily ascertained 1842.

Ledger (le·dʒəɹ). Also †**lidger, lieger, leiger,** etc. 1401. [Early forms *legger, lidger, ligger*, corresp. in sense to Du. *legger, ligger* (f. *leggen* LAY *v.*, *liggen* LIE *v.*[1]), on which the Eng. forms were prob. modelled with phonetic accommodation to ME. *legge* (le·dʒə) LAY *v.*, *ligge* (li·dʒə) LIE *v.*[1]; see -ER[1].]

A. *sb.* **1.** A book that lies permanently in some place; e.g. †a bible 1538; †a large copy of the breviary –1691; a register (now *U.S.*). **b.** *Comm.* The principal book of the set of books employed for recording mercantile transactions, in which all debtor-and-creditor accounts are set down 1588. **2.** A horizontal timber in a scaffolding, lying parallel to the face of the building and supporting the putlogs. (Cf. *ligger*.) 1571. **3.** A flat stone covering a grave 1510. **4.** The nether millstone. Now *dial.* 1530. **5.** *Angling.* Short for *ledger-bait* (see below). 1653. **6.** A resident ambassador; also, a papal nuncio. *Obs.* exc. *Hist.* in form *lieger.* 1548. **7.** *transf.* and *fig.* **a.** A (permanent) representative; a commissioner; an agent. *Obs.* or *arch.* in form *lieger.* 1603. †**b.** A resident in a place –1661.

6. A Nuncio differed from a Legate, almost as a Lieger from an extraordinary Ambassadour FULLER. 7. b. Hee's a lieger at Horne's ordinarie yonder B. JONS.

Comb.: **l.-bait,** a fishing bait which is made to remain in one place (also *attrib.*) WALTON; so *l.-hook, -line, -tackle*; **-blade,** in a cloth-shearing machine, the stationary straight-edged blade acting with a spiral revolving blade, and used to trim the nap and make it uniform; **-millstone** = sense 4; **-stone** = sense 3; **-wall** = *foot-wall* (FOOT *sb.* Combs. 2).

B. *adj.* **I.** In *attrib.* use. †**1.** *L.-ambassador* or *ambassador l.*: residenta mbassador 1550. †**2.** Resident in a place; permanent; stationary. Also *fig. L. side*: the side on which something lies. –1662. **3.** *Mus.* **Ledger line,** a short line added temporarily above or below the stave to extend its compass 1700.

2. *L.-jests*: standing, stock jests. Like a bruised Codling Apple a little corrupted on the Leiger side GAYTON.

II. In predicative use, esp. in *to be, lie l.* **1.** Resident as ambassador, commissioner, or agent. *Obs.* exc. *arch.* 1560. †**2.** Lying or resting in a place; stationary; resident –1661.

1. One that lay lieger at London for their dispatches HACKET. 2. Shiloh, where the Ark was long leiger FULLER.

Le·dger, *v.* Also **leger.** 1688. [f. LEDGER *sb.* (sense 5).] *intr.* To use a ledger-bait.

Le·dger-book. Now *Hist.* 1553. A book containing records; a register; a cartulary; a book of accounts.

Ledget, -it (le·dʒėt). 1805. [f. LEDGE *sb.* + -ET.] A projecting piece.

Ledgy (le·dʒi), *a.* 1779. [f. LEDGE *sb.* + -Y[1].] Abounding in or consisting of ledges or ridges of rock.

Lee (lī), *sb.*[1] Also *dial.* **lew.** [OE. *hlēo, hlēow-* = OFris. *hlī*, OS. *hleo* m., *hlea* fem., ON. *hlé* :- Gmc. **χlēw-* (whence **χlēwj-* in ON. *hlý*), not known outside Gmc. The naut. sense was mainly from ON. See LEW, LUKE *a.*] **1.** Protection, shelter, rarely *pl.* †Also, a resting-place. **2.** Chiefly *Naut.* The sheltered side of any object; hence, the side away from the wind ME. †**3.** A sheltered position or condition; hence, calmness, peace, tranquillity ME. **4.** *attrib.* **a.** Indicating that an object is on the lee-side of a vessel, or to leeward of some other object, e.g. *l.-bowline*, etc. 1513. **b.** Implying motion to leeward 1726.

1. Phr. *In, under (the) l. of.* Rob Roy's cave under the Lea of Ben Lomond 1847. 2. We run in as much under the l. of the point as we could DE FOE. Phr. †*At l.*: (*a*) windbound; (*b*) under shelter. †(*To bring, fall*) *by the l.*: to leeward; also *fig.* †(*To bring, lay, lie*) *upon the l.*: with sails aback. *On, under (the) l.*: to leeward = ALEE. 4. b. The leisurely weather-roll and l.-roll 1859.

Comb.: **l.-anchor,** the anchor on the leeward side; **-bow,** the bow of a vessel that is turned away from the wind; hence *lee-bow* vb., to run under the lee-bow of; **-gage** (see GAUGE *sb.* I. 5); **-latch,** 'dropping to leeward of the course' (Smyth); **-most** *a.*, farthest to leeward; **-port,** a sheltered port; **-wheel,** 'the assistant to the helmsman' (Smyth).

Lee (lī), *sb.*[2] *Obs.* exc. in *pl.* ME. [– OFr. *lie* = Pr., Sp., Pg. *lia*, med.L. pl. *liæ* (x) – Gaulish **liga* or **ligja* (cf. OIr. *lige*).] The sediment from wine and other liquids. †**a.** *sing.* Also *fig.* Also *upon the l., to drain to the l.* –1813. **b.** *pl.* ME. **c.** *fig.* Basest part, dregs, refuse 1593. **d.** *pl.* construed as *sing. Macb.* II. iii. 100.

c. In these Lees and Dregges of time 1621. Phr. *To drain, drink the lees, to the lees*, i.e. to the last drop; (*to settle*) *on* or *upon the lees.*

†**Lee,** *a.* Cf. LEW *a.* ME. [f. LEE *sb.*[1]] Sheltered from the wind –1674.

†**Lee-board**[1]. ME. [– ON. *hlé-borð*, f. *hlé* LEE *sb.*[1] + *borð* BOARD.] The lee side (of a vessel).

Lee-board[2] (lī·bōᵊɹd). 1691. [f. LEE *sb.*[1] + BOARD.] A strong frame of plank, fixed to the side of a flat-bottom vessel, and let down into the water to diminish her drift to leeward.

Leech (lītʃ), *sb.*[1] [OE. *lǣće* = OFris. *letza, leischa*, OS. *lāki*, OHG. *lāhhi*, OSw. *läkir*, Goth. *lēkeis* :- Gmc. **lǣkjaz* :- IE. **lēgios* (cf. Ir. *liaigh*).] **1.** A physician; one who practises healing. Now *arch.* (chiefly *poet.*) or *jocular.* Also *transf.* and *fig.* **2.** *attrib.*, as **l.-fee,** a physician's fee.

1. A farrier and bullock-leach 1776. Grudging the l. his growing bill 1839.

Leech (lītʃ), *sb.*[2] [OE. *lǣće*, Kentish *lȳce*, = MDu. *lake, lieke, leke*; orig. a distinct word from prec., but assim. to it.] One of the aquatic blood-sucking worms of the order *Hirudinea*; esp. one of the genus *Hirudo* or *Sanguisuga*, used medicinally for drawing blood. **b.** *Artificial l.*: an apparatus consisting of a scarifier and glass tube for drawing blood by suction 1858. **c.** *fig.* One who sticks to another to suck gain out of him 1784.

Phr. *To stick like a l.* c. The spendthrift, and the l. That sucks him COWPER.

Comb.: **l.-extract,** an extract prepared from leeches, used experimentally for intravenous or intraperitoneal injections; **-gaiter,** a kind of gaiter worn in Ceylon for protection against land-leeches; **-glass** *Surg.*, a glass tube to hold a l. which is to be applied to a particular spot.

Leech (lītʃ), *sb.*[3] ME. [Early forms *leche, lyche* Sc. *lek* (XV). Obscurely connected with ON. (naut.) *lik* (cf. Sw. *lik*, Da. *lig* bolt rope).] *Naut.* The perpendicular or sloping side of a sail. Also qualified, as *mast-l.*, etc. **b.** *attrib.* in **l.-line,** a rope attached to the l., serving to truss the sail close up to the yard; **-rope,** a name for that part of the bolt-rope to which the border or skirt of a sail is sewed.

Leech (lītʃ), *v.*[1] *arch.*, now *rare.* [Early ME., f. LEECH *sb.*[1]] *trans.* To cure, heal.

Leech, *v.*[2] 1828. [f. LEECH *sb.*[2]] *trans.* To apply leeches to medicinally. Also *absol.*

Leechcraft (lī·tʃ,kraft). *arch.* [OE. *lǣće-cræft*: see LEECH *sb.*[1], CRAFT.] The art of healing; medical science. †Also *concr.* Remedy, medicine. So **Lee·chdom** *arch.* [OE. *lǣćedōm*] remedy.

Lee·cher. *rare.* ME. [f. LEECH *v.*[1] + -ER[1].] One who leeches; a physician. So **Lee·chery** (*rare*), leechcraft.

Leef, obs. f. LIEF.

†**Lee·ful,** *a.* [ME. *leveful*, f. LEAVE *sb.* + -FUL.] Permissible, right, lawful; just –1814.

Leek (līk). [OE. *lēac*, corresp. to MDu. *looc* (Du. *look*), OHG. *louh* (G. *lauch*), ON. *laukr* :- Gmc. **laukaz, -am* (whence Finnish *laukka*, OSl. *luků*), of which no cognates are known outside Gmc.] **1.** A culinary herb, *Allium porrum*, allied to the onion, but having the bulbous part cylindrical and the leaves flat and broad. **2.** Referring to the colour of the leek, to its being the national emblem of the Welsh, etc. ME. **3.** *attrib.* ME.

1. The Leeke is hot and dry, and doth attenuate GERARDE. **Wild L.,** *Allium ursinum.* 2. Nowe cherrye redde, nowe pale and greene as leekes 1575. *To eat the* (or *one's*) *l.*: to pocket a deliberate affront. *Hen. V*, v. i. 10.

†**Leer,** *sb.*[1] [OE. *hlēor*, = OS. *hleor*, etc. ON. *hlýr* pl.] **1.** The cheek –1586. **2.** The face, countenance; hence, look, hue, complexion –1806.

2. *Tit. A.* IV. ii. 119.

Leer (līᵊɹ), *sb.*[2] 1598. [f. LEER *v.*] A side glance; a look or roll of the eye expressive of slyness, malignity, lasciviousness, etc.

Damn with faint praise, assent with civil l. POPE.

Leer, *sb.*[3] Also **lear, lier.** 1662. [Of unkn. origin.] *Glass-making.* An annealing-furnace. Also *attrib.*, as **l.-pan** = FRACHE.

Leer (līᵊɹ), *a.*[1] Also **lear.** [OE. **lǣre* (as in *lǣrnes* emptiness) = OS., OHG. *lāri* (Du. *laar*, G. *leer*) :- WGmc. **lāri*, of unkn. origin.] †**1.** Empty. Also, clear *of.* –1567. **2.** Having no burden or load; (of a horse) without a rider. *Obs.* exc. *dial.* ME. **3.** *dial.* Empty of food; hungry, faint for want of food 1848. Hence **Leerness,** emptiness.

2. Leir and sumpter horses 1688. A l. waggon 1787. 3. I'm rather lear at supper JEFFERIES.

†**Leer,** *a.*[2] 1629. [app. f. LEER *v.*] Looking askance; oblique; sly, underhand –1830.

Leer (līᵊɹ), *v.* 1530. [perh. f. LEER *sb.*[1], with sense 'to glance over one's cheek'.] **1.** *intr.* To look obliquely or askance. Now only, to glance with a sly, immodest, or malign expression in one's eye. †**2.** To walk stealthily or with averted looks –1878. **3.** *trans.* To give a leer with (the eye) 1835.

1. Here Fannia leering on her own good man POPE. 3. [A parrot] cocking his head, leering his eye, and working his black tongue D. JERROLD. Hence **Lee·ringly** *adv.*

Leery (līᵊ·ri), *a.*[1] *Obs.* exc. *dial.* 1676. [f. LEER *a.*[1] + -Y[1].] = LEER *a.*[1] in various senses.

Leery (līᵊ·ri), *a.*[2] *slang.* 1796. [perh. f. LEER *a.*[2] + -Y[1].] Wide-awake, knowing, 'fly'. Hence **Lee·rily** *adv.*

Lees, *pl.* (dregs): see LEE *sb.*[2]

†**Leese,** *v.* [OE. *-lēosan*, corresp. to OFris. *ur|liasa*, OS. *far|liosan* (Du. *verliezen*), OHG. *vir|liosan* (G. *verlieren*), Goth. *fra|liusan*; f. Gmc. base **leus- *laus- *los-*, repr. also by LEASING *sb.*, -LESS, LOOSE *a.* and *v.*, LOSS.] **1.** *trans.* = LOSE, in its various senses –1675. **2.** *absol.* and *intr.* To lose, be a loser –1610. **3.** *trans.* To destroy; to bring to ruin or perdition; to spoil. = L. *perdere* –1553. ¶**4.** Incorrectly used by Spenser in the str. pa. t. and pa. pple. (*lore, lorn*) with sense 'to forsake, desert, leave'.

1. Flowers Pressed or Beaten, do l. the Freshness and Sweetness of their Odour BACON. 4. SPENSER *F.Q.* I. iv. 2, III. i. 44. Hence †**Lee·ser,** a destroyer, a loser. †**Lee·sing** *vbl. sb.* losing, loss; *occas.* destruction, perdition.

Lee shore. 1579. [LEE *sb.*[1]] **1.** A shore that the wind blows upon. †**2.** A shore that shelters from the wind –1711.

Lee side. Also *dial.* **lew side.** 1577. [LEE *sb.*[1]] That side which is turned away from the wind. Opp. to *weather side.*

Leet (līt), *sb.*[1] *Obs.* exc. *Hist.* [ME. – AFr. *lete*, AL. *leta* (XI), of unkn. origin.] **1.** = COURT LEET. **2.** The jurisdiction of a court leet; the district over which this jurisdiction extended 1477. **3.** *attrib.* as *l.-jury*, etc. 1651.

Leet (līt), *sb.*[2] Now chiefly *Sc.* 1441. [Early forms *lite, lytte, lythe* (XV). Of obscure origin, but prob. – AFr., OFr. *lit(t)e*, var. of *liste* LIST *sb.*[2]] **1.** A list of persons designated as eligible for some office. **2.** *pl.* The candidates forming a leet 1533. Hence **Leet** *v.* (*Sc.*), to place in a l.

1. Phr. *To be in l., to be on the leets, to put in l., to put on the l.*, etc.

†**Leet,** *sb.*[3] 1571. [repr. OE. (*wega*) *ġelǣte* junction (of roads) :- Gmc. **ʒalǣtjam*, f. **ʒa-* Y- + **lǣt-*; see LET *v.*[1]] A meeting of ways; in *two-, three-, four-way l.* –1691.

Leet, obs. f. LET *v.*

Leetle (lī·t'l). 1687. A joc. hesitating or emphatic pronunciation of LITTLE.

Leeward (lī·wǫ̈ɹd, liū·əɹd), *a.* (*sb.*) and *adv.* 1549. [f. LEE *sb.*[1] + -WARD.] **A.** *adj.* †**1.** Of a ship: That makes much leeway –1769. **2.** *gen.* Situated, or having a direction, away from the wind. Opp. to *windward.* Const. *of.* Hence *occas.* Sheltered. 1666. **3.** *absol.* or quasi-*sb.* = LEE *sb.*[1] 2. 1549.

2. *L. shore* = LEE SHORE. *L.-tide*: a tide running the way the wind is blowing. *L.-way* = *Lee-way.* 3. Phr. *On, upon, to (the) l. of.*

B. *adv.* Toward the lee (LEE *sb.*[1] 2) 1785.

Hence **Lee·wardly** *a.* (of a ship) apt to fall to l. Opp. to *weatherly.* **Lee·wardmost** *a.* situated furthest to l. †**Lee·wardness,** tendency to fall to l.

Lee·-way, lee·way. 1669. [f. LEE *sb.*[1] + WAY.] The lateral drift of a ship to leeward of her course; the amount of deviation thus produced. Also *fig.*

Phr. *To make, fetch up, make up l. Angle of l.*: the angle made by the direction of a ship's keel with that of its actual course. *fig.* We have a great deal of leeway to make up with the Australians 1884.

Left (left). [ME. *lüft, lift, left* :– OE. **lyft* (as in *lyftādl* 'left disease', paralysis), Kentish *left* 'inanis'; the primary sense of 'weak, worthless' is found in EFris. *luf*, Du. dial. *loof*, and the derived sense in MDu., LG. *luchter, lucht, luft*, NFris. *leeft, leefter*; the ult. origin is unkn.] **A.** *adj.* **1.** Distinctive epithet of the hand which is normally the weaker (see LEFT HAND), and of the other parts on the same side of the body (occas. of their clothing, as in *l. boot, glove*, etc.); hence also of what pertains to the corresponding side of anything else. Opp. to *right*. **2.** That has the relative position of the left hand with respect to the right. In predicative use with const. *of*; in attrib. use now LEFT-HAND is usual. ME.

1. Who stooping op'nd my l. side, and took From thence a Rib MILT. *L. side*, †*half* (also LEFT HAND): The position or direction (relative to a person) to which the l. hand points. *Over the l. shoulder*, now *over the l.* simply, a slang phrase implying that the meaning is the reverse of what is said. **2.** *L. wing* (of an army), *l. branch* (of a stream). *L. bank* (of a river): that to the l. of a person looking down the stream. That part of the shield which appears on the l. side is called the dexter CUSSANS. *L. side, l. wing* in politics, = LEFT *sb.* 1 c. *L. centre*: in the French Chamber, those deputies of the centre (CENTRE *sb.* II. 4) who incline to the opinions of the Left and occupy seats adjacent to them.

B. *adv.* On or towards the left side ME. Squadrons—l. wheel! 1796.

C. *sb.* **1. a.** = LEFT HAND ME. **b.** *Mil.* The left wing (of an army). Also in *pl.*, the men whose place is on the left. 1707. **c.** In continental legislatures, the section of the members sitting on the left side of the chamber (as viewed from the president's chair), by custom those holding relatively liberal or democratic opinions. Hence *transf.* the more advanced or innovating section of a philosophical school, a religious sect, a political party, etc. 1837. **2.** A glove, etc., for the left hand, etc. 1864.

1. a. In her right a civic wreath, In her l. a human head TENNYSON. Cannon to l. of them, . . Volley'd and thunder'd TENNYSON. **b.** Their Centres and Lefts move up 1832.

Left (left), *ppl. a.* 1586. [pa. pple. of LEAVE *v.*[1]] **1.** In senses of LEAVE *v.*[1] Now rare exc. in *l.-luggage* (*office*, etc.). **2.** With advs. or advb. phr. 1783.

2. He came to thank me for some left-off clothes COWPER.

Left hand. ME. See LEFT *a.* 1. Also *attrib.* (usu. *left-hand*).

Phrases. *On, to the left hand (of)*: on the l. side (of), in the direction of the l. side; also *fig. To take the l. hand (of)*: to place oneself on the l. side (of). *To marry with the l. hand*, to marry morganatically; hence *a wife of the l. hand*; *(a daughter) by the l. hand*, one born of such a marriage; occas. an illegitimate daughter.

Comb.: **left-hand blow,** one delivered with the l. hand; **left-hand man,** †(*a*) a left-handed man; (*b*) one placed at one's left; **left-hand marriage** = *marriage with the left hand* (see above); so *left-hand wife, queen*; **left-hand rope,** rope laid up and twisted 'against the sun'; †**left-hand tongue,** a language written from right to left, as Hebrew.

Left-handed, *a.* (Stress variable.) 1485. [-ED[2].] **1.** Having the left hand more serviceable than the right; using the left hand by preference. **2.** *fig.* Awkward; clumsy, inapt 1613. **3.** Ambiguous, questionable. †In medical language: Spurious. 1612. **4.** Ill-omened, sinister. Of a deity: Unpropitious. (Cf. L. *lævus.*) ? *Obs.* 1609. **5.** Of a marriage: Morganatic (from the custom in Germany by which the bridegroom gave the bride his left hand in such marriages). Said also of the parties so married, and of their issue. Occas. applied also to fictitious or illegal marriages, or to unions without marriage, and to their offspring. 1642. **6.** Adapted to the left hand or arm, or for use by a left-handed person; (of a blow) delivered with the left hand 1629. **7.** Characterized by a direction or rotation to the left; producing such a rotation in the plane of a polarized ray. (Cf. LÆVO-.) 1812.

1. A left-handed bowler is nearly always a right-handed bat 1892. **2.** A good artist is left-handed to no profession FULLER. **3.** A very left-handed compliment 1881. **4.** The (Left-handed) stroaks of fortune 1650. **5.** The children of a left-handed alliance are not entitled to inherit H. WALPOLE. **6.** Hall met him with a left-handed facer 1814. **7.** Left-handed, or reversed varieties of spiral shells WOODWARD. Hence **Leftha·nded-ly** *adv.*, **-ness.**

Le·ft-ha·nder. 1861. [f. LEFT HAND + -ER[1].] A left-handed person or blow.

Left-handiness. [f. **left-handy* adj. (= LEFT-HANDED 2) + -NESS.] Awkward manner. Cf. Fr. *gaucherie*. CHESTERF.

Le·ftmost, *a.* Also **leftermost.** 1863. [f. LEFT *a.* + -MOST.] Situated furthest to the left.

Left-over. 1897. *adj.* and *sb.* (Something) left or remaining over; also, a survival (1911).

Leftward (le·ftwǫɹd), *adv.* and *a.* 1483. [f. LEFT *a.* + -WARD.] **1.** *adv.* On, or in the direction of, the left hand. **2.** *adj.* Situated on the left. Also *occas.*, Directed towards the left. 1813.

1. L. and behind us is the desert 1898. **2.** A l. bend 1886. So **Le·ftwards** *adv.* = LEFTWARD *adv.* 1844.

Leg (leg), *sb.* ME. [– ON. *leggr* :– **laȝjaz* (cf. Lombardic *lagi* thigh), of which there are no certain cognates elsewhere. Superseded *shank.*]

I. The limb. **1.** One of the organs of support and locomotion in an animal body; in narrower sense, the part of the limb between the knee and foot. Also *transf.* and *fig.* **2.** The leg cut from the carcass of an animal or bird for use as food 1533. **b. Leg-of-mutton** *adj. phr.*, resembling a leg of mutton, *esp.* in shape 1840. **3.** An obeisance made by drawing back one leg and bending the other; a bow, scrape. Now *arch.* or *joc.* 1589. **4.** Short for BLACK-LEG 2. 1815. **5.** *Cricket.* **a.** *L. before wicket*: the act of stopping with the leg a straight-pitched ball (a fault for which the batsman may be given 'out'). Also, simply, *l. before*. Abbrev. *l.b.w.* 1795. **b.** (Also *the l.*) (*a*) That part of the 'on' side of the field which lies behind, or about in a line with, the batsman. Chiefly in (a hit) *to (the) l.* 1843. (*b*) The side of the pitch on which the batsman stands 1843. **c.** Hence, the position of a fieldsman placed to stop balls hit 'to leg'; also, the fieldsman so placed 1816.

1. Vse your legs, take the start, run awaie SHAKS. *fig.* One l. by truth supported, one by lies, They sidle to the goal COWPER. Phrases. **a.** *All legs and wings*, said of an overgrown awkward young person; *Naut.* = overmasted. *On the l.*, (of a dog) long in the leg, leggy. *The boot is on the other l.* (see BOOT *sb.*[3]). *To pull* (or *draw* Sc.) *a person's l.*, to 'get at', befool him (colloq.). *To give a person a l. up*, to help him to climb up, mount (a horse, etc.), or get over an obstacle (*lit.* and *fig.*). *To have a bone in one's l.*: a feigned excuse to avoid the use of one's legs. *To lift* (or *heave up*) *the l.*: said of a dog voiding urine. **b.** *To change l.*, (of a horse) to change step. *To have the legs of*, to outrun. *To put* (or *set*) *one's best l. foremost*, to exert oneself to the utmost. *To shake a l.*, to dance. *To stretch one's legs*, to exercise them by walking. *To take to one's legs*, †*to take one's legs*, to run away. **c.** *On one's legs*: (*a*) standing, *esp.* to make a speech; so joc. *on one's hind legs*; (*b*) well enough to go about; (*c*) *fig.* in a prosperous condition, established, *esp.* in *to set* (a person) *upon his legs*; also *transf.* of things. *To fall on one's legs*: to get well out of a difficulty. *To get on one's hind legs*: *lit.* of a horse, hence *joc.* of a man, to go into a rage. *To stand upon one's own legs*: to be self-reliant. *Not a l. to stand on*: no support whatever. **d.** *On one's last legs*, near the end of one's life, or (*fig.*) resources; said also of things. **e.** *To dance (run, walk*, etc.) a person *off his legs*: to cause (him) to dance, etc. till he can do no more. **f.** Put for 'the power of using one's legs', as in *to feel, find one's legs. To keep one's legs*, to remain standing or walking. See also SEA LEGS. **2.** Then came up a l. of mutton DE FOE. **b. Leg-of-mutton sail,** a kind of triangular sail; so *leg-of-mutton rig.* **Leg-of-mutton sleeve,** one full and loose on the arm but close-fitting at the wrist. **3.** Phr. *To make a l.* **5. c.** *Long, short, square l.*, the fieldsman, or his position, far from or near to the wicket or about square with it.

II. Something more or less like a leg in shape or function. **1.** A representation of a leg; *esp.* in *Her.* 1500. **2.** An artificial leg ME. **3.** That part of a garment which covers the leg 1580. **4.** A bar, pole, etc. used as a support or prop; *esp.* in *Shipbuilding* and *Mining* 1430. **5.** One of the supports of a chair, table, stool, etc. 1680. **6.** One of the branches of a forked, jointed, or curved object 1683. **b.** One of the sides of a triangle, viewed as standing upon a base (so Gr. σκέλος); one of the two parts on each side of the vertex of a curve 1659. **7.** *Naut.* **a.** A name for various short ropes, which branch out into two or more parts 1627. **b.** A run made on a single tack. Chiefly in *long, short l., a good l.* 1867.

5. Mr. Pickwick grated the legs of his chair against the ground DICKENS. **7. b.** Valkyrie. . preferred a series of short legs off Wemyss Bay to weather the Skelmorlie 1895.

Comb.: **l.-bone,** the shin-bone, tibia; **-rest,** a contrivance for resting the l. of an invalid when seated; **-worm,** the GUINEA WORM (q.v.) which attacks the legs. **b.** in *Cricket*: **l. bail, stump,** that nearest the batsman; **l. ball, break,** a ball which pitches on or breaks from the l. side; **-bye** (see BYE 1 a); **l. hit, stroke,** a hit to l.; **-theory,** bowling to leg with fieldsmen massed on that side.

Leg (leg), *v.* 1601. [f. LEG *sb.*] **1.** *intr. To l. it*: To walk fast or run. †**2.** *To l. it*, to 'make a leg'. *To l. unto*, to bow to. *rare.* –1633. **3.** *trans.* To work (a boat) through a canal-tunnel by pressing with the feet against the top or sides of the tunnel; to navigate (a tunnel) thus; also *to l. through* 1836. **4.** To catch by, or hit on, the leg 1852. Hence **Le·gger** (in sense 3).

Legacy (le·găsi), *sb.* ME. [– OFr. *legacie* – med.L. *legatia* legateship, f. L. *legatus* LEGATE *sb.* In Branch II repr. also AL. *legantia* (XIII), f. *legare*; cf. LEGANTINE.]

†**I. 1.** The function or office of a delegate or deputy –1583. **b.** *spec.* The function or office of a papal legate. *To send in l.*: to send as legate. –1726. **2.** The message or business committed to a delegate or deputy –1654. **3.** A body of persons sent on a mission, or as a deputation, to a sovereign, etc.; also, the act of sending such a body –1598.

II. †**1.** = BEQUEST 1. –1606. **2.** A sum of money, etc. bequeathed to another: = BEQUEST 2. †Formerly also in gen. sense, what one bequeaths. 1460. **b.** *transf.* and *fig.*; esp. = anything handed down by an ancestor or predecessor 1586. **3.** *attrib.*, as *l.-duty*, etc.

2. You have paid. . his l., at the hazard of ruining the estate 'JUNIUS'. **b.** Leaving great legacies of thought TENNYSON. **3. L.-hunter, -monger,** one who pays court to old and rich persons in hope of obtaining a l.; so *legacy-hunting*.

Hence †**Le·gacy** *v.* to give or leave as a l.; to bequeath a l. to.

Legal (lī·găl), *a.* 1500. [– (O)Fr. *légal* or L. *legalis*, f. *lex, leg-* law; see -AL[1]. Cf. LEAL, LOYAL.] **1.** Of, pertaining to, or falling within the province of law 1529. **b.** Belonging to or characteristic of the profession of the law 1819. **c.** *nonce-uses.* Observant of law; devoted to law 1872. **2.** Such as is required or appointed by law 1610. **b.** Such as is recognized by 'law' as dist. from 'equity' 1818. **3.** Permitted, or not forbidden, by law; lawful 1647. **4.** *Theol.* **a.** Of, pertaining to, or based upon the Mosaic law. **b.** Of, pertaining to, or concerned with the law of works, i.e. salvation by works, not faith. 1500. **5.** quasi-*sb.* Something legal; a legal formality, etc.; *Sc. Law*, the legal period within which reversion is permitted 1526.

1. A l. artifice BOYLE. L. debt MILTON, advice 1898. Phr. *L. man* = Law Latin *legalis homo*, a man who has full l. rights. So *l. person*. **b.** A l. face BYRON, mind (*mod.*). **c.** Edward. . lived in a l. age STUBBS. **2.** L. possession 1751, tribunals 1844. *L. tender*: coin or other money, which a creditor is bound by law to accept, when tendered in payment of a debt. (See *Act* 33 *Vict.* c. 10 § 4.) **3.** It is as l. . . for the king to pardon, as for the party to accuse CLARENDON. Hence **Le·gally** *adv.*, **-ness** (*rare*).

Legalism (lī·găliz'm). 1838. [f. LEGAL + -ISM.] **1.** *Theol.* Adherence to the Law as opp. to the Gospel; the doctrine of justification by works, or teaching which savours of it. **2.** A disposition to exalt the importance of law or formulated rule 1878.

Legalist (lī·gălist). 1641. [f. LEGAL + -IST.] **1.** *Theol.* An adherent or advocate of legalism. **2.** A stickler for legality 1865. **3.** One who views things from a legal standpoint 1829. Hence **Le:gali·stic** *a.*

Legality (lĭgæ·lĭti). 1460. [– Fr. *légalité* or med.L. *legalitas*, f. L. *legalis*; see LEGAL, -ITY.] **1.** Attachment to law or rule. **b.** *Theol.* Insistence on the letter of the law; reliance on works for salvation, rather than on free grace. Also personified. 1678. **c.** The spirit of the legal profession 1880. **2.** The quality of being legal; lawfulness. In early use, Legitimacy. 1533.

1. c. L. delights in the ingenious contrivance of delays W. CORY. **2.** To try the l. of the proceedings..against him H. COX.

Legalize (lī·gălǝiz), *v.* 1716. [f. LEGAL + -IZE.] *trans.* To make legal; to authorize, justify, sanction.

A period..when oppression was legalised HOOK. Hence **Le:galiza·tion**, the action of legalizing.

Legantine (le·gæ̆ntin), *a.* 1533. [var. of LEGATINE, by substitution of *legant-*, pr. ppl. stem of *legare*, for the normal *legat-*; cf. the similar var., med.L. *legantia* (XIII) for *legatio* (XII) LEGACY.] = LEGATINE.

Legatary (le·gătări). 1542. [– L. *legatarius*, f. *legatum* bequest; see LEGATE *v.*, -ARY[1].] **A.** *adj.* Of or pertaining to, or of the nature of a bequest 1676. **B.** *sb.* One to whom a bequest is left; a legatee.

Legate (le·gĕt), *sb.* OE. [– (O)Fr. *légat* – L. *legatus*, subst. use of pa. pple. of *legare* depute, delegate; see -ATE[1].] **1.** An ecclesiastic deputed to represent the Pope and armed with his authority. **b.** The ruler of a LEGATION (sense 5) 1653. **2.** *gen.* An ambassador, delegate, messenger ME. **3.** *Rom. Hist.* The deputy or lieutenant of a general, or of the governor of a province; under the empire, the governor himself. Also *transf.* 1474.

1. *L. a* (or †*de*) *latere* (†also, *of latere*, *of the side*): a l. of the highest class, one whose acts are virtually those of the Pope himself. **2.** There stands The l. of the skies COWPER. Hence **Le·gateship.**

Legate (lĭgēi·t), *v.* 1546. [– *legat-*, pa. ppl. stem of L. *legare* bequeath as a legacy; see -ATE[3].] *trans.* To give by will, to bequeath. Hence **Le:gatee·**, one to whom a legacy has been bequeathed.

Legatine (le·gătin), *a.* 1450. [– med.L. *legatinus*, f. *legatus* papal legate; see LEGATE *sb.*, -INE. Cf. LEGANTINE.] Of, pertaining to, or having the authority of, a legate. (Earlier LEGANTINE and LEGATIVE.)

L. constitutions: ecclesiastical laws, enacted in national synods, held under legates from Pope Gregory IX and Pope Clement IV. *L. synod*: one held under the presidency of a (papal) legate.

Legation (lĭgēi·ʃǝn). 1460. [– (O)Fr. *légation* or L. *legatio*, f. *legat-*; see LEGATE *v.*, -ION.] **1.** The action of sending a deputy, esp. a (papal) legate; the fact of his being sent. **2.** His mission or commission 1470. **3.** *concr.* The body of deputies sent on a mission; a diplomatic minister (*now*, not being an 'ambassador') and his suite. Also *attrib.* 1603. **b.** The official residence of a diplomatic minister 1863. **4.** The dignity and office of a legate 1603. **5.** Formerly, one of the provinces of the Papal States, governed by a legate 1841.

1. The Divine L. of Moses WARBURTON. **3.** A secretary of l...supplying their place 1756. *attrib.* The L. buildings 1886. Hence **Lega·tionary** *a.* of or pertaining to a l.; qualified or ready to go on a l. CARLYLE.

Legative (le·gătiv), *a.* 1537. [– late L. *legativus*, f. as prec.; see -IVE.] **a.** In *l. bull, commission*: Deputing; conferring the authority of a legate. **b.** Of or pertaining to a legate, or (*rarely*) to an ambassador.

‖**Legato** (legā·to), *a.* (*adv.* and *sb.*) 1811. [It., pa. pple. of *legare* :– L. *ligare* bind.] *Mus.* A direction: Smooth and connected, without breaks. (Opp. to *staccato.*)

Legator (lĭgēi·tǒɹ). 1651. [– L. *legator*, f. *legat-*; see LEGATE *v.*, -OR 2.] One who gives something by will; a testator.

†**Le·gature.** [f. LEGATE *sb.* + -URE.] The dignity and office of a legate; legateship. CLARENDON.

Leg-bail. 1774. [See BAIL *sb.*[1] 5.] In *to give leg-bail*, to decamp. Hence *occas.* = 'French leave', etc.

Lege, obs. f. LEDGE *v.*[1]

Legend (le·dʒĕnd), *sb.* ME. [– (O)Fr. *légende* – med.L. *legenda*, prop. 'things to be read', n. pl. of gerundive of *legere* read, taken as fem. sing. For the formation cf. PREBEND.] **1.** The story of the life of a saint. **2.** A collection of saints' lives or of similar stories ME. †**3.** A story, history, account –1671. †**4.** A roll, list, record –1601. **5.** *Eccl.* A book of readings or lessons for use at divine service, containing passages from Scripture and the lives of saints. *Obs.* exc. *Hist.* 1440. **6.** An unauthentic story handed down by tradition and popularly regarded as historical 1613. **7.** An inscription or motto; chiefly *spec.*, the words or letters impressed on a coin or medal, the title affixed to a picture 1611. **b.** *gen.* Written character; writing (*rare*) 1822. ¶**8.** Misused for LEGION. *Merry W.* I. iii. 99.

2. A gloryous legende Of goode wemen CHAUCER. *The L.* (now usu. called *the Golden L.*), a 13th century collection of saints' lives written by Jacobus de Voragine, Archbishop of Genoa. I had rather beleeue all the fables in the L., and the Alcaron, then that this vniuersall frame is without a minde BACON. **6.** The l. which would attribute to Alfred the foundation of the University of Oxford HOOK. **7.** No l. or effigy marks the graves of these royal Ladies FREEMAN. Hence †**Le·gend** *v. trans.* to tell as a l.

Legendary (le·dʒĕndări). 1513. [– med.L. *legendarius* adj. (*-ium* sb.), f. *legenda*; see prec., -ARY[1].] **A.** *adj.* **1.** Pertaining to or of the nature of a legend; connected or concerned with legends; related in legend 1563. **b.** Of writers: Relating legends 1646. **2.** Containing the legend on a coin 1830.

1. *L. period, age*, one of which the accounts are mostly of the nature of legends. Relics of a mythical or l. past 1900.

B. *sb.* **1.** A collection of legends, esp. of lives of saints; *occas.* = The Golden Legend 1513. **2.** A writer of legends 1625.

Legendry (le·dʒĕndri). 1849. [f. LEGEND *sb.* + -RY.] Legends collectively.

†**Le·ger,** *a.* 1481. [– Fr. *léger* :– Gallo-Rom. **leviarius*, f. L. *levis* light.] Light, not heavy; slight, trifling. Also, nimble. –1598. Hence †**Le·gerly** *adv.*

Leger, obs. f. LEDGER.

Legerdemain (le:dʒǝɹdĭmēi·n). ME. [– Fr. *léger de main*, i.e. *léger* light, *de* of, *main* hand.] **1.** Sleight of hand; jugglery; conjuring tricks. **2.** *transf.* and *fig.* Trickery, hocus-pocus 1532; †a trick, a juggle –1663. †**3.** A conjurer. CIBBER. **4.** *attrib.* or *adj.* Pertaining to or of the nature of legerdemain; juggling, tricky 1576.

1. Will ye see any feates of activity, Some sleight of hand, leigerdemaine? BEAUM. & FL. **2.** There is a certain Knack or L. in argument SHAFTESB. **4.** L. Tricks 1707. Hence **Legerdemai·nist**, a conjurer.

†**Lege·rity.** 1561. [– Fr. *légèreté*; see LEGER *a.* and -ITY.] Lightness (*lit.* and *fig.*); nimbleness –1830.

†**Legge,** *v. rare.* ME. only. [aphet. f. ALLEGE *v.*[1]] To alleviate.

Legge, obs. f. LEDGE *v.*[1]

Legged (legd), *a.* 1470. [f. LEG *sb.* + -ED[2].] Having legs (*esp.* such or so many); as in BAKER-*l.*, *bare-l.*, BOW-LEGGED, *two-l.*, etc. In *Her.*, having legs of a specified tincture.

Leg'd like a man *Temp.* II. ii. 35.

†**Leggiadrous,** *a. rare.* 1648. [f. It. *leggiadro* light, sprightly + -OUS.] Graceful, elegant.

Legging (le·giŋ), *sb.* Chiefly *pl.* 1763. [f. LEG *sb.* + -ING[1] (but cf. -ING[3]).] In *pl.* A pair of outer coverings (usu. of leather or cloth) to protect the legs in bad weather, reaching from the ankle to the knee, or sometimes higher.

Legging (le·giŋ), *vbl. sb.* 1872. [f. LEG *v.* + -ING[1].] Making a leg or obeisance.

Leggy (le·gi), *a.* 1787. [f. LEG *sb.* + -Y[1].] Conspicuous for legs; lanky-legged.

†**Leg-harness.** ME. Armour for the leg –1840.

Leghorn (legǭ·ɹn, le·ghǭɹn). 1753. [f. place-name *Leghorn* – It. *Legorno* (XVI–XVII), now *Livorno* repr. L. *Liburnus*.] **1.** Name of a straw plaiting for hats and bonnets, made from a particular kind of wheat, cut green and bleached, and imported from Leghorn in Tuscany; a hat or bonnet made of this or straw like this. Also *attrib.*, as *L. bonnet, chip, plait*, etc. **2.** Name of a breed of the domestic fowl 1854.

Legible (le·dʒĭb'l), *a.* (*sb.*) ME. [– late L. *legibilis*, f. *legere* read; see -IBLE.] **a.** Of writing: Plain; easily made out. **b.** Of compositions: Accessible to readers (*nonce-use*); also, easy to read, readable (*rare*) 1676. **c.** *transf.* and *fig.* 1595.

a. A fair, fast, l. hand 1620. **c.** The trouble l. in my countenance LAMB. Hence **Legibi·lity. Le·gibly** *adv.*

Legific (lidʒi·fik), *a.* 1865. [f. L. *lex*, *leg-* law + -FIC.] Pertaining to the making of laws.

Legion (lī·dʒǝn). ME. [– OFr. *legiun*, *-ion* (mod. *légion*) – L. *legio*, *legion-*, f. *legere* choose, levy; see -ION.] **1.** *Rom. Antiq.* A body of infantry in the Roman army, ranging in number from 3,000 in early times to 6,000 under Marius, usually with a large complement of cavalry. **b.** Applied to certain bodies in modern armies 1598. **2.** Vaguely: A host of armed men ME. **3.** A vast host (of persons or things); *esp.* in the (inaccurate) phr. *their name is L.* = 'they are innumerable' (cf. Mark 5:9) ME. **4.** *L. of Honour* [= Fr. *Légion d'honneur*]: a French order of distinction, conferred for civil or military services, etc. 1827. **b.** *American L.*, a national association of ex-service men instituted in 1919. *British L.*, a similar association founded in 1921 and incorporated by Royal Charter in 1925. **5.** *Nat. Hist.* An occasional term repr. an assemblage of objects intermediate in extent between a class and an order 1859. **6.** *attrib.* or *adj.* Multitudinous 1678.

1. b. *Foreign l.* [= Fr. *légion étrangère*]: a body of foreign volunteers in the French army in the 19th c., employed in the colonies, etc. **3.** He..call'd His Legions, Angel Forms, who lay intrans't MILT. *P.L.* I. 301. A legioun is name to me; for we ben manye WYCLIF *Mark* 5:9.

Legionary (lī·dʒǝnări). 1577. [– L. *legionarius*, f. *legio*; see prec., -ARY[1].]

A. *adj.* **1.** Of or belonging to a legion. **b.** Of an inscription, mark, etc.: Designating a particular Roman legion 1851. **2.** Constituting or consisting of a legion or legions 1646.

1. The whole multitude of l. soldiers ARNOLD. **b.** The l. mark of the title 1863.

B. *sb.* A soldier of a legion, ancient or modern. Also a member of the Legion of Honour. 1598.

The cowering l., with whom to hear was to obey DE QUINCEY.

Legioned (lī·dʒǝnd), *a. poet.* 1818. [f. LEGION + -ED[2].] Arrayed in legions.

Legislate (le·dʒisleit), *v.* 1719. [Back-formation f. LEGISLATOR, LEGISLATION.] **1.** *trans.* To make laws for. D'URFEY. **2.** *intr.* To make or enact laws 1805. **3.** quasi-*trans.* To bring or drive by legislation *into* or *out of*. Also rarely *trans.* to bring about or control by legislation. 1845.

2. Solon, in legislating for the Athenians, had an idea of a more perfect Constitution than he gave them BP. WATSON. **3.** The legislated depreciation of this one estate..had cost him..£120,000. 1898.

Legislation (ledʒislēi·ʃǝn). 1655. [– late L. *legis latio*, i.e. *legis* gen. of *lex* law, *latio* proposing (a law); see -ION and LEGISLATOR.] **1.** The action of making or giving laws; the enactment of laws, lawgiving. **2.** The enactments of a legislator or legislature; enacted laws collectively 1838.

1. Pythagoras, who join'd L. to his Philosophy, and..pretended to Miracles..to give a more venerable Sanction to the Laws he prescribed LD. LYTTELTON. Hence **Legisla·tional** *a.* pertaining to l.

Legislative (le·dʒislĕtiv). 1641. [After LEGISLATION, LEGISLATOR; see -ATIVE. Cf. Fr. *législatif* (XIV).]

A. *adj.* **1.** That legislates; having the function of making laws 1651. **2.** Of or pertaining to the making of laws 1641; enacted or appointed by legislation 1855. Hence **Le·gislatively** *adv.* by legislation.

1. On the 30th of September [1791], this National Assembly..dissolved itself, and gave place to the succeeding L. National Assembly 1797. **2.** L. remedies 1855, penalties 1872, emancipation of Scotch industry LECKY.

B. *sb.* The power of legislating; the body in which this is vested, the legislature. Opp. to *executive.* Now *rare.* 1642.

Legislator (le·dʒisle^i tǝɹ). 1605. [– L. *legis lator*, i.e. *legis* gen. of *lex*, *lator* proposer, mover, agent-n. f. *latus*, pa. pple. of *tollere* raise; after phr. *legem ferre* propose a law.] One who makes laws (for a people or nation); a lawgiver; a member of a legislative body.
Legislators have long since discovered the absurdity of attempting to fix prices by law JEVONS. *transf.* The alleged l. of science BREWSTER. Hence **Le·gislatorship,** the position of l.

Legislatorial (ledʒislǎtōǝ·riǎl), *a.* 1774. [f. prec. + -AL[1]; see -ORIAL.] **1.** Having the power to legislate, acting as a legislator or legislature 1819. **2.** Of or pertaining to a legislator or legislation.

Legislatress (le·dʒisle^i trės). 1711. [f. LEGISLATOR + -ESS[1].] A female legislator.
Nature, a beneficent l. MAINE. So **Legisla·trix** 1677.

Legislature (le·dʒislětiŭɹ). 1655. [f. LEGISLATOR + -URE, after JUDICATURE.] **1.** 'The power that makes laws' (J.); a body of persons invested with the power of making the laws of a country or state; *spec.* (*U.S.*) the legislative body of a State or Territory, as dist. from Congress. †**2.** The exercise of the function of legislation –1765.
1. 'Twas April, as the bumpkins say, The l. called it May COWPER. **2.** It was very inconvenient to have both the l. and the execution in the same hands BURNET.

Legist (lī·dʒist). 1456. [– (O)Fr. *légiste* or med.L. *legista* (XII), f. L. *lex*, *leg-* law; see -IST.] One versed in the law. (Cf. JURIST.) So †**Le·gister** ME. –1555.

||**Le·git.** [L., pres. or pa. t. 3rd pers. sing. of *legere* read.] Claim to 'Benefit of Clergy' based upon the fact of being able to read a verse of the Bible. BAXTER.

Legitim: see LEGITIME.

Legitimacy (lǐdʒi·timǎsi). 1691. [f. LEGITIMATE; see -ACY.] **1.** The fact of being a legitimate child. **2.** Of a government or the title of a sovereign: The condition of being in accordance with law or principle. Now often, with reference to a sovereign's title: The fact of being derived by regular descent; *occas.* the principle of lineal succession to the throne. 1817. **3.** *gen.* Conformity to rule or principle, or (*Logic*) to sound reasoning 1836.
2. The Doctrine of Divine Right, which has now come back to us, like a thief from transportation, under the *alias* of L. MACAULAY. **3.** The l. of our assumption 1836.

Legitimate (lǐdʒi·timět), *a.* 1494. [– med.L. *legitimatus*, pa. pple. of *legitimare* legitimize, f. L. *lex*, *leg-* law; see -ATE[2].] **1.** Of a child: Having the status of one lawfully begotten; entitled to full filial rights. Said also of a parent, and of lineal descent. (The only sense in Johnson.) †**b.** *transf.* Genuine, real; opp. to 'spurious' –1818. **2.** Conformable to law or rule; lawful, proper 1638. **b.** Normal, regular; conformable to a standard type 1669. **c.** Of a sovereign's title: Resting on hereditary right. Hence, said of a sovereign, a kingdom, etc. 1821. **d.** Logically admissible 1797.
1. The common law had deemed all those bastards who were born before wedlock: By the canon law they were l. HUME. **2.** They [Moors] are a nation..without a l. country or a name W. IRVING. **b.** A l. English classic MACAULAY. *The l. drama*: the body of plays, Shakespearian or other, that have a recognized theatrical and literary merit; also ellipt. (*Theatr. slang*) *the l.* **b.** Both [methods] were l. logical processes MILL. Hence **Legi·timate-ly** *adv.*, **-ness.**

B. *sb.* **1.** A legitimate child 1583; a legitimate sovereign; also, one who supports the title of such sovereigns 1821. †**2.** Something to which one has a legitimate title. MILT.

Legitimate (lǐdʒi·time^i t), *v.* 1531. [– *legitimat-*, pa. ppl. stem of med.L. *legitimare*; see prec., -ATE[3].] **1.** *trans.* To render legitimate by authoritative declaration or decree. Also *fig.* 1597. **2.** To make legal by enactment. In early use, To give (a person) a legal claim *to* (something). 1531. **3.** To affirm or show to be legitimate; to justify 1611.
1. To l. the duke of Lancaster's ante-nuptial children HALLAM. **3.** Necessity legitimates my advice; for it is the only way to save our lives DE FOE.

Legitimation (lǐdʒitimē^i·ʃǝn). 1460. [– med.L. *legitimatio*, f. as prec.; see -ION. Cf. (O)Fr. *légitimation*.] **1.** The rendering or authoritatively declaring (a person) legitimate. †**2.** Legitimacy –1689. **b.** *transf.* Of a literary work: Authenticity, genuineness. Now *rare.* 1635. **3.** The action of making lawful; authorization 1660.
3. The l. of Money, and the giving it its denominated value 1799.

Legi·timatist. *rare.* 1860. [f. as next + -IST.] = LEGITIMIST.

Legitimatize (lǐdʒi·timǎtəiz), *v.* 1791. [f. LEGITIMATE *a.* + -IZE.] *trans.* To render legitimate or lawful, *esp.* to render (a child) legitimate.

Legitime (le·dʒǐtim). Also †**legitim.** ME. [– (O)Fr. *légitime* adj. and sb. – L. *legitimus*, f. *lex*, *leg-* LAW.] †**A.** *adj.* = LEGITIMATE *a.* –1795. **B.** *sb. Civil* and *Sc. Law.* The portion of his movable estate to which children are entitled on the death of their father. = L. *legitima* (*pars*) 1768.

Legitimism (lǐdʒi·timiz'm). 1877. [– Fr. *légitimisme*, f. *légitime*; see prec., -ISM.] In Fr. or Sp. politics: Adherence to the claim of the so-called 'legitimate pretender to the throne'.

Legitimist (lǐdʒi·timist). 1841. [– Fr. *légitimiste*, f. as prec.; see -IST.] A supporter of legitimate authority, esp. of a monarchical title claimed on the ground of direct descent; *spec.* in France, a supporter of the elder Bourbon line. Also *attrib.* or *adj.*

Legi·timize, *v.* 1833. [f. L. *legitimus* (see LEGITIME) + -IZE.] = LEGITIMATIZE. **Legi:timiza·tion.**

Legless (le·glės), *a.* ME. [f. LEG *sb.* + -LESS.] Having no legs.

Leglet (le·glėt). 1821. [f. LEG *sb.* + -LET.] **1.** A little leg. **2.** An ornament for the leg. (After *armlet*, etc.) 1836.

Leg-pull (le·gpul). *slang.* 1920. The act of 'pulling a person's leg' (see LEG *sb.* I. 1 phr.). So **Le·g-pu:ller, -pu:lling** (1908).

Leguleian (legiulī·ǎn). 1631. [f. L. *legulēius* pettifogger + -AN.]
A. *adj.* Pettifogging 1677. **B.** *sb.* A pettifogger. So **Legulei·ous** *a.* 1660.

Legume (le·gium, lǐgiū·m). 1676. [– Fr. *légume* – L. *legumen*, f. *legere* gather, so called because the fruit may be gathered by hand.] **1.** The fruit or edible part of a leguminous plant, e.g. beans, peas, pulse. Hence, A vegetable used for food; chiefly in *pl.* 1693. †**2.** A leguminous plant –1725. **3.** The pod of a leguminous plant 1785.

Legumen (lǐgiū·měn). *Pl.* **legumens,** ||**legumina.** ME. [– L. *legumen*; see prec.] = prec.

Legumin (lǐgiū·min). Also **-ine.** 1827. [f. LEGUME + -IN[1].] *Chem.* A proteid substance resembling casein, found in leguminous and other seeds.

Leguminous (lǐgiū·minǝs), *a.* 1656. [– mod.L. *leguminosus*, f. L. *legumen*, *-min-* pulse, bean; see LEGUME, -OUS.] **1.** Of, pertaining to, or of the nature of, pulse. **2.** *Bot.* Of or pertaining to the N.O. *Leguminosæ*, which includes peas, beans, and other plants bearing legumes or pods 1677. **b.** Like what pertains to a leguminous plant 1688.

Leibnitzian (ləibni·tsiǎn). Also **Leibnitian, -izian.** 1754. [f. the name of G. W. *Leibnitz* (1646–1716) + -IAN.] **A.** *adj.* Pertaining to Leibnitz or his philosophy or mathematical methods 1765. **B.** *sb.* A follower of Leibnitz.

Leicester (le·stǝɹ). 1834. [Name of an English county town.] Used *attrib.* and hence *ellipt.* as sb., to designate a long-woolled variety of sheep and a long-horned variety of cattle originally bred in Leicestershire.

Leiger, leigier: see LEDGER.

Leio- (ləi·o), also **lio-,** comb. f. Gr. λεῖος smooth; as in: **Leiophy·llous** [Gr. φύλλον] *a.*, *Bot.* having smooth leaves; **Leio·trichous** [Gr. τριχ-, θρίξ hair] *a.*, smooth-haired, belonging to the group ||**Leio·trichi,** one of the two so-called primary divisions of mankind.

Leip(o)-: see LIP(O)-.

Leister (lī·stǝɹ). 1533. [– ON. *ljóstr* (Norw. dial. *lioster*, Sw. *ljuster*, Da. *lyster*), f. *ljósta* strike.] A pronged spear for striking and taking salmon, etc. Hence **Lei·stėr** *v. trans.* to spear with a l.

Leisurable (le·ʒ^iŭrǎb'l, lī·-), *a.* 1540. [f. LEISURE + -ABLE; cf. *pleasurable*, etc.] **1.** Leisurely, deliberate. **2.** Not requiring haste; leisure (time). *rare.* 1607. Hence **Lei·surably** *adv.* (now *rare*).

Leisure (le·ʒ^iŭɹ, *local* lī·ʒ^iŭɹ). [ME. *leisour*, *-er* – AFr. *leisour*, OFr. *leisir* (mod. *loisir*); Rom. subst. use of L. *licēre* be permitted. Cf. PLEASURE.] †**1.** Freedom or opportunity to do something –1640. †**b.** An opportunity. ME. only. **2.** Opportunity afforded by unoccupied time ME. **b.** Time allowed before it is too late. Now *rare.* 1553. **3.** The state of having time at one's own disposal; free time ME. **b.** A spell of free time. Now *rare.* 1449. †**4.** Leisureliness, deliberation –1677. **5.** *attrib.* 1669.
2. If your l. seru'd, I would speake with you SHAKS. **b.** For whose sanction there was no l. to wait JAS. MILL. **3.** The Desire of L. is much more Natural, than of Business and Care TEMPLE. Phr. *To tarry, attend,* or *stay* (*upon*) a person's *l.*: to wait his time. Also *fig. arch.* **5.** Let us pass a l. hour in story telling JOWETT.
Phrases. *At l.*: with time at one's disposal; without haste, with deliberation. *At one's l.*: when one has time; at one's ease or convenience. †*By l.* (also *by good l.*): with deliberation: at one's l.; by degrees; slowly. Also (= Gr. σχολῇ), barely.

Leisured (le·ʒ^iŭɹd, lī·-), *a.* 1631. [f. LEISURE + -ED[2].] **1.** Characterized by leisure. **2.** Having ample leisure, esp. in *the l. class(es* 1794.

Leisurely (le·ʒ^iŭɹli, lī·-), *a.* 1604. [f. LEISURE + -LY[1].] **1.** Having leisure; proceeding without haste 1613. **2.** Of actions or agents: Performed or operating at leisure; deliberate.
1. The men of l. minds COLERIDGE. **2.** A l. journey across the south of France 1875. Hence **Lei·sureliness.** So **Lei·surely** *adv.* 1486.

||**Leitmotiv** (ləi·tmotī·f). Also **-motif, -motive.** 1876. [G., f. *leit-* leading + *motiv* MOTIVE.] *Mus.* In the musical drama of Wagner and his imitators, a theme associated throughout the work with a particular person, situation, or sentiment.

Lek (lek), *v.* 1884. [perh. – Sw. *leka* to play; see LAKE *v.*] *intr.* Said of grouse: To congregate. Also **Lek** *sb.* a gathering or congregating 1871.

Leman (le·mǎn, lī·mǎn). *arch.* [Early ME. *leofman*, *lefman*, *lemman*, f. *lēof*, *lēf* LIEF + MAN.] **1.** A lover or sweetheart; †*occas.* a husband or wife. **2.** In bad sense (cf. *paramour*): An unlawful lover or (chiefly in later archaistic use) mistress ME.
2. Yea! none did love him—not his lemans dear BYRON.

Leme, obs. f. LEAM *sb.*[1] and *v.*

Lemma[1] (le·mǎ). *Pl.* **lemmas,** ||**lemmata.** 1570. [– L. *lemma* – Gr. λῆμμα, pl. λήμματα something taken for granted or assumed, theme, argument, title, f. **lab-*, base of λαμβάνειν take.] **1.** *Math.*, etc. A proposition assumed or demonstrated, preliminary to the demonstration of some other. **2. a.** The argument or subject of a literary composition, prefixed as a heading or title; a motto appended to a picture, etc. **b.** The heading or theme of a scholium, annotation, or gloss. 1616.
2. b. He marks off the l. from the body of the note in cases in which a l. is given 1896.

Lemma[2] (le·mǎ). Pl. **lemmata** (le·mǎtǎ). 1880. [– Gr. λέμμα, f. λέπειν peel.] *Embryol.* The primary or outer layer of the germinal vesicle.

Lemming (le·miŋ). Also **leeming.** 1713. [– Norw. *lemming*, rel. to Sw. *lemmel*, †*lemb* (pl. *lemmar*), Norw. *lemende*.] A small arctic rodent, *Myodes lemmus*, resembling a fieldmouse, about 6 in. long, with a short tail, prolific, and remarkable for its annual migrations to the sea. Also *l.-mouse*, *-rat.*
Collared or **Snowy l.,** *Cuniculus torquatus.*

Lemnian (le·mniǎn), *a.* 1611. [f. L. *Lemnius*, Gr. Λήμνιος (f. Λῆμνος the island Lemnos) + -AN.] Of or pertaining to Lemnos.
L. earth (L. *terra Lemnia*), sigillated earth, sphragide. *L. reddle*, an ochre of a deep-red colour and firm consistence, occurring in conjunction with the Lemnian earth, and used as a pigment. *L. smith*; Hephæstus or Vulcan.

Lemniscate (lemni·skĕt). 1781. [– mod.L. *lemniscata*, fem. of L. *lemniscatus* adj., adorned with ribbons, f. *lemniscus*; see next, -ATE[2].] **a.** *Geom.* The designation of certain closed curves, having a general resemblance to the figure 8. **b.** *Alg.* Used *attrib.* in *l. function*, one of a class of elliptic functions first investigated by Gauss, in connection with formulæ relating to this class of curves.

‖**Lemniscus** (lemni·skŏs). *Pl.* **-ci** (-səi). Also †**lemnisc** (1706–18). 1849. [L. *lemniscus*, Gr. λημνίσκος ribbon.] **1.** The character ÷ used by ancient textual critics in annotations. **2.** One of the minute ribbon-like appendages of the generative pores of some entozoans 1855.

Lemon (le·mən), *sb.*[1] [ME. *lymon* – (O)Fr. *limon* (now restricted to the lime), corresp. to Sp. *limón*, Pg. *limão*, It. *limone*, med.L. *limo, limon-*; f. Arab. *līma*, collect. *līm* fruits of the citron kind. See LIME *sb.*[2]] **1.** An ovate fruit with a pale yellow rind, and an acid juice. The juice yields citric acid; the rind yields *oil* or *essence of lemons*, used in cookery and perfumery. **b.** *slang* (orig. *U.S.*). Something worthless or distasteful 1863. **2.** The tree (*Citrus limonum*) which bears this fruit 1615. **3.** The colour of the lemon; pale yellow. More fully *l.-colour*. 1796. **4.** *attrib.*, as *l.-bloom, l.-cake, l.-coloured*, etc. 1598. **5.** quasi-*adj.*, short for *lemon-coloured* 1875.

Comb.: **l.-balm**, *Melissa officinalis*; **-cheese**, a confection made from lemons, butter, and eggs; **-cutting**, the feat of cutting a suspended l. in two with a sword when riding at full speed; **-grass**, a fragrant E. Indian grass (*Andropogon schœnanthus*) yielding the grass oil used in perfumery; also *attrib.*; **-kali**, a mixture of tartaric acid and sodium bicarbonate, which when dissolved form an effervescing drink; **-plant** (*Aloysia citriodora*), the so-called lemon-scented verbena; **-squash**, a drink made from soda-water, lemon-juice, and sugar; **-squeezer**, an instrument for squeezing out the juice of lemons; **-thyme**, a lemon-scented variety of thyme; **-tree**, (*a*) = sense 2; (*b*) = *lemon-plant*; **-verbena** = *lemon-plant*; **-wood**, a New Zealand tree, the Tarata.

Hence **Le·mon** *v.* to flavour with l. **Le·mony** *a.*

Lemon (le·mən), *sb.*[2] 1835. [– Fr. *limande* (XIII), beside *lime* (cf. It. *lima, limanda*); of unkn. origin.] In **lemon-dab, lemon-sole**, names for certain species of plaice or flounder.

Lemonade (lemənē[1]·d). Also †**limonade.** 1663. [– Fr. *limonade*, f. *limon* lemon.] A drink made from lemons, with (aerated) water and sugar. So †**Lemona·do** 1640–76.

Lemur (lī·mɔ̆ɹ). *Pl.* **lemurs**, ‖**lemures** (le·miŭrīz). 1580. [– mod.L. *lemur* (Linnæus), deduced from L. pl. *lemures* shades of the departed; so named because of the spectre-like suggestion of the face.] **1.** *Rom. Myth.* In *pl.* The spirits of the dead. **2.** *Zool.* A genus of nocturnal mammals of the family *Lemuridæ*, found chiefly in Madagascar, allied to the monkeys, but having a pointed muzzle like that of a fox; an animal of this genus 1795.

1. The Lars, and Lemures moan with midnight plaint MILT. Hence **Lemu·ridous** *a.* belonging to the family *Lemuridæ*. **Le·murine** *a.* and *sb.* = next.

Lemuroid (le·miŭroid). 1873. [f. LEMUR + -OID.] **A.** *adj.* Resembling the lemurs; pertaining to the sub-order *Lemuroidea*, of which the genus *Lemur* is the type. **B.** *sb.* A lemuroid animal 1873.

†**Lend,** *sb.*[1] [OE. **lenden* (only in pl. *lendenu*) = OFris. *lenden*, OS. *lendin* loin, OHG. *lentin, lentī* kidney, loin, ON. *lend* loin; ult. rel. to L. *lumbus*.] Chiefly *pl.* The loins; also, the buttocks –1550.

Lend, *sb.*[2] *Sc.* 1575. [f. LEND *v.*[1]] A loan.

Lend (lend), *v.*[1] Pa. t. and pple. **lent.** OE. [Late ME. *lende* (XIV), superseding *lēne(n* :– OE. *lǣnan*, corresp. (with difference of conjugation) to OFris. *lēna, lēnia*, Du. *leenen*, OHG. *lēhanōn* (G. *lehnen* enfeoff); f. *lǣn* LOAN *sb.*[1] The substitution of *lend-* for *lēn-*, which became established in XV, arose from the fact that the pa. t. *lende* and pa. pple. *lent* of *lēne*, by assoc. with the conjugation of *bend, send, wend*, suggested an inf. *lende*.] **1.** *trans.* To grant temporary possession of (a thing) on condition of the return of the same or its equivalent. **b.** *spec.* To let out (money, etc.) at interest OE. **c.** *absol.* or *intr.* To make a loan or loans OE. **2.** To grant, bestow; to impart, afford (usu. something not in the possession of the subject, or something viewed as a temporary possession or attribute) OE. †**b.** To hold out (a hand) to be taken –1611. **c.** *To l. an ear* or *one's ears*: to listen ME. **d.** To afford the use or support of; esp. in *to l. a hand*, etc., to assist 1598. **e.** To give or deal (a blow). Now *dial.* 1460. **f.** To devote (one's strength) *to*. *rare.* 1697. **3.** *refl.* To accommodate oneself *to*. Of things: To admit of being applied *to* a purpose or subjected *to* a certain treatment 1854.

1. To lende one his house to solemnise a mariage 1573. To l. a volume of poems 1785, a lease for perusal 1893. **b.** Thou shalt not..l. him thy victuals for increase *Lev.* 25:37. **c.** Hee that hath pity vpon the poore, lendeth vnto the Lord *Prov.* 19:17. Phr. *To l. out*: = 1, 1 b; now esp. used of lending libraries. **2.** While Heaven lends us grace MILT. *Comus* 938. 'Tis distance lends enchantment to the view CAMPBELL. **b.** L. me thy hand, and I will giue thee mine SHAKS. **c.** The young king seemed to l. a willing ear GEO. ELIOT. **d.** Lend 's a Hand here MOTTEUX. **3.** None lends itself better to architectural purposes 1874.

Hence **Le·ndable** *a.* that may be lent.

†**Lend,** *v.*[2] *Obs.* [OE. *lendan* = OHG. *lenten*, ON. *lenda* :– Gmc. **landjan*, f. **landam* LAND *sb.* Superseded by LAND *v.*] *intr.* To arrive, light (*up*)*on*, remain, tarry –1535.

Lender (le·ndəɹ). Also †**lenner.** [orig. OE. *lǣnere*, f. *lǣnan* LEND *v.*[1]; later f. the vb. + -ER[1].] One who lends, esp. at interest.

Lending (le·ndiŋ), *vbl. sb.* ME. [f. LEND *v.*[1] + -ING[1].] **1.** The action of LEND *v.*[1]; *esp.* the letting out of money at interest. **2.** *concr.* Something lent 1602; †*spec. pl.*, money advanced to soldiers when the regular pay cannot be given –1637.

2. Mowbray hath receiu'd eight thousand Nobles, In name of lendings for your Highnesse Soldiers SHAKS.

Le·nding, *ppl. a.* 1586. [f. as prec. + -ING[2].] That lends.

L. library, one from which books are lent.

†**Lene,** *a.* and *sb.* 1751. [– L. *lenis* smooth.] *Phonetics.* Applied to the smooth breathing (*spiritus lenis*) in Greek; also to a stopped (esp. voiceless) consonant, opp. to *aspirate* –18..

Lene: see LEND *v.*[1]

†**Leng,** *adv.* [OE. *leng* = OS. *leng* :– Gmc. **lanȝiz* adverbial comparative of **lanȝaz* LONG *a.*] Longer –ME.

†**Lenger,** *a.* and *adv.* [OE. *lengra* :– Gmc. **lanȝizon*; compar. of *lang* LONG *a.*; see -ER[3].] **A.** *adj.* Longer –1561. **B.** *adv.* Longer –1590.

†**Lengest,** *a.* and *adv.* [OE. *lengest* :– Gmc. *lanȝistaz*; superl. of *lang*; see LONG *a.*, -EST.] **A.** *adj.* Longest, very long –1530. **B.** *adv.* Longest –1485.

Length (leŋþ), *sb.* [OE. *lengþu* (rare, the usual word being *lengu, lenge*, which survived till XVII) = Du. *lengte*, ON. *lengd* :– Gmc. *lanȝiþō*, f. *lanȝaz* LONG *a.*; see -TH[1].]

I. Quality of being long. **1.** Linear measurement of any thing from end to end; the greatest of the three dimensions of a body or figure. **2.** Extent from beginning to end, e.g. of a period of time, a series, a word, etc. ME. **3.** The quality or fact of being long; opp. to *shortness* ME.; prolixity (now *rare*) 1593. **b.** An instance of this; *esp.* a long period 1697. **4.** A distance as long as something specified ME. **b.** *Sport.* The length of a boat, a horse, etc., taken as a unit in stating the amount by which a race is won 1664. **5.** With a demonstrative or other defining word: Distance 1450. **b.** *fig.* in advb. phrases, as, *to go* (*to*) *the l. of, a* (*great*, etc.) *l.*, (*all*, etc.) *lengths* 1697. †**6.** Reach –1628. **7.** *Pros.* Quantity (of a sound or syllable). Also, long quantity (opp. to *shortness*). 1575. **8.** *Cricket.* The proper distance for pitching a ball in bowling. Also = *length ball*. 1776.

1. The full l. of the rope between us TYNDALL. Phr. *To find, get, know the l. of* (a person's) *foot*; see FOOT *sb.* *The l. of one's tether*; see TETHER. **2.** The lenght of the siege LD. BERNERS. **b.** To see a friend after a l. of absence LANDOR. **3.** Such Customes have their force, onely from L. of Time HOBBES. Excuse my l. BURKE. **4.** *At arm's l.*: see ARM *sb.*[1] *Cable('s) l.*: see CABLE *sb.* 2 b. *One's l.*; I fell all my l. 1870. **b.** The Oxford crew won by three and a half lengths 1894. **5.** He [Essex] had marched to the l. of Exeter CLARENDON. **b.** The cunningest of men, able to lie all lengths CARLYLE. **6.** If I can get him within my Pistol's l. SHAKS. **8.** How to stop a ball dropped rather short of a l. 1833.

II. Concrete senses. **1. a.** A long stretch or extent 1595. **b.** A piece of a certain or distinct length 1565. **2.** *Theatr. slang.* A portion of an actor's part, consisting of forty-two lines 1736. **3.** *Brewing.* The quantity of wort drawn off from a certain quantity of malt 1742.

1. Large lengths of seas and shores SHAKS. **2.** Kean said that 'Iago was three lengths longer than Othello' 1865.

Phr. **At length. a.** To the full extent; in full; without curtailment. Also *at full, great, some*, etc. *l.* **b.** After a long time; at or in the end. †**c.** (*a*) At a distance; (*b*) in an extended line; tandem-fashion; (*c*) of a portrait = FULL LENGTH 1. **d.** With the body fully extended. Now usu. *at* (*one's*) *full l.*

Comb. **l. ball** *Cricket*, a ball pitched a l. (see sense I. 8).

Hence †**Length** *v.* to make or become longer ME.

Lengthen (le·ŋþ'n). 1440. [f. LENGTH *sb.* + -EN[5].] **1.** *trans.* To make longer. Also with *out*. †**b.** Used for: To eke out, cause to last longer. Also with *out*. –1748. **2.** *intr.* To become longer 1695.

1. Then will I l. thy dayes 1 *Kings* 3:14. To l. a vowel 1755. **b.** We agreed for the Gallapagos to get Turtle to l. our Provisions 1712. **2.** Phr. *To l. out* (Mil.): to stride out.

Lengthful (le·ŋþfŭl), *a. poet.* (Now *rare.*) 1611. [f. LENGTH *sb.* + -FUL.] Of great length, long.

Lengthways (le·ŋþwē[i]z), *adv.* 1599. [f. LENGTH *sb.* + -WAYS.] In the direction of the length (*of* something).

Lengthwise (le·ŋþwəiz). 1580. [f. as prec. + -WISE.] **A.** *adv.* = prec. **B.** *adj.* Following the direction of the length 1871.

Lengthy (le·ŋþi), *a.* 1689. [f. LENGTH *sb.* + -Y[1]. Orig. an Americanism.] Characterized by length; having great length; often (of speeches, etc.) prolix, tedious.

I grow too minute and l. J. ADAMS. L. correspondence 1844, pleadings FREEMAN. A l. and stupendous cliff line H. M. STANLEY. Hence **Le·ngthily** *adv.* **Le·ngthiness.**

Lenience (lī·niĕns). 1796. [f. LENIENT; see -ENCE.] Lenient action or behaviour; indulgence.

Leniency (lī·niĕnsi). 1780. [f. LENIENT; see -ENCY.] The quality of being lenient.

Lenient (lī·niĕnt). 1652. [– *lenient-*, pr. ppl. stem of L. *lenire* soothe, f. *lenis* soft, mild; see -ENT. Cf. Fr. †*lénient*.]

A. *adj.* **1.** Softening, soothing, relaxing; emollient. Somewhat *arch.* **2.** Indisposed to severity; gentle, mild, tolerant 1787.

1. L. of grief and anxious thought MILT. The l. hand of time FOSTER. **2.** L. laws 1787, measures 1828. Hence **Le·niently** *adv.*

†**B.** *sb.* An emollient –1794.

Lenify (lī·nifəi), *v.* 1568. [– late L. *lenificare*, f. *lenis* soft, mild; see -FY.] †**1.** *trans.* To relax, make soft or supple (some part of the body); to render (cider) mellow. Also, to mitigate (a physical condition). 1574. **2.** To assuage, mitigate, soften, soothe (pain, suffering, etc.). Also, to mitigate (a sentence). Now *rare*.

Lenitive (le·nĭtiv). late ME. [– med.L. *lenitivus*, f. *lenit-*, pa. ppl. stem of L. *lenire* soften; see -IVE. Cf. (O)Fr. *lénitif, -ive*. In sense 2 as if f. LENITY + -IVE.]

A. *adj.* **1.** Tending to allay or soften; mitigating, soothing; gently laxative; esp. in *l. electuary*. †**2.** Of persons, etc.: Displaying leniency, gentle –1655.

1. Such Writers..use the most l. language in expressing distastfull matter FULLER. Hence **Le·nitive-ly** *adv.*, **-ness.**

B. *sb.* **1.** A lenitive medicine or appliance. Also *fig.* 1563. **2.** Anything that softens or soothes; a palliative 1614.

2. He hath under his greatest Misery the L. of Hope HALE.

Lenitude (le·nitiŭd). *rare.* 1627. [– L. *lenitudo*, f. *lenis* soft, mild; see -TUDE.] †**a.** In a material sense: Smoothness. **b.** = LENITY.

Lenity (le·nĭti). 1548. [– OFr. *lénité* or L. *lenitas*, f. as prec.; see -ITY.] Mildness, gentleness, mercifulness. Also, an instance of this.

Hee is the verie soule of lenitie 1592.

Leno (lī·no). 1804. [– Fr. *linon* (linon), f. *lin* flax; see LINE *sb.*[1], LINEN.] A kind of cotton gauze, used for caps, veils, curtains, etc. Also *attrib.*

†**Leno·cinant,** *a.* 1664. [– *lenocinant-*, pr. ppl. stem of L. *lenocinari* flatter, wheedle; see -ANT.] Inciting to evil. HY. MORE.

Lens (lenz). *Pl.* **lenses;** also formerly **lens, lens's,** and in L. form **lentes.** 1693. [– L. *lens* LENTIL; so called on account of its shape.] **1.** A piece of glass, or other transparent substance, with two curved surfaces, or one plane and one curved, serving to cause regular convergence or divergence of the rays of light passing through it. (Now sometimes applied to analogous contrivances, as *acoustic l., electric l.*) **b.** *spec.* A lens or combination of lenses used in photography 1841. **2.** *Anat.* **a.** = *crystalline lens* (see CRYSTALLINE *a.*) 1719. **b.** One of the facets of a compound eye 1868. **3.** *attrib.*, as *l.-shutter*, etc.; also, **l.-eye** = 2 b; **-form** = LENTIFORM 1787. Hence **Lensed** *a.* provided with a l. or lenses; **Le·nsless** *a.* having no l.

Lent (lent), *sb.*[1] ME. [Shortened from LENTEN.] **1.** The season of spring. *Obs.* exc. in *Comb.* ME. **2.** *Eccl.* The period including 40 weekdays extending from Ash-Wednesday to Easter-eve, kept as a time of fasting and penitence, in commemoration of Our Lord's fasting in the wilderness ME. **b.** *transf.* and *fig.* 1598. **c.** *pl.* At Cambridge: The Lent-term boat-races 1893. †**3.** Hence, **a.** A period of forty days, esp. in *l. of pardon*, an indulgence of forty days –1535. †**b.** A period of fasting prescribed by any religious system –1781.

2. What is a Ioynt of Mutton..in a whole L.? SHAKS.

attrib. and *Comb.*, as (sense 1) *l.-corn*, etc.; (sense 2) *L.-diet, -sermon*, etc.; **l.-lily,** the yellow daffodil, *Narcissus pseudonarcissus*; **l.-rose** = *lent-lily*; also, in S. Devon, *N. biflorus*; **L.-term** (at the Universities), the term in which L. falls.

†**Lent,** *sb.*[2] Also **lente.** ME. only. [– *lent-*, stem of L. *lens* LENTIL.] Lentils.

Lent (lent), *a.* Also **lente.** ME. [– (O)Fr. *lent* or L. *lentus.*] †**1.** Slow, sluggish; said esp. of a fever, a fire –1732. **2.** *Mus.* = LENTO. Now *rare.* 1724.

Lent (lent), *ppl. a.* ME. [pa. pple. of LEND *v.*[1]] In senses of LEND *v.*[1] (Formerly often = 'borrowed'.)

Lent, obs. pa. t. and pple. of LEAN *v.*

-lent, *suffix*, in adjs. from L. The L. ending *-lentus* nearly = Eng. -FUL. Normally it is preceded by *u*, as in *turbulentus* turbulent; exceptions are *pestilentus* pestilent, *violentus* violent, *sanguinolentus* bloody.

‖**Lentamente** (lentame·nte), *adv.* 1762. [It., f. *lento* slow.] *Mus.* Slowly, in slow time.

Lenten (le·nt'n), *sb.* and *a.* †Also *Sc.* and *north.* **lentern, lentrin, -on.** [OE. *lencten* str. masc.; prob. a derivative, through a shorter form appearing as MLG., MDu., Du. *lente*, Ger. *lenz*, etc., of **laŋgo-* LONG *a.*, with reference to the lengthening of the days in spring. The eccl. sense is peculiar to Eng.; in the other Teut. langs. the only sense is 'spring'. In attrib. use *lenten* is now apprehended as an adj., as if f. LENT + -EN[4].]

†**A.** As separate *sb.* *Obs.*; superseded by LENT *sb.*[1] **1.** Spring; = LENT *sb.*[1] 1. –ME. **2.** = LENT *sb.*[1] 2. –1553.

B. *attrib.* or *adj.* **1.** Of or pertaining to Lent, observed or taking place in Lent, as in *L. day, fast, sermon*, etc. OE. **2.** Appropriate to Lent; hence of provisions, etc., such as may be used in Lent, meagre; of clothing, looks, etc., mournful-looking, dismal 1577.

1. The Divell whipt St. Jerom in a l. dream, for reading Cicero MILT. **2.** L. fare WESLEY. Dabitur's l. face BROWNING.

Comb.: †**l.-chaps,** applied to a person having a lean visage; **L.-corn,** corn sown about Lent; **l. fig,** †(*a*) a dried fig; (*b*) a raisin; **L. lily** (*rare*) = *Lent-lily*; **l. pie,** a pie containing no meat.

Lenticel (le·ntisel). 1870. [– mod.L. *lenticella* (De Candolle, Fr. *lenticelle*), dim. f. L. *lens, lent-* lentil.] **1.** *Bot.* A lenticular corky spot on young bark, corresponding to one of the epidermal stomata. **2.** *Anat.* A lenticular gland 1888. So **Lentice·llate** *a.* producing lenticels; having corky spots on the bark 1855.

Lenticular (lenti·kiŭlăɹ). 1658. [– L. *lenticularis*, f. *lenticula*; see LENTIL, -AR[1].]

A. *adj.* **1.** Having the form of a lens or of a lentil; double convex. **2. a.** Of or pertaining to a lens 1875. **b.** Of or pertaining to the (crystalline) lens of the eye 1822.

L. bed *Geol.*, 'a bed which thins away in all directions' (Green); **l. ore,** beds of red argillaceous ore, so called from the flattened grains which compose it.

†**B.** *sb.* **a.** A lenticular glass or lens. **b.** A lenticular knife, i.e. a scraper used in osteotomy. –1802.

Hence **Lenti·cularly** *adv.* in a l. manner; after the fashion of a lens.

Lentiform (le·ntifǭɹm), *a.* 1706. [f. L. *lens, lent-* lentil + -FORM.] Having the form of a lentil or of a lens.

Lentigerous (lenti·dʒĕrəs), *a.* 1889. [f. L. *lens, lent-* lentil + -GEROUS.] Having a crystalline lens: said of the eyes of some molluscs.

‖**Lentigo** (lentəi·go). *Pl.* **lentigines** (lenti·dʒiniz). ME. [L., f. as prec.] A freckle or pimple; now usu. *collect.* for a freckly affection of the skin. Hence **Lenti·ginous** *a.* full of freckles; affected with l. 1597.

Lentil (le·ntil). [ME. *lentille* – (O)Fr. *lentille* :– Rom. **lentīcula*, f. L. *lenticula*, dim. of *lens, lent-* lentil.] **1.** Chiefly *pl.*, in early use occas. *collective sing.* The seed of a leguminous plant (*Ervum lens, Lens esculenta*); also the plant itself, cultivated for food. †**b.** = DUCKWEED (*Lemna*). More fully *Water l.* [= Fr. *lentilles d'eau*]. –1597. †**2.** *pl.* Freckles on the skin. (Cf. LENTIGO.) –1694. **3.** *attrib.*, as *l.-soup*, etc.; **l.-shell** (*Zool.*), the genus *Ervillia.* 1555.

‖**Lentiscus** (lenti·skŏs). *Pl.* **lentisci, lentiscus's.** 1587. [L.] = next.

Lentisk (le·ntisk). late ME. [– L. *lentiscus*, prob. of alien origin.] The mastic tree (*Pistacia lentiscus*).

Lentitude (le·ntitiud). 1623. [– L. *lentitudo*, f. *lentus* slow; see -TUDE.] Slowness, sluggishness.

Lento (le·nto). 1724. [It.] *Mus.* A direction: Slow; slowly.

Lentoid (le·ntoid), *a.* 1879. [f. L. *lens, lent-* (see LENS) + -OID.] Having the form of a lens or lentil.

Lentor (le·ntəɹ, le·ntǫɹ). 1615. [– L. *lentor* viscosity, f. *lentus*; see LENT *a.*, -OR 1. Cf. (O)Fr. *lenteur*, whence partly sense 2.] **1.** Of the blood, etc.: Clamminess, tenacity, viscidity. Now *rare.* †**b.** *concr.* A viscid component of the blood –1722. **2.** Slowness; want of vital activity 1763.

†**Le·ntous,** *a.* 1646. [f. L. *lentus* viscid + -OUS.] Clammy, viscid. SIR T. BROWNE.

L'envoy, lenvoy. ME. See ENVOY *sb.*[1] 1. *Pag.* Is not *lenuoy* a *salue*? *Ar.* No, Page, it is an epilogue SHAKS.

‖**Leo** (lī·o). OE. [L.; see LION.] The Lion, the zodiacal constellation lying between Cancer and Virgo. Also, the fifth sign of the zodiac (named from this constellation). *Leo Minor*, a minor constellation, lying between the Great Bear and Leo.

Leon, obs. f. LION.

Leonid (lī·ŏnid). Also *pl.* in L. form **Leonides** (li,ǫ·nidīz). 1876. [f. L. *leo, leon-* + -ID[3].] *Astron.* One of the meteors which appear to radiate from Leo.

Leonine (lī·ŏnəin, -nin), *a.*[1] ME. [– (O)Fr. *léonin, -ine* or L. *leoninus, -ina*, f. *leo, leon-* LION; see -INE[1].] **1.** Lion-like; resembling that of a lion. **2.** Of or relating to a lion 1500. Hence **Le·oninely** *adv.*

1. A man of l. aspect 1887. *L. monkey*: the *Macacus leoninus.*

L. convention or *partnership* (Rom. Law): one made 'on the terms that one should take all the profits and another bear all the loss' (Poste); held by Cassius to be not binding.

Leonine (lī·ŏnəin, -nin), *a.*[2] and *sb.* 1658. [f. proper name *Leo*; identical in form and ult. in origin with prec.] **A.** *adj.* **1.** Pertaining to one of the popes named Leo 1870., **2.** *L. verse*: Latin verse consisting of hexameters, or alternate hexameters and pentameters, in which the final word rhymes with that preceding the cæsural pause. So *l. poet, rhyme.* (For conjectures as to the identity of the inventor see Du Cange.) 1658. **B.** *sb. pl.* Leonine verse 1846.

L. city (mod.L. *Civitas Leonina*], that part of Rome, including the Vatican, which was walled and fortified by Leo IV (*c* 850).

‖**Leontiasis** (lī:ǫntəi·ăsis). 1753. [mod.L. – Gr. λεοντίασις, f. λέων, λεοντ- lion; see -ASIS.] *Med.* **1.** A form of leprosy in which the face looks somewhat lion-like. **2.** Hypertrophy of the bones of the face and skull, inducing a lion-like expression.

‖**Leontodon** (lī:ǫ·ntŏdǭn). 1807. [mod.L. f. as prec. + ὀδούς, ὀδοντ- tooth; tr. DANDELION.] A plant of the genus *Leontodon*, of which the Dandelion was the original type.

Leopard (le·pəɹd). [ME. *leopard*, also *lebard, lubard, libbard*, etc. – OFr. *leopard*, etc., (mod. *léopard*) – late L. *leopardus* – late Gr. λεόπαρδος, also λεοντόπαρδος, f. λέων, λεοντ- LION + πάρδος PARD[1]; so named because supposed to be a hybrid between lion and 'pard'.] **1.** A large carnivorous quadruped, *Panthera pardus*, also called the Panther, a native of Africa and southern Asia. Its coat is yellowish fawn shading to white under the body, with dark brown or black rosette-like spots. (In pop. language, the smaller varieties only are leopards, the larger being called panthers.) **2.** A figure of a leopard in painting, heraldry, etc. ME. **b.** *Anc. Her.* A lion passant guardant [Fr. *lion léopardé*], as in the Arms of England ME. **c.** A gold coin of Edward III having on the obverse a lion passant guardant. **3. Sea leopard** = *leopard-seal*: see SEA. **4.** *attrib.*, as *l. skin, whelp*, etc. ME.

1. American L., the jaguar, *Felis onca.* **Hunting L.,** the cheetah; **Snow L.,** the ounce, *F. irbis.* Can the blacke More change his skin? or the l. his spottes BIBLE (Genev.) *Jer.* 13:23. **2.** With Libbards head on knee *L.L.L.* v. ii. 551. **4. L. cat,** (*a*) the African wild cat, *Felis serval*; (*b*) the wild cat of India and the Malay Archipelago, *F. bengalensis*; (*c*) the American ocelot, *F. pardalis.* **L. wood,** the wood of a S. Amer. tree, *Brosimum aubletii.*

Hence **Leo·pardess,** a female l. 1567.

Leopard's bane. 1548. [See BANE *sb.*] A plant of the genus *Doronicum*, esp. *D. Pardalianches.* Also applied to *Arnica montana, Paris quadrifolia* (Herb Paris), etc.

Lep, obs. or Sc. f. LAP, LEAP.

Lepadoid (le·pădoid). 1843. [f. Gr. λέπας, λεπαδ- limpet + -OID.] **a.** *adj.* Resembling a barnacle. **b.** *sb.* A lepadoid animal.

Le·pal. 1835. [f. Gr. λεπίς scale, after *petal, sepal.*] *Bot.* A barren stamen transformed into a scale.

†**Le·per,** *sb.*[1] [ME. *lepre* – (O)Fr. *lèpre* – late L. *lepra*, cl. L. *lepræ* pl. (Pliny) – Gr. λέπρα, subst. use of fem. of λεπρός scaly, f. λέπος, λεπίς scale.] Leprosy –1588.

Leper (le·pəɹ), *sb.*[2] and *a.* ME. [prob. arising from attrib. use of prec.] **A.** *sb.* One affected with leprosy. Also *attrib.*, as **leper('s) window,** name given to a supposed hagioscope for lepers. **B.** *adj.* Leprous ME. Hence **Le·per** *v.* to affect with leprosy; *fig.* to taint (CLOUGH).

Lepid (le·pid), *a.* Now *rare.* 1619. [– L. *lepidus.*] Pleasant, jocose, facetious. Occas., Charming, elegant. Hence †**Lepi·dity,** facetiousness. **Le·pidly** *adv.*

Lepidine (le·pidəin). 1855. [ult. f. Gr. λεπίς, λεπιδ- scale + -INE[5].] *Chem.* A volatile oily base obtained by distilling quinine, cinchonine, and other alkaloids.

Lepido- (le·pido), repr. Gr. λεπιδο-, comb. f. λεπίς scale: **Le:pidode·ndroid** *a.*, pertaining to or resembling plants of the genus *Lepidodendron*; *sb.* a plant of this genus or of the group of which it is the type. ‖**Le:pidode·ndron** [Gr. δένδρον tree], a genus of fossil plants common in coal-measures, having leaf-scars on the trunk; a plant of this genus. **Le:pidoga·noid, -ganoi·dean** *adjs.* pertaining to the *Lepidoganoidei*, a group of ganoid fishes having regular scales instead of plates. **Le:pidomela·ne** [Gr. μέλας, μέλαν-ος black], *Min.* a highly ferruginous mica, usu. found in aggregations of small black scales. **Le:pidosau·rian** *a.*, pertaining to the subclass *Lepidosauria* of Reptiles, characterized by a scaly integument; *sb.* one of the *Lepidosauria.* **Le:pidosi·ren,** a genus of dipnoan fishes; a fish of this genus.

Lepidoid (le·pidoid). 1836. [f. Gr. λεπίς, λεπιδ- scale + -OID.] *adj.* and *sb.* Pertaining to, one of, the *Lepidoidei*, a family of fossil fishes having large rhomboidal scales.

Lepidolite (le·pidŏləit). 1796. [f. LEPIDO- + -LITE.] A variety of mica containing lithia.

‖**Lepidoptera** (lepidǫ·ptĕră), *sb. pl.* 1773. [mod.L., f. LEPIDO- + πτερόν wing.] *Entom.* A large order of insects having four membranous wings covered with scales; it comprises the butterflies and moths. Hence **Le·pidiopter,** one of the Lepidoptera. **Lepido·pteral, Lepido·pteran, Lepido·pterous** *adjs.*, of or pertaining to the L. **Lepido·pterist,** one who studies the Lepidoptera.

Lepidote (le·pidoᵘt), *a.* 1836. [– mod.L. *lepidotus* – Gr. λεπιδωτός, f. λεπίς, λεπιδ- scale.] *Bot.* Covered with scurfy scales; leprose, leprous. So **Le·pidoted** *a.*

Leporicide. [f. L. *lepus, lepor-* hare + -CIDE 1.] A killer of hares. BURKE.

Leporine (le·pŏrəin). 1656. [– L. *leporinus*, f. as prec.; see -INE¹.] **A.** *adj.* Pertaining to a hare or hares; of the nature or form of a hare; lagomorphic. **B.** *sb.* An alleged cross between a hare and a rabbit 1862.

‖**Lepra** (le·pră). ME. [Late L.; see LEPER *sb.*¹] *Path.* A skin disease characterized by desquamation: (*a*) formerly = psoriasis; (*b*) now applied to leprosy (*Lepra cutanea* or *Elephantiasis Græcorum*). **b.** *Bot.* 'A white mealy matter, which exudes or protrudes from the surface of some plants' (*Treas. Bot.*) 1866.

Lepre: see LEPER and LEPRY.

‖**Leprechaun** (leprĕχǭ·n). 1604. [Middle Irish *luchrupán*, altered f. OIrish *luchorpán*, f. *lu* small + *corp* body.] In Irish folk-lore, A pigmy sprite.

Leprose (le·proᵘs), *a.* 1856. [– late L. *leprosus*; f. LEPRA; see -OSE.¹] *Bot.* Having a scaly or scurfy appearance. Hence **Leproso-,** comb. f., meaning 'leprose and...'

Leprosery (le·prŏsəri). 1897. [– Fr. *léproserie*, f. *lépreux* or late L. *leprosus* LEPROUS: see -ERY.] A leper hospital or colony.

†**Lepro·sity.** 1555. [– OFr. *leprosite* or med.L. *leprositas*; see prec., -ITY.] Leprous quality or condition. In *Alch.*, metallic impurity. –1635.

Leprosy (le·prŏsi). 1535. [f. next + -Y³, repl. LEPRY.] **1.** A loathsome disease (*Elephantiasis Græcorum*), which slowly eats away the body, and forms shining white scales on the skin; common in mediæval Europe. (In the Eng. Bible, the Heb. and Gr. words rendered 'leprosy' were app. used as comprehensive terms for various skin diseases.) **2.** A leper-house (*rare*) 1834.

1. *fig.* Idleness is a moral l., which soon eats its way into the heart 1836.

Leprous (le·prəs), *a.* Also †**leperous,** etc. ME. [– OFr. *lepro(u)s* (mod. *lépreux*) – late L. *leprosus*, f. *lepra*; see LEPRA, -OUS.] **1.** Afflicted or tainted with leprosy. Also *fig.* †**b.** Inducing leprosy –1602. **c.** Pertaining to, resembling, or accompanying leprosy 1635. **2.** *transf.* Covered with white scales. In *Bot.* = LEPROSE. 1620.

1. The hous of Symon l. where as our lord dyned CAXTON. Behold, his hand was l. as snowe *Exod.* 4:6. **2.** One old l. screen of faded Indian leather DICKENS. Hence **Le·prous-ly** *adv.*, **-ness.**

†**Lepry.** ME. [f. LEPER *sb.*² + -Y³.] = LEPROSY. –1660.

Lepto-, comb. f. Gr. λεπτός fine, small, thin, delicate: used in various scientific terms, as *leptocepha·lic* narrow-skulled, *leptoda·ctyl* adj. and sb. (a bird) having slender toes.

Lepton (le·ptǫn). *Pl.* **lepta** (-ă), *erron.* **leptas.** 1727. [– Gr. λεπτόν (sc. νόμισμα coin), n. of λεπτός small.] **a.** An ancient Gr. coin worth about one-fourth of a farthing; the 'mite' of the N.T. **b.** The smallest coin ('centime') of modern Greece, being the one-hundredth part of a drachma.

†**Lere,** *v.* [OE. *lǣran* = OFris. *lēra*, OS. *lērian* (Du. *leeren*), OHG. *lēren* (G. *lehren*), ON. *læra*, Goth. *laisjan*; WGmc. **laiz-*, Gmc. *lais-*; see LORE *sb.*¹, LEARN.] **1.** *trans.* To teach; = LEARN *v.* II. 1. –1852. **2.** To inform; = LEARN *v.* II. 2. –1643. **3.** To learn, acquire knowledge of (something); to study, read (a book); to learn *to* do something –1818. **4.** *absol.* and *intr.* = LEARN *v.* I. 2, 3 b. –1721. Hence **Le·red** *ppl. a.* (*dial.*) = LEARNED.

Les, obs. f. LEASH.

Lesbian (le·zbiăn), *a.* 1601. [f. L. *Lesbius*, Gr. Λέσβιος + -AN.] **1.** Of or pertaining to the island of Lesbos, in the Grecian archipelago. **2.** *Lesbian vice*, SAPPHISM.

L. rule: a mason's rule made of lead, which could be bent to fit the curves of a moulding (Aristotle *Eth. Nic.* v. x. 7); *fig.*, a pliant principle of judgement. **2.** L. passion, as the Greeks called it 1908. Irais..A very scarce L. novel 1949. Hence **Le·sbianism.**

†**Lesed,** *pa. pple.* and *ppl. a.* ME. [f. L. *læsus*, pa. pple. of *lædere* to hurt + -ED¹.] Damaged, injured –1741.

Lese-majesty (lī·z,mæ·dʒĕsti). Also **leze-.** 1536. [– Fr. *lèse-majesté* – L. *læsa majestas* hurt or violated majesty, i.e. of the sovereign people; *læsa* pa. pple. of *lædere* injure (see next), *majestas* MAJESTY.] Any offence against the sovereign authority; treason. Also *transf.*

¶Both in Fr. and Eng., *lese-* has been treated as a vb.-stem, taking a sb. in an objective relation, as in *lese-humanity*, an outrage upon the dignity of humanity, etc.

Lesion (lī·ʒən). 1452. [– (O)Fr. *lésion* – L. *læsio*, f. *læs-*, pa. ppl. stem of *lædere* injure, hurt; see -ION.] **1.** Damage, injury; a hurt or flaw. **2.** Damage or detriment to one's property or rights. Now chiefly in *Civil* and *Scots Law*, as a ground for setting a contract aside. 1582. **3.** *Path.* Any morbid change in the exercise of functions or the texture of organs. Also *fig.* 1747.

Less (les), *a.* (*sb.*), *adv.*, and *conj.* [OE. *lǣssa* = OFris. *lēssa* :– Gmc. **laisizō*, f. **laisiz* (whence OE. *lǣs* = OFris. *lēs* adv.), compar. formation on **laisa-* :– IE. **loiso-* (cf. Gr. λοῖσθος last).] **A.** *adj.* As comparative of LITTLE.

I. In concord with sb. (expressed or implied). **1.** Of not so great size, extent, or degree (as something); smaller. Opp. (in mod. Eng.) to *greater*. Repl. by *smaller* with reference to material dimensions. **b.** Not so much; opp. to *more* ME. **c.** Fewer. Now regarded as incorrect. OE. **2.** Of lower station, condition, or rank; inferior. *Obs.* exc. as in *no less a person than*, etc. OE. **3.** Used *spec.* to characterize the smaller, inferior, or (after L. use) younger, of two persons or things of the same name; = L. *minor*. *Obs.* exc. in *James the Less*, and imitations of this. OE. **4.** Before (formerly also, after) a numeral, etc.; = MINUS. Also *transf.*, used (like *minus*) for 'not including', 'except'. OE. ¶**5.** Used by Shaks., in neg. expressions, where the sense requires 'more'.

1. Of too Evelis þe lasse Evill is to be chosyn 1440. **b.** I owe him little Dutie, and lesse Loue SHAKS. **2.** Phr. †*L. of, in*: inferior in point of. **3.** †*L. Britain*, †*Britain the l.*: Brittany. †*The l. world* = MICROCOSM. **4.** The space of a xi. wekes, thre dayes lesse LD. BERNERS. **5.** *Wint. T.* III. ii. 57, *Cymb.* I. iv. 23.

II. *absol.* (quasi-*sb.*) **1.** *The l.*: That which is smaller (of two things compared). Also of persons. ME. **2.** A less amount, quantity, or number (*than* one specified or implied) OE.

1. The haire that couers the wit, is more then the wit; for the greater hides the lesse SHAKS. **2.** Phr. *L. than no time*; joc. for a very short time. *Far, little, much, nothing, something l. No l.* = 'nothing less'. *Nothing l. than*: quite equal to, the same thing as; see also B.

B. *adv.* To a smaller extent; in a lower degree OE.

Much l., still l. (†formerly also simply *l.*); The world thou hast not seen, much l. her glory MILT. †*Nothing l.*: anything rather. *Nothing l. than*: anything rather than; = Fr. *rien moins que*. Now *rare*. 1548. *More or less*: see MORE.

†**C.** *conj.* Unless. In early use *l. than, l. that* 1422–1772.

And the mute Silence hist along, 'L. Philomel will daign a Song MILT. *Pens.* 56.

†**Less,** *v.* [ME. *lasse, lessi*, f. *lasse, lesse* LESS *a.*] To make or become less –1633.

-less (lès), *suffix*, forming adjs. The OE. *lēas* was used in the sense 'devoid (of)', 'free (from)', (*a*) in OE. only, as a separate adj., governing the genitive; (*b*) subseq., as a suffix, attached to sbs. to form adjs. with privative sense. On the supposed analogy of instances of (*b*) in which the sb. taking the suffix was of the same form with the stem of a related vb., as *countless, numberless*, the suffix has been appended to many verbs, as in *abashless, dauntless, resistless, tireless*, †*topless* (= not overtopped), etc.

Lessee (lesī·). 1495. [– AFr. *lessee*, OFr. *lessé*, pa. pple. of *lesser* (mod. *laisser* leave, let); see LEASE *v.*³, -EE¹.] A person to whom a lease is granted; a tenant under a lease. Hence **Lessee·ship.**

Lessen (le·s'n), *v.* ME. [f. LESS *a.* + -EN⁵; superseding LESS *v.*] **1.** *intr.* To become less; to decrease. **2.** To decrease in apparent size by the effect of distance, as a bird flying 1611. **3.** *trans.* To make less; to diminish ME. †**b.** *pass.* To suffer loss or curtailment *of*; to be reduced *in* –1793. **4.** To make less in estimation; to extenuate (faults); to disparage. *Obs.* or *arch.* 1585. †**5.** To humble; to degrade, lower –1788.

1. The river..lessened every step we went DE FOE. **2.** The sky-lark..lessening from the dazzled sight GRAY. **3.** To l. the value of money 1793, the hours of work JEVONS. **4.** To l. a heroic figure 1877. **5.** The making of new Lords lessens all the rest SELDEN.

Lesser (le·səɹ). 1459. [Double comparative, f. LESS *a.* + -ER³.] **A.** *adj.* **1.** = LESS *a.* Now only used *attrib.* **2.** In spec. or techn. use, opposed to *greater*. **a.** *Astron.*, as in *The Lesser Bear*. Also *Geog.* in *L. Asia* (now *arch.*), Asia Minor. 1551. **b.** *Mus.* = MINOR (intervals) 1674. **c.** In names of plants and animals, as *l. spotted woodpecker, l. celandine* 1678. **d.** *Anat.* 1842.

1. Woman is the l. man TENNYSON.

†**B.** adv. Less –1625.

†**Lesses,** *sb. pl.* ME. [– (O)Fr. *laisses* (mod. also *laissées*), *quasi* 'leavings', f. *laisser* leave.] The dung of a 'ravenous' animal, as a wild boar, wolf, or bear –1807.

Lessive (le·siv). *rare.* 1826. [– (O)Fr. *lessive* :– late L. *lixiva* lye, subst. use of n. pl. of L. *lixivus* adj. See LIXIVIUM.] A lye of wood-ashes, soap-suds, etc., used in washing.

Lessness (le·snès). *rare.* 1635. [f. LESS *a.* + -NESS.] Inferiority.

Lesson (le·sən, les'n), *sb.* ME. [– (O)Fr. *leçon* :– L. *lectio, -ōn-* LECTION.] †**1.** The action of reading. WYCLIF. †**b.** A public reading; a lecture; a course of lectures –1724. **2.** *Eccl.* A portion of Scripture or other sacred writing read at divine service; a lection. (Now chiefly, the portion of the O.T. ('first lesson') and that of the N.T. ('second lesson') read at Morning and Evening Prayer in the Church of England.) ME. **3.** A portion of a book or the like, to be studied by the pupil for repetition to the teacher. Hence something that is or is to be learnt. ME. **4.** A continuous portion of teaching given to a pupil or class at one time; one of the portions into which a course of instruction is divided. Hence occas. in text-books, a section of suitable length for continuous study. ME. **b.** *transf.* An instructive occurrence or example; a rebuke or punishment calculated to prevent a repetition of an offence 1586. †**5.** *Mus.* **a.** An exercise; a composition serving an educational purpose. **b.** A piece to be performed. –1811.

3. To learne Any hard L. that may do thee good SHAKS. **4.** *To give, take lessons*: to give, receive systematic instruction *in* a specified subject. Mr. Blagrave..did give me a l. upon the flageolette PEPYS. **b.** His self-denial..was a constant l. 1882. *attrib.*, *l. book*, (*a*) a book from which lessons are learnt; †(*b*) a lectionary.

Lesson (le·sən), *v.* 1555. [f. prec. sb.] **1.** *trans.* To give a lesson or lessons to, to instruct; to admonish, rebuke. Also, To bring *into* or *to* (a state) by lessoning. **2.** To teach (a thing) as a lesson 1821.

1. It ought to l. us into an abhorrence of the abuse of our own power in our own day BURKE.

Lessor (lesǭ·ɹ). 1487. [– AFr. *lesso(u)r*, f. *lesser*; see LEASE *v.*³ -OR 2.] One who grants a lease; one who lets property on lease.

Lest (lest), *conj.* [OE. *þȳ lǣs þe*, 'whereby less that' (*þȳ* THE *adv.*, *lǣs* less, *þe* relative particle), late OE. *þe lǣste*, whence ME. *lest(e*, by aphesis of the first word of the phr.; cf. for the meaning L. *quominus* 'whereby less', lest.] **1.** = L. *nē*, Eng. *that..not, for fear that.* †Also *l. that*, in the same sense. **2.**

Used after verbs of fearing, or the like, to introduce a clause expressing the event that is feared; often admitting of being replaced by *that* (without neg.) OE.

1. Take hede l. eny man deceave you TINDALE *Mark* 13:5. Lord God of Hosts, be with us yet, L. we forget, l. we forget R. KIPLING. **2.** Fearing l. they should succumb 1881.

Lest, obs. f. LAST, LEAST, LIST *sb.* and *v.*

Let (let), *sb.*[1] ME. [f. LET *v.*[2]] **1.** Hindrance, obstruction; also, something that hinders, an impediment. Now *arch.*: most common in *without l. or hindrance.* **2.** In *Bowls, Fives, Rackets*, etc. Obstruction of the ball in specified ways, requiring it to be served again 1608.

1. The enemy wrought his will without l. or hindrance FREEMAN.

Let (let), *sb.*[2] 1838. [f. LET *v.*[1]] A letting for hire or rent.

Let (let), *v.*[1] Pa. t. and pple. **let.** [OE. *lǣtan* = OFris. *lēta*, OS. *lātan* (Du. *laten*), OHG. *lāȥan* (G. *lassen*), ON. *láta*, Goth. *lētan* :- Gmc. (orig. reduplicating) vb., f. **lǣt-* (:- **lēd-*), rel. to **lat-* LATE *a.*]

I. To leave; to allow to pass. **†1.** *trans.* To allow to remain –1651. **†2.** To leave undone; to omit (in reading, etc.) –ME. **†b.** with *inf.* as *obj.*: To order or forbear *to* do something –1653. **†c.** *absol.* or *intr.* To desist, forbear –1554. **†3.** To leave *to* some one else –1612. **†4.** To quit, abandon, forsake; to abandon *to* (the flames) –1599. **†5.** To lose (one's life, honour, virtue, etc.) –1587. **6.** To allow (fluid) to escape; to shed (tears, blood); to emit (breath, etc.). Also, to discharge (a gun). *Obs.* or *dial.* OE. **7.** To grant the temporary possession and use of, in consideration of rent or hire. †Formerly also, to lend (money) at interest. OE. **b.** *intr.* in passive sense = *to be let* 1855. **†8.** To set free, liberate –1670. **9.** To allow to pass or go. ME.

1. *Wint. T.* I. ii. 41. **2. b.** SHAKS. *Lucr.* 10. **6.** *To l. blood* (Surg.): see BLOOD *sb.* I. 1. I'll..L. blood from her weasand SHELLEY. *To l. at* (now Sc.): to discharge missiles at; to assail; to aim at. *To l. into* (slang): to attack. **7.** To l. his labour where it would obtain a better reward 1833. **b.** The mortgaged houses would speedily l. 1885. **8.** Phr. *To l. free, at large.* **9.** They would not l. a single Englishman on board of her 1854.

Comb. with preps. *To l. into*: (*a*) to admit to, allow to enter (*lit.* and *fig.*); †also *absol.*; (*b*) to insert in the surface or substance of; (*c*) to introduce to the knowledge of, make acquainted with, inform about; also, †*to l. into one's knowledge.* *To l.* (a person) *off* a penalty, etc. (Cf. *let off* below.)

II. Uses requiring an inf. (normally without *to*). **1.** *trans.* To suffer, permit, allow OE. **b.** The use of *to* before the inf. occurs chiefly when *let* is used in the passive 1523. **2.** To cause. Now *arch.* exc. in *to l.* (a person) *know* = to inform (of something). OE. **3.** The imperative with sb. or pronoun as obj. often serves as an auxiliary ME. **b.** with ellipsis of *go.* (Freq. in Shaks.; now *arch.*) 1590.

1. I was not let see him J. H. NEWMAN. **b.** If they be..let to run wild KEBLE. **2.** Pray l. me know your mind in this, for I am utterly at a loss POPE. **3.** Leat vs call to memorie, the princes of times past LD. BERNERS. **b.** But com let's on MILT. *Comus* 599.

†III. To behave, appear, think. **1.** *intr.* To comport oneself; to have (a particular) behaviour or appearance; to make *as though* –1787 (*dial.*). **2.** To think (highly, etc.) *of* (occas. *by, to*). *To l. well of*: to be glad of. –1600. **3.** *trans.* with *complement.* To regard as. Also with obj. and inf., or clause: To consider *to be, that* (a person or thing) *is.* –1450.

Phraseological combs. **with adj. as complement.* **Let alone.** †**a.** To leave in solitude. **b.** To abstain from interfering with, attending to, or doing. *To l. well alone*: see WELL *a.* Also *absol.* **c.** *colloq.* in imper.: *Let me* (*him*, etc.) *alone to* (do so and so) = I (he, etc.) may be trusted to do, etc. Also with *for* and †*ellipt.* **d.** The imper. *let alone* is used colloq. with the sense 'not to mention'. (The obj. in this use follows the adj.). **e.** as *sb.* (*let-alone*); now only *attrib.* in the sense of 'laisser-aller'. **L. loose.** †**a.** To liberate, set free. **b.** To loose (one's hold, etc.), slacken (a bridle). **c.** To give free course to, allow to have full swing. †**d.** *intr.* To give way *to.*

***with a verb in the inf.* **L. be. a.** = *let alone*, b. **b.** *absol.* **c.** = *let alone*, d. Chiefly *Sc.* **L. fall. a.** To lower (a bridge, a veil, etc.); *Naut.* to drop an anchor; also, a sail loosed from its gaskets. **b.** To proceed no further with, drop (a business). ? *Obs.* **c.** To drop (a word, a hint), esp. inadvertently. **d.** To shed (tears). **e.** *Geom.* To draw (a perpendicular) to a line from a point outside it. **L. fly:** see FLY *v.*[1] **L. go. a.** *trans.* To set at liberty, release; to relax (one's hold); to drop (an anchor). **b.** *intr.* = to let go one's hold. Const. *of.* **c.** To dismiss from one's thoughts; to cease to attend to or control. †**d.** To fire off (ordnance), discharge (missiles). **e.** To cease to restrain. *To l. oneself go*: in recent use, to give free vent to one's enthusiasm. **f.** as *sb.* An act of letting go. **L. run.** *Naut.* 'To cast off at once' (Smyth). **L. slip. a.** To let go (*gen.*), e.g. to unloose (a knot), to let loose (a hound) from the leash. Also *fig.* **b.** To allow (an opportunity) to pass without profit.

****with advs.* †**L. abroad.** To permit or cause to get about. **L. down. a.** To lower (a drawbridge, steps of a carriage, etc.); in narrower sense, to cause or allow to descend by gradual motion or short stages. Also occas. *intr.* for *pass.* **b.** To lower in position, intensity, strength, †value; to abase, humble. Also, to disappoint. **c.** *techn.* (*a*) To lower the temper of (metal). (*b*) To reduce or dissolve (shellac, etc.) by means of a spirit solvents. **d.** *To be let down*: (of the claws of a hound), to be in contact with the ground. Also, of the sinew of a horse, to give way. **e.** *To l.* (a person) *down gently* or *softly*: to deal with him so as to spare his self-respect. **f.** as *sb.* (*let-down*). An act or instance of letting down: (*a*) a drawback; (*b*) a come-down; (*c*) a disappointment. *slang.* **L. in. a.** To admit; *esp.* to open the door of a house or room to; hence *refl.* to enter a building or room, usu. by means of a key. **b.** To give admittance to (light, water, air, etc.). Also *transf.* and *fig.* **c.** To insert into the surface or substance of a thing. **d.** To give rise to. *Obs.* or *arch.* **e.** Of ice, etc.: To give way and allow (a person) to fall through into the water. Hence *fig.* (colloq.) To involve in loss or difficulty, by fraud, etc. *To l. in for*: to involve in the performance, payment, etc. of. **L. off.** †**a.** *intr.* To cease. **b.** To discharge with an explosion. Hence *fig.* To 'fire off' (a joke, speech, etc.). **c.** To allow to escape; to excuse from punishment, service, etc. **d.** To allow or cause (fumes, sediment, etc.) to pass away. **e.** To lease in portions. **f.** as *sb.* (*let-off*). (*a*) A festivity. (*b*) An outlet. (*c*) A failure to utilize a chance in a game; e.g. in *Cricket*, to get a batsman out by a catch. (*d*) *Weaving.* The 'paying off' of the yarn from the beam; *concr.* a contrivance for regulating this; also *attrib.* **L. on.** *intr.* To disclose or betray a fact by word or look. *dial.* and *U.S.* **L. out. a.** To give egress to; to cause or allow to escape by an opening, esp. through a doorway (also *absol.*); to liberate. *To l. the cat out of the bag*: see BAG *sb.* **b.** To give vent to. †**c.** To allow to go forth freely to (an object). **d.** To make (a garment) looser. **e.** *Naut.* To shake out (a reef). **f.** To lend (money) at interest (? *obs.*); to put out to hire; to distribute among several tenants or hirers. **g.** To divulge; freq. with clause as obj. **h.** To strike out with (the fist, the heels, etc.). Chiefly *absol.* or *intr.* To strike or lash out. Hence, to use strong language. **i.** To give (a horse) his head. Also *absol.*, to ride with increased speed. *colloq.* **Let up.** *U.S. colloq.* **a.** To become less severe; to diminish, cease, stop; *to let up on*, to cease to have to do with 1882. **b.** as *sb.* (*let-up*). Cessation, pause, relaxation 1856.

Let (let), *v.*[2] [OE. *lettan* = OFris. *letta*, OS. *lettian* (Du. *letten*), OHG. *lezzen*, ON. *letja*, Goth. *latjan*, f. *lata-* slow; see LATE *a.* and prec.] **1.** *trans.* To hinder, stand in the way of (a person, thing, action, etc.). *arch.* **†b.** *absol.* To be a hindrance –1642. **†2.** *intr.* To withhold oneself, to desist, refrain; to omit *to do* (something) –1653. **†b.** To tarry, wait –ME.

1. Persons who wilfully l. or hinder any sheriff or constable 1799. 'Sir King, mine ancient wound is hardly whole, And lets me from the saddle' TENNYSON. **2. b.** And in that yle half a day he lette CHAUCER.

-let, *suffix*, appended to sbs. The oldest words in Eng. with this ending are adoptions of OFr. words formed by adding the dim. suffix *-et*, *-ete* (see -ET) to sbs. in *-el* (repr. the L. dim. suffix *-ellum*, *-ellam*, or the L. ending *-ale* of neut. adjs.; see -AL). Examples are *bracelet, chaplet, crosslet, frontlet, hamlet*, etc. Of these only *crosslet* suggests by its form and sense a dim. of an Eng. word. Possibly Fr. dims. were directly imitated by some Eng. writers.

An early dim. in *-let* is *armlet* (sense 2, 'little arm of the sea', recorded 1538); others are *townlet* (*a*1552), *ringlet* (Shaks.), *kinglet* (Florio, after Fr. *roitelet*). But the formation did not become common until the 18th c.

In a few words (*anklet, armlet, necklet*, etc.) the suffix is appended to sbs. denoting parts of the body, forming names for articles of ornament or attire. The oldest word of this type, *armlet*, was perh. suggested by a false analysis of *frontlet*; in the later words the analogy of *bracelet* has prob. been chiefly operative.

Let-alone, *sb.* and *attrib.*: see LET *v.*[1]

Letch (letʃ), *sb.*[1] *Sc.* and *n. dial.* [perh. f. OE. *leććan*, of which it would be the normal representative; see LEACH *v.*] A stream flowing through boggy land; a muddy ditch or hole; a bog.

Letch (letʃ), *sb.*[2] 1796. [perh. f. by-form of LATCH *v.*[1], but the transference of meaning is not clear.] A craving, longing.

The l. for blood which characterizes the savage 1862.

Letch, var. of LEACH *sb.*

Lethal (lī·pǎl), *a.* 1583. [– L. *lethalis*, f. *lēthum*, var. of *lētum* death, by assoc. with Gr. λήθη oblivion; see -AL[1].] **1.** That may or will cause death; deadly, mortal. Now *esp.* of a dose of poison: Sufficient to cause death. 1613. **2.** Causing or resulting in spiritual death; deadly 1583. **3.** Of or pertaining to death 1607.

1. *L. chamber*: a chamber containing gases for killing animals painlessly. **3.** On thy wan forehead starts the l. dew COLERIDGE. †**Le·thally** *adv.*

Lethality (lipæ·lĭti). *rare.* 1656. [f. LETHAL *a.* + -ITY.] Lethal condition or quality; deadliness.

Lethargic (lĭpā·ɹdʒik). ME. [– L. *lethargicus* – Gr. ληθαργικός, f. λήθαργος, f. ληθ- (cf. LETHE); see -IC.] **A.** *adj.* **1.** Affected with lethargy. **b.** *transf.* Dull, sleepy, sluggish, apathetic 1612. **2.** Of or belonging to lethargy 1595. **3.** Causing lethargy 1715.

3. Found to possess l. properties DICKENS.

B. *sb.* A lethargic person. ? *Obs.* 1470.

So **Letha·rgical** *a.*, **-ly** *adv.*, **-ness.** †**Letha·rgious** *a. rare*, lethargic.

Lethargize (le·pǎɹdʒəiz), *v.* 1614. [f. LETHARGY *sb.* + -IZE.] *trans.* To affect with lethargy.

Lethargy (le·pǎɹdʒi), *sb.* ME. [Earliest form *litargie* – OFr. *litargie* (mod. *léthargie*) – late L. *lethargia* (med. L. *litargia*, after med. Gr. pronunciation) – Gr. ληθαργία, f. λήθαργος forgetful, f. base of λανθάνεσθαι forget.] **1.** *Path.* Morbid drowsiness or prolonged and unnatural sleep. **2.** A condition of torpor, inertness, or apathy ME. Also *transf.*

2. Falling..into a carelessness and (as I may call it) a L. of thought DRYDEN. Hence †**Le·thargy** *v. rare*, to affect with l.

Lethargy, obs. f. LITHARGE.

‖**Lethe** (lī·pi). 1567. [L., a use of Gr. λήθη forgetfulness. No river is called Λήθη by the Greeks; the river is Λήθης ὕδωρ 'water of oblivion'.] **1.** *Gr. Myth.* A river in Hades, the water of which produced, in those who drank it, forgetfulness of the past. Hence, 'the waters of oblivion' or forgetfulness of the past. ¶**2.** [? Infl. by L. *let(h)um*.] Death. *Jul. C.* III. i. 206. **3.** *attrib.*, as *L.-flood*, etc. 1579.

3. The fat weede That rots it selfe in ease, on L. Wharfe *Haml.* I. v. 33. Hence **Lethe·an** *a.* pertaining to the river L.; hence, pertaining to or causing forgetfulness of the past.

†**Le·thied,** *a.* [app. for *Lethe'd* (as printed in mod. edd.), f. LETHE + -ED[2].] ? = LETHEAN. *Ant. & Cl.* II. i. 27.

Lethiferous (lĭpi·fěrəs), *a.* Also **letiferous.** 1651. [f. L. *let(h)ifer* (f. *let(h)um* death) + -OUS; see -FEROUS.] That causes or results in death; deadly. So **Lethi·feral** *a. rare.*

†**Lethy,** *a.* 1613. [f. LETHE + -Y[1].] = LETHEAN. Marston.

Let-off, *sb.*: see LET *v.*[1]

Let-pass (letpɑ·s). 1635. [f. phr. *let pass*, after Fr. *laissez-passer.*] A permission to pass; a permit.

Lett (let). 1831. [– G. *Lette* – native name *Latvi.*] **a.** One of a people who inhabit parts of the Baltic provinces of Russia. **b.** = LETTISH.

Lettable (le·tǎb'l), *a.* Also **letable.** 1611. [f. LET *v.*[1] + -ABLE.] That may be let.

Letter (le·təɹ), *sb.*[1] ME. [– (O)Fr. *lettre* :- L. *littera* letter of the alphabet, pl. epistle, written document, literature, culture.]

I. 1. A character representing one of the elementary sounds used in speech; an alphabetic symbol. **b.** *sing. collective* for *pl.* Now only in *before the l.* (= the more usual *before letters*): a proof taken from a plate before the lettering is added ME. **2.** *Printing.* A type;

usu. in *pl.* types; also, a style of printed characters; a fount of type; types collectively 1519.

1. Ouer whose hedde was written in letters of Romayn in gold, *faicte bonne chere quy voudra* HALL.

II. Something written. †**1. a.** *sing.* Anything written; an inscription, document, text; a written warrant –1534. **b.** *pl.* Writings, written records –1789. **2.** A missive in writing; an epistle ME. **b.** *pl.* with sing. meaning, after L. *litteræ* ME. **3.** The precise terms of a statement; the signification on the surface ME. **4.** *pl.* Literature; also, the study of literature, erudition, learning; occas. (later), the profession of literature ME.

1. a. Magicien was noon That koude expounde what this lettre mente CHAUCER. **2.** By penny-post to send a l. PRIOR. **b.** *Letters dimissory, patent, testimonial*, etc. (see the adjs.). *Letters of administration, horning*, etc. (see those words). **L. of advice** (Comm.), a letter notifying, e.g. the drawing of a bill on, or the consignment of goods to, the correspondent. **L. of attorney** = *power of attorney* (see ATTORNEY *sb.*[2]). **Letters of brotherhood** (or **fraternity**), letters granted by a convent or an order to its benefactors entitling those named in them to a share in the benefits of its prayers and good works. **3.** *The l.*: the literal tenor of a law or statement, opp. to *the spirit* (see 2 *Cor.* 3:6). *To the l.*: to the fullest extent; I shall obey you to the l. BYRON. **4. b.** *Man of letters* [= Fr. *homme de lettres*]: a scholar; now usu., a literary man, an author. *Commonwealth, republic of letters*, the whole body of those engaged in literary pursuits. Letters kept pace with art PRESCOTT.

attrib. and *Comb.* **1.** General: as *l.-bag, -clip, -post*, etc.; *l.-sorter*, etc.; *l.-copying, -writing*.

2. Special: as **l.-balance** a contrivance for weighing a l.; **-book**, a book in which letters are filed, or in which copies of letters are kept for reference; **-bound** *a.*, enslaved by the letter of a law; **-box**, one in which letters are posted or deposited on delivery; **-card** [Fr. *carte-lettre*, G. *Kartenbrief*], a folded card with gummed and perforated edges for writing a l. upon 1892; **-case**, a case to hold letters; **-cutter**, one who makes punches for type-founding; so *letter-cutting*; **-founder, -founding, -foundry** (see FOUNDER *sb.*[2] etc.); **-head**, a sheet of letter-paper with a printed or engraved heading giving address, date, etc.; **-high** *a.* (*Printing*), of the height of the ordinary printing-type; **-lock**, a lock which can be opened only by arranging letters on it so as to form the word to which the lock is set; **-paper**, quarto-size paper for writing letters, the smaller sizes being called *note-paper*; **-perfect** *a.* (*Theatr.*), knowing one's part to the l.; **-punch**, a steel punch used in making matrices for type; **-rack**, (*a*) a tray with divisions to hold types; (*b*) a small frame in which letters or papers are kept; **-stamp**, an official stamp for cancelling postage-stamps or for impressing notifications on letters or parcels; **-weight** = *paper-weight*; **-wood**, another name for *leopard-wood* (see LEOPARD); **-worship**, undue attention to the l. of a law, etc.; **-writer**, (*a*) one who writes letters (hence, a title for manuals of letter-writing 1759); (*b*) a machine for copying letters.

Le·tter, *sb.*[2] ME. [f. LET *v.*[1] + -ER[1].] One who lets (blood, property, loose, etc.).

†**Le·tter,** *sb.*[3] ME. [f. LET *v.*[2] + -ER[1].] One who lets or hinders –1616.

Letter (le·təɹ), *v.* 1460. [f. LETTER *sb.*[1]] †**1.** *trans.* To instruct in letters. **2.** To exhibit or distinguish by means of letters 1668. **3.** To affix a name or title in letters upon (a book, a shop, etc.); to inscribe (a name) in letters 1712.

2. Fraunhofer..lettered them and made accurate maps of them TYNDALL.

Lettered (le·təɹd), *ppl. a.* ME. [f. LETTER *sb.*[1] or *v.* + -ED.] **1.** Acquainted with letters; literate. **2.** Of or pertaining to learning or learned men; characterized by literary culture 1709. **3.** Composed of (so many) letters 1608. **4.** Inscribed with letters; *spec.* of a book: Having the title on the back in gilt or coloured letters 1665.

1. Mounsier, you are not lettred? *L. L. L.* v. i. 48. In lettered ease and calm content 1843. **2.** He was a man of l. tastes DISRAELI.

Lettering (le·təriŋ), *vbl. sb.* 1645. [f. LETTER *v.* or *sb.*[1] + -ING[1].] †**1.** Letter-writing –1813. **2.** Putting letters upon (anything) by inscribing, marking, painting, gilding, printing, stamping, etc. Also, the letters inscribed. 1811.

1. I hate l. BYRON.

Letterless (le·təɹlės), *a.* 1618. [f. LETTER *sb.*[1] + -LESS.] Devoid of letters. **1.** Illiterate. Also *absol.* **2.** Having no correspondence 1837. **3.** Having no letters inscribed 1881.

Lettern, obs. f. LECTERN.

Le·tter-press. 1758. [f. LETTER *sb.*[1]] **1.** (Now usu. *letterpress.*) Matter printed from letters or types, as dist. from plates. Also *attrib.*, as in *l. printing*. **2.** A letter-weight 1848. **3.** A copying-press 1901.

Letter(r)ure, var. of LETTRURE.

Lettic (le·tik), *a.* (*sb.*) 1872. [f. LETT + -IC.] = LETTISH. Also, in wider sense, applied to the Baltic group of langs., comprising Lettish, Lithuanian, and Old Prussian, and to the peoples speaking these. As *sb.*, the Lettic or Lettish language. Also **Letto-.**

‖**Lettiga** (letti·ga). 1805. [It. :– L. *lectica* a litter.] A kind of sedan chair carried by mules and seating two persons vis-à-vis.

Lettish (le·tiʃ), *a.* (*sb.*) 1831. [f. LETT + -ISH[1].] *adj.* Pertaining to the Letts or their language. *sb.* The language of the Letts.

†**Lettrure.** †Also **letterure.** ME. [– OFr. *let(t)rëure* :– L. *litteratura*, f. *littera* letter; see -URE.] **1.** A writing, a written book. *Holy lettrure* = Holy Scripture. –1450. **2.** Knowledge of letters; learning –1483.

Lettuce (le·tis). [ME. *letus(e*, obscurely rel. to OFr. *laitue* (mod. *laitue*) :– L. *lactuca*, f. *lac, lact-* milk, so called with ref. to the milky juice of the plant.] **1.** Any plant of the genus *Lactuca*; esp. *L. sativa* or Garden Lettuce, the leaves of which are used as a salad; often *collect.* in *sing.* for the plants or their leaves. **2.** *attrib.* 1540.

1. *Wild l.*: some plant of this genus growing wild; *spec.* in England, *L. scariola* and *L. virosa*; in U.S., *L. canadensis*. For *Cabbage, Cos, Hare, Lamb's L.*, etc., see the first member.

Comb.: **l. -opium**, the inspissated juice of various kinds of lettuce, used as a drug; **-water**, a decoction of l.

Letuare, -ie, -y(e, var. LECTUARY.

Let-up, *sb.*: see LET *v.*[1]

Leucæthiop (liusī·piǫp). Also **leucoethiop, leucœthiop.** 1819. [f. Gr. λευκός white (see LEUCO-) + Αἰθίοψ, Αἰθιοπ- an Ethiopian.] An albino of a negro race. So **Leu:cæthio·pia,** the constitution of a l. **Leu:cæthio·pic** *a.* characterized by leucæthiopia.

‖**Leuchæmia** (liukī·miă). Less correctly **leuc-, leukæmia.** 1855. [mod.L., f. Gr. λευκός white + αἷμα blood; see -IA[1].] *Path.* A disease in which there is an excess of white corpuscles in the blood; leucocythæmia. Hence **Leuchæ·mic** *a.*

Leucic (liū·sik), *a.* 1865. [f. LEUC(IN + -IC.] *Chem. L. acid*, a fatty acid obtained from leucin. *L. ether*, an oily liquid obtained by the action of zinc-ethyl on oxalic ether.

Leucin (liū·sin). Also **-ine.** 1826. [f. Gr. λευκός + -IN[1].] *Chem.* A white crystalline substance, produced by the decomposition of proteins; amido-caproic acid.

Leucite (liū·səit). Also †**leucit.** 1799. [– G. *leucit* (A. G. Werner, 1791), f. Gr. λευκός white; see -ITE[1] 2 b.] *Min.* A glassy silicate of aluminium and potassium, occurring in volcanic rocks. Hence **Leuci·tic** *a.* **Leu·citoid** (*Cryst.*), the trapezohedron or tetragonal trisoctahedron; so called as being the form of the mineral l.

Leuco- (liū·ko), bef. a vowel **leuc-,** – Gr. λευκο-, comb. f. λευκός white, as in:

Leuca·niline, *Chem.* a white crystalline substance obtained from rosaniline, etc. **Leuco·pathy** = ALBINISM. **Leu·cophyll** [Gr. φύλλον leaf], *Bot.* a colourless substance found in etiolated plants, capable of being transformed into chlorophyll. **Leu·coplast** [Gr. πλαστός moulded], **-pla·stid,** *Biol.* one of the colourless corpuscles found in the protoplasm of vegetable cells around which starch accumulates. **Leu·coscope,** an instrument contrived by Helmholtz for comparing the relative whiteness of lights or colours.

Leucocyte (liū·kŏsəit). 1870. [f. LEUCO- + -CYTE.] *Phys.* A colourless or 'white' corpuscle of the blood, lymph, etc. Hence **Leu:cocyto·sis,** Virchow's name for a temporary increase in the number of white corpuscles in the blood.

‖**Leucocythæmia** (liū:kosiþī·miă). Also **-themia.** 1852. [f. LEUCO- + -CYTE + Gr. αἷμα blood; see -IA[1].] *Path.* = LEUCHÆMIA.

Leucoethiop: see LEUCÆTHIOP.

Leucoline (liū·kŏləin). 1852. [f. LEUCO- + -OL + -INE[5].] A coal-tar base, identical with quinoline. Also **Leu·col (-kol)** 1844.

‖**Leucoma** (liukōu·mă). 1706. [mod.L. – Gr. λεύκωμα (Galen); see LEUCO-, -OMA.] *Path.* = ALBUGO.

Leucomaine (liukōu·meˌəin). 1887. [f. LEUCO- after *ptomaïne.*] *Physiol. Chem.* An alkaloid found in the living body as a decomposition product of a protein.

Leucophane (liū·kŏfēin). 1844. [f. late Gr. λευκοφανής, f. λευκός white + φαν-, φαίνεσθαι appear, from its showing whitish reflexions; named by Esmark, 1840.] *Min.* Silicate of glucium, calcium, and sodium. Also **Leuco·phanite.**

†**Leucophle·gmacy.** 1664. [– med.L. *leucophlegmasia*, var. of late L. *-matia* – Gr. λευκοφλεγματία; see LEUCO-, PHLEGMASIA.] *Path.* A dropsical tendency, denoted by a phlegmatic condition of body –1732. So **Leu:cophlegma·tic** *a.* 1668.

‖**Leucorrhœa** (liū:kŏrī·ă). 1797. [f. Gr. λευκός white + ῥοία flow; see DIARRHŒA.] *Path.* A mucous discharge from the female genital organs; the whites.

‖**Leucosis** (liukōu·sis). 1706. [– Gr. λεύκωσις, f. λευκοῦν make white, f. λευκός white; see -OSIS.] **a.** Albinism. **b.** Abnormal whitening of some part of the body.

Leucous (liū·kəs), *a.* 1842. [f. Gr. λευκός + -OUS.] White-skinned; blonde; albino.

Leud (liūd). *Hist.* Also in L. pl. form **leudes** (liū·dīz). 1756. [repr. med.L. *leudes* – OS. *liudi*; see LEDE.] In the Frankish kingdoms: A vassal or feudatory.

Leukæmia, var. (now the usual) sp. of LEUCHÆMIA.

Levancy (le·vănsi). 1695. [f. LEVANT *a.*; see -ANCY.] *Law.* In phr. *L. and couchancy*: the fact of being levant and couchant.

Levant (lĭvæ·nt), *sb.*[1] 1497. [– Fr. *levant*, pr. pple. of *lever*, used subst. for the point where the sun rises. (In Milt. stressed *le·vant.*)] **1.** *Geog.* †**a.** The countries of the East. **b.** *spec.* The eastern part of the Mediterranean, with its islands and the countries adjoining. **2.** An easterly wind blowing up the Mediterranean; a levanter. ? *Obs.* 1628. **3.** = *levant morocco* 1880. **4.** *attrib.* †**a.** = 'east-, eastern', as *l. sea, wind* 1601. **b.** (sense 1 b, 'coming from the Levant'), as *L. feathers, morocco*, etc. 1503.

1. a. *The High L.* = the Far East. **4. a.** Forth rush the L. and the Ponent Windes MILT. *P. L.* x. 704.

Levant (lĭvæ·nt), *sb.*[2] 1714. [transf. use of prec. 1. Cf. Fr. *'faire voile en Levant*, to bee stolne, filched, or purloyned away' (Cotgr.).] *To come the l., run* or *throw a l.*: to make a bet with the intention of absconding if it is lost.

Levant (le·vănt), *a.* 1496. [– Fr. *levant*, pr. pple. of *lever* to raise, *refl.* to rise.] *Law.* Only in phr. *Levant and couchant*: lit. 'rising up and lying down'; said of cattle.

Levant (lĭvæ·nt), *v.* 1760. [f. LEVANT *sb.*[2]] **1.** *intr.* To steal away, 'bolt'. Now *esp.* of a betting man: To abscond. 1781. †**2.** *trans.* To cheat by absconding 1776. In *L. me!*, a mild imprecation. FOOTE. Hence **Leva·nter**[2].

Levanter[1] (lĭvæ·ntəɹ). 1668. [f. LEVANT *sb.*[1] + -ER[1].] **1. a.** = LEVANTINE *sb.* 1 (*rare*). **b.** A ship trading to the Levant (*rare*). **2.** A strong and raw easterly wind in the Mediterranean (Smyth) 1790. Also *fig.*

Levantine (lĭvæ·ntin, le·văntin). 1649. [f. LEVANT *sb.*[1] + -INE[1], after Fr.] **A.** *adj.* Of or pertaining to the Levant; in early use, †eastern. Also, recalling or resembling the manners of the Levantines. Of a vessel: Trading to the Levant. **B.** *sb.* **1.** An inhabitant or native of the Levant 1706. **2.** [Fr. *levantine.*] A very rich stout twilled black silk material 1831.

†**Levation.** ME. [– OFr. *levation* or med. (eccl.)L. *levatio* elevation of Host, levy (of tax), in cl. L. raising, etc., f. *levare* lighten, raise, levy. Cf. next.] **1.** *Eccl.* The elevation of the Host –1559. **2.** *concr.* Something levied; a duty, tax 1690.

Levator (lĭvēi·tǒɹ). 1615. [mod.L. application of L. *levator* 'one who lifts', f. *levat-* pa. ppl. stem of *levare* raise; see -OR 2.] **1.** *Anat.* = ELEVATOR 1. †**2.** *Surg.* = ELEVATOR 2. –1789. Also †**Levatory** (in sense 2).

†**Leve,** *sb.* [OE. *ġelēafa* = OFris. *lāva*, OS. *gilobo* (Du. *geloof*), OHG. *giloubo* (G. *glaube*);

repl. by BELIEF; see BELIEVE.] Belief, faith; *occas.* trust –ME.

†**Leve**, *v.*[1] [OE. *lēfan*, WS. *līefan*, *lȳfan* = OFris. *bi|lēva*, OS. *gi|lōbian*, OHG. *gi-, irlouben* (G. *erlauben*), ON. *leyfa*, Goth. *us|laubjan*, f. Gmc. **laubō* LEAVE *sb.*] To allow, permit. Also (esp. of God or Christ), to grant. –1513.

And leue me nevere swich a cas be-falle CHAUCER.

†**Leve**, *v.*[2] [OE. *lēfan*, WS. *līefan*, shortened form of *ġelēfan*, *ġelīefan*; see BELIEVE.] **1.** *intr.* = BELIEVE I. 1. –1535. **2.** *trans.* = BELIEVE II. 1–3. –1570.

Leve, obs. f. LEAF, LIEF, LIVE *v.*

Levee (lĭvī·, le·vi), *sb.*[1] *U.S.* Also **levy.** 1718. [– Fr. *levée*, fem. of *levé*, pa. pple. of *lever* raise.] **1.** An embankment to prevent the overflow of a river. **2.** A landing-place, pier, quay 1842.

Levee (le·vi), *sb.*[2] Also †**levy, levée.** 1672. [– Fr. *levé*, var. of *lever* rising (subst. use of *lever* inf.); cf. COUCHEE. The pronunc. (lĭvī·) or (levī·) is preferred in the U.S.] †**1.** The action of rising, *spec.* from one's bed –1827. **2.** A reception of visitors on rising from bed; a morning assembly held by a prince, etc. 1672. **b.** In Great Britain and Ireland, an assembly held (in the early afternoon) by the sovereign or his representative, at which men only are received 1760. **c.** A miscellaneous assemblage of visitors, irrespective of the time of day; applied (*U.S.*) to the President's receptions 1766. †**3.** The company assembled at a levee –1771.

2. b. He goes to the Levée once a year THACKERAY. **c.** The evening l. of the Minister of the Home Department 1831.

Levee (lĭvī·), *v.*[1] *U.S.* 1858. [f. LEVEE *sb.*[1]] *trans.* To raise levees or embankments along (a river) or in (a district).

†**Le·vee**, *v.*[2] 1725. [f. LEVEE *sb.*[2]] *trans.* To attend the levees of; to pursue at levees –1770.

Leveful(le, var. of LEEFUL.

Level (le·vĕl), *sb.* [ME. *level*, *livel* – OFr. *livel*, later *nivel* (mod. *niveau*) – Rom. **libellum*, for L. *libella*, dim. of *libra* balance, scales.]

I. 1. An instrument which indicates a line parallel to the plane of the horizon, used in testing the relation to the horizontal of a surface to which it is applied. Also *fig.* †**2.** Level condition or position; horizontality –1726. **3.** Position as marked by a horizontal line; an imaginary line or plane at right angles to the plumb-line, considered as determining the position or one or more points or surfaces 1535. **4.** Position, plane, standard, in social, moral, or intellectual matters 1609. **5.** A level or flat surface 1634. **6.** A level tract of land; applied *spec.* (as a proper name) to *Bedford L.* or *the Great L.* in the fen district of England; *The Levels* (formerly *The L.*), the tract including Hatfield Chase in Yorkshire; etc. 1623. **7.** *Mining.* **a.** A nearly horizontal drift, passage, or gallery in a mine. 1606. **b.** A 'drift' for drainage purposes.

1. *fig.* We steal by lyne and leuell, and't like your grace *Temp.* IV. i. 239. **2.** Phr. *On, upon, a l.*, in a horizontal line or plane. *The l.*, the horizontal; *in l.*, on the ground (cf. L. *in plano*). **3.** Phr. *On a l. with*: in the same horizontal plane as. *To find one's* or *its l.*: said of persons or things arriving at their proper place with respect to those around or connected with them. †*To hold its l. with*: to be on an equality with (Shaks.). **4.** The calamity..had reduced all to one l. 1832. **5.** He..Came on the shining levels of the lake TENNYSON. *The l.*, the earth's surface (*rare*).

II. From the vb. †**1. a.** The action of aiming a gun, etc., aim –1718. †**b.** That which is aimed at; a mark –1600. †**c.** *fig.* Aim, purpose, design –1605. **2.** (*Surveying*) †*To make a l. of*: to ascertain the differences of elevation in (a piece of land). Also, *to take a l.* = LEVEL *v.* I. 4 (absol.). 1693.

1. As if that name shot from the dead leuell of a Gun, Did murder her *Rom. & Jul.* III. iii. 103.

Comb.: **l.-error**, 'the microscopic deviation of the axis of a transit instrument from the horizontal position' (Smyth); **-range** (in *Gunnery*), 'the same as Point-blank Shot, or the Distance that a piece of Ordinance carries a Ball in a direct Line' (Phillips); **-staff** = *levelling staff* (LEVELLING *vbl. sb.*).

Level (le·vĕl), *a., adv.* 1538. [f. LEVEL *sb.*]

A. *adj.* **1.** Having an even surface; 'not having one part higher than another' (J.). **b.** *fig.* Of quantities: Expressed in whole numbers. Of a race: Even. 1826. **2.** Horizontal; at right angles to the plumb-line 1559. **3.** On a level *with* something else. Also *fig.*, on an equality *with*; readily accessible or intelligible *to*. 1559. **4.** Of two or more things: Situated in the same level or plane. Also *fig.* 1601. **5.** Lying, moving, or directed in a (more or less) horizontal plane; esp. *poet.*, e.g. of the rays of the sun when it is low 1667. **6.** Of even quality, tone, or style; of even tenor 1655. **7.** †**a.** 'Equipoised, steady' (Schmidt). See 2 *Hen. IV*, II. i. 123, *Twel. N.* II. iv. 32. **b.** Well balanced: said of the head, etc. Orig. *U.S.* 1870. **8.** Plain, point-blank. KEATS. **9.** *One's l. best*: one's very best; one's utmost (*colloq.* or *slang*; orig. *U.S.*) 1851.

1. Along the l. Seas they flew POPE. **2.** Phr. *L. lines* (Shipbuilding), lines determining the shape of a ship's body horizontally, or square from the middle line of the ship. **3.** We should..apply ourselves to that which is l. to our capacities BUTLER. *L. crossing:* a place at which a road and a railway, or two railways, cross each other at the same l. **5.** The last l. rays were glittering on the stream 1832. **6.** A leisured and l. life 1899. **7. b.** To tell a woman her head is l. is apparently a compliment in America 1870. Hence **Le·vel-ly** *adv.*, **-ness.**

†**B.** *adv.* With direct aim; on a level *with* –1659.

As l. as the cannon to his blank *Haml.* IV. i. 42.

Level (le·vĕl), *v.* Inflected **levelled, levelling** (*U.S.* **leveled, leveling**). ME. [f. LEVEL *sb.*]

I. 1. *trans.* To make level or even; to remove inequalities in the surface of. †Also, to spread levelly. 1440. **b.** *Dyeing.* To make (colour) even 1874. **2.** To place on the same level or plane. Also *fig.* 1563. **3.** To bring to the level of the ground; to lay low, to raze 1614. **b.** To knock (a person) down 1760. **c.** *transf.* and *fig.* To reduce or remove (inequalities) 1642. **4.** *Surveying.* To ascertain the differences of level in (a piece of land); to 'run' a section of; hence, to lay out. Also *absol.* or *intr.*, to take levels. 1598.

1. Phr. *To l. out*: to extend on a level; †*fig.* to contrive, procure (an opportunity). The road that grandeur levels for his coach EMERSON. **2.** Gunpowder leveled peasant and prince 1863. Phr. *To l.* (a person or thing) *with* (now rare), *to*, †*unto*: to put on a level, equality, or par with. Also occas. *intr.* for *pass.* to be on a par with; With such Accomodation and besort As leuels with her breeding SHAKS. *To l. up, down*: to bring up, down to the level of something; Sir, your levellers wish to l. *down* as far as themselves; but they cannot bear levelling *up* to themselves JOHNSON. **3.** Phr. *To l. to* or *with the ground, in the dust.* **c.** The mercantile spirit levels all distinctions LAMB.

II. 1. To aim (a missile weapon); to lay (a gun) 1530. †**b.** To shoot (a missile) *out* (*of* a weapon) –1664. **c.** To direct (one's looks); to dart (rays) 1594. **d.** *fig.* To aim, direct, point 1576. **2.** *absol.* or *intr.* To aim with a weapon; †*occas.* said of the weapon. Also freq. *transf.* and *fig.* Somewhat *arch.* 1500. †**b.** To guess *at* –1596.

1. Phr. *To l. one's aim*; Each at the head Level'd his deadly aime MILT. **b.** [He] leuelled a quarrel out of a cros bowe STOW. **d.** This fellow's writings ..are levelled at the clergy FIELDING. **2.** To leuell at perfection 1626. **b.** *Merch. V.* I. ii. 41.

†**Level-coil.** 1594. [Corruptly – Fr. phr. (*faire*) *lever le cul* (*à quelqu'un*), to make a person rise from his seat (*lever* to raise, *cul* buttock). The Fr. name of the game is *lève-cul.*] A rough, noisy game, formerly played at Christmas, in which each player in turn is driven from his seat and supplanted by another. Hence = riotous sport, noisy riot; phr. *to keep level-coil.* Also *advb.* = turn and turn about. –1684.

Leveller (le·vĕləɹ). Also (now *U.S.*) **leveler.** 1598. [f. LEVEL *v.* + -ER[1].] **1.** One who or that which levels. **2.** One who would level all differences of position or rank among men 1607. **3.** *pl.* Name of a rebel secret society in Ireland in the 18th c. 1762.

1. Sleep is equally a l. with death JOHNSON.

Levelling (le·vĕliŋ), *vbl. sb.* Also (now *U.S.*) **leveling.** 1580. [f. LEVEL *v.* + -ING[1].] **1.** Aiming, aim. **2.** The action of bringing to a uniform horizontal surface, or of placing in a horizontal position by means of a level. Also *fig.* 1598. **3.** *Surveying.* 'The art of determining the relative heights of points on the surface of the ground as referred to a hypothetical surface which cuts the direction of gravity everywhere at right angles' (Gen. Walker) 1812.

Comb.: **l.-instrument,** an instrument consisting essentially of a telescope fitted with a spirit-level, used in surveying; **l. pole, rod, staff,** a graduated pole with a vane sliding upon it, used in levelling; **-stand** (*Photogr.*), an instrument used to support a glass plate in a horizontal position.

Le·velling, *ppl. a.* Also (now *U.S.*) **leveling.** 1635. [f. LEVEL *v.* + -ING[2].] That levels; also, of or pertaining to levellers and their principles.

Leven. ME. Clipped f. ELEVEN, ELEVENTH.

Leventh, clipped f. ELEVENTH.

Leven, var. of LEVIN; obs. f. LEAVEN.

Lever (lī·vəɹ), *sb.* ME. [– AFr. *lever*, (O)Fr. *levier*, alt. of OFr. *leveor* by substitution of suffix, f. *lever* raise.] **1.** A bar of iron or wood serving to prize up or dislodge some heavy or firmly fixed object; a crowbar, hand-spike, etc. Also *fig.* †**b.** *gen.* A bar, pole, or rod –1613. **2.** *Mech.* Name for a rigid structure of any shape (normally a straight bar) fixed at one point called the fulcrum, and acted on at two other points by two forces, tending to cause it to rotate about the fulcrum 1648.

The force to be resisted by the use of the lever is called the *weight*, and the force applied for this purpose the *power*. Levers are said to be of the *first, second*, or *third kind* or *order* according as the fulcrum, the weight, or the power is midmost of the three.

3. *spec.* **a.** *Steam-engine.* †(*a*) = BEAM *sb.* 10; (*b*) a starting-bar. 1758. **b.** The piece by which the barrel of a breech-loader is opened 1881. **c.** In *Dentistry* and *Surg.* = ELEVATOR 2. 1846. **d.** Short for *l.-watch.*

1. *fig.* Jealousy is a potent l. for quickening love 1831.

attrib. and *Comb.* **1.** General: **a.** with sense 'belonging to a l.', as *l.-pin*, etc. **b.** with sense 'acting as a l., worked by a l.', as *l.-corkscrew, -press*, etc. **2.** Special: as **l.-beam** (see BEAM *sb.* 10); **l. escapement** (*Watch-making*), an escapement in which the connection between the pallet and the balance is made by means of two levers; **l. watch,** a watch with a l. escapement; **-wood,** the Virginian hop-hornbeam or ironwood, *Ostrya virginica.*

Lever (lī·vəɹ), *v.* 1856. [f. LEVER *sb.*] **1.** *intr.* To apply, or work with, a lever. **2.** *trans.* To lift, push, or otherwise move with or as with a lever 1876.

Lever, obs. f. *liever*, compar. of LIEF *a.*

Leverage (lī·vərēdʒ). 1724. [f. LEVER *sb.* + -AGE.] **1.** The action of a lever; the arrangement by which lever-power is applied; *concr.* a system of levers. **2.** The power of a lever; the mechanical advantage gained by the use of a lever 1830. **b.** *fig.* Means of accomplishing a purpose; power of action 1858.

2. Phr. *L. of a force*: the distance of the direction of a force from the axis. **2. b.** With regard to such men the moralist has no l. whatever 1883.

Leveret (le·vərĕt). late ME. [– AFr. *leveret*, dim. of *levre*, (O)Fr. *lièvre* :– L. *lepus lepor-* hare; see -ET.] **1.** A young hare, esp. one in its first year. †**2.** *transf.* and *fig.* **a.** A pet, a mistress. **b.** A spiritless person. –1640. **3.** *attrib.*: **l.-skin,** a Japanese glaze, supposed to resemble a leveret's fur. (Rec. Dicts.)

2. b. Arrogant Boasters,..leverets in dangers 1630.

†**Le·vesel.** ME. [perh. repr. OE. **lēafsele*, f. *lēaf* LEAF + *sele* hall; cf. Sw. *löfsal*, Da. *løvsal.*] A bower of leaves; a canopy or lattice –1480.

†**Levet.** 1625. [perh. – It. *levata*, f. *levare* to raise.] A trumpet call or musical strain to rouse soldiers and others in the morning –1705.

Leviable (le·viăb'l), *a.* 1484. [f. LEVY *v.* + -ABLE.] **1.** Of a duty tax, etc.: That may be levied. **2.** Of a person: That may be called upon for contribution 1897. **b.** *U.S.* Of a thing: That may be levied upon (*rec.*).

Leviathan (lĭvəi·ăþăn). ME. [– L. (Vulg.) *leviathan* – Heb. *liwyātān.*] **1.** A (real or imaginary) sea monster, frequently mentioned in Hebrew poetry. **b.** *transf.*; esp. = a ship of huge size 1816. **c.** *fig.* A man of vast power or wealth 1607. †**2.** (After *Isa.*

27:1.) Satan –1595. **3.** Applied to the commonwealth as an organism 1651. **4.** *attrib.* or *adj.* Huge, monstrous 1624; applied recently to coarse kinds of material.

1. There is that Leuiathan, whom thou hast made, to take his pastyme therin COVERDALE *Ps.* 103[4]:26. **3.** The multitude so united in one person, is called a Commonwealth. .This is the generation of that great L. [etc.] HOBBES.

Levier (le·viəɹ). 1494. [f. LEVY *v.* + -ER¹.] One who levies (see LEVY *v.*).

Levigable (le·vigăb'l), *a.* 1670. [f. LEVIGATE *v.* + -ABLE.] That can be †(*a*) polished, (*b*) reduced to powder (*rare*).

†**Le·vigate,** *pple.* [– *levigatus,* pa. pple. of late L. *lĕvigare* make light, f. *lĕvis* light; see -ATE².] Lightened. ELYOT.

Levigate (le·vigĕt), *ppl. a.* Also *erron.* **læv-,** 1826. [– L. *lēvigatus,* pa. pple. of *lēvigare*; see next, -ATE².] *Bot.* and *Ent.* Smooth as if polished.

Levigate (le·vigeˡt), *v.* Also *erron.* **læv-.** 1612. [– *lēvigat-,* pa. ppl. stem of L. *lēvigare* polish, make smooth, f. *lēvis* smooth; see -ATE³.] †**1.** *trans.* To make smooth; to polish –1835. **2.** To reduce to a fine smooth powder; to rub down; to make a smooth paste of (*with* some liquid). Also *fig.* 1694.

2. Levigating it with the oil of sweet almonds 1782. So **Leviga·tion** [– L. *levigatio*], the action of the vb. 1471.

Levin (le·vin). *arch.* Also **leven.** [ME. *leuen(e,* first in Scandinavianized areas; prob. of ON. origin, and perh. based on OSw. *liughn|elder* (Sw. *ljung|eld,* Da. *lygn|ild*) lightning flash, f. **leux-* (see LIGHT *sb.*).] Lightning; a flash of lightning; any bright light or flame. **b.** *attrib.*, as *l.-brand* 1599.

Leviner, corrupt f. LIMER¹, kind of hound.

Levir (lī·vəɹ). 1865. [– L. *levir* brother-in-law, corresp. to OE. *tācor,* OSl. *děverĭ,* Homeric Gr. δαήρ, Skr. *devăr* -.] A brother-in-law, or one acting as such under the custom of the LEVIRATE.

Levirate (lī·vĭrĕt). 1725. [f. prec. + -ATE¹.] The custom among the Jews and some other nations, by which the brother or next of kin to a deceased man was bound under certain circumstances to marry the widow. Hence **Levira·tic, -al** *a.* **Levira·tion,** leviratical marriage.

Levitate (le·viteˡt), *v.* 1665. [f. L. *levis* light, after GRAVITATE *v.*] **1.** *intr.* To rise by virtue of lightness; opp. to GRAVITATE 2b. Now only with reference to 'spiritualism'. **2.** *trans.* †**a.** To make of less weight. **b.** To cause to rise in the air in consequence of lightness. Chiefly with reference to 'spiritualism'. 1686.

2. b. Tables turn, furniture dances, men are 'levitated' 1884. Hence **Levita·tion,** the action of levitating, in any sense 1668. **Le·vitative** *a.* **Le·vitator.**

Levite (lī·vəit). (Now with capital L.) ME. [– Chr. L. *levita, levites* – Gr. λευίτης, f. Λευί – Heb. *lēwî.*] **1.** *Israel. Hist.* **a.** One of the tribe of Levi. **b.** One of that portion of the tribe who acted as assistants to the priests in the temple-worship. †**2.** *transf.* A deacon –1604. †**3.** A clergyman (*disparaging*). Also, a domestic chaplain (cf. *Judges* 17:12). –1849. †**4.** A kind of loose dress. [After Fr. *lévite.*] H. WALPOLE.

3. A young L.—such was the phrase then in use —might be had for his board, a small garret, and ten pounds a year MACAULAY. Hence **Levi·tic** *a.* = next.

Levitical (lĭvi·tikăl), *a.* 1535. [f. late L. (Vulg.) *leviticus* – Gr. (LXX) λευιτικός; see -IC, -ICAL.] **1.** Pertaining to the Levites or the tribe of Levi. **2.** Of or pertaining to the ancient Jewish system of ritual administered by the Levites; also, pertaining to the book of Leviticus 1540. †**b.** Pertaining to ritual. MILT.

1. A L. city 1867. **2.** *L. degrees*: the degrees of consanguinity within which marriage is forbidden in *Lev.* 18:6–18. Hence **Levi·tical-ly** *adv.*, †**-ness.**

Leviticus (lĭvi·tikŏs). ME. [– late L. (Vulg.) *Leviticus* adj. (sc. *liber* book); see prec.] Name of the third book of the Pentateuch, which contains the Levitical law and ritual.

Levity¹ (le·vĭti). 1564. [– L. *lĕvitas,* f. *lĕvis* light; see -ITY. Cf. OFr. *levité* lightness.] **1.** The quality or fact of having comparatively little weight; lightness. Also *fig.* 1597. **b.** In pre-scientific physics, regarded as a positive property inherent in bodies in different degrees, in virtue of which they tend to rise. *Obs.* exc. *Hist.* or *allusively.* 1601. †**2.** Agility –1610. **3.** Want of serious thought; frivolity; unseasonable jocularity (the prevalent sense) 1564; instability, fickleness, inconstancy 1613; 'light' behaviour (said esp. of women) 1601.

1. Phr. †*Specific l.*: cf. *specific gravity* (GRAVITY II. 1. c). Hydrogen. .rises in the air on account of its l. 1869. **b.** Hee. .gave to every nature his proper forme; the forme of levitie to that which ascended RALEGH. **3.** Our grauer businesse Frownes at this leuitie *Ant. & Cl.* II. vii. 128. The Sarmatians soon forgot, with the l. of Barbarians, the services which they had so lately received GIBBON. Her elder sister. .had been distinguished by beauty and l. MACAULAY.

†**Le·vity**². 1613. [– L. *lēvitas,* f. *lēvis* smooth; see -ITY.] Smoothness.

Levo-, Levulin, var. LÆVO-, LÆVULIN.

Levy (le·vi), *sb.* ME. [– (O)Fr. *levée,* subst. use of fem. pa. pple. of *lever* :– L. *levare* raise, f. *levis* light; see -Y⁵.] **1.** The action of levying: **a.** an assessment, duty, tax, etc.; **b.** men for war or other purposes 1607. **2.** The amount or number levied: **a.** †A duty, impost, tax. In a benefit society, etc.: A call of so much per head. 1640. **b.** A body of men enrolled; also *pl.* the individual men 1611.

1. b. *L. in mass* [Fr. *levée en masse*]: a levy of all the able-bodied men. As to the levies, the men enlist unwillingly FROUDE. **2. a.** Great and heavy Leavies upon a poor people PETTY. **b.** The leuie was thirtie thousand men 1 *Kings* 5:13.

Comb. **l.-money,** †(*a*) bounty-money paid to recruits; (*b*) the proceeds of calls from the members of a trade or benefit society.

Levy (le·vi), *v.* ME. [f. LEVY *sb.*] **1.** *trans.* To raise (contributions, taxes); to impose (a rate, toll, etc.). Const. †*of, on, upon.* †**b.** To raise (a sum) as a profit or rent; to collect (a debt); also, to take the revenues of (land) –1768. **c.** To raise (a sum) by legal execution or process. Const. *on* (*the goods of*). Also, *To l. execution for* (a sum named). Also *absol.* 1506. **d.** To impose (service) *upon*; to require (a person's) attendance 1862. **2.** *Law. To l. a fine*: see FINE *sb.*¹ II. b. (See also sense 1.) **b.** To draw up (an objection, protest) in due form 1660. †**3. a.** To set up (a fence, weir, etc.); to erect (a house) –1741. **b.** To plan out (ground) 1500. **c.** To weigh (an anchor) 1648. **4.** To enlist, enrol (armed men); to muster the forces of (a district). Also *to l. up.* Also *fig.* 1500. **5.** To undertake, commence, make (war) 1471. †**6.** To raise (a siege); to break up (a camp) –1628. ¶**7.** Erron. used for LEVEL *v.* 1618.

1. The pension. .is levied by the emperor's officers SWIFT. A fine should be levied on the delinquent 1832. **4.** An army of twelve thousand men was suddenly levied HUME. **5.** The Syrian King. . Assassin-like had levied Warr, Warr unproclam'd MILT. **6.** Albeit hee saw that the siege was levied. .yet [etc.] P. HOLLAND.

Levyne (le·vin). 1825. Also **le·vynite** (1868). [Named by Brewster, 1825, after Prof. Armand *Levy*; see -INE⁵.] *Min.* A white or light-coloured silicate of aluminium and calcium.

Lew (liū, lū). Now *dial.* Also **loo(e.** [– OE. *hlēow-,* stem of *hlēo*; see LEE *sb.*¹] **A.** *adj.* **1.** †Warm; sunny (in OE.); lukewarm, tepid. **2.** Sheltered from the wind 1674. **B.** *sb.* **1.** Warmth, heat. *Obs.* exc. *Sc.* 1591. **2.** Shelter.

Lew, *v. Obs.* exc. *dial.* [OE. *hlīewan* make or become warm, f. *hlēo*; see prec.] **1.** To make or †become warm. **2.** To shelter 1664.

Lewd (liūd), *a.* [OE. *lǣwede,* of unkn. origin.] †**1.** Lay, not clerical. Also *absol.* –1819. †**2.** Unlearned, unlettered. Also *absol.* –1601. †**3.** Belonging to the lower orders; common, low, vulgar –1640. †**4.** Ignorant (implying a reproach); unskilful, bungling; ill-bred, ill-mannered –1710. †**5.** Of persons: Bad, wicked, base; unprincipled, ill-conditioned; good-for-nothing –1709. †**6.** Of things: Worthless, poor, sorry –1692. **7.** [From 5.] Lascivious, unchaste. (The surviving sense.) ME.

7. He had been seen in the company of l. women 1712. Hence **Lew·d-ly** *adv.*, **-ness.**

Lew·dster. [f. prec. + -STER.] A lewd person. *Merry W.* v. iii. 23.

-lewe, ME. *suffix,* OE. *-lǣwe,* with sense 'affected by, liable to, or characterized by' (something undesirable), as in COSTLEW, DRONKELEW. Etym. obscure.

Lewis (lū·is), *sb.*¹ 1743. [perh. f. the name *Lewis.*] An iron contrivance for raising heavy blocks of stone, consisting of three pieces dove-tailed together. Also called *lewisson.* Also *attrib.*, as **l.-hole,** the hole into which a lewis is fitted. **Lewis** *v.* to fit with a lewis.

Lewis (lū·is), *sb.*² 1835. [f. the inventor's name.] A kind of shears used in cropping woollen cloth.

Lewis gun. 1913. [f. the name of the inventor, Col. Isaac Newton *Lewis* of the U.S. army.] A kind of magazine-fed, gas-operated, and air-cooled machine-gun.

Lewth (lⁱūþ). Now *dial.* [OE. *hlēowþ,* f. *hlēow-* LEW *a.* + -TH¹.] Warmth; shelter.

Lew-warm, *a.* Now *dial.* Also **loo-.** 1450. [f. LEW *a.* (used advb.) + WARM *a.*] Lukewarm.

Lexical (le·ksikăl), *a.* 1836. [f. Gr. λεξικός pertaining to words, λεξικόν LEXICON + -AL¹.] **1.** Pertaining or relating to the words of a language. Often opp. to *grammatical.* **2.** Pertaining to, of the nature of, or connected with a lexicon 1873. Hence **Le·xically** *adv.* in respect of vocabulary; according to the lexicons; in the manner of a lexicon.

Lexicographer (leksikǫ·grăfəɹ). 1658. [f. late Gr. λεξικογράφος, f. λεξικόν LEXICON; see -GRAPHER.] A writer or compiler of a dictionary. So **Lexicogra·phic, -al** *a.* pertaining to lexicography; **-ally** *adv.* **Lexico·graphist** (*rare*), a l. **Lexico·graphy,** writing or compilation of a dictionary or dictionaries.

Lexicon (le·ksikǫn). 1603. [– mod.L. – Gr. λεξικόν (sc. βιβλίον), neut. sing. of λεξικός pertaining to words, f. λέξις phrase, word, f. λέγειν speak.] A word-book or dictionary; chiefly a dictionary of Greek, Hebrew, Syriac, or Arabic. **b.** *fig.* (*a*) A special vocabulary. (*b*) A list of words or names. 1647.

Lexigraphy (leksi·grăfi). 1828. [f. Gr. λέξις word, expression + -GRAPHY.] A system of writing in which each character represents a word. Hence **Lexigra·phic, -al** *a.*

‖**Lexiphanes** (leksi·fănīz). 1767. [– Gr. Λεξιφάνης phrase-monger (title of one of Lucian's dialogues), f. λέξις word, phrase + φαν-, φαίνειν to show.] One who uses bombastic phraseology. Hence **Lexipha·nic** *a.*

‖**Lex talionis** (leks tæliˌōᵘ·nis). 1597. [L.] The law of retaliation, 'an eye for an eye, a tooth for a tooth'.

Ley, obs. f. LAY, LEE *sb.* LYE.

Ley, dial. var. LEA *sb.*², *a.*; also, a laying down (see *lay down* i, LAY *v.*).

Leyden (ləi·dən). 1755. Name of a city in Holland, used in the names of certain electrical apparatus invented there in 1745–6: *L. jar* (formerly *phial* or *bottle*), an electrical condenser consisting of a glass bottle coated inside and outside with tinfoil, and having a brass rod surmounted by a knob passing through the cork, and communicating with the internal armature. Also *L. battery,* a battery consisting of several L. jars.

‖**Lhiamba, liamba.** 1861. [Native Afr. name.] Hemp.

‖**Li**¹ (lī). 1588. [Chinese.] The Chinese itinerary measure; $27\frac{4}{5}$ *li* = 10 miles.

‖**Li**² (lī). 1771. [Chinese.] A Chinese weight, one-thousandth part of a liang. (A li of silver = CASH *sb.*²)

li. 1450. Obs. abbrev. of L. *libra* pound, *libræ* pounds –1634.

Liability (ləiăbi·lĭti). 1794. [f. LIABLE + -ITY.] **1.** *Law.* The condition of being liable or answerable by law or equity. **2.** The condition of being subject *to* something, apt or likely *to do* something 1809. **3.** That for which one is liable; *pl.* debts, pecuniary obligations 1842.

1. *Limited l.* (Comm.): the being legally responsible only to a limited extent for the debts of a trading company of which one is a member. Also *attrib.* in *limited l. company.* Also *transf.* **2.** L. to error 1874, to military service FROUDE.

Liable (ləi·ăb'l), *a.* 1475. [– AFr. **liable,* f. (O)Fr. *lier* :– L. *ligare* bind; but if this is the origin the late appearance of the word and its absence from AFr. and AL. records are inexplicable.] **1.** *Law.* Bound or obliged by law or equity; answerable (*for*, also †*to*); legally subject or amenable *to*. **2. a.** Exposed or subject to or likely to suffer from (something prejudicial); in older use with wider sense, †subject to (any agency or change). Normally const. *to*. 1593. **b.** Const. *inf.* Subject to the possibility of (doing or undergoing something undesirable). 1682. ¶**3.** Erron. used for: Incident *to* 1631–1746. †**4.** Subject or subservient *to*; belonging *to* –1616. †**5.** Suitable, apt –1595. **6.** *U.S.* Likely 1901.

1. L. to serve on juries 1825, to income-tax 1867. **2. a.** Not l. to fear or flight or paine MILT. Reasons ..l. to dispute 1801. **b.** Difficulties may be l. to occur BENTHAM. Ground l. to be overflowed 1896. **5.** Apt, l. to be employ'd in danger SHAKS. Hence **Li·ableness** (now *rare*), liability.

‖**Liaison** (li,ē^i·zǫn, Fr. lyęzoṅ). 1648. [– Fr. *liaison*, f. *lier* bind; see prec., -ISON.] **1.** *Cookery.* A thickening for sauces; †also, the process of thickening. **2.** †**a.** *gen.* A close connection 1809. **b.** *spec.* An illicit intimacy between a man and a woman 1821. **3.** *Fr. Phonetics.* The joining of a final consonant (otherwise silent) to a following word beginning with a vowel or mute *h* 1884. **4.** *Milit.* Combination and co-operation of allied forces or arms of the same force. Hence *liaison-officer*. 1915.

Liana, liane (li,ā·nă, li,ā·n). 1796. [– Fr. *liane*, †*liene*, dial. *liorne*, *lierne* clematis (cf. LIERNE), perh. alteration, by crossing with *lier* bind, of dial. Fr. *viorne*, *vienne* :– L. *viburnum* wayfaring-tree. The form *liana* either is a latinization or has arisen from the notion that the word was of Sp. origin.] Name for the various climbing and twining plants in tropical forests.

‖**Liang** (lyæŋ). 1827. [Chinese.] A Chinese weight, about 1⅓ oz. avoirdupois; this weight in silver as a money of account. Also called *tael*.

Liar (ləi·əɹ). [OE. *lēogere* (= OHG. *liugari*, ON. *ljúgari*), f. *lēogan* LIE *v.*² + -ER¹. See -AR³.] One who lies; an untruthful person.

Lyers had nede to haue good memories *Provb.*

‖**Liard** (lyar). 1542. [Fr.; prob. subst. use of *liard* adj. grey (see LYARD, LYART *a.*).] A small French coin worth ¼ of a sou. Hence, typically, a coin of small value.

Liard, var. of LYARD, LYART, grey.

Lias (ləi·ăs). ME. [– (O)Fr. *liais* a hard limestone, prob. of Gmc. origin. (cf. OS. *leia*, MHG. *lei(e* rock, stone).] **1.** A blue limestone rock occurring in s.w. counties of England. **2.** *Geol.* The lower division of the Jurassic series, consisting of thin layers of blue argillaceous limestone 1833. Hence **Lia·ssic** *a.*, also **liasic**, pertaining to the l. formation.

Lib (lib), *v.*¹ Now *dial.* ME. [perh. repr. OE. *lybban = MDu. *lubben* maim, geld.] *trans.* To castrate.

†**Lib,** *v.*² *Cant.* 1567. [Of unkn. origin.] *intr.* To sleep –1859.

†**lib.,** abbrev. of L. *libræ* pounds. ME.

Li·bament. *arch.* 1582. [– L. *libamentum*, f. *libare*; see LIBATE *v.*, -MENT.] = LIBATION.

Libant (ləi·bănt), *a.* [– *libant-*, pr. ppl. stem of L. *libare* taste; see -ANT.] Tasting; touching lightly. LANDOR.

Libard, obs. form of LEOPARD.

Libate (ləibē^i·t), *v.* 1866. [– *libat-*, pa. ppl. stem of L. *libare* taste, pour as an offering, rel. to Gr. λείβειν pour drop by drop; see -ATE³.] **a.** *trans.* To pour out (wine, etc.) in honour of a god. Also, to make a libation to. **b.** *intr.* To pour out libations.

Libation (ləibē^i·ʃən). ME. [– L. *libatio*, f. as prec.; see -ION.] The pouring out of wine, etc., in honour of a god; the liquid poured out; a drink-offering. **b.** *transf.* (somewhat *joc.*) Liquid poured out to be drunk; hence, a potation 1751.

The solemne libations at sacrifices P. HOLLAND. **b.** Libations to his health, or, in plain english, bumpers 1751.

Libatory (ləi·bătŏri). 1609. [As adj., f. LIBATION, after *vibratory*/*vibration*. As sb. – eccl. L. (Vulg.) *libatorium*, f. as prec.; see -ORY¹ and ².] **A.** *adj.* Pertaining to or consisting of libations 1834. †**B.** *sb.* A libatory vessel. BIBLE (Douay) 1 *Macc.* 1:23.

Libbard, arch. var. of LEOPARD.

‖**Libeccio** (libe·tʃo, It. *libe·tʃo*). Also *erron.* **-ecchio.** 1667. [It., f. L. *Libs* (also *Lips*) – Gr. Λίψ, Λιβ-.] The south-west wind.

Libel (ləi·bĕl), *sb.* ME. [– OFr. *libel* (mod. *libelle*) – L. *libellus*, dim. of *liber* book; see -EL.] †**1.** A little book; a short writing –1715. †**b.** A written paper. *Occas.* = LABEL *sb.* –1689. **2.** A formal document; a written declaration. *Obs.* exc. *Hist.* and *Law.* ME. **3. a.** *Civil Law.* The writing of the plaintiff containing his allegations and instituting a suit. **b.** *Eccl. Law.* The first plea in a cause. **c.** *Sc. Law.* The form of complaint on which a prosecution takes place. ME. †**4.** A leaflet, bill, or pamphlet posted up or publicly circulated; *spec.* one defaming some person's character (orig. *famous l.* = Law L. *libellus famosus*) –1776. **5.** *Law.* Any published statement damaging to the reputation of a person. In wider sense, any treasonable, seditious, or immoral writing. Also, the act of publishing such a statement or writing. 1631. **b.** In pop. use: Any false and defamatory statement. Also *transf.* of an unsuccessful portrait, a thing or circumstance that brings undeserved discredit on a person, country, etc. 1618.

1. b. With his testament there were three litle libels or codicils 1603. **2.** Moses permitted a libell of diuorce 1565. **4.** Singeing a pig with a new purchased l. SWIFT. **5. b.** A rich knave's a l. on our laws YOUNG.

Libel (ləi·bĕl), *v.* 1561. [f. LIBEL *sb.*; cf. med.L. *libellare* (XIV) in sense 3.] †**1.** *intr.* To make libellous accusations; to spread defamation 1570–1637. **2.** *trans.* To defame by circulating libellous statements; to accuse falsely and maliciously; *spec.* in *Law*, to publish a libel against 1601. **3. a.** *Eccl.* and *Sc. Law.* To institute a suit against (a person) by means of a libel 1561. **b.** To bring suit in admiralty against (a vessel, a cargo, or its owner) 1805.

1. What's this but Libelling against the Senate? *Tit. A.* IV. iv. 17. **2.** Some wicked wits have libell'd all the fair POPE. Hence **Libellee·**, *Law*, one against whom a libel has been filed. **Libeller. Li·bellist.**

Libellant (ləi·bĕlănt). Also **libelant.** 1726. [f. LIBEL *v.* + -ANT; after *appellant*, etc.] *Law.* One who institutes a suit in an eccl. or admiralty court. Also as *adj.*

Libellous (ləi·bĕləs), *a.* 1619. [f. LIBEL *sb.* + -OUS.] Containing or constituting a libel, of the nature of a libel; also, engaged upon libels.

The l. pen of Martin Mar-prelate HALLAM. Hence **Li·bellously** *adv.*

‖**Liber** (ləi·bəɹ). 1753. [L., = 'bark'.] *Bot.* The inner bark of exogens; bast.

Liberal (li·bĕrăl). ME. [– (O)Fr. *libéral* – L. *liberalis*, f. *liber* free; see -AL¹.]

A. *adj.* **1.** Orig., epithet of those 'arts' or 'sciences' (see ART *sb.* II. 1) that were 'worthy of a free man'; opp. to *servile* or *mechanical*. Later, of conditions, pursuits, etc.: 'Becoming a gentleman' (J.). Now *rare*, exc. of education, etc.: Directed to general intellectual culture; not narrowly technical or professional. **2.** Free in giving; generous, open-hearted. Const. *of*. ME. **b.** Abundant, ample, large ME. †**3.** Free from restraint; free in speech or action. In 16–17th c. often: Licentious. –1709. **b.** Of construction, etc.: Not rigorous; free 1778. **4.** Free from narrow prejudice; open-minded 1781; *esp.* open to the reception of new ideas or proposals of reform 1846. **5.** Of political opinions: Favourable to changes and reforms tending in the direction of democracy. Hence, epithet of a party; opp. to *Conservative*. 1801. **6.** *Comb.*, as *liberal-minded* adj. JOHNSON.

1. L. habits HALLAM, curiosity MACAULAY. **2.** I see sir you are liberall in offers SHAKS. **b.** A l. gift 1602, foundation 1672, offer SCOTT. Women of l. outline 1897. **3.** Your liberall jests Upon his person 1613. **4.** *L. Christian*: in U.S. chiefly applied to the Unitarians and Universalists; in England to those who consider large parts of the traditional system of belief unessential; so *l. Christianity*, *l. theology*. **5.** The L. Government had outlived its popularity 1881. *L. Conservative*, a member of the Conservative party not prejudiced against reform. *L. Unionist*, a member of the party formed by those Liberals who refused to support the Irish Home Rule Bill in 1886.

B. *sb.* **1.** A member of the Liberal party (see A. 5): **a.** in continental politics 1820; **b.** in British politics 1822. **2.** One who holds liberal views in theology. Chiefly *U.S.* 1887.

1. a. Our travellers..continue to resort to Paris ..and occasionally take part with *Ultras* or with *Liberals* 1820.

Hence **Li·beralism,** the holding of l. opinions in politics or theology; the political tenets of a L. **Li·beralist,** an advocate of liberalism. **Liberali·stic** *a.* pertaining or tending to liberalism **Li·beral-ly** *adv.*, **-ness** (*rare*).

Liberality (libĕræ·lĭti). ME. [– (O)Fr. *libéralité* or L. *liberalitas*, f. *liberalis*; see prec., -ITY.] **1.** The quality of being liberal or free in giving; generosity, munificence. **b.** An instance of this (now *rare*) 1526. **2.** Freedom from bias or prejudice; liberal-mindedness 1808. ¶**3.** Liberalism; liberals collectively 1841.

1. His l. knew no bottom but an empty purse FULLER. **2.** Where look for l., if men of science are illiberal to their brethren? LYTTON.

Liberalize (li·bĕrăləiz), *v.* 1774. [f. LIBERAL + -IZE.] **1.** *trans.* To render liberal; to free from narrowness; to enlarge the intellectual range of. **b.** To make Liberal in politics 1853. **2.** *intr.* To be or become liberal 1791.

1. It [the law] is not apt..to open and to l. the mind BURKE. **2.** Russia must l., or be convulsed 1848. Hence **Li:beraliza·tion. Li·beralizer.**

‖**Liberate** (libĕrē^i·ti), *sb.* *Obs.* exc. *Hist.* 1475. [Subst. use of med.L. *liberate* deliver up (imper. pl. of L. *liberare* free, liberate), the word with which the writ commenced.] *Law.* **1. a.** A writ issued out of Chancery for the payment of a pension or other royal allowance. **b.** A writ to the sheriff of a county for the delivery of land and goods taken upon the forfeiture of a recognizance. **c.** A writ issued out of Chancery to a jailer for the delivery of a prisoner who has put in bail for his appearance. **2.** *attrib.*, as **l. roll,** the account formerly kept of pensions and other allowances under the great seal.

Liberate (li·bĕrē^it), *v.* 1623. [– *liberat-*, pa. ppl. stem of L. *liberare* set free, f. *liber* free; see -ATE³.] *trans.* To set free, set at liberty; to release *from* (something). *Chem.* To set free from combination 1805.

To l. the public revenue 1776, acid 1805, slaves 1867.

Liberation (libĕrē^i·ʃən). 1440. [– (O)Fr. *libération* or L. *liberatio*, f. as prec.; see -ION.] The action of liberating or condition of being liberated; setting free.

L. society: short for the 'Society for the L. of Religion from State Patronage and Control', which advocates disestablishment and disendowment of all established churches. Hence **Libera·tionist,** one who belongs to this society; an advocate of disestablishment. **Libera·tionism,** the principles or practice of liberationists.

Liberator (li·bĕrē^itəɹ). 1650. [– L. *liberator*, f. as prec.; see -OR 2.] One who liberates; a deliverer. So **Li·beratress, -trice, -trix,** a female l.

Liberatory (li·bĕrĕtŏri), *a.* *rare.* 1592. [f. as prec. + -ORY².] That liberates or favours liberation.

Libertarian (libəɹtē^ə·riăn), *sb.* (*a.*). 1789. [f. LIBERTY + -ARIAN, after *unitarian*, etc.] **1.** One who holds the doctrine of the freedom of the will. Opp. to *necessitarian*. Also *attrib.* or *adj.* **2.** One who approves of or advocates liberty 1878. Hence **Liberta·rianism,** l. principles or doctrines.

Liberticide (libə̄·ɹtisəid), *sb.*¹ and *a.* 1793. [– Fr. *liberticide*, f. *liberté*; see LIBERTY, -CIDE 1.]

A. *sb.* A killer or destroyer of liberty 1795. **B.** *adj.* Destructive of liberty.

A. Cæsar..the great l. SOUTHEY. Hence **Libe·rtici:dal** *a.*

Liberticide (libə̄·ɹtisəid), *sb.*² *rare.* 1819. [f. as prec.; see -CIDE 2.] Destruction of liberty.

Libertine (li·bəɹtin). ME. [– L. *libertinus*, f. *libertus* made free, f. *liber* free; in sense 2 after Fr. *libertin*; see -INE¹.]

A. *sb.* **1.** *Rom. Antiq.* A freedman; one manumitted from slavery; also, the son of a freedman. **2. a.** *pl.* The name given to certain antinomian sects of the early 16th c. **b.** Later, One who holds loose opinions about religion; a free-thinker. 1563. **c.** *transf.* One who goes his own way 1599. **3.** A man (†rarely a woman) who is not restrained by moral law; one who leads a licentious life 1593.

2. c. The Ayre, a Charter'd L. SHAKS. **3.** Like a puft, and reckless l. Himselfe, the Primrose path of dalliance treads *Haml.* I. iii. 49.

B. *adj.* **1.** Manumitted from slavery (*rare*) 1600. **2.** Acknowledging no law in religion or morals; free-thinking; antinomian. Also *occas.* Pertaining to the sects called 'Libertines'. 1577. **3.** Free or unrestrained generally. Now *rare* or *Obs.* 1589. **4.** Loose in morals; licentious, dissolute; characteristic of or resembling a libertine 1605.

3. The l. ant will choose her own settlement 1768. The transitions are as sudden as those in Pindar, but not so l. H. WALPOLE. **4.** That l. humanism which stamps the Renascence 1886. Hence **Li·bertinage** = LIBERTINISM 1, 2.

Libertinism (li·bəɹtiniz'm). 1611. [f. prec. + -ISM.] **1.** Free-thinking in religious matters 1641. **2.** Habitual licentiousness, *esp.* with regard to the relation of the sexes; the conduct or practice of a libertine 1611. **3.** Unrestrained liberty (*rare*) 1647.

1. Heathen false freedom and l. TRENCH. **2.** Thus are wickedness and l., called a knowledge of the world, a knowledge of human nature RICHARDSON. So †**Li·bertism** (in sense 1) 1644.

Liberty (li·bəɹti), *sb.* ME. [– (O)Fr. *liberté* – L. *libertas, -tat-*, f. *liber* free; see -TY¹.] **1.** Exemption or release from captivity, bondage, or slavery. **b.** In religious use ME. **2.** Freedom from arbitrary, despotic, or autocratic rule or control 1484. **3.** Faculty or power to do as one likes ME. **b.** *Philos.* Freedom from the control of fate or necessity. (Now chiefly in expressed antithesis to *necessity*.) 1538. **4.** Free opportunity or scope *to* do something; hence, leave, permission ME. **b.** *Naut.* Leave of absence 1758. **5.** Unrestrained action, conduct, or expression; licence. (*Occas.* personified.) Now only in sense: An instance of freedom; a licence. 1558. **6.** *Law.* **a.** = FRANCHISE *sb.* I. 2 b ME. **b.** *pl.* Privileges, immunities, or rights enjoyed by prescription or by grant ME. **c.** †Hence *occas.* a person's domain or property. The district over which a person's or corporation's privilege extends. Also (in England bef. 1850), a district within the limits of a county, but exempt from the jurisdiction of the sheriff, and having a separate commission of the peace. 1455. **7.** *L. of the tongue*: space for the tongue of a horse, made by the bit's arching in the middle 1727.

1. To proclaime libertie to the captives *Isa.* 61:1. **b.** Where is the spirit of God, there is liberte WYCLIF 2 *Cor.* 3:17. **2.** Fredome and lyberte is better than ony gold or syluer CAXTON. *Cap of l.*: see CAP *sb.*¹ *Natural l.*: the state in which every one is subject only to the laws of nature. *Civil l.*: natural l. restricted by the nature and necessities of the community. *L. of conscience*: freedom to follow without interference the dictates of conscience in matters of creed or worship. *L. of the press*: the right to print and publish whatever one pleases without previous governmental permission. **3.** I me reioysed of my libertee, That selde tyme is founde in mariage CHAUCER. **4.** There is no l. for causes to operate in a loose and stragling way SIR T. BROWNE. **5.** Libertie plucks Iustice by the nose SHAKS. Phr. *To take the l. to* do or *of* doing something: to go so far, be so presumptuous as to (etc.). *To take liberties*: to be unduly familiar (*with* a person; occas. *euphem.*); to deal freely *with* (rules, facts, etc.). The Mountain Nymph, sweet L. MILT. **6. b.** *Cor.* II. iii. 223. **c.** *L.* or *liberties of a city*: the district, extending beyond the bounds of the city, subject to the municipal authority. *Liberties of a prison*: the limits outside a prison, within which prisoners were occas. permitted to reside.

Phr. *At l.*: not in captivity or confinement; esp. in phr. *to set at l.*, to liberate. Also, free to act, move, think, etc. Also, (of persons or things) unoccupied, disengaged.

Comb.: **l. bond,** one of the interest-bearing bonds of the 'Liberty' loans issued by the U.S. government in 1917–19; **l.-cap** = *cap of liberty* (see CAP *sb.*¹); **-day** *Naut.*, a day on which part of a ship's crew are allowed to go ashore; so **-man; l. hall** (also with caps.), a place where one may do as one likes; **-party** *U.S. Hist.*, a political party which advocated the abolition of slavery; **-pole,** a tall mast or staff with a Phrygian cap or the like on the top; †**l. post,** a post marking the boundary of the Liberties of the City of London.

Hence **Li·berty** *v. trans.* to endow with liberties or privileges; to give liberty to. *Obs.* or *dial.*

Libethenite (libe·pĕnəit)¹. 1832. [Named (*Libethenit*) by Breithaupt, 1823, from *Libethen* in Hungary (now Czechoslovakia); see -ITE¹ 2 b.] *Min.* An olive-green phosphate of copper found in crystals and reniform masses.

L...occurs in quartz 1868.

†**Libi·dinist.** *rare.* 1628. [f. as next + -IST.] A lecher –1634.

Libidinous (libi·dinəs), *a.* 1447. [– L. *libidinosus*, f. *libido, libidin-* lust; see -OUS.] **1.** Given to, full of, or characterized by lust; lustful, lecherous, lewd. †**2.** Provocative of lust. P. HOLLAND. Hence †**Libidino·sity,** lustfulness. **Libi·dinous-ly** *adv.*, **-ness.**

Libken. *Old Cant.* Also †**libkin.** 1567. [f. LIB *v.*² + KEN *sb.*²] A place to sleep in.

‖**Libra** (ləi·bră). ME. [L. *libra* pound (12 ounces), balance, constellation so called. (In med.L. used for 'pound'; hence the abbrevs. £ = pound(s) sterling, lb. = pound weight.)] **1.** *Antiq.* A (Roman) pound. †**2.** Arm of a balance 1797. **3.** *Astron.* (with capital L.) **a.** A zodiacal constellation, lying between Virgo and Scorpio. **b.** The seventh sign of the zodiac (♎), which the sun enters on the 23rd of September. ME.

Libral (ləi·brăl), *a.* 1656. [– L. *libralis*, f. prec.; see -AL¹.] Pertaining to a libra, or to Libra. *L. as*: the Roman 'as' weighing a pound.

Librarian (ləibrēᵊ·riăn). 1670. [f. L. *librarius* concerned with books, bookseller or scribe + -AN.] †**1.** A scribe, copyist –1725. **2.** The custodian of a library 1713. †**3.** A dealer in books. NORTH. Hence **Libra·rianship.**

Library (ləi·brări). ME. [– (O)Fr. *librairie* (now only 'bookseller's shop') – Rom. **librāria*, alt. of L. *librāria* bookseller's shop, subst. use (sc. *taberna* shop) of *librarius* (see prec.), f. *liber* book; see -ARY¹, -Y³.] **1.** A place set apart to contain books for reading, study, or reference. **2.** The books contained in a library; 'a large collection of books, public or private' (J.) ME. **b.** Often a title for a series or set of books uniform in appearance and having something in common, as in 'The L. of Useful Knowledge', etc. 1692. **c.** *transf.* and *fig.*; esp. used to denote (*a*) a great mass of erudition; (*b*) the objects of study, the sources on which a person depends for instruction 1450. **3.** *attrib.*, as *l.-book* 1727, *-door* 1609, *-stairs* 1598.

1. I there saw his l., i.e. the Room which once contained his Books 1779. *Free l.*, a municipal or other l. for the use of the public without payment. *Circulating l.*: a private commercial establishment for the lending of books. **2.** Pisistratus..is said to have been the first person in Greece who collected a l. THIRLWALL. **c.** Tostatus..who was a living l. TRAPP. Cards and men formed the l. of the Duchess of Marlborough J. HAWTHORNE.

Librate (ləi·breⁱt), *sb. Hist.* 1610. [– med. L. *librata* (*terræ*) 'pounds' worth (of land)', f. *libra* pound; see -ATE¹.] A piece of land worth a pound a year.

Librate (ləi·breit), *v.* 1623. [– *librat-*, pa. ppl. stem of L. *librare*, f. *libra* balance; see -ATE³.] †**1.** *trans.* To weigh; to poise, balance; to cause libration in –1806. **2.** *intr.* To oscillate like the beam of a balance; to move from side to side or up and down 1694. **3.** Of a bird, etc.: To poise, balance itself 1786.

2. He..is librating between vice and virtue 1822. **3.** Made to flutter and l. like a kestrel over the place 1829.

Libration (ləibrēⁱ·ʃən). 1603. [– L. *libratio*, f. as prec.; see -ION.] **1.** The action of librating; the state of being balanced or in equipoise. Also *transf.* and *fig.* **2.** *Astron.* A real or apparent motion of an oscillating kind 1669. †**3.** Weighing (*lit.* and *fig.*) –1770.

1. Their pinions still, In loose l. stretched THOMSON. **2.** *L. of the moon*: an apparent irregularity of the moon's motion which makes it appear to oscillate in such a manner that the parts near the edge of the disc are alternately visible and invisible. (There are three kinds, called *l. in latitude, l. in longitude*, and *diurnal* or *parallactic l.*) The moon..is liable to librations depending upon the position of the spectator MRS. SOMERVILLE. Hence **Libra·tional** *a.* pertaining to (the moon's) l.

Libratory (ləi·brătŏri), *a.* 1668. [f. LIBRATION + -ORY².] Having a motion like that of the beam of a balance; oscillatory.

‖**Libretto** (libre·to). *Pl.* **-etti** (-e·ti). 1742. [It., dim. of *libro* book.] The text or words of an opera or extended musical composition. Hence **Libre·ttist,** a writer of librettos.

Libriform (ləi·brifǫɹm), *a.* 1877. [f. L. LIBER + -FORM.] *Bot.* Of the nature or character of liber.

Libyan (li·biăn). 1620. [f. L. *Libya* + -AN.] **A.** *adj.* Of or pertaining to ancient Libya. By some philologists applied to the Berber lang., or the group of mod. Hamitic langs. to which Berber belongs. **B.** *sb.* An inhabitant of Libya; the Libyan language. So **Libyo-,** comb. form = L. and —.

Lice, pl. of LOUSE.

Licence (ləi·sĕns), *sb.* Also **license.** ME. [– (O)Fr. *licence* – L. *licentia*, f. *licent-*, pr. ppl. stem of *licēre* be lawful; see -ENCE. The difference of sp. between sb. and vb. is in accordance with the usage exemplified in *practice* sb., *practise* vb., etc., which seems to be based on pairs like *advice* and *advise*, where the difference depends upon a historical phonetic distinction. The sp. *license* has no justification in the case of the sb.] **1.** Liberty (to do something), leave, permission. Now somewhat *rare.* †Also *occas.* exemption *from* (something). **2.** A formal permission from a constituted authority to do something, e.g. to marry, preach, carry on some trade, etc.; a permit ME. **b.** The document embodying this 1598. **c.** In some Univs., a certificate of competency in some faculty 1727. **3.** Liberty of action conceded or acknowledged; an instance of this ME. **b.** Excessive liberty; abuse of freedom; disregard of law or propriety 1450. **c.** Licentiousness, libertinism 1713. **4.** Deviation from form or rule by a writer, an artist, etc. 1530. **5.** *attrib.*, as *l.-duty*, etc. 1692.

1. And askeþ leue and lycence at londun to dwelle LANGL. Others would confine the license of disobedience to unjust laws MILL. **2.** Phr. *L. of mortmain* (see MORTMAIN). (*To marry*) *by l.* in opposition to *by banns.* Licences to dealers in spirits and wine BURKE. **3.** He..allowed great and public l. to his tongue 1868. **b.** They are for l., not for liberty SHEFFIELD. The intolerable l. with which the newspapers break..the rules of decorum BURKE. **c.** The license of the Restoration 1841. **4.** A lycence poetycall 1530. The poem..allows a metrical l. KINGSLEY.

License, licence (ləi·sĕns), *v.* ME. [f. LICENCE *sb.*, q.v. for the spelling.] **1.** *trans.* To give (a person) permission *to* (do something). Now *rare.* **b.** To permit (a thing) to be done; occas. with *dat.* of the person. Now *rare.* 1477. †**2.** [After Fr. *licencier.*] To give leave of departure to; to dismiss, set free *from*; to send away *to* –1814. **3.** To grant (a person) a licence to do something; *e.g.* to practise a trade, hold a curacy, keep a dog, carry a gun, etc. Const. *for, to,* and *to* with *inf.* ME. **b.** To grant a licence permitting (a house, theatre, etc.) to be used for a specified purpose 1777. **4.** To authorize the publication of (a book), the acting of (a play) 1628. **5.** To allow liberty or scope to; to privilege, tolerate. *Obs.* exc. in *ppl. a.* 1605.

3. Judith Kent, widow, 'Licenced..to vend tea, coffee, tobacco, and snuff' MISS MITFORD. **4.** This play was licensed on June 6th, 1634. 1858. Hence **Li·censable** *a.* **Licensee·**, one to whom a licence is granted.

Licensed (ləi·sĕnst), *ppl. a.* 1593. [f. LICENSE *v.* + -ED¹ or LICENCE *sb.* + -ED².] **1.** Provided with a licence. Now often *spec.* (of a house, etc.) licensed for the sale of alcoholic liquor. *L. victualler*: see VICTUALLER. 1632. **2.** Privileged, recognized, regular, tolerated 1593.

2. Clodius was a l. libertine FROUDE.

Licenser (ləi·sĕnsəɹ). 1644. [f. LICENSE *v.* + -ER¹.] One who licenses; esp. an official who authorizes the publication of books or papers (*l. of the press*), or the performance of plays (*l. of plays*), on being satisfied that law, public morals, or decency are not violated.

Licensure (ləi·sĕnsiuᵊɹ). *U.S.* 1846. [f. LICENSE *v.* + -URE.] A licensing; esp. to preach.

Licentiate (ləise·nʃiĕt), *sb.* ME. [– med.L. *licentiatus*, subst. use of pa. pple. (see next) of *licentiare*; see -ATE¹.] One who has obtained a licence to exercise some function; e.g. **a.** one who has received a formal attestation of professional competence or of proficiency in some art from some collegiate or other examining body; **b.** in the Presbyterian church: One who holds a licence to preach but as yet has no appointment; a probationer 1854.

a. *L. of the Royal College of Physicians* (abbrev. *L.R.C.P.*), *L. in Dental Surgery* (L.D.S.), *L. of the Royal Academy of Music* (L.R.A.M.), *L. of the College of Preceptors* (L.C.P.), etc.

†**Lice·ntiate,** *ppl. a.* 1424. [– med.L. *licentiatus*, pa. pple. of *licentiare*; see next, -ATE^2.] **1.** Allowed, licensed –1676. **2.** Freed from rules; assuming licence, unrestrained, licentious 1593–1656.

Licentiate (ləise·nʃieⁱt), *v.* 1560. [– *licentiat-*, pa. ppl. stem of med.L. *licentiare*, f. *licentia* authority, permission (in cl. L. liberty, freedom, licentiousness); see -ATE^3.] **1.** *trans.* To give liberty to; to allow, permit (something) *to* (a person), (a person) *to* (do something), or *that* (etc.) ? *Obs.* **2.** [After Fr. *licencier*.] To discharge (a servant). BYRON. Hence **Li:centia·tion,** the granting of a licence.

Licentious (ləise·nʃəs), *a.* 1535. [– L. *licentiosus*, f. *licentia* LICENCE; see -OUS.] Characterized by licence. **1.** Disregarding accepted rules, esp. in matters of grammar or style 1589. **2.** Unrestrained by law, decorum, or morality; lax. Now *rare.* 1535. **3.** Libertine, lascivious, lewd. Now the prevailing sense. 1555.

1. Verse..somewhat l. in number of syllables HALLAM. **2.** The lying and l. character of our newspapers JEFFERSON. **3.** Whose l. morals all good men detested W. ROBERTSON. Hence **Lice·ntious-ly** *adv.*, **-ness.**

Lich (litʃ). *Obs.* exc. *arch.* and in *Comb.* Also **lych, lyke.** [OE. *līċ* = OFris. *līk*, OS. *līc* (Du. *lijk*), OHG. *līh* (G. *leiche*), ON. *lík*, Goth. *leik* :– Gmc.* *līkam.*] = BODY. **a.** The living body. Also the trunk, as opp. to the limbs. **b.** A dead body; a corpse OE.

Comb.: †**l.-fowl** = LICH-OWL; **-house,** a mortuary; **-path** = *lich-way*; **-stone,** a stone to place the coffin on at the l.-gate; †**-wal, -wale,** a plant, the gromwell; †**-way,** a path along which a corpse has been carried to burial; †**-wort,** a plant, wall pellitory.

Lich, obs. f. LIKE.

Lichen (ləi·kĕn, li·tʃən), *sb.* 1601. [– L. *lichen* – Gr. λειχήν.] †**1.** = LIVERWORT –1759. **2.** One of a class of small cryptogamic plants, often of a green, grey, or yellow tint, which grow on the surface of rocks, trees, etc. Also *collect.* 1715.

According to the modern theory a lichen consists of a fungus and an alga symbiotically united.

3. *Path.* A skin disease, characterized by an eruption of reddish solid papules over a limited area 1601. †**4.** After a L. use in Pliny: = CHESTNUT 4. –1661.

Hence **Li·chen** *v.* to cover with lichens 1859. **Li·chenal** *a.* of or pertaining to a lichen or lichens; also as *sb.* 1846. **Liche·nic** *a.* pertaining to or obtained from lichens 1836. **Li·chenin** *Chem.* a kind of starch obtained from Iceland moss and other lichens 1835. **Li·chenism,** the symbiosis of alga and fungus in a lichen 1887. **Li·chenist** = *lichenologist* 1833. **Li·chenize** = *lichen* vb. 1839. **Li:cheno·graphy,** description of lichens; hence *licheno·grapher, -o·graphist*; *licheno-gra·phic, -al* a. 1824. **Li·chenoid** *a.* resembling a lichen or the disease lichen 1830. **Licheno·logy,** the science of lichens; hence *lichenolo·gic, -al* a.; *licheno·logist*, one versed in lichenology 1830. **Li·chenose** *a.* = next (*a*) 1855. **Li·chenous** *a.* (*a*) pertaining to, consisting of, resembling, or overgrown with lichens; (*b*) pertaining to or of the nature of the disease lichen 1822. **Li·cheny** *a.* overgrown with lichens 1826.

Lich-gate, lych-gate (li·tʃgeⁱt). *arch.* exc. *Arch.* 1482. [f. LICH corpse + GATE *sb.*^{1}] The roofed gateway to a churchyard under which the corpse is set down at a funeral, to await the clergyman's arrival.

Lichi, var. of LITCHI.

Li·ch-owl. 1585. [f. LICH + OWL.] The screech-owl, so called because its cry was supposed to portend death in the house.

Licht, Sc. f. LIGHT.

Licit (li·sit), *a.* 1483. [– L. *licitus*, pa. pple. of *licēre* be lawful.] Allowable, permitted, lawful.

The consumption of l. or duty-paid opium 1892. Hence **Li·cit-ly** *adv.*, **-ness.**

Licita·tion. *rare.* 1623. [– L. *licitatio*, f. *licitat-*, pa. ppl. stem of *licitari* bid at an auction; see -ION.] Exposing for sale to the highest bidder.

Lick (lik), *sb.* 1579. [f. LICK *v.*] **1.** An act of licking. Hence quasi-*concr.* a small quantity. **2.** *U.S.* A spot to which animals resort to lick salt or salt earth. Also *buffalo-l., salt-l.* 1751. **3.** A smart blow. Also *transf.* and *fig.* 1678. **4.** *dial.*, *U.S.* and *Austral.* A spurt, a spin; a spell of work 1837.

1. To have a l. at the Honey-pot DRYDEN. A l. of court white-wash GRAY. **3.** We're used to a l. of a stick every day S. LOVER. *fig.* A l. at the Laureat CIBBER. **4.** *Big licks* = hard work.

Lick (lik), *v.* [OE. *liccian* = OS. *liccon, leccon* (Du. *likken*), OHG. *leckōn* (G. *lecken*) :– WGmc. **likkōjan*; based ult. on IE. **ligh-* **leigh-* **loigh-*, repr. also by Gr. λείχειν, L. *lingere*.] **1.** *trans.* To pass the tongue over (something), e.g. in order to taste, moisten the surface, etc. Also *absol.* With *off*: To remove by licking. With *up*: To take up by licking. †**2.** To lap with the tongue; to drink, sip. Also *intr.* constr. *of, on.* –1791. **3.** *transf.* and *fig.* (from 1 and 2). **a.** Of persons and animals 1460. **b.** Of waves, flame, etc.: To lap, play lightly over, etc.; to take *up* (moisture, etc.) in passing over OE. **4.** *To l.* (*a person* or *thing*) *into shape*: To give form to; to mould, make presentable, 'as a Bear doth her Whelps' (Burton) 1612. **5.** *slang.* To beat, thrash. Also with *out of.* 1535. **b.** *slang.* To beat, get the better of; to excel 1800. **6.** *slang. intr.* To run or ride at full speed 1889.

1. The danger of licking adhesive stamps and envelopes 1885. Phr. *To l. one's fingers, to l. one's lips*, an action indicating relish or delighted anticipation of food. *To l. the ground, to l.* (another's) *shoe* or *spittle*, actions expressive of abject servility. How does thy honour? Let me licke thy shooe *Temp.* III. ii. 27. *To l. the dust*, †*the earth* [a Hebraism: Vulg. *terram lingere*], to fall prostrate, to suffer defeat. Betwixt them both, they lick't the platters clean RAY. **3. a.** †*To l. up* (an enemy's forces); to destroy, annihilate (after *Num.* 22:4); Yet sometyme thei wer slain, taken, and licked vp, or thei were ware HALL. **b.** The flames..licked up everything in their path 1893. **5.** Say you won't fag—they'll soon get tired of licking you HUGHES. **b.** Phr. *It licks me*: it is beyond my comprehension. *To l. into fits*: y.to defeat thoroughl

Licker (li·kəɹ). 1440. [f. LICK *v.* + -ER^1.] One who or something which licks. Also *licker-up*.

Lickerish, liquorish (li·kəriʃ), *a.* 1500. [Altered f. LICKEROUS, with -ISH^1 for *-ous*. Perverted (XVIII) to *liquorish* to express fondness for liquor.] †**1.** = LICKEROUS 1. Of a cook: Skilful in preparing dainties. –1728. **2.** = LICKEROUS 2, 2 b. 1500. **3.** = LICKEROUS 3. 1600. Hence **Li·ckerish-ly** *adv.*, **-ness.**

†**Li·ckerous,** *a.* ME. [– AFr. **likerous*, var. of *lecheros* LECHEROUS.] **1.** Pleasing to the palate; *gen.* and *fig.* sweet, pleasant, delightful –1603. **2.** Of persons, etc.: Fond of delicious food. Const. *of, after.* –1653. **b.** *gen.* and *fig.* Eagerly desirous, longing, greedy for something pleasant. Const. *of*; also *to* do. –1632. **3.** Lecherous, lustful, wanton –1611.

3. And sikerly she hadde a likerous eye CHAUCER. Hence †**Li·ckerous-ly** *adv.*, †**-ness.**

Licking (li·kiŋ), *vbl. sb.* ME. [f. LICK *v.* + -ING^1.] **1.** The action of LICK *v.* **b.** *concr.* in pl. 1851. **2.** *colloq.* A beating, thrashing (*lit.* and *fig.*) 1756. **3.** *attrib.*, as **l.-place** *U.S.* = LICK *sb.* 2; etc. 1597.

2. The power to take a l. is better worth having than the power to administer one G. MEREDITH.

†**Li·ckpenny.** late ME. [f. LICK *v.*] One who or that which 'licks up the pennies', i.e. makes the money go –1824.

Law is a lick-penny, Mr. Tyrrel SCOTT.

†**Li·ck-spigot.** 1599. [f. LICK *v.* + SPIGOT.] One who licks the spigot; a tapster (*contemptuous*); also, a parasite –1700.

Li·ck-spittle. 1818. [f. LICK *v.* + SPITTLE.] An abject parasite; a toady. Also *attrib.* So †**Lick-spit** 1757.

attrib. A..l. awe of rank THACKERAY.

Licorice, alternative f. LIQUORICE.

Licorous, licourous, var. LICKEROUS.

Licour, -ish, obs. ff. LIQUOR, LICKERISH.

Lictor (li·ktǫɹ). ME. [L., of unkn. origin, but pop. assoc. with *ligare* bind.] *Rom. Antiq.* An officer whose functions were to attend upon a magistrate, bearing the fasces before him, and to execute sentence of judgement upon offenders. Also *transf.*

Lid (lid). [OE. *hlid* = OFris. *hlid*, MLG. *lit* (-*d*-), Du. *lid*, OHG. (*h*)*lit* (now in G. (*augen*)-*lid* eyelid), ON. *hlið* gate, gateway, gap :– Gmc. **χliđam*, f. **χliđ-* cover.] **1.** That which covers the opening at the top of a vessel or closes the mouth of an aperture; the hinged upper part of a receptacle. **b.** The top crust of a pie (*dial.*) 1615. **2.** *Lid* (*of the eye*) = EYELID ME. **3.** Each of the covers of a book (*dial.*) 1459. **4.** *Bot.* and *Conch.* = OPERCULUM 1681. **5.** *attrib.*, as **l.-flower,** a tree or shrub of the genus *Calyptranthes* (N.O. *Myrtaceæ*), in which the upper part of the calyx forms a lid 1653.

1. Phr. (*slang* or *colloq.*) *To put the lid on*: to bring to a close or climax; so *with the lid off*, etc., with everything exposed to view.

Lidded (li·dĕd), *ppl. a.* [OE. *ġehlidod*, f. *hlid* (*ġehlid*) LID. In mod. use, f. LID + -ED.] **1.** Having a lid; covered with or as with a lid. **2.** Of the eyes: Having lids, covered with lids; as *heavy-, high-lidded*, etc. 1818.

Lidless (li·dlĕs), *a.* 1522. [f. LID + -LESS.] Without a lid. **b.** Of the eyes: Having no lids. Chiefly *poet.* = 'ever-watchful'. 1796.

b. Her l. dragon-eyes COLERIDGE.

Lie (ləi), *sb.*^{1} OE. [f. LIE *v.*^{2} (q.v.), repl. OE. *lyġe*.] An act or instance of lying; a false statement made with intent to deceive; a criminal falsehood. **b.** *transf.* An imposture 1560.

It was perhaps a l. invented by political malignity FROUDE. *White l.*: a consciously untrue statement deemed venial or praiseworthy in view of its motive. **b.** Men of high degree are a l. *Ps.* 62:9. Phr. *To give the l.* (*to*): to accuse (a person) to his face of lying. Also *transf.* of facts, actions, etc. Hence occas. *the l.* is used for: The charge of falsehood; He abhors to take the Lye but not to tell it BERKELEY. *Comb.* **l.-tea,** said to be a transl. of the Chinese name for teas coloured for the European market.

Lie (ləi), *sb.*^{2} 1697. [f. LIE *v.*^{1}] **1.** Manner of lying; direction or position in which something lies; direction and amount of slope or inclination. Also *fig.* the position or aspect (of affairs, etc.). **b.** *Golf.* (*a*) The inclination of a club when grounded for a stroke. (*b*) The situation of a ball, good or bad. 1857. **2.** *concr.* A mass that lies; a stratum, layer 1728. **3.** The place where an animal, etc. is accustomed to lie. Also, room for lying. 1869. **4.** *Railways.* A siding into which trucks may be run for loading or unloading. (Also *lye*.) 1855.

1. The general l. and disposition of the boughs RUSKIN. Friedrich understands well enough.. from the l. of matters, what his plan will be CARLYLE. **3.** A very favourite 'lie' for woodcock 1888.

Lie (ləi), *v.*^{1} Pa. t. **lay** (lēⁱ); pres. pple. **lying** (ləi·iŋ); pa. pple. **lain** (lēⁱn). [OE. *liċġan* = OFris. *lidz*(*i*)*a*, OS. *liggian* (Du. *liggen*), OHG. *liggen*, ON. *liggja* :– Gmc. **liʒjan*, f. base **leʒ-* **laʒ-* **lǣʒ-* :– IE. **legh-* **logh-* **lēgh-*, repr. also by Gr. λέκτρον, λέχος, L. *lectus* bed. The form *lie* (repl. normal ME. *liġġe* li·dʒə) is from the stem of the 2nd and 3rd pers. sing. pr. ind. OE. *liġ*(*e*)*st, list, liġ*(*e*)*þ, līþ*. Cf. LAY *v.*]

I. 1. *intr.* Of persons or animals: To be in a prostrate or recumbent position. **b.** To be extended on a bier or the like; to be buried (in a specified place) OE. **c.** To be in one's bed for the purpose of sleeping or resting ME. **2.** To assume a recumbent or prostrate position ME. **3.** To be or remain in a specified position of subjection, helplessness, misery, degradation, or captivity; to be kept *in* prison; to continue *in* sin, etc. †Also *simply* = 'to l. in prison'; occas. idiomatically *to l. by it.* OE. **4.** To remain in a state of inactivity or concealment (not necessarily prone or reclining) ME. **b.** *Shooting.* Of game-birds: To remain crouching upon the ground. (Also *to l. dead.*) 1797. **5.** To dwell or sojourn; *esp.* to sleep or pass the night (in a place), to lodge temporarily. Now *rare* or *arch.* ME. **b.** *spec.* of a host or army (or its leader): To be encamped, to have or take up a position in a field ME. †**c.** To live under specified circumstances or engaged in some specified occupation –1719. **6.** Idiomatic uses (see below).

1. As he lay and read The Tuscan poets on the lawn TENNYSON. Phr. *To l. asleep, sick, dead, in a fever.* **b.** *To l. in state*: see STATE. Two of us in the churchyard l., My sister and my brother WORDSW. **c.** You must l. on the bed which you have made for yourself THACKERAY. Phr. *To l. with* (also †*by*): to have sexual intercourse with (somewhat *arch.*). **3.** Phr. *To l. by the heels* (arch.): see HEEL *sb.*[1] The defendant..was lying in prison as a debtor MACAULAY. Phr. *To l. under*: to be subject to. To l. under a Vow 1701, a delusion ADDISON, a disadvantage 1748. **4.** Phr. *To l. close, low, perdu*, etc., see those adjs. *To l. in ambush, in wait* (see the sbs.). *To l. at catch* or *upon the catch* (? arch. or dial.): to be captious, to seek to entrap a person. *To l. on* or *upon one's arms, to l. on one's oars* (see the sbs.). **b.** Phr. *To l. to the dogs, to the gun*: to permit the approach of a dog or the sportsman without rising. **5.** He lay that night at the deanery MACAULAY. **b.** †*To l. in leaguer*: see LEAGUER *sb.*[1] 1. †**c.** To l. at rack and manger MASSINGER. **6.** †*To l. at* or *upon*: to importune, urge –1737. †*To l. heavy upon*: to oppress, harass –1676. *To l.* †*at, to*: to apply oneself steadily to 1583. †(*With gerund*): To keep on or continue *doing* something (*rare*) –1692.

II. Said of things. **1.** Of material things: To be placed or set horizontally or lengthwise or at rest on the ground or other surface OE. **b.** To be deposited, remain permanently in a specified place ME. **c.** Of a building, etc.: To be overthrown or fallen ME. **2.** To remain unworked, unused, untouched, or undiscovered ME. †**3.** Of the wind, the tongue: To be at rest, subside –1689. **4.** To be situated (in space), to have a specified position OE. **b.** To be spread out to the view 1764. **c.** Of a road, way, journey, etc.: To extend OE. **d.** Of the wind: To remain in a specified quarter 1604. **5.** *Naut.* **a.** Of a ship: To be stationed in a berth or anchorage OE. **b.** To steer in a specified direction 1574. **6.** *fig.* Of immaterial things: To exist, be found, have place, reside (in some specified place or quarter); to be set, fixed, or arranged in some specified position or order ME. †**b.** Of thoughts, inclinations etc.: To have a specified direction –1825. **c.** To rest or be imposed as a burden, charge, obligation, etc. *upon* a person; to press or weigh upon (one's mind or heart) ME. **d.** To be set *at stake*; to hang or depend *on* or *upon* a hazard, etc. 1590. **7.** (Chiefly in *Law.*) Of an action, charge, claim, etc.: To be admissible or sustainable ME.

1. Take as much as lies on a shilling of [etc.] WESLEY. **b.** A Petition from J. Macleod..was ordered to l. on the table 1804. Money lying in the bank (*mod.*). **c.** Phr. *To l. in ruin(s), in the dust.* How do thy towers in ruin l. KEBLE. *To l. heavy*: to be a heavy load *upon* (*lit.* and *fig.*: see HEAVY *a.*[1] I. 1). (Of food, etc.) *To l. heavy, cold*, etc. (†formerly, simply *to l.*) *on the stomach*: to be felt as oppressive. **2.** Phr. *To l. barren, fallow, hid, lea, waste*; also, *to l. on one's hands, at a stand.* Rarely within the living memory has so much of skill lain barren GLADSTONE. **4.** Within the manor of Collingham, where the lands lay CRUISE. **b.** What a future seemed to l. before him! J. PAYN. **c.** There lies your way SHAKS. **5. a.** The Zebra lay just off the pier 1851. **b.** The Success being to leeward, Captain Peard..lay across his hawse NELSON. *To l. the course* (quasi-*trans.*): (of a ship) to have her head in the direction wished. **6.** The fault lies at their own doors 1719. Their sympathies lay wholly with Gruffydd FREEMAN. Phr. *To l. in* (a person): to rest or centre in him; to depend upon him, be in his power (to do). (Now chiefly in phr. *as far as in* (*me*, etc.) *lies.*) *To l. in one's power, in* (or †*on*) *one's hands. To l. in*: to consist in, to have its ground or basis in; Pitt's strength lay in his character 1881. *To l. with*: to be the office or province of (some one) *to do* something. **b.** My humour lyes another way VILLIERS. **c.** These Things..lay upon my Mind DE FOE. With those charges lying upon him BURKE. **d.** He persists As if his life lay on 't SHAKS. **7.** There doth lye an Appeal to the Bishop PRIDEAUX.

¶**III.** *trans.* Used causatively or by mistake for LAY *v.* Now *rare.* ME.

The cloth was lain 1809.

Comb. with advs. **Lie about.** To lie here and there, esp. in disorder. †**L. abroad.** To lodge out of one's own house or abode; to reside in a foreign country; An Embassadour is an honest man, sent to lie abroad for the good of his Countrey WALTON. **L. along. a.** To lie outstretched on the ground (now *arch.*); to extend along a surface. **b.** *Naut.* Of a ship: To incline to one side under pressure of a wind abeam. **L. by. a.** *Naut.* = *lie to*; see BY *adv.* **b.** To remain unused, be laid up in store. **c.** To keep quiet; to remain inactive, rest. **L. down. a.** See sense I. 2 and DOWN *adv.* †**b.** To be brought to bed *of* a child. **c.** (*colloq.*) *To take* (a beating, etc.) *lying down*; to receive it with abject submission. **L. in. a.** To be brought to bed *of*, †*with*, a child; to be confined. Also *fig.* †**b.** To cost, 'to stand (a person) in' so much. **L. off. a.** *Naut.* Of a ship or boat: To stand some distance away from the shore, etc. **b.** To cease work for a time. **L. out. a.** To sleep out, now *dial.* of cattle, to be left unhoused at night. **b.** *To l. out of one's money*: to remain unpaid. **L. over. a.** To be held over to a future occasion. **b.** To remain unpaid after the time when payment is due. **L. to.** *Naut.* Of a ship: To come almost to a standstill, with her head as near the wind as possible, by backing or shortening sail. **L. up. a.** To go into or remain in retirement or retreat; to take to one's bed or keep one's room as an invalid; (of a ship) to go into dock. **b.** *To l. up in lavender*: to be in safe keeping or custody.

Lie (ləi), *v.*[2] Infl. **lying** (ləi·iŋ), **lied** (ləid). [OE. *lēogan* = OFris. *liāga*, OS. *liogan* (Du. *liegen*), OHG. *liogan* (G. *lügen*), ON. *ljúga*, Goth. *liugan*; Gmc. vb. f. **leuȝ-* **louȝ-* **luȝ-* (whence OE. *lyġe* LIE *sb.*[1]).] **1.** *intr.* To tell a lie or lies; to speak falsely. **2.** *fig.* Chiefly of inanimate objects: To convey a false impression; to be deceptive. ME. **3.** quasi-*trans.* with *adv.* or phr.: To take *away* by lying; to get (a person, etc.) *into* or *out of* by lying 1720.

1. He lies, and he knows he lies JOHNSON. Phr. *To l. of* (arch.), †*on*, †*upon*: to tell lies about. *To l. in one's teeth, throat, to l. like a trooper.* **2.** London's column, pointing at the skies, Like a tall bully, lifts the head, and lies POPE. **3.** Go on tamely to allow yourself to be lied into Party blindness 1884.

Lieberkühn (lī·bəɹkün). 1867. [f. the inventor J. N. *Lieberkühn* (1711–56), a Berlin anatomist.] *Optics.* A silver concave reflector· fixed on the object-glass end of a microscope to bring the light to focus on an opaque object. Hence **Lie:berküh·nian** *a.*, in *Lieberkühnian follicles* or *glands*, minute tubular cavities thickly distributed over the small intestines.

Liebig (lī·big). 1869. [f. Baron Justus von *Liebig* (1803–73).] More fully, *Liebig's extract* (*of beef*): A concentrated preparation of beef, containing the salts and extractive principles of the meat, without the albumen, gelatin, or fat.

Lief (līf), *a.* (*sb.*), and *adv.* [OE. *lēof* = OFris. *liāf*, OS. *liob*, *liof* (Du. *lief*), OHG. *liub*, *liup* (G. *lieb*), ON. *ljúfr*, Goth. *liufs* :– Gmc. **leuƀaz*; see LEAVE *sb.*, LOVE *sb.*]

A. *adj.* **1.** Beloved, dear, agreeable, acceptable, precious. Also *l. and dear. Obs.* or *arch.* **b.** In various constructions with *have* (see HAVE *v.*, and cf. Ger. *lieb haben*): *I* (*etc.*) *had* (occas. *have*) *as l. as* (= 'would as willingly'), *I had liefer* (= 'would rather'), †*liefest*, with object a *sb.*, *inf.* phr. (with or without *to*), or clause ME. †**2.** Desirous, willing, glad. Const. *of, to* with *inf.* –1500. **3.** Antithetically to *loath*, in senses 1 and 2. Also *absol. Obs.* or *arch.* OE. †**4. a.** *absol.* = Sir! Sire! Lord! OE. and ME. †**b.** quasi-*sb.* A dear one; a friend, sweetheart, mistress; occas. a wife. So in compar., one who is dearer. –1633.

1. Our sov'reign prince and liefest liege SHENSTONE. Quickly go again As thou art l. and dear TENNYSON. **b.** I had as l. have let it alone 1766. **3.** Now hence must I..be I loth or lief 1883.

B. *adv.* Dearly; gladly, willingly. Chiefly with *would*, pa. subj. Also in *as l.* (*as*), *the liefer*; *l. I were* = I would gladly be. (The advb. use is chiefly due to misinterpretation of the adj. use in *I had as l.*, *I had liefer*; see A. 1 b.) ME.

I would as l. go there as anywhere THACKERAY.

Liege (līdʒ). ME. [– (O)Fr. *lige*, (OFr. also *liege*) – med.L. *leticus*, *læticus*, **liticus*, f. *lētus*, *lītus*, prob. f. Gmc.] **A.** *adj.* **1. a.** Of the superior: Entitled to feudal allegiance and service. Now rare exc. in *l. lord.* **b.** Of the vassal: Bound to render feudal allegiance and service ME. **2.** Of or pertaining to the bond between superior and vassal ME.

1. b. A right to call on every l. subject to render assistance SCOTT. **2.** Homage l. and Feaute ME.

B. *sb.* **1.** = *liege lord* ME. **2.** A liege man. Hence, a loyal subject of the king. ME.

1. Nay, good my L., with patience hear ADDISON. **2.** The emperor's lieges AUSTIN. Hence **Lie·gedom. Lie·geful** *a.*, **-ly** *adv.* **Lie·geless** *a.*

Liege man, lie·geman. ME. [Cf. med.L. *homo ligeus* (XI), OFr. *home* (mod. *homme*) *lige.*] **1.** *Feudal Law.* A vassal sworn to the service and support of his superior lord. **2.** *transf.* and *fig.* A faithful follower or subject 1823.

2. Sworn liegemen of the Cross KEBLE.

Liegier, obs. f. LEDGER.

Lien (lī·ĕn, lĭn, ləi·ĕn). 1531. [– Fr. *lien*, OFr. *loien* :– L. *ligamen* bond, f. *ligare* bind.] †**1.** *Anat.* A tendon. COPLAND. **2.** *Law.* A right to retain possession of property until a debt due to the person detaining it is satisfied 1531. Also *fig.* Hence **Lienee·**, an owner of property on which another holds a lien. **Li·enor,** one who holds a l.

Lienal (ləi,ī·năl), *a.* 1879. [f. L. *lien* spleen + -AL[1].] *Anat.* Of the spleen; splenic.

‖**Lienculus** (ləi,e·ŋkiŭlŏs). 1897. [mod.L., dim. of L. *lien* spleen. See -CULE.] *Anat.* One of the small masses of splenic tissue found in the neighbourhood of the spleen; an accessory spleen.

‖**Lienitis** (ləiĕnəi·tis). 1845. [mod.L., f. L. *lien* spleen + -ITIS.] *Path.* = SPLENITIS.

Lieno- (ləi,ī·no), comb. f. L. *lien* spleen, in adjs. signifying 'pertaining to the spleen and —', as **Lieno-gastric** *a.* pertaining to the spleen and the stomach; **Lieno-intestinal** *a.*

Lientery (ləi·ĕntĕri). 1547. [– (O)Fr. *lientérie* or med.L. *lienteria* – Gr. λειεντερία, f. λεῖος smooth + ἔντερα bowels; see -Y[3].] *Path.* A form of diarrhœa, in which the food passes through the bowels partially or wholly undigested; an instance of this. var. **Lienteria.** Hence **Liente·ric** *a.* of or pertaining to l.

Lier (ləi·əɹ). 1583. [f. LIE *v.*[1] + -ER[1].] One who lies; see LIE *v.*[1]

There were liers in ambush against him *Joshua* 8:14.

Lierne (li,ɔ̄·ɹn). Also †**leyrn.** 1466. [– Fr. *lierne* (XVI), perh. transf. use of the term for climbing plants; see LIANE.] *Arch.* In vaulting, a short rib which neither springs from an impost nor runs along the ridge, but connects the bosses and intersections of the principal ribs. Also *attrib.*, in *l.-vault*, etc.

Lieu (l[i]ū). ME. [– (O)Fr. *lieu* :– L. *locus* place.] Place, stead.

Phr. *In* (*the*) *l. of*: in the place, room, or stead of; A quarter's rent in l. of notice 1891. *In l.* (used *absol.*) = INSTEAD 2 (*arch.*); A better in l. TUCKER.

Lieutenancy (lef-, lefte·nănsi). 1450. [f. LIEUTENANT; see -ANCY.] †**1.** Delegated authority. DONNE. **2.** The office of a lieutenant; e.g. that of deputy governor of a kingdom, etc., of Lord Lieutenant of a county; also, a lieutenant's commission in the army or navy 1450. **3.** The term of a lieutenant's office 1632. †**4.** The district or province governed by a lieutenant –1726. **5.** The body of deputy-lieutenants in a county. Also, in the city of London, the body of commissioners who perform the duties of a Lord Lieutenant with regard to the militia and volunteers 1679.

2. All your lordship can hope for, is only the l. of a county SWIFT.

Lieutenant (lef-, lefte·nănt, *U.S.* liute·nănt). ME. [– (O)Fr. *lieutenant*, f. *lieu* place + *tenant* holder (see LIEU, TENANT, and cf. LOCUM TENENS). Forms with *f*, to which the traditional Eng. pronunc. corresponds, appear in XIV, e.g. *leef-*, *leve-*, later *lief-*, *live-*, *liev.*] **1.** One who takes the place of another; usually, an officer, civil or military, who acts for a superior; a representative, substitute, vice-gerent. †Also *fig.* †**b.** Used as = L. *legatus*, *proconsul*, *suffectus*, Gr. ἡγεμών –1741. **2.** *Mil.* and *Naval.* (Often abbrev. *Lieut.*, and in combs. *Lt.*) **a.** In the army: The officer next in rank below captain 1578. **b.** In the navy: The officer next in rank and power below the commander 1626.

1. They are his Liefetenants, his vicegerents in his Church STUBBES. *L. of the Tower* (of London), title of the acting commandant delegated by the Constable. *L. of Ireland, of a county*: see LORD LIEUTENANT.

Comb.: †**l.-captain,** the officer who commands the company under the captain or in his absence;

-colonel, an army officer next in rank below a colonel, having the actual command of a regiment; hence **-colonelcy; -commander,** a naval officer, in rank next below a commander, and next above a lieutenant; **-governor,** the deputy of a governor, *esp.* (*a*) in the British colonies, the actual governor of a district or province in subordination to a governor-general; (*b*) in U.S., the deputy-governor of a state with certain independent duties and the right of succession to the governorship, in case of its becoming vacant; hence **-governorship,** the office, or the province, of a lieutenant-governor. Hence †**Lieute·nantry** 1552–1676 (chiefly *Sc.*). **Lieute·nantship** 1467 = LIEUTENANCY. Now *rare.*

Lieute·nant-ge·neral. 1483. [After Fr. *lieutenant général*, in which *général* was orig. an adj.] †**1.** *gen.* One who exercises a delegated rule or command; the vicegerent of a kingdom, etc. –1701. **2.** One who acts as deputy to a general. In the British army, an officer in rank next below a general, and next above a major-general. †Also *lieutenant-general of the ordinance.* (In the U.S. army the office is now in abeyance.) 1570.

Liever, var. of *liefer*, compar. of LIEF.

Lif, obs. f. LIEF.

Life (ləif), *sb.* [OE. *līf*, corresp. to OFris., OS. *līf* life, person (Du. *lijf* body), OHG. *līb* life (G. *leib* body), ON. *līf* life, body :– Gmc. **lībam* (**lībaz*), f. **līb-*, the weak grade of which appears in LIVE *v.*]

I. 1. a. Primarily, the condition, quality, or fact of being a living person or animal. **b.** More widely: The property which differentiates a living animal or plant, or a living portion of organic tissue, from dead or non-living matter; the assemblage of the functional activities by which the presence of this property is manifested. Often specialized, as in *animal, vegetable, psychical l.* 1567. **c.** Continuance of animate existence; opp. to *death* OE. **2.** *fig.* Used to designate a condition of power, activity, or happiness, in contrast to metaphorical 'death'. Chiefly in biblical and religious use: The condition of those who are 'alive unto righteousness'; the power or principle by which this condition is produced; also, the state of existence of the souls of the blessed departed. OE. **3.** Animate existence (esp. that of a human being) viewed as a possession of which one is deprived by death OE. **4.** Energy in action, thought, or expression; animation, vivacity, spirit 1583. **5.** The cause or source of living; the animating principle; one who or that which keeps a thing alive; soul; essence ME. **6.** *nonce-uses.* Vitality as embodied in an individual person or thing 1587. **b.** Living things in the aggregate 1728. **7.** (In early use commonly *the l.*) The living form or model; living semblance; life-size figure or presentation 1599.

1. a. The mouing creature that hath l. *Gen.* 2:20. **b.** L. is a state of ceaseless change *Nature*, 1889. **c.** *Tree, water, elixir,* etc. *of l.*, see these sbs. (*A matter,* etc.) *of l. and death*: (something) on which it depends whether a person shall live or die; hence *fig.* (a matter) of vital importance. *Staff of l.*, see STAFF *sb.*[1] *To come to l.*: to regain consciousness after a swoon. So *to bring to l.* **2.** Ȝour lyf is hid with Crist in God WYCLIF *Col.* 3:3. **3.** Phr. *To lose, save, lay down one's l. L. for l.*: a phrase expressing the *lex talionis*. [They] sold their lives very dearely EVELYN. Phr. *For (one's) l., for dear l.*, etc., so as to save, or, as if to save, one's l. (*I cannot*) *for my l., for the l. of me* (in trivial use). **4.** His preaching was without much l. or learning BURNET. **5.** Order, & distribution is the l. of dispatche BACON. *My l.*: my dearest (not now in familiar use). **6. b.** The noise of l. begins again TENNYSON. **7.** Phr. *After, from the l.*: (drawn) from the living model. *As large as l.*, life-size: hence *joc. To the l.*: with fidelity to the original.

II. 1. The period from birth to death OE. **b.** The term of duration of an inanimate thing 1703. **2.** In *Life assurance*: **a.** A person considered with regard to the probable future duration of his life. **b.** Any particular amount of expectation of life. **c.** An insurance on a person's life. 1692. **3.** *pl.* with reference to tenacity of life 1562. **4.** Transf. uses in games. *Cards* ('Commerce'). One of three counters, which each player has; so called because, when he has lost all of them, he falls out of the game. *Pool.* One of three chances which each player has. *Cricket.* The continuation of a batsman's innings after a chance of getting him out has been missed. 1806.

1. Phr. *All my* (*his*, etc.) *l.*: = in or during all my (etc.) l.; used advb. *For l.*: for all that remains of a person's l. *A lease, grant,* etc. *for* (*two, three,* etc.) *lives*: one which is to remain in force during the l. of the longest liver of (two, three, etc.) specified persons. Hence occas. the specified persons are called the *lives.* **b.** The average l. of the steel rails 1889. **2. a.** *A good l.*: one who is likely to live at least to the term assigned as the average 'expectation' at his age. **3.** A cat has nine lives *Provb.* **4.** (*Cricket*) The captain.. received a l...in the slips 1883.

III. 1. The series of actions and occurrences constituting the history of an individual from birth to death. In gen. sense, the course of human existence from birth to death. OE. **b.** A particular manner or course of living OE. **c.** In mod. use: The practical part of human existence; the business, active pleasures, or pursuits of the world. Often with reference to social gaieties or vicious pleasures; esp. in phr. *to see l.* 1771. **2.** A written account of a person's life; a biography ME.

1. (*Anything, nothing*) *in l.*: 'in the world', at all–Is L. worth living? MALLOCK. *This l.* (Vulg. *hæc vita*, Gr. ἡ ζωή αὐτή, 1 *Cor.* 15:19), also *the* or *this present l.*: the earthly state of human existence, as dist. from *the future l.*, the state of existence after death. **b.** *A good, bad, happy, wretched,* etc. *l.* The l. of Sparta was the l. of a camp JOWETT. **c.** To see me happily settled in l. DASENT. **2.** Few authors write their own lives JOHNSON.

IV. Phr. *On life, on live* = ALIVE. *Livesman,* etc.: see LIVE.

Comb. **1.** General: as *l.-experience, -germ,* etc.; *l.-bringing, -saving, -working* adjs.; *l.-teeming* adj.; (with sense 'in, of, for, with, or as l.') *l.-bereft, -weary* adjs.; *l.-struggle*; (with sense 'life-long; during one's whole l., for l.') *l.-annuity, -study,* etc.

2. Special: as **l.-arrow,** a barbed arrow with a line attached, which is fired from a gun to establish communication with a ship in distress; **-assurance** (see ASSURANCE 5); **-belt,** a belt of inflated india-rubber, of cork, or the like, used to support the body in the water; **-boat,** a boat specially constructed for saving l. at sea; **-breath,** the breath which supports l.; also *fig.*; **-buoy** (see BUOY *sb.* 1 b); **-cycle** *Biol.* = *life-history*; **-estate,** an estate held for a person's l.; **-force,** vital energy; **-history** *Biol.*, the series of developments of an organism from the egg to the adult state; also, an account of these; **-hold,** property held for a l. or lives; **-insurance** (see INSURANCE 4); **-interest,** an interest or estate which determines on the falling of a l.; **-jacket** (cf. *l.-belt*); **-line,** a rope used for saving l., e.g. that attached to a life-buoy, etc.; also, the line of life (LINE *sb.*[2] I.1 g); **-mortar,** a mortar for discharging a life-rocket; **-office,** an institution where life-insurances can be effected; **-peer,** a peer whose title lapses at his death; so *life-peerage*; **-raft,** a kind of raft for saving l. in a shipwreck; **-rate,** the rate at which a l. is insured; **-rocket** (cf. *life-arrow*); so **-shot; -spring,** the source of l.; **-string,** a string or nerve supposed to be essential to l.; *pl.* what is essential to the support of l.; **-table,** a table exhibiting statistics as to the probability of life at different ages; **-tenant,** a tenant for life **-work,** the work of a lifetime.

Li·fe-blood. 1590. **1.** The blood necessary to life. **2.** *transf.* and *fig.* The vital part or vitalizing influence 1596. **3.** (Also *live-blood.*) Popular name for an involuntary twitching of the lip or eyelid 1733.

2. A good Booke is the pretious life-blood of a master spirit MILT.

Lifeful (ləi·fˌfŭl), *a. rare.* ME. [f. LIFE *sb.* + -FUL.] Full of life; having or giving life or vitality. Hence **Li·feful-ly** *adv.*, **-ness.**

Life-giver. 1598. One who or that which gives life. So **Life-giving** *sb.* and *a.* 1561.

Li·fe-guard. 1648. [prob. after Du. †*lijfgarde*, G. *leibgarde* (in which the first element means 'body'), later assoc. with *life.*] **1.** A body-guard of soldiers; now *pl.* (written *Life Guards*), in the British army, two regiments of the household cavalry. Also *attrib.* **2.** The guard or protection of a person's life; a protecting agent or influence. ? *Obs.* 1648. **3.** A device attached to the front of a locomotive for sweeping up small obstructions 1864. **4.** *U.S.* A person employed to save bathers, etc. from drowning 1896.

1. *attrib.* **Life-guard-man,** a member of a life-guard; also *Life Guardsman,* one of the Life Guards.

Lifeless (ləi·fˌlės), *a.* [OE. *līflēas*; see LIFE *sb.*, -LESS.] Having no life: dead; insensible 1651; inanimate OE.; wanting vital quality or animation ME.; devoid of life or living beings 1728.

A l. carcass 1586. A liveless image HEYWOOD. This market is lagging again...Flax l. 1890. Treeless, herbless, l. mountain BROWNING. **Li·feless-ly** *adv.*, **-ness.**

Life-like, lifelike (ləi·fˌləik), *a.* 1514. **1.** Likely to live. Only in *phrase.* **2.** Resembling life; exactly like a real person or thing 1725. **3.** as *adv.* With animation or liveliness 1839. Hence **Li·felikeness.**

1. Here, mother..I'm living and l., thank God 1881.

Lifelong (ləi·fˌlǫŋ), *a.* 1757. [f. LIFE *sb.* + LONG.] †**1.** = LIVELONG *a.* 1. **2.** Continuing for a lifetime 1855. **3.** as *adv.* LOWELL.

†**Lifen,** *v.* [f. LIFE *sb.* + -EN[5].] To make lifelike. MARSTON.

Life-preserver. 1638. **1.** One who preserves life. SIR T. HERBERT. **2.** A contrivance, e.g. a life-belt, or the like, used in saving life at sea 1804. **3.** A stick or bludgeon loaded with lead, for self-defence 1837.

Lifer (ləi·fəɹ). *slang.* 1830. [f. LIFE *sb.* + -ER[1].] **1.** One sentenced to penal servitude (earlier, transportation) for life. **2.** A sentence for life 1832.

Liferent (ləi·fˌrent). 1491. *Sc. Law.* A rent which one receives for life, usually for support; the right to use and enjoy property during one's life. Hence **Li·fere:nter, Liferentrix.**

Life-size, *a.* 1841. (Of a picture or statue) equal in size to the original. **Life-sized** *a.*

Lifesome (ləi·fsŏm), *a. rare.* 1583. [f. LIFE *sb.* + -SOME[1].] †**1.** Fraught with life. **2.** Full of animation, lively 1688. Hence **Li·fesome-ly** *adv.*, **-ness.**

Lifetime (ləi·ftəim). ME. The time that life continues.

Liflod(e, obs. f. LIVELIHOOD[1].

Lift (lift), *sb.*[1] *Obs.* exc. *Sc.* and *poet.* [OE. *lyft*, corresp. to OS., OHG. *luft* (Du. *lucht*, G. *luft*), ON. *lopt* (see LOFT *sb.*), Goth. *luftus* :– Gmc. **luftuz* air, sky.] The sky, upper regions; †earlier also, the air, atmosphere. Also *pl.*, the (seven) heavens.

Lift (lift), *sb.*[2] ME. [f. LIFT *v.*]

I. 1. The action or an act of lifting (see also DEAD LIFT); a raising or rising; the distance through which anything is lifted and moved 1470. **b.** A help on the way given to a foot passenger by taking him into a vehicle 1712. **2.** *fig.* A 'rise'; promotion; a rise in price; an act of helping, or a circumstance that helps, to a better position 1622. †**b.** An emergency; = DEAD LIFT 2. –1632. **3.** An act of lifting or stealing; †a shift, trick. *Obs.* exc. *dial.* 1592. **4.** Elevated carriage (of the head, neck, etc.) 1835. **5.** *techn.* See below.

1. The Goat..gives the Fox a L., and so Out he Springs 1692. There was so much l. of sea 1857. **2.** The only l. to set him upon his legs PEPYS. A l. in the Navy BURKE. **5.** *Engineering.* The action of lifting a load through a vertical distance, or one of several successive distances. Hence *Coal-mining,* a series of workings being prosecuted to the rise at one time 1702. *Horology.* The amount of motion of a watch-balance produced by each impulse of vibration 1884. The extent to which anything rises, e.g. a safety-valve, the pestle of an ore stamp, the water in a canal lock 1829. *Aeronaut.* The upward pressure which the air exerts on a flying machine; the total weight which a flying machine can raise 1902.

†**II.** A person who lifts something; a thief (*slang*) –1630.

III. 1. *Naut.* pl. 'Ropes which reach from each mast-head to their respective yard-arms to steady and suspend the ends' (Smyth) 1485. **2.** *Shoemaking.* A layer of leather in the heel of a boot 1677. **3.** A hoist; = ELEVATOR 3 c. Also the well or vertical opening in which this works. 1851. **4.** A set of pumps in a mine; also, the section of a shaft occupied by one set 1849.

IV. 1. The quantity or weight that can be lifted at one time. Also *Sc.* a large quantity. ME. **2.** *dial.* A gate without hinges, that must be lifted 1674. **3.** *dial.* A particular joint or cut of meat, usu. of beef 1688. **4.** A rising ground 1825.

attrib. and *Comb.*, as (sense I. 1) *l.-capstan, -pulley,* (sense III. 3) *l.-attendant, -railway, -shaft, -well*; also, **l.-bridge,** a bridge that may be raised to let a boat pass, e.g. on a canal; **-gate** = sense IV. 2; **-hammer** = *tilt-hammer*; **-latch,** one that rises and falls; **-lock,** a canal lock; **-pump,** any pump other than a force-pump; **-tenter,** in windmills, a governor for regulating the speed, by adjusting the sails, or for adjusting the action of grinding machinery.

Lift (lift), *v.* ME. [– ON. *lypta* = MHG., G. *lüften* :– Gmc. *luftjan, f. *luftuz air, sky; see LIFT *sb.*[1]] **1.** *trans.* To raise into the air from the ground, or to a higher position; to elevate, heave, hoist. †Also, to erect (a building). Also with *up, aloft, away, off, out,* etc. **b.** *Sc.* To take up, pick up. Hence in *Golf*: To take up the ball. 1596. **c.** *colloq.* To bring (a constellation) above the horizon in sailing, etc. 1891. **2.** In immaterial sense and *fig.*: To elevate, raise. Also with *out, up,* etc. ME. **b.** To raise in dignity, rank, etc.; to exalt. Also with *up,* etc. Now *rare.* ME. **c.** Chiefly with *up*: To cheer, encourage. Also, to elate, puff up. 1450. **3.** *intr.* for *refl.* (also with *up*). To rise. Said *esp.* of a vessel riding on the waves. Also quasi-*pass.* (e.g. of a window): To admit of being raised. ME. **b.** Of clouds, fog, etc.: To rise and disperse. Also (*U.S.*) of rain: To cease temporarily. 1834. **c.** Of a floor, etc.: To swell or warp and rise 1793. †**4.** *To l. at*: **a.** To pull at (something) in trying to raise it (*lit.* and *fig.*). **b.** To rise in opposition to. –1704. **5.** *trans.* In various phrases, chiefly Hebraisms. See below. **6.** To bear or carry high 1671. **7.** To take up or collect (rents, etc.); to levy (contributions, fines, etc.); to draw (wages, profits, etc.). Now *dial.* ME. **8.** *slang.* To take up (a portable object) or drive away (cattle) with dishonest intentions; hence, to steal. Cf. *shop-lifting.* 1526. Also *transf.* †**9.** To carve (a swan). *techn.* 1500. **10.** *Cards. intr.* To cut (for deal). ? *Obs.* 1599. **11.** *trans.* To take up and remove; to drive (cattle) away or to market, to strike (a tent) 1670. **12.** To take up out of the ground; to dig up (potatoes) 1844. **13.** To hit (the ball) into the air; esp. in *Cricket* 1874.

1. He lifted his cane *in terrorem* SCOTT. **c.** She'll [a steamer] l. the Southern Cross in a week R. KIPLING. **2. b.** *absol.* The Lord..bringeth low, and lifteth vp 1 *Sam.* 2:7. **c.** His heart was lifted vp to his destruction 2 *Chron.* 26:16. **d.** To raise in price, value, or amount 1907. **5.** Phr. *To l. (up) one's eyes, brow, face, visage*: to look up (*lit.* and *fig.*). *To l. (up) the hand(s,* (occas. *one's arm*): (*a*) *gen.*; (*b*) in prayer, thanksgiving, etc.; (*c*) in taking an oath; (*d*) in hostility *against* (a person); (*e*) to do a stroke of work (*mod. slang*). *To l. up one's head*: (*a*) *literally*; (*b*) *fig.* to regain courage or energy; to rally; †*To l. up the head of* (a person): used in the Bible for: to bring out from prison. *To l. up one's heart, mind, soul*: to raise one's thoughts or desires; to exalt oneself (with pride). *To l. (up) a cry, one's voice,* etc.: to cry out loudly; also *fig.* *To l. up one's heel, horn* (see those sbs.). **8.** He took to his old courses, and lifted a purse here, and a watch there THACKERAY. **11.** Some hot-headed proposals were made, one being to l. tools at once 1896. **13.** W. G. lifted Spofforth (i.e. the ball bowled by him) round to the leg boundary 1882. Hence **Li·ftable** *a.*

Lifter (li·ftəɹ). 1535. [f. LIFT *v.* + -ER[1].] **1.** One who lifts or raises. Also with *up.* **b.** A thief. Cf. *cattle, shop-l.* 1592. **2.** Something which lifts or is used for lifting. Also with *up.* 1570. **b.** *Founding.* 'A tool for dressing the mould; also a contrivance attached to a cope to hold the sand together when the cope is lifted' (Webster) 1864.

Lifting (li·ftiŋ), *vbl. sb.* ME. [f. LIFT *v.* + -ING[1].] The action of LIFT *v.* Also *lifting up.*

attrib. and *Comb.* **a.** *gen.*, as *l. power*, etc.; **b.** a contrivance or portion of a machine adapted for lifting, as *l.-bar, -crane, -gear,* etc.; **l.-cam,** a cam or projection by which a l. movement is effected, e.g. in firearms; **-dog,** (*a*) = *lifting-cam*; (*b*) a claw-hook for grasping a column of bore-rods while raising or lowering them; **-jack** (see JACK *sb.*[1] II. 4.).

Lifting (li·ftiŋ), *ppl. a.* ME. [f. LIFT *v.* + -ING[2].] That lifts.

Comb.: **l.-bridge,** a bridge of which either a part or the whole may be drawn up at one end when needful; **-gate** = LIFT *sb.*[2] IV. 2; **-pump,** any pump other than a force-pump; **-sail,** a sail whose action tends to lift the bows out of the water; **-set,** the series of pumps by which water is raised from the bottom of a mine by successive lifts.

Lig, obs. and dial. f. LIE *v.*[1]

Ligament (li·gămĕnt). ME. [– L. *ligamentum*, f. *ligare* bind, tie; see -MENT.] **1.** Anything used in binding or tying; a band, tie; *Surg.* a bandage, ligature. *Obs.* in lit. sense. –1753. **b.** *fig.* Chiefly, a tie, bond of union ME. **2.** *Anat.* Any short band of tough, flexible, fibrous tissue which binds two bones of the body together. Hence, any membranous fold which supports an organ and keeps it in position. ME. **b.** A similar part in lower organisms 1797. **c.** *spec.* in *Conch.* The elastic substance which holds together the valves of a bivalve shell 1816.

Hence **Ligame·ntal, Ligame·ntary, Ligame·ntous** *adjs.*, of the nature of a l.; composed of the tissue proper to ligaments; of or pertaining to a l. **Ligame·ntously** *adv.* by ligaments.

Ligan, obs. f. LAGAN, wreckage.

Ligate (ləi·geit), *v.* 1599. [– *ligat-*, pa. ppl. stem of L. *ligare* tie, bind; see -ATE[3].] Chiefly *Surg.* To bind with a ligature or bandage; *spec.* to tie up (a bleeding artery, etc.).

Ligation (ləigēi·ʃən). 1597. [– late L. *ligatio*, f. as prec.; see -ION.] †**1.** The action or process of binding; the condition of being bound; suspension (of the faculties) –1684. **2.** The action of binding with a ligature; *esp.* in *Surg.*, the operation of tying up (a bleeding artery, etc.). Also, an instance of this. 1597. **3.** A ligature, bandage, bond, tie; also, the place of tying (*arch.*) 1597.

3. A bundle tied with tape, and sealed at each fold and l. with black wax SCOTT.

Ligature (li·gătiŭɹ), *sb.* ME. [– late L. *ligatura*, f. as prec.; see -URE. Cf. (O)Fr. *ligature*.] **1.** Anything used in binding or tying; a band, tie, etc. Chiefly *spec.* in *Surg.*, a thread or cord used to tie up a bleeding artery, etc. **b.** *fig.* A bond, tie 1627. **2.** = LIGAMENT 2. Not now in good use. ME. **3.** The action of tying; an instance of this. Also, a tie or the place of one 1541. **4.** *Mus.* A method of indicating the binding of notes into groups. In mod. notation: a TIE or SLUR. In *Counterpoint*: a SYNCOPATION. 1597. **5.** In *Writing* or *Printing*: A monogram. Also, a stroke connecting two letters. *In l.*, combined in one character or type. 1693. †**6.** Binding quality; also *concr.* –1727. Hence **Li·gature** *v.* to bind with a l. or bandage; *spec.* in *Surg.* to tie up (an artery, etc.).

Lige, obs. f. LIE *v.*[1], LIEGE.

Ligeance (ləi·dʒăns, lī·dʒăns). ME. [– OFr. *ligeance, legiance*, etc., in med.L. *ligantia, -entia, legantia* (XII), f. *lige* LIEGE; see -ANCE.] **1.** = ALLEGIANCE 2. *arch.* **2.** The sway of a sovereign over his subjects or lieges; the territories subject to a sovereign. Now only in legal use. ME. So †**Li·geancy.**

Ligge, obs. f. LIE *v.*[1]

Ligger (li·gəɹ), *sb. dial.* 1483. [f. *lig*, north. var. of LIE *v.*[1] + -ER[1]. Cf. LEDGER *sb.*, a doublet of this wd.] **1.** A coverlet. †**2.** = LEDGER *sb.* 2. –1518. †**3.** The nether millstone. PEGGE. **4.** A plank bridge 1840. **5.** *Angling.* A line with a float and bait which is left in the water 1825. Hence **Li·gger** *v.* to fish with a l.

Light (ləit), *sb.* [OE. *lēoht*, Angl. *līht* = OFris. *liācht*, OS., OHG. *lioht* (Du., G. *licht*) :– WGmc. *leuxta :– IE. *leuktom, f. *leuk- *louk- *lŭk- repr. in Gr. λευκός white, L. *lux* light.] **1.** The natural agent or influence which evokes the activity of the organ of sight. **a.** Viewed as the medium of visual perception. Also, the condition of space in which vision is possible. Opp. to *darkness.* **b.** Viewed as itself an object of perception. Also, an individual shining or appearance of light. OE. **c.** Viewed as residing in or emanating from a luminary OE. **d.** In scientific use (see below) 1704. **e.** The portion of light which illuminates a given space 1533. **f.** A gleam or sparkle in the eye, expressive of animation or the like 1593. **g.** In various fig. phrases (see below). **h.** *pl.* [after L. *lumina.*] Graces of style. ADDISON. **2.** *spec.* The illumination which proceeds from the sun in day-time; daylight. Also, day-time, day-break. (Usu. *the l.*; also, *the l. of day.*) OE. **3.** The state of being visible or exposed to view OE. **4.** Power of vision, eyesight (now *poet.* or *rhet.*). Also *pl.* = the eyes (now only *slang*). OE. **5.** A body from which illumination emanates: the sun or other heavenly body (after *Gen.* 1:16) OE.; an ignited candle, lamp, etc. OE.; *collect.* candles, etc. used to illuminate a particular place OE.; a signal-fire or beacon-lamp, e.g. on a ship or in a lighthouse; hence, the lighthouse 1604; †a linkman STEELE. **6.** Used *fig.* with reference to mental illumination or elucidation. **a.** In phrases (see below) 1420. **b.** Illumination or enlightenment as possessed by the mind, or as derivable from a particular source ME. **c.** *pl.* (*a*) Facts, discoveries, or suggestions which explain a subject. (*b*) The natural or acquired information and powers of an individual intellect. 1526. **d.** A suggestion that helps to the solution of a problem. Now *spec.* in an acrostic, each of the words to be guessed, their initials (or initials and finals) forming the answer to the puzzle. 1894. **7.** The brightness of Heaven, the illumination of the soul by divine truth, etc. OE. **b.** *spec.* Among Quakers, the inward revelation of Christ in the soul 1656. **8.** *fig.* (from sense 5): One who is eminent or conspicuous; a luminary 1592. **9.** *fig.* (from sense 1 e): A consideration which illuminates or points to a particular view of a subject. Hence, the aspect in which anything is viewed or judged 1689. **10.** A window or opening in a wall for the admission of light; *spec.* a perpendicular division of a mullioned window ME. **b.** *Gardening.* A glazed compartment in the side or roof of a greenhouse or the top of a frame 1733. **11.** *Mech.* An aperture or clear space 1776. **12.** *Painting.* Light or illuminated surface in a picture; any portion of a picture represented as lighted up 1622. Also *fig.* **13.** *Law.* The light falling on the windows of a house from the sky, interference with which by neighbours is illegal. (*Ancient Lights*, an inscription often put on the face or side of a house, to give warning against obstruction of the access of light.) 1768. **14.** A flame or spark serving to ignite any combustible substance; also, something used for igniting; e.g. a spill, taper, match 1684.

1. a. And God said, Let there be l.: and there was l. *Gen.* 1:3. **b.** The long l. shakes across the lakes TENNYSON. *Northern, Southern Lights* (= AURORA *Borealis, Australis*), *Zodiacal l.*: see the adjs. **c.** Phr. *To give l.* (said of a luminary). A goodly Bekon geuyng l. HALL. **d.** Senses in scientific use: (*a*) the thing (whether matter or energy) which is communicated from a luminous body to the body illuminated by it; The L. of the Sun 1704; (*b*) this thing regarded as producing sensation 1704; (*c*) the sensation produced 1800; (*d*) the process (variously conceived) by which the communication is made 1875; (*e*) certain characteristics of such processes (rays or waves) 1900; (*f*) physical energies and processes of the same type as those involved in the production of vision, but having possibly a different range of periods (e.g. Röntgen rays) 1865. **e.** The picture..is in a bad l. (i.e. imperfectly visible) 1797. Phr. *In l.*: lighted up. *One's l.*: the ordinary share of light which a person enjoys for seeing around him. *To stand in a person's l.* = to cut him off from this; hence *fig.* to prejudice his interests. So *to stand in one's own l.* **f.** Yet do I cease not to behold The love-light in her eye H. COLERIDGE. **g.** *To put out* or *quench* (one's) *l.*: to extinguish his 'vital spark'. Quench thou his l., Destruction dark! SCOTT. Phr. *L. of* one's *eye(s*: applied to a loved object. *The l. of God's countenance* (*Ps.* 4:6, etc.) = Divine favour. Hence, sarcastically *the l. of (a person's) countenance*: (his) sanction, approving presence. **2.** Phr. *To see the l.*: to be brought forth or published. **3.** Phr. *To come to l.*: to be made visible or made known. The thing that is hid bringeth he foorth to l. *Job* 28:11. **5.** Make we heuen & erth..and lyghtys fayre to se 1460. *Wax lights* = wax candles for lighting (now *rare* in this use). Phr. *Fixed, flashing, intermittent, revolving l.* (in a lighthouse). As a harbour l. reveals the port 1894. **6. a.** *To give (carry, bring) l.* (†*to* or *into* a subject). *To get, receive l.* Now usu. *to throw (cast, shed) l. upon.* **b.** *L. of nature*, the capacity of discerning divine truths without the help of revelation. The lycht of ressoun 1513. The men of England, the men, I mean, of l. and leading BURKE. **c.** He did his best; he worked according to his lights THACKERAY. *New light(s*: novel doctrines (esp. theol. and eccles.) the partisans of which lay claim to superior enlightenment 1650; hence *Old light(s*, the doctrines to which the 'new lights' are opposed; *Old Lights* (Sc. *Auld Lichts*) and *New Lights*, designations for persons holding the respective views: see O.E.D. He was afraid of Fox, for going after new lights SEWEL. **7.** *Angel* (or *spirit*) *of l.*, one who dwells in Heaven. Diuels soonest tempt resembling spirits of l. SHAKS. **8.** Joan of Arc, A l. of ancient France TENNYSON. **9.** Phr. *To set in a* (certain) *light. In the l. of*: (*a*) with the help given by (some fact); (*b*) viewed as being (so and so). In the l. of all that has been said and done 1893. **12.** The Italian masters universally make the horizon the chief l. of their picture RUSKIN. **14.** Phr. *To strike a l.*, to produce a flame, etc. with a match, etc. (see STRIKE *v.* V. 6a).

Comb.: **l.-ball** *Mil.*, a combustible fired from a mortar at night, to throw l. on the operations of the enemy; **-boat** = LIGHTSHIP; **-due, -duty,** a toll levied on ships for the upkeep of lights in lighthouses and lightships; **-head,** the top portion of a 'light' (sense 10); **-keeper,** one who has charge of the l. in a lighthouse, etc.; **-man,** (*a*) a light-keeper; (*b*) a linkman; hence **light-manship; -money** = *light-due*; **-port,** 'a scuttle made for showing a l. through' (Smyth); **-tower,** a lighthouse; **-vessel** = LIGHTSHIP; **-year** *Astron.*, the distance l. travels in a year, i.e. about 63,000 times the distance of the earth from the sun, taken as the unit of stellar distance.

Light (ləit), *a.*[1] [OE. *lēoht, līht* = OFris. *li(u)cht*, OS. *-līht* (Du. *licht*), OHG. *līht(i)* (G. *leicht*), ON. *léttr*, Goth. *leihts* :- Gmc. **liŋχtaz*, **-tjaz*, f. **liŋʒw-* :- IE. **leŋghw-*. See LUNG.] **I. 1.** Of little weight, not heavy. **b.** Deficient in weight ('*too* light') 1589. **2.** Of small specific gravity 1559. **3.** Bearing a small load. Of a vessel: Having a small burden, or (usu.) unladen, without cargo. 1573. Also *fig.* **4.** Chiefly *Mil.* Lightly armed or equipped. †Also, lightly clad. ME. **5.** Of a vehicle or vessel: Constructed for light loads and for swift movement OE. **6.** Of a building: Not looking heavy; graceful in form 1762. **7.** Boxing. *L. heavy-weight*, a boxer from 12 st. 7 to 11 st. 6.

1. My yoke is easie, and my burden is l. *Matt.* 11:30. Phr. *To lie l.* (cf. HEAVY *a.*[1] I. 1). *L. ice*, that which has but little depth in the water. *L. sails*, all above the topgallant sails; also the studding sails and flying jib. Wheat. .l. in the ear BURKE. **b.** Clipt and L. Money 1700. **2.** Hydrogen, the lightest gas LOCKYER. **3.** He di'd for heavines that his Cart went l. MILT. *L. engine*: an engine alone, without a train. *L. railway*: a railway constructed for l. traffic. *L. porter. L. water-line*, the water-line of a ship when just launched, or quite unladen. **4.** Phr. *In l. marching order*: i.e. carrying only arms and ammunition. **5.** *L. cart* = 'spring cart' (see CART *sb.* 3). **6.** Small l. spires 1850.

II. 1. Having little momentum or force; acting gently. Also *l. of touch.* OE. **2.** Having little density or cohesive force. Of soil: Friable, porous, workable. Of a cloud: Fleecy, evanescent. 1523. **b.** Of bread, etc.: That has risen properly; not heavy 1460. **3.** Of food or drink: Easy of digestion. Of wine, beer, etc.: Containing little alcohol. OE. **4.** *L. in the mouth* (of a horse): sensitive to the bit 1727. **5.** Of accent or syllables: Unemphatic. Hence, of rhythm, consisting of such syllables. 1575.

1. Waxe. .yeelds at last to euerie l. impression SHAKS. His l. walk GEO. ELIOT. A l. breeze 1885. **2.** There is a l. cloud by the moon BYRON.

III. 1. Of small consequence, not weighty; slight, trivial. Of a sin: Venial. OE. †**b.** Cheap. Of a price: Low. Also *l. cheap* = CHEAP *a.* and *adv.* –1647. †**c.** Of persons: Of small account –1548. **2.** Characterized by levity, frivolous ME. **b.** Chiefly of women: Wanton, unchaste ME.

1. This is no l. matter '*Junius' Lett.* Phr. *To set l. by* or *of* (a person or thing): to despise, slight, under-value. *To make l. of*: to treat as of small or no importance. The Natives make l. of such things as we call Colds 1698. **2.** That l. perpetual talk about him NEWMAN.

IV. 1. Moving readily; active, nimble, quick. *arch.* OE. **2.** That moves or is moved easily; pliant, fickle, unsteady; facile (of belief, etc.). Const. *of, to* with *inf.* Now *rare.* ME.

1. Phr. *L. of foot, of person*; †*l.-fingers.* **2.** Be not lyght of credence in no case SKELTON.

V. 1. Easy to bear or endure OE. **2.** Easy to accomplish, requiring little exertion; now only qualifying *task, work*, etc. OE. **3.** Of literature, plays, music, etc.: Requiring little mental effort; amusing 1597. **4.** Of sleep: Not heavy; easily shaken off. Hence *l. sleeper.* OE.

1. How l. and portable my paine seemes now! *Lear* III. vi. 115. **2.** The service will be l. and easy FRANKLIN. **3.** Phr. *L. comedian*: an actor of l. comedy. **4.** A man who at all times was a l. sleeper 1894.

VI. Free from the weight of care or sorrow; cheerful. *Obs.* exc. in *l. heart.* ME.

VII. Of the head: Dizzy, giddy. Also of persons: = LIGHT-HEADED 1590.

Is he not l. of Braine? *Oth.* IV. i. 280.

Light (ləit), *a.*[2] [OE. *lēoht, līht* = OFris. *liācht*, OS., OHG. *lioht* (Du., G. *licht*); see LIGHT *sb.*] **1.** †**a.** Bright, shining, luminous –1760. **b.** Having plenty of light, not dark. †Earlier: Brightly illuminated; *fig.* enlightened mentally. OE. **2.** Pale in hue. Also = *l.-coloured.* (Hyphened when prefixed to another adj. of colour used attrib.) ME.

1. a. *On* (*of, in*) *a l. fire*: in a blaze (common in 16–18th c.). All Sodome was of a l. fire 1652. **b.** When the morning is l., they practise it [euill] *Micah* 2:1. **2.** A l. bob Periwig 1686. Light-drab cloth MISS BRADDON.

†**Light,** *ppl. a.* 1495. [pa. pple. of LIGHT *v.*[2]] Lighted –1632.

Light (ləit), *adv.*[1] [OE. *lēohte* = OS., OHG. *līhto*, corresp. to the adjectival forms of LIGHT *a.*[1]] **1.** In a light manner; see LIGHT *a.*[1] **2.** *Comb.* (with pres. and pa. pples.) as *l.-bounding, -harnessed*, etc. 1533.

†**Light,** *adv.*[2] [OE. *lēohte* = OHG. *liohto*, f. *lēoht* LIGHT *a.*[2]] Brightly, clearly –1710.

Light (ləit), *v.*[1] [OE. *līhtan* = OFris. *lichta*, MDu. *lichten*, OHG. *līhten*, ON. *létta* :- Gmc. **liχtjan*, **liŋχtjan*; see LIGHT *a.*[1]] **I.** †**1.** *trans.* To make light, lessen the weight of. Also *fig.* –1600. **2.** To relieve *of* a (material) load; to unload (a ship). Also, to 'relieve' (a person) *of* his property. ? *Obs.* ME. †**3.** To relieve (*of* pain, sorrow, etc.); to comfort, cheer –1597. †Also *intr.* †**4.** To make of less effect 1619. **5. a.** *Naut.* 'To move or lift anything along' (Smyth). *trans.* and *absol.* 1841. **b.** ? Hence *to l. out* (*U.S. slang*): to decamp 1884.

2. We must. .l. this weary vessell of her lode SPENSER. **5. b.** And so when I couldn't stand it no longer, I lit out MARK TWAIN.

II. To descend. Cf. ALIGHT *v.*[1] [App. an absol. use of the vb. in sense I. 2 ('to relieve a horse, etc. of one's weight').] **1.** *intr.* To descend *from* a horse or vehicle; to dismount. †Sometimes conjugated with *to be.* OE. †**2.** Of persons: To descend. Occas. *refl.* –1533. **3.** To fall and settle on a surface, as a bird, a snowflake, etc. Also with *down.* ME. **4.** To have a particular place of incidence or arrival (see below) ME.

1. Stern Hassan. .from his horse Disdains to l. BYRON. **3.** Phr. *To l. on one's feet* or *legs* (fig.): to be fortunate or successful. I have made scores of new acquaintances and lighted on my legs as usual THACKERAY. **4. a.** Of a blow or weapon: To fall and strike; to fall (short, etc.) (now *rare*); There flies my Dart, l. where it will 1604. †**b.** To arrive *at* a point; to fall *into* a condition; to 'land' in a particular place or position –1697. **c.** *To l. on, upon*: to fall or descend upon; to fall to the lot of; *occas.* conjugated with *to be*; The plague of Egypt l. vppon you all 1607. **d.** Of persons. *To l. on* or *upon*: to chance upon; to meet with or discover; to come across 1470. **e.** To come or fall *into* a person's hands; to chance *into* a person's company. (Now *rare* or *obs.*) 1562. **f.** To turn out (well, happily); also *simply*, to happen. (Now *dial.*) 1607.

Light (ləit), *v.*[2] Pa. t. and pple. **lighted, lit;** pa. pple. pseudo-*arch.* **litten.** [OE. *līhtan* = OS. *liuhtian*, Goth. *liuhtjan* :- Gmc. **liuhtjan*, f. **leuχtam*; see LIGHT *sb.*] †**1.** *intr.* To give light; to shine; to be alight or burning. Also, to lighten. –1774. †**b.** Of day, etc.: To grow light –1596. **2.** *trans.* To set burning (a candle, etc., a fire, a combustible); to ignite. Also with *up.* OE. Also *transf.* and *fig.* **b.** *intr.* To take fire, be lighted; *transf.* to 'kindle' ME. **3.** *trans.* To give light to (a room, etc.); to illuminate; *esp.* to furnish with means of illumination. (Rarely with *up.*) ME. **b.** *transf.* (Chiefly with *up.*) To cause (the eyes, features, etc.) to brighten with animation. Also, to brighten up (writing). Also *intr.* for *refl.* or *pass.* 1766. **4.** To give light to (a person); hence, to show the way to (*lit.* and *fig.*). Also *absol.* ME. **5.** To illumine spiritually or intellectually. ? *Obs.* or *arch.* ME.

1. b. 1 *Hen. IV*, III. ii. 138. **2.** *transf.* Thine eyes were lit from other skies B. TAYLOR. absol. *To l. up*: to l. one's pipe, cigar, etc. (*colloq.*). **3.** The Globe, that lights the lower world SHAKS. St. Andrew's church. .is lighted with gas 1840. *absol.* (*colloq.*) Isn't it time to light up? Phr. *To l. up*: to furnish or fill with abundance of light; to illuminate in a special manner; to make prominent by means of light; Lit up by the rising moon W. IRVING. **b.** Her expressive features all lit up with Joy 1766. **4.** Here comes a candle to l. you to bed 18.. Hence **Li·ghtable** *a.* that can be lighted.

Lightage (ləi·tėdʒ). 1606. [f. LIGHT *sb.* + -AGE.] †**1.** A toll paid by a ship coming to a port where there is a lighthouse –1789. **2.** Provision of (artificial) light 1862.

Light-armed, *a.* 1579. [LIGHT *a.*[1]] Bearing light armour or arms. Also *fig.*

Li·ght-bob. 1785. [BOB *sb.*[7]] A soldier of the light infantry.

Lighten (ləi·t'n), *v.*[1] ME. [f. LIGHT *a.*[1] + -EN[5]; also, in sense 5, an extension of LIGHT *v.*[1]] **1.** *trans.* To reduce or remove the load of (a ship, etc.); to relieve *of* (a burden, etc.). Also *intr.* for *pass.* **2.** To remove a burden from, relieve (the heart or mind); †to cheer. Now *rare.* **b.** *intr.* for *refl.* or *pass.* Somewhat *rare.* ME. **3.** *trans.* To make lighter; to alleviate, mitigate 1483. †**b.** To lessen the pressure of –1797. **c.** To make nimble (*rare*) 1599. **4.** *intr.* To grow lighter 1720. †**5.** To descend, alight; to light *upon* –1704.

1. To l. the cart. .I descended and walked 1871. **2.** To l. his conscience MACAULAY. **3.** How we may light'n Each others burden in our share of woe MILT. **b.** Peraduenture hee will l. his hand from off you 1 *Sam.* 6:5. **c.** *Much Ado* V. iv. 120. **5.** O Lorde, let thy mercy l. upon us *Bk. Com. Prayer.*

Lighten (ləi·t'n), *v.*[2] ME. [f. LIGHT *a.*[2] + -EN[5].] **1.** *trans.* To give light to; to make bright or luminous; to light up. Also *fig.* **b.** To cause (the countenance or looks) to light up. Also *intr.* for *pass.* of the face, eyes, etc. 1795. †**2.** In Biblical lang.: To restore sight to (the eyes) –1535. **3.** To shed spiritual light upon (*arch.*) ME. †**4.** To kindle, ignite; = LIGHT *v.*[2] 2. –1645. **5.** *intr.* To shine, flash, burn brightly; to glow with light ME. **b.** To shine like light *on.* CARY. **6.** To emit flashes of lightning. Chiefly *impers.* 1440. **7.** *trans.* To cause to flash *out* or *forth*; to send *down* as lightning (*lit.* and *fig.*) 1586.

1. God. .l. his face on vs HAMPOLE *Ps.* 66:1. **b.** His eye lightened 1890. **2.** L. myne eyes, that I slepe not in death COVERDALE *Ps.* 12[3]:3. **3.** 2 *Hen. IV*, II. i. 208. **4.** As one Taper lightneth another HOWELL. **5.** His steely lance, that lighten'd as he pass'd POPE. **6.** Like skies that rain and l. BYRON.

Lighter (ləi·təɹ), *sb.*[1] ME. [f. LIGHT *v.*[1] (sense 2) + -ER[1], or – Du. *lichter.*] A boat, usu. a flat-bottomed barge, used in lightening or unloading (sometimes loading) ships that cannot be wharfed, and for transporting goods in harbour, etc. Also *attrib.*, as **Li·ghterman,** one employed on or owning a l. Hence **Li·ghterage,** transhipment or unloading of cargo by means of a l.; the charges for this.

Lighter (ləi·təɹ), *sb.*[2] 1553. [f. LIGHT *v.*[2] + -ER[1].] One who or that which lights or kindles.

Lighter (ləi·təɹ), *v.* 1840. [f. LIGHTER *sb.*[1]] *trans.* To remove or transport (goods) in or as in a lighter. Also *absol.* or *intr.*

Li:ghter-than-ai·r, designating aircraft of the balloon type that rise in the air by reason of lesser specific gravity 1909.

Light-fingered, *a.* 1547. Having light and nimble fingers. **a.** *gen.* 1804. **b.** Thievish, dishonest 1547. †**c.** Prompt in striking; pugnacious –1607.

Lightfoot (ləi·tfut), *a.* ME. [LIGHT *a.*[1]] **1.** *poet.* = LIGHT-FOOTED. (Common in 16th c.) 1440. †**2.** quasi-*sb.* A name for the hare and the deer –1815.

Light-footed, *a.* 1490. Having a light foot; treading lightly, active, nimble.

Lightful (ləi·tfŭl), *a.* ME. [f. LIGHT *sb.* + -FUL.] Full of light (*lit.* and *fig.*); luminous, bright.

Al thi body schal be liȝtful WYCLIF *Luke* 11:34. Hence **Li·ghtfulness.**

Light-handed, *a.* 1440. **a.** Having a light touch (*lit.* and *fig.*). **b.** Carrying little. **c.** Of a vessel or factory: = SHORT-HANDED. Hence **Light-ha·ndedness.**

Li·ghthead. 1751. A light-headed person. Also quasi-*adj.* = next.

Light-headed, *a.* ? 1537. **1.** Disordered in the head; giddy, delirious. **2.** Frivolous, thoughtless; fickle 1579. †**3.** quasi-*adv.* FULLER.

2. The light-headed doings of the Queen Dowager BURTON. Hence **Light-hea·ded-ly** *adv.*, **-ness.**

Light-hearted, *a.* ME. **1.** Having a light heart; cheerful, gay. **2.** Proceeding from a light heart 1841. Hence **Light-hea·rted-ly** *adv.*, **-ness** 1611.

Light-heeled, *a.* 1590. **1.** Brisk in walking or running; nimble. †**2.** Of a woman: Loose, unchaste –1796. †**Light-heels,** a loose woman.

Light horse. 1532. **1.** †**a.** *collect. sing* Light horsemen; a body of light cavalry. **b.** = LIGHT HORSEMAN. †**2.** A courtesan 1627.

Light horseman. 1548. **1.** A light-armed cavalry soldier. **2.** Slang name for one of a class of Thames thieves 1800. †**3.** 'The light boat, since called a gig' (Smyth) –1708. †**4.** A variety of fancy pigeons. R. HOLME. **5.** †**a.** An Australian sea-fish, prob. the Sweep, *Scorpis æquipennis.* **b.** A W. Indian fish of the genus *Ephippus.* 1789.

Li·ghthouse. 1622. [f. LIGHT *sb.* + HOUSE *sb.*[1]] A tower or other structure, with a powerful light or lights (orig. a beacon) at the top, erected at some important or dangerous point on or near the sea-coast for the guidance of mariners; a *pharos.*

Lightless (ləi·tlės), *a.* [OE. *lēohtlēas*; see LIGHT *sb.*, -LESS.] **1.** Receiving no light; dark. Also *fig.* **2.** Giving no light ME. Hence **Li·ghtlessness.**

Light-limbed, *a.* 1695. Having light limbs; agile.

The light-limbed Matadore BYRON.

Li·ghtly, *v.* Chiefly *Sc.* ME. [f. †*lightly* adj., contemptuous.] *trans.* To make light of, despise, disparage.

It's best no to l. them that have that character SCOTT.

Lightly (ləi·tli), *adv.* [OE. *lēohtliċe*; see LIGHT *a.*[1], -LY[2].] In a light manner. **1.** With little weight; with little pressure, force, or violence; gently. **2.** In no great quantity or thickness; to no great amount OE. †**b.** Slightly –1697. **3.** Without depression; cheerfully, gaily ME. **4.** Easily, readily. *Obs.* exc. *arch.* ME. **5.** Nimbly. †In early use, swiftly; *occas.* at once. ME. †**6.** Probably, perhaps –1672. †**b.** As is apt to happen; commonly, often –1676. **7. a.** Carelessly, indifferently. **b.** Slightingly. ME. **8.** For a slight cause; without careful consideration OE. †**9.** 'Not chastely'. SWIFT.

1. At the first he l. afflicted the land of Zebulun *Isa.* 9:1. I sleep l. enough 1852. **2.** They are but l. rewarded SHAKS. L. clad 1875. **3.** Try to bear l. what must needs be JOWETT. **4.** Credulous people believe l. whatever they hear CHESTERF. L. come, l. go *Provb.* **5.** L. vaulting off his saddle 1632. **7.** Thinking l. of the possession of gold JOWETT. **8.** These are opinions that I have not l. formed, or that I can l. quit BURKE.

Li·ghtmans. *Thieves' cant.* 1567. [f. LIGHT *a.*[2]; cf. DARKMANS.] The day.

Light-minded, *a.* 1611. Having a light mind; frivolous. Hence **Light-mi·ndedness.**

Lightness[1] (ləi·tnės). ME. [f. LIGHT *a.*[1] + -NESS.] The quality or fact of being light; see LIGHT *a.*[1]

Lightness[2] (ləi·tnės). [OE. *lihtnes*; see LIGHT *a.*[2], -NESS.] †**1.** Brightness, light (*lit.* and *fig.*) –1824. **2.** Illumination. Now only *lit.* ME.

1. An insane l. about the eyes SCOTT. **2.** The l. of an apartment LYTTON.

Lightning (ləi·tniŋ). ME. [spec. use of *lightening* vbl. sb. of LIGHTEN *v.*[2]; now differentiated in spelling.] **1.** The visible discharge of electricity between groups of clouds, or between the clouds and the ground. Also, A flash of lightning (now *rare*). **2.** *slang.* Gin 1781.

1. *Forked l., chain* or *chained l.*: designations of l. which assumes the form of a zigzag or divided line. *Sheet l.*: that which illuminates a wide surface at once. *Summer* or *heat l.*: sheet l. without audible thunder, the result of a distant storm. *Like l.*, with the speed of l. (hyperbolically for 'extremely swiftly'); This Notion ran like Lightening thro' the City DE FOE. Also, *like greased l.* (slang) *fig.* She..Makes wicked lightnings of her eyes TENNYSON. *attrib.* Her l. glance DISRAELI.

Comb.: **l.-arrester,** a device to protect telegraphic apparatus, etc. from l.; **-bone,** some kind of fossil bone; **-bug** = FIRE-FLY; **-conductor,** a metallic rod or wire fixed to an exposed point of a building, or the mast of a ship, to carry l. harmlessly into the earth or sea; **-discharger** = *lightning-arrester*; **-express** *U.S.*, name for certain very rapid trains; **-pains** *pl.*, sharp, shooting, momentary pains, felt by sufferers from locomotor ataxy; **-print,** an appearance sometimes found on the skin of men and animals and on clothing struck by l., pop. supposed to be photographs of surrounding objects; **-proof** *a.*, protected from l.; **-rod** = *lightning-conductor*; **-stone, -tube** = FULGURITE 1; **-strike,** a sudden strike (of workmen) without warning.

Light of love, light o' love. 1578. [See LIGHT *a.*[1] IV. 2.] **1.** As predicative phr.: Inconstant in love 1579. **2.** as *sb.* †**a.** Inconstancy in love 1578. **b.** A woman inconstant in love; also, a wanton, a harlot 1599. †**3.** Name of an old dance-tune –1612.

3. Best sing it to the tune of *Light O' Loue* SHAKS.

Lights (ləits), *sb. pl.* ME. [subst. use of LIGHT *a.*[1] Cf. LUNG.] The lungs. Now only the lungs of sheep, pigs, bullocks, etc., used as food (esp. for cats and dogs).

Li·ghtship. 1837. [f. LIGHT *sb.*] A vessel bearing a light, *esp.* one moored where a lighthouse cannot be placed; a floating light.

Li·ght-skirts. 1597. A woman of light character. Also *attrib.* (in form *light-skirt*).

Lightsome (ləi·tsŏm), *a.*[1] ME. [f. LIGHT *a.*[1] + -SOME[1].] **1.** Having the effect or appearance of lightness; light, graceful, elegant. †Also, in early use, easy. Somewhat *rare.* 1440. **2.** Light-hearted, cheerful; also, enlivening, entertaining ME. **b.** Flighty, frivolous 1533. **3.** Moving lightly; lively, quick 1601.

1. The lofty tower, straight and l. as a lily 1877. **2.** L. sangs SCOTT. **3.** As l. as a bird WORDSW. Hence **Li·ghtsome-ly** *adv.*[1], **-ness**[1].

Li·ghtsome, *a.*[2] ME. [f. LIGHT *sb.* + -SOME[1].] **1.** Light-giving, luminous 1440. Also *fig.* **2.** Of an apartment, a building, etc.: Well-lighted, bright 1538. Also *fig.* **3.** Clear, manifest. Now *rare.* 1532. †**4.** Light-hued –1674.

1. L. clouds and shining seas SHELLEY. **2.** His.. Roomes, so Large and L. BACON. Hence **Li·ghtsome-ly** *adv.*[2], **-ness**[2].

Li·ght-weight, light weight. 1773. [f. LIGHT *a.*[1]] **A.** *sb. Sporting.* A man or animal under the average weight; also of motorcycles; esp. in *Boxing*, a boxer from 9 st. 9 to 9 st. Also in *Racing* handicaps, a horse carrying light weights, or a jockey riding at a low weight. **B.** *adj.* Light in weight; said *esp.* of coins and cloth; cf. LIGHT *a.*[1] 1 b. Also *fig.* 1809.

Lightwood[1] (ləi·twud). 1685. [f. LIGHT *a.*[1]] A name for trees having light wood; in Australia esp. *Acacia melanoxylon.*

Li·ghtwood[2]. *N. Amer.* and *W. Ind.* 1693. [f. LIGHT *sb.* (or LIGHT *v.*[2]).] **a.** Any wood used in lighting a fire; esp. resinous pinewood. **b.** Any tree (e.g. *Amyris balsamifera*, candle-wood) the wood of which burns with a brilliant flame.

†**Li·ghty,** *a.* ME. [f. LIGHT *sb.* or *a.*[1] + -Y[1].] **1.** Full of light, bright. WYCLIF. **2.** Well-informed. TURNER.

Lign-aloes (ləin,æ·loᵘz). ME. [– late L. *lignum aloēs* 'wood of the aloe' (*aloēs*, gen. of *aloē*).] **a.** = ALOE 3. **b.** = ALOE 1. **c.** [= Sp. *linaloe.*] An aromatic wood obtained from a Mexican tree of the genus *Bursera.*

Ligneous (li·gniəs), *a.* 1626. [– L. *ligneus* (f. *lignum* wood) + -OUS; see -EOUS.] **1.** Of the nature of wood; woody; opp. to *herbaceous.* **2.** (A mod. use, chiefly *joc.*) Wooden. 1812.

1. That fossil, l. substance called peat 1792. **2.** *L. marble*, wood treated so as to resemble marble.

Ligni- (li·gni), comb. f. L. *lignum* wood, as in **Ligniferous** (-i·ferəs) *a.*, bearing or producing wood. **Li·gniform** *a.*, of the form or appearance of wood. **Lignipe·rdous** [L. *perdere*] *a.*, wood-destroying. **Ligni·vorous** [L. *-vorus*] *a.*, wood-devouring.

Lignify (li·gnifəi), *v.* 1828. [f. L. *lignum* wood + -FY.] To make or become ligneous. So **Lignifica·tion** 1808.

Lignin (li·gnin). Also **-ine.** 1822. [f. L. *lignum* wood + -IN[1].] *Chem.* An organic substance forming the essential part of woody fibre. *Comb.* **l.-dynamite,** wood-sawdust saturated with nitroglycerine, used as an explosive.

Lignite (li·gnəit). 1808. [– Fr. *lignite* (A. *Brongniart*, 1807), f. L. *lignum* wood; see -ITE[1] 2 b.] *Min.* A variety of brown coal bearing visible traces of its ligneous structure. **Ligni·tic** *a.* pertaining to, or of the nature of, l. **Ligniti·ferous** *a.* producing l.

Ligno- (li·gno), used as comb. f. L. *lignum* wood, as in **Lignoce·llulose,** lignin combined with cellulose. **Lignoce·ric** *a.*, in *lignoceric acid*, a fatty acid contained in paraffin and in beech-wood tar.

Lignose (li·gnoᵘs). 1698. [– L. *lignosus*, f. *lignum* wood; see -OSE[1].] **A.** *adj.* = LIGNEOUS. **B.** *sb.* **a.** *Chem.* One of the constituents of lignin 1878. **b.** An explosive consisting of wood fibre and nitroglycerine 1884.

Li·gnous, *a. rare* or *Obs.* 1664. [– L. *lignosus*, f. *lignum* wood; see -OUS.] = LIGNEOUS.

‖**Lignum** (li·gnŏm). ME. [L., = 'wood'.] †**1.** *Bot.* Woody tissue 1826. **2. l. aloes** (†occas. *aloe*) = LIGN-ALOES; **l. vitæ** (vəi·tī) = GUAIACUM 1–3.

‖**Ligula** (li·giŭlă). 1760. [L., 'strap', 'spoon', var. of *lingula*, f. *lingere* lick, assoc. with *lingua* tongue; see -ULE.] **a.** *Bot.* A ligule. **b.** *Zool.* A tongue-like structure forming part of the labium in insects, or of the parapodia in annelids. **c.** *Anat.* A band of white matter in the wall of the fourth ventricle of the brain.

Hence **Li·gular** *a.* pertaining to or like a l.

Ligulate (li·giŭlět), *a.* 1760. [f. LIGULA + -ATE[2].] **1.** *Bot.* Having the form of a ligula, strap-shaped, as the ray florets in composite flowers; furnished with a ligula, as a leaf. **2.** Of letters in an inscription: Connected by a band 1851.

1. The 5 segments that make up the l. floret of a Composita LINDLEY. So **Li·gulated** *a.* 1753.

Ligule (li·giul). 1862. [– L. LIGULA.] *Bot.* A thin appendage at the base of the blade of a leaf, esp. in grasses; a ligulate corolla in composites.

Liguli- (li·giŭli), comb. f. LIGULA in botanical terms, as *liguliflorate, -florous* (L. *flos, flor-*), having ligulate florets.

Ligurian (ləigiūᵊ·riăn, lig-), *a.* and *sb.* 1601. [f. L. *Liguria* + -AN.] **A.** *adj.* Belonging to the country anciently called *Liguria* in Cisalpine Gaul, including Genoa, parts of Piedmont and Savoy, etc. Sometimes as epithet of a race of mankind of which the Ligurians are the supposed type. 1632. **B.** *sb.* An inhabitant or native of Liguria; a person belonging to the Ligurian race; also, a Ligurian bee.

A. *L. bee*: a kind of honey-bee, *Apis ligustrica*, indigenous in southern Europe.

Ligustrin (ligɒ·strin). 1865. [f. L. *ligustrum* privet + -IN[1].] *Chem.* The bitter principle of privet.

Likable: see LIKEABLE.

Like (ləik), *sb.*[1] ME. [f. LIKE *v.*] †**1.** (One's) good pleasure. (Also *pl.*) –1615. †**2.** A liking (for). Const. *of.* NASHE. **3.** In mod. use pl. *likes* (coupled with *dislikes*): Feelings of liking; predilections 1851.

3. Her odd likes and dislikes W. BLACK.

Like (ləik), *a.*, *adv.*, (*conj.*), and *sb.*[2] Comp. **liker**; superl. **likest.** [ME. *lic, lik* – ON. *likr*, aphetic of *glikr* = OE. *ġelīc* ALIKE. The inflected compar. and superl. are now usu. *poet.* or *rhet.*]

A. *adj.* **1.** Having the same characteristics as some other person or thing; similar; resembling; analogous. Const. *to, unto* (arch.), now commonly with simple dative. **b.** With following regimen denoting a particular example of a class of which something is predicated 1627. **c.** Without construction: Resembling something already indicated or implied ME. **d.** Of two or more things: Mutually similar; in predicative use = alike (now *rare*) ME. **2.** In phraseological and proverbial expressions (see below). **3.** Of a portrait: Resembling the original. Now only *predicative.* 1561. **4.** *Math.* = *Similar*, exc. in *l. quantities* and *l. signs* (see below)

1557. **5.** *Golf.* (See quot.) 1887. **6.** †**a.** Apt, suitable, befitting. Chiefly predicative. –1592. **b.** Such as one might expect from 1667. **7.** *predicatively*, chiefly with the vbs. *feel, look, sound* 1654. **8.** In accordance with appearances, probable, likely. Now only *dial.* ME. **9.** *predicatively*, const. *to* with *inf.*: Likely *to*. *arch.* and *dial.* ME. **b.** (Now *colloq.* or *dial.*) Apparently on the point of 1560.

1. Wee also are men of l. passions with you *Acts* 14:15. Sweet sleep, were death l. to thee SHELLEY. Phr. *There is none* or *nothing l.* —, = 'so good or so wonderful as'; There is none like her, none TENNYSON. What we have The likest God within the soul TENNYSON. Phr. *What is he* (or *it*) *l.?* = 'What sort of a man is he?', 'What sort of a thing is it?' *To look l.* (occas. *to be l.*), = 'to have the appearance of being'; e.g. 'He looks l. a fool'. *L. that* (perh. = Fr. *comme cela*): of the nature, character, or habit indicated. **b.** A critic l. (= 'such as') you STEVENSON. **c.** *The l.*: such as have been mentioned. *In l. manner*, see MANNER; *in l. wise*, see LIKEWISE. **d.** Provb. *As l. as two peas*: see PEA[1]. Things which seem to be l. may be different JEVONS. **2.** *L. case* (advb. phr.): in the same way (now only *dial.*) 1534. *L. master, l. man* (as the master, so the man) 1548. *Anything l., nothing l., something l.*: anything, nothing, something approaching (another thing) in size or quality. *Something l.* (ellipt.) = something l. what he, it (etc.) should be, or what is aimed at (*colloq.*, as an emphatic expression of satisfaction) 1547. (These latter phrases are also used *adverbially*.) **3.** I got your photograph at last: it is a beastly thing: not a bit l. E. FITZGERALD. **4.** *L. Quantities* (in Algebra), such as are expressed by the same Letters, equally repeated in each Quantity. *L. Signs*, are when both are Affirmative, or both Negative. PHILLIPS. **5.** When both parties have played the same number of strokes they are said to be *like* 1887. **6. a.** The likest instruments to put a bad matter in execution 1592. **b.** That would be liker a Drunkard than a Gentleman 1703. **7.** The Forty Colonies.. are all pretty like (= giving promise of) rebelling just now CARLYLE. *To feel l.* (orig. U.S.): to be in the humour for (*rec. colloq.*). **9.** My graue is l. to be my wedding bed *Rom. & Jul.* I. v. 137. **b.** After the treaty had been l. to have been broken off STRYPE. Phr. *Had l. to* (for *was l. to*), chiefly with perf. inf.: = 'had come near to, narrowly missed (—ing)'.

Comb., as *l.-minded* (whence *like-mindedness*), etc.

B. *adv.* (quasi-*prep.*, *conj.*). **1.** (Const. as in A. 1.) In or after the manner of; in the same manner or to the same extent as; as in the case of; in the manner characteristic of. *L. that*: in that manner (cf. A. 1 quots.). ME. **2.** = ALIKE; in a like degree; equally. Now *arch.* or *poet.* (qualifying adj. or adv.) ME. **3.** In the manner of one who (or that which) is —. *Obs.* exc. in *l. mad* (see MAD *a.*) 1500. †**4.** In accordance with –1586. **5.** *L. as.* **a.** Introducing a clause: In the same way as, even as; (just) as if. Also, *l. as if.* ME. *arch.* or *dial.* **b.** With ellipsis of the vb. in the clause. *Obs.* exc. *poet.* 1489. **6.** Used as *conj.*: = 'like as', as. Now considered vulgar or slovenly 1530. †**b.** As well as; as also –1663. **c.** †As if, 'like as'. Also (now *dial.*) *as l.* 1493. **7.** *dial.* and *vulgar.* = 'as it were', 'so to speak' 1801. **8.** Likely, probably. Rare exc. in phr. *l. enough, very l.,* (*as*) *l. as not* (colloq. or dial.) 1563.

1. Featur'd l. him, l. him with friends possest SHAKS. What was the use of his talking l. that? 1872. Phr. *l. anything, l. a shot, l. fun, blazes*, etc. **2.** L. war-like as the Wolfe *Cymb.* III. iii. 41. **5. a.** I held the letter in my hand l. as if I was stupid COLERIDGE. **6.** To act l. Judith did with Holofernes 1715. There is more of morning visiting, like in country life in England W. IRVING. **b.** *Rich. III*, III. v. 9. **8.** Most l. I did SHAKS.

C. *absol.* and *sb.* **1.** With qualifying poss. pron., etc.: Counterpart, equal, match, analogue. Occas. in *pl.* (*his*, etc.) *likes*. ME. **2.** An instance of similarity ME. **3.** *The l.*: the same kind of thing. (Now chiefly in neg. contexts.) 1553. †**b.** = *that* or *those* (followed by *of*). *rare.* –1654. **4.** *Golf.* (See quot.) 1863.

1. His lyke is not in al y[e] world LD. BERNERS. **2.** Phr. *L.* (*will*) *to l., l. draws to l., l. begets l.*, etc.; *l. for l.; l. cures l.* **3.** Phr. *I never saw the l. And the l., or the l.*: = 'and so forth'. See also SUCH-LIKE. *The like*(*s of* (rarely *to*): such a person or thing as; now often depreciatory (*colloq.*). **b.** His death was accompanied by the l. of Orange EARL MONM. **4.** If your opponent has played one stroke more than you—i.e. 'the odd', your next stroke will be 'the like' 1881.

Like (ləik), *v.*[1] [OE. *līcian* = OFris. *līkia*, OS. *līkon* (Du. *lijken*), OHG. *līhhēn*, ON. *līka*, Goth. *leikan* :- Gmc. **līkǣjan*, **līkōjan*, f. **līkam* appearance, form. See LICH.] **1.** *intr.* To please, suit a person. Chiefly quasi-*trans.* with *dat.* Also *impers.*, as in *it likes me.* Now only *arch.* and *dial.* †**b.** *simply.* To be pleasing –1616. †**2.** *refl.* and *intr.* To please oneself, delight *in* (something) –1549. **3.** *intr.* To be pleased or glad ME. †**4.** To get on, do well, thrive. Chiefly with *well, better*, etc. –1681. **5.** To derive pleasure *of*, occas. *by, with* (a person or thing); to approve *of*, become fond *of*. Also with *well* or *ill*. *Obs.* exc. *dial.* ME. **6.** *trans.* (The current sense.) To find agreeable or congenial; to feel attracted to (a person); to have a taste or fancy for, take pleasure in (a thing, etc.). In early use *to l. well* (now *arch.*, though we say *to l. very well*), and *to l. ill* = to dislike. (Often contrasted with *love*, as expressing a weaker sentiment.) ME. Also *absol.* **b.** With inf. as obj.: To find it agreeable, feel inclined *to do* or *be* so and so ME. **c.** Often = *like to have* 1822. **d.** The neutral sense inferable from *to l. well* or *ill* (see below) survives in the interrog. use with *how*, as in 'How do you l. my new gown?', etc. 1596.

1. I rode sullenly Upon a certain path that liked me not ROSSETTI. **b.** If his Play doe not l., the Diuell is in't B. JONS. Phr. *To l. well* or *ill*: to be pleasing or the reverse: Where it liked her best she sought Her shelter WORDSW. **3.** Phr. *To l. ill*: to be displeased or sad (now only *Sc.*). **6.** I never lik'd thy talk MILT. *absol.* Looking [he] liked, and liking loved SCOTT. **b.** If you would l. to go, We'll visit him SHELLEY. Phr. *I should l.* (= Fr. *je voudrais bien*, G. *ich möchte gern*), often in conditional use, to express a desire; often derisively in *I should l. to see* (something not possible), *I should l. to know* (something unknowable). *To do as one likes* (ellipt.). **c.** Would you l. the armchair? (*mod.*). **d.** How l. you this old satire? TENNYSON.

Like, *v.*[2] ME. [f. LIKE *a.*] †**1.** *trans.* To fashion in a certain likeness; to compare *to*; to make a likeness of –1622. **2.** *intr.* (Const. *inf.*) †To seem, pretend; to look like or be near *to* doing (something) or *to* being treated (in a specified manner). Now *vulgar* and *dial.* ME.

1. If to gold I l. her Haire WITHER. **2.** Wee had likt to haue had our two noses snapt off with two old men without teeth *Much Ado* V. i. 115.

-like, *suffix*, forming adjs. and advs. These compounds of LIKE *a.* and *adv.* are entirely distinct from the derivs. formed with *-lik*(*e*, ME. dial. form of -LY[1], -LY[2]. Cf. ME. *gredilike* adv. (= greedily), and mod. Sc. *greedy-like.*

1. Appended to sbs. **a.** Forming adjs. with sense 'similar to —', 'befitting —'. Examples are *god-like, ladylike, clockworklike.* The hyphen is used in formations not generally current. late ME. **b.** Forming advs. with sense 'in or after the manner of —', 'so as to resemble —'. Examples are *gentlemanlike, bishoplike, Brutus-like*, etc. These advs. are now perh. archaistic or obs., recent examples being explicable as quasi-advb. uses of the adj. In this use *-like* is nearly always hyphened. 1530. **2.** Appended to adjs. **a.** Forming adjs. Common in Sc., but not in Eng.; the sense is usually 'resembling one that is —', as in *genteel-like.* 1470. **b.** Forming advs. with the sense 'like one that is —'. *Obs.* exc. in *Sc.* 1470.

Likeable, likable (ləi·kăb'l), *a.* 1730. [f. LIKE *v.*[1] + -ABLE.] Worthy of being liked; pleasing; agreeable; as, *l. people.* Hence **Likeabi·lity, Li·keableness,** l. quality.

†**Li·kehood.** [f. LIKE *a.* + -HOOD.] Likelihood, probability. G. HARVEY.

Li·kelihead. *arch.* ME. [f. LIKELY *a.* + -HEAD.] **1.** = next, 2. Chiefly in phr. *by* or *of l.* **2.** = next, 1. ME.

Likelihood (ləi·klihud). ME. [f. LIKELY *a.* + -HOOD.] †**1.** Likeness; resemblance. Also an instance of this. –1688. **2.** Probability; an instance of this 1449. †**3.** Something that is likely, a probability; hence, an indication, sign. Freq. in *pl.* –1656. **4.** Promise of success. Now only as an echo of Shaks. 1596.

1. There is no l. between pure light and black darkness RALEGH. **2.** There was a l. of rain JOHNSON. *The l.*: the probable fact, or probable amount. Now *rare* exc. *Sc.* **3.** *Two Gent.* V. ii. 43. **4.** A fellow of no marke, nor likelyhood SHAKS.

So **Li·keliness,** in all senses. ME.

Likely (ləi·kli), *a.* and *adv.* ME. [- ON. *likligr* (also *glikligr*), f. *likr* LIKE *a.* + *-ligr* -LY[1].]

A. *adj.* †**1.** Like, similar (*till, to*). Also, resembling the original. –1661. **2.** Having an appearance of truth or fact; seeming as if it would happen, or prove to be as stated; probable ME. **3.** Apparently suitable or qualified (*for* a purpose or an action); apparently able or fitted (*to do* or *to be* something) ME. **4.** (Now chiefly *U.S.*) **a.** Strong or capable looking. **b.** Giving promise of success or excellence; hopeful. 1454. **5.** [?Infl. by LIKE *v.*[1]] Comely, handsome. ? Now *U.S.* and *dial.* 1470. †**6.** Seemly, appropriate –1742. †**7.** *Was l.*, also catachr. *had l.*: came near *to do* or *be* (etc.); = *was* or *had like* –1652.

2. No likelier cause can be alleg'd MILT. 'Tis very l. you will never receive this 1710. Phr. *He is l. to* (with inf.) = 'it is likely that he will'. **3.** We are not yet come to a l. place WALTON. The likeliest place..to meet with us 1748. **4.** Tall, well-set, l. Fellows 1686. *Comb.*, as *l.-looking* adj.

B. *adv.* †**1. a.** Similarly. **b.** With close resemblance (in portraiture). –1600. **2.** Probably. (Now chiefly *most l., very l.*) ME. †**3.** In a fit manner, suitably, reasonably –1674.

2. You may be very l. right in that JOWETT.

Liken (ləi·k'n), *v.* ME. [f. LIKE *a.* + -EN[5].] **1.** *trans.* To represent as like; to compare (*to, unto, with*). Also, *to l. together.* **2.** To make like (*rare*) ME. †**3.** *intr.* To be, or become, like. Also *trans.* to symbolize, represent. –1838.

1. I likened him often..to sheet-lightning CARLYLE.

Likeness (ləi·knės). [OE. (*ġe*)*līknes*; see LIKE *a.*, -NESS.] **1.** Resemblance, similarity; an instance of this. Const. *to*; †formerly *of* (or gen. of pron.), *with.* ME. **2.** That which resembles an object; a semblance. Hence *gen.* form, shape, esp. in phr. *in l. of.* †In OE. = figure, stature. OE. **3.** A copy, counterpart, image, portrait. Of persons: One who closely resembles another. OE. †**4.** A comparison; hence, a parable –ME.

1. It was a l. to her little boy that had affected me so pleasantly 1866. **2.** An Enemy in the l. of a Friend 1692. **3.** Here, take my L. with you, whilst 'tis so COWLEY. Phr. *To take a person's l.*: to make a portrait of him. **4.** He seide to hem also a liknesse [Vulg. *similitudinem*] WYCLIF *Luke* 5:36.

Likerish, -ous: see LICKERISH, etc.

Likewalk: see LYKE-WAKE.

Likewise (ləi·kwəiz), *adv.* 1449. [abbrev. from *in like wise*; see LIKE *a.* and WISE *sb.*] †**1.** *In like wise*: in the same manner –1673. **2.** Similarly; = 1. *Obs.* exc. *arch.* in *to do l.* (after *Luke* 10:37). 1460. **3.** Also, as well as, moreover, too 1509.

2. Looke on mee, and doe l. *Judg.* 7:17. So †**Li·keways.**

‖**Likin** (lī·kīn). Also **lekin.** 1876. [Chin. *li-kin*, f. *li* LI[2] + *kin* money.] A Chinese provincial transit duty.

Liking (ləi·kiŋ), *vbl. sb.* [OE. *līcung*, f. *līcian*; see LIKE *v.*[1] and -ING[1].] †**1.** The fact of being to one's taste, or of being liked –1579. †**2.** Pleasure, enjoyment; an instance of this –1548. **3.** The bent of the will; (a person's) pleasure. Also *pl.* Now *rare.* ME. **4.** The condition of being fond of or not averse to (a person or thing); fancy for or inclination to (some object) ME. †**b.** Approval, consent 1607. **c.** *On* or *upon l.*: on approval or trial. Now *rare* in educated use. 1615. †**5.** An object liked; (one's) beloved –1667. †**6.** (Good or healthy) bodily condition –1774.

3. I leaue thee to thine own l. GREENE. Phr. *to* (rarely *after, in*) *one's l.*: to one's taste; A Gentleman, who would willingly marry, if he could find a Wife to his L. STEELE. **4.** Friendships begin with l. GEO. ELIOT. **c.** After spending a few months on l., I was unanimously chosen 1834. **6.** A bay Mare.., in good L. 1705.

†**Liking,** *ppl. a.* ME. [f. LIKE *v.*[1] + -ING[2].] **1.** Pleasant, agreeable, attractive; favourable. Const. *till, to.* –1610. **2.** 'In condition'; healthy, plump; (of a soil) rich –1656.

1. The wynd to hym was likyng HALL. **2.** Normandie is enriched with a fat and l. soil HEYLIN. Hence †**Li·kingly** *adv.* in a pleasing manner; to one's liking.

Lilac (ləi·lăk). Also **laylock** (now chiefly *dial.* or *U.S.*). 1625. [- Fr. †*lilac* (now *lilas*) - Sp. *lilac* - Arab. *līlāk* - Pers. *līlak*, var. of *nīlak* bluish, f. *nīl* blue; see NIL¹.] **1.** A shrub, *Syringa vulgaris*, with pale pinkish violet, or white, blossoms. Also, the flower of this shrub. Also *transf.* of other species of *Syringa* or plants of other genera. **2.** The colour of lilac blossom 1791. **b.** *attrib.* or *adj.* Of this colour 1801.

2. She brought us Academic silks, in hue The l. TENNYSON. **b.** L. ribbons 1801. *Comb.* **l.-moth,** a little chocolate-coloured moth (*Lazotænia ribeana*). Hence **Lilaceous** (ləilˈēˈʃəs) *a.*

Lilacin (ləi·lăsin). Also **-ine.** 1842. [f. LILAC + -IN¹.] *Chem.* = SYRINGIN.

Liliaceous (liliēˈ·ʃəs), *a.* 1730. [– late L. *liliaceus*, f. *lilium* LILY; see -ACEOUS.] Pertaining to or characteristic of the order *Liliaceæ*; lily-like.

Lilial (li·liăl). *Bot.* 1846. [– mod.L. *lilialis*, f. *lilium* LILY.] *adj.* Only in *L. alliance*: In Lindley's classification, the alliance which includes the *Liliaceæ*. *sb.* A member of this alliance.

Lilied (li·lid), *a.* 1614. [f. LILY + -ED².] **1.** Resembling a lily in hue. **2.** Covered with, or having many, lilies 1633; embellished with the heraldic lilies or fleur-de-lis 1795.

2. Dance no more By sandy Ladons Lillied banks MILT. The l. banner of France 1884.

†Lill, *v.* 1530. [Symbolic; see LOLL *v.*] *trans.* To loll or hang (the tongue) *out* (rarely *forth*); rarely *intr.* of the tongue. –1656.

Lillibullero (lilibŭliᵊ·ro). 1688. [perh. orig. burlesquing Irish words.] Part of refrain (hence, name and tune) of a song ridiculing the Irish, popular about 1688. Hence **Lillibulle·ro** *v.* to sing l. over. STERNE.

Lilliput (li·lipɒt). An imaginary country in *Gulliver's Travels* (1726), peopled by pygmies six inches high. *attrib.* = diminutive 1867.

Lilliputian (lilipiū·ʃⁱăn). 1726. [f. LILLIPUT + -IAN.] **A.** *sb.* An inhabitant of LILLIPUT; hence, a person of diminutive size, character, or mind.

Oh, Gemini! would I had been born a L.! FIELDING.

B. *adj.* Of or pertaining to Lilliput or its inhabitants; hence, diminutive; petty 1726.

The L. Statesmen rise To malice of gigantic size 1764.

Lilly-pilly. 1860. [Of unkn. origin.] An Australian timber-tree, *Eugenia smithii* (N.O. *Myrtaceæ*).

Lilt (lilt), *sb.* 1728. [f. LILT *v.*] **1.** A song or tune, *esp.* a cheerful one. Chiefly *Sc.* **2.** The swing of a tune or of verse. Chiefly *literary.* 1840. **3.** A springing action 1869.

1. Is't some words ye've learnt by rote, Or a l. o' dool and sorrow? *Jacobite Relics.* **2.** The lines go with a l., and sing themselves to music of their own STEVENSON.

Lilt (lilt), *v.* *Sc.*, *n. dial.*, and *literary.* [ME. *lilte* (in *†lilting horn* 'kind of trumpet', Chaucer), *lülte*, obscurely rel. to LG., Du. *lul* pipe (Du. *lullepijp* bagpipe; cf. rare Sc. *†liltpipe* XV and Sc. *lill*, *lilt* hole in a wind instrument XVIII).] **†1.** *trans.* To sound (an alarum); to lift up (the voice) –1513. **2.** *trans.* and *intr.* To sing cheerfully or merrily; to sing with a lilt 1786. **3.** *n. dial.* 'To move with a lively action' 1834.

1. L. up your pipes RAMSAY. **2.** Lilting a tune to supply the lack of conversation EMILY BRONTË. **3.** Whether the bird flit here or there, O'er table *lilt*, or perch on chair WORDSW.

Lily (li·li). [OE. *lilie* (wk. fem.) – L. *lilium* prob. – Gr. λείριον, but the L. and Gr. words may have a common Mediterranean origin.] **1.** Any plant (or its flower) of the genus *Lilium* (N.O. *Liliaceæ*) of bulbous plants bearing large showy white, reddish, or purplish flowers (often spotted inside) at the top of a tall slender stem; *esp.* the White or Madonna Lily (*L. candidum*). **b.** With qualification, applied to other plants of the genus *Lilium* or N.O. *Liliaceæ*, and to certain allied plants 1555. **c.** Used in all versions of the Bible to render Heb. *šûšan*, *šōšan*, *šōšannāh*, LXX and N.T. κρίνον. **2. L. of** (or **†in**) **the valley** or *vale* (now *poet.*), *†May l.*, *Convallaria majalis*, a spring-flowering plant having two largish leaves and racemes of white bell-shaped fragrant flowers 1538. **3.** *fig.* Applied to persons or things of exceptional whiteness, fairness, or purity; e.g. the white of a beautiful complexion (*sing.* and *pl.*; cf. *rose*) ME. **4.** A representation of the flower 1459; the heraldic fleur-de-lis, as in the arms of the old French monarchy; hence, the royal arms of France, the French (Bourbon) dynasty ME.; †the fleur-de-lis which marks the north on a compass –1661.

1. The wand-like l., which lifted up..its moonlight-coloured cup SHELLEY. **b.** *Flax, orange, panther, Persian, tiger, Turk's-cap l.* etc. (see the first element); also, belonging to N.O. *Amaryllidaceæ, belladonna, calla, Guernsey, Jacobean, lent, pond, sword l.*, etc. (see the first element). **African l.,** *Agapanthus umbellatus.* **Atamasco l.,** *Zephyranthes atamasco.* **Yellow l.,** the daffodil (*dial.*). **2.** That shy plant..the l. of the vale, That loves the ground WORDSW. **3.** A Virgin, A most vnspotted Lilly *Hen. VIII*, v. v. 62. **4.** Item, one box of silver..chased with liliis 1464. Great Edward, with the lilies on his brow From haughty Gallia torn GRAY.

attrib. and *Comb.* **1.** General: as *l.-bank, -crown, -root*, etc.; *l.-clear, -whitening* adjs.; *l.-like* adj. and adv.; *l.-cradled, -crowned* adjs.

2. Special: as **l.-beetle,** the beetle *Crioceris merdigera*, which infests lilies; **-encrinite,** an encrinite resembling a l. in shape; **-iron,** a harpoon with a detachable head used in killing sword-fish; **-pad** *U.S.*, the broad floating leaf of the water-lily; **-star,** (*a*) = *feather-star*, a crinoid of the family *Comatulidæ*; (*b*) the star-like flower of the water-lily.

b. In plant-names (little used): **l. asphodel, daffodil,** names for the genus *Amaryllis*; **-bind, -bine** *dial.*, bindweed; **l. hyacinth, †jacinth,** the genus *Scilla*, esp. *S. liliohyacinthus*; **l. pink,** the genus *Aphyllanthes*; **l. thorn,** the genus *Catesbæa*; **-worts,** Lindley's name for the N.O. *Liliaceæ*.

B. as *adj.* **a.** White or fair as a lily; lily-white; lily-like 15.. **b.** Pale, colourless, bloodless 1590.

a. Elaine, the l. maid of Astolat TENNYSON. A l.-fingered idler 1873. **b.** These Lilly Lips SHAKS. Thou Lilly-liuer'd Boy *Macb.* v. iii. 15.

Li·ly-flower. ME. The flower of the (white) lily; *occas.* the heraldic fleur-de-lis.

Li·ly-pot. 1540. **1.** A flower-pot with a lily growing in it; frequent as a symbolic accessory in pictures of the Annunciation. **2.** An ornamental vase imitating this; †*spec.* a tobacco-jar 1610.

Lily-white, *a.* (Stress variable.) ME. White as a lily. Hence **Lily-whiteness.**

Lim, obs. f. LIMB *sb.*¹, LIME *sb.*¹

Lima (lī·mă, ləi·mă), name of the capital of Peru, used *attrib.* in: **L. bark,** the bark of some species of *Cinchona*; a kind of Peruvian bark; **L. bean,** *Phaseolus lunatus*; also, *P. perennis*; **L.-wood,** a kind of Brazil-wood.

†Limace. *rare.* 1491. [– (O)Fr. *limace* or L. *limax, limac-* slug, snail.] A shell-snail –1592.

Limaceous (ləimēˈ·ʃəs), *a.* 1656. [f. L. *limax, limac-* slug, snail + -EOUS; see -ACEOUS.] Pertaining to slugs or snails; snail-like; now, pertaining to the genus *Limax* of slugs. So **Lima·ciform** *a.* having the form of a slug.

‖**Limaçon** (līmasoṅ). 1581. [Fr.. = snail-shell, spiral staircase, etc., f. *limace*; see LIMACE, -OON.] **†1.** A kind of military manœuvre. [So in OFr.] –1591. **2.** *Math.* Pascal's name for a certain curve of the fourth degree. **3.** A metallic gimp 1893.

Limail, lemel (lī·mĕl). ME. [– (O)Fr. *limaille* filings, f. *limer* :– L. *limare* file.] Metal filings.

An Ounce..Of siluer lemaille CHAUCER.

‖**Liman** (limā·n). 1858. [Russian; = 'estuary'.] A shallow narrow marsh at the mouth of a river, where salt is made.

Limation (ləimēˈ·ʃən). Now *rare.* 1612. [– late L. *limatio* (in med.L. 'filing, polishing'), f. *limat-*, pa. ppl. stem of L. *limare* file; see -ION.] Filing; *fig.* 'polishing up'. **†b.** *Astron.* Correction of errors in calculation or observation. FLAMSTEED.

Limb (lim), *sb.*¹ [OE. *lim*, corresp. to ON. *limr*; prob. rel. to OE. *liþ* LITH *sb.*] **1.** Any organ or part of the body. *Obs.* exc. *dial.* **2.** A part of an animal body distinct from the head or the trunk, e.g. a leg, arm, wing OE. Also *fig.* **b.** = LEG. Now only (esp. U.S.) in prudish use. ME. **3.** In uses originally *fig.* (cf. MEMBER). See below. OE. **4.** Transf. senses. **a.** A main branch of a tree OE. **b.** A projecting section of a building; one of the four branches of a cross; a member or clause of a sentence, or the like; a spur of a mountain range; one of the pieces forming the lock of a gun 1577. **†c.** [tr. med.L. *membrum.*] An estate, etc. dependent on another –1647.

1. Þe lyme of syȝte [L. *organum visus*] ME. **2.** Their weake limmes and failing ioyntes 1581. Phr. *Life and l., l. and carcase, l. and wind*, i.e. all the bodily faculties employed in certain connections. *To tear* or *pull* (*one*) *l. from l.* **b.** The poor brute [a horse]..fell..fracturing his l. 1858. **3. a.** A member (e.g. of the church, of Christ, etc.); a branch or section; a component part. *Obs.* exc. in nonce-uses. OE. An army is but the l. of a nation KINGLAKE. **b.** *L. of the devil, of Satan, of hell*: an agent or scion of the evil one; hence, a mischievous wicked person (now *dial.*) OE. **c.** Hence, *limb* alone = a mischievous young rascal (*colloq.*) 1625. **d.** *L. of the law*: a lawyer, a police officer, or other legal functionary (*derisive*). **†e.** Applied to things, as *a lim of Idolatry* –1661. **4.** A slender crosslet.. The shaft and limbs were rods of yew SCOTT. In another l. of the same sentence KINGLAKE.

Limb (lim), *sb.*² 1450. [– (O)Fr. *limbe* or its source L. *limbus*; see LIMBO, LIMBUS.] **†1.** *Sc.* = LIMBO 1. –1797. **†2.** An edging. DIGBY. **3.** In scientific use: The edge or boundary of a surface; the graduated edge of a quadrant or the like 1593; the edge of the disc of the sun, moon, etc. 1677. **b.** *Bot.* The lamina of a monopetalous corolla, of a petal or sepal. Also, the blade of a leaf. 1735.

3. The sun's lower l. was just free of the hill T. HARDY.

Limb (lim), *v.* 1623. [f. LIMB *sb.*¹] **1.** *trans.* To pull limb from limb, dismember. Also with *up.* 1674. **†2.** *refl.* To provide oneself with limbs MILT.

Limbate (li·mbeˈt), *a.* 1826. [– late L. *limbatus*, f. *limbus* LIMB *sb.*²] *Biol.* Of a part or organ: Having a limb or border; bordered; *Bot.* said of a flower having an edging of a different colour from the rest. Hence **Limba·tion,** the formation of a border; a border distinguished by colour or structure 1881.

Limbeck (li·mbek), *sb. arch.* ME. [Early forms *lambyke, lembike*; aphetic f. ALEMBIC.] = ALEMBIC. Also *fig.*

†Li·mbeck, *v.* 1598. [f. the sb.] **1.** *trans.* To treat as in an alembic; to distil. Chiefly *fig.*; esp. to rack (the brain) in the effort to extract ideas. –1661. **2.** To distil or extract (an essence, etc.) as by an alembic –1657.

1. Wasting my wits, and Limbeking my braines MABBE.

Limbed (limd), *a.* ME. [f. LIMB *sb.*¹ + -ED².] Having limbs. Usu. in comb., as *well-, straight-l.*, etc.

Perfet formes, Limb'd and full grown MILT.

Limber (li·mbəɹ), *sb.*¹ 1480. [Earliest forms *lymo(u)r*, perh. for **limmer*, **limner* (cf. Sc. *lymnar* XVI), subst. use of med.L. *limonarius* adj., f. *limo, limon-* shaft, of unkn. origin.] **1.** The shaft of a cart or carriage. *Obs.* exc. *dial.* **2.** *Mil.* (In early use *pl.*) The detachable fore part of a gun-carriage, consisting of two wheels and an axle, a pole for the horses, and a frame which holds one or two ammunition-chests 1497.

Comb.: **l.-box, -chest** *Mil.*, the ammunition box carried by a l.; **-hook,** the iron hook at the back of the l. to which the trail of the gun-carriage is attached; **-horse** *dial.*, the horse that is placed between the shafts; **-saddle,** a cart-saddle.

Limber (li·mbəɹ), *sb.*² 1626. [– (O)Fr. *lumière* light, hole (used in the same techn. sense) :– Rom. **luminaria*, fem. sing. use of pl. of L. *luminare* light, lamp, f. *lumen, lumin-* light.] *Naut. pl.* Holes cut through the floor-timbers on each side of the keelson to form a passage for water to the pump-well.

Comb.: **l.-board,** one of the short removable boards in a ship's floor above the limbers; **-chain,** a chain used like a limber-rope; **-passage,** the passage or channel formed by the limber-strakes on each side of the keelson; **-rope,** a rope passing through the limber-holes, by which they may be cleared of dirt; **-strake** (or **-streak**), the first course of inside planking next the keelson; **-tar,** the bilge-water or refuse found in the hold of a ship that imports tar.

Limber (li·mbəɹ), *a.* 1565. [perh. from LIMBER *sb.*¹ in allusion to the to-and-fro motion of shafts or a fore-carriage.] **1.** Easily bent; flexible, pliant, supple. **b.** Of persons, etc.: Lithe and nimble 1582. **†c.** Limp, flaccid, flabby –1747. **2.** *fig.* 1602.

1. The Bargeman that doth rowe with long and l. Oare TURBERV. **b.** A little child, a l. elf COLERIDGE. **c.** A rabbit, if stale, will be l. and slimy; if new, white and stiff MRS. GLASSE. **2.** Men of l. and pliable Consciences 1695. Hence **Li·mberness.**

Limber (li·mbəɹ), *v.*[1] 1748. [f. prec.] *trans.* To make limber, pliant, or supple.

Limber (li·mbəɹ), *v.*[2] 1843. [f. LIMBER *sb.*[1]] *Mil.* To attach the limber to (a gun); *absol.* to fasten together the two parts of a gun-carriage, in order to move away: usu. *to l. up.*

†**Li·mberha:m.** 1675. [f. LIMBER *a.* + HAM *sb.*[1]] **a.** One who has limber hams; *fig.* an obsequious person, lackey. **b.** A character like Dryden's '*Limberham*, a tame, foolish keeper' –1766.

Limbless (li·mlės), *a.* 1594. [f. LIMB *sb.*[1] + -LESS.] Having no limbs.

Limb-meal (li·m,mīl), *adv. Obs.* exc. *arch.* and *dial.* [OE. *limmǣlum*; see LIMB *sb.*[1], -MEAL.] Limb from limb, limb by limb; piecemeal.

O that I had her heere, to teare her Limb-meale SHAKS.

Limbo (li·mbo[u]). ME. [orig. in phr. *in limbo, out of limbo*, repr. med.L. *in limbo, e limbo*; abl. of L. *limbus*; see LIMBUS.] **1.** A region on the border of Hell, the abode of the just who died before Christ's coming, and of unbaptized infants. (More explicitly *limbo patrum, limbo infantum*; see LIMBUS.) Hence *gen.* †**b.** Hell, Hades –1637. **2.** *transf.* and *fig.* **a.** Prison, durance 1590. **b.** Any unfavourable place or condition, likened to Limbo 1642.

1. 'Tis a just Idea of a L. of the Infants CLEVELAND. *gen.* A L. large and broad, since calld The Paradise of Fools MILT. **2. a.** I haue some of 'em in *Limbo Patrum* SHAKS. **b.** L. of Lost Reputations MOORE (*title*). *Comb.* †**l.-lake,** the pit of Hell.

‖**Limbus** (li·mbŏs). 1400. [L., = edge, border; in med.L., a region on the border of Hell.] **1.** Occas. = LIMBO 1. *L. patrum* = 'the limbo of the fathers', i.e. of the just who died before Christ's coming. *L. infantum* = 'the limbo of infants'. **2.** Used *techn.* in lit. sense of 'border' or 'edge'; e.g. in *Bot.* = LIMB *sb.*[2] 3 b 1671.

2. Round the crater is the l., which is a decorated border of floral or other ornaments 1857.

Lime (ləim), *sb.*[1] [OE. *lim*, corresp. to MDu. *lîm* (Du. *lijm*), OHG. *lîm* (G. *leim*), ON. *lím*; f. Gmc. **līm-*, var. of **laim-* LOAM, ult. rel. to L. *limus* mud.] **1.** = BIRD-LIME. Now only *poet.* (In OE. any adhesive substance.) **2.** Usually coupled with *stone*: Mortar or cement used in building. Now *Sc.* OE. **3.** The alkaline earth which is the chief constituent of mortar; calcium oxide (CaO). It is obtained by calcining limestone (carbonate of lime), the heat driving off the carbonic acid, and leaving a brittle white solid, which is pure lime (or QUICKLIME). It is powerfully caustic, and combines readily with water, evolving great heat in the process, and forming hydrate of lime (*slaked lime*). †**4. a.** The CALX of metals. **b.** Any alkaline earth. –1796.

1. Toils for Beasts, and L. for Birds were found DRYDEN. You must lay l. to tangle her desires By walefull Sonnets *Two Gent.* III. ii. 68. **3.** You Rogue, heere's L. in this Sacke too SHAKS. *L. and hair*: a kind of plasterer's cement which added hair binds closely together.

Comb.: **l.-ash** *dial.*, a composition of ashes and l. used as a rough kind of flooring for kitchens, etc.; **-ball** (*light*), limelight; also *attrib.*; **-rock,** limestone (? now *U.S.*); **-wash,** *sb.* a mixture of l. and water, used for coating walls, etc.; *vb.* to whitewash with this; **-work,** a place where l. is made (also *pl.*).

b. In names of minerals, denoting the presence of l. or calcium, e.g. *l.-marl, -slate*; **l.-feldspar,** triclinic feldspar containing calcium.

Lime (ləim), *sb.*[2] 1622. [– Fr. *lime* – mod. Pr. *limo*, Sp. *lima* – Arab. *lima*; see LEMON *sb.*[1]] The globular fruit of the tree *Citrus medica*, var. *acida*, smaller and more acid than the lemon; *sour lime*. Its juice is much used as a drink. **Sweet L.,** *Citrus medica*, var. *limetta*.

Comb.: **l.-juice,** the juice of the l., used as a drink and as an antiscorbutic; **-punch,** punch made with lime-juice instead of lemon-juice; so **-squash.**

Lime (ləim), *sb.*[3] 1625. [unexpl. alt. of *line*, var. of LIND.] **1.** A tree of the genus *Tilia*, esp. *T. europæa*, an ornamental tree having heart-shaped leaves and small fragrant yellowish flowers. **2.** The seed of the lime-tree. MRS. GLASSE.

Lime (ləim), *v.*[1] OE. [f. LIME *sb.*[1]] **1.** *trans.* To cement. Chiefly *fig.* **2.** To smear (twigs, etc.) with bird-lime, for catching birds ME. **b.** To smear with a sticky substance (*rare*) ME. **3.** To catch with bird-lime. Often *fig.* ME. †**4.** To defile –1592. **5.** To treat or dress with lime 1598. †**b.** To coat with lime-wash –1615.

1. I will not ruinate my Father's House, Who gaue his blood to lyme the stones together SHAKS. **2.** My selfe haue lym'd a Bush for her SHAKS. **3.** He was..limed this time [matrimonially] 1870. **5.** *Merry W.* I. iii. 15. Then l. and sow with oats 1799. **b.** Houses newly limed 1615.

†**Lime,** *v.*[2] 1555. [Origin unkn. Cf. LINE *v.*[3]] *trans.* To impregnate (a bitch). Also *pass.* and *intr.* to copulate *with*, be coupled *to*. –1682.

Lime (-hound): see LYAM (-HOUND).

Li·me-burner. ME. [LIME *sb.*[1]] One who makes lime by burning limestone.

Lime-kiln (ləi·mkiln, -kil). ME. A kiln in which lime is made by calcining limestone. Also *transf.* and *fig.*

Limelight (ləi·mləit). 1826. [f. LIME *sb.*[1]] The intense white light produced by heating a piece of lime in an oxyhydrogen flame. Called also DRUMMOND LIGHT.

Phr. *In the l.* (orig. Theatr.): in a very conspicuous position. Hence **Li·melight** *v.*, to illuminate by l.

‖**Limen** (ləi·men). 1895. [L., = 'threshold'; introduced as equiv. of G. *schwelle* (Herbart *Psychol.* 1824). Cf. SUBLIMINAL.] *Psychol.* The limit below which a given stimulus ceases to be perceptible; the minimum amount of nerve-excitation required to produce a sensation. Also called THRESHOLD.

Li·me-pit. 1440. [f. LIME *sb.*[1]] **1. a.** A limestone quarry. **b.** A pit in which lime is burnt. **2.** A pit in which tanners dress skins with lime 1591.

Li·mer[1]. *arch.* ME. [– AFr. *limer* = OFr. *liemier* (mod. *limier*), f. OFr. *liem* (mod. *lien*) leash; see LIEN, LYAM.] A kind of hound; *prop.* a leash-hound; in early use (now *arch.*) a bloodhound; later, a mongrel.

Limer[2] (ləi·məɹ). 1611. [f. LIME *v.*[1] + -ER[1].] One who limes; one who snares with bird-lime; one who limewashes. Also, a brush for limewashing.

Limerick (li·mərik). 1898. [Said to be from a chorus 'Will you come up to Limerick?', following an extemporized 'nonsense-verse' sung by each member of a convivial party.] A form of nonsense-verse; erron. applied to that written by Lear.

†**Lime-rod.** ME. [f. LIME *sb.*[1]] = LIME-TWIG –1626.

Limestone (ləi·mstō[u]n). 1523. [f. LIME *sb.*[1] + STONE.] A rock which consists chiefly of carbonate of lime, and yields lime when burnt. (The crystalline variety is marble.)

Li·me-twig, *sb.* ME. [f. LIME *sb.*[1]] **1.** A twig smeared with bird-lime for catching birds. †**2.** *attrib.* or *adj.* Ensnaring; pilfering –1730. Hence †**Li·me-twig** *v. trans.* to catch as with a lime-twig; to entangle, ensnare.

Li·me-water. 1677. [f. LIME *sb.*[1]] A solution of lime in water, used medicinally and to clarify water.

Limicoline (ləimi·kŏləin, -in), *a.* 1872. [f. mod.L. *Limicolæ*, f. L. *limus* mud, after TERRICOLOUS, TERRICOLE; see -INE[1].] Of or pertaining to the *Limicolæ*, a family of shore or wading birds.

Liminal (li·minăl), *a.* 1884. [f. L. *limen, limin-* LIMEN + -AL[1].] Of or pertaining to a limen, or (*gen.*) to the initial stage.

Limit (li·mit), *sb.* ME. [– L. *limes, limit-* frontier; cf. Fr. *limite* (XVI).] **1.** A boundary, frontier; a landmark. Now only: A bounding line or terminal point; chiefly *pl.* bounds. **2.** One of the fixed points or values between which the possible or permissible range of anything is confined; a bound beyond which something ceases to be possible or allowable ME. **b.** *Math.* (*a*) A finite quantity to which the sum of a converging series progressively approximates, but to which it cannot become equal in a finite number of terms; a fixed value to which a function similarly approximates. (*b*) Each of the two values of a variable between which a definite integral is taken. (*c*) The ultimate position of the point of intersection of two lines, which, by their relative motion, are tending to coalescence. 1753. **c.** Astron. *L. of a planet*: its greatest heliocentric latitude 1704. **d.** *gen.* Limitation, restriction within limits. Chiefly in phr. *without l.* 1599. ¶**e.** Prescribed time; period of repose after child-bearing. SHAKS. **f.** A thing (or person) having some (usu. objectionable) quality or attribute in the highest possible or tolerable degree (*colloq.*, orig. *U.S.*) 1906. †**3.** The tract or region defined by a boundary; *pl.* the bounds, territories –1792. †**4.** *Logic.* = TERM (med.L. *terminus*) BLUNDEVIL.

1. Hence is the Water enforced to enlarge his limits 1625. A point may be the l. of a line BP. BERKELEY. **2.** Finding thy worth a limmit past my praise SHAKS. Nature has set limits to the pleasures of sense REID. **e.** *Rich. II*, I. iii. 151. *Wint. T.* III. ii. 107. **f.** Well, that's the limit! (*mod.*). **3.** At length into the limits of the North They came MILT. *P.L.* V. 755.

Limit (li·mit), *v.* ME. [– (O)Fr. *limiter* or L. *limitare*, f. as prec.] **1.** *trans.* To assign within limits; to appoint, fix definitely; to specify. Also with *away, over.* Const. *dat.*, or *to*, (*till*), *upon*, and *to* with *inf. Obs.* exc. in legal language. †**b.** To appoint (a person) to an office; to assign (a duty) to a person –1638. †**c.** To lot or plot *out*; to allot –1649. **2.** To confine within limits (*rarely* in material sense); to bound, restrict. Const. *to.* **b.** To serve as a limit or boundary to; to mark off *from.* Also *to l. in.* Now *rare.* 1582. †**3.** *intr.* To beg within specified limits. [f. LIMITER (sense 1).] 1577.

1. At the daye before lymytted and assygned 1494. A power..to l. other uses CRUISE. **2.** He thought a government limited by law was only a name BURNET. The commerce..was still mainly limited to the exportation of wool to Flanders GREEN. **b.** This rule thus fixed no tyme shall l., or hazard 1582. **3.** They [Popishe friers] go ydelly a limiting abrode 1577. Hence **Li·mitable** *a.* that may be limited. **Li·mitableness. Li·miting** *ppl. a.*

Limitanean (limitē[i]·niăn), *a.* 1839. [f. late L. *limitaneus* + -AN.] *Rom. Antiq.* Stationed on the border. So †**Li·mitany** *a.* 1611.

Limitarian (limitē[ə]·riăn), *a.* and *sb.* 1818. [f. LIMIT *sb.* + -ARIAN as in *unitarian*, etc.] A dyslogistic term applied to theologians who hold the doctrine of 'limited redemption'.

Limitary (li·mitări), *a.* and *sb.* 1620. [In sense 2 – L. *limitaris* of or situated on a boundary; in senses 1, 3, f. LIMIT *sb.* + -ARY[2].] **1.** Subject to limits; limited. **b.** Of a friar: Licensed to beg within certain limits. SCOTT. **2.** Of or pertaining to a boundary; situate on the boundary 1650. **3.** Serving as a boundary; limiting, confining, containing. Const. *of.* 1807. **4.** *sb.* = LIMITER 1. Heylin.

1. The poor l. creature calling himself a man of the world DE QUINCEY. **2.** This County (because a L.) did abound with Fortifications FULLER. **3.** The horizon's l. line 1807.

Limitate (li·mitē[i]t), *pa. pple.* and *ppl. a.* 1581. [– L. *limitatus*, pa. pple. of *limitare*; see LIMIT *v.*, -ATE[2].] †**A.** *pa. pple.* = LIMITED –1585. **B.** *ppl. a.* **a.** Of land: Parted off by boundaries (*rare*) 1853. **b.** *Bot.* Bounded by a distinct line 1871.

Limitation (limitē[i]·ʃən). ME. [– L. *limitatio*, f. *limitat-*, pa. ppl. stem of *limitare*; see LIMIT *v.*, -ION. Cf. (O)Fr. *limitation.*] **1.** The action of limiting (see the vb.); an instance of this. †**2. a.** An allotted space; the district or circuit of an itinerant officer or preaching friar; the region belonging to a particular nation; *fig.* one's allotted sphere –1552. †**b.** An allotted time. *Cor.* II. iii. 146. **3.** The condition of being limited 1597. **4.** A point or respect in which something is limited; a limiting provision, rule, or circumstance 1523. **5.** *Law.* **a.** The statutory specification of a period, or the period specified by statute, within which an action must be brought 1540. **b.** The specification of a period, or the period specified, for the continuance of an estate or the operation of a law 1767. **c.** The settlement of an estate by a special provision or with a special modification; the modification or provision itself

1767. **6.** = LIMIT 1, 2. Also *pl.* bounds. 1523.

1. A fresh l. of the succession to the throne 1863. **3.** The natural dulness and l. of our faculties BERKELEY. **4.** Most of the provinces coupled their acquiescence with limitations which rendered it of little worth PRESCOTT. **6.** She knew the limitations of her own powers too well to attempt [etc.] JANE AUSTEN.

Limitative (li·mitĕtiv). 1530. [– schol. L. *limitativus*, f. as prec.; see -IVE. Cf. Fr. *limitatif, -ive* (XVI).] **A.** *adj.* **1.** Limiting, restrictive. †**2.** Conditional 1682.

1. *L. judgement* (Logic): used by Kant to denote judgements of the type 'Every A is a not-B'; also *occas.* a judgement serving to limit or modify another.

B. *sb. Logic.* A limitative judgement. BOWEN.

Limited (li·mitĕd), *ppl. a.* 1551. [f. LIMIT *v.* + -ED¹.] **1.** In senses of the vb. **2.** quasi-*sb.* = *limited mail.* (*U.S. colloq.*) 1887.

1. *L. company*: short for *l. liability company* (see LIABILITY). *L. mail*: a mail train taking only a l. number of passengers. *L. monarchy*: one in which the functions of the monarch are exercised under constitutional restrictions; so *l. government, monarch, royalty.* Hence **Li·mited-ly** *adv.*, **-ness.**

Limiter (li·mitəɹ). Also **-or, -our.** ME. [f. LIMIT *v.* + -ER¹.] **1.** (Also *friar l.*) A friar licensed to beg within certain limits. *Obs.* exc. *Hist.* **2.** One who or that which limits (see the vb.) 1483.

1. A limitoure of the graye fryers, in the tyme of his limitation preached manye tymes and hadde but one Sermon LATIMER.

Limitless (li·mitlĕs), *a.* 1581. [f. LIMIT *sb.* + -LESS.] Having or admitting of no limits; illimitable; unbounded. Hence **Li·mitless-ly** *adv.*, **-ness.**

Limitor, -our, obs. ff. LIMITER.

Limitrophe (li·mitrōᵘf). 1589. [– Fr. *limitrophe* – late L. *limitrophus*, f. *limit-* LIMIT + Gr. -τροφος supporting (τρέφειν support, nourish), applied to lands set apart for the support of troops on the frontier.]

A. *adj.* Situated on the frontier; bordering on, adjacent *to* (another country) 1826.

The policy of a l. frontier with Russia revived 1881.

†**B.** *sb.* A border-land –1598.

Limmer (li·məɹ). *Sc.* and *n. dial.* 1456. [perh. conn. w. LIMB *sb.*¹] **A.** *sb.* **1.** A rogue, scoundrel. *arch.* **2.** A light woman; in weaker sense, a jade, hussy, minx 1566. **B.** *adj.* Knavish, scoundrelly 1500.

Limn (lim), *v.* Now *literary* and *arch.* ME. [contr. f. LUMINE.] †**1.** *trans.* To illuminate (letters, manuscripts, etc.). Also *absol.* –1588. †**2.** To embellish with gold or bright colour; to depict *in* (gold, etc.). Also (*rare*), to lay on (colour). –1653. **3.** To paint (a picture); to portray, depict (a subject). †Formerly *spec.* to paint in water-colour or distemper. 1592. **b.** *transf.* and *fig.* 1593. †**4.** *absol.* or *intr.* To paint; *esp.* in water-colour or distemper –1678.

3. Where Apelles limb'd to life Loathed Vulcans louely wife WITHER. *fig.* The..picture of a great man..limned in words SMILES. Provb. *To l. the water, to l.* (something) *on water*: said of something transient or futile. Hence **Limner** (li·mnəɹ), an illuminator of manuscripts (*Hist.*); a (portrait) painter. **Li·mnery,** the work of a limner.

Limonin (li·mŏnin). Also **-ine.** 1845. [f. mod.L. *limonum* (Fr. *limon*) LEMON + -IN¹.] *Chem.* The bitter principle contained in the pips of oranges, lemons, etc.

Limonite (ləi·mŏnəit). 1823. [Named by Hausman, 1813, probably from Gr. λειμών meadow, a rendering of its earlier German name *wiesenerz* 'meadow-ore'; see -ITE¹ 2 b.] *Min. Orig.*, bog iron ore; *now*, extended to all forms of hydrous sesquioxide of iron.

Limous (ləi·məs), *a.* ? *Obs.* ME. [– L. *limosus*, f. *limus* mud, slime; see -OUS.] Muddy; slimy.

Limousine (li·muzīn). 1902. [– Fr. *limousine*, f. *Limousin* name of a province of France; orig. caped cloak worn by natives of the province.] A motor-car with a closed body and a roofed place for the driver.

Limp (limp), *sb.*¹ 1818. [f. LIMP *v.*] The action of limping; a limping gait or walk.

Limp (limp), *sb.*² 1596. [Of unkn. origin.] *Mining.* An instrument for throwing off the refuse from the ore in the operation of jigging.

Limp (limp), *a.* 1706. [prob. of dial. origin; perh. ult. rel. to LIMP *v.*, the basic sense being 'hanging loose'.] **1.** Wanting in stiffness, flaccid; flexible, pliant. **b.** Used of a kind of binding without mill-board 1863. **2.** *transf.* and *fig.* Wanting in firmness, strictness, nervous energy, etc. 1853.

1. His [Byron's] l. collars 1897. **2.** Loose l. rhymes 1880. Hence **Li·mp-ly** *adv.*, **-ness.**

Limp (limp), *v.* ME. [prob. f. †*limphalt* lame, OE. *lempealt, læmpihalt*, f. **lamp-* :– IE. **lomb-* (cf. Skr. *lámbate* hangs down or loose, sinks) + *healt* HALT *a.*; cf. MHG. *limpfen* limp.] *intr.* To walk lamely, to halt. Occas. with cogn. obj. Also *fig.* Hence **Li·mper. Li·mpingly** *adv.*

Limpet (li·mpĕt). Also *Sc.* **lampit.** [ME. *lempet* :– OE. *lempedu* (cf. OHG. *lampfrīda*) – med.L. *lamprēda, -ida* limpet, LAMPREY.] A gasteropod mollusc of the genus *Patella* with a tent-shaped shell, adhering tightly to rocks. **b.** *fig.* A person, esp. a State employee, who clings to office 1905.

He..stuck like a lampit to a rock SCOTT.

Limpid (li·mpid), *a.* 1613. [– Fr. *limpide*, or L. *limpidus*, prob. conn. w. *lympha* clear liquid; see LYMPH.] Free from turbidity; pellucid, clear. Also *fig.*

L. waters DRYDEN, air COWPER, crystal 1834. A l. soprano 1847. *fig.* L. language GLADSTONE. So **Limpi·dity, Li·mpidness. Li·mpidly** *adv.*

Limuloid (li·miŭloid), *a.* (*sb.*) 1859. [f. mod.L. *Limulus*, f. L. *limulus* somewhat askance, f. *limus* askew; see -OID.] Of, pertaining to, or resembling the genus *Limulus* or king-crabs; also as *sb.*

Limy (ləi·mi), *a.* 1552. [f. LIME *sb.*¹ + -Y¹.] **1.** Besmeared with bird-lime. **2.** Consisting of or containing lime 1676. **3.** Resembling lime 1775.

†**Lin,** *v.* [OE. *linnan* = OHG. *bi|linnan*, ON. *linna*, Goth. *af|linnan*, f. Gmc. **lin-*; see LITHE *a.*] **1.** *intr.* To cease, leave off; desist *from.* Of the wind: To drop. As a command: 'Leave off!' 'Let go!' –1725. ¶**b.** Misused for: To fail, omit. M. PRIOR. **2.** *trans.* To cease from, leave off –1643.

Lin, obs. var. of LINN¹, waterfall.

Linable, lineable (ləi·năb'l), *a.* 1698. [f. LINE *sb.*² or *v.*² + -ABLE.] Ranged in a straight line.

Linage (ləi·nĕdʒ). Also **lineage.** 1883. [f. LINE *sb.*² + -AGE.] **a.** Position (of figures) in line. **b.** Quantity of printed or written matter estimated in lines 1884. **c.** Payment at so much per line 1888.

c. An editor..offered him [Mr. Swinburne] 'l.' for a poem 1888.

Linage, obs. f. LINEAGE.

Linarite (ləi·nărəit). 1844. [Named by Glocker, 1837, from *Linares*, Spain, where it is alleged to be found; see -ITE¹ 2 b.] *Min.* Sulphate of lead and copper, found in brilliant blue crystals.

Linch (linʃ), *sb.*¹ *Obs.* exc. in *Comb.* [ME. *lins* :- OE. *lynis* = WFris. *lins*, OS. *lunisa* (Du. *luns, lens*), MHG. *luns, lunse* (G. *lünse*); the base is seen also in ME. †*linnail* (XV), †*linpin*, perh. OE. **lyne* (:– **luni-*), rel. to OHG. *lun, luna* (G. dial. *lunn, lon*); cf. OHG. *luning* LINCH-PIN.] †**1.** = LINCH-PIN –1497. †**2.** *Naut.* ? A belaying-pin 1549.

Linch (linʃ), *sb.*² *dial.* 1591. [repr. OE. *hlinc*; see LINK *sb.*¹] A rising ground; also = LINCHET (1 and 2).

Linch (linʃ), *v.* 1898. [f. LINCH *sb.*¹] *trans.* To fasten with or as with a linch-pin.

Linchet (li·nʃĕt). Also **lynchet.** *dial.* 1674. [f. LINCH *sb.*²] **1.** A strip of green land between two pieces of ploughed land. **2.** A slope or terrace along the face of a chalk down 1797.

Li·nch-pin. ME. [f. LINCH *sb.*¹ + PIN.] A pin passed through the end of an axle-tree to keep the wheel in its place.

Lincoln (li·ŋkŏn). ME. [Name of the county town of Lincolnshire.] **1.** Used *attrib.* or *adj.*; esp. in **L. green,** a bright green stuff made at L. **2.** *ellipt.* as *sb.* in *pl.* A variety of sheep originally bred in Lincolnshire 1837.

Lincture (li·ŋktiŭɹ). 1621. [f. as next + -URE, perh. – med.L. **linctura.* Cf. contemp. LINGENCE.] = next.

Linctus (li·ŋktŏs). Pl. **linctuses.** 1681. [– med.L. **linctus* (cl. L. *linctus* licking, f. *lingere* lick); after late L. *electuarium* ELECTUARY.] A syrupy medicine to be licked up with the tongue.

†**Lind.** Also **lyne, line.** See also LINN². [OE. *lind, linde* lime-tree, shield, corresp. to OS. *lind(i)a* (Du. *linde*), OHG. *linta* (G. *linde*), ON. *lind*; prob. rel. to Gr. ἐλάτη silver fir.] = LINDEN *sb.* 1 –1796. Also *attrib.*, as *l.-grove*, etc. 1450.

Lindabrides (lindæ·bridīz). *arch.* 1640. The name of a lady in the 'Mirror of Knighthood' (1585), used allusively for: A lady-love, a mistress.

Linden (li·ndĕn), *sb.* 1577. [LINDEN *a.* used subst. In the comb. *linden-tree* – Du. *lindeboom*, †*lindenboom*, G. *lindenbaum*, f. *linde* (see LIND) + *boom, baum* tree.] **1.** The lime-tree (see LIME *sb.*³). Also *attrib.* **2.** *Antiq.* Used to render OE. *lind*, shield of lime-tree wood 1855.

†**Li·nden,** *a.* [OE. *linden*, f. *lind*; see LIND, -EN⁴.] Made of the wood of the lime-tree –ME.

Line (ləin), *sb.*¹ Now chiefly *dial.* [OE. *līn* = OS., OHG. *lîn* (Du. *lijn-*, G. *lein-*), ON. *lín*, Goth. *lein* :– Gmc. **līnam*, corresp. to or – L. *līnum* flax, rel. to Gr. λίνον.] **1.** = FLAX. †**a.** The fibre of flax. *Obs.* exc. as in b. **b.** In mod. techn. use, flax of a fine and long staple, which has been separated by the hackle from the tow 1835. **c.** The flax plant ME. **2.** Flax spun or woven; linen thread or cloth (now *rare* or *obs.*); †a napkin of linen; in *pl.* linen vestments OE. **3.** *attrib.*, as *l.-dresser, -spinner*, etc. ME.

2. Nor anie weauer, which his worke doth boast In dieper, in damaske, or in lyne SPENSER.

Line (ləin), *sb.*² [Two words of ult. identical etym. have coalesced: (1) OE. *līne* rope, line, series, rule = MDu. *line* (Du. *lijn*), OHG. *līna* (G. *leine* cord), ON. *lína*, prob. Gmc. – L. *linea*; (2) ME. *ligne, line* – (O)Fr. *ligne* :– Rom. **linja*, for L. *linea, līnia*, orig. subst. use (sc. *fibra* FIBRE) of fem. of *līneus* pert. to flax, f. *līnum*; see prec.]

I. Cord, etc. **1.** A rope, cord, string. *Obs.* in gen. sense; now chiefly *Naut.* or as short for *clothes-line*, etc. **b.** Cord, as a material 1797. †**c.** A 'cord' in the body (*rare*) –1780. **d.** Used of a spider's thread (*poet.*) 1732. **e.** A telegraph or telephone wire or cable. Also, a telegraph route, a telegraphic system. 1851. **f.** *pl.* Reins. *dial.* and *U.S.* 1852. †**g.** *L. of life*: the thread spun by the Fates, determining the length of a person's life –1681. **2.** A cord bearing a hook or hooks, for fishing. (Also *fishing-l.*) ME. †**3.** *pl.* Strings or cords laid for snaring birds –1753. **4.** A cord used by builders and others for taking measurements, or for making things level or straight ME. **b.** *pl.* Appointed lot in life; after *Ps.* 16:6; app. = land marked out for dwelling in 1611. †**5.** Rule, canon, precept; standard of life or practice (*rare*) –1611. **6.** *Hard lines* (colloq.): ill luck, bad fortune. (Prob. naut. in origin; often assoc. w. 4 b.) 1824.

1. And by her in a l. a milkewhite lambe she lad SPENSER. Shirts waving upon lines JOHNSON. **c.** COWPER *Table T.* 487. **e.** The American trans-Pacific l. 1854. **f.** He stepped into the carry-all and took the lines G. W. CABLE. **g.** Lo, thou a spanns length mad'st my living l. SIDNEY. **2.** *fig.* I am angling now, (Though you perceiue me not how I giue Lyne) SHAKS. It's policy to give 'em l. enough DICKENS. **4.** *L.-and-plummet* (attrib.): rigidly methodical. *fig.* This decencie is..the l. and leuell for al good makers to do their busines by PUTTENHAM. Phr. *By l., by l. and level, by rule and l.*, etc.: with methodical accuracy. **b.** The lines are fallen vnto mee in pleasant places; yea, I haue a goodly heritage *Ps.* 16:6. **5.** Their l. is gone out through all the earth, and their words to the end of the world *Ps.* 19:4.

II. A thread-like mark. **1.** A long and narrow stroke or mark, traced with a pen, a tool, etc. upon a surface ME. Also *fig.* **b.** *Mus.* One of the parallel strokes forming the stave, or placed above or below it (*ledger lines*) 1602. **c.** *Fine Art.* Applied *spec.* to the lines employed in a picture; chiefly *collect.* or in generalized sense, character of draughtsmanship, method of rendering form. Also *pl.* the distinctive features of composition in a picture. Also with reference to engraving (see *line engraving* in Combs.). 1616. **d.** In tennis, football, etc., *the line* denotes a particular line which marks the limit of legitimate or successful play 1546. **2.** Anything resembling a traced mark: e.g. a thin band of colour; a suture, seam, furrow, ridge, etc. ME. **b.** A furrow or seam in the face or hands. In *Palmistry*: A mark on the palm of the hand supposed to indicate one's fate, etc. 1538. **c.** A narrow region in a spectrum, appearing to the eye as a fine straight black or shining stroke transverse to the length of the spectrum. Called collect. *Fraunhofer's lines.* 1831. **3.** *Math.* A continuous extent (whether straight or curved) of length without breadth or thickness; the limit of a surface; the trace of a moving point 1559. **4.** A circle of the terrestrial or celestial sphere; e.g. †*ecliptic, equinoctial,* †*tropic l.* Now *rare.* ME. **b.** *The l.*: the equinoctial line; the equator. (Occas. written with a capital.) 1568. **5.** Often used for 'straight line' (sense II. 3); esp. in *Physics* and *techn.* (see below) ME. **6.** A direction as traced by marks on a surface or as indicated by a row of persons or objects 1500. **7.** Contour, outline; lineament 1590. **8.** *pl.* The outlines, plan, or draught of a building or other structure; *spec.* in *Shipbuilding*, the outlines of a vessel as shown in its horizontal, vertical, and oblique sections. (Also *fig.*) 1673. **b.** *fig.* Plan of construction, of action, or procedure; now chiefly in phr. *on* (such and such) *lines* 1757. **9.** [After Fr. *ligne.*] The twelfth part of an inch 1665. **10.** A limit, boundary; more fully, *l. of demarcation.* †**11.** Degree, rank, station –1785.

1. An expression of forms only by simple lines 1821. *fig.* The lines of his character are..broad and clear 1878. Phr. *L. of lines, of numbers,* Gunter's l. *L. of shadows*: = QUADRAT 1. **c.** Portraits..all beautifully engraved in l. 18.. Phr. *L. of beauty*: the curve (like a slender elongated S), which according to Hogarth is a necessary element in all beauty of form. **2.** Yon grey Lines, That fret the Clouds SHAKS. *Lines of growth* (Conch.): the eccentric striæ or lines, due to successive layers of shelly matter, by which the animal increases the shell. **b.** He does smile his face into more lynes, then is in the new Mappe SHAKS. Lines of premature age on the face 1895. Phr. *L. of life, of fortune, of the head, of the heart, of health* or *liver* (*hepatic l.*). **4. b.** Phr. *Under the l.*: on the equator; The straight of Malaca is vnder the l. 1588. **5.** Phr. *L. of fire*: the indefinite projection of the axis of the gun-barrel. *On the l.*: said of a picture in an exhibition so hung that its centre is about on a level with the eye. *As straight as a l., right as a* or *any l.*: straightforward; also, straightway. **6.** *To bring into* (*a*) *l.*: to align; *fig.* to make (persons) unanimous. The term *in l.* is applied to a battalion when its companies are deployed on the same alignment to their full extent, i.e. in two ranks. Columns are said to be *in l.* when their fronts are on the same alignment. VOYLE & STEVENSON. **b.** *To get a l. on* (U.S. colloq.): to acquire information about (a thing) 1903. **7.** The savage lines of his mouth MACAULAY. **10.** Phr. *To draw a* (or *the*) *line* (*fig.*): to determine the limit between two things; *mod. colloq.*, to lay down a definite limit of action beyond which one refuses to go. Also *to* †*lay, form a l. Mason and Dixon's l.*: the southern boundary of Pennsylvania, forming the line of demarcation between the free and the slave States. Named from the two astronomers who surveyed it. **11.** Women in the middle l. of life 1785.

III. Applied to things arranged along a (straight) line. **1.** A row or series of persons or things 1557. **2.** *Mil.* A trench or rampart; *pl.* (also *collect. sing.*), a connected series of field-works. Also, one of the rows of tents or huts in a camp, etc. 1645. **3.** *Mil.* and *Naut.* A row or rank of soldiers (dist. from a *column*); a row of ships in a certain order. Also occas. *collect. sing.* = ships of the line. 1704. **b.** *The l.*: in the British army, the regular and numbered troops as dist. from the guards and the auxiliary forces; in U.S., the regular fighting force of all arms 1802. **4.** A regular succession of public conveyances plying between certain places; e.g. the Cunard l. (of steamers), etc. 1848. **5.** A row of written or printed letters (see below) OE.

1. A l. of trading posts W. IRVING. The l. of festal light in Christ-Church hall M. ARNOLD. **2.** He took the French Lines without Bloodshed STEELE. **3.** Their L. consisted of 52 Ships and 24 Gallies 1704. *L. of battle*: see BATTLE *sb. Ship of the l.*: a l.-of-battle ship. *All along the l.*: at every point. **5. a.** *gen.* One row of letters in any piece of writing or letterpress; often, esp. in *pl.*, put for the contents of what is written or printed OE. Phr. *To read between the lines*: to discover a meaning or purpose not obvious or explicitly expressed in a piece of writing. **b.** *spec.* in *Printing.* A row of types or quads 1659. **c.** A few words in writing; a short letter 1647. Just a l. to say that all goes well MRS. CARLYLE. **d.** The portion of a metrical composition which is usually written in one line; a verse; *pl.* verses, poetry. Also *pl.*, (so many) lines of verse, etc. set to be written out as a school imposition. 1563. Marlowes mighty l. B. JONS. And ten low words oft creep in one dull line POPE. **e.** Short for *marriage lines*, certificate of marriage. Also *transf.* 1829. **f.** *pl.* The words of an actor's part 1882. **g.** *L. upon l.*: now taken as referring to reiteration of statements in successive lines (for the orig. meaning see I. 5) 1611.

IV. Serial succession. **1.** A continuous series of persons (rarely of things) in chronological succession. Chiefly with reference to family descent. ME. **2.** Lineage, stock, race. Somewhat *arch.* ME.

1. Purchases in the l. of the mother or grandmother CRUISE. Phr. *Male, female, direct l. Heir of l.* = *heir-at-law* (see HEIR *sb.* 1). †*By l.*: by lineal descent. **2.** The l. of Cyrus being extinct BANCROFT.

V. A direction. **1.** Track, course, direction; route ME. **b.** Short for *l. of rails, railway l., tram l.* 1825. **c.** *Hunting.* The straight course in the hunting field 1836. **2.** Course of action, procedure, life, thought, etc. ME. **3.** A department of activity; a branch of business, etc. 1638. †**4.** In *pl.*: = 'Goings on', caprices or fits of temper. (Cf. Warwickshire *on a l.* = in a rage.) SHAKS. **5.** *Comm.* An order for goods; the goods so ordered; also, the stock on hand of a particular class of goods 1882.

1. They ran on parallel lines that never met ZANGWILL. Phr. *L. of communication, of march, of operations.* **b.** A single track of rails, as in *the up l., the down l.*; a part of a railway system, as in *main l., branch l.*; an entire system, as in *the Midland l.* **c.** Phr. *To ride the l., to take, keep one's own l.* **2.** The Protectionists, as a party, have taken no l. in the matter LEWIS. **3.** Something in the l. of duty JOHNSON. Phr. *In* (or *out of*) *one's l.*: suited (or unsuited) to one's capacity, taste, etc. Her jokes aren't in my l. R. KIPLING. **4.** Your husband is in his olde lines (*Mod. edd.* lunes) againe *Merry W.* IV. ii. 22.

Combs. **1.** General: as *l. battalion, -guard, regiment, -room,* etc.; †in *Bot.* = *linear.*

2. Special: as **l.-bait,** bait used in line-fishing; **-boat,** a boat used for line-fishing; **-breeding** *U.S.*, breeding from stock of one strain or variety; **-co-ordinate** *Math.*, one of a set of quantities defining the position of a l.; **l. drawing,** a drawing done with a pen or pencil; **l. engraving,** the art of engraving 'in line', i.e. by lines incised on the plate, as dist. from etching and mezzotint; an engraving so executed; **-firing** *Mil.*, firing by a body of men in l.; **-hunter,** a hound which hunts by the l. of the scent alone; so **-hunting** *a.*; **-integral** *Math.*, the integral, taken along a l., of any differential that has a continuously varying value along that l.; **-integration,** the operation of finding a line-integral; **-rocket,** a small rocket attached to a l. or wire along which it is made to run; **-soldier,** a linesman; **-storm** *U.S.*, an equinoctial storm; **-wire** *Telegraphy*, the wire which connects the stations of a telegraph-line; **-work,** drawing or designing done with the pen or pencil (as opp. to wash, etc.).

Line (ləin), *v.*[1] ME. [f. LINE *sb.*[1]; with reference to frequent use of linen as lining material. Cf. med.L. *lineare, liniare* (XIII).] **1.** *trans.* To apply a second layer of (different) material to the inner side of (a garment; later, a box, culinary article, etc.); to cover on the inside. Also *transf.* and *fig.* †**2.** To reinforce, fortify. Also *fig.* –1761. **3.** To fill (one's purse, pocket, stomach, etc.); to cram, stuff 1514. **4.** To cover the outside of; to overlay, drape, pad (*lit.* and *fig.*); to face (a turf-slope). *Obs.* exc. *Naut.*, to add a layer of wood to. 1572. **5.** *techn.* (chiefly *to l. up*); see below. 1880. **6.** To serve as a lining for 1726.

1. A mode of lining culinary..articles with enamel YEATS. *transf.* Poplar that with silver lines his leaf COWPER. **2.** *Macb.* I. iii. 112. **3.** The Iustice, In faire round belly, with good Capon lin'd SHAKS. **5. a.** *Bookbinding.* To glue on the back of (a book) a paper covering continuous with the lining of the back of the cover. **b.** *Cabinet-making.* To put a moulding round (the top of a piece of furniture). **6.** These mortal lullabies of pain May bind a book, may l. a box TENNYSON.

Line (ləin), *v.*[2] ME. [f. LINE *sb.*[2]] **1.** *trans.* To tie with a line, string, or cord (*rare*). **2.** To measure or test with a line, to cut to a line; also *absol.* Occas. *fig.* to reach as with a measuring-line. *Obs.* exc. *techn.* ME. **3.** (*U.S.*) To angle with a hook and line (*rare*) 1833. **4.** To trace with, or as with, a line or lines; to delineate, sketch. Chiefly with advs. 1600. **5.** To mark with a line or lines; to cover with lines. Also with *off, out.* 1530. **6.** *U.S.* To follow the line of flight of (bees) 1827. **7. a.** *trans.* To bring (ships, soldiers, etc.) into a line or into line with others; also with *up.* Hence *U.S.* to assign (a person) *to* (certain work). 1796. **b.** *intr.* (*a*) To present to the eye a line of a specified kind 1794. (*b*) To form a (good) line with others; to fall into line; also with *out, up*; *fig.* to come *up to* a certain line 1790. (*c*) To run in line *with*; to border upon 1881. **8. a.** To arrange a line (orig. of troops) along (a hedge, road, etc.) 1647. **b.** To have or take one's place or to have a place in line along (a road, etc.) 1598.

4. Phr. *To l. in*: to put in with a hard pencil the permanent lines of (a freehand drawing); also, to insert (objects) in the outline of a picture. *To l. off*: to mark off by lines. *To l. out*: to trace the outlines of (something to be made); to forecast, adumbrate. **5.** Selfish cares..had lined his narrow brow SHELLEY. Phr. *To l. through*: to draw a line *through* (an entry). **8. a.** They having lined the hedges behind them with their reserve CLARENDON. **b.** The Streets were lin'd by the Militia 1707.

Line (ləin), *v.*[3] ME. [– (O)Fr. *ligner*, also *aligner*; identical with LINE *v.*[2], but the sense-development is obscure.] *trans.* Of a dog, wolf, etc.: To copulate with, cover.

Lineable, *a.*: see LINABLE.

Lineage (li·niėdʒ). Now only *literary.* [ME. *li(g)nage* – (O)Fr. *lignage*, †*linage* :– Rom. **lineaticum*, f. *linea* LINE *sb.*[2]; see -AGE. The sp. *lineage* (XVII) is due to assoc. with *line*; the pronunc. has followed it under the infl. of *lineal.*] **1.** Lineal descent from an ancestor; ancestry, pedigree. **2.** quasi-*concr.* (Chiefly *collect.*) †**a.** One's ancestors collectively. [So Fr. *lignage*, as opp. to *lignée* = descendants.] –1557. **b.** The descendants of a specified ancestor [= Fr. *lignée*] ME. †**c.** A tribe or clan –1604.

1. Norman l. was vulgarly regarded as the more honourable STUBBS. **2. b.** Of this Mariage ensued a plenteous lignage, to witt, three Sonnes and foure Daughters 1623.

Lineal (li·niăl). ME. [– (O)Fr. *linéal* – late L. *linealis*; see LINE *sb.*[2], -AL[1].] **A.** *adj.* **1.** Of or pertaining to a line or lines; consisting of lines. Of writing: Arranged in regular lines. **b.** Of measures: = LINEAR *a.* 3. 1696. **2.** That is in the direct line; opp. to *collateral* ME. **b.** Pertaining to or transmitted by lineal descent 1486. **c.** Lineally descended (*rare*); †legitimate 1590.

1. Phr. *L. translation*: one made line for line (*rare*). *L. number, perspective*: see LINEAR. **2.** I am the..lyneall heyre HALL. The Prime and Ancient Right of L. Succession LOCKE. **b.** As if they waged some l. feud with time BAILEY. **c.** For only you are l. to the throne DRYDEN.

†**B.** *sb.* One who is related in the direct line. FOOTE.

Hence **Linea·lity,** quality of being l.; uniformity of direction of writing. **Li·neally** *adv.* in a l. manner; *occas.* with regard to the lines or outline of anything; line for line.

Lineament (li·niămĕnt). ME. [– L. *lineamentum*, f. *lineare* make straight, in med.L. delineate, f. *linea* LINE *sb.*[2]; see -MENT.] †**1.** A line; a diagram, outline, sketch; *pl.* outlines, designs. *lit.* and *fig.* –1811. †**b.** A minute portion, a trace; *pl.* elements, rudiments –1811. †**2.** A portion of the body, considered with regard to its contour, a distinctive feature –1772. **b.** *fig.* in *pl.* Distinctive features or characteristics 1638. **3.** In narrower sense, a portion of the face viewed with respect to its outline; a feature 1513.

2. Man he seems In all his lineaments, though in his face The glimpses of his Fathers glory shine MILT. **b.** The principal lineaments of the law of contract STEPHEN. **3.** A single fine l. cannot make a handsom face 1702. Hence **Li:neamenta·tion,** representation in form or l.

Linear (li·niăɹ), *a.* 1642. [– L. *linearis*, f. *linea* LINE *sb.*[2]; see -AR[1]. Cf. (O)Fr. *linéaire.*] **1.** Of or pertaining to a line or lines 1656. **2.** Consisting of, or involving the use of, lines 1840. **3.** Extended in a line or in length;

spec. in *Math.* involving measurement in one dimension only 1706. **4.** Resembling a line; long, narrow, and of uniform breadth 1642; *spec.* in *Bot.* and *Zool.*, thread-like, narrow and elongated 1753.

1. *L. perspective*: that branch of perspective which is concerned with the apparent form, magnitude, and position of visual objects, as dist. from AERIAL *perspective*. **2.** L. design RUSKIN. **3.** *L. equation*, an equation of the first degree. **4.** L. leaf 1753. L. feathers 1874. Hence **Li·nearly** *adv.* †**Li·neary** *a.* (in senses 2, 3) 1551–1664.

Lineate (li·niĕt), *ppl. a.* and *sb.* 1643. [– L. *lineatus*, pa. pple. of *lineare* (see next); see -ATE².] **a.** *ppl. a.* Marked with lines, *spec.* in *Bot.* †**b.** *sb.* A figure formed of lines 1674.

Lineate (li·nieˈt), *v.* 1558. [– *lineat-*, pa. ppl. stem of L. *lineare* reduce to a line, in med.L. delineate, f. *linea* LINE *sb.*²; see -ATE³.] *trans.* **a.** To mark with lines. †**b.** To delineate, describe –1648. **Li·neated** *ppl. a.*

Lineation (liniēˈ·ʃən). ME. [– L. *lineatio*, f. as prec.; see -ION.] **1.** The action of drawing lines or marking with lines; a marking or line on a surface; such lines collectively. **2.** A division into lines (of verse) 1853.

†**Li·neature.** 1603. [f. LINEATE *v.* + -URE.] Something having an outline or shape; an outline; *Geom.* a periphery –1651.

Lineman (ləi·nmæ̆n). 1858. [f. LINE *sb.*² + MAN.] **1.** A man employed to attend to a railway, telegraph, or telephone line. **2.** One who carries the line in surveying. SIMMONDS.

Linen (li·nėn). [OE. *līnen*, *lînnen* = OFris. (Du.) *linnen*, OS., OHG. *līnīn* (G. *leinen*) :– WGmc. **līnīn*, f. **līnam* LINE *sb.*¹; see -EN⁴.] **A.** *adj.* Made of flax. In mod.Eng. felt as the sb. used attrib.: Made of linen.

Lappyng [it] in a clene lynnen clothe ME.

B. *sb.* **1.** Cloth woven from flax ME. **b.** *pl.* Kinds of linen; linen goods 1748. **2.** Something made of linen; a linen garment, etc. *Obs.* in *sing.*; the *pl.* is found in Sc. writers. 1566. **3.** *collect.* **a.** Garments, etc. made of linen, or, by extension, of calico, etc. Often *spec.* = undergarments, e.g. shirts; also = bed-, table-linen. ME. †**b.** Strips of linen, *esp.* for use as bandages; *pl.* graveclothes –1796.

1. Clothed in purple and fine linen *Luke* 16:19. **3. a.** *To wash one's dirty l. at home*: to say nothing in public about family scandals, etc.

Comb.: **l.-decency,** (*nonce-use*), outward conformity to convention; **-draper,** a retail dealer in linens, calicoes, etc.; **-fold, -pattern, -scroll,** a carved or moulded ornament for a panel, representing a fold or scroll of linen; **-panel,** one decorated with a linen-scroll; **-press,** a cupboard for linen.

Hence **Linene·tte,** an imitation l. 1894.

Linen-armourer. 1603. **a.** *Hist.* A maker of 'linen armour' (i.e. gambesons and similar adjuncts to armour). †**b.** *joc.* A tailor.

a. The Merchant-Taylors, then called Linnen-Armourers, were eminent not only in Peace, but War 1687.

†**Li·nener.** 1609. [f. LINEN *sb.* + -ER¹.] A linen-draper or shirt-maker –1625.

Lineolate (li·niŏleˈt), *a.* 1852. [f. L. *lineola*, dim. of *linea* LINE *sb.*² + -ATE² 2.] *Bot.* and *Zool.* Marked with minute lines. So **Li·neolated** *a.* 1819.

Line-out. 1900. [f. *line out*, LINE *v.*² 7 b (*b*).] *Rugby Football.* The arrangement of forwards opposite to one another when the ball is about to be thrown in from touch.

Liner¹ (ləi·nəɹ). 1611. [f. LINE *v.*¹ + -ER¹.] **1.** One who lines anything. **2.** *Mech.* Something which serves as a lining. **a.** An inside cylinder, or a vessel placed inside another 1886. **b.** A thin piece of metal, etc. placed between two parts to adjust them; a shim 1869. **c.** A slab on which pieces of marble, etc. are fastened for grinding or polishing 1875.

Liner² (ləi·nəɹ). ME. [f. LINE *sb.*² or *v.*²] **I.** Of persons. **1.** *Sc.* One who traces the boundaries of properties in burghs. **2.** One who paints lines on the wheels, etc. of carriages. Also *l.-out.* 1819. **3.** A writer of items for the newspapers, which are paid for at so much per line. (Cf. PENNY-A-LINER.) 1861. **4.** = LINESMAN 1. 1870.

II. Of things. †**1.** A thin plate of iron or brass, for showing whether any piece of work to which it is applied is straight or not. MOXON. **2. a.** A steam-ship, or other vessel, belonging to a 'line' of packets 1838. **b.** A line-of-battle ship 1858. **3.** *Baseball.* A ball which, when struck, flies through the air in a nearly straight line not far from the ground 1874. **4.** *colloq.* A picture hung 'on the line' (see LINE *sb.*² II. 5) 1887.

Linesman (ləi·nzmæ̆n). 1856. [f. *line's* (LINE *sb.*²) + MAN.] **1.** A soldier belonging to a regiment of the line. **2.** = LINEMAN 1. 1883. **3. a.** *Lawn Tennis.* An umpire posted near to one of the lines, to decide whether any particular ball falls within the court or not. **b.** *Association Football.* An official whose chief duty is to mark when and where the ball crosses the touch-line or the goal-line. 1890.

Line-up. 1889. [f. *line up*, LINE *v.*² 7 b (*b*).] An instance of bringing into line; the assembling of a number of persons in a line or file. Also *fig.*

Ling¹ (liŋ). [ME. *leng(e*, prob. of Du. or LG. origin; cf. Du. *leng*, earlier *lenghe*, *linghe*; rel. to LONG *a.* (cf. the synon. Scand. forms, ON. *langa*, Sw. *långa*, Da. *længe*).] **1.** A long slender gadoid fish, *Molva molva*, of N. Europe. It is largely used for food (usu. either salted or dried). **2.** In America, New Zealand, etc., the burbot, the cultus cod, etc. 1850. **3.** *attrib.* 1489.

Ling² (liŋ). ME. [– ON. *lyng*, of unkn. origin.] A name of kinds of Heather, esp. *Calluna vulgaris.* Also *attrib.*, as **l.-bird,** the meadow-pipit, *Anthus pratensis* 1814.

-ling (liŋ), *suffix*¹, forming sbs. A Com. Gmc. formative, arising from the addition of *-iŋga-z* -ING³ to noun-stems formed with *-ilo-* (-EL¹, -LE 1).

1. In OE., and subseq. in ME. and mod.E., *-ling* added to sbs. forms sbs. with sense 'a person or thing belonging to or connected with (the primary sb.)', as *hȳrling* hireling, etc. The derivs. from adjs. have the sense 'a person or thing that has the quality denoted by the adj.', e.g. *dēorling* darling, etc.; so from an adv., *underling* subordinate. The personal designations in *-ling* are now always contemptuous or unfavourable, as *courtling*, *earthling*, *worldling*, etc. A few words, e.g. *shaveling*, *starveling*, *stripling*, formed on vb.-stems, follow the analogy of *nursling*, where the first element is ambiguous. In these uses the suffix is no longer productive.

2. In ON. the suffix had a diminutive force. In Eng. this use appears first in *codling* (*c*1314), *gosling* (15th c.), *duckling*, etc. Hence many new dim. formations, chiefly contemptuous personal designations, as *lordling*, etc. In this use the suffix is still a living formative.

-ling², **-lin(g)s** *suffix*, forming advs., now mostly *dial.* The Gmc. root *liŋg- laŋg- luŋg-* to extend, appears in OE. (with or without advb. *-s*) added to sbs. forming advs. of direction or extent, as *on bæcling* backwards, *nihtlanges* for a night, *grundlunga*, *-linga* to the ground. ME. formations are *grufelyng* GROVELLING, *headling(s*, *noseling*, *sideling(s*; formations from adjs. denoting condition or position are more numerous later, as *darkling(s*, *flatling(s*, *hidlings*. (Cf. MLG. *sunderlingen*, *-es*, Du. *zondering* adj., EFris. *sirlings* sidelong, WFris. *sidjlongs*.)

‖**Lingam** (li·ŋgæ̆m), **linga** (li·ŋgă). 1719. [– Skr. *liṅgam* lit. mark, characteristic.] Among the Hindus, a phallus, worshipped as a symbol of the God Siva. Hence **Li·ngamism,** the worship of lingams.

Lingel, lingle¹ (li·ŋg'l). Now *dial.* 1440. [– OFr. *lignoel*, *ligneul* :– pop.L. **lineolum*, f. L. *linea* LINE *sb.*²] A shoemaker's waxed thread.

Lingel, lingle² (li·ŋg'l). Now *dial.* ME. [app. repr. AFr. **lengle* :– L. *lingula* strap, etc.; dim. of *lingua* tongue.] †**1.** *collect. sing.* The leather straps, etc. of a horse's harness. Only ME. **2.** A thong or latchet 1538. †**3.** A flat blade or spoon, a spatula –1611.

†**Lingence.** [f. L. *lingere* lick + -ENCE. Cf. the similar contemp. formation LINCTURE.] A linctus. FULLER.

Linger (li·ŋgəɹ), *v.* [Northern ME. *lenger*, frequent. (see -ER⁵) of †*leng* linger – ON. *lengja* = OE. *lenġan*, whence ME. *lenge* (le·ndʒə) = MLG. *lengen*, OHG. *lengen*, (G. *längen*) :– Gmc. **lanȝjan*, prop. make or be long, f. **lanȝ-* LONG *a.*] †**1.** *intr.* To stay (in a place). Only ME. **2.** To stay behind, loiter; to stay on or hang about in a place, esp. from reluctance to leave it 1530. **b.** To proceed at a slow pace, loiter. Also *fig.* 1826. **3.** 'To remain long in languor and pain' (J.); to continue barely alive 1534. **4.** To be tardy in doing or beginning anything; to delay; to dawdle 1548. **5.** *fig.* **a.** To be slow to pass away or disappear 1764. **b.** To be slow in coming or accruing 1842. **c.** To be protracted, to drag on 1836. **6.** quasi-*trans.*, esp. with advb. compl.: To draw out, prolong, protract by lingering, tarrying, or dallying 1550. †**7.** *trans.* To cause to linger; to protract, draw out; also, to defer –1633. †**b.** To put off (a person) –1606. **8.** *intr.* To hanker. Const. *after*; occas. with *inf.* 1641.

2. Then l. not, . . away, take horse SHAKS. **b.** *fig.* I l. round a subject STANLEY. **3.** He lingered for nearly two years 1898. **4.** Either Malcolm lingered in his preparations, or [etc.] FREEMAN. **5. a.** He has still a doubt lingering in his mind JOWETT. **b.** Knowledge comes, but wisdom lingers TENNYSON. **6.** 2 *Hen. IV*, I, ii. 265. Far from gay cities, and the ways of men, I l. life POPE. Hence **Li·ngerer.** **Li·ngeringly** *adv.*

‖**Lingerie** (læ̃nʒri). 1835. [Fr., f. *linge* linen.] Linen articles collectively; those in a woman's wardrobe or *trousseau*.

Linget, obs. f. LINGOT.

Lingism (li·ŋiz'm). 1879. [f. *Ling*, a Swedish physician + -ISM.] Ling's mode of treating certain diseases, as obesity, by gymnastics; kinesitherapy.

Lingo¹ (li·ŋgo). 1660. [prob. – Pg. *lingoa* :– L. *lingua* tongue.] A contemptuous word for: Foreign speech or language; the vocabulary of a special subject or jargon of a class of persons.

Lingo², **lingoa.** 1800. [Moluccan *lenggoa*, dial. var. of Malay *līgūh*.] A large leguminous tree, *Pterocarpus indicus*, or its wood, also called *Burmese rosewood*, *Amboyna wood*, *Kyabuka*, etc.

Lingot (li·ŋgǫ̈t). ? *Obs.* or *arch.* 1488. [– Fr. *lingot*; see INGOT.] = INGOT.

-lings: see -LING².

‖**Lingua** (li·ŋgwă). 1675. [L., = tongue; in sense 2 chiefly from It.] **1.** The tongue or a tongue-like organ; *spec.* in *Entom.* (*a*) the ligula; (*b*) a tongue-like prolongation of the hypopharynx; (*c*) the proboscis of a butterfly or moth. 1826. **2.** A language or 'lingo' 1675. **b. Lingua franca** [It., = 'Frankish tongue']: a mixed language or jargon used in the Levant, consisting largely of Italian words without their inflexions. Also *transf.* any mixed jargon used for intercourse between people speaking different languages.

2. b. Addressing himself to me. . in a most fluent lingua-franca, half Italian and half Portuguese BECKFORD.

Linguadental: see LINGUO-.

Lingual (li·ŋgwăl). ME. [– med.L. *lingualis*, f. L. *lingua* tongue; see -AL¹.] **A.** *adj.* †**1.** Tongue-shaped. Only ME. **2.** *Anat.*, *Zool.*, etc. Of or pertaining to the tongue, or to any tongue-like part (see LINGUA 1) 1650. **3.** *Phonetics.* Of sounds: Formed by the tongue. ? *Obs.* exc. as = CEREBRAL (e.g. in Whitney's *Skr. Grammar*). 1668. **4. a.** Pertaining to the tongue as the organ of speech. **b.** Pertaining to language or languages. 1774.

2. *L. nerve*, a tactile and sensory nerve, supplying the tongue. *L. ribbon*, in molluscs, = ODONTOPHORE. *L. teeth*, the chitinous band of teeth which is borne upon the odontophore.

B. *sb.* **1.** A lingual sound (see A. 3) 1668. **2.** *Anat.* The lingual nerve 1877.

Hence **Lingua·lity,** l. quality. **Li·ngualize** *v. trans.* to make l. **Li·ngually** *adv.*

Linguet, var. of LANGUET.

Linguiform (li·ŋgwifǭɹm), *a.* Also erron. **lingua-, linguæ-.** 1753. [f. LINGUA; see -FORM.] Shaped like the tongue.

Linguist (li·ŋgwist). 1588. [f. L. *lingua* language + -IST.] **1.** One skilled in other tongues besides his own. Often qualified, as a *good*, *bad*, *perfect l.*, etc. 1591. †**2.** A student of language; a philologist –1817. †**3.** An interpreter. (Formerly much used in the East.) –1882. †**4.** One who knows how to talk; a master of language –1691.

1. He was a l., a mathematician, and a poet MACAULAY. **4.** Ile dispute with him. Hee's a rare l. WEBSTER. Hence **Li·nguistry** (*rare*), study of language.

Linguistic (liŋgwi·stik), *a.* and *sb.* 1837. [f. LINGUIST + -IC.] **A.** *adj.* Of or pertaining to the knowledge or study of languages. Also used *erron.* for: Of or pertaining to language or languages. 1856. **B.** *sb.* [-IC 2.] The science of languages; philology 1837; *pl.* **lingui·stics** 1855. So **Lingui·stical** *a.* 1823. Hence **Lingui·stically** *adv.*

Lingula (li·ŋgiŭlă). Pl. **-læ** (-lī). 1664. [L., dim. of *lingua* tongue. Cf. LIGULA.] **1.** A little tongue or tongue-like part. Now only *spec.* in *Anat.* **2.** A genus of bivalve molluscs, including many fossil species; any shell of the genus 1836.

2. *L. flags*, micaceous flagstones and slates of N. Wales, containing the l. in large quantities. Hence **Li·ngular** *a. Anat.*, of or pertaining to a l.

Lingulate (li·ŋgiŭlĕ[1]t), *a.* 1849. [– L. *lingulatus*; see LINGULA, -ATE[2].] Tongue-shaped. So **Li·ngulated** 1797.

Linguo-, †**lingua-**, used as comb. f. L. *lingua* (the correct form would be *lingui-*, but see -O-), in **Linguo-**, †**linguade·ntal** *a.*, of or formed by tongue and teeth; also *sb.*, a sound so formed.

Liniment (li·nimĕnt). ME. [– late L. *linimentum*, f. *linere* smear, anoint; see -MENT.] †**1.** Something used for smearing or anointing –1691. **2.** An embrocation usually made with oil 1543.

Lining (ləi·niŋ), *vbl. sb.*[1] ME. [f. LINE *v.*[1] + -ING[1].] **1.** *concr.* The stuff with which garments are lined. Also *fig.* **b.** *pl.* Drawers; underclothing (*dial.*) 1614. **2.** Any material occurring or placed next beneath the outside one 1713. **3.** *fig.* Contents; that which is inside ME. **4.** The action of LINE *v.*[1] Also *l. up*, in bookbinding and carpentry. 1839. **5.** *attrib.*, as *l. paper*, etc. 1585.

2. I have found unvalued repositories of learning in the l. of bandboxes POPE. **3.** The l. of his coffers shall make Coates To decke our souldiers for these Irish warres SHAKS.

Li·ning, *vbl. sb.*[2] 1478. [f. LINE *v.*[2]] Alignment; the use of a measuring line for alignment; the tracing of lines; etc. 1598. **b.** *Sc.* The authoritative fixing of the boundaries of burghal properties.

Link (liŋk), *sb.*[1] [OE. *hlinc* (whence also LINCH *sb.*[2]), perh. *k-* derivative of the base of OE. *hlinian* LEAN *v.*[1]] **a.** Rising ground; a ridge or bank. *Obs.* exc. *dial.* **b.** *pl.* (*Sc.* and *north.*) More or less level or gently undulating sandy ground near the sea-shore, covered with turf, coarse grass, etc. **c.** *pl.* The ground on which golf is played, often resembling that in b (also *a links* as sing.).

Link (liŋk), *sb.*[2] 1440. [– ON. **hlenkr* (Icel. *hlekkr*, OSw. *lænker*) :– Gmc. **χlaŋkjaz*, rel. to OE. *hlencan* pl. armour, MLG. *lenkhake* pot-hook, MHG. *gelenke* (collect.) flexible parts of the body, *gelenk* joint, link; cf. LANK *a.*] **1.** A single ring or loop of a chain. †Also, *pl.* chains, fetters. 1450. †**b.** *sing.* A chain. Also *transf.* and *fig.* –1730. **c.** One division, being a hundredth part, of the chain used in surveying (see CHAIN *sb.* II. 3); used as a measure of length. (In Gunter's chain the link is 7·92 inches.) 1661. **d.** Short for *sleeve-link* 1807. **2.** Something looped, or forming part of a chain-like arrangement. **a.** A loop (in knitting); a segment of a cord, etc.; a lock of hair. In *Angling*, one of the segments of a hair-line. 1440. **b.** A division of a chain of sausages, etc. (Chiefly *pl.*) Now *dial.* 1440. **c.** *pl.* Windings of a stream; also, the ground lying along these. *Sc.* 1700. **3.** A connecting part; a thing (*occas.* a person) that connects others; a member of a series; a means of connection 1548. **b.** Any intermediate rod or piece transmitting motive power from one part of a machine to another. Also = *link-motion* (Dicts.). 1825. **4.** A machine for linking or joining together the loops of fabrics 1892.

1. Linkes of Iron *Jul. C.* I. iii. 94. **2.** Sir, a new linke to the Bucket must neede bee had SHAKS. **c.** The lairdship of the bonny Links of Forth 1700. **3.** *Missing l.*: see MISSING *ppl. a.*

attrib. and *Comb.*, as *l.-belt, -chain*, etc.; **l.-block** *Steam-engine*, the block actuated by the link-motion and giving motion to a valve-stem; **-motion**, (*a*) *Steam-engine*, a valve-gear for reversing the motion of the engine, etc., consisting of two eccentrics and their rods, which give motion to a slide-valve by means of a 'link'; (*b*) *Geom.*, a linkage in which all the points describe definite curves in the same plane or in parallel planes; **-staff** *Surveying*, = *offset-staff* (see OFFSET *sb.*); **-structure** *Math.*, a linkage or link-work; **-work**, (*a*) work composed of or arranged in links; (*b*) *Mech.*, that species of gearing by which motions are transmitted by links; (*c*) *Geom.*, a system of lines, pivoted together so as to rotate about one another; **-worming**, protection of a rope by worming it with chains.

Link (liŋk), *sb.*[3] 1526. [perh. – med.L. *linchinus*, alt. of *lichinus* wick, match – Gr. λύχνος light, lamp.] **1.** A torch made of tow and pitch, etc., formerly used for lighting people along the streets. **b.** A link-boy 1845. †**2.** ? The material of 'links' used as blacking 1596.

1. In the strong glare of the l. DICKENS. **2.** There was no Linke to Colour Peters hat SHAKS.

Link (liŋk), *v.* ME. [f. LINK *sb.*[2]] **1.** *trans.* To couple or join with or as with a link (*in* or *into* a chain, *in* amity, etc.). Also *absol.* **a.** things, persons *together*. **b.** one thing (*in*) *with* or (*on*) *to* another ME. **c.** To pass (one's arm) *through* or *in* another's 1843. **2.** *intr.* To be coupled, joined, or connected (e.g. in friendship, etc.) 1540. **3.** *To link up* (*trans.* and *intr.*): to connect, combine, etc. 1897.

1. Linked together by many promises and professions, and by an entire conjunction in guilt CLARENDON. **b.** Strong fetters l. him to the rock SOUTHEY. **2.** No one generation could l. with the other BURKE. Hence **Linked** *ppl. a.*; *spec.* in *Mil.* of two infantry battalions (or regiments) which are coupled together to form a regimental district. **Li·nker**, one who or that which links or joins.

Linkage (li·ŋkėdʒ). 1874. [f. LINK *sb.*[2] or *v.* + -AGE.] The condition or manner of being linked; a system of links.

Applied e.g. (*Chem.*) to the union of atoms or radicals in a molecule; (*Geom.*) to a system of straight lines, etc. pivoted together so as to rotate about one another.

Li·nk-boy. 1660. A boy employed to carry a link (LINK *sb.*[3] 1). So **Li·nkman** 1716.

Lin-lan-lone. A formation echoic of the sound of a chime of three bells. TENNYSON.

Linn[1] (lin). Chiefly *Sc.* [– Gael. *linne*, Ir. *linn* (earlier *lind*) = W. *llyn*, Corn. *lin*, Breton* *lenn.*] **1.** A torrent running over rocks; a waterfall. **2.** A pool, esp. one into which a cataract falls 1577. **3.** A ravine with precipitous sides 1799.

Linn[2]. Now *dial.* 1475. [Altered f. LIND.] The linden or lime; also, the wood of this tree; *attrib.* in *l.-bark*, etc.

‖**Linnæa** (linī·ă). 1862. [mod.L., so named by Gronovius, 1749, after C. F. *Linné*; see next, -A 2.] *Bot.* A slender evergreen flowering plant (*L. borealis*) of the north temperate and frigid zones.

Linnæan, Linnean (linī·ăn). 1753. [f. *Linnæus*, latinized form of the surname of Carl von *Linné*, Sw. naturalist (1707–78); see -AN. The sp. *Linnæan* is usual, but the Linnean Society adopts the other form.] **A.** *adj.* Of or pertaining to Linnæus or his system; given or instituted by Linnæus; adhering to his system. **B.** *sb.* A follower of Linnæus or his system 1772.

Linnæite (linī·əit). 1849. [Named after *Linnæus*, who first described it; see prec., -ITE[1] 2 b.] *Min.* Sulphide of cobalt, containing some nickel and copper.

Linnet (li·nėt). 1530. [– OFr. (Walloon, Picard) *linette*, earlier *linot* (mod. *linot*, *linotte*), f. *lin* flax (see LINEN).] **1.** A song-bird, *Linota* (or *Linaria*) *cannabina*, of the family *Fringillidæ*. Its plumage is brown or warm grey; but in summer the breast and crown of the cock (when wild) become crimson or rose-colour. Allied species are the Mountain-Linnet or Twite (*Linota flavirostris* or *L. montium*) and the Lesser Redpoll (*L. rufescens*). **2.** Applied, with qualifications, to birds of other genera 1868. **3.** *Mining. pl.* Oxidized lead ores 1881.

2. *Green l.*, the greenfinch. *Pine l.*, a siskin of N. America, *Chrysomitris* (or *Spinus*) *pinus*.

Lino (ləi·no). Abbrev. of LINOLEUM, LINOTYPE.

Linocut (ləi·nŏkɒt). 1923. [f. LINO(LEUM + CUT *sb.*[2]] A design cut in relief on a block of linoleum; a print obtained from this.

Linoleic (linolī·ik), *a.* 1857. [f. L. *linum* flax + *oleum* oil + -IC.] *Chem. L. acid*: an acid found as a glyceride in linseed and other oils. Hence **Lino·leate**, a salt of l. acid.

Linoleum (linōᵘ·liŏm). Patented by F. Walton, 1860 and 1863. [f. L. *linum* flax + *oleum* oil.] A kind of floor-cloth of canvas coated with a preparation of oxidized linseed-oil.

Linotype (ləi·nŏtəip). 1888. [= *line o' type.*] *Printing.* **a.** A type-bar or -line. **b.** (= *l.-machine*) a machine for producing stereotyped lines or bars of words, etc., as a substitute for type-setting.

Linsang (li·nsæŋ). 1885. [– Javanese *linsang*, *wlinsang*, erron. rendered 'otter' in Dicts.] A kind of civet cat, *Linsang* (or *Prionodon*) *gracilis*, of Borneo and Java.

Linseed (li·nsīd). Also **lintseed** (*n. dial.*). [OE. *līnsǣd*, i.e. *līn* LINE *sb.*[1] + SEED.] The seed of flax, well known as the source of linseed-oil, and as a medicament. †Occas. the flax-plant.

attrib. and *Comb.*, as **l. cake**, l. pressed into cakes in extracting the oil, used as food for cattle; **-meal**, l. ground in a mill; **-oil**, the oil expressed from l.; **l. poultice**, one made of l. or linseed-meal; **-tea**, an infusion of l., used as a demulcent.

Linsey (li·nzi). ME. [prob. f. name of *Lindsey* (near Kersey) in Suffolk, where the manufacture is said to have originated. Cf. KERSEY.] Orig., perh. some coarse linen fabric. Later, = next. Also *attrib.*

Linsey-woolsey (li·nzi wu·lzi). 1483. [f. prec. + WOOL, with jingling ending.] **1.** Orig., a textile material, of mixed wool and flax; now, a dress material of coarse inferior wool, woven upon a cotton warp. Also *pl.* pieces or kinds of this. **2.** *fig.*, etc., *esp.* a strange medley in talk or action; nonsense 1592. **3.** *attrib.* or *adj.* 1618. **b.** *fig.*: chiefly = 'neither one thing nor the other' 1565.

2. What linsie wolsy hast thou to speake to vs againe? *All's Well* IV. i. 13. **3. b.** An asse in a rocket, a lince wolse bishop T. STAPLETON.

Linstock (li·nstǫk). *Obs.* exc. *Hist.* 1560. [In XVI *lintstocke* – Du. *lontstok*, f. *lont* match + *stok* stick; assim. to LINT.] A staff about three feet long, having a pointed foot to stick in the deck or ground, and a forked head to hold a match.

Their master gunner..confronts me with his linstock, readie to giue fire B. JONS.

Lint (lint). [ME. *lyn(n)et*, perh. – (O)Fr. *linette* (known only in the sense 'linseed'), f. *lin* flax; see LINE *sb.*[1], -ETTE, -ET.] **1.** (Now only *Sc.*) The flax-plant 1458. **2.** (Chiefly *Sc.*) Flax prepared for spinning. Also, flax refuse, used as a combustible. ME. **3.** A soft material for dressing wounds (formerly also burnt for tinder), prepared by ravelling or scraping linen cloth. †In *pl.*, pieces of this. ME. **b.** Fluff (*rare*) 1611. **4.** Now only *dial.* or *U.S.* Netting for fishing-nets 1615.

attrib. and *Comb.*, as **l.-doctor** *Calico-printing*, a sharp-edged ruler for removing fibres which may have come off the calico in the act of printing; **-scraper**, a person employed to scrape lint (for hospital use); also (*slang*) a young surgeon; **-white** *a.*, white as l.; flaxen. Hence **Li·nty** *a.*

Lintel (li·ntĕl). ME. [– OFr. *lintel* (mod. *linteau*), alt. of **linter*, *lintier* :– Rom. **limitaris*, alt. of *liminaris* pertaining to the threshold (used subst.), by crossing of *limes*, *limit-* LIMIT with *limen*, *limin-* threshold.] **1.** A horizontal piece of timber, stone, etc. placed over a door, window, or other opening to discharge the superincumbent weight. **2.** *attrib.*, as *l.-piece*, etc. 1575. Hence **Li·ntelled** *a.* furnished with a l.

Linter (li·ntəɹ). *U.S.* 1890. [f. LINT + -ER[1].] A machine for removing short-staple cotton-fibre from cotton-seed after ginning; the fibre thus obtained, used in making mattresses, etc.

Lintie (li·nti). *Sc.* Also **linty.** 1795. [f. *lint* in LINTWHITE + dim. ending -IE (-Y[6]).] = LINNET.

Lintseed, -stock: see LINSEED, -STOCK.

Lintwhite (li·nt,hwəit). Chiefly *Sc.* [OE. *līnetwiġe*, ME. *lynkwhyte*, Sc. *lyntquhyte*, f. *līn* flax, LINE *sb.*[1] + **twig-* (as in OHG. *zwigōn* pluck; cf. OE. *þisteltwiġe* thistle-finch, and TWITE.] = LINNET.

The l. and the throstlecock Have voices sweet and clear TENNYSON.

‖**Linum** (ləi·nŏm). 1867. [mod.L. use of L. *linum* LINE *sb.*[1]] *Bot.* A genus of plants including flax, and various ornamental species.

Liny, liney (ləi·ni), *a.* 1807. [f. LINE *sb.*[2] +

-Y[1].] **1.** Of the nature of or resembling a line, thin, meagre. **2.** Full of, or marked with, lines 1817.

2. The leaf being..rendered l. by bold markings of its ribs RUSKIN.

Lion (ləi·ən). [ME. *liun, lioun, leoun* – AFr. *liun* (Fr. *lion*) – L. *leo, leon-* – Gr. λέων. In OE. *lēo* – L. *leo.*] **1.** A large carnivorous quadruped, *Panthera leo*, now found native only in Africa and southern Asia, of a tawny colour, and having a tufted tail, and in the male usu. a flowing shaggy mane. **b.** Extended to other animals of the genus *Felis*, as the *American mountain l.*, the puma or cougar 1630. **2.** *fig.* (chiefly after biblical usage; cf. *Rev.* 5:5; also *Ps.* 35:17, 57:4, etc.). See quots. ME. **3.** *pl.* Things of note (in a town, etc.); sights worth seeing; esp. in phr. *to see* or *show the lions.* (This use is derived from the practice of taking visitors to see the lions formerly kept in the Tower of London.) 1590. **b.** Hence: A person of note who is much sought after 1715. **c.** *Oxford slang.* A visitor to Oxford 1785. **4.** An image or picture of a lion. (Often a sign for inns and taverns; usu. *Red, White,* etc. *L.*) ME. **5.** The constellation and zodiacal sign LEO. Also *Little L.*: Leo Minor. ME. †**6.** Alchemy. *Green l.*: a 'spirit' of great transmuting power; occas. identified with the philosophical mercury. *Red l.*: the tincture of gold. –1664. **7.** *attrib.* or *adj.* = 'lion-like' 1614.

1. The L. is (beyond dispute) Allow'd the most majestic brute GAY. Provbs. and phr. *A l. in the way* (or *path*): after *Prov.* 26:13, applied to a danger or obstacle, esp. an imaginary one. *The lion's mouth*: a place of great peril. (Cf. *Ps.* 22:21, 2 *Tim.* 4:17.) *The lion's share*: the largest or choicest portion. *The lion's skin* (with reference to the fable of the ass in the lion's skin; see also *Hen. V*, IV. iii. 93). *The lion's provider*: = JACKAL (*lit.* and *fig.*). *To twist the lion's tail*: frequent in (chiefly U.S.) journalistic use with reference to insults to or encroachments on the rights of Great Britain. †*Cotswold l.*: a sheep 1450. **2.** He, my Lyon, and my noble Lord SPENSER. A Lyon among sheepe and a sheepe among Lyons PUTTENHAM. *The L. of the North*, Gustavus Adolphus. **3.** The churches were the best lions we met with in our way MALKIN. †*To have seen the lions*: in early use, to have had experience of life (B. JONS. *Cynthia's Rev.* V. ii). **b.** The literary l. who likes to be petted LYTTON. **4.** Hark, countrymen! either renew the fight, Or tear the lions out of England's coat SHAKS. *British L.*, the l. as the national emblem of Great Britain; hence *fig.* the British nation. So *Scottish l.* **7.** Strong mother of a Lion-line TENNYSON.

Comb.: **l.-ant,** the same as ANT-LION; **-dog** [after Fr. *chien-lion* (Buffon)], a variety of dog having a flowing mane; **-dragon,** a heraldic beast having the fore part like a l. and the hind part like a wyvern; **-hunter,** one who hunts lions; one who is given to lionizing celebrities; so **-hunting** (*lit.* and *fig.*); **-lizard,** the basilisk, its crest being compared to a lion's mane; **-monkey,** the marikina or silky marmoset; **-tailed** *baboon, monkey,* the wanderoo (*Macacus silenus*); **-tamer** (1798).

Lion, Lion Herald, etc.: see LYON.

Lionced, leonced (ləi·ŏnst), *a.* 1828. [irreg. f. LIONC(EL + -ED[2].] *Her.* Adorned with lions' heads, as a cross, etc.

Lioncel (ləi·ŏnsel). 1610. [– OFr. *lioncel* (mod. *lionceau*), dim. of *lion* LION; see -EL.] A small or young lion; chiefly *Her.* var. ||**Li·onceau** late ME. –1610.

†**Lion-drunk,** *a.* 1592. Said of a man in the second of the four stages of drunkenness, in which he becomes violent and quarrelsome.

Lionel (ləi·ŏnĕl). 1661. [– OFr. *lionel*, dim. of *lion* LION; see -EL.] *Her.* = LIONCEL.

Lioness (ləi·ŏnės). ME. [– OFr. *lion(n)esse, leonesse* (mod. *lionne*), f. *lion* LION; see -ESS[1].] **1.** The female of the lion. Also *fig.* of persons. **2.** A woman who is lionized; a lady visitor to Oxford (*slang*) 1808.

Li·onet. 1586. [– OFr. *lionet*, dim. of *lion* LION; see -ET.] A young lion.

Li·on-heart. 1665. †**a.** A heart like that of a lion, i.e. courageous. **b.** A lion-hearted person; used as tr. *Cœur de Lion.*

b. What songs..The lion-heart, Plantagenet, Sang looking thro' his prison bars TENNYSON. So **Lion-hearted** *a.* courageous.

Li·onhood. 1833. [f. LION + -HOOD.] The condition of being a 'lion'.

Lionism (ləi·ŏniz'm). 1835. [f. LION + -ISM.] The practice of lionizing; the condition of being lionized.

Lionize (ləi·ŏnəiz), *v.* 1809. [f. LION + -IZE.] **1.** *trans.* To visit the 'lions' of (a place); to go over (a place of interest) 1838. **2. a.** To show the 'lions' to (a person). Also *absol.* **b.** To show the 'lions' of (a place). 1830. **3.** *intr.* To see the 'lions' of a place 1825. **4.** *trans.* To treat (a person) as a 'lion'; to make a 'lion' of 1809. **5.** *intr.* To be a 'lion' 1834.

3. We sailed forth to l...which is the Oxford term for gazing about, usually applied to strangers 1825.

Li·on-like, *a.* (*adv.*) 1556. [See -LIKE.] **1.** Resembling a lion or what belongs to one. So **Li·only** *a.* (now *rare*). **2.** *adv.* 1610.

Lionne (lyon). ME. [– Fr. *lionne*, fem. of *lion* LION. Cf. LIONESS.] †**1.** A lioness. Only ME. ||**2.** A woman of the highest fashion 1846.

Lionship (ləi·ənʃip). 1769. [f. LION + -SHIP.] The quality or condition of being a lion; also as a mock title.

Lip (lip), *sb.* [OE. *lippa* = OFris. *lippa*, MLG., MDu. *lippe* (whence G. *lippe*) :– Gmc. **lipjon*, rel. to synon. OS. *lepor*, OHG. *leffur, lefs* (G. dial. *lefze*) :– Gmc. **lepaz, lefs*; f. **lep-* :– IE. **leb-*, rel. to L. *labia, labra* n.pl. lips.]

I. 1. Either of the two fleshy structures which form the edges of the mouth. Dist. as *upper* and *lower*, also *under*. **2.** Chiefly *pl.* Considered as one of the organs of speech; often in fig. contexts OE. †**b.** *sing.* Language (*lit.* and *fig.*) –1695. **c.** *slang.* Impudent or saucy talk 1821.

1. When she drinkes, against her lips I bob SHAKS. Phr. (*Immersed, steeped*) *to the lips.* *To bite one's l.*, (*a*) to show vexation; (*b*) to repress emotion. *To carry* or *keep a stiff upper l.*, not to lose heart; in bad sense, to be hard or obstinate. *To curl one's l.*, to bend or raise the upper lip slightly on one side, as an expression of contempt or scorn. †*To hang the l.*, to look vexed. *To lick one's lips* (see LICK *v.* 1). *To smack one's lips*, to express relish for food, *fig.* to express delight. **2.** Atheisme is rather in the L., than in the Heart of Man BACON. Phr. *To escape* (a person's) *lips* (see ESCAPE *v.* 2 b.). *To hang on* (a person's) *lips*: to listen with rapt attention to his words. **b.** *Phr. Of one l.* (a Hebraism); also, agreeing in one story.

II. 1. The margin of a cup, a bell, etc. 1592. **b.** The edge of an opening or cavity 1726. **c.** Any edge or rim, esp. one that projects 1608. **2.** In scientific and techn. uses. See below.

1. b. Every stream of lava descending from the lips of the crater LYELL. **c.** The l. of the hammer of a gun 1813. **2. a.** *Surg.* One of the edges of a wound ME. **b.** *Anat.* and *Zool.* = LABIUM or LABRUM 1597. **c.** *Bot.* (*a*) One of the two divisions of a bilabiate corolla or calyx. (*b*) = LABELLUM 1. 1776. **d.** *Conch.* One of the edges of the opening of a spiral shell 1681. **e.** *Mech.* The helical blade on the end of an auger 1884. **f.** *Organ-building.* One of the two edges above and below the mouth of an organ-pipe 1727.

attrib. and *Comb.* **1.** General: as *l.-favour, -smile*, etc.; (in sense 'not heartfelt', 'of the lips only') *l.-comfort, -comforter, -devotion, -homage, -love, -religion, -service, -wisdom, -worship*, etc.; *l.-born* adj.

2. Special: as **l.-auger,** one having pod and l., as dist. from the screw auger; **-bit,** a boring tool used in a brace, and having a cutting l. projecting beyond the end of the barrel; **-hook,** the upper hook of several on a line, which is put through the l. of a live bait; **-language,** (for the deaf and dumb) language communicated by movements of the lips; **-pipe** *Organ-building*, a flue-pipe; **-reading,** (in the case of the deaf and dumb) the apprehending of what another says by watching the movements of his lips; so **-speaking; -stick,** a stick of cosmetic for colouring the lips; **-tooth,** a tooth on the l. of a shell; **-vein,** a labial vein; **-work** = LIP-LABOUR.

Lip (lip), *v.*[1] 1604. [f. LIP *sb.*] **1.** *trans.* To touch with the lips, apply the lips to 1826. **b.** To kiss (*poet.*) 1604. **c.** *transf.* Of water: To kiss, to lap 1842. **2.** To pronounce with the lips only; to murmur softly; to utter (? *obs.*); (*slang*) to sing (a song) 1789. **3. a.** *trans.* To serve as a lip or margin to 1845. **b.** *Golf.* To hit the ball just to the lip or edge of (a hole) 1899.

1. Or the bubble on the wine, which breaks Before you l. the glass PRAED. **b.** A hand that Kings Haue lipt, and trembled kissing SHAKS. **3. a.** The margin..lips the pool with gentleness 1880.

†**Lip,** *v.*[2] [Late ME. *lyp*, perh. repr. OE. **lyppan* :– **lup-*; see LOP *v.*[1]] *trans.* To cut off (the head of an animal); to prune (a root); to shear (a sheep) –1607.

Lipæmia: see LIPO-.

Liparite (li·părəit). 1865. [f. Gr. λιπαρός shining + -ITE[1] 2 b.] *Min.* = FLUORITE.

Lipic (li·pik), *a.* 1838. [f. Gr. λίπος fat + -IC.] *Chem.* In *l. acid*: a crystallizable acid produced by the action of nitric acid upon a fatty acid.

Li·p-labour. 1538. Labour of the lips: empty talk; *esp.* vain repetition in prayer; †kissing –1665.

Liplet (li·plėt). 1816. [f. LIP *sb.* + -LET.] A little lip or (*Entom.*) lip-like projection.

Lipo- (lipo) (bef. a vowel **lip-**), comb. f. Gr. λίπος fat; as in ||**Li:pohæ·mia** (also *lipæmia*) [Gr. αἷμα blood], *Path.* prevalence of fatty matter in the circulation.

Lipogram (li·pŏgræm). 1711. [Back-formation f. Gr. λιπογράμματος *adj.*, wanting a letter, f. λιπ-, wk. stem of λείπειν leave, be wanting + γράμμα, γραμματ- letter; see -GRAM.] A composition from which all words that contain a certain letter or letters are omitted. Hence **Li:pogramma·tic** *a.*, of, pertaining to, or of the nature of a l. So **Lipogra·mmatist,** a writer of lipograms.

||**Lipoma** (lipō^u·mă). Pl. **-mata** (-mătă). 1830. [mod.L.; see LIPO-, -OMA.] *Path.* A fatty tumour. **Lipo:mato·sis,** excess of fat in a tissue. **Lipo·matoid, Lipo·matous** *adjs.* resembling, or of the nature of, a l.

Lipothymy (lipǫ·þimi), **lipothymia** (lipŏþəi·miă). 1603. [– mod.L. *lipothymia* – Gr. λιποθυμία, f. λιπ-, weak base of λείπειν leave, fail, be lacking + θυμός animation, spirit; see -Y[3]. Cf. Fr. *lipothymie* (XVI).] Fainting, swooning, syncope.

fig. When nature is in a lipothymie JER. TAYLOR. So **Lipothy·mial, Lipothy·mic** *adjs.* of or pertaining to l.: characterized by l.

Lipped (lipt), *ppl. a.* ME. [f. LIP *sb.* or *v.*[1] + -ED.] **1.** Having or furnished with a lip or lips. Often qualified, as *blubber-, red-, thick-l.* **2.** *Bot.* = LABIATE; also, having a labellum 1731.

Lippen (li·pĕn), *v.* Chiefly *Sc.* [Early ME. *lipnen, lipnien*, of unkn. origin.] **1.** *intr.* To confide, rely, trust. **2.** *trans.* To entrust ME. **3.** To expect confidently ME.

Lippitude (li·pitiud). Now *rare.* 1626. [– Fr. *lippitude* (XVI) or L. *lippitudo*, f. *lippus* blear-eyed; see -TUDE.] Soreness of the eyes; blearedness.

Lipsalve (li·p,sāv). 1591. [f. LIP *sb.* + SALVE *sb.*[1]] Salve or ointment for the lips; an example of this; *fig.* flattering speech.

Lipse, obs. var. of LISP *v.*

†**Li·quable.** 1460. [– L. *liquabilis*, f. *liquare*; see LIQUATE *v.*, -ABLE.] **A.** *adj.* That can be liquefied. Also, soluble (in a liquid). –1768. **B.** *sb.* [sc. *substance.*] –1612.

Liquate (ləi·kwe[i]t), *v.* 1669. [– *liquat-*, pa. ppl. stem of L. *liquare* make liquid, cogn. w. *liquor* LIQUOR; see -ATE[3].] †**1.** *trans.* To make liquid, cause to flow. Also *intr.*, to melt. –1728. **2.** *Metall.* To separate metals or free them from impurities by liquefying. Also to *l. out.* 1864.

Liquation (likwē[i]·ʃən). 1471. [– late and med.L. *liquatio* melting, f. as prec.; see -ION.] **1.** The making or becoming liquid; the condition or capacity of being melted 1612. **2.** *Metall.* The action of separating metals by fusion.

Liquefacient (likwĭfē[i]·ʃ[i]ĕnt). 1853. [– *liquefacient-*, pr. ppl. stem of L. *liquefacere*; see LIQUEFY, -ENT.]

A. *adj.* Making liquid 1889.

B. *sb.* Something which serves to liquefy; *spec.* in *Med.*, an agent (e.g. mercury and iodine) supposed to have the power of liquefying solid deposits 1853. Also, an agent which increases the amount of fluid secretions 1889.

Liquefaction (likwĭfæ·kʃən). Also †**liqui-.** late ME. [– Fr. *liquéfaction* or late L. *liquefactio*, f. *liquefact-*, pa. ppl. stem of L. *liquefacere*; see LIQUEFY, -ION.] The action or process of liquefying, or the state of being liquefied; reduction to a liquid state. †Also *fig.* of the 'melting' of the soul –1711.

Liquefactive (likwĭfæ·ktiv), *a.* 1877. [f.

prec. + -IVE.] Having the effect of liquefying.

Liquefy (li·kwĭfəi), *v.* Also †**liquify.** 1483. [– Fr. *liquéfier* – L. *liquefacere* make liquid, melt (pass. *liquefieri*), f. *liquēre*; see LIQUOR, -FY.] **1.** *trans.* To reduce (a solid, air, gas) into a liquid condition. †Formerly, to dissolve (in a liquid). 1547. **2.** *fig.* To 'melt' with spiritual ardour. Also *intr.* for *pass.* 1483. **3.** *intr.* To become liquid; †*rarely* to dissolve (in water) 1583.

3. The ice liquefying rapidly TYNDALL. Hence **Li·quefi·able** *a.* **Li·quefier.**

Liquescent (likwe·sĕnt), *a.* 1727. [– *liquescent-*, pr. ppl. stem of L. *liquescere*, f. *liquēre*; see LIQUOR, -ESCENT.] In process of becoming liquid; apt to become liquid. Hence **Lique·scence** (*rare*).

‖**Liqueur** (likōr; often likiū·ɹ), *sb.* 1742. [Fr.; = LIQUOR *sb.*] **1.** A strong alcoholic liquor sweetened and flavoured with aromatic substances. **b.** A mixture (of sugar and certain wines or alcohol) used to sweeten and flavour champagne 1872. **2.** Short for *liqueur-glass*.

Comb. **l. brandy,** a brandy of special bouquet, consumed in small quantities as a l.; **-glass,** a very small drinking glass used for liqueurs; **-wine** [= Fr. *vin de liqueur*], one of the strong and delicate-flavoured wines that have the character of liqueurs. Hence **Liqueu·r** *v.* to flavour (champagne) with a l.

Liquid (li·kwid). ME. [– L. *liquidus*, f. *liquēre*; see LIQUOR, -ID[1]. Cf. (O)Fr. *liquide*.] **A.** *adj.* **I.** Said of a material substance in that condition in which its particles move freely over each other (so that its masses have no determinate shape), but do not tend to separate as do those of a gas; not solid nor gaseous; resembling water, oil, alcohol, etc. in their normal condition. Hence, composed of a substance in this condition. **b.** Watery, *poet.* and *rhet.* 1606.

L. sap SPENSER, fire SHAKS. **b.** Behold The strong ribb'd Barke through l. Mountaines cut SHAKS.

II. Transf. and fig. senses. **1.** Of light, fire, the air: Clear, transparent, bright 1590. **2.** Of sounds: Flowing, pure and clear in tone; not harsh or grating. Also in *Phonetics*, Vowel-like (see B. 2). 1637. †**3.** Of proofs, exposition, etc.: Clear, manifest –1726. **b.** Of an account or debt: Undisputed 1660. **4.** Not fixed or stable. Of movement: Facile, unconstrained. 1835. **5.** Of assets, securities, etc.: Promptly convertible into cash 1818.

1. They That wing the l. Air, or swim the Sea DRYDEN. **2.** The l. and gurgling notes of the bobolink 1879. **4.** The l. nature, so to speak, of its technical terms. They mean anything and everything 1867.

B. *sb.* **1.** A liquid substance (see A. I). In *pl.* often = *liquid food*. 1708. **2.** *Phonetics.* A name applied to the sounds of *l*, *m*, *n*, *r*, or (by some writers) only to those of *l* and *r*. Cf. Fr. *mouillé* lit. 'wet'. 1530.

2. It [L] melteth in the sounding, and is therefore called a l., the tongue striking the root of the palate gently B. JONS.

Hence **Li·quidless** *a.* **Li·quid-ly** *adv.*, **-ness.** **Li·quidize** *v. trans.* to make l.

Liquidambar (likwidæ·mbăɹ). Also **liquid amber.** 1598. [– mod.L. *liquidambar*, app. irreg. f. L. *liquidus* + med.L. *ambar* AMBER.] **1.** A resinous gum which exudes from the bark of the tree *Liquidambar styraciflua*. Called also *copalm balsam*. **2.** *Bot.* A genus of trees, N.O. *Hamamelideæ*, consisting of two species, *L. orientalis* of Asia Minor (which yields the balsam liquid storax), and *L. styraciflua*, the Sweet-gum tree of N. America; a tree of this genus 1843.

Li·quidate, *pa. pple.* and *ppl. a.* *Law.* 1574. [– med.L. *liquidatus*, pa. pple. of *liquidare*; see next, -ATE[2].] Ascertained and fixed in amount.

Liquidate (li·kwideⁱt), *v.* 1575. [– *liquidat-*, pa. ppl. stem of med.L. *liquidare*, f. L. *liquidus*; see LIQUID, -ATE[3]. The financial senses are due to It. *liquidare*, Fr. *liquider*.] †**1.** *trans.* To make clear or plain; to render unambiguous; to settle (differences, etc.) –1780. **b.** To clear away (objections). *rare.* 1620. **2.** To determine and apportion by agreement or by litigation; to set out clearly (accounts). Now *U.S.* **3.** To clear off, pay (a debt). Also *absol.* in *U.S. slang.* 1755. **4.** *Law* and *Comm.* **a.** *trans.* To ascertain and set out clearly the liabilities of (a company or firm) and to apportion the assets; to wind up. **b.** *intr.* To go into liquidation. 1870. **5.** *trans.* To make liquid (*rare*) 1656.

1. Ere we l. our differences by the sword H. WALPOLE. **2.** Agreed to pay the debt on its being liquidated 1798. **3.** To l. the National Debt 1834. Hence **Li·quidator,** a person appointed to wind up a company.

Liquidation (likwidēⁱ·ʃən). 1575. [– Fr. *liquidation*, f. *liquider*; see prec., -ATION; (partly f. LIQUIDATE *v.*). Cf. med.L. *liquidatio* making clear, explaining (XV).] **1.** *Law.* The action or process of ascertaining and apportioning the amounts of a debt, etc. **2.** The clearing off or settling (of a debt) 1786. **3.** The action or process of winding up a company; the state or condition of being wound up; *esp.* in phr. *to go into l.* 1869. **4.** *U.S. slang.* The taking of liquid refreshment. 1889.

2. The l. of Debt is a national duty LUBBOCK.

Liquidity (likwi·dĭti). 1620. [– Fr. *liquidité* or med.L. *liquiditas*; partly f. LIQUID + -ITY.] The quality or condition of being liquid.

Liquor (li·kəɹ), *sb.* [ME. *licur, licour* – OFr. *licur, licour* (mod. *liqueur*) – L. *liquor*, rel. to *liquare* liquefy, filter, *liqui* flow, *liquēre* be fluid.] †**1.** A liquid; matter in a liquid state; *occas.* a fluid –1701. **b.** The liquid constituent of a secretion or the like; the liquid product of a chemical operation 1565. **2.** A prepared solution used as a wash or bath, and in industrial processes, e.g. in *Tanning* 1583. **b.** *Brewing.* Water 1691. **3.** Liquid for drinking. Now usu. *spec.* a drink produced by fermentation or distillation. ME. Also *fig.* **b.** *slang.* (Chiefly *U.S.*) A drink (of an intoxicating beverage). Also, *a liquor-up*. 1860. **4.** The water in which meat has been boiled; the fat in which bacon, fish, etc. has been fried; the liquid contained in oysters ME. **5.** The liquid produced by infusion (in testing tea) 1870. ‖**6.** The L. word, pronounced ləi·kwǫɹ and li·kwǫɹ, used (*a*) in *Pharmacy* and *Med.* in the names of solutions of specified medicinal substances in water; (*b*) in *Physiol.*, as *l. sanguinis*, the blood-plasma, etc. 1796.

1. b. Phr. *L. of flints* = *liquor silicum* (see below); *l. of the Hollanders*, the chloride of olefiant gas; *l. of Libavius*, bichloride of tin. **3.** Neither shal he drinke any l. of grapes *Num.* 6:3. *Malt l. Spirituous l. Vinous l.* Phr. *Disguised with l. To be* (*the*) *worse for l.*: to be overcome by drink. **6.** (*a*) *Liquor ammoniæ*, strong solution of ammonia. *Liquor potassæ*, an aqueous solution of hydrate of potash. *Liquor silicum*, soluble glass. (*b*) *Liquor amnii*, the fluid contained in the sac of the amnion.

Comb.: **l.-pump,** a portable pump for emptying casks, etc.; **-thief,** a tube which is let down through the bung-hole of a cask in sampling spirits.

Liquor (li·kəɹ), *v.* 1502. [f. LIQUOR *sb.*] **1.** *trans.* To cover or smear with a liquor; *esp.* to lubricate with grease or oil 1573. **2.** *esp.* To dress (leather, boots, etc.) with oil or grease 1502. **3.** To steep in or soak with a liquor; to steep (malt) in water 1743. **4.** To supply with liquor to drink; to ply with liquor. Also *to l. up.* Now *slang.* 1560. **5.** *intr.* (*slang.*) To drink alcoholic liquor. Also *to l. up.* 1839.

2. They would melt mee out of my fat drop by drop, and l. Fishermen's boots with me SHAKS.

Liquorice, licorice (li·kŏris). ME. [– AFr. *lycorys*, OFr. *licoresse*, *-ece* – (with assim. to *licor* LIQUOR) late L. *liquiritia* – Gr. γλυκύρριζα, f. γλυκύς sweet + ῥίζα root.] **1.** The rhizome (also called *liquorice-root*) of the plant *Glycyrrhiza glabra*. Also, a black substance (used medicinally and as a sweetmeat) prepared from the evaporated juice of this; also called *Spanish l.*, *Spanish juice*, etc. **2.** The plant itself. Also other species, esp. *G. echinata*. 1548. **3.** With qualification, used of plants the roots of which resemble or are used as substitutes for the true liquorice, as *mountain, wild l.*, etc. 1548.

3. L., Wild, *Astragalus*; *Caperaria*; *Glycine* J. LEE. Wild L., *Abrus*; also an American name for *Galium circæzans* (Treas. Bot.).

Comb.: **l. vetch,** *Astragalus glycyphyllus*; **l. weed,** a tropical plant, *Scoparia dulcis*.

Liquorish (li·kəriʃ), *a.* 1789. [f. LIQUOR *sb.* + -ISH[1]. A sense-perversion of LICKERISH.] Fond of or indicating fondness for liquor. Hence **Li·quorish-ly** *adv.*, **-ness.**

Liquorist (li·kərist). 1839. [– Fr. *liquoriste*, f. LIQUEUR; see -IST.] A maker of liqueurs.

‖**Lira** (lī·ră). *Pl.* ‖**lire** (lī·re), *rarely* **liras.** 1617. [It. – Pr. *liura* = Fr. *livre*, It. *libbra* :– L. *libra* pound.] An Italian silver coin, the unit of monetary value in Italy: equal in value to the French franc, and containing 100 centesimi.

Lire (ləiᵊɹ). *Obs.* exc. *Sc.* and *n. dial.* [OE. *līra*, rel. to ON. *lær*, Sw. *lår* thigh, ON. *leggr* leg.] Flesh, muscle, brawn. Hence **Li·ry** *a.* fleshy.

‖**Lirella** (lire·lă). 1839. [mod.L., = Fr. *lirelle*, dim. f. L. *lira* furrow.] *Bot.* The narrow shield or apothecium, with a furrow along the middle, found in some lichens. Hence **Lire·lliform** *a.* shaped like a l.

Li·ripipe, li·ripoop. *Obs.* exc. *Hist.* 1546. [– med.L. *liripipium*, *leropipium*, variously explained as 'tippet of a hood', 'cord', 'shoe-lace', etc., of unkn. origin. The earliest forms, *liripoop*, etc., are unexpl.] **1.** In early academical costume: The long tail of a graduate's hood 1737. †**2.** One's 'lesson', 'rôle', or 'part'; chiefly in phr. *to know* or *have* (one's) *liripoop*, *to teach* (a person) *his l.* –1633. †**3.** A silly person –17..

Lis (līs). *Pl.* **lis, lisses.** 1611. [– Fr. *lis* lily.] *Her.* = FLEUR-DE-LIS 2.

Lisbon (li·zbən). 1767. [The capital of Portugal.] **a.** A white wine of the province of Estremadura. **b.** Clayed sugar 1767. **c.** A kind of lemon 1897.

Lisle (ləil). 1851. Name of a French town (now *Lille*): *attrib.* in *L. glove*, a fine thread glove for summer wear; *L. thread*, a hard twisted cotton thread, orig. made at L.; etc.

Lisp (lisp), *sb.* 1625. [f. LISP *v.*] The action or an act of lisping; *transf.* rippling of water, rustling of leaves, etc.

A young lady of sixty-five..with an engaging l. DICKENS.

Lisp (lisp), *v.* Pa. t. and pple. **lisped** (lispt). [OE. *wlispian* (only in *āwlyspian*), f. *wlisp*, *wlips* adj. lisping; cf. MLG. *wlispen*, *wilspen* (Du. *lispen*), OHG. *lisp* stammering, *lispen* lisp (G. *lispeln*); imitative.] **1.** *intr.* To substitute for s and z sounds approaching þ and ð in speaking; either from a defect in the organs of speech or as an affectation. Also, *loosely*, to speak with childlike utterance. **2.** *trans.* To utter with a lisp (also with *out*); to utter with childlike, imperfect, or faltering articulation (also *fig.*) 1620.

1. He can carue too, and lispe SHAKS. As little children l., and tell of Heaven KEBLE. **2.** To l. mysteries to those that would be deterred by any other way of expressing them BOYLE. *fig.* The light wave lisps 'Greece' BROWNING. Hence **Li·sper. Li·spingly** *adv.*

Lispound (li·spaund). 1502. [– LG., Du. *lispund*, for *livsch pund* 'Livonian pound'.] A unit of weight (12 to 30 lb.) used in the Baltic trade, and in Orkney and Shetland.

†**Liss.** [OE. *lips*, *liss*, f. *līþe* gentle, soft; see LITHE *a.*] **1.** Release; mitigation; hence, cessation –1802. **2.** Tranquillity, peace, rest; joy –ME.

Lissom (li·səm), *a.* Also **lissome.** 1800. [Of dial. origin; for **lithsom*, f. LITHE *a.* + -SOME[1], with shortening of the first syllable; cf. LITHESOME.] Supple, limber; agile; lithesome.

Straight, but as lissome as a hazel wand TENNYSON. Hence **Li·ssomness.**

†**List,** *sb.*[1] [OE. *hlyst* = OS., ON. *hlust* :– Gmc. **χlustiz* :– IE. **klustis*, f. **klus-* extension of **klu-* hear; see LITHE *v.*[2]] **1.** Hearing; the sense of hearing –ME. **2.** The ear –1535.

List (list), *sb.*[2] [OE. *līste* = MDu. *lijste* (Du. *lijst*), OHG. *līsta* (G. *leiste*) :– Gmc. **listōn*. In its application to tilting repr. OFr. *lisse* (mod. *lice*).]

I. Border, edging, strip. †**1.** *gen.* A border, hem, bordering strip –1696. †**b.** Applied to the lobe of the ear –1631. **2.** *spec.* The selvage or border of a cloth, usu. of different material from the body. Also *fig.* ME. **b.** Such selvages collectively; the material of which the selvage of cloth consists 1567. **c.** *attrib.* (quasi-*adj.*) = Made of list, as *l.*

slippers, etc. 1661. **3.** A strip of cloth or other fabric ME. **4.** A band or strip of any material; a line or band conspicuously marked on a surface. ? *Obs.* ME. **b.** One of the divisions of a head of hair, of a beard. [Cf. It. *lista.*] 1859. **5.** A stripe of colour. 1496. **6.** *Arch.* A small square moulding or ring encircling the foot of a column, between the torus below and the shaft above. Cf. LISTEL. 1663. **7. a.** *Carpentry.* The upper rail of a railing. **b.** *Carpentry.* A strip cut from the edge of a plank. **c.** *Tin-plating.* The wire of tin left on the under edge of a tinned plate, and removed by plunging the plate into the list-pot. 1688.

II. Boundary. **†1.** A limit, boundary. Often *pl.* –1645. **2.** *spec.* in *pl.* The palisades or other barriers enclosing a space set apart for tilting; *hence*, a space so enclosed in which tournaments, etc. were held. Occas., the arena in which bulls fight or wrestlers contend, etc. ME. **b.** *transf.* and *fig.* A place of combat or contest. Phr. *To enter (the) lists.* 1579. **†3. a.** *sing.* and *pl.* A railed or staked enclosure. **b.** *pl.* The starting-place of a race (= L. *carceres*). Also *sing.* A race-course or exercising ground for horses. –1737.

1. I am bound to your Neece sir: I meane she is the l. of my voyage SHAKS. **2.** Cambalo That faught in listes with the bretheren two For Canacee CHAUCER. When the Lists set wide, Gave room to the fierce Bulls DRYDEN. **b.** See, Chloris, how the clouds Tilt in the azure lists DRUMM. OF HAWTH.

Comb. **l.-pot**, a cast-iron trough containing a small quantity of melted tin, in which the tinned plates are plunged to remove the l. (sense I. 7 c).

List (list), *sb.*[3] ME. [f. LIST *v.*[1]] **†1.** Pleasure, joy, delight –1573. **2.** Appetite, craving; desire; inclination. *arch.* ME. **3.** (One's) desire or wish; (one's) good pleasure. Phr. *at (one's) l. arch.* ME.

2. I had little l. or leisure to write FULLER.

List (list), *sb.*[4] †Also (*Naut.*) **lust.** 1633. [Of unkn. origin.] **1.** *Naut.* The careening or inclination of a ship to one side. **2.** *transf.* A leaning over (of a building, etc.) 1793.

1. The cargo shifted giving the ship a l. to port 1881.

List (list), *sb.*[5] 1602. [– Fr. *liste* (XVI) = Sp., It. *lista*, presumably identical with LIST *sb.*[2], the special application being developed from 'strip' (of paper).] A catalogue or roll of names, figures, words, or the like. In early use, *esp.* a catalogue of the names of persons having the same duties; *spec.* a catalogue of the soldiers of an army or of a particular arm. **b.** *Racing slang.* Short for: The list of geldings in training. Hence *to put on the l.* = to castrate. 1890.

Active l., a l. of officers in the army or navy liable to be called upon for active service. *Free l.*, (*a*) a l. of persons admitted free to a theatre, etc.; (*b*) a l. of articles which are duty-free. *Army-l.*, CIVIL LIST, *retired l.*, *sick-l.*, etc. (see the first wds.).

List (list), *v.*[1] *arch.* [OE. *lystan* = OS. *lustian* (Du. *lusten*), OHG. *lusten* (G. *lüsten*), ON. *lysta* :– Gmc. **lustjan*, f. **lust-* pleasure, LUST *sb.*] **1.** *impers. trans.* To be pleasing to: *Me list* (occas. *listeth*): I please, like, care, or desire. **2.** With *personal* construction: To desire, like, wish, choose (with or without dependent inf.) ME. **†3.** *trans.* To desire or wish for (something) –1587.

1. The lestyth nat a louere be CHAUCER. To do as me listeth with myne awne TINDALE *Matt.* 20:15. **2.** If we l. to speake *Haml.* I. v. 177. The winde bloweth where it listeth *John* 3:8.

List (list), *v.*[2] *arch.* [OE. *hlystan*, f. *hlyst* LIST *sb.*[1]] = LISTEN *v.* 1, 2.

L., l., I hear Som far off hallow break the silent Air MILT. *Comus* 480. Wilt then l. to me? COWPER. I l. no more the tuck of drum SCOTT.

List (list), *v.*[3] ME. [f. LIST *sb.*[2]; cf. OFr. *lister* to put a list on (cloth); G. *leisten*, Du. *lijsten.*] **†1.** *trans.* To put a list, border, or edge round (an object); to border, edge. Also, to put as a list *upon.* –1703. **b.** To fix list upon the edge of (a door) 1860. **†2.** To enclose; to rail *in* –1565. **†b.** To bound. HOOKER. **3.** *Carpentry.* To cut away the sappy edge of a board; to shape a block or stave by chopping 1635.

1. A Danish curtaxe, listed with gold or silver MILT. **b.** Monsieur Leclerc. .listed the doors against approaching winter breezes 1881.

List (list), *v.*[4] 1614. [f. LIST *sb.*[5] In senses 3 and 4 now aphet. f. *enlist*, and often written *'list.*] **1.** *trans.* To set down in a list; to catalogue, register. **b.** To set down in a special or official list (e.g. of cases for trial, of stocks, etc.) 1702. **†2.** To comprise in a list or catalogue; to enrol; to put in the same category *with* –1777. **3.** To appoint formally (an officer); also in *pass.* to be appointed or gazetted as (captain, etc.). Later, only = ENLIST *v.* 1 1643. Also *transf.* and *fig.* **4.** *refl.* and *intr.* (for *refl.*) = ENLIST *v.* 3. Phr. *To l. (oneself) a soldier* or *for a soldier.* 1643. Also *transf.* and *fig.*

1. About one hundred species of butterflies have been listed 1887. **3.** He listed me when I was out of my senses SOUTHEY. *fig.* He that is born, is listed; life is war YOUNG. **4.** He listed at last for a sodger STEVENSON. *transf.* Merely that they [M.P.'s] may l. under party banners 1845.

List (list), *v.*[5] 1626. [f. LIST *sb.*[4]] *intr.* Of a ship: To careen, heel, or incline to one side. Also with *off.*

She listed to port and filled rapidly 1885.

Listel (li·stĕl). 1598. [– It. *listello* (whence also Fr. *listel* XVII), dim. of *lista* = LIST *sb.*[2]] *Arch.* A small list or fillet.

Listen (li·s'n), *sb.* 1803. [f. next.] The action or an act of listening; a spell of listening. Chiefly in phr. *On* or *upon the l.*

Listen (li·s'n), *v.* [OE. *hlysnan*, corresp. to MHG. *lüsenen* :– WGmc. **χlusinōjan* (cf. OE. *hlosnian* listen :– **χlusnōjan*), f. Gmc. **χlus-*; see LIST *sb.*[1]] **1.** *trans.* To hear attentively; to give ear to; to pay attention to. Now *arch.* or *poet.* **2.** *intr.* To make an effort to hear something; to give ear ME.

1. At which I ceas't, and listen'd them a while MILT. **2.** They will be sure to l. if they find that you are a good speaker JOWETT. *To l. to (unto)*: to give ear to (= sense 1); also, to allow oneself to be persuaded by. List'n not to his Temptations MILT. *To l. for*, *†after*: to be eager or make an effort to catch the sound of. *To l. in*: to listen to concert performances, news, etc. transmitted by wireless. Hence **Li·stener,** one who listens; an attentive hearer. **Li·stening** *vbl. sb.*; *spec.* in **Listening gallery** *Fortif.*, a gallery run out under and beyond the glacis in the direction of the besiegers' works, to enable the besieged to hear and estimate the distance the besiegers have mined.

†Lister[1]. ME. [– OFr. *listre*, altered f. *litre* :– L. *lector* (see LECTOR).] A reader or lector –1555.

Lister[2] (li·stəɹ). 1678. [f. LIST *v.*[4] + -ER[1].] **1.** An enlister. **2.** One who makes out a list, *spec.* (*U.S.*) of taxable property 1716.

Lister, var. of LEISTER.

Listerian (listīᵊ·riăn), *a.* 1880. Applied to the system of antiseptic surgery invented by Lord Lister. So **Listerine** (li·sterin), a proprietary antiseptic solution named after Lister 1889. **Li·sterism,** the system of antiseptic surgery originated by Lister 1880. **Li·sterize** *v.* to treat on Listerian methods 1902.

Listful (li·stfŭl), *a. arch.* 1595. [f. LIST *v.*[2] + -FUL.] Inclined to listen, attentive.

Listing (li·stiŋ), *sb.* ME. [f. LIST *sb.*[2] + -ING[1].] **1.** Selvage; the material of which the list of cloth is composed. **2.** *Naut.* A narrow strip cut out off the edge of a plank to show its condition, or in order to put in a new piece 1846. *Comb.* **l.-pot** = *list-pot*: see LIST *sb.*[2]

Listless (li·stlĕs), *a.* 1440. [f. LIST *sb.*[3] + -LESS.] **†a.** Destitute of relish or inclination for some object or pursuit; const. *of.* **b.** Unwilling to move, act, or make any exertion; languid, indifferent.

b. A dull discourse naturally produces a l. audience 1766. Hence **Li·stless-ly** *adv.*, **-ness.**

Lit, *sb. Obs.* exc. *dial.* [Early ME. *lit* – ON. *litr* colour. See LITMUS.] Dye, dye-stuff. Hence **Lit** *v.*, to dye.

Lit (lit), *ppl. a.* 1820. [pa. pple. of LIGHT *v.*[2]] Lighted, illumined; also with *up.* (Also in *comb.*, as *sun-lit.*)

Lit, pa. t. of LIGHT *v.*[1] and [2].

Litany (li·tăni). [ME. *letanie* (later assim. to L.) – OFr. *letanie* (mod. *litanie*) – eccl.L. *litania* (whence OE. *letania*) – Gr. λιτανεία prayer, entreaty, f. λιτανός suppliant, f. λιτή supplication, λιτέσθαι entreat.] **1.** *Eccl.* A form of public prayer, usually penitential, consisting of a series of petitions, in which the clergy lead and the people respond. A litany may be used either as part of a service or by itself, in the latter case often in procession. **b.** *The L.*: that form of 'general supplication' appointed for use in the Book of Common Prayer 1544. **2.** *transf.* A form of supplication resembling a litany; also, a continuous repetition or long enumeration resembling those of litanies ME.

1. *attrib.*, as *l. desk.* **2.** Lord deliver me from my self, is a part of my Letany SIR T. BROWNE. Hear them mumble Their l. of curses SHELLEY.

Litarge, -y, obs. ff. LITHARGE.

Litchi (lītʃī·). 1588. [Chinese *li-chi.*] The fruit of the *Nephelium litchi* (N.O. *Sapindaceæ*), a tree introduced from China into Bengal.

Lite, *sb.*, *a.*, and *adv. Obs.* exc. *arch.* or *dial.* [Partly repr. OE. *lȳt* sb., adj., adv. (= OS. *lūt* sb.), and partly the synon. ON. *litt* adv., contr. of *litit*, n. of *litill*; see LITTLE.] **A.** *sb.* **1.** Little, not much. **2.** Few OE. **B.** *adj.* (Uninflected in OE.) **1.** Few OE. **2.** Little in amount ME. **3.** Small ME. **C.** *adv.* Little: in a small degree OE.

-lite (= Fr. *-lite*, G. *-lith*, *-lit*), ending of names of minerals, repr. Gr. λίθος stone. The form *-lite*, instead of -LITH, is due to the example of the French geologists.

Liter, var. of LITRE.

Literacy (li·tĕrăsi). 1883. [f. LITERATE; see -ACY. (Formed as an antithesis to *illiteracy.*)] Quality or state of being literate.

‖**Literæ humaniores** (li·tarī hiumēⁱniōᵘ·rīz). 1747. See HUMANE *a.* 2, LETTER *sb.*[1] II. 4; *spec.* the name of a School in the University of Oxford. (Abbrev. *Lit. Hum.*)

Literal (li·tĕrăl). ME. [– (O)Fr. *litéral* or late L. *lit(t)eralis*, f. *lit(t)era* LETTER; see -AL[1].] **A.** *adj.* **1.** Of or pertaining to letters of the alphabet; of the nature of letters; expressed by letters. †Of a verse: ALLITERATIVE. **b.** Of a misprint, etc.: Affecting a letter 1606. **2.** Of a translation, version, transcript, etc.: Representing the very words of the original; verbally exact 1599. **3. a.** *Theol.* Pertaining to the 'letter' (of Scripture); in interpretation, applied to taking the words of a text, etc., in their natural and customary meaning, and using the ordinary rules of grammar; opp. to *mystical, allegorical*, etc. †Also *occas.* of a law, etc.: That is to be interpreted literally. ME. **b.** Hence, applied to taking words in their etymological or primary sense, or in the sense expressed by the actual wording of a passage, without recourse to any metaphorical or suggested meaning 1597. **c.** Of persons: Prosaic, matter-of-fact 1778. **4.** Used to denote that the accompanying sb. has its literal sense, without metaphor, exaggeration, or inaccuracy; literally so called 1646. **†5.** Epistolary –1657. **†6.** = LITERARY –1604.

1. The art of expressing their thoughts by l. characters 1733. The l. notation of numbers JOHNSON. **b.** 'Twas a l. fault in that Copy, which Casaubon used BENTLEY. **2.** The common way. . is not a l. Translation, but a kind of Paraphrase DRYDEN. **3. a.** Where a litterall construction will stand, the farthest from the letter is commonly the worst HOOKER. **b.** I see very few people; and, in the l. sense of the word, I hear nothing CHESTERF.

B. *sb.* **†1.** A literal interpretation or meaning –1646. **2.** *Printing.* A literal misprint 1622.

Hence **Li·teralness,** quality of being l.

Literalism (li·tĕrăliz'm). 1644. [f. prec. + -ISM.] **1.** The disposition to take and interpret words in their literal sense. **2.** A peculiarity of expression due to literality 1903. **3.** *Fine Arts.* The disposition to represent objects or interpret representations faithfully, without idealization 1863. So **Li·teralist,** one who adheres to the letter of a text or statement. Also, in art and literature, an exact copyist. **Literali·stic** *a.* pertaining to or characteristic of a literalist; having the character of l.

Literality (litĕræ·līti). 1643. [f. LITERAL + -ITY.] The quality or fact of being literal; literalness. †Also, a literal meaning.

Literalize (li·tĕrăləiz), *v.* 1826. [f. LITERAL + -IZE.] *trans.* To represent or accept as literal.

To l. poetical allegory 1827, metaphors 1856. Hence **Literaliza·tion, Li·teralizer.**

Literally (li·tĕrăli), *adv.* 1533. [f. LITERAL

+ -LY².] **1.** In the very words, word for word. Also *transf.* 1646. **2.** In the literal sense 1533. **b.** Used to indicate that the following word or phrase must be taken in its literal (now often *erron.*, in its strongest admissible) sense 1687.

1. Which are l. thus translated SIR T. BROWNE. **2.** It is found that the Act does not mean l. what it says 1895. **b.** The singular fate of dying l. of hunger HUME. Literally worn to a shadow 1825. For the last four years..I l. coined money 1863.

Literary (li·tĕrări). *a.* 1646. [– L. *lit(t)erarius*, f. *lit(t)era* LETTER; see -ARY¹.] †**1.** Pertaining to the letters of the alphabet –1793. †**2.** Carried on by letters; epistolary. SMOLLETT. **3.** Of or pertaining to, or of the nature of, literature, polite learning, or books and written compositions; pertaining to that kind of written composition which has value on account of its qualities of form 1749. **4.** Versed in literature; *spec.* engaged in literature as a profession. Of a society, etc.: Consisting of literary men. 1791.

3. *L. history* (e.g. of a legend, an event, etc.): the history of the treatment of, and references to, the subject in literature. *L. property*: (*a*) property which consists in written or printed compositions; (*b*) the exclusive right of publication as recognized and limited by law. A man of l. merit GOLDSM. A l. reputation JOHNSON, conflict MACAULAY. Hence **Li·terarily** *adv.* **Li·terariness. Li·teraryism,** addiction to l. forms; an instance of this.

‖**Literata** (litĕrēi·tă). *Pl.* **-tæ.** [L. fem. of *lit(t)eratus*: see next.] A learned or literary lady. COLERIDGE.

Literate (li·tĕrĕt). ME. [– L. *lit(t)eratus*, f. *lit(t)era* LETTER; see -ATE².] **A.** *adj.* **1.** Acquainted with letters; educated, learned. In early use, const. *in*. **2.** Literary 1648.

1. A polite and l. Court CHESTERF. **2.** To beguile,..with some l. diversion, the tedious length of those days 1651. Hence †**Literated** *a.* learned.

B. *sb.* **1.** A liberally educated or learned person 1550. **2.** *spec.* In the Church of England, one admitted to holy orders without having a university degree 1824. **3.** One who can read and write. Opp. to *illiterate*. 1894.

1. Callista was a Greek; a l., or blue-stocking J. H. NEWMAN.

‖**Literati** (litĕrēi·təi), *sb. pl.* Also †**litterati.** 1621. [L., pl. of *lit(t)eratus* LITERATE.] Men of letters; the learned class as a whole.

To be..examined & approued as the l. in China BURTON.

‖**Literatim** (litĕrēi·tim), *adv.* 1643. [med. L., after L. GRADATIM.] Letter for letter; literally.

Literation (litĕrēi·ʃən). [f. L. *littera* + -ATION.] The action or process of representing (sounds or words) by letters. (Mod. Dicts.)

‖**Literato** (litĕră·to). 1704. [It. *litterato* – L. *lit(t)eratus* LITERATE.] One of the literati; a man of letters; a learned man.

Literator (li·tĕrēitŏɹ). 1635. [– L. *lit(t)erator* teacher of ABC, grammarian, smatterer, sciolist, f. *lit(t)era* LETTER; see -ATOR.] †**1.** A pretender to learning, a sciolist –1641. **2.** A literary man; = LITTÉRATEUR 1791. **3.** †A bibliographer. Also, a grammarian, critic (*rare*) 1727.

2. [French] preceptors..a set of pert petulant literators BURKE.

Literature (li·tĕrătiŭɹ). ME. [– (partly through Fr. *littérature*) L. *lit(t)eratura*, f. *lit(t)era* LETTER; see -URE.] **1.** Acquaintance with 'letters' or books; literary culture. Now *rare* or *obsol.* **2.** Literary work or production; the activity or profession of a man of letters; the realm of letters 1779. **3.** Literary productions as a whole; the writings of a country or period, or of the world in general. Now also, less widely, writings esteemed for beauty of form or emotional effect. 1812. **b.** The body of books, etc. that treat of a subject 1860. **c.** *colloq.* Any printed matter 1895.

1. Another person of infinite l. [Selden] 1693. **2.** L., the most seductive, the most deceiving, the most dangerous of professions MORLEY. **3.** Their l., their works of art offer models that have never been excelled SIR H. DAVY. *Light l.*: see LIGHT *a.*¹ V. 3.

‖**Literatus** (litĕrēi·tŏs). *rare.* 1704. [L.; see LITERATE.] One of the LITERATI.

Our bright ideal of a l. may chance to be married DE QUINCEY.

Lites, var. sp. of LIGHTS.

Lith (liþ), *sb. Obs.* exc. *arch.* or *dial.* [OE. *liþ* = OFris., OS. *lith* (Du. *lid*), OHG. *lid* (G. *glied*), ON. *liðr*, Goth. *liþus* :– Gmc. **liþu-*; prob. rel. to OE. *lim* LIMB.] **1.** A limb. **2.** A joint; freq. in *l. and limb* OE. **3.** *Sc.* A division (of an orange, etc.); one of the rings round the base of a cow's horn 1795.

Lith, obs. 3rd sing. pres. ind. of LIE.

-lith, terminal element repr. Gr. λίθος stone, used chiefly in *Biol.* and *Path.*, as *coccolith*, etc. In *Min.* -LITE is the usual form.

‖**Lithæmia** (liþī·miă). 1874. [mod.L., f. Gr. λίθος stone + αἷμα blood; see -IA¹.] *Path.* The condition in which lithic or uric acid is in excess in the blood; formerly called *uricæmia*. Hence **Lithæ·mic** *a.*

Lithagogue (li·păgọg). 1844. [f. Gr. λίθος stone + ἀγωγός drawing forth.] *Path. adj.* and *sb.* (A medicine) having the power to expel calculi from the kidneys or bladder.

Lithanode (li·pănōᵘd). 1887. [f. as prec. + ANODE.] *Electr.* A hard compact form of peroxide of lead, used in storage batteries.

Litharge (li·păɹdʒ). [ME. *litarge* – OFr. *litarge* (mod. *litharge*) – L. *lithargyrus* – Gr. λιθάργυρος, f. λίθος stone + ἄργυρος silver.] **1.** Monoxide of lead (PbO) prepared by exposing melted lead to a current of air. †**2.** = WHITE *lead* or RED LEAD –1800.

1. †*L. of gold*: l. when coloured red by mixture of red lead. †*L. of silver*: a name given to l. as being a by-product in the separation of silver from lead.

Lithate (li·pēᵗt). 1821. [f. LITHIC *a.*¹ + -ATE⁴.] *Chem.* A salt of lithic acid.

Lithe (ləið), *a.* [OE. *līþe* = OS. *līthi*, OHG. *lindi* (G. *lind*) soft, gentle :– WGmc. **linþja-*, f. Gmc., IE. **len-*, whence ON. *linr* soft, yielding, OE. *linnan*; see LIN *v.*] †**1.** Of persons, their actions, etc.: Gentle, meek –ME. **2.** Of things: Mild, soft; agreeable, mellow, pleasant. Of a medicine: Gentle in operation. *Obs.* exc. *dial.* OE. **3.** Easily bent; flexible, limber, pliant, supple. (The current sense.) ME.

3. Th' unwieldy Elephant..wreathd His L. Proboscis MILT. Hence **Li·the-ly** *adv.*, **-ness.**

†**Lithe,** *v.*¹ [OE. *līþan*, f. *līþe* LITHE *a.*] *trans.* To render 'lithe', i.e. gentle or mild; to influence gently; to relax; to mitigate; to relieve; to render supple; to bend, subdue –1642.

Lithe (ləið), *v.*² *Obs.* exc. *arch.* and *dial.* ME. [– ON. *hlýða*, f. *hljóð* listening, sound, rel. to Goth. *hliuma* sense of hearing, OE. *hlēoþor* sense of hearing, music, OHG. *hliudar*, f. **χleu-*, strong grade of **χlu-*; see LIST *sb.*¹] *intr.* To hearken, listen. Also, to hear *of* (a thing).

Lither (li·ðəɹ). [OE. *lȳþre* (:– **liuþri-*), the first element of MHG., G. *liederlich* (= late OE. *lȳðerlić*); cf. MLG. *lüder* lewd fellow.] **A.** *adj.* †**1.** Of persons, etc.: Bad, wicked; base, rascally. Of an animal: Ill-tempered. –1546. †**2.** Of things: Bad (chiefly in physical senses). Of a part of the body: Withered, impotent. –1622. †**b.** Of the air: Pestilential. Only ME. **3.** Lazy, sluggish, spiritless. Now *dial.* 1460. **4.** Pliant, supple; (of the air, sky) yielding (*arch.*) 1565.

4. The l. Skie SHAKS. †**Li·ther-ly** *a.* and *adv.*, **-ness.**

†**B.** *adv.* Badly, wickedly; ill, poorly –ME.

Lithesome (ləi·ðsŏm), *a.* 1768. [f. LITHE *a.* + -SOME¹.] = LISSOM.

Lithia¹ (li·piă). 1818. [mod.L., alteration, after *soda*, *potassa*, of mod.L. *lithion* (as if – Gr. λίθειον, n. of λίθειος stony, f. λίθος stone), applied to the fixed alkali to designate its mineral origin.] *Chem.* The oxide of lithium, LiO. Also *attrib.* **b.** *colloq.* Short for *lithia water* 1893.

Lithia water is..prescribed to gouty..persons 1878.

‖**Lithia**² (li·piă). 1822. [mod.L., f. Gr. λίθος stone. See -IA¹.] *Path.* The formation of sandy or stony concretions in the body, *esp.* in the Meibomian follicles of the eye. (Cf. next.)

‖**Lithiasis** (lipəi·ăsis). 1657. [med.L. – Gr. λιθίασις, f. λίθος stone; see -ASIS.] *Path.* The formation of stony concretions in the body, *esp.* in the urinary passages.

Lithic (li·pik), *a.*¹ 1797. [– Gr. λιθικός, f. λίθος stone; see -IC.] **1.** *Chem.* and *Path.* Of or pertaining to 'stone' or calculi in the bladder. **2.** *gen.* Of, pertaining to, or consisting of stone 1862.

1. †*L. acid*: uric acid. The uric, or l., acid calculus 1876. **2.** *L. age*, the 'stone age' of Archæology. L. ornaments 1865.

Lithic (li·pik), *a.*² 1839. [f. LITH(IUM + -IC.] *Chem.* Pertaining to lithium.

Lithiophilite (lipiọ·filəit). 1878. [f. LITHIUM + Gr. φίλος friend + -ITE¹ 2 b.] *Min.* A mineral containing a large proportion of lithium.

Lithium (li·piŏm). 1818. [f. LITHIA¹; see -IUM.] *Chem.* A metallic element of the alkaline group occurring in small quantities in various minerals. Symbol Li.

Litho (li·po). 1890. Techn. abbrev. of LITHOGRAPH.

Litho- (lipo), bef. a vowel **lith-**, comb. f. Gr. λίθος stone; in various scientific and technical words, as **Litho·genous** [Gr. -γενής producing + -OUS] *a.*, stone-producing, applied to those animals which produce coral. **Litho·phagous** [Gr. -φάγος eating] *a.*, stone-eating, as certain molluscs which bore through stones. **Li·thophane** [Gr. -φανής appearing], a kind or ornamentation produced by impressing upon porcelain-glass in a soft state figures which are made visible by transmitted light; so **Lithopha·nic** *a.*; **Litho·phany,** the art of making this. **Li·thotint,** the art or process of printing tinted pictures from lithographic stones; a picture so printed.

Lithochromatic (li:pokromæ·tik). 1846. [f. LITHO- + CHROMATIC.] *adj.* Pertaining to lithochromatics. *sb. pl.* The art or process of applying oil colours to stone and taking impressions therefrom. So **Li·thochrome,** chromolithography 1854. **Li·thochromy,** painting on stone 1829; also, chromolithography 1885.

Lithoclast (li·pŏklast). 1829. [f. LITHO- + Gr. -κλάστης breaker, f. κλᾶν break.] †**1.** A stone-breaker. **2.** *Surg.* An instrument for breaking up stone in the bladder 1847. Hence **Lithocla·stic** *a.*

Lithocyst (li·pŏsist). 1859. [f. LITHO- + CYST.] **1.** *Zool.* One of the sacs containing mineral particles found in certain Medusæ, and supposed to be organs of hearing. **2.** *Bot.* A cell containing crystals of calcium carbonate in the leaves of certain plants. VINES.

Lithodomous (lipọ·dŏməs), *a.* 1862. [f. mod.L. generic name *Lithodomus* – Gr. λιθοδόμος mason + -OUS.] *Zool.* Boring in stone, as mussels of the genus *Lithodomus*.

Lithoglyph (li·pŏglif). 1842. [f. LITHO- + GLYPH.] An incision or engraving on stone.

Lithograph (li·pŏgraf), *sb.* 1839. [Back-formation from LITHOGRAPHY.] **1.** A lithographic print. **2.** An inscription on stone 1859.

Li·thograph, *v.* 1825. [f. as prec.] **1.** *trans.* To print from stone; to produce by lithography. **2.** To write or engrave on stone (*rare*) 1872. So **Litho·grapher,** †one who writes about stones 1685; one who practises lithography 1828. †**Litho·graphize** *v.*

Lithographic (lipŏgræ·fik), *a.* 1813. [f. LITHOGRAPHY + -IC.] **1.** Pertaining to, employed in, or produced by lithography; engraved on or printed from stone. **2.** Descriptive of stones or rocks (*rare*) 1820.

1. L. impressions from drawings 1813. L. chalk and l. ink 1839. *L. limestone, slate, stone*: a compact yellowish slaty limestone used in lithography. So **Lithogra·phical** *a.* pertaining to lithography (*rare*); lithological.

Lithography (lipọ·grăfi). 1708. [In sense 1 – mod.L. *lithographia*; in sense 2 – G. *lithographie*; see LITHO-, -GRAPHY.] †**1.** A description of stones or rocks. **2.** The art or process of making a drawing, design, or writing on lithographic stone, so that impressions in ink can be taken from it 1813.

2. The process of l. consists essentially in the applications of a greasy ink on to a damp stone 1879.

Lithoid (li·poid), *a.* 1833. [– Gr. λιθοειδής, f. λίθος stone; see -OID.] Of the nature or structure of stone. So **Lithoi·dal** *a.* 1833.

Lithology (lipọ·lŏdʒi). 1716. [See LITHO-

and -LOGY.] **1.** The science of the nature and composition of stones and rocks. **2.** The department of medical science concerned with calculi in the human body. Also, a treatise on calculi. 1802.

Hence **Litholo·gic, -al** *a.* **Litholo·gically** *adv.* **Litho·logist,** one versed in l.

Lithomancy (li·þŏmænsi). 1646. [f. Gr. λίθος stone; see -MANCY.] Divination from stones.

Lithomarge (li·þŏmāɹdʒ). 1753. [– mod. L. *lithomarga* (also used), f. Gr. λίθος stone + L. *marga* marl.] *Geol.* 'An early name for several kinds of soft clay-like minerals, including kaolin' (A. H. Chester).

Lithontriptic (liþǫntri·ptik), **lithonthryptic** (-þri·ptik). 1646. [– Fr. *lithontriptique* or mod.L. *lithontripticus* (corrected later to *-thrypticus*), repr. Gr. (φάρμακα τῶν ἐν νεφροῖς) λίθων θρυπτικά (drugs) comminutive of stones (in kidneys); assoc. with τρίβειν ('rub') suggested 'wearing down'.] *Med. adj.* and *sb.* (A medicine) having the property of breaking up stone in the bladder.

Lithophyte (li·þŏfəit). 1774. [f. LITHO- + -PHYTE.] **1.** *Zool.* A polyp the substance of which is stony or calcareous, as some corals. **2.** *Bot.* A plant growing on stone or rock 1895. **Lithophy·tic, -phy·tous** *adjs.*

Lithotome (li·þŏtoᵘm). 1758. [– Gr. λιθοτόμον, n. of λιθοτόμος adj. stone-cutting, f. λίθος stone + -τομος cutting. Cf. Fr. *lithotome* (XVII).] *Surg.* An instrument for cutting the bladder in lithotomy; prop. called a *cystotome.* Hence **Lithoto·mic, -al** *a.*

Lithotomy (liþǫ·tŏmi). 1721. [– late L. *lithotomia* – Gr. λιθοτομία, f. λίθος stone; see -TOMY.] The operation, art, or process of cutting for stone in the bladder. So **Litho·tomist,** one who practises l. 1663; also, one who cuts inscriptions on stone 1713. **Litho·tomize** *v. trans.* to subject to l. 1836.

Lithotripsy (li·þŏtripsi). 1834. [f. LITHO- + Gr. τρῖψις rubbing.] The operation of rubbing down or crushing stone in the bladder. So **Lithotri·ptic** (refash, f. LITHONTRIPTIC, as if f. Gr. -τριπτικός, f. τρίβειν to rub] *a.* = LITHONTRIPTIC 1847. **Lithotri·ptor** 1847 (**lithon-** 1825) *Surg.* an instrument for lithotripsy.

Lithotritor (li·þŏtrəitǫɹ). 1828. [– Fr. *lithotriteur* (also used), f. Gr. λίθος stone + L. *tritor* rubber (f. *terere* rub).] *Surg.* = LITHOTRIPTOR. So **Li·thotrite,** a form of lithotriptor for crushing stone into minute particles which can be voided 1839. **Litho·tri·tic** *a.* 1830. **Litho·tritist,** one who practises lithotrity 1836. **Litho·tritize** *v. trans.* to subject to lithotrity 1842. **Litho·trity,** lithotripsy, esp. by means of a lithotrite 1827.

Lithotype (li·þŏtəip), *sb.* 1875. [f. LITHO- + -TYPE.] **1.** A stereotype plate made with gum-shellac, sand, tar, and linseed-oil. **2.** An etched stone surface for printing 1875. **3.** A lithographed finger-print. CONAN DOYLE. So **Li·thotype** *v. trans.* to prepare for printing by lithotypy. **Lithoty·pic** *a.* **Litho·typy,** the process of making lithotypes (sense 1); also printing from etched stone.

Lithsman (li·þs,mæ̆n). *Hist.* [OE. *liðsmann* – ON. *liðsmað-r* (accus. *-mann*), f. *lið*, genit. of *lið* host + *maðr* MAN.] A sailor in the navy under the Danish kings of England.

Lithuanian (liþiu,ēⁱ·niăn), *a.* and *sb.* 1555. [f. *Lithuania* + -AN.] Belonging to (a native of) Lithuania, its people or language; *sb.* also, the Lithuanian language. So **Lithuanic** (liþiu,æ·nik) 1841.

Lithy (li·ði), *a. dial.* [OE. *liþig* = ON. *liðugr* yielding, nimble, MDu. *ledech*, G. *ledig* unoccupied, vacant; ult. etym. unkn.] Pliable, flexible, supple; soft, unresisting.

Litigable (li·tigăb'l), *a.* 1764. [f. LITIGATE + -ABLE.] That may be litigated; disputable.

Litigant (li·tigănt). 1638. [– Fr. *litigant*, – *litigant-*, pr. ppl. stem of L. *litigare*; see LITIGATE, -ANT.] **A.** *adj.* Engaged in a lawsuit or in a dispute. Only in connection with *party.* **B.** *sb.* A person engaged in a lawsuit or dispute 1659.

A The parties l. are agreed that [etc.] CHILLINGW. **B.** Poverty is no bar to the l. 1885.

Litigate (li·tigeⁱt), *v.* 1615. [– *litigat-*, pa. ppl. stem of L. *litigare*, f. *lis, lit-* strife, lawsuit; see -ATE³.] **1.** *intr.* To be a party to a lawsuit; to go to law. Also †*gen.* to dispute. **2.** *trans.* To contest at law; to plead for or against 1741. **b.** *gen.* To dispute, contest (a point, etc.) 1739.

2. My grandfather's estate is to be litigated with me 1748. Hence **Li·tigator,** one who litigates.

Litigation (litigēⁱ·ʃən). 1567. [– late L. *litigatio*, f. as prec.; see -ION.] **1.** The action of carrying on a suit in law or equity; legal proceedings 1647. **b.** The practice of going to law 1785. **2.** Disputation (now *rare*) 1567.

1. Phr. *In l.*: in process of investigation before a court of law. **b.** The spirit of l. TROLLOPE.

Litigious (liti·dʒəs), *a.* ME. [– (O)Fr. *litigieux* or L. *litigiosus*, f. *litigium* litigation; see -OUS.] **1. a.** Fond of disputes, contentious (now *rare*). **b.** Fond of going to law. †**2.** Disputable, questionable; productive of contention –1648. **b.** Disputable at law; that is or is liable to become the subject of a lawsuit, esp. of a benefice 1568. **3.** Of or pertaining to lawsuits 1589.

1. a. Socrates hade ii. l. and malicious wifes ME. **b.** They [Hindus] are very l... They will persevere in a law-suit till they are ruined ELPHINSTONE. **2.** The time of his birth seemeth to him to be l. 1615. **3.** Pleasing thoughts of l. terms, fat contentions, and flowing fees MILT. **Liti·gious-ly** *adv.*, **-ness.**

Litmus (li·tmŏs). 1502. [– ONorw. *litmosi*, f. ON. *litr* sb., *lita* vb. (see LIT *sb.*) + *mosi* MOSS.] A blue colouring matter obtained from various lichens, esp. archil, *Roccella tinctoria.* (It is turned red by acids, and turned blue again by alkalis.) Also *attrib.*

L. blue, a blue pigment prepared from l.; **l. paper,** unsized paper stained blue with l., used as a test for acids; when reddened by an acid, it serves as a test for alkalis.

‖**Litotes** (ləi·totīz, li·t-). 1657. [late L. – Gr. λιτότης, f. λιτός single, simple, meagre.] *Rhet.* A figure, in which an affirmative is expressed by the negative of the contrary; an instance of this; e.g. *a citizen of no mean city.*

Litre (lī·təɹ, Fr. litr). Also *U.S.* **liter.** 1810. [– Fr. *litre* (1793), suggested by †*litron* old measure of capacity, f. med.L. *litra* – Gr. λίτρα Sicilian money of account.] The unit of capacity in the metric system, represented by a cube whose edge is the tenth of a metre, and = about 1¾ pints.

Li·tster. *Obs.* exc. *Hist.* ME. [f. LIT *v.* + -STER.] A dyer.

Litten (lit'n), *ppl. a.* 1849. [pseudo-arch. pa. pple. of LIGHT *v.*²] Lighted; as, *red-l.*, etc.

Litter (li·təɹ), *sb.* ME. [– AFr. *litere*, (O)Fr. *litière* :– med.L. *lectaria*, f. L. *lectus* (Fr. *lit*) bed.] †**1.** A bed –1481. **b.** In techn. use: A bed or substratum of various materials 1848. **2. a.** A vehicle containing a couch shut in by curtains, and carried on men's shoulders or by animals. **b.** A framework supporting a bed or couch for transporting the sick and wounded. ME. **3.** Straw, rushes, or the like, serving as bedding. †**a.** For human beings –1774. **b.** For animals. (Now also, the straw and dung together.) ME. **c.** Hence applied to straw, etc. †for plaster, †for thatch, or for the protection of plants 1453. **4.** Odds and ends, miscellaneous rubbish; a state of untidiness; a disorderly accumulation of things lying about 1730. **5.** The young brought forth at a birth 1486; also *transf.* and *fig.* (*contemptuous*) 1565; †an act of bringing forth young (said of animals only) –1794.

2. He ordeyned lyttyers for the wounded knyghtes MALORY. To keep himself close shut up in his l. 1734. **3. a.** Phr. *To make l. of* (one's life): to sacrifice lavishly (= Fr. *faire litière de*). **b.** The l. of a farmyard gathered under the windows of his bed-chamber MACAULAY. **4.** She was ashamed to be seen in such a pickle,..her house was in such a l. FIELDING. **5.** The l. is lyke to the syre and the damme HEYWOOD. Phr. *At a* or *one l.* Hence **Li·ttery** *a.* of or pertaining to l.; untidy.

Litter (li·təɹ), *v.* ME. [f. LITTER *sb.*] †**1.** *trans.* To carry in a litter 1713. **2.** To furnish (a horse, etc.) with litter or straw for his bed. Also *to l. down.* ME. **3.** *intr.* To lie down on a bed or on litter (*rare*) 1634. **4.** *trans.* To cover with litter. Also with *down.* 1700. **5.** To cover as with litter, to strew *with* objects scattered in disorder. Also with *about, on, over* 1713. **6.** Chiefly of animals: To bring forth (young). Also *absol.* or *intr.* 1484.

2. Tell them how they l. their Jades..in the House of God HACKET. **4.** But, for his ease, well littered was the floor DRYDEN. **5.** Dinner was over. The floor was littered with rushes and fragments of rolls and broken meat FROUDE. **6.** Saue for the Son, that she did littour heere, A frekelld whelpe, hag-borne *Temp.* I. ii. 282.

‖**Littérateur** (litᵉratör). 1806. [Fr. (XV) – L. *litterator* in its later (med.L.) application to a literary man; see LITERATOR 2.] A literary man, a writer of literary works. So ‖**Littératrice,** a literary woman, an authoress.

Little (li·t'l), *a.*, *adv.*, and *sb.* [OE. *lȳtel*, *lytel* = OS. *luttil* (Du. *luttel*), OHG. *luzzil* (MHG., G. dial. *lützel*) :– WGmc. **lŭttila*, f. *lŭt*, repr. also by OE. *lyt* adv. little.] **A.** *adj.* The opposite of *great* or *much.* Compar. LESS, LESSER; superl. LEAST. (In certain uses the adj. has no recognized mode of comparison; for these a synonym (as *smaller, smallest*) is used, or occas. the dial. or illiterate *littler, littlest.*)

I. Opp. to *great.* Often synonymous with *small*, but capable of emotional implications, which *small* is not. In mod. Eng. usu. in antithesis to *great* or *big*, not to *large.* **1.** Small in size, not large or big; (of persons) short in stature. **b.** Used to designate the smaller or smallest of two or more species, countries, places, things, etc. bearing the same name ME. **2.** Used *spec.* of young children or animals OE. **3.** Used with an implication of endearment or depreciation, or of tender feeling on the part of the speaker 1567. **4.** Of collective unities: Small in number OE. **5.** Of immaterial things, in respect of their quantity, length in series, etc. ME. **6.** Of dimension, distance, or time: Short OE.; †bare, scarcely complete (16–17th c.). **7.** Of qualities, conditions, occurrences, etc.: Small in extent or degree ME. **b.** With sb. indicating occupation, etc.: That is such on a small scale 1440. **c.** Now often playful, indicating amusement on the speaker's part 1885. **8.** Not important; trivial OE.; not distinguished (now *rare*) ME. **9.** Paltry, contemptible; little-minded 1483.

1. My l. body is wearie of this great world SHAKS. **b.** L. Mouse-tail 1776. The L. Auk 1876. †*L. Britain*, Brittany. *L. Malvern. The L. Bear.* (With superl. meaning) *L. finger, toe.* **2.** My l. sonne SHAKS. *L. one* (often pl.): child, young one. My wife! my l. ones! Destitute, helpless SHELLEY. *L. language*: Swift's name for the infantine dialect which he used in talk and correspondence with 'Stella'. **3.** He [a dog] had the dearest l. ways (*mod.*). Bless your l. heart 1903. **4.** Our Court shall be a l. Achademe SHAKS. What l. town by river or sea shore..Is emptied of this folk, this pious morn? KEATS. **5.** I said thou hadst a fine wit: true saies she, a fine l. one SHAKS. **6.** Our l. life Is rounded with a sleepe SHAKS. A l. half league broad 1697. **7.** Where l. feares grow great, great loue growes there SHAKS. **b.** A much larger capital than any l. farmer can possess A. YOUNG. **c.** So this is your l. game (*mod.*). I understand his l. ways (*mod.*). **8.** Constant attention in the littlest things DICKENS. No patronising condescension to l. people LYTTON. **9.** The l. cunning of l. minds 1863.

II. Opp. to *much.* **1.** Not much; barely any. (Often *but l.* Also in phr. *l. or no*..) OE. **2.** *A l.*: a small quantity of; some, though not much. Prob. orig. *a l. of* (see B. II. 1 b), with ellipsis of *of.* ME. †**b.** *Rarely* without *a* in this sense (SHAKS.). †**3.** With pl. and collect. sing.: = FEW –1660.

1. I haue l. wealth to loose SHAKS. God help me for my l. wit! WORDSW. **2.** A litul stale ale 1450. A l. learning is a dang'rous thing POPE. **b.** O do not sweare, Hold l. faith, though thou hast too much feare *Twel. N.* v. i. 174.

Phr. **L. Englander,** one who advocates a 'little England', that is, desires to restrict the dimensions of the Empire. So **L. Englandism. L. giant,** 'a jointed iron nozzle used in hydraulic mining' (Raymond). **L. hours,** the 'hours' of prime, terce, sext, and none (Fr. *les petites heures*). **L. people,** fairies.

Comb.: **l.-endian** *a.* and *sb.*, the designation of the orthodox party in Lilliput on the question at which end an egg should be opened (Swift *Gulliver* iv); hence *allusively*; **-thrift,** a wastrel.

B. *absol.* and *sb.*

I. The adj. used *absol.* **1.** Chiefly with *the*: Those that are little OE. **2.** *The l.*: that which is little; the little qualities, aspects, etc. 1791. **3.** Not much; only a small amount: often *but l., very, rather l.* ME.

1. They came all to mete her, litle & greate COVERDALE *Judith* 13 : 13. **2.** The great and l. of thy lot COWPER. **3.** *L. or nothing*: hardly anything. *To make l. of* or *set l. by*, etc.: see the vbs. Man wants but l. here below, Nor wants that l. long GOLDSM. Of political sagacity he had very l. 1903. The l. of his poems which remains GROTE.

II. *sb.* (With *a* or in *pl.*) **1.** A small quantity, piece, portion; a small thing; a trifle ME. **b.** Const. *of.* (In early use with *genitive.*) OE. **c.** Used advb.: To a slight extent; in a small degree; somewhat, rather ME. **2.** A short time or distance OE. **b.** Used *advb.* For or at a short time or distance ME. †**3.** *But a l.* = 'but little' (see I. 3) –1628.

1. When a man's being shaved, what a l. will make him laugh D. JERROLD. **b.** Let me recommend you a l. of this pike DISRAELI. **c.** *Not a l.*: a good deal, extremely. We are not a l. hungry, I can tell you MARRYAT. **2.** Phr. *After a l., for a l., in a l.* We will go for a l. into the garden 1881. **b.** A l. onward lend thy guiding hand To these dark steps, a l. further on MILT. **3.** *Tam. Shr.* I. ii. 61.

Phrases, chiefly with repetition of *little*, having the sense: By small degrees; a little at a time; gradually. **a.** *By l. and l.* †**b.** *L. and l.* **c.** *L. by l.* Also *In l.*: on a small scale; formerly esp. with reference to *Painting* = in miniature.

C. *adv.* **1.** To only a small extent; not much, not very OE. **b.** When preceding and qualifying the vbs. *know, think, care,* and the like, *little* becomes an emphatic negative, as in *he l. knows* = 'he is very far from knowing' ME. †**2.** A little time (before); for a little time –1604.

1. They liked us as l. as they did one another ADDISON. **b.** They l. know How dearly I abide that boast so vaine MILT. *P.L.* IV. 86.

†**Li·ttle,** *v.* [OE. *lȳtlian*, f. *lȳtel* LITTLE *a.*] To make or become little –1642.

Little-ease. Now *Hist.* or *arch.* 1529. A place of little ease for him who occupies it; *spec.* the name of a dungeon in the Tower of London, etc. Also, the pillory, stocks.

Worthy to be cast in bocardo or lytle ease LATIMER.

Little-go. 1795. [f. LITTLE *a.* + GO *sb.* Cf. GREAT-GO.] **1.** A private and illegal lottery. Now *Hist.* **2.** *Univ. colloq.* The popular name (still current at Cambridge) for the first examination for the B.A. degree 1820.

Little man. ME. **1.** The little finger. *Obs.* exc. *dial.* **2.** A small landowner or capitalist 1811. **3.** *pl.* Fairies, 'little folk' 1850.

Little master. ME. †**1.** A sub-master. WYCLIF. **2.** *pl.* A group of 16th c. German engravers, followers of Dürer, so called from the smallness of their prints 1837. **3.** A manufacturer in a small way of business, who works as a journeyman 1870.

Littleness (li·t'lnės). [OE. *lȳtelnes*; see LITTLE *a.* and -NESS.] The attribute of being little (see LITTLE *a.*). Also with *a* and *pl.*

I confess, I love L. almost in all things, A little convenient Estate, a little chearful House, a little Company, and a very little Feast COWLEY. L. of soul 1779. Vainglorious littlenesses H. WALPOLE.

Little-worth, *a.* (*sb.*) Now *arch.* and *Sc.* ME. Of little worth; esp. *Sc.* = of worthless character.

Littoral (li·tŏrăl). Also **litoral.** 1656. [– L. *littoralis*, var. of *litoralis*, f. *litus, litor-* shore; see -AL[1].] **A.** *adj.* Of or pertaining to the shore; existing, taking place upon, or adjacent to the shore. **b.** *Zool., Geol.*, etc.: Growing, living, or deposited on the 'littoral zone' (see quot. 1876) 1661.

The l. extent of Italy 1869. **b.** The Littoral [zone] lies between high and low water mark 1876.

B. *sb.* A littoral district; the region lying along the shore. [After It. *littorale*, Fr. *littoral.*] 1828.

The towns along the Mediterranean l. 1859.

Liturgic (litɒ̆·ɹdʒik). 1656. [– med.L. *liturgicus* – Gr. λειτουργικός; see LITURGY, -IC.] **A.** *adj.* = LITURGICAL. **b.** *Gr. Antiq.* (Cf. LITURGY 3.) 1849. **B.** *sb. pl.* †**1.** ? Liturgical books. BARROW. **2. a.** The study of liturgies, their form, origin, etc. **b.** That part of pastoral theology which deals with the conduct of public worship. 1855.

Liturgical (litɒ̆·ɹdʒikăl), *a.* 1641. [f. as prec.; see -ICAL.] Pertaining to or connected with public worship; having to do with liturgies, or *spec.* with the Liturgy or Eucharistic service. Also, pertaining to liturgics.

L. day: a day on which mass was celebrated. **Litu·rgically** *adv.* from a l. point of view; in a liturgy.

Liturgiology (litɒ̆ɹdʒiǫ·lŏdʒi). 1863. [f. LITURGY + -LOGY.] The science which treats of liturgies. Hence **Litu:rgiolo·gical** *a.* **Liturgio·logist,** one skilled in l.

Liturgist (li·tɒɹdʒist). 1649. [f. LITURGY + -IST.] **1.** One who uses or favours the use of a liturgy. **2.** An authority on liturgies; a compiler of a liturgy or liturgies 1657. **3.** One who celebrates divine worship 1848.

1. The lip-work of every Prelatical L. MILT.

Liturgy (li·tɒ̆ɹdʒi). 1560. [– Fr. *liturgie* or late L. *liturgia* – Gr. λειτουργία public service, worship of the gods, f. λειτουργός public servant, minister, f. *λεῖτος public, prob. var. of λήιτος public, f. ληός, Ionic form of λαός people, + -εργος performing.] **1.** The service of the Holy Eucharist; prop. that of the Eastern Church. In liturgics, used *spec.* of the different types of Eucharistic service. **2.** A form of public worship; a collection of formularies for the conduct of this 1593. Also *fig.* **b.** Chiefly with *the*: The Book of Common Prayer 1629. **3.** *Gr. Antiq.* At Athens, a public office or duty discharged by the richer citizens at their own expense 1836.

2. *fig.* The Liturgie of Loue, *Ouid de arte amandi* B. JONS.

‖**Lituus** (li·tiu,ɒ̆s). 1611. [L.] **1.** *Rom. Antiq.* **a.** The crooked staff borne by an augur. **b.** A curved trumpet, a clarion. **2.** *Math.* A spiral represented by the polar equation $r^2\theta = a$. 1758.

Livable: see LIVEABLE.

Live (ləiv), *a.* 1542. [Aphetic f. ALIVE, repl. older LIVES.] **1.** That is alive; living, as opp. to 'dead'. **b.** *joc.*, esp. in 'a real live —' (*slang*) 1887. **2.** *transf.* and *fig.* Full of life or active power 1647; full of energy; up to date; of present interest and importance; not obsolete or exhausted (chiefly *U.S.*) 1877. **3.** Of combustibles: Flaming, glowing; also *transf.* and *fig.* 1611. **4.** Containing unexpended energy; (of a shell) unexploded; (of a rail, wire, etc.) charged with electricity; (of a cartridge) containing a bullet 1799. **5. a.** Of a mineral, a rock: Native, unwrought; = L. *vivus.* **b.** Of air: In its native state, pure. 1661. **6.** Said of machines or parts which either themselves move or impart motion to others 1825. **7.** Of or pertaining to a living being 1613.

1. The importation of l. cattle 1897. *L. hair, feathers*: hair or feathers pulled from a living animal. Phr. *A l. certainty*: put for *a dead certainty* THACKERAY. **b.** A real l. glass milk-jug 1887, philosopher 1890. **2.** The l. murmur of a summer's day M. ARNOLD. A new type of 'live' newspaper BRYCE. A l. issue 1900. **3.** L. coal 1611, embers BOWEN. **4.** *L. wire* (*fig.*), a highly energetic person (orig. *U.S.*). **5. b.** His essences turn'd the l. air sick TENNYSON. **6.** *L. axle*, one communicating power, as dist. from a dead or blind axle KNIGHT. *L. ring*, a circular gang of wheels, as used in the turn-tables of draw-bridges, and in those for locomotives KNIGHT. **7.** *L. weight*, the weight of an animal while living.

Combs., etc.: **l.-birth,** the fact of a child's being born alive; **-hole** *Brickmaking*, the flue; **l. load,** the load to which a structure (or vehicle) is subjected in addition to its own weight; **-matter** *Printing*, type in page or column ready for printing; **-steam,** (*a*) steam from the boiler at its full pressure; dist. from *dead-steam*; (*b*) steam from the boiler; dist. from *exhaust-steam.* **b.** In names of contrivances for holding living objects or for examining them microscopically, as *l.-box, -trap, -well.*

Live (liv), *v.* Pa. t. and pple. **lived** (livd). [OE. (i) *libban* (pa. t. *lifde*), (ii) *lifian* (pa. t. *lifode*), corresp. to OFris. *libba, liva,* OS. *libbian, lebon,* OHG. *lebēn* (G. *leben*), ON. *lifa* live, remain, Goth. *liban*; f. Gmc. base **lib-* remain, continue; see LIFE, LEAVE *v.*[1]] **1.** *intr.* To be alive; to have life either as an animal or as a plant; to be capable of vital functions. (In this sense the compound present *is living*, not the simple present, is now usual.) **b.** *fig.* Of things: To exist, be found (*poet.*) 1593. **2.** To feed, subsist (†*by*, †*of, on, upon,* †*with*, rarely †*in* the actual food or the means of providing it) OE. Also *fig.* **3.** To procure oneself the means of subsistence (*by*, †*of, on* or *upon*, †*with*) OE. **4.** To pass life in a specified fashion, indicated by an adv. or advb. phr. (see below) OE. **5.** quasi-*trans.* with cognate *obj.* = 4. OE. **b.** *transf.* in *Hunting.* To keep up (the pace). Also *absol.* in phr. *to l. with hounds* 1840. **6.** quasi-*trans. To l. down*: †**a.** To outlive (*nonce-use*). **b.** To silence, wear out (prejudice, slander, etc.) by a blameless course of life. **c.** To lose hold of (a fancy) as life goes on. 1731. **7.** *trans.* To express in one's life 1542. **8.** To have life that deserves the name; to enjoy or use one's life abundantly 1606. **9.** To continue in life; to have one's life prolonged OE. **b.** *fig.* (*poet.* and *rhet.*) Of things: To survive, continue in operation 1768. **10.** Chiefly of a vessel: To escape destruction; to remain afloat. Also quasi-*trans.* of persons. 1601. **11.** To continue in the memory of men; to escape oblivion 1586. **12.** To dwell, reside. Also, to cohabit ME. Also *fig.*

1. And Ioseph said..Doeth my father yet liue? *Gen.* 45:3. **b.** No glory liues behinde the backe of such *Much Ado* III. i. 110. **2.** A man lyueth not in breed aloon WYCLIF *Matt.* 4:4. To liue vpon other mens labours 1583. To l. on one's means 1852. **3.** Every one..must l. by his trade 1796. Phr. *To l. from* HAND TO MOUTH. *To l. by one's wits*: see WIT. Provb. *L. and let. l.* **4.** Wych tyme he lyuyd more vertuesly T. STARKEY. We l. in quite a small way 1836. They saw no society; lived wholly to their work CARLYLE. Phr. *To l. in clover* (see CLOVER). *To l. fast* (see FAST *adv.*). *To l. well*: (*a*) to feed luxuriously; (*b*) to be well to do; (*c*) to live a virtuous life. *To l. in* (or *within*) *oneself*: to rely upon oneself for occupation and diversion, not upon 'society'. †*To l. up*: *fig.* to live on a high level (DRYDEN). *To l. up to*: not to fall below (principles, rules, etc.). Also, to push expenditure to the limits of (one's fortune). **5.** This is no life for men at armes to liue MARLOWE & NASHE. **7.** Our Minister lives Sermons FULLER. To l. a lie 1770. **8.** He was living up to the last days of his life THACKERAY. **9.** To the use of A. for 99 years, if he should so long l. CRUISE. While the tree lived, he in these fields lived on M. ARNOLD. Phr. *To l. out*: to complete (a term of life); to survive the end of (a period). *To l. to* (be or do so and so). *Long l.* (formerly simply *l.*) *the king!* **b.** E'en in our Ashes l. their wonted Fires GRAY. **10.** It was impossible for the Boat to l. any longer in that Sea 1671. The savages in the boat never could l. out the storm DE FOE. **11.** Mens euill manners, liue in Brasse, their Vertues We write in Water SHAKS. **12.** It was admitted that they lived together 1891. Phr. *To l. in*: (of shop-assistants) to reside in the establishment; opp. to *to l. out. To l. in* (a room, etc.): to treat as one's ordinary abode. *To l. out* (U.S. colloq): to be in domestic service.

Comb. **L. (for) ever,** (*a*) = LIVELONG *sb.* 1 and 2; (*b*) Everlasting Flower.

Liveable, livable (li·văb'l), *a.* 1664. [f. LIVE *v.* + -ABLE.] †**1.** Conducive to (comfortable) living. PEPYS. **2.** Of a house, room, locality: That may be lived in; suitable for living in 1814. **3.** Of life: That can be lived; supportable 1841. **4.** Of persons (also *liveable with*): That may be lived with; companionable 1860.

2. His rooms at the top of the Albany are very liveable 1849. Hence **Li·veableness,** l. quality.

Lived (ləivd), *a.* 1589. [f. LIFE *sb.* + -ED[2].] Having (such or so long) life.

†**Li·velihead.** 1412. [f. LIVELY + -HEAD.] **1.** Liveliness; vivacity –1717. **b.** Living form. Also, condition of being alive. –1596. **2.** Means of living; also, inheritance –1590.

Livelihood[1] (ləi·vlihud). OE. [Alteration, by assim. to LIVELY and -HOOD, of *liflode* course of life, maintenance, sustenance, OE. *liflād*, f. *līf* LIFE + *lād* course, way (see LODE, LOAD *sb.*).] †**1.** Lifetime; manner of life; conduct –1581. **2.** Means of living, maintenance ME. †**b.** Food, victuals –1688. †Also *fig.* †**3.** Income, revenue, stipend *pl.* emoluments –1621. †**4.** Property yielding an income; an estate, inheritance, patrimony –1627.

2. Phr. *To earn, gain, get, make, seek a l.* Fishermen who gain their l. on its waters HERSCHEL.

†**Li·velihood**[2]. 1566. [f. LIVELY *a.* + -HOOD.] Liveliness, in various senses –1646.

The tirrany of her sorrowes takes all liuelihood from her cheeke SHAKS.

Livelong, live-long (li·vlǫŋ), *sb.* 1578. [f. LIVE *v.* + LONG *adv.*] A name of plants. **1.** *Sedum telephium*, ORPINE. **†2.** American Cudweed, *Antennaria margaritacea* –1656.

Livelong (li·vlǫŋ), *a. poet.* and *rhet.* Also *Sc.* **lee-lang.** [ME. *lefe longe, leve longe*, i.e. LIEF, LONG *a.*[1]; cf. G. *die liebe lange nacht*. In XVI apprehended as f. LIVE *a.* or *v.*, and consequently altered in form.] **1.** Emotional intensive of *long*. Chiefly in *the l. day, night*. **2.** *nonce-use*. That lives long; lasting 1630. **¶3.** Taken as = LIFELONG 2 (prob. with pronunc. ləiv-) FREEMAN.

1. He watched there the lee-lang night HOGG. **2.** Thou in our wonder and astonishment Hast built thy self a l. Monument MILT.

Lively (ləi·vli), *a.* [OE. *līflīć*, f. *līf* LIFE + *-līć* -LY[1].] **†1.** = LIVE *a.* 1, LIVING –1638. **†b.** = LIVE *a.* 3, 5, LIVING –1632. **†c.** Of or pertaining to a living person. Of instruction, etc.: Imparted *viva voce*. –1709. **†2.** Necessary to life, vital –1640. **3.** Of an image, picture, etc.: Life-like, animated, vivid. (Cf. 4.) ME. **4.** Full of life; see quots. ME. **5.** Of colour, light, etc.: Vivid, brilliant, fresh ME. **6.** Gay, sprightly 1580. **7.** *Naut.* Of a vessel: Capable of rising lightly to the sea 1697.

1. What shall I doe Now I behold thy liuely body so? SHAKS. **c.** This [*sc.* Moses] is he..who receiued the liuely oracles [λόγια ζῶντα], to giue vnto vs *Acts* 7:38. **3.** Full l. is the semblaunt, though the substance dead SPENSER. A l. description of [etc.] 1849. **4.** A man..of l. parts LAW. A l. remembrance 1769, consciousness of the truth M. ARNOLD. A more l. combustion 1854. A pretty l. week 1887. *joc.* Things are getting l. 1891. **5.** Her liuelie colour kil'd with deadlie cares SHAKS. **6.** An entertaining and l. Essay 1756. L. in conversation 1868. Hence **Li·velily** *adv.* **Li·veliness.**

Lively (ləi·vli), *adv.* Now *rare.* [OE. *līflīće*, f. as prec. + -LY[2]; re-formed in XIV.] **†1.** (OE. only.) So as to impart life. **†2.** As a living person or thing –1590. **3.** With animation, actively, briskly, vigorously ME. **4.** In a life-like manner; vividly ME.; †clearly, plainly –1673. **†5.** Of a vessel: (Floating) in a lively manner (see LIVELY *a.* 7). SMEATON.

3. You must act l.; do it without distraction CROMWELL. **4.** Wel koude he peynten lifly that it wroghte CHAUCER.

Liven (ləi·v'n), *v. colloq.* 1884. [f. LIFE + -EN[5]. Cf. ENLIVEN.] To make or become lively; to brighten. Also with *up*.

Live-oak (ləi·v,ōᵘ·k). 1610. [LIVE *a.*] An American evergreen tree (*Quercus virens*) growing in the southern Atlantic States. Applied to some other species in the Pacific States.

Liver[1] (li·vəɹ). [OE. *lifer* = OFris. *livere*, MDu. *lever* (Du. *lever*), OHG. *libara* (G. *leber*), ON. *lifr* :– Gmc. **librō*, having no certain cognates.] **1.** A large glandular organ in vertebrate animals, serving to secrete bile and to purify the venous blood. Also, the flesh of this, *e.g.* used as food. (Its colour is usually dark reddish-brown.) **b.** Applied to analogous organs or tissues in invertebrates 1841. **2.** *fig.* and *allusive*. **a.** As a vital organ of the body (coupled with *brain* and *heart*); also, as the supposed seat of love and violent passion. (Now only *arch.*) **b.** A *white l.* is spoken of as characterizing a coward; whence *white-livered*. ME. **3.** Liver-complaint. Often qualified as *bronze, cirrhotic, hobnailed l.* 1805. **4.** *Old Chem.* Applied (tr. L. *hepar*) to certain liver-coloured substances, e.g. metallic sulphides, and compounds of a metal or of sulphur with an 'alkali' 1664. **5.** *Agric.* 'Livery' soil 1803. **6.** *adj.* Liver-coloured 1868.

1. A fry'd l. and bacon GOLDSM. *Line of the l.*, also *l.-line* (Palmistry): the line which stretches from the wrist to the base of the little finger. **2. a.** To quench the coale which in his liuer glowes SHAKS. *Lucr.* 47. To you (the Liuer, Heart, and Braine of Britaine) By whom (I grant) she liues *Cymb.* v. v. 15. **b.** How manie cowards..Who inward searcht, haue lyuers white as milke SHAKS. **3.** Dyspeptic troubles..usually attributed to l. 1898. **4.** *L. of antimony*, Antimony open'd by Salt-peter and Fire PHILLIPS.

attrib. and *Comb.*, as *l. abscess, attack, colour, disease, disorder*, etc.; *l.-coloured* adj.; **l.-brown** *a.*, dark brownish red; **-complaint,** disease of the l.; **l. fluke,** a trematoid worm infesting the l.; **†-grown** *a.*, having an enlarged l.; also, adherent as an enlarged l.; (*fig.* in MILT.); **-leaf** *U.S.* = LIVERWORT 2; **-pyrites,** hepatic pyrites; **-shark,** the basking shark (*Cetorhinus maximus*); **-spots,** yellowish brown patches or spots of chloasma; **-stone** = HEPATITE[1]; **†-vein,** the basilic vein; also *allusively*, 'the style and manner of men in love' (Schmidt); **-weed,** *Hepatica triloba*; **-wing,** the right wing of a fowl, etc., which, when dressed for cooking, has the l. tucked under it; hence *joc.*, the right arm.

Hence **Li·verish** *a.* resembling l.; having the symptoms of disordered l.

Liver[2] (li·vəɹ). ME. [f. LIVE *v.* + -ER[1].] **1.** One who is alive; a living creature. Now *rare.* Also, an inhabitant (chiefly *U.S.*). **b.** One who lives (in a specified way, for a long time, etc.) ME. **2.** One who lives a life of pleasure (= Fr. *viveur*). R. S. SURTEES.

1. A L. on Sasquehanna River 1747. **b.** The Queen..will be no long l. SWIFT. A loose l. 1836. *Good l.*: (*a*) one who leads a good life; (*b*) one given to good living.

Liver[3] (ləi·vəɹ). 1668. [Back-formation from *Liverpool*.] A name arbitrarily given to the bird figured in the arms of the city of Liverpool. (It was orig. intended for the eagle of St. John the Evangelist.)

Liver, etc., aphetic f. DELIVER, etc.

Liveried (li·vəɹid), *a.* 1634. [f. LIVERY *sb.* + -ED[2].] Dressed in, furnished with, or wearing a livery.

Liverpudlian (livəɹpʊ·dliăn). 1833. [f. *Liverpool* (with joc. substitution of *puddle* for *pool*) + -IAN.] *adj.* Belonging to Liverpool. *sb.* A native or inhabitant of Liverpool.

Liverwort (li·vəɹwɒ̄ɹt). ME. [tr. med.L. HEPATICA (applied to plants having liver-shaped parts or used in liver diseases).] A name of various plants. **1.** = HEPATICA 2. Sometimes called Stone L. **2.** *Anemone* (*Hepatica*) *triloba*; = HEPATICA 1. Formerly called Noble L., Three-leaf L. (In U.S. *liver-leaf.*) 1578. **†3.** Agrimony –1617.

Livery (li·vəri), *sb.* ME. [– AFr. *liveré*, (O)Fr. *livrée*, subst. use of fem. pa. pple. of *livrer* dispense, deliver (:– L. *liberare*; see LIBERATE *v.*), in med.L. *liberare* deliver up, hand over; see -Y[5].] **1. a.** The dispensing of food, provisions, or clothing to retainers or servants; hence *gen.* provision, allowance. **b.** The food or provisions so dispensed; a ration. Now *Hist.* **c.** Allowance of provender for horses. Now *rare* or *Obs.* exc. in LIVERY-STABLE. 1440. **2.** A distinctive suit or badge bestowed by a person upon his retainers or servants; a distinctive badge or suit worn by a servant or official, a member of a company, etc.; the distinctive uniform style of dress worn by a person's servants, etc. (now only men-servants) ME. Also *transf.* and *fig.* **†3.** *collect. sing.* **a.** Retainers or servants in livery. ME. **b.** Following, faction –1613. **c.** = *livery company* or the liverymen of a company 1521. **†4.** Lodging; quarters –1525. **5.** *Law.* **a.** The legal delivery of property into a person's possession. **b.** The writ by which possession is obtained from the court of wards. ME. **†6.** *gen.* The action of handing over; delivery (of goods, money, etc., of a writ) –1745. **7.** A particular sort of wool, that which comes from the breech of the animal 1837. **8.** *U.S.* A livery-stable.

1. There he made large lyueray, Bothe of ale and of wyne 1492. **c.** Phr. *At l.*: (of a horse) kept for the owner, and fed and groomed at a fixed charge. **2.** Phr. *In l.*: wearing a particular l. *Out of l.*: (of a servant) not dressed in l.; wearing plain clothes. A Servant out of l. leaped from the box LYTTON. *fig.* Now..Twilight gray Had in her sober Liverie all things clad MILT. **3. c.** Phr. *To take up one's l.* (orig. in sense 2): to become a liveryman of a City company. **5. a.** Phr. *To have, give, take l. To sue* (also *sue for, sue out*) *one's l.*: to institute a suit as heir in the court of wards to obtain possession of lands. *L. of seisin* (often erron *l. and seisin*): the delivery of property into the corporal possession of a person; e.g. of a house, by giving him the key, or the like; of land, by handing him a twig or a piece of turf, etc. (Now virtually abolished by 8 & 9 Vict. cap. 106 § 2.)

attrib. and *Comb.*, esp. in sense 'kept at livery or for hire', as *l. horse, nag*; transf. *l. friend, mistress*, etc.; also **l. company,** one of the London City companies which had formerly a distinctive costume used on special occasions; **l. fine,** the payment due from those who become liverymen in a London company; **l. servant,** a servant who wears l.; **†l. table,** a table on which 'liveries' or rations were put; hence, a side table.

Hence **†Li·very** *v.* to array in or as in a l. SHAKS.

Livery (li·vəri), *a.* 1778. [f. LIVER[1] + -Y[1].] **1.** Of the consistency or colour of liver; *dial.* (of soil) heavy, tenacious. **2.** *colloq.* Liverish (*mod.*).

Li·very-man, li·veryman. 1682. **†1.** A liveried retainer or servant –1711. **2.** A freeman of the City of London entitled to wear the livery of his company, and to exercise other privileges 1682. **3.** A keeper of or attendant at a livery-stable 1841.

2. All freemen or Liverymen of this city hath a Right to Choose their sherriffs 1710.

Livery-stable. 1705. A stable where horses are kept at livery, or are let out for hire. (Also *l. and bait stable.*)

†Lives. [OE. *līfes*, gen. sing. of *līf* LIFE *sb.*; see LIVE *a.*] **a.** *pred.* = alive; *occas.* as *sb.*, the living –ME. **b.** *attrib.* = live, living –1600.

b. No lyues creature Be it of fyssh, or bryd, or beest, or man CHAUCER.

Live stock, li·ve-stock. 1775. Domestic animals generally; any animals kept or dealt in for use or profit. Also *transf.*

Livid (li·vid), *a.* *a*1500. [– Fr. *livide* or L. *lividus*, f. *livēre* be bluish; see -ID[1].] Of a bluish leaden colour; discoloured as by a bruise; black and blue.

There followed no Carbuncle, no purple or liuide Spots BACON. So **Livi·dity** (1477), **Li·vidness** (1656), l. quality or condition; a pale-bluish discoloration.

Living (li·viŋ), *vbl. sb.* ME. [f. LIVE *v.* + -ING[1].] **1.** The action of LIVE *v.* in various senses. **2.** The action, process, or method of gaining one's livelihood 1538. **3.** The means of living; livelihood, maintenance; †also, an endowment ME. **b.** Food; †*pl.* victuals ME. **†4.** Property, esp. landed estate; *pl.* estates, possessions –1813. **†b.** A tenement –1819. **5.** *Eccl.* A benefice. More fully *ecclesiastical, spiritual l.* ME.

1. There would be no l. for me in a cave DE FOE. Plain l. and high thinking are no more WORDSW. **2.** To..fynd to them some honest lyvyngs 1538. **3.** Phr. *To earn, get, make a l.* **4.** Men whose liuing lieth together in one Shire BACON. **5.** To take a l. only to get a l., is an horrid impiety 1703.

attrib. and *Comb.*, as *l.-room, -wagon*, etc.; *l.-broker*; **l.-wage,** a wage on which a worker can live; so *l. price*.

Living (li·viŋ), *ppl. a.* OE. [f. LIVE *v.* + -ING[2].] **1.** *Predicatively*, or *attrib.* following the sb.: Alive, or when alive. **2.** *attrib.* That lives or has life. **a.** Said of the Deity OE. **b.** of human beings, etc. In mod. use, 'now (or then) existing or living', 'contemporary' ME. **c.** *transf.* (*a*) In phrases of biblical origin. Of water: Constantly flowing; also, refreshing. (*b*) Of coals: Burning, flaming. Cf. LIVE *a.* 3. (*c*) Of rock, stone: Native. ME. **d.** Of a language: Still in vernacular use. (Cf. *dead language.*) 1706. **e.** *fig.* ME. **3.** Of or pertaining to a living person or what is living 1676. **4.** = LIVELY *a.* 4–6. 1718.

1. Where a testator..gives to his four children then l. JARMAN. **2. a.** The Church of the liuing God 1 *Tim.* 3:15. **b.** He was generally esteemed the greatest l. master of the art of war MACAULAY. Phr. *The l.* (absol.): those who are alive. *The land of the l.* (see *Ps.* 27:13, 52:5, etc.). *L. skeleton*: a person of very emaciated frame. **c.** In a spacious cave of l. stone DRYDEN. The fish ponds..were fed by a l. stream 1843. **e.** The l. question of the hour O. W. HOLMES. The l. fact 1871. Phr. *L. death*: a state of misery not fit to be called life. **3.** Phr. *Within l. memory*: within the recollection of persons still alive. *L. force* = *Vis viva* (VIS). **4.** A l. image of the man 1888. *L. gale* (Naut.): a tremendous gale. Hence **Li·ving-ly** *adv.*, **-ness.**

Livor (ləi·vǫɹ). 1607. [– L. *livor*, in both senses.] **1.** *Path.* Lividness, discoloration of the skin 1656. **†2.** Ill-will, malignity –1675.

‖Livre (līvr). 1553. [Fr. :– L. *libra* pound; cf. LIRA, LITRE.] An old French money of account, divided into 20 sols (or sous), and about equal to the present franc.

‖Lixivium (liksi·viŏm). *Pl.* **-ia.** 1612. [– late L. *lixivium*, subst. use of L. *lixiv(i)us* made into lye, f. *lix* ashes, lye.] Water impregnated with alkaline salts extracted from wood ashes (or other substances); lye. Hence **Lixi·vial** *a.* of or pertaining to l.; obtained by lixiviation; †also formerly, alkaline. †**Lixi·viate** *a.* obtained by lixiviation; of or pertaining to a l. or to lixivial salts; alkaline; *sb.* a l.; **Lixi·viate** *v. trans.* to impregnate with l.; to subject to lixiviation; **Lixivia·tion,** the action or process of separating a soluble from an insoluble substance by percolation of water, as salts from wood ashes. **Lixi·vious** *a.* = *lixivial.*

Lizard (li·zăɹd). [ME. *lesard(e* – OFr. *lesard, -arde* (mod. *lézard, -arde*), repr. L. *lacertus, lacerta,* which appears to be identical with *lacertus* muscle; cf. the etym. of MUSCLE.] **1.** A small reptile of the genus *Lacerta* or other genera of the order *Lacertilia,* having an elongated body, a long tail, four legs, and a scaly or granulated hide; in scientific use, any reptile of this order; sometimes extended to the larger saurians, as the crocodiles. **2.** A figure of a lizard; esp. in *Her.* 1455. **3.** A fancy variety of the canary. In full *l. canary.* 1865. **4.** *Naut.* A piece of rope having a thimble or block spliced into one or both ends 1794. **5.** A piece of timber with a forked end, used in dragging a heavy stone, etc. 1875.

attrib. and *Comb.,* as **l.-bird, dragon,** animals half l. and half bird or dragon; **l. canary** (see 3); †**l. fish,** (*a*) the horse-mackerel or scad; (*b*) a fish of the genus *Synodus*; **-green,** a colour like that of the green l. (*Lacerta viridis*); also as adj.; **-skin** *a.,* made of the skin of a l. **b.** with **lizard's,** as **lizard's tail,** a N. Amer. plant of the genus *Saururus,* with small white flowers in a slender spike; in the W. Indies, applied to *Heckeria peltata.*

'll (l; after a consonant 'l). 1576. Contr. f. WILL, after pronouns ending in a vowel; occas., colloq., after other words, as in *that'll do.* Formerly also **'le,** as in *Ile* or *I'le,* etc.

LL. Contr. for L. *legum* of laws, in degrees, as LL.B. = *Legum Baccalaureus,* Bachelor of Laws, LL.D. = *Legum Doctor,* Doctor of Laws.

Llama (lā·mă, Sp. lya·ma). 1600. [– Sp. *llama,* cited as Peruvian in 1535 and 1560.] A S. Amer. ruminant quadruped, *Auchenia llama,* closely allied to the camel, but smaller, humpless, and woolly-haired; used as a beast of burden in the Andes. **b.** (Material made of) its wool 1882.

‖**Llano** (lā·no, Sp. lya·no). 1613. [Sp. :– L. *planum* PLAIN.] A level treeless plain or steppe in the northern parts of S. America.

Lloyd's (loidz). [f. the name of Edward *Lloyd* who opened a coffee-house in London in 1688, a resort of shipping underwriters.] The incorporated society of marine underwriters in London (1871).

L.'s Register, an annual alphabetic list of ships assigned to various classes; see also A IV. 2.

Lo (lōu), *int. arch.* [(i) ME. *lō* :– OE. *lā,* excl. of surprise, grief, or joy (with voc.) O!; (ii) ME. *lō,* prob. short for *lōke* :– OE. *lōca,* imper. of *lōcian* LOOK.] †**a.** In early use, a vague exclam. = mod. O! or Oh! **b.** = Look! See! Behold! Also freq. in mod. use, *Lo and behold.*

Lo! He comes with clouds descending WESLEY.

Loach (lōutʃ). ME. [– (O)Fr. *loche,* in AL. *lochia* (*c*1200); of unkn. origin.] **1.** A small European freshwater fish, *Cobitis* (*Nemachilus*) *barbatula* (*-us*), esteemed for food; also, any fish of the family *Cobitidæ.* †**2.** *fig.* A simpleton –1620.

Load (lōud), *sb.* [OE. *lād* way, journey, conveyance = OHG. *leita* course, leading, procession (G. *leite*), ON. *leið* way, course :– Gmc. **laiðō,* whence **laiðjan* LEAD *v.*[1] The development of meaning has been infl. by assoc. with LADE *v.* Cf. LODE.] †**1.** Carriage. Also, an act of loading. –1523. **2.** That which is to be carried; a burden. Also, the amount usually carried; e.g. *cart-l., wagon-l.,* etc. ME. **b.** Hence, this customary quantity, taken as a unit of measure or weight for certain substances ME. **c.** The charge of a fire-arm 1692. **3.** A material object or a force, acting or conceived as a weight, clog, or the like 1593. **4.** *Mech.,* etc. **a.** Amount of pressure on a structure due either to its own weight or to a superimposed weight 1871. **b.** Amount of external resistance to be overcome by a machine or prime mover 1895. **c.** *Electr.* The amount of current supplied by a dynamo or generating station at any given time 1902. **5.** *fig.* A burden (of affliction, sin, responsibility, etc.) 1593. **6.** *Loads*: superabundance, 'heaps' (*colloq.*) 1606.

2. Æneas bare a liuing loade SHAKS. **b.** As a measure, a l. of wheat is usually 40 bushels, of lime 64 (in some districts 32) bushels, of timber 50 cubic feet, of hay 36 trusses (= 18 cwt.), etc. A l. of lead ore (in the Peak, Derbyshire) = 9 dishes (see DISH *sb.* 6 b). Wheat futures are usually dealt with in 'loads'. A l. is a thousand quarters 1898. **3.** 2 *Hen. VI,* I. ii. 2. **5.** Our life's a l. DRYDEN.

attrib. and *Comb.,* as **l. displacement, draught,** the displacement or draught of a vessel when laden; **l. factor,** the ratio of the average to the maximum amount of work, power, etc., of consumption to production, etc.; **l.-line** = LOAD-WATER-LINE.

Load (lōud), *v.* Pa. pple. **loaded;** *dial.* **loaden.** 1495. [f. LOAD *sb.*] **1.** *trans.* To put a load on or in; to furnish with a burden, cargo, or lading; to charge *with* a load. Freq. in pa. pple. 1503. **2.** To place on or in a vehicle as a load for transport; to put on board as cargo 1495. **b.** *absol.* or *intr.* To take in one's load or cargo. Also with *up.* 1720. **3.** To add a weight to, to add to the weight of; to be a burden upon; to oppress *with* a material weight; to weight, *spec.* with lead; to increase the resistance in the working of (a machine) by the addition of a weight 1578. **b.** To adulterate with something to increase the weight or 'body' of 1860. **4.** To supply in excess or overwhelming abundance *with.* Chiefly in pa. pple. 1577. **5.** To put the charge into (a firearm); also *absol.* 1626. **6.** *fig.* To weigh down, burden, oppress (*with* something immaterial) 1526. **b.** To overwhelm *with* abuse, reproaches, etc. 1662. **7.** To pile *on* (*rare*) 1580. **b.** *Painting.* To lay (colour) on thickly in opaque masses 1859. **8.** *intr.* To collect into a heap; to become clogged 1806. **9.** *refl.* and *intr.* (*Stock-exchange.*) To buy heavily of stock. Also *To be loaded up*: to have large quantities of a thing in hand as security. 1885. **10.** *Life-insurance.* To increase (a premium) by adding a charge (called the 'loading') for contingencies, etc.; to charge (a life) with a 'loaded' premium 1867.

1. A large Dutch ship..loaden with tea 1775. **2.** We were to l. mahogany for home 1900. **3.** Trees loaden with fairest Fruit MILT. A bat loaded with lead 1802. A stomach loaded with food. A table loaded with delicacies (*mod.*). **b.** To l. paper, i.e. to adulterate it with clay or cheap fibres 1887. Loaded claret THACKERAY. **4.** *Loaded with*: charged, fraught, or heavily laden with; Loaded with Riches and Honours STEELE. **6.** Lest so stern a solitude should l. And break thy being J. H. NEWMAN.

Loaded (lōu·dėd), *ppl. a.* 1661. [f. LOAD *v.* + -ED[1].] **1.** In senses of LOAD *v.* **b.** Weighted, esp. with lead, as a *l. stick, whip* 1771. ¶**c.** Charged with magnetism. [After LOAD-STONE.] PRIOR. **2.** *techn.* Of wine: Adulterated so as to appear full-bodied. Of the tongue: Thickly furred. Of the liver: Charged with excess of bile. Of the urine: Surcharged with salts, etc. 1860. **3.** *U.S. slang.* Drunk 1890.

1. Where ease my l. Heart? OTWAY. **b.** *L. dice*: dice so weighted with lead as to fall oftenest with a particular face upwards.

Loaden (lōu·d'n), *v. Obs.* exc. *dial.* 1568. [f. LOAD *sb.* + -EN[5].] *trans.* = LOAD *v.*

Loader (lōu·dəɹ). 1476. [f. LOAD *v.* + -ER[1].] **1.** One who or that which loads. **b.** An attendant whose business it is to load guns for a man who is shooting game 1869. †**2.** App. a dicing term; a doublet. Also *fig.* DRYDEN. **3.** A gun which is loaded in a particular way, as in BREECH-LOADER, MUZZLE-*loader, single-loader* 1858.

Loading (lōu·diŋ), *vbl. sb.* 1494. [f. LOAD *v.* + -ING[1].] **1.** The action of LOAD *v.* 1523. **2.** *Life-insurance.* The practice of making an addition to the pure premium for expenses and contingencies. Hence, the difference between the premium payable by the assured and the net premium deducible from any table at the time in use. 1867. **3.** *concr.* A load, lading, cargo. Now *rare.* 1494.

1. Phr. †*Bill of l.* = bill of lading.

Loading (lōu·diŋ), *ppl. a.* 1625. [f. LOAD *v.* + -ING[2].] **1.** That loads 1891. **2.** †*fig.* Burdensome, oppressive –1642. **3.** That is loaded in a specified way; as in *breech-loading* 1858.

Loadstar: see LODESTAR.

Loadstone, lodestone (lōu·dstōun). 1515. [f. *load* LODE + STONE *sb.* Literally 'way-stone', from the use of the magnet in guiding mariners.] **1.** Magnetic oxide of iron; a piece of this used as a magnet. **2.** *fig.* Something which attracts 1577.

2. Load-star of love, and load-stone of all hearts 1649.

†**Loa·dum.** Also **lodam(e,** etc. 1591. [Origin unc.] A game of cards; in one form, called *losing l.,* the loser won the game –1755.

Load-water-line. 1769. The line of floatation of a ship when she has her full cargo on board. (Called also *load-line, Plimsoll's mark,* etc.) Hence **Load-water-draught, -length. Load-water-section,** a horizontal section at the load-water-line in the ship-builder's draught.

Loaf (lōuf), *sb.*[1] Pl. **loaves** (lōuvz). [OE. *hlāf* = OHG. *leip* (G. *laib,* †*leib*), ON. *hleifr* loaf, Goth. *hlaifs* bread :– Gmc. **χlaibaz.*] **1.** Bread. *Obs.* exc. *dial.* **2.** A portion of bread baked in one mass; one of the portions, of uniform size and shape, into which a batch of bread is divided OE. **3.** A moulded conical mass of sugar; a sugar-loaf ME. †**4.** A mass or lump (of anything) –1694. **5.** A head (of a cabbage) 1585.

2. *Brown l.,* a l. of BROWN BREAD. *White l.,* one made of fine wheaten flour only. *Prov.* For better is halfe a lofe than no bread 1546. Phr. *Loaves and fishes* (fig. after John 6:26): pecuniary benefit as a motive for religious profession (or, *occas.,* for a show of public spirit). *Comb.*: **l.-cake** *U.S.,* a plain cake made in the form of a loaf.

Loaf (lōuf), *v.*[1] 1578. [f. LOAF *sb.*[1] 5.] *intr.* To form a loaf or head.

Loaf (lōuf), *v.*[2] *slang.* 1838. [prob. back-formation from contemp. *loafer,* which may be based on G. *landläufer* vagabond, tramp (whence U.S. *landloafer*), f. *land* LAND *sb.* + *laufen* (dial. *lofen*) run.] *intr.* To spend time idly. Also quasi-*trans.* To idle *away* (time). So **Loaf** *sb.*[2], the action of loafing 1855. **Loa·fer** 1835.

Loaf-sugar. 1440. Sugar refined and moulded into a loaf or conical mass.

Loam (lōum), *sb.* [OE. *lām* = (M)Du. *leem,* MLG. *lēm* (whence G. *lehm*), rel. to OHG. *leimo* (G. dial. *leimen*) :– WGmc. **laima,* **laimo,* f. **lai-,* **lī-* be sticky; see LIME *sb.*[1]] †**1.** Clay, clayey earth, mud –1657. **b.** *loosely,* Earth, ground, soil (*arch.*) ME. **2.** Clay moistened with water so as to form a paste; *spec.* a composition of moistened clay and sand with chopped straw, etc., used in making bricks and casting-moulds, plastering walls, grafting, etc. 1395. **3.** A rich soil composed chiefly of clay and sand with an admixture of decomposed vegetable matter 1664. **4.** *attrib.* or *adj.* Made or consisting of loam 1536.

1. A House of Clay best fits a Guest of Lome 1633. **2.** But we wash a wall of l.; we labour in vain HOOKER. **3.** The fruity district of deep l. T. HARDY. Hence **Loam** *v.* to cover, plaster, or dress with l. **Loa·my** *a.* of, pertaining to, consisting of, or resembling l.

Loan (lōun), *sb.*[1] ME. [– ON. *lán,* corresp. to OE. *lǣn* (see LEND *v.*[1]), MDu. *lēne* (Du. *leen*), OHG. *lēhan* (G. *lehn, lehen*) :– Gmc. **laixwniz-, -az-*; cogn. w. LEND *v.*[1]] †**1.** A gift or grant from a superior –1470. **2.** A thing lent; *esp.* a sum of money lent for a time, to be returned in money or money's worth, and usually at interest ME. **b.** *fig.* Said, in recent use, of a word, a custom, etc. 'borrowed' or adopted by one people from another 1891. **3.** The action, or an act, of lending ME. **4.** *National finance.* **a.** A contribution of money, formerly often forced, from individuals or public bodies, towards the expenses of the state, acknowledged by the government as a debt 1439. **b.** An arrangement or contract by which a government receives upon its own credit advances of money on specified conditions, esp. the payment of a stipulated interest 1765.

2. Security for a pecuniary l. 1844. **3.** I am promis'd the l. of it [a book] HEARNE. **4. a.** Since Juarez triumphed, there have been no forced loans, no exactions G. DUFF. **b.** It had been thought necessary to offer..ten per cent. per annum, on a l. 1844.

Comb.: **l.-collection,** a collection of works of art, curiosities, or the like, lent by their owners for exhibition; **-holder,** one who holds debentures or other acknowledgements of a l.; a mortgagee; **-money,** money payable as a contribution to a government loan; money advanced as a loan; **-monger,** a loan-contractor (*contemptuous*); **-society,** a body of persons who pay periodical subscriptions to form a fund from which loans may be made to members of others; **-word** [after G. *lehnwort* 1856], a word adopted from another language 1861.

Loan (lōᵘn), *sb.*² Now only *Sc.* and *dial.* ME. [See LANE *sb.*] **1.** A lane, a by-road. **2.** = LOANING 2. 1715.

Loan (lōᵘn), *v.* Now chiefly *U.S.* ME. [f. LOAN *sb.*¹] *trans.* To grant the loan of; to lend. Also with *out.* Hence **Loa·nable** *a.* that may be loaned or lent; (of capital, etc.) available for use in loans.

Loaning (lōᵘ·niŋ). *Sc.* and *n. dial.* ME. [f. LOAN *sb.*² + -ING¹.] **1.** = LOAN *sb.*² 1. **2.** An open uncultivated piece of ground near a farm-house or village, on which the cows are milked 1750.

2. But now they are moaning on ilka green l. *The Flowers of the Forest.*

Loa·n-o:ffice. 1720. **1.** An office for lending money to private borrowers. **2.** An office for receiving subscriptions to a government loan 1777.

†**Loath,** *sb.* [OE. *lāþ*, orig. neut. of *lāþ* LOATH *a.* In sense 2 f. LOATHE *v.*] **1.** Something hateful or harmful –1460. **2.** Dislike, hatred, ill will; later, physical disgust, loathing –1728.

Loath, loth (lōᵘþ), *a.* [OE. *lāþ* = OFris. *lēd*, OS. *lēð* (Du. *leed*), OHG. *leid* (cf. G. *leid* sorrow, pain, *leider* prop. compar. unfortunately), ON. *leiðr* :– Gmc. **laipaz*.] †**1.** Hostile, angry, spiteful –ME. †**2.** Repulsive, hateful, loathsome –1592. †**3.** Ugly –1546. **4.** Averse, disinclined, unwilling. **b.** Sometimes quasi-*adv.* Phr. *Nothing l.*: not at all unwilling. ME.

4. She lyueth loþ of this lyf CHAUCER. The residue shewed themselues unwilling and loath to depart HAKLUYT. I..would be loth he should not do well PEPYS. **Loath to depart.** Orig. the tune of a song (prob. containing those words) expressive of regret for departure; *transf.* any tune played as a farewell. Hence **Loa·thness,** the quality or condition of being l.

Loathe (lōᵘð), *v.* [OE. *lāþian* = OS. *lēthon*, ON. *leiða* :– **laipōjan*, f. **laip-* LOATH *a.*] †**1.** *intr.* To be hateful, displeasing, or offensive. Const. *dat.* or *to.* –1597. †**b.** *impers.* –1596. †**2.** To be or become disgusted, to feel disgust. Const. *at, for, of, with.* –1609. †**3.** *trans.* To excite loathing or disgust in (a person, etc.) Const. *of.* Also, to render loath *to* (do something) or averse *from* (something). –1661. **4.** To feel aversion or dislike for; to be reluctant *to* (do something). Now only: To have an intense aversion for; to regard with utter disgust. ME. **b.** To feel a disgust for (food, etc.) ME.

3. They are..good for nothing but to loath pious souls 1661. **4.** In my soul I loath All affectation COWPER. Mother, I l. him HT. MARTINEAU. **b.** The full soule loatheth an honie combe *Prov.* 27:7. Hence **Loa·ther. Loa·thingly** *adv.*

Loathful (lōᵘ·ðfŭl), *a.* Also *Sc.* **laithfu'.** 1450. [f. LOATH *sb.* + -FUL.] **1.** That is an object of loathing; hateful, loathsome. Now *rare.* **2.** Reluctant, bashful. Now *Sc.* 1561.

1. And lothefull idlenes he doth detest SPENSER. **2.** But blate and laithfu', scarce can weel behave BURNS. Hence **Loa·thful-ly** *adv.*, **-ness.**

Loathing (lōᵘ·ðiŋ), *vbl. sb.* ME. [f. LOATHE *v.* + -ING¹.] The action of LOATHE *v.*; abhorrence; strong distaste (for food).

L. of remuneration 1792, for venison 1901.

Loathly (lōᵘ·ðli), *a.* [OE. *lāþlić*, f. *lāþ* LOATH *a.* + *-lić* -LY¹.] Hateful, disgusting, loathsome, repulsive, hideous, horrible. Revived in 19th c. as a literary word.

Thou art so loothly, and so oold also CHAUCER. A l. worm BESANT. Hence **Loa·thliness** (now *rare*).

Loathly (lōᵘ·ðli), *adv.* [OE. *lāþlīće*, f. *lāþ* LOATH *a.* + *-līće* -LY².] †**1.** In a manner to cause loathing; foully, hideously –1600. †**b.** With detestation. *Lear* II. i. 31. **2.** Reluctantly, unwillingly. Now *rare.* 1547.

1. With dust and blood his locks were l. dight 1600. **2.** The child goes, but l. 1880.

Loathsome (lōᵘ·ðsŏm), *a.* ME. [f. LOATH *sb.* + -SOME¹.] **1.** Exciting disgust or loathing; noisome, sickening; odious, repulsive, shocking. †**2.** Affected with loathing or disgust. Const. *of.* –1579.

1. A Gouty scrofulous Substance, very loathsom to look upon 1703. Errors which make some of Rousseau's confessions l. STEPHEN. Hence **Loa·thsome-ly** *adv.*, **-ness.**

Loathy (lōᵘ·ði). *a. arch.* 1481. [f. LOATH *sb.* + -Y¹.] = prec.

Lob (lǫb), *sb.*¹ ME. [prob. of LDu. origin and repr. adoptions of various dates and sources; cf. EFris. *lob*(*be* hanging lump of flesh, MLG., †Du. *lobbe, lubbe* hanging lip, Du. *lobbes* bumpkin, gawk.] †**1.** The pollack –1769. **2.** A country bumpkin; a lout. Now *dial.* 1533. **3.** Something pendulous, e.g. the wattles of a fowl, hanging ornaments, etc. (*rare*) 1688. **4.** A lump, a large piece; a nugget (of gold), etc. Chiefly *dial.* 1825. **5.** *Brewing.* A thick mixture. (Cf. LOBLOLLY, LOBSCOUSE.] 1839. **6.** *attrib.* or *adj.* Rustic; loutish; clumsy. Also *appos.* as quasi-proper name. 1508.

2. Farewell thou L. of spirits, Ile be gon SHAKS. This L. too was made principal Prolocutor 1658. **6.** A Giant..that was cal'd Lob-lie-by-the-fire 1613.

Lob (lǫb), *sb.*² Also **lobb.** 1681. [Of unkn. origin.] *Mining. pl.* Steps in a mine. Also applied to an irregular vein of ore resembling a flight of steps.

Lob (lǫb), *sb.*³ 1875. [f. LOB *v.*] **1.** *Cricket.* A slow underhand ball. Also *attrib.* **2.** *Lawn-tennis.* 'A ball tossed high in the air, and, if possible, over the opponent's head.' Also *attrib.* in *l.-volley.* 1890.

Lob (lǫb), *v.* Infl. **lobbed** (lǫbd), **lobbing.** 1596. [f. LOB *sb.*¹] †**1.** *intr.* To behave like a lout. J. SMYTH. **2.** *trans.* To cause or allow to hang heavily; to droop. ? *Obs.* exc. *slang.* 1599. **3.** *intr.* To move heavily or clumsily (often with *along*). Of a cabman: To crawl or prowl in search of a fare. 1819. **4.** *trans.* To throw heavily or clumsily; to toss or bowl with a slow movement. In *Lawn-tennis,* to strike (a ball) well into the air so as to fall at the back of the opponent's court. 1847. **5.** *Brewing.* To add 'lob' to (see LOB *sb.*¹ 5) 1838. **6.** *Mining.* To break into small pieces, as ore preliminary to hand sorting 1875.

2. Their poore Iades L. downe their heads SHAKS. **3.** The enemy's shells came lobbing into it [the trench] L. OLIPHANT.

Lobar (lōᵘ·bǎɹ), *a.* 1856. [f. LOBE + -AR¹.] Pertaining to a lobe.

Lobate (lōᵘ·beⁱt), *a.* 1760. [f. LOBE + -ATE².] *Nat. Hist.* Having or characterized by lobes; lobed. So **Lo·bated** *a.* 1703. Hence **Lo·bately** *adv.* so as to form lobes. **Loba·tion,** the formation of lobes; the condition of being l.

Lobato- (loᵘbēⁱ·to), comb. f. LOBATE with sense 'lobate and..', as *l.-digitate,* etc.

†**Lo·bbish,** *a.* 1567. [f. LOB *sb.*¹ + -ISH¹.] Like a lob; clownish –1586.

Lobby (lǫ·bi), *sb.* 1553. [– med.L. *lobium, lobia* (see LODGE); prob. orig. in monastic use.] †**1.** ? A covered walk, cloister (in a monastery). BECON. **2.** A passage or corridor; often used as a waiting-place or ante-room 1575. †**b.** *Naut.* An apartment or passage-way in the fore part of a cabin under the quarter-deck 1815–50. **c.** *Agric.* A small enclosure for cattle adjoining the farm-yard 1777. **3.** *spec.* In the House of Commons and other houses of legislature, a large entrance-hall open to the public, and chiefly used for interviews between members and non-members of the House; also (in full *division l.*), one of the two corridors to which members retire to vote 1640. **b.** *collect.* Those who frequent the lobbies of the House or who vote in a particular lobby; *U.S.* those who frequent the lobby in order to influence members of the legislature; the body of lobbyists 1859. **4.** *attrib.*, as *l.-correspondent,* etc. 1650.

2. The box l. of a theatre DICKENS. **3.** If the hon. member divides, I shall go into the same l. with him BRIGHT. **b.** The l. and corruption are legitimate subjects for satire 1884. *Comb.* **l.-member,** a lobbyist.

Lobby (lǫ·bi), *v.* orig. *U.S.* 1832. [f. LOBBY *sb.*] **1.** *intr.* To frequent the lobby of a legislative assembly for the purpose of influencing members' votes; to solicit the votes of members. **2.** *trans.* To influence (members of a house of legislature) in the exercise of their functions by frequenting the lobby. Also, to get (a measure) *through* Congress by means of such influence. 1850.

Lobbyist (lǫ·bi,ist). Chiefly *U.S.* 1863. [f. LOBBY *sb.* + -IST.] One who frequents the lobbies of the House of Representatives in order to influence members in their votes. Also *occas.*, a journalist, etc., who frequents the lobby of the House of Commons. So **Lo·bbyism,** the system of lobbying.

Lobcock (lǫ·bkǫk). Now *dial.* 1553. [f. LOB *sb.*¹ + COCK *sb.*¹] A country bumpkin; a clown; a blundering fool.

Lobe (lōᵘb). 1541. [– late L. *lobus* – Gr. λοβός lobe of the ear or the liver, capsule, pod.] **1.** A roundish projecting part, usu. one of two or more separated by a fissure: *spec.* **a.** One of the divisions of the liver or lungs formed by the fissures. **b.** The lower soft pendulous part of the external ear 1719. **c.** *Bot.* and *Zool.* A rounded projection or part of a leaf or other organ 1671. **d.** One of the divisions of the brain 1672. **e.** The larger and projecting part of a cam-wheel 1855.

Comb.: **l.-foot,** a lobe-footed bird; **-footed** *a.*, having lobate feet, as some birds. Hence **Lobed** (lōᵘbd) *a.*, having a lobe or lobes; lobate (chiefly *Nat. Hist.*) 1787. **Lobelet** (lōᵘ·b,lėt), a small lobe, a lobule 1836.

Lobelia (lobī·liǎ). 1739. [f. name of Matthias de *Lobel* (1538–1616), botanist to James I; see -IA¹.] A genus of herbaceous (rarely shrubby) plants, having blue, scarlet, or purple flowers, with deeply cleft spurless corolla; a plant of this genus, or its flower. **b.** *Pharmacy.* The herb *L. inflata* 1858.

Lobeliaceous (-ēⁱ·ʃəs), *a.* 1830. [f. mod.L. *Lobeliaceæ* (f. LOBELIA) + -OUS; see -ACEOUS.] *Bot.* Belonging to the N.O. *Lobeliaceæ.*

Lobeline (lōᵘ·bĭləin). Also **lobeli(i)n.** 1836. [f. LOBELIA + -INE⁵.] *Chem.* An oily alkaloid with a pungent tobacco-like taste obtained from *Lobelia inflata* (Indian tobacco).

Loblolly (lǫ·blǫli). Now *dial.* 1597. [perh. f. dial. *lob* eat or drink up noisily + *lolly* broth, soup.] **1.** Thick gruel or spoon-meat, as used by seamen, etc.; burgoo. **2.** A bumpkin, rustic, boor 1604.

Comb.: **l. bay,** an ornamental tree, *Gordonia lasianthus,* of the southern U.S.; **l. boy,** a surgeon's attendant on shipboard; also *dial.* an errand boy, man of all work; **l. pine,** the tree *Pinus tæda,* growing in swamps in the southern U.S.; **l. tree** = *loblolly wood*; **l. wood,** *Cupania glabra*; also *Pisonia cordata* (*Treas. Bot.*).

Lobose (lōᵘ·boᵘs), *a.* 1885. [– mod.L. *lobosus,* f. *lobus* LOBE.] Having many or large lobes; *spec.* pertaining to the order *Lobosa* of Rhizopods.

Lobscouse (lǫ·bskaus). *Naut.* and *dial.* 1706. [= Du. *lapskous,* Da., Norw., G. *lapskaus*; of unkn. origin.] A sailor's dish of meat stewed with vegetables and ship's biscuit, or the like.

Lobsided, var. of LOP-SIDED.

Lob's pound. Now *dial.* 1597. [See LOB *sb.*¹ 2.] Prison; jail; the lock-up. Also *fig.*, an entanglement, difficulty.

Lobster (lǫ·bstəɹ). [OE. *loppestre, lopystre, lopustre* – L. *locusta* crustacean, LOCUST, with unexpl. *p* for *c*, and *-stre* after agent-nouns in *-stre* -STER (cf. OE. *myltestre* – L. *meretrix*).] **1.** A large marine stalk-eyed ten-footed long-tailed crustacean of the genus *Homarus,* much used for food; it is greenish or bluish black when raw, and red when boiled; the first pair of feet form the characteristic 'claws'. **b.** The flesh of this, as food 1789. †**2.** An opprobrious name (? for a red-faced man) –1609. **3.** A contemptuous name for: A British soldier; orig. referring to the jointed plate-armour (called *lobster-tail*) worn by Roundhead cuirassiers; later, to the red coat. Also *boiled l.* 1643. **4.** Short for *lobster-caterpillar, -moth* 1869.

1. Norway l., *Nephrops norvegicus.* **Spiny** or **thorny l.,** *Palinurus vulgaris* = CRAYFISH 3 b. Gauntlets..were..oftener of small plates of iron rivetted together, in imitation of the lobster's tail GROSE. **2.** You whorson L. B. JONS. **3.** *Raw* (or *unboiled*) *l.*: a policeman; so called on account of his blue uniform.

attrib. and *Comb.*, as *l.-fishery, -sauce*, etc.; **l.-box** *slang*, (*a*) a transport ship; (*b*) barracks; **-clad** *a.*, clad in jointed armour suggesting a lobster's shell; **-coated** *a.*, red-coated; **-crab,** a crustacean of the family *Porcellanidæ*; a porcelain-crab; **-creel** = *lobster-pot*; **-joint,** a joint in an instrument resembling a joint in a lobster's claws; **-louse,** a parasite of the l., *Nicothoe astaci*; **-moth,** the bombycid moth *Stauropus fagi*; **-pot,** a basket, etc., serving as a trap to catch lobsters; **-smack** *joc.*, a military transport; **-tail,** a piece of armour jointed after the manner of a lobster's tail; also *attrib.*; **-tailed** *a.*, wearing 'lobster-tail' armour.

Lobular (lǫ·biŭlăɹ), *a.* 1822. [f. LOBULE + -AR¹.] *Anat.*, etc. Pertaining to or having the form of a lobule or lobules. Of pneumonia: Affecting the lobules of the lungs.

Lobulate (lǫ·biŭlět), *a.* 1838. [f. LOBULE + -ATE².] Having or consisting of lobules. **Lo·bulated** *a.* 1783. **Lobula·tion,** the formation of lobules; a lobulated condition 1861. **Lobulato-,** comb. f. = 'lobulate and..' 1846.

Lobule (lǫ·biul). 1682. [f. LOBE + -ULE, after *globule*, etc. Also in latinized form *lobulus*.] A small lobe. Chiefly *Anat.*

Lob-worm (lǫ·bˌwɒ̈ɹm). 1651. [f. LOB *sb.*¹] **a.** A large earthworm used for bait by anglers. **b.** The lug-worm (see LUG *sb.*³) 1854.

‖**Local** (lokal), *sb.*¹ Commonly *erron.* **locale** (lokā·l), fem. 1772. [Fr. *local*, subst. use of the adj.; see next.] A place or locality; esp. a place considered with reference to some particular event or particular operations.

Local (lōᵘ·kăl), *a.* and *sb.*² ME. [– (O)Fr. *local* – late L. *localis*, f. L. *locus* place; see -AL¹.] **A.** *adj.* **1.** Pertaining to or concerned with place or position in space. Now chiefly in *l. situation*. 1485. †**b.** Having spatial position –1729. †**c.** *L. motion*, movement from place to place, locomotion –1707. **d.** *Grammar.* Relating to place or situation 1842. **2.** Belonging to, existing in, or peculiar to a particular place or places ME. **b.** Belonging to a town or other limited region, as dist. from the country as a whole 1688. **c.** In various specific collocations (see below) 1772. **3.** *Law.* (In renderings of AFr. *chose local, trespas local*) 1598. **4.** Pertaining to a particular place in a system, series, etc., or to a particular portion of an object (see below). **5.** Pertaining to places (in the geographical sense) or to an individual place as such 1605. **6.** *Math.* Pertaining to a locus 1704.

1. c. Plants have no l. or progressive Motion 1707. **2.** *L. time*: the time of day or night reckoned from the instant of transit of the mean sun over the l. meridian. Truth is not l. COWPER. Mr. Yeo, the l. lawyer 1891. **b.** *L. government*, the administration of the affairs of a town, etc. by the inhabitants, as dist. from the state at large. *L. Government Board*: a former department of state acting as the central authority for Local Government in England and Wales. **c.** *L. examination*, one held in a number of different places under the direction of a central board at one of the Universities. *L. preacher* (among the Methodists), a layman authorized to preach in the district in which he resides. *L. rank*, the rank given to an officer in his Majesty's service serving in a foreign land with other troops, whereby he is equalized in rank with officers whose first commissions are of the same date, but who have been more fortunate in promotion. *L. veto*: the prohibition of the sale of liquors in a district, under the system of l. option. **Local option.** The principle of allowing localities to decide whether the trade in liquor, etc. shall be prohibited within the district 1868. **4. a.** Pertaining to, or affecting, a particular part or organ of the body 1541: I employed only l. means for their cure ABERNETHY. A l. inflammation 1899. **b.** Electr. and Magnetism. *L. action*, action between different parts of a plate in an electric battery, as dist. from the general action of the battery. *L. attraction*, the effect of the iron in a ship on her compasses. *L. battery*, the battery of a l. circuit. *L. circuit*, one which includes only the apparatus in the office, and is closed by a relay. 1841. **c. Local colour:** (*a*) In *Painting*, the colour natural to each object or part of a picture 1706. (*b*) Hence, in art and literature, the representation in vivid detail of the manners, dress, scenery, etc. of a particular period or country 1721. Hence **Lo·cally** *adv.* in a l. manner.

B. *sb.* (the adj. used *absol.*) **1.** A person attached by his occupation, etc. to, or an inhabitant of, a particular locality. Chiefly *pl.* 1835. **b.** *esp.* A local preacher 1824. **2.** Something local: an item of local news in a newspaper 1869; a postage-stamp of only local currency 1870; *Telegr.* a local battery or circuit 1875; a local train 1902; a local examination 1893.

Locale, erron. f. LOCAL *sb.*¹

Localism (lōᵘ·kăliz'm). 1823. [f. LOCAL *a.* + -ISM.] Attachment to a locality; limitation of ideas, sympathies, and interests resulting from this; disposition to favour what is local 1843. **2.** A local idiom, custom, or the like.

2. All talk scandal, gossip, localisms 1858.

Localist (lōᵘ·kălist). 1683. [f. LOCAL *a.* + -IST.] One who treats or regards things as local; a student of what is local; one who assigns a local origin to (diseases).

'Localists' attributed the epidemics to local conditions, atmospheric changes, [etc.] 1901. Hence **Locali·stic** *a.* (of a theory) attributing a local nature or origin.

Locality (lokæ·lĭti). 1628. [– Fr. *localité* or late L. *localitas, -tat-*, f. *localis*; see LOCAL *a.*, -ITY.] **1.** The fact or quality of having a place, i.e. of having position in space. †**2.** The fact of being local. Also *pl.* local characteristics, feelings, or prejudices. –1802. **3.** *pl.* The features of a particular place. [So Fr.] 1828. **4. a.** The place in which an object (e.g. a plant, a mineral, etc.) is, or is to be found 1834. **b.** A district as the site occupied by certain persons or things, or as the scene of certain activities 1830. **5.** *Law.* Limitation to a county, district, or place. BLACKSTONE. **6.** *Phrenol.* The faculty of recognizing and remembering places 1815. **7.** *Psychol.* in phr. *sense of l.* 1888.

1. That the Soul and Angels..have nothing to do with grosser l., is generally opinion'd GLANVILL. **4. a.** A blind man..feeling all around him with his cane, so as to find out his l. HAWTHORNE. **5.** The l. of trial 1768. **7.** *L., sense of*, the faculty of distinguishing the part of a sensory surface to which a stimulus is applied (*Syd. Soc. Lex.*) 1888.

Localization (lōᵘkăləizēⁱ·ʃən). 1816. [f. LOCALIZE *v.* + -ATION.] **1.** The action of localizing; the fact of being localized 1853. **b.** *Phys.* The process of fixing, or fact of being fixed, in some particular part or organ of the body 1855. **2.** Assignment to a particular place or locality. Also, the determination of the locality of an object. 1816.

1. Centralization or l. of administrative power 1853. **2.** The localisation of a bullet in a wound 1881.

Localize (lōᵘ·kăləiz), *v.* 1600. [f. LOCAL *a.* + -IZE.] †**1.** *intr.* To act in accordance with the custom of the place. G. HARVEY. **2.** *trans.* To make local; to invest with local characteristics 1792. **3.** To fix in a particular place, or in a particular part of a whole or system. Usu.: To attach or restrict *to* a particular locality. 1798. **4.** To attribute to a particular place; to find a locality for, determine the locality of. Occas. constr. *to*. 1816.

4. The Romans appropriated and localised every tale and tradition H. COLERIDGE. **Lo·calizable** *a.*

‖**Locanda** (loka·nda). 1838. [It. – med. L. (*camera, domus*) *locanda* (room, house) to be let.] A lodging-house or inn.

Locate (lōᵘ·kēⁱt, lokēⁱ·t), *v.* 1652. [– *locat-*, pa. ppl. stem of L. *locare* place, let for hire, f. *locus* place; see -ATE³.] **1.** *trans.* To fix the situation or site of (lands granted, a building, etc.). Chiefly *U.S.* 1765. **2.** To survey and define the limits of; to lay out (a road); to enter on or take possession of (a land-claim, a gold-mine, etc.). *U.S.* 1739. **3.** To fix or establish in a place; to settle. Chiefly *U.S.* 1807. **b.** *pass.* Of a quality, faculty, etc.: To have its seat 1829. **4.** *intr.* for *refl.* To establish oneself in a place, to settle 1652. **5.** To allocate, allot, apportion 1816. **6.** To refer to a particular place; to state the locality of 1807. **7.** To discover the exact locality of (a person or thing) 1882. **8.** *Civil Law.* As tr. L. *locare*: To let out, hire out. 1880.

2. He..located a valuable claim near the Pyramid Mountains 1885. **3.** The motives that led me to l. myself at Tunbridge 1807. **6.** That large Philosophy which embraces and locates truth of every kind J. H. NEWMAN. **7.** The gunboats yesterday..located the enemy's position at Kerreri 1898.

Location (lokēⁱ·ʃən). Now chiefly *U.S.* 1592. [– L. *locatio*, f. as prec.; see -ION.] **1.** *Civil* and *Sc. Law.* The action of letting for hire (correl. w. CONDUCTION) 1592. **2.** The action of placing; the fact or condition of being placed; settlement in a place 1623. **3.** Local position, situation. Also, position in a series. 1597. **4.** The marking out or surveying of a tract of land (*esp.* of a claim) or a settlement; the laying out of a road or the like. *U.S.* 1718. **5.** *concr.* (*U.S.*) A tract of land marked out or surveyed; *spec.* a mining claim. Also in the S. African colonies, the quarters set apart for natives. 1792. **b.** *Austral.* A farm or station 1828. **6.** Place of settlement or residence. Chiefly *U.S.* 1827.

1. Phr. *Contract of l.*: a contract by which the use of a chattel is agreed to be given, or by which a person agrees to give his services, for hire. **3.** The l. of the praetorium 1883. **5. b.** Rides about the l. 1863. **6.** They visited Windsor. Mr. Beck said that if he had such a l. he should always live there BESANT & RICE.

Locative (lǫ·kătiv). 1804. [f. as prec. + -IVE, after *nominative, accusative*, etc. In med.L. *locativus* localizing (XIV) (cf. sense A2); first used in treating of Skr. grammar.] **A.** *adj.* Pertaining to location. **1.** *Gram.* Name of the case-form denoting 'place where'; e.g. L. *domī* = at home. Also, pertaining to this case. 1841. **2.** Serving to locate the position of something 1817. **B.** *sb.* *Gram.* The locative case 1804.

Locator (lokēⁱ·tǫ̆ɹ). 1607. [In sense 1 – late L. *locator* one who lets or hires out (cf. L. 'contractor'); in sense 2, f. LOCATE *v.* 2 + -OR 2.] **1.** One who lets for hire; esp. in *Civil* and *Sc. Law.* **2.** *U.S.* One who or a thing which locates (see LOCATE *v.* 2) 1817.

Loch (lǫχ). *Sc.* ME. [– Gael. *loch*; see LOUGH².] A lake; also, an arm of the sea, *esp.* when narrow or partially landlocked.

Loch, var. of LOHOCH.

Lochaber (lǫχæ·bəɹ). 1618. [Name of a district in Inverness-shire.] *attrib.* in *L.-axe* (Antiq.): 'A sort of halbert of a large size, having a strong hook behind for laying hold of the object assaulted' (Jam.).

Lochage (lǫ·kědʒ). Also quasi-L. ‖**lochagus** (lokēⁱ·gǒs). 1808. [– Gr. λοχαγός, f. λόχος LOCHUS + ἀγ-, ἄγειν to lead.] *Gr. Antiq.* The commander of a lochus.

Lochan (lǫ·χăn). *Sc.* 1789. [– Gael. *lochan*, dim. of *loch* LOCH.] A small loch or lake.

Loche, var. of LOACH.

‖**Lochia** (lǫ·kiă). *pl.* 1685. [mod.L. – Gr. λόχια, subst. use of n.pl. of λόχιος pertaining to childbirth, f. λόχος lying-in; in earliest use in Fr. form *lochies*.] *Path.* The discharge from the uterus and vagina which follows child-birth. Hence **Lo·chial** *a.* of or pertaining to the l.

‖**Lochus** (lǫ·kǒs). Pl. **lochi** (lǫ·kəi). 1832. [mod.L. – Gr. λόχος.] *Gr. Antiq.* A division of the army, in Sparta and other states.

Lock (lǫk), *sb.*¹ [OE. *locc*, corresp. to OFris., OS. *lok*, MDu. *locke* (Du. *lok*), OHG. *loc* (G. *locke*), ON. *lokkr* :– Gmc. **lokkaz*, **lukkaz*. Formally coincident and perh. ult. identical with next.] **1.** One of the natural divisions of a head of hair, a beard, etc.; a tress. In *pl.* = the hair of the head. †**b.** A lovelock; also, a tress of artificial hair –1688. **c.** *transf.* and *fig.* (of foliage, etc.) 1567. **2.** A tuft or flock (of wool, cotton, etc.) ME. **3.** A (small) quantity of hay, straw, etc.; a handful, armful. Now *dial.* 1440.

1. With these..the Spirits Elect Bind thir resplendent locks MILT. **c.** The locks of the approaching storm SHELLEY. **2.** A l. of wooll falls without noise BP. HALL. **3.** A l. of bacon 1843, of straw T. HARDY.

Lock (lǫk), *sb.*² [OE. *loc* = OFris. *lok* lock, OS. *lok* hole, OHG. *loh* (G. *loch*) hole, ON. *lok* lid, end, conclusion (Goth. has *us|luk* opening) :– Gmc. **lokam*, **lukam*, f. **luk-* **lūk-* close, enclose, whence OE. *lūcan* str. vb., which was repl. by a new derivative (see next).]

I. A contrivance for fastening. **1.** An appliance for fastening a door, lid, etc., consisting of a bolt or bolts which can be propelled and withdrawn by means of a key or similar instrument. (In OE. applied to a bar, bolt, latch, or the like.) OE. **2.** A cotter, a forelock 1875. †**3.** A hobble or shackle for a horse's foot; a horse-lock 1486. **4.** A contrivance to keep a wheel from turning 1884. **5.** In fire-arms, the piece of mechanism by means of which the charge is exploded. (See also FIRELOCK, FLINT-LOCK, MATCHLOCK.) 1547. **6.** Short for ROWLOCK 1850.

1. *fig.* I kept a l. upon my lips CARLYLE. Phr. *L. and key*: a typical expression for appliances for fastening or securing. *Under l. and key*: securely locked up. **5.** Phr. *L., stock, and barrel* = the entirety of anything: The whole thing, l., stock, and barrel, isn't worth one big yellow sea-poppy R. KIPLING.

II. A barrier, an enclosure. †**1.** A barrier on a river, which can be opened or closed at will –1758. †**2.** The waterway between the piers of a bridge –1813. **3.** On a canal or river: A portion of the channel shut off above and below by folding gates provided with sluices to let the water out and in, and thus raise or lower boats from one level to another 1577. †**b.** A lift on a railway, for raising and lowering vehicles from one level to another –1825. **4.** *Engineering.* An antechamber giving access to a chamber in which work is carried on in compressed air; an *air-lock* 1874.

III. f. LOCK *v.* **1.** A locking together, interlocking; an assemblage of objects jammed together, now esp. a 'block', 'jam' of carriages in the streets 1550. †**2.** A grapple, grip, or trick in wrestling; hence *fig.* a dodge; a difficulty, dilemma 1608. **3.** The swerving (to right or left) of the wheels of the fore-carriage of a vehicle from the line of direction of the hind-wheels 1851. **4.** *Thieves' slang.* (App. short for *lock-all-fast.*) A receiver of stolen goods; also, a house where stolen goods are received 1700.

1. Stopped on the road from Epsom in a l. of carriages THACKERAY. **2.** The Enemy is at his old l. CROMWELL.

IV. (More fully *Lock-hospital.*) A hospital for the treatment of venereal diseases. (Now usually with capital L.) 1700.

attrib. and *Comb.* **1.** General: as (sense I. 1) *l.-maker, -staple*, etc.; (sense I. 5) *l.-action*, etc.; (sense II. 3) *l.-bank, -duty, -house, -keeper*, etc.

2. Special: as **l.-bay,** the space of water between the gates of a canal-lock; **-chamber,** the space enclosed between the side-walls and gates of a l.; **-nut,** a nut screwed down upon another to prevent its breaking loose, a check-nut; **-pulley,** two pulleys that can be worked separately or together; **-rail,** in doors, the rail nearest the l.; **-spring,** the spring by means of which the case of a watch is opened or closed; **-step** *Mil.*, a step in which the heel of one man is brought nearly in contact with the joint of the great toe of another; hence *lock-step* adv. and vb.; **-stitch,** a sewing-machine stitch, in which two threads are locked firmly together; also *attrib.*

Lock (lǫk), *v.* Pa. t. and pple. **locked** (lǫkt). ME. [f. LOCK *sb.*², repl. OE. *lūcan* (see prec.).] **1.** *trans.* To fasten (a door, box, drawer, etc.) with a lock and key; occas. with *up.* Hence (chiefly with *up*), to secure (a chamber, building, enclosure) by locking the doors. **b.** *intr.* Of a door: To be locked; to admit of being locked 1590. **2.** *trans.* To shut up with a lock; to put under lock and key. Const. *in, into, within.* Also with advs. *in, up.* ME. **3.** *transf.* **a.** To enclose, hem in. Chiefly with *in.* ME. **b.** To keep securely, as if in a locked receptacle. Chiefly with *up.* 1562. **c.** Comm. and Finance. *To l. up*: To invest (capital) *in* something not easily convertible into money 1692. **d.** Of sleep, enchantment, etc.: To hold fast, overpower completely. Also with *up.* 1725. **4.** To shut off with or as with a lock *from* (a person); to preclude *from* (something) by or as by locking. Also with *up.* 1601. **5.** To fasten, make or set fast, fix; *techn.* to fasten or engage (one part of a machine) *to* another; in *pass.* (of a joint), to be rendered rigid 1670. **b.** To put a lock on the foot of (a horse); to fasten (a wheel) so as to keep it from turning 1694. **c.** *intr.* for *refl.* Of mechanism, a joint: To become fixed or set fast. †Of an animal's flanks: To draw together 1658. **6.** To fix or join firmly by interlacing or fitting of parts into each other. Also with *together, up.* 1592. Also *intr.* for *refl.* 1688. **b.** *Fencing.* To seize the adversary's sword-arm, by turning one's left arm round it, in order to disarm him 1782. **c.** *To l. horns*: (of cattle) to entangle horns with horns in fighting. Hence *fig.* U.S., to engage in combat *with* (some one). 1839. **d.** To embrace closely; also, to grapple in combat. Now only *passive. lit.* and *fig.* 1611. **7.** *Mil.* (*absol.* and *passive*) *To l. up,* to take the closest possible order in line or in file 1802. **8.** *intr.* Of a vehicle: To admit of the fore-wheels passing askew under the body of the carriage. Said also of the wheel. 1669. **9.** *Engineering* and *Navigation.* **a.** *intr.* Of a canal: To pass by a lock *into.* Also of the vessel: To pass *down, in,* or *out* through a lock. Of persons: To pass *out* through an air-lock. 1795. **b.** *trans.* To pass (a vessel) *down, in, out,* or *through* by means of a lock 1840. **c.** *trans.* To furnish (a canal) with locks; to shut *off* (a portion of a river) by means of a lock 1892.

1. Were not my doores lockt vp, and I shut out? SHAKS. *fig.* And David's Lips are lock't FITZ-GERALD. Phr. *To l. up* (absol.): to l. up the house, l. the doors. **2.** To l. up wine POPE. **3. a.** A still salt pool, lock'd in with bars of sand TENNYSON. **b.** Prudent men l. up their motives SHENSTONE. **d.** I lay fast locked in sleep for eight hours TYNDALL. **4.** To locke it [*sc.* life] From Action and Adventure *Cymb.* IV. iv. 2. Phr. **L. out:** (*a*) to turn (a person) out and l. the door against him; (*b*) to keep out (persons) by locking the door; hence (of an employer) to refuse employment to (operatives) in an industrial dispute. **5.** *To l. up a forme* (Printing): to fix the types or pages in a metal frame so as to prepare them for press, etc. **6.** Pray you, l. hand in hand SHAKS.

-lock, *suffix,* surviving in mod. Eng. only in WEDLOCK, repr. OE. *-lāc* 'actions or proceeding, practice', which appears in about a dozen compounds, e.g. *brȳdlāc* nuptials, *feohtlāc* warfare, *rēaflāc* robbery, *wedlāc* pledge-giving, the first three of which survived into early ME., and the other into mod. Eng. with altered meaning.

Lockage (lǫ·kėdʒ). 1770. [f. LOCK *sb.*² and *v.* + -AGE.] †**1.** The means of locking (pieces of timber) together. PLOT. **2. a.** The amount of rise and fall effected by a lock or series of locks on a canal or river. **b.** The passage of a vessel through a lock; the toll paid for this 1771. **c.** The construction and working of locks; also, aggregate of locks constructed 1809. **3.** *attrib.*, as *l. water*, etc. 1816.

Locked (lǫkt), *ppl. a.* 1470. [f. LOCK *v.* + -ED¹.] In senses of LOCK *v.* Also with *up.*

Locked jaw: (*a*) a jaw set fast by spasmodic contraction of the muscles; (*b*) = LOCK-JAW, and occas. = JAW-FALL 2.

Locker (lǫ·kəɹ). ME. [f. LOCK *sb.*² or *v.* + -ER¹. Sense 3 is prob. of LDu. origin (cf. Flem. *loker*, Kilian); for the formation cf. *drawer.*] **1.** One who locks; *spec.* an officer at the Custom House, in charge of a locked-up warehouse, acting under the warehouse-keeper 1735. Also with *up, out.* **2.** *techn.* Something that locks or closes; e.g. a stop to a bell ME. **3.** A box or chest with a lock; also, a small cupboard, e.g. one placed under a window-seat 1440. **b.** *Naut.* A chest or compartment for containing clothes, stores, ammunition, etc. Often specified, as *chain-, shot-l.* 1626. **4.** A compartment in a pigeon-house, a pigeon-hole 1600. **b.** *Eccl.* A cupboard, recess, or niche in a wall, usually near an altar, fitted with a door and lock, for the reservation of the Sacrament, etc. 1517.

3. b. fig. phr. (*Not*) *a shot in the l.*: (no) money in one's pocket, (not) a chance left. *Laid in the lockers*, dead. *Davy Jones's l.*: see DAVY JONES.

Locket (lǫ·kėt). ME. [– OFr. *locquet* (mod. *loquet* latch), dim. of (chiefly AFr.) *loc* latch, lock, f. the Gmc. source of LOCK *sb.*²] †**1.** One of the iron cross-bars of a window –1598. **2.** One of the metal plates or bands on a scabbard 1562. †**3.** A fastening or socket. BUTLER. †**4.** A group of small jewels set in a pattern –1706. **5.** †**a.** 'A small lock; any catch or spring to fasten a necklace or other ornament' (J.) –1765. Hence **b.** A small case of gold or silver, containing a miniature, a lock of hair, etc., and worn as an ornament 1679.

Lockfast (lǫ·kfɑst), *a.* 1453. [(1) f. LOCK *sb.*² + FAST *a.*; (2) f. LOCK *v.* + FAST *adv.*] **1.** Chiefly *Sc.* Fastened or secured by a lock. Also as quasi-*sb.* A safe. **2.** *Mech.* Adapted for locking something fast; fast-locking 1881.

Lockian (lǫ·kiăn). 1858. [f. the name of the English philosopher John *Locke* (1632–1704) + -IAN.] *adj.* Of or pertaining to Locke or his followers. *sb.* A follower of Locke. Hence **Lo·ckianism,** the doctrines of Locke or his followers. So **Lo·ckist** *sb.* 1705.

Lo·ck-jaw. 1803. [Altered f. *locked jaw*: see LOCKED *ppl. a.*] Pop. name for trismus, or tonic spasm of the muscles of mastication; a variety of tetanus. Also = TETANUS. Hence **Lo·ck-jawed** *ppl. a.* having the jaws fixed; *fig.* unable to speak 1801.

Lockless (lǫ·klės), *a.* 1591. [f. LOCK *sb.*² + -LESS.] Having no lock.

Lockman (lǫ·kmæ̆n). Also **locksman.** 1470. [f. LOCK *sb.*² + MAN *sb.*] †**a.** In Scotland: A public executioner, hangman –1818. **b.** In the Isle of Man: A coroner's summoner 1863. **c.** A man employed at a canal or river lock 1846.

Lo·ck-out. Pl. **lock-outs** (*erron.* **locks-out**). 1860. [f. phr. *lock out*; see LOCK *v.* 4.] An act of locking out a body of operatives; *i.e.* a refusal on the part of an employer, or employers acting in concert, to furnish work to their operatives except on conditions to be accepted by the latter collectively.

Lockram (lǫ·krăm). *Obs.* exc. *Hist.* 1483. [– Fr. *locrenan*, f. *Locronan* (lit. 'cell of St. Ronan'), name of a village in Brittany, where formerly made. For the *m*, cf. BUCKRAM.] A linen fabric of various qualities; an article made of this; *pl.*, pieces of this. Also *attrib.*

Locksmith (lǫ·ksmiþ). ME. [f. LOCK *sb.*² + SMITH.] An artificer whose occupation is to make or mend locks.

Lo·ck-up, *sb.* (*a.*) 1767. [f. LOCK *v.* + UP *adv.*] **1.** The action of locking up a school, etc. for the night; also, the time of this 1871; the action of locking up capital; also, an amount locked up 1822. **2.** (Short for *lock-up house* or *room.*) An apartment or building that can be locked up; *esp.* a house or room for the (temporary) detention of offenders 1859.

attrib. or *adj.*, with sense 'capable of being locked up'; as *lock-up coach-house, room*, etc.; **lock-up house,** a house of detention 1767; **lock-up shop,** a detached apartment used as a shop and locked up at night.

Locky (lǫ·ki), *a.* 1611. [f. LOCK *sb.*¹ + -Y¹.] Of or pertaining to locks (of hair); having locks in plenty.

Loco¹ (lōᵘ·ko). *U.S.* 1883. [A use of Sp. *loco* insane.] One of several leguminous plants (chiefly species of *Astragalus*) found in the western and south-western U.S., which, when eaten by cattle, produce *loco-disease.* More fully *l.-plant, l.-weed.* **b.** = *loco-disease.* *Comb.* **l.-disease,** a disease in horses, affecting the brain, caused by eating l.

Loco². 1896. Short for LOCOMOTIVE *sb.*

Lo:co-descri·ptive, *a.* 1815. [f. *loco-*, taken as the comb. form of L. *locus* place (quasi 'local').] Descriptive of local scenery, etc.

Loco-foco (lōᵘ·ko,fōᵘ·ko). *U.S.* 1834. [An invented word; said by some to be made up of *loco* in *locomotive*, imagined to mean 'self-moving', and *foco* for It. *fuoco* or Sp. *fuego* fire.] †**1.** 'A self-igniting cigar or match' (Bartlett). More fully *loco-foco cigar, match.* –1852. **2.** *U.S. Polit. Hist.* Used *attrib.* as the designation of the 'Equal Rights' section of the Democratic party (for the origin of the name see O.E.D.). Hence *absol.*, a member of this party. 1837. Hence **Lo:cofo·coism.**

Locomobile (lōᵘkŏmōᵘ·bil). 1889. [f. L. *loco* (see LOCOMOTIVE) + *mobilis* MOBILE.] **a.** *adj.* Having the power to move about, as *a locomobile crane.* **b.** *sb.* A locomobile vehicle, engine, etc. 1902.

Locomote (lōᵘ·kŏmōᵘt), *v.* 1846. [Back-formation from next.] *intr.* To move about from place to place. (Orig. *slang*; now in biological use.)

Locomotion (lōᵘkŏmōᵘ·ʃən). 1646. [f. L. *loco* (see next) + *motio* MOTION.] **1.** The action or power of moving from place to place; progressive motion of an animal. **2.** Movement from place to place, esp. by artificial means; travel; the means of travelling 1788. **3.** Progressive movement of an inanimate body 1851.

1. Movement..of the body as a whole..is termed

l. HUXLEY. 2. I have no taste whatever for l., by earth, air, or sea MRS. CARLYLE.

Locomotive (lōᵘ·kǒmōᵘtiv, lōᵘkǒmōᵘ·tiv). 1612. [– mod.L. *locomotivus*, f. L. *loco*, abl. of *locus* place + late L. *motivus* MOTIVE, after schol. L. *in loco movēri* = *movēri localiter* move by change of position in space (cf. Aristotle's ἡ κατὰ τόπον κίνησις).]

A. *adj.* **1.** Of or pertaining to locomotion, or (*joc.*) to travel. **2.** Having the power of locomotion 1657; *joc.* (of a person) given to locomotion 1732; (of a vehicle or piece of machinery) moving by its own power 1815. **3.** Adapted for or used in locomotion 1841.

1. *L. faculty, power*, the faculty or power of movement from place to place by an act of the will. In these l. days one is too apt to forget one's neighbours HELPS. 2. A caterpillar then may be regarded as a l. egg 1816. *L. tailor* (slang), a tramping workman FARMER. *L.* (*steam*) *engine*: an engine constructed for movement from place to place by its own power (as opp. to 'stationary' engine); *esp.* a steam-engine adapted to draw a train of carriages along a railway; a railway-engine. Now generally shortened to *locomotive*.

B. *sb.* **1.** = *Locomotive engine* (see above) 1829. **b.** *slang. pl.* The legs 1841. **2.** An animal having powers of locomotion 1872.

Comb. **l.-car** *U.S.*, a l. and a car combined in one vehicle; a dummy engine (Webster).

Hence **Locomo·tive-ly** *adv.*, **-ness.** **Lo:co-moti·vity**, the quality or fact of being l.

Locomotor (lōᵘ·kǒmōᵘtəɹ). 1822. [f. L. *loco* (see prec.) + MOTOR; as adj. after Fr. *locomoteur.*] **A.** *sb.* One who or that which has locomotive power. **B.** *adj.* (Chiefly *Phys.*) Of, pertaining to, or concerned with locomotion 1870.

L. ataxy: see ATAXY 2.

Locomotory (lōᵘkǒmōᵘ·tǒri), *a.* 1835. [f. as prec. + MOTORY.] Pertaining to, or having the power of, locomotion.

‖**Loculus** (lǫ·kiŭləs). *Pl.* **-li** (-ləi). 1858. [L., dim. of *locus*; see -CULE.] **1.** A small chamber or cell in an ancient tomb for corpses or urns. **2.** *Zool.*, *Anat.*, and *Bot.* One of a number of small cavities or cells separated by septa 1861.

So **Lo·culament** = LOCULUS 2. 1656. **Lo·cular** (1847), **Lo·culate** (1866), **Lo·culated** (1801) *adjs.* having or divided into loculi; **Locula·tion** (1819). **Lo·culicidal** *a.* of a carpel, etc., that dehisces through the back or dorsal suture of the loculus 1819. **Loculici·dally** *adv.* 1847. **Lo·culose** (1855), **Loculous** (1840) *adjs.* full of or divided into loculi.

‖**Locum tenens** (lōᵘ·kǒm tī·nenz). 1641. [med.L. (XIII; cf. contemp. *locum tenēre*) 'one holding the place (of another)'; L. *locum*, acc. of *locus* place, and *tenens*, pr. pple. of *tenēre* hold; cf. LIEUTENANT, TENANT.] One filling an office temporarily in place of another, *esp.* a doctor or a clergyman; a deputy, substitute. Hence **Lo·cum-te·nency**, the position of being a *locum tenens*.

‖**Locus** (lōᵘ·kǒs). *Pl.* **loci** (lōᵘ·səi). 1715. [L., = 'place'.] **1.** Place of something, locality. **2.** A subject, head, topic. [So in L. writers, after Gr. τόπος.] 1753. **3.** *Math.* The curve or figure constituted by all the points which satisfy a particular equation of relation between co-ordinates, or generated by a point, line, or surface moving in accordance with mathematically defined conditions 1727.

Latin phrases: **l. classicus,** a standard passage which is authoritative on a subject; **l. communis,** a COMMONPLACE; **l. in quo,** the locality of an event, etc.; in *Law*, the land on which trespass has been committed; **l. pœnitentiæ** (after Heb. 12:17), a place of repentance; in *Law*, an opportunity allowed to a person to recede from some engagement, so long as some decisive step has not been taken; **l. standi,** lit. 'place of standing', recognized position; in *Law*, a right to appear in court. Also GENIUS *loci*.

Locust (lōᵘ·kǒst), *sb.* ME. [– (O)Fr. *locuste* – L. *locusta* locust, lobster or crayfish. See LOBSTER.] **1.** An orthopterous saltatorial insect of the family *Acridiidæ* (characterized by short horns), esp. *Œdipoda migratoria* (or *Pachytylus migratorius*), the Migratory Locust, well known for its ravages in Asia and Africa, where, migrating in myriads, it often eats up every green thing. In many countries used for food. **2.** *fig.* A person of devouring or destructive propensities 1546. **3. a.** The fruit of the carob-tree. **b.** A cassia-pod. 1615. **4.** = LOCUST-TREE 1640.

1. The white ant can destroy fleets and cities, and the locusts erase a province DISRAELI. 2. Those locusts called middle-men COBBETT.

attrib. and *Comb.*, as *l.-swarm*, etc.; *l. fruit, timber*, etc.; **l.-bean,** the fruit of the carob-tree; **-beetle** = *locust-borer*; **-bird,** the rose-coloured starling, *Pastor roseus*, which devours locusts; **-borer,** a longicorn beetle, *Cyllene robiniæ*, whose larva destroys the, locust-tree; **-eater,** a bird of the genus *Gryllivora*.

Hence **Locust** *v. intr.* to swarm and devour as locusts do (TENNYSON).

Lo·cust-tree. 1623. [In sense 1 f. LOCUST *sb.* In the other applications the identity of the word is somewhat doubtful.] **1.** The carob-tree, *Ceratonia siliqua*. **2.** = ACACIA[1] 2. 1640. **3.** The COURBARIL of Guiana and the West Indies 1629. **4.** A leguminous plant of New Zealand (*Sophora tetraptera*) 1872.

Bastard Locust-tree of the W. Indies, *Clethra tinifolia*. **Honey Locust-tree,** a N. Amer. ornamental tree, *Gleditschia triacanthos*. **Swamp** or **Water Locust-tree,** *G. monosperma*.

Locution (lokiū·ʃən). ME. [– (O)Fr. *locution* or L. *locutio*, f. *locut-*, pa. ppl. stem of *loqui* talk, speak; see -ION.] †**1.** The act of speaking –1767. **2.** Speech as the expression of thought; discourse; also, style of discourse, expression. Now *rare* or *Obs.* 1519. **3.** A phrase, expression ME.

2. I hate these figures in l., These about phrases forc'd by ceremonie MARSTON. 3. A..figurative loquucion 1547.

Locutory (lǫ·kiŭtǒri). 1450. [– med. L. *locutorium*, f. as prec.; see -ORIUM.] An apartment in a monastery set apart for conversation, a parlour; *occas.* a grille at which conversation is allowed with those outside.

Lode (lōᵘd). [OE. *lād* LOAD, of which *lode* is a spelling-variant.] **1.** †Way, journey; *dial.* a road. **2.** A water-course; an aqueduct, channel; an open drain in fenny districts. Now *local.* 1572. †**3.** Leading, guidance. ME. only. **4.** A loadstone 1509. **5.** *Mining.* A vein of metal ore 1602.

2. Down that long dark l...he..skated home KINGSLEY. 4. As with the Loade The Steele we touch DRAYTON.

†**Lodeman.** [OE. *lādmann*, f. *lād* LODE + *mann* MAN; in AL. *lodmannus* XIII, also *lodesmannus* XIV, Eng. *lodesman* (XIII).] In OE., a leader, guide; later, only *spec.* a pilot –1536. So †**Lo·desman** ME. –1594.

Lodemanage (lōᵘ·dmǎnědʒ). *Obs.* or *Hist.* ME. [– AFr. *lodmanage*, f. as prec. + -AGE; in AL. *lod(es)managium* XIII.] Pilotage.

Lodestar, loadstar (lōᵘ·dstāɹ). ME. [f. *load*, LODE + STAR *sb.*[1]; cf. ON. *leiðastjarna*, MHG. *leit(e)sterne.*] **1.** A star that shows the way; *esp.* the pole-star. **2.** *fig.* A guiding star; that on which one's attention or hopes are fixed ME.

2. Your eyes are loadstarres SHAKS. France [became] the lode-star of Continental democracy M. ARNOLD.

Lodestone: see LOADSTONE.

Lodge (lǫdʒ), *sb.* [ME. *log(g)e* – OFr. *loge* arbour, summer-house, hut (in mod. Fr. hut, cottage, box at a theatre, etc.) :– med.L. *laubia, lobia* (see LOBBY) – Gmc. **laubja* (G. *laube* arbour, summer-house), prob. f. **laubam* LEAF.] **1.** A small dwelling; a hut or booth; a tent, arbour, or the like. Now *dial.* †**b.** A cell, prison –1704. **c.** An out-house (*dial.*) 1706. **2.** A house in a forest or other wild place, e.g. in the Highlands of Scotland, occupied in the hunting or shooting season 1465. **3.** A house or cottage at the entrance of a park or in the grounds belonging to a mansion, occupied by a caretaker, keeper, gardener, etc.; the room or 'box' occupied by the porter of a college, a factory, etc. 1500. **4.** *gen.* A lodging, abode, esp. a temporary one; †formerly also *transf.* a place to hold something 1571. **5.** The workshop of a body of 'freemasons' (see FREEMASON 1). *Obs.* exc. *Hist.* ME. **6.** *Freemasonry*, etc. The place of meeting for members of a branch; hence, the members composing a branch; also, a meeting of a 'lodge' 1686. **7.** The residence of the head of a college at Cambridge 1769. **8.** The den or lair of an animal; now only of a beaver or an otter 1567. **9.** The tent of a N. Amer. Indian; a wigwam. Also, the number usually occupying one tent, as a unit of enumeration, reckoned at from four to six. 1805. †**10.** A collection of objects lodged close together DE FOE. **11.** †**a.** = LOGGIA –1813. **b.** = LOGE 2 (*rare*) 1730. **12.** *Mining.* A room or flat adjoining the shaft, for discharging ore, etc. 1881.

1. So to the Silvan L. They came MILT. 2. As melancholy as a L. in a Warren SHAKS. 4. [A raven's] airy l. COWPER. 6. Phr. *Grand l.*, the governing body of the freemasons (and of other societies), presided over by the grand-master. *Orange l.* (see ORANGE *sb.*[2] 2). 10. The Maldives, a famous l. of islands 1720.

Comb.: **l.-book,** a book recording the doings of a masonic l.; **-gate,** the gate of a park, etc. at which there is a l.

Lodge (lǫdʒ), *v.* ME. [– OFr. *logier* (mod. *loger*), f. *loge* LODGE *sb.*]

I. *trans.* †**1.** To place in tents or the like; to encamp, station (an army). Often *refl.* –1598. **2.** To provide with temporary quarters; to receive into one's house for the night. Also, to provide with a habitation; to place as a resident *in* a building; also in *pass.*, to be (well or ill) accommodated with regard to house-room. ME. †Also *fig.* **b.** To serve as a lodging or habitation for. Often *transf.* and *fig.* of things: To contain; in *pass.*, to be contained *in* something. 1449. **c.** To have as a lodger 1741. **3.** To place, deposit. See below. **4.** To discover the lodge of (a buck) 1576. **5.** To lay flat. Now only of wind or rain: To beat down (crops). 1593.

2. Be not forgetfull to l. straungers COVERDALE *Heb.* 13:2. You l. your horses more magnificently than yourself LYTTON. *fig. Rich. III*, II. i. 65. **b.** The Memory [can] l. a greater store of Images, than all the Senses can present at one time CHEYNE. 3. **a.** To put and leave in a place of custody or security 1666. To l. [a person] in..a state prison MAR. EDGEWORTH, money in the hands of a banker 1882. **b.** To deposit in court or with an official a formal statement of (an information, complaint, objection, etc.). Hence, *pop.*, to allege (an objection). 1708. The impeachment which the king had lodged against him HUME. **c.** To vest, cause to reside, *in* a person or thing, place (power, etc.) *with* or *in the hands of* a person 1670. The power of the Crown is always lodged in a single person HUME. **d.** To get (a thing) into the intended place 1611. Wounded..By a bullet lodged in the thorax SHERIDAN. **e.** To throw (something) so that it is caught in its fall; to cause to 'lodge' or be intercepted; (of a current, etc.) to deposit in passing 1606. To l. sand, clay, etc. in a crate filled with stone 1808. †**f.** To set or fasten in a socket or the like –1825. 4. The deer is lodg'd. I've track'd her to her covert ADDISON.

II. *intr.* †**1.** To encamp –1603. **2.** To dwell temporarily in a place; *esp.* to pass the night. Now *rare.* ME. **b.** To dwell, reside. Later, chiefly *transf.* and *fig.* of a thing = to have its seat, reside. Now *rare.* ME. **c.** *spec.* To be a lodger, to live in lodgings 1749. **3.** To be arrested in fall or progress; to stick in a position 1611. **4.** *Hunting.* Of a buck: *intr.* To betake himself to his lodge or lair. Also quasi-*pass.*, to be in his lodge. 1470. **5.** Of corn: = *to be lodged* (see sense I. 5) 1630.

2. He lodged in the cottage of a peasant GIBBON. **b.** Sure something holy lodges in that brest MILT. *Comus* 246. 3. The ball lodged in the shoulder LYTTON. 5. As corn lodgeth by too great abundance 1630. Hence **Lo·dgeable** *a.* that may be lodged in; that may or can be lodged.

Lodged (lǫdʒd), *ppl. a.* 1580. [f. prec. + -ED[1].] In senses of LODGE *v.* 1596. **b.** *Her.* Of a buck, hart, etc.: Represented as lying on the ground.

b. Arms.—Sable, a buck l. Argent 1580.

Lodgement, lodgment (lǫ·dʒměnt). 1598. [– (O)Fr. *logement*, f. *loger*; see LODGE *v.*, -MENT.] **1.** A place or building in which persons or things are lodged; a place of shelter or protection; in early use *Mil.*, quarters for soldiers. ? Now *rare* or *Obs.* **b.** A lodging-place; a lodging-house; lodgings. Now *rare.* 1703. **c.** *Gunnery.* 'The hollow or cavity in the under part of the bore, where the shot rests when rammed home' (Voyle) 1872. **2.** *Mil.* A temporary defensive work made on a captured portion of the enemy's fortifications 1677. **3. a.** The action of making good a position on an enemy's ground, or obtaining a foothold; hence, a stable position gained, a foothold. Also *transf.* and *fig.* 1702. **b.** The action of depositing (money, securities, etc.); *concr.* a deposit of money. Now only *legal.* 1760. **c.** The lodging of a thing or the accumulation of matter intercepted in fall or transit; *concr.* a mass of matter so lodged 1739. **4.** Accommodation in a lodging-place; provision of lodgings; lodging (*rare*) 1805.

3. a. Phr. *To make* or *find a lodgement.* My friend, who had found a lodgment upon the edge of a rock TYNDALL. **b.** A decree for..lodgment in Court of a sum [etc.] 1884. **c.** Some [rain] finding lodgment in little hollows of the rock HUXLEY.

Lodger (lǫ·dʒəɹ). ME. [f. LODGE *v.* + -ER¹.] One who, or that which, lodges. **b.** *esp.* One who occupies hired rooms in another person's house 1596.

attrib. **l.-franchise,** a right to vote conferred by statute upon persons occupying lodgings.

Lodging (lǫ·dʒiŋ), *vbl. sb.* ME. [f. LODGE *v.* + -ING¹.] **1.** The action of LODGE *v.* 1480. †**2.** Dwelling, abode –1611. **3.** Accommodation for rest at night or for residence; now only, accommodation in hired rooms or in a lodging-house ME. †**b.** Material to lie or sleep upon –1691. **4.** *concr.* A dwelling-place, abode; †military quarters, encampment. (In sense of 'hired rooms', the pl. *lodgings* is now usual.) ME. Also *transf.* and *fig.* †**b.** *Hunting.* The lair of a buck, stag, etc. –1610. **5.** Specialized uses of the *plural.* See below. 1475.

2. They haue taken vp their l. at Geba *Isa.* 10:29. **3.** My l. it is on the Cold ground DAVENANT. Phr. *Board and l.* **4.** He lives in a L. of Ten Shillings a Week STEELE. *fig.* Christians..acknowledged their Bodies to be the L. of Christ SIR T. BROWNE. **5.** †**a.** Military quarters –1677. Very cold Lodgings, hard Marches, Scarcity of Provisions 1677. **b.** A room or rooms hired for residence in the house of another (*now,* not in an inn or hotel) 1640. Wits take lodgings in the sound of Bow POPE. **c.** An official residence 1661. The Provost's Lodgings (Queen's College, Oxford) 1827. *Judges' lodgings*: the house occupied by the judges (in some assize towns) during the assizes.

Comb.: **l.-house,** †(*a*) a dwelling-house; (*b*) a house, other than an inn or hotel, in which lodgings are let 1766; also *transf.* and *fig.*; **-money,** an allowance made by government to all officers and soldiers for whom there is no room in barracks (Voyle); **-room,** a sleeping apartment, bedroom (now *local*).

Lodicule (lǫ·dikiul). 1864. [– L. *lodicula,* dim. of *lodix, lodic-* coverlet; see -CULE.] *Bot.* The hypogynous scale of a grass.

Loess (lōᵘ·es, Ger. lös). Also **löss,** *erron.* **loëss.** 1833. [– G. *löss,* f. Swiss G. *lösch* 'loose', f. *lösen* loosen.] *Geol.* A deposit of fine yellowish-grey loam found in the Rhine and other river valleys.

Lof, Loff(e, obs. f. LUFF, LAUGH.

Loft (lǫ̆ft), *sb.* [Late OE. *loft* – ON. *lopt* (pronounced loft) air, upper room, balcony; see LIFT *sb.*¹] †**1.** Air, sky, upper region –1590. **2.** An upper chamber, an attic; any apartment ME. **b.** The apartment over a stable. (Cf. HAYLOFT.) 1530. **c.** A pigeon-house. Hence, a flock (of pigeons). 1735. **3.** A gallery in a church or public room. (Cf. *organ-, rood-l.*) 1504. **4.** A floor or story in a house 1465. *Obs.* exc. *U.S.* One of the upper floors of a warehouse or business building 1890. †**5.** A layer, stage, stratum. Also *transf.* of the lateral branches of trees. –1686. **6.** *Golf.* In the head of a club: Slope backward from the vertical. Also, the action of lofting; a lofting stroke. 1887.

1. Phr. †*On, upon (the) l.*: (*a*) = ALOFT; (*b*) in a high voice, loudly. **2.** I preached at five in a large l. WESLEY. **5.** And hills of Snow and lofts of piled Thunder MILT. *Comb.* **l.-dried** *adj.*

†**Loft,** *a. rare.* ME. [app. deduced from ALOFT, as LIVE *a.* from *alive.*] Elated, elevated –1590.

Loft (lǫ̆ft), *v.* 1518. [f. LOFT *sb.*] **1.** *trans.* †To insert a layer of planks in (a building) so as to separate the lofts or stories –1646. Also, to furnish with an upper story or loft. †**2.** To store in a loft –1785. **3.** *Golf.* To hit (a ball) into the air so as to clear an obstacle; to hit the ball over (an obstacle). 1857. Hence **Lo·fter,** a club for lofting the ball.

3. If there is a high face to l. 1887.

Lo·fting, *vbl. sb.* 1537. [f. LOFT *sb.* or *v.* + -ING¹.] A roofing, ceiling, or flooring.

Lofty (lǫ̆·fti), *a.* ME. [f. LOFT *sb.* (in *on loft, aloft*) + -Y¹.] **1.** Of imposing altitude, towering (not said of persons); soaring 1590. **2.** *fig.*, etc. **a.** Haughty, overweening, proud 1485. **b.** Exalted in rank, character, quality. Of aims, desires, etc.: Directed to high objects 1548. **c.** Of compositions, etc. (hence of writers or speakers): Elevated in style or sentiment 1565. **d.** Of majestic sound 1596.

1. Vpon a loftie and high mountaine hast thou set thy bed *Isa.* 57:7. Of loftiest stature COWPER. Birds of l. Wing WESLEY. **2. a.** The eyes of the loftie shall be humbled *Isa.* 5:15. Inclined to treat everybody..with a sort of l. good humour BLACK. **b.** The High and loftie One that inhabiteth eternitie *Isa.* 57:15. **c.** He knew Himself to sing, and build the l. rhyme MILT. **d.** Sound all the l. Instruments of Warre SHAKS. Hence **Lo·ftily** *adv.* **Lo·ftiness.**

Log (lǫg), *sb.*¹ [First recorded in Trevisa (1398), but cf. AL. *loggiare* cut into logs (1205), *loggum* log (1306); of unkn. origin.]

I. *gen.* **1.** A bulky mass of wood; now usu. an unhewn portion of a felled tree, or a length cut off for firewood. **b.** *fig.* 1579. **c.** *Mining.* A balance weight, placed near the end of the pit-rope, to prevent its running back over the pulley 1860. †**d.** In Old St. Paul's, a block or bench on which serving-men sat –1639. **2.** A heavy piece of wood, fastened to a man's or beast's leg, to impede his movements. †Also *fig.* 1589. **b.** A former military punishment. *Obs.* exc. *Hist.* 1830. **3.** *pl. Austral. slang.* A jail or lock-up. (Formerly built of logs. Cf. *log-house.*) 1888.

1. Bring in great logs and let them lie, To make a solid core of heat TENNYSON. Phr. *In the l.*: in unhewn condition. **b.** [The ship] being no other then a logge in the sea HAWKINS. To sleep like a l. 1886. Phr. *To have a log to roll*: see LOG-ROLLING. **2.** Here I am tied like a l. to you DICKENS. Phr. *King L.*: the l. which Jupiter in the fable made king over the frogs; used as the type of inertness on the part of rulers, as 'King Stork' typifies an excess of activity.

II. *Naut.*, etc. **1.** An apparatus for ascertaining the rate of a ship's motion, consisting of a thin quadrant of wood, loaded so as to float upright, and fastened to a line wound on a reel. Said also of other appliances for the same purpose. 1574. **2.** Short for LOG-BOOK 1825. **b.** *Mech.* The record of an engine, boiler, etc. in which a series of observations have been taken 1875. **c.** = LOG-BOOK 3. 1882. **3.** *Tailoring.* A document fixing the number of hours to be credited to journeymen for making each description of garment; the scale of computation embodied in this 1861.

1. During the chace we ran per l. seventy miles 1805. Phr. *To heave, throw the l.*, (*to sail* or *calculate one's way*) *by the l.*

Combs.: **l.-board,** a hinged pair of boards on which the particulars of a ship's l. are noted for transcription into the log-book; **-cabin,** a small house built of rough logs (*U.S.*); **-canoe,** one hollowed out of a single tree; **-chip** = *log-ship*; **-house,** a house built of logs; in early use (*U.S.*), a prison; **-juice** *slang,* cheap port wine; **-knot** *Naut.*, a knot made in a log-line to indicate a specified length; **-line** *Naut.*, a line of 100 fathoms or more to which the l. is attached; also the sort of line used for this purpose; **-man,** †(*a*) one employed to carry logs; (*b*) one employed in cutting and carrying logs to a mill (*local U.S.*); **-perch,** a freshwater fish, *Percina caprodes,* of N. America; **-reel,** the reel on which the log-line is wound; **-ship,** also *log-chip,* a flat piece of wood in the form of a quadrant, which is loaded so as to keep upright in the water; **-slate,** a double slate used instead of the *log-board*; **-work,** (*a*) the arrangement of logs in the walls of a building; (*b*) the keeping of a l. or log-book.

‖**Log** (lǫg, lōᵘg), *sb.*² 1530. [Heb. *lōg.*] A Hebrew measure for liquids, the twelfth part of a hin, = about ⅚ of a pint.

Log (lǫg), *v.*¹ 1622. [f. LOG *sb.*¹] **1.** *trans.* †To deprive (a tree) of branches; to cut (timber) into logs. Also *absol.* 1699. **2.** *Naut.* To enter (esp. the distance run by a ship) in the log-book; hence *gen.*, to record 1823. **b.** Of a ship: To run (a certain distance) by log-measurements 1883. **c.** To enter the name of (a man as an offender) in a log-book, with a penalty attached. Hence, to fine. 1889.

2. b. This day we logged 160 miles 1883.

Log (lǫg), *v.*² 1808. [Of unkn. origin.] *trans.* and *intr.* To rock, oscillate.

Log, abbrev. of LOGARITHM, LOGARITHMIC.

Loganberry (lōᵘ·gănbe:ri). 1900. [Named after J. H. *Logan,* of U.S.A., by whom it was first grown in 1881.] A fruit obtained by a cross between the raspberry and blackberry.

Logan-stone (lǫ·gănstōᵘn). Also **loggan-stone, logan.** 1759. [f. *logan* logging (f. LOG *v.*²) + STONE.] A rocking-stone.

Logaœdic (lǫgă,ī·dik), *a.* 1844. [– late L. *logaœdicus* – Gr. λογαοιδικός, f. λόγος speech + ἀοιδή song; see LOGOS, ODE, -IC.] *Prosody.* Composed of dactyls combined with trochees, or anapæsts with iambs. As *sb.*, a logaœdic verse.

Logarithm (lǫ·găriþ'm). 1615. [– mod.L. *lŏgarithmus* (Napier 1614), f. Gr. λόγος ratio + ἀριθμός number (cf. LOGOS, ARITHMETIC); perh. based on Gr. ἀριθμῶν λόγος ratio of numbers (Archimedes III B.C.).] *Math.* One of a class of arithmetical functions, invented by John Napier of Merchiston (died 1617), and tabulated for use in abridging calculation. Abbreviated *log* (no period).

The sum of the logarithms of any two or more numbers is the logarithm of their product; hence a table of logarithms enables one to substitute addition and subtraction for multiplication and division, and multiplication and division for involution and evolution. *Natural, hyperbolic,* or *Napierian logarithms,* those of which the base is the incommensurable quantity *e* (2·71828+), used in analytical investigations. *Common, decimal,* or *Briggsian logarithms* those invented by Henry Briggs (died 1630), of which the base is 10, used in practical calculations. *Logistic logarithms*: see LOGISTIC.

Logarithmic (lǫgări·þmik), *a.* (and *sb.*) 1698. [f. LOGARITHM + -IC.] *Math.* **1.** Of or pertaining to logarithms. Also = 'logarithm (increased by ten) of', as in *log sine, tangent, secant,* etc.; opp. to *natural.* **b.** Pertaining to the logarithmic curve 1875. **2.** *sb.* = *logarithmic curve* or *line* 1753.

1. *L. curve* (or *line*), a curve having its ordinates in geometrical progression and its abscissas in arithmetical progression, so that the abscissas are the logarithms of the corresponding ordinates. *L. spiral,* a spiral which intersects all its radiants at the same angle. So **Logari·thmical** *a.* 1631. Hence **Logari·thmically** *adv.*

Lo·g-book. 1679. **1.** *Naut.* A book in which the particulars of a ship's voyage (including her rate of progress as measured by the log) are entered daily from the log-board. Hence *transf.* and *fig.*, a journal of travel. **2.** *Tailoring.* = LOG *sb.*¹ II. 3. 1869. **3.** A kind of journal of proceedings to be kept by the master of a public elementary school 1872.

‖**Loge** (lōᵘʒ). 1749. [Fr.; see LODGE *sb.*] **1.** A booth, stall. CHESTERF. **2.** A box in a theatre or opera-house 1768.

-loger (lŏdʒəɹ), a word-ending repr. Gr. -λόγος (L. *-logus*); see -LOGUE, -LOGY. The oldest word with this ending is *astrologer* (XIV); it may be either f. L. *astrologus* + -ER¹ (a type of derivation afterwards common), or f. *astrology* + -ER¹ (cf. *astronomyer, astronomer*). On the analogy of this word, *-loger* was applied in a few instances to form personal designations correlative with words in *-logy, -logic-al,* as in *chronologer, philologer,* etc.; but it is now superseded by -LOGIST.

Lo·ggat, lo·gget. *Obs.* exc. *Hist.* 1541. [app. f. LOG *sb.*¹] **1.** An old game, played by throwing pieces of wood at a stake fixed in the ground; the player who is nearest the stake wins. **2.** A pole, heavy stake 1600.

1. *Haml.* v. i. 100. **2.** Beating of fruit downe with long poales, loggets, or such like MARKHAM.

Logged (lǫgd), *ppl. a.* 1820. [f. LOG *v.*¹ + -ED¹.] **a.** Reduced to the condition of a log (*lit.* and *fig.*). Of water: Stagnant. Of a vessel: Water-logged. **b.** Of land: Cleared by hewing the timber into logs.

Logger (lǫ·gəɹ). *N. Amer.* 1734. [f. LOG *v.*¹ + -ER¹.] One who fells timber or cuts it into logs; a lumberman.

Loggerhead (lǫ·gəɹhed). 1588. [prob. f. *logger* hobble for horses (recorded only in mod. dialects but prob. earlier), a deriv. of LOG + HEAD.] **1.** A block-head. **2.** A head out of proportion to the body; a large or 'thick' head. Chiefly *fig.* 1598. **3.** An iron instrument with a long handle and a ball or bulb at the end, used, when heated, for melting pitch, etc. 1687. **4.** A stout wooden post, built into the stern of a whale-boat, 'for catching a turn of the line to' (Smyth). Also *transf.* 1840. **5.** As pop. name of heavy-headed animals. **a.** (Also *l. turtle,* †*tortoise.*) A species of turtle, *Thalassochelys caretta* 1657. **b.** Applied to species of birds; *esp.* a N. American shrike, *Lanius ludovicianus* or *carolinensis* 1657. **6.** *pl.* A plant of the genus *Centaurea* 1829.

1. A pitifull, sneaking, whining Puritan, related to yᵉ L. at Lambeth HEARNE. '*We three* loggerheads be': an inscription under a common public-house sign, in which two wooden heads are shown, the spectator being the third. See MALONE on *Twel. N.* II. iii. 17. **2.** Let us retire, and lay our two loggerheads together RICHARDSON.

Phr. †*To fall, get, go to loggerheads*: to come to blows. *To be at loggerheads*: to be in contention about differences of opinion; also, rarely, *to come to l.*

Comb. **l.-sponge**, a W. Indian sponge of inferior quality; probably named from Loggerhead Key. Hence **Lo·gger-headed** *a.* thick-headed, stupid; (of animals) having a large head.

‖**Loggia** (lǫ·dʒiă; It. lǭ·ddʒa). *Pl.* **loggias**, It. **loggie.** 1742. [– It. *loggia*; see LODGE *sb.*] A gallery or arcade having one or more of its sides open to the air.

Logging (lǫ·giŋ), *vbl. sb.* 1706. [f. LOG *v.*¹ + -ING¹.] The action of felling timber or hewing it into logs. Also *concr.* A quantity of timber felled. Also *attrib.*

-logian (lōᵘ·dʒiăn), an ending occurring first in *astrologian* (-(*i*)*en* CHAUCER), – OFr. *astrologien*, f. *astrologie*: see -AN, -IAN, and hence in a few mod. wds. correlative to names of sciences in -LOGY. Now usu. repl. by -LOGIST.

Logic (lǫ·dʒik). ME. [– (O)Fr. *logique* – late L. *logica* – Gr. λογική (Cicero), for ἡ λογικὴ τέχνη the art of reasoning; λογική, fem. of λογικός, f. λόγος reasoning, discourse (see LOGOS).] **1.** The branch of philosophy that treats of the forms of thinking in general, and esp. of inference and scientific method. **b.** *pl.* in the same sense. Not now in general use. 1637. **c.** Name of a class in Roman Catholic schools 1705. **d.** With reference to Hegel: The fundamental science of thought and its categories (including metaphysics or ontology) 1838. **2.** A system of logic; a treatise on logic. Also, the science or art of reasoning as applied to a department of knowledge. ME. **3.** Logical argumentation; a mode of argumentation viewed as good or bad according to its conformity or want of conformity to logical principles. Also, logical pertinence or propriety. 1601. **b.** *transf.* A means of convincing or proving 1682. **4.** *attrib.* Of or pertaining to logic 1440.

1. L. may be most briefly defined as the Science of Reasoning JEVONS. **2.** The logick of taste, if I may be allowed the expression BURKE. The empirical l. of Mill, the formal l. of Kant 1882. **3.** England, as Mr. Disraeli once said, is not governed by l. 1891. To argue with more learning than l. (*mod.*). **b.** Bonner's Logick, Fire and Faggot 1682. **4.** Questions..deeper than any of our Logic-plummets hitherto will sound CARLYLE. *Comb.* †**l.-fisted** *a.*, having the hand clenched, like L. in personification (see Bacon *Adv. Learn.* II. xviii § 5).

-logic (lǫ·dʒik), **-logical** (lǫ·dʒikăl), endings orig. repr. Gr. -λογικός in adjs. derived from adjs. and sbs. in -λογος, -λογον, having derivative nouns in -λογία, Eng. -LOGY. Such adjs. are commonly apprehended as if f. *-logy* + -IC. Hence, with few exceptions (e.g. *apology*), a sb. in *-logy* now implies a possible correlative adj. in *-logical*. See further -ICAL, and cf. GEOLOGIC.

Logical (lǫ·dʒikăl), *a.* (and *sb.*) 1500. [– med.L. *logicalis* – late and med.L. *logica* LOGIC; see -AL¹.] **1.** Of or pertaining to logic; also, of the nature of formal argument. **2.** That is in conformity with the laws of correct reasoning 1689. **3.** That follows as a reasonable inference; that is in accordance with the logic of events, of human character, etc. 1860. **4.** Of persons: Capable of reasoning correctly; also, reasoning correctly (in a particular case) 1664. **5.** *nonce-use.* Rational 1652. **6.** *sb. pl.* The subjects which are studied in a course of instruction in logic. *Obs.* exc. *Hist.* 1551.

1. L. Demonstrations 1707, writers WHATELY, generalizations 1851. **2.** A process of l. reasoning D. STEWART. **3.** In France accordingly feudal government runs its l. career STUBBS. **4.** A clear and L. Head ADDISON. **6.** *Little* or *small logicals*: certain minor questions treated in the *Parva Logicalia* of Petrus Hispanus and others. Hence **Logica·lity. Lo·gically** *adv.*

Logician (lǒdʒi·ʃăn). ME. [– (O)Fr. *logicien*, f. *logique*; see LOGIC, -ICIAN.] **1.** A writer on logic; a student of logic. **b.** A member of the school class called Logic 1705. **2.** One skilled in reasoning 1592. So †**Logi·cianer** 1548.

Logicize (lǫ·dʒisəiz), *v. rare.* 1835. [f. LOGIC + -IZE, after *criticize*.] **1.** *intr.* To employ logic. **2.** *trans.* To turn into logic 1865.

Logie (lōᵘ·gi). 1860. [f. name of XIX inventor, David *Logie*.] *Theatr.* Ornament of zinc to simulate jewellery.

‖**Logion** (lǫ·giǫn). *Pl.* **logia** (lǫ·giă). 1875. [Gr. λόγιον oracle, f. λόγος word. Cf. late L. *logion, logium* oracle.] A traditional maxim of a religious teacher or sage. Chiefly used with reference to sayings of Jesus not recorded in the Gospels.

-logist (lǒdʒist), f. -LOGY + -IST, forming sbs. 'one who is versed in —logy'. The only living formative with this function.

Logistic (lodʒi·stik). 1628. [– late L. *logisticus* – Gr. λογιστικός, f. λογίζεσθαι reckon, f. λόγος calculation; see LOGOS, -ISTIC.]

A. *adj.* †**1.** ? Pertaining to reasoning –1644. **2.** Pertaining to reckoning or calculation 1706. **3.** *Math.* **a.** In *l. curve*, etc. = logarithmic. **b.** *L. logarithms*: logarithms of sexagesimal numbers, used in astronomical calculations. **c.** *L. numbers*: old name for ratios or fractions. 1727. So **Logi·stical** *a.* 1570.

B. *sb.* †**1.** A calculator. W. ROBINSON. **2.** *Math.* A logistic curve 1727. **3.** *pl.* (rarely *sing.*) **a.** The art of arithmetical calculation; the elementary processes of arithmetic 1656. **b.** Logistical or sexagesimal arithmetic 1801.

Logistics, *sb. pl.*¹: see LOGISTIC B. 3.

Logistics (lodʒi·stiks), *sb. pl.*² 1879. [– Fr. *logistique*, f. *loger* quarter, LODGE; see -ICS.] The art of moving and quartering troops (i.e. quarter-master's work), now esp. of organizing supplies.

Logocracy (lǒgǫ·krăsi). 1804. [f. Gr. λόγος word + -CRACY.] A community or system of government in which words are the ruling powers.

†‖**Logodæ·dalus.** *Pl.* **-i.** Also **logodædale.** 1611. [mod.L. – Gr. λογοδαίδαλος, f. λόγος word + δαίδαλος cunning.] One who is cunning in words –1664. So **Logodæ·dalist** 1654. **Logodæ·daly** (*rare*), cunning in words.

Logogram (lǫ·gǒgræm). 1820. [f. Gr. λόγος word + -GRAM.] **1.** = LOGOGRIPH. **2.** A sign or character representing a word; in *Phonography*, a word-letter; a single stroke which represents a word 1840.

Logograph (lǫ·gǒgrɑf), *sb.* 1797. [f. as prec. + -GRAPH.] ¶**1.** Used erron. for LOGOGRIPH. **2.** *Phonography.* = LOGOGRAM 2. 1888. **3.** = LOGOTYPE 1872. **4.** = LOGOGRAPHER 2. 1862. **5.** An instrument for giving a graphic representation of speech-sounds 1879. Hence **Lo·gograph** *v. trans.* to print with logotypes.

Logographer (lǒgǫ·grăfəɹ). 1656. [f. late L. *logographus* accountant – Gr. λογογράφος prose-writer, f. λόγος word; see -GRAPHER.] †**1.** A lawyer's clerk; an accountant–1735. **2.** *Gr. Antiq.* A writer of traditional history in prose 1846. **3.** *Gr. Antiq.* A professional speech-writer 1853. **4.** One who practises logography 1860.

Logography (lǒgǫ·grăfi). 1783. [f. *logo-*, comb. form of Gr. λόγος word + -GRAPHY.] **1.** A method of printing with entire words, instead of single letters. **2.** A method of longhand reporting in which several reporters were employed, each taking down a few words in succession 1842. Hence **Logogra·phic, -al** *a.* pertaining to l. (sense 1); consisting of characters or signs, each of which represents an entire word. **Logogra·phically** *adv.*

Logogriph (lǫ·gǒgrif). 1597. [– Fr. *logogriphe*, f. Gr. λόγος word + γρῖφος fishing-basket, riddle.] A kind of enigma, in which a certain word, and other words that can be formed out of all or any of its letters, are to be guessed from synonyms of them introduced into a set of verses. Occas.: Any anagram or puzzle involving anagrams. Hence **Logogri·phic** *a.* of or pertaining to logogriphs, of the nature of a l.

Logomachy (lǒgǫ·măki). 1569. [– Gr. λογομαχία, f. λόγος word; see -MACHY.] **1.** Contention about words; an instance of this. **2.** ? *U.S.* A game of word-making (Webster).

1. This quarrel tending to vain logomachies.. ended in confusion SEWEL. **Lo·gomach, Logoma·chic, -ical** *a.*, **Logo·machist, Logo·machize** *v.*

Logometric (lǫgǒme·trik), *a.* 1813. [f. Gr. λόγος ratio + μέτρον measure + -IC.] Indicating ratios by measurement. Applied by Wollaston to his 'scale' for chemical equivalents.

‖**Logos** (lǫ·gǫs). 1587. [Gr. λόγος account, ratio, reason, argument, discourse, saying, (rarely) word, rel. to λέγειν gather, choose, recount, say.] A term used by Hellenistic and Neo-platonist philosophers in certain senses developed from its ordinary senses 'reason' and 'word'; in the N.T. rendered 'Word', as a designation of Jesus Christ; hence used by Christian theologians for the Second Person of the Trinity. By mod. writers used untranslated, esp. in discussions of the doctrine of the Trinity in its philosophical aspects.

Logothete (lǫ·gǒþīt). 1781. [– med.L. *logotheta* or its source Gr. λογοθέτης auditor, f. λόγος account; cf. NOMOTHETE.] Any of various functionaries under the Byzantine emperors; also a chancellor, esp. in Sicily.

Logotype (lǫ·gǒtəip). 1816. [f. Gr. λόγος word + TYPE.] *Printing.* A type containing a word, or two or more letters, cast in one piece. Hence **Lo·gotypy** = LOGOGRAPHY 1.

Lo·g-roll, *v.* 1835. [Back-formation from LOG-ROLLING.] **a.** *trans.* To procure the passing of (a bill) by log-rolling. **b.** *intr.* To engage in log-rolling.

The leading politicians who..log-roll the railway bills 1865. **b.** To log-roll with everybody who was willing to work with him 1879.

Lo·g-ro:ller. 1864. [f. LOG *sb.*¹ + ROLLER.] **1.** One who engages in political or literary log-rolling. **2.** *U.S.* A sawmill device for loading logs 1884.

Lo·g-ro:lling. 1823. [f. LOG *sb.*¹ + ROLLING *vbl. sb.*] **1.** *U.S.* The action of rolling logs to any spot; a meeting for co-operation in doing this 1848. **2.** *U.S. slang.* Combination for political or other co-operation. (Suggested by the phr. 'You roll my log and I'll roll yours'.) 1823. **b.** Mutual puffing in literary publications ? 1845.

2. Our log-rolling, our stumps and their politics.. are yet unsung EMERSON.

-logue (lǫg), repr. Gr. -λογος, -λογον in adapted wds. (mostly through Fr.), as *analogue, catalogue, dialogue*. The wds. with this ending which designate persons, e.g. *Assyriologue, ideologue*, are now little used, derivs. in *-loger, -logist*, or *-logian* being preferred.

Logwood (lǫ·gwud). 1581. [f. LOG *sb.*¹ + WOOD.] †**1.** Logs stored for fuel. PEPYS. **2.** The heartwood of an American tree (*Hæmatoxylon campechianum*); so called because imported in logs; also, the dye or drug extracted from this 1581. **b.** The tree itself 1652. **3.** *attrib.*, as *l. red* 1752.

Logy (lōᵘ·gi), *a. U.S.* 1859. [Of unkn. origin. Cf. Du. *log* heavy, dull.] Dull and heavy in motion or thought. **b.** as *sb.*: A heavy fish. R. KIPLING.

-logy (lǒdʒi), earlier *-logie*, an ending occurring orig. in wds. adapted from Gr. words in -λογία (the earliest, e.g. *theology*, through Fr. *-logie*, med.L. *-logia*). In some instances the terminal element is λόγος word, discourse (e.g. in τετραλογία tetralogy, τριλογία trilogy); more commonly it is the root λογ- (ablaut-var. of λεγ-, λέγειν to speak; cf. LOGOS). In this latter case, the sbs. in -λογία usually denote the character, action, or department of knowledge of a person described by an adj. or sb. in -λόγος, meaning either '(one) who speaks (in a certain way)', or '(one) who treats of (a certain subject)'. Hence (1) wds. anglicized as *brachylogy, cacology, eulogy, tautology*, etc.; and (2) names of sciences or departments of study, e.g. *theology, astrology*, etc. Words of the last-mentioned class, in which the first element is always a sb., have *o* for their combining vowel, following the Gr. analogy; exceptions are *petralogy* and *mineralogy*. All mod. formations in *-logy* may imply correlative formations in -LOGICAL and -LOGIST (or in the case of some of the older wds. -LOGER or -LOGIAN).

Lohoch (lōᵘ·hǫk). 1544. Also †**loch,** dial. **loach.** [– med.L. *lohoc* – Arab. *laʻūḳ*, f. *laʻiḳa* lick.] *Med.* A linctus.

Loin (loin). ME. [– OFr. *loigne*, eastern var. of *longe* (in mod. Fr., loin of veal) :– Rom. **lumbia*, fem. of **lumbeus* LUMBAR, f. L. *lumbus* loin.] **1.** Chiefly *pl.* The part or parts of a human being or quadruped, situated on both sides of the vertebral column, between the false ribs and the hip-bone. **b.** As food; chiefly, the joint of meat which includes the vertebræ of the loins ME. **2.** Chiefly *Biblical* and *poet.* This part of the body, **a.** as that about which the clothes are bound 1526. **b.** as the seat of strength and generative power. †Hence occas. = 'sire', 'offspring', 'descendants'. Also *fig.* 1535.

2. a. Phr. *To gird (up) the loins* (lit. and fig.), to prepare for strenuous exertion. **b.** Loe now, his strength is in his loynes *Job* 40:16. A multitude, like which the populous North Pour'd never from her frozen loyns MILT. *attrib.* **l.-cloth** 1859.

Loir (loiᵊɹ). 1774. [– (O)Fr. *loir* :– pop.L. **lēr-* (*lerus* in glosses), for L. *glīs, glīr-* dormouse.] The Fat Dormouse (*Myoxus glis.*)

Loiter (loi·təɹ), *v.* [Late ME. *lotere* (XIV), *loytre* (XV), later *leut(e)re* (XVI); perh. introduced by vagrants from the Low Countries, and – MDu. *loteren* wag about, Du. *leuteren* shake, totter, dawdle (*oi* repr. Du. *ö*), f. base repr. also in MDu. *lutsen* wag about. Cf. G. *lottern.*] **1.** *intr.* To idle. Now only: To linger indolently on one's way; to hang idly about a place; to dawdle over a task. **b.** To travel indolently and with frequent pauses. With advs. or advb. phrases. 1728. **2.** *trans.* **a.** To allow (time, etc.) to pass idly. Const. *away.* †**b.** To postpone getting or giving 1549.

1. Sir John, you loyter heere too long SHAKS. Officers..loitered in the hall, as if waiting for orders SCOTT. **b.** The Avon loiters past the churchyard HAWTHORNE. **2.** We loitered away the rest of the day 1903. Hence **Loi·terer,** one who loiters; †a vagabond. **Loi·teringly** *adv.*

Loke (lōᵘk). *dial.* 1787. [repr. OE. *loca*, f. root of *lūcan* (pa. pple. *locen*) to lock; see LOCK *sb.*²] A lane; a 'cul-de-sac'; a grass road; a private lane or road.

Loll (lǫl), *sb.* 1582. [f. LOLL *v.*] **1.** The action or posture of lolling 1709. **2.** One who or that which lolls, e.g. a tongue 1582. **3.** A pet, a spoilt child 1728.

Loll (lǫl), *v.* ME. [Symbolic; perh. f. a base ult. identical with that of LILL *v.*; the orig. meaning may have been 'allow to hang loose'.] **1.** *intr.* To hang down loosely; to droop, dangle. Also with *down. Obs.* or *arch.* †**2.** *trans.* To let droop or dangle –1650. **3.** To thrust, hang *out* (the tongue) 1611. **b.** *intr.* for *refl.* Of the tongue: To protrude. Usu. with *out.* 1801. **4.** *intr.* To lean idly; to recline or rest in a relaxed attitude, resting against something. Also with *about, back, out.* (The chief current sense.) ME. **b.** *trans.* To allow to rest idly (*rare*). Also, to pass *away* (time) in lolling about. 1696. †**5.** *intr.* To saunter (*rare*) –1678.

1. A great white feather lolling down 1849. **3.** Fierce Tigers couch'd around, and loll'd their fawning Tongues. DRYDEN. **4.** And, among the rest, Duncomb, lolling, with his heels upon another chair PEPYS. Hence **Lo·ller**¹. **Lo·llingly** *adv.*

Lollard (lǫ·lăɹd). Now *Hist.* ME. [– MDu. *lollaerd*, lit. 'mumbler, mutterer', f. *lollen* mumble; see -ARD.] **1.** A name of contempt given in the 14th c. to certain heretics, who were either followers of Wyclif or held opinions similar to his. ¶**2.** [Assoc. w. LOLL *v.*] One who lolls; an idler. *Obs. rare.* –1659.

1. *attrib.* Jack Sharp, l. rebel, was a weaver of Abingdon 1897. **2.** A pulpited divine..a l. indeed over his elbow-cushion MILT. Hence **Lo·llardist. Lo·llardism,** the tenets and practice of the Lollards. **Lo·llardry** (now *rare*), **Lo·llardy** *sbs.*, the tenets of the Lollards. **Lo·llardy** *a.* characteristic of the Lollards. var. †**Lo·ller**².

Lollipop (lǫ·lipǫp). *colloq.* 1796. [perh. f. dial. *lolly* tongue + POP.] **a.** *dial.* A kind of sweetmeat, consisting chiefly of sugar or treacle, that dissolves easily in the mouth. **b.** *pl.* (formerly also *collect. sing.*) Sweet-meats in general. Also shortened **Lo·lly** *Austral.* and *dial.*

Lollop (lǫ·ləp), *v. colloq.* 1745. [prob. f. LOLL, by assoc. with TROLLOP.] **1.** *intr.* To lounge or sprawl; to go with a lounging gait. **2.** To bob up and down 1851. Hence **Lo·llop** *sb.* 1834.

2. To l. about in the trough of a heavy sea 1878.

Loll-shraub (lǫl,ʃrǭb). Also **-shrob.** 1816. ['Englishman's Hindustani *lāl-shrāb* red wine' (Yule).] 'The universal name for claret in India' (Yule).

Lombard (lǫ·mbăɹd, lɒ·mbăɹd), *sb.*¹ and *a.* ME. [– MDu., MLG. *lombaerd* or Fr. *lombard* – It. *lombardo* (med.L. *lombardus*), repr. med.L. *Lango-, Longobardus,* L. *langobardi* (Tacitus) – Gmc. **Laŋʒobarðaz, -on* (OE. pl. *Langbeardas, -an,* ON. *Langbarðar*), f. **laŋʒa-* LONG *a.* + ethnic name *Bardi.*] **A.** *sb.* **1. a.** *Hist.* A person belonging to the Germanic people (L. *Langobardi*) who conquered Italy in the 6th c., whence the name of Lombardy. **b.** A native of Lombardy. 1480. †**2.** A native of Lombardy engaged as a banker, money-changer, or pawnbroker; hence *gen.* a banker, pawnbroker, etc. –1709. †**3.** A bank, money-changer's or money-lender's office; a pawnshop –1799.

2. They are fallen to the L., left at the Brokers GREENE. **3.** No sooner got I coine..But to the bancke or lumbard straight it went MARKHAM.

B. *adj.* **1.** Belonging to the Lombards or to Lombardy; Lombardic 1500. †**2.** *Cookery.* In **l. pie** (see LUMBER-PIE).

Hence †**Lombardee·r,** 'an usurer or broaker' (Blount); **Lombarde·sque** *a.*, resembling the L. school of painters; **Lo·mbardism,** a Lombardic idiom; **Lomba·rdo-,** comb. form with sense 'Lombardic combined with..'.

Lombard (lǫ·mbăɹd), *sb.*² *Hist.* 1838. [– obs. Sp. *lombarda.* Cf. late Gr. λουμπάρδα, app. synonymous with βουμβάρδα BOMBARD.] A military engine used in Spain in the 16th c.

Lombardic (lǫmbā·ɹdik), *a.* 1697. [f. LOMBARD *sb.*¹ + -IC.] Pertaining to Lombardy or the Lombards. Applied *spec.* to the architecture of northern Italy from the 7th to the 13th century; to a type of handwriting found in Italian MSS. during the same period; and to the school of painters, including Leonardo da Vinci, Mantegna, and Luini, which flourished in Lombardy during the 15th and 16th centuries. **b.** *absol.* Lombardic writing 1893.

Lo·mbard-street. 1598. Name of a street in London, orig. occupied by Lombard bankers, and still containing many banks. *fig.* The 'money market'; the body of financiers.

'It is Lombard Street to a China orange', quoth Uncle Jack LYTTON.

Loment (lōᵘ·ment). ME. [– L. *lomentum* bean-meal (orig. a wash made of bean-meal), f. *lo-, lavare* to wash.] †**1.** Bean-meal. Only ME. **2.** *Bot.* = LOMENTUM 1814.

‖**Lomentum** (lome·ntǒm). *Pl.* **-ta.** 1836. [L.; see prec.] A legume which is contracted in the spaces between the seeds, breaking up when mature into one-seeded joints. Hence **Lomenta·ceous** *a.* of the nature of or resembling a l.; characterized by lomenta; belonging to the N.O. *Lomentaceæ*, a former sub-order of *Cruciferæ.*

Lomonite, early var. LAUMONTITE.

Lond(e, obs. f. LAND.

London (lɒ·ndən), name of the capital of England, used *attrib.*:

L. clay, a geological formation belonging to the lower division of the Eocene tertiary, in the south-east of England and esp. at and near London; **L. particular** *colloq.*, a L. fog; **L. paste,** a caustic composed of equal parts of quicklime and caustic soda mixed with alcohol; **L. rocket,** the plant *Sisymbrium irio*, which sprang up abundantly on the ruins of the great fire of London in 1666.

Hence **Lo·ndoner,** a native (or inhabitant) of London 1460; †a ship belonging to London 1764. **Lo·ndonism,** a habit, manner, or peculiarity of speech belonging to Londoners 1803. **Lo·ndonize** *v. trans.* to make like London or Londoners 1778; *intr.* to visit or frequent London LAMB.

Lo·ndon pri·de. 1629. **a.** The Sweet William, *Dianthus barbatus.* Now *dial.* **b.** *Lychnis chalcedonica.* Now *dial.* 1688. **c.** *Saxifraga umbrosa,* having pretty pink flowers on long stalks, commonly grown in towns; also called *none-so-pretty.*

Lone (lōᵘn), *a.* 1530. [aphet. f. ALONE.] **1.** Having no companions; solitary. Chiefly *poet.* and *rhet.* **b.** Lonesome 1839. **2.** Unmarried; single or widowed. Now only of women, with mock-pathetic reference to sense 1. 1548. **3.** Standing apart from others of its kind; isolated. Formerly *esp.* in phr. *l. house.* 1667. **4.** *poet.* Of places: Lonely; unfrequented, uninhabited 1712.

1. As some l. miser, visiting his store GOLDSM. Phr. *To play, hold a l. hand*: in Quadrille and Euchre, to play against all the other players, or without help from one's partner. Hence *l. hand, l. player* = a person playing such a game. **2.** Queen Elizabeth being a l. woman, and having few friends, refusing to marry 1642. **3.** At some l. ale-house in the Berkshire moors M. ARNOLD. **4.** In l. Glenartney's hazel shade SCOTT. Hence **Lo·neness** (now *rare* or *dial.*).

Lonely (lōᵘ·nli), *a.* 1607. [f. LONE *a.* + -LY¹.] **1.** Having no companionship; solitary, lone. **2.** *poet.* = LONE 3. 1632. **3.** = LONE 4. 1629. **4.** Dejected at the consciousness of being alone; having a feeling of solitariness 1811. **b.** *poet.* Imparting a feeling of loneliness; dreary 1813.

1. To give due light To the misled and l. Travailer MILT. *Comus* 200. **2.** That l. tree against the western sky M. ARNOLD. **3.** An isle..the loneliest in a l. sea TENNYSON. Hence **Lo·nelihood** (*poet.*), loneliness. **Lo·nelily** *adv.* **Lo·neliness.**

Lonesome (lōᵘ·nsǒm), *a.* 1647. [f. LONE *a.* + -SOME¹.] **1.** Of persons, etc.: Solitary, lonely. In later use: Feeling lonely or forlorn. **b.** *By* (or *on*) *one's lonesome*, all alone 1908. **2.** Of localities: Solitary, unfrequented, desolate; also, making one feel forlorn 1647.

1. The l. Bittern shall possess This fenny seat BLACKMORE. You must..not be l. because I'm not at home DICKENS. **2.** Like one that on a l. road Doth walk in fear and dread COLERIDGE. Hence **Lo·nesome-ly** *adv.*, **-ness.**

Long (lǫŋ), *a.*¹ and *sb.* [OE. *lang, long* = OFris., OS. *lang, long,* OHG. *lang* (Du., G. *lang*), ON. *langr,* Goth. *laggs* :– Gmc. **laŋʒaz.*]

A. *adj.* **I.** With reference to spatial measurement. **1.** Great in measurement from end to end. Opp. to *short.* **b.** Tall. Now *rare* exc. *joc.* OE. **c.** Qualifying a sb. denoting a measure of length, to indicate an extent greater than that expressed by the sb. 1619. **d.** Of action, vision, etc.: Extending to a great distance. (Cf. *l. sight*, below.) 1604. **2.** Having (more or less, or a specified) extension from end to end; often with adv. or advb. phr. OE. **3.** Elongated 1551.

1. A l. and large difference CHAUCER. The l. low line of the Dutch coast 1893. A l. distance, journey 1903. Phr. *L. arm, hand*: used *transf.* and *fig.* of extent of reach; The l. arm of coincidence 1899. *A l. face* (colloq.): a dismal or solemn expression 1786. *A l. head*: one of more than normal length from back to front; *fig.* capacity for calculation and forethought. *To make a l. nose* (slang): to put the thumb to the nose in mockery. *A l. tongue* (fig.): loquacity. *L. litter*: long straw, etc. serving as bedding. *L. forage*: straw and green fodder, as dist. from hay, oats, etc. *A l. drink* (colloq.): *lit.* of liquor in a l. glass; hence, a large measure of liquor. **c.** A l. mile from Launceston 1697. **d.** Phr. *At l. weapons*: (fighting) at long range. So, *at l. bowls* or *balls*: said of ships exchanging shots at a distance. *L. train* = *l. distance train.* **2.** A mark 30 feet long by 20. 1854. Phr. *It's as l. as it's broad* (see BROAD *a.*). **3.** Phr. *L. square*: an oblong rectangle. *L. in the* TOOTH.

II. With reference to serial extent or duration. **1.** Of a series, enumeration, speech, sentence, word, etc.: Having a great extent from beginning to end OE. **b.** *colloq.* Of numbers, and of things numbered: Large. Chiefly in *l. family, odds, price.* 1746. **2.** Of a period of time, or a process, state, or action viewed with reference to time: Having a great extent in duration OE. **3.** Having (more or less, or a specified) extension serially or temporally ME. **4.** Continuing too long; lengthy, prolix, tedious ME. **5.** Qualifying a sb. denoting a period of time, a number, or quantity, to indicate an extent greater than that expressed by the sb.; also, to indicate that the time is felt by the speaker to be excessive or unusual in duration 1592. **6.** That has continued or will continue in action, operation, or obligation for a long period. Freq. applied to feelings, dispositions, etc.;

hence also, to persons exhibiting these. ME. **7.** Of a point of time: Distant, remote. Now only in *l. date*, and in the legal phr. *a l. day*. ME. **b.** Of bills, promissory notes, etc.: Of long date, having a long time to run 1861. **8.** *Phonetics* and *Prosody*. Applied to a vowel (now also to a cons.) when its utterance has the greater of the two measures of duration recognized in speech-sounds. Also, in *Prosody*, of a syllable: Occupying a longer time (e.g. two time-units) in utterance than a *short* syllable. OE. **9.** *Comm.* Said of the market (e.g. in cotton) when consumers have made large contracts in advance against an anticipated scarcity 1859.

1. Phr. *L. bill*: one containing many items; hence, one in which the charges are excessive. *L. hour*: one indicated by many strokes; Before the l. hour of midnight all was hush 1827. **b.** Phr. *L. suit* (in Card games): one in which more than three cards are held; *fig.* (*colloq.*), a thing at which one excels. **2.** Enjoy..Short pleasures, for l. woes are to succeed MILT. *L. of life* = 'of l. life' (now *rare*). *L. time, while*, etc.: often used advb. (now, exc. *poet.*, always with *a*) = LONG *adv.* 1. *This l. time* or *while*: for a l. time down to the present. Similarly with preceding prep., *for, of* (*arch.* or *dial.*); now always with *a*. I have not seen him for a long time (*mod.*). **3.** *Mids. N.* v. i. 61. **4.** I cou'd be l. in Precepts DRYDEN. Phr. †*It were (too) l. to*, etc. *To think l.* (chiefly *Sc.*): to grow weary or impatient; Haue I thought l. to see this mornings face, And doth it giue me such a sight as this? SHAKS. **5.** Phr. *L. years*: = 'many years'. *At (the) l. last*: see LAST *a.* II. *L. dozen, hundred*: see the sbs. **6.** A l. farewell to all my Greatnesse SHAKS. His recollections..contained some..surprises to his longest friends 1882. Phr. *L. memory*: one that remembers events for a l. period. *A l. word* (colloq.): one that indicates a l. time; 'Never' is a l. word 1883. **7. b.** Rates given for l. paper, as compared with those for bills on demand 1861. **8.** Phr. *L. mark*: the mark (¯) placed over a vowel letter to indicate l. quantity. In ordinary language 'the long *a, e, i, o, u*' denotes that sound of the letter which is used as its alphabetical name, while 'the short *a, e, i, o, u*' denotes the sound which the letter most commonly has in a stressed short syllable. O.E.D.

Comb., etc.: **l.-axed** *a.*, having a l. axis; **-bowls,** the game of ninepins; **-butt** *Billiards*, a cue for reaching a ball beyond the range of the half-butt; **l. card,** one of a suit remaining in one hand after the others of the suit are played; **l.-clothes,** the garments of a baby in arms; **-dated** *a.*, extending to a distant date; chiefly of an acceptance, falling due at a distant date; **l. division, home, jump** (see the sbs.); **l. firm** *slang*, a swindling business concern; **l. measure,** (*a*) lineal measure, the measure of length; (*b*) a table of lineal measures; (*c*) = next; **l. metre,** the metre of a hymn-stanza in iambic rhythm of four lines of eight syllables each; **l. nine** *U.S.*, a cheap cigar; **L. Parliament,** the Parliament which sat from Nov. 1640 to March 1653, and again for a short time in 1659, and was dissolved in 1660; †also, the second Parliament of Charles II (1661–1678); **l.-pig,** tr. cannibal's name for human flesh; **l. primer** *Printing* (see PRIMER); **l. service** *Mil.*, 'the maximum period a recruit can enlist for in any branch of the service, viz. for 12 years' (Voyle); **l. ship** *Hist.*, a ship of great length, built to accommodate a considerable number of rowers; a ship of war, a galley; = L. *navis longa*; **l.-shot,** (*a*) a shot fired at a distance; (*b*) a distant range; **l. sight,** power of seeing distant objects; also, the defect of sight by which only distant objects are seen distinctly; **l.-sixes,** long candles, six to the pound; **-staple** *a.* having a long fibre: applied to cotton of a superior grade; **l. stone,** a menhir; **l. sword** (see SWORD); **l.-threads,** warp; **L. Vacation,** summer vacation at the Law-Courts and Universities; **l.-wall, way,** used *attrib.* to imply a method of working in which all available coal is extracted at once; **l. wave** *Wireless*, a wave having a wave-length of (about) 800 metres and upwards; **l. whist** (see WHIST *sb.*); **-wool,** (*a*) a long-stapled wool, suitable for combing or carding; (*b*) a long-woolled sheep; **l. writ** = PREROGATIVE-*w.*

b. In names of animals, as **l.-bill,** a bird with a l. bill, *e.g.* a snipe; **l. clam,** (*a*) *Mya arenaria* (see CLAM *sb.*[2] 1 c); (*b*) the razor-clam, *Ensis americana*; **l.-horn,** (*a*) one of a breed of long-horned cattle; (*b*) the long-eared owl, *Otus vulgaris*; **-nose,** the Garfish; **-wing,** the swift.

c. In names of plants, etc., as †**l.-bean** = KIDNEY BEAN; **-flax,** flax to be spun its natural length without cutting; **-leek,** the ordinary leek (*Allium porrum*); **-pod,** a variety of broad bean which produces a very l. pod; **l. purples,** (*a*) the early purple orchis, *O. mascula* SHAKS.; (*b*) *Lythrum salicaria*; (*c*) *Vicia cracca* TENNYSON.

d. *Cricket*: **l. field (off, on),** the position of a fieldsman who stands at a distance behind the bowler, either to his left or right; **l.-hop,** a ball that makes a long flight after pitching, before reaching the wicket; **l. off, on,** short for *long field off, on*; **l.-stop,** a fieldsman who stands behind the wicket-keeper to stop balls that pass him; hence *long-stop* vb., to field as long-stop. Also *long leg, long slip* (see the sbs.).

B. Quasi-*sb.* and *sb.* **I.** The adj. used *absol.* **1.** In various phrases with preps. See below. ME. **2.** Without prep.: Much time. Now chiefly in *to take l.* 1470. **b.** as the predicate of an impersonal clause (see below) OE. **3.** *The l. and the short of* (*it*, etc.): the sum total, substance, upshot 1500.

1. *Before l.* (short for †*before it be long*): soon. So *ere long*. Perhaps we may meet ere l. 1760. I'll be here again before l. TROLLOPE. *For l.*: throughout a l. period; also *predicatively*, destined or likely to continue l. The children..had been restless for l. 1895. *At (the) longest*: on the longest estimate. Short, at the longest, were the life of man PUSEY. **2.** Phr. *That l.* (colloq.): that length of time. **b.** Phr. *It is (was, will be*, etc.) *l. before, since, to* (something); *it will be l. first: ere it be l.* **3.** The l. and the short of it..is that you must pay me this money 1898.

II. As *sb.* (with *a* and *pl.*) **1.** *Mus.* A long note; *spec.* in the early notation, a note equivalent to two or three breves, according to the rhythm employed 1460. **2.** *Prosody.* A long syllable 1548. **3.** Building. *Longs and shorts*: long and short blocks placed alternately in a vertical line; the style of masonry to which this arrangement belongs 1845. **4.** (*colloq.*) = *Long Vacation* (see A. Combs.) 1885. **5.** *pl.* = *long-clothes* 1841. **6.** *Comm.* One who has bought in expectation of future demand 1881.

2. Phr. *Longs and shorts*: quantitative (esp. Latin or Greek) verses or versification. Hence **l.-and-short** *v.* to make Gr. or L. verses (BYRON). **6.** Wheat fell off owing to longs unloading 1890.

Long (lǫŋ), *a.*[2] ME. [aphet. f. ME. *ilong*, OE. *ġelang* ALONG *a.*[1]] Phr. *L. of* (†*l. on*): attributable to, owing to, 'along of'. Now *arch.* and *dial.*

That all these Have fallen out profitless, 'tis l. of you SWINBURNE.

Long (lǫŋ), *adv.* Comp. **longer** (lǫ·ŋgəɹ), **longest** (lǫ·ŋgėst). [OE. *lange, longe* = OFris. *lang(e, long(e*, OS., OHG. *lango* (Du. *lang*, G. *lange*), f. Gmc. **lanȝaz*, LONG *a.*[1]] **1.** For or during a long time. **2.** In expressions like *to be l. about one's work*, the adv. *long* becomes a quasi-adj. = 'occupying a long time', 'delaying long' ME. **3.** With an agent-noun, as *l.-liver*. Also *longer, longest liver*, in legal use for 'the survivor, the last survivor' 1485. **4.** Followed by *after, before, ere, since*, etc.: = At, from, or to a point of time far distant from the time indicated ME. **5.** The compar. (chiefly with *any, no, much*, etc.) has the sense: After the point of time indicated by the context (= L. *amplius*). *No longer*: not now as formerly. ME. **6.** Throughout the length of (a period specified). [Cf. G. *sein leben lang*.] ME. †**7.** At or to a great or a specified distance in space; far (*rare*) –1586.

1. Man wants but little here below, Nor wants that little l. GOLDSM. To cling to your profession as l. as you can THIRLWALL. *So* (or *as*) *l. as*: often = 'provided that', 'if only'. *So l.* (colloq.): good-bye, 'au revoir' 1834. **2.** Ile not be l. before I call vpon thee SHAKS. I advise to be l. a chusing a kind of life 1671. The opportunity was not l. in coming 1894. Phr. *Not to be l. for this world*: to have only a short time to live. **4.** Such is life—as Mrs. Harris l. since observed SWINBURNE. **5.** There was no longer any room for doubt 1894. **6.** He traveyled all night l. to Winchester warde 1568.

Long (lǫŋ), *v.*[1] [OE. *langian* = OS. *langon*, MDu. *langen* seem long, desire, extend, offer (Du. *langen* offer, present), OHG. *langēn* impers. (G. *langen* reach, extend, suffice), ON. *langa* (impers. and pers.) desire, long :– Gmc. **lanȝōjan, -ǣjan*, f. **lanȝaz* LONG *a.*[1]] †**1.** To lengthen, *trans.* and *intr.* –1500. †**2.** *impers.* with accus. *Me longs* (*longeth*): I have a yearning desire; I long –ME. **3.** *intr.* To have a yearning desire; to wish earnestly. Const. *for* (*after*), or *to* with inf. ME.

3. I haue longed after thy precepts *Ps.* 119:40. This man longed for her TROLLOPE.

Long (lǫŋ), *v.*[2] *arch.* ME. [f. *lang, long*, aphet. f. OE. *ġelang* at hand, dependent on, ALONG *a.*[1] Now repl. by BELONG *v.*] **1.** *intr.* To be appropriate *to*; to refer or relate *to*; to be a part, appendage, or dependency; to belong. Now only *poet.* as a rare archaism (written *'long*). †**b.** To concern (a person); hence, to befit, beseem –1564. †**2.** (Const. *to, unto*.) = BELONG *v.* 3. –1608.

1. b. She durste never seyn ne do But that thing that hir longed to CHAUCER.

Long, aphet. f. ALONG.

-long (lǫŋ), †**-longs** *suffix*, forming advs. The earliest instance, *endlong*, from ON. *endlangr* adj., 'extending from end to end', is prop. a compound of LONG *a.*[1]; but in Eng. it was used as an adv. with the sense 'endwise', 'end foremost'. The ending *-long* thus became a var. of -LING *suffix*[2].

†**Long-acre.** 1607. App. a proper name for a long narrow field containing an acre. (Still in use as the name of a well-known London street.) *allusively*, One's estate or patrimony –1659.

Long-ago. 1834. Attrib. use of advb. phr. *long ago* (see AGO): That has long gone by; that belongs to the distant past. Also quasi-*sb.* and *sb.*, the distant past or its events.

Longan (lǫ·ŋgăn). 1732. [Chinese *lungyen*, lit. 'dragon's eye', f. *lung* dragon + *yen* eye.] The fruit of an evergreen tree, *Nephelium longanum*, cultivated in China and the E. Indies; also, the tree.

Longanimity (lǫŋgăni·mĭti). Now *rare.* 1450. [– late L. *longanimitas, -tat-*, f. *longanimis* (f. *longus* long, *animus* mind), after Gr. μακροθυμία; see -ITY.] Long-suffering; forbearance or patience. So **Longa·nimous** *a.* 1620.

Lo·ng-boat. 1515. The largest boat belonging to a sailing vessel.

Long-bow (lǫ·ŋbōᵘ). 1500. [See BOW *sb.*[1] 4.] The bow drawn by hand and discharging a long feathered arrow (cf. CROSS-BOW). †*occas.* A soldier armed with a long bow.

Phr. *To draw* or *pull the* (or *a*) *long-bow*: to make exaggerated statements (*colloq.*).

Long-breathed (-breþt), *a.* 1568. [See BREATHED II.] Long of breath (*lit.* and *fig.*).

Long cloth, lo·ng-cloth. 1545. A kind of cotton cloth or calico made in long pieces.

Long coat, lo·ng-coat. 1603. **a.** A coat reaching to the ankles; also in *pl.* = *long-clothes*. **b.** One who wears a long coat.

Long-drawn, *a.* 1646. **1.** Prolonged to a great or inordinate length. Also *long-drawn-out*. **2.** Having great longitudinal extension. Chiefly *poet.* 1750.

1. A longdrawn carol TENNYSON. **2.** The long-drawn Isle and fretted Vault GRAY.

Longe: see LUNGE.

Long-eared, *a.* 1591. **1.** Having long ears; *spec.* in names of animals. **2.** Asinine 1605.

1. The long-eared owl 1831. **2.** An evil, heavy-laden, long-eared age CARLYLE.

†**Longee.** 1678. = LUNGE *sb.*[2] BUTLER.

Longeval, longæval (lǫndʒī·văl), *a.* 1597. [f. L. *longævus* LONGEVOUS + -AL[1].] Long-lived, long-lasting. So †**Longe·ve, longæ·ve** *a.* 1673–8.

Longevity (lǫndʒe·vĭti). Also †**-ævitie,** etc. 1615. [– late L. *longævitas, -tat-*, f. L. *longævus* (after Gr. μακραίων), f. *longus* long + *ævum* age; see -ITY.] Long life; long duration of existence.

Young men are careless of l. HAMERTON.

Longevous, -ævous (lǫndʒī·vəs), *a.* Now *rare.* 1680. [f. L. *longævus* (see prec.) + -OUS.] Long-lived; living or having lived to a great age.

Lo·ng-hand, lo·nghand. 1666. Handwriting of the ordinary character, as dist. from shorthand.

Long-head. 1650. [f. LONG *a.*[1]] One who has a skull of more than average length; *spec.* one the breadth of whose head is less than four-fifths of its length; a dolichocephalic person.

Long-headed, *a.* 1700. **1.** Having a long head 1875. **2.** Of great discernment or foresight; shrewd.

1. Long-headed glands DARWIN, men 1888. **2.** Long-headed customers, knowing dogs DICKENS. Hence **Long-hea·dedness.**

Longi- (lǫ·ndʒi), comb. f. L. *longus* LONG *a.*[1], in various terms, chiefly scientific, as **Lo·ngicorn** [mod.L. *longicornis*], *adj.* pertaining to the *Longicornes* or *Longicornia*, a group of beetles having very long antennæ; *sb.* one of these 1848. †**Longila·teral** *a.*, long-sided; of the form of a long parallelogram 1658.

Longiloquence (lǫndʒi·lŏkwĕns). *rare*. 1836. [f. LONGI-, after BREVILOQUENCE.] Speaking at great length.

American l. in oratory F. HALL.

Longimanous (lǫndʒi·mănəs), *a. rare*. 1646. [f. late L. *longimanus* (f. L. *longus* long + *manus* hand), or its source, Gr. μακρόχειρ 'long-armed', a surname of Artaxerxes, King of Persia.] Long-handed; *Zool.* applied to certain apes. †*fig.* Far-reaching.

Longimetry (lǫndʒi·mĭtri). *rare*. 1674. [f. LONGI-, after contemp. ALTIMETRY (in med.L. *altimetria* XII); cf. Fr. *longimétrie* (XVII).] The measuring of distances. Hence **Longime·tric** *a.*

Longing (lǫ·ŋiŋ), *vbl. sb.* [OE. *langung*, f. *langian* LONG *v.*[1]] **1.** The action of LONG *v.*[1]; yearning desire. Const. *for, after*, or with *inf.* **2.** *Path.* The fanciful cravings incident to womęn during pregnancy. Chiefly *pl.* 1552.

1. Giue me my Robe, put on my Crowne, I haue Immortall longings in me *Ant. & Cl.* v. ii. 284.

Lo·nging, *ppl. a.* 1509. [f. LONG *v.*[1] + -ING[2].] That longs; characterized by yearning desire.

Nor cast one l. ling'ring Look behind! GRAY. Hence **Lo·nging-ly** *adv.*, **-ness.**

Longinquity (lǫndʒi·ŋkwĭti). Now *rare*. 1549. [– L. *longinquitas, -tat-*, f. *longinquus* distant, f. *longus* long; see -ITY.] **1.** Long distance; remoteness. **2.** Remoteness or long continuance (of time) 1623.

Longish (lǫ·ŋiʃ), *a.* 1611. [f. LONG *a.*[1] + -ISH[1].] Somewhat long.

Longitude (lǫ·ndʒitiūd). ME. [– L. *longitudo, -din-*, f. *longus* long; see -TUDE. Cf. (O)Fr. *longitude*.] **1.** Length, longitudinal extent; *occas.* a length; a long figure. †Also, tallness. Now chiefly *joc.* **2.** Length (of time, etc.); long continuance. Now *rare*. 1607. **3.** *Geog.* †**a.** The extent lengthwise (i.e. from east to west) of the habitable world as known to the ancients. **b.** Distance east or west on the earth's surface, measured by the angle which the meridian of a particular place makes with a standard meridian, as that of Greenwich. It is reckoned to 180° east or west, and is expressed either in degrees, etc., or in time (15° being equivalent to 1 hour). Abbrev. *long.* ME. **4.** *Astron.* The distance of a heavenly body reckoned (in degrees, etc.) eastward on the ecliptic from the vernal equinoctial point to a circle at right angles to the ecliptic through that heavenly body. ME.

1. A petticoat, of scanty l. SCOTT. **3.** *Circle of l.*: see CIRCLE *sb.* 2.

Comb. **l. star,** any of the fixed stars which have been selected for finding the l. by lunar observations.

Longitudinal (lǫndʒitiū·dinăl). 1541. [f. as prec. + -AL[1]. Cf. med.L. (*diameter*) *longitudinalis* (XIII).] **A.** *adj.* **1.** Of or pertaining to length; (extent) in length 1765. **2.** Extending or proceeding lengthwise 1715. **b.** *Acoustics.* Of vibrations: Produced in the direction of the vibrating body; also, executed in the direction in which the sound travels 1867. **3.** Pertaining to longitude 1874. Hence **Longitu·dinally** *adv.*

B. *sb.* †**1.** *Anat.* A name for two muscles of the epigastrium 1541. **2.** *Ship-building.* In iron and steel ships, a plate (nearly) parallel to the vertical keel 1869. **3.** A railway sleeper lying parallel with the rail 1864.

Lo·ng-leg. 1585. †**1.** = BUPRESTIS 1. –1783. **2. Long-legs. a.** The stilt; the 'long-legged plover' 1713. **b.** = DADDY-LONG-LEGS 1753. Hence **Long-legged** *a.* having long legs; *Naut.* of a ship, drawing much water.

Long-line. 1755. **1.** A deep-sea fishing-line 1876. **2.** *attrib.* **a.** Written or printed with long lines. **b.** Furnished with or using long-lines (sense 1). 1755. Hence **Long-lining,** fishing with long-lines.

Long-lived (-ləivd, -livd), *a.* ME. [f. LONG *a.*[1] + *live*, LIFE *sb.* + -ED[2].] Having a long life or existence; lasting a long time; longeval.

The long-lived summer days JEFFERIES.

Longly (lǫ·ŋli), *adv.* ME. [f. LONG *a.*[1] + -LY[2].] †**1.** = LONG *adv.* 1. –1605. **2.** At considerable length. Now *Sc.* ME. **3.** To a considerable length (in space). *rare*. 1662.

Long-necked, *a.* 1605. Having a long neck; used *spec.* in names of animals.

Longness (lǫ·ŋnĕs). Now *rare*. [OE. *langnes*, f. *lang* LONG *a.*[1] + *-nes* -NESS.] Length; †protractedness.

Long-nosed, *a.* 1552. Having a long nose; used *spec.* in names of animals.

Longobard (lǫ·ŋgŏbaɹd), *sb.* and *a.* 1598. [– L. *Longobardi* (see LOMBARD *sb.*[1]).] = LOMBARD. So **Longoba·rdic** *a.* Lombardic.

Long robe. 1601. [Cf. Fr. '*gens de robbe longue*' (COTGR.).] Put symbolically for: The legal profession; esp. in *gentlemen*, etc., *of the long robe* = lawyers, barristers. Also *occas.* = The priesthood or ministry. (Cf. GOWN *sb.*)

Long run, lo·ng-run. 1627. Phr. *in* (also †*at*, †*on*, †*upon*) *the long run*: in the end; when things have run their full course; as the outcome of many vicissitudes. (Cf. Fr. *à la longue*.)

Longshanks (lǫ·ŋʃæŋks). 1590. [See SHANK.] **1.** A nickname given to Edward I of England on account of his long legs. **2.** A stilt or long-legged plover 1817.

Lo·ng-shore, *attrib. phr.* 1822. [aphet. f. ALONGSHORE.] Existing on or frequenting the shore; found or employed along the shore. Hence **Lo·ngshoreman,** a man employed in loading and unloading ships, or in fishing for oysters, etc. along the shore.

Long-sighted, *a.* 1790. **1.** Having 'long sight' (see LONG *a.*[1]); able to see objects distinctly at a distance but not close at hand; hypermetropic. **2.** *fig.* Far-seeing 1791. Hence **Longsi·ghtedness.**

Longsome (lǫ·ŋsəm), *a.* Now chiefly *dial.* and *arch.* [OE. *langsum*, f. *lang* LONG *a.*[1] + *-sum* -SOME[1]. Cf. OS., OHG. *langsam* (Du. *langzaam*, G. *langsam*).] Long, lengthy; long-lasting; *esp.* tediously long; †dilatory.

The way there was a little l. STEVENSON.

Long standing. 1601. Continuance for a long time in a settled position, rank, etc. Chiefly in phr. *of long standing*. Also *attrib.*

Long sufferance. *arch.* ME. = next.

Long-suffering. *sb.* 1526. (Tindale). Patient endurance of provocation or trial; longanimity.

The riches of his goodnesse, and forbearance, and long suffering *Rom.* 2:4. So **Long-suffering** *a.* 1535 (Coverdale).

Long sword. *Obs.* exc. *Hist.* 1593. A sword with a long cutting blade. Often *fig.* or *allusive*. Also cognomen (AFr. *Longespei*) of William, son of Henry II and Fair Rosamond.

Lo·ng-tail. 1575. **1.** A long-tailed animal; *spec.* a greyhound; formerly, a horse or dog with the tail uncut. **2.** A nickname for: †**a.** A native of Kent –1701. **b.** A Chinaman 1867. **3.** *attrib.* 1848.

1. *Cut and long-tail*: *lit.* horses and dogs with cut tails and long tails; *fig.* in sense 'riff-raff'. So **Long-tailed** *a.* having a long tail; (of words) having a long termination (*joc.*) 1500.

Long Tom. 1854. **1.** *dial.* A name for the long-tailed titmouse, etc. **2.** A kind of gold-washing cradle 1855. **3.** A gun of large size and long range 1867.

Lo·ng-tongue. 1731. A person or animal with a long tongue, e.g. the wryneck (*dial.*). So **Long-tongued** *a.* chattering, babbling 1553.

Long-waisted, *a.* 1647. **1.** Having a long waist, as a person, a ship, etc. 1653. †**2.** *fig.* Easy; loose –1658.

Longways (lǫ·ŋwē[i]z), *adv.* 1588. [f. LONG *a.*[1] + -WAYS.] Lengthways, longitudinally.

Long-winded, *a.* 1589. **1.** Long-breathed 1596. Also *fig.* **2.** Of persons: Tediously long in speech or dilatory in action. Of speech, etc.: Tediously long.

1. Men of endurance,—deep-chested, long-winded, tough EMERSON. **2.** Such a long-winded Discourse 1652. Hence **Longwi·nded-ly** *adv.*, **-ness.**

Longwise (lǫ·ŋwəiz), *adv.* (*a.*) 1544. [f. LONG *a.*[1] + -WISE.] Lengthwise, longitudinally.

Loo (lū̦), *sb.*[1] 1675. [abbrev. f. LANTERLOO.] **1.** A round card-game. In three-card loo the cards have the same value as in whist; in five-card loo the Jack of Clubs ('Pam') is the highest card. A player who fails to take a trick or breaks any of the laws of the game is 'looed', i.e. required to pay a certain sum or 'loo' to the pool. **b.** The fact of being looed. **c.** The sum added to the pool by a player who is looed. **2.** A party playing at loo 1760. †**3.** Party, set –1774.

1. *Limited l.*: l. in which the l. or penalty is limited to a fixed sum. *Unlimited l.*: l. in which each player looed has to put in the amount there was in the pool. *Comb.* **l.-table,** a table for playing l. upon; now the trade name of a particular form of round table, orig. devised for this purpose.

Loo, *sb.*[2] *Obs.* exc. *Hist.* 1690. [– Fr. *loup*; see LOUP *sb.*[2]] A velvet mask partly covering the face, formerly worn by women to protect the complexion.

Loo (lū), *v.*[1] 1680. [f. LOO *sb.*[1]] *trans.* To subject to a forfeit at loo. Also *transf.* and *fig.*

A flush. .*loos the board*, i.e. the holder receives the amount of a loo from every one, and the hand is not played 1883.

Loo, *v.*[2] *Obs.* exc. *dial.* 1666. [aphet. f. HALLOO *v.*] *trans.* To urge on with shouts.

Loo (lū), *int.* 1605. [aphet. f. HALOO *int.*] A cry to incite a dog to the chase; = HALLOO *int.* Also *l. in!* Also quasi-*sb.*

Loob (lūb). 1674. [Of unkn. origin.] *Tin-mining.* **1.** A pit or vessel into which the dross and earth is delivered by the trough. RAY. **2.** *pl.* Slime containing ore 1778.

Looby (lū·bi). Now chiefly *dial.* ME. [Of unkn. origin; prob. rel. to LOB *sb.*[1]] A lazy hulking fellow; a lout; a clown. Also *attrib.* Hence †**Loo·bily** *a.* looby-like.

Looch, var. of LOHOCH.

Loof (lūf), *sb.*[1] *Sc.* and *n. dial.* ME. [– ON. *lófi* = Goth. *lofa*.] The palm of the hand.

Loof, *sb.*[2] and *v.*: see LUFF *sb.* and *v.*

Loof (lūf), *sb.*[3] 1865. [– Arab. *lūf* (see next).] = next.

Loofah (lū·fă). 1887. [– Egyptian Arab. *lūfa*, a plant of this species, which collectively is called *lūf*.] The fibrous substance of the pod of the plant *Luffa ægyptiaca*, used as a sponge or flesh-brush. Also *attrib.*, as *l.-tree*.

Look (luk), *sb.* ME. [f. LOOK *v.*] **1.** The action or an act of looking; a glance of the eyes; a particular direction of the eyes or face. **2. a.** Appearance, aspect (of the countenance, of things) ME. **b.** *pl.* as sing. Occas. = good looks. 1564.

1. For lookes kill loue, and loue by lookes reuiueth SHAKS. Phr. *To have a look at* (colloq.): to look at for the purpose of examining; In the meantime I shall have a l. at Warsaw 1885. With sick and scornful looks averse TENNYSON. **2. a.** A man may bee knowen by his looke *Ecclus.* 19:29. **b.** Lean are their Looks DRYDEN. Catherine was in very good looks (= was looking well) JANE AUSTEN. *To have a l. of*: to resemble vaguely.

Comb., as *l.-back, -down, -forward, -on, -up*, corresponding to phrases under the vb.

Look (luk), *v.* [OE. *lōcian* = OFris. **lōkia* (WFris. *loaitsje*), OS. *lōkon*, MDu. *loeken* :– WGmc. **lōkōjan*, parallel to **lōʒǣjan*, whence OHG. *luogēn* (G. dial. *lugen*) see, look, spy; no further cognates are known.]

I. To direct one's sight. **1.** *intr.* To give a direction to one's sight; to apply one's power of vision; to direct one's eyes *at* (*on, upon* arch.). **b.** *occas.* To give a look of surprise, to stare. Now *colloq.* 1610. **c.** quasi-*trans.*, as in *to l.* (a person or thing) *in the face* ME. **d.** with cogn. obj. 1592. **e.** *trans.* with complement or prep.: To bring by one's looks into a certain place or condition. Now *rare*. 1611. **f.** To express by a look or glance, or by one's countenance 1727. **2.** With indirect question: To apply one's sight to ascertain (*who, what, how, whether*, etc.). Now only when a single glance will give an answer. ME. **3.** *fig.* **a.** 'To direct the intellectual eye' (J.); to turn or fix one's attention or regard. Now usu. const. *at*; formerly *on* or *upon*. 1548. **b.** To take care, make sure, see (*that* or *how* something is done); also with *that* omitted). Now *arch.* OE. **c.** To expect. Const. *to* with *inf.* 1513. †**d.** with indirect question: To consider, ascertain (*who, when, whether*, etc.); to try (*if* something can be done). Also *simply*, to consider the matter, make inquiry. –1692. **4.** Idiomatic uses of the imperative. **a.** = 'see', 'behold', 'lo' OE. †**b.** Prefixed to interrog. pron. or adv., or relative conj., forming indef. relatives = *whoever, whatever, however*, etc. OE. –1625. **5. Look sharp.** Orig. (with *sharp* as adv.) = 'keep strict watch'. In later use, 'lose no time' (with vb. in sense of branch III, and *sharp* as complementary adj.; now merely *colloq.*). 1711. **6.** Trans. uses, chiefly = intr. uses with preps. See below. ME.

1. Looking neither to the right nor left 1797. She could not l. on the sweet heaven TENNYSON. Phr. (*Fair*, etc.) *to l. at, †on, †upon*: with respect to appearance. *To l. at him* (*me, it*, etc.): *colloq.* = judging from his (my, etc.) appearance. *Not to l. at* (*†on, upon*): often emphatically for 'not to touch, taste, meddle with'. Looke therfore ere thou leape 1550. Wherefore looke ye so sadly to-day? *Gen.* 40:7. **b.** Yes, you may l.! 1903. **c.** To l. death in the face SOUTH. An eye that looks one through and through 1891. Phr. *To look a gift horse in the mouth*: see HORSE *sb.* **d.** Such lookes as none could looke but beauties queen SHAKS. **e.** Thou shalt l. us out of pain G. HERBERT. **f.** She *look'd* a lecture, Each eye a sermon, and her brow a homily BYRON. Phr. *To l. daggers*: see DAGGER *sb.* 2. **2.** I will l. what time the train starts (*mod.*). †*L. else*: see whether it be not so. *Go l.* = 'find it out'; a contemptuous refusal to say (now *dial.*). **3. a.** He that made vs with such large discourse, Looking before and after *Haml.* IV. iv. 37 (1604 Qo.). Instead of reforming others..let him l. at home BENTHAM. The whole mode and manner of looking at things varies with every age M. PATTISON. **b.** Look't be done *Oth.* IV. iii. 8. **c.** By whom we l. to be protected HOBBES. **4. a.** *L. you* (mod. colloq.) = 'mind this'. *L. here*, a brusque preface to an order, expostulation, reprimand, etc. Now, l. here, my man..I'll have no feelings here DICKENS. **5.** Glass of ale, young woman; and l. sharp, please! 1874. **6. a.** To look at; to view, inspect, examine. Now *dial.* †*To l. babies*: to gaze at the reflection of one's face in another's eyes. ME. †**b.** To consult or refer to; to 'turn up'. In the imper. = VIDE. Also, to search for (a word, etc.) in a book of reference. (Cf. *l. up.*) –1813. L. Lord Bacon in his life FULLER. †**c.** To seek, search for; to *l. for*. Also, to seek or search out. –1821. He hath bin all this day to looke you SHAKS. †**d.** To expect, look for –1611. His fortune gives him more than he could looke DANIEL.

II. To face a certain way. **1.** *intr.* To have a certain outlook; to face, front, or be turned *towards, into, on to*, etc. 1555. **b.** Of parts of the body, etc.: To face or turn 1648. **2.** To show a tendency; to tend, point 1647. †**b.** To tend *to*, promise *to*. SHAKS.

1. Pisgah, which looketh toward Ieshimon *Num.* 21:20. **b.** The florets looking downwards 1776. **2.** All the facts l. the other way 1881. **b.** *Cor.* III. iii. 29.

III. To have a certain appearance. [Cf. similar use in passive sense of *smell, taste, feel.*] **1.** *intr.* To have the appearance of being; to seem ME. **b.** with adv. of manner: To have a certain look or appearance ME. (Now *rare* exc. with *well, ill, badly.*) ME. **c.** Const. *inf.* To seem to the view (*lit.* and *fig.*) 1775. **d.** Quasi-*trans.* To have an appearance corresponding with (one's character, condition, etc.) 1828. **2. Look like. a.** To have the appearance of being 1440. **b.** with gerund, vbl. sb., or sb.: To give promise of, show a likelihood of 1593.

1. Phr. *To l. well, ill*, i.e. 'in good, bad health'. *To l. black, blue*, etc. (fig.): see the adjs. 'You made me l. rather a fool, Arminius', I began M. ARNOLD. **b.** The skies looke grimly SHAKS. **c.** A.. hat that looked to be made of beaver 1890. Phr. *To l. as if*—: to have an appearance suggesting that—. Often *it looks* (or *things l.*) *as if* —. It looks as if there was going to be a free fight 1892. **d.** Phr. *To l. one's age*: to have the appearance of being as old as one is. *To l. oneself*: to appear to be in one's usual health. **2. a.** This looks like a lad of spirit GOLDSM. **b.** Later on..he..looked like biting 1883. It looks like rain 1888.

Spec. uses with preps. **L. about** —. **a.** To make searches in various parts of (a room, etc.); to go about observing in (a country, town, etc.). **b.** *To l. about one*: to turn one's eyes to surrounding objects; to examine one's position and circumstances; to be apprehensive. **L. after** —. **a.** To follow with the eye. †Also, to observe the course of (a person). †**b.** To search for. †**c.** To anticipate; to look forward to. **d.** To seek for, demand (qualities). **e.** To busy oneself about; to consider. **f.** To attend to; to take care of; to 'see to'. **L. behind** —. With pron. used refl. *Not* or *never to l. behind one* (colloq.): to have an uninterrupted career of advancement. **L. for** —. **a.** To expect, hope for, be on the watch for. **b.** To seek, search for. **L. into** —. **a.** To direct one's sight to the interior of. Also, to consult (a book) in a cursory manner. **b.** To examine minutely, investigate. **c.** To enter (a house, etc.) for a moment in passing. **L. on** —. **a.** To pay regard to; to respect. Now *dial.* **b.** To regard *as.* **c.** To regard with a specified feeling. **L. over** —. **a.** To inspect cursorily; †to examine. **b.** To ignore. Now only, to overlook (a fault). **L. through** —. **a.** To direct one's sight through; also *fig.* †**b.** To be visible through (*Haml.* IV. vii. 152). **c.** To direct one's view over the whole of; to glance through. **L. to** —. **a.** To direct a look to. **b.** To direct one's attention to. In Bibl. use, *occas.* to regard with favour. **c.** To attend to, take care of; †to nurse. **d.** In the *imperative*, etc.: To direct one's solicitude to (something endangered). **e.** *To l. to it*: to beware. Often with *cl.*, to see *that.* **f.** To keep watch upon. **g.** To rely on (a person, etc.) *for* something. **h.** To look forward to; to count upon. **L. toward(s** —. See simple senses and TOWARD(S. **b.** *To l. towards a person*: to drink his health (now *joc.*). **L. unto** —. *arch.* = *Look to* (senses a–f). **L. upon** —. †**a.** = *look on* (sense a). **b.** = *look on* (senses b, c). †Also, *to l. upon it*; to be of opinion *that.*

Spec. uses with advs. **L. about.** *intr.* See simple senses and ABOUT *adv.*; *fig.* to be on the look-out. Also const. *for* (*†after*): to be in search of. **L. around.** *intr.* To l. in several directions; *fig.* to take a comprehensive view of things. **L. back.** *intr.* **a.** To turn and l. at something in the direction from which one is going. **b.** To think on the past. Const. *into, on, upon, to.* †**c.** *trans.* = *look back to.* (*Ant. & Cl.* III. xi. 53.) **d.** *colloq.* in neg. contexts; To show signs of interrupted progress. **L. down. a.** *intr.* See simple senses and DOWN *adv.* **b.** *fig.* *To l. down on, upon*: to scorn; to consider oneself superior to. **c.** To quell by one's looks. **L. downward.** *intr.* = *look down.* **L. forth.** *intr.* To l. out (of a window, etc., on to something). Now *arch.* and *poet.* **L. in. a.** See simple senses and IN *adv.* **b.** To enter a room, etc. to see something; hence, now, to make a call (*upon* a person); to 'drop in'. **L. on.** *intr.* To direct one's looks towards an object; often, to be a mere spectator. *To look on ahead*; to look forward into the future. **b.** colloq. *To l. on* (*with*): to read from a book, etc. at the same time (with another person). **L. out. a.** *intr.* To look from within to the outside; also, to put one's head out of a window, etc. **b.** To show itself. SHAKS. **c.** To be on the look out; to take care. **d.** *To l. out for*: to be on the look out for; to await vigilantly. **e.** To have or afford an outlook. **f.** *trans.* To find or choose out by looking. **L. over.** *trans.* To cast one's eyes over; to examine (papers, etc.). **L. round.** *intr.* **a.** To l. about in every direction. **b.** *fig.* To search about *for.* **L. through. a.** *trans.* To penetrate with a glance. **b.** To examine exhaustively. †**c.** *intr.* To become visible. SHAKS. **L. up. a.** To raise the eyes, turn the face upwards. †**b.** To take courage. SHAKS. **c.** *To l. up to*: (*a*) to direct the look up towards; to raise the eyes towards, in adoration, supplication, etc.; (*b*) *fig.* to respect or venerate. **d.** *slang.* To improve. Chiefly *Comm.* **e.** To search for (something) in a dictionary, among papers, or the like; to consult (books). **f.** To call on (a person) in order to see him. *colloq.* **g.** To search for. **h.** *To l.* (a person) *up and down*: to scrutinize his appearance from head to foot.

Loo·k-down. *U.S.* 1882. [f. phr. *look down.*] The Horse-head or Moon-fish, *Selene vomer.*

Looker (lu·kəɹ). ME. [f. LOOK *v.* + -ER[1].] **1.** One who looks *at, on, to, upon*, etc. **2.** One who looks after anything; a guardian, keeper, shepherd, farm-bailiff. Now *local.* ME. **3.** A handsome person (esp. *U.S. colloq.*) 1904.

1. **Looker on, l.-on,** one who looks on; a beholder, spectator, eyewitness. Often, one who merely looks on. Cf. *onlooker.*

Look-in, *sb.* 1847. [f. LOOK *sb.* + IN *adv.*] **1.** A hasty glance. Hence, a short visit. **2.** *Sport. slang.* A chance of success 1870.

Looking (lu·kiŋ), *vbl. sb.* ME. [f. LOOK *v.* + -ING[1].] **1.** The action of LOOK *v.* †**2.** Look, expression of countenance, appearance –1610. **3.** *attrib.* 1519.

2. Wherefore this ghastly l.? *Temp.* II. i. 309.

Looking (lu·kiŋ), *ppl. a.* 1590. [f. as prec. + -ING[2].] **1.** That looks or gazes (*rare*) 1649. **2.** Forming combs., as *good-, ill-looking, westward-looking.*

Loo·king-gla:ss. 1526. [f. LOOKING *vbl. sb.* + GLASS.] **1.** A glass to look in, in order to see one's own face or figure; a mirror made of glass coated with an amalgam of quicksilver. **2.** Plate glass, or glass silvered for use as a mirror 1682. **3.** *Lady's* or *Venus' l.*, the plant *Campanula speculum.*

1. *fig.* The Eyes, the Looking-glasses of Nature 1658. *Comb.*: **l. plant,** an Asiatic tree, *Heritiera littoralis*; **l. writing,** writing done backwards, so as to be legible by means of a mirror.

Loo:k ou·t, look-out. *Pl.* **look-outs.** 1699. [f. phr. *look out.*] **1.** The action of looking out (*lit.* and *fig.*). Orig. *Naut.* 1748. **2.** *concr.*: see quots. 1699. **3.** A more or less distant view 1779; a prospective condition, an outlook 1825. **4.** with possessive sb. or pron., *That is —'s look-out* (colloq.): i.e. that concerns only his interest, he must see to that himself 1844. **5.** *attrib.*, as *look-out man*, etc. 1781.

1. Phr. *To keep a* (*good*, etc.) *look-out*; *to be, place, put on* or *upon the look out*; const. *for, to*, or *to* with *inf.* The gamekeeper..was upon the look-out for poachers 1815. **2.** The Look-out formerly built on Sullivan's Island 1700. One man on deck as a lookout R. H. DANA. Ere the channel was full enough for the look-outs (= look-out vessels) to intercept her 1841. **3.** This leads to a little tower.. The look-out charming 1779. It seemed a rather blue look-out 1889.

Look-see (lu·ksī). *slang.* 1883. [perh. orig. Pidgin-English.] An inspection, survey.

Loom (lūm), *sb.*[1] [ME. *lōme*, aphetic f. OE. *ġelōma* utensil, implement, f. collect. *ġe-* Y- + **lōma*, as in *andlōman* pl. apparatus, furniture.] **1.** An implement or tool of any kind. *Obs.* exc. *Sc.* and *n. dial.* **2.** An open vessel of any kind, as a bucket, tub, vat, etc. *Obs.* exc. *Sc.* ME. **3.** A machine in which yarn or thread is woven into fabric by the crossing of threads called respectively the warp and weft ME. Also *fig.* †**b.** *transf.* Attributed to a spider or caterpillar; *occas.* (*poet.*) the web itself –1647. **4.** The art, business, or process of weaving 1676.

3. The shaft of his speare was like a weauers lome (app. = beam of a l.) COVERDALE 1 *Sam.* 17:7. **4.** In the L. unskill'd DRYDEN.

Loom (lūm), *sb.*[2] 1694. [– ON. *lómr.*] A name given to species of the Guillemot and the Diver, esp. *Alca bruennichi* and *Colymbus septentrionalis* (Red-throated Diver).

Loom (lūm), *sb.*[3] 1697. Also **lum.** [Scand.; cf. Norw. *lom, lumm*, Icel. *hlumr, hlummr.*] The shaft of an oar; also, limited to the part between the rowlock and the hands in rowing; also, loosely, the handle.

Loom (lūm), *sb.*[4] 1836. [f. LOOM *v.*[2]] A seaman's term for the indistinct and exaggerated appearance of land on the horizon, an object seen through mist or darkness, etc.

Loom (lūm), *v.*[1] *rare.* 1548. [f. LOOM *sb.*[1]] **1.** *trans.* To weave (a fabric). **2.** *To l. the web*: to mount the warp on the loom 1827.

Loom (lūm), *v.*[2] 1591. [prob. of LDu. origin; cf. EFris. *lōmen* (whence Sw. dial. *loma*) move slowly, rel. to MHG. *lüemen* be weary, f. *lüeme* slack, soft.] †**1.** Of a ship at sea: To move slowly up and down (*rare*) –1678. **2.** *intr.* To appear indistinctly; to come into view in an exaggerated and indefinite form. Also with *up.* **b.** *fig.* of immaterial things 1591.

2. Men are magnified to giants, and brigs 'l. up' ..into ships of the line KANE. **b.** Cash affairs l. well in the offing SCOTT.

Loon[1] (lūn). Chiefly *Sc.* and *n. dial.* 1450. [orig. north. and Sc. in forms showing the pronunc. (*ū*), which has been preserved in the transference to Southern Eng.] **1.** A rogue, scamp; an idler. **b.** A strumpet, concubine 1560. **2.** A man of low condition; in phr. *lord and l.* Now only *arch.* 1535. **3.** A boor, lout, clown 1619. **4.** A boy, lad, youth 1560.

Loon[2] (lūn). 1634. [prob. alt. of LOOM *sb.*[2], perh. by assim. to prec.] A name for certain aquatic birds. **1.** Any bird of the genus *Colymbus*, esp. *C. glacialis.* **2.** The Great Crested Grebe; the Little Grebe or Dabchick 1678.

Loony, luny (lū·ni). *vulgar.* 1872. [Shortened f. LUNATIC + -Y[1].] *adj.* Lunatic, crazed, silly. *sb.* A lunatic.

Loop (lūp), *sb.*[1] ME. [Of unkn. origin.] **1.** The doubling or return into itself of a portion of a string, cord, thong, or the like, so as to leave an aperture between the parts; the portion so doubled, usu. fastened at the ends. **2.** A ring or curved piece of metal, etc., for the insertion of a bolt, ramrod, or rope, as a handle, etc.; *dial.* a door-hinge 1674. **3.** Something in the form of a loop, e.g. a line traced on paper, a bend of a river, etc. 1668. **4.** In specific applications: see below 1846.

1. There are rows of buttons and loops down the breast of the tunic 1815. We should speak of a *mesh* in netting, a *loop* in knitting 1880. **3.** I wish ..you would..open the loops of your l's SCOTT. **4. a.** *Anat.* A looped vessel or fibre. *L. of Henle*,

the looped part of a uriniferous tubule 1846. **b.** *Zool.* In brachiopods, the folding of the brachial appendages 1851. **c.** *Acoustics.* The portion of a vibrating string, column of air, etc. between two nodes 1878. **d.** *Railways* and *Telegraphy.* A line of rails or a telegraph wire diverging from, and afterwards returning to, the main line or circuit 1863. **e.** The circuit in a centrifugal railway, along the upper portion of which the passenger travels head downwards 1900. *To loop the l.*, to travel along such a circuit, or in a similar course through the air in an aeroplane. **f.** *Electr.* A complete electric circuit; a multiple or branch circuit.

Comb.: **l.-knot,** †(*a*) a reef-knot; (*b*) a single knot tied in a double cord, so as to leave a l. beyond the knot; **-lace,** (*a*) a series of loops as an ornament; (*b*) a kind of lace consisting of patterns worked on a ground of fine net; hence **-laced** *a.*; **-line,** see 4 d.; **-stitch,** a kind of fancy stitch consisting of loops.

Loop (lūp), *sb.*[2] ME. [Identical with AL. *lupa* (XIII), *loupa* (XIV) loop-hole, embrasure, of unkn. origin.] = LOOP-HOLE.

Loop (lūp), *sb.*[3] ME. [– (O)Fr. *loupe.* Cf. G. *luppe.*] **1.** *Metall.* A mass of iron in a pasty condition ready for the tilt-hammer or rolls; a bloom 1674. †**2.** A precious stone of imperfect brilliancy, *esp.* a sapphire –1548.

Loop (lūp), *v.*[1] 1832. [f. LOOP *sb.*[1] Cf. LOOPED *a.*[1], which is much earlier.] **1.** *trans.* To form into a loop or loops; also with *round* 1856. **2.** *intr.* To form a loop; *spec.* of certain larvæ 1832. **3.** *trans.* To put or form loops upon 1894. **4.** To enclose *in* or *with* something formed into a loop 1840. **5.** Chiefly with *adv.* or *phr.*: To fasten (*back, up*) by forming into, or by means of, a loop; to connect by means of a loop or loops. Also *intr.* for *refl.* 1837. **6.** *Electr.* To connect so as to form a loop. **7.** Phr. *to l. the loop* (see LOOP *sb.*[1] 4e) 1904.

1. The other end is already looped, or as sailors would say, 'doubled in a bight' KANE. **5.** She had an abundance of dark hair looped up BLACK.

†**Loop,** *v.*[2] 1674. [f. LOOP *sb.*[3]] *intr.* Of heated iron-ore: To form a loop (LOOP *sb.*[3]).

Looped (lūpt), *a.*[1] 1513. [f. LOOP *sb.*[1] and *v.*[1] + -ED.] **1.** Coiled or wreathed in loops; †intertwined. †**2.** Having, or fastened with, a loop. Of a dart: Furnished with a thong for throwing. –1609. **3.** Of lace: Wrought upon a ground of fine net 1698. **4.** Held in a loop, held *up* by a loop 1869.

Looped (lūpt), *a.*[2] 1605. [f. LOOP *sb.*[2] + -ED[2].] Having loop-holes.

Your loopt and windowed raggednes SHAKS.

Looper (lū·pəɹ). 1731. [f. LOOP *v.*[1] + -ER[1].] One who or that which makes loops. **1.** The larva of any geometrid moth, which in crawling bends the middle of its body into a loop. **2.** A contrivance in a machine for making loops or looping pieces together 1857.

Loop-hole, loophole (lū·phoᵘl), *sb.* 1591. [f. LOOP *sb.*[2] + HOLE *sb.* In sense 3 perh. infl. by Du. *loopgat*, f. *loopen* run + *gat* way, GATE *sb.*[1]] **1.** *Fortif.* A narrow vertical opening, usually widening inwards, cut in a wall, etc., for shooting through. †**b.** *Naut.* A port-hole –1769. **2.** A similar opening to look through, or to admit light and air 1591. **3.** *fig.* An outlet or means of escape 1663.

2. *fig.* 'Tis pleasant through the loopholes of retreat To peep at such a world COWPER. **3.** The Test Act..left loopholes through which schismatics sometimes crept into civil employments MACAULAY.

Loo·p-hole, *v.* 1810. [f. prec.] *trans.* To cut loop-holes in the walls of; to provide with loop-holes.

Looping (lū·piŋ), *vbl. sb.* 1480. [f. LOOP *v.*[1] + -ING[1].] The action of LOOP *v.*[1] **b.** *concr.* Material formed into loops; loops as a trimming 1647.

Looping (lū·piŋ), *ppl. a.* 1854. [f. LOOP *v.*[1] + -ING[2].] That forms loops.

L. caterpillar = LOOPER 1. *L.-snail*, a snail of the genus *Truncatella.*

Loopy (lū·pi), *a.* 1824. [f. LOOP *sb.*[1] + -Y[1].] **1.** Full of or characterized by loops 1856. **2.** *Sc.* Deceitful, crafty. SCOTT.

Loord, var. of LOURD *Obs.*

Loos, obs. f. LOSE, LOSS.

Loose (lūs), *sb.* 1519. [f. LOOSE *v.* and *a.*] **1.** *Archery.* The act of discharging an arrow. †**2.** The close of a matter; the upshot, issue –1647. **3.** A condition of looseness, laxity, or unrestraint; hence, free indulgence; unrestrained action or feeling. *Obs.* exc. in phr. *to give a l.* (occas. *give l.*) *to*, to give full vent to; to free from restraint; *occas.*, to give (a horse) the rein. 1593. †**4.** Liberation, release –1734. †**5.** An impetuous course or rush –1737.

1. *fig.* To allow me a L. at the Crimes of the Guilty DE FOE. **2.** Phr. *At* (or *in*) *the* (*very*) *l.*: at the last moment (*L.L.L.* v. ii. 752). **3.** The little boy..gave a l. to his innocent tongue, and asked many questions THACKERAY. **4.** Phr. *To make a l. from*: to get away from the company of.

Loose (lūs), *a.* and *adv.* [ME. *lōs* (north. *lous*) – ON. *lauss* = OE. *lēas* lying, untrue, OFris. *lās*, OS., OHG. *lōs*, Goth. *laus* :– Gmc. **lausaz*, f. **laus-* **leus-* **lus-*; see LEASE *a.*]

A. *adj.* **1.** Unbound, unattached. **a.** Free from bonds or physical restraint. Now used only in implied contrast. **b.** *transf.* and *fig.*, e.g. of the tongue: Not 'tied', free to speak. 1726. **c.** Freed from an obligation, etc.; at liberty. *Obs.* exc. *dial.* 1553. †**d.** Free *from* or *of*; released *from*; unattached *to* –1821. †**e.** Ungirt; naked –1709. **f.** Of an inanimate thing: Detached. Phr. *To come, get l.* 1728. **g.** Not joined to anything else. Of a chemical element: Free, uncombined 1828. **h.** Having an end or ends hanging free. (See also LOOSE END.) 1781. **i.** Not bound together; not tied up or secured 1488. **j.** Unconnected; rambling; detached, stray, random. Now *rare.* 1681. **k.** Free for disposal; unattached, unappropriated, unoccupied. *Obs.* exc. *joc.* 1479. **2.** Not rigidly fixed in place; ready to shift or come apart ME. †**b.** Of the eyes: Not fixed, roving –1751. **3.** Not tense or stretched; slack, relaxed 1460. **b.** Of clothes: Loosely fitting 1463. **4.** Not close or compact in arrangement or structure ME. **b.** *Bot.* = LAX *a.* 3b. Also, 'of a soft cellular texture' (Lindley). 1776. **c.** Of handwriting: Straggling 1711. **d.** Applied to exercise or play in which the players, etc. act more independently 1802. **5.** Wanting in retentiveness or power of restraint ME. **b.** Of the bowels: Relaxed 1508. **6.** Of qualities, actions, statements, ideas, etc.: Not rigid, strict, correct, or careful; hence, inexact, indefinite, vague 1606. †**b.** Of conditions, undertakings, etc.: Lacking security, unsettled –1687. **c.** *Cricket.* Of bowling: Not accurate in pitch. Of fielding, etc.: Slack, careless. 1859. **7.** Of persons, etc.: Lax in principle, conduct, or speech; chiefly in narrower sense, unchaste, dissolute, immoral 1470. **8.** Applied to a stable in which animals are kept without being fastened up. So also *l. box* (see BOX *sb.*[2] II. 4) 1813.

1. a. You are afraid you see the Beare l. SHAKS. He got one hand l. 1903. **b.** Murder is l. 1879. **f.** Some of the pages have come l. 1903. **h.** As to Logic, its chain of conclusions hangs l. at both ends J. H. NEWMAN. **i.** Her haire not l. nor ti'd in formall plat SHAKS. **j.** A good deal of l. information CARLYLE. **k.** I hope you read..at l. hours, other books JOHNSON. *L. card*: a card in a hand that is of no value, and consequently the properest to throw away (HOYLE). **2.** His bridge was only l. planks DE FOE. **3.** The labour'd Oxe In his l. traces MILT. My knees l. under me STEVENSON. Phr. *With a l. rein* (fig.): slackly, without rigour. **b.** Men in l. flannel jackets 1901. **4.** The Ashes with Aire between, lie looser BACON. The l. assault of the Mexicans 1777. **5.** A rash young fool; carries a l. tongue CARLYLE. **6.** L. and negligent curiosity MILT. L., exaggerated calculations HUME. L. tradition and reports PALEY. A l. construction 1872. L. thinkers and l. talkers 1875. **7.** A l. liuer 1591.

Spec. collocations: **l. box,** a stable in which a horse is allowed to move about freely; **l. fish** (*colloq.*), a person of irregular habits; **l.-leaf** *a.*, of a ledger, etc.: with each leaf separate and detachable; **l. pulley,** a pulley running loosely on the shaft on which it is journaled; also *fast and l. pulley* (see FAST *a.*).

Comb.: **l.-bodied** *a.*, (of a dress) loose-fitting; **-tongued** *a.*, blabbing.

B. quasi-*sb.* and *sb.* **1.** *absol.* **a.** *On the l.*: 'on the spree' 1849. **b.** *In the l.*: not made up or prepared 1898. **2.** *Rugby Football.* That part of the play in which the ball travels freely from player to player 1892.

C. *adv.* Loosely; with a loose hold 1591.

Phr. *To sit l.* (fig.): to be independent or indifferent; to hold loosely *to*, not to be enslaved *to*; *occas.* not to weigh heavily *upon.* *To hold l.*: to be indifferent. *To play fast and l.*: see FAST AND LOOSE b.

Hence **Loo·se-ly** *adv.*, **-ness. Loo·sish** *a.* somewhat l.

Loose (lūs), *v.* ME. [f. LOOSE *a.*] **1.** *trans.* To let loose, set free; to release from bonds or constraint. **2.** To undo, untie (fetters, a knot); to break (a seal). Now *dial.* or *poet.* ME. Also *fig.* **b.** To detach, cast loose, let go; chiefly *Naut.* ME. **3.** †*To l. the anchor*: to weigh anchor 1450. **b.** Hence *absol.* To weigh anchor; *occas.* with *up* 1526. **4.** To let fly (an arrow); to let off (a gun). Also *absol.* or *intr.* ME. **b.** *trans.* (*transf.* and *fig.*) To give vent to, emit; to cause or allow to proceed from one 1508. **5.** = LOOSEN *v.* 3. Also *intr.* for *pass.* Now only *arch.* ME. **6.** To make loose or slack; †*pass.* (of nerves) to be unstrung. Now *arch.* exc. in *to l. hold* (colloq.): to let go. 1440. †**b.** *transf.* To relax or loosen (the bowels). Also *absol.* –1651. †**7.** [Cf. L. *solvere.*] To break up, dissolve, do away with. Chiefly *fig.* –1819. †**8.** To solve, explain –1660. **9.** *pass.* and *intr.* To finish working; (of a school, factory, etc.) to close, disperse, break up (*dial.*) 1813.

1. The captiue exile hasteneth that he may be loosed *Isa.* 51:14. The wine loosed the tongues of the guests 1902. **2. b.** She loosed the boat from its moorings GEO. ELIOT. **4. b.** L. now and then A scattred smile, and that Ile liue vpon *A. Y. L.* III. v. 103.

Loose end. 1546. An end of a string, etc., left hanging loose; *fig.* of something left disconnected, undecided, or unguarded. Chiefly *pl.*

Phr. *At* (*after, on*) *a loose end*: having no regular occupation; not knowing what to be at. Also (*to leave a matter*) *at a loose end*: unsettled. *colloq.*, orig. *dial.* 1851.

Loosen (lū·s'n), *v.* ME. [f. LOOSE *a.* + -EN[5].] To make loose or looser. **1.** *trans.* = LOOSE *v.* 1. **2.** To undo, unfasten (bonds, a knot, etc.). Now usu.: To render looser or less tight. ME. **3.** To weaken the adhesion or attachment of; to unfix, detach 1667. †Also *fig.* Also *intr.* for *refl.* or *pass.* **4.** *trans.* To make less coherent 1697. **5.** To relax (the bowels) 1587; to render (a cough) looser 1833. **6.** To relax in severity or strictness 1798.

1. *fig.* By degrees her tongue was loosened TROLLOPE. The fragrance of the valley was loosened 1893. **3.** From thir foundations loosning to and fro They pluckt the seated Hills MILT. Phr. *To l.* (a person's) *hide* (slang): to flog. **4.** He struck the snow with his baton to l. it TYNDALL. **6.** The men neither straggled nor loosened their discipline 1899. Hence **Loo·sener,** one who or that which loosens.

Loosestrife (lū·sˌstrəif). 1548. [f. LOOSE *v.* + STRIFE *sb.*, a mistransl. of L. *lysimachia*, also *-machion*, taken as if directly f. the adj. λυσίμαχος 'loosing' (i.e. ending) strife (f. λυσι-, λύειν + μάχη), instead of as – Gr. λυσιμάχιον, f. the personal name Λυσίμαχος Lysimachus, its discoverer.] The name of two tall upright plants growing in moist places: **a.** *Lysimachia vulgaris* (N.O. *Primulaceæ*), Golden or Yellow L., flowering in July, and bearing racemes of golden-yellow flowers. **b.** *Lythrum salicaria* (N.O. *Lythraceæ*), Red, Purple, or Spiked L., blooming in summer, with a showy spike of purplish-red flowers. Also a book-name for the genera *Lysimachia* and *Lythrum*, and extended to plants of other genera.

b. When through the Wytham flats, Red l. and blond meadow-sweet among..We tracked the shy Thames shore M. ARNOLD.

Loot (lūt), *sb.* 1839. [– Hindi *lūṭ*, repr. either Skr. *lōtra*, *lōptra* booty, spoil (f. *lup* = *rup* break), or Skr. *luṇṭ* rob.] Goods taken from an enemy, a captured city, etc. in time of war; also, something taken by force; booty, plunder, spoil; occas. *transf.*, illicit gains, 'pillage' (e.g. by a public servant). Also, the action of looting.

The talismanic gathering-word *Loot* (plunder) 1839.

Loot (lūt), *v.* 1842. [f. prec. sb.] *trans.* To plunder, sack (a city, building) 1845; to carry off as loot or booty 1847; also *absol.*

To l. a village 1845, cattle and grain 1887. Hence **Loo·ter.**

Loover, obs. f. LOUVER.

†**Lop** (lǫp), *sb.*[1] [OE. *loppe*, also *lobbe*; of unkn. origin.] A spider –ME.

Lop (lǫp), *sb.*[2] Now *dial.* 1440. [prob. – ON. **hloppa*, f. root of *hlaupa* LEAP *v.*] A flea.

Lop (lǫp), *sb.*^{3} ME. [f. LOP *v.*^{1} Cf. AL. *loppa* (pl.) XIV.] **1.** The smaller branches and twigs of trees; faggot-wood, loppings. Also, a branch lopped off. **†2.** A lopped tree or part –1656. **†3.** The action of lopping a tree or its boughs –1600.

1. Phr. *L. and top, l. and crop.*

Lop (lǫp), *sb.*^{4} 1829. [Of imit. origin. Cf. LOP *v.*^{3}] *Naut.* A state of the sea in which the waves are short and lumpy.

Lop (lǫp), *sb.*^{5} 1868. [Short for *lop-rabbit*; see LOP *v.*^{2}] A variety of rabbit with long drooping ears. Also *full-, half-l.*, etc.

Lop (lǫp), *v.*^{1} 1480. [:– OE. **loppian*, implied in pa. pple. *lopped* (*æt loppede thorne*); cf. AL. *loppare* (XV); perh. f. *lup-* (cf. LIP *v.*^{2}), and rel. to Lith. *lùpti* strip, peel.] **1.** *trans.* To cut off the branches, twigs, etc., *rarely* the top or 'head', of (a tree); to trim. **b.** *transf.* and *fig.* †Also with *away, off.* 1602. **2.** To cut off (the branches, twigs, etc.) from a tree; to shorten by cutting off the extremities. Now chiefly with *away, off.* 1593. **b.** *transf.* and *fig.* To cut off (a person's limbs or head). Also *gen.*, to cut off, reduce by cutting. Also with *away, down, off.* 1586. **c.** *absol.* or *intr.* 1588.

1. In the moneth of December..l. hedges and trees MARKHAM. **b.** When our grandsire great.. Lop'd the French lillies DRAYTON. **2.** He lopped off the tops as they sprang up N. BACON. **b.** His leg was lopp'd CRABBE. To l. off part of a visit 1864.

Lop (lǫp), *v.*^{2} 1578. [rel. to LOB *v.*] **1.** *intr.* To hang loosely or limply; to droop; to sway limply about. **b.** *trans.* To droop (the ears) 1828. **2.** *intr.* To slouch; to hang idly about 1587. **3.** To move with short irregular bounds. Cf. LOPE *v.* 1895.

3. Lopping easily along, a fox crosses through the teazles 1902. *Comb.*: **l.-eaves**, eaves which hang down at the sides; **-rabbit** (see LOP *sb.*^{5}).

Lop (lǫp), *v.*^{3} 1897. [Of imit. origin; cf. LOP *sb.*^{4}] *intr.* Of water: To break in short lumpy waves.

Lope (lōᵘp), *sb.* ME. [– ON. *hlaup*; see LEAP *v.*, LOUP *sb.*^{1}] **†1.** = LEAP *sb.*^{1} –1734. **2.** A long bounding stride (chiefly of animals) 1846.

2. The easy l. of the 'rickshaw coolie R. KIPLING.

Lope (lōᵘp), *v.* 1483. [var. of LOUP *v.* – ON. *hlaupa* LEAP *v.* – ON. *hlaup*; see LEAP *sb.*^{1}, LOUP *sb.*^{1}] **1.** *intr.* To leap, jump, spring. Also with *about. Obs.* exc. *dial.* **2.** *intr.* To run, run away. Now only *slang* and *dial.* 1572. **3.** To run with a long bounding stride. (Said chiefly of animals.) 1825.

3. The larger wolves..l. hungrily around 1848.

Lop-ear (lǫ·p,iᵊ·ɹ), *sb.* (and *a.*) 1692. [LOP *v.*^{2}] **1.** *pl.* Ears that droop or hang down. **2.** A kind of rabbit with such ears. Also *attrib.* 1877. So **Lo·p-eared** *a.* having ears which hang loosely down 1687.

†Lo·peman. [– Du. *loopman* (obs.), f. *loopen* to run + *man* MAN *sb.*] A runner. FLETCHER.

Loper (lōᵘ·pəɹ). 1483. [f. LOPE *v.* + -ER^1.] **†1.** A leaper, dancer. **2.** *Ropemaking.* A swivel upon which yarns are hooked at one end while being twisted into cordage. [Cf. Du. *looper* runner.] 1794.

Lopho- (lǫ·fǒ, lofǫ·), bef. a vowel **loph-**, comb. f. Gr. λόφος crest: in various scientific terms, as **Lo·phobranch** (-bræŋk), **-bra·nchiate** [Gr. βράγχια gills] *Ichthyol.* **a.** *adj.* having the gills disposed in tufts; **b.** *sb.* a l. fish 1834. **Lo·phophore** [Gr. -φόρος bearing] **a.** *Zool.* in Polyzoa, the oral disc at the free end of the polypide, bearing the tentacles 1850; **b.** a bird of the genus *Lophophorus*, with crested crown and brilliant plumage 1883.

Lophodont (lǫ·fodǫnt). 1887. [f. LOPHO- + Gr. ὀδούς, ὀδοντ- tooth.] Characterized by having ridges on the crowns of the molar teeth.

Lopped (lǫpt), *ppl. a.* 1570. [f. LOP *v.*^{1} + -ED^1.] In senses of the vb. *Bot.* and *Zool.* Truncate. **b.** *Her.* Cut so as to show the thickness; snagged 1828.

Lopper (lǫ·pəɹ), *sb.* 1538. [f. LOP *v.*^{1} + -ER^1.] One who lops (a tree).

Lopper (lǫ·pəɹ), *v.* Now only *Sc.* and *n. dial.* ME. [perh. a deriv. (with suffix -ER^5) of ON. *hlaup* coagulation (of milk or blood).] **1.** *intr.* Of milk: To curdle. **2.** 'To dabble, to besmear, or to cover so as to clot' (Jam.) 1818.

Lopping (lǫ·piŋ), *vbl. sb.* 1480. [f. LOP *v.*^{1} + -ING^1.] **1.** The action of LOP *v.*^{1} (The cant term of the Rye House conspirators for the killing of the King and the Duke of York.) **2.** Chiefly *pl.* Branches and shoots lopped from a tree. Also, material for lopping. 1589. **3.** *attrib.* 1659.

2. He shall gather vp the loppings to make fewell of SURFLET.

Lo·ppy, *a.* 1855. [f. LOP *v.*^{2} + -Y^1.] That hangs loosely; limp.

Lopseed (lǫ·psīd). 1850. [f. LOP *v.*^{2}] A North American perennial herb, *Phryma leptostachya*, with small purple flowers and spikes of strongly reflexed fruits.

Lop-sided, lopsided (lǫ·p,səi·dėd), *a.* 1711. [f. LOP *v.*^{2} + SIDE *sb.* + -ED^2.] That lops or leans on or towards one side; having one side lower or smaller than the other. Orig. *Naut.* (of a ship): Disproportionately heavy on one side.

Loquacious (lokwēⁱ·ʃəs), *a.* 1667. [f. L. *loquax, loquaci-*, f. *loqui* speak; see -OUS, -ACIOUS.] **1.** Given to much talking; talkative. **2.** *transf.* Of birds, water, etc.: Chattering, babbling. Chiefly *poet.* 1697.

1. The chief Exercise of the Female l. Faculty STEELE. **2.** L. Frogs DRYDEN. Hence **Loqua·cious-ly** *adv.*, **-ness.**

Loquacity (lokwæ·sĭti). 1596. [– Fr. *loquacité* or L. *loquacitas*, f. as prec.; see -ITY, -ACITY.] The condition or quality of being loquacious; talkativeness.

The only limit to his l. was his strength BUCKLE.

Loquat (lōᵘ·kwæt). 1814. [– Chinese *luh kwat*, lit. 'rush orange'.] The fruit of *Eriobotrya japonica*, a native of China and Japan, introduced into southern Europe, India, and Australia. Also, the tree itself. Also *l. tree.*

Lor', lor (lǭɹ), *int. vulgar.* 1835. A clipped form of LORD, used as an exclam.

Loral (lōᵊ·răl), *a.* (and *sb.*) 1874. [f. LORE *sb.*^{2} + -AL^1.] *Zool.* Pertaining to the lore. Hence as *sb.* = *l. shield* or *plate* (see LORE *sb.*^{2}).

Lorate (lōᵊ·reⁱt), *a.* 1836. [f. L. *lorum* (LORE *sb.*^{2}) + -ATE^2.] Strap-shaped.

Lorcha (lǭ·ɹtʃă), **lorch** (lǭɹtʃ). 1653. [– Pg. *lorcha*, of unkn. origin.] A light Chinese sailing vessel with the hull after a European model, but a Chinese rig, usually carrying guns.

Lord (lǭɹd), *sb.* [OE. *hlāford*, once *hlāfweard* :– **χlaibward-*, f. **χlaib-* LOAF + **ward-* keeper, WARD *sb.* The etymol. sense expresses the relation of the head of a household to his dependants who 'eat his bread' (cf. OE. *hlāfǣta* 'bread-eater', servant, and the similar G. *brotherr* 'bread-lord', employer, Sw. *matmoder*, etc., 'meat-mother', mistress). The word is, like LADY, a peculiarly Eng. formation. It was reduced to one syll. (XV) by the fall of *v* in *lōverd* and coalescence of the vowels. The development of sense has been largely influenced by the adoption of the word as the customary rendering of L. *dominus*.]

I. A master, ruler. **†1.** A master of servants; the male head of a household –1611. **2.** One to whom service and obedience are due; a master, chief, prince, sovereign. Now only *rhet.* Also *l. and master.* OE. **b.** *fig.* One who or something which has the mastery or pre-eminence ME. **c.** An owner, possessor, proprietor (of land, houses, etc.). Now only *poet.* or *rhet.* ME. **d.** A 'magnate' in some particular industry. (Cf. *King.*) 1823. **3.** *spec.* A feudal superior; the proprietor of a fee, manor, etc. OE. **4.** A husband. Now only *poet.* or *joc.* OE. **5.** [Cf. 2 b.] *Astrol.* The planet that has a dominant influence over an event, period, region, etc. ME. **6. The Lord** (vocatively **Lord**): God OE. **b.** As an exclam. of surprise. Now only in profane or trivial use. ME. **7.** As a title of Jesus Christ. Commonly *Our L.*; also *the L.* ME.

1. *Matt.* 24:46. **2.** Man over men He made not L. MILT. transf. *L.L.L.* IV. i. 38. **b.** *Lords of (the) creation*: mankind; now *joc.*, men as opp. to women. My bosomes L. sits lightly in his throne SHAKS. **c.** L. of few Acres, and those barren too DRYDEN. **d.** The cotton lords are not more popular than the landlords COBDEN. **3.** *L. of the Manor* (see MANOR). *L. mesne, paramount* (see those wds.). **4.** *Tam. Shr.* V. ii. 131. **6.** The L. increase this businesse SHAKS. Phr. *(The) L. knows who, what, how*, etc.: a flippant expression of one's own ignorance of a matter. *L. have mercy (on us)*: (*a*) a prayer (chalked on house-doors in time of plague); (*b*) in trivial use (vulgarly *lord-a-mercy*, etc.), as an exclam. of astonishment. So (in trivial use only) *L. bless me.* **b.** O L. I must laugh SHAKS. **7.** How loyal in the following of thy L.! TENNYSON. Phr. *(In) the year of our L.*, †*of our Lord's incarnation*: = ANNO DOMINI. *Comb.*, etc. **The Lord's Prayer** [= L. *oratio Dominica*], the prayer taught by Jesus to His disciples (see *Matt.* 6:9–13); the paternoster. **The Lord's Supper** [= L. *cena Dominica*, Gr. τὸ κυριακὸν δεῖπνον 1 *Cor.* 11:24], the Holy Communion. **The Lord's table** [= Gr. τραπέζα κυρίου 1 *Cor.* 10:21]: cf. ALTAR 2 b; hence, the Holy Communion.

II. As a designation of rank, etc. **1.** In early use employed vaguely for any man of exalted position, and in a narrower sense applied to barons (see BARON 1). Now, = NOBLEMAN: A peer of the realm, or one who by courtesy is entitled to the prefix Lord, or some higher title, as a part of his ordinary appellation ME. **2.** pl. *The Lords*: the lords of parliament, temporal and spiritual, as constituting one of the two bodies composing the legislature of the United Kingdom 1451. **3.** Applied, with defining word, to the individual members of a Board appointed to perform the duties of some high office of state that has been put in commission (see below) 1642. **4.** Forming part of various official titles (see below) 1598. **b.** In ceremonious use, prefixed to the titles of bishops, whether lords of parliament or not 1639. **5.** As a prefixed title, forming part of a person's customary appellation. Abbrev. Ld., Lo. 1455.

Now used as follows. In substitution for 'Marquis', 'Earl', or 'Viscount' (whether denoting a peer, or applied 'by courtesy' to the eldest son of a peer of higher rank); the word *of* being dropped. Thus 'Lord Hartington' may be used instead of 'The Marquis of Hartington', etc. A baron is always called 'Lord —', as 'Lord Tennyson'; the Christian name, if used, comes first, as 'Alfred, Lord Tennyson'. The younger sons of dukes and marquises have the courtesy title of 'Lord' followed by the Christian name and surname, as 'Lord John Russell'.

The Lord, the early form of the prefixed title, still survives in certain formal uses, and in the superscription of letters.

6. Jocular uses. See below. 1556. **b.** *slang.* A hunchback 1700. **7. My Lord** (usu. pronounced milǭ·ɹd). **a.** Prefixed to a name or title. (*a*) Formerly used where we now use simply 'Lord' (see II. 5), with or without *of.* (Now only *arch.*) (*b*) *My L. of* (*London*, etc.): a respectful mode of referring to a bishop (*obs.* or *arch.*). (*c*) Prefixed to a title of rank or office; now only *vocatively*; as in *my L. Mayor, my L. Duke*, etc. 1440. **b.** Used separately. (*a*) The usual polite and respectful form of address to a nobleman under the rank of a duke, and to a bishop; also in speaking of them. (*b*) In courts of law used in addressing a judge of the Supreme Court; in Scotland and Ireland in addressing a judge of any of the superior courts. (In affected pronunciation *my Lud, m'lud*: see LUD.) **c.** pl. *My lords*: (*a*) form of address to a number of noblemen or bishops, and to two or more of the superior judges sitting in court together; (*b*) in departmental correspondence, used as a collective designation for the ministers composing the department.

1. The Englishman of to-day still dearly loves a l. 1900. Phr. *To live like a l.*: to fare sumptuously. *To treat* (a person) *like a l.*: to entertain sumptuously, to treat with great deference. Phr. *Drunk as a l.*; *to swear like a l. Lord-in-waiting, L. of the Bed-chamber*, any nobleman holding certain offices in attendance on the person of the sovereign, called 'in waiting' if the sovereign is a queen, 'of the bedchamber' if a king. **2.** The Lords..suspended the sitting until eleven at night 1879. *The Lords Temporal*, the temporal or lay peers. *The Lords Spiritual*: the bishops who are lords of parliament, and, formerly, the mitred abbots. *House of Lords* (see HOUSE *sb.*^{1} 4 d). **3.** *Lords Commissioners* (now simply *Lords*) *of the Admiralty, of the Treasury*; *Lords Commissioners of the Great Seal.* Also *Lords Justices* (*of Ireland*): the commissioners to whom, in the early 18th c., the viceregal authority was entrusted. *Civil L.*: the one civilian member (besides the First L.) of the Board of Admiralty, the others being *Naval Lords*. **4.** *L.* (*High*) *Admiral*, *L. Chamberlain*, *L.* (*High*) *Chancellor*, *L. Chief Justice*, *L. High Commissioner*, *L. Deputy*, *L. Marshal*, *L. President*, *L. Privy Seal*, *L. Treasurer*, *L. Warden*, etc. **Lord-rector,** an honorary title for the elected chief in certain Scotch Universities; hence *Lord-rectorship*. **5.** *The L. Harry*: see HARRY *sb.* **6.** *L. of Misrule* (see MISRULE), etc. **b.** His pupil..was..on account of his hump, distinguished by the title of My Lord SMOLLETT.

Lord (lǭɹd), *v.* ME. [f. LORD *sb.*] **1.** *intr.* †**a.** To exercise lordship –1489. **b.** To play the lord (now usu. with *over*); to assume airs of grandeur; to rule tyrannically, domineer ME. **2.** *trans.* To be or act as lord of; to control, manage, rule (*rare*) 1586. **3.** To confer the title of lord upon 1610; to address as 'Lord' 1636.

1. *To l. it*; They..l. it as they list SPENSER.

Lording (lǭ·ɹdiŋ). [OE. *hlāfording*; see LORD *sb.*, -ING³.] **1.** = LORD *sb.* I. 2. Rarely *sing.* = Sir! freq. in *pl.* = Sirs! Gentlemen! *Obs.* exc. *arch.* **2.** As dim. of LORD: A little lord, a petty lord; usu. *contemptuous* 1577. **3.** A kind of apple or pear 1664.

1. It was a Lordings daughter SHAKS. **2.** When you were Boyes: You were pretty Lordings then? SHAKS.

Lo·rdkin. [f. LORD *sb.* + -KIN.] A little or young lord. THACKERAY.

Lordless (lǭ·ɹdlės), *a.* [OE. *hlāfordlēas*, f. *hlāford* LORD *sb.* + *-lēas* -LESS.] Without a lord. Of a woman: Husbandless.

Lo·rd-lieute·nant. *Pl.* **lords-lieutenant(s, lord-lieutenants.** 1557. **a.** In Ireland (before the establishment of the Irish Free State in 1922): The Viceroy 1614. **b.** In a county: The chief executive authority and head of the magistracy, appointed by the sovereign by patent. Under him and of his appointing are deputy-lieutenants. 1557. Hence **Lo·rd-lieute·nancy.**

Lordlike (lǭ·ɹdləik). 1470. [-LIKE.] **a.** *adj.* Befitting or like a lord; lordly. Now *rare.* †**b.** *adv.* After the fashion of a lord; domineeringly; sumptuously –1727.

Lordling (lǭ·ɹdliŋ). ME. [f. LORD *sb.* + -LING¹.] **1.** A little or puny lord; often *contemptuous*. Occas. = LORDING *sb.* 1. †**2.** A kind of apple 1727.

Lordly (lǭ·ɹdli). [OE. *hlāfordlīć*, f. LORD *sb.* + -LY¹.]

A. *adj.* **1.** Of or pertaining to a lord; consisting of, or administered by, lords. Now *rare.* **2.** Having the character, attributes, appearance, or demeanour of a lord. Of actions: Befitting a lord; honourable. ME. **b.** Haughty, imperious, lofty, disdainful ME. **3.** Of things: Suitable for a lord; hence, grand, magnificent, noble 1535. **4.** *absol.* 1470.

1. A l. prelacy 1862. **2.** A l. spectacle CARLYLE. **b.** The L. domineering of the English 1665. **3.** I built my soul a l. pleasurehouse TENNYSON. Hence **Lo·rdlily** *adv.* **Lo·rdliness,** †the condition or state of a lord; l. disposition.

B. *adv.* After the manner of a lord; in a lordly manner ME.

Lord Mayor. 1554. A title, orig. of the mayors of London, York, and Dublin only, but now also of some other large towns.

Lord Mayor's Day, Nov. 9, when the Lord Mayor goes in procession with the city dignitaries to and from Westminster, where he receives from the Lord Chancellor the assent of the Crown to his election. *Lord Mayor's Show*, the procession on Lord Mayor's Day.

Lordolatry (lǫɹdǫ·lătri). *joc.* 1846. [f. LORD *sb.* + -LATRY.] Worship of lords.

The..prevalence of L. in this country THACKERAY.

‖**Lordosis** (lǫɹdōᵘ·sis). 1704. [mod.L. – Gr. λόρδωσις, f. λορδός bent backwards.] *Path.* Anterior curvature of the spine, producing convexity in front.

Lords and ladies. 1760. A popular name for the wild arum (*Arum maculatum*), in reference to the dark and light spadices.

Lord's day or **Day.** ME. [Properly, *The Lord's Day* = eccl. L. *dies Dominicus*, *d. Dominica* (whence Fr. *dimanche*, Sp. *domingo*, It. *domenica*), Gr. ἡ κυριακὴ ἡμέρα, *Rev.* 1:10.] A Christian appellation for Sunday.

Lord's day (without the article) is no longer used, except by some Nonconformists. *The Lord's day* is the form now current.

Lordship (lǭ·ɹdʃip). [OE. *hlāfordsćipe*; see LORD *sb.*, -SHIP.] **1.** The dignity and functions of a lord; dominion, rule; ownership *of* or dominion †*on*, *over*; rarely *pl.* **2.** The land or territory of a lord; a domain, estate, manor, seignory ME. †**b.** A government, province, district –1578. **3.** The personality of a lord, esp. with possess. prons. 1489. **b.** *joc.* (as a mock complimentary designation for ordinary persons or animals) 1892. **4.** *Sc.* A royalty 1861.

1. Our first parent had L. over Sea, and Land, and Air MILT. **3.** *Your lordship(s*: a form of address to noblemen (except archbishops and dukes), and to judges. **b.** His l. [the donkey] 1892.

Lore (lōᵊɹ), *sb.*¹ [OE. *lār* = OFris. *lāre*, OS., OHG. *lēra* (Du. *leer*, G. *lehre*) :– WGmc. **laiza* (= Gmc. **laizō*), f. *lais-* LEARN.] **1.** The act of teaching; the condition of being taught; instruction; a piece of instruction; a lesson. Now *arch.* and *dial.* **2.** That which is taught; doctrine. Applied chiefly to religious doctrine. Now *poet.* or *arch.* OE. †**b.** *pl.* Doctrines, precepts, ordinances –1580. †**c.** A creed, religion –1550. †**3.** Advice, counsel; instruction, command, order –1667. **4.** That which is learned; learning, scholarship, erudition. Now only *arch.* and *Sc.* Also, recently: The body of traditional facts or beliefs relating to some subject; as, *animal, bird, fairy, plant l.* ME.

1. She finish'd, and the suttle Fiend his l. Soon learnd MILT. **2.** Her [Vertue's] l. MILT. The l. of Christ TRENCH. **4.** Skill'd in legendary l. GOLDSM.

Lore (lōᵊɹ), *sb.*² 1621. [– L. *lorum* strap, thong.] †**1.** A strap, thong, rein (*rare*) –1636. **2.** *Nat. Hist.* A strap-like appendage or part in certain insects, birds, and snakes 1817.

Lore, str. pa. t. and pple. of LEESE *v.*

Loreal (lōᵊ·riăl), *a.* and *sb.* 1849. [app. irreg. f. LORE *sb.*² + -AL¹; cf. LORAL.] = LORAL.

†**Lorel.** [ME. *lorel*, f. *loren*, pa. pple. of LEESE, *v.*, as LOSEL from the var. *losen.*] A worthless person, rogue, blackguard; = LOSEL. In 16th c. often opp. to *lord*.

Cock Lorel. See *Cocke Lorelles Bote* (printed by Wynkyn de Worde *c*1515). *allusively*, Rogue, reprobate.

Loren, pa. pple. of LEESE *v.*

‖**Lorgnette** (lǫɹnye·t). 1820. [Fr., f. *lorgner* to squint; see -ETTE.] **a.** A pair of eye-glasses held in the hand, usu. by a long handle. **b.** An opera-glass.

‖**Lorgnon** (lǭ·ɹnyoṅ). 1846. [Fr., f. as prec.; see -OON.] **a.** A single or double eye-glass; a lorgnette. **b.** An opera-glass.

Lori, var. of LORIS.

‖**Lorica** (lŏrəi·kă). 1706. [L., 'breast-plate', f. *lorum* strap.] **1.** *Rom. Antiq.* A cuirass or corslet of leather. **2.** *Old Chem.* A kind of lute or paste for coating vessels before subjecting them to heat 1753. **3.** *Zool.* The protective case or sheath of some infusorians and rotifers; also applied to the carapace of crustaceans 1856. **4.** *Bot.* The integument of seeds. LINDLEY.

Loricate (lǫ·rikeᶦt). 1826. [– L. *loricatus*, pa. pple. of *loricare*; see next, -ATE².] *Zool.* **A.** *adj.* Covered with 'armour' or adjoining plates or scales; having a lorica. So **Lo·ricated** *a.* 1623. **B.** *sb. pl.* (repr. mod.L. *Loricati* or *Loricata.*) Applied to various groups of animals having such an integument, as those represented by the armadillos, crocodiles, and certain infusorians 1855.

Loricate (lǫ·rikeᶦt), *v.* 1623. [– *loricat-*, pa. ppl. stem of L. *loricare*, f. *lorica*; see LORICA, -ATE³.] *trans.* To enclose in or cover with a protective coating. Hence **Lorica·tion,** the action of loricating; *concr.* a defensive covering or casing 1706.

Lorikeet (lǫrikī·t). 1772. [f. LORY + *-keet* in PARAKEET.] Name for small brightly-coloured parrots of the Malay Archipelago, comprehending the genera *Charmosyna*, *Loriculus*, and *Coriphilus*.

Lorimer, loriner (lǫ·rimǝɹ, lǫ·rinǝɹ). Now *Hist.* ME. [– OFr. *loremier, lorenier*, f. *lorain* strap of harness :– Rom. **loranum*, f. L. *lorum* strap, thong; see -ER² 2. For the vars. *-m-*, *-n-*, cf. LATIMER.] A maker of bits and metal mountings for horses' bridles; also, a spurrier, and (generally) a maker of small iron ware, etc. (Now only in the title of a London livery company.)

†**Lo·ring,** *vbl. sb.* [f. LORE *sb.*¹ + -ING¹.] Teaching, instruction. SPENSER.

Loriot (lǫ·riǫ̆t). 1601. [– Fr. *loriot*, for *l'oriot*, with def. art. incorporated; *oriot* is an unexpl. alt. of *oriol* ORIOLE.] The Golden Oriole, *Oriolus galbula*.

Loris (lōᵊ·ris). Also *erron.* **lori, lory.** 1774. [– Fr. *loris* (Buffon), said to be – Du. †*loeris* booby, clown.] A small slender tailless nocturnal climbing lemur of Ceylon (*Loris gracilis*); also extended to the related genus *Nycticebus*.

Lorn (lǭɹn), *ppl. a.* ME. [pa. pple. of LEESE *v.*] †**1.** Lost, perished, ruined; doomed –1805. **2.** = FORLORN 4, 5. 1475.

1. If thou readest, thou art l.! SCOTT. **2.** Left lone and l. 1876.

Lorry, lurry (lǫ·ri, lʋ·ri). 1838. [Of north-country origin; the sp. *laurie* in the minutes of a meeting of the Liverpool and Manchester Railway of 3 Dec. 1834 suggests that the vehicle was called after an inventor named *Laurie.*] **1.** A long flat wagon without sides, or with low sides, running on four low wheels. Also, a truck or wagon running on railways or tramways. **2.** *Mining.* A running bridge over a pit 1883.

Lory (lōᵊ·ri). 1692. [– Malay *lūrī*, dial. var. of *nūrī*, whence synon. †*newry, nori* (XVII); earlier *lourey, lowry*, the present *lory* being due to Buffon's form *lori.*] A parrot-like bird of the family *Loriinæ*, with brilliant plumage, from South-eastern Asia and Australia. Also the S. African touraco, *Turacus albicristatus*.

Losable, loseable (lū·zăb'l), *a.* 1611. [f. LOSE *v.* + -ABLE.] Capable of being lost.

Losang(e, obs. f. LOZENGE.

†**Lose,** *sb.* ME. [– OFr. *los, loz, loos* :– L. *laudes*, pl. of *laus* praise.] Praise, renown, fame. Also (good or bad) reputation; *occas.* ill fame. *Out of lose*: to one's dispraise. –1825.

Lose (lūz), *v.*¹ [OE. *losian*, f. *los* LOSS, used mostly *intr.* (sense 1). Later, synonymous with the cognate LEESE *v.*, which it finally superseded. The normal phonetic repr. of *losian* would be (lōᵘz), which is found dial. and is reflected by the sp.; the pronunc. (lūz) is presumably due to the influence of *loose.*] †**1.** *intr.* To perish; to be lost –ME. †**2.** *trans.* To destroy, ruin; to be the ruin of –1628. **b.** To ruin in estimation (*rare*) 1605. **c.** *pass.* To be brought to destruction, ruin, or misery; to be killed; to be damned. Of a ship, etc.: To perish at sea. OE. **3.** To incur the privation of (something that one possesses or has control of); to part with through negligence or misadventure; to be deprived of. See below. ME. **4.** *absol.* or *intr.* To suffer loss; to cease to possess something; to be deprived of or part with some of one's or its possessions, attributes, or qualities; to become deteriorated or incur disadvantage ME. **b.** Of an immaterial thing: To be deprived of its power or force (*rare*) 1794. **5.** To become unable to find; to cease to know the whereabouts of OE. **b.** To fail to keep in sight. Also, *to l. sight of.* Also *occas.*, to cease to hear (*poet.*); to fail to follow in argument (*obs.* or *arch.*) 1587. **c.** To draw away from; to leave hopelessly behind in a race 1704. †**d.** To fail to retain in the mind or memory; to forget –1712. **e.** To cease to follow (the right track); also, to cease to find (traces of a person, etc.). Chiefly in *to l. one's way* (lit. and fig.). 1530. **6.** To spend unprofitably; to waste, get no return or result for (one's labour or efforts); to let slip (opportunities); to waste (time) ME. **7.** To fail to obtain (e.g. a prize); *occas.* const. *to*. Also, to fail to catch (a train, etc.). ME. **b.** To fail to apprehend; not to 'catch' (words, etc.) 1599. **c.** *Hunting.* To fail to catch (an animal) 1567. **8.** To forfeit (a stake); to be defeated in (a game, battle, lawsuit); to fail to carry (a motion). In *Cricket*: To have (a wicket) taken. Const. *to*. 1440. **9.** *causal.* To cause the loss of; often const. *dative* of the person suffering loss ME. **10.** *refl.* (and corresponding *pass.*). **a.** To go astray. Also *fig.* 1535. **b.** To become merged (*in* something else). Also *fig.* 1604. **c.** To become engrossed (*in* thought, etc.); to be overwhelmed (*in* wonder); †to be distracted (from excitement, etc.) 1604. **d.** To become obscured (*in* clouds, etc.) 1697.

2. b. *Lear* I. i. 236. **c.** The Woman that Deliberates is lost ADDISON. **3. a.** To l. lands, goods, a right, quality, a place, etc. ME. **b.** To l. a limb, faculty, one's life, etc. *To l. one's head*: see HEAD *sb. To l. heart*: to become discouraged. *To l. one's heart*: to fall in love. *To l. one's legs* (slang): to get drunk. **c.** To l. a relative, friend, servant, etc. by death, men in battle ME. To l. a patient 1882. **d.** *To l. patience, one's temper, to l. caste, hold, one's balance*, etc. *To l. ground*: to fail to keep one's position; esp. *fig.* to decline in reputation, favour, health, etc. **e.** To l. an ague 1677, one's fears 1742, a sense of misery 1859. **f.** To l. (a portion of itself, a quality, or appurtenance) ME. Til that the brighte sonne loste his hewe CHAUCER. Her household duties had lost their interest 1894. **g.** The *passive* is often used without any reference to a determinate person or thing as 'losing'; e.g. (of an art, etc.) to cease to be known or practised; (of a quality, etc.) to cease to be present 1667. **4.** Both armies lost heavily (*mod.*). **c.** *To l. out* (*U.S.*): to be unsuccessful, to fail 1889. **5.** Like a Schoole-boy that had lost his A.B.C. SHAKS. **c.** His great stride and iron legs..enabled him, in the language of the turf, to l. his antagonist 1886. **d.** Being ouerfull of selfe-affaires, My minde did l. it SHAKS. I am in great danger of losing my English 1718. **6.** There is no time to be lost MARRYAT. *To be lost on* or *upon*: to have no effect upon: Your kindness is not lost upon me 1833. **7.** Hee shall in no wise l. his reward *Matt.* 10:42. **b.** I did not l. a word of his speech 1903. **8.** If we loose the Field, We cannot keepe the Towne SHAKS. *absol.* A captiue victor that hath lost in gaine SHAKS. **9.** The crimes of John lost him all the northern part of his French possessions FREEMAN. **10. a.** I love to l. my selfe in a mystery SIR T. BROWNE. **b.** All surprise was shortly lost in other feelings JANE AUSTEN. **c.** I.. l. myself in melancholy musings W. IRVING. **d.** Woody mountains half in vapours lost POPE.

†**Lose**, *v.*² [f. LOSE *sb.*, or perh. aphetic f. ALOSE *v.*] *trans.* To praise. Only in ME.

Losel (lōᵘ·zĕl). *arch.* and *dial.* ME. [app. f. *losen*, pa. pple. of LEESE *v.* (cf. LOREL from the more usual *loren*, and BROTHEL from OE. *broþen*, pa. pple. of *brēoþan* be ruined). The etymol. sense is thus 'one who is lost', 'a son of perdition'.] **A.** *sb.* A worthless person; a profligate, rake, scoundrel; in weaker sense, a ragamuffin, ne'er-do-well. **B.** *adj.* Good-for-nothing, worthless 1601. Hence **Lo·selry**, profligacy, debauchery, rascality (*rare*).

†**Losenger.** ME. [– OFr. *losengeour* (nom. *-ere*), f. *losengier*, f. *losange* (mod. *louange* praise) flattery.] **1.** A false flatterer, a lying rascal, a deceiver –1616. ¶**2.** *Sc.* A sluggard. DOUGLAS. †**Losengery**, flattery, deceit.

Loser (lū·zəɹ). ME. [f. LOSE *v.*¹ + -ER¹.] **1.** One who loses (see LOSE *v.*¹). **b.** A horse that loses in a race 1902. **2.** *Billiards.* A losing hazard 1873. **3.** *Tennis.* A losing stroke 1928. **4.** *Bridge.* A losing card 1918.

Losing (lū·ziŋ), *vbl. sb.* OE. [f. LOSE *v.*¹ + -ING¹.] The action of LOSE *v.*¹

attrib. in **l.-money**, a payment allowed to the loser in certain competitions.

Lo·sing, *ppl. a.* 1519. [f. LOSE *v.*¹ + -ING².] That loses, or results in loss.

L. game, (*a*) a game played with ill success (usu. *fig.*); (*b*) a game in which the loser wins the stakes. **L. hazard**, see the sb. **Lo·singly** *adv.*

Loss (lǫs) [From XIV prob. back-formation from *lost*, pa. pple. of LOSE *v.*¹; cf. the synon. contemp. LOST *sb.* (Chaucer, Trevisa); not continuing OE. *los* (only in phr. *to lose* to destruction).] **1.** The condition or fact of being lost, destroyed, or ruined. Now only with mixture of other senses. OE. **2.** The fact of losing. See senses of LOSE *v.*¹ Const. with *of* or objective genitive. ME. †**3.** *occas.* Cause or occasion of ruin or deprivation –1548. **4.** An instance of losing. Also, a person, thing, or amount lost. ME. **5.** Detriment or disadvantage resulting from deprivation or change of conditions; an instance of this. (Opp. to *gain*.) ME. **6.** *Mil.* The losing of men by death, wounds, or capture; also (*sing.* and *pl.*) the number of men so lost ME. †**7.** Lack, default –1632. †**8.** *Tennis.* A lost chase (see CHASE *sb.*¹ 7) –1619.

1. Thou hast..quitted all to save A World from utter l. MILT. **2.** The l. of power 1620, of sight MILT. The L. of a Mother STEELE. The battle's l. SHELLEY. The l. of an hour TYNDALL, of a train 1903. *L. of life*: the being put to death (as a punishment). Also, the 'sacrifice' of human lives. **3.** Womman was the los of al mankynde CHAUCER. **4.** A rich fellow enough, goe to, and a fellow that hath had losses SHAKS. **5.** L. and gain NEWMAN (*title*). He is no l. 1903. Phr. *To have a great l. in* (or *of*): to suffer severely by losing. **6.** They were repulsed with l. GROTE. **7.** Phr. *In the l. of question*: provided there is no dispute. *Meas. for M.* II. iv. 90.

Phrase. **At a loss**, †**at l.** Of a hound: Having lost the track or scent; at fault. Hence of persons: At fault; puzzled what to say or do. *At a l. for*: unable to discover or obtain (something needed).

Comb.: **l.-leader** *U.S.*, an article sold below cost for the purpose of attracting buyers.

†**Lost**, *sb.* ME. [app. f. *lost*, pa. pple. of LOSE *v.*¹; see prec.] = LOSS *sb.* –1671.

Lost (lǫst), *ppl. a.* 1500. [pa. pple. of LOSE *v.*¹] **1.** That has perished or been destroyed; ruined, esp. morally or spiritually; (of the soul) damned 1533. **2.** Not retained in possession; no longer to be found. Also, of a person or animal: Having gone astray, having lost his or its way 1526. **3.** Of time, labour, space: Not used advantageously; spent in vain; †hence, vain. Of opportunities: Missed. 1500. **4.** Of a battle, game: In which one has been defeated. Also *transf.* Of a person: Defeated (*poet.*). 1724.

1. A l. man BURNET, ship FALCONER. **2.** The thought..of l. happiness MILT. The L. Leader BROWNING (*title*). A 'Lost Ball' 1849. *To give* (*over* or *up*) *for l.*, to consider, set down as lost. **3.** It were l. sorrow to waile one that's l. SHAKS. To make up for l. time 1889. **4.** In the l. battle, borne down by the flying SCOTT.

Phr. *To be l. to*: **a.** to have passed from the possession of; **b.** (of a person) to have no sense of (right, shame, etc.); also *rarely*, to have lost all interest in; †to be forgotten by, unknown to (the world).

Lot (lǫt), *sb.* [OE. *hlot* portion, choice, decision, corresp. to OFris. *hlot*, MLG., (M)Du. *lot*, ON. *hlutr*, *hluti*; f. **χlut-* (also in OE. *hlȳt* lot), rel. to **χleut-*, in OE. *hlēotan*, OS. *hliotan*, OHG. *liozan*, ON. *hljóta* cast lots, obtain by lots, and to **χlaut-*, in OE. *hlīet* (:– **χlautiz*), OS. *hlōt*, OHG. (*h*)*lōz* (G. *loos*, *los*), Goth. *hlauts* lot; the primary Gmc. sense is unkn.] **1.** An object (usu. a piece of wood) used in an ancient method of selection or decision by chance; a number of these being placed in a receptacle and shaken or drawn out. Nearly always in phr. *to cast* or (arch.), *draw* (†*send*, †*throw*, etc.) *lots* (or †*lot*). **b.** In abstract sense: The use of this, or any equivalent process, to obtain a decision. Chiefly in phr. *by l.* ME. **c.** The choice resulting from a casting of lots ME. †**d.** *sing.* and *pl.* Applied to games of chance or to divinatory appeals to chance –1777. **2.** What falls to a person by lot OE. **b.** *fig.* One's destiny, fortune, or portion in this life; condition (good or bad) in life ME. **3.** A tax, due, custom; esp. in *scot and lot* (see SCOT *sb.*²). **b.** *Derbyshire Mines.* See quots. 1631. †**4.** A prize in a lottery –1711. Also in the card-game LOTTERY. **5. a.** (Now chiefly *U.S.*) A plot or portion of land assigned by the state to a particular owner. Hence, any piece of land divided off, e.g. for building or pasture. **b.** One of the plots in which a tract of land is divided when offered for sale. 1450. **6.** An article, or set of articles, offered separately at a general sale; *esp.* each of the items at a sale by auction 1704. **b.** *transf.* of a person (*colloq.*); chiefly in *a bad l.* 1862. **7.** *gen.* A number or quantity of persons or things associated in some way; also, a quantity (of anything). Now only *colloq.*, exc. of goods, live stock, etc. Often slightly depreciatory. 1725. **8.** *colloq.* A considerable number or quantity; a good deal, a great deal. Used in sing. (*a l.*) and pl.; also as quasi-adv. Often absol. Also with adj., as *a good l.*, *a great l.* 1812.

1. Phr. *To cast* (rarely *throw*) *in one's l. with*: to associate oneself with the fortunes of. **b.** Good Counsell comes not by L., nor by Inheritance HOBBES. **c.** Phr. *The l. falls on* (a person or thing). **2.** Now cometh thy l. (= 'turn'), now comestow on the rynge CHAUCER. The lott is fallen vnto me in a fayre grounde COVERDALE *Ps.* 15[6]:6. Phr. *To fall to the l. of*. *To have neither part nor l. in*, after Acts 8:21. **b.** Bewailing His l. unfortunate in nuptial choice MILT. Phr. *The l. falls* (*to* a person), (*it*) *falls to the l. of* (a person), *it falls to* (him) *as his l.* (to have or to do something). **3. b.** The Duty called L...shall be One Thirteenth Part of all Ore raised within the Jurisdiction of the Barmote Courts 1851. **4.** *Great l.*, *chief l.*, the highest prize. **6.** L. after lt was disposed of..at..good prices 1859. **7.** Two several lots of children 1854. A large l. of ore RAYMOND. Phr. *The l.* = the whole number or quantity. A shilling for the l. 1877. **8.** I've lots to do 1891. I would give a l. to [etc.] 1901.

Comb.: **l.-mead, -meadow**, a common meadow, the shares in which are apportioned by l.; **-seller**, one who sells a variety of small articles, or 'a lot', all for 1*d.*; so **-selling.**

Lot (lǫt), *v.* 1449. [f. LOT *sb.* Cf. Fr. *lotir* cast lots, etc.]

I. *intr.* **1.** To cast lots. Const. interrog. cl., or *for*. *rare.* 1483. **2.** *To l. upon*: to count upon, expect. Now *U.S.* 1642.

II. *trans.* **1.** To assign *to* one as his portion; to assign as one's lot or destiny. Also with *out*. 1524. **2.** To divide (land) into lots. Usu. with *out*: To portion out and allot (*to* a person or persons). 1449. **3.** To divide or group into lots for sale. Also with *out*. 1709. **4.** To cast lots for; to apportion or distribute by lot. Now *rare*. 1703. **5.** To choose (pressed men) by lot for service. *Obs.* exc. *Hist.* 1758.

‖**Lota, lotah** (lōᵘ·tă). *Anglo-Ind.* Also **lootah, loto.** 1809. [Hindi *loṭa*.] A spheroidal water-pot, usu. of polished brass.

Lote (lōᵘt), *sb. arch.* 1510. Anglicized form of LOTUS, in various senses. So **Lote-tree,** *arch.* 1548.

†**Lote**, *v.* ME. only. [perh. repr. OE. **lotian*, f. **lut-*, grade-var. of **lūt* in synon. OE. *lūtian* = OHG. *lūzzēn*; prob. f. same base as that in OE. *lūtan* LOUT *v.*¹] *intr.* To lurk, lie concealed. Hence †**Lo·teby**, a lover, a paramour ME.

Loth, alternative f. LOATH.

Lothario (loþēᵊ·riˌo). 1756. [A character in Rowe's *Fair Penitent*.] A libertine, gay deceiver, rake. (With capital L.)

The gay L. dresses for the fight 1756.

Lotion (lōᵘ·ʃən). ME. [– (O)Fr. *lotion* or L. *lotio*, *-ion-* washing, f. *lōt-*, *laut-*, pa. ppl. stem of *lavare* LAVE *v.*¹; see -ION.] †**1.** The action of washing (the body); washing with a medicinal preparation; *pl.* ritual ablutions –1797. †**2.** The washing of metals, medicines, etc. in water to cleanse them –1796. **3.** *Pharm.* A liquid preparation used externally to heal wounds, relieve pain, beautify the skin, etc. ME. **4.** *slang.* Alcoholic drink 1876.

Loto: see LOTA, LOTTO.

‖**Lotophagi** (lōᵘtǫ·fădʒəi), *sb. pl.* 1601. [L. – Gr. Λωτοφάγοι, f. λωτός LOTUS + φαγεῖν eat.] The lotus-eaters; a people in Greek legend who lived on the fruit of the lotus, which caused a dreamy forgetfulness in those who ate it. So **Loto·phagous** *a. rare*, lotus-eating, resmbling the L. 1855.

Lottery (lǫ·təri). 1567. [prob. – Du. *loterij* (early XVI), whence mod.L. *loteria*; cf. Fr. *loterie* – Du., or It. *lotteria*; see LOT *sb.*, -ERY.] **1.** An arrangement for the distribution of prizes by chance among persons purchasing tickets. Slips or lots, bearing the same numbers as the tickets, and representing either prizes or blanks, are drawn from a wheel. Also *transf.* and *fig.* †**2.** Sortilege, appeal to the lot; also, chance, issue of events as determined by chance –1663. †**3.** Something which comes by lot or fortune. *Ant. & Cl.* II. ii. 248. **4.** A round game at cards, in which certain cards carry prizes 1830.

Comb.: **l.-wheel,** a vertical wheel bearing on its axis a drum by the revolution of which the numbered slips are shuffled before being drawn.

Lotto, loto (lǫ·to, lōᵘ·to). 1778. [– It. *lotto* or its deriv., Fr. *loto*.] A game played with cards divided into numbered and blank squares and numbered discs to be drawn on the principle of a lottery.

A disc is drawn from a bag, and its number called; a counter is placed on the square so numbered, the player whose card first gets one row covered being the winner.

Lotus (lōᵘ·tǫs), **lotos** (lōᵘ·tǫs). *Pl.* **lotuses.** 1540. [– L. *lotus* – Gr. λωτός, of Semitic origin.] **1.** The plant yielding the fruit eaten by the LOTOPHAGI; represented by Homer (*Od.* ix. 90 ff.) as producing a state of dreamy forgetfulness and loss of all desire to return home. (Identified by some with the jujube-tree, *Zizyphus lotus*.) Hence *allusively*. **2.** A tree mentioned by ancient writers, having hard, black wood; prob. the nettle-tree, *Celtis australis* 1551. **3.** The water-lily of Egypt and

Asia, *Nymphæa lotus* (and other species), and *Nelumbium speciosum* 1584. **b.** *Arch.* An ornament repr. the Egyptian water-lily. **4.** Some kind of clover or trefoil (in Homer, food for horses) 1562. **5.** Name of a genus of leguminous plants, including the Bird's-foot Trefoil, *Lotus corniculatus* 1753.

1. Eating the Lotos day by day TENNYSON. **4.** When with rush-grass tall, Lotus and all sweet herbage, every one Had pastured been SHELLEY.

Lotus-eater. Also **lotos-.** 1832. One of the LOTOPHAGI; *transf.* one who gives himself up to dreamy and luxurious ease. So **Lotus-eating** *vbl. sb.* and *ppl. a.* 1861.

‖**Louche** (lūʃ), *a. rare.* 1819. [Fr. *louche* squinting.] Oblique, not straightforward.

Loud (laud), *a.* [OE. *hlūd* = OFris. *(h)lūd*, OS. *hlūd* (Du. *luid*), OHG. *hlūt* (G. *laut*) :- WGmc. **χluða* :- IE. **klūtós*, pa. pple. of **kleu-* **klu-* hear, a base of very wide extent, whence also Gr. *κλύειν* hear, *κλυτός* famous, L. *cluēre* be famed.] **1.** Of sounds or voices: Strongly audible; striking forcibly on the sense of hearing. Hence, with agent-n.: That speaks, sings, etc. with a loud voice. **b.** Giving a forcible sound, sonorous. **c.** Of a place, etc.: Full of noise, re-echoing 1595. **2.** *fig.* **a.** Clamorous, noisy; emphatic, vehement in expression 1530. †**b.** Manifest, palpable, flagrant. Chiefly of a lie. –1700. **3.** *transf.* Of smell or flavour: Powerful, offensive. Now chiefly *U.S. colloq.* 1641. **4.** Of colours, dress, etc.: Vulgarly obtrusive. Opp. to *quiet*. 1849.

1. A l. halloo SCOTT, speaker 1855. **b.** L. wyndes ME., seas 1898. **c.** Streets and factories l. with life 1878. **3.** The strong breath and l. stench of avarice MILT. **4.** The l. pattern of his trousers 1878. *Comb.* **l. speaker** *Wireless Telephony*, any one of several similar instruments for converting electrical impulses into sounds loud enough to be heard at a distance. **Lou·dish** *a.* somewhat l. **Lou·d-ly** *adv.*, **-ness.**

Loud (laud), *adv.* [OE. *hlude*, f. *hlūd* (prec.) with adverbial suffix.] **1.** Loudly; aloud. **2.** Of smell: Strongly, offensively 1871. *Comb.* **l.-spoken** *a.* given to loud speaking.

Louden (lau·d'n), *v.* 1848. [f. LOUD *a.* + -EN⁵.] To become or make loud or louder.

†**Lough**¹. [ME. *lowe, loȝe, lou(g)h*, repr. OE. (Northumb.) *luh* pool, strait, gulf – Ir. *loch*; the normal pronunc. of the Eng. word has been superseded by that of Ir. *loch*.] A lake, pool. In ME. poetry *occas.*, Water, sea. –1829. *attrib.*, as **l.-diver, -plover,** names for the female smew 1678.

Lough² (lǫχ). ME. [– Irish *loch* (see LOCH), with spelling of prec.] A lake or arm of the sea (in Ireland); = Sc. LOCH.

‖**Louis** (lū·i). *Hist.* Pl. **louis.** Also †**lewis,** *pl.* **lewis('s.** 1689. [Fr. *louis*, use of the Christian name of many French kings.] = LOUIS D'OR.

‖**Louis d'or** (lūidǭ·ɹ). *Hist.* 1689. [Fr., lit. 'gold louis'; see prec.] A gold coin issued in the reign of Louis XIII and subsequently till the time of Louis XVI. After the Restoration applied to the 20-franc piece or Napoleon.

‖**Louis Quatorze** (lūikætǭ·ɹz). 1842. Louis XIV, King of France, 1643–1715. Used as adj. to designate the styles in architecture, furniture, etc. of his reign. So **Louis Quinze** (-kæṅz), Louis XV, 1715–74. **Louis Seize** (-sēz), Louis XVI, 1774–93. **Louis Treize** (-trēz), Louis XIII, 1610–43.

Lounge (laundʒ), *sb.* 1775. [f. LOUNGE *v.*] **1.** An act, spell, or course of lounging; a saunter, stroll; also, a lounging gait 1806. **b.** *slang* (Eton and Cambridge), 'a treat, a chief meal' 1844. **2.** A place where one can lounge; esp. applied to a sitting-room for guests in a hotel, etc.; a gathering of loungers 1775. **3.** A kind of sofa or easy chair on which one can lie at length 1852. **4.** *attrib.* 1800.

2. But pray, Mr. Fag, what kind of a place is this Bath?..*Fag*...'tis a good l. SHERIDAN. *attrib.* **l. lizard,** one who frequents hotel lounges, e.g. as a professional dancing partner.

Lounge (laundʒ), *v.* 1508. [perh. f. LUNGIS.] **1.** *intr.* To move indolently, resting betweenwhiles, or the like. **2.** To recline lazily, to loll 1746. **3.** To idle 1671. **4.** *trans.* To pass (time, etc.) *away* (rarely *out*) with lounging 1776. Hence **Lou·nger.**

4. To l. away whole months 1776.

attrib. **l. suit,** a suit comprising a short coat designed for ordinary wear.

Loup (laup), *sb.*¹ *Sc.* ME. [– ON. *hlaup*; see LEAP *sb.*¹, LOPE *sb.*] = LEAP *sb.*¹ So **Loup** *v.* [– ON. *hlaupa*].

‖**Loup** (lū), *sb.*² 1834. [– Fr. *loup*, lit. 'wolf'.] A light mask or half-mask of silk or velvet worn by women.

Loup, obs. f. LOOP.

‖**Loup cervier** (lu sę̄rvye). 1725. [Fr. – L. *lupus cervarius* (Pliny) the lynx (*lupus* wolf, *cervarius* that hunts stags, f. *cervus* stag).] The Canada Lynx (*Lynx canadensis*).

Lour, lower (lauᵊɹ, lau·əɹ), *sb.* ME. [f. LOUR *v.*] **1.** A gloomy or sullen look; a scowl. **2.** Of the sky, etc.: Gloominess, threatening appearance 1596.

1. In one smile or lowre of thy sweet eye Consists my life DRAYTON. **2.** The tempest's lower J. WILSON. Hence **Lou·ry, low·ery** *a.* dull, gloomy 1648.

Lour, lower (lauᵊɹ, lau·əɹ), *v.* ME. [Of unkn. origin.] **1.** *intr.* To frown, scowl; to look angry or sullen. **b.** quasi-*trans.* To express by frowning. WESLEY. **2.** *transf.* and *fig.* Of the clouds, sky, etc.: To look dark and threatening 1450.

1. Nor from that right to part an hour, Smile she or lowre MILT. **b.** To lour defiance 1746. **2.** A shadow lour'd on the fields M. ARNOLD. Hence **Lou·ringly, Low·eringly** *adv.* gloomily, threateningly.

†**Lourd.** ME. [– (O)Fr. *lourd* heavy, †foolish.] **A.** *adj.* Sluggish, dull, sottish, stupid –1681. **B.** *sb.* A sottish fellow, a lout 1579–90.

Louse (laus), *sb.* Pl. **lice** (ləis). [OE. *lūs*, pl. *lȳs*, = MLG., MDu., OHG. *lūs* (Du. *luis*, G. *laus*), ON. *lús*.] **1.** A parasitic insect of the genus *Pediculus*, infesting the human hair and skin. Applied also to other kinds of insects parasitic on mammals, birds, and plants, and to the degraded crustaceans which infest fishes; often differentiated, as *bird-, fish-, plant, sea-l.* **2.** *transf.* Applied in scorn to human beings 1633.

1. 'Tis not that I value the money three skips of a l. SWIFT.

Comb.: **l.-disease,** PHTHIRIASIS; **lousewort,** †(*a*) Stinking Hellebore, *Helleborus fœtidus*; (*b*) any plant of the genus *Pedicularis*, esp. *P. palustris* and *P. sylvatica*; (*c*) Yellow Rattle, *Rhinanthus cristagalli*; (*d*) *Delphinium staphisagria*.

Louse (lauz), *v.* 1440. [f. LOUSE *sb.*] **1.** *trans.* To clear (a person, oneself, a garment) of lice. Also *intr.* for *refl.* †**2.** *intr.* To be infested with lice. *Lear* III. ii. 29.

Lousy (lau·zi), *a.* ME. [f. LOUSE *sb.* + -Y¹.] **1.** Full of lice, infested by lice. †**b.** Characterized by the presence of lice –1830. **2.** *fig.* Dirty, filthy, obscene. Also: Mean, sorry, scurvy, vile, contemptible. Now *slang*. ME.

1. I do not give to a l. Tibetan KIPLING. **b.** †*L. disease, evil* = PHTHIRIASIS. **2.** A l. story 1893. Hence **Lou·sily** *adv.*, **Lou·siness.**

Lout (laut), *sb.* 1548. [perh. f. LOUT *v.*¹] **1.** An awkward fellow; a bumpkin, clown. **2.** *Rugby School slang.* A common fellow, 'cad' 1857.

1. 'Tis no trusting to yond foolish Lowt SHAKS. Hence **Lou·tish** *a.* like a l. **Lou·tish-ly** *adv.*, **-ness.**

Lout (laut), *v.*¹ Pa. t. and pple. **louted.** Now *arch., poet.*, and *dial.* [OE. *lūtan* (str. vb.), corresp. to ON. *lúta*, f. Gmc. base **leut-* **laut-* **lŭt-*. Cf. LOTE *v.*] *intr.* (occas. *refl.*) To bend, bow, make obeisance; to stoop; also with *down*. **b.** *fig.* To bow, stoop, submit (*to*) ME.

He faire the knight saluted, louting low SPENSER.

Lout, *v.*² 1530. [perh. f. LOUT *sb.*] **1.** *trans.* To treat with contumely, mock. (Cf. FLOUT *v.*) **2.** *intr.* To act as a lout; to loll about 1807.

1. 1 *Hen. VI*, IV. iii. 13.

Louver (lū·vəɹ). Also **louvre, luffer.** [ME. *luver, lover* – OFr. *lover, lovier* skylight, prob. – Gmc. form related to **laubja* LODGE *sb.*] **1.** A domed turret-like erection on the hall-roof, etc. of a mediæval building, with lateral openings for the passage of smoke or light. (Cf. LANTERN 3.) †**2.** A dovecote of this construction –1661. **3.** Chiefly *pl.* An arrangement of overlapping boards, laths, or slips of glass, admitting air, but excluding rain 1555.

1. Ne lightned was with window, nor with louer SPENSER. *Comb.* **l.** (*luffer*) **boards** (see 3). Hence **Louvered** *ppl. a.* arranged like louvers, provided with a l. or louvers.

†‖**Louvre** (lūvr). 1729. [Fr.; named after the *Louvre*, the palace of the French kings at Paris.] Some kind of dance –1772.

Lovable, loveable (lɒ·văb'l), *a.* ME. [f. LOVE *v.*¹ + -ABLE.] Deserving of being loved; amiable; attractive.

'She is..very loveable—that is the exact word.' 'I fear it is not English', said Miss Hauton MAR. EDGEWORTH. Hence **Lov(e)abi·lity, Lo·v(e)ableness. Lo·v(e)ably** *adv.*

Lovage (lɒ·vėdʒ). [ME. *lov(e)ache*, alt. (as if *love-ache* 'love parsley': see ACHE *sb.*²) of OFr. *levesche, luvesche* (mod. *livèche*) :- late L. *levisticum* (sc. *apium*), for earlier *ligusticum*, n. of *ligusticus* Ligurian.] The umbelliferous herb *Levisticum officinale*, used as a domestic remedy; also applied, with or without defining word, to other umbellifers.

Love (lɒv), *sb.* [OE. *lufu* = OFris. *luve*, OHG. *luba*, Goth. *brōþru|lubō* brotherly love :- Gmc. **lubō*, f. weak grade of **leub-* **laub-* **lub-*, repr. also by OS. *lubig* loving, OHG. *gilob* precious, and OE., OS., ON. *lof*, OHG. *lob* praise; for the other grades see LIEF, LEAVE *sb.*, BELIEF, BELIEVE. Outside Gmc. the base appears in L. *lubet* it is pleasing, *lubido* desire, OSl. *ljubŭ* dear, *ljubiti* love, Skr. *lúbhyati* desires.] **1.** That state of feeling with regard to a person which arises from recognition of attractive qualities, from sympathy, or from natural ties, and manifests itself in warm affection and attachment. **b.** An instance of affection. †Also, an act of kindness. OE. **2.** In religious use, applied to the paternal benevolence and affection of God, to the affectionate devotion due to God from His creatures, and to the affection of one created being to another thence arising OE. **3.** Strong predilection *for* or devotion *to* (something) OE. **4.** That feeling of attachment which is based upon difference of sex; the affection between lover and sweetheart OE. **b.** An instance of being in love. Also *collect. pl.* love-affairs 1589. **5.** (With capital.) The personification of sexual affection; usu. masculine, = Eros, Amor, or Cupid; formerly also = Venus ME. **b.** with *pl.* A Cupid; any one of the many nameless gods of love imagined by mythologists; a figure or representation of the god of love 1594. **6.** The sexual instinct and its gratification ME. **7.** A beloved person; *esp.* a sweetheart. (Often used as a term of endearment.) ME. Also *transf.* of animals. †**b.** A paramour (man or woman) –1613. **c.** The object of love; the beloved (of..) 1734. **d.** A charming or delightful person or thing; a 'duck' (*colloq.*) 1814. **8. a.** *For l.*: without stakes, for nothing 1678. **b.** In scoring in various games, as tennis, rackets, etc.: No score, nothing; *l. all*, no score on either side. 1742. **c.** A form of euchre 1886. †**9.** A game of guessing the number of fingers held up in a quick movement of the hand; = MORA² –1725. †**10.** 'A kind of thin silk stuff' (J.), formerly used when in mourning; a border of this. Also *love-hood*. 1650–1829. **11.** A name for Traveller's Joy, *Clematis vitalba* 1640.

1. Thy loue hath bene more speciall vnto me, then the loue of wemen COVERDALE 2 *Sam.* 1:26. Loue doth moue the mynde to mercie 1557. Phr. (*Give*) *my l. to..*, or *L. to..*: convey a message of affection to (a third person). Also *to send one's l.* **b.** What good loue may I performe for you? SHAKS. **2.** God is loue 1 *John* 4:16. This is the loue of God, that we keepe his commandements *Ibid.* 5: 3. **3.** Blynde auarice and loue of money HALL. The l. of ease and the l. of occupation FOWLER. **4.** It is commonly a weak man who marries for l. JOHNSON. The greatest weakness of the play is in the scenes of l. JOHNSON. **b.** I suppose, the Colonel was cross'd in his first L. SWIFT. **5.** In peace, L. tunes the shepherd's reed; In war, he mounts the warrior's steed SCOTT. **b.** The little Loves, that waited by, Bow'd COWLEY. **6.** Come, let vs take our fill of loue vntill the morning *Prov.* 7:18. **7.** Liue with me and be my Loue MARLOWE. **d.** The tiniest teacups you ever beheld—perfect loves! 1864.

Phrases. *For the l. of*: for the sake of, on account of. Now chiefly in adjurations. †*For* or *of all* (*the*) *loves, of all l.*: a phr. of strong entreaty. *For l. or money*: at any price, by any means. (In neg. contexts.) *In l.* (*with*): enamoured (of); *transf.* very fond (of) or much addicted (to). *Out of l.* (*with*):

the opposite of *in l.* (*with*); disgusted with. *To fall in l.*: to become enamoured; *transf.* to become very fond of. Const. *with. To make l.*: to pay amorous attention; with *to* = to court, woo. **b.** Proverbs, etc. *L. is blind. Labour of l.*: work that one delights in, or work undertaken to benefit a person one loves. *L. in a cottage*: marriage with insufficient means. *There's no l. lost between them*: an ambiguous phrase, meaning: †(*a*) Their affection is mutual; (*b*) *now*, They have no l. for each other.

Combs. **a.** General: as *l.-adept*; *l.-inspiring*; *l.-stricken*; and many others, of obvious meaning. **b.** Special: **l.-affair,** orig. *pl.* the experiences connected with being in l.; now *sing.* an amour; **-begotten** *a.*, illegitimate; **-call,** a call or note used as a means of amorous communication between the sexes; **-child,** a child born out of wedlock 1805; **-cup,** †(*a*) a philtre; (*b*) a loving-cup; **-dart,** an organ found in certain snails, the *spiculum amoris*; **-drink,** a drink to excite l., a philtre; **-favour** (see FAVOUR *sb.* 6); †**-juice,** a juice which dropped on the eyes has the effect of a philtre; **-letter,** a letter of courtship; **-making,** amorous proposals or intercourse, courtship; **-match,** a marriage for l., not for money or convenience; **-mate,** one with whom one is mated in love, a lover or sweetheart; **-philtre,** = PHILTRE; **-potion,** a philtre; **-scene,** a scene, esp. in a story or play, consisting of an interview between lovers; **-song,** an amorous song ME.; **-story,** a story about the affection between lovers; **-token,** something given as a token of love OE.

In names of plants and animals: **l.-bind,** Traveller's Joy; **-entangle, -entangled** = *love-in-a-mist* (*a*); **-grass,** a grass of the genus *Eragrostis*; **l.-in-a-mist,** (*a*) the Fennel-flower, *Nigella damascena*; (*b*) a W. Indian plant, *Passiflora fœtida*; **l.-in-idleness** (also †**l.-in-idle**), the Heartsease, *Viola tricolor* (cf. IDLE *sb.* 1, IDLENESS 1); **l.-lies-(a)-bleeding,** the garden-plant *Amaranthus caudatus*, having a long drooping purplish-red spike of bloom; **l.-parrakeet, -parrot** = LOVE-BIRD; **-tree,** the Judas-tree, *Cercis siliquastrum*; also *tree of love*; **-vine,** the Dodder.

Love (lɒv), *v.*[1] [OE. *lufian*, f. *lufu* LOVE *sb.*] **1.** *trans.* To bear love to; to entertain a great regard for; to hold dear. **2.** *absol.* and *intr.* To entertain a strong affection; *spec.* to be in love ME. **3.** *trans.* **a.** To be unwilling to part with (life, honour, etc.) OE. **b.** To be fond of; to be devoted or addicted to. In U.S. a frequent vulgarism for *like*. ME. **c.** To take pleasure in the existence of (a virtue, a practice, a state of things) ME. **4.** Of plants or animals: To tend to thrive in (a certain kind of situation) 1573. **5.** Const. *inf.* To have great pleasure in doing something; †with negative, not to like. †Also *rarely* of things (= L. *amare*, Gr. φιλεῖν) to be accustomed. ME. **6.** To caress, embrace affectionately. (A childish use.) 1877.

1. Whom forsothe the Lord looueth, he chastiseth WYCLIF *Prov.* 3:12. I neuer knew woman loue man so SHAKS. L. me, l. my dog *Provb.* (*Lord*) *l. you* (*or your heart*), etc.: a vulgar ejaculation. *I l. my love with an A, with a B*, etc.: a formula used in games of forfeits. **2.** One that lou'd not wisely, but too well SHAKS. Loue (= l. one another), and be Friends *Jul. C.* IV. iii. 131. **3. a.** No man styrre and he l. his lyfe 1530. **b.** Loue not sleepe, lest thou come to pouertie *Prov.* 20:13. **c.** I l. firm government BURKE. **4.** The violet loves a sunny bank B. TAYLOR. **5.** They don't l. to be told the Truth 1704.

†**Love,** *v.*[2] [OE. *lofian* = OS. *lobon* (Du. *loven*), OHG. *lobōn, lobēn* (G. *loben*), ON. *lofa* :- Gmc. *lobōjan, lobǣjan*, f. *lob-*; see LOVE *sb.*] To praise –1596.

Lo·ve-apple. ? *Obs.* Also **apple of love.** 1578. [tr. Fr. *pomme d'amour*, G. *liebesapfel*.] The fruit of the TOMATO, *Lycopersicum esculentum*. †Formerly also the BRINJAL.

Lo·ve-bird. 1595. A very small bird of the parrot tribe, esp. the W. African Lovebird, *Agapornis pullarius*, remarkable for the affection it shows for its mate. Also applied to other species of parrot.

†**Lo·veday.** ME. [tr. med.L. *dies amoris* (XIII).] **1.** A day appointed for a meeting for the amicable settlement of a dispute; hence, an agreement entered into at such a meeting –1655. **2.** A day for love-making. GREENE.

†**Love-drury.** ME. only. [f. LOVE *sb.* + DRU(E)RY.] = DRUERY 1, 2.

Lovee (lɒvī·). *nonce-wd.* 1754 (Richardson). [f. LOVE *sb.* + -EE[1].] One who is loved.

Lo·ve-feast. 1580. **1.** *Eccl. Antiq.* Used as tr. Gr. ἀγάπη, Eccl. L. AGAPE. Among the early Christians, a meal partaken of in token of brotherly love; app. orig. in connection with the Eucharist; *transf.* a parochial feast at a festival time. **2.** Among Methodists, etc. a religious service in imitation of this 1738.

Loveful (lɒ·vfŭl), *a.* ME. [f. LOVE *sb.* + -FUL.] †**1.** Lovable –1596. **2.** Abounding in love (now *rare*) ME.

Lo·ve-knot. ME. A knot or bow of ribbon tied in a peculiar way, supposed to be a love token. Cf. *true-love knot*.

Loveless (lɒ·vlės), *a.* ME. [f. LOVE *sb.* + -LESS.] **1. a.** Not feeling love. **b.** Not loved. †**2.** Unlovely. P. HOLLAND. Hence **Lo·velessly** *adv.*, **-ness.**

Lovelihead (lɒ·vlihed). *rare.* 1633. [f. LOVELY *a.* + -HEAD.] Loveliness.

Lovelock (lɒ·vlǫk). 1592. [f. LOVE *sb.* + LOCK *sb.*[1]] A particular curl worn by courtiers in the time of Elizabeth and James I; later, any curl or tress of a striking character.

Lo·ve-lorn, *a.* 1634. [f. LOVE *sb.* + LORN *ppl. a.*] Forsaken by one's love; pining from love.

The love-lorn Nightingale MILT.

Lovely (lɒ·vli), *a.* [OE. *luflić*, f. *lufu* LOVE + *-lić* -LY[1].] †**1.** Loving, kind, affectionate –1602. †**b.** Amorous –1599. **2.** Lovable; having qualities that attract love OE. **3.** Lovable on account of beauty; beautiful. Now with emotional sense: Exquisitely beautiful. ME. **b.** with ref. to moral or spiritual beauty 1805. **4.** *colloq.* Delightful, highly excellent 1614.

1. b. Sweet Cytherea..Did court the Lad with many a louely looke SHAKS. **2.** Being beloued in all companies for his louely qualities SIDNEY. **3.** Til the teares..Like enuious flouds ore-run her louely face SHAKS. The loveliest and best That Time and Fate of all their Vintage prest E. FITZGERALD. L. all times she [Oxford] lies, l. tonight M. ARNOLD. **4.** Come my friend Coridon, this Trout looks l. WALTON. Hence **Lo·velily** *adv.* **Lo·veliness.**

†**Lo·vely,** *adv.* [OE. *luflīće*, f. *lufu* LOVE *sb.* + *-līće* -LY[2].] **1.** Lovingly, affectionately –1596. **2.** Lovably, beautifully –1811.

2. Oh thou weed: Who art so louely faire SHAKS.

Lover (lɒ·vəɹ). Also †**lovyer(e,** etc. ME. [f. LOVE *v.* + -ER[1].] One who loves. **1.** A friend or wellwisher. Now *rare*. **2.** One who is in love with or enamoured of a person of the other sex; now (exc. in *pl.*) usu. applied to the male ME. **b.** One who loves illicitly; a paramour 1611. **3.** One who has an affection, a fancy, or liking for (something) ME.

1. Ionathas and Dauid are sworne louers 1535. L. of souls! great God! I look to Thee J. H. NEWMAN. **2.** A louyer, and a lusty Bacheler CHAUCER. **b.** *Jer.* 3:1. **3.** He was a great l. of his country CLARENDON. Lovers of Liberty HUME, of Selborne 1901.

Lover, obs. f. LOUVER.

Loverly (lɒ·vəɹli). 1875. [f. LOVER + -LY.] **A.** *adj.* Like a lover. **B.** *adv.* In the manner of a lover. So **Lo·verwise** *adv.* in the manner of a lover.

Lovery, obs. f. LOUVER.

Lovesick (lɒ·vsik), *a.* 1530. [f. LOVE *sb.* + SICK *a.*] Languishing for or with love.

Purple the Sailes; and so purfumed that The Windes were Loue-sicke with them SHAKS. Where Nightingales their Love-sick Ditty sing DRYDEN. Hence **Lovesickness.**

Lovesome (lɒ·vsɒ̆m), *a.* Now *arch.* or *dial.* [OE. *lufsum*, f. *lufu* LOVE *sb.*; see -SOME[1].] = LOVELY *a.* in all senses. Hence **Lo·vesomeness.**

Loveworthy (lɒ·vwɒ̄:ɹði), *a.* ME. [f. LOVE *sb.* + WORTHY *a.*] Worthy to be loved. Hence **Loveworthiness.**

Lovey (lɒ·vi). Also **lovy.** 1731. [f. LOVE *sb.* + -Y[6].] A term of affection: = 'Dear love', 'darling'. Also **Lo·vey-do·vey** *sb.* and *a.*

And what would Dovey do if Lovey were to die? *Punch* 1884.

Loving (lɒ·viŋ), *ppl. a.* OE. [f. LOVE *v.* + -ING[2].] **1.** That loves; affectionate. **2.** Manifesting love; proceeding from love 1450.

1. *Your l. friend* (in 16th c. an ordinary form of subscription for letters). *Our l. subjects* (a usual phrase in royal proclamations). **2.** They continue that louing custome [widow burning] deuoutly to this day SIR T. HERBERT. **Loving cup,** a large drinking vessel, usu. of silver, passed from hand to hand, generally at the close of a banquet, for each guest to drink from in turn 1808. **Loving-ly** *adv.*, **-ness.**

Loving-kindness (lɒ·viŋ,kəi·ndnės) 1535 (Coverdale). [f. LOVING *ppl. a.* + KINDNESS. Orig. two wds.] Affectionate and tender consideration. *Ps.* 89:33.

Low (lōᵘ), *sb.*[1] [OE. *hlāw, hlǣw*, corresp. to OS. *hlēo, hlēw-*, OHG. *hleo*, Goth. *hlaiw* :- Gmc. **χlaiwaz-*, **χlaiwiz-* :- IE. **kloiwos-, -es-*, f. **kloi-* slope (see LEAN *v.*[1]). Cf. LAW *sb.*[2]] **1.** = LAW *sb.*[2] 1. *arch.* **2.** A tumulus. ? *Obs.* OE.

Low, lowe (lōᵘ), *sb.*[2] Chiefly *Sc.* and *n. dial.* ME. [- ON. *logi* = OFris. *loga* :- Gmc. **loʒon*, **luʒon* :- *lukón*, rel. to MHG., G. *lohe* (also in *lichterloh* in a blaze) :- **luχō* :- **lúkā*, f. *luk-* ; see LIGHT *sb.*] Flame; a flame, a blaze.

Low (lōᵘ), *sb.*[3] 1549. [f. LOW *v.*[3]] The action of LOW *v.*[3]; the ordinary sound uttered by an ox or cow.

Bull Ioue, sir, had an amiable l. SHAKS.

Low (lōᵘ), *a.* and *sb.*[4] [Early ME. *lāh*, inflected *lāʒe* – ON. *lágr* = OFris. *lēge, lēch*, MDu. *lage, laech, lege, leech* (Du. *laag*), MHG. *læge* (G. dial. *läg*) flat :- Gmc. **lǣʒjaz*, f. **lǣʒ-*, see LIE *v.*[1]]

A. *adj.* (Usu. the opposite of *high.*) **I. 1.** Of small upward extent; not tall; little, short. (Now rarely of persons.) **b.** Rising but little from a surface. *L. relief* = BAS-RELIEF 1711. **c.** Of a woman's dress: Cut so as to leave the neck, etc. exposed. See also *l. neck*. 1857. **2.** Not elevated in position. †Formerly, as in *Low Germany, L. Egypt* (*obs.*), denoting the part near the sea-shore (now only in the compar. LOWER). Also LOW-COUNTRY. ME. **b.** Of a heavenly body: Near the horizon 1676. **c.** Lying dead, or dead and buried. Now only *predicative*. ME. **d.** Of an obeisance: Profound, deep 1548. **e.** *Phonetics.* Of a vowel sound: Produced with the tongue or some part of it in a low position 1876. **3.** Of a liquid: Less in vertical measurement than the normal; shallow. Hence: Containing or yielding less water than usual. *Low tide* = LOW WATER. (For *low ebb*, see EBB *sb.*) 1440.

1. Apes With foreheads villanous l. SHAKS. Of a l. stature 1724. L. buildings PARKER. **2.** Trees growing in l. and shady places BP. BERKELEY. **b.** There was a l. moon 1889. **c.** The last great Englishman is l. TENNYSON. **3.** The Springs and Rivers are very l. 1695.

II. Transf. and fig. senses. **1.** Of humble rank, position, or estimation. (Only in *compar.* and *superl.* exc. *contemptuously*.) ME. **2.** Of inferior quality or style; wanting in elevation, commonplace, mean ME. **b.** Of style, words, expressions, a writer: The opposite of sublime; undignified 1672. **c.** Little advanced in civilization or organization 1859. **3. a.** Abject, mean 1559. **b.** Degraded, dissolute 1599. **c.** Coarse, vulgar; not 'respectable' 1759. **4.** Wanting in vigour; poorly nourished, weak ME. **b.** Dejected, dispirited, dull, esp. in phr. *l. spirits* 1737. **c.** Of diet: Not stimulating; poor 1715. **5.** Not high in amount or degree of intensity. (Often with reference to position in a graduated scale.) ME. **b.** *Geog.* Of latitude: Denoted by a low number; not far from the equator 1748. **c.** Of things: Having a low value, price, or degree of some quality. Of a playing-card: Of small numerical value. 1727. **d.** Of condition: Not flourishing or advanced 1596. **6. a.** Of musical sounds: Produced or characterized by slow vibrations; grave ME. **b.** Of the voice, a sound: Not loud 1440. **7.** Humble, lowly, meek. Now *rare*. ME. **8.** (Cf. sense I. 3.) Of one's pockets, money, etc.: Nearly empty or exhausted 1700. **9.** Of an opinion, estimate: Depreciatory, disparaging (*mod.*). **10.** Of a date: Recent. Chiefly in *compar.* and *superl.* (*mod.*). **11.** Of religious doctrine: The opposite of *high* (see HIGH *a.* II. 11); often *colloq.* = LOW CHURCH 1854.

1. Men l. in the social scale DEUTSCH. **2.** Much parliamentary ability of a l. kind MACAULAY. **b.** And ten l. words oft creep in one dull line POPE. **c.** Germs of bacteria and other l. organisms TYNDALL. **3. a.** Flattery or fawning or other l. arts 1799. **b.** L. woomene 1599. **c.** She has evidently kept l. company MME. D'ARBLAY. **4.** She..grew l. from loss of appetite 1783. **c.** Such l. diet as sour milk and potatoes BERKELEY. **5.** The fever is kept l. 1789. Chinese workmen.. work for l. wages 1885. **c.** In general a l. card is to be played second hand 1885. **d.** My Creditors grow cruell, my estate is very l. SHAKS. **6. b.** Her voice was euer soft, Gentle, and l. SHAKS. **8.** Phr. *To be l. in pocket.* **9.** I have a l. opinion of his abilities 1903.

Phrases. *To lay l.*: **a.** To lay flat; to overthrow, to stretch lifeless. **b.** To bury. **c.** *fig.* To abase, humble. *To lie l.*: **a.** *lit.* To lie in a l. position or on a l. level; also, to crouch. **b.** To lie on or in the ground, lie prostrate or dead; *fig.* to be humbled, abased. **c.** *Mod. slang.* To keep quiet, remain in hiding; to bide one's time. Also *To burn l.*: to burn feebly or with reduced flame; *to run l.*: to be nearly exhausted, to become scanty.

Combs. **1.** General: in concord with sbs. forming combs. used attrib. or quasi-adj., as *l.-blast, -flash, -grade, -pressure*, etc.; *l.-arched, -priced, -rented* adjs.; **l.-necked,** (of a dress) cut l. in the neck or bosom; *l.-lying*, etc.

2. Special: as **l. celebration**, the administration of the Holy Communion without assistant ministers and choir; **l. comedian**, an actor of l. comedy; **l. comedy,** (*a*) comedy in which the subject and treatment border upon farce; (*b*) *Theatr. slang* = *low comedian*; **L. Dutch** (see DUTCH); hence *Low-Dutchman*; **L. German** (see GERMAN); **L. Latin** *a.* and *sb.* [= Fr. *bas-latin*], late Latin or mediæval Latin; hence **L.-Latinist**, a scholar in Low Latin; **l. mass** (see MASS *sb.*[1]); **l. milling** (see MILLING *vbl. sb.*); **l.-sail,** easy sail (EASY *a.* 5); **l. side window,** a small window lower than the other windows, found in some old churches, a leper window 1847; **l. tea,** *U.S.*, a plain tea; **L. Week,** the week following Easter week, beginning with LOW SUNDAY.

B. quasi-*sb.* and *sb.* **1.** What is low, a low position, place, or area ME. †**2.** With preps. *At, in, on l.*: down low, on the ground, below, on earth –1460. **3.** (with *a* and *pl.*) **a.** A piece of low-lying land 1790. **b.** An area of low barometric pressure 1878. **4.** In *All-fours*: The deuce of trumps, or the lowest trump dealt 1818. **5.** *U.S.* A low level or figure 1911.

Low (lō^u), *adv.* [ME. *laȝe, lahe, loȝe*, f. the adj.] **1.** In a low position; on or under the ground; little above some base ME. **b.** *fig.* Humbly; in a low condition or rank; on poor diet; at a low rate ME. **2.** To a low point, position, or posture; along a low course, in a low direction ME. **3.** In a low tone, gently, softly; at a low pitch, on low notes ME. **4.** With reference to time: Far down, or to a point far down; late 1625.

1. The towne standeth lowe HALL. Ears hung l. COWPER. **b.** Live cool for a time, and rather l. CHESTERF. Phr. *To play l.*: to play for small stakes. **2.** Thou shalt come downe very l. *Deut.* 28:43. Party fights are won by aiming l. O. W. HOLMES. *fig.* Verse cannot stoop so l. as thy desert COWPER. **3.** Your true loues coming, That can sing both high and l. SHAKS. He read his sermon..so brokenly and l., that nobody could hear at any distance PEPYS. **4.** As l. as the restoration SWIFT.

Low (lō^u), *v.*[1] *Obs.* exc. *dial.* ME. [f. LOW *a.*] **1.** *trans.* To make or bring low; to abase, humble, lower. **2.** To diminish, lessen; to depreciate ME. **3.** To lower; to lower the level of (ground) 1450.

Low (lō^u), *v.*[2] *Obs.* exc. *dial.* ME. [– ON. *loga*, f. *logi* LOW *sb.*[2]] *intr.* To flame, blaze, glow; *fig.* to be on fire with passion, etc. Also with *up*.

Low (lō^u), *v.*[3] [OE. *hlōwan* = OS. *hlōian*, (Du. *loeien*) whence *hlōwinga* roaring, OHG. *hluoen*, redupl. str. vb., f. Gmc. **χlō-* :– IE. **klā-*, as in L. *clamare* shout.] **1.** *intr.* Of cattle: To utter their cry; to moo. Also *transf.* **2.** *trans.* To utter in a voice like that of cattle; to bellow *forth* 1547.

1. The sober herd that lowed to meet their young GOLDSM.

†**Low·bell, low-bell,** *sb.* 1578. [perh. f. LOW *a.* + BELL.] **1.** A small bell, *esp.* a cow-bell or sheep-bell; *joc.*, any bell –1664. **2.** A bell used in fowling at night. (The birds are stupefied with the noise of the bell and the sudden glare from lights in a tin-lined box, and a net is then thrown over them.) Also *fig.* –1821.

1. A bell hanged about sheepe or goates, a lowe-bell FLORIO. **2.** Some he catches..with frights (as Black-birds with..a Low-Bell) BOYLE. Hence **Low·bell** *v.* †to catch (birds) by the use of a l.; *transf.* to scare as the lowbeller does birds 1581–1660; to deride by jangling of tins, etc. (*dial.*). **Low·beller**, one who does this.

Low·-born, *a.* ME. Born in a low station.

Low-bred, *a.* 1757. [f. LOW *adv.* + BRED *ppl. a.*; cf. †*to breed low* (LOW *adv.* 1 b).] Brought up in a low, inferior, vulgar fashion; characterized by low breeding, conduct, or manners.

Low·-browed, *a.* 1632. [f. LOW *a.* + BROW *sb.*[1] + -ED[2].] **1.** Having a low brow 1868. **2.** *transf.* Of rocks: Beetling. Of a building, doorway, etc.: Having a low entrance; dark, gloomy. **3.** Not being, or claiming to be, highly intellectual. Hence **Low·brow** *sb.* and *a.* 1913.

2. There under..low-brow'd Rocks..In dark Cimmerian desert ever dwell MILT.

Low Church. 1702. [app. from *Low-Churchman*, and used attrib. as in *Low Church party*, and then subst.] **A.** *adj.* or *attrib. phr.* Of, belonging to, or characteristic of Low-Churchmen, or their principles and practices 1710. **B.** *sb.* [orig. short for *L. C. party, L. C. principles.*] The party or principles of the Low-Churchmen. Hence **Low-Chu·rchism.**

Low-Churchman. 1702. [Cf. HIGH-CHURCHMAN.] A member of the Church of England holding opinions which give a low place to the authority and claims of the Episcopate and the priesthood, to the inherent grace of the sacraments, and to matters of eccl. organization, thus differing little from the opinions held by Protestant Nonconformists. (In later use, mostly = EVANGELICAL.)

Low-country. 1530. **1.** A region whose level is lower than that of the surrounding country. **2.** *pl.* **Low Countries,** the district now forming the kingdoms of Holland and Belgium, and the grand duchy of Luxemburg; the Netherlands in the wider sense 1548. **b.** *attrib.*, quasi-*adj.* Belonging to (†or having served in) the Low Countries 1625.

Low down, *a.* and *adv.* 1548. [f. LOW *a.* and *adv.* + DOWN *adv.*] **a.** Used as emphatic for the adj. in predicative use, and for the adv. **b.** In attrib. use (*low-down*); orig. *U.S.* degraded, abject 1865. **c.** *sb.* (*U.S. slang.*) The actual facts; inside information 1926.

a. They had played it rather low down on the preacher 1890. **b.** A beautiful low-down catch 1882. So much better than he could have expected from his 'low-down' relative 1811. Hence **Low-downer** *U.S.* a 'poor white' of the southern States 1871.

Lower (lō^u·əɹ), *a.* (*sb.*) and *adv.* ME. [f. LOW *a.* + -ER[3].]

A. *adj.* **1.** The comparative of LOW *a.*, q.v. **2.** Used as the specific designation of an object, a class or group of objects, a part or parts of some whole (with reference either to local situation or to rank, dignity, or place in classification); occas. in partitive concord (= 'the lower part of'). Cf. UPPER, HIGHER. 1590. **3.** quasi-*sb.* One lower; an inferior ME.

1. And in the lowest deep a l. deep Still MILT. At a l. period than the apostolic age 1839. A l. class, l. pay MACAULAY. I feel l. and sadder than ever 1873. Keep that l. in tone 1895. **2.** L. Syria SHAKS., Asia 1631. Every l. facultie Of sense MILT. The l. sort in the camp BURKE. Merchants from the L. Danube MACAULAY. The L. Cambrian, Silurian 1873.

Spec. collocations: **l. boy,** a boy in the *lower school* (see below); **l.-case** *Printing* (see CASE *sb.*[2] 6); **l. chamber** = *lower house*; **l. classes,** those below the middle rank in society; **l. criticism,** verbal or textual criticism; so **l. critic**, one occupied with this; **l. deck,** the deck immediately over the hold, orig. only of a ship with two decks; **L. Empire** [= Fr. *Bas-Empire*], the later Roman Empire; now usually, from the reign of Constantine; **l. fourth, fifth,** etc., the l. division of the fourth, fifth, etc. form in a public school; **l. house,** the inferior branch of a legislature consisting of two houses; also of the convocation of the Church of England; **l.** †**order** or **orders** = *lower classes*; **l. school,** in public schools, usually the forms below the fifth; (*the* or *this*) **l. world,** earth as opp. to heaven.

B. *adv.* Comparative of LOW *adv.* 1548.

Then he fell to play l. 1648. Still farther north [the snow line] reaches yet l. HUXLEY.

Lower (lō^u·əɹ), *v.* 1606. [f. LOWER *a.*] **1.** *trans.* To cause or allow to descend, to let down gradually (e.g. a boat, a drawbridge, etc.); to haul down (a sail, a flag). Also with *away* (Naut.), *down*. 1659. Also *absol.* **b.** To diminish the height of 1858. **c.** *Wood-engraving.* To remove by cutting or scraping, or to depress (the surface of a block) 1839. **2.** *intr.* To descend, sink (also *fig.*). Often with *down*. Also *Naut.* of a yard: To admit of being let down. 1606. **b.** To slope downwards 1813. **3. a.** *trans.* To diminish in amount, price, proportion, etc. 1690. **b.** *intr.* To become lower in price 1697. **4.** *trans.* To make lower in quality or degree; to lessen the intensity or elevation of 1780. Also *intr.* †**b.** To reduce the strength or quality of (a liquid, the air) –1844. **c.** *Mus.* To depress in pitch 1889. **5.** *trans.* To bring down in rank, station, or estimation; to degrade, dishonour 1771. Also *intr.* for *refl.* **6.** *trans.* To bring down to a lower position on a graduated scale 1860.

1. The workmen have to be lowered by ropes down the face of the cliff 1895. **2.** Smoke lowering down from chimney-pots DICKENS. **3. a.** They lowered the rents 1886. **b.** Meat will l. in price 1823. **4.** The Mahratta government..might have been induced to l. its tone JAS. MILL. Lowering his voice 1834. **5.** His letter has lowered him in my opinion 1771. **6.** To l. the freezing point 1871.

Lower: see LOUR *sb.* and *v.*

Lowermost (lō^u·əɹmo^ust), *a.* 1561. [f. LOWER *a.* + -MOST.] = LOWEST *a.*

Lowest (lō^u·ėst), *a.* (*sb.*) and *adv.* ME. [f. LOW *a.* + -EST.]

A. *adj.* The superlative of LOW *a.*, q.v.

You would sound mee from my lowest Note to the top of my Compasse SHAKS. Harsh Thunder, that the l. bottom shook Of Erebus MILT. At the l. ebb 1681, price 1780.

B. *absol.* or as *sb.* **1.** The lowest part, position, or pitch. *Obs.* exc. with *at*. ME. **2.** One who or that which is lowest 1785.

1. When taste was almost at its l. in England 1897.

C. *adv.* The superlative of LOW *adv.* ME. The salary of our l.-paid Judges 1834.

Lowish (lō^u·iʃ), *a.* 1689. [f. LOW *a.* + -ISH[1].] Somewhat low.

Lowland (lō^u·lǣnd). 1508. [f. LOW *a.* + LAND.] **A.** *sb.* **1.** Low or level land; land lying lower than the surrounding country. Usu. *pl.* 1693. **2.** *spec.* (Now always *pl.*) The less mountainous part of Scotland, lying south and east of the Highlands 1631.

1. *sing.* The cities of the l. R.V. *Jer.* 33:13.

B. *attrib.* or *adj.* **1.** Of, pertaining to, or inhabiting low land or a level district 1567. **2.** *spec.* Of, belonging to, or characteristic of the Lowlands of Scotland 1508.

Hence **Low·lander**, an inhabitant of a low-lying country or district 1835; *spec.* a native of the Lowlands of Scotland 1692.

Lowlihead (lō^u·lihed). *arch.* ME. [f. LOWLY *a.* + -HEAD.] Humility, lowliness. So **Low·lihood** (*rare*).

Low-lived (lō^u·ləi·vd), *a.* Also †**low-lifed.** 1760. [f. LOW *a.* + *live-*, LIFE + -ED[2].] Of persons: Living a low life; vulgar, mean. Hence of actions, etc.

Lowly (lō^u·li), *a.* Somewhat *arch.* ME. [f. LOW *a.* + -LY[1].] **1.** Humble in feeling or demeanour; not proud or ambitious. **2.** Humble in condition or quality; modest, unpretending 1634. **3.** Low in situation or growth 1593. **b.** ? Lying low. 1 *Hen. VI*, III. iii. 47. ¶**4.** *occas.* Low in character, mean 1741.

1. Take my yoke vpon you, and learne of me, for I am meeke and l. in heart *Matt.* 11:29. **2.** Courtesie..is sooner found in l. sheds..then in tapstry Halls MILT. **3.** L. Shrubs DRYDEN, Lands POPE. In lowliest depths of bosky dells 1852. Hence **Low·lily** *adv.* **Low·liness.**

Lowly (lō^u·li), *adv.* ME. [f. LOW *a.* + -LY[2].] **1.** In a lowly manner; humbly, reverently; modestly. **2.** In a low manner or degree ME.

1. L. they bow'd adoring MILT. **2.** I will show my self highly fed, and l. taught SHAKS. Sadly and l. singing 1839.

Lo·wman, low man. 1592. [f. LOW *a.* + MAN. Cf. HIGHMAN.] Usu. *pl.* Dice loaded so as to turn up low numbers.

Lown(e, var. of LOON[1].

Lowness (lō^u·nės). ME. [f. LOW *a.* + -NESS.] **1.** The quality or condition of being LOW, q.v. **2.** As a mock title of dignity 1771.

Low-pitched, *ppl. a.* 1622. [In sense 1 f. LOW *adv.* + PITCHED *ppl. a.*; in sense 2 f. LOW *a.* + PITCH *sb.*[2] + -ED[2].] **1.** Pitched in a low key or tone (*lit.* and *fig.*); little elevated; of low quality. **2.** Of a roof: Having but a slight angular elevation. Hence of a room: Having a low ceiling. 1833.

1. Poor and low-pitched desires MILT.

Lowry (lau^ə·ri). 1875. [Cf. LORRY.] *U.S. Railways.* An open box-car.

Low-spirited, *a.* 1588. [f. LOW *a.* + SPIRIT *sb.* + -ED[2].] Having low spirits. †**a.** Mean in spirit; abject, cowardly, paltry

–1795. **b.** Wanting in animation; dejected, dispirited 1753. Hence **Low-spi·ritedness.**

Low Sunday. ME. The Sunday next after Easter Sunday.

Low water. late ME. The state of the tide when the water is lowest; the time of lowest ebb. Also, a low stage of the water in a river, lake, etc. **b.** *fig.* Chiefly in phr. *in low water*: 'hard up' 1785.

b. His lordship was in low water financially 1886.

Low-wa·ter mark. **a.** *lit.* The line on the shore reached by the tide or by a river at low water; a mark to indicate this 1526. **b.** *fig.* The lowest point reached in number, quantity, quality, etc. 1651.

b. My ink is at low water-mark for all my acquaintance H. WALPOLE.

Lowy. *Obs.* exc. *Hist.* 1389. [– OFr. *louée, lieuée* :– med.L. *leucata, leugata*, f. late L. *leuca, leuga*; see LEAGUE *sb.*[1], -Y[5].] A liberty extending for about a league outside a town.

Loxodromic (lǫksodrǫ·mik). 1679. [– Fr. *loxodromique*, f. Gr. λοξός oblique + δρόμος course; see -IC.] **A.** *adj.* Pertaining to oblique sailing, or sailing by the rhumb 1702. **B.** *sb.* = *L. line, table* 1679. **b. Loxodromics:** the art of oblique sailing 1704.

L. chart, projection, another name for Mercator's projection. *L. curve, line, spiral*, a rhumb-line. *L. tables*, traverse tables.

Hence **Lo·xodrome** = *l. line* 1880. **Loxodro·mical** *a.* 1704, **-ly** *adv.* 1752. **Loxo·dromism,** the tracing of or moving in a loxodromic line or curve 1853. **Loxo·dromy,** a loxodromic line or course; also = *loxodromics* 1656.

Loy (loi). [– Ir. *laighe.*] **a.** *Anglo-Ir.* A kind of spade used in Ireland 1763. **b.** *U.S.* A similar tool with a broad chisel point for making post-holes (*mod.*).

Loyal (loi·ăl), *a.* (*sb.*) 1531. [– Fr. *loyal*, OFr. *loial, leial* – L. *legalis* LEGAL. Cf. LEAL.] **1.** True to obligations of duty, love, etc.; faithful to plighted troth 1604. **2.** Faithful in allegiance to the sovereign or constituted government. Also, *now*, enthusiastically devoted to the sovereign's person and family. 1531. **3.** Of things, actions, etc.: Exhibiting loyalty 1598. †**4.** = LEGAL. **a.** Of a child: Legitimate. **b.** Of money: Genuine. **c.** Of goods: Of the legal standard of quality. –1690. **5.** *sb. pl.* †**a.** Liege subjects 1540–1602. **b.** In recent use: Loyal, as opp. to disaffected, subjects 1885.

1. Your true and loyall wife *Oth.* IV. ii. 35. L. to his word TENNYSON. L. friendships 1871. **2.** We [*sc.* French Canadians] are l. because we are free SIR W. LAURIER. **3.** 'Loyal and patriotic' toasts DICKENS. Hence **Loy·alism,** the principles or actions of a loyalist; loyalty. **Loy·alist,** one who is l.; one who adheres to his sovereign or to constituted authority, *esp.* in times of revolt; one who supports the existing form of government. **Loy·alize** *v.* to make l.; to restore to faithful allegiance; to attach to the loyalist party. **Loy·al-ly** *adv.*, **-ness.**

Loyalty (loi·ălti). ME. [– OFr. *loialté* (mod. *loyauté*), f. *loial* LOYAL; see -TY[1].] **1.** Faithful adherence to one's promise, oath, word, etc.; †conjugal fidelity. **2.** Faithful adherence to the sovereign or lawful government. Also, *now*, enthusiastic devotion to the sovereign's person and family. 1531. †**3.** Legality (of marriage). R. COKE.

1. And piety with wishes placed above, And steady l., and faithful love GOLDSM. **2.** Under the rule of Elizabeth l. became more and more a passion GREEN.

†**Loyn.** ME. [– OFr. *loigne*, var. of *longe* (cf. LOIN), shortening of *allonge*; see LUNGE *sb.*[1] In med.L., AL. *longia, loignia* (XIII).] A length (of cord); a leash for a hawk –1575.

Lozenge (lǫ·zėndʒ). ME. [– OFr. *losenge* (mod. *losange*); prob. deriv. of the word repr. by Pr. *lausa*, Sp. *losa*, Pg. *lousa* slab, tomb-stone, and late L. *lausiæ* (*lapides*) stone slabs, slates, of Gaulish or Iberian origin.] **1.** A plane rectilineal figure with four equal sides and two acute and two obtuse angles; a rhomb, 'diamond'. In *Her.*, such a figure used as a bearing (cf. FUSIL[1]), and placed with its longer axis vertical. **b.** A lozenge-shaped shield bearing the arms of a spinster or widow 1797. **c.** *Math.* = RHOMBUS. Now only in *spherical l.* 1551. **d.** A lozenge-shaped facet of a precious stone when cut 1750. **2.** A small cake or tablet, orig. diamond-shaped, of medicated or flavoured sugar, concentrated meat, etc., to be dissolved in the mouth 1530. **3.** A lozenge-shaped pane of glass in a casement 1656. **4.** *attrib.* or *adj.* Lozenge-shaped; composed of lozenges 1658.

4. Gravers are of two sorts, square and l. IMISON. L. brickwork BROWNING, ornament 1870. *L. moulding, L. fret*, a kind of moulding characterized by lozenge-shaped ornaments.

Comb.: **l.-coach,** a coach with the owner's coat of arms emblazoned on a l., a dowager's or widow's coach (H. Walpole). Hence **Lo·zenged** *a.* = LOZENGY *a.* 1523.

Lozengy (lǫ·zėndʒi), *a.* 1562. [– OFr. *losengié*, f. *losenge*; see prec., -Y[5].] *Her.*, etc. Covered with lozenges of alternate tinctures; divided into lozenges; also, lozenge-shaped.

L. s. d., £. s. d. (e:lesdī·), abbrev. for 'pounds, shillings, and pence' (see the letters L, S, D); hence often = 'money'. Hence **L. S. Deism** (*joc.*), worship of money.

Lu, obs. f. LOO *sb.*[1]

Lubbard (lɒ·băɹd). *Obs.* exc. *Sc.* and *n. dial.* 1586. [Altered f. LUBBER; see -ARD.] = LUBBER *sb.* **b.** *attrib.* Lubberly 1679.

Lubber (lɒ·bəɹ), *sb.* [ME. *lobre, lobur*, perh. – OFr. *lobeor* swindler, parasite, f. *lober* deceive, sponge upon, mock (perh. – Frank. *lobon* praise) with assim. in sense to LOB *sb.*[1]] **1.** A big, clumsy, stupid fellow; esp. one who does nothing; a lout. Now *arch.* or *dial.* **b.** A sailor's term for: A clumsy seaman. (Cf. LAND-LUBBER.) 1579. †**c.** A drudge, scullion –1706. **2.** *attrib.* or *adj.* (In *l. lips* perh. a different wd.) 1530.

1. If you will measure your lubbers length againe, tarry SHAKS. **b.** He swore woundily at the lieutenant, and called him..swab and l. SMOLLETT. **2.** Then narrow court and l. King, farewell! TENNYSON.

Comb.: **l.-grasshopper,** a name for two large-bodied clumsy insects of the U.S.; (*a*) *Brachystola magna*, of the western plains; (*b*) *Romalea microptera*, of the Gulf States; **-head,** a blockhead; **lubber's line, mark, point** *Naut.*, a vertical line inside a compass-case, indicating the direction of the ship's head.

Hence **Lu·bber** *v.* to behave like a l.; to navigate a boat like a l. 1530. **Lu·bberland,** an imaginary land of plenty without labour 1598.

Lubber fiend. 1632 (Milton). [Cf. LUBBER *sb.* 1 c.] A beneficent goblin who performs some of the drudgery of a household or farm during the night; a 'Lob-lie-by-the-fire'.

Lubberly (lɒ·bəɹli). 1573. [f. LUBBER *sb.* + -LY.] **A.** *adj.* **1.** Of the nature of a lubber; loutish; clumsy; lazy; stupid; sometimes *transf.* of animals and inanimate things. Also of things: Appropriate to or characteristic of a lubber. **2.** In naut. use: Resembling, pertaining to, or characteristic of a lubber; unseamanlike 1795.

1. Great l. Southdowns [sheep] 1847, l. barges 1862. A l., yellow-haired boy of twelve 1859. **2.** A case of l. navigation 1884. Hence **Lu·bberliness.**

B. *adv.* In a lubberly manner; like a lubber; unskilfully, clumsily 1594.

Lubber's hole. Also †**lubber-hole.** 1772. *Naut.* A hole in the ship's top, close to the mast, affording an easier way of ascent or descent than by climbing the futtock shrouds.

Lubric (l[i]ū·brik), *a.* 1490. [– (O)Fr. *lubrique* or L. *lubricus* slippery.] **1.** Smooth and slippery. Now *rare.* †**2.** *fig.* Slippery, shifty; unsteady; prone to danger or error –1660. **3.** Lascivious 1490.

2. Lubrick is the estate of Favorites 1646. **3.** This lubrique and adult'rate age DRYDEN. So **Lu·brical** *a.* 1601.

Lubricant (l[i]ū·brikănt). 1822. [– *lubricant-* pr. ppl. stem of L. *lubricare*; see next, -ANT.] **A.** *adj.* Lubricating. **B.** *sb.* An oil, or other material, used to lubricate machinery. Hence *transf.* **a.** A fluid which makes motion or action smooth or removes friction. **b.** (*joc.*) Any oily or greasy substance. 1828.

Paraffin-oil..had been found the best of all anti-friction lubricants 1882.

Lubricate (l[i]ū·brike[i]t), *v.* 1623. [– *lubricat-*, pa. ppl. stem of L. *lubricare*, f. *lubricus*; see LUBRIC, -ATE[3].] **1.** *trans.* To make slippery or smooth by applying a fluid or unguent. **b.** To apply oil or other unguent to (a machine) in order to minimize friction 1742. **c.** *gen.* To oil or grease 1791. **d.** *fig.* 1784. **2.** *absol.* or *intr.* To act as a lubricant 1726.

1. b. Man's..balmy bath, That supples, lubricates, and keeps in play, The various movements of this nice machine YOUNG. **d.** Here rills of oily eloquence in soft Meanders l. the course they take COWPER. Hence **Lu·bricating** *vbl. sb.* and *ppl. a.* (esp. in *l. oil*). **Lubrica·tion.**

Lubricator (l[i]ū·brike[i]təɹ). 1756. [f. prec. + -OR 2.] **1.** One who or that which lubricates Also *fig.* **2.** An oil-cup or other contrivance for lubricating a machine or instrument 183..

1. Water is . . a great . . l. of the fibres BURKE.

Lubricity (l[i]ubri·sĭti). 1491. [– (O)Fr. *lubricité* or late L. *lubricitas*, f. *lubricus*; see LUBRIC, -ITY.] **1.** Slipperiness, smoothness; oiliness 1547. **2.** *fig.* Slipperiness, shiftiness; instability; elusiveness 1613. **3.** Lasciviousness, lewdness, wantonness 1491.

1. The scented l. of soap SYD. SMITH. **2.** The l. of mundan greatnesse HOWELL. **3.** Mens vaine pleasures and idle lubricities 1593.

Lubricous (l[i]ū·brikəs), *a.* 1535. [f. L. *lubricus* LUBRIC + -OUS.] = LUBRIC. So **Lubri·cious** *a.* 1583.

Lubrify (l[i]ū·brifəi), *v.* Now *rare.* 1611. [– Fr. *lubrifier*, irreg. f. L. *lubricus*; see LUBRIC, -FY.] *trans.* To make slippery or smooth; to lubricate. So **Lubrifa·ction** (1542) [see -FACTION], **Lubrifica·tion** (1611), lubrication.

Lucan (l[i]ū·kăn), *a.* Also **Lukan.** 1876. [f. eccl. L. *Lūcās*, Gr. *Λουκᾶς* + -AN.] Pertaining to St. Luke.

Lucarne (l[i]ukā·ɹn). 1548. [–(O)Fr. *lucarne*, OFr. also *lucane* – Pr. *lucana*; of obsc. origin.] A skylight, a dormer or garret window. (Now only as Fr.) Also *l. window.*

Luce (l[i]ūs). ME. [– OFr. *lus, luis* :– late L. *lucius.*] The pike (*Esox lucius*), *esp.* when full grown.

Lucent (l[i]ū·sěnt), *a.* 1500. [– *lucent-*, pr. ppl. stem of L. *lucēre* shine; see -ENT.] **1.** Shining, bright, luminous. Also *fig.* **2.** Translucent; clear 1820.

1. The Sun's l. Orbe MILT. **2.** L. syrops, tinct with cinnamon KEATS. Hence **Lu·cency,** luminosity 1656.

Lucern[1] (l[i]usə·ɹn). *Obs.* exc. *Hist.* 1532. [prob. – early mod.G. *lüchsern* adj., pertaining to the lynx, f. *luchs* lynx; app. orig. a name for the fur; cf. MARTEN.] **1.** The lynx. **b.** The skin or fur of the lynx, formerly much valued. ¶**2.** A kind of hunting dog. CHAPMAN.

†**Lucern**[2]. [app. erron. f. LUCE, after prec.] The full-grown pike. MARKHAM.

Lucernal (l[i]usə·ɹnăl). *a.* 1787. [f. L. *lucerna* lamp + -AL[1].] Pertaining to a lamp; *l. microscope*, a microscope in which the object is illuminated by a lamp or other artificial light.

Lucerne, lucern (l[i]usə·ɹn). 1626. (In 17th and 18th c. agricultural books often *la lucerne*, with Fr. def. article.) [– Fr. *luzerne* – mod.Pr. *luzerno*, transf. use of *luzerno* glow-worm, with ref. to the shiny seeds.] The leguminous plant *Medicago sativa*, resembling clover, cultivated for fodder; purple medick.

Lucian (lū·ʃ[i]ăn). [repr. Gr. *Λουκιανός*, L. *Lucianus.*] The name of a celebrated writer of Greek dialogues (c160 A.D.); *allusively*, a witty scoffer (1750). Hence **Lucia·nic** (1820), †**-ical** (1561) *a.* pertaining to or like L. and his style; marked by a scoffing wit. **Lucia·nically** *adv.* 1592. †**Lucianist,** a disciple of L. 1585–92.

Lucid (l[i]ū·sid), *a.* 1591. [– Fr. *lucide* or It. *lucido* – L. *lucidus*, f. *lucēre* shine; see -ID[1].] **1.** Bright, shining, luminous, resplendent. Now *poet.* and *techn. Entom.* and *Bot.* = Smooth and shining. *Astr.* Of a star: Visible to the naked eye. **2.** Translucent, pellucid, clear 1620. **3. Lucid interval** [med.L. *lucida intervalla* (pl.), also in early use in English]: **a.** A period of temporary sanity occurring between attacks of lunacy. †Formerly also, an interval of apparent health between the periods of a malady. 1645. **b.** *transf.* and *fig.* A period of calm in the midst of tumult or confusion 1622. **c.** In etymol. sense: An interval of sunshine in a storm 1749. **4.** Clear in reasoning, expression, or arrangement; easily intelligible; also *transf.* of a person in reference to reasoning or statement 1786. **5.** Of persons: Clear in intellect; rational 1843.

1. The l. firmament SPENSER. **2.** The l. wave POPE. **3. a.** She had a l. interval, while making the will 1839. **b.** Which [dissensions] although they had had..l. intervals.., yet [etc.] BACON. **4.** The sermon was long but l. 1876. A l. reasoner

1879. **5.** Two apparently l. people 1859. **Lu·cid·ity. Lu·cid-ly** *adv.*, **-ness.**

‖**Lucida** (lⁱū·sidă). 1727. [L. (sc. *stella* star).] *Astr.* The brightest star of the constellation, group, etc. mentioned.

Lucifer (lⁱū·sifəɹ). OE. [– L. *lucifer* light-bringing; used as proper name of the morning star; f. *lux, luc-* light + *-fer* bearing (cf. -FEROUS). Cf. the equivalent Gr. φωσφόρος, after which it was prob. formed.] **1.** The morning star; the planet Venus when she appears in the sky before sunrise. Now only *poet.* **2.** The rebel archangel whose fall from heaven was supposed to be referred to in Isa. 14:12; Satan, the Devil. Now chiefly in the phr. *As proud as L.* †**b.** *allusively.* One who seeks to dethrone God; *occas.* one who presumptuously rebels against an earthly sovereign –1618. **3.** (Orig. **lucifer match**) A friction match made usually of a splint of wood tipped with an inflammable substance ignited on a prepared surface 1831.

1. After the lucifere the day sterre hath chasyd awey the dirke nyht CHAUCER. **2.** And when he falles, he falles like L., Neuer to hope againe SHAKS.

†**Luciferian** (lⁱūsifiᵊ·riăn), *a.*¹ and *sb.*¹ 1570. [f. LUCIFER + -IAN.] **A.** *adj.* Of or pertaining to Lucifer; Satanic, devilish; as proud as Lucifer –1773. **B.** *sb.* A Luciferian or Satanic person. TRAPP. So †**Luciferine** *a.* 1546–88, †**Luciferous** *a.*¹ 1554–93.

Lucife·rian, *a.*² and *sb.*² 1550. [f. L. proper name *Lucifer* (see below) + -IAN.] Of or pertaining to (An adherent of) the sect founded by Lucifer, bishop of Cagliari in the fourth century, who separated from the Church because it was too lenient towards Arians who repented of their heresy 1607.

Luciferous (lⁱusi·fĕrəs), *a.*² 1648. [f. L. *lucifer* light-bearing (see LUCIFER) + -OUS.] **1.** That brings, conveys, or emits light. Now *rare.* 1656. **2.** *fig.* Luminous, illuminating.

2. So L. an Experiment BOYLE. Hence **Luci·ferous-ly** *adv.*, **-ness.**

Lucific (lⁱusi·fik), *a.* 1701. [– late L. *lucificus*, f. *lux, luc-* light; see -FIC.] Light-producing.

Luciform (lⁱū·sifǭɹm), *a.* Now *rare.* 1668. [– med.L. *luciformis* (repr. Gr. αὐγοειδής); f. as prec.; see -FORM.] Having the character of light, luminous; applied *spec.* to the 'vehicle' of the soul (αὐγοειδὲς ὄχημα) imagined by the Neo-Platonists; *occas.* to the spiritual body of the Resurrection.

Lucifugous (lⁱusi·fiŭgəs), *a.* 1654. [f. L. *lucifugus*, f. as prec. + *fugere* flee; see -OUS.] Shunning the light.

Bats and other such shy and l. creatures 1865.

Lucimeter (lⁱusi·mĭtəɹ). 1825. [f. as prec. + -METER.] **a.** An instrument for measuring the intensity of light; a photometer. **b.** An instrument for measuring the evaporative effect of sunlight 1890.

‖**Lucina** (lⁱusəi·nă). ME. [L. fem. of *lucinus* adj., f. *lux, luc-* light; see -INE¹.] In Roman mythology, the goddess of childbirth, sometimes identified with Juno or with Diana; hence, a midwife. **b.** By identification with Diana: The moon (*poet.*) 1500.

Death must be the L. of life SIR T. BROWNE.

Luck (lɒk). late ME. [prob. orig. a gambling term; – LG. *luk*, aphetic of *geluk*, in MDu. *ghelucke* (Du. *geluk*) = MHG. *gelücke* (G. *glück* good fortune, happiness), f. *ge-* Y- + a base of unkn. origin; the LG. word was adopted in Icel., OSw. *lukka*, etc.] **1.** Fortune good or ill; the fortuitous happening of events affecting the interests of a person; a person's condition with regard to the favourable or unfavourable character of such events. Often with adj., as *bad, evil, good, hard l.*, ILL LUCK. Also, the fancied tendency of chance (esp. in gambling) to produce a run of favourable or unfavourable events; the disposition ascribed to chance at a particular time. 1481. **b.** Chance as a cause or bestower of success and failure. Occas. *personified.* 1534. **2.** Good fortune; success, prosperity or advantage coming by chance ME. **b.** *occas.* A name given to an object on which the prosperity of a family, etc. is supposed to depend 1800. †**3.** An omen –1600.

1. It hath beene my l. alwayes to beat the bush, while another kild the Hare 1602. Better l. next time 1791. The l. turns at last 1856. **b.** L., in the great game of war, is undoubtedly lord of all 1899. **2.** No man can have lucke alwayes at playe 1583. Phr. *To have the l.*, to be so fortunate as (*to* be or do something). **b.** 'The L. of Eden Hall': an oriental glass goblet (of the 15th c. or earlier) in the possession of the Musgraves of Eden, Cumberland, so called with reference to the words, 'If this glass will break or fall, Farewell the l. of Eden-hall'.

Phrases. *Bad l. to* (a person or thing)*!*: a vulgar expression of ill will, disgust, or disappointment. *Down on* (occas. *in*) *one's l.*: in ill luck, in misfortune (*slang*). *For l.*: in order to bring good l. *In l.*: enjoying good l. *Out of l.*: having bad l., in misfortune. *To try one's l.*: see TRY *v.* *Worse l.*: unfortunately, 'more's the pity' (*colloq.*). *Run, stroke of l.*: see the sbs.

Comb. **l.-money, -penny,** a piece of money given or kept for l., esp. in the sale of live-stock.

Luckily (lɒ·kili), *adv.* 1482. [f. LUCKY *a.* + -LY².] **1.** In a lucky manner; successfully, prosperously, happily. Now *rare.* **2.** Qualifying the sentence as a whole, indicating that the fact or circumstance is a lucky one 1717.

2. Climbing a long snow-slope which was l. in fair order L. STEPHEN.

Luckiness (lɒ·kinės). 1561. [f. LUCKY *a.* + -NESS.] The quality or condition of being lucky.

Luckless (lɒ·klės), *a.* 1563. [f. LUCK + -LESS.] **1.** Having no luck or good fortune; unlucky, hapless, ill-starred, unfortunate. †**2.** Ominous of ill –1637.

1. I, and ten thousand in this lucklesse Realme SHAKS. **2.** The shreikes of lucklesse Owles B. JONS. Hence **Lu·ckless-ly** *adv.*, **-ness.**

Lucky (lɒ·ki), *sb.*¹ *Sc.* Also **luckie.** 1717. [f. LUCKY *a.* 5.] A familiar name for an elderly woman; *spec.* a grandmother. Also applied, joc. or affectionately, to a woman of any age; a wife, mistress. **b.** *spec.* The mistress of an ale-house.

Lucky (lɒ·ki), *sb.*² *slang.* 1834. [Of unkn. origin.] In phr. *To cut* or *make one's l.*: to escape, decamp.

Lucky (lɒ·ki), *a.* 1502. [f. LUCK + -Y¹.] **1.** Attended by good luck. In early use, Fortunate, successful, prosperous. Now: Favoured by chance. **b.** Of a literary composition: Having an unstudied felicity 1700. **2.** Of the nature of good luck; occurring by chance and producing happy results 1547. **3.** Presaging or likely to promote good luck; well-omened 1549. **4.** Occurring by chance; casual, fortuitous 1691. **5.** *Sc.* Used as a term or address of endearment, esp. to a woman. [Cf. Icel, *heill* good luck, used similarly.] 1555.

1. A dexterous and l. player MACAULAY. A l. guess CRABBE. **b.** Genius now and then produces a l. trifle JOHNSON. **2.** L. legacies JOHNSON. **3.** They say, a Fool's hansel is l. B. JONS. *L. penny, sixpence* (usu. one bent or perforated, carried as a charm). *L. stone* (often, one with a natural hole through it). *Comb.* **l.-proach** *Sc.* = FATHER-LASHER.

Lu·cky-bag. 1825. [f. prec. adj.] A bag, at fairs and bazaars, in which, on paying a small sum, one dips one's hand and draws an article of greater or less value. Often *fig.*

Lucrative (lⁱū·krătiv), *a.* ME. [– L. *lucrativus*, f. *lucrari*, f. *lucrum* gain; see -ATIVE.] **1.** Yielding gain or profit; gainful. †**2.** Of persons, etc.: Bent upon or directed towards making of gain; avaricious, covetous –1797.

1. A l. contract warded off the blow for a time SCOTT. A l. traffic with the coast of Guinea 1874. Hence **Lu·crative-ly** *adv.*, **-ness.**

Lucre (lⁱū·kəɹ). ME. [– Fr. *lucre* or L. *lucrum* gain.] **1.** Gain, profit, pecuniary advantage. Now only in bad sense: Gain viewed as a low motive for action; 'pelf'. **2.** Const. *of.* †**a.** Gain or profit derived from (something). **b.** Acquisition of (something profitable) (*arch.*) ME.

1. His sonnes. . turned aside after l., and tooke bribes 1 *Sam.* 8:3. *Filthy l.*: see FILTHY. **2. b.** I am going to make a book for the l. of gain SOUTHEY.

Lucretian (lⁱukrī·ʃⁱăn), *a.* (*sb.*) 1712. [f. *Lucretius*, Latin poet and Epicurean philosopher + -AN.] Pertaining to, characteristic of, or resembling Lucretius or his philosophy. As quasi-*sb.* A follower of Lucretius 1881.

The L. comfort is none to me TUCKER.

†**Lucta·tion.** 1651. [– L. *luctatio*, f. *luctari* wrestle; see -ATION.] Struggling, wrestling –1698. **b.** *transf.* Agitation due to chemical reaction. Also, a struggling for breath. –1693.

Lu·ctual, *a.* 1613. [f. L. *luctus* mourning + -AL¹.] Mournful –1655.

Lucubrate (lⁱū·kiubreⁱt), *v.* 1623. [– *lucubrat-*, pa. ppl. stem of L. *lucubrare*, f. *lux, luc-* light; see -ATE³.] **1.** *intr.* Literally, To work by artificial light. In mod. use, to produce lucubrations. **2.** *trans.* To produce (literary compositions) by laborious study. (Rec. Dicts.) Hence **Lu·cubrator,** a nocturnal student; one who produces lucubrations. †**Lucubratory** *a.* meditative; *sb.* (*joc.*) a 'thinking-shop'.

Lucubration (lⁱūkiubrēⁱ·ʃən). 1595. [– L. *lucubratio*, f. as prec.; see -ION.] **1.** The action of lucubrating; nocturnal study or meditation; study in general. **2.** quasi-*concr.* Usu. *pl.* The product of this; hence, a literary work showing signs of careful elaboration. Now suggesting something pedantic or over-elaborate. 1611.

1. The well-earned harvest of. . many a midnight l. GIBBON. **2.** Tons of dusty lucubration CARLYLE.

Luculent (lⁱū·kiŭlĕnt), *a.* ME. [– L. *luculentus*, f. *lux, luc-* light.] **1.** Full of light; bright, shining. Now *rare.* **2.** †**a.** Of oratory, writings: Brilliant. Hence of a writer, etc. **b.** Of evidence, arguments: Clear, cogent. Of explanations: Lucid. 1548. **3.** Of persons: Brilliant, illustrious –1620.

1. L. along The purer rivers flow THOMSON. **2. b.** The most l. testimonies that Christian Religion hath HOOKER. **3.** Most debonaire, and L. Ladie B. JONS. Hence **Lu·culently** *adv.*

Lucullian, -ean (lⁱukɒ·liăn, lⁱū:kɒlī·ăn), *a.* 1601. [– L. *Lucullianus* (see -IAN), or f. L. *Luculleus* (f. *Lucullus*) + -OUS.] Pertaining to or characteristic of L. Licinius Lucullus, a wealthy Roman famous for the luxury of his banquets.

†*Lucullean marble*: some kind of black marble.

‖**Lucumo** (lⁱū·kiumo). Also **-on.** 1837. [L. *lucumo, -on-*, an Etruscan title.] One of the Etruscan nobles, who were at once priests and princes.

Lud (lɒd). 1725. Minced form of LORD *sb.*

O l.! he has almost cracked my head GOLDSM. 'My Lud', said Mr. Caterham, 'my case is completed' 1898.

Luddite (lɒ·dəit). 1811. [Said (but without confirmation) to be f. Ned *Lud*, a lunatic living about 1779, who in a fit of rage smashed up two frames belonging to a Leicestershire 'stockinger'. See -ITE¹ 1.] A member of an organized band of mechanics and their friends, who (1811–16) went about destroying machinery in the midlands and north of England.

Are you not near the Luddites? And down with all kings but King Ludd? BYRON. **Lu·ddism** 1812.

Ludibrious (lⁱudi·briəs), *a.* 1563. [– L. *ludibriosus*, f. *ludibrium* sport, jest, f. *ludere* play; see -OUS.] †**1.** Apt to be a subject of jest or mockery –1675. **2.** Full of scorn; inclined to scoff; mocking. Now *rare.* 1641. So †**Lu·dibry,** derision 1637–1723.

Ludicro- (lⁱū·dikro), used as comb. f. L. *ludicrus* LUDICROUS, in sense 'ludicrous and..', as *l.-pathetic*, etc.

Ludicrous (lⁱū·dikrəs), *a.* 1619. [f. L. *ludicrus*, f. *ludicrum* stage play, f. *ludere* play; see -OUS.] †**1.** Pertaining to play; sportive; jocular, derisive –1781. †**2.** Given to jesting; frivolous; also, witty, humorous –1827. **3.** Ridiculous; laughably absurd 1782.

3. The Duke was in a state of l. distress MACAULAY. Hence **Lu·dricrous-ly** *adv.*, **-ness.**

Ludification (lⁱūdifikēⁱ·ʃən). Now *rare.* late ME. [– L. *ludificatio*, f. *ludificare* delude, f. *ludus* sport; see -FICATION.] A deception or mocking. So †**Ludificatory** *a.* deceptive. BARROW.

Ludo (lⁱū·do). 1898. [– L. *ludo* I play.] A game played with dice and counters on a special board.

‖**Lues** (lⁱū·īz). 1634. [L., = 'plague'.] A plague or pestilence; a spreading disease, *esp.* syphilis (*L. venerea*); also, a contagious disease among cattle. Hence **Lue·tic** *a.* [badly formed], pertaining to, or affected with, l.

Luff (lɒf), *sb.* [ME. *lo(o)f* – OFr. *lof*, prob. of LG. or Du. origin; so also Sp., Pg. *ló*, G. *luv*, Sw. *luf*, Da. *luv*, used of the weather side of a ship or sail (in Eng. from XIV); ult. origin and orig. sense obscure.] *Naut.* †**1.** Some contrivance for altering the course of a ship; e.g. a rudder, a paddle, or some kind of machine for working on the sails –1485. †**2.** The weather-gauge, or part of a ship towards the wind –1622. **3.** The weather-part of a fore-and-aft sail, i.e. the side next the mast or stay 1513. **4.** The fullest part of a ship's bow, where the sides begin to curve in towards the stem 1624.

Phr. *To turn, wend the l.*: to change one's course; also *fig.* *L. a l.*: hugging the wind closely. *To keep one's l.*: to keep close to the wind; to keep to windward, keep one's distance. *To spring one's l.*: to bring the ship's head closer to the wind.

Comb., etc.: **l.-tackle,** a purchase composed of a double and a single block, used for various purposes; **l. upon l.,** a luff-tackle attached to the fall of another, to increase the purchase.

Luff (lɒf), *v.* ME. [f. LUFF *sb.*; perh. immed. – Du. *loeven.*] *Naut.* **1.** *intr.* To bring the head of a ship nearer to the wind; to steer or sail nearer the wind; to sail in a specified direction with the head kept close to the wind. **2.** *trans.* To bring the head of (a vessel) nearer to the wind. Also with *up.* 1606. **3.** In yacht-racing: To get the windward side of (an opponent). Also with *away.* 1894.

1. *To l. round* or *alee*: to make the excess of the movement of luffing, in order to throw the ship's head up in the wind, for the purpose of tacking her, etc. **2.** *L. the helm,* the call or order to the steersman.

Luffer, var. of LOUVER.

Lug (lɒg), *sb.*[1] Now *dial.* ME. [Of unkn. origin.] **1.** A long stick or pole; the branch or limb of a tree. **2.** A measure **a.** of length; a pole or perch, varying locally; usu. of 16½ feet 1562; **b.** of surface: a square pole or perch 1602.

Lug (lɒg), *sb.*[2] Chiefly *Sc.* and *n. dial.* 1495. [prob., like LUG *v.*, of Scand. origin; cf. Sw. *lugg* forelock, nap of cloth.] **1.** One of the flaps or lappets of a cap or bonnet, covering the ears. **2.** = EAR *sb.*[1] 1 and 4. 1507. **3.** An object resembling the external ear: **a.** The handle of a pitcher, etc. Also *techn.*, an appendage by which an object may be lifted or suspended. 1624. **b.** The side-wall (of a fireplace or other recess); a (chimney) corner 1784. **c.** *Electr.* A fitting of copper or brass to which electrical wires are connected. **4.** *Comb.* **l.-mark** *sb.* and *v.* = EAR-MARK.

Lug (lɒg), *sb.*[3] Also **log.** 1602. [Cf. LURG.] A large marine worm (*Arenicola marina*) much used for bait. Also **l.-worm.**

Lug (lɒg), *sb.*[4] 1830. Short for LUGSAIL.

Lug, *sb.*[5] 1616. [f. LUG *v.*] The act of lugging; *concr.* (*U.S.*) that which is lugged.

Lug (lɒg), *v.* ME. [prob. of Scand. origin; cf. Sw. *lugga* pull a person's hair; see LUG *sb.*[2]] **1.** *trans.* To pull, give a pull to; to tease, worry, bait (a bear, bull, etc.). *Obs.* exc. *dial.* **2.** *intr.* To pull, tug. Of a horse: To press heavily *on* (the bit or reins). ME. †**b.** To take a pull *at* (liquor, the breast). Also *trans.* To pull at (the breast). –1617. **c.** To move *about, along,* heavily and slowly; to drag. Now only *techn.* ME. **3.** *trans.* To drag, tug with violent effort ME. **b.** *colloq.* hyperbolically 1652. **4.** *fig.* To drag in forcibly or irrelevantly 1721.

3. I lugged this Money home to my Cave, and laid it up DE FOE. **b.** Boswell..succeeded in lugging him [Johnson] into the wilds of the Highlands L. STEPHEN. **4.** Counsel..had lugged in every thing he could to prejudice the case 1901.

L. out. a. *trans.* See prec. senses and *out.* ME. **b.** *absol.* or *intr.* To draw one's sword; to pull out money or a purse. *arch.* 1684.

Luge (lūʒ), *sb.* 1907. [Fr.] A kind of toboggan used in Switzerland. Also *vb.*

Luggage (lɒ·gėdʒ). 1596. [f. LUG *v.* + -AGE, after *baggage.*] **1.** †In early use: What has to be lugged about; inconveniently heavy baggage. Also, the baggage of an army. Now, The baggage belonging to a traveller or passenger. **2.** †**a.** With *a.* An encumbrance –1693. **b.** *pl.* *nonce-use* = IMPEDIMENTA. Carlyle.

1. A Boy of the House, who rode after us with the L. SWIFT. *fig.* The cumbersome l. of riches LAMB.

Lugger (lɒ·gəɹ). 1795. [f. LUG(SAIL; see -ER[1] 1.] A vessel carrying a lugsail or lugsails, with one, two, or three masts.

Lu·gsail. 1677. [prob. f. LUG *sb.*[2]] A four-cornered sail, bent upon a yard which is slung at about one-third or one-fourth of its length from one end, and so hangs obliquely.

Lugubrious (lⁱugiū·briəs), *a.* 1601. [f. L. *lugubris*, f. *lugēre* mourn; see -IOUS.] Characterized by mourning; doleful, dismal, sorrowful. Hence **Lugu·brious-ly** *adv.*, **-ness.** var. †**Lugu·brous** 1632–1708.

Lug-worm: see LUG *sb.*[3]

Luke (lⁱūk), *a. Obs.* exc. *dial.* [The ME. variants *leuk, hleuk* suggest deriv. from LEW, OE. **hlēow* (in *ġehlēow* warm, *un|hlēow* cold, *hlēowe* warmly), = ON. *hlýr* warm, mild, rel. obscurely to OHG. *lāo* (G. *lau*). Cf. LEE *sb.*[1], LEW.] = next.

Nine penn'orth o' brandy and water l. DICKENS.

Lukewarm (lⁱū·k,wǭɹm), *a.* (*sb.*) ME. [f. LUKE *a.* + WARM *a.*] **1.** Moderately warm, tepid. **2.** Of persons, etc.: Having little warmth or depth of feeling, lacking zeal or enthusiasm, indifferent 1522. **3.** *sb.* A lukewarm person 1693.

1. Apply the Collyrium luke-warm 1658. **2.** Our l. Temper 1718. L. advocate 1771, accents 1804. Hence **Lu·kewarm-ly** *adv.*, **-ness.** **Lu·kewarmth** (now *rare*) 1598.

Lull (lɒl), *sb.*[1] 1659. [f. LULL *v.*] **1.** That which lulls; a lulling sound, etc. 1719; †soothing drink, 'nepenthe' 1659. **2.** A lulled or stupefied condition 1822. **3.** A short intermission in a storm, etc. 1815.

Lull, *sb.*[2] 1820. [– Du. *lul* tube.] *Whaling.* A tube to convey blubber into the hold.

Lull (lɒl), *v.* ME. [imit. of the repetition of (lu lu) or similar sounds (cf. *lully, lulla, lullay* XV) appropriate to singing a child to sleep; cf. Sw. *lulla,* Da. *lulle* hum a lullaby, Du. *lullen,* and further MDu. *lollen* mutter (see LOLLARD) and L. *lallare* sing to sleep.] **1.** *trans.* To soothe with sounds or caresses; to induce to sleep or to pleasing quiescence. **2.** *fig.* To quiet (suspicion) by deception; to delude into a sense of security 1601. **3.** *trans.* To quiet (winds, sea, etc.) 1680. **4.** *intr.* Of the sea or wind: To become gradually diminished in force or power. Also *fig.* 1808.

1. The Virgin voyce That Babies l. a-sleepe SHAKS. **3.** Lull'd like the depth of ocean when at rest BYRON. **4.** The wind lulled, the rain came down in a deluge MARRYAT.

Lullaby (lɒ·lăbəi), *int.* and *sb.* 1560. [f. as prec. + *-by* as in *by-by* BYE-BYE[1]; cf. *hush-aby, rockaby.*] **1.** *int.* A soothing refrain, used to quiet an infant or esp. send it to sleep. Also *gen.* †**b.** Used for 'farewell', 'good-night'. SHAKS. **2.** *sb.* A song sung to a child to put it to sleep. Also, any soothing song. 1588. **b.** *transf.* and *fig.* 1611.

1. L., oh, l.! The brat will never shut an eye HOOD. **b.** *Twel. N.* v. i. 48. **2. b.** The bees have hummed their noontide l. ROGERS. Hence **Lu·llaby** *v.* to soothe with a l.; to sing to sleep. Also *absol.* or *intr.* 1592.

Lum (lɒm). *n. dial.* and *Sc.* 1507. [perh. an application of OFr. *lum* light (:– L. *lumen*); cf. the uses of Fr. *lumière* in the sense of 'aperture, passage'.] †**1.** ? A skylight. **2.** A chimney; also, a chimney-top 1697.

Lumachella (lⁱūmăke·lă). Also **lumachel(le,** etc. 1727. [– It. *lumachella* little snail, f. *lumaca.*] *Min.* A dark-coloured compact limestone containing shells which frequently emit fire-like reflections; fire-marble.

Lumbago (lɒmbē·go), *sb.* 1693. [– L. *lumbago,* f. *lumbus* loin.] *Med.* A rheumatic affection in the lumbar region of the body. So **Lumba·ginous** *a.* pertaining to, resembling, or afflicted with l. 1620. **Lumba·go** *v.* to afflict with l. 1796.

Lumbar (lɒ·mbăɹ). 1656. [– med.L. *lumbaris,* f. L. *lumbus* LOIN; see -AR[1].] **A.** *adj.* Of, belonging to, or situated in the loin; as *l. arteries, vein,* etc. **B.** *sb.* [The adj. used ellipt.] An artery, nerve, vein, or vertebra situated in the loin 1858. var. †**Lu·mbal** *a.* and *sb.* 1696.

Lumber (lɒ·mbəɹ), *sb.*[1] 1552. [perh. f. LUMBER *v.*[1]; but at one time assoc. w. LUMBER *sb.*[2]] **1.** Disused articles of furniture and the like, which only take up room; useless odds and ends. **b.** *fig.* Useless or cumbrous material 1649. **2.** Superfluous fat, esp. in horses 1806. **3.** *N. Amer.* Timber sawn into rough planks or otherwise roughly prepared for the market 1662.

1. Stands, dishes, formes, chaires, stoles, and other lumbar 1587. **b.** The bookful blockhead.. With loads of learned l. in his head POPE.

Comb.: **l.-carrier,** a vessel employed in the lumber-trade; **-man,** one who works among l., esp. in felling and dressing rough timber in the forest; **-mill,** a sawmill for cutting up l.; **-room,** a room for l. or disused chattels; **-trade,** the trade in rough timber; **-wood,** a wood where l. is cut.

†**Lu·mber,** *sb.*[2] 1617. [var. of LOMBARD *sb.*[1]] **1.** A pawnbroking establishment –1749. **2.** Money due with respect to articles pawned. BUTLER.

1. Phr. *To put to l.*: to put in pawn. *To be in l.* (slang): to be imprisoned.

Lumber (lɒ·mbəɹ), *v.*[1] [ME. *lomere* (XIV), perh. of symbolic origin. Cf. synon. LUMPER *v.* (XVI), LUMP *v.*[2] 5 (XIX).] **1.** *intr.* To move in a clumsy or blundering manner; now only, to move heavily by reason of bulk and mass. †**2.** To rumble. 1529–1621.

1. Hush! I hear him lumbering in! FOOTE.

Lumber (lɒ·mbəɹ), *v.*[2] 1642. [f. LUMBER *sb.*[1]] **1.** *trans.* To cover, fill up, or obstruct with lumber; to encumber. Occas. with *over, up.* **b.** *intr.* To lie as lumber 1850. **2.** *trans.* To heap or place together as lumber 1678. **3.** *intr.* (*N. Amer.*) To cut forest timber and prepare it for the market. Occas. *trans.* 1809.

1. Empty bottles lumbered the bottom of every closet W. IRVING. Hence **Lu·mberer** (*N. Amer.*), one employed in the lumber or timber trade.

Lu·mber, *v.*[3] *slang.* 1812. [f. LUMBER *sb.*[2]] To deposit (property) in pawn; hence in *passive,* to be placed away privily, to be imprisoned.

†**Lumber-pie.** Also **lumbar-pie.** 1656. [See LOMBARD *a.* 2.] A savoury pie made of meat or fish and eggs.

Lumbo- (lɒ·mbo), used as comb. f. L. *lumbus* loin, as **l.-abdominal** *a.,* pertaining to the loins and the abdomen; so *l.-costal, -sacral,* etc.

Lumbrical (lɒmbrəi·kăl, lɒ·mbrikăl). 1694. [– mod.L. *lumbricalis*; see LUMBRICUS, -AL[1].] *Nat. Hist.* **A.** *adj.* Pertaining to or resembling a lumbricus or worm; *Anat.* applied to certain fusiform muscles in the hand and the foot which assist in flexing the digits. **B.** *sb.* Often in L. form **lumbricalis,** pl. **-es.** A lumbrical muscle 1706.

Lumbriciform (lɒmbr(ə)i·sifǭɹm), *a.* 1828. [See LUMBRICUS and -FORM.] Resembling a lumbricus; vermiform.

Lumbricoid (lɒmbrəi·koid, lɒ·mbrikoid). 1849. [– mod.L. *lumbricoides*; see LUMBRICUS and -OID.] *Zool.* **A.** *adj.* Resembling the lumbricus or earth-worm. **B.** *sb.* The round-worm.

‖**Lumbricus** (lɒmbrəi·kɒ̆s). *Pl.* **-ci** (-səi). ME. [L. *lumbrĭcus* worm.] **a.** The earth-worm, *L. terrestris.* **b.** The round-worm which infests the intestines, *Ascaris lumbricoides.*

‖**Lumen** (lⁱū·men). *Pl.* **lumina** (lⁱū·mină). 1873. [L., = light; an opening.] **1.** *Anat., Bot.,* etc. A cavity or space enclosed by the walls of a tube, cell, or the like. **2.** *Photom.* A unit of light flux.

Luminant (lⁱū·minănt). 1884. [– *luminant-,* pr. ppl. stem of L. *luminare*; see LUMINATE, -ANT.] **A.** *adj.* Illuminating, luminous 1891. **B.** *sb.* An illuminant.

Lu·minance, luminousness 1880.

Luminarist (lⁱū·minărist). 1888. [– Fr. *luminariste,* f. L. *lumen, lumin-,* light.] A painter who treats light effectively, or whose colour is luminous. So **-ism.**

That..subtle l. Adrian van Ostade 1888.

Luminary (lⁱū·minări), *sb.* 1450. [– OFr. *luminarie* (mod. *-aire*) or late L. *luminarium,* f. *lumen, lumin-* light; see -ARY[1].] **1.** A natural light-giving body, *esp.* the sun or the moon 1489. **2.** An artificial light; †in 17th c. *pl.,* illuminations betokening rejoicing (so med.L. *luminaria*) 1483. **3.** *fig.* A source of intellectual, moral, or spiritual light; a person of 'light and leading' 1450.

1. Where the great Luminarie..Dispenses Light from farr MILT. **2.** There were extraordinary luminaries in all the windows in the publick streets 1692. **3.** A late happy Discovery by two great Luminaries of this Island BENTLEY. So **Lu·minary** *a.* (*rare*), pertaining to light 1794.

Luminate (l^{i}ū·mine^{i}t), *v. Obs.* or *arch.* 1623. [– *luminat-*, pa. ppl. stem of L. *luminare*, f. *lumen, lumin-* light; see -ATE[3].] *trans.* To light up, illuminate. Hence **Lumina·tion** (*rare*), a shedding or emission of light; †*concr.* an illumination 1654.

Lumine (l^{i}ū·min), *v.* Now *rare* or *Obs.* ME. [– OFr. *luminer* – L. *luminare*, f. as prec. See LIMN *v.*, ILLUMINE *v.*] *trans.* To light up, illumine. †In early use, to illuminate (manuscripts, etc.). So †**Luminer,** illuminator.

Luminescent (l^{i}ūmine·sĕnt), *a.* 1889. [f. L. *lumen, lumin-* + -ESCENT.] **a.** Emitting light otherwise than as a result of incandescence. **b.** Pertaining to luminescence. Hence **Lumine·sce** *v. intr.* to become l. **Lumine·scence,** l. condition or quality.

Luminiferous (l^{i}ūmini·fĕrəs), *a.* 1801. [f. as prec. + -FEROUS.] Producing or transmitting light; *esp.* in *l. ether* (see ETHER 5).

Luminist (l^{i}ū·minist). *rare.* 1901. [f. as prec. + -IST.] = LUMINARIST. So **-ism.**

Luminous (l^{i}ū·minəs), *a.* ME. [– (O)Fr. *lumineux* or L. *luminosus*, f. as prec.; see -OUS.] **1.** Full of light; emitting light; shining, bright. **b.** Of a room: Well lighted 1610. **2.** *transf.* and *fig.*: esp. of writers, etc. 1450.

1. The phaenomenon of the l. sea 1792. Some of the cuttle-fishes are slightly l. 1851. *spec.* Applied to paint, etc. which shows up in the dark. **b.** The library..is elegant and l. JOHNSON. **2.** The l. page of Gibbon SHERIDAN. L. eloquence MACAULAY. Hence **Lumino·sity,** the quality or condition of being l.; also *concr.* 1634. **Lu·minous-ly** *adv.*, **-ness.**

Lummy (lɒ·mi), *a. slang.* 1838. First-rate.

Lump (lɒmp), *sb.*[1] ME. [Of unkn. origin. Cf. Da. *lump(e* lump, Norw., Sw. dial. *lump* block, stump, log; but the presumably orig. sense of 'shapeless piece' is seen also in Du. *lomp*, †*lompe* rag, Du. *lomp*, LG. *lump* coarse, rude (whence G. *lumpen* rag).] **1.** A compact piece or mass with no particular shape; often with implication of excessive size, protuberant outline, or clumsiness. **b.** A great quantity; a 'lot', 'heap'. Also *pl.* 'lots', 'heaps'. *slang* or *dial.* 1523. **2.** Applied *spec.* (chiefly *fig.* in Biblical use) to the mass of clay taken up by a potter or sculptor for one operation, and to the mass of dough intended for one baking 1526. †**b.** Hence, *allusively*, the whole mass or quantity of anything. Also, the 'mass', 'bulk', great majority. –1711. †**3.** An aggregate of units; a congeries, heap, clump, cluster; *occas.* a group (of persons) –1781. **4.** A protuberance, swelling, or excrescence, *esp.* one caused by disease or injury in an animal body 1475. **5.** Applied to persons. *colloq.* **a.** A heavy, dull person 1597. **b.** A big sturdy creature 1630. **6.** *techn.* **a.** A bloom or loop of malleable iron 1686. **b.** A kind of thickish paving brick or tile 1787. **c.** A barge or lighter used in dockyards 1796. **d.** In firearms: (*a*) The nipple-seat on a gun-barrel; (*b*) a steel projection under the barrel on a break-joint breech-loader which descends into a recess in the action. 1844.

1. A l. of Sugar SWIFT, of lead, iron, etc. TYNDALL. *transf.* Thou lumpe of fowle Deformitie SHAKS. Phr. *A l. in one's throat*: (*a*) a swelling in the throat; (*b*) a feeling of tightness in the throat due to emotion (*popular*). *L. of clay*: the human body; a soulless person (*disparaging*). **b.** A l. of money 1869. **2.** 1 *Cor.* 5:6. Before that sin turned..all our l. to leaven G. HERBERT. **3.** Take a lumpe of figs 2 *Kings* 20:7.

Phrases. *By the l.* (rarely *by l.*): = *in the lump.* †*In a l.*: the whole together. *In the l.*: in the mass; in gross; wholesale. *All of a l.*: altogether, in a heap; also, swollen so as appear one l.

Comb.: **l.-coal,** coal including the largest lumps as they come from the mine; **l. gold,** gold in nuggets; **l. sugar,** loaf sugar broken into lumps or cut into cubes 1623; **l. sum,** a sum which covers a number of items.

Lump (lɒmp), *sb.*[2] 1545. [– MLG. *lumpen*, MDu. *lumpe* (whence mod.L. *lumpus*), perh. identical with LUMP *sb*[1].] **1.** An uncouth-looking spiny-finned fish of a leaden-blue colour, *Cyclopterus lumpus*, having a suctorial disc on its belly with which it adheres strongly to objects; the sea-owl. **2.** *Comb.*: **l.-fish, l. sucker,** = 1.

Lump (lɒmp), *v.*[1] 1577. [Of symbolic sound: cf. *dump, grump, thump, mump*.] **1.** *intr.* To look sulky or disagreeable. **2.** *trans.* In antithesis with *like*: To be displeased at (something that must be endured). *colloq.* 1833.

2. If you don't like it you may l. it HALIBURTON.

Lump (lɒmp), *v.*[2] 1624. [f. LUMP *sb.*[1] With sense 5 cf. LUMPER *v.*, LUMBER *v.*[1] 1.] **1.** *trans.* **a.** To melt down into a lump. **b.** To form or raise into lumps. **c.** To cover with lumps. 1797. **2.** To put together in one lump, mass, sum, or group; to consider or deal with in the lump without regard for particulars or details 1624. **3.** To lay the whole of (a particular sum of money) *on* a single object 1864. **4.** *intr.* To collect *together* into a lump; to be formed or raised into lumps 1720. **5.** To move heavily *along*; to drop *down* like a lump 1861.

2. They always l. the petty officers and common seamen MARRYAT. The premium and the principal are lumped in one sum SIR J. BACON. **3.** He lumped it all upon an outsider *Derby Day* (1864). **4.** The old one [cushion], which used to l. up all in a heap 1856.

Lumper (lɒ·mpəɹ), *sb.* 1785. [f. LUMP *v.* + -ER[1].] **1.** A labourer employed in loading and unloading cargoes, esp. timber. **2.** *slang.* A small contractor, sweater 1851. **3.** One who lumps things together 1852. **4.** *Ireland.* A coarse variety of potato 1837.

3. It is good to have hair-splitters and lumpers DARWIN.

Lu·mper, *v. Obs.* exc. *dial.* 1581. [Cf. synon. LUMBER *v.*[1] 1, LUMP *v.*[2] 5.] *intr.* To move clumsily; to blunder along.

Lump-fish: see LUMP *sb.*[2]

Lu·mping, *ppl. a.* ME. [f. LUMP *sb.*[1] or *v.*[2] + -ING[2].] †**1.** Coagulating. LAVINGTON. †**2.** Weighing heavy. ME. only. **b.** Hence *colloq.*: Great, big 1705. **c.** Of movement: Heavy, clumsy. Also of the noise so produced. 1884. **3.** Characterized by taking things in a lump without regard for detail 1793.

2. **b.** *L. pennyworth* (now *dial.*) = 'plenty for one's money'. *L. weight*, good or full weight. **3.** L. methods of cost-keeping 1896.

Lumpish (lɒ·mpiʃ), *a.* 1528. [f. LUMP *sb.*[1] (and in part LUMP *v.*[1]) + -ISH[1].] †**1.** Heavy and unwieldy. –1727. **2.** Heavy and clumsy in appearance, shape, or movement 1555. **3.** Stupidly dull or heavy; sluggishly inactive; unapprehensive 1528. †**4.** Low-spirited, dejected, melancholy –1741. **5.** Of sound: Dull and heavy 1742. **6.** In lumps, lumpy. *Obs.* (exc. as nonce-use). 1735.

4. She is l., heauy, mellancholly SHAKS. Hence **Lu·mpish-ly** *adv.*, **-ness.**

Lumpkin (lɒ·mᵖkin). *dial.* 1901. [f. LUMP *sb.*[1] + -KIN. (Cf. the character Tony Lumpkin in Goldsmith's *She Stoops to Conquer*.)] A clumsy, blundering person.

Lump sucker: see LUMP *sb.*[2]

Lumpy (lɒ·mpi), *a.* 1707. [f. LUMP *sb.*[1] + -Y[1].] **1.** Full of lumps. **b.** Of water: Cut up by the wind into small waves 1857. **2.** Having an outline or shape characterized by lumps 1708. **3.** *slang.* Drunk 1810. Hence **Lu·mpily** *adv.*, **Lu·mpiness.**

‖**Luna** (l^{i}ū·nă). ME. [L., = moon. (In senses 1 and 2 written with capital L as proper name.)] **1.** The moon (personified) 1529. **2.** †**a.** *Alch.* Silver. **b.** *Her.* A name for argent in blazoning the arms of sovereigns. ME. **c.** **L. cornea** = HORN-SILVER, chloride of silver fused. Also *Lunæ* (erron. *Luna*) *cornua*. 1706. **3.** *Eccl.* A lunette. **4.** In full *luna-moth*: A large moth of N. America, *Actias luna*, having crescent-shaped spots on the wings 1884.

1. And L. hides her selfe to pleasure vs KYD. **2.** **a.** Sol gold is, and L. silver we threpe CHAUCER.

Lunacy (l^{i}ū·năsi). 1541. [f. LUNATIC; see -ACY 3.] The condition of being a lunatic; intermittent insanity as formerly attributed to the changes of the moon; now *gen.* any form of insanity (idiocy usually excepted). In *Law*, such mental unsoundness as interferes with civil rights or transactions. †Also, an attack of this. **b.** *transf.* and *fig.* Mad folly 1588.

Commission of l., a commission, issuing from a court, authorizing inquiry into a person's sanity. *Commissioner in l.*, now, a member of a board inspecting asylums and granting licences to private persons who undertake the charge of lunatics. *Master in l.*, an officer who investigates cases of alleged lunacy and makes orders dealing with the persons and estate of lunatics.

This disease of lunacie, is a disease whose distemper followeth the course of the moon 1635. *attrib.* The L. Acts 1881. **b.** The wicked lunacies of the gaming-table COLERIDGE.

Lunar (l^{i}ū·năɹ). 1626. [– L. *lunaris*, f. *luna* moon; see -AR[1].] **A.** *adj.* **1.** Of or belonging to the moon; situated in the moon; †influenced by or dependent on the moon, or supposed to be so. **2.** *transf.* and *fig.* **a.** Monthly, menstrual (*rare*) 1683. **b.** Like the moon; not warmly bright; pale, pallid 1742. **3.** Crescent-shaped, LUNATE. Also, marked with crescent-shaped spots, as *l. underwing*. 1635. **4.** Of or containing silver 1800.

1. **L. cycle:** see CYCLE *sb.* 2 (quot.). **L. day,** the interval between two successive crossings of the meridian by the moon. **L. distance,** in *Naut. Astr.*, the distance of the moon from the sun, a planet, or a fixed star, which is used in calculating longitude at sea. **L. month,** the interval from one new moon to the next, about 29½ days; in pop. language, 28 days (four weeks). **L. rainbow,** one formed by the moon's rays. **L. tables,** tables for showing or calculating the true place of the moon at any time. **L. theory,** the deduction of the moon's motion from the law of gravitation. **L. year,** a period of 12 l. months (about 354⅓ days). **2.** **b.** Even the lustre of Partridge [in *Tom Jones*] is pallid and l. beside the noontide glory of Micawber SWINBURNE. **3.** *L. bone* (= medical L. *os lunare*): = B. 3. **4.** **Lunar caustic,** nitrate of silver fused.

B. *sb.* †**1.** A moon-like body, a satellite 1651. **2.** A l. distance or observation 1830. **3.** A bone of the wrist, shaped like a half-moon. Also in L. form **lunare** (l^{i}unē^ə·ri). 1854.

Lunarian (l^{i}unē^ə·riăn). 1708. [f. L. *lunaris* + -IAN.] **A.** *adj.* Inhabiting the moon. LOCKYER. **B.** *sb.* **1.** A dweller in the moon 1708. **2.** One who observes or describes the moon; one who used the lunar method in finding longitude 1817.

Lunary (l^{i}ū·nări). *sb.* †Also in L. form **lunaria.** ME. [– med.L. *lunaria*, f. *luna* moon; see -ARY[1] 3. Cf. late L. *lunaria* henbane (Dioscurides Latinus VI).] **a.** The garden plant HONESTY, *Lunaria biennis*. **b.** The fern called MOONWORT, *Botrychium lunaria*.

Lunary (l^{i}ū·nări), *a.* 1561. [– L. *lunaris*, f. *luna*; see -ARY[2]. Cf. Fr. *lunaire*.] = LUNAR *a.*, in various senses.

Lunate (l^{i}ū·nĕt), *a.* 1777. [– L. *lunatus* crescent-shaped, f. *luna* moon; see -ATE[2].] Crescent-shaped. Chiefly *Nat. Hist.*

L. eyes 1828, leaves 1870. So **Lu·nated** *a.* (now *rare*) 1673.

Lunatic (l^{i}ū·nătik). ME. [– (O)Fr. *lunatique* – late L. *lunaticus*, f. *luna* moon; see -ATIC.]

A. *adj.* **1.** Orig., affected with the intermittent insanity formerly attributed to the changes of the moon. In mod. use, = INSANE. Not now employed technically by physicians. **b.** Of things: Indicating lunacy; crazy 1605. **c.** *fig.* Madly foolish, idiotic, 'mad' 1571. †**2.** Influenced by the moon –1593. †**b.** *Farriery.* Moon-blind –1737.

1. He was..euery moneth once Lunaticke LYDG. The House of Castile..terminated in a l. girl 1889. **c.** No policy can be more l. than the policy of annexation BRIGHT. So **Luna·tical** *a.* (*rare*) 1599.

B. *sb.* A person of unsound mind; a madman ME. **b.** *fig.* A madly foolish person 1602.

The Lunaticke, the Louer, and the Poet, Are of imagination all compact SHAKS. *attrib.* **l. asylum** (also **l. hospital,** †**house**), a hospital for the reception and treatment of lunatics.

Lunation (l^{i}unē^i·ʃən). ME. [– med.L. *lunatio*, f. L. *luna* moon; see -ATION.] **1.** The time from one new moon to the next, a lunar month (about 29½ days). †**2.** The time of full moon –1686. **3.** A menstruation (*rare*) 1822.

Lunch (lɒnʃ), *sb.* 1591. [In sense 1 perh. – Sp. *lonja* slice. Sense 2 is a shortening of LUNCHEON 2.] †**1.** A piece, a thick piece; a hunch –1785. **2.** Colloq. for LUNCHEON *sb.* 2. (Now the usual word exc. in formal use.) 1829.

2. *U.S.* A light repast taken at any time in the twenty-four hours. Hence **Lunch** *v. intr.* to take l. 1823; *trans.* (*colloq.*) to provide l. for 1892.

Luncheon (lɒ·nʃən), *sb.* 1580. [Sense 1 is prob. an extension of LUNCH *sb.* 1 on the analogy of *punch* and *puncheon*, *trunch* and *truncheon*. Sense 2 appears XVII, and first in the forms *lunchin(g)*.] †**1.** = LUNCH *sb.* 1.

–1824. **2.** Orig., a slight repast taken between two meal-times, *esp.* in the morning. Still so applied by those who dine at midday; with others, *luncheon* denotes a less ceremonious midday meal than dinner. Now somewhat *formal.* 1652.

1. A large l. of brown bread H. BROOKE. **2.** *U.S.* (cf. LUNCH *sb.* 2 quots.). *attrib.* A l. bar 1891. L.-baskets 1903. Hence **Lu·ncheon** *v. intr.* to lunch.

Lundyfoot (lʌ·ndifut). 1811. [f. *Lundy Foot*, a Dublin tobacconist.] A kind of snuff.

Lune[1] (l[i]ūn). 1470. [var. of LOYN.] *Hawking.* A leash for a hawk.

Lune[2] (l[i]ūn). *arch.* 1611. [– L. *luna* moon, in med.L. also 'fit of lunacy', whence also Fr. *lune*, MHG. *lūne* (G. *laune* whim, caprice).] *pl.* Fits of lunacy; mad freaks or tantrums.

Lune[3] (l[i]ūn). 1704. [– Fr. *lune* :– L. *luna* moon, crescent.] **1.** *Geom.* The figure formed on a sphere or on a plane by two arcs of circles that enclose a space. **2.** Anything in the shape of a crescent or half-moon 1706.

Lunel (l[i]une·l). 1770. [f. *Lunel* (Hérault) a town in France.] A sweet muscat wine. Also *l.-wine.*

Lunette (l[i]une·t). †Also **lunet(t.** 1580. [– Fr. *lunette*, dim. of *lune* moon; see -ETTE.] †**1.** A little moon, a satellite. BP. HALL. †**2.** The figure of a crescent moon –1787. **3.** *Farriery.* A horseshoe consisting of the front semicircular portion only. Also *l.-shoe.* 1580. **4.** *Arch.* **a.** An arched aperture in a concave ceiling for the admission of light 1613. **b.** A crescent-shaped or semicircular space in a ceiling, dome, etc., decorated with paintings or sculptures; a piece of decoration filling this 1722. **5.** *Fortif.* A work larger than a redan, consisting of two faces and two flanks 1704. **6.** A blinker for a horse 1652. **7.** †**a.** *pl.* Spectacles –1796. **b.** A kind of concavo-convex lens for spectacles 1855. **8.** A watch-glass of flattened shape 1832. **9.** In the guillotine, the circular hole for the victim's neck 1859. **10.** *Glass-making.* A flue in the side of a furnace, to admit smoke and flame to the arch; a linnet-hole 1839. **11.** A forked iron plate into which the stock of a field-gun carriage is inserted 1875. **12.** *Eccl.* A circular crystal case to hold the consecrated Host 1890.

Lung (lʌŋ). [OE. *lungen* = OFris. *lungen*, MLG. *lunge*, MDu. *longe* (Du. *long*), OHG. *lungun* (G. *lunge*), corresp. to ON. *lunga*; f. Gmc. **lunʒ-* :– IE. **lṇgh-*; see LIGHT *a.*[1] The lungs were so named because of their lightness; cf. LIGHTS.] **1.** Each of the two breathing organs in man and many vertebrates, placed within the cavity of the thorax, one on each side of the heart, and communicating with the trachea or windpipe. **b.** *transf.* and *fig.* 1651. **2.** Applied to analogous organs in other animals 1889. †**3.** *pl.* One who blows the fire; a chemist's assitant –1663. **4. Lungs of (the) oak, †oak-lungs** = LUNGWORT c. 1650.

1. Gentlemen,..of such sensible and nimble Lungs that they always vse to laugh at nothing SHAKS. **b.** *Lungs of (London*, etc.), open spaces within or adjacent to a city 1808.

Comb.: **l.-fever**, pneumonia; **-fish**, a fish having lungs as well as gills, a dipnoan; **-flower**, the Marsh Gentian (Gerarde); †**lung(s)-growing**, a disease in cattle, in which the lungs adhere to the side; so †**l.-grown** *a.*; **l. lichen** = LUNGWORT c; **-power**, power of voice; **-worm**, a parasite infesting the lungs of cattle.

Lunge, longe (lʌndʒ), *sb.*[1] 1607. [– (O)Fr. *longe*, var. of OFr. *loigne*; see LOYN.] †**1.** *gen.* A thong, cord. TOPSELL. **2.** A long rope used in training horses; it is fastened at one end to the horse's head and held at the other by the trainer, who causes the horse to canter in a circle 1720. **3. a.** The use of the lunge in training horses. **b.** A circular exercising-ground in which the lunge is used. 1833.

Lunge (lʌndʒ), *sb.*[2] Also **lounge.** 1748. [Aphetic f. ALLONGE *sb.*[1] 1 – Fr. *allonger* lengthen (in phr. *allonger un coup d'épée* give a sword-thrust), f. *à* AD- + *long* LONG *a.*] **1.** A thrust with a sword (spec. in *Fencing*) or other weapon. **2.** A sudden forward movement; a plunge, rush 1873.

Lunge (lʌndʒ), *sb.*[3] *Amer.* Also **longe, 'longe, 'lunge.** 1882. [Short for *maskalonge*, etc., var. of MASKINONGE.] The Great Lake trout (*Salvelinus namaycush*).

Lunge (lʌndʒ), *v.*[1] Also **lounge.** 1735. [f. LUNGE *sb.*[2]] **1.** *intr.* **a.** *Fencing.* To make a thrust with a foil or rapier. **b.** *Boxing.* To deliver a straightforward blow. 1809. **c.** quasi-*trans.* with cognate obj. To deliver (a kick, etc.); also with *out* 1735. **2.** *trans.* To drive or thrust with or as with a lunge 1841. **3.** *intr.* To move with a lunge; to make a sudden forward movement; to rush 1821.

1. c. The Mulligan..lunged out a kick THACKERAY.

Lunge, longe (lʌndʒ), *v.*[2] Also **lounge.** 1806. [f. LUNGE *sb.*[1]] **1.** *trans.* To put (a horse) through his paces by the use of the lunge; to make a horse go round the lunge. **2.** *intr.* Of the horse: To go round the lunge in a specified direction 1833.

Lunged (lʌŋd), *ppl. a.* 1693. [f. LUNG + -ED[2].] Having lungs, or something resembling lungs; as *small-, weak-l.*, etc.

Lungeous (lʌ·ndʒəs), *a. dial.* 1787. [f. LUNGE sb.[2] or *v.*[1] + -OUS.] Rough-mannered, violent (in play).

‖**Lungi** (lu·ngī). 1616. [Urdu (Pers.) *lungī*, f. *lung* of the same meaning.] A loin-cloth. Also, the material of this.

†**Lu·ngis.** 1560. [– Fr. *longis* (XVI) :– L. *Longinus*, apocryphal name of the centurion who pierced our Lord with a spear, pop. assoc. w. L. *longus* long.] **a.** A long, slim, awkward fellow; a lout. **b.** A laggard, a lingerer. –1706.

Lungwort (lʌ·ŋwʌɹt). [OE. *lungenwyrt*, f. *lungen* LUNG + *wyrt* WORT[1].] The Eng. name of various plants; *esp.* **a.** The boraginaceous plant *Pulmonaria officinalis* (Common Lungwort), having leaves with white spots (fancied to resemble the spots in a diseased lung) 1538. †**b.** The Great Mullein, *Verbascum thapsus* –1706. **c.** A species of lichen (*Sticta pulmonacea* or *pulmonaria*), otherwise known as Lungs of Oak (see LUNG 4) and Tree Lungwort 1578.

Luniform (l[i]ū·nifǫɹm), *a.* 1826. [f. L. *luna* moon; see -FORM.] Moon-shaped; *spec.* in *Nat. Hist.*

Lunisolar (l[i]ū:niˌsōᵘ·lăɹ), *a.* 1691. [f. L. *luna* + SOLAR.] *Astr.* Pertaining to the mutual relations of the sun and moon, or resulting from their combined action.

L. period: a cycle of 532 years (= 19 × 28, the numbers of years in the cycles of the moon and sun respectively). *L. year*: a year divided into lunar months, but whose average length is determined by the sun.

Lunistice (l[i]ū·nistis). 1650. [f. L. *luna* moon, after *solstice.*] *Astr.* The point or time at which the moon is furthest north or south in her monthly course.

Luniti·dal, *a.* 1851. [f. L. *luna* + TIDAL.] Pertaining to the movements of the tide dependent on the moon.

L. interval: the interval between the culmination of the moon and the time of high water.

Lunt (lʌnt), *sb. Sc.* 1550. [– Du. *lont* match. Cf. LINSTOCK.] **1.** A slow match; also, a torch. **2.** Smoke without flame, as that from a pipe. Also, hot vapour. 1785. Hence **Lunt** *v. intr.* to smoke, emit smoke; also, (of smoke) to curl; quasi-*trans.* to smoke (a pipe); *trans.* to kindle, light *up.*

‖**Lunula** (l[i]ū·niŭlă). 1571. [L., dim. of *luna*; see -ULE.] = LUNULE. Hence **Lu·nular** *a.* pertaining to or resembling a lunule, crescent-shaped 1727; †*sb.* a crescent-shaped figure 1570–1789. **Lu·nulate** (1760), **-ated** (1705) *adjs.* crescent-shaped; marked with crescent-shaped spots.

Lunule (l[i]ū·niul). 1737. [– L. *lunula*; see prec., -ULE.] *Nat. Hist.* and *Geom.* A crescent-shaped mark, body, or figure. So **Lu·nulet** *Nat. Hist.* a small lunule 1826.

Lunulite (l[i]ū·niŭləit). 1845. [– mod.L. *lunulites* (J. Parkinson, 1822), f. L. LUNULA, see- ITE[1] 2 a.] *Geol.* A small fossil coral, more or less circular in shape.

Luny, var. of LOONY.

‖**Lupercal** (l[i]ū·pəɹkăl), *sb.* 1513. [L., subst. form of *lupercale*, neut. of *lupercalis* pertaining to Lupercus, the Roman Pan.] *Rom. Antiq.* **1.** A grotto on the Palatine sacred to Lupercus. **2.** A festival held annually in February in honour of Lupercus. Also *pl.* **Lupercalia.** 1600.

2. You all did see, that on the Lupercall, I thrice presented him a Kingly Crowne *Jul. C.* III. ii. 200. So †**Lupe·rcal** *a. rare*, pertaining to the Lupercal or Lupercalia 1607–56.

Lupine, lupin (l[i]ū·pin), *sb.* ME. [– L. *lupinus, lupinum*, prob. rel. to *lupus* wolf.] **1.** Any plant of the leguminous genus *Lupinus*; in early use, chiefly *L. albus*, cultivated for the seed and for fodder; later, species of various colours cultivated in flower-gardens. **2.** *pl.* The seed of this plant.

Lupine (l[i]ū·pəin), *a.* 1660. [– L. *lupinus*, f. *lupus* wolf; see -INE[1].] Having the nature or qualities of a wolf.

Lupinin (l[i]ū·pinin). 1839. [– Fr. *lupinine*; see LUPINE *sb.* and -IN[1].] *Chem.* A bitter glucoside obtained from the seeds of *Lupinus albus.*

Lupulin (l[i]ū·piŭlin). 1826. [f. mod.L. (*Humulus*) *lupulus* hop-plant (– med.L. *lupulus* (XIII) hop) + -IN[1].] **1.** *Bot.* The resinous yellow powder found under the scales of the calyx of the hop. **2.** *Chem.* The bitter principle obtained from this powder 1839. Hence **Lupuli·nic** *a.* relating to lupulin.

‖**Lupus** (l[i]ū·pŏs). 1590. [L., = wolf.] **1.** *Med.* A disease of the skin, usually tubercular and ulcerous, eating into the substance and leaving deep scars. **2.** *Astr.* The Wolf, a constellation south of Scorpio 1706. **3.** The pike or luce 1706. Hence **Lu·pous** *a.* pertaining to or affected with l. 1883.

Lurch (lɒɹtʃ), *sb.*[1] 1533. [app. –Fr. †*lourche* (also *l'ourche*) game resembling backgammon, also in phr. *demeurer lourche* be discomfited (orig. in the game), prob. – MHG. *lurz* (mod. dial. *lurtsch*) left (hand), wrong, in mod.G. *lurz werden* fail in a game; cf. MHG. *lürzen* deceive and OE. *belyrtan.*] †**1.** A game supposed to have resembled backgammon –1693. **2.** Used in some games to denote a state of the score in which the winner is far ahead of the loser; often, a 'maiden set' or love-game; at cribbage, a game in which the winner scores 61 before the loser has scored 31; in whist, a treble. Now *rare* or *Obs.* 1570. **3.** Discomfiture; disadvantage. *Obs.* exc. in phr. *to leave in the l.*, to leave in adverse circumstances without assistance. 1584. †**4.** [f. LURCH *v.*[1] 2] A cheat, swindle –1616.

2. Phr. *To save the l.*: in whist, to prevent one's adversary from scoring a treble. **3.** Phr. †*To give* (a person) *the l.*: to get the better of.

Lurch (lɒ̄ɹtʃ), *sb.*[2] 1568. [f. LURCH *v.*[1]] **1.** An act of lurching or getting the start in obtaining food, profit, etc. **2.** phr. *To lie at* (*on, upon the*) *l.*: to lie concealed; to lie in wait 1578.

Lurch (lɒ̄ɹtʃ), *sb.*[3] 1819. [app. orig. in *lee-lurch*, prob. alt. of *lee-larch* (Falconer, 1769), for *lee-latch* (1708) drifting to leeward, f. LEE *sb.*[1] + †*latch* (XVII) ? leeway, ? lurch, perh. f. Fr. *lâcher* let go.] **1.** (Orig. *Naut.*) A sudden leaning over to one side, as of a ship, a person staggering, etc. Also, a lurching gait **2.** *U.S.* A propensity, leaning 1854.

1. Here the ship gave a l., and he grew sea-sick BYRON.

Lurch (lɒ̄ɹtʃ), *v.*[1] ME. [perh. var. of LURK *v.*, infl. in meaning by LURCH *sb.*[1]] †**1.** *intr.* To remain in or about a place furtively –1790. **b.** Of a greyhound: To run cunning, and let the opponent do the work 1824. **2.** *trans.* To get the start of (a person) so as to prevent him from obtaining a fair share of food, profit, etc. Later, to defraud, cheat, rob. *arch.* 1530. †**3.** To be beforehand in securing (something); to engross, monopolize (commodities); later, to pilfer, filch, steal –1660. **4.** To catch (rabbits) by means of lurchers 1727.

1. I my selfe..am faine to shuffle, to hedge, and to l. SHAKS. **2.** You haue lurch'd your friends of the better halfe of the garland B. JONS. **3.** *absol.* Wherein had he been a thiefe, if he had not.. meant to l. out of the common Treasury? BP. HALL.

Lurch (lɒ̄ɹtʃ), *v.*[2] ME. [f. LURCH *sb.*[1]] **1.** *trans.* To defeat by a lurch, as in cribbage, etc. (see LURCH *sb.*[1] 2). †**b.** *fig.* To defeat 1716–1829. †**2.** To leave in the lurch, disappoint, deceive 1651–1810.

Lurch (lɒ̄ɹtʃ), *v.*[3] (orig. *Naut.*) 1833. [f. LURCH *sb.*[3]] **1.** *intr.* Of a ship, etc.: To make a lurch; to lean suddenly over to one side; to move with lurches. **2.** To move suddenly, unsteadily, and without purpose in any direction; to stagger 1851.

1. The boat lurched through the breakers like a log 1845. **2.** Where the tipsy trainband-man is lurching against the post THACKERAY.

Lurcher (lɒ̄·ɹtʃəɹ). 1528. [f. LURCH *v.*[1] + -ER[1].] †**1.** One who forestalls others of their fair share of food; hence, a glutton –1616. **2.** One who filches in a mean fashion; a petty thief, swindler, rogue 1528. **3.** One who loiters or lies hidden in a suspicious manner; a spy 1706. **4.** A cross-bred dog, properly between the collie and the greyhound; much used by poachers for catching hares and rabbits 1668. **b.** *slang.* A bumbailiff 1785.

Lurdan (lɒ̄·ɹdăn). *arch.* or *Sc.* and *dial.* ME. [– OFr. *lourdin*, f. *lourd* heavy, OFr. *lort* foolish :– L. *luridus* yellow, LURID, which in Rom. assumes many divergent meanings.] **A.** *sb.* A term of abuse; a sluggard, vagabond, loafer. **B.** *adj.* Worthless, ill-bred, lazy ME.

Lure (l[i]ū[ə]ɹ), *sb.*[1] ME. [– OFr. *luere* (mod. *leurre*) – Gmc. *lōþr- (cf. MHG. *luoder*, G. *luder* bait), prob. rel. to *lapōn invite.] **1.** An apparatus used by falconers to recall their hawks, being a bunch of feathers attached to a cord, within which, during its training, the hawk finds its food 1440. **2.** *Her.* A representation of this, consisting of two birds' wings with the points downwards, and joined above by a ring attached to a cord 1572. **3.** (orig. *fig.*) Something which allures, entices, or tempts ME. **4.** A means of alluring animals to be captured; in *Angling* a more general term than *bait* 1700. ¶**b.** Erron.: A trap or snare (*fig.*) 1463. **5.** The cry of a falconer recalling his hawk; *fig.* any alluring cry 1653.

1. As Faulcons to the l., away she flies SHAKS. Phr. *To alight on the l., to bring, call, come, stoop to* (*the* or *one's*) *l.* **3.** How many have with a smile made small account Of beauty and her lures? MILT.

Lure (l[i]ū[ə]ɹ), *sb.*[2] *techn.* Also **lewer.** 1858. [Shortened from VELURE.] A pad of silk or velvet used by hatters for smoothing.

Lure (l[i]ū[ə]ɹ), *v.* ME. [f. LURE *sb.*[1]] **1.** *trans.* To recall (a hawk) by casting the lure; to call (a hawk) to the lure. **2.** *intr.* To call to a hawk while casting the lure 1530; †to call loudly –1626. **3.** To allure, entice, tempt ME.

3. Lured into a snare by treachery 1855.

Lurg (lɒ̄ɹg). *local.* 1880. [Cf. LUG *sb.*[3]] A British marine worm used for bait; the white-rag worm.

Lurid (l[i]ū[ə]·rid), *a.* 1656. [– L. *luridus*, f. *luror* wan or yellowish colour; see -ID[1].] **1.** Pale and dismal in colour; wan; ghastly of hue. **2.** Shining with a red glow or glare amid darkness 1727. **3.** *fig.* (from 1 or 2), with connotation of 'terrible', 'ominous', 'ghostly', 'sensational'; also, marked by violent passion or crime 1850. **4.** In scientific use: Of a dingy-brown or yellowish-brown colour 1767.

1. A leaden glare..makes the snow and ice more l. SYMONDS. **2.** At night also the l. reflection of immense fires hung in the sky W. IRVING. A softness gathered over the l. fires of her eye 1852. **3.** He adds one fact more which casts a l. light on the annals of the persecution 1879. Hence **Lu·rid-ly** *adv.*, **-ness.**

Lurk (lɒ̄ɹk), *sb.* 1829. [f. LURK *v.*] **1.** The action of prowling about. In phr. *on the l.* **2.** *slang.* A method of fraud 1851.

2. The 'bereavement lurk' is a lucrative one—(i.e.) the pretended loss of a wife [etc.] 1875.

Lurk (lɒ̄ɹk), *v.* Now *literary.* ME. [perh. f. *lur-* LOUR *v.* + frequent. suffix *-k* as in *talk*. Cf. LG. *lurken* shuffle along, Norw. *lurka* sneak away, etc.] **1.** *intr.* To hide oneself; to lie in ambush. (Now only with indication of place.) †**b.** To shirk work; to idle –1792. **2.** *transf.* and *fig.* Of things: To escape observation, to be concealed or latent ME. **3.** To move about furtively; to steal *along, away, out.* Now *rare.* ME.

1. Shaftesbury..had left his house and secretly lurked in the city HUME. **2.** The Vices that l. in the secret Corners of the Soul ADDISON.

Lurry (lɒ·ri). *Obs.* exc. *dial.* 1580. [Short f. LIRIPOOP.] **1.** Something said by rote; a lesson, set speech, 'patter'; *fig.* a cant formula. **2.** A confusion of voices; babel, hubbub 1649. **3.** A confused assemblage (of persons) or mass (of things) 1607.

1. Then was the Priest set to con his motions, and his Postures, his Liturgies, and his Lurries MILT.

Lurry: see LORRY.

Luscious (lɒ·ʃəs), *a.* ME. [perh. orig. aphetic f. DELICIOUS, but the earliest forms of the present word, *looshious, lousious, lussyous* (XVI) remain obscure.] **1.** Sweet and highly pleasant in taste or smell. **2.** Sweet to excess, cloying, sickly 1530. **3.** Of immaterial things, esp. of language, literary style, etc.: Sweet and highly pleasing to the eye, ear, or mind. Chiefly dyslogistic. 1651. †**4.** Of tales, talk, writing, etc.: Lascivious, voluptuous, wanton –1815.

1. L. woodbine SHAKS. The most l. fruits JOHNSON. *fig.* The l. sweets of sin BOYLE. **3.** A l. Style stuffed with gawdy Metaphors and Fancy 1738. The groups of children,..l. in colour and faint in light RUSKIN. Hence **Lu·scious-ly** *adv.*, **-ness.**

Luser(a)n, var. of LUCERN[1].

Lush (lɒʃ), *sb. slang.* 1790. [perh. joc. application of LUSH *a.*] Liquor, drink; a drinking bout. Hence **Lu·shy** *a.* drunk.

Lush (lɒʃ), *a.* 1440. [perh. var. of LASH *a.* (sense 3) by assoc. with *luscious.*] **1.** Lax, flaccid; soft, tender. *Obs.* exc. *dial.* **2.** Of grass, etc.: Succulent and luxuriant in growth 1610. Also *fig.* **b.** Of a season: Of luxuriant vegetation 1818. ¶**3.** Erron. applied to colour (a misapprehension of Shakespeare's use): Deep, not pale and faint 1744.

2. How l. and lusty the grasse lookes SHAKS. In the warm hedge grew l. eglantine SHELLEY. **3.** The l. rose lingers late T. MARTIN.

Lush (lɒʃ), *v. slang.* 1811. [f. LUSH *sb.*] **1.** *trans.* To ply with 'lush' or drink 1821. **2.** *intr.* and *trans.* To drink 1811. Hence **Lushing** *vbl. sb.* (in *pl.* abundance; cf. *lashings*).

†**Lu·shburg.** ME. [Anglicized name of Luxemburg.] An imitation of the English silver penny, imported from Luxemburg in the reign of Edward III. Also *L. sterling.* –1716.

God woot no lussheburgh payen ye CHAUCER.

Lusitanian (l[i]ūsitē[i]·niăn). 1607. [f. L. *Lusitania* (see below) + -AN.] **A.** *adj.* Of or belonging to Lusitania, an ancient name of the region roughly corresponding to modern Portugal; hence (usu. *poet.*), of or pertaining to Portugal 1720. **B.** *sb.* An inhabitant of Lusitania; hence, a Portuguese.

†**Lusk,** *sb.* ME. [f. LUSK *v.*] A lazy fellow; a sluggard –1694. Hence **Lusk** *a.* lazy, sluggish 1775. †**Lu·skish** *a.* 1530, **-ly** *adv.*, **-ness.**

†**Lusk,** *v.* ME. [The sense agrees with that of OHG. *loscēn*, which would correspond to an OE. *loscian. For the phonology cf. DUSK.] *intr.* To lie hid; to lie idly or at ease, skulk –1662.

Lusory (l[i]ū·səri), *a.* 1653. [f. L. *lusorius* belonging to a player (*lusor*) + -OUS.] Used as a pastime; of the nature of play; written in a playful style.

A refined species of comic poetry,—l. yet elegant D'ISRAELI. So †**Luso·rious** *a.* 1613–1697.

Lust (lɒst), *sb.* Now *literary.* [OE. *lust* corresp. to OFris., OHG. (G.) *lust*, ON. *losti*, Goth. *lustus*, f. Gmc. *lust-; cf. LIST *v.*[1]] †**1.** Pleasure, delight; also, a source of pleasure –1607. †**2.** Desire, appetite, relish or inclination for something –1627. †**b.** (One's) desire or wish; (one's) good pleasure –1677. **3.** *spec.* in Biblical and Theol. use: Sensuous appetite or desire, as sinful OE. **4.** Sexual appetite or desire. Now only: Libidinous desire, degrading animal passion. (The chief current use.) OE. **5.** In mod. rhet. use: Lawless and passionate desire *of* or *for* some object. In poetry occas.: Overmastering desire (esp. of battle). 1678. †**6.** Vigour, lustiness; fertility (of soil) –1682.

2. Litle leysure, and lesse l., either to heare Sermons or to read bookes FOXE. **3.** Phr. *The lusts of the flesh, fleshly lusts.* **4.** He never spared man in his anger, nor woman in his l. NAUNTON. **5.** A l. of power 1786, of applause H. WALPOLE, of accumulation RUSKIN.

Lust (lɒst), *v. literary* and *arch.* ME. [f. LUST *sb.*] †**1.** *trans.* To please, delight (also *absol.*). ME. *only.* †**2.** *intr.* To desire, choose, wish –1618. **3.** To have a strong, excessive, or inordinate desire (*arch.*) 1530. **b.** *spec.* of sexual desire 1526.

3. If we be an hungred, we l. for bread 1563. **b.** Yet dost thou l. after the daughter of our despised race LYTTON. Hence **Lu·ster,** one who lusts. A l. after power C. BRONTË.

Luster, obs. and U.S. f. LUSTRE.

Lustful (lɒ·stfŭl), *a.* [OE. *lustfull*; see LUST *sb.* and -FUL.] **1.** Having a strong or excessive desire (for something). Also with *of* or *to do. Obs.* or *arch.* **2.** Vigorous, lusty (*arch.*) 1561. **3.** Full of or characterized by lust; pertaining to or manifesting sensual desire; libidinous 1579. †**4.** Provocative of lust –1667.

2. This want of lustfull health 1561. **3.** Bred..to the taste Of l. appetence MILT. **4.** Not all the l. Shell-fish of the Sea [etc.] COWLEY. Hence **Lu·stful-ly** *adv.*, **-ness.**

†**Lu·stick,** *a.* and *adv.* Also **-ique.** 1601. [– Du. *lustig.*] **a.** *adj.* Merry, jolly; chiefly with reference to drinking. **b.** *adv.* Merrily, jovially –1691.

Lustihood (lɒ·stihud). *arch.* 1599. [f. LUSTY + -HOOD.] Lustiness, vigour of body; †lustfulness. So **Lu·stihead** [-HEAD] ME., now *arch.*

Lustily (lɒ·stili), *adv.* ME. [f. LUSTY + -LY[2].] In a lusty or vigorous manner; †lustfully –1589.

Lustiness (lɒ·stinės). ME. [f. LUSTY + -NESS.] †Pleasure, delight –1550; vigour ME.; †lustfulness, libidinousness –1619.

Lustless (lɒ·stlės), *a.* Now *rare* or *Obs.* ME. [f. LUST *sb.* + -LESS. Cf. LISTLESS.] †**1.** Without vigour or energy, listless –1612. †**2.** Joyless –1586. **3.** Without lust or sexual appetite 1586.

Lustra, pl. of LUSTRUM.

Lustral (lɒ·străl), *a.* 1533. [– L. *lustralis*, f. LUSTRUM; see -AL[1].] **1.** Pertaining to the Roman lustrum or purificatory sacrifice; hence, purificatory. **2.** Quinquennial 1781.

1. The assistants were sprinkled with l. water GIBBON.

Lustrate (lɒ·strē[i]t), *v.* 1623. [– *lustrat-*, pa. ppl. stem of L. *lustrare* purify by lustral rites, go round, etc., f. LUSTRUM; see -ATE[3].] **1.** *trans.* To purify by a propitiatory offering; *gen.* to purify 1653. †**2. a.** *intr.* To pass or go *through* (a place). **b.** *trans.* To pass through or traverse. –1721. †**3.** *trans.* To view, survey –1648.

1. There was..a great Plague; the Oracle advis'd them to l. the City 1655. Hence **Lu·strative** *a.* pertaining to lustration, purification, or (*joc.*) washing. **Lu·stratory** *a.* (*rare*), lustral, expiatory.

Lustration (lɒstrē[i]·ʃən). 1614. [– L. *lustratio*, f. as prec.; see -ION.] **1.** The action of lustrating; the performance of an expiatory sacrifice or a purificatory rite. **b.** *gen.* Washing. Chiefly *joc.* 1825. **2.** *fig.* Purification, *esp.* spiritual or moral 1655. **3.** The action of going round, viewing, or surveying a place; the review (of an army) 1614. Now *rare.* †**4.** An inspection, census. SIR T. BROWNE. *rare.* **5.** = LUSTRE *sb.*[2] 1853. *rare.*

1. Signatures of the cross, and lustrations by holy water TUCKER. **2.** Let them [the prelates] perform a l.; let them purify..this country from this sin CHATHAM.

Lustre (lɒ·stəɹ), *sb.*[1] Formerly (still *U.S.*) **luster.** 1522. [– Fr. *lustre* – It. *lustro*, f. *lustrare* :– L. *lustrare* light up :– *lucstrare, f. *lux, luc-* LIGHT *sb.*] **1.** The quality of shining by reflected light; sheen, refulgence; gloss. Often with adj., as *metallic, pearly, silky, waxy l.* **b.** rarely in *pl.* Appearances of lustre 1614. **c.** A composition used to impart a lustre to manufactured articles 1727. **2.** Luminosity, brilliancy, bright light 1549; *concr.* a shining body or form 1742. **3.** *transf.* Radiant beauty or splendour (of the countenance, of natural objects, etc.) 1602. **4.** *fig.*, esp. Brilliance or splendour of renown; glory. Also, splendid beauty (of language, etc.). 1555. †**b.** Something that adds lustre; a glory –1647. †**c.** External splendour –1674. **5. a.** One of the prismatic glass pendants attached to a chandelier, etc. **b.** A chandelier [the usual sense in Fr.]. 1716. **6.** A thin light dress material having a cotton (formerly also silk or linen) warp and woollen weft and a lustrous surface 1831.

1. All stones of l. shoot their vivid ray GRAY. **2.** And now the scorching Sun was mounted high, In all its l. ADDISON. **3.** Virgins are like the fair flower in its l. GAY. **4.** The pomp and l. of his language J. WARTON. Mythical l. illumined all the historic facts of Abraham's life 1874. **c.** Solemnizing Nativities and Deaths with equal L. SIR T. BROWNE.

Comb.: **l. mottling,** the peculiar mottling seen in pœcilitic rocks; **l. ware,** cheap pottery with surface ornamentation in bright metallic colours. Hence **Lu·streless** *a.*

Lustre (lʊ·stəɹ), *sb.*^{2} Formerly (still *U.S.*) **luster.** ME. [Anglicized f. L. *lustrum.*] A period of five years.

Come eight more lustres, and your heads will be bald like mine THACKERAY.

†Lu·stre, *v.*^{1} *rare.* 1541. [– L. *lustrare.*] = LUSTRATE *v.* 1, 3. –1645.

Lustre (lʊ·stəɹ), *v.*^{2} 1582. [f. LUSTRE *sb.*^{1}; in sense 3 – Fr. *lustrer* in same sense (but cf. LUSTRE *sb.*^{1} 1 c).] **†1.** *trans.* **a.** To render illustrious. **b.** To illustrate. **c.** To make specious or attractive. –1644. **2.** *intr.* To be or become lustrous. Now *rare.* 1582. **3.** *trans.* To put a lustre upon (cloth, pottery, etc.) 1883.

Lustring (lʊ·striŋ). *Obs.* exc. *arch.* (See also LUTESTRING^2.) 1697. [– Fr. *lustrine* or its source It. *lustrino* (said to have been first made at Genoa), f. *lustro* LUSTRE *sb.*^{1}, with assim. to -ING^3. Cf. LUTESTRING^2.] A glossy silk fabric. var. **Lu·strine** 1851.

Lustrous (lʊ·strəs), *a.* 1601. [f. LUSTRE *sb.*^{1} + -OUS.] Having lustre, sheen, or gloss.

Where beauty cannot keep her l. eyes KEATS. Hence **Lu·strous-ly** *adv.*, **-ness.**

‖**Lustrum.** *Pl.* **lustra, lustrums.** 1590. [L., of obscure origin.] **1.** *Rom. Antiq.* A purificatory sacrifice made quinquennially, after the census had been taken 1598. **2.** A period of five years 1590.

Lusty (lʊ·sti), *a.* Now *dial.* or *rare arch.* ME. [f. LUST *sb.* + -Y^1. Cf. MHG. *lustic*, ON. *lostigr.*] **†1.** Joyful, merry; lively –1621. **†2.** Pleasing, pleasant. Of persons: Gaily dressed –1610. **†3.** Full of desire, desirous –1657. **†4.** Full of sexual desire; lustful –1697. **5.** Full of healthy vigour; strong ME. **†6.** Insolent, arrogant, self-confident –1674. **†7.** Of a fire, wine, poison, a disease, etc.: Strong, powerful –1692. **†b.** Of a ship: Sailing well –1669. **8.** Of actions: Vigorous. Of a meal, etc.: Hearty, abundant. 1672. **†9.** Massive, substantial, large –1842. **10.** Of persons: Massively built. Hence, corpulent, fat. 1772.

5. A mery herte maketh a l. age COVERDALE *Prov.* 17:22. Like a l. flower in June's caress KEATS. *transf.* The l. young democracy BLACKIE. **8.** The Turk..gave him two or three l. kicks on the seat of honour BURKE.

‖**Lusus naturæ** (l^{i}ū·sŏs nĕtiū^ə·rī). Also simply **lusus.** 1661. [L., = a sport of nature.] A sport or freak of nature; a markedly abnormal natural production.

Lutanist, lutenist (l^{i}ū·tănist, -ĕnist). 1600. [– med.L. *lutanista*, f. *lutana* lute; see -IST.] A lute-player.

†Luta·rious, *a.* [f. L. *lutarius* (f. *lutum* mud) + -OUS.] Inhabiting mud. GREW. So **†Lu·tary** *a.* (*rare*) 1661.

†Luta·tion. 1611. [f. LUTE *v.*^{2} + -ATION. Cf. Fr. *lutation* luting of a tube.] The process of luting; the material used in luting –1657.

Lute (l^{i}ūt), *sb.*^{1} ME. [– Fr. *†lut* (mod. *luth*), earlier *leüt*, prob. – Pr. *laüt* – Arab. *al-'ūd* (see AL-^{2}).] A stringed musical instrument, formerly much in vogue, the strings of which were struck with the fingers of the right hand and stopped on the frets with the left. **b.** The name of a stop in some forms of the harpsichord 1879.

Comb.: **l.-backed** *a.*, having a back shaped like a l.; **-pin,** one of the pegs or screws for turning the strings of the l.

Lute (l^{i}ūt), *sb.*^{2} ME. [–(O)Fr. *lut* or med.L. *lutum*, spec. use of L. *lutum* mud, potter's clay.] **1.** Tenacious clay or cement, used to stop an orifice, to make a joint air-tight, to coat a retort, etc., and to protect a graft. **†2.** Mud –1756. **3.** A packing-ring of india-rubber for making jars airtight 1875.

Lute (l^{i}ūt), *sb.*^{3} *U.S.* 1875. [– Du. *loet.*] *Brickmaking.* A straight-edged piece of wood for scraping off superfluous clay from a brick-mould.

Lute (l^{i}ūt), *v.*^{1} Now *rare.* ME. [f. LUTE *sb.*^{1}] **a.** *intr.* To play on the lute; quasi-*trans.* to express by means of the lute. **b.** *intr.* To sound like a lute. KEATS.

a. Thanne luted Loue in a loude note, *Ecce quam bonum et quam iocundum, etc.* LANGL.

Lute (l^{i}ūt), *v.*^{2} late ME. [– L. *lutare* bedaub with mud, f. *lutum* LUTE *sb.*^{2} Cf. Fr. *luter.*] *trans.* To close, seal, or cover with lute; to fasten or fix with lute.

Before they distill, luting the Limbeck 1594. The lids were luted down 1879.

Luteic (l^{i}utī·ik), *a.* 1892. [f. L. *luteus* yellow + -IC.] *Chem.* In *l. acid*: a yellow colouring matter prepared from the flowers of *Euphorbia cyparissias.*

Lutein (l^{i}ū·tīin). Also **-ine.** 1869. [f. L *luteum* yolk of egg (neut. of *luteus* yellow) + -IN^1.] *Chem.* A substance of a deep yellow colour found in the yolk of eggs and the ovaries of animals.

Lutenist: see LUTANIST.

Luteo- (l^{i}ū·tīo), used as comb. f. L. *luteus* LUTEOUS, signifying the presence of a yellow colour with some other. **Lu:teo-coba·ltic** *a.* *Chem.*, containing a compound of cobalt with a yellow colour. **Lu:teo-fu·lvous** *a.* *Bot.*, of a tawny yellow colour.

Luteolin (l^{i}ū·tīŏlin). Also **-ine.** 1839. [– Fr. *lutéolin*, f. mod.L. *(reseda) luteola* weld.] *Chem.* The yellow colouring matter of weld (*Reseda luteola*).

Luteous (l^{i}ū·tīəs), *a.* 1657. [f. L. *luteus* (f. *lutum* yellow weed) + -OUS.] *Nat. Hist.* Of a deep orange yellow colour.

Luter (l^{i}ū·təɹ). *Obs.* exc. *Hist.* 1474. [f. LUTE *v.*^{1} + -ER^1.] A lute-player.

Lutescent (l^{i}ute·sĕnt), *a.* 1819. [f. L. *luteus* yellow + -ESCENT.] *Nat. Hist.* Inclining to yellow.

Lu·te-string^1. 1530. [f. LUTE *sb.*^{1} + STRING *sb.*] **1.** A string of a lute. **2.** A noctuid moth having lines resembling the strings of a lute on its wings 1819.

Lutestring^2 (l^{i}ū·tstriŋ). 1471. [app. alt. of LUSTRING, which however is evidenced rather later.] A kind of glossy silk fabric; a dress or a ribbon of this.

Lutheran (l^{i}ū·þərăn). 1521. [f. proper name *Luther* + -AN.] **A.** *adj.* Pertaining to Martin Luther (1483–1546), his opinions and followers. (In 16th c. used by Roman Catholics as coextensive with PROTESTANT. Now chiefly applied to doctrinal views peculiar to Luther, and to churches which accept the Augsburg Confession.) 1530. **B.** *sb.* A follower of Luther; an adherent of his doctrines; a member of the Lutheran church 1521.

B. I know her for A spleeny L. SHAKS. Hence **Lu·theranism,** the body of L. doctrine; the holding of L. opinions 1560. **Lu·theranize** *v.* to make or become L. 1845. var. **†Luthe·rian** *a.* and *sb.* 1526–89.

Lutherism (l^{i}ū·þeriz'm). 1695. [f. *Luther* + -ISM. So mod.L. *Lutherismus* (XVI).] **a.** = LUTHERANISM. **b.** Something characteristic of Luther, or done or said in imitation of him.

Luthern (l^{i}ū·þəɹn). 1669. [perh. corrupt f. LUCARNE.] A dormer-window. Also *l.-light, -window.*

Lutist (l^{i}ū·tist). 1627. [f. LUTE *sb.*^{1} + -IST. Cf. LUTANIST.] A lute-player. Also, a maker of lutes.

Lutose (l^{i}ū·tō^{u}s), *a.* 1826. [– L. *lutosus*, f. *lutum* mud; see -OSE^1.] Covered with mud; miry. So **Luto·sity** 1650.

Lutulent (l^{i}ū·tiŭlĕnt), *a. rare.* 1600. [– L. *lutulentus*, f. *lutum* mud.] Muddy, turbid. Hence **Lu·tulence** (*rare*), muddiness; mud, dirt 1727.

†Lux, *v.* 1708. [– Fr. *luxer* or L. *luxare.*] = LUXATE *v.* –1775.

†Lu·xate, *ppl. a.* 1597. [– L. *luxatus*, pa. pple. of *luxare*; see -ATE^2.] Luxated –1661.

Luxate (lʊ·kse^{i}t), *v.* 1623. [– *luxat-*, pa. ppl. stem of L. *luxare*; see -ATE^3.] *trans.* To dislocate, put out of joint. So **Luxa·tion** *Surg.*, dislocation 1552.

Luxe. 1558. [– Fr. *luxe* – L. *luxus*; see LUXURY.] **†1.** Luxury –1746. ‖**2.** As Fr.: Luxuriousness, sumptuous elegance; esp. in *édition de luxe, train de luxe* 1819.

Luxuriance (lʊgziū^ə·riăns, -ʒū-, lʊksiū^ə·riăns). 1728. [f. LUXURIANT; see -ANCE.] The condition of being luxuriant; superabundant growth or development; exuberance. Also quasi-*concr.*

The faults which grow out of the l. of freedom BURKE. So **Luxu·riancy** (now *rare*) 1648.

Luxuriant (lʊgziū^ə·riănt, -ʒū-, lʊksiū^ə·riănt), *a.* 1540. [– L. *luxurians, -ant-*, pr. pple. of *luxuriare*; see next, -ANT.] **1.** Producing abundantly, prolific. Now *rare.* **2.** Of plants, etc.: Growing profusely, exuberant, rank 1661. **b.** *spec.* in *Bot.* Applied where the organs of nutrition are more developed than those of fructification 1760. **3.** Exuberantly productive, as genius, fancy, etc.; profuse, excessive, as speech, action, etc.; (of ornamentation) excessively rich 1625. ¶**4.** Misused for LUXURIOUS 1671.

1. The growth of the l. year POPE. **2.** Wit's like a L. Vine COWLEY. **3.** The irish jig, which they can dance with a most l. expression A. YOUNG. The l. (= excessively prosperous) great ones of the world GOLDSM. Hence **Luxu·riantly** *adv.*

Luxuriate (lʊgziū^ə·rie^{i}t, -ʒū-, lʊksiū^ə·rie^{i}t), *v.* 1621. [– *luxuriat-*, pa. ppl. stem of L. *luxuriare* grow rank, f. *luxuria*; see LUXURY, -ATE^3.] **1.** *intr.* Of a plant: To grow rank. Now *rare.* Also *fig.* †Of a writer: To write at exuberant length. **†b.** *fig.* To grow or develop exuberantly *into* (error, folly, etc.) 1651–1808. **2.** To indulge in luxury; to feast, enjoy oneself. Now only with *in, on.* 1621. **b.** To take great delight, revel *in* (something) 1650.

1. The vineyards hereabouts are..left to l. 1832. **2.** A huge crocodile luxuriating in the slime 1832. **b.** The Oriental mind..luxuriates in dreams 1880. Hence **Luxuria·tion** 1839.

†Luxuriety. [f. LUXURIOUS, after *variety*, etc.] Luxuriance. STERNE.

Luxurious (lʊgziū^ə·riəs, -ʒū-, lʊksiū^ə·riəs), *a.* ME. [– OFr. *luxurios* (mod. *-eux*) – L. *luxuriosus*, f. *luxuria*; see LUXURY, -OUS.] **†1.** Lascivious, lecherous, unchaste –1697. **†2.** Outrageous, extravagant, excessive –1665. **3. a.** Of persons, etc.: Given to luxury or self-indulgence 1606. **b.** Of things: Of or pertaining to luxury; characterized by luxury 1650. ¶**4.** = LUXURIANT **2.** Now *rare.* 1644.

3. a. Corinth..was..excessively proud and l. 1691. **b.** L. wealth MILT., provisions 1879. **4.** L. Vines 1653, grass 1801. Hence **Luxu·rious-ly** *adv.*, **-ness.**

Lu·xurist. *Obs.* or *arch.* 1689. [f. LUXURY + -IST.] One addicted to luxury.

Luxury (lʊ·kʃŭri, lʊ·ksiŭri). ME. [– OFr. *luxurie*, var. of (also mod.) *luxure* – L. *luxuria*, f. *luxus* abundance, sumptuous enjoyment; see -Y^3.] **†1.** Lasciviousness, lust; *pl.* lusts –1812. **†2.** = LUXURIANCE 1611–1695. **3.** Habitual use of what is choice or costly, whether food, dress, furniture, or appliances 1633. **4.** *transf.* Refined and intense enjoyment 1715. **5.** quasi-*concr.* Sumptuous and exquisite food or surroundings 1704. **b.** Something which conduces to enjoyment over and above the necessaries of life. Hence, now, something which is desirable but not indispensable 1780. **6.** *abstr.* Luxuriousness 1849.

1. Grov'lling in the sty..of shameless l. CRABBE. **3.** I never knew or want or luxurie P. FLETCHER. **4.** And learn the l. of doing good GOLDSM. **5.** Tables covered with l. JOHNSON. **6.** Necessaries come always before luxuries BENTHAM.

LXX. 1662. The Roman numeral symbol for Seventy; hence, abbrev. for SEPTUAGINT.

-ly, *suffix*^{1}, appended to sbs. to form adjs., represents OE. *-lić*, ME. *-lich, -lik, -li*, corresp. to OFris., OS. *-līk*, OHG. *-līh* (Du. *-lijk*, G. *-lich*), ON. *-ligr, -legr*, Goth. *-leiks.* (The vowel was shortened in OE., ON., and G.; the Eng. forms in *-li, -ly* are due to ON.) The primitive force of the suffix is therefore 'having the appearance or form indicated by the first element of the word'.

The most general senses of the suffix are 'having the qualities appropriate to', 'characteristic of', 'befitting'; e.g. *beastly, beggarly, cowardly, kingly, scholarly, soldierly.* Another use is to form adjs. denoting periodic recurrence, as *daily, hourly, yearly,* etc.

-ly, *suffix*^{2}, forming advs., represents OE. *-līće*, ME. *-liche, -līke, -liȝe, -li(e* = OFris. *-līke*, OS. *-līko*, OHG. *-līhho* (Du. *-lijk*, G. *-lich*), ON. *-liga*, Goth. *-leikō*: f. -LY^1 with advb. suffix *-ō.

In Gmc. an adv. with this suffix must have implied the existence of an adj. with the suffix corresponding to -LY[1]. In OE., however, there are instances (e.g. *bealdlīċe* boldly, *swētlīċe* sweetly) in which an adv. has been formed from a simple adj. without the intervention of an adj. in *-lic*, and this became the regular mode of forming an adv. of manner. Down to the 17th c., *-ly* was frequently attached even to adjs. in *-ly*, as *godlily, kindlily, lowlily, statelily*; but these formations are now generally avoided by recourse to some periphrastic form of expression. In *daily, hourly*, etc., the adj. and the adv. are identical in form. *Partly* and *purposely* are examples of an adv. f. sb. + *-ly*[2] with no related adj. Advs. in *-ly* were in several cases app. formed in ME. in imitation of OFr. adverbs in *-ment*, before the corresponding adjective existed in English. Since the 16th c. the suffix has been added to ordinal numerals to form advs. denoting serial position, as *firstly, secondly*, etc., after Fr. *premièrement*, etc.

When *-ly* is attached to a disyllabic or polysyllabic adj. in *-le*, the word is contracted, as *ably, simply*, etc.; monosyllables in *-le* retain the *e* in writing, as *solely*; *wholly* is peculiar. Adjs. of more than one syll. ending in *y* change *y* to *i* bef. *-ly*, as *merrily*; in formations from monosyllabic adjs. the usage varies, e.g. *slily, slyly*. In *duly, truly*, the *e* is dropped. Adjs. in *-ic* nearly always form advs. in -ICALLY.

Lyam (ləi·ăm), **lyme** (ləim). *Obs.* exc. *Hist.* ME. [– OFr. *liem* (mod. *lien*) :– L. *ligamen* LIEN.] **1.** A leash for hounds, or (*Her.*) a representation of this. **2.** Short for LYAM-HOUND 1486.

Lyam-hound, lyme-hound. *Obs.* exc. *Hist.* 1527. [f. LYAM + HOUND.] A bloodhound. Also *fig.*

Lyard, lyart, *a. Obs.* exc. *dial.* ME. [– OFr. *liart* grey, in med. L. *liardus* (XII).] Grey, silvery grey approaching white. Applied by Burns to the colour of withered leaves.

The bandsters are lyart and runkled and grey *The Flowers of the Forest.*

Lycanthropy (ləikæ·nþrŏpi). 1594. [– mod. L. *lycanthropia* – Gr. λυκανθρωπία, f. λυκάνθρωπος, f. λύκος wolf + ἄνθρωπος man; see -Y[3].] **1.** A kind of insanity in which the patient imagines himself to be a wolf, or, loosely, a beast of any kind. **2.** The kind of witchcraft in which human beings were supposed to assume the form and nature of wolves 1830.

Hence **Lycanthrope** (ləi·kănþrōᵘp, ləikæ·nþrop), one afflicted with l. 1621; also used as a synonym of werewolf 1831. **Lycanthro·pic** *a.* of, belonging to, or suffering from l. 1829. **Lyca·nthropist**, a lycanthrope 1727.

‖**Lycée** (lise). 1865. [Fr. – L. *Lyceum* LYCEUM.] In France, a secondary school maintained by the State, as dist. from a *collège* or secondary school maintained by a municipality.

Lyceum (ləisī·ŏm). Also *erron.* **Lycæum.** 1579. [– L. *Lyceum* – Gr. Λύκειον (sc. γυμνάσιον GYMNASIUM), n. of Λύκειος, epithet of Apollo, to whose temple the Lyceum was adjacent.] **1.** (With cap. L.) Name of a garden with covered walks at Athens, in which Aristotle taught. Hence, the Aristotelian philosophy and its adherents. Also *transf.* **2.** Adopted as the title of literary institutions, and of the buildings erected for them, usu. including lecture-rooms, classrooms, and a library 18.. **3.** = LYCÉE 1827. **4.** *U.S.* An institution in which popular lectures are delivered on literary and scientific subjects 1820.

Lych(e, obs. f. LIKE.

Lychee, var. of LITCHI.

Lych-gate: see LICH-GATE.

‖**Lychnis** (li·knis). *Pl.* **lychnides** (li·knidīz). 1601. [L. – Gr. λυχνίς some red flower, f. λύχνος lamp.] *Bot.* A genus of caryophyllaceous plants, including the Campion and the Ragged Robin.

Lychnoscope (li·knŏskōᵘp). 1843. [f. Gr. λύχνος lamp + -σκόπος -SCOPE.] *Arch.* A name given to the low side window (see LOW *a. Combs.* 2) on the supposition that its purpose was to allow lepers to see the altar lights.

†**Lycium.** 1597. [L. *lycium* kind of thorn (Pliny) – Gr. λύκιον, orig. n. of Λύκιος Lycian.] The shrub Box-thorn (*L. barbarum*), its fruit, or the juice extracted from it –1839.

‖**Lycoperdon** (ləikŏpə̄·ɹdŏn). 1756. [mod. L.; irreg. f. Gr. λύκος wolf + πέρδεσθαι break wind.] *Bot.* The fungus Puff-ball, *L. bovista.*

Lycopodium (ləikŏpōᵘ·diŏm). 1706. [mod. L., f. Gr. λύκος wolf + πούς, ποδ- foot; see -IUM.] **1.** *Bot.* A plant of the cryptogamous genus *Lycopodium*; a club-moss. **2.** A fine inflammable powder, also called 'vegetable brimstone', consisting of the spores of *Lycopodium*, used in surgery as an absorbent, and in theatres for making stage lightning 1836.

Hence **Ly·copod,** a club-moss 1846. **Ly:copodia·ceous** *a.* pertaining to the N.O. *Lycopodiaceæ* 1852. **Lyco·podite,** a fossil l. 1839.

Lyddite (li·dəit). 1888. [f. *Lydd* in Kent, where first tested; see -ITE[1] 4 a.] A high explosive, composed chiefly of picric acid; used in making explosive shells.

Lydian (li·diăn). 1545. [f. L. *Lydius*, Gr. Λύδιος + -AN.] **A.** *adj.* **1.** Pertaining to the Lydians, a people of Asia Minor, or to Lydia 1584. **2.** *spec.* in *Mus.* **a.** A mode in ancient Greek music of a soft and effeminate character. **b.** The third of the authentic ecclesiastical modes, having F for its 'final', and C for its 'dominant' 1579.

2. a. Lap me in soft L. aires, Married to immortal verse MILT. *Comb.* **L.-stone** *Min.*, a black variety of jasper (basanite), used by jewellers as a touchstone for testing gold.

B. *sb.* An inhabitant of Lydia; also, the anguage of the Lydians 1545.

Lye (ləi), *sb.* [OE. *lēaġ* = MDu. *lōghe* (Du. *loog*), OHG. *louga* (G. *lauge*) lye, ON. *laug* hot bath :– Gmc. **lauʒō*, f. **lau-* (cf. LATHER) :– IE. **lou-* wash, LAVE.] **1.** Alkalized water made by the lixiviation of vegetable ashes; also applied to any strong alkaline solution, esp. one used for washing. **b.** Any detergent; a cleansing substance. Also *fig.* ME. **2.** Water impregnated with salts by decoction or lixiviation. Now *rare.* 1634. **3.** *attrib.*, as *l.-ashes*, etc. 1601.

Lye, var. of LIE.

Lying (ləi·iŋ), *vbl. sb.*[1] ME. [f. LIE *v.*[1] + -ING[1].] **1.** The action of LIE *v.*[1] **2.** *concr.* With qualification (as *dry, soft*, etc. *l.*): Accommodation for repose 1853.

Lying (ləi·iŋ), *vbl. sb.*[2] ME. [f. LIE *v.*[2] + -ING[1].] The action of LIE *v.*[2]; the telling of ies.

Lying (ləi·iŋ), *ppl. a.*[1] OE. [f. LIE *v.*[1] + -ING[2].] That lies (see the vb.).

Comb.: **l.-dog,** a setter; **-panel,** †(*a*) one which occupies the lowest place in a series; (*b*) one whose largest dimension, or whose grain, lies horizontally; **-wall** *Mining* = *foot-wall* (FOOT *sb. Combs.* 2).

Lying (ləi·iŋ), *ppl. a.*[2] ME. [f. LIE *v.*[2] + -ING[2].] That lies; mendacious; deceitful, false. Hence **Ly·ingly** *adv.*

Ly·ing-i·n. ME. [LYING *vbl. sb.*[1]] The being in childbed; accouchement. Also *attrib.* as *l. hospital.*

Lyken, obs. f. LIKE *v.*

Ly·ke-wake, ly·kewake (ləi·kˌwēⁱk). ME. [perh. – ON. **líkavaka*; see LICH, WAKE *sb*[1].] The watch kept at night over a dead body.

Lym, Lymail(le, obs. ff. LEAM *sb.*[1], LIMAIL.

Ly·me-grass. 1776. [perh. f. LIME *sb.*[1] with reference to its binding quality, the spelling being infl. by *Elymus.*] The name for grasses of the genus *Elymus*, esp. *E. arenarius*, which is planted on sand to keep it from shifting.

Lymph (limf). 1630. [– Fr. *lymphe* or L. *lympha*, prob. hellenized form (by assoc. with Gr. νυμφή nymph) of *lumpa, limpa* (cf. LIMPID).] **1.** Pure water; water in general; a stream. Only *poet.* and *rhet.* Also *fig.* and *transf.* †**2.** *Bot.* The sap in plants –1830. **3.** *Phys.* A colourless alkaline fluid, derived from various tissues and organs of the body, resembling blood but containing no red corpuscles 1725. **4. a.** The exudation from a sore, etc. **b.** Now often *spec.* for *vaccine l.*, the matter taken from cow-pox vesicles, etc. to be used in vaccination; also extended to any morbid matter similarly used as a prophylactic. 1800. **5.** *attrib.*, as *l.-cell, -corpuscle*; *l.-secretion*; *l.-forming* adj.; **l.-heart,** in some lower vertebrates, one of a number of contractile muscular sacs which pump the l. forward.

Lymphad (li:mfæd). Also †**lang-, lum-, lime-.** 1536. [Gael. *longfhada* (= *long* ship + *fada* long).] A one-masted galley propelled by oars. Now only *Hist.*, and *Sc. Her.*

‖**Lymphadenitis** (limfædĭnəi·tis). 1879. [mod.L., f. LYMPH + ADENITIS.] *Path.* Inflammation of the lymphatic glands. So **Lympha·denoid** *a.* resembling the tissue of a lymphatic gland 1877. ‖**Ly:mphadeno·ma,** a tumour consisting of lymphoid tissue 1873.

‖**Lymphangitis** (limfændʒəi·tis). 1861. [mod.L., f. L. *lympha* LYMPH + Gr. ἀγγεῖον vessel + -ITIS.] *Path.* Inflammation of the walls of the lymphatic vessels.

Lymphatic (limfæ·tik). 1649. [– L. *lymphaticus* mad, adaptation of Gr. νυμφόληπτος seized by nymphs (cf. νυμφιᾶν be frenzied); in mod. scientific Latin the ending has prob. been assoc. with *spermatic.*] **A.** *adj.* †**I.** Frenzied, mad –1822. **II.** In senses conn. w. LYMPH. **1. a.** *Phys.* and *Anat.* Pertaining to or concerned in the secretion or conveyance of lymph, as in *l. gland, vessel.* Also, of the nature of lymph, as *l. fluid, humour* (rare). 1649. †**b.** *Bot.* Containing or conveying sap –1836. **2.** Having the characteristics (flabby muscles, pale skin, sluggishness) formerly attributed to an excess of lymph in the system 1834.

1. a. *L. system*, the l. vessels and glands collectively. *L. heart* = *lymph-heart.* **2.** In..persons of a l. habit, the skin becomes white J. FORBES.

B. *sb.* †**1.** A lunatic, a madman –1763. **2.** Chiefly *pl.* Vessels similar to veins, whose function is the conveyance of lymph. †Also applied to the sap-vessels in plants. 1667.

Lymphoid (li·mfoid), *a.* 1867. [f. LYMPH + -OID.] *Phys.* Resembling lymph, lymph-corpuscles, or the tissue of lymphatic glands.

‖**Lymphoma** (limfōᵘ·mă). *Pl.* **-mata.** 1873. [mod.L., f. LYMPH + -OMA.] *Path.* A tumour having the structure of a lymphatic gland. Hence **Lympho·matous** *a.*

Lymphous (li·mfəs), *a.* 1672. [f. LYMPH + -OUS.] *Phys.* Containing, of the nature of, or resembling lymph.

Lymphy (li·mfi), *a.* 1848. [f. LYMPH + -Y[1].] Of the nature of or resembling lymph.

Lyn, obs. f. LINN.

Lyncean (linsī·ăn), *a.* 1622. [f. L. *Lyncēus* (– Gr. λύγκειος, f. λύγξ LYNX) + -AN. Occas. used with a reference to *Lynceus*, an Argonaut, famous for his sharp sight.] Lynx-like; sharp-sighted.

Lynch (linʃ), *v.* Orig. *U.S.* 1836. [f. *Lynch*; see LYNCHLAW.] *trans.* To condemn and punish by lynch law. Orig., to whip, tar and feather, or the like; now only, to inflict sentence of death by lynch law.

Lynchet, variant of LINCHET.

Lynch law. Orig. *U.S.* In early use **Lynch's (Linch's) law.** 1811. The practice of inflicting summary punishment upon an offender, by a self-constituted court without legal authority; now limited to the summary execution of one charged with a flagrant offence. (The capital L is still often used.)

The originator of Lynch law was Captain William Lynch of Pittsylvania in Virginia. According to A. Ellicott (*Life and Lett.*, 1908, 200) 'this self-created judicial tribunal was first organised in the state of Virginia about the year 1776'; another authority gives the date definitely as 1780.

Lynch law, however shocking it may seem to Europeans, is far removed from arbitrary violence BRYCE. **Judge Lynch,** the imaginary authority from whom the sentences of lynch law are said to proceed.

Lynn. Common U.S. var. of LINN[2].

Lynx (liŋks). ME. [– L. *lynx* – Gr. λύγξ, rel. to OE. *lox*, OHG. *luhs* (G. *luchs*), OSw. *lō.*] **1.** Any animal of the sub-genus *Lynx* of the genus *Felis*, having a tufted ear-tip, short tail, and spotted fur. **2.** The fur of the lynx 1839. **3.** A northern constellation 1798.

1. A black l. snarled and pricked a tufted ear BROWNING. *Comb.* **l.-eye,** an eye as keen as that of a l.; so **-eyed** *a.*, having eyes like those of a l.. keen-sighted.

Lyo- (ləi·o, ləiǫ·), used as comb. form of Gr. λύειν to loosen, solve, in the sense of 'solvent', as **Lyophilic** (-fi·lik) *a.*, of a colloid which is readily dispersed in an appropriate medium; **Lyophobic** (-fōᵘ·bik) *a.*, that resists solvents.

Lyon, short form, with early spelling, of *Lyon King of Arms* (see KING-OF-ARMS), the title of the chief herald in Scotland; so named from the lion on the royal shield. Also *Lyon Herald* (see HERALD *sb.*), *Lyon King.*

‖**Lyra** (ləi³·ră). 1586. [L. – Gr. λύρα.] †**1.** A lyre –1724. **2.** *Astr.* (With cap. L.) An ancient northern constellation; = HARP *sb.* 2. 1658. **3.** *Anat.* A part of the under surface of the corpus callosum of the brain, marked with lines suggesting the strings of a lyre 1756.

Lyraid (ləi³reˌid), **Lyrid** (ləi³·rid). 1883. [f. LYRA + -ID³.] *Astr.* One of a group of meteors apparently radiating from Lyra.

Lyrate (ləi³·reⁱt), *a.* 1760. [f. L. *lyra* LYRE + -ATE².] *Nat. Hist.* Shaped like a lyre. In *Bot.*, of a leaf: Pinnatifid, with the upper lobes much larger than the lower. So **Ly·rated** *a.* 1753. Hence **Ly·rately** *adv.* in a l. form.

Lyre (ləi³ɹ). ME. [– OFr. *lire* (mod. *lyre*) – L. *lyra* – Gr. λύρα.] **1.** A stringed instrument of the harp kind, used by the Greeks for accompanying song and recitation. **b.** *fig.* esp. as the symbol of lyric poetry 1683. **2.** *Astr.* = LYRA 2. 1868. **3.** *Anat.* = LYRA 3. 1900.

1. b. Make me thy l. even as the forest is SHELLEY.

Comb.: **l.-bat,** a species of bat, *Megaderma lyra*; **-bird,** an Australian bird, *Menura superba* or *M. novæ-hollandiæ*, resembling a pheasant, with a beautiful lyre-shaped tail; **-pheasant, -tail** = *lyre-bird*; **-turtle** *U.S.*, the leather-back or trunk-turtle, *Dermochelys coriaceus.*

Lyric (li·rik). 1581. [– (O)Fr. *lyrique* or L. *lyricus* – Gr. λυρικός; see prec., -IC.]

A. *adj.* **1.** Of or pertaining to the lyre; meant to be sung; pertaining to or characteristic of song. Now the name for short poems, usually divided into stanzas or strophes, and directly expressing the poet's own thoughts and sentiments. Hence, applied to the poet. 1589. **2.** Of persons: Given to song, singing (*poet.*) 1814.

1. L. poetry is the expression by the poet of his own feelings RUSKIN. *L. drama, l. stage,* the opera.

B. *sb.* **1.** *absol.* (with *the*): That which is lyrical; lyric style, verse, etc. 1586. †**2.** A lyric poet –1839. **3.** A lyric poem. Also *pl.*, verses in lyric metre. 1581.

1. From the high l. down to the low rational BYRON. **3.** An Eton boy follows..Horace in lyrics 1849.

Lyrical (li·rikăl), *a.* 1581. [f. as LYRIC *a.* + -AL¹; see -ICAL.] **1.** = LYRIC *a.* Also, having the qualities of lyric poetry. **2.** Resembling what is found in lyric poetry 1817.

1. L. Ballads (*title*) 1798. Hence **Ly·rical-ly** *adv.*, **-ness.**

Lyricism (li·riciz'm). 1760. [f. LYRIC + -ISM.] Lyric character or style; the pursuit or eulogy of the same; (with *pl.*) a lyrical expression or characteristic. *Occas.* (after Fr. *lyrisme*), affectation of high-flown sentiment or poetic enthusiasm.

Lyrid: see LYRAID.

Lyriform (ləi³·rifǫɹm), *a.* 1856. [f. L. *lyra* + -FORM.] Lyre-shaped.

Lyrism (ləi³·riz'm, li·riz'm). 1859. [– Fr. *lyrisme* or Gr. λυρισμός playing on the lyre, f. λύρα LYRE.] = LYRICISM.

Lyrist (li·rist). 1656. [– L. *lyrista* – Gr. λυριστής, f. λύρα LYRE.] **1.** A player on the lyre, or a singer who accompanies himself on the lyre. **2.** A lyric poet 1813.

2. From her wilds Ierne sent The sweetest l. of her saddest wrong SHELLEY.

‖**Lysis** (ləi·sis). 1822. [L. – Gr. λύσις loosening.] **1.** *Arch.* 'A plinth or step above the cornice of the podium of ancient temples, which surrounded or embraced the stylobate' (Gwilt) 1842. **2.** *Path.* An insensible or gradual solution or termination of a disease or disorder. Opp. to CRISIS 1. **3.** *Med.* Dissolution of a cell by a **Ly·sin,** as in infection or immunization. Hence **Ly·tic** *a.* 1902.

-lysis, formative element, repr. Gr. λύσις loosening, used in various scientific terms, as *electrolysis*, etc. The corresp. adjs. end in **-lytic** [Gr. λυτικός].

Lysol (ləi·sǫl). 1891. [Trade name, f. Gr. λύσις (see prec.) + -OL.] A saponified mixture of creosol and oil, used as a disinfectant.

Lythe (ləið). *Sc.* 1769. [Of unkn. origin.] The pollack.

M

M (em), the thirteenth letter of the modern and twelfth of the ancient Roman alphabet, represents historically Gr. *mū* and Semitic *mēm*. The Phœnician form of the letter is 𐤌, whence the early Gr. and L. ᴍ, ᴍ, **M.** In Eng. it has always expressed what was doubtless its original sound, that of the bilabial nasal consonant. It is capable of being used as a sonant or vowel, denoted by ('m) in the notation here followed; but in Eng. this occurs only after (ð) and (z) at the end of words, as *rhythm, spasm, schism,* and the suffix *-ism*; in these words many speakers substitute (-əm). It is never silent, exc. initially bef. *n* in Gr. derivs., as *mnemonic.*

I. 1. The letter and its sound. **b. M roof:** a kind of roof formed by the junction of two ordinary gable roofs with a valley between them, making the section resembling the letter M. **2.** *Printing.* = EM.

II. Symbolical uses. **1.** Used to denote serial order; applied e.g. to the thirteenth, or more usually the twelfth (I or J being omitted) group or section, the twelfth sheet of a book, etc. **2.** The Roman numeral symbol for: A thousand. (Now *rare*, exc. in dates.)

III. Abbrevs. M. = Mark, Margaret, etc.; = †Majesty, in ancient criminal proceedings; = Member, as in M.P. (q.v.), M.C., Member of Congress (*U.S.*), M.R.C.P., Member of the Royal College of Physicians; *Mus.* = metronome; *Math.* = modulus; (M. or m.) in astronomical tables, etc. = meridian or meridional; also (after *twelve*) = L. *meridies* noon; cf. A.M. (= *ante meridiem*) before noon, P.M. (= *post m.*) after noon; m. = mass, in *Mech.*; = molar, in dental formulæ; = minute, metre (mm. = millimetre); in log-books = mist; *Mus.* It. *mano* or Fr. *main* (as *mano destra, main droite*), *mezzo* (as mf = *mezzoforte*), in organ music, *manual.* See also M.B., M.D., M.S.

b. Abbrev. for Master: †(*a*) generally, = the later MISTER, MR. (*b*) Used for *master* or L. *magister* in academical degrees, as M.A. or A.M. (*magister artium*), Master of Arts; M.Ch. (*magister chirurgiæ*), Master of Surgery; also in M.C., Master of the ceremonies; M.F.H., Master of fox-hounds.

‖**c.** = MONSIEUR (q.v.) as prefixed title.

-m, in I'M = I am; see BE *v.*

Ma (mā). 1829. Vulg. abbrev. of MAMMA.

Maad, obs. f. MADE.

Ma'am (mæm; usu. unstressed məm, 'm). Also written as vulgar **marm, mem, mim, mum, 'm.** 1668. A colloq. shortening of MADAM, now used only parenthetically or at the end of a sentence.

Formerly the ordinary respectful form of address to a (married) woman: now used at Court in addressing the Queen or a royal princess, and by servants to their mistresses. Hence **Ma'am** *v. trans.*, to address as 'ma'am' 1813.

Maat, obs. f. MATE.

†**Mab,** *sb.* 1557. [Cf. *map*, XVII form of MOP *sb.*¹; also *Mab*, short for *Mabel.*] A slattern; a woman of loose character –1725. So †**Mab** *v. intr.* to dress untidily 1691–1829.

†**Mabble,** *v.* Also **mable.** [Cf. MOBLE *v.*] *trans.* To wrap or muffle up (the head). G. SANDYS.

Mac (mæk). Also **Mack.** 1500. [Ir., Gael. *mac* :– OCelt. **makkos*, rel. to W. *mab*, OW. *map* :– OCelt. **makwos.*] The Gaelic word for 'son', occurring as a prefix in Sc. and Ir. names, and thus = Eng. *-son.* Hence, a person whose name contains the prefix *Mac*; †also contempt.: A Celtic Irishman.

Mac. Colloq. abbrev. of MACKINTOSH 2.

‖**Macabre** (makā·br), *a.* ME. [repr. Fr. *macabre* (XIX), error for OFr. *macabré* (*danse macabrée aux Innocens* XV), perh. alt. of OFr. *Macabé* Maccabæus (cf. †*Judas Macabré*, med.L. *chorea Maccabæorum* dance of the Maccabees XV); the orig. ref. may have been to a miracle play in which the slaughter of the Maccabees under Antiochus Epiphanes was enacted.] **1.** *Danse Macabre*, also †*dance (of) Machabree, -bray* (obs.), *dance Macaber*: the Dance of Death (see DANCE *sb.*). **2.** Gruesome, like the *danse Macabre*; applied to literary or artistic productions 1889.

Macaco¹ (măkēⁱ·ko). 1771. [– Pg. *macaco* – native (Fiot) *makaku* some monkeys, f. *ma* numerical sign + *kaku* monkey.] Orig., a S. African monkey described by Marcgrave (1648); now, any monkey of the genus *Macacus*; = MACAQUE.

Macaco² (măkēⁱ·ko). 1751. [– Fr. *mococo* (Buffon). Cf. MAKI.] A name given to certain lemurs, *esp.* to the genus *Lemur.*

‖**Macacus** (măkēⁱ·kŏs). *Pl.* **-ci.** (-səi). 1871. [mod.L. – Fr. *macaque*; see MACAQUE.] A genus of Old World catarrhine monkeys of the family *Cercopithecidæ*; now restricted to species resembling the bonnet macaque or toque; a monkey of this genus.

Macadam (mækæ·dăm). 1824. **1.** The name of John Loudon *McAdam* (1756–1836) used *attrib.* to designate a kind of roadway and of material advocated by him; see MACADAMIZE. **2.** The material of which a macadamized road is made 1826. Hence **Maca·damite** *sb.* one who practises or advocates this system of road-making; *adj.* pertaining to this system of road-making.

Macadamize (mækæ·dăməiz), *v.* 1825. [f. prec. + -IZE.] **1.** *trans.* To make or repair (a road) according to McAdam's system, by compacting into a solid mass successive layers of stone broken into pieces of nearly uniform size; hence extended to similar methods of road-making 1826. **b.** *fig.* To render level; to level, raze 1826. **2.** To convert into road-metal 1841. **b.** *transf.* and *fig.* To break up (something hard) *into* pieces. ? *Obs.* 1825.

Hence **Maca:damiza·tion,** the process, system, or practice of making macadamized roads; also, the converting of stone into road-metal. **Maca·damizer,** one who makes, or one who keeps to, macadamized roads.

†**Maca·o.** Also **makao.** 1778. [f. *Macao*, a Pg. settlement on the coast of China, noted for gambling.] A gambling game at cards resembling vingt-et-un.

Macao, obs. f. MACAW¹.

Macaque (măkā·k). 1698. [– Fr. *macaque* – Pg. *macaco*; see MACACO¹.] †**1.** Some Brazilian species of monkey. FROGER. **2.** A monkey of the genus MACACUS 1840.

Macarize (mæ·kărəiz), *v. rare.* Also **macarise, makarize.** 1816. [f. Gr. μακαρίζειν, f. μάκαρ blessed; see -IZE.] *trans.* To account or call happy or blessed. So **Ma·carism** [Gr. μακαρισμός], an accounting happy; also, = BEATITUDE 2. 1818.

Macaroni (mækărōᵘ·ni). *Pl.* **-ies.** Also †**maccaroni,** etc. 1599. [– It. *maccaroni*, later *maccheroni*, pl. of *macca-, maccherone*, f. late Gr. μακαρία barley food (Hesychius).] **1.** A kind of wheaten paste, of Italian origin, formed into long slender tubes and dried for use as food. **2. a.** *Hist.* One of a class of 18th c. exquisites, consisting of young men who had travelled and affected continental tastes and fashions. **b.** *dial.* A fop, dandy. 1764. **3.** A species of crested penguin, *Eudyptes chrysolophus.* In full *m. penguin.* 1838. **4.** A medley (such as a macaronic poem) 1884. **5.** = *macaroni tool* 1867.

2. You are a delicate Londoner; you are a maccaroni; you can't ride BOSWELL. *Comb.* **m. cheese,** a savoury of m. and cheese baked; **m. tool,** a square-cutting tool used in wood-carving. Hence †**Macaro·nian** *a.* = MACARONIC 1727–1788. **Macaro·nism,** dandyism 1775.

Macaronic (mækărǫ·nik). 1611. [– mod.L. *macaronicus* – It. †*macaronico* (*maccheronico*), joc. f. *macaroni* (see prec.).] **A.** *adj.* **1.** Used to designate a form of verse containing vernacular words in a Latin context with Latin terminations and in Latin constructions. Also *transf.*; and applied *loosely* to any form of verse in which two or more langs. are jumbled together. Hence: Resembling the mixed jargon of macaronic poetry. 1638. †**2.** Of the nature of a medley –1816. **B.** *sb.* **1. a.** Macaronic language or composition. **b.** *pl.*

Macaronic verses. 1668. †**2.** A medley. COTGR.

Macaroon (mækărū·n). 1611. [– Fr. *macaron* – It. *maccarone* MACARONI.] **1.** A small cake or biscuit made chiefly of ground almonds, white of egg, and sugar. †**2.** = MACARONI 1. –1753. †**3.** A buffoon; a dolt. Also *dial.* a fop. –1825.

Macartney (măkā·ɹtni). 1834. [The name of George, Earl *Macartney* (1737–1806).] A pheasant of the genus *Euplocamus*, esp. *E. ignitus*.

Macassar (măkæ·səɹ). 1666. [Name (= native *Mangkasara*) of a district in the island of Celebes.] **Macassar oil,** an unguent for the hair, said to consist of ingredients obtained from Macassar. Also applied commercially to other oils, etc. imported from the East.

Macauco, var. of MACACO.

Macaw[1] (măkǭ·). 1668. [– Pg. *macao*, of unkn. origin.] Any parrot of the genus *Ara*, inhabiting tropical and subtropical America and remarkable for their gaudy plumage.

Macaw[2] (măkǭ·). 1657. [Carib; cf. Arawak *mocoya, macoya*.] W. Indian name for palms of the genus *Acrocomia*. Now only *attrib.* in *m.-berry, -palm, -tree*; also **m.-bush,** a W. Indian plant, *Solanum mammosum*.

Macco (mæ·ko). ?*Obs.* 1809. [perh. var. of MACAO.] = MACAO.

Maccoboy (mæ·kŏboi). Also **maccaboy, mackabaw,** etc. 1740. [f. *Macouba*, a district in Martinique.] A kind of snuff, usually scented with attar of roses.

Mace[1] (mēⁱs). ME. [– OFr. *masse, mace* (mod. *masse* large hammer, etc.) :– Rom. **mattea* club.] **1.** A heavy staff or club, either all of metal or metal-headed, often spiked; formerly a weapon of war. †In early use also, any club. **2.** A staff of office resembling this, borne before certain officials. †Also formerly = the sceptre of sovereignty 1440. **b.** A mace-bearer 1663. **3.** A stick with a flat square head, used in *Bagatelle*, and formerly in *Billiards*, for propelling the ball 1727. **4.** *Tanning.* A knobbed mallet used in dressing leather to make it supple 1839.

1. Then cam Treason with hir mas Hevy as a clobbe of leed LYDG. *fig.* O Murd'rous slumber! Layest thou thy Leaden M. vpon my Boy? SHAKS. **2. b.** And here upon a M. was sent to bring Cromwell into the Court 1663. *Comb.* **Ma·ce-bearer,** an official who carries a mace, as a symbol of authority, before some high functionary 1552.

Mace[2] (mēⁱs). [ME. *macis* – AFr. *macis* (XIII) or (O)Fr. *macis* (XIV) – L. *macir* red spicy bark from India (Pliny); the form *macis* being apprehended as a pl., a new sing. *mace* was formed from it.] A spice consisting of the dried outer covering of the nutmeg.

Mace[3] (mēⁱs). 1598. [– Malay *mās*, said to repr. Skr. *māsha* weight of about 17 grains.] A weight and money of account equal to one-tenth of a tael.

‖**Macédoine** (mæsedwān). 1846. [Fr.] A dish of fruit or vegetables embedded in jelly.

Macedon (mæ·sĭdǫn). ME. [– L. *Macedo, -don-*, Gr. Μακεδών, -ον-.] †**1.** One of the people (esp. Alexander the Great) that inhabited Macedonia –1700. †**b.** quasi-*adj.* Macedonian –1710. **2.** Macedonia 1584.

1. The valiant M.. Lamented that there were no more [worlds] to conquer MASSINGER. **2.** Phillip of M. BACON.

Macedonian (mæsĭdōᵘ·niăn), *a.*[1] and *sb.*[1] 1556. [f. L. *Macedonius* (= Gr. Μακεδόνιος, f. Μακεδών; see prec.) + -AN.] Pertaining to (A native or inhabitant of) Macedonia.

Macedonian (mæsĭdōᵘ·niăn), *a.*[2] and *sb.*[2] 1449. [– eccl.L. *Macedonianus*, f. L. *Macedonius*; see -AN.] Applied to the followers of Macedonius, a heretical Bishop of Constantinople in the 4th c. Hence **Macedo·nianism.**

Macer (mēⁱ·səɹ). ME. [– OFr. *maissier, massier*, f. *masse* MACE[1]; see -ER[2].] A mace-bearer; *spec.* in Scotland, an official who keeps order in courts of law. Hence **Ma·cership.**

Macerate (mæ·sĕrēⁱt), *v.* 1547. [– *macerat-*, pa. ppl. stem of L. *macerare*, prob. cogn. with Gr. μάσσειν knead; see -ATE[3].] **1.** *trans.* To soften by steeping in a liquid, with or without heat; to wear away or separate the soft parts of, by steeping 1563. **b.** *intr.* for *pass.* To undergo maceration 1610. **2.** *trans.* To cause (the body, flesh, etc.) to waste or wear away, esp. by fasting 1547. †**b.** *fig.* To oppress, crush –1640. †**3.** To fret, vex, worry –1761.

2. To..m. his body for his owne sinnes PURCHAS. **3.** A city so macerated with expectation STERNE. Hence **Macera·tion,** the action or process of macerating or condition of being macerated 1612. **Ma·cerator,** one who macerates; a vessel used for maceration 1891.

†**Machecoled,** *pa. pple.* ME. [– OFr. *machecollé*.] Machicolated –1500. Hence †**Machecoling** *vbl. sb.* machicolation 1491.

Machet(t)e, macheto, vars. of MATCHET.

Machiavel (mæ·kiăvel). 1570. [Anglicized name of Niccolò *Machiavelli*, a Florentine statesman and writer of the work *Del Principe*.] One who acts on the principles of Machiavelli; an intriguer, an unscrupulous schemer.

Am I subtle? Am I a Machiuell? SHAKS.

Machiavellian (mæ:kiăve·liăn). 1568. [f. prec. or *Machiavelli* + -AN.] **A.** *adj.* Of, pertaining to, or characteristic of Machiavelli, or his alleged principles; preferring expediency to morality; practising duplicity, *esp.* in statecraft; astute, cunning, intriguing 1579.

Divide et regna is an old Matchiavilian maxime and trick 1637.

B. *sb.* A follower of Machiavelli; one who adopts his principles in statecraft or in general conduct.

Hence **Ma:chiave·llianism,** the principles and practice of Machiavelli or of the Machiavellians. So **Ma:chiave·llism,** Machiavellianism 1592. **Ma:chiave·llist,** a Machiavellian 1589.

Machicolation (mătʃikŏlēⁱ·ʃən). 1788. [f. *machicolate* v. (see below), f. OFr. *machicoler*, AL. *machicollare*, ult. f. Pr. *machacol* (for **macacol*), f. *macar* beat, crush + *col* neck; see -ATION.] *Arch.* An opening between the corbels which support a projecting parapet, or in the floor of a gallery or the roof of a portal, through which combustibles, molten lead, stones, etc., were dropped upon assailants. Also, a projecting structure containing such openings. So **Machi·colate** *v. trans.* to furnish with m.; chiefly in *pa. pple.* and *ppl. a.* 1773.

Machinate (mæ·kineⁱt), *v.* 1600. [– *machinat-*, pa. ppl. stem of L. *machinari* contrive, f. *machina* MACHINE; see -ATE[3].] **1.** *intr.* To lay plots; to intrigue, scheme. **2.** *trans.* To contrive, plan, plot. Now *rare.* 1602.

1. A Tyrant conspires, machinates, [etc.] 1689. Hence **Ma·chinator** 1611.

Machination (mækinēⁱ·ʃən). ME. [– (O)Fr. *machination* or L. *machinatio*, f. as prec.; see -ION.] **1.** The action or process of contriving or planning; contrivance, intrigue, plotting. Now *rare.* 1549. **2.** An instance of this; an intrigue, plot, scheme. Usu. in bad sense. 1477. †**3.** The use or construction of machinery –1711. †**4.** Something contrived or constructed, e.g. a weapon, a framework or apparatus –1680.

1. By secret m., or by confederacy with others HOBBES. **2.** This machinacion fayling, another.. was put on foote 1678.

Machine (măʃī·n), *sb.* 1549. [– (O)Fr. *machine* – L. *machina* device, contrivance, engine – μαχανά, Doric form of Gr. μηχανή, f. μῆχος contrivance, rel. to Gmc. **maʒan* have power; see MAY *v.*[1]] **1.** A structure of any kind, material or immaterial; a fabric, an erection. Now *rare.* **b.** *spec.* A vehicle of any kind (usu. wheeled). *Obs.* exc. *Sc.* 1687. **2.** A military engine, siege-tower, or the like. Now *rare.* (= L. *machina.*) 1656. †**3.** An apparatus, appliance, instrument –1741. **4.** An apparatus for applying mechanical power, consisting of a number of parts, each having a definite function 1673. **b.** Often short for *sewing-m., printing-m.*, or any machine in question. Also, for a bicycle or tricycle. 1841. **c.** Applied to the human and animal frame as a combination of several parts 1602. **d.** A combination of parts moving mechanically, as contrasted with a being acting voluntarily. Hence applied to a person who acts mechanically, without intelligence, or to one whose actions exhibit a machine-like regularity 1692. **5.** *Mech.* Any instrument for transmitting force, or modifying its application 1704. **6.** *Theatr.* [= L. *machina.*] A contrivance for the production of stage effects. Also in *pl.* stage machinery. Now *rare.* 1658. **7.** Hence in literary use: A contrivance for dramatic presentation; a supernatural agency or personage introduced into a poem; the interposition of one of these 1678. **8.** *Politics* (orig. *U.S.*). The controlling organization of a political party; often used disparagingly 1876.

1. b. Your very kind letter of the 15th,.. I received by the machine BURKE. **4.** *fig.* The great state wheels in all the political machines of Europe FIELDING. **c.** Thine euermore most deere Lady, whilst this M. is to him SHAKS. **d.** The nearer the soldiers approach to machines, perhaps the better 1779. **5.** *Simple m.*: one in which there is no combination of parts, e.g. a lever. *Compound m.*: one whose efficiency depends on the combined action of two or more parts. **7.** The episodes of Circe, of the Sirens, and of Polyphemus, are machines 1897.

attrib. and *Comb.*, as **m. bolt,** a machine screw; esp. a bolt with a square or hexagonal head and the upper portion of the shank not threaded; **-gun,** a mounted gun which is mechanically operated, delivering a continuous fire 1870; **-man,** one who manages a m.; **-minder** (*Print.*); **m. screw,** a screw adapted for screwing into metal rather than into wood; **-shop,** a workshop for making or repairing machines; **-tool,** a m. for cutting or shaping wood, metals, etc., by means of a tool, esp. one used in a machine-shop; **-twist** *U.S.*, a kind of silk twist, made especially for the sewing-m.; **-work,** †(*a*) poetic or dramatic 'machinery'; (*b*) work done by a m., as dist. from that done by hand.

Machine (măʃī·n), *v.* 1450. [orig. – Fr. *machiner*, – L. *machinari* (see MACHINATE); later, f. MACHINE *sb.*] †**1. a.** *trans.* To contrive, plot; also, to resolve *that*. **b.** *intr.* To plot (*against* a person). –1679. **2.** *trans.* To form, make, or operate upon by means of a machine 1827. **3.** *nonce-use. fig.* To work (a project, etc.) like a machine 1881. †**4.** *intr.* To appear, as a god, from a 'machine'; to serve as a poetic 'machine' 1697.

2. Making shirts, machining men's coats [etc.] 1886.

Machiner (măʃī·nəɹ). 1798. [f. MACHINE *sb.* + -ER[1].] **1.** A horse employed to draw a 'machine' or vehicle. **2.** One who works a machine 1827.

Machinery (măʃī·nĕri). 1687. [f. MACHINE *sb.* + -ERY.] **1.** *Theatr.* and *literary.* †**a.** Stage appliances and contrivances. (Cf. MACHINE *sb.* 6.) **b.** The assemblage of machines (MACHINE *sb.* 7) employed in a poem. **2.** Machines, or their parts, taken collectively; the mechanism or works of a machine or machines 1731. **b.** A system or kind of machinery (*lit.* and *fig.*) 1849.

1. The M., Madam, is a term invented by the Critics, to signify that part which the Deities, Angels, or Dæmons, are made to act in a Poem POPE. **2.** *fig.* The whole m. of government was out of joint 1855.

Machinist (măʃī·nist). 1706. [orig. – Fr. *machiniste*, f. *machine*; later f. MACHINE *sb.* + -IST.] **1.** One who invents, makes, or controls machines; an engineer. **b.** *Theatr.* One who makes or manages the stage machinery. Now *rare.* 1739. **2.** One who works a machine, esp. a sewing-machine 1879. **3.** *U.S.* A supporter of machinism in politics; a member of a political machine 1883. So **Machi·nism,** management of parties by political machines.

-machy, in actual use **-omachy** (ǫ·măki), repr. Gr. -μαχία, the ending of certain Gr. sbs. with the general sense 'fighting, warfare', from adjs. in -μάχος 'that fights'. Eng. examples are *logomachy, angelomachy*, etc.

Macilent (mæ·silĕnt), *a.* Now *rare.* 1535. [– L. *macilentus*, f. *macer* thin, MEAGRE, after *gracilentus* (f. *gracilis*); see -LENT.] Lean, shrivelled, thin; *fig.* of verses: Jejune, poor. Hence **Ma·cilency** (now *rare*), leanness 1632.

Macintosh: see MACKINTOSH.

Mack. Colloq. abbrev. MACKINTOSH 2.

Mackerel[1] (mæ·korel). ME. [– AFr. *makerel*, OFr. *maquerel* (mod. *maquereau*), first recorded in med.L. *macarellus* (XII), from Flanders; of unkn. origin. See -REL.] **1.** A sea-fish, *Scomber scombrus*, marked on the back with dark stripes; much used for food. Also applied with qualifying word to other fishes of the same genus or family; esp. **Spanish m.,** the tunny, *S. colias*. **2.** *Angling.* Short for *mackerel-fly* 1799.

1. Bad fortunes are like m. at midsummer 1623. *attrib.* and *Comb.*: **m.-back, -backed** *adjs.*, †(*a*) *slang*, long-backed; (*b*) said of clouds, sky (see *mackerel-sky*); **-bird,** local name for the wryneck and the young kittiwake; so called because they usually appear about the same time as the m.; **-breeze, -gale,** a (strong) breeze that ruffles the water, so as to favour the catching of m.; **-clouds** (see *mackerel-sky*); **-cock,** the Manx Shearwater (*local*); **-fly** *Angling*, a species of May-fly, also an artificial fly imitating this; **-guide,** the garfish (*local*); **-gull,** U.S. name for the tern; **-midge,** the young of the rockling (*Motella*); **-plough,** a knife used for creasing the sides of lean m. in order to improve their appearance; **-shark,** the porbeagle; **-sky,** a sky dappled with small white fleecy clouds 1669.

†Ma·ckerel[2]. ME. [– OFr. *maquerel* (mod. *maquereau, -elle*), metath. f. **makeler* – MDu. *makelaer* (Du. *-aar*) broker, whence also OFr. *makelare*.] A procurer or procuress –1700.

Mackinaw (mæ·kinǭ). 1841. The name (also written *Mackinac*) of an island in the strait between Lakes Huron and Michigan.

Comb.: **M. blanket,** also simply **M.,** a thick blanket, such as used to be distributed to the Indians of the North-west by the U.S. government. **M. (boat),** a large flat-bottomed sharp-ended boat, used on the Great Lakes. **M. trout,** the lake trout.

Mackintosh (mæ·kintǫʃ). Also **macintosh.** 1835. **1.** The name of Charles *Macintosh* (1766–1843), used *attrib.* (or in genitive) to designate garments made of the waterproof material patented by him, consisting of layers of cloth cemented with india-rubber. Now taken as an attrib. use of 3, and written with a small initial. **2.** Short for *M. cloak, coat*, etc. 1836. (Colloq. abbrev. *mack.*) **3.** The material of which 'Mackintosh' garments are made; now any cloth made waterproof by a coating of india-rubber. Also *attrib.* 1880.

Mackle, macle (mæ·k'l), *sb.* 1706. [– Fr. *macule* – L. *macula* spot.] *Printing.* A blur in printing; a doubling of the impression; also, a blurred sheet. So **Ma·ckle, ma·cle** *v.* to blur or become blurred; now usu. *trans.* to print (a page) blurred or double 1594.

Macle (mæ·k'l). 1680. [– Fr. *macle* – L. *macula* spot, mesh.] **1.** *Cryst.* A twin crystal. Also *attrib.* 1801. **2.** *Min.* A dark spot in certain minerals 1839. **3.** = CHIASTOLITE 1821. **4.** *Her.* = MASCLE 2. 1680. Hence **Ma·cled, ma·ckled** *ppl. a.* (of a crystal) twin; marked like chiastolite; *Her.* mascled.

Macramé (măkrā·me). Also **-mi.** 1869. [– Turk. *makrama* bedspread – Arab. *miḳrama* bedspread.] A fringe or trimming of knotted thread or cord; knotted-work; the art of making this. Also *attrib.*

Macro- (mæ·kro), bef. a vowel **macr-,** repr. Gr. μακρο-, comb. f. μακρός long, large, in various scientific uses.

a. *Anat.* and *Path.* in sbs. denoting excessive development of some parts, as *macrocheilia* (of the lips), *-glossia* (of the tongue), *-melia* (of a limb); also MACROCEPHALY.
b. In sbs. (chiefly in antithesis with *micro-*) indicating either an individual of unusual size, or one containing a number of smaller individuals; as *macro-cyst*, etc.
c. *Cryst.* **Ma:crodia·gonal** *sb.* the longer of the diagonals of a rhombic prism; *adj.* pertaining to this diagonal. **Ma·crodome,** a dome (see DOME *sb.* 5 b) parallel to the macrodiagonal. **Macropi·nacoid,** a pinacoid parallel to the vertical and macrodiagonal axes. **Ma·croprism,** a prism o an orthorhombic crystal between the macro pinacoid and the unit prism. **Ma:cropy·ramid,** a pyramid corresponding to the macroprism.
d. in adjs., with sense 'containing or possessed of some object in a largely developed form', as **Macroda·ctyl, -dacty·lic, -da·ctylous** [Gr. δάκτυλος] *adjs.*, having long fingers or toes. **Ma·crodont** [Gr. ὀδοντ-, ὀδούς] *a.*, having long teeth. **Macrogna·thic, Macro·gnathous** [Gr. γνάθος] *adjs.*, having long or protruding jaws. **Ma:cropleu·ral** [Gr. πλευρά rib, side] *a.*, having long pleuræ. **Ma:crosty·lous** *a.*, *Bot.* having a long style.

Macrobiotic (mæ:krobəiǫ·tik). 1797. [f. Gr. μακροβίοτος (f. μακρός long + βίοτος life) + -IC.] **A.** *adj.* Inclined or tending to prolong life; relating to the prolongation of life. **B.** *sb. pl.* The science of prolonging life.

Macrocephalic (mæ:kro₁sĭfæ·lik), *a.* 1851. [f. Gr. μακροκέφαλος (f. μακρός long + κεφαλή head) + -IC.] Having a long or large head; also said of the head or skull. So **Macroce·phalous** *a.* long-headed; in *Bot.* said of dicotyledonous embryos whose cotyledons are consolidated 1835. **Macroce·phaly,** excessive length or size of the head 1889.

Macrocosm (mæ·krokǫz'm). 1600. [– med.L. *macrocosmus*, repr. Gr. *μακρὸς κόσμος 'great world'. Cf. (O)Fr. *macrocosme*.] The 'great world' or universe, as dist. from the 'little world' or MICROCOSM, i.e. from man as an epitome of the universe. Also *transf.*

The microcosm repeats the m. HUXLEY. Hence **Ma:croco·smic** *a.* of or pertaining to the m.

Macrology (mǣkrǫ·lŏdʒi). 1616. [– late L. *macrologia* – Gr. μακρολογία; see MACRO-, -LOGY.] *Rhet.* The use of redundant words or phrases. *gen.* Prolixity of speech.

Macromere (mæ·kromīᵊɹ). 1877. [f. Gr. μακρός long + μέρος part.] *Embryol.* The larger of the two masses into which the vitellus of the developing ovum of *Lamellibranchiata* divides; cf. MICROMERE. Hence **Macrome·ral, Macrome·ric** *adjs.*

Macrometer (mækrǫ·mǐtəɹ). 1825. [f. MACRO- + -METER.] An instrument for measuring distant or inaccessible objects.

‖**Macron** (mæ·krǫn, mēⁱ·krǫn). 1851. [– Gr. μακρόν, n. of μακρός long.] A straight horizontal line (¯) placed over a vowel to indicate that it is 'long'.

Macropod (mæ·krŏpǫd). 1864. [f. MACRO- + -POD.] *adj.* Long-footed. *sb.* A long-footed animal, e.g. a spider-crab. **Macro·podal** (1830), **-ous** (1852) *adjs. Bot.*, of a monocotyledonous embryo: Having the radicle large in proportion to the cotyledon. **Macropo·dian** *Zool.*, one of a tribe of brachyurous decapod crustaceans 1839.

Macroscopic (mæ:kro₁skǫ·pik), *a.* 1872. [f. MACRO- after MICROSCOPIC.] Visible to the naked eye; opp. to MICROSCOPIC. So **Ma:crosco·pical** *a.*, **-ly** *adv.*

Macrospore (mæ·krospōᵊɹ). 1859. [f MACRO- + SPORE.] *Bot.* and *Zool.* One of the larger spores in certain flowerless plants and unicellular animals; opp. to MICROSPORE. So **Ma:crospora·nge, -a·ngium** *Bot.* the sporange containing macrospores 1875.

Macrurous, macrourous (măkrū·rəs), *a.* 1826. [f. mod.L. *macrura* n. pl. (f. Gr. μακρός + οὐρά tail) + -OUS.] *Zool.* Belonging to the *Macrura* or long-tailed tribe of Decapod Crustacea (lobsters, etc.). So **Macru·ral, -ou·ral, Macru·ran, -ou·ran** *adjs.* and *sbs.*

Mactation (mæktēⁱ·ʃən). 1640. [– late L. *mactatio*, f. *mactat-*, pa. ppl. stem of L. *mactare* slay; see -ION.] The action of killing a sacrificial victim.

‖**Macula** (mæ·kiŭlă). *Pl.* **-æ.** ME. [L.] A spot or stain: *Astron.* a dark spot in the sun; *Min.* a spot in a mineral due to the presence of particles of some other mineral; *Path.* a spot or stain in the skin, *esp.* a permanent one. Hence **Ma·cular** *a.* of, pertaining to, or marked by the presence of maculæ 1822.

Maculate (mæ·kiŭlĕt), *ppl. a.* 1490. [– L. *maculatus*, pa. pple. of *maculare*, f. *macula* spot; see -ATE[2].] Maculated. Now only in antithesis to *immaculate*.

Maculate (mæ·kiŭleⁱt), *v.* ME. [– *maculat-*, pa. ppl. stem of L. *maculare*; see prec., -ATE[3].] *trans.* To spot, stain, soil, defile, pollute. Hence **Ma·culated** *ppl. a.* spotted, stained; also, marked with maculæ. So **Macula·tion,** the action of spotting or staining or the condition of being spotted or stained ME.; also, the state of being marked with, or a particular arrangement of, maculæ 1826.

Macule (mæ·kiul), *sb.* 1483. [– Fr. *macule* or its source L. *macula* spot.] A blemish, spot. *Obs.* in gen. sense. **b.** *Path.* = MACULA 1863. **c.** *Printing.* = MACKLE *sb.* 1841. So **Macule** [Fr. *maculer*] *v. trans.* †To spot, stain ME.; *Printing.* = MACKLE *v.* 1841.

Maculose (mæ·kiŭlōᵘs), *a.* 1727. [– L. *maculosus*, f. *macula* spot; see -OSE[1].] Full of spots; spotted. So **Ma·culous** *a.* 1688.

†Mad, *sb.* 1573. [var. of MATHE.] **1.** A maggot or grub; *esp.* the larva of the blow-fly, which causes a disease in sheep. Also *pl.*, the disease so caused. –1688. **2.** An earth-worm –1691.

Mad (mæd), *a.* [Aphetic of early ME. *ȝamad*, repr. OE. *ġemǣd(d, ġemǣded*, pa. pple. of **ġemǣdan* render insane, f. *ġemād* insane = OS. *gimēd* foolish, OHG. *gameit* foolish, vain, boastful, Goth. *gamaiþs* crippled :- Gmc. **ȝamaiðaz*, f. **ȝa-* Y- + **maiða-*.] **1.** Suffering from mental disease; out of one's mind; insane, lunatic. In mod. use chiefly: Maniacal, frenzied. **†b.** Causing madness (*rare*) –1676. **2.** Foolish, unwise. Now only: Wildly foolish; ruinously imprudent. OE. **3.** Carried away by enthusiasm or desire; wildly excited; infatuated ME. **b.** Wildly desirous *to* do something (now *rare*) 1627. **4.** Beside oneself with anger; furious. Now only *colloq.* (In many dialects and in U.S. the ordinary word for 'angry'.) ME. **5.** Of an animal: Rabid 1538. **6.** Uncontrolled by reason; extravagant in gaiety; wild 1597. **b.** *transf.* of storm, wind 1836.

1. And then to hear a dead man chatter Is enough to drive one m. TENNYSON. Phr. *To go, run m. Like m.*: lit., in the manner of one who is m.; hence, furiously, violently. **b.** It's [new Wine's] m. Fumes DRYDEN. **2.** A Mad World my Masters MIDDLETON. The chief justice..was not m. enough to risk a quarrel on such a subject MACAULAY. **3.** The World is running m. after Farce DRYDEN. We are now m. about tar-water H. WALPOLE. **b.** All m. to speak, and none to hearken SWIFT. **4.** They that are m. against me, are sworne against me *Ps.* 102:8. **5.** The dog, to gain some private ends, Went m., and bit the man GOLDSM. **6.** In m. spirits 1777.

Provbs. *As m. as a buck, a hatter, a March hare.*

Mad (mæd), *v.* ME. [f. MAD *a.*] **1.** *trans.* To make mad (see MAD *a.*). Now *rare* exc. *U.S. colloq.*, to exasperate. **2.** *intr.* To be or to become mad; to act like a madman. Now *rare.* ME. **†b.** To become infatuated –1624.

1. Sin..Mads the ill-counsell'd heart 1850. **2.** Far from the madding crowd's ignoble strife GRAY.

Madagass, Also **Madegass.** 1793. [var. of MALAGASH.] **1.** A native or inhabitant of Madagascar. **2.** A light-complexioned negro of Jamaica 1873.

Madam (mæ·dəm), *sb.* ME. [– OFr. *ma dame* (in mod.Fr. MADAME), lit. 'my lady'. Generally written *madam* when used as English, otherwise MADAME. Pl. MESDAMES; the Eng. pl. (exc. in sense 2) beings obs.] **1.** A form of polite address to a woman (substituted for the name), orig. used by servants in speaking to their mistress, and the like, and by people generally in speaking to a lady. In oral use now chiefly employed by salesmen and saleswomen in addressing adult female customers or by those in the position of servants to the public. From the 17th c., the title normally used in beginning or subscribing a letter to a woman of any station, except where the use of the name (as in 'Dear Mrs. A.', etc.) is permitted. (Corresponding to SIR.)

As a prefixed title. **†a.** Prefixed to a first or sole name –1749. **b.** Prefixed to a surname: (*a*) Now in U.S., and perh. formerly in England, the style of a woman who has a married son (whose wife is styled 'Mrs.'). (*b*) *dial.* The style of a married woman of position, e.g. the squire's wife.
2. (with *pl.*) A woman who is addressed as 'madam'. **†a.** A lady of rank or station. Also *fig.* –1632. **b.** (*a*) An affected fine lady 1598. †(*b*) A kept mistress, a prostitute –1761. (*c*) A hussy, minx 1802.

‖**Madame** (madam; often mădā·m, or anglicized mæ·dəm). Also **madam.** Pl. MESDAMES. 1599. [Fr.; see prec.] **1.** The title prefixed to the surname of a French married woman (= Eng. 'Mrs.', 'Lady', etc.). Abbrev. *Mme.* (In Eng. use often assumed (instead of Mrs.) by singers or musicians, dressmakers, etc.) **†2.** The title given to female members of the French royal family; a French princess; *spec.* the eldest daughter of the French king or of the dauphin; in the reign of Louis XIV, the wife of MONSIEUR, the king's only brother –1798. **†3.** A French married woman; a Frenchman's wife –1765.

1. Mrs. Skelton, daughter to Madam Orfeur 1706.

Madapollam (mædăpǫ·lăm). 1832. [The name of a suburb of Narsapur, Madras presidency.] A kind of cotton cloth, orig. manufactured at Madapollam.

Ma·d-apple. 1597. [tr. L. *malum insanum*, a corruption of an oriental word (cf. BRINJAL).] The fruit of the EGG-PLANT.

Mad-brained, *a.* 1577. Having a mad brain; hot-headed, uncontrolled. So **Ma·d-brain,** a mad-brained person; also *attrib.* or *adj.* 1570.

Madcap (mæ·dkæp). 1588. [f. MAD *a.* + CAP *sb.*] **A.** *sb.* †**a.** A madman, maniac (*rare*). **b.** One who acts like a maniac; a reckless, wildly impulsive person. Often applied playfully to young women. 1589. **B.** *attrib.* or *adj.* Mad; reckless, wildly impulsive.

A. Come-on you mad-cap: Ile to the Ale-house with you SHAKS. **B.** That last is Beroune, the mery mad-cap Lord SHAKS.

Madden (mæ·d'n), *v.* 1735. [f. MAD *a.* + -EN[5].] To become or make mad.

My fierce steed maddens to be gone 1811. Fierce spirits..maddened by fanaticism MACAULAY. Hence **Ma·ddeningly** *adv.*

Madder (mæ·dəɹ), *sb.* [OE. *mædere*, corresp. to OHG. *matara*, ON. *maðra* in place-names (Sw. *madra*, Norw. *modra*, *maure*), obscurely rel. to synon. WFris. *miede*, MLG., MDu. *mēde* (Du. *mede*, *mee*).] **1.** A herbaceous climbing plant, *Rubia tinctorum*, with rough hairy stems and small yellowish flowers; cultivated for the dye obtained from it. With qualifying words applied to plants allied to or resembling this. **2.** The root of this plant, used medicinally and as a source of dye-stuff; the dye-stuff or pigment prepared from this ME. **3.** The colour obtained from madder dyes or pigments, as *crimson m.*, etc. 1861. Hence **Ma·dder** *v. trans.* to dye or treat with madder 1461.

Maddish (mæ·diʃ), *a.* 1573. [f. MAD *a.* + -ISH[1].] Somewhat mad.

Ma·d-do·ctor. 1703. [f. MAD *a.* used *absol.*] A physician who treats mental diseases; an alienist.

Made (mē[i]d), *ppl. a.* ME. [pa. pple. of MAKE *v.*] **1.** Produced or obtained by 'making'. **2.** Of which the making has taken place ME.

1. Phr. *M. earth, ground*: solid ground that has been 'made' by filling up a marsh, embanking a river, etc. *M. dish* (Cookery): a dish composed of several ingredients. *M. gravy*: a gravy artificially compounded. *M. mast* (Naut.): one composed of several pieces of timber. *M. block*: a pulley-block composed of several parts joined together. *M. wines*: name for 'British wines' (as currant, gooseberry, etc. wine). **2.** None but m. soldiers..would be employed 1796. Teach a boy arithmetic thoroughly, and he is a m. man SMILES.

Comb. **made-up**, †(*a*) consummate, accomplished; (*b*) put together; composed of parts from various sources; (*c*) artificially contrived or prepared, esp. in order to deceive; (*d*) of a person's mind, resolved, decided; (*e*) of articles of trade, ready-made.

†**Ma·defy**, *v.* ME. [– Fr. *madéfier* – L. *madefacere*, f. *madēre* be wet; see -FY.] *trans.* To make wet; to moisten –1671. So **Madefa·ction** [Fr. *madéfaction*], a wetting or moistening (now *rare*) 1581.

Madeira (mădī[ə]·ră). 1585. [– Pg.; so called because formerly thickly wooded (Pg. *madeira* = Sp. *madera* timber :– L. *materia* MATTER *sb.*).] **1.** (With capital M.) An island in the Atlantic Ocean. Used *attrib.* in names of things produced in or connected with the island, as *M. lace*; **M. chair**, a kind of cane chair; **M. nut** *U.S.*, the common European walnut; **M. wine** = sense 2. 1664. **2.** A white wine produced in the island of Madeira 1585. *Comb.* **m. cake**, a kind of sponge-cake.

‖**Mademoiselle** (madəmwazẹl; often anglicized mædəmwəze·l). 1450. [Fr.; orig. *ma* my, *demoiselle* DAMSEL.] **1.** The title applied to an unmarried Frenchwoman. In English often used *absol.* as the designation of a French governess or the French teacher in a girls' school. Abbrev. *Mlle.* Pl. **mesdemoiselles** (medəmwazẹl), abbrev. *Mlles.* 1696. **2.** *Fr. Hist.* The title (as a substitute for the name) of the eldest daughter of 'Monsieur', the eldest brother of the king. Subseq. applied to the eldest daughter of the king, or, if he had none, to the first princess of the blood, while unmarried 1679. **3.** *occas.* A person usually referred to as 'mademoiselle', an unmarried Frenchwoman, *spec.* a French governess 1642. **4.** *U.S.* A sea fish, *Sciæna punctata* 1882.

Madge (mædʒ). 1591. [prop., pet-name for *Margaret*.] **1.** The Barn-Owl, *Aluco flammeus*. Also *m.-owl*. **2.** The Common Magpie, *Pica caudata* 1823.

Mad-headed, *a.* 1567. = MAD-BRAINED.

Madhouse (mæ·dhous). Now *rhet.* or *derisive.* 1687. [f. MAD *a.* used *absol.*] A house for the reception and detention of the insane; a lunatic asylum.

‖**Madia** (mē[i]·diă). 1839. [mod.L. – Chilian *madi.*] A composite plant, *Madia sativa*, native in Chili; cultivated for the oil (*m. oil*) obtained from its seeds.

Madid (mæ·did), *a.* Now *rare.* 1615. [– L. *madidus*, f. *madēre* be wet; see -ID[1].] Wet, moist.

Madly (mæ·dli), *adv.* ME. [f. MAD *a.* + -LY[2].] In an insane or foolish manner.

Madman (mæ·dmæ̆n). ME. [orig. two words.] One who is insane; a lunatic. Also, one who behaves like a lunatic, a wildly foolish person.

I have been a m. and a fool 1843.

†**Ma·dnep.** Also **-nip.** 1597. [f. MAD *a.* + *nep*, *nip* NEEP.] The Cow Parsnip, *Heracleum sphondylium* –1712.

Madness (mæ·dnės). ME. [f. MAD *a.* + -NESS.] **1.** Mental disease, insanity; mania. Also (in animals) rabies. **2.** Extravagant folly ME. **3.** Ungovernable anger, rage, fury 1665. **4.** Extravagant excitement; ecstasy 1596.

2. To advance towards London would have been m. MACAULAY. **3.** The m. of the people soon subsided GIBBON. **4.** Such a hare is m. the youth, to skip ore the meshes of good counsaile the cripple SHAKS.

Madonna (mădǫ·nă). 1584. [– It. *madonna*, i.e. *ma*, old unstressed form of *mia* my (:– L. *mea*), *donna* lady (:– L. *domina*); cf. MADAM.] ‖**1.** †**a.** As an Italian form of address or title: My lady, madam –1827. †**b.** An Italian lady –1639. **2. a.** An Italian designation of the Virgin Mary; usu. with *the*. **b.** A picture or statue of the Virgin Mary. 1644.

2. A faire Madonna of Pietro Perugino, painted on the wall EVELYN. 'Ave Mary' was her moan, 'M., sad is night and morn' TENNYSON.

attrib. and *Comb.*, as **M.-braided** *a.*, (of the hair) braided on each side of the face, after the manner of the M. in Italian representations; **M. lily**, the White Lily, *Lilium candidum*, as in pictures of the M.

Madras (mădrɑ·s). 1833. **1.** Name of a city and province of India; used *attrib.* in the names of things produced there or originally connected therewith: **Madras (net) muslin**, a handsome, but coarse make of muslin, produced in several varieties; **M. work**, the work executed upon M. handkerchiefs; etc. 1864. **2.** In full *M. handkerchief*: a bright-coloured handkerchief of silk and cotton worn by the negroes of the W. Indies as a head-dress, 'formerly exported from Madras' (Yule).

‖**Madrasah** (mădræ·sa), **medresseh** (medre·se). 1630. [Different pronunciations of Arab. *madrasa*, f. *darasa* study.] A Moslem college.

Madre-perl. *rare.* [– It. *madreperla*, f. *madre* mother + *perla* PEARL.] Mother-of-pearl. LONGF.

Madrepore (mæ·drĭpo[ə]ɹ). 1751. [– Fr. *madrépore* or mod.L. *madrepora* – It. *madrepora*, presumably f. *madre* mother (perh. in allusion to the prolific growth of the 'plant') + *poro*, L. *porus* PORE *sb.*, or L. *pōrus* – Gr. πῶρος calcareous stone, stalactite.] Formerly, any perforate coral; now usually, a polypidom of the genus *Madrepora* or family *Madreporidæ*; also, the animal producing this.

Hence **Madropo·ric** *a.* pertaining or related to, consisting or characteristic of, madrepore coral; resembling madrepore coral, as certain structures in echinoderms 1817. **Ma:drepo·riform** *a.* having the form or characters of madrepore coral 1840. **Madrepo·rite**, †(*a*) *Palæont.* fossil madrepore –1843; (*b*) *Min.* a calcareous rock resembling madrepore 1802; (*c*) *Zool.* a madreporic body in echinoderms 1877.

‖**Madrier** (mæ·driəɹ). 1704. [Fr.] *Fortif.* A thick plank used for various purposes, as to receive the mouth of a petard, to support the earth in mines or fortifications, etc.

Madrigal (mæ·drigăl). 1588. [– It. *madrigale* :– med.L. *matricalis* mother- (cf. med.L. *ecclesia matrix* mother church); see MATRIX.] **1.** A short lyrical poem of amatory character. **2.** *Mus.* An old style of contrapuntal unaccompanied part-song for several voices; also *loosely*, applied to other part-songs 1588. **3.** *transf.* and *fig.* A song, ditty 1589.

1. He [Clément Marot] was..the restorer of the m. WARTON. **2.** And who shall silence all the airs and madrigalls that whisper softnes in chambers MILT. **3.** By shallow Rivers, to whose fals Melodious birds sing Madrigals MARLOWE. Hence **Madriga·lian** *a.* pertaining to, consisting or characteristic of, or dealing with madrigals 1848. **Ma·drigalist**, a writer or composer of madrigals 1789.

‖**Madroño** (madrō·n[y]o). Also **madrona, madrone.** 1850. [Sp.] A handsome evergreen tree of western N. America, *Arbutus Menziesii*, having a very hard wood and bearing yellow berries.

Madwort (mæ·d,wɒɹt). 1597. [perh. tr. L. *alyssum* – Gr. ἄλυσσον, f. ἀ- A *pref.* 14 + λύσσα rabies.] **1.** A herb of the genus *Alyssum*. **2.** The Trailing Catchweed, *Asperugo procumbens*. (Also called *German m.*) 1760.

Mæcenas (misī·næs). *Pl.* **Mæcenases**, †**Mæcenates** (-ē[i]·tīz). 1561. A Roman knight, the patron of Horace and Virgil. Hence: A generous patron of literature or art; occas. *gen.* a patron.

Maelstrom (mē[i]·lstrŏm). 1682. [– early mod.Du. *maelstrom* (now *maalstroom*), f. *maalen* grind, whirl round + *stroom* STREAM, whence the Scand. forms, e.g. Sw. *malström*.] A famous whirlpool on the west coast of Norway, formerly supposed to suck in and destroy all vessels within a long radius. Also *transf.* a great whirlpool. Also *fig.*

Mænad (mī·næd). 1579. [– L. *Mænas*, *Mænad-* – Gr. Μαινάς, Μαιναδ-, f. μαίνεσθαι rave.] A Bacchante. Hence **Mæna·dic** *a.* characteristic of a M.; infuriated.

‖**Maestoso** (maẹstō·so). 1724. [It., = majestic.] *Mus.* A direction: To be executed majestically.

‖**Maestro** (maẹ·stro). 1797. [It., = master.] A master in music; a great composer, teacher, or conductor.

†**Maffick** (mæ·fik), *v.* 1900 (no longer used). [Back-formation from *mafficking* (= the place-name *Ma·feking* treated joc. as a pres. pple.).] *intr.* A journalistic word, used to designate the extravagant behaviour of the London crowds on the relief of Mafeking (17 May, 1900); also *transf.*

Maffle (mæ·f'l), *v.* *Obs.* exc. *dial.* ME. [Cf. early mod.Du. *maffelen* move the jaws.] **1.** *intr.* To stammer; to mumble. **2.** To bungle; to delay, waste time 1781. **3.** *trans.* To confuse, bewilder, muddle 1820. Hence **Ma·ffler. Ma·fflingly** *adv.*

‖**Mafia** (mafī·a). Also **maffia.** 1875. [Sicilian.] In Sicily, the spirit of hostility to law and its ministers, often manifesting itself in vindictive crimes. Also, the body of those who share in this spirit.

Mag (mæg), *sb.*[1] ME. [Short for *Margaret*.] Used as a personal name in various prov. phr.; also, as a proper name for a magpie, hence = MAGPIE.

Mag (mæg), *sb.*[2] *slang.* Also **meg.** 1781. [Of unkn. origin.] A halfpenny.

Mag (mæg), *sb.*[3] 1801. Abbrev. of MAGAZINE (sense 5 b). So **Maga** (mæ·gă), abbrev. for Blackwood's Magazine 1825.

Mag, *sb.*[4] 1920. Abbrev. of MAGNETO.

Mag (mæg), *v.* Also **meg.** 1810. [f. MAGPIE. Cf. MAG *sb.*[1]] *intr.* To chatter. So **Mag** *sb.*[5] chatter, talk; a chatterbox 1778.

Magazine (mægăzī·n), *sb.* 1583. [– Fr. *magasin* – It. *magazzino* – Arab. *makẕin*, pl. of *makzan* store-house, f. *ḵazana* store up.] **1.** A storehouse or repository for goods or merchandise; a warehouse, depot. Now *rare.* Also *fig.* **b.** *transf.* of a country or district 1596. **c.** A portable receptacle for articles of value. Now *rare.* 1768. **2.** *Mil.* **a.** *gen.* A building in which are stored arms, ammunition, and provisions for an army. **b.** *spec.* A powder magazine. 1596. Also *fig.* **3. a.** *Mil.* The contents of a magazine; a store. Also *collect. pl.* Stores, provisions, munitions of war; armament, military equipment 1589. Also *fig.* **b.** *gen.* A store, heap; †a wardrobe 1615. Also *fig.* †**4.** A victualling ship; more fully *magazine(s ship* 1624. **5.** †**a.** Used in the titles of books, with sense: A storehouse of information –1802. **b.** A periodical publication containing articles by various writers, intended chiefly for the general reader 1731. **6. a.** A chamber in a repeating rifle, machine-gun, etc., containing a supply of cartridges which are fed automatically to the breech 1867. **b.** A case for carrying a supply of cartridges 1892. **c.** A reservoir or supply-chamber in a machine, stove, battery, etc. 1873.

1. b. Constantinople..Aleppo..and grand Cayro ..are the three Maggezzines of the whole Empire LITHGOW. **2.** Here Irish wit is seen! When nothing's left that's worth defence, We build a m. SWIFT. **3. a.** A corps of 5000 men..had carried away a m. of arms WELLINGTON. **b.** A..m. of flesh, milk, butter, and cheese DE FOE.

attrib. and *Comb.*, as *m. article*, *-editor*; *m. rifle*; **m. gun,** a gun (i.e. either a cannon or rifle, etc.) provided with a 'magazine' (sense 6 a); **-stove,** one having a fuel-chamber which supplies coal to the fire by some self-feeding process. Hence **Magazi·ne** *v.* (now *rare*) *trans.* to lay up in or as in a magazine 1643; *intr.* to conduct a magazine 1763. **Magazi·ner** (1758), **-i·nist** (1821) one who writes for magazines. **Magazi·nish** *a.* 1794.

Magdalen, Magdalene (mæ·gdălĕn, -līn). ME. [From *the Magdalen* (XIV, Chaucer), after (O)Fr. *la Madeleine* – eccl.L. (*Maria*) *Magdalēna*, *-lēnē* – Gr. (Μαρία ἡ) Μαγδαληνή (Mary) of *Magdala*, a town on the Sea of Galilee in Palestine. The vernacular form of the word (adopted through Fr.) is MAUDLIN, whence the pronunc. (mǭ·dlin) in the names of Magdalen and Magdalene Colleges.] **1. a.** *The Magdalen(e*: a disciple of Christ named Mary (Luke 8:2), commonly identified with the 'sinner' of Luke 7:37, and therefore appearing in Western hagiology as a repentant harlot elevated to saintship. **b.** A picture of Mary Magdalen 1661. **2.** *transf.* One whose history resembles that of the Magdalen; *spec.* a reformed prostitute 1693. **3.** [Short for *M. hospital.*] A home for the reformation of prostitutes 1766. **4.** A kind of peach 1706.

Comb.: **M. day,** the feast of St. Mary Magdalen, 22 July; **M. asylum, charity, home, hospital, house** = sense 3.

†Magdaleon. 1450. [– med.L. *magdaleo*, *-on-* (also late and med.L. *-io*, *-ium*), whence Fr. *magdaléon* (XVI), f. Gr. μαγδαλία dough or bread-crumb (Galen).] *Pharmacy.* A cylindrical roll of plaster, salve, or any medicinal substance.

Mage (mēⁱdʒ), *arch.* ME. [Anglicized f. MAGUS. Cf. (O)Fr. *mage.*] **1.** A magician; *transf.* a person of wisdom and learning. **2.** *pl.* The Magi 1584.

Magellan (măge·lăn). 1638. Eng. form of the name of Fernão de *Magalhães* (? 1470–1521), the Portuguese navigator who first passed through the Straits of M. into the Pacific Ocean; used *attrib.* (or in possessive) = MAGELLANIC. Hence **Magella·nic** *a.* [mod.L. *Magellanicus*] pertaining to or named after Magellan 1602.

M. clouds, two large globular cloudy spots formed of nebulæ and clusters of stars, visible in the southern hemisphere.

Magenta (mădʒe·ntă). 1860. Name of a brilliant crimson aniline dye, discovered shortly after the date, 1859, of the battle of Magenta, in Northern Italy. Also *attrib.* or *adj.*

Magged (mægd), *a.* 1867. [Of unkn. origin.] *Naut.* Worn, fretted; as, a *m. brace.*

Maggot (mæ·gǫt). ME. [perh. AFr. alt. of ME. *maddo(c)k*, earlier *maðek* (cf. *maked* XV) – ON. *maðkr* (Da. *madike*), a *k*-derivative (see -OCK and cf. MAWKISH) of the base of OE. *maþa*, *maþu* = OS. *matho*, OHG. *mado* (Du., G. *made*), Goth. *maþa* :- Gmc. **maþon*, **maþō*, of unkn. origin. For the change of k to g cf. *flagon*, *sugar*.] **1.** A worm or grub; chiefly applied to the larva of the cheese-fly and the flesh-fly or blue-bottle. Also *fig.* **2.** A whimsical fancy; a crotchet 1625. **3.** A whimsical or capricious person 1681.

1. *Red m.*: the larva of the wheat-midge. **2.** She's got some m. in her head about being loved for her own sake 1898. Hence **Ma·ggoty** *a.* full of maggots.

Ma·ggot-pie. *Obs.* exc. *dial.* 1573. [f. ME. *Magote* – Fr. *Margot*, pet name for *Marguerite* Margaret + PIE *sb.*] A magpie.

Magi (mēⁱ·dʒəi), *sb. pl.*: see MAGUS.

Magian (mēⁱ·dʒiăn). 1578. [f. L. MAGUS + -IAN.] **A.** *sb.* One of the Magi; a follower of or believer in the Magi; a magician, wizard. **B.** *adj.* Of or pertaining to the Magi 1716; magical (KEATS). Hence **Ma·gianism,** the tenets or doctrines of the Magi 1716.

Magic (mæ·dʒik), *sb.* ME. [– OFr. *magique* (superseded by *magie*) – late L. *magica* (*magicē* Pliny) – Gr. μαγική, subst. use (sc. τέχνη art) of μαγικός, f. μάγος MAGUS.] **1.** The pretended art of influencing the course of events by compelling the agency of spiritual beings, or by bringing into operation some occult controlling principle of nature; sorcery, witchcraft. Also, the practice of this art. **†b.** A magical procedure or rite; also *concr.* a charm, fetish –1814. **2.** *fig.* A secret and over-mastering influence, resembling magic in its effects 1611. **3.** *transf.* The art of producing (by legerdemain, optical illusion, etc.) surprising phenomena resembling the results of 'magic'; conjuring 1831.

1. M., which means the unnatural interference with nature 1884. *Black m.* [= Fr. *magie noire*]: modern name for the kind of m. that involved the invocation of devils; opp. to *white m.* [= Fr. *magie blanche*]. *Natural m.*: that which did not involve recourse to the agency of personal spirits. **2.** Oh Royall Peece: There's Magick in thy Maiestie SHAKS.

Magic (mæ·dʒik), *a.* ME. [– (O)Fr. *magique* – L. *magicus* – Gr. μαγικός, lit. pertaining to the Magi, f. μάγος; see MAGUS, -IC.] **1.** Of or pertaining to magic. Also, working or produced by enchantment. Not used predicatively. **b.** Of a material object, a diagram, etc.: Employed in magic rites, endued with magic powers, enchanted 1697. **2.** Producing appearances or results like those of sorcery 1696.

1. To magike artes against my will I bend SURREY. **b.** *M. glass, mirror*: one in which the spectator is supposed to see the representation of future events or distant scenes; often *fig.* **2.** Longings..that..the m. curtain [would] once more arise SCOTT.

Phr. *M. square*: a square divided into smaller squares, each containing a number, so arranged that the sum of the figures in a row, vertical, horizontal, or diagonal, is always the same. *M. circle*: an arrangement of numbers in concentric circles with radial divisions, with arithmetical properties similar to those of the magic square.

So **Ma·gical** *a.* magic; resembling magic in action or effect; produced as by magic 1555. **Ma·gically** *adv.*

Magician (mădʒi·ʃăn). ME. [– (O)Fr. *magicien*, f. late L. *magica* MAGIC *sb.*; see -ICIAN.] One skilled in magic; a necromancer, wizard. Also *occas.*, a conjuror.

fig. The M. of the North [i.e. Walter Scott] 1877.

Ma·gic la·ntern. 1696. [tr. mod.L. *laterna magica.*] An optical instrument by means of which a magnified image of a picture on glass is thrown upon a white screen or wall in a darkened room.

Magilp, var. of MEGILP.

Magism (mēⁱ·dʒiz'm). 1844. [f. L. *magus* + -ISM.] The beliefs, principles, and practices of the Magi.

‖**Magister** (mădʒi·stəɹ). 1756. A mediæval and mod.L. title of academic rank, usu. rendered by MASTER, but occas. employed *Hist.* or in speaking of foreign universities.

Magisterial (mædʒistīᵊ·riăl), *a.* 1632. [– med.L. *magisterialis*, f. late L. *magisterius*, f. L. *magister* MASTER *sb.*¹; see -AL¹, -IAL.] Of or pertaining to a master or a magistrate. **†1.** Of or pertaining to a master-workman; displaying a master's skill –1683. **2.** Of or pertaining to one qualified to speak with authority; authoritative. Of persons: Having the bearing or authority of a master; *occas.* dictatorial. 1632. **3.** Of, pertaining to, or proper to a magistrate or magistrates. Of persons: Holding the office of a magistrate. Of an inquiry: Conducted by magistrates. 1660. **†4.** *Alch.* and *Med.* = MAGISTRAL 2. –1722. **†5.** quasi-*sb.* or *sb.* = MAGISTERY 3. –1662.

2. These M. Propositions don't Dispute for Belief, but demand it COLLIER. A M. Air and too much Heat and Passion appear in their Writings BENTLEY. **3.** The m. inquiry into the charge of arson 1885. Hence **†Magisteriality,** mastership, authoritative position. **Ma:giste·rial-ly** *adv.*, **†-ness.**

‖**Magisterium** (mædʒistīᵊ·riŏm). 1593. [L., = next.] **†1.** *Alch.* = MAGISTERY 3 a. –1675. **2.** *R. C. Theol.* The teaching function of the Church 183..

Magistery (mæ·dʒistĕri). *Obs.* exc. *Hist.* 1566. [– L. *magisterium* the office of a master; in med.L. the philosopher's stone; f. *magister* MASTER *sb.*; see -ERY.] **†1.** = MAGISTRACY 2, 3. –1585. **†2.** The quality or functions of a master; mastership, authoritative appearance. **b.** The office of a (Grand) Master. –1706. **3.** *Alch.*, *Med.*, etc. **a.** A master principle of nature; a potent transmuting or curative quality or agency; a substance that has this quality, e.g. the philosopher's stone 1594. **b.** A product or result of transmutation 1605. **c.** The concentrated essence of a substance 1641. **d.** The residuum obtained by precipitation from an acid solution, e.g. *m. of bismuth*, etc.; a precipitate 1602. **e.** A specific 1669.

Magistracy (mæ·dʒistrăsi). 1577. [f. MAGISTRATE; see -ACY.] **†1.** The condition of being a magistrate –1693. **2.** The office of a magistrate; *occas.* conduct in office as a magistrate. Now *rare.* 1577. **3.** Magistrates collectively 1601.

Magistral (mădʒi·străl). 1572. [– Fr. *magistral* or L. *magistralis*, f. *magister*; see MASTER, -AL¹.] **A.** *adj.* **1.** Of, pertaining to, or befitting a master; authoritative, dogmatic. Now *rare.* 1605. **2.** *Pharmacy.* Of a remedy, a formula; Devised by a physician for a particular case; opp. to OFFICINAL 1605. **†b.** By some writers taken to mean: Sovereign, supremely effective –1678. **3.** *Fortif.* Leading, principal, master –1828. **4.** *occas.* Having the title of 'Master'; of or pertaining to a master or masters 1837.

1. Your assertion..is more Magistrall, then true 1641. **2.** Some Magistrall Opiate 1638. **3.** *M. line*: in field fortifications, the interior crest line; in permanent fortifications, usually the line of the top of the escarp of each work. **4.** The men are rebuked, in the m. homilies, for their ingratitude in striking RUSKIN.

B. *sb.* **†1.** *Pharmacy.* A magistral preparation or formula –1670. **2.** *Fortif.* = *Magistral line.* (See A. 3.) 1853. ‖**3.** *Metallurgy.* [Sp. (maχistra·l).] Roasted copper pyrites used in the reduction of silver ore 1839.

Hence **†Magistra·lity,** the quality or condition of being m.; quasi-*concr.* a dogmatic utterance; in *Med.* a special prescription. **†Magi·strally** *adv.*

Magistrand (mæ·dʒistrænd). *Sc.* 1642. [– med.L. *magistrandus*, gerund. pple. of *magistrari* become a Master (of Arts).] Orig., in Scottish Universities, an Arts student in the fourth, or highest, class; later, one in the fourth year. Now, in official use, only at Aberdeen.

Magistrate (mæ·dʒistrĕt). ME. [– L. *magistratus*, f. *magister*; see MASTER, -ATE¹ 1 a. Cf. Fr. *magistrat.*] **†1.** The office and dignity of a magistrate –1530. **2.** A civil officer charged with the administration of the laws, a member of the executive government ME. **3.** *spec.* A 'justice of the peace' (see JUSTICE *sb.* III. 3); also applied to salaried officials having criminal jurisdiction of the first instance; as, *police*, *stipendiary*, and, in Ireland, *resident m.* 1688.

2. The king was too eminent a m. to be trusted with discretionary power HUME. *Chief m.*, *first m.*: in a monarchy, the sovereign; in a republic usually the president. Hence **Ma·gistrateship. †Magistra·tic, Magistra·tical** *a.* of, pertaining to, or befitting a m. or magistrates. **Magistra·tically** *adv.*

Magistrature (mæ·dʒistrĕtiŭɹ). 1672. [– Fr. *magistrature*, f. *magistrat*; see prec., -URE.] **1.** The dignity or office of a magistrate; *occas.* the exercise of the office; with *a* and *pl.* an individual office. **b.** The term of a magistrate's office 1720. **2.** *collect.* = MAGISTRACY 3. 1679.

Magma (mæ·gmă). ME. [– L. *magma* (sense 1), Gr. μάγμα, f. root of μάσσειν knead.] **†1.** The dregs that remain from a semi-liquid substance after the liquid part has been removed by pressure or evaporation –1856. **2.** Any crude mixture of mineral or organic matters in the state of a thin paste 1681. **3.** *Geol.* **a.** One of two or more supposed strata of fluid or semi-fluid matter lying beneath the earth's crust. **b.** The amorphous basis of certain porphyritic rocks. 1804. Hence **Magma·tic** *a.*

Magna Charta, Magna Carta (mæ·gnă kā·ɹtă). 1568. [med.L., = 'great charter'.] The Great Charter of English personal and political liberty, obtained from King John in 1215. Also *transf.* and *fig.*

†‖**Magna·le,** *pl.* **-alia.** 1623. [sing. deduced from eccl.L. *magnalia* miracles, subst. use of n. pl. of *magnalis* wonderful, f. L. *magnus* great; see -AL[1].] A great or wonderful thing –1702; *pl.* wonders 1645–81.

†**Magna·lity.** [f. eccl.L. *magnalia* (see prec.) + -ITY.] A great or wonderful thing. SIR T. BROWNE.

Magnanimity (mægnăni·mĭti). ME. [– (O)Fr. *magnanimité* – L. *magnanimitas*, f. *magnanimus*; see next, -ITY.] †**1.** The (vague) name of a virtue in mediæval ethics –1526. †**2.** Lofty courage; fortitude –1801. **3.** As tr. Aristotle's μεγαλοψυχία 'greatness of soul' (see *Eth. N.* iv. 3). Also, loftiness of thought or purpose. Now *rare.* 1598. **4.** Nobility of feeling; superiority to petty resentment or jealousy 1771. **b.** *pl.* Instances of this 1639. †**5.** Magnificence. SIR T. BROWNE.

4. It may be m. in Lord Mansfield to despise attacks made upon himself BURKE.

Magnanimous (mægnæ·nimǝs), *a.* Also †**-ious.** 1584. [f. L. *magnanimus* (f. *magnus* great + *animus* mind; repr. Gr. μεγαλόψυχος) + -OUS.] **1.** Great in courage; nobly valiant. Also, proceeding from or manifesting high courage. ?*Obs.* **2.** High-souled; lofty of purpose; noble in feeling or conduct. Now esp.: Superior to petty resentment or jealousy. 1598.

1. The incouragement, that the magnanimious Cesar gaue vnto his souldiours 1584. **2.** Pitch thy behaviour low, thy projects high; So shalt thou humble and m. be G. HERBERT. They knew.. what strength was, that would not bend But in m. meekness WORDSW. Hence **Magna·nimous-ly** *adv.*, **-ness** (*rare*).

Magnate (mæ·gnēɪt). Chiefly *pl.* ME. [– late L. (Vulg.) pl. *magnates*, f. *magnus* great; perh. infl. in XVIII by Fr. *magnat.*] **1.** A great man; a noble; a person of great influence or eminence in any sphere; now *spec.* one prominent in the management of a large industry or enterprise, as, an *oil magnate* (U.S.). **2.** In Hungary, and formerly in Poland, a member of the Upper House in the Diet 1797.

Magne- (mæ·gni), irreg. comb. form for MAGNETO-, as in **Ma:gne-cry·stal,** a crystal acted upon by magnetism; etc. 1831.

†**Magnes.** ME. [– L. *magnes* – Gr. μάγνης, for ὁ Μάγνης λίθος (also ὁ Μαγνήτης λίθος, ἡ λίθος Μαγνῆτις) the Magnesian stone. See MAGNET.] A magnet, loadstone –1750. Also *m.-stone* **b.** *transf.* Magnetic virtue. EVELYN.

Magnesia (mægnī·ʃ'ă). ME. [– med.L. *magnesia* – Gr. (ἡ) Μαγνησία (λίθος) 'the Magnesian stone'; see prec.] †**1.** *Alch.* A mineral said to be an ingredient of the philosopher's stone –1610. †**2.** = MANGANESE 1. Also *black m.* (opp. to †*white m.* = mod.L. *magnesia alba* = 3) –1797. **3. a.** Orig., and still pop., applied to hydrated magnesium carbonate, a white earthy powder, used as an antacid and cathartic. **b.** In mod. *Chemistry*, an alkaline earth, now recognized as the oxide of magnesium (MgO). 1755. Hence **Magne·sian** *a.* of, pertaining to, or containing m.; in **M. limestone** *Geol.* = DOLOMITE.

Magnesic (mægnī·sik), *a.* 1877. [f. MAGNESIA and MAGNESIUM + -IC.] **a.** Containing magnesia. **b.** Of, pertaining to, or containing magnesium.

Magnesite (mæ·gnĭsǝit). 1815. [f. MAGNESIA + -ITE[1] 2 b.] *Min.* Carbonate of magnesium, occurring commonly in compact white masses, but occas. crystalline.

Magnesium (mægnī·ziŏm, -ī·ʃ'ŏm). 1808. [f. MAGNESIA; see -IUM.] *Chem.* †**1.** = MANGANESE 1. Sir H. Davy. **2.** A chemical element, one of the 'metals of the alkaline earths', being the base of magnesia. Symbol Mg. Found only in composition. 1812.

Comb.: **m. light,** a brilliant light produced by the combustion of m.; **m. ribbon, thread, wire,** a thin strip or wire of m. prepared for burning.

Magnet (mæ·gnėt). 1440. [– L. *magneta* (whence OFr. *magnete*, perh. in part the source), acc. of *magnes* MAGNES.] **1.** *Min.* = LOADSTONE; a variety of magnetic (proto-sesquioxide of iron) having the power of attracting iron and steel, and other properties. **2.** A piece of loadstone; also, a piece of iron or steel to which the characteristic properties of loadstone have been imparted by contact, by induction, or by means of an electric current. When a magnet is suspended freely, one of its poles (hence called the north pole) points approximately north, and the other (the south pole) approximately south. 1625. **b.** Any body possessing the properties characteristic of a magnet 1797. **3.** *fig.* Something which attracts 1655.

1. In midst of this white City stands a Castle built of M. MILT. **2.** *Bar m.*, a polarized rod of iron, now much used in the construction of electro-magnetic apparatus. *Natural m.*: one consisting of loadstone; opp. to *artificial m.* **3.** Two magnets, heaven and earth, allure to bliss, The larger loadstone that, the nearer this DRYDEN.

attrib. and *Comb.*, as **m. core,** the rod or bar of soft magnetized iron placed in the middle of an electro-magnet; **m. helix,** a coil of wire such as surrounds the core of an electro-magnet.

Magnetic (mægne·tik). 1632. [– late L. *magneticus*, f. L. *magneta*; see MAGNET, -IC.] **A.** *adj.* **1.** Having the properties of a magnet; pertaining to a magnet or to magnetism; producing, caused by, or operating by means of magnetism 1634. **2.** *fig.* Having powers of attraction; very seductive. Now often with a tinge of sense 4. 1632. **3.** Applied to all bodies which are acted upon by the loadstone; also, = PARAMAGNETIC 1837. **4.** Pertaining to animal magnetism; mesmeric 1800.

2. That m. influence which irresistibly draws our feet to spots on which our imagination had long fed M. PATTISON. **4.** As if he had been in a m. slumber DICKENS.

B. *sb.* †**1.** = MAGNET –1671. **2. a.** Any metal which is acted upon by the loadstone 1847. **b.** A paramagnetic body 1890. **3. Magnetics:** the science of magnetism 1786. So **Magne·tical** *a.*; **-ly** *adv.*, †**-ness.**

Magnetico- (mægne·tiko), used (*rarely*) as comb. form of MAGNETIC = 'magnetic and..'.

Magneti·ferous, *a.* 1832. [f. MAGNET + -FEROUS.] Producing or conducting magnetism.

Magnetism (mæ·gnėtiz'm). 1616. [– mod.L. *magnetismus*; see MAGNET, -ISM.] **1.** The characteristic properties of the magnet; magnetic phenomena and their laws. Also, the natural agency concerned in producing these phenomena; now regarded as a modification of energy. **b.** *fig.* Attractive power, esp. personal charm or ascendancy; *occas.* with a tinge of sense 3. 1655. **2.** The science which treats of magnetic phenomena 1828. **3.** Short for *animal magnetism* (see ANIMAL) = MESMERISM 1785.

1. *Terrestrial m.*: the magnetic properties of the earth, consisting as a whole. **b.** Now, m. is among the highest qualities which an American popular leader can possess BRYCE.

Magnetist (mæ·gnėtist). 1761. [f. MAGNET + -IST.] **1.** One skilled in the science of magnetism. **2.** One who practises animal magnetism; a mesmerist. Also *animal m.* 1802.

Magnetite (mæ·gnėtǝit). 1851. [– G. *magnetit* (Haidinger, 1845); see MAGNET, -ITE[1] 2 b.] *Min.* Proto-sesquioxide of iron, which is readily attracted by the magnet; magnetic oxide of iron.

Magnetizable (mæ·gnėtǝizăb'l), *a.* 1797. [f. MAGNETIZE + -ABLE.] Capable of being magnetized. Hence **Ma:gnetizabi·lity.**

Magnetize (mæ·gnėtǝiz), *v.* 1785. [f. MAGNET + -IZE.] **1.** *trans.* To charge with magnetic properties 1801. **2.** *intr.* To become magnetic. (Ducts.) **3.** *trans.* To attract as a magnet does. Chiefly *fig.* (with mixture of sense 4), to subdue or win by personal charm. 1835. **4.** To influence by animal magnetism; to mesmerize. Also *fig.* 1785.

1. To m. a steel bar 1801. **3.** External Nature is ..an enchantress who magnetises the human spirit MOZLEY. Hence **Ma:gnetiza·tion,** the action of magnetizing or condition of being magnetized. **Ma·gnetizer,** one who or that which magnetizes; *esp.* a mesmerist.

Magneto (mægnī·to), *sb.* 1882. Colloq. abbrev. for *magneto-electric machine*; *spec.* the ignition apparatus of internal combustion engines.

Magneto- (mægnī·to-), repr. comb. form of Gr. μάγνης, μάγνητ-, MAGNET denoting processes carried on by magnetic means, or the application of magnetism to departments of art or industry; as in **m.-therapy,** the treatment of disease by the external application of metal plates inducing magnetic electricity; etc.

Magne:to-ele·ctric, *a.* 1831. Pertaining to electric phenomena involving electric currents induced in conductors by the relative motion of these conductors with respect to either permanent magnets or electro-magnets; as, *magneto-electric induction.*

Magneto-electric machine: first used by Faraday, in 1831, to denote a machine generating currents by magneto-electric induction; by later writers employed in various limited senses, and in recent times commonly limited to the machines with permament steel magnets; see O.E.D. So **Magne:to-ele·ctrical** *a.*

Magne:to-electri·city. 1832. Electricity generated by the relative movement of electric conductors and magnets of any kind.

Magne·togram. 1884. [f. MAGNETO- + -GRAM.] The automatic record of magnetic needles.

Magnetograph (mægnī·tograf). 1847. [f. MAGNETO- + -GRAPH.] **1.** An instrument recording automatically the movements of the magnetometer. Also *attrib.* **2.** = MAGNETOGRAM. (U.S. Dicts.)

Magnetometer (mægnĭtǫ·mĭtǝɹ). 1827. [– Fr. *magnétomètre*; see MAGNETO-, -METER.] An instrument for measuring magnetic forces, esp. terrestrial magnetism. Hence **Magne:tome·tric, -al** *a.* of, pertaining to, or measured by the m. **Magneto·metry,** measurement by means of the m.

Magne:tomo·tor. 1823. [f. MAGNETO- + MOTOR.] A voltaic series of large plates producing a great quantity of electricity of low intensity, adapted to the exhibition of electro-magnetic phenomena.

Magnifiable (mæ·gnifǝiˌăb'l), *a.* [f. MAGNIFY + -ABLE.] Capable of being magnified. SIR T. BROWNE.

Magnific (mægni·fik), *a.* Now *literary* and *arch.* Also †**magnifique.** 1490. [– (O)Fr. *magnifique* or L. *magnificus*, f. *magnus* great; see -FIC.] †**1.** Renowned, glorious –1669. †**2.** = MAGNIFICENT 2. –1655. **3.** = MAGNIFICENT 3, 4. 1490. **4.** Imposing by vastness or dignity. Of language, etc.: Exalted, sublime; *occas.* in derisive sense, grandiloquent. 1558. †**5.** Of compositions, titles, etc.: Serving to magnify or extol –1667.

3. The pillared dome m. heaved Its ample roof THOMSON. **4.** Power..God's gift m. BROWNING.

Magnifical (mægni·fikăl), *a.* 1538. [f. as prec. + -AL[1].] = MAGNIFIC. Hence **Magni·fically** *adv.* (*arch.*).

‖**Magnificat** (mægni·fikæt). ME. [L., 3rd pers. sing. pres. ind. of *magnificare* MAGNIFY.] **1.** The hymn of the Virgin Mary in *Luke* 1:46–55 (in the Vulgate beginning *Magnificat anima mea Dominum*), used as a canticle. **2.** *transf.* A song of praise; a pæan 1614.

†**Magni·ficate,** *v.* 1598. [– *magnificat-*, pa. ppl. stem of L. *magnificare*; see MAGNIFY, -ATE[3].] *trans.* = MAGNIFY *v.* –1672.

Magnification (mæ:gnifikēɪ·ʃǝn). 1625. [In sense 'laudation' – eccl.L. *magnificatio*, f. as prec.; see -ION. In sense 'apparent enlargement' f. MAGNIFY; see -FICATION.] The action of magnifying or condition of being magnified; laudation; enlargement. Also quasi-*concr.* a magnified reproduction.

Magnificence (mægni·fisĕns). ME. [– Fr. *magnificence* or L. *magnificentia*; see next, -ENCE.] **1.** The name of one of the Aristotelian and scholastic 'virtues', repr. Gr. μεγαλοπρέπεια, liberality of expenditure combined with good taste. †**2.** Sovereign bounty or munificence –1647. †**3.** Glory; greatness of nature or reputation –1667. **4.** Sumptuousness or splendour of surroundings or appointments ME. †**b.** An instance of this; a splendid ceremony –1674. **5.** Grandeur or imposing beauty of appearance. †Also *pl.* features of magnificence. ME. **6.** A title of honour, applied to kings and other distinguished persons. *Obs.* exc. *Hist.* or as a foreign title. ME.

1. Thanne comth M., that is to seyn, whan a man dooth and perfourneth grete werkes of goodnesse CHAUCER. **4.** Nor doth this grandeur and majestic show Of luxury, though call'd m.,..allure mine eye MILT. **5.** Not Babilon, Nor great Alcairo such m. Equal'd in all thir glories MILT. So **Magni·ficency;** also with *a* and *pl.*

Magnificent (mægni·fisĕnt), *a.* 1513. [– Fr.

magnificent or L. *magnificent-*, alt. stem of *magnificus*, after *benevolens* (var. of *-volus*); see MAGNIFIC, -ENT.] **1.** Characterized by greatness of achievement or by conduct befitting lofty position. *Obs.* exc. as a titular epithet, e.g. in Lorenzo the M., etc. **2.** Royally lavish or munificent (now *rare*) 1579. **3.** Splendid, stately; living in splendour and pomp 1526. **4.** Sumptuously constructed or adorned; also, imposingly beautiful 1540. **5.** Of immaterial things: Imposing, exalted 1639. **6.** Used to express admiration 1704.

2. A Prince is neuer so m., As when hee's sparing to inrich a few With th' iniuries of many MASSINGER. **4.** That m. Temple of Salomon 1540. **6.** The day was m. 1860. Hence **Magni·ficently** *adv.*

||**Magnifico** (mægni·fiko). 1573. [It., = MAGNIFIC.] Title bestowed upon the magnates of Venice; also *transf.*

Magnifier (mæ·gnifəiəɹ). 1550. [f. MAGNIFY *v.* + -ER[1].] One who or that which magnifies. Also *fig.*

Magnify (mæ·gnifəi), *v.* ME. [– (O)Fr. *magnifier* or L. *magnificare*, f. *magnificus*; see MAGNIFIC, -FY. Sense 4 is in Eng. only.] **1.** *trans.* To speak or act for the glory of (a person or thing); to laud, extol (*arch.*). **2.** To make greater in size, status, importance, or qualities; to enlarge, augment. Now *rare.* ME. **3.** *trans.* To represent as great or greater; to exaggerate 1759. **4.** To increase the apparent size of an object by artificial means. Also *absol.* 1665. **5.** *intr.* 'A cant word for *to have effect*' (J.); to signify. Now *dial.* 1712.

1. If the invention of the ship was thought so noble..how much more are letters to be magnified, which as ships pass through the vast seas of time BACON. **4.** *fig.* The effects of fogs upon our estimation of dimension..are well known: men are magnified to giants KANE.

Magnifying glass, a glass lens, or combination of lenses, used to increase the apparent size of any object seen through it 1665.

Magniloquence (mægni·lǒkwěns). 1623. [f. next; see -ENCE.] The quality of being magniloquent.

Magniloquent (mægni·lǒkwěnt), *a.* 1656. [f. L. *magniloquus* (f. *magnus* great + *-loquus* speaking) + -ENT.] Lofty or ambitious in expression, grandiloquent. Also, *occas.*, talking big, boastful. Hence **Magni·loquently** *adv.* So †**Magni·loquous** *a.*

Magnitude (mæ·gnitiud). ME. [– L. *magnitudo*, f. *magnus* great, large, rel. to Gr. μέγας, Gmc. **mikil-* (see MUCH); see -TUDE.] **1.** = GREATNESS, in various senses; see quots. **2.** Size, whether great or small; in *Geom.*, the measure or extent of a line, area, volume, or angle 1570. **3.** A class in a system of classification determined by size: *esp.* each of the classes into which the fixed stars have been arranged according to their degree of brilliancy 1641. **b.** *Of the first m.* (fig.): of the utmost greatness or importance 1693.

1. [Boadicea's] orations..wherein is expressed all m. of a spirit, breathing to the libertie and redemption of her Countrie B. JONS. The height, and strength, and m. of their building DE FOE. The m. of his crimes '*Junius Lett.*' **2.** quasi-*concr.* A long m., we terme a Line 1570. **3.** The stars 'of the first m.' are the most brilliant; the 'sixth m.' includes those that are barely visible to the naked eye; the seventh and lower magnitudes are telescopic only. The classification into 'magnitudes', ..is now a matter of photometric measurement. O.E.D.

Magnolia (mægnōᵘ·liă). 1748. [– mod.L. *magnolia*, f. name of Pierre *Magnol* (latinized *Magnolius*), professor of botany at Montpellier, 1638–1715; see -IA[1].] A genus of large (rarely shrubby) trees (the typical genus of the N.O. *Magnoliaceæ*) cultivated for their foliage and flowers. Hence **Magnolia·ceous** *a.* of or belonging to the N.O. *Magnoliaceæ*.

Magnum (mæ·gnǒm). 1788. [n. sing. of L. *magnus* large, used subst.] A bottle containing two quarts of wine or spirits; also, as a measure of liquor. **b.** A large glass (of spirits). DICKENS.

A..partiality for..magnums of old port 1893.

Magnum bonum (mæ·gnǒm bōᵘ·nǒm). 1721. [n. sing. of L. *magnus* great, *bonus* good, used subst.] **1.** A kind of large yellow cooking-plum. Also *magnum bonum plum.* **2.** = MAGNUM. 1800. **3.** A kind of potato 1882. **4.** A large-barrelled steel pen 1851.

||**Magnum opus.** See OPUS.

||**Magot** (mæ·gǫt, mago). 1707. [Fr.] **1.** A species of ape (*Macacus inuus*); the tailless Barbary Ape. **2.** A small grotesque figure of porcelain, ivory, etc. of Chinese or Japanese workmanship 1844.

Magpie (mæ·gpəi). 1605. [f. MAG *sb.*[1] + PIE *sb.*[1] Cf. MAGGOT-PIE.] **1.** A common European bird, *Pica caudata*, of the family *Corvidæ*, with a long pointed tail and black-and-white plumage; distinguished for its chattering voice and thievish habits. **b.** *Austral.* Applied to the black-and-white Crow-shrike (*Gymnorrhina*); also, in Tasmania, to the genus *Strepera* 1859. **2.** *transf.* An idle or impertinent chatterer 1632. **3.** †**a.** A derisive term for an Anglican bishop, from his black chimere and white rochet. **b.** Now, a joc. name for this episcopal costume. 1704. **4. a.** = *magpie moth* 1749. **b.** A kind of potato 1794. **c.** A variety of the domestic pigeon 1868. **5.** *slang.* A halfpenny. DICKENS. **6.** *Mil. slang.* A shot from a rifle that strikes the outermost division but one of a target, and is signalled by a black and white flag 1884.

1. And only hear the M. gossip Garrulous under a roof of pine TENNYSON.

attrib. and *Comb.*, as **m. diver,** (*a*) the Golden-eye Duck, *Clangula glaucion*; (*b*) the Smew, *Merganser albellus*; **m. lark,** a small Australian bird, *Grallina picata*; **m. moth,** a white moth, patched with black and some yellow spots, *Abraxas grossulariata.*

Ma·gsman. *slang.* 1838. [f. MAG *sb.*[5]] A street swindler, 'confidence man'.

||**Maguari** (măgwā·ri). 1678. [Tupi *mbaguári.*] A S. American Stork, *Euxenura maguari*, with a forked tail.

||**Maguey** (mæ·gweⁱ; Sp. magē·y). 1555. [Sp. – Haytian.] The American aloe, *Agave americana.*

||**Magus** (mēⁱ·gǒs). *Pl.* **Magi** (mēⁱ·dʒəi). ME. [L. – Gr. μάγος – OPers. *magus.* Cf. MAGE.] **1.** *Hist.* A member of the ancient Persian priestly caste. Hence, one skilled in Oriental magic and astrology, an ancient magician or sorcerer. **b.** Applied to the heathen sorcerers who opposed St. Patrick 1822. **2.** *spec. The* (*three*) *Magi*: the three 'wise men' who came from the East (see WISE MAN 3) ME.

Magyar (ma·dʸar, mæ·gyar). 1797. [Native name.] **A.** *sb.* **1.** A member of the race now forming the predominant section of the inhabitants of Hungary. **2.** The Ural-Altaic language of the Magyars; Hungarian 1828. **B.** *adj.* Of or pertaining to the Magyars, or to their language 1828. **b.** Applied recently to a type of female dress in which bodice and sleeves are cut in one piece. Hence **Ma·gyarize** *v. trans.* to assimilate to the M. type; to translate (names) into M.

||**Mahal** (măhā·l). *Indian.* 1623 (**mawle**). [Urdu – Arab. *maḥall*, f. *ḥalla* dismount, pass a night.] **1.** Private apartments or lodgings. **2.** A summer house or palace 1625. **3.** A territorial division in India; a ward of a town. Also, a division of an estate or tract of land for farming, hunting, etc. 1793.

Mahaleb (mā·hăleb). 1558. [orig. *macaleb* – Fr. *macaleb* (now *mah-*) – Arab. *maḥlab*, pl. *maḥālib*; later assim. to Arab. in form.] A kind of cherry, *Prunus mahaleb*, the kernels of which are used by perfumers.

||**Maharaj** (maharā·dʒ). 1826. [Hindi *mahārāj*, f. *mahā* great + *rāj* sovereignty, sovereign.] = next.

||**Maharaja(h)** (maharā·dʒa). 1698. [Hindi *mahārājā*, f. *mahā* great + *rājā* RAJA(H.] The title of certain Indian princes. So ||**Maharanee** (maharā·nī) [Hindi *mahārānī*, see RANEE], the wife of a maharajah 1862.

Mahatma (măhæ·tmă). 1884. [– Skr. *mahātman*, f. *mahā* great + *ātmán* soul.] In Esoteric Buddhism, one of a class of persons with preternatural powers, supposed to exist in India and Tibet.

||**Mahdi** (mā·di). 1792. [Arab. *mahdīy*, lit. 'he who is guided aright', pass. pple. of *hadā* lead in the right way.] A spiritual and temporal leader expected by the Moslems to appear in the latter days. Applied from about 1880 to insurrectionary leaders in the Sudan, who claimed to be the expected Mahdi. Hence **Ma·hd(i)ism,** the rebel movements in the Soudan about 1880. **Ma·hd(i)ist.**

Mah Jong (mā dʒǫ·ŋ). 1923. [Chinese, f. *ma* sparrow, *djung* play.] An old Chinese game, played usu. by four persons with 136 or 144 'tiles'.

Mahlstick, var. of MAULSTICK.

Mahoe (măhōᵘ·). 1666. [Carib *mahou*; in Fr. *mahot* (also used in Eng.).] The name of several trees. (Also *m.-tree.*) **a.** A sterculiaceous tree or large shrub (*Sterculia caribæa*), a native of the W. Indies. **b.** A malvaceous shrub or tree (*Paritium tiliaceum* and *P. elatum*), found in many tropical countries. **c.** Applied with qualifications to species of *Hibiscus, Ochroma*, etc.

Mahogany (măhǫ·găni). 1671. [Of unkn. origin; adopted as bot.L. by Linnæus (1762) in the form *mahagoni*, whence the various Continental forms.] **1.** The wood of *Swietenia mahagoni* (N.O. *Cedrelaceæ*), a tree indigenous to the tropical parts of America. Its colour varies from yellow to a rich red brown, it is very hard and fine-grained, and takes a high polish. Also differentiated as *Baywood, Cuba, Honduras, Jamaica, Spanish m.* **b.** The tree itself 1759. **2.** *transf.* Applied to woods resembling mahogany, and to the trees producing them. In Australia mainly used for species of *Eucalyptus*, esp. the Jarrah (*E. marginata*). 1842. **3.** *colloq.* A table, esp. a dining-table 1840. **4.** *dial.* A Cornish beverage compounded of gin and treacle 1791. **5.** *attrib.* and quasi-*adj.* **a.** Made of mahogany 1730. **b.** Of the colour of mahogany, polished reddish-brown 1737.

3. Other families did not welcome us to their m. THACKERAY.

Mahomet (măhǫ·mėt; in verse occas. mēⁱ·homet). See also MAUMET. [ME. *Mac-(h)amete, Mako-* – (O)Fr. *Mahomet*, †*Mach-*, med.L. *Ma(c)hometus.*] **1.** The pop. rendering of Arabic *Muḥammad* MOHAMMED (now the lit. form). †**2.** An idol –1553. †**3.** = MAHOMETAN –1747. **4.** A kind of pigeon. ?*Obs.* 1735.

1. If the Hill will not come to M., M. wil go to the hil BACON.

Mahometan (măhǫ·mėtăn), *a.* and *sb.* 1529. [– med.L. *Ma(c)hometanus*, etc.; see prec., -AN.] = MOSLEM. Hence **Maho·metanism** = ISLAM. So †**Maho·metism** 1597; also †**Maho·metist,** a MOSLEM 1553.

Mahometry (măhǫ·mėtri). *Obs.* exc. *arch.* 1481. [f. MAHOMET + -RY. Cf. MAUMETRY.] = ISLAM. In 16th c. misused for 'idolatry'.

†||**Mahone.** 1572. [Occurs as Fr. *mahonne*, Sp. *mahona*, It. *maona*, Turk. *māvuna*, *mavna.*] A flat-bottomed sailing vessel formerly used by the Turks –1658.

Mahound (măhū·nd, măhau·nd). [Early ME. *Mahun, -um* – OFr. *Mahun, -um*, shortening of *Mahomet*. Cf. MAUMET.] **1.** The 'false prophet' Mohammed. Now only *arch.* †**2.** *gen.* A false god; an idol. (Cf. MAUMET.) ME. only. **3.** *Sc.* A name for the devil. Also *transf. Obs.* (? exc. *dial.*) ME. †**4.** *attrib.* Pagan, heathen. FLETCHER.

1. The Carle..by Turmagant and M. swore SPENSER. **4.** Who's this? my Mauhound cousin? 1624.

||**Mahout** (măhau·t). *Indian.* 1662. [Hindi *mahāut, mahāwat* :– Skr. *mahāmātra* high official, lit. 'great in measure'.] An elephant-driver.

Mahratta, Mahratti: see MARATHA, MARATHI.

||**Mahseer** (mā·siᵊɹ). 1854. [Hindi *mahāsir.*] A large Indian freshwater cyprinoid fish, *Barbus tor*, resembling the barbel.

†**Ma·hu.** 1603. [perh. suggested by MAHOUND,] Used as the name of a devil. *Lear* III. iv. 149.

||**Mahwa** (mā·wa). 1687. [Hindi *mahwa*, repr. Skr. *madhūka*, f. *madhu* sweet.] **1.** An E. Indian timber tree, *Bassia latifolia*; also *B. butyracea.* **2.** An ardent spirit distilled from the flowers of the Mahwa tree 1810; also *m. arrack.*

Maid (mēⁱd). ME. [Shortened from MAIDEN; not identical w. OE. *mæġeþ* (see MAIDEN) = G. *magd.* For the loss of final *n* cf. *clue, eve, game.*] **1.** A girl; a young (unmarried) woman. Now only (exc. *dial.*) *arch.* or *playful.* **2.** A virgin; *spec.* of the Virgin

Mary. *Obs.* or *arch.* ME. **b.** *Hist.* As a title of Joan of Arc, *The M.* (*of God, of Orleans*), tr. Fr. *la Pucelle* 1548. †**c.** *transf.* A man that has never had sexual intercourse. (Cf. Gr. *παρθένος*.) –1710. **3.** An unmarried woman, spinster. (Now *rare* exc. in OLD MAID.) 1603. **4.** A MAIDSERVANT; often differentiated as *bar-, chamber-, house-, nurse-, servant-m.*, etc., q.v.; *lady's maid* (see LADY) ME. **5.** *dial.* **a.** = MAIDEN *sb.* 5. 1677. **b.** A clothes-horse 1795. **6.** A name for the Skate and Thornback (*Raia batis* and *R. clavata*) when young, and the Twait Shad, *Alosa finta* 1579.

1. Faire and fresh of hewe, As a mayde in hir beaute LYDG. **2.** Who serueth our lord, And the mayde marye CAXTON. **c.** He Dy'd a *Maid* 1710. **3.** A m. almost a hundred yeare old 1648. **4.** We kept no m.:—and I had much to do 1835. *M.-of-all-work*, a female servant who does all kinds of house-work.

‖**Maidan** (məidā·n). *Indian.* 1625. [Urdu *maydān* – Arab. *maydān*.] An open space in or near a town; an esplanade or parade-ground.

Maiden (mē^i·d'n), *sb.* and *a.* [OE. *mæġden* n. = OHG. *magatīn* :– Gmc. **mazadīnam*, dim. (see -EN^1), f. **mazadiz* maid, virgin, which is repr. by OE. *mæġ(e)þ*, OS. *magath*, OHG. *magad* (G. *magd*, whence dim. *mägdchen*, now *mädchen* girl), Goth. *magaþs*, and is rel. to Gmc. **mazuz* :– IE. **moghus* boy, young man, whence OE., OS. *magu*, ON. *mǫgr*, Goth. *magus* son, young man, OIr. *mug* slave, Av. *magu* young man. Cf. MAC, MAY *sb.*^{1}] **A.** *sb.* **1.** = MAID 1. (Not now in colloq. use exc. *dial.*) **2.** = MAID 2. Now *rare*. OE. †**b.** *transf.* = MAID 2 c. –1497. **3.** = MAID 3. *Obs.* exc. *dial.* 1775. **4.** A maidservant, a female attendant (*arch.* and *dial.*) OE. **5.** The instrument, similar to a guillotine, formerly used in Edinburgh for beheading criminals 1581. **6.** *dial.* A clothes-horse 1859. **7.** Short for *maiden horse, over, race, tree* (see B).

1. A m. of our century, yet most meek TENNYSON. **2.** Why then you are no m. SHAKS. **4.** As the eyes of a m. [looke] vnto the hand of her mistresse *Ps.* 123:2. *Comb.* **m. plum** (**tree**), a name of the W. Indian trees, (*a*) *Comocladia integrifolia*; (*b*) *Chrysobalanus*.

B. *adj.* (the sb. in appositive and attrib. uses). **I.** Literal uses. **1.** Unmarried; as, *m. aunt, lady, sister* ME. **2.** Of or pertaining to a maiden, or to maidenhood; befitting, or having the qualities of, a maiden 1591. **3.** Of female animals; Uncoupled, unmated 1840.

1. M. aunts with small fortunes JOHNSON. **2.** *M. name*: the surname of a married woman before marriage.

II. Fig. uses. **1.** That has yielded no results. **a.** Of an assize, circuit, session: Formerly, one at which no prisoner was condemned to death; now, one at which there are no cases for trial. **b.** Of a game, esp. *Cricket*, of an over: One in which no runs are scored. **c.** Of a tide: One on which no vessels enter or leave the dock. **d.** Of a horse, etc.: That has never won a prize. Hence of a prize or a race: Open to maiden horses, etc. 1760. **2.** That has not been conquered, tried, worked, etc.; *esp.* **a.** Of a town, castle, fortress, etc.: That has never been taken 1593; **b.** Of a plant or tree: That has grown from seed, not from a stock 1649; **c.** Of a soldier, a weapon, etc.: Untried 1603. **3.** That is the first of its kind; made, used, etc. for the first time. Occas. in sense *early, earliest*. 1555.

1. b. An occasional 'maiden over' 1893. **2. a.** She was a m. City, bright and free WORDSW. **c.** A m. knight—to me is given Such hope, I know not fear TENNYSON. **3.** A m. trip 1884, m. speech (= the first delivered in the House by a member of parliament).

†**Maiden** (mē^i·d'n), *v.* 1597. [f. MAIDEN *sb.*] In phr. *To m. it*: to act like a maiden, be coy. BP. HALL.

Maidenhair (mē^{i}d'n,hē^{ə}ɹ). ME. [f. MAIDEN *sb.* + HAIR.] The name of certain ferns having fine hair-like stalks and delicate fronds: **a.** *Adiantum capillus-veneris*, or True M., formerly much used in medicine 1450; **b.** *Asplenium trichomanes*, or Common or English M. ME.; **c.** *Asplenium ruta-muraria*, or White M. 1597.

Comb.: **m. grass,** *Briza media*; **-tree,** the ginkgo.

Maidenhead (mē^i·d'nhed). *arch.* ME. [f. MAIDEN *sb.* + -HEAD.] **1.** The condition of a maiden; virginity; said occas. of a man. †**2.** *transf.* and *fig.*, *esp.* the first stage or first-fruits of anything; the first example, proof, trial, or use –1775.

2. The maiden head of my industrie I yeelded to a noble Mecenas (renoumed Lecester) FLORIO.

Maidenhood (mē^i·d'nhud). [OE. *mæġdenhād*; see MAIDEN, -HOOD.] The condition of being a maiden; the time of life during which one is a maiden. Formerly also = MAIDENHEAD 2.

Mai·denlike. 15.. [f. MAIDEN *sb.* + -LIKE.] **a.** *adj.* Such as is usual with maidens; befitting a maiden. **b.** *adv.* After the manner of a maiden.

Maidenly (mē^i·d'nli), *a.* and *adv.* 1450. [f. as prec. + -LY.] **A.** *adj.* **1.** Of or pertaining to a maiden or to maidenhood. †**2.** Resembling a maiden in action or bearing; gentle, modest, timid –1672. **3.** Proper to, or characteristic of a maiden 1532.

1. Her m. bloom fresh-glowing 1871. **2.** 2 *Hen. IV*, II. ii. 82. **3.** M. reserve 1748, modesty 1849.

B. *adv.* In a maidenly manner 1596.

Hence **Mai·denliness,** m. quality.

Maiden's blush. 1648. Used as a name for a delicate pink colour. Hence, a rose of this colour.

Mai·denship. 1602. [f. MAIDEN *sb.* + -SHIP.] The personality of a maiden; chiefly in *Your M.*, as a playful form of address.

Maidhood (mē^i·d,hud). ME. [f. MAID + -HOOD. In the earliest examples repr. OE. *mæġ(e)þhād*, f. *mæġ(e)þ* (see MAIDEN).] = MAIDENHOOD.

Maid Marian. 1525. A female personage in the May-game and morris-dance. In the later forms of the story of Robin Hood, the companion of the outlaw.

Maid of honour. 1586. **1.** An unmarried lady who attends upon a queen or princess. **2.** A kind of cheesecake 1769. **3.** The principal bridesmaid at a wedding (*U.S.*) 1906.

Mai·dse:rvant. 1526. [f. MAID + SERVANT.] A female servant, usu. a domestic servant.

Maieutic (mē^{i}iū·tik), *a.* (*sb.*) 1655. [– Gr. *μαιευτικός* (*lit.* 'obstetric'; used *fig.* by Socrates), f. *μαιεύεσθαι*, f. *μαῖα* midwife; see -IC.] Pertaining to (intellectual) midwifery, *i.e.* to the Socratic process of helping a person to bring into full consciousness conceptions previously latent in his mind. **b.** *sb. pl.* The maieutic art 1885. So †**Maieutical** *a.* CUDWORTH.

Maigre (mē^i·gəɹ), *sb.* Also **meagre.** 1835. [– Fr. *maigre*.] A large fish, *Sciæna aquila*, common in the Mediterranean.

‖**Maigre** (mēgr, mē^i·gəɹ), *a.* 1683. [(O)Fr., lit. lean; see MEAGRE *a.*] **1.** Of soup, etc.: Not containing flesh or its juices; proper for 'maigre' days 1787. **2.** Applied to those days on which, according to ecclesiastical rule, flesh may not be eaten 1683. †**3.** *To eat, keep, live m.*: to live on maigre diet –1778.

1. A common m. dish 1787.

Mail (mē^{i}l), *sb.*^{1} ME. [– (O)Fr. *maille* :– L. *macula* spot, mesh.] †**1.** One of the metal rings or plates of which mail-armour was composed –1706. **2.** *collect.* Armour composed of interlaced rings or chain-work or of overlapping plates fastened upon a groundwork ME. †**b.** A piece of mail-armour –1617. **c.** *transf.* of the protective shell or scales of some animals 1714. **d.** *fig.* 1813. **3.** *Hawking.* The breast-feathers of a hawk when the feathers are full-grown. Occas. applied to the plumage of other birds. 1486. **4.** *Rope-making.* A kind of steel chain-work, flat, and fastened upon leather, for rubbing off the loose hemp that remains on white cordage 1750.

2. *Coat of m.*: see COAT *sb.* Also CHAIN-*mail*, RING-*mail*. **c.** Where the sea-snakes coil and twine, Dry their m. and bask in the brine M. ARNOLD. **d.** She was clad in the m. of endurance 1866.

attrib. and *Comb*, as *m.-armour, -plate, -shirt*, etc.; *m.-clad* adj.; **m.-shell,** a name for the genus *Chiton*.

Mail (mē^{i}l), *sb.*^{2} Now only *Sc.* [north. repr. of late OE. *māl* – ON. *mál* speech, agreement = OE. *mæl* speech; prob. contr. f. the word appearing in OE. *mæþel* meeting, discussion, OS., OHG. *mahal* assembly, judgement, treaty, Goth. *maþl* meeting-place; in sense the Eng. word corresponds rather to ON. *máli* stipulation, stipulated pay. See also BLACK MAIL.] Payment, tax, tribute, rent. (Cf. BLACK MAIL.)

Phr. *Mails and duties*: the rents of an estate, whether in money or grain.

Mail (mē^{i}l), *sb.*^{3} [ME. *male* – OFr. *male* (mod. *malle* bag, trunk) – Gmc. (cf. OHG. *mal(a)ha* wallet, bag, MDu. *male*, Du. *maal*).] **1.** A bag, pack, or wallet; a travelling bag. Now only *Sc.* and *U.S.* in *pl.* = baggage. **2.** A bag or packet of letters or dispatches for conveyance by post, more fully *m. of letters* 1654. **b.** orig. *U.S.* (A person's) batch of letters 1890. **3.** The person, vehicle, or train that carries the mail or postal matter; often short for *m.-coach, m.-train*, etc. Hence, the system of transmission of letters by post; the POST. (So now in *U.S.* In England the word signifies only the dispatch of letters abroad, as the *Indian m.*, etc., or is short for mail-train, as the *night m.*, etc.) 1654.

1. A male tweyfold on his croper lay CHAUCER. **2.** The arrival and distribution of a m. of letters 1893. *The m.*, all the postal matter conveyed on one occasion. **b.** That official was opening his m. 1890.

attrib. and *Comb.*: **m.-bag,** a large bag in which the m. is carried; **-box,** (*a*) a box in which the mail-bags were placed on a mail-coach; (*b*) *U.S.*, a letter-box; **-cart,** (*a*) a vehicle in which the m. is carried by road; (*b*) a light vehicle to carry children, pushed or pulled by hand; **-catcher** *U.S.*, a contrivance attached to a railroad car for catching a mail-bag while the train is in motion; **m. contractor,** one who contracts with the government for the conveyance of the mails; **-guard,** the guard of a mail-coach; **-phaeton,** a high two-seated phaeton drawn by a pair of horses; **-stage** *U.S.* = MAIL-COACH; **-train,** a fast train which carries the mails.

†**Mail,** *sb.*^{4} *Obs.* exc. as alien (may). Also **maill(e;** and see MALL. 1670. [– (O)Fr. *mail* :– L. *malleus* hammer.] The game of pall-mall; a place where it was played; hence (from the 'Mail' at Paris), a public promenade bordered by trees. *The Mail* (in St. James's Park, London): now the MALL.

Mail (mē^{i}l), *v.*^{1} 1795. [f. MAIL *sb.*^{1}; partly back-formation from MAILED *a.*] *trans.* To clothe or arm with or as with mail.

Mail (mē^{i}l), *v.*^{2} 1570. [Of unkn. origin; sense 2 may perh. be the orig. use; cf. MAIL *sb.*^{1} and *sb.*^{3}] †**1.** *trans.* To tie (*up*), wrap up (goods, a parcel, etc.); to envelop. Also *fig.* –1660. **2.** *spec.* in *Hawking.* To wrap (a hawk) up in a handkerchief, either to tame her, or to keep her quiet during an operation 1575.

Mail (mē^{i}l), *v.*^{3} *U.S.* 1828. [f. MAIL *sb.*^{3}] *trans.* To send by post, to post. Hence **Mai·lable** *a.* that may be sent by post; **-abi·lity.**

Mai·l-coach. 1787. [MAIL *sb.*^{3} 2.] **1.** A stage-coach used primarily for the conveyance of the mail. Later, a coach employed by the Post Office for carrying parcels by road. **2.** A railway carriage carrying the mail 1838.

Mailed (mē^{i}ld), *a.* ME. [f. MAIL *sb.*^{1} + -ED^2.] †**1.** Covered with or composed of mail –1856. **2.** Mail-clad. Of a vessel: Ironclad. 1596. Also *fig.* **3.** *transf.* of animals, etc.: Having a skin or outer covering resembling mail-armour 1681. **4.** Of a hawk: Having breast-feathers (of a specified colour) 1575.

2. The mayled Mars shall on his Altar sit Vp to the eares in blood SHAKS. Phr. *The m. fist* [tr. G. *die gepanzerte faust*], (symbolically) armed force.

Mailing (mē^i·liŋ). *Sc.* 1452. [f. MAIL *sb.*^{2} + -ING^1.] **1.** A rented farm. **2.** The rent paid for a farm 1725.

2. Let the creatures stay at a moderate m. SCOTT.

Maim (mē^{i}m), *sb. Obs.* or *arch.* [ME. *maheym* (rare), *maime*, later also *maine*, Sc. †*manyie* – OFr. *mayhem, mahaing, main(e*, f. *mahaignier, mayner*; see MAIM *v.*, MAYHEM.] An injury to the body which causes the loss of a limb, or of the use of it; loss or permanent disablement of a limb; *transf.* and *fig.* mutilation or disablement; hence, any injury or hurt 1543.

Your Father's sicknesse is a mayme to vs SHAKS. They are so eminent in their generations, that their omission would make a m. in history FULLER.

Maim (mē^{i}m), *a. rare.* 1475. [rel. to prec.;

cf. OFr. *mehaigne*, mod. Fr. dial. *mécaigne*.] Maimed.

His own life being m. R. L. STEVENSON.

Maim (mē^{i}m), *v.* [– OFr. *mahaignier*, *mayner* :– Rom. **mahagnare*, of unkn. origin. See MAIM *sb.*] *trans.* To deprive of the use of some member; to mutilate, cripple. †Earlier, to disable, hurt, wound, disfigure. **b.** *fig.* To mutilate, cripple, render powerless or essentially incomplete; †to deprive *of* ME.

By the antient law of England he that maimed any man, whereby he lost any part of his body, was sentenced to lose the like part BLACKSTONE. **b.** Thereby is England main'd And faine to go with a staffe SHAKS. Hence **Mai·med-ly** *adv.*, **-ness.**

Main (mē^{i}n), *sb.*[1] [OE. *mæġen* = OS. *megin*, OHG. *magan*, *megin*, ON. *magn*, *meg(i)n*, f. Gmc. base **maӡ-* have power; see MAY *v.*[1]]

I. Physical strength, force, or power. *Obs.* exc. in phr. *with might and m.* †Also *fig.*

He gan aduaunce With huge force and insupportable mayne SPENSER.

II. Absol. uses of MAIN *a.* **1.** *ellipt.* for *main land*, MAINLAND (*arch.*) 1555. **b.** Short for SPANISH *Main*, q.v. 1890. **2.** *ellipt.* for MAIN SEA: The high sea, the ocean. Now *poet.* 1579. †**b.** *transf.* A broad expanse –1667. **3.** The most important part; the chief matter or principal thing in hand 1602. **b.** Const. *of.* The principal part (*of* some whole); the important or essential point 1595. †**4.** The object aimed at; end, purpose –1657. **5.** (for *main drain*, etc.) A principal channel, duct, or conductor for conveying water, sewage, gas, or electricity, e.g. along the street of a town 1727. **6.** Short for *mainmast* 1894. **7.** *techn.* A main line of railway 1892.

1. The island..was separated from the m. by a channel half a mile broad THIRLWALL. **b.** Drake.. sailed once more for the M. CORBETT. **2.** To gaze O'er land and m. TENNYSON. **b.** Natiuity once in the maine of light, Crawles to maturity SHAKS. **3.** We let the M. go, while we grasp at the accessories 1702. Phr. *In the m.*, in all essential points; mainly. **b.** The m. of life is composed of small incidents JOHNSON. **6.** The German flag flying at the main 1894.

Main (mē^{i}n), *sb.*[2] 1567. [prob. by ellipsis from MAIN CHANCE 1 c.] **1.** In the game of hazard, a number (from 5 to 9 inclusive) called by the caster before the dice are thrown 1575. †**b.** *fig.* esp. coupled with or opp. to *by* (see BY *sb.*[2]) –1781. **2.** A match fought between cocks; also *locally*, a match at bowls, etc. 1760 (cf. *main match* 1716, opp. to *by-battle*.)

1. Diceplayers, that gaine more by the bye then by the maine 1598. He likes to throw a m. of an evening THACKERAY. *fig.* 1 *Hen. IV*, IV. i. 47. **2.** My lord would ride twenty miles..to see a m. fought THACKERAY.

Main (mē^{i}n), *a.* [Partly repr. OE. *mæġen* MAIN *sb.*, in compounds; partly – ON. *megenn*, *megn*, or (in combination) *megin* strong, powerful.] **1.** Strong, vigorous, mighty; manifesting, or exerting, great physical strength or force. †**2.** Of an army, host, etc.: Great in numbers; 'mighty'; powerful in arms; †completely equipped ME. **3.** Of great size or bulk. *Obs.* exc. *dial.* ME. **4.** Said of a continuous stretch of land or water; occas. also of void space 1548. †**b.** Of earth, rock: Forming the principal mass; solid –1647. †**5.** Highly important. Rarely const. *to.* –1671. **6.** Very great (in degree, value, etc.); highly remarkable; very considerable of its kind. *Obs.* exc. *dial.* ME. **7.** Chief in size or extent; constituting the bulk; the chief part of (what is denoted by the sb.) 1584. †**b.** General –1638. **8.** Of preeminent importance; principal, chief, leading 1476. †**9.** *Main flood*: **a.** High water. **b.** A large or full-flowing body of water. Also *m. tide.* **c.** The ocean or MAIN SEA. –1605. **10.** *Naut.* Pertaining to, connected with, or near the mainmast or mainsail 1485.

1. That Maine, which by maine force Warwicke did winne SHAKS. It was a maine (= violent) storme DIGBY. Soaring on m. wing MILT. Phr. *By* (†*with*) *m. force*: by force exerted to the full. †*A m. pace* or *speed* = at full speed. **2.** *M. battle*: a pitched battle, opp. to skirmishing. **3.** On thir heads M. Promontories flung MILT. **4.** Over all the face of Earth M. Ocean flow'd MILT. **5.** That, which thou aright Beleivst so m. to our success MILT. **6.** It's a m. untruth SCOTT. A m. fool 1860. **7.** *M. body*, †*battle*: the body of troops which form the bulk of an armed force, marching between the vanguard and the rear. **b.** Which is no further, Then the maine voyce of Denmarke goes withall SHAKS. **8.** The statements may be grouped under two m. heads FREEMAN. *M. drain, pipe, stream, root, line* (of a railway), etc.

Special collocations: **m. centre,** in side-lever engines, the strong shaft upon which the side-levers vibrate; **m. couple** *Arch.*, the principal truss in a roof; **m. earth,** the chief earth in which the fox kennels; **m. keel,** the principal keel of a ship, as dist. from the false keel and the kelson; **m. piece** *Shipbuilding*, the principal timber in certain parts of a wooden ship, like the rudder, windlass, etc.

Main (me^{i}n), *adv.* Now *dial.* 1632. [f. MAIN *a.* Cf. MIGHTY *adv.*] Very, exceedingly.

I was m. stupid indeed, and much disposed to sleep SCOTT.

Mai·n-brace[1]. 1487. [MAIN *a.*, BRACE *sb.*[3]] *Naut.* The brace attached to the main-yard.

Phr. *To splice the main-brace* (*Naut. slang*): to serve out grog; hence, to drink freely 1805.

Mai·n-brace[2]. 1794. [MAIN *a.*, BRACE *sb.*[2]] A principal brace; *Mech.* in a system of braces, that which resists the main strain.

Main chance. 1579. [MAIN *a.*] †**1.** = MAIN *sb.*[2] 1; usu. *fig.* or *allusive.* **a.** The likeliest course to obtain success. **b.** The general probability as to a future event or the success of an undertaking. **c.** The most important point at stake; also, the general outcome of a series of events; the whole fortunes of a person, a nation, etc. –1703. **2.** That which is of principal importance in life; now *esp.* one's own interests 1584.

1. a. Phr. *To look, have an eye*, etc., *to the main chance*: to be solicitous (for some object). **2.** Be careful still of the main Chance, my Son DRYDEN.

Main-course. 1515. [MAIN *a.*, COURSE *sb.* 20.] *Naut.* The mainsail (of a square-rigged ship).

Main-deck. 1748. [MAIN *a.*, DECK *sb.* 2.] **a.** In a man-of-war, the deck next below the spar-deck. **b.** In a merchantman, that part of the upper deck which lies between the poop and the forecastle. Also *fig.*

Main-guard. 1653. **1.** *Fortif.* The keep of a castle; also, the building within a fortress in which the 'main-guard' (sense 2 b) is lodged. **2.** *Mil.* **a.** A guard of cavalry posted on the wings of a camp towards the enemy. **b.** In fortresses, a guard having the custody of all disturbers of the peace, drunkards, etc. 1706.

Mainland (mē^i·nlænd). ME. [MAIN *a.* 4; cf. ON. *meginland*.] A continuous body of land; dist. from *island* or *peninsula.* †Formerly *occas.* = land as opp. to sea, *terra firma.* **b.** Applied to the largest island of the Shetlands, also of the Orkneys (Pomona) 1596. Also *attrib.*

Pillars of chalk have thus been separated from the m. HUXLEY. Hence **Mai·nlander** 1860.

Mainly (mē^i·nli), *adv.* ME. [f. MAIN *a.* + -LY[2].] †**1.** With force, vigour, or violence; mightily –1656. †**2.** In a great degree; greatly, very much, a great deal. Also *occas.* entirely, perfectly. –1800. **b.** Used as an intensive with adjs. and advs. = MAIN *adv.* Now *dial.* 1670. **3.** For the most part; chiefly, principally 1667.

2. I think we should suit one another m. LAMB.

Mainmast (mē^i·nmɑst, -məst). 15.. [f. MAIN *a.* (sense 10) + MAST *sb.*[1]] The principal mast in a ship. Also *attrib.*

Mai·nour, ma·nner. *Obs.* exc. *Hist.* or *arch.* 1472. [orig. *manor, maner*, in law-book spelling *mainour* – AFr. *mainoure, meinoure, mainoevere*, OFr. *maneuvre*; see MANŒUVRE.] **1.** *Law.* The stolen thing which is found in a thief's possession when arrested; chiefly in phr. *taken, found with the m.* **2.** *With* (later *in*) *the mainour* (usu. *manner*): in the act of doing something unlawful, 'in flagrante delicto' 1530.

2. If..there be no witnesse against her, neither she be taken with the maner *Num.* 5:13.

Mainpernor. *Obs.* exc. *Hist.* or *arch.* ME. [– AFr. *mainpernour* (for *-prenour*), f. *mainprendre*, f. *main* hand + *prendre* take, the equiv. of med.L. *manucapere* 'take in the hand', assume responsibility for.] *Law.* A surety for a prisoner's appearance in court on a specified day; one who gives mainprize for another.

So †**Mainpernable** *a.*, capable of being mainprized 1456–1772.

Mainprize (mē^i·npraiz), *sb. Obs.* exc. *Hist.* ME. [– AFr., OFr. *mein-, mainprise*, f. *mainprendre*; see prec., PRIZE *sb.*[3]] **1.** *gen.* Suretyship 1447. **2.** *spec.* The action of procuring the release of a prisoner by becoming surety ('mainpernor') for his appearance in court at a specified time ME. Also *fig.* **3.** *concr.* One's mainpernor or mainpernors ME.

2. *Writ of m.*: a writ directed to the sheriff, commanding him to take sureties for the prisoner's appearance, usually called mainpernors, and to set him at large (Blackstone). **3.** Resolv'd to leave the Squire for Bail And M. for him to the Goal BUTLER. Hence †**Mai·nprize** *v.* to procure or grant the release of (a prisoner) by m.; to accept mainpernors for the appearance of. Often *fig.* ME. –1681.

Mains (mē^{i}nz), *sb. pl. Sc.* and *n.* 1479. [aphet. f. pl. of DOMAIN, DEMESNE.] The farm attached to a mansion house; a home farm. (Retained in Scotland in the names of farms, e.g. the Mains of Forthar.)

Mainsail (mē^i·nsē^{i}l, -s'l). 1485. [See MAIN *a.* 10.] The principal sail of a ship: in square-rigged vessels, that bent to the main-yard; in fore-and-aft rigged vessels, that set on the after part of the mainmast.

They..hoysed vppe the mayne sayle to the wynde TINDALE *Acts* 27:40.

Main sea. *arch.* 1526. [See MAIN *a.* 4. Cf. ON. *meginsjór*.] The high sea. Also *fig.*

Main-sheet, mai·nsheet. 1485. [f. MAIN *a.* 10 + SHEET *sb.*[2]] *Naut.* The rope which secures the mainsail when set.

Mainspring (mē^i·nspriŋ). 1591. [MAIN *a.* 8.] **1.** A principal spring in a piece of mechanism. **a.** In a gun-lock, the spring which drives the hammer 1616. **b.** The principal coiled spring of a watch, clock, etc. 1591. **2.** *fig.* The chief motive power or incentive 1695.

Mainstay (mē^i·nstē^i). 1485. [See MAIN *a.* 8, 10.] **1.** *Naut.* The stay which extends from the maintop to the foot of the foremast. Also *attrib.* **2.** Chief support 1787.

1. *attrib.* **mainstaysail,** a storm-sail set on the m. **2.** Direct record is the m. of History TYLOR.

Mainswear, obs. f. MANSWEAR.

Maintain (mē^{i}n-, mĕntē^i·n), *v.* [ME. *maintene, -teine* repr. tonic stem of (O)Fr. *maintenir* (AFr. *maintener*) :– Rom. **manutenēre*, f. L. *manu*, abl. of *manus* hand + *tenēre* hold.] †**1.** *trans.* To practise habitually (an action, etc.); to observe (a rule, custom) –1611. **2.** †**a.** *gen.* To continue, persevere in –1545. **b.** To carry on, keep up; to have ground for sustaining (an action) ME. **c.** To continue in, preserve, retain (a condition, position, attitude, etc.) 1837. **3.** To keep in being; to preserve unimpaired (a cause, right, state of things, etc.) ME. **4.** To cause (a person) to continue *in* a state, relation, position, possession of property, etc. ME. **b.** *Comm.* To keep (stock) from declining in price 1881. †**5.** To keep in good order, to rule (a people, country); to preserve *in* (a state of peace, etc.) –1602. **6.** To support (one's state in life) by expenditure, etc.; to sustain (life) by nourishment ME. †**b.** To afford –1605. **7.** To provide with means of subsistence or necessaries of life. †Also, to keep *in* (clothing). ME. **8.** To pay or furnish the means for the keeping up of; to keep supplied or equipped (e.g. a ship, a garrison); to keep (a road, a building) in repair ME. **9.** To back up (a cause, one's side or interest, a party, etc.); to support or uphold *in* (an action) ME. †**b.** In bad sense: To aid or abet *in* (wrong-doing); to back up *in* (error, etc.) –1552. **c.** *Law.* To give support to (a suitor) in an action in which one is not concerned 1716. **10.** To hold (a place, position, possession) against hostility or attack ME. **11.** To uphold, defend (an opinion, statement, tenet, etc.); to assert to be true or right ME.

1. *Titus* 3:14. **2. b.** To m. the doubtful combat DRYDEN, Correspondence HEARNE, an action at law CRUISE. **c.** Pitt maintained a stately..reserve 1898. **3.** The necessity of justice to m. peace and order HUME. He had a reputation to m. JOWETT. **4.** The limb was maintained in this state of tension for several seconds 1874. **6.** Sufficeth, that I haue maintaines my state SHAKS. **b.** *Tam. Shr.* v. i. 79. **7.** A time..When every rood of ground maintained its man GOLDSM. **8.** Tenne talents yeerely, to maintaine the burnt offerings vpon the Altar euery day 1 *Esdras* 4:52. **9.** Who single hast maintaind Against revolted multitudes the Cause Of Truth MILT. **c.** Where one maintains one Side, to have Part of the Thing in Suit, which is called Champerty 1716. **10.** Phr. *To m. one's ground* (often *fig.*). **11.** And he ones saye a thyng, he wyll mayntayne it to dye for it PALSGR. He.. Maintains the Multitude can never err DRYDEN. Hence **Maintai·nable** *a.* **Maintai·ner.**

Maintenance (mē^i·ntėnăns). ME. [– (O)Fr. *maintenance*, f. *maintenir*; see prec., -ANCE.] †**1.** Bearing, deportment, behaviour –1596. **2.** The action of maintaining; the state or fact of being maintained; means of sustentation ME. **3.** The action of wrongfully aiding and abetting litigation; *spec.* sustentation of a suit or suitor at law by a party who has no interest in the proceedings or who acts from any improper motive ME. **4.** *Cap* (or †*hat*) *of m.*: a kind of hat or cap formerly worn as a symbol of official dignity or high rank, or carried before a sovereign, or a high dignitary in processions 1485.

1. She had so stedfaste countenaunce, So noble porte and meyntenaunce CHAUCER. **2.** For the maintenaunce of theyr authoritie SIR T. MORE. M. of troops BURKE, of opinions 1875. A comfortable m. LAW. Phr. *Separate m.*: support given by a husband to a wife when the parties are separated. **3.** Actions for m. are in modern times rare though possible 1901. **4.** *Her.* Applied to a cap with two horn-like points behind, borne as a charge or in place of a wreath.

‖**Maintenon** (mæ̃ntənoṅ). 1805. The name of the Marquise de Maintenon, secretly married to Louis XIV in 1685; used *attrib.* in *M. bonnet, chop, cutlet*, etc.

Main-top (mē^i·n,tǫp). 1485. [f. MAIN *a.* 10 + TOP *sb.*[1] III. 1.] *Naut.* The TOP of the mainmast; a platform just above the head of the lower mainmast. Often = *main-topgallant-masthead.* Also *attrib.*, as *main-top bowline, -man.*

Main-topgallant (mē^i:n,tǫpgæ·lănt). 1626. [See MAIN *a.* 10 and TOPGALLANT.] *Naut.* Used *attrib.* in **main-topgallant-mast,** the mast above the main-topmast; so *main-topgallant-mast-head, -sail* (*-yard*), *-yard*, etc. Similarly **Main-topmast** (mē^in,tǫ·pmast, -məst), the mast next above the lower mainmast; also *attrib.* 1495; **Main-topsail** (mē^in,tǫ·psē^il, -s'l), the sail above the mainsail; also *attrib.* 1618.

Main-yard (mē^i·n,yāɹd). 1485. [f. MAIN *a.* 10 + YARD *sb.*[2] 5.] *Naut.* The yard on which the mainsail is extended.

‖**Maison(n)ette** (mē^izǫne·t). 1818. [Fr. (*-nn-*), dim. of *maison* house; see -ETTE.] A small house; in recent use, a portion of a house used as a self-contained dwelling.

Maister, -ery, var. of MASTER, -ERY.

Maistres(se, obs. f. MISTRESS.

‖**Maître d'hôtel** (mętr' dotęl). 1540. [Fr., = 'house-master'.] A major-domo, a steward or butler. **b.** A hotel manager 1891.

Maize (mē^iz). 1565. [– Fr. *maïs*, †*mahiz*, or its source Sp. *maiz*, †*mahiz*, *-is*, †*mayz*, of Carib origin.] **1.** An American graminaceous plant (*Zea mays*) or the grain produced by it; = INDIAN CORN. **2.** = *m.-yellow* 1890.

Comb.: **m.-bird, -thief,** an American blackbird of the subfamily *Agelæinæ*, so called from its fondness for m.; **-eater,** a S. American maize-bird; **-sugar,** glucose; **-yellow,** a yellow like that of m. Hence **Maize·na,** maize-starch prepared for food 1862.

Majestatic (mædʒėstæ·tik), *a.* Now *rare.* 1659. [– med.L. *majestaticus*, f. *majestat-* MAJESTY; see -IC.] Pertaining to the majesty of God. So †**Majesta·tical** *a.* 1694.

Majestic (mădʒe·stik), *a.* 1601. [f. MAJESTY + -IC.] Possessing or characterized by majesty; of imposing dignity or grandeur.

He was grave and m., and carried it something like a king DE FOE. Virgil's great majestick lines 1704. So **Maje·stical** *a.* majestic 1579; **-ly** *adv.*

Majesty (mæ·dʒėsti). ME. [– (O)Fr. *majesté* (earlier *maesté*) – L. *majestas, -tat-*, f. **majes-*, var. of **majos-* (*majus, major*); see MAJOR *a.*, -ITY.] **1.** The dignity or greatness of a sovereign; sovereign power, sovereignty. Also, the person or personality of a sovereign. **b.** *spec.* The greatness and glory of God. (The earliest use) ME. **c.** *transf.* of other beings. **d.** *Rom. Hist.* As tr. L. *majestas*: The sovereign power and dignity of the Roman people, *esp.* considered with reference to offences against it 1565. (Cf. LESE-MAJESTY.) **2.** Preceded by a poss., *Your, His, Her, the King's, the Queen's*: used as an honorific title in speaking to or of a king, queen, emperor, or empress. ME. †**3.** The external magnificence befitting a sovereign –1667. **4.** Kingly or queenly dignity of look, bearing, or appearance 1531. **b.** *transf.* of natural objects, etc. 1555. **5.** Impressive stateliness of character, expression, or action 1597. **6.** *Religious Art.* A figure of the Father or the Son (occas. the Virgin Mary) represented in glory within a nimbus [1485], 1847.

1. A man who..was known to have free access to m. MACAULAY. **b.** That far-beaming blaze of M. MILT. **2.** *Your M.*, a respectful substitute for *you. His, Her M.* (abbrev. H.M.) may be either prefixed to *the King, the Queen, King Goerge V*, etc., or substituted for them; so *Their Majesties*, when more than one is meant. (In the syntax of this word, as of *highness, grace*, etc., the neut. pronouns *it, its, which*, cannot be used with reference to a foregoing (*Your, His, Her*) *Majesty*; either the titular form is repeated, or the pronoun is the same as if 'you', or 'the king', 'the queen' had been used instead of the periphrastic form.) **4.** Some great Potentate..such Majestie Invests him coming MILT. **b.** The Moon Rising in clouded Majestie MILT.

Majolica, maiolica (mădʒǫ·likă, măyǫ·likă). 1555. [– It. *majolica*, f. name of the island Majorca, formerly †*Majolica*, where according to J. C. Scaliger (1557) the best ware of this kind was made; cf. Fr. *majolique, maïolique*, †*majorique*.] Orig., a name for a fine kind of Italian pottery coated with an opaque white enamel ornamented with metallic colours; later, applied to all kinds of glazed Italian ware. Also, a modern imitation ware. Also *attrib.*

Major (mē^i·dʒəɹ), *sb.*[1] 1643. [– Fr. *major*, short for *sergent-major* SERGEANT-MAJOR, orig. a much higher grade than now.] **1.** In the army: An officer next below the rank of a lieutenant-colonel and above that of a captain. **2.** A full wig tied back in one curl. *Obs.* exc. *Hist.* 1753. **3.** *Angling.* An artificial salmon-fly 1867.

Major (mē^i·dʒəɹ), *a.* and *sb.*[2] ME. [– L. *major* compar. of *magnus* great. Some uses may depend on Fr. *majeur*, †*maiour*, learned var. of OFr. *maour*, acc. of *maire* MAYOR.] **A.** *adj.* **I.** = GREATER (but not followed by *than*). **1.** Distinctive epithet of the greater of two things, species, etc., that have a common designation; also applied to those members of a class that form a subdivision on the ground of being greater than the rest; opp. to *minor.* **2.** *Mus.* **a.** Applied to intervals greater by a chromatic semitone than those called *minor*, i.e. to the normal or perfect intervals; as *m. third, sixth, seventh* (and, occas. in recent use, *m. fourth* and *fifth*). Hence also applied to the note distant by a major interval from a given note. **b.** Applied to a common chord or triad containing a major third between the root and the second note; hence to a cadence ending on such a chord. **c.** Denoting those keys, or that mode, in which the scale has a major third (and also a major sixth and seventh). (In naming a key, *major* follows the letter, as *C major.*) 1694. **3.** That constitutes the majority; now only with *part, portion*, or the like. †Also, preponderating in quantity. 1594. †**4.** Paramount to all other claims. *Tr. & Cr.* V. i. 49. **5.** Following the sb. qualified (see below) 1616. **6.** Of full age, out of (one's) minority 1646.

1. *M. excommunication* (= greater e.), *orders, prophets.* †*M. Fellow* (Cambridge): a senior Fellow. *M. epilepsy*: epilepsy proper, as dist. from the 'petit mal'. *M. point* (Football): a goal (opp. to a *minor point*, i.e. a try). *M. alcaics*, etc.: the longer of the two types of alcaics, etc. *M. term* (Logic): the term which enters into the predicate of the conclusion of a syllogism. *M. premiss, proposition*: that premiss which contains the major term. *M. axis* (Math.): the axis (of a conic section) which passes through the foci; also called *transverse axis.* †*M. circle* (Astron.) = great circle (see CIRCLE *sb.* 2). **3.** When they are the m. part of a general assembly HOOKER. **5. a.** *Quart, Quint, Tierce m.*: see QUART *sb.*[2], QUINT *sb.*[2], TIERCE; also DRUM-MAJOR, SERGEANT-MAJOR, etc. **b.** *Bob- m.* (Bell-ringing): a bob (BOB *sb.*[5]) rung upon eight bells. **c.** In boys' schools, appended to a surname to distinguish the elder or senior of two boys of the same surname. Brown m. had a trick of bringing up unpleasant topics 1866.

B. *sb.* **1.** A 'major' individual of a specified class 1626. **2.** *Logic.* The major premiss in a syllogism 1530. **3.** Short for *major key, mode*, etc. (see A. 2) 1667. **4.** One who has 'come of age' 1616.

5. *U.S.* A subject to which special attention is given during a certain period of study 1890. Hence **Ma·jor** *v. intr.* (*U.S.*), to take, or qualify *in*, a m. 1927.

‖**Majorat** (maʒora). 1827. [– Fr. *majorat* – med.L. *majoratus* right of primogeniture (in late L. 'leading position'), f. L. *major*; see prec., -ATE[1].] *Continental Law.* The right of primogeniture; also, an estate going with this right.

†**Majorate,** *v. rare.* 1656. [– *majorat-*, pa. ppl. stem of late and med.L. *majorare* enlarge; see MAJOR *a.*, -ATE[3].] To make greater; to cause to increase or develop –1660. So †**Majora·tion** 1626–73.

Major-domo (mē^i·dʒəɹ,dō^u·mo). 1589. [Earliest forms *maior-*, *mayordome* – (partly through Fr. *mayordome*) Sp. *mayordomo*, It. *maggiordomo* – med.L. *major domus* (*domūs*, gen. of *domus* house) highest official of the royal household under the Merovingians, 'mayor of the palace'. Cf. earlier *majores domus regiæ* at the court of Theodoric (Cassiodorus).] In early use, the chief official of an Italian or Spanish princely household, often having some functions of a minister of state; later, applied to the head servant of a wealthy household in foreign countries, and (joc.) to an English house-steward or butler.

Ma·jor-ge·neral. 1642. [– Fr. *major général*, where *major* is sb. and *général* adj. The fuller form *sergeant-major general* is earlier (XVI) in Eng. use.] **1.** An officer of the lowest grade of general officers, ranking below a lieutenant-general. **2.** *Hist.* One of the officers placed in command of an administrative district under Cromwell's system of military government (1655–1657).

Majority (mădʒǫ·riti). 1552. [– Fr. *majorité* – med.L. *majoritas*; see MAJOR *a.*, -ITY.] †**1.** The state or fact of being greater; superiority; pre-eminence –1741. **2.** The state of being 'major' or of age 1565. **3.** The greater number or part; more than half; *spec.* the larger party voting together in a deliberative assembly or electoral body 1691. **4.** The number by which, in voting, the votes cast on one side exceed those cast on the other 1743. †**5.** Ancestry. [After L. *majores* ancestors.] SIR T. BROWNE. **6.** [Prop. a distinct word; see MAJOR *sb.*[1]] The rank or office of a major 1760.

2. The M. of Mr. C. L. A..has been celebrated [etc.] 1867. **3.** In a House of Commons all things are determin'd by a M. POPE. *Absolute m.*: a majority that includes more than half of the votes cast or of the possible voters. *The m.*: the dead. *To join, go*, or *pass over to the m.* [After L. phr. *abiit ad plures.*] **4.** Carried by a very small m. THIRLWALL. **6.** Promoted to a half-pay m. 1900.

Majorize (mē^i·dʒərəiz), *v.* [f. MAJOR *sb.*[2] + -IZE.] *Rugby Football.* To convert a try into a goal, i.e. to increase the points from three to five.

Majorship (mē^i·dʒəɹʃip). 1717. [f. MAJOR *sb.*[1] + -SHIP.] The office or rank of a major; majority.

Majuscule (mădʒɒ·skiul). 1727. [– Fr. *majuscule* – L. *majusculus* somewhat larger, dim. of *major*, n. *majus*; see MAJOR *a.*, -CULE.] **A.** *adj.* †**a.** *Printing.* Of a letter: Capital. **b.** *Palæogr.* Of a letter: Large (whether capital or uncial). Also, written in majuscules. **B.** *sb.* †**a.** *Printing.* A large or capital letter. **b.** *Palæogr.* A large letter, whether capital or uncial. 1825.

Hence **Maju·scular** *a.* of the nature of a m.; composed of majuscules.

Make (mē^ik), *sb.*[1] *Obs.* exc. *dial.* [OE. *ġemaca*, corresp. to OS. *gimaco* fellow, equal, OHG. *gimahho* 'socius' :– WGmc. **ʒamako*; rel. to OE. *ġemæċċa* MATCH *sb.*[1]] **1.** An (or one's) equal, peer, match; one's like. **2.** A mate, companion. (*occas.* The opponent with whom a fighter is matched.) ME. **3.** Of animals, esp. birds: A mate (male or female) OE. **4.** Of human beings: A mate, consort; a husband or wife, lover or mistress ME.

4. Like a widdow hauing lost her m. SIDNEY.

Make (mē^{i}k), *sb.*[2] ME. [f. MAKE *v.*] †**1.** Doing, action –1535. **2.** The manner in which a thing is made. **a.** Style of construction, kind of composition ME. **b.** Form or composition, structure, constitution. Often of the body: Build. ME. **c.** Of immaterial things: Form, fashion; hence, sort, character, nature 1660. **3.** Mental or moral constitution, disposition, or character 1674. **4.** Kind, sort, species (*dial.*) 1740. **5.** The action or process of making or manufacture. Now *rare* exc. *techn.* 1743. **6.** Amount manufactured; quantity produced 1865. **7.** *Electr.* The action of making contact in an electric circuit; the position in which contact is made (in phr. *at m.*) 1875.

2. a. The caps and bonnets were of quite a new m. 1833. A slow m. of bromide paper 1889. **b.** A huge man, with the m. and muscles of a prize-fighter MRS. H. WARD. **3.** Deeming there were more in the World of my m. 1674. **5.** Qualified by poss. denoting the manufacturer, with implication of style or quality. Are these shoes your own m.? Phr. *On the m.*: intent on profit or advancement. *slang.* (orig. *U.S.*)

Make (mē^{i}k), *v.* Pa. t. and pple. **made** (mē^{i}d). [OE. *macian* = OFris. *makia*, OS. *makon* (Du. *maken*), OHG. *mahhōn* (G. *machen*) :– WGmc. **makōjan*, f. **mak-* fitting. Cf. MATCH *sb.*[1]]

I. 1. *trans.* To produce by combination of parts, or by giving a certain form to a portion of matter; to construct, frame, fashion, bring into existence. Also *absol.*, esp. in phr. *m. or mend.* **2.** To compose, write as the author (a book, poem, verses, poetry, etc.) ME. †Also *absol.* or *intr.* **b.** To draw up (a legal document) ME. **3.** To put together materials for (a fire) and light them ME. **4.** To set apart and prepare the site for (a garden, park, road, etc.) late ME.

1. The beaver makes its hole, the bee makes its cell 1852. That dress, made full. .suits you 1865. An Indian can m. almost anything out of bamboo 1859. Let me m. the tea DICKENS. Do you know who made you? MRS. STOWE. She. .said. .that you were made (= naturally fitted) for your vocation 1870. The drums were made of metal 1892. **2.** Would you. .have me marry a woman that makes verses? 1803. *absol.* I m. to please my selfe, and not for them WITHER. **b.** He may. . have time to make a written will 1797. **4.** How changed is here each spot man makes or fills! M. ARNOLD.

II. 1. To cause to exist; to produce by action, bring about ME. †**b.** Const. dat. of the person, or with *to*, *unto*: To cause to happen to; to cause to experience; to bring into a person's possession or power –1725. **2.** To give rise to; to have as a result or consequence ME. **3.** *Gram.* Of a word: To form (a case, tense, etc.) in a specified manner; to change into (a specified form) when inflected OE. **4.** To establish (a rule, etc.); to enact (a law); to impose (a rate); †to institute (a religious order, etc.) OE. †**b.** To arrange (a match) –1752. **5. a.** To appoint (an officer), ordain (a minister) ME. **b.** *Naut.* To promote in rank 1795. **c.** *gen.* To cause to become (what is specified by the object) 1594. **d.** To fix (a price). Now only *Comm.* 1567. **6.** To provide (a meal, feast), give (a dinner, etc.). *Obs.* exc. *arch.* OE. **7.** To form by collection of individuals (see below) ME. **8.** To bring forth; to have as a product ME. **9.** Used with const. *of* or *out of* to designate the action of causing what is denoted by the object of the prep. to become what is denoted by the object of the verb ME.

1. He makes a solitude, and calls it—peace! BYRON. To m. a corner in rice 1897. *To m. melody, minstrelsy*; *to m. a note*, etc.; *to m. ado*, (*a*) *commotion, fun, a fuss, game, an impression, a row, a sensation, sport, a stir*, etc.; *to m. room, way*: see the substantives. *To m. peace*: (*a*) to bring about a condition of peace. (*b*) to conclude a treaty of peace. **2.** One Fool makes many SWIFT. *To m. a difference. To m. work*: to occasion the necessity for work to be done; to give trouble. **4.** A receiving order is 'made' on the day it is pronounced, not when it is drawn up 1898. **5. a.** The fourme and maner of makynge and consecratynge, Bishoppes, Priestes and Deacons 1552. He [Rich. II] then made nine Knights, and created four Earls 1641. **b.** Frank is made. He was yesterday raised to the rank of Commander JANE AUSTEN. **c.** He was. .a man to make both friends and enemies J. H. NEWMAN. **6.** He made a feast, drank fierce and fast [etc.] M. ARNOLD. **7.** The greatest strength and power that he can m. SHAKS. *To make a head* (see HEAD *sb.*). *To m. a House*: to ensure the presence of the number (now 40) of members required to constitute a sitting of the House (of Commons). So *to m. a quorum. To m. a bag* (Sporting): to kill a number of game. *To m. the bag*: to contribute most of the total of the game killed. *To m. a book* (Betting): to arrange a series of bets on the same race or event, with odds calculated with a view to a gain on the whole transaction. **8.** *To m. water*, †*urine*: see the sbs. **9.** He is going to m. a night of it 1809. *To m. a business, practice, trade of*; *to m. an example, a fool of*; *to m. an ass, a beast, an exhibition of oneself*: see the sbs. *To m.* (much, little, something, nothing, etc.) *of*: to turn to (much or little) account. *To m. the best, the most of*: see BEST *sb.*, MOST *sb. To m. a hash, mess, muddle of*: to bungle (a business).

III. 1. To entertain (doubt, scruple, question, etc.) in the mind; to formulate mentally; to form (a judgement) ME. **b.** To recognize in classification (a certain number of kinds, species, etc.) 1562. **c.** *legal.* To formulate, set out (a case, title) 1883. **2.** Used with const. as in II. 9 in idiomatic expressions relating to questions of estimation, calculation, or meaning: see below ME. **3.** *Naut.* To descry or discern; to come in sight of 1565.

1. I m. no doubt every one. .has practised similar stratagems 1844. *To m.* (*great*, etc.) *account of*: to have a high opinion of. **b.** Our School-men. .m. nine kinds of bad Spirits BURTON. **c.** To m. a good title 1891. **2.** *To m. head or tail* (also *top or tail*) *of*, *to m. sense of*: see the sbs. *To m.* (much, little, nothing, etc.) *of*: to have a (high, low, etc.) opinion of; to value at a (high, low, etc.) rate; to treat with (much, no, etc.) consideration. *To m. much of*: often, to treat with marked courtesy and show of affection. *To m. nothing of* (doing something): to find no difficulty in or feel no scruples at. *To m. light of*: see LIGHT *a.*[1] III. 1. *To m. of* (intr.): = *to m. much of.* (*Obs.* exc. *dial.*) *What do you m. of that?*: what do you understand to be the meaning of that? **3.** We. .made the Coast of Galway, in Ireland, the 10th DE FOE.

IV. Said of constituent parts or material. **1.** To amount to. Also, of the latest item added, to bring up the sum to (a certain amount). ME. **2.** To be sufficient to constitute ME. **3.** To amount to, signify (much, little, nothing, etc.) in relation to the question in point. Const. *for*, *to*. Now *rare.* 1456. †**b.** Of arguments or evidence: To avail (much, little, etc.) *for*, *against* –1690. **4.** To count as, form, be (a part or unit in an aggregate, a particular member in a series) ME. **5.** To be the material or components of; to be made or admit of being made into ME. **6.** To become by development or training 1572.

1. Nine Taylors m. but one man 1672. Twice one makes two 1892. **2.** One swalowe maketh not sommer HEYWOOD. Worth makes the man POPE. **3.** The course which he intended made much for the glory of God A. V. *Transl. Pref.* ¶ 3. *To m. no matter* (somewhat *arch.*): not to matter. **4.** You came in and made the fourteenth 1892. *To m. one* (*of*): often, to take part in a combined action, be present at a meeting, etc.; also, to assimilate oneself to one's company. **5.** She was fit to have made a Spouse for Jupiter himself 1699. They [frogs] m. a good soup 1787. **6.** She will make him a good wife 1885.

V. 1. To gain, acquire, or earn (money, reputation, etc.) by labour, business, or the like. Const. *of*, *out of.* ME. **b.** To fetch (a certain price) 1868. **2.** *Cards.* To win (a trick); to play (a card) to advantage. Also *intr.* of a card: to take a trick. 1608. **b.** In games: To secure (a certain score); to score (a point in the game); to perform (a stroke) successfully 1680. **3.** To gain, put on (weight). Also of a tree, to produce a growth of (timber). *To m. water* (Naut.): to take in water by a leak. 1832.

1. *To m. a* (or *one's*) *fortune, capital out of, a living, a name* (for oneself): see the sbs. **2.** In the third round you m. your Queen HOYLE. His partner. .has his last trump drawn, and the ace and king of diamonds m. 'CAVENDISH'. **b.** He made ten fours, six threes, and two twos 1890.

VI. †**1.** To bring *to* a specified condition, reduce *to* –1692. **2.** *intr.* To attempt or 'offer' (*to do* something) 1880. **3.** With ellipsis of verb of motion: To prepare to go; to proceed in a certain direction 1488. **4.** To prepare (a bed) for sleeping in ME. **5.** To shut, close, bar (a door). Now *arch.* and *dial.* ME. **6.** *Cards.* To shuffle 1876. **7.** Naut. *To m. sail*: (*a*) to spread a sail or sails; hence, to set sail, to sail; (*b*) to spread additional sails 1450. **8.** To train (a hawk, dog, horse) ME. **9.** To secure the advancement of; to 'be the making of'; chiefly, to set up (*esp.* in *pass.*) ME.

1. Phr. †*To m. to death*; †*to m. away, out of the way, hence* = make away with. **2.** He makes to follow, then stops 1900. **3.** I made steadily but slowly towards them STEVENSON. **5.** M. the doores vpon a womans wit, and it will out at the casement SHAKS. **8.** A Setting-dog that he has *made* himself ADDISON. **9.** Bismarck has made Germany 1890. Phr. *To m. or mar* (occas. *to m. or break*): to cause either the complete success or ruin of (a person or thing). Also *absol.*

VII. 1. To cause to be, render OE. Also *absol.* **2.** With sb. as complement. **a.** To cause (a person or thing) to be or become (what is denoted by the complement) OE. **b.** *spec.* To appoint to the office of; to raise to the dignity of; to create (a person) a noble, etc. ME. **c.** To determine (a thing, occas. a person) to be (what is expressed by the complement); to set down as (a law, penalty, etc.) 1500. **d.** To transform into something else. Chiefly in *pass.*, after L. *fieri.* ME. **3.** To convert *into* 1583. **4.** To regard as, consider or compute to be; to represent as (so-and-so); to cause to appear as ME. **b.** *Naut.* To announce or indicate (a particular time) by sounding a bell or otherwise; often in the order *make it so* 1835.

1. His generosity made him courted by many dependents JOHNSON. I wish you had made (= arranged so as to pass through) London in your way LAMB. *To m. English*: to translate into English. *To m. even, fast, good, ready, sure, unready, void, waste*; *to m. it hot, warm, m. things lively*; *to m. oneself scarce, to m. ready, sure*: see the adjs. **2. a.** It's pity that fellow was not made a soldier 1603. **b.** She made Marlborough a duke 1890. **c.** I made it my pride to keep aloof STEVENSON. **d.** I will make the riuers Ilands *Isa.* 42:15. **3.** Fresh curds newly pressed, and made into little cheeses MORYSON. **4.** What time may you m. it, Mr. Twemlow? DICKENS. What do you make the time? I make it half-past five (*mod.*). Macbeth is not half so bad as the play makes him 1879. **b.** Noon was made; the captain dined STEVENSON.

VIII. Causative uses. **1.** To cause (something to happen); to bring it about *that*. *Obs.* exc. *arch.* OE. **2.** With obj. and inf.: To cause a person or thing to do something; to have something done to a person or thing (inf. without *to* when both *make* and the dependent verb are in the active voice; otherwise *arch.*) ME. **3.** To constrain *to do* something; to compel, force (now always without *to* bef. the inf. when *make* is active) 1592. **b.** with ellipsis of inf. (*colloq.*) 1888. **4.** To consider, represent, or allege *to* be or do something 1594.

2. I wonder what makes these Bells ring SWIFT. The two statements can hardly be made to agree (*mod.*). Phr. *To m. both ends meet* (END *sb.* Phrases 2), *one's hair stand on end*, etc. *To m. believe*: †(*a*) [after Fr. *faire croire*] to cause people to believe; (*b*) in mod. use (often with hyphen, *make-believe*), to pretend *to do* something; to simulate a belief *that*. **3.** He made me stay and sup with him 1662. **b.** The enemy will not play the game. .and there are none to m. him 1888. **4.** What do you m. that bird to be? 1825. Most of the Chronicles m. Richard die in 1026 FREEMAN.

IX. 1. †**a.** To work (a miracle); to commit (a crime, sin, fault), tell (a lie); to do (justice, mercy); to give (alms) –1715. **b.** To wage (WAR) ME. **c.** To perform (a bodily movement or gesture) ME. **d.** To enter into, conclude (a bargain, contract). So, *to m. a marriage* (now only *legal*). ME. **e.** *Eccl.*, in *to m. one's confession, one's communion.* Also, †to do (penance). ME. **f.** With reference to locomotion or travel (see below) ME. **g.** To deliver orally (a speech, an oration). **2.** In questions introduced by *what*, e.g. *What m. you here?* = What are you doing here? What is your business, right, or purpose? Now *arch.* ME. **3.** With sbs. expressing the action of vbs., *make* forms phrases equivalent to those vbs. (see exx. below) ME. **4.** To eat (a meal) 1542. **5.** To offer, present, render. Const. *to* or *dative.* ME. **b.** *Law.* Of a court, a judge: To render, give (a decision, judgement). Still *U.S.* 1804. **6.** To put forth (an effort) 1456. **7.** To incur, suffer (something undesirable) 1453. **8.** To accomplish (a distance) by travelling, etc. 1564. **b.** orig. *Naut.* To reach, arrive at (a place); *slang*, to catch (a train, etc.) 1624. **9.** In phrases like *to m.*

long hours (i.e. to work many hours a day). Also, *to m. good time*: to accomplish a distance in a short time. 1887.

1. b. To m. the campaign was the dearest wish of Harry's life THACKERAY. c. *To m. a* (or *one's*) *bow, m. a curtsy, m. a face (at), m. a leg, m. (an) obeisance, a salaam*, etc.: see the sbs. f. *To m. an excursion, an expedition, a journey, a tour, a trip, a voyage, to m. one's way, to m. a circuit*: see the sbs. 3. *To m. (one's) abode, an acquisition, an assertion, an award, a blunder, (an) excuse, a motion, (an) oath, a promise, (a) reply, a slip, a start, a venture, a vow*, etc. 4. He made his simple morning meal 1890. 5. *To m. amends, love, satisfaction*: see the sbs. *To m. head*: see HEAD *sb.* 7. *To m. shipwreck* (arch.), *a loss*. 8. I must m. the distance on foot 1899.

X. 1. *intr.* (the obj. *it* being omitted); in OE. with adv.; later with adj., in *to m. bold, free, merry*, etc. (see the adjs.). **2.** *To m. as if, as though* (arch. *as*): to behave as if; to pretend that ME. **3.** To have to do *with* (a person or thing); to interfere *in* (a matter). *dial.* 1564. **4.** *Naut.* Of the flood or ebb tide: To begin to flow or ebb; also, to be in progress. Hence of the tide: To flow towards the land; also, to flow in a specified direction. 1651. **5.** Of arguments, evidences, influences: To 'tell' (on one side or the other). Chiefly with *for, with, against*. 1892.

2. He..beckons, and makes as he would speak LONGF. 3. And so, Sir, pray don't meddle or m. with the maids 1756. 4. The tide made to the westward DE FOE. The ebb was now making 1883. 5. He had the highest opinion of..precedents—when they made in his own favour 1892.

In specialized senses with preps. **Make after —.** To pursue, follow (*arch.*). **M. against —. a.** To 'tell' against. †**b.** To go to attack. **M. at —.** To make a hostile movement towards. Now somewhat *arch.* **M. for —. a.** To operate in favour of; to favour, further, aid. **b.** To go in the direction of; also, to 'go for'. **M. to —.** †**a.** To tend to support; to be conducive to. †**b.** To be pertinent to. †**c.** To proceed towards. **M. with —.** †**a.** To side with. Of things: To tell in favour of. †**b.** To select as one's adversary.

With adverbs. **M. away.** (Now repl. in trans. senses by *make away with*.) †**a.** *trans.* To put out of the way, put to death; also, to put an end to (a person's life). †**b.** To destroy. †**c.** To alienate; to dispose of, get rid of. **d.** *intr.* To run away; = *make off* (c). **M. away** *with*. **a.** = prec. a. **b.** To remove from its rightful place or ownership; to get rid of; to squander; to destroy fraudulently. **M. in.** *intr.* To go in; to intervene; to join in a fray; in *Hawking*, (of the falconer), to go up to a hawk after it has killed. **M. off.** †**a.** *trans.* To dispose of. **b.** *Farming.* To fatten (lambs) for the market. **c.** *intr.* To depart suddenly, often with a disparaging implication; to hasten away; to decamp. **d.** *To m. off with*: to decamp with (something) in one's possession. **M. on.** *intr.* To proceed; to hasten on. **M. out. a.** To draw up (a list, a document, etc.); to make a draft of; to write out (a bill, cheque, etc.). **b.** (*a*) To succeed in accomplishing; to effect. Now *Sc.* (*b*) To manage, make shift *to do* something. Also *absol.* to get along; to get on (well, badly). Also *to m. it out*. Chiefly *U.S.* **c.** †To compensate; to eke out. Also *intr.* to make up, compensate *for*. **d.** To make complete; to get together with difficulty. **e.** To fill up (the time). ? *Obs.* **f.** To represent clearly or in detail; now only in *Art.* **g.** To demonstrate, prove. Also *colloq.* **h.** To represent, pretend. **i.** To arrive at an understanding of; to decipher. Also (with clause or obj. and inf.) to discover, find out. **j.** To succeed in perceiving or identifying. **k.** To start forth; to get away. ? Now only *dial.* **M. over. a.** *trans.* To transfer (*prop.* by a formal agreement) the possession of (a thing) *to* another. **b.** To remake, refashion. Now only *U.S.* **M. up.** †**a.** To build up; to repair by filling up gaps. **b.** (*a*) To make complete. Also, to raise (a sum) *to* a larger sum. (*b*) To make good; to supply (a deficiency). (*c*) *intr.* To compensate *for*, atone *for*. **c.** To fill up (a gap, etc.); to stop up (a passage, etc.); to shut up (a door, a house). Now chiefly *dial.* **d.** To wrap up (an article); to put together (a parcel) *of* goods. **e.** To put together into a particular form; to fit together (pieces) to form a garment; to make (cloth) into clothing; also quasi-*pass.* to admit of being made up; *trans.* to compound (medicines, etc.); to mix (dough); to get together (a company, a sum); *Printing*, to arrange into columns or pages; to add fuel to (a fire) so as to keep it up. **f.** To compile (a list, etc.); to concoct (a story, lie); to improvise (verses). **g.** Of component parts: To compose (a sum, total, or whole). **h.** To prepare (an actor) for his part by dressing him, giving him false hair, etc. Also *intr.* for *refl.* To prepare (a bed) for a particular occasion. Also, to 'do up' (a room) (? *local*). **i.** To set out the items of (an account) in order; to add up and balance (an account). **j.** *To m. up one's mind*: to come to a decision or conclusion. Hence, *to m. up one's mind for, to*, or *to do* (something): to be reconciled to the thought of, to be prepared for. **k.** To arrange (a marriage, a treaty, etc.); to settle (a dispute, etc.); *intr.* (also often *to m. it up*) to be reconciled after a dispute. **l.** *intr.* (*a*) To advance in a certain direction; now only in *to m. up to*, to draw near to. (*b*) *To m. up to* (fig.): to make advances to; to pay court or make love to.

Make-, the stem of MAKE *v.* in comb., as in **m.-play** = MAKE-SPORT; **-rhyme**, a phrase introduced merely for rhyme; **-talk**, something said for the sake of talking; **-way**, an event which leads up to another; etc.

Makebate (mē̆ⁱ·kbē̆ⁱt). 1529. [f. MAKE *v.* + BATE *sb.*[1]] One who or that which creates contention; a breeder of strife. †Also *attrib.*

Ma·ke-belie:f. *rare.* 1833. Substituted for next on the erron. assumption that *make-believe* is incorrect.

Ma·ke-believe. 1811. [The phr. *make believe* used subst.] **1.** Pretence. Also with *a* and *pl.* **2.** One who makes believe or pretends 1863. **3.** *attrib.* or *adj.* Of the nature of make-believe 1824.

1. Her mourning is all make-believe 1811. 3. Here again I am met with a make-believe reply GLADSTONE.

†**Ma·ke-game.** 1762. = MAKE-SPORT. –1817.

Ma·keless, *a.* *Obs.* exc. *dial.* ME. [f. MAKE *sb.*[1] + -LESS.] **1.** Matchless, peerless. **2.** Mateless ME.

Ma·ke-peace. 1516. [See MAKE *v.* II. 1.] A peace-maker.

Maker (mē̆ⁱ·kəɹ). ME. [f. MAKE *v.* + -ER[1].] **1.** One who makes, fashions, constructs, prepares for use, etc.; a manufacturer. **2.** Qualified by *the*, or an attrib. phr.: Applied to God as the Creator of the universe. (Now with capital M.) ME. **3.** One who brings about a condition, effect, state of mind, etc. ME. **4.** A poet. *Obs.* exc. *arch.* (Cf. Gr. ποιητής.) ME. **5.** 'The person who signs a promissory note' (Wharton).

2. Let vs knele before the Lorde oure m. COVERDALE *Ps.* 94[5]:6. †*To receive* or *take one's M.*: to make one's communion.

Make-ready. 1887. [f. phr. *make ready*.] *Printing.* The operation of making a form ready to be printed; the form so made ready, or the sheet or sheets used to effect this.

Makeshift (mē̆ⁱ·kˌʃift). 1565. [f. phr. *to make shift*.] †**1.** One given to making shifts; a shifty person, a rogue –1608. **2.** That with which one makes shift; a temporary and inferior substitute 1802. **3.** The action of making shift 1870. **4.** *attrib.* or *adj.* With which one makes shift 1683. **b.** *transf.* Characterized by makeshifts 1824.

2. The cottage was a sorry antediluvian makeshift of a building LAMB. 4. A make-shift dinner 1809.

†**Make-sport.** 1582. [See MAKE *v.* II. 1.] One who or that which provides sport for others; a laughing-stock –1661.

Ma·ke-up. 1821. [f. phr. *make up* (see MAKE *v.*).] **1.** The way in which anything is put together; composition, constitution. **2.** Chiefly *Theatr.* An appearance of face, dress, etc. assumed in impersonating a character 1858. **3.** *Printing.* The process of making up type into columns and pages; the matter so made up. Also, an editor's selection of articles to form a number of a periodical. 1852. **4.** A made-up story 1844. **5.** *attrib.* (sense 2) 1885.

1. Something in the..make-up of their clothes H. SPENCER.

Make-weight, makeweight (mē̆ⁱ·kˌwē̆ⁱt). 1695. [See MAKE *v.* IV. 1.] **1.** A small quantity added to make up a certain weight; *spec.* a small candle. **2.** *fig.* A person or thing of little account thrown in to make up a deficiency or fill a gap 1776. **3.** A counterpoise 1787. **4.** *attrib.* Serving as a make-weight 1701.

2. The mines..are now thrown in as a make-weight in the scale BURKE.

Maki (mē̆ⁱ·ki, mæ·ki). 1774. [– Fr., repr. Malagasy *maka*.] French name of the LEMUR.

Making (mē̆ⁱ·kiŋ), *vbl. sb.* [OE. *macung*, f. *macian*; see MAKE *v.* and -ING[1].] **1.** The action of MAKE *v.*; fabrication, production, preparation; institution, appointment; doing, performance (of an action); conversion into something; etc. Also occas., the process of being made. **2.** *spec.* in techn. uses: The training or bringing to the required condition (of an animal); the preparation (of hay); the curing (of fish) ME. †**3.** Poetical composition. Also *pl.* = poems. –1614. **4.** Advancement, success. *Obs.* exc. in *to be the m. of*: to be what ensures the success of. 1470. †**5.** The way in which a thing is made; 'make' –1669. **6.** *concr.* Something that has been made; a product of manufacture. Also, the quantity made at one time. ME. **b.** *pl.* Earnings, profits (*colloq.*) 1837. **7.** The material out of which something may be made; the potentiality of becoming something; in phr. *to have* or *to be the making(s of* 1613.

1. The m. of the world 1842, of a codicil 1891, of several engineers 1897. Phr. *Of* (so-and-so's) *m.* = made by (so-and-so); A poet of Nature's own m. CARLYLE. *In the m.*: used adjectively, to designate something as existing in an undeveloped state; Opinion in good men is but knowledge in the m. MILT. 7. She had all the Royall makings of a Queene SHAKS.

Comb. **m.-iron,** a kind of grooved chisel used by caulkers to finish off seams.

Making-up. 1593. In the senses of *make up* (see MAKE *v.*); completion; compounding; reconcilation; dressing up for the impersonation of a character; the balancing of accounts at the end of a period. Also *attrib.*

Mal- (mæl), *prefix*, formerly often written **male-** (but pronounced as one syllable), repr. Fr. *mal* adv. :– L. *male* ill, badly. It occurs orig. in adoptions from Fr., as *maltreat, malfeasance*; also, *maladroit, malcontent* (= the reverse of *adroit, content*), etc. In English formations it conveys the sense 'ill', 'wrong', 'improper(ly', as in *malpractice, malformation, malodorous*, etc.

Malabar (mæ·lăbāɹ), name of a sea-board district in the S.W. of India, used attrib.; as in **M. nut**, an acanthaceous plant, *Justicia adhatoda*; **M.-oil**, an oil obtained from the livers of various fishes found on the M. coast.

Malacaton, -catoon, var. ff. MELOCOTON.

Malacca (mălæ·kă). 1611. Name of a town and district on the Malay peninsula in the S.E. of Asia; used attrib.; as in **M. apple** = *Malay apple* (see MALAY *a.*); **M. cane** (also simply *Malacca*), a walking-cane of a rich brown colour, often clouded or mottled, made of the stem of the palm *Calamus scipionum*.

Malachite (mæ·lăkəit). 1567. [– OFr. *melochite* (mod. *malachite*) – L. *molochites* (Pliny) – Gr. μολοχῖτις, f. μολόχη, var. of μαλάχη MALLOW.] Hydrous carbonate of copper, occurring as a mineral of a green colour, susceptible of a high polish. Also, a specimen of this. **b.** *Blue m.* = AZURITE 1821. *Comb.* **M.-green,** (*a*) = malachite; (*b*) a dye of the colour of m.

Malaco- (mæ·lăko), comb. f. Gr. μαλακός soft, in many scientific terms, as: **Ma·lacoderm** [Gr. δέρμα skin] *Nat. Hist.* *a.* having a soft skin; *sb.* a soft-skinned animal, esp. of the *Malacodermata* (*-derma, -dermi*), a division in old classification of reptiles, of beetles, and of *Anthozoa* 1835; hence **Malacode·rmatous** *a.* **Ma·lacolite** [-LITE] *Min.* = DIOPSIDE 1823. **Malaco·logy** [Fr. *malacologie*], that branch of zoology which treats of molluscs 1836; hence **Malacolo·gical** *a.*; **Malaco·logist**, one versed in m. **Ma:lacoptery·gian** [Gr. πτέρυξ wing] *a.* of or pertaining to the *Malacopterygii* or soft-finned fishes; *sb.* one of these; so **Ma:lacoptery·gious** *a.* ‖**Malaco·steon** [Gr. ὀστέον bone] *Path.* = OSTEOMALACIA 1801. **Malaco·stomous** [mod.L. *malacostomus*; Gr. στόμα mouth] *a.* of fishes: having a soft mouth (i.e. toothless jaws) 1753. **Malaco·stracan** [Gr. μαλακόστρακα; ὄστρακον shell] *a.* of or belonging to the *Malacostraca*, an order of *Crustacea*; *sb.* one of these 1835; so **Malaco·stracous** *a.* **Malacozo·ic** [Gr. ζῷον animal] *a.* applied by Huxley to the series of animals from the *Polyzoa* to the *Mollusca* 1877.

Ma:ladapta·tion. 1877. [f. MAL- + ADAPTATION.] Faulty adaptation.

Maladive (mæ·lădiv), *a.* *rare.* 1481. [– (O)Fr. *maladif, -ive*, f. *malade* sick; see MALADY, -IVE.] Sickly.

Maladju·stment. 1833. [f. MAL- + ADJUSTMENT.] Faulty adjustment.

Maladminister (mælǣdmi·nistəɹ), *v.* 1705.

[f. MAL- + ADMINISTER.] To administer inefficiently or badly.

Maladministration (mæ:lædministrēi·ʃən). Also †**male-**. 1644. [f. MAL- + ADMINISTRATION.] Faulty administration; inefficient or improper management of affairs, esp. public affairs.

‖**Maladresse** (mælădre·s). Also **maladdress.** 1804. [Fr., f. *maladroit* (see next) after *adroit, adresse.*] Want of dexterity or tact; awkwardness.

Maladroit (mæ·lădroit), *a.* 1685. [– Fr. *maladroit*, f. *mal* MAL- + *adroit* ADROIT.] Wanting in adroitness; awkward, bungling. Hence **Ma·ladroit-ly** *adv.*, **-ness.**

Malady (mæ·lădi). ME. [– (O)Fr. *maladie*, f. *malade* sick, ill :– Rom. **male habitus* 'badly conditioned', in med.L. *male habēre* be ill (IX), i.e. L. *male* badly + *habitus* (cf. Massurius Sabinus, *equum nimis strigosum et male habitum*), pa. pple. of *habēre* have, hold.] **1.** †Ill health, disease; an ailment, a disease. **2.** *fig.* A morbid or depraved condition; something that calls for a remedy ME.

1. Abstinence ingenders maladies SHAKS. **2.** Astrology is another m. of weak minds 1786.

‖**Mala fide** (mēi·le fəi·di). 1681. [L., = 'in bad faith'. Cf. BONA FIDE.] *adv.* In bad faith. *adj.* Chiefly with agent-nouns: Acting in bad faith; pretended, sham. So **Ma·la fi·des** *Law*, bad faith, intent to deceive 1681.

Malaga (mæ·lăgă). 1608. Name of a seaport in the south of Spain. Used *attrib.* in *M. raisins, sack, wine.* Also as sb. (short for *M. wine*), a white wine exported from M.

Ma·lagash. 1711. [See next.] Var. of next.

Malagasy (mælăgæ·si). 1835. [f. *Malegass, -gash*, vars. of *Madegass, -cass*, after or parallel with Fr. *malgache, madécasse*, adj. f. the name of the island, which is found as *Madagascar* in XVII.] *adj.* and *sb.* Of or pertaining to, a native of, Madagascar. **b.** The language spoken there.

Malaguetta (mælăge·tă). 1568. [Early forms *manguetta, manegete, mellegette* – Fr. *maniguette*, †*-guete*, alt. of *malaguette* – Sp. *malagueta*; cf. med.L. *melegeta*, perh. dim. of It. *melica* millet.] The capsules or seeds of *Amomum meliguetta* of W. Africa, used as a spice and in medicine; also known as *Grains of Paradise* and *Guinea Grains.* Also *attrib.*, as *m. pepper.*

‖**Malaise** (mæ·lēiz, Fr. malẹ̄z). 1768. [Fr., f. OFr. *mal* bad, ill (L. *malus*) + *aise* EASE *sb.*] A condition of bodily discomfort, *esp.* a condition of lassitude, without the development of specific disease. Also *fig.*

Malander, mallender (mæ·lĕndəɹ). Now only *pl.* late ME. [– (O)Fr. *malandre* :– L. *malandria* (pl.) pustules on the neck.] A dry scabby eruption behind the knee in horses.

Malapert (mæ·lăpə̄rt). *Obs.* exc. *arch.* late ME. [– OFr. *malapert*, f. *mal-* (indicating the opposite) + *apert*, var. of *espert* EXPERT, but apprehended as if f. MAL- improperly + *apert* bold, PERT.] **A.** *adj.* Presumptuous, impudent, saucy. **B.** *sb.* A presumptuous or saucy person 1622.

His malepert boldnes might peraduenture be punished SIR T. MORE. Hence **Ma·lapert-ly** *adv.*, **-ness.**

Malaprop (mæ·lăprǫp). 1823. [f. Mrs. *Malaprop* (after MALAPROPOS), in Sheridan's play, *The Rivals* (1775).] *sb.* = MALAPROPISM. *adj.* = MALAPROPIAN. So **Malapropian** (mælăprǫ·piăn), *a.* of the nature of, or given to, malapropisms 1860. **Malapropism** (mæ·lăprǫpiz'm), ludicrous misuse of words; an instance of this 1849.

Mr. Lewes is sending what a Malapropian friend once called a 'missile' to Sara GEO. ELIOT.

Malapropos (malaprọpo, mælæprǒ·pōu·), *adv.*, *a.*, and *sb.* Also written **mal à propos, mal-a-propos, mal apropos,** etc. 1668. [Fr. *mal à propos*, f. *mal* ill + *à* to + *propos* purpose; see MAL- and APROPOS.] **A.** *adv.* In an inopportune or awkward manner; unseasonably, inappropriately. **B.** *adj.* Inopportune, inappropriate 1711. **C.** *sb.* Something inopportune or inappropriate 1868. Hence **Malapropo·ism** = MALAPROPISM 1834.

Malar (mēi·lăɹ), *a.* (and *sb.*) 1782. [– mod.L. *malaris*, f. L. *mala* jaw, cheek-bone, cheek; see -AR¹.] **1.** Of or belonging to the cheek. **2.** *sb.* (or *absol.* = *m. bone*) The cheek-bone 1866.

Malaria (mălē·riă). 1740. [– It. *mal' aria* for *mala aria* 'bad air'.] **a.** The unwholesome atmosphere which results from the exhalations of marshy districts. **b.** (= *m. fever*) A febrile disease (formerly attributed to this) caused by a blood-parasite (*m. parasite*), conveyed by the bite of a mosquito. Also *transf.* and *fig.*

Ma:lassimila·tion. 1865. [MAL-.] Imperfect assimilation; *esp.* in *Path.* imperfect absorption of nutriment into the system.

Malate (mēi·lĕt). 1794. [f. MALIC *a.* + -ATE⁴.] *Chem.* A salt of malic acid.

†**Malax,** *v.* late ME. [– L. *malaxare*; see MALAXATE.] *trans.* To rub or knead (a plaster, etc.) to softness; *gen.* to soften –1764.

Malaxate (mæ·lækseit), *v.* 1657. [– *malaxat-*, pa. ppl. stem of L. *malaxare* – Gr. μαλάσσειν make soft; see -ATE³.] *trans.* To soften by kneading or mixing, or by means of an emollient. Hence **Malaxa·tion,** the action of reducing to a soft mass by kneading or rolling. **Ma·laxator,** a mixing-mill.

Malay (mălēi·). 1598. [repr. the native name *malāyu.*] **A.** *sb.* **1.** One of a race predominating in Malacca and the Eastern Archipelago, a Malayan. **2.** The Malay language 1598. **3.** Short for *M. fowl* 1830.

1. In person the Malays are short, squat, and robust 1840.

B. *adj.* Of, pertaining to, or characteristic of the Malays or their country 1779. **b.** In names of plants, animals, etc., e.g. **M. apple,** a myrtaceous tree, *Jambosa* (*Eugenia*) *malaccensis*, with an edible fruit; **M. fowl,** a large variety of domestic fowl introduced from the Malay Peninsula; etc. 1820.

Hence **Mala·yan** *a.* and *sb.*, in same senses.

Malayalam (mælăyā·læm). [Native name.] Name of a cultivated Dravidian dialect, closely related to Tamil.

Malaysian (mălēi·siăn), *a.* 1883. [f. *Malaysia*, i.e. the Malay archipelago + -AN.] Of or belonging to Malaysia.

Malco·nduct. Also †**male-.** 1741. [MAL-.] Improper conduct; *esp.* improper or dishonest administration of an office, business, etc.

Ma:lco:nforma·tion. 1776. [MAL-.] Bad or faulty conformation.

Malcontent (mæ·lkǫ̆ntent). Also †**male-.** 1581. [– (O)Fr. *malcontent*; see MAL-, CONTENT *a.*] **A.** *adj.* Discontented, dissatisfied. Now chiefly in political use: Inclined to rebellion or mutiny; restless and disaffected 1586.

You stand pensiue, as halfe malecontent SHAKS.

B. *sb.* **1.** A malcontent person (see A.) 1581. †**2.** The state of being discontented. [Really a distinct word; see CONTENT *sb.*] –1663.

2. A necessity of sadnesse and malecontent MILT. Hence †**Malconte·nted** *a.*, †**-ly** *adv.*, †**-ness.**

Male (mēil). [ME. *masle* – OFr. *male, masle* (mod. *mâle*) :– L. *masculus* (f. *mas* male person), whence MASCULINE *a.*]

A. *adj.* **I. 1.** Of or belonging to the sex which begets offspring, or performs the fecundating function. Used: **a.** of persons ME. **b.** of animals ME. **c.** of certain plants (of diœcious species) the flowers of which contain only the fecundating organs ME. **d.** of certain plants to which sex was formerly attributed on account of some peculiarity of habit, colour, etc. 1562. **2.** Of or pertaining to a man or men, or to male animals; peculiar to men; composed or consisting of men 1631. **b.** Adapted to or meant for the use of a man 1788. †**3.** *transf.* **a.** Said of precious stones, on account of depth, brilliance, or other accident of colour; also of other stones, with reference to their hardness or other esteemed qualities. [Gr. ἄρρην, L. *masculus.*] –1855. †**b.** Used to distinguish the harder and more compact kind of sand or gravel 1601–1813. †**4. Male incense.** [So in L. and Fr.] A superior quality of incense, known by the greater size of the 'tears' in which it is collected; frankincense 1598–1727. **5.** Of rhyme: see under MASCULINE *a.* 3. 1581. **6.** Said of the external layer of bark on a tree 1884.

1. a. Caine, the first male-childe SHAKS. Phr. *Heir, issue, line, tail m.* (Law). **b.** There is no more mercy in him, then there is milke in a male-Tyger SHAKS. **c.** The catkins which appear in January are the m. parts of a nut-tree 1791. **d. M. fern,** *Asplenium* (*Nephrodium*) *filix-mas.* **2.** They keep as good female company as I do m. SWIFT. **b.** M. Hospital 1828. **3.** Lordly male-sapphires BROWNING.

II. A distinctive epithet for that part of an instrument or contrivance which is adapted to penetrate or fill the corresponding female part 1669.

Phr. *M. gauge*: the outer gauge or screw of a printing-press. *M. screw*: the spiral pin or rod which fits the spirally bored circular socket of the female screw.

B. *sb.* **1.** A male animal ME. **2.** A male person; a boy or man. Only in expressed or implied antithesis with *female* ME.; *occas.* a male plant 1548. **3.** *Comb.* **m. impersonator,** a female who personates a male on the stage.

Male, obs. f. MAIL.

Male-: see MAL-.

Maledicent (mælĭdəi·sĕnt). Now *rare.* 1599. [– *maledicent-*, pr. ppl. stem of L. *maledicere* speak evil of; see -ENT.] **A.** *adj.* Given to evil-speaking; of the nature of evil-speaking, slanderous. **B.** *sb.* One who speaks evil of another 1657. Hence †**Maledi·cency,** the practice of speaking evil 1653.

Maledict (mæ·lĭdikt), *a.* (*sb.*) *arch.* 1550. [– L. *maledictus*, pa. pple. of *maledicere*; see prec.] Accursed. Also as *sb.*

Malediction (mælĭdi·kʃən). 1447. [– L. *maledictio*, f. as prec.; see -ION. Cf. Fr. *malédiction.*] **1.** The utterance of a curse; the being under a ban or curse. **2.** Reviling, slander; the condition of being reviled or slandered 1526.

1. I. .loaded him with maledictions SCOTT.

Malefa·ction. 1602. [– med.L. *malefactio*, f. after late L. *benefactio* BENEFACTION, partly deduced from *malefactor* (see next). In late and med.L. *malefactio* = swooning, also (med.L.) illness.] Evil-doing; an instance of this.

Malefactor (mæ·lĭfæktəɹ). 1440. [– (partly through OFr. *malfaicteur*) L. *malefactor*, f. *malefacere*, f. *male* MAL- + *facere* do.] **1.** One guilty of a heinous offence against the law; a felon, a criminal. Also *transf.* **2.** An evil-doer; one who does ill towards another; opp. to *benefactor* 1483. So **Ma·lefactress,** a female m. 1647.

Malefeazance: see MALFEASANCE.

Malefic (măle·fik). 1652. [– L. *maleficus*, f. *male* ill; see -FIC.] **A.** *adj.* Productive of disaster or evil; baleful. Said esp. of stellar influences and magical practices. **B.** *sb.* **a.** *Astrol.* A malefic aspect or body. †**b.** A malefic doer; a malign wizard. 1652. So †**Male·fical** *a.*, **-ly** *adv.*

Malefice (mæ·lĭfis). late ME. [– L. *maleficium* evil deed, sorcery, f. *maleficus* MALEFIC. Cf. (O)Fr. *maléfice* (XIV) sorcery, which may be partly the source.] **1.** A wicked enchantment; sorcery (*arch.*) **2.** An evil deed; mischief. *Obs.* or *arch.* 1591. †**3.** *Astrol.* Malefic character. GAULE.

Maleficent (măle·fisĕnt), *a.* 1678. [Analogical formation on earlier *maleficence* (XVI), after *malevolent, malevolence.*] **1.** Of things, etc.: Working harm, hurtful, malefic. Const. *to.* **2.** Of persons, etc.: Wrong-doing, criminal 1760. So **Male·ficence.**

†**Malefi·cial,** *a.* 1601. [In XVII f. MALEFICE, or its source L. *maleficium*; see -AL¹, -IAL; cf. *malefical* (see MALEFIC). In mod. use an analogical f. after BENEFICIAL.] Malefic, maleficent –1831.

Malefi·ciate, *v.* 1621. [– med.L. *maleficiare* bewitch, f. L. *maleficium*; see MALEFICE, -ATE³.] *trans.* To bewitch; *spec.* to render impotent by spells –1693. Hence †**Maleficia·tion.**

Maleic (mălī·ik), *a.* 1838. [– Fr. *maléique* (Pelouze 1834), formed by alt. of *malique* MALIC, to indicate that this acid was related to malic acid.] *Chem.* In *m. acid*: a product of the dry distillation of malic acid.

†**Malengin.** late ME. [– (O)Fr. †*malengin*, f. *mal* evil + *engin* contrivance; see ENGINE

sb.] Evil machination, ill intent; fraud, deceit, guile –1726.

‖**Mal-entendu** (malantandü). 1780. [Fr., f. *mal* ill + *entendu* understood.] A misunderstanding.

‖**Maleo** (mæ·lĭ,o). 1869. [Native name.] A megapode bird, *Megacephalon maleo*, inhabiting Celebes.

Maletolt. *Obs.* exc. *Hist.* Also **-tot(e**, etc. 1514. [– AFr. *maletoute*, OFr. *maletote, maltolte, maletoute* (mod. *maltôte*), repr. med.L. *mala tolta*, i.e. *mala* fem. evil, bad, *tolta* (unjust) tax, f. *tolt-*, med.L. pa. ppl. stem of L. *tollere*, OFr. *tolir, toudre* take.] *Law.* An unjust or burdensome tax.

Malevolence (măle·vŏlĕns). 1489. [– OFr. *mali-, malevolence* – L. *malevolentia*; see next, -ENCE.] The attribute of being malevolent; ill-will. So †**Malevolency.**

Malevolent (măle·vŏlĕnt), *a.* (*sb.*) 1509. [– OFr. *malivolent* or L. *mali-, malevolens, -ent-*, f. *male* ill + *volens, -ent-* willing, pr. pple. of *velle* will, wish.] **1.** Of persons, etc.: Desirous of evil to others; indicative of ill-will; disposed or addicted to ill-will. †**b.** *transf.* 1719. †**2.** *Astrol.* Exercising a baleful influence. Also *transf.* and *fig.* –1696. †**3.** *sb.* A person of evil wishes or designs –1670.

1. b. To secure plants from m. winds 1719. Hence **Male·volently** *adv.* So †**Male·volous** *a.* (in sense 1) 1536–1727.

Malfeasance (mælfī·zăns). Also †**male-.** 1696. [– AFr. *malfaisance*, f. *mal* MAL- + OFr. *faisance* act, action, also spec. FEASANCE. Cf. MISFEASANCE, NON-FEASANCE.] **1.** *Law.* Evil-doing; *spec.* official misconduct in public affairs. **2.** *gen.* Wrong-doing; an instance of this 1856. So **Malfea·sant,** a malefactor 1882.

Malforma·tion. 1800. [MAL-.] Faulty or anomalous formation or structure of parts. Also *fig.* So **Malfo·rmed** *a.* badly formed; marked by m.; also *transf.* and *fig.* 1817.

‖**Malgré** (malgre), *prep.* 1608. [Fr.; see MAUGRE.] In spite of, notwithstanding. Also †‖**Malgra·do** [It.] 1590.

Malic (mē^{i}·lik), *a.* 1797. [– Fr. *malique*, f. L. *malum* apple; see -IC.] *Chem.* In *m. acid*: an acid, $C_4H_6O_5$, derived from the apple, the berries of the mountain-ash, and other fruits.

Malice (mæ·lis), *sb.* ME. [– (O)Fr. *malice* – L. *malitia*, f. *malus* bad; see MAL-, -ICE.] †**1.** Badness; wickedness –1605. †**2.** Harmfulness; harmful action or effect. Of a disease, poison, etc.: Virulence. –1685. **3.** Active ill-will or hatred. In mod. use occas.: Desire to tease (cf. Fr. *malice*). ME. **b.** *fig.* Attributed to fortune, or impersonal agencies 1660. †**4.** Malicious conduct; a malicious act or device –1669. **5.** *Law.* Wrongful intention; *esp.* that kind of evil intent which aggravates the guilt of certain offences (esp. of murder) 1547.

1. It seemeth the children of time do take after the nature and m. of the father BACON. **2.** Our Cannons m. vainly shall be spent SHAKS. **3.** God forbid any M. should preuayle SHAKS. Phr. *To bear m.*: to feel ill-will; now usually, to keep alive revengeful feelings on account of some injury. **4.** *Cor.* II. ii. 36. **5.** In the best known definitions of m. it is scarcely distinguishable from intention MARKBY. *M. aforethought* := *malice prepense* (see PREPENSE *a*).

†**Ma·lice,** *v.* 1547. [f. prec.] **1.** *trans.* To regard with malice –1694. **2.** *intr.* To entertain malice –1592.

Malicious (măli·ʃəs), *a.* ME. [– OFr. *malicius* (mod. *malicieux*) – L. *malitiosus*; see MALICE *sb.*, -OUS.] **1.** Given to malice; addicted to sentiments or acts of ill-will. Now occas.: Inclined to tease. Also *absol.* **2.** Proceeding from or characterized by malice. Earlier often: †Evil, wicked. Now occas.: 'Mischievous'. ME. **3.** *Law.* Characterized by 'malice prepense', as in *m. damage, prosecution, waste*, etc. 1530. †**4.** *Med.* Malignant, virulent –1720. †**5.** Artful –1590.

1. Either you must Confesse your selues wondrous M., Or be accus'd of Folly SHAKS. **2.** The private whisper of a m. groundlesse lye 1651. Hence **Mali·cious-ly** *adv.*, **-ness.**

Malign (mălai·n), *a.* ME. [– OFr. *maligne*, fem. of (O)Fr. *malin*, or its source L. *malignus*, f. *malus* evil. For the ending, cf. *benign.*] **1.** Characterized by ill-will; desiring, or rejoicing in, the suffering of others; malignant, malevolent. Now *rare.* 1450. **2.** Of things: Baleful ME. **3.** Of diseases: Malignant 1541. **4.** *Astrol.* Having a baleful influence. Also *transf.* 1605.

1. Some tempers are so m., that they wish ill to all, and believe ill of all 1674. **2.** A struggle between two forces, the one beneficent, the other m. BRYCE. **3.** Old and maligne vlcers GALE. **4.** Saturn which is a planet Maligne BACON. **Mali·gn-ly** *adv.*

Malign (mălai·n), *v.* late ME. [– OFr. *malignier* – late L. *malignare* contrive maliciously, f. *malignus*; see prec.] †**1.** *intr.* To speak evil, entertain malice, plot, contrive (*against*). †**2.** *trans.* To regard with hatred. Also, to resent, take amiss. –1667. †**3.** To regard with envy; to begrudge –1706. **4.** To speak ill of (one), to traduce, slander 1647.

3. Strangers conspired together against him, and maligned him in the wildernesse *Ecclus.* 45:18. The envious Gods Maligne our happinesse 1638. **4.** No religion was ever so maligned, age after age 1758.

Mali·gnance. 1641. [See -ANCE.] = next.

Malignancy (măli·gnănsi). 1601. [f. MALIGNANT *a.*; see -ANCY.] The quality of being malignant. **1.** Disaffection to rightful authority. *Obs.* exc. *Hist.* [Cf. MALIGNANT B.) 1644. **2.** *Path.* Of a disease, tumour, etc. 1685. **3.** Baleful character; unpropitiousness; noxiousness 1601. **4.** Malignant disposition; intense malevolence; desire to inflict injury or suffering 1640. **5.** An instance of malignancy 1652.

1. The m., which at that time began to appear in people MAY. **3.** My starres shine darkely ouer me; the malignancie of my fate, might perhaps distemper yours SHAKS. **4.** Penetration gives her more artifice and m. 1706.

Malignant (măli·gnănt), *a.* and *sb.* 1542. [– *malignans, malignant-*, pr. pple. of late L. *malignare*; see MALIGN *v.*, -ANT.] **A.** *adj.* †**1.** Disposed to rebel; disaffected, malcontent –1659. Also *absol.* **b.** *spec.* Applied between 1641 and 1660 by the supporters of the Parliament and the Commonwealth to their adversaries 1641. **2.** Of a disease: Virulent; exceptionally contagious or infectious. Now used to differentiate a definite variety of a disease, as *m. cholera, m. smallpox*, etc. 1568. **3.** Having an evil influence. Chiefly *Astrol.*, etc. = MALIGN. Formerly also: Poisonous, deleterious. 1591. **4.** Characterized by malignity; keenly desirous of the misfortune of another, or of others generally 1592.

1. In Aleppo once, Where a m., and a Turbond-Turke Beate a Venetian SHAKS. *The church m.*: applied to the followers of antichrist, and by early Protestants to the Church of Rome. **2.** *M. growth, tumour*: in mod. use one which tends to spread and recur and so prove fatal. **3.** O m. and ill-boading Starres SHAKS. A witch. . charged with having. . a m. touch 1765. **4.** So shall the Worlde goe on, To good m., to bad men benigne MILT.

B. *sb.* A malcontent 1597. **b.** Used by opponents as a designation for a supporter of Charles I against the Parliament; a Royalist, Cavalier. Also, applied by Puritans and Covenanters to their eccl. opponents. Now *Hist.* 1642.

Hence **Mali·gnantly** *adv.* in a m. manner.

Maligner (mălai·nəɹ). late ME. [f. MALIGN *v.* + -ER[1].] One who maligns; a traducer, a slanderer.

Malignify (măli·gnifəi), *v. rare.* 1613. [f. L. *malignus* MALIGN *a.*; see -FY.] *trans.* To render malign.

Malignity (măli·gnĭti). late ME. [– OFr. *malignité* or L. *malignitas*, f. *malignus*; see MALIGN *a.*, -ITY.] **1.** Deep-rooted ill-will; persistent desire to cause suffering to another person; propensity to this feeling. **b.** *pl.* Malignant feelings or actions 1529. **2.** Wickedness, heinousness (*arch.*) 1534. **3.** Noxiousness (*arch.*) 1605. **4.** Of diseases, etc.: Malignant character 1646.

1. Thanne comth malignitee thurgh which a man anoyeth his neighebor priuely CHAUCER. **3.** The m. of the atmosphere 1858.

Malinger (măli·ŋgəɹ), *v.* 1820. [Back-formation f. next.] *intr.* To pretend illness, or to produce or protract disease, in order to escape duty; said esp. of soldiers and sailors.

Malingerer (măli·ŋgərəɹ). 1768 (in form **maligner**), 1785 (**malingeror**). [app. f. (O)Fr. *malingre* (as a personal name XIII), perh. f. *mal-* MAL- + *haingre* weak, thin, prob. of Gmc. origin.] One who malingers.

Malison (mæ·lisən). *arch.* and *dial.* ME. [– OFr. *malison, maleison* – L. *maledictio, -on-* MALEDICTION; cf. BENISON and see -ISON.] A curse, malediction.

Malkin, mawkin (mǭ·kin). *Obs.* exc. *dial.* ME. [dim. of ME. *Malde* Maud, Matilda (OFr. *Mahault* – Gmc. *Mahthildis* 'strength-battle'); see -KIN.] †**1.** A female personal name; applied typically to a woman of the lower classes –1670. †**b.** Proper name of a female spectre or demon –1605. **2.** A slut, slattern; *occas.* a lewd woman 1586. **3.** A mop; a bundle of rags fastened to the end of a stick ME. **b.** *Naut.* 'A joint-staff sponge, for cleaning out a piece of ordnance' (Smyth). **4.** A scarecrow (also *fig.*); a guy 1633. **5.** A designation, or quasi-proper name for: **a.** a cat (*dial.*) 1673; **b.** a hare (*Sc.* and *n. dial.*) 1724.

Mall[1] (mǭl). †Also **mell, maul.** 1662. [A use of *mall* MAUL *sb.*[1], in certain XVII senses of Fr. *mail.* Cf. PALL-MALL.] **1.** The mallet used in the game of 'mall' or 'pall-mall'; = PALL-MALL 1. **2.** The game; = PALL-MALL 2. 1675. **3.** The alley in which the game was played; = PALL-MALL 3. 1687. **4.** *The Mall* (mæl): a walk bordered by trees in St. James's Park, London, which was orig. a 'mall' in sense 3. 1674. **b.** *transf.* A sheltered walk serving as a promenade 1737.

Mall[2]: see MAUL, MAW.

Mallard (mæ·lăɹd). ME. [– OFr. *mallard*, (also mod.) *malart*, prob. for **maslart*, f. *masle* MALE; see -ARD.] **1.** The male of the wild duck (*Anas boscas*). †Formerly also = DRAKE[2]. **2.** Used for either sex ME. **b.** The flesh of this bird 1440. **3.** *The M.*: a festival celebrated on the 14th Jan. at All Souls College, Oxford 1632.

Malleable (mæ·lĭ,ăb'l), *a.* late ME. [– OFr. *malleable* – med.L. *malleabilis*, f. L. *malleare* to hammer, f. *malleus*; see MAUL *sb.*[1], -ABLE.] **1.** That can be deprived of form by hammering or pressure, without a tendency to return to it, or to fracture; applied to metals, etc. **2.** *transf.* and *fig.* Capable of being fashioned or adapted 1612.

1. *M. iron*: iron which has been decarburized by oxidation under prolonged heat and rendered capable of being malleated in a slight degree. Hence **Ma:lleabi·lity, Ma·lleableness,** the property of being m. **Ma·lleableize, ma·lleablize** *v. trans.* to render m.

Mallear (mæ·lĭ,ăɹ), *a.* 1889. [f. MALLEUS + -AR[1].] Pertaining to the malleus.

Malleate (mæ·lĭ,ĕt), *a.* 1884. [f. MALLEUS + -ATE[2].] *Zool.* Furnished with a malleus.

Malleate (mæ·lĭ,e^{i}t), *v.* Now *rare.* 1597. [– *malleat-*, pa. ppl. stem of L. (also med.L.) *malleare* hammer, f. *malleus*; cf. MALLEABLE, see -ATE[3].] *trans.* To beat with a hammer; *spec.* to beat (metal) thin or flat.

Malleation (mælĭ,ē^{i}·ʃən). 1596. [– med.L. *malleatio*, f. as prec.; see -ION.] **1.** The action of malleating or condition of being malleated. Now *rare.* Also *fig.* **2.** *Path.* A convulsive disorder characterized by the hammering one part of the body against another; occurring as a symptom in chorea and insanity 1822.

Mallecho: see MICHING MALICHO.

‖**Mallee**[1] (mǭ·lĭ). *Anglo-Ind.* 1759. [Hindi *mālī.*] One of the gardener caste in India; hence, any native gardener.

Mallee[2] (mæ·lĭ). 1848. [Native Austral.] Any one of several scrubby species of eucalyptus; esp. *Eucalyptus dumosa* and *E. oleosa.*

M. bird, fowl, hen, an Australian mound-bird, *Leipoa ocellata.*

Mallein (mæ·lĭ,in). Also **-ine.** 1892. [f. late L. *malleus* glanders + -IN[1].] A sterilized culture of the bacillus of glanders, used for inoculation.

‖**Mallemuck.** Also **mallemoke, -mock,** etc. 1694. [– Du. *mallemok*, f. *mal* foolish + *mok* gull.] The fulmar, *Fulmarus glacialis*; also applied to similar or related birds.

Mallender, var. f. MALANDER.

‖**Malleolus** (mělī·ŏlŏs). *Pl.* **-i.** 1693. [L., dim. of *malleus* hammer.] **1.** *Anat.* Either of the two bony eminences of the leg bone at the ankle. (The *internal m.* belongs to the tibia, the *external m.* to the fibula.) **2.** *Hort.* A layer which when separated from the parent stem presents a hammer-shape 1706.

Mallet (mæ·lėt), *sb.*[1] late ME. [– (O)Fr. *maillet*, f. *mailler* to hammer, f. *mail* hammer, MAUL *sb.*[1]] A kind of hammer, usually of wood, smaller than a maul or beetle. **b.** *Games.* The wooden hammer used for striking the balls in croquet or polo; also *transf.* the player who uses this 1868. †**c.** *fig.* A person or agency that smites, beats down, or crushes. [After L. *malleus.*] –1823.

c. Sometimes like a m., to strike the Israelites 1561. *Comb.* **m.-shoot**, a hammer-shaped slip of a tree for planting.

†**Ma·llet,** *sb.*[2] *rare.* 1612. [– Sp. *maleta* = Fr. *mallette*, dim. of *malle* MAIL *sb.*[3]] A little portmanteau.

Mallet (mæ·lėt), *v. Obs.* exc. *arch.* 1594. [f. MALLET *sb.*[1]] *trans.* To beat, hammer.

‖**Malleus** (mæ·lĭ,ŏs). *Pl.* **-ei** (-ĭ,əi). 1669. [L., lit. 'hammer'.] *Anat.* **1.** The outermost of the three small bones (*malleus, incus,* and *stapes*) in the ear of mammals, which transmits the vibrations of the tympanum to the incus or 'anvil'. **2.** One of two organs of the trophi or mouth-apparatus in *Rotifera*, which work upon the incus 1850.

Mallophagous (mælǫ·făgəs), *a.* 1890. [f. mod.L. *mallophagus* (f. Gr. μαλλός lock of wool + -φάγος -PHAGOUS) + -OUS.] *Entom.* Of an insect: Devouring wool, hair, feathers, etc.; applied to the *Mallophaga*, a group of apodous parasitic insects.

Mallow (mæ·loᵘ). [OE. *mealuwe, -(e)we* – L. *malva*, rel. to Gr. μαλάχη, μολόχη and prob. of Mediterranean origin.] **1.** (Also *pl.* const. as *sing.*) A common wild plant, *Malva sylvestris* (N.O. *Malvaceæ*), with hairy stems and leaves and reddish-purple flowers; it is very mucilaginous. Called also *Common, Field, Wild m.* Hence extended to other plants of the genus *Malva* or N.O. *Malvaceæ*. **2.** = MARSH-MALLOW, *Althæa officinalis*. Called also *Water, White M.* ME. **3.** The Syrian Mallow, *Hibiscus syriacus* ME. **4.** *Garden* or *Rose M.*, the hollyhock, *Althæa rosea* 1577. **5.** The leaf or fibre of the mallow used for writing upon. COWLEY.

1. Indian m., (*a*) *Abutilon avicennæ,* (*b*) any plant of the genera *Urena* or *Sida.* **Jews' m.,** *Corchorus olitorius.* Also MARSH MALLOW, q.v. **Tree m.,** *Lavatera arborea.* **Yellow m.** = *Indian mallow.*

‖**Mallum** (mæ·lŏm), **mallus** (mæ·lŏs). 1844. [– med.L. (Lex Salica) – OFrankish *mahl*; see MAIL *sb.*[2]] *Hist.* The hundred-court among the Franks.

Malm (mām), *sb.* [OE. **mealm* (in *mealmstān* friable stone, and *mealmiht* sandy) = ON. *malmr* ore, metal, Goth. *malma* sand, f. **mal-* **mel-* grind; see MEAL *sb.*[1]] **1. a.** A soft friable rock, consisting largely of chalky material. **b.** The light loamy soil formed by the disintegration of this. 1477. **2.** Short for *malm-brick* 1858. **3.** *attrib.*: **m.-brick,** the best kind of brick; **-rock** *Geol.* = GREENSAND 1 c.; **-stone** = sense 1 a. OE. Hence **Ma·lmy** *a.* of a loamy character.

Malm (mām), *v.* 1619. [f. prec.] *trans.* †**a.** To treat (land) with malm. **b.** To convert (clay) into artificial malm for brickmaking; to cover (brick-earth) with artificial malm.

‖**Malmag** (mæ·lmæg). 1838. [repr. *malmay* in Sp. dialect of the Philippines.] The Spectre, *Tarsius spectrum*, a small lemuroid animal, native of Borneo and the Philippines.

Malmaison (mælmē^i·zǫn). 1892. [Short for *Souvenirs de Malmaison* (Fr. 'recollections of Malmaison', the château of the empress Josephine).] *Hort.* A variety of the carnation.

Malmsey (mā·mzi). late ME. [– MDu., MLG. *malmesie, -eye* (in med.L. *malmasia*, f. Gr. place-name *Monemvasia* (Μονεμβασία) in the Morea, of which the var. *Malvasia* gave MALVOISIE.] **1.** A strong sweet wine, orig. from Monemvasia (Napoli di Malvasia) in the Morea; but now also from Spain, the Azores, etc. Also *attrib.* **2.** A kind of grape, from which this wine was originally made 1511.

Malnutrition (mælniutri·ʃən). 1862. [MAL-.] Insufficient nutrition.

Mal-observa·tion. 1886. Defective observation.

Malodorous (mælōᵘ·dŏrəs), *a.* 1850. [f. MAL- + ODOROUS.] Evil-smelling. Hence **Malo·dorous-ly** *adv.*, **-ness.**

Malodour (mælōᵘ·dəɹ). 1825. [f. MAL- + ODOUR.] An evil smell, a stench.

Malpighian (mælpi·giăn), *a.* 1847. [f. name of Marcello *Malpighi*, an Italian physician (1628–1694) + -AN.] **1.** *Anat.* Distinctive epithet of certain structures (esp. in the substance of the kidneys) discovered by Malpighi, and of others connected with these. **2.** *Bot.* In *M. cells*: those which compose the outer layer of the seed in *Malpighiaceæ* 1900.

Malposi·tion. 1836. [f. MAL- + POSITION.] Misplacement 1862. **b.** *spec.* in *Obstetrics.* Faulty position of a part or organ, esp. of the fœtus in the uterus.

Malpra·ctice. 1671. [f. MAL- + PRACTICE.] **1.** *Law.* **a.** Improper treatment or culpable neglect of a patient by a physician. **b.** Illegal action by which a person seeks a benefit for himself, while in a position of trust 1758. **2.** *gen.* A criminal or overtly mischievous action; wrong-doing 1772.

1. b. Malpractices begin with the prospectus and continue till liquidation 1895. So **Malpra·xis.**

Malt (mǫlt), *sb.* [OE. *malt*, (*mealt*) = OS. *malt* (Du. *mout*), (O)HG. *malz*, ON. *malt* :– Gmc. **maltaz* n. (whence Finnish *maltas* and OSl. *mlato*), rel. to the base of MELT *v.*] **1.** Barley or other grain prepared for brewing or distilling by steeping, germinating, and kiln-drying, or by gelatinization, etc. **2.** *transf.* Used for: Malt liquor (*slang* or *colloq.*) 1718.

1. *Extract of m.*, a preparation of m. used as food for invalids. Provb. *The m. is above the meal*, said of a person under the influence of drink.

attrib. and *Comb.*, as *m.-spirits*; *m-cellar, -meal*, etc.; **m. extract**, a saccharine and mucilaginous substance obtained from wort: also = *extract of m.*; **-floor,** (*a*) a floor on which the malt is spread to germinate; (*b*) a perforated floor in the malt-kiln, through which heat ascends from a furnace below to dry the barley laid upon it; **-kiln,** a kiln in which the m. is dried after steeping and couching; **m. liquor,** liquor made from m. by fermentation, as ale, beer, stout, etc.; **-sugar** = MALTOSE; **-tax,** a tax on m., now replaced by the beer-duty; **m. vinegar,** vinegar made from the fermentation of m.

Malt (mǫlt), *v.* 1440. [f. MALT *sb.*] **1.** *trans.* To convert (grain) into malt. Also *absol.* **b.** *intr.* To admit of being malted 1766. **2.** *transf.* (*pass.* and *intr.*) Of seeds: To come to the condition of malt owing to germination being checked by drought 1733. **3.** *trans.* To make (liquor) with malt 1605. **4.** *intr.* To drink malt liquor (*vulgar*) 1813.

3. A man of worship, whose beere was better hopped than maulted CAMDEN.

Malta (mǫ·ltă). 1651. Name of an island in the Mediterranean; used *attrib.*, as †**M. cross** = *Maltese cross*; **M. fever,** a complicated fever of long duration, common in M.

†**Ma·ltalent.** ME. [– OFr., f. *mal* evil + *talent* disposition, temper (see TALENT).] Ill-will, malevolence –1828.

Malt-dust. 1512. The refuse which falls from the grain in malting.

Maltese (mǫltī·z), *a.* and *sb. sing.* and *pl.* 1615. [f. MALTA + -ESE.] **A.** *adj.* Of or pertaining to Malta and its inhabitants, or to the Knights of Malta 1797.

M. cat, a short-haired blue-coloured variety of the domestic cat; **M. cross,** see CROSS *sb.* 13; **M. dog,** a small kind of spaniel, with a roundish muzzle, and long, silky, generally white hair; **M. lace,** a lace having arabesque or geometric patterns, said to have been orig. made in Malta; **M. orange,** the 'blood' orange, much grown in southern Italy.

B. *sb.* **1. a.** A native or an inhabitant of Malta. **b.** A Knight of Malta. 1615. **2.** The language of the natives of Malta, a corrupt Arabic 1828. **3.** Short for *Maltese lace* 1900.

Maltha (mæ·lþă). late ME. (**malthe**). [– L. *maltha* – Gr. μάλθα, μάλθη mixture of wax and pitch.] **1.** A kind of cement made by mixing pitch and wax, or lime and sand, with other ingredients. **2.** The name anciently given to some viscid form of bitumen; applied variously to asphaltum, to mineral tar, and to ozocerite (Kirwan's 'mineral tallow') 1601.

†**Ma·lt-horse.** 1561. A heavy kind of horse used by maltsters; occas., as a term of abuse –1616.

Mome, M., Capon, Coxcombe, Idiot SHAKS.

Malt-house (mǫ·lt,haus). OE. A building in which malt is prepared and stored; a malting.

Malthusian (mælþiū·ziăn). 1812. [f. T. R. *Malthus* + -IAN.] **A.** *adj.* Pertaining to T. R. Malthus (1766–1835) or his teaching 1821. **B.** *sb.* A follower or supporter of T. R. Malthus in his views on population. Hence **Malthusianism** (mælþiū·ziănizm), the teaching of Malthus and his followers, who held that, as population increases faster than the means of subsistence, its increase should be checked, mainly by moral restraint: popularly viewed as a proposal to check marriage 1833.

Maltine (mǫ·ltīn). 1889. [f. MALT *sb.* + -INE[5].] Commercial name for various preparations of malt.

Malting (mǫ·ltiŋ), *vbl. sb.* 1440. [f. MALT *v.* + -ING[1].] **1.** In senses of MALT *v.* **2.** A MALT-HOUSE 1846. **3.** *attrib.*, as **m.-floor, -kiln,** etc. = *malt-floor, -kiln,* etc. 1467.

Maltman (mǫ·ltmæ̆n). ME. A maltster.

Maltose (mǫ·ltōᵘs). 1862. [– Fr. *maltose* (Dubrunfaut); see MALT *sb.*, -OSE[2].] *Chem.* Sugar produced from starch-paste as by the action of malt.

Maltreat (mæltrī·t), *v.* 1708. [– Fr. *maltraiter*; see MAL- and TREAT *v.*] *trans.* To abuse, ill-use; to handle roughly or rudely. Hence **Maltrea·tment** 1721.

Maltster (mǫ·ltstəɹ). ME. [f. MALT *sb.* + -STER.] One whose occupation is to make malt.

Ma·lt-worm. 1440. †**1.** A weevil which infests malt. **2.** *transf.* A toper 1550.

Malty (mǫ·lti), *a.* 1819. [f. MALT *sb.* + -Y[1].] Addicted to, affected by, or containing malt (liquor). Also *slang*, drunk. **b.** Of the nature of or resembling malt 1830.

Malvaceous (mælvē^i·ʃəs), *a.* 1699. [f. L. *malvaceus* (Pliny), f. *malva* MALLOW; see -ACEOUS.] *Bot.* Pertaining to the genus *Malva* (the Mallow), or to the N.O. *Malvaceæ*.

Malval (mæ·lvăl), *a.* 1836. [f. L. *malva* MALLOW + -AL[1].] *Bot.* Only in *M. alliance, exogens*: an alliance embracing the N.O. *Malvaceæ* and other orders (Lindley).

Malversation (mælvəɹsē^i·ʃən). 1549. [– Fr. *malversation*, f. *malverser* – L. *male versari* (*male* ill, MAL- + *versari* behave).] Corrupt behaviour in a position of trust; an instance of this. **b.** Corrupt administration *of* something 1706.

b. Cardonnel was turned out of the House of Commons..for m. of public money THACKERAY.

Malvoisie (mæ·lvoizi). *Obs.* exc. *arch.* [ME. *malvesin, malvesie* – OFr. *malvesie*, from the Fr. form (cf. It. *Malvasia*) of the place-name *Monemvasia*; see MALMSEY.] **1.** = MALMSEY 1. **2.** = MALMSEY 2. 1517.

Mam (mæm). *colloq.* 1500. [See MAMMA[1].] A childish word for mother; corresp. to DAD.

Mama, var. of MAMMA[1].

‖**Mamamouchi.** 1672. A mock-Turkish title, from Molière's play *Le Bourgeois Gentilhomme* IV. iii. Hence occas.: A pompous-sounding title; also, one assuming such a title.

This ridiculous M. [The Duke of Newcastle] H. WALPOLE.

Mamelon (mæ·mĕlǫn). 1830. [– Fr. *mamelon* nipple, f. (O)Fr. *mamelle* :– L. *mamilla*, dim. of *mamma* breast; see -ELLE, -OON.] **1.** A rounded eminence or hummock. **2.** A small hemispherical tubercle 1872. Hence **Ma·melonated** *a.* covered with rounded protuberances.

‖**Mameluco** (mæmĕl^iū·ko). 1863. [Pg., lit. a mameluke; see next.] A cross-breed between a white and a Brazilian Indian.

Mameluke (mæ·mĕl^iūk). *Obs.* exc. *Hist.* 1511. [– Fr. *mameluk* (OFr. *mamelus*), ult. – Arab *mamlūk* slave, subst. use of pa. pple. of *malaka* possess.] **1.** A member of the military body, originally composed of Circassian slaves, which seized the throne of Egypt in 1254, and continued to form the ruling class in that country until exterminated by Mohammed Ali in 1811. **2.** A slave (in Moslem countries) 1600. **3.** *fig.* A 'fighting slave' of the Pope, etc. 1531.

3. The Assumptionists are mere mamelukes of the Vatican 1902.

||**Mamilla** (mæmi·lă). Also **mammilla.** 1693. [L., dim. of *mamma* breast, teat.] **1.** The nipple of the female breast; also, the male mamma. **2.** *transf.* (*Anat., Bot.,* etc.) Any nipple-shaped organ or protuberance; a papilla 1818. Hence **Ma·m(m)illar** *a.* = MAMILLARY 2. **Mami·lliform, Ma·milloid** *adjs.* resembling a m.

Mamillary (mæ·milări), *a.* Also **mamm-.** 1615. [f. prec. + -ARY².] **1.** Of or pertaining to the breast; †having mammæ 1669. **2.** Of the form of a mamma 1615. **b.** Having mammiform protuberances 1813.

2. *M. brooch* (Antiq.): one consisting of two cup-shaped pieces connected by a handle 1862.

Ma·millate, *a.* Also **mamm-.** 1826. [f. as prec. + -ATE²] = next.

Mamillated (mæ·mileⁱtėd), *ppl. a.* Also **mamm-.** 1741. [f. as prec. + -ED¹.] **1.** Having rounded protuberances; covered with mammiform excrescences. *spec.* in *Path., Geol.,* and *Min.* **2.** Having a nipple-shaped process or part 1839.

Mamillation (mæmilēⁱ·ʃən). Also **mamm-.** 1856. [f. as prec. + -ION.] **1.** The condition of being mamillated. **2.** *concr.* in *pl.* Rounded bosses 1863.

Mamma¹ (mămā·). Also **mama.** 1579. [A reduplication of *ma*, an instinctive infantine utterance. The spelling *mama* is now rare. In U.S. commonly stressed *ma·mma*; in educated Eng. use always on the last syllable.] = Mother; used chiefly in the vocative, or with a possess. pronoun (as 'my mamma'); also without article in the manner of a proper name (e.g. 'Mamma is well').

||**Mamma**² (mæ·mă). *Pl.* **-æ.** OE. [L.] The milk-secreting organ of the female in mammalia. Also the corresponding structure in males. Hence **Ma·mmary** *a.* of or belonging to the m.; having the form of a m. **Mammi·ferous** *a.* mammalian; (of a part of the body) bearing the mammæ. **Ma·mmiform** *a.*, also *erron.* **mammæform,** having the form of a m.

Mammal (mæ·măl). 1826. [First used in pl. as an anglicized form of MAMMALIA.] An animal of the class mammalia. Also *attrib.*

||**Mammalia** (mămēⁱ·liă), *sb. pl.* 1773. [mod.L. (Linnæus), n. pl. of L. *mammalis,* f. *mamma*; see MAMMA², -AL¹, -IA².] A class of animals characterized by the possession of mammæ in which milk is secreted for the nourishment of their young.

The *Mammalia* are divided into the *placental* and the *implacental* mammalia (see the adjs.), the latter comprising only the marsupials and the monotremes. Except the monotremes, all mammalia are viviparous.

Hence **Mammali·ferous** *a. Geol.* containing mammalian remains.

Mammalian (mămēⁱ·liăn). 1835. [f. prec. + -AN.] **A.** *adj.* Of or belonging to the mammalia. **B.** *sb.* One of the mammalia.

Mammalogy (mămæ·lŏdʒi). 1835. [irreg. f. MAMMALIA + -LOGY, after Fr. *mammalogie.*] The science of mammals. Hence **Mammalo·gical** *a.* pertaining to m. **Mamma·logist,** one versed in m.

Mammato- (mămēⁱ·to), comb. form of L. *mammatus* (f. MAMMA²) in meteorological terms descriptive of clouds resembling rounded festoons, as *m.-ci·rrus, -cu·mulus.*

Mammee (mæmī·). 1572. [– Sp. *mamei* (whence Fr. *mamey*), of Haytian origin, whence mod.L. *mammea* (Linnæus).] A large tree (*Mammea americana,* N.O. *Guttiferæ*) of tropical America which bears a large fruit with a yellow pulp of pleasant taste. Also, the fruit of this tree; also called **mammee-apple.**

†**Ma·mmer,** *v.* late ME. [imit., with frequent. suffix -ER⁵. Cf. *mumble, stammer.*] *intr.* To stammer, mutter; also, to vacillate –1842.

Mammet, var. of MAUMET.

Mammifer (mæ·mifəɹ). Now *rare.* 1832. [– Fr. *mammifère,* orig. used in pl. as – mod.L. *mammifera*; see next.] = MAMMAL.

||**Mammifera** (mămi·fĕră). *rare.* 1827. [mod.L. (n. pl.), f. L. *mamma* MAMMA² + *-fer* (see -FEROUS). Substituted by French naturalists *a*1800 for Linnæus' *mammalia.*] = MAMMALIA.

Mammock (mæ·mək), *sb. arch.* and *dial.* 1529. [Of unkn. origin; see -OCK.] A scrap, shred, broken or torn piece. Also *fig.* Hence **Ma·mmock** *v. trans.* to break, cut, or tear into fragments or shreds.

Mammodi (mæ·mŏdi). 1828. [– Urdu (Pers.) *maḥmūdī* a sort of fine muslin.] A kind of muslin or fine linen.

Mammon (mæ·mən). late ME. [orig. *Mammona* (XIV), as a proper name for 'the devil of covetousness', – late L. (Vulg.) *mam(m)ōna, mam(m)on* – N.T. Gr. μαμ(μ)ωνᾶς (*Matt.* 6:24, *Luke* 16:9, 11, 13) – Aram. *māmōnā, māmōn* riches, gain.] A term of opprobrium for wealth regarded as an idol or evil influence. Usu. more or less personified.

Ye cannot serue God and M. *Matt.* 6:24. Hence **Ma·mmonish** *a.* influenced by or devoted to m. **Ma·mmonism,** devotion to the pursuit of riches. **Ma·mmonist, Ma·mmonite,** a worshipper of m. **Ma·mmonitish** *a.* mammon-like. **Ma·mmonize** *v. rare,* to influence through m.; whence **Ma:mmoniza·tion.**

Mammose (mæ·mōᵘs), *a.* 1856. [mod., f. L. *mamma* breast + -OSE¹.] Having breast-like protuberances.

Mammoth (mæ·mŏþ), *sb.* (*a.*) 1706. [– Russ. *mamont, mamot,* prob. of Siberian origin.] **1.** A large extinct species of elephant (*Elephas primigenius*) formerly native in Europe and northern Asia; its remains are often found in the alluvial deposits in Siberia. Also *fig.* **b.** *U.S.* Often applied to the fossil mastodon 1816. **2.** *adj.* Resembling the mammoth in size; huge 1814.

†**Mammothrept.** 1599. [– late L. *mammothreptus* – Gr. μαμμόθρεπτος, f. μάμμη grandmother + θρεπτός vbl. adj., f. τρέφειν to bring up.] A spoilt child; a nursling –1651.

You are a meere m. in judgement B. JONS.

Mammy (mæ·mi). 1523. [dim. of MAM; see -Y⁶.] **1.** A child's word for mother. **2.** In southern U.S.: A coloured woman having the care of white children 1859.

Mamsell (mæmze·l). *colloq.* [– Fr. *mam'selle,* contr. of MADEMOISELLE.] = MADEMOISELLE 3. Thackeray.

†**Mamzer.** 1562. [– late L. *mamzer,* a Heb. word adopted by the Vulgate in *Deut.* 23:2.] A bastard –1865.

Man (mæn), *sb. Pl.* **men.** [OE. *man(n, mon(n,* pl. *menn* (:– **manniz*), also *manna, monna,* corresp. to OFris. *man, mon,* OS. *man,* OHG. *man* sing. and pl. (Du. *man,* G. *mann*), ON. *maðr,* rarely *mannr,* Goth. *manna*; the various forms belong to two Gmc. stems **mann-*, **mannon-*; a third stem **manno-* is repr. by the tribal names *Allemanni, Marcomanni*; a pre-Gmc. **manw-*, **mane-* appears in *Mannus* (Tacitus), a founder of the West Gmc. peoples, and links with the base of Skr. *mánu-* man-, mankind.]

I. 1. A human being; = L. *homo.* OE. and occas. later. Now surviving in general or indef. applications in the sense 'person' (e.g. with *every, any, no,* and in the pl. with *all, any, some,* etc.). **2.** In generic sense, without article: The human creature regarded abstractly; hence, the human race or species, mankind. In *Zool.*: The human creature or race viewed as a genus of animals (*Homo*: in the present classification consisting of only one species, *H. sapiens*). OE. **3.** In biblical, etc. use, with *inner, inward, outer, outward*: The spiritual and material parts (respectively) of a human person; hence applied *joc.* to parts of the physical frame of man. **b.** With *old, new*: used to denote the spiritual condition of the unregenerate and the regenerate. OE.

1. He deserueth it as lytell as euer dyd man 1530. The Lord had but one paire of men in Paradise 1597. Measuring other mens actions and consciences SANDERSON. Phr. *To be, become, be made m.*: to have or assume human nature. **2.** Man is said to live without food for seven days GOLDSM. Men are weak, but M. is strong LOWELL. **3.** To clothe the outer man; to refresh the inner man (*mod.*).

II. 1. An adult male person OE. **b.** generically (without article). The male human being. Also *predicatively.* 1591. **c.** with special ref. to adult age. (Sometimes, A male who has attained his majority) ME. **d.** without express contrast ME. **e.** In the vocative, usually implying contempt or impatience. late ME. **f.** Phrases (see below). ¶**2.** Applied to beings other than human, e.g. God, the Devil, Death –17.. **3.** In pregnant sense: An adult male eminently endowed with manly qualities. late ME. †**b.** Manliness, courage –1605. **4.** A person of position, importance, or note 1541. **5.** A husband. Now only *Sc.* and *dial.,* exc. in phr. *m. and wife.* ME. **6.** A LIEGEMAN or vassal. Now *Hist.* †Also *fig.* OE. **7.** A manservant; a valet ME. **b.** As correl. of *master.* Now commonly applied (chiefly in *pl.*) to workmen as dist. from their employers. late ME. **8.** Applied (chiefly in *pl.*) to members of a fighting force; now esp. to the common soldiers as dist. from the officers ME. **9.** In universities, etc.: An undergraduate or student 1803.

1. They speake..here the Hebrew tongue, man, woman and child 1632. **b.** Woman is not undevelopt m., But diverse TENNYSON. **c.** The Child is father of the M. WORDSW. *M. and boy*: †(*a*) one and all; (*b*) (advb. phr.): from boyhood upwards. †*To write m.*: to be entitled by years to call oneself a m. †(*To grow up,* etc.) *to m.*: to adult age. **d.** [He] was hand and glove with some of the best men in town THACKERAY. *The m.*: occas. used for 'he', with a tinge of depreciation, sympathy, or the like: so *the good m., the poor m.,* etc. The late earl was not much liked; the present m. is more popular (*mod.*). **e.** Here, read it, read it, m. DISRAELI. **f.** *Little m.*: a term (now joc. or affectionate) for a young male child. *A m.* = 'one' or 'any one', but implies a reference to the male sex only. So †*a man's self, a man's own.* In *M. by m., between m. and m., m for m., per m., as one m.* (app. orig. a Hebraism = with one accord, †altogether), *to a m.* (= without exception), *man* = 'individual (male) person'. *As a m.*: (considered) in regard to his personal character exclusively. So *The m.*: what one is merely 'as a m.' *The* (*very*) *m.* (ellipt. in predicative use): the man most suitable *for* or *to do* something. *The m. for me* (colloq. *for my money*; see MONEY): the man whom I should choose to employ or support. *My, your,* etc. *m.*: the person one needs, or with whom one has to do. *To be one's own m.*: (*a*) to be in full possession of one's senses, faculties, or powers; (*b*) to be at one's own disposal. (*Every, not a*) *m. Jack*: see JACK *sb.*¹ I. 2. *University, Oxford, Cambridge,* etc. *m.*: one who is or has been a member of a (particular) university, public school, etc. *Best m., handy m., reading m.,* etc., see the adjs. **2.** But was the Diuell a proper m., Gossip? B. JONS. **3.** He [Cromwell] was a m. MORLEY. Pym, the m. of men BROWNING. Phr. *To play the m.* **b.** Hauing more m. then wit about me SHAKS. **4.** [To] set him upon his legs, and make him a m. for ever SANDERSON. **7.** **a.** Find out..who's master, who's m. SWIFT. *M. Friday*: a servile follower; a factotum. (After Robinson Crusoe's 'man Friday'.) **b.** The masters had locked out the men..from seventeen factories 1860. **8.** The English had lost more than 2,400 officers and men 1880.

III. Transf. uses. **1.** One of the pieces in chess, draughts, and backgammon. late ME. **2.** With qualification: A ship 1473. **3.** Applied to any representation of a man 1636. *M. of straw* (fig.): see STRAW *sb.* **4.** In Cumberland, Westmorland, and Lonsdale: A cairn marking a summit or prominent point of a mountain; cf. *Low Man, High M.* as local names for particular cairns 1800.

1. The cheste-bourde and men 1562. **2.** They chased a Barbadoes and a Jamaica m. into Limrick 1665.

Phrases and combs. **a.** Phrases. **M. of Belial,** a worthless or wicked m. (cf. 1 *Sam.* 25:25); **m. of blood** (Hebraism), one who is laden with blood-guiltiness; **m. in blue** *slang,* a policeman; **m. of God** (Hebraism), (*a*) a saint, (*b*) an ecclesiastic; **m. of Kent,** one of the inhabitants of Kent east of the river Medway (cf. KENTISH *man*); †**m. of Rome,** the Pope.

b. Obvious combs., as *m.-famine,* etc.; *m.* (='male') *cook, m. nurse,* etc.; *one-man* (show), etc.; *m.-stealer*; *m.-stealing*; *m.-worthy* adj.; *m.-made* ppl. adj.; *m.-fashion* adv.

c. Special combs.: **m.-ape,** an anthropoid ape; **-engine,** a kind of lift for lowering and raising men in a shaft, consisting essentially of a reciprocating vertical rod with platforms at intervals; **-machine** = *man-engine*; **-mountain,** the name given to Gulliver by the Lilliputians; **-power,** (*a*) the power exerted by a man; as a unit, one-eighth of a horsepower; (*b*) the amount of men available for state or other services; **-rope, a**

rope on either side of a gangway or ladder, used in ascending and descending a ship's side, etc.

Man (mæn), *v.* [Late OE. (*ġe*)*mannian*, with corresp. forms in other Gmc. languages.] **1.** *trans.* (*Mil.* and *Naut.*) To furnish (a fort, ship, etc.) with men. Said also of the men. **b.** *Naut.* To place men at or on (a particular part of a ship), as at the capstan to heave anchor, or on the yards to salute a distinguished person. Said also of the men; hence *transf.* to exert force upon (a rope, etc.). 1697. †**c.** To equip and send (a boat, occas. an army) with its complement of men *out*, *forth*, etc. –1774. **2.** To supply with a man, men, or inhabitants. late ME. †**3.** To escort (esp. a woman) –1688. **4.** To make manly or manlike 1615. **5.** *Falconry.* To accustom (a hawk, etc.) to the presence of men. Hence (*transf.* and *gen.*) to make tame or tractable 1575.

1. M. the Pinnace, and get her by the Ship's Side 1694. **b.** Manned Ship and cheered Sir John Jervis 1796. **2.** To be mand with one bare Page CHAPMAN. The pulpits were manned with seditious preachers SOUTHEY. **4.** My Soul's up in Arms, and Mans each part about me DRYDEN.

Manace, obs. f. MENACE *sb.* and *v.*

Manacle (mæ·năk'l), *sb.* [ME. *manicle* – (O)Fr. *manicle* handcuff, also (as in mod. Fr.) gauntlet – L. *manicula* little hand, handle, in med.L. gauntlet, dim. of *manus* hand; later assim. to words in *-acle*.] A fetter for the hand; usu. *pl.* **b.** Chiefly *pl.*, bonds, restraints 1587.

1. Wee'le put you..in Manacles, Then reason safely with you SHAKS. **b.** The Manacles Of the all-building-Law SHAKS. Hence **Ma·nacle** *v. trans.* to fetter or confine (the hands); *loosely*, to fetter; to fasten, secure. Also *fig.*

Manage (mæ·nėdʒ), *sb.* Also (in senses 1–3) MANÈGE. 1577. [– It. *maneggio* (whence Fr. *manège*), f. *maneggiare* :– Rom. **manidiare*, f. L. *manus* hand.] **1.** The training of a horse in its paces. *Obs.* exc. *arch.* (Now usually MANÈGE.) Also *transf.* and *fig.* 1586. **2.** The action and paces of a trained horse; *spec.* a short gallop at full speed. *Obs.* exc. *arch.* 1577. **3.** A riding-school 1655. **4.** The skilful handling of (a weapon) 1611. †**5.** Management; conduct (of affairs); administration, direction, control –1756. †**6.** Treatment –1626.

1. Speake tearmes of m. to thy bounding Steed SHAKS. **2.** His horses..are taught their mannage SHAKS. **5.** Young men in the conduct and mannage of Actions, embrace more then they can hold BACON. **6.** Quick-silver will not endure the Mannage of the Fire BACON.

Manage (mæ·nėdʒ), *v.* 1561. [– It. *maneggiare*; see prec.] **1.** *trans.* To train (a horse) in his paces; to put through the exercises of the manège. Now merged in senses 2 and 7. †**b.** *intr.* Of a horse: To perform the exercises of the manège –1719. **2.** *trans.* To handle, wield (a weapon, tool, etc.). Now only, to make (a weapon, instrument, etc.) serve one's purpose (well or ill). 1586. **b.** To handle, work (a ship or boat) 1600. **3.** To conduct (a war, an undertaking, etc.). Now, To carry on successfully or otherwise; to control the course of (affairs) by one's own action. 1579. Also *absol.* **4.** *trans.* To control the affairs of (a household, institution, state, etc.); to take charge of (cattle, etc.) 1609. **5.** To administer (finances, provisions, etc.) 1649. **6.** To deal with carefully; to husband. ? *Obs.* 1649. †**b.** To treat (persons) with indulgence or consideration. Also *absol.* –1796. **7.** To cause (persons, animals, etc.) to submit to one's control 1594. **8.** To bring over to one's wishes by artifice, flattery, etc. 1706. **9.** To operate upon; to treat (land) 1655. **10.** To bring to pass by contrivance; hence, to succeed in accomplishing. Also with *inf.* as obj.; often ironically, to be so unskilful or unlucky as *to do* something. 1722. **b.** *absol.* To contrive to get along or pull through (under disadvantages). *colloq.* 1899.

2. Put vp thy Sword, Or m. it to part these men with me SHAKS. **3.** So you see,..they m. these things better in France LADY MORGAN. *absol.* If I had not managed very cleverly 1791. Her father.. Hadn't a head to m. TENNYSON. **6.** I am obliged to m. my health, and I have many things to do BP. BERKELEY. **8.** Managing mankind, by studying their tempers and humouring their weaknesses DISRAELI. **10.** I managed to lose..£2,500 1838.

Manageable (mæ·nėdʒăb'l), *a.* 1598. [f. prec. + -ABLE.] That can be managed; tractable; workable; capable of being accomplished by contrivance; etc.

A meek and m. child E. B. BROWNING. Hence **Manageabi·lity, Ma·nageableness,** the condition or quality of being m. **Ma·nageably** *adv.*

Management (mæ·nėdʒmĕnt). 1598. [f. MANAGE *v.* + -MENT.] **1.** The action or manner of managing (see the vb.). †In early use sometimes in pl. **b.** *spec.* The working (of land); hence *dial.* manuring; *concr.* manure. †**c.** An instance of managing –1676. **a.** The use of contrivance for effecting some purpose; often in bad sense, implying deceit or trickery 1666. †Also with *a* and *pl.* †**3.** A negotiation –1715. **4.** Power of managing; administrative skill; also, †tact, ingenuity 1715. †**5.** Indulgence or consideration shown towards a person; politic moderation; an instance of this [= Fr. *ménagement.*] –1818. **6.** *collect.* A governing body, e.g. a board of directors, a board of governors, etc. 1739. **7.** *attrib.*, as *m. expenses*, etc. 1903.

1. In contracts and m. of State affaires HOLLAND. **2.** Talent for intrigue or 'management' BRYCE. **3.** He [the Duke of Savoy] had great Managements with several Ecclesiasticks before he turn'd Hermite ADDISON. **5.** When I have any thing to object to persons in power,..I use no sort of m. towards them BURKE.

Manager (mæ·nėdʒəɹ). 1588. [f. MANAGE *v.* + -ER¹.] **1.** One who manages (something specified). Now *rare* in general sense. **2.** One skilled in managing affairs, money, etc. 1670. **3.** One who manages a business, an institution, etc. 1705. **4.** One of several members of either house of parliament appointed for the performance of some duty in which both houses are concerned 1667. **5.** *Law.* A person appointed, usu. by a court of chancery, to manage a business for the benefit of creditors or others; usu. *receiver and m.* 1793.

2. She is not what is called a good m. 1806. **4.** The conference [between Lords and Commons] is conducted by 'Managers' for both houses 1840. Hence **Ma·nageress,** a woman m., e.g. of a theatre or hotel. **Manage·rial** *a.* of, pertaining to, or characteristic of a m. **Ma·nagership,** the office, or the control, of a m.

†**Ma·nagery.** 1633. [f. MANAGE *sb.* or *v.* + -ERY; but often infl. by Fr. *ménagerie.*] **1.** Domestic or agricultural administration –1734. **b.** Economy –1705. **2.** The art of managing (weapons, implements) 1654–93. **3.** Managership; an administrative office 1643–1734. **4.** Cunning or adroit management; an instance of this – 1734. **5.** = MANAGE *sb.* 1, 3. –1782.

Ma·naging, *ppl. a.* 1715. [-ING².] That manages. **1.** Addicted to scheming or to assuming the direction of affairs. **2.** Economical 1754. **3.** Having executive control 1766.

1. That brisk, m., lively, imperious woman THACKERAY. **3.** You want a firstrate m. man DISRAELI.

Manakin (mæ·năkin). Also **-ikin.** 1743. [var. of MANIKIN.] One of the small gaily-coloured birds of the passerine family *Pipridæ*, inhabiting tropical America.

Man-at-arms. Orig. †**man-of-arms.** late ME. [tr. OFr. *homme d'armes, homme a armes*; cf. med.L. *homo ad arma* (XIII).] A soldier; *esp.* a heavy-armed soldier on horseback.

Manatee (mænătī·). Also **manati, manatin.** 1555. [– Sp. *manati* – Carib *manattouï*.] *Zool.* A large aquatic herbivorous cetacean of the genus *Manatus* (order *Sirenia*), esp. *M. americanus*; it inhabits the shallow waters of rivers and estuaries on the Atlantic shores within the tropics. Also LAMANTIN.

Comb. **m.-grass,** a marine plant of the W. Indies, *Thalassia testudinum.*

†**Mana·tion.** 1656. [– L. *manatio*, f. *manat-*, pa. ppl. stem of *manare* flow; see -ION.] The action of flowing out –1814.

Manav(i)lins (mănæ·v(i)linz), *sb. pl. slang.* Now *rare.* 1865. [Cf. *manarvel* (sailors' slang) pilfer small stores.] Odds and ends.

Manbote (mæ·nbōᵘt). *Obs.* exc. *Hist.* [OE. *mannbōt*: see MAN *sb.*, BOOT *sb.*¹] A fine paid to an overlord for the loss of a man.

Manche, maunche (mānʃ). late ME. [– (O)Fr. *manche* :– L. *manica*, f. *manus* hand.] **1.** A sleeve. *Obs.* exc. as used by antiquaries. **2.** *Her.* A sleeve used as a charge, esp. the hanging sleeve of the 14th c. 1486.

Manchester (mæ·ntʃėstəɹ). 1552. Name of a city in Lancashire, the chief seat of the cotton manufacture. **1.** Used *attrib.* or as *adj.* in *M. cottons*, etc. **M. wares,** cotton goods manufactured at M.; hence *M. warehouse, warehouseman.* **2.** *M. School*: a name first applied by Disraeli to Cobden and Bright and their followers, who, before the repeal of the Corn Laws, held their meetings at M. and advocated free trade. Also in *M. policy*, etc., used to designate a policy of laissez-faire and self-interest 1848.

Manchet (mæ·ntʃėt). *Obs.* exc. *dial.* or *Hist.* late ME. [perh. f. †*maine* (XV), aphetic f. *demaine*, in *pain-demaine* (– AFr. *pain demeine, demaine*, med.L. *panis dominicus* 'lord's bread' XIII, *p. de dominico* XI) + CHEAT *sb.*², or dim. of AFr. **menche* for †*demenche* :– L. *dominica*, fem. of *dominicus* DOMINICAL.] †**1.** The finest kind of wheaten bread –1791. **2.** A small loaf or roll of this. Now only *arch.* or *dial.* 1481. **b.** *Her.* 1640. **3.** *attrib.*, as *m. bread*, etc.

Ma·n-child. *Pl.* **men-children.** late ME. A male child.

Manchineel (mæntʃinī·l). 1630. [– Fr. *mancenille* – Sp. *manzanilla*, dim. of *manzana* apple.] A W. Indian tree, *Hippomane mancinella*, having a poisonous and caustic milky sap, and acrid fruit resembling an apple. Also *m. tree.*

Bastard m., a W. Indian tree, *Cameraria latifolia.*

Manchu (mæntʃū·). 1736. [Manchu, 'pure', the name of a tribe descended from the Nü-chên Tartars.] (One) of the native Mongolian race of Manchuria which formed the ruling class in China from 1644 to 1912.

†**Ma·ncipate,** *ppl. a.* 1502. [– L. *mancipatus*, pa. pple. of *mancipare*; see next, -ATE².] Made subject (*to*) –1687.

Mancipate (mæ·nsipeⁱt), *v.* 1574. [– *mancipat-*, pa. ppl. stem of L. *mancipare*, f. *manceps* purchaser, f. *manus* hand + base of *capere* take; see -ATE³.] **1.** *Roman Law.* (*trans.*) To hand over by MANCIPATION 1656. †**2.** To make subject, enslave (*to, unto*) –1756. Hence **Ma·ncipatory** *a.* pertaining to or involving mancipation. So **Ma·ncipable** *a.* 1875.

Mancipation (mænsipēⁱ·ʃən). 1577. [– L. *mancipatio*, f. as prec.; see -ION.] **1.** The ceremonial process by which certain kinds of property (called *res mancipi*) were transferred 1656. **2.** *gen.* The action of enslaving; the state of being enslaved.

1. M...is performed by recital of certain words of style, in presence of a balance-holder and five witnesses 1880.

Manciple (mæ·nsip'l). ME. [– AFr., OFr. *manciple*, var. of *mancipe* :– L. *mancipium* purchase, slave (orig. one obtained by legal purchase), f. *manceps*; see MANCIPATE *v.*] **1.** An officer or servant who buys provisions for a college, an inn of court, a monastery, etc. †**2.** A bondslave, servant. [= L. *mancipium.*] –1587.

Mancus (mæ·ŋkŏs). *Obs.* exc. *Hist.* [OE. *mancus* = OS. *mancus*, OHG. (acc. pl.) *manchussa* – med.L. *mancusus* (XI) – Arab. *manḳūš*, subst. use (sc. *dīnār* DINAR) of pa. pple. of *naḳaša* paint, carve, engrave.] An OE. money of account of the value of thirty pence.

-mancy, a terminal element, repr. OFr. *-mancie*, late L. *-mantia*, Gr. *μαντεία* divination; as *chiromancy, necromancy, hydromancy*, etc. The related adjs. end in -MANTIC.

Mandæan (mændī·ăn), *a.* and *sb.* 1875. [f. Mandæan Aram. *mandaiia* (rendering Gr. *γνωστικοί* Gnostics; f. *manda* knowledge) + -AN.] The designation of a Gnostic sect still surviving in Mesopotamia, and of the Aramaic dialect of their sacred books.

‖**Mandamus** (mændēⁱ·mŏs). 1535. [L., = 'we command'.] *Law.* A term applied orig. to writs, letters missive, or mandates issued by the sovereign directing the performance of certain acts, but subseq. restricted to the judicial writ issued in the king's name from the Court of King's Bench (now, from the Crown side of the King's Bench Division of the High Court of Justice) and directed to an inferior court, a corporation, an officer, etc., commanding some specified thing to be done.

'Its general object is to enforce the performance of some public duty in respect of which there is no specific legal remedy' (G. H. B. Kenrick).

Mandarin[1] (mæ·ndărin). 1589 (**mandeline**). [– Pg. *mandarim* – Malay *mantrī* – Hindi *mantrī* :– Skr. *mantrin* counsellor, f. (ult.) root *man* think.] **1.** A generic name for all grades of Chinese officials, of which there were nine, each distinguished by a particular kind of button. (The Chinese name is *Kwan.*) †Formerly extended to other Asiatic officials. **b.** A grotesque toy figure in Chinese costume, that goes on nodding after it is shaken 1781. **2.** The language spoken in China by officials and educated people 1727. **3.** Short for *mandarin porcelain* 1873.

1. c. *transf.* A pedantic official, bureaucrat. *Combs.*, etc.: **m. duck,** a duck of bright and gay plumage, *Aix galericulata*, native to China; **m. jar,** a jar of m. porcelain; **m. porcelain,** Japanese porcelain decorated with figures of mandarins; **m. vase,** a vase of m. porcelain. Hence **Ma·ndarinate,** the office of a m.; mandarins as a body; government by mandarins. **Mandari·nic** *a.* pertaining to a m. **Ma·ndarinism,** the m. system, government by mandarins. **Ma·ndarinship.**

Mandarin[2], **mandarine** (mæ·ndărin, -īn). 1816. [– Fr. *mandarine* (sc. *orange*; cf. Sp. *naranja mandarina*), fem. of *mandarin* (see prec.); prob. so named from the yellow of mandarins' costume.] **1.** A small flattened deep-coloured orange, with sweet pulp and thin easily-separable rind. Also *m. orange*. Also *attrib.* **2.** A colour (obtained from coal-tar) resembling that of the mandarin orange. Also *m.-orange*, *-yellow*. 1883. **3.** A liqueur 1882. Hence **Ma·ndarining** *vbl. sb.* the process of giving an orange colour to silk or wool by the action of nitric acid 1839.

Mandatary (mæ·ndătəri). 1611. [– late L. *mandatarius*, f. *mandat-*; see next, -ARY[1].] †**1.** One who is appointed to a benefice by a papal mandate –1726. **2.** = MANDATORY *sb.* 1656.

Mandate (mæ·ndět), *sb.* 1552. [– L. *mandatum*, subst. use of n. pa. pple. of *mandare* enjoin, commit, f. *manus* hand + **dō* (*dare*) give; see -ATE[1].] **1.** *gen.* A command, order, injunction. Now *poet.* and *rhet.* 1576. **2.** *spec.* A judicial or legal command from a superior to an inferior 1552. **b.** A papal rescript, esp. with reference to preferment to a benefice 1611. **c.** A command from the sovereign to elect a fellow of a college or to confer a degree (*Hist.*) 1617. †**d.** A pastoral letter –1824. **3. a.** *Rom. Law.* A commission by which one person requested another to act for him gratuitously, undertaking to indemnify him against loss 1756. **b.** *Scots Law.* A contract by which one person employs another to act for him in his affairs 1681. **c.** A contract of gratuitous bailment 1781. **4.** *Politics.* [After Fr. *mandat.*] The instruction as to policy supposed to be given by the electors to a parliament or a member of parliament. Also *transf.* 1774. **5.** A commission from the League of Nations to a power (*the mandatory*) to administer, etc. a territory 1919. **6.** †*attrib.* = MAUNDY 1546.

2. b. Mandates for deposing sovereigns BURKE.

Mandate (mæ·ndeɪt), *v.* 1724. [– *mandat-*, pa. ppl. stem. of L. *mandare*; see prec., -ATE[3].] **1.** To commit (a sermon) to memory *Sc.* **2.** To hand over (a territory) to a mandatory (chiefly *pa. pple.*) 1922.

Mandative (mæ·ndătiv), *a. rare.* 1651. [– late L. *mandativus*, f. as prec.; see -IVE.] Pertaining to command.

‖**Mandator** (mændē·tǫɹ). 1681. [L., f. as prec.; see -OR 2.] One who gives a mandate, esp. in the legal senses.

Mandatory (mæ·ndătəri). 1576. [– late L. *mandatorius* adj., f. as prec.; see -ORY[2]. In med.L. (XIII) also as sb., 'agent'; see -ORY[1].] **A.** *adj.* Of the nature of, pertaining to, or conveying a command or mandate. **b.** Of actions: Obligatory, esp. in consequence of a command 1818. **c.** Concerning which the League of Nations has issued a mandate 1921. **B.** *sb.* One to whom a mandate is given (esp. in *Law*) 1661; see also MANDATE *sb.* 5.

‖**Manda·tum.** 1547. [L.] = MANDATE.

Mandelic (mænde·lik), *a.* 1844. [f. G. *mandel* almond + -IC.] *Chem.* In *m. acid* (G. *mandelsäure*): an acid formed by the action of hydrochloric acid upon amygdalin.

Manderelle, -il, obs. ff. MANDREL.

Mandible (mæ·ndib'l). Now only *Anat.* and *Zool.* 1548. [– OFr. *mandible*, later *mandibule*, or its source late L. *mandibula*, *-ulum*, f. *mandere* chew.] A jaw or jawbone; *esp.* the lower jaw (in mammals and fishes). **b.** In birds, (usually) either part, upper or lower, of the beak 1686. **c.** In insects, either half of the upper or anterior pair of jaws 1826. So **Mandi·bular, -ary** *adjs.* belonging to or connected with a m. **Mandi·buliform** *a. Entom.* shaped like a m.

Mandibulate (mændi·biŭleɪt), *a.* (*sb.*) 1826. [f. late L. *mandibula* (prec.) + -ATE[2].] **1.** Provided with mandibles; applied to a group of insects (the *Mandibulata*) which have the organs of the mouth adapted for mastication. **b.** *sb.* One of these. **2.** Of organs: Adapted for mastication 1835. So **Mandi·bulated** *a.*

Mandibulo- (mændi·biŭlo), irreg. comb. form of late L. *mandibula* MANDIBLE, used with sense 'pertaining to the mandible and ...', as *m.-hyoid*, etc.

Mandil (mæ·ndil). 1662. [– Sp. *mandil* – Arab. *mandīl* sash, turban cloth, handkerchief – med.Gr. μανδήλιον – L. *mantelium*, *-tēlum* MANTLE.] A turban.

Mandilion (mændi·liǫn). *Obs.* exc. *Hist.* 1577. [– Fr. *mandilion* – It. *mandiglione*, augm. of *mandiglia* – Fr. *mandille*, earlier *mandil* – Sp. *mandil*; see prec.] A loose coat or cassock, in later times sleeveless, formerly worn as a kind of overcoat.

Mandioca, var. MANIOC.

†**Mandment.** ME. [– OFr. *mandement* :– med.L. *mandamentum*, f. L. *mandare* command; see -MENT.] A commandment; that which is commanded. Also, command, rule. –1567.

Mandola (mændōᵘ·lă), **mandora** (mændōᵊ·ră). 1758. [– It. *mandola*, *mandora*; see next.] A larger variety of the mandolin.

Mandolin, -ine (mæ·ndŏlin). 1707. [– Fr. *mandoline* – It. *mandolino*, dim. of *mandola*, var. of *mandora*; see prec., next; cf. BANDORE.] An intrument of the lute kind having four to six metal strings stretched upon a deeply-rounded body. Hence **Ma·ndolinist,** a performer on the m.

Mandore (mændōᵊ·ɹ). 1823. [– Fr. *mandore* – It. *mandora*; see prec.] = MANDOLA.

Mandragora (mændræ·gŏră). OE. [In OE. in med.L. form; in ME. anglicized or – (O)Fr. *mandragore* – med.L. *mandragora*, L. *-as* – Gr. μανδραγόρας, prob. of pre-Hellenic origin. The form with *-ora* has been established since SHAKS.] **1. a.** The plant MANDRAKE. Now only *Hist.* **b.** *Bot.* The genus to which this plant belongs. **c.** As the type of a narcotic (Shaks.). †**2.** *Chinese mandragoras*: ginseng –1741.

1. c. *Oth.* III. iii. 330. I haue..drunke Lethe and M. to forget you CHAPMAN. Hence **Mandra·gorite,** one who is habitually under the influence of m.

Mandrake (mæ·ndreɪk). [ME. *mandrag(g)e*, (also *-drake*), prob. – MDu. *mandrage*, *mandragre* – med.L. MANDRAGORA; alt. to *mandrake* was prob. in allusion to the man-like form of the root of the plant, and assoc. with DRAKE[1] dragon (cf. the var. *mandragon*) because of the plant's supposed magical properties.] **1.** Any plant of the genus *Mandragora*, having very short stems, thick, fleshy, often forked, roots, and fetid lance-shaped leaves.

The mandrake is poisonous, having emetic and narcotic properties. Its forked root was thought to resemble the human form, and was fabled to shriek when plucked up from the ground.

†**b.** in allusive and fig. uses –1676. **2.** The root of White Bryony 1585. **3.** *U.S.* The May-apple, *Podophyllum peltatum* 1845. **4.** *attrib.* 1563.

1. And shrikes like Mandrakes torne out of the earth SHAKS. **b.** Thou horson M. SHAKS. He stands as if his Legs had taken root; A very M.! DAVENANT. **4. M. apple,** the fruit of the m.

Mandrel, mandril (mæ·ndrĕl, -ɪl). 1516. [Of unkn. origin; senses 2 and 3 are identical with those of Fr. *mandrin* (late XVII).] **1.** A miner's pick. **2.** In a lathe, an arbor or spindle to which work is secured while it is being turned. Also, a similar part in a circular saw or cutter. 1665. **3.** A cylindrical rod, core, or spindle round which metal or other material is forged, cast, moulded, or shaped 1790. **4.** *attrib.* 1825.

4. *M.-lathe*, a lathe adapted for turning hollow work, which is clasped by a chuck on the end of the mandrel in the head-stock (KNIGHT).

Mandrill (mæ;ndril). Also **-il.** 1744. [app. f. MAN *sb.* + DRILL *sb.*[3]] The largest, most hideous, and most ferocious of the baboons, *Cynocephalus maimon* or *mormon*, of W. Africa.

Manducable (mæ·ndiŭkăb'l), *a. Obs.* or *arch.* 1614. [– late L. *manducabilis* eatable, f. L. *manducare*; see next, -ABLE.] Capable of being manducated; eatable.

Manducate (mæ·ndiŭkeɪt), *v.* 1623. [– *manducat-*, pa. ppl. stem of L. *manducare* chew; see -ATE[3].] *trans.* To chew, eat. So **Manduca·tion,** the action of eating (chiefly *Theol.*, as *carnal*, *literal*, *spiritual m.*, etc.); the action of chewing 1551. **Ma·nducatory** *a.* (chiefly *Phys.*), pertaining to or fitted for manducation.

Mane (mēɪn). [OE. *manu* = OFris. *mana*, (M)Du. *mane*, OHG. *mana* (G. *mähne*), ON. *mǫn* :– Gmc. **manō*.] **1.** The long hair on the back of the neck and the shoulders of various animals, esp. the horse and the lion. Also *fig.* and *transf.* †**2.** The hackles of a game-cock 1614–1727. **3.** *Agric.* A ridge or tuft of grass or stubble, left by the mowers 1523. Hence **Maned** *ppl. a.* having a m.; in *Her.* = CRINED.

-mane (mēɪn), the ending of some words adopted from Fr., as *Anglomane*, etc. Viewed as a Gallicism; the Eng. *-maniac* is preferred.

Ma·n-ea:ter. 1600. [MAN *sb.*] **1.** A cannibal. **2.** An animal that eats or has a propensity for eating men; e.g. a shark (esp. *Carcharodon rondeleti*) 1837; a tiger, lion, hyena 1862. So **Ma·n-ea:ting** *vbl. sb.* and *ppl. a.*

‖**Manège, manege** (manę̄ʒ). 1644. [Fr. form of the word earlier adopted as MANAGE *sb.*] **1.** A riding-school. **2.** The movements proper to a trained horse; the art or practice of training horses; horsemanship 1776.

‖**Maneh** (mā·ne). 1611. [Heb. *māneh*; see MINA[1].] *Heb. Antiq.* A Heb. coin and weight, equal to from sixty to one hundred shekels.

Maneless (mēɪ·nɪlĕs), *a.* 1828. [f. MANE + -LESS.] Without or destitute of a mane.

Manequin(e, obs. f. MANIKIN.

Manerial (mănīᵊ·riăl), *a.* 1765. [– med.L. *manerialis* (XIV), f. *manerium* MANOR; see -AL[1].] = MANORIAL *a.*

‖**Manes** (mēɪ·nīz), *sb. pl.* late ME. [L. *manes* pl.] The deified souls of departed ancestors (as beneficent spirits). Also, the shade of a departed person, as an object of reverence, or as demanding to be propitiated by vengeance.

The m. of my son shall smile this day, While I, in blood, my vows of vengeance pay DRYDEN.

Manful (mæ·nfŭl), *a.* late ME. [f. MAN *sb.* + -FUL.] **1.** = MANLY *a.* 2. †**2.** *occas.* = MANLY *a.* 3. FULLER.

1. A stoute and m. minde 1576. Hence **Ma·nful-ly** *adv.*, **-ness.**

Mangabey (mæ·ngăbēɪ). 1774. [Name of a region of Madagascar. The erron. application is due to Buffon.] A monkey of the African genus *Cercocebus*; esp. the Sooty M., *C. fuliginosus*.

Mangan-, repr. MANGANESE (G. *mangan*) in compound names of minerals, as **m.-amphibole** = RHODONITE; etc.

Manganate (mæ·ŋgănĕt). 1839. [f. MANGANIC + -ATE[4].] *Chem.* A salt of manganic acid. So †**Mangane·sate** 1819.

Manganese (mæ·ŋgănīz). 1676. [– Fr. *manganèse* – It. *manganese*, unexpl. alt. of med.L. *magnesia* (also *mangnesia*) MAGNESIA.] **1.** A black mineral (now recognized as an oxide of a metal; see sense 2) used in glass-making and other processes. Also called **black m.** **2.** *Chem.* The metallic element (symbol Mn) of which 'black manganese' is the oxide 1783. (Also called †**Manganes(i)um.**).

1. The black m. of commerce is usually a mixture of various oxides, but the term is applied esp. to m. dioxide, MnO_2, which is the valuable ingredient in the mixture (O.E.D.).

attrib. and *Comb.*, as **m. bronze,** (*a*) a bronze dye, (*b*) an alloy of copper and zinc with m.; **m. green,** an unstable green dye derived from manganate of barium; **m. steel,** a malleable mixture of iron and m.

Manganesian (mæŋgănī·ziăn), *a.* 1795. [f. prec. + -IAN.] Pertaining to manganese, or characterized by its presence. So †**Manganesic** *a.*; *m. acid* = manganic acid 1819; **Mangane·s(e)ous** *acid,* manganous acid.

Manganic (mæŋgæ·nik), *a.* 1836. [f. MANGANESE + -IC.] *Chem.* Applied to compounds containing manganese in its higher valency.

M. acid: an acid (H_2MnO_4) not known exc. in comb. with alkalis, with which it forms *manganates.*

Manganiferous (mæŋgăni·fĕrəs), *a.* 1851. [f. MANGANESE + -FEROUS.] *Min.* Containing or yielding manganese. So **Manganin** (mæ·ŋgănin) [-IN[1]], *Metall.* an alloy of copper, manganese, and nickel, much used in the construction of standard resistance coils 1902. **Manganite** (mæ·ŋganəit), [-ITE[1]], *Min.* a hydrated sesquioxode of manganese, occurring massive and in pseudo-crystals; grey manganese ore 1827; *Chem.* a salt of manganous acid 1865. ||**Manganium** (mæŋgē·niŏm) [mod.L.] *Chem.* = MANGANESE 2. 1850.

Manganous (mæ·ŋgănəs), *a.* 1823. [f. MANGANESE + -OUS.] **a.** Of the nature of, or containing, manganese. **b.** *Chem.* Containing manganese in its lower valency.

Mange (mēindʒ). [Late ME. *maniewe*, later *mangie*, shortened to *mange* (XVI) – OFr. *manjue, mangeue* itch, f. *manju-*, pres. ind. sing. stem of *mangier* (mod. *manger*) eat :– L. *manducare* MANDUCATE.] A cutaneous disease occurring in many hairy and woolly animals, caused by an arachnidan parasite. Also *loosely*, a dirty, scabby or scurfy condition of the skin. †**b.** *fig.* A restless desire, an itch to do something –1790.

b. If yet thy head possess the M. of Writing WOLCOT.

Mangel (mæ·ŋg'l), **mangold** (mæ·ŋgŏld). 1856. Short for next.

Mangel - wurzel, mangold - wurzel (mæ·ŋg'l-, mæ·ŋgŏld,wɒ̄·ɹz'l). 1779. [– G. *mangoldwurzel*, f. *mangold*, †*manegolt* beet + *wurzel* root (cf. WORT[1]). The altered form G. *mangelwurzel*, due to assoc. with *mangel* want, was sometimes translated 'root of scarcity' (so Fr. *racine de disette*).] A variety of beet, with a root larger than that of the garden beet; cultivated as a food for cattle. By some considered as a hybrid between the red and the white beet. Also *attrib.*

Manger (mē·ndʒəɹ). [ME. *manyour, maniore* – (O)Fr. *mangeoire*, f. *mangeure* :– Rom. **manducatoria*, f. L. *manducat-*; see MANDUCATE.] **1.** A box or trough in a stable or cowhouse, from which horses and cattle eat. **2.** *Naut.* A small berthing in the bows of a ship, intended to keep the water entering the hawse-holes from flooding the deck 1627.

Mangle (mæ·ŋg'l), *sb.*[1] 1613. [– Sp. *mangle* (Oviedo 1535); see MANGROVE.] = MANGROVE.

Mangle (mæ·ŋg'l), *sb.*[2] 1774. [– Du. *mangel*, short for synon. *mangelstok*, f. *mangelen* mangle + *stok* staff, roller, STOCK *sb.*[1]; ult. from Gr. μάγγανον (see MANGONEL).] A machine for rolling and pressing linen and cotton clothing, etc. after washing; now consisting of two or more cylinders working one upon another.

Comb.: **m.-wheel,** a wheel which, by an ingenious adjustment of rack and pinion, causes the movable part of a m. to travel backwards and forwards, while the wheel itself rotates in only one direction; applied also to a similar wheel in textile machines; similarly **m. pinion, rack.**

Mangle (mæ·ŋg'l), *v.*[1] late ME. [– AFr. *mangler*, **mahangler* (cf. med.L. *mangulare* XIV), prob. frequent. of *mahaignier* MAIM *v.*; see -LE.] **1.** *trans.* To hack, cut, or lacerate by repeated blows; to reduce thus to a more or less unrecognizable condition. Also *transf.* and *fig.* **2.** To cut or hack (a thing) roughly, so as to damage and disfigure 1530. **3.** *fig.* Now chiefly: To make (words) unrecognizable by mispronunciation; to spoil (a quotation, text, etc.) by gross blundering or falsification. Formerly often: To mutilate, deprive of essential parts. 1533.

1. A human head was found severed from the body..and so frightfully mangled that no feature could be recognised MACAULAY. **2.** The bench.., Though mangled, hacked, and hewed, not yet destroyed COWPER. **3.** Remember how they m. our British names abroad MILT.

Mangle (mæ·ŋg'l), *v.*[2] 1775. [f. MANGLE *sb.*[2]] **1.** *trans.* To press smooth with a mangle. **2.** To beat (lead) flat on a roller 1880.

Mango (mæ·ŋgo[u]), *sb.*[1] *Pl.* **mangoes, -gos** (mæ·ŋgo[u]z). 1582. [orig. *manga* – Pg. *manga* (whence mod.L. *mangas*), later altered to the Du. form *mango* – Malay *maŋgā* – Tamil *mānkāy*, f. *mān* mango-tree + *kāy* fruit.] **1.** The fruit of *Mangifera indica* (N.O. *Anacardiaceæ*); it is a fleshy drupe, having in the wild state a turpentine flavour; the best kinds are eaten ripe; the green fruit is used for pickles and conserves. **2.** The tree 1678. **3.** *Cookery.* A pickle, esp. of melons or cucumbers, resembling that made of green mangoes 1699. **4.** Short for *mango-bird, m.-fish* 1819.

Comb.: **m.-bird,** (*a*) an oriole (*Oriolus kundoo*), native of India; (*b*) a humming-bird (*Lampornis mango*), native of Jamaica; **-fish,** a golden-coloured fish, *Polynemus paradiseus* or *risua*, inhabiting the tropical seas between India and the Malay archipelago; **m. (tree) trick,** an Indian juggling trick in which a mango-tree appears to spring up and bear fruit within an hour or two.

†**Ma·ngo,** *sb.*[2] [– L. *mango.*] A slave-dealer. B. JONS.

Mangold (-wurzel): see MANGEL (-WURZEL).

Mangonel (mæ·ŋgŏnel). *Obs.* exc. *Hist.* ME. [– OFr. *mangonel, -elle* (mod. *mangonneau*) – med.L. *manganellus, -gon-*, dim. of late L. *manganum* – Gr. μάγγανον engine of war, axis of a pulley.] A military engine for casting stones, etc.

†**Ma·ngonism.** 1656. [– Fr. †*mangonisme*, f. L. *mango, mangon-* broker, dealer in vamped-up goods; see -ISM.] **1.** The craft of setting out saleable things to advantage. BLOUNT. **2.** A method of treating plants contrary to nature, in order to produce changes in their growth –1722. So †**Ma·ngonist,** one who furbishes up inferior wares for sale 1605–98. †**Ma:ngonization,** the action of tricking out for sale 1660–78. †**Ma·ngonize** *v. trans.* to furbish up (inferior wares) for sale 1623; *intr.* to traffic in slaves 1601.

Mangosteen (mæ·ŋgǫstīn). Also **-stan,** etc. 1598. [– Malay *manggustan* (now *manggis*).] **1.** The fruit of the E. Indian tree *Garcinia mangostana* (N.O. *Guttiferæ*). It is about the size of an apple, with a thick reddish-brown rind, and a white juicy pulp of delicious flavour. **2.** The tree 1734. **3.** **Wild m. (tree),** *Embryopteris glutinifera* 1753.

Mangrove (mæ·ŋgrō[u]v). 1613. [Early forms *mangrowe, mangrave*, later assim. to GROVE; obscurely connected with Pg. *mangue*, Sp. *mangle* (whence Fr. *mangle*), all recorded XVI, from a Haytian Arawak language.] **1.** Any tree or shrub of the genus *Rhizophora*, or the allied genus *Bruguiera*; esp. the Common M., *R. mangle.*

The species are all tropical, growing in the mud on the sea-shore down to low-water-mark; they have large masses of interlacing roots above ground, which intercept mud and weeds, and thus cause the land to encroach on the sea.

2. Applied to plants of similar habit and appearance; *esp.* the White Mangrove (*Avicennia officinalis*) found in Brazil and Australia, and the Black or Olive Mangrove (*A. nitida*) of tropical America and Africa 1683. **3.** *attrib.*, as *m. jungle, root, swamp, tree*, etc. 1672.

||**Mangue** (mæŋ). 1840. [– Fr., perh. a colonial shortening of *mangouste* MONGOOSE.] The KUSIMANSE (*Crossarchus obscurus*).

Mangy (mē·ndʒi), *a.* late ME. [f. MANGE + -Y[1].] **1.** Having the mange; of the nature of or caused by the mange. †Also formerly: Scabby. **2.** Squalid, shabby 1529. **3.** Beggarly, mean, 'lousy'. Common in 17th c. 1538. Hence **Ma·ngily** *adv.* **Ma·nginess.**

Manhad(d)en, var. of MENHADEN.

Man-ha·ndle, *v.* 1457. [f. MAN *sb.* + HANDLE *v.*] †**1.** *trans.* To handle a tool. **2.** *Naut.*, etc. 'To move by force of men, without levers or tackles' (Smyth) 1867. **3.** *slang* To handle roughly; to pull or hustle about 1865.

†**Ma·nhead.** ME. [f. MAN *sb.* + -HEAD.] = MANHOOD, in various senses –1588.

Ma·n-hole. 1793. A hole or opening in a floor, pavement, boiler, sewer, etc., through which a man may pass. Also, a recess in a wall, etc., used as a place of refuge, e.g. to avoid passing trains.

Manhood (mæ·nhud). ME. [f. MAN *sb.* + -HOOD.] **1.** The state or condition of being human; human nature. **2.** The state of being a man, as opp. to childhood or to womanhood ME. **3.** The qualities eminently becoming a man; manliness, courage, valour (*arch.*) ME. †**4.** Humanity, humaneness –1571. **5.** Men collectively 1588. **6.** *attrib.* 1873.

2. Children, as they grow to m. FROUDE. **3.** Peace hath higher tests of m. Than battle ever knew 1853. **5.** The whole m. of Greece fought the battell of Salamis P. HOLLAND. **6. M. suffrage:** suffrage granted to all male citizens of lawful age not disqualified by crime, insanity, etc.

Ma·n-hu:nter. 1555. A hunter of men; usually a contemptuous term for cannibals, slave-dealers, brigands, etc.

Mania (mē·niă). late ME. [– late L. *mania* – Gr. μανία, rel. to μαίνεσθαι be mad, f. **men-*; see MIND *sb.*, -IA[1].] **1.** *Nosology.* Mental derangement characterized by excitement, hallucinations, and, in its acute stage, by great violence. **2.** Chiefly with *a* or *the*: A vehement passion or desire; also (after Fr. *manie*), a craze, a rage. Const. *for, of.* Also a period of excitement affecting a body of persons. 1689.

2. The m. of land speculation 1807. The tulip m. in Holland 1777. Hence **Manic** (mæ·nik) *a.*

-mania, a terminal element, repr. Gr. μανία MANIA in composition, with the general sense 'a certain kind of madness', as *kleptomania, megalomania*; or 'the state of being mad after some object', as *bibliomania, Anglomania*, etc. The sbs. in *-mania* have, or may have, correlative sbs. in *-maniac*; the words in -MANE are few, and are viewed as Gallicisms.

†**Ma·niable,** *a.* 1483. [– (O)Fr. *maniable*, f. *manier* handle, ult. f. L. *manus* hand; see -ABLE.] **1.** Easy to handle; manageable –1727. **2.** That may be handled, palpable –1686.

Maniac (mē·niæk). 1604. [– late L. *maniacus* – late Gr. μανιακός, f. μανία; see MANIA, -AC.] **A.** *adj.* **1.** Affected with mania. **2.** Of, pertaining to, or characterized by mania; characteristic of a maniac 1727. **b.** Frantic 1809.

2. b. The performance of a m. hornpipe DICKENS.

B. *sb.* One who is affected with mania 1763. So **Mani·acal** *a.* 1678, **-ly** *adv.*

-maniac: see -MANIA.

Manicate (mæ·nikeit), *a.* 1832. [– L. *manicatus* furnished with long sleeves, f. *manica*; see MANCHE, -ATE[2].] *Bot.* Covered with hairs interwoven into a mass that can be easily separated from the surface.

Manichæan, Manichean (mænikī·ăn). 1556. [f. late L. *Manichæus* (see next) + -AN.] *adj.* Of or pertaining to the Manichees or their doctrine; characteristic of a Manichee. *sb.* = MANICHEE. Also *transf.* So **Ma·nichæism, Ma·nicheism,** the doctrine or principles of the Manichees. **Ma·nichæist** = MANICHEE.

Manichee (mænikī·). late ME. [– late L. *Manichæus* (late Gr. Μανιχαῖος), f. name of the founder of the sect, *Manes* or *Manichæus.*] An adherent of a religious system widely accepted from the 3rd to the 5th century, composed of Gnostic Christian, Mazdean, and pagan elements, and representing Satan as co-eternal with God.

Leo said that the Devil reigned in all other heresies, but had rais'd his very throne in that of the Manichees 1702.

Manichord (mæ·nikǭɹd). *Obs.* exc. *Hist.* 1668. [– Fr. *manichordion* XV (†*manicorde*, *-cordon*, also OFr. *monacorde* XII) – med.L. *monochordium* – late Gr. μονοχόρδιον, Gr. -χορδον MONOCHORD; the word was assoc. with L. *manus* hand.] = CLAVICHORD.

†**Ma·nicon.** [– L. *manicon* (Pliny) – Gr. μανικόν, f. μανία MANIA; see -IC.] A kind of nightshade, supposed to cause madness *Hudibras* III. i. 324.

Manicure (mæ·nikiuᵊɹ), *sb.* 1880. [– Fr. *manicure* (1877), f. L. *manus* hand + *cura* care. Cf. earlier PEDICURE.] **1.** One who undertakes professionally the treatment of the hands and finger-nails. **2.** The treatment of the hands and finger-nails 1887. Hence **Ma·nicure** *v. trans.* and *intr.* to apply m. treatment (to). **Ma·nicurist** = sense 1.

†**Manie.** late ME. [– Fr. *manie* – L. *mania* MANIA.] = MANIA –1623.

Manifest (mæ·nifest), *sb.* 1561. [– It. *manifesto*; see MANIFESTO.] **1.** *gen.* A manifestation, indication. Now *rare.* **2.** A public declaration; an open statement; a manifesto. *Obs.* exc. as gallicism. **3.** The list of a ship's cargo, signed by the master, for the use of officers of customs 1706.

Manifest (mæ·nifest), *a.* late ME. [–(O)Fr. *manifeste* or L. *manifestus*, earlier *manufestus*, f. *manus* hand + **festus* struck (cf. *infestus* dangerous), f. base of *defendere* DEFEND.] **1.** Evident to the eye, mind, or judgement; obvious. †**2.** Having evident signs *of*; evidently possessed *of* or guilty *of*. [Const. after L.] –1725.

1. That the works of God should be made m. in him *John* 9:3. **2.** Calisto there stood m. of shame DRYDEN. Hence **Ma·nifest-ly** *adv.*, **-ness.**

Manifest (mæ·nifest), *v.* late ME. [–(O)Fr. *manifester* or L. *manifestare*, f. *manifestus*; see prec.] **1.** *trans.* To make evident to the eye or to the mind; to show plainly. **b.** Of things: To be evidence of, prove 1508. †**2.** To clear up (a matter) –1669. **3. a.** To display (a quality, condition, feeling, etc.); to reveal the presence of, evince 1567. **b.** *refl.* Of a thing: To reveal itself as existing or operative 1808. **4.** To record in a ship's manifest 1541. **5.** *intr.* To make a public expression of opinion 1898. **6.** *Spiritualism.* Of a ghost (*refl.* or *intr.*): To reveal its presence, appear 1858. **7.** *Hist.* In Spanish law, to protect by a MANIFESTATION (sense 4) 1818.

1. [He] manifested forth his glory *John* 2:11. **b.** Thy Life did m., thou lou'dst me not SHAKS. **3. b.** No tendency, in general, to dysentery, manifested itself at this time 1808.

Manifestation (mænifestē¹·ʃən). late ME. [– late L. *manifestatio*, f. *manifestat-*, pa. ppl. stem of L. *manifestare*; see prec., -ION.] **1.** The action of manifesting or the fact of being manifested. **b.** An instance of this; hence, that by which something is manifested 1785. **2.** A public act on the part of a government intended as a display of its power and determination to enforce some demand; also, a collective action (e.g. a procession, public meeting, etc.) undertaken by a political party, etc., in order to call attention to its views 1844. **3.** *Spiritualism.* A phenomenon by which the presence of a spirit is supposed to be rendered perceptible 1853. **4.** *Hist.* In Spanish law, a process by which an accused person might be protected from the action of judges and removed to a special prison out of their reach. Also, this prison (= Sp. *carcel de los manifestados.*). 1769.

1. The matter..requireth more wordes for the m. thereof than I may now affoorde 1570. **b.** The first m. of thought is speech MAX-MÜLLER.

Manifesto (mænife·sto), *sb.* 1644. [– It. *manifesto*, f. *manifestare* – L. *manifestare*; see MANIFEST *v.*] †**1.** A proof, a piece of evidence –1686. **2.** A public declaration by a sovereign prince or state, or by an individual or body of individuals whose proceedings are of public importance, making known past actions and explaining the motives for actions announced as forthcoming 1647.

2. The manifestoes of modern agrarianism 1839. Hence **Manife·sto** *v. rare*, to issue a m. or manifestos.

Manifold (mæ·nifōᵘld), *a.*, *adv.*, and *sb.*¹ Now *literary.* [OE. *maniġfeald* = OFris. *manichfald*, OHG. *managfalt* (G. *mannigfalt*), Goth. *managfalþs*; Gmc. f. MANY + -FOLD.] **A.** *adj.* **1.** Having various forms, features, relations, applications, etc.; †complex. **b.** Qualifying a personal designation: That is such in many ways or in many relations ME. **2.** Qualifying pl. sb.: Numerous and varied. †Formerly simply: Numerous. OE.

1. They..m. in sin, deserv'd to fall MILT. **b.** The m. Linguist, and the army-potent souldier SHAKS. **2.** Overwhelmed by m. vexations 1849.

†**B.** *adv.* In many ways, modes, degrees, etc. –1593. †**b.** In the proportion of many to one, *Luke* 18:30.

C. *absol.* and *sb.* †**1.** Phr. *By* (rarely *on*) *m.*: many times over –1596. **2.** That which is manifold. **a.** *spec.* In the Kantian philosophy, the sum of the particulars furnished by sense before they have been unified by the understanding 1855. **b.** *gen.* 1856. **3.** *Math.* A general conception of which time and space are particular varieties 1890. **4.** A copy made by a manifold writer 1884. **5.** *Mech.* A pipe or chamber with several outlets or valves forming connections with other pipes, etc. 1891.

2. b. The picturesque m. of life 1902.

D. *Comb.*: **m.-paper**, carbonized paper used in making several copies of a writing at one time; **m. writer**, an apparatus fitted with carbonized paper for doing this; so **m. writing.**

Ma·nifold, *sb.*² *dial.* Also **manifolds.** ME. [f. MANY *a.* + FOLD *sb.*² Cf. MANYPLIES.] The intestine or bowels; *spec.* the manyplies or third stomach of a ruminant.

Manifold (mæ·nifōᵘld), *v.* [OE. *maniġfealdian*, f. the adj.; see MANIFOLD *a.* The word became obsolete in ME. and was subsequently formed afresh from the adj.] *trans.* To make manifold, multiply. *rare* exc. as in b. **b.** *spec.* To make copies (of), as by a manifold writer 1865.

b. The Home Secretary received such precise and timely information that he was enabled to have it manifolded 1881.

Ma·nifoldly, *adv.* Now only *literary.* [OE. *maniġfealdlīċe*; see MANIFOLD *a.*, -LY².] In manifold ways; †*occas.* in the proportion of many to one.

Manifoldness (mæ·nifōᵘldnės). [OE. *maniġfealdnis*; see MANIFOLD *a.*, -NESS.] **1.** The quality or condition of being manifold; varied character; multiplicity. **2.** *Math.* = MANIFOLD C. 3. [A transl. of G. *mannigfaltigkeit.*] 1873.

Maniform (mæ·nifǭɹm), *a.* 1826. [f. L. *manus* hand + -FORM.] Having the form of a hand; *Entom.* chelate.

Manihot, var. of MANIOC.

Manikin (mæ·nikin). 1570. [– Du. *manneken*, dim. of *man* MAN *sb.*; see -KIN. Cf. MANNEQUIN.] **1.** A little man (often *contemptuous*); a dwarf, pygmy. Also *fig.* 1601. **2. a.** An artist's lay figure 1570. **b.** A model of the human body used for exhibiting the anatomical structure or for demonstrating surgical operations 1831. **3.** *attrib.* or *adj.* Dwarf, pygmy, undersized; puny 1840.

2. Thus, of a Manneken (as the Dutch painters terme it) in the same Symmetrie, may a Giant be made 1570. **3.** The m. grasp of the English ministry DISRAELI.

Manikin, var. of MANAKIN.

Manilio, var. of next, and of MANILLE.

Manilla¹ (mǎni·lǎ). 1556. [– Sp. *manilla*, prob. dim. of *mano* hand.] A ring of metal worn on the arm or wrist by some African tribes and used as a medium of exchange.

Manillas..are regularly manufactured at Birmingham for the African traders 1851.

Manilla², **Manila** (mani·lǎ). 1697. [Native name; the form *Manila* is correct, but rare.] **1.** Name of the capital of the Philippine Islands, used attrib. in *M. copal, grass, tobacco*, etc., products of those islands. **2.** (In full *M. hemp.*) A fibrous material, obtained from the leaves of *Musa textilis* (see ABACA), for ropes, matting, textile fabrics, paper, etc. Hence *M. cable, hat, paper, rope*, etc. 1814. **3.** (In full *M. cheroot.*) A kind of cheroot manufactured in Manila 1839.

Manille (mǎni·l). 1674. [– Fr. *manille* – Sp. *malilla*, dim. of *mala* used in the same sense, fem. (sc. *carta* card) of *malo* bad.] *Cards.* In quadrille and ombre, the second best trump.

Man in the moon. ME. **1.** The fancied semblance of a man (or a man's face) in the disc of the moon. **2.** Referred to as the type of an imaginary person (e.g. the person who supplies money for illicit expenditure at elections) 1596.

1. Which he knows no more then the Man in the Moon MARVELL.

Manioc (mæ·niǫk). Also **mandioc**, etc. 1568. [Earliest form *manihot*, from Fr. (but *manioch* is found XVII); repr. Tupi *mandioca*, Guarani *mandio.*] = CASSAVA 1, 2.

Maniple (mæ·nip'l). ME. [– OFr. *maniple* (mod. *manipule*) or L. *manipulus* handful, troop of soldiers, f. *manus* hand + an unkn. element.] †**1.** A handful (*lit.* and *fig.*) 1632–1829. **2.** *Rom. Antiq.* A subdivision of the Roman legion, of which a cohort contained three, numbering 120 men each among the *hastati* and *principes*, and 60 each among the *triarii* 1533. †**b.** In mod. warfare, a small band of soldiers of more or less definite number –1644. **3.** *Eccl.* In the Western Church, one of the Eucharistic vestments, consisting now of a strip of stuff two to four feet in length worn hanging from the left arm; said to have been orig. a napkin ME.

Manipular (mǎni·piŭlǎɹ), *a.* (*sb.*) 1623. [– L. *manipularis*, f. *manipulus*; see prec., -AR¹.] **1.** Pertaining to the MANIPLE (sense 2); characterized by formation in maniples. **2.** = MANIPULATIVE. [Not a justifiable sense.] 1831. **3.** *sb.* A soldier of a maniple 1862.

2. An unequivocal m. token of resentment 1831.

Manipulate (mǎni·piŭlēⁱt), *v.* 1827. [Back-formation from MANIPULATION, after Fr. *manipuler.*] **1.** *trans.* To handle, esp. with dexterity; to treat by manual (and, hence, any mechanical) means 1831. **b.** *absol.* or *intr.* in *Chem.* 1827. **2.** To handle or treat (questions, artistic matter, resources, etc.) with skill 1856. **3.** To manage by dexterous (esp. unfair) contrivance or influence 1864.

1. To m. guillotines CARLYLE. **2.** The art of manipulating money FROUDE. **3.** It will be possible for firms to m. their books 1893. Hence **Mani·pulative, Mani·pulatory** *adjs.* pertaining to or involving manipulation. **Mani·pulator,** one who or that which manipulates or facilitates manipulation.

Manipulation (mǎnipiulē¹·ʃən). 1727. [– Fr. *manipulation* (= Sp. *-ción*, It. *-zione*) – mod.L. **manipulatio*, *-on-*, f. **manipulare*, f. *manipulus* handful (spec. of chemical ingredients); see MANIPLE, -ATION.] †**1.** The method of digging silver ore. (Only in Dicts.) **2.** *Chem.* The method of handling apparatus, etc. in experiments. In *Pharmacy*, 'the preparation of drugs' (Webster 1828). 1796. **3.** *gen.* The handling of objects for a particular purpose; in *Surgery*, the manual examination of a part of the body. Also, manual action. 1826. **4.** Dexterous (esp. unfair) management of persons or things 1828.

2. The various sources of inaccuracy to which chemical manipulations are liable 1805. **3.** The m. of a musket 1846. **4.** The third estate..was only too susceptible of royal m. STUBBS.

‖**Manis** (mē¹·nis). 1770. [mod.L. (Linn.), said to be a spurious sing. of MANES.] *Zool.* The typical genus of the family *Manidæ* (scaly ant-eaters); any one of these, a pangolin.

‖**Manitou** (mæ·nitu). Also **manito, manitu (-ido), moneto.** 1671. [– Algonquin *manitu*, *manito*, f. *manit* active pa. pple. of a vb. meaning 'surpass' + predic. suffix ('he or it is *manit*').] Among some American Indians, a spirit (of good or of evil) which is an object of religious awe; also, anything having supernatural power, as a fetish.

Manitrunk (mæ·nitrɒŋk). 1826. [f. L. *manus* taken as 'fore-leg' + *truncus* trunk.] *Entom.* The anterior segment of the thorax.

Ma·n-keen, *a.* Now *dial.* 1568. [f. MAN *sb.* + KEEN *a.*] Of animals (*rarely* of persons): Inclined to attack men; fierce, savage.

Mankin. 1820. [f. MAN *sb.* + -KIN.] A manikin.

Mankind, *sb.* and *a.*[1] ME. [repl. †*mankin,* OE. *mancynn* (MAN *sb.*, KIN), by substitution of KIND *sb.*] **A.** *sb.* **I.** (Now mænkəi·nd.) **1.** The human species. Now only *collect.* and with pl. concord. †**2.** Human nature –1567. †**b.** Humanity. B. JONS.

1. M. never suffer any work to be lost which tends to make them more wise or happy GOLDSM.

II. (Now mæ·nkəind.) The male sex; persons of the male sex 1526.

The..silliness of m. and womankind at large 1874.

B. *adj.* †**1.** Human 1584. †**2.** Male –1638. †**3.** Of woman: Masculine, virago-like –1635.

†**Ma·nkind,** *a.*[2] 1519. [perh. a perversion of MAN-KEEN, though that form does not appear until later.] = MAN-KEEN –1672.

Manks, obs. f. MANX.

Manless (mæ·nlės), *a.* OE. [f. MAN *sb.* + -LESS.] **1.** Having no men. †**2.** Unmanly –1653; inhuman 1611. Hence †**Ma·nless-ly** *adv.*, **-ness.**

Ma·nlihood. *rare.* 1641. [f. MANLY *a.* + -HOOD.] Manliness.

Manlike (mæ·nləik), *a.* (*adv.*) 1450. [f. MAN *sb.* + -LIKE.] **1.** Having the qualities proper to a man. Of women: Having masculine qualities; mannish. **b.** Befitting a man 1561. **2.** Resembling a man 1590. **3.** *adv.* = MANFULLY 1560.

1. That m. nation 1579. The m. Amazons POPE **b.** Glaring Chloe's m. Taste and Mien SHENSTONE. **2.** The M. apes HUXLEY. **3.** M. let him turn and face it [the danger] EMERSON. Hence **Ma·n-like-ly** *adv.*, **-ness.**

Manling (mæ·nliŋ). 1575. [-LING[1].] A little man; sometimes *depreciatory.*

Manly (mæ·nli), *a.* ME. [f. MAN *sb.* + LY[1].] †**1.** Belonging to human beings; human –1625. **2.** Possessing the virtues proper to a man; chiefly, courageous, independent, frank, upright ME. **b.** Of a woman; Possessing qualities characteristic of a man 1511. **c.** *transf.* and *fig.* 1697. **3.** Befitting or belonging to a man ME. †**4.** Grown up; adult, mature –1691.

2. Be stronge now and m. ye Philistynes..Be m. and fighte COVERDALE 1 *Sam.* 4:9. **3.** I saw the wound,..here on his m. brest SHAKS. M. sports 1851. Hence **Ma·nlily** *adv.* **Ma·nliness.**

Manly (mæ·nli), *adv.* [OE. *mannlīċe*; see MAN *sb.* and -LY[2].] **1.** In a manly manner; manfully; courageously, with valour or energy. †**2.** Like a human being; humanely. **b.** Like fallen man; unregenerately. –1547. †**3.** Excellently, 'bravely'. *Macb.* IV. iii. 235.

1. Our Souldiers..stood m. to it LITHGOW.

Ma·n-mi·dwife. Now *rare.* Pl. **men-midwives.** 1625. An accoucheur.

Ma·n-mi·lliner. *Pl.* **men-, man-milliners.** 1792. A man who makes or vends millinery; in contemptuous use, a man who occupies himself excessively with embellishments of dress or ornaments. So **Ma·n-mi·llinery,** a contemptuous term for clothing or apparel (e.g. uniforms, vestments) to which men devote too much attention.

Manna (mæ·nă). OE. [– late L. *manna* – Hellenistic Gr. μάννα (LXX, N.T.) – Aram. *mannā* – Heb. *mān*, corresp. to Arab. *mann*, Egyptian *mannu*, the word being prob. anciently current in the Sinaitic wilderness for the exudation of the tree *Tamarix gallica*. Traditionally derived (cf. Ex. 16:15) from Aram. *mān hū* what is it?]

I. Biblical, etc. uses. **1.** The substance miraculously supplied to the Israelites during their progress through the Wilderness. (See *Exod* 16.) Also *transf.* and *fig.* **2.** Spiritual nourishment; food divinely supplied, *esp.* the Holy Communion. late ME.

1. *fig.* His Tongue Dropt M., and could make the worse appear The better reason MILT.

II. In *Pharmacy*, etc. **1.** A sweet pale yellow or whitish concrete juice obtained from incisions in the bark of the Manna ash, *Fraxinus ornus*, chiefly in Calabria and Sicily; used as a gentle laxative. Also, any similar exudation. 1533. †**2.** In early *Chem.*: A white powder –1706. **3.** = *manna seeds* 1785. **4.** A species of grass. *Setaria* (*Panicum*) *italica*, better known as Italian or Hungarian millet 1897. †**5.** A grain (of frankincense); frankincense in grains. [Strictly another wd.] –1753.

1. Australian m., a secretion of certain species of Eucalyptus, esp. *E. viminalis*. **Briançon m.,** a substance secreted by the common larch. **Hebrew, Jews', Mount Sinai, Persian m.,** the product of *Alhaga maurorum* or of *Tamarix gallica*, var. *mannifera*.

attrib. and *Comb.*, as **m. ash (tree),** the tree *Fraxinus ornus*; **m.-grass,** †(*a*) = DEW-GRASS; (*b*) the aquatic grass *Glyceria fluitans*; **m. seeds,** the seeds of manna-grass, *Glyceria fluitans*; **m. sugar** = MANNITE; **m. tree** = *manna ash*.

Manna-croup (mæ·năkrūˑp). 1843. [– Russ. *mánnaya krupá* lit. groats of manna.] **a.** A coarse granular meal consisting of the large hard grains of wheat-flour not ground into fine flour by the mill-stones; used for making puddings, soups, etc. **b.** A similar meal made from the seeds of the manna-grass.

Mannequin (mæ·nėkwin, -kin). 1902. [– Fr. *mannequin* MANIKIN.] A dressmaker's live model for exhibiting new fashions.

Mannequin, var. of MANIKIN.

Manner (mæ·nəɹ), *sb.*[1] [ME. *manere* – AFr. *manere*, (O)Fr. *manière* :– Rom. **manuaria* subst. use of fem. of L. *manuarius* pertaining to the hand, in Gallo-Rom. handy, convenient, f. *manus* hand; see -ER[2] 2.] **1.** The way in which something is done or takes place; mode of action or procedure. **2.** Customary mode of acting or behaviour; habitual practice; usage, custom, fashion. Now only *literary* or *arch.* ME. **3.** *collect. pl.* †**a.** A person's habitual behaviour or conduct; moral character, morals –1794. †**b.** Conduct in its moral aspect; also, morality as a subject of study; the moral code embodied in general custom or sentiment –1776. **c.** The modes of life, rules of behaviour, conditions of society, prevailing in a people ME. **d.** Good customs or way of living 1579. †**e.** *Literary criticism.* Character, distinctive varieties of disposition and temperament, as portrayed in epic or dramatic poetry; the portraiture of character, as an element of poetic art. (After Aristotle's use of ἦθη.) –1780. †**f.** Habits (of animals). Cf. Fr. *mœurs*. –1831. **4.** Outward bearing. With reference to a speaker: Characteristic style of attitude, gesture, and utterance. ME. **b.** A distinguished or fashionable air 1694. **5.** *pl.* (†formerly also *sing.*) External behaviour in social intercourse. late ME. **6.** Polite behaviour or deportment; habits indicating good breeding. Usu. in *pl.* late ME. **b.** Forms of politeness or respect. *Obs.* exc. *arch.* or *dial.* in *To do* or *make one's manners*. 1596. **7. a.** Method or style of execution in art or literature 1662. **b.** *spec.* The method or style characteristic of a particular artist, etc.; often = mannerism 1706. **8.** Species, kind, sort. Now only *arch.* in *What m.* (*of*)...? ME. **b.** *sing.* with pl. construction, qualified by *all, many, these*, or a numeral. Now only in *all m. of* = all sorts of. ME. †**9.** [= L. *modus*.] Measure, moderation. *In m.*: in due measure. –1502.

1. God spake at sondrie tymes & in diuers maners in the olde tyme to our fathers by the Prophetes N.T. (Geneva) *Heb.* 1:1. Phr. *In like m. M. of speaking* [cf. Fr. *manière de parler*]: form of expression. *In a m. of speaking*: so to speak. *Adverb of m.* (Gram.): one which answers, or asks, the question *how?* †*In* (*the*) *m. of*: after the fashion of, in the guise of. *In a m.* (formerly †*in m.*): in some way, so to speak, as it were. **2.** Here Ctesippus, as his m. was, burst into a roar of laughter JOWETT. Phr. *To the m. born*: In *Haml.* I. iv. 15, destined by birth to be subject to the custom; later often: Naturally fitted for some position or employment. **3. a.** Euell speakinges corruppe good maners COVERDALE 1 *Cor.* 15:33. **b.** The rule of faith and manners TILLOTSON. **c.** To study the manners of the age D'ISRAELI. **d.** Oh! raise us up, return to us again; And give us manners, virtue, freedom, power WORDSW. **4.** Something in the boy's m. attracted the banker's interest FROUDE. **5.** Hugh..was in manners and bearing an Englishman GREEN. **6.** We could not, in manners, refuse him 1760. **7. a.** M. is all in all, whatever is writ, The substitute for genius, sense, and wit COWPER. **b.** A picture of Raphael in his first m. H. WALPOLE. **8.** What m. of Fellow was hee that robb'd you? SHAKS. **b.** These externall m. of Laments SHAKS. Phr. *No* (or *any*) *m. of*..: periphrastic for 'no, any (person or thing) whatever'. (†*Of* formerly omitted.) *By no* (or *any*) *m. of means*: see MEAN *sb.*

Comb. **manners-bit** *dial.*, a portion of a dish left by the guests that the host may not think he has provided too little.

Manner, *sb.*[2] (*taken with the m.*): see MAINOUR.

Mannered (mæ·nəɹd), *a.* late ME. [f. MANNER *sb.*[1] + -ED[2].] **1.** Having manners of a specified kind (as *evil-, gentle-, rough-m.*, etc.). †**b.** Of a literary work, etc.: Exhibiting manners or character. (Cf. Horace, *A.P.* 319 *morataque recte fabula*.) –1789. **2.** Marked by manner or mannerism, esp. in art or literature 1801.

1. Giue her Princely training, that she may be manere'd as she is borne SHAKS. **2.** That Spohr was too doctrinaire and m. [etc.] 1884.

Mannerism (mæ·nəriz'm). 1803. [f. MANNER *sb.*[1] + -ISM.] Excessive or affected addiction to a distinctive manner, esp. in art and literature. **b.** An instance of this; a trick of manner 1819.

Mr. Stewart's style..has character without m., or eccentricity 1803. So **Ma·nnerist** [orig. after Fr. *maniériste*], one who is addicted to m. 1695. **Manneri·stic, -al** *a.* marked by m. 1830.

Ma·nnerless, *a.* 1460. [f. MANNER *sb.*[1] + -LESS.] Without manners.

Mannerly (mæ·nəɹli), *a.* ME. [f. MANNER *sb.*[1] + -LY[1].] †**1.** Seemly, respectable –1697. †**2.** Moral, well-conducted –1549. **3.** Well-mannered; polite 1529.

3. Criticism must be truthful, but it may also be m. 1887. Hence **Ma·nnerliness,** m. quality.

Ma·nnerly, *adv.* ME. [f. MANNER *sb.*[1] + -LY[2].] †**1.** In a seemly manner, properly –1647. **2.** Politely, courteously 1519.

2. Eate the thinge that is set before the, manerly COVERDALE *Ecclus.* 31:16.

Mannide (mæ·nəid). 1862. [f. MANNA + -IDE.] *Chem.* A syrupy substance obtained by heating mannite with butyric acid.

Mannish (mæ·niʃ), *a.* [OE. *mennisć* (see MAN *sb.*, -ISH[1]); in XIV re-formed on MAN *sb.*] †**1.** Of or belonging to mankind; human –1674. **2.** Of a woman, etc.: Masculine. Chiefly *contemptuous.* ME. **3.** Pertaining to or characteristic of a grown man (often opp. to *childish*); aping manhood 1530. **4.** Characteristic of a man as dist. from a woman 1748. †**5.** quasi-*adv.* Like a man, CHAUCER.

2. A woman impudent and m. growne, Is not more loth'd, then an effeminate man SHAKS. **3.** Why must every thing smack of man and m.? Is the world all grown up? LAMB. **4.** Oh! what a m. room 1884. Hence **Ma·nnish-ly** *adv.*, **-ness.**

Mannite (mæ·nəit). 1830. [f. MANNA + -ITE[1] 4.] *Chem.* A substance, $C_6H_{14}O_6$, obtained chiefly from manna; = manna sugar. Hence **Manni·tic** *a.* derived from m.; as *mannitic acid* $C_6H_{12}O_7$.

Manœuvre (mănūˑvəɹ), *sb.* Also *U.S.* **manœuver, -euver.** 1479. [– Fr. *manœuvre* (OFr. *manuevre*), f. *manœuvrer*; see next.] †**1.** Hand-labour (*rare*). **2.** *Mil.* and *Naval.* The planned movement or evolution of troops or vessels of war; a device in navigation; exercise or a movement in military or naval tactics 1758. **b.** Skilful management *of* 1834. **3.** A deceptive or elusive movement made by a person, animal, etc. 1774. **4.** *transf.* and *fig.* An artful plan; an adroit move; also, management of affairs by scheming 1774. †**5.** A method of working –1789.

4. These Acts of Parliament and ministerial manœuvres will injure me 1774. **5.** I do not understand the m. of sugar H. WALPOLE.

Manœuvre (mănūˑvəɹ), *v.* Forms: see prec. sb. 1777. [– Fr. *manœuvrer* :– med.L. *manuoperare*, for L. *manu operari* (*-are*) work with the hand, f. *manus* hand; see OPERATE.] **1.** *intr. Mil.* and *Naval.* To perform manœuvres; to make changes of position in the disposition of troops, vessels, etc. Also *to m. it.* **b.** *transf.* and *fig.*, esp.: To manage by artifice, to scheme 1809. **c.** To drive (a person) *into* or *out of* by manœuvring 1817. **2.** *trans. Mil.* and *Naval.* To cause (troops or vessels) to perform manœuvres; to handle (a boat) 1777. **b.** *transf.* and *fig.* To manipulate adroitly. Also *occas.* to effect by stratagem. 1815.

1. b. I remember her manœuvring to gain a husband, and then manœuvring to manage him MAR. EDGEWORTH. **c.** When she had manœuvred him into a fever of passionate love, she often felt and always assumed indifference PEACOCK. Hence **Manœu·vrer.**

Man of the world. ME. †**a.** A secular person. **b.** A worldly or irreligious person (after Ps. 17:14). **c.** A man versed in the ways of the world and prepared to accept its conventions.

c. A true, fashionable, unprincipled man of the world 1778.

Man-of-war (mæ:nəvwǭ·ɹ). *Pl.* **men-of-war.** late ME. [In sense 1 app. after Fr. *homme de guerre*; for sense 2 cf. MAN sb. III. 2.] **1.** A fighting man; a soldier. *Obs.* exc. *arch.* or *joc.* **2.** A vessel equipped for warfare; an armed ship belonging to the recognized navy of a country. Also *attrib.* 1484. †**3.** (In full *man-of-war bird* or *hawk.*) The frigate-bird, *Fregata aquila.* Also applied to the albatross and occas. to species of skua (Newton). –1885.

1. The Lord is a man of warre *Exod.* 15:3. **2.** *Man-of-war's man*: a sailor serving on a man-of-war. Phr. *Portuguese man-of-war*: A marine hydrozoan of the genus *Physalia*; so called from its floating on the sea with a sail-like crest displayed.

Manometer (mănǫ·mĭtəɹ). 1730. [– Fr. *manomètre*, f. Gr. μανός thin, rare; see -METER.] An instrument for ascertaining the elastic force of gases or vapours. Hence **Manome·tric** (1873), **Manome·trical** (1777) *a.*

Manometric flame, a flame arranged to pulsate under the influence of sound-waves, used in an apparatus for analysing sounds.

Manor (mæ·nəɹ). [ME. *maner(e* – AFr. *maner*, OFr. *maneir*, (now) *manoir* dwelling, habitation (latinized *manerium*, *-eria*), subst. use of *maneir* dwell :– L. *manēre* remain, in Rom. dwell; see MANSION. The sp. with *-or* (XVI) is alt. of *mannor*, which succeeded to *manner, manoir*.] †**1.** A mansion, habitation; the principal house of an estate –1610. †Also *fig.* †**2.** The mansion of a lord with the land belonging to it; hence, a landed possession –1600. **3.** A unit of English territorial organization, orig. of the nature of a feudal lordship. It now consists of the lord's demesne (if any) and of lands from the holders of which he has the right to exact certain fees and fines, and within which he has certain privileges. 1538. **b.** Applied to certain districts in the U.S. which were manors in colonial times 1639. **4.** *attrib.*, as *m.-court*, etc. 1667.

3. By an ancient custom of this m. [Mansfield], the heirs were declared of age as soon as born 1797. *Lord of the m.*, the person or corporation having the seignorial rights of a m.

Hence **Mano·rial** *a.* of or pertaining to a m. or manors; incidental to a m. 1785.

Manor-house (mæ·nəɹ,haus). 1575. [f. MANOR + HOUSE *sb.*[1]] The mansion of the lord of a manor. So **Ma·nor-place** 1426.

‖**Manqué** (maŋke). 1841. [Fr., pa. pple. of *manquer* fall short (of).] That might have been but is not.

Manqueller (mæ·nkweləɹ). *Obs.* exc. *arch.* ME. [f. MAN *sb.* + QUELLER.] A murderer.

†**Ma·nred.** [OE. *mannrǣden*, f. *mann* MAN *sb.* + *-rǣden* -RED.] **1.** Homage –1679. **2.** Vassals collectively; the men whom a lord can call upon in time of war; a supply of men for warfare –1630. **3.** The 'conduct' (of an army) –1581. So **Manrent.** *Sc.* Now *Hist.*

Mansard (mæ·nsăɹd). 1734. [– Fr. *mansarde* (*toit en mansarde*), f. name of François *Mansard*, French architect, 1598–1666.] *Arch.* A form of curb-roof, in which each face of the roof has two slopes, the lower one steeper than the other. Usu. *m. roof.*

Manse (mæns). 1490. [– med.L. *mansus*, *mansa*, *mansum* dwelling, house, measure of land, f. *mans-*; see MANSION.] †**1.** A mansion-house or 'capital messuage' –1781. **2.** A measure of land regarded as sufficient for the support of a family. *Obs.* exc. *Hist.* 1597. **3.** An ecclesiastical residence; now *esp.* the house of the minister of a parish in Scotland 1534.

2. A monastery founded at Ripon and endowed with xxx manses of land MILMAN. **3.** The castle of St. Andrews..had been the Bishop of St. Andrews his manse 1683.

Ma·n-se:rvant. *Pl.* **men-servants.** 1551. A male servant.

Mansion (mæ·nʃən), *sb.* ME. [– (O)Fr. *mansion* – L. *mansio* stay, station, abiding-place, quarters (whence Fr. *maison* house), f. *mans-*, pa. ppl. stem of L. *manēre* remain, stay.] †**1.** The action of remaining, dwelling, or staying in a place. Also, continuance in a position or state. –1722. **2.** A place of abode, an abiding-place. Now *arch.* ME. Also *transf.* and *fig.* †**b.** Chiefly *pl.* A separate dwelling-place or apartment in a large house or enclosure –1697. **3.** †**a.** *gen.* A house, tent, etc. –1781. **b.** In early use: The chief residence of a lord; a manor-house. Hence, later, a large and stately residence. 1512. **c.** *fig.* (e.g. of the body as enclosing the soul) 1526. **d.** Used in *pl.* of large buildings divided into flats 1901. †**4.** A halting-place in a journey; a stage –1737. **5.** *Astrol.* **a.** = HOUSE *sb.*[1] 8. **b.** Each of the twenty-eight divisions of the ecliptic, which are occupied by the moon on successive days. ME. †**6.** Used as tr. med.L. *mansa, mansus* a hide of land; see MANSE 2. –1809. **7.** *attrib.* †*m.-place* = senses 3 b, c, 4. 1473.

1. Phr. *To have, keep, make, take* (one's) *m.* = to abide, dwell. These poets near our Princes sleep, And in one grave their m. keep DENHAM. **2.** Where the bleak Swiss their stormy m. tread GOLDSM. *fig.* When thy mind Shall be a m. for all lovely forms WORDSW. **b.** In my fathers housse are many mansions TINDALE *John* 14:2. Hell it self will pass away, And leave her dolorous mansions to the peering day MILT. **3. b.** The lordly M. of its pride Is stripped WORDSW.

Hence †**Ma·nsion** *v. rare*, to reside 1638–1711.

Ma·nsion-house. 1533. †**a.** A house in which a person resides –1755. **b.** The house of the lord of a manor, the chief residence of a landed proprietor; hence (now only U.S.) a great house 1641. **c.** An official residence. Now *spec.* the official residence of the Lord Mayor of London. 1546.

a. He took his present Lodging in St. John Street, at the Mansion-House of a Taylor's Widow STEELE.

Mansionry (mæ·nʃənri). *rare.* 1605. [f. MANSION *sb.* + -RY.] ? Mansions collectively. In *Macb.* I. vi. 5 perh. mispr. for *masonry.*

Manslaughter (mæ·nslǭtəɹ). ME. [f. MAN *sb.* + SLAUGHTER. The earlier word was *manslaught* (OE. *mannslæht*).] **1.** †**a.** Homicide; chiefly criminal homicide, *esp.* murder –1611. **b.** The 'slaughtering' of human beings 1450. **2.** *Law.* Criminal homicide without malice aforethought 1447.

2. In this there are also degrees of guilt, which divide the offence into m., and murder BLACKSTONE.

Manslayer (mæ·nslēˈ,əɹ). ME. One who kills a man; a homicide; *occas.* one who commits manslaughter. So **Ma·n-slaying** *vbl. sb.*

Mansuete (mænswī·t, mæ·nswīt), *a. Obs.* or *arch.* late ME. [– L. *mansuetus* gentle, f. *manus* hand + *suetus* accustomed.] Gentle, mild; tame, not wild or fierce.

Mansuetude (mæ·nswĭtiud). *arch.* late ME. [– (O)Fr. *mansuétude* or L. *mansuetudo*, f. *mansuetus*; see prec., -TUDE. Cf. *desuetude.*] Gentleness, meekness.

Manswear (mæ·nsweᵊɹ), *v. Obs.* exc. *arch.* and *dial.* Pa. t. **-swore,** pa. pple. **-sworn.** [OE. *mānswerian*, f. *mān* wickedness (= OFris., OS. *mēn*, OHG. *mein*, surviving in *meineid* perjury, ON. *mein*) + *swerian* SWEAR.] **1.** *intr.* To swear falsely. **2.** *refl.* To perjure oneself ME. †**3.** To swear falsely by (a god) –1567.

Mansworn (mæ·nswǭɹn), *ppl. a. Obs.* exc. *Sc.* and *n. dial.* ME. [pa. pple. of prec.] Forsworn, perjured.

Manteau. *Obs.* exc. *Hist.* 1671. [– Fr. *manteau*; see MANTLE.] A loose upper garment formerly worn by women; also, a mantle or cloak.

Mantel (mæ·nt'l). 1489. [var. of MANTLE *sb.*] †**1.** = MANTELET 2 a –1578. **2. a.** = MANTEL-TREE 1. ? *Obs.* 1519. **b.** = MANTELPIECE 1. 1532. **c.** = MANTELSHELF 1742. **d.** *attrib.* **m.-board,** a wooden shelf, usu. draped, fixed upon a mantelshelf.

Mantelet, mantlet (mæ·ntlėt). late ME. [– OFr. *mantelet*, dim. of *mantel* (mod. *manteau*) MANTLE, MANTEL.] **1.** A kind of short, loose, sleeveless mantle covering the shoulders. †**b.** A woollen covering for a horse –1548. **2. a.** *Mil.* A movable shelter for men-at-arms when attacking a fortified place. *Obs.* exc. *Hist.* 1524. **b.** A screen, now usually of rope, to protect men working a gun 1859. **c.** A bullet-proof shelter from which firing results can be observed and signalled 1874.

Ma·ntelpiece. 1686. [f. MANTEL + PIECE *sb.*] **1.** The ornamental structure of wood, marble, etc. above and around a fire-place. **2.** = MANTELSHELF 1827.

Ma·ntelshelf. 1828. [f. MANTEL + SHELF.] That projecting part of a mantelpiece which serves as a shelf.

Ma·ntel-tree. 1482. [f. MANTEL + TREE.] **1.** A beam across the opening of a fireplace, supporting the masonry above; in later use, a stone or arch serving the same purpose. **2.** = MANTELPIECE 1, 2. 1634.

Mantic (mæ·ntik), *a.* 1850. [– Gr. μαντικός, f. μάντις soothsayer, f. root *man-*; see MANIA, -IC.] Pertaining to divination.

Revelation knows nothing of this m. fury TRENCH.

-mantic, repr. Gr. μαντικός (see prec.) in comb., is the ending of adjs. related to sbs. in -MANCY, as in *geomantic*, etc.

Manticore (mæ·ntikoᵊɹ). *Obs.* exc. *Hist.* Also **mantiger.** ME. [– L. *manticora*, repr. Gr. μαντιχώρας, a corrupt reading in Aristotle *Hist. Anim.* II. i. 53 for μαρτιχόρας, app. an OPers. word for 'man-eater'.] **1.** A fabulous monster having the body of a lion, the head of a man, porcupine's quills, and the tail or sting of a scorpion. **2.** *Her.* A monster figured with the body of a beast of prey, the head of a man with spiral or curved horns, and sometimes the feet of a dragon 1562.

Mantilla (mænti·lă). 1717. [– Sp. *mantilla*, dim. of *manta* mantle.] **1.** A large veil worn by women over the head and the shoulders. **2.** A small cape or mantle 1859.

‖**Mantis** (mæ·ntis). 1658. [mod.L. – Gr. μάντις prophet (also, some insect); see MANTIC *a.*] *Entom.* An orthopterous insect of the genus *Mantis* or family *Mantidæ*; *esp.* the Praying Mantis, *M. religiosa*, which holds its forelegs in a position suggesting hands folded in prayer. **b.** *attrib.*, as **m.-crab, -shrimp,** a stomatopodous crustacean, *Squilla mantis* and other species.

Mantissa (mænti·să). 1641. [– L. *mantis(s)a* make-weight, said to be of Etruscan origin.] †**1.** An addition of trivial importance, esp. to a discourse –1671. **2.** *Math.* The decimal part of a logarithm 1865.

Mantle (mæ·nt'l), *sb.* [ME. *mantel* – OFr. *mantel* (mod. *manteau*) :– L. *mantellum*, var. of *mantēlum* and rel. to *mantēlium*, *-ēle*, *mantīlium*, *-īle* towel, napkin, table-cloth, with shortened deriv., late L. *mantus*, med.L. *mantum*, **manta* short cloak, whence Sp. *manto* cloak, *manta* blanket, *mantilla* woman's veil. Not continuous with OE *mentel* – L.] **1.** A loose sleeveless cloak of varying length. **b.** Used allusively with reference to the descent of Elijah's mantle (2 Kings 2:13) 1660. **c.** *Her.* = MANTLING *vbl. sb.* 2. 1577. **2.** *transf.* and *fig.* A covering ME. †**b.** *spec.* The foam that covers the surface of liquor; the green vegetable coating on standing water –1605. †**3.** A kind of woollen cloth; a blanket of this –1582. †**4.** A measure of quantity of furs, containing from 30 to 100 skins according to size –1662. **5.** *Mech.* A covering, envelope, or shade employed in various mechanical contrivances (see below) 1609. **6.** *Zool.*, *Bot.*, etc. Applied to various coverings or envelopes, as that enclosing the viscera in molluscs (see quots.) 1460; *Ornith.* the plumage of the back and folded wings when distinct in colour, etc. from the rest. (So Fr. *manteau.*) 1840.

1. As she fled, her m. she did fall SHAKS. **b.** On Heine..the largest portion of Goethe's m. fell M. ARNOLD. **c.** The m. upon the panels [of Mr. Glossin's coach] only bore a plain cipher of G. G. 1815. **2.** Well couer'd with the Nights black M. SHAKS. Ruins, over which vegetation had thrown a wild m. of ivy SCOTT. **b.** *Lear* III. iv. 139. **5. a.** A linen cloth employed in the swarming of bees 1609. **b.** The leather hood of an open carriage 1794. **c.** An enclosed chute which leads the water from a fore-bay to a water-wheel 1875. **d.** The outer wall and casing of an iron blast furnace, above the hearth 1881. **e.** A fragile lace-like tube, which, fixed around a burning gas jet, becomes incandescent and gives a brilliant light 1887. **6.** An Ascidian consists..of an external membranous bag or 'mantle', within which is a Muscular envelope 1874. Each one of the inner layers..of this m. has its initial group above the apex of the pterome 1884. **7.** *Comb.* **m.-knot,** a clasp, composed of a number of precious stones [cf. Fr. *nœud de diamants*].

Mantle (mæ·nt'l), *v.* late ME. [Partly f. prec. sb., partly – OFr. *manteler*.] **1.** *trans.* To clothe or wrap in or as in a mantle. Also with *up*, *over*. 1450. **b.** Said of wings. MILT. *P. L.* v. 279. **2.** *transf.* and *fig.* To cover or conceal; to envelop; †to cloak (a fault) late ME. **3.** *Falconry. refl.* and *intr.* To spread first one wing and then the other over the corresponding outstretched leg for exercise, as a perched hawk does. *Obs.* exc. *Hist.* 1486. **4.** *intr.* Of liquids: To be or become covered with a coating or scum; to form a 'head' or froth; to cream. Also *transf.* and *fig.* 1596. **5.** Of the blood: To suffuse the cheeks with a blush. Said also of a blush, etc. (rarely *trans.*). Of the face: To flush. 1707. **6.** *intr.* To form a mantle or covering; to spread over a surface 1634.

1. The mourning-stole no more Mantled her form M. ARNOLD. **2.** The ignorant fumes that m. Their clearer reason SHAKS. Mountains..mantled and capped with snow 1890. **3.** *fig.* There my fraile fancy, fed with full delight, Doth bath in blisse, and mantleth most at Ease SPENSER. **4.** *fig.* There are a sort of men, whose visages Do creame and m. like a standing pond SHAKS. **5.** Her rich face mantling with emotion DISRAELI.

Mantlet, var. of MANTELET.

Mantling (mæ·ntliŋ), *vbl. sb.* 1507. [f. MANTLE *sb.* or *v.* + -ING[1].] †**1.** The action of making a mantle. **2.** *Her.* The ornamental accessory of drapery or scroll-work frequently depicted behind and around an achievement; a lambrequin 1591. **3.** What serves the purpose of a mantle; a covering, envelope, etc. 1652. **4.** The action of the vb. (senses 3–5) 1652.

‖**Manto** (mæ·nto). 1679. [It. or Sp.; see MANTLE *sb.*] A (Spanish, etc.) cloak or mantle.

†**Manto·logy.** *rare.* 1774. [Badly f. Gr. μάντις + -LOGY.] The art or practice of divination. Hence **Manto·logist,** a diviner 1864.

Manton (mæ·ntən). 1816. A fowling-piece made by Joseph *Manton* (?1766–1835), a noted gunsmith. Also *Joe Manton*.

‖**Mantra** (mæ·ntră). *Indian.* 1808. [Skr. *mantra*, lit. 'instrument of thought', f. *man* think.] A sacred text or passage, esp. one from the Vedas used as a prayer or incantation.

Ma·n-trap. 1788. A trap for catching men, esp. trespassers in private grounds.

Mantua (mæ·ntiuă). *Obs.* exc. *Hist.* 1678. [Corruption of MANTEAU, infl. by the place-name *Mantua*.] **1.** = MANTEAU. †**2.** = *mantua silk* –1787. **3.** *attrib.*, as *m. gown*, *petticoat*, *silk*. So **Ma·ntua-ma:ker,** one who makes mantuas; later, a dress-maker 1694.

Mantuan (mæ·ntiuăn). 1588. [– L. *Mantuanus*, f. *Mantua*; see -AN.] **A.** *adj.* Of or belonging to Mantua in northern Italy where Virgil was born; hence, Virgilian 1709. **B.** *sb.* A native or inhabitant of Mantua.

The m., *the M. Muse*, *Swan*, Virgil.

Manual (mæ·niuăl). late ME. [Earliest form *manuel* (later assim. to L.) – (O)Fr. *manuel* – L. *manualis*, f. *manus* hand.] **A.** *adj.* **1.** Of, pertaining to, or done with the hands. Now esp. of (physical) labour. **b.** Of a signature, etc.: Autograph. Chiefly in SIGN MANUAL. 1476. **c.** Of a weapon, tool, etc.: That is used or worked with the hands. Now *rare* exc. in *m.* (*fire*) *engine* as dist. from *steam* (*fire*) *engine*. 1591. **2.** *Law.* Of occupation, possession: Actual, not merely prospective 1538. **3.** That works with the hands (*arch.*) 1658. †**4.** Furnished with hands. SIR T. BROWNE. **5.** Of a book, etc.: Of the nature of a manual 1881.

1. Patron of industry and m. arts POPE. I expressed my ideas by m. signs TYLOR. Phr. *M. exercise* (*Mil.*), drill in handling a rifle. *M. alphabet*, the finger alphabet. Hence **Ma·nually** *adv.*

B. *sb.* **1.** A small book for handy use. **a.** In the mediæval Church, a book containing the forms to be observed in administration of the sacraments. late ME. **b.** A handbook 1533. **2.** Short for *manual exercise* 1762. **3.** Short for *manual fire-engine* 1872. **4.** A key-board of an organ played with the hands, as dist. from the *pedals* 1852.

2. The corporal went through his *manual* with exactness STERNE.

Ma·nualist. 1592. [f. prec. + -IST.] †**1.** One who labours with the hands. **2.** One who favours the manual method of teaching the deaf 1883.

Manuary (mæ·niuări). 1576. [– L. *manuarius*, f. *manus* hand; see -ARY[1].] **A.** *adj.* **1.** = MANUAL *a.* 1. *Obs.* exc. in affected use. †**2.** = MANUAL *a.* 3. –1678. **B.** *sb.* †**1.** One who works with his hands –1656. †**2.** Manual work –1616.

‖**Manubrium** (mănū·bri₁ŏm). *Pl.* **-ia, -iums.** 1660. [L., = haft.] †**1.** A handle or haft. **2.** *Anat.* and *Zool.* A handle-like part. **a.** The broad upper division of the sternum of mammals, with which the two first ribs articulate. **b.** The handle-like bony process of the malleus of the ear in man and many mammals. **c.** A small process, often bifurcate, at the root of the keel of the sternum in birds. **d.** The lower part of the malleus in rotifers. **e.** A peduncle which depends from the roof of the gonocalyx of hydroids or of the swimming-bell of medusæ. 1848. **3.** *Bot.* A process projecting from each of the shields forming the inner wall of the antheridium in characeous plants 1875. Hence **Manubrial** *a.* 1835.

Manucaption (mæniukæ·pʃən). *Obs.* exc. *Hist.* 1588. [– med.L. *manucaptio*, f. *manucapere* (*-capt-*) lit. 'take by the hand'; see MAINPRIZE.] *Law.* **a.** = MAINPRIZE. **b.** A writ directing the bringing in of a person charged with a felony. So **Manuca·ptor** = MAINPERNOR 1581.

Manucode (mæ·niŭkōᵘd). 1835. [– Fr. *manucode* (Buffon), shortening of next.] †**a.** = next. **b.** Any bird of either of the genera *Manucodia* and *Phonygama*, inhabiting the Papuan region, and formerly classed with the birds of paradise.

†‖**Manucodiata.** 1555. [mod.L. – Malay *mānuq dēwāta* 'bird of the gods'.] A bird of paradise –1691.

Manuduction (mæniudɒ·kʃən). 1502. [– med.L. *manuductio*, f. *manu ducere* lead by the hand, guide.] **1.** Guidance, introduction, direction. **2.** Means or instrument of guidance; a guide or introduction 1624. So †**Manuductor,** a guide, director 1657–1677; the conductor of a band or choir –1852.

†**Manufactor.** 1649. [f. as next; see -OR 2.] A manufacturer or artificer –1812.

Manufactory (mæniufæ·ktŏri), *sb.* and *a.* 1618. [f. next (by suffix-substitution), after FACTORY; see -ORY[1] and [2].] **A.** *sb.* †**1.** = MANUFACTURE *sb.* 2 –1786. †**2.** MANUFACTURE 1 b. –1846. **3.** A factory or workshop, as a *cotton m.* 1692. **B.** *adj.* Pertaining to, of the nature of, or engaged in manufacture –1741.

Manufacture (mæniufæ·ktiŭɹ), *sb.* 1567. [– Fr. *manufacture* (XVI) – It. *manifattura* (XIV), with refash. after L. *manu factum* made by hand.] **1.** †**a.** The action or process of making by hand. BACON. **b.** The making of articles or material (now, on a large scale) by physical labour or mechanical power. 1622. **c.** A branch of productive industry 1683. **d.** In depreciatory sense, production of a merely mechanical kind. Also *fig.* applied, e.g. to literary work, or to the fabrication of false statements on a large scale for the market. 1829. **2.** *concr.* †**a.** A person's handiwork. Also *fig.* –1726. **b.** A product of physical labour or machinery 1611. †**3.** Working with the hands; a manual occupation, handicraft –1699. †**4.** A manufacturing establishment or business –1783.

1. b. A single article, either of domestic or foreign growth or m. MCCULLOCH. **1. c.** *Linen*, *woollen*, *worsted m.* **2. b.** Colchester baize, a coarse rug-like m. DE FOE. Hence **Manufa·ctural** *a.* pertaining to m.

Manufacture (mæniufæ·ktiŭɹ), *v.* 1683. [f. prec.] **1.** *trans.* To work up (material) into forms suitable for use. **2.** To produce by labour (now esp. on a large scale) 1755. **b.** *transf.* Said of natural agencies 1876. **3.** *fig.* In disparaging sense: To fabricate, invent; also, to produce (literary work) mechanically 1762. **4.** To admit of being manufactured 1763.

2. b. Poisons manufactured within the system 1899. **3.** The speech is evidently manufactured by the historian GIBBON. Hence **Manufa·cturer,** †an operative in a manufactory; the owner of a manufactory; also *transf.* and *fig.* **Manufa·cturing** *ppl. a.* engaged or concerned in manufacture.

†**Manumise, manumiss,** *v.* 1523. [– *manumiss-*, pa. ppl. stem of L. *manumittere* MANUMIT.] = MANUMIT *v.* –1819.

Manumission (mæniumi·ʃən). *Obs.* exc. *Hist.* late ME. [– (O)Fr. *manumission* or L. *manumissio*, f. as prec.; see -ION.] The action of manumitting, or the fact of being manumitted; an act or instance of this. Also *transf.* and *fig.*

M. is properly when the Lord makes a deed to his villeine to enfranchise him by this word (*Manumittere*) which is the same as to put him out of the hands and power of another COKE.

Manumit (mæniumi·t), *v.* late ME. [– L. *manumittere*, ante-cl. *manu emittere*, lit. 'to send forth from one's hand', i.e. from one's control.] *trans.* To release from slavery; to liberate from bondage or servitude; to set free. Also *transf.* and *fig.* Also *absol.*

Christian masters were not bound to m. their slaves JER. TAYLOR.

Manurable (măniūᵊ·răb'l), *a.* 1628. [f. MANURE *v.* + -ABLE.] †**1.** *Law.* Admitting of being held in corporeal possession –1767. †**2.** Of land: That can be worked or cultivated –1756. **3.** That can be manured 1828.

Manurance (măniūᵊ·răns). 1468. [f. MANURE *v.* + -ANCE.] **1.** Tenure, occupation (of land, etc.); control, management. Now only in *Law*. **2.** †Cultivation (of land), †tillage; manuring 1572. †**b.** *fig.* Cultivation (of the character or faculties) –1615.

2. b. The culture and m. of minds in youth BACON.

Manure (măniūᵊ·ɹ), *sb.* 1549. [f. MANURE *v.* Formerly *ma·nure*, and so still in Cowper (1784); and still *dial.* (mæ·nəɹ).] **1.** Dung or compost spread over or mixed with soil to fertilize it. †**2.** Manuring; cultivation –1696. **3.** *attrib.*, as *m.-heap*, etc. 1766.

Manure (măniūᵊ·ɹ), *v.* late ME. [Earliest forms *maynoyre*, *-oure*, *manour* – AFr. *mainoverer*, OFr. *mano(u)vrer* MANŒUVRE *v.*; assim. in ending to -URE.] †**1.** *trans.* To hold, occupy (land, etc.); to administer, manage –1645. †**2.** To till, cultivate (land) –1774. †**b.** To cultivate, train (a plant, the body or mind, etc.) –1797. **3.** [f. MANURE *sb.* 1] To enrich (land) with fertilizing material; to apply manure to 1599. †**4.** To work up –1575; to manœuvre (a ship) 1569.

1. That which is manually occupied, manured and possessed COKE. **2.** A barren Sand, not capable of being manur'd by either Spade or Plow 1700. **b.** Who like a nut tree must be manured by beating FULLER. **3.** The Corps of half her Senate M. the Fields of Thessaly ADDISON. Hence **Manu·rer.**

†**Manurement.** 1639. [f. MANURE *v.* + -MENT.] Cultivation (*lit.* and *fig.*) –1707.

Manurial (măniūᵊ·riăl), *a.* 1861. [irreg. f. MANURE *sb.* + -IAL.] Pertaining to, or of the nature of manure.

Manuring (măniūᵊ·riŋ), *vbl. sb.* late ME. [f. MANURE *v.* + -ING[1].] †**a.** Occupation, tenure. †**b.** Cultivation, tillage. **c.** Fertilization by means of manure; †occas. *concr.* = manure.

‖**Manus** (mēⁱ·nŏs). 1826. [L., = hand.] **1.** *Anat.* The terminal or distal segment of the fore limb of a vertebrate animal. Also, the claw of a crustacean; *Entom.* the tarsus of the anterior leg; *Ichth.* the pectoral fin. **2.** *Rom. Law.* The power or authority of a husband over his wife 1854. †**3.** *Manus Christi* [= 'hand of Christ'], a cordial 1516–1706.

Manuscript (mæ·niu₁skript). 1597. Abbrev. MS. (*pl.* MSS.). [– med.L. *manuscriptus* adj., i.e. *manu* with the hand, abl. of *manus* and *scriptus* pa. pple. of *scribere* write; cf. med.L. *manuscriptum* sb. document written with a person's own hand (cf. CHIROGRAPH).] **A.** *adj.* Written by hand, not printed.

Manvscript Poems of great Antiquitie 1597.

B. *sb.* **1.** A book, document, or the like, written by hand; a writing of any kind, as dist. from printed matter. Also *transf.* and *fig.* 1600. **2.** Writing (as opp. to print); also, (a person's) handwriting 1849.

1. John Mill..borrowed the m. [of the 'French Revolution'] as it was thrown off, that he might make notes and suggestions FROUDE. *fig.* Alas,.. That Youth's sweet-scented M. should close! FITZGERALD. *attrib.* Special Assistant in the MS. Department. Hence **Manuscri·ptal** *a. rare*, of or pertaining to a m. or manuscripts; found or occurring in a m. So **Manuscri·ption** *rare*, the action of writing by hand; a written inscription LAMB.

†**Manutenency.** 1633. [– med.L. *manutenentia* (whence OFr. *manutenance*), f. pr. ppl. stem of Rom. **manutenēre* MAINTAIN; see -ENCY.] Support, maintenance –1699. So †**Manute·ntion** 1603–1657.

Manward (mæ·nwǫ̈ɹd). late ME. [See -WARD.] **A.** *adv.* (In early use *to m.*, also *to menward.*) **a.** Towards man, in the direction of man. **b.** In relation to man. **B.** *adj.* Tending or directed towards man 1867.

Manx (mæŋks). 1572. [Earlier *Manks* – (with metathesis) ON. **Manskr* (whence immed. †*maniske* XVI), f. *Man-* (nom. *Mǫn* :– **Manu* – OIr. *Manu*) + *-skr* -ISH[1].] **A.** *adj.* Of or pertaining to the Isle of Man, its inhabitants, language, etc. **B.** *sb.* **1.** (As *pl.*) The people of the Isle of Man 1688. **2.** The Celtic language spoken in the Isle of Man 1672. Hence **Ma·nxman,** a native of the Isle of Man.

M. cat: a tailless variety of cat, indigenous to the Isle of Man. *M. penny*: a coin stamped with the device of three legs.

Many (me·ni), *a.* and *sb.* [OE. *maniġ, moniġ*, later *mæniġ*, corresp. to OFris. *man(i)ch, monich, menich*, OS. *manag*, MDu. *menech*, Du. *menig*, OHG. *manag, menig* (G. *manch*), ON. **mangr* (OSw. *mangher*), Goth. *manags* :– Gmc. **manaʒaz*, **maniʒaz.*] **A.** *adj.* The adjectival designation of great indefinite number. **1.** Used *distributively* with a *sing.* (Formerly sometimes with pl. vb.) **2.** With *pl. sb.* OE. **3.** *ellipt.* and *absol.* in pl. sense: Many individuals of the kind specified (often *many of*); also (as quasi-pron.), many persons OE. **4.** With As, How, So, Too (q.v.), the adj. only expresses the notion of number in the abstract. With *pl. sb.*; also *ellipt.* and *absol.* = '(as, etc.) many persons'. OE.

1. To m. a youth, and m. a maid MILT. M. a more unlikely thing has happened 1809. *M. a(n) one*: = 'many a person'. Now chiefly *colloq.* **2.** We must drink m. happy returns to her DICKENS. *M. times, m. ways, (on) m. wise*, advb. phr.; see the sbs. **3.** I see, one Fool makes m. SWIFT. M. of his ideas..did not belong to him peculiarly MORLEY. Phr. *The m.* (= Gr. οἱ πολλοί): the great body of people; the multitude. **4.** As m. words as make an even line CRABBE. *As m. as*: idiomatic for 'all who'. *As m.*: the same number of. *One too m.*: used predicatively of something not wanted. *Too m. for*: more than a match for 1692. (Prop. with a pl. subject, but said *joc.* of a single person or thing 1708.)

Comb. **a.** parasynthetic (unlimited in number), as *m.-acred, -fountained, -voiced*, etc. **b.** *poet.* with pples. in quasi-advb. sense = 'in many ways, many times, much', as *m.-beaming, -blossoming*, etc.

B. quasi-*sb.* and *sb.* **1.** quasi-*sb.* On the analogy of *a few* (see FEW *a.* 2), *a many* has from the 16th c. been followed by a pl. sb. or used *absol.* in pl. sense. Without adj. now *arch.*; formerly with various adjs., now only *a good many, a great many*. In such collocations *many* may be interpreted as a sb., meaning 'a great number'. (Cf. MEINIE.) **a.** with pl. sb. (or *people*) immediately following 1590. **b.** Const. *of*; now only followed by a definite sb. or pron. 1525. **c.** *ellipt.* and *absol.* SHAKS. †**2.** By confusion with MEINIE: Company, host, flock; (one's) retinue or following –1700. **3.** *Philos.* A multitude, plurality. Opp. to *one.* 1619.

1. a. A m. such miracles HY. MORE. **b.** He..had invited a m. of his kindred and friends 1652. **c.** A good m. died of hardship and fatigue 1875. **2.** The manie begins to march along; thronging one another for haste 1609. **3.** One idea, throughout all manys, wrapt up in one T. TAYLOR. Hence **Ma·nyness** plurality (*rare*) 1609.

Many-: see MANI-.

Many-headed, *a.* (Stress variable.) 1586. Having many heads.

Keep nothing sacred; 'tis but just The many-headed beast (= the people) should know TENNYSON.

Manyplies (me·niplɔiz), *sb. pl.* Chiefly *dial.* 1774. [f. MANY + *plies*, pl. of PLY; modelled on synon. *manifolds* MANIFOLD *sb.*[2]] The omasum or third stomach of a ruminant.

Many-sided, *a.* (Stress variable.) 1660. **1.** Having many sides; multilateral. **2.** *fig.* Having many aspects, capacities, or possibilities 1843.

2. Raleigh was..a many-sided man; soldier, sailor, statesman, historian, and poet GARDINER. Hence **Manysi·dedness.**

Manyways *adv.*: see WAY.

Manywise *adv.*: see WISE *sb.*

‖**Manzanilla** (mænzăni·lă, Sp. manþani·lʸa). 1843. [Sp., f. *manzanilla* camomile.] A dry light sherry with a bitterish flavour.

‖**Manzanita** (mænzănī·tă, Sp. manþanī·ta). 1872. [Sp., dim. of *manzana* apple.] One of the berry-bearing shrubs of the genus *Arctostaphylos* found in the U.S.; the bearberry.

Maori (ma·ŏri, mauᵊ·ri), *sb.* (*a.*) *Pl.* **Maori, Maori(e)s.** 1843. [Native name; said to mean 'of the usual kind' (Morris).] **1.** An individual of the brown race inhabiting New Zealand. Also *attrib.* or *adj.* pertaining to this race or their language; *absol.* the language. **2.** A New South Wales fish, *Coris lineolatus* 1882.

Map (mæp), *sb.* 1527. [– med.L. *mappa*, short for *mappa mundi* 'sheet of the world', i.e. *mappa* (in class. L. table-cloth, NAPKIN), *mundi* gen. of *mundus* world.] **1.** A representation of the earth's surface or a part of it, its physical and political features, etc., or of the heavens, delineated on a flat surface of paper, etc., according to a definite scale or projection. Also *transf.* **2.** *fig.* A detailed representation in epitome; a circumstantial account of a state of things. Now *rare* or *Obs.* 1586. †**b.** The very picture (*of* a virtue, vice, character, etc.). (So Sp. *mapa.*) –1698.

1. Colloq. phr. *Off the map*: of no account, obsolete. *On the map*: of some account or importance. **2.** I don't know the m. of their situation BURKE. **b.** What were man if he were once left to himselfe? A m. of misery 1591.

Comb.: **m. lichen,** a lichen, *Lecidea geographica*, the thallus of which has markings resembling a m.

Map (mæp), *v.* Infl. **mapped** (mæpt), **mapping.** 1586. [f. MAP *sb.*] **1.** *trans.* To make a map of; to represent on a map 1602. Also *transf.* and *fig.* **2. M. out. a.** To represent in detail on a map 1656. **b.** *fig.* †To record minutely 1619; to plan out (a course of conduct, one's time, etc.) 1883. **c.** To divide (a country) *into* districts, as by lines on a map 1860.

1. *transf.* I am neere to th' place where they should meet, if Pisanio haue mapp'd it truely SHAKS. **2. c.** The Continent was not then mapped out with tourists' routes 1870. Hence **Mapping** *vbl. sb.* (also *attrib.* as **m. pen**).

Maple (mēⁱ·p'l). [In OE. *mapeltrēow, mapulder* maple-tree; cf. OS. *mapulder*, MLG. (with alt. of final element) *mapeldorn*. The simplex is first recorded XIV (Chaucer).] **1.** Any tree or shrub of the genus *Acer*, many of which are grown for shade or ornament, for their wood, or for a sugar product. The Common Maple is *Acer campestre*. The fruit of these trees is a double-winged samara or 'key'. **2.** The light, hard, close-grained wood of any of these trees. late ME.

1. Bird's-eye M. = *sugar maple.* **Red, Scarlet,** or **Swamp M.,** *A. rubrum.* **Silver, Silver-leaved,** or **White M.,** *A. dasycarpum*, of eastern North America. **Sugar M.,** *A. saccharinum* of North America, which yields maple-sugar. **Sycamore M.,** *A. pseudo platanus* (see SYCAMORE).

attrib. and *Comb.*, as *m. leaf*, etc.; **m.-honey** *U.S.*, the uncrystallized part of the sap of the sugar m.; **m. molasses, syrup** *U.S.*, a syrup obtained by evaporating maple sap or dissolving maple sugar; **m. sugar,** the sugar obtained by evaporation from the sap of certain maples.

Mappemonde (mæpmōᵘ·nd). Now only *Hist.* late ME. [– (O)Fr. *mappemonde* – med.L. *mappa mundi*; see MAP *sb.*] The map of the world; in early use, the world itself.

‖**Maqui** (ma·kī). 1704. [Chilean Sp.] The Chilean shrub *Aristotelia maqui* (N.O. *Tiliaceæ*), yielding a valuable fibre, and producing berries used in the adulteration of wine.

Mar (māɹ), *sb.* ME. [f. MAR *v.*] †**1.** A hindrance; an impediment in speech –1824. **2.** Something that mars; a drawback *to*. In early use, †a fault. 1551.

Mar (māɹ), *v.* [OE. *merran* (WS. *mierran*) = OFris. *meria*, OS. *merrian* hinder (Du. *marren* fasten, tie up, loiter), OHG. *marren, merren* hinder, ON. *merja* bruise, crush, Goth. *marzjan* cause to stumble (tr. Gr. σκανδαλίζειν).] **1.** *trans.* To hinder, interrupt, or stop (a person, event, or thing). *Obs.* exc. *Sc.* **2.** To spoil, impair OE. **3.** *trans.* To harm, injure (a person, etc.); to disfigure (now *arch.*); †to ruin; to damage morally ME.

2. Striuing to better, oft we marre what's well SHAKS. The wine is spilled, and the bottles will bee marred *Mark* 2:22. Phr. *To make or m.* (see MAKE *v.* VI. 9). **3.** Mend your speach..lest it m. your fortunes SHAKS. Digby Lord Gerard..was utterly mar'd by keeping company with base lewd fellowes WOOD.

Mar, north. and Sc. f. MORE.

Mar-, *vbl. stem*, prefixed to sbs., with sense 'one who or something which mars', and *adjs.*, with sense 'that mars'; as *mar-all* sb. and adj., *mar-feast*, etc. **b.** *esp.* in **mar-prelate,** first used in the pseudonym 'Martin Marprelate', the writer of certain tracts issued in 1588–1589; hence *attrib.*

Marabou (mæ·răbū). Also **marabout, marabu.** 1823. [– Fr. *marabout* – Arab. *murābiṭ*; see next (the stork is said to be *mrabt* holy).] **1.** A large stork or heron, *Leptoptilus marabou* or *crumenifer*, a native of Western Africa. Now applied also to the adjutant-bird of India, *L. dubius* or *argala*. 1826. **2.** In full *m. feather, plume*. A tuft or plume of down from under the wings and tail of these birds, used for trimming hats and dresses; *collect. sing.* trimming made of these feathers 1823. **3.** An exceptionally white kind of raw silk which can be dyed without first removing the natural gum 1835.

2. A m. feather which she wears in her turban THACKERAY.

‖**Marabout** (mæ·răbūt). 1623. [The present form is – Fr. *marabout* – Pg. *marabuto* – Arab. *murābiṭ* hermit, holy man, orig. one who betook himself to a frontier station (*ribāṭ*) to acquire merit against the infidel.] **1.** A Moslem hermit or holy man, esp. amongst the Moors and Berbers of N. Africa. **2.** A shrine marking the burial-place of a marabout 1859.

‖**Marah** (mā·ră). late ME. [Heb. *mārāh*, fem. of *mar* bitter.] The Heb. word for 'bitter' or 'bitterness', used as a proper name (*Exod.* 15:23 and *Ruth* 1:20); hence allusively.

Never had any writer so vast a command of the whole eloquence of scorn, misanthropy, and despair. That M. was never dry MACAULAY.

Maranatha (mærănæ·þă). late ME. [The Aram. phr. (in Gr. form μαραναθά) is variously interpreted as *māran 'aṯā* our Lord has come, or *māranā ṯā* O our Lord, come thou.] An Aramaic phrase occurring in 1 Cor. 16:22; see ANATHEMA MARANATHA. As an abbrev. of this formula used subst. for: A terrible curse.

‖**Marasca** (măræ·skă). 1864. [It., aphetic f. *amarasca*, f. *amaro* bitter.] A small black cherry, *Prunus avium*, grown in Dalmatia.

‖**Maraschino** (mæraskī·no). 1791. [It., f. *marasca*; see prec. Cf. Fr. *marasquin*.] A liqueur distilled from the marasca cherry.

‖**Marasmus** (măræ·zmŏs). 1656. [mod.L. – Gr. μαρασμός, f. μαραίνειν to waste.] Wasting of the body. Hence **Mara·smic** *a.*

‖**Maratha, Mahratta** (mărā·tă, măræ·tă). 1758. [Hindi *Marhaṭṭa* :– Skr. *Māhārāshṭra* 'great kingdom'.] **1.** One of a warlike Hindu race occupying the central and south-western parts of India 1763. **2.** *attrib.* or *adj.* Pertaining to the Marathas 1758.

‖**Marathi** (mărā·tī). 1698 (**Moratty**). [f. *Maratha*; see prec.] The language of the Marathas.

Marathon (mæ·răþǫn). 1896. [Name of Greek city, the scene of a victory of the Athenians over the Persians (490 B.C.), the news of which was conveyed by a runner to Athens, a distance of about 20 miles.] *attrib.* in *m.-race*, etc., a long-distance race.

Maraud (mărǭ·d), *v.* 1708. [– Fr. *marauder*, f. *maraud* rogue, vagabond, scoundrel, or back-formation f. *marauder* (– Fr. *maraud-*

eur).] **1.** *intr.* To make a raid for the purpose of plundering. **2.** *trans.* To plunder; to harry 1829.

1. They met with a Party of French that had been Marauding ADDISON. Hence **Marau·d** *sb.* the act of marauding. **Marau·der** 1698.

Maravedi (mærăvē·di). *Obs.* exc. *Hist.* late ME. [- Sp. *maravedi*, a deriv. of Arab. *murābiṭīn* (oblique case pl. of *murābiṭ*; see MARABOUT), name of a Moorish dynasty at Cordova (1087–1147).] **1.** An old Spanish gold coin, weighing about 60 grains and worth fourteen shillings 1643. **2.** A former Spanish copper coin and money of account, valued at about ⅙ of a penny sterling.

2. I will strip thee of every m. thou hast in the world SCOTT.

Marble (mā·ɹb'l), *sb.* [ME. *marbel, marbre* - OFr. *marble*, dissim. f. (O)Fr. *marbre* :- L. *marmor* - Gr. μάρμαρος shining stone, orig. stone, block of rock, but later assoc. with μαρμαίρειν shine.] **I. 1.** Limestone in a crystalline (or, less strictly, also a granular) state and capable of taking a polish; occurring in many varieties; much used in sculpture and architecture. **b.** A kind or variety of marble 1640. **c.** As a type of something hard, inflexible, durable, or smooth 1586. **d.** As the material of which a tomb or tombstone is made (*poet.*) 1613. **2.** A piece, block, or slab of marble; a marble monument. Also *fig.* ME. **†b.** A marble tomb or tombstone –1730. **c.** *Antiq.* (*pl.*) Applied to certain collections of sculptures, etc. 1667. **3.** A small ball, orig. of marble, now of baked clay, porcelain, etc., used in a children's game; hence in *pl.* the game itself. Also a small ball of glass, etc., used in other games. 1694. **4.** *Bookbinding.* The marbled pattern or paper used in ornamenting books 1699.

1. *Black, fibrous, green, grey, red, variegated, white m.*; *Carrara, Egyptian, English, Genoese, Italian,* PARIAN, *Pentelican, Purbeck m.* Also RUIN, VERD ANTIQUE *m.*, etc. **c.** Writing all injuries in m. PURCHAS. **d.** When I am forgotten..And sleepe in dull cold M. SHAKS. **2.** An Inscription on a M. LEONI. **c.** *Arundel, Arundelian,* or *Oxford marbles*, a collection of sculptures, etc. made by the Earl of Arundel (died 1646) and presented to the University of Oxford. *Elgin marbles*, a collection (now in the British Museum) of ancient sculptures from the Parthenon, which was sold by Lord Elgin to the nation in 1816.

II. *attrib.* or *adj.* **a.** Made or consisting of marble. Also, like that of marble. ME. **b.** White, hard, cold, or rigid like marble. (Rarely used *predicatively.*) 1591. **c.** Enduring as marble, or as if carved in marble 1596. **d.** *poet.* Smooth as marble 1557. **e.** Of a variegated or mottled colour; marbled. late ME.

a. A m. Madona like a Colosse EVELYN. **b.** His M., obdurate Heart SOUTH. Her m. brow, and eager lips SHELLEY. **d.** Through the pure m. Air MILT. **e.** Countless m.-covered octavos HAN. MORE. Phr. *†m. colours*: used *fig.* by Drummond to express ostentatious splendour. Hence **Ma·rbly** *a.* resembling marble 1439.

Marble (mā·ɹb'l), *v.* 1628. [f. prec. sb. Cf. (O)Fr. *marbrer.*] **1.** *trans.* To stain or colour (paper, edges of books, soap, etc.) so as to make them look like variegated marble. **2.** To make white like marble (*rare*) 1791.

2. Features, marbled by the moon B. TAYLOR. Hence **Ma·rbling** *vbl. sb.* the action of the vb.; also *concr.* 1686.

Marbled (mā·ɹb'ld), *ppl. a.* 1599. [f. MARBLE *sb.* and *v.* + -ED.] **1.** In occas. uses: Portrayed in marble; having buildings, etc. of marble; turned into marble (*fig.*); decorated or covered with marble. **2. a.** Coloured or stained with variegated patterns like those of marble 1671. **b.** Veined, mottled, or dappled (*with* markings of various colours). Chiefly *Nat. Hist.* and *Path.* 1694. **c.** Of meat: Having the lean streaked with thin layers of fat. (A sign of the best quality.) 1770. **3.** Used as the specific designation of various animals and plants having mottled or dappled markings 1699.

1. Sunium's m. steep BYRON. **2. a.** Common m. paper 1699. **b.** The m. Sky 1719. **3. M. beauty,** the moth *Bryophila perla.*

Marbleize (mā·ɹbləiz), *v. U.S.* 1875. [f. MARBLE *sb.* + -IZE.] *trans.* To colour in imitation of marble.

Marbler (mā·ɹbləɹ). 1402. [f. MARBLE *sb.* and *v.* + -ER[1].] **†1.** A hewer of marble –1538. **†2.** One who carves, or works in, marble –1720. **3.** One who marbles paper, etc.; an instrument for marbling paper 1835.

Marc (māɹk). 1601. [- Fr. *marc*, f. *marcher* MARCH *v.*[2]] The refuse which remains after the pressure of grapes or other fruits.

Marc, obs. f. MARK, MARQUE.

†Marcantant. [repr. It. *mercatante.*] A merchant. *Tam. Shr.* IV. ii. 63.

Marcasite (mā·ɹkăsəit). 1471. [- med.L. *marcasita* - Arab. *marḳašīṯā* - Pers.; assoc. with -ITE[1] 2 b.] *Min.* **1.** Pyrites, *esp.* the crystallized forms of iron pyrites used in the 18th c. for ornaments; by some restricted to the arsenical varieties; in recent use, white iron pyrites (iron disulphide). **2.** A specimen of marcasite; an ornament made of crystallized iron pyrites 1555.

The 'marcasites' of gold and silver were app. specimens of copper and iron pyrites with the lustre of gold and silver O.E.D.

2. Half the ladies of our acquaintance..carry their jewels to town, and bring nothing but paste and marcasites back GOLDSM. Hence **Marcasi·tical** *a.* pertaining to or containing m.

‖Marcassin (ma·ɹkæsin). 1727. [Fr.] *Her.* A young wild boar, used as a charge.

Marcel (maɹse·l). 1906. [f. name of Paris hairdresser.] Applied to a method of waving the hair; as *m.-wave, -waved*, adj. Also as vb.

‖Marcel(l)ine (mā·ɹsĕlin). 1835. [Fr.; prob. f. personal name.] A silk fabric used for linings.

Marcella, marsella (maɹse·lă). 1812. [Anglicized pronunc. of MARSEILLES.] A kind of twilled cotton or linen cloth used for waistcoats, etc.

Marcescent (maɹse·sĕnt), *a.* (*sb.*) 1727. [- *marcescens, -ent-*, pr. pple. of L. *marcescere*, inceptive of *marcēre* be faint or languid; see -ESCENT.] *Bot.* Of parts of a plant: withering but not falling off. **b.** *sb.* A plant having marcescent parts 1859. Hence **Marce·scence,** m. condition.

Marcgrave: see MARGRAVE.

†March, *sb.*[1] [OE. *merece* = OS. *merka*, OHG. *merch*, ON. *merki.*] Smallage or wild celery, *Apium graveolens* –1632.

March (māɹtʃ), *sb.*[2] ME. [- OFr. *march(e*, north-eastern var. of *marz*, (also mod.) *mars* :- L. *Martius* (sc. *mensis* month; lit. month of Mars).] The third month of the year in the Julian and Gregorian calendar. Abbrev. Mar.

The Ides of M. are come SHAKS. Hair More black that ashbuds in the front of M. TENNYSON. *attrib.* One bushell of m. dust is worth a kynges raunsome HEYWOOD.

Comb.: **M. ale, beer,** a strong ale or beer brewed in M.; **M. brown,** a fly used in angling; **M. hare,** a proverbial type of madness; **†M. mad** = mad as a M. hare; **M. violet,** the garden violet, *Viola odorata.*

March (māɹtʃ), *sb.*[3] ME. [- (O)Fr. *marche* - Rom. (med.L.) *marca* - OFrank. **marka* :- Gmc. **markō* MARK *sb.*[1]] **1.** Boundary, frontier, border. **a.** The border of a country. Hence, a tract of land on the border of a country, or a tract of debatable land separating two countries. Often *collect. pl.*, esp. with ref. to the borderland of England and Scotland, and England and Wales. Now *Hist.* **b.** The boundary of an estate. Chiefly *Sc.* 1540. **2.** Country, territory. *Obs.* exc. in ref. to continental names, as It. *Marca* (cf. MARK *sb.*[1] I. 3).

1. The lord Hunsdon lord warden of the east marches, and gouernor of Berwike HOLINSHED. Granted in fief..as a m. or border territory FREEMAN. **2.** The olde marche of Brandenburg 1758. The Marches comprise the M. of Ancona.. and the M. of Fermo.

attrib. and *Comb.*, as (sense 1 b) *m.-balk, -dike, -ditch*, etc.; (sense 1 a) *m.-law, -treason* (arch.), etc.

March (māɹtʃ), *sb.*[4] 1572. [f. MARCH *v.*[2] or - Fr. *marche*, f. *marcher* (see MARCH *v.*[2]).] **1.** *Mil.* The action of marching; the regular forward movement together and in time of a body of troops. Also, any orderly forward movement. 1590. **b.** Steady progression on a long journey; a long and toilsome walk 1691. **2.** *transf.* and *fig.* Advance, forward movement, progress, e.g. of time, events, population, knowledge, etc. 1625. **3.** *Mil.* The distance covered by troops in a single day 1594. **4.** The regular and uniform step of a body of men, esp. of troops. Also qualified, as *double, quick, slow m.* 1773. **b.** *fig.* Of verse: Rhythmic movement 1635. **5.** *Mil.* A beating of the drum in a particular rhythm as an accompaniment to the marching of troops 1572. **6.** *Mus.* A tune or composition of marked rhythm (usu. including the rhythmical drum-beats, sense 5), designed to accompany the marching of troops, etc.; also any similar composition; usually in common time, and with a subsidiary intermediate section or 'trio'. So also *m. past.* 1603. **7.** *Games.* **a.** *Euchre.* A taking of all five tricks 1886. **b.** *Chess*, etc. The move of a 'man' 1672.

1. Two mightier Troopes..Which ioyn'd with him, and made their m. for Burdeaux SHAKS. Phr. *Column of m.*, a formation assumed by troops on the line of m. *Line of m.*: direction or route of marching; *transf.* way. *M. past*, the marching past of a body of men, esp. in review. **2.** The regular m. of history H. WALPOLE. And drill the raw world for the m. of mind, Till crowds at length be sane and crowns be just TENNYSON. **3.** The army are.. within two or three marches of the Ebro WELLINGTON. Phr. *To gain, get a m. on* or *upon*: to get ahead of to the extent of a m. *To steal a m.* (*on* or *upon*): to gain a m. by stealth; often *fig.* **6.** Each regiment in the British service has its special m. for marching past 1876. *Dead m.*: see DEAD *Combs.* 2; also *funeral m. Rogue's m., wedding m.* (see ROGUE, WEDDING).

March (māɹtʃ), *v.*[1] ME. [- OFr. *marchir*, f. *marche* MARCH *sb.*[3]] *intr.* To border *upon, on*; to have a common frontier *with* (*to*, *†unto*). Said of countries, estates, etc., and hence of their rulers, owners, or inhabitants.

The frontiers of Dakota, Montana, and Washington m. with the Canadian Dominion 1889.

March (māɹtʃ), *v.*[2] 1515. [- (O)Fr. *marcher* walk, orig. tread, trample :- Gallo-Rom. **marcare*, f. late L. *marcus* hammer.] **1.** *intr.* To walk in a military manner with regular and measured tread; to walk in step. Also, to begin to walk in step (esp. in commands, as *Quick march!*), to set out from quarters. Freq. with advs., as *away, forth, off, on, out, past.* **b.** quasi-*trans.* To go upon (a warfare); to traverse (a distance) in marching 1619. **2.** To walk, proceed *off, on, out*, in a steady and deliberate manner 1572. **3.** *transf.* and *fig.* See quots. 1600. **4.** *trans.* (causatively). To cause to march or move in military order 1595; to force (a person) to go; to *march off* 1884.

1. Men that in battle array,..M. with banner and bugle and fife, To the death for their native land TENNYSON. The word *March*, given singly, at all times denotes that 'slow time' is to be taken 1833. **2.** Miss Ophelia marched straight to her own chamber MRS. STOWE. **3.** Without a strain the great ship marches by CLOUGH. It was the president who made the enterprise m. SKRINE. **4.** I should be glad to m. you to the gate 1896.

Marcher[1] (mā·ɹtʃəɹ). *Obs.* exc. *Hist.* 1440. [f. MARCH *sb.*[3] + -ER[1].] **†1.** One whose territory adjoins that of another. ME. only. **2.** An inhabitant of a march or border district 1470.

2. *Lord M.* (pl. *Lords Marchers*), a lord who enjoyed royal liberties and had exclusive jurisdiction over territory in the marches which he obtained by border warfare. Hence *Lordship M.*, territory so obtained and held.

Marcher[2] (mā·ɹtʃəɹ). 1611. [f. MARCH *v.*[2] + -ER[1].] One who marches or walks.

‖Marchese (markē·ze). 1517. [It.; see MARQUIS.] In Italy: A marquis. So **‖Marchesa** (markē·za), a marchioness 1797.

Marchet, obs. f. MARKET.

Marching (mā·ɹtʃiŋ), *vbl. sb.* 1560. [f. MARCH *v.*[2] + -ING[1].] The action of MARCH *v.*[2]

attrib. and *Comb.*: **m. money,** the additional pay received by officers and soldiers when marching from one place to another; **m. order,** equipment for marching; *pl.* orders to march. So **Ma·rching** *ppl. a.*, esp. in *m. regiment*, one which had not any permanent quarters, but was liable to be sent anywhere 1667.

Marchioness (mā·ɹʃənės). 15.. [- med.L. *marchionissa*, f. *marchio, -on-*, prop. captain of the marches, f. *marca* MARK *sb.*[1], MARCH *sb.*[3]] **1.** The wife or widow of a marquis, or a lady holding in her own right the position equal to that of marquis. **b.** *allusive.* A maid-of-all-work. (See DICKENS *Old C. Shop* lvii.) 1883. **2.** A kind of pear 1706. **3.** A size of slate, 22 inches by 11, or 20 by 12. 1878.

Ma·rch-land. 1536. [f. MARCH *sb.*[3] +

LAND *sb.* Cf. OE. *mearc-land* in same sense.] A border territory; border-land, frontier-land.

Ma·rch-man. *Obs.* exc. *Hist.* late ME. [f. MARCH *sb.*³ + MAN *sb.*] An inhabitant of the marches or borders.

Marchpane (mā·ɹtʃpeⁱn). Superseded by MARZIPAN. 1494. [The various forms, *march-*, *marts-*, *maza-*, *-pain(e*, *-pan(e*, represent diverse Continental forms, as Fr. †*marcepain* (mod. *massepain*), It. *marzapane*, Sp. *mazapan*, G. *marzipan* MARZIPAN.] **1.** A paste of pounded almonds, sugar, etc., made up into cakes, etc.; a cake or fancy form of this. †**b.** *fig.* –1652. **2.** *attrib.* 1587. †**b.** quasi-*adj.* Dainty, superfine –1649.

†**Ma·rcid,** *a.* 1656. [– L. *marcidus*, f. *marcēre* wither; see -ID¹.] **1. a.** Withered, wasted, decayed. **b.** Weak, exhausted. –1822. **2.** *M. fever*: a fever that causes wasting –1684.

Marcionite (mā·ɹʃⁱŏnəit). 1540. [– eccl. L. *Marcionita* (Tertullian), f. *Marcion*; see -ITE¹ 1.] An adherent of the sect founded at Rome by Marcion of Sinope, an ascetic gnostic of the 2nd c. Also †**Ma·rcionist** 1449.

Marcion accepted as sacred books ten of St. Paul's epistles and a garbled form of the gospel of St. Luke, and regarded the creation of the world and the revelation of the Old Testament as the work of a finite and imperfect God, whose authority is abrogated by the manifestation of the supreme God in Jesus Christ.

Marconi (maɹkōᵘ·ni). 1897. Name of the inventor (born 1874) of a system of wireless telegraphy; used *attrib.* of this system, and of things connected with it. Hence **Marconi** *v.*, to send a marconigram (*intr.* and *trans.*) 1919. **Marco·nigram,** a wireless telegram 1902. **Marco·nigraph,** the apparatus used for transmitting marconigrams 1903; also as vb.

Marcor (mā·ɹkǫɹ). 1646. [– L. *marcor*, f. *marcēre* wither; see -OR 1.] †**a.** *gen.* Decay. **b.** *Path.* Emaciation of the body.

Marcosian (maɹkōᵘ·ziăn). 1587. [f. eccl. Gr. Μαρκώσιος (app. f. Syriac *Marqūs* Marcus) + -AN.] *Hist.* An adherent of a Gnostic system founded by one Marcus in the 2nd c. Also *adj.*

‖**Mardi gras** (mardi gra). 1848. [Fr. 'fat Tuesday'.] Shrove Tuesday; *U.S.* as observed in New Orleans.

Mare¹ (mēᵊɹ). [Early ME. *mâre*, with stem-vowel from obl. cases of OE. *mearh* horse, finally superseding *mēre*, *mūre*, OE. **mēre*, **mīere*, **mȳre* :- Gmc. **marχjōn* (OFris., MLG., MDu. *mer(r)ie*, OHG. *mar(i)ha*, Du. *merrie*, G. *mähre*, ON. *merr*), f. **marχaz* horse (OHG. *marah*, ON. *marr*) :- **markos*, repr. also by Gaulish acc. sing. *markan* (Pausanias), Gaelic *marc*, W. *march*. Cf. MARSHAL.] **1.** The female of any equine animal, esp. of the domestic horse (*Equus caballus*). **2.** *transf.*, chiefly with implication of 'riding' 1568. **3.** A throw in wrestling. Also *flying m.* 1602.

1. *Grey m.* (see GREY *a.* 4). **2.** The two or three-legg'd M. (= 'the gallows') 1694. See also SHANK.

†**Mare**². [ME. *mare*, OE. *mære* incubus, corresp. to MLG. *mar*, MDu. *mare*, *maer*, OHG. *mara* (G. *mahr*), ON. *mara* :- Gmc. **maron*, **marōn*.] **1.** = NIGHTMARE. **2.** A spectre, hag –1529.

1. The Incubus, which we call the M. BACON.

†**Marechal.** 1676. [app. an application of Fr. *maréchal* or *maréchale*.] A scent or perfume; a hair powder scented with it –1852.

‖**Maréchal Niel** (mareʃal nīl). 1867. Also anglicized **Marshal Niel** (ma·ɹʃăl nīl). [Fr., named after Adolphe *Niel* (1802–1869), Marshal of France.] A yellow climbing rose.

‖**Maremma** (măre·mă). *Pl.* **maremme.** 1832. [– It. *maremma* :- L. *maritima*, fem. of *maritimus* MARITIME.] Low marshy insalubrious country by the sea shore.

Mareschal, obs. f. MARSHAL.

Mare's nest. 1619. [MARE¹.] Orig. in phr. *to have found a mare's nest*; to imagine that one has discovered something wonderful.

Mare's tail, mares-tail (mēᵊ·ɹzteⁱl). 1762. **1.** A book-name for aquatic or marsh plants of the N.O. *Halorageæ*, esp. *Hippuris vulgaris*. **2.** *pl.* Long straight streaks of cirrus, supposed to foretoken bad weather 1775.

Margaret (mā·ɹgărĕt). ME. [– OFr. *Margarete*, *-ite* (mod. *Marguerite*) – late L. *Margarita*, an application of L. *margarita* pearl: see MARGARITE¹.] **1.** A female name. †**2.** A daisy; called also *herb M.* –1640. **3.** A variety of apple, and also of pear 1664.

Margaric (maɹgæ·rik), *a.* 1819. [– Fr. *margarique*, f. Gr. μάργαρον = μαργαρίτης pearl + *-ique*, -IC, in reference to the pearly lustre of the crystals or scales.] *Chem.* In **Margaric acid:** †**a.** orig. the name given by Chevreul to one of the three fatty acids (*oleic, margaric, stearic*), the glyceryl derivs. of which were thought to form the chief constituents of animal fats. So *m. ether.*

It was shown by Heintz in 1852 that the three fatty acids of animal fat are the oleic, palmitic, and stearic, and that the 'margaric' of Chevreul was really a mixture of palmitic and stearic acid.

b. Now, applied to an acid of composition $C_{17}H_{34}O_2$, artificially prepared 1865. Hence **Ma·rgarate,** a salt of m. acid.

Margarin (mā·ɹgărin). Also **-ine.** 1836. [– Fr. *margarine*, f. *margarique* MARGARIC; see -IN¹.] *Chem.* The margarate of glyceryl or glyceride of margaric acid. †**a.** Orig. applied to a fatty substance in certain animal and vegetable oils, supposed to be the glyceride of the 'margaric acid' of Chevreul, really a mixture of stearin and palmitin. **b.** Now, the glyceride of margaric acid in its later application (see prec. b).

Margarine (mā·ɹgărīn, *pop.* māɹdʒərī·n). 1873. [– Fr. *margarine*, a misapplication of the chemical term: see prec.] The legal name (by Act 50 and 51 Vict. c. 29) for any substitute for butter made from OLEO-MARGARINE (q.v.), and for all substances made in imitation of butter, and offered for sale.

Margaritaceous (māɹgăritēⁱ·ʃəs), *a.* 1826. [f. L. *margarita* + -ACEOUS.] *Nat. Hist.* Pearly.

Margarite¹ (mā·ɹgărəit). *Obs.* exc. *arch.* ME. [– OFr. *margarite* (mod. *marguerite*), – L. *margarita* – Gr. μαργαρίτης, f. μάργαρον pearl, μάργαρος pearl-oyster + -ίτης; see -ITE¹ 1.] **1.** A pearl. †**2.** = MARGARET 2.

Margarite² (mā·ɹgărəit). 1823. [f. Gr. μάργαρον pearl + -ITE¹ 2 b.] *Min.* 'Pearl mica', a hydrous silicate found in scales having a pearly lustre.

Margaritic (māɹgări·tik), *a.* 1819. [f. L. *margarita* pearl + -IC.] *Chem. M. acid*: †**a.** used for Chevreul's 'margaric acid' (MARGARIC a); **b.** the name given to one of the fatty acids resulting from the saponification of castor oil.

Margaritiferous (māɹgăriti·fĕrəs), *a.* 1656. [f. L. *margaritifer* (Pliny), f. *margarita*; see MARGARITE¹, -FEROUS.] Producing pearls.

Margarodite (mā·ɹgărŏdəit). 1849. [– G. *margarodit* (Schafhäutl, 1843), f. late Gr. μαργαρώδης, f. μάργαρον pearl; see -ITE¹ 2 b.] *Min.* A variety of potash mica having a pearly lustre.

‖**Margaux** (mā·ɹgōᵘ, Fr. margo). Also †**margose.** 1705. Claret produced in the commune of Margaux (Gironde), France.

Margay (mā·ɹgeⁱ). 1781. [– Fr. *margay* (Buffon), alt. of *margaia* (Claude d'Abbeville, 1614) – Tupi *mbaracaïa*.] A S. American tiger cat, *Felis tigrina*.

Marge (māɹdʒ), *sb.* Now *poet.* or *rhet.* 1551. [– (O)Fr. *marge* :- L. *margo*, *margin-* MARGIN.] = MARGIN *sb.* 1, 3.

In-il'd on mighty Neptune's m. DRAYTON.

Margent (mā·ɹdʒĕnt), *sb.* Now *arch.* and *poet.* 1485. [alt. f. MARGIN *sb.*; cf. *ancient, pageant, peasant, pheasant, tyrant.*] **1.** = MARGIN *sb.* 1. 1538. **2.** = MARGIN *sb.* 3. 1485. †**b.** The margin of a book as being the place for a commentary or summary; hence the commentary or summary itself 1579–1733. **4.** quasi-*adj.* = marginal 1555.

1. By slow Meander's m. green MILT. **2. b.** And what obscur'd in this faire volume lies, Find written in the M. of his eyes SHAKS. Hence †**Margent** *v. trans.* to insert as a marginal note, to add marginal notes to 1610–1663.

Margin (mā·ɹdʒin), *sb.* ME. [– L. *margo*, *margin-*, rel. to MARK *sb.*¹] **1.** That part of a surface which lies immediately within its boundary; also, the space immediately adjacent to a well, a river, or piece of water; an edge, border, or brink. **b.** *Nat. Hist.* The contour or boundary line of a body, or a distinct border differing in texture, etc. from the main body 1760. **2.** *fig.* **a.** The limit below or beyond which something ceases to be possible or desirable 1863. **b.** An amount (of space, time, money, material, etc.) in addition to what is strictly necessary, serving as a provision for contingencies, or the like 1852. **c.** *Stockbroking* and *Comm.* A certain sum deposited with a broker to cover the risk of loss on a transaction on account 1882. **d.** *Life-insurance.* = LOADING *vbl. sb.* 2. 1881. **3.** The space on a page between the extreme edge and the main body of written or printed matter. Often restricted to the margins at the sides of the page ('inner' and 'outer' margins). ME. **4. a.** *Joinery.* The flat part of the stiles and rails of framed work. **b.** *Building*, etc. That part of a course of slates, plates, etc. which is not covered by the next course 1678.

1. On the M. of a Lake, close to the Edge of the Water 1774. **2. a.** No tax can be levied from those who are on the m. of bare subsistence ROGERS. **b.** The narrow m. of profit ROGERS. *Comb.* **m. draft, draught** = DRAFT *sb.* 6 a.

Margin (mā·ɹdʒin), *v.* 1607. [f. prec. sb.] **1.** *trans.* To furnish with marginal notes. **2.** To specify in the margin of a page 1640. **3.** To provide with a margin, edge, or border 1715. **4.** *Stockbroking.* To deposit a margin upon (stock) 1889.

Marginal (mā·ɹdʒinăl). 1576. [– med.L. *marginalis*, f. L. *margo*, *margin-*; see MARGIN *sb.*, -AL¹. Cf. Fr. *marginal.*] **A.** *adj.* **1.** Written or printed in the margin of a page, as *m. note, reference*; also, having marginal notes. **2.** Pertaining to an edge, border, or boundary; situated at the extreme edge (of an area, etc.) 1658. **3.** That is on the margin below or beyond which something ceases to be possible or desirable 1887.

1. †*M. finger*: a finger or hand set in the margin to call attention to something; hence *fig.* **2.** A m. growth of willow and flag BLACK. **3.** M. prices 1887.

B. *sb.* A marginal note, reference, or decoration. Now *rare.* 1602. Hence **Ma·rginal** *v. trans.* = MARGENT *v.* **Ma·rginally** *adv.*

‖**Marginalia** (māɹdʒinēⁱ·liă), *sb. pl.* 1832. [med. L. n. pl. of *marginalis*; see prec., -IA².] Marginal notes.

Marginate (mā·ɹdʒinĕt), *a.* 1777. [– L. *marginatus* furnished with a margin or border; see MARGIN *sb.*, -ATE².] *Nat. Hist.* and *Path.* Having a distinct margin. So **Ma·rginated** *ppl. a.* 1727.

Marginate (mā·ɹdʒineⁱt), *v.* 1609. [In sense 2 – L. *marginare* furnish with a border; see MARGIN *sb.*, -ATE³. In sense 1 app. f. MARGIN *v.* + -ATE³.] †**1.** *trans.* To annotate with marginal notes. **2.** To furnish with a margin or border 1623. Hence **Margina·tion,** a marginated appearance or marking.

Margined (mā·ɹdʒind), *a.* 1826. [f. MARGIN *sb.* or *v.* + -ED.] Chiefly *Nat. Hist.* and *Bot.* Having a margin; marginate. (Often as pple. followed by 'with'.)

Marginicidal (mā·ɹdʒinisəi·dăl), *a.* 1889. [f. L. *margo*, *margin-* (see MARGIN) + *-cīd-* (*cædere* cut) + -AL¹.] *Bot.* Dehiscent by the disjunction of the united margins of the carpels.

‖**Margosa** (maɹgōᵘ·să). 1813. [Short for Pg. *amargosa*, fem. of *amargoso* bitter.] An E. Indian tree, *Melia azadirachta*, yielding a bitter oil.

Margravate (mā·ɹgrĕvĕt). 1802. [f. next + -ATE¹.] = MARGRAVIATE.

Margrave (mā·ɹgreⁱv). *Hist.* Also **mark-grave, mar(k)graf,** etc. 1551. [– MDu. *markgrave* = OHG. *marcgrāvo* (G. *markgraf*); see MARK *sb.*¹, GRAVE *sb.*³] A German title, orig. of a military governor of a border province; subseq. the hereditary title of certain princes of the Holy Roman Empire.

Margraviate (māɹgrēⁱ·viĕt). 1702. [Like the later MARGRAVATE, f. MARGRAVE + -(*i*)ATE¹, the *-i-* being analogical, or suggested by med.L. *margravius* MARGRAVE.] The territory ruled by a margrave.

Margravine (mā·ɹgrĕvin). 1692. [– Du. *markgravin*, fem. of *markgraaf* MARGRAVE.] The wife of a margrave.

Marguerite (mā·ɹgĕ̆rīt). 1866. [– Fr. *marguerite* (see MARGARET).] The Ox-eye Daisy, *Chrysanthemum leucanthemum*; also *C. frutescens* or Paris Daisy. **Blue M.,** *Agathæa (Detris) cœlestis.*

Marian (mēᵊ·riăn), *sb.*¹ 1567. A female name. See also MAID MARIAN.

Marian (mēᵊ·riăn), *a.* and *sb.*² 1608. [f. L. *Marīa* Mary + -AN.] **A.** *adj.* **1.** Pertaining to the Virgin Mary 1701. **2.** Pertaining to Mary Queen of England or her time (1553–58) 1608. **3.** Relating to Mary Queen of Scots (1542–87) 1902. **B.** *sb.* **1.** A worshipper of the Virgin Mary 1635. **2.** An adherent of Mary Queen of Scots 1893. **3.** An English Roman Catholic of Queen Mary's reign 1899.

A. 2. The M. persecution in England 1608.

Marie, obs. f. MARRY.

†**Mariet.** 1597. [– Fr. †*mariette*, f. *Marie* Mary; see -ET, -ETTE.] The Canterbury Bell, *Campanula medium* –1658.

Marigenous (mări·dʒĭnəs), *a.* 1599. [f. L. *mare* sea + -GEN + -OUS.] Produced in or by the sea.

Marigold (mæ·rigōᵘld). ME. [f. proper name *Mary* (presumably with ref. to the Virgin Mary) + (dial.) *gold*, OE. *golde*, prob. rel. to GOLD.] **1.** The name of several plants having golden or bright yellow flowers. **a.** A plant of the genus *Calendula* (N.O. *Compositæ*), esp. *C. officinalis*, common in country gardens. **b.** Any plant of the genus *Tagetes*, native to S. America and Mexico, and much cultivated in gardens. **African m.,** *T. erecta*; **French m.,** *T. patula*. 1548. **c.** *Chrysanthemum segetum*; usu. CORN- *m.*, also *field, wild, yellow m.* 1578. **d.** *Fig m.* (see FIG *sb.*¹). Also MARSH MARIGOLD. **2.** A variety of apple (in full *m. apple*). ? *Obs.* 1577.

Comb.: **m. apple** (see 2); **m. bird, finch,** the golden-crested wren or kinglet, *Regulus cristatus*; **m. window** *Arch.*, a rose window.

‖**Marikina** (mærikī·nă). 1774. [repr. Tupi *miriquiná*.] The silky tamarin, *Midas rosalia*.

‖**Marimba** (mări·mbă). 1704. [Congo.] A kind of xylophone, used by natives in Africa.

‖**Marimonda** (mærimǫ·ndă). 1758. [Amer. Sp.] A spider-monkey of tropical America, *Ateles belzebuth*.

‖**Marina** (mărī·nă). Also *erron.* **-o.** 1805. [It. and Sp., fem. of *marino* MARINE *a.*] A promenade or esplanade by the sea.

Marinade (mærinēⁱ·d), *sb.* 1704. [– Fr. *marinade* – Sp. *marinada*, f. *marinar* to pickle in brine, f. *marino* MARINE *a.*] A pickle, generally composed of wine and vinegar, with herbs and spices, in which fish or meat is steeped; also, the fish or meat thus pickled. So **Ma·rinade** *v.* to steep in m.; to marinate 1682.

Marinate (mæ·rineⁱt), *v.* 1654. [– It. *marinare* or Fr. *mariner*; see prec., -ATE³.] *trans.* To pickle (fish, etc.) with marinade.

Marine (mărī·n). ME. [– (O)Fr. *marin*, fem. *marine* :– L. *marinus*, f. *mare* sea; see -INE¹.] **A.** *adj.* **1.** Of or belonging to, found in, or produced by the sea; *Zool.* inhabiting the deep sea, pelagic. †**b.** Of sculptured figures, etc.: Representing sea-gods, fishes, sea-shells, etc. –1741. **c.** Of a painter: That depicts sea subjects 1883. †**2.** Belonging to, or situated at, the sea-side; maritime –1728. **3.** Connected with the sea; pertaining to shipping, a navy, or naval force; relating to naval matters 1551. **4.** Of soldiers: Serving on board ship, as *m. force* 1690. **5.** Used or for use at sea 1704.

1. M. denudation is not equally active at all depths of the sea HUXLEY. *M. rainbow*: a rainbow formed on sea-spray. †*M. acid* (Old Chem.): the acid obtained from m. salt, hydrochloric acid. **3.** *M. board*: an establishment at a port for carrying into effect the provisions of the Merchant Shipping Act. *M. insurance*, insurance against perils at sea. **5.** *M.* *barometer, chronometer, galvanometer, watch.* **M. glue,** an adhesive composition used in ship carpentry.

B. *sb.* †**1.** [= Fr. *marine.*] The sea-coast; a promenade by the sea; also, the country or district near the coast –1703. **2.** [= Fr. *marine.*] The shipping, fleet, navy, or naval service of a country; sea-going vessels collectively, esp. with reference to nationality or class, as *mercantile m.* (now the chief use) 1669. ‖**3.** The continental counterpart of the English Admiralty (as a department of the government) 1784. **4.** One who serves on board ship. †**a.** A mariner –1634. **b.** A soldier who serves on board a man-of-war; one of a body of troops enlisted to do military service on board ship, at dockyards, etc.; also in *pl.* used collectively 1672. **5.** *Painting.* A sea piece 1846.

1. In the summer time every evening the m. is full with all sorts of people with musick, singing, and dancing 1687. **2.** France knew that America had the largest mercantile m. COBDEN. **4. b.** *Royal Marines*, troops who serve on British men-of-war. Phr. *Tell that to the marines*: a colloq. expression of disbelief. **5.** One of the marines of Salvator RUSKIN.

Marined (mărī·nd), *a.* 1823. [f. MARINE *a.* + -ED¹.] *Her.* An epithet for an animal that has the lower part of the body like a fish.

Mariner (mæ·rinəɹ). ME. [– AFr. *mariner*, (O)Fr. *marinier* :– med.L. *marinarius*, f. L. *marinus*; see MARINE *a.*, -ER² 2.] **1.** A sailor, seaman; in law, any person employed on a ship. †**2.** = MARINE *sb.* 4 b. 1642–1699.

1. *Master m.*: †a captain of a merchant vessel; a skilled seaman certified as competent to command a merchant vessel. *Comb.* **mariner's compass, needle** (see these words). Hence †**Ma·rinership,** seamanship 1542–1613.

Marine store(s. 1831. **1.** *pl.* Old ship's materials as an object of merchandise 1831. **2.** *sing.* A shop where such old odds and ends (old iron, bottles, etc.) are sold 1837.

attrib. as *marine store dealer.*

Mariolatry (mēᵊriǫ·lătri). 1612. [f. L. *Maria* (the Virgin) Mary + -LATRY, after IDOLATRY.] The idolatrous worship of the Virgin Mary. Hence **Mario·later,** one who practises Mariolatry. **Mario·latrous** *a.* characterized by Mariolatry.

Marionette (mæriǒne·t). 1620. [– Fr. *marionnette*, f. *Marion*, dim. of *Marie* MARY; see -ETTE.] **1.** A puppet actuated by strings and used to represent persons (or animals) in action. Also *fig.* **2.** The buffle-headed duck, *Bucephala albeola* 1838. **3.** *attrib.* 1856.

3. The m.-players will please the children JOWETT.

Mariposa lily (mæripōᵘ·să,li:li). 1882. [f. Sp. *mariposa* butterfly.] A plant of the genus *Calochortus*, native to California and Mexico.

Marish (mæ·riʃ). *poet.* and *dial.* [ME. *mar(r)eis, mar(r)ais* (XIV) – (O)Fr. *marais*, †*mareis* – med.L. *mariscus*; see MARSH. The present form dates from XVI.] **A.** *sb.* = MARSH. **B.** *adj.* Marshy; such as is produced in a marsh 1543.

A. As Ev'ning Mist Ris'n from a River o're the m. glides MILT. B. ¶App. associated with L. *mare* sea, and hence = salt. Her cheekes o'reflowne With m. teares QUARLES.

Marist (mēᵊ·rist). 1877. [– Fr. *Mariste*, f. *Marie* Mary; see -IST.] A member of the Roman Catholic Society of Mary, devoted to the work of foreign missions and to teaching.

Marital (mæ·rităl), *a.* 1603. [– L. *maritalis*, f. *maritus* husband; see -AL¹.] **1.** Pertaining or relating to a husband; husbandly 1616. **2.** Of or pertaining to marriage; matrimonial. Hence **Marita·lity,** excessive affection of a wife for her husband. **Ma·ritally** *adv.* as if married.

Maritime (mæ·ritəim). Also †**-ayne, -an(e, -in(e** (after OFr. variant forms). 1550. [– (partly through Fr. *maritime*) L. *maritimus*, f. *mare*, *mari-* sea + *-timus*, as in *finitimus* neighbouring, etc.] **A.** *adj.* **1.** Bordering on the sea; living near the sea coast 1598. **b.** Living or found near the sea 1608. **2.** Connected with the sea; relating to or dealing with matters of commerce or navigation on the sea 1591. **3.** Of a fighting force: Intended for service at sea 1550. **4.** Of, pertaining to, arising from, or existing in, the sea. Now *rare* or *Obs.* 1624. **5.** Nautical 1743.

1. Brittany (a marittime part of France) SIR T. HERBERT. A m. people 1854. **b.** The coarse m. cabbage 1856. **2. M. insurance** = *marine insurance.* **M. interest,** premium or interest on a bottomry bond. **5.** He was far from having a m. appearance DICKENS.

B. *sb.* †**1.** The sea-coast; a country or district adjoining the sea –1657. †**2.** A person living near the sea 1655.

Marjoram (mā·ɹdʒərəm). [ME. *majorane, mageram* (XIV) – OFr. *majorane* (mod. *marjolaine*, through **marjoraine*) – med.L. *majorana*, of doubtful origin.] Any plant of the genus *Origanum* (N.O. *Labiatæ*); esp. the Wild M., *O. vulgare*, and the Sweet M., *O. Majorana*, an aromatic herb used in cookery.

Mark (māɹk), *sb.*¹ [OE. (Anglian) *merc*, (WS.) *mearc* = OFris. *merke*, OS. *marka* (Du. *mark*), OHG. *marc(h)a* (G. *mark*), ON. *mǫrk*), Goth. *marka* :– Gmc. **markō* (beside **markam* sign, landmark, standard), rel. to L. *margo* MARGIN. Branch IV is from MARK *v.* Cf. MARCH *sb.*³]

I. Boundary. **1.** A boundary, frontier, limit; rarely in *pl.* †territories. *Obs.* exc. *Hist.* or *arch.* **2.** *Hist.* Name in mediæval Germany for the tract of land held in common by a village community. Hence applied to tracts of land similarly held in primitive Germanic times. Also *attrib.*, as in *m.-system*, etc. 1848. **3.** Used to represent G. *Mark* as the name of certain principalities, esp. the Mark of Brandenburg 1726.

2. Each community occupied a territory or m., which was divided into three, or rather four portions 1876.

II. Sign of a boundary, position, etc. †**1.** = LANDMARK 1. –1697. †**2.** A stone or other monument set up or standing as a memorial, or as a guide –1591. **3.** A target, butt, or other object set up to be aimed at. Hence *transf.* the thing that is aimed at in shooting or throwing. ME. †**b.** The quarry of a hawk, etc. –1691. **c.** *Boxing slang.* The pit of the stomach, the 'wind' 1747. **d.** *fig.* 1549. **e.** *Bowls.* The jack. Also, a proper bowling distance or a position allowed for the jack. 1630. **4.** A post, etc. placed to indicate the terminal point of a race; a goal. Often *fig.*, an object desired. ME. **5.** An object on shore or at sea serving as a guide to travellers, *esp.* a LANDMARK, *leading-mark*, SEA-MARK. Also *fig.* late ME.

1. COVERDALE *Deut.* 27:17. **3.** Do not look from the m. to the arrow and back again 'STONEHENGE'. **d.** A m. to wrath, and hate, and wrong assign'd 1586. Phr. *Easy m.* (colloq.): a thing easily attained. *Beside, far from, near, short of, wide of the m.*; *to hit, miss the m.*, to attain or miss some desired object or end. **4.** Let this be our perpetual marke, to aide all men faithfully 1561. **5.** Men that have past by a Rock at Sea, set up some m., thereby to remember their former danger, and avoid it HOBBES.

III. A sign, indication. **1.** A sign, token, symptom (*of* something) OE. **b.** A characteristic property; a criterion 1522. **c.** *spec.* A depression caused by a fold in the enamel of a horse's incisor tooth, which gives some indication of the age of the animal. Also *m. of mouth.* Also *fig.* late ME. **2.** A sign affixed or impressed for distinction. **a.** A device, stamp, seal, label, brand, inscription, written character, or the like, indicating ownership, quality, etc. ME. **b.** A badge, brand, etc., assumed by or imposed on a person; *occas.* in *pl.* †insignia ME. **c.** A cross, or the like, used by illiterate persons in place of a signature OE. **d.** A written symbol 1787. **e.** (*a*) *Good, bad m.*: a written character used to indicate an instance of good or bad conduct respectively; hence *fig.* a point noted to a person's credit or discredit. (*b*) The unit of the numerical award given by a teacher or examiner to a candidate in a competitive examination, etc. 1829. †**f.** In schools, a badge worn by the pupil who had last committed some particular fault 1832–1855. **g.** *Her.* A small charge added to a coat of arms as a sign of distinction; esp. in *m. of* CADENCY 1702. **h.** *Freemasonry.* Used *attrib.* (with reference to sense III. 2 a), to designate a degree, grade, or rank immediately superior to that of a free and accepted mason (see *Combs.*). **3.** A line, dot, object, etc. intended to record or indicate position 1460. **b.** *Naut.* A measured notification on a hand lead-line, indicated by a piece of white, blue, or red bunting, a piece of leather, or a knot 1769. **c.** *fig.* 1765. **d.** *Rugby Football.* The heel-mark on the ground, made by a player who has obtained a fair catch 1867. **4.** A visible trace or impression diversifying a surface, as a line, dot, stain, discoloration, scar, or the like ME. **5.** That which is signified by a mark. †**a.** Those who bear a particular mark or stamp (*fig.*); a person's race, sect, etc. –1555. **b.** A particular brand, make, quality, or size of an article 1488. **c.** *vulgar.* That which suits one's taste 1760. **6.** (*Gòd*) *bless* (or *save*) *the m.*: an exclam., prob. originally a formula to avert an evil omen, and hence used by way of apology for mentioning anything horrible, disgusting, or profane. In mod. literary use (after Shaks.), an expression of impatient scorn. 1591. **7.** A die or stamp for impressing a manufacturer's mark on goods 1797.

1. Is it not a great Marque of Honor? GALE. Marks of Truth, of Falsehood WATTS. **2. a.** The first of these [Hall-marks] was the *King's mark*—a leopard's or lion's head crowned 1885. EAR-, HALL-, TRADEMARK, q.v. **b.** *God's m.*, *m. of clergy, of holy church*: the tonsure. *M. of the Beast*: see *Rev.* 16:2 and BEAST *sb.* 5. **d.** A m. of interrogation (?) 1862. **3.** *Plimsoll's m.*: a load-line required by the Merchant Shipping Act, 1876, to be placed upon the hull of a British vessel. *To be above, beneath, near, under, up to, within the m.*: to be above (etc.) a fixed or recognized standard. *Athletics.* A line indicating the starting-point. **4.** *To leave, make a m.*: to leave or make a permanent, important, or obvious impression. *To make one's m.*: to attain distinction. **5. a.** Moore wikkednesse Than all the m. of Adam may redresse CHAUCER.

IV. Remark, notice. †**1.** Attention, notice –1823. **2.** *Of m.*: noteworthy, important, conspicuous. Also *of great, little*, etc. *m.* 1590.

2. A fellow of no marke, nor likelyhood SHAKS.

V. *attrib.* and *Comb.*: **m.-boat,** a boat moored at a particular spot as a sea-mark; **m.-book,** a book for recording marks; **-lodge,** a lodge of mark masons; **m. man, m. mason, m. master (mason),** a freemason holding a certain rank in mark masonry (cf. III. 2 h); **m. tooth,** the tooth of a horse containing the m. (cf. III. 1 c); **-vessel** = *mark-boat.*

Mark (māɹk), *sb.*² [OE. *marc*, corresp. to OFris. *merk*, MDu. *marc* (Du. *mark*), MHG. *marke* (G. *mark*), ON. *mǫrk*; the Gmc. forms, which vary in gender, are prob. all – med.L. *marcus, marca* (whence also Fr., Pr. *marc*, Sp. *marco*, It. *marco, -a*), perh. ult. identical with MARK *sb.*[1]] **1.** A denomination of weight (chiefly for gold and silver); usu. regarded as = 8 ounces. Now used only to represent its continental equivalent. **2.** A money of account, orig. representing the value of a mark weight of pure silver. **a.** In England, = 13*s.* 4*d.* or ⅔ of the £ sterling. *Obs.* exc. *Hist.* OE. **b.** In Scotland, = 13*s.* 4*d.* Scots, 13⅓*d.* English. 1480. **c.** Repr. the continental word in its various forms, as a name of foreign moneys of account 1475. **3.** As the name of a coin. **a.** In Scotland, a coin worth 13*s.* 4*d.* Scots. *Obs.* exc. *Hist.* 1480. **b.** Used as the name of various coins on the Continent, *esp.* a silver coin of the German Empire first issued in 1875, and formerly worth slightly less than the Eng. shilling 1727.

Mark (māɹk), *v.* [OE. *mearcian* = OFris. *merkia*, OS. (*gi*)*markon* appoint, observe (Du. *marken*), OHG. *marchōn* plan, ON. *marka* mark, observe :– WGmc. **markōjan*, f. Gmc. *markō* MARK *sb.*[1]]

I. To put a mark upon. **1.** *trans.* To trace out boundaries for; to plot out (ground); to set out the ground plan of (a building); *fig.* to plan out, design. Also with *out.* **2.** To make a mark or marks on (anything) OE. Also *absol.* **b.** *spec.* To put an identifying mark on linen, etc. 1530. **c.** *Comm.* To attach to (an article) figures or signs indicating the price 1894. **d.** *pass.* To have or bear natural marks. Also *fig.* ME. **3.** To form or portray by making marks ME. **4.** *fig.* To designate as if by placing a mark upon; to destine. †Also with complement, to designate as being so and so). OE. Also with *out.* **b.** To separate *from* something else as by a line or distinctive mark. Now chiefly with *off.* 1703. **5.** To express or indicate by marks or signs OE. **b.** In games: To record (the points gained by the players). Chiefly *absol.*, and in phr. *to m. the game.* 1816. **c.** Of a graduated instrument: To show, register (so many degrees, etc.) 1882. **6.** In immaterial sense: **a.** To make perceptible by some indication 1904. **b.** To manifest (one's approval, displeasure, etc.) by some act, or by reward or punishment 1791. **7.** To be a mark of or upon 1687. **b.** *pass.* Of lines, features, etc.: To be (more or less) strikingly noticeable 1824. **c.** To be a distinguishing mark or feature of. Often *pass.*, to be characterized, distinguished, or made remarkable (now only const. *by*) 1661. **8.** *Mil.* **a.** To indicate the pivots, formations, etc. in military evolutions 1796. **b.** *To m. time*: to move the feet as in marching, but without advancing. Also *transf.* and *fig.* 1833.

2. My bodie's mark'd With Roman Swords SHAKS. I can get no pen that will m. SHELLEY. **c.** Phr. *To m. down*: to label (goods) with a lower figure; to reduce the indicated price of. So *To m. up*: to mark at a higher price. **4.** If we are markt to die SHAKS. Melancholy mark'd him for her own GRAY. **5.** He draws the chart and marks the sunken reefs 1879. **b.** One large round one [counter] that marks 500 'CAVENDISH'. Phr. *To m. up* (colloq.): to add (an item) to an existing tavern score; hence, to give credit for. **6. a.** To m. the..accent by a..prolongation of the first note of the bar 1904. **5.** Wolf's coming to Halle in 1783..marks an era [etc.] M. ARNOLD. **c.** No triumph—no exultation..marks her manner COWDEN CLARKE.

II. †**1.** To direct (one's way). Also *refl.* and *intr.* to proceed, advance. –1596. †**2.** To aim a blow or missile at; to strike, hit –1529.

III. 1. To notice or keep the eye upon; to observe. Now *poet.* and *rhet.* ME. **2.** To consider; to give heed or attention to. Often with *well.* ME. **3.** *Sport.* **a.** *trans.* To note and keep in mind the spot to which (the game) has retired after being 'put up'. Also *to m. down.* 1450. **3.** *Football.* To keep close to (an opponent) in order to hamper him if he receives the ball 1887. **4.** *absol.* or *intr.* To take notice; to fix (one's) attention; to consider. Occas.: To ascertain by observation (*what, whether*, etc.). 1526.

1. So near that..I could m. him well, Myself unseen WORDSW. She quickened her pace to m. him in the glory of the battle MEREDITH. **2.** Marke the perfect man, and behold the vpright: for the end of that man is peace *Ps.* 37:37. **4.** Marke, I pray you, and see how this man seeketh mischiefe 1 *Kings* 20:7.

Marked (māɹkt), *ppl. a.* OE. [f. MARK *sb.*[1] and *v.* + -ED.] **1.** Having a visible mark. Also, affixed as a mark; expressed by a mark. **2.** *Marked man*: one whose doings are watched with suspicion or hostility 1833. **3.** Easy to distinguish or recognize 1795.

m. bar, a particular form of pig-iron; **m. iron** = *marked bar*; **m. proof,** an impression of an engraving in which some detail is left unfinished as a mark of an early state of the plate. Hence **Marked-ly** (mā·ɹkėdli) *adv.*, **-ness.**

Marker (mā·ɹkəɹ). 1486. [f. MARK *v.* + -ER[1].] **1.** One who marks (see MARK *v.*). **a.** One who marks game. **b.** One who records the score in games, esp. billiards, or at target practice 1532. **2.** An implement for marking 1725. **3.** A book-marker 1852. **4.** *U.S.* A tablet or other permanent memorial 1906.

Market (mā·ɹkėt), *sb.* [Early ME. *market* (XII, Peterborough Chron.), recorded earlier in the late OE. comp. *ġēarmarkett* (XI), in which *ġēar* YEAR corresponds to the gen. of the native term *ġēares ćīeping* 'year's market'; both simplex and comp. appear to be – OS. *iārmarket* = OHG. *iārmarchāt*, of which the second element – L. *mercatus* (in Rom. **marcatus*, whence OFr. *marchiet*, mod. *marché*, Pr. *markat-z*), f. *mercari* buy, f. *merz, merc-* merchandise.] **1.** The meeting together of people for the purchase and sale of provisions or live stock, publicly exposed, at a fixed time and place; the time of this; also, the company assembled. **2.** *Law.* The privilege granted to the lord of a manor, a municipality or other body, to establish a meeting of persons to buy and sell OE. **3.** An open space or covered building in which cattle, provisions, etc. are exposed for sale; a market-place, market-house ME. **4.** The action or business of buying and selling; a purchase or sale; a (good or bad) bargain (*lit.* and *fig.*). *Obs.* exc. as in phrases (see below). 1525. †**b.** The marketing *of* (a commodity) –1680. **5.** Sale as controlled by supply and demand; hence, demand 1689. **6.** Opportunity of buying or selling 1684. **7.** Price in the market, market value. Also *fig.* 1535. **8.** A place or seat of trade; a country, district, etc. in which there is a demand for articles of trade; hence, the trade of such a country, etc. 1615.

1. †*High m.*: the time when the m. is busiest. *fig.* Sell when you can, you are not for all markets SHAKS. Phr. *To bring to m.*: to offer for sale (*lit.* and *fig.*). *To bring one's eggs* (or *one's hogs*) *to a bad m.*: to fail in one's schemes. *M. overt* (in *Law*): open m.; the exposal of vendible goods in an open place so that any one who passes by may see them. **4.** The Juncto..willing to make the best of a bad m., prepare for war 1660. *To make a* or *one's market of* (something): to make (it) an object of bargaining or profit. *To mar another's*, or *one's own m.*: to spoil his or one's own trade (*lit.* and *fig.*). *To mend one's m.*: to improve one's bargain. **b.** *Haml.* IV. iv. 34 (Qo. 2). **5.** The extra quantity can only find a m., by calling forth an additional demand equal to itself MILL. Phr. *To make a m.* (Stock Exchange): to induce active dealing in a stock or shares, by being both a buyer and a seller at about the same price; to bring an enterprise to the notice of the public by interesting dealers in it (by means of options or otherwise) 1899. **6.** Phr. *To lose one's m.*: to miss one's chance of doing business. *To overstand one's m.*: to stand out about terms till the opportunity is lost. *The m.*: the particular trade or traffic in the commodity specified in the context. Chiefly *in* or *on the m.* *To be in the m.*: (of a person) to be a buyer; (of a possession) to be offered for sale (so *to come into the m.*). *To engross the m.*: to buy up the stock of any commodity in order to sell it again at an enhanced price. **7.** These lands at present would sell at a low m. BURKE. **8.** Wars for a m. 1891.

Comb.: **m. bell,** a bell rung to announce the commencement of a m.; **m. cross,** a cross erected in a m.-place; **-custom,** the dues levied on goods brought to m.; **-garden,** a piece of land on which vegetables are grown for the m.; hence *m.-gardener*; **m. man,** one who deals in a m.; **-place, square,** a square or wide open space where a m. is held; **-rate,** the current value of a commodity; **-stead** *arch.* = *market-place*; **m. town,** a town which has the privilege of holding a m.; **-value,** saleable value.

Market (mā·ɹkėt), *v.* 1455. [f. prec. sb.] **1.** *trans.* To sell; also, to bring or send to market. **2.** *intr.* To buy and sell in a market; to go to market with produce, to purchase provisions 1635.

1. The Treasurer..for a Price Mercates his Maister, to extend his Purse G. DANIEL.

Marketable (mā·ɹkėtăb'l), *a.* 1600. [f. prec. + -ABLE.] **1.** Capable of being marketed; that finds a ready market; saleable. **2.** Concerned with trade. Of price, value: That may be obtained in buying or selling. 1602.

1. One of them Is a plaine Fish, and no doubt m. SHAKS. Unpossessed of any m. talent 1851. **2.** To enlarge the m. area by [etc.] 1872.

Marketeer (māɹkėtīᵊ·ɹ). *U.S.* 1832. [See -EER.] One who sells in a market.

Marketer (mā·ɹkėtəɹ). *U.S.* 1787. [f. MARKET *v.* + -ER[1].] One who goes to market; one who buys or sells in a market.

Marketing (mā·ɹkėtiŋ), *vbl. sb.* 1561. [f. MARKET *v.* + -ING[1].] **1.** The action of MARKET *v.* **2. a.** Something bought in the market 1701. **b.** Produce to be sold in the market; also, a consignment of such produce 1883.

‖**Markhor**(**e** (mā·ɹkǫɹ). Also **markhoor.** 1867. [– Pers. *mār-ḵwār* lit. 'serpent-eater', f. *mār* serpent + *ḵwār* -eating.] A large wild goat (*Capra falconeri*), of N. India.

Marking (mā·ɹkiŋ), *vbl. sb.* ME. [f. MARK *v.* + -ING[1].] **1.** The action of MARK *v.* **2.** *concr.* A mark or pattern of marks ME.

1. I doe confesse much of the hearing of it, but little of the m. of it SHAKS.

attrib. and *Comb.*: **m. board,** (*a*) a board for registering the score in certain games; (*b*) a board in the Stock Exchange upon which transactions are posted; **m. ink,** (*a*) an indelible ink for marking linen, etc.; (*b*) a mixture for marking packing-cases with a stencil, etc.; **m. iron,** a branding iron; **m.-nut,** the fruit of the tree *Semecarpus anacardium*, the juice of which makes an indelible black stain on linen, etc.

Markis, etc., obs. var. of MARQUIS, etc.

Marksman (mā·ɹksmæ̆n). 1660. [f. *mark's*, genitive of MARK *sb.*[1] + MAN *sb.*] **1.** One skilled or practised in aiming at a mark; *spec.* one who reaches a certain recognized degree of proficiency in rifle practice. **2.** One who makes a mark in place of a signature 1777. Earlier †**Ma·rkman** 1577–1654.

2. The..drover who signed the contract was a m. 1885. Hence **Ma·rksmanship,** the function, quality, or art of a m.

Ma·rkworthy, *a.* 1827. [f. MARK *sb.*[1] + WORTHY *a.*, after G. *merkwürdig.*] Worthy of note.